# METRICATION TABLES

**Conversion to Metric Units**   **Conversion from Metric Units**

## LINEAR MEASURE (LENGTH)

| To convert | Multiply by | To convert | Multiply by |
|---|---|---|---|
| inches to millimeters | 25.4 | millimeters to inches | 0.039 |
| inches to centimeters | 2.54 | centimeters to inches | 0.394 |
| feet to meters | 0.305 | meters to feet | 3.281 |
| yards to meters | 0.914 | meters to yards | 1.094 |
| miles to kilometers | 1.609 | kilometers to miles | 0.621 |

## SQUARE MEASURE (AREA)

| To convert | Multiply by | To convert | Multiply by |
|---|---|---|---|
| sq. inches to sq. centimeters | 6.452 | sq. centimeters to sq. inches | 0.155 |
| sq. feet to sq. meters | 0.093 | sq. meters to sq. feet | 10.764 |
| sq. yards to sq. meters | 0.836 | sq. meters to sq. yards | 1.196 |
| acres to hectares | 0.405 | hectares to acres | 2.471 |

## CUBIC MEASURE (VOLUME)

| To convert | Multiply by | To convert | Multiply by |
|---|---|---|---|
| cu. inches to cu. centimeters | 16.387 | cu. centimeters to cu. inches | 0.061 |
| cu. feet to cu. meters | 0.028 | cu. meters to cu. feet | 35.315 |
| cu. yards to cu. meters | 0.765 | cu. meters to cu. yards | 1.308 |

## LIQUID MEASURE (CAPACITY)

| To convert | Multiply by | To convert | Multiply by |
|---|---|---|---|
| fluid ounces to liters | 0.03 | liters to fluid ounces | 33.814 |
| quarts to liters | 0.946 | liters to quarts | 1.057 |
| gallons to liters | 3.785 | liters to gallons | 0.264 |
| imperial gallons to liters | 4.546 | liters to imperial gallons | 0.220 |

## WEIGHTS (MASS)

| To convert | Multiply by | To convert | Multiply by |
|---|---|---|---|
| ounces avoirdupois to grams | 28.35 | grams to ounces avoirdupois | 0.035 |
| pounds avoirdupois to kilograms | 0.454 | kilograms to pounds avoirdupois | 2.205 |
| tons to metric tons | 0.907 | metric tons to tons | 1.102 |

## TEMPERATURE

| Fahrenheit thermometer | | Celsius (or Centigrade) thermometer |
|---|---|---|
| 32°F | freezing point of water | 0°C |
| 212°F | boiling point of water | 100°C |
| 98.6°F | body temperature | 37°C |

To find degrees Celsius, subtract 32 from degrees Fahrenheit and divide by 1.8.
To find degrees Fahrenheit, multiply degrees Celsius by 1.8 and add 32.

SECOND CONCISE EDITION

# WEBSTER'S NEW WORLD DICTIONARY

## SECOND CONCISE EDITION

# WEBSTER'S NEW WORLD DICTIONARY

David B. Guralnik, GENERAL EDITOR

## SIMON AND SCHUSTER

WEBSTER'S NEW WORLD DICTIONARY, Second Concise Edition

This book is based upon and includes material from WEBSTER'S NEW WORLD DICTIONARY, Second College Edition, copyright © 1970, 1972, 1974, 1976, 1978, 1979, 1980, 1982 by Simon & Schuster, a Division of Gulf & Western Corporation.

Published by New World Dictionaries/Simon and Schuster
A Simon & Schuster Division of Gulf & Western Corporation
Simon & Schuster Building
Rockefeller Center
1230 Avenue of the Americas
New York, New York 10020
SIMON AND SCHUSTER, TREE OF KNOWLEDGE, WEBSTER'S NEW WORLD and colophons
are trademarks of Simon & Schuster.

Manufactured in the United States of America

5 7 9 10 8 6 4

LIBRARY OF CONGRESS CATALOG CARD NO.: 81-85761
Webster's New World Dictionary.

New York: Simon & Schuster
882 p. Concise ed.
8201        811119

ISBN 0-671-41816-5 plain edged
ISBN 0-671-41817-3 indexed

Dictionary Editorial Offices: New World Dictionaries,
850 Euclid Avenue, Cleveland, Ohio 44114

Previous editions of this book were published by The World Publishing Company, William Collins +World Publishing Co., Inc. and William Collins Publishers, Inc.

PRINTED IN THE UNITED STATES OF AMERICA

# CONTENTS

# EDITORIAL STAFF

| | |
|---|---|
| *Editor in Chief* | David B. Guralnik |
| *Managing Editor* | Samuel Solomon |
| *Associate Editors* | Clark C. Livensparger *(Supervising)*, Thomas Layman, Andrew N. Sparks, Christopher T. Hoolihan, Paul B. Murry, Ruth Kimball Kent |
| *Assistant Editors* | Eleanor Rickey Stevens, Jonathan L. Goldman, Roslyn Block, Lois Engintunca, Thomas V. Sullivan |
| *Office Assistants* | Virginia C. Becker, Dorothy H. Benedict, Cynthia Sadonick, Joan McDaniel, Sharon Preisler, Gertrude Tullar |
| *Chief Proofreader* | Shirley M. Miller |
| *Illustrator* | Anita S. Rogoff |

# FOREWORD

The *Second Concise Edition* of WEBSTER'S NEW WORLD DICTIONARY is still another addition to the family of word reference books that have been serving America's dictionary needs for over two decades. It has been prepared by the same permanent lexicographical staff that brought out the highly acclaimed *Second College Edition*, using the same data base compiled for that work. The success of the earlier *Concise Edition*, first published in 1956, has made it clear that there are many professional and business people, secondary-school students, office workers, word-game addicts, learners of English as a second language, and others who want a comprehensive and up-to-date dictionary, but who have less need for the extensive etymologies, highly technical or arcane terms, rare meanings, and certain other features found in the *Second College Edition*. For such persons, the *Second Concise Edition* should prove highly serviceable.

The word stock of this edition, over 105,000 vocabulary entries, was selected on the basis of frequency of occurrence in general publications and books of general interest. It is of primary importance that a contemporary dictionary make every effort to incorporate the burgeoning vocabulary that reflects our rapidly expanding technology and the changes that are taking place in our life styles. That very term *life style* typifies the kind of coinage that the lexicographer must be constantly on the alert to identify and to incorporate in the ongoing record of language usage that we term a dictionary. In selecting for inclusion in this *Second Concise Edition* items from our vast citation file, we have been careful to cull only those terms that have acquired a stability of form and meaning and that show some promise of surviving in the language, at least for a time. We have equally sought to avoid expending space on the merely faddish or ephemeral terms that appear suddenly and then die within a year or two.

Obsolete and archaic terms and senses that are frequently found in the Bible or in standard works of literature have been included. Also, such technical terms and meanings of specialized fields as are encountered in general writings have been entered, usually prefaced by a field label. The abbreviations for these various labels will be found in the List of Abbreviations immediately preceding the first page of the vocabulary. With the aid of the United States Trademark Association, every effort has been made to establish the status of terms suspected of being trademarks and to properly label those so identified.

A great many prefixes, suffixes, and combining forms have been entered, and these will enable the user of this dictionary to determine the meanings of thousands of additional words that are themselves too specialized for entry in a work of this scope. In the interest of conserving space, many words derived from main words, such as nouns ending in *-tion*, *-er*, or *-ness*, adjectives ending in *-like* or *-less*, and adverbs ending in *-ly* have been run in at the end of the entry for the base word. Such run-ins are syllabified and, where necessary, pronounced, and irregular inflected forms, if any, are shown. The meaning of any such run-in can easily be determined from the meanings of the base word and the suffix. Any derivative that has an important meaning not readily inferred from its separate parts is entered separately and defined.

Among the words whose spelling offers difficulty to many people are the principal parts of so-called irregular verbs, plurals that are formed in some way other than by adding *-s* or *-es*, and comparisons of adjectives that may or may not double the consonant before adding *-er* and *-est*. Rather than leave these forms to guesswork or to reliance on a number of rules to which many exceptions exist, we have shown them in full or in shortened form immediately after the appropriate part-of-speech label.

As a convenience to the user of this dictionary, all vocabulary entries, including proper names as of persons and places, abbreviations, affixes, and unnaturalized foreign terms frequently met up with in English contexts, have been entered in one alphabetical listing. There is no need to rummage among a number of appendixes in order to find lexical information of any sort. The pages following the dictionary proper have been restricted to useful nonlexical aids, such as tables of weights and measures and guides to punctuation, spelling, and the like.

The continuing popular interest in language resulted in our decision to include brief etymologies within these entries. The history of the origin and development of a word, in addition to satisfying the curiosity that many people have about the language they speak, can often help one to understand more clearly the current meaning of the word and to remember that meaning when the word is reencountered. Those who seek even more detailed etymologies, including the ultimate Indo-European roots from which most of our vocabulary derives, can find that information in the *Second College Edition* of WEBSTER'S NEW WORLD DICTIONARY.

The pronunciations recorded here are those that at the present time are most frequently used by cultivated speakers of the major dialects of the American language. Common variants are also shown, as well as native pronunciations of foreign words and proper names. Transcription is in a simple, easily read key that is nevertheless phonemically precise, and a short form of that key appears on every right-hand page of the dictionary text. A more detailed explanation will be found in the introductory Guide to the Dictionary and inside the front cover of this book.

Through the use of the latest technological advances in composition, this dictionary has been set by computer in modern type that is clear, attractive, and of the largest practicable size. To help the reader find more quickly the information he is seeking, various type faces are used for the different elements within the entry. More than 500 illustrations have been included where it was felt that a picture would help to expand or sharpen the definition. The actual sizes of animals have been given in feet or inches, and tools and instruments have been shown in use to make even clearer their function and relative size.

To help the user get the full benefit of the language information included in this dictionary, we have prepared a detailed *Guide to the Use of the Dictionary*, which appears on the following pages. You are urged to read it.

David B. Guralnik

# GUIDE TO THE USE OF THE DICTIONARY

## I. THE MAIN ENTRY WORD

### A. Arrangement of Entries

All main entries, including single words, hyphenated and unhyphenated compounds, proper names, prefixes, suffixes, and abbreviations, are listed in strict alphabetical order and are set in large, boldface type.

**black** (blak) *adj.* . . .
**black-and-blue** (-ən blōō′) *adj.* . . .
**black·ber·ry** (-ber′ē) *n.* . . .
**black flag** . . .
**Black Forest** . . .
**Black·pool** (blak′pōōl′) . . .
**-blast** (blast) . . .
**bldg.** . . .
**bleach** (blēch) *vt., vi.* . . .

Note that in the biographical entry only the last, or family, name (that part coming before the comma) has been considered in alphabetization. When two or more persons with the same family name are entered, they are dealt with in a single entry block, arranged in alphabetical order by first names. Biographical and geographical names that are identical in spelling are kept in separate blocks.

**Jack·son** (jak′s'n) [after A. JACKSON] capital of Miss., in the SW part: pop. 154,000
**Jack·son** (jak′s'n) **1. Andrew,** 1767–1845; 7th president of the U.S. (1829–37) **2. Thomas Jonathan,** (nickname *Stonewall Jackson*) 1824–63; Confederate general in the Civil War

Strict alphabetical order is followed for "Saint" and "St." when they appear as a part of proper names that are not the names of canonized persons.

**Saint Agnes's Eve**
**Saint Bernard** (dog)
**sainted**
**Saint-Gaudens, Augustus**
**stain**
**St. George's Channel**
**stick**
**St. John** (city)

Canonized persons are entered by their given names, which appear in the regular alphabetical listing. Thus **Augustine,** the saint, will be found in the A's, but **St. Augustine,** the city in Florida, will be found in the S's.

### B. Variant Spellings & Forms

When variant spellings of a word are some distance apart in alphabetical listing, the definition appears at the spelling most frequently used. Other spellings of the word are cross-referred to that spelling. Sometimes such a cross-reference indicates that the variant is British, dialectal, slang, obsolete, or the like.

**ae·on** . . . *n. same as* EON
**kerb** . . . *n. Brit. sp. of* CURB (*n.* 4)
**shew** . . . *n., vt., vi.* . . . *archaic sp. of* SHOW

If two variant spellings would appear close to each other in alphabetical order and are used with nearly equal frequency, they are placed together at the head of the entry. Neither spelling is considered to be "more correct," even though the one listed first may be used somewhat more often.

**the·a·ter, the·a·tre** . . . *n.* . . .

If a variant spelling is close in alphabetical order to the main-entry spelling and pronounced exactly like it but is used less often, such a spelling or spellings are given at the end of the entry block or pertinent definition.

**Az·er·bai·jan** . . . Also sp. **Azerbaidzhan, Azerbaydzhan**
**co·op·er·a·te, co-op·er·ate** . . . *vi.* . . . : also **co·öp′er·ate′**

When related words with the same meaning would appear in alphabetical order close to each other, the less frequently used word is placed at the end of the entry block or pertinent definition for the more common word.

**laud·a·to·ry** . . . *adj.* . . . : also **laud′a·tive**
**in·fu·so·ri·an** . . . *n.* . . . —*adj.* . . . : also **in′fu·so′ri·al**

### C. Cross-references

In all entries or senses that consist simply of a cross-reference to another entry having the same meaning, the entry cross-referred to is shown in small capitals.

**gay·e·ty** . . . *n.* . . . *same as* GAIETY
**ca·ble** . . . *n.* **1.** . . . **2.** . . . **3.** *same as* CABLE LENGTH
**aer·o·plane** . . . *n.* . . . *Brit. var. of* AIRPLANE
**chaunt** . . . *n., vt., vi. archaic var. of* CHANT
**lark·spur** . . . *n. a common name for* DELPHINIUM
**ma·jor·ette** . . . *n. short for* DRUM MAJORETTE
**re·pro** . . . *n. shortened form of* REPRODUCTION PROOF
**lib** . . . *n. clipped form of* LIBERATION

### D. Homographs

Main entries that are spelled exactly alike but are different in meaning and origin, as **bat** (a club), **bat** (the animal), and **bat** (to wink), are entered in separate blocks and are marked with small, raised numerals just after the boldface spellings.

**bat¹** . . . *n.* . . .
**bat²** . . . *n.* . . .
**bat³** . . . *vt.* . . .

Cross-references to such entries are identified by these small, raised numerals.

**Indian corn** *same as* CORN¹ (sense 2)

### E. Foreign Terms

Foreign words and phrases that appear fairly often in English speech and writing but are not yet felt as a part of the English vocabulary, are marked with a double dagger (‡) at the beginning of the entry. This mark indicates that such a term is usually printed in italic type.

**‡au na·tu·rel** . . . [Fr.] . . .

### F. Prefixes, Suffixes, & Combining Forms

Prefixes and combining forms used at the beginning of words are indicated in the dictionary by a hyphen placed after the entry form.

**re-** . . . *a prefix meaning:* **1.** back [*repay*] **2.** again, anew [*reappear*] . . .

Suffixes and combining forms used at the end of words are indicated in the dictionary by a hyphen placed before the entry form.

**-hood** . . . *a suffix meaning:* **1.** state, quality, condition [*childhood*] **2.** the whole group of (a specified class, profession, etc.) [*priesthood*]

Many such forms are entered here and make it possible for the reader to figure out the meaning of words that are made with these forms but that are not entered in the dictionary.

### G. Syllabification

Center dots in the entry words indicate where the words can be divided if they need to be broken at the end of a written or printed line. In actual copy, a hyphen is used in place of the center dot. For example, **car·niv·o·rous** can be broken at the end of a line in the following ways (*car-* or *carniv-* or *carnivo-*), depending on how much space is available.

If the stress given to the syllables of a word shifts when that word is used as another part of speech, the syllabification shown may properly apply only to the use of the word as the first part of speech given. In the case of a word such as *progress*, the writer may wish to change the syllabification from **prog·ress** when the noun is meant to **pro·gress** when the verb is meant; the pronunciation shown for the verb serves as a guide for this change.

All the syllables of a word are marked (for example, **might·y, a·ban·don**) although it is not customary in written or printed matter to break a word after the first syllable or before the last if that syllable consists of only a single letter or generally, in the case of a long word, of only two letters.

## II. PRONUNCIATION

### A. Introduction

The pronunciations recorded in this dictionary are for the most part those found in the normal, relaxed conversation of educated speakers. For some words, pronunciations that are dialectal, British, Canadian, etc. are given along with the usual American pronunciation.

**neph·ew** (nef′yoo; *chiefly Brit.* nev′-) . . .

### B. Key to Pronunciation

An abbreviated form of this key appears at the bottom of every right-hand page of the vocabulary.

| Symbol | Key Words | Symbol | Key Words |
|---|---|---|---|
| a | ask, fat, parrot | b | bed, fable, dub |
| ā | ape, date, play | d | dip, beadle, had |
| ä | ah. car, father | f | fall, after, off |
| | | g | get, haggle, dog |
| e | elf, ten, berry | h | he, ahead, hotel |
| ē | even, meet, money | j | joy, agile, badge |
| | | k | kill, tackle, bake |
| i | is, hit, mirror | l | let, yellow, ball |
| ī | ice, bite, high | m | met, camel, trim |
| | | n | not, flannel, ton |
| ō | open, tone, go | p | put, apple, tap |
| ô | all, horn, law | r | red, port, dear |
| o͞o | ooze, tool, crew | s | sell, castle, pass |
| o͝o | look, pull, moor | t | top, cattle, hat |
| yo͞o | use, cute, few | v | vat, hovel, have |
| yo͝o | united, cure, globule | w | will, always, swear |
| oi | oil, point, toy | y | yet, onion, yard |
| ou | out, crowd, plow | z | zebra, dazzle, haze |
| | | | |
| u | up, cut, color | ch | chin, catcher, arch |
| ʉr | urn, fur, deter | sh | she, cushion, dash |
| | | th | thin, nothing, truth |
| ə | a in ago | *th* | then, father, lathe |
| | e in agent | zh | azure, leisure |
| | i in sanity | ŋ | ring, anger, drink |
| | o in comply | ’ | [see explanatory note |
| | u in focus | | below and also *Foreign* |
| ər | perhaps, murder | | *sounds* below] |

The symbols in the key above can be easily understood from the key words in which they are shown, and a speaker of any dialect of American English will automatically read his own pronunciation into any symbol shown here. Explanatory notes on some of these symbols follow.

**ä** This symbol represents the vowel of *car*. Some words shown with **ä**, such as *alms* (ämz), *hot* (hät), *rod* (räd), etc., are heard in the speech of some persons with the vowel sound **ô** (ômz), (hôt), (rôd). Such variations may be assumed although they are not recorded in this dictionary.

**e** This symbol represents the vowel of *ten*. It is also used, followed by **r**, to represent the vowel sound of *care* (ker); for this sound, vowels ranging from **ā** (kār *or* kā′ər) to **a** (kar) are sometimes heard and may be assumed as variants although they are not recorded in this dictionary.

**ē** This symbol represents the vowel of *meet* and is also used for the vowel in the unstressed final syllable of such words as *lucky* (luk′ē), *pretty* (prit′ē), etc.

**i** This symbol represents the vowel of *hit* and is also used for the vowel in the unstressed syllables of such words as *garbage* (gär′bij), *goodness* (good′nis), *preface* (pref′is), *deny* (di nī′), *curate* (kyoor′it), etc. In such unstressed syllables, the schwa (ə) is often heard (gär′bəj), (good′nəs), etc. and may be assumed as a variant although not recorded in this dictionary. This symbol is also used, followed by **r**, to represent the vowel sound of *dear* (dir); for this sound, vowels ranging to ē (dēr *or* dē′ər) are sometimes heard and, although not here recorded, may be assumed as variants.

**ô** This symbol represents the vowel of *all*. When followed by **r**, as in *more* (môr), vowels ranging to ō (môr *or* mō′ər) are often heard and, although not here recorded, may be assumed as variants. In certain words shown with **ô**, such as *cough* (kôf), *lawn* (lôn), etc., vowel sounds ranging all the way to ä (käf), (län), etc. are heard and may be assumed as variants although not generally recorded in this dictionary.

**ʉr** and **ər** These two symbols represent, in order, the stressed and the unstressed r-colored vowels heard in the two syllables of *murder* (mʉr′dər). Where these symbols are shown, some speakers, especially in the South and along the Eastern seaboard, will "drop their *r*'s" in pronouncing them.

**ə** This symbol, called the schwa, represents the neutral vowel heard in the unstressed syllables of *ago*, *agent*, *focus*, etc. In many words, such as *colitis*, this vowel is sometimes heard as **i** (kō līt′is).

**ŋ** This symbol represents the nasal sound indicated in spelling by the *ng* of *sing* and occurring also for **n** before the consonants **k** and **g**, as in *drink* (driŋk) and *finger* (fiŋ′gər).

**’** The apostrophe occurring before **l**, **m**, and **n** indicates that the following consonant is a syllabic consonant, with little or no vowel sound accompanying it, as in *apple* (ap′′l) or *happen* (hap′′n). Some persons pronounce such words with a vowel sound close to the schwa (ə), as in *happen* (hap′ən), but such variants are not entered in this dictionary.

### Foreign Sounds

Most of the symbols in the key above have been used to transcribe pronunciations in foreign languages, although it should be understood that these sounds will vary somewhat from language to language. The additional symbols below will cover those situations that cannot be adequately dealt with using the general key.

**à** This symbol, representing the *a* in French *bal* (bàl) can best be described as intermediate between (a) and (ä).

**ë** This symbol represents the sound of the vowel cluster in French *coeur* (kër) and can be approximated by rounding the lips as for (ô) and pronouncing (e).

**ö** This symbol variously represents the sound of *eu* in French *feu* (fö) or of *ö* (or *oe*) in German *Göthe* (or *Goethe*) (gö′tə) and can be approximated by rounding the lips as for (ō) and pronouncing (ā).

**ô** This symbol represents a range of sounds varying from (ō) to (ô) and heard with such varying quality in French *coq* (kôk), German *doch* (dôkh), Italian *poco* (pô′kô), Spanish *torero* (tô re′rô), etc.

**ü** This symbol variously represents the sound of *u* in French *duc* (dük) and in German *grün* (grün) and can be approximated by rounding the lips as for (o͞o) and pronouncing (ē).

**kh** This symbol represents the sound heard in German *doch* (dôkh). It can be approximated by arranging the speech organs as for (k) but allowing the breath to escape in a stream, as in pronouncing (h).

**H** This symbol represents a sound similar to the preceding but formed by friction against the forward part of the palate, as in German *ich* (iH). It is sometimes misheard, and hence pronounced, by English speakers as (sh).

**n** This symbol indicates that the vowel sound immediately preceding it is nasalized; that is, the nasal passage is left open so that the breath passes through both the mouth and nose in voicing the vowel, as in French *mon* (mōn).

**r** This symbol represents any of various sounds used in languages other than English for the consonant *r*. It may represent the tongue-point trill or uvular trill of the *r* in French *reste* (rest) or *sur* (sür), German *Reuter* (roi′tər), Italian *ricotta* (rē kôt′tä), Russian *gorod* (gô′rôd), etc.

**’** The apostrophe is used after final *l* and *r*, in certain French pronunciations, to indicate that they are voiceless after an unvoiced consonant, as in *lettre* (let′r′). In Russian words the "soft sign" in the Cyrillic spelling is indicated by (y′). The sound can be approximated by pronouncing an unvoiced (y) directly after the consonant involved, as in *Sevastopol* (se′väs tô′pəl y′).

### C. General Styling of Pronunciation

Pronunciations are given inside parentheses, immediately following the boldface entry. A single space is used between syllables. A primary, or strong, stress is indicated by a heavy stroke (′) immediately following the syllable so stressed. A secondary, or weak, stress is indicated by a lighter stroke (′) following the syllable so stressed. All notes, labels, or other matter inside the parentheses are in italics.

### D. Truncation

Variant pronunciations are truncated wherever possible, with only that syllable or those syllables in which change occurs shown. A hyphen after the truncated variant shows that it is the beginning of the word; one before the variant, that it is the end; and hyphens before and after the variant, that it is within the word.

**ac·cept** (ək sept′, ak-) . . .
**rec·ti·tude** (rek′tə tood′, -tyood′) . . .
**fu·tu·ri·ty** (fyoo toor′ə tē, -tyoor′-, -choor′-) . . .

Truncations of variant pronunciations involving different parts of speech in the same entry block appear as follows:

**pre·cip·i·tate** (pri sip′ə tāt′; *also, for adj. & n.*, -tit) . . .

Truncated pronunciations are also given for a series of words having the same first part, after the pronunciation of this first part has been established.

**le·git·i·ma·tize** (lə jit′ə mə tīz′) . . .
**le·git·i·mist** (-mist) . . .
**le·git·i·mize** (-mīz′) . . .

Similarly, with a series made up of compounds and derived forms:

**time-hon·ored** (tīm′än′ərd) . . .
**time-keep·er** (-kē′pər) . . .
**time-lapse** (-laps′) . . .
**time·less** (-lis) . . .
**time loan** . . .
**time·ly** (-lē) . . .

Full pronunciations are given with words in a series of the following kind when the stress in the first part is changed in some way.

**bi·o·as·tro·nau·tics** (bī′ō as′trə nô′tiks) . . .
**bi·o·chem·is·try** (-kem′is trē) . . .
**bi·o·cide** (bī′ə sīd′) . . .
**bi·o·de·grad·a·ble** (bī′ō di grā′də b'l) . . .
**bi·o·en·gi·neer·ing** (-en′jə nir′iŋ) . . .

### E. Variants

Where two or more pronunciations for a single word are given, the order in which they are entered does not necessarily mean that the first is preferred or is more correct. In most cases, the order indicates that on the basis of available information, the form given first is the one more frequent in general cultivated use. Unless a variant is qualified, as by *now rarely* or *occasionally* or some such note, it is understood that any pronunciation here entered represents a standard use.

## III. PART-OF-SPEECH LABELS

Part-of-speech labels are given for lower-case main entries that are solid or hyphenated forms, except for prefixes, suffixes, and abbreviations. The following labels for the parts of speech into which words are classified in traditional English grammar are used in this dictionary. They appear in boldface italic type following the pronunciations.

| | | | |
|---|---|---|---|
| *n.* | noun | *prep.* | preposition |
| *vt.* | transitive verb | *conj.* | conjunction |
| *vi.* | intransitive verb | *pron.* | pronoun |
| *adj.* | adjective | *interj.* | interjection |
| *adv.* | adverb | | |

In addition, the following labels are sometimes used:

| | |
|---|---|
| *n.pl.* | plural noun |
| *v.aux.* | auxiliary verb |
| *v.impersonal* | impersonal verb |
| *n.fem.* | feminine noun |
| *n.masc.* | masculine noun |

When an entry word is used as more than one part of speech, long dashes introduce each different part of speech in the entry block and each part-of-speech label appears in boldface italic type.

**round¹** . . . *adj.* . . . —*n.* . . . —*vt.* . . . —*vi.* . . . —*adv.* . . . — *prep.* . . .

Two or more part-of-speech labels are given jointly for an entry when the definition or definitions, or the cross-reference, will suffice for both or all.

**lip-read** . . . *vt., vi.* . . . to recognize (a speaker's words) by lip reading . . .
**hal·lo, hal·loa** . . . *interj., n., vi., vt. same as* HALLOO

Part-of-speech labels are not used for names of persons and places, or for given names, figures in religion, mythology, literature, etc. However, usages have sometimes developed from these that can be classified as parts of speech and these are indicated.

**A·don·is** . . . *Gr. Myth.* a young man loved by Aphrodite —*n.* any very handsome young man . . .

It is theoretically possible to use almost any word as whatever part of speech is required. Thus any transitive verb can be used absolutely as an intransitive verb, with the object understood ("Shall I *use* this lotion?" "Yes, but *use* sparingly.") Such absolute uses are entered only when they are relatively common. In the same way nouns used as adjectives (a *cloth* cover; a *family* affair) are indicated only for the most frequent uses.

## IV. INFLECTED FORMS

Inflected forms regarded as irregular or offering difficulty in spelling are entered in small boldface immediately following the part-of-speech labels. They are truncated where possible, and syllabified and pronounced where necessary.

### A. Plurals of Nouns

Plurals formed regularly by adding -*s* to the singular (or -*es* after *s, x, z, ch*, and *sh*), as *bats, boxes*, are not normally indicated.

Plurals are shown when formed irregularly, as for nouns with a -*y* ending that changes to -*ies*, and for those with an -*o* ending, those inflected by some change within the word, those having variant forms, those having different forms for different meanings, compound nouns, etc.

**cit·y** . . . *n., pl.* **cit′ies** . . .
**bo·le·ro** . . . *n., pl.* **-ros** . . .
**tooth** . . . *n., pl.* **teeth** (tēth) . . .
**a moo ba** *n. pl.* **-has, -bae** (-bē) . . .
**die²** . . . *n., pl.*, for 1 **dice** (dīs); for 2 **dies** (dīz) . . .
**son-in-law** . . . *n., pl.* **sons′-in-law′** . . .

If an irregular plural is so altered in spelling that it would appear at some distance from the singular form, it is entered additionally in its proper alphabetical place.

**lice** . . . *n. pl. of* LOUSE

### B. Principal Parts

Verb forms regarded as regular and not normally indicated include:

*a)* present tenses formed by adding -*s* to the infinitive (or -*es* after *s, x, z, ch*, and *sh*), as *waits, searches;*

*b)* past tenses and past participles formed by simply adding -*ed* to the infinitive with no other changes in the verb form, as *waited, searched;*

*c)* present participles formed by simply adding -*ing* to the infinitive with no other change in the verb form, as *waiting, searching.*

Principal parts are given for irregular verbs, including those in which the final *e* is dropped in forming the present participle.

Where two inflected forms are given for a verb, the first is the form for the past tense and the past participle, and the second is the form for the present participle.

**make** . . . *vt.* **made, mak′ing** . . .
**sip** . . . *vt., vi.* **sipped, sip′ping** . . .

Where three forms are given, separated from one another by commas, the first represents the past tense, the second the past participle, and the third the present participle.

**swim** . . . *vi.* **swam, swum, swim′ming** . . .

Where there are alternative forms for any of the principal parts, these are indicated as follows:

**trav·el** . . . *vi.* **-eled** or **-elled, -el·ing** or **el·ling**
**drink** . . . *vt.* **drank** or archaic **drunk, drunk** or now colloq. **drank** or archaic **drunk′en, drink′ing** . . .

If a principal part of a verb is so altered in spelling that it would appear at some distance from the infinitive form, it is entered additionally in its proper alphabetical place.

**said** . . . *pt. & pp. of* SAY

### C. Comparatives & Superlatives of Adjectives & Adverbs

Comparatives and superlatives formed by simply adding -*er* or -*est* to the base, as *taller, tallest*, are not indicated.

Those formed irregularly, as by adding *-r* and *-st* (*rare, rarer, rarest*), by changing final *-y* to *-i-* (*happy, happier, happiest*), or by some radical change in form (*good, better, best* or *well, better, best*), are indicated with the positive form.

The positive form is also noted at the comparative and superlative forms when these are entered and defined at some distance from it.

**best** ... *adj. superl. of* GOOD ... —*adv. superl. of* WELL² ...

## V. THE ETYMOLOGY

Brief etymologies, or little histories of the words in this dictionary have been included so that they may help the user to a clearer understanding of the current meanings of these words. The etymology will be found immediately before the definition, set off in heavy brackets. The symbols, as < for "derived from," and the abbreviations of language labels, etc. used in the etymologies are dealt with in full in the list of Abbreviations and Symbols immediately preceding page 1 of the vocabulary.

**ex·er·cise** (ek′sər sīz′) *n.* [< OFr. < L. < pp. of *exercere*, to drive out (farm animals to work) < *ex-*, out + *arcere*, to enclose] **1.** active use or operation ...
**es·cape** (ə skāp′, e-) *vi.* **-caped′, -cap′ing** [< ONormFr. < L. *ex-*, out of + *cappa*, cloak (i.e., leave one's cloak)] **1.** to get free; get away ...

For some words etymologies are shown by means of cross-references (in small capitals) to the elements of which they are formed and which are dealt with separately in the dictionary.

**en·dog·a·my** (en däg′ə mē) *n.* [ENDO- + -GAMY] **1.** the custom of marrying only within one's own tribe, clan, etc.; inbreeding ...
**ra·don** (rā′dän) *n.* [RAD(IUM) + -ON] a radioactive gaseous chemical element ...

No etymology is shown where one is not needed, as because the elements making up the word are immediately apparent to the user (**precondition**) or because the definition that follows clearly explains the derivation (see **bluebottle**).

Where no etymology is known for certain, that fact is indicated by the following: [< ?]

A special effort has been made to include as many etymologies as possible for place names in the United States.

## VI. THE DEFINITIONS

### A. Order of Senses

The definitions, or senses, of a longer entry have been arranged in an order which shows how the word has developed from its etymology and its earliest meanings and how the meanings of the word are related to one another. Senses that need to be labeled as colloquial, slang, archaic, obsolete, or the like are given after the general senses. Next, any technical senses are given, arranged in alphabetical order according to their special field labels. Sometimes an obsolete sense may be given first, preceded by "originally" (abbreviated "orig.") or "formerly," to serve as a link between the etymology and the current senses.

### B. Numbering & Grouping of Senses

Senses are numbered consecutively within any given part of speech in boldface numerals. A new series of numerals is used for each new part of speech and for each idiomatic phrase.

**tap²** ... *n.* **1.** ... **2.** ... **3.** ... —*vt.* **1.** ... **2.** ... **3.** ... —**on tap 1.** ... **2.** ...

Where a primary sense of a word can easily be subdivided into several closely related meanings, this has been done; such meanings are indicated by italicized letters after the pertinent numbered or labeled sense. The words "especially" or "specifically" (abbreviated "esp." and "specif.") are often used after an introductory definition to introduce such a grouping of related senses.

**bind·er** ... *n.* **1.** a person who binds; specif., a bookbinder **2.** a thing that binds; specif., *a)* a band, cord, etc. *b)* a substance, as tar, that binds things together *c)* a detachable cover for holding sheets of paper together **3.** a device attached to a reaper ...

### C. Capitalization

If a main-entry word is capitalized in all its senses, the entry word itself is printed with a capital letter.

**Eur·a·sian** (-zhən; *chiefly Brit.* -shən) *adj.* **1.** of Eurasia **2.** of mixed European and Asian descent —*n.* a person with one European parent and one Asian parent ...

If a capitalized main-entry word has a sense or senses that are uncapitalized, these are marked with the corresponding lower-case letter enclosed in brackets, sometimes with a qualifying word, such as "usually," "often," "also," etc.

**Pur·i·tan** ... *n.* ... **1.** ... **2.** [p-] ... —*adj.* **1.** ... **2.** [p-] ...

If a lower-case main-entry word has a sense or senses that are capitalized, these are marked with the corresponding upper-case letter enclosed in brackets, sometimes with a qualifying word, such as "usually," "often," "also," etc.

**north** ... *n.* ... **1.** ... **2.** ... **3.** [*often* N-] ... —*adj.* **1.** ... **2.** ... **3.** [N-] ...

### D. Plural Forms

The designation "[*pl.*]" (or "[*often pl.*]," "[*usually pl.*]," etc.) before a definition indicates that it is the plural form of the entry word (or *often* or *usually* the plural form) that has the meaning given in the definition.

**lim·it** ... *n.* ... **1.** ... **2.** [*pl.*] bounds ...
**look** ... *vi.* ... —*n.* **1.** ... **2.** ... **3.** [Colloq.] *a)* [*usually pl.*] appearance ... *b)* [*pl.*] personal appearance, esp. of a pleasing nature ...

If such a plural sense is construed as singular, the designation "*with sing. v.*" is added inside the brackets.

**bone** ... *n.* ... **6.** [*pl.*] *a)* flat sticks used as clappers in minstrel shows *b)* [*with sing. v.*] the end man in a minstrel show ...

The note "*usually used in pl.*" at the end of a singular noun definition means that although the definition applies to the given singular form of the entry word, the word is usually used in the plural and with a plural meaning.

**ex·trem·i·ty** (ik strem′ə tē) *n.*, *pl.* **-ties** ... **5.** an extreme measure; strong action: *usually used in pl.* ...

If a plural noun entry is construed as singular, the designation "[*with sing. v.*]" is placed after the *n.pl.* label or, in some cases, with the numbered sense to which it applies.

**ger·i·at·rics** ... *n.pl.* [*with sing. v.*] ... the branch of medicine that deals with the diseases and hygiene of old age ...
**a·cous·tics** ... *n.pl.* **1.** the qualities of a room, etc. that have to do with how clearly sounds can be heard in it **2.** [*with sing. v.*] the branch of physics dealing with sound

### E. Prepositions Accompanying Verbs

Where certain verbs are, in usage, always or usually followed by a specific preposition or prepositions, this has been indicated in the following ways: the preposition has been worked into the definition, italicized and enclosed in parentheses, or a note has been added in parentheses indicating that the preposition is so used.

**strike** ... —*vi.* ... **9.** to come suddenly (*on* or *upon*) [*we struck on an idea*] ... **16.** *U.S. Navy* to be in training (*for a specified rating*) ...
**hit** ... —*vi.* ... **4.** to come by accident or after search (with *on* or *upon*) ...

*Note:* Such uses of verbs with specific prepositions should not be confused with verb sets consisting of a verb form with an adverb, which are entered as idiomatic phrases under the key verb (**make out, make over,** and **make up** at the entry **make**).

### F. Objects of Transitive Verbs

In definitions of transitive verbs the specific or generalized objects of the verb, where given, are enclosed in parentheses since such objects are not part of the definition.

**ob·serve** ... *vt.* ... **1.** to adhere to or keep (a law, custom, duty, etc.) **2.** to celebrate (a holiday, etc.) according to custom **3.** *a)* to notice or perceive (something) *b)* to pay special attention to ...

In some cases the transitive verb can be defined jointly with the intransitive verb.

**chis·el** ... —*vi., vt.* ... **1.** to cut or shape with a chisel ...

### G. Additional Information & Notes

Additional information or any note or comment on the definition proper is preceded by a colon.

**Cau·ca·soid** ... *adj.* ... designating or of one of the major groups of mankind that includes the native peoples of Europe, North Africa, the Near East, India, etc.: loosely called the *white race*, although skin color varies ...
**ma·ture** ... *adj.* ... **4.** due: said of a note, bond, etc. ...
**mil·li·gram** ... *n.* ...: also, chiefly Brit. sp., **mil′·li·gramme′**

If the note or comment applies to all the senses or parts of speech preceding it, it begins with a capital letter and no colon introduces it.

**rest**[2] ... *n.* ... **1.** what is left; remainder **2.** [*with pl. v.*] the others Used with *the* ...

### H. Illustrative Examples of Entry Words in Context

Examples of a word in use have been given where such examples help make the meaning clearer or show more exactly the differences in meaning among the different senses. Such examples of usage are enclosed in slanted brackets, and the word being defined is set in italics.

**spir·it** ... *n.* ... **5.** an individual person or personality [*a brave* spirit] **6.** [*usually pl.*] disposition; mood [*high* spirits] **7.** vivacity, courage, enthusiasm, etc. **8.** enthusiasm and loyalty [*school* spirit] **9.** real meaning; true intention [*to follow the* spirit *if not the letter of the law*] **10.** an essential quality or prevailing tendency [*the* spirit *of the Renaissance*] **11.** ...

### I. Cross-references

Entry words (or tables, illustrations, etc.) to which the reader is being cross-referred are given in small capitals.

**cap·i·tal**[1] ... —*n.* ... **8.** ...: distinguished from LABOR
**ca·tab·o·lism** ... *n.* ...: opposed to ANABOLISM
**civil disobedience** ... : see also NONCOOPERATION, PASSIVE RESISTANCE
**clause** ... *n.* ... **1.** ...: cf. MAIN CLAUSE, SUBORDINATE CLAUSE **2.** ...
**ev·o·lu·tion** ... *n.* ... **5.** ...: see DARWINIAN THEORY
**Gem·i·ni** ... : see ZODIAC, illus.
**Holy Land** *same as* PALESTINE (sense 1)
**sol**[1] ... *n.* ... *see* MONETARY UNITS, table (Peru)

## VII. USAGE LABELS & NOTES

It is generally understood that usage varies among groups of people according to locality, level of education, social environment, occupation, etc. More specifically, usage can vary in the speech of any person depending upon the particular situation in which he is involved and the purpose his language must serve. The language that a scientist uses in preparing a report on his work may be quite different from the language he uses in writing a letter to a friend. What is good usage in a literary essay may not be the best usage in the lyrics to a popular song or in casual conversation. Certain occasions call for language that is more or less formal, and others, language that is more or less informal.

Dictionaries can reasonably be expected to assign usage labels, as, for example, to those terms that the record shows are regularly used in informal or highly informal contexts. The conventional usage labels are so well known that they can be used if their meaning is clearly understood in advance. The labels, and what they are intended to indicate, are given below. If the label, which is placed in brackets (and in some cases abbreviated), occurs directly after a part-of-speech label or after a boldface entry term, it applies to all senses given with that part of speech or that term; if it occurs after a numeral or letter, it applies only to the sense so numbered or lettered.

Colloquial: The term or sense is generally characteristic of conversation and informal writing. It is not to be regarded as substandard or illiterate.
Slang: The term or sense is not generally regarded as conventional or standard usage but is used, even by the best speakers, in highly informal contexts. Slang consists of both coined terms and of new or extended meanings at-tached to established terms. Slang terms tend either to pass into disuse in time or to move toward standard usage.
Obsolete: The term or sense is no longer used but occurs in earlier writings.
Archaic: The term or sense is rarely used today except in certain restricted contexts, as in church ritual, but occurs in earlier writings.
Poetic: The term or sense is used chiefly in poetry, especially in earlier poetry, or in prose where a poetic quality is desired.
Dialect: The term or sense is used regularly only in some geographical areas or in a certain designated area (*South, Southwest, West*, etc.) of the United States.
British (or Canadian, Scottish, etc.): The term or sense is characteristic of British (or Canadian, etc.) English rather than of that spoken in the United States. When preceded by *chiefly*, the label indicates an additional, though less frequent, American usage. *British dialect* indicates that the term or sense is used regularly only in certain geographical areas of Great Britain, usually in northern England.

In addition to the above usage labels, additional information is often given after the definition, indicating whether the term or sense is generally regarded as vulgar, substandard, or derogatory, or used for ironic, familiar, or exaggerated effect, etc. Where there are some objections to common usages, that fact is also indicated (for example, **who, whom**).

## VIII. FIELD LABELS

Labels for specialized fields of knowledge and activity appear in italics (in abbreviated form where practical) immediately before the sense involved. In long entry blocks having many general and specialized senses, these labels, arranged in alphabetical order, help the user to quickly find the special sense or senses he is seeking.

**base**[1] ... *n.* ... **8.** *Chem.* ... **9.** *Geom.* ... **10.** *Linguis.* ... **11.** *Math.* ...

## IX. IDIOMATIC PHRASES

Idiomatic phrases are run in on an entry block in alphabetical order after the definition or definitions of the main-entry word. The entry for each phrase is set in small boldface with a dash preceding it. Such phrases have been entered wherever possible under the key word.

**busi·ness** ... *n.* ... —**business is business** ... —**do business with** ... —**give** (or **get**) **the business** ... —**mean business** ...

Alternative forms are indicated inside parentheses, as above in **give** (or **get**) **the business.** In the phrase **(at) full tilt** under the entry **tilt,** both the longer phrase, **at full tilt,** and the shorter, **full tilt,** are being recorded.

## X. RUN-IN DERIVED ENTRIES

It is possible in English to form an almost infinite number of derived forms simply by adding certain prefixes or suffixes to the base word. This dictionary includes as run-in entries in small boldface type only those words one might reasonably expect to meet up with in literature or ordinary usage, and then only when the meaning of such derived words can be immediately understood from the meanings of the base word and the affix. Thus, **greatness, liveliness,** and **newness** are run in at the end of the entries for **great, lively,** and **new,** the meanings of the derived forms being clearly understood from the base word and the suffix **-ness,** which is found as a separate entry in this dictionary and means "state, quality, or instance of being." Many words formed with common suffixes such as **-able, -er, -less, -like, -ly, -tion,** etc. are similarly treated as run-in entries with the base word from which they are derived. All such entries are syllabified and either accented to show stress in pronunciation or, where necessary, pronounced in full or in part. Each run-in derived form is preceded by a dash.

If two run-in derived forms have the same meaning and share a part-of-speech label, the more frequently used form appears first and the part-of-speech label is given after the second form. Note the plural form following the first run-in:

**prac·ti·cal** ... *adj.* ... —**prac′ti·cal′i·ty** (-kal′ə tē), *pl.* **-ties, prac′ti·cal·ness** *n.*

When a derived word has a meaning or meanings different from those which can be deduced from the sum of its parts, it has been entered in a block of its own, pronounced, and fully defined (for example, **producer**).

# ABBREVIATIONS AND SYMBOLS USED IN THIS DICTIONARY

abbrev. abbreviated; abbreviation
abl. ablative
acc. accusative
adj. adjective
adv. adverb
Aeron. Aeronautics
Afr. African
Afrik. Afrikaans
alt. alternative
Am. American
AmFr. American French
AmInd. American Indian
AmSp. American Spanish
Anat. Anatomy
Anglo-Fr. Anglo-French
Anglo-Ind. Anglo-Indian
Anglo-Ir. Anglo-Irish
Anglo-L. Anglo-Latin
Anglo-N. Anglo-Norse
Anglo-Norm. Anglo-Norman
Ar. Arabic
Aram. Aramaic
Archaeol. Archaeology
Archit. Architecture
Arith. Arithmetic
Arm. Armenian
art. article
assoc. associated
Assyr. Assyrian
Astrol. Astrology
Astron. Astronomy
at. no. atomic number
at. wt. atomic weight
Bab. Babylonian
Beng. Bengali
Biochem. Biochemistry
Biol. Biology
Bohem. Bohemian
Bot. Botany
Braz. Brazilian
Bret. Breton
Brit. British
Bulg. Bulgarian
C Celsius; Central
c. century (in etym.); circa
Canad. Canadian
CanadFr. Canadian French
cap. capital
Celt. Celtic
cent. century; centuries
cf. compare
Ch. Chaldean; Church
Chem. Chemistry
Chin. Chinese
Chr. Chronicles
Col. Colossians
comp. compound
compar. comparative
conj. conjunction
contr. contracted; contraction
Cop. Coptic
Cor. Corinthians
Corn. Cornish
cu. cubic
Cym. Cymric
Dan. Daniel; Danish
dat. dative
deriv. derivative
Deut. Deuteronomy
Dial., dial. dialectal
dim. diminutive
Du. Dutch
E East; eastern
E. East; English (in etym. & pronun.
Early ModDu. Early modern Dutch
Early ModG. Early modern German
EC east central
Eccl. Ecclesiastes
Eccles. Ecclesiastical
Ecol. Ecology
Econ. Economics

Educ. Education
e.g. for example
Egypt. Egyptian
Elec. Electricity
Eng. English
Eph. Ephesians
equiv. equivalent
Esk. Eskimo
esp. especially
est. estimated
Esth. Esther
Eth. Ethiopic
etym. etymology
Ex. example; Exodus
exc. except
Ezek. Ezekiel
F Farenheit
fem. feminine
ff. following (entry, sense, etc.)
fig. figurative; figuratively
Finn. Finnish
Fl. Flemish
fl. flourished
Fr. French
Frank. Frankish
freq. frequentative
Fris. Frisian
ft. feet
fut. future
G. German (in etym. & pronun.)
Gael. Gaelic
Gal. Galatians
gal. gallon; gallons
Gaul. Gaulish
Gen. Genesis
gen. genitive
Geog. Geography
Geol. Geology
Geom. Geometry
Ger. German
ger. gerund
Gmc. Germanic
Goth. Gothic
Gr. Greek
Gram. Grammar
Hab. Habakkuk
Hag. Haggai
Haw. Hawaiian
Heb. Hebrew; Hebrews
Hort. Horticulture
Hos. Hosea
Hung. Hungarian
hyp. hypothetical
Ice. Icelandic
i.e. that is
imper. imperative
imperf. imperfect
in. inch; inches
incl. including
Ind. Indian
indic. indicative
inf. infinitive
infl. influenced
intens. intensive
interj. interjection
Ir. Irish
Iran. Iranian
IrGael. Irish Gaelic
irreg. irregular
Isa. Isaiah
It. Italian
Jap. Japanese
Jas. James
Jer. Jeremiah
Josh. Joshua
Judg. Judges
KJV King James Version
L Late
L. Latin
Lam. Lamentations
lb. pound

# Abbreviations and Symbols

**Lev.** Leviticus
**LGr.** Late Greek
**Linguis.** Linguistics
**lit.** literally
**Lith.** Lithuanian
**LL.** Late Latin
**LME.** Late Middle English
**LXX** Septuagint
**M** Middle; Medieval
**Mal.** Malachi
**Math.** Mathematics
**Matt.** Matthew
**MDu.** Middle Dutch
**ME.** Middle English
**Mech.** Mechanics
**Med.** Medicine; Medieval
**met.** metropolitan
**Meteorol.** Meteorology
**Mex.** Mexican
**MexSp.** Mexican Spanish
**MFr.** Middle French
**MGr.** Medieval Greek
**MHG.** Middle High German
**mi.** mile; miles
**Mic.** Micah
**Mil.** Military
**ML.** Medieval Latin
**MLowG.** Middle Low German
**Mod, Mod.** Modern
**ModE.** Modern English
**ModGr.** Modern Greek
**ModHeb.** Modern Hebrew
**ModL.** Modern Latin
**Mongol.** Mongolic
**Myth.** Mythology
**N** North; northern
**N.** North
**n.** noun
**Nah.** Nahum
**Naut., naut.** nautical usage
**NC** north central
**NE** northeastern
**Neh.** Nehemiah
**neut.** neuter
**n.fem.** feminine form of noun
**n.masc.** masculine form of noun
**nom.** nominative
**Norm, Norm.** Norman
**Norw.** Norwegian
**n.pl.** plural form of noun
**n.sing.** singular form of noun
**N.T.** New Testament
**Num.** Numbers
**NW** northwestern
**O** Old
**Ob.** Obadiah
**Obs, obs.** obsolete
**occas.** occasionally
**OE.** Old English
**OFr.** Old French
**OHG.** Old High German
**OIr.** Old Irish
**OIt.** Old Italian
**OL.** Old Latin
**ON.** Old Norse
**ONormFr.** Old Norman French
**orig.** origin; originally
**OS.** Old Saxon
**O.T.** Old Testament
**oz.** ounce
**P** Primitive
**p.** page
**part.** participle
**pass.** passive
**Per.** Persian
**perf.** perfect
**pers.** person
**Peruv.** Peruvian
**Pet.** Peter
**Phil.** Philippians
**Philem.** Philemon
**Philos.** Philosophy
**Phoen.** Phoenician
**Phonet.** Phonetics
**Photog.** Photography
**phr.** phrase
**Phys. Ed.** Physical Education
**Physiol.** Physiology
**PidE.** Pidgin English
**pl.** plural
**Poet.** Poetic
**Pol.** Polish

**pop.** popular; population
**Port.** Portuguese
**poss.** possessive
**pp.** pages; past participle
**Pr.** Provençal
**prec.** preceding
**prep.** preposition
**pres.** present
**prin. pts.** principal parts
**prob.** probably
**pron.** pronoun
**pronun.** pronunciation
**Prov.** Proverbs; Provincial
**prp.** present participle
**Ps.** Psalms
**pseud.** pseudonym
**Psychol.** Psychology
**pt.** past tense
**qt.** quart; quarts
**R.C.Ch.** Roman Catholic Church
**redupl.** reduplication
**refl.** reflexive
**Rev.** Revelation
**Rom.** Roman; Romans
**R.S.F.S.R.** Russian Soviet Federated Socialist Republic
**RSV** Revised Standard Version
**Russ.** Russian
**S** South; southern
**S.** South
**Sam.** Samuel
**Sans.** Sanskrit
**SC** south central
**Scand.** Scandinavian
**Scot, Scot.** Scottish
**ScotGael.** Scottish Gaelic
**SE** southeastern
**Sem.** Semitic
**Serb.** Serbian
**sing.** singular
**Sinh.** Sinhalese
**Slav.** Slavic
**S. of Sol.** Song of Solomon
**Sp.** Spanish
**sp.** spelled; spelling
**specif.** specifically
**sq.** square
**S.S.R.** Soviet Socialist Republic
**subj.** subjunctive
**superl.** superlative
**SW** southwestern
**Sw.** Swedish (in etym. & pronun.)
**Swed.** Swedish
**Syr.** Syriac
**Tag.** Tagalog
**Theol.** Theology
**Thess.** Thessalonians
**Tim.** Timothy
**Tit.** Titus
**transl.** translation
**Turk.** Turkish
**TV** television
**ult.** ultimately
**UN** United Nations
**U.S.** United States
**U.S.S.R.** Union of Soviet Socialist Republics
**v.** verb
**var.** variant; variety
**v.aux.** auxiliary verb
**Vet.** Veterinary Medicine
**vi.** intransitive verb
**VL.** Vulgar Latin
**voc.** vocative
**vt.** transitive verb
**Vulg.** Vulgate
**W** West; western
**W.** Welsh; West
**WAfr.** West African
**WC** west central
**WGmc.** West Germanic
**WInd.** West Indian
**yd.** yard; yards
**Yid.** Yiddish
**Zech.** Zechariah
**Zeph.** Zephaniah
**Zool.** Zoology

‡ foreign word or phrase
\* hypothetical
+ plus
< derived from
? uncertain; possibly; perhaps
& and

# A

**A, a** (ā) *n., pl.* **A's, a's** **1.** the first letter of the English alphabet **2.** a sound of *A* or *a* **3.** *a symbol for* the first in a sequence or group

**A** (ā) *n.* **1.** *Educ.* a grade indicating excellence **2.** *Music* a) the sixth tone in the ascending scale of C major b) the scale having A as the keynote —*adj.* shaped like *A*

**a** (ə; *stressed* ā) *adj., indefinite article* [form of AN¹] **1.** one; one sort of **2.** each; any one *A* connotes a thing not previously noted or recognized; *the,* a thing previously noted or recognized **3.** [orig. a prep. < OE. *an,* in, on, at] to each; in each; per [*once a day*] Before words beginning with a consonant sound or a sounded *h, a* is used [*a child, a home, a uniform*]; before words beginning with a vowel sound or a silent *h, an* is used [*an eye, an ultimatum, an honor*]

**a-¹** [weakened form of OE. *an, on,* in, on, at] *a prefix meaning:* **1.** in, into, on, at, to [*abed, ashore*] **2.** in the act or state of [*asleep*]

**a-²** *a prefix of various origins and meanings:* **1.** [OE. *a-,* out of, up] up, out: now generally an intensive [*awake, arise*] **2.** [OE. *of-, af-*] off, of [*akin*] **3.** [Gr. *a-, an-,* not] not, without [*atypical*]: before vowels *an-* is used [*anastigmatic*]

**A.** **1.** Absolute **2.** angstrom

**a.** **1.** about **2.** acre(s) **3.** adjective **4.** alto **5.** ampere **6.** anode **7.** anonymous **8.** answer

**AA, A.A.** **1.** Alcoholics Anonymous **2.** antiaircraft

**AAA, A.A.A.** American Automobile Association

**Aa·chen** (ä′kən; *G.* ä′khən) city in W West Germany, on the Belgian border: pop. 177,000

**aard·vark** (ärd′värk′) *n.* [obs. Afrik., earth pig] a burrowing African mammal that feeds on ants and termites: it has a long snout

**aard·wolf** (-wŏŏlf′) *n., pl.* **-wolves′** (-wŏŏlvz′) [Afrik., earth wolf] a mammal of S and E Africa resembling the hyena but feeding chiefly on termites and insect larvae

**Aar·on** (er′ən) [LL. < Gr. < Heb. *aharōn,* lit., the exalted one] **1.** a masculine name **2.** *Bible* the older brother of Moses and first high priest of the Hebrews

AARDVARK
(c. 2 ft. high at shoulder)

**Ab** (äb; *Heb.* äv) *n.* [Heb.] the eleventh month of the Jewish year: see JEWISH CALENDAR

**ab-** [L.] *a prefix meaning* away, from, from off, down [*abdicate*]: shortened to a- before *m, p,* and *v;* often *abs-* before *c* or *t* [*abstract*]

**A.B.** [ML. *Artium Baccalaureus*] Bachelor of Arts

**a·ba** (ä′bə) *n.* [Ar.] **1.** a fabric of wool or hair fiber with a felted finish **2.** a loose, sleeveless robe worn by Arabs

**a·ba·cá** (ab′ə kə) *n.* [Tag.] **1.** *same as* MANILA HEMP (sense 1) **2.** the Philippine plant yielding Manila hemp

**a·back** (ə bak′) *adv.* **1.** [Archaic] backward; back **2.** backward against the mast, as sails in a wind from ahead —**taken aback** startled and confused

**ab·a·cus** (ab′ə kəs, ə bak′əs) *n., pl.* **-cus·es, -ci′** (-sī′) [L. < Gr. *abax*] **1.** a frame with beads or balls sliding back and forth on wires or in slots, for doing arithmetic **2.** *Archit.* a slab forming the uppermost part of the capital of a column

**A·ba·dán** (ä′bä dän′) city in W Iran, on an island in the Shatt-al-Arab: pop. 302,000

**a·baft** (ə baft′) *adv.* [< OE. *on,* on + *bæftan* < *be,* by + *æftan,* behind] at or toward the stern of a ship; aft —*prep. Naut.* behind

ABACUS

**ab·a·lo·ne** (ab′ə lō′nē) *n.* [AmSp. < AmInd. *aulun*] a sea mollusk with an oval, somewhat spiral shell lined with mother-of-pearl

**a·ban·don** (ə ban′dən) *vt.* [ < OFr. < *mettre a bandon,* to put under (someone else's) ban] **1.** to give up (something) completely **2.** to forsake; desert **3.** to yield (oneself) completely, as to a feeling —*n.* unrestrained freedom of action or emotion —**a·ban′don·ment** *n.*

**a·ban·doned** (-dənd) *adj.* **1.** forsaken; deserted **2.** shamefully wicked **3.** unrestrained

**a·base** (ə bās′) *vt.* **a·based′, a·bas′ing** [< OFr. < ML. *abassare,* to lower < L. *ad-,* to + LL. *bassus,* low] to humble or humiliate —**a·base′ment** *n.*

**a·bash** (ə bash′) *vt.* [OFr. *esbahir,* to astonish < L. *ex* + *ba,* interj. of surprise] to make ashamed and ill at ease —**a·bashed′** *adj.*

**a·bate** (ə bāt′) *vt.* **a·bat′ed, a·bat′ing** [ < OFr. *abattre,* to beat down: see AD- & BATTER¹] **1.** to make less in amount, degree, etc. **2.** to deduct **3.** *Law* to put a stop to; end —*vi.* to become less; subside —**a·bate′ment** *n.*

**ab·a·tis, ab·at·tis** (ab′ə tis) *n., pl.* **-a·tis, -at·tis** [Fr.: see prec.] a barricade of felled trees with branches facing the enemy

**ab·at·toir** (ab′ə twär′, ab′ə twär′) *n.* [Fr.: see ABATE] a slaughterhouse

**ab·ba·cy** (ab′ə sē) *n., pl.* **-cies** an abbot's position, jurisdiction, or term of office

**ab·bé** (a′bā; *Fr.* à bā′) *n.* [Fr. < LL.: see ABBOT] a French title of respect for a priest, minister, etc.

**ab·bess** (ab′əs) *n.* [< LL.: see ABBOT] a woman who is head of an abbey of nuns

**ab·bey** (ab′ē) *n.* **1.** a monastery headed by an abbot or a convent of nuns headed by an abbess **2.** the monks or nuns in such a place, collectively **3.** a church or building belonging to an abbey

**ab·bot** (ab′ət) *n.* [< OE. < LL. < Gr. < Aram. *abba,* father] a man who heads an abbey of monks

**abbr., abbrev.** **1.** abbreviated **2.** abbreviation

**ab·bre·vi·ate** (ə brē′vē āt′) *vt.* **-at′ed, -at′ing** [< LL. pp. of *abbreviare* < L. < *ad-,* to + *brevis,* short] **1.** to make shorter **2.** to shorten (a word or phrase) by leaving out or substituting letters —**ab·bre′vi·a′tor** *n.*

**ab·bre·vi·a·tion** (ə brē′vē ā′shən) *n.* **1.** a making shorter **2.** the state or fact of being made shorter **3.** a shortened form of a word or phrase, as *N.Y.* for *New York, Mr.* for *Mister, lb.* for *pound*

**A B C** (ā′ bē′ sē′) *n., pl.* **A B C's** **1.** [*usually pl.*] the alphabet **2.** the basic elements (*of* a subject); rudiments

**ABC** American Broadcasting Company

**ABC soil** a vertical section of soil in three distinct layers: the top layer (*A-horizon*) is mostly humus, the middle layer (*B-horizon*) is of clay and other oxidized material, and the bottom layer (*C-horizon*) consists of loose rock and other mineral materials

**ab·di·cate** (ab′də kāt′) *vt., vi.* **-cat′ed, -cat′ing** [< L. pp. of *abdicare* < *ab-,* off + *dicare,* to proclaim] **1.** to give up formally (a high office, etc.) **2.** to surrender (a right, responsibility, etc.) —**ab′di·ca′tion** *n.* —**ab′di·ca′tor** *n.*

**ab·do·men** (ab′də mən, ab dō′-) *n.* [L.] **1.** the part of the body between the diaphragm and the pelvis, containing the intestines, etc.; belly **2.** in insects and crustaceans, the hind part of the body —**ab·dom·i·nal** (ab däm′ə n'l) *adj.*

**ab·duct** (ab dukt′) *vt.* [<L. pp. of *abducere* < *ab-,* away + *ducere,* to lead] **1.** to kidnap (a person) **2.** to move (a part of the body) away from the median axis of the body —**ab·duc′tion** *n.* —**ab·duc′tor** *n.*

**a·beam** (ə bēm′) *adv.* abreast (*of*) the middle of a ship's side

**a·bed** (ə bed′) *adv., adj.* in bed; on a bed

**A·bel** (ā′b'l) [L. < Gr. < Heb. *hebel,* lit., breath] **1.** a

---

fat, āpe, cär; ten, ēven; is, bīte; gō, hôrn, tōōl, lŏŏk; oil, out; up, fur; get; joy; yet; chin; she; thin, then; zh, leisure; ŋ, ring; ə for *a* in *ago, e* in *agent, i* in *sanity, o* in *comply, u* in *focus*; ′ as in *able* (ā′b'l); Fr. bål; ë, Fr. coeur; ö, Fr. feu; Fr. mon; ô, Fr. coq; ü, Fr. duc; r, Fr. cri; H, G. ich; kh, G. doch; ‡foreign; *hypothetical; < derived from. See inside front cover.

masculine name **2.** *Bible* the second son of Adam and Eve, killed by his brother Cain: Gen. 4

**Ab·é·lard** (á bā lár'), **Pierre** (pyer) 1079–1142; Fr. philosopher & teacher: Eng. name Peter **Ab·e·lard** (ab'ə lärd') : see also HÉLOÏSE

**Ab·er·deen** (ab'ər dēn') seaport in E Scotland, on the North Sea: pop. 182,000 —**Ab'er·do'ni·an** (-dō'nē ən) *adj., n.*

**ab·er·rant** (a ber'ənt) *adj.* [< L. prp. of *aberrare* < *ab-*, from + *errare*, to wander] deviating from what is true, normal, or typical —**ab'er'rance, ab·er'ran·cy** *n.*

**ab·er·ra·tion** (ab'ər ā'shən) *n.* **1.** a departure from what is right, true, etc. **2.** a deviation from the normal or typical **3.** mental derangement or lapse **4.** *Optics a)* the failure of light rays from one point to converge to a single focus *b)* an error in a lens or mirror causing this

**a·bet** (ə bet') *vt.* **a·bet'ted, a·bet'ting** [< OFr. *abeter*, to incite < *a-*, to + *beter*, to BAIT] to incite or help, esp. in wrongdoing —**a·bet'ment** *n.* —**a·bet'tor, a·bet'ter** *n.*

**a·bey·ance** (ə bā'əns) *n.* [< Anglo-Fr. < OFr. *abeance*, expectation < *a-*, at + *bayer*, to gape] temporary suspension, as of an activity or function

**ab·hor** (ab hôr', ab-) *vt.* **-horred', -hor'ring** [< L. *abhorrere* < *ab-*, away, from + *horrere*, to shudder] to shrink from in disgust or hatred; detest —**ab·hor'rence** *n.*

**ab·hor·rent** (-ənt) *adj.* **1.** causing disgust, hatred, etc.; detestable **2.** opposed (*to*) [*abhorrent* to his principles] —**ab·hor'rent·ly** *adv.*

**a·bide** (ə bīd') *vi.* **a·bode'** or **a·bid'ed, a·bid'ing** [OE. *abidan* < *a-* (intens.) + *bidan*, to remain] **1.** to stand fast; remain **2.** [Archaic] to stay; reside (*in* or *at*) —*vt.* **1.** to await 2. to submit to; put up with —abide by **1.** to live up to (a promise, etc.) **2.** to submit to and carry out (a rule, decision, etc.) —**a·bid'ance** *n.*

**a·bid·ing** (ə bīd'iŋ) *adj.* enduring; lasting —**a·bid'ing·ly** *adv.*

**Ab·i·djan** (äb'i jän') seaport and capital of the Ivory Coast: pop. 282,000

**Ab·i·gail** (ab'ə gāl') [Heb. *abīgayil*, lit., father is rejoicing] a feminine name: dim. *Abby, Gail*

**Ab·i·lene** (ab'ə lēn') [ult. < Luke 3:1] city in C Tex.: pop. 98,000

**a·bil·i·ty** (ə bil'ə tē) *n., pl.* **-ties** [see ABLE] **1.** a being able; power to do **2.** skill or talent

**-a·bil·i·ty** (ə bil'ə tē) *pl.* **-ties** [L. *-abilitas:* see -ABLE & -ITY] *a suffix used to form nouns from adjectives ending in* -ABLE [*durability*]

**ab·i·o·gen·e·sis** (ab'ē ō jen'ə sis) *n.* [ModL. < Gr. *a-*, without + BIOGENESIS] *same as* SPONTANEOUS GENERATION

**ab·ject** (ab'jekt, ab jekt') *adj.* [< L. pp. of *abjicere* < *ab-*, away, from + *jacere*, to throw] **1.** of the lowest degree; miserable [*abject* poverty] **2.** lacking self-respect; degraded —**ab'ject·ly** *adv.* —**ab'ject·ness, ab·jec'tion** *n.*

**ab·jure** (əb joor', ab-) *vt.* **-jured', -jur'ing** [< L. *abjurare* < *ab-*, away, from + *jurare*, to swear] **1.** to give up (rights, allegiance, etc.) on oath; renounce **2.** to give up (opinions) publicly; recant —**ab·ju·ra·tion** (ab'jə rā'shən) *n.* —**ab·jur'er** *n.*

**ab·late** (ab lāt') *vt.* **-lat'ed, -lat'ing** [back-formation < *ablation* < LL. < L. *ablatus:* see ff.] **1.** to remove, as by surgery **2.** *Astrophysics* to melt, vaporize, etc. (surface material) during high-speed movement through the atmosphere —*vi.* to become ablated —**ab·la'tion** *n.*

**ab·la·tive** (ab'lə tiv; *for adj. 2* ab lāt'iv) *n.* [< L. < *ablatus*, pp. of *auferre* < *ab-*, away + *ferre*, to carry] **1.** the grammatical case in Latin and some other languages expressing removal, deprivation, direction from, or source, cause, etc. **2.** a word in this case —*adj.* **1.** of or in the ablative **2.** *Astrophysics* that ablates

**ab·laut** (äb'lout, ab'-; *G.* äp'lout) *n.* [G. < *ab-*, off, from + *laut*, sound] the change of base vowels in related words to show changes in tense, meaning, etc. (Ex.: drink, drank, drunk) —*adj.* of or characterized by ablaut

**a·blaze** (ə blāz') *adj.* **1.** flaming; gleaming **2.** greatly excited; eager

**a·ble** (ā'b'l) *adj.* **a'bler** (-blər), **a'blest** (-blist) [< OFr. < L. *habilis*, handy < *habere*, to have, hold] **1.** having enough power, skill, etc. (*to do* something) **2.** having much power of mind; skilled; talented —**a'bly** *adv.*

**-a·ble** (ə b'l) [< OFr. < L. *-abilis*] *a suffix meaning:* **1.** able to [*durable*] **2.** capable of being [*drinkable*] **3.** worthy of being [*lovable*] **4.** having qualities of [*comfortable*] **5.** tending or inclined to [*peaceable*]

**a·ble-bod·ied** (ā'b'l bäd'ēd) *adj.* healthy and strong

**able-bodied seaman** a trained, skilled sailor

**a·bloom** (ə blōōm') *adj.* in bloom; in flower

**ab·lu·tion** (ab lōō'shən, əb-) *n.* [< L. *ablutio < abluere < ab-*, off + *luere*, to LAVE] a washing of the body, esp. as a religious ceremony

**-a·bly** (ə blē) *a suffix used to form adverbs from adjectives ending in* -ABLE [*peaceably*]

**ABM** anti-ballistic missile

**ab·ne·gate** (ab'nə gāt') *vt.* **-gat'ed, -gat'ing** [< L. pp. of *abnegare < ab-*, away, from + *negare*, to deny] to give up (rights, claims, etc.); renounce —**ab'ne·ga'tion** *n.* —**ab'ne·ga'tor** *n.*

**Ab·ner** (ab'nər) [L. < Heb. *'abnēr*, lit., the father is a light] a masculine name

**ab·nor·mal** (ab nôr'm'l) *adj.* [earlier *anormal* < Fr. < LL. < Gr. *anōmalos* (see ANOMALOUS) infl. by L. *abnormis* < *ab-*, from + *norma*, NORM] not normal; not average; not typical; irregular, esp. to a considerable degree —**ab·nor'mal·ly** *adv.*

**ab·nor·mal·i·ty** (ab'nôr mal'ə tē) *n.* **1.** the condition of being abnormal **2.** *pl.* **-ties** an abnormal thing

**a·board** (ə bôrd') *adv.* **1.** on board; on, in, or into a ship, airplane, etc. **2.** alongside —*prep.* on board of; on; in —**all aboard!** get on! get in!: a warning that the train, car, etc. will start soon

**a·bode¹** (ə bōd') *n.* [see ABIDE] a place where one lives or stays; home; residence

**a·bode²** (ə bōd') *alt. pt. and pp. of* ABIDE

**a·bol·ish** (ə bäl'ish) *vt.* [< OFr. < L. *abolescere*, to decay < L. *abolere*, to destroy] to do away with; put an end to; annul —**a·bol'ish·ment** *n.*

**ab·o·li·tion** (ab'ə lish'ən) *n.* **1.** an abolishing or being abolished; annulment **2.** [*occas.* A-] the abolishing of slavery in the U.S. —**ab'o·li'tion·ar'y** *adj.*

**ab·o·li·tion·ist** (-ist) *n.* one in favor of abolishing some law, custom, etc.; specif., [*occas.* A-] one who favored the abolition of slavery in the U.S. —**ab'o·li'tion·ism** *n.*

**ab·o·ma·sum** (ab'ə mā'səm) *n., pl.* **-ma'sa** (-sə) [ModL. < L. *ab-*, from + *omasum*, paunch] the fourth, or digesting, chamber of the stomach of a cud-chewing animal, as the cow

**A-bomb** (ā'bäm') *n. same as* ATOMIC BOMB —*vt.* to attack with an atomic bomb

**a·bom·i·na·ble** (ə bäm'ə nə b'l) *adj.* [see ABOMINATE] **1.** disgusting; vile; loathsome **2.** disagreeable; very bad —**a·bom'i·na·bly** *adv.*

**Abominable Snowman** a large, hairy, manlike animal reputed to live in the Himalayas

**a·bom·i·nate** (ə bäm'ə nāt') *vt.* **-nat'ed, -nat'ing** [< L. pp. of *abominari*, to regard as an ill omen] **1.** to feel hatred and disgust for; loathe **2.** to dislike very much —**a·bom'i·na'tor** *n.*

**a·bom·i·na·tion** (ə bäm'ə nā'shən) *n.* **1.** hatred and disgust **2.** anything hateful and disgusting

**ab·o·rig·i·nal** (ab'ə rij'ə n'l) *adj.* **1.** existing from earliest days; first; indigenous **2.** of aborigines

**ab·o·rig·i·ne** (ab'ə rij'ə nē') *n., pl.* **-nes'** [L. < *ab-*, from + *origine*, the beginning] **1.** any of the earliest known inhabitants of a region; native **2.** [*pl.*] the native animals or plants of a region

**a·born·ing** (ə bôr'niŋ) *adv.* while being born or created [the plan died *aborning*]

**a·bort** (ə bôrt') *vi.* [< L. pp. of *aboriri*, to miscarry] **1.** to have a miscarriage **2.** to fail to be completed —*vt.* **1.** to cause to have an abortion **2.** to check (a disease) before fully developed **3.** to cut short (an operation of an aircraft, missile, etc.) as because of an equipment failure

**a·bor·tion** (ə bôr'shən) *n.* **1.** expulsion of a fetus from the womb before it is viable; miscarriage **2.** an aborted fetus **3.** anything immature and incomplete —**a·bor'tion·ist** *n.*

**a·bor·tive** (ə bôr'tiv) *adj.* **1.** coming to nothing; unsuccessful **2.** *Biol.* rudimentary **3.** *Med.* causing abortion —**a·bor'tive·ly** *adv.*

**ABO system** the system of classifying human blood types in accordance with their compatibility for transfusion: there are four major types (A, B, AB, and O), determined by the antigens inherited

**a·bound** (ə bound') *vi.* [< OFr. < L. *abundare*, to overflow < *ab-*, away + *undare*, to rise in waves < *unda*, a wave] **1.** to be plentiful **2.** to have plenty; be rich (*in*) or teem (*with*)

**a·bout** (ə bout') *adv.* [< OE. *onbutan*, around, on the outside (of)] **1.** all around [*look about*] **2.** here and there [*travel about*] **3.** near [it is somewhere *about*] **4.** in the opposite direction [turn it *about*] **5.** in succession or rotation [play fair—turn and turn *about*] **6.** nearly [*about* four years old] **7.** [Colloq.] almost [just *about* ready] —*adj.* [*used only in the predicate*] **1.** active [he is up and *about* again] **2.** in the vicinity [typhoid is *about*] —*prep.* **1.** around; on all sides of **2.** here and there in; everywhere in **3.** near to **4.** with; on (one's person) [have your wits *about* you] **5.** attending to [go *about* your business] **6.** intending; on the point of [he is *about* to speak] **7.** having to do with; concerning **8.** in connection with —**how** (or **what**) **about** [Colloq.] what is your wish or opinion concerning? —**how about that!** [Colloq.] isn't that interesting!

**a·bout-face** (ə bout'fās'; *for v.* ə bout'fās') *n.* **1.** a sharp turn to the opposite direction, esp. in response to a military command **2.** a sharp change, as in opinion —*vi.* **-faced', -fac'ing** to turn or face in the opposite direction

**a·bove** (ə buv′) *adv.* [OE. *abufan*] **1.** in, at, or to a higher place; overhead; up **2.** in or to heaven **3.** at a previous place (in a piece of writing) **4.** higher in power, status, etc. —*prep.* **1.** higher than; over **2.** beyond; past *[the road above the town]* **3.** at a point upstream of **4.** better than *[above the average]* **5.** more than *[above fifty dollars]* —*adj.* placed, found, mentioned, etc. above or earlier —*n.* something that is above —**above all** most of all; mainly

**a·bove·board** (-bôrd′) *adv., adj.* without dishonesty or concealment

**ab·ra·ca·dab·ra** (ab′rə kə dab′rə) *n.* [LL.] **1.** a word supposed to have magic powers, used in incantations, etc. **2.** foolish or meaningless talk

**ab·rade** (ə brād′) *vt., vi.* -rad′ed, -rad′ing [< L. *abradere* < *ab-*, away + *radere*, to scrape] to rub off; wear away by scraping —**ab·rad′er** *n.*

**A·bra·ham** (ā′brə ham′) [Heb., lit., father of many] **1.** a masculine name: dim. *Abe;* var. *Abram* **2.** *Bible* the first patriarch and ancestor of the Hebrews

**a·bran·chi·ate** (ā bran′kē it, -āt′) *adj.* [< Gr. *a-*, not + *branchia*, gills + -ATE¹] without gills —*n.* an animal without gills   Also **a·bran′chi·al** (-əl)

**ab·ra·sion** (ə brā′zhən) *n.* **1.** a scraping or rubbing off, as of skin **2.** an abraded spot or area

**ab·ra·sive** (ə brā′siv) *adj.* causing abrasion —*n.* a substance used for grinding, polishing, etc.

**a·breast** (ə brest′) *adv., adj.* [A-¹ + BREAST] **1.** side by side *[walking four abreast]* **2.** informed *(of)* or conversant *(with)* recent developments

**a·bridge** (ə brij′) *vt.* **a·bridged′, a·bridg′ing** [< OFr. < LL. *abbreviare:* see ABBREVIATE] **1.** to reduce in scope, extent, etc. **2.** to shorten by using fewer words but keeping the main contents **3.** to lessen (rights, authority, etc.) —**a·bridg′a·ble, a·bridge′a·ble** *adj.* —**a·bridg′er** *n.*

**a·bridg·ment, a·bridge·ment** (ə brij′mənt) *n.* **1.** an abridging or being abridged **2.** an abridged form of a book, etc.

**a·broad** (ə brôd′) *adv.* **1.** broadly; far and wide **2.** circulating *[a report is abroad that he is ill]* **3.** outdoors *[to stroll abroad]* **4.** to or in foreign countries —**from abroad** from a foreign land

**ab·ro·gate** (ab′rə gāt′) *vt.* -gat′ed, -gat′ing [< L. pp. of *abrogare*, to repeal < *ab-*, away + *rogare*, to propose] to cancel or repeal by authority; annul —**ab′ro·ga·ble** (-gəb′l) *adj.* —**ab′ro·ga′tion** *n.* —**ab′ro·ga′tive** *adj.* —**ab′ro·ga′tor** *n.*

**a·brupt** (ə brupt′) *adj.* [< L. pp. of *abrumpere* < *ab-*, off + *rumpere*, to break] **1.** sudden; unexpected **2.** curt or brusque **3.** very steep **4.** jumping from topic to topic; disconnected —**a·brupt′ly** *adv.* —**a·brupt′ness** *n.*

**Ab·sa·lom** (ab′sə ləm) *Bible* David's favorite son, who rebelled against his father: II Sam. 18

**ab·scess** (ab′ses) *n.* [< L. < *abscidere* < *ab(s)-*, from + *cedere*, to go] a swollen, inflamed area in body tissues, in which pus gathers —*vi.* to form an abscess —**ab′scessed** *adj.*

**ab·scis·sa** (ab sis′ə) *n., pl.* -sas, -sae (-ē) [L. *abscissa* (*linea*), (a line) cut off < pp. of *abscindere* < *ab-*, from, off + *scindere*, to cut] *Math.* in a system of coordinates, the distance of a point from the vertical axis as measured along a line parallel to the horizontal axis: cf. ORDINATE

y-AXIS

x   P

y

x-AXIS

ABSCISSA
(x, the abscissa of P;
y, the ordinate of P)

**ab·scond** (ab skänd′, ab-) *vi.* [< L. *abscondere* < *ab(s)-*, from, away + *condere*, to hide] to run away and hide, esp. in order to escape the law

**ab·sence** (ab′s'ns) *n.* **1.** the state of being absent, or away **2.** the time of being away **3.** the fact of being without; lack *[in the absence of proof]*

**ab·sent** (ab′s'nt; *for v.* ab sent′) *adj.* [< OFr. < L. prp. of *abesse* < *ab-*, away + *esse*, to be] **1.** not present; away **2.** not existing; lacking **3.** not attentive; absorbed in thought —*vt.* to keep (oneself) away *[he absents himself from classes]* —**ab′sent·ly** *adv.*

**ab·sen·tee** (ab′s'n tē′) *n.* a person who is absent, as from work —*adj.* designating or of a landlord who lives away from the property he owns

**ab·sen·tee·ism** (-iz'm) *n.* absence from work, school, etc., esp. when deliberate or habitual

**ab·sent-mind·ed** (ab′s'nt mīn′did) *adj.* **1.** so lost in thought as not to pay attention to what is going on around one **2.** habitually forgetful —**ab′sent-mind′ed·ly** *adv.* —**ab′sent-mind′ed·ness** *n.*

**ab·sinthe, ab·sinth** (ab′sinth) *n.* [< OFr. < L. < Gr. *apsinthion* < OPer.] **1.** wormwood **2.** a green liqueur with the flavor of wormwood and anise

**ab·so·lute** (ab′sə lōōt′, ab′sə lōōt′) *adj.* [< L. pp. of *absolvere:* see ABSOLVE] **1.** perfect; complete *[absolute silence]* **2.** not mixed; pure **3.** not limited; unrestricted *[an absolute ruler]* **4.** positive; definite **5.** actual; real *[an absolute truth]* **6.** without reference to anything else **7.** *Gram. a)* forming part of a sentence, but not in the usual relations of syntax *[in the sentence "The weather being good, they went," the weather being good is an absolute construction] b)* with no expressed object: said of a verb usually transitive *c)* used alone, with the noun understood: said of a pronoun or an adjective, such as *ours* and *brave* in the sentence "Ours are the brave." —*n.* something that is absolute —**ab′so·lute′ly** *adv.* —**ab′so·lute′ness** *n.*

**absolute pitch** the ability to identify the pitch of any tone, or to sing a given tone, without having a known pitch sounded beforehand

**absolute temperature** temperature measured from absolute zero

**absolute zero** a point of temperature theoretically equal to −273.15° C or −459.67° F: the hypothetical point at which a substance would have no molecular motion and no heat

**ab·so·lu·tion** (ab′sə lōō′shən) *n.* [<OFr. < L. *absolutio* < *absolvere:* see ABSOLVE] **1.** a formal freeing *(from* guilt); forgiveness **2.** *a)* remission *(of* sin or its penalty); specif., in some churches, such remission formally given by a priest in the sacrament of penance *b)* the formula stating such remission

**ab·so·lut·ism** (ab′sə lōō′tiz'm) *n.* government in which the ruler has unlimited powers; despotism —**ab′so·lut′ist** *n., adj.*

**ab·solve** (ab zälv′, ab-; -sälv′) *vt.* -solved′, -solv′ing [< L. *absolvere* < *ab-*, from + *solvere*, to loose] **1.** to pronounce free from guilt or blame; acquit **2.** *a)* to give religious absolution to *b)* to remit (a sin) **3.** to free (someone *from* an obligation) —**ab·solv′ent** *adj., n.* —**ab·solv′er** *n.*

**ab·sorb** (ab zôrb′, ab-; -sôrb′) *vt.* [< L. *absorbere* < *ab-*, from + *sorbere*, to drink in] **1.** to suck up *[sponges absorb water]* **2.** to take up fully the attention of; engross **3.** to take in and incorporate; assimilate **4.** to take in (a shock, jolt, etc.) with little or no recoil or reaction **5.** to take in and not reflect (light, sound, etc.) —**ab·sorbed′** *adj.* —**ab·sorb′ing** *adj.* —**ab·sorb′ing·ly** *adv.*

**ab·sorb·ent** (ab zôr′b'nt, ab-; -sôr′-) *adj.* capable of absorbing moisture, light, etc. —*n.* a thing that absorbs moisture, etc. —**ab·sorb′en·cy** *n.*

**ab·sorp·tion** (ab zôrp′shən, ab-; -sôrp′-) *n.* **1.** an absorbing or being absorbed **2.** great interest; engrossment **3.** *Biol.* the passing of nutrient material into the blood or lymph —**ab·sorp′tive** *adj.* —**ab′sorp·tiv′i·ty** *n.*

**ab·stain** (ab stān′, ab-) *vi.* [< OFr. < L. *abstinere* < *ab(s)-*, from + *tenere*, to hold] to do without voluntarily; refrain *(from)* —**ab·stain′er** *n.*

**ab·ste·mi·ous** (ab stē′mē əs, ab-) *adj.* [< L. < *ab(s)-*, from + root of *temetum*, strong drink] moderate, esp. in eating and drinking; temperate —**ab·ste′mi·ous·ly** *adv.* —**ab·ste′mi·ous·ness** *n.*

**ab·sten·tion** (ab sten′shən, ab-) *n.* an abstaining; specif., a refraining from voting on some issue

**ab·sti·nence** (ab′stə nəns) *n.* **1.** an abstaining from some or all food, drink, or other pleasures **2.** an abstaining from alcoholic liquors —**ab′sti·nent** *adj.* —**ab′sti·nent·ly** *adv.*

**ab·stract** (ab strakt′; *also, and for n.* 1 & *v.* 4 *always,* ab′strakt) *adj.* [< L. pp. of *abstrahere* < *ab(s)-*, from + *trahere*, to draw] **1.** thought of apart from any particular instances or material objects **2.** expressing a quality so thought of *["beauty" is an abstract word]* **3.** not easy to understand; abstruse **4.** theoretical; not practical or applied **5.** designating or of art that does not depict objects realistically but in patterns or forms of lines, masses, or colors —*n.* **1.** a brief statement of the essential thoughts of a book, article, etc.; summary **2.** an abstract thing, condition, etc. —*vt.* **1.** to take away **2.** to steal **3.** to think of (a quality) apart from any particular instance or from any object that has it **4.** to summarize; make an abstract of —**in the abstract** in theory as apart from practice —**ab·stract′er** *n.* —**ab·stract′ly** *adv.* —**ab·stract′ness** *n.*

**ab·stract·ed** (ab strak′tid) *adj.* **1.** removed or separated *(from* something) **2.** withdrawn in mind; preoccupied —**ab·stract′ed·ly** *adv.*

**abstract expressionism** a style of painting popular after World War II, in which the artist's self-expression is carried out by applying paint freely in compositions that do not represent known objects

**ab·strac·tion** (ab strak′shən) *n.* **1.** an abstracting or being abstracted **2.** formation of an idea, as of the qualities of a thing, by separating it mentally from any particular instances or material objects **3.** an idea so formed, or a word for it /"honesty" is an *abstraction*/ **4.** an unrealistic notion **5.** mental withdrawal; preoccupation **6.** a picture, sculpture, etc. that is wholly or partly abstract —**ab·strac'tion·ism** n. —**ab·strac'tion·ist** n.

**ab·struse** (ab strōōs') *adj.* [< L. pp. of *abstrudere* < *ab(s)-*, away + *trudere*, to thrust] hard to understand; deep —**ab·struse'ly** *adv.* —**ab·struse'ness** n.

**ab·surd** (əb surd', ab-; -zurd') *adj.* [< Fr. < L. *absurdus*, not to be heard of < *ab-*, intens. + *surdus*, dull, deaf] so clearly untrue or unreasonable as to be laughable or ridiculous —**ab·surd'ly** *adv.* —**ab·surd'ness** n.

**ab·surd·i·ty** (əb sur'də tē, ab-; -zur'-) n. **1.** the quality or state of being absurd; foolishness **2.** *pl.* **-ties** an absurd idea or thing

**a·bun·dance** (ə bun'dəns) n. [< OFr. < L. prp. of *abundare:* see ABOUND] **1.** a great supply; more than sufficient quantity **2.** wealth —**a·bun'dant** *adj.* —**a·bun'dant·ly** *adv.*

**a·buse** (ə byōōz'; *for* n. ə byōōs') *vt.* **a·bused', a·bus'ing** [< OFr. < L. pp. of *abuti*, to misuse < *ab-*, away, from + *uti*, to use] **1.** to use wrongly; misuse **2.** to mistreat **3.** to use insulting language about or to; revile **4.** [Obs.] to deceive —n. **1.** wrong or excessive use **2.** mistreatment; injury **3.** a bad or corrupt custom or practice **4.** insulting language —**a·bus'er** n.

**a·bu·sive** (ə byōōs'iv) *adj.* **1.** abusing; mistreating **2.** insulting in language; scurrilous —**a·bu'sive·ly** *adv.* —**a·bu'sive·ness** n.

**a·but** (ə but') *vi.* **a·but'ted, a·but'ting** [< OFr. < *a-*, to + *bout*, end] to end (*on*) or lean (*upon*) at one end; border (*on*) —*vt.* to border upon

**a·but·ment** (-mənt) n. **1.** an abutting **2.** that part of a support which carries the weight of an arch **3.** the supporting structure at either end of a bridge

**a·but·ter** (-ər) n. the owner of an abutting, or adjacent, piece of land

**a·buzz** (ə buz') *adj.* **1.** filled with buzzing **2.** full of activity, talk, etc.

**a·bysm** (ə biz''m) n. [Poet.] *same as* ABYSS

**a·bys·mal** (ə biz'm'l) *adj.* **1.** of or like an abyss; bottomless **2.** immeasurably bad /*abysmal* poverty/ —**a·bys'mal·ly** *adv.*

**a·byss** (ə bis') n. [< L. < Gr. < *a-*, without + *byssos*, bottom] **1.** a deep fissure in the earth; bottomless gulf; chasm **2.** anything too deep for measurement /an *abyss* of shame/ **3.** the ocean depths **4.** *Theol.* the primeval chaos before the Creation —**a·bys·sal** (ə bis''l) *adj.*

**Ab·ys·sin·i·a** (ab'ə sin'ē ə) *same as* ETHIOPIA —**Ab'ys·sin'·i·an** *adj., n.*

**-ac** (ak, ək) [Fr. *-aque* < L. *-acus* < Gr. *-akos* (or directly < any of these)] *a suffix meaning:* **1.** characteristic of /*elegiac*/ **2.** of; relating to /*cardiac*/ **3.** affected by or having /*maniac*/

**Ac** *Chem.* actinium

**AC, A.C., a.c.** alternating current

**A/C, a/c** *Bookkeeping* **1.** account **2.** account current

**a·ca·cia** (ə kā'shə) n. [< OFr. < L. < Gr. *akakia*, thorny tree; prob. < *akē*, a point] **1.** a tree or shrub of the legume family, with clusters of yellow or white flowers; some yield gum arabic or dyes **2.** the flower**3.** *same as* LOCUST (sense 3)

**ac·a·dem·ic** (ak'ə dem'ik) *adj.* [see ACADEMY] **1.** of colleges, universities, etc.; scholastic **2.** having to do with liberal rather than technical or vocational education **3.** following fixed rules; formalistic **4.** merely theoretical /an *academic* question/ Also **ac'a·dem'i·cal** —n. a teacher or student at a college or university —**ac'a·dem'i·cal·ly** *adv.*

**academic freedom** freedom of a teacher or student to hold and express views without fear of arbitrary interference by officials

**a·cad·e·mi·cian** (ə kad'ə mish'ən, ak'ə də-) n. a member of an academy (sense 3)

**a·cad·e·my** (ə kad'ə mē) n., *pl.* **-mies** [< Fr. < L. < Gr. *akadēmeia*, the grove of *Akadēmos* (legendary figure), where Plato taught] **1.** a private secondary or high school **2.** a school offering training in a special field **3.** an association of scholars, writers, artists, etc., for advancing literature, art, or science

**A·ca·di·a** (ə kā'dē ə) [< Fr., prob. < native name of Nova Scotia] French colony (1604–1713) that became Nova Scotia and New Brunswick —**A·ca'di·an** *adj., n.*

**a·can·thus** (ə kan'thəs) n., *pl.* **-thus·es, -thi** (-thī) [L. < Gr. *akantha*, thorn < *akē*, a point] **1.** a thistlelike Mediterranean plant with lobed, often spiny leaves **2.** *Archit.* a conventional representation of its leaf, esp. on the capitals of Corinthian columns —**a·can'thine** (-thin) *adj.*

**a cap·pel·la** (ä' kə pel'ə) [It., in chapel style < L. *ad*, to +

ML. *capella*, CHAPEL] without instrumental accompaniment: said of choral singing

**acc. 1.** accompanied **2.** account **3.** accusative

**ac·cede** (ak sēd') *vi.* **-ced'ed, -ced'ing** [< L. *accedere* < *ad-*, to + *cedere*, to yield] **1.** to enter upon the duties (of an office); attain (*to*) **2.** to give assent; give in; agree (*to*) —**ac·ced'ence** n. —**ac·ced'er** n.

**ac·cel·er·an·do** (ak sel'ə ran'dō; *It.* ät che'le rän'dō) *adv., adj.* [It.] *Music* with gradually quickening tempo

**ac·cel·er·ate** (ak sel'ə rāt', ak-) *vt.* **-at'ed, -at'ing** [< L. pp. of *accelerare* < *ad-*, to + *celerare*, to hasten < *celer*, swift] **1.** to increase the speed of **2.** to cause to progress more rapidly **3.** *Physics* to cause a change in the rate of velocity of (a moving body) **4.** to cause to happen sooner —*vi.* to go or progress faster —**ac·cel'er·a'tive** *adj.*

**ac·cel·er·a·tion** (ak sel'ə rā'shən, ak-) n. **1.** an accelerating or being accelerated **2.** change in velocity, or the rate of such change

**ac·cel·er·a·tor** (ak sel'ə rāt'ər, ak-) n. **1.** one that accelerates **2.** a device, as the foot throttle of an automobile, for speeding up something **3.** *Chem.* a substance that speeds up a reaction **4.** *Nuclear Physics* a device that accelerates charged particles to high energies

**ac·cent** (ak'sent; *for v. also* ak sent') n. [Fr. < L. < *ad-*, to + *cantus*, pp. of *canere*, to sing] **1.** the emphasis given to a particular syllable or word in speaking it **2.** a mark used to show this emphasis, as primary (′) and secondary (′) accents **3.** a mark used to distinguish between various sounds of the same letter /in French there are acute (ˊ), grave (ˋ), and circumflex (ˆ) *accents*/ **4.** a distinguishing regional or national way of pronouncing **5.** [*pl.*] [Poet.] speech; words /in *accents* mild/ **6.** something that lends emphasis, as by contrast with its surroundings **7.** special emphasis /to put the *accent* on safety/ **8.** *Music* emphasis or stress on a note or chord **9.** *Prosody* rhythmic stress or beat —*vt.* **1.** to pronounce with special stress **2.** to mark with an accent **3.** to emphasize

**ac·cen·tu·al** (ak sen'choo wəl) *adj.* **1.** of or having to do with accent **2.** having rhythm based on stress, as some poetry —**ac·cen'tu·al·ly** *adv.*

**ac·cen·tu·ate** (ak sen'choo wāt') *vt.* **-at'ed, -at'ing** **1.** to pronounce or mark with an accent or stress **2.** to emphasize —**ac·cen'tu·a'tion** n.

**ac·cept** (ak sept', ak-) *vt.* [< OFr. < L. *acceptare* < *accipere* < *ad-*, to + *capere*, to take] **1.** to take (what is offered or given); receive willingly **2.** to receive favorably; approve **3.** to agree or give assent to **4.** to believe in **5.** to understand as having a certain meaning **6.** to reply affirmatively to; say "yes" to /to *accept* an invitation/ **7.** *Business* to agree to pay —*vi.* to accept something offered —**ac·cept'er** n.

**ac·cept·a·ble** (ək sep'tə b'l, ak-) *adj.* worth accepting; satisfactory or, sometimes, merely adequate —**ac·cept'a·bil'i·ty** n. —**ac·cept'a·bly** *adv.*

**ac·cept·ance** (ək sep'təns, ak-) n. **1.** an accepting or being accepted **2.** approving reception; approval **3.** belief in; assent **4.** a written order to pay a certain sum at a set future time

**ac·cep·ta·tion** (ak'sep tā'shən) n. the generally accepted meaning (of a word or expression)

**ac·cept·ed** (ək sep'tid, ak-) *adj.* generally regarded as true, proper, etc.; conventional; approved

**ac·cess** (ak'ses) n. [< OFr. < L. pp. of *accedere*, ACCEDE] **1.** a coming toward; approach **2.** a means of approaching, using, etc. **3.** the right to enter, approach, or use **4.** increase **5.** an outburst /an *access* of anger/ **6.** the onset (of a disease) —*vt.* to gain or have access to /branch officials can *access* the central data bank/

**ac·ces·sa·ry** (ək ses'ər ē, ak-) *adj., n., pl.* **-ries** *same as* ACCESSORY

**ac·ces·si·ble** (ak ses'ə b'l) *adj.* [see ACCESS] **1.** that can be approached or entered **2.** easy to approach or enter **3.** obtainable **4.** open to the influence of (with *to*) /not *accessible* to pity/ —**ac·ces'si·bil'i·ty** n. —**ac·ces'si·bly** *adv.*

**ac·ces·sion** (ak sesh'ən) n. [see ACCESS] **1.** the act of attaining (a throne, power, etc.) **2.** assent **3.** *a)* increase by addition *b)* an item added, as to a library —**ac·ces'sion·al** *adj.*

**ac·ces·so·rize** (ak ses'ə rīz', ak-) *vt.* **-rized', -riz'ing** to equip, decorate, supplement, etc. with accessories

**ac·ces·so·ry** (ak ses'ər ē, ak-) *adj.* [< ML. < L. pp. of *accedere*, ACCEDE] **1.** helping in a secondary way; extra; additional **2.** *Law* helping in an unlawful act —n., *pl.* **-ries** **1.** something extra added to help in a secondary way; specif., *a)* an article to complete one's costume, as a purse, gloves, etc. *b)* a piece of optional equipment for convenience, comfort, etc. **2.** *Law* an accomplice —**accessory before** (or **after**) **the fact** one who, though absent at the commission of a felony, aids the accused before (or after) its commission —**ac·ces·so·ri·al** (ak'sə sôr'ē əl) *adj.*

**access time** in computers, the time between the moment when information is requested from (or presented for) storage and the moment of its delivery (or storage)

**ac·ci·dence** (ak′sə dəns) *n.* [see ff.] the part of grammar dealing with inflection of words

**ac·ci·dent** (ak′sə dənt) *n.* [< OFr. < L. prp. of *accidere*, happen < *ad-*, to + *cadere*, to fall] 1. a happening that is not expected, foreseen, or intended 2. an unintended happening that results in injury, loss, etc. 3. chance [to meet by *accident*] 4. an attribute that is not essential

**ac·ci·den·tal** (ak′sə den′t′l) *adj.* 1. happening by chance 2. belonging but not essential; incidental —*n.* 1. a nonessential quality 2. *Music a*) a sign, as a sharp or flat, placed before a note to show a chromatic change of pitch *b*) the tone of such a note —**ac′ci·den′tal·ly** *adv.*

**ac·ci·dent-prone** (ak′sə dənt prōn′) *adj.* tending to become involved in accidents

**ac·claim** (ə klām′) *vt.* [< L. *acclamare* < *ad-*, to + *clamare*, to cry out] 1. to greet with loud applause or strong approval 2. to announce with much applause or praise; hail [they *acclaimed* him president] —*n.* loud applause or strong approval

**ac·cla·ma·tion** (ak′lə mā′shən) *n.* 1. an acclaiming or being acclaimed 2. loud applause or strong approval 3. an enthusiastic approving vote by voice without an actual count —**ac·clam·a·to·ry** (ə klam′ə tôr′ē) *adj.*

**ac·cli·mate** (ak′lə māt′, ə klī′mət) *vt., vi.* -**mat′ed**, -**mat′ing** [< Fr.: see AD- & CLIMATE] to accustom or become accustomed to a different climate or environment —**ac′cli·ma′tion** *n.*

**ac·cli·ma·tize** (ə klī′mə tīz′) *vt., vi.* -**tized′**, -**tiz′ing** *same as* ACCLIMATE —**ac·cli′ma·ti·za′tion** *n.*

**ac·cliv·i·ty** (ə kliv′ə tē) *n., pl.* -**ties** [< L. < *ad-*, up + *clivus*, hill] an upward slope of ground —**ac·cli·vous** (ə kli′vəs) *adj.*

**ac·co·lade** (ak′ə lād′) *n.* [Fr. < Pr. < It. pp. of *accollare*, to embrace < L. *ad*, to + *collum*, neck] 1. formerly, an embrace (now, a touch with a sword) used in conferring knighthood 2. anything done or given as a sign of great respect, appreciation, etc.

**ac·com·mo·date** (ə käm′ə dāt′) *vt.* -**dat′ed**, -**dat′ing** [< L. pp. of *accommodare* < *ad-*, to + *com-*, with + *modus*, a measure] 1. to adjust; adapt 2. to reconcile (differences) 3. to help by supplying (*with* something) 4. to do a favor for 5. to have room for —*vi.* to become adjusted, as the lens of the eye in focusing —**ac·com′mo·da′tive** *adj.* —**ac·com′mo·da′tor** *n.*

**ac·com·mo·dat·ing** (-dāt′iŋ) *adj.* ready to help; obliging —**ac·com′mo·dat′ing·ly** *adv.*

**ac·com·mo·da·tion** (ə käm′ə dā′shən) *n.* 1. adaptation (*to* a purpose); adjustment 2. reconciliation of differences 3. willingness to do favors 4. a help or convenience 5. [*pl.*] lodgings or space, as in a hotel, on a ship, etc. 6. the self-adjustment of the lens of the eye in focusing

**ac·com·pa·ni·ment** (ə kump′ni mənt, ə kum′pə nē-mənt) *n.* 1. anything that accompanies something else 2. *Music* a part performed, as on a piano, together with the main part, as with a vocal solo

**ac·com·pa·nist** (ə kum′pə nist) *n.* a person who plays an accompaniment

**ac·com·pa·ny** (ə kum′pə nē, ə kump′nē) *vt.* -**nied**, -**ny·ing** [< MFr. < *ac-*, to + OFr. *compagnon*: see COMPANION[1]] 1. to go or be together with 2. to supplement [to *accompany* words with acts] 3. to play an accompaniment for or to

**ac·com·plice** (ə käm′plis) *n.* [< A-[1] + OFr. *complice* < LL. *complex*, accomplice: see COMPLEX] a person who knowingly helps another in an unlawful act

**ac·com·plish** (ə käm′plish) *vt.* [< OFr. < L. *ad-*, intens. + *complere*: see COMPLETE] to do; succeed in doing; complete —**ac·com′plish·a·ble** *adj.*

**ac·com·plished** ·(-plisht) *adj.* 1. done; completed 2. skilled; proficient 3. trained in the social arts or skills; polished

**ac·com·plish·ment** (-plish mənt) *n.* 1. an accomplishing or being accomplished; completion 2. something done successfully; achievement 3. a social art or skill: *usually used in pl.*

**ac·cord** (ə kôrd′) *vt.* [< OFr. < L. *ad-*, to + *cor* (gen. *cordis*), heart] 1. to make agree; reconcile 2. to grant or concede —*vi.* to agree or harmonize (*with*) —*n.* 1. mutual agreement; harmony 2. an informal agreement, as between nations 3. harmony of sound, color, etc. —**of one's own accord** willingly, without being asked —**with one accord** all agreeing

**ac·cord·ance** (-′ns) *n.* agreement; conformity —**ac·cord′ant** *adj.* —**ac·cord′ant·ly** *adv.*

**ac·cord·ing** (-iŋ) *adj.* agreeing; in harmony —**according as** to the degree that —**according to** 1. in agreement with 2. in the order of [seated *according to* age] 3. as stated by

**ac·cord·ing·ly** (-iŋ lē) *adv.* 1. in a way that is fitting and proper 2. therefore

**ac·cor·di·on** (ə kôr′dē ən) *n.* [< G., prob. < It. *accordare*, be in tune] a musical instrument with a bellows which is pulled out and pressed together to produce tones by forcing air through metal reeds opened by fingering keys —*adj.* having folds, or folding, like an accordion's bellows —**ac·cor′di·on·ist** *n.*

ACCORDION

**ac·cost** (ə kôst′, -käst′) *vt.* [< Fr. < It. < L. < *ad-*, to + *costa*, rib, side] to approach and speak to, esp. in a bold or forward manner

**ac·couche·ment** (ə kōōsh′mənt; *Fr.* ä kōōsh män′) *n.* [Fr. < OFr. *acoucher:* see AD- & COUCH] confinement for giving birth to a child; childbirth

**ac·count** (ə kount′) *vt.* [< OFr. < *a-*, to + *conter*, to tell < L. *computare:* see COMPUTE] to consider to be; deem —*vi.* 1. to furnish a reckoning of money received and paid out 2. to make satisfactory amends (*for*) [made to *account* for his crime] 3. to give satisfactory reasons or an explanation (*for*) 4. to be the cause or source of (with *for*) 5. to do away with as by killing (with *for*) —*n.* 1. *a*) a record of the financial transactions of a person, business, etc. *b*) *same as* CHARGE ACCOUNT *c*) a business that is a customer or client, esp. on a credit basis 2. *same as* BANK ACCOUNT 3. worth; importance [a thing of small *account*] 4. an explanation 5. a report; description —**call to account** 1. to demand an explanation of 2. to reprimand —**give a good account of oneself** to acquit oneself well —**on account** as partial payment —**on account of** because of —**on no account** under no circumstances —**take account of** 1. to allow for 2. to take notice of —**take into account** to take into consideration —**turn to account** to get use from

**ac·count·a·ble** (-ə b′l) *adj.* 1. obliged to account for one's acts; responsible 2. that can be accounted for; explainable —**ac·count′a·bil′i·ty** *n.* —**ac·count′a·bly** *adv.*

**ac·count·an·cy** (ə kount′'n sē) *n.* the work of an accountant

**ac·count·ant** (ə kount′'nt) *n.* a person whose work is to inspect or keep financial accounts: see CERTIFIED PUBLIC ACCOUNTANT

**ac·count·ing** (ə koun′tiŋ) *n.* 1. the principles or practice of setting up and auditing financial accounts 2. a settling or balancing of accounts

**ac·cou·ter** (ə kōōt′ər) *vt.* [Fr., prob. < L. *con-*, together + *suere*, to sew] to equip or attire: also **ac·cou′tre** -**tred**, -**tring**

**ac·cou·ter·ments, ac·cou·tre·ments** (ə kōōt′ər mənts, -kōō′trə-) *n.pl.* 1. clothes; dress 2. equipment; furnishings; trappings

**Ac·cra** (ə krä′) capital of Ghana, on the Atlantic: pop. 533,000

**ac·cred·it** (ə kred′it) *vt.* [< Fr.: see CREDIT] 1. to bring into credit or favor 2. to give credentials to 3. to take as true 4. to certify as meeting certain standards 5. to attribute; credit —**ac·cred′it·a′tion** (-ə tā′shən) *n.*

**ac·cre·tion** (ə krē′shən) *n.* [< L. *accretio* < *accrescere* < *ad-*, to + *crescere*, to grow] 1. growth in size, esp. by addition or accumulation 2. a growing together of separate parts 3. accumulated matter 4. a part added separately 5. a whole resulting from such growth —**ac·cre′tive** *adj.*

**ac·crue** (ə krōō′) *vi.* -**crued′**, -**cru′ing** [< OFr. < L.: see ACCRETION] 1. to come as a natural growth, advantage, or right (*to*) 2. to be added periodically as an increase: said esp. of interest on money —**ac·cru′al** *n.*

**acct.** account

**ac·cul·tu·rate** (ə kul′chə rāt′) *vi., vt.* -**rat′ed**, -**rat′ing** to undergo, or alter by, acculturation

**ac·cul·tu·ra·tion** (ə kul′chə rā′shən) *n.* [AC- (see AD-) + CULTUR(E) + -ATION] 1. the conditioning of a child to the patterns of a culture 2. a becoming adapted to a different culture 3. the mutual influence of different cultures in close contact

**ac·cu·mu·late** (ə kyōōm′yə lāt′) *vt., vi.* -**lat′ed**, -**lat′ing** [< L. pp. of *accumulare* < *ad-*, to + *cumulare*, to heap] to pile up or collect, esp. over a period of time —**ac·cu′mu·la·ble** (-lə b′l) *adj.*

**ac·cu·mu·la·tion** (ə kyōōm′yə lā′shən) *n.* 1. an accumulating; collection 2. accumulated or collected material

**ac·cu·mu·la·tive** (ə kyōōm′yə lāt′iv) *adj.* 1. resulting from accumulation 2. tending to accumulate —**ac·cu′mu·la′tive·ly** *adv.* —**ac·cu′mu·la′tive·ness** *n.*

**ac·cu·mu·la·tor** (-lāt′ər) *n.* 1. one that accumulates

**2.** [Brit.] a storage battery **3.** a device, as in a computer, that stores a quantity and that will add to that quantity others, storing the sum

**ac·cu·ra·cy** (ak′yər ə sē) *n.* the quality or state of being accurate; precision

**ac·cu·rate** (ak′yər it) *adj.* [< L. pp. of *accurare*, to take care < *ad-*, to + *cura*, care] **1.** careful and exact **2.** free from errors; precise **3.** adhering closely to a standard —**ac′cu·rate·ly** *adv.* —**ac′cu·rate·ness** *n.*

**ac·curs·ed** (ə kʉr′sid, -kʉrst′) *adj.* **1.** under a curse; ill-fated **2.** deserving to be cursed; damnable Also **ac·curst′** (-kʉrst′) —**ac·curs′ed·ly** *adv.* —**ac·curs′ed·ness** *n.*

**ac·cu·sa·tion** (ak′yə zā′shən) *n.* **1.** an accusing or being accused **2.** the wrong that one is accused of

**ac·cu·sa·tive** (ə kyōō′zə tiv) *adj.* [< L. < pp. of *accusare:* see ACCUSE] **1.** designating or in the grammatical case, as in Latin, used for the direct object of a verb and after certain prepositions **2.** accusatory —*n.* **1.** the accusative case **2.** a word in this case —**ac·cu′sa·ti′val** (-tī′v′l) *adj.* —**ac·cu′sa·tive·ly** *adv.*

**ac·cu·sa·to·ry** (-tôr′ē) *adj.* making or containing an accusation; accusing

**ac·cuse** (ə kyōōz′) *vt.* -**cused′**, -**cus′ing** [< OFr. < L. *accusare* < *ad-*, to + *causa*, a cause or lawsuit] **1.** to find at fault; blame **2.** to bring formal charges against (*of* breaking the law, etc.) —**the accused** *Law* the person formally charged with committing a crime —**ac·cus′er** *n.* —**ac·cus′ing·ly** *adv.*

**ac·cus·tom** (ə kus′təm) *vt.* to make used (*to* something) as by custom or regular use; habituate

**ac·cus·tomed** (-təmd) *adj.* **1.** customary; usual; characteristic **2.** used (*to*); in the habit of

**ace** (ās) *n.* [< L. *as*, unit] **1.** a playing card, domino, etc. marked with one spot **2.** *a)* a serve, as in tennis, that one's opponent is unable to return *b)* the point thus made **3.** *Golf* a hole in one: see entry HOLE **4.** a combat pilot who has destroyed many enemy planes **5.** an expert —*adj.* [Colloq.] first-rate; expert [*an* ace *salesman*] —*vt.* **aced** (āst), **ac′ing** to score an ace against (an opponent) in tennis, or on (a hole) in golf —**within an ace of** on the verge of

**-a·ce·a** (ā′shə, ā′shē ə) [L., neut. pl. of *-aceus*] a plural suffix used in forming zoological names of classes or orders: see -ACEOUS

**-a·ce·ae** (ā′si ē′) [L., fem. pl. of *-aceus*] a plural suffix used in forming botanical names of families: see -ACEOUS

**ace-high** (ās′hī′) *adj.* [orig. a poker term] [Colloq.] highly esteemed; respected

**ace in the hole 1.** *Stud Poker* an ace dealt and kept face down until the deal is over **2.** [Slang] any advantage held in reserve

**-a·ceous** (ā′shəs) [L. *-aceus*] a suffix meaning of the nature of, like, belonging to, producing, etc.: often used to form adjectives corresponding to nouns ending in -ACEA, -ACEAE

**ac·er·bate** (as′ər bāt′) *vt.* -**bat′ed**, -**bat′ing** [< L. pp. of *acerbare*] **1.** to make sour or bitter **2.** to irritate; vex

**a·cer·bi·ty** (ə sʉr′bə tē) *n., pl.* -**ties** [< Fr. < L. < *acerbus*, bitter] **1.** a sour, astringent quality **2.** sharpness or harshness of temper, words, etc.

**ac·e·tab·u·lum** (as′ə tab′yoo ləm) *n., pl.* -**la** (-lə), -**lums** [L., orig. vinegar cup < *acetum:* see ACETO-] *Anat.* the cup-shaped socket of the hipbone

**ac·e·tal** (as′ə tal′) *n.* [ACET(O)- + -AL] a colorless, volatile liquid, $C_6H_{14}O_2$, used as a hypnotic

**ac·et·an·i·lide** (as′ə tan′ə līd′, -′l id) *n.* [ACET(O)- + ANIL(INE) + -IDE] a white, crystalline organic substance, $C_8H_9NO$, used to lessen pain and fever

**ac·e·tate** (as′ə tāt′) *n.* [ACET(O)- + -ATE²] **1.** a salt or ester of acetic acid **2.** *same as* CELLULOSE ACETATE —**ac′e·tat′ed** *adj.*

**a·ce·tic** (ə sēt′ik, -set′-) *adj.* [< L. *acetum:* see ACETO-] of, like, containing, or producing acetic acid or vinegar

**acetic acid** a sour, colorless liquid, $C_2H_4O_2$, having a sharp odor: it is found in vinegar

**a·cet·i·fy** (ə set′ə fī′, -sēt′-) *vt., vi.* -**fied′**, -**fy′ing** to change into vinegar or acetic acid —**a·cet′i·fi·ca′tion** *n.*

**ac·e·to-** [< L. *acetum*, vinegar] a combining form meaning of or from acetic acid: also, before a vowel, **ac·et-**

**ac·e·tone** (as′ə tōn′) *n.* [ACET(O)- + -ONE] a colorless, flammable, volatile liquid, $C_3H_6O$, used as a solvent for certain oils, etc. —**ac′e·ton′ic** (-tän′ik) *adj.*

**ac·e·to·phe·net·i·din** (ə set′ō fə net′ə din) *n.* [ACETO- + PHEN(O)- + ET(HYL) + -ID(E) + -IN¹] a white, crystalline powder, $C_{10}H_{13}O_2N$, used to reduce fever and to relieve headaches and muscular pains; phenacetin

**a·cet·y·lene** (ə set′'l ēn′) *n.* [ACET(O)- + -YL + -ENE] a colorless, poisonous, highly flammable gaseous hydrocarbon, $C_2H_2$, used for lighting and, with oxygen, in blowtorches, etc.

**ac·e·tyl·sal·i·cyl·ic acid** (ə set′'l sal′ə sil′ik, as′ə t′l-) *same as* ASPIRIN

**ace·y-deuc·y** (ā′sē dōō′sē) *n.* [< ACE + DEUCE¹] a variation of backgammon

**A·chae·an** (ə kē′ən) *adj.* **1.** of Achaea, an ancient province in the Peloponnesus, or its people **2.** loosely, Greek —*n.* **1.** a native or inhabitant of Achaea **2.** loosely, a Greek

**A·cha·tes** (ə kāt′ēz) in Virgil's *Aeneid*, a loyal friend of Aeneas —*n.* a loyal friend

**ache** (āk) *vi.* **ached**, **ach′ing** [OE. *acan*] **1.** to have or give dull, steady pain **2.** to feel pity, etc. (*for*) **3.** [Colloq.] to yearn or long: with *for* or an infinitive —*n.* a dull, continuous pain

**a·chene** (ā kēn′) *n.* [< ModL. < Gr. *a-*, not + *chainein*, to gape] any small, dry, one-seeded fruit that ripens without bursting —**a·che′ni·al** *adj.*

**a·chieve** (ə chēv′) *vt.* **a·chieved′**, **a·chiev′ing** [< OFr. < *a-*, to + *chief:* see CHIEF] **1.** to succeed in doing; accomplish **2.** to get by exertion; attain; gain —*vi.* to bring about a desired result —**a·chiev′a·ble** *adj.* —**a·chiev′er** *n.*

**a·chieve·ment** (-mənt) *n.* **1.** an achieving **2.** a thing achieved, esp. by skill, work, etc.; feat

**A·chil·les** (ə kil′ēz) *Gr. Myth.* Greek hero in the Trojan War, who killed Hector and was killed by Paris with an arrow that struck his vulnerable heel: he is the hero of Homer's *Iliad*

**Achilles' heel** (one's) vulnerable spot

**Achilles' tendon** the tendon connecting the back of the heel to the muscles of the calf of the leg

**ach·ro·mat·ic** (ak′rə mat′ik) *adj.* [< Gr. < *a-*, without + *chrōma*, color + -IC] **1.** colorless **2.** refracting white light without breaking it up into its component colors **3.** forming visual images whose outline is free from prismatic colors [*an achromatic* lens] **4.** *Music same as* DIATONIC —**ach′ro·mat′i·cal·ly** *adv.*

**a·chro·mic** (ā krō′mik) *adj.* [< Gr. < *a-*, without + *chrōma*, color + -IC] without color: also **a·chro′mous** (-məs)

**ach·y** (āk′ē) *adj.* **ach′i·er**, **ach′i·est** having an ache, or dull, steady pain

**ac·id** (as′id) *adj.* [L. *acidus*, sour] **1.** sharp and biting to the taste; sour **2.** sharp or sarcastic in speech, etc. **3.** of or being an acid **4.** having too much acid —*n.* **1.** a sour substance **2.** [Slang] *same as* LSD **3.** *Chem.* any compound that reacts with a base to form a salt, produces hydrogen ions in water solution, and turns blue litmus red —**ac′id·ly** *adv.* —**ac′id·ness** *n.*

**a·cid·ic** (ə sid′ik) *adj.* **1.** forming acid **2.** acid

**a·cid·i·fy** (ə sid′ə fī′) *vt., vi.* -**fied′**, -**fy′ing** **1.** to make or become sour or acid **2.** to change into an acid —**a·cid′i·fi′a·ble** *adj.* —**a·cid′i·fi·ca′tion** *n.* —**a·cid′i·fi′er** *n.*

**a·cid·i·ty** (-tē) *n., pl.* -**ties 1.** *a)* acid quality or condition; sourness *b)* the degree of this **2.** *same as* HYPERACIDITY

**ac·i·do·sis** (as′ə dō′sis) *n. Med.* a condition in which the body's alkali reserve is below normal —**ac′i·dot′ic** (-dät′ik) *adj.*

**acid test** [orig., a *test* of gold by *acid*] a crucial, final test of value or quality

**a·cid·u·late** (ə sij′oo lāt′) *vt.* -**lat′ed**, -**lat′ing** to make somewhat acid or sour —**a·cid′u·la′tion** *n.*

**a·cid·u·lous** (-ləs) *adj.* [< L. dim. of *acidus*, sour] **1.** somewhat acid or sour **2.** somewhat sarcastic Also **a·cid′u·lent** (-lənt)

**ac·i·nus** (as′i nəs) *n., pl.* -**ni′** (-nī′) [L., a grape] *Anat.* any of the small sacs of a compound gland —**ac′i·nar** (-nər), **ac′i·nous** (-nəs) *adj.*

**-a·cious** (ā′shəs) [< L. *-ax* (gen. *-acis*) + -OUS] a suffix meaning characterized by, inclined to, full of [*tenacious*]

**-ac·i·ty** (as′ə tē) a suffix corresponding to -ACIOUS [*tenacity*]

**ack-ack** (ak′ak′) *n.* [echoic; prob. expansion of abbrev. *A.A.*, antiaircraft artillery] [Slang] an antiaircraft gun or its fire

**ac·knowl·edge** (ək näl′ij, ak-) *vt.* -**edged**, -**edg·ing** [< ME. *knowleche* (see KNOWLEDGE); infl. by ME. *aknowen* < OE. *oncnawan*, to understand] **1.** to admit to be true; confess **2.** to recognize the authority or claims of **3.** to recognize and answer (a greeting or introduction) **4.** to express thanks for **5.** to state that one has received (a letter, gift, etc.) **6.** *Law* to certify in legal form [*to acknowledge* a deed] —**ac·knowl′edge·a·ble** *adj.*

**ac·knowl·edg·ment, ac·knowl·edge·ment** (-mənt) *n.* **1.** an acknowledging; admission **2.** something done or given in acknowledging, as thanks **3.** recognition of the authority or claims of **4.** a legal avowal or certificate

**ACLU, A.C.L.U.** American Civil Liberties Union

**ac·me** (ak′mē) *n.* [Gr. *akmē*, a point, top] the highest point; peak

**ac·ne** (ak′nē) *n.* [ModL., ? orig. error for Gr. *akmē:* see prec.] a common skin disease characterized by chronic inflammation of the sebaceous glands, usually causing pimples on the face, etc.

**ac·o·lyte** (ak′ə līt′) *n.* [< ML. < Gr. *akolouthos*, follower] **1.** *R.C.Ch.* a member of the highest of the four minor orders, who serves at Mass **2.** *same as* ALTAR BOY **3.** an attendant

**A·con·ca·gua** (ä′kŏn kä′gwä) mountain of the Andes in W Argentina: 22,835 ft.

**ac·o·nite** (ak′ə nīt′) *n.* [< L. < Gr. *akoniton*]  **1.** any of a genus of plants of the buttercup family, with blue, purple, or yellow hoodlike flowers: most species are poisonous  **2.** a drug made from the dried roots of one species, formerly used in medicine

**a·corn** (ā′kôrn′) *n.* [< OE. *æcern*, nut]  the fruit of the oak tree; oak nut

**acorn squash** a kind of winter squash, acorn-shaped with a dark-green, ridged skin

**a·cous·tic** (ə kōōs′tik) *adj.* [< Fr. < Gr. < *akouein*, to hear]  **1.** having to do with hearing or with sound as it is heard  **2.** of acoustics  Also **a·cous′ti·cal** —**a·cous′ti·cal·ly** *adv.*

**a·cous·tics** (-tiks) *n.pl.*  **1.** the qualities of a room, etc. that have to do with how clearly sounds can be heard in it  **2.** [*with sing. v.*] the branch of physics dealing with sound

**ac·quaint** (ə kwānt′) *vt.* [< OFr. < ML. < L. *ad*, to + *cognitus*, pp. of *cognoscere*, to know thoroughly]  **1.** to let know; make aware  **2.** to cause to know personally; make familiar (*with*)

**ac·quaint·ance** (-′ns) *n.*  **1.** knowledge (of something) got from personal experience or study  **2.** the state of being acquainted (*with* someone)  **3.** a person whom one knows only slightly —**ac·quaint′ance·ship′** *n.*

**ac·qui·esce** (ak′wē es′) *vi.* **-esced′, -esc′ing** [< Fr. < L. *acquiescere* < *ad*-, to + *quiescere:* see QUIET]  to consent quietly without protest, but without enthusiasm (often with *in*) —**ac′qui·es′cence** *n.* —**ac′qui·es′cent** *adj.* —**ac′qui·es′cent·ly** *adv.*

**ac·quire** (ə kwīr′) *vt.* **-quired′, -quir′ing** [L. *acquirere* < *ad*-, to + *quaerere*, to seek]  **1.** to get or gain by one's own efforts or actions  **2.** to get as one's own —**ac·quir′a·ble** *adj.*

**acquired character** *Biol.* a modification of structure or function caused by environmental factors: now generally regarded as not inheritable: also **acquired characteristic**

**ac·quire·ment** (ə kwīr′mənt) *n.*  **1.** an acquiring  **2.** something acquired, as a skill, etc.

**ac·qui·si·tion** (ak′wə zish′ən) *n.*  **1.** an acquiring or being acquired  **2.** something acquired

**ac·quis·i·tive** (ə kwiz′ə tiv) *adj.* eager to acquire; good at getting and holding wealth, ideas, etc. —**ac·quis′i·tive·ly** *adv.* —**ac·quis′i·tive·ness** *n.*

**ac·quit** (ə kwit′) *vt.* **-quit′ted, -quit′ting** [< OFr. < ML. *acquitare*, to settle a claim < L. *ad*, to + *quietare*, to quiet]  **1.** to release from a duty, etc.  **2.** to declare not guilty of a charge; exonerate  **3.** to conduct (oneself); behave —**ac·quit′tal** *n.* —**ac·quit′ter** *n.*

**ac·quit·tance** (-′ns) *n.*  **1.** a settlement of, or release from, debt or liability  **2.** a record of this; receipt

**a·cre** (ā′kər) *n.* [OE. *æcer*, field; akin to L. *ager*]  **1.** a measure of land, 43,560 sq. ft.  **2.** [*pl.*] specific holdings in land; lands

**a·cre·age** (ā′kər ij, ā′krij) *n.* acres collectively

**ac·rid** (ak′rid) *adj.* [< L. *acris*, sharp; form infl. by ACID]  **1.** sharp, bitter, or irritating to the taste or smell  **2.** bitter or sarcastic in speech, etc. —**a·crid·i·ty** (a krid′ə tē, ə-), **ac′rid·ness** *n.* —**ac′rid·ly** *adv.*

**ac·ri·mo·ny** (ak′rə mō′nē) *n.* [< L. < *acer*, sharp]  bitterness or harshness of manner or speech; asperity —**ac′ri·mo′ni·ous** *adj.*

**ac·ro-** [< Gr. *akros*, at the end or top]  *a combining form* meaning highest, at the extremities [*acrogen*]

**ac·ro·bat** (ak′rə bat′) *n.* [< Fr. < Gr. *akrobatos*, walking on tiptoe < *akros* (see prec.) + *bainein*, to go]  an expert performer of tricks in tumbling or on the trapeze, tightrope, etc.; skilled gymnast —**ac′ro·bat′ic** *adj.* —**ac′ro·bat′i·cal·ly** *adv.*

**ac·ro·bat·ics** (ak′rə bat′iks) *n.pl.* [*also with sing. v.*]  **1.** the skill or tricks of an acrobat  **2.** tricks requiring great skill [*mental acrobatics*]

**ac·ro·gen** (ak′rə jən) *n.* [ACRO- + -GEN]  a plant, such as a fern or moss, having a perennial stem with the growing point at the tip —**a·crog·e·nous** (ə kräj′ə nəs), **ac′ro·gen′ic** (-jen′ik) *adj.*

**ac·ro·meg·a·ly** (ak′rō meg′ə lē) *n.* [< Fr.: see ACRO- & MEGALO-]  abnormal enlargement of the bones of the head, hands, and feet, resulting from overproduction of growth hormone by the pituitary gland —**ac′ro·me·gal′ic** (-məgal′ik) *adj.*

**ac·ro·nym** (ak′rə nim) *n.* [< ACRO- + Gr. *onyma*, name]  a word formed from the first (or first few) letters of a series of words, as *radar*, from *radio detecting and ranging* —**ac′ro·nym′ic** *adj.*

**ac·ro·pho·bi·a** (ak′rə fō′bē ə) *n.* [ACRO- + PHOBIA]  an abnormal fear of being in high places

**a·crop·o·lis** (ə kräp′′l is) *n.* [< Gr. < *akros* (see ACRO-) + *polis*, city]  the fortified upper part of an ancient Greek city, esp. [A-] that of Athens, on which the Parthenon was built

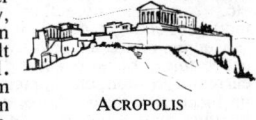
ACROPOLIS

**a·cross** (ə krôs′) *adv.*  **1.** crossed; crosswise  **2.** from one side to the other  **3.** on or to the other side —*prep.*  **1.** from one side to the other of; so as to cross  **2.** on or to the other side of; over  **3.** into contact with by chance [he came *across* a friend]

**a·cros·tic** (ə krôs′tik) *n.* [< Gr. < *akros* (see ACRO-) + *stichos*, line of verse]  a verse or arrangement of words in which certain letters in each line, as the first or last, when taken in order spell out a word, motto, etc. —*adj.* of or like an acrostic —**a·cros′ti·cal·ly** *adv.*

**a·cryl·ic fiber** (ə kril′ik) [ult. < ACR(ID) + -YL + -IC]  any of a group of synthetic fibers derived from a compound of hydrogen cyanide and acetylene, and made into fabrics

**acrylic resin** any of a group of transparent thermoplastic resins, as Lucite

**act** (akt) *n.* [< Fr. < L. *actus*, a doing, *actum*, thing done, pp. of *agere*, to do]  **1.** a thing done; deed  **2.** an action; doing  **3.** a decision (of a court, legislature, etc.)  **4.** a document formally stating what has been done, etc.  **5.** one of the main divisions of a drama or opera  **6.** any of the separate performances on a variety program  **7.** insincere behavior, put on just for effect —*vt.*  **1.** to play the part of  **2.** to perform in (a play)  **3.** to behave like [don't act the child] —*vi.*  **1.** to perform on the stage; play a role  **2.** to behave as though playing a role  **3.** to behave; comport oneself  **4.** to do something  **5.** to serve or function  **6.** to serve as spokesman (*for*)  **7.** to have an effect [acids act on metal]  **8.** to appear to be —**act up** [Colloq.]  **1.** to be playful  **2.** to misbehave  **3.** to become inflamed, painful, etc.

**act·a·ble** (ak′tə b′l) *adj.* that can be acted: said of a play, a role, etc. —**act′a·bil′i·ty** *n.*

**ACTH** [<*a*(dreno)*c*(ortico)*t*(rophic) *h*(ormone)]  a hormone secreted by the anterior lobe of the pituitary gland, that stimulates the growth and hormone production of the adrenal cortex

**act·ing** (ak′tiŋ) *adj.*  **1.** adapted for performance [an *acting* version of a play]  **2.** that acts; functioning  **3.** temporarily taking over the duties of a position [the *acting* chairman] —*n.* the art or occupation of performing in plays

**ac·tin·ic** (ak tin′ik) *adj.* having to do with actinism —**ac·tin′i·cal·ly** *adv.*

**actinic rays** violet or ultraviolet rays that produce chemical changes, as in photography

**ac·ti·nide series** (ak′tə nīd′)  a group of radioactive chemical elements from element 89 (actinium) through element 103 (lawrencium)

**ac·tin·ism** (ak′tən iz′m) *n.* [< Gr. *aktis* (gen. *aktinos*), ray & -ISM]  that property of ultraviolet light, X-rays, etc. by which chemical changes are produced

**ac·tin·i·um** (ak tin′ē əm) *n.* [ModL. < Gr. *aktis* (gen. *aktinos*), ray]  a radioactive chemical element found in pitchblende and other minerals: symbol, Ac; at. wt., 227 (?); at. no., 89

**ac·ti·noid** (ak′tə noid′) *adj.* star-shaped

**ac·ti·no·my·cin** (ak′ti nō mī′s′n) *n.* [< ModL. *Actinomyces*, a genus of bacteria]  any of various antibiotic substances derived from soil bacteria

**ac·ti·no·zo·an** (ak′ti nō zō′ən) *n.* [< Gr. *aktis* (gen. *aktinos*), ray + *zōion*, animal]  same as ANTHOZOAN

**ac·tion** (ak′shən) *n.* [< OFr. < L. *actio* < pp. of *agere*: see ACT]  **1.** the doing of something; a being in motion  **2.** an act or thing done  **3.** [*pl.*] behavior; habitual conduct  **4.** bold and energetic activity  **5.** an effect [the *action* of a drug]  **6.** the way of moving, working, etc., as of a machine  **7.** the moving parts or mechanism, as of a gun, piano, etc.  **8.** the happenings in a story or play  **9.** a legal proceeding; lawsuit  **10.** military combat  **11.** [Slang] activity or excitement —**bring action** to start a lawsuit —**see action** to take part in military combat —**take action**  **1.** to become active  **2.** to start a lawsuit

**ac·tion·a·ble** (-ə b′l) *adj. Law* that gives cause for an action, or lawsuit

**ac·ti·vate** (ak′tə vāt′) *vt.* **-vat′ed, -vat′ing**  **1.** to make active  **2.** to put (an inactive military unit) on an active status  **3.** to make radioactive  **4.** to make capable of reacting or of accelerating a chemical reaction  **5.** to treat (sewage) with air so that aerobes will purify it —**ac′ti·va′tion** *n.* —**ac′ti·va′tor** *n.*

**activated carbon** a highly porous carbon that can adsorb gases, vapors, and colloidal particles

**ac·tive** (ak′tiv) *adj.* [< OFr. < L. *activus* < base *act-* as in *actus:* see ACT] **1.** acting, functioning, working, moving, etc. **2.** capable of acting, functioning, etc. **3.** causing motion or change **4.** full of action; lively, busy, quick, etc. [an *active* mind, an *active* boy] **5.** involving action [an *active* role] **6.** necessitating action [*active* sports] **7.** in current operation, effect, etc. **8.** *Gram.* denoting the voice or form of a verb whose subject is shown as performing the action of the verb —*n. Gram.* the active voice —**ac′tive·ly** *adv.*
**ac·tiv·ism** (ak′tə viz′m) *n.* the doctrine or policy of taking positive, direct action, esp. for political or social ends —**ac′tiv·ist** *adj., n.*
**ac·tiv·i·ty** (ak tiv′ə tē) *n., pl.* **-ties 1.** the state of being active; action **2.** energetic action; liveliness **3.** an active force **4.** any specific action [recreational *activities*]
**ac·tiv·ize** (ak′tə vīz′) *vt.* **-ized′, -iz′ing** *same as* ACTIVATE
**act of God** *Law* an occurrence, esp. a disaster, that is due to the forces of nature and could not reasonably have been prevented
**Ac·ton** (ak′t′n), Lord (*John Emerick Edward Dalberg-Acton*) 1834–1902; Eng. historian
**ac·tor** (ak′tər) *n.* **1.** a person who does something **2.** a person who acts in plays, movies, etc.
**ac·tress** (ak′tris) *n.* a woman or girl who acts in plays, movies, etc.
**Acts** (akts) a book of the New Testament, ascribed to Luke: full title, **The Acts of the Apostles**
**ac·tu·al** (ak′choo wəl) *adj.* [< LL. < L. *actus:* see ACT] **1.** existing in reality or fact; not merely possible, but real **2.** existing at present or at the time
**ac·tu·al·i·ty** (ak′choo wal′ə tē) *n.* **1.** the state of being actual; reality **2.** *pl.* **-ties** an actual thing or condition; fact
**ac·tu·al·ize** (ak′choo wə līz′) *vt.* **-ized′, -iz′ing** to make actual or real —**ac′tu·al·i·za′tion** *n.*
**ac·tu·al·ly** (ak′choo wəl ē, ak′chə lē) *adv.* as a matter of actual fact; really
**ac·tu·ar·y** (ak′choo wer′ē) *n., pl.* **-ar′ies** [L. *actuarius,* clerk < *actus:* see ACT] a person who calculates risks, premiums, etc. for insurance —**ac′tu·ar′i·al** *adj.* —**ac′tu·ar′i·al·ly** *adv.*
**ac·tu·ate** (ak′choo wāt′) *vt.* **-at′ed, -at′ing 1.** to put into action or motion **2.** to cause to take action —**ac′tu·a′tion** *n.* —**ac′tu·a′tor** *n.*
**a·cu·i·ty** (ə kyōō′ə tē) *n.* [< Fr. < L. *acus,* a needle] keenness, as of thought or vision; acuteness
**a·cu·men** (ə kyōō′mən, ak′yoo-) *n.* [L., a point < *acuere,* to sharpen] keenness and quickness of mind
**a·cu·mi·nate** (ə kyōō′mə nit; *for v.* -nāt′) *adj.* [< L. pp. of *acuminare* < *acumen:* see prec.] pointed; tapering to a point —*vt.* **-nat′ed, -nat′ing** to make sharp or pointed —**a·cu′mi·na′tion** *n.*
**ac·u·punc·ture** (ak′yoo puŋk′chər) *n.* [< L. *acus,* needle + PUNCTURE] the ancient practice, esp. as carried on by the Chinese, of piercing parts of the body with needles in seeking to treat disease or relieve pain
**a·cute** (ə kyōōt′) *adj.* [< L. pp. of *acuere:* see ACUMEN] **1.** having a sharp point. keen or quick of mind; shrewd **3.** sensitive [*acute* hearing] **4.** severe and sharp, as pain, jealousy, etc. **5.** severe but of short duration, as some diseases; not chronic **6.** very serious; critical [an *acute* shortage] **7.** of less than 90° [an *acute* angle] —**a·cute′ly** *adv.* —**a·cute′ness** *n.*

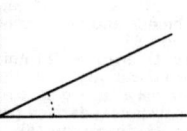

ACUTE ANGLE

**acute accent** a mark (′) used to show: **1.** the quality or length of a vowel, as in French *idée* **2.** primary stress, as in *týpewriter*
**-a·cy** (ə sē) [variously < Fr. < L. < Gr. *-ateia*] a suffix meaning quality, condition, position, etc. [*celibacy, curacy*]
**ad¹** (ad) *n.* [Colloq.] an advertisement
**ad²** (ad) *n. Tennis* advantage; the first point scored after deuce
**ad-** [L., to, at, toward; akin to AT] a prefix meaning variously motion toward, addition to, nearness to [*admit, adjoin, adrenal*]: assimilated in words of Latin origin to **ac-, af-, ag-, al-, an-, ap-, ar-, as-, at-,** and **a-** before certain consonants
**A.D.** [L. *Anno Domini,* in the year of the Lord] of the Christian era: used with dates
**A·da, A·dah** (ā′də) [Heb. *'adha,* beauty] a feminine name
**ad·age** (ad′ij) *n.* [Fr. < L. < *ad-,* to + *aio,* I say] an old saying that has been popularly accepted as a truth
**a·da·gio** (ə dä′jō, -jē ō) *adv.* [It. *ad agio,* lit., at ease] *Music* slowly and leisurely —*adj.* slow —*n., pl.* **-gios 1.** a slow movement in music **2.** a slow ballet dance, esp. by a mixed couple
**Ad·am** (ad′əm) [Heb. < *adam,* a human being] **1.** a masculine name **2.** *Bible* the first man: Gen. 1–5 —**not know (a person) from Adam** not know (a person) at all

**ad·a·mant** (ad′ə mənt, -mant′) *n.* [OFr. < L. < Gr. *adamas* (gen. *adamantos*) < *a-,* not + *daman,* to subdue] a substance of unbreakable hardness —*adj.* **1.** too hard to be broken᾿ **2.** not giving in or relenting; unyielding —**ad·a·man′tine** (-man′tēn, -tīn, -tin) *adj.* —**ad′a·mant·ly** *adv.*
**Ad·ams** (ad′əmz) **1. Henry (Brooks),** 1838–1918; U.S. historian & writer **2. John,** 1735–1826; 2d president of the U.S. (1797–1801) **3. John Quin·cy** (kwin′sē), 1767–1848; 6th president of the U.S. (1825–29): son of *prec.* **4. Samuel,** 1722–1803; Am. statesman & Revolutionary leader
**Adam's apple** the projection formed in the front of the throat by the thyroid cartilage, seen chiefly in men
**A·da·na** (ä′dä nä′) city in S Turkey: pop. 290,000
**a·dapt** (ə dapt′) *vt.* [< Fr. < L. *adaptare* < *ad-,* to + *aptare,* to fit] **1.** to make fit or suitable by changing or adjusting **2.** to adjust (oneself) to new or changed circumstances —*vi.* to adjust oneself —**a·dapt′a·bil′i·ty** *n.* —**a·dapt′a·ble** *adj.* —**a·dapt′er, a·dap′tor** *n.*
**ad·ap·ta·tion** (ad′əp tā′shən) *n.* **1.** an adapting or being adapted **2.** a thing resulting from adapting [a movie *adaptation* of a novel] **3.** *Biol.* a change in structure, function, etc. of a plant or animal that produces better adjustment to the environment Also **a·dap·tion** (ə dap′shən)
**a·dap·tive** (ə dap′tiv) *adj.* **1.** showing adaptation **2.** able to adapt —**a·dap′tive·ly** *adv.*
**A·dar** (ä där′) *n.* [Heb.] the sixth month of the Jewish year: see JEWISH CALENDAR
**A.D.C., ADC** aide-de-camp
**add** (ad) *vt.* [< L. *addere* < *ad-,* to + *dare,* to give] **1.** to join or unite (*to*) so as to increase the quantity, number, etc. **2.** to state further **3.** to combine (numbers) into a sum or total —*vi.* **1.** to cause an increase (*to*) **2.** to figure a total —**add up** to seem reasonable —**add up to 1.** to reach a total of **2.** to mean; signify
**Ad·dams** (ad′əmz), **Jane** 1860–1935; U.S. social worker & writer
**ad·dax** (ad′aks) *n.* [L. < native Afr. word] a large antelope of N Africa, with long, twisted horns
**ad·dend** (ad′end, ə dend′) *n.* [< ff.] a number or quantity to be added to another
**ad·den·dum** (ə den′dəm) *n., pl.* **-da** (-də) [L., gerundive of *addere:* see ADD] a thing added; esp., an appendix or supplement
**ad·der** (ad′ər) *n.* [ME. < *nadder* (by faulty separation of *a nadder*) < OE. *nædre*] **1.** a small poisonous snake of Europe; common viper **2.** any of various other snakes, as the puff adder (sense 1), the milk snake, etc.
**ad·der's-tongue** (ad′ərz tuŋ′) *n.* **1.** *same as* DOGTOOTH VIOLET **2.** a fern with a narrow spike
**ad·dict** (ə dikt′; *for n.* ad′ikt) *vt.* [< L. pp. of *addicere,* to give assent < *ad-,* to + *dicere,* to say] **1.** to give (oneself) up (*to* some strong habit): usually in the passive **2.** to make an addict of —*n.* one addicted to a habit, esp. to the use of a narcotic drug —**ad·dic′tion** *n.* —**ad·dic′tive** *adj.*
**Ad·dis A·ba·ba** (ä′dis ä′bə bə) capital of Ethiopia: pop. 644,000
**Ad·di·son** (ad′ə s′n), **Joseph** 1672–1719; Eng. essayist & poet —**Ad′di·so′ni·an** (-sō′nē ən) *adj.*
**Ad·di·son's disease** (ad′ə s′nz) [after T. *Addison,* 19th-c. Eng. physician] a disease of the adrenal glands, characterized by weakness, skin discolorations, etc.
**ad·di·tion** (ə dish′ən) *n.* **1.** an adding of numbers to get a number called the sum **2.** a joining of a thing to another thing **3.** a thing or part added **4.** a room or rooms added to a building —**in addition (to)** besides; as well (as) —**ad·di′tion·al** *adj.* —**ad·di′tion·al·ly** *adv.*
**ad·di·tive** (ad′ə tiv) *adj.* **1.** showing or relating to addition **2.** to be added —*n.* a substance added to another in small quantities for a desired effect, as a preservative added to food
**ad·dle** (ad′′l) *adj.* [< OE. *adela,* mire, mud] **1.** rotten: said of an egg **2.** muddled; confused: often in compounds [*addlebrained*] —*vt., vi.* **-dled, -dling 1.** to make or become rotten **2.** to make or become muddled or confused
**ad·dle·brained** (-brānd′) *adj.* having an addle brain; muddled: also **ad′dle·head′ed, ad′dle·pat′ed** (-pāt′id)
**ad·dress** (ə dres′; *for n.* esp. 2, 3, & 4, also ad′res) *vt.* [< OFr. < *a-,* to + *dresser,* to direct < L. *dirigere:* see DIRECT] **1.** to direct (spoken or written words *to*) **2.** to speak to or write to **3.** to write the destination on (a letter or parcel) **4.** to use a proper form in speaking to **5.** to apply (oneself) or direct (one's energies) **6.** to take a stance, as in aiming the club at (a golf ball), facing (a target), etc. —*n.* **1.** a speech, esp. a formal one **2.** the place to which mail can be sent to one; place where one lives or works **3.** the writing on mail showing its destination **4.** the location in a computer's storage compartment of an item of information **5.** social skill and tact **6.** conversational manner —**ad·dress′er, ad·dres′sor** *n.*
**ad·dress·ee** (ad′res ē′) *n.* the person to whom mail, etc. is addressed
**ad·duce** (ə dōōs′, -dyōōs′) *vt.* **-duced′, -duc′ing** [< L. *ad-*

*ducere* < *ad-*, to + *ducere:* see DUCT]  to give as a reason or proof; cite —**ad·duc′er** *n.* —**ad·duc′i·ble, ad·duce′a·ble** *adj.*

**ad·duct** (a dukt′, ə-) *vt.* [< L. pp. of *adducere:* see prec.] to pull (a part of the body) toward the median axis: said of a muscle —**ad·duc′tor** *n.*

**ad·duc·tion** (a duk′shən, ə-) *n.*   1. an adducing or citing   2. an adducting

**-ade** (ād) [ult. < L. *-ata*]  *a suffix meaning:*   1. the act of *[blockade]*   2. the result or product of *[pomade]*   3. participant(s) in an action *[brigade]*   4. [after LEMONADE] drink made from *[limeade]*

**Ad·e·laide** (ad′'l ād′) [< Fr. < G. < OHG. *Adalheit*, lit., nobility]   1. a feminine name: dim. *Addie;* var. *Adeline, Adelina, Adele*   2. city in S Australia: pop. 727,000

**A·den** (äd′'n, ād′-)   1. former Brit. colony in SW Arabia: now part of YEMEN (sense 2)   2. seaport in this region: pop. 250,000   3. Gulf of, arm of the Arabian Sea, between S Arabia and E Africa

**ad·e·nine** (ad′'n ēn′) *n.* [ADEN(O)- + -INE⁴] a white, crystalline purine base, C₅H₅N₅, found in nucleic acid in the spleen, pancreas, etc.

**ad·e·no-** [< Gr. *adēn*, gland]  *a combining form meaning* of a gland or glands: also, before a vowel, **aden-**

**ad·e·noi·dal** (ad′'n oid′'l) *adj.*   1. *a)* glandular *b)* of or like lymphoid tissue: also **ad′e·noid′**   2. having adenoids   3. having the characteristic difficult breathing or nasal tone due to enlarged adenoids

**ad·e·noids** (ad′'n oidz′) *n.pl.* [< ADEN(O)- & -OID] lymphoid growths in the throat behind the nose: they can swell up and obstruct breathing

**ad·e·no·ma** (ad′'n ō′mə) *n.* [ADEN(O)- + -OMA] a benign tumor of glandular origin or glandlike cell structure

**a·den·o·sine** (ə den′ə s'n, -sēn′) *n.* [arbitrary blend < ADENINE + RIBOSE] a white crystalline powder, C₁₀H₁₃N₅O₄, obtained from the hydrolysis of yeast nucleic acid: see also ADP, ATP

**ad·ept** (ə dept′; *for n.* ad′ept) *adj.* [< L. pp. of *adipisci* < *ad-*, to + *apisci*, to pursue, attain]  highly skilled; expert —*n.* an expert —**ad·ept′ly** *adv.* —**ad·ept′ness** *n.*

**ad·e·quate** (ad′ə kwət) *adj.* [< L. pp. of *adaequare* < *ad-*, to + *aequare*, to make equal < *aequus*, level]   1. enough or good enough; sufficient; suitable   2. barely satisfactory —**ad′e·qua·cy** (-kwə sē), **ad′e·quate·ness** *n.* —**ad′e·quate·ly** *adv.*

**ad·here** (əd hir′, ad-) *vi.* **-hered′, -her′ing** [< L. *adhaerere* < *ad-*, to + *haerere*, to stick]   1. to stick fast; stay attached   2. to stay firm in supporting or approving —**ad·her′er** *n.*

**ad·her·ence** (əd hir′əns, ad-) *n.* an adhering; attachment or devotion (*to* a person, cause, etc.)

**ad·her·ent** (-ənt) *adj.*   1. sticking fast; attached   2. *Bot.* grown together —*n.* a supporter or follower (*of* a person, cause, etc.)

**ad·he·sion** (əd hē′zhən, ad-) *n.* [Fr. < L. *adhaesio* < *adhaerere:* see ADHERE]   1. a sticking or being stuck together   2. devoted attachment; adherence   3. *Med. a)* the joining together, by fibrous tissue, of bodily parts normally separate *b)* such fibrous tissue   4. *Physics* the force that holds together the molecules of unlike substances in surface contact: distinguished from COHESION

**ad·he·sive** (əd hē′siv, ad-; -ziv) *adj.*   1. sticking and not coming loose; clinging   2. gummed; sticky —*n.* an adhesive substance, as glue —**ad·he′sive·ly** *adv.* —**ad·he′sive·ness** *n.*

**adhesive tape** tape with a sticky substance on one side, used for holding bandages in place, etc.

**ad hoc** (ad′ häk′) [L., to this]  for a special case or purpose only *[an ad hoc committee]*

**ad·i·a·bat·ic** (ad′ē ə bat′ik) *adj.* [< Gr. < *a-*, not + *dia*, through + *bainein*, to go]  *Physics* involving expansion or compression without loss or gain of heat —**ad′i·a·bat′i·cal·ly** *adv.*

**a·dieu** (ə dyōō′, -dōō′; *Fr.* à dyö′) *interj., n., pl.* **a·dieus′;** *Fr.* **a·dieux′** (-dyö′) [Fr. < OFr. < L. *ad*, to + *Deus*, God]  goodbye

**ad in·fi·ni·tum** (ad in′fə nīt′əm) [L., to infinity]  endlessly; forever; without limit

**ad in·ter·im** (ad in′tər im) [L.]   1. in the meantime   2. temporary

**a·di·os** (a′dē ōs′, ä′-; *Sp.* ä dyôs′) *interj.* [Sp. *adiós* < L. *ad*, to + *Deus*, God]  goodbye

**ad·i·pose** (ad′ə pōs′) *adj.* [< ModL. < L. *adeps* (gen. *adipis*), fat]  of, like, or containing animal fat; fatty —*n.* animal fat in the connective tissue —**ad′i·pos′i·ty** (-päs′ə tē) *n.*

**Ad·i·ron·dack Mountains** (ad′ə rän′dak)  mountain range of the Appalachians, in NE N.Y.: also **Ad′i·ron′dacks**

**ad·it** (ad′it) *n.* [< L. pp. of *adire* < *ad-*, to + *ire*, to go]  an approach or entrance

**adj.**   1. adjective   2. adjourned   3. adjutant

**ad·ja·cent** (ə jā′s'nt) *adj.* [< L. prp. of *adjacere* < *ad-*, to + *jacere*, to lie]  near or close (*to* something); adjoining —**ad·ja′cen·cy** *n.* —**ad·ja′cent·ly** *adv.*

**adjacent angles** two angles having the same vertex and a side in common

**ad·jec·tive** (aj′ik tiv) *n.* [< L. < pp. of *adjicere*, to add to < *ad-*, to + *jacere*, to throw]   1. any of a class of words used to limit or qualify a noun or other substantive *[good, every,* and *Aegean* are *adjectives]*   2. any phrase or clause similarly used —*adj.* of, or having the nature or function of, an adjective —**ad′jec·ti′val** (-ti′v'l) *adj.* —**ad′jec·ti′val·ly** *adv.*

**ad·join** (ə join′) *vt.* [< OFr. < L. *adjungere* < *ad-*, to + *jungere:* see JOIN]  to be next to; be contiguous to —*vi.* to be next to each other; be in contact —**ad·join′ing** *adj.*

**ad·journ** (ə jurn′) *vt.* [< OFr. < *a*, at + *jorn*, day < L. *diurnum*, daily < *dies*, day]  to put off or suspend until a future day —*vi.*   1. to close a session or meeting for a time   2. [Colloq.] to go (*to* another place) *[let's adjourn to the patio]* —**ad·journ′ment** *n.*

**ad·judge** (ə juj′) *vt.* **-judged′, -judg′ing** [< OFr. < L. *adjudicare* < *ad-*, to + *judicare*, to judge < *judex*, JUDGE]   1. to judge or decide by law   2. to declare or order by law   3. to award (costs, etc.) by law   4. [Rare] to regard; deem

**ad·ju·di·cate** (ə jōō′də kāt′) *vt.* **-cat′ed, -cat′ing** [< L. pp. of *adjudicare:* see prec.]  *Law* to hear and decide (a case); adjudge —*vi.* to serve as a judge (*in* or *on* a matter) —**ad·ju′di·ca′tion** *n.* —**ad·ju′di·ca′tive** *adj.* —**ad·ju′di·ca′tor** *n.* —**ad·ju′di·ca·to′ry** (-kə tôr′ē) *adj.*

**ad·junct** (aj′uŋkt) *n.* [< L. pp. of *adjungere:* see ADJOIN]   1. a thing added to something else, but secondary   2. a subordinate associate   3. *Gram.* a modifier —*adj.* connected in a subordinate way —**ad·junc·tive** (ə juŋk′tiv) *adj.* —**ad·junc′tive·ly** *adv.* —**ad′junct·ly** *adv.*

**ad·jure** (ə jōōr′) *vt.* **-jured′, -jur′ing** [< L. *adjurare* < *ad-*, to + *jurare:* see JURY¹]   1. to charge solemnly, often under oath or penalty   2. to entreat earnestly —**ad·ju·ra·tion** (aj′oo rā′shən) *n.* —**ad·jur′a·to′ry** (-ə tôr′ē) *adj.* —**ad·jur′er, ad·ju′ror** *n.*

**ad·just** (ə just′) *vt.* [< OFr. < *a-*, to + *j(o)uster* (see JOUST); infl. by OFr. *juste* < L. *justus*, JUST¹]   1. to change so as to fit, conform, make suitable, etc.   2. to regulate *[to adjust a watch]*   3. to settle or arrange rightly   4. to resolve or bring into accord   5. to decide how much is to be paid on (an insurance claim) —*vi.* to adapt oneself, as to one's surroundings —**ad·just′a·ble** *adj.* —**ad·just′er, ad·jus′tor** *n.*

**ad·just·ment** (-mənt) *n.*   1. an adjusting or being adjusted   2. a means by which parts are adjusted to one another   3. the settlement of a claim

**ad·ju·tant** (aj′ə tənt) *n.* [< L. prp. of *adjutare* < *adjuvare* < *ad-*, to + *juvare*, to help]   1. an assistant   2. *Mil.* a staff officer who is an administrative assistant to the commanding officer   3. a large stork of India and Africa

**adjutant general** *pl.* **adjutants general**   1. an army officer who is the chief administrative assistant of a commanding general   2. [A- G-] *U.S. Army* the general in charge of the department that handles records, correspondence, etc.

**ad-lib** (ad′lib′) *vt., vi.* **-libbed′, -lib′bing** [< ff.] [Colloq.] to improvise (words, etc. not in the script); extemporize —*n.* [Colloq.] an ad-libbed remark: also **ad lib** —*adj.* spoken or done extemporaneously —*adv.* [Colloq.] extemporizing freely: also **ad lib**

**ad lib·i·tum** (ad′ lib′i təm) [ML. < L. *ad*, at + *libitum* < *libet*, it pleases]  at pleasure; as one pleases: used esp. as a musical direction that a section may be altered to suit the performer

**Adm.**   1. Admiral   2. Admiralty

**ad·man** (ad′man′) *n., pl.* **-men′** (-men′) a man whose work or business is advertising: also **ad man**

**ad·meas·ure** (ad me′zhər) *vt.* **-ured, -ur·ing** [see AD- & MEASURE] to measure out shares of; apportion —**ad·meas′ure·ment** *n.*

**ad·min·is·ter** (əd min′ə stər, ad-) *vt.* [< OFr. < L. *administrare* < *ad-*, to + *ministrare*, to serve]   1. to manage or direct   2. to give out or dispense (punishment, etc.)   3. to give or apply (medicine, etc.)   4. to direct the taking of (an oath, pledge, etc.)   5. *Law* to act as executor or administrator of (an estate) —*vi.*   1. to act as manager or administrator   2. to furnish help or be of service —**ad·min′is·tra·ble** (-ə strə b'l) *adj.* —**ad·min′is·trant** (-ə strənt) *n., adj.*

**ad·min·is·trate** (əd min′ə strāt′, ad-) *vt.* **-trat′ed, -trat′ing** *same as* ADMINISTER

ADJU-
TANT
STORK
(to 60
in. high)

**ad·min·is·tra·tion** (əd min'ə strā'shən, ad-) *n.* **1.** management, specif. of the affairs of a government, business, etc. **2.** *a*) [*often* A-] the executive officials of a government, business, etc., and their policies *b*) their term of office **3.** the administering (*of* medicine, an oath, etc.) **4.** *Law* the management and settling (*of* an estate) —**ad·min'is·tra'tive** *adj.* —**ad·min'is·tra'tive·ly** *adv.*

**ad·min·is·tra·tor** (əd min'ə strāt'ər, ad-) *n.* **1.** one who administers, or manages affairs **2.** *Law* one appointed by a court to settle an estate: cf. EXECUTOR —**ad·min'is·tra'trix** (-strā'triks) *n.fem., pl.* -tra'tri·ces' (-tri sēz'), -trix·es

**ad·mi·ra·ble** (ad'mər ə b'l) *adj.* inspiring or deserving admiration or praise; splendid —**ad'mi·ra·bil'i·ty** *n.* —**ad'mi·ra·bly** *adv.*

**ad·mi·ral** (ad'mər əl) *n.* [< OFr. < Ar. *amîr a' âli*, high leader; sp. infl. by ADMIRABLE] **1.** the commanding officer of a navy or fleet **2.** a naval officer of the highest rank **3.** [orig. ADMIRABLE] any of certain colorful butterflies

**ad·mi·ral·ty** (-tē) *n., pl.* -ties **1.** the rank, position, or authority of an admiral **2.** *a*) [*often* A-] the governmental department for naval affairs, as in England *b*) maritime law or court

**ad·mi·ra·tion** (ad'mə rā'shən) *n.* **1.** an admiring **2.** wonder, delight, and pleased approval at anything fine, skillful, beautiful, etc. **3.** a thing or person inspiring such feelings

**ad·mire** (əd mīr', ad-) *vt.* -mired', -mir'ing [< OFr. < L. *admirari* < *ad-*, at + *mirari*, to wonder] **1.** to regard with wonder, delight, and approval **2.** to have high regard for **3.** [Dial.] to like or wish (*to* do something) —**ad·mir'er** *n.* —**ad·mir'ing·ly** *adv.*

**ad·mis·si·ble** (əd mis'ə b'l, ad-) *adj.* [Fr. < L. pp. of *admittere*, ADMIT] **1.** that can be properly accepted or allowed **2.** that ought to be admitted —**ad·mis'si·bil'i·ty** *n.* —**ad·mis'si·bly** *adv.*

**ad·mis·sion** (əd mish'ən, ad-) *n.* **1.** an admitting or being admitted **2.** the right to enter **3.** an entrance fee **4.** a conceding, or granting **5.** an acknowledging or confessing **6.** a thing conceded, acknowledged, or confessed —**admis'sive** *adj.*

**ad·mit** (əd mit', ad-) *vt.* -mit'ted, -mit'ting [< L. *admittere* < *ad-*, to + *mittere*, to send] **1.** to permit to enter or use **2.** to entitle to enter **3.** to allow, or leave room for **4.** to have room for; hold **5.** to concede; grant **6.** to acknowledge or confess **7.** to permit to practice [*admitted* to the bar] —*vi.* **1.** to give entrance (*to* a place) **2.** to allow or warrant (with *of*)

**ad·mit·tance** (-'ns) *n.* **1.** an admitting or being admitted **2.** permission or right to enter **3.** *Elec.* the reciprocal of impedance

**ad·mit·ted·ly** (əd mit'id lē) *adv.* by admission or agreement; confessedly [*admittedly* afraid]

**ad·mix** (ad miks') *vt., vi.* [< ff.] to mix (a thing) in; mix with something

**ad·mix·ture** (-chər) *n.* [< L. pp. of *admiscere* < *ad-*, to + *miscere*, to mix + -URE] **1.** a mixture **2.** a thing or ingredient added in mixing

**ad·mon·ish** (əd män'ish, ad-) *vt.* [< OFr. < L. *admonere* < *ad-*, to + *monere*, to warn] **1.** to caution against specific faults; warn **2.** to reprove mildly **3.** to urge or exhort **4.** to inform or remind, by way of a warning —**ad·mon'ish·ing·ly** *adv.* —**ad·mon'ish·ment** *n.*

**ad·mo·ni·tion** (ad'mə nish'ən) *n.* **1.** an admonishing, or warning to correct some fault **2.** a mild rebuke; reprimand

**ad·mon·i·tor** (əd män'ə tər, ad-) *n.* a person who admonishes —**ad·mon'i·to'ry** (-tôr'ē) *adj.*

**ad nau·se·am** (ad' nô'zē əm, -shē-, -sē-) [L., to nausea] to the point of disgust

**a·do** (ə dōō') *n.* [ME. < dial. inf. *at do*, to do] fuss; trouble; excitement

**a·do·be** (ə dō'bē) *n.* [Sp. < Ar. < Coptic *tôbe*, brick] **1.** unburnt, sun-dried brick **2.** the clay of which such brick is made **3.** a building made of adobe, esp. in the Southwest

**ad·o·les·cence** (ad'l es''ns) *n.* **1.** the state or quality of being adolescent **2.** the time of life between puberty and maturity

**ad·o·les·cent** (-'nt) *adj.* [Fr. < L. prp. of *adolescere*, to mature < *ad-*, to + *alescere*, to increase, grow up < *alere*, to feed] **1.** developing from childhood to maturity; growing up **2.** of or characteristic of adolescence; youthful, exuberant, immature, etc. —*n.* a boy or girl from puberty to adulthood; person in his teens

**Ad·olph** (ad'älf, ā'dôlf) [< L. < OHG. < *adal*, nobility + *wolf*, wolf] a masculine name

**A·don·is** (ə dän'is, -dō'nis) *Gr. Myth.* a young man loved by Aphrodite —*n.* any very handsome young man —**A·don'ic** (-ik) *adj.*

**a·dopt** (ə däpt') *vt.* [< L. *adoptare* < *ad-*, to + *optare*, to choose] **1.** to choose and bring into a certain relationship; specif., to take into one's own family by legal process and

raise as one's own child **2.** to take up and use (an idea, etc.) as one's own **3.** to choose and follow (a course) **4.** to vote to accept (a motion, etc.) **5.** to select as a required textbook —**a·dopt'a·ble** *adj.* —**a·dopt'er** *n.* —**a·dop'tion** *n.*

**a·dop·tive** (ə däp'tiv) *adj.* **1.** of adoption **2.** having become so by adopting [*adoptive* parents]

**a·dor·a·ble** (ə dôr'ə b'l) *adj.* **1.** [Now Rare] worthy of adoration **2.** [Colloq.] delightful; charming —**a·dor'a·bil'i·ty** *n.* —**a·dor'a·bly** *adv.*

**ad·o·ra·tion** (ad'ə rā'shən) *n.* **1.** a worshiping or paying homage **2.** great love or devotion

**a·dore** (ə dôr') *vt.* **a·dored', a·dor'ing** [< OFr. < L. *adorare* < *ad-*, to + *orare*, to speak] **1.** to worship as divine **2.** to love or honor greatly; idolize **3.** [Colloq.] to like very much —**a·dor'er** *n.* —**a·dor'ing·ly** *adv.*

**a·dorn** (ə dôrn') *vt.* [< OFr. < L. *adornare* < *ad-*, to + *ornare*, to deck out] **1.** to be an ornament to; add beauty or distinction to **2.** to put decorations on; ornament —**a·dorn'ment** *n.*

**ADP** [A(DENOSINE) *d*(*i*)*p*(*hosphate*)] a vital substance, $C_{10}H_{15}N_5O_{10}P_2$, of all living cells, that is essential to the energy processes of life

**ad·re·nal** (ə drē'n'l) *adj.* [AD- + RENAL] **1.** near the kidneys **2.** of or from the adrenal glands —*n. same as* ADRENAL GLAND

**adrenal gland** either of a pair of endocrine organs lying immediately above the kidney and producing a variety of hormones

**Ad·ren·al·in** (ə dren''l in) [ADRENAL + -IN¹] *a trademark for* EPINEPHRINE —*n.* [a-] epinephrine: also **ad·ren'al·ine** (-in)

**ad·re·no-** *a combining form meaning:* **1.** adrenal glands **2.** epinephrine Also, before a vowel, **adren-**

**A·dri·at·ic (Sea)** (ā'drē at'ik) arm of the Mediterranean between Italy and Yugoslavia

**a·drift** (ə drift') *adv., adj.* **1.** floating freely without being steered; drifting **2.** without any particular aim or purpose

**a·droit** (ə droit') *adj.* [Fr. *à*, to + *droit*, right < L. pp. of *dirigere*, DIRECT] skillful in a physical or mental way; clever —**a·droit'ly** *adv.* —**a·droit'ness** *n.*

**ad·sorb** (ad sôrb', -zôrb') *vt.* [< AD- + L. *sorbere* (cf. ABSORB)] to collect (a gas, liquid, or dissolved substance) in condensed form on a surface —**ad·sorb'a·ble** *adj.* —**ad·sor'bent** *adj., n.*

**ad·sorp·tion** (ad sôrp'shən, -zôrp'-) *n.* adhesion of the molecules of a gas, liquid, or dissolved substance to a surface —**ad·sorp'tive** *adj.*

**ad·u·late** (aj'ə lāt') *vt.* -lat'ed, -lat'ing [< L. pp. of *adulari*, to fawn upon] to praise or flatter too greatly —**ad'u·la'tion** *n.* —**ad'u·la'tor** *n.* —**ad'u·la·to'ry** (-lə tôr'ē) *adj.*

**a·dult** (ə dult', ad'ult) *adj.* [< L. pp. of *adolescere*: see ADOLESCENT] **1.** grown up; fully developed in size, strength, mind, etc. **2.** of or for adult persons —*n.* **1.** a mature person **2.** a mature animal or plant **3.** a person who has reached the age at which he has full legal rights and responsibilities —**a·dult'hood** *n.* —**a·dult'ness** *n.*

**a·dul·ter·ant** (ə dul'tər ənt) *n.* a substance used to adulterate something —*adj.* adulterating

**a·dul·ter·ate** (ə dul'tə rāt') *vt.* -at'ed, -at'ing [< L. pp. of *adulterare*, to falsify < *ad-*, to + *alter*, other] to make inferior, impure, etc. by adding a harmful, inferior, or unnecessary substance —**a·dul'ter·a'tion** *n.* —**a·dul'ter·a·tor** *n.*

**a·dul·ter·er** (ə dul'tər ər) *n.* a person (esp. a man) who commits adultery —**a·dul'ter·ess** *n.fem.*

**a·dul·ter·ous** (-əs) *adj.* of, or having committed, adultery —**a·dul'ter·ous·ly** *adv.*

**a·dul·ter·y** (ə dul'tər ē) *n., pl.* -ter·ies [L. *adulterium* < *adulter*: see ADULTERATE] voluntary sexual intercourse between a married person and another not the spouse

**ad·um·brate** (ad um'brāt, ad'əm brāt') *vt.* -brat·ed, -brat·ing [< L. pp. of *adumbrari* < *ad-*, to + *umbra*, shade] **1.** to outline vaguely; sketch **2.** to foreshadow vaguely **3.** to obscure; overshadow —**ad'um·bra'tion** *n.* —**ad·um'·bra·tive** *adj.*

**adv.** **1.** adverb **2.** adverbial **3.** advertisement **4.** advisory **5.** advocate

**ad va·lo·rem** (ad' və lôr'əm) [L.] in proportion to the value: said of duties levied on imports according to their invoiced value: abbrev. **ad val.**

**ad·vance** (əd vans') *vt.* -vanced', -vanc'ing [< OFr. *avancer* < L. *ab-*, from + *ante*, before] **1.** to bring or move forward **2.** to raise in rank, importance, etc. **3.** to help; further **4.** to put forward; propose **5.** to cause to happen earlier **6.** to raise the rate of **7.** to pay (money) before due **8.** to lend —*vi.* **1.** to go forward **2.** to improve; progress; develop **3.** to rise in rank, importance, price, etc. —*n.* **1.** a moving forward **2.** an improvement; progress **3.** a rise in value or cost **4.** [*pl.*] approaches to gain favor, become acquainted, etc. **5.** a payment made before due, as of wages **6.** a loan —*adj.*

**1.** in front [advance guard] **2.** beforehand [advance information] —**in advance 1.** in front **2.** ahead of time

**ad·vanced** (əd vanst′) adj. **1.** in advance; in front **2.** far on in life; old **3.** ahead or beyond in progress, complexity, etc. [advanced studies] **4.** higher than usual [advanced prices]

**ad·vance·ment** (əd vans′mənt) n. **1.** an advancing or being advanced **2.** promotion, as to a higher rank **3.** progress or improvement; furtherance

**ad·van·tage** (əd van′tij) n. [< OFr. < avant, before < L. ab ante, from before] **1.** a more favorable position; superiority or a better chance **2.** a favorable circumstance, event, etc. **3.** gain or benefit **4.** Tennis the first point scored after deuce —vt. **-taged, -tag·ing** to give an advantage to —**take advantage of 1.** to use for one's own benefit **2.** to impose upon —**to advantage** producing a good effect

**ad·van·ta·geous** (ad′vən tā′jəs) adj. favorable; profitable —**ad′van·ta′geous·ly** adv.

**Ad·vent** (ad′vent) n. [< L. pp. of advenire < ad-, to + venire, to come] **1.** the period including the four Sundays just before Christmas **2.** Theol. a) Christ's birth b) same as SECOND COMING **3.** [a-] a coming or arrival

**Ad·vent·ist** (ad′vən tist) n. a member of a Christian sect based on the belief that Christ's second coming will soon occur —**Ad′vent·ism** n.

**ad·ven·ti·tious** (ad′vən tish′əs) adj. [< L., coming from abroad: see ADVENT] **1.** added from outside; accidental **2.** Biol. occurring in unusual or abnormal places [adventitious leaves on a plant] —**ad′ven·ti′tious·ly** adv. —**ad′ven·ti′tious·ness** n.

**ad·ven·tive** (ad ven′tiv) adj. Bot. not native to the environment

**ad·ven·ture** (əd ven′chər) n. [< OFr. < L. advenire: see ADVENT] **1.** the encountering of, or a liking for, danger **2.** an exciting and dangerous undertaking **3.** an unusual, stirring experience, often of a romantic nature **4.** a business venture or speculation —vt. **-tured, -tur·ing** to risk or venture —vi. **1.** to engage in adventure **2.** to take a risk

**ad·ven·tur·er** (-ər) n. **1.** a person who has or likes to have adventures **2.** same as SOLDIER OF FORTUNE **3.** a financial speculator **4.** a person who seeks to become rich, powerful, etc. by dubious schemes —**ad·ven′tur·ess** n.fem.

**ad·ven·ture·some** (-səm) adj. willing to take risks; adventurous

**ad·ven·tur·ism** (-iz′m) n. actions, esp. in international relations, regarded as reckless and risky —**ad·ven′tur·ist** n., adj.

**ad·ven·tur·ous** (-əs) adj. **1.** fond of adventure; daring **2.** full of danger; risky —**ad·ven′tur·ous·ly** adv. —**ad·ven′·tur·ous·ness** n.

**ad·verb** (ad′vurb) n. [< L. adverbium < ad-, to + verbum, a word] **1.** any of a class of words used to modify a verb, adjective, or another adverb, by expressing time, place, manner, degree, cause, etc. **2.** any phrase or clause similarly used —**ad·ver′bi·al** adj., n. —**ad·ver′bi·al·ly** adv.

**ad·ver·sar·y** (ad′vər ser′ē) n., pl. **-sar′ies** [< OFr. < L. < adversus, ADVERSE] a person who opposes or fights against another; opponent; enemy

**ad·ver·sa·tive** (ad vur′sə tiv, əd-) adj. [< LL. < L. pp. of adversari, to be opposed to] expressing opposition or antithesis —n. an adversative word, such as but, yet, however

**ad·verse** (ad vurs′, əd-; ad′vərs) adj. [< OFr. < L. adversus, turned opposite to, pp. of advertere: see ADVERT] **1.** opposite in position or direction **2.** unfavorable; harmful —**ad·verse′ly** adv.

**ad·ver·si·ty** (ad vur′sə tē, əd-) n. **1.** a state of wretchedness; poverty and trouble **2.** pl. **-ties** a disaster; calamity

**ad·vert** (ad vurt′, əd-) vi. [< OFr. < L. advertere < ad-, to + vertere, to turn: see VERSE] to pay attention (to); refer

**ad·vert·ent** (-'nt) adj. attentive; heedful —**ad·vert′ence, ad·vert′en·cy** n. —**ad·vert′ent·ly** adv.

**ad·ver·tise** (ad′vər tīz′) vt. **-tised′, -tis′ing** [< OFr. advertir, to call attention to < L. advertere: see ADVERT] **1.** to tell about or praise (a product, etc.), as through newspapers, radio, or the like, so as to promote sales **2.** to make known —vi. **1.** to call the public's attention to things for sale, for rent, etc., as by printed notices **2.** to ask (for) publicly by printed notice, etc. [advertise for a maid] —**ad′ver·tis′er** n.

**ad·ver·tise·ment** (ad′vər tīz′mənt, əd vur′tiz mənt) n. **1.** the act of advertising **2.** a public announcement, usually paid for, as of things for sale, needs, etc.

**ad·ver·tis·ing** (ad′vər tī′ziŋ) n. **1.** printed or spoken matter that advertises **2.** the business or work of preparing and issuing advertisements

**ad·ver·tize** (ad′vər tīz′) vt., vi. **-tized′, -tiz′ing** same as ADVERTISE —**ad′ver·tize′ment** n.

**ad·vice** (əd vīs′) n. [< OFr. < ML. advisum < pp. of ad-

videre < L. < ad-, at + videre, to look] **1.** opinion given as to what to do; counsel **2.** [usually pl.] information or report

**ad·vis·a·ble** (əd vī′zə b'l) adj. proper to be advised or recommended; being good advice —**ad·vis′a·bil′i·ty** n. —**ad·vis′a·bly** adv.

**ad·vise** (əd vīz′) vt. **-vised′, -vis′ing** [< OFr. < ML. advisum: see ADVICE] **1.** to give advice to; counsel **2.** to offer as advice; recommend **3.** to notify; inform —vi. **1.** to discuss or consult (with) **2.** to give advice —**ad·vis′er, ad·vi′sor** n.

**ad·vised** (əd vīzd′) adj. showing or resulting from thought or advice: now chiefly in WELL-ADVISED, ILL-ADVISED

**ad·vis·ed·ly** (əd vī′zid lē) adv. with due consideration; deliberately

**ad·vise·ment** (əd vīz′mənt) n. careful consideration —**take under advisement** to consider carefully

**ad·vi·so·ry** (əd vī′zər ē) adj. **1.** advising or empowered to advise **2.** relating to, or containing, advice —n., pl. **-ries** a warning, esp. one about weather conditions

**ad·vo·ca·cy** (ad′və kə sē) n. an advocating; a speaking or writing in support (of something)

**ad·vo·cate** (ad′və kit, -kāt′; for v. -kāt′) n. [< OFr. < L. advocatus, a counselor < ad-, to + vocare, to call] **1.** a person who pleads another's cause; specif., a lawyer **2.** a person who speaks or writes in support of something —vt. **-cat′ed, -cat′ing** to speak or write in support of; be in favor of —**ad′vo·ca′tor** n.

**advt.** pl. **advts.** advertisement

**adz, adze** (adz) n. [OE. adesa] an axlike tool for trimming and smoothing wood, etc., with a curved blade at right angles to the handle

**A.E.C., AEC** Atomic Energy Commission

**a·ë·des** (ā ē′dēz) n., pl. **a·ë′des** [ModL. < Gr. aēdēs < a-, not + hēdys, sweet] the mosquito that carries the virus of yellow fever

ADZ

**ae·dile** (ē′dīl) n. [< L. < aedes, building] in ancient Rome, an official in charge of buildings, roads, public games, etc.

**Ae·ge·an (Sea)** (ē jē′ən) sea between Greece and Turkey: an arm of the Mediterranean

**ae·gis** (ē′jis) n. [L. < Gr. aigis, goatskin] **1.** Gr. Myth. a shield borne by Zeus and, later, by Athena **2.** a protection **3.** sponsorship; auspices

**Ae·ne·as** (i nē′əs) Gr. & Rom. Myth. a Trojan warrior who escaped from ruined Troy and wandered for years before coming to Latium

**Ae·ne·id** (i nē′əd) a Latin epic poem by Virgil, about Aeneas and his adventures

**Ae·o·li·an** (ē ō′lē ən) adj. **1.** of Aeolus **2.** [often a-] of the wind

**aeolian harp** a boxlike stringed instrument that makes musical sounds when air blows on it

**Ae·o·lus** (ē′ə ləs) Gr. Myth. the god of the winds

**ae·on** (ē′ən, ē′än) n. same as EON

**ae·o·ni·an** (ē ō′nē ən) adj. lasting for eons; eternal

**aer·ate** (er′āt′, ā′ər-) vt. **-at′ed, -at′ing** [AER(O)- + -ATE[1]] **1.** to expose to air, or cause air to circulate through **2.** to supply oxygen to (the blood) by respiration **3.** to charge (liquid) with gas, as in making soda water —**aer·a′tion** n. —**aer′a′tor** n.

**aer·i-** same as AERO-

**aer·i·al** (er′ē əl; occas. for adj. ā ir′ē əl) adj. [< L. aerius < aer (see AIR) + -AL] **1.** of, in, or by the air **2.** like air; light as air **3.** not substantial; unreal; imaginary **4.** high up **5.** of, for, or by means of aircraft or flying **6.** growing in the air instead of in soil or water —n. an antenna (sense 2) —**aer′i·al·ly** adv.

**aer·i·al·ist** (er′ē əl ist) n. an acrobat who performs on a trapeze, high wire, etc.

**aer·ie** (er′ē, ir′ē) n. [< OFr. < ML. aeria, area; sp. & meaning infl. by L. aer, air & ME. ei, egg] **1.** the nest of an eagle or other bird of prey that builds in a high place **2.** a house or stronghold on a high place

**aer·o-** (er′ō, ā′ə rō′) adj. of or for aeronautics or aircraft

**aer·o-** [< Gr. aēr, air] a combining form meaning: **1.** air; of the air [aerolite] **2.** of aircraft or flying [aerostatics] **3.** of gases [aerodynamics]

**aer·obe** (er′ōb) n. [< AERO- + Gr. bios, life] a microorganism that can live and grow only where free oxygen is present

**aer·o·bic** (er ō′bik) adj. **1.** of, characteristic of, or produced by aerobes **2.** designating or involving exercise, such as running, that increases the efficiency of oxygen intake by the body —n. [pl.] aerobic exercises

**aer·o·drome** (erʹə drōm′) *n. Brit. var. of* AIRDROME

**aer·o·dy·nam·ics** (erʹō dī namʹiks) *n.pl.* [*with sing. v.*] the branch of aeromechanics dealing with the forces exerted by air or other gases in motion —**aerʹo·dy·namʹic** *adj.* —**aerʹo·dy·namʹi·cal·ly** *adv.*

**aer·o·em·bo·lism** (erʹō em′bə liz′m) *n.* 1. *same as* DECOMPRESSION SICKNESS 2. nitrogen bubbles formed in the blood during decompression sickness

**aer·o·lite** (erʹə līt′) *n.* [AERO- + -LITE] a stony meteorite — **aerʹo·litʹic** (-litʹik) *adj.*

**aer·ol·o·gy** (er älʹə jē) *n.* [AERO- + -LOGY] the branch of meteorology concerned with the study of air, esp. in the upper atmosphere

**aer·o·me·chan·ics** (erʹō mə kanʹiks) *n.pl.* [*with sing. v.*] the branch of mechanics dealing with air or other gases in motion or equilibrium: it includes aerodynamics and aerostatics —**aerʹo·me·chanʹic** *adj.*

**aer·o·nau·tics** (erʹō nôtʹiks) *n.pl.* [*with sing. v.*] [AERO- + Gr. *nautēs,* sailor + -ICS] the science, art, or work of designing, making, and operating aircraft —**aerʹo·nauʹti·cal, aerʹo·nauʹtic** *adj.* —**aerʹo·nauʹti·cal·ly** *adv.*

**aer·o·pause** (erʹō pôz′) *n.* a region at the upper level of the earth's atmosphere, regarded as the boundary between the atmosphere and outer space

**aer·o·plane** (erʹə plān′) *n. Brit. var. of* AIRPLANE

**aer·o·pulse** (-puls′) *n.* [AERO- + PULSE!] *same as* PULSEJET (ENGINE)

**aer·o·sol** (-sôl′, -säl′, -sōl′) *n.* [AERO- + SOL³] a suspension of colloidal particles in a gas —*adj.* of or dispensed by a container in which gas under pressure is used to aerate liquid and eject it as a spray or foam

**aer·o·space** (erʹō spās′) *n.* [altered < AIR + SPACE] the earth's atmosphere and the space outside it, considered as one continuous field

**aer·o·stat** (-stat′) *n.* [< Fr.: see AERO- & -STAT] a dirigible, balloon, or other airship that is lifted by a contained gas lighter than air

**aer·o·stat·ics** (erʹō statʹiks) *n.pl.* [*with sing. v.*] the branch of aeromechanics dealing with the equilibrium of air or other gases, and with the equilibrium of solid bodies floating in air or other gases —**aerʹo·statʹic** *adj.*

**aer·y** (erʹē, irʹē) *n. same as* AERIE

**Aes·chy·lus** (esʹkə ləs) 525?-456 B.C.; Gr. writer of tragedies —**Aesʹchy·leʹan** (-lēʹən) *adj.*

**Aes·cu·la·pi·us** (esʹkyoo lāʹpē əs) *Rom. Myth.* the god of medicine and of healing: identified with the Greek god Asclepius —**Aesʹcu·laʹpi·an** *adj.*

**Ae·sir** (āʹsir, ēʹ-) *n.pl.* [ON., pl. of *ass,* a god] the principal gods of Norse mythology

**Ae·sop** (ēʹsäp, -səp) real or legendary Gr. author of fables: supposed to have lived 6th cent. B.C. —**Ae·so·pi·an** (ē sōʹpē ən) *adj.*

**aes·thete** (esʹthēt′) *n.* [Gr. *aisthētēs,* one who perceives] 1. a person highly sensitive to art and beauty 2. a person who artificially cultivates artistic sensitivity or makes a cult of art and beauty —**aesʹthet·i·cism** (es thetʹə siz′m) *n.*

**aes·thet·ic** (es thetʹik) *adj.* 1. of aesthetics 2. of beauty 3. sensitive to art and beauty; artistic Also **aes·thetʹi·cal** —*n.* the aesthetic principle —**aes·thetʹi·cal·ly** *adv.*

**aes·thet·ics** (-iks) *n.pl.* [*with sing. v.*] the study or theory of beauty and of the psychological responses to it; specif., the branch of philosophy dealing with art and its forms, effects, etc.

**aes·ti·vate** (esʹtə vāt′) *vi.* -vatʹed, -vatʹing *same as* ESTIVATE

**aet., aetat.** [L. *aetatis*] at the age of

**ae·ther** (ēʹthər) *n. earlier var. of* ETHER

**Aet·na** (etʹnə) *same as* ETNA

**a.f., A.F.** audio-frequency

**a·far** (ə fär′) *adv.* [Poet. or Archaic] at or to a distance — **from afar** from a distance

**AFB** Air Force Base

**A.F.C., AFC** automatic frequency control

**a·feard, a·feared** (ə fird′) *adj.* [< OE. < *a-* (intens.) < *faeran,* to frighten] [Dial. or Archaic] frightened; afraid

**af·fa·ble** (afʹə b'l) *adj.* [< L. *affabilis* < *ad-,* to + *fari,* to speak: see FAME] 1. easy to approach and talk to; friendly 2. gentle and kindly [an *affable* smile] —**afʹfa·bilʹi·ty** *n.* — **afʹfa·bly** *adv.*

**af·fair** (ə fer′) *n.* [< OFr. < *a faire,* to do < L. *ad-,* to + *facere,* to do] 1. a thing to be done; business 2. [*pl.*] matters of business or concern 3. any matter, occurrence, or thing 4. an event arousing public controversy 5. a social gathering 6. a sexual relationship outside of marriage

**af·fect¹** (ə fektʹ: *for n.* afʹekt) *vt.* [< L. *affectare,* to strive after < pp. of *afficere,* to influence < *ad-,* to + *facere,* to do] 1. to have an effect on; influence 2. to move or stir the emotions of —*n. Psychol.* emotion or emotional response

**af·fect²** (ə fektʹ) *vt.* [< OFr. < L. *affectare,* AFFECT¹] 1. to like to have, use, wear, etc. [she *affects* plaid coats] 2. to

pretend to have, feel, like, etc.; feign [to *affect* indifference]

**af·fec·ta·tion** (af′ek tāʹshən) *n.* 1. an affecting or pretending to like, have, etc.; show or pretense 2. artificial behavior meant to impress others

**af·fect·ed¹** (ə fekʹtid) *adj.* 1. attacked by disease 2. influenced; acted upon 3. emotionally moved

**af·fect·ed²** (ə fekʹtid) *adj.* 1. assumed for effect; artificial 2. behaving in an artificial way to impress people —**af·fectʹed·ly** *adv.* —**af·fectʹed·ness** *n.*

**af·fect·ing** (ə fekʹtiŋ) *adj.* emotionally touching; causing one to feel pity, sympathy, etc.

**af·fec·tion** (ə fekʹshən) *n.* 1. a tendency or disposition 2. fond or tender feeling; warm liking 3. a disease; ailment 4. an affecting or being affected

**af·fec·tion·ate** (-it) *adj.* full of affection; tender and loving —**af·fecʹtion·ate·ly** *adv.*

**af·fec·tive** (ə fekʹtiv) *adj.* of affects, or feelings; emotional —**af·fecʹtive·ly** *adv.* —**af·fec·tiv·i·ty** (afʹek tivʹə tē) *n.*

**af·fer·ent** (afʹər ənt) *adj.* [< L. prp. of *afferre* < *ad-,* to + *ferre,* to BEAR¹] *Physiol.* bringing inward to a central part; specif., designating nerves that transmit impulses toward a nerve center: opposed to EFFERENT

**af·fi·ance** (ə fīʹəns) *vt.* -anced, -anc·ing [< OFr. *afier* < ML. < *ad-,* to + *fidare,* to trust] to betroth

**af·fi·ant** (ə fīʹənt) *n.* [< prp. of OFr. *afier:* see prec.] a person who makes an affidavit

**af·fi·da·vit** (afʹə dāʹvit) *n.* [ML., he has made oath] a written statement made on oath as before a notary public

**af·fil·i·ate** (ə filʹē āt′; *for n.* -it) *vt.* -atʹed, -atʹing [< ML. pp. of *affiliare,* to adopt as a son < L. *ad-,* to + *filius,* son] 1. to take in as a member or branch 2. to connect or associate (oneself *with*) —*vi.* to associate oneself; join —*n.* an affiliated person or organization —**af·filʹi·aʹtion** *n.*

**af·fin·i·ty** (ə finʹə tē) *n., pl.* -ties [< OFr. < L. < *affinis,* adjacent < *ad-,* to + *finis,* end] 1. relationship by marriage 2. close relationship; connection 3. a similarity of structure implying common origin 4. a natural liking; esp., a mutual attraction between a man and a woman 5. a person of the opposite sex who especially attracts one 6. the force that causes the atoms of certain elements to combine and stay combined —**af·finʹi·tive** *adj.*

**af·firm** (ə furm′) *vt.* [< OFr. < L. *affirmare* < *ad-,* to + *firmare,* to make firm] 1. to declare positively; assert to be true 2. to confirm; ratify (a law, decision, or judgment) — *vi. Law* to declare solemnly, but not under oath —**af·firmʹa·ble** *adj.* —**af·firmʹer,** *Law* **af·firmʹant** *n.*

**af·fir·ma·tion** (afʹər māʹshən) *n.* 1. an affirming 2. a positive declaration; assertion 3. *Law* a solemn declaration, but not under oath, made by one having conscientious objections to taking oaths

**af·firm·a·tive** (ə furʹmə tiv) *adj.* 1. answering "yes" 2. bold or positive, as in asserting —*n.* 1. a word or expression indicating assent or agreement 2. an affirmative statement —**the affirmative** the side upholding the proposition being debated —**af·firmʹa·tive·ly** *adv.*

**affirmative action** a policy or program for correcting the effects of discrimination in the employment or education of members of certain groups, as women, blacks, etc.

**af·fix** (ə fiks′; *for n.* afʹiks) *vt.* [< L. pp. of *affigere* < *ad-,* to + *figere,* FIX] 1. to fasten; attach 2. to add at the end —*n.* 1. a thing affixed 2. a prefix, suffix, or infix —**afʹfix·al** *adj.*

**af·fla·tus** (ə flātʹəs) *n.* [L. < pp. of *afflare* < *ad-,* to + *flare,* to blow] inspiration, as of an artist

**af·flict** (ə flikt′) *vt.* [< L. *afflictare* < pp. of *affligere* < *ad-,* to + *fligere,* to strike] to cause pain or suffering to; distress very much

**af·flic·tion** (ə flikʹshən) *n.* 1. pain; suffering 2. anything causing pain or distress; calamity

**af·flic·tive** (-tiv) *adj.* causing pain or misery —**af·flicʹtive·ly** *adv.*

**af·flu·ence** (afʹloo wəns; *now sometimes* af lōō′-) *n.* [< L. < *affluere* < *ad-,* to + *fluere,* to flow] 1. great plenty; abundance 2. abundant riches; wealth; opulence

**af·flu·ent** (-wənt) *adj.* 1. plentiful; abundant 2. wealthy; rich —*n.* a stream flowing into a river; tributary —**afʹflu·ent·ly** *adv.*

**af·ford** (ə fôrd′) *vt.* [OE. *geforthian,* to advance < *forthian,* to further] 1. to have enough or the means for; bear the cost of without serious inconvenience: usually with *can* or *be able* 2. to be able (*to* do something) with little risk 3. to give; yield; furnish [it *affords* much pleasure]

**af·fray** (ə frā′) *n.* [< OFr. < *esfraer,* to frighten < L. *ex,* out of + Gmc. base *frithu-,* peace] a noisy brawl or quarrel

**af·fri·cate** (afʹrə kit) *n.* [< L. pp. of *affricare* < *ad-,* to + *fricare,* to rub] *Phonet.* a sound produced when a slowly released stop is followed immediately by a fricative, as the (ch) in *latch* —**af·fric·a·tive** (ə frikʹə tiv) *n., adj.*

**af·fright** (ə frīt′) *vt.* [Archaic] to frighten; terrify —*n.* [Archaic] great fright or terror

**af·front** (ə frunt′) *vt.* [< OFr. *afronter*, to encounter < ML. < *ad-*, to + *frons*, forehead] **1.** to insult openly or on purpose **2.** to confront defiantly —*n.* an open or intentional insult

**Af·ghan** (af′gan, -gən) *n.* **1.** a native of Afghanistan. any of a breed of hunting dog with silky hair and a long, narrow head **3.** [a-] a soft blanket or shawl, crocheted or knitted, esp. in a geometrical design —*adj.* of Afghanistan, its people, etc.

**af·ghan·i** (af gan′ē) *n., pl.* **-is** see MONETARY UNITS, table (Afghanistan)

**Af·ghan·i·stan** (af gan′ə stan′) country in SW Asia, between Iran and Pakistan: 250,000 sq. mi.; pop. 16,516,000; cap. Kabul

**a·fi·cio·na·do** (ə fish′ə nä′dō, -fis′ē ə-; *Sp.* ä fē′syð nä′thð) *n., pl.* **-dos** (-dōz; *Sp.* -thðs) [Sp., pp. of *aficionar*, to be devoted to < L. *affectio*, warm liking] a devoted follower of some sport, art, etc.; fan

**a·field** (ə fēld′) *adv.* **1.** in, on, or to the field **2.** away (from home) **3.** off the right path; astray

**a·fire** (ə fīr′) *adv., adj.* **1.** on fire **2.** greatly excited

**a·flame** (ə flām′) *adv., adj.* **1.** in flames **2.** glowing **3.** greatly excited

**AFL-CIO** American Federation of Labor and Congress of Industrial Organizations

**a·float** (ə flōt′) *adv.* **1.** floating freely **2.** on board ship; at sea **3.** flooded /the deck is *afloat*/ **4.** drifting about **5.** in circulation; current /rumors are *afloat*/ **6.** free of trouble, debt, etc.

**a·flut·ter** (ə flut′ər) *adv., adj.* in a flutter

**a·foot** (ə foot′) *adv.* **1.** on foot; walking **2.** in motion or operation; in progress; astir

**a·fore** (ə fôr′) *adv., prep., conj.* [Archaic or Dial. except in compounds and nautical use] before

**a·fore·men·tioned** (ə fôr′men′shənd) *adj.* mentioned before or previously

**a·fore·said** (-sed′) *adj.* spoken of before; mentioned previously

**a·fore·thought** (-thôt′) *adj.* thought out beforehand; premeditated

**a for·ti·o·ri** (ā fôr′tē ôr′ē, -shē ôr′ī) [L., for a stronger (reason)] all the more: said of a conclusion following with even greater logical necessity another already accepted

**a·foul** (ə foul′) *adv., adj.* in a collision or a tangle —**run (or fall) afoul of** to get into trouble with

**Afr. 1.** Africa **2.** African

**a·fraid** (ə frād′) *adj.* [< ME. pp. of *affraien*, to frighten: see AFFRAY] feeling fear; frightened (with *of, that,* or an infinitive): often used colloquially to indicate regret /I'm *afraid* I can't go/

**A-frame** (ā′frām′) *n.* a structural framework, as of a house, with steeply angled sides meeting at the top like the sides of the letter A

**a·freet** (af′rēt, ə frēt′) *n.* [Ar. *'ifrīt*] Arabic Myth. a strong, evil demon: also sp. **af′rit**

**a·fresh** (ə fresh′) *adv.* again; anew

**Af·ri·ca** (af′ri kə) second largest continent, in the Eastern Hemisphere, south of Europe: c. 11,500,000 sq. mi.; pop. c. 345,000,000

**Af·ri·can** (-kən) *adj.* of Africa, its peoples (esp. Negro peoples), their cultures, etc. —*n.* **1.** a member of an indigenous ethnic group of Africa, esp. a Negro **2.** any native or inhabitant of Africa

**African violet** any of several tropical African plants with hairy, dark-green leaves, often grown as house plants

**Af·ri·kaans** (af′ri känz′, -käns′, -kanz′) *n.* [Afrik. < *Afrika*, Africa] an official language of South Africa, a development from 17th-cent. Dutch

**Af·ri·ka·ner** (af′ri kän′ər) *n.* [Du.] a South African of European, esp. Dutch, ancestry; Boer

**Af·ro** (af′rō) *adj.* [< ff.] designating or of a full, bouffant hair style, as worn by some Negroes

**Af·ro-** *a combining form meaning:* **1.** Africa **2.** African Also, before a vowel, **Afr-**

**Af·ro-A·mer·i·can** (af′rō ə mer′ə kən) *adj.* of Negro Americans, their culture, etc. —*n.* a Negro American

**aft** (aft) *adv.* [< OE. < *afta*, behind] at, near, or toward the stern of a ship or rear of an aircraft

**af·ter** (af′tər) *adv.* [OE. *æfter* < *of*, off + *-ter*, old compar. suffix] behind in place or time; later or next —*prep.* **1.** behind in place **2.** behind in time; later than **3.** in search of **4.** as a result of /after what has happened, he won't go/ **5.** in spite of /after all his bad luck, he is still cheerful/ **6.** following next to in rank or importance **7.** in the manner of /a novel *after* Dickens' style/ **8.** for; in honor of /named *after* Lincoln/ **9.** concerning /she asked *after* you/ —*conj.* following the time when —*adj.* **1.** next; later **2.** nearer the rear (esp. of a ship or aircraft)

**af·ter·birth** (-burth′) *n.* the placenta and fetal membranes expelled from the womb after childbirth

**af·ter·burn·er** (-bur′nər) *n.* **1.** a device for obtaining additional thrust in a jet engine by using the hot exhaust gases to burn extra fuel **2.** a device, as on an incinerator, for burning undesirable exhaust gases

**af·ter·damp** (-damp′) *n.* an asphyxiating gas left in a mine after an explosion of firedamp

**af·ter·ef·fect** (-ə fekt′) *n.* an effect coming later, or as a secondary result

**af·ter·glow** (-glō′) *n.* **1.** the glow remaining after a light has gone, as after sunset **2.** a pleasant feeling after an enjoyable experience

**af·ter·im·age** (-im′ij) *n.* a visual image that continues after the external stimulus is withdrawn

**af·ter·math** (-math′) *n.* [AFTER + dial. *math* < OE. *mæth*, cutting of grass] a result or consequence, esp. an unpleasant one

**af·ter·most** (-mōst′) *adj.* **1.** hindmost; last **2.** nearest to the stern

**af·ter·noon** (af′tər nōōn′, af′tər nōōn′) *n.* the time of day from noon to evening —*adj.* of, in, or for the afternoon

**af·ter·noons** (-nōōnz′) *adv.* during every afternoon or most afternoons

**af·ter·taste** (af′tər tāst′) *n.* **1.** a taste lingering on in the mouth, as after eating **2.** the feeling remaining after an experience

**af·ter·thought** (-thôt′) *n.* **1.** an idea, explanation, etc. coming or added later **2.** a thought coming too late to be apt, useful, etc.

**af·ter·ward** (-wərd) *adv.* at a later time; subsequently: also **af′ter·wards**

**Ag** [L. *argentum*] *Chem.* silver

**AG** Adjutant General

**Ag.** August

**A.G.** Attorney General

**a·gain** (ə gen′; chiefly Brit. -gān′) *adv.* [OE. *ongegn* < *on-*, toward + *gegn*, direct] **1.** [Rare] in return /answer *again*/ **2.** back into a former condition **3.** once more; anew **4.** besides; further **5.** on the other hand —**again and again** often; repeatedly —**as much again** twice as much

**a·gainst** (ə genst′; chiefly Brit. -gānst′) *prep.* [see AGAIN] **1.** in opposition to /against my will/ **2.** toward so as to strike /throw the ball *against* the wall/ **3.** opposite to the direction of /drive *against* the traffic/ **4.** in contrast with /green *against* the gold/ **5.** next to; adjoining **6.** in preparation for /we provided *against* a poor crop/ **7.** as a charge on /a bill was entered *against* his account/ —**over against 1.** opposite to **2.** as compared with

**Ag·a·mem·non** (ag′ə mem′nän, -nən) *Gr. Myth.* king of Mycenae and commander in chief of the Greek army in the Trojan War

**A·ga·ña** (ä gän′yə) capital of Guam: pop. 900

**a·gape¹** (ə gāp′) *adv., adj.* [A-¹ + GAPE] **1.** with the mouth wide open, as in wonder **2.** wide open

**ag·a·pe²** (ä′gä pā′, ag′ə pē) *n.* [< LL. < Gr. *agapē*, love] Christian Theol. **1.** God's love for man **2.** spontaneous, altruistic love

**a·gar-a·gar** (ä′gär ä′gär, ag′ər ag′ər) *n.* [Malay] a gelatinous extract of seaweed, used for bacterial cultures, as a laxative, etc.: also **a′gar**

**ag·ar·ic** (ə ger′ik, ag′ər ik) *n.* [< L. < Gr. < *Agaria*, ancient E European town] any gill fungus, as the common edible mushroom, etc.

**Ag·as·siz** (ag′ə sē), (Jean) Louis (Rodolphe) 1807–73; U.S. zoologist & geologist, born in Switzerland

**ag·ate** (ag′ət) *n.* [OFr. < L. < Gr. *achatēs* < ?] **1.** a hard, semiprecious stone, a variety of chalcedony, with striped or clouded coloring **2.** a little ball made of this stone or of glass, used in playing marbles **3.** a small size of type, 5½ point

**Ag·a·tha** (ag′ə thə) [L. < Gr. *Agathē*, lit., good, fem. of *agathos*, good] a feminine name

**a·ga·ve** (ə gä′vē) *n.* [ModL. < Gr. *Agauē*, a proper name, lit., illustrious] any of several American desert plants, as the century plant, having tall flower stalks and fleshy leaves: some agaves yield a rope fiber

**a·gaze** (ə gāz′) *adv., adj.* gazing

**age** (āj) *n.* [< OFr. < L. *aetas*] **1.** the time that a person or thing has existed since birth or beginning **2.** the lifetime **3.** a stage of life /the awkward *age*/ **4.** the condition of being old /bent with *age*/ **5.** a generation **6.** a period in history or in prehistoric or geologic time **7.** [often pl.] [Colloq.] a long time —*vi.* **aged, ag′ing or age′ing** to grow old or become mature —*vt.* to make old or cause to become mature —**of age** having reached the age of full legal rights

**-age** (ij, əj) [OFr. < LL. *-aticum*, belonging to] *a noun-forming suffix meaning:* **1.** the act, condition, or result of *[usage]* **2.** amount or number of *[acreage]* **3.** cost of *[postage]* **4.** place of *[steerage]* **5.** collection of *[peerage]* **6.** home of *[hermitage]*

**a·ged** (ā′jid *for 1 & 2;* ājd *for 3 & 4*) *adj.* **1.** grown old **2.** of old age **3.** brought to a desired state of aging **4.** of the age of *[a boy aged ten]* —**the aged** (ā′jid) old people

**age·ism** (āj′iz′m) *n.* [AGE + (RAC)ISM] discrimination against people on the basis of age; specif., discrimination against, and prejudicial stereotyping of, older people — **age′ist** *adj., n.*

**age·less** (āj′lis) *adj.* **1.** seemingly not growing older **2.** eternal —**age′less·ly** *adv.*

**age·long** (-lôŋ′) *adj.* lasting a very long time

**age-mate** (-māt′) *n.* a person or animal of the same age, or nearly the same age, as another

**a·gen·cy** (ā′jən sē) *n., pl.* **-cies** [see AGENT] **1.** action; power **2.** means; instrumentality **3.** the business or place of business of any person, firm, etc. authorized to act for another **4.** an administrative division of government

**a·gen·da** (ə jen′də) *n., pl.* **-das** [L., pl. of *agendum* < *agere*, ACT] program of things to be done; specif., a list of things to be dealt with at a meeting: also **a·gen′dum** (-dəm), *pl.* **-da** (-də), **-dums**

**a·gent** (ā′jənt) *n.* [< L. *agens* (gen. *agentis*), prp. of *agere*, ACT] **1.** a person or thing that performs an action **2.** a force or substance that produces an effect *[chemical agent]* **3.** a person, firm, etc. authorized to act for another **4.** a representative of a government agency **5.** [Colloq.] a traveling salesman —**a·gen·tial** (ā jen′shəl) *adj.*

**‡a·gent pro·vo·ca·teur** (à zhän′ prô vô kà tër′) *pl.* **a·gents pro·vo·ca·teurs** (à zhän′ prô vô kà tër′) [Fr.] a secret agent hired to join some group in order to incite its members to commit unlawful acts

**age of consent** *Law* the age of a girl, specified by law, before which sexual intercourse with her may be classified as statutory rape

**age-old** (āj′ōld′) *adj.* ages old; ancient

**ag·er·a·tum** (aj′ə rāt′əm) *n.* [ModL. < Gr. < *agēratos*, not growing old < *a-*, not + *gēras*, old age] a plant of the composite family, with small bluish flowers

**ag·glom·er·ate** (ə gläm′ə rāt′; *for adj. & n.* -ər it) *vt., vi.* **-at′ed, -at′ing** [< L. pp. of *agglomerare* < *ad-*, to + *glomerare*, to form into a ball] to gather into a mass or ball —*adj.* gathered into a mass or ball —*n.* a jumbled heap, mass, etc. —**ag·glom′er·a′tion** *n.* —**ag·glom′er·a′tive** *adj.*

**ag·glu·ti·nant** (ə glo̅o̅t′'n ənt) *adj.* [see ff.] sticking together —*n.* a sticky substance

**ag·glu·ti·nate** (ə glo̅o̅t′'n it; *for v.* -āt′) *adj.* [< L. pp. of *agglutinare* < *ad-*, to + *gluten*, glue] **1.** stuck together, as with glue **2.** *Linguis.* forming words by agglutination —*vt., vi.* **-nat′ed, -nat′ing** **1.** to stick together, as with glue **2.** *Linguis.* to form (words) by agglutination **3.** *Med. & Bacteriology* to clump, as blood cells, microorganisms, etc. suspended in fluid —**ag·glu′ti·na′tive** *adj.*

**ag·glu·ti·na·tion** (ə glo̅o̅t′'n ā′shən) *n.* **1.** an agglutinating or being agglutinated **2.** a mass of agglutinated parts **3.** *Linguis.* the combining of words into compounds without marked change of form or loss of meaning

**ag·gran·dize** (ə gran′dīz′, ag′rən-) *vt.* **-dized′, -diz′ing** [< Fr. < *a-*, to + *grandir*, to increase < L. *grandire* < *grandis*, great] **1.** to make (esp. oneself) greater, more powerful, richer, etc. **2.** to make seem greater —**ag·gran′dize·ment** (-diz mənt) *n.* —**ag·gran′diz′er** *n.*

**ag·gra·vate** (ag′rə vāt′) *vt.* **-vat′ed, -vat′ing** [< L. pp. of *aggravare* < *ad-*, to + *gravis*, heavy] **1.** to make worse; make more burdensome, troublesome, etc. **2.** [Colloq.] to exasperate; annoy —**ag′gra·va′tion** *n.*

**ag·gre·gate** (ag′rə gət; *for v.* -gāt′) *adj.* [< L. pp. of *aggregare* < *ad-*, to + *gregare*, to herd < *grex* (gen. *gregis*), a herd] gathered into, or considered as, a whole; total —*n.* a group or mass of distinct things gathered into, or considered as, a whole; total —*vt.* **-gat′ed, -gat′ing** **1.** to gather into a whole or mass **2.** to amount to; total —**in the aggregate** taken all together; on the whole —**ag′gre·ga′tion** *n.*

**ag·gress** (ə gres′) *vi.* [< L. pp. of *aggredi*, to attack < *ad-*, to + *gradi*, to step] to start a quarrel or make an attack

**ag·gres·sion** (ə gresh′ən) *n.* **1.** an unprovoked attack or warlike act **2.** the practice or habit of being aggressive, or quarrelsome **3.** *Psychiatry* forceful or hostile behavior

**ag·gres·sive** (ə gres′iv) *adj.* **1.** aggressing or inclined to aggress **2.** ready to engage in direct action **3.** full of enterprise; bold and active —**ag·gres′sive·ly** *adv.*

**ag·gres·sor** (-ər) *n.* a person, nation, etc. that is guilty of aggression, or makes an unprovoked attack

**ag·grieve** (ə grēv′) *vt.* **-grieved′, -griev′ing** [< OFr. < L. *aggravare*, AGGRAVATE] **1.** to cause grief or injury to; offend **2.** to injure in one's legal rights

**a·ghast** (ə gast′) *adj.* [< ME. < *a-* (intens.) + *gastan* < OE. *gæstan*, to terrify < *gast*, GHOST] feeling great horror or dismay; horrified

**ag·ile** (aj′'l; *chiefly Brit.* -īl) *adj.* [Fr. < L. < *agere*, ACT] **1.** quick and easy of movement; nimble **2.** keen and lively *[an agile wit]* —**ag′ile·ly** *adv.* —**a·gil·i·ty** (ə jil′ə tē) *n.*

**ag·ism** (āj′iz′m) *n.* same as AGEISM —**ag′ist** *adj., n.*

**ag·i·tate** (aj′ə tāt′) *vt.* **-tat′ed, -tat′ing** [< L. pp. of *agitare*, to put in motion < *agere*, ACT] **1.** to move violently; stir up or shake up **2.** to disturb the feelings of —*vi.* to stir up support through speeches and writing so as to produce changes *[to agitate for reform]* —**ag′i·tat′ed·ly** *adv.*

**ag·i·ta·tion** (aj′ə tā′shən) *n.* **1.** an agitating or being agitated; violent motion **2.** emotional disturbance **3.** discussion meant to stir up people and produce changes

**‡a·gi·ta·to** (ä′jē tä′tô) *adj., adv.* [It.: see AGITATE] *Music* fast and with excitement

**ag·i·ta·tor** (aj′ə tāt′ər) *n.* **1.** a person who tries to stir up people in support of a social or political cause: often used in disapproval **2.** an apparatus for shaking or stirring

**ag·it·prop** (aj′it präp′) *adj.* [< Russ. *agit(atsiya) prop(aganda)*, agitation propaganda] of or for agitating and propagandizing

**a·gleam** (ə glēm′) *adv., adj.* gleaming

**a·gley** (ə glē′, -glī′, -glā′) *adv.* [Scot.] awry

**a·glow** (ə glō′) *adv., adj.* in a glow (of color or emotion)

**Ag·nes** (ag′nis) [< Fr. < L. < Gr. *hagnē*, fem. of *hagnos*, chaste] a feminine name: dim. *Aggie*

**ag·nos·tic** (ag näs′tik) *n.* [< Gr. < *a-*, not + base of *gignōskein*, to know] a person who believes that one cannot know whether there is a God, or anything beyond material phenomena —*adj.* of or characteristic of an agnostic —**ag·nos′ti·cal·ly** *adv.* —**ag·nos′ti·cism** *n.*

**Ag·nus De·i** (ag′noos dā′ē; ag′nəs dē′ī) [L., Lamb of God] **1.** a representation of Christ as a lamb, often holding a cross or flag **2.** *R.C.Ch.* a prayer in the Mass, beginning *Agnus Dei*, or music for it

**a·go** (ə gō′) *adj.* [< OE. *agan* < *a-*, away + *gan*, go] gone by; past *[years ago]* —*adv.* in the past *[long ago]*

**a·gog** (ə gäg′) *adv., adj.* [OFr. < *a-*, to + *gogue*, joyfulness] with eager interest or excitement

**-a·gogue, -a·gog** (ə gäg′, -gôg′) [< Gr. prp. of *agein*, to lead] *a combining form meaning* leading, directing, inciting *[demagogue]*

**ag·o·nize** (ag′ə nīz′) *vi.* **-nized′, -niz′ing** **1.** to make convulsive efforts; struggle **2.** to be in agony —*vt.* to torture —**ag′o·niz′ing·ly** *adv.*

**ag·o·ny** (ag′ə nē) *n., pl.* **-nies** [< L. < Gr. *agōnia*, a contest < *agōn*, an assembly < *agein*, to lead] **1.** very great mental or physical pain **2.** death pangs **3.** a convulsive struggle **4.** a sudden, strong outburst (*of* emotion)

**ag·o·ra¹** (ag′ə rə) *n., pl.* **-rae** (-rē′), **-ras** [Gr. < *ageirein*, to assemble] in ancient Greece, an assembly or a place of assembly, esp. a marketplace

**ag·o·ra²** (ä′gô rä′) *n., pl.* **-rot′** (-rōt′) [ModHeb. *'agōrāh*] *see* MONETARY UNITS, table (Israel)

**ag·o·ra·pho·bi·a** (ag′ər ə fō′bē ə) *n.* [AGORA¹ + -PHOBIA] an abnormal fear of being in open spaces

**a·gou·ti, a·gou·ty** (ə go̅o̅′tē) *n., pl.* **-tis, -ties:** see PLURAL, II, D, 1 [Fr. < Sp. < Guarani] a rodent related to the guinea pig, found in tropical America

**A·gra** (ä′grə) city in N India: site of the Taj Mahal: pop. 509,000

**a·grar·i·an** (ə grer′ē ən) *adj.* [< L. < *ager*, a field, land] **1.** relating to land or to the ownership or division of land **2.** of agriculture —*n.* a person who favors a more even division of land among those who work it — **a·grar′i·an·ism** *n.*

AGOUTI
(17–25 in. long)

**a·gree** (ə grē′) *vi.* **-greed′, -gree′ing** [< OFr. < *a gre*, favorably < L. *ad*, to + *gratus*, pleasing] **1.** to consent or accede (*to*) **2.** to be in harmony **3.** to be of the same opinion; concur (*with*) **4.** to arrive at a satisfactory understanding (*about* prices, etc.) **5.** to be suitable, healthful, etc. (followed by *with*) *[the climate agrees with him]* **6.** *Gram.* to be inflected so as to correspond in number, person, case, or gender —*vt.* to grant or acknowledge *[we agreed that it was true]*

**a·gree·a·ble** (-ə b'l) *adj.* **1.** pleasing or pleasant **2.** willing or ready to consent **3.** conformable; in accord —**a·gree′a·bil′i·ty, a·gree′a·ble·ness** *n.* —**a·gree′a·bly** *adv.*

**a·greed** (ə grēd′) *adj.* settled by mutual consent *[pay the agreed price]*

**a·gree·ment** (ə grē′mənt) *n.* **1.** an agreeing, or being in harmony **2.** an understanding between two or more people, countries, etc. **3.** a contract

**ag·ri·busi·ness** (ag′rə biz′nis) *n.* [AGRI(CULTURE) + BUSINESS] farming and the businesses associated with farming

**ag·ri·cul·ture** (ag′ri kul′chər) *n.* [Fr. < L. < *ager*, a field (see ACRE) + *cultura*, cultivation] the science and art of farming; work of cultivating the soil, producing crops, and raising livestock —**ag′ri·cul′tur·al** *adj.* —**ag′ri·cul′tur·al·ly** *adv.*

**ag·ri·cul·tur·ist** (ag′ri kul′chər ist) *n.* 1. an expert in agriculture 2. a farmer Also **ag′ri·cul′tur·al·ist**

**ag·ri·mo·ny** (ag′rə mō′nē) *n., pl.* **-nies** [< OE. & OFr. < L. < Gr. *argemōnē*] a plant of the rose family, having little yellow flowers on spiky stalks and bearing burlike fruits

**ag·ro·bi·ol·o·gy** (ag′rō bī ä l′ə jē) *n.* the science of plant growth and nutrition as applied to improvement of crops and control of soil

**a·gron·o·my** (ə grän′ə mē) *n.* [< Fr. < Gr. < *agros*, field + *nemein*, to manage] the science and economics of crop production; management of farm land —**ag·ro·nom·ic** (ag′rə näm′ik), **a·gron′o·mist** *n.*

**a·ground** (ə ground′) *adv., adj.* on or onto the shore, a reef, etc. *[the ship ran aground]*

**agt.** agent

**a·gue** (ā′gyōō) *n.* [< OFr. < ML. (*febris*) *acuta*, violent (fever)] 1. a fever, usually that of malaria, marked by regularly recurring chills 2. a chill; fit of shivering

**ah** (ä, ô) *interj.* an exclamation expressing pain, delight, regret, disgust, surprise, etc.

**a·ha** (ä hä′) *interj.* an exclamation expressing satisfaction, pleasure, triumph, etc., often mixed with irony or mockery

**A·hab** (ā′hab) *Bible* a wicked king of Israel, husband of Jezebel: I Kings 16:29

**a·head** (ə hed′) *adv., adj.* 1. in or to the front 2. forward; onward 3. in advance 4. winning or leading 5. having something as a profit or advantage —**get ahead** to advance socially, financially, etc. —**get ahead of** to outdo or excel

**a·hem** (ə hem′; *conventionalized pronun.*) *interj.* a cough or similar sound made to get attention, fill a pause, etc.

**a·him·sa** (ə him′sə) *n.* [< Sans. < *a-*, not + *himsā*, injury] the Buddhist and Hindu principle of not harming any living creature

**Ah·med·a·bad, Ah·mad·a·bad** (ä′məd ə bäd′) city in W India: pop. 1,206,000

**A·ho·ri·zon** (ā′hə rī′z′n) *n.* see ABC SOIL

**a·hoy** (ə hoi′) *interj. Naut.* a call used in hailing *[ship ahoy!]*

**A·hu·ra Maz·da** (ä′hōo rə maz′də) *same as* ORMAZD

**a·i** (ä′ē) *n., pl.* **a′is** (-ēz) [Tupi *ai hai* < the animal's cry] a S. American sloth with three toes

**aid** (ād) *vt., vi.* [< OFr. < L. *adjutare:* see ADJUTANT] to give help (to); assist —*n.* 1. help; assistance 2. a helper; assistant 3. a helpful device 4. *same as* AIDE-DE-CAMP

**aide** (ād) *n.* [Fr.: see AID] 1. an assistant 2. *same as* AIDE-DE-CAMP

**aide-de-camp** (ād′də kamp′) *n., pl.* **aides-de-camp** [Fr., lit., camp assistant] an officer in the army, navy, etc. serving as assistant and confidential secretary to a superior

**aid·man** (ād′man′) *n., pl.* **-men** (-men′) an enlisted man in a medical corps in a combat area

**ai·grette, ai·gret** (ā′gret, ā gret′) *n.* [SEE EGRET] 1. the long, white plumes of the egret, once worn for ornament by women 2. any ornament like this

**Ai·ken** (āk′'n), **Conrad** (**Potter**) 1889-1973; U.S. poet & fiction writer

**ail** (āl) *vt.* [< OE. *eglian*, to afflict with dread, trouble < *egle*, harmful] to be the cause of pain to; trouble —*vi.* to be in poor health; be ill

**ai·lan·thus** (ā lan′thəs) *n., pl.* **-thus·es** [ModL. < native name in Malacca] a tree with pointed leaflets, fine-grained wood, and greenish flowers with an unpleasant odor

**Ai·leen** (ī lēn′, ā-) *var. of* EILEEN

**ai·le·ron** (ā′lə rän′) *n.* [Fr. < OFr. < *aile* < L. *ala*, wing] a movable hinged section of an airplane wing for controlling rolling movements

**ail·ing** (āl′iŋ) *adj.* in poor health; sickly

**ail·ment** (āl′mənt) *n.* an illness, esp. a mild one

**aim** (ām) *vi., vt.* [< OFr. *aesmer* < L. < *ad-*, to + *aestimare*, to estimate] 1. to point (a weapon) or direct (a blow, remark, etc.) 2. to direct (one's efforts) 3. to try or intend (*to do or be*) —*n.* 1. the act of aiming 2. the direction of a missile, blow, etc. 3. intention or purpose —**take aim** to point a weapon, as by viewing along a sight

**aim·less** (ām′ləs) *adj.* having no aim or purpose —**aim′less·ly** *adv.* —**aim′less·ness** *n.*

**ain't** (ānt) [early assimilation of *amn't*, contr. of *am not*; later confused with *a'nt* (*are not*), *i'nt* (*is not*), *ha'nt* (*has not*, *have not*)] [Colloq.] am not: also a dialectal or substandard contraction for *is not*, *are not*, *has not*, and *have not:* ain't was formerly standard for *am not* and is still sometimes defended as a useful contraction for *am not* in questions *[I'm going too, ain't I?]*

**Ai·nu** (ī′nōō) *n.* [Ainu, lit., man] 1. *pl.* **-nus, -nu** a member of a native, light-skinned people of Japan 2. their language, unrelated to any other

**air** (er) *n.* [< OFr. < L. *aer* < Gr. *aēr*, air, mist] 1. the elastic, invisible mixture of gases (chiefly nitrogen and oxygen, as well as hydrogen, carbon dioxide, etc.) that surrounds the earth; atmosphere 2. space above the earth; sky 3. a movement of air; breeze; wind 4. *same as* COMPRESSED AIR 5. an outward appearance *[an air of luxury]* 6. a person's manner or bearing 7. *[pl.]* affected, superior manners 8. public expression *[give air to your opinions]* 9. transportation by aircraft 10. the medium through which radio signals are transmitted: a figurative use 11. a song or melody —*adj.* of aircraft, air forces, etc. —*vt.* 1. to let air into or through 2. to publicize —*vi.* to become aired, dried, etc. —**give** (or **get**) **the air** [Slang] to reject (or be rejected) —**in the air** 1. prevalent 2. not decided —**on** (or **off**) **the air** *Radio & TV* that is (or is not) broadcasting or being broadcast —**take the air** to go outdoors, as for fresh air —**up in the air** not settled or decided —**walk on air** to feel very happy or exalted

**air bag** a bag of nylon, plastic, etc. that inflates automatically within an automobile at the impact of a collision, to protect riders from being thrown forward

**air base** a base of operations for military aircraft

**air bladder** a sac with air or gas in it, found in most fishes and in some other animals and some plants

**air·borne** (er′bôrn′) *adj.* 1. carried by or through the air 2. aloft or flying

**air brake** 1. a brake operated by the action of compressed air on a piston 2. any flap on an airplane for reducing its speed in flight

**air·brush** (er′brush′) *n.* a kind of atomizer operated by compressed air and used for spraying on paint or other liquid: also **air brush** —**air′brush′** *vt.*

**air chamber** a cavity or compartment full of air, esp. one used in hydraulics

**air command** *U.S. Air Force* the largest organizational unit

**air conditioning** a method of filtering air and regulating its humidity and temperature in buildings, cars, planes, etc. —**air′con·di′tion** *vt.* —**air conditioner**

**air-cooled** (er′kōold′) *adj.* cooled by having air passed over, into, or through it —**air′-cool′** *vt.*

**air·craft** (er′kraft′) *n., pl.* **-craft′** any machine designed for flying, whether heavier or lighter than air; airplane, balloon, helicopter, etc.

**aircraft carrier** a warship that carries aircraft, with a large, flat deck for taking off and landing

**air curtain** (or **door**) a downward draft of air at an open entrance for maintaining even temperatures within

**air·drome** (er′drōm′) *n.* [AIR + -DROME] the physical facilities of an air base

**air·drop** (-dräp′) *n.* the delivery of supplies or troops by parachute from an aircraft —*vt.* **-dropped′, -drop′ping** to deliver by airdrop

**Aire·dale** (er′dāl′) *n.* [after *Airedale* in Yorkshire, England] a large terrier having a hard, wiry, tan coat with black markings

**air·field** (er′fēld′) *n.* a field where aircraft can take off and land

**air·foil** (-foil′) *n.* a part with a flat or curved surface, as a wing, rudder, etc., used to keep an aircraft up or control its movements

**air force** 1. the aviation branch of the armed forces 2. *U.S. Air Force* a unit lower than an air command

**air gun** 1. a gun operated by compressed air 2. a gunlike device used to spray paint, insecticide, etc. by compressed air

AIREDALE
(23 in. high
at shoulder)

**air hole** 1. a hole that permits passage of air 2. an unfrozen or open place in the ice covering a body of water

**air·i·ly** (er′ə lē) *adv.* in an airy or gay, light manner; jauntily; breezily

**air·i·ness** (-ē nis) *n.* 1. a being airy, or full of fresh air 2. gay lightness; jauntiness

**air·ing** (-iŋ) *n.* 1. exposure to the air, as for drying 2. exposure to public knowledge 3. a walk or ride outdoors

**air lane** a prescribed route for travel by air; airway

**air·less** (-lis) *adj.* 1. without air or without fresh air 2. without wind or breeze

**air·lift** (-lift′) *n.* a system of transporting troops, supplies, etc. by aircraft, as when ground routes are blocked —*vt.* to transport by airlift

**air·line** (-līn′) *n.* 1. a direct line; beeline: also **air line** 2. a system or company for moving freight and passengers by aircraft **3.** a route for travel by air —*adj.* of or on an airline

**air·lin·er** (-lī′nər) *n.* a large aircraft for carrying passengers

**air lock** an airtight compartment, with adjustable air pressure, between places that do not have the same air pressure

**air·mail** (-māl′) *n.* **1.** the system of transporting mail by aircraft **2.** mail so transported —*vt.* to send by airmail

**air·man** (-mən) *n., pl.* **-men 1.** an aviator **2.** an enlisted man or woman in the U.S. Air Force

**air mass** *Meteorol.* a large body of air having virtually uniform conditions of temperature and moisture in a horizontal cross section

**air-mind·ed** (er′mīn′dəd) *adj.* interested in or promoting aviation, aircraft, air power, etc.

**air·plane** (er′plān′) *n.* an aircraft, heavier than air, that is kept aloft by the aerodynamic forces of air upon its wings and is driven forward by a screw propeller, by jet propulsion, etc.

**air pocket** an atmospheric condition that causes an aircraft to make sudden, short drops

**air·port** (-pôrt′) *n.* a place where aircraft can land and take off, usually with facilities for repair, accommodations for passengers, etc.

**air power** total capacity of a nation for air war

**air pressure** the pressure of atmospheric or compressed air

**air·proof** (-prōōf′) *adj.* not penetrable by air —*vt.* to make airproof

**air pump** a machine for removing or compressing air or for forcing it through something

**air raid** an attack by aircraft, esp. bombers

**air rifle** a rifle in which the force of compressed air is used to shoot BB's, etc.

**air sac** any of the air-filled cavities in a bird's body, having connections to the lungs

**air shaft 1.** a passage through which fresh air can enter a tunnel, mine, etc. **2.** *same as* AIR WELL

**air·ship** (-ship′) *n.* any self-propelled aircraft that is lighter than air and can be steered

**air·sick** (-sik′) *adj.* sick or nauseated from traveling in an aircraft —**air′sick′ness** *n.*

**air·space** (-spās′) *n.* **1.** space for maneuvering an aircraft **2.** the space extending upward above a particular land area

**air·speed** (-spēd′) *n.* the speed of an aircraft relative to the air rather than to the ground

**air·strip** (-strip′) *n.* a hard-surfaced area used as a temporary airplane runway

**air taxi** a small commercial airplane that carries passengers to places not regularly served by scheduled airlines

**air·tight** (er′tīt′) *adj.* **1.** too tight for air or gas to enter or escape **2.** giving no opening for attack; without weak points *[an airtight alibi]*

**air·waves** (-wāvz′) *n.pl.* the medium through which radio signals are transmitted

**air·way** (-wā′) *n.* **1.** *same as:* a) AIR SHAFT (sense 1) b) AIR LANE c) *[pl.]* AIRWAVES **2.** a passage for air, as to the lungs

**air well** an open shaft passing through the floors of a building, for ventilation

**air·wor·thy** (-wur′*the*) *adj.* fit and safe to fly: said of aircraft —**air′wor′thi·ness** *n.*

**air·y** (er′ē) *adj.* **air′i·er, air′i·est 1.** in the air; high up **2.** of air **3.** open to the air; breezy **4.** unsubstantial as air; visionary **5.** light as air; delicate; graceful **6.** lighthearted; gay **7.** flippant **8.** [Colloq.] putting on airs; affected

**aisle** (īl) *n.* [< OFr. *aile:* see AILERON: the *-s-* is through confusion with ISLE] **1.** a part of a church set off by a row of columns or piers **2.** a passageway, as between rows of seats —**aisled** (īld) *adj.*

**Aisne** (ān) river in N France: 175 mi.

**A·jac·cio** (ä yät′chō) chief city of Corsica: birthplace of Napoleon: pop. 41,000

**a·jar**[1] (ə jär′) *adv., adj.* [ME. *on char* < OE. *cier*, a turn: see CHORE] slightly open, as a door

**a·jar**[2] (ə jär′) *adv., adj.* [A-[1], on + JAR, *v.*] not in harmony

**A·jax** (ā′jaks) *Gr. Myth.* a Greek hero in the Trojan War

**AK** Alaska

**a·kim·bo** (ə kim′bō) *adv., adj.* [ME. *in kenebowe*, lit., in keen bow; a folk etym. < ON. < *keng*, bent + *bogi*, a bow] with hands on hips and elbows bent outward *[with arms akimbo]*

**a·kin** (ə kin′) *adj.* **1.** of one kin; related **2.** having similar qualities; similar

**Ak·ron** (ak′rən) [< Gr. *akron*, highest point] city in N Ohio: pop. 237,000 (met. area 660,000)

**-al** (əl, 'l) [< Fr. < L. *-alis*] **1.** *an adj.-forming suffix meaning* of, like, or suitable for *[comical, hysterical]* **2.** a suffix of nouns originally adjectives *[perennial, annual]* **3.** a *n.-forming suffix meaning* the act or process of *[avowal]* **4.** [AL(DEHYDE)] *Chem.* a *n.-forming suffix denoting:* a) an aldehyde *[chloral]* b) a barbiturate *[phenobarbital]*

**Al** *Chem.* aluminum

**a·la** (ā′lə) *n., pl.* **a′lae** (-lē) [L., a wing] **1.** *Zool.* a wing **2.** a winglike structure, as the ear lobe

**à la, a la** (ä′lə, -lä; al′ə) [Fr.] **1.** to, in, or at the **2.** in the manner or style of **3.** according to

**Al·a·bam·a** (al′ə bam′ə) [< Fr. < AmInd. tribal name] Southern State of SE U.S.: 51,609 sq. mi.; pop. 3,890,000; cap. Montgomery: abbrev. **Ala., AL** —**Al′a·bam′i·an** (-ē ən) *adj., n.*

**al·a·bas·ter** (al′ə bas′tər) *n.* [< OFr. < L. < Gr., prob. < Egypt. name for "vessel of (the goddess) Bast"] **1.** a translucent, whitish, fine-grained variety of gypsum **2.** a streaked or mottled variety of calcite —**al′a·bas′trine** (-trin) *adj.*

**a la carte** (ä′lə kärt′, al′ə-) [Fr., by the bill of fare] with a separate price for each item on the menu: opposed to TABLE D'HÔTE

**a·lack** (ə lak′) *interj.* [A(H) + LACK] [Archaic] an exclamation of regret, surprise, dismay, etc.

**a·lac·ri·ty** (ə lak′rə tē) *n.* [< OFr. < L. < *alacer*, lively] eager willingness or readiness, often shown by quick, lively action —**a·lac′ri·tous** *adj.*

**A·lad·din** (ə lad′'n) a boy in *The Arabian Nights* who found a magic lamp and a magic ring

**à la king** (ä′lə kiŋ′) [lit., in kingly style] diced and served in a sauce containing mushrooms, pimentos, and green peppers

**Al·a·me·da** (al′ə mē′də, -mā′-) [Sp. < *álamo*, poplar tree] city on an island in San Francisco Bay, Calif.: pop. 64,000

**Al·a·mo** (al′ə mō′) [see prec.] Franciscan mission at San Antonio, Tex.: scene of a siege and massacre of Texans by Mexican troops (1836)

**a la mode** (al′ə mōd′, ä′lə mōd′) [Fr. *à la mode*] **1.** in the fashion; stylish **2.** made or served in a certain style, as (pie) with ice cream, or (beef) braised with vegetables in sauce Also **à la mode, alamode**

**Al·an** (al′ən) [ML. *Alanus*, of Breton origin] a masculine name

**a·lar** (ā′lər) *adj.* [< L. < *ala*, a wing] **1.** of or like a wing **2.** having wings

**A·lar·cón** (ä′lär kōn′), **Pe·dro An·to·nio de** (pe′thrō än tō′nyō de) 1833–91; Sp. writer

**Alarcón y Men·do·za** (ē men dō′thä), **Juan Ru·iz de** (hwän rōō′ēth de) 1581?–1639; Sp. dramatist

**Al·a·ric** (al′ə rik) 370–410 A.D.; king of the Visigoths (395?–410): captured Rome (410)

**a·larm** (ə lärm′) *n.* [< OFr. < It. *all'arme*, to arms] **1.** [Archaic] a sudden call to arms **2.** a signal, sound, etc. to warn of danger **3.** a mechanism designed to warn of danger or trespassing *[a burglar alarm]* **4.** the bell, buzzer, etc. of an alarm clock **5.** fear caused by the sudden realization of danger —*vt.* **1.** to warn of approaching danger **2.** to frighten

**alarm clock** a clock that can be set to ring, buzz, or flash a light at any particular time, as to awaken a person from sleep

**a·larm·ing** (-iŋ) *adj.* that alarms, or makes suddenly afraid; frightening —**a·larm′ing·ly** *adv.*

**a·larm·ist** (-ist) *n.* **1.** one who habitually spreads alarming rumors, etc. **2.** one who usually expects the worst to happen —*adj.* of or like an alarmist

**a·lar·um** (ə ler′əm, -lär′-) *n. archaic var. of* ALARM (esp. sense 1)

**a·las** (ə las′) *interj.* [< OFr. < *a*, ah + *las*, wretched < L. *lassus*, weary] an exclamation of sorrow, pity, regret, etc.

**A·las·ka** (ə las′kə) [< Esk. *Alákshak*] **1.** State of the U.S. in NW N. America: 586,400 sq. mi.; pop. 400,000; cap. Juneau: abbrev. **Alas., AK 2.** Gulf of, inlet of the Pacific in the S coast of Alaska —**A·las′kan** *adj., n.*

**Alaska Highway** highway between E British Columbia, Canada, and Fairbanks, Alas.: 1,523 mi.

**Alaska Range** mountain range in SC Alaska: highest peak, Mount McKINLEY

**Alaska Standard Time** *see* STANDARD TIME

**a·late** (ā′lāt) *adj.* [< L. < *ala*, a wing] having wings or winglike attachments: also **a′lat·ed**

**alb** (alb) *n.* [< OE. *albe*, ult. < L. *albus*, white] a long, white linen robe with sleeves tapering to the wrist, worn by a priest at Mass

**al·ba·core** (al′bə kôr′) *n., pl.* **-cores′, -core′:** see PLURAL, II, D, 1 [Port. < Ar. *al*, the + *bakūrah*, albacore] **1.** *a)* a warm-water tuna with unusually long pectoral fins *b) same as* TUNA[1] **2.** any of several related saltwater fishes, as the bonito

**Al·ba·ni·a** (al bā′nē ə, -bän′yə) country in the W Balkan Peninsula, on the Adriatic: 11,099 sq. mi.; pop. 2,019,000; cap. Tirana —**Al·ba′ni·an** *adj., n.*

**Al·ba·ny** (ôl′bə nē) [after the Duke of York and *Albany*, later JAMES II] **1.** capital of N.Y., on the Hudson: pop. 102,000 **2.** city in SW Ga.: pop. 74,000

**al·ba·tross** (al′bə trôs′, al′bə träs′) *n., pl.* **-tross′es, -tross′:** see PLURAL, II, D, 1 [<

ALB

Spanish < Port. < Ar. *al qādūs*, water container < Gr. *kados*, cask; prob. < Heb. *kad*, water jug] **1.** any of several large, web-footed sea birds related to the petrel **2.** [from the bird used as a guilt symbol in a poem by S. T. COLERIDGE] a source of worry or trouble, esp. when it keeps one from doing things effectively: often in the phrase **an albatross around one's neck**

**al·be·it** (ôl bē′it, al-) *conj.* [ME. *al be it*, al(though) it be] although; even though

**Al·bé·niz** (äl bā′nith, -nis), **Isaac (Manuel Francisco)** 1860–1909; Sp. composer & pianist

**Al·bert** (al′bərt) [Fr. < OHG. *Adalbrecht*, lit., bright through nobility] **1.** a masculine name: dim. *Al, Bert;* var. *Adelbert, Elbert* **2.** Prince, (*Albert of Saxe-Coburg Gotha*) 1819–61; husband of Queen Victoria of England

**Al·ber·ta** (al bɜr′tə) [fem. of ALBERT] **1.** a feminine name: var. *Albertina, Albertine* **2.** [after Princess Louise *Alberta,* 4th daughter of Queen Victoria] province of SW Canada: 255,285 sq. mi.; pop. 1,838,000; cap. Edmonton: abbrev. Alta.

**Al·ber·tus Mag·nus** (al bɜr′təs mag′nəs), Saint (*Count von Bollstädt*) 1193?–1280; Ger. scholastic philosopher

**Al·bi·gen·ses** (al′bə jen′sēz) *n.pl.* a religious sect in France c.1020–1250 A.D.: it was suppressed for heresy —**Al′bigen′si·an** (-sē ən) *adj., n.*

**al·bi·no** (al bī′nō) *n., pl.* -**nos** [< Port. < L. *albus,* white] **1.** a person whose skin, hair, and eyes lack normal coloring: albinos have a white skin, whitish hair, and pink eyes **2.** any animal or plant abnormally lacking in color —**albin′ic** (-bin′ik) *adj.* —**al·bi·nism** (al′bə niz′m) *n.*

**Al·bi·on** (al′bē ən) *poet. name for* ENGLAND

**al·bum** (al′bəm) *n.* [L., neut. of *albus,* white] **1.** a book with blank pages for mounting pictures, clippings, stamps, etc., or for collecting autographs **2.** *a)* a booklike holder for phonograph records *b)* a set of records in such a holder *c)* a single long-playing record, not part of a set **3.** an anthology, picture book, or the like

**al·bu·men** (al byoo′mən) *n.* [L. < *albus,* white] **1.** the white of an egg **2.** the nutritive protein substance in germinating plant and animal cells **3.** *same as* ALBUMIN

**al·bu·min** (al byoo′mən) *n.* [ALBUM(EN) + -IN¹] any of a class of water-soluble proteins found in milk, egg, muscle, blood, and in many plants

**al·bu·mi·nous** (-mə nəs) *adj.* of, like, or containing albumin or albumen

**Al·bu·quer·que** (al′bə kɜr′kē) [after the Duke of *Albuquerque,* Mex. Viceroy (1702–11)] city in C N.Mex.: pop. 332,000

**al·bur·num** (al bɜr′nəm) *n.* [< L. < *albus,* white] *same as* SAPWOOD

**al·cai·de, al·cay·de** (al kī′dē; *Sp.* äl kä′ē *the*) *n.* [Sp. < Ar. < *qāda,* to lead] **1.** a governor of a Spanish fortress **2.** a warden of a Spanish prison

**al·cal·de** (al kal′dē; *Sp.* äl käl′de) *n.* [Sp. < Ar. < *qada,* to judge] the mayor of a Spanish or Spanish-American town, who also acts as a judge

**Al·ca·traz** (al′kə traz′) [< Sp. *Isla de Alcatraces,* Island of Pelicans] small island in San Francisco Bay: site of a Federal prison (1934–63)

**al·caz·ar** (al′kə zär′, al kaz′ər; *Sp.* äl kä′thär) *n.* [Sp. < Ar. *al-qasr,* the castle] a palace or fortress of the Moors in Spain; specif., [A-] such a palace in Seville, later used by the Spanish kings

**al·che·mist** (al′kə mist) *n.* one who practiced alchemy —**al′che·mis′tic** (-mis′tik) *adj.*

**al·che·my** (al′kə mē) *n.* [< OFr. < ML. < Ar. *al-kīmiyā* < ? Gr. *cheein,* to pour] **1.** an early form of chemistry studied in the Middle Ages: its chief aims were to change the baser metals into gold and to find the elixir of perpetual youth **2.** a means of transmutation; esp., the seemingly miraculous change of a thing into something better —**al·chem·ic** (al kem′ik), **al·chem′i·cal** *adj.* —**al·chem′i·cal·ly** *adv.*

**Alc·me·ne** (alk mē′nē) *see* AMPHITRYON

**al·co·hol** (al′kə hôl′, -häl′) *n.* [ML. < Ar. *al kuhl,* powder of antimony] **1.** a colorless, volatile, pungent liquid, C₂H₅OH: it can be burned as fuel, is used in industry and medicine, and is the intoxicating element in whiskey, wine, beer, etc.: also called *ethyl alcohol* **2.** any intoxicating liquor with this liquid in it **3.** any of a series of similarly constructed organic compounds with a hydroxyl group, as methyl (or wood) alcohol

**al·co·hol·ic** (al′kə hôl′ik, -häl′-) *adj.* **1.** of, containing, or caused by alcohol **2.** suffering from alcoholism —*n.* one who has chronic alcoholism

**al·co·hol·ism** (al′kə hôl′iz′m, -häl′-) *n.* the habitual drinking of alcoholic liquor to excess, or a diseased condition caused by this

**al·co·hol·ize** (al′kə hôl īz′, -häl-) *vt.* -**ized′, -iz′ing 1.** to saturate or treat with alcohol **2.** to convert into alcohol

**Al·cott** (ôl′kət), **Louisa May** 1832–88; U.S. novelist

**al·cove** (al′kōv) *n.* [Fr. < Sp. < Ar. < *al,* the + *qubba,* an arch, vault] **1.** a recessed section of a room **2.** a secluded bower in a garden

**Ald., Aldm.** Alderman

**Al·deb·a·ran** (al deb′ər ən) a brilliant red star in the constellation Taurus

**al·de·hyde** (al′də hīd′) *n.* [< AL(COHOL) + L. *de,* without + HYD(ROGEN)] **1.** a colorless, volatile fluid, CH₃CHO, with a strong, unpleasant odor, obtained from alcohol by oxidation **2.** any of a class of organic compounds containing the CHO group —**al′de·hy′dic** (-hī′dik) *adj.*

**Al·den** (ôl′d′n), **John** 1599?–1687; Pilgrim settler in Plymouth Colony

**al·der** (ôl′dər) *n.* [< OE. *alor*] any of a group of trees and shrubs of the birch family, having durable wood and growing in cool, moist regions

**al·der·man** (ôl′dər mən) *n., pl.* -**men** [< OE. < *eald,* old + *man,* man] **1.** in some U.S. cities, a member of the municipal council, usually representing a certain district or ward **2.** in England and Ireland, a senior member of a county or borough council —**al′der·man·cy** (-sē) *n.* —**al′der·man·ic** (-man′ik) *adj.*

**Al·der·ney** (ôl′dər nē) *n., pl.* -**neys** any of a breed of small dairy cattle originally from Alderney, one of the Channel Islands

**ale** (āl) *n.* [< OE. *ealu*] a fermented drink made from malt and hops, like beer, but produced by rapid fermentation at a relatively high temperature

**a·le·a·to·ry** (ā′lē ə tôr′ē) *adj.* [< L. < *alea,* chance] depending on chance or luck: also **a′le·a·to′ric**

**a·lee** (ə lē′) *adv., adj. Naut.* on or toward the lee; leeward

**ale·house** (āl′hous′) *n.* a place where ale is sold and served; saloon; tavern

**A·leich·em, Sho·lom** *see* SHOLOM ALEICHEM

**Alembert, Jean le Rond d'** *see* D'ALEMBERT

**a·lem·bic** (ə lem′bik) *n.* [< OFr. < ML. < Ar. < *al,* the + *anbīq,* a still < Gr. *ambix,* a cup] **1.** an apparatus of glass or metal, formerly used for distilling **2.** anything that refines or purifies

**a·leph** (ä′lif) *n.* [Heb., lit., ox, leader] the first letter of the Hebrew alphabet

**A·lep·po** (ə lep′ō) city in NW Syria: pop. 563,000

**a·lert** (ə lɜrt′) *adj.* [< Fr. < It. *all' erta,* on the watch < L. *erigere,* to ERECT] **1.** watchful; vigilantly ready **2.** quick and active; nimble —*n.* **1.** a warning signal, as of an expected air raid **2.** the period when such a warning is in effect —*vt.* to warn to be ready or watchful [the troops were *alerted*] —**on the alert** watchful; vigilant —**a·lert′ly** *adv.* —**a·lert′ness** *n.*

**A·leut** (ə loot′, al′oot) *n.* [< Russ. < ? native name] **1.** *pl.* **A·leuts′, A·leut′** any of a native people of the Aleutian Islands and parts of mainland Alaska **2.** either of their two languages

**A·leu·tian** (ə loo′shən) *adj.* **1.** of the Aleutian Islands **2.** of the Aleuts, their culture, etc. —*n. same as* ALEUT

**Aleutian Islands** chain of islands of Alaska, extending c. 1,200 miles from the SW coast

**ale·wife** (āl′wīf′) *n., pl.* -**wives** (-wīvz′) [< ?] an edible N. American fish resembling the herring

**Al·ex·an·der** (al′ig zan′dər) [< L. < Gr. < *alexein,* to defend + *andros,* gen. of *anēr,* man] **1.** a masculine name: dim. *Alex* **2. Alexander II** 1818–81; czar of Russia (1855–81): son of NICHOLAS I

**Alexander Nev·ski** (nef′skē) 1220?–63; Russ. military hero, statesman, & saint

**Alexander the Great** 356–323 B.C.; king of Macedonia (336–323); military conqueror

**Al·ex·an·dri·a** (al′ig zan′drē ə) **1.** seaport in Egypt, on the Mediterranean: pop. 1,513,000 **2.** [< prec., but with allusion to the *Alexander* family, owners of the town site] city in NE Va., near Washington, D.C.: pop. 103,000

**al·ex·an·drine** (al′ig zan′drin, -drēn) *n.* [*occas.* A-] *Prosody* an iambic line having six feet; iambic hexameter —*adj.* of an alexandrine or alexandrines

**a·lex·i·a** (ə lek′sē ə) *n.* [ModL. < Gr. *a-,* without + *lexis,* speech < *legein,* to speak] a loss of the ability to read, caused by brain injury

**al·fal·fa** (al fal′fə) *n.* [Sp. < Ar. *al-fasfasah,* the best fodder] a deep-rooted plant of the legume family, used extensively in the U.S. for fodder, pasture, and as a cover crop

**‡al fi·ne** (äl fē′ne) [It.] *Music* to the end (of a repeated section)

**Al·fred** (al′frid) [OE *Ælfred,* lit., wise counselor] a masculine name: dim. *Al, Alf*

**Alfred the Great** 849–900? A.D.; king of Wessex (871–900?)

**al·fres·co** (al fres′kō) *adv.* [It. < *al* (for *a il*), in the + *fresco,* fresh, cool] in the open air; outdoors —*adj.* outdoor Also **al fresco**

**Alg. 1.** Algeria **2.** Algerian

**alg.** algebra

**al·gae** (al′jē) *n.pl., sing.* **al′ga** (-gə) [pl. of L. *alga,* seaweed] a group of plants, variously one-celled or colonial, containing chlorophyll and other pigments, and having no true root, stem, or leaf: algae are found in water or damp places and include seaweeds —**al′gal** (-gəl) *adj.*

**al·ge·bra** (al′jə brə) *n.* [ML. < Ar. < *al,* the + *jabr,* reunion of broken parts] a mathematical system used to generalize certain arithmetical operations by permitting letters or other symbols to stand for numbers: it is used esp. in the solution of polynomial equations —**al′ge·bra′ic** (-brā′ik), **al′ge·bra′i·cal** *adj.* —**al′ge·bra′i·cal·ly** *adv.* —**al′ge·bra′-ist** *n.*

**Al·ger** (al′jər), **Horatio** 1832–99; U.S. writer of boys' stories

**Al·ge·ri·a** (al jir′ē ə) country in N Africa, on the Mediterranean: c. 919,000 sq. mi.; pop. 13,547,000; cap. Algiers —**Al·ge′ri·an** *adj., n.*

**Al·ger·non** (al′jər nən) [prob. < OFr. *al grenon,* with a mustache] a masculine name: dim. *Algie, Algy*

**-al·gi·a** (al′jə, -jē ə) [< Gr. *algos,* pain] *a n.-forming suffix meaning pain [neuralgia]*

**al·gid** (al′jid) *adj.* [< Fr. < L. *algidus*] cold; chilly —**al·gid′i·ty** (al jid′ə tē) *n.*

**Al·giers** (al jirz′) capital of Algeria; seaport on the Mediterranean: pop. 943,000

**Al·gon·qui·an** (al gäŋ′kē ən, -kwē-) *adj.* designating or of a widespread family of languages used by a number of N. American Indian tribes, including the Arapaho, Cheyenne, Blackfoot, etc. —*n.* **1.** this family of languages **2.** a member of any tribe using one of these languages

**Al·gon·quin** (al gäŋ′kwin, -kin) *n.* [< AmInd.] **1.** a member of a tribe of Algonquian Indians who live in the area of the Ottawa River, Canada **2.** their Algonquian language

**al·go·rism** (al′gər iz′m) *n.* [< ME. & OFr. < ML. *algorismus* < name of 9th-c. Ar. mathematician] **1.** the Arabic, or decimal, system of counting **2.** any method of computing

**al·go·rithm** (-ith′m) *n.* [altered (after ARITHMETIC) < prec.] *Math.* any special method of solving a certain kind of problem; specif., the repetitive calculations used in finding the greatest common divisor of two numbers

**Al·ham·bra** (al ham′brə) [Sp. < Ar. *al hamrā′,* lit., the red (house)] **1.** early palace of the Moorish kings near Granada, Spain **2.** city in SW Calif.: pop. 65,000 —**Al′·ham·bresque′** (-bresk′) *adj.*

**a·li·as** (ā′lē əs, āl′yəs) *n., pl.* **a′li·as·es** [< L. < *alius,* other] an assumed name; another name —*adv.* otherwise named; called by the assumed name of [Bell *alias* Jones]

**A·li Ba·ba** (ä′lē bä′bə, al′ē bab′ə) in *The Arabian Nights,* a poor woodcutter who finds the treasure of forty thieves in a cave

**al·i·bi** (al′ə bī′) *n., pl.* **-bis′** [L., contr. < *alius ibi,* elsewhere] **1.** *Law* the plea or fact that an accused person was elsewhere than at the scene of the crime **2.** [Colloq.] an excuse —*vi.* **-bied′, -bi′ing** [Colloq.] to offer an excuse

**Al·ice** (al′is) [< OFr. < OHG. *Adalheit:* see ADELAIDE] a feminine name: dim. *Elsie;* var. *Alicia*

**al·ien** (āl′yən, -ē ən) *adj.* [< OFr. < L. *alienus* < *alius,* other] **1.** belonging to another country or people; foreign **2.** not natural; repugnant (*to*) [ideas *alien* to him] **3.** of aliens —*n.* **1.** a foreigner **2.** a foreign-born resident in a country who is not a naturalized citizen **3.** an outsider

**al·ien·a·ble** (-ə bl) *adj.* capable of being transferred to a new owner —**al′ien·a·bil′i·ty** *n.*

**al·ien·ate** (-āt′) *vt.* **-at′ed, -at′ing 1.** to transfer the ownership (of property) to another **2.** to make unfriendly; estrange [behavior that *alienated* his friends] **3.** to cause to be withdrawn or detached, as from society **4.** to cause a transference (of affection) —**al′ien·a′tor** *n.*

**al·ien·a·tion** (āl′yə nā′shən, -ē ə-) *n.* **1.** an alienating or being alienated **2.** insanity

**al·ien·ee** (āl′yə nē′, āl′ē ə-) *n.* a person to whom property is transferred or conveyed

**al·ien·ist** (āl′yən ist, āl′ē ən-) *n.* a psychiatrist, esp. one who testifies in a law court

**al·ien·or** (-ôr′, -ər) *n.* a person from whom property is transferred or conveyed

**al·i·form** (al′ə fôrm′, ā′lə-) *adj.* [< L. *ala,* a wing + -FORM] shaped like a wing

**a·light**[1] (ə līt′) *vi.* **a·light′ed** or **a·lit′, a·light′ing** [< ME. < *a-,* out, off + *lihtan,* to dismount] **1.** to get down or off; dismount **2.** to come down after flight **3.** [Rare] to come (*on* or *upon*) accidentally

**a·light**[2] (ə līt′) *adj.* lighted up; glowing

**a·lign** (ə līn′) *vt.* [< Fr. < *a,* to + *ligner* < *ligne,* LINE[1]] **1.** to bring into a straight line **2.** to bring (parts, as the wheels of a car) into proper coordination **3.** to bring into agreement, close cooperation, etc. [he *aligned* himself with the liberals] —*vi.* to come into line; line up

**a·lign·ment** (-mənt) *n.* **1.** an aligning or being aligned; esp., *a*) arrangement in a straight line *b*) a condition of close cooperation **2.** a line or lines formed by aligning

**a·like** (ə līk′) *adj.* [< OE. *gelic, onlike:* see A-[1] & LIKE[1]] like one another; similar: usually in the predicate —*adv.* **1.** in the same manner; similarly **2.** to the same degree; equally —**a·like′ness** *n.*

**al·i·ment** (al′ə mənt; *for v.* -ment′) *n.* [L. *alimentum* < *alere,* to nourish] **1.** anything that nourishes; food **2.** means of support —*vt.* to nourish —**al′i·men′tal** (-men′t'l) *adj.*

**al·i·men·ta·ry** (al′ə men′tər ē) *adj.* [see prec.] **1.** connected with food or nutrition **2.** nourishing **3.** furnishing support or sustenance

**alimentary canal** (or **tract**) the passage in the body through which food passes to be digested: it extends from the mouth to the anus

**al·i·men·ta·tion** (al′ə men tā′shən) *n.* **1.** nourishment; nutrition **2.** support; sustenance —**al′i·men′ta·tive** (-men′tə tiv) *adj.*

**al·i·mo·ny** (al′ə mō′nē) *n.* [< L. < *alere,* to nourish] an allowance paid, esp. to a woman, by the spouse or former spouse after a legal separation or divorce

**a·line** (ə līn′) *vt., vi.* **a·lined′, a·lin′ing** same as ALIGN —**a·line′ment** *n.*

**al·i·quant** (al′ə kwənt) *adj.* [< L. < *alius,* other + *quantus,* how much] *Math.* that does not divide a number evenly but leaves a remainder [8 is an *aliquant* part of 25]: cf. ALIQUOT

**al·i·quot** (al′ə kwət) *adj.* [L. < *alius,* other + *quot,* how many] *Math.* that divides a number evenly and leaves no remainder [8 is an *aliquot* part of 24]: cf. ALIQUANT

**Al·i·son** (al′ə s'n) [< OFr.: see ALICE] a feminine name

**a·lit** (ə lit′) *alt. pt. & pp. of* ALIGHT[1]

**a·live** (ə līv′) *adj.* [< OE. *on,* in + *life,* life] [*usually used in the predicate*] **1.** having life; living **2.** in existence, operation, etc. [to keep his memory *alive*] **3.** lively; alert [*Alive* is used as an interjection in such phrases as *man alive! sakes alive!* etc. —**alive to** fully aware of; perceiving —**alive with** teeming with; full of

**a·liz·a·rin** (ə liz′ər in) *n.* [G., ult. < Ar. *al asārah,* the juice < *asara,* to press] a reddish-yellow crystalline compound, $C_{14}H_8O_4$, used in dyes: also **a·liz′a·rine** (-in, -ēn′)

**al·ka·li** (al′kə lī′) *n., pl.* **-lies′, -lis′** [< Ar. *al,* the + *qili,* ashes (of saltwort)] **1.** any base or hydroxide, as soda, potash, etc., that gives a high concentration of hydroxyl ions in solution **2.** any soluble mineral salt or mixture of salts found in desert soils and capable of neutralizing acids

**alkali metals** the group of metallic chemical elements consisting of lithium, sodium, potassium, rubidium, cesium, and francium

**al·ka·line** (al′kə lin, -līn′) *adj.* of, like, or containing an alkali; basic —**al′ka·lin′i·ty** (-lin′ə tē) *n.*

**al·ka·line-earth metals** (al′kə lin ʉrth′, -līn′-) a group of metallic chemical elements, including calcium, strontium, barium, and sometimes beryllium, magnesium, and radium: the oxides of these metals are called **alkaline earths**

**al·ka·lin·ize** (al′kə lə nīz′) *vt.* **-ized′, -iz′ing** same as ALKALIZE —**al′ka·lin·i·za′tion** *n.*

**al·ka·lize** (al′kə līz′) *vt.* **-lized′, -liz′ing** to make alkaline —**al′ka·li·za′tion** *n.*

**al·ka·loid** (-loid′) *n.* [ALKAL(I) + -OID] any of a number of colorless, bitter, basic organic substances, as caffeine, morphine, quinine, etc., found in certain plants —**al′ka·loid′al** *adj.*

**Al·ko·ran** (al′kō ran′, -rän′) *n.* the Koran

**al·kyd** (al′kid) *n.* [ult. < ALKALI + ACID] any of several synthetic resins used as coatings, and in paints, varnishes, etc.: also **alkyd resin**

**all** (ôl) *adj.* [OE. *eall*] **1.** the whole quantity, extent, or number of [*all* the gold, *all* day] **2.** every one of [*all* men must eat] **3.** the greatest possible [said in *all* sincerity] **4.** any; any whatever [true beyond *all* question] **5.** every [*all* manner of men] **6.** alone; only [life is not *all* pleasure] **7.** seeming to be nothing but [he was *all* arms and legs] —*pron.* **1.** [with *pl. v.*] everyone [*all* are present] **2.** [with *pl. v.*] every one [*all* of us are going] **3.** everything [*all* is over between them] **4.** every part or bit [*all* of it is eaten] —*n.* **1.** everything one has [give your *all*] **2.** a totality; whole —*adv.* **1.** wholly; entirely [*all* worn out] **2.** apiece [a score of thirty *all*] —**after all** nevertheless; in spite of everything —**all but 1.** all except **2.** nearly; almost —**all in** [Colloq.] very tired —**all in all 1.** considering everything **2.** as a whole —**all over 1.** ended **2.** everywhere; in every part of; throughout **3.** [Colloq.] typically [that's Mary *all over*] —**all the (better, worse,** etc.) so much the (better, worse, etc.) —**all the (farther, closer,** etc.) [Colloq. or Dial.]

as (far, close, etc.) as —**all the same 1.** nevertheless **2.** of no importance —**at all 1.** in the least **2.** in any way **3.** under any conditions —**for all** in spite of —**in all** altogether

**all-** *a combining form meaning:* **1.** wholly; entirely *[all-American]* **2.** for every *[all-purpose]* **3.** of every part *[all-inclusive]*

**Al·lah** (al′ə, ä′lə, ä lä′) [Ar. *Allāh < al,* the + *ilāh,* god] *the Moslem name for* GOD

**Al·la·ha·bad** (al′ə hä bäd′) city in N India, on the Ganges: pop. 431,000

**all-A·mer·i·can** (ôl′ə mer′ə kən) *adj.* **1.** made up wholly of Americans or of American elements **2.** representative of the U.S. as a whole, or chosen as best in the U.S. **3.** of all the Americas —*n.* **1.** a hypothetical football (or other) team of college players voted the best of the year in the U.S. **2.** a player chosen for such a team

**Al·lan** (al′ən) *var. of* ALAN

**all-a·round** (ôl′ə round′) *adj.* having many abilities, talents, or uses; versatile

**al·lay** (ə lā′) *vt.* **-layed′, -lay′ing** [< OE. < *a-,* down + *lec-gan,* to lay] **1.** to put (fears, etc.) to rest; calm **2.** to lessen or relieve (pain, etc.)

**all-clear** (ôl′klir′) *n.* a siren or other signal that an air raid or practice alert is over

**al·le·ga·tion** (al′ə gā′shən) *n.* **1.** an alleging **2.** something alleged; assertion **3.** an assertion made without proof **4.** *Law* an assertion which its maker proposes to support with evidence

**al·lege** (ə lej′) *vt.* **-leged′, -leg′ing** [ME. *aleggen,* to produce as evidence < OFr., ult. < L. *ex-,* out of + *litigare:* see LITIGATE] **1.** to declare or assert **2.** to assert or declare without proof **3.** to give as a plea, excuse, etc. —**al·lege′a·ble** *adj.* —**al·leg′er** *n.*

**al·leged** (ə lejd′, ə lej′id) *adj.* **1.** so declared, but without proof *[the alleged assassin]* **2.** so-called *[his alleged friends]* —**al·leg′ed·ly** *adv.*

**Al·le·ghe·ny** (al′ə gā′nē) [< AmInd. < ?] river in W Pa., joining the Monongahela to form the Ohio: 325 mi.

**Allegheny Mountains** mountain range of the Appalachians, in C Pa., Md., Va., and W.Va.: also **Al′le·ghe′nies**

**al·le·giance** (ə lē′jəns) *n.* [< OFr. *a-,* to + *ligeance < liege:* see LIEGE] **1.** the obligation of support and loyalty to one's ruler, government, or country **2.** loyalty or devotion, as to a cause, person, etc. —**al·le′giant** (-jənt) *adj., n.*

**al·le·gor·i·cal** (al′ə gôr′i k'l, -gär′-) *adj.* **1.** of or characteristic of allegory **2.** that is or contains an allegory Also **al′le·gor′ic** —**al′le·gor′i·cal·ly** *adv.*

**al·le·go·rist** (al′ə gôr′ist, -gər ist) *n.* one who writes allegories —**al′le·go·ris′tic** *adj.*

**al·le·go·rize** (al′ə gə rīz′) *vt.* **-rized′, -riz′ing 1.** to make into or treat as an allegory **2.** to interpret in an allegorical sense —*vi.* to make or use allegories —**al′le·go·ri·za′tion** *n.* —**al′le·go·riz′er** *n.*

**al·le·go·ry** (al′ə gôr′ē) *n., pl.* **-ries** [< L. < Gr. < *allos,* other + *agoreuein,* to speak < *agora,* AGORA¹] **1.** a story in which people, things, and events have a symbolic meaning: allegories are used for teaching or explaining ideas, moral principles, etc. **2.** the presenting of ideas by such stories **3.** any symbol or emblem

**al·le·gret·to** (al′ə gret′ō) *adj., adv.* [It., dim. of ALLEGRO] *Music* moderately fast; somewhat slower than *allegro* —*n., pl.* **-tos** an allegretto movement or passage

**al·le·gro** (ə leg′rō, -lā′grō) *adj., adv.* [It. < L. *alacer,* brisk] *Music* fast, but not so fast as *presto* —*n., pl.* **-gros** a fast movement or passage

**al·lele** (ə lēl′) *n.* [G. *allel* < Gr. *allēlōn,* of one another] either of a pair of genes in the same position on both members of a pair of chromosomes and bearing characters inherited alternatively according to Mendelian law: also **al·le·lo·morph** (ə lel′ə môrf′, ə lē′lə-) —**al·le′lic** *adj.*

**al·le·lu·ia** (al′ə lōō′yə) *interj., n. same as* HALLELUJAH

**Al·len** (al′ən) *var. of* ALAN

**Al·len·town** (al′ən toun′) [after Wm. *Allen,* the founder] city in E Pa.: pop. 104,000

**al·ler·gen** (al′ər jən) *n.* [G. < *allergie,* ALLERGY + -*gen,* -GEN] a substance inducing an allergic state or reaction —**al′ler·gen′ic** (-jen′ik) *adj.*

**al·ler·gic** (ə lur′jik) *adj.* **1.** of or caused by allergy **2.** having an allergy **3.** unwilling or not inclined (*to*): a humorous usage *[allergic to study]*

**al·ler·gist** (al′ər jist) *n.* a doctor who specializes in treating allergies

**al·ler·gy** (al′ər jē) *n., pl.* **-gies** [< G. < Gr. *allos,* other + *-ergeia,* as in *energeia* (see ENERGY)] **1.** abnormal sensitivity to a specific substance (such as a food, pollen, dust, etc.) or condition (as heat or cold) which in like amounts is harmless to most people **2.** a strong dislike

**al·le·vi·ate** (ə lē′vē āt′) *vt.* **-at′ed, -at′ing** [< LL. pp. of *alleviare < L. < ad-,* to + *levis,* light] **1.** to make less hard to bear; relieve (pain, etc.) **2.** to reduce or decrease *[to alleviate poverty]* —**al·le′vi·a′tion** *n.* —**al·le′vi·a′tive** *adj.* —**al·le′vi·a′tor** *n.* —**al·le′vi·a′to·ry** (-ə tôr′ē) *adj.*

**al·ley** (al′ē) *n., pl.* **-leys** [< OFr. *alee,* a going < *aler* (Fr. *aller*), to go < ML. < L. *ambulare,* to walk] **1.** a lane in a garden or park **2.** a narrow street or walk; specif., a lane behind a row of buildings **3.** *Bowling a)* the long, narrow lane along which the balls are rolled: now usually LANE *b)* *[occas. pl.]* a bowling establishment —**up** (or **down**) **one's alley** [Slang] suited to one's tastes or abilities

**al·ley·way** (al′ē wā′) *n.* **1.** an alley between buildings **2.** any narrow passageway

**All Fools′ Day** *same as* APRIL FOOLS′ DAY

**all hail** [Archaic] all health: a greeting

**All·hal·lows** (ôl′hal′ōz) *n.* [< OE. *ealle halgan:* see ALL & HALLOW¹] [Archaic] *same as* ALL SAINTS′ DAY: also called **All′hal′low·mas** (-hal′ō məs)

**al·li·ance** (ə lī′əns) *n.* [< OFr. < *alier:* see ALLY] **1.** an allying or being allied; specif., a union, as of families by marriage **2.** *a)* a close association for a common goal, as of nations, parties, etc. *b)* the agreement for such an association *c)* the countries, groups, etc. in such association **3.** similarity or relationship in characteristics

**al·lied** (ə līd′; *also, esp. for 3,* al′īd) *adj.* **1.** united by kinship, treaty, etc. **2.** closely related *[allied sciences]* **3.** [A-] of the Allies

**Al·lies** (al′īz, ə līz′) *n.pl.* **1.** in World War I, the nations allied by treaty against Germany and the other Central Powers; orig., Great Britain, France, and Russia, later joined by the U.S., Italy, Japan, etc. **2.** in World War II, the nations associated against the Axis; esp., Great Britain, the Soviet Union, and the U.S.: see UNITED NATIONS

**al·li·ga·tor** (al′ə gāt′ər) *n.* [< Sp. *el,* the + *lagarto* < L. *lacerta,* LIZARD] **1.** a large reptile of the crocodile group, found in tropical rivers and marshes of the U.S. and in China **2.** a leather made from its hide

**ALLIGATOR**
**(8–12 ft. long)**

**alligator pear** *same as* AVOCADO

**all-im·por·tant** (ôl′im pôr′t'nt) *adj.* essential

**al·lit·er·ate** (ə lit′ə rāt′) *vi., vt.* **-at′ed, -at′ing** to show or cause to show alliteration

**al·lit·er·a·tion** (ə lit′ə rā′shən) *n.* [< ML. < L. *ad-,* to + *littera,* letter] repetition of a beginning sound, usually of a consonant, in two or more words of a phrase, line of poetry, etc. (Ex.: "Sing a song of sixpence")

**al·lit·er·a·tive** (ə lit′ə rāt′iv, -ər ə tiv) *adj.* of, showing, or using alliteration —**al·lit′er·a′tive·ly** *adv.* —**al·lit′er·a′tive·ness** *n.*

**al·lo-** (al′ō) [< Gr. *allos,* other] *a combining form signifying* variation or reversal *[allotropy]*

**al·lo·cate** (al′ə kāt′) *vt.* **-cat′ed, -cat′ing** [< ML. pp. of *allocare < L. ad-,* to + *locus,* a place] **1.** to set apart for a specific purpose **2.** to distribute in shares; allot **3.** to locate —**al′lo·ca·ble** (-kə b'l) *adj.* —**al′lo·ca′tion** *n.*

**al·lom·er·ism** (ə läm′ər iz′m) *n.* [< ALLO- + Gr. *meros,* part + -ISM] variation in chemical makeup without change in crystalline form —**al·lom′er·ous** (-əs) *adj.*

**al·lo·path** (al′ə path′) *n.* a person who practices or advocates allopathy: also **al·lop·a·thist** (ə läp′ə thist)

**al·lop·a·thy** (ə läp′ə thē) *n.* [< G.: see ALLO- & -PATHY] treatment of disease by remedies that produce effects different from those produced by the disease: opposed to HOMEOPATHY —**al·lo·path·ic** (al′ə path′ik) *adj.* —**al′lo·path′i·cal·ly** *adv.*

**al·lo·phone** (al′ə fōn′) *n.* [ALLO- + -PHONE¹] *Linguis.* any of the variant forms of a phoneme

**al·lot** (ə lät′) *vt.* **-lot′ted, -lot′ting** [OFr. *aloter < a-,* to + *lot,* lot] **1.** to distribute by lot or in shares; apportion **2.** to give or assign as one's share *[each speaker is allotted five minutes]* —**al·lot′ta·ble** *adj.* —**al·lot′ter** *n.*

**al·lot·ment** (-mənt) *n.* **1.** an allotting or being allotted **2.** a thing allotted; portion **3.** *Mil.* a regular deduction from one's pay

**al·lo·trope** (al′ə trōp′) *n.* an allotropic form

**al·lo·trop·ic** (al′ə träp′ik) *adj.* of or having allotropy: also **al′lo·trop′i·cal** —**al′lo·trop′i·cal·ly** *adv.*

**al·lot·ro·py** (ə lät′rə pē) *n.* [< Gr. < ALLO- + *tropos,* way, manner] the property that certain chemical elements have of existing in two or more different forms: also **al·lot′ro·pism**

**al·lot·tee** (ə lät′ē′) *n.* a person to whom something is allotted

**all-out** (ôl′out′) *adj.* complete or wholehearted [an *all-out* effort]

**al·low** (ə lou′) *vt.* [< OFr. *alouer* < ML. < L. < *ad-*, to + *locus*, a place: associated with OFr. *alouer* < L. *ad-*, to + *laudare*, to praise] 1. to let do, happen, etc.; permit [*allowed* to rot] 2. to let have [*allowed* no vacation] 3. to let enter [dogs not *allowed*] 4. to admit (a claim or the like); acknowledge as true 5. to provide or allot (an amount, period, etc.) for a purpose [*allow* an inch for shrinkage] 6. [Dial.] *a*) to think; give as one's opinion *b*) to intend —**allow for** to keep in mind [*allow for* the difference in time] —**allow of** to be subject to

**al·low·a·ble** (-ə b'l) *adj.* that can be allowed; permissible —**al·low′a·bly** *adv.*

**al·low·ance** (-əns) *n.* 1. an allowing, permitting, etc. 2. something allowed, as an amount of money, food, etc. given regularly, as to a child, or for a specific purpose, as to a soldier 3. a reduction in price in consideration of a large order, a trade-in, etc. —*vt.* -anced, -anc·ing 1. to put on an allowance 2. to apportion economically —**make allowance** (or **allowances**) to take circumstances into consideration —**make allowance** (or **allowances**) **for** 1. to excuse because of mitigating factors 2. to leave room, time, etc. for

**al·low·ed·ly** (ə lou′id lē) *adv.* admittedly

**al·loy** (al′oi; *also, and for v. usually,* ə loi′) *n.* [< Anglo-Fr. < OFr. < L. *alligare*: see ALLY] 1. a substance that is a mixture of two or more metals, or of a metal and something else 2. *a*) formerly, a less valuable metal mixed with a more valuable one, often to give hardness *b*) something that lowers the value of another thing when mixed with it —*vt.* 1. to make (a metal) less pure by mixing with a less valuable metal 2. to mix (metals) to form an alloy 3. to debase by mixing with something inferior

**all-pur·pose** (ôl′pur′pəs) *adj.* useful in many ways

**all-right** (-rīt′) *adj.* [Slang] honest, honorable, good, etc. [an *all-right* guy]

**all right** 1. satisfactory; adequate 2. unhurt; safe 3. correct 4. yes; very well 5. [Colloq.] certainly [he's the one, *all right*]

**all-round** (ôl′round′) *adj. same as* ALL-AROUND

**All Saints' Day** an annual church festival (November 1) in honor of all the saints

**All Souls' Day** in some Christian churches, a day (usually November 2) of prayer for the dead

**all-spice** (ôl′spīs′) *n.* 1. the berry of a West Indian tree of the myrtle family 2. the spice made from this berry: its flavor seems to combine the tastes of several spices: the tree itself

**all-star** (-stär′) *adj.* made up entirely of outstanding or star performers

**all-time** (-tīm′) *adj.* unsurpassed up to the present time [an *all-time* record]

**al·lude** (ə lood′) *vi.* -lud′ed, -lud′ing [L. *alludere*, to jest < *ad-*, to + *ludere*, to play] to refer in a casual or indirect way (*to*)

**al·lure** (ə loor′) *vt., vi.* -lured′, -lur′ing [< OFr. < *a-*, to + *lurer*, to LURE] to tempt with something desirable; attract; entice —*n.* the power of alluring; fascination —**al·lure′-ment** *n.* —**al·lur′er** *n.*

**al·lur·ing** (ə loor′iŋ) *adj.* tempting strongly; highly attractive; charming —**al·lur′ing·ly** *adv.*

**al·lu·sion** (ə loo′zhən) *n.* 1. an alluding 2. an indirect reference; casual mention

**al·lu·sive** (ə loos′iv) *adj.* 1. containing an allusion 2. using allusion; full of allusions —**al·lu′sive·ly** *adv.* —**al·lu′sive·ness** *n.*

**al·lu·vi·al** (ə loo′vē əl) *adj.* of, composed of, or found in alluvium —*n. same as* ALLUVIUM

**al·lu·vi·um** (ə loo′vē əm) *n.* -vi·ums, -vi·a (-vē ə) [< L. < *alluere* < *ad-*, to + *luere*, to LAVE] sand, clay, etc. gradually deposited by moving water, as along a river bed

**al·ly** (ə lī′; *also, and for n. usually,* al′ī) *vt.* -lied′, -ly′ing [< OFr. *alier* < L. *alligare* < *ad-*, to + *ligare*, to bind] 1. to unite for a specific purpose, as families by marriage or nations by treaty 2. to relate by similarity of structure, qualities, etc.: usually in the passive [the onion is *allied* to the lily] —*vi.* to become allied —*n., pl.* -lies 1. a country or person joined with another for a common purpose: see also ALLIES 2. a plant, animal, or thing closely related in structure, etc. to another 3. an associate; helper

**Al·ma** (al′mə) [L. fem. of *almus*, nourishing] a feminine name

**Al·ma-A·ta** (äl′mə ä′tə) capital of the Kazakh S.S.R.: pop. 673,000

**al·ma ma·ter** (al′mə mät′ər, mät′ər) [L., fostering mother] 1. the college or school that one attended 2. its anthem, or hymn

**al·ma·nac** (ôl′mə nak′, al′-) *n.* [< ML. < LGr. *almenichiaka*, calendar] 1. a calendar with astronomical data, weather forecasts, etc. 2. a book published annually, containing information, usually statistical, on many subjects

**al·might·y** (ôl mīt′ē) *adj.* [< OE. < *eal*, all + *mihtig*, mighty] 1. having unlimited power; all-powerful 2. [Slang] great; extreme —*adv.* [Slang] extremely —**the Almighty** God —**al·might′i·ly** *adv.* —**al·might′i·ness** *n.*

**al·mond** (ä′mənd, am′ənd, al′mənd) *n.* [< OFr. < L. < Gr. *amygdalē*] 1. the edible, nutlike kernel of a small, dry, peachlike fruit 2. the tree bearing this fruit —**al′mond-like′** *adj.*

**al·mon·er** (al′mən ər, ä′mən-) *n.* one who distributes alms, as for a church, etc.

**al·most** (ôl′mōst, ôl′mōst′) *adv.* [OE. *eallmæst*: see ALL & MOST] very nearly; all but

**alms** (ämz) *n., pl.* **alms** [< OE. < LL. < Gr. *eleēmosynē*, alms < *eleos*, pity] money, food, etc. given to poor people —**alms′giv′er** *n.*

**alms·house** (-hous′) *n.* formerly, a home for people too poor to support themselves; poorhouse

**al·oe** (al′ō) *n., pl.* -oes [< L. < Gr. *aloē* < ? Heb.] 1. a South African plant of the lily family, with fleshy, spiny leaves 2. [*pl., with sing. v.*] a laxative drug made from the juice of certain aloe leaves

**a·loft** (ə lôft′) *adv.* [ME. *o, on,* on + *loft* < ON. *lopt*: see LOFT] 1. far above the ground 2. in the air; flying 3. high above a ship's deck

**a·lo·ha** (ä lō′ə, ä lō′hä) *n., interj.* [Haw., lit., love] a word used as a greeting or farewell

**a·lone** (ə lōn′) *adj., adv.* [ME. < *al*, ALL + *one*, ONE] 1. apart from anything or anyone else [the hut stood *alone* in the woods] 2. without any other person [to walk *alone*] 3. with nothing more; only [the box *alone* weighs two pounds] 4. without equal or peer —**let alone** 1. to refrain from bothering 2. not to mention [we hadn't a dime, *let alone* a dollar] —**let well enough alone** to be content with things as they are —**a·lone′ness** *n.*

**a·long** (ə lôŋ′) *prep.* [< OE. *andlang*, along < *and-*, over against + *-lang*, long] 1. on or beside the length of [*along* the wall is a hedge] 2. in conformity with [to think *along* certain lines] —*adv.* 1. in a line; lengthwise 2. progressively onward [he walked *along* by himself] 3. as a companion [come *along* with us] 4. with one [she took her book *along*] 5. advanced [well *along* in years] 6. [Colloq.] approaching [*along* toward evening] —**all along** from the very beginning —**along with** 1. together with 2. in addition to —**be along** [Colloq.] to come or arrive [I'll be *along* soon] —**get along** 1. to go forward 2. to contrive 3. to succeed 4. to agree 5. [Colloq.] to go away

**a·long·shore** (ə lôŋ′shôr′) *adv.* along the shore; near or beside the shore

**a·long·side** (-sīd′) *adv.* at or by the side; side by side —*prep.* at the side of; side by side with —**alongside of** at the side of; beside

**a·loof** (ə loof′) *adv.* [*a-*, on + *loof* < Du. *loef*, LUFF, to windward] at a distance but in view; apart —*adj.* 1. at a distance; removed 2. distant in sympathy, interest, etc. [an *aloof* manner] —**a·loof′ly** *adv.* —**a·loof′ness** *n.*

**a·loud** (ə loud′) *adv.* 1. loudly 2. with the normal voice [read the letter *aloud*]

**Al·o·ys·i·us** (al′ə wish′əs) [< ML.; prob. < OFr. *Loeis*: see LOUIS] a masculine name

**alp** (alp) *n.* [< L. *Alpes*, the Alps] a high mountain, esp. in Switzerland: see ALPS

**al·pac·a** (al pak′ə) *n., pl.* -pac′as, -pac′a: see PLURAL, II, D, 1 [Sp. < SAmInd. *allpaca*] 1. a domesticated S. American mammal related to the llama, with long, fleecy wool 2. this wool 3. a cloth woven from this wool, often mixed with other fibers 4. a glossy cloth of cotton and wool

**al·pen·horn** (al′pən hôrn′) *n.* [G., Alpine horn] a curved, wooden, powerful-sounding horn, from five to twelve feet long, used by Swiss Alpine herdsmen for signaling: also **alp′horn′**

**al·pen·stock** (-stäk′) *n.* [G., Alpine staff] an iron-pointed staff used by mountain climbers

**al·pha** (al′fə) *n.* [Gr. < Phoen. name whence Heb. *āleph*: see ALEPH] 1. the first letter of the Greek alphabet (A, α) 2. the beginning of anything 3. the brightest star in a constellation

**alpha and omega** 1. the first and last letters of the Greek alphabet 2. the beginning and the end

**al·pha·bet** (al′fə bet′) *n.* [< LL. < LGr. < Gr.: see ALPHA & BETA] 1. the letters of a language, arranged in a traditional order 2. a system of signs or symbols to indicate letters or speech sounds 3. the first elements, as of a subject

**al·pha·bet·i·cal** (al′fə bet′i k'l) *adj.* 1. of or using an alphabet 2. in the usual order of the alphabet Also **al′-pha·bet′ic** —**al′pha·bet′i·cal·ly** *adv.*

**al·pha·bet·ize** (al′fə bə tīz′) *vt.* -ized′, -iz′ing 1. to arrange in alphabetical order 2. to express by or provide with an alphabet —**al′pha·bet·i·za′tion** (-bet′i zā′shən) *n.*

**al·pha·nu·mer·ic** (al′fə noo mer′ik, -nyoo′-) *adj.* [AL-PHA(BET) + NUMERIC(AL)] having or using both alphabetical and numerical symbols

**alpha particle** a positively charged particle given off by certain radioactive substances: it consists of two protons and two neutrons

**alpha ray** **1.** *same as* ALPHA PARTICLE **2.** a stream of alpha particles, less penetrating than a beta ray

**Al·pine** (al′pīn) *adj.* **1.** of the Alps or their inhabitants **2.** [**a-**] *a*) of or like high mountains *b*) growing in high altitudes

**al·pin·ist** (al′pə nist) *n.* [*also* A-] a mountain climber

**Alps** (alps) mountain system of SC Europe: highest peak, Mont BLANC

**al·read·y** (ôl red′ē) *adv.* **1.** by or before the given or implied time **2.** even now or even then

**al·right** (ôl rīt′) *adv. var. of* ALL RIGHT: a disputed sp., but in common use

**Al·sace** (al sās′, al′sas; *Fr.* al zàs′) former province of NE France —**Al·sa′tian** (-sā′shən) *adj., n.*

**Al·sace-Lor·raine** (-lô rān′; *Fr.* -lô ren′) region in NE France consisting of the former provinces of Alsace and Lorraine

**al·so** (ôl′sō) *adv.* [< OE. < *eal*, all + *swa*, so] in addition; too: sometimes used in place of *and*

**al·so-ran** (-ran′) *n.* [Colloq.] any loser in a race, competition, election, etc.

**alt.** **1.** alternate **2.** altitude **3.** alto

**Alta.** Alberta (Canada)

**Al·ta·ic** (al tā′ik) *adj.* **1.** of the Altai Mountains or the people living there **2.** designating or of a family of languages including Turkic and Mongolic

**Al·tai Mountains** (al′tī, al tī′) mountain system in SC U.S.S.R., NW China, and W Mongolia

**Al·ta·ir** (al tā′ir) [Ar. *al tā′ir*, the bird] the brightest star in the constellation Aquila

**al·tar** (ôl′tər) *n.* [< OE. & OFr.; both ult. < L. < *altus*, high] **1.** a raised platform where sacrifices are made to a god, etc. **2.** a table, stand, etc. used for sacred purposes in a place of worship, as the Communion table in Christian churches —**lead to the altar** to marry

**altar boy** a boy or man who helps a priest, vicar, etc. at religious services, esp. at Mass

**al·tar·piece** (-pēs′) *n.* an ornamental carving, painting, etc. above and behind an altar

**al·ter** (ôl′tər) *vt.* [< ML. *alterare* < L. *alter*, other] **1.** to make different in details; modify **2.** to resew parts of (a garment) for a better fit **3.** to castrate or spay —*vi.* to become different; change —**al′ter·a·ble** *adj.* —**al′ter·a·bly** *adv.*

**al·ter·ant** (-ənt) *adj.* causing alteration —*n.* a thing that causes alteration

**al·ter·a·tion** (ôl′tə rā′shən) *n.* **1.** an altering or being altered **2.** the result of this; change

**al·ter·a·tive** (ôl′tə rāt′iv, -tər ə tiv) *adj.* **1.** causing alteration **2.** *Med.* gradually restoring to health —*n.* an alterative medicine or treatment

**al·ter·cate** (ôl′tər kāt′) *vi.* -**cat′ed**, -**cat′ing** [< L. pp. of *altercari*, to dispute < *alter*, other] to argue angrily; quarrel

**al·ter·ca·tion** (ôl′tər kā′shən) *n.* an angry or heated argument

**al·ter e·go** (ôl′tər ē′gō, eg′ō) [L., lit., other I] **1.** another aspect of oneself **2.** a very close friend or constant companion

**al·ter·nate** (ôl′tər nit, al′-; *for v.* -nāt′) *adj.* [< L. pp. of *alternare*, to do by turns < *alternus*, one after the other < *alter*, other] **1.** succeeding each other; first one and then the other **2.** every other [*alternate* Fridays] **3.** being one of two or more choices; alternative **4.** *Bot.* growing along the stem singly at intervals —*n.* a person chosen to take the place of another if necessary; substitute —*vt.* -**nat′ed**, -**nat′**ing to do, use, or make happen by turns —*vi.* **1.** to act, happen, etc. by turns **2.** to take turns **3.** to exchange places, etc. regularly **4.** *Elec.* to reverse direction periodically: said of a current —**al′ter·nate·ly** *adv.* —**al′ter·na′tion** *n.*

**alternate angles** two angles at opposite ends and on opposite sides of a line crossing two others

**alternating current** an electric current that reverses its direction periodically

**al·ter·na·tive** (ôl tur′nə tiv, al-) *adj.* providing or being a choice between two (or, less strictly, among more than two) things —*n.* **1.** a choice between two or more things **2.** any of the things to be chosen —**al·ter′na·tive·ly** *adv.*

ALTERNATE ANGLES (B,C)

**al·ter·na·tor** (ôl′tər nāt′ər, al′-) *n.* an electric generator or dynamo producing alternating current

**al·the·a, al·thae·a** (al thē′ə) *n.* [< L. < Gr. *althaia*, wild mallows] **1.** any of a genus of plants in the mallow family, as the hollyhock **2.** *same as* ROSE OF SHARON (sense 1)

**alt·horn** (alt′hôrn′) *n.* a brass-wind instrument, the alto saxhorn: also **alto horn**

**al·though** (ôl thō′) *conj.* [ME. < *all, al*, even (emphatic) + *though*] in spite of the fact that; though: now sometimes sp. **altho**

**al·tim·e·ter** (al tim′ə tər; *chiefly Brit.* al′tə mēt′ər) *n.* [< L. *altus*, high + -METER] an instrument for measuring altitude; esp., in aircraft, an aneroid barometer that tells how high the craft is flying —**al·tim′e·try** *n.*

**al·ti·tude** (al′tə tōōd′, -tyōōd′) *n.* [< L. < *altus*, high] **1.** height; esp., the height of a thing above the earth's surface or above sea level **2.** a high place or region: *usually in pl.* **3.** a high level, rank, etc. **4.** *Astron.* the angular height of a planet, star, etc. above the horizon **5.** *Geom.* the perpendicular distance from the base of a figure to its highest point or to the side parallel to the base —**al′ti·tu′di·nal** (-′n əl) *adj.*

**al·to** (al′tō) *n., pl.* -**tos** [It. < L. *altus*, high] **1.** the range of the lowest female voice or, esp. formerly, the highest male voice **2.** a voice or singer with such range **3.** an instrument with the second highest range within a family of instruments, as the alto saxophone **4.** a part for such a voice or instrument —*adj.* of, in, for, or having this range

**alto clef** *see* C CLEF

**al·to·geth·er** (ôl′tə geth′ər, ôl′tə geth′ər) *adv.* [see ALL & TOGETHER] **1.** wholly; completely [*altogether* right] **2.** in all [he wrote six books *altogether*] **3.** on the whole [*altogether* a success] Distinguished from **all together** —**in the altogether** [Colloq.] nude

**Al·too·na** (al tōō′nə) [< *Altona*, former Ger. seaport] city in C Pa.: pop. 57,000

**al·tru·ism** (al′trōō iz′m) *n.* [< Fr. < It. *altrui*, of or to others < L. *alter*, another] unselfish concern for the welfare of others —**al′tru·ist** *n.*

**al·tru·is·tic** (al′trōō is′tik) *adj.* of or motivated by altruism —**al′tru·is′ti·cal·ly** *adv.*

**al·um** (al′əm) *n.* [< OFr. < L. *alumen*] **1.** a hydrated double sulfate of a trivalent metal and a univalent metal; esp., a double sulfate of potassium and aluminum, used in medicine and in making dyes, paper, etc. **2.** aluminum sulfate: erroneous use

**a·lu·mi·na** (ə lōō′mi nə) *n.* an oxide of aluminum, $Al_2O_3$, present in bauxite and clay and found as different forms of corundum, including emery, sapphires, rubies, etc.

**a·u·min·i·um** (al′yōō min′yəm, -ē əm) *n. Brit. var. of* ALUMINUM

**a·lu·mi·nize** (ə lōō′mə nīz′) *vt.* -**nized′**, -**niz′ing** to cover, or treat, with aluminum

**a·lu·mi·nous** (-nəs) *adj.* of or containing alum, alumina, or aluminum

**a·lu·mi·num** (ə lōō′mə nəm) *n.* [ModL. < L. *alumen*, alum] a silvery, lightweight, metallic chemical element that is easily worked, resists corrosion, and is found abundantly, but only in combination: symbol, Al; at. wt., 26.9815; at. no., 13 —*adj.* of, containing, or made of aluminum

**aluminum oxide** *same as* ALUMINA

**a·lum·na** (ə lum′nə) *n., pl.* -**nae** (-nē) [L., fem. of ff.] a girl or woman alumnus

**a·lum·nus** (-nəs) *n., pl.* -**ni** (-nī) [L., foster son < *alere*, to nourish] a person, esp. a boy or man, who has attended or is a graduate of a particular school, college, etc.

**al·ve·o·lar** (al vē′ə lər) *adj.* **1.** of or like an alveolus; socketlike **2.** *Anat. a*) of the part of the jaws containing the sockets of the teeth *b*) designating the ridge of the gums behind the upper front teeth *c*) of the air pockets in the lungs **3.** *Phonet.* formed, as English *t, d, s*, by touching or approaching the alveolar ridge with the tip of the tongue —*n. Phonet.* an alveolar sound

**al·ve·o·late** (-lit) *adj.* full of small cavities: also **al·ve′o·lat′ed** (-lāt′id) —**al·ve′o·la′tion** *n.*

**al·ve·o·lus** (al vē′ə ləs) *n., pl.* -**li** (-lī′) [L., dim. of *alveus*, a cavity < *alvus*, the belly] **1.** *Anat., Zool.* a small cavity or hollow, as an air cell of a lung, a tooth socket, etc. **2.** [*usually pl.*] the alveolar ridge

**Al·vin** (al′v′n) [< G. < OHG. *adal*, nobility + *wini*, friend] a masculine name

**al·way** (ôl′wā) *adv.* [Archaic] always

**al·ways** (ôl′wiz, -wāz) *adv.* [see ALL & WAY] **1.** in every instance; invariably [he's *always* late] **2.** all the time; forever [*always* present in the atmosphere] **3.** at any time [you can *always* leave]

**a·lys·sum** (ə lis′əm) *n.* [ModL. < Gr. < *alyssos*, curing madness < *a-*, without + *lyssa*, rage] **1.** any of a genus of plants of the mustard family, with white or yellow flowers **2.** *same as* SWEET ALYSSUM

---

fat, āpe, cär, ten, ēven, is, bīte; gō, hôrn, tōōl, look; oil, out; up, fur; get; joy; yet; chin; she; thin, *th*en; zh, leisure; ŋ, ring; ə for *a* in *ago, e* in *agent, i* in *sanity, o* in *comply, u* in *focus;* ′ as in *able* (ā′b′l); Fr. bàl; ë, Fr. coeur; ö, Fr. feu; Fr. mon; ô, Fr. coq; ü, Fr. duc; r, Fr. cri; H, G. ich; kh, G. doch; ‡foreign; *hypothetical; < derived from. See inside front cover.

**am** (am; *unstressed* əm) [OE. *eom:* see BE] *1st pers. sing., pres. indic., of* BE

**Am** *Chem.* americium

**AM** amplitude modulation

**Am.** 1. America 2. American

**A.M., AM** [L. *Artium Magister*] master of arts

**A.M., a.m., AM** [L. *ante meridiem*] before noon: used to designate the time from midnight to noon

**AMA, A.M.A.** American Medical Association

**a·mah** (ä′mə) *n.* [Anglo-Ind. < Port. *ama*] in the Orient, a woman servant, esp. one who serves as a baby's nurse

**a·main** (ə mān′) *adv.* [A-¹, on + MAIN¹] [Archaic or Poet.] 1. forcefully; vigorously 2. at or with great speed 3. hastily; suddenly 4. greatly

**a·mal·gam** (ə mal′gəm) *n.* [< ML., prob. < Ar. < Gr. *malagma,* an emollient < *malassein,* to soften] 1. any alloy of mercury with another metal or metals [silver *amalgam* is used as a dental filling] 2. any mixture or blend

**a·mal·ga·mate** (-gə māt′) *vt., vi.* -**mat′ed, -mat′ing** 1. to combine in an amalgam 2. to join together into one; unite —**a·mal′gam·a·ble** (-gəm ə b'l) *adj.* —**a·mal′ga·ma′tion** *n.* —**a·mal′ga·ma′tive** *adj.* —**a·mal′ga·ma′tor** *n.*

**A·man·da** (ə man′də) [L., lit., worthy to be loved < *amare,* to love] a feminine name: dim. *Mandy*

**a·man·dine** (ä′mən dēn′, am′ən-) *adj.* [Fr. < *amande,* almond + *-ine,* -INE¹] prepared or garnished with thinly sliced almonds [*trout amandine*]

**a·man·u·en·sis** (ə man′yoo wen′sis) *n., pl.* -**ses** (-sēz) [L. < *a-* (*ab*), from + *manus,* a hand + *-ensis,* relating to] an assistant who takes dictation or copies something already written; secretary: now somewhat jocular

**am·a·ranth** (am′ə ranth′) *n.* [< L. < Gr. *amarantos,* unfading < *a-,* not + *marainein,* to die away] 1. any of a genus of plants, usually with colorful leaves, including love-lies-bleeding, etc. 2. [Poet.] an imaginary flower that never fades or dies 3. a dark purplish red —**am′a·ran′thine** (-ran′thin) *adj.*

**Am·a·ril·lo** (am′ə ril′ō) [Sp., yellow] city in NW Texas: pop. 149,000

**am·a·ryl·lis** (am′ə ril′əs) *n.* [< L. & Gr.; conventional name for a shepherdess] 1. a bulb plant bearing several white, purple, pink, or red lilylike flowers on a single stem 2. any of several plants closely related to this

**a·mass** (ə mas′) *vt.* [< Fr. < ML. < *a-,* to + VL. *massare,* to pile up < L. *massa,* a MASS] 1. to pile up; collect together 2. to accumulate (esp. wealth) —**a·mass′er** *n.* —**a·mass′ment** *n.*

**am·a·teur** (am′ə chər, -toor, -tyoor) *n.* [Fr. < L. *amator,* a lover < *amare,* to love] 1. a person who engages in some art, science, sport, etc. for pleasure rather than as a profession; specif., an athlete who is forbidden by rule to profit from his athletic activity 2. a person who does something without professional skill —*adj.* 1. of or done by or as by an amateur or amateurs 2. being an amateur or made up of amateurs

**am·a·teur·ish** (am′ə choor′ish, -toor′-, -tyoor′-) *adj.* like an amateur; unskillful; not expert —**am′a·teur′ish·ly** *adv.* —**am′a·teur′ish·ness** *n.*

**am·a·teur·ism** (am′ə chər iz′m, -toor-, -tyoor-) *n.* 1. an amateurish method or quality 2. the nonprofessional status of an amateur

**am·a·to·ry** (am′ə tôr′ē) *adj.* [< L. pp. of *amare,* to love] of or showing love, esp. sexual love

**a·maze** (ə māz′) *vt.* **a·mazed′, a·maz′ing** [< OE. *amasian:* see MAZE] to fill with great surprise or sudden wonder; astonish —*n.* [Poet.] amazement —**a·maz′ed·ly** (-id lē) *adv.* —**a·maz′ing·ly** *adv.*

**a·maze·ment** (-mənt) *n.* an amazed condition; great wonder; astonishment

**Am·a·zon** (am′ə zän′, -zən) river in S. America, flowing from the Andes in Peru across N Brazil into the Atlantic: c. 3,300 mi. —*n.* [L. < Gr. < ?, but derived by folk etym. < *a-,* without + *mazos,* breast, hence the story that the Amazons cut off one breast to facilitate archery] 1. *Gr. Myth.* any of a race of female warriors supposed to have lived in Scythia 2. [a-] a large, strong, masculine woman —**Am′a·zo′ni·an** (-zō′nē ən) *adj.*

**am·bas·sa·dor** (am bas′ə dər) *n.* [< MFr. < OIt. < Pr. < hyp. *ambaissa,* task, mission] 1. the highest-ranking diplomatic representative appointed by a government to represent it in another country: an **ambassador-at-large** is one accredited to no particular country; an **ambassador extraordinary** is one on a special diplomatic mission; an **ambassador plenipotentiary** has the power to make treaties 2. an official messenger with a special mission —**am·bas′sa·do′ri·al** (-dôr′ē əl) *adj.* —**am·bas′sa·dor·ship′** *n.*

**am·ber** (am′bər) *n.* [< OFr. < Ar. ′*anbar,* ambergris] 1. a yellow or brownish-yellow translucent fossil resin used in jewelry, pipestems, etc. 2. the color of amber —*adj.* 1. made of or like amber 2. having the color of amber

**am·ber·gris** (-grēs′, -gris′) *n.* [< OFr. < *ambre gris,* gray AMBER] a grayish, waxy substance from the intestines of sperm whales, found floating in tropical seas and used in some perfumes

**am·ber·jack** (-jak′) *n.* [AMBER + JACK (fish): from its color] any of several food and game fishes found in warm seas

**am·bi-** [< L. < *ambo,* both] *a combining form meaning both* [*ambidextrous*]

**am·bi·ance** (am′bē əns) *n.* [Fr.: see AMBIENT] an environment or milieu: also **am′bi·ence**

**am·bi·dex·trous** (am′bə dek′strəs) *adj.* [< L. AMBI- + *dexter,* right hand + *-OUS*] 1. able to use both hands with equal ease 2. very skillful or versatile 3. deceitful; double-dealing —**am′bi·dex·ter′i·ty** (-dek stər′ə tē) *n.* —**am′bi·dex′trous·ly** *adv.*

**am·bi·ent** (am′bē ənt) *adj.* [< L. prp. of *ambire* < *ambi-,* around + *ire,* to go] surrounding; on all sides

**am·bi·gu·i·ty** (am′bə gyōō′ə tē) *n.* 1. the quality or state of being ambiguous 2. *pl.* -**ties** an ambiguous word, statement, etc.

**am·big·u·ous** (am big′yoo wəs) *adj.* [< L. < *ambigere,* to wander < *ambi-,* around + *agere,* to ACT] 1. having two or more possible meanings 2. not clear; indefinite; vague —**am·big′u·ous·ly** *adv.* —**am·big′u·ous·ness** *n.*

**am·bi·tion** (am bish′ən) *n.* [< OFr. < L. *ambitio,* a going around (to solicit votes) < pp. of *ambire:* see AMBIENT] 1. a strong desire for success, fame, power, wealth, etc. 2. the thing so desired

**am·bi·tious** (-əs) *adj.* 1. full of or showing ambition 2. greatly desirous (*of* something) 3. needing great effort, skill, enterprise, etc. —**am·bi′tious·ly** *adv.* —**am·bi′tious·ness** *n.*

**am·biv·a·lence** (am biv′ə ləns) *n.* [AMBI- + VALENCE] simultaneous conflicting feelings toward a person or thing, as love and hate —**am·biv′a·lent** *adj.* —**am·biv′a·lent·ly** *adv.*

**am·ble** (am′b'l) *vi.* -**bled, -bling** [< OFr. < L. *ambulare,* to walk] 1. to move at a smooth, easy gait by raising first both legs on one side, then both on the other: said of a horse, etc. 2. to walk in a leisurely manner —*n.* 1. a horse's ambling gait 2. a leisurely walking pace —**am′bler** *n.*

**Am·brose** (am′brōz) [< L. < Gr. < *ambrotos:* see ff.] a masculine name

**am·bro·sia** (am brō′zhə) *n.* [L. < Gr. < *ambrotos* < *a-,* not + *brotos,* mortal] 1. *Gr. & Rom. Myth.* the food of the gods and immortals 2. anything that tastes or smells delicious —**am·bro′sial** (-zhəl), **am·bro′sian** (-zhən) *adj.*

**am·bu·lance** (am′byə ləns) *n.* [< Fr. (*hôpital*) *ambulant* < L. prp. of *ambulare,* to walk] 1. orig., a mobile field hospital 2. a specially equipped vehicle for carrying the sick or wounded

**am·bu·lance-chas·er** (-chās′ər) *n.* [Slang] a lawyer who encourages victims of accidents to sue for damages as his clients

**am·bu·lant** (am′byə lənt) *adj.* moving; walking

**am·bu·late** (am′byə lāt′) *vi.* -**lat′ed, -lat′ing** [< L. pp. of *ambulare,* to walk] to move about; walk —**am′bu·la′tion** *n.*

**am·bu·la·to·ry** (-lə tôr′ē) *adj.* 1. of or for walking 2. able to walk and not confined to bed 3. moving from one place to another; movable 4. *Law* that can be changed or revoked —*n., pl.* -**ries** any sheltered place for walking, as in a cloister

**am·bus·cade** (am′bəs kād′; *also for n.* am′bəs kād′) *n., vt., vi.* -**cad′ed, -cad′ing** [< Fr. < OFr. *embuschier:* see ff.] *same as* AMBUSH —**am′bus·cad′er** *n.*

**am·bush** (am′boosh) *n.* [< OFr. *embuschier* < ML. *imboscare,* to set an ambush < *in-,* in + *boscus,* woods] 1. an arrangement of persons in hiding to make a surprise attack 2. *a)* the persons in hiding *b)* their place of hiding 3. the act of so lying in wait to attack —*vt., vi.* 1. to hide in ambush 2. to attack from ambush —**am′bush·ment** *n.*

**a·me·ba** (ə mē′bə) *n., pl.* -**bas, -bae** (-bē) *same as* AMOEBA —**a·me′bic, a·me′ban** *adj.* —**a·me′boid** *adj.*

**amebic dysentery** a form of dysentery caused by an amoeba

**a·meer** (ə mir′) *n. same as* AMIR

**A·me·lia** (ə mēl′yə, -ē ə) [of Gmc. origin; lit., ? diligent < base of *amal,* work] a feminine name

**a·mel·io·rant** (ə mēl′yər ənt) *n.* a thing that ameliorates

**a·mel·io·rate** (ə mēl′yə rāt′) *vt., vi.* -**rat′ed, -rat′ing** [< Fr. < OFr. *ameillorer* < *a-,* to + *meillor* < L. *melior,* better] to make or become better; improve —**a·mel′io·ra·ble** (-yər ə b'l) *adj.* —**a·mel′io·ra′tion** *n.* —**a·mel′io·ra′tive** *adj.* —**a·mel′io·ra′tor** *n.*

**A·men** (ä′mən) *same as* AMON

**a·men** (ā′men′, ä′-) *interj.* [< L. < Gr. < Heb. *āmēn,* truly, certainly] may it be so! so it is!: used after a prayer or to express approval —*n.* a speaking or writing of "amen"

**a·me·na·ble** (ə mē′nə b'l, -men′ə-) *adj.* [Anglo-Fr. < OFr. < *a-,* to + *mener,* to lead < L. *minare,* to drive (animals)] 1. responsible or answerable 2. able to be controlled or influenced; responsive; submissive [*amenable* to suggestion] 3. that can be tested by (with *to*) [*amenable* to the laws of physics] —**a·me′na·bil′i·ty** *n.* —**a·me′na·bly** *adv.*

**amen corner** in some rural Protestant churches, the seats to the minister's right, once occupied by those leading the responsive amens

**a·mend** (ə mend′) *vt.* [< OFr. < L. *emendare*, to correct: see EMEND] **1.** to make better; improve **2.** to remove the faults of; correct **3.** to change or revise (a legislative bill, a law, etc.) —*vi.* to improve one's conduct —**a·mend′a·ble** *adj.* —**a·mend′a·to′ry** *adj.* —**a·mend′er** *n.*

**a·mend·ment** (ə mend′mənt) *n.* **1.** a change for the better; improvement **2.** a correction of errors, faults, etc. **3.** a revision or addition proposed or made in a bill, law, constitution, etc.

**a·mends** (ə mendz′) *n.pl.* [< OFr., pl. of *amende*, a fine: see AMEND] [*sometimes with sing. v.*] something given or done to make up for injury, loss, etc. that one has caused [to make *amends* for rudeness by apologizing]

**a·men·i·ty** (ə men′ə tē, -mē′nə-) *n., pl.* **-ties** [< OFr. < L. *amoenitas* < *amoenus*, pleasant] **1.** pleasant quality; attractiveness **2.** *a)* an attractive or desirable feature, as of a place, climate, etc. *b)* anything that adds to one's comfort; convenience **3.** [*pl.*] the courtesies of polite social behavior

**a·men·or·rhe·a, a·men·or·rhoe·a** (ā men′ə rē′ə) *n.* [ModL. < Gr. *a-*, not + *mēn*, month + *rheein*, to flow] abnormal absence or suppression of menstruation

**am·ent** (am′ənt, ā′mənt) *n.* [< L. *amentum*, thong] *same as* CATKIN —**am·en·ta·ceous** (am′ən tā′shəs) *adj.*

**a·men·tia** (ā men′shə) *n.* [L., madness < *amens* (gen. *amentis*) < *a-* (*ab*), away + *mens*, mind] severe congenital mental deficiency: cf. DEMENTIA

**a·merce** (ə murs′) *vt.* **a·merced′, a·merc′ing** [< Anglo-Fr. < OFr. *a merci*, at the mercy of] **1.** to punish by imposing an arbitrary fine **2.** to punish generally —**a·merce′ment** *n.*

**A·mer·i·ca** (ə mer′ə kə) [name traditionally associated with *Amerigo* VESPUCCI, but < ? Sp. *Amerrique* (< AmInd. *Americ*), name of a Nicaraguan mountain range] **1.** North America and South America considered together **2.** either North America or South America **3.** the United States —**the Americas** America (sense 1)

**A·mer·i·can** (ə mer′ə kən) *adj.* **1.** of or in America **2.** of, in, or characteristic of the U.S., its people, etc. —*n.* **1.** a native or inhabitant of America; specif., *a)* an American Indian *b)* a citizen of the U.S. **2.** the English language spoken in the U.S.

**A·mer·i·ca·na** (ə mer′ə kan′ə, -kä′nə) *n.pl.* [see -ANA] books, papers, objects, etc. having to do with America, its people, and its history

**American cheese** a kind of fairly hard, mild Cheddar cheese, popular in the U.S.

**American Indian** *same as* INDIAN (*n.* 2)

**A·mer·i·can·ism** (ə mer′ə kən iz′m) *n.* **1.** a custom, characteristic, or belief of or originating in the U.S. **2.** a word, phrase, or usage originating in or peculiar to American English **3.** devotion or loyalty to the U.S., or to its traditions, etc.

**A·mer·i·can·ize** (-īz′) *vt., vi.* **-ized′, -iz′ing** to make or become American in character, manners, methods, ideals, etc.; assimilate to U.S. customs, speech, etc. —**A·mer′i·can·i·za′tion** *n.*

**American plan** a system of hotel operation in which the charge to guests covers room, service, and meals: distinguished from EUROPEAN PLAN

**American Revolution** **1.** a sequence of actions (1763-83) by American colonists against British domination, culminating in the Revolutionary War **2.** the Revolutionary War (1775-83), fought by the American colonies to gain independence from England

**American Samoa** *see* SAMOA

**American Standard Version** a revision of the King James Version of the Bible, published in the U.S. in 1901

**am·er·ic·i·um** (am′ə rish′ē əm, -ris′-) *n.* [ModL. < AMERICA] a chemical element, one of the transuranic elements produced from plutonium: symbol, Am; at. wt., 243.13; at. no., 95

**Am·er·ind** (am′ə rind′) *n.* [AMER(ICAN) + IND(IAN)] an American Indian or Eskimo —**Am′er·in′di·an** *adj., n.* —**Am′er·in′dic** *adj.*

**am·e·thyst** (am′ə thist) *n.* [< OFr. < L. < Gr. < *a-*, not + *methystos*, drunken (from the notion that it prevented intoxication)] **1.** a purple or violet variety of quartz, used in jewelry: popularly, a purple corundum, used in jewelry: also called *Oriental amethyst* **3.** purple or violet —**am′e·thys′tine** (-this′tin, -tēn) *adj.*

**Am·har·ic** (am har′ik, äm här′-) *n.* the Semitic language used officially in Ethiopia

‡**a·mi** (à mē′) *n., pl.* **a·mis′** (-mē′) [Fr.] a (man or boy) friend —**a·mie′** *n. fem., pl.* **a·mies′** (-mē′)

**a·mi·a·ble** (ā′mē ə b'l) *adj.* [< OFr. < LL. *amicabilis*, friendly < L. *amicus*, friend] having a pleasant, friendly disposition; good-natured —**a′mi·a·bil′i·ty** *n.* —**a′mi·a·bly** *adv.*

**am·i·ca·ble** (am′i kə b'l) *adj.* [< LL. *amicabilis*: see AMIABLE] friendly in feeling; showing good will; peaceable [an *amicable* discussion] —**am′i·ca·bil′i·ty** *n.* —**am′i·ca·bly** *adv.*

**am·ice** (am′is) *n.* [< OFr. < L. *amictus*, a cloak] an oblong cloth of white linen worn about the neck and shoulders by a priest at Mass

**a·mi·cus cu·ri·ae** (ə mī′kəs kyoor′i ē′) [L., friend of the court] *Law* a person who offers, or is called in, to advise a court on some legal matter

**a·mid** (ə mid′) *prep.* [ME. < *on*, at + *middan*, middle] in the middle of; among

**am·ide** (am′īd, -id) *n.* [AM(MONIA) + -IDE] **1.** any of a group of organic compounds containing the CO·NH₂ radical or an acid radical in place of one hydrogen atom of an ammonia molecule **2.** any of the ammono bases in which one hydrogen atom of the ammonia molecule is replaced by a metal —**a·mid·ic** (ə mid′ik) *adj.*

**am·i·dol** (am′ə dōl′, -dôl′) *n.* [< AMID(E) + (PHEN)OL] a colorless, crystalline compound used as a developer in photography

**a·mid·ships** (ə mid′ships) *adv., adj.* in or toward the middle of a ship: also **a·mid′ship**

**a·midst** (ə midst′) *prep. same as* AMID

**a·mi·go** (ə mē′gō; *Sp.* ä mē′gô) *n., pl.* **-gos** (-gōz; *Sp.* -gôs) [Sp.] a friend

**a·mine** (ə mēn′; am′ēn, -in) *n.* [AM(MONIA) + -INE⁴] *Chem.* a derivative of ammonia in which hydrogen atoms have been replaced by radicals containing hydrogen and carbon atoms

**a·mi·no** (ə mē′nō) *adj.* [< prec.] of or containing the NH₂ radical in combination with certain organic radicals

**amino acids** a group of organic compounds that contain the amino radical and serve as units of structure of the proteins

**a·mir** (ə mir′) *n.* [Ar.] in some Moslem countries, a ruler, prince, or commander: see also EMIR

**Am·ish** (ä′mish, am′ish) *n.pl.* [after Jacob Ammann (or Amen), the founder] Mennonites of a sect founded in the 17th cent. —*adj.* of this sect

**a·miss** (ə mis′) *adv.* [ME.: see A-¹ & MISS¹] in a wrong way; astray, wrongly, faultily, etc. —*adj.* wrong, faulty, improper, etc.: used predicatively

**a·mi·to·sis** (ā′mī tō′sis, am′ə-) *n.* [A-² (sense 3) + MITOSIS] *Biol.* cell division by simple constriction of the nucleus into two halves: opposed to MITOSIS —**am′i·tot′ic** (-tät′ik) *adj.*

**am·i·ty** (am′ə tē) *n., pl.* **-ties** [< OFr. *amistie* < L. *amicus*, friend] friendly, peaceful relations, as between nations; friendship

**Am·man** (äm′än) capital of Jordan: pop. 330,000

**am·me·ter** (am′mēt′ər) *n.* [AM(PERE) + -METER] an instrument for measuring the strength of an electric current in terms of amperes

**am·mo** (am′ō) *n.* [Slang] ammunition

**Am·mon** (am′ən) Amon, the ancient Egyptian god: identified by the Greeks (and Romans) with Zeus (and Jupiter)

**am·mo·nia** (ə mōn′yə) *n.* [< (SAL) AMMONIAC] **1.** a colorless, pungent gas, NH₃, used in fertilizers, cleaning fluids, etc. **2.** a water solution of this gas: in full, **ammonia water**

**am·mo·ni·ac** (ə mō′nē ak′) *n.* [< L. < Gr. *ammōniakon*, gum resin said to come from near the temple of Jupiter AMMON in Libya] an Asian gum resin used in perfumes, porcelain cements, etc.

**am·mo·ni·ate** (ə mō′n ē āt′; *for n.* -it) *vt.* **-at′ed, -at′ing** to mix or combine with ammonia —*n.* any of several compounds containing ammonia —**am·mo′ni·a′tion** *n.*

**am·mo·ni·fi·ca·tion** (ə mō′nə fi kā′shən, -män′ə-) *n.* **1.** an ammoniating **2.** the forming of ammonia by bacterial action in the decay of nitrogenous organic matter —**am·mo′ni·fy′** *vt., vi.* **-fied′, -fy′ing**

**am·mo·nite** (am′ə nīt′) *n.* [< L. (*cornu*) *Ammonis*, (horn) of Ammon] any of the coiled fossil shells of a Mesozoic mollusk

**am·mo·ni·um** (ə mō′nē əm) *n.* the radical NH₄, present in salts produced by the reaction of ammonia with an acid

**ammonium chloride** a white, crystalline compound, NH₄Cl: it is used in medicine, and also in dry cells, dyes, etc.: also called **sal ammoniac**

**ammonium hydroxide** an alkali, NH₄OH, formed by dissolving ammonia in water

**ammonium sulfate** an ammonium salt, (NH₄)₂SO₄, used in making fertilizers, in treating water, etc.

**am·mo·no** (am′ə nō′) *adj.* of, containing, or derived from ammonia

**am·mu·ni·tion** (am′yə nish′ən) *n.* [< Fr., by faulty separation of *la munition:* see MUNITIONS] **1.** anything hurled by a weapon or exploded as a weapon, as bullets, shells, bombs, grenades, etc. **2.** any means of attack or defense

**am·ne·sia** (am nē′zhə, -zhē ə) *n.* [ModL. < Gr. < *a-*, not + *mnasthai*, to remember] partial or total loss of memory caused by brain injury, or by shock, repression, etc. —**am·ne′si·ac′** (-zē ak′), **am·ne′sic** (-sik, -zik) *adj., n.*

**am·nes·ty** (am′nəs tē) *n., pl.* **-ties** [< Fr. < L. < Gr. *amnēstia*, a forgetting: see prec.] a general pardon, esp. for political offenses —*vt.* **-tied, -ty·ing** to grant amnesty to; pardon

**am·ni·on** (am′nē ən, -än′) *n., pl.* **-ni·ons, -ni·a** (-ə) [Gr., dim. of *amnos*, lamb] the innermost membrane of the sac enclosing the embryo of a mammal, reptile, or bird: it is filled with a watery fluid (**amniotic fluid**) —**am′ni·ot′ic** (-ät′ik) *adj.*

**a·moe·ba** (ə mē′bə) *n., pl.* **-bas, -bae** (-bē) [ModL. < Gr. *amoibē* < *ameibein*, to change] **1.** a microscopic, one-celled animal found usually in stagnant water: it moves by making continual changes in its shape and multiplies by fission **2.** a similar animal that is a parasite in higher animals and man

**a·moe·bic** (-bik) *adj.* **1.** of or like an amoeba or amoebas **2.** caused by amoebas Also **a-moe′ban** (-bən)

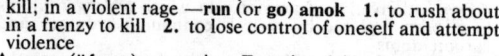

NUCLEUS

VACUOLE

PSEUDOPODIUM

AMOEBA

**a·mok** (ə muk′) *adj., adv.* [Malay *amoq*] in a frenzy to kill; in a violent rage —**run** (or **go**) **amok 1.** to rush about in a frenzy to kill **2.** to lose control of oneself and attempt violence

**A·mon** (ä′mən) an ancient Egyptian deity, later identified with the sun god: see AMON-RE

**a·mong** (ə muŋ′) *prep.* [OE. *on gemang*, in the company (of) < *on*, in + *gemang*, a crowd < *gemengan*, to mingle] **1.** in the company of; surrounded by [*among* friends] **2.** from place to place in [*pass among* the crowd] **3.** in the group or class of [fairest *among* women] **4.** by or with many of [rebellion *among* the youth] **5.** as compared with [one *among* thousands] **6.** with a share for each of [divided *among* us] **7.** with one another [talking *among* ourselves] **8.** by the joint action of

**a·mongst** (ə muŋst′) *prep. same as* AMONG

**A·mon-Re** (ä′mən rā′) the ancient Egyptian sun god: also **A′mon-Ra′** (-rä′)

**a·mon·til·la·do** (ə män′tə lä′dō) *n.* [Sp. < *Montilla*, a town in Spain] a pale, rather dry sherry

**a·mor·al** (ā môr′əl, -mär′-) *adj.* **1.** not to be judged by moral values; neither moral nor immoral **2.** without moral sense or principles —**a·mor·al·i·ty** (ā′mə ral′ə tē) *n.* —**a·mor′al·ly** *adv.*

**am·o·rous** (am′ər əs) *adj.* [< OFr. < LL. *amorosus* < L. *amor*, love < *amare*, to love] **1.** fond of making love **2.** in love; enamored or fond (*of*) **3.** full of or showing love or sexual desire [*amorous* words] **4.** of sexual love or lovemaking —**am′o·rous·ly** *adv.* —**am′o·rous·ness** *n.*

**a·mor·phous** (ə môr′fəs) *adj.* [< ModL. < Gr. < *a-*, without + *morphē*, form] **1.** without definite form; shapeless **2.** indefinite, unorganized, vague, etc. **3.** *Biol.* without specialized structure **4.** *Chem., Mineralogy* not crystalline —**a·mor′phism** *n.* —**a·mor′phous·ly** *adv.* —**a·mor′phous·ness** *n.*

**am·or·tize** (am′ər tīz′, ə môr′-) *vt.* **-tized′, -tiz′ing** [< OFr. *amortir*, to extinguish < ML. < L. *ad*, to + *mors, death*] **1.** to put money aside at intervals, as in a sinking fund, for gradual payment of (a debt, etc.) **2.** *Accounting* to write off (expenditures) by prorating over a fixed period Chiefly Brit. sp. **am′or·tise′, -tised′, -tis′ing** —**am′or·tiz′a·ble** *adj.* —**am′or·ti·za′tion** *n.*

**A·mos** (ä′məs) [Heb. *'āmōs*, lit., borne (by God?)] **1.** a masculine name **2.** *Bible a)* a Hebrew prophet of the 8th cent. B.C. *b)* the book containing prophecies attributed to him

**a·mount** (ə mount′) *vi.* [< OFr. *amonter* < *amont*, upward < *a-* (L. *ad*), to + *mont* < L. *mons*, mountain] **1.** to add up; total [the bill *amounts* to $4.50] **2.** to be equal in meaning, value, or effect [her reply *amounts* to a refusal] —*n.* **1.** the sum of two or more quantities; total **2.** a principal sum plus its interest **3.** a quantity

**a·mour** (ə moor′) *n.* [< Pr. < L. *amor*, love] a love affair, esp. one that is illicit or secret

**‡a·mour-pro·pre** (ȧ mōōr prō′pr′) *n.* [Fr.] self-love

**amp. 1.** amperage **2.** ampere(s)

**am·per·age** (am′pər ij, am pir′-) *n.* the strength of an electric current, measured in amperes

**am·pere** (am′pir) *n.* [after A. M. *Ampère* (1775-1836), Fr. physicist] the standard unit for measuring the strength of an electric current; rate of flow of charge of one coulomb per second

**am·per·sand** (am′pər sand′) *n.* [< *and per se and*, lit., (the sign) & by itself (is) *and*] a sign (& or &), meaning *and*

**am·phet·a·mine** (am fet′ə mēn′, -min) *n.* [alpha-methyl-beta-phenyl-ethyl-*amine*] a compound, $C_9H_{13}N$, used as a drug to overcome depression, fatigue, etc. and to lessen the appetite

**am·phi-** [< Gr.] *a prefix meaning:* **1.** on both sides or ends **2.** of both kinds **3.** around; about

**am·phib·i·an** (am fib′ē ən) *n.* [see ff.] **1.** any of a class of vertebrates, including frogs, toads, salamanders, etc., that usually begin life in the water as tadpoles with gills, and later develop lungs: they are coldblooded and scaleless **2.** any amphibious animal or plant **3.** an aircraft that can take off from and come down on either land or water **4.** a vehicle that can travel on either land or water —*adj.* **1.** of the amphibians **2.** *same as* AMPHIBIOUS

**am·phib·i·ous** (am fib′ē əs) *adj.* [< Gr. < *amphi-*, AMPHI- + *bios*, life] **1.** that can live both on land and in water **2.** that can operate on both land and water **3.** of or for a military operation involving the landing of troops from seaborne transports —**am·phib′i·ous·ly** *adv.*

**am·phi·bole** (am′fə bōl′) *n.* [Fr. < LL. *amphibolus*, ambiguous < Gr. *amphiballein*, to be uncertain < AM-PHI- + *ballein*, to throw] any of a group of rock-forming minerals, as hornblende or asbestos, composed largely of silica, calcium, iron, and magnesium —**am′phi·bol′ic** (-bäl′ik) *adj.*

**am·phi·ox·us** (am′fē äk′səs) *n.* [< AMPHI- + Gr. *oxys*, sharp] *same as* LANCELET

**am·phi·pro·style** (am′fə prō′stīl, am fip′rə stīl′) *adj.* [< L. < Gr.: see AMPHI- & PROSTYLE] *Archit.* having rows of columns only at the front and back —*n.* an amphiprostyle building

**am·phi·the·a·ter, am·phi·the·a·tre** (am′fə thē′ə tər) *n.* [< L. < Gr.: see AMPHI- & THEATER] **1.** a round or oval building with an open space (arena) surrounded by rising rows of seats **2.** a scene of contest **3.** a level place surrounded by rising ground

**Am·phi·tri·te** (am′fi trīt′ē) *Gr. Myth.* goddess of the sea and wife of Poseidon

**Am·phi·try·on** (am fit′rē ən) *Gr. Myth.* a king of Thebes: his wife, Alcmene, became the mother of Hercules by Zeus

**am·pho·ra** (am′fər ə) *n., pl.* **-rae** (-ē), **-ras** [L. < Gr. < *amphi-*, AMPHI- + *pherein*, to bear] a tall jar with a narrow neck and base and two handles, used by the ancient Greeks and Romans

**am·pho·ter·ic** (am′fə ter′ik) *adj.* [< Gr. < *amphō*, var. of AMPHI-] *Chem.* having both acid and basic properties

**am·ple** (am′p'l) *adj.* **-pler, -plest** [OFr. < L. *amplus*] **1.** large in size, extent, etc. **2.** more than enough; abundant **3.** enough; adequate —**am′ple·ness** *n.*

**am·plex·i·caul** (am plek′sə kôl′) *adj.* [< L. pp. of *amplectari*, to twine around + *caulis*, stem] *Bot.* growing directly from the main stem and encircling it, as corn leaves

**am·pli·fi·ca·tion** (am′plə fi kā′shən) *n.* **1.** an amplifying or being amplified **2.** additional details **3.** a statement, etc. with something added

**am·pli·fi·er** (am′plə fī′ər) *n.* **1.** a person or thing that amplifies **2.** *Electronics* a device, esp. one with electron tubes or semiconductors, used to increase electrical signal strength

**am·pli·fy** (am′plə fī′) *vt.* **-fied′, -fy′ing** [< OFr. < L. *amplificare* < *amplus*, AMPLE + *facere*, to make] **1.** to make stronger; increase (power, authority, etc.) **2.** to develop more fully, as with details, examples, etc. **3.** *Electronics* to strengthen (an electrical signal) by means of an amplifier —*vi.* to speak or write at length; expatiate

**am·pli·tude** (am′plə tōōd′, -tyōōd′) *n.* [< L. < *amplus*, AMPLE] **1.** extent; largeness **2.** abundance; fullness **3.** scope or breadth, as of mind **4.** the extreme range of a fluctuating quantity, from the average or mean to the extreme

**amplitude modulation** the changing of the amplitude of the transmitting radio wave in accordance with the signal being broadcast: distinguished from FREQUENCY MODULATION

**am·ply** (am′plē) *adv.* to an ample degree

**am·pul** (am′pool, -pul) *n.* [Fr. < L. *ampulla*, AMPULLA] a small, sealed glass container for one dose of a medicine to be injected hypodermically: also **am′pule** (-pyool), **am′poule** (-pōōl)

**am·pul·la** (am pul′ə, -pool′ə) *n., pl.* **-pul′lae** (-ē) [< OE. < L. *ampulla*, dim. of AMPHORA] **1.** a nearly round bottle with two handles, used by the ancient Greeks and Romans **2.** a container used in churches for holy oil, consecrated wine, etc.

**am·pu·tate** (am′pyə tāt′) *vt.* **-tat·ed, -tat′ing** [< L. pp. of *amputare* < *am-*, for AMBI- + *putare*, to prune] to cut off (an arm, leg, etc.), esp. by surgery —**am′pu·ta′tion** *n.* —**am′pu·ta′tor** *n.*

**am·pu·tee** (am′pyə tē′) *n.* [see -EE] a person who has had a limb or limbs amputated

**Am·rit·sar** (əm rit'sər) city in Punjab, N India: pop. 398,000

**Am·ster·dam** (am'stər dam') constitutional capital of the Netherlands: pop. 868,000: see also The HAGUE

**amt.** amount

**amu, AMU** atomic mass unit

**a·muck** (ə muk') *adj., adv. same as* AMOK

**am·u·let** (am'yə lit) *n.* [< Fr. < L.] something worn on the body as a charm against evil

**A·mund·sen** (ä'mŏŏn sən), **Ro·ald** (rō'äl) 1872–1928; Norw. polar explorer

**A·mur** (ä mŏŏr') river in NE Asia, flowing along the U.S.S.R.–China border: c. 2,700 mi.

**a·muse** (ə myŏŏz') *vt.* **a·mused', a·mus'ing** [< Fr. < *à,* at + OFr. *muser,* to stare fixedly] **1.** to keep pleasantly occupied; entertain **2.** to make laugh, smile, etc. by being humorous —**a·mus'a·ble** *adj.* —**a·mus'er** *n.*

**a·muse·ment** (-mənt) *n.* **1.** the condition of being amused **2.** something that amuses or entertains

**amusement park** an outdoor place with devices for entertainment, as a merry-go-round, etc.

**a·mus·ing** (ə myŏŏ'ziŋ) *adj.* **1.** entertaining; diverting **2.** causing laughter —**a·mus'ing·ly** *adv.*

**A·my** (ā'mē) [< OFr. *Amee,* lit., beloved < pp. of *aimer,* to love < L. *amare*] a feminine name

**a·myg·da·lin** (ə mig'də lin) *n.* [< L. *amygdala,* almond + -IN[1]] a glucoside, $C_{20}H_{27}NO_{11}$, present in bitter almonds and used as a flavoring agent

**am·yl** (am'il) *n.* [AM(YLUM) + -YL] any of various isomeric forms of the monovalent radical $C_5H_{11}$ —**a·myl·ic** (ə mil'ik) *adj.*

**am·y·la·ceous** (am'ə lā'shəs) *adj.* [< AMYLUM + -ACEOUS] of or like starch

**am·yl·ase** (am'ə lās') *n.* an enzyme that helps change starch into sugar: it is found in saliva, pancreatic juice, etc.: see also DIASTASE

**am·y·loid** (am'ə loid') *n.* a starchy substance

**am·y·lop·sin** (am'ə läp'sin) *n.* [< ff. + TRYPSIN] the enzyme (amylase) of pancreatic juice

**am·y·lum** (am'ə ləm) *n.* [< L. < Gr.] *Chem. a* technical name for STARCH

**an**[1] (ən; *stressed* an) *adj., indefinite article* [weakened variant of ONE < OE. *an,* the numeral one] **1.** one; one sort of [*an* apple pie] **2.** each; any one [*pick an* apple] **3.** to each; in each; for each; per [*two an* hour] See also A[1]

**an**[2], **an'** (an) *conj.* [< *and*] **1.** [Dial.] and **2.** [Archaic] if

**an-** *same as* A-[2] (not, without): used before vowels

**-an** (ən, 'n) [< L. *-anus*] an *adj.-forming and n.-forming suffix meaning:* **1.** (one) belonging to or having some relation to [*diocesan*] **2.** (one) born in or living in [*American*] **3.** (one) believing in or following [*Mohammedan*]

**an.** **1.** [L. *anno*] in the year **2.** anonymous

**an·a-** [L. < Gr. *ana,* up, on, again] a *prefix meaning:* **1.** up [*anadromous*] **2.** back, backward [*anagram*] **3.** again [*Anabaptist*] **4.** throughout [*analysis*] **5.** according to, similar to [*analogy*]

**-a·na** (an'ə, ä'nə, ā'nə) [neut. pl. of L. *-anus*] a *n.-forming suffix meaning* sayings, writings, anecdotes, or facts of [*Americana*]

**An·a·bap·tist** (an'ə bap'tist) *n.* [< LL. < Gr. < *ana-,* again + *baptizein,* to baptize] a member of a 16th-cent. Swiss sect of the Reformation, that rejected infant baptism and practiced baptism of adults —*adj.* of this sect —**An'a·bap'tism** *n.*

**A·nab·a·sis** (ə nab'ə sis) [Gr. < *anabainein,* to go up < *ana-,* up + *bainein,* to go] **1.** the unsuccessful military expedition (401–400 B.C.) of Cyrus the Younger to overthrow Artaxerxes II **2.** a book about this by Xenophon —*n.* [a-] *pl.* **-ses'** (-sēz') any large military expedition

**an·a·bat·ic** (an'ə bat'ik) *adj.* [Gr. *anabatikos:* see prec.] moving upward: said of air currents

**an·a·bi·o·sis** (an'ə bī ō'sis) *n.* [ModL. < Gr. < *anabioein,* to come to life again] a state of suspended animation, as in certain arthropods when desiccated —**an'a·bi·ot'ic** (-ät'ik) *adj.*

**a·nab·o·lism** (ə nab'ə liz'm) *n.* [< Gr. *anabolē,* a rising up + -ISM] the process in a plant or animal by which food is changed into living tissue; constructive metabolism: opposed to CATABOLISM —**an·a·bol·ic** (an'ə bäl'ik) *adj.*

**a·nach·ro·nism** (ə nak'rə niz'm) *n.* [< MGr. *anachronizein,* to refer to a wrong time < *ana-,* against + *chronos,* time] **1.** the representation of something as existing or occurring at other than its proper time **2.** anything out of its proper time in history —**a·nach'ro·nis'tic, a·nach'ro·nous** (-nəs) *adj.* —**a·nach'ro·nis'ti·cal·ly** *adv.*

**an·a·co·lu·thon** (an'ə kə lŏŏ'thän) *n., pl.* **-tha** (-thə), **-thons** [Gr. < *anakolouthos,* inconsequent < *an-,* not + *akolouthos,* following] a change from one grammatical con-

struction to another within the same sentence, sometimes as a rhetorical device —**an'a·co·lu'thic** *adj.*

**an·a·con·da** (an'ə kän'də) *n.* [< ? Singhalese *henakandayā,* whip snake] **1.** a long, heavy S. American snake of the boa family **2.** any similar large snake that crushes its victim in its coils

ANACONDA (to 30 ft. long)

**a·nad·ro·mous** (ə nad'rə məs) *adj.* [< Gr. < *ana-,* upward + *dramein,* to run] going up rivers to spawn: said of salmon, shad, etc.

**a·nae·mi·a** (ə nē'mē ə, -myə) *n. same as* ANEMIA —**a·nae'mic** *adj.*

**an·aer·obe** (an er'ōb, an'ə rōb') *n.* [< ff.] a microorganism that can live and grow where there is no free oxygen —**an·aer·o·bic** (an'er ō'bik, -ə rō'-) *adj.*

**an·aer·o·bi·um** (an'er ō'bē əm, -ə rō'-) *n., pl.* **-bi·a** (-bē ə) [ModL. < Gr. *an-,* AN- + *aero-,* AERO- + *bios,* life] *same as* ANAEROBE

**an·aes·the·sia** (an'əs thē'zhə) *n. same as* ANESTHESIA —**an'·aes·thet'ic** (-thet'ik) *adj., n.* —**an·aes·the·tist** (ə nes'thə tist) *n.* —**an·aes'the·tize** *vt.* **-tized', -tiz'ing**

**an·a·gram** (an'ə gram') *n.* [< ModL. < Gr. *anagrammatizein,* to transpose letters < *ana-,* back + *gramma,* letter < *graphein,* to write] **1.** a word or phrase made from another by rearranging its letters (Ex.: *now — won*) **2.** [*pl.,* with *sing. v.*] a game in which players seek to form words by arranging letters drawn at random from a stock of them —**an'a·gram·mat'ic** (-grə mat'ik), **an'a·gram·mat'i·cal** *adj.* —**an'a·gram·mat'i·cal·ly** *adv.*

**an·a·gram·ma·tize** (an'ə gram'ə tīz') *vt.* **-tized', -tiz'ing** to make an anagram of

**An·a·heim** (an'ə hīm') [< Santa *Ana* (St. Anne, reputed mother of the Virgin Mary) + G. *heim,* home] city in SW Calif.: pop. 222,000

**a·nal** (ā'n'l) *adj.* **1.** of or near the anus **2.** *Psychoanalysis* of an early stage of psychosexual development focusing on excretory functions —**a'nal·ly** *adv.*

**an·a·lects** (an'ə lekts') *n.pl.* [< L. < Gr. *analegein,* to collect < *ana-,* up + *legein,* to gather] collected literary excerpts: also **an'a·lec'ta** (-lek'tə) —**the Analects** a collection of Confucius' teachings

**an·a·lep·tic** (an'ə lep'tik) *adj.* [< Gr. < *analambanein,* to recover < *ana-,* up + *lambanein,* to take] *Med.* restorative —*n.* an analeptic drug

**an·al·ge·si·a** (an'l jē'zē ə, -sē ə) *n.* [ModL. < Gr. *an-,* without + *algēsia,* pain] a state of not feeling pain although fully conscious

**an·al·ge·sic** (-zik, -sik) *adj.* of or causing analgesia —*n.* a drug producing analgesia

**analog computer** an electronic computer that uses voltages to represent the numerical data of physical quantities: cf. DIGITAL COMPUTER

**an·a·log·i·cal** (an'ə läj'i k'l) *adj.* of, expressing, or based upon analogy —**an'a·log'i·cal·ly** *adv.*

**a·nal·o·gize** (ə nal'ə jīz') *vi.* **-gized', -giz'ing** to use, or reason by, analogy —*vt.* to explain or liken by analogy —**a·nal'o·gist** (-jist) *n.*

**a·nal·o·gous** (-gəs) *adj.* [see ANALOGY] **1.** similar or comparable in certain respects **2.** *Biol.* similar in function but not in origin and structure —**a·nal'o·gous·ly** *adv.*

**an·a·logue** (an'ə lôg', -läg') *n.* a thing or part that is analogous —*adj.* of or by means of an analog computer: usually **analog**

**a·nal·o·gy** (ə nal'ə jē) *n., pl.* **-gies** [< ME. & OFr. < L. < Gr. *analogia,* proportion < *ana-,* according to + *logos,* ratio: see LOGIC] **1.** similarity in some respects; partial resemblance **2.** a comparing of something point by point with something similar **3.** *Biol.* similarity in function but not in origin and structure **4.** *Logic* the inference that certain resemblances imply probable further similarity

**a·nal·y·sand** (ə nal'ə sand') *n.* a person who is undergoing psychoanalysis

**an·a·lyse** (an'ə līz') *vt.* **-lysed', -lys'ing** chiefly *Brit. sp.* of ANALYZE

**a·nal·y·sis** (ə nal'ə sis) *n., pl.* **-ses'** (-sēz') [ML. < Gr., a dissolving < *ana-,* up, throughout + *lysis,* a loosing < *lyein,* to loose] **1.** *a)* a breaking up of any whole into its parts so as to find out their nature, function, etc. *b)* a statement of these findings **2.** *same as* PSYCHOANALYSIS **3.** *Chem.* the separation of compounds and mixtures into their constituent substances to determine the nature (*qualitative analysis*) or the proportion (*quantitative analysis*) of the constituents **4.** *Linguis.* the use of word order and function words rather than inflection to express syntactic relationships

**an·a·lyst** (an′ə list) *n.* **1.** a person who analyzes *[a news analyst]* **2.** *same as* PSYCHOANALYST

**an·a·lyt·ic** (an′ə lit′ik) *adj.* **1.** *Linguis.* characterized by analysis rather than inflection **2.** *same as* ANALYTICAL

**an·a·lyt·i·cal** (-i k′l) *adj.* **1.** of analysis or analytics **2.** skilled in or using analysis **3.** *same as* ANALYTIC (sense 1) —**an′a·lyt′i·cal·ly** *adv.*

**an·a·lyt·ics** (-iks) *n.pl.* [*with sing. v.*] the part of logic having to do with analyzing

**an·a·lyze** (an′ə līz′) *vt.* **-lyzed′, -lyz′ing** [ < Fr. < *analyse,* ANALYSIS] **1.** to separate into parts so as to find out their nature, function, etc. **2.** to examine in detail so as to determine the nature or tendencies of **3.** to psychoanalyze —**an′a·lyz′a·ble** *adj.* —**an′a·lyz′er** *n.*

**an·a·pest, an·a·paest** (an′ə pest′) *n.* [ < L. < Gr. < *ana-,* back + *paiein,* to strike] a metrical foot consisting of two unaccented syllables followed by an accented one, as in English verse (Ex.: "Ănd thĕ shéen/ŏf thĕir spéars/wăs lĭke stárs/ŏn thĕ séa") —**an′a·pes′tic, an′a·paes′tic** *adj.*

**a·naph·o·ra** (ə naf′ər ə) *n.* [L. < Gr. < *ana-,* up, back + *pherein,* to BEAR] the repetition of a word or phrase at the beginning of successive clauses or sentences as a rhetorical device

**an·aph·ro·dis·i·ac** (an af′rə diz′ē ak) *adj.* that lessens sexual desire —*n.* a drug, etc. that lessens sexual desire

**an·ar·chic** (an är′kik) *adj.* **1.** of, like, or promoting anarchy **2.** without controls; lawless Also **an·ar′chi·cal** —**an·ar′chi·cal·ly** *adv.*

**an·ar·chism** (an′ər kiz′m) *n.* [ANARCH(Y) + -ISM] **1.** the theory that all forms of government interfere unjustly with individual liberty and should be replaced by a system of voluntary cooperation **2.** resistance, sometimes by terrorism, to government

**an·ar·chist** (-kist) *n.* **1.** a person who believes in anarchism **2.** a promoter of anarchy —**an′ar·chis′tic** *adj.*

**an·ar·chy** (-kē) *n., pl.* **-chies** [ < Gr. < *an-,* without + *archos,* leader] **1.** the complete absence of government **2.** political disorder and violence **3.** disorder in any sphere of activity

**An·a·sta·sia** (an′ə stā′shə, -zhə) [LL. < Gr. *Anastasios,* lit., of the resurrection] a feminine name

**an·as·tig·mat·ic** (an as′tig mat′ik, an′ə stig-) *adj.* free from, or corrected for, astigmatism

**a·nas·to·mose** (ə nas′tə mōz′) *vt., vi.* **-mosed′, -mos′ing** to join by anastomosis

**a·nas·to·mo·sis** (ə nas′tə mō′sis) *n., pl.* **-ses** (-sēz) [ModL. < Gr. *anastomōsis,* opening < *ana-,* again + *stoma,* mouth] **1.** interconnection as between blood vessels or veins of a leaf **2.** a surgical joining of one hollow or tubular organ to another

**a·nas·tro·phe** (ə nas′trə fē) *n.* [Gr. < *ana-,* back + *strephein,* to turn] reversal of the usual word order of a sentence (Ex.: "Came the dawn")

**anat. 1.** anatomical **2.** anatomist **3.** anatomy

**a·nath·e·ma** (ə nath′ə mə) *n., pl.* **-mas** [LL. < Gr., thing devoted to evil < *anatithenai,* to dedicate < *ana-,* up + *tithenai,* to set] **1.** a thing or person accursed **2.** a thing or person greatly detested **3.** a formal curse, as in excommunicating a person from a church **4.** any strong curse

**a·nath·e·ma·tize** (ə nath′ə mə tīz′) *vt., vi.* **-tized′, -tiz′ing** to utter an anathema (against); curse

**An·a·to·li·a** (an′ə tō′lē ə) **1.** formerly, Asia Minor **2.** the part of modern Turkey that is in Asia —**An′a·to′li·an** *adj., n.*

**an·a·tom·i·cal** (an′ə täm′i k′l) *adj.* **1.** of or connected with anatomy **2.** structural Also **an′a·tom′ic** —**an′a·tom′i·cal·ly** *adv.*

**a·nat·o·mist** (ə nat′ə mist) *n.* **1.** a person skilled in anatomy **2.** a person who anatomizes

**a·nat·o·mize** (-mīz′) *vt., vi.* **-mized′, -miz′ing** [see ff.] **1.** to dissect (an animal or plant) in order to examine the structure **2.** to analyze in great detail

**a·nat·o·my** (ə nat′ə mē) *n., pl.* **-mies** [ < ME. & OFr. < LL. < Gr. < *ana-,* up + *temnein,* to cut] **1.** the dissecting of an animal or plant in order to study its structure **2.** the science of the structure of animals or plants **3.** the structure of an organism or body **4.** a detailed analysis

**An·ax·ag·o·ras** (an′ak sag′ər əs) 500?-428? B.C.; Gr. philosopher

**-ance** (əns, 'ns) [ < Fr. < L. *-antia, -entia,* or directly < L.] a suffix meaning: **1.** the act of *[utterance]* **2.** the quality or state of being *[vigilance]* **3.** a thing that *[conveyance]* **4.** a thing that is *[dissonance, inheritance]*

**an·ces·tor** (an′ses′tər) *n.* [ < ME. & OFr. < L. *antecessor,* one who goes before < *ante-,* before + *cedere,* to go] **1.** any person from whom one is descended; forebear **2.** an early type of animal from which later kinds have evolved **3.** a precursor or predecessor **4.** *Law* the person from whom an estate has been inherited —**an′ces′tress** (-trəs) *n.fem.*

**an·ces·tral** (an ses′trəl) *adj.* of or inherited from ancestors —**an·ces′tral·ly** *adv.*

**an·ces·try** (an′ses′trē) *n., pl.* **-tries 1.** family descent or lineage **2.** ancestors collectively

**an·chor** (aŋ′kər) *n.* [ < OE. < L. < Gr. *ankyra,* a hook] **1.** a heavy object, usually a shaped iron weight with flukes, lowered to the bottom of water by cable or chain to keep a ship from drifting **2.** any device that holds something else secure **3.** anything regarded as giving stability or security —*vt.* **1.** to hold secure by or as by an anchor **2.** to act as an anchorman on —*vi.* **1.** to lower the anchor overboard **2.** to be or become fixed —**at anchor** anchored —**drop** (or **cast**) **anchor 1.** to lower the anchor overboard **2.** to settle (*in a place*) —**weigh anchor 1.** to raise the anchor **2.** to leave; go away

ANCHOR

**An·chor·age** (aŋ′kər ij, aŋ′krij) seaport in S Alas.: pop. 173,000

**an·chor·age** (aŋ′kər ij) *n.* **1.** money charged for the right to anchor **2.** an anchoring or being anchored **3.** a place to anchor **4.** something that can be relied on

**an·cho·rite** (aŋ′kə rīt′) *n.* [ < OFr. < LL. < Gr. *ana-chōrētēs* < *ana-,* back + *chōrein,* to retire] a person who lives alone for religious meditation; hermit: also **an′cho·ret** (-rit) —**an′cho·ress** *n.fem.* —**an′cho·rit′ic** (-rit′ik) *adj.*

**an·chor·man** (aŋ′kər man′) *n.* **1.** the final contestant, as on a relay team **2.** *Radio & TV* that member of a team of newscasters who coordinates various reports —**an′chor·wom′an** *n.fem., pl.* **-wom′en**

**an·chor·per·son** (-pʉr′s'n) *n. same as* ANCHORMAN: used to avoid the masculine implication of *anchorman*

**an·cho·vy** (an′chō′vē, -chə-; an′chō′vē) *n., pl.* **-vies, -vy:** see PLURAL, II, D, 1 [ < Port. *anchova,* prob. ult. < Gr. *aphyē,* small fry] a very small, herringlike fish: anchovies are usually canned in oil or made into a salty paste

**an·chy·lose** (aŋ′kə lōs′) *vt., vi.* **-losed′, -los′ing** *same as* AN-KYLOSE —**an′chy·lo′sis** (-lō′sis) *n.*

‡**an·cien ré·gime** (än syan′ rā zhēm′) [Fr., old order] the former social and political system, esp. that in France before the Revolution of 1789

**an·cient** (ān′shənt) *adj.* [ < OFr., ult. < L. *ante,* before] **1.** of times long past; esp., of the time before the end of the Western Roman Empire in 476 A.D. **2.** very old **3.** antiquated —*n.* **1.** a person who lived in ancient times **2.** an aged person —**the ancients** the people who lived in ancient times; esp., the classical writers and artists of Greco-Roman times —**an′cient·ness** *n.*

**an·cient·ly** (-lē) *adv.* in ancient times

**an·cil·lar·y** (an′sə ler′ē) *adj.* [ < L. < *ancilla,* maidservant] **1.** subordinate (*to*) **2.** auxiliary

**an·con** (aŋ′kän) *n., pl.* **an·co·nes** (aŋ kō′nēz) [L. < Gr. < *ankos,* a bend] a bracketlike projection supporting a cornice

**-an·cy** (ən sē, 'n sē) *same as* -ANCE

**and** (and, ən, 'n; *stressed* and) *conj.* [OE.] **1.** also; in addition; as well as: used to join elements of equal grammatical value *[apples and pears, to beg and borrow]* **2.** plus *[6 and 2 equals 8]* **3.** as a result *[he told her and she wept]* **4.** [Colloq.] to *[try and get it]* **5.** [Archaic] then *[and it came to pass]* **6.** [Obs.] if

**An·da·lu·sia** (an′də loo′zhə, -shə) region of S Spain

**an·dan·te** (än dän′tā, an dan′tē) *adj., adv.* [It., prp. of *an-dare,* to walk] *Music* moderate in tempo —*n.* an andante movement or passage

**an·dan·ti·no** (än′dän tē′nō, an′dan-) *adj., adv.* [It., dim. of *andante*] *Music* slightly faster than andante —*n., pl.* **-nos** an andantino movement or passage

**An·der·sen** (an′dər s'n), **Hans Christian** 1805-75; Dan. novelist & writer of fairy tales

**An·der·son** (an′dər s'n) [after a Delaware Indian, Chief *Anderson*] city in EC Ind.: pop. 65,000

**An·des** (Mountains) (an′dēz) mountain system along the length of W S.America: highest peak, ACONCAGUA —**An·de·an** (an dē′ən, an′dē-) *adj.*

**and·i·ron** (and′ī′ərn) *n.* [ < OFr. *andier* (with ending altered after IRON)] either of a pair of metal supports with front uprights, used to hold the wood in a fireplace

**and/or** either *and* or *or;* according to what is meant *[personal and/or real property]*

**An·dor·ra** (an dôr′ə, -där′ə) republic in the E Pyrenees, between Spain and France: 180 sq. mi.; pop. 19,000 —**An·dor′ran** *adj., n.*

**Andrea del Sarto** see SARTO

ANDIRONS

**An·drew** (an′drōō) [ < OFr. < L. < Gr. *Andreas,* lit., manly < *anēr* (gen. *andros*), man] **1.** a masculine name: dim. *Andy* **2.** *Bible* one of the twelve apostles

**an·dro-** [ < Gr. *anēr* (gen. *andros*), man] *a combining form meaning:* **1.** man, male, masculine **2.** anther, stamen

**An·dro·cles** (an′drə klēz′) *Rom. Legend* a slave spared in the arena by a lion that recognized him as the man who had once pulled a thorn from its paw

**an·droe·ci·um** (an drē′shē əm, -sē-) *n., pl.* **-ci·a** (-ə) [ModL. < ANDRO- + Gr. *oikos*, house] *Bot.* the stamens and the parts belonging to them, collectively

**an·dro·gen** (an′drə jən) *n.* [ANDRO- + -GEN] a male sex hormone that can give rise to masculine characteristics — **an′dro·gen′ic** (-jen′ik) *adj.*

**an·drog·y·nous** (an dräj′ə nəs) *adj.* [< L. < Gr. < *anēr* (gen. *andros*), man + *gynē*, woman] **1.** hermaphroditic **2.** *Bot.* bearing both staminate and pistillate flowers in the same cluster —**an·drog′y·ny** (-ə nē) *n.*

**an·droid** (an′droid) *n.* [ANDR(O)- + -OID] in science fiction, an automaton that looks human

**An·drom·a·che** (an dräm′ə kē) *Gr. Myth.* the wife of Hector

**An·drom·e·da** (an dräm′ə də) **1.** *Gr. Myth.* an Ethiopian princess whom Perseus rescued from a sea monster and then married **2.** *Astron.* a N constellation just south of Cassiopeia

**an·dros·ter·one** (an dräs′tə rōn′) *n.* [ANDRO- + STER(OL) + -ONE] a steroid that is a male sex hormone

**-an·drous** (an′drəs) [< Gr. *anēr:* see ANDRO-] *a suffix meaning* having stamens

**-ane** (ān) [arbitrary formation] *a suffix denoting* a hydrocarbon of the paraffin series *[methane]*

**an·ec·dote** (an′ik dōt′) *n.* [Fr. < ML. < Gr. *anekdotos*, unpublished < *an-*, not + *ek-*, out + *didonai*, to give] a short, entertaining account of some happening, usually personal or biographical —**an′ec·dot′al** (-dōt′’l) *adj.* —**an′ec·dot′ist** (-dōt′ist) *n.*

**an·e·cho·ic** (an′e kō′ik) *adj.* [AN- + ECHOIC] free from echoes *[an anechoic recording chamber]*

**a·ne·mi·a** (ə nē′mē ə, -myə) *n.* [ModL. < Gr. < *a-*, *an-*, without + *haima*, blood] **1.** a condition in which there is a reduction of red blood corpuscles or of hemoglobin (or of both) in the bloodstream **2.** lack of vigor; lifelessness — **a·ne′mic** (-mik) *adj.* —**a·ne′mi·cal·ly** *adv.*

**a·nem·o·graph** (ə nem′ə graf′) *n.* [< Gr. *anemos*, the wind + -GRAPH] an instrument for recording the velocity and direction of the wind

**an·e·mom·e·ter** (an′ə mäm′ə tər) *n.* [< Gr. *anemos*, the wind + -METER] a gauge for determining the force or speed of the wind, and sometimes its direction —**an′e·mo·met′ric** (-mō met′rik) *adj.* —**an′e·mom′e·try** *n.*

**a·nem·o·ne** (ə nem′ə nē′) *n.* [L. < Gr., infl. by *anemos*, wind] **1.** any of various plants of the buttercup family, with cup-shaped flowers, usually white, purple, or red **2.** *same as* SEA ANEMONE

**a·nent** (ə nent′) *prep.* [< OE. *on efen*, lit., on even (with), with (with)] concerning; as regards

**an·er·oid** (an′ər oid) *adj.* [< Gr. *a-*, without + *nēros*, liquid + -OID] not using liquid

**aneroid barometer** a barometer consisting of a box in which a partial vacuum is maintained: changes in atmospheric pressure cause its elastic top to bend in or out, thus moving a pointer

**an·es·the·sia** (an′əs thē′zhə, -zhē ə) *n.* [< Gr. < *an-*, without + *aisthēsis*, feeling] **1.** a partial or total loss of the sense of pain, temperature, touch, etc. produced by disease **2.** a loss of sensation induced by an anesthetic and limited to a specific area ( **local anesthesia** ) or producing unconsciousness ( **general anesthesia** )

**an·es·the·si·ol·o·gist** (an′əs thē′zē äl′ə jist) *n.* a doctor who specializes in anesthesiology

**an·es·the·si·ol·o·gy** (-jē) *n.* the science of anesthesia and anesthetics

**an·es·thet·ic** (an′əs thet′ik) *adj.* **1.** of or with anesthesia **2.** producing anesthesia —*n.* a drug, gas, etc. used to produce anesthesia, as before surgery —**anesthetic to** incapable of feeling or responding to —**an′es·thet′i·cal·ly** *adv.*

**an·es·the·tist** (ə nes′thə tist) *n.* a nurse or other person trained to administer anesthetics

**an·es·the·tize** (-tīz′) *vt.* **-tized′, -tiz′ing** to cause anesthesia in as by giving an anesthetic —**an·es′the·ti·za′tion** *n.*

**an·eu·rysm, an·eu·rism** (an′yər iz′m) *n.* [ModL. < Gr. < *ana-*, up + *eurys*, broad] a sac formed when the wall of an artery, weakened by disease or injury, becomes enlarged — **an′eu·rys′mal, an′eu·ris′mal** (-yə riz′m’l) *adj.*

**a·new** (ə nōō′, -nyōō′) *adv.* **1.** once more; again **2.** in a new manner or form

**an·ga·ry** (aŋ′gə rē) *n.* [L. *angaria*, enforced service < Gr. < *angaros*, a mounted courier] *International Law* the right of a belligerent to use or destroy a neutral's property if necessary, provided that indemnification is made

**an·gel** (ān′j’l) *n.* [< OFr. or OE. < L. *angelus* < Gr. *angelos*, messenger < Iran.] **1.** *Theol. a)* a messenger of God *b)* a supernatural being, either good or bad, of more than human power, intelligence, etc. **2.** a guiding spirit *[one's good angel]* **3.** a conventionalized image of a figure in human form with wings and a halo **4.** a person regarded as beautiful, good, etc. **5.** [Colloq.] a supporter who provides money, as for producing a play —*vt.* [Slang] to support with money

**An·ge·la** (an′jə lə) [< ML. < L. *angelicus*, angelic] a feminine name: var. *Angelica, Angelina*

**angel dust** [*also* A- D-] [Slang] a phenyl-based hallucinogenic drug, sometimes sniffed in powder form

**An·gel·e·no** (an′jə lē′nō) *n., pl.* **-nos** [AmSp.] a native or inhabitant of Los Angeles

**an·gel·fish** (ān′j’l fish′) *n., pl.* **-fish′, -fish′es:** see FISH **1.** a shark with winglike pectoral fins **2.** any of a number of bright-colored tropical fishes with spiny fins

**angel food cake** a light, spongy, white cake made with egg whites and no shortening: also **angel cake**

**an·gel·ic** (an jel′ik) *adj.* **1.** of an angel or the angels **2.** like an angel in beauty, goodness, etc. Also **an·gel′i·cal** — **an·gel′i·cal·ly** *adv.*

**an·gel·i·ca** (an jel′i kə) *n.* [ML. (*herba*) *angelica*, lit., the angelic (herb)] a plant of the parsley family, with roots and fruit used in flavoring, medicine, etc.

**An·gel·i·co** (an jel′ə kō′), **Fra** (frä) (*Giovanni da Fiesole*) 1387-1455; It. painter

**An·ge·lus** (an′jə ləs) *n.* [L.: see ANGEL] [*also* a-] *R.C.Ch.* **1.** a prayer said at morning, noon, and evening in commemoration of the Incarnation **2.** a bell rung to announce the time for this

**an·ger** (aŋ′gər) *n.* [ON. *angr*, distress, sorrow] a feeling of displeasure and hostility resulting from injury, mistreatment, opposition, etc. —*vt.* to make angry; enrage —*vi.* to become angry

**An·ge·vin, An·ge·vine** (an′jə vin) *adj.* [Fr.] of Anjou or the Plantagenets —*n.* **1.** a native of Anjou **2.** any of the Plantagenets

**an·gi·na** (an jī′nə, an′jə-) *n.* [L., quinsy < Gr. < *anchein*, to squeeze] **1.** any inflammatory disease of the throat, esp. one characterized by fits of suffocation **2.** a localized spasm of pain **3.** *same as* ANGINA PECTORIS —**an·gi′nal, an·gi·nose** (an′jə nōs′), **an′gi·nous** (-nəs) *adj.*

**angina pec·to·ris** (pek′tər is) [L., angina of the breast] a condition marked by recurrent pain in the chest and left arm, caused by a sudden decrease of blood to the heart

**an·gi·o·ma** (an′jē ō′mə) *n., pl.* **-ma·ta** (-mə tə), **-mas** [< Gr. *angeion*, vessel + -OMA] a tumor made up mainly of blood vessels and lymph vessels

**an·gi·o·sperm** (an′jē ə spurm′) *n.* [< Gr. *angeion*, capsule + -SPERM] any flowering plant having the seeds enclosed in an ovary

**Angl. 1.** Anglican **2.** Anglicized

**an·gle¹** (aŋ′g’l) *n.* [ME. & OFr. < L. *angulus*, a corner < Gr. *ankylos*, bent] **1.** *a)* the shape made by two straight lines or plane surfaces that meet *b)* the space between such lines or surfaces *c)* the degrees of difference in direction between them **2.** a sharp corner **3.** point of view *[consider this from all angles]* **4.** [Colloq.] a selfish motive or tricky plan —*vt., vi.* **-gled, -gling 1.** to move or bend at an angle **2.** [Colloq.] to give a specific point of view to (a story, report, etc.)

**an·gle²** (aŋ′g’l) *vi.* **-gled, -gling** [OE. *angul*, fishhook] **1.** to fish with a hook and line **2.** to use tricks to get something *[angling for attention]*

**angle iron** an angled piece of iron or steel used for joining or reinforcing two beams, girders, etc.

**angle of incidence** the angle that a light ray or electromagnetic wave striking a surface makes with a line perpendicular to the surface

**an·gler** (aŋ′glər) *n.* [< ANGLE²] **1.** a fisherman **2.** a schemer **3.** a saltwater fish that feeds on other fish attracted by a filament on its head

ANGLE IRON

**An·gles** (aŋ′g’lz) *n.pl.* a Germanic people that settled in E England in the 5th cent. A.D. — **An′gli·an** (-glē ən) *adj., n.*

**an·gle·worm** (aŋ′g’l wurm′) *n.* an earthworm: so called because used as fishing bait

**An·gli·can** (aŋ′gli kən) *adj.* [< ML. < *Anglicus*, of England, of the Angles] **1.** of England; English **2.** of the Church of England or any related church with the same faith and forms —*n.* a member of an Anglican church — **An′gli·can·ism** *n.*

**An·gli·cism** (aŋ'glə siz'm) *n.* **1.** a word or idiom peculiar to English, esp. British English; Briticism **2.** a typically English trait, custom, etc. **3.** the quality of being English

**An·gli·cize** (aŋ'glə sīz') *vt., vi.* **-cized', -ciz'ing** [*also* a-] to change to English idiom, pronunciation, customs, etc. — **An'gli·ci·za'tion** *n.*

**An·gli·fy** (-fī') *vt.* **-fied', -fy'ing** *same as* ANGLICIZE

**an·gling** (aŋ'gliŋ) *n.* the act of fishing with hook and line

**An·glo-** [< L. *Anglus*, sing. of *Angli*, ANGLES] *a combining form meaning* English *[Anglophile]*

**An·glo-A·mer·i·can** (aŋ'glō ə mer'ə kən) *adj.* English and American —*n.* an American of English birth or ancestry

**An·glo-French** (-french') *adj.* English and French —*n.* the French spoken in England from the Norman Conquest through the Middle Ages: see NORMAN FRENCH

**An·glo-In·di·an** (-in'dē ən) *adj.* **1.** of England and India **2.** of Anglo-Indians or their English speech —*n.* **1.** a person of English and Indian ancestry **2.** words borrowed into English from the languages of India

**An·glo·ma·ni·a** (-mā'nē ə) *n.* an exaggerated liking for and imitation of English customs, manners, institutions, etc. —**An'glo·ma'ni·ac'** (-ak') *n.*

**An·glo-Nor·man** (-nôr'mən) *adj.* English and Norman — *n.* **1.** a Norman settler in England after the Norman Conquest **2.** the Anglo-French dialect of such settlers

**An·glo·phile** (aŋ'glə fīl') *n.* [*often* a-] a person characterized by Anglophilia

**An·glo·phil·i·a** (aŋ'glə fil'ē ə) *n.* [*often* a-] extreme admiration for England, its people, customs, etc.

**An·glo·phobe** (aŋ'glə fōb') *n.* [*often* a-] a person characterized by Anglophobia

**An·glo·pho·bi·a** (aŋ'glə fō'bē ə) *n.* [*often* a-] hatred or fear of England, its people, customs, etc. —**An'glo·pho'bic** (-fō'bik) *adj.*

**An·glo-Sax·on** (aŋ'glō sak's'n) *n.* [< ML.: see ANGLES & SAXON] **1.** a member of the Germanic peoples (Angles, Saxons, and Jutes) living in England at the time of the Norman Conquest **2.** *same as* OLD ENGLISH **3.** plain, blunt language of Old English origin **4.** a person of English nationality or descent —*adj.* **1.** of the Anglo-Saxons or their language **2.** of their descendants; English

**An·go·la** (aŋ gō'lə, an-) country on the W coast of Africa: formerly a Port. territory: 481,351 sq. mi.; pop. 6,761,000

**An·go·ra** (aŋ gôr'ə, an-) *n.* [former name of ANKARA] **1.** a kind of cat with long, silky fur **2.** *a)* a kind of goat raised for its long, silky hair *b)* a cloth made from this hair; mohair **3.** *a)* a long-eared rabbit, raised for its long, silky hair *b)* a soft yarn made from this hair Also **angora** for senses 2b, 3b

**an·gos·tu·ra** (**bark**) (aŋ'gəs toor'ə, -tyoor'-) [after *Angostura*, former name of Ciudad Bolívar, city in Venezuela] a bitter bark used as a tonic and as a flavoring in bitters

**an·gry** (aŋ'grē) *adj.* **-gri·er, -gri·est 1.** feeling, showing, or resulting from anger **2.** wild and stormy **3.** inflamed and sore —**an'gri·ly** (-grə lē) *adv.* —**an'gri·ness** *n.*

**ang·strom** (aŋ'strəm) *n.* [after A. J. *Ångström*, 19th-c. Swed. physicist] one hundred-millionth of a centimeter, a unit used in measuring the length of light waves: also **ang·strom unit**

**an·guish** (aŋ'gwish) *n.* [< OFr. < L. *angustia*, tightness < *angustus*, narrow] great suffering, as from grief or pain; agony —*vi., vt.* to feel or make feel anguish —**an'guished** (-gwisht) *adj.*

**an·gu·lar** (aŋ'gyə lər) *adj.* **1.** having or forming an angle or angles; having sharp corners **2.** measured by an angle *[angular distance]* **3.** lean; bony; gaunt **4.** without ease or grace; awkward *[an angular stride]* —**an'gu·lar·ly** *adv.*

**an·gu·lar·i·ty** (aŋ'gyə lar'ə tē) *n., pl.* **-ties 1.** the quality of being angular **2.** [*pl.*] angular forms; angles

**An·gus** (aŋ'gəs) [< Gael. & Ir. < *aon*, one] a masculine name

**an·hy·dride** (an hī'drīd) *n.* [< Gr. *anhydros* (see ff.) + -IDE] **1.** an oxide that reacts with water to form an acid or a base **2.** any compound formed by the removal of water, usually from an acid

**an·hy·drous** (-drəs) *adj.* [Gr. *anhydros* < *an-*, without + *hydōr*, water] **1.** without water **2.** *Chem.* having no water of crystallization

**an·il** (an'il) *n.* [Fr. < Port. < Ar. *al*, the + *nīl*, blue] **1.** a West Indian shrub from which indigo is made **2.** *same as* INDIGO

**an·i·line** (an'l in, -ēn', -īn') *n.* [prec. + -INE⁴] a colorless, poisonous, oily liquid, $C_6H_5NH_2$, a derivative of benzene, used in making dyes, synthetic resins, rocket fuel, etc.

**aniline dye 1.** any dye made from aniline **2.** commonly, any synthetic dye made from coal tar

**an·i·ma** (an'ə mə) *n.* [L.] life principle; soul

**an·i·mad·ver·sion** (an'ə mad vur'zhən, -shən) *n.* [see ff.]

**1.** a critical, esp. unfavorable, comment (*on* or *upon* something) **2.** the act of criticizing adversely

**an·i·mad·vert** (-vurt') *vi.* [< L. < *animus*, mind + *advertere*, to turn: see ANIMUS & ADVERT] to comment (*on* or *upon*), esp. with disapproval; criticize adversely

**an·i·mal** (an'ə m'l) *n.* [L. < *anima, animus*, breath, life principle, soul] **1.** any living organism except a plant or bacterium: most animals can move about voluntarily and are unable to make their own food by photosynthesis, as plants do **2.** any such organism other than a human being, esp. a mammal or, sometimes, any four-footed creature **3.** a brutish person —*adj.* **1.** of, like, or from an animal **2.** gross, bestial, sensual, etc. —**an'i·mal·ly** *adv.*

**an·i·mal·cule** (an'ə mal'kyool) *n.* [< ModL., dim. of prec.] a very small or microscopic animal: also **an'i·mal'cu·lum** (-kyə ləm) *n., pl.* **-la** (-lə) —**an'i·mal'cu·lar** *adj.*

**animal husbandry** the raising of domesticated animals, as cattle, sheep, horses, etc.

**an·i·mal·ism** (an'ə m'l iz'm) *n.* **1.** the activity, appetites, nature, etc. of animals **2.** the doctrine that man is a mere animal with no soul —**an'i·mal·ist** *n.* —**an'i·mal·is'tic** *adj.*

**an·i·mal·i·ty** (an'ə mal'ə tē) *n.* **1.** animal characteristics or nature **2.** the animal kingdom; animal life **3.** the animal instincts or nature in man

**an·i·mal·ize** (an'ə mə līz') *vt.* **-ized', -iz'ing** to make (a person) resemble a beast; brutalize; dehumanize —**an'i·mal·i·za'tion** *n.*

**animal magnetism 1.** *old term for* HYPNOTISM **2.** the power to attract others in a sensual way

**animal spirits** healthy, lively vigor

**an·i·mate** (an'ə māt'; *for adj.* -mit) *vt.* **-mat'ed, -mat'ing** [< L. pp. of *animare*, to make alive < *anima:* see ANIMAL] **1.** to give life to; bring to life **2.** to make gay or spirited; enliven **3.** to cause to act; inspire **4.** to give motion to *[a breeze animating the leaves]* **5.** to make move so as to seem lifelike *[to animate puppets]* **6.** to produce as an animated cartoon —*adj.* **1.** living; having life, esp. animal life **2.** lively; spirited —**an'i·ma'tor, an'i·mat'er** *n.*

**an·i·mat·ed** (-māt'id) *adj.* **1.** alive or seeming alive; living **2.** lively; spirited —**an'i·mat'ed·ly** *adv.*

**animated cartoon** a motion picture made by filming a series of drawings, each slightly changed from the one before, so that the figures in them seem to move when the film is projected

**an·i·ma·tion** (an'ə mā'shən) *n.* **1.** an animating or being animated **2.** life **3.** vivacity; liveliness **4.** the making of animated cartoons **5.** *same as* ANIMATED CARTOON

**‡a·ni·ma·to** (ä'nē mä'tô) *adj., adv.* [It.] *Music* with animation

**an·i·mism** (an'ə miz'm) *n.* [< Fr. & G. < L. *anima:* see ANIMAL & -ISM] **1.** the doctrine that all life is produced by a spiritual force **2.** the belief that all natural objects and phenomena have souls **3.** a belief in the existence of spirits, demons, etc. —**an'i·mist** *n.* —**an'i·mis'tic** *adj.*

**an·i·mos·i·ty** (an'ə mäs'ə tē) *n., pl.* **-ties** [< L. *animositas*, spirit < *animus:* see ff.] strong hostility; hostility

**an·i·mus** (an'ə məs) *n.* [L., soul, mind, passion: see ANIMAL] **1.** an animating force; intention **2.** a feeling of ill will; animosity

**an·i·on** (an'ī'ən) *n.* [< Gr. neut. prp. of *anienai*, to go up < *ana-*, up + *ienai*, to go] a negatively charged ion: in electrolysis, anions move toward the anode —**an·i·on·ic** (an'ī än'ik) *adj.*

**an·ise** (an'is) *n.* [< ME. & OFr. < L. < Gr. *anēson*] **1.** a plant of the parsley family, with fragrant seeds used for flavoring **2.** *same as* ANISEED

**an·i·seed** (an'ə sēd') *n.* the seed of anise

**an·i·sette** (an'ə set', -zet') *n.* [Fr., dim. < *anis:* see ANISE] a sweet, anise-flavored liqueur

**A·ni·ta** (ə nēt'ə) [Sp. dim. of *Ana*, equiv. of ANNA] a feminine name

**An·jou** (an'jōō; *Fr.* än zhōō') former province of W France

**An·ka·ra** (aŋ'kə rə, än'-) capital of Turkey: pop. 906,000

**ankh** (aŋk) *n.* [Egypt., life, soul] a cross with a loop at the top, an ancient Egyptian symbol of life

**an·kle** (aŋ'k'l) *n.* [OE. *anclew*] **1.** the joint that connects the foot and the leg **2.** the part of the leg between the foot and calf

**an·kle·bone** (-bōn') *n.* the bone of the ankle; talus

**an·klet** (aŋ'klit) *n.* **1.** anything worn around the ankle as an ornament or fetter **2.** a short sock

**an·ky·lose** (aŋ'kə lōs') *vt., vi.* **-losed', -los'ing** to stiffen or join by ankylosis

**an·ky·lo·sis** (aŋ'kə lō'sis) *n.* [Gr. < *ankyloun*, to stiffen < *ankylos*, bent] *Med.* an abnormal growing together and stiffening of a joint —**an'ky·lot'ic** (-lät'ik) *adj.*

**ann. 1.** annual **2.** annuity

**An·na** (an'ə) [< Fr. < L. < Gr. < Heb. *hannāh*, lit., grace] a feminine name: var. *Ann, Anne, Hannah*

**an·na** (an′ə, ä′nə) *n.* [Hindi *ānā*] a former coin of India, Pakistan, and Burma, equal to 1/16 of a rupee

**An·na·bel, An·na·belle** (an′ə bel′) [? altered < *Amabel* < L. *amabilis*, lovable < *amare*, to love] a feminine name

**an·nal·ist** (an′'l ist) *n.* a writer of annals —**an′nal·is′tic** *adj.*

**an·nals** (an′'lz) *n.pl.* [< L. < *annus*, year] **1.** a written account of events year by year in chronological order **2.** historical records; history **3.** any journal containing reports of a society, etc.

**An·nam** (an am′, an′am) region in EC Vietnam —**An′na·mese′** (-ə mēz′) *adj., n., pl.* **-mese′**

**An·nap·o·lis** (ə nap′ə lis) [< ANNA + Gr. *polis*, city] capital of Md., on Chesapeake Bay: pop. 32,000

**An·na·pur·na** (än′ə poor′na, an′ə pur′-) mountain mass of the Himalayas, C Nepal: highest peak, 26,500 ft.

**Ann Ar·bor** (an är′bər) [prob. after *Ann* Allen, early settler] city in SE Mich.: pop. 107,000

**Anne** (an) **1.** a feminine name: see ANNA **2.** 1665–1714; queen of Great Britain & Ireland (1702–14)

**an·neal** (ə nēl′) *vt.* [OE. *anælan*, to burn < *an-*, on + *ælan*, to burn < *æl*, fire] **1.** to heat (glass, metals, etc.) and then cool slowly to prevent brittleness **2.** to temper (the mind, will, etc.) —**an·neal′er** *n.*

**an·ne·lid** (an′'l id) *n.* [< Fr. < L. *annellus*, dim. of *anulus*, a ring: see ANNULAR] a worm with a body made of joined segments, as the earthworm —*adj.* of such worms

**An·nette** (an et′, ə net′) [Fr. dim. of *Anne*] a feminine name

**an·nex** (ə neks′; *for n.* an′eks) *vt.* [< OFr. < L. pp. of *annectere* < *ad-*, to + *nectere*, to tie, bind] **1.** to add on or attach, esp. to something larger **2.** to add as a condition, consequence, etc. **3.** to incorporate into a state, etc. the territory of (another state, etc.) **4.** to take, esp. without asking —*n.* something added on; esp., an addition to a building —**an·nex′a·ble** *adj.* —**an·nex·a·tion** (an′ek sā′shən) *n.* —**an′nex·a′tion·ist** *n.*

**An·nie Oak·ley** (an′ē ōk′lē) *n.* [after woman rifle expert (1860–1926) ? because her targets resembled punched tickets] [Slang] a free ticket; pass

**an·ni·hi·late** (ə nī′ə lāt′) *vt.* **-lat′ed, -lat′ing** [< L. pp. of *annihilare*, to bring to nothing < *ad-*, to + *nihil*, nothing] **1.** to destroy completely; demolish **2.** to kill **3.** to conquer decisively —**an·ni′hi·la·ble** (-lə b'l) *adj.* —**an·ni′hi·la′tion** *n.* —**an·ni′hi·la′tive** *adj.* —**an·ni′hi·la′tor** *n.*

**an·ni·ver·sa·ry** (an′ə vur′sər ē) *n., pl.* **-ries** [< L. < *annus*, year + pp. of *vertere*, to turn] **1.** the date on which some event occurred in an earlier year **2.** the celebration of such a date —*adj.* of or connected with an anniversary

‡**an·no Do·mi·ni** (an′ō dō′mə nē, an′ō däm′ə nī) [L., lit., in the year of (the Lord)] in the (given) year since the beginning of the Christian Era

**an·no·tate** (an′ə tāt′, -ō-) *vt., vi.* **-tat′ed, -tat′ing** [< L. pp. of *annotare* < *ad-*, to + *notare*, to mark < *nota:* see NOTE] to provide critical or explanatory notes for (a literary work, etc.) —**an′no·ta′tive** *adj.* —**an′no·ta′tor** *n.*

**an·no·ta·tion** (an′ə tā′shən, -ō-) *n.* **1.** an annotating or being annotated **2.** a critical or explanatory note or notes

**an·nounce** (ə nouns′) *vt.* **-nounced′, -nounc′ing** [< OFr. < L. *annuntiare* < *ad-*, to + *nuntiare*, to report < *nuntius*, messenger] **1.** to give notice of publicly; proclaim **2.** to say or tell **3.** to make known the arrival, etc. of **4.** *Radio & TV* to be an announcer for —*vi.* **1.** to serve as an announcer **2.** to declare one's candidacy or endorsement (with *for*) —**an·nounce′ment** *n.*

**an·nounc·er** (-ər) *n.* a person who announces; specif., one who introduces radio or television programs, identifies the station, reads the news, etc.

**an·noy** (ə noi′) *vt.* [< OFr. < VL. < *in odio habere*, to have in hate: see ODIUM] **1.** to irritate, bother, or make somewhat angry **2.** to harm by repeated attacks; harass —*vi.* to be annoying —**an·noy′er** *n.* —**an·noy′ing** *adj.* —**an·noy′ing·ly** *adv.*

**an·noy·ance** (-əns) *n.* **1.** an annoying or being annoyed **2.** a thing or person that annoys

**an·nu·al** (an′yoo wəl) *adj.* [< ME. & OFr. < L. < *annus*, year] **1.** of or measured by a year **2.** happening once a year; yearly **3.** for a year's time, work, etc. *(an annual wage)* **4.** living for only one year or season —*n.* **1.** a yearly publication; specif., a yearbook of a school senior class **2.** a plant that lives only one year or season —**an′nu·al·ly** *adv.*

**an·nu·i·tant** (ə noo′ə tənt, -nyoo′-) *n.* a person receiving an annuity

**an·nu·i·ty** (ə noo′ə tē, -nyoo′-) *n., pl.* **-ties** [< ME. & OFr. < ML. < L. *annus*, year] **1.** a payment of a fixed sum of money at regular intervals, esp. yearly **2.** an investment yielding such payments

**an·nul** (ə nul′) *vt.* **-nulled′, -nul′ling** [< OFr. < LL. *annullare*, to bring to nothing < *ad-*, to + *nullum*, nothing: see NULL] **1.** to do away with **2.** to invalidate; cancel —**an·nul′la·ble** *adj.*

**an·nu·lar** (an′yoo lər) *adj.* [< L. < *anulus*, a ring] of, like, or forming a ring —**an·nu·lar′i·ty** (-lar′ə tē) *n.* —**an′nu·lar·ly** *adv.*

**annular eclipse** an eclipse in which a ring of sunlight can be seen around the disk of the moon

**annular ligament** the ligament surrounding the ankle joint or wrist joint

**an·nu·late** (an′yoo lit, -lāt′) *adj.* [see ANNULAR] marked with, or made up of, rings: also **an′nu·lat′ed** —**an′nu·la′tion** *n.*

**an·nu·let** (an′yoo lət) *n.* [< L. *anulus*, a ring + -ET] **1.** a small ring **2.** *Archit.* a ringlike molding near the top of a column

**an·nul·ment** (ə nul′mənt) *n.* **1.** an annulling or being annulled **2.** an invalidation, as of a marriage, by the decree of a court

**an·nu·lus** (an′yoo ləs) *n., pl.* **-li** (-lī′), **-lus·es** [L. *anulus*] any ringlike part or mark

**an·nun·ci·ate** (ə nun′sē āt′, -shē-) *vt.* **-at′ed, -at′ing** [< L. pp. of *annuntiare*] to announce —**an·nun′ci·a′tor** *n.*

**an·nun·ci·a·tion** (ə nun′sē ā′shən, -shē-) *n.* **1.** an announcing or being announced **2.** [A-] *a)* the angel Gabriel's announcement to Mary that she was to give birth to Jesus: Luke 1:26–38 *b)* the church festival (March 25) commemorating this

**an·ode** (an′ōd) *n.* [< Gr. < *ana-*, up + *hodos*, way] **1.** a positively charged electrode, as in an electrolytic cell, electron tube, etc. **2.** the negative electrode in a battery supplying current

**an·o·dize** (an′ə dīz′) *vt.* **-dized′, -diz′ing** to put a protective oxide film on (a light metal) by an electrolytic process in which the metal serves as the anode

**an·o·dyne** (an′ə dīn′) *adj.* [< L. < Gr. < *an-*, without + *odynē*, pain] relieving or lessening pain —*n.* anything that relieves pain or soothes —**an′o·dyn′ic** (-din′ik) *adj.*

**a·noint** (ə noint′) *vt.* [< OFr. < L. *inungere* < *in-*, on + *ungere*, to smear] **1.** to rub oil or ointment on **2.** to put oil on in a ceremony of consecration —**a·noint′er** *n.* —**a·noint′ment** *n.*

**Anointing of the Sick** *R.C.Ch.* the sacrament in which a priest prays for and anoints a person dying or critically ill

**a·nom·a·lis·tic** (ə näm′ə lis′tik) *adj.* **1.** tending to be anomalous **2.** of an anomaly

**a·nom·a·lous** (ə näm′ə ləs) *adj.* [< L. < Gr. < *an-*, not + *homalos* < *homos*, the same] **1.** deviating from the general rule; abnormal **2.** being, or seeming to be, inconsistent or improper —**a·nom′a·lous·ly** *adv.* —**a·nom′a·lous·ness** *n.*

**a·nom·a·ly** (-lē) *n., pl.* **-lies** [< L. < Gr. < *anōmalia*, inequality: see prec.] **1.** departure from the regular arrangement or usual method; abnormality **2.** anything anomalous

**an·o·mie, an·o·my** (an′ə mē) *n.* [< Fr. < Gr. < *a-*, without + *nomos*, law] lack of purpose, identity, or ethical values in a person or in a society; rootlessness —**a·nom′ic** (ə näm′ik) *adj.*

**a·non** (ə nän′) *adv.* [OE. *on an*, in one, straightway] **1.** soon; shortly; also, at another time: now nearly archaic **2.** [Archaic] at once —**ever and anon** now and then

**anon.** anonymous

**an·o·nym** (an′ə nim) *n.* [Fr. < Gr.: see ANONYMOUS] **1.** a person whose name is not known **2.** a pseudonym

**an·o·nym·i·ty** (an′ə nim′ə tē) *n.* the condition or fact of being anonymous

**a·non·y·mous** (ə nän′ə məs) *adj.* [< Gr. < *an-*, without + *onyma*, name] **1.** with no name known or acknowledged **2.** given, written, etc. by a person whose name is withheld or unknown **3.** lacking in distinctive features —**a·non′y·mous·ly** *adv.*

**a·noph·e·les** (ə näf′ə lēz′) *n.* [ModL. < Gr. *anōphelēs*, harmful < *an-*, without + *ophelēs*, use] the mosquito that can carry the malaria parasite and transmit the disease —**a·noph′e·line′** (-līn′, -lin) *adj.*

**an·o·rex·i·a** (an′ə rek′sē ə) *n.* [ModL. < Gr. < *an-*, without + *orexis*, a desire for] lack of appetite for food; specif., **anorexia ner·vo·sa** (nər vō′sə), a personality disorder, chiefly in young women, characterized by aversion to food, obsession with weight loss, etc.

**an·oth·er** (ə nuth′ər) *adj.* [ME. *an other*] **1.** one more; an additional **2.** a different **3.** one of the same kind as *(another* Caesar*)* —*pron.* **1.** one additional **2.** a different one **3.** one of the same kind

**an·ox·i·a** (an äk′sē ə) *n.* [AN- + OX(YGEN) + -IA] th̶̶̶̶̶̶̶ tion of not having enough oxygen in the body tissu̶̶̶̶

**ans.** answer

**an·ser·ine** (an'sər īn', -in) *adj.* [< L. < *anser*, goose] 1. of or like a goose 2. stupid; foolish

**an·swer** (an'sər) *n.* [< OE. < *and-*, against + *swerian*, to SWEAR] 1. something said or written in return to a question, letter, etc. 2. any act in response or retaliation 3. a solution to a problem 4. *Law* a defense —*vi.* 1. to reply in words, by an action, etc. 2. to respond (*to*) [the horse *answered* to its rider's touch] 3. to be sufficient 4. to be responsible (*to* a person *for* an action, etc.) 5. to correspond (*to*) [he *answers* to the description] —*vt.* 1. to reply to in some way 2. to respond to the signal of (a telephone, doorbell, etc.) 3. to comply with; serve [to *answer* a purpose] 4. to refute (an accusation, criticism, etc.) 5. to suit [he *answers* the description] —**answer back** [Colloq.] to reply rudely or impertinently

**an·swer·a·ble** (-ə b'l) *adj.* 1. responsible; accountable 2. that can be answered or shown to be wrong [an *answerable* argument]

**ant** (ant) *n.* [OE. *æmete*] any of a family of insects, generally wingless, that live in colonies with a complex division of labor

WORKER ANT

**-ant** (ənt, 'nt) [Fr. < L. *-antem* or *-entem*, acc. prp. ending] *a suffix meaning:* 1. that has, shows, or does [*defiant*, *radiant*] 2. a person or thing that [*occupant*, *accountant*]

**ant.** 1. antenna 2. antonym

**ant·ac·id** (ant'as'id) *adj.* counteracting acidity —*n.* an antacid substance

**an·tag·o·nism** (an tag'ə niz'm) *n.* [see ANTAGONIZE] 1. the state of being opposed or hostile to another or to each other; opposition or hostility 2. an opposing force, principle, etc.

**an·tag·o·nist** (-nist) *n.* 1. an adversary; opponent 2. a muscle, drug, etc. that counteracts another

**an·tag·o·nis·tic** (an tag'ə nis'tik) *adj.* showing antagonism; acting in opposition —**an·tag'o·nis'ti·cal·ly** *adv.*

**an·tag·o·nize** (an tag'ə nīz') *vt.* -nized', -niz'ing [< Gr. < *anti-*, against + *agōn*, a contest: see AGONY] 1. to oppose or counteract 2. to incur the dislike of; make an enemy of

**ant·al·ka·li** (ant al'kə lī') *n., pl.* -lies', -lis' a substance that counteracts alkalinity

**ant·arc·tic** (ant ärk'tik, -är'-) *adj.* [< OFr. < L. < Gr. < *anti*, opposite + *arktikos*, ARCTIC] of or near the South Pole or the region around it —**the Antarctic** *same as* ANTARCTICA

**Ant·arc·ti·ca** (-ti kə) land area about the South Pole, covered by ice: c. 5,000,000 sq. mi.

**Antarctic Circle** [*also* a- c-] an imaginary circle parallel to the equator, 66°33' south of it

**Antarctic Ocean** the parts of the Atlantic, Pacific, and Indian oceans surrounding Antarctica

**An·tar·es** (an ter'ēz) the brightest star in the constellation Scorpio

**ant bear** a large anteater of tropical S. America

**an·te** (an'tē) *n.* [L., before] 1. *Poker* the stake that each player must put into the pot before receiving cards 2. [Colloq.] the amount one must pay as his share —*vt., vi.* -ted *or* -teed, -te·ing 1. *Poker* to put in (one's stake) 2. [Colloq.] to pay (one's share) —**ante up** to ante one's stake or share

**an·te-** [< L. *ante*, before] *a prefix meaning:* 1. before, prior (to) [*antecedent*, *ante*-Victorian] 2. before, in front (of) [*anteroom*]

**ant·eat·er** (ant'ēt'ər) *n.* any of several mammals that feed mainly on ants: anteaters have a long, sticky tongue and a long snout

**an·te·bel·lum** (an'ti bel'əm) *adj.* [L.] before the war; specif., before the American Civil War

**an·te·cede** (an'tə sēd') *vt., vi.* -ced'ed, -ced'ing [< L. *antecedere* < *ante*, before + *cedere*, to go] to go before; precede

**an·te·ced·ence** (-sēd''ns) *n.* [see prec.] a being prior; precedence: also **an'te·ced'en·cy** (-'n sē)

**an·te·ced·ent** (-sēd''nt) *adj.* [see ANTECEDE] prior; previous —*n.* 1. any thing prior to another 2. anything logically preceding 3. [*pl.*] one's ancestry, past life, etc. 4. *Gram.* the word, phrase, or clause to which a pronoun refers 5. *Math.* the first term of a ratio —**an'te·ced'ent·ly** *adv.*

**an·te·cham·ber** (an'ti chām'bər) *n.* [< Fr.: see ANTE- & CHAMBER] a smaller room leading into a larger or main room

**an·te·date** (-dāt') *vt.* -dat'ed, -dat'ing 1. to put a date on that is earlier than the actual date 2. to come before 3. to set an earlier date for —*n.* a date fixed for an event, etc. that is earlier than the actual one

**an·te·di·lu·vi·an** (an'ti də loo'vē ən) *adj.* [< ANTE- + L. *diluvium*, a flood + -AN] 1. of the time before the Biblical Flood 2. very old or old-fashioned —*n.* an antediluvian person or thing

**an·te·lope** (an'tə lōp') *n., pl.* -lopes', -lope': see PLURAL, II, D, 1 [< ME. & OFr. < ML. < MGr. *antholops*, deer] 1. *a)* any of a group of swift, cud-chewing, hollow-horned, deerlike animals related to oxen, sheep, and goats *b)* same as PRONGHORN 2. leather made from an antelope's hide

**an·te me·ri·di·em** (an'tē mə rid'ē əm) [L.] before noon: abbrev. A.M., a.m., AM

**an·ten·na** (an ten'ə) *n.* [< L. < *antemna*, sail yard] 1. *pl.* -nae (-ē), -nas either of a pair of movable sense organs in the head of an insect, crab, etc.; feeler 2. *pl.* -nas *Radio & TV* an arrangement of wires, metal rods, etc. used in sending and receiving electromagnetic waves; aerial

ANTELOPE (to 70 in. high at shoulder)

**an·te·pe·nult** (an'ti pē'nəlt) *n.* [see ANTE- & PENULT] the third last syllable in a word, as *-lu-* in *an·te·di·lu·vi·an*

**an·te·pe·nul·ti·mate** (-pi nul'tə mit) *adj.* third last; third from the end —*n.* 1. anything third from the end 2. an antepenult

**an·te·ri·or** (an tir'ē ər) *adj.* [L., compar. of *ante*, before] 1. at or toward the front; forward: opposed to POSTERIOR 2. coming before in time, order, etc.; earlier —**an·te'ri·or·ly** *adv.*

**an·te·room** (an'ti rōōm', -room') *n.* a room leading to a larger one; waiting room

**an·them** (an'thəm) *n.* [< OE. *antefn* < ML. < Gr. *antiphōnos*, sounding back < *anti-*, over against + *phōnē*, voice] 1. a religious choral song usually based on words from the Bible 2. a song of praise or devotion, as to a nation, college, etc.

**an·ther** (an'thər) *n.* [< Fr. < ModL. < Gr. *antheros*, blooming < *anthos*, a flower] the part of a stamen that contains the pollen

**an·ther·id·i·um** (an'thə rid'ē əm) *n., pl.* -id'i·a (-ə) [ModL. < prec. + Gr. dim. suffix *-idion*] in flowerless and seedless plants, the organ in which the male sex cells are developed —**an'ther·id'i·al** *adj.*

**ant·hill** (ant'hil') *n.* the soil carried by ants from their underground nest and heaped around its entrance

**an·thol·o·gize** (an thäl'ə jīz') *vi.* -gized', -giz'ing to make anthologies —*vt.* to make an anthology of or include in an anthology —**an·thol'o·gist** *n.*

**an·thol·o·gy** (an thäl'ə jē) *n., pl.* -gies [< Gr. *anthologia*, a garland < *anthos*, flower + *legein*, to gather] a collection of poems, stories, etc. —**an·tho·log·i·cal** (an'thə läj'i k'l) *adj.*

**An·tho·ny** (an'thə nē; *also, for 1 & 2*, -tə-) [< L. *Antonius*, name of a Roman gens] 1. a masculine name: dim. *Tony*; var. *Antony* 2. Mark, see ANTONY 3. Susan B(rownell), 1820–1906; U.S. leader in the women's suffrage movement

**an·tho·zo·an** (an'thə zō'ən) *n.* [< ModL. < Gr. *anthos*, flower + *zōion*, animal + -AN] any of a class of sea organisms, comprising corals, sea anemones, etc. —*adj.* of the anthozoans

**an·thra·cene** (an'thrə sēn') *n.* [< Gr. *anthrax*, coal + -ENE] a crystalline hydrocarbon, $C_{14}H_{10}$, a product of coal-tar distillation used in making dyes and as a radiation detector

**an·thra·cite** (-sīt') *n.* [< Gr. < *anthrax*, coal] hard coal, which gives much heat but little flame and smoke —**an'thra·cit'ic** (-sit'ik) *adj.*

**an·thrax** (an'thraks) *n.* [L. < Gr., (burning) coal, hence carbuncle] 1. an infectious disease of wild and domesticated animals, esp. cattle and sheep, that can be transmitted to man: it is characterized by black pustules 2. any such pustule

**an·thro·po-** [< Gr. *anthrōpos*, man] *a combining form meaning* man, human [*anthropology*]: also, before a vowel, **anthrop-**

**an·thro·po·cen·tric** (an'thrə pə sen'trik) *adj.* [prec. + CENTRIC] 1. that considers man as the central fact, or final aim, of the universe 2. viewing everything in terms of human values

**an·thro·po·gen·e·sis** (-jen'ə sis) *n.* the study of man's origin and development: also **an'thro·pog'e·ny** (-päj'ə nē) —**an'thro·po·ge·net'ic** (-jə net'ik) *adj.*

**an·thro·poid** (an'thrə poid') *adj.* [ANTHROP(O)- + -OID] 1. resembling man; manlike; esp., designating or of any of the most highly developed apes, as the chimpanzee and gorilla 2. apelike —*n.* any anthropoid ape —**an'thro·poi'dal** *adj.*

**an·thro·pol·o·gist** (an'thrə päl'ə jist) *n.* a student of or specialist in anthropology

**an·thro·pol·o·gy** (-päl'ə jē) *n.* [ANTHROPO- + -LOGY] the study of man, esp. of the variety, distribution, characteristics, cultures, etc. of mankind —**an'thro·po·log'i·cal** (-pə läj'i k'l), **an'thro·po·log'ic** *adj.* —**an'thro·po·log'i·cal·ly** *adv.*

**an·thro·pom·e·try** (-päm′ə trē) *n.* [ANTHROPO- + -METRY] the science dealing with measurement of the human body in comparing individual and group differences —**an′thro·po·met′ric** (-pə met′rik), **an′thro·po·met′ri·cal** *adj.* —**an′thro·po·met′ri·cal·ly** *adv.*

**an·thro·po·mor·phic** (-pə môr′fik) *adj.* of, characterized by, or resulting from anthropomorphism —**an′thro·po·mor′phi·cal·ly** *adv.*

**an·thro·po·mor·phism** (-pə môr′fiz′m) *n.* [ANTHROPO-MORPH(OUS) + -ISM] the attributing of human shape or characteristics to a god, animal, or inanimate thing —**an′thro·po·mor′phist** *n.*

**an·thro·po·mor·phous** (-pə môr′fəs) *adj.* [< Gr. < *anthrōpos*, a man + *morphē*, form, shape] having human shape and appearance

**an·thro·poph·a·gi** (-päf′ə jī′) *n.pl., sing.* **-a·gus** (-ə gəs) [L. < Gr. < *anthrōpos*, man + *phagein*, to eat] cannibals

**an·thro·poph·a·gy** (-päf′ə jē) *n.* [see prec.] cannibalism —**an′thro·poph′a·gous** (-gəs), **an′thro·po·phag′ic** (-pə-faj′ik) *adj.*

**an·thu·ri·um** (an thoor′ē əm) *n.* [ModL. < Gr. *anthos*, flower + *oura*, tail] a tropical American plant having a long spike with a flaring, heart-shaped spathe around its base

**an·ti** (an′tī, -tē) *n., pl.* **-tis** [< ff.] [Colloq.] a person opposed to some policy, proposal, etc. —*prep.* [Colloq.] opposed to; against

**an·ti-** (an′ti; *also variously* -tē, -tī, -tə) [< Gr. < *anti*, against] *a prefix meaning:* **1.** against; hostile to [*antilabor*] **2.** that operates against [*antiaircraft*] **3.** that prevents, cures, or neutralizes [*antitoxin*] **4.** opposite; reverse [*antimatter*] **5.** rivaling [*antipope*]

**an·ti·air·craft** (an′tē er′kraft, -tī-) *adj.* used for defense against hostile aircraft [*antiaircraft* gun]

**an·ti·bac·te·ri·al** (-bak tir′ē əl) *adj.* that checks the growth or effect of bacteria

**an·ti·bal·lis·tic missile** (-bə lis′tik) a ballistic missile intended to intercept and destroy another ballistic missile in flight

**an·ti·bi·o·sis** (-bī ō′sis) *n.* [ModL. < ANTI- + Gr. *biōsis*, way of life < *bios*, life] *Biol.* an association between organisms which is harmful to one of them

**an·ti·bi·ot·ic** (-bī ät′ik, -bē-) *adj.* **1.** of antibiosis **2.** destroying, or stopping the growth of, bacteria and other microorganisms —*n.* an antibiotic substance produced by various microorganisms, as by bacteria or fungi

**an·ti·bod·y** (an′ti bäd′ē) *n., pl.* **-bod′ies** a protein produced in the body in response to contact of the body with an antigen, serving to neutralize the antigen, thus creating immunity

**an·tic** (an′tik) *adj.* [< It. < L. *antiquus:* see ANTIQUE] **1.** [Archaic] fantastic and queer **2.** odd and funny —*n.* **1.** a playful or silly act, trick, etc.; caper **2.** [Archaic] a clown or buffoon —*vi.* **-ticked, -tick·ing** to perform antics; caper

**an·ti·christ** (an′ti krīst′, -tī-) *n.* an opponent of Christ —[A-] *Bible* the great antagonist of Christ: I John 2:18

**an·tic·i·pant** (an tis′ə pənt) *adj.* expecting; anticipating (with *of*) —*n.* a person who anticipates

**an·tic·i·pate** (an tis′ə pāt′) *vt.* **-pat′ed, -pat′ing** [< L. pp. of *anticipare* < *ante-*, before + *capere*, to take] **1.** to look forward to; expect **2.** to prevent by action in advance; forestall [to *anticipate* an opponent's blows] **3.** to foresee and take care of in advance [to *anticipate* a request] **4.** to use or enjoy in advance [to *anticipate* a legacy] **5.** to be ahead of in doing or achieving something —**an·tic′i·pa′tor** *n.*

**an·tic·i·pa·tion** (an tis′ə pā′shən) *n.* **1.** an anticipating or being anticipated **2.** something anticipated or expected **3.** foreknowledge; presentiment

**an·tic·i·pa·tive** (an tis′ə pāt′iv) *adj.* of or full of anticipation —**an·tic′i·pa′tive·ly** *adv.*

**an·tic·i·pa·to·ry** (-pə tôr′ē) *adj.* of or expressing anticipation —**an·tic′i·pa·to′ri·ly** *adv.*

**an·ti·cler·i·cal** (an′ti kler′ə k′l, -tī-) *adj.* opposed to the influence of the clergy or church in public affairs —**an′ti·cler′i·cal·ism** *n.*

**an·ti·cli·max** (-klī′maks) *n.* **1.** a sudden drop from the dignified or important to the commonplace or trivial **2.** a final event which is in disappointing contrast to those coming before —**an′ti·cli·mac′tic** (-mak′tik) *adj.*

**an·ti·cline** (an′ti klīn) *n.* [< ANTI- + Gr. *klinein*, to incline] *Geol.* a fold of stratified rock in which the strata slope downward in opposite directions from the central axis: opposed to SYNCLINE —**an′ti·cli′nal** *adj.*

**an·ti·co·ag·u·lant** (an′ti kō ag′yə lənt, -tī-) *n.* a drug or substance that delays or prevents the clotting of blood

**an·ti·cy·clone** (-sī′klōn) *n.* an extensive atmospheric condition of high barometric pressure, with the winds at the edge blowing outward —**an′ti·cy·clon′ic** (-klän′ik) *adj.*

**an·ti·de·pres·sant** (-di pres′ənt) *adj.* designating or of any drug used to treat emotional depression —*n.* an antidepressant drug

**an·ti·dote** (an′tə dōt′) *n.* [ME. & OFr. < L. < Gr. < *anti-*, against + *dotos*, given < *didonai*, to give] **1.** a remedy to counteract a poison **2.** anything that works against an evil or unwanted condition —**an′ti·dot′al** *adj.*

**An·tie·tam** (an tēt′əm) [AmInd. < ?] creek in W Md.: site of a Civil War battle (1862)

**an·ti·fed·er·al·ist** (an′ti fed′ər ə list, -tī-; -fed′rə-) *n.* **1.** one opposed to federalism **2.** [A-] one who opposed the Federalists and the adoption of the U.S. Constitution

**an·ti·freeze** (an′ti frēz′, -tī-) *n.* a substance of low freezing point added esp. to the water in automobile radiators to prevent freezing

**an·ti·gen** (an′tə jən) *n.* [ANTI- + -GEN] an enzyme, toxin, etc. to which the body reacts by producing antibodies —**an′ti·gen′ic** (-jen′ik) *adj.*

**An·tig·o·ne** (an tig′ə nē′) *Gr. Myth.* daughter of Oedipus: she defied her uncle by performing funeral rites for her brother

**An·ti·gua** (an tē′gə, -gwə) self-governing island under Brit. protection, in the Leeward group of the West Indies: 108 sq. mi.; pop. 57,000

**an·ti·he·ro** (an′ti hir′ō, -tī-) *n.* the main character of a novel, play, etc. who lacks the virtues of a traditional hero

**an·ti·his·ta·mine** (an′ti his′tə mēn′, -tī-; -mən) *n.* any drug used to minimize the action of histamine in such allergic conditions as hay fever and hives —**an′ti·his′ta·min′ic** (-min′ik) *adj.*

**an·ti·knock** (an′ti näk′, -tī-) *n.* a substance added to the fuel of internal-combustion engines to do away with noise caused by too rapid combustion

**an·ti·la·bor** (an′ti lā′bər, -tī-) *adj.* opposed to labor unions or to the interests of workers

**An·til·les** (an til′ēz) main island group of the West Indies: see GREATER ANTILLES, LESSER ANTILLES —**An·til′le·an** (-ē ən, an′tə lē′ən) *adj.*

**an·ti·log·a·rithm** (an′ti lôg′ə rith′m, -tī-; -läg′-) *n.* the number corresponding to a given logarithm [the *antilogarithm* of 1 is 10]

**an·ti·ma·cas·sar** (an′ti mə kas′ər) *n.* [ANTI- + *macassar* (*oil*), a former hair oil] a small cover to protect the back or arms of a chair, etc. from soiling

**an·ti·mag·net·ic** (an′ti mag net′ik, -tī-) *adj.* made of metals that resist magnetism [an *antimagnetic* watch]

**an·ti·ma·lar·i·al** (-mə ler′ē əl) *adj.* preventing or relieving malaria —*n.* an antimalarial drug

**an·ti·mat·ter** (an′ti mat′ər, -tī-) *n.* a form of matter in which the electrical charge or other property of each constituent particle is the reverse of that in the usual matter of our universe

**an·ti·mis·sile** (-mis′′l) *adj.* designed as a defense against ballistic missiles

**an·ti·mo·ny** (an′tə mō′nē) *n.* [< OFr. < ML. *antimonium*] a silvery-white, brittle, metallic chemical element, found only in combination: used to harden alloys, etc.: symbol, Sb; at. wt., 121.75; at. no., 51 —**an′ti·mo′nic** *adj.* —**an′ti·mo′nous** *adj.*

**An·ti·och** (an′tē äk′) capital of ancient Syria: now, a city in S Turkey: pop. 46,000

**an·ti·par·ti·cle** (an′ti pär′tə k′l, an′tī-) *n.* any of the constituent particles of antimatter

**an·ti·pas·to** (an′ti pas′tō, -päs′-) *n.* [It. < *anti-* (L. *ante*), before + *pasto* < L. *pastus*, food] a dish of salted fish, meat, olives, etc. served as an appetizer

**an·ti·pa·thet·ic** (an′ti pə thet′ik) *adj.* **1.** having antipathy **2.** opposed or antagonistic in character, tendency, etc. Also **an′ti·pa·thet′i·cal** —**an′ti·pa·thet′i·cal·ly** *adv.*

**an·tip·a·thy** (an tip′ə thē) *n., pl.* **-thies** [< L. < Gr. < *anti-*, against + *patheia* < *pathein*, to feel] **1.** a strong dislike **2.** the object of such dislike

**an·ti·per·son·nel** (an′ti pur′sə nel′, -tī-) *adj.* directed against, or intended to destroy, people rather than material objects [*antipersonnel* mines]

**an·ti·per·spir·ant** (-pur′spər ənt) *n.* a substance applied to the skin to reduce perspiration

**an·ti·phlo·gis·tic** (-flə jis′tik) *adj.* counteracting inflammation —*n.* an antiphlogistic substance

**an·ti·phon** (an′tə fän′) *n.* [< ML. < Gr.: see ANTHEM] a hymn, psalm, etc. chanted or sung in responsive, alternating parts —**an·tiph′o·nal** (-tif′ə n′l), **an′ti·phon′ic** *adj.*

**an·tiph·o·nar·y** (an tif′ə ner′ē) *n., pl.* **-nar′ies** a book of antiphons

**an·ti·pode** (an′tə pōd′) *n.* [back-formation of ff.] an exact opposite

**an·tip·o·des** (an tip′ə dēz′) *n.pl.* [ML. < L. < Gr., pl. of *antipous* < *anti-*, opposite + *pous*, foot] **1.** any two places directly opposite each other on the earth **2.** [*with pl. or sing. v.*] a place on the opposite side of the earth: in British usage, New Zealand and Australia **3.** two opposite or contrary things —**an·tip′o·dal** *adj.* —**an·tip′o·de′an** (-dē′ən) *adj., n.*

**an·ti·pope** (an′ti pōp′, -ti-) *n.* a pope set up against the one chosen by church laws, as in a schism

**an·ti·py·ret·ic** (an′ti pī ret′ik, -ti-) *adj.* reducing fever —*n.* anything that reduces fever

**antiq.** **1.** antiquarian **2.** antiquity; antiquities

**an·ti·quar·i·an** (an′tə kwer′ē ən) *adj.* **1.** of antiques or antiquities **2.** of antiquaries **3.** of, or dealing in, rare old books —*n.* an antiquary

**an·ti·quar·y** (an′tə kwer′ē) *n., pl.* **-quar′ies** one who collects or studies relics and ancient art

**an·ti·quate** (-kwāt′) *vt.* **-quat′ed, -quat′ing** [< L. pp. of *antiquare* < *antiquus*: see ANTIQUE] to make old or obsolete; cause to become old-fashioned —**an′ti·quat′ed** *adj.* —**an′ti·qua′tion** *n.*

**an·tique** (an tēk′) *adj.* [Fr. < L. *antiquus*, ancient < *ante*, before] **1.** of ancient times; ancient **2.** out-of-date; old-fashioned **3.** in the style of classical antiquity **4.** of, or in the style of, a former period **5.** dealing in antiques —*n.* **1.** an ancient relic **2.** the ancient style, esp. of Greek or Roman sculpture, etc. **3.** a piece of furniture, silverware, etc. of a former period **4.** *Printing* a variety of boldface type —*vt.* **-tiqued′, -tiqu′ing** to make look antique —**an·tique′ly** *adv.* —**an·tique′ness** *n.*

**an·tiq·ui·ty** (an tik′wə tē) *n., pl.* **-ties** [see prec.] **1.** the early period of history, esp. before the Middle Ages **2.** great age; oldness [*a statue of great antiquity*] **3.** the people of ancient times **4.** [*pl.*] *a)* relics, monuments, etc. of the distant past *b)* ancient manners, customs, etc.

**an·ti·scor·bu·tic** (an′ti skôr byōō′tik, -ti-) *adj.* that cures or prevents scurvy

**an·ti-Se·mit·ic** (-sə mit′ik) *adj.* **1.** having or showing prejudice against Jews **2.** discriminating against or persecuting Jews —**an′ti-Sem′ite** (-sem′īt) *n.* —**an′ti-Sem′i·tism** (-sem′ə tiz′m) *n.*

**an·ti·sep·sis** (an′tə sep′sis) *n.* [ANTI- + SEPSIS] **1.** the technique of preventing infection, the growth of microorganisms, etc. **2.** the condition of being antiseptic **3.** the use of antiseptics

**an·ti·sep·tic** (-sep′tik) *adj.* **1.** preventing infection, decay, etc. by inhibiting the action of microorganisms **2.** using antiseptics **3.** free from infection; sterile **4.** untouched by life, its problems, etc. —*n.* any antiseptic substance —**an′ti·sep′ti·cal·ly** *adv.* —**an′ti·sep′ti·cize′** *vt.* **-cized′, -ciz′ing**

**an·ti·se·rum** (an′ti sir′əm) *n.* a serum with antibodies in it

**an·ti·slav·er·y** (an′ti slā′vər ē, -ti-) *adj.* against slavery

**an·ti·so·cial** (-sō′shəl) *adj.* **1.** unsociable **2.** harmful to the welfare of the people generally

**an·ti·spas·mod·ic** (-spaz mäd′ik) *adj.* relieving spasms —*n.* an antispasmodic drug

**an·ti·stat·ic** (-stat′ik) *adj.* reducing static electric charges, as on textiles, polishes, etc.

**an·tis·tro·phe** (an tis′trə fē) *n.* [L. < Gr. < *anti-*, opposite + *strephein*, to turn] **1.** *a)* the return movement, left to right, made by the chorus of an ancient Greek play in answering a strophe *b)* the part of a choric song performed during this **2.** a stanza following a strophe, often in the same form —**an·ti·stroph·ic** (an′tə sträf′ik) *adj.*

**an·ti·tank** (an′ti taŋk′, -ti-) *adj.* for use against tanks in war

**an·tith·e·sis** (an tith′ə sis) *n., pl.* **-ses′** (-sēz′) [L. < Gr. < *anti-*, against + *tithenai*, to place] **1.** a contrast of thoughts, usually in two phrases, clauses, etc. (Ex.: "Man proposes, and God disposes") **2.** a contrast or opposition **3.** the exact opposite [*joy is the antithesis of sorrow*] —**an·ti·thet·i·cal** (an′tə thet′i k'l) *adj.* —**an′ti·thet′i·cal·ly** *adv.*

**an·ti·tox·in** (an′ti täk′sin, -ti-) *n.* **1.** an antibody formed by the body to act against a specific toxin **2.** a serum containing an antitoxin: taken from the blood of an immunized animal, such a serum is injected into a person to prevent a specific disease, such as diphtheria or tetanus —**an′ti·tox′ic** *adj.*

**an·ti·trades** (an′ti trādz′) *n.pl.* winds that blow above and opposite to the trade winds

**an·ti·trust** (an′ti trust′, -ti-) *adj.* opposed to or regulating trusts, or business monopolies

**an·ti·ven·in** (-ven′ən) *n.* [ANTI- + VEN(OM) + -IN¹] **1.** an antitoxin for venom, as of snakes, produced by gradually increased injections of the specific venom **2.** a serum containing this antitoxin

**an·ti·viv·i·sec·tion** (-viv′ə sek′shən) *n.* opposition to medical research on living animals —**an′ti·viv′i·sec′tion·ist** *n., adj.*

**ant·ler** (ant′lər) *n.* [< OFr. < L. < *ante-*, before + *ocularis*, of the eyes] **1.** the branched, deciduous horn of any animal of the deer family **2.** any branch of such a horn —**ant′lered** *adj.*

**ant lion** **1.** the large-jawed larva of certain winged insects that digs a pit for trapping ants, etc. on which it feeds **2.** the adult insect

**An·toi·nette** (an′twə net′, -tə-) **1.** a feminine name: dim. *Nettie, Netty* **2. Marie,** see MARIE ANTOINETTE

**An·to·ny** (an′tə nē) **1.** *var. of* ANTHONY **2. Mark** or **Marc,** (L. name *Marcus Antonius*) 83?-30 B.C.; Rom. general & statesman

MOOSE ANTLERS

**an·to·nym** (an′tə nim′) *n.* [< Gr. < *anti-*, opposite + *onyma*, name] a word that is opposite in meaning to another word ["sad" is an *antonym* of "happy"] —**an·ton·y·mous** (an tän′ə məs) *adj.*

**an·trum** (an′trəm) *n., pl.* **-tra** (-trə), **-trums** [L. < Gr. *antron*, cave] *Anat.* a cavity; esp., either of a pair of sinuses in the upper jaw

**Ant·werp** (an′twərp) seaport in N Belgium, on the Scheldt River: pop. 240,000

**A·nu·bis** (ə nyōō′bis, -nōō′-) an Egyptian god, depicted with the head of a jackal, who led the dead to judgment

**an·u·re·sis** (an′yoo rē′sis) *n.* [ModL. < AN- + Gr. *ourēsis*, urination] the condition of being unable to pass one's urine

**a·nus** (ā′nəs) *n., pl.* **a′nus·es, a′ni** (-nī) [L., a ring] the opening at the lower end of the alimentary canal

**an·vil** (an′vəl) *n.* [< OE. *anfilt* < *an-*, on + hyp. *filtan*, to beat] **1.** an iron or steel block on which metal objects are hammered into shape **2.** the incus, one of the three bones of the middle ear

**anx·i·e·ty** (aŋ zī′ə tē) *n., pl.* **-ties** [see ff.] **1.** a state of being uneasy or worried about what may happen **2.** an eager but often uneasy desire [*anxiety* to do well]

**anx·ious** (aŋk′shəs, aŋ′-) *adj.* [L. *anxius* < *angere*, to choke] **1.** uneasy in mind; worried **2.** causing or full of anxiety [*an anxious hour*] **3.** eagerly wishing —**anx′ious·ly** *adv.* —**anx′ious·ness** *n.*

**an·y** (en′ē) *adj.* [< OE. *ænig* < *an*, ONE] **1.** one, no matter which, of more than two [*any* pupil may answer] **2.** some, no matter what amount or kind [he hasn't *any* food] **3.** without limit [enter *any* number of times] **4.** every [*any* child can do it] —*pron. sing. & pl.* any one or ones; any amount or number —*adv.* to any degree or extent; at all [is he *any* better?]

**an·y·bod·y** (-bud′ē, -bäd′ē) *pron.* **1.** any person; anyone **2.** a person of fame, importance, etc.

**an·y·how** (-hou′) *adv.* **1.** no matter in what way **2.** in any case **3.** carelessly

**an·y·more** (-môr′) *adv.* now; nowadays: in standard use, only in negative constructions [he doesn't live here *anymore*]: also **any more**

**an·y·one** (-wun′) *pron.* any person; anybody

**any one** any single (person or thing)

**an·y·place** (en′ē plās′) *adv.* [Colloq.] in, at, or to any place; anywhere —**get anyplace** [Colloq.] to succeed

**an·y·thing** (-thiŋ′) *pron.* any object, event, fact, etc. —*n.* a thing, no matter of what kind —*adv.* in any way; at all —**anything but** not at all

**an·y·way** (-wā′) *adv.* **1.** in any manner or way **2.** in any case; anyhow **3.** haphazardly; carelessly

**an·y·where** (-hwer′, -wer′) *adv.* **1.** in, at, or to any place **2.** [Colloq.] at all; to any extent —**get anywhere** [Colloq.] to have any success

**an·y·wise** (-wīz′) *adv.* in any manner; at all

**A/O, a/o** account of

**A-OK** (ā′ō kā′) *adj.* [A(LL) OK] [Colloq.] excellent, fine, in working order, etc.: a generalized term of commendation: also **A′-O·kay′**

**A one** (ā′ wun′) [Colloq.] first-class; first-rate; superior: also **A 1, A number 1**

**a·or·ta** (ā ôr′tə) *n., pl.* **-tas, -tae** (-tē) [ModL. < Gr. *aeirein*, to raise] the main artery of the body carrying blood from the left ventricle of the heart to arteries in all organs and parts —**a·or′tic, a·or′tal** *adj.*

**a·ou·dad** (ä′oo dad′) *n.* [Fr. < Moorish *audad*] a wild North African sheep with large, curved horns and a heavy growth of hair on the chest

**a·pace** (ə pās′) *adv.* at a fast pace; swiftly

**A·pach·e** (ə pach′ē) *n.* [AmSp., prob. < Zuñi *ápachu*, enemy] **1.** *pl.* **A·pach′es, A·pach′e** a member of a group of tribes of Indians of N Mexico and the SW U.S. **2.** any of their Athapascan languages

**a·pache** (ə pash′, -päsh′; Fr. à pàsh′) *n., pl.* **a·pach′es** (-iz; Fr. à pàsh′) [Fr., lit., APACHE] a gangster of Paris —*adj.* designating a dance which represents an apache handling his girl brutally

**a·part** (ə pärt′) *adv.* [< OFr. < L. *ad*, to, at + *partem*, acc.

of *pars*, a part, side] **1.** to one side; aside **2.** away in place or time **3.** separately in function, use, etc. [*viewed apart*] **4.** in or to pieces **5.** aside; notwithstanding [*all joking apart*] —*adj.* [*used only in the predicate*] separated —**apart from** other than; besides —**take apart** to reduce (a whole) to its parts —**tell apart** to distinguish one from another

**a·part·heid** (ə pärt′hāt, -hīt) *n.* [Afrik., apartness] in South Africa, the policy of strict racial segregation and discrimination imposed on Negroes and other colored peoples

**a·part·ment** (ə pärt′mənt) *n.* [< Fr. < It. < *appartare*, to separate < *parte*, PART] a room or suite of rooms to live in **apartment house** a building divided into a number of apartments: also **apartment building**

**ap·a·thet·ic** (ap′ə thet′ik) *adj.* [< APATHY, after PATHETIC] **1.** feeling no emotion; unmoved **2.** not interested; indifferent —**ap′a·thet′i·cal·ly** *adv.*

**ap·a·thy** (ap′ə thē) *n., pl.* **-thies** [< Fr. < L. < Gr. < *a-*, without + *pathos*, emotion] **1.** lack of emotion **2.** lack of interest; indifference

**APC tablet** a tablet containing aspirin, phenacetin, and caffeine, for relieving headaches, etc.

**ape** (āp) *n.* [OE. *apa*] **1.** any of a family of large, tailless monkeys; specif., a chimpanzee, gorilla, orangutan, or gibbon **2.** any monkey **3.** a person who imitates; mimic **4.** a coarse, uncouth person —*vt.* **aped, ap′ing** to imitate or mimic —**ape′like′** *adj.*

**ape-man** (-man′) *n.* any of several extinct primates, with structural characteristics between those of man and the higher apes

**Ap·en·nines** (ap′ə nīnz′) mountain range in C Italy: highest peak, 9,560 ft.

**a·pe·ri·ent** (ə pir′ē ənt) *adj., n.* [< L. prp. of *aperire*: see APERTURE] *same as* LAXATIVE

**a·pe·ri·od·ic** (ā′pir ē äd′ik) *adj.* **1.** occurring irregularly **2.** *Physics* without periodic vibrations

**a·pe·ri·tif** (ä′pā rə tēf′) *n.* [< Fr. < L. *apertus*: see ff.] an alcoholic drink, esp. a wine, taken before meals to stimulate the appetite

**ap·er·ture** (ap′ər chər) *n.* [< L. < *apertus*, pp. of *aperire*, to open] **1.** an opening; hole; gap **2.** the diameter of the opening in a camera, etc., through which light passes into the lens

**a·pet·a·lous** (ā pet′'l əs) *adj. Bot.* without petals

**a·pex** (ā′peks) *n., pl.* **a′pex·es, ap′i·ces** (ap′ə sēz′, ā′pə-) [L., a point] **1.** the highest point; peak; vertex **2.** the pointed end; tip **3.** a climax

**a·pha·si·a** (ə fā′zhə, -zhē ə) *n.* [ModL. < Gr. < *a-*, not + *phanai*, to speak] a total or partial loss of the power to use or understand words —**a·pha′sic** (-zik), **a·pha′si·ac′** (-zē ak′) *adj., n.*

**a·phe·li·on** (ə fē′lē ən) *n., pl.* **-li·ons, -li·a** (-ə) [ModL. < Gr. *apo*, from + *helios*, sun] the point farthest from the sun in the orbit around it of a planet, comet, or man-made satellite: cf. PERIHELION

**a·phid** (ā′fid, af′id) *n.* [ModL. *aphis* (pl. *aphides*) < Gr. *apheides*, lavish] any of a group of small insects that suck the juice from plants; plant louse: also **a·phis** (ā′fis, af′is), *pl.* **aph·i·des** (af′ə dēz′) —**a·phid·i·an** (ə fid′ē ən) *adj., n.*

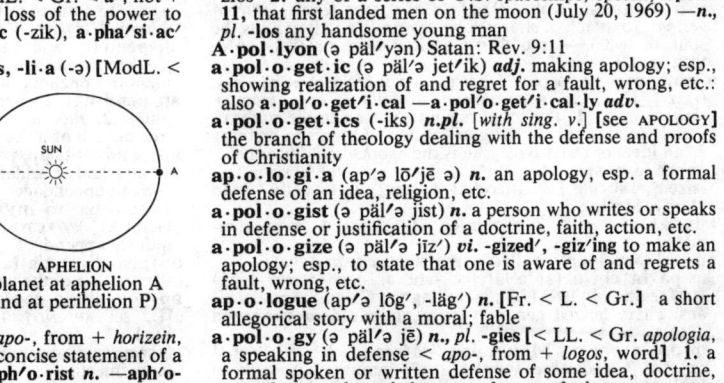

APHELION
(planet at aphelion A and at perihelion P)

**aph·o·rism** (af′ə riz′m) *n.* [< Fr. < Gr. < *aphorizein*, to divide < *apo-*, from + *horizein*, to bound: see HORIZON] **1.** a short, concise statement of a principle **2.** a maxim or adage —**aph′o·rist** *n.* —**aph′o·ris′tic** *adj.* —**aph′o·ris′ti·cal·ly** *adv.*

**aph·ro·dis·i·ac** (af′rə diz′ē ak′) *adj.* [< Gr. < ff.] arousing or increasing sexual desire —*n.* any aphrodisiac drug or other agent

**Aph·ro·di·te** (af′rə dīt′ē) *Gr. Myth.* the goddess of love and beauty: identified with the Roman Venus

**a·pi·a·rist** (ā′pē ə rist, -er′ist) *n.* a person who keeps bees —**a′pi·ar′i·an** (-er′ē ən) *adj.*

**a·pi·ar·y** (ā′pē er′ē) *n., pl.* **-ar′ies** [< L. < *apis*, bee] a place where bees are kept for their honey

**ap·i·cal** (ap′i k'l, ā′pi-) *adj.* of, at, or constituting the apex

**ap·i·ces** (ap′ə sēz′, ā′pə-) *n.* alt. *pl.* of APEX

**a·pi·cul·ture** (ā′pə kul′chər) *n.* [< L. *apis*, bee + CULTURE] the raising and care of bees; beekeeping —**a′pi·cul′tur·al** *adj.* —**a′pi·cul′tur·ist** *n.*

**a·piece** (ə pēs′) *adv.* [see A & PIECE] for each one

**ap·ish** (āp′ish) *adj.* **1.** like an ape **2.** foolishly imitative **3.** silly, affected, mischievous, etc. —**ap′ish·ly** *adv.* —**ap′ish·ness** *n.*

**a·plen·ty** (ə plen′tē) *adj., adv.* [Colloq.] in abundance

**a·plomb** (ə pläm′, -plum′) *n.* [Fr., lit., perpendicularity < *à*, to + *plomb*, a PLUMB] self-possession; poise

**ap·o-** [< Gr. *apo*, off] *a prefix meaning* off, from, or away from [*apogee*]

**APO** Army Post Office

**Apoc. 1.** Apocalypse **2.** Apocrypha

**a·poc·a·lypse** (ə päk′ə lips′) *n.* [< L. < Gr. < *apokalyptein*, to disclose] any of various religious writings depicting symbolically the end of evil and the triumph of good; specif., [A-] the last book of the New Testament; book of Revelation —**a·poc′a·lyp′tic** (-lip′tik), **a·poc′a·lyp′ti·cal** *adj.* —**a·poc′a·lyp′ti·cal·ly** *adv.*

**a·po·car·pous** (ap′ə kär′pəs) *adj. Bot.* having separate or partially joined carpels

**a·poc·o·pe** (ə päk′ə pē′) *n.* [< Gr. < *apo-*, from + *koptein*, to cut off] the dropping of a sound or sounds at the end of a word (Ex.: *mos′* for *most*)

**a·poc·ry·pha** (ə päk′rə fə) *n.pl.* [< LL. < Gr. *apokryphos*, hidden, obscure < *apo-*, away + *kryptein*, to hide] **1.** any writings, anecdotes, etc. of doubtful authenticity or authorship **2.** [A-] fourteen books of the Septuagint that are rejected in Judaism and regarded by Protestants as not canonical: eleven are fully accepted in the Roman Catholic canon

**a·poc·ry·phal** (-f'l) *adj.* **1.** of doubtful authorship or authenticity **2.** not genuine; false; counterfeit **3.** [A-] of or like the Apocrypha

**a·pod·o·sis** (ə päd′ə sis) *n., pl.* **-ses** (-sēz′) [Gr., a giving back] the clause expressing result in a conditional sentence: opposed to PROTASIS

**ap·o·gee** (ap′ə jē′) *n.* [< Fr. < L. < Gr. < *apo-*, from + *gē*, earth] **1.** the point farthest from the earth, the moon, or another planet, in the orbit of a satellite or spacecraft around it **2.** the highest or farthest point —**ap′o·ge′an** (-jē′ən), **ap′o·ge′al** *adj.*

**a·po·lit·i·cal** (ā′pə lit′ə k'l) *adj.* not concerned with political matters —**a′po·lit′i·cal·ly** *adv.*

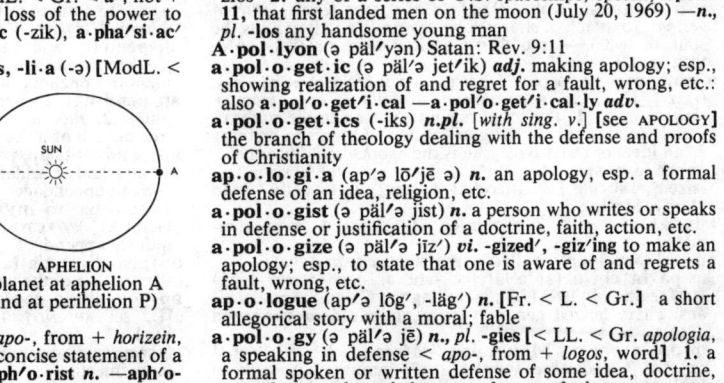

APOGEE
(moon at apogee A and at perigee P)

**A·pol·lo** (ə päl′ō) **1.** *Gr. & Rom. Myth.* the god of music, poetry, prophecy, and medicine: later identified with HELIOS **2.** any of a series of U.S. spaceships; specif., **Apollo 11,** that first landed men on the moon (July 20, 1969) —*n., pl.* **-los** any handsome young man

**A·pol·lyon** (ə päl′yən) Satan: Rev. 9:11

**a·pol·o·get·ic** (ə päl′ə jet′ik) *adj.* making apology; esp., showing realization of and regret for a fault, wrong, etc.: also **a·pol′o·get′i·cal** —**a·pol′o·get′i·cal·ly** *adv.*

**a·pol·o·get·ics** (-iks) *n.pl.* [with *sing. v.*] [see APOLOGY] the branch of theology dealing with the defense and proofs of Christianity

**ap·o·lo·gi·a** (ap′ə lō′jē ə) *n.* an apology, esp. a formal defense of an idea, religion, etc.

**a·pol·o·gist** (ə päl′ə jist) *n.* a person who writes or speaks in defense or justification of a doctrine, faith, action, etc.

**a·pol·o·gize** (ə päl′ə jīz′) *vi.* **-gized′, -giz′ing** to make an apology; esp., to state that one is aware of and regrets a fault, wrong, etc.

**ap·o·logue** (ap′ə lôg′, -läg′) *n.* [Fr. < L. < Gr.] a short allegorical story with a moral; fable

**a·pol·o·gy** (ə päl′ə jē) *n., pl.* **-gies** [< LL. < Gr. *apologia*, a speaking in defense < *apo-*, from + *logos*, word] **1.** a formal spoken or written defense of some idea, doctrine, etc. **2.** an acknowledgment of some fault, wrong, etc., with an expression of regret **3.** an inferior substitute [he is a poor *apology* for an actor]

**ap·o·phthegm** (ap′ə them′) *n. same as* APOTHEGM

**ap·o·plec·tic** (ap′ə plek′tik) *adj.* **1.** of, like, or causing apoplexy **2.** having apoplexy **3.** seemingly about to have apoplexy [*apoplectic* with rage] Also **ap′o·plec′ti·cal** —*n.* a person having or likely to have apoplexy —**ap′o·plec′ti·cal·ly** *adv.*

**ap·o·plex·y** (ap′ə plek′sē) *n.* [< ME. & OFr. < L. < Gr. < *apo-*, down + *plēssein*, to strike] sudden paralysis with some loss of consciousness and feeling, caused when a blood vessel in the brain breaks or becomes clogged; stroke

**a·port** (ə pôrt′) *adv. Naut.* on or to the left, or port, side

**a·pos·ta·sy** (ə päs′tə sē) *n., pl.* **-sies** [< LL. < Gr. < *apo-*, away + *stasis*, a standing] an abandoning of something that one once believed in, as a faith, cause, etc.

**a·pos·tate** (-tāt′, -tit) *n.* a person guilty of apostasy; renegade —*adj.* guilty of apostasy

**a·pos·ta·tize** (-tə tīz′) *vi.* **-tized′, -tiz′ing** to become an apostate

**a pos·te·ri·o·ri** (ā′ päs tir′ē ôr′ī, -ôr′ē) [ML., lit., from what comes later] **1.** from effect to cause, or from particular instances to a generalization; inductive or inductively **2.** based on observation or experience; empirical  Opposed to A PRIORI

**a·pos·tle** (ə päs′'l) *n.* [< OE. & OFr. < LL. < Gr. *apostolos*, one sent forth < *apo-*, from + *stellein*, to send] **1.** a person sent out on a special mission; specif., [*usually* A-] any of the twelve disciples sent out by Jesus to teach the gospel **2.** the first Christian missionary in a place **3.** any of a group of early Christian missionaries **4.** an early advocate or leader, as of a reform movement **5.** any of the twelve administrative officials of the Mormon Church —a·pos′tle·ship′ *n.*

**Apostles' Creed** an early statement of belief in the basic Christian doctrines, formerly thought to have been composed by the twelve Apostles

**a·pos·to·late** (ə päs′t'l it, -tə lāt′) *n.* the office, duties, or period of activity of an apostle

**ap·os·tol·ic** (ap′əs täl′ik) *adj.* **1.** of an apostle **2.** of the Apostles, their teachings, work, or times **3.** held to derive from the Apostles in a direct line of succession **4.** [*often* A-] of the Pope; papal  Also **ap′os·tol′i·cal**

**Apostolic See** *R.C.Ch.* the Pope's see at Rome

**a·pos·tro·phe¹** (ə päs′trə fē) *n.* [L. < Gr. *apostrophē*, a turning away to address one person < *apo-*, from + *strephein*, to turn] words addressed to a person or thing, whether absent or present —**ap·os·troph·ic** (ap′ə sträf′ik) *adj.*

**a·pos·tro·phe²** (ə päs′trə fē) *n.* [Fr. < LL. < Gr. *apostrophos* (*prosōdia*), averted (accent): see prec.] the mark (′) used: **1.** to show the omission of a letter or letters from a word (Ex.: *it's* for *it is*) **2.** to indicate the possessive case (Ex.: *Mary's* dress, the *girls'* club) **3.** in forming some plurals, as of figures and letters (Ex.: five *6's*, dot the *i's*)

**a·pos·tro·phize** (-fīz′) *vt., vi.* **-phized′, -phiz′ing** to speak or write an apostrophe (to)

**apothecaries' measure** a system of units used in measuring liquids in pharmacy: see TABLES OF WEIGHTS AND MEASURES in the Supplements

**apothecaries' weight** a system of weights used in pharmacy: see TABLES OF WEIGHTS AND MEASURES in the Supplements

**a·poth·e·car·y** (ə päth′ə ker′ē) *n., pl.* **-car′ies** [< OFr. < ML. < L. < Gr. *apothēkē*, storehouse < *apo-*, away + *tithenai*, to put] a pharmacist, or druggist: apothecaries formerly also prescribed drugs

**ap·o·thegm** (ap′ə them′) *n.* [< Gr. < *apo-*, from + *phthengesthai*, to utter] a short, pithy saying (Ex.: "Brevity is the soul of wit") —**ap′o·theg·mat′ic** (-theg mat′ik), **ap′o·theg·mat′i·cal** *adj.*

**a·poth·e·o·sis** (ə päth′ē ō′sis, ap′ə thē′ə sis) *n., pl.* **-ses′** (-sēz′) [L. < Gr. < *apotheoun*, to deify < *apo-*, from + *theos*, a god] **1.** the act of raising a person to the status of a god; deification **2.** the glorification of a person or thing **3.** an ideal or exact type [she is the *apotheosis* of beauty]

**a·poth·e·o·size** (ə päth′ē ə sīz′, ap′ə thē′ə sīz′) *vt.* **-sized′, -siz′ing** [APOTHEOS(IS) + -IZE] **1.** to deify **2.** to glorify; idealize

**app. 1.** appendix **2.** appointed **3.** approved **4.** approximate

**ap·pal** (ə pôl′) *vt.* **-palled′, -pal′ling** *same as* APPALL

**Ap·pa·la·chi·a** (ap′ə lā′chə, -chē ə; -lach′ə) the highland region of the E U.S., including the C and S Appalachians: characterized generally by economic depression and poverty

**Ap·pa·la·chi·an Mountains** (-lā′chən, -chē ən; -lach′-ən) [< ? *Apalachee* Indians < ?] mountain system in E N. America, extending from S Quebec to N Ala.: highest peak, 6,684 ft.: also **Appalachians** —**Ap′pa·la′chi·an** *adj.*

**ap·pall** (ə pôl′) *vt.* [< OFr. *apalir* < *a-*, to + *palir*, to grow pale < L. *pallidus*, pale] to fill with horror or dismay; shock

**ap·pall·ing** (-iŋ) *adj.* causing horror, shock, or dismay —**ap·pall′ing·ly** *adv.*

**ap·pa·loo·sa** (ap′ə lōō′sə) *n.* [altered < *a palouse*, after the *Palouse* Indians of the NW U.S.] any of a sturdy breed of Western saddle horses with spotted markings on the rump and loins

**ap·pa·nage** (ap′ə nij) *n.* [< Fr. < ML. < L. *ad*, to + *panis*, bread] **1.** money, land, etc. granted by a monarch for the support of his younger children **2.** a benefit that is a perquisite or adjunct

**ap·pa·ra·tus** (ap′ə rat′əs, -rāt′-) *n., pl.* **-ra′tus, -ra′tus·es** [L., a making ready < *apparare* < *ad-*, to + *parare*, to prepare] **1.** the instruments, equipment, etc. for a specific use **2.** any complex device or system **3.** *Physiol.* a set of organs having a specific function [the digestive *apparatus*.]

**ap·par·el** (ə per′əl, -par′-) *n.* [< OFr., ult. < L. *apparare*: see prec.] clothing; attire —*vt.* **-eled** or **-elled, -el·ing** or **-el·ling 1.** to clothe; dress **2.** to adorn; bedeck

**ap·par·ent** (ə per′ənt, -par′-) *adj.* [< OFr. < L. prp. of *apparere*, APPEAR] **1.** readily seen; visible **2.** readily understood; obvious **3.** appearing to be real or true; seeming  See also HEIR APPARENT —**ap·par′ent·ly** *adv.* —**ap·par′ent·ness** *n.*

**ap·pa·ri·tion** (ap′ə rish′ən) *n.* [< OFr. < ML. < L. *apparere*: see APPEAR] **1.** anything that appears unexpectedly or remarkably **2.** a ghost; phantom **3.** the act of appearing —**ap′pa·ri′tion·al** *adj.*

**ap·peal** (ə pēl′) *vt.* [< OFr. < L. *appellare*, to accost, appeal < *ad-*, to + *pellere*: see COMPEL] to make a request to a higher court for the rehearing of (a case) —*vi.* **1.** to appeal a law case to a higher court **2.** to make an urgent request (*to* a person *for* help, sympathy, etc.) **3.** to resort (*to*) for decision, etc. **4.** to be attractive, interesting, etc. —*n.* **1.** a call upon some authority for a decision, etc. **2.** an urgent request for help, etc. **3.** a quality that arouses interest, sympathy, etc.; attraction **4.** *Law  a)* a request that a case be transferred to a higher court for rehearing or review *b)* the right to request this —**ap·peal′a·ble** *adj.* —**ap·peal′ing** *adj.* —**ap·peal′ing·ly** *adv.*

**ap·pear** (ə pir′) *vi.* [< OFr. < L. *apparere* < *ad-*, to + *parere*, to come forth] **1.** to come into sight **2.** to come into being **3.** to become understood [it *appears* he left] **4.** to seem; look **5.** to present oneself formally, as in court **6.** to come before the public [he *appeared* in Hamlet.] **7.** to be published

**ap·pear·ance** (-əns) *n.* **1.** an appearing **2.** the outward aspect of anything **3.** an outward show; pretense **4.** [*pl.*] the way things seem to be —**keep up appearances** to try to give the impression of being proper, well-off, etc. —**put in an appearance** to be present for a short time, as at a party

**ap·pease** (ə pēz′) *vt.* **-peased′, -peas′ing** [< OFr. < *a-*, to + *pais* < L. *pax*, PEACE] **1.** to make peaceful or quiet, esp. by giving in to the demands of **2.** to satisfy or relieve [water *appeases* thirst] —**ap·peas′a·ble** *adj.* —**ap·peas′er** *n.*

**ap·pease·ment** (-mənt) *n.* **1.** an appeasing or being appeased **2.** the policy of giving in to demands of a hostile power in an attempt to keep peace

**ap·pel·lant** (ə pel′ənt) *adj. Law* relating to appeals; appealing —*n.* a person who appeals, esp. to a higher court

**ap·pel·late** (-it) *adj.* [< L. pp. of *appellare*, APPEAL] *Law* relating to, or having jurisdiction to review, appeals [an *appellate* court]

**ap·pel·la·tion** (ap′ə lā′shən) *n.* [< L. < pp. of *appellare*, APPEAL] **1.** the act of calling by a name **2.** a name or title; designation

**ap·pel·la·tive** (ə pel′ə tiv) *adj.* of appellation; naming —*n.* **1.** a name or title **2.** a common noun: earlier usage —**ap·pel′la·tive·ly** *adv.*

**ap·pend** (ə pend′) *vt.* [< OFr. < L. *appendere* < *ad-*, to + *pendere*, to suspend] to attach or affix; add as a supplement or appendix

**ap·pend·age** (ə pen′dij) *n.* **1.** anything appended; adjunct **2.** *Biol.* any secondary, external organ or part, as a tree branch or a dog's tail

**ap·pend·ant, ap·pend·ent** (-dənt) *adj.* [Fr.: see APPEND] **1.** attached or added **2.** associated with as a consequence —*n.* an appendage

**ap·pen·dec·to·my** (ap′ən dek′tə mē) *n., pl.* **-mies** [APPEND(IX) + -ECTOMY] the surgical removal of the vermiform appendix

**ap·pen·di·ci·tis** (ə pen′də sīt′əs) *n.* [< ff. + -ITIS] inflammation of the vermiform appendix

**ap·pen·dix** (ə pen′diks) *n., pl.* **-dix·es, -di·ces′** (-də sēz′) [L.: see APPEND] **1.** additional material at the end of a book **2.** *Anat.* an outgrowth of an organ; esp., a small sac (**vermiform appendix**) extending from the cecum of the large intestine

**ap·per·ceive** (ap′ər sēv′) *vt.* **-ceived′, -ceiv′ing** [< OFr. < L. *ad*, to + *percipere*, PERCEIVE] *Psychol.* to assimilate and interpret (a new perception) by the help of past experience

**ap·per·cep·tion** (ap′ər sep′shən) *n.* [< Fr. < *apercevoir*, APPERCEIVE] **1.** an apperceiving **2.** the state of the mind in being conscious of its own consciousness —**ap′per·cep′tive** *adj.*

**ap·per·tain** (ap′ər tān′) *vi.* [< OFr. < L. *appertinere* < *ad-*, to + *pertinere*: see PERTAIN] to belong properly as a function, part, etc.; pertain

**ap·pe·ten·cy** (ap′ə tən sē) *n., pl.* **-cies** [< L. prp. of *appetere*: see ff.] **1.** a strong desire **2.** a propensity **3.** an affinity  Also **ap′pe·tence**

**ap·pe·tite** (ap′ə tīt′) *n.* [< ME. & OFr. < L. *appetitus*, pp. of *appetere* < *ad-*, to + *petere*, to seek] a desire or craving, esp. for food or for a specific food —**ap′pe·ti′tive** (-tīt′iv) *adj.*

**ap·pe·tiz·er** (-tī′zər) *n.* a small portion of a tasty food or a drink to stimulate the appetite at the beginning of a meal

**ap·pe·tiz·ing** (-tī′ziŋ) *adj.* **1.** stimulating the appetite **2.** savory; tasty —**ap′pe·tiz′ing·ly** *adv.*

**ap·plaud** (ə plôd′) *vt., vi.* [L. *applaudere* < *ad-*, to + *plaudere*, to clap hands] **1.** to show approval (of) by clapping the hands, cheering, etc. **2.** to praise; approve —**applaud'er** *n.*

**ap·plause** (ə plôz') *n.* approval or praise, esp. as shown by clapping hands, cheering, etc.

**ap·ple** (ap''l) *n.* [OE. *æppel*] **1.** *a)* a round, firm, fleshy, edible fruit with a red, yellow, or green skin and a seed core, growing on any of a genus of trees in temperate regions *b)* any of these trees **2.** any of various plants bearing apple-like fruits, as the May apple

**apple butter** a kind of jam made from apples stewed with spices

**ap·ple·jack** (-jak') *n.* brandy distilled from apple cider

**apple of one's eye 1.** the pupil of one's eye **2.** any person or thing that one cherishes

**ap·ple-pie order** (ap''l pī') [Colloq.] neat order

**apple polisher** [Slang] a person who curries favor by gifts, flattery, etc.

**ap·ple·sauce** (-sôs') *n.* **1.** apples cooked to a pulp in water **2.** [Slang] nonsense; hokum

**Ap·ple·seed** (ap''l sēd'), **Johnny** (nickname of *John Chapman*) 1775-1845; U.S. frontiersman who planted apple trees throughout the Midwest

**Ap·ple·ton** (ap''l tən) [after S. *Appleton*, 19th-c. Boston philanthropist] city in E Wis.: pop. 59,000

**ap·pli·ance** (ə plī'əns) *n.* a device or machine for performing a specific task, esp. one worked mechanically or by electricity

**ap·pli·ca·ble** (ap'li kə b'l) *adj.* that can be applied; appropriate; suitable —**ap'pli·ca·bil'i·ty** *n.* —**ap'pli·ca·bly** *adv.*

**ap·pli·cant** (ap'li kənt) *n.* a person who applies, as for employment, help, etc.

**ap·pli·ca·tion** (ap'lə kā'shən) *n.* **1.** the act or a way of applying or being applied **2.** anything applied, esp. a remedy **3.** a request, or the form filled out in making a request [an *application* for employment] **4.** continued effort; diligence **5.** relevance or practicality [this idea has no *application* to the case]

**ap·pli·ca·tor** (ap'lə kāt'ər) *n.* any device for applying medicine or paint, polish, etc.

**ap·pli·ca·to·ry** (-kə tôr'ē) *adj.* that can be applied or used; practical: also **ap'pli·ca'tive** (-kāt'iv)

**ap·plied** (ə plīd') *adj.* used in actual practice or to work out practical problems [applied science]

**ap·pli·qué** (ap'lə kā') *n.* [Fr. < L. *applicare:* see ff.] a decoration made of one material attached by sewing, etc. to another —*adj.* applied as such a decoration —*vt.* -**quéd'**, -**qué'ing** **1.** to decorate with appliqué **2.** to put on as appliqué

**ap·ply** (ə plī') *vt.* -**plied'**, -**ply'ing** [< OFr. < L. *applicare,* to attach to < *ad-*, to + *plicare,* to fold] **1.** to put on [to *apply* salve] **2.** to use practically [to *apply* one's knowledge] **3.** to refer to a person or thing with (an epithet, etc.) **4.** to concentrate (one's faculties); employ (oneself) diligently —*vi.* **1.** to make a formal request **2.** to be suitable or relevant [this rule *applies* to everyone] —**ap·pli'er** *n.*

APPLIQUÉ

**ap·pog·gia·tu·ra** (ə päj'ə toor'ə) *n.* [It. < *appoggiare,* to lean, ult. < L. *ad-*, to + *podium*, PODIUM] *Music* an auxiliary note like a grace note but rhythmically more prominent than the melodic note that it precedes

**ap·point** (ə point') *vt.* [< OFr. *apointer,* to make ready, ult. < L. *ad,* to + *punctum,* a POINT] **1.** to set (a date, place, etc.); decree **2.** to name for an office, etc. [to *appoint* a chairman] **3.** to furnish and arrange: now usually in *well-appointed,* etc. —**ap·point·ee** (ə poin'tē') *n.*

**ap·point·ive** (ə poin'tiv) *adj.* to which one is appointed, not elected [an *appointive* office]

**ap·point·ment** (ə point'mənt) *n.* **1.** an appointing or being appointed; specif., a naming for an office, etc. **2.** a person so named **3.** an office held in this way **4.** an arrangement to meet a person; engagement **5.** [pl.] furnishings

**Ap·po·mat·tox (Court House)** (ap'ə mat'əks) [< Algonquian tribal name] former village in C Va., where Lee surrendered to Grant (April 9, 1865), ending the Civil War

**ap·por·tion** (ə pôr'shən) *vt.* [< OFr.: see AD- & PORTION] to divide and distribute in shares according to a plan

**ap·por·tion·ment** (-mənt) *n.* **1.** an apportioning **2.** a proportional distribution, as of U.S. Representatives among the States

**ap·pose** (ə pōz') *vt.* -**posed'**, -**pos'ing** [< Fr. < L. *appositus,* pp. of *apponere* < *ad-*, near + *ponere,* to put] to put side by side, next, or near —**ap·pos'a·ble** *adj.*

**ap·po·site** (ap'ə zit) *adj.* [see prec.] appropriate; apt —**ap'po·site·ly** *adv.* —**ap'po·site·ness** *n.*

**ap·po·si·tion** (ap'ə zish'ən) *n.* **1.** an apposing or being apposed **2.** the position resulting from this **3.** *Gram. a)* the placing of a word or expression beside another so that the second explains and has the same grammatical construction as the first *b)* the relationship between such terms ["my cousin" is in *apposition* with "Mary" in "Mary, my cousin, is here"] —**ap'po·si'tion·al** *adj.*

**ap·pos·i·tive** (ə päz'ə tiv) *adj.* of or in apposition —*n.* a word, phrase, or clause in apposition —**ap·pos'i·tive·ly** *adv.*

**ap·prais·al** (ə prā'z'l) *n.* **1.** an appraising **2.** an appraised value; esp., an expert valuation as for taxation or sale Also **ap·praise'ment**

**ap·praise** (ə prāz') *vt.* -**praised'**, -**prais'ing** [< OFr. < LL. *appretiare* < L. *ad,* to + *pretium,* PRICE; Eng. sp. infl. by PRAISE] **1.** to set a price for; decide the value of, esp. officially **2.** to estimate the quantity or quality of —**ap·prais'er** *n.* —**ap·prais'ing·ly** *adv.*

**ap·pre·ci·a·ble** (ə prē'shə b'l, -shē ə-) *adj.* enough to be perceived; noticeable; measurable [an *appreciable* difference] —**ap·pre'ci·a·bly** *adv.*

**ap·pre·ci·ate** (ə prē'shē āt') *vt.* -**at'ed**, -**at'ing** [< LL. pp. of *appretiare*, APPRAISE] **1.** to think well of; enjoy; esteem **2.** to recognize gratefully **3.** to estimate the quality or worth of **4.** to be fully or sensitively aware of **5.** to raise the price of: opposed to DEPRECIATE —*vi.* to rise in value —**ap·pre'ci·a'tor** *n.* —**ap·pre'ci·a·to'ry** (-shə tôr'ē, -shē ə-) *adj.*

**ap·pre·ci·a·tion** (ə prē'shē ā'shən) *n.* **1.** an appreciating; specif., *a)* proper estimation *b)* grateful recognition, as of a favor *c)* sensitive awareness or enjoyment, as of art *d)* an evaluation **2.** a rise in value or price

**ap·pre·ci·a·tive** (ə prē'shə tiv, -shē ə-; -shē āt'iv) *adj.* feeling or showing appreciation —**ap·pre'ci·a·tive·ly** *adv.* —**ap·pre'ci·a·tive·ness** *n.*

**ap·pre·hend** (ap'rə hend') *vt.* [< L. *apprehendere,* to take hold of < *ad-*, to + *prehendere,* to seize] **1.** to take into custody; arrest **2.** to perceive or understand **3.** to anticipate with anxiety; dread

**ap·pre·hen·si·ble** (-hen'sə b'l) *adj.* that can be apprehended —**ap'pre·hen'si·bil'i·ty** *n.*

**ap·pre·hen·sion** (-hen'shən) *n.* **1.** capture or arrest **2.** perception or understanding **3.** anxiety or dread

**ap·pre·hen·sive** (-hen'siv) *adj.* **1.** perceptive **2.** uneasy or fearful about the future —**ap'pre·hen'sive·ly** *adv.* —**ap'pre·hen'sive·ness** *n.*

**ap·pren·tice** (ə pren'tis) *n.* [< OFr. < *aprendre,* to teach < L. *apprehendere,* APPREHEND] **1.** a person under legal agreement to work a specified length of time for a master craftsman in a craft or trade in return for instruction and, formerly, support **2.** a person, usually a member of a labor union, learning a trade, etc. under specified conditions **3.** any learner or beginner —*vt.* -**ticed**, -**tic·ing** to place or accept as an apprentice —**ap·pren'tice·ship'** *n.*

**ap·prise¹, ap·prize¹** (ə prīz') *vt.* -**prised'** or -**prized'**, -**pris'ing** or -**priz'ing** [< Fr. pp. of *apprendre,* to teach, inform < L. *apprehendere,* APPREHEND] to inform or notify

**ap·prize², ap·prise²** (ə prīz') *vt.* -**prized'** or -**prised'**, -**priz'ing** or -**pris'ing** same as APPRAISE

**ap·proach** (ə prōch') *vi.* [< OFr. < LL. *appropiare* < L. *ad,* to + *propius,* compar. of *prope,* near] to come closer or draw nearer —*vt.* **1.** to come near or nearer to **2.** to be similar to; approximate **3.** to bring near (to something) **4.** to make advances, a proposal, or a request to **5.** to begin dealing with [to *approach* a task] —*n.* **1.** a coming closer **2.** an approximation **3.** an advance or overture (to someone): *often used in pl.* **4.** a way of getting to a person, place, or thing; path; road; access **5.** *Golf* a shot to drive the ball from the fairway onto the putting green —**ap·proach'a·bil'i·ty** *n.* —**ap·proach'a·ble** *adj.*

**ap·pro·ba·tion** (ap'rə bā'shən) *n.* [< L. < *approbare,* APPROVE] official approval, permission, or praise —**ap'pro·ba'tive, ap·pro·ba·to·ry** (ə prō'bə tôr'ē) *adj.*

**ap·pro·pri·ate** (ə prō'prē āt'; *for adj.* -it) *vt.* -**at'ed**, -**at'ing** [< LL. pp. of *appropriare* < L. < *ad-*, to + *proprius,* one's own] **1.** to take for one's own use **2.** to take improperly, as without permission **3.** to set aside for a specific use [to *appropriate* funds for schools] —*adj.* right for the purpose; suitable —**ap·pro'pri·ate·ly** (-it lē) *adv.* —**ap·pro'pri·ate·ness** *n.* —**ap·pro'pri·a'tive** (-āt'iv) *adj.* —**ap·pro'pri·a'tor** *n.*

**ap·pro·pri·a·tion** (ə prō'prē ā'shən) *n.* **1.** an appropriating or being appropriated **2.** a thing appropriated; esp., money set aside for a specific use

**ap·prov·al** (ə prōō'v'l) *n.* **1.** an approving **2.** favorable attitude or opinion **3.** formal consent or permission —**on**

fat, āpe, cär, ten, ēven, is, bīte; gō, hôrn, tōol, look; oil, out; up, fur; get; joy; yet; chin; she; thin, then; zh, leisure; ŋ, ring; ə for *a* in *ago, e* in *agent, i* in *sanity, o* in *comply, u* in *focus;* as in *able* (ā'b'l); Fr. bàl; ë, Fr. coeur; ö, Fr. feu; Fr. mon; ô, Fr. coq; ü, Fr. duc; r, Fr. cri; H, G. ich; kh, G. doch; ‡foreign; *hypothetical; < derived from. See inside front cover.

**approval** for the customer to examine and decide whether to buy or return

**ap·prove** (ə prōōv′) *vt.* **-proved′, -prov′ing** [< OFr. < L. *approbare* < *ad-*, to + *probare*, to try, test < *probus*, good] **1.** to give one's consent to; sanction **2.** to be favorable toward; judge to be good, satisfactory, etc. —*vi.* to have a favorable opinion (*of*) —**ap·prov′er** *n.* —**ap·prov′ing·ly** *adv.*

**approx. 1.** approximate **2.** approximately

**ap·prox·i·mate** (ə präk′sə mit; *for v.* -māt′) *adj.* [< LL. pp. of *approximare* < L. *ad*, to + *proximus*, superl. of *prope*, near] **1.** near in position **2.** much like; resembling **3.** not exact, but almost so —*vt.* **-mat′ed, -mat′ing 1.** to come near to; be almost the same as *[a painting that approximates reality]* **2.** to bring near (*to* something) —*vi.* to come near; be almost the same —**ap·prox′i·mate·ly** *adv.*

**ap·prox·i·ma·tion** (ə präk′sə mā′shən) *n.* **1.** an approximating **2.** a fairly close estimate, etc.

**ap·pur·te·nance** (ə pʉr′t'n əns) *n.* [< Anglo-Fr. < OFr. < L. prp. of *appertinere*, APPERTAIN] **1.** something added to a more important thing; adjunct **2.** [*pl.*] accessories **3.** *Law* an additional, subordinate right or privilege —**ap·pur′te·nant** *adj., n.*

**a·prax·i·a** (ə prak′sē ə) *n.* [ModL. < Gr. *apraxia*, nonaction] loss of memory of how to perform complex muscular movements, resulting from brain damage —**a·prax′ic** (-prak′sik), **a·prac′tic** (-prak′tik) *adj.*

**a·près** (a′prā′; *Fr.* à pre′) *prep.* [Fr.] after: often in hyphenated compounds *[an après-ski party]*

**a·pri·cot** (ap′rə kät′, ā′prə-) *n.* [< Fr. < Port. < Ar. < MGr. < L. *praecoquus*, early matured (fruit)] **1.** a small, yellowish-orange fruit related to the peach **2.** the tree it grows on **3.** yellowish orange

**A·pril** (ā′prəl) *n.* [< OFr. < L. *apero-*, second (in the ancient Rom. calendar, the year began with March)] the fourth month of the year, having 30 days: abbrev. **Apr.**

**April fool** a victim of jokes on April Fools' Day

**April Fools' Day** April 1, All Fools' Day, when practical jokes are traditionally played

**a pri·o·ri** (ā′prē ôr′ē, ā′prī ôr′ī) [L., from something prior] **1.** from cause to effect or from a generalization to particular instances; deductive or deductively **2.** based on theory instead of on experience or experiment **3.** before examination or analysis Opposed to A POSTERIORI

**a·pron** (ā′prən, -pərn) *n.* [by faulty separation < ME. *a napron* < OFr. *naperon* < *nape*, a cloth < L. *mappa*, a napkin] **1.** a garment worn over the front part of the body, usually to protect one's clothes **2.** anything like an apron; specif., *a)* a protective covering for or edging on a structure, machine, etc. *b)* the hard-surfaced area in front of a hangar *c)* a broadened part of a driveway *d)* the part of a stage in front of the curtain —*vt.* to put an apron on or provide an apron for

**apron string** a string for tying an apron on —**tied to one's mother's** (or **wife's,** etc.) **apron strings** dominated by one's mother (or wife, etc.)

**ap·ro·pos** (ap′rə pō′) *adv.* [Fr. *à propos*, to the purpose] at the right time; opportunely —*adj.* relevant; apt —**apropos of** with regard to

**apse** (aps) *n.* [< L. < Gr. *hapsis*, an arch, fastening < *haptein*, to fasten] a semicircular or polygonal projection of a building, esp. one at the east end of a church, with a domed or vaulted roof —**ap′si·dal** (ap′sid 'l) *adj.*

**apt** (apt) *adj.* [< ME. & OFr. < L. *aptus*, pp. of *apere*, to fasten] **1.** appropriate; fitting *[an apt remark]* **2.** tending or inclined; likely *[apt to rain]* **3.** quick to learn or understand *[an apt student]* —**apt′ly** *adv.* —**apt′ness** *n.*

**apt.** *pl.* **apts.** apartment

**ap·ter·ous** (ap′tər əs) *adj.* [< Gr. < *a-*, without + *pteron*, a wing] *Biol.* having no wings; wingless

**ap·ter·yx** (ap′tər iks) *n.* [< Gr. *a-*, without + *pteryx*, wing] *same as* KIWI

**ap·ti·tude** (ap′tə tōōd′, -tyōōd′) *n.* [< ML. < L. *aptus*: see APT] **1.** the quality of being appropriate; fitness **2.** a natural tendency, inclination, or ability **3.** quickness to learn or understand

**aq·ua** (ak′wə, äk′-) *n., pl.* **aq′uas, aq′uae** (-wē) [L.] water; esp., *Pharm.* a solution of a substance in water —*adj.* [< AQUAMARINE] bluish-green

**aq·ua·cul·ture** (ak′wə kul′chər, äk′-) *n.* [prec. + CULTURE] cultivation of water plants and animals for human use —**aq′ua·cul′tur·al** *adj.*

**aqua for·tis** (fôr′təs) [L., strong water] *same as* NITRIC ACID

**Aq·ua-lung** (ak′wə luŋ′, äk′-) [AQUA + LUNG] a trademark for a kind of self-contained underwater breathing apparatus: see SCUBA —*n.* an apparatus of this kind: usually **a′qua·lung′**

**aq·ua·ma·rine** (ak′wə mə rēn′, äk′-) *n.* [L. *aqua marina*, sea water] **1.** a transparent, pale bluish-green variety of beryl, used in jewelry **2.** its color —*adj.* bluish-green

**aq·ua·naut** (ak′wə nôt′, äk′-) *n.* [AQUA + (ASTRO)NAUT] **1.** any of a group of persons using a watertight underwater chamber as a base for oceanographic experiments **2.** *same as* SKIN DIVER

**aq·ua·plane** (ak′wə plān′, äk′-) *n.* [AQUA + PLANE⁴] a board on which one rides standing up as it is pulled over water by a motorboat —*vi.* **-planed′, -plan′ing** to ride on such a board as a sport

**aqua re·gi·a** (rē′jē ə) [L., lit., kingly water: it dissolves the "noble metals," gold and platinum] a mixture of nitric and hydrochloric acids

**a·quar·ist** (ə kwer′ist) *n.* the keeper of an aquarium

**a·quar·i·um** (ə kwer′ē əm) *n., pl.* **-i·ums, -i·a** (-ē ə) [L., neut. of *aquarius*, of water < *aqua*, water] **1.** a tank, usually with glass sides, or a pool, bowl, etc., for keeping live water animals and water plants **2.** a building where such collections are exhibited

**A·quar·i·us** (ə kwer′ē əs) [L., the water carrier] **1.** a large S constellation **2.** the eleventh sign of the zodiac: see ZODIAC, illus.

**a·quat·ic** (ə kwät′ik, -kwat′-) *adj.* [< L. < *aqua*, water] **1.** growing or living in or upon water **2.** done in or upon the water *[aquatic sports]* —*n.* **1.** an aquatic plant or animal **2.** [*pl.*, *often with sing. v.*] aquatic sports or performances —**a·quat′i·cal·ly** *adv.*

**aq·ua·tint** (ak′wə tint′, äk′-) *n.* [< Fr. < It. *acqua tinta*, dyed in water] **1.** a process by which spaces rather than lines are etched with acid to produce an etching that looks like a water color **2.** such an etching —*vt.* to etch in this way

**aqua vi·tae** (vīt′ē) [L., water of life] **1.** *Alchemy* alcohol **2.** brandy or other strong liquor

**aq·ue·duct** (ak′wə dukt′) *n.* [< L. < *aqua*, water + pp. of *ducere*, to lead] **1.** a large pipe or conduit for bringing water from a distant source **2.** a bridgelike structure for carrying a water conduit or canal across a river or valley

**a·que·ous** (ā′kwē əs, ak′wē-) *adj.* [see AQUA & -OUS] **1.** of, like, or containing water; watery **2.** *Geol.* formed by the action of water

**aqueous humor** a watery fluid in the space between the cornea and the lens of the eye

**aq·ui·cul·ture** (ak′wi kul′chər, äk′-) *n.* *same as* AQUACULTURE —**aq′ui·cul′tur·al** *adj.*

**Aq·ui·la** (ak′wi lə) [L., eagle] a N constellation in the Milky Way

**aq·ui·line** (ak′wə līn′, -lən) *adj.* [< L. < *aquila*, eagle] **1.** of or like an eagle **2.** curved or hooked like an eagle's beak *[an aquiline nose]*

**A·qui·nas** (ə kwī′nəs), Saint **Thomas** 1225?–74; It. theologian & philosopher

**Aq·ui·taine** (ak′wə tān′) region of SW France

**-ar** (ər) [< ME. < OFr. < L. *-aris* or *-arius*; or directly < L.] **1.** *a suffix meaning* of, relating to, like, of the nature of *[singular, polar]* **2.** *a suffix denoting* agency *[bursar, vicar]*

**Ar** *Chem.* argon

**AR 1.** Airman Recruit **2.** Arkansas **3.** Army Regulation

**Ar. 1.** Arabic **2.** Aramaic

**ar. 1.** arrival **2.** arrives

**A.R.** Autonomous Republic

**A·ra** (ā′rə) [L., an altar] a S constellation

**Ar·ab** (ar′əb) *n.* **1.** a native or inhabitant of Arabia **2.** any of a Semitic people originating in Arabia; commonly, a Bedouin **3.** any of a breed of swift, graceful horses native to Arabia —*adj. same as* ARABIAN

**ar·a·besque** (ar′ə besk′) *n.* [Fr. < It. < *Arabo*, Arab < Ar. *'arab*: with reference to Moorish designs] **1.** an elaborate design of intertwined flowers, foliage, geometrical patterns, etc. **2.** *Ballet* a position in which one leg is extended back and the arms are extended, usually one back and one forward **3.** *Music* a light, whimsical composition —*adj.* of or done in arabesque; fantastic and elaborate

ARABESQUE

**A·ra·bi·a** (ə rā′bē ə) peninsula, largely a desert, in SW Asia: also **Arabian Peninsula**

**A·ra·bi·an** (-ən) *adj.* of Arabia or the Arabs —*n. same as* ARAB (senses 1 & 3)

**Arabian Nights, The** a collection of ancient tales from Arabia, India, Persia, etc.

**Arabian Sea** part of the Indian Ocean, between India and Arabia

**Ar·a·bic** (ar′ə bik) *adj.* **1.** of Arabia **2.** of the Arabs, their language, culture, etc. —*n.* the Semitic language of the Arabs, spoken in Arabia, Syria, Jordan, Iraq, northern Africa, etc.

**Arabic numerals** the figures 1, 2, 3, 4, 5, 6, 7, 8, 9, and the 0 (zero), orig. used in India

**ar·a·ble** (ar′ə b'l) *adj.* [Fr. < L. < *arare*, to plow] suitable for plowing and producing crops —*n.* arable land —**ar'a·bil'i·ty** *n.*

**Arab League** a confederation of a number of Arabic-speaking nations

**Ar·a·by** (ar'ə bē) [Archaic or Poet.] Arabia

**a·rach·nid** (ə rak'nid) *n.* [ModL. < Gr. *arachnē*, spider] any of a large group of arthropods, including spiders, scorpions, and mites, with four pairs of legs and with breathing tubes or lunglike sacs —**a·rach'ni·dan** (-ni dən) *adj., n.*

**Ar·a·gon** (ar'ə gän') region in NE Spain —**Ar'a·go·nese'** (-gə nēz') *adj., n., pl.* **-nese'**

**ar·ak** (ar'ək) *n. same as* ARRACK

**Ar·al Sea** (ar'əl) inland body of salt water in SW Asiatic U.S.S.R., east of the Caspian Sea: also **Lake Aral**

**Ar·am** (ar'əm) [Heb.] *Biblical name for* ancient Syria —**Ar·a·mae·an, Ar·a·me·an** (ar'ə mē'ən) *adj., n.*

**Aram.** Aramaic

**Ar·a·ma·ic** (ar'ə mā'ik) *n.* a group of northwestern Semitic languages of Biblical times, including that of Palestine

**A·rap·a·ho** (ə rap'ə hō') *n.* [< ? Crow, lit., enemy] **1.** *pl.* **-hos'**, **-ho'** any member of a tribe of Indians orig. from the area between the upper Platte and Arkansas rivers **2.** their Algonquian language

**Ar·a·rat** (ar'ə rat') mountain in E Turkey: supposed landing place of Noah's Ark (Gen. 8:4)

**ar·ba·lest, ar·ba·list** (är'bə list) *n.* [< OFr. < L. < *arcus*, a bow + *ballista*, BALLISTA] a medieval crossbow with a steel bow

**ar·bi·ter** (är'bə tər) *n.* [L., orig., one who goes to a place, a witness < *ad-*, to + *baetere*, to go] **1.** a person selected to judge a dispute; umpire; arbitrator **2.** a person fully authorized to judge or decide —**ar'bi·tral** (-trəl) *adj.* —**ar'bi·tress** *n.fem.*

**ar·bi·tra·ble** (är'bə trə b'l) *adj.* that can be arbitrated; subject to arbitration

**ar·bit·ra·ment** (är bit'rə mənt) *n.* **1.** arbitration **2.** an arbitrator's verdict or award

**ar·bi·trar·y** (är'bə trer'ē) *adj.* [< L. < *arbiter*, ARBITER] **1.** not fixed by rules but left to one's own choice **2.** based on one's whim or notion; capricious **3.** absolute; despotic —**ar'bi·trar'i·ly** *adv.* —**ar'bi·trar'i·ness** *n.*

**ar·bi·trate** (är'bə trāt') *vt.* **-trat'ed, -trat'ing** [< L. pp. of *arbitrari*, to give a decision < *arbiter*, ARBITER] **1.** to give to an arbitrator to decide **2.** to decide (a dispute) as an arbitrator —*vi.* **1.** to act as an arbitrator (*in* a dispute, *between* persons) **2.** to submit a dispute to arbitration

**ar·bi·tra·tion** (är'bə trā'shən) *n.* settlement of a dispute by someone chosen to hear both sides and come to a decision —**ar'bi·tra'tion·al** *adj.*

**ar·bi·tra·tor** (är'bə trāt'ər) *n.* a person chosen to arbitrate a dispute

**ar·bor¹** (är'bər) *n.* [< OFr. < LL. *herbarium*, HERBARIUM] a place shaded by trees, shrubs, or vines: Brit. sp. **ar'bour** —**ar'bored** *adj.*

**ar·bor²** (är'bər) *n., pl.* **ar'bo·res'** (-bə rēz') [L.] *Bot.* a tree

**ar·bor³** (är'bər) *n.* [< Fr. *arbre* < L. *arbor*, tree, beam] *Mech.* **1.** a shaft; beam **2.** a spindle; axle **3.** a bar that holds cutting tools

**Arbor Day** a tree-planting day observed in most States of the U.S., usually in April

**ar·bo·re·al** (är bôr'ē əl) *adj.* **1.** of or like a tree **2.** living in trees

**ar·bo·res·cent** (är'bə res''nt) *adj.* treelike in form or growth; branching —**ar'bo·res'cence** *n.*

**ar·bo·re·tum** (är'bə rēt'əm) *n., pl.* **-tums, -ta** (-ə) [L.] a place where many kinds of trees and shrubs are grown for exhibition or study

**ar·bor·vi·tae** (är'bər vīt'ē) *n.* [L., tree of life] any of several evergreen trees related to the cypress, with flattened sprays of scalelike leaves

**ar·bu·tus** (är byoōt'əs) *n.* [L., wild strawberry tree] **1.** a tree or shrub of the heath family, with dark-green leaves and berries like strawberries **2.** a related trailing plant with clusters of white or pink flowers

**arc** (ärk) *n.* [OFr. < L. *arcus*, a bow, arch] **1.** a bowlike curved line or object **2.** *Elec.* the band of sparks or incandescent light formed when an electric discharge is conducted from one electrode or conducting surface to another **3.** *Geom. a)* any part of a curve, esp. of a circle *b)* the angular measurement of this —*vi.* **arced** or **arcked, arc'ing** or **arck'ing 1.** to move in a curved course **2.** *Elec.* to form an arc

**Arc, Jeanne d'** (zhän dàrk') *see* JOAN OF ARC

**ARC, A.R.C.** American Red Cross

**ar·cade** (är kād') *n.* [Fr. < Pr. < ML. < L. *arcus*, arch] **1.** a covered passageway, as through a building, often with an arched roof; esp., such a passage with shops along the

sides **2.** a line of arches and their supporting columns —*vt.* **-cad'ed, -cad'ing** to make into or provide with an arcade

**Ar·ca·di·a** (är kā'dē ə) a pastoral district of ancient Greece —*n.* any place of rural peace and simplicity Also [Poet.] **Ar·ca·dy** (är'kə dē) —**Ar·ca·di·an** (är kā'dē ən) *adj., n.*

**ar·cane** (är kān') *adj.* [see ff.] **1.** hidden or secret **2.** esoteric

**ar·ca·num** (-kā'nəm) *n., pl.* **-na** (-nə), **-nums** [L., hidden < *arcere*, to shut up] a secret; mystery

**arch¹** (ärch) *n.* [< OFr. < ML. < L. *arcus*, a bow, arch] **1.** a curved structure, as of masonry, that supports the weight of material over an open space, as in a bridge, doorway, etc. **2.** the form of an arch **3.** anything shaped like an arch *[the arch of the foot]* —*vt.* **1.** to provide with an arch or arches **2.** to form into an arch —*vi.* **1.** to form an arch **2.** to span as an arch

**arch²** (ärch) *adj.* [< ff.] **1.** main; chief **2.** gaily mischievous; pert —**arch'ly** *adv.* —**arch'ness** *n.*

ARCHES (A, semicircular; B, horseshoe; C, pointed)

**arch-** [< OE. < L. < Gr. *archos*, ruler] *a prefix meaning* main, chief *[archbishop, archduke]*

**-arch** (ärk; *occas.* ərk) [< Gr. *archos*, ruler] *a suffix meaning* ruler *[matriarch]*

**arch.** **1.** archaic **2.** archaism **3.** archipelago **4.** architect **5.** architectural **6.** architecture

**ar·chae·ol·o·gy** (är'kē äl'ə jē) *n.* [< Gr. *archaios*, ancient < *archē*, the beginning + -LOGY] the scientific study of the life and culture of ancient peoples, as by excavation of ancient cities, artifacts, etc. —**ar'chae·o·log'i·cal** (-ə läj'i k'l) *adj.* —**ar'chae·o·log'i·cal·ly** *adv.* —**ar'chae·ol'o·gist** *n.*

**ar·cha·ic** (är kā'ik) *adj.* [< Gr. < *archaios*, ancient] **1.** ancient **2.** antiquated; old-fashioned **3.** that is now seldom used except in poetry, church ritual, etc., as the word *thou* —**ar·cha'i·cal·ly** *adv.*

**ar·cha·ism** (är'kē iz'm, -kā-) *n.* **1.** the use or imitation of archaic words, technique, etc. **2.** an archaic word, usage, etc. —**ar'cha·ist** *n.* —**ar'cha·is'tic** *adj.* —**ar'cha·is'ti·cal·ly** *adv.*

**arch·an·gel** (ärk'ān'j'l) *n.* a chief angel

**Arch·an·gel** (ärk'ān'j'l) seaport in NW R.S.F.S.R., on the White Sea: pop. 313,000

**arch·bish·op** (ärch'bish'əp) *n.* a chief bishop, who presides over an archbishopric or archdiocese

**arch·bish·op·ric** (-bish'ə prik') *n.* the office, rank, term, or church district of an archbishop

**arch·dea·con** (ärch'dē'k'n) *n.* [see ARCH- & DEACON] a church official ranking just below a bishop, as in the Anglican Church —**arch'dea'con·ry** *n., pl.* **-ries**

**arch·di·o·cese** (-dī'ə sis, -sēs') *n.* the diocese of an archbishop —**arch'di·oc'e·san** (-dī äs'ə sən) *adj.*

**arch·du·cal** (-dōōk''l, -dyōōk''l) *adj.* of an archduke or archduchy

**arch·duch·ess** (-duch'is) *n.* **1.** the wife or widow of an archduke **2.** a princess of the former Austrian royal family

**arch·duch·y** (-duch'ē) *n., pl.* **-ies** the territory of an archduke or of an archduchess

**arch·duke** (-dōōk', -dyōōk') *n.* a chief duke, esp. a prince of the former Austrian royal family

**ar·che·go·ni·um** (är'kə gō'nē əm) *n., pl.* **-ni·a** (-nē ə) [ModL. < Gr. *archos*, first + *gonos*, offspring] the flask-shaped female reproductive organ in mosses, ferns, etc. —**ar'che·go'ni·al** *adj.*

**arch·en·e·my** (ärch'en'ə mē) *n., pl.* **-mies** a chief enemy —**the archenemy** Satan

**ar·che·ol·o·gy** (är'kē äl'ə jē) *n. same as* ARCHAEOLOGY

**arch·er** (är'chər) *n.* [< ME. & OFr. < VL. < L. < *arcus*, bow] a person who shoots with bow and arrow; bowman —[A-] the constellation Sagittarius

**arch·er·y** (är'chər ē) *n.* **1.** the practice, art, or sport of shooting with bow and arrow **2.** an archer's equipment **3.** archers collectively

**ar·che·type** (är'kə tīp') *n.* [< L. < Gr. < *archos*, first + *typos*: see TYPE, *n.*] **1.** the original pattern or model of something; prototype **2.** a perfect example of a type or group —**ar'che·typ'al** (-tīp'əl), **ar'che·typ'i·cal** (-tīp'i-k'l) *adj.*

**arch·fiend** (ärch'fēnd') *n.* a chief fiend —**the archfiend** Satan

**Ar·chi·bald** (är'chə bôld') [of Gmc. origin, prob. nobly bold] a masculine name

---

fat, āpe, cär; ten, ēven; is, bīte; gō, hôrn, tōōl, look; oil, out; up, fur; get; joy; yet; chin; she; thin, then; zh, leisure; ŋ, ring; ə for *a* in *ago, e* in *agent, i* in *sanity, o* in *comply, u* in *focus*; ' as in *able* (ā'b'l); Fr. bàl; ë, Fr. coeur; ö, Fr. feu; Fr. mon; ô, Fr. coq; ü, Fr. duc; r, Fr. cri; H, G. ich; kh, G. doch; ‡foreign; *hypothetical; < derived from. See inside front cover.

**ar·chi·di·ac·o·nal** (är′kə dī ak′ə n′l) *adj.* of an archdeacon or archdeaconry —**ar′chi·di·ac′o·nate** (-nit) *n.*

**ar·chi·e·pis·co·pal** (är′kē ə pis′kə p′l) *adj.* of an archbishop or archbishopric —**ar′chi·e·pis′co·pate** (-pət, -pāt′) *n.*

**Ar·chi·me·des** (är′kə mē′dēz) 287?–212 B.C.; Gr. mathematician & inventor —**Ar′chi·me′de·an** (-mē′dē ən, -midē′ən) *adj.*

**ar·chi·pel·a·go** (är′kə pel′ə gō′) *n., pl.* -goes′, -gos′ [< It. < MGr. < Gr. *archi*-, chief + *pelagos*, sea] **1.** a sea with many islands **2.** such a group of islands —**ar′chi·pe·lag′ic** (-pə laj′ik) *adj.*

**ar·chi·tect** (är′kə tekt′) *n.* [< L. < Gr. < *archi*-, chief + *tektōn*, carpenter] **1.** a person whose profession is designing plans for buildings, bridges, etc. and generally administering construction **2.** any planner, builder, or creator

**ar·chi·tec·ton·ic** (är′kə tek tän′ik) *adj.* [see prec.] **1.** of architecture or architectural methods, etc. **2.** having structure or design like that of architecture —*n.* same as ARCHITECTONICS

**ar·chi·tec·ton·ics** (-tän′iks) *n.pl.* [with sing. v.] **1.** the science of architecture **2.** structural design, as of a symphony

**ar·chi·tec·ture** (är′kə tek′chər) *n.* [Fr. < L. *architectura*: see ARCHITECT] **1.** the science, art, or profession of designing and constructing buildings, etc. **2.** a building, or buildings collectively **3.** a style of construction *[modern architecture]* **4.** design and construction **5.** any framework, system, etc. —**ar′chi·tec′tur·al** *adj.* —**ar′chi·tec′-tur·al·ly** *adv.*

**ar·chi·trave** (är′kə trāv′) *n.* [Fr. < It. < L. *archi*-, first + *trabs*, a beam] *Archit.* **1.** the lowest part of an entablature, a beam resting directly on the tops of the columns **2.** the molding around a doorway, window, etc.

**ar·chives** (är′kīvz) *n.pl.* [Fr. < L. < Gr. *archeion*, town hall < *archē*, the beginning] **1.** a place where public records, documents, etc. are kept **2.** the public records, documents, etc. kept there —**ar·chi·val** (är′kī′v′l, är kī′v′l) *adj.*

**ar·chi·vist** (är′kə vist, är′kī′vist) *n.* a person having charge of archives

**ar·chon** (är′kän′) *n.* [< Gr. < *archein*, to be first, rule] **1.** one of the nine chief magistrates of ancient Athens **2.** a ruler

**arch·priest** (ärch′prēst′) *n.* a chief priest

**arch·way** (ärch′wā′) *n.* a passage under an arch

**-ar·chy** (är kē, ər kē) [< Gr. < *archein*, to rule] *a suffix meaning* a ruling, or that which is ruled *[matriarchy, monarchy]*

**arc lamp** a lamp in which the light is produced by an arc between electrodes: also **arc light**

**arc·tic** (ärk′tik, är′-) *adj.* [< OFr. < L. < Gr. *arktikos*, lit., of the (constellation of the) Bear (Gr. *arktos*), northern] **1.** of, characteristic of, or near the North Pole or the region around it **2.** very cold —**the Arctic** the region around the North Pole

**Arctic Circle** [also a- c-] an imaginary circle parallel to the equator, 66°33′ north of it

**Arctic Ocean** ocean surrounding the North Pole, north of the Arctic Circle

**arc·tics** (ärk′tiks, ärk′-) *n.pl.* [< ARCTIC] high, warm, waterproof overshoes, usually with buckles

**Arc·tu·rus** (ärk toor′əs, -tyoor′-) [L. < Gr. *Arktouros* < *arktos*, a bear + *ouros*, a guard] a giant red star of the first magnitude, the brightest in the constellation Boötes

**arc welding** the welding of metal parts using the extreme heat of an electric arc

**-ard** (ərd) [OFr. < MHG. *hart*, bold] *a suffix denoting* one who carries an action too far or has too much of some quality *[sluggard, drunkard]*

**ar·dent** (är′d′nt) *adj.* [< L. prp. of *ardere*, to burn] **1.** warm or intense in feeling; passionate **2.** intensely enthusiastic or devoted; zealous **3.** glowing; radiant **4.** burning; aflame —**ar′den·cy** (-d′n sē) *n.* —**ar′dent·ly** *adv.*

**ar·dor** (är′dər) *n.* [< OFr. < L. < *ardere*, to burn] **1.** emotional warmth; passion **2.** enthusiasm; zeal **3.** intense heat; fire

**ar·dour** (är′dər) *n. Brit. sp. of* ARDOR

**ar·du·ous** (är′joo wəs) *adj.* [L. *arduus*, steep] **1.** difficult to do; laborious **2.** using much energy; strenuous **3.** steep; hard to climb —**ar′du·ous·ly** *adv.* —**ar′du·ous·ness** *n.*

**are**[1] (är; *unstressed* ər) [OE. (Northumbrian) *aron*] *pl. & 2d pers. sing., pres. indic., of* BE

**are**[2] (er, är) *n.* [Fr. < L. *area*: see ff.] a unit of surface measure in the metric system, equal to 100 square meters (119.6 sq. yd.)

**ar·e·a** (er′ē ə) *n.* [L., vacant place, courtyard] **1.** orig., a level surface **2.** a part of the earth's surface; region **3.** the size of a surface, in square units **4.** a yard of a building **5.** a particular part of a house, city, etc. *[dining area, slum area]* **6.** a part of any surface **7.** scope or extent, as of an operation —**ar′e·al** *adj.*

**ar·e·a·way** (-wā′) *n.* **1.** a sunken yard leading into a cellar **2.** a passage between buildings

**a·re·na** (ə rē′nə) *n.* [L., sand, sandy place, arena] **1.** the central part of an ancient Roman amphitheater, for gladiatorial contests **2.** any place like this **3.** any sphere of struggle

**arena theater** a theater having a central stage without a proscenium, surrounded by seats

**aren't** (ärnt) are not: also, occas., a substitute for a contraction of *am not* in questions: see also AIN'T

**a·re·o·la** (ə rē′ə lə) *n., pl.* -lae′ (-lē′), -las [L., dim. of *area*: see AREA] **1.** a small space, as between the veins of a leaf **2.** *Anat.* a small, surrounding area, as the dark ring around a nipple Also **ar·e·ole** (ar′ē ōl′) —**a·re′o·lar** (-lər) *adj.* —**a·re′o·late** (-lit) *adj.* —**ar·e·o·la·tion** (ar′ē-ə lā′shən, ə rē′ə-) *n.*

**Ar·e·op·a·gus** (ar′ē äp′ə gəs) [L. < Gr. < *Areios*, of Ares + *pagos*, hill] a rocky hill northwest of the Acropolis in Athens —*n.* the high court of justice that met there

**Ar·es** (er′ēz) *Gr. Myth.* the god of war: identified with the Roman god Mars

**ar·ga·li** (är′gə lē) *n., pl.* -lis, -li: see PLURAL, II, D, 1 [Mongol.] a wild sheep of Asia, with large, curved horns

**ar·gent** (är′jənt) *n.* [Fr. < L. *argentum*, silver] [Archaic or Poet.] silver —*adj.* [Poet.] of silver: also **ar·gen′tal** (-jen′t′l)

**ar·gen·tif·er·ous** (är′jən tif′ər-əs) *adj.* [see prec. & -FEROUS] containing silver, as ore

**Ar·gen·ti·na** (är′jən tē′nə) country in S S. America: 1,084,120 sq. mi.; pop. 23,983,000; cap. Buenos Aires —**Ar′gen·tine**′ (-tēn′, -tīn′), **Ar′gen·tin′e·an** (-tin′ē ən) *adj., n.*

ARGALI (3–4 ft. high at shoulder)

**ar·gen·tine** (är′jən tin, -tīn′, -tēn′) *adj.* of or like silver —*n.* silver or a silvery substance

**ar·gil·la·ceous** (är′jə lā′shəs) *adj.* [< L. *argilla*, clay < Gr. < *argos*, white] like or containing clay

**Ar·give** (är′gīv, -jiv) *adj., n.* Greek

**Ar·go** (är′gō) *Gr. Myth.* the ship on which Jason sailed to find the Golden Fleece

**ar·gon** (är′gän) *n.* [Gr., inert < *a-*, without + *ergon*, work] one of the chemical elements, an inert, odorless, colorless gas forming nearly one percent of the atmosphere: it is used in radio tubes, welding, etc.: symbol, Ar; at. wt., 39.948; at. no., 18

**Ar·go·naut** (är′gə nôt′) *n.* [< L. < Gr. < ARGO + *nautēs*, sailor] *Gr. Myth.* any of the men who sailed with Jason to search for the Golden Fleece

**Ar·gonne** (är′gän; *Fr.* är gôn′) wooded region in NE France, near the Belgian border

**ar·go·sy** (är′gə sē) *n., pl.* -sies [earlier *ragusy* < It. (*nave*) *Ragusea*, (vessel of) Ragusa, ancient Dalmatian port; sp. infl. by ARGO] [Poet.] **1.** a large ship **2.** a fleet of such ships

**ar·got** (är′gō, -gət) *n.* [Fr., orig. (in thieves' jargon), the company of beggars < *argoter*, to beg, prob. < *ergot*, claw] the specialized vocabulary and idioms of a particular group, as the secret jargon of criminals

**ar·gue** (är′gyōō) *vi.* -gued, -gu·ing [< OFr. < L. *argutare*, to prattle, freq. of *arguere*, to prove] **1.** to give reasons (*for* or *against* a proposal, etc.) **2.** to have a disagreement; quarrel —*vt.* **1.** to give reasons for and against; debate **2.** to try to prove by giving reasons; contend **3.** to give evidence of; indicate **4.** to persuade (*into* or *out of* an opinion, etc.) by giving reasons —**ar′gu·a·ble** *adj.* —**ar′-gu·a·bly** *adv.* —**ar′gu·er** *n.*

**ar·gu·fy** (är′gyə fī′) *vt., vi.* -fied′, -fy′ing [< ARGU(E) + -FY] [Colloq. or Dial.] to argue, esp. merely for the sake of arguing

**ar·gu·ment** (är′gyə mənt) *n.* **1.** a reason or reasons offered for or against something **2.** the offering of such reasons; reasoning **3.** discussion in which there is disagreement; dispute; debate **4.** a short statement of subject matter; summary

**ar·gu·men·ta·tion** (är′gyə men tā′shən) *n.* **1.** the process of arguing **2.** debate; discussion

**ar·gu·men·ta·tive** (-men′tə tiv) *adj.* **1.** controversial **2.** apt to argue Also **ar′gu·men′tive** —**ar′gu·men′ta·tive·ly** *adv.* —**ar′gu·men′ta·tive·ness** *n.*

**Ar·gus** (är′gəs) [L. < Gr. < *argos*, bright] *Gr. Myth.* a giant with a hundred eyes, killed by Hermes —*n.* an alert watchman

**Ar·gus-eyed** (-īd′) *adj.* keenly observant; vigilant

**ar·gyle** (är′gīl) *adj.* [orig. a clan tartan of *Argyll*, county of Scotland] knitted or woven in a pattern of diamond-shaped figures of different colors —*n.* [*pl.*] argyle socks

**a·ri·a** (är′ē ə, er′-) *n.* [It. < L. *aer*, AIR] an air or melody in an opera, cantata, or oratorio, esp. for solo voice with instrumental accompaniment

**-a·ri·a** (er′ē ə, ā′rē ə) [ModL. < L. *-arius*] *Biol.* a plural suffix *used in* names of taxonomic groups

**Ar·i·ad·ne** (ar′ē ad′nē) *Gr. Myth.* King Minos' daughter, who gave Theseus the thread by which he found his way out of the Labyrinth

**Ar·i·an¹** (er′ē ən, ar′-) *n., adj. same as* ARYAN

**Ar·i·an²** (er′ē ən, ar′-) *adj.* of Arius or Arianism —*n.* a believer in Arianism

**-ar·i·an** (er′ē ən, ar′-) [L. *-arius* + *-anus*] a suffix denoting: **1.** age [*octogenarian*] **2.** sect [*Unitarian*] **3.** social belief [*utilitarian*] **4.** occupation [*antiquarian*]

**Ar·i·an·ism** (er′ē ə niz′m, ar′-) *n.* the doctrines of Arius, who taught that Jesus was not of the same substance as God

**ar·id** (ar′id, er′-) *adj.* [< L. < *arere,* to be dry] **1.** dry and barren **2.** not interesting; dull —**a·rid·i·ty** (ə rid′ə tē), ar′·id·ness *n.* —**ar′id·ly** *adv.*

**Ar·i·el** (er′ē əl, ar′-) in Shakespeare's *The Tempest,* an airy spirit who is Prospero's servant

**Ar·i·es** (er′ēz, ar′-; -i ēz′) [L., the Ram] **1.** a N constellation **2.** the first sign of the zodiac: see ZODIAC, illus.

**a·right** (ə rīt′) *adv.* in a right way; correctly

**ar·il** (ar′il, er′-) *n.* [ModL. *arillus* < ML., dried grape] an additional covering that forms on certain seeds after fertilization —**ar′il·late′** (-ə lāt′) *adj.*

**a·ri·o·so** (är′ē ō′sō) *adj., adv.* [It. < *aria,* ARIA] like an aria —*n.* an arioso composition

**a·rise** (ə rīz′) *vi.* **a·rose′, a·ris′en** (-riz′'n), **a·ris′ing** [OE. < *a-,* out + *risan,* to rise] **1.** to get up, as from sleeping or sitting; rise **2.** to move upward; ascend **3.** to come into being; originate **4.** to result or spring (*from* something)

**Ar·is·ti·des** (ar′ə stī′dēz) 530?–468? B.C.; Athenian general & statesman

**ar·is·toc·ra·cy** (ar′ə stäk′rə sē) *n., pl.* **-cies** [< L. < Gr. < *aristos,* best + *kratein,* to rule] **1.** orig., government by the best citizens **2.** government by a privileged minority, usually of inherited wealth and social position **3.** a country with such government **4.** a privileged ruling class; nobility **5.** those considered the best in some way

**a·ris·to·crat** (ə ris′tə krat′, ar′is-) *n.* **1.** a member of the aristocracy; nobleman **2.** a person with the manners, beliefs, etc. of the upper class **3.** a supporter of aristocracy in government

**a·ris·to·crat·ic** (ə ris′tə krat′ik, ar′is-) *adj.* **1.** of or favoring aristocracy in government **2.** of an aristocracy or upper class **3.** like an aristocrat —**a·ris′to·crat′i·cal·ly** *adv.*

**Ar·is·toph·a·nes** (ar′ə stäf′ə nēz′) 448?–380? B.C.; Gr. writer of satirical comedies

**Ar·is·to·te·li·an** (ar′is tə tēl′yən, -tē′lē ən) *adj.* of Aristotle or his philosophy —*n.* **1.** a follower of Aristotle **2.** a person who is empirical or practical in his thinking —**Ar′·is·to·te′li·an·ism** *n.*

**Ar·is·tot·le** (ar′ə stät′'l) 384–322 B.C.; Gr. philosopher, pupil of Plato

**a·rith·me·tic** (ə rith′mə tik; *for adj.* ar′ith met′ik) *n.* [OFr. < L. < Gr. < *arithmein,* to count < *arithmos,* number] **1.** the science of computing by positive, real numbers, specif. by adding, subtracting, multiplying, and dividing **2.** skill in this science —*adj.* of or using arithmetic: also **ar′·ith·met′i·cal** —**ar′ith·met′i·cal·ly** *adv.*

**a·rith·me·ti·cian** (ar′ith mə tish′ən, ə rith′mə-) *n.* a person skilled in arithmetic

**arithmetic mean** the average obtained by dividing a sum by the number of its addends

**arithmetic progression** a sequence of terms each of which, after the first, is derived by adding to the preceding one a constant quantity (Ex.: 5, 9, 13)

**A·ri·us** (ə rī′əs, er′ē əs) 256?–336 A.D.: Christian theologian of Alexandria: see ARIANISM

**Ar·i·zo·na** (ar′ə zō′nə) [AmSp. < AmInd. *Arizonac,* "little springs"] State of the SW U.S., on the Mexican border: 113,909 sq. mi.; pop. 2,718,000; cap. Phoenix: abbrev. **Ariz., AZ** —**Ar′i·zo′nan, Ar′i·zo′ni·an** (-nē ən) *adj., n.*

**ark** (ärk) *n.* [< OE. *earc* < L. *arca* < *arcere,* to enclose] **1.** *Bible* the huge boat in which Noah, his family, and two of every kind of creature survived the Flood: Gen. 6–9 **2.** formerly, a large, flat-bottomed river boat **3.** a place of refuge **4.** *same as* ARK OF THE COVENANT

**Ar·kan·sas** (är′k'n sô′; *for 2, also* är kan′zəs) [< Fr. < Siouan tribal name] **1.** State of the SC U.S.: 53,104 sq. mi.; pop. 2,286,000; cap. Little Rock: abbrev. **Ark., AR 2.** river flowing from Colorado southeast into the Mississippi: 1,450 mi. —**Ar·kan′san** (-kan′z'n) *adj., n.*

**ark of the covenant** *Bible* the chest containing the stone tablets inscribed with the Ten Commandments: Ex. 25:10

**Ark·wright** (ärk′rīt′), Sir **Richard** 1732–92; Eng. inventor of a cotton-spinning machine

**Ar·ling·ton** (är′liŋ tən) [orig. after a place name in England] **1.** urban county in Va., near Washington, D.C.: pop. 153,000: site of a national cemetery (**Arlington National Cemetery**) **2.** city in NE Tex.: suburb of Fort Worth: pop. 160,000

**arm¹** (ärm) *n.* [OE. *earm*] **1.** an upper limb of the human body **2.** anything like this in structure or function; esp., *a*) the forelimb of a vertebrate animal *b*) any limb of an octopus, starfish, etc. *c*) a branch of a tree **3.** anything commonly in contact with the human arm; esp., *a*) a sleeve *b*) a support for the arm, as on a chair **4.** anything armlike, esp. in being connected with something larger [an *arm* of the sea] **5.** power to seize, control, etc. [the *arm* of the law] —**arm in arm** with arms interlocked —**at arm's length** at a distance; aloof —**with open arms** in a warm and friendly way —**arm′less** *adj.* —**arm′like′** *adj.*

**arm²** (ärm) *n.* [< OFr. *armes,* pl. < L. *arma,* implements, weapons] **1.** any weapon: *usually used in pl.:* see also SMALL ARMS **2.** [*pl.*] warfare; fighting **3.** [*pl.*] heraldic insignia: see COAT OF ARMS **4.** any combatant branch of the military forces —*vt.* **1.** to provide with weapons, tools, etc. **2.** to prepare for or against attack **3.** to equip with needed parts —*vi.* to equip oneself with weapons, etc., esp. for war —**bear arms** to serve in the armed forces —**take up arms 1.** to go to war **2.** to enter a dispute —**to arms!** get ready to fight! —**under arms** equipped with weapons —**up in arms 1.** prepared to fight **2.** indignant

**ar·ma·da** (är mä′də, -mā′-) *n.* [Sp. < L. *armata,* fem. pp. of *armare,* to arm < *arma:* see ARM²] **1.** *a*) a fleet of warships *b*) [A-] such a fleet sent against England by Spain in 1588 but destroyed: also **Spanish Armada 2.** a fleet of military aircraft

**ar·ma·dil·lo** (är′mə dil′ō) *n., pl.* **-los** [Sp., dim. of *armado:* see prec.] any of a family of burrowing, chiefly nocturnal mammals of Texas and Central and South America, having an armorlike covering of bony plates

**Ar·ma·ged·don** (är′mə ged′'n) *Bible* the place described as the scene of the last, deciding battle between good and evil: Rev. 16:16

**ar·ma·ment** (är′mə mənt) *n.* [< L. < *armare:* see ARMADA] **1.** [*often pl.*] all the military forces and equipment of a nation **2.** a combat force **3.** all the military equipment of a warship, fortification, etc. **4.** an arming or being armed for war **5.** anything serving to protect or defend

**ar·ma·ture** (är′mə chər) *n.* [< L. *armatura,* arms, equipment < pp. of *armare:* see ARMADA] **1.** any protective covering; armor **2.** any part of an animal useful for offense or defense **3.** a soft iron bar placed across the poles of a magnet **4.** *a*) the laminated iron core wound around with wire, usually a revolving part, in a generator or motor *b*) the vibrating part in an electric relay, bell, etc. **5.** *Sculpture* a framework for supporting the clay, etc. in modeling

**arm·chair** (ärm′cher′) *n.* a chair with supports at the sides for one's arms or elbows

**armed** (ärmd) *adj.* **1.** provided with arms (weapons), armor, etc. **2.** having arms (limbs) of a specified kind [*long-armed*]

**armed forces** all the military, naval, and air forces of a country or group of countries

**Ar·me·ni·a** (är mē′nē ə, -mēn′yə) **1.** former kingdom of SW Asia, south of the Caucasus Mts. **2.** republic of the U.S.S.R., including most of this region: 11,500 sq. mi.; pop. 2,300,000; cap. Yerevan: in full, **Armenian Soviet Socialist Republic** —**Ar·me′ni·an** *adj., n.*

**arm·ful** (ärm′fool) *n., pl.* **-fuls** as much as the arms or one arm can hold

**arm·hole** (-hōl′) *n.* an opening for the arm in a garment

**Ar·min·i·us, Ja·co·bus** (jə kō′bəs är min′ē əs) 1560–1609; Du. theologian, whose doctrines (**Ar·min′i·an·ism**) stress man's free will as against Calvinistic predestination —**Ar·min′i·an** *adj., n.*

**ar·mi·stice** (är′mə stis) *n.* [Fr. < L. *arma,* arms + *sistere,* to cause to stand] a temporary stopping of warfare by mutual agreement; truce

**Armistice Day** November 11, the anniversary of the armistice of World War I in 1918: see VETERANS DAY

**arm·let** (ärm′lit) *n.* **1.** a band worn for ornament around the upper arm **2.** a small inlet of the sea

**arm·lock** (-läk′) *n. Wrestling* a hold in which one contestant's arm is locked by the other's arm

**ar·moire** (är mwär′) *n.* [Fr. < OFr. < L. *armarium,* chest for arms] a large cupboard or clothespress

**ar·mor** (är′mər) *n.* [< OFr. < L. *armatura:* see ARMATURE] **1.** covering worn to protect the body against weapons **2.** any defensive or protective covering, as the shell of a turtle or the metal plating on warships **3.** armored forces, as tanks **4.** a quality, etc. serving as a defense difficult to penetrate —*vt.,vi.* to put armor on

**ar·mor·bear·er** (-ber′ər) *n.* a person who carried the armor or weapons of a warrior

**ar·mored** (är′mərd) *adj.* **1.** covered with armor **2.** equipped with tanks and other armored vehicles

**ar·mor·er** (är′mər ər) *n.* **1.** formerly, one who made or repaired armor **2.** a maker of firearms **3.** *Mil.* an enlisted man in charge of small arms

**ar·mo·ri·al** (är môr′ē əl) *adj.* of coats of arms; heraldic

**armor plate** a protective covering of steel plates, as on a tank —**ar′mor-plat′ed** *adj.*

**ar·mor·y** (är′mər ē) *n., pl.* **-mor·ies** [< OFr. < *arme:* see ARM²] **1.** an arsenal **2.** a building housing the drill hall and offices of a National Guard unit **3.** a place where firearms are made

**ar·mour** (är′mər) *n., vi., vt. Brit. sp. of* ARMOR

**arm·pit** (ärm′pit′) *n.* the hollow under the arm where it joins the shoulder; axilla

**arm·rest** (-rest′) *n.* a support for one's arm

**ar·my** (är′mē) *n., pl.* **-mies** [< OFr. < L. *armata:* see ARMADA] **1.** a large, organized body of soldiers for waging war **2.** a military unit of two or more corps **3.** [*often* A-] a large organization of persons for a specific cause [the Salvation *Army*] **4.** any large number of persons, animals, etc.

**army ant** any of certain ants that travel in large groups and devour insects and animals

**army worm** any of the larvae of certain moths that travel in large groups, ruining crops

**Arn·hem** (ärn′hem) city on the Rhine, in E Netherlands: pop. 135,000

**ar·ni·ca** (är′ni kə) *n.* [ModL.] **1.** any of a number of plants bearing bright yellow flowers **2.** a preparation made from certain of these plants, formerly used for treating sprains, bruises, etc.

**Ar·nold** (är′nəld) [< G. < Gmc. bases *aran*, eagle + *wald*, power] **1.** a masculine name **2. Benedict,** 1741–1801; Am. Revolutionary general who became a traitor **3. Matthew,** 1822–88; Eng. poet, essayist, & critic

**a·roint** (ə roint′) *vt.* [< ?] [Obs.] begone!: used in the imperative, usually followed by *thee*

**a·ro·ma** (ə rō′mə) *n.* [LL. < Gr. *arōma*, sweet spice] **1.** a pleasant, often spicy odor; fragrance, as of a plant, cooking, etc. **2.** a characteristic quality or atmosphere

**ar·o·mat·ic** (ar′ə mat′ik) *adj.* **1.** of or having an aroma **2.** *Chem.* containing one or more benzene rings in the molecule —*n.* an aromatic plant, substance, or chemical —**ar′o·mat′i·cal·ly** *adv.*

**a·ro·ma·tize** (ə rō′mə tīz′) *vt.* **-tized′, -tiz′ing** to make aromatic —**a·ro′ma·ti·za′tion** *n.*

**a·rose** (ə rōz′) *pt. of* ARISE

**a·round** (ə round′) *adv.* [ME. < *a-*, on + *round*] **1.** round; esp., *a*) in a circle; along a circular course *b*) in or through a course or circuit *c*) in every direction *d*) in circumference *e*) in or to the opposite direction, belief, etc. *f*) in various places *g*) in sequence [his turn came *around*] *h*) throughout **2.** [Colloq.] nearby [stay *around*] **3.** [Colloq.] to a (specified) place [come *around* to see us] —*prep.* **1.** round; esp., *a*) so as to encircle or envelop *b*) on the border of *c*) on all sides of *d*) in various places in or on *e*) so as to rotate about (a center) **2.** close to; about [*around* 1890] —*adj.* [*used only in the predicate*] **1.** on the move; about [he's up and *around* now] **2.** existing [when dinosaurs were *around*] Cf. ROUND —**have been around** [Colloq.] to have had wide experience; be sophisticated See also phrases under BRING, COME, GET, etc.

**a·rouse** (ə rouz′) *vt.* **a·roused′, a·rous′ing** [A-² (sense 1) + ROUSE] **1.** to awaken, as from sleep **2.** to stir, as to action **3.** to bring forth or work up (some action or feeling); excite —*vi.* to become aroused —**a·rous′al** *n.*

**ar·peg·gio** (är pej′ō, -pej′ē ō) *n., pl.* **-gios** [It. < *arpeggiare*, to play on a harp < *arpa*, a harp] **1.** the playing of the notes of a chord in quick succession instead of simultaneously **2.** a chord so played

**ar·que·bus** (är′kwə bəs) *n. same as* HARQUEBUS

**arr. 1.** arranged **2.** arrival

**ar·rack** (ar′ək) *n.* [< Fr. < Ar. *'araq*, sweat, liquor] in the Orient, strong alcoholic drink, esp. that made from rice, molasses, or coconut milk

**ar·raign** (ə rān′) *vt.* [< OFr. < ML. < L. *ad*, to + *ratio*, reason] **1.** to bring before a law court to hear and answer charges **2.** to call to account; accuse —**ar·raign′er** *n.* —**ar·raign′ment** *n.*

**ar·range** (ə rānj′) *vt.* **-ranged′, -rang′ing** [< OFr. < *a-*, to + *renc*, rank: see RANGE] **1.** to put in the correct or suitable order **2.** to classify **3.** to prepare or plan **4.** to settle or adjust (matters) **5.** *Music* to adapt (a composition) to other instruments or voices than those for which it was written, or to the style of a certain band or orchestra —*vi.* **1.** to come to an agreement (*with* a person, *about* a thing) **2.** to make plans **3.** *Music* to write arrangements —**ar·range′a·ble** *adj.* —**ar·rang′er** *n.*

**ar·range·ment** (-mənt) *n.* **1.** an arranging or being arranged **2.** the way in which something is arranged **3.** something made by arranging parts in a particular way **4.** [*usually pl.*] a plan or preparation [*arrangements* for the party] **5.** a settlement or adjustment **6.** *Music* an adaptation of a composition for other instruments, voices, etc.

**ar·rant** (ar′ənt) *adj.* [var. of ERRANT] that is plainly such; out-and-out [an *arrant* fool] —**ar′rant·ly** *adv.*

**ar·ras** (ar′əs) *n.* [after *Arras*, city in France, where it was made] **1.** an elaborate kind of tapestry **2.** a wall hanging, esp. of tapestry

**ar·ray** (ə rā′) *vt.* [< OFr. < ML. *arredare*, to put in order < *ad-*, to + Gmc. base *raid-*, order] **1.** to put in the proper order; marshal (troops, etc.) **2.** to dress in finery —*n.* **1.** an orderly grouping, esp. of troops **2.** a military force so grouped **3.** an impressive display of persons or things **4.** fine clothes —**ar·ray′al** *n.* —**ar·ray′er** *n.*

**ar·rear·age** (ə rir′ij) *n.* arrears or the state of being in arrears

**ar·rears** (ə rirz′) *n.pl.* [< OFr. *ariere*, backward < VL. < L. *ad*, to + *retro*, behind] **1.** overdue debts **2.** unfinished work, etc. —**in arrears** (or **arrear**) behind in paying a debt, in one's work, etc.

**ar·rest** (ə rest′) *vt.* [< OFr. < L. *ad-*, to + *restare*, to stop] **1.** to stop or check **2.** to seize or take into custody by authority of the law **3.** to catch and keep (one's attention, etc.) —*n.* an arresting or being arrested —**under arrest** in legal custody, as of the police —**ar·rest′er, ar·res′tor** *n.*

**ar·rest·ing** (-iŋ) *adj.* attracting attention; interesting; striking —**ar·rest′ing·ly** *adv.*

**Ar·rhe·ni·us** (ä rā′nē oos), **Svan·te Au·gust** (svän′te ou′goost) 1859–1927; Swed. chemist

**ar·rhyth·mi·a** (ə rith′mē ə) *n.* [ModL. < Gr. *a-*, without + *rhythmos*, measure] any irregularity in the rhythm of the heart's beating —**ar·rhyth′mic, ar·rhyth′mi·cal** *adj.* —**ar·rhyth′mi·cal·ly** *adv.*

**ar·ris** (ar′əs) *n.* [< OFr. < L. *arista*, awn of grain] the edge made by two surfaces coming together at an angle, as in a molding

**ar·riv·al** (ə rī′v′l) *n.* **1.** the act of arriving **2.** a person or thing that arrives or has arrived

**ar·rive** (ə rīv′) *vi.* **-rived′, -riv′ing** [< OFr. < L. *ad-*, to + *ripa*, shore] **1.** to reach one's destination; come to a place **2.** to come [the time has *arrived*] **3.** to attain fame, etc. —**arrive at 1.** to reach by traveling **2.** to reach by thinking, etc.

‡**ar·ri·ve·der·ci** (ä rē′ve der′chē) *interj.* [It.] until we meet again; goodbye

‡**ar·ri·viste** (á rē vēst′) *n.* [Fr. < *arriver* (see ARRIVE) + *-iste*, -IST] *same as* PARVENU

**ar·ro·gance** (ar′ə gəns) *n.* [see ff.] overbearing pride or self-importance: also **ar′ro·gan·cy**

**ar·ro·gant** (-gənt) *adj.* [OFr. < L. prp. of *arrogare*, ARROGATE] full of or due to arrogance; overbearing; haughty —**ar′ro·gant·ly** *adv.*

**ar·ro·gate** (-gāt′) *vt.* **-gat′ed, -gat′ing** [< L. pp. of *arrogare* < *ad-*, for + *rogare*, to ask] **1.** to claim or seize without right **2.** to ascribe or attribute without reason —**ar′ro·ga′tion** *n.*

‡**ar·ron·disse·ment** (á rōn dēs män′) *n., pl.* **-ments′** (-män′) [Fr. < *arrondir*, to make round] in France, **1.** the largest subdivision of a department **2.** a municipal subdivision, as of Paris

**ar·row** (ar′ō) *n.* [OE. *earh, arwe*] **1.** a slender shaft, usually pointed at one end and feathered at the other, for shooting from a bow **2.** anything like an arrow in form, etc. **3.** a sign (←) used to indicate direction —**ar′row·y** *adj.*

**ar·row·head** (-hed′) *n.* **1.** the pointed tip of an arrow **2.** anything shaped like an arrowhead, as an indicating mark **3.** a marsh plant with arrow-shaped leaves and small, white flowers

**ar·row·root** (-rōōt′, -root′) *n.* [from its use as an antidote for poisoned arrows] **1.** a tropical American plant with starchy roots **2.** the edible starch made from its roots

**ar·roy·o** (ə roi′ō) *n., pl.* **-os** [Sp. < L. *arrugia*, mine shaft] [Southwest] **1.** a dry gully **2.** a rivulet or stream

**ar·se·nal** (är′s'n əl, -snəl) *n.* [It. *arsenale*, a dock < Ar. *dār* (*ęș*) *șind'a*, wharf, workshop] **1.** a place for making or storing weapons and other munitions **2.** a store or collection [an *arsenal* of facts used in a debate]

**ar·se·nate** (är′s'n āt′, -it) *n.* [ARSEN(IC) + -ATE²] a salt or ester of arsenic acid

**ar·se·nic** (är′s'n ik, -snik; *for adj.* är sen′ik) *n.* [OFr. < L. < Gr. *arsenikon*, a yellow sulfide of arsenic; ult. < Per. *zar*, gold] **1.** a silvery-white, brittle, very poisonous chemical element, compounds of which are used in making insecticides, medicines, etc.: symbol, As; at. wt., 74.9216; at. no., 33 **2.** loosely, arsenic trioxide, a poisonous, tasteless, white powder, used to exterminate insects and rodents —*adj.* of or containing arsenic, esp. with a valence of five

**arsenic acid** a white, poisonous crystalline compound, $H_3AsO_4$, used in insecticides, etc.

**ar·sen·i·cal** (är sen′ə k′l) *adj.* of or containing arsenic —*n.* an arsenical drug, insecticide, etc.

**ar·se·ni·ous** (är sē′nē əs) *adj.* of or containing arsenic, esp. with a valence of three: also **ar·se·nous** (är′s′n əs)

**‡ars gra·ti·a ar·tis** (ärz′ grä′shē ə är′tis; grä′tē ə) [L.] art for art's sake

**ar·son** (är′s′n) *n.* [OFr. < L. pp. of *ardere*, to burn] the crime of purposely setting fire to a building or property —**ar′son·ist** *n.*

**art¹** (ärt) *n.* [< OFr. < L. *ars* (gen. *artis*), art] **1.** human creativity **2.** skill **3.** any specific skill or its application **4.** any craft or profession, or its principles *[the cobbler's art]* **5.** a making or doing of things that have form and beauty; creative work: see also FINE ART **6.** any branch of creative work, esp. painting, drawing, sculpture, etc. **7.** products of creative work; paintings, statues, etc. **8.** a branch of learning; specif., *[pl.]* the liberal arts as distinguished from the sciences **9.** cunning **10.** trick; wile: *usually used in pl.* —*adj.* of or for works of art or artists

**art²** (ärt) *archaic 2d pers. sing., pres. indic., of* BE: *used with* thou

**-art** (ərt) *same as* -ARD

**art.** **1.** article **2.** artificial

**ar·te·fact** (är′tə fakt′) *n. var. sp. of* ARTIFACT

**Ar·te·mis** (är′tə mis) *Gr. Myth.* the goddess of the moon and hunting, Apollo's twin sister: identified with the Roman goddess Diana

**ar·te·ri·al** (är tir′ē əl) *adj.* **1.** of or like an artery or arteries **2.** designating or of the bright-red, oxygenated blood in the arteries **3.** of or being a main road with many branches —**ar·te′ri·al·ly** *adv.*

**ar·te·ri·al·ize** (-īz′) *vt.* -ized′, -iz′ing to change (venous blood) into arterial blood by oxygenation —**ar·te′ri·al·i·za′tion** *n.*

**ar·te·ri·ole** (är tir′ē ōl′) *n.* a small artery

**ar·te·ri·o·scle·ro·sis** (är tir′ē ō sklə rō′sis) *n.* [see ff. & SCLEROSIS] a thickening, and loss of elasticity, of the walls of the arteries, as in old age —**ar·te′ri·o·scle·rot′ic** (-rät′ik) *adj.*

**ar·ter·y** (är′tər ē) *n., pl.* -ter·ies [< L. < Gr.; prob. < *aeirein*, to raise] **1.** any of the system of tubes carrying blood from the heart to all parts of the body: cf. VEIN **2.** a main road or channel

**ar·te·sian well** (är tē′zhən) [Fr. *artésien*, lit., of Artois, former Fr. province] a well in which ground water is forced up by hydrostatic pressure

**art·ful** (ärt′fəl) *adj.* **1.** skillful or clever, esp. in achieving a purpose **2.** sly or cunning **3.** using or showing considerable art or skill **4.** artificial; imitative —**art′ful·ly** *adv.* —**art′ful·ness** *n.*

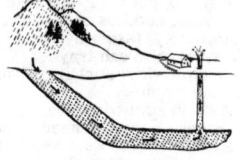
ARTESIAN WELL

**ar·thral·gia** (är thral′jə) *n.* [see ff. & -ALGIA] neuralgic pain in a joint or joints

**ar·thri·tis** (är thrīt′əs) *n.* [Gr. < *arthron*, a joint + -ITIS] inflammation of a joint or joints —**ar·thrit′ic** (-thrit′ik) *adj.* —**ar·thrit′i·cal·ly** *adv.*

**ar·thro·pod** (är′thrə päd′) *n.* [< Gr. *arthron*, a joint + -POD] any member of a large group of invertebrate animals with jointed legs and a segmented body, as insects, crustaceans, arachnids, etc. —**ar·throp·o·dal** (är thräp′ə d′l), **ar·throp′o·dous** (-dəs) *adj.*

**Ar·thur** (är′thər) [ML. *Arthurus*] **1.** a masculine name: dim. *Art* **2.** a legendary 6th-cent. king of Britain who led the knights of the Round Table **3.** Chester Alan, 1830–86; 21st president of the U.S. (1881–85) —**Ar·thu′ri·an** (-thoor′ē ən) *adj.*

**ar·ti·choke** (är′tə chōk′) *n.* [< It. < Sp. < Ar. *al-ḥaršūf*] **1.** a thistlelike plant **2.** its flower head, cooked as a vegetable **3.** *short for* JERUSALEM ARTICHOKE

**ar·ti·cle** (är′ti k′l) *n.* [OFr. < L. *articulus*, dim. of *artus*, a joint] **1.** any of the sections of a written document, as of a treaty **2.** a complete piece of writing that is part of a newspaper, magazine, or book **3.** a separate item *[an article of luggage]* **4.** a commodity **5.** *Gram.* any one of the words *a, an,* or *the* (and their equivalents in other languages), used as adjectives —*vt.* -cled, -cling to bind by the articles of an agreement or contract

**ar·tic·u·lar** (är tik′yə lər) *adj.* [< L. < *articulus:* see prec.] of a joint or joints *[an articular inflammation]*

**ar·tic·u·late** (är tik′yə lit; *for v.* -lāt′) *adj.* [< L. pp. of *articulare*, to disjoint < *articulus:* see ARTICLE] **1.** jointed: usually **ar·tic′u·lat′ed** **2.** made up of distinct syllables or words that have meaning **3.** able to speak **4.** expressing

oneself easily and clearly **5.** well formulated —*vt.* -lat′ed, -lat′ing **1.** to put together by joints **2.** to correlate **3.** to pronounce carefully; enunciate **4.** to express clearly —*vi.* **1.** to speak distinctly **2.** to be jointed —**ar·tic′u·late·ly** *adv.* —**ar·tic′u·late·ness** *n.* —**ar·tic′u·la′tive** *adj.* —**ar·tic′u·la′tor** *n.*

**ar·tic·u·la·tion** (är tik′yə lā′shən) *n.* **1.** a jointing or being jointed **2.** the way in which parts are joined together **3.** enunciation **4.** a spoken sound **5.** a joint between bones or similar parts **6.** *Bot.* a node, or a space between two nodes

**ar·ti·fact** (är′tə fakt′) *n.* [< L. *ars* (gen. *artis*), ART¹ + *factum*, thing made (see FACT)] any object made by human work; esp., a primitive tool, etc.

**ar·ti·fice** (är′tə fis) *n.* [Fr. < L. < *ars*, ART¹ + *facere*, to make] **1.** skill or ingenuity **2.** trickery or craft **3.** a sly or artful trick

**ar·tif·i·cer** (är tif′ə sər) *n.* [see prec. & -ER] **1.** a skilled craftsman **2.** an inventor **3.** a military mechanic

**ar·ti·fi·cial** (är′tə fish′əl) *adj.* [< OFr. < L.: see ARTIFICE] **1.** made by human work or art; not natural **2.** made in imitation of something natural; simulated *[artificial teeth]* **3.** unnatural in an affected way *[an artificial smile]* —**ar′ti·fi′ci·al′i·ty** (-fish′ē al′ə tē) *n., pl.* -ties —**ar′ti·fi′cial·ly** *adv.* —**ar′ti·fi′cial·ness** *n.*

**artificial insemination** the impregnation of a female by the introduction of semen without sexual intercourse

**artificial respiration** the artificial maintenance of breathing, as by forcing breath into the mouth

**ar·til·ler·y** (är til′ər ē) *n.* [< OFr. < Pr. *artilla*, fortifications; ult. < L. *ars*, ART¹] **1.** heavy mounted guns, as cannon or missile launchers **2.** the science of guns; gunnery **3.** [Slang] small arms: a facetious usage —**the artillery** the military branch specializing in the use of artillery —**ar·til′ler·ist**, **ar·til′ler·y·man** (-mən) *n., pl.* -men

**ar·ti·san** (är′tə z′n, -s′n) *n.* [Fr. < It.; ult. < L. *ars*, ART¹] a skilled workman; craftsman

**art·ist** (är′tist) *n.* [ML. *artista*, craftsman < L. *ars*, ART¹] **1.** a person who is skilled in any of the fine arts, esp. in painting, sculpture, etc. **2.** a person who does anything very well, with a feeling for form, etc. **3.** *same as* ARTISTE

**ar·tiste** (är tēst′) *n.* [Fr.] **1.** a professional in any of the performing arts **2.** a person very skilled in his work: often humorous or facetious

**ar·tis·tic** (är tis′tik) *adj.* **1.** of art or artists **2.** done skillfully and tastefully **3.** keenly sensitive to aesthetic values —**ar·tis′ti·cal·ly** *adv.*

**art·ist·ry** (är′tis trē) *n.* artistic work or skill

**art·less** (ärt′lis) *adj.* **1.** lacking skill or art **2.** uncultured; ignorant **3.** simple; natural **4.** without guile or deceit; ingenuous —**art′less·ly** *adv.* —**art′less·ness** *n.*

**‡art nou·veau** (àr nōō vō′) [Fr., lit., new art] an art movement of the late 19th and early 20th cent., emphasizing stylized curvilinear designs

**art·sy-craft·sy** (ärt′sē kraft′sē) *adj.* [Colloq.] of arts and crafts: usually a disparaging term connoting faddishness, amateurishness, etc.

**art·y** (ärt′ē) *adj.* **art′i·er**, **art′i·est** [Colloq.] showing artistic pretensions —**art′i·ness** *n.*

**ar·um** (er′əm, ar′-) *n.* [L. < Gr. *aron*, the wake robin] any of a family of plants bearing small flowers on a fleshy spike enclosed by a hoodlike leaf, as the jack-in-the-pulpit

**A.R.V.** American (Standard) Revised Version (of the Bible), printed in 1901

**-ar·y** (er′ē; *chiefly Brit.* ər i) [L. *-arius, -aria, -arium*] **1.** *a suffix meaning: a)* related to; connected with *[auxiliary] b)* a person or thing connected with *[missionary] c)* a place for *[granary]* **2.** [L. *-aris*] *a suffix meaning* like; of the same kind *[military]*

**Ar·y·an** (er′ē ən, ar′-) *adj.* [< Sans. *ārya*, noble, lord (used as a tribal name)] **1.** *earlier term for* INDO-EUROPEAN **2.** *same as* INDO-IRANIAN **3.** of the Aryans —*n.* **1.** formerly, the hypothetical language from which all Indo-European languages are supposed to be descended **2.** a person belonging to, or supposed to be a descendant of, the prehistoric peoples who spoke this language **3.** loosely, as in Nazi usage, a non-Jewish Caucasoid, a Nordic, etc.

**as¹** (az; *unstressed* əz) *adv.* [weakened form of ALSO < OE. *ealswa*, quite so, just as: see ALSO] **1.** to the same amount or degree; equally *[he's just as happy at home]* **2.** for instance; thus *[a card game, as bridge]* **3.** when related in a specified way *[romanticism as contrasted with classicism]* —*conj.* **1.** to the same amount or degree that *[fly straight as an arrow]* **2.** in the same manner that *[do as he does]* **3.** at the same time that *[she wept as she spoke]* **4.** because *[as you object, we won't go]* **5.** that the consequence is *[a question so obvious as to need no reply]* **6.** though *[full as he was, he kept eating]* **7.** [Colloq.] that

[I don't know *as* I should] —*pron.* 1. a fact that [he is tired, *as* anyone can see] 2. that (preceded by *such* or *the same*) [the same color *as* yours (is)] —*prep.* 1. in the role, function, capacity, or sense of [he poses *as* a friend] 2. like [the same *as* mine] —*as . . . as* a correlative construction used to indicate the equality or sameness of two things [*as* large *as*, *as* many *as*, etc.] —*as for* with reference to; concerning —*as if* (or *though*) 1. as it (or one) would if 2. that [it seems *as if* she's never home] —*as is* [Colloq.] just as it is; without any changes: said of damaged goods for sale —*as it were* as if it were so; so to speak —*as of* up to, on, or from (a specified time) —*as to* 1. concerning 2. as if to

**as²** (as) *n., pl.* **as′ses** (-əz, -ēz) [L.] 1. an ancient Roman unit of weight equal to about twelve ounces 2. an ancient Roman coin of copper alloy

**As** *Chem.* arsenic

**AS., A.S., A.-S.** Anglo-Saxon

**as·a·fet·i·da, as·a·foet·i·da** (as′ə fet′ə də) *n.* [ML. *asa* < Per. *āzā*, gum + L *f(o)etida*, FETID] a bad-smelling gum resin obtained from various Asiatic plants of the parsley family, formerly used in folk medicine to repel disease

**as·bes·tos, as·bes·tus** (as bes′təs, az-) *n.* [< L. < Gr. *asbestos*, inextinguishable < *a-*, not + *sbennynai*, to extinguish] a grayish mineral, esp. an amphibole, that separates into long, threadlike fibers: some varieties resist heat and chemicals and are used in fireproof curtains, roofing, etc.

**as·ca·rid** (as′kə rid) *n.* [< Gr. *askaris*] a roundworm that is a parasite in mammals

**as·cend** (ə send′) *vi.* [< OFr. < L. < *ad-*, to + *scandere*, to climb] 1. to go up; move upward; rise 2. to slope or lead upward —*vt.* 1. to move upward along; climb 2. to succeed to (a throne) —**as·cend′a·ble, as·cend′i·ble** *adj.* —**as·cend′er** *n.*

**as·cend·an·cy, as·cend·en·cy** (-ən sē) *n.* a position of control or power; supremacy; domination: also **as·cend′ance, as·cend′ence**

**as·cend·ant, as·cend·ent** (-ənt) *adj.* 1. rising; ascending 2. in control; dominant; superior —*n.* 1. a dominating position; ascendancy 2. *Astrol.* the sign of the zodiac just above the eastern horizon at any given moment —**in the ascendant** at or approaching the height of power, fame, etc.

**as·cen·sion** (ə sen′shən) *n.* 1. an ascending; ascent 2. [A-] *same as* ASCENSION DAY —**the Ascension** *Bible* the bodily ascent of Jesus into heaven on the fortieth day after the Resurrection: Acts 1:9 —**as·cen′sion·al** *adj.*

**Ascension Day** the fortieth day after Easter, celebrating the Ascension

**as·cent** (ə sent′) *n.* 1. an ascending or rising 2. an advancement, as in rank, fame, etc. 3. *a)* an upward slope *b)* the degree of such slope 4. a going back in time or genealogy

**as·cer·tain** (as′ər tān′) *vt.* [< OFr. < *a-*, to + *certain*, CERTAIN] to find out with certainty —**as′cer·tain′a·ble** *adj.* —**as′cer·tain′ment** *n.*

**as·cet·ic** (ə set′ik) *adj.* [< Gr. < *askein*, to train the body] of or characteristic of ascetics or their way of life; self-denying; austere: also **as·cet′i·cal** —*n.* a person who leads a life of contemplation and rigorous self-denial, esp. for religious purposes —**as·cet′i·cal·ly** *adv.* —**as·cet′i·cism** *n.*

**as·cid·i·an** (ə sid′ē ən) *n.* [< Gr. *askidion*: see ff.] any of a class of sea animals that are sac-shaped and have a tough outer covering

**as·cid·i·um** (-əm) *n., pl.* **-i·a** (-ə) [ModL. < Gr. dim. of *askos*, a bag, bladder] *Bot.* a pitcherlike leaf or structure, as of the pitcher plant

**As·cle·pi·us** (as klē′pē əs) *Gr. Myth.* the god of healing and medicine: identified with the Roman god Aesculapius

**as·co·my·cete** (as′kə mī sēt′) *n.* [< Gr. *askos*, bladder + *mykēs*, fungus] any of a class of fungi, including the mildews, yeasts, etc., that develop spores in a saclike structure —**as′co·my·ce′tous** *adj.*

**a·scor·bic acid** (ə skôr′bik) [A-² (sense 3) + SCORB(UTIC) + -IC] a water-soluble vitamin, $C_6H_8O_6$, occurring in citrus fruits, tomatoes, etc.: it prevents and cures scurvy; vitamin C

**as·cot** (as′kət, -kät′) *n.* 1. [A-] an annual horse-racing meet at Ascot Heath, Berkshire, England 2. a necktie or scarf with very broad ends hanging from the knot, one upon the other

**as·cribe** (ə skrīb′) *vt.* **-cribed′, -crib′ing** [< OFr. < L. < *ad-*, to + *scribere*, to write] 1. to put down (*to* a supposed cause); attribute 2. to regard as belonging (*to*) or coming from someone [poems ascribed to Homer] —**as·crib′a·ble** *adj.*

**as·crip·tion** (ə skrip′shən) *n.* 1. the act of ascribing 2. a statement that ascribes

**-ase** (ās, āz) [< (DIAST)ASE] *a suffix denoting* an enzyme, esp. one of vegetable origin [*amylase*]

ASCOT

**a·sep·sis** (ā sep′sis, ə-) *n.* 1. the condition of being aseptic 2. aseptic treatment or technique

**a·sep·tic** (-tik) *adj.* not septic; free from microorganisms that cause disease —**a·sep′ti·cal·ly** *adv.*

**a·sex·u·al** (ā sek′shoo wəl) *adj.* 1. having no sex or sexual organs; sexless 2. of reproduction without the union of male and female germ cells —**a·sex′u·al′i·ty** (-wal′ə tē) *n.* —**a·sex′u·al·ly** *adv.*

**As·gard** (as′gärd, az′-) *Norse Myth.* the home of the gods and slain heroes: also **As′garth** (-gärth)

**ash¹** (ash) *n.* [OE. *æsce*] 1. the white or grayish powder left after something has been thoroughly burned 2. fine, volcanic lava 3. the silvery-gray color of wood ash See also ASHES

**ash²** (ash) *n.* [OE. *æsc*] 1. a timber and shade tree of the olive family, having tough, elastic, straight-grained wood 2. the wood

**a·shamed** (ə shāmd′) *adj.* 1. feeling shame 2. feeling humiliated or embarrassed 3. reluctant because fearing shame beforehand —**a·sham·ed·ly** (ə shā′mid lē) *adv.*

**A·shan·ti** (ə shän′tē, -shan′-) region in C Ghana, orig. a native kingdom —*n.* 1. *pl.* **-ti, -tis** any member of the W African people of Ashanti 2. their language

**ash·can** (ash′kan′) *n.* a can for ashes and trash

**ash·en¹** (ash′ən) *adj.* 1. of ashes 2. like ashes, esp. in color; pale; pallid

**ash·en²** (ash′ən) *adj.* [Archaic] of the ash tree or its wood

**ash·es** (ash′iz) *n.pl.* 1. the unburned particles and grayish powder left after a thing has been burned 2. human remains, esp. after cremation 3. the ruins or remains of something destroyed

**Ashe·ville** (ash′vil) [after S. *Ashe* (1725-1813), governor of N.C.] city in W N.C.: pop. 58,000

**Ash·ke·naz·im** (äsh′kə naz′im, äsh′kə näz′im) *n.pl., sing.* **-naz′, -naz′i** (-ē) [Heb.: cf. Jer. 51:27] the Jews who settled in C and N Europe after the Diaspora, or their descendants: cf. SEPHARDIM —**Ash′ke·naz′ic** *adj.*

**ash·lar, ash·ler** (ash′lər) *n.* [< OFr. < L. *assis*, board] 1. a square, hewn stone used in building 2. a thin, dressed, square stone used for facing masonry walls 3. masonry made of either kind of ashlar

**a·shore** (ə shôr′) *adv., adj.* 1. to or on the shore 2. to or on land

**ash·ram** (ash′rəm) *n.* [< Sans. < *ā*, toward + *śrama*, fatigue, penance] a secluded place for a community of Hindus leading a life of religious meditation

**Ash·to·reth** (ash′tə reth′) the ancient Phoenician and Syrian goddess of love and fertility: identified with ASTARTE

**ash·tray** (ash′trā′) *n.* a container for smokers' tobacco ashes: also **ash tray**

**A·shur** (ä′shoor) *Assyr. Myth.* the chief deity, god of war and empire

**Ash Wednesday** the first day of Lent: from the putting of ashes on the forehead in penitence

**ash·y** (ash′ē) *adj.* **ash′i·er, ash′i·est** 1. of, like, or covered with ashes 2. of ash color; pale

**A·sia** (ā′zhə, -shə) largest continent, situated in the Eastern Hemisphere and separated from N Europe by the Ural Mountains: 16,900,000 sq. mi.; pop. 2,035,000,000 —**A′sian, A·si·at·ic** (ā′zhē at′ik) *adj., n.*

**Asia Minor** large peninsula in W Asia, between the Black Sea and the Mediterranean

**Asian influenza** a widespread influenza caused by a strain of virus first isolated in Singapore in 1957: also **Asian flu**

**Asiatic cholera** an acute, infectious disease characterized by severe diarrhea, cramps, and loss of water from the body

**a·side** (ə sīd′) *adv.* 1. on or to one side 2. away; in reserve [put this *aside* for me] 3. out of the way; out of one's mind 4. apart; notwithstanding [joking *aside*, I mean it] —*n.* an actor's words spoken as to the audience and supposedly not heard by the other actors —**aside from** 1. with the exception of 2. apart from; besides

**as·i·nine** (as′ə nīn′) *adj.* [< L. < *asinus*, ass] like an ass; esp., having qualities thought of as asslike; stupid, silly, obstinate, etc. —**as′i·nine′ly** *adv.* —**as′i·nin′i·ty** (-nin′ə tē) *n., pl.* **-ties**

**ask** (ask) *vt.* [OE. *ascian*] 1. to use words in seeking the answer to (a question); inquire about 2. to put a question to (a person); inquire of 3. to request; solicit; beg 4. to demand or expect as a price 5. to be in need of or call for (a thing) 6. to invite —*vi.* 1. to make a request (*for*) 2. to inquire (*about, after*, or *for*) 3. to behave so as to appear to be looking (*for* trouble, etc.) —**ask′er** *n.* —**ask′ing** *n.*

**a·skance** (ə skans′) *adv.* [< ME. *askoin* < *a-*, on + *skwyn* < Du. *schuin*, sidewise] 1. with a sidewise glance; obliquely 2. with suspicion, disapproval, etc. Also [Archaic or Poet.] **a·skant′**

**a·skew** (ə skyoo′) *adv.* to one side; awry; crookedly —*adj.* on one side; awry

**asking price** the price asked by a seller, esp. when he will accept less after bargaining

**a·slant** (ə slant′) *adv.* on a slant; slantingly —*prep.* on a slant across —*adj.* slanting

**a·sleep** (ə slēp′) *adj.* **1.** in a condition of sleep; sleeping **2.** inactive; dull; sluggish **3.** numb except for a prickly feeling [my arm is *asleep*] **4.** dead —*adv.* into a sleeping or inactive condition

**a·slope** (ə slōp′) *adv., adj.* at a slant

**As·ma·ra** (äs mä′rä) capital of Eritrea, in N Ethiopia: pop. 146,000

**a·so·cial** (ā sō′shəl) *adj.* **1.** not social; characterized by withdrawal from others **2.** selfish

**asp** (asp) *n.* [< OFr. < L. < Gr. *aspis*] any of several small, poisonous snakes of Africa and Europe, as the horned viper

**as·par·a·gus** (ə spar′ə gəs) *n.* [L. < Gr. *asparagos*, a sprout] **1.** a plant of the lily family, with small, scalelike leaves and many needlelike branches **2.** the tender shoots of this plant, eaten as a cooked vegetable

**as·par·kle** (ə spär′k'l) *adj.* sparkling

**A.S.P.C.A.** American Society for the Prevention of Cruelty to Animals

**as·pect** (as′pekt) *n.* [< L. pp. of *aspicere* < *ad-*, to, at + *specere*, to look] **1.** the way a person or thing appears or looks to another; appearance **2.** the appearance of an idea, problem, etc. regarded from a specific viewpoint **3.** a facing in a given direction **4.** a side facing in a given direction [the eastern *aspect* of the house] **5.** *Astrol.* the position of stars in relation to each other or to the observer, as it supposedly influences human affairs

**as·pen** (as′pən) *n.* [OE. *æspe*] a kind of poplar tree with leaves that flutter in the least breeze —*adj.* of or like an aspen; esp., fluttering; trembling

**as·per·i·ty** (as per′ə tē) *n., pl.* -ties [ME. & OFr. < L. < *asper*, rough] **1.** roughness or harshness, as of surface, sound, etc. **2.** sharpness of temper

**as·perse** (ə spurs′) *vt.* -persed′, -pers′ing [< L. pp. of *aspergere* < *ad-*, to + *spargere*, to sprinkle] to spread false or damaging rumors about; slander —**as·pers′er** *n.*

**as·per·sion** (ə spur′zhən, -shən) *n.* **1.** a defaming **2.** a damaging or disparaging remark; slander

**as·phalt** (as′fôlt) *n.* [< ML. < Gr.; prob. < *a-*, not + *sphallein*, to cause to fall] **1.** a brown or black tarlike substance, a variety of bitumen, found in a natural state or obtained by evaporating petroleum **2.** a mixture of this with sand or gravel, for paving, roofing, etc. —*vt.* to pave, roof, etc. with asphalt —**as·phal′tic** *adj.*

**as·phal·tum** (as fôl′təm) *n. same as* ASPHALT

**as·pho·del** (as′fə del′) *n.* [< L. < Gr. *asphodelos*] a plant of the lily family, having fleshy roots and white or yellow flowers

**as·phyx·i·a** (as fik′sē ə) *n.* [ModL. < Gr., a stopping of the pulse < *a-*, not + *sphyzein*, to throb] loss of consciousness as a result of too little oxygen and too much carbon dioxide in the blood: suffocation causes asphyxia —**asphyx′i·ant** *adj., n.*

**as·phyx·i·ate** (-āt′) *vt.* -at′ed, -at′ing **1.** to cause asphyxia in **2.** to suffocate —*vi.* to undergo asphyxia —**asphyx′i·a′tion** *n.* —**as·phyx′i·a′tor** *n.*

**as·pic** (as′pik) *n.* [Fr. < OFr. *aspe*, ASP] **1.** [Archaic] an asp **2.** [Fr., from its asplike colorfulness] a jelly of meat juice, tomato juice, etc., molded, often with meat, seafood, etc., and eaten as a relish

**as·pi·dis·tra** (as′pə dis′trə) *n.* [ModL. < Gr. *aspis*, a shield + *astron*, a star] a plant of the lily family, with stiff, glossy evergreen leaves

**as·pir·ant** (as′pər ənt, ə spīr′ənt) *adj.* aspiring —*n.* a person who aspires, as after honors, etc.

**as·pi·rate** (as′pə rāt′; *for n. & adj.* -pər it) *vt.* -rat′ed, -rat′ing [< L. pp. of *aspirare*: see ASPIRE] **1.** to begin (a word or syllable) with the sound of English *h* **2.** to follow (a consonant) with a puff of suddenly released breath **3.** to suck in or draw in, as by inhaling **4.** *Med.* to remove (fluid or gas), as from a body cavity, by suction —*n.* **1.** the speech sound represented by English *h* **2.** an expiratory breath puff —*adj.* preceded or followed by an aspirate: also **as′pi·rat′ed**

**as·pi·ra·tion** (as′pə rā′shən) *n.* **1.** *a)* strong desire or ambition, as for honor, etc. *b)* the thing so desired **2.** an aspirating **3.** an aspirate

**as·pi·ra·tor** (as′pə rāt′ər) *n.* a suction apparatus for removing air, fluids, etc. as from a body cavity

**as·pir·a·to·ry** (ə spīr′ə tôr′ē) *adj.* of or suited for breathing or suction

**as·pire** (ə spīr′) *vi.* -pired′, -pir′ing [< L. *aspirare* < *ad-*, to + *spirare*, to breathe] **1.** to be ambitious (*to* get or do something lofty); yearn or seek (*after*) **2.** [Archaic] to rise high; tower —**as·pir′er** *n.* —**as·pir′ing·ly** *adv.*

**as·pi·rin** (as′pər in, as′prin) *n.* [G. < *a(cetyl)* + *spir(säure)*, salicylic acid + -IN[1]] a white, crystalline powder, acetylsalicylic acid, $C_9H_8O_4$, used for reducing fever, relieving headaches, etc.

**a·squint** (ə skwint′) *adv., adj.* [ME. *of skwyn* (see ASKANCE): infl. by SQUINT] with a squint; out of the corner of the eye

**ass** (as) *n.* [OE. *assa* < L. *asinus*] **1.** an animal related to the horse but having longer ears and a shorter mane: donkeys and burros are domesticated asses **2.** a stupid or silly person; fool

**as·sa·fet·i·da, as·sa·foet·i·da** (as′ə fet′ə də) *n. same as* ASAFETIDA

**‡as·sa·i** (äs sä′ē) *adv.* [It.] *Music* very: used in indicating tempo [*adagio assai*]

**as·sail** (ə sāl′) *vt.* [< OFr. < L. *assilire* < *ad*, to + *salire*, to leap] **1.** to attack physically and violently **2.** to attack with arguments, etc. **3.** to begin working on (a task, etc.) with vigor **4.** to have a forceful effect on —**as·sail′a·ble** *adj.* —**as·sail′er** *n.* —**as·sail′ment** *n.*

**as·sail·ant** (-ənt) *n.* a person who assails; attacker

**As·sam** (a sam′, as′am) state of NE India, between Bhutan and Bangladesh: 47,091 sq. mi.; pop. 11,873,000 —**Assa·mese** (as′ə mēz′, -mēs′) *adj., n., pl.* -mese′

**as·sas·sin** (ə sas′'n) *n.* [Fr. < Ar. *hash-shāshīn*, hashish users < *hashish*, hemp] **1.** [A-] a member of a secret cult of Moslems who killed Crusaders, supposedly while under the influence of hashish **2.** a murderer who strikes suddenly; esp., the killer of a politically important person

**as·sas·si·nate** (-āt′) *vt.* -nat′ed, -nat′ing **1.** to murder (esp. a politically important person) **2.** to harm or ruin (a reputation, etc.), as by slander —**as·sas′si·na′tion** *n.*

**as·sault** (ə sôlt′) *n.* [< OFr. < L. *ad*, to + *saltare*, to leap] **1.** a violent attack, either physical or verbal; sometimes, specif., rape **2.** *Law* an unlawful threat or unsuccessful attempt to physically harm another —*vt., vi.* **1.** to make an assault (upon) **2.** to rape —**as·sault′ive** *adj.*

**assault and battery** *Law* the carrying out of threatened physical harm or violence

**as·say** (as′ā, a sā′; *for v.* a sā′, ə-) *n.* [OFr. *essai*, trial, test < L. *exagium*, a weighing < *ex-*, out + *agere*, to ACT] **1.** an examination or testing **2.** the analysis of an ore, etc. to find out the nature and proportion of the ingredients **3.** a substance to be analyzed in this way **4.** the result or report of such analysis —*vt.* **1.** to make an assay of; test; analyze **2.** to try; attempt —**as·say′er** *n.*

**as·sem·blage** (ə sem′blij) *n.* **1.** an assembling or being assembled **2.** a group of persons or things gathered together; assembly **3.** a form of art in which a number of unrelated objects are arranged together to form a kind of sculptural collage

**as·sem·ble** (ə sem′b'l) *vt., vi.* -bled, -bling [< OFr. < L. < *ad-*, to + *simul*, together] **1.** to gather into a group; collect **2.** to fit or put together the parts of —**as·sem′bler** *n.*

**as·sem·bly** (ə sem′blē) *n., pl.* -blies **1.** an assembling or being assembled **2.** a group of persons gathered together, as for a meeting **3.** [A-] in some States, the lower house of the legislature **4.** *a)* a fitting together of parts to form a complete unit *b)* such parts **5.** a call, as by bugle or drum, for soldiers to assemble in ranks

**assembly line** in many factories, an arrangement by which each worker does a single operation in assembling the work as it is passed along, often on a slowly moving belt or track

**as·sem·bly·man** (ə sem′blē mən) *n., pl.* -men (-mən, -men′) a member of a legislative assembly, esp. [A-] of a State Assembly

**as·sent** (ə sent′) *vi.* [< OFr. < L. < *assentire* < *ad-*, to + *sentire*, to feel] to express acceptance of an opinion, proposal, etc.; agree (*to*); concur —*n.* consent or agreement —**as·sent′er** *n.*

**as·sen·ta·tion** (as′en tā′shən) *n.* immediate and usually flattering or hypocritical assent

**as·sert** (ə surt′) *vt.* [< L. pp. of *asserere* < *ad-*, to + *serere*, to join] **1.** to state positively; declare **2.** to insist on or defend (one's rights, a claim, etc.) —**assert oneself** to insist on one's rights, or on being recognized —**as·sert′er, as·ser′tor** *n.*

**as·ser·tion** (ə sur′shən) *n.* **1.** an asserting **2.** a positive statement; declaration

**as·ser·tive** (-tiv) *adj.* positive or confident in a persistent way —**as·ser′tive·ly** *adv.* —**as·ser′tive·ness** *n.*

**as·sess** (ə ses′) *vt.* [< OFr. < ML. *assessare*, to set a rate < L. pp. of *assidere*, to sit beside, assist < *ad-*, to + *sedere*, to sit] **1.** to set an estimated value on (property, etc.) for taxation **2.** to set the amount of (damages, a fine, etc.) **3.** to impose a fine, tax, etc. on (a person or property) **4.** to impose (an amount) as a fine, tax, etc. **5.** to estimate the importance or value of

**as·sess·ment** (-mənt) *n.* **1.** an assessing **2.** an amount assessed

**as·ses·sor** (-ər) *n.* a person who assesses property, etc. for taxation —**as·ses·so·ri·al** (as'ə sôr'ē əl) *adj.* —**as·ses'sor·ship'** *n.*

**as·set** (as'et) *n.* [< Anglo-Fr. *assetz*, enough < OFr.; ult. < L. *ad*, to + *satis*, enough] **1.** anything owned that has exchange value **2.** a valuable or desirable thing [charm is her chief *asset*] **3.** [*pl.*] *a*) *Accounting* the entries on a balance sheet showing all the resources of a person or business, as accounts and notes receivable, cash, property, etc. *b*) *Law* property, as of a bankrupt

**as·sev·er·ate** (ə sev'ə rāt') *vt.* -**at'ed**, -**at'ing** [< L. pp. of *asseverare* < *ad*-, to + *severus*, earnest] to state seriously or positively; assert —**as·sev'er·a'tion** *n.*

**as·si·du·i·ty** (as'ə dyoo'ə tē, -doō'-) *n., pl.* -**ties 1.** the quality or condition of being assiduous; diligence **2.** [*pl.*] constant personal attention

**as·sid·u·ous** (ə sij'oo wəs) *adj.* [< L. < *assidere*: see AS-SESS] working with constant and careful attention; diligent; persevering —**as·sid'u·ous·ly** *adv.* —**as·sid'u·ous·ness** *n.*

**as·sign** (ə sīn') *vt.* [< OFr. < L. *assignare*, to allot < *ad*-, to + *signare*, SIGN] **1.** to set apart or mark for a specific purpose; designate **2.** to place at some task or duty **3.** to give out as a task; allot **4.** to ascribe (a motive, reason, etc.) **5.** *Law* to transfer (a claim, property, etc.) to another —*vi.* *Law* to transfer property, etc. to another —*n.* [*usually pl.*] an assignee —**as·sign'a·bil'i·ty** *n.* —**as·sign'a·ble** *adj.* —**as·sign'er**, *Law* **as·sign'or** (-ər, -ôr') *n.*

**as·sig·na·tion** (as'ig nā'shən) *n.* **1.** an assigning **2.** anything assigned **3.** an appointment to meet, esp. one made secretly by lovers; rendezvous

**as·sign·ee** (ə sī'nē') *n.* *Law* a person to whom a claim, property, etc. is transferred

**as·sign·ment** (ə sīn'mənt) *n.* **1.** an assigning or being assigned **2.** anything assigned, as a lesson, task, etc. **3.** *Law a*) a transfer of a claim, property, etc. *b*) a deed, etc. authorizing this

**as·sim·i·late** (ə sim'ə lāt') *vt.* -**lat'ed**, -**lat'ing** [< L. pp. of *assimilare* < *ad*-, to + *similare*, make similar to < *similis*, like] **1.** to absorb (food) into the body **2.** to absorb and incorporate into one's thinking **3.** to absorb (groups of different cultures) into the main culture **4.** to make like or alike (with *to*) —*vi.* to become assimilated —**as·sim'i·la·bil'i·ty** *n.* —**as·sim'i·la·ble** *adj.* —**as·sim'i·la'tor** *n.*

**as·sim·i·la·tion** (ə sim'ə lā'shən) *n.* an assimilating or being assimilated; specif., *a*) the absorption of a minority group into the main culture *b*) *Phonet.* the process by which a sound tends to become like a neighboring sound [the *p* in *cupboard* has been lost by assimilation to *b*] *c*) *Physiol.* the change of digested food into the protoplasm of an animal; also, the absorption of nutritive elements by plants

**as·sim·i·la·tive** (ə sim'ə lāt'iv) *adj.* of or causing assimilation; assimilating: also **as·sim·i·la·to·ry** (ə sim'l ə tôr'ē)

**as·sist** (ə sist') *vt.* [< OFr. < L. *assistere* < *ad*-, to + *sistere*, to make stand < *stare*, to stand] **1.** to give help to; aid **2.** to work as an assistant to —*vi.* to give help; aid —*n.* **1.** an instance or act of helping **2.** *Baseball* a defensive play by a fielder enabling a teammate to make a putout **3.** *Hockey* the passing of the puck in such a way as to enable a teammate to score a goal —**assist at** to be present at; attend

**as·sis·tance** (ə sis'təns) *n.* the act of assisting or the help given; aid

**as·sis·tant** (-tənt) *adj.* assisting; helping —*n.* **1.** a person who assists another or serves in a lower position; helper **2.** a thing that aids

**as·size** (ə sīz') *n.* [< OFr. < L. *assidere*: see ASSESS] **1.** orig., a legislative assembly or any of its decrees **2.** [*pl.*] *a*) court sessions held periodically in each county of England to try civil and criminal cases *b*) the time or place of these

**assn.** association

**assoc. 1.** associate **2.** associated **3.** association

**as·so·ci·ate** (ə sō'shē āt', -sē-; *for n. & adj., usually* -it) *vt.* -**at'ed**, -**at'ing** [< L. pp. of *associare* < *ad*-, to + *sociare*, to join < *socius*, companion] **1.** to join together; connect; combine **2.** to bring into relationship as companion, partner, friend, etc. **3.** to connect in the mind [to *associate* rain with grief] —*vi.* **1.** to join (*with*) as a companion, partner, friend, etc. **2.** to join together; unite —*n.* **1.** a friend, partner, fellow worker, etc. **2.** a member of less than full status, as of a society **3.** anything joined with another thing or things **4.** a degree granted by a junior college to those completing the regular two-year course —*adj.* **1.** joined with others, as in some work **2.** of less than full status

**as·so·ci·a·tion** (ə sō'sē ā'shən, -shē-) *n.* **1.** the act of associating **2.** companionship; fellowship; partnership **3.** an organization of persons having the same interests, purposes, etc.; society **4.** a connection in the mind between ideas, feelings, etc. —**as·so'ci·a'tion·al** *adj.*

**association football** *British name for* SOCCER

**as·so·ci·a·tive** (ə sō'shē āt'iv, -sē-; -shə tiv) *adj.* **1.** of, characterized by, or causing association **2.** *Math.* of an operation, as multiplication of three numbers, in which the result is the same regardless of the way the elements are grouped

**as·so·nance** (as'ə nəns) *n.* [Fr. < L. prp. of *assonare* < *ad*-, to + *sonare*, to sound] **1.** likeness of sound, as in a series of words or syllables **2.** a partial rhyme in which the stressed vowel sounds are alike but the consonant sounds are unlike, as in *late* and *make* —**as'so·nant** *adj., n.*

**as·sort** (ə sôrt') *vt.* [< OFr. < *a*- (L. *ad*), to + *sorte*, SORT] **1.** to separate into classes according to sorts or kinds; classify **2.** to supply with an assortment of goods —*vi.* **1.** to match or harmonize (*with*) **2.** to associate (*with*) —**as·sort'a·tive** *adj.* —**as·sort'er** *n.*

**as·sort·ed** (-id) *adj.* **1.** of different sorts; miscellaneous **2.** sorted into groups according to kind **3.** matched [a poorly *assorted* pair]

**as·sort·ment** (-mənt) *n.* **1.** an assorting or being assorted; classification **2.** an assorted, or miscellaneous, group or collection; variety

**ASSR, A.S.S.R.** Autonomous Soviet Socialist Republic

**asst.** assistant

**as·suage** (ə swāj') *vt.* -**suaged'**, -**suag'ing** [< OFr. < L. *ad*, to + *suavis*, sweet] **1.** to lessen (pain, distress, etc.); allay **2.** to calm (passion, anger, etc.); pacify **3.** to satisfy or slake (thirst, etc.) —**as·suage'ment** *n.* —**as·suag'er** *n.*

**as·sume** (ə soom', -syoom') *vt.* -**sumed'**, -**sum'ing** [< L. *assumere*, to claim < *ad*-, to + *sumere*, to take] **1.** to take on or put on (the appearance, form, role, etc. *of*) **2.** to seize; usurp [to *assume* control] **3.** to take upon oneself; undertake **4.** to take for granted; suppose **5.** to pretend to have; feign —**as·sum'a·ble** *adj.* —**as·sum'a·bly** *adv.* —**as·sum'ed·ly** *adv.* —**as·sum'er** *n.*

**as·sum·ing** (ə soo'miŋ, -syoo'-) *adj.* taking too much for granted; presumptuous

**as·sump·tion** (ə sump'shən) *n.* **1.** the act of assuming **2.** anything taken for granted; supposition **3.** presumption; impudence **4.** [A-] *R.C.Ch. a*) the taking up of the body and soul of the Virgin Mary into heaven after her death *b*) a church festival on August 15 celebrating this —**as·sump'tive** *adj.*

**as·sur·ance** (ə shoor'əns) *n.* **1.** the act of assuring **2.** a being assured; sureness; confidence **3.** something that inspires confidence, as a promise, positive statement, etc.; guarantee **4.** self-confidence **5.** impudent forwardness; presumption **6.** [Chiefly Brit.] insurance

**as·sure** (ə shoor') *vt.* -**sured'**, -**sur'ing** [< OFr. < ML. *assecurare* < L. *ad*, to + *securus*, SECURE] **1.** to make (a person) sure of something; convince **2.** to give confidence to [the news *assured* us] **3.** to declare to or promise confidently **4.** to make (a doubtful thing) certain; guarantee **5.** [Brit.] to insure against loss —**as·sur'er** *n.*

**as·sured** (ə shoord') *adj.* **1.** made sure; certain **2.** confident **3.** insured —*n.* **1.** the person to whom an insurance policy is payable **2.** the person whose life or property is insured —**as·sur·ed·ly** (ə shoor'id lē) *adv.* —**as·sur'ed·ness** *n.*

**As·syr·i·a** (ə sir'ē ə) ancient empire in SW Asia in the region of the upper Tigris River

**As·syr·i·an** (-ən) *adj.* of Assyria, its people, language, etc. —*n.* **1.** a native or inhabitant of Assyria **2.** the Semitic language of the Assyrians

**As·tar·te** (as tär'tē) a Semitic goddess of fertility and sexual love

**as·ta·tine** (as'tə tēn') *n.* [< Gr. *astatos*, unstable + -INE⁴] a radioactive chemical element formed from bismuth bombarded by alpha particles: symbol, At; at. wt., 210 (?); at. no., 85

**as·ter** (as'tər) *n.* [L. < Gr. *astēr*, star] a plant of the composite family, with purplish, blue, pink, or white daisylike flowers

**-as·ter** (as'tər) [L. dim. suffix] *a suffix meaning* inferior or worthless [poetaster]

**as·ter·isk** (as'tər isk) *n.* [< LL. < Gr. dim. of *astēr*, a star] a starlike sign (*) used in printing to indicate footnote references, omissions, etc. —*vt.* to mark with this sign

**as·ter·ism** (as'tər iz'm) *n.* [< Gr. < *astēr*, star] *Astron.* a group or cluster of stars

**a·stern** (ə sturn') *adv.* **1.** behind a ship or aircraft **2.** at or toward the back of a ship or aircraft **3.** backward; in a reverse direction

**as·ter·oid** (as'tə roid') *adj.* [< Gr. < *astēr*, star + -OID] like a star or starfish —*n.* **1.** any of the many small planets with orbits between those of Mars and Jupiter; planetoid **2.** a starfish

NEW ENGLAND ASTER

**as·the·ni·a** (as thē'nē ə) *n.* [ML. < Gr. < *a-*, without + *sthenos*, strength] bodily weakness —**as·then'ic** (-then'ik) *adj.*

**asth·ma** (az'mə) *n.* [Gr.] a chronic disorder characterized by wheezing, coughing, difficulty in breathing, and a suffocating feeling

**asth·mat·ic** (az mat'ik) *adj.* of or having asthma: also **asth·mat'i·cal** —*n.* a person who has asthma —**asth·mat'ical·ly** *adv.*

**as·tig·mat·ic** (as'tig mat'ik) *adj.* **1.** of or having astigmatism **2.** correcting astigmatism **3.** having a distorted view or judgment —**as'tig·mat'i·cal·ly** *adv.*

**a·stig·ma·tism** (ə stig'mə tiz'm) *n.* [< Gr. *a-*, without + *stigma*, a mark + -ISM] **1.** an irregularity in the curvature of a lens, esp. of the eye, so that light rays do not meet in a single focal point and images are distorted **2.** a distorted view or judgment, as because of prejudice

**a·stir** (ə stur') *adv., adj.* **1.** in motion; in excited activity **2.** out of bed

**as·ton·ish** (ə stän'ish) *vt.* [< OFr. < L. < *ex-*, emphatic + *tonare*, to thunder] to fill with sudden wonder or great surprise; amaze —**as·ton'ish·ing** *adj.* —**as·ton'ish·ing·ly** *adv.*

**as·ton·ish·ment** (-mənt) *n.* **1.** a being astonished; great amazement **2.** anything that astonishes

**As·tor** (as'tər), **John Jacob** 1763–1848; U.S. fur merchant & financier, born in Germany

**as·tound** (ə stound') *vt.* [< ME. pp. of *astonien*, ASTONISH] to astonish greatly; amaze —**as·tound'ing** *adj.* —**astound'ing·ly** *adv.*

**a·strad·dle** (ə strad''l) *adv.* in a straddling position

**As·tra·khan** (as'trə kan'; *Russ.* äs'trə khän'y') seaport in S European R.S.F.S.R.: pop. 376,000

**as·tra·khan** (as'trə kən) *n.* **1.** a loosely curled fur from the pelt of very young lambs orig. bred near Astrakhan **2.** a wool fabric made to look like this  Also sp. **as'tra·chan**

**as·tral** (as'trəl) *adj.* [< L. < Gr. *astron*, star < *astēr*, star] **1.** of, from, or like the stars **2.** *Theosophy* of a substance supposedly existing at a level just beyond normal human perception

**a·stray** (ə strā') *adv.* **1.** off the right path **2.** so as to be in error

**a·stride** (ə strīd') *adv.* **1.** with a leg on either side; astraddle **2.** with legs far apart —*prep.* **1.** with a leg on either side of (a horse, etc.) **2.** extending over or across

**as·trin·gent** (ə strin'jənt) *adj.* [< L. prp. of *astringere*, to contract < *ad-*, to + *stringere*, to draw] **1.** that contracts body tissues and checks secretions, capillary bleeding, etc. **2.** having a harsh, biting quality —*n.* an astringent substance —**as·trin'gen·cy** *n.* —**as·trin'gent·ly** *adv.*

**as·tro-** [< Gr. *astron*: see ASTRAL] a combining form meaning of a star or stars [*astrophysics*]

**as·tro·dome** (as'trə dōm') *n.* a transparent dome on top of an aircraft fuselage for the navigator

**astrol. 1.** astrologer **2.** astrology

**as·tro·labe** (as'trə lāb') *n.* [< OFr. < ML. < Gr. < *astron*, a star + *lambanein*, to take] an instrument once used to find the altitude of stars, etc.

**as·trol·o·gy** (ə sträl'ə jē) *n.* [< L. & Gr. *astron*, star + *-logia*, -LOGY] **1.** orig., primitive astronomy **2.** a pseudoscience based on the notion that the positions of the moon, sun, and stars affect human affairs and that one can foretell the future by studying the stars, etc. —**as·trol'o·ger** *n.* —**as·tro·log·i·cal** (as'trə läj'i k'l) *adj.* —**as'tro·log'i·cal·ly** *adv.*

**astron. 1.** astronomer **2.** astronomy

**as·tro·naut** (as'trə nôt') *n.* [< Fr.: see ff.] a person trained to make rocket flights in outer space

**as·tro·nau·tics** (as'trə nôt'iks) *n.pl.* [with *sing. v.*] [< Fr.: see ASTRO- & AERONAUTICS] the science that deals with spacecraft and with travel in outer space —**as'tro·nau'ti·cal** *adj.*

**as·tro·nom·i·cal** (as'trə näm'i k'l) *adj.* **1.** of or having to do with astronomy **2.** extremely large, as the numbers or quantities used in astronomy  Also **as'tro·nom'ic** —**as'tro·nom'i·cal·ly** *adv.*

**astronomical unit** a unit of length equal to the mean radius of the earth's orbit (c. 93 million mi.) used in measuring distances in astronomy

**as·tron·o·my** (ə strän'ə mē) *n.* [< ME. & OFr. < L. < Gr. < *astron*, star + *nomos*, system of laws < *nemein*, to arrange] the science of the stars, planets, and all other heavenly bodies, dealing with their composition, motion, relative position, size, etc. —**as·tron'o·mer** *n.*

**as·tro·phys·ics** (as'trō fiz'iks) *n.pl.* [with *sing. v.*] the science of the physical properties and phenomena of the stars, planets, etc. —**as'tro·phys'i·cal** *adj.* —**as'tro·phys'i·cist** (-ə sist) *n.*

**as·tute** (ə stoot', -styoot') *adj.* [< L. < *astus*, craft, cunning] having or showing a clever or shrewd mind; keen —**as·tute'ly** *adv.* —**as·tute'ness** *n.*

**A·sun·ción** (ä soon syōn') capital of Paraguay, on the Paraguay River: pop. 305,000

**a·sun·der** (ə sun'dər) *adv.* [see SUNDER] **1.** into parts or pieces **2.** apart or separate

**As·wan** (äs wän', as-; as'wän') city on the Nile, in SE Egypt: pop. 48,000: a dam (**Aswan High Dam**) has been built just south of this city

**a·sy·lum** (ə sī'ləm) *n.* [L. < Gr. *asylon*, asylum < *a-*, without + *sylē*, right of seizure] **1.** formerly, a sanctuary, as a temple, where criminals, etc. were safe from arrest **2.** any refuge **3.** the protection given by one country to refugees from another **4.** *an old term for* a place for the care of the mentally ill, or of the aged, poor, etc.

**a·sym·me·try** (ā sim'ə trē) *n.* lack of symmetry —**a·sym·met·ri·cal** (ā'sə met'ri k'l), **a'sym·met'ric** *adj.* —**a'sym·met'ri·cal·ly** *adv.*

**as·ymp·tote** (as'im tōt') *n.* [ModL. < Gr. < *a-*, not + *syn-*, together + *piptein*, to fall] a straight line always approaching but never meeting a curve —**as'ymp·tot'ic** (-tät'ik), **as'ymp·tot'i·cal** *adj.*

ASYMPTOTE
(A, asymptote of curve C)

**at¹** (at; *unstressed* ət) *prep.* [OE. *æt*] **1.** on; in; near; by [*at* the office] **2.** to or toward [look *at* her] **3.** through [enter *at* the gate] **4.** from [get the facts *at* their source] **5.** attending [*at* the party] **6.** occupied in; busy with [*at* work] **7.** in a state of [*at* war] **8.** in the manner of [*at* a trot] **9.** because of [terrified *at* the sight] **10.** according to [*at* his discretion] **11.** with reference to [good *at* tennis] **12.** in the amount, degree, price, etc. of [*at* five cents each] **13.** from an interval of [*at* half a mile] **14.** on or close to the time or age of [*at* five o'clock] **15.** during the period of [to happen *at* night]

**at²** (ät, at) *n., pl.* **at** *see* MONETARY UNITS, table (Laos)

**At** *Chem.* astatine

**at. 1.** airtight **2.** atmosphere **3.** atomic

**At·a·brine** (at'ə brin, -brēn') [G. *atebrin*] *a trademark for* a synthetic drug used in treating malaria and other diseases —*n.* [a-] this drug

**At·a·lan·ta** (at''l an'tə) *Gr. Myth.* a beautiful, swift-footed maiden who offered to marry any man able to defeat her in a race

**at·a·rac·tic** (at'ə rak'tik) *n.* [< Gr. < *ataraxia*, calmness < *a-*, not + *tarassein*, to disturb] a tranquilizing drug —*adj.* of tranquilizing drugs or their effects  Also **at'a·rax'ic** (-rak'sik)

**at·a·vism** (at'ə viz'm) *n.* [< Fr. < L. *atavus*, ancestor < *at-*, beyond + *avus*, grandfather] **1.** the appearance in an individual of a characteristic found in an early ancestor but not in more recent ones **2.** *a)* such a characteristic *b)* an individual with such a characteristic: also **at'a·vist** —**at'a·vis'tic** *adj.* —**at'a·vis'ti·cal·ly** *adv.*

**a·tax·i·a** (ə tak'sē ə) *n.* [Gr., disorder < *a-*, not + *tassein*, to arrange] inability to coordinate voluntary muscular movements —**a·tax'ic** *adj., n.*

**A·te** (ā'tē) *Gr. Myth.* the goddess personifying criminal folly or reckless ambition

**ate** (āt; *Brit.*, or *U.S. dial.*, et) *pt. of* EAT

**-ate¹** (āt *for 1;* it, āt *for 2 & 3*) [< L. *-atus*, pp. ending] **1.** *a suffix meaning: a)* to become [*maturate*] *b)* to cause to become [*sublimate*] *c)* to produce [*salivate*] *d)* to provide or treat with [*vaccinate*] *e)* to put in the form of [*triangulate*] *f)* to arrange for [*orchestrate*] *g)* to combine or treat with [*oxygenate*] **2.** *a suffix meaning: a)* of or characteristic of [*roseate*] *b)* having or filled with [*passionate*] *c)* *Biol.* having or characterized by [*spatulate*] **3.** *a suffix roughly equivalent to the past participial ending* -ed [*animate, animated*]

**-ate²** (āt, it) [L. *-atus*, a noun ending] *a suffix denoting:* **1.** a function, agent, or official [*directorate, potentate*] **2.** [L. *-atum*, neut. of *-atus*] *Chem.* a salt made from (an acid with a name ending in -ic) [*acetate, nitrate*]

**at·el·ier** (at''l yā') *n.* [Fr., ult. < L. *assula*, dim. of *assis*, board] a studio or workshop

**a tem·po** (ä tem'pō) [It.] *Music* in time: a direction to return to the original tempo

**Ath·a·na·sius** (ath'ə nā'shəs), **Saint** 296?–373 A.D.; Alexandrian bishop, who opposed Arianism —**Ath'a·na'sian** (-zhən) *adj., n.*

**Ath·a·pas·can, Ath·a·pas·kan** (ath'ə pas'kən) *adj.* [< Cree *athap-askaw*, lit., grass here and there] designating or of the most widely scattered linguistic family of N. American Indians, including the Navajos and Apaches —*n.*

---

fat, āpe, cär; ten, ēven; is, bīte; gō, hôrn, tōōl, look; oil, out; up, fur; get; joy; yet; chin; she; thin, then; zh, leisure; ŋ, ring; ə for *a* in *ago*, *e* in *agent*, *i* in *sanity*, *o* in *comply*, *u* in *focus*; ' as in *able* (ā'b'l); Fr. bal; ë, Fr. coeur; ö, Fr. feu; Fr. mon; ô, Fr. coq; ü, Fr. duc; r, Fr. cri; H, G. ich; kh, G. doch; ‡foreign; *hypothetical; < derived from. See inside front cover.

an Athapascan Indian or language Also **Ath′a·bas′can, Ath′a·bas′kan** (-bas′-)

**a·the·ism** (ā′thē iz′m) *n.* [< Fr. < Gr. < *a-*, without + *theos*, god] the belief that there is no God —**a′the·ist** (-ist) *n.* —**a′the·is′tic, a′the·is′ti·cal** *adj.*

**A·the·na** (ə thē′nə) *Gr. Myth.* the goddess of wisdom, skills, and warfare, identified with the Roman goddess Minerva: also **A·the′ne** (-nē)

**Ath·e·nae·um, Ath·e·ne·um** (ath′ə nē′əm) the temple of Athena at Athens, where writers and scholars met —*n.* [a-] 1. a literary or scientific club 2. a library or reading room

**Ath·ens** (ath′′nz) capital of Greece: pop., of met. area, 2,540,000: the ancient center of Greek culture and capital of ancient Attica —**A·the·ni·an** (ə thē′nē ən) *adj., n.*

**ath·er·o·scle·ro·sis** (ath′ər ō sklə rō′sis) *n.* [ModL. < Gr. *athērōma*, tumor filled with grainy matter + SCLEROSIS] a thickening, and loss of elasticity, of the walls of arteries, with the formation of fatty nodules —**ath′er·o·scle·rot′ic** (-rät′ik) *adj.*

**a·thirst** (ə thurst′) *adj.* 1. thirsty 2. eager; longing *[athirst for knowledge]*

**ath·lete** (ath′lēt′) *n.* [< L. < Gr. < *athlein*, to contest for a prize < *athlon*, a prize] a person trained in exercises, games, or contests requiring physical strength, skill, speed, etc.

**athlete's foot** a common fungous infection of the skin of the feet; ringworm of the feet

**ath·let·ic** (ath let′ik) *adj.* 1. of, like, or proper to athletes or athletics 2. physically strong, skillful, muscular, etc. —**ath·let′i·cal·ly** *adv.*

**ath·let·i·cism** (-ə siz′m) *n.* 1. addiction to athletics 2. an athletic quality

**ath·let·ics** (-iks) *n.pl.* *[sometimes with sing. v.]* sports, games, etc. requiring physical strength, skill, stamina, speed, etc.

**at-home** (ət hōm′) *n.* an informal reception at one's home, usually in the afternoon

**a·thwart** (ə thwôrt′) *prep.* 1. from one side to the other of; across 2. in opposition to; against 3. *Naut.* across the course or length of —*adv.* 1. crosswise 2. so as to block or thwart

**-at·ic** (at′ik) [< Fr. or L. < Gr. *-atikos*] a suffix meaning of, of the kind of *[lymphatic, chromatic]*

**a·tilt** (ə tilt′) *adj., adv.* tilted

**a·tin·gle** (ə tin′g′l) *adj.* tingling; excited

**-a·tion** (ā′shən) [< Fr. or L.] a suffix meaning: 1. the act of *[alteration]* 2. the condition of being *[gratification]* 3. the result of *[compilation]*

**-a·tive** (ə tiv, āt′iv) [< Fr. or L.] a suffix meaning of or relating to, serving to, tending to *[demonstrative, informative, talkative]*

**At·lan·ta** (ət lan′tə, at-) [< Western & *Atlantic* Railroad] capital of Ga., in the NC part: pop. 425,000 (met. area 2,010,000)

**at·lan·tes** (ət lan′tēz) *n.pl., sing.* **at·las** (at′ləs) [L. < Gr. pl. of ATLAS] supporting columns in the form of standing or kneeling figures of men

**At·lan·tic** (ət lan′tik, at-) [< L. *Atlanticum* (*mare*), Atlantic (ocean) < *Atlanticus*, of the Atlas Mts.] ocean touching the American continents to the west and Europe and Africa to the east —*adj.* of, in, on, or near this ocean

**Atlantic City** city & ocean resort in N.J., on the Atlantic: pop. 40,000

**Atlantic Standard Time** *see* STANDARD TIME

**At·lan·tis** (ət lan′tis, at-) legendary island or continent west of Gibraltar, supposed to have sunk in the Atlantic —**At·lan·te·an** (at′lan tē′ən) *adj.*

**At·las** (at′ləs) [L. < Gr.; ult. < *tlan*, bearing] *Gr. Myth.* a Titan forced to hold the heavens on his shoulders —*n.* [a-] 1. a book of maps 2. a book of tables, charts, etc. on a specific subject

**Atlas Mountains** mountain system in NW Africa, extending across Morocco, Algeria, and Tunisia

**atm.** 1. atmosphere 2. atmospheric

**at·man** (ät′mən) *n.* [Sans., breath, soul] *Hinduism* 1. the individual soul or ego 2. [A-] the universal soul; source of all individual souls

**at·mos·phere** (at′məs fir′) *n.* [< ModL. < Gr. *atmos*, vapor + *sphaira*, sphere] 1. all the air surrounding the earth, consisting of oxygen, nitrogen, and other gases 2. the gaseous mass surrounding any star, etc. 3. the air in any given place 4. the general feeling or spirit of a place; mood 5. [Colloq.] an interesting effect produced by decoration, etc. 6. *Physics* a unit of pressure equal to 14.69 lb. per sq. in.

**at·mos·pher·ic** (at′məs fer′ik, -fir′-) *adj.* 1. of or in the atmosphere 2. caused or produced by the atmosphere 3. creating an atmosphere, or mood Also **at′mos·pher′i·cal** —**at′mos·pher′i·cal·ly** *adv.*

**at·mos·pher·ics** (-iks) *n.pl.* same as STATIC (*n.* 1)

**at. no.** atomic number

**at·oll** (a′tôl, ā′-; -tàl) *n.* [< Maldive Is. term] a ring-shaped coral island nearly or completely surrounding a lagoon

**at·om** (at′əm) *n.* [< OFr. < L. < Gr. *atomos*, uncut < *a-*, not + *temnein*, to cut] 1. orig., any of the tiny particles that ancient philosophers imagined as the basic component of all matter 2. a tiny particle; jot 3. *Chem. & Physics* any of the smallest particles of an element that combine with similar particles of other elements to produce compounds: atoms consist of electrons revolving about a positively charged nucleus —**the atom** same as ATOMIC ENERGY

ATOLL

**atom bomb** same as ATOMIC BOMB —**at′om-bomb′** *vt.*

**a·tom·ic** (ə täm′ik) *adj.* 1. of an atom or atoms 2. of or using atomic energy or atomic bombs 3. having its atoms in an uncombined form 4. very small; minute —**a·tom′i·cal·ly** *adv.*

**Atomic Age** the period since the creation of the first self-sustaining nuclear chain reaction on December 2, 1942

**atomic bomb** an extremely destructive type of bomb, the power of which comes from the very great quantity of energy that is suddenly released when a chain reaction of nuclear fission is set off: first used in warfare in 1945 by the United States

**atomic clock** a highly accurate clock regulated by the unvarying vibrational frequency of the atoms or molecules of certain substances

**atomic cocktail** a dose of medicine to be swallowed, containing a radioactive element and used as in diagnosing or treating cancer

**atomic energy** the energy released from an atom in nuclear fission or nuclear fusion, or by radioactive decay

**at·o·mic·i·ty** (at′ə mis′ə tē) *n.* 1. the state of being made up of atoms 2. *Chem. a)* the number of atoms in a molecule *b)* same as VALENCE

**atomic mass unit** a unit of mass, exactly one twelfth of the mass of an atom of the most common isotope of carbon

**atomic number** *Chem.* a number representing the relative position of an element in the periodic table; number representing the number of protons in the nucleus of the atom of an element

**atomic pile** *early name for* NUCLEAR REACTOR

**atomic theory** the theory that all material objects and substances are composed of atoms

**atomic weight** *Chem.* a number representing the weight of one atom of an element as compared with an arbitrary number representing the weight of one atom of another element taken as the standard (now usually carbon at 12)

**at·om·ize** (at′ə mīz′) *vt.* -ized′, -iz′ing 1. to separate into atoms 2. to reduce (a liquid) to a fine spray 3. to destroy by atomic weapons 4. to disintegrate; break up —**at′om·i·za′tion** *n.*

**at·om·iz·er** (-mī′zər) *n.* a device used to shoot out a fine spray, as of medicine or perfume

**atom smasher** *same as* ACCELERATOR (sense 3)

**a·ton·al** (ā tōn′′l) *adj.* having atonality —**a·ton′al·ism** *n.* —**a·ton′al·ist** *n.* —**a·ton′al·is′tic** *adj.* —**a·ton′al·ly** *adv.*

**a·to·nal·i·ty** (ā′tō nal′ə tē) *n. Music* lack of tonality through intentional disregard of key; also, use of chromatic tones without relation to a central keynote

**a·tone** (ə tōn′) *vi.* **a·toned′, a·ton′ing** [ME. *at-onen*, become reconciled < *at one*, in accord] to make amends (*for* wrongdoing, etc.) —**a·ton′er** *n.*

**a·tone·ment** (-mənt) *n.* 1. an atoning 2. satisfaction given for wrongdoing, etc.; expiation 3. [A-] *Theol.* the reconciliation of God to man by means of Jesus' sufferings and death

**a·top** (ə täp′) *adv.* on the top; at the top —*prep.* on the top of

**-a·to·ry** (ə tôr′ē, ə tō′rē) [< L. *-atorius*] a suffix meaning of, characterized by, produced by *[accusatory]*

**ATP** [A(DENOSINE) *t(ri)p(hosphate)*] a vital substance, $C_{10}H_{16}P_3O_{13}N_5$, found in all living cells: it is the immediate source of muscular energy

**at·ra·bil·ious** (a′trə bil′yəs) *adj.* [< L. *atra bilis*, black bile: cf. MELANCHOLY] melancholy, morose, cross, etc.: also **at′ra·bil′iar** (-yər)

**a·tri·um** (ā′trē əm) *n., pl.* **a′tri·a** (-ə), **a′tri·ums** [L.] 1. the main room of an ancient Roman house 2. a hall or entrance court 3. *Anat.* a chamber or cavity, esp. either of the upper chambers of the heart —**a′tri·al** (-əl) *adj.*

**a·tro·cious** (ə trō′shəs) *adj.* [< L. *atrox* (gen. *atrocis*), fierce < *ater*, black + -OUS] 1. very cruel, evil, etc. 2. appalling or dismaying 3. [Colloq.] very bad, offensive, inferior, etc. —**a·tro′cious·ly** *adv.* —**a·tro′cious·ness** *n.*

**a·troc·i·ty** (ə träs′ə tē) *n., pl.* -ties 1. atrocious behavior, brutality, etc. 2. an atrocious act 3. [Colloq.] a very offensive thing

**at·ro·phy** (at′rə fē) *n.* [< Fr. < L. < Gr. < *a-*, not + *trephein*, to nourish] a wasting away, or the failure to grow, of an organ, etc., because of insufficient nutrition —*vi.* **-phied, -phy·ing** to waste away or fail to develop —*vt.* to cause atrophy in —**a·troph·ic** (ə träf′ik) *adj.*

**at·ro·pine** (at′rə pēn′, -pin) *n.* [< ModL. < Gr. *Atropos* (see ff.) + -INE⁴] a poisonous, crystalline alkaloid obtained from belladonna and similar plants, used to relieve spasms or to dilate the pupil of the eye: also **at′ro·pin** (-pin)

**At·ro·pos** (at′rə päs′) *Gr. & Rom. Myth.* that one of the three Fates who cuts the thread of life

**att.** 1. attention 2. attorney

**at·tach** (ə tach′) *vt.* [< OFr. < *estachier* < *estache*, a post] 1. to fasten by tying, etc. 2. to join (often used reflexively) [he *attached* himself to us] 3. to connect by ties of affection, etc. 4. to affix (a signature, etc.) 5. to ascribe 6. to appoint by order 7. *Law* to take (property or a person) into custody by writ 8. *Mil.* to join (troops, etc.) temporarily to another unit —*vi.* to be joined; belong —**at·tach′a·ble** *adj.*

**at·ta·ché** (at′ə shā′; *chiefly Brit.* ə tash′ā; *Fr.* à tà shā′) *n.* [Fr., pp. of *attacher*, ATTACH] a person with special duties on the staff of an ambassador or minister

**attaché case** a flat, rectangular case for carrying documents, papers, etc.

**at·tach·ment** (ə tach′mənt) *n.* 1. the act of attaching something 2. anything that attaches; fastening 3. devotion 4. anything attached 5. an accessory for an electrical appliance, etc. 6. *Law* a taking of a person, property, etc. into custody, or a writ for this

**at·tack** (ə tak′) *vt.* [< Fr. < It. < ATTACH] 1. to use force against in order to harm 2. to speak or write against 3. to begin working on energetically 4. to begin acting upon harmfully —*vi.* to make an assault —*n.* 1. an attacking; onslaught 2. an onset or recurrence of a disease 3. a beginning of a task, undertaking, etc. —**at·tack′er** *n.*

**at·tain** (ə tān′) *vt.* [< OFr. < L. *attingere* < *ad-*, to + *tangere*, to touch] 1. to gain through effort; achieve 2. to reach or come to; arrive at —*vi.* to succeed in reaching or coming (*to* a goal) —**at·tain′a·bil′i·ty, at·tain′a·ble·ness** *n.* —**at·tain′a·ble** *adj.*

**at·tain·der** (ə tān′dər) *n.* [OFr. *ataindre*, to attain] the loss of a person's civil rights and property because he has been sentenced to death or outlawed: see BILL OF ATTAINDER

**at·tain·ment** (ə tān′mənt) *n.* 1. an attaining or being attained 2. anything attained, as a skill

**at·taint** (ə tānt′) *vt.* to punish by attainder —*n.* an attainder

**at·tar** (at′ər) *n.* [< Per. < Ar. ′*itr*, perfume] a perfume made from the petals of flowers, esp. of damask roses (**attar of roses**)

**at·tempt** (ə tempt′) *vt.* [< OFr. < L. *attemptare* < *ad-*, to + *temptare*, to try] to try to do, get, etc.; endeavor —*n.* 1. a try; endeavor 2. an attack, as on a person's life —**attempt the life of** to try to kill —**at·tempt′a·ble** *adj.*

**at·tend** (ə tend′) *vt.* [< OFr. < L. *attendere*, to give heed to < *ad-*, to + *tendere*, to stretch] 1. [Now Rare] to take care or charge of 2. *a)* to wait on; serve *b)* to serve as doctor to during an illness 3. to go with 4. to accompany as a result [success *attended* his efforts] 5. to be present at —*vi.* 1. to pay attention 2. to wait (*on* or *upon*) 3. to devote oneself (*to*) 4. to give the required care or attention (*to*)

**at·tend·ance** (ə ten′dəns) *n.* 1. an attending 2. the number of persons attending 3. the degree of regularity in attending

**at·tend·ant** (-dənt) *adj.* 1. attending or serving 2. being present 3. accompanying [attendant difficulties] —*n.* 1. one who attends or serves 2. a person present 3. an accompanying thing

**at·ten·tion** (ə ten′shən) *n.* 1. *a)* the act of keeping one's mind closely on something; concentration *b)* readiness for concentration 2. notice 3. care or consideration 4. *a)* thoughtful consideration for others *b)* an act of consideration, courtesy, etc.: *usually used in pl.* 5. *Mil. a)* the erect, motionless posture of soldiers in readiness for a command *b)* a command to assume this posture

**at·ten·tive** (ə ten′tiv) *adj.* 1. paying attention 2. courteous, devoted, etc. —**at·ten′tive·ly** *adv.* —**at·ten′tive·ness** *n.*

**at·ten·u·ate** (ə ten′yoo wāt′) *vt.* **-at′ed, -at′ing** [< L. pp. of *attenuare* < *ad-*, to + *tenuare* < *tenuis*, thin] 1. to make slender or thin 2. to dilute; rarefy 3. to lessen or weaken —*vi.* to become thin, weak, etc. —**at·ten′u·a·ble** *adj.* —**at·ten′u·a′tion** *n.*

**at·test** (ə test′) *vt.* [< Fr. < L. *attestari* < *ad-*, to + *testari*, to bear witness < *testis*, a witness] 1. to declare to be true or genuine 2. to certify, as by oath 3. to serve as proof of —*vi.* to bear witness; testify (*to*) —**at·tes·ta·tion** (at′es tā′shən) *n.* —**at·test′er, at·tes′tor** *n.*

**At·tic** (at′ik) *adj.* 1. of Attica 2. Athenian 3. classical in a simple, restrained way [an *Attic* style] —*n.* 1. the Greek dialect of Attica, the literary language of ancient Greece 2. an Athenian

**at·tic** (at′ik) *n.* [< Fr. < prec.] 1. a low wall or story above the cornice of a classical façade 2. the room or space just below the roof of a house; garret

**At·ti·ca** (at′i kə) province of SE Greece: in ancient times, a region dominated by Athens

**At·ti·cism** (at′ə siz′m) *n.* [also a-] an Attic idiom, style, custom, etc. —**At′ti·cize′** (-sīz′) *vt., vi.* **-cized′, -ciz′ing**

**Attic salt, Attic wit** graceful, piercing wit

**At·ti·la** (at′l ə, ə til′ə) 406?-453 A.D.; king of the Huns (433?-453)

**at·tire** (ə tīr′) *vt.* **-tired′, -tir′ing** [< OFr. *atirier*, put in order < *a* (L. *ad*), to + *tire*, row, order] to dress, esp. in fine garments; clothe; array —*n.* clothes, esp. rich apparel; finery

**at·ti·tude** (at′ə tōōd′, -tyōōd′) *n.* [Fr. < It. < LL. *aptitudo* < L. *aptus*, APT] 1. the posture of the body in connection with an action, mood, etc. 2. a way of acting, feeling, or thinking; one's disposition, mental set, etc. 3. the position of an aircraft or spacecraft in relation to a given line or plane —**at′ti·tu′di·nal** *adj.*

**at·ti·tu·di·nize** (at′ə tōōd′′n īz′, -tyōōd′-) *vi.* **-nized′, -niz′ing** to pose for effect

**at·to-** [< Dan. *atten*, eighteen] *a combining form meaning* one quintillionth ($10^{-18}$) [*attosecond*]

**at·tor·ney** (ə tur′nē) *n., pl.* **-neys** [< OFr. < *a-* (L. *ad*), to + *torner*: see TURN] any person having the legal power to act for another; esp. (*also* **attorney at law**), a lawyer

**attorney general** *pl.* **attorneys general, attorney generals** 1. the chief law officer of a national or State government 2. [A- G-] the head of the U.S. Department of Justice

**at·tract** (ə trakt′) *vt.* [< L. pp. of *attrahere* < *ad-*, to + *trahere*, to draw] 1. to draw to itself or oneself [a magnet *attracts* iron] 2. to get the admiration, attention, etc. of; allure —*vi.* to be attractive —**at·tract′a·ble** *adj.* —**at·tract′er, at·trac′tor** *n.*

**at·trac·tion** (ə trak′shən) *n.* 1. an attracting or the power of attracting; esp., charm or fascination 2. anything that attracts 3. *Physics* the mutual action by which bodies or particles of matter tend to draw together or cohere: opposed to REPULSION

**at·trac·tive** (-tiv) *adj.* that attracts or has the power to attract; esp., charming, pretty, etc. —**at·trac′tive·ly** *adv.* —**at·trac′tive·ness** *n.*

**attrib.** 1. attribute 2. attributive

**at·trib·ute** (ə trib′yoot; *for n.* a′trə byoot′) *vt.* **-ut·ed, -ut·ing** [< L. pp. of *attribuere* < *ad-*, to + *tribuere*, to assign < *tribus*: see TRIBE] 1. to think of as belonging to or coming from a particular person or thing; assign or ascribe (*to*) 2. to ascribe as a characteristic or quality —*n.* 1. a characteristic or quality of a person or thing 2. an object used in the arts as a symbol for a person, office, etc. 3. a word or phrase used as an adjective —**at·trib′ut·a·ble** *adj.* —**at′tri·bu′tion** *n.*

**at·trib·u·tive** (ə trib′yoo tiv) *adj.* 1. attributing 2. of or like an attribute 3. *Gram.* joined directly to the substantive it modifies, esp., in English, coming just before it: said of an adjective —*n.* an attributive adjective, as *black* in *black cat* —**at·trib′u·tive·ly** *adv.*

**at·tri·tion** (ə trish′ən) *n.* [< L. < pp. of *atterere* < *ad-*, to + *terere*, to rub] 1. a wearing away by friction 2. any gradual wearing, or weakening 3. loss of personnel in the normal course of events, as because of death, retirement, etc.

**at·tune** (ə tōōn′, -tyōōn′) *vt.* **-tuned′, -tun′ing** 1. to tune 2. to bring into harmony or agreement

**atty.** attorney

**at. wt.** atomic weight

**a·typ·i·cal** (ā tip′i k'l) *adj.* not typical; not characteristic: also **a·typ′ic** —**a·typ′i·cal·ly** *adv.*

**Au** [L. *aurum*] *Chem.* gold

**au·burn** (ô′bərn) *adj., n.* [< OFr. < L. *alburnus* < *albus*, white; meaning infl. by ME. *brun*, brown] reddish brown

**Auck·land** (ôk′lənd) seaport on North Island, New Zealand: pop. 152,000 (met. area 577,000)

**†au cou·rant** (ō kōō rän′) [Fr., lit., with the current] fully informed; up-to-date

**auc·tion** (ôk′shən) *n.* [< L. < pp. of *augere*, to increase] 1. a public sale at which each item is sold to the highest bidder 2. *same as* AUCTION BRIDGE —*vt.* to sell at auction

**auction bridge** a variety of the game of bridge in which the players bid for the right to say what suit shall be trump or to declare no-trump

---

fat, āpe, cär; ten, ēven; is, bīte; gō, hôrn, tool, look; oil, out; up, fur; get; joy; yet; chin; she; thin, then; zh, leisure; ŋ, ring; ə for *a* in *ago*, *e* in *agent*, *i* in *sanity*, *o* in *comply*, *u* in *focus*; ′ as in *able* (ā′b′l); Fr. bal; ë, Fr. coeur; ö, Fr. feu; Fr. mon; ô, Fr. coq; ü, Fr. duc; r, Fr. cri; H, G. ich; kh, G. doch; ‡foreign; *hypothetical; < derived from. See inside front cover.

**auc·tion·eer** (ôk'shə nir′) *n.* one whose work is selling things at auction —*vt.* to auction

**auc·to·ri·al** (ôk tôr′ē əl) *adj.* [< L. *auctor,* author] of or by an author

**aud.** 1. audit 2. auditor

**au·da·cious** (ô dā′shəs) *adj.* [< L. < *audax,* bold < *audere,* to dare] 1. bold or daring; fearless 2. rudely bold; brazen; insolent —**au·da′cious·ly** *adv.* —**au·da′cious·ness** *n.*

**au·dac·i·ty** (ô das′ə tē) *n.* 1. bold courage; daring 2. brazen boldness; insolence 3. *pl.* -ties an audacious act or remark

**Au·den** (ôd′'n), **W(ystan) H(ugh)** 1907–73; U.S. poet, born in England

**au·di·ble** (ô′də b'l) *adj.* [< ML. < L. *audire,* to hear] loud enough to be heard —**au′di·bil′i·ty** *n.* —**au′di·bly** *adv.*

**au·di·ence** (ô′dē əns) *n.* [ME. & OFr. < L. *audientia,* a hearing < prp. of *audire,* to hear] 1. a group assembled to see and hear a play, concert, etc. 2. those who are tuned in to a certain radio or TV program or who read a certain book 3. those who pay attention to what one writes or says 4. the act or state of hearing 5. an opportunity to be heard; hearing 6. a formal interview with a person in high position

**au·di·o** (ô′dē ō) *adj.* [< L. *audire,* hear] 1. of frequencies corresponding to sound waves that are normally audible 2. of or relating to sound reproduction, esp. to the sound phase of TV

**au·di·o-fre·quen·cy** (ô′dē ō frē′kwən sē) *adj.* of the band of audible sound frequencies or corresponding electric current frequencies, from about 20 to 20,000 hertz

**au·di·ol·o·gy** (ô′dē äl′ə jē) *n.* the science of hearing; esp., evaluation of hearing defects and rehabilitation of those who have such defects —**au′di·o·log′i·cal** (-ə läj′i k'l) *adj.* —**au′di·ol′o·gist** *n.*

**au·di·om·e·ter** (ô′dē äm′ə tər) *n.* an instrument for measuring hearing

**au·di·o·phile** (ô′dē ə fīl′) *n.* a devotee of high-fidelity sound reproduction

**au·di·o-vis·u·al** (ô′dē ō vizh′oo wəl) *adj.* 1. involving both hearing and sight 2. designating or of such teaching aids as filmstrips, radio, etc.

**au·dit** (ô′dit) *n.* [< L. pp. of *audire,* to hear] 1. a formal, often periodic examination and checking of accounts or financial records 2. a settlement or adjustment of accounts 3. an account thus examined and adjusted, or a statement of this —*vt., vi.* 1. to examine (accounts, claims, etc.) 2. to attend (a college course) as a listener receiving no credits

**au·di·tion** (ô dish′ən) *n.* 1. the act or sense of hearing 2. a hearing to test the ability or fitness of an actor, musician, etc. —*vt.* to give an audition to —*vi.* to perform in an audition

**au·di·tor** (ô′də tər) *n.* 1. a hearer or listener 2. a person who is authorized to audit accounts 3. a person who audits a college course

**au·di·to·ri·um** (ô′də tôr′ē əm) *n.* 1. a room for an audience, as in a school, library, etc. 2. a building or hall for speeches, concerts, etc.

**au·di·to·ry** (ô′də tôr′ē) *adj.* of hearing or the sense of hearing —**au′di·to′ri·ly** *adv.*

**Au·du·bon** (ô′də bän′), **John James** 1785–1851; U.S. ornithologist, naturalist, & painter

‡**auf Wie·der·se·hen** (ouf vē′dər zā′ən) [G.] till we see each other again; goodbye

**Aug.** August

**Au·ge·an** (ô jē′ən) *adj.* 1. *Gr. Legend* of King Augeas or his large, filthy stable, which Hercules cleaned in one day 2. very filthy

**au·ger** (ô′gər) *n.* [by faulty separation of ME. *a nauger* < OE. *nafu,* nave (of a wheel) + *gar,* a spear] 1. a tool for boring holes in wood 2. a similar but larger tool, as for boring in the earth

**aught** (ôt) *n.* [OE. *awiht* < *a,* one + *wiht,* a creature, WIGHT] 1. anything whatever [for aught I know] 2. [< *a naught* (see NAUGHT), wrongly divided *an aught*] a zero —*adv.* [Archaic] to any degree

TYPES OF AUGER

**aug·ment** (ôg ment′) *vt., vi.* [< OFr. < L. *augmentare* < *augere,* to increase] to make or become greater; increase —**aug·ment′a·ble** *adj.* —**aug·ment′er** *n.*

**aug·men·ta·tion** (ôg′men tā′shən) *n.* 1. an augmenting or being augmented 2. an addition; increase

**aug·men·ta·tive** (ôg men′tə tiv) *adj.* augmenting —*n.* an intensifying word or affix

**au gra·tin** (ō grät′'n, ô-; -grat′-) [Fr., lit., with scrapings] made with a lightly browned crust of bread crumbs and grated cheese

**Augs·burg** (ôgz′bərg; *G.* ouks′boŏrk) city in Bavaria, S West Germany: pop. 211,000

**au·gur** (ô′gər) *n.* [L., orig., a priest at rituals of fertility; prob. < *augere* (see AUGMENT)] 1. in ancient Rome, any of a group of officials who interpreted omens as favorable or unfavorable for an undertaking 2. a fortuneteller; soothsayer; prophet —*vt., vi.* 1. to foretell or prophesy from omens 2. to be an omen (of) —**augur ill** (or **well**) to be a bad (or good) omen

**au·gu·ry** (ô′gyər ē) *n., pl.* -ries 1. the rite conducted by an augur 2. an omen; indication

**Au·gust** (ô′gəst) [L. < AUGUSTUS (Caesar)] a masculine name —*n.* the eighth month of the year, having 31 days: abbrev. Aug., Ag.

**au·gust** (ô gust′) *adj.* [L. *augustus,* orig., prob. "consecrated by the augurs"] 1. inspiring awe and reverence; imposing 2. worthy of respect; venerable —**au·gust′ly** *adv.* —**au·gust′ness** *n.*

**Au·gus·ta** (ô gus′tə) [L., fem. of AUGUSTUS] 1. a feminine name 2. city in E Ga.: pop. 60,000 3. capital of Me.: pop. 22,000

**Au·gus·tan** (ô gus′tən) *adj.* 1. of or characteristic of Augustus Caesar, his reign (27 B.C.–14 A.D.), or his times 2. of or like any similar age; classical; elegant —*n.* a writer living in an Augustan age

**Au·gus·tine** (ô′gəs tēn′, ô gus′t'n) [< L. dim. of AUGUSTUS] 1. a masculine name: var. *Austin, Augustin* 2. Saint *a)* 354–430 A.D.; Christian church father & bishop in North Africa *b)* ?–604? A.D.; Roman monk sent to convert the English to Christianity —**Au′gus·tin′i·an** (-tin′ē ən) *adj., n.*

**Au·gus·tus** (ô gus′təs) [L. < *augustus,* AUGUST] 1. a masculine name: dim. *Gus* 2. (*Gaius Julius Caesar Octavianus*) 63 B.C.–14 A.D.; 1st Roman emperor (27 B.C.–14 A.D.): grandnephew of Julius Caesar: also called *Octavian*

**au jus** (ō zhoō′, ō joōs′; *Fr.* ō zhü′) [Fr., with the juice] served in its natural gravy: said of meat

**auk** (ôk) *n.* [dial. *alk* < ON. *alka*] any of a number of related diving birds of the northern seas, with webbed feet and short wings used as paddles

‡**au lait** (ō le′) [Fr.] with milk

**auld** (ôld) *adj.* [Dial. & Scot.] old

**auld lang syne** (ôld′ laŋ′ zīn′, sīn′) [Scot., lit., old long since] old times; the good old days

‡**au na·tu·rel** (ō ná tü rel′) [Fr.] 1. in the natural state 2. naked 3. prepared simply

**aunt** (ant, änt) *n.* [< ME. & OFr. < L. *amita,* paternal aunt] 1. a sister of one's mother or father 2. the wife of one's uncle

**GREAT AUK**
**(to 30 in. high)**

**aunt·ie, aunt·y** (an′tē, än′-) *n.* aunt: a familiar or affectionate form

**au·ra** (ôr′ə) *n., pl.* -ras, -rae (-ē) [L. < Gr., akin to *aēr,* air] 1. an invisible emanation 2. a particular atmosphere or quality that seems to arise from and surround a person or thing

**au·ral** (ôr′əl) *adj.* [< L. *auris,* ear + -AL] of or received through the ear or the sense of hearing —**au′ral·ly** *adv.*

**au·re·ate** (ôr′ē it) *adj.* [< LL. < L. *aureus < aurum,* gold] 1. golden; gilded 2. splendid or brilliant, often affectedly so

**Au·re·li·us** (ô rē′lē əs, -rēl′yəs), **Marcus** (*Marcus Aurelius Antoninus*) 121–180 A.D.; Roman emperor (161–180) & Stoic philosopher

**au·re·ole** (ôr′ē ōl′) *n.* [< L. *aureola* (*corona*), golden (crown) < *aureus:* see AUREATE] 1. a halo 2. the sun's corona Also **au·re·o·la** (ô rē′ə lə)

**Au·re·o·my·cin** (ôr′ē ō mīs′'n) [< L. *aureus,* golden + Gr. *mykēs,* fungus + -IN¹] *a trademark for* CHLORTETRACYCLINE

**au re·voir** (ō′rə vwär′) [Fr. < re-, again + *videre,* to see] until we meet again; goodbye

**au·ri·cle** (ôr′ə k'l) *n.* [< L. *auricula,* dim. of *auris,* ear] 1. *Anat. a)* the external part of the ear; pinna *b)* an atrium of the heart 2. *Biol.* an earlike part or organ

**au·ric·u·lar** (ô rik′yoo lər) *adj.* 1. of or near the ear, or having to do with the sense of hearing 2. spoken directly into the ear 3. ear-shaped 4. *Anat.* of an auricle —**au·ric′u·lar·ly** *adv.*

**au·rif·er·ous** (ô rif′ər əs) *adj.* [< L. < *aurum,* gold + *ferre,* to BEAR¹ + -OUS] bearing or yielding gold

**au·ri·form** (ôr′ə fôrm′) *adj.* ear-shaped

**au·rochs** (ô′räks) *n., pl.* **au′rochs** [G. *auerochs* < OHG. *urohso* < *uro,* aurochs + *ohso,* ox] 1. the wild ox of Europe, now extinct 2. the nearly extinct European bison

**Au·ro·ra** (ô rôr′ə, ə-) [L., lit., dawn] 1. *Rom. Myth.* the goddess of dawn 2. [immediately or ult. < prec.] *a)* city in NE Ill., near Chicago: pop. 81,000 *b)* city in NC Colo. near Denver: pop. 159,000 —*n.* [a-] *pl.* -ras, -rae (-ē)

the dawn **2.** *same as* AURORA AUSTRALIS or AURORA BOREALIS —au·ro'ral, au·ro're·an (-ē ən) *adj.*

**aurora aus·tra·lis** (ô strā'lis) [L.: see prec. & AUSTRAL] luminous bands of light like the aurora borealis, but in the Southern Hemisphere

**aurora bo·re·a·lis** (bôr'ē al'is) [AL.: see AURORA & BOREAS] luminous bands or streamers of light sometimes appearing in the night sky of the Northern Hemisphere; northern lights

**Au·schwitz** (ou'shvits) city in SW Poland: site of a Nazi concentration camp notorious as an extermination center: Pol. name, OŚWIĘCIM

**aus·cul·ta·tion** (ôs'kəl tā'shən) *n.* [< pp. of L. *auscultare*, to listen] **1.** a listening **2.** a listening, often with a stethoscope, to sounds in the chest, abdomen, etc., as in diagnosis —aus'cul·tate' *vt., vi.* -tat'ed, -tat'ing —aus'cul·ta'tor *n.*

**aus·land·er** (ous'lan'dər, ôs'-) *n.* [G. *ausländer* < *aus*, out + *land*, land] a foreigner; outsider

**aus·pice** (ôs'pis) *n., pl.* **-pi·ces'** (-pə sēz') [Fr. < L. *auspicium*, omen] **1.** an omen, esp. a favorable one **2.** [*pl.*] guiding sponsorship; patronage

**aus·pi·cious** (ôs pish'əs) *adj.* **1.** of good omen; favorable **2.** favored by fortune; successful —aus·pi'cious·ly *adv.* —aus·pi'cious·ness *n.*

**Aus·ten** (ôs'tən), **Jane** 1775–1817; Eng. novelist

**aus·tere** (ô stir') *adj.* [< OFr. < L. < Gr. *austēros* < *auos*, dry] **1.** having a stern manner; forbidding **2.** showing strict self-discipline; ascetic **3.** very plain —aus·tere'ly *adv.* —aus·tere'ness *n.*

**aus·ter·i·ty** (ô ster'ə tē) *n., pl.* **-ties 1.** an austere quality, state, act, or practice **2.** tightened economy, as from shortages of goods

**Aus·tin** (ôs'tən) **1.** a masculine name: see AUGUSTINE **2.** [after S. F. *Austin*, Am. pioneer in Tex.] capital of Tex., on the Colorado River: pop. 345,000 (met. area 533,000)

**aus·tral** (ôs'trəl) *adj.* [< L. < *auster*, the south] **1.** southern; southerly **2.** [A-] Australian

**Aus·tral·a·sia** (ôs'trə lā'zhə, -shə) the islands of the SW Pacific; specif., *a)* Australia, New Zealand, and adjacent islands *b)* Australia, New Zealand, the Malay Archipelago, and Oceania —Aus'tral·a'sian *adj., n.*

**Aus·tral·ia** (ô strāl'yə) [< L. (*terra*) *australis*, southern (land)] **1.** island continent between the S Pacific and Indian oceans **2.** country comprising this continent and Tasmania: a member of the Commonwealth: 2,971,081 sq. mi.; pop. 12,446,000; cap. Canberra —Aus·tral'ian *adj., n.*

**Australian ballot** an official ballot listing candidates for election to public office, marked by the voter in secrecy

**Aus·tra·loid** (ôs'trə loid') *adj.* [AUSTRAL(IA) + -OID] designating or of an ethnic group of mankind that includes the Australian aborigines, the Ainu, etc. —*n.* any member of this group

**Aus·tri·a** (ôs'trē ə) country in C Europe: 32,375 sq. mi.; pop. 7,371,000; cap. Vienna: Ger. name, ÖSTERREICH —Aus'tri·an *adj., n.*

**Aus·tri·a-Hun·ga·ry** (-huŋ'gər ē) former monarchy in C Europe (1867–1918) —Aus·tro-Hun·gar·i·an (ôs'trō huŋ ger'ē ən) *adj.*

**Aus·tro-**[1] *a combining form meaning* Austria

**Aus·tro-**[2] [< L. *auster*, south] *a combining form meaning* South, Southern

**Aus·tro-A·si·at·ic** (ôs'trō ā'zhē at'ik) *adj.* of a family of languages widely scattered throughout SE Asia, including Vietnamese

**Aus·tro·ne·sia** (ôs'trō nē'zhə, -shə) island area extending from Madagascar east to Hawaii and Easter Island

**Aus·tro·ne·sian** (-zhən, -shən) *adj.* **1.** of Austronesia, its people, etc. **2.** *same as* MALAYO-POLYNESIAN

**au·tar·chy** (ô'tär kē) *n., pl.* **-chies** [< Gr. < *autarchos*, absolute ruler < *autos*, self + *archos*, first, ruler] **1.** absolute rule; autocracy **2.** a country under such rule **3.** *same as* AUTARKY —au·tar'chic, au·tar'chi·cal *adj.*

**au·tar·ky** (ô'tär kē) *n.* [Gr. *autarkeia* < *autos*, self + *arkein*, to suffice] economic self-sufficiency as a national policy —au·tar'kic, au·tar'ki·cal *adj.*

**auth. 1.** author **2.** authority **3.** authorized

**au·then·tic** (ô then'tik) *adj.* [< OFr. < LL. < Gr. *authentikos* < *authentēs*, one who does things himself] **1.** that can be believed; reliable [an *authentic* report] **2.** genuine; real [an *authentic* antique] **3.** legally executed, as a deed —au·then'ti·cal·ly *adv.* —au·then·tic·i·ty (ô'thən tis'ə tē) *n.*

**au·then·ti·cate** (-tə kāt') *vt.* **-cat'ed, -cat'ing** to establish as authentic, or true, valid, genuine, etc. —au·then'ti·ca'tion *n.* —au·then'ti·ca'tor *n.*

**au·thor** (ô'thər) *n.* [< OFr. < L. *auctor* < *augere*, to increase] **1.** one who makes or originates something; creator **2.** the writer (*of* a book, article, etc.) —*vt.* to be the au-

thor of —au'thor·ess [Now Rare] *n.fem.* —au·tho·ri·al (ô thôr'ē əl) *adj.*

**au·thor·i·tar·i·an** (ə thôr'ə ter'ē ən, -thär'-) *adj.* believing in or characterized by unquestioning obedience to authority rather than individual freedom —*n.* a person who believes in or enforces such obedience —au·thor'i·tar'i·an·ism *n.*

**au·thor·i·ta·tive** (ə thôr'ə tāt'iv, -thär'-) *adj.* **1.** having authority; official **2.** reliable because coming from an authority or expert **3.** asserting authority; dictatorial —au·thor'i·ta'tive·ly *adv.* —au·thor'i·ta'tive·ness *n.*

**au·thor·i·ty** (ə thôr'ə tē, -thär'-) *n., pl.* **-ties** [< OFr. < L. *auctoritas* < *auctor*: see AUTHOR] **1.** *a)* the power or right to give commands, enforce obedience, take action, or make final decisions; jurisdiction *b)* the position of one having such power [the man in *authority*] *c)* such power as delegated; authorization **2.** power or influence resulting from knowledge, prestige, etc. **3.** a writing, decision, etc. cited in support of an opinion, action, etc. **4.** *a)* [*pl.*] persons, esp. in government, having the power to enforce orders, laws, etc. *b)* a government agency that administers a project **5.** an expert whose opinion is considered reliable **6.** self-assurance based on expertness

**au·thor·ize** (ô'thə rīz') *vt.* **-ized', -iz'ing 1.** to give official approval to or permission for **2.** to give power or authority to; empower; commission **3.** to give justification for; warrant —au'thor·i·za'tion *n.* —au'thor·iz'er *n.*

**Authorized Version** the revised English translation of the Bible published in England in 1611 with the authorization of King James I: also called *King James Version*

**au·thor·ship** (ô'thər ship') *n.* **1.** the profession of a writer **2.** the origin (of a book, idea, etc.) with reference to its author or originator [a story of unknown *authorship*]

**au·tism** (ô'tiz'm) *n.* [AUT(O)- + -ISM] *Psychol.* a state of mind characterized by self-absorption, fantasy, and a disregard of external reality —au·tis'tic *adj.*

**au·to** (ôt'ō) *n., pl.* **-tos** an automobile —*vi.* **-toed, -to·ing** to go by automobile: an earlier usage

**au·to-** [Gr. *autos*, self] *a combining form meaning:* **1.** of or for oneself; self [*autobiography*] **2.** by oneself or itself [*automobile*] Also, before a vowel, **aut-**

‡**Au·to·bahn** (ou'tō bän'; E. ôt'ə bän') *n., pl.* **-bahn'en** (-bä'nən); E. **-bahns'** [G.] in Germany, an automobile expressway

**au·to·bi·og·ra·phy** (ôt'ə bī äg'rə fē, -bē-) *n., pl.* **-phies** the story of one's own life written or dictated by oneself —au'to·bi·og'ra·pher *n.* —au'to·bi'o·graph'i·cal (-bī'ə graf'i k'l), au'to·bi'o·graph'ic *adj.* —au'to·bi'o·graph'i·cal·ly *adv.*

**au·to·clave** (ôt'ə klāv') *n.* [Fr. < *auto-*, AUTO- + L. *clavis*, a key] a container for sterilizing, cooking, etc. by superheated steam under pressure —*vt.* **-claved', -clav'ing** to sterilize, etc. in this

**au·toc·ra·cy** (ô täk'rə sē) *n., pl.* **-cies** [< Gr. < *autokratēs*: see ff.] **1.** a government in which one person has supreme power; dictatorship **2.** unlimited power or authority over others

**au·to·crat** (ôt'ə krat') *n.* [< Fr. < Gr. *autokratēs*, absolute ruler < *autos*, self + *kratos*, power] **1.** a ruler with absolute power; dictator; despot **2.** anyone having unlimited power over others **3.** any domineering, self-willed person —au'to·crat'ic, au'to·crat'i·cal *adj.* —au'to·crat'i·cal·ly *adv.*

**au·to-da-fé** (ôt'ō də fā', out'-) *n., pl.* **au'tos-da-fé'** [Port., lit., act of the faith] **1.** the public ceremony in which the Inquisition judged and sentenced those tried as heretics **2.** the execution of the sentence; esp., the public burning of a heretic

**au·tog·a·my** (ô täg'ə mē) *n.* [AUTO- + -GAMY] self-fertilization, as in a flower receiving pollen from its own stamens —au·tog'a·mous *adj.*

**au·to·gi·ro, au·to·gy·ro** (ôt'ə jī'rō) *n., pl.* **-ros** [orig. a trademark < AUTO- + Gr. *gyros*, a circle] an earlier kind of aircraft having both a propeller and a large horizontal rotor

**au·to·graph** (ôt'ə graf') *n.* [< L. < Gr. *autographos* < *autos*, self + *graphein*, to write] **1.** a person's own signature or handwriting **2.** a thing written in one's own handwriting; holograph —*vt.* **1.** to write (something) with one's own hand **2.** to write one's signature on or in —au'to·graph'ic *adj.* —au'to·graph'i·cal·ly *adv.*

**au·to·hyp·no·sis** (ôt'ō hip nō'sis) *n.* a hypnotizing of oneself or the state of being so hypnotized

**au·to·in·tox·i·ca·tion** (-in täk'sə kā'shən) *n.* poisoning by toxic substances ( autotoxins ) formed within the body —au'to·tox'ic *adj.*

**au·to·mat** (ôt'ə mat') *n.* [see AUTOMATIC] a restaurant in which patrons get food from small compartments opened by putting coins into slots

---

fat, āpe, cär, ten, ēven, is, bīte; gō, hôrn, tool, look; oil, out; up, fur; get; joy; yet; chin; she; thin, *then*; zh, leisure; ŋ, ring; ə for *a* in *ago*, *e* in *agent*, *i* in *sanity*, *o* in *comply*, *u* in *focus*; ' as in *able* (ā'b'l); Fr. bal; ë, Fr. coeur; ö, Fr. feu; Fr. mon; ô, Fr. coq; ü, Fr. duc; r, Fr. cri; H, G. ich; kh, G. doch; ‡foreign; *hypothetical; < derived from. See inside front cover.

**au·to·mate** (ôt′ə māt′) *vt.* **-mat′ed, -mat′ing** [backformation < AUTOMATION] **1.** to convert (a factory, process, etc.) to automation **2.** to use the techniques of automation in

**au·to·mat·ic** (ôt′ə mat′ik) *adj.* [Gr. *automatos*, self-moving] **1.** done without conscious thought or volition, as if mechanically, or from force of habit **2.** involuntary or reflex, as some muscle action **3.** *a)* moving, operating, etc. by itself *[automatic machinery] b)* done with automatic equipment **4.** *Firearms* using the force of the explosion of a shell to eject, reload, and fire again, so that shots continue in rapid succession with one trigger pull: cf. SEMIAUTOMATIC —*n.* **1.** an automatic pistol, rifle, etc. **2.** any automatic machine —**au′to·mat′i·cal·ly** *adv.*

**au·to·ma·tion** (-mā′shən) *n.* [AUTOMA(TIC) + -TION] **1.** in manufacturing, a system or method in which many or all of the processes are automatically performed or controlled by machinery, electronic devices, etc. **2.** any system using equipment to replace people **3.** the state of being automated

**au·tom·a·tism** (ô täm′ə tiz′m) *n.* **1.** the quality or condition of being automatic **2.** automatic action **3.** *Physiol.* action independent of outside stimulus or of conscious control

**au·tom·a·tize** (-tīz′) *vt.* **-tized′, -tiz′ing 1.** to make automatic **2.** *same as* AUTOMATE

**au·tom·a·ton** (ô täm′ə tän′, -tən) *n., pl.* **-tons′, -ta** (-tə) [Gr., neut. of *automatos:* see AUTOMATIC] **1.** anything that can move or act of itself **2.** an apparatus that works or moves by responding to preset controls or computerized instructions **3.** a person acting in a mechanical way

**au·to·mo·bile** (ôt′ə mə bēl′, -mō-; ôt′ə mə bēl′; ôt′ə-mō′bēl) *n.* [Fr.: see AUTO- & MOBILE] a passenger car propelled by an engine, esp. an internal-combustion engine, and used for traveling on streets or roads; motorcar

**au·to·mo·tive** (ôt′ə mōt′iv) *adj.* [AUTO- + -MOTIVE] **1.** moving by its own power; self-moving **2.** of or having to do with motor vehicles

**au·to·nom·ic** (-näm′ik) *adj.* **1.** of or controlled by the autonomic nervous system **2.** *Biol.* resulting from internal causes —**au′to·nom′i·cal·ly** *adv.*

**autonomic nervous system** the divisions of the nervous system that control the motor functions of the heart, lungs, intestines, smooth muscles, glands, etc.

**au·ton·o·mous** (ô tän′ə məs) *adj.* [< Gr. < *autos*, self + *nomos*, law] **1.** of an autonomy **2.** *a)* having self-government *b)* functioning independently **3.** *Biol.* functioning independently of other parts

**au·ton·o·my** (-mē) *n.* **1.** self-government **2.** *pl.* **-mies** any state that governs itself

**au·top·sy** (ô′täp′sē) *n., pl.* **-sies** [< ML. & Gr. *autopsia*, a seeing with one's own eyes < *autos*, self + *opsis*, a sight] an examination and dissection of a dead body to discover the cause of death, damage done by a disease, etc.; postmortem

**au·to·sug·ges·tion** (ôt′ō səg jes′chən) *n.* suggestion to oneself arising within oneself and having effects on one's thinking and bodily function

**au·tumn** (ôt′əm) *n.* [< OFr. < L. *autumnus;* prob. of Etruscan origin] **1.** the season that comes between summer and winter; fall **2.** any period of maturity or of beginning decline —*adj.* of, in, characteristic of, or like autumn —**au·tum′nal** (ô tum′n'l) *adj.* —**au·tum′nal·ly** *adv.*

**aux.** auxiliary

**aux·il·ia·ry** (ôg zil′yər ē, -zil′ər-) *adj.* [< L. < *auxilium*, aid < pp. of *augere*, AUGMENT] **1.** giving help or aid; assisting **2.** acting in a subsidiary, or subordinate, capacity **3.** additional; supplementary; reserve —*n., pl.* **-ries 1.** an auxiliary person or thing **2.** *[pl.]* foreign troops aiding a country at war **3.** a supplementary group or organization *[a women's auxiliary]*

**auxiliary verb** a verb that helps form tenses, moods, or voices of other verbs, as *have, be, may, can, must, do, shall, will*

**Av., av.** avenue

**av.** **1.** average **2.** avoirdupois

**A.V.** Authorized Version (of the Bible)

**a.v., a/v, A/V** ad valorem

**a·vail** (ə vāl′) *vi., vt.* [< OFr. *a* (L. *ad*), to + *valoir* < L. *valere*, to be strong] to be of use, help, worth, or advantage (to), as in accomplishing an end —*n.* effective use or help; advantage *[of no avail]* —**avail oneself** *[of or to]* take advantage of (an opportunity, etc.)

**a·vail·a·ble** (ə vā′lə b'l) *adj.* **1.** that can be used **2.** that can be got, had, or reached; accessible **3.** qualified and willing to run for public office —**a·vail′a·bil′i·ty** *n.* —**a·vail′a·bly** *adv.*

**av·a·lanche** (av′ə lanch′) *n.* [Fr. (altered after *avaler*, to descend) < *lavanche* < LL. < L. < *labi*, to slip, glide down] **1.** a large mass of loosened snow, earth, rocks, etc. suddenly and swiftly sliding down a mountain **2.** anything that comes suddenly in overwhelming number *[an avalanche of

mail] —vi., vt.* **-lanched′, -lanch′ing** to come down (on) like an avalanche

**a·vant-garde** (ä vänt′gärd′; *Fr.* à vän gàrd′) *n.* [Fr., lit., advance guard] the leaders in new or unconventional movements, esp. in the arts; vanguard —*adj.* of such movements, ideas, etc. —**a·vant′-gard′ism** *n.* —**a·vant′-gard′-ist** *n.*

**av·a·rice** (av′ər is) *n.* [< OFr. < L. < *avarus*, greedy < *avere*, to desire] too great a desire to have wealth; greed for riches; cupidity —**av·a·ri·cious** (av′ə rish′əs) *adj.* —**av′a·ri′cious·ly** *adv.* —**av′a·ri′cious·ness** *n.*

**a·vast** (ə vast′) *interj.* [< Du. *houd vast*, hold fast] *Naut.* stop! cease! halt!

**av·a·tar** (av′ə tär′) *n.* [Sans. *avatāra*, descent] **1.** *Hinduism* a god's coming down in bodily form to the earth; incarnation **2.** any embodiment

**a·vaunt** (ə vônt′, -vänt′) *interj.* [< OFr. < L. *ab*, from + *ante*, before] [Archaic] begone! go away!

**avdp.** avoirdupois

**a·ve** (ä′vā, ä′vē) *interj.* [L., imperative of *avere*, to be well] **1.** hail! **2.** farewell! —*n.* **1.** the salutation *ave* **2.** [A-] the prayer AVE MARIA

**Ave., ave.** avenue

**A·ve Ma·ri·a** (ä′vä mə rē′ə, -vē) [L. (Luke 1:28)] **1.** "Hail, Mary," the first words of a prayer to the Virgin Mary used in the Roman Catholic Church **2.** this prayer **3.** a musical setting of this

**a·venge** (ə venj′) *vt., vi.* **a·venged′, a·veng′ing** [< OFr. < *a-* (L. *ad*), to + *vengier* < L. *vindicare*, to claim: see VINDICATE] **1.** to get revenge for (an injury, wrong, etc.) **2.** to take vengeance on behalf of, as for a wrong —**a·veng′er** *n.*

**av·e·nue** (av′ə nōō′, -nyōō′) *n.* [Fr. < L. *advenire:* see ADVENT] **1.** a road, path, or drive, often bordered with trees **2.** a way of approach to something **3.** a street, esp. a wide, principal one

**a·ver** (ə vur′) *vt.* **a·verred′, a·ver′ring** [< OFr. *averrer* < L. *ad*, to + *verus*, true] **1.** to declare to be true; affirm **2.** *Law* to state or declare formally; assert; allege —**a·ver′-ment** *n.*

**av·er·age** (av′rij, -ər ij) *n.* [< Fr. *avarie*, damage to ship < It. < Ar. *'awâr*, damaged goods; sense development from *n.* 4] **1.** the numerical result obtained by dividing the sum of two or more quantities by the number of quantities; an arithmetic mean **2.** any similar value *[a grade average of C]* **3.** the usual or normal kind, amount, quality, etc. **4.** *Marine Law a)* a loss incurred by damage to a ship or its cargo *b)* the equitable division of such a loss among the interested parties —*adj.* **1.** being a numerical average **2.** usual; normal; ordinary —*vi.* **-aged, -ag·ing 1.** to be or amount to on the average **2.** to buy or sell more shares, goods, etc. at intervals so as to get a better average price —*vt.* **1.** to calculate the average or mean of **2.** to do, take, etc. on the average **3.** to divide proportionately among more than two —**average out** to arrive at an average eventually —**on the** (or **an**) **average** as an average quantity, rate, etc. —**av′er·age·ness** *n.*

**a·verse** (ə vurs′) *adj.* [< L. pp. of *avertere:* see AVERT] not willing; reluctant; opposed (*to*) —**a·verse′ly** *adv.* —**a·verse′ness** *n.*

**a·ver·sion** (ə vur′zhən, -shən) *n.* **1.** a strong or definite dislike; antipathy; repugnance **2.** the object arousing such dislike

**a·vert** (ə vurt′) *vt.* [< L. *avertere* < *a-* (*ab-*), from + *vertere*, to turn] **1.** to turn away *[to avert one's eyes]* **2.** to keep from happening; avoid; prevent *[to avert a catastrophe]* —**a·vert′i·ble** *adj.*

**A·ves·ta** (ə ves′tə) *n.* [< Per.] the sacred writings of Zoroastrianism, in an ancient Iranian language —**A·ves′-tan** *adj., n.*

**avg.** average

**a·vi·an** (ā′vē ən) *adj.* [< L. *avis*, bird + -AN] of or having to do with birds

**a·vi·ar·y** (-er′ē) *n., pl.* **-ar′ies** [< L. < *avis*, bird] a large cage or building for keeping many birds

**a·vi·a·tion** (ā′vē ā′shən) *n.* [Fr. < L. *avis*, bird] **1.** the art or science of flying airplanes **2.** the development and operation of heavier-than-air craft

**a·vi·a·tor** (ā′vē āt′ər) *n.* an airplane pilot; flier —**a′vi·a′-trix** (-ā′triks) *n.fem.*

**av·id** (av′id) *adj.* [L. *avidus* < *avere*, to desire] **1.** having an intense desire or craving; greedy *[avid for power]* **2.** eager and enthusiastic *[an avid reader]* —**a·vid·i·ty** (ə vid′ə tē) *n.* —**av′id·ly** *adv.*

**A·vi·gnon** (à vē nyôn′) city in SE France: seat of the papacy (1309–77): pop. 73,000

**a·vi·on·ics** (ā′vē än′iks) *n.pl.* [AVI(ATION) + (ELECTR)ON-ICS] *[with sing. v.]* the branch of electronics dealing with the use of electronic equipment in aviation and astronautics —**a′vi·on′ic** *adj.*

**av·o·ca·do** (av′ə kä′dō, äv′-) *n., pl.* **-dos** [Sp. < MexSp. *aguacate* < Nahuatl *ahuacatl*] **1.** a thick-skinned, pear-shaped tropical fruit, yellowish green to purplish black, with a single large seed and yellow, buttery flesh, used in salads; alligator pear  2. the tree that it grows on

**av·o·ca·tion** (av'ə kā'shən) *n.* [< L. pp. of *avocare* < *ab-*, away + *vocare*, to call] something one does in addition to his regular work, and usually for pleasure; hobby —**av'o·ca'tion·al** *adj.*

**av·o·cet** (av'ə set') *n.* [< Fr. < It.] a long-legged wading bird with webbed feet and a slender bill that curves upward

**a·void** (ə void') *vt.* [< Anglo-Fr. < OFr. *esvuidier*, to empty < *es-* (< L. *ex*), out + *vuidier:* see VOID] 1. to make void; annul, invalidate, or quash (a plea, etc. in law)  2. to keep away from; shun [to *avoid* crowds]  3. to keep from happening [to *avoid* breakage] —**a·void'a·ble** *adj.* —**a·void'a·bly** *adv.* —**a·void'ance** *n.*

**av·oir·du·pois** (av'ər də poiz', av'ər də poiz') *n.* [< OFr. *aveir de peis*, goods having weight] 1. *same as* AVOIRDUPOIS WEIGHT  2. [Colloq.] heaviness or weight, esp. of a person

**avoirdupois weight** an English and American system of weights based on a pound of 16 ounces: see TABLES OF WEIGHTS AND MEASURES in Supplements

**a·vouch** (ə vouch') *vt.* [< OFr. *avochier* < L. *advocare:* see ADVOCATE] 1. to vouch for; guarantee  2. to declare the truth of; affirm  3. to acknowledge openly; avow —**a·vouch'ment** *n.*

**a·vow** (ə vou') *vt.* [< OFr. *avouer* < L. *advocare:* see AD-VOCATE] 1. to declare openly or admit frankly  2. to acknowledge or claim (oneself) to be [he *avowed* himself a patriot] —**a·vowed'** *adj.* —**a·vow·ed·ly** (ə vou'id lē) *adv.* —**a·vow'er** *n.*

**a·vow·al** (-əl) *n.* open acknowledgment or declaration; frank admission

**a·vun·cu·lar** (ə vuŋ'kyə lər) *adj.* [< L. *avunculus*, maternal uncle, dim. of *avus*, ancestor] of, like, or in the relationship of, an uncle

**aw** (ô, ä) *interj.* an exclamation of protest, dislike, disgust, sympathy, etc.

**a·wait** (ə wāt') *vt.* [< ONormFr. < *a-* (L. *ad*), to + *waitier*, WAIT] 1. to wait for; expect  2. to be in store for; be ready for —*vi.* to wait

**a·wake** (ə wāk') *vt.* **a·woke'** or **a·waked'**, **a·waked'**, **a·wak'ing**; occas. Brit. pp. **a·woke'** or **a·wok'en** [< OE. *awacan* (on- + *wacan*, to arise, awake) & OE. *awacian* (on- + *wacian*, to be awake, watch)] 1. to rouse from sleep; wake  2. to rouse from inactivity; stir up  3. to call forth (memories, etc.) —*vi.* 1. to come out of sleep; wake  2. to become active  3. to become aware (with *to*) —*adj.* 1. not asleep  2. active or alert

**a·wak·en** (ə wāk'n) *vt., vi.* to awake; wake up; rouse —**a·wak·en·er** *n.*

**a·wak·en·ing** (-iŋ) *n., adj.* 1. (a) waking up  2. (an) arousing, as of impulses, interest, etc.

**a·ward** (ə wôrd') *vt.* [< Anglo-Fr. < ONormFr. < *es-* (< L. *ex*) + Gmc. hyp. *wardon:* see GUARD] 1. to give by the decision of a law court or arbitrator  2. to give as the result of judging, as in a contest [*award* prizes] —*n.* 1. a decision, as by a judge or arbitrator  2. something awarded; prize

**a·ware** (ə wer') *adj.* [< OE. *gewær* < *wær*, cautious] 1. orig., on one's guard  2. knowing or realizing; conscious; informed —**a·ware'ness** *n.*

**a·wash** (ə wôsh', -wäsh') *adv., adj.* 1. just above the surface of the water and washed over by it  2. floating on the water  3. flooded with water

**a·way** (ə wā') *adv.* [< OE. *aweg* < *on*, on + *weg*, way] 1. from any given place; off [to run *away*]  2. in another place, esp. the proper place [put tools *away*]  3. in another direction [look *away*]  4. far [*away* behind]  5. off; aside [to clear snow *away*]  6. from one's possession [give it *away*]  7. out of existence [to fade *away*]  8. at once [fire *away*]  9. without stopping [to work *away* all night]  10. into action [*away* we go!] —*adj.* 1. absent; gone [he is *away*]  2. at a distance [a mile *away*]  3. *Baseball* out [one *away* in this inning] —*interj.* 1. begone!  2. let's go! —**away with** 1. take away  2. go or come away —**do away with** 1. to get rid of  2. to kill

**awe** (ô) *n.* [ON. *agi*] a mixed feeling of reverence, fear, and wonder, caused by something sublime, etc. —*vt.* **awed, aw'ing** to inspire awe in; fill with awe —**stand** (or **be**) **in awe of** to respect and fear —**awe'less, aw'less** *adj.*

**·weigh** (ə wā') *adj. Naut.* clearing the bottom; being weighed: said of an anchor

**awe·some** (ô'səm) *adj.* 1. inspiring awe  2. showing awe —**awe'some·ly** *adv.* —**awe'some·ness** *n.*

**we-struck** (ô'struk') *adj.* filled with awe or wonder: also **awe'·strick'en** (-strik'ən)

**w·ful** (ô'fəl) *adj.* [see AWE & -FUL] 1. inspiring awe

2. causing fear; terrifying  3. [Colloq.] *a)* very bad, unpleasant, etc. [an *awful* joke] *b)* great [an *awful* bore] —*adv.* [Colloq.] very; extremely [*awful* happy] —**aw'ful·ness** *n.*

**aw·ful·ly** (ô'fə lē, ô'flē) *adv.* 1. in a way to inspire awe  2. [Colloq.] badly or offensively [to behave *awfully*]  3. [Colloq.] very; extremely

**a·while** (ə wil', -hwil') *adv.* for a while; for a short time

**awk·ward** (ôk'wərd) *adj.* [< ON. *ofugr*, turned backward + OE. *-weard*, -WARD] 1. not having grace or skill; clumsy; bungling  2. hard to handle and use; unwieldy  3. inconvenient; uncomfortable [an *awkward* position]  4. embarrassed or embarrassing [an *awkward* remark]  5. not easy to deal with; delicate [an *awkward* situation] —**awk'ward·ly** *adv.* —**awk'ward·ness** *n.*

**awl** (ôl) *n.* [< OE. *æl, awel*] a small, pointed tool for making holes in wood, leather, etc.

**awn** (ôn) *n.* [ON. *ogn*, chaff] any of the bristly fibers on a head of barley, oats, etc., or, usually, such fibers collectively; beard —**awned** *adj.* —**awn'less** *adj.*

AWN

**awn·ing** (ô'niŋ) *n.* [< ? MFr. *auvans*, pl. of *auvent*, window shade] a structure of canvas, metal, etc. extended before a window or door or over a patio, deck, etc. as a protection from sun or rain

**a·woke** (ə wōk') alt. pt. & occas. Brit. pp. of AWAKE

**a·wok·en** (ə wōk'n) occas. Brit. pp. of AWAKE

**A·WOL, a·wol** (ā'wôl') *adj.* [*a(bsent)* w(ith)o(ut) l(eave)] *Mil.* absent without leave, but without intention of deserting —*n.* one who is AWOL

**a·wry** (ə rī') *adv., adj.* [see A-¹ (sense 1) & WRY] 1. with a twist to a side; askew  2. wrong; amiss [our plans went *awry*]

**ax, axe** (aks) *n., pl.* **ax'es** [OE. *eax, æx*] 1. a tool with a long handle and a bladed head, for chopping trees and splitting wood  2. any similar tool or weapon, as a battle-ax —*vt.* **axed, ax'ing** 1. to trim, split, etc. with an ax  2. to get rid of —**get the ax** [Colloq.] 1. to be beheaded  2. to be discharged from one's job —**have an ax to grind** [Colloq.] to have an object of one's own to promote

**ax·es¹** (ak'siz) *n. pl. of* AX

**ax·es²** (ak'sēz) *n. pl. of* AXIS

**ax·i·al** (ak'sē əl) *adj.* 1. of, like, or forming an axis  2. around or along an axis —**ax'i·al·ly** *adv.*

**ax·il** (ak'sil) *n.* [< L. *axilla:* see ff.] the upper angle between a leaf, twig, etc. and the stem from which it grows

**ax·il·la** (ak sil'ə) *n., pl.* **-lae** (-ē), **-las** [L., armpit] 1. the armpit  2. *Bot.* an axil

**ax·il·lar** (ak'sə lər) *adj. same as* AXILLARY —*n.* any of the stiff feathers on the underside of a bird's wing where it joins the body

**ax·il·la·ry** (ak'sə ler'ē) *adj.* 1. *Anat.* of or near the axilla  2. *Bot.* of, in, or growing from an axil —*n., pl.* **-ries** *same as* AXILLAR

**ax·i·om** (ak'sē əm) *n.* [< Fr. < L. < Gr. *axiōma*, authority < *axios*, worthy] 1. a statement widely accepted as true; truism  2. an established principle or law of a science, art, etc.  3. *Logic, Math.* a statement that needs no proof because its truth is obvious; self-evident proposition

**ax·i·o·mat·ic** (ak'sē ə mat'ik) *adj.* 1. of or like an axiom; self-evident  2. full of axioms; aphoristic —**ax'i·o·mat'i·cal·ly** *adv.*

**ax·is** (ak'sis) *n., pl.* **ax'es** (-sēz) [L.] 1. a real or imaginary straight line on which an object rotates or is regarded as rotating [the earth's *axis*]  2. a real or imaginary straight line around which the parts of a thing, system, etc. are symmetrically or evenly arranged  3. a straight line for reference or measurement, as in a graph [*x-axis, y-axis*]  4. *Bot., Zool.* any of various axial or central parts, as the main stem of a plant —**the Axis** Germany and Italy (**Rome-Berlin Axis**), and later Japan, etc. (**Rome-Berlin-Tokyo Axis**), as allies in World War II

**ax·le** (ak's'l) *n.* [< ff.] 1. a rod on which a wheel turns, or one connected to a wheel so that they turn together  2. a bar connecting opposite wheels, as of an automobile

**ax·le·tree** (-trē') *n.* [< ON. < *qxull*, axle + *tre*, tree, beam] a bar connecting two opposite wheels of a carriage, wagon, etc.

**Ax·min·ster** (aks'min stər) *n.* [< *Axminster*, town in England] a type of carpet with a cut pile

**ax·o·lotl** (ak'sə lät''l) *n.* [< Nahuatl, lit., water toy] a salamander of Mexico and the W U.S. that matures sexually while remaining in the larval stage

**ax·on** (ak'sän) *n.* [ModL. < Gr. *axōn*, axis] that part of a

---

at, āpe, cär; ten, ēven; is, bīte; gō, hôrn, tōol, look; oil, out; up, fur; get; joy; yet; chin; she; thin, then; zh, leisure; ŋ, ring; ə for *a* in *ago*, *e* in *agent*, *i* in *sanity*, *o* in *comply*, *u* in *focus*; ' as in *able* (ā'b'l); Fr. bâl; ë, Fr. coeur; ö, Fr. feu; Fr. mon; Fr. coq; ü, Fr. duc; r, Fr. cri; H, G. ich; kh, G. doch; ‡foreign; *hypothetical; < derived from. See inside front cover.

nerve cell through which impulses travel away from the cell body

**ay·ah** (ä′yə) n. [< Hindi < Port. aia, governess] a native nursemaid or lady's maid in India

**ay·a·tol·lah** (ī′ə tō′lə) n. [Ar., lit., sign of God] a leader of one of the sects of the Moslem religion, serving as teacher, judge, and administrator

**aye[1]** (ā) adv. [ON. ei] [Poet.] always; ever: also sp. ay

**aye[2]** (ī) adv. [< ? prec.] yes; yea —n. an affirmative vote or voter Also sp. ay

**aye-aye** (ī′ī′) n. [Fr. < Malagasy: echoic of its cry] a lemur of Madagascar, with shaggy fur, large ears, fingerlike claws, and a long, bushy tail

**AZ** Arizona

**a·zal·ea** (ə zāl′yə) n. [ModL. < Gr. fem. of azaleos, dry: because it thrives in dry soil] 1. any of several rhododendrons, having variously colored flowers and leaves that are usually shed in the fall 2. the flower of any of these plants

**Az·er·bai·jan** (äz′ər bī jän′, az′-) 1. region of NW Iran 2. republic of the U.S.S.R., on the Caspian Sea: 33,436 sq. mi.; pop. 4,900,000; cap. Baku: in full, **Azerbaijan Soviet Socialist Republic** Also sp. **Azerbaidzhan, Azerbaydzhan**

AYE-AYE
(34–41 in. long, including tail)

**Az·er·bai·ja·ni** (-jä′nē) n., pl. **-nis, -ni** 1. a native or inhabitant of Azerbaijan 2. the Turkic dialect spoken there

**az·i·muth** (az′ə məth) n. [< OFr. < Ar. as-sumūt < al, the + sumūt, pl. of samt, way, path] Astron., Surveying, etc. distance in angular degrees in a clockwise direction from the north point or, in the Southern Hemisphere, south point —az′i·muth′al (-muth′əl) adj.

**az·o** (az′ō, ā′zō) adj. [< azote, obs. name for nitrogen] containing the nitrogen radical -N:N- [azo dyes] : used also as a prefix, az·o-

**A·zores** (ā′zôrz, ə zôrz′) group of Portuguese islands in the N Atlantic, west of Portugal

**A·zov** (ā′zôf; Russ. ä′zôf), **Sea of** northern arm of the Black Sea, in S European U.S.S.R.

**Az·tec** (az′tek) n. [< Nahuatl Aztatlán, name of their legendary place of origin] 1. pl. **-tecs, -tec** a member of a people who lived in Mexico and had an advanced civilization before the conquest of Mexico by Cortés in 1519 2. their Uto-Aztecan language, usually called Nahuatl —adj. of the Aztecs, their language, culture, etc.: also **Az′tec·an**

**az·ure** (azh′ər) adj. [OFr. azur < Ar. < Per. lāzhuward, lapis lazuli] of or like the color of a clear sky; sky-blue —n. 1. sky blue or any similar blue 2. [Poet.] the blue sky

**az·u·rite** (azh′ə rīt′) n. [AZUR(E) + -ITE] 1. a brilliant blue mineral, $2CuCO_3 \cdot Cu(OH)_2$, an ore of copper 2. a semiprecious gem cut from it

**az·y·gous** (az′i gəs) adj. [Gr.] not one of a pair; unpaired; odd

# B

**B, b** (bē) n., pl. **B's, b's** 1. the second letter of the English alphabet 2. the sound of B or b 3. a symbol for the second in a sequence or group

**B[1]** (bē) n. 1. Chem. boron 2. Educ. a grade indicating above-average work 3. Music a) the seventh tone in the ascending scale of C major b) the scale having B as the keynote

**B[2]** Chess bishop

**B-** bomber

**B.** 1. Bible 2. British 3. Brotherhood

**B., b.** 1. bachelor 2. bacillus 3. Baseball base(man) 4. Music bass 5. bay 6. book 7. born 8. brother

**Ba** Chem. barium

**B.A.** [L. Baccalaureus Artium] Bachelor of Arts

**baa** (bä) n. [echoic] the cry of a sheep or goat —vi. to make this cry; bleat

**Ba·al** (bā′əl, bāl) n., pl. **Ba′al·im** (-im), **Ba′als** 1. among some ancient Semitic peoples, any of several fertility gods; later, a chief god 2. a false god; idol —**Ba′al·ism** n. —**Ba′al·ist, Ba′al·ite′** (-īt′) n.

**bab·bitt[1]** (bab′it) n. same as BABBITT METAL

**bab·bitt[2], Bab·bitt** (bab′it) n. [after the title character of a novel by Sinclair Lewis (1922)] a smugly conventional person interested chiefly in business and social success and indifferent to cultural values —**bab′bitt·ry, Bab′bitt·ry** n.

**Babbitt metal** [after Isaac Babbitt (1799–1862), U.S. inventor] a soft alloy of tin, copper, and antimony, used to reduce friction in bearings, etc.

**bab·ble** (bab′'l) vi. **-bled, -bling** [of echoic origin] 1. to make incoherent sounds, as a baby does; prattle 2. to talk foolishly or too much 3. to make a low, bubbling sound [a babbling brook] —vt. 1. to say indistinctly or incoherently 2. to say foolishly; blab —n. 1. confused, incoherent vocal sounds 2. foolish or meaningless talk 3. a low, bubbling sound —**bab′bler** n.

**babe** (bāb) n. 1. a baby 2. a naive, gullible, or helpless person: also **babe in the woods** 3. [Slang] a girl or young woman

**Ba·bel** (bā′b'l, bab′'l) Bible a city where people tried to build a tower to the sky and were stopped by God, who caused them suddenly to speak in different languages: Gen. 11:1–9 —n. [also b-] 1. a confusion of voices, languages, or sounds; tumult 2. a place of such confusion

**ba·biche** (ba bēsh′) n. [< CanadFr. < Algonquian] [Chiefly Canad.] thongs or lacings as of rawhide, used for tying or weaving, esp. in snowshoes

**bab·i·rus·sa, bab·i·rous·sa, bab·i·rus·sa** (bab′ə rōōs′ə, bä′bə-) n. [Malay bābī, hog + rūsa, deer] a wild hog of the East Indies, with large, curving tusks: the upper pair grow through the skin of the snout and curve backwards

**Bab·ism** (bäb′iz′m) n. a Persian religion founded c. 1844: cf. BAHAISM —**Bab′ist, Bab′ite** n., adj.

**ba·boon** (ba bōōn′) n. [< OFr. babuin, ape, fool < baboue, lip (of animals) < bab, echoic] any of various large and fierce, short-tailed monkeys of Africa and Arabia, having a doglike snout, cheek pouches, and bare calluses on the rump —**ba·boon′er·y** n. —**ba·boon′ish** adj.

**ba·bu, ba·boo** (bäb′ōō) n. [Hindi bābu] 1. a Hindu title equivalent to Mr. or Sir 2. a native clerk in India who can write English

**ba·bush·ka** (bə bōosh′kə) n. [Russ., grandmother] a scarf worn on the head by a woman or girl and tied under the chin

BABOON
(35–58 in. long, including tail)

**ba·by** (bā′bē) n., pl. **-bies** [ME. babi] 1. a very young child; infant 2. a person who behaves like an infant 3. a very young animal 4. the youngest or smallest in a group 5. [Slang] a) a girl or young woman b) any person or thing —adj. 1. of or for an infant 2. extremely young 3. small of its kind 4. infantile or childish —vt. **-bied, -by·ing** 1. to treat like a baby; pamper; coddle 2. [Colloq.] to handle with great care —**ba′by·hood′** n. —**ba′by·ish** adj. —**ba′by·ish·ly** adv. —**ba′by·like′** adv.

**baby beef** meat from a heifer or steer fattened for butchering when one to two years old

**baby carriage** a light carriage for wheeling a baby about: also **baby buggy**

**baby grand** a small grand piano

**Bab·y·lon** (bab′ə lən, -län′) ancient capital of Babylonia, famous for wealth, luxury, and wickedness

**Bab·y·lo·ni·a** (bab′ə lō′nē ə) ancient empire in SW Asia, in the lower valley of the Tigris & Euphrates rivers: flourished c. 2100–538 B.C. —**Bab′y·lo′ni·an** adj., n.

**ba·by's breath** (bā′bēz breth′) 1. any of several plants of the pink family, having small, delicate, white or pink flowers 2. any of several other plants with small, sweetly scented flowers: also **ba′bies′ breath**

**ba·by-sit** (bā′bē sit′) vi., vt. **-sat′, -sit′ting** to act as a baby sitter (to)

**baby sitter** a person hired to take care of a child or children, as when parents are away for an evening

**bac·ca·lau·re·ate** (bak′ə lôr′ē it) n. [< ML. < baccalaris, vassal farmer, squire (n. 1) < ? L. baculum, staff] 1. the degree of Bachelor of Arts (or Science, etc.) 2. a speech to a graduating class at commencement: also **baccalaureate address** (or **sermon**)

**bac·ca·rat, bac·ca·ra** (bak′ə rä′, bäk′-) n. [Fr. < ?] a gambling game played with cards

**bac·cha·nal** (bak′ə nəl, -nal′; bak′ə nal′) *n.* [L., place devoted to Bacchus] **1.** a worshiper of Bacchus **2.** a drunken carouser **3.** [*pl.*] the Bacchanalia **4.** a drunken party; orgy —*adj.* **1.** of Bacchus or his worship **2.** carousing

**Bac·cha·na·li·a** (bak′ə näl′yə, -nā′lē ə) *n.pl.* **1.** an ancient Roman festival honoring Bacchus **2.** [b-] a drunken party; orgy —**bac′cha·na′li·an** *adj., n.*

**bac·chant** (bak′ənt, bə kant′) *n., pl.* **-chants, -chan′tes** (-kan′tēz) **1.** a priest or worshiper of Bacchus **2.** a drunken carouser —*adj.* **1.** worshiping Bacchus **2.** given to carousing —**bac·chan·te** (bə kan′tē, -kant′) *n.fem.*

**Bac·chus** (bak′əs) an ancient Greek and Roman god of wine and revelry: earlier called *Dionysus* by the Greeks —**Bac′chic, bac′chic** *adj.*

**bach** (bach) *vi.* [< BACHELOR] [Slang] to live alone or keep house for oneself, as a bachelor: usually in phr. **bach it** —*n.* [Slang] a bachelor

**Bach** (bäkh; *E. also* bäk) **1. Jo·hann Sebastian** (yō′hän), 1685–1750; Ger. organist & composer **2. Karl Philipp Emanuel,** 1714–88; Ger. composer: son of *prec.*

**bach·e·lor** (bach′'l ər, bach′lər) *n.* [< OFr. < ML. *baccalaris:* see BACCALAUREATE] **1.** orig., a young knight who served under another's banner **2.** a man who has not married **3.** a person who is a BACHELOR OF ARTS (or SCIENCE, etc.) —*adj.* of or for a bachelor —**bach′e·lor·hood′** *n.*

**Bachelor of Arts** (or **Science,** etc.) **1.** a degree given by a college or university to one who has completed a four-year course in the humanities (or in science, etc.) **2.** one who has this degree

**bachelor's button** any of several plants of the composite family, as the cornflower, with button-shaped flowers

**ba·cil·lar·y** (bas′ə ler′ē, bə sil′ər ē) *adj.* [ModL. *bacillarius:* see ff.] **1.** rod-shaped: also **ba·cil·li·form** (bə sil′ə fôrm′) **2.** consisting of rodlike structures **3.** of, like, or caused by bacilli Also **ba·cil·lar** (bə sil′ər)

**ba·cil·lus** (bə sil′əs) *n., pl.* **-cil′li** (-ī) [ModL. < LL. < L. dim. of *baculus,* a stick] **1.** any of the rod-shaped bacteria **2.** [*usually pl.*] loosely, any of the bacteria, esp. those causing disease

**back** (bak) *n.* [< OE. *bæc*] **1.** the part of the body opposite to the front; in man and other animals, the part from the nape of the neck to the end of the spine **2.** the backbone **3.** the part of a chair that supports one's back **4.** the part of a garment that fits on the back **5.** the rear part of anything **6.** the part or side that is less often used, seen, etc. **7.** the part of a book where the sections are fastened together **8.** *Sports* a player or position behind the front line —*adj.* **1.** at the rear; behind **2.** distant or remote **3.** of or for a time in the past [*back* pay] **4.** backward; reversed **5.** *Phonet.* with the tongue toward the back of the mouth —*adv.* **1.** at, to, or toward the rear **2.** to or toward a former position **3.** into or toward a previous condition **4.** to or toward an earlier time **5.** in concealment [to hold *back* information] **6.** in return [to pay one *back*] —*vt.* **1.** to cause to move backward (often with *up*) **2.** to stand behind **3.** to support or help **4.** to bet on **5.** to get on the back of; mount **6.** to provide with a back or backing **7.** to form the back of —*vi.* **1.** to go backward **2.** to shift counterclockwise: said of the wind **3.** to have the back facing —**back and forth** to and fro —**back down** to withdraw from a position, etc.: also **back water** —**back out (of) 1.** to withdraw from an enterprise **2.** to break a promise or engagement —**back up 1.** to support **2.** to go backward: also **back away, back out,** etc. **3.** to accumulate as the result of a stoppage [traffic *backed up*] —**be (flat) on one's back** to be ill, bedridden, etc. —**behind one's back** without one's knowledge or consent —**get off one's back** (or **case**) [Slang] to stop nagging or harassing one —**get** (or **put**) **one's back up** to make or be obstinate —**go back on** [Colloq.] **1.** to betray **2.** to fail to keep (a promise, etc.) —**(in)** back of behind —**turn one's back on** to desert; fail —**with one's back to the wall** in a desperate position

**back·ache** (bak′āk′) *n.* an ache or pain in the back

**back·bench·er** (bak′ben′chər) *n.* a legislator who is not a leader in his party

**back·bite** (-bīt′) *vt., vi.* **-bit′, -bit′ten** or **-bit′, -bit′ing** to slander (an absent person) —**back′bit′er** *n.*

**back·board** (-bôrd′) *n. Basketball* a board or flat surface just behind the basket

**back·bone** (-bōn′) *n.* **1.** the column of bones (vertebrae) along the center of the back; spine **2.** main support **3.** a main ridge of mountains **4.** willpower, courage, etc.

**back·break·ing** (-brāk′iŋ) *adj.* very tiring

**back burner** [from the idea of keeping a pot and its contents warm on a back burner of a stove] a state of temporary suspension, low priority, etc.: usually in phr. **on the back burner,** in or into such a state

**back court 1.** *Basketball* a team's defensive half of the court **2.** *Tennis* the area from the service line to the base line on either side of the net

**back·down** (-doun′) *n.* [Colloq.] a backing down; withdrawal from a position, claim, etc.

**back·drop** (-dräp′) *n.* a curtain hung at the back of a stage, often a painted scene

**backed** (bakt) *adj.* having a (specified kind of) back [canvas-*backed*]

**back·er** (bak′ər) *n.* **1.** a patron; supporter **2.** a person who bets on a contestant

**back·field** (-fēld′) *n. Football* the players stationed behind the line of scrimmage; esp., the offensive unit

**back·fill** (-fil′) *vt.* to refill (an excavation), as with earth previously removed

**back·fire** (-fīr′) *n.* **1.** a fire started to stop a prairie fire or forest fire by creating a burned area in its path **2.** a premature explosion in a cylinder of an internal-combustion engine **3.** an explosive force toward the breech of a firearm —*vi.* **-fired′, -fir′ing 1.** to use or set a backfire **2.** to explode as a backfire **3.** to go awry; boomerang

**back-for·ma·tion** (-fôr mā′shən) *n.* **1.** a word formed from, but looking as if it were the base of, another word (Ex.: *burgle* from *burglar*) **2.** the forming of such a word

**back·gam·mon** (-gam′ən) *n.* [BACK + GAMMON²] a game played on a special board by two people, with pieces moved according to the throw of dice

**back·ground** (-ground′) *n.* **1.** the part of a scene or picture toward the back **2.** surroundings behind something, providing harmony or contrast **3.** an unimportant position **4.** the whole of one's study, training, and experience **5.** events or conditions leading up to or surrounding something, helping to explain it **6.** music (in full, **background music**) or sound effects accompanying action, as in movies

**back·hand** (-hand′) *n.* **1.** handwriting that slants up to the left **2.** a backhand catch, stroke, etc. —*adj.* **1.** done with the back of the hand turned inward, as for a baseball catch, or forward, as for a tennis stroke, and with the arm across the body **2.** written in backhand —*adv.* in a backhand way —*vt.* to hit, catch, swing, etc. backhand

**back·hand·ed** (-han′did) *adj.* **1.** same as BACKHAND **2.** not direct and open; equivocal or sarcastic [a *backhanded* compliment] —*adv.* in a backhanded way

**back·hoe** (-hō′) *n.* an excavating machine with a hinged bucket on a long, jointed arm: it digs by drawing the bucket toward its power unit

BACKHAND
STROKE

**back·ing** (-iŋ) *n.* **1.** something forming a back for support or strength **2.** support given to a person or cause **3.** those giving such support **4.** [Slang] a musical accompaniment

**back·lash** (-lash′) *n.* **1.** a quick, sharp recoil **2.** a sudden, strong reaction, as to a political or social movement **3.** a snarl in a reeled fishing line, from an imperfect cast

**back·log** (-lôg′, -läg′) *n.* **1.** a large log at the back of a fireplace **2.** a reserve **3.** an accumulation of unfilled orders, unfinished work, etc. —*vi., vt.* **-logged′, -log′ging** to accumulate as a backlog

**back number** an old issue of a periodical

**back order** an order not yet filled

**back·pack** (-pak′) *n.* a knapsack, often on a lightweight frame, worn by campers or hikers —*vi.* to hike wearing a backpack —*vt.* to carry in a backpack —**back′pack′er** *n.*

**back·ped·al** (-ped′'l) *vi.* **-aled** or **-alled, -al·ing** or **-al·ling 1.** to press backward on bicycle pedals in braking **2.** to move backward quickly in boxing to avoid a blow **3.** to retreat from a previously held opinion

**back road** a road that is away from the main road; country road, esp. an unpaved one

**back seat** a secondary or inconspicuous position

**back-seat driver** (-sēt′) an automobile passenger who offers unwanted advice about driving

**back·side** (bak′sīd′) *n.* **1.** the back or hind part **2.** the rump; buttocks

**back·slide** (-slīd′) *vi.* **-slid′, -slid′** or **-slid′den, -slid′ing** to slide backward in morals or religion —**back′slid′er** *n.*

**back·space** (-spās′) *vi.* **-spaced′, -spac′ing** to move a typewriter carriage back a space at a time by depressing a certain key (**backspacer**)

**back·spin** (-spin′) *n.* a backward spin given to a ball, etc., making it come back as upon hitting the ground

**back·stage** (-stāj′) *adv.* in the wings or dressing rooms of a theater —*adj.* **1.** situated backstage **2.** of the life of people in show business

**back·stairs** (-sterz′) *adj.* involving intrigue or scandal

**back·stay** (-stā′) *n.* a stay or rope extending aft from a masthead to the side or stern of the ship

**back·stop** (-stäp′) *n.* **1.** a screen, etc., as behind a baseball catcher, to stop balls from going too far **2.** anything that supports or bolsters

**back·stretch** (-strech′) *n.* the part of a race track farthest from the grandstand

**back·stroke** (-strōk′) *n.* **1.** a backhand stroke **2.** a stroke made by a swimmer lying face upward, stretching the arms alternately over the head —*vi.* **-stroked′, -strok′ing** to perform a backstroke —*vt.* to hit with a backstroke

**back talk** [Colloq.] saucy or insolent retorts

**back-to-back** (bak′tə bak′) *adj.* [Colloq.] one right after another; consecutive

**back·track** (-trak′) *vi.* **1.** to return by the same path **2.** to withdraw from a position, etc.

**back·up, back-up** (-up′) *adj.* **1.** alternate or auxiliary *[a backup pilot]* **2.** supporting *[a backup effort]* —*n.* a backing up; specif., *a)* an accumulation because of a stoppage *b)* a support

**back·ward** (-wərd) *adv.* **1.** toward the back; behind **2.** with the back or rear foremost **3.** in reverse **4.** in a way contrary to normal **5.** into the past **6.** from a better to a worse state Also **back′wards** —*adj.* **1.** turned or directed toward the rear or in the opposite way **2.** hesitant or shy, as in meeting people **3.** late in developing; retarded —**bend** (or **lean**) **over backward 1.** to try earnestly (to please, pacify, etc.) **2.** to offset a tendency, bias, etc. by an effort in the opposite direction —**back′ward·ly** *adv.* —**back′ward·ness** *n.*

**back·wash** (-wôsh′, -wäsh′) *n.* **1.** water moved backward, as by a ship, an oar, etc. **2.** a backward current, as of air from an airplane propeller

**back·wa·ter** (-wôt′ər, -wät′-) *n.* **1.** water moved backward or held back by a dam, etc. **2.** stagnant water in a stream **3.** a place or condition where there is no progress or growth —*adj.* stagnant; backward

**back·woods** (-woodz′) *n.pl.* [*occas. with sing. v.*] **1.** heavily wooded areas far from centers of population **2.** any remote, thinly populated place —*adj.* in, from, or like the backwoods: also **back′wood′** —**back′woods′man** *n., pl.* **-men**

**ba·con** (bāk′n) *n.* [OFr. < OS. *baco*, side of bacon] salted and smoked meat from the back or sides of a hog —**bring home the bacon** [Colloq.] **1.** to earn a living **2.** to succeed; win

**Ba·con** (bāk′n) **1. Francis,** 1561–1626; Eng. philosopher, essayist, & statesman **2. Roger,** 1214?–94; Eng. philosopher & scientist

**bac·te·ri·a** (bak tir′ē ə) *n.pl., sing.* **-ri·um** (-əm) [ModL. < Gr. dim. of *baktron*, a staff] typically one-celled microorganisms which have no chlorophyll, multiply by simple division, and occur in various forms, chiefly as cocci, bacilli, and spirilla: some bacteria cause diseases, but others are necessary for fermentation, nitrogen fixation, etc. —**bac·te′ri·al** *adj.* —**bac·te′ri·al·ly** *adv.*

**bac·te·ri·cide** (bak tir′ə sīd′) *n.* [BACTERI(O)- + -CIDE] an agent that destroys bacteria —**bac·te′ri·ci′dal** *adj.*

**bac·te·ri·o-** a combining form meaning of bacteria

**bac·te·ri·ol·o·gy** (bak tir′ē äl′ə jē) *n.* the study of bacteria, as in medicine, or for food processing, agriculture, etc. —**bac·te′ri·o·log′ic** (-ē ə läj′ik), **bac·te′ri·o·log′i·cal** *adj.* —**bac·te′ri·o·log′i·cal·ly** *adv.* —**bac·te′ri·ol′o·gist** *n.*

**bac·te·ri·o·phage** (bak tir′ē ə fāj′) *n.* [BACTERIO- + -PHAGE] any virus that is parasitic upon certain bacteria, disintegrating them

**bac·te·ri·um** (-əm) *n. sing. of* BACTERIA

**Bac·tri·an camel** (bak′trē ən) [< *Bactria*, ancient country in W Asia] a camel with two humps, native to C Asia, shorter and hairier than the dromedary

**bad¹** (bad) *adj.* **worse, worst** [ME.] **1.** not good; not as it should be **2.** defective in quality **3.** unfit; unskilled **4.** not pleasant; unfavorable **5.** rotten; spoiled **6.** incorrect; faulty *[bad spelling]* **7.** *a)* wicked; immoral *b)* mischievous **8.** causing injury; harmful **9.** severe *[a bad storm]* **10.** ill; in poor health **11.** sorry; distressed *[he feels bad about it]*: cf. BADLY **12.** *Law* not valid —*adv.* [Colloq.] badly —*n.* **1.** anything bad; bad quality or state **2.** wickedness —**in bad** [Colloq.] in trouble or disfavor —**not bad** [Colloq.] good; fairly good: also **not half bad, not so bad** —**bad′ness** *n.*

**bad²** (bad) *archaic pt. of* BID

**bad blood** a feeling of (mutual) enmity

**bade** (bad; *occas.* bād) *alt. pt. of* BID

**bad egg** [Slang] a mean or dishonest person: also **bad actor, bad apple, bad hat, bad lot,** etc.

**Ba·den** (bäd′'n) **1.** region in SW West Germany **2.** city & health resort there: in full, **Baden-Baden**

**badge** (baj) *n.* [ME. *bage*] **1.** a token, emblem, or sign worn to show rank, membership, etc. **2.** any distinguishing mark or symbol —*vt.* **badged, badg′ing** to provide or mark with a badge

**badg·er** (baj′ər) *n., pl.* **-ers, -er:** *see* PLURAL, II, D, 1 [< ? obs. n. & personal name *badger*, grain dealer] **1.** a carnivorous, burrowing mammal with thick, short legs, and long claws on the forefeet **2.** its fur —*vt.* to nag at

**bad·i·nage** (bad′ə näzh′, bad′'n ij) *n.* [Fr. < *badiner*, to jest < Pr. < ML. *badare*, to gape] playful, teasing talk; banter —*vt.* **-naged′, -nag′ing** to tease with playful talk

**bad·lands** (bad′landz′) *n.pl.* **1.** any section of barren land where deep erosion has cut the dry soil or soft rocks into strange shapes **2.** [B-] any section like this in the W U.S., esp. in SW S.Dak.: also **Bad Lands**

**bad·ly** (bad′lē) *adv.* **1.** in a bad manner **2.** [Colloq.] very much; greatly Also used informally as an adjective meaning "sorry" or "distressed"

**bad·man** (bad′man′) *n., pl.* **-men′** (-men′) a cattle thief; desperado, or hired gunman of the old West

**bad·min·ton** (bad′min t'n) *n.* [ after *Badminton*, estate of the Duke of Beaufort] a game in which a feathered cork (*shuttlecock*) is batted back and forth with light rackets across a net

**bad-tem·pered** (bad′tem′pərd) *adj.* having a bad temper or cranky disposition; irritable

**Bae·de·ker** (bā′də kər) *n.* **1.** any of a series of guidebooks to foreign countries first published in Germany by Karl Baedeker (1801–59) **2.** loosely, any guidebook

**baf·fle** (baf′'l) *vt.* **-fled, -fling** [16th-c. Scot.; prob. respelling of obs. Scot. *bauchle*] **1.** to confuse so as to keep from understanding or solving; puzzle; confound **2.** to hinder; impede **3.** to check the interference of (sound waves) by a baffle —*n.* **1.** a baffling or being baffled **2.** a wall or screen to deflect the flow of liquids, gases, etc.: also **baf′fle-plate′ 3.** a mounting that checks the transmission of sound waves between the front and rear of a loudspeaker —**baf′fle·ment** *n.* —**baf′fler** *n.* —**baf′fling** *adj.*

**bag** (bag) *n.* [ON. *baggi*] **1.** a nonrigid container made of fabric, paper, leather, etc., with an opening at the top that can be closed; sack **2.** the amount a bag holds **3.** a piece of hand luggage **4.** a woman's handbag; purse **5.** *a)* a container for game *b)* the amount of game caught or killed **6.** anything shaped or bulging like a bag *[bags under the eyes]* **7.** an udder or sac **8.** [Slang] one's special sphere of interest, talent, obsession, etc. **9.** [< BAGGAGE 3*a*] [Slang] an unattractive woman **10.** *Baseball* a base —*vt.* **bagged, bag′ging 1.** to make bulge **2.** to enclose within a bag **3.** to capture **4.** to kill in hunting **5.** [Slang] to get —*vi.* **1.** to swell **2.** to hang loosely —**bag and baggage** [Colloq.] **1.** with all one's possessions **2.** entirely —**be left holding the bag** [Colloq.] to be left to suffer the bad consequences or the blame —**in the bag** [Slang] having its success assured—**bag′ful′** *n., pl.* **-fuls′**

**ba·gasse** (bə gas′) *n.* [Fr. < Pr. *bagasso*, refuse from processing grapes, etc. < L. *baca*, berry] the part of sugar cane left after the juice has been extracted, or the residue of certain other processed plants: used for making fiberboard, etc.

**bag·a·telle** (bag′ə tel′) *n.* [Fr. < It. *bagatella*, dim. < L. *baca*, berry] **1.** something of little value; trifle **2.** a game somewhat like billiards, played with nine balls on a table

**Bag·dad** (bag′dad, bäg däd′) *same as* BAGHDAD

**ba·gel** (bā′g'l) *n.* [< Yid., ult. < G. *beugen*, to bend] a hard, doughnut-shaped bread roll that is simmered in water before being baked

**bag·gage** (bag′ij) *n.* [< OFr. < *bagues*, baggage < ML. *baga*, chest] **1.** the bags and other equipment of a traveler **2.** the supplies and gear of an army **3.** *a)* [< Fr. *bagasse*, harlot, ult. < Ar. *bagīja*, adulteress; infl. by "army baggage," i.e., "camp follower"] formerly, a prostitute *b)* a saucy girl **4.** burdensome or superfluous ideas, practices, etc.

**bag·gy** (bag′ē) *adj.* **-gi·er, -gi·est 1.** puffed in a baglike way **2.** hanging loosely *[baggy trousers]* —**bag′gi·ly** *adv.* —**bag′gi·ness** *n.*

**Bagh·dad** (bag′dad, bäg däd′) capital of Iraq, on the Tigris River: pop. c. 1,000,000

**bag·man** (bag′mən) *n., pl.* **-men 1.** [Brit.] a traveling salesman **2.** [Slang] a go-between, as in the numbers racket, etc.

**bagn·io** (ban′yō, bän′-) *n., pl.* **-ios** [< It. < L. < Gr. *balaneion*, bath] a house of prostitution; brothel

**bag·pipe** (bag′pīp′) *n.* [*often pl.*] a shrill-toned musical instrument with a double-reed, fingered pipe and drone pipes, all sounded by air forced from a leather bag: now chiefly Scottish —**bag′pip′er** *n.*

**ba·guette, ba·guet** (ba get′) *n.* [< Fr. < It. < L. *baculum*, a staff] **1.** a gem, etc. cut in the shape of a narrow oblong **2.** this shape **3.** *Archit.* a small, convex molding

**bah** (bä, ba) *interj.* an exclamation expressing contempt, scorn, or disgust

**Ba·hai** (bə hī′, bə hä′ē) *n., pl.* **Ba·hais′ 1.** a believer in Bahaism **2.** *same as* BAHAISM —*adj.* of Bahaism or a Bahai Also written **Baha'i**

BAGPIPE

**Ba·ha·ism** (bə hä′iz′m, -hī′-) *n.* [Ar. *ba-hā*, splendor + -ISM] a modern religion, developed orig. in Iran from Babism, that advocates universal brotherhood, social equality, etc. —**Ba·ha′ist** *n., adj.*

**Ba·ha·mas** (bə hä′məz, -hä′-) country consisting of a group of islands (**Bahama Islands**) in the West Indies: a member of the Commonwealth: 4,404 sq. mi.; pop. 180,000; cap. Nassau —**Ba·ha′mi·an** *adj., n.*

**Bah·rain, Bah·rein** (bä rän′) independent Arab sheikdom consisting of a group of islands in the Persian Gulf: a member of the Commonwealth: 231 sq. mi.; pop. 200,000

**baht** (bät) *n., pl.* **bahts, baht** [Thai *bāt*] *see* MONETARY UNITS, table (Thailand)

**Bai·kal** (bī käl′), **Lake** lake in SE Siberia: 12,000 sq. mi.

**bail**[1] (bāl) *n.* [OFr., power, control < *baillir*, keep in custody < L. *bajulare*, bear a burden < *bajulus*, porter] **1.** money or credit deposited with the court to get an arrested person released until his trial **2.** the release thus brought about **3.** the person giving bail —*vt.* **1.** to set (an arrested person) free on bail or have (an arrested person) set free by giving bail (often with *out*) **2.** to help out of financial or other difficulty (often with *out*) —**go bail for** to furnish bail for —**bail′a·ble** *adj.*

**bail**[2] (bāl) *n.* [< OFr. < VL. hyp. *bajula*, vessel < *bajulare:* see prec.] a bucket, etc. for dipping up water from a boat —*vi., vt.* **1.** to remove water from (a boat) as with a bail **2.** to dip out (water, etc.) as with a bail —**bail out** to make a parachute jump from an aircraft —**bail′er** *n.*

**bail**[3] (bāl) *n.* [< ON. *beygla < beygia*, to bend] **1.** a hoop-shaped support, as for a canopy **2.** a hoop-shaped handle for a bucket, etc. **3.** a bar on a typewriter to hold the paper against the platen

**bail**[4] (bāl) *n.* [< OFr., ult. < L. *bajulus*, porter] *Cricket* either of two pieces of wood laid across the three stumps to form a wicket

**bai·lie** (bā′lē) *n.* [Scot. < OFr. < *bailif:* see ff.] in Scotland, a municipal official corresponding to an alderman in England

**bai·liff** (bā′lif) *n.* [OFr. *bailif < baillir:* see BAIL[1]] **1.** a deputy sheriff who serves processes, etc. **2.** a court officer who guards jurors, keeps order in the courtroom, etc. **3.** in England, an administrative official of a district **4.** [Chiefly Brit.] an overseer or steward of an estate

**bai·li·wick** (bā′lə wik) *n.* [ME. < *bailif*, BAILIFF + *wik* < OE. *wic*, village] **1.** a bailiff's district **2.** one's particular area of activity, authority, etc.

**bail·out** (bāl′out′) *n.* [see BAIL[1], *vt.* 2] a helping out of one in serious financial or other difficulty; specif., a providing of government assistance, including loans, to a failing company, municipality, etc.

**bails·man** (bālz′mən) *n., pl.* **-men** a person who acts as surety or gives bail for another

**bairn** (bern) *n.* [< OE. < *beran*, to BEAR[1]] [Scot.] a child

**bait** (bāt) *vt.* [ON. *beita*, to make bite, caus. < *bīta*, to bite] **1.** to set attacking dogs against for sport *[to bait bears]* **2.** to torment or harass with unprovoked, repeated attacks **3.** to tease or goad **4.** to put food, etc. on (a hook or trap) so as to lure animals or fish **5.** to lure; tempt; entice —*n.* **1.** food, etc. put on a hook or trap to lure fish or animals **2.** any lure; enticement —**bait′er** *n.*

**bait-and-switch** (bāt′'n swich′) *adj.* of or using an unethical sales technique in which a seller lures customers by advertising an often nonexistent bargain item and then tries to switch their attention to more expensive items

**baize** (bāz) *n.* [< OFr. pl. of *baie* < L. *badius*, chestnut-brown] a feltlike, thick woolen cloth, often green, used to cover billiard tables, etc.

**Ba·ja Ca·li·for·nia** (bä′hä kä′lē fôr′nyä) peninsula in Mexico, between the Pacific & the Gulf of California: 55,634 sq. mi.

**bake** (bāk) *vt.* **baked, bak′ing** [OE. *bacan*] **1.** to cook (food) by dry heat, esp. in an oven **2.** to dry and harden (esp. glazed stoneware) by heat —*vi.* **1.** to bake bread, etc. **2.** to become baked —*n.* **1.** a baking **2.** a product of baking **3.** a social affair at which a baked food is served

**Ba·ke·lite** (bā′kə līt′) [after L. H. *Baekeland* (1863–1944), U.S. chemist] *a trademark for* a synthetic resin and plastic

**bak·er** (bāk′ər) *n.* **1.** one whose work or business is baking bread, etc. **2.** a small, portable oven

**baker's dozen** thirteen

**Bak·ers·field** (bāk′ərz fēld′) [after Col. *Baker*, early landowner] city in SC Calif.: pop. 106,000

**bak·er·y** (bāk′ər ē) *n.* **1.** *pl.* **-er·ies** a place where bread, pastries, etc. are baked or sold **2.** baked goods

**bake·shop** (bāk′shäp′) *n.* a bakery

**baking powder** a leavening agent containing baking soda and an acid substance, such as cream of tartar, which together produce carbon dioxide in the presence of water

**baking soda** sodium bicarbonate, $NaHCO_3$, used as a leavening agent and as an antacid

**bak·sheesh, bak·shish** (bak′shēsh) *n.* [via Turk. or Ar. < Per. < *bakhshidan*, to give] in Turkey, Egypt, India, etc., a tip, gratuity, or alms

**Ba·ku** (bä ko͞o′) capital of the Azerbaijan S.S.R., on the Caspian Sea: pop. 1,224,000

**bal.** balance

**Ba·laam** (bā′ləm) *Bible* a prophet rebuked by his donkey after he had beaten it: Num. 22–24

**bal·a·lai·ka** (bal′ə lī′kə) *n.* [Russ.] a Russian stringed instrument like a guitar, but with a triangular body

**bal·ance** (bal′əns) *n.* [OFr. < ML. < LL. *bilanx*, having two scales < L. *bis*, twice + *lanx*, a scale] **1.** an instrument for weighing, esp. one with two matched pans hanging from either end of a poised lever; scales **2.** a state of equilibrium or equipoise; equality in weight, value, importance, etc. **3.** bodily equilibrium */he kept his balance on the tightrope/* **4.** mental or emotional stability **5.** the pleasing harmony of various elements in a work of art; harmonious proportion **6.** a weight, force, etc. that counteracts another or causes equilibrium **7.** the point along an object's length at which there is equilibrium: in full, **balance point 8.** *a)* equality of debits and credits in an account *b)* the difference between credits and debits **9.** the amount still owed after a partial settlement **10.** a remainder **11.** a balancing **12.** *same as* BALANCE WHEEL —*vt.* **-anced, -anc·ing 1.** to weigh in or as in a balance **2.** to compare as to relative importance, value, etc. **3.** to counterpoise or counteract; offset **4.** to put or keep in a state of equilibrium; poise **5.** to bring into proportion, harmony, etc. **6.** to make or be equal to in weight, force, etc. **7.** *a)* to find any difference between the debit and credit sides of (an account); also, to equalize the debit and credit sides of (an account) *b)* to settle (an account) —*vi.* **1.** to be in equilibrium **2.** to be equal in value, weight, etc. **3.** to have the credit and debit sides equal **4.** to waver slightly —**in the balance** in a critical, undecided state —**bal′ance·a·ble** *adj.* —**bal′anc·er** *n.*

**balance beam** a long, horizontal wooden beam raised about four feet above the floor, on which women gymnasts perform balancing exercises of jumps, turns, steps, etc.

**balance of (international) payments** a balance estimated for a given period showing an excess or deficit in total payments of all kinds between one country and another country or other countries

**balance of power** an even distribution of military and economic power among nations that keeps any one of them from being too strong or dangerous

**balance of trade** the difference in value between the imports and exports of a country

**balance sheet** a summarized statement showing the financial status of a business

**balance wheel** a wheel that swings back and forth to regulate the movement of a timepiece, etc.

**bal·a·ta** (bal′ə tə) *n.* [Sp. < Tupi] **1.** a tropical American tree **2.** its dried sap, a rubberlike gum used commercially

**bal·bo·a** (bal bō′ə) *n.* [Sp., after ff.] *see* MONETARY UNITS, table (Panama)

**Bal·bo·a** (bal bō′ə; *Sp.* bäl bō′ä), **Vas·co Nú·ñez de** (väs′kô no͞o′nyeth *the*) 1475?–1517?; Sp. explorer: first European to discover the Pacific Ocean

**bal·brig·gan** (bal brig′ən) *n.* [after *Balbriggan*, Ireland] a knitted cotton material used for hosiery, underwear, etc.

**bal·co·ny** (bal′kə nē) *n., pl.* **-nies** [< It., akin to OHG. *balcho*, a beam] **1.** a platform projecting from a building and enclosed by a balustrade **2.** an upper floor of seats in a theater, etc., often jutting out over the main floor

**bald** (bôld) *adj.* [ME. *balled* < ?] **1.** having white fur or feathers on the head, as some animals and birds **2.** having no hair on all or part of the scalp **3.** not covered by natural growth *[bald hills]* **4.** plain; unadorned **5.** frank and blunt —**bald′ly** *adv.* —**bald′ness** *n.*

**bald·cy·press** (bôld′sī′pris) *n.* a cone-bearing tree of SE U.S. swamps, that sheds its needles in the fall

**bald eagle** a large, strong eagle of N. America, with a white-feathered head and neck

**Bal·der** (bôl′dər) *Norse Myth.* the god of light, peace, virtue, and wisdom: also sp. **Baldr**

**bal·der·dash** (bôl′dər dash′) *n.* [orig., a senseless mixture of liquids] nonsensical talk or writing

**bald·faced** (bôld′fāst′) *adj.* brazen; shameless

**bald·head** (-hed′) *n.* **1.** a person who has a bald head **2.** a bald (sense 1) bird —**bald′head′ed** *adj.*

**bald·ing** (bôl′diŋ) *adj.* becoming bald

**bald·pate** (bôld′pāt′) *n.* **1.** a baldheaded person **2.** a N. American duck with a white crown

**bal·dric** (bôl′drik) *n.* [< OFr., ult. < L. *balteus*, a girdle] a belt worn over one shoulder and across the chest to support a sword, etc.

**Bald·win** (bôld′win) *n.* [after Col. L. *Baldwin* (1740–1807), Mass. apple grower] a moderately tangy, red winter apple

**bale¹** (bāl) *n.* [OFr. < OHG. *balla,* a ball] a large bundle, esp. a standardized quantity, as of cotton, hay, or straw, compressed and bound —*vt.* **baled, bal′ing** to make into bales —**bal′er** *n.*

**bale²** (bāl) *n.* [OE. *bealu*] [Poet.] 1. evil; harm 2. woe

**Bal·e·ar·ic Islands** (bal′ē er′ik) group of Sp. islands in the Mediterranean, east of Spain

**ba·leen** (bə lēn′) *n.* [ < OFr. < L. *ballaena,* a whale] *same as* WHALEBONE

**bale·ful** (bāl′fəl) *adj.* harmful or evil; sinister —**bale′ful·ly** *adv.* —**bale′ful·ness** *n.*

**Ba·li** (bä′lē, bal′ē) island of Indonesia, east of Java: 2,100 sq. mi. —**Ba′li·nese′** (bä′lə nēz′, bal′ə-) *adj., n.*

**balk** (bôk) *n.* [OE. *balca,* a bank, ridge] 1. a ridge of unplowed land between furrows 2. a roughly hewn piece of timber 3. a check, hindrance, disappointment, etc. 4. *Baseball* an illegal motion by the pitcher, as an uncompleted motion to throw, entitling base runners to advance one base —*vt.* 1. to miss or let slip by 2. to obstruct or foil —*vi.* 1. to stop and refuse to move or act 2. to hesitate or recoil (*at*) 3. to make a balk in baseball —**balk′er** *n.*

**Bal·kan** (bôl′kən) *adj.* 1. of the Balkans, their people, etc. 2. of the Balkan Mountains

**Balkan Mountains** mountain range extending across C Bulgaria, from Yugoslavia to the Black Sea

**Balkan Peninsula** peninsula in SE Europe, between the Adriatic & the Black seas

**Bal·kans** (bôl′kənz) countries of the Balkan Peninsula (Yugoslavia, Bulgaria, Albania, Greece, & the European part of Turkey) & Romania: also **Balkan States**

**balk·line** (bôk′līn′) *n.* a line across one end of a billiard table, from behind which opening shots are made

**balk·y** (bôk′ē) *adj.* **balk′i·er, balk′i·est** stubbornly refusing to move or act —**balk′i·ness** *n.*

**ball¹** (bôl) *n.* [ME. *bal,* akin to OHG. *balla*] 1. any round object; sphere; globe 2. a planet or star, esp. the earth 3. *a)* a round or egg-shaped object used in various games *b)* any of several such games, esp. baseball 4. a throw or pitch of a ball *[a fast ball]* 5. a solid missile for a cannon or firearm 6. a rounded part of the body *[the ball of the foot]* 7. *Baseball* a pitch that is wide of the plate or goes above the armpit or below the knee of the batter and is not struck at by him —*vi., vt.* to form into a ball —**ball up** [Slang] to muddle or confuse —**be on the ball** [Slang] to be alert; be efficient —**carry the ball** [Colloq.] to assume responsibility —**get (or keep) the ball rolling** [Colloq.] to start (or maintain) some action —**have something on the ball** [Slang] to have ability —**play ball** 1. to begin or resume playing a ball game 2. to begin or resume any activity 3. [Colloq.] to cooperate

**ball²** (bôl) *n.* [Fr. *bal* < OFr. < LL. *ballare,* to dance < Gr. *ballein,* to throw] 1. a formal social dance 2. [Slang] an enjoyable time or experience

**bal·lad** (bal′əd) *n.* [ < OFr. *ballade,* dancing song, ult. < LL. *ballare:* see prec.] 1. a romantic or sentimental song with the same melody for each stanza 2. a song or poem, usually of unknown authorship and handed down orally, that tells a story in short stanzas and simple words, with repetition, refrain, etc. 3. a slow, sentimental popular song —**bal′lad·eer′** *n.* —**bal′lad·ry** *n.*

**bal·lade** (bə läd′) *n.* [Fr.: see prec.] 1. a verse form with three stanzas of eight or ten lines each and an envoy of four or five lines 2. a romantic musical composition

**ball-and-sock·et joint** (bôl′′n säk′it) a joint, as that of the hip, formed by a ball in a socket, allowing limited movement in any direction

**bal·last** (bal′əst) *n.* [LowG. < ODan. *barlast* < *bar,* bare + *last,* a load] 1. anything heavy carried in a ship, aircraft, or vehicle to give stability or in an airship to help control altitude 2. anything giving stability and firmness to character, human relations, etc. 3. crushed rock or gravel, as that used to make a firm bed for railroad ties —*vt.* 1. to furnish with ballast; stabilize 2. to fill in (a railroad bed, etc.) with ballast

BALL-AND-SOCKET JOINT

**ball bearing** 1. a bearing in which the moving parts revolve on freely rolling metal balls so that friction is reduced 2. any of these balls

**bal·le·ri·na** (bal′ə rē′nə) *n.* [It. < LL. *ballare:* see BALL²] a woman ballet dancer

**bal·let** (bal′ā, ba lā′) *n.* [ < Fr. < It. *balletto,* dim. < *ballo,* a dance: see BALL²] 1. an intricate group dance (or dancing) using pantomime and conventionalized movements to tell a story 2. ballet dancers —**bal·let·ic** (ba let′ik) *adj.*

**bal·lis·ta** (bə lis′tə) *n., pl.* **-tae** (-tē) [L. < Gr. *ballein,* to

throw] a device used in ancient warfare to hurl heavy stones, etc.

**bal·lis·tic** (bə lis′tik) *adj.* 1. of or connected with ballistics 2. of the motion and force of projectiles

**ballistic missile** a long-range missile guided in the first part of its flight, but free-falling as it approaches its target

**bal·lis·tics** (bə lis′tiks) *n.pl.* [*with sing. v.*] 1. the science dealing with the motion and impact of projectiles, such as bullets, rockets, bombs, etc. 2. the study of the effects of firing on a firearm or bullet, etc.

**bal·loon** (bə lōōn′) *n.* [ < Fr. < It. *pallone* < *palla,* a ball] 1. a large, airtight bag that rises above the earth when filled with a gas lighter than air 2. a bag of this sort with an attached car for passengers or instruments 3. a small, inflatable rubber bag, used as a toy 4. the outline enclosing spoken words in a comic strip —*vt.* to cause to swell like a balloon —*vi.* 1. to ride in a balloon 2. to swell; expand —*adj.* like a balloon —**bal·loon′ist** *n.*

**bal·lot** (bal′ət) *n.* [It. *ballotta, pallotta,* dim. of *palla,* a ball] 1. orig. a ball, now a ticket, paper, etc., by which a vote is registered 2. act or method of voting, esp. secret voting by the use of ballots or voting machines 3. the right to vote 4. the total number of votes cast in an election 5. a list of candidates for office; ticket —*vi.* to decide by means of the ballot; vote —**bal′lot·er** *n.*

**ball·park** (bôl′pärk′) *n.* a stadium for playing baseball —*adj.* [Colloq.] reasonably accurate *[a ballpark estimate]* —**in the ballpark** [Colloq.] 1. reasonably accurate 2. fairly close to what is required

**ball·play·er** (-plā′ər) *n.* a baseball player

**ball point pen** a pen having instead of a point a small ball bearing that rolls over an ink reservoir: also **ball′-point′, ball′point′** *n.*

**ball·room** (-rōōm′) *n.* a large hall for dancing

**ballroom dancing** dancing in which two people dance as partners to a waltz, fox trot, etc.

**bal·ly·hoo** (bal′ē hōō′; *also, for v.* bal′ē hōō′) *n.* [ < ?] 1. loud talk; uproar 2. loud or sensational advertising or propaganda —*vt., vi.* **-hooed′, -hoo′ing** [Colloq.] to advertise or promote by sensational methods —**bal′ly·hoo′er** *n.*

**balm** (bäm) *n.* [ < OFr. < L. < Gr. *balsamon*] 1. an aromatic gum resin obtained from certain trees and plants and used as medicine; balsam 2. any fragrant ointment or oil 3. anything healing or soothing, esp. to the mind or temper 4. any of various aromatic plants of the mint family 5. pleasant odor; fragrance

**balm of Gilead** 1. *a)* a small evergreen tree native to Asia and Africa *b)* an aromatic ointment formerly prepared from its resin 2. anything healing or soothing 3. *same as* BALSAM FIR 4. a hybrid poplar of the northern U.S.

**balm·y** (bäm′ē) *adj.* **balm′i·er, balm′i·est** 1. having the qualities of balm; soothing, mild, pleasant, etc. 2. [var. of BARMY] [Chiefly Brit. Slang] crazy or foolish —**balm′i·ly** *adv.* —**balm′i·ness** *n.*

**ba·lo·ney** (bə lō′nē) *n.* [altered < ? *bologna,* sausage] 1. *same as* BOLOGNA 2. [Slang] nonsense —*interj.* [Slang] nonsense!

**bal·sa** (bôl′sə) *n.* [Sp.] 1. a tropical American tree that yields an extremely light and buoyant wood used for rafts, etc. 2. the wood 3. a raft, esp. one made up of a frame on cylindrical floats

**bal·sam** (bôl′səm) *n.* [OE. < L.: see BALM] 1. any of various aromatic resins obtained from certain trees 2. any of various aromatic, resinous oils or fluids 3. anything healing or soothing; balm 4. any of various trees that yield balsam, as the balsam fir 5. any of various species of the impatiens —**bal·sam·ic** (bôl sam′ik) *adj.*

**balsam fir** an evergreen fir of Canada and the northern U.S. with a soft wood used for pulpwood

**Bal·tic** (bôl′tik) *adj.* 1. of the Baltic Sea 2. of the Baltic States —*n.* the Baltic Sea

**Baltic Sea** sea in N Europe, south & east of Scandinavia & west of the U.S.S.R.

**Baltic States** former independent countries of Latvia, Lithuania, & Estonia

**Bal·ti·more** (bôl′tə môr′) [after Lord *Baltimore,* George Calvert (1580?–1632), Eng. founder of Md.] seaport in N Md., on Chesapeake Bay: pop. 787,000 (met. area 2,166,000)

**Baltimore oriole** [from the colors of the coat of arms of Lord *Baltimore:* see prec.] a N. American oriole that has an orange body with black on the head, wings, and tail

**bal·us·ter** (bal′əs tər) *n.* [ < Fr. < It. < L. < Gr. *balaustion,* flower of the wild pomegranate: from some resemblance in shape] any of the small posts supporting a railing, as on a staircase

**bal·us·trade** (bal′ə strād′) *n.* a railing held up by balusters

**Bal·zac** (bàl zàk′; E. bôl′zak), **Ho·no·ré de** (ô nô rā′ də) 1799–1850; Fr. novelist

**bam·bi·no** (bam bē′nō) *n., pl.* **-nos, -ni** (-nē) [It., dim. of *bambo,* childish] 1. a child; baby 2. any image of the infant Jesus

**bam·boo** (bam bo͞o′) *n.* [Malay *bambu*] any of a number of treelike, semitropical or tropical grasses with springy, jointed, often hollow stems, sometimes growing to heights of 120 feet: the stems are used for furniture, canes, etc., and the young shoots of some species are eaten

**bamboo curtain** [*often* **B- C-**] the barrier of political and ideological differences that separate China from the West

**bam·boo·zle** (bam bo͞o′z′l) *vt.* -zled, -zling [< ?] **1.** to deceive or cheat by trickery **2.** to confuse or puzzle —**bam·boo′zle·ment** *n.* —**bam·boo′zler** *n.*

**ban¹** (ban) *vt.* **banned, ban′ning** [OE. *bannan*, to summon] to prohibit or forbid, as by official order —*n.* [< the *v.;* also < OFr. *ban*, decree < OHG. *bann*] **1.** an excommunication or condemnation by church authorities **2.** a curse **3.** an official prohibition **4.** strong public disapproval **5.** a sentence of outlawry

**ban²** (bän) *n., pl.* **ba·ni** (bä′nē) *see* MONETARY UNITS, table (Romania)

**ba·nal** (bā′n′l; bə nal′, -näl′) *adj.* [Fr. < *ban*: see BAN¹] dull or stale because of overuse; trite; hackneyed —**ba·nal·i·ty** (bə nal′ə tē) *n., pl.* -ties —**ba·nal′ly** *adv.*

**ba·nan·a** (bə nan′ə) *n.* [Sp. & Port. < native name in W Africa] **1.** any of a genus of tree-like, tropical plants, with long, broad leaves and large clusters of edible fruit **2.** the fruit: it is narrow and somewhat curved, and has a sweet, creamy flesh covered by a yellow or reddish skin

**banana oil 1.** a colorless liquid acetate with a bananalike odor, used in flavorings, in making lacquers, etc. **2.** [Old Slang] insincere talk

**banana republic** any small Latin American country whose economy is controlled by foreign capital

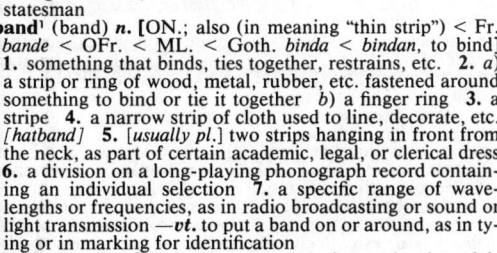

BANANA

**Ban·croft** (ban′krôft, baŋ′-), **George** 1800–91; U.S. historian & statesman

**band¹** (band) *n.* [ON.; also (in meaning "thin strip") < Fr. *bande* < OFr. < ML. < Goth. *binda* < *bindan*, to bind] **1.** something that binds, ties together, restrains, etc. **2.** *a)* a strip or ring of wood, metal, rubber, etc. fastened around something to bind or tie it together *b)* a finger ring **3.** a stripe **4.** a narrow strip of cloth used to line, decorate, etc. [*hatband*] **5.** [*usually pl.*] two strips hanging in front from the neck, as part of certain academic, legal, or clerical dress **6.** a division on a long-playing phonograph record containing an individual selection **7.** a specific range of wavelengths or frequencies, as in radio broadcasting or sound or light transmission —*vt.* to put a band on or around, as in tying or in marking for identification

**band²** (band) *n.* [Fr. *bande*, a troupe (orig., prob., those following the same sign) < It. *banda* < Goth. *bandwa*, a sign] **1.** a group of people united for a common purpose **2.** a group of musicians playing together, esp. upon wind and percussion instruments [*a dance band*] —*vi., vt.* to unite for a common purpose (usually with *together*)

**band·age** (ban′dij) *n.* [Fr. < *bande*, BAND¹] a strip of cloth or other dressing used to bind or cover an injured part of the body —*vt.* -aged, -ag·ing to put a bandage on

**Band-Aid** (ban′dād′) [BAND(AGE) + AID] *a trademark for a* small prepared bandage of gauze and adhesive tape —*n.* [**b- a-**] a bandage of this type: also **band′aid′**

**ban·dan·na, ban·dan·a** (ban dan′ə) *n.* [Hindi *bāndhnū*, method of dyeing] a large, colored handkerchief, usually with a printed pattern

**band·box** (band′bäks′) *n.* a light box of wood or pasteboard to hold hats, collars, etc.

**ban·deau** (ban dō′, ban′dō) *n., pl.* -deaux′ (-dōz′, -dōz) [Fr.] **1.** a narrow ribbon, esp. one worn around the head to hold the hair in place **2.** a narrow brassiere giving little support

**ban·de·role, ban·de·rol** (ban′də rōl′) *n.* [Fr. < It. dim. of *bandiera*, banner] a narrow flag or pennant, as one attached to a lance

**ban·di·coot** (ban′di ko͞ot′) *n.* [< Telugu *pandikokku*, pig rat] **1.** a very large rat found esp. in India and Ceylon **2.** a ratlike animal of Australia that carries its young in a pouch

**ban·dit** (ban′dit) *n., pl.* -dits, ban·dit·ti (ban dit′ē) [It. *bandito* < *bandire*, to outlaw, akin to OHG. *bann* (see BAN¹, *n.*)] **1.** a robber, esp. one who robs travelers on the road; brigand **2.** anyone who cheats, steals, etc. —**ban′dit·ry** *n.*

**band·mas·ter** (band′mas′tər) *n.* the leader or conductor of a military or brass band

**ban·do·leer, ban·do·lier** (ban′də lir′) *n.* [< Fr. < Sp. <

*banda*, a scarf, ult. < Goth. *bandwa*: see BAND²] a broad shoulder belt with pockets for carrying ammunition, etc.

**band saw** a power saw consisting of an endless, toothed steel belt running over pulleys

**band shell** an outdoor platform for concerts, having a concave back serving as a sounding board

**bands·man** (bandz′mən) *n., pl.* -men a member of a band of musicians

**band·stand** (band′stand′) *n.* **1.** an outdoor, usually roofed platform for a band or orchestra **2.** any platform for a musical band, as in a ballroom

**Ban·dung** (bän′doͦŋ, ban doͦŋ′) city in W Java, Indonesia: pop. 973,000

**band·wag·on** (band′wag′ən) *n.* a wagon for the band to ride in, as in a parade —**on the bandwagon** [Colloq.] on the popular or apparently winning side, as in an election

**band·width** (-width′) *n.* the range of frequencies within a radiation band needed to transmit a particular signal

**ban·dy¹** (ban′dē) *vt.* -died, -dy·ing [Fr. *bander*, to bandy at tennis] **1.** to toss or hit (a ball, etc.) back and forth **2.** to pass (gossip, etc.) about carelessly **3.** to exchange (words), as in arguing

**ban·dy²** (ban′dē) *adj.* [< Fr. pp. of *bander*, to bend (as a bow)] bent or curved outward

**ban·dy·leg·ged** (-leg′id, -legd′) *adj.* having bandy legs; bowlegged

**bane** (bān) *n.* [OE. *bana*, slayer] **1.** [Poet.] ruin **2.** the cause of distress, death, or ruin **3.** deadly poison: now obs. except in *ratsbane*, etc.

**bane·ber·ry** (bān′ber′ē) *n., pl.* -ries **1.** any of a genus of plants of the buttercup family, with clusters of berries, some of which are poisonous **2.** the berry of any of these plants

**bane·ful** (-fəl) *adj.* causing distress, death, or ruin —**bane′ful·ly** *adv.*

**bang¹** (baŋ) *vt.* [ON. *banga*, to pound] **1.** to hit hard and noisily **2.** to shut (a door, etc.) noisily **3.** to handle violently —*vi.* **1.** to make a sharp, loud noise **2.** to strike sharply (*against, into*, etc.) —*n.* **1.** a hard blow or loud knock **2.** a sudden, loud noise **3.** *a)* [Colloq.] a display of enthusiasm or vigor [*to start with a bang*] *b)* [Slang] a thrill —*adv.* **1.** hard and noisily **2.** suddenly or exactly —**bang up** to do physical damage to

**bang²** (baŋ) *vt.* [< ?] to cut (hair) short and straight across —*n.* [*usually pl.*] banged hair worn across the forehead

**Ban·ga·lore** (baŋ′gə lôr′) city in S India: pop. 1,207,000

**Bang·ka** (bäŋ′kä) island of Indonesia, off the E coast of Sumatra: 4,610 sq. mi.

**Bang·kok** (baŋ′käk) capital of Thailand, a seaport in the S part: pop. 1,669,000

**Bang·la·desh** (bäŋ′glə desh′) country in S Asia, at the head of the Bay of Bengal: a member of the Commonwealth: 55,134 sq. mi.; pop. 50,840,000; cap. Dacca

**ban·gle** (baŋ′g′l) *n.* [Hindi *baṅgrī*, glass bracelet] **1.** a decorative bracelet, armlet, or anklet **2.** a disk-shaped ornament

**bang·tail** (baŋ′tāl′) *n.* [Slang] a racehorse

**bang-up** (baŋ′up′) *adj.* [Colloq.] excellent

**ban·ian¹** (ban′yən) *n. same as* BANYAN

**ban·ian²** (ban′yən) *n.* [Port., ult. < Sans. *vaṇij*, merchant] a Hindu merchant

**ban·ish** (ban′ish) *vt.* [< extended stem of OFr. *banir* < *ban*: see BAN¹] **1.** to send into exile **2.** to send or put away; dismiss —**ban′ish·ment** *n.*

**ban·is·ter** (ban′əs tər) *n.* [altered < BALUSTER] **1.** [*often pl.*] a railing and the balusters supporting it, as on a staircase **2.** the railing itself

**ban·jo** (ban′jō) *n., pl.* -jos, -joes [of Afr. origin] a stringed musical instrument having a long neck and a circular body covered with taut skin —**ban′jo·ist** *n.*

**bank¹** (baŋk) *n.* [< Fr. < It. *banca*, orig. a (moneylender's) table < OHG. *bank*, bench: see ff.] **1.** *a)* an establishment for receiving, lending, or, sometimes, issuing money *b)* its building **2.** *same as* PIGGY BANK **3.** the fund held, as by the dealer, in some gambling games **4.** *Med. a)* any place for gathering and distributing blood for transfusions or body parts for transplantation *b)* any reserve thus gathered —*vi.* **1.** to put money in or do business with a bank **2.** to manage a bank **3.** to keep the bank, as in some gambling games —*vt.* to deposit (money) in a bank —**bank on** [Colloq.] to depend on; rely on —**bank′a·ble** *adj.*

BANJO

**bank²** (baŋk) *n.* [< ON. *bakki,* akin to OHG. *bank* & OE. *benc,* BENCH] **1.** a long mound or heap; ridge **2.** a steep slope, as of a hill **3.** a stretch of rising land at the edge of a stream, etc. **4.** a shoal or shallow place, as in a sea **5.** the sloping of an airplane laterally to avoid slipping sideways on a turn **6.** the sloping of a road laterally along a curve — *vt.* **1.** to heap dirt around for protection from cold, etc. **2.** to cover (a fire) with ashes and fuel so that it will burn longer **3.** to pile up so as to form a bank **4.** to construct (a curve in a road, etc.) so that it slopes up from the inside edge **5.** to slope (an airplane) laterally on a turn **6.** *Billiards* to stroke (a ball) so that it recoils from a cushion — *vi.* **1.** to form a bank or banks **2.** to bank an airplane

**bank³** (baŋk) *n.* [< OFr. < OHG. *bank:* see prec.] **1.** a bench for rowers in a galley **2.** a row of oars **3.** a row or tier of objects **4.** a row of keys in a keyboard or console — *vt.* to arrange in a bank

**bank account** money deposited in a bank and subject to withdrawal by the depositor

**bank·book** (baŋk'book') *n.* the book in which the account of a depositor in a bank is recorded

**bank·er** (baŋ'kər) *n.* **1.** one who owns or manages a bank **2.** the keeper of the bank in some gambling games

**bank·ing** (-kiŋ) *n.* the business of a bank

**bank note** a promissory note issued by a bank, payable on demand: it is a form of paper money

**bank·roll** (baŋk'rōl') *n.* a supply of money —*vt.* [Colloq.] to finance

**bank·rupt** (baŋk'rupt', -rəpt) *n.* [< Fr. < It. < *banca,* bench (see BANK¹) + *rotta,* broken < L. pp. of *rumpere,* to break] a person legally declared unable to pay his debts: his property is divided among his creditors —*adj.* **1.** that is a bankrupt **2.** lacking in some quality [morally *bankrupt]* **3.** that has failed completely [a *bankrupt* foreign policy] —*vt.* to make bankrupt

**bank·rupt·cy** (-rupt'sē, -rəp sē) *n., pl.* **-cies** **1.** the state or an instance of being bankrupt **2.** complete failure; ruin; destitution

**ban·ner** (ban'ər) *n.* [< OFr. *baniere* (< WGmc. *banda,* a sign), altered after *banir,* to announce (see BANISH)] **1.** a piece of cloth bearing a design, motto, etc. **2.** a flag **3.** a headline extending across a newspaper page —*adj.* foremost; leading

**ban·nis·ter** (ban'əs tər) *n. same as* BANISTER

**ban·nock** (ban'ək) *n.* [< Gael. *bannach,* a cake] [Scot.] a flat cake of oatmeal or barley meal

**banns** (banz) *n.pl.* [see BAN¹] the proclamation, generally made in church on three successive Sundays, of an intended marriage

**ban·quet** (baŋ'kwit, ban'-) *n.* [Fr. < It. *banchetto,* dim. of *banca:* see BANK¹] **1.** a feast **2.** a formal dinner, usually with speeches —*vt.* to honor with a banquet —*vi.* to dine at a banquet —**ban'quet·er** *n.*

**ban·quette** (baŋ ket') *n.* [Fr., dim. < Norm. *banque,* earthwork < Du. *bank,* BANK²] **1.** a gunners' platform along the inside of a trench or parapet **2.** [South] a sidewalk **3.** an upholstered bench along a wall

**ban·shee, ban·shie** (ban'shē) *n.* [< Ir. < *bean,* woman + *sith,* fairy] *Ir. & Scot. Folklore* a female spirit believed to wail to warn of an impending death in the family

**ban·tam** (ban'təm) *n.* [after *Bantam,* former Du. residency in Java] **1.** [*often* B-] any of various dwarf varieties of breeds of domestic fowl **2.** a small but aggressive person — *adj.* like a bantam; small and aggressive

**ban·tam·weight** (-wāt') *n.* a boxer or wrestler between a flyweight and a featherweight (in boxing, 113–118 pounds)

**ban·ter** (ban'tər) *vt.* [17th-c. slang < ? BANDY¹] to tease in a playful way —*vi.* to exchange banter (*with* someone) —*n.* good-natured teasing or joking —**ban'ter·ing·ly** *adv.*

**bant·ling** (bant'liŋ) *n.* [< G. *bänkling,* bastard < *bank,* a bench] [Archaic] a young child; brat

**Ban·tu** (ban'tōō) *n.* [Bantu *ba-ntu,* mankind] **1.** *pl.* **-tus, -tu** any member of a large group of Negroid tribes of equatorial and southern Africa **2.** any of the group of languages of these peoples —*adj.* of the Bantus or their languages

**ban·yan** (ban'yən) *n.* [from a tree of this kind under which the *banians* (see BANIAN²) had built a pagoda] an East Indian fig tree whose branches take root and become new trunks

**ban·zai** (bän'zī') *interj.* a Japanese greeting or shout, meaning "May you live ten thousand years!"

**ba·o·bab** (bā'ō bab', bā'-) *n.* [prob. EAfr. native name] a tall tree of Africa and India, with a thick trunk and gourdlike, edible fruit

**bap·tism** (bap'tiz'm) *n.* [< OFr. < L. < Gr. < *baptizein,* to immerse] **1.** the rite or sacrament of admitting a person into a Christian church by dipping him in water or sprinkling water on him **2.** any experience that initiates, tests, or purifies —**bap·tis'mal** (-tiz'm'l) *adj.*

**bap·tist** (bap'tist) *n.* **1.** a person who baptizes; specif., [**B-**] JOHN THE BAPTIST **2.** [**B-**] a member of a Protestant denomination holding that baptism should be given only after confession of faith and only by immersion

**bap·tis·ter·y** (bap'tis trē, -tis tər ē) *n., pl.* **-ter·ies** a place, esp. a part of a church, used for baptizing: also **bap'tis·try** (-trē), *pl.* **-tries**

**bap·tize** (bap'tīz, bap tīz') *vt.* **-tized, -tiz·ing** **1.** to administer baptism to **2.** to purify; initiate **3.** to christen —*vi.* to administer baptism —**bap'tiz·er** *n.*

**bar¹** (bär) *n.* [OFr. *barre* < ML. *barra,* barrier] **1.** any piece of wood, metal, etc. longer than it is wide or thick, often used as a barrier, lever, etc. **2.** *a)* an oblong piece [*bar* of soap] *b)* a small metal strip worn to show military or other rank **3.** anything that obstructs, hinders, or prevents **4.** a strip, band, or broad line **5.** the part of a law court, enclosed by a railing, where the judges or lawyers sit, or where prisoners are brought to trial **6.** *a)* a law court *b)* any place of judgment **7.** *a)* lawyers collectively *b)* the legal profession **8.** *a)* a counter at which alcoholic drinks are served *b)* a place with such a counter **9.** a handrail held onto while doing ballet exercises **10.** the mouthpiece of a horse's bit **11.** *Music a)* any of the vertical lines across a staff, dividing it into measures *b)* a measure —*vt.* **barred, bar'ring** **1.** to fasten in or as with a bar **2.** to obstruct; shut off; close **3.** to oppose, prevent, or forbid **4.** to keep out; exclude **5.** to set aside [*barring* certain possibilities] — **prep.** excluding; excepting [the best, *bar* none] —**cross the bar** to die

**bar²** (bär) *n.* [G. < Gr. *baros,* weight] a metric unit of pressure equal to one million dynes per square centimeter

**bar.** **1.** barometer **2.** barrel **3.** barrister

**barb¹** (bärb) *n.* [< OFr. < L. *barba,* a beard] **1.** a beardlike growth near the mouth of certain animals **2.** a sharp point projecting away from the main point of a fishhook, arrow, etc. **3.** a cutting remark **4.** any of the hairlike projections from the shaft of a feather —*vt.* to provide with a barb or barbs —**barbed** *adj.*

**barb²** (bärb) *n.* [< Fr. < It. < Ar. *Barbar,* Berber] a horse of a breed native to Barbary

**Bar·ba·dos** (bär bā'dōz, -dōs) country on the easternmost island of the West Indies, northeast of Trinidad: a member of the Commonwealth: 166 sq. mi.; pop. 253,000 —**Barba'di·an** (-dē ən) *adj., n.*

**Bar·ba·ra** (bär'bər ə, -brə) [L., fem. of *barbarus,* foreign, strange] a feminine name

**bar·bar·i·an** (bär ber'ē ən) *n.* [see BARBAROUS] **1.** orig., a foreigner; esp., a non-Greek or non-Roman **2.** a member of a people with a civilization regarded as primitive, etc. **3.** a person who lacks culture **4.** a coarse or unmannerly person; boor **5.** a savage, cruel person; brute —*adj.* of or like a barbarian; esp., uncivilized, cruel, rude, etc. —**bar·bar'i·an·ism** *n.*

**bar·bar·ic** (-ik) *adj.* **1.** of or like barbarians; uncivilized; primitive **2.** wild; crude —**bar·bar'i·cal·ly** *adv.*

**bar·ba·rism** (bär'bər iz'm) *n.* **1.** *a)* the use of words and expressions not standard in a language *b)* a word or expression of this sort (Ex.: "youse" for "you") **2.** the state of being primitive or uncivilized **3.** a barbarous act, custom, etc.

**bar·bar·i·ty** (bär ber'ə tē) *n., pl.* **-ties** **1.** cruel or brutal behavior **2.** a cruel or brutal act **3.** a crude or coarse taste, manner, etc.

**bar·ba·rize** (bär'bə rīz') *vt., vi.* **-rized', -riz'ing** to make or become barbarous —**bar·ba·ri·za'tion** *n.*

**bar·ba·rous** (-bər əs) *adj.* [< L. < Gr. *barbaros,* foreign; prob. < echoic word describing unintelligible speech] **1.** orig., foreign or alien; esp., in the ancient world, non-Greek or non-Roman **2.** characterized by substandard usages in speaking or writing **3.** uncivilized **4.** uncultured, crude, coarse, etc. **5.** cruel; brutal —**bar'ba·rous·ly** *adv.* — **bar'ba·rous·ness** *n.*

**Bar·ba·ry** (bär'bər ē) region in N Africa, west of Egypt, inhabited chiefly by Berbers: its coast ( **Barbary Coast** ) was once a center of piracy

**Barbary ape** a tailless, apelike monkey of North Africa and Gibraltar

**bar·bate** (bär'bāt) *adj.* [< L. < *barba,* a beard] bearded

**bar·be·cue** (bär'bə kyōō') *n.* [< Sp. < Haitian Creole *barbacoa,* framework] **1.** orig., a framework for smoking, drying, or broiling meat **2.** a hog, steer, etc. roasted whole over an open fire **3.** any meat broiled over an open fire **4.** a party or picnic at which such meat is served **5.** a portable outdoor grill —*vt.* **-cued', -cu'ing** **1.** to prepare (meat) outdoors by broiling on a spit or over a grill **2.** to cook (meat) with a highly seasoned sauce (**barbecue sauce**)

**barbed wire** twisted wire with sharp points all along it, used for barriers

**bar·bel** (bär'b'l) *n.* [OFr., ult. < L. *barba,* a beard] **1.** a threadlike growth from the jaws of certain fishes: it is an organ of touch  **2.** any of several large European fresh-water fishes with such growths

**bar·bell** (bär′bel′) *n.* [BAR¹ + (DUMB)BELL] a metal bar to which disks of varying weights are attached at each end, used for weight-lifting exercises: also **bar bell, bar-bell**

**bar·ber** (bär′bər) *n.* [OFr. *barbour*, ult. < L. *barba*, a beard] a person whose work is cutting hair, shaving and trimming beards, etc. —*vt.* to cut the hair of, shave, etc. —*vi.* to work as a barber

**barber pole** a pole with spiral stripes of red and white, a symbol of the barber's trade

**bar·ber·ry** (bär′ber′ē) *n., pl.* **-ries** [< ML. *barberis* < Ar. *barbāris*] **1.** a spiny shrub with sour, red berries  **2.** the berry

**bar·ber·shop** (bär′bər shäp′) *n.* a barber's place of business —*adj.* [Colloq.] designating, characterized by, or like the close harmony of male voices *[a barbershop quartet]*

**bar·bi·can** (bär′bi kən) *n.* [< OFr., prob. < Per. *barbarkhānah*, house on a wall] a fortification at the gate or bridge leading into a town or castle

**bar·bi·cel** (bär′bə sel′) *n.* [< ModL. < L. *barba*, a beard] any of the tiny, hairlike extensions growing from the barbules of a feather

**bar·bi·tal** (bär′bi tôl′) *n.* [BARBIT(URIC ACID) + -AL] a drug, $C_8H_{12}O_3N_2$, in the form of a white powder, used to induce sleep

**bar·bi·tu·rate** (bär bich′ər it, bär′bə tyoor′it) *n.* any salt or ester of barbituric acid, used as a sedative or to induce sleep

**bar·bi·tu·ric acid** (bär′bə tyoor′ik, -toor′-) [< G. *barbitursäure* + -IC] a crystalline acid, $C_4H_4O_3N_2$, derivatives of which are used to induce sleep

**bar·bule** (bär′byōōl) *n.* [< L. *barba*, a beard] **1.** a very small barb  **2.** any of the threadlike parts fringing each barb of a feather

**barb·wire** (bärb′wīr′) *n. same as* BARBED WIRE

**bar·ca·role, bar·ca·rolle** (bär′kə rōl′) *n.* [Fr. < It. < *barca*, boat] **1.** a song sung by Venetian gondoliers  **2.** a piece of music imitating this

**Bar·ce·lo·na** (bär′sə lō′nə; *Sp.* bär′the lō′nä) seaport in NE Spain: pop. 1,697,000

**bard** (bärd) *n.* [Gael. & Ir.] **1.** an ancient Celtic poet  **2.** any poet —**bard′ic** *adj.*

**Bard of Avon** William Shakespeare: so called from his birthplace, Stratford-on-Avon

**bare¹** (ber) *adj.* [OE. *bær*] **1.** *a)* without the customary covering *[bare floors] b)* without clothing; naked  **2.** without equipment or furnishings; empty  **3.** simple; plain  **4.** without tools or weapons *[to use one's bare hands]*  **5.** threadbare  **6.** mere *[a bare wage]* —*vt.* **bared, bar′ing** to make bare; uncover; strip —**lay bare** to uncover; expose —**bare′ness** *n.*

**bare²** (ber) *archaic pt. of* BEAR¹

**bare·back** (ber′bak′) *adv., adj.* on a horse with no saddle

**bare·faced** (-fāst′) *adj.* **1.** with the face uncovered or beardless  **2.** unconcealed; open  **3.** shameless; brazen; audacious —**bare′fac′ed·ly** (-fās′id lē) *adv.* —**bare′fac′ed·ness** *n.*

**bare·foot** (-foot′) *adj., adv.* without shoes and stockings —**bare′foot′ed** *adj.*

**bare·hand·ed** (-han′did) *adj., adv.* **1.** with hands uncovered  **2.** without weapons or other means

**bare·head·ed** (-hed′id) *adj., adv.* wearing no hat or other head covering

**bare·leg·ged** (-leg′id, -legd′) *adj., adv.* with the legs bare; without stockings on

**bare·ly** (ber′lē) *adv.* **1.** openly; plainly  **2.** only just; scarcely  **3.** scantily *[barely furnished]*

**barf** (bärf) *vi., vt.* [echoic] [Slang] to vomit

**bar·fly** (bär′flī′) *n., pl.* **-flies′** [Slang] one who spends much time drinking in barrooms

**bar·gain** (bär′g'n) *n.* [< OFr. < *bargaignier*, to haggle < Frank.] **1.** a mutual agreement between parties on what should be given or done by each  **2.** such an agreement in terms of its worth to one of the parties *[a bad bargain]*  **3.** something sold at a price favorable to the buyer —*vi.* **1.** to talk over a transaction, contract, etc., trying to get the best possible terms —*vt.* to barter —**bargain for 1.** to try to get cheaply  **2.** to expect; count on: also **bargain on** —**into the bargain** in addition —**bar′gain·er** *n.*

**barge** (bärj) *n.* [< OFr. < ML. *barga*] **1.** a large, flat-bottomed boat for carrying freight on rivers, etc.  **2.** a large pleasure boat, used for pageants, etc.  **3.** a flagship's boat for use by flag officers —*vt.* **barged, barg′ing** to carry by barge —*vi.* **1.** to move slowly and clumsily  **2.** to come or go *(in or into)* in a rude, abrupt way  **3.** to collide *(into)* —**barge′man** *n., pl.* **-men**

**bar graph** a graph with parallel bars representing in proportional lengths the figures given in the data

**Ba·ri** (bä′rē) seaport in SE Italy, on the Adriatic: pop. 345,000

**bar·ite** (ber′īt) *n.* [< Gr. *barys*, weighty + -ITE] a white, crystalline mineral composed mainly of barium sulfate

**bar·i·tone** (bar′ə tōn′) *n.* [< It. < Gr. < *barys*, deep + *tonos*, tone] **1.** the range of a male voice between bass and tenor  **2.** a voice or singer with such a range  **3.** any wind instrument with a similar range  **4.** a part for such a voice or instrument —*adj.* of, in, for, or having this range

**bar·i·um** (ber′ē əm) *n.* [ModL. < Gr. *barys*, heavy] a silver-white, metallic chemical element: symbol, Ba; at. wt., 137.34; at. no., 56

**bark¹** (bärk) *n.* [ON. *bọrkr*] the outside covering of the stems and roots of trees and woody plants —*vt.* **1.** to tan (hides) with a bark infusion  **2.** to take the bark off (a tree)  **3.** [Colloq.] to scrape some skin off *[to bark one's shin]*

**bark²** (bärk) *vi.* [OE. *beorcan:* echoic] **1.** to make the sharp, abrupt cry of a dog  **2.** to make a sound like this *[the engine barked]*  **3.** to speak or shout sharply; snap  **4.** [Colloq.] to cough  **5.** [Slang] to work as a barker —*vt.* to say with a bark or a shout —*n.* a sound made in barking —**bark up the wrong tree** to misdirect one's attack, energies, etc.

**bark³** (bärk) *n.* [< Fr. < It. & L. *barca* < Gr. < Coptic *bari*, small boat] **1.** [Poet.] any boat, esp. a small sailing boat  **2.** a sailing vessel with its two forward masts square-rigged and its rear mast rigged fore-and-aft

**bar·keep·er** (bär′kēp′ər) *n.* **1.** an owner or manager of a bar  **2.** a bartender  Also **bar′keep′**

**bark·en·tine** (bär′kən tēn′) *n.* [< BARK³ after BRIGANTINE] a sailing vessel with its foremast square-rigged and its other two masts rigged fore-and-aft

**bark·er** (bär′kər) *n.* one that barks; esp., a person in front of a sideshow, etc. who tries to attract customers by loud, lively talk about it

**bar·ley** (bär′lē) *n.* see PLURAL, II, D, 3 [< OE. *bærlic, adj.* < *bere,* barley] **1.** a cereal grass  **2.** its grain, used in making malts, in soups, and as a feed for animals

**bar·ley·corn** (-kôrn′) *n.* barley or a grain of barley: see also JOHN BARLEYCORN

**barm** (bärm) *n.* [OE. *beorma*] the foamy yeast that appears on the surface of fermenting malt liquors

**bar·maid** (bär′mād′) *n.* a waitress who serves alcoholic drinks in a bar

**bar·man** (-mən) *n., pl.* **-men** a bartender

**bar mitz·vah, bar miz·vah** (bär mits′və) [Heb. *bar mitswāh,* son of the commandment] *[also* B- M-] **1.** a Jewish boy who has arrived at the age of religious responsibility, thirteen years  **2.** the ceremony celebrating this event

**barm·y** (bär′mē) *adj.* **-i·er, -i·est 1.** full of barm; foamy  **2.** [Brit. Slang] silly; idiotic

**barn** (bärn) *n.* [< OE. *bern, berern < bere,* barley + *ærn,* a building] **1.** a farm building for sheltering harvested crops, livestock, etc.  **2.** a large building for housing street-cars, trucks, etc.

**bar·na·cle** (bär′nə k'l) *n.* [< Fr. *bernicle* & Bret. *bernik,* kind of shellfish] any of a number of saltwater shellfish that attach themselves to rocks, ship bottoms, etc. —**bar′na·cled** *adj.*

**barn dance** a party, orig. held in a barn, at which people dance square dances

**barn owl** a species of brown and gray owl with a spotted white breast, commonly found in barns

**barn·storm** (bärn′stôrm′) *vi., vt.* [BARN + STORM, *vi.* 3: from occas. use of barns as auditoriums] to tour in small towns and rural districts, performing plays, giving campaign speeches, etc. —**barn′storm′er** *n.* —**barn′storm′ing** *adj., n.*

**barn swallow** a common swallow with a long, deeply forked tail: it usually nests in barns

**Bar·num** (bär′nəm), **P(**hineas**) T(**aylor**)** 1810-91; U.S. showman & circus operator

**barn·yard** (bärn′yärd′) *n.* the yard or ground near a barn —*adj.* **1.** of a barnyard  **2.** like or fit for a barnyard; earthy, smutty, etc.

**bar·o-** [< Gr. *baros,* weight] *a prefix meaning* of pressure, esp. atmospheric pressure *[barograph]*

**bar·o·gram** (bar′ə gram′) *n.* the linear record traced by a barograph

**bar·o·graph** (-graf′) *n.* a barometer that records variations in atmospheric pressure automatically on a revolving cylinder —**bar′o·graph′ic** *adj.*

**ba·rom·e·ter** (bə räm′ə tər) *n.* [BARO- + -METER] **1.** an instrument for measuring atmospheric pressure, as by a graduated glass tube (**mercury barometer**) in which a column of mercury rises or falls as the pressure changes (see also ANEROID BAROMETER): barometers are used in forecast-

---

ing the weather or finding height above sea level  **2.** anything that indicates change —**bar·o·met·ric** (bar'ə-met'rik), **bar'o·met'ri·cal** *adj.* —**bar'o·met'ri·cal·ly** *adv.*
**barometric pressure** the pressure of the atmosphere as indicated by a barometer: in a mercury barometer it averages 29.92 inches at sea level
**bar·on** (bar'ən) *n.* [OFr. < Frank. hyp. *baro*, freeman, man]  **1.** a member of the lowest rank of the British hereditary peerage  **2.** a European or Japanese nobleman of like rank  **3.** a powerful businessman or industrialist; magnate —**ba·ro·ni·al** (bə rō'nē əl) *adj.*
**bar·on·age** (bar'ə nij) *n.*  **1.** barons as a class  **2.** the peerage  **3.** the rank, title, etc. of a baron
**bar·on·ess** (-nis) *n.*  **1.** a baron's wife or widow  **2.** a lady with a barony in her own right
**bar·on·et** (-nit, -net') *n.* a man holding the lowest hereditary British title, below a baron but above a knight —**bar'on·et·cy** (-sē) *n., pl.* **-cies**
**ba·ro·ni·al** (bə rō'nē əl) *adj.* of or fit for a baron [a *baronial* mansion]
**bar·on·y** (bar'ə nē) *n., pl.* **-on·ies**  **1.** a baron's domain  **2.** the rank or title of a baron
**ba·roque** (bə rōk') *adj.* [Fr. < Port. *barroco*, imperfect pearl]  **1.** *a)* of or like a style of art and architecture with much ornamentation and curved rather than straight lines *b)* of or like a style of music with highly embellished melodies and fugal or contrapuntal forms  **2.** of the period in which these styles flourished (c. 1550–1750)  **3.** *same as* ROCOCO  **4.** overdecorated, or too ornate  **5.** irregular in shape: said of pearls —*n.* baroque style, baroque art, etc.
**bar·o·scope** (bar'ə skōp') *n.* [BARO- + -SCOPE] an instrument indicating but not measuring changes in atmospheric pressure —**bar'o·scop'ic** (-skäp'ik) *adj.*
**ba·rouche** (bə rōōsh') *n.* [< G. < It. < LL. *birotus* < *bi-*, two + *rota*, a wheel] a four-wheeled carriage with a collapsible hood, two double seats opposite each other, and a driver's seat in front
**barque** (bärk) *n. same as* BARK³
**bar·quen·tine** (bär'kən tēn') *n. same as* BARKENTINE
**Bar·qui·si·me·to** (bär kē'sē mā'tō) city in NW Venezuela: pop. 235,000
**bar·rack** (bar'ik) *n.* [< Fr. < Sp. < *barro*, clay < VL. hyp. *barrum*, clay] [*pl., often with sing. v.*]  **1.** a building or group of buildings for housing soldiers  **2.** a large, plain building for housing workmen, etc. —*vt., vi.* to house in barracks
**barracks bag** a large cloth bag to hold a soldier's equipment and personal possessions
**bar·ra·cu·da** (bar'ə kōō'də) *n., pl.* **-da, -das:** see PLURAL, II, D, 2 [Sp., prob. < native WInd. name] a fierce, pikelike fish of tropical seas
**bar·rage** (bə räzh', -räj'; *for n. 3* bär'ij) *n.* [Fr. < *barrer*, to stop < *barre*, BAR¹]  **1.** a curtain of artillery fire laid down to keep enemy forces from moving, or to cover one's own forces, esp. in attack  **2.** a prolonged attack of words, blows, etc.  **3.** a man-made barrier in a river; dam —*vi., vt.* **-raged'**, **-rag'ing** to lay down a barrage (against)
**bar·ran·ca** (bə ran'kə) *n.* [Sp.] a deep ravine or a steep cliff: also **bar·ran'co** (-kō), *pl.* **-cos**
**Bar·ran·qui·lla** (bä'rän kē'yä) seaport in NW Colombia: pop. 498,000
**bar·ra·tor, bar·ra·ter** (bar'ə tər) *n.* [< OFr. *barater*, to cheat < *barate*, fraud < ON. *baratta*, quarrel] a person guilty of barratry
**bar·ra·try** (-trē) *n.* [see prec.]  **1.** the criminal offense of habitually bringing about quarrels or lawsuits  **2.** fraud or negligence on the part of a ship's officers or crew that results in a loss to the owners —**bar'ra·trous** *adj.*
**barred** (bärd) *adj.*  **1.** having bars or stripes  **2.** closed off with bars  **3.** forbidden or excluded
**bar·rel** (bar'əl) *n.* [< OFr. *baril* < ML. *barillus* < ?]  **1.** a large, wooden, cylindrical container with slightly bulging sides and flat ends, made usually of staves bound together with hoops  **2.** the capacity of a standard barrel (in the U.S., usually 31½ gal.)  **3.** any somewhat similar cylinder, drum, etc. [the *barrel* of a windlass]  **4.** the tube of a gun, through which the projectile is fired —*vt.* **-reled** or **-relled**, **-rel·ing** or **-rel·ling** to put or pack in a barrel or barrels —*vi.* [Slang] to go at a high speed —**have (someone) over a barrel** [Slang] to have (someone) completely at one's mercy, esp. financially
**bar·rel-chest·ed** (-ches'tid) *adj.* having an especially broad, deep chest for one's height
**barrel organ** a mechanical musical instrument having a revolving cylinder studded with pins which open pipe valves, producing a tune
**barrel roll** a complete revolution made by an airplane around its longitudinal axis while in flight
**bar·ren** (bar'ən) *adj.* [< OFr. *baraigne*, orig. used of land]  **1.** that cannot produce offspring; sterile  **2.** not producing crops or fruit; having little or no vegetation  **3.** unproductive; unprofitable  **4.** lacking appeal, interest, or meaning;

dull; boring  **5.** empty; devoid [*barren* of creative spirit] —*n.*  **1.** an area of unproductive land  **2.** [*usually pl.*] land with shrubs, brush, etc. and sandy soil —**bar'ren·ly** *adv.* —**bar'ren·ness** *n.*
**bar·rette** (bə ret', bä-) *n.* [Fr., dim. of *barre*, BAR¹] a small bar or clasp for holding a girl's or woman's hair in place
**bar·ri·cade** (bar'ə kād'; *also, esp. for v.,* bar'ə kād') *n.* [Fr. < It. pp. of *barricare*, to fortify]  **1.** a barrier thrown up hastily for defense  **2.** any barrier or obstruction —*vt.* **-cad'ed, -cad'ing  1.** to shut in or keep out with a barricade  **2.** to put up barricades in; obstruct
**Bar·rie** (bar'ē), **Sir James M(atthew)** 1860–1937; Scot. novelist & playwright
**bar·ri·er** (bar'ē ər) *n.* [< OFr. < *barre*, BAR¹]  **1.** an obstruction, as a fence or wall  **2.** anything that holds apart or separates [*racial barriers*]
**barrier reef** a long ridge of coral parallel to the coastline, separated from it by a lagoon
**bar·ring** (bär'iŋ) *prep.* unless there should be; excepting [*barring* rain, we leave tonight]
**bar·ri·o** (bär'ē ō) *n., pl.* **-os** [Sp. < Ar. < *barr*, open country] in Spanish-speaking countries, a district or suburb of a city
**bar·ris·ter** (bar'is tər) *n.* [< BAR¹ (*n.* 6) + *-ister*, as in MINISTER] in England, a counselor-at-law who presents and pleads cases in court: distinguished from SOLICITOR
**bar·room** (bär'rōōm') *n.* a room with a bar at which alcoholic drinks are sold
**bar·row¹** (bar'ō) *n.* [< OE. < *beran*, BEAR¹]  **1.** *same as: a)* HANDBARROW  *b)* WHEELBARROW  **2.** a small cart with two wheels, pushed by hand; pushcart
**bar·row²** (bar'ō) *n.* [OE. *beorg*, hill] a heap of earth or rocks marking an ancient grave
**Bar·row** (bar'ō), **Point** [after Sir J. *Barrow*, 19th-c. Eng. geographer] northernmost point of Alas.; cape on the Arctic Ocean
**bar sinister** *same as* BEND SINISTER
**Bart.** Baronet
**bar·tend·er** (bär'ten'dər) *n.* a man who mixes and serves alcoholic drinks at a bar
**bar·ter** (bär'tər) *vi.* [< OFr. *barater:* see BARRATOR] to trade by exchanging goods or services without using money —*vt.* to exchange (goods, etc.); trade —*n.*  **1.** the act or practice of bartering  **2.** anything bartered —**bar'ter·er** *n.*
**Barth** (bärt), **Karl** 1886–1968; Swiss theologian
**Bar·thol·o·mew** (bär thäl'ə myōō') [< LL. < Gr. *Bartholomaios* < Aram., lit., son of Talmai] a masculine name
**bar·ti·zan** (bär'tə zən, bär'tə zan') *n.* [altered < ME. *bretasce*, a parapet < OFr., prob. < OHG. *bret*, a board] a small, overhanging turret on a tower or battlement
**Bart·lett pear** (bärt'lət) [after E. *Bartlett* of Roxbury, Mass., the distributor] a large, juicy variety of pear
**Bar·tók** (bär'tôk), **Bé·la** (bā'lä) 1881–1945; Hung. composer
**Bar·ton** (bär't'n), **Clara** 1821–1912; U.S. philanthropist: founder of the American Red Cross
**bar·y·on** (bar'ē än') *n.* [< Gr. *barys*, heavy + (ELECTR)ON] one of a class of heavy atomic particles, including the proton and neutron
**ba·ry·tes** (bə rīt'ēz) *n. same as* BARITE
**bar·y·tone** (bar'ə tōn') *adj., n. same as* BARITONE
**bas·al** (bā's'l) *adj.*  **1.** of, at, or forming the base  **2.** basic; fundamental —**bas'al·ly** *adv.*
**basal metabolism** the quantity of energy used by any organism at rest, measured by the rate (**basal metabolic rate**) at which heat is given off by the organism
**ba·salt** (bə sôlt'; bäs'ôlt, bas'-) *n.* [< L. *basaltes*, a dark marble] a dark, tough, fine-grained to dense, volcanic rock —**ba·sal'tic** *adj.*
**bas·cule** (bas'kyōōl) *n.* [Fr.] any device balanced like a seesaw
**bascule bridge** a drawbridge counterweighted so that it can be raised and lowered easily
**base¹** (bās) *n., pl.* **bas'es** (-əz) [< OFr. *bas* < L. *basis*, BASIS]  **1.** the thing or part on which something rests; foundation  **2.** the main part, as of a plan, system, etc., on which the rest depends  **3.** the principal or essential ingredient [paint with an oil *base*]  **4.** a basis  **5.** a goal or place of safety in certain games, as baseball  **6.** the point of attachment of a part of the body  **7.** a center of operations or source of supply; headquarters  **8.** *Chem.* any compound that reacts with an acid to form a salt, produces hydroxyl ions in water solutions, and turns red litmus blue  **9.** *Geom.* the line or plane upon which a figure is thought of as resting  **10.** *Linguis.* any morpheme to which prefixes, suffixes, etc. are added; root  **11.** *Math. a)* the number that is raised to various powers to produce the main counting units of a number system [10 is the *base* of the decimal system]  *b)* the number that when raised to the logarithm of a given number produces the given number  *c)* in business, etc., a figure or sum upon which certain calculations are made —*adj.* forming a base —*vt.* **based, bas'ing  1.** to make a

base for **2.** to put or rest (on) as a base or basis **3.** to place or station (in or at a base) —**off base 1.** Baseball not touching the base **2.** [Slang] taking an unsound or wrong position, attitude, etc.

**base²** (bās) adj. [< OFr. < VL. bassus, low] **1.** with little or no honor, courage, or decency; mean; contemptible **2.** of a menial or degrading kind **3.** inferior in quality **4.** of comparatively low worth /iron is a base metal, gold a precious one/ **5.** debased or counterfeit **6.** [Archaic] of servile or humble birth —**base′ly** adv. —**base′ness** n.

**base·ball** (bās′bôl′) n. **1.** a game played with a rawhide-covered ball and a bat by two opposing teams of nine players each, on a field with four bases forming a diamond **2.** the ball used in this game

**base·board** (-bôrd′) n. a board or molding covering the edge of a wall next to the floor

**base·born** (-bôrn′) adj. **1.** of humble birth or origin **2.** of illegitimate birth **3.** mean or ignoble

**base·burn·er, base-burn·er** (-bur′nər) n. any stove, etc. in which more coal is fed automatically from above when that at the base is consumed

**base hit** Baseball a play in which the batter hits the ball and gets on base without benefit of an opponent's error and without forcing a runner

**Ba·sel** (bä′z'l) city in NW Switzerland, on the Rhine: pop. 212,000

**base·less** (bās′lis) adj. having no basis in fact; unfounded —**base′less·ness** n.

**base line 1.** a line serving as a base **2.** Baseball the lane between any two consecutive bases **3.** Tennis the line at the back at either end of a court

**base·man** (-mən) n., pl. **-men** Baseball an infielder stationed at first, second, or third base

**base·ment** (bās′mənt) n. [BASE¹ + -MENT] the lowest story of a building, below the main floor and wholly or partly below the surface of the ground

**ba·sen·ji** (bə sen′jē) n. [Bantu < ba-, plural prefix + senji < Fr. singe, a monkey] any of an African breed of small dog with a reddish-brown coat

**base on balls** Baseball same as WALK

**base runner** Baseball any member of the team at bat who is on base or is trying to reach a base

**bas·es¹** (bās′əz) n. pl. of BASE¹

**ba·ses²** (bā′sēz) n. pl. of BASIS

**bash** (bash) vt. [echoic; akin to (< ?) ON. hyp. basca, to strike] [Colloq.] to strike with a violent blow; smash (in) — n. **1.** [Colloq.] a violent blow **2.** [Slang] a gala party

**bash·ful** (bash′fəl) adj. [(A)BASH + -FUL] **1.** timid, shy, and easily embarrassed **2.** showing an embarrassed timidity —**bash′ful·ly** adv. —**bash′ful·ness** n.

**bas·ic** (bā′sik) adj. **1.** of, at, or forming a base; fundamental **2.** introductory or elementary **3.** Chem. of, having the nature of, or containing a base; alkaline —n. a basic principle, factor, etc.: usually used in pl. —**bas′i·cal·ly** adv.

**Basic English** a copyrighted simplified form of English for international communication and for first steps into full English, devised by C. K. Ogden (1889–1957)

**ba·sid·i·o·my·cete** (bə sid′ē ō mī′sēt, -mī sēt′) n. [< ModL. < Gr. basis, base + ModL. dim. suffix -idium + -MYCETE] any of a class of fungi, including the mushrooms, rusts, etc., that reproduce through spores borne on a club-shaped structure

**Bas·il** (baz′'l, bā′z'l) [< L. < Gr. Basileios, lit., kingly < basileus, king] a masculine name

**bas·il** (baz′'l, bā′z'l) n. [< OFr. < ML. < Gr. basilikon (phyton), lit., royal (plant) < basileus, king] a fragrant herb of the mint family, whose leaves are used for flavoring in cooking

**bas·i·lar** (bas′ə lər) adj. of or at the base, esp. of the skull: also **bas′i·lar′y** (-ler′ē)

**ba·sil·i·ca** (bə sil′i kə) n. [L. < Gr. basilikē (stoa), royal (portico)] **1.** in ancient Rome, a rectangular building with a broad nave flanked by colonnaded aisles, used as a courtroom, etc. **2.** a Christian church in this style

**bas·i·lisk** (bas′ə lisk′) n. [< L. < Gr. dim. of basileus, king] **1.** a mythical, lizardlike monster with fatal breath and glance **2.** a tropical American lizard with a crest on its back and tail

**ba·sin** (bās′'n) n. [< OFr. < VL. < bacca, water vessel] **1.** a) a wide, shallow container, as for liquid b) its contents or capacity **2.** a washbowl or sink **3.** any shallow, esp. water-filled hollow, as a pond **4.** a bay or harbor **5.** all the land drained by a river and its branches **6.** a great hollow in the earth's surface filled with an ocean

**ba·sis** (bā′sis) n., pl. **ba′ses** (-sēz) [L. < Gr., a base, pedestal] **1.** the base or foundation of anything **2.** a prin-

cipal constituent **3.** the basic principle or theory, as of a system of knowledge

**bask** (bask) vi. [ME. basken, to wallow (in blood) < ?] **1.** to warm oneself pleasantly, as in sunlight **2.** to enjoy any pleasant or warm feeling /he basked in her favor/

**bas·ket** (bas′kit) n. [ME. < ?] **1.** a container made of interwoven cane, strips of wood, etc. **2.** the amount that a basket will hold **3.** anything used or shaped like a basket **4.** the structure hung from a balloon to carry persons, etc. **5.** Basketball a) the goal, a round net open at the bottom and hanging from a metal ring b) a score made by tossing the ball through this net

**bas·ket·ball** (-bôl′) n. **1.** a game played by two teams of five players each, in a zoned floor area: points are scored by tossing a ball through a basket at the opponent's end of the court **2.** the large, inflated ball used in this game

**basket case** [Slang] **1.** a person lacking all four limbs **2.** any helpless or emotionally distraught person **3.** anything that cannot function as it should

**bas·ket·ry** (bas′kə trē) n. **1.** the craft of making baskets **2.** same as BASKETWORK

**basket weave** a weave of fabrics resembling the weave used in basketwork

**bas·ket·work** (bas′kit wurk′) n. work that is interlaced or woven like a basket

**ba·so·phile** (bā′sə fīl′, -fil′) n. [< BASIC + -PHILE] a cell or tissue that is readily stained with basic dyes: also **ba′so·phil′** (-fil′) —**ba′so·phil′ic** adj.

**Basque** (bask) n. **1.** any member of a certain people living in the W Pyrenees **2.** their unique language —adj. of the Basques, their language, etc.

**basque** (bask) n. [Fr. < Pr. basto < ?] a woman's tightfitting bodice or tunic

**Bas·ra** (bus′rə, buz′-) port in SE Iraq: pop. 328,000

**bas-re·lief** (bä′rə lēf′) n. [Fr. < It. basso-rilievo: see BASSO & RELIEF] sculpture in which figures are carved in a flat surface so that they project only a little from the background

**bass¹** (bās) n. [ME. bas, BASE²] **1.** the range of the lowest male voice **2.** a voice or singer with such a range **3.** an instrument of the lowest range; specif., same as DOUBLE BASS **4.** a part for such a voice or instrument —adj. of, in, for, or having this range

**bass²** (bas) n., pl. **bass, bass′es:** see PLURAL, II, D, 2 [< OE. bærs] a spiny-finned food and game fish of fresh or salt water

**bass³** (bas) n. same as: **1.** BAST **2.** BASSWOOD

**bass clef** (bās) Music a sign on a staff, indicating the position of F below middle C on the fourth line

**bass drum** (bās) the largest and lowest-toned of the double-headed drums

**bas·set** (bas′it) n. [OFr., orig., dim. of bas, BASE²] a kind of hunting hound with a long body, short legs, and long, drooping ears: also **basset hound**

**bass horn** (bās) same as TUBA

**bas·si·net** (bas′ə net′) n. [< Fr. bercelonnette, dim. of berceau, cradle] an infant's basketlike bed, often hooded and set on a stand having casters

**bass·ist** (bās′ist) n. a person who plays the double bass

**bas·so** (bas′ō; It. bäs′sô) n., pl. **bas′sos;** It. **bas′si** (-sē) [It. < VL. bassus, low] a bass voice or singer

**bas·soon** (bə sōōn′, ba-) n. [Fr. basson < It. < prec.] a double-reed bass woodwind instrument having a long, curved stem attached to the mouthpiece —**bas·soon′ist** n.

**bas·so-re·lie·vo** (bas′ō rə lē′vō) n., pl. **-vos** same as BAS-RELIEF

**bass viol** (bās) same as: **1.** VIOLA DA GAMBA **2.** DOUBLE BASS

**bass·wood** (bas′wood′) n. **1.** any of several trees of the U.S. and Canada, with fragrant, yellowish flowers and light, soft wood **2.** the wood

**bast** (bast) n. [OE. bæst] **1.** same as PHLOEM **2.** fiber obtained from phloem, for making ropes, etc.

BASSOON

**bas·tard** (bas′tərd) n. [< OFr. < ?] **1.** a person born of parents not married to each other **2.** anything spurious, inferior, or varying from standard **3.** a person regarded with contempt, hatred, pity, etc. or, sometimes, with playful affection: a vulgar usage —adj. **1.** of illegitimate birth or uncertain origin **2.** of a size or shape not standard **3.** not genuine or authentic; inferior; spurious —**bas′tard·ly** adj. —**bas′tard·y** n., pl. **-ies**

**bas·tard·ize** (bas′tər dīz′) vt. **-ized′, -iz′ing 1.** to make, declare, or show to be a bastard **2.** to make corrupt or inferior —**bas′tard·i·za′tion** n.

**baste¹** (bāst) vt. **bast′ed, bast′ing** [< OFr. < OHG. bastjan, to sew with bast] to sew with long, loose stitches so as to keep the parts together until properly sewed —**bast′er** n.

**baste²** (bāst) vt. **bast′ed, bast′ing** [< OFr. < bassiner, to moisten < bassin, BASIN] to moisten (meat) with melted butter, drippings, etc. during roasting —**bast′er** n.

**baste³** (bāst) vt. **bast′ed, bast′ing** [ON. beysta] **1.** to beat soundly **2.** to attack with words; abuse

**bas·tille, bas·tile** (bas tēl′) n. [Fr. < OFr. bastir, to build: see BASTION] a prison —**the Bastille** a state prison in Paris until destroyed (July 14, 1789) in the French Revolution

**bas·ti·na·do** (bas′tə nā′dō, -nā′dō) n., pl. **-does** [< Sp. < bastón, a stick] **1.** a beating with a stick, usually on the soles of the feet, esp. as a punishment **2.** a rod or stick Also **bas′ti·nade′** (-nād′) —vt. **-doed, -do·ing** to inflict a bastinado on

**bast·ing** (bās′tiŋ) n. **1.** the act of sewing with loose, temporary stitches **2.** loose, temporary stitches or the thread used for them

**bas·tion** (bas′chən; occas. -tē ən) n. [Fr. < It. < bastire, to build < Gmc. bastjan, to make with bast, build] **1.** a projection from a fortification **2.** any strong defense or bulwark —**bas′tioned** adj.

**bat¹** (bat) n. [< OE. batt, cudgel (prob. < W. bat) & < OFr. battre, BATTER¹] **1.** any stout club or stick **2.** a club used to strike the ball in baseball and cricket **3.** a turn at batting, as in baseball /to be at bat/ **4.** [Brit.] a batsman at cricket **5.** [Colloq.] a blow or hit **6.** [Old Slang] a spree —vt. **bat′ted, bat′ting 1.** to strike with or as with a bat **2.** to have a batting average of —vi. to take a turn at batting —**bat around** [Slang] to consider or discuss (an idea, plan, etc.) —**go to bat for** [Colloq.] to intervene on behalf of; defend —**(right) off the bat** [Colloq.] immediately

**bat²** (bat) n. [altered < ME. bakke < Scand.] a mouselike mammal with a furry body and membranous wings, usually seen flying at night —**blind as a bat** quite blind —**have bats in the (or one's) belfry** [Slang] to be insane; have crazy notions

**bat³** (bat) vt. **bat′ted, bat′ting** [ME. baten, to flap (wings) < OFr. battre, BATTER¹] [Colloq.] to wink; blink; flutter —**not bat an eye (or eyelash)** [Colloq.] not show surprise

**Ba·ta·vi·a** (bə tā′vē ə) former name of JAKARTA

**batch** (bach) n. [OE. bacan, to bake] **1.** the amount (of bread, etc.) produced at one baking **2.** the quantity of anything needed for or made in one operation or lot **3.** a number of things or persons taken as a group

**bate** (bāt) vt., vi. **bat′ed, bat′ing** [< ABATE] to abate or lessen —**with bated breath** with the breath held in because of fear, excitement, etc.

**ba·teau** (ba tō′) n., pl. **-teaux′** (-tōz′) [Fr. < OFr. batel < OE. bat, boat] a lightweight, flat-bottomed river boat with tapering ends

**bat·fish** (bat′fish′) n., pl. **-fish′, -fish′es:** see FISH any of certain marine fishes with expanded or extended pectoral fins

**Bath** (bath) city in SW England: a health resort with hot springs: pop. 85,000

**bath** (bath) n., pl. **baths** (bathz, baths) [OE. bæth] **1.** a washing or dipping of a thing, esp. the body, in water or other liquid, steam, etc. **2.** water or other liquid for bathing, or for dipping, soaking, regulating temperature, etc. **3.** a container for such liquid **4.** a bathtub **5.** a bathroom **6.** a building or set of rooms for bathing **7.** [often pl.] a resort where bathing is part of the medical treatment —vt., vi. [Brit.] same as BATHE

**bathe** (bāth) vt. **bathed, bath′ing** [OE. bathian < bæth, bath] **1.** to put into a liquid; immerse **2.** to give a bath to; wash **3.** to wet or moisten **4.** to cover as if with a liquid /trees bathed in moonlight/ —vi. **1.** to take a bath **2.** to go into or be in water so as to swim, cool oneself, etc. **3.** to soak oneself in some substance or influence —n. [Brit.] a swim or dip —**bath′er** n.

**bath·house** (bath′hous′) n. **1.** a public building where people can take baths **2.** a building used by bathers for changing clothes

**Bath·i·nette** (bath′ə net′) [< BATH, BASSINET] a trademark for a portable folding bathtub for babies, made of rubberized cloth, etc. —n. [b-] a bathtub of this kind

**bathing cap** a tightfitting cap of rubber, etc., worn to keep the hair dry as while swimming

**bathing suit** a garment worn for swimming

**bath·mat** (bath′mat′) n. a mat used in or next to a bathtub, as to prevent slipping

**ba·thos** (bā′thäs, -thôs) n. [Gr., depth] **1.** an abrupt change from the lofty to the ordinary or trivial in writing or speech; anticlimax **2.** false pathos; sentimentality **3.** triteness —**ba·thet·ic** (bə thet′ik) adj. —**ba·thet′i·cal·ly** adv.

**bath·robe** (bath′rōb′) n. a long, loose coat for wear to and from the bath, in lounging, etc.

**bath·room** (-rōōm′) n. a room with a bathtub, toilet, washstand, etc.

**bath·tub** (-tub′) n. a tub, now usually a bathroom fixture, in which to take a bath

**bath·y·scaph** (bath′ə skaf′) n. [Fr. < Gr. bathys, deep + skaphē, boat] a deep-sea diving compartment for reaching great depths without a cable

**bath·y·sphere** (bath′ə sfir′) n. [< Gr. bathys, deep + -SPHERE] a round, watertight observation chamber lowered by cables into sea depths

**ba·tik** (bə tēk′, bat′ik) n. [Malay] **1.** a method of dyeing designs on cloth by coating with removable wax the parts not to be dyed **2.** cloth so decorated or a design made in this way —adj. of or like batik

**ba·tiste** (ba tēst′, bə-) n. [Fr. < OFr. baptiste: after the supposed original maker, Baptiste of Cambrai] a fine, thin cloth of cotton, linen, rayon, etc.

**bat mitz·vah, bat miz·vah** (bät mits′və) [Heb. bat mitswāh, daughter of the commandment] [also B- M-] **1.** a Jewish girl who undergoes a ceremony analogous to that of a bar mitzvah **2.** the ceremony itself

**ba·ton** (bə tän′, ba-) n. [Fr. < OFr. < VL. hyp. basto, a stick] **1.** a staff serving as a symbol of office **2.** a slender stick used by a conductor in directing an orchestra, choir, etc. **3.** a hollow metal rod twirled in a showy way, as by a drum majorette **4.** the short rod passed from one runner to the next in a relay race

**Bat·on Rouge** (bat′'n rōōzh′) [Fr. transl. of Choctaw ītuúma, red (boundary) pole] capital of La., on the Mississippi: pop. 219,000

**ba·tra·chi·an** (bə trā′kē ən) adj. [< ModL. < Gr. < batrachos, frog] of, like, or concerning amphibians without tails, as frogs and toads —n. an amphibian without a tail; frog or toad

**bats·man** (bats′mən) n., pl. **-men** the batter in cricket

**bat·tal·ion** (bə tal′yən) n. [< Fr. < It. < VL. battalia, BATTLE] **1.** a large group of soldiers arrayed for battle **2.** any large group joined together in some activity **3.** U.S. Army a tactical unit made up of three or more companies, batteries, or similar units

**bat·ten¹** (bat′'n) n. [var. of BATON] **1.** a sawed strip of wood, flooring, etc. **2.** a strip of wood put over a seam between boards as a fastening or covering **3.** a strip used to fasten canvas over a ship's hatchways —vt. to fasten or supply with battens —**batten down the hatches** to fasten canvas over the hatches, esp. in preparing for a storm

**bat·ten²** (bat′'n) vi. [ON. batna, to improve] to grow fat; thrive —vt. to fatten up; overfeed

**bat·ter¹** (bat′ər) vt. [OFr. batre, battre < VL. < L. battuere, to beat; also, in part, freq. of BAT¹, v.] **1.** to beat or strike with blow after blow; pound **2.** to injure by pounding, hard wear, or use —vi. to pound noisily and repeatedly

**bat·ter²** (bat′ər) n. the player whose turn it is to bat in baseball or cricket

**bat·ter³** (bat′ər) n. [< OFr., prob. < batre: see BATTER¹] a flowing mixture of flour, milk, eggs, etc. for making cakes, pancakes, etc.

**bat·ter·ing ram** (bat′ər iŋ ram′) **1.** an ancient military machine having a heavy wooden beam for battering down gates, walls, etc. **2.** any bar, log, etc. used like this to force entrance

**bat·ter·y** (bat′ər ē, bat′rē) n., pl. **-ter·ies** [< Fr. < battre: see BATTER¹] **1.** a battering or beating **2.** a group of similar things arranged, connected, or used together; set or series **3.** Baseball the pitcher and the catcher **4.** Elec. a connected group of cells (or popularly, a single cell) storing an electrical charge and capable of furnishing a current **5.** Law any illegal beating of another person: see ASSAULT AND BATTERY **6.** Mil. a) an emplacement or fortification equipped with heavy guns b) a set of heavy guns, rockets, etc. c) the men who operate such a set: usually the basic unit of artillery

**bat·ting** (bat′iŋ, bat′'n) n. [< BAT¹] fiber of cotton, wool, or synthetic fiber wadded into sheets and used in bandages, quilts, etc.

**batting average 1.** a measure of a baseball player's batting effectiveness, figured by dividing the number of safe hits by the number of times at bat **2.** [Colloq.] the average level of competence or success reached in any activity

**bat·tle** (bat′'l) n. [< OFr. < VL. battalia < L. < battuere: see BATTER¹] **1.** a large-scale fight between armed forces **2.** armed fighting; combat or war **3.** any fight or struggle; conflict —vt., vi. **-tled, -tling** to oppose, fight, or struggle —**give (or do) battle** to engage in battle; fight —**bat′tler** n.

**bat·tle-ax, bat·tle-axe** (-aks′) n. **1.** a heavy ax formerly used as a weapon of war **2.** [Slang] a woman who is harsh, domineering, etc.

**battle cruiser** a large warship with longer range and greater speed than a battleship, but less heavily armored

**battle cry** a cry or slogan used to encourage those in a battle, struggle, contest, etc.

**bat·tle·dore** (bat′'l dôr′) n. [< ? Pr. batedor, beater] **1.** a paddle or racket used to hit a shuttlecock back and forth in a game (called **battledore and shuttlecock**) like badminton **2.** this game

**battle fatigue** *same as* COMBAT FATIGUE

**bat·tle·field** (bat''l fēld') *n.* **1.** the place where a battle is fought or was fought **2.** any area of conflict Also **bat'tle-ground'**

**bat·tle·ment** (-mənt) *n.* [< OFr. *batailler*, to fortify] **1.** a low wall, as on top of a tower, with open spaces for shooting **2.** an architectural decoration like this —**bat'tle·ment'ed** (-men'tid) *adj.*

**battle royal** *pl.* **battles royal** **1.** a fight involving many contestants; free-for-all **2.** a bitterly fought battle **3.** a heated dispute

**bat·tle·ship** (-ship') *n.* any of a class of large warships with the biggest guns and very heavy armor: also [Slang] **bat'tle·wag'on**

**bat·ty** (bat'ē) *adj.* **-ti·er, -ti·est** [< BAT² + -Y²] [Slang] **1.** insane; crazy **2.** odd; eccentric

**bau·ble** (bô'b'l) *n.* [< OFr. *baubel, belbel*, prob. redupl. of *bel* < L. *bellus*, pretty] a showy but worthless thing; trinket; trifle

BATTLEMENTS

**Baude·laire** (bōd ler'), **(Pierre) Charles** (shȧrl) 1821–67; Fr. poet & essayist

**baulk** (bôk) *n., vt., vi. same as* BALK

**baux·ite** (bôk'sīt, bō'zīt) *n.* [Fr. < (*Les*) *Baux*, town in SE France] the claylike ore from which aluminum is obtained

**Ba·var·i·a** (bə ver'ē ə) state of S West Germany: cap. Munich —**Ba·var'i·an** *adj., n.*

**bawd** (bôd) *n.* [< ? OFr. *baud*, gay, licentious (< Frank. *bald*, bold)] [Now Literary] **1.** a person, esp. a woman, who keeps a brothel **2.** a prostitute

**bawd·y** (bô'dē) *adj.* **bawd'i·er, bawd'i·est** [see prec.] indecent, obscene, etc. —**bawd'i·ly** *adv.* —**bawd'i·ness** *n.*

**bawd·y·house** (-hous') *n.* a house of prostitution

**bawl** (bôl) *vi., vt.* [< ML. *baulare*, to bark & ? ON. *baula*, to low like a cow] **1.** to shout or call out noisily; bellow **2.** to weep loudly —*n.* **1.** an outcry; bellow **2.** a noisy weeping —**bawl out** [Slang] to scold angrily —**bawl'er** *n.*

**bay¹** (bā) *n.* [< OFr. < ML. *baia*] a part of a sea or lake, indenting the shoreline; wide inlet

**bay²** (bā) *n.* [< OFr. *baer* < VL. *batare*, to gape] **1.** *a*) an opening or alcove marked off by columns, etc. *b*) a recess in a wall, as for a window *c*) *same as* BAY WINDOW **2.** a wing of a building **3.** a compartment or space: cf. BOMB BAY **4.** *same as* SICK BAY

**bay³** (bā) *vi.* [< OFr., ult. < VL. *batare*, to gape] to bark in long, deep tones —*vt.* **1.** to bark at **2.** to bring to or hold at bay —*n.* **1.** the sound of baying **2.** the situation of or as of a hunted animal forced to turn and fight —**at bay** **1.** with escape cut off; cornered **2.** held off /the bear kept the hunters *at bay*/ —**bring to bay** to force into a situation that makes escape impossible

**bay⁴** (bā) *n.* [< OFr. < L. *baca*, berry] **1.** *same as* LAUREL (*n.* 1) **2.** [*pl.*] *a*) a wreath of bay leaves, a classical token of honor given to poets and conquerors *b*) honor; fame

**bay⁵** (bā) *adj.* [< OFr. < L. *badius*] reddish-brown: said esp. of horses —*n.* **1.** a horse, etc. of this color **2.** reddish brown

**Ba·ya·món** (bä yä mōn') city in NE Puerto Rico, near San Juan: pop. 196,000

**bay·ber·ry** (bā'ber'ē) *n., pl.* **-ries** **1.** *a*) any of several shrubs, as the wax myrtle, having a small, wax-covered, berrylike fruit *b*) this fruit **2.** a tropical American tree yielding an aromatic oil used in bay rum

**Bay·ern** (bī'ərn) *Ger. name of* BAVARIA

**bay leaf** the aromatic leaf of the laurel, dried and used as a spice in cooking

**bay lynx** a wildcat of temperate N. America

**bay·o·net** (bā'ə nit, -net'; bā'ə net') *n.* [< Fr. < *Bayonne*, city in France] a detachable, daggerlike blade put on the muzzle end of a rifle, for hand-to-hand fighting —*vt., vi.* **-net'ed** or **-net'ted, -net'ing** or **-net'ting** to stab, prod, or kill with a bayonet

**Ba·yonne** (bā yōn') [after a city in SW France] city in NE N.J.: pop. 65,000

**bay·ou** (bī'ōō, -ō) *n.* [AmFr. < Choctaw *bayuk*, small stream] in the southern U.S., a marshy inlet or outlet of a lake, river, etc.

**bay rum** an aromatic liquid formerly obtained from leaves of a bayberry tree, now made of certain oils, water, and alcohol: it is used in medicines and cosmetics

**bay window** **1.** a window or set of windows jutting out from the wall of a building **2.** [Slang] a large, protruding belly

**ba·zaar** (bə zär') *n.* [Per. *bāzār*] **1.** in Oriental countries, a market or street of shops **2.** a shop for selling various kinds of goods **3.** a sale of various articles, usually to raise money for a club, church, etc.

**ba·zoo·ka** (bə zōōk'ə) *n.* [term orig. coined for a comic musical horn] a weapon of metal tubing, for aiming and launching electrically fired, armor-piercing rockets

**b.b., bb** base on balls

**B.B.A.** Bachelor of Business Administration

**BBC** British Broadcasting Corporation

**bbl.** *pl.* **bbls.** barrel

**BB** (shot) ) [a designation of the size] a size of shot measuring .18 of an inch in diameter, fired from an air rifle (**BB gun**) or shotgun

**B.C.** **1.** before Christ **2.** British Columbia

**bch.** *pl.* **bchs.** bunch

**bd.** *pl.* **bds.** **1.** board **2.** bond **3.** bound

**B/D** bank draft

**B.D.** Bachelor of Divinity

**bd. ft.** board foot (or feet)

**bdl.** *pl.* **bdls.** bundle

**be** (bē; *unstressed* bi) *vi.* **was** or **were, been, be'ing** [OE. *beon*] **1.** to exist; live /Caesar *is* no more/ **2.** to happen or occur /the party *is* tonight/ **3.** to remain or continue /will he *be* here long?/ **4.** to come to; belong /peace *be* with you/ **5.** to have a place or position /the door *is* on your left/ Note: *be* is often used to link its subject to a predicate nominative, adjective, or pronoun and is sometimes equivalent to the mathematical sign (=) (Ex.: he *is* brave, that hat *is* ten dollars, let x *be* y); *be* is also used as an auxiliary: (1) with the past participle of a transitive verb to form the passive voice /he will *be* paid/ (2) with the past participle of certain intransitive verbs to form an archaic perfect tense /Christ *is* risen/ (3) with the present participle of another verb to express continuation /the motor *is* running/ (4) with the present participle or infinitive of another verb to express futurity, possibility, obligation, intention, etc. /he *is* going next week, she *is* to wash the dishes/ *Be* is conjugated in the present indicative: (I) **am**, (he, she, it) **is**, (we, you, they) **are**; in the past indicative: (I, he, she, it) **was**, (we, you, they) **were**; archaic forms are (thou) **art, wert, wast**; the present subjunctive is **be**, the past subjunctive **were** —**be off** go away

**be-** [OE. < *be, bi*, about, near] *a prefix used variously with verbs, nouns, and adjectives to mean:* **1.** around [*besprinkle, beset*] **2.** completely; thoroughly [*bedeck, besmear*] **3.** away [*bereave, betake*] **4.** about [*bethink, bemoan*] **5.** make [*besot, bepretty*] **6.** furnish with; affect by [*befriend, bedizen, becloud*] **7.** covered with; furnished with (to excess) [*bemedaled, bewhiskered*]

**Be** *Chem.* beryllium

**B/E, b.e.** bill of exchange

**beach** (bēch) *n.* [E. dial., orig., pebbles, shingles] **1.** a nearly level stretch of pebbles and sand beside a sea, lake, etc., often washed by high water; sandy shore **2.** an area of shore as for swimmers, sunbathers, etc. —*vt., vi.* to ground (a boat) on a beach —**on the beach** **1.** not aboard a ship; ashore **2.** unemployed

**beach·comb·er** (-kō'mər) *n.* **1.** a long wave rolling ashore; comber **2.** a man who loafs on beaches or wharves, living on what he can beg or find

**beach·head** (-hed') *n.* **1.** a position established by invading troops on an enemy shore **2.** a position secured as a starting point for any action

**bea·con** (bēk''n) *n.* [OE. *beacen*] **1.** a signal fire, esp. one on a hill, pole, etc. **2.** any light for warning or guiding **3.** a lighthouse **4.** a radio transmitter that sends out signals for guiding aircraft, as at night **5.** a person or thing that warns, offers guidance, etc. —*vt.* **1.** to light up (darkness, etc.) **2.** to provide or mark with beacons —*vi.* to shine or serve as a beacon

**bead** (bēd) *n.* [ME. *bede*, prayer bead < OE. *bed* < *biddan*, to pray] **1.** a small, usually round piece of glass, wood, metal, etc., pierced for stringing **2.** [*pl.*] *a*) a string of beads; necklace *b*) a rosary **3.** any small, round object, as the front sight of a rifle **4.** a drop or bubble **5.** foam, as on beer **6.** the inner edge of a rubber tire where it fits on the rim **7.** a narrow, half-round molding —*vt.* **1.** to decorate or string with beads **2.** to string like beads —*vi.* to form a bead or beads —**draw a bead on** to take careful aim at —**say** (or **tell** or **count**) **one's beads** to say prayers with a rosary —**bead'ed** *adj.*

**bead·ing** (-iŋ) *n.* **1.** beads or decorative work in beads **2.** a molding or edge resembling a row of beads **3.** a narrow, half-round molding **4.** *a*) a narrow trimming of lacelike loops *b*) an openwork trimming through which a ribbon can be run

**bea·dle** (bē'd'l) *n.* [< OFr. < Frank. *bidal*, messenger] formerly, a minor parish officer in the Church of England, who kept order in church

**beads·man** (bēdz′mən) *n., pl.* **-men** [see BEAD] **1.** a person who prays for another's soul, esp. one hired to do so **2.** a person in a poorhouse —**beads′wom′an** *n.fem., pl.* -wom′en

**bead·y** (bē′dē) *adj.* **bead′i·er, bead′i·est 1.** small, round, and glittering like a bead [the *beady* eyes of a snake] **2.** decorated with beads

**bea·gle** (bē′g'l) *n.* [< ? Fr. *bégueule*, wide-throat] a small hound with a smooth coat, short legs, and drooping ears

**beak** (bēk) *n.* [< OFr. < L. *beccus* < Gaul.] **1.** a bird's bill, esp. the large, sharp, horny bill of a bird of prey **2.** the beaklike mouthpart of various insects, fishes, etc. **3.** the spout of a pitcher **4.** the metal-covered ram projecting from the prow of an ancient warship **5.** [Slang] the nose — **beaked** (bēkt) *adj.* —**beak′less** *adj.* —**beak′like′** *adj.*

BEAGLE
(13–15 in. high at shoulder)

**beak·er** (bē′kər) *n.* [< ON. *bikarr*, a cup < VL. < LL. < L. *bacar*, wine glass] **1.** a large or ornate cup; goblet **2.** a jarlike container of glass or metal with a lip for pouring, used by chemists, druggists, etc. **3.** its contents or capacity

**beam** (bēm) *n.* [< OE., akin to G. *baum*, a tree] **1.** a long, thick piece of wood, or of metal or stone, esp. one used as a horizontal support for a ceiling **2.** the part of a plow to which the handles, share, etc. are attached **3.** the crossbar of a balance, or the balance itself **4.** any of the heavy, horizontal crosspieces of a ship **5.** a ship's breadth at its widest point **6.** the side of a ship or the direction out sidewise from a ship **7.** a slender shaft of light or other radiation, as of X-rays **8.** a radiant look, smile, etc. **9.** a stream of radio or radar signals sent continuously in one direction as a guide for aircraft or ships —*vt.* **1.** to give out (shafts of light); radiate **2.** to direct or aim (a radio signal, program, etc.) —*vi.* **1.** to shine brightly **2.** to smile warmly —**off the beam 1.** not following a guiding beam, as an airplane **2.** [Colloq.] wrong; incorrect —**on the beam 1.** at right angles to the ship's keel **2.** following a guiding beam, as an airplane **3.** [Colloq.] working or functioning well; alert, keen, quick, etc. —**beam′ing** *adj.* —**beam′ing·ly** *adv.*

**beamed** (bēmd) *adj.* having exposed beams [a *beamed* ceiling]

**beam-ends** (bēm′endz′) *n.pl.* the ends of a ship's beams —**on the beam-ends 1.** tipping so far to the side as to be in danger of overturning **2.** at the end of one's resources, money, etc.

**beam·y** (-ē) *adj.* **beam′i·er, beam′i·est 1.** sending out beams of light; radiant **2.** beamlike; broad

**bean** (bēn) *n.* [OE. *bean*] **1.** any of various plants of the legume family, with edible, smooth, kidney-shaped seeds **2.** any such seed **3.** a pod with such seeds, eaten as a vegetable when still unripe **4.** any of various beanlike seeds [coffee *beans*] **5.** [Slang] the head or brain **6.** [*pl.*] [Slang] even a little amount [doesn't know *beans* about music] —*vt.* [Slang] to hit on the head, specif. with a pitched baseball —**full of beans** [Slang] **1.** lively; ebullient **2.** mistaken; in error —**spill the beans** [Colloq.] to divulge secret information —**bean′like′** *adj.*

**bean·bag** (bēn′bag′) *n.* a small cloth bag filled with beans, and thrown in some games

**bean·er·y** (bē′nər ē) *n., pl.* **-er·ies** [< baked *beans*, a chief dish] [Colloq.] a cheap restaurant

**bean·ie** (bē′nē) *n.* [Colloq.] any of various kinds of skullcap worn by children, etc.

**bean·pole** (bēn′pōl′) *n.* **1.** a tall pole for bean plants to climb on **2.** [Colloq.] a tall, lean person

**bean·stalk** (-stôk′) *n.* the main stem of a bean plant

**bear[1]** (ber) *vt.* **bore** or archaic **bare, borne** or **born** (see vt. 3), **bear′ing** [OE. *beran*, akin to L. *ferre*, Gr. *pherein*] **1.** to carry; transport **2.** to have or show [the letter *bore* his signature] **3.** to give birth to: the passive past participle in this sense is **born** when *by* does not follow **4.** to produce or yield [fruit-*bearing* trees] **5.** to support or sustain **6.** to sustain the burden of [to *bear* the cost] **7.** to put up with; tolerate [to *bear* pain] **8.** to call for; require [his actions *bear* watching] **9.** to carry or conduct (oneself) **10.** to carry over or hold (a sentiment) [to *bear* a grudge] **11.** to bring and tell (a message, tales, etc.) **12.** to move or push as if carrying [the crowd *bore* us along] **13.** to give or supply [to *bear* witness] —*vi.* **1.** to be productive [the tree *bears* well] **2.** *a)* to lie or move in a given direction *b)* to point toward (with *on* or *upon*) **3.** to have bearing (*on*); have a relation [his story *bears* on the crime] **4.** to tolerate; put up patiently (*with*) **5.** to be oppressive; weigh [grief *bears* heavily on her] —**bear down 1.** to press or

push down **2.** to make a strong effort —**bear down on 1.** to exert pressure on **2.** to make a strong effort toward accomplishing **3.** to approach —**bear out** to support or confirm —**bear up** to endure, as under a strain —**bring to bear on** (or **upon**) to cause to have an effect on

**bear[2]** (ber) *n., pl.* **bears, bear:** see PLURAL, II, D, 1 [OE. *bera*] **1.** a large, heavy mammal with shaggy fur and a very short tail, native to temperate and arctic zones **2.** [B-] either of two N constellations, the **Great Bear** and the **Little Bear 3.** a person who is clumsy, rude, etc. **4.** one who sells stock-market shares, etc. in the expectation of buying them later at a lower price —*adj.* falling in price [a *bear* market] —**be a bear for punishment** to be able to withstand rough treatment, hardship, etc. —**bear′like′** *adj.*

**bear·a·ble** (-ə b'l) *adj.* that can be borne or endured; tolerable —**bear′a·bly** *adv.*

**beard** (bird) *n.* [OE., akin to G. *bart*] **1.** the hair growing on the lower part of a man's face; whiskers **2.** any beardlike part, as of certain animals **3.** a hairy outgrowth on the head of certain grains, etc.; awn **4.** anything that projects like a beard; barb or hook —*vt.* **1.** to face or oppose courageously, as if grasping by the beard; defy **2.** to provide with a beard —**beard′ed** *adj.*

**beard·less** (bird′lis) *adj.* **1.** having no beard **2.** too young to have a beard **3.** young, callow, etc.

**Beards·ley** (birdz′lē), **Aubrey Vincent** 1872–98; Eng. artist & illustrator

**bear·er** (ber′ər) *n.* **1.** a person or thing that bears, carries, or supports **2.** a plant or tree that bears fruit **3.** a person presenting for payment a check, note, money order, etc. —*adj.* made out to the bearer [*bearer* bonds]

**bear·ing** (ber′iŋ) *n.* **1.** way of carrying and conducting oneself; carriage; manner **2.** a support or supporting part **3.** *a)* the act, power, or period of producing young, fruit, etc. *b)* that which is produced, as a crop **4.** endurance **5.** *a)* [*sometimes pl.*] direction or position with reference to the compass, some known points, etc. *b)* [*pl.*] awareness of one's position or situation [to lose one's *bearings*] **6.** relevant meaning; application; relation [the evidence has no *bearing* on the case] **7.** *Heraldry* any figure in a coat of arms **8.** *Mech.* any part of a machine in or on which another part revolves, slides, etc. —*adj.* that bears, or supports weight

**bear·ish** (ber′ish) *adj.* **1.** bearlike; rough, surly, etc. **2.** directed toward or causing a lowering of prices in the stock exchange —**bear′ish·ly** *adv.* —**bear′ish·ness** *n.*

**bear·skin** (ber′skin′) *n.* **1.** the pelt or hide of a bear **2.** a rug, coat, etc. made of this

**beast** (bēst) *n.* [< OFr. < L. *bestia*] **1.** orig., any animal except man **2.** any large, four-footed animal **3.** a person who is brutal, gross, vile, etc.

**beast·ly** (bēst′lē) *adj.* **-li·er, -li·est 1.** of or like a beast; bestial, brutal, etc. **2.** [Colloq.] disagreeable; unpleasant —*adv.* [Brit. Colloq.] very [*beastly* bad news] —**beast′li·ness** *n.*

**beast of burden** any animal used for carrying things

**beast of prey** any animal that hunts and kills other animals for food

**beat** (bēt) *vt.* **beat, beat′en, beat′ing** [OE. *beatan*] **1.** to strike repeatedly; pound **2.** to punish by so striking; flog **3.** to dash repeatedly against [waves *beat* the shore] **4.** to form (a path, etc.) by repeated treading or riding **5.** to shape by hammering; forge **6.** to mix by stirring or striking repeatedly with a utensil; whip **7.** to move (esp. wings) up and down; flap **8.** to hunt through; search [the posse *beat* the countryside] **9.** to make or force, as by flailing or pounding [to *beat* one's way through a crowd] **10.** *a)* to defeat in a contest or struggle *b)* to outdo or surpass *c)* to act, arrive, or finish before **11.** to mark (time) by tapping, etc. **12.** to sound or signal, as by a drumbeat **13.** [Colloq.] to baffle or puzzle **14.** [Colloq.] to cheat or trick **15.** [Slang] to avoid the penalties associated with (a charge, indictment, etc.) —*vi.* **1.** to strike repeatedly **2.** to move or sound rhythmically; throb, pulsate, etc. **3.** to hunt through woods, etc. for game **4.** to take a beating or stirring [this cream doesn't *beat* well] **5.** to make a sound by being struck, as a drum **6.** [Colloq.] to win **7.** *Naut.* to progress by tacking into the wind —*n.* **1.** a beating, as of the heart **2.** any of a series of blows or strokes **3.** a pulsating movement or sound; throb **4.** a habitual route [a policeman's *beat*] **5.** *a)* the unit of musical rhythm [four *beats* to a measure] *b)* the accent in the rhythm of verse or music *c)* the gesture of the hand, baton, etc. used to mark this **6.** *same as* BEATNIK **7.** *Journalism* a publishing of news before rival newspapers; scoop —*adj.* **1.** [Slang] tired out; exhausted **2.** of or belonging to a group of alienated young persons, esp. of the 1950's, rebelling against conventional attitudes, dress, speech, etc. —**beat about** to hunt or look through or around —**beat back** to force to retreat —**beat down 1.** to shine with dazzling light and intense heat **2.** to put down; suppress **3.** [Colloq.] to force to a lower price —**beat it!** [Slang] go away! —**beat off**

drive back; repel —**beat up (on)** [Slang] to give a beating to; thrash —**to beat the band** (or **hell, the devil,** etc.) [Slang] vigorously; fast and furiously —**beat′er** *n.*

**beat·en** (bēt′'n) *adj.* **1.** struck with repeated blows; whipped **2.** shaped by hammering **3.** flattened by treading *[a beaten path]* **4.** *a)* defeated *b)* crushed in spirit by defeat **5.** tired out —**off the beaten track** (or **path**) unusual, unfamiliar, etc.

**be·a·tif·ic** (bē′ə tif′ik) *adj.* [see BEATIFY] **1.** making blissful or blessed **2.** full of bliss or joy *[a beatific smile]* —**be′a·tif′i·cal·ly** *adv.*

**be·at·i·fi·ca·tion** (bē at′ə fi kā′shən) *n.* [see ff.] *R.C.Ch.* the process of declaring a certain dead person to be among the blessed in heaven: he is then entitled to public veneration

**be·at·i·fy** (bē at′ə fī′) *vt.* **-fied′, -fy′ing** [ < Fr. < LL. *beatificare* < L. *beatus,* happy + *facere,* to make] **1.** to make blissfully happy **2.** *R.C.Ch.* to pronounce the beatification of by papal decree

**beat·ing** (bēt′iŋ) *n.* **1.** the act of one that beats **2.** a whipping **3.** a throbbing **4.** a defeat

**be·at·i·tude** (bē at′ə tood′, -tyood′) *n.* [ < Fr. < L. < *beatus,* happy] perfect blessedness or happiness —**the Beatitudes** the blessings on the meek, the peacemakers, etc. in the Sermon on the Mount: Matt. 5:3–12

**beat·nik** (bēt′nik) *n.* [BEAT, *adj.* 2 + Russ. (via. Yid.) *-nik,* equiv. to -ER] a member of the beat group

**Be·a·trice** (bē′ə tris) [It. < L. *beatrix,* she who makes happy < *beatus,* happy] a feminine name: var. *Beatrix*

**beat-up** (bēt′up′) *adj.* [Slang] in a worn-out condition; dilapidated, battered, shabby, etc.

**beau** (bō) *n., pl.* **beaus, beaux** (bōz) [Fr. < *beau,* pretty < L. *bellus,* pretty] the sweetheart of a woman or girl

**Beau Brum·mell** (brum′əl) **1.** (*George Bryan Brummell*), 1778–1840; Eng. gentleman famous for his fashionable dress and manners **2.** a dandy; fop

**Beau·fort scale** (bō′fərt) [after Sir Francis *Beaufort* (1774–1857), Brit. naval officer] *Meteorol.* a scale of wind velocities ranging from 0 (calm) to 17 (hurricane)

‡**beau geste** (bō zhest′) *pl.* **beaux gestes** (bō zhest′) [Fr.] **1.** a fine gesture **2.** an act or offer that seems fine, noble, etc., but is empty

**beau i·de·al** (ī dē′əl) [Fr.] **1.** ideal beauty **2.** the perfect type or conception (*of* something)

**beau monde** (bō′mänd′) [Fr.] fashionable society

**Beau·mont** (bō′mänt) [ult. < Fr., lit., beautiful hill] city in SE Tex.: pop. 118,000

**beaut** (byoot) *n.* [Slang] one that is beautiful or superlative in some way: often used ironically

**beau·te·ous** (byoot′ē əs) *adj. same as* BEAUTIFUL —**beau′te·ous·ly** *adv.*

**beau·ti·cian** (byoo tish′ən) *n.* a person who does hair styling, manicuring, etc. in a beauty shop

**beau·ti·ful** (byoot′ə fəl) *adj.* having beauty; very pleasing to the eye, ear, mind, etc. —**beau′ti·ful·ly** *adv.* —**beau′ti·ful·ness** *n.*

**beau·ti·fy** (byoot′ə fī′) *vt., vi.* **-fied′, -fy′ing** to make or become beautiful or more beautiful —**beau′ti·fi·ca′tion** *n.* —**beau′ti·fi′er** *n.*

**beau·ty** (byoot′ē) *n., pl.* **-ties** [ < OFr. < L. *bellus,* pretty] **1.** the quality attributed to whatever pleases the senses or mind, as by line, color, form, tone, behavior, etc. **2.** a thing having this quality **3.** good looks **4.** a very good-looking woman **5.** any very attractive feature —*adj.* [Slang] best, nicest, etc. *[the beauty part]*

**beauty shop** (or **salon** or **parlor**) a place where women go for hair styling, manicuring, etc.

**beauty spot 1.** a tiny black patch formerly applied by women to the face or back to emphasize whiteness of skin **2.** a natural mark or mole on the skin **3.** any place noted for its beauty

**beaux** (bōz; *Fr.* bō) *n. alt. pl. of* BEAU

‡**beaux-arts** (bō zàr′) *n.pl.* [Fr.] the fine arts

**bea·ver**¹ (bē′vər) *n.* [OE. *beofor*] **1.** *pl.* **-vers, -ver:** see PLURAL, II, D, 1 *a)* a large rodent with soft, brown fur, webbed hind feet, and a flat, broad tail: it can live on land or in water *b)* its fur **2.** a man's high silk hat **3.** a heavy cloth of felted wool **4.** [Colloq.] a hard-working, conscientious person

**bea·ver**² (bē′vər) *n.* [OFr. *baviere,* ult. < *bave,* saliva] **1.** orig., a piece of armor to protect the mouth and chin **2.** later, the visor of a helmet

**BEAVER**
**(32–47 in. long, including tail)**

**Bea·ver·board** (-bôrd′) *a trademark for* artificial board made of wood fiber, used for walls, etc. —*n.* [b-] fiberboard of this kind

**be·calm** (bi käm′) *vt.* **1.** to make calm **2.** to make (a sailing ship) motionless from lack of wind

**be·came** (bi kām′) *pt. of* BECOME

**be·cause** (bi kôz′, -kuz′) *conj.* [ < ME. *bi,* by + *cause*] for the reason or cause that; since —**because of** by reason of; on account of

‡**bêche-de-mer** (besh də mer′) *n.* [Fr., worm of the sea < Port. *bicho do mar,* sea slug] **1.** *pl.* **bêches-de-mer′** (besh-) *same as* TREPANG **2.** a pidgin English spoken in island areas of the SW Pacific

**beck** (bek) *n.* [ < BECKON] a beckoning gesture of the hand, head, etc. —*vt., vi.* [Archaic] to beckon —**at the beck and call of** at the service of

**Beck·et** (bek′ət), Saint Thomas à 1118?–70; Eng. prelate; archbishop of Canterbury

**beck·on** (bek′'n) *vi., vt.* [OE. *beacnian* < *beacen,* a beacon] **1.** to call or summon by a gesture **2.** to attract; lure —*n.* a summoning gesture

**be·cloud** (bi kloud′) *vt.* to cloud over; obscure

**be·come** (bi kum′) *vi.* **-came′, -come′, -com′ing** [OE. *becuman:* see BE- & COME] **1.** to come to be *[to become ill]* **2.** to grow to be *[the tadpole becomes a frog]* —*vt.* to be right for or suitable to *[that hat becomes you]* —**become of** to happen to; be the fate of

**be·com·ing** (bi kum′iŋ) *adj.* **1.** that is suitable or appropriate; fit **2.** suitable to the wearer *[a becoming gown]* —**becom′ing·ly** *adv.*

**Bec·que·rel** (be krel′), **An·toine Hen·ri** (än twán′ än rē′) 1852–1908; Fr. physicist

**bed** (bed) *n.* [OE.] **1.** a piece of furniture for sleeping or resting on, consisting typically of a bedstead, spring, mattress, and bedding **2.** *same as* BEDSTEAD **3.** any place or thing used for sleeping or reclining, or for sexual intercourse **4.** *a)* a plot of soil where plants are raised *b)* such plants **5.** *a)* the bottom of a river, lake, etc. *b)* a place on the ocean floor where things grow *[oyster bed]* **6.** rock, etc. in which something is embedded **7.** any flat surface used as a base or support **8.** a pile or heap resembling a bed **9.** a geological layer *[a bed of coal]* —*vt.* **bed′ded, bed′ding 1.** to provide with a sleeping place **2.** to put to bed **3.** to have sexual intercourse with **4.** to embed **5.** *a)* to plant in a bed of earth *b)* to make (earth) into a bed for plants **6.** to arrange in layers —*vi.* **1.** to go to bed; rest **2.** to form in layers —**bed and board 1.** sleeping accommodations and meals **2.** the married state —**bed down** to prepare and use a sleeping place —**get up on the wrong side of the bed** to be cross or grouchy —**put to bed 1.** to get (a child, etc.) ready for sleep **2.** [Slang] to get (a newspaper, etc.) ready for the press —**take to one's bed** to go to bed because of illness, etc.

**be·daub** (bi dôb′) *vt.* **1.** to make daubs on; smear over **2.** to overdecorate

**be·daz·zle** (bi daz′'l) *vt.* **-zled, -zling** to dazzle thoroughly; bewilder; confuse

**bed·bug** (bed′bug′) *n.* a small, wingless, reddish-brown, bloodsucking insect that infests beds, etc.

**bed·cham·ber** (-chām′bər) *n. same as* BEDROOM

**bed·clothes** (-klōz′, -klō*th*z′) *n.pl.* sheets, blankets, comforters, etc. used on a bed

**bed·ding** (-iŋ) *n.* **1.** mattresses and bedclothes **2.** straw, hay, etc., used to bed animals **3.** a bottom layer **4.** *Geol.* stratification

**be·deck** (bi dek′) *vt.* to decorate; adorn

**be·dev·il** (bi dev′'l) *vt.* **-iled** or **-illed, -il·ing** or **-il·ling 1.** to plague diabolically; torment **2.** to bewitch **3.** to confuse completely; muddle **4.** to corrupt; spoil —**be·dev′il·ment** *n.*

**be·dew** (bi doo′, -dyoo′) *vt.* to make wet with or as if with drops of dew

**bed·fast** (bed′fast′) *adj. same as* BEDRIDDEN

**bed·fel·low** (-fel′ō) *n.* **1.** a person who shares one's bed **2.** an associate, ally, etc.

**be·dight** (bi dīt′) *adj.* [pp. of obs. *bedight* < ME. < *bi-,* BE- + *dighten,* to set in order < OE. *dihtan,* to compose < L. *dictare:* see DICTATE] [Archaic or Poet.] bedecked; arrayed

**be·dim** (bi dim′) *vt.* **-dimmed′, -dim′ming** to make (the eyes or vision) dim; darken or obscure

**be·di·zen** (bi dī′z'n, -diz′'n) *vt.* [BE- + DIZEN] to dress in a cheap, showy way —**be·di′zen·ment** *n.*

**bed jacket** a woman's short, loose upper garment sometimes worn in bed over a nightgown

**bed·lam** (bed′ləm) *n.* [ < *Bedlam,* altered < (St. Mary of) Bethlehem, old insane asylum in London] **1.** [Archaic] an insane asylum **2.** any place or condition of noise and confusion —**bed′lam·ite′** (-īt′) *n.*

**bed linen** bed sheets, pillowcases, etc.

**bed of roses** [Colloq.] a situation or position of ease and luxury

---

fat, āpe, cär, ten, ēven, is, bīte; gō, hôrn, tool, look; oil, out; up, fur; get; joy; yet; chin; she; thin, *then;* zh, leisure; ŋ, ring; ə for *a* in *ago, e* in *agent, i* in *sanity, o* in *comply, u* in *focus;* ′ as in *able* (ā′b'l); Fr. bàl; ë, Fr. coeur; ö, Fr. feu; Fr. mon; ô, Fr. coq; ü, Fr. duc; r, Fr. cri; H, G. ich; kh, G. doch; ‡foreign; *hypothetical; < derived from. See inside front cover.

**Bed·ou·in** (bed′ōō win) *n., pl.* **-ins, -in** [< Fr. < Ar. *badā-wīn*, dwellers in the desert] [*also* b-] **1.** an Arab of any of the nomadic desert tribes of Arabia, Syria, or N Africa **2.** any wanderer or nomad —*adj.* of or like the Bedouins
**bed·pan** (bed′pan′) *n.* **1.** *same as* WARMING PAN **2.** a shallow pan for use as a toilet by a person confined to bed
**be·drag·gle** (bi drag′'l) *vt.* **-gled, -gling** to make wet, limp, and dirty, as by dragging through mud —**be·drag′gled** *adj.*
**bed·rid·den** (bed′rid′'n) *adj.* having to stay in bed, usually for a long period, because of illness, infirmity, etc.: also **bed′rid′**
**bed·rock** (-räk′) *n.* **1.** solid rock beneath the soil and superficial rock **2.** a secure foundation **3.** the very bottom **4.** basic principles
**bed·roll** (-rōl′) *n.* a portable roll of bedding, generally for sleeping outdoors
**bed·room** (-rōōm′) *n.* a room to sleep in —*adj.* **1.** dealing with sex or sexual affairs [a *bedroom* farce] **2.** housing those who work days in a nearby metropolis [*bedroom* suburbs]
**bed·side** (-sīd′) *n.* the side of a bed; space beside a bed —*adj.* **1.** beside a bed **2.** as regards patients [a doctor's *bedside* manner]
**bed·sore** (-sôr′) *n.* a sore on the body of a bedridden person, caused by chafing or pressure
**bed·spread** (-spred′) *n.* a cover spread over the blanket on a bed, mainly for ornament
**bed·spring** (-spriŋ′) *n.* **1.** a framework of springs in a bed to support the mattress **2.** any such spring
**bed·stead** (-sted′) *n.* a framework for supporting the spring and mattress of a bed
**bed·straw** (-strô′) *n.* [from its former use as straw for beds] a small plant of the madder family, with whorled leaves and small, white or colored flowers
**bed·time** (-tīm′) *n.* one's usual time for going to bed
**bed-wet·ting** (-wet′iŋ) *n.* urinating in bed
**bee¹** (bē) *n.* [OE. *beo*] a four-winged, hairy insect that gathers pollen and nectar: some bees live in organized colonies and make honey —**have a bee in one's bonnet 1.** to be preoccupied or obsessed by an idea **2.** to be not quite sane
**bee²** (bē) *n.* [ult. < OE. *ben*, compulsory service] a meeting of people to work together or to compete [a sewing *bee*, spelling *bee*]
**bee·bread** (-bred′) *n.* a yellowish-brown mixture of pollen and honey, made and eaten by some bees
**beech** (bēch) *adj.* [OE. *boece, bece*] designating a family of trees including the beeches, oaks, and chestnuts —*n.* **1.** a tree of the beech family, with smooth bark, hard wood, dark-green leaves, and edible nuts **2.** its wood —**beech′en** *adj.*
**Bee·cher** (bē′chər), **Henry Ward** 1813–87; U.S. clergyman & lecturer
**beech·mast** (bēch′mast′) *n.* beechnuts, esp. as they lie on the ground: also **beech mast**
**beech·nut** (-nut′) *n.* the small, three-cornered, edible nut of the beech tree
**beef** (bēf) *n., pl.* **beeves;** also, and for 5 always, **beefs** [< OFr. *boef* < L. *bovis,* gen. of *bos,* ox] **1.** a full-grown ox, cow, bull, or steer, esp. one bred for meat **2.** meat from such an animal; specif., a dressed carcass **3.** such animals collectively **4.** [Colloq.] *a)* human flesh or muscle *b)* strength; brawn **5.** [Slang] a complaint —*vi.* [Slang] to complain —**beef up** [Colloq.] to strengthen by addition, reinforcement, etc.

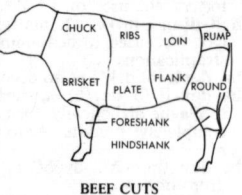

BEEF CUTS

**beef cattle** cattle bred and fattened for meat
**beef·eat·er** (-ēt′ər) *n.* **1.** an eater of beef, typified as portly, ruddy, etc. **2.** *same as* YEOMAN OF THE GUARD **3.** a guard at the Tower of London **4.** [Slang] an Englishman
**beef·steak** (-stāk′) *n.* a slice of beef, esp. from the loin, cut thick for broiling or frying
**beef tea** a drink made from beef extract or by boiling lean strips of beef
**beef·y** (bēf′ē) *adj.* **beef′i·er, beef′i·est** fleshy and solid; very muscular; brawny —**beef′i·ness** *n.*
**bee·hive** (bē′hīv′) *n.* **1.** a box or other shelter for a colony of bees, where they make and store honey **2.** a place of great activity
**bee·keep·er** (-kēp′ər) *n.* a person who keeps bees for producing honey —**bee′keep′ing** *n.*
**bee·line** (-līn′) *n.* a straight, direct route —**make a beeline for** [Colloq.] to go straight toward
**Be·el·ze·bub** (bē el′zə bub′) *Bible* the chief devil; Satan: also **Be·el′ze·bul′** (-bool′)
**bee moth** a moth whose larvae, hatched in beehives, eat the wax of the honeycomb
**been** (bin, ben; *chiefly Brit.* bēn) *pp.* of BE

**beep** (bēp) *n.* [echoic] **1.** the brief, high-pitched sound of a horn, as on an automobile **2.** a brief, high-pitched electronic signal, used in warning, direction-finding, etc. —*vi., vt.* to make or cause to make such a sound
**beer** (bir) *n.* [OE. *beor*] **1.** an alcoholic, fermented beverage made from grain, esp. malted barley, and flavored with hops **2.** any of various soft drinks made from root and plant extracts [root *beer*]
**Beer·she·ba** (bir shē′bə) city in S Israel, in the Negev: pop. 70,000
**beer·y** (bir′ē) *adj.* **beer′i·er, beer′i·est 1.** of or like beer **2.** showing the effects of drinking beer; drunken, maudlin, etc. —**beer′i·ness** *n.*
**beest·ings** (bēs′tiŋz) *n.pl.* [*often with sing. v.*] [OE. *bysting* < *beost,* beestings] the first milk of a cow after having a calf
**bees·wax** (bēz′waks′) *n.* wax secreted and used by bees to build their honeycomb: see WAX¹ (sense 1)
**beet** (bēt) *n.* [< OE. < L. *beta*] **1.** a plant with edible leaves and a thick, fleshy, white or red root **2.** this root: some varieties are eaten as a vegetable, others as a source of sugar
**Bee·tho·ven** (bā′tō vən), **Lud·wig van** (lōōt′viH vän) 1770–1827; Ger. composer
**bee·tle¹** (bēt′'l) *n.* [OE. *bitela* < *bitan,* to bite] an insect with biting mouthparts and hard front wings that cover the membranous hind wings when these are folded
**bee·tle²** (bēt′'l) *n.* [OE. *betel,* ult. connected with BEAT] **1.** a heavy, wooden mallet **2.** a household mallet or pestle for mashing or beating —*vt.* **-tled, -tling** to pound with a beetle
**bee·tle³** (bēt′'l) *vi.* **-tled, -tling** [prob. < ff.] to project or jut; overhang —*adj.* jutting; overhanging: also **bee′tling**
**bee·tle-browed** (bēt′'l broud′) *adj.* [ME. < ? *bitel,* sharp + *brouwe,* BROW] **1.** having bushy or overhanging eyebrows **2.** frowning; scowling
**beet sugar** sugar extracted from sugar beets
**beeves** (bēvz) *n. alt. pl. of* BEEF
**be·fall** (bi fôl′) *vi.* **-fell′, -fall′en, -fall′ing** [< OE. < *be- + feallan,* to fall] to come to pass; happen —*vt.* to happen to [what *befell* them?]
**be·fit** (bi fit′) *vt.* **-fit′ted, -fit′ting** to be suitable or proper for —**be·fit′ting·ly** *adv.*
**be·fog** (bi fôg′, -fäg′) *vt.* **-fogged′, -fog′ging 1.** to cover with fog; make foggy **2.** to make obscure or muddled; confuse [to *befog* an issue]
**be·fore** (bi fôr′) *adv.* [< OE. < *be-,* by + *foran,* before] **1.** ahead; in front **2.** in the past; previously [I've seen him *before*] **3.** earlier; sooner [come at ten, not *before*] —*prep.* **1.** ahead of in time, space, rank, or importance **2.** just in front of [he paused *before* the door] **3.** in the sight, notice, presence, etc. of [to stand *before* a judge] **4.** being considered, judged, or decided by [the bill *before* the assembly] **5.** earlier than [he left *before* noon] **6.** in preference to [death *before* dishonor] —*conj.* **1.** earlier than the time that [drop in *before* you go] **2.** rather than [I'd die *before* I'd halt]
**be·fore·hand** (-hand′) *adv., adj.* **1.** ahead of time; in advance **2.** in anticipation
**be·foul** (bi foul′) *vt.* **-got′** to dirty or sully; foul
**be·friend** (-frend′) *vt.* to act as a friend to; help
**be·fud·dle** (-fud′'l) *vt.* **-dled, -dling 1.** to fuddle or confuse (the mind, a person, etc.) **2.** to stupefy with alcoholic liquor —**be·fud′dle·ment** *n.*
**beg** (beg) *vt.* **begged, beg′ging** [< Anglo-Fr. < OFr. *begard,* beggar < MDu. *beggaert*] **1.** to ask for as charity [he *begged* a dime] **2.** to ask for earnestly as a kindness or favor —*vi.* **1.** to ask for alms; be a beggar **2.** to entreat —**beg off** to ask to be released from —**beg the question 1.** to use an argument that assumes as proved the very thing one is trying to prove **2.** loosely, to evade the issue —**go begging** to be unwanted
**be·gan** (bi gan′) *pt.* of BEGIN
**be·get** (bi get′) *vt.* **-got′** or archaic **-gat′** (-gat′), **-got′ten** or **-got′, -get′ting** [< OE. *begitan,* to acquire: see BE- & GET] **1.** to be the father of; procreate **2.** to bring into being; produce [tyranny *begets* rebellion] —**be·get′ter** *n.*
**beg·gar** (beg′ər) *n.* [< OFr. *begard:* see BEG] **1.** a person who begs; esp., one who lives by begging **2.** a very poor person; pauper **3.** a person; fellow [a cute little *beggar*] —*vt.* **1.** to make a beggar of; make poor **2.** to make seem inadequate or useless [her beauty *beggars* description] —**beg′gar·dom** (-dəm) *n.*
**beg·gar·ly** (-lē) *adj.* like or fit for a beggar; very poor, inadequate, etc. —**beg′gar·li·ness** *n.*
**beg·gar·y** (beg′ər ē) *n.* **1.** extreme poverty **2.** the act of begging
**be·gin** (bi gin′) *vi.* **be·gan′, be·gun′, be·gin′ning** [< OE. *beginnan*] **1.** to start doing something; get under way **2.** to come into being; arise **3.** to have a first part [the Bible *begins* with Genesis] **4.** to be or do in the slightest degree [they don't *begin* to compare] —*vt.* **1.** to cause to start;

commence **2.** to bring into being; originate **3.** to do or be the first part of

**be·gin·ner** (-ər) *n.* **1.** one who begins anything **2.** one just beginning to do or learn a thing; novice

**be·gin·ning** (-iŋ) *n.* **1.** a starting or commencing **2.** the time or place of starting; birth; origin; source **3.** the first part *[the beginning of a book]* **4.** *[usually pl.]* an early stage

**be·gird** (bi gurd') *vt.* **-girt'** or **-gird'ed, -girt', -gird'ing 1.** to bind around; gird **2.** to encircle

**be·gone** (bi gôn', -gän') *interj., vi.* (to) be gone; go away; get out

**be·gon·ia** (bi gōn'yə) *n.* [after M. *Bégon* (1638–1710), Fr. governor of the Dominican Republic] a plant with showy flowers and ornamental leaves

**be·got** (bi gät') *pt. & alt. pp. of* BEGET

**be·got·ten** (-'n) *alt. pp. of* BEGET

**be·grime** (bi grīm') *vt.* **-grimed', -grim'ing** to cover with grime; make dirty; soil

**be·grudge** (bi gruj') *vt.* **-grudged', -grudg'ing 1.** to feel ill will or resentment at the possession or enjoyment of (something) by another *[to begrudge* another's fortune*]* **2.** to give with reluctance *[he begrudges* her every cent*]* **3.** to regard with displeasure **—be·grudg'ing·ly** *adv.*

**be·guile** (bi gīl') *vt.* **-guiled', -guil'ing 1.** to mislead by guile; deceive **2.** to deprive *(of or out of)* by deceit; cheat **3.** to pass (time) pleasantly; while away *[he beguiled his day with reading]* **4.** to charm or delight **—be·guile'ment** *n.* **—be·guil'er** *n.* **—be·guil'ing·ly** *adv.*

**be·guine** (bi gēn') *n.* [< Fr. *béguin,* infatuation] a native dance of Martinique or its music

**be·gum** (bē'gəm) *n.* [< Hindi *begam,* lady] in India, a Moslem princess or lady of high rank

**be·gun** (bi gun') *pp. of* BEGIN

**be·half** (bi haf') *n.* [< OE. *be,* by + *healf,* side, half] support, interest, side, etc. *[speak in his behalf]* **—in** (or **on**) **behalf of** in the interest of; for **—on behalf of** speaking for; representing

**be·have** (bi hāv') *vt., vi.* **- haved', -hav'ing** [see BE- & HAVE] **1.** to conduct (oneself or itself) or act in a specified way **2.** to conduct (oneself) properly; do what is right

**be·hav·ior** (bi hāv'yər) *n.* **1.** the way a person behaves or acts; conduct **2.** an organism's observable responses to stimulation **3.** the way a machine, element, etc. acts or functions **—be·hav'ior·al** *adj.* **—be·hav'ior·al·ly** *adv.*

**behavioral science** any of the sciences, as sociology, psychology, or anthropology, that study human behavior

**be·hav·ior·ism** (bi hāv'yər iz'm) *n.* the doctrine that observed behavior provides the only valid data of psychology: it rejects the concept of mind **—be·hav'ior·ist** *n., adj.* **—be·hav'ior·is'tic** *adj.*

**be·hav·iour** (bi hāv'yər) *n. Brit. sp. of* BEHAVIOR

**be·head** (bi hed') *vt.* to cut off the head of

**be·held** (bi held') *pt. & pp. of* BEHOLD

**be·he·moth** (bi hē'məth, bē'ə-) *n.* [Heb. *behēmōth,* intens. pl. of *behēmāh,* beast] **1.** a huge animal, assumed to be the hippopotamus: Job 40:15–24 **2.** any huge animal or thing

**be·hest** (bi hest') *n.* [OE. *behæs,* a vow] an order, command, or earnest request

**be·hind** (bi hīnd') *adv.* [OE. *behindan:* see BE- & HIND¹] **1.** in or to the rear or back *[walk behind]* **2.** in a former time, place, condition, etc. *[the girl he left behind]* **3.** into a retarded state *[to drop behind in one's studies]* **4.** into arrears *[to fall behind in one's dues]* **5.** slow in time; late **—prep. 1.** remaining after *[the sons he left behind him]* **2.** in back of *[sit behind her]* **3.** lower than in rank, achievement, etc. **4.** later than *[behind schedule]* **5.** on the other or farther side of *[behind the hill]* **6.** gone by or ended for *[his schooling is behind him]* **7.** supporting or advocating *[Congress is behind the plan]* **8.** hidden by; not yet revealed *[the story behind the news]* **—adj.** that follows *[the person behind]* **—n.** *[Colloq.]* the buttocks

**be·hind·hand** (-hand') *adv., adj.* **1.** behind in paying debts, rent, etc. **2.** behind time; late **3.** behind or slow in progress, advancement, etc.

**be·hold** (bi hōld') *vt.* **-held', -held'** or archaic **-hold'en, -hold'ing** [OE. *bihealdan,* to hold: see BE- & HOLD¹] to hold in view; look at; regard **—interj.** look! see!

**be·hold·en** (-ən) *adj.* obliged to feel grateful; owing thanks; indebted

**be·hoof** (bi hōōf') *n.* [OE. *behof,* profit] behalf, benefit, interest, advantage, sake, etc.

**be·hoove** (-hōōv') *vt.* **-hooved', -hoov'ing** [OE. *behofian,* to need] to be necessary for or incumbent upon *[it behooves you to do this]*

**be·hove** (-hōv') *vt.* **-hoved', -hov'ing** *chiefly Brit. var. of* BEHOOVE

**beige** (bāzh) *n.* [Fr.] **1.** a soft, unbleached and undyed, wool fabric **2.** its characteristic sandy color; grayish tan **—adj.** grayish-tan

**be·ing** (bē'iŋ) *n.* [see BE] **1.** existence; life **2.** basic or essential nature **3.** one that lives or exists, or is assumed to do so *[a human being,* a divine *being]* **—being as** (or **that**) [Dial. or Colloq.] since; because **—for the time being** for now

**Bei·rut** (bā rōōt', bā'rōōt) capital of Lebanon: pop. c. 500,000

**be·jab·bers** (bi jab'ərz) *interj.* [< *by Jesus*] an exclamation used to express surprise, pleasure, anger, etc.: also used as a slang noun of indefinite meaning in **beat** (or **scare**) **the bejabbers out of:** also **be·ja'bers** (-jā'bərz), **be·je'sus** (-jē'zəs)

**be·jew·el** (bi jōō'əl) *vt.* **-eled** or **-elled, -el·ing** or **-el·ling** to decorate with or as with jewels

**be·la·bor** (-lā'bər) *vt.* **1.** to beat severely **2.** to attack verbally **3.** *popularly, same as* LABOR, *vt.*

**be·lat·ed** (-lāt'id) *adj.* late or too late; tardy **—be·lat'ed·ly** *adv.* **—be·lat'ed·ness** *n.*

**be·lay** (-lā') *vt., vi.* **-layed', -lay'ing** [< OE. < *be-* + *lecgan,* to lay] **1.** to make (a rope) secure by winding around a pin **(belaying pin),** cleat, etc. **2.** [Naut. Colloq.] to hold; stop *[belay* there!*]* **3.** to secure by a rope

**bel can·to** (bel' kän'tō) [It., lit., beautiful song] a style of singing with brilliant vocal display and purity of tone

**belch** (belch) *vi., vt.* [OE. *bealcian*] **1.** to expel (gas) through the mouth from the stomach **2.** to utter (curses, etc.) violently **3.** to throw forth (its contents) violently *[the volcano belched flame]* **—n.** a belching

**bel·dam, bel·dame** (bel'dəm) *n.* [*bel-* < Fr. *belle* (see BELLE) + DAME] an old woman; esp., a hag

**be·lea·guer** (bi lē'gər) *vt.* [Du. *belegeren* < *legeren,* to camp < *leger,* a camp] **1.** to besiege by encircling, as with an army **2.** to beset; harass

**Be·lém** (bə len') seaport in NE Brazil: pop. 402,000

**Bel·fast** (bel'fast) seaport & capital of Northern Ireland: pop. 398,000

**bel·fry** (bel'frē) *n., pl.* **-fries** [altered (after BELL¹) < OFr. *berfroi* < OHG. < *bergen,* to protect + *frid,* peace] **1.** a bell tower **2.** the part of a steeple that holds the bell or bells **—bel'fried** *adj.*

**Belg. 1.** Belgian **2.** Belgium

**Bel·gium** (bel'jəm) kingdom in W Europe, on the North Sea: 11,779 sq. mi.; pop. 9,660,000; cap. Brussels: Fr. name **Bel·gique** (bel zhēk'); Fl. name **Bel·gi·ë** (bel'gē ə) **—Bel'·gian** *adj., n.*

**Bel·grade** (bel'grād, -gräd; bel grād', -gräd') capital of Yugoslavia, on the Danube: pop. 598,000

**Be·li·al** (bē'lē əl, bēl'yəl) *n.* [< LL. < Heb. *belīya'al,* worthlessness] *Bible* wickedness as an evil force (in the *New Testament,* personified as Satan)

**be·lie** (bi lī') *vt.* **-lied', -ly'ing 1.** to give a false idea of; misrepresent *[his smile belies* his anger*]* **2.** to leave unfulfilled *[war belied* hopes for peace*]* **3.** to show to be untrue *[her cruelty belied* her kind words*]* **—be·li'er** *n.*

**be·lief** (bə lēf') *n.* [ME. < *bi-,* BE- + *-leve* < OE. *geleafa,* belief] **1.** the state of believing; conviction **2.** faith, esp. religious faith **3.** trust or confidence *[I have belief* in his ability*]* **4.** anything believed or accepted as true; esp., a creed, tenet, etc. **5.** an opinion; expectation *[my belief* is that he'll come*]*

**be·lieve** (bə lēv') *vt.* **-lieved', -liev'ing** [ME. < *bi-,* BE- + *-leven* < OE. *geliefan,* believe] **1.** to take as true, real, etc. **2.** to have confidence in a statement or promise of (another person) **3.** to suppose or think **—vi. 1.** to have trust or confidence *(in)* **2.** to have religious faith **3.** to suppose or think **—be·liev'a·bil'i·ty** *n.* **—be·liev'a·ble** *adj.* **—be·liev'·a·bly** *adv.* **—be·liev'er** *n.*

**Be·lin·da** (bə lin'də) [< Gmc. *Betlindis* < ?] a feminine name

**be·lit·tle** (bi lit''l) *vt.* **-tled, -tling** to make seem little, less important, etc.; depreciate **—be·lit'tle·ment** *n.*

**Be·lize** (bə lēz') self-governing Brit. territory in Central America: 8,867 sq. mi.; pop. 127,000

**bell¹** (bel) *n.* [OE. *belle*] **1.** a hollow object, usually cuplike and of metal, which rings when struck **2.** the sound made by a bell **3.** anything shaped like a bell, as a flower, the flare of a horn, etc. **4.** *Naut. a)* a bell rung every half hour to mark the periods of the watch *b)* any of these periods **—vt. 1.** to attach a bell to **2.** to shape like a bell **—vi.** to flare out like a bell

**bell²** (bel) *n., vi., vt.* [< OE. *bellan*] bellow; roar; bay

**Bell** (bel), **Alexander Graham** 1847–1922; U.S. inventor of the telephone, born in Scotland

**bel·la·don·na** (bel'ə dän'ə) *n.* [ModL. < It. *bella donna,* beautiful lady, a folk etym. for ML. *bladona,* nightshade] **1.** a poisonous plant with purplish, bell-shaped flowers and black berries; deadly nightshade: it yields atropine **2.** *same as* ATROPINE

**bell-bot·tom** (bel'bät'əm) *adj.* designating trousers flaring at the ankles: also **bell'-bot'tomed**

**bell·boy** (-boi') *n. same as* BELLMAN (sense 2)

**bell buoy** a buoy with a warning bell rung by the motion of the waves

**Belle** (bel) [Fr.: see ff.] a feminine name

**belle** (bel) *n.* [Fr., fem. of *beau:* see BEAU] a pretty woman or girl; often, one who is the prettiest or most popular [the *belle* of the ball]

**belles-let·tres** (bel let'rə) *n.pl.* [Fr.] literature as a fine art; fiction, poetry, drama, etc. as distinguished from technical and scientific writings —**bel·let·rist** (bel let'rist) *n.* —**bel'·le·tris'tic** (-lə tris'tik) *adj.*

**Belle·vue** (bel'vyōō') [Fr., lit., beautiful view] city in NW Wash.: suburb of Seattle: pop. 74,000

**Bell·flow·er** (bel'flou'ər) city in SW Calif.: suburb of Los Angeles: pop. 53,000

**bell·flow·er** (bel'flou'ər) *n.* any of a large genus of plants, with showy, bell-shaped flowers of white, pink, or blue

**bell·hop** (bel'häp') *n. same as* BELLMAN (sense 2)

**bel·li·cose** (bel'ə kōs') *adj.* [< L. < *bellicus,* of war < *bellum,* war] of a quarrelsome nature; eager to fight; warlike —**bel'li·cose'ly** *adv.* —**bel'li·cos'i·ty** (-käs'ə tē) *n.*

**bel·lied** (bel'ēd) *adj.* having a belly, esp. of a specified kind [the yellow-*bellied* sapsucker]

**bel·lig·er·ence** (bə lij'ər əns) *n.* belligerent or aggressively hostile attitude or quality

**bel·lig·er·en·cy** (-ən sē) *n.* **1.** the state of being at war or of being recognized as a belligerent **2.** *same as* BELLIGERENCE

**bel·lig·er·ent** (bə lij'ər ənt) *adj.* [< L. prp. of *belligerare* < *bellum,* war + *gerere,* to carry on] **1.** recognized under international law as being at war **2.** of war; of fighting **3.** warlike **4.** showing readiness to fight or quarrel —*n.* a belligerent person or nation —**bel·lig'er·ent·ly** *adv.*

**Bel·li·ni** (bel lē'nē), **Gio·van·ni** (jô vän'nē) 1430?–1516; Venetian painter

**bell jar** a bell-shaped container or cover made of glass, used to keep gases, air, moisture, etc. in or out: also **bell glass**

**bell·man** (bel'mən) *n., pl.* **-men 1.** *same as* TOWN CRIER **2.** a man or boy employed by a hotel, etc. to carry luggage and do errands

**bel·low** (bel'ō) *vi.* [OE. *bylgan*] **1.** to roar with a reverberating sound, as a bull **2.** to cry out loudly, as in anger or pain —*vt.* to utter loudly or powerfully —*n.* a bellowing sound; roar

**Bel·low** (bel'ō), **Saul** 1915– ; U.S. novelist

**bel·lows** (bel'ōz, -əz) *n.sing. & pl.* [ME. *belwes,* orig. pl. of *beli:* see BELLY] **1.** a device that produces a stream of air through a narrow tube when its sides are pumped together: used for blowing fires, in pipe organs, etc. **2.** anything like a bellows, as the folding part of some cameras

**bell-shaped curve** (bel'shapt') a statistical curve, as of probability, which in graphic representation resembles the outline of a cuplike bell standing on its flared lip: also **bell curve**

**bell·weth·er** (bel'weth'ər) *n.* a male sheep, usually wearing a bell, that leads the flock

**bel·ly** (bel'ē) *n., pl.* **-lies** [ME. *beli* < OE. *belg,* leather bag, bellows] **1.** the lower front part of the human body between the chest and thighs; abdomen **2.** the underside of an animal's body **3.** the abdominal cavity **4.** the stomach **5.** the deep interior [the *belly* of a ship] **6.** any part, surface, or section that curves outward or bulges —*vt., vi.* **-lied, -ly·ing** to swell out; bulge

**bel·ly·ache** (-āk') *n.* pain in the abdomen or bowels —*vi.* **-ached', -ach'ing** [Slang] to complain —**bel'ly·ach'er** *n.*

**bel·ly·band** (-band') *n.* a girth around an animal's belly for keeping a saddle, etc. in place

**bel·ly·but·ton** (-but''n) *n.* [Colloq.] the navel: also **belly button**

**belly dance** a dance of eastern Mediterranean origin characterized by a twisting of the abdomen, sinuous hip movements, etc. —**bel'ly-dance'** *vi.* **-danced', -danc'ing** —**belly dancer**

**bel·ly-flop** (-fläp') *vi.* **-flopped', -flop'ping** [Colloq.] **1.** to dive awkwardly, with the belly striking flat against the water **2.** to throw oneself on a sled, with the belly downward, and coast, as down a hill Also **bel'ly-bump'**, **bel'ly-whop'**, **bel'ly-slam'**, etc.

**bel·ly·ful** (-fool') *n.* **1.** enough or more than enough to eat **2.** [Slang] all that one can bear

**belly laugh** [Colloq.] a hearty laugh

**Be·lo Ho·ri·zon·te** (be'lô rē zôn'te) city in SE Brazil: pop. 693,000

**be·long** (bi lôŋ') *vi.* [ME. < *be-,* intens. + OE. *langian,* belong] **1.** to have a proper or fitting place [the book *belongs* on his desk] **2.** to be part of; be related (*to*) **3.** to be a member (with *to*) **4.** to be owned (with *to*) **5.** [Slang] to be the owner (with *to*) [who *belongs* to this hat?]

**be·long·ing** (-iŋ) *n.* **1.** a thing that belongs to one **2.** [*pl.*] possessions; property **3.** close relationship; affinity [a sense of *belonging*]

**be·lov·ed** (bi luv'id, -luvd') *adj.* dearly loved —*n.* a dearly loved person

**be·low** (bi lō') *adv., adj.* [see BE- & LOW¹] **1.** in or to a lower place; beneath **2.** in a lower place on the page or on a later page (of a book, etc.) **3.** in hell **4.** on earth **5.** on or to a lower floor or deck **6.** in or to a lesser rank, function, etc. —*prep.* **1.** lower than, as in position, rank, worth, etc. **2.** unworthy of [it is *below* her to do that]

**Bel·shaz·zar** (bel shaz'ər) *Bible* the last king of Babylon: Dan. 5

**belt** (belt) *n.* [OE., ult. < L. *balteus,* a belt] **1.** a band of leather, etc., worn about the waist to hold clothing up, support tools, etc., or as an ornament: see also SAFETY BELT **2.** any encircling thing like this **3.** an endless band for transferring motion from one wheel or pulley to another, or for carrying things **4.** an area or zone with some distinctive feature [the corn *belt*] **5.** an encircling road or route **6.** [Slang] a hard blow; cuff **7.** [Slang] *a)* a drink or big gulp, esp. of liquor *b)* a thrill —*vt.* **1.** to surround or encircle as with a belt **2.** to fasten or attach as with a belt **3.** to hit hard, as with a belt **4.** [Colloq.] to sing (*out*) lustily —**below the belt** unfair(ly); foul —**tighten one's belt** to live more thriftily —**under one's belt** [Colloq.] as part of one's experience [ten years at sea *under his belt*]

**belt·ed** (bel'tid) *adj.* **1.** wearing a belt, esp. as a mark of distinction **2.** marked by a band or stripe

**belt·ing** (-tiŋ) *n.* **1.** material for making belts **2.** belts collectively **3.** [Slang] a beating

**be·lu·ga** (bə lōō'gə) *n., pl.* **-ga, -gas:** see PLURAL, II, D, 2 [< Russ. < *byeli,* white] **1.** a large, white sturgeon of the Black and Caspian seas **2.** a large, white dolphin of northern seas; white whale

**be·moan** (bi mōn') *vt., vi.* to moan about or lament (a loss, grief, etc.) [to bemoan one's fate]

**be·muse** (bi myōōz') *vt.* **-mused', -mus'ing** [BE- + MUSE] **1.** to muddle, confuse, or stupefy **2.** to plunge in thought; preoccupy —**be·mused'** *adj.*

**bench** (bench) *n.* [OE. *benc* (cf. BANK²)] **1.** a long, hard seat for several persons, with or without a back **2.** the place where judges sit in a court **3.** [sometimes **B-**] *a)* the status or office of a judge *b)* judges collectively *c)* a law court **4.** *a)* a seat on which the players on a sports team sit when not on the field *b)* auxiliary players collectively **5.** a stand for exhibiting a dog at a dog show **6.** a strong table on which work with tools is done; worktable —*vt.* **1.** to provide with benches **2.** to place on a bench, esp. an official one **3.** *Sports* to keep (a player) out of a game —**on the bench 1.** presiding in a law court **2.** *Sports* not taking part in the game, as an auxiliary player

**bench mark 1.** a surveyor's mark made on a permanent landmark for use as a reference point in determining other altitudes **2.** a standard in judging quality, value, etc. Also **bench'mark'** *n.*

**bench warrant** an order issued by a judge or law court for the arrest of a person

**bend¹** (bend) *vt.* **bent** or archaic **bend'ed, bend'ing** [OE. *bendan,* to bind with a string; hence, to bend (a bow)] **1.** to force (an object) into a curved or crooked form, or (*back*) to its original form **2.** to turn from a straight line [to *bend* one's steps from a path] **3.** to make (someone) submit or give in, as to one's will **4.** to turn or direct (one's attention, etc. *to*) **5.** to incline or tend (*to* or *toward*) **6.** *Naut.* to fasten (sails or ropes) into position —*vi.* **1.** to turn or be turned as from a straight line **2.** to yield by curving or crooking, as from pressure **3.** to crook or curve the body; stoop (*over* or *down*) **4.** to give in; yield [he *bent* to her wishes] —*n.* **1.** a bending or being bent **2.** a bending or curving part, as of a river —**bend'a·ble** *adj.*

**bend²** (bend) *n.* [ME. < prec.] any of various knots used in tying ropes —**the bends** [Colloq.] *same as* DECOMPRESSION SICKNESS

**bend³** (bend) *n.* [< OFr. < Goth. *bindan,* to bind] *Heraldry* a band or stripe on a coat of arms, from the upper left to the lower right corner

**bend·er** (ben'dər) *n.* **1.** a person or thing that bends **2.** [Slang] a drinking bout; spree

**bend sinister** *Heraldry* a band or stripe on a coat of arms, from the upper right to the lower left corner: a sign of bastardy in the family line

**be·neath** (bi nēth') *adv., adj.* [< OE. < *be-* + *neothan,* down] **1.** in a lower place **2.** just below something; underneath —*prep.* **1.** lower than; below **2.** directly under; underneath **3.** inferior to in rank, quality, worth, etc. **4.** unworthy of [it is *beneath* him to cheat]

**ben·e·dic·i·te** (ben'ə dis'ə tē'; *for n. 2 usually* bā'nā dē'chē tā') *interj.* [L.] bless you! —*n.* **1.** the invocation of a blessing **2.** [B-] a canticle praising God

**Ben·e·dict** (ben'ə dikt') [< L. *Benedictus*, blessed] **1.** a masculine name **2.** Saint, 480?–543? A.D.; It. monk: founder of the Benedictine order

**ben·e·dict** (ben'ə dikt') *n.* [< *Benedick*, a bachelor in Shakespeare's *Much Ado About Nothing*] a newly married man, esp. one who seemed to be a confirmed bachelor

**Ben·e·dic·tine** (ben'ə dik'tin; *also, and for n. 2 usually,* -tēn) *adj.* **1.** of Saint Benedict **2.** designating or of the monastic order based on his teachings —*n.* **1.** a Benedictine monk or nun **2.** [b-] a liqueur, orig. made by Benedictine monks

**ben·e·dic·tion** (ben'ə dik'shən) *n.* [< L. < *bene*, and *dicere*, to speak] **1.** a blessing **2.** an invocation of divine blessing, esp. ending a religious service **3.** blessedness — **ben'e·dic'to·ry** *adj.*

**ben·e·fac·tion** (ben'ə fak'shən, ben'ə fak'shən) *n.* [< LL. < L. *benefacere* < *bene*, well + *facere*, to do] **1.** the act of doing good or helping those in need **2.** money or help freely given

**ben·e·fac·tor** (ben'ə fak'tər) *n.* a person who has given help, esp. financial help; patron —**ben'e·fac'tress** (-tris) *n.fem.*

**ben·e·fice** (ben'ə fis) *n.* [OFr. < L. *beneficium*, a kindness: see BENEFACTION] **1.** an endowed church office providing a living for a vicar, rector, etc. **2.** its income —*vt.* **-ficed, -fic·ing** to provide with a benefice

**be·nef·i·cence** (bə nef'ə s'ns) *n.* [< L.: see BENEFACTION] **1.** the fact or quality of being kind or doing good **2.** a charitable act or generous gift

**be·nef·i·cent** (-s'nt) *adj.* **1.** showing beneficence; doing good **2.** resulting in benefit Also **be·nef·ic** (bə nef'ik) — **be·nef'i·cent·ly** *adv.*

**ben·e·fi·cial** (ben'ə fish'əl) *adj.* producing benefits; advantageous; favorable —**ben'e·fi'cial·ly** *adv.*

**ben·e·fi·ci·ar·y** (ben'ə fish'ē er'ē, -fish'ər ē) *adj.* of or holding a benefice —*n., pl.* **-ar·ies 1.** a holder of a benefice **2.** anyone receiving benefit **3.** a person named to receive the income or inheritance from a will, insurance policy, trust, etc.

**ben·e·fit** (ben'ə fit) *n.* [< OFr. < L.: see BENEFACTION] **1.** [Archaic] a charitable act **2.** anything helping to improve conditions; advantage **3.** [*often pl.*] payments made by an insurance company, public agency, etc. as during sickness or retirement **4.** a public performance, dance, etc. whose proceeds go to help a certain person, cause, etc. —*vt.* **-fit·ed, -fit·ing** to do good to or for; aid —*vi.* to receive advantage; profit

**benefit of clergy 1.** the exemption which the medieval clergy had from trial or punishment except in a church court **2.** the rites or approval of the church [marriage without *benefit of clergy*]

**be·nev·o·lence** (bə nev'ə ləns) *n.* [ME. & OFr. < L. < *bene*, well + *volens*, prp. of *velle*, to wish] **1.** an inclination to do good; kindliness **2.** a kindly, charitable act or gift; beneficence

**be·nev·o·lent** (-lənt) *adj.* **1.** doing or inclined to do good; kindly; charitable **2.** characterized by benevolence —**be·nev'o·lent·ly** *adv.*

**Beng.** Bengali

**Ben·gal** (ben gôl', beŋ-) **1.** region in the NE Indian peninsula, divided (1947) into **East Bengal** (now *Bangladesh*) and **West Bengal** (a state of India) **2. Bay of,** part of the Indian Ocean, east of India and west of Burma and the Malay Peninsula —**Ben'ga·lese'** (-gə lēz') *adj., n., pl.* **-lese'**

**Ben·gal·i** (ben gôl'ē, beŋ-) *n.* **1.** a native of Bengal **2.** the Indo-European, Indic language of Bengal —*adj.* of Bengal, its people, or their language

**ben·ga·line** (beŋ'gə lēn', beŋ'gə lēn') *n.* [Fr. < *Bengal*] a heavy, corded cloth of silk, rayon, etc. and either wool or cotton

**Ben·gha·zi** (ben gä'zē, beŋ-) seaport in Libya & one of its two capitals: pop. 140,000

**be·night·ed** (bi nīt'id) *adj.* **1.** surrounded by darkness or night **2.** intellectually or morally backward; unenlightened —**be·night'ed·ness** *n.*

**be·nign** (bi nīn') *adj.* [OFr. < L. < *bene*, well + *genus*, birth] **1.** good-natured; kindly **2.** favorable; beneficial **3.** *Med.* doing little or no harm; not malignant —**be·nign'ly** *adv.*

**be·nig·nant** (bi nig'nənt) *adj.* [< prec., by analogy with MALIGNANT] **1.** kindly or gracious **2.** favorable; beneficial —**be·nig'nan·cy** *n., pl.* **-cies**

**be·nig·ni·ty** (-nə tē) *n., pl.* **-ties 1.** benignancy; kindliness **2.** a kind act; favor

**Be·nin** (be nēn') country in WC Africa, on the Atlantic: 44,696 sq. mi.; pop. 3,112,000

**ben·i·son** (ben'ə z'n, -s'n) *n.* [< OFr. < L.: see BENEDICTION] a blessing; benediction

**Ben·ja·min** (ben'jə mən) [Heb. *binyāmīn*, lit., son of the right hand; hence, favorite son] **1.** a masculine name: dim. *Ben, Benjie, Benny* **2.** *Bible a*) Jacob's youngest son *b*) the tribe of Israel descended from him

**ben·ny** (ben'ē) *n., pl.* **-nies** [Slang] an amphetamine pill, esp. Benzedrine, used as a stimulant

**bent¹** (bent) *pt. and pp. of* BEND¹ —*adj.* **1.** made curved or crooked; not straight **2.** strongly determined (with *on*) [she is *bent* on going] **3.** set in a course; bound [westward *bent*] —*n.* **1.** an inclining; tendency **2.** a mental leaning; propensity [a *bent* for art] —**to** (or at) **the top of one's bent** to (or at) the limit of one's ability

**bent²** (bent) *n.* [OE. *beonot*] **1.** any of various wiry, low-growing grasses much used for lawns and golf greens: also called **bent'grass' 2.** the stiff flower stalk of certain grasses

**Ben·tham** (ben'thəm), **Jeremy** 1748–1832; Eng. philosopher & economist

**Ben·tham·ism** (-iz'm) *n.* the utilitarian philosophy of Jeremy Bentham, which holds that the greatest happiness of the greatest number should be the main goal of society

**ben·ton·ite** (ben'tə nīt') *n.* [after Fort *Benton*, Montana, where found] a porous clay, formed by the decomposition of volcanic ash

**bent·wood** (bent'wood') *adj.* designating furniture made of wood permanently bent into various forms by heat, moisture, and pressure

**be·numb** (bi num') *vt.* **1.** to make numb **2.** to deaden the mind, will, or feelings of

**Ben·ze·drine** (ben'zə drēn') *a trademark for* AMPHETAMINE —*n.* [b-] this drug

**ben·zene** (ben'zēn, ben zēn') *n.* [BENZ(OIC) + -ENE] a clear, flammable, poisonous liquid, C₆H₆, obtained from coal tar and used as a solvent for fats and in making varnishes, dyes, etc.

BENTWOOD CHAIR

**benzene ring** a structural unit thought to exist in the molecules of benzene and derivatives of benzene, consisting of a ring of six carbon atoms with alternate double bonds between them

**ben·zine** (ben'zēn, ben zēn') *n.* [BENZ(OIC) + -INE⁴] a colorless, flammable liquid obtained in the fractional distillation of petroleum and used as a motor fuel, a solvent in dry cleaning, etc.

**ben·zo·ate** (ben'zō āt') *n.* a salt or ester of benzoic acid

**ben·zo·caine** (ben'zə kān') *n.* [BENZO(IN) + (CO)CAINE] a white, odorless powder, C₉H₁₁NO₂, used in ointments as an anesthetic and to protect against sunburn

**ben·zo·ic** (ben zō'ik) *adj.* [BENZO(IN) + -IC] of or derived from benzoin

**benzoic acid** a white, crystalline organic acid, C₆H₅COOH, used as an antiseptic, preservative, etc.

**ben·zo·in** (ben'zō in, -zoin) *n.* [< Fr. < It. *benzoino* < Ar. *lubān jāwī*, incense of Java] the balsamic resin from certain tropical Asiatic trees, used in medicine, perfumes, etc.

**ben·zol** (ben'zōl, -zôl) *n.* [BENZ(OIN) + -OL¹] *same as* BENZENE: sometimes, a mixture distilling below 100° C that is 70 percent benzene

**Be·o·wulf** (bā'ə woolf') the hero of an Old English folk epic of that name (c. 700 A.D.)

**be·queath** (bi kwēth', -kwēth') *vt.* [OE. *becwethan*, to give by will < *be-* + *cwethan*, to say: see QUOTH] **1.** to leave (property) to another by last will and testament **2.** to hand down; pass on —**be·queath'al** (-əl) *n.*

**be·quest** (-kwest') *n.* [< *be-* + OE. *cwis* < *cwethan*: see prec.] **1.** a bequeathing **2.** anything bequeathed

**be·rate** (bi rāt') *vt.* **-rat'ed, -rat'ing** [BE- + RATE²] to scold or rebuke severely

**Ber·ber** (bur'bər) *n.* **1.** any of a Moslem people living in N Africa **2.** their language —*adj.* of the Berbers, their culture, or their language

**ber·ceuse** (ber sooz'; *Fr.* ber söz') *n., pl.* **-ceus'es** (-sooz'iz; *Fr.* -söz') [Fr. < *bercer*, to rock] **1.** a lullaby **2.** a piece of instrumental music that has a lulling effect

**be·reave** (bi rēv') *vt.* **-reaved'** or **- reft'** (-reft'), **-reav'ing** [OE. *bereafian* < *be-* + *reafian*, to rob] **1.** to deprive of or rob: now usually in the pp. (bereft) [*bereft* of hope] **2.** to leave in a sad or lonely state, as by death —**the bereaved** the survivors of a recently deceased person —**be·reave'ment** *n.*

---

fat, āpe, cär, ten, ēven, is, bīte; gō, hôrn, to͞ol, look; oil, out; up, fur; get; joy; yet; chin; she; thin, then; zh, leisure; ŋ, ring; ə for *a* in *ago, e* in *agent, i* in *sanity, o* in *comply, u* in *focus;* ' as in *able* (ā'b'l); Fr. bàl; ë, Fr. coeur; ö, Fr. feu; Fr. mon; δ, Fr. coq; ü, Fr. duc; r, Fr. cri; H, G. ich; kh, G. doch; ‡foreign; *hypothetical; < derived from. See inside front cover.

**be·ret** (bə rā′) *n.* [< Fr. < Pr. < LL.: see BIRETTA] a flat, round cap of felt, wool, etc.

**berg** (bʉrg) *n. same as* ICEBERG

**ber·ga·mot** (bʉr′gə mät′) *n.* [< Fr. < It. < Turk. *beg-armûdī,* prince's pear] **1.** *a)* a pear-shaped citrus fruit grown in S Europe for its oil, used in perfumery *b)* this oil **2.** any of several aromatic N. American herbs of the mint family

BERET

**Ber·gen** (ber′gən; *E.* bʉr′-) seaport in SW Norway: pop. 117,000

**Berg·son** (berg sōn′; *E.* berg′sən), Hen·ri (än rē′) 1859–1941; Fr. philosopher —Berg·so·ni·an (berg sō′nē ən) *adj., n.* —Berg′son·ism *n.*

**ber·i·ber·i** (ber′ē ber′ē) *n.* [Singh. *beri,* weakness] a disease caused by lack of thiamine (vitamin B₁) in the diet and characterized by nerve disorders, body swelling, etc.

**Ber·ing Sea** (ber′iŋ, bir′-) part of the N Pacific Ocean, between NE Siberia & Alaska

**Bering Standard Time** *see* STANDARD TIME

**Bering Strait** strait between Siberia & Alaska: average width, c. 50 mi.

**Berke·ley** (bʉr′klē) [after ff.] city in Calif., just north of Oakland: pop. 103,000

**Berke·ley** (bär′klē, bʉr′-), George 1685–1753; Ir. philosopher & bishop —Berke′le·ian (-klē ən, bər klē′ən) *adj.*

**berke·li·um** (bʉr′klē əm) *n.* [< U. of California at BERKELEY, where first isolated] a radioactive chemical element: symbol, Bk; at. wt., 248 (?); at. no., 97

**Berk·shire Hills** (bʉrk′shir, -shər) region of wooded hills and mountains in W Mass.: also **Berk′shires**

**Ber·lin** (bər lin′; *G.* ber lēn′) city in E Germany: capital of Germany (1871–1945): now divided into EAST BERLIN and WEST BERLIN

**ber·lin** (bər lin′, bʉr′lin) *n.* [after prec.] **1.** a four-wheeled, closed carriage with a footman's platform behind **2.** [*sometimes* B-] a fine, soft wool yarn: also called **Berlin wool**

**Ber·li·oz** (ber′lē ōz′; *Fr.* ber lyôz′), (Louis) Hector 1803–69; Fr. composer

**berm, berme** (bʉrm) *n.* [Fr. < MDu. *baerm*] a ledge or shoulder, as along the edge of a paved road

**Ber·mu·da** (bər myōō′də) self-governing Brit. colony on a group of islands in the W Atlantic, c. 580 mi. southeast of N.C.: 20 sq. mi.; pop. 52,000 —Ber·mu′dan, Ber·mu′di·an *adj., n.*

**Bermuda grass** a creeping perennial grass widely grown in warm climates for lawns or pasture

**Bermuda onion** a large onion with a mild flavor, grown in Texas, California, etc.

**Bermuda shorts** short trousers reaching just above the knee

**Bermuda triangle** triangular area in the Atlantic Ocean, bounded by Bermuda, Puerto Rico, and Florida, where ships and aircraft are rumored, since the 1940's, to have disappeared mysteriously

**Bern, Berne** (bʉrn; *Fr.* bern) capital of Switzerland, in the WC part: pop. 167,000

**Ber·nard** (bər närd′, bʉr′nərd; *for 2* ber nàr′) [Fr. < OHG. *bero,* BEAR² + *hart,* bold] **1.** a masculine name: dim. *Bernie* **2.** Claude (klōd), 1813–78; Fr. physiologist

**Bernard of Clair·vaux** (kler vō′), Saint 1090?–1153; Fr. Cistercian monk & theological writer —Ber·nard·ine (bʉr′nər din, -dēn′) *adj.*

**Bern·hardt** (bʉrn′härt′; *Fr.* ber nàr′), Sarah (born *Rosine Bernard*) 1844–1923; Fr. actress

**Ber·nice** (bər nēs′, bʉr′nis) [< L. < Gr. *Berenikē,* lit., victory-bringing] a feminine name: var. *Berenice*

**ber·ret·ta** (bə ret′ə) *n. same as* BIRETTA

**ber·ry** (ber′ē) *n., pl.* **-ries** [OE. *berie*] **1.** any small, juicy, fleshy fruit, as a raspberry, blueberry, etc. **2.** the dry seed or kernel of various plants, as a coffee bean **3.** an egg of a lobster, crayfish, etc. **4.** *Bot.* a fleshy fruit with a soft wall and thin skin, as the tomato, grape, etc. —*vi.* **-ried, -ry·ing 1.** to bear berries **2.** to pick berries —**ber′ry·like′** *adj.*

**ber·serk** (bər sʉrk′, -zʉrk′; bʉr′sərk) *n.* [ON. *berserkr,* warrior in bearskin < *ber,* a bear + *serkr,* coat] *Norse Legend* a frenzied warrior: also **ber·serk′er** —*adj., adv.* in or into a state of violent or destructive rage or frenzy

**berth** (bʉrth) *n.* [< base of BEAR¹] **1.** *Naut. a)* enough space to keep clear of another ship, the shore, etc. *b)* space for anchoring *c)* a place of anchorage **2.** a position, office, job, etc. **3.** *a)* a built-in bed or bunk on a ship, train, etc. *b)* any sleeping place —*vt.* **1.** to put into a berth **2.** to furnish with a berth —*vi.* to come into or occupy a berth —**give a wide berth to** to stay well away from

**Ber·tha** (bʉr′thə) [G. < OHG. < *beraht,* shining] a feminine name —*n.* [b-] [Fr. *berthe* < *Berthe,* Bertha] a woman's wide collar, often of lace, usually extending over the shoulders

**Ber·til·lon system** (bʉr′tə län′; *Fr.* ber tē yōn′) [after A. *Bertillon* (1853–1914), Fr. anthropologist] a system of iden-

tifying people through records of measurements, coloring, fingerprints, etc.

**Ber·tram** (bʉr′trəm) [G. < OHG. < *beraht,* shining + *hraban,* raven] a masculine name

**Ber·trand** (-trənd) *var. of* BERTRAM

**Ber·wyn** (bʉr′win) [after *Berwyn* Mts., Wales] city in NE Ill., near Chicago: pop. 47,000

**ber·yl** (ber′əl) *n.* [< OFr. < L. < Gr. *bēryllos*] beryllium aluminum silicate, a very hard, crystalline mineral: emerald and aquamarine are two gem varieties of beryl

**be·ryl·li·um** (bə ril′ē əm) *n.* [ModL. < prec.] a hard, rare, metallic chemical element: symbol, Be; at. wt., 9.0122; at. no., 4

**be·seech** (bi sēch′) *vt.* **-sought′** or **-seeched′, -seech′ing** [< OE. *besecan:* see BE- & SEEK] **1.** to ask (someone) earnestly; implore **2.** to ask for earnestly; beg for —**be·seech′ing·ly** *adv.*

**be·seem** (bi sēm′) *vi.* to be suitable or appropriate (to)

**be·set** (bi set′) *vt.* **-set′, -set′ting** [< OE. *besettan:* see BE- & SET] **1.** to set thickly with; stud **2.** to attack from all sides; harass or besiege **3.** to surround or hem in —**be·set′ment** *n.*

**be·set·ting** (-iŋ) *adj.* constantly harassing or attacking [a *besetting* temptation]

**be·shrew** (bi shrōō′) *vt.* [< ME.: see BE- & SHREW] [Archaic] to curse: used mainly in mild oaths

**be·side** (bi sīd′) *prep.* [ME.: see BY & SIDE] **1.** by or at the side of; alongside; near **2.** in comparison with [*beside* yours, my share seems small] **3.** in addition to; besides **4.** other than; aside from [*beside* him, who cares?] **5.** not pertinent to [*beside* the point] —*adv.* [Archaic] in addition —**beside oneself** wild with fear, rage, etc.

**be·sides** (-sīdz′) *adv.* [ME. < prec. + adv. gen. -(e)s] **1.** in addition; as well **2.** except for that mentioned; else **3.** moreover; furthermore —*prep.* **1.** in addition to; as well as **2.** other than; except

**be·siege** (bi sēj′) *vt.* **-sieged′, -sieg′ing** [ME. < *be-* + *segen,* to lay siege to < *sege,* SIEGE] **1.** to hem in with armed forces, esp. for a sustained attack **2.** to close in on; crowd around **3.** to overwhelm or beset [*besieged* with queries] —**be·sieg′er** *n.*

**be·smear** (bi smir′) *vt.* to smear over; soil

**be·smirch** (bi smʉrch′) *vt.* [BE- + SMIRCH] **1.** to make dirty; soil **2.** to bring dishonor to; sully

**be·som** (bē′zəm) *n.* [< OE. *besma,* broom, rod] **1.** a broom, esp. one made of twigs tied to a handle **2.** *same as* BROOM (*n.* 1)

**be·sot** (bi sät′) *vt.* **-sot′ted, -sot′ting 1.** to make a sot of; stupefy, as with alcoholic drink **2.** to make silly or foolish —**be·sot′ted** *adj.*

**be·sought** (bi sôt′) *alt. pt. and pp. of* BESEECH

**be·span·gle** (bi spaŋ′g'l) *vt.* **-gled, -gling** to cover with or as with spangles

**be·spat·ter** (bi spat′ər) *vt.* to spatter, as with mud or slander; soil or sully by spattering

**be·speak** (bi spēk′) *vt.* **-spoke′** (-spōk′) or archaic **-spake** (-spāk′), **-spo′ken** or **-spoke′, -speak′ing 1.** to speak for or engage in advance; reserve **2.** to be indicative of; show [a mansion that *bespeaks* wealth] **3.** to foreshadow; point to **4.** [Archaic or Poet.] to speak to; address

**be·spec·ta·cled** (bi spek′tə k'ld) *adj.* wearing eyeglasses

**be·spread** (bi spred′) *vt.* **-spread′, -spread′ing** to spread over or cover

**be·sprin·kle** (bi spriŋ′k'l) *vt.* **-kled, -kling** to sprinkle over (with something)

**Bess** (bes) a feminine name: see ELIZABETH

**Bes·sa·ra·bi·a** (bes′ə rä′bē ə) region in SW European Russia —**Bes′sa·ra′bi·an** *adj., n.*

**Bes·se·mer process** (bes′ə mər) [after Sir Henry *Bessemer* (1813–98), Eng. inventor] a method of making steel by blasting air through molten pig iron in a large container (**Bessemer converter**) to burn away the impurities

**best** (best) *adj. superl. of* GOOD [OE. *betst*] **1.** of the most excellent sort; above all others in worth or ability **2.** most suitable, most desirable, etc. **3.** being almost the whole; largest [the *best* part of an hour] —*adv. superl. of* WELL² **1.** in the most excellent or most suitable manner **2.** in the highest degree; most —*n.* **1.** the person or people, thing, condition, action, etc. of the greatest excellence, worth, suitability, etc. **2.** the utmost [to do one's *best*] **3.** one's finest clothes —*vt.* to win out over; defeat or outdo —**all for the best** turning out to be fortunate after all —**as best one can** as well as one can —**at best 1.** under the most favorable conditions **2.** at most —**at one's best** in one's best mood, form, health, etc. —**get (or have) the best of 1.** to outdo or defeat **2.** to outwit —**had best ought to** —**make the best of** to do as well as one can with

**be·stead** (bi sted′) *adj.* [< ME. < *bi-,* be + *stad,* placed < ON. *staddr,* prp. of *stethja,* to place] [Archaic] situated; placed —*vt.* **-stead′ed, -stead′, -stead′ing** [Archaic] to help; avail

**bes·tial** (bes′chəl, -tyəl; bēs′-) *adj.* [OFr. < LL. *bestialis*]

1. of beasts 2. like a beast; brutish, savage, vile, etc. —**bes·ti·al·i·ty** (bes′chē al′ə tē, bēs′-) n., pl. **-ties** —**bes′tial·ly** adv.

**bes·tial·ize** (bes′chə līz′, -tyə-; bēs′-) vt. **-ized′, -iz′ing** to make bestial; brutalize

**bes·ti·ar·y** (bes′chē er′ē, bēs′-) n., pl. **-ar′ies** [< ML. < L. < bestia, beast] a type of medieval natural history book with moralistic or religious fables about real and mythical animals

**be·stir** (bi stur′) vt. **-stirred′, -stir′ring** to stir to action; exert or busy (oneself)

**best man** the principal attendant of the bridegroom at a wedding

**be·stow** (bi stō′) vt. [see BE- & STOW] 1. to give or present as a gift (often with on or upon) 2. to apply; devote 3. [Archaic] to put or place, as in storage 4. [Obs.] to give in marriage —**be·stow′al** n.

**be·strew** (bi strōō′) vt. **-strewed′, -strewed′** or **-strewn′, -strew′ing** 1. to cover over (a surface); strew 2. to scatter or lie scattered over or about

**be·stride** (bi strīd′) vt. **-strode′** (-strōd′), **-strid′den** (-strid′'n), **-strid′ing** 1. to sit on, mount, or stand over with a leg on each side; straddle 2. [Archaic] to stride over

**best seller** a book, phonograph record, etc. currently outselling most others

**bet** (bet) n. [prob. < ABET] 1. an agreement between two persons that the one proved wrong about the outcome of something will do or pay what is stipulated; wager 2. a) the thing or sum thus staked b) the thing, contestant, etc. that something is staked on 3. a person, thing, or action likely to bring about a desired result [he's the best bet for the job] —vt. **bet** or **bet′ted, bet′ting** 1. to declare in or as in a bet [I bet he'll be late] 2. to stake (money, etc.) in a bet 3. to wager with (someone) —vi. to make a bet —**you bet (you)!** [Colloq.] certainly!

**be·ta** (bāt′ə; chiefly Brit. bēt′ə) n. [L. < Gr. bēta < Heb. bēth, lit., house; of Phoen. origin] 1. the second letter of the Greek alphabet (B, β) 2. the second of a group or series

**beta blocker** any of a class of drugs used to control heartbeat, relieve angina pectoris, reduce anxiety, etc. by inhibiting adrenal gland secretions

**be·take** (bi tāk′) vt. **-took′, -tak′en, -tak′ing** 1. to go (used reflexively) [he betook himself to his castle] 2. to direct or devote (oneself)

**beta particle** an electron or positron ejected at high velocity from the nucleus of an atom undergoing radioactive disintegration

**beta ray** 1. same as BETA PARTICLE 2. a stream of beta particles

**be·ta·tron** (bāt′ə trän′) n. [BETA (RAY) + (ELEC)TRON] an electron accelerator that uses a rapidly changing magnetic field to accelerate the particles to high velocities

**be·tel** (bēt′'l) n. [Port. < Malay vettilai] a tropical Asian climbing plant of the pepper family, whose leaf is chewed by some Asians

**Be·tel·geuse, Be·tel·geux** (bet′'l jōōz′, bēt′-) [< Fr. < Ar. bayt al jauza, lit., house of the twins] a very large, red, first-magnitude star, second brightest in the constellation Orion

**betel nut** the fruit of the betel palm, chewed together with lime and leaves of the betel (plant) by some Asians

**betel palm** a palm grown in SE Asia

**bête noire** (bāt′ nwär′) pl. **bêtes noires** (bāt′ nwärz′) [Fr., lit., black beast] a person or thing feared, disliked, and avoided

**beth** (bāth, beth; Heb. bāt, bās) n. [Heb. bēth: see BETA] the second letter of the Hebrew alphabet

**Beth·a·ny** (beth′ə nē) ancient town in Palestine, near Jerusalem

**Beth·el** (beth′əl) ancient town in Palestine, just north of Jerusalem

**beth·el** (beth′əl) n. [LL. < Heb. bēth 'ēl, house of God] 1. a holy place 2. a church or other place of worship for seamen

**be·think** (bi thiŋk′) vt. **-thought′, -think′ing** to bring (oneself) to think of, consider, or recollect; remind (oneself)

**Beth·le·hem** (beth′lə hem′, -lē əm) 1. ancient town in Judea: birthplace of Jesus 2. city in E Pa.: pop. 70,000

**be·tide** (bi tīd′) vi., vt. **-tid′ed, -tid′ing** [< ME. < be- + OE. tidan, to happen < tid, time] to happen (to); befall

**be·times** (bi tīmz′) adv. [ME. < bi-, by + time, TIME + adv. gen. -(e)s] 1. early or early enough 2. [Archaic] promptly or quickly

**be·to·ken** (bi tō′k'n) vt. [< ME. < be- + toknen < OE. tacnian, to mark < tacen, TOKEN] 1. to be a token or sign of; show 2. to show beforehand

**be·tray** (bi trā′) vt. [< ME. < be- + traien, betray < OFr.

< L. tradere, to hand over] 1. to help the enemy of (one's country, cause, etc.); be a traitor to 2. to break faith with; fail to uphold [to betray a trust] 3. to lead astray; specif., to seduce and then desert 4. to reveal unknowingly 5. to reveal or show signs of 6. to disclose (secret information, etc.) —**be·tray′al** n. —**be·tray′er** n.

**be·troth** (bi trōth′, -trôth′) vt. [< ME. < be- + treuthe < OE. treowth, truth] 1. to promise in marriage 2. [Archaic] to promise to marry

**be·troth·al** (-əl) n. a betrothing or being betrothed; mutual pledge to marry; engagement

**be·trothed** (-trōthd′, -trôtht′) adj. engaged to be married —n. the person to whom one is betrothed

**bet·ta** (bet′ə) n. [ModL.] a brightly colored, tropical, freshwater fish of SE Asia: some species are kept in aquariums

**bet·ted** (bet′id) alt. pt. and pp. of BET

**bet·ter** (bet′ər) adj. compar. of GOOD [< OE. betera] 1. more excellent; above another or others in worth or ability 2. more suitable, more desirable, etc. 3. being more than half; larger [the better part of an hour] 4. improved in health or disposition —adv. compar. of WELL[2] 1. in a more excellent or more suitable manner 2. in a higher degree 3. more [it took better than an hour] —n. 1. a person superior in authority, position, etc. 2. the thing, condition, etc. that is more excellent, etc. —vt. 1. to outdo; surpass 2. to make better; improve —vi. to become better —**better off** in a better condition —**for the better** to a better condition —**get (or have) the better of** 1. to outdo 2. to outwit —**had better** ought to

**better half** [Slang] one's wife or, less often, one's husband

**bet·ter·ment** (-mənt) n. 1. a making or being made better; improvement 2. Law an improvement, other than repairs, that increases the value of property

**bet·tor, bet·ter** (bet′ər) n. a person who bets

**be·tween** (bi twēn′) prep. [< OE. < be, by + tweon(um), by twos, in pairs] 1. in or through the space that separates (two things) 2. in or of the time, amount, or degree that separates (two things); intermediate to 3. that connects or relates to [a bond between friends] 4. along a course that connects [a road between here and there] 5. by the joint action of [between them they landed the fish] 6. in or into the combined possession of [they had fifty dollars between them] 7. from one or the other of [choose between love and duty] 8. because of the combined effect of [between work and study he has no time left] Between is sometimes used of more than two, if the relationship is thought of as individual with each of the others [a treaty between four powers] —adv. in an intermediate space, position, or function —**between ourselves** in confidence; as a secret: also **between you and me** —**in between** in an intermediate position

**be·tween·times** (-tīmz′) adv. in the intervals: also **between′·whiles**′

**be·twixt** (bi twikst′) prep., adv. [< OE. betwix < be- + a form related to twegen, TWAIN] between: now archaic except in **betwixt and between**, neither altogether one nor altogether the other

**Beu·lah** (byōō′lə) [Heb. be 'ūlāh, married: a Biblical name for the land of Israel] a feminine name

**bev, Bev** (bev) n., pl. **bev, Bev** [B(ILLION) + E(LECTRON)-V(OLTS)] a unit of energy equal to one billion electron-volts

**bev·a·tron** (bev′ə trän′) n. [< BEV + (CYCLO)TRON] a synchrotron for raising atomic particles to a level of six or more bev

**bev·el** (bev′'l) n. [prob. < OFr. hyp. baivel, dim. < baif, gaping: see BAY[2]] 1. a tool that is a rule with a movable arm, for measuring or marking angles, etc.: also **bevel square** 2. an angle other than a right angle 3. a sloping edge between parallel surfaces —adj. sloped; beveled —vt. **-eled** or **-elled, -el·ing** or **-el·ling** to cut to an angle other than a right angle —vi. to slope at an angle

**bevel gear** a gearwheel meshed with another so that their shafts are at an angle

**bev·er·age** (bev′rij, -ər ij) n. [< OFr. < bevre < L. bibere, IMBIBE] any liquid for drinking, esp. other than plain water

**Bev·er·ley, Bev·er·ly** (bev′ər lē) [< ME. bever, BEAVER[1] + ley, lea] a feminine name

**bev·y** (bev′ē) n., pl. **bev′ies** [< Anglo-Fr. bevée < OFr., a drinking bout < bevre: see BEVERAGE] 1. a group, esp. of girls or women 2. a flock: now chiefly of quail

**be·wail** (bi wāl′) vt. to wail over or complain about; lament; mourn —**be·wail′er** n.

**be·ware** (bi wer′) vi., vt. **-wared′, -war′ing** [prob. < OE. < be- + warian, to be wary] to be wary or careful (of); be on one's guard (against)

**be·wil·der** (bi wil′dər) vt. [BE- + archaic wilder, to lose

BEVEL GEAR

one's way] to confuse hopelessly, as by something complicated; befuddle; puzzle —be·wil′dered *adj.* —be·wil′der·ing *adj.* —be·wil′der·ing·ly *adv.* —be·wil′der·ment *n.*

**be·witch** (bi wich′) *vt.* [< ME. < *be-* + *wicchen* < OE. < *wicca:* see WITCH] **1.** to cast a spell over **2.** to enchant; fascinate; charm —be·witch′ing *adj.*—be·witch′ing·ly *adv.*
**be·witch·ment** (-mənt) *n.* **1.** power to bewitch **2.** a bewitching or being bewitched **3.** a spell that bewitches Also be·witch′er·y (-ər ē), *pl.* -er·ies
**be·wray** (bi rā′) *vt.* [< ME. < *be-* + OE. *wregan*, to inform] [Archaic] to divulge; reveal; betray
**bey** (bā) *n.* [Turk. *bey, beg*] **1.** in the Ottoman Empire, the governor of a Turkish province **2.** a Turkish title of respect and former title of rank **3.** the former native ruler of Tunis
**be·yond** (bi yänd′) *prep.* [< OE. < *be-* + *geond*, yonder] **1.** on or to the far side of; farther on than **2.** later than [*beyond* noon] **3.** outside the reach or understanding of [*beyond* help] **4.** more or better than; exceeding [*success beyond* one's hopes] —*adv.* **1.** farther away **2.** in addition —the (great) beyond whatever follows death
**bez·el** (bez′'l) *n.* [< OFr. hyp. *bisel* (Fr. *biseau*), sloping edge] **1.** a sloping surface, as the cutting edge of a chisel **2.** the slanting faces of a cut jewel, esp. those of the upper half **3.** the groove and flange holding a gem or a watch crystal in place
**be·zique** (bi zēk′) *n.* [Fr. *bésigue*] a card game resembling pinochle
**bf, b.f.** boldface
**B/F** brought forward
**bg.** *pl.* **bgs.** bag
**bhang** (baŋ) *n.* [Hindi < Sans. *bhangā*, hemp] **1.** the hemp plant **2.** its dried leaves and flowers, or a preparation, such as hashish, made from these and used for its intoxicating properties
**Bha·rat** (bu′rut) *Hindu name for* INDIA (sense 2)
**B-horizon** *n. see* ABC SOIL
**Bhu·tan** (bōō tän′) country in the Himalayas: c. 18,000 sq. mi.; pop. 750,000 —**Bhu·tan·ese** (bōōt′'n ēz′) *adj., n., pl.* -ese′
**bi-** (bī) [L. *bi-* < OL. *dui-*] *a prefix meaning:* **1.** having two [*biangular*] **2.** doubly [*biconvex*] **3.** happening every two [*biweekly*] **4.** happening twice during every [*bimonthly*]: in this sense, now usually *semi-* or *half-* **5.** using two or both [*bilabial*] **6.** joining or involving two [*bilateral*] **7.** *Chem.* having twice as many atoms or chemical equivalents for a definite weight of the other constituent of the compound [sodium *bicarbonate*]: in organic compounds, usually replaced by *di-*
**Bi** *Chem.* bismuth
**Bi·a·fra** (bē äf′rə) region in E Nigeria: fought an unsuccessful war for independence (1967–70)
**bi·an·gu·lar** (bī aŋ′gyoo lər) *adj.* having two angles
**bi·an·nu·al** (bī an′yoo wəl, -yool) *adj.* coming twice a year; semiannual: see also BIENNIAL —bi·an′nu·al·ly *adv.*
**bi·as** (bī′əs) *n., pl.* **bi′as·es** [Fr. *biais*, a slant] **1.** a slanting or diagonal line, cut or sewn across the weave of cloth **2.** a mental leaning; partiality; prejudice; bent —*adj.* slanting; diagonal —*adv.* diagonally —*vt.* **-ased** or **-assed, -as·ing** or **-as·sing** to cause to have a bias; prejudice —on the bias diagonally
**bi·ax·i·al** (bī ak′sē əl) *adj.* having two axes, as some crystals —bi·ax′i·al·ly *adv.*
**bib** (bib) *n.* [< L. *bibere*, to drink] **1.** an apronlike cloth tied under a child's chin at meals **2.** the front upper part of an apron or overalls
**Bib.** **1.** Bible **2.** Biblical
**bib and tucker** [Colloq.] an outfit of clothes
**bibb lettuce** (bib) [after J. *Bibb* (1789–1884), Kentucky horticulturist] a kind of lettuce in loose heads of dark-green leaves
**bib·cock** (bib′käk′) *n.* a faucet whose nozzle is bent downward
‡**bi·be·lot** (bē blō′) *n.* [Fr. < OFr. < *belbel*, BAUBLE] a small object whose value lies in its beauty or rarity
**Bibl., bibl.** **1.** Biblical **2.** bibliographical
**Bi·ble** (bī′b'l) *n.* [< OFr. < ML. < Gr. *biblia*, collection of writings, pl. of *biblion*, book < *biblos*, papyrus] **1.** the sacred book of Christianity; Old Testament and New Testament **2.** the Holy Scriptures of Judaism, identical with the Old Testament of Christianity **3.** any collection of writings sacred to a religion [the Koran is the Moslem *Bible*] **4.** [b-] any book regarded as authoritative See also AUTHORIZED VERSION, REVISED STANDARD VERSION, DOUAY BIBLE, VULGATE, SEPTUAGINT, APOCRYPHA
**Bib·li·cal** (bib′li k'l) *adj.* [*also* b-] **1.** of or in the Bible **2.** in keeping with or according to the Bible; like that in the Bible —Bib′li·cal·ly *adv.*
**Bib·li·cist** (-sist) *n.* **1.** a person who takes the words of the Bible literally **2.** a specialist in Biblical literature —Bib′li·cism *n.*

**biblio-** [< Gr. *biblion:* see BIBLE] *a combining form meaning:* **1.** book; of books [*bibliophile*] **2.** of the Bible [*bibliomancy*]
**bib·li·og·ra·phy** (bib′lē äg′rə fē) *n., pl.* -phies [< Gr. see BIBLE & -GRAPHY] **1.** the study of the editions, dates authorship, etc. of books and other writings **2.** a list o writings on a given subject, by a given author, etc. **3.** a lis of the books, articles, etc. referred to by an author —bib′li og′ra·pher *n.* —bib′li·o·graph′ic (-ə graf′ik), bib′li·o graph′i·cal *adj.* —bib′li·o·graph′i·cal·ly *adv.*
**bib·li·o·man·cy** (bib′lē ə man′sē) *n.* [BIBLIO- + -MANCY] prediction based on a Bible verse chosen at random
**bib·li·o·ma·ni·a** (bib′lē ə mā′nē ə, -nyə) *n.* [BIBLIO- -MANIA] a craze for collecting books, esp. rare one —bib′li·o·mane′ (-mān′) *n.* —bib′li·o·ma′ni·ac *n., adj.*
**bib·li·o·phile** (bib′lē ə fīl′) *n.* [BIBLIO- + -PHILE] **1.** on who loves or admires books, esp. for their style of bind ing, printing, etc. **2.** a book collector Also bib′li·o·phil (-fil′), bib·li·oph·i·list (bib′lē äf′ə list) —bib′li·o·phil′i (-ə fil′ik) *adj.* —bib′li·oph′i·lism (-äf′ə liz′m), bib′li oph′i·ly (-äf′ə lē) *n.*
**bib·li·o·pole** (-pōl′) *n.* [< L. < Gr. < *biblion*, a book + *pō lein*, to sell] a bookseller, esp. one dealing in rare works also bib·li·op·o·list (bib′lē äp′ə list) —bib′li·o·pol′i (-ə päl′ik) *adj.* —bib′li·op′o·ly (-äp′ə lē), bib′li·op′o lism *n.*
**bib·u·lous** (bib′yoo ləs) *adj.* [< L. < *bibere*, to drink **1.** highly absorbent **2.** fond of alcoholic liquor —bib′u lous·ly *adv.* —bib′u·lous·ness *n.*
**bi·cam·er·al** (bī kam′ər əl) *adj.* [< BI- + L. *camera*, chamber] made up of or having two legislative chamber —bi·cam′er·al·ism *n.*
**bi·car·bon·ate** (bī kär′bə nit, -nāt′) *n.* an acid salt of car bonic acid containing the radical HCO₃
**bicarbonate of soda** *same as* SODIUM BICARBONATE
**bi·cen·te·nar·y** (bī′sen ten′ər ē, bī sen′tə ner′ē) *adj., n. pl.* -nar·ies *same as* BICENTENNIAL
**bi·cen·ten·ni·al** (bī′sen ten′ē əl) *adj.* **1.** happening once in a period of 200 years **2.** lasting for 200 years —*n* a 200th anniversary or its celebration
**bi·ceps** (bī′seps) *n., pl.* -ceps or -ceps·es [L. < *bis*, two + *caput*, head] **1.** a muscle having two heads, or points o origin; esp., the large muscle in the front of the uppe arm or the corresponding muscle at the back of the thigh **2.** strength or muscular development, esp. of the arm
**bi·chlo·ride** (bī klôr′īd) *n.* **1.** a binary compound containing two atoms of chlorine for each atom of another element **2.** *same as* MERCURIC CHLORIDE
**bichloride of mercury** *same as* MERCURIC CHLORIDE
**bi·chro·mate** (bī krō′māt) *n. same as* DICHROMATE
**bick·er** (bik′ər) *vi.* [ME. *bikeren*] **1.** to have a petty quarrel; squabble **2.** to flicker, twinkle, etc. —*n.* a petty quarrel —bick′er·er *n.*
**bi·col·or** (bī′kul′ər) *adj.* of two colors: also bi′col′ored
**bi·con·cave** (bī′kän kāv′, bī kän′kāv) *adj.* concave on both surfaces [a biconcave lens]
**bi·con·vex** (bī′kän veks′, bī kän′veks) *adj.* convex on both surfaces [a biconvex lens]
**bi·cus·pid** (bī kus′pid) *adj.* [< BI- + L. *cuspis*, pointed end] having two points [a bicuspid tooth]: also bi·cus′pi·date′ (-pi dāt′) —*n.* any of eight adult teeth with two-pointed crowns

BICUSPID

**bi·cy·cle** (bī′si k'l) *n.* [Fr.: see BI- & CY-CLE] a vehicle consisting of a metal frame mounted on two wheels, one behind the other, and equipped with handlebars, a saddlelike seat, and, usually, foot pedals —*vi., vt.* -cled, -cling to ride on a bicycle —bi′cy·clist, bi′cy·cler *n.*
**bid** (bid) *vt.* bade or bid or archaic bad, bid′den or bid, bid′ding; for vt. 2, 6, & for vi., the pt. & pp. are always bid [< OE. *biddan*, to urge & OE. *beodan*, to command] **1.** to command, ask, or tell **2.** to offer (a certain amount) as the price that one will pay or accept **3.** to declare openly [to *bid* defiance] **4.** to express in greeting or taking leave [to *bid* farewell] **5.** [Archaic or Dial.] to invite **6.** *Card Games* to state (the number of tricks one expects to take) and declare (a suit or no-trump) —*vi.* to make a bid —*n.* **1.** a bidding of an amount **2.** the amount bid **3.** a chance to bid **4.** an attempt or try [a *bid* for fame] **5.** [Colloq.] an invitation, esp. to become a member **6.** *Card Games* a) the act of bidding b) the number of tricks stated c) a player's turn to bid —bid fair to seem likely —bid in at an auction, to bid more than the best offer on one's own property in order to keep it —bid up to raise the amount bid —bid′der *n.*
**bid·ding** (bid′iŋ) *n.* **1.** a command or request **2.** an invitation or summons **3.** the bids or the making of bids in a card game or auction
**bid·dy** (bid′ē) *n., pl.* -dies **1.** a hen **2.** [Slang] a woman, esp. an elderly, gossipy one

# bide 73 billabong

**bide** (bīd) *vi.* **bode** or **bid'ed, bid'ed, bid'ing** [OE. *bīdan*] [Archaic or Dial.] **1.** to stay; continue **2.** to dwell; reside **3.** to wait —*vt.* [Archaic or Dial.] to endure or tolerate —**bide one's time** *pt.* **bid'ed** to wait patiently for an opportunity

**bi·den·tate** (bī den'tāt) *adj.* having two teeth or toothlike parts

**bi·det** (bi dā') *n.* [Fr.] a low, bowl-shaped bathroom fixture with running water, used for bathing the crotch

**bi·en·ni·al** (bī en'ē əl) *adj.* [< L. < *bis,* twice + *annus,* year + -AL] **1.** happening every two years **2.** lasting for two years —*n.* **1.** a biennial event **2.** *Bot.* a plant that lasts two years, usually producing flowers and seed the second year —**bi·en'ni·al·ly** *adv.*

**bier** (bir) *n.* [OE. *bær,* a bed] **1.** a portable framework on which a coffin or corpse is placed **2.** a coffin and its supporting platform

**Bierce** (birs), **Ambrose** 1842–1914?; U.S. writer

**biff** (bif) *n.* [prob. echoic] [Slang] a blow; strike; hit —*vt.* [Slang] to strike; hit

**bi·fid** (bī'fid) *adj.* [< L. < *bis,* twice + *findere,* to cleave] divided into two equal parts by a cleft; forked —**bi·fid'i·ty** (-ə tē) *n.* —**bi'fid·ly** *adv.*

**bi·fo·cal** (bī fō'k'l, bī'fō'k'l) *adj.* adjusted to two different focal lengths —*n.* a lens with one part ground to adjust the eyes for close focus, and the rest ground for distant focus

**bi·fo·cals** (bī'fō'k'lz) *n.pl.* a pair of glasses with bifocal lenses

**bi·fur·cate** (bī'fər kāt', bī fur'kāt; *for adj. also* -kit) *adj.* [< ML. < L. < *bi-* + *furca,* FORK] having two branches; forked —*vt., vi.* **-cat'ed, -cat'ing** to divide into two branches —**bi'fur·cate'ly** *adv.* —**bi'fur·ca'tion** *n.*

**big** (big) *adj.* **big'ger, big'gest** [ME.; akin to L. *bucca,* puffed cheek] **1.** *a)* of great size, extent, or capacity; large *b)* great in force or intensity *[a big wind]* **2.** *a)* full-grown *b)* elder *[his big sister]* **3.** *a)* far advanced in pregnancy (*with*) *b)* filled or swelling (*with*) **4.** loud **5.** important or outstanding *[to do big things]* **6.** boastful; extravagant *[big talk]* **7.** generous; noble *[a big heart] Big* is much used in combination to form adjectives *[big-bodied, big-souled]* —*adv.* [Colloq.] **1.** pompously; boastfully *[to talk big]* **2.** impressively **3.** in a broad way; showing imagination *[think big!]* —**big'ness** *n.*

**big·a·my** (big'ə mē) *n., pl.* **-mies** [< OFr. < LL. < *bis,* twice + Gr. *gamos,* marriage] the act of marrying a second time while a previous marriage is still legally in effect: when done knowingly, it is a criminal offense —**big'a·mist** *n.* —**big'a·mous** *adj.* —**big'a·mous·ly** *adv.*

**Big Apple** *nickname for* NEW YORK CITY

**big-bang theory** a theory of cosmology holding that the expansion of the universe began with a gigantic explosion

**Big Ben** **1.** the great bell in the Parliament clock tower in London **2.** the clock itself

**Big Dipper** a dipper-shaped group of stars in the constellation Ursa Major (Great Bear)

**big game** **1.** large wild animals hunted for sport, as lions, tigers, etc. **2.** the object of any important or dangerous undertaking

**big·head** (big'hed') *n.* [Colloq.] conceit; egotism: also **big head**

**big·heart·ed** (big'här'tid) *adj.* generous or magnanimous —**big'heart'ed·ly** *adv.*

**big·horn** (-hôrn') *n., pl.* **-horns', -horn'** see PLURAL, II, D, 1 an animal with large horns, esp. a large, wild, shaggy-haired sheep of the Rocky Mountains

**big house, the** [Slang] a penitentiary

**bight** (bīt) *n.* [ME. *byht*] **1.** a loop or slack part in a rope **2.** *a)* a curve in a river, coastline, etc. *b)* a bay formed by such a curve —*vt.* to fasten with a bight

**big-league** (big'lēg') *adj.* [after the *big* (i.e., major) *leagues* in professional baseball] [Colloq.] of or at the top level in a field of activity

**big lie, the** **1.** a gross distortion of facts, constantly repeated to make it seem credible **2.** a propaganda technique using this device

**big mouth** [Slang] a person who talks too much

**big·no·ni·a** (big nō'nē ə) *n.* [after the Abbé *Bignon,* 18th-c. Fr. librarian] a tropical American vine with trumpet-shaped flowers

**big·ot** (big'ət) *n.* [Fr. < OFr., a term of insult used of Normans] a narrow-minded person who is intolerant of other creeds, opinions, races, etc. —**big'ot·ed** *adj.* —**big'ot·ed·ly** *adv.* —**big'ot·ry** (-ə trē) *n., pl.* **-ries**

**big shot** [Slang] an important, influential person: also **big noise, big wheel,** etc.

**big stick** [< use of term by T. ROOSEVELT] [*also* B- S-] a policy of acting or negotiating from a position backed by a show of strength

**big time** [Slang] **1.** formerly, vaudeville in the top-ranking theatrical circuits **2.** the highest level in any profession, etc. —**big'-time'** *adj.*

**big top** [Colloq.] **1.** the main tent of a circus **2.** the life or work of circus performers

**big tree** a giant Sequoia tree related to the redwood and found in the high Sierras

**big·wig** (big'wig') *n.* [Colloq.] *same as* BIG SHOT

**bi·jou** (bē'zhōō) *n., pl.* **-joux** (-zhōōz) [Fr. < Bret. *bizou,* a ring < *biz,* a finger] **1.** a jewel **2.** an exquisite trinket

**bi·ju·gate** (bī'jōō gāt', bī jōō'git) *adj.* [BI- + JUGATE] having two pairs of leaflets, as some pinnate leaves: also **bi'ju·gous** (-gəs)

**bike** (bīk) *n., vt., vi.* **biked, bik'ing** [< BICYCLE] [Colloq.] **1.** bicycle **2.** motorcycle

**bike·way** (-wā') *n.* a path or lane for bicycle riders only

**bi·ki·ni** (bi kē'nē) *n.* [< *Bikini,* atoll in the Marshall Islands] an extremely brief two-piece bathing suit for women

**bi·la·bi·al** (bī lā'bē əl) *adj.* **1.** *same as* BILABIATE **2.** *Phonet.* made by stopping or constricting the airstream with the lips, as the English stops *p* and *b* —*n.* a bilabial sound

**bi·la·bi·ate** (-bē it, -āt') *adj.* [BI- + LABIATE] *Bot.* having two lips, as the corolla of some flowers

**bi·lat·er·al** (bī lat'ər əl) *adj.* [BI- + LATERAL] **1.** of, on, or having two sides, factions, etc. **2.** affecting both sides equally; reciprocal *[a bilateral trade pact]* **3.** symmetrical on both sides of an axis —**bi·lat'er·al·ism** *n.* —**bi·lat'er·al·ly** *adv.*

**Bil·ba·o** (bil bä'ō) seaport in N Spain: pop. 372,000

**bil·ber·ry** (bil'ber'ē) *n., pl.* **-ries** [ult. < ON. *bollr,* BALL[1] + *ber,* berry] a N. American blueberry or its fruit

**bil·bo** (bil'bō) *n., pl.* **-boes** [after BILBAO] **1.** [*pl.*] a long iron bar with shackles, for fettering a prisoner's feet **2.** [Archaic] a sword

**bile** (bīl) *n.* [Fr. < L. *bilis*] **1.** the bitter, yellow-brown or greenish fluid secreted by the liver and found in the gallbladder: it helps in digestion, esp. of fats **2.** [< ancient belief in bile as the humor causing anger] bad temper; anger

**bilge** (bilj) *n.* [var. of BULGE] **1.** the bulge of a cask **2.** the rounded, lower part of a ship's hold **3.** stagnant, dirty water that gathers there: also **bilge water 4.** [Slang] worthless talk or writing; nonsense —*vt., vi.* **bilged, bilg'ing** to break open in the bilge: said of a ship

**bil·i·ar·y** (bil'ē er'ē, bil'yər ē) *adj.* [Fr. *biliaire*] **1.** of or involving the bile **2.** bile-carrying **3.** bilious

**bi·lin·gual** (bī liŋ'gwəl) *adj.* [< L. < *bis,* two + *lingua,* tongue] **1.** of or in two languages **2.** capable of using two languages, esp. with equal facility —**bi·lin'gual·ism** *n.* —**bi·lin'gual·ly** *adv.*

**bil·ious** (bil'yəs) *adj.* **1.** of the bile **2.** having, appearing to have, or resulting from some ailment of the bile or the liver **3.** bad-tempered; cross; irritable —**bil'ious·ly** *adv.* —**bil'ious·ness** *n.*

**bilk** (bilk) *vt.* [? altered < BALK] **1.** to cheat or swindle; defraud **2.** to get away without paying (a debt, etc.) **3.** to elude —*n.* **1.** a bilking or being bilked **2.** a cheat or swindler —**bilk'er** *n.*

**bill[1]** (bil) *n.* [< Anglo-L. *billa,* altered < ML. *bulla,* sealed document < L. *bulla,* knob] **1.** a statement of charges for goods or services; invoice **2.** a list, as a menu, theater program, ship's roster, etc. **3.** a poster or handbill, esp. one announcing a circus, show, etc. **4.** the entertainment offered in a theater **5.** a draft of a law proposed to a lawmaking body **6.** a bill of exchange **7.** any promissory note **8.** *a)* a bank note or piece of paper money *b)* [Slang] a hundred dollars or a hundred-dollar bill **9.** *Law* a written declaration of charges filed in a legal action —*vt.* **1.** to make out a bill of (items); list **2.** to present a statement of charges to **3.** *a)* to advertise by bills or posters *b)* to book (a performer or performance) **4.** to post bills or placards throughout (a town, etc.) **5.** to enter on a bill of consignment; book for shipping —**fill the bill** [Colloq.] to meet the requirements —**bill'a·ble** *adj.*

**bill[2]** (bil) *n.* [OE. *bile*] **1.** the horny jaws of a bird, usually pointed; beak **2.** a beaklike mouthpart, as of a turtle **3.** [Colloq.] the peak or visor of a cap —*vi.* **1.** to touch bills together **2.** to caress lovingly: now only in **bill and coo,** to kiss, talk softly, etc. in a loving way

**bill[3]** (bil) *n.* [OE. *bill*] **1.** an ancient weapon having a hook-shaped blade with a spike at the back **2.** *same as* BILLHOOK

**bill·a·bong** (bil'ə bäŋ') *n.* [native term < *billa,* water + ?] in Australia, **1.** a backwater channel that forms a lagoon or pool **2.** a river branch that reenters the main stream

---

fat, āpe, cär, ten, ēven, is, bīte; gō, hôrn, tōol, look; oil, out; up, fur; get; joy; yet; chin; she; thin, *th*en; zh, leisure; ŋ, ring; ə for a in ago, e in agent, i in sanity, o in comply, u in focus; ' as in able (ā'b'l); Fr. bal; ë, Fr. coeur; ö, Fr. feu; Fr. mon; ö, Fr. coq; ü, Fr. duc; r, Fr. cri; H, G. ich; kh, G. doch; ‡foreign; *hypothetical; < derived from. See inside front cover.

**bill·board** (bil'bôrd') *n.* a large signboard, usually outdoors, for advertising posters

**bil·let**[1] (bil'it) *n.* [< Anglo-Fr., dim. of *bille,* BILL[1]] **1.** *a)* a written order to provide lodging for military personnel, as in private buildings *b)* the quarters thus occupied *c)* the sleeping place assigned to a sailor on ship **2.** a position or job —*vt.* to assign to lodging by billet —*vi.* to be billeted or quartered

**bil·let**[2] (bil'it) *n.* [OFr. *billette,* dim. of *bille,* tree trunk] **1.** *a)* a short, thick piece of firewood *b)* [Obs.] a wooden club **2.** a small, unfinished metal bar, esp. of iron or steel

**bil·let-doux** (bil'ē dōō'; *Fr.* bẽ ye dōō') *n., pl.* **bil·lets-doux** (bil'ē dōōz'; *Fr.* bẽ ye dōō') [Fr., lit., sweet letter] a love letter

**bill·fold** (bil'fōld') *n.* same as WALLET

**bill·hook** (-hŏŏk') *n.* a tool with a curved or hooked blade at one end, for pruning and cutting

**bil·liard** (bil'yərd) *adj.* of or for billiards —*n.* a point scored in billiards by a carom

**bil·liards** (-yərdz) *n.* [Fr. *billard;* orig., a cue < *bille:* see BILLET[2]] any of several games played with hard balls on an oblong, cloth-covered table with raised, cushioned edges: a cue is used to hit and move the balls: see also POOL[2]

**bill·ing** (bil'iŋ) *n.* the listing or the order of listing of actors' names on a playbill, marquee, etc.

**Bil·lings** (bil'iŋz) [after F. *Billings* (1823–90), railroad executive] city in S Mont.: pop. 67,000

**bil·lings·gate** (bil'iŋz gāt') *n.* [after a fish market in London] foul, vulgar, abusive talk

**bil·lion** (bil'yən) *n.* [Fr. contr. < *bi-,* BI- + *million*] **1.** a thousand millions (1,000,000,000) **2.** formerly, in Great Britain, a million millions (1,000,000,000,000) **3.** an indefinite but very large number —*adj.* amounting to one billion in number —**bil'lionth** *adj., n.*

**bil·lion·aire** (bil'yə ner') *n.* one whose wealth comes to at least a billion dollars, pounds, etc.

**bill of attainder** a legislative enactment pronouncing a person guilty, without a trial, of an alleged crime (esp. treason) and inflicting the punishment of death and attainder upon him: prohibited in the U.S. by the Constitution

**bill of exchange** a written order to pay a certain sum of money to the person named; draft

**bill of fare** a list of the foods served; menu

**bill of goods** a shipment of goods sent to an agent for sale —**sell (someone) a bill of goods** [Colloq.] to persuade (someone) by deception or misrepresentation to accept, believe, or do something

**bill of health** a certificate stating whether there is infectious disease aboard a ship or in the port sailed from —**clean bill of health 1.** a bill of health certifying the absence of infectious disease **2.** [Colloq.] a good record; favorable report, as after an investigation

**bill of lading** a contract issued to a shipper by a transportation agency, listing the goods received for shipment and promising their delivery

**bill of rights 1.** a list of the rights and freedoms regarded as essential to a people **2.** [B- R-] the first ten amendments to the Constitution of the U.S., which guarantee certain rights to the people, as freedom of speech, assembly, and worship

**bill of sale** a written statement transferring the ownership of something by sale

**bil·low** (bil'ō) *n.* [ON. *bylgja:* see BELLY] **1.** a large wave; great swell of water **2.** any large, swelling mass or surge, as of smoke, sound, etc. —*vi., vt.* to surge, swell, or cause to swell like or in a billow

**bil·low·y** (bil'ə wē) *adj.* **-low·i·er, -low·i·est** swelling in or as in a billow —**bil'low·i·ness** *n.*

**bill·post·er** (bil'pōs'tər) *n.* a person hired to fasten advertisements on walls, billboards, etc.

**bil·ly** (bil'ē) *n., pl.* **-lies** [< BILLET[2]] a club or heavy stick, esp. one carried by a policeman

**billy goat** a male goat

**bi·lo·bate** (bī lō'bāt) *adj.* having or divided into two lobes: also **bi·lo'bat·ed, bi·lobed'**

**bi·man·u·al** (bī man'yōō wəl) *adj.* using or requiring both hands —**bi·man'u·al·ly** *adv.*

**bi·met·al** (bī'met''l) *n.* a bimetallic substance

**bi·me·tal·lic** (bī'mə tal'ik) *adj.* **1.** containing or using two metals, often two metals bonded together **2.** of or based on bimetallism

**bi·met·al·lism** (bī met''l iz'm) *n.* **1.** the use of two metals, usually gold and silver, as the monetary standard, with fixed values in relation to each other **2.** the actions or policies supporting this —**bi·met'al·list** *n.*

**bi·month·ly** (bī munth'lē) *adj., adv.* **1.** once every two months **2.** twice a month: in this sense, *semimonthly* is the preferred term —*n., pl.* **-lies** a publication appearing once every two months

**bin** (bin) *n.* [OE., manger, crib] a box or enclosed space, esp. for storing foods or other things —*vt.* **binned, bin'ning** to store in a bin

**bi·na·ry** (bī'nər ē) *adj.* [< L. < *bini,* two by two < *bis,* double] **1.** made up of two parts or things; twofold; double **2.** designating or of a number system that has 2 as its base **3.** *Chem.* composed of two elements or radicals or of one element and one radical —*n., pl.* **-ries 1.** something made up of two parts or things **2.** same as BINARY STAR

**binary star** two stars revolving around a common center of gravity; double star

**bi·nate** (bī'nāt) *adj.* [see BINARY] *Bot.* occurring in pairs *[binate* leaves] —**bi'nate·ly** *adv.*

**bi·na·tion·al** (bī nash'ə n'l) *adj.* composed of or involving two nations or two nationalities

**bin·au·ral** (bī nôr'əl, bi-) *adj.* [see BI- & AURAL] **1.** having two ears **2.** of or involving the use of both ears **3.** of sound reproduction or transmission using at least two sources of sound to give a stereophonic effect

**bind** (bīnd) *vt.* **bound, bind'ing** [< OE. *bindan*] **1.** to tie together; make fast, as with a rope **2.** to hold or restrain as if tied *[bound* by convention] **3.** to gird or encircle with a belt, etc. **4.** to bandage (often with *up*) **5.** to make stick together **6.** to constipate **7.** to strengthen or ornament the edges of by a band, as of tape **8.** to fasten together printed sheets of (a book) and enclose within a cover **9.** to secure or make firm (a bargain, contract, etc.) **10.** to obligate, as by duty **11.** to compel, as by oath or legal restraint **12.** to make an apprentice of (often with *out* or *over*) **13.** to unite or hold, as by loyalty or love —*vi.* **1.** to do the act of binding **2.** to grow hard or stiff **3.** to be constricting or restricting **4.** to be obligatory —*n.* **1.** anything that binds **2.** [Colloq.] a difficult situation —**bind over** to put under bond to appear, as before a law court

**bind·er** (bīn'dər) *n.* **1.** a person who binds; specif., a bookbinder **2.** a thing that binds; specif., *a)* a band, cord, etc. *b)* a substance, as tar, that binds things together *c)* a detachable cover for holding sheets of paper together **3.** a device attached to a reaper, for tying grain in bundles **4.** *Law* a temporary memorandum of a contract, in effect pending execution of the final contract

**bind·er·y** (bīn'dər ē, -drē) *n., pl.* **-er·ies** a place where books are bound

**bind·ing** (-diŋ) *n.* **1.** the action of one that binds **2.** a thing that binds, as *a)* the fastenings on a ski for the boot *b)* a band or bandage *c)* tape used in sewing for strengthening seams, edges, etc. *d)* the covers and backing of a book **3.** a cohesive substance for binding a mixture —*adj.* that binds; esp., that holds one to an agreement, etc.; obligatory

**bind·weed** (bīnd'wēd') *n.* any of a number of twining vines related to the morning glory

**bine** (bīn) *n.* [dial. form of BIND] any climbing, twining stem, as of the hop

**Bi·net-Si·mon test** (bi nā' sī'mən) [after its Fr. devisers, A. *Binet* (1857–1911) and T. *Simon* (1873–1961)] any of a series of tests seeking to measure intelligence in children: also **Binet test**

**binge** (binj) *n.* [? < dial. *binge,* to soak] [Colloq.] a drunken or unrestrained spree

**Bing·ham·ton** (biŋ'əm tən) [after W. *Bingham* (1752–1804), land donor] city in SC N.Y.: pop. 56,000

**bin·go** (biŋ'gō) *n.* [< ?] a gambling game, like lotto, usually with many players

**bin·na·cle** (bin'ə k'l) *n.* [formerly *bittacle* < Port. < L. *habitaculum,* dwelling place < *habitare,* to inhabit] the case enclosing a ship's compass

**bin·oc·u·lar** (bī näk'yə lər; *also, esp. for n.,* bi-) *adj.* [< L. *bini,* double + *oculus,* an eye] using, or for the use of, both eyes at the same time —*n.* [*usually pl.*] a binocular instrument, as field glasses or opera glasses —**bin·oc'u·lar'i·ty** (-lar'ə tē) *n.* —**bin·oc'u·lar·ly** *adv.*

**bi·no·mi·al** (bī nō'mē əl) *n.* [< LL. < *bi-* + Gr. *nomos,* law + -AL] **1.** a mathematical expression consisting of two terms connected by a plus or minus sign **2.** a two-word scientific name of a plant or animal —*adj.* **1.** composed of two terms **2.** of binomials

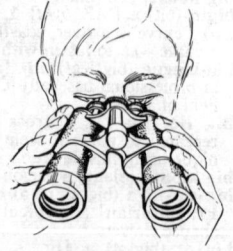

BINOCULARS

**bi·o** (bī'ō) *n., pl.* **bi'os** [Colloq.] a biography, often a very brief one

**bi·o-** [Gr. < *bios,* life] a combining form meaning life, of living things, biological *[biography]*

**bi·o·as·tro·nau·tics** (bī'ō as'trə nô'tiks) *n.pl.* [*with sing. v.*] the science dealing with the effects of space travel upon living organisms

**bi·o·chem·is·try** (-kem'is trē) *n.* the branch of chemistry that deals with plants and animals and their life processes —**bi'o·chem'i·cal** *adj.* —**bi'o·chem'ist** *n.*

**bi·o·cide** (bī′ə sīd′) *n.* [BIO- + -CIDE] any substance that can kill living organisms

**bi·o·de·grad·a·ble** (bī′ō di grā′də b'l) *adj.* [BIO- + DEGRAD(E) + -ABLE] that can be readily decomposed by biological, esp. bacterial, action, as some detergents

**bi·o·en·gi·neer·ing** (-en′jə nir′iŋ) *n.* a science dealing with the application of engineering science to problems of biology and medicine

**bi·o·feed·back** (-fēd′bak′) *n.* a technique of seeking to control emotional states, as anxiety, by training oneself, with the aid of electronic devices, to modify involuntary body functions, as blood pressure

**biog.** 1. biographer 2. biographical 3. biography

**bi·o·gen·e·sis** (bī′ō jen′ə sis) *n.* [BIO- + GENESIS] 1. the principle that living organisms derive only from other similar organisms 2. such generation of organisms —**bi′o·ge·net′ic** (-jə net′ik), **bi′o·ge·net′i·cal** *adj.*

**bi·og·ra·phee** (bī äg′rə fē′, bē-) *n.* a person who is the subject of a biography

**bi·og·ra·phy** (bī äg′rə fē, bē-) *n.* [< Gr.: see BIO- & -GRAPHY] 1. *pl.* **-phies** an account of a person's life written by another 2. such writings, collectively, as a branch of literature —**bi·og′ra·pher** *n.* —**bi′o·graph′i·cal** (bī′ə graf′i k'l), **bi′o·graph′ic** *adj.* —**bi′o·graph′i·cal·ly** *adv.*

**bi·o·haz·ard** (bī′ō haz′ərd) *n.* a danger to life or health, esp. that resulting from biological experimentation

**biol.** 1. biological 2. biologist 3. biology

**bi·o·log·i·cal** (bī′ə läj′i k'l) *adj.* 1. of or connected with biology 2. of the nature of living matter 3. used in or produced by practical biology Also **bi′o·log′ic** —*n.* a biological product —**bi′o·log′i·cal·ly** *adv.*

**biological warfare** the use of disease-spreading microorganisms, toxins, etc. as a weapon of war

**bi·ol·o·gy** (bī äl′ə jē) *n.* [BIO- + -LOGY] 1. the science that deals with the origin, history, life processes, structure, etc. of plants and animals: it includes botany, zoology, and their subdivisions 2. animal and plant life, as of a given area —**bi·ol′o·gist** *n.*

**bi·o·med·i·cine** (bī′ō med′ə s'n) *n.* a branch of medicine combined with research in biology —**bi′o·med′i·cal** *adj.*

**bi·o·met·rics** (-met′riks) *n.pl.* [*with sing. v.*] that branch of biology which deals with its data statistically —**bi′o·met′ric, bi′o·met′ri·cal** *adj.* —**bi′o·met′ri·cal·ly** *adv.*

**bi·on·ic** (bī än′ik) *adj.* 1. designating an artificial replacement for a bodily part 2. furnished with such a replacement part or parts, specif. in science fiction, so that strength, abilities, etc. are greatly enhanced

**bi·on·ics** (bī än′iks) *n.pl.* [*with sing. v.*] [< Gr. *bion*, living + -ICS] the science of designing instruments or systems modeled after living organisms

**bi·o·phys·ics** (bī′ō fiz′iks) *n.pl.* [*with sing. v.*] the study of biological phenomena in relation to physics —**bi′o·phys′i·cal** *adj.* —**bi′o·phys′i·cist** *n.*

**bi·op·sy** (bī′äp′sē) *n., pl.* **-sies** [see BIO- & -OPSIS] the removal of bits of living tissue, fluids, etc. from the body for diagnostic examination

**bi·o·rhythm** (bī′ō rith′′m, -rith′əm) *n.* any of three separate biological cycles in terms of which, according to a theory, a person's physical, emotional, and intellectual energy levels regularly and predictably rise and fall

**bi·os·co·py** (bī äs′kə pē) *n.* [BIO- + -SCOPY] a medical examination to find out whether life is present

**-bi·o·sis** (bī ō′sis, bē-) [< Gr. *biōsis*, way of life < *bios*, life] *a combining form meaning* way of living [*symbiosis*]

**bi·o·sphere** (bī′ə sfir′) *n.* [BIO- + SPHERE] that portion of the earth and its atmosphere containing living organisms

**bi·o·tin** (bī′ə tin) *n.* [< Gr. *bios*, life + -IN¹] a bacterial growth factor, $C_{10}H_{16}O_3N_2S$, one of the vitamin B group, found in liver, egg yolk, and yeast

**bi·par·ti·san** (bī pär′tə z′n, -s′n) *adj.* of or representing two parties —**bi·par′ti·san·ship′** *n.*

**bi·par·tite** (bī pär′tīt) *adj.* [< L. < *bi-*, two + *partire*, to divide] 1. having two (corresponding) parts 2. with two involved 3. *Bot.* divided in two nearly to the base, as some leaves —**bi·par′tite·ly** *adv.* —**bi′par·ti′tion** (-tish′ən) *n.*

**bi·ped** (bī′ped) *n.* [< L. < *bi-* + *pedis*, gen. of *pes*, foot] any two-footed animal —*adj.* two-footed: also **bi·ped′al**

**bi·pet·al·ous** (bī pet′'l əs) *adj.* having two petals

**bi·pin·nate** (bī pin′āt, -it) *adj.* having pinnate leaflets on stems that grow opposite each other on a main stem

**bi·plane** (bī′plān′) *n.* an airplane with two sets of wings, one above the other

**bi·po·lar** (bī pō′lər) *adj.* 1. of or having two poles 2. of or involving both of the earth's polar regions 3. characterized by two opposed opinions, natures, etc. —**bi·po·lar·i·ty** (bī′pō lar′ə tē) *n.*

**bi·ra·cial** (bī rā′shəl) *adj.* consisting of or involving two races, esp. blacks and whites

**birch** (burch) *n.* [OE. *beorc*] 1. a tree having smooth bark easily peeled off in thin sheets, and hard, closegrained wood 2. this wood 3. a birch rod or bunch of twigs used for whipping —*vt.* to beat with a birch —*adj.* of birch

**bird** (burd) *n.* [OE. *bridd*, young bird] 1. any of a class of warmblooded, two-legged, egg-laying vertebrates with feathers and wings 2. a small game bird 3. same as CLAY PIGEON 4. a shuttlecock 5. [Slang] a person, esp. a mildly eccentric one 6. [Slang] a sound of disapproval made by fluttering the lips 7. [Slang] a rocket or guided missile —*vi.* 1. to shoot or catch birds 2. to engage in bird watching —**bird in the hand** something sure because already in one's possession: opposed to **bird in the bush**, something unsure, etc. —**birds of a feather** people with the same characteristics or tastes —**for the birds** [Slang] ridiculous, worthless, etc.

**bird·bath** (-bath′) *n.* a basinlike garden ornament for birds to bathe in

**bird·brain** (-brān′) *n.* [Colloq.] a stupid or silly person

**bird·call** (-kôl′) *n.* 1. the sound or song of a bird 2. an imitation of this 3. a device for imitating bird sounds

**bird dog** 1. a dog trained for hunting birds, as a pointer 2. [Colloq.] a person whose work is searching, as for missing persons, etc.

**bird·ie** (bur′dē) *n.* 1. a small bird: child's word 2. *Golf* a score of one stroke under par for a hole

**bird·lime** (burd′līm′) *n.* 1. a sticky substance spread on twigs to catch birds 2. anything that snares

**bird of paradise** 1. any of a number of brightly colored birds found in and near New Guinea 2. a tropical plant with brilliant orange and blue flowers in a form resembling a bird in flight

**bird of passage** 1. any migratory bird 2. anyone who travels or roams about constantly

**bird of prey** any bird, as the hawk, owl, etc., that kills and eats mammals and other birds

**bird·seed** (-sēd′) *n.* seed for feeding caged birds

**bird's-eye** (burdz′ī′) *n.* a cotton or linen cloth with a woven pattern of small, diamond-shaped figures —*adj.* 1. *a)* seen from above *b)* general; cursory 2. having markings like birds' eyes

**bird·shot** (burd′shät′) *n.* small shot for shooting birds

**bird watching** the hobby of observing wild birds in their habitat —**bird watcher**

**bi·re·frin·gence** (bī′ri frin′jəns) *n.* [< BI- + L. prp. of *refringere*: see REFRACT] the splitting of a light ray, generally by a crystal, into two components which travel at different velocities within the crystal —**bi′re·frin′gent** *adj.*

**bi·reme** (bī′rēm) *n.* [< L. < *bi-* + *remus*, oar] a galley having two rows of oars on each side

**bi·ret·ta** (bə ret′ə) *n.* [< It. < LL. dim. of L. *birrus*, a hood, cloak] a square cap with three projections and a tassel on top, worn by Roman Catholic clergy

**Bir·ken·head** (bur′k'n hed′) seaport in W England, at the mouth of the Mersey River: pop. 142,000

**birl** (burl) *vt., vi.* [? echoic, after *whirl, purl,* etc.] to revolve (a floating log) by treading

**birl·ing** (-iŋ) *n.* a competition among loggers in which each tries to keep his balance while revolving a floating log with his feet —**birl′er** *n.*

**Bir·ming·ham** (bur′miŋ əm *for 1;* -ham′ *for 2)* 1. city in C England: pop. 1,075,000 2. [after prec.] city in NC Ala.: pop. 284,000 (met. area 834,000)

**birr** (bur) *n., pl.* **birr′otch** (-äch) [Amharic, silver] *see* MONETARY UNITS, table Ethiopia

**birth** (burth) *n.* [< OE. *byrde* < *beran*, to BEAR¹] 1. the act of bringing forth offspring 2. the act of being born 3. origin or descent [a Spaniard *by birth*] 4. the beginning of anything 5. an inherited or natural inclination or talent [an actor *by birth*] —*vi., vt.* [Dial.] to give birth (to) —**give birth to** 1. to bring forth (offspring) 2. to be the cause or origin of; originate

**birth control** control of how many children a woman will have, as by contraception

**birth·day** (-dā′) *n.* 1. the day of a person's birth or a thing's beginning 2. the anniversary of this

**birth·mark** (-märk′) *n.* a skin blemish present at birth

**birth·place** (-plās′) *n.* 1. the place of one's birth 2. the place where something originated

**birth·rate** (-rāt′) *n.* the number of births per year per thousand of population in a given group: sometimes other units of time or population are used

**birth·right** (-rīt′) *n.* the rights that a person has because he was born in a certain family, nation, etc. or because he was the firstborn son

BIRETTA

fat, āpe, cär, ten, ēven, is, bīte; gō, hôrn, tool, look; oil, out; up, fur; get; joy; yet; chin; she; thin, *then*; zh, leisure; ŋ, ring; ə for *a* in *ago, e* in *agent, i* in *sanity, o* in *comply, u* in *focus;* as in *able* (ā′b'l); Fr. bål; ë, Fr. coeur; ö, Fr. feu; Fr. mon; ô, Fr. coq; ü, Fr. duc; r, Fr. cri; H, G. ich; kh, G. doch; ‡foreign; *hypothetical; < derived from. See inside front cover.

**birth·stone** (-stōn') *n.* a precious or semiprecious gem symbolizing the month of one's birth

**Bis·cay** (bis'kā, -kē), **Bay of** part of the Atlantic, north of Spain & west of France

**bis·cuit** (bis'kit) *n., pl.* **-cuits, -cuit** [OFr. *bescuit* < ML. < L. *bis*, twice + *coctum*, pp. of *coquere*, to cook] 1. [Chiefly Brit.] a cracker or cookie 2. a quick bread baked in small pieces 3. light brown; tan 4. pottery after the first firing and before glazing

**bi·sect** (bī sekt', bī'sekt) *vt.* [< ML. pp. of *bisecare* < L. *bi-* + *secare*, to cut] 1. to cut in two 2. *Geom.* to divide into two equal parts —*vi.* to divide; fork —**bi·sec'tion** *n.* —**bi·sec'tion·al** *adj.* —**bi·sec'tor** *n.*

**bi·sex·u·al** (bī sek'shoo wəl) *adj.* 1. of both sexes 2. having both male and female organs; hermaphroditic 3. sexually attracted to both sexes —*n.* one that is bisexual —**bi·sex'u·al'i·ty** (-wal'ə tē), **bi·sex'u·al·ism** *n.* —**bi·sex'u·al·ly** *adv.*

**bish·op** (bish'əp) *n.* [< OE. *bisceop* < LL. < Gr. *episkopos*, overseer < *epi-*, upon + *skopein*, to look] 1. a highranking Christian clergyman usually supervising a diocese or church district 2. a chessman that can move only diagonally

**bish·op·ric** (bish'ə prik) *n.* the district, office, authority, or rank of a bishop

**Bis·marck** (biz'märk) [after ff.] capital of N.Dak., on the Missouri River: pop. 44,000

**Bis·marck** (biz'märk), **Prince Otto von** 1815–98; Prussian chancellor of Germany (1871–90)

**bis·muth** (biz'məth) *n.* [< G. *wismut* < ?] a hard, brittle, metallic chemical element used in low-melting alloys, medical compounds, etc.: symbol, Bi; at. wt., 208.980; at. no., 83

**bi·son** (bī's'n, -z'n) *n., pl.* **bi'sons** [Fr. < L. < Gmc. hyp. *wisunt*] any of several four-legged bovine mammals with a shaggy mane, short, curved horns, and a humped back, as the American buffalo

**bisque¹** (bisk) *n.* [Fr.] 1. a rich, thick, creamy soup made from shellfish or from rabbit, fowl, etc. 2. a thick, strained, creamy vegetable soup

**bisque²** (bisk) *n.* 1. biscuit ceramic ware left unglazed in the finished state 2. a red-yellow color

**bis·ter, bis·tre** (bis'tər) *n.* [Fr. *bistre*] 1. a yellowish-brown to dark-brown pigment made from the soot of burned wood 2. a color in this range

BISON (5½–6 ft. high at shoulder)

**bis·tro** (bis'trō, bēs'-) *n., pl.* **-tros** [Fr.] a small nightclub or bar

**bi·sul·fate** (bī sul'fāt) *n.* an acid sulfate; compound containing the monovalent HSO₄– radical

**bi·sul·fide** (bī sul'fīd) *n.* same as DISULFIDE

**bit¹** (bit) *n.* [< OE. *bite*, a bite < *bitan*, to bite] 1. the metal mouthpiece on a bridle, used for controlling the horse 2. anything that curbs or controls 3. the part of a key that actually turns the lock 4. the cutting part of any tool 5. a drilling or boring tool for use in a brace, drill press, etc. —*vt.* **bit'ted, bit'ting** to put a bit into the mouth of (a horse)

**bit²** (bit) *n.* [< OE. *bita*, a piece < *bitan*, to bite] 1. *a)* a small piece or quantity *b)* a limited degree: used with *a* and having adverbial force [a *bit* bored] *c)* a short time 2. [Colloq.] an amount equal to 12½ cents: now usually in *two bits, four bits*, etc. 3. a small part, as in a play —*adj.* very small [a *bit* role] —**bit by bit** little by little; gradually —**do one's bit** to do one's share —**every bit** altogether; entirely

**bit³** (bit) *n.* [*b(inary) (dig)it*] a single character in a binary number system; specif., a unit of information equal to the amount of information obtained by learning which of two equally likely events occurred

**bitch** (bich) *n.* [< OE. *bicce*] 1. the female of the dog, wolf, etc. 2. a bad-tempered, malicious, or promiscuous woman: a coarse term of contempt 3. [Slang] a complaint —*vi.* [Slang] to complain —**bitch'i·ness** *n.* —**bitch'y** *adj.* **bitch'i·er, bitch'i·est**

**bite** (bīt) *vt.* **bit** (bit), **bit·ten** (bit''n) or **bit, bit'ing** [< OE. *bitan*] 1. to seize or cut with or as with the teeth 2. to cut into, as with a sharp weapon 3. to sting, as an insect 4. to hurt in a sharp, stinging way 5. to eat into; corrode 6. to seize or possess [*bitten* by a lust for fame] —*vi.* 1. *a)* to press or snap the teeth (*into, at*, etc.) *b)* to have a tendency to do this 2. to cause a biting sensation 3. to press hard; grip [the tires *bit* into the snow] 4. to seize a bait 5. to be caught, as by a trick —*n.* 1. the act of biting 2. biting quality; sting 3. a wound or sting from biting 4. *a)* a mouthful *b)* a light meal or snack 5. a tight hold or grip 6. the way the upper and lower teeth meet 7. [Colloq.] an amount cut off or sum deducted —**bite the bullet** to confront a painful situation with fortitude or stoicism —**put the**

**bite on** [Slang] to press for a loan, gift, or bribe of money —**bit'er** *n.*

**bit·ing** (bīt'iŋ) *adj.* 1. cutting; sharp 2. sarcastic —**bit'ing·ly** *adv.*

**biting midge** a tiny fly which has piercing and sucking mouthparts

**bitt** (bit) *n.* [< ?] *Naut.* any of the deck posts, usually in pairs, around which ropes or cables are fastened —*vt.* to wind around a bitt

**bit·ter** (bit'ər) *adj.* [< OE. < base of *bitan*, to bite] 1. having a sharp, often unpleasant taste; acrid 2. causing or showing sorrow, pain, etc. 3. sharp; harsh; piercing 4. characterized by hatred, resentment, etc. —*adv.* in a bitter way —*n.* 1. something bitter [take the *bitter* with the sweet] 2. [Brit.] bitter, strongly hopped ale: cf. BITTERS —**bit'ter·ly** *adv.* —**bit'ter·ness** *n.*

**bit·tern** (bit'ərn) *n., pl.* **-terns, -tern**: see PLURAL, II, D, 1 [< OFr. *butor*, prob. < L. *butio*] a wading bird of the heron family, the male of which has a resounding, thumping call

**bit·ter·root** (bit'ər rōōt', -root') *n.* a plant of W N. America having fleshy, edible roots and white or pink flowers

**bit·ters** (bit'ərz) *n.pl.* a liquor containing bitter herbs, roots, etc. and usually alcohol, used as a tonic and for flavoring in some cocktails

**bit·ter·sweet** (bit'ər swēt') *n.* 1. a N. American woody vine bearing clusters of orange fruits which open to expose the red seeds 2. an old-world climbing vine of the nightshade family, with purple flowers and poisonous, red berries —*adj.* 1. both bitter and sweet 2. pleasant with sad overtones

**bi·tu·men** (bi tōō'mən, bī-; -tyōō'-) *n.* [L. < Celt.] any of several substances obtained as asphaltic residue in the distillation of coal tar, petroleum, etc., or occurring as natural asphalt —**bi·tu'mi·nize'** (-mə nīz') *vt.* **-nized', -niz'ing** —**bi·tu'mi·nous** *adj.*

**bituminous coal** coal that yields pitch or tar when it burns; soft coal

**bi·va·lent** (bī vā'lənt, biv'ə-) *adj.* 1. having two valences 2. having a valence of two —**bi·va'lence, bi·va'len·cy** *n.*

**bi·valve** (bī'valv') *n.* any mollusk having a shell of two parts, or valves, hinged together, as a mussel, clam, etc. —*adj.* having such a shell: also **bi'valved'**

**biv·ou·ac** (biv'wak, -oo wak') *n.* [Fr. < OHG. *biwacht*, outpost < *bi-*, by + *wacht*, a guard] a temporary encampment (esp. of soldiers) in the open, with only improvised shelter —*vi.* **-acked, -ack·ing** to encamp in the open

**bi·week·ly** (bī wēk'lē) *adj., adv.* 1. once every two weeks 2. twice a week: in this sense, *semiweekly* is the preferred term —*n., pl.* **-lies** a publication that appears once every two weeks

**bi·year·ly** (bī yir'lē) *adj., adv.* 1. once every two years; biennial(ly) 2. twice a year: in this sense, *semiyearly, semiannual(ly)*, or *biannual(ly)* is preferred

**bi·zarre** (bi zär') *adj.* [Fr. < It. < Sp. *bizarro*, bold < Basque *bizar*, a beard] 1. odd in manner, appearance, etc.; grotesque; queer; eccentric 2. unexpected and unbelievable; fantastic —**bi·zarre'ly** *adv.* —**bi·zarre'ness** *n.*

**Bi·zet** (bē zā'), **Georges** (zhôrzh) (born *Alexandre César Léopold Bizet*) 1838–75; Fr. composer

**Bk** *Chem.* berkelium

**bk.** *pl.* **bks.** 1. bank 2. block 3. book

**bkg.** banking

**bkt.** 1. basket(s) 2. bracket

**bl.** 1. bale(s) 2. barrel(s) 3. black

**B/L** *pl.* **BS/L** bill of lading

**B.L.** Bachelor of Laws

**blab** (blab) *vt., vi.* **blabbed, blab'bing** [ME. *blabben*: see ff.] 1. to give away (a secret) in idle chatter 2. to chatter; prattle —*n.* 1. loose chatter; gossip 2. a person who blabs

**blab·ber** (-ər) *vt., vi.* [ME. *blabberen*, freq. of *blabben*, of echoic origin] [Dial. or Colloq.] to blab or babble —*n.* a person who blabs: also [Colloq.] **blab'ber·mouth'** (-mouth')

**black** (blak) *adj.* [OE. *blæc*] 1. opposite to white; of the color of coal: see COLOR 2. having dark-colored skin and hair; esp., Negro 3. *a)* totally without light; in complete darkness *b)* very dark 4. without cream, milk, etc.: said of coffee 5. soiled; dirty 6. wearing black clothing 7. evil; wicked 8. disgraceful 9. sad; dismal 10. sullen or angry 11. without hope [a *black* future] 12. humorous or satirical in a morbid or cynical way [*black* comedy] —*n.* 1. *a)* black color *b)* a black pigment, dye, etc. 2. black clothes, esp. when worn in mourning 3. a person with dark-colored skin; esp., a Negro: *black* is now the generally preferred term 4. complete darkness —*vt., vi.* 1. to blacken 2. to polish with blacking —**black out** 1. to cover (writing, etc.) as with black pencil marks 2. to cause a blackout in 3. to lose consciousness —**in the black** operating at a profit —**black'ish** *adj.* —**black'ly** *adv.* —**black'ness** *n.*

**black-and-blue** (-ən blōō') *adj.* discolored from congestion of blood under the skin, as a bruise

**black and white** writing or print /to put an agreement down in *black and white]*

**black art** *same as* BLACK MAGIC

**black·ball** (-bôl′) *n.* a secret ballot or vote against a person or thing —*vt.* **1.** to vote against; esp., to vote to exclude **2.** to ostracize

**black bass** (bas) any of various freshwater game fishes of N. America

**black bear 1.** the common N. American bear **2.** any of several dark-colored bears of Asia

**black belt** a black-colored belt awarded to an expert in judo or karate

**black·ber·ry** (-ber′ē) *n., pl.* **-ries 1.** the fleshy, purple or black, edible fruit of various brambles of the rose family **2.** a bush or vine bearing this fruit

**black·bird** (-burd′) *n.* any of various birds the male of which is almost entirely black, as the red-winged blackbird, English thrush, etc.

**black·board** (-bôrd′) *n.* a smooth, usually dark surface of slate or other material on which to write with chalk

**black·bod·y** (-bäd′ē) *n.* an ideal surface or body that can absorb all radiation striking it

**black book** a book with the names of those blacklisted

**black·cap** (-kap′) *n.* **1.** a bird with a black crown, as the chickadee **2.** *same as* BLACK RASPBERRY

**black·cock** (-käk′) *n., pl.* **-cocks′, -cock′:** see PLURAL, II, D, 1 the male of the black grouse

**black·damp** (-damp′) *n.* a suffocating gas, a mixture of carbon dioxide and nitrogen, found in mines

**Black Death** a deadly disease, probably bubonic plague, which devastated Europe and Asia in the 14th cent.

**black·en** (blak′′n) *vi.* to become black or dark —*vt.* **1.** to make black; darken **2.** to slander; defame; vilify —**black′-en·er** *n.*

**black eye 1.** a discoloration of the skin surrounding an eye, resulting from a sharp blow or contusion **2.** [Colloq.] bad reputation; dishonor

**black-eyed pea** (blak′īd′) *same as* COWPEA (sense 2)

**black-eyed Susan** a N. American wildflower with yellow ray flowers about a dark, cone-shaped center

**black·face** (blak′fās′) *adj.* having a black face —*n.* black makeup used by performers, as in minstrel shows, in gross caricature of Negroes

**black flag** the flag of piracy, usually with a white skull and crossbones on a black background

**Black·foot** (-foot′) *n.* **1.** *pl.* **-feet′, -foot′** any member of an Indian tribe consisting of three subtribes of Montana, Alberta, and Saskatchewan **2.** their Algonquian language

**Black Forest** heavily wooded, mountainous region in SW Germany

**black grouse** a large grouse of Europe and Asia: the male is almost entirely black

**black·guard** (blag′ärd, -ärd) *n.* [BLACK + GUARD] a scoundrel; villain —*adj.* vulgar, abusive, etc. —*vt.* to abuse with words; revile —**black′guard·ly** *adj., adv.*

**black·head** (blak′hed′) *n.* **1.** any of various birds black about the head **2.** a black-tipped plug of dried fatty matter clogging a skin pore

**black·heart·ed** (-här′tid) *adj.* wicked; evil

**Black Hills** mountainous region in SW S.Dak. & NE Wyo.

**black hole** a hypothetical body in space, supposed to be an invisible collapsed star so condensed that neither light nor matter can escape its gravitational field

**black·ing** (-in) *n.* a black polish, as for shoes

**black·jack** (-jak′) *n.* [see JACK-] **1.** a small, leathercovered bludgeon with a flexible handle **2.** the card game TWENTY-ONE —*vt.* **1.** to hit with a blackjack **2.** to coerce

**black·list** (-list′) *n.* a list of censured persons being discriminated against, refused employment, etc. —*vt.* to put on a blacklist

**black lung (disease)** a disease of the lungs caused by the continual inhalation of coal dust

**black magic** magic with an evil purpose; sorcery

**black·mail** (-māl′) *n.* [lit., black rent < OE. *mal*, lawsuit < ON. *mal*, discussion; infl. by OFr. *maille*, a coin] **1.** payment extorted to prevent disclosure of information that could bring disgrace **2.** extortion of such payment —*vt.* **1.** to get or try to get blackmail from **2.** to coerce (*into* doing something) as by threats —**black′mail′er** *n.*

**black mark** an unfavorable item in one's record

**black market** a place or system for selling goods illegally, esp. in violation of rationing —**black′-mar′ket** *vt., vi.* —**black marketeer (or marketer)**

**Black Muslim** a member of a militant Islamic sect of American blacks that advocates racial separation: members of the sect call themselves simply "Muslims"

**black nationalism** a movement for establishing a separate nation of blacks within the U.S.

**black·out** (-out′) *n.* **1.** the extinguishing of all stage lights to end a play or scene **2.** a concealing of all lights that might be visible to enemy air raiders at night **3.** a temporary loss of electricity in an area because of a failure in its generation or transmission **4.** a temporary loss of consciousness **5.** a loss of memory of an event **6.** suppression or concealment, as of news by censorship

**black pepper** a hot seasoning made by grinding the whole dried, black berries of the pepper plant

**Black·pool** (blak′pool′) city in NW England, on the Irish Sea: pop. 148,000

**black power** political and economic power sought by black Americans in the struggle for civil rights

**black raspberry** a shrub of the rose family, bearing juicy, purple-black fruits

**Black Sea** sea surrounded by the European U.S.S.R., Asia Minor, & the Balkan Peninsula

**black sheep** a person regarded as not so respectable as the rest of his family or group

**Black Shirt** a member of any fascist organization (specif., of the Italian Fascist party) having a black-shirted uniform: also **Black′shirt′** *n.*

**black·smith** (blak′smith′) *n.* a smith who works in iron, making and fitting horseshoes, etc.

**black·snake** (-snāk′) *n.* a slender, harmless, black or dark-colored snake of the U.S.

**Black·stone** (blak′stōn′; *Brit.* -stən), Sir **William** 1723–80; Eng. jurist & writer on law

**black·strap molasses** (blak′strap′) crude, dark molasses

**black tea** tea withered and fermented before being dried by heating

**black·thorn** (-thôrn′) *n.* **1.** a thorny, white-flowered shrub with blue-black, plumlike fruit; sloe **2.** a walking stick made of its stem

**black tie 1.** a black bow tie, properly worn with a tuxedo **2.** a tuxedo and the proper accessories

**black·top** (blak′täp′) *n.* a bituminous mixture, usually asphalt, used as a surface for roads, etc. —*vt.* **-topped′, -top′-ping** to cover with blacktop

**black walnut 1.** a tall walnut tree of E N. America **2.** its hard, heavy, dark-brown wood, used in making furniture, etc. **3.** its edible, oily nut

**black widow** an American spider the female of which has a black body with red markings underneath, and a very poisonous bite: the female sometimes eats its mate

**blad·der** (blad′ər) *n.* [OE. *blæddre*] **1.** a bag of membranous tissue in the bodies of many animals, that inflates to receive and contain liquids or gases; esp., the **urinary bladder** in the pelvic cavity, which holds urine flowing from the kidneys **2.** a bag, etc. resembling this **3.** an air sac, as in some water plants —**blad′der·y** *adj.*

**blad·der·wort** (-wurt′) *n.* a plant growing in or near water and having leaves with bladders on them that trap small insects and crustaceans

**blade** (blād) *n.* [OE. *blæd*] **1.** *a)* the leaf of a plant, esp. of grass *b)* the flat, expanded part of a leaf; lamina **2.** a broad, flat surface, as of an oar **3.** a flat bone /the shoulder *blade]* **4.** the cutting part of a knife, tool, etc. **5.** the metal runner of an ice skate **6.** a sword or a swordsman **7.** a gay, dashing young man **8.** *Phonet.* the flat part of the tongue, behind the tip —*adj.* designating or of various cuts of meat from the shoulder blade section —**blad′ed** *adj.*

**blah** (blä) *n., interj.* [Slang] nonsense —*adj.* [Slang] **1.** unappetizing **2.** dull, lifeless, etc.

**blain** (blān) *n.* [< OE. *blegen*] a pustule or blister

**Blake** (blāk) **William** 1757–1827; Eng. poet & artist

**blam·a·ble, blame·a·ble** (blām′ə b'l) *adj.* that deserves blame; culpable —**blam′a·bly** *adv.*

**blame** (blām) *vt.* **blamed, blam′ing** [< OFr. < LL. *blasphemare*, BLASPHEME] **1.** to accuse of being at fault; condemn (*for* something) **2.** to find fault with **3.** to put the responsibility of (an error, fault, etc. *on*) —*n.* **1.** a blaming; condemnation **2.** responsibility for a fault or wrong **3.** [Archaic] fault —**be to blame** to be blamable —**blame′ful** *adj.* —**blame′ful·ly** *adv.* —**blame′ful·ness** *n.* —**blame′less** *adj.* —**blame′less·ly** *adv.* —**blame′less·ness** *n.*

**blame·wor·thy** (blām′wur′thē) *adj.* deserving to be blamed —**blame′wor′thi·ness** *n.*

**Blanc** (blän), **Mont** (môn) mountain in E France: highest peak in the Alps: 15,781 ft.

**blanch** (blanch) *vt.* [OFr. *blanchir* < *blanc*: see BLANK] **1.** to make white; bleach **2.** to make pale **3.** to scald (vegetables, almonds, etc.), as for removing the skins —*vi.* to turn white or pale —**blanch′er** *n.*

**Blanche, Blanch** (blanch) [Fr., lit., white, fem. of *blanc*: see BLANK] a feminine name

**blanc·mange** (blə mänzh′, -mänj′) *n.* [Fr. < *blanc*, white + *manger*, to eat] a sweet, molded, jellylike dessert made with starch or gelatin, milk, etc.

**bland** (bland) *adj.* [< L. *blandus*, mild] **1.** pleasantly smooth; agreeable; suave **2.** *a)* mild and soothing; not sharp, harsh, etc. *b)* tasteless, insipid, dull, etc. —**bland′ly** *adv.* —**bland′ness** *n.*

**blan·dish** (blan′dish) *vt., vi* [< OFr. < L. *blandiri*, to flatter < prec.] to flatter or coax in persuading; cajole —**blan′dish·er** *n.* —**blan′dish·ment** *n.*

**blank** (blaŋk) *adj.* [OFr. *blanc*, white < Frank.] **1.** *a)* not written on; not marked *[a blank paper]* *b)* having empty spaces to be filled in **2.** having an empty or vacant look **3.** empty of thought *[a blank mind]* **4.** utter; complete *[a blank denial]* **5.** lacking certain elements or characteristics —*n.* **1.** an empty space, esp. one to be filled out in a printed form **2.** such a printed form **3.** an empty place or time; void **4.** a piece of metal, etc. to be finished by stamping or marking **5.** a lottery ticket that fails to win **6.** a powder-filled cartridge without a bullet: in full, **blank cartridge** —*vt.* to hold (an opponent) scoreless in a game —**blank out** to cancel or obscure as by covering over —**draw a blank** [Colloq.] **1.** to be unsuccessful in an attempt **2.** to be unable to remember a particular thing —**blank′ly** *adv.* —**blank′ness** *n.*

**blank check** a check carrying a signature only and allowing the bearer to fill in any amount

**blan·ket** (blaŋ′kit) *n.* [< OFr. dim. of *blanc*, white] **1.** a large, soft piece of cloth used for warmth, esp. as a bed cover **2.** anything like a blanket *[a blanket of leaves]* —*adj.* covering a group of conditions or items *[a blanket insurance policy]* —*vt.* **1.** to cover, as with a blanket **2.** to apply uniformly to: said of rates **3.** to suppress; obscure *[a powerful radio station blankets a weaker one]*

**blank verse** unrhymed verse; esp., unrhymed verse having five iambic feet per line

**blare** (bler) *vt., vi.* **blared, blar′ing** [ME. *bleren*, to bellow] **1.** to sound out with loud, trumpetlike tones **2.** to exclaim loudly —*n.* **1.** a loud, brassy sound **2.** harsh brilliance or glare

**blar·ney** (blär′nē) *n.* [see ff.] smooth talk used in flattering or coaxing —*vt., vi.* **-neyed, -ney·ing** to use blarney (on)

**Blarney stone** a stone in Blarney Castle in the county of Cork, Ireland, said to impart skill in blarney to those who kiss it

**bla·sé** (blä zā′, blä′zā) *adj.* [Fr., pp. of *blaser*, to satiate] having indulged in pleasure so much as to be unexcited by it; satiated and bored

**blas·pheme** (blas fēm′, blas′fēm) *vt.* **-phemed′, -phem′ing** [< OFr. < LL. < Gr. *blasphēmein*, to speak evil of] **1.** to speak irreverently or profanely of or to (God or sacred things) **2.** to curse or revile —*vi.* to utter blasphemy —**blas·phem′er** *n.*

**blas·phe·my** (blas′fə mē) *n., pl.* **-mies** [see prec.] **1.** words or action showing disrespect or scorn for God or anything held sacred **2.** any irreverent or disrespectful remark or action —**blas′phe·mous** *adj.* —**blas′phe·mous·ly** *adv.*

**blast** (blast) *n.* [< OE. *blæst*] **1.** a gust of wind; strong rush of air **2.** the sound of a sudden rush of air or gas, as through a trumpet **3.** the steady current of air forced into a blast furnace **4.** an abrupt and damaging influence; blight **5.** *a)* an explosion, as of dynamite *b)* a charge of explosive causing this **6.** [Slang] a gay, hilarious time; esp., a wild party —*vi.* **1.** to make a loud, harsh sound **2.** to set off explosives, gunfire, etc. **3.** to suffer from a blight —*vt.* **1.** to damage or destroy by or as if by a blight; wither **2.** to blow up with an explosive; explode **3.** [Colloq.] to criticize sharply **4.** *Sports* to hit (a ball) with great, driving force —**blast off** to take off with explosive force and begin its flight, as a rocket —**(at) full blast** at full speed or capacity —**blast′er** *n.*

**-blast** (blast) [< Gr. *blastos*, a sprout] *a combining form meaning* formative, embryonic

**blast·ed** (blas′tid) *adj.* **1.** blighted; withered; destroyed **2.** damned; confounded

**blast furnace** a smelting furnace into which a blast of air is forced from below for intense heat

**blast·off, blast-off** (blast′ôf′) *n.* the launching of a rocket, space vehicle, etc.

**blas·tu·la** (blas′choo lə) *n., pl.* **-las, -lae′** (-lē′) [ModL. dim. < Gr. *blastos*, a germ, sprout] an embryo at the stage of development in which it consists typically of a single layer of cells around a central cavity —**blas′tu·lar** *adj.*

**blat** (blat) *vi.* **blat′ted, blat′ting** [var. of BLEAT] to bleat —*vt.* to blurt out —*n.* a blatting sound

**bla·tant** (blāt′'nt) *adj.* [coined by E. Spenser; prob. < L. *blaterare*, to babble] **1.** disagreeably loud; noisy **2.** glaringly conspicuous or obtrusive —**bla′tan·cy** *n., pl.* **-cies** —**bla′tant·ly** *adv.*

**blath·er** (blath′ər) *n.* [ON. *blathr*] foolish talk —*vi., vt.* to chatter foolishly —**blath′er·er** *n.*

**blath·er·skite** (-skīt′) *n.* a talkative, foolish person

**blaze¹** (blāz) *n.* [< OE. *blæse*] **1.** a brilliant burst of flame; strongly burning fire **2.** any very bright light or glare **3.** a sudden or spectacular outburst *[a blaze of oratory]* **4.** a brightness; vivid display —*vi.* **blazed, blaz′ing 1.** to burn rapidly or brightly **2.** to give off a strong light; glare **3.** to be deeply stirred, as with anger —**blaze away** to fire a gun rapidly several times

**blaze²** (blāz) *n.* [< ON. *blesi*] **1.** a white spot on an animal's face **2.** a mark made on a tree by cutting off a piece of bark —*vt.* **blazed, blaz′ing** to mark (a tree or trail) with blazes —**blaze a way** (or **path**, etc.) in to pioneer in

**blaze³** (blāz) *vt.* **blazed, blaz′ing** [ME. *blasen*, to blow < OE. or ON.] to make known publicly

**blaz·er** (blā′zər) *n.* [< BLAZE¹ + -ER] a lightweight sports jacket, often brightly colored or striped

**bla·zon** (blā′z'n) *n.* [OFr. *blason*, a shield] **1.** a coat of arms **2.** showy display —*vt.* **1.** to make widely known; proclaim (often with *forth, out,* or *abroad*) **2.** to describe or portray (coats of arms) **3.** *a)* to portray in colors *b)* to adorn colorfully or showily —**bla′zon·er** *n.* —**bla′zon·ment** *n.* —**bla′zon·ry** *n., pl.* **-ries**

**bldg.** building

**bleach** (blēch) *vt., vi.* [OE. *blæcan* < *blac*, pale] to make or become white or colorless by means of chemicals or by exposure to sunlight —*n.* **1.** a bleaching **2.** a substance used for bleaching —**bleach′er** *n.*

**bleach·ers** (-ərz) *n.pl.* [< prec., in reference to the effects of exposure] seats or benches in tiers without a roof, for spectators at sporting events

**bleak** (blēk) *adj.* [< ON. *bleikr*, pale] **1.** exposed to wind and cold; unsheltered **2.** cold and cutting; harsh **3.** not cheerful or hopeful; gloomy —**bleak′ly** *adv.* —**bleak′ness** *n.*

**blear** (blir) *adj.* [< ME. *bleren*, to have watery eyes] **1.** made dim by tears, mucus, etc.: said of eyes **2.** blurred; dim —*vt.* **1.** to dim (the eyes) with tears, mucus, etc. **2.** to blur

**blear·y** (-ē) *adj.* **blear′i·er, blear′i·est 1.** dim or blurred **2.** having blurred vision —**blear′i·ly** *adv.* —**blear′i·ness** *n.*

**blear·y-eyed** (-īd′) *adj.* having bleary eyes or blurred vision: also **blear′eyed′**

**bleat** (blēt) *vi.* [< OE. *blætan*] **1.** to make the cry of a sheep, goat, or calf **2.** to make a sound like this cry —*vt.* to say in a bleating voice —*n.* a bleating cry or sound —**bleat′er** *n.*

**bleed** (blēd) *vi.* **bled** (bled), **bleed′ing** [< OE. *bledan* < *blod*, blood] **1.** to emit or lose blood **2.** to suffer wounds or die in a battle or cause **3.** to feel pain, grief, or sympathy; suffer **4.** to ooze sap, juice, etc., as bruised plants **5.** to run together, as dyes in wet cloth **6.** to come through a covering coat of paint —*vt.* **1.** to draw blood from **2.** to ooze (sap, juice, etc.) **3.** to empty of liquid, air, or gas **4.** to take sap or juice from **5.** [Colloq.] to extort money from

**bleed·er** (-ər) *n.* a person who bleeds profusely; hemophiliac

**bleeding heart 1.** a plant with fernlike leaves and drooping clusters of pink, heart-shaped flowers **2.** a person regarded as too sentimental or too liberal in his approach to social problems

**bleep** (blēp) *n., vi.* [echoic] *same as* BEEP —*vt.* to censor (something said), as in a telecast, by substituting a beep

**blem·ish** (blem′ish) *vt.* [<OFr. *blesmir*, to injure] to mar, as by some flaw or fault —*n.* **1.** a mark that mars the appearance, as a stain or nick **2.** any flaw, defect, or shortcoming

**blench¹** (blench) *vt., vi.* [var. of BLANCH] to make or become pale; whiten

**blench²** (blench) *vi.* [< OE. *blencan*, to deceive] to shrink back, as in fear; flinch

**blend** (blend) *vt.* **blend′ed** or **blent, blend′ing** [< OE. *blendan* & ON. *blanda*, to mix] **1.** to mix or mingle (varieties of tea, tobacco, etc.) **2.** to mix or fuse thoroughly, so the parts are no longer distinct —*vi.* **1.** to mix or merge **2.** to shade gradually into each other, as colors **3.** to go well together; harmonize —*n.* **1.** a blending **2.** a mixture of varieties *[a blend of coffee]* **3.** *Linguis.* a word formed by combining parts of other words (Ex.: *smog*) —**blend′er** *n.*

**blende** (blend) *n.* [G. < *blenden*, to blind, deceive] sphalerite or any of certain other sulfides

**blended whiskey** whiskey that is a blend of straight whiskey and neutral spirits or of two or more straight whiskeys

**blen·ny** (blen′ē) *n., pl.* **-nies, -ny:** see PLURAL, II, D, 1 [< L. < Gr. < *blenna*, slime] any of a number of small ocean fishes having long dorsal fins and a tapering body covered with a slimy substance —**blen′ni·oid′** (-ē oid′) *adj.*

**bless** (bles) *vt.* **blessed** or **blest, bless′ing** [< OE. *bletsian*, orig. to consecrate with blood < *blod*, blood] **1.** to make holy; hallow **2.** to ask divine favor for · **3.** to favor or endow (with) *[blessed* with health] **4.** to make happy or prosperous **5.** to praise or glorify **6.** to make the sign of the cross over or upon **7.** to protect from evil, harm, etc. —**bless me** (or **you, him,** etc.)! an exclamation of surprise, dismay, etc.

**bless·ed** (bles′id; *occas.* blest) *adj.* **1.** holy; sacred **2.** blissful; fortunate **3.** of or in eternal bliss: a title applied to one who has been beatified **4.** bringing joy —**bless′ed·ly** *adv.* —**bless′ed·ness** *n.*

**bless·ing** (-iŋ) *n.* **1.** an invocation or benediction **2.** a grace said before or after eating **3.** the gift of divine favor **4.** good wishes or approval **5.** a special benefit or favor

**blest** (blest) *alt. pt. & pp. of* BLESS —*adj.* blessed

**bleu cheese** (bloo; *Fr.* blö) *[Fr. bleu,* blue] *same as* BLUE CHEESE

**blew** (bloo) *pt. of* BLOW[1] & BLOW[3]

**blight** (blīt) *n.* [? < ON. *blikja,* turn pale] **1.** any parasite, insect, etc. that destroys or stunts plants **2.** any of several plant diseases, as mildew **3.** anything that destroys, prevents growth, frustrates, etc. —*vt.* **1.** to wither **2.** to destroy **3.** to frustrate —*vi.* to suffer blight

**blimp** (blimp) *n.* [echoic coinage] [Colloq.] a small, nonrigid or semirigid airship

**blind** (blīnd) *adj.* [OE.] **1.** without the power of sight; sightless **2.** of or for sightless persons **3.** not able or willing to notice or understand **4.** done without adequate directions or knowledge *[a blind* search] **5.** disregarding evidence, sound logic, etc. *[blind* faith] **6.** reckless; unreasonable **7.** hard to see; hidden *[a blind* driveway] **8.** dense; impenetrable *[a blind* hedge] **9.** closed at one end *[a blind* alley] **10.** not controlled by intelligence *[blind* destiny] **11.** *Aeron.* by the use of instruments only *[blind* flying] **12.** *Archit.* having no opening —*vt.* **1.** to make sightless **2.** to dazzle **3.** to deprive of the power of insight or judgment **4.** to make dim; obscure **5.** to hide —*n.* **1.** anything that obscures or prevents sight **2.** *a)* anything that keeps out light, as a window shade *b) same as* VENETIAN BLIND **3.** a place of concealment **4.** a decoy —*adv.* **1.** blindly **2.** recklessly **3.** sight unseen *[to buy a thing blind]* —**the blind** blind people —**blind′ly** *adv.* —**blind′ness** *n.*

**blind date** [Colloq.] **1.** a date arranged for a man and a woman previously unacquainted **2.** either of these persons

**blind·er** (blīn′dər) *n.* either of two flaps on a horse's bridle that shut out the side view

**blind·fold** (blīnd′fōld′) *vt.* [altered (after FOLD[1]) < ME. *blindfeld,* struck blind: see BLIND & FELL[2]] to cover the eyes of, as with a cloth —*n.* something used to cover the eyes —*adj.* **1.** with the eyes covered **2.** reckless

**blind·man's buff** (blīnd′manz buf′) *[buff,* contr. < BUFFET[1]] a game in which a blindfolded player has to catch and identify another: also **blind′man's bluff′** (bluf′)

**blind spot 1.** the small area, insensitive to light, in the retina of the eye where the optic nerve enters **2.** an area where vision is obscured **3.** a prejudice, or area of ignorance, that one has but is often unaware of

**blind trust** an arrangement whereby a person, as a public official, in an effort to avoid conflicts of interest places certain personal assets under the control of an independent trustee with the provision that the person is to have no knowledge of how those assets are managed

**blink** (bliŋk) *vi.* [ME. *blenken* (see BLENCH[2])] **1.** to wink quickly one or more times **2.** to flash on and off; twinkle **3.** to look with eyes half shut and winking —*vt.* to cause (eyes, light, etc.) to wink or blink —*n.* **1.** a blinking **2.** a glimmer —**blink at** to ignore or condone (a mistake) —**on the blink** [Slang] not working right; out of order

**blink·er** (-ər) *n.* **1.** a flashing warning light at crossings **2.** *same as* BLINDER

**blintz** (blints) *n.* [< Yid. < Russ. < *blin,* pancake] a thin pancake rolled with a filling of cottage cheese, etc.

**blip** (blip) *n.* [echoic of a brief sound] **1.** a luminous image on an oscilloscope **2.** a quick, sharp sound —*vt.* **blipped, blip′ping** *same as* BLEEP

**bliss** (blis) *n.* [OE. *bliths < blithe,* BLITHE] **1.** great joy or happiness **2.** spiritual joy —**bliss′ful** *adj.* —**bliss′ful·ly** *adv.* —**bliss′ful·ness** *n.*

**blis·ter** (blis′tər) *n.* [< Du. *bluister* or OFr. *blestre* < ON. *blastr]* **1.** a raised patch of skin filled with watery matter and caused by burning or rubbing **2.** anything resembling a blister —*vt.* **1.** to raise blisters on **2.** to lash with words —*vi.* to have or form blisters —**blis′ter·y** *adj.*

**blithe** (blīth, blith) *adj.* [OE.] gay; cheerful; carefree —**blithe′ly** *adv.* —**blithe′ness** *n.*

**blith·er·ing** (blith′ər iŋ) *adj. [blither,* var. of BLATHER] talking without sense; jabbering

**blithe·some** (blīth′səm, blith′-) *adj.* blithe; gay —**blithe′some·ly** *adv.* —**blithe′some·ness** *n.*

**B.Litt., B.Lit.** [L. *Baccalaureus Lit(t)erarum*] Bachelor of Letters (or Literature)

**blitz** (blits) *n.* [< ff.] a sudden, overwhelming attack —*vt.* to subject to a blitz; overwhelm

**blitz·krieg** (-krēg′) *n.* [G. < *blitz,* lightning + *krieg,* war] **1.** sudden, swift, large-scale offensive warfare intended to win a quick victory **2.** any sudden, overwhelming attack

**bliz·zard** (bliz′ərd) *n.* [dial. *bliz,* violent blow (? akin to G. *blitz,* lightning) + -ARD] a violent storm with driving snow and very cold winds

**blk.** **1.** black **2.** block **3.** bulk

**bloat**[1] (blōt) *vt., vi* [< ON. *blautr,* soaked] **1.** to swell, as with water or air **2.** to puff up, as with pride

**bloat**[2] (blōt) *vt.* [< ME. *blote,* soft with moisture < ON. *blautr:* see prec.] to cure (herring, etc.) by soaking in salt water and smoking

**bloat·er** (-ər) *n.* a fat herring or mackerel that has been bloated, or cured

**blob** (bläb) *n.* [echoic] **1.** a small drop or mass **2.** something of indefinite form

**bloc** (bläk) *n.* [Fr. & OFr. < LowG. *block,* log] a bipartisan group of legislators, or a group of nations, acting together in some common cause

**block** (bläk) *n.* [< MDu. or OFr. < LowG. *block:* see prec.] **1.** any large, solid piece of wood, stone, or metal **2.** a blocklike stand on which chopping, etc. is done **3.** an auctioneer's platform **4.** a mold upon which hats, etc. are shaped **5.** an obstruction or hindrance **6.** an interruption of a normal body function **7.** a pulley in a frame **8.** a large, hollow building brick **9.** a child's wooden or plastic toy brick **10.** a group of buildings **11.** *a)* a city square *b)* one side of a city square **12.** any number of things regarded as a unit **13.** *Printing* a piece of engraved wood, etc. with a design or picture **14.** *Sports* a legal thwarting of an opponent's play or movement —*vt.* **1.** to impede the passage or progress of; obstruct **2.** to stand in the way of; hinder **3.** to shape or mold on a block **4.** to strengthen or support with blocks **5.** to sketch with little detail (often with *out*) **6.** *Med.* to deaden (a nerve), esp. by anesthesia **7.** *Sports* to hinder (an opponent or his play) —**on the block** up for sale or auction —**block′age** *n.*

**block·ade** (blä kād′) *n.* [BLOCK + -ADE] **1.** a shutting off of a port or region by hostile troops or ships to prevent passage **2.** the troops or ships so used **3.** any strategic barrier —*vt.* **-ad′ed, -ad′ing** to subject to a blockade —**run the blockade** to go through a blockade —**block·ad′er** *n.*

**block and tackle** pulley blocks and ropes or cables, used for hoisting large, heavy objects

**block·bust·er** (-bus′tər) *n.* [Colloq.] **1.** a large, highly destructive aerial bomb **2.** a successful, heavily promoted movie, novel, etc.

**block·bust·ing** (-bus′tiŋ) *n.* [Colloq.] the practice of inducing the quick sale of homes by creating fear about a minority group moving into the neighborhood

**block·head** (-hed′) *n.* a stupid person

**block·house** (-hous′) *n.* **1.** formerly, a strong wooden fort with a projecting second story and openings in the walls to shoot from **2.** any building of squared timber or logs **3.** *Mil.* a small structure of concrete for defense or observation

**block·ish** (-ish) *adj.* stupid; dull —**block′ish·ly** *adv.*

**block·y** (-ē) *adj.* **block′i·er, block′i·est** **1.** having contrasting blocks or patches **2.** stocky; chunky —**block′i·ness** *n.*

**Bloem·fon·tein** (bloom′fän tān′) city in C South Africa: pop. 146,000

**bloke** (blōk) *n.* [< ?] [Chiefly Brit. Slang] a fellow; chap

**blond** (bländ) *adj.* [Fr. < ? Gmc.] **1.** having yellow or yellowish-brown hair, often with fair skin and blue or gray eyes **2.** yellow or yellowish-brown: said of hair **3.** light-colored *[blond* furniture] —*n.* a blond person —**blond′ness** *n.*

**blonde** (bländ) *adj. same as* BLOND —*n.* a blond woman or girl

**blood** (blud) *n.* [< OE. *blod]* **1.** *a)* the fluid, usually red, circulating in the heart, arteries, and veins of vertebrates *b)* a similar fluid in invertebrates **2.** the spilling of blood; murder **3.** the essence of life; lifeblood **4.** the sap of a plant **5.** passion, temperament, or disposition **6.** parental heritage; family line; lineage; ancestry **7.** kinship; family rela-

BLOCKHOUSE

---

tionship **8.** descent from nobility **9.** a descent from pure-bred stock **10.** a dandy **11.** people, esp. youthful people *[new blood in the firm]* —**bad blood** anger; hatred —**in cold blood 1.** with cruelty; unfeelingly **2.** dispassionately; deliberately —**make one's blood boil** to make one angry —**make one's blood run cold** to terrify one

**blood bank 1.** a place where whole blood or plasma is stored for future use in transfusion **2.** any reserve of such blood

**blood bath** a massacre; slaughter

**blood brother 1.** a brother by birth **2.** a person bound to one by the ceremony of mingling his blood with one's own —**blood brotherhood**

**blood count** the number of red corpuscles and white corpuscles in a given volume of blood

**blood·cur·dling** (-kurd′liŋ) *adj.* very frightening

**blood·ed** (blud′id) *adj.* **1.** having (a specified kind of) blood *[hot-blooded]* **2.** of fine stock or breed

**blood group** any of several groups into which human blood is classified

**blood·hound** (-hound′) *n.* any of a breed of large, keen-scented dogs used in tracking fugitives, etc.

**blood·less** (-ləs) *adj.* **1.** without blood **2.** without bloodshed **3.** anemic or pale **4.** having little energy or vitality —**blood′less·ly** *adv.* —**blood′less·ness** *n.*

**blood·let·ting** (-let′iŋ) *n.* **1.** the opening of a vein to remove blood; bleeding **2.** *same as* BLOODSHED

**blood·mo·bile** (-mō bēl′, -mə-) *n.* [BLOOD + (AUTO)MOBILE] a traveling unit equipped for collecting blood from donors for blood banks

**blood money 1.** money paid to a hired killer **2.** money paid as compensation for a murder **3.** money gotten ruthlessly through others' suffering

**blood poisoning** any of various diseases in which the blood contains microorganisms, their toxins, or other poisonous matter; septicemia

**blood pressure** the pressure exerted by the blood against the inner walls of the blood vessels

**blood pudding** a large sausage made of pig's blood and suet, enclosed in a casing

**blood·root** (-rōōt′, -root′) *n.* a N. American wildflower of the poppy family, with a white flower and a rootstock that yields a red juice

**blood·shed** (-shed′) *n.* the shedding of blood; killing

**blood·shot** (-shät′) *adj.* red because the small blood vessels are swollen or broken: said of an eye

**blood·stained** (-stānd′) *adj.* **1.** soiled or discolored with blood **2.** guilty of murder

**blood·stone** (-stōn′) *n.* a dark-green variety of quartz spotted with red jasper, used as a gem

**blood·stream** (-strēm′) *n.* the blood flowing through the circulatory system of a body

**blood·suck·er** (-suk′ər) *n.* **1.** an animal that sucks blood, esp. a leech **2.** a person who extorts from others all that he can —**blood′suck′ing** *adj., n.*

**blood·thirst·y** (-thur′stē) *adj.* eager to kill; murderous

**blood type** *same as* BLOOD GROUP

**blood typing** the classification of blood to determine compatible blood groups for transfusion

**blood vessel** a tube through which the blood circulates in the body; artery, vein, or capillary

**blood·y** (blud′ē) *adj.* **blood′i·er, blood′i·est 1.** of, like, or containing blood **2.** covered or stained with blood **3.** involving bloodshed **4.** bloodthirsty **5.** [Brit. Slang] cursed; damned: a vulgar usage —*adv.* [Brit. Slang] very: a vulgar usage —*vt.* **blood′ied, blood′y·ing** to cover or stain with blood —**blood′i·ly** *adv.* —**blood′i·ness** *n.*

**Bloody Mary** a drink of vodka with tomato juice

**bloom** (blōōm) *n.* [< ON. *blomi*, flowers] **1.** a flower; blossom **2.** flowers collectively, as of a plant **3.** the state or time of flowering **4.** the state or time of most health, vigor, etc. **5.** a youthful, healthy glow, as of the cheeks **6.** *a)* the powdery coating on some fruits or leaves *b)* a similar coating, as on new coins —*vi.* **1.** to bear flowers; blossom **2.** to be in one's prime; flourish **3.** to glow as with health —**bloom′ing** *adj.*

**bloom·er¹** (blōō′mər) *n.* **1.** a plant with reference to its blooming *[an early bloomer]* **2.** a person in his prime

**bloom·er²** (blōō′mər) *n.* [after Amelia J. *Bloomer* (1818–94), U.S. feminist who advocated it] **1.** formerly, a woman's costume consisting of a short skirt and loose trousers gathered at the ankles **2.** *[pl.] a)* baggy trousers gathered at the knee, formerly worn by women for athletics *b)* an undergarment somewhat like this

**Bloom·ing·ton** (blōō′miŋ tən) [? from abundance of flowering plants orig. found there] city in E Minn., near Minneapolis: pop. 82,000

**bloop** (blōōp) *vt.* [Slang] *Baseball* **1.** to hit (a ball) as a blooper **2.** to get (a hit) in this way

**bloop·er** (blōōp′ər) *n.* [echoic of a vulgar noise] [Slang] **1.** a

stupid mistake **2.** *Baseball* a ball batted so that it drops between the infield and outfield, usually for a hit

**blos·som** (bläs′əm) *n.* [< OE. *blostma*] **1.** a flower or bloom, esp. of a fruit-bearing plant **2.** a state or time of flowering —*vi.* **1.** to have or open into blossoms; bloom **2.** to begin to thrive or flourish; develop —**blos′som·y** *adj.*

**blot** (blät) *n.* [< ?] **1.** a spot or stain, esp. of ink **2.** anything that spoils or mars something **3.** a moral stain; disgrace —*vt.* **blot′ted, blot′ting 1.** to spot; stain **2.** to erase or get rid of *[memories blotted from one's mind]* **3.** to dry, as with blotting paper —*vi.* **1.** to make blots **2.** to become blotted **3.** to be absorbent —**blot out 1.** to darken or obscure **2.** to destroy

**blotch** (bläch) *n.* [? extension of BLOT] **1.** a discolored patch or blemish on the skin **2.** any large blot or stain —*vt.* to mark with blotches —**blotch′y** *adj.* **blotch′i·er, blotch′i·est**

**blot·ter** (blät′ər) *n.* **1.** a piece of blotting paper **2.** a book for recording events as they occur *[a police blotter is a record of arrests, etc.]*

**blotting paper** a thick, soft, absorbent paper used to dry a surface freshly written on in ink

**blouse** (blous, blouz) *n.* [Fr., workman's or peasant's smock] **1.** a loose, shirtlike garment extending to the waist, worn by women and children **2.** the coat or jacket of a military uniform **3.** a sailor's jumper —*vi., vt.* **bloused, blous′ing** to gather in and drape at the waistline

**blow¹** (blō) *vi.* **blew, blown, blow′ing** [< OE. *blawan*] **1.** to move with some force: said of the wind **2.** to send forth air, as with the mouth **3.** to pant; be breathless **4.** to sound by blowing or being blown **5.** to spout water and air, as whales do **6.** to be carried by the wind *[the paper blew away]* **7.** to be stormy **8.** to burst suddenly, as a tire, or melt, as a fuse (often with *out)* **9.** to lay eggs: said of flies **10.** [Colloq.] to brag; boast **11.** [Slang] to go away —*vt.* **1.** to force air from (a bellows, etc.) **2.** to send out (breath, etc.) from the mouth **3.** to force air onto, into, or through **4.** to drive by blowing **5.** *a)* to sound (a wind instrument) by blowing *b)* to make (a sound) by blowing **6.** to shape or form by blown air or gas **7.** to clear by blowing through **8.** to burst by an explosion **9.** to cause (a horse) to pant **10.** to melt (a fuse, etc.) **11.** [Colloq.] to spend (money) freely **12.** [Colloq.] to forget (one's lines) in a show **13.** [Slang] to go away from **14.** [Slang] to bungle and fail in —*n.* **1.** a blowing **2.** a blast of air **3.** a strong wind; gale —**blow hot and cold** to be favorable toward and then opposed to; vacillate —**blow in** [Slang] to arrive —**blow off** [Colloq.] to give vent to one's feelings, as by loud talking —**blow one's stack (or top or lid)** [Slang] to lose one's temper —**blow out 1.** to put out or be put out by blowing **2.** to blow (*vi.* 8) **3.** to dispel (itself) after a time: said of a storm —**blow over 1.** to move away, as rain clouds **2.** to be forgotten —**blow up 1.** to fill with air or gas **2.** to explode **3.** to arise and become intense, as a storm **4.** to enlarge (a photograph) **5.** to exaggerate (an incident, etc.) **6.** [Colloq.] to lose one's temper —**blow′er** *n.*

**blow²** (blō) *n.* [ME. *blowe*, akin to G. *bleuen*, to strike] **1.** a hard hit or stroke, as with the fist **2.** a sudden attack or forcible effort **3.** a sudden calamity or misfortune; shock —**at a (or one) blow** by one action —**come to blows** to begin fighting

**blow³** (blō) *vi.* **blew, blown, blow′ing** [OE. *blowan*] [Poet.] to bloom; blossom —*n.* a mass of blossoms

**blow-by** (-bī′) *adj.* designating or of a crankcase device that returns unburned gases to the engine for combustion so as to reduce air pollution

**blow-by-blow** (-bī′blō′) *adj.* told in great detail *[a blow-by-blow description]*

**blow-dry** (-drī′) *vt.* **-dried′, -dry′ing** to dry (wet hair) with an electric device (**blow′-dry′er**) that sends out a powerful stream of heated air —*n.* the act of blow-drying the hair

**blow·fish** (-fish′) *n., pl.* **-fish′, -fish′es:** see FISH *same as* PUFFER (sense 2)

**blow·fly** (-flī′) *n., pl.* **-flies′** [BLOW¹ (*vi.* 9) + FLY²] any of various two-winged flies that deposit eggs in meat, open wounds, etc.

**blow·gun** (-gun′) *n.* a long, tubelike weapon through which darts or pellets are blown

**blow·hard** (-härd′) *n.* [Slang] a loudly boastful person

**blow·hole** (-hōl′) *n.* **1.** a nostril in the top of the head of whales, etc., used for breathing **2.** a hole through which gas or air can escape **3.** a hole in the ice to which seals, etc. come for air

**blown** (blōn) *pp.* of BLOW¹ & BLOW³ —*adj.* **1.** swollen or bloated **2.** out of breath, as from exertion **3.** made by blowing or by using a blowpipe, etc.

**blow·out** (blō′out′) *n.* **1.** the bursting of a tire **2.** the melting of an electric fuse **3.** [Slang] a party, banquet, etc.

**blow·pipe** (-pīp′) *n.* **1.** a tube for forcing air or gas into a flame to increase its heat **2.** a metal tube used in blowing glass **3.** *same as* BLOWGUN

**blow·torch** (-tôrch′) *n.* a small gasoline torch that shoots out a hot flame intensified by a blast of air: used to melt metal, remove old paint, etc.

**blow·up** (-up′) *n.* **1.** an explosion **2.** an enlarged photograph **3.** [Colloq.] a hysterical outburst

**blow·y** (-ē) *adj.* **blow′i·er, blow′i·est** windy

**blowz·y** (blou′zē) *adj.* **blowz′i·er, blowz′i·est** [< obs. *blouze*, wench] **1.** fat, ruddy, and coarse-looking **2.** slovenly; sloppy Also **blows′y**

**BLS** Bureau of Labor Statistics

**bls. 1.** bales **2.** barrels

**B.L.S.** Bachelor of Library Science

**BLT** bacon, lettuce, and tomato (sandwich)

**blub·ber**[1] (blub′ər) *n.* [ME. *blober*, a bubble; prob. echoic] **1.** the fat of the whale and other sea mammals **2.** unsightly fat on the human body —**blub′ber·y** *adj.*

**blub·ber**[2] (blub′ər) *vi.* [ME. *bloberen*, to bubble (see prec.)] to weep loudly, like a child —*vt.* to say while blubbering —*n.* loud weeping —*adj.* thick or swollen —**blub′ber·er** *n.*

**blu·cher** (blōō′chər, -kər) *n.* [after G. L. von *Blücher* (1742–1819), Prussian field marshal] a kind of shoe in which the upper laps over the vamp, which is of one piece with the tongue

**bludg·eon** (bluj′n) *n.* [? altered < MFr. dim. of *bouge*, a club] a short club with a thick, heavy, or loaded end —*vt., vi.* **1.** to strike with or as with a bludgeon **2.** to bully or coerce

**blue** (blōō) *adj.* [< OFr. *bleu* < Frank. *blao*] **1.** having the color of the clear sky or the deep sea **2.** livid: said of the skin **3.** sad and gloomy; depressed or depressing **4.** puritanical; rigorous **5.** [Colloq.] indecent; risqué —*n.* **1.** the color of the clear sky or the deep sea **2.** any blue pigment or dye **3.** anything colored blue **4.** *a*) [*often* B-] one who wears a blue uniform *b*) [*pl.*] a sailor's blue uniform **5.** [*pl.*] [Colloq.] a depressed, unhappy feeling (with *the*) **6.** [*pl., also with sing. v.*] *a*) Negro folk music, or the jazz evolved from it, with minor harmonies, slow tempo, and melancholy words (often with *the*) *b*) a song in this style —*vt.* **blued, blu′ing** or **blue′ing 1.** to make blue **2.** to use bluing on or in —*vi.* to become blue —**once in a blue moon** very seldom —**out of the blue** as if from the sky; unexpectedly —**the blue 1.** the sky **2.** the sea —**blue′ness** *n.*

**blue baby** a baby born with cyanosis

**Blue·beard** (-bird′) a legendary character who married and murdered one wife after another

**blue·bell** (-bel′) *n.* any of various plants with blue, bell-shaped flowers

**blue·ber·ry** (-ber′ē, -bər ē) *n., pl.* **-ries 1.** a shrub bearing small, edible, blue-black berries with tiny seeds **2.** any of the berries

**blue·bird** (-bʉrd′) *n.* any of several small N. American songbirds: the male has a blue or bluish back and an orange or reddish breast

**blue blood 1.** descent from nobility or royalty **2.** a person of such descent; aristocrat: also **blue′blood′** *n.*

**blue·bon·net** (-bän′it) *n.* **1.** a wildflower with blue blossoms, common in the SW U.S. **2.** [Chiefly Scot.] a cornflower with blue blossoms Also **blue bonnet**

**blue book 1.** a book listing socially prominent people **2.** a blank booklet with a blue cover in which students write examination answers: also **blue′book′** *n.*

**blue·bot·tle** (-bät′'l) *n.* **1.** any of several plants with blue, bottle-shaped flowers, as the cornflower, grape hyacinth, etc. **2.** a large blowfly with a steel-blue abdomen

**blue cheese** a cheese similar to Roquefort, but usually made of cow's milk

**blue-chip** (-chip′) *adj.* [after the high-value *blue chips* of poker] **1.** designating a high-priced stock with a good record of earnings and price stability **2.** [Colloq.] excellent, valuable, etc.

**blue·coat** (-kōt′) *n.* a policeman

**blue-col·lar** (-käl′ər) *adj.* [from the color of many work shirts] designating or of industrial workers, esp. the semi-skilled and unskilled

**Blue Cross** a nonprofit health-insurance organization offering hospitalization, etc. to subscribers

**blue·fish** (-fish′) *n., pl.* **-fish′, -fish′es:** see FISH a bluish food fish, common along the Atlantic coast of N. America

**blue flag** any iris with blue flowers

**blue fox 1.** a mutant of the arctic fox, having bluish or smoky-gray fur **2.** this fur

**blue·gill** (-gil′) *n.* a bluish, freshwater sunfish

**blue·grass** (-gras′) *n.* **1.** any of various forage grasses, as Kentucky bluegrass **2.** [*often* B-] Southern string-band folk music

**blue gum** a large Australian tree, grown extensively in California, with aromatic leaves and a smooth bark that peels off in strips

**blue·ing** (-in) *n. same as* BLUING

**blue·ish** (-ish) *adj. same as* BLUISH

**blue·jack·et** (-jak′it) *n.* an enlisted man in the U.S. or British navy

**blue jay** a noisy, often crested, American bird with a bluish upper part: also **blue′jay′** *n.*

**blue law** a puritanical law, esp. one prohibiting certain activities on Sunday

**blue·nose** (-nōz′) *n.* [Colloq.] a puritanical person

**blue-pen·cil** (-pen′s'l) *vt.* **-pen′ciled** or **-pen′cilled, -pen′cil·ing** or **-pen′cil·ling** to edit, cross out, etc. with or as with a blue pencil

**blue·point** (-point′) *n.* [< *Blue Point*, Long Island] a small oyster, usually eaten raw

**blue·print** (-print′) *n.* **1.** a photographic reproduction in white on a blue background, as of architectural plans **2.** any detailed plan —*vt.* to make a blueprint of

**blue-rib·bon** (-rib′ən) *adj.* [Colloq.] **1.** outstanding of its kind **2.** specially selected, as a jury

**blue ribbon** first prize in a competition

**Blue Ridge Mountains** easternmost range of the Appalachians, extending from S Pa. to N Ga.

**blue·stock·ing** (-stäk′in) *n.* [from the blue stockings worn at literary meetings in 18th-c. London] a learned, bookish, or pedantic woman

**blue streak** [Colloq.] anything thought of as like a streak of lightning in speed, vividness, etc.

**blu·et** (blōō′it) *n.* [< Fr. dim. of *bleu*, blue] a small plant having little, pale-blue flowers

**blue whale** a whalebone whale with a dark blue-gray body: the largest animal that has ever lived

**bluff**[1] (bluf) *vt., vi.* [prob. < Du. *bluffen*, to baffle] **1.** to mislead by a false, bold front **2.** to frighten by threats that cannot be made good **3.** to manage to get (one's way) by bluffing —*n.* **1.** a bluffing **2.** a person who bluffs: also **bluff′er**

**bluff**[2] (bluf) *adj.* [< Du. *blaf*, flat] **1.** having a broad, flat front that slopes steeply **2.** having a rough, frank, but affable manner —*n.* a high, steep bank or cliff —**bluff′ly** *adv.*

**blu·ing** (blōō′in) *n.* a blue liquid, powder, etc. used in rinsing white fabrics to prevent yellowing

**blu·ish** (-ish) *adj.* somewhat blue

**blun·der** (blun′dər) *vi.* [< ON. *blunda*, to shut the eyes] **1.** to move clumsily or carelessly; flounder; stumble **2.** to make a foolish mistake —*vt.* **1.** to say stupidly or confusedly; blurt (*out*) **2.** to do clumsily or poorly; bungle —*n.* a foolish or stupid mistake —**blun′der·er** *n.* —**blun′der·ing·ly** *adv.*

**blun·der·buss** (-bus′) *n.* [Du. *donderbus*, thunder box: altered after prec.] **1.** an obsolete short gun with a broad muzzle **2.** a person who blunders

**blunt** (blunt) *adj.* [< ?] **1.** slow to perceive; dull **2.** having a dull edge or point **3.** plain-spoken and abrupt —*vt.* **1.** to make dull or insensitive **2.** to make less effective —*vi.* to become dull —**blunt′ly** *adv.* —**blunt′ness** *n.*

**blur** (blʉr) *vt., vi.* **blurred, blur′ring** [? akin to BLEAR] **1.** to smear or smudge **2.** to make or become less distinct or clear **3.** to dim or dull —*n.* **1.** the state of being blurred **2.** an obscuring stain or blot **3.** anything indistinct to the sight or mind —**blur′ri·ness** *n.* —**blur′ry** *adj.*

**blurb** (blʉrb) *n.* [arbitrary coinage (c. 1907) by Gelett Burgess (1866–1951), U.S. humorist] [Colloq.] an advertisement, as on a book jacket, esp. a very laudatory one

**blurt** (blʉrt) *vt.* [prob. echoic] to say suddenly, without stopping to think (with *out*)

**blush** (blush) *vi.* [< OE. *blyscan*, to shine] **1.** to become red in the face from shame, embarrassment, etc. **2.** to be ashamed or embarrassed (*at* or *for*) **3.** to be or become rosy —*n.* **1.** a reddening of the face, as from shame **2.** a rosy color [the *blush* of youth] —*adj.* rosy [*blush-*pink] —**at first blush** at first sight; without further thought —**blush′ful** *adj.* —**blush′ing·ly** *adv.*

**blush·er** (-ər) *n.* **1.** a person who blushes, esp. one who blushes readily **2.** any of various cosmetic powders, gels, creams, etc. applied to the face to give it color

**blus·ter** (blus′tər) *vi.* [< or akin to LowG. *blüstern*] **1.** to blow stormily: said of wind **2.** to speak or behave in a noisy, swaggering, or bullying way —*vt.* **1.** to force by blustering **2.** to say noisily and aggressively —*n.* **1.** noisy commotion **2.** noisy swaggering or bullying talk —**blus′ter·er** *n.* —**blus′ter·ing·ly** *adv.* —**blus′ter·y, blus′ter·ous** *adj.*

**blvd.** boulevard

**BM 1.** bench mark **2.** [Colloq.] bowel movement
**BMR** basal metabolic rate
**BO, B.O. 1.** body odor **2.** box office
**b.o. 1.** back order **2.** branch office
**bo·a** (bō'ə) *n.* [L.] **1.** any of a number of tropical snakes that crush their prey in their coils, as the anaconda **2.** a woman's long, fluffy scarf, as of feathers
**boa constrictor** a species of boa that is 10 to 15 feet long
**boar** (bôr) *n., pl.* **boars, boar:** see PLURAL, II, D 1 [OE. *bar*] **1.** an uncastrated male hog or pig **2.** a wild hog of Europe, Africa, and Asia
**board** (bôrd) *n.* [< OE. *bord*, plank & OFr. *bord*, side of a ship] **1.** a long, broad, flat piece of sawed wood ready for use **2.** a flat piece of wood or other material for some special use *[a bulletin board, diving board]* **3.** *a)* a construction material used in thin, flat, rectangular sheets *[fiberboard] b)* pasteboard or stiff paper, often used in book covers **4.** *a)* a table for meals *b)* food served at a table; esp., meals provided regularly for pay **5.** a council table **6.** a group of administrators; council **7.** a stock exchange or its listings **8.** the side of a ship *[overboard]* **9.** a rim or border *[seaboard]* —*vt.* **1.** to cover or close (*up*) with boards **2.** to provide with meals, or room and meals, regularly for pay **3.** to come onto the deck of (a ship) **4.** to get on (an airplane, bus, etc.) —*vi.* to receive meals, or room and meals, regularly for pay —**across the board 1.** *Horse Racing* to win, place, and show: said of betting **2.** including all classes or groups —**go by the board 1.** to be swept overboard **2.** to be got rid of, lost, etc. —**on board** on or in a ship, aircraft, bus, etc. —**the boards** the stage (of a theater)
**board·er** (bôr'dər) *n.* **1.** one who boards at a boardinghouse, etc. **2.** one who boards a ship, etc.
**board foot** *pl.* **board feet** a unit of measure of lumber, equal to a board one foot square and one inch thick
**board·ing·house** (-hous') *n.* a house where meals, or room and meals, can be had for pay: also **boarding house**
**boarding school** a school providing lodging and meals for the pupils
**board of health** a local government agency that supervises public health
**board·walk** (bôrd'wôk') *n.* a walk made of boards, esp. one elevated and placed along a beach
**boast** (bōst) *vi.* [< Anglo-Fr.] **1.** to talk about deeds, abilities, etc. with too much pride and satisfaction; brag **2.** to be vainly proud; exult —*vt.* **1.** to brag about **2.** to glory in having or doing (something); be proud of —*n.* **1.** the act of one who boasts **2.** anything boasted of —**boast'er** *n.* —**boast'ing·ly** *adv.*
**boast·ful** (-fəl) *adj.* inclined to brag; boasting —**boast'ful·ly** *adv.* —**boast'ful·ness** *n.*
**boat** (bōt) *n.* [OE. *bat*] **1.** a small, open vessel or watercraft propelled by oars, sails, or engine **2.** a large vessel; ship: landsman's term **3.** a boat-shaped dish *[a gravy boat]* —*vt.* to lay or carry in the boat *[boat the oars]* —*vi.* to row, sail, or cruise in a boat —**in the same boat** in the same unfavorable situation —**miss the boat** [Colloq.] to fail to make the most of an opportunity —**rock the boat** [Colloq.] to disturb the status quo —**boat'er** *n.*
**boat·house** (bōt'hous') *n.* a building for storing a boat or boats
**boat·ing** (-in) *n.* rowing, sailing, or cruising
**boat·load** (-lōd') *n.* **1.** all the freight or passengers that a boat can carry or contain **2.** the load carried by a boat
**boat·man** (-mən) *n., pl.* **-men** a man who operates, works on, rents, or sells boats
**boat·swain** (bō's'n) *n.* a ship's warrant officer or petty officer in charge of the deck crew, the rigging, anchors, etc.
**bob**[1] (bäb) *n.* [ME. *bobbe*, hanging cluster; senses 4 & 5 < the *v.*] **1.** a knoblike weight hanging as at the end of a plumb line **2.** a docked tail, as of a horse **3.** a woman's or girl's short haircut **4.** a quick, jerky motion **5.** a float on a fishing line: now usually **bob'ber** —*vt.* **bobbed, bob'bing** [ME. *bobben*, to knock against] **1.** to move, esp. up and down, with short, jerky motions **2.** to cut (hair, a tail, etc.) short —*vi.* **1.** to move with short, jerky motions **2.** to try to catch hanging or floating fruit with the teeth (with *for*) —**bob up** to appear unexpectedly or suddenly
**bob**[2] (bäb) *n., pl.* **bob** [< ? *Bob*, nickname for ROBERT] [Brit. Slang] a shilling
**bob·bin** (bäb'in) *n.* [Fr. *bobine*] a reel or spool for thread or yarn, used in spinning, weaving, machine sewing, etc.
**bob·ble** (bäb''l) *n.* [< BOB[1], *v.*] **1.** a bobbing, up-and-down movement **2.** [Colloq.] an awkward juggling of a ball in trying to catch it —*vi.* **-bled, -bling** to move jerkily; bob —*vt.* [Colloq.] to deal with awkwardly; specif., to make a bobble with (a ball); muff; bungle
**bob·by** (bäb'ē) *n., pl.* **-bies** [after Sir Robert (*Bobby*) Peel (1788–1850), who reorganized the London police force] [Brit. Colloq.] a policeman

**bobby pin** [from use with *bobbed* hair] a metal hairpin with the sides pressing close together
**bobby socks** (or **sox**) [< BOB[1] (*vt.* 2)] [Colloq.] girls' socks that reach just above the ankle
**bob·cat** (bäb'kat') *n., pl.* **-cats', -cat':** see PLURAL, II, D, 1 [< its short tail] *same as* BAY LYNX
**bob·o·link** (bäb'ə link') *n.* [echoic, after its call] a migratory songbird of N. America
**bob·sled** (-sled') *n.* a long sled with two sets of runners one behind the other, steering apparatus, and brakes: it is ridden by a team of four or two men in races down a prepared run —*vi.* **-sled'ded, -sled'ding** to ride or race on a bobsled

BOBSLED

**bob·stay** (-stā') *n.* a rope or chain for tying down a bowsprit to keep it from bobbing
**bob·tail** (-tāl') *n.* **1.** a tail cut short; docked tail **2.** a horse or dog with a bobtail —*adj.* **1.** having a bobtail **2.** cut short; abbreviated —*vt.* **1.** to dock the tail of **2.** to cut short; curtail
**bob·white** (bäb'hwīt', -wīt') *n., pl.* **-whites', -white':** see PLURAL, II, D, 1 [echoic, after its call] a small N. American quail having markings of brown and white on a gray body
**Boc·cac·cio** (bō kä'chē ō'; *It.* bō kät'chō), **Gio·van·ni** (jō-vän'nē) 1313–75; It. writer
**boc·cie, boc·ce, boc·ci** (bäch'ē) *n.* [It. *bocce*] an Italian game similar to bowls
**bock** (bäk) *n.* [G. < *bockbier* < *Einbecker bier* < *Einbeck*, Hanover, where first brewed] a dark beer traditionally drunk in the spring: also **bock beer**
**bode**[1] (bōd) *vt.* **bod'ed, bod'ing** [< OE. < *boda*, messenger] to be an omen of; presage —**bode ill** (or **well**) to be a bad (or good) omen
**bode**[2] (bōd) *alt. pt. of* BIDE
**bod·ice** (bäd'is) *n.* [altered < *bodies*, pl. of *body*] **1.** the upper part of a woman's dress **2.** a kind of vest worn over a blouse or dress by women or girls, usually laced in front
**bod·ied** (bäd'ēd) *adj.* having a body or substance, esp. of a specified kind *[able-bodied]*
**bod·i·less** (-ē lis) *adj.* without a body; having no material substance; incorporeal
**bod·i·ly** (-'l ē) *adj.* of, in, by, or to the body —*adv.* **1.** in person; in the flesh **2.** as a single body; in entirety
**bod·kin** (bäd'k'n) *n.* [ME. *boidekyn* < ?] **1.** a pointed instrument for making holes in cloth **2.** a long, ornamental hairpin **3.** a thick, blunt needle **4.** [Obs.] a dagger
**bod·y** (bäd'ē) *n., pl.* **bod'ies** [< OE. *bodig*, trunk, orig. sense "cask"] **1.** the whole physical substance of a person, animal, or plant **2.** *a)* the trunk or torso of a man or animal *b)* the part of a garment that covers the trunk **3.** a dead person; corpse **4.** the flesh, as opposed to the spirit **5.** [Colloq.] a person **6.** a group of people or things regarded as a unit *[an advisory body]* **7.** the main or central part of anything **8.** a portion or mass of matter *[a body of water]* **9.** density or consistency, as of a liquid, fabric, etc. **10.** richness of tone or flavor —*vt.* **bod'ied, bod'y·ing** to give a body or substance to —**body forth** to give shape or form to —**keep body and soul together** to stay alive
**body English** [cf. ENGLISH (*n.* 3)] a follow-through motion of the body, as after bowling a ball, in a joking effort to control its movement
**bod·y·guard** (-gärd') *n.* a person or persons, usually armed, assigned to guard someone
**body language** gestures, unconscious body movements, facial expressions, etc. which serve as nonverbal communication or as accompaniments to speech
**body politic** the people who collectively constitute a political unit under a government
**body stocking** a tightfitting garment, usually of one piece, that covers the torso and, sometimes, the legs
**bod·y·suit** (-soot') *n.* a one-piece, tightfitting, sleeved or sleeveless garment that covers the torso, usually worn with slacks, a skirt, etc.: also **body shirt**
**bod·y·surf** (-surf') *vi.* to engage in the sport of surfing, lying prone on the wave without the use of a surfboard
**Boe·o·tia** (bē ō'shə) region in EC Greece: in ancient times, a region dominated by Thebes —**Boe·o'tian** *adj., n.*
**Boer** (bôr, boor, bō'ər) *n.* [Du. *boer*, peasant: see BOOR] a South African whose ancestors were Dutch colonists
**bog** (bäg, bôg) *n.* [< Gael. & Ir. *bog*, soft, moist] wet, spongy ground; a small marsh or swamp —*vt., vi.* **bogged, bog'ging** to sink or become stuck in or as in a bog (often with *down*); mire —**bog'gi·ness** *n.*
**bo·gey** (bō'gē) *n., pl.* **-geys 1.** *same as* BOGY **2.** [after Colonel *Bogey*, imaginary first-rate golfer] *Golf* par or, now usually, one stroke more than par on a hole —*vt.* **-geyed, -gey·ing** *Golf* to score one over par on (a hole)
**bog·gle** (bäg''l) *vi.* **-gled, -gling** [< Scot. *bogle*, specter;

now associated with BUNGLE] **1.** to be startled or frightened (*at*); shy away **2.** to hesitate (*at*); have scruples **3.** to be or become confused —*vt.* **1.** to bungle; botch **2.** to confuse or stagger (the mind) —*n.* a boggling

**bo·gie** (bō′gē) *n., pl.* **-gies** [< Brit. Dial.] **1.** an undercarriage on a railroad car **2.** any of the wheels supporting the tread of an armored tank

**Bo·go·tá** (bō′gə tä′) capital of Colombia, in the C part: pop. 2,148,000

**bo·gus** (bō′gəs) *adj.* [< ?] not genuine; counterfeit

**bo·gy** (bō′gē, boog′ē) *n., pl.* **-gies** [see BOGGLE] **1.** an imaginary evil spirit; goblin **2.** anything causing great, often needless, fear; bugbear

**bo·gy·man, bo·gey·man** (bō′gē man′, boog′ē-) *n., pl.* **-men′** (-men′) an imaginary frightful being, esp. one used as a threat in disciplining children

**Bo·he·mi·a** (bō hē′mē ə) region and former province of W Czechoslovakia: earlier, a kingdom

**Bo·he·mi·an** (-ən) *n.* **1.** a native or inhabitant of Bohemia **2.** *same as* CZECH (*n.* 2) **3.** a gypsy **4.** [*often* b-] an artist, poet, etc. who lives in an unconventional, nonconforming way —*adj.* **1.** of Bohemia, its people, or their language; Czech **2.** [*often* b-] like or characteristic of a Bohemian (*n.* 4) —**Bo·he′mi·an·ism** *n.*

**Bohr** (bôr), **Niels (Henrik David)** (nēlz) 1885-1962; Dan. theoretical physicist

**boil**[1] (boil) *vi.* [< OFr. < L. < *bulla*, a bubble] **1.** to bubble up and vaporize by being heated **2.** to seethe like boiling liquids **3.** to be agitated, as with rage **4.** to cook in boiling water or other liquid —*vt.* **1.** to heat to the boiling point **2.** to cook or process in boiling water, etc. —*n.* the act or state of boiling —**boil away** to evaporate by boiling —**boil down 1.** to lessen in quantity by boiling **2.** to condense; summarize —**boil over 1.** to come to a boil and spill over the rim **2.** to lose one's temper

**boil**[2] (boil) *n.* [< OE. *byl*] an inflamed, painful, pus-filled swelling on the skin, caused by infection

**boil·er** (boi′lər) *n.* **1.** a container in which things are boiled or heated **2.** a tank in which water is turned to steam for heating or power **3.** a tank for heating water and storing it

**boil·er·mak·er** (-mā′kər) *n.* **1.** a worker who makes or repairs boilers **2.** [Colloq.] a drink of whiskey in beer or with beer as a chaser

**boiling point** the temperature at which a specified liquid boils: water at sea level boils at 212°F or 100°C

**Boi·se** (boi′sē, -zē) [< Fr. *boisé*, wooded] capital of Ida.: pop. 102,000: also **Boise City**

**bois·ter·ous** (bois′tər əs) *adj.* [ME. *boistreous*, crude, coarse < *boistous*, violent] **1.** rough and stormy **2.** *a)* noisy and unruly *b)* loud and exuberant —**bois′ter·ous·ly** *adv.* —**bois′ter·ous·ness** *n.*

**bok choy** (bäk choi) [Cantonese, white vegetable] a variety of CHINESE CABBAGE

**bo·la** (bō′lə) *n.* [Sp., a ball < L. *bulla*, a bubble] a throwing weapon made of a long cord or thong with heavy balls at the ends: also **bo′las** (-ləs)

**bold** (bōld) *adj.* [< OE. *beald*] **1.** daring; fearless **2.** taking liberties; impudent **3.** steep or abrupt **4.** prominent and clear /to write a *bold* hand/ —**make bold** to dare (*to*) —**bold′ly** *adv.* —**bold′ness** *n.*

**bold·face** (bōld′fās′) *n.* a printing type with a heavy, dark face (Ex.: **face**)

**bold·faced** (-fāst′) *adj.* impudent; forward

**bole** (bōl) *n.* [ON. *bolr*] a tree trunk

**bo·le·ro** (bə ler′ō, bō-) *n., pl.* **-ros** [Sp.] **1.** a Spanish dance in 3/4 time **2.** music for this **3.** a sleeveless or sleeved jacket that ends at the waist and is open in front

**bo·lí·var** (bō lē′vär, bäl′ə vər) *n., pl.* **bo·lí·va·res** (bō′li vä′rēs), **bo·lí′vars** [after ff.] *see* MONETARY UNITS, table (Venezuela)

**Bol·í·var** (bäl′ə vər; *Sp.* bô lē′vär), **Si·món** (*Sp.* sē môn′) 1783-1830; S. American general & revolutionary leader

**Bo·liv·i·a** (bə liv′ē ə) country in WC S. America: 424,000 sq. mi.; pop. 4,804,000; capitals, La Paz & Sucre —**Bo·liv′i·an** *adj., n.*

**boll** (bōl) *n.* [< OE. *bolla*, a bowl] the roundish seed pod of a plant, esp. of cotton or flax

**bol·lix** (bäl′iks) *vt.* [< OE. *beallucas*, testicles] [Slang] to bungle or botch (usually with *up*)

**boll weevil** a small, grayish weevil whose larvae destroy the cotton bolls in which they are hatched

**bo·lo** (bō′lō) *n., pl.* **-los** [Sp. < native name] a large, single-edged knife used in the Philippines

**Bo·lo·gna** (bə lō′nyä; *E.* bə lō′nə) city in NC Italy: pop. 485,000 —*n.* [*usually* b-] (bə lō′nē, -nyə, -nə) a large, smoked sausage of various meats: also **bologna sausage**

**bo·lo tie** (bō′lō) [altered from *bola tie*: see BOLA] a man's string tie held together with a slide device

**Bol·she·vik** (bōl′shə vik′, bäl′-) *n., pl.* **-viks′**, **Bol′she·vi′ki** (-vē′kē) [Russ. < *bolshe*, the majority] [*also* b-] **1.** orig., a member of a majority faction of the Social Democratic Party of Russia, which formed the Communist Party after seizing power in the 1917 Revolution **2.** a Communist, esp. of the Soviet Union **3.** loosely, any radical: hostile usage —*adj.* [*also* b-] of or like the Bolsheviks or Bolshevism —**Bol′she·vism** *n.* —**Bol′she·vist** *n., adj.* —**Bol′she·vize′** (-vīz′) *vt.* **-vized′, -viz′ing**

**bol·ster** (bōl′stər) *n.* [OE.] **1.** a long, narrow cushion or pillow **2.** a soft pad **3.** any bolsterlike object or support —*vt.* to prop up as with a bolster; support or strengthen (often with *up*)

**bolt**[1] (bōlt) *n.* [OE.] **1.** an arrow with a thick, blunt head, shot from a crossbow **2.** a flash of lightning **3.** a sudden dash or movement **4.** a sliding bar for locking a door, etc. **5.** a similar bar in a lock, moved by a key **6.** a metal rod with a head, threaded and used with a nut to hold parts together **7.** a roll (*of* cloth, paper, etc.) of a given length **8.** a withdrawal from one's party or group **9.** *Firearms* a sliding bar that pushes the cartridge into place and extracts the empty cartridge case after firing —*vt.* **1.** [Archaic] to shoot (an arrow, etc.) **2.** to say suddenly; blurt (*out*) **3.** to swallow (food) hurriedly; gulp down **4.** to fasten as with a bolt **5.** to roll (cloth, etc.) into bolts **6.** to abandon (a party, group, etc.) —*vi.* **1.** to dash or spring away suddenly; dart **2.** to withdraw support from a party, group, etc. —*adv.* straight; erectly /to sit *bolt* upright/ —**bolt from the blue** a sudden, unforeseen occurrence, often an unfortunate one —**shoot one's bolt** to exhaust one's capabilities —**bolt′er** *n.*

**bolt**[2] (bōlt) *vt.* [< OFr. *buleter* < ?] **1.** to sift (flour, grain, etc.) so as to separate and grade **2.** to examine closely —**bolt′er** *n.*

**bo·lus** (bō′ləs) *n., pl.* **bo′lus·es** [L. < Gr. *bōlos*, a lump] **1.** a small, round lump, as of chewed food **2.** a large pill

**bomb** (bäm) *n.* [< Fr. < It. < Gr. *bombos*, hollow sound] **1.** a container filled with an explosive, incendiary, or other chemical, for dropping or hurling, or for detonating by a timing mechanism **2.** a sudden, surprising occurrence **3.** an aerosol container **4.** a shielded device containing radioactive material, used in radiotherapy /a cobalt *bomb*/ **5.** [Slang] a complete failure: said esp. of a performance or show —*vt.* to attack or destroy with a bomb or bombs —*vi.* [Slang] to have a complete failure

**bom·bard** (bäm bärd′; *for n.* bäm′bärd) *vt.* [< Fr. < *bombarde*, mortar < *bombe*, BOMB] **1.** to attack with or as with artillery or bombs **2.** to keep attacking with questions, suggestions, etc. **3.** to direct a stream of particles, as neutrons, against —*n.* an early type of cannon, hurling stones —**bom·bard′ment** *n.*

**bom·bar·dier** (bäm′bə dir′, -bər-) *n.* a person who releases the bombs in a bomber

**bom·bast** (bäm′bast) *n.* [< OFr. < ML. < *bambax*, cotton < LGr. < Per. *pambak*, cotton] pompous, high-sounding talk or writing

**bom·bas·tic** (bäm bas′tik) *adj.* using or characterized by high-sounding but unimportant or meaningless language; pompous —**bom·bas′ti·cal·ly** *adv.*

**Bom·bay** (bäm′bā′) seaport in W India, on the Arabian Sea: pop. 4,152,000

**bomb bay** a compartment in the fuselage of a bomber that can be opened to drop bombs

**bom·ba·zine** (bäm′bə zēn′, bäm′bə zēn′) *n.* [< Fr. < ML. < *bambax*: see BOMBAST] a twilled cloth of silk or rayon with worsted, often dyed black

**bomb·er** (bäm′ər) *n.* **1.** an airplane designed for dropping bombs **2.** a person who uses bombs as for illegal purposes

**bomb·proof** (bäm′prōōf′) *adj.* capable of withstanding the force of ordinary bombs

**bomb·shell** (-shel′) *n. same as* BOMB (*n.* 1, 2)

**bomb·sight** (-sīt′) *n.* an instrument on a bomber for aiming the bombs

**bo·na fi·de** (bō′nə fīd′, bän′ə; bō′nə fī′dē) [L.] in good faith; without fraud or deceit

**bo·nan·za** (bə nan′zə, bō-) *n.* [Sp., prosperity, ult. < Gr. *malakia*, a calm at sea] **1.** a rich vein of ore **2.** any source of wealth or profits

**Bo·na·parte** (bō′nə pärt′; *Fr.* bô nà pàrt′) Corsican family including NAPOLEON I & LOUIS NAPOLEON

**bon·bon** (bän′bän′) *n.* [Fr. *bon*, good] a small piece of candy, esp. one with a creamy filling

**bond**[1] (bänd) *n.* [ME. *bond, band*: see BAND[1]] **1.** anything that binds, fastens, or unites; specif., glue, solder, etc. **2.** [*pl.*] *a)* fetters; shackles *b)* [Archaic] imprisonment **3.** a binding or uniting force; tie; link **4.** a binding agreement; covenant **5.** the status of goods kept in a warehouse until taxes are paid **6.** *same as* BOND PAPER **7.** *Chem.* the means by which atoms or groups of atoms are combined in molecules **8.** *Finance* an interest-bearing certificate issued by a government or business, promising to pay the holder a specified sum on a specified date **9.** *Law* a) a written obligation to pay specified sums, do or not do specified things, etc. b) an amount paid as surety or bail c) [Archaic] a bondsman —*vt.* **1.** to fasten or unite as with a bond **2.** to furnish a bond, or bail, and thus become a surety for (someone) **3.** to place (goods) under bond **4.** to issue bonds (sense 8) on; mortgage **5.** to put under bonded debt —*vi.* to hold together by or as by a bond —**bottled in bond** bottled and stored in bonded warehouses for the length of time stated on the label, as some whiskey —**bond'a·ble** *adj.* —**bond'er** *n.*

**bond²** (bänd) *n.* [see ff.] [Obs.] a serf or slave —*adj.* in serfdom or slavery

**bond·age** (bän'dij) *n.* [< Anglo-L. < OE. *bonda* < ON. *bonde* < *bua*, to inhabit] **1.** serfdom; slavery **2.** subjection to some force or influence

**bond·ed** (-did) *adj.* **1.** subject to or secured by a bond or bonds **2.** placed in a government-certified, or bonded, warehouse pending payment of taxes

**bond·hold·er** (bänd'hōl'dər) *n.* an owner of bonds issued by a company, government, or person

**bond·man** (-mən) *n.*, *pl.* **-men 1.** a feudal serf **2.** a man or boy bondservant —**bond'maid'** *n.fem.* —**bond'wom'an** *n.fem.*, *pl.* **-wom'en**

**bond paper** a strong, superior stock of paper, esp. of rag pulp, used for documents, letterheads, etc.

**bond·ser·vant** (-sur'vənt) *n.* **1.** a person bound to service without pay **2.** a slave

**bonds·man** (bändz'mən) *n.*, *pl.* **-men 1.** same as BONDMAN **2.** a person who takes responsibility for another by furnishing a bond; surety

**bone** (bōn) *n.* [OE. *ban*] **1.** any of the pieces of hard tissue forming the skeleton of most vertebrate animals **2.** this hard tissue **3.** [*pl.*] a) the skeleton b) the body **4.** a bonelike substance or part **5.** a thing made of bone, plastic, etc.; specif., a) a corset stay b) [*pl.*] [Colloq.] dice **6.** [*pl.*] a) flat sticks used as clappers in minstrel shows b) [*with sing. v.*] an end man in a minstrel show **7.** same as BONE WHITE —*vt.* **boned, bon'ing 1.** to remove the bones from **2.** to put whalebone, etc. into — *vi.* [Slang] to study hard and hurriedly; cram (usually with *up*) —**feel in one's bones** to be certain without any real reason —**have a bone to pick** to have something to quarrel about —**make no bones about** [Colloq.] to make no attempt to hide; admit freely —**bone'like'** *adj.*

**bone-dry** (bōn'drī') *adj.* dry as bone; very dry

**bone·head** (-hed') *n.* [Slang] a stupid person

**bone·less** (-lis) *adj.* without bones; specif., with the bones removed

**bone meal** crushed or finely ground bones, used as feed for stock or as fertilizer

**bon·er** (bōn'ər) *n.* [Slang] a stupid blunder

**bone·set** (-set') *n.* a plant of the composite family, with flat clusters of white flowers: used in folk medicine

**bone white** any of various shades of grayish-white or yellowish-white

**bon·fire** (bän'fīr') *n.* [ME. *banefyre*, bone fire; later, funeral pyre] a large fire built outdoors

**bong** (bôŋ, bäŋ) *n.* [echoic] a deep, ringing sound, as of a large bell —*vi.* to make this sound

**bon·go** (bäŋ'gō) *n.*, *pl.* **-gos** [AmSp. < ?] either of a pair of small joined drums, of different pitch, struck with the fingers: in full, **bongo drum**

**bon·ho·mie, bon·hom·mie** (bän'ə-mē'; Fr. bô nô mē') *n.* [Fr. < *bon*, good + *homme*, man] good nature; pleasant, affable manner; amiability

**bo·ni·to** (bə nēt'ō) *n.*, *pl.* **-tos, -toes, -to:** see PLURAL, II, D, 1 [Sp.] any of several saltwater fishes of the mackerel family, related to the tuna

BONGO DRUMS

**‡bon jour** (bôn zhōōr') [Fr.] good day; hello

**bon mot** (bôn'mō'; Fr. bōn mō') *pl.* **bons mots** (bōn'mōz'; Fr. bôn mō') [Fr., lit., good word] an apt, clever, or witty remark

**Bonn** (bän) capital of West Germany, on the Rhine: pop. 138,000

**bon·net** (bän'it) *n.* [OFr. *bonet*] **1.** a flat, brimless cap, worn by men and boys in Scotland **2.** a) a hat with a chin ribbon, worn by babies or girls b) [Colloq.] any hat for a woman or girl **3.** short for WAR BONNET **4.** a) a metal covering, as over a fireplace b) [Brit.] an automobile hood —*vt.* to put a bonnet on

**bon·ny, bon·nie** (bän'ē) *adj.* **-ni·er, -ni·est** [< Fr. *bon*, good < L. *bonus*] [Now Chiefly Scot. or Eng. Dial.] **1.** handsome or pretty, with a healthy, cheerful glow **2.** fine; pleasant —**bon'ni·ly** *adv.* —**bon'ni·ness** *n.*

**bon·sai** (bän sī') *n.* [Jap., lit., tray arrangement] **1.** the art of dwarfing and shaping trees, shrubs, etc. **2.** *pl.* **bonsai'** such a tree or shrub

**‡bon soir** (bôn swär') [Fr.] good evening

**bo·nus** (bō'nəs) *n.*, *pl.* **bo'nus·es** [L., good] anything given or paid in addition to the customary or required amount as an incentive, reward, etc.

**bon vi·vant** (bän' vi vänt'; Fr. bōn vē vän') *pl.* **bons vivants** (bän' vi vänts'; Fr. bōn vē vän') [Fr.] one who enjoys good food and other luxuries

**bon voy·age** (bän'voi äzh'; Fr. bōn vwä yàzh') [Fr.] pleasant journey: a farewell to a traveler

**bon·y** (bō'nē) *adj.* **bon'i·er, bon'i·est 1.** of or like bone **2.** having many bones **3.** having protruding bones **4.** thin; emaciated —**bon'i·ness** *n.*

**boo** (bōō) *interj., n., pl.* **boos** [echoic] a prolonged sound made to show disapproval, scorn, etc., or, more abruptly, to startle —*vi., vt.* **booed, boo'ing** to make this sound (at)

**boob** (bōōb) *n.* [Slang] a booby; foolish person

**boo-boo, boo·boo** (bōō'bōō') *n., pl.* **-boos' 1.** [Slang] a stupid or foolish mistake **2.** a minor injury or bruise: child's usage

**boo·by** (bōō'bē) *n., pl.* **-bies** [prob. < Sp. *bobo*, stupid] **1.** a stupid or foolish person **2.** a tropical, diving sea bird related to the gannet **3.** the one doing worst in a game, contest, etc.

**booby prize** a prize, usually ridiculous, given in fun to whoever has done worst in a game, race, etc.

**booby trap 1.** any device for tricking a person unawares **2.** a mine set to be exploded by some action of the unsuspecting victim —**boo'by-trap'** *vt.* **-trapped', -trap'ping**

**boo·dle** (bōō'd'l) *n.* [< Du. *boedel*, property] [Slang] **1.** the entire lot; caboodle **2.** something given as a bribe **3.** the loot taken in a robbery

**boo·gie-woo·gie** (bōōg'ē wōōg'ē) *n.* [? echoic of the characteristic "walking" bass] a style of jazz piano playing in which repeated bass figures in 8/8 rhythm accompany the melodic variations

**boo·hoo** (bōō'hōō') *vi.* **-hooed', -hoo'ing** [echoic] to weep noisily —*n., pl.* **-hoos'** noisy weeping

**book** (book) *n.* [OE. *boc*, pl. *bec*, akin to OE. *bece*, beech: runes were first carved on beech tablets] **1.** a) a number of sheets of paper, etc. with writing or printing on them, fastened together along one edge, usually between protective covers b) a relatively long literary work, scientific writing, etc. **2.** a main division of a literary work **3.** a) a number of blank or ruled sheets or printed forms bound together [an account *book*] b) a record or account kept in this **4.** the words of an opera, etc.; libretto **5.** a booklike package, as of matches or tickets **6.** a record of bets, as on horse races **7.** *Bridge*, etc. a specified number of tricks that must be won before scoring can take place —*vt.* **1.** to record in a book; list **2.** to engage (rooms, performers, etc.) ahead of time **3.** to record charges against on a police record —*adj.* in, from, or according to books or accounts —**bring to book 1.** to force to explain **2.** to reprimand —**by the book** according to the rules —**close the books** *Bookkeeping* to make no further entries —**in one's book** in one's opinion —**keep books** to keep a record of business transactions —**know like a book** to know well or fully —**make book** [Slang] to make or accept bets —**on the books 1.** recorded **2.** enrolled —**the Book** the Bible —**throw the book at** [Slang] **1.** to place all possible charges against (an accused person) **2.** to give the maximum punishment to —**book'er** *n.*

**book·bind·ing** (-bīn'diŋ) *n.* the art, trade, or business of binding books —**book'bind'er** *n.* —**book'bind'er·y** *n., pl.* **-er·ies**

**book·case** (-kās') *n.* a set of shelves or a cabinet for holding books

**book club** an organization that sells books, usually at reduced prices, to members who undertake to buy a minimum number of them annually

**book·end** (-end') *n.* an ornamental weight or bracket at the end of a row of books to keep them upright

**book·ie** (-ē) *n.* [Slang] same as BOOKMAKER (sense 2)

**book·ing** (-iŋ) *n.* an engagement, as for a lecture, performance, etc.

**book·ish** (-ish) *adj.* **1.** of books **2.** inclined to read and study; scholarly **3.** having mere book learning; pedantic; stodgy —**book'ish·ness** *n.*

**book·keep·ing** (-kēp'iŋ) *n.* the work of keeping a systematic record of business transactions —**book'keep'er** *n.*

**book learning** knowledge gained from reading or formal education rather than from practical experience: also **book'lore'** *n.*

**book·let** (-lit) *n.* a small, often paper-covered book

**book·mak·er** (-māk'ər) *n.* **1.** a maker of books **2.** a person in the business of taking bets, as on horse races —**book'mak'ing** *n.*

**book·mark** (-märk') *n.* anything slipped between the pages of a book to mark a place

**book·mo·bile** (-mō bēl′, -mə-) *n.* [BOOK + (AUTO)MOBILE] a traveling lending library moved from place to place in a truck

**Book of Common Prayer** the official book of services and prayers used in Anglican churches

**book·plate** (-plāt′) *n.* a label pasted in a book to identify its owner

**book·rest** (-rest′) *n. same as* BOOKSTAND (sense 1)

**book review** an article or talk in which a book is discussed and critically analyzed

**book·sell·er** (-sel′ər) *n.* the owner or manager of a bookstore

**book·shelf** (-shelf′) *n., pl.* **-shelves′** a shelf on which books are kept

**book·stack** (-stak′) *n.* a series of bookshelves, one over the other, as in a library

**book·stall** (-stôl′) *n.* a stand, booth, or counter, often one outdoors, where books are sold

**book·stand** (-stand′) *n.* **1.** a stand for holding a book open before a reader **2.** *same as* BOOKSTALL

**book·store** (-stôr′) *n.* a store where books are sold: also **book′shop′**

**book value** the value as shown in account books; specif., the value of the capital stock of a business as shown by the excess of assets over liabilities

**book·worm** (-wurm′) *n.* **1.** an insect or insect larva that harms books by feeding on the binding, paste, etc. **2.** one who reads or studies much

**boom¹** (bōōm) *vi.* [echoic] to make a deep, hollow, resonant sound —*vt.* to utter with such a sound —*n.* a booming sound, as of thunder, heavy guns, etc.

**boom²** (bōōm) *n.* [Du., a tree, beam] **1.** a spar extending from a mast to hold the bottom of a sail outstretched **2.** a long beam extending as from an upright to lift and guide something **3.** a barrier of chains or timbers to keep ships out or to keep floating logs in **4.** *Aeron.* a retractable metal tube for transferring fuel from one plane to another in flight —*vt.* **1.** to stretch out (sails) with a boom **2.** to place a boom in (a river, etc.) —*vi.* to sail or move at top speed (usually with *along*) —**lower the boom** [Colloq.] to act forcefully in punishing, criticizing, etc.

**boom³** (bōōm) *vi.* [< ? prec. *vi.*; later associated with BOOM¹] to increase suddenly or grow swiftly; flourish [business *boomed*] —*vt.* **1.** to cause to flourish **2.** to promote vigorously —*n.* a period of business prosperity, etc. —*adj.* of or resulting from a boom in business [a *boom* town]

**boom·er·ang** (bōōm′ə raŋ′) *n.* [< Australian native name] **1.** a flat, curved stick that can be thrown so that it will return to the thrower: used as a weapon by Australian aborigines **2.** something that goes contrary to the expectation of its originator and results in his disadvantage or harm —*vi.* to act as a boomerang

**boon¹** (bōōn) *n.* [ON. *bon*, a petition] **1.** a welcome benefit; blessing **2.** [Archaic] a request or favor

**boon²** (bōōn) *adj.* [< OFr. < L. *bonus*, good] **1.** [Archaic or Poet.] kind, generous, pleasant, etc. **2.** merry; convivial: now only in **boon companion**

**boon·docks** (bōōn′däks′) *n.pl.* [orig. military slang < Tag. *bundok*, mountain] [Colloq.] **1.** a wild, heavily wooded area; wilderness **2.** any remote rural region; hinterland Used with *the*

**boon·dog·gle** (bōōn′dôg′′l, -däg′-) *vi.* **-gled, -gling** [orig. sense, ornamental leather strap] [Colloq.] to do trifling, pointless work —*n.* trifling, pointless work or a useless project —**boon′dog′gler** *n.*

**Boone** (bōōn), **Daniel** 1734-1820; Am. frontiersman

**boor** (boor) *n.* [Du. *boer* < MDu. *gheboer*, fellow dweller < *ghe-*, with, co- + *bouwen*, to cultivate] **1.** orig., a peasant or farm worker **2.** a rude, awkward, or ill-mannered person —**boor′ish** *adj.* —**boor′ish·ly** *adv.* —**boor′ish·ness** *n.*

**boost** (bōōst) *vt.* [< ?] **1.** to raise by or as by a push from behind or below **2.** to urge others to support; promote **3.** to increase in amount, power, etc. —*n.* **1.** a push to help a person or thing upward or forward **2.** an act that helps or promotes **3.** an increase in amount, power, etc.

**boost·er** (bōōs′tər) *n.* **1.** one who boosts; ardent supporter **2.** any device providing added power, thrust, etc. **3.** any of the early stages of a multistage rocket; also, a rocket system that launches a spacecraft, etc.: also **booster rocket**

**booster shot** (or **injection**) a later injection of a vaccine for maintaining immunity

**boot¹** (bōōt) *n.* [OFr. *bote*] **1.** *a)* a protective covering of leather, rubber, etc. for the foot and part of the leg *b)* an overshoe **2.** a boot-shaped instrument of torture **3.** a patch for the inner surface of an automobile tire **4.** [Brit.] the trunk of an automobile **5.** *a)* a kick *b)* [Colloq.] pleasurable excitement; thrill **6.** [Slang] a navy or marine recruit —*vt.* **1.** to put boots on **2.** to kick **3.** [Slang] to

dismiss **4.** *Baseball* to fumble (a grounder) —**die with one's boots on** to die in action —**lick the boots of** to be servile toward —**the boot** [Slang] dismissal; discharge

**boot²** (bōōt) *n., vt., vi.* [< OE. *bot*, advantage] [Archaic] profit —**to boot** besides; in addition

**boot·black** (-blak′) *n.* a person whose work is shining shoes and boots

**boot camp** [Colloq.] a station where navy or marine recruits receive basic training

**boot·ee, boot·ie** (bōōt′ē, bōō tē′) *n.* **1.** a short boot or light overshoe worn by women and children **2.** a baby's soft, knitted or cloth shoe

**Bo·ö·tes** (bō ō′tēz) [L. < Gr. *boōtēs*, lit., plowman] a N constellation including the star Arcturus

**booth** (bōōth) *n., pl.* **booths** (bōōthz) [< ON. *buth*, temporary dwelling < *bua*, to dwell, akin to BONDAGE] **1.** a stall for the sale or display of goods, as at a market **2.** a small enclosure for voting at elections **3.** a small structure to house a sentry, public telephone, etc. **4.** a small, partially enclosed compartment with a table and seats, as in some restaurants

**Booth** (bōōth), **1. Edwin (Thomas)**, 1833-93; U.S. actor **2. John Wilkes** (wilks), 1838-65; U.S. actor, brother of *prec.*: assassin of Abraham Lincoln **3. William**, 1829-1912; Eng. founder of the Salvation Army

**boot·jack** (bōōt′jak′) *n.* a device to grip a boot heel, for helping a person to pull off boots

**boot·leg** (-leg′) *vt., vi.* **-legged′, -leg′ging** [in allusion to concealing objects in the leg of a boot] to make, carry, or sell (esp. liquor) illegally —*adj.* bootlegged; illegal —*n.* bootlegged liquor —**boot′leg′ger** *n.*

**boot·less** (-lis) *adj.* [BOOT² + -LESS] useless —**boot′less·ly** *adv.* —**boot′less·ness** *n.*

**boot·lick** (-lik′) *vt., vi.* [Colloq.] to try to gain favor with (someone) by fawning, servility, etc. —**boot′lick′er** *n.*

**boot·strap** (-strap′) *n.* a strap on a boot for pulling it on —*adj.* undertaken without others' help [a *bootstrap* operation] —**lift** (or **raise**) **oneself by the** (or **one's own**) **bootstraps** to achieve success by one's own unaided efforts

**boo·ty** (bōōt′ē) *n., pl.* **-ties** [< MLowG. *bute;* infl. by BOOT²] **1.** spoils of war **2.** any loot **3.** any valuable gain; prize: a humorous usage

**booze** (bōōz) *vi.* **boozed, booz′ing** [< Du. *buizen*] [Colloq.] to drink too much alcoholic liquor —*n.* [Colloq.] alcoholic liquor —**booz′er** *n.* —**booz′y** *adj.* **-i·er, -i·est**

**bop¹** (bäp) *n., vt.* **bopped, bop′ping** [echoic] [Slang] hit; punch

**bop²** (bäp) *n.* [< earlier *be-bop* < ?] a style of jazz with complex rhythms and harmonies, etc.

**bo·rac·ic** (bə ras′ik) *adj. same as* BORIC

**bor·age** (bôr′ij, bur′-) *n.* [< OFr. < ML. < ? *burra*, coarse hair] an annual plant with brilliant blue flowers and hairy leaves

**bo·rate** (bôr′āt) *n.* a salt or ester of boric acid —*vt.* **-rat·ed, -rat·ing** to treat or mix with borax or boric acid —**bo′rat·ed** *adj.*

**bo·rax** (bôr′aks) *n.* [< OFr. < ML. < Ar. < Per. *būrah*] a white, crystalline salt, $Na_2B_4O_7$, used as a flux and in glass, soaps, etc.

**Bor·deaux** (bôr dō′) seaport in SW France: pop. 267,000 —*n.* red or white wine from the region around Bordeaux

**bor·der** (bôr′dər) *n.* [< OFr. < OHG. *bord*, margin] **1.** an edge or a part near an edge; margin **2.** a dividing line between countries, etc.; frontier **3.** a narrow, ornamental strip along an edge —*vt.* **1.** to provide with a border **2.** to bound —*adj.* of, forming, or near a border —**border on** (or **upon**) **1.** to be next to **2.** to be like; be nearly —**bor′dered** *adj.*

**bor·der·land** (-land′) *n.* **1.** land forming or near a border **2.** a vague, uncertain condition

**bor·der·line** (-līn′) *n.* a boundary —*adj.* on the boundary of what is acceptable, normal, etc.

**bore¹** (bôr) *vt.* **bored, bor′ing** [< OE. < *bor*, auger] **1.** to make a hole in or through with a drill, etc. **2.** to make (a hole, tunnel, etc.) as by drilling **3.** to force (one's way), as through a crowd **4.** to weary by being dull or monotonous —*vi.* to bore a hole or passage —*n.* **1.** a hole made by or as by boring **2.** *a)* the hollow part of a tube, gun barrel, etc. *b)* its inside diameter; caliber **3.** a tiresome, dull person or thing

**bore²** (bôr) *n.* [< ON. *bara*, a billow] a high, abrupt tidal wave in a narrow channel

**bore³** (bôr) *pt. of* BEAR¹

**bo·re·al** (bôr′ē əl) *adj.* [LL. *borealis* < ff.] **1.** northern **2.** of the northern zone of plant and animal life lying just below the tundra

**Bo·re·as** (bôr′ē əs) **1.** *Gr. Myth.* the god of the north wind **2.** the north wind personified

**bore·dom** (bôr′dəm) *n.* the condition of being bored or uninterested; ennui

**bor·er** (bôr′ər) *n.* **1.** a tool for boring **2.** an insect or worm that bores holes in trees, fruit, etc.

**bore·some** (bôr′səm) *adj.* boring; tiresome

**Bor·glum** (bôr′gləm), **(John) Gut·zon** (gut′s′n) 1867–1941; U.S. sculptor

**bo·ric** (bôr′ik) *adj.* of or containing boron

**boric acid** a white, crystalline, weakly acid compound, H₃BO₃, used as a mild antiseptic

**Bor·is** (bôr′is) [Russ., lit., fight] a masculine name

**born** (bôrn) *alt. pp. of* BEAR¹ —*adj.* **1.** brought into life or being **2.** by birth [French-*born*] **3.** having certain qualities innately; natural [a *born* athlete]

**born-a·gain** (bôrn′ə gen′) *adj.* having undergone a spiritual conversion, esp. to evangelical Christianity

**borne** (bôrn) *alt. pp. of* BEAR¹

**Bor·ne·o** (bôr′nē ō) large island in the Malay Archipelago, southwest of the Philippines: the S part is in Indonesia & the N part is composed of Brunei & two states of Malaysia: 288,000 sq. mi.

**Bo·ro·din** (bôr′ə din; *Russ.* bồ′rồ dyēn′), **A·lek·san·dr Por·fir·e·vich** (ä′lyik sän′dr′ pồr fir′yi vich) 1833–87; Russ. composer

**bo·ron** (bôr′än) *n.* [< BOR(AX) + *-on* as in (CARB)ON] a non-metallic chemical element occurring only in combination, as with sodium and oxygen in borax: symbol, B; at. wt., 10.811; at. no., 5

**boron carbide** a compound of boron and carbon, B₄C, almost as hard as diamond: used as an abrasive and in control rods for nuclear reactors

**bor·ough** (bʉr′ō) *n.* [< OE. *burg,* town, fortress] **1.** in certain States, a self-governing, incorporated town **2.** any of the five administrative units of New York City **3.** in England *a)* a town with a municipal corporation granted by royal charter *b)* a town that sends representatives to Parliament

**bor·row** (bär′ō, bôr′ō) *vt., vi.* [< OE. *borgian,* to borrow, lend] **1.** to take or receive (something) with the understanding that one will return it or an equivalent **2.** to adopt (something) as one's own [to *borrow* a theory] **3.** to adopt (a word) from another language **4.** *Arith.* in subtraction, to take from the next higher denomination in the minuend and add to the next lower —**borrow trouble** to worry prematurely —**bor′row·er** *n.*

**borsch** (bôrsh, bôrshch) *n.* [Russ. *borshch*] a Russian beet soup, served hot or cold, usually with sour cream: also **borsht** (bôrsht)

**bort** (bôrt) *n.* [< ? OFr. *bourt,* bastard] a poorly crystallized variety of diamond used as an abrasive in industry: also **bortz** (bôrts)

**bor·zoi** (bôr′zoi) *n.* [Russ., swift] any of a breed of large dog with a narrow head, long legs, and silky coat

**bos·cage** (bäs′kij) *n.* [OE. < Frank. *busk,* forest] a natural growth of trees or shrubs

**Bosch** (bäs, bôs), **Hier·on·y·mus** (hi rän′ə məs) 1450?–1516; Du. painter

**bosh** (bäsh) *n., interj.* [Turk., empty, worthless] [Colloq.] nonsense

**bosk** (bäsk) *n.* [ME. *bosk,* BUSH¹] a small wooded place; thicket

**bosk·y** (bäs′kē) *adj.* covered with trees or shrubs

**bo's'n** (bōs′′n) *n. contracted form of* BOATSWAIN

**Bos·ni·a and Her·ce·go·vi·na** (bäz′nē ə ənd hert′sə gō vē′na) republic of Yugoslavia, in the C part: 19,745 sq. mi.; cap. Sarajevo

**bos·om** (booz′əm, boo′zəm) *n.* [OE. *bosm*] **1.** the human breast; specif., a woman's breasts **2.** a thing thought of as like this [the *bosom* of the sea] **3.** the breast regarded as the source of feelings **4.** the enclosing space formed by the breast and arms in embracing **5.** the midst [in the *bosom* of one's family] **6.** the part of a garment that covers the breast —*vt.* **1.** to embrace **2.** to conceal —*adj.* close; intimate [a *bosom* companion]

**bos·om·y** (-ē) *adj.* having large breasts

**Bos·po·rus** (bäs′pər əs) strait between the Black Sea & Sea of Marmara: also **Bos′pho·rus** (-fər əs)

**boss¹** (bôs, bäs) *n.* [Du. *baas,* a master] **1.** a person in authority over employees, as an employer or supervisor **2.** a person who controls a political organization: often **political boss** —*vt.* **1.** to act as boss of **2.** [Colloq.] to order (a person) about; act bossy with —*adj.* **1.** [Colloq.] chief **2.** [Slang] fine

**boss²** (bôs, bäs) *n.* [< OFr. *boce,* a swelling] **1.** a raised part on a flat surface; esp., a decorative knob, stud, etc. **2.** *Mech.* the enlarged part of a shaft —*vt.* to decorate with knobs, studs, etc.

**boss·ism** (bôs′iz′m, bäs′-) *n.* control by bosses, esp. of a political machine or party

**boss·y¹** (bôs′ē, bäs′ē) *adj.* **boss′i·er, boss′i·est** [BOSS¹ + -Y²] [Colloq.] domineering or dictatorial —**boss′i·ly** *adv.* —**boss′i·ness** *n.*

**boss·y²** (-ē) *n. a pet name for* a cow

**Bos·ton** (bôs′t′n, bäs′-) [after *Boston,* port in NE England] capital of Mass., on the Atlantic: pop. 563,000 (met. area 2,760,000) —**Bos·to′ni·an** (-tō′nē ən) *adj., n.*

**Boston brown bread** a dark, steamed bread made of cornmeal, rye flour, etc. and molasses

**Boston fern** a fern having pinnately compound leaves of various forms, used as a house plant

**Boston ivy** a climbing vine of the grape family, with shield-shaped leaves and purple berries: often grown to cover walls

**Boston terrier** any of a breed of small dog having a smooth, dark coat with white markings

**bo·sun** (bōs′′n) *n. same as* BOATSWAIN

**Bos·well** (bäz′wel, -wəl), **James** 1740–95; Scot. writer: biographer of Samuel Johnson

**bot** (bät) *n.* [< ? Gael. < *boiteag,* maggot] the larva of the botfly

**bot.** **1.** botanical **2.** botanist **3.** botany

**bo·tan·i·cal** (bə tan′i k′l) *adj.* [< ML. < Gr. < *botanē,* a plant] **1.** of plants and plant life **2.** of or connected with the science of botany Also **bo·tan′ic** —*n.* a vegetable drug prepared from roots, herbs, etc. —**bo·tan′i·cal·ly** *adv.*

**bot·a·nize** (bät′′n īz′) *vi.* **-nized′, -niz′ing** **1.** to gather plants for botanical study **2.** to study plants, esp. in their natural environment —*vt.* to investigate the plant life of (a region)

**bot·a·ny** (bät′′n ē) *n.* [BOTAN(ICAL) + -Y³] **1.** the science, a branch of biology, that deals with plants, their life, structure, growth, etc. **2.** the plant life of an area **3.** the characteristics of a plant or plant group —**bot′a·nist** *n.*

**Botany Bay** bay on the SE coast of Australia: site of a former Brit. penal colony

**botch** (bäch) *vt.* [ME. *bocchen,* to repair < ? Du. *botsen,* to patch] **1.** to repair or patch clumsily **2.** to bungle —*n.* **1.** a badly patched place or part **2.** a bungled piece of work —**botch′er** *n.* —**botch′y** *adj.*

**bot·fly** (bät′flī′) *n., pl.* **-flies′** [see BOT] a fly whose larvae are parasitic in horses, sheep, etc.

**both** (bōth) *adj., pron.* [< OE. *ba tha,* both these] the two (of them) [*both* birds) sang] —*conj., adv.* together; equally: used correlatively with *and* [*both* tired *and* sick]

**both·er** (bäth′ər) *vt., vi.* [prob. Anglo-Ir. for POTHER] **1.** to worry, trouble, annoy, etc. **2.** to bewilder **3.** to concern or trouble (oneself) —*n.* **1.** worry; trouble **2.** a person who gives trouble —*interj.* a mild expression of annoyance, irritation, etc.

**both·er·a·tion** (bäth′ə rā′shən) *n., interj.* [Colloq.] *same as* BOTHER

**both·er·some** (bäth′ər səm) *adj.* causing bother; annoying; troublesome; irksome

**Bot·swa·na** (bät swä′nə) country in S Africa: a member of the Commonwealth: 222,000 sq. mi.; pop. 629,000

**bott** (bät) *n. same as* BOT

**Bot·ti·cel·li** (bät′ə chel′ē), **San·dro** (sän′drō) (born *Alessandro di Mariano dei Filipepi*) 1445?–1510; It. Renaissance painter

**bot·tle** (bät′′l) *n.* [< OFr. < ML. *butticula,* a bottle < LL. *buttis,* a cask] **1.** a container, esp. for liquids, usually of glass or plastic, with a relatively narrow neck **2.** the amount that a bottle holds **3.** milk from an infant's nursing bottle —*vt.* **-tled, -tling** **1.** to put into a bottle or bottles **2.** to store under pressure in a cylinder, etc. [bottled gas] —**bottle up** **1.** to shut in (enemy troops, etc.) **2.** to hold in or suppress (emotions) —**hit the bottle** [Slang] to drink much alcoholic liquor —**bot′tle·ful′** *n., pl.* **-fuls′** —**bot′tler** *n.*

**bot·tle·neck** (-nek′) *n.* **1.** a place, as a narrow road, where traffic is slowed up or halted **2.** any point at which progress is slowed up

**bot·tle·nose** (-nōz′) *n.* a kind of dolphin, gray or greenish, with a bottle-shaped snout

**bot·tom** (bät′əm) *n.* [< OE. *botm, bodan,* ground] **1.** the lowest part **2.** *a)* the lowest or last position *b)* *Baseball* the second half (of an inning) **3.** the part on which something rests; base **4.** the side or end that is underneath **5.** the seat of a chair **6.** the ground beneath a body of water **7.** [often *pl.*] *same as* BOTTOM LAND **8.** *a)* a ship's keel *b)* a ship **9.** [usually *pl.*] pajama trousers **10.** basic meaning or cause; source **11.** stamina **12.** [Colloq.] the buttocks —*adj.* of, at, or on the bottom; lowest; last, etc. —*vt.* **1.** to provide (a chair, etc.) with a bottom **2.** to understand; fathom **3.** to place or base (on or upon) —*vi.* **1.** to reach the bottom **2.** to be based —**at bottom** fundamentally; actually —**be at the bottom of** to be the real reason for —**bottom out** to level off at a low point, as prices —**bottoms up!** [Colloq.] drink deep!: a toast

**bottom land** low land through which a river flows, rich in alluvial deposits; flood plain

**bot·tom·less** (-lis) *adj.* **1.** having no bottom **2.** very deep, endless, etc.

**bottom line** **1.** the bottom line of the earnings report of a company, on which net profit per share of stock is shown **2.** [Colloq.] profits or losses **3.** [Slang] the basic or most important factor, meaning, etc.

**bot·u·lism** (bäch′ə liz′m) *n.* [< G. < L. *botulus*, sausage + *-ismus*, -ISM: from early German cases involving sausages] poisoning resulting from the toxin produced by a certain bacillus sometimes found in foods improperly canned or preserved

**bou·clé, bou·cle** (bōō klā′) *n.* [Fr., pp. of *boucler*, to buckle, curl] **1.** a curly yarn that gives a fabric a tufted or knotted texture **2.** fabric made from this yarn

**bou·doir** (bōōd′wär) *n.* [Fr., lit., pouting room < *bouder*, to pout, sulk] a woman's bedroom, dressing room, or private sitting room

**bouf·fant** (bōō fänt′) *adj.* [Fr., prp. of *bouffer*, to puff out] puffed out; full, as some skirts

**bou·gain·vil·le·a, bou·gain·vil·lae·a** (bōō′gən vil′ē ə) *n.* [ModL., after L. A. de *Bougainville* (1729–1811), Fr. explorer] a woody tropical vine having flowers with large, showy, purple or red bracts

**bough** (bou) *n.* [OE. *bog*, shoulder, hence branch] a branch of a tree, esp. a main branch

**bought** (bôt) *pt. & pp. of* BUY —*adj.* [Dial.] *same as* BOUGHTEN

**bought·en** (-'n) *adj.* [Dial.] bought at a store and not home-made

**bouil·la·baisse** (bōōl′yə bās′; *Fr.* bōō yȧ bes′) *n.* [Fr. < Pr. < *bouli*, to boil + *abaissa*, to settle] a chowder made with several kinds of fish

**bouil·lon** (bōōl′yän, -yən; *Fr.* bōō yōn′) *n.* [Fr. < *bouillir*, to boil] a clear broth, esp. of beef

**Boul·der** (bōl′dər) [from the abundance of large rocks there] city in NC Colo.: pop. 77,000

**boul·der** (bōl′dər) *n.* [< ME. *bulderstan* < Scand., as in Sw. *bullersten*, lit., noisy stone] any large rock worn smooth and round by weather and water

**Boulder Dam** *former name of* HOOVER DAM

**boule** (bōōl) *n.* [Fr., ball] **1.** [*usually pl.*] a French game similar to bowls **2.** a gambling game like roulette **3.** a small rounded mass, as of synthetic ruby, produced by the fusion of alumina

**boul·e·vard** (bōōl′ə värd′) *n.* [Fr. < MDu. *bolwerc*, bulwark] a broad street, often lined with trees, plots of grass, etc.

**bounce** (bouns) *vt.* **bounced, bounc′ing** [akin to Du. *bonzen* & LowG. *bunsen*, to thump] **1.** orig., to bump or thump **2.** to cause to hit against a surface so as to spring back **3.** [Slang] *a)* to put (a person) out by force *b)* to discharge from employment —*vi.* **1.** to spring back after striking a surface; rebound **2.** to jump; leap [*bounce* out of bed] **3.** [Slang] to be returned to the payee by a bank: said of a worthless check —*n.* **1.** *a)* a bouncing; rebound *b)* a leap or jump **2.** capacity for bouncing **3.** [Colloq.] energy; zest —**bounce back** [Colloq.] to recover strength, spirits, etc. quickly —**the bounce** [Slang] dismissal or forcible ejection —**bounc′y** *adj.*

**bounc·er** (boun′sər) *n.* [Slang] a man hired to remove disorderly people from a nightclub, etc.

**bounc·ing** (-siŋ) *adj.* big, healthy, strong, etc.

**bouncing Bet** (bet) a perennial plant with pinkish flowers

**bound¹** (bound) *vi.* [Fr. *bondir*, to leap, orig., to echo < LL. < L. *bombus*, a humming (see BOMB)] **1.** to move with a leap or series of leaps **2.** to bounce or rebound, as a ball —*vt.* to cause to bound or bounce —*n.* **1.** a jump; leap **2.** a bounce

**bound²** (bound) *pt. & pp. of* BIND —*adj.* **1.** tied **2.** closely connected **3.** certain; destined [*bound* to win] **4.** obliged [legally *bound* to pay] **5** constipated **6.** provided with a binding, as a book **7.** [Colloq.] determined; resolved —**bound up in** (or **with**) **1.** devoted to **2.** involved in

**bound³** (bound) *adj.* [ME. < *boun*, ready < ON. *buinn*, pp. of *bua*: see BONDAGE] ready to go or going; headed [*bound* for home]

**bound⁴** (bound) *n.* [< OFr. < ML. *bodina*, boundary] **1.** a boundary; limit **2.** [*pl.*] a place near or enclosed by a boundary —*vt.* **1.** to limit; confine **2.** to be a limit or boundary to **3.** to name the boundaries of (a state, etc.) —*vi.* to have a boundary (*on* another country, etc.) —**out of bounds 1.** beyond the boundaries or limits **2.** not to be entered or used; forbidden

**-bound** (bound) *a combining form meaning* going or headed in (a specified direction) [*southbound*]

**bound·a·ry** (boun′drē, -dər ē) *n.*, *pl.* **-ries** [altered after BOUND⁴ < ML. *bunnarium*] any line or thing marking a limit; bound; border

**bound·en** (boun′dən) *adj.* [old pp. of BIND] **1.** under obligation **2.** obligatory [*bounden* duty]

**bound·er** (-dər) *n.* [BOUND¹ + -ER] [Chiefly Brit. Colloq.] an ill-mannered fellow; cad

**bound·less** (bound′lis) *adj.* having no bounds; unlimited —**bound′less·ly** *adv.* —**bound′less·ness** *n.*

**boun·te·ous** (boun′tē əs) *adj.* [< OFr. *bontive*: see BOUNTY] *same as* BOUNTIFUL —**boun′te·ous·ly** *adv.* —**boun′te·ous·ness** *n.*

**boun·ti·ful** (-tə f'l) *adj.* **1.** giving freely and graciously; generous **2.** abundant; plentiful —**boun′ti·ful·ly** *adv.*

**boun·ty** (-tē) *n.*, *pl.* **-ties** [< OFr. < L. < *bonus*, good] **1.** generosity **2.** a generous gift **3.** a reward or premium, as one given by a government for the performance of certain services

**bou·quet** (bō kā′; *also, & for 2 usually,* bōō-) *n.* [Fr.] **1.** a bunch of cut flowers **2.** a fragrant smell or aroma, esp. of a wine or brandy

**Bour·bon** (boor′bən) the ruling family at various times of France, Spain, Naples, Sicily, etc. —*n.* [*also* b-] a political and social reactionary —**Bour′bon·ism** *n.*

**bour·bon** (bʉr′bən, boor′-) *n.* [< *Bourbon* County, Ky.] [*sometimes* B-] a whiskey made from a mash of at least 51% corn and aged for not less than two years —*adj.* of or made with such whiskey

**bour·geois** (boor zhwä′, boor′zhwä) *n.*, *pl.* **-geois′** [Fr. < OFr. < ML. < LL. *burgus*, castle] **1.** a shopkeeper **2.** a member of the bourgeoisie **3.** a person whose beliefs, attitudes, etc. are middle-class —*adj.* of or characteristic of the bourgeoisie; middle-class, conventional, smug, materialistic, etc. —**bour·geoise′** (-zhwäz′) *n.fem.*

**bour·geoi·sie** (boor′zhwä zē′) *n.* [*with sing. or pl. v.*] **1.** the social class between the aristocracy or very wealthy and the working class; middle class **2.** in Marxist doctrine, capitalists as a social class antithetical to the proletariat

**bour·geon** (bʉr′jən) *n.*, *vt.*, *vi.* *same as* BURGEON

**bourn¹, bourne¹** (bôrn, boorn) *n.* [OE. *burna*, a stream] a brook or stream

**bourn², bourne²** (bôrn, boorn) *n.* [< Fr. < OFr. < ML. *bodina*: see BOUND⁴] [Archaic] **1.** a limit; boundary **2.** a goal; objective **3.** a domain

**Bourne·mouth** (bôrn′məth, boorn′-) resort city in S England: pop. 151,000

**bour·rée** (bōō rā′) *n.* [Fr. < *bourrir*, to whir] **1.** a lively, 17th-cent. French dance in duple time **2.** music for this

**bourse** (boors) *n.* [Fr., a purse < OFr. < ML. *bursa*, a bag < Gr. *byrsa*, a hide] a stock exchange; specif., [B-] the stock exchange of Paris

**bout** (bout) *n.* [for earlier *bought* < ME. *bught*] **1.** a struggle; contest or match **2.** a period of time taken up by some activity, illness, etc.

**bou·tique** (bōō tēk′) *n.* [Fr. < Gr. *apothēkē*: see APOTHECARY] a small shop, or a small department in a store, selling fashionable, expensive items

**bou·ton·niere, bou·ton·nière** (bōōt′'n ir′, -yer′) *n.* [Fr. *boutonnière*, a buttonhole] a flower or flowers worn in a buttonhole, as of a lapel

**bou·var·di·a** (bōō vär′dē ə) *n.* [ModL., after C. *Bouvard*, 17th-c. Fr. physician] a plant of the madder family, having showy flowers often used in brides' bouquets

**bou·vi·er des Flan·dres** (bōō′vē ā′ də flan′dərz) [Fr., cowherd of Flanders] a large, strong dog with a rough, wiry coat: first used in Flanders for herding cattle

**bou·zou·ki** (bōō zōō′kē) *n.* [< ModGr., prob. < Turk.] a stringed musical instrument of Greece, somewhat like a mandolin

**bo·vine** (bō′vīn, -vin, -vēn) *adj.* [< LL. < L. *bovis*, gen. of *bos*, ox] **1.** of an ox or cow **2.** slow, dull, stupid, stolid, etc. —*n.* an ox, cow, etc.

**bow¹** (bou) *vi.* [< OE. *bugan*, to bend] **1.** [Dial.] to bend or stoop **2.** to bend the head or body in respect, greeting, agreement, etc. **3.** to yield, as to authority —*vt.* **1.** [Dial.] to bend **2.** to bend (the head) in respect, prayer, shame, etc. **3.** to indicate (agreement, thanks, etc.) by bowing **4.** to weigh (*down*); overwhelm —*n.* a bending of the head or body, as in respect, greeting, etc. —**bow and scrape** to be too polite and ingratiating —**bow out 1.** to leave or retire formally **2.** (or **in**) to usher out (or in) with a bow —**take a bow** to acknowledge applause, etc. as by bowing

**bow²** (bō) *n.* [< OE. *boga* < *bugan*, BOW¹] **1.** anything curved or bent [a *rainbow*] **2.** a curve; bend **3.** a device for shooting arrows, a flexible, curved strip of wood, etc. with a taut cord connecting the two ends **4.** an archer **5.** a slender stick strung along its length with horsehairs, drawn across the strings of a violin, cello, etc. to play it **6.** *same as* BOWKNOT **7.** either of the sidepieces for the ears on a pair of glasses; temple —*vt.*, *vi.* **1.** to bend in the shape of a bow **2.** to play (a violin, etc.) with a bow

**bow³** (bou) *n.* [< LowG. or Scand.] **1.** the front part of a ship, etc.; prow **2.** the oarsman nearest the bow —*adj.* of or near the bow

**bowd·ler·ize** (boud′lə rīz′, bōd′-) *vt.* -ized′, -iz′ing [after Thomas *Bowdler*, who in 1818 published an expurgated Shakespeare] to expurgate —**bowd′ler·ism** *n.* —**bowd′ler·i·za′tion** *n.*

**bow·el** (bou′əl, boul) *n.* [< OFr. < ML. < L. *botellus*, dim. of *botulus*, sausage] **1.** an intestine, esp. of a human being; gut; entrail: *usually used in pl.* **2.** [*pl.*] the inner part [*the bowels* of the earth] **3.** [*pl.*] [Archaic] tender emotions —*vt.* -eled or -elled, -el·ing or -el·ling to disembowel —**move one's bowels** to pass waste matter from the large intestine; defecate

**bowel movement 1.** the act of defecating **2.** defecated matter; feces

**bow·er** (bou′ər) *n.* [< OE. *bur*, a dwelling] **1.** a place enclosed as by leafy boughs; arbor **2.** [Archaic] a boudoir —*vt.* to enclose in a bower —**bow′er·y** *adj.*

**Bow·er·y** (bou′ər ē, bou′rē) a street in New York City, a center of cheap hotels, saloons, etc.

**bow·fin** (bō′fin′) *n.* a primitive freshwater fish of E N. America, with a rounded tail fin

**bow·ie knife** (bōō′ē, bō′ē) [after Col. J. *Bowie*, Am. frontiersman] a long sheath knife with a single edge, orig. carried by frontiersmen

**bow·knot** (bō′nät′) *n.* a decorative knot, usually with two loops, untied by pulling the ends

**bowl¹** (bōl) *n.* [< OE. *bolla*] **1.** a deep, hollow, rounded dish **2.** a large drinking cup **3.** convivial drinking **4.** a thing or part shaped like a bowl, as the hollowed-out part of a smoking pipe, a hollow land formation, or an amphitheater **5.** the contents of a bowl —**bowl′like′** *adj.*

**bowl²** (bōl) *n.* [< OFr. < L. *bulla*, a bubble] **1.** a heavy ball used in the game of bowls **2.** a roll of the ball in bowling or bowls —*vi.*, *vt.* **1.** to roll (a ball) or participate in bowling or bowls **2.** to move or cause to move swiftly and smoothly, as on wheels **3.** *Cricket* to throw (a ball) to the batsman —**bowl over 1.** to knock over **2.** [Colloq.] to astonish and confuse —**bowl′er** *n.*

**bowl·der** (bōl′dər) *n.* same as BOULDER

**bow·leg** (bō′leg′) *n.* a leg that is bowed or curved outward —**bow′leg′ged** (-leg′id, -legd′) *adj.*

**bowl·er** (bōl′ər) *n.* [< *Bowler*, name of 19th-c. London hat manufacturer] [Brit.] a derby hat

**bow·line** (bō′lin, -lin′) *n.* [ME. *bouline*, prob. < Scand.] **1.** a rope used to keep the sail taut when sailing into the wind **2.** a knot used to tie off a loop: also **bowline knot**

**bowl·ing** (bōl′iŋ) *n.* **1.** a game in which a heavy ball is bowled along a wooden lane (**bowling alley**) in an attempt to knock over wooden pins, now usually ten, set upright at the far end **2.** *same as* BOWLS **3.** the playing of either game

**bowls** (bōlz) *n.* **1.** a game played on a smooth lawn (**bowling green**) with wooden balls which are rolled in an attempt to make them stop near a target ball (the *jack*) **2.** ninepins, tenpins, or skittles

**bow·man** (bō′mən) *n.*, *pl.* -men an archer

**bow·shot** (-shät′) *n.* the distance an arrow can travel when shot from a bow

**bow·sprit** (bou′sprit, bō′-) *n.* [prob. < Du. < *boeg*, BOW³ + *spriet*, SPRIT] a large, tapered spar extending forward from the bow of a sailing vessel

**bow·string** (bō′striŋ′) *n.* a cord stretched from one end of an archer's bow to the other

**bow tie** (bō) a small necktie tied in a bowknot

BOWSPRIT

**box¹** (bäks) *n.* [OE. < ML. *buxis* < L. *pyxos*, boxwood] **1.** any of various kinds of containers, usually lidded, made of cardboard, wood, or other stiff material; case; carton **2.** the contents of a box **3.** [< the tool *box* under the seat] the driver's seat on a coach **4.** any boxlike thing, as *a*) a small, enclosed group of seats in a theater, stadium, etc. *b*) a small booth *c*) a large, enclosed stall, for a horse, etc.: in full, **box stall** *d*) a space for a certain person or group [a jury *box*] **5.** a short newspaper article enclosed in borders **6.** *Baseball* any of the designated areas for the batter, pitcher, catcher, and coaches **7.** *Mech.* a protective casing for a part [a journal *box*] —*vt.* **1.** to provide with a box **2.** to put into a box —*adj.* **1.** shaped or made like a box **2.** packaged in a box —**box in** (or **up**) to shut in or keep in —**box the compass 1.** to name the thirty-two points of the compass in order: compasses were kept in boxes **2.** to make a complete circuit —**in a box** [Colloq.] in difficulty or a dilemma —**box′like′** *adj.*

**box²** (bäks) *n.* [< ?] a blow struck with the hand or fist, esp. on the ear —*vt.* **1.** to strike such a blow **2.** to fight in a boxing match with —*vi.* to fight with the fists; engage in boxing

**box³** (bäks) *n.* [OE. < L. *buxus* < Gr. *pyxos*] an evergreen shrub or small tree with small, leathery leaves

**box·car** (-kär′) *n.* a fully enclosed railroad freight car

**box elder** a fast-growing N. American maple with compound leaves

**Box·er** (bäk′sər) *n.* a member of a Chinese society that led an unsuccessful uprising (the **Boxer Rebellion,** 1900) against foreigners in China

**box·er** (bäk′sər) *n.* **1.** a man who boxes; pugilist; prizefighter **2.** a medium-sized dog with a sturdy body and a smooth, fawn or brindle coat

**box·ing** (-siŋ) *n.* [< BOX²] the skill or sport of fighting with the fists, esp. in padded leather mittens (**boxing gloves**)

**box office 1.** a place where admission tickets are sold, as in a theater **2.** [Colloq.] the power of a show or performer to attract an audience

**box pleat** a double pleat with the under edges folded toward each other

**box score** a statistical summary of a baseball game, showing the hits, runs, errors, etc.

**box seat** a seat in a box at a theater, etc.

**box turtle** a N. American land turtle with a hinged under shell that can be completely closed

**box·wood** (bäks′wood′) *n.* **1.** the wood of the box (shrub or tree) **2.** the box (shrub or tree)

**box·y** (bäk′sē) *adj.* -i·er, -i·est like a box, as in squarish form, confining quality, etc.

**boy** (boi) *n.* [ME. *boie*] **1.** a male child from birth to physical maturity **2.** an immature or callow man **3.** any man; fellow: familiar term **4.** a man servant, porter, etc.: a patronizing term **5.** [Colloq.] a son —*interj.* [Slang] an exclamation of pleasure, surprise, etc.: often **oh, boy!** —**boy′ish** *adj.* —**boy′ish·ly** *adv.* —**boy′ish·ness** *n.*

**boy·cott** (boi′kät) *vt.* [after Captain C. C. *Boycott,* Irish land agent so treated in 1880] **1.** to join together in refusing to deal with, so as to punish, coerce, etc. **2.** to refuse to buy, sell, or use (something) —*n.* the act of boycotting

**boy·friend** (boi′frend′) *n.* [Colloq.] **1.** a sweetheart, beau, or escort of a girl or woman **2.** a boy who is one's friend

**boy·hood** (-hood′) *n.* [see -HOOD] **1.** the time or state of being a boy **2.** boys collectively

**boy scout** a member of the **Boy Scouts,** a worldwide boys' organization that stresses outdoor life and service to others

**boy·sen·ber·ry** (boi′z'n ber′ē) *n.*, *pl.* -ries [after Rudolph *Boysen*, U.S. horticulturist] a large, purple berry, a cross of the raspberry, loganberry, and blackberry

**bp. 1.** birthplace: also **bpl. 2.** bishop

**B/P, BP, b.p.** bills payable

**b.p. 1.** below proof **2.** boiling point

**Br** *Chem.* bromine

**Br. 1.** Breton **2.** Britain **3.** British

**br. 1.** branch **2.** bronze **3.** brother **4.** brown

**B/R, BR, b.r.** bills receivable

**bra** (brä) *n.* [< BRA(SSIERE)] an undergarment worn by women to support and shape the breasts

**brace** (brās) *vt.* **braced, brac′ing** [< OFr. < L. *brachia,* pl. of *brachium,* an arm] **1.** to tie or bind on firmly **2.** to tighten, esp. by stretching **3.** to strengthen or make firm by supporting the weight of, etc.; prop up **4.** to equip with braces **5.** to make ready for an impact, shock, etc. **6.** to stimulate **7.** to get a firm hold with (the hands or feet) —*n.* **1.** a couple; pair **2.** a device that clasps or connects; fastener **3.** [*pl.*] [Brit.] suspenders **4.** a device for maintaining tension, as a guy wire **5.** either of the signs { }, used to connect words, lines, or staves of music **6.** a device, as a beam, used as a support, to resist strain, etc.; prop **7.** *a*) any of various devices for supporting a weak or deformed part of the body *b*) [*often pl.*] a device for irregular teeth to force them into proper occlusion **8.** a tool for holding and rotating a drilling bit —**brace up** [Colloq.] to call forth one's courage, etc.

**brace and bit** a tool for boring, consisting of a removable drill (*bit*) in a rotating handle (*brace*)

**brace·let** (brās′lit) *n.* [< OFr. < L. < *brachium,* an arm] **1.** an ornamental band or chain worn about the wrist or arm **2.** [Colloq.] a handcuff: *usually used in pl.*

**brac·er** (brā′sər) *n.* **1.** a person or thing that braces **2.** [Slang] a drink of alcoholic liquor

**bra·ce·ro** (brə ser′ō) *n.*, *pl.* -ros [Sp. < *brazo*, an arm < L. *brachium*] a Mexican farm laborer brought into the U.S. temporarily for migrant work in harvesting crops

**bra·chi·o-** [< L. < Gr. *brachiōn*, an arm] *a combining form meaning* of an arm or the arms [*brachiopod*]: also **bra′chi-**

BRACE AND BIT

**bra·chi·o·pod** (brā′kē ə päd′, brak′ē-) *n.* [prec. + -POD] any of a number of related marine animals with hinged upper and lower shells and two armlike parts with tentacles

**bra·chi·um** (brā′kē əm, brak′ē-) *n., pl.* **-chi·a** (-ə) [L.] **1.** the part of the arm from the shoulder to the elbow **2.** *Biol.* any armlike part —**bra′chi·al** *adj.*

**brach·y-** [< Gr. *brachys*, short] *a combining form meaning short* [*brachycephalic*]

**brach·y·ce·phal·ic** (brak′i sə fal′ik) *adj.* [BRACHY- + -CEPHALIC] having a relatively short or broad head: also **brach′y·ceph′a·lous** (-sef′ə ləs): see CEPHALIC INDEX —**brach′y·ceph′a·ly** (-sef′ə lē) *n.*

**brac·ing** (brās′iŋ) *adj.* invigorating; stimulating —*n.* **1.** a device that braces **2.** braces

**brack·en** (brak′'n) *n.* [< ON.] **1.** a large, coarse fern, as the brake **2.** a growth of such ferns

**brack·et** (brak′it) *n.* [< Fr. dim. of *brague*, knee pants, ult. < Gaul. *braca*, pants] **1.** an architectural support projecting from a wall **2.** any angle-shaped support, esp. one in the form of a right triangle **3.** a wall shelf held up by brackets **4.** a wall fixture, as for a small electric lamp **5.** either of the signs [ ], used to enclose words, figures, etc. **6.** the part of a classified grouping that falls within specified limits [a $5 to $10 price *bracket*] —*vt.* **1.** to support with brackets **2.** to enclose in brackets **3.** to classify together

**brack·ish** (brak′ish) *adj.* [earlier Scot. *brack* < MDu. *brak*, salty + -ISH] **1.** somewhat salty, as water in some marshes near the sea **2.** having an unpleasant taste; nauseating —**brack′ish·ness** *n.*

**bract** (brakt) *n.* [L. *bractea*, thin metal plate] a modified leaf, usually small and scalelike, growing at the base of a flower or on its stalk —**brac·te·al** (brak′tē əl) *adj.* —**brac′te·ate** (-it) *adj.*

**bract·let** (-lit) *n.* a secondary bract at the base of a flower: also **brac·te·ole** (brak′tē ōl′)

**brad** (brad) *n.* [ON. *broddr*, a spike] a thin wire nail with a small or off-center head —*vt.* **brad′ded, brad′ding** to fasten with brads

**Brad·ford** (brad′fərd) city in N England, in Yorkshire: pop. 294,000

**Brad·ford** (brad′fərd), **William** 1590–1657; 2d governor of Plymouth Colony

**Bra·dy** (brā′dē), **Mat·hew B.** (math′yōō) 1823?–96; U.S. photographer

**brae** (brā) *n.* [ON. *bra*, eyelid, brow] [Scot.] a sloping bank; hillside

**brag** (brag) *vt., vi* **bragged, brag′ging** [prob. < OFr. *braguer;* ? akin to BRAY] to boast —*n.* **1.** boastful talk or manner **2.** [Colloq.] anything boasted of; boast **3.** a braggart —**brag′ger** *n.*

**brag·ga·do·ci·o** (brag′ə dō′shē ō, -dō′shō) *n., pl.* **-os** [coined by Spenser < BRAG + It. ending] **1.** a braggart **2.** noisy boasting or bragging

**brag·gart** (brag′ərt) *n.* [< OFr.: see BRAG] an offensively boastful person —*adj.* boastful

**Bra·he** (brä′ə), **Ty·cho** (tü′kō) 1546–1601; Dan. astronomer

**Brah·ma** (brä′mə; *for n.* brā′-) [Hindi < Sans. *brahman*, worship] *Hinduism* **1.** the supreme essence or spirit of the universe **2.** the chief member of the trinity (Brahma, Vishnu, and Siva) and creator of the universe —*n. same as* BRAHMAN (sense 2)

**Brah·man** (brä′mən; *for 2* brā′-) *n., pl.* **-mans** [see prec.] **1.** a member of the priestly Hindu caste, the highest **2.** a breed of domestic cattle developed from the zebu of India —**Brah·man·ic** (brä man′ik), **Brah·man′i·cal** *adj.*

**Brah·man·ism** (-iz′m) *n.* the religious doctrines and system of the Brahmans

**Brah·min** (brä′mən) *n.* **1.** *same as* BRAHMAN (sense 1) **2.** a cultured, upper-class person, esp. of New England, regarded as haughty or conservative —**Brah·min·ic** (brä-min′ik), **Brah·min′i·cal** *adj.*

**Brah·min·ism** (-iz′m) *n.* **1.** *same as* BRAHMANISM **2.** the characteristic attitude, etc. of Brahmins

**Brahms** (brämz), **Jo·han·nes** (yō hän′əs) 1833–97; Ger. composer

**braid** (brād) *vt.* [< OE. *bregdan*, to move quickly] **1.** to interweave three or more strands of (hair, straw, etc.) **2.** to make by such interweaving **3.** to arrange (the hair) in a braid or braids **4.** to trim or bind with braid —*n.* **1.** a band or strip formed by braiding **2.** a length of braided hair **3.** a woven band of tape, ribbon, etc. used to bind or decorate clothing —**braid′er** *n.* —**braid′ing** *n.*

**Braille** (brāl) *n.* [after L. *Braille* (1809–52), Fr. teacher who devised it] [*also* b-] **1.** a system of printing and writing for the blind, using raised dots felt by the fingers **2.** the characters used in this system —*vt.* **Brailled, Brail′ling** [*also* b-] to print or write in such characters

**brain** (brān) *n.* [OE. *brægen*] **1.** the mass of nerve tissue in the cranium of vertebrate animals: it is the center of thought and receives and transmits impulses: cf. GRAY MATTER, WHITE MATTER **2.** *a)* [*often pl.*] intelligence; mental ability *b)* [Colloq.] a person of great intelligence *c)* [Colloq.] the main organizer of a group activity —*vt.* **1.** to dash out the brains of **2.** [Slang] to hit hard on the head —**beat** (or **rack, cudgel,** etc.) **one's brains** to try hard to remember, understand, etc. —**have on the brain** to be obsessed by

**brain·case** (-kās′) *n. same as* BRAINPAN

**brain·child** (-chīld′) *n.* [Colloq.] an idea, plan, etc. regarded as produced by one's mental labor

**brain drain** [Colloq.] depletion of the intellectual or professional resources of a country, etc., esp. through emigration

**brain·less** (-lis) *adj.* foolish or stupid —**brain′less·ly** *adv.* —**brain′less·ness** *n.*

**brain·pan** (-pan′) *n.* the part of the cranium containing the brain

**brain·pow·er** (-pou′ər) *n.* mental ability

**brain·storm** (-stôrm′) *n.* [Colloq.] a sudden inspiration or idea —*vi.* to engage in brainstorming

**brain·storm·ing** (-stôr′miŋ) *n.* the unrestrained offering of ideas by all members of a conference to seek solutions to problems

**brain trust** a group of experts acting as administrative advisers —**brain truster**

**brain·wash** (-wôsh′, -wäsh′) *vt.* [Colloq.] to indoctrinate so intensively and thoroughly as to effect a radical transformation of beliefs

**brain wave** rhythmic electric impulses given off by nerve centers in the brain during rest

**brain·y** (-ē) *adj.* **brain′i·er, brain′i·est** [Colloq.] intelligent; mentally bright —**brain′i·ness** *n.*

**braise** (brāz) *vt.* **braised, brais′ing** [Fr. *braiser* < *braise* (< Gmc. *brasa*), live coals] to cook (meat) by browning in fat and then simmering in a covered pan with a little liquid

**brake¹** (brāk) *n.* [prob. taken as sing. of BRACKEN] a large, coarse fern, a variety of bracken

**brake²** (brāk) *n.* [< MLowG. *brake* or ODu. *braeke* < *breken*, to break] **1.** a device for beating flax or hemp so that the fiber can be separated **2.** any device for slowing or stopping the motion of a vehicle or machine, as by causing a block or band to press against a moving part —*vt.* **braked, brak′ing, 1.** to break up (flax, etc.) into smaller pieces **2.** to slow down or stop as with a brake —*vi.* **1.** to operate a brake **2.** to be slowed down or stopped by a brake —**brake′less** *adj.*

**brake³** (brāk) *n.* [< or akin to MLowG. *brake*, stumps] a clump of brushwood, briers, etc.

**brake⁴** (brāk) *archaic pt. of* BREAK

**brake band** a band with a lining (**brake lining**) of asbestos, fine wire, etc., that creates friction when tightened about the drum of a brake

**brake·man** (-mən) *n., pl.* **-men** a railroad worker who operated the brakes on a train, but is now chiefly an assistant to the conductor

**brake shoe** a block curved to fit the shape of a wheel and forced against it to act as a brake

**bram·ble** (bram′b'l) *n.* [< OE. *bræmel* < *brom*, broom] **1.** any prickly shrub of the rose family, as the raspberry, blackberry, etc. **2.** any prickly shrub or vine —**bram′bly** *adj.* **-bli·er, -bli·est**

**bran** (bran) *n.* [OFr. *bren*] the skin or husk of grains of wheat, rye, oats, etc. separated from the flour, as by sifting

**branch** (branch) *n.* [< OFr. *brance* < LL. *branca*, a paw] **1.** any woody extension from the trunk or main stem, or from a main limb, of a tree or shrub **2.** anything like a branch, as a tine of a deer's antler **3.** any of the streams into which a river may divide or which flow into it **4.** *same as* BRANCH WATER **5.** *a)* a division of a body of learning *b)* a division of a family *c)* a separately located unit of an organization [a *branch* of a library] —*vi.* **1.** to put forth or divide into branches; ramify **2.** to come out (*from* the trunk or stem) as a branch —*vt.* to separate into branches —**branch off 1.** to separate into branches; fork **2.** to go off in another direction; diverge —**branch out 1.** to put forth branches **2.** to extend the scope of interests, activities, etc. —**branched** *adj.* —**branch′like** *adj.*

**bran·chi·ae** (braŋ′ki ē′) *n.pl., sing.* **-chi·a** (-ə) [< L. < Gr. *branchia*, fins] the gills of a fish —**bran′chi·al** *adj.* —**bran′chi·ate** (-kē it) *adj.*

**branch water 1.** water from a small stream **2.** water as used for mixing with whiskey, etc.

**brand** (brand) *n.* [< OE., flame, sword < base of *biernan*, *vi.*, to burn] **1.** a stick that is burning or partially burned **2.** *a)* a mark burned on the skin with a hot iron, formerly used to punish and identify criminals, now used on cattle to show ownership *b*) the iron thus used **3.** a mark of disgrace; stigma **4.** *a*) an identifying mark or label on products; trademark *b*) the kind or make of a commodity [a *brand* of cigars] *c*) a special kind [a *brand* of nonsense] **5.** [Archaic] a sword —*vt.* **1.** to mark with or as with a brand **2.** to mark as disgraceful —**brand′er** *n.*

**Bran·deis** (bran′dīs), **Louis Dem·bitz** (dem′bits) 1856–1941; U.S. Supreme Court justice

**Bran·den·burg** (bran′dən burg′; *G.* brän′dən boork′) region in E Germany, surrounding Berlin

**bran·dish** (bran′dish) *vt.* [< OFr. < Gmc. *brand:* see BRAND] to wave or shake menacingly or exultantly; flourish —*n.* a brandishing of something

**brand name** the name by which a brand or make of commodity is known —**brand′name′** *adj.*

**brand-new** (brand′nŏŏ′, -nyŏŏ′) *adj.* [orig., fresh from the fire: see BRAND] **1.** entirely new; recently made **2.** recently acquired

**bran·dy** (bran′dē) *n., pl.* **-dies** [earlier *brandywine* < Du. *brandewijn,* lit., burnt (i.e., distilled) wine] **1.** an alcoholic liquor distilled from wine **2.** a similar liquor distilled from fermented fruit juice [cherry *brandy*] —*vt.* **-died, -dy·ing** to flavor, mix, or preserve with brandy

**bran·ni·gan** (bran′ə gən) *n.* [prob. < surname *Brannigan*] [Slang] a noisy quarrel or fight; brawl

**brant** (brant) *n., pl.* **brants, brant:** see PLURAL, II, D, 1 [< ?] any of a number of related small, dark wild geese of Europe and N. America

**Brant·ford** (brant′fərd) city in SE Ontario, Canada: pop. 60,000

**Braque** (bråk), **Georges** (zhôrzh) 1882–1963; Fr. painter

**brash** (brash) *adj.* [< ?] **1.** brittle, as some wood **2.** reckless; rash **3.** bold, presumptuous, impudent, etc. —**brash′ly** *adv.* —**brash′ness** *n.*

**bra·sier** (brā′zhər) *n. same as* BRAZIER

**Bra·sil** (brä zēl′) *Port. sp. of* BRAZIL

**Bra·si·lia** (brä zē′lyä) capital of Brazil, in the EC part: pop. 400,000

**brass** (bras) *n., pl.* **brass′es:** *see* PLURAL, II, D, 3 [OE. *bræs*] **1.** a yellowish metal that is essentially an alloy of copper and zinc **2.** things made of brass **3.** [*often pl.*] brass-wind musical instruments **4.** [Colloq.] bold impudence **5.** [*often with pl. v.*] [Slang] *a*) military officers of high rank: see BRASS HAT *b*) any high officials —*adj.* made of brass

**bras·sard** (brə särd′, bras′ärd) *n.* [Fr., ult. < *bras,* an arm] **1.** armor for the upper arm: also **bras·sart** (bras′ärt) **2.** an identifying arm band

**brass band** a band of esp. brass-wind instruments

**brass hat** [< the gold braid on the cap] [Slang] **1.** a military officer of high rank **2.** any high official

**brass·ie** (bras′ē) *n.* [orig. made with a *brass* sole] a golf club with a wooden head, used for long fairway shots: now usually called *number 2 wood*

**bras·siere, bras·sière** (brə zir′) *n.* [Fr., orig. arm guard < *bras,* an arm] *same as* BRA

**brass knuckles** linked metal rings or a metal bar with finger holes, worn for rough fighting

**brass tacks** [Colloq.] basic facts; practical details: usually in **get (or come) down to brass tacks**

**brass·ware** (bras′wer′) *n.* articles made of brass

**brass winds** (windz) musical instruments made of coiled metal tubes and having a cup-shaped mouthpiece —**brass′-wind′** *adj.*

**brass·y** (-ē) *adj.* **brass′i·er, brass′i·est** **1.** of or decorated with brass **2.** like brass **3.** tawdry **4.** loud and blaring **5.** impudent; brazen —**brass′i·ly** *adv.* —**brass′i·ness** *n.*

**brat** (brat) *n.* [OE. *bratt,* a cloak < Gael. *bratt,* a cloth, rag < ?] a child, esp. an impudent, unruly child: scornful or playful term —**brat′ti·ness, brat′tish·ness** *n.* —**brat′ty, brat′tish** *adj.*

**Bra·ti·sla·va** (bra′ti slä′və) city in S Czechoslovakia, on the Danube: pop. 277,000

**brat·wurst** (brat′wərst; *G.* brät′voorsht) *n.* [G. < OHG. < *brato,* lean meat + *wurst,* sausage] highly seasoned, fresh sausage of veal and pork

**bra·va·do** (brə vä′dō) *n.* [< Sp. *bravada* < *bravo,* BRAVE] pretended courage or feigned confidence

**brave** (brāv) *adj.* [Fr. < It. *bravo,* brave, fine, orig., wild, savage < L. *barbarus,* BARBAROUS] **1.** not afraid; having courage; valiant **2.** [Poet.] splendid [*brave* new world] —*n.* **1.** any brave man **2.** [< 17th-c. NAmFr.] a N. American Indian warrior —*vt.* **braved, brav′ing** **1.** to face with courage **2.** to defy; dare —**brave′ly** *adv.* —**brave′ness** *n.*

**brav·er·y** (brā′vər ē) *n.* **1.** courage; valor **2.** fine appearance, show, or dress

**bra·vo′** (brä′vō) *interj.* [It.: see BRAVE, *adj.*] well done! very good! excellent! —*n., pl.* **-vos** a shout of "bravo!" —**bra′va** (-vä) *interj., n.fem.*

**bra·vo²** (brä′vō) *n., pl.* **-voes, -vos;** It. **-vi** (-vē) [It.: see BRAVE] a hired killer; assassin

**bra·vu·ra** (brə vyoor′ə) *n.* [It., spirit < *bravo,* BRAVE] **1.** a display of daring; dash **2.** *Music a*) a brilliant passage or piece that displays the performer's skill and technique *b*) brilliant technique —*adj.* characterized by bravura

**braw** (brô, brä) *adj.* [< BRAVE] [Scot.] **1.** finely dressed **2.** fine; excellent

**brawl** (brôl) *vi.* [< ? Du. *brallen,* to boast] to quarrel or fight noisily —*n.* **1.** a noisy quarrel or fight; row **2.** [Slang] a noisy party —**brawl′er** *n.*

**brawn** (brôn) *n.* [< OFr. *braon,* muscular part < Frank. *brado,* meat, calf (of leg)] **1.** strong, well-developed muscles **2.** muscular strength —**brawn′i·ness** *n.* —**brawn′y** *adj.* **brawn′i·er, brawn′i·est**

**bray** (brā) *vi.* [< OFr. < VL. *bragire,* to cry out] to make the loud, harsh cry of a donkey, or a sound, esp. a laugh, like this —*vt.* to utter loudly and harshly —*n.* the loud, harsh cry of a donkey, or a sound like this

**braze′** (brāz) *vt.* **brazed, braz′ing** [Fr. *braser,* to solder, var. of *braiser,* BRAISE] to solder with a metal having a high melting point, esp. with an alloy of zinc and copper —**braz′er** *n.*

**braze²** (brāz) *vt.* **brazed, braz′ing** [< OE. *bræsian* < *bræs,* BRASS] **1.** to make of, or coat with, brass **2.** to make hard like brass —**braz′er** *n.*

**bra·zen** (brā′z′n) *adj.* [OE. *bræsen* < *bræs,* BRASS] **1.** of brass **2.** like brass in color, etc. **3.** showing no shame; bold; impudent **4.** harsh and piercing —**brazen it out** to act boldly as if one need not be ashamed —**bra′zen·ly** *adv.* —**bra′zen·ness** *n.*

**bra·zier′** (brā′zhər) *n.* [Fr. *brasier* < *braise:* see BRAISE] a metal pan, bowl, etc. to hold burning coals or charcoal

**bra·zier²** (brā′zhər) *n.* [see BRASS] a person who works in brass

**Bra·zil** (brə zil′) country in C & SE S. America: c. 3,287,000 sq. mi.; pop. 90,990,000; cap. Brasília —**Bra·zil′ian** (-yən) *adj., n.*

**Brazil nut** **1.** a hard-shelled, three-sided, oily, edible seed of a tall S. American tree **2.** this tree, on which the seeds grow clustered in capsules

**Braz·za·ville** (brä′zə vil′) capital of the Congo, on the Congo River: pop. 156,000

**breach** (brēch) *n.* [< OE. < *brecan,* to break] **1.** orig., a breaking or being broken **2.** a failure to observe a law, a contract, etiquette, public peace, etc. **3.** an opening made by breaking through a wall, defense, etc. **4.** a break in friendly relations —*vt.* to make a breach in; break through

BRAZIL NUTS

**breach of promise** a breaking of a promise to marry

**bread** (bred) *n.* [OE. *bread,* crumb, morsel] **1.** a food baked from a leavened, kneaded dough made with flour or meal, water, yeast, etc. **2.** any baked food like bread but made with a batter [quick *breads*] **3.** food generally **4.** one's livelihood **5.** [Slang] money —*vt.* to cover with bread crumbs before cooking —**bread and butter** one's means of subsistence; livelihood —**break bread** to partake of food; eat —**cast one's bread upon the waters** to do good deeds without expecting something in return —**know which side one's bread is buttered on** to know what is to one's economic interest

**bread-and-but·ter** (-′n but′ər) *adj.* **1.** of the product, work, etc. basically relied on for earnings **2.** basic, commonplace, everyday, etc. **3.** expressing thanks, as a letter to one's host after a visit

**bread·bas·ket** (-bas′kit) *n.* **1.** a region supplying much grain **2.** [Slang] the stomach or abdomen

**bread·fruit** (-frōōt′) *n.* **1.** a large, round fruit with a starchy pulp, that is like bread when baked **2.** the tropical tree on which it grows

**bread line** a line of people waiting to be given food as government relief or private charity

**bread·stuff** (-stuf′) *n.* **1.** ground grain or flour for making bread **2.** bread

**breadth** (bredth) *n.* [OE. *brædu* < *brad,* broad + -TH¹] **1.** the distance from side to side of a thing; width **2.** a piece of a given and regular width [a *breadth* of linoleum] **3.** lack of narrowness [*breadth* of knowledge]

**breadth·ways** (-wāz′) *adv., adj.* in the direction of the breadth: also **breadth′wise′** (-wiz′)

**bread·win·ner** (bred′win′ər) *n.* a person who supports dependents by his earnings

**break** (brāk) *vt.* **broke, bro′ken, break′ing** [OE. *brecan*] **1.** to cause to come apart by force; smash; burst **2.** to cut open the surface of (soil, the skin, etc.) **3.** to cause the failure of by force [to *break* a strike] **4.** to make inoperative by cracking, disrupting, etc. **5.** to make obedient with or as with force **6.** to get rid of (a habit) or to cause to get rid of (of a habit) **7.** to lower in rank or grade; demote **8.** *a)* to reduce to poverty or bankruptcy *b)* to wreck the health, spirit, etc. of **9.** to surpass (a record) **10.** to violate (a law, agreement, etc.) **11.** to escape from by force *[to break* prison*]* **12.** to disrupt the order or completeness of *[to break* ranks*]* **13.** to interrupt (a journey, electric circuit, etc.) **14.** to reduce the force of by interrupting (a fall, etc.) **15.** to bring to a sudden end *[to break* a tie*]* **16.** to penetrate (silence, darkness, etc.) **17.** to make known; disclose **18.** *a)* to decipher (a code, etc.) *b)* to solve *[to break* a criminal case*]* **19.** to make (a will) invalid **20.** to prove (an alibi) false **21.** to begin; open **22.** to exchange (a bill or coin) for smaller units —*vi.* **1.** to split into pieces; come apart; burst **2.** to scatter; disperse *[break* and run*]* **3.** to force one's way *(through)* **4.** to stop associating *(with)* **5.** to become inoperative **6.** to rise, fall, turn, shift, etc. suddenly **7.** to move away suddenly **8.** to begin suddenly to perform, etc. *[break* into song*]* **9.** to come into being, evidence, or general knowledge *[the story broke]* **10.** *a)* to fall apart slowly; disintegrate *b)* to dash apart, as a wave on the shore **11.** to curve near the plate: said of a pitched baseball **12.** [Colloq.] to happen in a certain way *[things were breaking* badly*]* —*n.* **1.** a breaking; breach; fracture **2.** *a)* a breaking in, out, or forth *b)* a sudden move; rush; dash **3.** a broken place; separation; crack **4.** a beginning or appearance *[break* of day*]* **5.** an interruption of something regular **6.** a gap; interval; omission **7.** a breach in friendly relations **8.** a sudden change **9.** an escape, as from prison **10.** a lowering or drop, as of prices **11.** [Colloq.] an improper or untimely action or remark **12.** [Slang] a chance piece of luck, specif. of good luck **13.** *Music a)* the point where one register changes to another *b)* a transitional phrase in a piece of jazz music —**break down 1.** to go out of working order **2.** to give way to tears or emotion **3.** to have a physical or nervous collapse **4.** to analyze —**break in 1.** to enter forcibly **2.** to interrupt **3.** to train (a beginner) **4.** to work the stiffness out of (new equipment) —**break off 1.** to stop abruptly **2.** to stop being friendly —**break out 1.** to begin suddenly **2.** to escape **3.** to become covered with pimples or a rash **4.** to bring out for use *[break out* the gear*]* —**break up 1.** to disperse: also, esp. as a command, **break it up 2.** to take apart **3.** to put a stop to **4.** [Colloq.] to end a relationship **5.** [Colloq.] to distress; upset **6.** [Colloq.] to laugh or make laugh uncontrollably —**break'a·ble** *adj.*

**break·age** (-ij) *n.* **1.** a breaking **2.** things or quantity broken **3.** loss or damage due to breaking, or the sum allowed for this

**break·down** (-doun') *n.* **1.** a breaking down; specif., *a)* a failure to function properly *b)* a failure of health *c)* decomposition *d)* a separating into parts; analysis **2.** a lively, shuffling dance

**break·er** (-ər) *n.* **1.** a person or thing that breaks; specif., a wave that breaks into foam

**break·fast** (brek'fəst) *n.* the first meal of the day —*vi.* to eat breakfast —*vt.* to give breakfast to —**break'fast·er** *n.*

**break·front** (brāk'frunt') *adj.* having a front with a projecting section —*n.* a breakfront cabinet

**breaking point** the point at which material, or one's endurance, etc., collapses under strain

**break·neck** (brāk'nek') *adj.* likely to cause an accident; highly dangerous *[breakneck* speed*]*

**break·out** (-out') *n.* **1.** a sudden, forceful escape, as from prison **2.** a skin eruption

**break·through** (-throo') *n.* **1.** the act or place of breaking through against resistance **2.** a strikingly important advance or discovery

**break·up** (-up') *n.* a breaking up; specif., *a)* a dispersion *b)* a disintegration or decay *c)* a collapse *d)* a stopping or ending

**break·wa·ter** (-wôt'ər, -wät'-) *n.* a barrier to break the impact of waves, as before a harbor

**bream** (brēm; *also, esp. for 2,* brim) *n., pl.* **bream, breams:** see PLURAL, II, D, 2 *[< OFr. bresme < Frank. brahsima]* **1.** a European freshwater fish related to the minnows **2.** any of various saltwater fishes **3.** any of various freshwater sunfishes

**breast** (brest) *n.* [OE. *breost*] **1.** either of two milk-secreting glands at the upper, front part of a woman's body **2.** a corresponding gland in other animals **3.** the upper, front part of the body; chest **4.** the part of a garment, etc. that is over the breast **5.** the breast regarded as the center of emotions **6.** anything likened to the breast *[the breast* of the sea*]* —*vt.* to face, esp. firmly —**beat one's breast to** make an exaggerated display of feeling, as of guilt —**make a clean breast of** to confess (guilt, etc.) fully

**breast·bone** (-bōn') *n.* same as STERNUM

**breast-feed** (-fēd') *vt.* **-fed'** (-fed'), **-feed'ing** to feed (a baby) milk from the breast; suckle

**breast·pin** (-pin') *n.* an ornamental pin or brooch worn on a dress, near the throat

**breast·plate** (-plāt') *n.* a piece of armor for the breast

**breast stroke** a swimming stroke in which both arms are simultaneously brought out sideways from a position close to the chest

**breast·work** (-wurk') *n.* a low wall put up quickly as a defense, esp. to protect gunners

**breath** (breth) *n.* [OE. *bræth*, odor, exhalation] **1.** air taken into the lungs and then let out **2.** breathing; respiration **3.** the power to breathe easily **4.** life or spirit **5.** air carrying fragrance or odor **6.** a puff or whiff, as of air; slight breeze **7.** moisture produced by a condensing of the breath, as in cold air **8.** a whisper or murmur **9.** the time taken by a single respiration; moment **10.** a slight pause or rest **11.** a faint hint or indication **12.** *Phonet.* a voiceless exhalation of the airstream, as in pronouncing (s) or (p) —**below** (or **under**) **one's breath** in a whisper or murmur —**catch one's breath 1.** to gasp or pant **2.** to pause or rest —**in the same breath** almost simultaneously —**out of breath** breathless, as from exertion —**save one's breath** to refrain from talking —**take one's breath away** to thrill

**breathe** (brēth) *vi., vt.* **breathed, breath'ing** [< ME. < *breth*, BREATH] **1.** to take (air) into the lungs and let it out again; inhale and exhale **2.** to live **3.** to give out (an odor) **4.** to instill *[to breathe* confidence*]* **5.** to blow softly **6.** to speak or sing softly; whisper **7.** to give or take time to breathe; rest **8.** to pant or cause to pant, as from exertion —**breathe again** (or **freely**) to have a feeling of relief or reassurance —**breathe one's last** to die —**breath·a·ble** (brē'thə b'l) *adj.*

**breath·er** (brē'thər) *n.* **1.** one who breathes in a certain way **2.** a small vent, as for releasing moisture **3.** [Colloq.] a pause as for rest

**breath·ing** (brē'thiŋ) *adj.* that breathes; living; alive —*n.* **1.** respiration **2.** a single breath or the time taken by this **3.** a pause for rest **4.** the sound of *h* in *hit, hope,* etc.; aspirate

**breath·less** (breth'lis) *adj.* **1.** without breath **2.** no longer breathing; dead **3.** out of breath; gasping **4.** unable to breathe easily because of excitement, fear, etc. **5.** still and heavy, as the air —**breath'less·ly** *adv.* —**breath'less·ness** *n.*

**breath·tak·ing** (-tāk'iŋ) *adj.* **1.** that takes one's breath away **2.** very exciting; thrilling —**breath'tak'ing·ly** *adv.*

**breath·y** (-ē) *adj.* with too much, audible letting out of breath —**breath'i·ly** *adv.* —**breath'i·ness** *n.*

**brec·ci·a** (brech'ē ə, bresh'-) *n.* [It.] rock consisting of sharp-cornered bits cemented together by sand, clay, or lime

**Brecht** (breHt; *E.* brekt), **Ber·tolt** (ber'tôlt) 1898–1956; Ger. playwright

**bred** (bred) *pt. & pp. of* BREED

**breech** (brēch; *for vt. 1, usually* brich) *n.* [< OE. *brec,* pl. of *broc]* **1.** the buttocks; rump **2.** the lower or back part of a thing **3.** the part of a gun behind the barrel —*vt.* **1.** to clothe with breeches **2.** to provide (a gun) with a breech

**breech·cloth** (-klôth') *n.* a cloth worn about the loins; loincloth: also **breech'clout'** (-klout')

**breech·es** (brich'iz) *n.pl.* [see BREECH] **1.** trousers reaching to the knees **2.** [Colloq.] any trousers

**breeches buoy** (brēch'iz, brich'-) a device for rescuing people at sea, consisting of a pair of short canvas breeches suspended from a life preserver that is run along a rope from ship to shore or to another ship

**breech·ing** (brich'iŋ, brēch'-) *n.* a harness strap around a horse's hindquarters

**breech·load·er** (brēch'lōd'ər) *n.* any gun loaded at the breech —**breech'-load'ing** *adj.*

**breed** (brēd) *vt.* **bred, breed'ing** [< OE. *bredan* < *brod,* a hatching, fetus] **1.** to bring forth (offspring) **2.** to be the source of; produce *[ignorance breeds* prejudice*]* **3.** to cause to reproduce; raise *[to breed* dogs*]* **4.** to bring up or train **5.** to produce (fissionable material) in a breeder reactor —*vi.* **1.** to be produced; originate **2.** to reproduce —*n.* **1.** a stock of animals or plants descended from common ancestors **2.** a kind; sort; type —**breed'er** *n.*

BREECH-ES

**breeder reactor** a nuclear reactor that produces more fissionable material than it consumes

**breed·ing** (-iŋ) *n.* **1.** the producing of young **2.** the rearing of young **3.** good upbringing or training **4.** the producing of plants and animals, esp. so as to develop new or better types

**breeze** (brēz) n. [< Fr. brise, prob. < EFris. brisen, to blow fresh and strong] **1.** a wind, esp. a gentle wind **2.** [Brit. Colloq.] commotion **3.** [Colloq.] a thing easy to do **4.** Meteorol. any wind ranging in speed from 4 to 31 miles per hour —vi. **breezed, breez'ing** [Slang] to move or go quickly, jauntily, etc. —**in a breeze** [Colloq.] easily —**shoot** (or **bat**) **the breeze** [Slang] to chat idly

**breeze·way** (-wā') n. a covered passageway, as between a house and garage

**breez·y** (brē'zē) adj. **breez'i·er, breez'i·est 1.** slightly windy **2** lively and carefree [breezy talk] —**breez'i·ly** adv. —**breez'i·ness** n.

**Bre·men** (brem'ən; G. brā'mən) port in N West Germany: pop. 604,000

**Bren·ner Pass** (bren'ər) mountain pass across the Alps at the border between Italy & Austria

**Bre·scia** (bre'shä) city in N Italy, at the foot of the Alps: pop. 201,000

**Bres·lau** (bres'lou) Ger. name of WROCŁAW

**breth·ren** (breth'rən, -ərn) n.pl. brothers: now chiefly in religious use

**Bret·on** (bret''n) adj. [Fr., ult. same word as BRITON] of Brittany, its people, or their language —n. **1.** a native or inhabitant of Brittany **2.** the Celtic language of the people of Brittany

**Breu·ghel** (brü'gəl; occas. broi'-) same as BRUEGEL

**breve** (brev, brēv) n. [It. < L. brevis, brief] **1.** a mark (˘) put over a short vowel or short or unstressed syllable **2.** Music a note (|o|) equal to two whole notes

**bre·vet** (brə vet'; chiefly Brit. brev'it) n. [< OFr., a note < ML. breve, letter < L. brevis, brief] Mil. a commission giving an officer a higher honorary rank without more pay —adj. held by brevet —vt. **-vet'ted** or **-vet'ed, -vet'ting** or **-vet'ing** to give a brevet to —**bre·vet'cy** n., pl. **-cies**

**bre·vi·ar·y** (brē'vē er'ē, brev'yər ē) n., pl. **-ar'ies** [< ML. brevarium, abridgment, ult. < L. brevis, brief] R.C.Ch. a book of the daily prayers, hymns, etc. prescribed for priests and other clerics

**brev·i·ty** (brev'ə tē) n. [< L. < brevis, brief] **1.** briefness of time **2.** conciseness; terseness

**brew** (broō) vt. [< OE. breowan] **1.** to make (beer, ale, etc.) from malt and hops by steeping, boiling, and fermenting **2.** to make (tea, coffee, etc.) by steeping or boiling **3.** to plan (mischief, trouble, etc.); plot —vi. **1.** to brew beer, ale, etc. **2.** to begin to form: said of a storm, trouble, etc. —n. **1.** a brewed beverage **2.** an amount brewed —**brew'er** n.

**brew·er·y** (broō'ər ē) n., pl. **-er·ies** an establishment where beer, ale, etc. are brewed

**brew·ing** (broō'iŋ) n. **1.** the preparation of a brew **2.** the amount of brew made at one time

**Bri·an** (brī'ən) [Celt., ? strong] a masculine name

**bri·ar¹** (brī'ər) n. same as BRIER¹ —**bri'ar·y** adj.

**bri·ar²** (brī'ər) n. **1.** same as BRIER² **2.** a tobacco pipe made of brierroot

**bri·ar·root** (-root', -root') n. same as BRIERROOT

**bri·ar·wood** (-wood') n. same as BRIERWOOD

**bribe** (brīb) n. [< OFr., morsel of bread given to beggars < briber, to beg] **1.** anything given or promised to induce a person to do something illegal or wrong **2.** anything given or promised as an inducement —vt. **bribed, brib'ing 1.** to offer or give a bribe to **2.** to get or influence by bribing —vi. to give bribes —**brib'a·ble** adj. —**brib'er** n.

**brib·er·y** (brī'bər ē) n., pl. **-er·ies** the giving, offering, or taking of bribes

**bric-a-brac** (brik'ə brak') n. [< Fr. < à bric et à brac, by hook or crook] small, rare, or artistic objects, or knick-knacks, placed about a room for ornament

**brick** (brik) n. [< MDu. bricke & OFr. brique, a fragment] **1.** a substance made from clay molded into oblong blocks and baked, used in building, etc. **2.** any of these blocks **3.** bricks collectively **4.** anything shaped like a brick **5.** [Colloq.] a fine fellow —adj. **1.** built or paved with brick **2.** like brick [brick red] —vt. to build or pave with brick —**brick up** (or **in**) to wall in with brick

**brick·bat** (-bat') n. **1.** a piece of brick used as a missile **2.** an unfavorable or critical remark

**brick cheese** a ripened semihard American cheese shaped like a brick

**brick·lay·ing** (-lā'iŋ) n. the act or work of building with bricks —**brick'lay'er** n.

**brick red** yellowish or brownish red —**brick'-red'** adj.

**brick·work** (-wurk') n. anything built of bricks

**brick·yard** (-yärd') n. a place where bricks are made or sold

**brid·al** (brīd''l) n. [< OE. bryd ealo, marriage feast < bryd, bride + ealo, ale] a wedding —adj. **1.** of a bride **2.** of a wedding

**bridal wreath** a cultivated shrub of the rose family, with many small, white double flowers

**bride** (brīd) n. [OE. bryd] a woman who has just been married or is about to be married

**bride·groom** (brīd'grōōm', -groom') n. [< OE. brydguma,

suitor < bryd, bride + guma, man; altered by folk etym. after GROOM] a man who has just been married or is about to be married

**brides·maid** (brīdz'mād') n. any of the young women who attend the bride at a wedding

**bridge¹** (brij) n. [< OE. brycge] **1.** a structure built over a river, railroad, etc. to provide a way across for vehicles or pedestrians **2.** a thing that provides connection or contact **3.** a) the upper, bony part of the nose b) the curved bow of a pair of glasses fitting over the nose **4.** the thin, arched piece over which the strings are stretched on a violin, etc. **5.** a raised platform on a ship for the commanding officer **6.** Dentistry a fixed or removable mounting for false teeth, attached to real teeth **7.** Music a connecting passage between two sections of a composition —vt. **bridged, bridg'ing 1.** to build a bridge on or over **2.** to provide a connection, transition, etc. across or between —**burn one's bridges** (**behind one**) to commit oneself to a course from which there is no retreat —**bridge'a·ble** adj.

**bridge²** (brij) n. [earlier biritch, "Russian whist," altered after prec.; ? of Russ. origin] any of various card games that developed from whist: see AUCTION BRIDGE, CONTRACT BRIDGE

**bridge·head** (-hed') n. **1.** a fortified position established by an attacking force on the enemy's side of a bridge, river, etc. **2.** same as BEACHHEAD (sense 2)

**Bridge·port** (brij'pôrt) [after the bridge across a local river] seaport in SW Conn.: pop. 143,000

**bridge·work** (-wurk') n. a dental bridge or bridges

**bri·dle** (brīd''l) n. [< OE. < bregdan, to pull] **1.** a head harness for guiding a horse: it consists of headstall, bit, and reins **2.** anything that controls or restrains —vt. **-dled, -dling 1.** to put a bridle on **2.** to curb as with a bridle —vi. **1.** to pull one's head back quickly with the chin drawn in, as in showing anger, scorn, etc. **2.** to take offense (at)

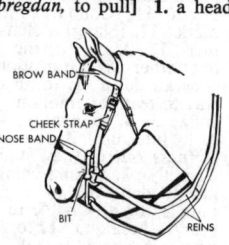

BROW BAND

CHEEK STRAP

NOSE BAND

BIT

REINS

BRIDLE

**bridle path** a path for horseback riding

**brief** (brēf) adj. [< OFr. bref < L. brevis] **1.** of short duration or extent **2.** terse; concise **3.** curt or abrupt —n. **1.** a summary or abstract **2.** a concise statement of the main points of a law case for use in court **3.** [pl.] closefitting, legless underpants —vt. **1.** to summarize **2.** to supply with all the pertinent instructions or information **3.** [Brit.] a) to furnish with a legal brief b) to hire as counsel —**hold a brief for** to argue for or be in favor of —**in brief** in a few words —**brief'ing** n. —**brief'ly** adv. —**brief'ness** n.

**brief·case** (-kās') n. a flat, flexible case, usually of leather, for carrying papers, etc.

**bri·er¹** (brī'ər) n. [< OE. brer] **1.** any thorny bush, as a bramble, wild rose, etc. **2.** a growth of such bushes —**bri'er·y** adj.

**bri·er²** (brī'ər) n. [Fr. bruyère, white heath] **1.** a heath native to S Europe **2.** its root, or a tobacco pipe made from the root: usually sp. **bri'ar**

**bri·er·root** (-root', -root') n. the root wood of the brier, or a pipe made of this

**bri·er·wood** (-wood') n. same as BRIERROOT

**brig¹** (brig) n. [< BRIGANTINE] a two-masted ship with square sails

**brig²** (brig) n. [< ?] **1.** a prison on a U.S. warship **2.** [Mil. Slang] the guardhouse; prison

**bri·gade** (bri gād') n. [Fr. < It. brigata, troop < brigare, to contend < briga, strife] **1.** a large unit of soldiers **2.** U.S. Army a military unit composed of two or more battalions **3.** a group of people organized to function as a unit in some work [a fire brigade] —vt. **-gad'ed, -gad'ing** to organize into a brigade

**brig·a·dier** (brig'ə dir') n. a brigade commander

**brigadier general** pl. **brigadier generals** U.S. Mil. an officer ranking just above a colonel: abbrev. **Brig. Gen.**

**brig·and** (brig'ənd) n. [< OFr. < It. brigante < brigare: see BRIGADE] a bandit, usually one of a roving band —**brig'and·age** (-ij) n.

**brig·an·tine** (brig'ən tēn') n. [< Fr. < It. brigantino, pirate vessel: see BRIGAND] a two-masted ship with the foremast square-rigged and a fore-and-aft mainsail

**bright** (brīt) adj. [OE. bryht, earlier beorht] **1.** shining with light that is radiated or reflected; full of light **2.** clear or brilliant in color or sound; vivid or intense **3.** lively; vivacious; cheerful **4.** mentally quick; clever **5.** a) full of happiness or hope b) favorable; auspicious **6.** glorious or splendid; illustrious —adv. in a bright manner —**bright'ly** adv. —**bright'ness** n.

**bright·en** (brīt''n) vt., vi. **1.** to make or become bright or brighter **2.** to gladden; cheer up

**Brigh·ton** (brīt''n) resort city in S England: pop. 165,000

**Bright's disease** (brīts) [after R. *Bright* (1789–1858), Eng. physician] chronic nephritis

**bril·liance** (bril'yəns) *n.* great brightness, radiance, splendor, intelligence, etc.: also **bril'lian·cy**

**bril·liant** (-yənt) *adj.* [< Fr. prp. of *briller* < It. *brillare*, to sparkle] 1. shining brightly; sparkling 2. vivid; intense 3. very splendid or distinguished 4. highly intelligent, talented, or skillful —*n.* a gem, esp. a diamond, cut with many facets to increase its sparkle —**bril'liant·ly** *adv.*

**brim** (brim) *n.* [OE. *brim*, sea] 1. the topmost edge of a cup, bowl, etc. 2. a projecting rim or edge, as of a hat —*vt., vi.* **brimmed, brim'ming** to fill or be full to the brim —**brim'less** *adj.*

**brim·ful** (brim'fool') *adj.* full to the brim

**brim·stone** (-stōn') *n.* [< OE. *brynstan:* see BURN¹ & STONE] *same as* SULFUR

**brin·dle** (brin'd'l) *adj. same as* BRINDLED

**brin·dled** (-d'ld) *adj.* [prob. < ME. *brended* < *brennen*, to burn] gray or tawny, streaked or spotted with a darker color [a *brindled* cow]

**brine** (brīn) *n.* [OE.] 1. water full of salt 2. *a)* the water of the sea *b)* the sea; ocean —*vt.* **brined, brin'ing** to soak in or treat with brine

**bring** (briŋ) *vt.* **brought, bring'ing** [OE. *bringan*] 1. to carry or lead (a person or thing) to the place thought of as "here" or to a place the speaker wishes 2. to cause to be, happen, appear, etc. [war *brings* death] 3. to lead, persuade, or influence along a course of action or belief 4. to sell for [to *bring* a high price] 5. *Law a)* to present in a law court [to *bring* charges] *b)* to advance (evidence, etc.) —**bring about** to make happen; effect —**bring around** (or **round**) 1. to persuade by arguing, urging, etc. 2. to bring back to consciousness —**bring forth** 1. to produce (offspring, fruit, etc.) 2. to make known; disclose —**bring forward** to introduce; show —**bring in** 1. to import 2. to produce (income or revenue) —**bring off** to accomplish —**bring on** to cause to be, happen, or appear —**bring out** 1. to reveal; make clear 2. to publish (a book), produce (a play), etc. 3. to introduce (a girl) formally to society —**bring to** 1. to revive (an unconscious person) 2. to cause (a ship) to stop —**bring up** 1. to take care of during childhood; raise; rear 2. to introduce, as into discussion 3. to cough up 4. to vomit 5. to stop abruptly

**brink** (briŋk) *n.* [< MLowG. or Dan., shore, bank] the edge, esp. at the top of a steep place; verge: often used figuratively [at the *brink* of war]

**brink·man·ship** (briŋk'mən ship') *n.* [BRINK + *-manship*, as in *statesmanship*] the policy of pursuing a hazardous course of action to the brink of catastrophe: also **brinks'man·ship'** (briŋks'-)

**brin·y** (brīn'ē) *adj.* **brin'i·er, brin'i·est** of or like brine; very salty —**the briny** [Slang] the ocean —**brin'i·ness** *n.*

**bri·o** (brē'ō) *n.* [It.] animation; vivacity; zest

**bri·oche** (brē ōsh', -ôsh') *n.* [Fr.] a light, rich roll made with flour, butter, eggs, and yeast

**bri·quette, bri·quet** (bri ket') *n.* [< Fr. dim. of *brique*, brick] a brick made of compressed coal dust, etc., used for fuel or kindling

**Bris·bane** (briz'bān, -bən) seaport on the E coast of Australia: pop. 719,000

**brisk** (brisk) *adj.* [< ? Fr. *brusque*, BRUSQUE] 1. quick in manner; energetic 2. cool, dry, and bracing [*brisk* air] 3. pungent, keen, sharp, etc. [a *brisk* flavor] 4. active; busy [*brisk* trading] —**brisk'ly** *adv.* —**brisk'ness** *n.*

**bris·ket** (bris'kit) *n.* [ME. *brusket*, akin to Dan. *bryske*] 1. the breast of an animal 2. meat cut from this part

**bris·ling** (bris'liŋ, briz'-) *n.* [Norw. dial. < older Dan. *bretling*] *same as* SPRAT (sense 1)

**bris·tle** (bris''l) *n.* [< OE. *byrst*] any short, stiff, prickly hair; esp., any of the hairs of a hog, etc., used for brushes —*vi.* **-tled, -tling** 1. to become stiff and erect, like bristles 2. to have the bristles become erect, as in fear 3. to become tense with fear, anger, etc. 4. to be thickly covered (with) —*vt.* 1. to make stand up like bristles 2. to make bristly

**bris·tly** (bris'lē) *adj.* **-tli·er, -tli·est** 1. having bristles; rough with bristles 2. bristlelike; prickly —**bris'tli·ness** *n.*

**Bris·tol** (bris't'l) 1. seaport in SW England: pop. 428,000 2. [after prec.] city in C Conn.: pop. 57,000

**Bristol board** [after BRISTOL, England] a fine, smooth pasteboard, used by artists, printers, etc.

**Bristol Channel** arm of the Atlantic, between S Wales & SW England

**Brit** (brit) *adj.* [Slang] British —*n.* [Slang] Britisher

**Brit.** 1. Britain 2. Britannia 3. British

**Brit·ain** (brit''n) *same as* GREAT BRITAIN

**Bri·tan·ni·a** (bri tan'yə, -tan'ē ə) 1. *Roman name for*

GREAT BRITAIN (sense 1), esp. the southern part 2. *same as* BRITISH EMPIRE

**britannia metal** [*also* B-] an alloy of tin, copper, and antimony, used in tableware, like pewter

**Bri·tan·nic** (bri tan'ik) *adj.* of Britain; British

**britch·es** (brich'iz) *n.pl.* [Colloq.] *same as* BREECHES (sense 2)

**Brit·i·cism** (brit'ə siz'm) *n.* a word, phrase, or idiom peculiar to British English: also **Brit'ish·ism**

**Brit·ish** (brit'ish) *adj.* [< OE. *Bryttisc* < *Bret*, a Celt. inhabitant of Britain < *Celt.*] 1. of Great Britain or its people 2. of the British Commonwealth —*n.* the English language as spoken and written in England —**the British** the people of Great Britain

**British Columbia** province of SW Canada: 366,255 sq. mi.; pop. 2,467,000; cap. Victoria: abbrev. **B.C.**

**British Commonwealth (of Nations)** confederation of independent nations, including the United Kingdom and dominions, former colonies, etc. that were once part of the British Empire, united under the British crown: official name, **the Commonwealth**

**British Empire** formerly, the United Kingdom and British dominions, colonies, etc.

**Brit·ish·er** (-ər) *n.* a native of Great Britain, esp. an Englishman

**British Honduras** *former name of* BELIZE

**British Isles** group of islands consisting of Great Britain, Ireland, & adjacent islands

**British thermal unit** the quantity of heat required to raise the temperature of one pound of water one degree Fahrenheit

**British West Indies** Brit. possessions in the West Indies, including the Bahamas, British Virgin Islands, etc.

**Brit·on** (brit''n) *n.* [< OFr. < L. *Brit(t)o;* of Celt. origin: see BRITISH] 1. a member of an early Celtic people living in S Britain at the time of the Roman invasion 2. a native or inhabitant of Great Britain, esp. an Englishman

**Brit·ta·ny** (brit''n ē) peninsula of NW France

**brit·tle** (brit''l) *adj.* [< OE. *breotan*, to break] 1. easily broken or shattered because hard and inflexible 2. having a sharp, hard quality [*brittle* tones] 3. stiff and unbending in manner —*n.* a brittle, crunchy candy with nuts in it [peanut *brittle*] —**brit'tle·ly, brit'tly** *adv.* —**brit'tle·ness** *n.*

**Br·no** (bur'nō) city in C Czechoslovakia: pop. 333,000

**bro.** *pl.* **bros.** brother

**broach** (brōch) *n.* [< OFr. < ML. *brocca*, a spike < L. *broccus*, with projecting teeth] 1. a spit for roasting meat 2. a tapered bit for enlarging or shaping holes 3. *same as* BROOCH —*vt.* 1. to make a hole in so as to let out liquid 2. to start a discussion of; bring up —**broach'er** *n.*

**broad** (brôd) *adj.* [< OE. *brad*] 1. of large extent from side to side; wide 2. spacious [*broad* prairies] 3. clear; open; full [*broad* daylight] 4. plain to the mind; obvious [a *broad* hint] 5. strongly marked [a *broad* accent] 6. coarse or ribald [a *broad* joke] 7. tolerant; liberal [a *broad* view] 8. wide in range; not limited [a *broad* survey] 9. main or general; not detailed [in *broad* outline] 10. *Phonet.* pronounced with the tongue held low and flat in the mouth; open, esp. as the (ä) of *father* —*n.* 1. the broad part of anything 2. [Slang] a woman: a vulgar term —**broad'ly** *adv.* —**broad'ness** *n.*

**broad·ax, broad·axe** (-aks') *n.* an ax with a broad blade, used as a weapon or tool

**broad·cast** (-kast') *vt.* **-cast'** or, in radio, occas. **-cast'ed, -cast'ing** 1. to scatter (seed) widely 2. to spread (information, etc.) widely 3. to transmit by radio or TV —*vi.* to broadcast radio or TV programs —*adj.* 1. widely scattered 2. of, for, or by radio or TV broadcasting —*n.* 1. a broadcasting 2. a radio or TV program —*adv.* far and wide —**broad'cast'er** *n.*

**Broad Church** that part of the Anglican Church holding a doctrinal position between the ritualism and formality of the High Church and the evangelism of the Low Church —**Broad'-Church'** *adj.*

**broad·cloth** (-klôth') *n.* 1. a fine, smooth woolen cloth: it originally was made on broad looms 2. a fine, smooth cotton or silk cloth, used for shirts, pajamas, etc.

**broad·en** (-'n) *vt., vi.* to make or become broad or broader; widen; expand

**broad gauge** a width (between the rails of a railroad) greater than standard gauge or width (56 1/2 inches) —**broad'-gauge', broad'-gauged'** *adj.*

**broad jump** earlier term for LONG JUMP

**broad·loom** (-lōōm') *adj.* woven on a broad loom, as in widths of 6, 9, 12, 15, or 18 feet

**broad-mind·ed** (-mīn'did) *adj.* tolerant of others' opinions and behavior; not bigoted; liberal —**broad'-mind'ed·ly** *adv.* —**broad'-mind'ed·ness** *n.*

**broad·side** (-sīd′) *n.* **1.** the entire side of a ship above the waterline **2.** *a)* all the guns that can be fired from one side of a ship *b)* their simultaneous firing **3.** an abusive attack in words **4.** a large sheet of paper printed as with advertising and often folded —*adv.* **1.** with the length turned (*to* an object) **2.** directly in the side **3.** indiscriminately [to level charges *broadside*]

**broad-spec·trum** (-spek′trəm) *adj.* effective against a wide variety of microorganisms

**broad·sword** (-sôrd′) *n.* a sword with a broad blade, for slashing rather than thrusting

**broad·tail** (-tāl′) *n.* **1.** *same as* KARAKUL (sense 1) **2.** the glossy, wavy pelt of the karakul lamb, esp. of one prematurely born

**Broad·way** (brôd′wā′) street in New York City, the axis of the city's entertainment section

**Brob·ding·nag** (bräb′diŋ nag′) in Swift's *Gulliver's Travels*, a land of giants —**Brob′ding·nag′i·an** *adj.*, *n.*

**bro·cade** (brō kād′) *n.* [Sp. *brocado* < It. pp. of *broccare*, to embroider: see BROACH] a rich cloth with a raised design, as of silk, velvet, gold, or silver, woven into it —*vt.* **-cad′ed, -cad′ing** to weave a raised design into (cloth)

**broc·co·li** (bräk′ə lē) *n.* [It., pl. of *broccolo*, a sprout, dim. of *brocco*: see BROACH] a plant related to the cauliflower but bearing tender shoots with greenish buds, cooked as a vegetable

**bro·chette** (brō shet′) *n.* [Fr., dim. of *broche*: see BROACH] a small spit, as for broiling kebabs

**bro·chure** (brō shoor′, -shyoor′) *n.* [Fr. < *brocher*, to stitch] a pamphlet

**Brock·ton** (bräk′tən) [after I. *Brock* (1769–1812), Lt. Gov. of Canada] city in E Mass.: pop. 95,000

**bro·gan** (brō′g′n) *n.* [Ir., dim of *brōg*] a heavy work shoe, fitting high on the ankle

**brogue¹** (brōg) *n.* [prob. < Ir. *barrōg*, a hold, grip (esp. on the tongue)] dialectal pronunciation, esp. that of English as spoken by the Irish

**brogue²** (brōg) *n.* [Gael. & Ir. *brōg*, a shoe] **1.** a coarse shoe of untanned leather, formerly worn in Ireland **2.** a man's heavy oxford shoe, usually a kind of blucher with decorative perforations

**broil¹** (broil) *vt.* [OFr. *bruillir*, prob. by confusion of *bruir*, to burn & *usler*, to singe] **1.** to cook by exposing to direct heat **2.** to expose directly to intense heat —*vi.* **1.** to become broiled **2.** to become heated or angry —*n.* a broiling

**broil²** (broil) *n.* [ME. *broilen*, to quarrel < OFr. *brouillier*, to dirty] a noisy or violent quarrel; brawl —*vi.* to take part in a broil

**broil·er** (broil′ər) *n.* **1.** a pan, grill, etc. for broiling **2.** the part of a stove designed for broiling **3.** a young chicken suitable for broiling

**broke** (brōk) *pt. & archaic pp. of* BREAK —*adj.* [Colloq.] having no money; bankrupt —**go broke** [Colloq.] to become bankrupt —**go for broke** [Slang] to risk everything in a venture

**bro·ken** (brō′k'n) *pp. of* BREAK —*adj.* **1.** splintered, fractured, burst, etc. **2.** not in working condition **3.** violated [a *broken* promise] **4.** disrupted as by divorce [a *broken* home] **5.** sick, weakened, or beaten **6.** bankrupt **7.** not even; interrupted **8.** not complete [*broken* sizes] **9.** imperfectly spoken, esp. with reference to grammar and syntax [*broken* English] **10.** subdued and trained; tamed **11.** [Colloq.] demoted in rank For phrases, see BREAK —**bro′ken·ly** *adv.* —**bro′ken·ness** *n.*

**bro·ken-down** (-doun′) *adj.* **1.** sick or worn out, as by old age or disease **2.** out of order; useless

**bro·ken·heart·ed** (-här′tid) *adj.* crushed by sorrow, grief, or disappointment; inconsolable

**bro·ker** (brō′kər) *n.* [< ONormFr. < OFr. *brochier*, to broach, tap; orig. sense "wine dealer"] **1.** a person hired to act as an agent in making contracts or sales **2.** *same as* STOCKBROKER

**bro·ker·age** (-ij) *n.* **1.** the business of a broker **2.** a broker's fee

**bro·mide** (brō′mīd) *n.* [BROM(INE) + -IDE] **1.** a compound of bromine with another element or with a radical **2.** potassium bromide, KBr, used in medicine as a sedative **3.** a trite saying or remark

**bro·mid·ic** (brō mid′ik) *adj.* [see prec.] using or containing a trite remark or remarks; dull

**bro·mine** (brō′mēn) *n.* [Fr. *brome* < Gr. *brōmos*, stench + -INE⁴] a chemical element, usually a reddish-brown, corrosive liquid volatilizing to form an irritating vapor: symbol, Br; at. wt., 79.909; at. no., 35

**bron·chi** (bräŋ′kī) *n. pl. of* BRONCHUS

**bron·chi·al** (-kē əl) *adj.* of the bronchi or bronchioles

**bronchial tubes** the bronchi and the tubes branching from them

**bron·chi·ole** (bräŋ′kē ōl′) *n.* any of the small subdivisions of the bronchi

**bron·chi·tis** (bräŋ kīt′əs) *n.* [BRONCH(O)- + -ITIS] an inflam-

mation of the mucous lining of the bronchial tubes —**bron·chit′ic** (-kit′ik) *adj.*

**bron·cho-** [< Gr. *bronchos*, windpipe] *a combining form meaning* having to do with the bronchi [*bronchoscope*] : also, before a vowel, **bronch-**

**bron·cho·scope** (bräŋ′kə skōp′) *n.* [BRONCHO- + -SCOPE] an instrument for examining the bronchi, or for removing foreign bodies from them

**bron·chus** (bräŋ′kəs) *n., pl.* **-chi** (-kī) [ModL. < Gr. *bronchos*, windpipe] either of the two main branches of the trachea, or windpipe

**bron·co** (bräŋ′kō) *n., pl.* **-cos** [MexSp. < Sp., rough] a wild or partially tamed horse or pony of the western U.S.: also sp. **bron′cho,** *pl.* **-chos**

**bron·co·bust·er** (-bus′tər) *n.* [Colloq.] a cowboy who tames broncos —**bron′co·bust′ing** *n.*

**Bron·të** (brän′tē) **1. Charlotte,** 1816–55; Eng. novelist **2. Emily Jane,** 1818–48; Eng. novelist: sister of *prec.*

**bron·to·sau·rus** (brän′tə sôr′əs) *n., pl.* **-sau′rus·es, -sau′ri** (-ī) [ModL. < Gr. *brontē*, thunder + -SAURUS] a huge, plant-eating American dinosaur of the Jurassic Period: also **bron′to·saur′** (-sôr′)

**Bronx** (bräŋks) [after J. *Bronck,* early settler] N borough of New York City: pop. 1,169,000

**Bronx cheer** [Slang] a noisy vibration of the lips and extended tongue, as to show derision

BRONTOSAURUS
(to 75 ft. long)

**bronze** (bränz) *n.* [Fr. < It. *bronzo*] **1.** an alloy consisting chiefly of copper and tin **2.** an article, esp. a sculpture, made of bronze **3.** a reddish-brown color like that of bronze —*adj.* of or like bronze —*vt.* **bronzed, bronz′ing** to give a bronze color to —**bronz′y** *adj.*

**Bronze Age** a phase of human culture (c. 3500–1000 B.C.) characterized by bronze tools and weapons

**brooch** (brōch, brōōch) *n.* [see BROACH] a large ornamental pin with a clasp

**brood** (brōōd) *n.* [< OE. *brod*] **1.** a group of birds or fowl hatched at one time and cared for together **2.** all the children in a family **3.** a group of a particular breed or kind —*vt.* **1.** to sit on and hatch (eggs) **2.** to hover over or protect (offspring, etc.) —*vi.* **1.** to brood eggs or offspring **2.** to keep thinking about something in a troubled way; worry (often with *on, over,* or *about*) —*adj.* kept for breeding [a *brood* mare] —**brood′ing·ly** *adv.*

**brood·er** (-ər) *n.* **1.** one that broods **2.** a heated shelter for raising young fowl

**brood·y** (-ē) *adj.* **brood′i·er, brood′i·est 1.** ready to brood, as poultry **2.** inclined to dwell moodily on one's own thoughts —**brood′i·ly** *adv.* —**brood′i·ness** *n.*

**brook¹** (brook) *n.* [OE. *broc*] a small stream, usually not so large as a river

**brook²** (brook) *vt.* [OE. *brucan,* to use] to put up with; endure [he will *brook* no interference]

**brook·let** (-lit) *n.* a little brook

**Brook·lyn** (brook′lən) [< Du.] borough of New York City, on W Long Island: pop. 2,231,000 —**Brook′lyn·ite′** (-lə nīt′) *n.*

**brook trout** a mottled trout native to NE N. America, but introduced elsewhere as a game fish

**broom** (brōōm, broom) *n.* [OE. *brom,* brushwood] **1.** a shrub of the legume family, with many, usually yellow, flowers **2.** a bundle of long, stiff fibers or straws (orig. twigs of broom) fastened to a long handle and used for sweeping —*vt.* to sweep as with a broom

**broom·corn** (-kôrn′) *n.* a cultivated variety of sorghum: the stiff stems of the flower clusters are used in making brooms and brushes

**broom·stick** (-stik′) *n.* the handle of a broom

**bros.** brothers

**broth** (brôth) *n.* [OE.] a clear, thin soup made by boiling meat, etc. in water

**broth·el** (brôth′əl, bräth′-) *n.* [ME., wretched person < OE. pp. of *breothan,* to go to ruin] a house of prostitution

**broth·er** (bruth′ər) *n., pl.* **broth′ers;** chiefly religious, **breth′ren** [OE. *brothor*] **1.** a male as he is related to the other children of his parents **2.** a close friend who is like a brother **3.** a fellow man **4.** a fellow member of the same race, creed, profession, organization, etc. **5.** a lay member of a men's religious order —*vt.* to treat or address as a brother

**broth·er·hood** (-hood′) *n.* **1.** the state of being a brother or brothers **2.** an association of men united in a common interest, work, creed, etc.

**broth·er-in-law** (-in lô′) *n., pl.* **broth′ers-in-law′ 1.** the brother of one's husband or wife **2.** the husband of one's sister **3.** the husband of the sister of one's wife or husband

**broth·er·ly** (-lē) *adj.* **1.** of or like a brother **2.** friendly, kind, loyal, etc. —**broth′er·li·ness** *n.*

**brougham** (brōōm; brōō'əm, brō'-) *n*. [after Lord *Brougham* (1778–1868), Brit. statesman] **1.** a closed carriage with the driver's seat outside **2.** any of various styles of automobile

**brought** (brôt) *pt. & pp. of* BRING

BROUGHAM

**brow** (brou) *n*. [< OE. *bru*] **1.** the eyebrow **2.** the forehead **3.** the facial expression *[an angry brow]* **4.** a projecting edge, as of a cliff

**brow·beat** (-bēt') *vt*. **-beat'**, **-beat'en**, **-beat'ing** to intimidate with harsh, stern looks and talk

**brown** (broun) *adj*. [< OE. *brun*] **1.** having the color of chocolate or coffee, a mixture of red, black, and yellow **2.** tanned or dark-skinned —*n*. **1.** a brown color **2.** a brown pigment or dye —*vt., vi.* to make or become brown, as by exposure to sunlight or heat —**do up brown** [Slang] to do completely or perfectly —**brown'ish** *adj*. —**brown'ness** *n*.

**Brown, John** 1800–59; U.S. abolitionist: hanged for raiding an arsenal at Harpers Ferry (W.Va.)

**brown bet·ty** (bet'ē) *[also* b- B-*]* a baked apple pudding made with bread crumbs, butter, etc.

**brown bread** **1.** any bread made of dark flour **2.** *same as* BOSTON BROWN BREAD

**brown coal** *same as* LIGNITE

**Browne** (broun) **1. Charles Far·rar** (far'ər), *see* Artemus WARD **2. Sir Thomas**, 1605–82; Eng. physician & writer

**Brown·i·an movement** (broun'ē ən) [after R. *Brown* (1773–1858), Brit. botanist who described it] the constant, random, zigzag movement of small particles dispersed in a fluid medium, caused by collision with molecules of the fluid

**brown·ie** (broun'ē) *n*. **1.** a small, helpful, brown elf or goblin in folk tales **2.** [B-] a Girl Scout of the youngest group, those seven and eight years old **3.** any of the small bars cut from a flat, rich chocolate cake with nuts in it

**Brown·ing** (broun'iŋ) **1. Elizabeth Bar·rett** (bar'it), 1806–61; Eng. poet **2. Robert**, 1812–89; Eng. poet: husband of *prec.*

**brown·out** (-out') *n*. partial elimination of lights in a city, as during an electric power shortage

**brown rice** rice that has not been polished

**brown shirt** **1.** *[often* B- S-*]* a storm trooper in Nazi Germany **2.** any Nazi

**brown·stone** (-stōn') *n*. **1.** a reddish-brown sandstone, used for building **2.** a house with a façade of brownstone: also **brownstone front**

**brown study** [< early sense of BROWN, gloomy] deep absorption in thought; reverie

**brown sugar** soft sugar prepared so that the crystals retain a brown coating of dark syrup

**Browns·ville** (brounz'vil) [after a Major *Brown*, killed there] seaport in S Tex.: pop. 85,000

**browse** (brouz) *n*. [< OFr. < OS. *brustian*, to sprout] **1.** leaves, twigs, and young shoots of trees or shrubs, which animals feed on **2.** the act of browsing —*vt*. **browsed**, **brows'ing** **1.** to nibble at **2.** to graze on **3.** to examine casually —*vi*. **1.** to nibble at leaves, twigs, etc. **2.** to glance through a book, etc. casually **3.** to look casually over articles for sale —**brows'er** *n*.

**Bruce** (brōōs) [Scot. < Fr. *Brieuse*, locality in France] **1.** a masculine name **2. Robert (the)**, 1274–1329; Scot. patriot &, as *Robert I*, king of Scotland (1306–29)

**bru·cel·lo·sis** (brōō'sə lō'sis) *n*. [after Sir David *Bruce* (1855–1931), Scot. physician + -OSIS] a disease, esp. in man and cattle, caused by bacteria: see UNDULANT FEVER

**Brue·gel, Brue·ghel** (brü'gəl; *occas.* broi'-), **Pie·ter** (pē'tər) 1522?–69; Fl. painter

**Bru·in** (brōō'ən) [Du., brown] *[also* b-*]* a name for the bear in fable and folklore

**bruise** (brōōz) *vt*. **bruised**, **bruis'ing** [ME. *bruisen* (infl. by OFr. *bruisier*, to break) < OE. *brysan*, to crush] **1.** to injure (body tissue) without breaking the skin but causing discoloration **2.** to injure the surface of (fruit, etc.) **3.** to crush as with a pestle in a mortar **4.** to hurt (the feelings, spirit, etc.) —*vi*. to be or become bruised —*n*. **1.** a bruised area of tissue, of a surface, etc. **2.** an injury to one's feelings, etc.

**bruis·er** (brōōz'ər) *n*. a strong, pugnacious man; specif., a professional boxer

**bruit** (brōōt) *vt*. [< OFr. < *bruire*, to rumble, prob. < L. *rugire*, to roar] to spread (*about*) a rumor of

**brunch** (brunch) *n*. [BR(EAKFAST) + (L)UNCH] [Colloq.] a meal combining breakfast and lunch

**Bru·nei** (brōō nī') Brit.-protected sultanate on the NW coast of Borneo: 2,226 sq. mi.; pop. 116,000

**bru·net** (brōō net') *adj*. [< OFr., dim. of *brun* < OHG. *brun*, brown] **1.** having black or dark-brown hair, often along with dark eyes and a dark complexion **2.** having a dark color: said of hair, eyes, or skin —*n*. a brunet person

**bru·nette** (-net') *adj*. [Fr., fem. of *prec.*] *same as* BRUNET —*n*. a brunette woman or girl

**Brun·hild** (brōōn'hild) in the *Nibelungenlied*, a queen of Iceland: see also BRÜNNHILDE, BRYNHILD

**Brünn·hil·de** (broon hil'də; G. brün-) in Wagner's *Die Walküre*, a Valkyrie whom Siegfried releases from enchantment: see also BRUNHILD, BRYNHILD

**Bru·no** (brōō'nō) [OHG. < *brun*, brown] a masculine name

**Bruns·wick** (brunz'wik) **1.** region in C Germany **2.** city in this region: pop. 229,000

**brunt** (brunt) *n*. [< ? ON. *bruni*, heat] **1.** the shock (of an attack) or impact (of a blow) **2.** the heaviest or hardest part

**brush**[1] (brush) *n*. [< OFr. *broce*, bush < VL. *bruscia* < Gmc.] **1.** *same as* BRUSHWOOD **2.** sparsely settled, scrubby country **3.** *a)* a device for cleaning, polishing, painting, etc., having bristles, hairs, or wires fastened into a back, with or without a handle *b)* a device of wires spread from a handle, used as on drums for a swishing effect **4.** the act of brushing **5.** a light, grazing stroke **6.** a bushy tail, esp. that of a fox **7.** [Slang] *same as* BRUSHOFF **8.** *Elec.* a piece or bundle of carbon, copper, etc. used as a conductor between an external circuit and a revolving part —*vt*. **1.** to clean, polish, paint, etc. with a brush **2.** to apply, remove, etc. with a stroke or strokes as of a brush **3.** to touch or graze in passing —*vi*. to graze past something —**brush aside** (or *away*) to dismiss from consideration —**brush off** [Slang] to dismiss or get rid of abruptly —**brush up 1.** to clean up **2.** to refresh one's memory or skill (often with *on*)

**brush**[2] (brush) *vi*. [ME. *bruschen* < ?] to move with a rush; hurry —*n*. a short, quick fight or quarrel

**brush fire** **1.** a fire in brushwood **2.** a flare-up that threatens to intensify unless controlled

**brush·off** (-ôf') *n*. [Slang] an abrupt dismissal: esp. in the phrase **give** (or **get**) **the brushoff**

**brush·wood** (-wood') *n*. **1.** chopped-off tree branches **2.** a thick growth of small trees and shrubs

**brush·y** (-ē) *adj*. **brush'i·er**, **brush'i·est** **1.** rough and bristly **2.** covered with brushwood or underbrush

**brusque** (brusk) *adj*. [Fr. < It. *brusco* < ML. *bruscus*, brushwood] rough and abrupt in manner or speech; curt: also **brusk** —**brusque'ly** *adv*. —**brusque'ness** *n*.

**Brus·sels** (brus'lz) capital of Belgium, in the C part: pop. 1,079,000

**Brussels sprouts** **1.** a plant of the mustard family that bears miniature cabbagelike heads on an erect stem **2.** these edible heads

**bru·tal** (brōōt''l) *adj*. **1.** like a brute; cruel and unfeeling; savage, violent, ruthless, etc. **2.** very harsh *[a brutal winter]* **3.** plain and direct, but disturbing *[brutal facts]* —**bru'tal·ly** *adv*.

**bru·tal·i·ty** (brōō tal'ə tē) *n*. **1.** the quality of being brutal **2.** *pl.* **-ties** a brutal act

**bru·tal·ize** (brōōt''l īz') *vt*. **-ized'**, **-iz'ing** **1.** to make brutal **2.** to treat brutally —*vi*. to become brutal —**bru'tal·i·za'tion** *n*.

**brute** (brōōt) *adj*. [OFr. *brut* < L. *brutus*, irrational] **1.** lacking the ability to reason *[a brute beast]* **2.** lacking consciousness *[the brute force of nature]* **3.** of or like an animal; brutal, cruel, sensual, stupid, etc. —*n*. **1.** an animal **2.** a person who is brutal or stupid, sensual, etc.

**brut·ish** (brōōt'ish) *adj*. of or like a brute; savage, stupid, sensual, etc. —**brut'ish·ly** *adv*. —**brut'ish·ness** *n*.

**Bru·tus** (brōōt'əs), (**Marcus Junius**) 85?–42 B.C.; Rom. statesman who helped kill Julius Caesar

**Bry·an** (brī'ən) **1.** *var. of* BRIAN **2. William Jen·nings** (jen'iŋz), 1860–1925; U.S. politician & orator

**Bry·ant** (brī'ənt), **William Cul·len** (kul'ən) 1794–1878; U.S. poet & journalist

**Bryn·hild** (brin'hild) *Norse Legend* a Valkyrie awakened from an enchanted sleep by Sigurd: see also BRUNHILD, BRÜNNHILDE

**bry·ol·o·gy** (brī äl'ə jē) *n*. [< Gr. *bryon*, moss + -LOGY] the branch of botany dealing with bryophytes —**bry'o·log'i·cal** (-ə läj'i k'l) *adj*. —**bry·ol'o·gist** *n*.

**bry·o·ny** (brī'ə nē) *n., pl.* **-nies** [< L. < Gr. < *bryein*, to swell] a vine of the gourd family, with large, fleshy roots and greenish flowers

**bry·o·phyte** (-fīt') *n*. [< Gr. *bryon*, moss + -PHYTE] any moss or liverwort —**bry'o·phyt'ic** (-fit'ik) *adj*.

**Bry·thon·ic** (bri thän'ik) *adj., n.* [W., ult. < same word as BRITON] see CELTIC

**B/s, b/s** **1.** bags **2.** bales

**B.S.** Bachelor of Science

**b.s.** **1.** balance sheet **2.** bill of sale

**B.S.A.** Boy Scouts of America

**B.Sc.** [L. *Baccalaureus Scientiae*] Bachelor of Science
**B.S.Ed.** Bachelor of Science in Education
**Bs/L** bills of lading
**Bt.** Baronet
**B.Th., B.T.** [L. *Baccalaureus Theologiae*] Bachelor of Theology
**btry** battery (of artillery)
**B.t.u.** British thermal unit(s): also **B.T.U., b.t.u., Btu, btu**
**bu.** 1. bureau 2. bushel(s)
**bub·ble** (bub′'l) *n.* [echoic] 1. a very thin film of liquid forming a ball around air or gas [soap *bubbles*] 2. a tiny ball of air or gas in a liquid or solid 3. anything shaped like a bubble, sphere, or hemisphere 4. any scheme, etc. that seems plausible but proves to be worthless 5. the act or sound of bubbling —*vi.* **-bled, -bling** 1. to rise in bubbles; boil; foam 2. to make a gurgling sound —*vt.* to form bubbles in; make bubble —**bubble over** 1. to overflow, as boiling liquid 2. to be unrestrained in one's enthusiasm, etc. —**bub′bly** *adj.*
**bubble bath** 1. a bath perfumed and softened by a solution, crystals, or powder that forms surface bubbles 2. such a solution, powder, etc.
**bubble gum** a kind of chewing gum that can be blown into large bubbles
**bu·bo** (byōō′bō, bōō′-) *n., pl.* **-boes** [< ML. < Gr. *boubōn*, groin] an inflamed swelling of a lymph gland, esp. in the groin —**bu·bon′ic** (-bän′ik) *adj.*
**bubonic plague** a contagious disease characterized by buboes, fever, and delirium: fleas from infected rats are the carriers
**buc·cal** (buk′'l) *adj.* [L. *bucca*, cheek + -AL] 1. of the cheek or cheeks 2. of the mouth
**buc·ca·neer** (buk′ə nir′) *n.* [Fr. *boucanier*, user of a *boucan*, native Brazilian grill for roasting meat; orig. applied to Fr. hunters in Haiti] a pirate, or sea robber
**Bu·chan·an** (byōō kan′ən), James 1791-1868; 15th president of the U.S. (1857-61)
**Bu·cha·rest** (bōō′kə rest′, byōō′-) capital of Romania, in the S part: pop. 1,415,000
**Buch·en·wald** (bōō′k'n wôld′; *G.* bōōkh′ən vält′) village in C Germany: site of a notorious Nazi concentration camp & extermination center
**buck¹** (buk) *n.* [< OE. *bucca*, male goat] 1. *pl.* **bucks, buck:** see PLURAL, II, D, 1 a male deer, goat, etc. 2. the act of bucking 3. *same as* BUCKSKIN 4. [Colloq.] a young man: sometimes a patronizing term —*vi.* 1. to rear upward quickly in an attempt to throw off a rider: said of a horse, etc. 2. to plunge forward with lowered head, as a goat 3. [Colloq.] to resist something as if plunging against it 4. [Colloq.] to move jerkily —*vt.* 1. to charge against, as in football 2. to throw by bucking 3. [Colloq.] to resist stubbornly —*adj.* 1. male 2. of the lowest military rating [buck sergeant] —**buck for** [Slang] to work eagerly for (a promotion, etc.) —**buck up** [Colloq.] to cheer up —**buck′er** *n.*
**buck²** (buk) *n.* [< Du. *zaagbok*] 1. a sawbuck; sawhorse 2. a gymnastic apparatus somewhat like a sawhorse, with a padded top, for vaulting over
**buck³** (buk) *n.* [prob. < BUCKHORN: a knife with a buckhorn handle was used as a counter] 1. *Poker* a counter placed before a player as a reminder to deal next, etc. 2. [Slang] a dollar —**pass the buck** [Colloq.] to seek to make someone else take the blame or responsibility
**buck and wing** a complicated, fast tap dance
**buck·a·roo** (buk′ə rōō′, buk′ə rōō′) *n., pl.* **-roos′** [prob. < Gullah *buckra*, white man, altered after Sp. *vaquero*, cowboy] a cowboy
**buck·board** (buk′bôrd′) *n.* [< ?] a four-wheeled, open carriage with the seat carried on a flooring of long, flexible boards whose ends rest directly on the axles
**buck·et** (buk′it) *n.* [< Anglo-Fr. *buket*, dim. of OE. *buc*, pitcher] 1. a round container with a curved handle, for carrying water, coal, etc.; pail 2. the amount held by a bucket: also **buck′et·ful′**, *pl.* **-fuls′** 3. a

BUCKBOARD

thing like a bucket, as a scoop on a steam shovel 4. [Slang] the buttocks —*vt., vi.* to carry or lift in a bucket —**kick the bucket** [? < obs. *bucket*, beam on which a slaughtered pig was hung] [Slang] to die
**bucket seat** a single contoured seat whose back can be tipped forward, as in some sports cars
**buck·eye** (buk′ī′) *n.* [BUCK¹ + EYE: from the appearance of the seed] 1. a tree of the horse-chestnut family, with large, spiny capsules enclosing shiny brown seeds 2. the seed 3. [B-] [Colloq.] a native or inhabitant of Ohio (the **Buckeye State**)
**buck·horn** (-hôrn′) *n.* the horn of a buck, used for knife handles, etc.

**Buck·ing·ham Palace** (buk′iŋ əm) the official residence in London of British sovereigns
**buck·le¹** (buk′'l) *n.* [< OFr. < LL. < L. *buccula*, cheek strap of a helmet, dim. of *bucca*, cheek] 1. a clasp for fastening a strap, belt, etc. 2. a clasplike ornament, as for shoes —*vt., vi.* **-led, -ling** to fasten with a buckle —**buckle down** to apply oneself energetically
**buck·le²** (buk′'l) *vt., vi.* **-led, -ling** [prob. < Du. *bukken*, to bend] to bend, warp, or crumple —*n.* a bend, bulge, kink, etc. —**buckle under** to give in; yield; submit
**buck·ler** (buk′lər) *n.* [OFr. *bocler* < *bocle*, the boss, in its center] 1. a small, round shield worn on the arm 2. any protection or defense
**buck·o** (buk′ō) *n., pl.* **-oes** [< BUCK¹] a bully
**buck-pass·er** (-pas′ər) *n.* [Colloq.] a person who regularly seeks to shift blame or responsibility to someone else —**buck′-pass′ing** *n.*
**buck·ram** (buk′rəm) *n.* [< OFr., prob. < *Bokhara*, in Asia Minor] a coarse cloth stiffened with glue or other size, for use in bookbinding, for lining clothes, etc. —*adj.* of or like buckram
**buck·saw** (buk′sô′) *n.* [see BUCK²] a saw set in a frame and held with both hands in cutting wood
**buck·shot** (buk′shät′) *n.* a large lead shot for shooting deer and other large game
**buck·skin** (-skin′) *n.* 1. a soft, usually napped, yellowish-gray leather made from the skins of deer or sheep 2. [pl.] clothes or shoes made of buckskin —*adj.* made of buckskin
**buck·thorn** (-thôrn′) *n.* [BUCK¹ + THORN] 1. a tree or shrub with small, greenish flowers and purple drupes 2. any of a genus of trees of the sapodilla family, native to the southern U.S.
**buck·tooth** (-tōōth′) *n., pl.* **-teeth′** [BUCK¹ + TOOTH] a projecting front tooth —**buck′toothed′** *adj.*
**buck·wheat** (-hwēt′, -wēt′) *n.* [< ME. *bok-* (< OE. *boc-*), BEECH + WHEAT: from the beechnut-shaped seeds] 1. a plant grown for its black, tetrahedral grains 2. the grain of this plant, from which a dark flour is made 3. this flour
**bu·col·ic** (byōō käl′ik) *adj.* [< L. < Gr. < *boukolos*, herdsman < *bous*, ox] 1. of shepherds; pastoral 2. of country life; rustic —*n.* a pastoral poem —**bu·col′i·cal·ly** *adv.*
**bud** (bud) *n.* [ME. *budde*, seedpod] 1. *a)* a small swelling on a plant, from which a shoot, cluster of leaves, or flower develops *b)* a partly opened flower 2. any immature person or thing —*vi.* **bud′ded, bud′ding** 1. to put forth buds 2. to begin to develop 3. to be young, promising, etc. —*vt.* 1. to cause to bud 2. to graft by inserting a bud of (a plant) into the bark of another sort of plant —**nip in the bud** to check at the earliest stage —**bud′der** *n.* —**bud′like′** *adj.*
**bud²** (bud) *n.* [Slang] *short for* BUDDY: used in addressing a man or boy
**Bu·da·pest** (bōō′də pest′) capital of Hungary, on the Danube: pop. 1,990,000
**Bud·dha** (bood′ə, bōō′də) [Sans., the enlightened one] Siddhartha Gautama, a religious philosopher who lived in India 563?-483? B.C. and was the founder of Buddhism
**Bud·dhism** (bood′iz'm, bōō′diz'm) *n.* a religion of central and eastern Asia, founded in India by Buddha: it teaches that right living and self-denial will enable the soul to reach Nirvana, a divine state of release from bodily pain and sorrow —**Bud′dhist** *n., adj.* —**Bud·dhis′tic** *adj.*
**bud·dy** (bud′ē) *n., pl.* **-dies** [< ? Brit. dial. *butty*, companion] [Colloq.] 1. a companion; comrade 2. either of two persons paired off in an arrangement (**buddy system**) for mutual help
**budge** (buj) *vt., vi.* **budged, budg′ing** [Fr. *bouger*, to move, ult. < L. *bulla:* see BOIL¹] 1. to move even a little 2. to yield or cause to yield
**budg·er·i·gar** (buj′ə ri gär′) *n.* [native name] an Australian parakeet with a greenish-yellow body and bright blue on the cheeks and tail feathers
**budg·et** (buj′it) *n.* [< OFr. *bougette*, dim. of *bouge*, a bag < L. *bulga*, leather bag] 1. a collection of items; stock 2. a plan adjusting expenses to the expected income during a certain period 3. the estimated cost of living, operating, etc. 4. the amount of money needed for a specific use —*vt.* 1. to put on or in a budget 2. to plan in detail; schedule [budget your time] —*vi.* to make a budget —**budg′et·ar′y** *adj.* —**budg′et·er** *n.*
**budg·ie** (buj′ē) *n.* [Colloq.] *same as* BUDGERIGAR
**Bue·na Park** (bwā′nə) [Sp. *buena*, good + PARK] city in SW Calif., near Los Angeles: pop. 64,000
**Bue·nos Ai·res** (bwā′nəs er′ēz, ī′rēz; *Sp.* bwe′nôs ī′res) capital of Argentina, on the Río de la Plata: pop. 2,967,000
**buff¹** (buf) *n.* [earlier *buffe*, buffalo < It. *bufalo*, BUFFALO] 1. a heavy, soft, brownish-yellow leather made from the skin of a buffalo or from other animal hides 2. a military coat made of this leather 3. a stick, small block, or wheel (**buffing wheel**) covered with leather or cloth, used for cleaning or shining 4. a dull brownish yellow 5.

[Colloq.] a devotee; fan *[a jazz buff]* —*adj.* **1.** made of buff **2.** of the color buff —*vt.* to shine with a buff —**in the buff** naked

**buff**[2] (buf) *vt.* [OFr. *buffe:* see BUFFET[1]] to lessen the force of —*vi.* to serve as a buffer

**Buf·fa·lo** (buf′ə lō′) [transl. of the name of a Seneca Indian who lived there] city in W N.Y., on Lake Erie: pop. 358,000 (met. area 1,241,000)

**buf·fa·lo** (buf′ə lō′) *n., pl.* **-loes′, -los′, -lo′:** see PLURAL, II, D, 1 [It. *bufalo* < LL. < Gr. < *bous,* ox] **1.** any of various wild oxen, sometimes domesticated, as the water buffalo of India, Cape buffalo of Africa, etc. **2.** popularly, the American bison —*vt.* **-loed′, -lo′ing** [Slang] to baffle, bluff, or overawe

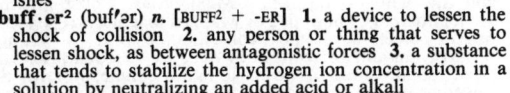

WATER BUFFALO (55–70 in. high at shoulder)

**Buffalo Bill** *nickname of* William CODY

**buffalo grass** a low, creeping range grass of the Great Plains, used for forage

**buff·er**[1] (buf′ər) *n.* [BUFF[1], *v.* + -ER] a person or thing that buffs or polishes

**buff·er**[2] (buf′ər) *n.* [BUFF[2] + -ER] **1.** a device to lessen the shock of collision **2.** any person or thing that serves to lessen shock, as between antagonistic forces **3.** a substance that tends to stabilize the hydrogen ion concentration in a solution by neutralizing an added acid or alkali

**buf·fet**[1] (buf′it) *n.* [< OFr. < *buffe,* a blow] **1.** a blow with the hand or fist **2.** any blow or shock —*vt.* **1.** to punch or slap **2.** to thrust about **3.** to struggle against —*vi.* to struggle

**buf·fet**[2] (bə fā′, boo-) *n.* [Fr. < OFr. *buffet,* a bench] **1.** a piece of furniture with drawers and cupboards for dishes, table linen, silver, etc. **2.** a counter where refreshments are served, or a restaurant with such a counter **3.** a meal at which guests serve themselves as from a buffet

‡**buf·fo** (boof′fō; *E.* boo′fō) *n., pl.* **-fi** (-fē) [It., comic: see ff.] an opera singer, generally a bass, in a comic role

**buf·foon** (bə foon′) *n.* [< Fr. < It. < *buffare,* to jest] a person who is always clowning and trying to be funny —**buf·foon′er·y** *n.* —**buf·foon′ish** *adj.*

**bug** (bug) *n.* [prob. < W. *bwg,* hobgoblin] **1.** any of various insects with sucking mouthparts and with forewings thickened toward the base **2.** any insect or small, insectlike animal, specif. one regarded as a pest **3.** [Colloq.] a germ or virus **4.** [Slang] a tiny microphone hidden to record conversation secretly **5.** [Slang] a defect, as in a machine **6.** [Slang] a hobbyist or devotee —*vt.* **bugged, bug′ging** [Slang] **1.** to hide a microphone in (a room, etc.) for secretly recording conversation **2.** to annoy, anger, etc. —*vi.* [Slang] to bulge or open wide: said of the eyes —**bug off** [Slang] to stop annoying someone and leave

**bug·a·boo** (bug′ə boo′) *n., pl.* **-boos′** a bugbear

**bug·bear** (-ber′) *n.* [BUG + BEAR[2]] **1.** an imaginary hobgoblin or terror **2.** a cause of needless fear or anxiety

**bug-eyed** (-īd′) *adj.* [Slang] with bulging eyes

**bug·gy**[1] (bug′ē) *n., pl.* **-gies** [< ?] **1.** a light, one-horse carriage with one seat **2.** *same as* BABY CARRIAGE

**bug·gy**[2] (bug′ē) *adj.* **-gi·er, -gi·est 1.** infested or swarming with bugs **2.** [Slang] mentally ill

**bug·house** (-hous′) *n.* [Slang] an insane asylum —*adj.* [Slang] mentally ill

**bu·gle** (byoo′g'l) *n.* [< OFr. < L. *buculus,* young ox, dim. of *bos,* ox] a brass-wind instrument like a trumpet but smaller, and usually without keys or valves: used chiefly for military calls —*vi., vt.* **-gled, -gling** to call or signal by blowing a bugle —**bu′gler** *n.*

**bugs** (bugz) *adj.* [Slang] mentally ill

**bug·shah** (bug′shə, -shô) *n., pl.* **-shah, -shahs** see MONETARY UNITS, table (Yemen Arab Rep.)

**build** (bild) *vt.* **built** or *archaic* **build′ed, build′ing** [< OE. *byldan* < base of *bold,* a house] **1.** to make, or direct the making of, by putting together materials, parts, etc.; construct **2.** to make a basis for; establish *[to build a theory on facts]* **3.** to create, develop, promote, strengthen, etc. —*vi.* **1.** *a)* to put up buildings *b)* to have a house, etc. built **2.** to grow or intensify —*n.* the way a thing is built or shaped; form or figure *[a stocky build]*

**build·er** (bil′dər) *n.* **1.** one that builds **2.** a person in the business of constructing buildings

**build·ing** (-diŋ) *n.* **1.** anything that is built with walls and a roof **2.** the act, process, work, or business of constructing houses, ships, etc.

**build-up, build·up** (bild′up′) *n.* [Colloq.] **1.** favorable publicity or praise **2.** growth or expansion *[a military buildup]*

**built-in** (bilt′in′) *adj.* **1.** made as part of the building *[a built-in bathtub]* **2.** intrinsic; inherent

**built-up** (-up′) *adj.* **1.** made higher, stronger, etc. by the addition of parts **2.** having many buildings on it: said of an area

**bulb** (bulb) *n.* [< L. < Gr. *bolbos*] **1.** an underground bud that sends down roots and has a very short stem covered with leafy scales, as in a lily, onion, etc. **2.** a corm, tuber, or tuberous root resembling a bulb, as in a crocus **3.** a plant that grows from a bulb **4.** anything shaped like a bulb *[an electric light bulb]* —**bul·bar** (bul′bər) *adj.* —**bulbed** *adj.*

**bul·ba·ceous** (bəl bā′shəs) *adj. same as* BULBOUS

**bul·bous** (bul′bəs) *adj.* **1.** of, having, or growing from bulbs **2.** shaped like a bulb

**Bul·gar·i·a** (bəl ger′ē ə, bool-) country in SE Europe, on the Black Sea, south of Romania: 42,796 sq. mi.; pop. 8,436,000; cap. Sofia —**Bul·gar′i·an, Bul·gar** (bul′gär, bool′-) *adj., n.*

**bulge** (bulj) *n.* [ME., var. of *bouge:* see BUDGET] **1.** an outward swelling; protuberance **2.** a projecting part **3.** [Colloq.] a sudden increase —*vi., vt.* **bulged, bulg′ing** to swell or bend outward; protrude —**bulg′y** (-ē) *adj.*

**bul·gur (wheat)** (bool′gər, bul′-) [Turk.] wheat cooked and dried, then coarsely ground: often cooked like pilaf

**bulk** (bulk) *n.* [ON. *bulki,* a heap, cargo] **1.** size, mass, or volume, esp. if great **2.** the main mass or body; largest part *[the bulk of one's fortune]* **3.** soft, bulky matter that passes through the intestines unabsorbed —*vi.* **1.** to form into a mass **2.** to increase in size, importance, etc. **3.** to have size or importance —*vt.* to cause to bulk; give more bulk to —*adj.* **1.** total; aggregate **2.** not put up in individual packages —**in bulk 1.** not put up in individual packages **2.** in large amounts

**bulk·head** (bulk′hed′) *n.* [< ON. *balkr,* partition + HEAD] **1.** any of the upright partitions separating parts of a ship, airplane, etc. as for protection against fire or leakage **2.** a wall or embankment for holding back earth, fire, water, etc. **3.** a boxlike structure built over an opening, as at the head of a staircase, elevator shaft, etc.

**bulk·y** (bul′kē) *adj.* **bulk′i·er, bulk′i·est 1.** *a)* having great bulk; large; massive *b)* relatively large for its weight **2.** awkwardly large; big and clumsy —**bulk′i·ly** *adv.* —**bulk′i·ness** *n.*

**bull**[1] (bool) *n.* [< OE. *bula,* a steer] **1.** the adult male of any bovine animal, as the ox, buffalo, etc. **2.** the adult male of certain other large animals, as the elephant, moose, walrus, whale, etc. **3.** a person who buys stocks, etc. expecting, or seeking to bring about, a rise in their prices **4.** a person regarded as like a bull in size, strength, etc. **5.** [Slang] a policeman or detective **6.** [Slang] foolish or insincere talk; nonsense —[B-] *same as* TAURUS —*vt.* to make (one's way) with force —*adj.* **1.** male **2.** like a bull in size, strength, etc. **3.** rising in price *[a bull market]* —**shoot the bull** [Slang] to talk idly —**take the bull by the horns** to deal boldly with a danger or difficulty —**bull′ish** *adj.* —**bull′ish·ly** *adv.* —**bull′ish·ness** *n.*

**bull**[2] (bool) *n.* [< OFr. < LL. *bulla,* a seal (L., bubble)] an official document or decree from the Pope

**bull**[3] (bool) *n.* [ult. < L. *bulla,* bubble] a mistake in statement that is illogical in a ludicrous way

**bull-** [< BULL[1]] *a combining form meaning:* **1.** of a bull or bulls *[bullfight]* **2.** like a bull or bull's *[bullhead]* **3.** large or male *[bullfrog]*

**bull·dog** (bool′dôg′, -däg′) *n.* [BULL- + DOG] a short-haired, square-jawed, heavily built dog noted for its strong, stubborn grip —*adj.* like or characteristic of a bulldog —*vt.* **-dogged′, -dog′ging** to throw (a steer) by seizing its horns and twisting its neck

**bull·doze** (-dōz′) *vt.* **-dozed′, -doz′ing** [< *bull* (Botany Bay slang), a flogging of 75 lashes + DOSE] **1.** [Colloq.] to force or frighten by threatening; intimidate **2.** to move, make level, dig out, etc. with a bulldozer

**bull·doz·er** (-dō′zər) *n.* **1.** a person who bulldozes **2.** a tractor with a large, shovellike blade on the front, for pushing or moving earth, debris, etc.

**bul·let** (bool′it) *n.* [Fr. *boulette,* dim. of *boule,* a ball < L. *bulla:* see BULL[2]] **1.** a small, shaped piece of lead, metal alloy, etc. to be shot from a firearm **2.** anything like a bullet in shape, action, etc.

**bul·le·tin** (bool′ət 'n) *n.* [Fr. < It. dim. of LL. *bulla:* see BULL[2]] **1.** a brief statement of the latest news **2.** a regular publication, as for members of a society —*vt.* to announce in a bulletin

**bulletin board** a board or wall area on which notices or displays are put up

**bul·let·proof** (bool′it proof′) *adj.* that bullets cannot pierce —*vt.* to make bulletproof

---

**bull·fight** (bool'fīt') *n.* a public show in which a bull is first provoked in various ways and then usually killed with a sword by a matador —**bull'fight'er** *n.* —**bull'fight'ing** *n.*

**bull·finch** (-finch') *n.* [BULL- + FINCH] **1.** a European songbird with a black head and white rump **2.** any of various other small songbirds

**bull·frog** (-frôg', -fräg') *n.* [BULL- + FROG] a large N. American frog with a deep, loud croak

**bull·head** (-hed') *n.* [see BULL-] **1.** any of various N. American freshwater catfishes **2.** any of various similar fishes of fresh or salt waters

**bull·head·ed** (-hed'id) *adj.* blindly stubborn —**bull'-head'ed·ly** *adv.* —**bull'head'ed·ness** *n.*

**bull·horn** (-hôrn') *n.* [BULL- + HORN] a portable electronic voice amplifier

**bul·lion** (bool'yən) *n.* [< Du. < OFr. *billon,* small coin < *bille,* a stick: see BILLET²] **1.** gold and silver regarded as raw material **2.** bars of gold or silver, as before coinage

**bull-necked** (-nekt') *adj.* having a short, thick neck

**bull·ock** (bool'ək) *n.* [< OE. *bulluc,* dim. of *bula:* see BULL¹] a castrated bull; steer

**bull·pen** (-pen') *n.* **1.** a fenced enclosure for bulls **2.** [Colloq.] an enclosure in a jail, where prisoners are herded temporarily **3.** *Baseball* an area where relief pitchers practice and warm up

**bull·ring** (-riŋ') *n.* an arena for bullfighting

**Bull Run** [< ?] small stream in NE Va.: site of two Union defeats (1861 & 1862) in the Civil War

**bull's-eye** (boolz'ī') *n.* **1.** a thick, circular glass in a roof, ship's deck, etc., for admitting light **2.** *a)* the central mark of a target *b)* a direct hit **3.** *a)* a convex lens for concentrating light *b)* a lantern with such a lens **4.** a hard, round candy

**bull terrier** a strong, lean, white dog, developed by crossing the bulldog and the terrier

**bull·whip** (bool'hwip', -wip') *n.* [BULL- + WHIP] a long, heavy whip, formerly used by cattle drivers, etc. —*vt.* **-whipped', -whip'ping** to whip with a bullwhip

**bul·ly¹** (bool'ē) *n., pl.* **-lies** [orig., sweetheart < Du. < MHG. *buole* (G. *buhle*), lover; later infl. by BULL¹] a person who hurts, frightens, or browbeats those who are smaller or weaker —*vt., vi.* **-lied, -ly·ing** to behave like a bully (toward) —*adj.* **1.** dashing, hearty, or jolly **2.** [Colloq.] fine; very good —*interj.* [Colloq.] good! well done!

**bul·ly²** (bool'ē) *n.* [< Fr. < *bouillir,* to boil] canned or corned beef: also **bully beef**

**bul·ly·rag** (-rag') *vt.* **-ragged', -rag'ging** [see BULLY¹, *vt.* & RAG², *vt.*] [Dial. or Colloq.] to bully or intimidate

**bul·rush** (bool'rush') *n.* [< OE. *bol,* BOLE + *risc,* a rush] **1.** a marsh plant of the sedge family **2.** [Brit.] the cattail **3.** the papyrus or other aquatic plant like a bulrush: cf. Ex. 2:3

**bul·wark** (bool'wərk, bul'-) *n.* [< MDu. *bolwerc:* see BOLE & WORK] **1.** an earthwork or defensive wall; rampart **2.** a defense or protection **3.** [*usually pl.*] a ship's side above the deck —*vt.* **1.** to provide bulwarks for **2.** to be a bulwark to

**bum** (bum) *n.* [prob. < G. *bummler,* loafer < *bummeln,* to go slowly] [Colloq.] **1.** a vagrant, tramp, beggar, or derelict **2.** any shiftless or irresponsible person **3.** a devotee, as of golf or skiing, who neglects all else —*vi.* **bummed, bum'-ming** [Colloq.] **1.** to live as a bum **2.** to live by sponging on people —*vt.* [Slang] to get by sponging; cadge —*adj.* **bum'mer, bum'mest** [Slang] **1.** poor in quality **2.** false or not valid [*a bum steer*] **3.** lame or ailing —**give** (or **get**) **the bum's rush** [Slang] to eject (or be ejected) forcibly —**on the bum** [Colloq.] **1.** living as a vagrant **2.** out of repair; broken —**bum'mer** *n.*

**bum·ble·bee** (bum'b'l bē') *n.* [altered (after ME. *bomblen,* to buzz) < ME. *humbul-be,* bumblebee] a large, hairy, yellow-and-black social bee

**bum·bling** (bum'bliŋ) *adj.* [prp. of bumble, buzz: see prec.] self-important in a blundering way

**bump** (bump) *vt.* [echoic] **1.** to hit against; collide lightly with **2.** [Slang] to displace, as from a job, plane reservation, etc. —*vi.* **1.** to collide with a jolt **2.** to move with jolts —*n.* **1.** a light blow or jolt **2.** a swelling or lump, esp. one caused by a blow —**bump into** [Colloq.] to meet unexpectedly —**bump off** [Slang] to murder

**bump·er¹** (bum'pər) *n.* a device for absorbing some of the shock of a collision; specif., a metal bar across the front or back of an automobile

**bump·er²** (bum'pər) *n.* [prob. < obs. *bombard,* liquor jug, altered after BUMP] **1.** a cup or glass filled to the brim **2.** [Colloq.] anything unusually large of its kind —*adj.* unusually abundant [*a bumper* crop]

**bump·kin** (bump'kən, bum'-) *n.* [prob. < MDu. *bommekijn,* small cask] an awkward or simple person from the country

**bump·tious** (bump'shəs) *adj.* [prob. < BUMP] disagreeably conceited, arrogant, or forward —**bump'tious·ly** *adv.* —**bump'tious·ness** *n.*

**bump·y** (bum'pē) *adj.* **bump'i·er, bump'i·est** full of bumps; rough —**bump'i·ly** *adv.* —**bump'i·ness** *n.*

**bun** (bun) *n.* [ME. *bunne,* wheat cake, prob. < OFr. *buigne,* a swelling] **1.** a small roll, usually somewhat sweetened and often spiced **2.** hair worn in a roll or knot

**bunch** (bunch) *n.* [ult. < Fl. *boudje,* dim. of *boud,* bundle] **1.** a cluster of things growing together [*a bunch* of grapes] **2.** a collection of things of the same kind fastened, grouped, or thought of together [*a bunch* of keys] **3.** [Colloq.] a group of people —*vt., vi.* to gather together in a mass or in loose folds, wads, etc. (often with *up*) —**bunch'i·ness** *n.* —**bunch'y** *adj.*

**bun·co** (buŋ'kō) *n., pl.* **-cos** [< Sp. *banca,* card game < It. *banca,* BANK¹] [Colloq.] a swindle, esp. at a card game; confidence game —*vt.* **-coed, -co·ing** [Colloq.] to swindle; cheat

**bun·combe** (buŋ'kəm) *n.* [< *Buncombe* county, N.C., whose Congressman (1819–21) regularly made "a speech for Buncombe"] [Colloq.] talk that is empty, insincere, or merely for effect; humbug

**bund, Bund** (boond; *G.* boont) *n., pl.* **bunds;** *G.* **Bun·de** (bün'də) [G.] **1.** a league or confederation **2.** the German-American Bund, a former pro-Nazi organization in the U.S. —**bund'ist** *n.*

**bun·dle** (bun'd'l) *n.* [prob. < MDu. *bondel* < *binden,* BIND] **1.** a number of things tied or wrapped together **2.** a package or parcel **3.** a bunch, collection, or group **4.** [Slang] a large amount of money **5.** *same as* VASCULAR BUNDLE —*vt.* **-dled, -dling 1.** to make into a bundle; wrap (often together **2.** to send hastily (*away, off, out,* or *into*) —*vi.* **1.** to move or go hastily; bustle **2.** to lie in the same bed with one's sweetheart without undressing: a former courting custom, esp. in New England —**bundle up** to put on plenty of warm clothing —**bun'dler** *n.*

**bung** (buŋ) *n.* [< MDu. *bonge*] **1.** a cork or other stopper for the hole in a barrel, cask, or keg **2.** a bunghole —*vt.* **1.** to close (a bunghole) with a stopper **2.** to stop up **3.** [Slang] to bruise or damage (with *up*)

**bun·ga·low** (buŋ'gə lō') *n.* [< Hindi *bānglā,* thatched house, lit., Bengalese] a small house or cottage, usually of one story and an attic

**bung·hole** (buŋ'hōl') *n.* a hole in a barrel or keg through which liquid can be drawn out

**bun·gle** (buŋ'g'l) *vt.* **-gled, -gling** [< ? Sw. *bangla,* to work ineffectually] to spoil by clumsy work; botch —*vi.* to do things badly or clumsily —*n.* **1.** a bungling, or clumsy, act **2.** a bungled piece of work —**bun'gler** *n.* —**bun'gling·ly** *adv.*

**bun·ion** (bun'yən) *n.* [prob. < ME. *boni,* swelling, boil < OFr. *buigne:* see BUN] an inflammation and swelling at the base of the big toe

**bunk¹** (buŋk) *n.* [prob. < Scand. cognate of BENCH] **1.** a shelflike bed or berth built into or against a wall, as in a ship **2.** [Colloq.] any sleeping place, as a narrow cot —*vi.* **1.** to sleep in a bunk **2.** [Colloq.] to use a makeshift sleeping place —*vt.* to provide a sleeping place for

**bunk²** (buŋk) *n.* [Slang] *same as* BUNCOMBE

**bunk bed** a pair of twin beds linked one above the other, often with a detachable ladder

**bunk·er** (buŋ'kər) *n.* [Scot. < ?] **1.** a large bin or tank, as for a ship's fuel **2.** a weapon emplacement of steel and concrete in an underground fortification system **3.** a sand trap or mound of earth serving as an obstacle on a golf course —*vt. Golf* to hit (a ball) into a bunker

**Bun·ker Hill** (buŋ'kər) hill in Boston, Mass., near which a battle of the American Revolution was fought in 1775

**bunk·house** (buŋk'hous') *n.* a barracks for ranch hands, migratory farm workers, etc.

**bun·ko** (buŋ'kō) *n., pl.* **-kos,** *vt.* **-koed, -ko·ing** *same as* BUNCO

**bun·kum** (buŋ'kəm) *n. same as* BUNCOMBE

**bun·ny** (bun'ē) *n., pl.* **-nies** [dim. of dial. *bun,* rabbit] a rabbit: pet name used by children

**Bun·sen burner** (bun's'n) [after R. W. *Bunsen,* 19th-c. Ger. chemist] a small, tubular gas burner that produces a hot, blue flame

**bunt** (bunt) *vt., vi.* [< ? base of Bret. *bounta,* to butt] **1.** [Brit. Dial.] to strike or butt with or as with horns **2.** *Baseball* to bat (a pitched ball) lightly without swinging so that it does not go beyond the infield, usually in attempting a sacrifice play —*n.* **1.** a butt or shove **2.** *Baseball a)* the act of bunting *b)* a bunted ball

**bun·ting¹** (bun'tiŋ) *n.* [< ? ME. *bonting,* sifting (cloth)] **1.** a thin cloth used in making flags, etc. **2.** flags, or strips of cloth in the colors of the flag, used as decorations **3.** a baby's garment of soft, warm cloth made into a kind of hooded blanket that can be closed

**bun·ting²** (bun'tiŋ) *n.* [< ?] any of various small, brightly colored birds having a stout bill

**bunt·line** (bunt'lin, -lin') *n.* [*bunt,* middle part of a sail + LINE¹] one of the ropes attached to the foot of a square sail to prevent the sail from bellying when drawn up to be furled

**Bun·yan** (bun'yən) **1.** John, 1628–88; Eng. writer & preacher **2.** see PAUL BUNYAN

**Buo·na·par·te** (bwô'nä pär'te) *It. sp. of* BONAPARTE

**buoy** (boo'ē, boi; *for v., usually* boi) *n.* [< OFr. *buie*, chain < L. *boia*, fetter: prob. first applied to the chain anchoring the float] **1.** a floating object anchored in water to warn of rocks, shoals, etc. or to mark a channel **2.** *short for* LIFE BUOY —*vt.* **1.** to mark or provide with a buoy **2.** to keep afloat: usually with *up* **3.** to lift or keep up in spirits; encourage: usually with *up*

**buoy·an·cy** (boi'ən sē, boo'yən-) *n.* [< ff.] **1.** the ability or tendency to float or rise in liquid or air **2.** the power to keep something afloat **3.** lightness of spirit; cheerfulness

**buoy·ant** (-ənt, -yənt) *adj.* [< ? Sp. < *boyar*, to float] having or showing buoyancy —**buoy'ant·ly** *adv.*

**bur** (bur) *n.* [ME. *burre* < Scand.] **1.** the rough, prickly seedcase or fruit of certain plants **2.** a weed or other plant with burs **3.** anything that clings like a bur **4.** *Dentistry* a cutting or drilling bit **5.** *same as* BURR¹ & BURR² —*vt.* **burred, bur'ring 1.** to remove burs from **2.** to burr

**bur.** bureau

**Bur·bank** (bur'baŋk) [after Dr. D. *Burbank*, one of the city planners] city in SW Calif.: suburb of Los Angeles: pop. 85,000

**Bur·bank** (bur'baŋk), **Luther** 1849–1926; U.S. horticulturist: bred numerous varieties of plants

**bur·ble** (bur'b'l) *vi.* -**bled, -bling** [echoic] **1.** to make a gurgling or bubbling sound **2.** to babble as a child does

**bur·bot** (bur'bət) *n., pl.* -**bot, -bots:** see PLURAL, II, D, 2 [< OFr. *borbote*, ult. < L. *barba*, a beard] a freshwater fish of the cod family, with barbels on the nose and chin

**bur·den¹** (burd''n) *n.* [< OE. *byrthen* < base of *beran:* see BEAR¹] **1.** anything that is carried; load **2.** a heavy load, as of work, responsibility, sorrow, etc. **3.** the carrying of loads [a beast of *burden*] **4.** the carrying capacity of a ship, or the weight of its cargo —*vt.* to put a burden on; load; oppress

**bur·den²** (burd''n) *n.* [< OFr. *bourdon*, a humming < ML. *burdo*, DRONE¹, wind instrument] **1.** a chorus or refrain of a song **2.** a repeated, central idea; theme [the *burden* of a speech]

**burden of proof** the obligation to prove what is asserted and in dispute

**bur·den·some** (-səm) *adj.* hard to bear; heavy; oppressive —**bur'den·some·ly** *adv.*

**bur·dock** (bur'däk') *n.* [BUR + DOCK³] a plant of the composite family, with large leaves, and purple-flowered heads covered with hooked prickles

**bu·reau** (byoor'ō) *n., pl.* -**reaus, -reaux** (-ōz) [Fr., desk < OFr. *burel*, coarse cloth (as table cover) < LL. *burra*, ragged (woolen) garment] **1.** [Brit.] a desk with drawers for papers **2.** a chest of drawers, often with a mirror, for clothing, etc. **3.** an agency providing specified services for clients [a travel *bureau*] **4.** a government department or a subdivision of this

**bu·reau·cra·cy** (byoo rä'krə sē) *n., pl.* -**cies** [< Fr. < *bureau* + -*cratie*, -CRACY] **1.** the administration of government through departments managed by officials following an inflexible routine **2.** the officials collectively **3.** governmental officialism or inflexible routine **4.** concentration of authority in a complex structure of administrative bureaus

**bu·reau·crat** (byoor'ə krat') *n.* an official in a bureaucracy, esp. one who follows a routine strictly, insisting on proper forms, petty rules, etc. —**bu'reau·crat'ic** *adj.* —**bu'reau·crat'i·cal·ly** *adv.*

**bu·reau·cra·tize** (byoo rä'krə tīz') *vt., vi.* -**tized', -tiz'ing** to make or become bureaucratic —**bu·reau'cra·ti·za'tion** *n.*

**bu·rette, bu·ret** (byoo ret') *n.* [Fr. < OFr. dim. of *buire*, flagon] a graduated glass tube with a stopcock at the bottom, for measuring small quantities of liquid or gas

**burg** (burg) *n.* [var. of BOROUGH] **1.** orig., a fortified town **2.** [Colloq.] a city, town, or village, esp. one regarded as quiet, unexciting, etc.

**-burg** (burg) *a suffix meaning* burg or borough [*Vicksburg*]: also **-burgh** [*Pittsburgh*]

**bur·geon** (bur'jən) *vi.* [< OFr. < *burjon*, a bud] **1.** to put forth buds, shoots, etc. **2.** to grow or develop rapidly; flourish [the *burgeoning* suburbs]

**-bur·ger** (bur'gər) [< (HAM)BURGER] *a combining form meaning:* **1.** sandwich of a patty of ground meat, fish, etc. [*turkeyburger*] **2.** hamburger and [*cheeseburger*]

**Bur·ger** (bur'gər), **Warren Earl** 1907– ; U.S. jurist; chief justice of the U.S. (1969– )

**bur·gess** (bur'jis) *n.* [OFr. *burgeis:* see BOURGEOIS] a member of the lower house of the legislature of Md. or Va. before the American Revolution

**burgh** (burg; *Scot.* bu'rə) *n.* [Scot. var. of BOROUGH] **1.** [Brit.] a borough **2.** in Scotland, a chartered town

**burgh·er** (bur'gər) *n.* an inhabitant of a borough or town; now, esp., a middle-class townsman

**bur·glar** (bur'glər) *n.* [< Anglo-L. *burglator*, altered after L. *latro*, thief < OFr. *burgeor*, burglar] a person who commits burglary

**bur·glar·i·ous** (bər gler'ē əs) *adj.* of, given to, or being burglary —**bur·glar'i·ous·ly** *adv.*

**bur·glar·ize** (bur'glə rīz') *vt.* -**ized', -iz'ing** [Colloq.] to commit burglary in or upon

**bur·gla·ry** (bur'glər ē) *n., pl.* -**ries** [BURGLAR + -Y⁴] **1.** the act of breaking into a house at night to commit theft or other felony **2.** a breaking into any building at any time to commit theft, etc.

**bur·gle** (bur'g'l) *vt., vi.* -**gled, -gling** [< BURGLAR] [Colloq.] to commit burglary (in)

**bur·go·mas·ter** (bur'gə mas'tər) *n.* [< MDu. < *burg*, town + *meester*, master] the mayor or head magistrate of a city or town in the Netherlands, Flanders, Austria, or Germany

**Bur·gun·dy** (bur'gən dē) region in SE France: formerly a province, duchy, & kingdom of varying extent —*n.* [occas. b-] *pl.* -**dies 1.** a kind of wine, either red or white, made in the Burgundy region **2.** a similar red wine made elsewhere —**Bur·gun·di·an** (bər gun'dē ən) *adj., n.*

**bur·i·al** (ber'ē əl) *n.* the burying of a dead body; interment —*adj.* of or connected with burial

**burial ground** a cemetery; graveyard

**bu·rin** (byoor'in) *n.* [Fr. < It. < Gmc. *boro*, borer] a pointed cutting tool used by engravers or marble workers

**Burke** (burk), **Edmund** 1729–97; Brit. statesman, orator, & writer, born in Ireland

**burl** (burl) *n.* [< OFr. < VL. < LL. *burra:* see BUREAU] **1.** a knot in wool, thread, yarn, etc. that gives a nubby appearance to cloth **2.** a kind of knot on some tree trunks —*vt.* to finish (cloth) by taking out the burls, etc. —**burled** *adj.*

BURIN

**bur·lap** (bur'lap) *n.* [< ? ME. *borel*, coarse cloth (< OFr. *burel:* see BUREAU) + *lappa*, LAP¹] a coarse cloth made of jute or hemp, used for making sacks, etc.

**bur·lesque** (bər lesk') *n.* [Fr. < It. < *burla*, a jest] **1.** any broadly comic or satirical imitation; parody **2.** (*also, facetiously,* bur'li kyoo') a sort of vaudeville characterized by low comedy, striptease acts, etc. —*adj.* **1.** comically imitating; parodying **2.** of or connected with burlesque (sense 2) —*vt., vi.* -**lesqued', -lesqu'ing** to imitate comically or derisively; parody

**bur·ley** (bur'lē) *n.* [< ? a proper name] [*also* B-] a thin-leaved tobacco grown esp. in Kentucky

**bur·ly** (bur'lē) *adj.* -**li·er, -li·est** [ME. *borlich*, excellent, handsome < ? OE. *borlice*, very, excellently] **1.** big and strong; heavy and muscular **2.** rough and hearty in manner —**bur'li·ness** *n.*

**Bur·ma** (bur'mə) country in SE Asia, on the Indochinese peninsula: 261,783 sq. mi.; pop. 26,980,000; cap. Rangoon —**Bur·mese** (bər mēz') *adj., n., pl.* -**mese'**

**burn¹** (burn) *vt.* **burned** or **burnt, burn'ing** [< ON. & OE.: ON. *brenna*, to burn, light; OE. *biernan*] **1.** to set on fire or subject to combustion **2.** to destroy by fire **3.** to injure or damage by fire, friction, or acid; scorch, scald, etc. **4.** to consume as fuel **5.** to transform into energy by metabolism **6.** to sunburn **7.** to cauterize **8.** to harden or glaze (bricks, pottery, etc.) by fire; fire **9.** to cause by fire, heat, etc. [to *burn* a hole in a coat] **10.** to cause a sensation of heat in [horseradish *burns* the throat] **11.** [Slang] *a)* to cheat, swindle, or rob *b)* to cause to suffer through misplaced trust: usually used in the passive —*vi.* **1.** to be on fire; flame; blaze **2.** to undergo combustion **3.** to give out light or heat; shine; glow **4.** to be destroyed by fire or heat **5.** to be injured or damaged by or as by fire or heat **6.** to feel hot **7.** to be excited or inflamed, as with anger or desire —*n.* **1.** an injury caused by fire, heat, wind, etc. **2.** the process or result of burning —**burn down** to burn to the ground —**burn oneself out** to exhaust oneself by too much work or dissipation —**burn up 1.** to burn completely **2.** [Slang] to make or become angry

**burn²** (burn) *n.* [see BOURN¹] [Scot.] a brook

**burn·a·ble** (-ə b'l) *adj.* that can be burned —*n.* something, esp. refuse, that can be burned

**burn·er** (bur'nər) *n.* **1.** the part of a stove, furnace, etc. from which the flame comes **2.** an apparatus for burning fuel or trash

**burn·ing** (bur'niŋ) *adj.* **1.** that burns **2.** intense; critical [a *burning* issue]

**bur·nish** (bʉr′nish) *vt., vi.* [< OFr. *brunir*, to make brown < *brun*, brown] to make or become shiny by rubbing; polish —*n.* a gloss or polish —**bur′nish·er** *n.*

**bur·noose, bur·nous** (bʉr nōōs′, bʉr′nōōs) *n.* [< Fr. < Ar. *burnus*, prob. < Gr. *birros*, a cloak] a long cloak with a hood, worn by Arabs and Moors

**Burns** (bʉrnz), **Robert** 1759–96; Scot. poet

**burn·sides** (bʉrn′sīdz′) *n.pl.* [after A. E. *Burnside*, Union general in the Civil War] a style of beard with full side whiskers and mustache, but with the chin clean-shaven

**burnt** (bʉrnt) *alt. pt. and pp. of* BURN[1]

**burnt sienna** *see* SIENNA

**burnt umber** *see* UMBER

**burp** (bʉrp) *n., vi.* [echoic] [Colloq.] belch —*vt.* to cause (a baby) to relieve itself of stomach gas, as by patting its back

**burp gun** [echoic] [Mil. Slang] any of various automatic pistols or submachine guns

**burr**[1] (bʉr) *n.* [var. of BUR] **1.** a rough edge left on metal, etc. by cutting or drilling **2.** *same as* BUR (senses 1, 2, 3) —*vt.* **1.** to form a rough edge on **2.** to remove burrs from (metal)

**burr**[2] (bʉr) *n.* [prob. echoic] **1.** the trilling of *r*, with uvula or tongue [a Scottish *burr*] **2.** a whirring sound —*vi.* **1.** to speak with a burr **2.** to make a whir —*vt.* to pronounce with a burr

**Burr** (bʉr), **Aaron** 1756–1836; U.S. political leader: killed Alexander Hamilton in a duel

**bur·ro** (bʉr′ō, boor′ō) *n., pl.* -ros [Sp. < LL. *burricus*, small horse] [Southwest] a donkey

**bur·row** (bʉr′ō, -ə) *n.* [see BOROUGH] **1.** a hole dug in the ground by an animal **2.** any similar hole for shelter, etc. —*vi.* **1.** to make a burrow **2.** to live or hide in or as in a burrow **3.** to delve or search, as if by digging —*vt.* **1.** to make burrows in **2.** to make by burrowing

**bur·ry**[1] (bʉr′ē) *adj.* -ri·er, -ri·est **1.** full of burs **2.** like a bur or burs; prickly

**bur·ry**[2] (bʉr′ē) *adj.* -ri·er, -ri·est having a burr in speech

**bur·sa** (bʉr′sə) *n., pl.* -sae (-sē) -sas [ML., a bag < Gr. *byrsa*, a hide] *Anat.* a sac or cavity, esp. one containing a fluid that reduces friction, as between a tendon and bone —**bur′sal** *adj.*

**bur·sar** (bʉr′sər) *n.* [ML. *bursarius* < *bursa:* see prec.] a treasurer, as of a college

**bur·si·tis** (bər sīt′əs) *n.* [< BURSA + -ITIS] inflammation of a bursa

**burst** (bʉrst) *vi.* burst, burst′ing [< OE. *berstan* & ON. *bresta*] **1.** to come apart suddenly and violently; break open or out; explode **2.** to give sudden expression to some feeling; break [into tears, laughter, etc.) **3.** to go, come, start, etc. suddenly and with force [he *burst* into the room] **4.** *a)* to be as full or crowded as possible *b)* to be filled (with anger, pride, etc.) —*vt.* to cause to burst —*n.* **1.** a bursting; explosion **2.** the result of a bursting; break **3.** a sudden, violent display of feeling **4.** a sudden action; spurt [a *burst* of speed] **5.** a single series of shots from an automatic firearm —**burst′er** *n.*

**bur·then** (bʉr′thən) *n., vt. archaic var. of* BURDEN[1]

**Bur·ton** (bʉr′tən), Sir **Richard Francis** 1821–90; Eng. writer, translator, & explorer

**Bu·run·di** (boo roon′dē, -run′-) country in EC Africa, east of Zaire: 10,745 sq. mi.; pop. 3,475,000 —**Bu·run′di·an** *adj., n.*

**bur·y** (ber′ē) *vt.* bur′ied, bur′y·ing [OE. *byrgan*, akin to *beorgan*, conceal] **1.** to put (a dead body) into the earth, a tomb, the sea, etc.; inter **2.** *a)* to hide (something) in the ground *b)* to cover up so as to conceal **3.** to put away [to *bury* a feud] **4.** to get deeply in [to *bury* oneself in one's work]

**bus** (bus) *n., pl.* bus′es, bus′ses [< (OMNI)BUS] **1.** a large motor coach for carrying many passengers, usually along a regular route; omnibus **2.** [Slang] an automobile —*vt.* **bused** or **bussed, bus′ing** or **bus′sing** to transport by bus —*vi.* **1.** to go by bus **2.** to do the work of a busboy

**bus.** business

**bus·boy** (-boi′) *n.* a waiter's assistant who clears tables, brings water, etc.

**bus·by** (buz′bē) *n., pl.* -bies [prob. < the name *Busby*] a tall fur hat worn by hussars, British guardsmen, etc.

**bush**[1] (boosh) *n.* [ME., of WGmc. orig.] **1.** a woody plant having many stems branching out low instead of one main stem; shrub **2.** anything resembling a bush; esp., a thickly furred tail **3.** shrubby woodland or uncleared country —*vi.* to spread out like a bush —**beat around the bush** to talk around a subject without getting to the point

**bush**[2] (boosh) *n.* [MDu. *busse*, box < ML. *buxis:* see BOX[1]] *same as* BUSHING —*vt.* to fit with a bushing

**bushed** (boosht) *adj.* [Colloq.] tired; fatigued

**bush·el**[1] (boosh′'l) *n.* [< OFr. *boissel* < *boisse*, grain measure] **1.** a unit of dry measure for grain, fruit, etc., equal to 4 pecks or 32 quarts **2.** a container holding one

bushel **3.** [Colloq.] a large amount Abbrev. **bu.** —**bush′el·bas′ket** *n.*

**bush·el**[2] (boosh′'l) *vt., vi.* -eled or -elled, -el·ing or -el·ling [< ? G. *bosseln*, to repair] to repair or alter (garments)

**Bu·shi·do** (boo′shē dō′) *n.* [Jap., way of the warrior] [*also* b-] the chivalric code of the samurai of feudal Japan

**bush·ing** (boosh′iŋ) *n.* [< BUSH[2]] a removable metal sleeve for reducing the effect of friction on a bearing or for decreasing the diameter of a hole

**bush league** [Slang] *Baseball* a small or second-rate minor league —**bush′-league′** *adj.*

**bush leaguer** [Slang] **1.** a player in a bush league **2.** any second-rate performer

**bush·man** (boosh′mən) *n., pl.* -men **1.** a person who lives in the Australian bush **2.** a backwoodsman **3.** [B-] a member of a nomadic people of SW Africa

**bush·mas·ter** (-mas′tər) *n.* a large, poisonous snake of Central and South America

**bush·rang·er** (-rān′jər) *n.* [< BUSH[1] (*n.* 3) + RANGER] **1.** a person who lives in the bush **2.** in Australia, an outlaw who makes the bush his hide-out

**bush·whack** (-hwak′, -wak′) *vi.* [prob. < BUSH[1] + WHACK] **1.** to beat or cut one's way through bushes **2.** to engage in guerrilla fighting, attacking from ambush —*vt.* to ambush —**bush′whack′er** *n.* —**bush′whack′ing** *n.*

**bush·y** (boosh′ē) *adj.* bush′i·er, bush′i·est **1.** covered or overgrown with bushes **2.** thick and spreading out like a bush —**bush′i·ness** *n.*

**bus·i·ly** (biz′ə lē) *adv.* in a busy manner

**busi·ness** (biz′nis) *n.* [OE. *bisignes:* see BUSY & -NESS] **1.** one's work, occupation, or profession **2.** rightful concern or responsibility **3.** a matter, affair, activity, etc. **4.** the buying and selling of goods and services; commerce; trade **5.** a commercial or industrial establishment; store, factory, etc. **6.** action in a drama to take up a pause in dialogue, etc. —*adj.* of or for business —**business is business** sentiment, friendship, etc. cannot be allowed to interfere with profit making —**do business with 1.** to engage in commerce with **2.** to have dealings with —**give (or get) the business** [Slang] to subject (or be subjected) to rough treatment, practical joking, etc. —**mean business** [Colloq.] to be in earnest

**business college** (or **school**) a school offering instruction in secretarial skills, business administration, etc.

**busi·ness·like** (-līk′) *adj.* efficient, methodical, etc.

**busi·ness·man** (-man′) *n., pl.* -men′ (-men′) a man in business, esp. as an owner or executive —**busi′ness·wom′an** *n.fem., pl.* -wom′en

**bus·ing, bus·sing** (bus′iŋ) *n.* the act of transporting children by bus to a school outside of their neighborhood, esp. in order to desegregate the school

**bus·kin** (bus′kin) *n.* [< ? OFr. < MDu. *brosekin*, small leather boot] **1.** a boot reaching to the calf or knee, worn long ago **2.** *a)* the high, thick-soled, laced boot worn by actors in ancient Greek and Roman tragedy *b)* tragic drama; tragedy —**bus′kined** *adj.*

**bus·man** (bus′mən) *n., pl.* -men the operator of a bus

**busman's holiday** a holiday in which one's recreation is very similar to one's daily work

**buss** (bus) *n., vt., vi.* [? akin to G. dial. (or W. & Gael.) *bus*] [Archaic or Dial.] kiss

**bus·ses** (bus′iz) *n.* alt. pl. of BUS

**bust**[1] (bust) *n.* [< Fr. < It. *busto*] **1.** a piece of sculpture representing a person's head, shoulders, and upper chest **2.** a woman's bosom

BUSKINS

**bust**[2] (bust) *vt., vi.* [orig., dial. var. of BURST] [Slang] **1.** to burst or break **2.** to make or become penniless or bankrupt **3.** to demote or become demoted **4.** to tame (esp. broncos) **5.** to hit **6.** to arrest —*n.* [Slang] **1.** a failure **2.** a financial collapse **3.** a punch **4.** a spree **5.** an arrest —**bust′ed** *adj.*

**bus·tard** (bus′tərd) *n.* [< OFr., ult. < L. *avis tarda*, lit., slow bird] a large, long-legged, old-world game bird

**bus·tle**[1] (bus′'l) *vi., vt.* -tled, -tling [< ME. *busken*, to prepare < ON.] to hurry busily or with much fuss and bother —*n.* busy and noisy activity —**bus′tling·ly** *adv.*

**bus·tle**[2] (bus′'l) *n.* [late 18th c. < ? G. *buschel*, a bunch, pad] a framework or padding worn at the back by women to puff out the skirt

**bus·y** (biz′ē) *adj.* bus′i·er, bus′i·est [< OE. *bisig*] **1.** occupied; at work; not idle **2.** full of activity **3.** *a)* in use at the moment, as a telephone line *b)* indicating such use [the *busy* signal] **4.** meddlesome **5.** displeasingly crowded with detail, colors, etc. —*vt.* bus′ied, bus′y·ing to make or keep busy —**bus′y·ness** *n.*

**cab·i·net** (kab′ə nit, kab′nit) *n.* [Fr., dim. of *cabine;* origin obscure] **1.** a case with drawers or shelves for holding or storing things **2.** a boxlike enclosure for a record player, radio, television, etc. **3.** formerly, a private council room **4.** [*often* C-] a body of official advisers to a president, king, governor, etc.: in the U.S., the heads of certain governmental departments —*adj.* **1.** of a kind usually kept in a cabinet **2.** of a political cabinet

**cab·i·net·mak·er** (-māk′ər) *n.* a workman who makes fine furniture, etc. —**cab′i·net·mak′ing** *n.*

**cab·i·net·work** (-wurk′) *n.* **1.** articles made by a cabinetmaker **2.** the work or art of a cabinetmaker Also **cab′i·net·ry** (-rē)

**ca·ble** (kā′b'l) *n.* [OFr. < LL. *capulum* < L. *capere*, to take hold] **1.** a thick, heavy rope, now often of wire **2.** a ship's anchor chain **3.** *same as* CABLE LENGTH **4.** a bundle of insulated wires through which an electric current can be passed **5.** *same as* CABLEGRAM —*vt.* **-bled, -bling 1.** to fasten with a cable **2.** to transmit by undersea cable **3.** to send a cablegram to —*vi.* to send a cablegram

**cable car** a car drawn by a moving cable

**ca·ble·gram** (-gram′) *n.* a message sent by undersea cable

**cable length** a unit of nautical measure variously equal to 720 feet (120 fathoms) or 600 feet (100 fathoms): also **cable's length**

CABLES

**cable railway** a street railway on which cars are pulled by a continuously moving underground cable

**ca·bob** (kə bäb′) *n. same as* KEBAB

**ca·boo·dle** (kə bōō′d'l) *n.* [*ca*-, colloq. intens. prefix + BOODLE] [Colloq.] lot; group [the whole *caboodle*]

**ca·boose** (kə bōōs′) *n.* [< MDu. *kabuys, kambuis* (< ?), cabin house, ship's galley] **1.** [Brit.] a ship's galley or kitchen **2.** the trainmen's car on a freight train, usually at the rear

**Cab·ot** (kab′ət), **John** (It. name *Giovanni Caboto*) 1450?–98; It. explorer in the service of England: discovered coast of N. America (1497)

**ca·bret·ta** (kə bret′ə) *adj.* [< Sp. *cabra*, goat + It. dim. suffix -*etta*] designating or of a soft leather made from a special kind of sheepskin

**cab·ri·o·let** (kab′rē ə lā′, -let′) *n.* [Fr., dim. of *cabriole*, a leap < It. *capriola*] **1.** a light, two-wheeled carriage, usually with a hood that folds, drawn by one horse **2.** a former style of automobile like a convertible coupe

**cab·stand** (kab′stand′) *n.* a place where cabs are stationed for hire

**ca·ca·o** (kə kā′ō, -kä′-) *n., pl.* **-ca′os** [Sp. < Nahuatl *cacauatl*, cacao seed] **1.** a tropical American tree, bearing large, elliptical seedpods **2.** the seeds (**cacao beans**) of this tree, from which cocoa and chocolate are made

**cac·cia·to·re** (kach′ə tôr′ē) *adj.* [It., lit., a hunter < pp. of *cacciare*, to hunt] cooked in a casserole with olive oil and tomatoes, onions, spices, etc. [chicken *cacciatore*]

**cach·a·lot** (kash′ə lät′, -lō′) *n.* [Fr. < Sp. < ? Port. *cachola*, big head] *same as* SPERM WHALE

**cache** (kash) *n.* [Fr. < *cacher*, conceal < L. *coactare*, constrain] **1.** a place in which stores of food, supplies, etc. are hidden **2.** a safe place for hiding things **3.** anything so hidden —*vt., vi.* **cached, cach′ing** to hide or store in a cache

**cache·pot** (kash′pät, -pō) *n.* [Fr., lit., hide-pot < *cacher*, to hide + *pot*, pot] a decorative pot, jar, etc., esp. for house plants: also **cache pot**

**ca·chet** (ka shā′, kash′ā) *n.* [Fr. < *cacher:* see CACHE] **1.** a seal or stamp on an official letter **2.** *a)* a mark indicating genuine or superior quality *b)* prestige **3.** a commemorative design, slogan, etc. stamped on mail

**cach·in·nate** (kak′ə nāt′) *vi.* **-nat′ed, -nat′ing** [< L. pp. of *cachinnare*, prob. echoic] to laugh loudly or too much —**cach′in·na′tion** *n.*

**ca·cique** (kə sēk′) *n.* [Sp. < native word] **1.** in Spanish America, an Indian chief **2.** in Spanish America and Spain, a local political boss

**cack·le** (kak′'l) *vi.* **-led, -ling** [akin to Du. *kokkelen*, of echoic origin] **1.** to make the shrill, broken, vocal sounds of a hen **2.** to laugh or chatter with similar sounds —*vt.* to utter in a cackling manner —*n.* **1.** a cackling **2.** cackling laughter or chatter

**cac·o-** [< Gr. *kakos*, bad, evil] *a combining form meaning* bad, poor, harsh [*cacography*]: also, before a vowel, **cac-**

**ca·cog·ra·phy** (kə käg′rə fē) *n.* [CACO- + -GRAPHY] **1.** bad handwriting **2.** incorrect spelling —**cac′o·graph′ic** (kak′ə graf′ik) *adj.*

**ca·coph·o·ny** (kə käf′ə nē) *n., pl.* **-nies** [< ModL. < Gr. < *kakos*, bad + *phōnē*, voice] harsh, jarring sound; dissonance —**ca·coph′o·nous** *adj.* —**ca·coph′o·nous·ly** *adv.*

**cac·tus** (kak′təs) *n., pl.* **-tus·es, -ti** (-tī) [L. < Gr. *kaktos*, kind of thistle] any of various new-world desert plants with fleshy stems, reduced or spinelike leaves, and often showy flowers

**cad** (kad) *n.* [< CADDIE & CADET] a man or boy whose behavior is not gentlemanly

**ca·dav·er** (kə dav′ər) *n.* [L., prob. < *cadere*, to fall] a dead body, esp. of a person; corpse, as for dissection —**ca·dav′er·ic** *adj.*

**ca·dav·er·ous** (-ər əs) *adj.* of or like a cadaver; esp., pale, ghastly, or gaunt and haggard —**ca·dav′er·ous·ly** *adv.*

**cad·die** (kad′ē) *n.* [Scot. form of Fr. *cadet:* see CADET] **1.** a person who attends a golf player, carrying his clubs, etc. **2.** a small, wheeled cart —*vi.* **-died, -dy·ing** to act as a caddie

**cad·dis fly** (kad′is) [see CADDIS WORM] a small, mothlike insect with two pairs of wings, a soft body, and long legs

**cad·dish** (kad′ish) *adj.* like or characteristic of a cad; ungentlemanly —**cad′dish·ly** *adv.* —**cad′dish·ness** *n.*

**cad·dis worm** (kad′is) [< OFr. *cadas*, floss silk (with reference to the case)] the wormlike larva of the caddis fly that lives in a case made of twigs, grains of sand, etc. cemented together with its secreted silk: used as bait by anglers

**cad·dy¹** (kad′ē) *n., pl.* **-dies** [< Malay *kati*, weight equivalent to a little more than a pound] **1.** a small container used for tea **2.** any of various devices for holding or storing certain articles

**cad·dy²** (kad′ē) *n., vi. same as* CADDIE

**-cade** (kād) [< (CAVAL)CADE] *a suffix meaning* procession, parade [motorcade]

**ca·dence** (kād′'ns) *n.* [ult. < L. prp. of *cadere*, to fall] **1.** fall of the voice in speaking **2.** inflection or modulation in tone **3.** a rhythmic flow of sound **4.** measured movement, as in marching, or the beat of such movement **5.** *Music* the harmonic ending, final trill, etc. of a phrase or movement Also **ca′den·cy** —**ca′denced** *adj.*

**ca·den·za** (kə den′zə) *n.* [It.: see prec.] **1.** an elaborate, often improvised musical passage played by the solo instrument in a concerto, usually near the end of the first movement **2.** any brilliant flourish in an aria or solo passage

**ca·det** (kə det′) *n.* [Fr. < Gascon *capdet*, chief < Pr. < LL. dim. of L. *caput:* see CAPTAIN] **1.** a younger son or brother **2.** a student at an armed forces academy **3.** a student at a military school **4.** any trainee, as a practice teacher or a junior business associate —**ca·det′ship** *n.*

**cadge** (kaj) *vt., vi.* **cadged, cadg′ing** [ME. *caggen*, to tie; ? var. of *cacchen*, to catch] to beg or get by begging; sponge —**cadg′er** *n.*

**ca·di** (kä′dē, kā′-) *n.* [Ar. *qādi*] a minor Moslem magistrate or judge

**Cá·diz** (kə diz′, kā′diz; *Sp.* kä *thēth′*) seaport in SW Spain, on the Atlantic: pop. 133,000

**Cad·me·an** (kad mē′ən) *adj.* of or like Cadmus

**Cadmean victory** a victory won with great losses to the victors

**cad·mi·um** (kad′mē əm) *n.* [ModL. < L. *cadmia*, zinc ore < Gr. *kadmeia*] a blue-white, malleable, ductile, metallic chemical element occurring in zinc ores: it is used in some alloys, electroplating, etc.: symbol, Cd; at. wt., 112.40; at. no., 48 —**cad′mic** (-mik) *adj.*

**Cad·mus** (kad′məs) *Gr. Myth.* a Phoenician prince who killed a dragon and sowed its teeth, from which many armed men rose and fought, five surviving to help him build Thebes

**ca·dre** (kad′rē) *n.* [Fr. < It. < L. *quadrum*, a square] **1.** a framework **2.** an operational unit around which an expanded organization, as a military unit, can be built; nucleus

**ca·du·ce·us** (kə dōō′sē əs, -dyōō′-) *n., pl.* **-ce·i′** (-sē ī′) [L.] **1.** the staff of an ancient herald; esp., the winged staff with two serpents twined about it, carried by Mercury **2.** a staff like this twined with one or two serpents, used as a symbol of the medical profession —**ca·du′ce·an** *adj.*

**cae·cum** (sē′kəm) *n., pl.* **-ca** (-kə) *same as* CECUM —**cae′cal** *adj.*

**Caed·mon** (kad′mən) fl. late 7th cent. A.D.; first Eng. poet whose name is known

**Cae·sar** (sē′zər) *n.* [after ff. < ? L. pp. of *caedere*, to cut] **1.** the title of the Roman emperors from Augustus to Hadrian **2.** any emperor or dictator

**Cae·sar** (sē′zər), **(Gaius) Julius** 100?–44 B.C.; Roman general & statesman

**Cae·sar·e·an, Cae·sar·i·an** (si zer′ē ən) *adj.* of Julius Caesar or the Caesars —*n. same as* CAESAREAN SECTION

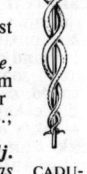

CADUCEUS

**Caesarean section** [after Julius *Caesar*, supposedly born in this way] [*also* c- s-] a surgical operation for delivering a baby by cutting through the mother's abdominal and uterine walls

**cae·si·um** (sē′zē əm) *n. same as* CESIUM

**cae·su·ra** (si zhŏŏr′ə, -zyŏŏr′ə) *n., pl.* **-ras, -rae** (-ē) [L., a cutting < pp. of *caedere*, to cut] **1.** a break or pause in a line of verse: in Greek and Latin verse, the caesura falls within the metrical foot; in English verse, it is usually about the middle of the line **2.** a pause showing rhythmic division of a melody —**cae·su′ral** *adj.*

**ca·fé, ca·fe** (ka fā′, kə-) *n.* [Fr. < It. *caffé*, COFFEE] **1.** coffee **2.** a coffeehouse **3.** a small restaurant, esp. one serving alcoholic drinks and sometimes providing entertainment **4.** a barroom

‡**ca·fé au lait** (kà fā ō lā′) [Fr.] **1.** coffee with an equal part of hot milk **2.** pale brown

**café curtains** short, straight curtains hung from a rod by sliding rings

‡**ca·fé noir** (kà fā nwàr′) [Fr.] black coffee

**caf·e·te·ri·a** (kaf′ə tir′ē ə) *n.* [AmSp., coffee store] a restaurant in which food is displayed on counters and patrons serve themselves

**caf·feine, caf·fein** (kaf′ēn, -ē in; ka fēn′) *n.* [< G., ult. < It. *caffé*, COFFEE + *-in*, -INE⁴] an alkaloid, $C_8H_{10}N_4O_2$, present in coffee, tea, and kola: it is a stimulant to the heart and central nervous system

**caf·tan** (kaf′tən, käf tän′) *n.* [Turk. *qaftān*] a long-sleeved robe with a girdle, worn in eastern Mediterranean countries

**cage** (kāj) *n.* [OFr. < L *cavea*, hollow place < *cavus*, hollow] **1.** a box or structure of wires, bars, etc. for confining birds or animals **2.** an openwork structure, as some elevator cars **3.** *Baseball* a backstop used in batting practice, etc. **4.** *Basketball* the basket **5.** *Hockey* the network frame that is the goal —*vt.* **caged, cag′ing** to put or confine, as in a cage

**ca·gey, ca·gy** (kā′jē) *adj.* **ca′gi·er, ca′gi·est** [< ?] [Colloq.]. **1.** sly; tricky; cunning **2.** careful not to get caught or fooled —**ca′gi·ly** *adv.* —**ca′gi·ness** *n.*

**Ca·glia·ri** (kä′lyä rē′) capital of Sardinia; seaport on the S coast: pop. 216,000

**Ca·guas** (kä′gwäs) city in EC Puerto Rico: pop. 63,000

**ca·hoots** (kə hŏŏts′) *n.pl.* [< ?] [Slang] partnership; league —**go cahoots** [Slang] to share alike —**in cahoots** [Slang] in league: usually applied to questionable dealing

**cai·man** (kā′mən) *n., pl.* **-mans** [Sp. < Carib native name] a reptile of Central or South America similar to the alligator and crocodile

**Cain** (kān) *Bible* the oldest son of Adam and Eve: he killed his brother Abel: Gen. 4 —*n.* any murderer —**raise Cain** [Slang] to cause a great commotion or much trouble

**ca·ique, ca·ïque** (kä ēk′) *n.* [Fr. < It. < Turk. *qayiq*] **1.** a light rowboat used on the Bosporus **2.** a sailboat used esp. in the eastern Mediterranean

**cairn** (kern) *n.* [Scot. < Gael. *carn*, an elevation] a conical heap of stones built as a monument or landmark —**cairned** *adj.*

**Cai·ro** (kī′rō) capital of Egypt, at the head of the Nile delta: pop. 3,346,000

**cais·son** (kā′sän, käs′'n) *n.* [Fr. < It. < *cassa* < L. *capsa*, a box, CASE²] **1.** a chest for holding ammunition **2.** a two-wheeled wagon for transporting ammunition **3.** a watertight enclosure inside which men can do construction work under water **4.** a watertight box for raising sunken ships

**caisson disease** *same as* DECOMPRESSION SICKNESS

**cai·tiff** (kāt′if) *n.* [OFr. *caitif*, a captive < L. *captivus*, CAPTIVE] a mean, evil, or cowardly person —*adj.* mean, evil, or cowardly

**ca·jole** (kə jōl′) *vt., vi.* **-joled′, -jol′ing** [< Fr. < ? blend of OFr. *cage*, CAGE + *jaole, gaole*, prison: see JAIL] to coax with flattery and insincere talk; wheedle —**ca·jole′ment**, **ca·jol′er·y** *n.* —**ca·jol′er** *n.* —**ca·jol′ing·ly** *adv.*

**Ca·jun, Ca·jan** (kā′jən) *n.* [< Acadian Fr.] **1.** a native of Louisiana originally descended from Acadian French immigrants: sometimes used contemptuously **2.** the dialect of the Cajuns

**cake** (kāk) *n.* [< ON. *kaka*] **1.** a small, flat mass of dough or batter, or of some hashed food, that is baked or fried **2.** a mixture of flour, eggs, milk, sugar, etc. baked as in a loaf and often covered with icing **3.** a shaped, solid mass, as of soap, ice, etc. **4.** a hard crust or deposit —*vt., vi.* **caked, cak′ing** to form into a hard mass or a crust —**take the cake** [Slang] to win the prize; excel: ironic usage —**cak′y** *adj.* **cak′i·er, cak′i·est**

**cakes and ale** the good things of life

**cake·walk** (-wôk′) *n.* **1.** an elaborate step or walk formerly performed by Negroes in the South competing for the prize of a cake **2.** a strutting dance developed from this —*vi.* to do a cakewalk

**Cal.** **1.** California **2.** large calorie(s)

**cal.** **1.** calendar **2.** caliber **3.** small calorie(s)

**cal·a·bash** (kal′ə bash′) *n.* [< Fr. < Sp. *calabaza* < ?] **1.** a tropical American tree or its large, gourdlike fruit **2.**

*a)* a tropical vine bearing white flowers, or its bottle-shaped gourd *b)* a large smoking pipe made from the neck of this gourd **3.** the dried, hollow shell of a calabash, used as a bowl, cup, etc.

**cal·a·boose** (kal′ə bŏŏs′) *n.* [Sp. *calabozo*] [Slang] a prison; jail

**ca·la·di·um** (kə lā′dē əm) *n.* [ModL. < Malay *kélády*, kind of plant] a tropical American plant of the arum family, with brilliantly colored leaves

**Cal·ais** (ka lā′, kal′ā) seaport in N France, on the Strait of Dover: pop. 75,000

**cal·a·mine** (kal′ə mīn′, -min) *n.* [Fr. < ML. *calamina* < L. *cadmia*: see CADMIUM] a pink powder consisting of zinc oxide mixed with a little ferric oxide, used in skin lotions and ointments

**ca·lam·i·tous** (kə lam′ə təs) *adj.* bringing or causing calamity —**ca·lam′i·tous·ly** *adv.* —**ca·lam′i·tous·ness** *n.*

**ca·lam·i·ty** (-tē) *n., pl.* **-ties** [< Fr. < L. *calamitas*] **1.** deep trouble or misery **2.** any extreme misfortune; disaster

**cal·a·mon·din** (kal′ə män′din) *n.* [Tag. *kalamunding*] a small, spicy orange of the Philippines

**cal·a·mus** (kal′ə məs) *n., pl.* **-mi′** (-mī′) [L. < Gr. *kalamos*, a reed] **1.** *same as* SWEET FLAG **2.** the quill of a feather

**ca·lash** (kə lash′) *n.* [Fr. *calèche* < G. < Czech *kolésa*; prob. < *kolo*, a wheel] **1.** a light, low-wheeled carriage, usually with a folding top **2.** a folding top of a carriage **3.** a folding hood or bonnet, worn by women in the 18th cent.

**cal·ca·ne·us** (kal kā′nē əs) *n., pl.* **-ne·i′** (-nē ī′) [LL. < L. < *calx*, the heel] the heel bone: also **cal·ca′ne·um** (-əm), *pl.* **-ne·a** (-ə) —**cal·ca′ne·al** *adj.*

**cal·car·e·ous** (kal ker′ē əs) *adj.* [< L. < *calx*, lime] of, like, or containing calcium carbonate, calcium, or lime —**cal·car′e·ous·ness** *n.*

**cal·ces** (kal′sēz) *n. alt. pl.* of CALX

**cal·ci-** [< L. *calx* (gen. *calcis*), lime] *a combining form meaning* calcium or lime [*calcify*]

**cal·cif·er·ol** (kal sif′ə rôl′, -rōl′) *n.* [CALCIF(EROUS) + (ER-GOST)EROL] vitamin D₂: it is a crystalline alcohol, $C_{28}H_{43}OH$

**cal·cif·er·ous** (-ər əs) *adj.* [CALCI- + -FEROUS] producing or containing calcite

**cal·ci·fy** (kal′sə fī′) *vt., vi.* **-fied′, -fy′ing** [CALCI- + -FY] to change into a hard, stony substance by the deposit of lime or calcium salts —**cal′ci·fi·ca′tion** *n.*

**cal·ci·mine** (-mīn′, -min) *n.* [< L. *calx*, lime] a white or colored liquid of whiting or zinc white, glue, and water, used as a wash for plastered surfaces —*vt.* **-mined′, -min′-ing** to cover with calcimine

**cal·cine** (kal′sīn, kal sīn′) *vt., vi.* **-cined, -cin·ing** [< OFr. < ML. *calcinare* (an alchemists' term)] **1.** to change to calx or powder by heat **2.** to burn to ashes or powder —**cal·ci·na′tion** (kal′sə nā′shən) *n.*

**cal·cite** (kal′sīt) *n.* calcium carbonate, $CaCO_3$, a mineral found as limestone, chalk, and marble

**cal·ci·um** (kal′sē əm) *n.* [ModL. < L. *calx*, lime] a soft, silver-white, metallic chemical element found in limestone, marble, chalk, etc.: symbol, Ca; at. wt., 40.08; at. no., 20

**calcium carbide** a dark-gray, crystalline compound, $CaC_2$, used to produce acetylene, etc.

**calcium carbonate** a white powder or colorless, crystalline compound, $CaCO_3$, found mainly in limestone, marble, and chalk, and in bones, teeth, shells, and plant ash: used in making lime

**calcium chloride** a white, crystalline compound, $CaCl_2$, used in making ice, for dehydrating, etc.

**calcium hydroxide** slaked lime, $Ca(OH)_2$, a white, crystalline compound, used in making alkalies, bleaching powder, etc.

**calcium oxide** a white, soft, caustic solid, CaO, prepared by heating calcium carbonate; lime: used in mortar and plaster, in ceramics, etc.

**calcium phosphate** any of a number of phosphates of calcium found in bones, teeth, etc.

**calc·spar** (kalk′spär′) *n. same as* CALCITE

**cal·cu·la·ble** (kal′kyə lə b'l) *adj.* that can be calculated —**cal′cu·la·bil′i·ty** *n.* —**cal′cu·la·bly** *adv.*

**cal·cu·late** (kal′kyə lāt′) *vt.* **-lat′ed, -lat′ing** [< L. pp. of *calculare*, to reckon < *calculus*, pebble used in counting, dim. of *calx*, limestone] **1.** to determine by using mathematics; compute **2.** to determine by reasoning; estimate **3.** to plan or intend [a tale *calculated* to fool us] **4.** [Colloq.] to think; suppose —*vi.* **1.** to make a computation **2.** to rely or count (*on*)

**cal·cu·lat·ed** (-lāt′id) *adj.* **1.** undertaken after the probable results have been estimated [*calculated* risk] **2.** deliberately planned [*calculated* cruelty] **3.** apt or likely —**cal′cu·lat′ed·ly** *adv.*

**cal·cu·lat·ing** (-iŋ) *adj.* shrewd or scheming

**cal·cu·la·tion** (kal′kyə lā′shən) *n.* **1.** a calculating **2.** something deduced by calculating; estimate; plan **3.**

careful planning or forethought, esp. with selfish motives —**cal′cu·la′tive** *adj.*

**cal·cu·la·tor** (kal′kyə lāt′ər) *n.* **1.** a person who calculates **2.** a machine for doing rapid addition, subtraction, multiplication, and division: also **calculating machine**

**cal·cu·lous** (kal′kyə ləs) *adj. Med.* caused by or having a calculus or calculi

**cal·cu·lus** (kal′kyə ləs) *n., pl.* **-li′** (-lī′), **-lus·es** [L.: see CALCULATE] **1.** any abnormal stony mass or deposit formed in the body, as in a kidney **2.** *Math. a)* a method of calculation using symbols *b)* a method of mathematical analysis using the combined methods of DIFFERENTIAL CALCULUS and INTEGRAL CALCULUS

**Cal·cut·ta** (kal kut′ə) seaport in NE India, in the Ganges delta: pop. 2,927,000

**cal·dron** (kôl′drən) *n.* [< OFr. < L. *caldaria,* warm bath < *calidus,* warm] a large kettle or boiler

**Ca·leb** (kā′ləb) [Heb. *kālēb,* lit., dog: hence, faithful] a masculine name

**ca·lèche, ca·leche** (kȧ lesh′) *n. same as* CALASH

**Cal·e·do·ni·a** (kal′ə dōn′yə, -dō′nē ə) [L.] *poet. name for* SCOTLAND —**Cal′e·do′ni·an** *adj., n.*

**cal·en·dar** (kal′ən dər) *n.* [L. *kalendarium,* account book < *kalendae,* CALENDS] **1.** a system for arranging time into days, weeks, months, and years **2.** a table or chart that shows such an arrangement, usually for a single year **3.** a list or schedule, as of pending court cases —*adj.* that appears on popular calendars [*calendar* art] —*vt.* to enter in a calendar; schedule

**calendar year** the period of time from Jan. 1 through Dec. 31: distinguished from FISCAL YEAR

**cal·en·der** (kal′ən dər) *n.* [< Fr. < ML. < L. *cylindrus,* CYLINDER] a machine with rollers between which paper, cloth, etc. is run, as to give it a smooth or glossy finish —*vt.* to process (paper, etc.) in a calender

**cal·ends** (-əndz) *n.pl.* [*often with sing. v.*] [< L. *kalendae* < *calare,* to proclaim < Gr. *kalein*] the first day of each month in the ancient Roman calendar

**ca·len·du·la** (kə len′jə lə) *n.* [ModL. < L. *kalendae,* calends: prob. because the plants flower in most months] any of a genus of plants of the composite family, with yellow or orange flowers

**ca·les·cent** (kə les′′nt) *adj.* [< L. < *calescere,* to grow warm] getting warm or hot —**ca·les′cence** *n.*

**calf¹** (kaf) *n., pl.* **calves;** esp. for 3, **calfs** [< OE. *cealf* & ON. *kalfr*] **1.** a young cow or bull **2.** the young of some other large animals, as the elephant, whale, hippopotamus, seal, etc. **3.** leather from the hide of a calf; calfskin **4.** [Colloq.] an awkward or silly youth —**kill the fatted calf** to make a feast of welcome: Luke 15:23

**calf²** (kaf) *n., pl.* **calves** [ON. *kalfi*] the fleshy back part of the leg below the knee

**calf′s-foot jelly** (kafs′fŏŏt′) an edible gelatin made by boiling calves' feet

**calf·skin** (kaf′skin′) *n.* **1.** the skin of a calf **2.** a soft, flexible leather made from this

**Cal·ga·ry** (kal′gər ē) city in S Alberta, Canada: pop. 470,000

**Cal·houn** (kal hōōn′), **John Cald·well** (kôld′wel) 1782–1850; U.S. statesman

**Ca·li** (kä′lē) city in SW Colombia: pop. 638,000

**Cal·i·ban** (kal′ə ban′) a deformed, savage creature in Shakespeare's *The Tempest*

**cal·i·ber, cal·i·bre** (kal′ə bər) *n.* [< Fr. & Sp. < *calibo* < Ar. *qālib,* a mold] **1.** the size of a bullet or shell as measured by its diameter **2.** the diameter of the bore of a gun measured in hundredths of an inch or in millimeters **3.** the diameter of the inside of any cylinder **4.** quality or ability

**cal·i·brate** (-brāt′) *vt.* **-brat′ed, -brat′ing 1.** to determine the caliber of **2.** to fix, check, or correct the scale of (a measuring instrument, as a thermometer) —**cal′i·bra′tion** *n.* —**cal′i·bra′tor** *n.*

**cal·i·co** (kal′ə kō′) *n., pl.* **-coes′, -cos′** [< *Calicut* (now Kozhikode), city in India where first obtained] any of several kinds of cotton cloth, usually coarse and printed —*adj.* **1.** of calico **2.** spotted like calico [*a calico* cat]

**ca·lif** (kā′lif, kal′if) *n. same as* CALIPH

**Cal·i·for·ni·a** (kal′ə fôr′nyə, -nē ə) [Sp., name of a fabled island] **1.** State of the SW U.S., on the Pacific coast: 158,693 sq. mi.; pop. 23,669,000; cap. Sacramento: abbrev. **Calif., CA, Cal. 2.** Gulf of, arm of the Pacific, between Baja California & the Mexican mainland —**Cal′i·for′ni·an** *adj., n.*

**cal·i·for·ni·um** (kal′ə fôr′nē əm) *n.* [< University of *California*] a radioactive chemical element produced by intense neutron irradiation of plutonium or curium: symbol, Cf; at. wt., 251 (?); at. no., 98

**Ca·lig·u·la** (kə lig′yŏŏ lə) (born *Gaius Caesar*) 12–41 A.D.; Roman emperor (37–41 A.D.)

**cal·i·per** (kal′ə pər) *n.* [var. of CALIBER] **1.** [*usually pl.*] an instrument consisting of a pair of movable, curved legs fastened together at one end, used to measure the thickness or diameter of something: there are **inside calipers** and **outside calipers 2.** *same as* CALIPER RULE —*vt., vi.* to measure with calipers

**caliper rule** a graduated rule with one sliding jaw and one that is stationary

**ca·liph** (kā′lif, kal′if) *n.* [< OFr. < Ar. *khalīfa*] supreme ruler: the title taken by Mohammed's successors as heads of Islam

**cal·iph·ate** (kal′ə fāt′, -fit) *n.* the rank, reign, or dominion of a caliph: also **cal′if·ate′**

**cal·is·then·ics** (kal′əs then′iks) *n.pl.* [< Gr. *kallos,* beauty + *sthenos,* strength] **1.** exercises to develop a strong, trim body; simple gymnastics **2.** [*with sing. v.*] the art of developing bodily strength and gracefulness by such exercises —**cal′is·then′ic, cal′is·then′i·cal** *adj.*

**calk¹** (kôk) *vt. same as* CAULK —**calk′er** *n.*

**calk²** (kôk) *n.* [OE. *calc,* shoe < L. *calx,* a heel] **1.** the part of a horseshoe that projects downward to prevent slipping **2.** a metal plate with spurs, fastened to the sole of a shoe to prevent slipping —*vt.* to fasten calks on

**call** (kôl) *vt.* [< OE. *ceallian* & (or <) ON. *kalla*] **1.** to say or read in a loud tone; shout; announce **2.** to ask to come; summon **3.** to summon to a specific duty, etc. [the army *called* him] **4.** to convoke [to call a meeting] **5.** to give or apply a name to [call the baby Ann] **6.** to consider or declare to be as specified [I *call* it silly] **7.** to awaken [call me at six] **8.** to communicate with by telephone **9.** to give orders for [to call a strike] **10.** to stop [game *called* because of rain] **11.** to demand payment of (a loan or bond issue) **12.** to utter directions for (a square dance) **13.** in pool, to describe (the shot one plans to make) **14.** *a) Poker* to require (a player) to show his hand by equaling his bet *b)* to force to account for something said or done *c)* to expose (someone's bluff) by such action —*vi.* **1.** to speak in a loud tone; shout **2.** to utter its characteristic cry, as a bird or animal **3.** to visit for a short while **4.** to telephone **5.** *Poker* to require a player to show his hand by equaling his bet —*n.* **1.** an act or instance of calling **2.** a loud utterance; shout **3.** the distinctive cry of an animal or bird, or a device imitating this **4.** a summons to a meeting, etc. **5.** a signal on a bugle, etc. **6.** an economic demand, as for a product **7.** an inner urging toward a certain action or profession, esp. to be a priest, minister, etc. **8.** power to attract [the *call* of the wild] **9.** need; occasion [no *call* for tears] **10.** an order or demand for payment **11.** a brief visit, esp. a formal or professional visit **12.** *Sports* an official's decision —**call back 1.** to ask or command to come back **2.** to telephone again or in return —**call down 1.** to invoke **2.** [Colloq.] to scold sharply —**call for 1.** to demand **2.** to come and get; stop for —**call forth** to bring into play —**call in 1.** to summon for help or consultation **2.** to take out of circulation, as coin —**call off 1.** to order away **2.** to read aloud in order from a list **3.** to cancel (a scheduled event) —**call on 1.** to visit briefly **2.** to ask (a person) to speak —**call out 1.** to shout **2.** to summon into action —**call time** *Sports* to suspend play temporarily —**call up 1.** to make one remember **2.** to summon, esp. for military duty **3.** to telephone —**on call 1.** available when summoned **2.** payable on demand

**cal·la** (kal′ə) *n.* [ModL. (named by Linnaeus) < L., a kind of plant] any of several plants of the arum family, with a large spathe surrounding a yellow spadix: also **calla lily**

**call·board** (kôl′bôrd′) *n. Theater* a bulletin board backstage for posting instructions, etc.

**call·boy** (-boi′) *n.* **1.** a boy who calls actors when it is time for them to go on the stage **2.** *same as* BELLMAN (sense 2)

**call·er** (-ər) *n.* **1.** a person or thing that calls **2.** a person who makes a short visit

**call girl** a prostitute who is called by telephone to assignations

**cal·lig·ra·phy** (kə lig′rə fē) *n.* [< Gr. < *kallos,* beauty + *graphein,* to write] **1.** beautiful handwriting **2.** handwriting —**cal·lig′ra·pher, cal·lig′ra·phist** *n.* —**cal·li·graph·ic** (kal′ə graf′ik) *adj.*

**call·ing** (kôl′iŋ) *n.* **1.** the action of one that calls **2.** one's occupation, profession, or trade

**calling card** a small card with one's name and, sometimes, one's address, used in making visits

**Cal·li·o·pe** (kə lī′ə pē; for *n.,* also kal′ē ōp′) [L. < Gr. *Kalliopē* < *kallos,* beauty + *ops,* voice] *Gr. Myth.* the Muse of eloquence and epic poetry —*n.* [c-] a keyboard instrument like an organ, having a series of steam whistles

**cal·li·per** (kal′ə pər) *n., vt., vi. same as* CALIPER

**cal·lis·then·ics** (kal'əs then'iks) *n.pl. same as* CALISTHENICS —**cal'lis·then'ic** *adj.*

**call loan** a loan that must be repaid on demand

**cal·los·i·ty** (ka läs'ə tē, kə-) *n.* **1.** the quality or state of being callous, hardened, or unfeeling **2.** *pl.* **-ties** a hardened, thickened place on skin or bark; callus

**cal·lous** (kal'əs) *adj.* [< L. < *callum,* hard skin] **1.** *a)* having calluses *b)* thick and hardened **2.** lacking pity, mercy, etc.; unfeeling; insensitive —*vt., vi.* to make or become callous —**cal'lous·ly** *adv.* —**cal'lous·ness** *n.*

**cal·low** (kal'ō) *adj.* [< OE. *calu,* bald] **1.** still lacking the feathers needed for flying **2.** young and inexperienced; immature —**cal'low·ness** *n.*

**cal·lus** (kal'əs) *n., pl.* **-lus·es** [L., var. of *callum,* hard skin] **1.** a hardened, thickened place on the skin **2.** the hard substance that forms at the break in a fractured bone so as to reunite the parts **3.** a mass of undifferentiated cells that develops over cuts or wounds on plants —*vi., vt.* to develop or cause to develop a callus

**calm** (käm; *occas.* kälm) *n.* [< OFr. < It. < LL. *cauma,* heat of the day (hence, in It., time to rest: cf. SIESTA) < Gr. *kauma,* heat] **1.** lack of wind or motion; stillness **2.** lack of excitement; tranquillity; serenity —*adj.* **1.** without wind or motion; still; quiet **2.** not excited; tranquil —*vt., vi.* to make or become calm (often with *down*) —**calm'ly** *adv.* —**calm'ness** *n.*

**cal·o·mel** (kal'ə mel', -məl) *n.* [Fr. < Gr. *kalos,* beautiful + *melas,* black] mercurous chloride, HgCl, a white, tasteless powder, formerly used as a cathartic, for intestinal worms, etc.

**ca·lor·ic** (kə lôr'ik, -lär'-) *n.* [< Fr. < L. *calor,* heat] [Archaic] heat —*adj.* **1.** of heat **2.** of or pertaining to calories —**ca·lor'i·cal·ly** *adv.*

**cal·o·rie** (kal'ə rē) *n.* [Fr. < L. *calor,* heat] **1.** the amount of heat needed to raise the temperature of one gram of water one degree centigrade: also **small calorie 2.** [*occas.* C-] the amount of heat needed to raise the temperature of one kilogram of water one degree centigrade: also **large calorie 3.** a unit equal to the large calorie, used for measuring energy produced by food when oxidized in the body Also sp. **cal'o·ry,** *pl.* **-ries**

**cal·o·rif·ic** (kal'ə rif'ik) *adj.* [< Fr. < L. < *calor,* heat + *facere,* to make] producing heat

**cal·o·rim·e·ter** (kal'ə rim'ə tər) *n.* [< L. *calor,* heat + -METER] an apparatus for measuring amounts of heat, as in chemical combination, friction, etc.

**cal·o·rim·e·try** (kal'ə rim'ə trē) *n.* [< L. *calor,* heat + -METRY] measurement of the quantity of heat —**cal·o·ri·met·ric** (kal'ə ri met'rik, kə lôr'ə-), **cal'o·ri·met'ri·cal** *adj.*

**cal·u·met** (kal'yə met', kal'yə met') *n.* [Fr.; ult. < L. *calamus,* a reed] a long-stemmed ceremonial pipe, smoked by N. American Indians as a token of peace

**ca·lum·ni·ate** (kə lum'nē āt') *vt., vi.* **-at'ed, -at'ing** [< L. pp. of *calumniari,* to slander < *calumnia,* CALUMNY] to spread false and harmful statements about; slander —**ca·lum'ni·a'tion** *n.* —**ca·lum'ni·a'tor** *n.*

CALUMET

**ca·lum·ni·ous** (kə lum'nē əs) *adj.* full of calumnies; slanderous —**ca·lum'ni·ous·ly** *adv.*

**cal·um·ny** (kal'əm nē) *n., pl.* **-nies** [< Fr. < L. *calumnia,* trickery, slander] **1.** a false and malicious statement meant to hurt someone's reputation **2.** the uttering of such a statement; slander

**Cal·va·ry** (kal'vər ē) [< LL. < L. *calvaria,* skull; transl. of Aram. *gulgūlthā,* Golgotha, lit., skull] *Bible* the place near Jerusalem where the crucifixion of Jesus took place: Luke 23:33, Matt. 27:33

**calve** (kav, käv) *vt., vi.* **calved, calv'ing** [< OE. *cealfian*] to give birth to (a calf)

**calves** (kavz, kävz) *n. pl. of* CALF

**Cal·vin** (kal'vin) [< ModL. < Fr., prob. < L. *calvus,* bald] **1.** a masculine name **2. John,** (born *Jean Cau(l)vin* or *Chauvin*) 1509–64; Fr. Protestant reformer

**Cal·vin·ism** (-iz'm) *n.* the theological system of John Calvin and his followers, which emphasizes the doctrines of predestination and salvation solely by God's grace: associated, in practice, with a stern moral code —**Cal'vin·ist** *n., adj.* —**Cal'vin·is'tic, Cal'vin·is'ti·cal** *adj.* —**Cal'vin·is'ti·cal·ly** *adv.*

**calx** (kalks) *n., pl.* **calx'es, cal·ces** (kal'sēz) [L., small stone, lime] the ashy powder left after a metal or mineral has been calcined

**Ca·lyp·so** (kə lip'sō) in Homer's *Odyssey,* a sea nymph who kept Odysseus on her island for seven years

**ca·lyp·so** (kə lip'sō) *adj.* [< ? prec.] designating or of satirical ballads improvised and sung as originally by natives of Trinidad and characterized by wrenched syllabic stress and syncopated rhythms —*n.* a calypso song or calypso music

**ca·lyx** (kā'liks, kal'iks) *n., pl.* **ca'lyx·es, ca·ly·ces** (kā'lə sēz', kal'ə-) [L., outer covering, pod < Gr. *kalyx*] **1.** the outer whorl of protective leaves, or sepals, of a flower, usually green **2.** *Zool.* a cuplike part or cavity

**cal·zo·ne** (kal zō'nē, -zōn') *n.* [It.] a kind of turnover filled variously with cheese, meat, and vegetables

**cam** (kam) *n.* [Du. *cam,* orig., comb] a wheel, projection on a wheel, etc. which gives an eccentric or reciprocating motion to another wheel, a shaft, etc., or receives such motion from it

**ca·ma·ra·de·rie** (käm'ə räd'ər ē, kam'-) *n.* [Fr. < *camarade,* comrade] loyalty and warm, friendly feeling among comrades; comradeship

CAM

**cam·a·ril·la** (kam'ə ril'ə; *Sp.* kä'mä rēl'yä) *n.* [Sp. dim. of *camara,* chamber < L. *camera,* a vault] a group of secret or confidential advisers; cabal

**cam·ass, cam·as** (kam'əs) *n.* [Chinook < *chamas,* sweet] any of a genus of N. American plants of the lily family, with sweet, edible bulbs and racemes of bluish flowers

**cam·ber** (kam'bər) *n.* [OFr., dial. var. of *chambre,* bent < L. *camur,* arched] **1.** a slight convex curve of a surface, as of a road, a beam, etc. **2.** a slight tilt given to each of a pair of automobile wheels by aligning them so that the bottoms are closer together than the tops **3.** *Aeron.* the arching curve of an airfoil from the leading edge to the trailing edge —*vt., vi.* to arch slightly

**cam·bi·um** (kam'bē əm) *n.* [LL., change] a layer of formative cells between the wood and bark in woody plants: the cells increase by division and differentiate to form new wood and bark

**Cam·bo·di·a** (kam bō'dē ə) country in the S Indochinese peninsula: 69,884 sq. mi.; pop. 6,701,000; cap. Phnom Penh: official name *Democratic Kampuchea* —**Cam·bo'di·an** *adj., n.*

**Cam·bri·a** (kam'brē ə) *poet.* name for WALES

**Cam·bri·an** (-ən) *adj.* **1.** of Cambria; Welsh **2.** designating or of the first geological period in the Paleozoic Era —*n.* a native or inhabitant of Cambria; Welshman —**the Cambrian** the Cambrian Period or its rocks: see GEOLOGY, chart

**cam·bric** (kām'brik) *n.* [< *Kambryk,* Fl. name of *Cambrai,* city in N France] **1.** a very fine, thin linen **2.** a cotton cloth like this

**cambric tea** a hot drink of milk, sugar, and water or, often, weak tea

**Cam·bridge** (kām'brij) **1.** city in EC England: pop. 100,000: site of Cambridge University **2.** city in E Mass., near Boston: pop. 95,000

**Cam·den** (kam'dən) [after C. Pratt, Earl of *Camden* (1714–94)] city in SW N.J.: pop. 85,000

**came** (kām) *pt. of* COME

**cam·el** (kam'l) *n.* [< OE. or OFr. < L. *camelus* < Gr. *kamēlos* < Heb. *gāmāl* (or) < Egypt. *kamál*] either of two species of large, domesticated, cud-chewing mammals with a humped back, long neck, and large, cushioned feet: capable of storing water in its body tissue, the camel is the common beast of burden in Asian and African deserts: see BACTRIAN CAMEL and DROMEDARY

**cam·el·eer** (kam'ə lir') *n.* a camel driver

**ca·mel·li·a** (kə mēl'yə, -mē'lē ə) *n.* [after G. J. *Kamel* (1661–1706), Jesuit missionary to the Far East] **1.** any of a genus of Asian evergreen trees and shrubs with glossy evergreen leaves and waxy, roselike flowers **2.** the flower

**ca·mel·o·pard** (kə mel'ə pärd') *n.* [< LL. < L. < Gr. < *kamēlos,* camel + *pardalis,* leopard: from its camellike neck and leopardlike spots] *early name for the* GIRAFFE

**Cam·e·lot** (kam'ə lät') the legendary English town where King Arthur had his court

**camel's hair 1.** the hair of the camel **2.** cloth made of this hair, sometimes mixed with wool, etc. —**cam'el's-hair', cam'el-hair'** *adj.*

**camel's-hair brush** an artist's small brush, made of hair from a squirrel's tail

**Cam·em·bert (cheese)** (kam'əm ber') [from *Camembert,* in Normandy] a soft, creamy, rich cheese

**cam·e·o** (kam'ē ō') *n., pl.* **-os'** [< It. < ML. *camaeus* < ?] **1.** a carving in relief on certain stratified gems or shells so that the raised design, often a head in profile, is usually in a layer of different color from its background: opposed to INTAGLIO **2.** a gem, shell, etc. so carved **3.** *a)* a choice bit role, esp. when played by a notable actor *b)* a fine bit of descriptive writing

**cam·er·a** (kam'ər ə, kam'rə) *n., pl.* **-er·as;** also for 1, **-er·ae'** (-ə rē') [L., a vault < Gr. *kamara,* vaulted chamber] **1.** a chamber; specif., the private office of a judge **2.** a device for taking photographs, consisting of a closed box containing a sensitized plate or film on which an image is formed when light enters the box through a lens **3.** *TV* that part of the transmitter which consists of a lens and a special cathode-ray tube containing a plate on which the image to be televised is projected for transformation into electrical signals —**in camera** in privacy or secrecy

**cam·er·a·man** (-man′, -mən) *n., pl.* **-men′** (-men′, -mən) an operator of a camera, esp. of a motion-picture or television camera

**cam·er·a·shy** (-shī′) *adj.* unwilling to be photographed

**Cam·e·roun** (kam′ə rōōn′) country in WC Africa, on the Atlantic: 183,000 sq. mi.; pop. 5,562,000: also sp. **Cameroon** —**Cam′e·roun′i·an** *adj., n.*

**Ca·mille** (kə mēl′) [Fr. < L. *camilla,* virgin of unblemished character] a feminine name: var. **Ca·mil′la** (-mil′ə)

**cam·i·sole** (kam′ə sōl′) *n.* [Fr. < Sp. dim. of *camisa,* shirt: see CHEMISE] **1.** a woman's sleeveless underwaist, orig. a corset cover, now worn under a sheer blouse **2.** a woman's short negligee

**cam·o·mile** (kam′ə mīl′, -mēl′) *n.* same as CHAMOMILE

**cam·ou·flage** (kam′ə fläzh′, -fläj′) *n.* [Fr. < *camoufler,* to disguise] **1.** the disguising of troops, ships, guns, etc. to conceal them from the enemy, as by the use of paint, nets, leaves, etc. in patterns merging with the background **2.** a disguise or concealment of this kind **3.** any device or action used to conceal or mislead; deception —*vt., vi.* **-flaged′, -flag′ing** to disguise or conceal by camouflage —**cam′ou·flag′er** *n.*

**camp** (kamp) *n.* [< Fr. < It. < L. *campus,* a field] **1.** *a)* a place where tents, huts, barracks, etc. are put up, as for soldiers in training or in bivouac *b)* military life **2.** *a)* a group of people who support or advance a common opinion, cause, etc. *b)* the position taken by such a group **3.** a tent, cabin, etc., or a group of these, used for temporary lodging, as by hunters, fishermen, etc. **4.** a place in the country for vacationers, esp. children, with outdoor recreation, often organized and supervised **5.** the people living in a camp **6.** [Slang] [orig., homosexual jargon] banality, mediocrity, artifice, etc. so extreme as to amuse or have a perversely sophisticated appeal —*adj.* [Slang] characterized by camp (*n.* 6) —*vi.* **1.** to set up a camp **2.** to live or stay in or as if in a camp (often with *out*) —*vt.* to put into a camp —**break camp** to pack up camping equipment and go away —**camp it up** [Slang] to behave in a camp way

**cam·paign** (kam pān′) *n.* [Fr. *campagne,* open country < It. < LL. < L. *campus,* a field] **1.** a series of military operations with a particular objective in a war **2.** a series of organized, planned actions for a particular purpose, as for electing a candidate —*vi.* to participate in, or go on, a campaign —**cam·paign′er** *n.*

**cam·pa·ni·le** (kam′pə nē′lē) *n., pl.* **-les, -li** (-lē) [It. < LL. *campana,* a bell] a bell tower, esp. one that stands apart from another building

**cam·pan·u·la** (kam pan′yoo lə) *n.* [ModL. < LL., dim. of *campana,* a bell] any of a genus of plants with bell-shaped flowers; bellflower

**camp chair** a lightweight folding chair

**camp·craft** (kamp′kraft′) *n.* the art or practice of camping outdoors

**cam·pea·chy wood** (kam pē′chē) [< *Campeche,* state of SE Mexico] same as LOGWOOD (sense 1)

**camp·er** (kamp′ər) *n.* **1.** a person who vacations at a camp **2.** any of various motor vehicles or trailers equipped for camping out

**‡cam·pe·si·no** (käm′pe sē′nô) *n., pl.* **-nos** (-nôs) [Sp.] a peasant or farm worker

**camp·fire** (kamp′fīr′) *n.* **1.** an outdoor fire at a camp **2.** a social gathering around such a fire

**campfire girl** a member of the **Camp Fire Girls,** a girls' organization, founded in 1910, to promote activities that build health and character

**camp·ground** (-ground′) *n.* **1.** a place where a camp is set up **2.** a place where a camp meeting or religious revival is held

**cam·phor** (kam′fər) *n.* [< OFr. < LL. < Ar. < Sans. *karpurah,* camphor tree] a volatile, crystalline substance, $C_{10}H_{16}O$, with a strong characteristic odor, derived chiefly from the wood of an Asian laurel (**camphor tree**): used as a moth repellent, in making cellulose plastics, and in medicine as an irritant, etc. —**cam·phor′ic** (-fôr′ik) *adj.*

**cam·phor·ate** (kam′fə rāt′) *vt.* **-at·ed, -at·ing** to put camphor in or on [*camphorated* oil]

**camphor ball** same as MOTHBALL

**camphor ice** an ointment made of white wax, camphor, spermaceti, and castor oil, used for dry, chapped skin

**cam·pi·on** (kam′pē ən) *n.* [prob. ult. < L. *campus,* field] any of various flowering plants of the pink family, with white or pink flowers

**camp meeting** a religious gathering held outdoors or in a tent, etc., usually lasting several days

**camp·site** (kamp′sīt′) *n.* **1.** any site for a temporary camp **2.** an area in a public or private park set aside for camping, often equipped with water, toilets, picnic stoves, etc.

**camp·stool** (-stōōl′) *n.* a light folding stool

**cam·pus** (kam′pəs) *n., pl.* **-pus·es** [L., a field] the grounds, sometimes including the buildings, of a school or college —*adj.* **1.** on or of the campus **2.** of a school or college [*campus* politics]

**camp·y** (kam′pē) *adj.* **camp′i·er, camp′i·est** [Slang] characterized by camp (*n.* 6)

**cam·shaft** (kam′shaft′) *n.* a shaft to which a cam is fastened

**can¹** (kan; *as an auxiliary, usually* kən, k′n) *vi. pt.* **could** [< OE. < *cunnan,* to know, be able] **1.** to know how to **2.** to be able to **3.** to be likely to [*can* it be true?] **4.** to have the right to **5.** [Colloq.] to be permitted to; may —**can but** can only

**can²** (kan) *n.* [< OE. *canne,* a cup] **1.** a container of various kinds, usually made of metal with a separate cover [a milk *can,* a garbage *can*] **2.** a container made of tinned iron or other metal, in which foods or other perishable products are sealed for preservation **3.** the contents of a can; canful **4.** [Slang] *a)* a prison *b)* the buttocks *c)* a toilet —*vt.* **canned, can′ning 1.** to put up in airtight cans or jars for preservation **2.** [Slang] *a)* to dismiss; discharge *b)* to make a recording of

**Can. 1.** Canada **2.** Canadian **3.** Canon

**Ca·naan** (kā′nən) Promised Land of the Israelites, between the Jordan & the Mediterranean

**Ca·naan·ite** (-īt′) *n.* **1.** one of the original inhabitants of Canaan **2.** their Semitic language —**Ca′naan·it′ish** (-īt′ish), **Ca′naan·it′ic** (-it′ik) *adj.*

**Canad.** Canadian

**Can·a·da** (kan′ə də) country in N North America: a member of the Commonwealth: 3,852,000 sq. mi.; pop. 20,015,000; cap. Ottawa

**Canada balsam** a thick, yellow, resinous fluid from the balsam fir

**Canada goose** a large wild goose of Canada and the northern U.S., gray, with black head and neck

**Ca·na·di·an** (kə nā′dē ən) *adj.* of Canada or its people —*n.* a native or inhabitant of Canada

**Ca·na·di·an·ism** (-iz′m) *n.* **1.** a custom, belief, etc. originating in Canada **2.** a word or phrase originating in or peculiar to Canadian English

**ca·naille** (kə nāl′; *Fr.* kà näl′y) *n.* [Fr. < It. *canaglia* < L. *canis,* a dog] the mob; rabble

**ca·nal** (kə nal′) *n.* [< OFr. < L. *canalis,* a channel < *canna,* a reed] **1.** an artificial waterway for transportation or irrigation **2.** *Anat.* a tubular passage or duct —*vt.* **-nalled′** or **-naled′, -nal′ling** or **-nal′ing** to build a canal through or across

**ca·nal·boat** (-bōt′) *n.* a long, narrow freight-carrying boat, used on canals: also **canal boat**

**can·a·lic·u·lus** (kan′ə lik′yoo ləs) *n., pl.* **-li** (-lī′) [L., dim. of *canalis,* a groove] *Anat., Bot., Zool.* a very small groove, as in bone —**can′a·lic′u·late** (-lit, -lāt′) *adj.*

**ca·nal·i·za·tion** (kə nal′ə zā′shən, kan′′l ə-) *n.* **1.** a canalizing **2.** a system of canals or channels

**ca·nal·ize** (kə nal′īz, kan′ə līz′) *vt.* **-ized, -iz·ing 1.** to make a canal through **2.** to change into or make like a canal **3.** to provide an outlet for, esp. by directing into a specific channel

**Canal Zone** *former name of* the strip of land in Panama that extends 5 miles on either side of the Panama Canal: it was leased to the U.S., which governed it (1904–79)

**ca·na·pé** (kan′ə pē, -pā′) *n.* [Fr.] a small piece of bread or toast or a cracker spread with spiced meat, fish, cheese, etc., served as an appetizer

**ca·nard** (kə närd′) *n.* [Fr., a duck, hoax] a false, malicious report, fabricated as by a newspaper

**ca·nar·y** (kə ner′ē) *n., pl.* **-nar′ies** [< CANARY ISLANDS] **1.** a small, yellow songbird of the finch family **2.** a light yellow: also **canary yellow 3.** a sweet wine like madeira, of the Canary Islands

**Canary Islands** group of Sp. islands in the Atlantic, off the NW coast of Africa

**ca·nas·ta** (kə nas′tə) *n.* [Sp., basket] a double-deck card game for two to six players

**Ca·na·ver·al** (kə nav′ər əl), **Cape** [Sp. *cañaveral,* canebrake] cape on the E coast of Fla.: U.S. proving ground for missiles and spacecraft

**Can·ber·ra** (kan′bər ə) capital of Australia, in the SE part: pop. 92,000

**canc. 1.** cancel **2.** canceled **3.** cancellation

**can·can** (kan′kan′) *n.* [Fr.] a lively dance with much high kicking performed by women entertainers, orig. in Paris dance halls in the late 19th cent.

**can·cel** (kan's'l) *vt.* **-celed** or **-celled**, **-cel·ing** or **-cel·ling** [< Anglo-Fr. < L. *cancellare*, to draw latticelike lines across < *cancer*, lattice] **1.** to cross out with lines or mark over, as in deleting written matter or marking a postage stamp, check, etc. as used **2.** to make invalid; annul **3.** to do away with; abolish, withdraw, etc. [to *cancel* an order] **4.** to neutralize or balance; offset (often with *out*) **5.** *Math.* to remove (a common factor from both terms of a fraction, equivalents on opposite sides of an equation, etc.) —*vi.* to offset or cancel each other (with *out*) —*n.* a cancellation —**can'cel·er, can'cel·ler** *n.*

**can·cel·la·tion** (kan'sə lā'shən) *n.* **1.** the act of canceling **2.** something canceled **3.** the mark showing that something is canceled

**can·cer** (kan'sər) [< L., a crab; later, malignant tumor] **1.** [C-] a N constellation **2.** [C-] the fourth sign of the zodiac: see ZODIAC, illus. —*n.* **1.** a malignant new growth, or tumor, anywhere in the body: cancers tend to spread: see also CARCINOMA, SARCOMA **2.** anything bad or harmful that spreads and destroys —**can'cer·ous** *adj.*

**can·de·la** (kan dē'lə) *n.* [L., candle] *same as* CANDLE (*n.* 3)

**can·de·la·brum** (kan'də lä'brəm, -lab'rəm, -lā'brəm) *n., pl.* **-bra** (-brə), **-brums** [L.: see CHANDELIER] a large branched candlestick: also **can'de·la'bra,** *pl.* **-bras**

**can·des·cent** (kan des''nt) *adj.* [< L. prp. of *candescere* < *candere,* to shine] glowing; incandescent —**can·des'·cence** *n.*

**can·did** (kan'did) *adj.* [L. *candidus,* white, sincere < *candere:* see prec.] **1.** free from bias; fair; impartial **2.** very honest or frank in speech or writing **3.** unposed and informal [a *candid* photograph] —**can'did·ly** *adv.* —**can'did·ness** *n.*

**can·di·da·cy** (kan'də də sē) *n., pl.* **-cies** the fact or state of being a candidate: also [Brit.] **can'di·da·ture** (-di chər, -dā'chər)

**can·di·date** (kan'də dāt', -dit) *n.* [L. *candidatus,* white-robed < *candidus* (see CANDID): office seekers in Rome wore white gowns] **1.** a person who seeks, or has been proposed for, an office, an award, etc. **2.** a person or thing apparently destined for a certain end [a *candidate* for fame]

**candid camera** a camera, usually small, with a fast lens, used to take informal, unposed pictures

**can·died** (kan'dēd) *adj.* **1.** cooked in or with sugar or syrup, esp. to preserve, glaze, or encrust **2.** crystallized into sugar **3.** sugary in expression

**can·dle** (kan'd'l) *n.* [< OE. < L. *candela,* a torch < *candere,* to shine] **1.** a cylinder of tallow or wax with a wick through its center, which gives light when burned **2.** anything like this in form or use **3.** a unit of luminous intensity equal to 1/60 of the luminous intensity of one square centimeter of a blackbody at the temperature of solidification of platinum —*vt.* **-dled, -dling** to examine (eggs) for freshness, fertilization, etc. by holding in front of a light —**burn the candle at both ends** to work or, esp., play too much so that one's energy is dissipated —**not hold a candle to** to be not nearly so good as —**not worth the candle** not worth doing —**can'dler** *n.*

**can·dle·ber·ry** (-ber'ē) *n., pl.* **-ries** *same as:* **1.** BAYBERRY (sense 1) **2.** CANDLENUT

**can·dle·light** (-līt') *n.* **1.** subdued light given by or as by candles **2.** twilight; evening

**Can·dle·mas** (kan'd'l məs) *n.* [< OE.: see CANDLE & MASS] a church feast, Feb. 2, commemorating the purification of the Virgin Mary: candles for sacred uses are blessed then: also **Candlemas Day**

**can·dle·nut** (kan'd'l nut') *n.* **1.** a tree growing in the Pacific Islands, whose fruit the natives burn as candles **2.** its fruit

**can·dle·pow·er** (-pou'ər) *n.* the luminous intensity of a light source expressed in candles

**can·dle·stick** (-stik') *n.* a cupped or spiked holder for a candle or candles

**can·dor** (kan'dər) *n.* [L., whiteness, openness < *candere:* see CANDESCENT] **1.** the quality of being fair and unprejudiced **2.** sharp honesty in expressing oneself Also, Brit. sp., **can'dour**

**can·dy** (kan'dē) *n., pl.* **-dies** [< *sugar candy* < OFr. < It. < Ar. < Per. *qand,* cane sugar] **1.** crystallized sugar made by evaporating boiled cane sugar, syrup, etc. **2.** *a)* a sweet food, usually made from sugar or syrup, in small pieces, with flavoring, fruit, chocolate, nuts, etc. added *b)* a piece of such food —*vt.* **-died, -dy·ing 1.** to cook in or with sugar or syrup, esp. to preserve, glaze, or encrust **2.** to crystallize into sugar **3.** to sweeten; make pleasant —*vi.* to become candied (in senses 1 & 2)

**can·dy-striped** (-strīpt') *adj.* having diagonal, colored stripes like those on a stick of candy

**cane** (kān) *n.* [< OFr. < It. < L. *canna* < Gr. *kanna*] **1.** the slender, jointed, usually flexible stem of any of certain plants, as bamboo, rattan, etc. **2.** any plant with such a stem, as sugar cane, sorghum, etc. **3.** the woody stem of a fruiting plant, as the blackberry **4.** a stick used for flogging **5.** *same as* WALKING STICK (sense 1) **6.** split rattan, used in weaving chair seats, etc. —*vt.* **caned, can'ing 1.** to flog with a cane **2.** to make or furnish (chairs, etc.) with cane —**can'er** *n.*

**cane·brake** (kān'brāk') *n.* [CANE + BRAKE³] a dense growth of cane plants

**cane sugar** sugar (*sucrose*) from sugar cane

**ca·nine** (kā'nīn) *adj.* [L. *caninus* < *canis,* a dog] **1.** of or like a dog **2.** of the family of animals that includes dogs, wolves, jackals, and foxes —*n.* **1.** a dog or other canine animal **2.** a sharp-pointed tooth on either side of the upper jaw and lower jaw, between the incisors and the bicuspids: in full, **canine tooth**

**Ca·nis Ma·jor** (kān'is mā'jər) [L., the Greater Dog] a S constellation southeast of Orion, containing the Dog Star, Sirius

**Canis Mi·nor** (mī'nər) [L., the Lesser Dog] a N constellation east of Orion, containing the bright star Procyon

**can·is·ter** (kan'is tər) *n.* [< L. *canistrum,* wicker basket < Gr. *kanistron* < *kanna,* a reed] **1.** a small box or can for coffee, tea, etc. **2.** a boxlike vacuum cleaner **3.** the part of a gas mask with chemicals for filtering the air

**can·ker** (kaŋ'kər) *n.* [< OFr. < L. *cancer:* see CANCER] **1.** an ulcerlike sore, esp. in the mouth, that spreads **2.** a disease of plants that causes decay **3.** anything that corrupts —*vt.* **1.** to attack or infect with canker **2.** to infect or debase with corruption —*vi.* to become cankered —**can'ker·ous** *adj.*

**can·ker·worm** (-wurm') *n.* any of several moth larvae harmful to fruit and shade trees

**can·na** (kan'ə) *n.* [L., a reed] any of a genus of broad-leaved tropical plants, often grown for its striking foliage and brilliant flowers

**can·na·bis** (kan'ə bis) *n.* [L., hemp < Gr. *kannabis*] **1.** *same as* HEMP **2.** the female flowering tops of the hemp

**canned** (kand) *adj.* **1.** preserved in cans or jars **2.** [Slang] *a)* recorded for reproduction, as on radio [*canned* commercials] *b)* prepared for publication in a newspaper chain [a *canned* editorial]

**can·nel (coal)** (kan''l) [< ? *candle coal*] a variety of bituminous coal that burns with a bright flame and has a high volatile content

**can·nel·lo·ni** (kan'ə lō'nē; *It.* kän'nel lô'nē) *n.* [It., pl. of *cannellone,* hollow noodle] tubular casings of dough filled with ground meat, baked, and served in a tomato sauce

**can·ner·y** (kan'ər ē) *n., pl.* **-ner·ies** a factory where foods are canned

**Cannes** (kan, kanz; *Fr.* kàn) city in SE France, on the Riviera: pop. 67,000

**can·ni·bal** (kan'ə b'l) *n.* [Sp. *canibal,* a savage (term used by Columbus) < *Caniba,* a cannibal people, prob. < Carib *galibi,* lit., strong men] **1.** a person who eats human flesh **2.** an animal that eats its own kind —*adj.* of, resembling, or having the habits of, cannibals —**can'ni·bal·ism** *n.* —**can'·ni·bal·is'tic** *adj.*

**can·ni·bal·ize** (-īz') *vt., vi.* **-ized', -iz'ing 1.** to strip (old or worn equipment) of parts for use in other units **2.** to take personnel or components from (one organization) for use in building up another **3.** to devour (another of the same kind): used figuratively —**can'ni·bal·i·za'tion** *n.*

**can·ni·kin** (kan'ə k'n) *n.* [< CAN² + -KIN] **1.** a small can; cup **2.** [Dial.] a wooden bucket

**can·ning** (kan'iŋ) *n.* the act, process, or work of putting food in cans or jars for preservation

**can·non** (kan'ən) *n., pl.* **-nons, -non:** see PLURAL, II, D, 4 [< OFr. < It. < L. *canna:* see CANE] **1.** *a)* a large, mounted piece of artillery; sometimes, specif., a large gun with a relatively short barrel, as a howitzer *b)* an automatic gun, now usually of 20-mm. caliber, mounted on an aircraft **2.** *same as* CANNON BONE —*vt., vi.* to cannonade

**can·non·ade** (kan'ə nād') *n.* a continuous firing of artillery —*vi., vt.* **-ad'ed, -ad'ing** to fire artillery (at)

**can·non·ball** (kan'ən bôl') *n.* **1.** a heavy ball, esp. of iron, formerly used as a projectile in cannon: also **cannon ball 2.** [Colloq.] a fast express train —*adj.* [Slang] fast; rapid —*vi.* [Slang] to move very rapidly

**cannon bone** the bone between hock or knee and fetlock in a four-legged, hoofed animal

**can·non·eer** (kan'ə nir') *n.* an artilleryman

**cannon fodder** soldiers, sailors, etc. thought of as being expended (i.e., killed or maimed) or expendable in war

**can·non·ry** (kan'ən rē) *n., pl.* **-ries 1.** cannons collectively; artillery **2.** cannon fire

**can·not** (kan'ät, -ət; kə nät') can not —**cannot but** have no choice but to

**can·ny** (kan'ē) *adj.* **-ni·er, -ni·est** [< CAN¹] **1.** careful and shrewd in one's actions and dealings; clever and cautious **2.** wise and well-informed **3.** careful with money; thrifty —**can'ni·ly** (-'l ē) *adv.* —**can'ni·ness** (-ē nis) *n.*

**ca·noe** (kə nōō′) *n.* [< Sp. *canoa* < the Carib name] a narrow, light boat with its sides meeting in a sharp edge at each end: it is moved by paddles —*vi.* **-noed′, -noe′ing** to paddle, or go in, a canoe —*vt.* to transport by canoe —**ca·noe′ist** *n.*

**can·on¹** (kan′ən) *n.* [< OE. & OFr. < L., a rule < Gr. *kanōn*, rod, bar < *kanna:* see CANE] **1.** a law or body of laws of a church **2.** *a)* an established or basic rule, principle, or criterion [the *canons* of good taste] *b)* a body of rules, principles, criteria, etc. **3.** *a)* a list of books of the Bible officially accepted as genuine *b)* a list of the genuine works of an author [the Shakespearean *canon*] **4.** *a)* [often C-] *Eccles.* the fundamental part of the Mass, between the Preface and the Communion *b)* a list of recognized saints as in the Roman Catholic Church **5.** *Music* a polyphonic composition in which a melody is repeated at delayed intervals in the same or a related key

**can·on²** (kan′ən) *n.* [< OE. & OFr. < LL. *canonicus*, one living by the canon: see prec.] **1.** a member of a clerical group living according to a canon, or rule **2.** a clergyman serving in a cathedral or collegiate church

**ca·ñon** (kan′yən; *Sp.* kä nyôn′) *n. same as* CANYON

**ca·non·ic** (kə nän′ik) *adj.* **1.** *same as* CANONICAL **2.** of a musical canon

**ca·non·i·cal** (kə nän′i k′l) *adj.* **1.** of, according to, or ordered by church canon **2.** authoritative; accepted **3.** belonging to the canon of the Bible **4.** of a canon (clergyman) —**ca·non′i·cal·ly** *adv.*

**canonical hour** any of the seven periods of the day assigned to prayer and worship

**ca·non·i·cals** (-k′lz) *n.pl.* the clothes prescribed by canon for a clergyman when conducting services

**can·on·ic·i·ty** (kan′ə nis′ə tē) *n.* the fact or condition of being canonical

**can·on·ist** (kan′ən ist) *n.* an expert in canon law —**can′on·is′tic** *adj.*

**can·on·ize** (kan′ə nīz′) *vt.* **-ized′, -iz′ing** [< LL. *canonizare:* see CANON¹ + -IZE] **1.** to declare (a dead person) a saint in formal church procedure **2.** to glorify **3.** to put in the Biblical canon **4.** to give church sanction to —**can′on·i·za′tion** *n.*

**canon law** the laws governing the ecclesiastical affairs of a Christian church

**can·on·ry** (kan′ən rē) *n., pl.* **-ries 1.** the benefice or office of a canon **2.** canons collectively

**can·o·py** (kan′ə pē) *n., pl.* **-pies** [< ML. < L. < Gr. *kōnōpeion*, bed with mosquito nets, dim. of *kōnōps*, gnat] **1.** a covering of cloth, etc. fastened above a bed, throne, etc. or held on poles over a person or sacred thing **2.** a canvas structure forming a sheltered walk to a building entrance **3.** anything that covers or seems to cover like a canopy, as the sky **4.** the transparent hood over an airplane cockpit **5.** a rooflike projection over a door, pulpit, etc. —*vt.* **-pied, -py·ing** to place or form a canopy over; cover; shelter

**canst** (kanst; *unstressed* kənst) *archaic 2d pers. sing., pres. indic., of* CAN¹: *used with* thou

**cant¹** (kant) *n.* [< L. *cantus:* see CHANT] **1.** whining, singsong speech, esp. as used by beggars **2.** the secret slang of beggars, thieves, etc.; argot **3.** the special words and phrases used by those in a certain sect, occupation, etc.; jargon **4.** insincere, trite talk, esp. when pious or moral —*vi.* to use cant; speak in cant —*adj.* of, or having the nature of, cant —**cant′er** *n.*

**cant²** (kant) *n.* [< OFr. < LL. < L. *cant(h)us*, tire of a wheel < Celt.] **1.** a corner or outside angle **2.** a slanting surface; beveled edge **3.** a sudden movement that causes tilting, turning, or overturning **4.** the tilt, turn, or slant thus caused —*vt.* **1.** to give a sloping edge to; bevel **2.** to tilt or overturn **3.** to pitch; toss —*vi.* **1.** to tilt or turn over **2.** to slant —*adj.* **1.** with canted sides or corners **2.** slanting

**can't** (kant) cannot

**can·ta·bi·le** (kän tä′bi lā′) *adj., adv.* [< It. < L. < *cantare:* see CHANT] *Music* in any easy, flowing manner; songlike —*n.* music in this style

**Can·ta·brig·i·an** (kan′tə brij′ē ən, -brij′ən) *adj.* [< ML. *Cantabrigia*, Cambridge] of Cambridge, England, or Cambridge University —*n.* **1.** a student or graduate of Cambridge University **2.** any inhabitant of Cambridge, England

**can·ta·loupe, can·ta·loup** (kan′tə lōp′) *n.* [< Fr. < It. < *Cantalupo*, near Rome, where first grown in Europe] **1.** a muskmelon with a hard, rough rind and sweet, juicy flesh **2.** any muskmelon

**can·tan·ker·ous** (kan taŋ′kər əs) *adj.* [prob. < ME. *contakour*, a troublemaker (< *contek*, strife, quarrel) + -OUS] bad-tempered; quarrelsome —**can·tan′ker·ous·ly** *adv.* —**can·tan′ker·ous·ness** *n.*

**can·ta·ta** (kən tät′ə) *n.* [< It. pp. of *cantare:* see CHANT] a musical composition with vocal solos, choruses, etc., telling a story that is sung but not acted

**can·teen** (kan tēn′) *n.* [< Fr. < It. *cantina*, wine cellar] **1.** *same as* POST EXCHANGE **2.** *a)* a place where refreshments can be obtained, as by employees or visitors *b)* such a place serving as a social center [a youth *canteen*] **3.** a place where cooked food is dispensed to people in distress, as in a disaster area **4.** a small flask for carrying drinking water

**can·ter** (kan′tər) *n.* [contr. < *Canterbury gallop*, the riding pace of the medieval Canterbury pilgrims] a smooth, easy pace like a moderate gallop —*vi., vt.* to ride or move at a canter

**Can·ter·bur·y** (kan′tər ber′ē, -bər ē) city in SE England: site of a famous cathedral: pop. 33,000

**Canterbury bells** a cultivated bellflower with white, pink, or blue, cuplike flowers

**cant hook** [see CANT²] a pole with a movable hooked arm at or near one end, for catching hold of logs and rolling them

**can·thus** (kan′thəs) *n., pl.* **-thi** (-thī) [ModL. < Gr. *kanthos*] either corner of the eye, where the eyelids meet

**can·ti·cle** (kan′ti k′l) *n.* [< L. dim. of *canticum*, song < *cantus*] **1.** a song or chant **2.** a liturgical hymn with words from the Bible

**Can·ti·cles** (-k′lz) *same as* SONG OF SOLOMON: also (in the Douay Bible) **Canticle of Canticles**

**can·ti·le·na** (kan′tə lē′nə) *n.* [It. < L., a song < *cantare*, to sing] a smooth, flowing, lyrical passage of vocal, or sometimes instrumental, music

**can·ti·le·ver** (kan′t′l ē′vər, -ev′ər) *n.* [as if < CANT² + LEVER] **1.** a large bracket or block projecting from a wall to support a balcony, cornice, etc. **2.** a projecting beam or structure supported only at one end, which is anchored as to a pier or wall —*vt.* to support by means of cantilevers —**can′ti·le′vered** *adj.*

**cantilever bridge** a bridge whose span is formed by two cantilevers projecting toward each other

CANTILEVER

**can·til·la·tion** (kan′t′l ā′shən) *n.* [< L. *cantillare*, to hum < *cantare:* see CHANT] in Jewish liturgy, a chanting with certain prescribed musical phrases indicated by notations —**can′til·late′** (-āt′) *vt., vi.* **-lat′ed, -lat′ing**

**can·ti·na** (kan tē′nə) *n.* [Sp.] [Southwest] a saloon or barroom

**can·tle** (kan′t′l) *n.* [< OFr. < ML. dim. of L. *cantus:* see CANT²] the upward-curving rear part of a saddle

**can·to** (kan′tō) *n., pl.* **-tos** [It. < L. *cantus:* see CHANT] any of the chapterlike divisions of certain long poems

**Can·ton** (kan tän′; *for 2* kan′tən) **1.** *former name of* KWANGCHOW **2.** [ult. after prec. sense] city in EC Ohio: pop. 95,000

**can·ton** (kan′tən, -tän, kan tän′; *for vt. 2* kan tän′, -tōn′) *n.* [Fr. < It. < LL. *cantus*, corner: see CANT²] any of the political divisions of a country or territory; specif., any of the states in the Swiss Republic —*vt.* **1.** to divide into cantons **2.** to assign quarters to (troops, etc.) —**can′ton·al** *adj.* —**can·ton′ment** *n.*

**Can·ton·ese** (kan′tə nēz′) *adj.* of Canton, China, or its people —*n.* **1.** *pl.* **-ese** a native or inhabitant of Canton **2.** the Chinese dialect spoken in and around Canton

**can·tor** (kan′tər) *n.* [L., singer < *canere:* see CHANT] **1.** a church choir leader **2.** a singer of liturgical solos in a synagogue, who leads the congregation in prayer —**can·to′ri·al** (-tôr′ē əl) *adj.*

**Ca·nuck** (kə nuk′) *n., adj.* [< ?] [Colloq.] (a) Canadian; sometimes specif., (a) French Canadian

**Ca·nute** (kə nōōt′, -nyōōt′) 994?–1035; Dan. king of England (1017–35) & of Denmark (1018–35) & of Norway (1028–35): also called **Canute the Great**

**can·vas** (kan′vəs) *n.* [< OFr. < It. < L. *cannabis*, hemp] **1.** a closely woven, coarse cloth of hemp, cotton, or linen, used for tents, sails, etc. **2.** a sail or set of sails **3.** *a)* a specially prepared piece of canvas on which an oil painting is made *b)* such a painting **4.** a tent or tents, esp. circus tents **5.** any loosely woven, coarse cloth for embroidery, etc. —**the canvas** the canvas-covered floor of a boxing or wrestling ring —**under canvas 1.** in tents **2.** with sails unfurled **3.** by means of sails

**can·vas·back** (-bak′) *n., pl.* **-backs′, -back′** : see PLURAL, II, D,1 a large, N. American wild duck with a brownish-red head and dark back

**can·vass** (kan′vəs) *vt.* [< *canvas:* ? because used for sifting] **1.** to examine or discuss in detail **2.** to go through (places) or among (people) asking for (votes, opinions, orders, etc.) —*vi.* to try to get votes, orders, etc. —*n.* the act of canvassing, esp. in an attempt to estimate the outcome of an election, sales campaign, etc. —**can′vass·er** *n.*

**can·yon** (kan′yən) *n.* [Sp. *cañon*, a canyon, tube < L. *canna*, a reed: see CANE] a long, narrow valley between high cliffs, often containing a stream

**caou·tchouc** (kou chŏŏk′, kŏŏ′chŏŏk) *n.* [Fr. < obs. Sp. *cauchuc* < Quechua] crude, natural rubber

**cap** (kap) *n.* [OE. *cæppe* < LL. *cappa*, a cloak] 1. any close-fitting head covering, brimless or visored 2. *a)* a head covering worn as a mark of occupation, rank, etc. /a cardinal's *cap/ b)* a mortarboard (sense 2) 3. a caplike part or thing; cover or top 4. *same as* PERCUSSION CAP —*vt.* **capped, cap′-ping** 1. to put a cap on 2. to present ceremoniously with a cap, as at a graduation /to *cap* a nurse/ 3. to cover the top or end of /snow *capped* the hills/ 4. to match, surpass, or top 5. to bring to a high point; climax —**cap the climax** to be or do more than could be expected or believed

**CAP, C.A.P.** Civil Air Patrol

**cap.** 1. capacity 2. *pl.* **caps.** capital 3. capitalize

**ca·pa·bil·i·ty** (kā′pə bil′ə tē) *n., pl.* **-ties** 1. the quality of being capable; practical ability 2. a capacity for being used or developed 3. [*pl.*] abilities, features, etc. not yet developed

**ca·pa·ble** (kā′pə b'l) *adj.* [Fr. < LL. *capabilis* < L. *capere*, to take] having ability; able; skilled; competent —**capable of** 1. admitting of; open to 2. having the ability or qualities necessary for 3. able or ready to /*capable of* telling a lie/ —**ca′pa·ble·ness** *n.* —**ca′pa·bly** *adv.*

**ca·pa·cious** (kə pā′shəs) *adj.* [< L. *capax* (gen. *capacis*) < *capere*, to take + -OUS] able to contain or hold much; spacious —**ca·pa′cious·ly** *adv.* —**ca·pa′cious·ness** *n.*

**ca·pac·i·tance** (kə pas′ə təns) *n.* [CAPACIT(Y) + -ANCE] *Elec.* the quantity of electric charge that can be stored in a capacitor, expressed, in farads, as the ratio of the charge to the potential difference between the plates —**ca·pac′i·tive** *adj.*

**ca·pac·i·tor** (-tər) *n. Elec.* a device consisting of two or more conducting plates separated by insulating material and used for storing an electric charge; condenser

**ca·pac·i·ty** (kə pas′ə tē) *n., pl.* **-ties** [< OFr. < L. < *capax:* see CAPACIOUS] 1. the ability to contain, absorb, or receive 2. the amount of space that can be filled; content or volume 3. mental ability 4. aptitude; capability; potentiality 5. maximum output or producing ability /operating at *capacity/* 6. position, function, status, etc. /acting in the *capacity* of adviser/ 7. *Elec. same as* CAPACITANCE 8. *Law* legal authority or competency

**cap and bells** a fool's cap with little bells on it

**cap-a-pie, cap-à-pie** (kap′ə pē′) *adv.* [< OFr. < L. *caput*, head + *pes*, foot] from head to foot

**ca·par·i·son** (kə par′ə s'n) *n.* [< Fr. < Pr. *caparasso*, large cloak < ff.] 1. an ornamented covering for a horse; trappings 2. clothing, equipment, and ornaments; outfit —*vt.* to adorn, as with trappings or rich clothing

**cape¹** (kāp) *n.* [Fr. < Pr. *capa* < LL. *cappa*, mantle, cloak] a sleeveless garment fastened at the neck and hanging over the back and shoulders

**cape²** (kāp) *n.* [OFr. < ML. *caput*, headland < L., head] a piece of land projecting into a body of water —**the Cape** *same as* 1. Cape of GOOD HOPE 2. Cape COD

**Ca·pek** (chä′pek), **Ka·rel** (kär′əl) 1890–1938; Czech playwright & novelist

**ca·per¹** (kā′pər) *vi.* [prob. < CAPRIOLE] to skip about in a playful manner —*n.* 1. a gay, playful jump or leap 2. a wild, foolish prank 3. [Slang] a criminal act, esp. a robbery —**cut a caper** (or **capers**) 1. to caper 2. to play tricks

**ca·per²** (kā′pər) *n.* [< L. < Gr. *kapparis*] 1. a prickly, trailing Mediterranean bush whose green flower buds are pickled and used to flavor sauces, etc. 2. any of these buds

**Ca·pe·tian** (kə pē′shən) *adj.* the French dynasty (987–1328 A.D.) founded by Hugh **Ca·pet** (kā′pit, kap′it) —*n.* a member of this dynasty

**Cape Town** seat of the legislature of South Africa, a seaport on the SW coast: pop. 807,000: also, esp. formerly, **Cape′-town′**

**Cape Verde** country on a group of islands in the Atlantic, west of Cape Verde, Senegal: 1,557 sq. mi.; pop. 294,000

**cap·ful** (kap′fool′) *n., pl.* **-fuls** as much as the cap of the bottle can hold

**ca·pi·as** (kā′pē əs, kap′ē-) *n.* [< ML. < L., 2d pers. sing., pres. subj., of *capere*, to take] *Law* a writ issued by a court directing an officer to arrest the person named

**cap·il·lar·i·ty** (kap′ə ler′ə tē) *n.* 1. capillary state 2. the property of exerting or having capillary attraction 3. *same as* CAPILLARY ATTRACTION

**cap·il·lar·y** (kap′ə ler′ē) *adj.* [< L. < *capillus*, hair] 1. of or like a hair; very slender 2. having a very small bore 3. in or of capillaries —*n., pl.* **-lar′ies** 1. a tube with a very small bore: also **capillary tube** 2. any of the tiny blood vessels connecting the arteries with the veins

**capillary attraction** a force that is the resultant of adhesion, cohesion, and surface tension in liquids which are in contact with solids, as in a capillary tube, causing the liquid surface to rise or be depressed in the tube: also **capillary action**

**cap·i·tal¹** (kap′ə t'l) *adj.* [< OFr. < L. < *caput*, head] 1. involving or punishable by death /a *capital* offense/ 2. most important or most serious; principal; chief /a *capital* virtue/ 3. being the seat of government /a *capital* city/ 4. of or having to do with capital, or wealth 5. first-rate; excellent /a *capital* idea/ See also CAPITAL LETTER —*n.* 1. *same as* CAPITAL LETTER 2. a city or town that is the official seat of government of a state, nation, etc. 3. a city where a certain industry, etc. is centered /the rubber *capital/* 4. money or property owned or used in business by a person, corporation, etc. 5. an accumulation of such wealth, or its value 6. wealth used to produce more wealth 7. any source of benefit 8. [*often* C-] capitalists collectively: distinguished from LABOR —**make capital of** to make the most of; exploit

**cap·i·tal²** (kap′ə t'l) *n.* [< OFr. < L. dim. of *caput*, head] the top part of a column or pilaster

**cap·i·tal·ism** (-iz'm) *n.* 1. the economic system in which the means of production and distribution are privately owned and operated for profit, originally under fully competitive conditions 2. the principles, power, etc. of capitalists

**cap·i·tal·ist** (-ist) *n.* 1. a person who has capital; owner of wealth used in business 2. an upholder of capitalism —*adj.* capitalistic

**cap·i·tal·is·tic** (kap′ə t'l is′tik) *adj.* 1. of or characteristic of capitalists or capitalism 2. upholding, preferring, or practicing capitalism —**cap′i·tal·is′ti·cal·ly** *adv.*

**cap·i·tal·i·za·tion** (-ə zā′shən) *n.* 1. the act or process of converting something into capital 2. the total capital funds of a corporation, represented by stocks, bonds, undivided profit, etc. 3. the total value of the stocks and bonds outstanding of a corporation 4. the act or system of using capital letters in writing and printing

**cap·i·tal·ize** (kap′ə t'l īz′) *vt.* **-ized′, -iz′ing** 1. to use as capital; convert into capital 2. to establish the capital stock of (a business firm) at a certain figure 3. to supply capital to or for (an enterprise) 4. to print or write (a word or words) in capital letters 5. to begin (a word) with a capital letter —**capitalize on (something)** to use (something) to one's own advantage

**capital letter** a large letter of a kind used to begin a sentence or proper name, as A, B, C

**cap·i·tal·ly** (kap′ə t'l ē) *adv.* excellently; very well

**capital punishment** penalty of death for a crime

**capital ship** formerly, an armored war vessel carrying guns exceeding a caliber of a specified size

**capital stock** 1. the capital of a corporation, divided into negotiable shares 2. the total par or stated value of the issued shares of stock

**cap·i·ta·tion** (kap′ə tā′shən) *n.* [< LL. < L. *caput*, the head] a tax or fee of so much per head

**Cap·i·tol** (kap′ə t'l) [< OFr. < L. *Capitolium*, the temple of Jupiter] 1. the temple of Jupiter in Rome 2. the building in which the U.S. Congress meets, at Washington, D.C. — *n.* [*usually* c-] the building in which a State legislature meets

**Cap·i·to·line** (kap′ə t'l īn′) one of the SEVEN HILLS OF ROME —*adj.* 1. of this hill 2. of the temple of Jupiter which stood there

**ca·pit·u·late** (kə pich′ə lāt′) *vi.* **-lat′ed, -lat′ing** [< LL. pp. of *capitulare*, to draw up in chapters] 1. to give up (*to* an enemy) on prearranged conditions 2. to give up

**ca·pit·u·la·tion** (kə pich′ə lā′shən) *n.* 1. a statement of the main parts of a subject 2. a conditional surrender 3. a document containing terms of surrender, etc.; treaty

**ca·pon** (kā′pän, -pən) *n.* [< OE. & OFr. < L. *capo*] a castrated rooster fattened for eating —**ca′pon·ize′** (-pə nīz′) *vt.* **-ized′, -iz′ing**

**ca·pote** (kə pōt′) *n.* [Fr., dim. of *cape*, CAPE¹] a long cloak, usually with a hood

**Ca·pri** (kä prē′, kä′prē) island near the entrance to the Bay of Naples: 5 sq. mi.

**ca·pric·ci·o** (kä prē′chē ō; *It.* kä prēt′chō) *n., pl.* **-ci·os**; *It.* **-pric′ci** (-chē) [It.: see ff.] 1. a whim; caprice 2. a lively musical composition of irregular form

**ca·price** (kə prēs′) *n.* [Fr. < It. *capriccio* < *capo*, head + *riccio*, curl, lit., hedgehog] 1. a sudden, impulsive change

CAPITAL

in thought or action; freakish notion; whim **2.** a capricious quality or nature **3.** *Music* *same as* CAPRICCIO

**ca·pri·cious** (kə prish′əs) *adj.* subject to caprices; erratic; flighty —**ca·pri′cious·ly** *adv.* —**ca·pri′cious·ness** *n.*

**Cap·ri·corn** (kap′rə kôrn′) [< OFr. < L. < *caper*, goat + *cornu*, a horn] **1.** a S constellation **2.** the tenth sign of the zodiac: see ZODIAC, illus.

**cap·ri·fi·ca·tion** (kap′rə fi kā′shən) *n.* [< L. < *caprificare*, to ripen figs by caprification] the pollination of certain cultivated figs by a species of small wasps

**cap·ri·ole** (kap′rē ōl′) *n.* [Fr. < It., ult. < L. *caper*, goat] **1.** a caper; leap **2.** an upward leap made by a horse without going forward —*vi.* -**oled′**, -**ol′ing** to make a capriole

**caps.** capitals (capital letters)

**cap·si·cum** (kap′sə kəm) *n.* [ModL. < L. *capsa*, a box] **1.** any of various red peppers whose pungent, fleshy pods are the chili peppers, cayenne peppers, etc. of commerce **2.** these pods prepared as condiments, or, in medicine, as a gastric stimulant

**cap·size** (kap′sīz, kap sīz′) *vt.*, *vi.* -**sized**, -**siz·ing** [? < Sp. *cabezar*, lit., to sink by the head] to overturn or upset: said esp. of a boat

**cap·stan** (kap′stən) *n.* [Fr. & Pr. *cabestan* < ? L. < *capere*, to take] an apparatus, mainly on ships, consisting of an upright cylinder around which cables or hawsers are wound, by machinery or by hand, for hoisting anchors, etc.

**capstan bar** any of the poles inserted in a capstan and used as levers in turning it by hand

**cap·stone** (-stōn′) *n.* the uppermost stone of a structure

**cap·sule** (kap′s′l, -syool) *n.* [Fr. < L. dim. of *capsa*, chest] **1.** a

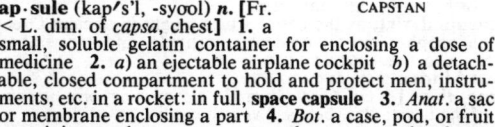
CAPSTAN

small, soluble gelatin container for enclosing a dose of medicine **2.** *a)* an ejectable airplane cockpit *b)* a detachable, closed compartment to hold and protect men, instruments, etc. in a rocket: in full, **space capsule 3.** *Anat.* a sac or membrane enclosing a part **4.** *Bot.* a case, pod, or fruit containing seeds, spores, or carpels, esp. one that bursts when ripe —*adj.* in a concise form [a *capsule* biography] —*vt.* -**suled**, -**sul·ing** to condense —**cap′su·lar** *adj.* —**cap′su·late′**, **cap′su·lat′ed** *adj.*

**cap·sul·ize** (-īz′) *vt.* -**ized′**, -**iz′ing 1.** to enclose in a capsule **2.** to condense

**Capt.** Captain

**cap·tain** (kap′tən) *n.* [< OFr. < LL. < L. *caput*, the head] **1.** a chief or leader **2.** the head of a group or division; esp., *a)* *U.S. Mil.* an officer ranking above a first lieutenant *b)* *U.S. Navy* an officer ranking above a commander *c)* the commander or master of a ship *d)* the pilot of a commercial airplane *e)* the leader of a team, as in sports *f)* a precinct commander in a police or fire department —*vt.* to be captain of —**cap′tain·cy** (-sē), *pl.* -**cies**, **cap′tain·ship′** *n.*

**cap·tion** (kap′shən) *n.* [< OFr. < L. < pp. of *capere*, to take] **1.** a heading, as of a newspaper article, or a legend, as under an illustration **2.** *same as* SUBTITLE (*n.* 2) —*vt.* to supply a caption for

**cap·tious** (-shəs) *adj.* [< L. *captiosus* < prec.] **1.** made for the sake of argument or faultfinding; sophistical **2.** quick to find fault; quibbling —**cap′tious·ly** *adv.* —**cap′tious·ness** *n.*

**cap·ti·vate** (kap′tə vāt′) *vt.* -**vat′ed**, -**vat′ing** [< LL., ult. < L. *captivus*, CAPTIVE] **1.** orig., to take captive **2.** to capture the attention or affection of; charm —**cap′ti·vat′ing·ly** *adv.* —**cap′ti·va′tion** *n.* —**cap′ti·va′tor** *n.*

**cap·tive** (kap′tiv) *n.* [L. *captivus* < pp. of *capere*, to take] a person caught and held, as a prisoner in war, or captivated, as by love —*adj.* **1.** *a)* taken or held prisoner *b)* unable to act independently *c)* forced to listen, willing or not [a *captive* audience] **2.** of captivity

**cap·tiv·i·ty** (kap tiv′ə tē) *n.*, *pl.* -**ties** the condition or time of being captive; imprisonment

**cap·tor** (kap′tər) *n.* [L.] a person who captures

**cap·ture** (kap′chər) *n.* [Fr. < L. *captura* < pp. of *capere*, to take] **1.** a taking or being taken by force, surprise, or skill **2.** that which is thus taken **3.** the absorption of a bombarding particle by an atomic nucleus, often causing radiation —*vt.* -**tured**, -**tur·ing 1.** to take or seize by force, surprise, or skill **2.** to represent (something immaterial, etc.) in more or less permanent form [to *capture* her charm on canvas] **3.** to effect the capture of (a subatomic particle)

**Cap·u·chin** (kap′yoo shin, -chin; kə pyoo′-) *n.* [< Fr. < *capuce* (It. *cappuccio*), a cowl] **1.** a monk of a branch of

the Franciscan order that adheres strictly to the original rule **2.** [c-] a woman's cloak with a hood **3.** [c-] a new-world monkey with a hoodlike crown of hair

**car** (kär) *n.* [< ONormFr. < LL. < L. *carrus*, two-wheeled chariot < Gaul. *carros*] **1.** any vehicle on wheels **2.** [Poet.] a chariot **3.** a vehicle that moves on rails, as a streetcar **4.** an automobile **5.** an elevator cage **6.** the part of a balloon or airship for carrying people and equipment

**ca·ra·bao** (kär′ə bou′) *n.*, *pl.* -**baos**, -**bao′**: see PLURAL, II, D, 1 [Sp. < Malay *karbau*] *same as* WATER BUFFALO

**car·a·bi·neer, car·a·bi·nier** (kar′ə bə nir′) *n.* [Fr. *carabinier*] a cavalryman armed with a carbine

**ca·ra·ca·ra** (kär′ə kär′ə) *n.* [Sp. < Tupi] a large, vulturelike hawk of S. America

**Ca·ra·cas** (kə räk′əs, -rak′-; *Sp.* kä rä′käs) capital of Venezuela, in the NC part: pop. 1,000,000

**car·a·cole** (kar′ə kōl′) *n.* [Fr. < Wal. < Sp. *caracol*, shell of a snail < Catal. < Fr. *escargot*, snail] a half turn to the right or left made by a horse with a rider —*vi.* -**coled′**, -**col′ing** to make a caracole or caracoles

**car·a·cul** (kar′ə kəl) *n. same as* KARAKUL

**ca·rafe** (kə raf′, -räf′) *n.* [Fr. < It. *caraffa*, prob. < Ar. *gharafa*, to draw water] a bottle of glass or metal for water, coffee, etc.

**car·a·mel** (kar′ə m′l, -mel′; kär′m′l) *n.* [Fr. < OFr., ult. < L. *canna mellis*, sugar cane] **1.** burnt sugar used to color or flavor food **2.** a chewy candy made from sugar, milk, etc.

**car·a·mel·ize** (-mə līz′) *vt.*, *vi.* -**ized′**, -**iz′ing** to turn into caramel

**car·a·pace** (kar′ə pās′) *n.* [Fr. < Sp. *carapacho*] an upper case or shell, as of the turtle

**car·at** (kar′ət) *n.* [Fr. < It. < Ar. < Gr. *keration*, carat, dim. of *keras*, horn] **1.** a unit of weight for precious stones, equal to 200 milligrams **2.** *same as* KARAT

**Ca·ra·vag·gio** (kä′rä väd′jō), **(Michelangelo da)** (born *Michelangelo Merisi*) 1573–1610; It. painter

**car·a·van** (kar′ə van′) *n.* [< Fr. < OFr. < Per. *kārwān*, caravan] **1.** a company of merchants, pilgrims, etc. traveling together for safety, as through a desert **2.** a number of vehicles traveling together **3.** a large covered vehicle for passengers, circus animals, etc.; van

**car·a·van·sa·ry** (kar′ə van′sə rē) *n.*, *pl.* -**ries** [< Fr. < Per. < *kārwān*, caravan + *sarāī*, palace] in the Orient, a kind of inn with a large central court, where caravans stop for the night

**car·a·vel** (kar′ə vel′) *n.* [< Fr. < Port. < LL. < Gr. *karabos*, kind of light ship] a fast, small sailing ship used in the 16th cent.

**car·a·way** (kar′ə wā′) *n.* [< Ar. *karawiyā* < ? Gr. *karon*, caraway] **1.** an herb with spicy, strong-smelling seeds **2.** the seeds, used to flavor bread, cakes, cheese, etc.

**car·bide** (kär′bīd) *n.* [CARB(O)- + -IDE] a compound of an element, usually a metal, with carbon; esp., calcium carbide

**car·bine** (kär′bīn, -bēn) *n.* [< Fr., ult. < *scarabée*, a beetle] **1.** a rifle with a short barrel **2.** *U.S. Armed Forces* a semiautomatic or automatic .30-caliber rifle

**car·bi·neer** (kär′bə nir′) *n. same as* CARABINEER

**car·bo-** *a combining form meaning* carbon: also, before a vowel, **carb-**

**car·bo·hy·drate** (kär′bə hī′drāt) *n.* [CARBO- + HYDRATE] any of a group of organic compounds, including the sugars and starches, composed of carbon, hydrogen, and oxygen: carbohydrates form an important class of foods

**car·bo·lat·ed** (kär′bə lāt′id) *adj.* containing or treated with carbolic acid

**car·bol·ic acid** (kär bäl′ik) [CARB(O)- + -OL[1] + -IC] *same as* PHENOL (sense 1)

**car·bo·lize** (kär′bə līz′) *vt.* -**lized′**, -**liz′ing** [see prec.] to treat or sterilize with phenol

**car·bon** (kär′bən) *n.* [< Fr. < L. *carbo*, coal] **1.** a nonmetallic chemical element found in many inorganic compounds and all organic compounds: diamond and graphite are pure carbon; carbon is also present in coal, coke, etc.: symbol, C; at. wt., 12.01115; at. no., 6: a radioactive isotope (**carbon 14**) is used in biochemical research and in dating archaeological specimens, etc. **2.** a sheet of carbon paper **3.** a copy, as of a letter, made with carbon paper: in full, **carbon copy 4.** *Elec. a)* a stick of carbon used in an arc lamp *b)* a carbon plate or rod used in a battery —*adj.* of carbon

**car·bo·na·ceous** (kär′bə nā′shəs) *adj.* of, consisting of, or containing carbon

**car·bon·ate** (kär′bə nit; *also, and for v. always,* -nāt′) *n.* a salt or ester of carbonic acid —*vt.* -**at′ed**, -**at′ing 1.** to charge with carbon dioxide [*carbonated* drinks] **2.** to form into a carbonate —**car′bon·a′tion** *n.*

**carbon black** finely divided carbon produced by the incomplete burning of oil or gas, used esp. in rubber and ink

**car·bon-date** (kär′bən dāt′) *vt.* **-dat′ed, -dat′ing** to establish the approximate age of (fossils, etc.) by measuring the carbon 14 content

**carbon dioxide** a colorless, odorless gas, $CO_2$: it passes out of the lungs in respiration, and is absorbed by plants in photosynthesis

**car·bon·ic** (kär bän′ik) *adj.* of, containing, or obtained from carbon or carbon dioxide

**carbonic acid** a weak, colorless acid, $H_2CO_3$, formed by the solution of carbon dioxide in water

**car·bon·if·er·ous** (kär′bə nif′ər əs) *adj.* [< CARBON + -FEROUS] **1.** producing or containing carbon or coal **2.** [C-] designating or of a great coal-making period of the Paleozoic Era: the warm, damp climate produced great forests, which later formed rich coal seams —**the Carboniferous 1.** the Carboniferous Period **2.** the rock and coal strata formed then See GEOLOGY, chart

**car·bon·ize** (kär′bə nīz′) *vt.* **-ized′, -iz′ing 1.** to change into carbon, as by partial burning **2.** to treat, cover, or combine with carbon —*vi.* to become carbonized —**car′bon·i·za′tion** *n.*

**carbon monoxide** a colorless, odorless, highly poisonous gas, CO, produced by the incomplete combustion of carbon

**carbon paper** very thin paper coated on one side with a carbon preparation: placed between sheets of paper, it is used to make copies of letters, etc.

**carbon tet·ra·chlo·ride** (tet′rə klôr′īd) a nonflammable, colorless liquid, $CCl_4$, used in fire extinguishers, cleaning mixtures, etc.

**Car·bo·run·dum** (kär′bə run′dəm) [CARB(ON) + (C)ORUNDUM] *a trademark for* a very hard, abrasive substance, esp. a carbide of silicon, used in grindstones, abrasives, etc.

**car·boy** (kär′boi) *n.* [< Per. *qarābah*] a large glass bottle enclosed in basketwork or in a wooden crate: used as a container for corrosive liquids

**car·bun·cle** (kär′buŋ k'l) *n.* [< OFr. < L. dim. of *carbo*, coal] **1.** a smooth, convex-cut garnet **2.** a painful, pus-bearing inflammation of the tissue beneath the skin, more severe than a boil and having several openings —**car·bun′cu·lar** (-kyoo lər) *adj.*

**car·bu·ret** (kär′bə rāt′, -ret′; -byoo-) *vt.* **-ret′ed** or **-ret′ted, -ret′ing** or **-ret′ting** [< obs. *carburet*, carbide] **1.** to combine chemically with carbon **2.** to mix or charge (gas or air) with volatile carbon compounds —**car′bu·re′tion** (-rā′shən) *n.*

**car·bu·ret·or** (kär′bə rāt′ər, -byoo-) *n.* a device in which air is mixed with gasoline spray to make an explosive mixture in an internal-combustion engine: Brit. sp. **car′bu·ret′tor** (-byoo ret′ər)

**car·ca·jou** (kär′kə joo′, -zhoo′) *n.* [CanadFr. < Algonquian] *same as* WOLVERINE

**car·cass** (kär′kəs) *n.* [< OFr. & Fr. < ?] **1.** the dead body of an animal, often specif. of a slaughtered animal dressed as meat **2.** the human body, living or dead: scornful or humorous usage **3.** the worthless remains of something **4.** a framework or shell Also, Brit. var., **car′case** (-kəs)

**car·cin·o·gen** (kär sin′ə jən) *n.* [< ff. + -GEN] any substance that produces cancer —**car·ci·no·gen·e·sis** (kär′sə nō jen′ə sis) *n.* —**car′ci·no·gen′ic** *adj.*

**car·ci·no·ma** (kär′sə nō′mə) *n., pl.* **-mas, -ma·ta** (-mə tə) [L. < Gr. *karkinōma*, cancer < *karkinos*, a crab] a cancerous growth made up of epithelial cells —**car′ci·nom′a·tous** (-näm′ə təs, -nō′mə-) *adj.*

**car coat** a short overcoat, mid-thigh in length

**card¹** (kärd) *n.* [< OFr. < L. *charta* < Gr. *chartēs*, leaf of paper] **1.** a flat, stiff piece of thick paper or thin pasteboard, usually rectangular; specif., *a)* one of a pack of playing cards: see also CARDS *b)* a pasteboard with small articles attached for sale [*a card* of thumbtacks] *c)* same as CALLING CARD, COMPASS CARD, POST CARD, SCORE CARD *d)* a card bearing a message or greeting [a birthday *card*] *e)* a card to advertise or announce *f)* a card identifying a person as an agent, member, patron, etc. *g)* any of a series of cards on which information is recorded [a file *card*] **2.** a series of events making up a program, as in boxing **3.** an event or attraction [a drawing *card*] **4.** [Colloq.] a comical person —*vt.* **1.** to provide with a card **2.** to put or list on a card or cards —**card up one's sleeve** a plan or resource kept secret or in reserve —**in** (or **on**) **the cards** likely or seemingly destined to happen —**put** (or **lay**) **one's cards on the table** to reveal frankly, as one's intentions

**card²** (kärd) *n.* [< Fr. < Pr. < L. *carere*, to card; sp. infl. by L. *carduus*, thistle] **1.** a metal comb or wire brush for raising nap or combing fibers of wool, cotton, etc. **2.** a machine with rollers covered with wire teeth, used to brush, clean, and straighten such fibers —*vt.* to use a card on (fibers) in preparation for spinning —**card′er** *n.* —**card′ing** *n., adj.*

**car·da·mom** (kär′də məm) *n.* [< L. < Gr. *kardamon*, cress + *amōmon*, spice plant] **1.** an Asiatic plant with aromatic seeds **2.** its seeds, used in medicine and as a spice Also **car′da·mon** (-mən)

**card·board** (kärd′bôrd′) *n.* stiff, thick paper, or pasteboard, used for cards, boxes, etc.

**card file** cards containing data or records, arranged systematically: also **card catalog**

**car·di·ac** (kär′dē ak′) *adj.* [< Fr. < L. < Gr. < *kardia*, the heart] **1.** of, near, or affecting the heart **2.** relating to the part of the stomach connected with the esophagus —*n.* a person with a heart disorder

**Car·diff** (kär′dif) seaport in SE Wales, on the Bristol Channel: pop. 287,000

**car·di·gan** (kär′də gən) *n.* [after 7th Earl of *Cardigan* (1797–1868), Eng. general] a sweater or jacket, usually knitted, that opens down the front: also **cardigan sweater** (or **jacket**)

**car·di·nal** (kärd′'n əl) *adj.* [< OFr. < L. *cardinalis*, chief < *cardo*, hinge] **1.** of main importance; principal; chief **2.** bright-red —*n.* **1.** one of the Roman Catholic officials appointed by the Pope to his council **2.** bright red **3.** a bright-red, crested American songbird: in full, **cardinal bird 4.** *same as* CARDINAL NUMBER —**car′di·nal·ly** *adv.* —**car′di·nal·ship′** *n.*

CARDIGAN

**car·di·nal·ate** (-āt′) *n.* the position, dignity, or rank of a cardinal

**cardinal flower 1.** the bright-red flower of a N. American plant that grows in damp, shady places or in shallow water **2.** this plant

**cardinal number** any number used in counting or showing how many (e.g., two, forty, 627, etc.): distinguished from ORDINAL NUMBER

**cardinal points** the four principal points of the compass; north, south, east, and west

**cardinal virtues** the basic virtues taught in ancient Greek philosophy: justice, prudence, fortitude, and temperance: see also THEOLOGICAL VIRTUES

**card index** *same as* CARD FILE

**car·di·o-** [< Gr. *kardia*, heart] *a combining form meaning* of the heart: also, before a vowel, **cardi-**

**car·di·o·gram** (kär′dē ə gram′) *n. same as* ELECTROCARDIOGRAM —**car′di·o·graph′** (-graf′) *n.* —**car′di·og′ra·phy** (-äg′rə fē) *n.*

**car·di·ol·o·gy** (kär′dē äl′ə jē) *n.* the branch of medicine dealing with the heart, its functions, and its diseases —**car′di·ol′o·gist** *n.*

**car·di·o·vas·cu·lar** (kär′dē ō vas′kyoo lər) *adj.* of the heart and the blood vessels as a system

**cards** (kärdz) *n.pl.* **1.** a game or games played with a deck of cards, as bridge, rummy, poker, etc. **2.** the playing of such games; card playing

**card shark** [Colloq.] **1.** an expert card player **2.** *same as* CARDSHARP

**card·sharp** (kärd′shärp′) *n.* [Colloq.] a professional cheater at cards: also **card′sharp′er**

**care** (ker) *n.* [< OE. *caru*, sorrow] **1.** *a)* worry or concern *b)* a cause of this **2.** close attention or careful heed **3.** a liking or regard (*for*) **4.** charge; protection; custody **5.** something to watch over or attend to —*vi.* **cared, car′ing 1.** to have objection, worry, regret, etc.; mind **2.** to feel concern or interest **3.** to feel love or a liking (*for*) **4.** to look after; provide (*for*) **5.** to wish (*for*); want —**care of** at the address of —**have a care** to be careful: also **take care** —**take care of 1.** to be responsible for; attend to **2.** to provide for

**ca·reen** (kə rēn′) *vt.* [< Fr. < It. < L. *carina*, keel] **1.** to cause (a ship) to lean or lie on one side, as for repairs **2.** to cause to lean sideways; tip; tilt —*vi.* **1.** to lean sideways **2.** to lurch from side to side —*n.* a careening

**ca·reer** (kə rir′) *n.* [Fr. *carrière*, racecourse < It. < *carro*, CAR] **1.** a swift course **2.** one's progress through life or in a particular vocation **3.** a profession or occupation —*adj.* pursuing a normally temporary activity as a lifework [a *career* soldier] —*vi.* to move at full speed; rush wildly —**in full career** at full speed

**ca·reer·ist** (-ist) *n.* a person interested chiefly in his own professional ambitions, to the neglect of other things —**career′ism** *n.*

**care·free** (ker′frē′) *adj.* free from troubles or worry

**care·ful** (-fəl) *adj.* **1.** acting or working in a thoughtful, painstaking way **2.** cautious or wary **3.** accurately or thoroughly done [a *careful* analysis] —**care′ful·ly** *adv.* —**care′ful·ness** *n.*

**care·less** (-lis) *adj.* **1.** carefree; untroubled **2.** not paying enough attention; not thinking before one acts or speaks; inconsiderate **3.** done without enough attention, precision, etc. —**care′less·ly** *adv.* —**care′less·ness** *n.*

**ca·ress** (kə res′) *vt.* [< Fr. < It., ult. < L. *carus*, dear] to touch or stroke lovingly or gently; also, to embrace or kiss —*n.* an affectionate touch or gesture —**ca·ress′er** *n.* —**ca·ress′ing·ly** *adv.* —**ca·res′sive** *adj.* —**ca·res′sive·ly** *adv.*

**car·et** (kar′it, ker′-) *n.* [L., lit., there is lacking] a mark (∧) used in writing or in correcting proof, to show where something is to be added

**care·tak·er** (ker′tāk′ər) *n.* a person hired to take care of something, as a house, estate, etc.

**care·worn** (-wôrn′) *adj.* showing the effects of troubles and worry; haggard

**car·fare** (kär′fer′) *n.* the price of a ride on a streetcar, bus, etc.

**car·go** (kär′gō) *n., pl.* **-goes, -gos** [< Sp. < *cargar,* to load < VL. *carricare:* see CHARGE] the load of commodities carried by a ship, airplane, truck, etc.; freight

**car·hop** (kär′häp′) *n.* [CAR + (BELL)HOP] one who serves customers in cars at a drive-in restaurant

**Car·ib** (kar′ib) *n.* [< Sp. *caribal,* altered < *canibal:* see CANNIBAL] **1.** a member of an Indian people of the S West Indies and the N coast of S. America **2.** the family of languages of the Caribs —**Car′ib·an** *adj., n.*

**Car·ib·be·an** (kar′ə bē′ən, kə rib′ē ən) *same as* CARIBBEAN SEA —*adj.* **1.** of the Caribs, their language, culture, etc. **2.** of the Caribbean Sea, its islands, etc. —*n. same as* CARIB (sense 1)

**Car·ib·be·an Sea** (kar′ə bē′ən, kə rib′ē ən) part of the Atlantic, bounded by the West Indies, Central America, & South America

**ca·ri·be** (kə rē′bä) *n.* [AmSp., lit., Carib (see CANNIBAL)] *same as* PIRANHA

**car·i·bou** (kar′ə bōō′) *n., pl.* **-bous′, -bou′:** see PLURAL, II, D, 1 [CanadFr. < Algonquian name] a large, northern N. American deer

**car·i·ca·ture** (kar′ə chər, -choor′) *n.* [Fr. < It. < *caricare,* to load, exaggerate] **1.** a picture or imitation of a person, literary style, etc. that exaggerates certain features or mannerisms for satirical effect **2.** the art of making caricatures **3.** a poor imitation —*vt.* **-tured, -tur·ing** to depict as in a caricature —**car′i·ca·tur·ist** *n.*

**car·ies** (ker′ēz) *n.* [L., decay] decay of bones, or, esp., of teeth

**car·il·lon** (kar′ə län′; *occas.* kə·ril′yən) *n.* [Fr., chime of (orig. four) bells, ult. < L. *quattuor,* four] **1.** a set of stationary bells, each producing one tone of the chromatic scale **2.** a melody played on such bells **3.** an organ stop producing a carillonlike sound

**car·il·lon·neur** (kar′ə lə nur′) *n.* [Fr.] a carillon player

**car·i·ole** (kar′ē ōl′) *n.* [< Fr. < It. dim. of *carro,* CAR] **1.** a small carriage drawn by one horse **2.** a light, covered cart **3.** [Canad.] a dog sled

**car·i·ous** (kar′ē əs) *adj.* [L. *cariosus*] having caries; decayed —**car′i·os′i·ty** (-äs′ə tē) *n.*

**cark** (kärk) *vt., vi.* [< ONormFr. var. of OFr. *chargier:* see CHARGE] [Archaic] to worry or be worried —*n.* [Archaic] distress; anxiety

**Carl** (kärl) *var. of* CHARLES

**carl, carle** (kärl) *n.* [OE. < ON. *karl*] **1.** [Archaic or Obs.] a peasant, bondman, or villein **2.** [Scot.] a boor **3.** [Scot.] a sturdy fellow

**car·load** (kär′lōd′) *n.* a load that fills a car, esp. a freight car

**car·load·ings** (-iŋz) *n.pl.* the number of railroad carloads shipped within a given period

**Car·lot·ta** (kär lät′ə) *var. of* CHARLOTTE

**Car·lyle** (kär lil′, kär′lil), **Thomas** 1795–1881; Brit. writer, born in Scotland

**car·ma·gnole** (kär′mən yōl′) *n.* [Fr., altered < older *carmignole,* kind of cap] **1.** the costume worn by French Revolutionaries (1792) **2.** a song and dance popular during the French Revolution

**car·man** (kär′mən) *n., pl.* **-men** (-mən) a streetcar conductor or motorman

**Car·mel·ite** (kär′mə līt′) *n.* a friar or nun of the order of Our Lady of Mount Carmel, founded in Syria about 1160 —*adj.* of this order

**car·min·a·tive** (kär min′ə tiv, kär′mə nāt′iv) *adj.* [ModL. < L. pp. of *carminare,* to card, cleanse] causing gas to be expelled from the stomach and intestines —*n.* a carminative medicine

**car·mine** (kär′min, -mīn) *n.* [< Fr. < ML. *carminium* < Ar. *qirmiz,* crimson] **1.** a red or purplish-red pigment obtained mainly from cochineal **2.** its color —*adj.* red or purplish-red; crimson

**car·nage** (kär′nij) *n.* [< Fr. < It., ult. < L. *caro* (gen. *carnis,* flesh) bloody and extensive slaughter, esp. in battle; massacre; bloodshed

**car·nal** (-n′l) *adj.* [OFr. < LL. *carnalis* < L. *caro:* see prec.] **1.** in or of the flesh; material or worldly, not spiritual **2.** sensual; sexual —**car·nal·i·ty** (kär nal′ə tē) *n., pl.* **-ties** —**car′nal·ly** *adv.*

**car·na·tion** (kär nā′shən) *n.* [Fr. < LL. *carnatio* < *caro:* see CARNAGE] **1.** formerly, rosy pink; now, deep red **2.** a plant of the pink family, with white, pink, or red flowers that smell like cloves

**car·nau·ba** (kär nô′bə, -nou′-) *n.* [Braz. Port. < Tupi native name] a Brazilian palm yielding a hard wax used in polishes, lipsticks, etc.

**Car·ne·gie** (kär′nə gē′, kär nā′gē), **Andrew** 1835–1919; U.S. industrialist & philanthropist, born in Scotland

**car·nel·ian** (kär nēl′yən) *n.* [altered (after L. *caro:* see CARNAGE) < CORNELIAN] a red variety of chalcedony, used in jewelry

**car·ni·val** (kär′nə vəl) *n.* [< Fr. or It. < ML. < hyp. *carnem levare,* to remove meat] **1.** the period of feasting and revelry just before Lent **2.** a reveling; festivity; merrymaking **3.** a traveling entertainment with rides, games, etc. **4.** a program of contests, etc. *[sports carnival]*

**car·ni·vore** (-vôr′) *n.* [Fr.: see ff.] **1.** any of an order of fanged, flesh-eating mammals, including the dog, wolf, cat, lion, bear, seal, etc.: opposed to HERBIVORE **2.** a plant that ingests insects

**car·niv·o·rous** (kär niv′ə rəs) *adj.* [< L. < *caro* (see CARNAGE) + *vorare,* to eat] **1.** *a)* flesh-eating: opposed to HERBIVOROUS *b)* insect-eating, as certain plants **2.** of the carnivores —**car·niv′o·rous·ly** *adv.* —**car·niv′o·rous·ness** *n.*

**car·ny, car·ney, car·nie** (kär′nē) *n., pl.* **-nies** [Slang] **1.** *same as* CARNIVAL (sense 3) **2.** a worker in such a carnival

**Car·ol** (kar′əl) *var. of:* **1.** CAROLINE **2.** CHARLES

**car·ol** (kar′əl) *n.* [< OFr. < L. < Gr. < *choros,* dance + *aulein,* to play on the flute] a song of joy or praise; esp., a Christmas song —*vi.* **-oled** or **-olled, -ol·ing** or **-ol·ling 1.** to sing in joy; warble **2.** to sing carols, esp. Christmas carols, in unison —*vt.* **1.** to sing (a tune, etc.) **2.** to praise in song —**car′ol·er, car′ol·ler** *n.*

**Car·o·li·na¹** (kar′ə li′nə) [L. fem. adj. of *Carolus* (see CAROLINE), in honor of CHARLES I] English colony including what is now N.Carolina, S.Carolina, Ga., & N Fla. —**the Carolinas** N.Carolina & S.Carolina

**Ca·ro·li·na²** (kä′rō lē′nä) city in NE Puerto Rico, near San Juan: pop. 95,000

**Car·o·line** (kar′ə lin′, -lən) [G. & Fr. < It. *Carolina,* fem. < ML. *Carolus,* CHARLES] a feminine name

**Caroline Islands** group of islands in the W Pacific: see Trust Territory of the PACIFIC ISLANDS

**Car·o·lin·i·an** (kar′ə lin′ē ən) *adj.* of North Carolina or South Carolina —*n.* a native or inhabitant of North Carolina or South Carolina

**Car·o·lyn** (kar′ə lin) *var. of* CAROLINE

**car·om** (kar′əm) *n.* [< Fr. < Sp. *carambola*] **1.** *Billiards* a shot in which the cue ball successively hits the two object balls **2.** a hitting and rebounding, as of a ball striking a surface —*vi.* **1.** to make a carom **2.** to hit and rebound

**car·o·tene** (kar′ə tēn′) *n.* [< L. *carota,* CARROT + -ENE] any of three red or orange-colored isomeric hydrocarbons, $C_{40}H_{56}$, found in carrots and some other vegetables, and changed into vitamin A in the body: also **car′o·tin** (-tin)

**ca·rot·e·noid, ca·rot·i·noid** (kə rät′′n oid′) *n.* any of several red and yellow pigments related to and including carotene —*adj.* **1.** of or like carotene **2.** of the carotenoids

**ca·rot·id** (kə rät′id) *adj.* [Gr. *karōtides,* the carotids < *karoun,* to plunge into sleep: compression of these arteries causes unconsciousness] designating, of, or near either of the two principal arteries, one on each side of the neck, which convey the blood to the head —*n.* a carotid artery

**ca·rous·al** (kə rou′zəl) *n. same as* CAROUSE

**ca·rouse** (kə rouz′) *vi.* **-roused′, -rous′ing** [< Fr. < G. *gar aus*(*trinken*), (to drink) quite out] to drink much alcoholic liquor, esp. along with others having a noisy, merry time —*n.* a noisy, merry drinking party —**ca·rous′er** *n.*

**car·ou·sel** (kar′ə sel′, -zel′) *n. same as* CARROUSEL

**carp¹** (kärp) *n., pl.* **carp, carps:** see PLURAL, II, D, 2 [OFr. *carpe* < Gmc. *carpa*] **1.** any of a group of edible freshwater fishes living in ponds **2.** any of various similar fishes, as the goldfish

**carp²** (kärp) *vi.* [< ON. *karpa,* to brag] to find fault in a petty or nagging way —**carp′er** *n.*

**-carp** (kärp) [< Gr. *karpos,* fruit] *a terminal combining form meaning* fruit *[endocarp]*

**car·pal** (kär′pəl) *adj.* [ModL. *carpalis*] of the carpus —*n.* a bone of the carpus: also **car·pa′le** (-pä′lē), *pl.* **-li·a** (-ə)

**Car·pa·thi·an Mountains** (kär pā′thē ən) mountain

system in C Europe, extending from S Poland into NE Romania: also **Car·pa'thi·ans**

‡**car·pe di·em** (kär'pe dē'em, dī'-) [L., lit., seize the day] make the most of present opportunities

**car·pel** (kär'pəl) *n.* [ModL. dim. < Gr. *karpos*, fruit] **1.** a simple pistil, regarded as a single ovule-bearing leaf or modified leaflike structure **2.** any of the segments of a compound pistil —**car'pel·lar'y** (-pə ler'ē) *adj.* —**car'pel·late'** (-pə lāt') *adj.*

**car·pen·ter** (kär'pən tər) *n.* [Anglo-Fr. < LL. *carpentarius* < L. *carpentum*, a cart < Gaul.] a workman who builds and repairs wooden articles, buildings, etc. —*vt.* to do a carpenter's work —*vt.* to make or repair as by carpentry

**car·pen·try** (-trē) *n.* the work or trade of a carpenter

**car·pet** (kär'pit) *n.* [< OFr. < ML. *carpita*, woolen cloth < L. pp. of *carpere*, to card] **1.** a heavy fabric for covering a floor, stairs, etc., usually in a strip, or several joined strips **2.** anything like a carpet [a carpet of snow] —*vt.* to cover as with a carpet —**on the carpet 1.** under consideration **2.** being, or about to be, reprimanded

**car·pet·bag** (-bag') *n.* an old-fashioned type of traveling bag, made of carpeting —*vi.* **-bagged', -bag'ging** to act as a carpetbagger

**car·pet·bag·ger** (-bag'ər) *n.* a Northern politician or adventurer who went South to take advantage of unsettled conditions after the Civil War: contemptuous term

**carpet beetle** (or **bug**) a small beetle whose larvae feed on furs and woolens, esp. carpets

**car·pet·ing** (-iŋ) *n.* carpets or carpet fabric

**carpet sweeper** a hand-operated device with a revolving brush for sweeping carpets and rugs

**-car·pic** (kär'pik) *same as* -CARPOUS

**carp·ing** (kär'piŋ) *adj.* tending to carp, or find fault; captious —**carp'ing·ly** *adv.*

**car pool** an arrangement by a group to rotate the use of their cars, as for going to work

**car·port** (kär'pôrt') *n.* a shelter for an automobile, consisting of a roof extended from the side of a building, sometimes with an additional wall

**-car·pous** (kär'pəs) [< Gr. *karpos*, fruit] a terminal combining form meaning fruited, having fruit

**car·pus** (kär'pəs) *n.*, *pl.* **-pi** (-pī) [ModL. < Gr. *karpos*, wrist] the wrist, or the wrist bones

**car·rack** (kar'ək) *n.* [< OFr. < Sp. < Ar. pl. of *qurqūr*, merchant ship] *same as* GALLEON

**Car·ra·ra** (kə rä'rə; *It.* kär rä'rä) city in NW Italy: a fine, white marble (**Carrara marble**) is quarried in nearby mountains: pop. 67,000

**car·rel, car·rell** (kar'əl) *n.* [< ML. *carula*, small study in a cloister] a small enclosure in the stack room of a library, for study or reading

**car·riage** (kar'ij; *for* 2, *usually* kar'ē ij) *n.* [< Anglo-Fr. < *carier*, CARRY] **1.** a carrying; transportation **2.** the cost of carrying **3.** manner of carrying the head and body; posture **4.** *a)* a four-wheeled passenger vehicle, usually horse-drawn *b)* *same as* BABY CARRIAGE **5.** a wheeled support [a gun *carriage*] **6.** a moving part (as on a typewriter) for supporting and shifting something

**Car·rie** (kar'ē) a feminine name

**car·ri·er** (kar'ē ər) *n.* **1.** a person or thing, as a mailman or a train, that carries something **2.** one in the transportation business **3.** a messenger or porter **4.** something in or on which something else is carried or conducted **5.** *same as* AIRCRAFT CARRIER **6.** a person or animal that carries and transmits disease germs, esp. a person immune to the germs **7.** *Electronics* the steady transmitted wave whose amplitude, frequency, or phase is modulated by the signal

**carrier pigeon** a homing pigeon trained to carry a written message fastened to its leg

**car·ri·ole** (kar'ē ōl') *n. same as* CARIOLE

**car·ri·on** (kar'ē ən) *n.* [< Anglo-Fr., ult. < L. *caro*, flesh] **1.** the decaying flesh of a dead body **2.** anything very repulsive —*adj.* **1.** of or like carrion **2.** feeding on carrion

**carrion crow** the common crow of Europe

**Car·roll** (kar'əl), **Lewis** (pseud. of *Charles Lutwidge Dodgson*) 1832–98; Eng. writer

**car·rom** (kar'əm) *n.*, *vi. same as* CAROM

**car·rot** (kar'ət) *n.* [< Fr. < L. < Gr. *karōton*] **1.** a plant of the parsley family with a fleshy, orange-red root, eaten as a vegetable **2.** the root

**car·rou·sel** (kar'ə sel', -zel') *n.* [Fr. < It. dial. *carusiello*, prob. < *carro*, CAR] **1.** *same as* MERRY-GO-ROUND **2.** something that revolves like a merry-go-round, as a revolving tray from which slides are fed into a projector, or a circular conveyor in an airport from which passengers pick up their luggage

**car·ry** (kar'ē) *vt.* **-ried, -ry·ing** [< Anglo-Fr. *carier* < VL. *carricare*: see CHARGE] **1.** to hold or support while moving **2.** to take from one place to another; transport, as in a vehicle **3.** to hold, and direct the motion of [a pipe *carrying* water] **4.** to lead or impel **5.** to transmit [air *carries* sound] **6.** to transfer or extend [to *carry* a pipe to a sewer]

**7.** to transfer (a figure, entry, etc.) from one column, time, etc. to the next **8.** to bear the weight of **9.** to be pregnant with **10.** to have as a quality, consequence, etc. [to *carry* a guarantee] **11.** to keep with one [to *carry* a watch] **12.** to hold or conduct (oneself) in a specified way **13.** to include as part of its contents or program: said of a newspaper, TV station, etc. **14.** to have or keep on a list or register **15.** to capture (a fortress, etc.) **16.** to win over or influence (a group) **17.** *a)* to win (an election, argument, etc.) *b)* to gain a majority of the votes in (a district, state, etc.) **18.** *Commerce a)* to keep in stock *b)* to keep on one's account books, etc. **19.** *Music* to sing the notes of (a melody or part) accurately —*vi.* **1.** to act as a bearer, conductor, etc. **2.** to have or cover a range [his voice *carries* well] **3.** to have an intended effect **4.** to win approval [the motion *carried*] —*n.*, *pl.* **-ries 1.** the range or distance covered by a gun, golf ball, etc. **2.** a portage between two navigable bodies of water **3.** a carrying —**be** (or **get**) **carried away** to be moved to unreasoning enthusiasm —**carry off 1.** to kill [disease *carries off* many] **2.** to win (a prize, etc.) **3.** to handle (a situation), esp. with success —**carry on 1.** to engage in; conduct **2.** to continue as before **3.** [Colloq.] to behave in a wild or childish way **4.** [Colloq.] to engage in an illicit love affair —**carry out 1.** to put (plans, etc.) into practice **2.** to get done; accomplish —**carry over 1.** to have or be remaining **2.** to transfer, hold over for, or extend to another place or later time **3.** to postpone; continue —**carry through 1.** to get done; accomplish **2.** to keep (a person) going; sustain

**car·ry·all**[1] (-ôl') *n.* [< Fr. *carriole* (see CARIOLE); sp. infl. by CARRY & ALL] a light, covered carriage with seats for several people

**car·ry·all**[2] (-ôl') *n.* a large bag, basket, etc.

**carrying charge 1.** interest paid on the balance owed in installment buying **2.** the costs associated with property ownership, as taxes, upkeep, etc.

**car·ry·ings-on** (kar'ē iŋz än') *n.pl.* [Colloq.] wild, extravagant, or immoral behavior

**car·ry-on** (kar'ē än') *adj.* designating lightweight luggage to be carried onto an airplane by a passenger, esp. if small enough to fit under an airplane seat

**car·ry-out** (kar'ē out') *adj.* designating a service, as of a restaurant, by which food and beverages may be taken out to be eaten elsewhere

**car·ry-o·ver** (-ō'vər) *n.* something carried over, as a remainder of crops or goods

**car·sick** (kär'sik') *adj.* nauseated from riding in an automobile, bus, etc. —**car'sick'ness** *n.*

**Car·son** (kär's'n) [after ff.] city in SW Calif.: suburb of Los Angeles: pop. 81,000

**Car·son** (kär's'n), **Kit** (kit) (full name *Christopher Carson*) 1809–68; U.S. frontiersman

**Carson City** [after prec.] capital of Nev., near Lake Tahoe: pop. 32,000

**cart** (kärt) *n.* [< ON. *kartr*] **1.** a small, strong, two-wheeled vehicle drawn by a horse, etc. **2.** a small, wheeled vehicle, drawn or pushed by hand —*vt.*, *vi.* to carry or deliver, as in a cart, truck, etc. —**put the cart before the horse** to do things backwards —**cart'er** *n.*

**cart·age** (kär'tij) *n.* **1.** the act or work of carting **2.** the charges made for carting

**carte blanche** (kärt' blänsh', blänch') *pl.* **cartes blanches** (kärts' blänsh', kärt blän'shəz) [Fr., lit., white (i.e., blank) card] **1.** full authority **2.** freedom to do as one thinks best

**car·tel** (kär tel') *n.* [Fr. < It. *cartello*, dim. of *carta*, CARD[1]] **1.** a written challenge, as to a duel **2.** a written agreement between nations at war, esp. as to exchange of prisoners **3.** [G. *kartell* < Fr.] an association of business firms establishing a national or international monopoly

**Car·ter** (kär'tər), **Jim·my** (jim'ē) (full name *James Earl Carter, Jr.*) 1924– ; 39th president of the U.S. (1977–81)

**Car·te·sian** (kär tē'zhən) *adj.* [< *Cartesius*, Latinized form of DESCARTES] of Descartes or his philosophical or mathematical ideas —*n.* a follower of Descartes

**Cartesian coordinates** a pair of numbers that locate a point by its distances from two lines intersecting usually at right angles

**Car·thage** (kär'thij) ancient city-state in N Africa, founded by the Phoenicians near the site of modern Tunis: destroyed by the Romans, 146 B.C. —**Car'tha·gin'i·an** (-thə jin'ē ən) *adj.*, *n.*

**Car·thu·sian** (kär thōō'zhən, -thyōō'-) *n.* [< ML. < L. name for Chartreuse] a monk or nun of a very strict order founded at Chartreuse, France, in 1084 —*adj.* of the Carthusians

**Car·tier** (kár tyā'), **Jacques** (zhák) 1491–1557; Fr. explorer in North America

**car·ti·lage** (kärt''l ij) *n.* [OFr. < L. *cartilago*] **1.** a tough, elastic, whitish tissue forming part of the skeleton; gristle **2.** a part or structure consisting of cartilage

**car·ti·lag·i·nous** (kärt''l aj'ə nəs) *adj.* **1.** of or like cartilage **2.** having a skeleton made up mainly of cartilage

**cart·load** (kärt'lōd') *n.* as much as a cart holds

**car·tog·ra·phy** (kär täg'rə fē) *n.* [< ML. *carta* (see CARD¹) + -GRAPHY] the art or work of making maps or charts —**car·tog'ra·pher** *n.* —**car·to·graph·ic** (kär'tə graf'ik), **car'to·graph'i·cal** *adj.*

**car·ton** (kärt'ʼn) *n.* [Fr. < It. *cartone* < *carta:* see CARD¹] 1. a cardboard box or container 2. its full contents

**car·toon** (kär tōōn') *n.* [Fr. *carton* < It. *cartone:* see prec.] 1. a drawing that caricatures, often satirically, some situation or person 2. a full-size sketch of a design or picture to be copied in a fresco, tapestry, etc. 3. *a)* a humorous drawing, often with a caption *b) same as* COMIC STRIP 4. *same as* ANIMATED CARTOON —*vt.* to draw a cartoon of —*vi.* to draw cartoons —**car·toon'ist** *n.*

**car·tridge** (kär'trij) *n.* [altered < Fr. *cartouche* < It. < *carta:* see CARD¹] 1. a cylindrical case of cardboard, metal, etc. containing the charge and primer, and usually the projectile, for a firearm 2. a small container holding a supply of material for insertion into a larger device 3. a protected roll of camera film 4. a replaceable stylus unit in a phonograph pickup

**cartridge clip** a metal container for cartridges, inserted in certain types of firearms

**cart·wheel** (kärt'hwēl', -wēl') *n.* 1. a kind of handspring performed sidewise 2. [Slang] a silver dollar

**Ca·ru·so** (kə rōō'sō; *It.* kä rōō'zō), **En·ri·co** (en rē'kō) 1873–1921; It. operatic tenor

**carve** (kärv) *vt.* **carved, carv'ing** [< OE. *ceorfan*] 1. to make or shape by or as by cutting, chipping, etc. [*carve* a statue, *carve* a career] 2. to decorate the surface of with cut designs 3. to divide by cutting; slice —*vi.* 1. to carve statues or designs 2. to carve meat —**carv'er** *n.*

**car·vel** (kär'vəl) *n. same as* CARAVEL

**carv·en** (kär'v'n) *adj.* [Archaic or Poet.] carved

**Car·ver** (kär'vər), **George Washington** 1864–1943; U.S. botanist & chemist

**carv·ing** (kär'viŋ) *n.* 1. the work or art of a person who carves 2. a carved figure or design

**carving knife** a large knife for carving meat, used with a large, two-tined fork ( **carving fork** )

**car·wash** (kär'wôsh', -wäsh') *n.* a facility for washing and polishing automobiles

**car·y·at·id** (kar'ē at'id) *n., pl.* **-ids, -i·des'** (-ə dēz') [< L. < Gr. *karyatides,* priestesses at Karyai, in Macedonia] a supporting column that has the form of a draped female figure

**car·y·o-** *same as* KARYO-

**ca·sa·ba** (kə sä'bə) *n.* [< *Kassaba,* town near Smyrna, Asia Minor] a cultivated melon with a hard, yellow rind and sweet, usually white flesh

**Ca·sa·blan·ca** (kas'ə blaŋ'kə, kä'sə bläŋ'kə) seaport in NW Morocco: pop. 1,177,000

**Ca·sals** (kə sälz', -salz'; *Sp.* kä säls'), **Pa·blo** (päb'lō) 1876–1973; Sp. cellist & composer

**Ca·sa·no·va** (kas'ə nō'və; *It.* kä'zä nô'vä), **Gio·van·ni (Jacopo)** (jô vän'nē) 1725–98; It. adventurer, noted for his *Memoirs*

**as·bah** (käz'bä, kas'-) *n.* [Fr. < Ar. dial. *qaṣba* < Ar. *qaṣaba,* fortress] 1. in N Africa, a fortress 2. the old, crowded quarter of a N African city, esp. [C-] of Algiers

**as·cade** (kas kād') *n.* [Fr. < It. *cascata* < L. *cadere,* to fall] 1. a small, steep waterfall, esp. one of a series 2. a shower of sparks, or rippling fall of lace, etc. —*vt., vi.* **-cad'ed, -cad'ing** to fall or drop in a cascade

**Cascade Range** [after cascades on the Columbia River] mountain range extending from N Calif., through Oreg. and Wash., into British Columbia

**as·car·a** (kas ker'ə) *n.* [Sp. *cáscara,* bark] 1. a small buckthorn of the U.S. Pacific coast 2. a laxative made from its bark: in full, **cascara sa·gra·da** (sə grä'də, -grä'-)

**ase¹** (kās) *n.* [< OFr. *cas,* an event < L. *casus,* an accident, pp. of *cadere,* to fall] 1. an example or instance [a *case* of measles] 2. a person being treated or helped, as by a doctor or social worker 3. any matter undergoing observation, study, etc. 4. a statement of the facts, as in a law court 5. convincing arguments [he has no *case*] 6. a lawsuit 7. [Colloq.] a peculiar person 8. [Colloq.] an infatuation 9. *Gram. a)* an inflected form taken by a noun, pronoun, or adjective to show syntactic relationship *b)* such relationship —*vt.* **cased, cas'ing** [Slang] to look over carefully, esp. for an intended robbery —**in any case** anyhow —**in case** in the event that —**in case of** in the event of —**in no case** by no means; never

**ase²** (kās) *n.* [< ONormFr. *casse* < L. *capsa,* a box < *capere,* to hold] 1. a container, as a box, sheath, etc. 2. a protective cover [a *watchcase*] 3. a full box or its contents 4. a set or pair [a *case* of pistols] 5. a frame, as for a win-

dow 6. *Printing* a shallow tray in which type is kept: the **upper case** is for capitals, the **lower case** for small letters —*vt.* **cased, cas'ing** 1. to put in a container 2. to cover or enclose

**ca·se·fy** (kā'sə fī') *vt., vi.* **-fied', -fy'ing** [< L. *caseus,* CHEESE¹ + -FY] to make or become cheeselike

**case·hard·en** (kās'här'd'n) *vt.* 1. *Metallurgy* to form a hard, thin surface on (an iron alloy) 2. to make callous or unfeeling —**case'hard'ened** *adj.*

**case history** (or **study**) collected information about an individual or group, for use in sociological, medical, or psychiatric studies

**ca·se·in** (kā'sē in, kā'sēn) *n.* [< L. *caseus,* CHEESE¹ + -IN¹] a protein that is one of the chief constituents of milk and the basis of cheese

**case knife** 1. *same as* SHEATH KNIFE 2. a table knife

**case law** law based on previous judicial decisions, or precedents: distinguished from STATUTE LAW

**case·load** (kās'lōd') *n.* the number of cases being handled by a court, a social or welfare agency, a caseworker, etc.

**case·mate** (kās'māt') *n.* [Fr. < It. < Gr. *chasmata,* pl. of *chasma,* CHASM] a shellproof or armored enclosure with openings for guns, as in a fortress or on a warship —**case'mat'ed** *adj.*

**case·ment** (kās'mənt) *n.* [< OFr. *encassement,* a frame: see CASE²] 1. a hinged window frame that opens outward: a **casement window** often has two such frames, opening like French doors 2. a casing; covering —**case'ment·ed** *adj.*

**ca·se·ous** (kā'sē əs) *adj.* [< L. *caseus,* cheese] of or like cheese

**ca·sern, ca·serne** (kə zurn') *n.* [< Fr. < Pr. *cazerna,* small hut < LL. *quaterna,* four each < *quattuor,* four] a military barracks in a fortified town

**case·work** (kās'wurk') *n.* social work in which the worker investigates a case of personal or family maladjustment and gives guidance —**case'work'er** *n.*

**cash¹** (kash) *n.* [< Fr. *caisse,* money box < Pr. < L. *capsa:* see CASE²] 1. money that a person actually has; esp., ready money 2. bills and coins 3. money, a check, etc. paid at the time of purchase —*vt.* to give or get cash for —*adj.* of, for, or requiring cash [a *cash* sale] —**cash in** 1. to turn into cash 2. [Slang] to die —**cash in on** to get profit or profitable use from

**cash²** (kash) *n., pl.* **cash** [Port. *caixa* < Tamil *kasu* < Sans. *karṣa*] any of several Chinese or Indian coins of small value

**cash-and-car·ry** (kash'ən kar'ē) *adj.* with cash payments and no deliveries

**cash·book** (-book') *n.* a book in which all receipts and payments of money are entered

**cash discount** a discount allowed a purchaser paying within a specified period

**cash·ew** (kash'ōō, kə shōō') *n.* [< Fr. < Port. < Tupi *acajú*] 1. a tropical tree bearing edible, kidney-shaped nuts 2. the nut: also **cashew nut**

**cash flow** the pattern of expenses and income of a company, government, etc. that determines how much cash, if any, is available at any given time

**cash·ier¹** (ka shir') *n.* [< Fr. *caissier*] a person in charge of cash transactions for a bank, store, etc.

**cash·ier²** (ka shir') *vt.* [< MDu. < OFr. < LL. *cassare* (see QUASH¹) & L. *quassare* (see QUASH²)] 1. to dismiss, esp. in dishonor, from a position of command, trust, etc. 2. to discard or reject

**cashier's check** a check drawn by a bank on its own funds and signed by the cashier

**cash·mere** (kazh'mir, kash'-) *n.* [< *Cashmere,* former sp. of KASHMIR] 1. a fine carded wool from goats of Kashmir and Tibet 2. a soft, twilled cloth of this or similar wool 3. a cashmere shawl, sweater, coat, etc.

**cash register** a business machine, usually with a money drawer, that registers visibly the amount of each sale

**cas·ing** (kās'iŋ) *n.* 1. a protective covering; specif., *a)* a membrane used to encase processed meats *b)* a pneumatic rubber tire exclusive of an inner tube and often of the tread *c)* the steel pipe used to line an oil or gas well 2. a frame, as of a window or door

**ca·si·no** (kə sē'nō) *n., pl.* **-nos** [It., dim. of *casa,* house < L., hut] 1. a room or building for dancing, or, esp., gambling 2. *same as* CASSINO

**cask** (kask, käsk) *n.* [< Fr. *casque* < Sp. *casco,* ult. < L. *quassare:* see QUASH²] 1. a barrel of any size, made of staves, esp. one for liquids 2. the contents of a full cask; barrelful

**cas·ket** (kas'kit) *n.* [prob. < OFr. dim. of *casse* (see CASE²)] 1. a small box or chest, as for valuables 2. a coffin —*vt.* to put into a casket

**Cas·pi·an Sea** (kas'pē ən) inland sea between Caucasia and Asiatic U.S.S.R. —**Cas'pi·an** *adj.*

---

**casque** (kask) *n.* [Fr.: see CASK] a helmet —**casqued** (kaskt) *adj.*

**cas·sa·ba** (kə sä′bə) *n. same as* CASABA

**Cas·san·dra** (kə san′drə) *Gr. Myth.* Priam's daughter: Apollo gave her prophetic power but decreed no one should believe her prophecies —*n.* a person whose warnings of misfortune are disregarded

**cas·sa·va** (kə sä′və) *n.* [< Fr. < Sp. < native Indian *casávi*] **1.** any of several tropical American plants with edible starchy roots **2.** a starch taken from the root, used to make bread and tapioca

**cas·se·role** (kas′ə rōl′) *n.* [Fr., dim. of *casse*, a bowl < Pr. < VL. < Gr. dim. of *kyathos*, a bowl] **1.** an earthenware or glass baking dish, often with a cover, in which food can be cooked and served **2.** the food baked in such a dish

**cas·sette** (ka set′, kə-) *n.* [Fr., dim. < ONormFr. *casse*, a CASE²] **1.** a case with roll film in it, for loading a camera quickly and easily **2.** a similar case with magnetic tape, for use in a tape recorder

**cas·sia** (kash′ə) *n.* [< L. < Gr. *kasia*, kind of cinnamon < Heb. *qeṣīʿāh*] **1.** *a)* the bark (**cassia bark**) of a tree native to SE Asia: used as a source of cinnamon *b)* this tree **2.** *a)* any of a genus of herbs, shrubs, etc. of the legume family, common in tropical countries: the pods (**cassia pods**) of some of these plants have a mildly laxative pulp (**cassia pulp**); from others the drug senna is extracted *b)* cassia pods *c)* cassia pulp

**cas·si·mere** (kas′ə mir′) *n.* [var. of CASHMERE] a woolen cloth, twilled or plain, used for men's suits

**cas·si·no** (kə sē′nō) *n.* [see CASINO] a simple card game for two to four players

**Cas·si·o·pe·ia** (kas′ē ə pē′ə) **1.** *Gr. Myth.* the mother of Andromeda **2.** a N constellation near Andromeda

**Cassiopeia's Chair** five stars in the constellation Cassiopeia, supposedly outlining a chair

**Cas·si·us** (Longinus) (kash′əs, kas′ē əs), (Gaius) ?–42 B.C.; Rom. general & conspirator against Caesar

**cas·sock** (kas′ək) *n.* [< Fr. < Per. *kazhāghand*, a jacket < *kazh*, raw silk] a long, closefitting vestment, usually black, worn as an outer garment or under the surplice by clergymen, choristers, etc.

**cas·so·war·y** (kas′ə wer′ē) *n., pl.* -**war′ies** [Malay *kasuāri*] any of a genus of large, flightless birds of Australia and New Guinea, somewhat like the ostrich, but smaller

**cast** (kast) *vt.* **cast, cast′ing** [< ON. *kasta*, to throw] **1.** to throw with force; fling; hurl **2.** to deposit (a ballot or vote) **3.** *a)* to cause to fall or turn; direct [to *cast* one's eyes on a thing] *b)* to give forth [to *cast* light, gloom, etc.] **4.** to throw out or drop (a net, anchor, etc.) at the end of a rope or cable **5.** to throw out (a fly, etc.) at the end of a fishing line **6.** to draw (lots) or shake (dice) out of a container **7.** to throw off; shed [the snake *casts* its skin] **8.** to add up (accounts) **9.** to calculate (a horoscope, tides, etc.) **10.** to formulate **11.** *a)* to form (molten metal, plastic, etc.) by pouring or pressing into a mold *b)* to make by such a method **12.** *a)* to choose actors for (a play or movie) *b)* to select (an actor) for (a role) —*vi.* **1.** to throw dice **2.** to throw out a fly, etc. on a fishing line —*n.* **1.** a casting; a throw; specif., *a)* a throw of dice; also, the number thrown *b)* a turn of the eye; glance; look *c)* a throw of a fishing line, net, etc. **2.** a quantity or thing cast in a certain way; specif., *a)* something formed in a mold, as a statue; also, the mold *b)* a mold taken of an object *c)* a plaster form to immobilize a broken arm, leg, etc. *d)* the set of actors in a play or movie **3.** the form in which a thing is cast; specif., *a)* an appearance, as of features *b)* kind; quality *c)* a tinge; shade [a reddish *cast*] *d)* a turn or twist to one side *e)* a slight turning in or out of the eye —**cast about 1.** to search (*for*) **2.** to devise —**cast aside** (or **away**) to discard —**cast back** to refer to something past —**cast down 1.** to turn downward **2.** to sadden; discourage —**cast off 1.** to discard; disown **2.** to set free **3.** to free a ship from a dock, quay, etc., as by releasing the lines **4.** *Knitting* to make the last row of stitches —**cast on** *Knitting* to make the first row of stitches —**cast out** to expel —**cast up 1.** to throw up **2.** to turn upward **3.** to total **4.** to construct by digging [to *cast up* earthworks]

**cas·ta·nets** (kas′tə nets′) *n.pl.* [< Fr. < Sp. *castañeta*, dim. < L. *castanea*, chestnut: from the shape] a pair of small, hollowed pieces of hard wood, ivory, etc. held in the hand and clicked together in time to music, esp. in Spanish dances

**cast·a·way** (kas′tə wā′) *n.* **1.** a person or thing cast out or off, esp. an outcast **2.** a shipwrecked person —*adj.* **1.** thrown away; discarded **2.** cast adrift or stranded, as by shipwreck

**caste** (kast) *n.* [Fr. < Port. *casta*, a breed < L. *castus*, pure] **1.** any of the distinct, hereditary Hindu social classes, each by tradition, but no longer officially, excluded from social dealings with the others

CASTANETS

**2.** any exclusive social or occupational class or group **3.** rigid class distinction based on birth, wealth, etc., operating as a social system or principle **4.** any of the differentiated types of social insects in a colony —**lose caste** to lose social status or rank

**cas·tel·lat·ed** (kas′tə lāt′id) *adj.* [< ML. < L. *castellum*, CASTLE] built with turrets and battlements, like a castle —**cas′tel·la′tion** *n.*

**cast·er** (kas′tər) *n.* **1.** a person or thing that casts **2.** *a)* a small bottle or container for serving vinegar, salt, etc. at the table *b)* a stand for holding such containers **3.** a wheel or freely rolling ball set in a frame and attached to each leg, bottom corner, etc. of a piece of furniture, etc. so that it can be moved easily

**cas·ti·gate** (kas′tə gāt′) *vt.* -**gat′ed**, -**gat′ing** [< L. pp. of *castigare*, to purify, chastise < *castus*, pure] to punish or rebuke severely, esp. by public criticism —**cas′ti·ga′tion** *n.* —**cas′ti·ga′tor** *n.* —**cas′ti·ga·to′ry** (-gə tôr′ē) *adj.*

**Cas·tile** (kas tēl′) region and former kingdom in N and C Spain

**Castile soap** [< *Castile*, where first made] [*also* c- s-] a fine, mild, hard soap made from olive oil and sodium hydroxide

**Cas·til·ian** (kas til′yən) *adj.* of Castile, its people, language, or culture —*n.* **1.** a native or inhabitant of Castile **2.** the dialect spoken in Castile, now the standard form of Spanish

**cast·ing** (kas′tiŋ) *n.* **1.** the action of one that casts **2.** anything, esp. of metal, that has been cast in a mold **3.** *Zool.* anything thrown off, excreted, etc.

**casting vote** (or **voice**) the deciding vote cast by the presiding officer in the event of a tie

**cast-i·ron** (kast′ī′ərn) *adj.* **1.** made of cast iron **2.** very hard, rigid, strong, healthy, etc.

**cast iron** a hard, unmalleable alloy of iron made by casting: it has a high proportion of carbon

**cas·tle** (kas′'l) *n.* [< OE. & Anglo-Fr. < L. *castellum*, dim. of *castrum*, fort] **1.** a large building or group of buildings fortified with thick walls, turrets, and often a moat: castles were strongholds for noblemen in the Middle Ages **2.** any massive dwelling like this **3.** a safe, secure place **4.** *Chess same as* ROOK² —*vt.* -**tled**, -**tling 1.** to furnish with a castle **2.** *Chess* to move (a king) two squares to either side and then, in the same move, set the castle in the square skipped by the king —*vi. Chess* **1.** to castle a king **2.** to be castled: said of a king

**castle in the air** an imaginary scheme unlikely to be realized; daydream: also **castle in Spain**

**cast·off** (kast′ôf′) *adj.* thrown away; discarded —*n.* a person or thing cast off

**Cas·tor** (kas′tər) **1.** *Gr. & Rom. Myth.* the mortal twin of Pollux **2.** one of the two bright stars in the constellation Gemini

**cas·tor¹** (kas′tər) *n.* [Fr. < L. < Gr. *kastōr*, beaver] **1.** a strong-smelling, oily substance obtained from the beaver used in perfumery: also **cas·to′re·um** (-tôr′ē əm) **2.** a hat of beaver or rabbit fur

**cas·tor²** (kas′tər) *n. same as* CASTER (senses 2 & 3)

**cas·tor-oil plant** (kas′tər oil′) a tropical plant with large, beanlike seeds (**castor beans**) from which oil (**castor oil**) is extracted: this oil is used as a cathartic and lubricant

**cas·trate** (kas′trāt) *vt.* -**trat·ed**, -**trat·ing** [< L. *castratus*, pp. of *castrare*] **1.** to remove the testicles of; emasculate; geld **2.** to deprive of real vigor or meaning by mutilation, expurgation, etc.; emasculate —**cas·tra′tion** *n.*

**cast steel** steel formed by casting, not by rolling or forging —**cast′-steel′** *adj.*

**cas·u·al** (kazh′ōō wəl) *adj.* [< OFr. < LL. *casualis*, by chance < L. *casus*, chance] **1.** happening or governed by chance; not planned [a *casual* visit] **2.** happening, active, etc. at irregular intervals; occasional [a *casual* worker] **3.** slight or superficial [a *casual* acquaintance] **4.** careless or nonchalant **5.** *a)* informal or relaxed [a *casual* atmosphere] *b)* designed for informal occasions or use [*casual* clothes] —*n.* **1.** one who does something only occasionally or temporarily, esp. a casual worker **2.** [*pl.*] shoes, clothes, etc. for informal occasions **3.** *Mil.* a person temporarily attached to a unit —**cas′u·al·ly** *adv.* —**cas′u·al·ness** *n.*

**cas·u·al·ty** (kazh′əl tē, -ōō wəl-) *n., pl.* -**ties** [see prec.] **1.** an accident, esp. a fatal one **2.** a member of the armed forces killed, wounded, captured, etc. **3.** anyone hurt or killed in an accident **4.** anything lost, destroyed, or made useless by some unfortunate or unforeseen happening

**cas·u·ist** (kazh′ōō wist) *n.* [< Fr. < L. *casus*, CASE¹] a person expert in, or apt to resort to, casuistry —**cas′u·is′tic, cas′u·is′ti·cal** *adj.* —**cas′u·is′ti·cal·ly** *adv.*

**cas·u·ist·ry** (kazh′ōō wis trē) *n., pl.* -**ries** [prec. + -RY] **1.** the solving of specific cases of right and wrong in conduct by applying general principles of ethics **2.** subtle but misleading or false reasoning, esp. about moral issues; sophistry

‡**ca·sus bel·li** (kā′səs bel′ī) [L.] an event provoking war or used as a pretext to make war

**cat** (kat) *n., pl.* **cats, cat:** see PLURAL, II, D, 1 [OE.] **1.** any of a family of flesh-eating, predacious mammals, including the lion, tiger, leopard, etc.; *specif.*, a small, lithe, soft-furred animal of this family, often kept as a pet or for killing mice **2.** a person regarded as a cat in some way, esp. a woman who makes spiteful remarks **3.** *same as* CAT-O'-NINE-TAILS **4.** a catfish **5.** [C-] *same as* CATERPILLAR (tractor) **6.** [Slang] *a)* a jazz musician or enthusiast *b)* any person, esp. a man **7.** *Naut.* tackle to hoist an anchor to the cathead —*vt.* **cat′ted, cat′ting** to hoist (an anchor) to the cathead —**let the cat out of the bag** to let a secret be found out

**cat.** **1.** catalog **2.** catechism

**cat·a-** (kat′ə) [< Gr. *kata,* down] *a prefix meaning:* **1.** down, downward [*catabolism*] **2.** away, completely [*catalysis*] **3.** against [*catapult*] Also, before a vowel, **cat-**

**cat·ab·o·lism** (kə tab′ə liz'm) *n.* [< CATA- + Gr. *ballein,* to throw + -ISM] the process in a plant or animal by which living tissue is changed into waste products of a simpler composition; destructive metabolism: opposed to ANABOLISM —**cat·a·bol·ic** (kat′ə bäl′ik) *adj.*

**ca·tab·o·lize** (-līz′) *vi., vt.* **-lized′, -liz′ing** to change by catabolism

**cat·a·chre·sis** (kat′ə krē′sis) *n., pl.* **-ses** (-sēz) [L. < Gr. < *kata-,* against + *chrēsthai,* to use] incorrect use of a word or words —**cat′a·chres′tic** (-kres′tik), **cat′a·chres′ti·cal** *adj.* —**cat′a·chres′ti·cal·ly** *adv.*

**cat·a·clysm** (kat′ə kliz'm) *n.* [< L. < Gr. < *kata-,* down + *klyzein,* to wash] **1.** a great flood; deluge **2.** any great upheaval or sudden, violent change, as an earthquake, war, etc. —**cat′a·clys′mic** (-kliz′mik), **cat′a·clys′mal** *adj.*

**cat·a·comb** (kat′ə kōm′) *n.* [< LL. *catacumba* < L. < *cata* (< Gr. *kata*), by + *tumba,* TOMB] any of a series of galleries in an underground burial place: *usually used in pl.*

**cat·a·falque** (kat′ə falk′, -fôlk′) *n.* [Fr. < It. < L. *cata* (< Gr. *kata*), by + *fala,* a scaffold] a wooden framework, usually draped, on which the body in a coffin awaiting burial lies in state

**Cat·a·lan** (kat′'l an′, -'l ən) *adj.* of Catalonia, its people, or their language —*n.* **1.** a native or inhabitant of Catalonia **2.** the Romance language of Catalonia, closely akin to Provençal

**cat·a·lep·sy** (kat′'l ep′sē) *n.* [< LL. < Gr. *katalēpsis,* a seizing < *kata-,* down + *lambanein,* to seize] a condition in which consciousness and feeling are suddenly and temporarily lost, and the muscles become rigid: it may occur in epilepsy, schizophrenia, etc. —**cat′a·lep′tic** *adj., n.*

**cat·a·lo** (kat′'l ō′) *n., pl.* **-loes′, -los′** (BUFF)ALO] an animal bred by crossing the American buffalo, or bison, with domestic cattle

**cat·a·log, cat·a·logue** (kat′'l ôg′, -äg′) *n.* [Fr. < LL. *catalogus,* list < Gr. < *kata,* down + *legein,* to count] a complete list; esp., *a)* an alphabetical card file, as of the books in a library *b)* a list of things exhibited, articles for sale, school courses offered, etc., usually with comments and illustrations *c)* a book or pamphlet with such a list —*vt., vi.* **-loged′** or **-logued′, -log′ing** or **-logu′ing** **1.** to enter in a catalog **2.** to make a catalog of —**cat′a·log′er** or **cat′a·logu′er, cat′a·log′ist** or **cat′a·logu′ist** *n.*

**Cat·a·lo·ni·a** (kat′'l ō′nē ə) region in NE Spain, on the Mediterranean —**Cat′a·lo′ni·an** *adj., n.*

**ca·tal·pa** (kə tal′pə) *n.* [< AmInd. (Creek) *kutuhlpa*] a tree of America and Asia with large, heart-shaped leaves, showy trumpet-shaped flowers, and slender, beanlike pods

**ca·tal·y·sis** (kə tal′ə sis) *n., pl.* **-ses′** (-sēz′) [Gr. *katalysis,* dissolution < *kata-,* down + *lyein,* to loose] the speeding up or, sometimes, slowing down of the rate of a chemical reaction by the addition of some substance which itself undergoes no permanent chemical change thereby

**cat·a·lyst** (kat′'l ist) *n.* **1.** any substance serving as the agent in catalysis **2.** a person or thing that is a stimulus in producing or hastening results —**cat′a·lyt′ic** *adj., n.* —**cat′a·lyt′i·cal·ly** *adv.*

**catalytic converter** a device that is part of the exhaust system of an automotive vehicle and contains a chemical catalyst to reduce polluting emissions

**cat·a·lyze** (kat′'l īz′) *vt.* **-lyzed′, -lyz′ing** to change or bring about as a catalyst —**cat′a·lyz′er** *n.*

**cat·a·ma·ran** (kat′ə mə ran′) *n.* [Tamil *kaṭṭumaram* < *kaṭṭu,* tie + *maram,* log] **1.** a log raft or float propelled by sails or paddles **2.** a boat with two parallel hulls

**cat·a·mount** (kat′ə mount′) *n.* [< CAT + obs. *a,* of + MOUNT(AIN)] any of various wildcats; esp., *a)* the puma; cougar *b)* the lynx

**Ca·ta·nia** (kä tä′nyä; *E.* kə tän′yə) seaport on the E coast of Sicily: pop. 407,000

**cat·a·pult** (kat′ə pult′, -poolt′) *n.* [< L. < Gr. *katapeltēs* < *kata-,* down + *pallein,* to hurl] **1.** an ancient military device for throwing or shooting stones, spears, etc. **2.** a slingshot **3.** a mechanism for launching an airplane, rocket, etc., as from a ship's deck —*vt.* to shoot from or as from a catapult; hurl —*vi.* to be catapulted; leap

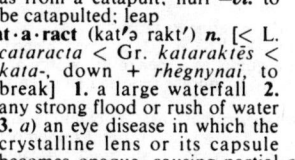

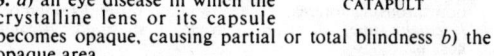

**cat·a·ract** (kat′ə rakt′) *n.* [< L. *cataracta* < Gr. *kataraktēs* < *kata-,* down + *rhēgnynai,* to break] **1.** a large waterfall **2.** any strong flood or rush of water **3.** *a)* an eye disease in which the crystalline lens or its capsule becomes opaque, causing partial or total blindness *b)* the opaque area

**ca·tarrh** (kə tär′) *n.* [< Fr. < LL. < Gr. < *kata-,* down + *rhein,* to flow] inflammation of a mucous membrane, esp. of the nose or throat, causing an increased flow of mucus: a term not now in use —**ca·tarrh′al, ca·tarrh′ous** *adj.*

**ca·tas·tro·phe** (kə tas′trə fē) *n.* [< L. < Gr. *katastrophē,* an overthrowing < *kata-,* down + *strephein,* to turn] **1.** the culminating event of a drama, esp. of a tragedy, by which the plot is resolved **2.** a disastrous end **3.** any sudden, great disaster **4.** a total failure —**cat·a·stroph·ic** (kat′ə sträf′ik) *adj.* —**cat′a·stroph′i·cal·ly** *adv.*

**cat·a·ton·ic** (kat′ə tän′ik) *adj.* [< CATA- + Gr. *tonos,* tension] of or in a state of schizophrenia marked esp. by stupor or catalepsy

**Ca·taw·ba** (kə tô′bə) *n.* [after name of a Choctaw Indian tribe] [*often c-*] **1.** a reddish grape of the E U.S. **2.** a wine made from this grape

**cat·bird** (kat′burd′) *n.* a slate-gray N. American songbird with a black crown and tail: its call is similar in sound to the mew of a cat

**cat·boat** (-bōt′) *n.* a catrigged sailboat, usually having a centerboard

**cat burglar** [Slang] a burglar who climbs up to openings in upper stories, roofs, etc. to enter

**cat·call** (-kôl′) *n.* a shrill shout or whistle expressing derision or disapproval, as of a speaker, actor, etc. —*vt., vi.* to make catcalls (at)

**catch** (kach, kech) *vt.* **caught, catch′ing** [< Anglo-Fr. *cachier* < VL. < L. *captare,* to try to seize < pp. of *capere,* to take] **1.** to seize and hold, as after a chase; capture **2.** to take by or as by a trap, snare, etc. **3.** to deceive; ensnare **4.** to surprise in the act [to be *caught* stealing] **5.** to hit [the blow *caught* him in the eye] **6.** to get to in time [to *catch* a train] **7.** to lay hold of; grab [to *catch* a ball] **8.** *a)* to get as by chance or quickly [to *catch* a glimpse] *b)* [Colloq.] to manage to see, hear, etc. [to *catch* a newscast] **9.** to get as by exposure to others infected [to *catch* the mumps] **10.** *a)* to understand; apprehend *b)* to show an understanding of by depicting [the statue *catches* her beauty] **11.** to captivate; charm **12.** to cause to be entangled [to *catch* one's heel in a rug] **13.** *Baseball* to act as catcher for (a specified pitcher) —*vi.* **1.** to become held, fastened, or entangled **2.** to take fire or start burning **3.** to take and keep hold, as a lock **4.** to act as a catcher —*n.* **1.** the act of catching **2.** a thing that catches or holds **3.** the person or thing caught **4.** the amount caught **5.** a person worth catching, esp. as a husband or wife **6.** a snatch, scrap, or bit [*catches* of old tunes] **7.** an emotional break in the voice **8.** a simple game of throwing and catching a ball **9.** [Colloq.] a hidden qualification; tricky condition [a *catch* in his offer] **10.** *Music* a round for three or more voices **11.** *Sports* a catching [of a ball in a specified manner] —*adj.* **1.** tricky; deceptive [a *catch* question on an exam] **2.** attracting or meant to attract attention or interest —**catch as catch can** with any hold, approach, etc.: orig. said of a style of wrestling —**catch at 1.** to try to catch **2.** to reach for eagerly —**catch it** [Colloq.] to receive a scolding or other punishment —**catch on 1.** to understand **2.** to become fashionable, popular, etc. —**catch oneself** to hold oneself back abruptly from saying or doing something —**catch up 1.** to take up suddenly; snatch **2.** to show to be in error **3.** to heckle **4.** to come up even, as by hurrying or by extra work **5.** to fasten in loops —**catch up on** to engage in more (work, sleep, etc.) so as to compensate for earlier neglect

**catch·all** (-ôl′) *n.* a place for holding all sorts of things [one drawer was a *catchall*]

**catch basin** a sievelike device at the entrance to a sewer to catch, or stop, bulky matter

**catch·er** (-ər) *n.* **1.** one that catches **2.** *Baseball* the player stationed behind home plate, who catches pitched balls not hit away by the batter

**catch·fly** (-flī′) *n., pl.* **-flies′** *same as* CAMPION

**catch·ing** (-iŋ) *adj.* **1.** contagious; infectious **2.** attractive; catchy

**catch·pen·ny** (-pen′ē) *adj.* cheap and flashy; worthless —*n., pl.* **-nies** a catchpenny commodity

**catch phrase** a phrase that catches or is meant to catch popular attention

**catch·up** (kech′əp, kach′-) *n. same as* KETCHUP

**catch·word** (kach′wʉrd′, kech′-) *n.* **1.** a word placed to catch attention and be a guide, as either of the words at the top of this page **2.** a word or phrase repeated so often that it becomes a slogan

**catch·y** (-ē) *adj.* **catch′i·er, catch′i·est 1.** catching attention; arousing interest **2.** easily taken up and remembered [a *catchy* tune] **3.** meant to trick **4.** spasmodic —**catch′i·ness** *n.*

**cat·e·chet·i·cal** (kat′ə ket′i k'l) *adj.* **1.** of or like a catechism **2.** teaching by questions and answers Also **cat′e·chet′ic** —**cat′e·chet′i·cal·ly** *adv.*

**cat·e·chism** (kat′ə kiz'm) *n.* [< LL. < Gr. < *katēchizein,* to catechize < *kata-,* thoroughly + *ēchein,* to sound] **1.** a handbook of questions and answers for teaching the principles of a religion **2.** any similar handbook for teaching the fundamentals of a subject **3.** a series of questions; close questioning —**cat′e·chis′mal** *adj.* —**cat′e·chis′tic** (-kis′tik), **cat′e·chis′ti·cal** *adj.*

**cat·e·chist** (-kist) *n.* a person who catechizes

**cat·e·chize** (-kīz′) *vt.* **-chized′, -chiz′ing** [see CATECHISM] **1.** to teach (esp. religion) by the use of questions and answers **2.** to question searchingly Also sp. **cat′e·chise′** —**cat′e·chi·za′tion** *n.* —**cat′e·chiz′er** *n.*

**cat·e·chu** (kat′ə chōō′) *n.* [Malay *kachu*] a water-soluble, astringent substance obtained from several Asiatic trees: used in dyeing, tanning, etc.

**cat·e·chu·men** (kat′ə kyōō′mən) *n.* [< LL. < Gr. *katēchoumenos:* see CATECHISM] a person being instructed in Christian fundamentals before baptism or confirmation

**cat·e·gor·i·cal** (kat′ə gôr′i k'l, -gär′-) *adj.* **1.** unqualified; unconditional; absolute; positive: said of a statement, theory, etc. **2.** of, as, or in a category Also **cat′e·gor′ic** —**cat′e·gor′i·cal·ly** *adv.*

**cat·e·go·rize** (kat′ə gə rīz′) *vt.* **-rized′, -riz′ing** to place in a category —**cat′e·go·ri·za′tion** *n.*

**cat·e·go·ry** (kat′ə gôr′ē) *n., pl.* **-ries** [< LL. < Gr. < *katēgorein,* to accuse < *kata-,* against + *agoreuein,* to declaim] **1.** a class or division in a scheme of classification **2.** *Logic* any of the basic concepts into which knowledge is classified

**cat·e·nate** (kat′'n āt′) *vt.* **-nat′ed, -nat′ing** [< L. < *catena,* chain] to form into a chain or series; link —**cat′e·na′tion** *n.*

**ca·ter** (kā′tər) *vi.* [< OFr. < *achater,* to buy, ult. < L. *ad-,* to + *capere,* to take] **1.** to provide food; act as a caterer **2.** to seek to gratify another's desires (with *to*) —*vt.* to serve as caterer for (a banquet, party, etc.)

**cat·er-cor·nered** (kat′ē kôr′nərd, kit′-) *adj.* [ME. *cater,* four (ult. < L. *quattuor,* FOUR) + CORNERED] diagonal —*adv.* diagonally Also **cat′er-cor′ner**

**ca·ter·er** (kāt′ər ər) *n.* one who caters; esp., one whose business is providing food and service as for parties

**cat·er·pil·lar** (kat′ər pil′ər, kat′ə-) *n.* [< ONormFr. *catepilose* < L. *catta pilosa,* hairy cat] the wormlike larva of various insects, esp. of a butterfly or moth —**[C-]** *a trademark for* a tractor having on each side an endless roller belt over cogged wheels, to move over rough or muddy ground

**cat·er·waul** (kat′ər wôl′) *vi.* [ME. *cater* (prob. < MDu. *kater,* tomcat) + *w(r)awlen, v.,* prob. echoic] to make a shrill, howling sound like that of a cat; wail; scream —*n.* such a sound

**cat·fish** (kat′fish′) *n., pl.* **-fish′, -fish′es:** see FISH any of a group of scaleless fishes with long barbels about the mouth

**cat·gut** (-gut′) *n.* [CAT + GUT: reason for *cat* unc.] a tough thread made from dried intestines, as of sheep, and used for surgical sutures, musical instruments, etc.

**cath-** (kath) *same as* CATA-: used before an aspirate

**Cath. 1.** Catholic **2.** [*also* c-] cathedral

**ca·thar·sis** (kə thär′sis) *n.* [ModL. < Gr. < *katharsis* < *katharos,* pure] **1.** purgation, esp. of the bowels **2.** the purifying or relieving of the emotions, esp. by art **3.** *Psychiatry* the relieving of fears, problems, etc. by bringing them to consciousness or giving them expression

**ca·thar·tic** (-tik) *adj.* of or effecting catharsis; purging: also **ca·thar′ti·cal** —*n.* a medicine for purging the bowels

**Ca·thay** (ka thā′, ka-) *poet. or archaic name of* CHINA

**cat·head** (kat′hed′) *n.* a projecting beam near the bow of a ship, to which the anchor is fastened

**ca·the·dra** (kə thē′drə, kath′i-) *n.* [LL. < L. < Gr. *kathedra* < *kata-,* down + *hedra,* a seat] **1.** the bishop's throne in a cathedral **2.** the episcopal see See EX CATHEDRA

**ca·the·dral** (kə thē′drəl) *n.* **1.** the main church of a bishop's see, containing the cathedra **2.** loosely, any large, imposing church —*adj.* **1.** of, like, or containing a cathedra **2.** official **3.** of or like a cathedral

**Cath·er·ine** (kath′rin, -ər in) [Fr. < L. *Catharina* < Gr. *Aikaterinē;* infl. by *katharos,* pure] **1.** a feminine name: dim. *Cathy, Kate, Kit, Kitty* **2. Catherine II** 1729–96; German-born empress of Russia (1762–96): called **Catherine the Great**

**cath·e·ter** (kath′ə tər) *n.* [LL. < Gr. *kathetēr* < *kata-,* down + *hienai,* to send] a slender tube inserted into a body passage, etc. for passing fluids, making examinations, etc., esp. for draining urine from the bladder

**cath·e·ter·ize** (-īz′) *vt.* **-ized′, -iz′ing** to insert a catheter into —**cath′e·ter·i·za′tion** *n.*

**cath·ode** (kath′ōd) *n.* [< Gr. *kathodos,* descent < *kata-,* down + *hodos,* way] **1.** in an electrolytic cell, the negative electrode, from which current flows **2.** in a vacuum tube, the negatively charged electron emitter **3.** the positive terminal of a battery —**ca·thod′ic** (ka thäd′ik) *adj.*

**cathode rays** streams of electrons projected from the surface of a cathode: cathode rays produce X-rays when they strike solids

**cathode-ray tube** a vacuum tube in which the electrons can be focused on a fluorescent screen, producing a visible pattern on the exterior face: used as oscilloscopes, television picture tubes, etc.

**cath·o·lic** (kath′ə lik, kath′lik) *adj.* [L. *catholicus,* universal < Gr. < *kata-,* completely + *holos,* whole] **1.** of general scope or value; all inclusive; universal **2.** broad in sympathies, tastes, etc.; liberal **3.** [*often* C-] of the universal Christian church **4.** [C-] of the Christian church headed by the Pope; Roman Catholic —*n.* **1.** [*often* C-] a member of the universal Christian church **2.** [C-] *same as* ROMAN CATHOLIC —**ca·thol·i·cal·ly** (kə thäl′i k'l ē, -ik lē) *adv.*

**Ca·thol·i·cism** (kə thäl′ə siz'm) *n.* the doctrine, faith, practice, and organization of a Catholic church, esp. of the Roman Catholic Church

**cath·o·lic·i·ty** (kath′ə lis′ə tē) *n.* **1.** broadness of taste, sympathy, etc.; liberality, as of ideas **2.** universality **3.** [C-] Catholicism

**ca·thol·i·cize** (kə thäl′ə sīz′) *vt., vi.* **-cized′, -ciz′ing 1.** to make or become catholic **2.** [C-] to convert or be converted to Catholicism

**cat·i·on** (kat′ī′ən) *n.* [coined by Faraday < Gr. < *kata,* down + *ion,* prp. of *ienai,* to go] a positive ion: in electrolysis, cations move toward the cathode —**cat·i·on·ic** (kat′ī än′ik) *adj.*

**cat·kin** (kat′kin) *n.* [< Du. dim. of *katte,* cat] a drooping, scaly spike of unisexual flowers without petals, as on poplars or walnuts; ament

**cat·nap** (kat′nap′) *n.* a short, light sleep; doze —*vi.* **-napped′, -nap′ping** to take a catnap

**cat·nip** (-nip′) *n.* [CAT + *nip* (dial. for catnip) < L. *nepeta*] a plant of the mint family, with downy leaves and bluish flowers: cats like its odor

**Ca·to** (kāt′ō) **1.** (Marcus Porcius), 234–149 B.C.; Rom. statesman: called *the Elder* **2.** (Marcus Porcius), 95–46 B.C.; Rom. statesman & Stoic philosopher: great-grandson of *prec.:* called *the Younger*

**cat-o'-nine-tails** (kat′ə nīn′tālz′) *n., pl.* **-tails′** a whip made of nine knotted cords attached to a handle, formerly used for flogging

**cat rig** a rig, esp. of a catboat, consisting of one large sail on a mast well forward in the bow —**cat′rigged′** (-rigd′) *adj.*

**CAT scan** (kat) [c(*omputerized*) a(*xial*) t(*omography*)] tomography is an X-ray technique] **1.** a method for diagnosing disorders of the soft tissues, esp. of the brain: it uses a computerized combination of many X-rays to form an image **2.** the image —**CAT scanner —CAT scanning**

**cat's cradle** a child's game in which a string looped over the fingers is transferred back and forth on the hands of the players to form designs

**cat's-eye** (kats′ī′) *n.* any gem, stone, etc. that reflects light in a way suggestive of a cat's eye, as a child's marble, a glass reflector, etc.

**Cats·kill Mountains** (kat′skil′) [Du., cat stream] mountain range in SE N.Y.: also **Cats′kills′**

**cat's-paw** (kats′pô′) *n.* **1.** a person used by another to do distasteful or unlawful work; dupe **2.** a light breeze rippling the surface of water

**cat·sup** (kech′əp, kat′səp; kat′səp) *n. same as* KETCHUP

**cat·tail** (kat′tāl′) *n.* a tall marsh plant with reedlike leaves and long, brown, fuzzy, cylindrical flower spikes

**cat·ta·lo** (kat′'l ō′) *n., pl.* **-loes′, -los′** *same as* CATALO

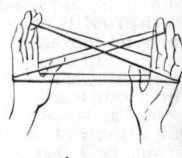

CAT'S CRADLE

cat·tish (kat'ish) *adj.* 1. like a cat; feline 2. *same as* CATTY —cat'tish·ly *adv.* —cat'tish·ness *n.*

cat·tle (kat'l) *n.* [< Anglo-Fr. *catel* < ML. *captale*, property < L. < *caput*, the head] 1. [Archaic] farm animals 2. domesticated bovine animals collectively; cows, bulls, steers, or oxen 3. people in the mass: contemptuous term

cat·tle·man (-mən) *n., pl.* -men a man who tends cattle or raises them for market

cat·ty (kat'ē) *adj.* -ti·er, -ti·est 1. of or like a cat 2. spiteful, mean, malicious, etc. —cat'ti·ly *adv.* —cat'ti·ness *n.*

cat·ty-cor·nered (kat'ē kôr'nərd, kit'-) *adj., adv. same as* CATER-CORNERED: also cat'ty-cor'ner

cat·walk (kat'wôk') *n.* a high, narrow walk, as along the edge of a bridge or over a machine

Cau·ca·sia (kô kā'zhə) *same as* CAUCASUS (sense 1)

Cau·ca·sian (kô kā'zhən) *adj.* 1. of the Caucasus, its people, their languages, etc. 2. *same as* CAUCASOID Also Cau·cas'ic (-kas'ik) —*n.* 1. a native of the Caucasus 2. *same as* CAUCASOID 3. the Caucasian languages; Circassian, Georgian, etc.

Cau·ca·soid (kôk'ə soid') *adj.* [from the erroneous notion that the original home of the hypothetical Indo-Europeans was the Caucasus] designating or of one of the major groups of mankind that includes the native peoples of Europe, North Africa, the Near East, India, etc.: loosely called the *white race*, although skin color varies —*n.* a member of the Caucasoid group

Cau·ca·sus (kôk'ə səs) 1. region in SE European U.S.S.R., between the Black Sea and the Caspian: often called the Caucasus 2. mountain range in this region: in full, Caucasus Mountains

cau·cus (kôk'əs) *n.* [< ? *Caucus* Club, 18th-c. social and political club; ult. < MGr. *kaukos*, drinking cup] a private meeting of leaders or a committee of a political party or faction to decide on policy, candidates, etc., esp. prior to an open meeting —*vi.* -cused or -cussed, -cus·ing or -cus·sing to hold, or take part in, a caucus

cau·dal (kôd'l) *adj.* [< L. *cauda*, tail] 1. of or like a tail 2. at or near the tail —cau'dal·ly *adv.*

cau·date (kô'dāt) *adj.* [< L. *cauda*, tail] having a tail or taillike part: also cau'dat·ed

cau·dle (kôd'l) *n.* [< Anglo-Fr., ult. < L. *cal(i)dus*, warm] a warm drink for invalids; esp., a spiced and sugared gruel with wine or ale added

caught (kôt) *pt. & pp. of* CATCH

caul (kôl) *n.* [OE. *cawl*, basket, net] a membrane sometimes enveloping the head of a child at birth

caul·dron (kôl'drən) *n. same as* CALDRON

cau·li·flow·er (kôl'ə flou'ər, käl'-) *n.* [< It. *cavolfiore*, after L. *caulis*, cabbage] 1. a variety of cabbage with a compact white head of fleshy flower stalks 2. the head of this plant, eaten as a vegetable

cauliflower ear an ear permanently deformed by injuries from repeated blows, as in boxing

cau·lis (kô'lis) *n., pl.* -les (-lēz) [L., akin to Gr. *kaulos*] *Bot.* the main stem of a plant

caulk (kôk) *vt.* [< OFr. < L. *calcare*, to tread < *calx*, a heel] 1. to make (a boat, etc.) watertight by filling the seams or cracks with oakum, tar, etc. 2. to stop up (cracks of window frames, etc.) with a filler —caulk'er *n.*

caus·al (kôz'l) *adj.* 1. of, like, or being a cause 2. relating to cause and effect 3. expressing a cause or reason —caus'al·ly *adv.*

cau·sal·i·ty (kô zal'ə tē) *n., pl.* -ties 1. causal quality or agency 2. the interrelation or principle of cause and effect

cau·sa·tion (kô zā'shən) *n.* 1. the act of causing 2. anything producing an effect; cause 3. causality

caus·a·tive (kôz'ə tiv) *adj.* 1. producing an effect; causing 2. expressing causation, as the verb *fell* (to cause to fall) —*n.* a causative word or form —caus'a·tive·ly *adv.*

cause (kôz) *n.* [< OFr. (or) < L. *causa*] 1. anything producing an effect or result 2. a person or thing that brings about an effect or result 3. a reason, motive, or ground for some action, feeling, etc.; esp., sufficient reason [*cause* for complaint] 4. any objective or movement that a person or group is interested in and supports, esp. one involving social reform 5. *Law* an action or question to be resolved by a court of law —*vt.* caused, caus'ing to be the cause of; bring about; effect —make common cause with to join forces with —caus'a·ble *adj.* —cause'less *adj.*

‡cause cé·lè·bre (kôz' sā leb'r'; *E.* kôz' sə leb') [Fr.] a celebrated law case, trial, or controversy

cause of action *Law* the right by which a party seeks a remedy against another in a court of law

cau·se·rie (kō'zə rē') *n.* [Fr. < *causer*, to chat < VL. < *causari*, to plead < *causa*, cause] 1. an informal talk; chat 2. a short, conversational piece of writing

cause·way (kôz'wā') *n.* [< Brit. dial. *causey*, ult. < L. *calx*, limestone + WAY] 1. a raised path or road, as across a marsh 2. a paved way or road; highway

caus·tic (kôs'tik) *adj.* [< L. < Gr. *kaustikos* < *kaiein*, to burn] 1. that can burn or destroy tissue by chemical action; corrosive 2. cutting or sarcastic in utterance —*n.* any caustic substance —caus'ti·cal·ly *adv.* —caus·tic'i·ty (-tis'ə tē) *n.*

caustic potash *same as* POTASSIUM HYDROXIDE

caustic soda *same as* SODIUM HYDROXIDE

cau·ter·ize (kôt'ər īz') *vt.* -ized', -iz'ing [< LL. < Gr. < *kautērion*, branding iron < *kaiein*, to burn] to burn with a hot iron or needle, or with a caustic substance, so as to destroy dead tissue, etc. —cau'ter·i·za'tion *n.*

cau·ter·y (kôt'ər ē) *n., pl.* -ter·ies 1. an instrument or substance for cauterizing: also cau'ter·ant 2. the act of cauterizing

cau·tion (kô'shən) *n.* [< L. *cautio* < same base as *cavere*, to be wary] 1. a warning; admonition 2. a word, sign, etc. by which warning is given 3. the act or practice of being cautious; wariness 4. [Colloq.] a person or thing provoking notice, etc. —*vt.* to urge to be cautious; warn; admonish

cau·tion·ar·y (-er'ē) *adj.* urging caution; warning

cau·tious (kô'shəs) *adj.* full of caution; careful to avoid danger; circumspect; wary —cau'tious·ly *adv.* —cau'tious·ness *n.*

cav·al·cade (kav'l kād', kav'l kād') *n.* [Fr. < It. < *cavalcare*, to ride < VL. < L. *caballus*, horse, nag] 1. a procession of horsemen or carriages 2. *a)* any procession *b)* a sequence of events, etc.

cav·a·lier (kav'ə lir') *n.* [Fr. < It. *cavaliere* < LL. < L. *caballus*, horse, nag] 1. an armed horseman; knight 2. a gallant gentleman, esp. one serving as a lady's escort 3. [C-] a partisan of Charles I of England in his struggles with Parliament (1641–49); Royalist —*adj.* 1. [C-] of the Cavaliers 2. *a)* free and easy; gay *b)* casual or indifferent toward matters of some importance *c)* haughty; arrogant; supercilious —cav'a·lier'ly *adv., adj.* —cav'a·lier'ness *n.*

cav·al·ry (kav'l rē) *n., pl.* -ries [< Fr. < It. < *cavaliere*: see CAVALIER] combat troops mounted originally on horses but now often on motorized armored vehicles —cav'al·ry·man (-mən) *n., pl.* -men

cave (kāv) *n.* [< OFr. < L. < *cavus*, hollow] a hollow place inside the earth; cavern —*vt.* caved, cav'ing to make a hollow in —*vi.* [Colloq.] 1. to cave in 2. to explore caves —cave in 1. to collapse 2. to make collapse 3. [Colloq.] to give way; give in; yield —cav'er *n.*

ca·ve·at (kā'vē at', kav'ē-; kā'vē ät') *n.* [L., let him beware] 1. *Law* a notice that an interested party files with the proper officers directing them to stop an action until he can be heard 2. a warning

caveat emp·tor (emp'tôr) [L.] let the buyer beware (i.e., one buys at his own risk)

cave-in (kāv'in') *n.* 1. a caving in 2. a place where the ground, a mine, etc. has caved in

cave man 1. a prehistoric human being of the Stone Age who lived in caves: also cave dweller 2. a man who is rough and crudely direct

cav·ern (kav'ərn) *n.* [< Fr. < L. *caverna* < *cavus*, hollow] a cave, esp. a large cave —*vt.* 1. to enclose in or as in a cavern 2. to hollow (out)

cav·ern·ous (kav'ər nəs) *adj.* 1. full of caverns 2. full of cavities; porous 3. like a cavern; deep-set, hollow, etc. —cav'ern·ous·ly *adv.*

cav·i·ar, cav·i·are (kav'ē är', käv'-; kav'ē är') *n.* [Fr. < It. < Turk. < Per. *khaviyār*] the salted eggs of sturgeon, salmon, etc. eaten as an appetizer

cav·il (kav'l) *vi.* -iled or -illed, -il·ing or -il·ling [< OFr. < L. *cavillari* < *cavilla*, a jest] to object when there is little reason; resort to trivial faultfinding; carp (*at* or *about*) —*n.* a trivial objection; quibble —cav'il·er, cav'il·ler *n.*

cav·i·ty (kav'ə tē) *n., pl.* -ties [< Fr. < LL. *cavitas* < L. *cavus*, hollow] 1. a hole or hollow place, as in a tooth 2. a natural hollow place within the body [the abdominal *cavity*]

ca·vort (kə vôrt') *vi.* [< ? ] 1. to leap about; prance or caper 2. to romp about happily; frolic

ca·vy (kā'vē) *n., pl.* -vies [< Carib *cabiai*] any of several short-tailed S. American rodents, as the guinea pig

caw (kô) *n.* [echoic] the harsh, strident cry of a crow or raven —*vi.* to make this sound

Cax·ton (kak'stən), William 1422?–91; 1st Eng. printer

cay (kā, kē) *n.* [Sp. *cayo*: see KEY[2]] a low island, coral reef, or sandbank off a mainland

cay·enne (kī en', kā-) *n.* [< Tupi *kynnha*] a very hot red pepper made from the dried fruit of a pepper plant, esp. of the capsicum: also cayenne pepper

cay·man (kā'mən) *n., pl.* -mans *same as* CAIMAN

at, āpe, cär; ten, ēven; is, bīte; gō, hôrn, tōol, look; oil, out; up, fur; get; joy; yet; chin; she; thin, then; zh, leisure; ŋ, ring; ' for *a* in *ago, e* in *agent, i* in *sanity, o* in *comply, u* in *focus;* ' as in *able* (ā'b'l); Fr. bal; ë, Fr. coeur; ö, Fr. feu; Fr. mon; , Fr. coq; ü, Fr. duc; r, Fr. cri; H, G. ich; kh, G. doch; ‡foreign; *hypothetical; < derived from. See inside front cover.

**Ca·yu·ga** (kā yōō'gə, kī-) *n.* **1.** *pl.* **-gas, -ga** any member of a tribe of Iroquoian Indians who lived around Cayuga Lake and Seneca Lake in N.Y. **2.** their Iroquoian dialect

**Cay·use** (kī'ōōs, kī ōōs') *n., pl.* **-us·es;** for 1 *a,* also **-use 1.** *a)* a member of a tribe of Oregonian Indians *b)* their language **2.** [c-] a small Western horse used by cowboys

**CB** (sē'bē') *adj.* [CITIZENS' BAND] designating or having to do with shortwave radio that uses citizens' band frequencies **—***n., pl.* **CB's** a shortwave radio using citizens' band frequencies

**CBC** Canadian Broadcasting Corporation

**CBS** Columbia Broadcasting System

**cc.chapters**

**cc., c.c.** cubic centimeter(s)

**C.C., c.c.** carbon copy

**CCC** Commodity Credit Corporation

**C clef** *Music* a sign on a staff indicating that C is the note on the third line (*alto clef*) or on the fourth line (*tenor clef*)

**Cd** *Chem.* cadmium

**CD, C.D.** Civil Defense

**CDR, Cdr.** Commander

**Ce** *Chem.* cerium

**C.E. 1.** Church of England **2.** Civil Engineer

**cease** (sēs) *vt., vi.* **ceased, ceas'ing** [< OFr. < L. *cessare* < *cedere,* to yield] to end; stop; discontinue **—***n.* a ceasing: chiefly in **without cease**

**cease-fire** (sēs'fīr') *n.* a temporary cessation of warfare by mutual agreement of the participants

**cease·less** (-lis) *adj.* unceasing; continual **—cease'less·ly** *adv.*

**Ce·bu** (sā bōō') **1.** seaport on an island in the SC Philippines: pop. 310,000 **2.** this island

**Ce·cil** (sēs''l, ses''l) [L. *Caecilius,* prob. < *caecus,* dimsighted, blind] a masculine name

**Ce·cil·ia** (sə sēl'yə) [L. < fem. of *Caecilius:* see prec.] a feminine name: var. **Cecile, Cecily**

**ce·cro·pi·a moth** (si krō'pē ə) [< *Cecrops,* legendary Gr. king] the largest moth of the U.S., having wide wings, each with a crescent-shaped spot

**ce·cum** (sē'kəm) *n., pl.* **-ca** (-kə) [< L. (*intestinum*) *caecum,* blind (intestine)] the pouch that is the beginning of the large intestine **—ce'cal** *adj.*

**ce·dar** (sē'dər) *n.* [< OFr. < L. < Gr. *kedros*] **1.** any of certain coniferous trees of the pine family, having durable, fragrant wood, as the **cedar of Lebanon 2.** any of various trees like this, as the juniper **3.** the wood of any of these **—***adj.* of cedar

**Cedar Rapids** [after the rapids of nearby Cedar River] city in EC Iowa: pop. 110,000

**cedar waxwing** a brownish-gray, crested American bird, with red, waxlike tips on its secondary wing feathers: also **ce'dar·bird'** *n.*

**cede** (sēd) *vt.* **ced'ed, ced'ing** [< Fr. < L. *cedere,* to yield] **1.** to give up one's rights in; surrender **2.** to transfer the title or ownership of

**ce·di** (sā'dē) *n., pl.* **-dis** [< native word *sedie,* cowrie, formerly used as money] *see* MONETARY UNITS, table (Ghana)

**ce·dil·la** (si dil'ə) *n.* [< Fr. < Sp. *cedilla,* dim. of *zeda* (< Gr. *zēta,* zeta)] a hooklike mark put under *c* in some French words (Ex.: *façade*) to show that it is to be sounded like a voiceless *s*

**Ced·ric** (sed'rik, sē'drik) [< ? Celt.] a masculine name

**ceil** (sēl) *vt.* [< OFr. < L. *celare,* to hide; prob. infl. by L. *caelum,* heaven] to build a ceiling in or over

**ceil·ing** (-iŋ) *n.* [< prec.] **1.** the inside top part of a room, opposite the floor **2.** an upper limit set on anything [a ceiling on prices] **3.** *Aeron. a)* a cloud cover limiting vertical visibility, or the height of its lower surface *b)* the maximum height at which an aircraft can normally fly **—hit the ceiling** [Slang] to lose one's temper

**cel·an·dine** (sel'ən dīn', -dēn') *n.* [< OFr. < L. < Gr. *chelidōn,* a swallow] **1.** a weedy plant related to the poppy, with yellow flowers **2.** a plant of the buttercup family, with yellow flowers

**-cele** (sēl) [< Gr. *kēlē*] **1.** *a combining form meaning* tumor, hernia, or swelling **2.** *same as* -COELE

**ce·leb** (sə leb') *n.* clipped form of CELEBRITY (sense 2)

**Cel·e·bes** (sel'ə bēz', sə lē'bēz) island of Indonesia, east of Borneo: 69,277 sq. mi.

**cel·e·brant** (sel'ə brənt) *n.* [see ff.] **1.** a person who performs a religious rite, as the priest officiating at Mass **2.** a celebrator

**cel·e·brate** (-brāt') *vt.* **-brat'ed, -brat'ing** [< L. pp. of *celebrare,* to frequent, honor < *celeber,* populous] **1.** to perform (a ritual, etc.) publicly and formally; solemnize **2.** to commemorate (an anniversary, etc.) with ceremony or festivity **3.** to honor or praise publicly **4.** to mark (a happy occasion) with a pleasurable activity **—***vi.* **1.** to observe a holiday, anniversary, etc. with festivities **2.** to perform a religious ceremony **3.** [Colloq.] to have a good time **—cel'e·bra'tor** *n.* **—ce·leb·ra·to·ry** (sə leb'rə tôr'ē) *adj.*

**cel·e·brat·ed** (-id) *adj.* famous; renowned

**cel·e·bra·tion** (sel'ə brā'shən) *n.* **1.** the act or an instance of celebrating **2.** that which is done to celebrate

**ce·leb·ri·ty** (sə leb'rə tē) *n.* **1.** wide recognition; fame **2.** *pl.* **-ties** a celebrated person

**ce·ler·i·ty** (sə ler'ə tē) *n.* [< Fr. < L. *celeritas* < *celer,* swift] swiftness in acting or moving; speed

**cel·er·y** (sel'ər ē, sel'rē) *n.* [Fr. *céleri* < It. < L. < Gr. *selinon,* parsley] a plant of the parsley family, with long, crisp leafstalks eaten as a vegetable

**celery salt** a seasoning made of celery seed and salt

**ce·les·ta** (sə les'tə) *n.* [< Fr. < *céleste,* celestial] a small keyboard instrument with hammers that strike metal plates to make bell-like tones

**Ce·leste** (sə lest') [Fr. *Céleste:* see prec.] a feminine name

**ce·les·tial** (sə les'chəl) *adj.* [OFr. < L. *caelestis* < *caelum,* heaven] **1.** of the heavens, or sky **2.** *a)* of heaven; divine [*celestial beings*] *b)* highest; perfect [*celestial bliss*] **—ce·les'tial·ly** *adv.*

**celestial equator** the great circle of the celestial sphere formed by projecting the plane of the earth's equator on the celestial sphere

**celestial sphere** an imaginary sphere of infinite diameter containing the whole universe and on which all celestial bodies appear to be projected

**Ce·lia** (sēl'yə) [L. fem. of *Caelius,* name of a Roman clan] a feminine name

**ce·li·ac** (sē'lē ak') *adj.* [L. *coeliacus* < Gr. < *koilos,* hollow] of or in the abdominal cavity

**cel·i·ba·cy** (sel'ə bə sē) *n.* [see ff.] **1.** the state of being unmarried, esp. that of one under a vow not to marry **2.** complete sexual abstinence

**cel·i·bate** (sel'ə bət, -bāt') *adj.* [< L. *caelebs,* unmarried] of or in a state of celibacy **—***n.* a celibate person

**cell** (sel) *n.* [< OFr. *celle* < L. *cella*] **1.** a small room or cubicle, as in a convent or prison **2.** a very small hollow, cavity, or enclosed space, as in a honeycomb, or in a plant ovary **3.** any of the smallest organizational units of a group or movement, as of a Communist party **4.** *Biol.* a small unit of protoplasm, usually with a nucleus, cytoplasm, and an enclosing membrane: all plants and animals are made up of one or more cells **5.** *Elec.* a receptacle used either for generating electricity by chemical reactions or for decomposing compounds by electrolysis **—celled** *adj.*

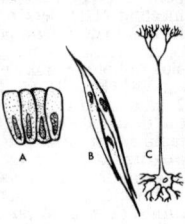

CELLS
(A, epithelial;
B, smooth muscle;
C, nerve)

**cel·lar** (sel'ər) *n.* [< OFr. < L. *cellarium* < *cella,* small room] **1.** a room or rooms below ground level and usually under a building, often used for storing fuel, wines, provisions, etc. **2.** a stock of wines kept in a cellar **—***vt.* to store in a cellar **—the cellar** [Colloq.] the lowest position

**cel·lar·age** (-ij) *n.* **1.** space of or in a cellar **2.** the fee for storage in a cellar

**cel·lar·er** (-ər) *n.* a person in charge of a cellar or provisions, as in a monastery

**cel·lar·et** (sel'ə ret') *n.* [CELLAR + -ET] a cabinet for bottles of wine or liquor, glasses, etc.

**Cel·li·ni** (chə lē'nē), **Ben·ve·nu·to** (ben'və nōō'tō) 1500–71; It. sculptor & goldsmith

**cel·lo** (chel'ō) *n., pl.* **-los, -li** (-ē) [< VIOLONCELLO] an instrument of the violin family, between the viola and double bass in size and pitch: also sp. **'cel·lo —cel'list** *n.*

**cel·lo·phane** (sel'ə fān') *n.* [< CELLULOSE + Gr. *phainein,* appear] a thin, transparent material made from cellulose, used as moistureproof wrapping for foods, etc.

**cel·lu·lar** (sel'yoo lər) *adj.* of, like, or containing a cell or cells **—cel'lu·lar'i·ty** (-lar'ə tē) *n.*

**cel·lu·lite** (sel'yoo līt') *n.* [Fr.] fatty deposits on the hips and thighs: a nonmedical term

**Cel·lu·loid** (sel'yoo loid') [CELLUL(OSE) + -OID] *a trademark for* a flammable substance made from pyroxylin and camphor, used for toilet articles, etc. and, formerly, for photographic films **—***n.* [c-] this substance

**cel·lu·lose** (sel'yoo lōs') *n.* [Fr.: see CELLULE & -OSE[1]] the chief substance composing the cell walls or fibers of all plant tissue: used in the manufacture of paper, textiles, explosives, etc. **—cel'lu·los'ic** (-lō'sik) *adj.,* *n.*

**cellulose acetate** a cellulose resin used in making acetate fiber, plastics, lacquers, etc.

**Cel·si·us** (sel'sē əs) *adj.* [after A. Celsius (1701–44), Swed. astronomer] designating or of a thermometer on which 0° is the freezing point and 100° is the boiling point of water; centigrade: abbrev. C

**Celt** (selt, kelt) *n.* [< Fr. < L. *Celta,* pl. *Celtae* (Gr. *Keltoi*), the Gauls] **1.** a person who speaks Celtic: the Bretons, Irish, Welsh, and Highland Scots are Celts **2.** an ancient Gaul or Briton

**Cel·tic** (sel′tik, kel′-) *adj.* of the Celts, their languages, culture, etc. —*n.* an Indo-European subfamily of languages with a Goidelic branch (Irish Gaelic, Scottish Gaelic, Manx) in Ireland, the Scottish Highlands, and the Isle of Man, and a Brythonic branch (Welsh, Breton, and the extinct Cornish) in Wales and Brittany

**ce·ment** (si ment′) *n.* [< OFr. < L. *caementum,* rough stone < *caedere,* to cut] **1.** a powdered substance made of burned lime and clay, mixed with water and sand to make mortar or with water, sand, and gravel to make concrete: the mixture hardens like stone when it dries **2.** any soft substance that fastens things together firmly when it hardens, as glue **3.** a cementlike substance used in dentistry as to fill cavities **4.** anything that joins together or unites; bond **5.** *same as* CEMENTUM —*vt.* **1.** to join or unite as with cement **2.** to cover with cement —*vi.* to become cemented —**ce·men·ta·tion** (sē′men tā′shən) *n.* —**ce·ment′er** *n.* —**ce·ment′like′** *adj.*

**ce·men·tum** (si men′təm) *n.* [< L.: see prec.] the hard, bony outer tissue of the root of a tooth

**cem·e·ter·y** (sem′ə ter′ē) *n., pl.* **-ter′ies** [< LL. < Gr. *koimētērion* < *koiman,* to put to sleep] a place for the burial of the dead; graveyard

**cen·o·bite** (sen′ə bīt′, sē′nə-) *n.* [< LL. *coenobita* < Gr. < *koinos,* common + *bios,* life] a member of a religious order in a monastery or convent —**cen′o·bit′ic** (-bit′ik), **cen′o·bit′i·cal** *adj.* —**cen′o·bit·ism** (-bit iz′m) *n.*

**cen·o·taph** (sen′ə taf′) *n.* [< Fr. < L. < Gr. < *kenos,* empty + *taphos,* a tomb] a monument honoring a dead person whose body is somewhere else

**Ce·no·zo·ic** (sē′nə zō′ik, sen′ə-) *adj.* [< Gr. *kainos,* recent + ZO- + -IC] designating or of the geologic era following the Mesozoic and including the present —**the Cenozoic** the Cenozoic Era or its rocks: see GEOLOGY, chart

**cen·ser** (sen′sər) *n.* [< OFr. < *encens:* see INCENSE¹] a container in which incense is burned

**cen·sor** (sen′sər) *n.* [L. < *censere,* to tax, value] **1.** one of two Roman magistrates appointed to take the census and, later, to supervise public morals **2.** an official with the power to examine publications, movies, mail, etc. and to remove or prohibit anything considered obscene, objectionable, etc. —*vt.* to subject (a book, letter, writer, etc.) to censorship —**cen·so·ri·al** (sen sôr′ē əl) *adj.*

**cen·so·ri·ous** (sen sôr′ē əs) *adj.* [see prec.] inclined to find fault; harshly critical —**cen·so′ri·ous·ly** *adv.* —**cen·so′ri·ous·ness** *n.*

**cen·sor·ship** (sen′sər ship′) *n.* **1.** the act or a system of censoring **2.** the work or position of a censor

**cen·sure** (sen′shər) *n.* [L. *censura* < *censor,* CENSOR] **1.** a condemning as wrong; strong disapproval **2.** an official expression of disapproval, specif. as passed by a legislature —*vt.* **-sured, -sur·ing** to express strong disapproval of; condemn as wrong —**cen′sur·a·ble** *adj.* —**cen′sur·er** *n.*

**cen·sus** (sen′səs) *n.* [L., orig. pp. of *censere:* see CENSOR] **1.** in ancient Rome, a count of the people and evaluation of their property for taxation **2.** an official, usually periodic, count of population and recording of economic status, age, sex, etc.

**cent** (sent) *n.* [< OFr. < L. *centum,* a hundred] **1.** a 100th part of a dollar, or a coin of this value; penny: symbol, ¢ **2.** a 100th part of a guilder, rand, etc.: see MONETARY UNITS, table

**cent. 1.** centigrade **2.** centimeter **3.** century

**cen·tare** (sen′ter, -tär) *n. same as* CENTIARE

**cen·taur** (sen′tôr) *n.* [< L. < Gr. *Kentauros*] *Gr. Myth.* any of a race of monsters with a man's head, trunk, and arms, and a horse's body and legs

**cen·ta·vo** (sen tä′vō) *n., pl.* **-vos** [Sp. < L. *centum,* a hundred] a unit of currency equal to 1/100 of a peso in Mexico, the Philippines, etc. and to 1/100 of a Brazilian cruzeiro, a Portuguese escudo, etc.: see MONETARY UNITS, table

**cen·te·nar·i·an** (sen′tə ner′ē ən) *adj.* **1.** of 100 years; of a centenary **2.** of a centenarian —*n.* a person at least 100 years old

**cen·te·nar·y** (sen ten′ər ē, sen′tə ner′ē) *adj.* [< L. < *centum,* a hundred] **1.** of a century, or period of 100 years **2.** of a centennial —*n., pl.* **-nar·ies 1.** a century; period of 100 years **2.** *same as* CENTENNIAL

**cen·ten·ni·al** (sen ten′ē əl) *adj.* [< L. *centum,* a hundred + *annus,* year + -AL] **1.** of 100 years **2.** happening once in 100 years **3.** 100 years old **4.** of a 100th anniversary —*n.* a 100th anniversary or its celebration —**cen·ten′ni·al·ly** *adv.*

**cen·ter** (sen′tər) *n.* [< OFr. < L. *centrum* < Gr. *kentron,* sharp point] **1.** a point equally distant from all points on the circumference of a circle or surface of a sphere **2.** the point around which anything revolves; pivot **3.** a place at which an activity or complex of activities is carried on *[a shopping center],* from which ideas, influences, etc. emanate *[Paris, the fashion center],* or to which many people are attracted *[a center of interest]* **4.** the approximate middle point, place, or part of anything **5.** a group of nerve cells regulating a particular function **6.** in some sports, a player near the center of the line or playing area, who often puts the ball or puck into play **7.** *Mil.* that part of an army between the flanks **8.** *[often* C-*] Politics* a position or party between the left (radicals and liberals) and the right (conservatives and reactionaries) —*vt.* **1.** to place in, at, or near the center **2.** to draw or gather to one place —*vi.* to be centered; be concentrated or focused

**cen·ter·board** (-bôrd′) *n.* a movable, keellike board that is lowered through a slot in the floor of a sailboat to prevent drifting to leeward

**cen·ter·fold** (-fōld′) *n.* the center facing pages of a magazine, frequently with an extra fold or folds, given over to a photograph, often of a nude young woman or man

**center of gravity** that point in a body or system around which its weight is evenly distributed or balanced and may be assumed to act

**cen·ter·piece** (sen′tər pēs′) *n.* an ornament, bowl of flowers, etc. for the center of a table

**cen·tes·i·mal** (sen tes′ə məl) *adj.* [< L. *centesimus* < *centum,* a hundred] **1.** hundredth **2.** of or divided into hundredths —**cen·tes′i·mal·ly** *adv.*

**cen·tes·i·mo** (sen tes′ə mō′; *Sp.* -ē mō′; *It.* chen te′sē mō′) *n., pl.* **-mos′** (-mōz′; *Sp.* -mōs′); *It.* **-mi′** (-mē′) [It. & Sp. < L.: see prec.] a unit of currency equal to 1/100th of an Italian lira, a Uruguayan peso, etc.: see MONETARY UNITS, table

**cen·ti-** [L. < *centum*] *a combining form meaning:* **1.** hundred or hundredfold **2.** a 100th part of

**cen·ti·are** (sen′tē er′, -är′) *n.* [Fr.: see CENTI- & ARE²] a 100th part of an are (unit of land measure)

**cen·ti·grade** (sen′tə grād′) *adj.* [Fr. < L. *centum,* a hundred + *gradus,* a degree] **1.** consisting of or divided into 100 degrees **2.** *same as* CELSIUS: the preferred term until the international adoption of *Celsius* in 1948

**cen·ti·gram** (-gram′) *n.* [Fr.: see CENTI- & GRAM¹] a unit of weight, equal to 1/100 gram: also, chiefly Brit. sp., **cen′ti·gramme′** : abbrev. **cg., cgm.**

**cen·ti·li·ter** (sen′tə lēt′ər) *n.* [Fr.: see CENTI- & LITER] a unit of capacity, equal to 1/100 liter: also, chiefly Brit. sp., **cen′ti·li′tre:** abbrev. **cl.**

**cen·time** (sän′tēm; *Fr.* sän tēm′) *n.* [Fr. < L.: see CENTESIMAL] the 100th part of a franc, the Algerian dinar, etc.: see MONETARY UNITS, table

**cen·ti·me·ter** (sen′tə mēt′ər) *n.* [< Fr.: see CENTI- & METER¹] a unit of measure, equal to 1/100 meter (.3937 inch): also, chiefly Brit. sp., **cen′ti·me′tre:** abbrev. **cm., c., C., cent.**

**cen·ti·me·ter-gram-sec·ond** (-gram′sek′ənd) *adj.* designating or of a system of measurement in which the centimeter, gram, and second are used as the units of length, mass, and time, respectively

**cen·ti·mo** (sen′tə mō′) *n., pl.* **-mos′** [see CENTIME] the 100th part of a Spanish peseta, a Venezuelan bolívar, etc.: see MONETARY UNITS, table

**cen·ti·pede** (sen′tə pēd′) *n.* [Fr. < L. < *centum,* a hundred + *pes* (gen. *pedis*), a foot] a many-segmented arthropod with a pair of legs to each segment

**cen·tral** (sen′trəl) *adj.* [L. *centralis*] **1.** in, at, or near the center **2.** of or forming the center **3.** equally distant or accessible from various points **4.** main; basic; principal **5.** of or having to do with a single source that controls all activity in an organization or system **6.** designating or of that part of the nervous system consisting of the brain and spinal cord (of a vertebrate) —*n.* formerly, a telephone exchange, esp. the main one, or the telephone operator —**cen·tral′i·ty** (-tral′ə tē) *n.* —**cen′tral·ly** *adv.*

**Central African Republic** country in C Africa, south of Chad: 238,224 sq. mi.; pop. 2,370,000

**Central America** part of N. America between Mexico and S. America —**Central American**

**central city** the principal municipality of a metropolitan area, surrounded by suburbs; esp., the crowded, industrial, often blighted area

**cen·tral·ism** (-iz′m) *n.* the principle or system of centralizing power or authority —**cen′tral·ist** *adj., n.*

**cen·tral·ize** (-sen′trə līz′) *vt.* **-ized′, -iz′ing 1.** to make central; bring to or focus on a center; gather together **2.** to organize under one control —*vi.* to become centralized —**cen′tral·i·za′tion** *n.* —**cen′tral·iz′er** *n.*

**Central Powers** in World War I, Germany, Austria-Hungary, Turkey, and Bulgaria

**Central Standard Time** *see* STANDARD TIME

**cen·tre** (sen'tər) *n.*, *vt.*, *vi.*, -tred, -tring *chiefly Brit. sp. of* CENTER

**cen·tri-** *same as* CENTRO-

**cen·tric** (sen'trik) *adj.* **1.** in, at, or near the center; central **2.** of or having a center Also **cen'tri·cal** —**cen'tri·cal·ly** *adv.* —**cen·tric'i·ty** (-tris'ə tē) *n.*

**-cen·tric** (sen'trik) *a combining form meaning:* **1.** having a center or centers (of a specified kind or number) [polycentric] **2.** having (a specified thing) as its center [geocentric]

**cen·trif·u·gal** (sen trif'yə gəl, -ə gəl) *adj.* [< ModL. < CENTRI- + L. *fugere*, to flee + -AL] **1.** moving or tending to move away from a center **2.** using or acted on by centrifugal force —*n.* a centrifuge —**cen·trif'u·gal·ly** *adv.*

**centrifugal force** the force tending to pull a thing outward when it is rotating rapidly around a center

**cen·trif·u·gal·ize** (-īz') *vt.* -ized', -iz'ing to subject to or as to the action of a centrifuge —**cen·trif'u·gal·i·za'tion** *n.*

**cen·tri·fuge** (sen'trə fyōōj') *n.* a machine using centrifugal force to separate particles of varying density, as cream from milk —*vt.* -fuged', -fug'ing to subject to the action of a centrifuge

**cen·trip·e·tal** (sen trip'ət 'l) *adj.* [< ModL. < CENTRI- + L. *petere*, to seek + -AL] **1.** moving or tending to move toward a center **2.** using or acted on by centripetal force —**cen·trip'e·tal·ly** *adv.*

**centripetal force** the force tending to pull a thing inward when it is rotating rapidly around a center

**cen·trist** (sen'trist) *n.* a member of a political party of the center

**cen·tro-** [< L. *centrum*, CENTER] *a combining form meaning* center

**cen·tro·some** (sen'trə sōm') *n.* [CENTRO- + -SOME³] a very small body near the nucleus in most animal cells: it divides in mitosis —**cen'tro·som'ic** (-säm'ik, -sōm'-) *adj.*

**cen·tu·ri·on** (sen tyoor'ē ən, -toor'-) *n.* [< L. *centuria*: see ff.] the commanding officer of a Roman century

**cen·tu·ry** (sen'chər ē) *n.*, *pl.* -ries [L. *centuria* < *centum*, a hundred] **1.** any period of 100 years, esp. as reckoned from the beginning of the Christian Era **2.** in ancient Rome *a)* a military unit, originally made up of 100 men *b)* a subdivision of the people made for voting purposes —**cen·tu·ri·al** (sen tyoor'ē əl, -toor'-) *adj.*

**century plant** a tropical American agave having fleshy leaves and a tall stalk that bears greenish flowers only once after 10 to 30 years: mistakenly thought to bloom only once a century

**ce·phal·ic** (sə fal'ik) *adj.* [< L. < Gr. < *kephalē*, the head] **1.** of the head, skull, or cranium **2.** in, on, near, or toward the head —**ce·phal'i·cal·ly** *adv.*

**-ce·phal·ic** (sə fal'ik) *a combining form meaning* head or skull [dolichocephalic]

**cephalic index** a measure of the human head computed by dividing its maximum breadth by its maximum length and multiplying by 100

**ceph·a·lo-** [see CEPHALIC] *a combining form meaning* the head, skull, or brain: also, before a vowel, **cephal-**

**ceph·a·lo·pod** (sef'ə lə päd') *n.* [prec. + -POD] any of a class of mollusks having a distinct head with a beak, and muscular tentacles about the mouth, as the octopus, squid, and cuttlefish

**ceph·a·lo·tho·rax** (sef'ə lə thôr'aks) *n.* the head and thorax united as a single part, in certain crustaceans and arachnids

**-ceph·a·lous** (sef'əl əs) [see CEPHALIC] *a combining form meaning* -headed [microcephalous]

**ce·ram·ic** (sə ram'ik) *adj.* [< Gr. *keramos*, clay, pottery] **1.** of pottery, earthenware, tile, porcelain, etc. **2.** of ceramics —*n.* **1.** [pl., with sing. v.] the art or work of making objects of baked clay **2.** such an object —**ce·ram·ist** (sə ram'ist, ser'ə mist), **ce·ram'i·cist** (-ə sist) *n.*

**Cer·ber·us** (sur'bər əs) *Gr. & Rom. Myth.* the three-headed dog guarding the gate of Hades

**cere** (sir) *n.* [< Fr. < L. < Gr. *kēros*, wax] a waxy, fleshy area at the base of the beak of some birds, as the parrot, eagle, etc. —*vt.* cered, cer'ing to wrap in a cerecloth

**ce·re·al** (sir'ē əl) *adj.* [< L. *Cerealis*, of Ceres] of grain or the grasses producing grain —*n.* **1.** any grain used for food, as wheat, oats, etc. **2.** any grass producing such grain **3.** food made from grain, esp. breakfast food, as oatmeal

**cer·e·bel·lum** (ser'ə bel'əm) *n.*, *pl.* -lums, -la (-ə) [L., dim. of *cerebrum*, the brain] the section of the brain behind and below the cerebrum: it is the coordinating center for muscular movement

**cer·e·bral** (ser'ə brəl, sə rē'-) *adj.* of the brain or the cerebrum —**cer·e'bral·ly** *adv.*

**cerebral palsy** any of several disorders of the central nervous system resulting from brain damage and characterized by spastic paralysis

**cer·e·brate** (ser'ə brāt') *vi.* -brat'ed, -brat'ing [< L. *cerebrum* (see CEREBELLUM) + -ATE¹] to use one's brain; think —**cer'e·bra'tion** *n.*

**cer·e·bro-** [< L. *cerebrum*, the brain] *a combining form meaning* the brain (and); cerebrum (and)

**cer·e·bro·spi·nal** (ser'ə brō spī'n'l, sə rē'brō-) *adj.* of or affecting the brain and the spinal cord

**cer·e·brum** (ser'ə brəm, sə rē'-) *n.*, *pl.* -brums, -bra (-brə) [L.: see CEREBELLUM] the upper, main part of the brain of vertebrate animals, consisting of two equal hemispheres and, in man, controlling conscious and voluntary processes

**cere·cloth** (sir'klôth') *n.* [< *cered cloth:* see CERE] cloth treated with wax or a similar substance, formerly used to wrap a dead person for burial

**cer·e·ment** (ser'ə mənt, sir'mənt) *n.* [see CERE] **1.** a cerecloth; shroud **2.** [usually pl.] any burial clothes

**cer·e·mo·ni·al** (ser'ə mō'nē əl, -nyəl) *adj.* of, for, or consisting of ceremony; ritual; formal —*n.* **1.** an established system of rites or formal actions connected with an occasion; ritual **2.** a rite or ceremony —**cer'e·mo'ni·al·ism** *n.* —**cer'e·mo'ni·al·ist** *n.* —**cer'e·mo'ni·al·ly** *adv.*

**cer·e·mo·ni·ous** (-nē əs, -nyəs) *adj.* **1.** ceremonial **2.** full of ceremony **3.** characterized by conventional usages or formality; very polite —**cer'e·mo'ni·ous·ly** *adv.* —**cer'e·mo'ni·ous·ness** *n.*

**cer·e·mo·ny** (ser'ə mō'nē) *n.*, *pl.* -nies [L. *caerimonia*] **1.** a formal act or set of formal acts established as proper to a special occasion, such as a wedding, religious rite, etc. **2.** a conventionally courteous act **3.** behavior that follows rigid etiquette **4.** formality or formalities **5.** empty or meaningless formality —**stand on ceremony** to behave with or insist on formality

**Ce·res** (sir'ēz) **1.** *Rom. Myth.* the goddess of agriculture: identified with the Greek goddess Demeter **2.** the first asteroid discovered (1801)

**ce·re·us** (sir'ē əs) *n.* [L., wax taper: from its shape] any of various cactuses, esp. night-blooming varieties, of the SW U.S. and Mexico

**ce·rise** (sə rēs', -rēz') *n.*, *adj.* [Fr.: see CHERRY] bright red; cherry red

**ce·ri·um** (sir'ē əm) *n.* [after the asteroid *Ceres*] a gray, metallic chemical element: symbol, Ce; at. wt., 140.12; at. no., 58

**ce·ro-** [< L. < Gr. *kēros*, wax] *a combining form meaning* wax

**ce·ro·plas·tic** (sir'ə plas'tik) *adj.* [< Gr. < *kēros*, wax + *plassein*, to mold] **1.** having to do with wax modeling **2.** modeled in wax

**cert. 1.** certificate **2.** certified

**cer·tain** (surt'n) *adj.* [< OFr. < L. *certus*, determined < *cernere*, to decide] **1.** fixed, settled, or determined **2.** inevitable **3.** not to be doubted [the evidence is *certain*] **4.** reliable; dependable [a *certain* cure] **5.** controlled; unerring [his *certain* aim] **6.** sure; positive [I'm *certain* he's here] **7.** not named or described, though definite [a *certain* person] **8.** some, but not very much; appreciable [to a *certain* extent] —**for certain** without doubt

**cer·tain·ly** (-lē) *adv.* beyond a doubt; surely

**cer·tain·ty** (-tē) *n.* **1.** the quality, state, or fact of being certain **2.** *pl.* -ties anything certain; definite fact

**cer·tes** (sur'tēz) *adv.* [< OFr. < L. *certus*, CERTAIN] [Archaic] certainly; verily

**cer·tif·i·cate** (sur tif'ə kit; *for v.* -kāt') *n.* [< OFr. < ML. < LL. pp. of *certificare*, CERTIFY] a written or printed statement testifying to a fact, qualification, ownership, etc. —*vt.* -cat'ed, -cat'ing to attest by a certificate; issue a certificate to —**cer·tif'i·ca'tor** *n.* —**cer·tif'i·ca·to'ry** (-kə tôr'ē) *adj.*

**cer·ti·fi·ca·tion** (sur'tə fi kā'shən) *n.* **1.** a certifying or being certified **2.** a certified statement

**cer·ti·fied** (sur'tə fīd') *adj.* **1.** vouched for; guaranteed **2.** having, or attested to by, a certificate

**certified check** a check certified by a bank as genuine, or which it guarantees payment

**certified mail** a postal service which provides a receipt to the sender of first-class mail and a record of its delivery: also, mail sent by this

**certified public accountant** a public accountant certified by a State examining board after meeting the requirements of State law

**cer·ti·fy** (sur'tə fī') *vt.* -fied', -fy'ing [< OFr. < LL. *certificare* < L. *certus*, CERTAIN + *facere*, to make] **1.** to declare (a thing) true, accurate, certain, etc. by formal statement; verify **2.** to declare officially insane **3.** to guarantee; vouch for **4.** to issue a certificate to **5.** [Archaic] to assure; make certain —*vi.* to testify (*to*) —**cer'ti·fi'a·ble** *adj.* —**cer'ti·fi'a·bly** *adv.* —**cer'ti·fi'er** *n.*

**cer·ti·o·ra·ri** (sur'shē ə rer'ē, -rär'-) *n.* [LL., to be made more certain] *Law* a writ from a higher court to a lower one, or to a board or official with judicial power, requesting the record of a case for review

**cer·ti·tude** (sur'tə tōod', -tyōod') *n.* [< OFr. < LL. *certitudo*] **1.** a feeling absolutely sure **2.** inevitability

**ce·ru·le·an** (sə rōo'lē ən) *adj.* [< L., prob. < dim. of *caelum*, heaven] sky-blue; azure

**ce·ru·men** (sə rōō′mən) *n.* [< L. *cera*, wax, after ALBUMEN] *same as* EARWAX

**Cer·van·tes (Saavedra)** (thēr vän′tes; *E.* sər van′tēz), **Mi·guel de** (mē gel′ *the*) 1547–1616; Sp. writer: author of *Don Quixote*

**cer·vi·cal** (sur′viks kəl) *adj.* of the neck or cervix

**cer·vix** (sur′viks) *n., pl.* -vi·ces′ (sur′və sēz′, sər vī′-), -vix·es [L., the neck] 1. the neck, esp. the back of the neck 2. a necklike part, esp. of the uterus

**Ce·sar·e·an, Ce·sar·i·an** (si zer′ē ən) *adj., n. same as* CAESAREAN

**ce·si·um** (sē′zē əm) *n.* [ModL., neut. of L. *caesius*, bluishgray] a soft, silver-white, ductile, metallic chemical element, used in photoelectric cells: symbol, Cs; at. wt., 132.905; at. no., 55

**ces·sa·tion** (se sā′shən) *n.* [< L. < pp. of *cessare*, CEASE] a ceasing, either final or temporary; stop

**ces·sion** (sesh′ən) *n.* [OFr. < L. < pp. of *cedere*, to yield] a ceding or giving up (of rights, territory, etc.) to another

**cess·pool** (ses′pōōl′) *n.* [< It. *cesso*, privy < L. *secessus*, place of retirement] 1. a tank or deep hole in the ground to receive drainage or sewage from the sinks, toilets, etc. of a house 2. a center of moral filth and corruption

**ces·tus** (ses′təs) *n.* [L. *caestus* < *caedere*, to strike] a device of leather straps, sometimes weighted with metal, worn on the hand by boxers in ancient Rome

**ce·su·ra** (si zhoor′ə, -zyoor′ə) *n., pl.* -ras, -rae (-ē) *same as* CAESURA

**ce·ta·cean** (si tā′shən) *n.* [L. *cetus*, whale < Gr. *kētos*] any of an order of nearly hairless, fishlike water mammals with paddlelike forelimbs, including whales, porpoises, and dolphins —*adj.* of the cetaceans: also **ce·ta′ceous** (-shəs)

CESTUS

**ce·vi·tam·ic acid** (sē′vī tam′ik, -vi-) [< C + VITAM(IN) + -IC] *same as* ASCORBIC ACID

**Cey·lon** (sə län′, sā-, sī-) country on an island off the SE tip of India: a member of the Commonwealth: 25,332 sq. mi.; pop. 12,240,000; cap. Colombo: official name *Sri Lanka* — **Cey·lo·nese** (sel′ə nēz′) *adj., n.*

**Cé·zanne** (sā zàn′), **Paul** 1839–1906; Fr. impressionist & postimpressionist painter

**Cf** *Chem.* californium

**cf.** [L. *confer*] compare

**CG, C.G.** Coast Guard

**cg, cg., cgm, cgm.** centigram(s)

**cgs, c.g.s., C.G.S.** centimeter-gram-second

**Ch.** 1. Chaldean 2. China 3. Chinese

**Ch., ch.** 1. chain 2. champion 3. chapter 4. child; children 5. church

**cha·conne** (shä kôn′) *n.* [Fr. < Sp. *chacona*] 1. a slow, stately dance of 17th- and 18th-cent. Europe 2. music for this dance, or a musical form based on this dance

**Chad** (chad) 1. country in NC Africa, south of Libya: 495,000 sq. mi.; pop. 3,361,000 2. Lake, lake at the juncture of the Chad, Niger, and Nigeria borders —**Chad′i·an** *adj., n.*

**chafe** (chāf) *vt.* chafed, chaf′ing [< OFr. *chaufer*, to warm < L. < *calere*, to be warm + *facere*, to make] 1. to rub so as to make warm 2. to wear away by rubbing 3. to make sore by rubbing 4. to annoy; irritate —*vi.* 1. to rub (on or against) 2. to be vexed —*n.* an injury or irritation caused by rubbing —**chafe at the bit** to be impatient

**chaf·er** (chāf′ər) *n.* [OE. *ceafor*] any of various beetles that feed on plants

**chaff** (chaf) *n.* [OE. *ceaf*] 1. threshed or winnowed husks of wheat or other grain 2. anything worthless 3. goodnatured teasing; banter —*vt., vi.* to tease or ridicule in a good-natured way —**chaff′y** *adj.* **chaff′i·er, chaff′i·est**

**chaf·fer** (chaf′ər) *vi.* [< OE. *ceap*, a purchase] [Now Rare] to haggle over price; bargain —**chaf′fer·er** *n.*

**chaf·finch** (chaf′finch′) *n.* [OE. *ceaffinc*: see CHAFF + FINCH: it eats chaff] a small European songbird, often kept in a cage as a pet

**chaf·ing dish** (chāf′iŋ) [see CHAFE] a pan with a heating apparatus beneath it, to cook food at the table or to keep food hot

**Cha·gall** (shä gäl′), **Marc** 1889– ; Russ. painter, esp. in France

**cha·grin** (shə grin′) *n.* [Fr., grief, prob. < OFr. *graignier*, to sorrow < Gmc. *gram*, sorrow] a feeling of embarrassment and distress caused by failure or disappointment —*vt.* -grined′, -grin′ing to cause to feel chagrin

**chain** (chān) *n.* [OFr. *chaine* < L. *catena*, a chain] 1. a flexible series of joined links, usually of metal 2. [*pl.*] *a)* bonds, shackles, etc. *b)* captivity; bondage 3. a chainlike measuring instrument, or its measure of length: a *surveyor's chain* is 66 feet; an *engineer's chain* is 100 feet 4. a connected series of things or events 5. a number of stores, restaurants, etc. owned by one company 6. *Chem.* a linkage of atoms in a molecule —*vt.* 1. to fasten or shackle with chains 2. to hold down, restrain, confine, etc.

**chain gang** a gang of prisoners chained together, as when working

**chain letter** a letter to be circulated among many people by being copied and passed to others

**chain mail** flexible armor made of metal links

**chain-re·act** (-rē akt′) *vi.* to be involved in or subjected to a chain reaction

**chain reaction** 1. a self-sustaining series of chemical or nuclear reactions in which the products of the reaction contribute directly to the propagation of the process 2. any sequence of events, each of which results in the following

**chain saw** a portable power saw with an endless chain that carries cutting teeth

**chain-smoke** (-smōk′) *vt., vi.* -smoked′, -smok′ing to smoke (cigarettes) one right after the other —**chain smoker, chain′-smok′er** *n.*

**chain stitch** a fancy stitch in which the loops are connected in a chainlike way, as in crocheting —**chain′-stitch′** *vt.*

**chain store** any of a chain of retail stores

**chair** (cher) *n.* [OFr. *chaiere* < L. *cathedra*: see CATHEDRA] 1. a piece of furniture for one person to sit on, having a back and, usually, four legs 2. a seat of authority or dignity 3. the position of a player in an instrumental section of a symphony orchestra 4. an important or official position, as a professorship 5. a person who presides over a meeting; chairman 6. *same as: a)* SEDAN CHAIR *b)* ELECTRIC CHAIR —*vt.* 1. to place in a chair; seat 2. to place in authority 3. to preside over as chairman —**take the chair** to preside as chairman

**chair·lift** (-lift′) *n.* a line of seats suspended from a powerdriven endless cable, used esp. to carry skiers up a slope

**chair·man** (-mən) *n., pl.* -men a person who presides at a meeting or heads a committee, board, etc. —*vt.* -maned or -manned, -man·ing or -man·ning to preside over as chairman —**chair′man·ship′** *n.* —**chair′wom′an** *n.fem., pl.* -wom′en

**chair·per·son** (-pur′s'n) *n. same as* CHAIRMAN: used to avoid the masculine implication of *chairman*

**chaise** (shāz) *n.* [Fr., var. of *chaire*, CHAIR] 1. any of certain lightweight carriages, some with a collapsible top, having two or four wheels 2. *same as* CHAISE LONGUE

**chaise longue** (shāz′ lôŋ′; *often also* lounj′—*see next entry*) *pl.* **chaise** (or **chaises**) **longues** (shāz′ lôŋz′; loun′jəz) [Fr., lit., long chair] a couchlike chair with a support for the back and a seat long enough to support the outstretched legs

**chaise lounge** (lounj) *pl.* **chaise lounges** [by folk etym. < prec.] *same as* CHAISE LONGUE

**cha·la·za** (kə lā′zə) *n., pl.* -zae (-zē), -zas [ModL. < Gr. *chalaza*, hailstone] either of the spiral bands of dense albumen extending from the yolk toward the lining membrane at each end of a bird's egg

**chal·ced·o·ny** (kal sed′n ē, kal′sə dō′nē) *n., pl.* -nies [< OFr. < LL. < Gr. *chalkēdōn*, a precious stone < ?] a kind of quartz with the luster of wax, variously colored

**Chal·de·a, Chal·dae·a** (kal dē′ə) 1. ancient province of Babylonia, at the head of the Persian Gulf 2. Babylonia: so called from the supremacy of Chaldea (6th cent. B.C.) —**Chal·de′an, Chal·dae′an, Chal·da′ic** (-dā′ik), **Chal′dee** (-dē) *adj., n.*

**cha·let** (sha lā′, shal′ē) *n.* [Swiss-Fr., prob. ult. < L. *casa*, a house] 1. a herdsman's hut or cabin in the Swiss Alps 2. *a)* a type of Swiss house, with balconies and overhanging eaves *b)* any building in this style

**chal·ice** (chal′is) *n.* [OFr. < L. *calix*, a cup] 1. a cup; goblet 2. the cup for the wine of Holy Communion 3. a cupshaped flower —**chal′iced** *adj.*

**chalk** (chôk) *n.* [OE. *cealc* < L. *calx*, limestone] 1. a white or gray limestone that is soft and easily pulverized, composed mainly of minute seashells 2. any substance like chalk 3. a piece of chalk, often colored, used for writing on a blackboard, etc. —*adj.* made or drawn with chalk —*vt.* 1. to rub or smear with chalk 2. to make pale 3. to write, draw, or mark with chalk —*vi.* to become chalky or powdery —**chalk out** 1. to mark out as with chalk 2. to outline; plan —**chalk up** 1. to score, get, or achieve 2. to charge or credit —**walk a chalk line** [Colloq.] to behave with strict propriety —**chalk′·ness** *n.* —**chalk′y** *adj.* **chalk′i·er, chalk′i·est**

**chal·lenge** (chal′ənj) *n.* [< OFr. < L. *calumnia*, CALUMNY] 1. a demand for identification /a sentry gave the *challenge*/ 2. a calling into question /a *challenge* to an assertion/ 3. a call or dare to take part in a duel, contest, etc. 4. anything that calls for special effort or dedication 5. an exception to a vote or to someone's right to vote 6. *Law* a formal objection or exception to a person chosen as a prospective juror —*vt.* **-lenged, -leng·ing** 1. to call to a halt for identification 2. *a)* to call to account *b)* to make an objection to; call into question 3. to call or dare to take part in a duel, contest, etc.; defy 4. to call for; make demands on /to *challenge* the imagination/ 5. to take exception to (a vote or voter) as not being valid or qualified 6. to take formal exception to (a prospective juror) —*vi.* to issue or offer a challenge —**chal′lenge·a·ble** *adj.* —**chal′leng·er** *n.*

**chal·lis, chal·lie** (shal′ē) *n.* [< ?] a soft, lightweight, usually printed fabric of wool, cotton, etc.

**cha·lyb·e·ate** (kə lib′ē ət, -āt′) *adj.* [< L. *chalybs* < Gr. *chalyps*, steel] 1. containing salts of iron 2. tasting like iron —*n.* a chalybeate liquid

**cham·ber** (chām′bər) *n.* [< OFr. < LL. *camera*: see CAMERA] 1. a room in a house, esp. a bedroom 2. [*pl.*] [Brit.] a suite of rooms used by one person 3. [*pl.*] a judge's office near the courtroom 4. an assembly hall 5. a legislative or judicial body or division /the *Chamber* of Deputies/ 6. a council or board /a *chamber* of commerce/ 7. an enclosed space in the body 8. a compartment; specif., the part of a gun that holds the charge or cartridge —*vt.* to provide a chamber or chambers for —**cham′bered** *adj.*

**cham·ber·lain** (-lin) *n.* [< OFr. < OHG. < *chamara* (< L. *camera*) + dim. suffix *-linc*: see CAMERA & -LING¹] 1. an officer in charge of the household of a ruler or lord; steward 2. a high official in certain royal courts 3. [Brit.] a treasurer

**cham·ber·maid** (-mād′) *n.* a woman whose work is taking care of bedrooms, as in hotels

**chamber music** music for performance by a small group, as a string quartet, orig. in a small hall

**chamber of commerce** an association established to further the business interests of its community

**chamber pot** a portable container kept in a bedroom and used as a toilet

**cham·bray** (sham′brā) *n.* [var. of CAMBRIC] a smooth fabric of cotton, made by weaving white or unbleached threads across a colored warp

**cha·me·le·on** (kə mēl′yən, -mē′lē ən) *n.* [< L. < Gr. *chamai*, on the ground + *leōn*, lion] 1. any of various lizards that can change the color of their skin 2. a changeable or fickle person —**cha·me′le·on′ic** (-mē′lē än′ik) *adj.*

**cham·fer** (cham′fər) *n.* [< Fr. < L. *cantum frangere*: see CANT² & FRAGILE] a beveled edge or corner, esp. one cut at a 45° angle —*vt.* 1. to cut a chamfer on; bevel 2. to make a groove or fluting in

CHAMELEON (to 24 in. long, including tail)

**cham·ois** (sham′ē) *n., pl.* **-ois** [Fr. < VL. *camox*] 1. a small, goatlike antelope of the mountains of Europe and the Caucasus 2. *a)* a soft leather made from the skin of chamois, or of sheep, deer, goats, etc. *b)* a piece of this leather, used as a polishing cloth: also **cham·my** (sham′ē), *pl.* **-mies** —*adj.* 1. made of chamois 2. yellowish-brown —*vt.* **cham′oised** (-ēd), **cham′ois·ing** (-ē iŋ) to polish with a chamois skin

**cham·o·mile** (kam′ə mīl′, -mēl′) *n.* [< OFr. < Gr. *chamaimēlon* < *chamai*, on the ground + *mēlon*, apple] any of several plants with strong-smelling foliage; esp., a plant whose dried, daisylike flower heads have been used in a medicinal tea

**champ¹** (champ) *vt., vi.* [earlier *cham*: prob. echoic] to chew hard and noisily; munch —*n.* the act of champing —**champ at the bit** 1. to bite upon its bit repeatedly and restlessly: said of a horse 2. to be restless

**champ²** (champ) *n.* [Slang] *same as* CHAMPION

**cham·pagne** (sham pān′) *n.* 1. orig., any of various wines produced in Champagne, a region in NE France 2. now, any effervescent white wine: a symbol of luxury 3. pale, tawny yellow

**Cham·paign** (sham pān′) [see ff.] city in EC Ill.: pop. 58,000

**cham·paign** (sham pān′) *n.* [< OFr. *champaigne*: see CAMPAIGN] a broad plain; flat, open country —*adj.* of or like a champaign

**cham·pi·on** (cham′pē ən) *n.* [< OFr. < LL. *campio*, gladiator < L. *campus*, a field] 1. a person who fights for another or for a cause; defender; supporter 2. a winner of first place in a competition —*adj.* winning first place; excelling over all others —*vt.* to fight for; defend; support

**cham·pi·on·ship** (-ship′) *n.* 1. a championing 2. the position or title of a champion

**Cham·plain** (sham plān′), Lake [after S. de *Champlain*, 17th-c. Fr. explorer] lake between N.Y. and Vt.

**Champs É·ly·sées** (shän zā lē zā′) [Fr., lit., Elysian fields] famous avenue in Paris

**Chan., Chanc.** 1. Chancellor 2. Chancery

**chan.** channel

**chance** (chans) *n.* [< OFr. < ML. < L. prp. of *cadere*, to fall] 1. the happening of events without apparent cause; fortuity; luck 2. an unpredictable event or accidental happening 3. a risk or gamble 4. a ticket in a lottery or raffle 5. an opportunity /a *chance* to go/ 6. a possibility or probability /a *chance* that he will live/ 7. *Baseball* a fielding opportunity —*adj.* happening by chance; accidental —*vi.* **chanced, chanc′ing** 1. to have the fortune (to) 2. [Archaic] to happen by chance —*vt.* to leave to chance /let's *chance* it/ —**by chance** accidentally —**chance on** (or **upon**) to find by chance —**on the (off) chance** relying on the (remote) possibility

**chan·cel** (chan′s'l) *n.* [< OFr. < LL. < L. *cancelli*, pl., lattices: see CANCEL] that part of a church around the altar, reserved for the clergy and the choir: it is sometimes set off by a railing

**chan·cel·ler·y** (chan′sə lə rē, -slə rē) *n., pl.* **-ler·ies** 1. the position of a chancellor 2. a chancellor's office or the building that houses it 3. the office of an embassy or consulate Also sp. **chan′cel·lor·y**

**chan·cel·lor** (-lər) *n.* [< OFr. < LL. *cancellarius*, keeper of the barrier: see CANCEL] 1. [usually C-] any of several high officials in the British government 2. the title of the president or a high officer in some universities 3. the prime minister in certain countries 4. a chief judge of a court of chancery or equity in some States 5. a high church official —**chan′cel·lor·ship′** *n.*

**chance-med·ley** (chans′med′lē) *n.* [see CHANCE & MEDDLE] 1. accidental homicide 2. haphazard action

**chan·cer·y** (chan′sər ē) *n., pl.* **-cer·ies** [< OFr. < ML. *cancellaria*: see CHANCELLOR] 1. a division of the High Court of Justice in England and Wales 2. a court of equity 3. equity law 4. a court of record 5. *same as* CHANCELLERY (senses 2 & 3) 6. *R.C.Ch.* the diocesan office in charge of certain documents, secretarial services, etc. for the bishop —**in chancery** 1. in process of litigation in a court of equity 2. in a helpless situation

**chan·cre** (shaŋ′kər) *n.* [Fr.: see CANCER] a venereal sore or ulcer; primary lesion of syphilis —**chan′crous** (-krəs) *adj.*

**chan·croid** (-kroid) *n.* [CHANCR(E) + -OID] a nonsyphilitic venereal ulcer: also called **soft chancre**

**chanc·y** (chan′sē) *adj.* **chanc′i·er, chanc′i·est** risky; uncertain

**chan·de·lier** (shan′də lir′) *n.* [Fr. < OFr. < L. *candelabrum* < *candela*, CANDLE] a lighting fixture hanging from a ceiling, with branches for candles, electric bulbs, etc.

**chan·dler** (chan′dlər) *n.* [< OFr. < L. *candela*, CANDLE] 1. a maker or seller of candles 2. a retailer of supplies, equipment, etc. of a certain kind /ship *chandler*/ —**chan′·dler·y** (-ē) *n., pl.* **-dler·ies**

**Chang·chun** (chäŋ′choon′) city in NE China: pop. 1,800,000

**change** (chānj) *vt.* **changed, chang′ing** [< OFr. < LL. < L. *cambire*, to barter < Celt.] 1. to put or take (a thing) in place of something else; substitute /to *change* one's clothes/ 2. to exchange /let's *change* seats/ 3. *a)* to make different; alter *b)* to undergo a variation of /leaves *change* color/ 4. to give or receive the equivalent of (a coin or bank note) in currency of lower denominations or in foreign money 5. to put a fresh covering, as a diaper, on —*vi.* 1. *a)* to alter; vary /the scene *changes*/ *b)* to undergo alteration or replacement 2. to become lower in range, as the male voice at puberty 3. to leave one train, bus, etc. and board another 4. to put on other clothes 5. to make an exchange —*n.* 1. the act or process of substitution, alteration, or variation 2. variety 3. something of the same kind but new or fresh 4. another set of clothes 5. *a)* money returned as the difference between the purchase price and the larger sum given in payment *b)* a number of coins or bills whose total value equals a single larger coin or bill *c)* small coins 6. a place where merchants meet to do business; exchange: also **'change** 7. [*usually pl.*] *Bell Ringing* any order in which the bells may be rung —**change off** to take turns —**ring the changes** 1. to ring a set of bells with all possible variations 2. to do or say a thing in many and various ways —**change′ful** *adj.* —**change′ful·ly** *adv.* —**change′ful·ness** *n.* —**chang′er** *n.*

**change·a·ble** (chānj′ə b'l) *adj.* 1. that can change or be changed; alterable 2. having a changing appearance or color —**change′a·bil′i·ty, change′a·ble·ness** *n.* —**change′a·bly** *adv.*

**change·less** (chānj′lis) *adj.* unchanging; immutable —**change′less·ly** *adv.* —**change′less·ness** *n.*

**change·ling** (-liŋ) *n.* a child secretly put in the place of another, esp., in folk tales, by fairies

**change of life** *same as* MENOPAUSE

**change·o·ver** (-ō′vər) *n.* a complete change, as in goods produced, equipment, etc.

**change ringing** the art of ringing a series of unrepeated changes on a set of bells tuned together

**chan·nel** (chan′'l) *n.* [< OFr.: see CANAL] **1.** the bed of a river, etc. **2.** the deeper part of a river, harbor, etc. **3.** a body of water joining two larger bodies of water **4.** a tube-like passage for liquids **5.** any means of passage or transmission **6.** [*pl.*] the proper or official course of action [to make a request through army *channels*] **7.** a long groove or furrow **8.** a narrow frequency band within which a radio or television transmitting station must keep its signal —*vt.* **-neled** or **-nelled, -nel·ing** or **-nel·ling 1.** to make a channel or channels in **2.** to send through or direct into a channel

**Channel Islands** group of Brit. islands in the English Channel, off the coast of Normandy

‡**chan·son** (shän sôn′; *E.* shan′sən) *n., pl.* **-sons′** (-sôn′; *E.* -sənz) [Fr.] a song

**chant** (chant) *n.* [Fr. < L. *cantus*, song < the *v.*] **1.** a song; melody **2.** *a*) a simple liturgical song in which a series of syllables or words is sung to each tone *b*) words, as of a psalm, to be sung in this way **3.** *a*) a singsong way of speaking *b*) anything uttered in this way —*vi.* [< OFr. < L. *cantare*, freq. of *canere*, to sing] **1.** to sing a chant; intone **2.** to speak monotonously or repetitiously —*vt.* **1.** to sing **2.** to celebrate in song **3.** to say monotonously **4.** to intone

**chan·teuse** (shan tōōz′) *n.* [Fr.] a woman singer

**chan·tey** (shan′tē, chan′tē) *n., pl.* **-teys** [< ? Fr.: see CHANT] a song that sailors sing in rhythm with their motions while working: also **chan′ty,** *pl.* **-ties**

**chan·ti·cleer** (chan′tə klir′) *n.* [< OFr.: see CHANT & CLEAR] a rooster: name used in fable and folklore

**Cha·nu·kah** (khä′nōō kä′) *n.* same as HANUKA

**cha·os** (kā′äs) *n.* [L. < Gr. *chaos*, space, chaos (sense 1)] **1.** the disorder of formless matter and infinite space, supposed to have existed before the ordered universe **2.** extreme confusion or disorder

**cha·ot·ic** (kā ät′ik) *adj.* in a state of chaos; in a completely confused or disordered condition —**cha·ot′i·cal·ly** *adv.*

**chap¹** (chäp, chap) *n.* [prob. < ME. *cheppe* < ?] *same as* CHOP²

**chap²** (chap) *n.* [< CHAPMAN] [Colloq.] a man or boy; fellow

**chap³** (chap) *vt., vi.* **chapped** or **chapt, chap′ping** [ME. *chappen*, var. of *choppen* (see CHOP¹)] to crack open or roughen, as the skin from exposure to cold —*n.* a chapped place in the skin

**chap. 1.** chaplain **2.** chapter

**cha·pa·re·jos, cha·pa·ra·jos** (chap′ə rā′hōs, shap′-) *n.pl.* [MexSp.] *same as* CHAPS¹

**chap·ar·ral** (chap′ə ral′, shap′-) *n.* [Sp. < *chaparro*, evergreen oak] [Southwest] a thicket of shrubs, thorny bushes, etc., orig. of evergreen oaks

**chap·book** (chap′book′) *n.* [< CHAP(MAN): chapmen peddled such books] a small book or pamphlet of poems, ballads, religious tracts, etc.

**cha·peau** (sha pō′) *n., pl.* **-peaus′, -peaux′** (-pōz′) [Fr. < OFr. < VL. *capellus*, dim. of LL. *cappa:* see CAPE¹] a hat

**chap·el** (chap′'l) *n.* [< OFr. < ML. < VL. (see prec.): orig. sanctuary in which cloak of St. Martin was preserved] **1.** a place of Christian worship smaller than a church **2.** a room or building used as a place of worship, as in a school **3.** a small room in a church, having its own altar **4.** a religious service, as in a chapel **5.** in Great Britain, any place of worship for those who are not members of an established church

**chap·er·on, chap·er·one** (shap′ə rōn′) *n.* [Fr. < OFr., hood (hence, protector) < *chape*, COPE²] a person, esp. an older or married woman, who accompanies young unmarried people in public or attends their parties, etc. for propriety or to supervise their behavior —*vt., vi.* **-oned′, -on′-ing** to act as chaperon (to) —**chap′er·on·age** *n.*

**chap·fall·en** (chäp′fô′lən, chap′-) *adj.* [CHAP¹ + FALLEN] **1.** having the lower jaw hanging down, as from fatigue **2.** disheartened, depressed, or humiliated

**chap·lain** (chap′lən) *n.* [< OFr. < ML.: see CHAPEL] **1.** a clergyman attached to a chapel, as of a royal court **2.** a minister, priest, or rabbi serving in a religious capacity with the armed forces or in a prison, hospital, etc. **3.** a clergyman, or sometimes a layman, appointed to perform religious functions in a public institution, club, etc. —**chap′lain·cy,** *pl.* **-cies, chap′lain·ship′** *n.*

**chap·let** (chap′lit) *n.* [< OFr. dim. of *chapel* < VL. *capellus:* see CHAPEAU] **1.** a garland for the head **2.** *a*) a string of prayer beads one third the length of a full rosary *b*) the prayers said with such beads **3.** any string of beads —**chap′let·ed** *adj.*

**Chap·lin** (chap′lin), Sir **Charles Spencer** 1889–1977; Eng. motion-picture actor & producer

**chap·man** (chap′mən) *n., pl.* **-men** [< OE. < *ceap*, trade + *man*] [Brit.] a peddler; hawker

**chaps¹** (chaps, shaps) *n.pl.* [< CHAPAREJOS] leather trousers without a seat, worn over ordinary trousers by cowboys to protect their legs

**chaps²** (chäps, chaps) *n.pl.* [see CHAP¹] *same as* CHOPS

**chap·ter** (chap′tər) *n.* [< OFr. *chapitre* < L. CAPITULUM, dim. of *caput*, head] **1.** a main division, as of a book **2.** a thing like a chapter; part; episode **3.** *a*) a formal meeting of canons of a church or of the members of a religious order *b*) the group of such canons, etc. **4.** a local branch of a club, fraternity, etc. —*vt.* to divide into chapters

**char¹** (chär) *vt., vi.* **charred, char′ring** [< CHARCOAL] **1.** to burn to charcoal **2.** to scorch —*n.* anything charred

**char²** (chär) *n.* [< CHARWOMAN] [Brit.] a charwoman —*vi.* **charred, char′ring** [Chiefly Brit.] to work as a charwoman

**char³** (chär) *n., pl.* **chars, char:** see PLURAL, II, D, 1 [< Gael. *ceara*, red] any of a genus of trouts with a red belly

**char·a·banc, char-à-banc** (shar′ə baŋk′, -baŋ′) *n.* [Fr., lit., car with bench] [Brit.] a sightseeing bus

**char·ac·ter** (kar′ik tər) *n.* [< L. < Gr. *charaktēr*, an engraving instrument < *charattein*, to engrave] **1.** a distinctive mark **2.** any figure, letter, or symbol used in writing and printing **3.** a distinctive trait or quality **4.** nature; kind or sort **5.** the pattern of behavior or personality found in an individual or group **6.** moral strength; self-discipline, fortitude, etc. **7.** *a*) reputation *b*) good reputation **8.** status; position **9.** a personage [great *characters* in history] **10.** a person in a play, novel, etc. **11.** [Colloq.] an odd, eccentric, or noteworthy person **12.** *Biol.* any attribute, as color, shape, etc., caused by the action of one or more genes —**in** (or **out of**) **character** consistent with (or inconsistent with) the role or general character

**character actor** an actor usually cast in the role of a person with pronounced or eccentric characteristics —**character actress** *fem.*

**char·ac·ter·is·tic** (kar′ik tə ris′tik) *adj.* of or constituting the special character; typical; distinctive —*n.* **1.** a distinguishing trait, feature, or quality **2.** the whole number, or integral part, of a logarithm, as 4 in the logarithm 4.7193: cf. MANTISSA —**char′ac·ter·is′ti·cal·ly** *adv.*

**char·ac·ter·ize** (kar′ik tə rīz′) *vt.* **-ized′, -iz′ing 1.** to describe or portray the particular traits of **2.** to be the distinctive character of; distinguish —**char′ac·ter·i·za′tion** *n.*

**cha·rade** (shə rād′) *n.* [Fr. < Pr. *charrada* < *charrar*, to gossip] **1.** [*often pl.*] a game in which a word or phrase is to be guessed is acted out in pantomime **2.** a pretense or fiction that can be seen through readily

**char·broil, char-broil** (chär′broil′) *vt.* [CHAR(COAL) + BROIL] to broil over a charcoal fire

**char·coal** (chär′kōl′) *n.* [ME. *char cole*, prob. < *charren*, to turn + *cole*, coal] **1.** a form of carbon produced by partially burning organic matter, as wood, in kilns from which air is excluded **2.** a pencil made of this substance **3.** a drawing made with such a pencil **4.** a very dark gray or brown, almost black —*vt.* to draw with charcoal

**chard** (chärd) *n.* [Fr. *carde* < L. *carduus*, thistle] a kind of beet whose large leaves and thick stalks are used as food

**chare** (cher) *n.* [OE. *cierr*, a turn, job < *cierran*, to turn] a chore, esp. a household chore —*vi.* **chared, char′ing 1.** to do chores **2.** *same as* CHAR²

**charge** (chärj) *vt.* **charged, charg′ing** [< OFr. *chargier* < VL. *carricare*, to load < L. *carrus*, car, wagon] **1.** to load or fill with the required material [*charged* with gunpowder] **2.** to saturate with another substance [air *charged* with steam] **3.** to add carbon dioxide to (water, etc.) **4.** to add an electrical charge to (a battery, etc.) **5.** to give as a task, duty, etc. to **6.** to give instructions to or command authoritatively **7.** to accuse of wrongdoing; censure [he *charged* her with negligence] **8.** to make liable for (an error, etc.) **9.** to ask as a price or fee [to *charge* $20 for labor] **10.** to record as a debt against a person or his account [to *charge* a purchase] **11.** to attack vigorously —*vi.* **1.** to ask payment (*for*) [to *charge* for a service] **2.** to attack vigorously or move forward as if attacking —*n.* **1.** the amount, as of fuel, gunpowder, etc., used to load or fill something **2.** *a*) the amount of chemical energy stored in a battery and dischargeable as electrical energy *b*) a change from the condition of electrical neutrality by the accumulation of electrons (*negative charge*) or by the loss of electrons (*positive charge*) **3.** [Slang] a thrill **4.** responsibility or duty (*of*) **5.** care or custody (*of*) **6.** a person or thing entrusted to someone's care **7.** instruction or command, esp. instructions given by a judge to a jury **8.** accusation; indictment [*charges* of cruelty] **9.** the cost or price of an article, service, etc. **10.** a debt **11.** *same as* CHARGE ACCOUNT **12.** *a*) an attack, as by troops *b*) the signal for this **13.** *Heraldry* a bearing —**charge off 1.** to regard as a loss **2.** to ascribe —**in charge** having the responsibility or control —**charge′a·ble** (chär′jə b'l) *adj.*

**charge account** an arrangement by which a customer may pay for purchases within a specified future period

**char·gé d'af·faires** (shär zhā′ də fer′) *pl.* **char·gés d'af·faires** (shär zhāz′ də fer′, shär zhā′ də fer′) [Fr.] **1.** a diplomat substituting for a minister or ambassador **2.** a diplomat ranking below an ambassador or minister

**charge plate** a metal or plastic plate embossed with the owner's name and address, for stamping his bills when he makes purchases on credit: also **charge card**

**charg·er¹** (chär′jər) *n.* **1.** one that charges **2.** a horse ridden in battle or on parade **3.** an apparatus for charging storage batteries

**charg·er²** (chär′jər) *n.* [ME. *chargeour*] [Archaic] a large, flat dish; platter

**char·i·ly** (cher′ə lē) *adv.* in a chary manner

**char·i·ness** (-ē nis) *n.* the quality of being chary

**char·i·ot** (char′ē ət) *n.* [< OFr. < VL. *carricare:* see CHARGE] a horse-drawn, two-wheeled cart used in ancient times for war, racing, etc. —*vt., vi.* to drive or ride in a chariot

**char·i·ot·eer** (char′ē ə tir′) *n.* a chariot driver

**cha·ris·ma** (kə riz′mə) *n., pl.* **-ma·ta** (-mə tə) [< Gr., favor, grace] **1.** *Christian Theol.* a divinely inspired gift or talent, as

CHARIOT

for prophesying **2.** a special quality of leadership that inspires great popular allegiance Also **char·ism** (kar′iz'm)

**char·is·mat·ic** (kar′iz mat′ik) *adj.* **1.** having or resulting from charisma **2.** designating or of any religious group or movement that stresses direct divine inspiration —*n.* **1.** a member of a charismatic group or movement **2.** a person who supposedly has some divinely inspired power, as the ability to prophesy

**char·i·ta·ble** (char′i tə b'l) *adj.* **1.** kind and generous in giving help to those in need **2.** of or for charity **3.** kind and forgiving in judging others —**char′i·ta·bly** *adv.*

**char·i·ty** (char′ə tē) *n., pl.* **-ties** [< OFr. < L. *caritas*, affection < *carus*, dear] **1.** *Christian Theol.* the love of God for man or of man for his fellow men **2.** an act of good will **3.** benevolence **4.** kindness in judging others **5.** a voluntary giving of money, etc. to those in need **6.** a welfare institution, organization, etc.

**cha·ri·va·ri** (shə riv′ə rē′, shiv ə rē′, shiv′ə rē) *n.* [Fr. < LL. < Gr. *karēbaria*, heavy head] *same as* SHIVAREE

**char·la·tan** (shär′lə t'n) *n.* [Fr. < It. *ciarlatano* < LL. *cerretanus*, seller of papal indulgences] one who pretends to have expert knowledge or skill that he does not have; fake —**char′la·tan·ism, char′la·tan·ry,** *pl.* **-ries** *n.*

**Char·le·magne** (shär′lə mān′) 742–814 A.D.; king of the Franks (768–814); emperor of the Holy Roman Empire (800–814): also called **Charles the Great**

**Charles** (chärlz) [Fr. < ML. *Carolus* (or) < Gmc. *Karl*; lit., full-grown] **1.** a masculine name: dim. *Charley, Charlie* **2. Charles I** *a*) 1600–49; king of England, Scotland, & Ireland (1625–49) *b*) *same as* CHARLEMAGNE **3. Charles II** 1630–85; king of England, Scotland, & Ireland (1660–85): son of *Charles I* **4. Charles V** 1500–58; Holy Roman Emperor (1519–56) &, as **Charles I,** king of Spain (1516–56)

**Charles's Wain** (chärl′ziz) [Brit.] *same as* BIG DIPPER

**Charles·ton** (chärl′stən) [after CHARLES I of England] **1.** capital of W.Va., in the W part: pop. 64,000 **2.** seaport in S.C.: pop. 70,000 —*n.* [< the seaport] a lively dance in 4/4 time, characterized by a twisting step

**char·ley horse** (chär′lē) [Colloq.] a cramp in the leg or arm muscles, caused by strain

**char·lock** (chär′lək) *n.* [OE. *cerlic*] a weed of the mustard family, with yellow flowers

**Char·lotte** (shär′lət) [Fr., fem. of *Charlot*, dim. of *Charles*] **1.** a feminine name **2.** [after Queen *Charlotte*, wife of GEORGE III] city in S N.C.: pop. 314,000 (met. area 632,000)

**char·lotte** (shär′lət) *n.* [Fr. < prec.] a dessert made of fruit, gelatin, custard, etc. in a mold lined with strips of bread, cake, etc.

**Charlotte A·ma·lie** (ə mäl′yə, ə mäl′ē) capital of the Virgin Islands of the U.S.: pop. 12,000

**charlotte russe** (rōōs) [Fr., Russian charlotte] a charlotte of whipped cream, custard, etc. in a spongecake mold

**Char·lotte·town** (shär′lət toun′) capital of Prince Edward Island, Canada: pop. 18,000

**charm** (chärm) *n.* [< OFr. < L. *carmen*, song, charm] **1.** a chanted word or verse, an action, or an object assumed to have magic power to help or hurt **2.** a trinket on a bracelet, watch chain, etc. **3.** a quality or feature that attracts or delights —*vt.* **1.** to act on as though by magic **2.** to attract or please greatly; fascinate; delight —*vi.* to be charming —**charm′er** *n.*

**charm·ing** (chärm′iŋ) *adj.* attractive; fascinating; delightful —**charm′ing·ly** *adv.*

**char·nel** (chär′n'l) *n.* [OFr. < LL. *carnale*, graveyard; neut. of *carnalis*, CARNAL] a building or place where corpses or bones are deposited: in full, **charnel house** —*adj.* of, like, or fit for a charnel

**Cha·ron** (ker′ən) *Gr. Myth.* the boatman who ferried souls of the dead across the river Styx to Hades

**charr** (chär) *n., pl.* **charrs, charr:** *see* PLURAL, II, D, 1 *same as* CHAR³

**char·ry** (chär′ē) *adj.* **-ri·er, -ri·est** like charcoal

**chart** (chärt) *n.* [OFr. < ML. < L. *charta:* see CARD¹] **1.** a map, esp. one for marine or air navigation **2.** an outline map on which special information, as on weather, is plotted geographically **3.** *a*) a group of facts set up in the form of a diagram, graph, etc. *b*) such a diagram, graph, etc., or a sheet with diagrams, etc. —*vt.* **1.** to make a chart of **2.** to plan (a course of action) **3.** to show by, on, or as by a chart —**chart′less** *adj.*

**char·ter** (chär′tər) *n.* [< OFr. < L. dim. of *charta:* see CARD¹] **1.** a franchise or written grant of specified rights given by a government or ruler to a person, corporation, etc. **2.** *a*) a document setting forth the aims and principles of a united group, as of nations *b*) a document embodying a city constitution **3.** a document authorizing the organization of a local chapter of a society **4.** the hire or lease of a ship, bus, etc. —*vt.* **1.** to grant a charter to **2.** to hire for exclusive use —**char′ter·er** *n.*

**charter member** one of the founders or original members of an organization

**Char·tres** (shär′tr′; *E.* shärt) city in NC France: site of a Gothic cathedral: pop. 31,000

**char·treuse** (shär trōōz′, -trōōs′; *Fr.* shår tröz′) *n.* [Fr., Carthusian] **1.** a yellow, pale-green, or white liqueur made by Carthusian monks **2.** pale, yellowish green

**char·wom·an** (chär′woom′ən) *n., pl.* **-wom′en** [see CHARE, CHORE] a woman who does cleaning or scrubbing, as in office buildings

**char·y** (cher′ē, char′ē) *adj.* **char′i·er, char′i·est** [OE. *cearig* < *cearu,* care] **1.** not taking chances; cautious **2.** not giving freely; sparing

**Cha·ryb·dis** (kə rib′dis) whirlpool off the NE coast of Sicily: see SCYLLA

**chase¹** (chās) *vt.* **chased, chas′ing** [< OFr. *chacier, cachier:* see CATCH] **1.** to follow quickly or persistently so as to catch or harm **2.** to run after; follow **3.** to make away; drive —*vi.* **1.** to go in pursuit **2.** [Colloq.] to go hurriedly; rush —*n.* **1.** a chasing; pursuit **2.** the hunting of game for sport (often with *the*) —**give chase** to chase

**chase²** (chās) *n.* [OFr. *châsse,* a frame, ult. < L. *capsa:* see CASE²] **1.** a groove; furrow **2.** a rectangular metal frame in which pages or columns of type are locked —*vt.* **chased, chas′ing** to make a groove or furrow in; indent

**chase³** (chās) *vt.* **chased, chas′ing** [< Fr. *enchâsser,* enshrine] to ornament (metal) by engraving, embossing, etc.

**chas·er** (chā′sər) *n.* **1.** one that chases or hunts **2.** [Colloq.] a mild drink, as water, taken after or with whiskey

**chasm** (kaz′'m) *n.* [L. & Gr. *chasma* < Gr. *chainein,* to gape] **1.** a deep crack in the earth's surface; abyss; gorge **2.** any break or gap **3.** a wide divergence of feelings, interests, etc.; rift —**chas′mal** (-m'l), **chas′mic** (-mik) *adj.*

**chas·seur** (sha sur′) *n.* [Fr.] **1.** a hunter **2.** a soldier, esp. one of certain French troops, trained for rapid action **3.** a uniformed attendant

**Chas·sid·im** (has′i dim; *Heb.* khä sē′-) *n.pl., sing.* **Chas′sid** *same as* HASIDIM —**Chas·sid′ic** *adj.* —**Chas′sid·ism** *n.*

**chas·sis** (chas′ē, shas′ē) *n., pl.* **-sis** (-ēz) [Fr. *châssis:* see CHASE²] **1.** the frame, wheels, etc. of a motor vehicle, but not the body and engine **2.** the frame supporting the body of an airplane **3.** *Radio & TV a*) the framework to which the parts of a receiver, amplifier, etc. are attached *b*) the assembled frame and parts **4.** [Slang] the body; figure

**chaste** (chāst) *adj.* [OFr. < L. *castus,* pure: see CASTE] **1.** not indulging in unlawful sexual activity; virtuous: said esp. of women **2.** sexually abstinent; celibate **3.** pure; decent; modest **4.** restrained and simple in style —**chaste′ly** *adv.* —**chaste′ness** *n.*

**chas·ten** (chās′'n) *vt.* [< OFr. < L. *castigare,* to punish < *castus,* pure + *agere,* to lead] **1.** to punish so as to correct; chastise **2.** to restrain from excess; subdue **3.** to refine in style —**chas′ten·er** *n.*

**chas·tise** (chas tīz′, chas′tīz) *vt.* **-tised′, -tis′ing** [see prec.] **1.** to punish, esp. by beating **2.** to scold or condemn sharply —**chas·tise′ment** *n.* —**chas·tis′er** *n.*

**chas·ti·ty** (chas′tə tē) *n.* [see CHASTE] the quality or state of being chaste; specif., *a)* virtuousness *b)* sexual abstinence *c)* decency *d)* simplicity of style

**chas·u·ble** (chaz′yoo b'l, chas′-) *n.* [OFr. < ML. *casubla,* hooded garment] a sleeveless outer vestment worn over the alb by priests at Mass

**chat** (chat) *vi.* **chat′ted, chat′ting** [< CHATTER] to talk or converse in a light, easy, informal way —*n.* **1.** light, easy, informal conversation **2.** any of various birds with a chattering call

**chât·eau** (sha tō′) *n., pl.* **-teaux′** (-tōz′, -tō′), **-teaus′** [Fr. < OFr. < L. *castellum,* CASTLE] **1.** a French feudal castle **2.** a large country house, esp. in France Also **cha·teau′**

**cha·teau·bri·and** (shà tō brē än′) *n.* [after F. R. de *Chateaubriand* (1768–1848), Fr. statesman] a thick beef fillet from the center of the tenderloin

CHASUBLE

**chat·e·laine** (shat′'l ān′) *n.* [Fr., ult. < L. *castellum,* CASTLE] **1.** the mistress of a castle or of any large household **2.** a woman's ornamental chain or clasp, esp. for the waist, with keys, a watch, etc. fastened to it

**Chat·ta·noo·ga** (chat′ə nōō′gə) [< AmInd.] city in SE Tenn., on the Ga. border: pop. 170,000

**chat·tel** (chat′'l) *n.* [OFr. *chatel:* see CATTLE] **1.** *a)* a movable item of personal property, as a piece of furniture: in full, **chattel personal** *b)* any interest in real estate less than a freehold: in full, **chattel real 2.** [Archaic] a slave

**chattel mortgage** a mortgage on personal property

**chat·ter** (chat′ər) *vi.* [echoic] **1.** to make short, indistinct sounds in rapid succession, as birds, apes, etc. **2.** to talk fast, incessantly, and foolishly **3.** to click together rapidly, as the teeth do from fright or cold —*vt.* to utter with a chattering sound —*n.* **1.** the act or sound of chattering **2.** rapid, foolish talk —**chat′ter·er** *n.*

**chat·ter·box** (-bäks′) *n.* an incessant talker

**chat·ty** (chat′ē) *adj.* **-ti·er, -ti·est 1.** fond of chatting **2.** light, familiar, and informal: said of talk —**chat′ti·ly** *adv.* —**chat′ti·ness** *n.*

**Chau·cer** (chô′sər), **Geoffrey** 1340?–1400; Eng. poet: author of *The Canterbury Tales* —**Chau·ce′ri·an** (-sir′ē ən) *adj.*

**chauf·feur** (shō′fər, shō fur′) *n.* [Fr., lit., stoker < *chauffer,* to heat: see CHAFE] a person hired to drive a private automobile for someone else —*vt.* to act as chauffeur to

**chaunt** (chônt) *n., vt., vi.* archaic var. of CHANT

**chau·tau·qua** (shə tô′kwə) *n.* [< the summer schools inaugurated at Chautauqua, N.Y., in 1874] an educational and recreational assembly with a program of lectures, etc.

**chau·vin·ism** (shō′və niz′m) *n.* [< Fr. < N. *Chauvin,* Napoleonic soldier, notorious for his fanatical patriotism] **1.** militant, boastful, and fanatical patriotism **2.** unreasoning devotion to one's race, sex, etc., the opposite sex, etc. —**chau′vin·ist** *n., adj.* —**chau′vin·is′tic** *adj.* —**chau′vin·is′ti·cal·ly** *adv.*

**chaw** (chô) *n. dial. var. of* CHEW (*n.* 2)

**cheap** (chēp) *adj.* [< *good cheap,* good bargain < OE. *ceap,* a bargain] **1.** low in price; not expensive **2.** charging low prices **3.** spending little **4.** worth more than the price **5.** easily got **6.** of little or no value **7.** contemptible **8.** [Colloq.] stingy; miserly **9.** lowered in buying power or available at low interest rates: said of money —*adv.* at low cost —**cheap′ly** *adv.* —**cheap′ness** *n.*

**cheap·en** (chēp′'n) *vt., vi.* to make or become cheap or cheaper —**cheap′en·er** *n.*

**cheap-jack** (-jak′) *n.* [CHEAP + JACK] a peddler of cheap, inferior articles —*adj.* cheap, inferior, base, etc. Also **cheap′-john′** (-jän′)

**cheap·skate** (-skāt′) *n.* [Slang] a miserly person

**cheat** (chēt) *n.* [< ME. *eschete:* see ESCHEAT] **1.** a fraud; deception **2.** one who deceives or defrauds others; swindler —*vt.* **1.** to defraud; swindle **2.** to deceive by trickery; fool **3.** to foil or escape by tricks or good luck [to *cheat* death] —*vi.* **1.** to practice fraud or deception **2.** [Slang] to be sexually unfaithful (often with *on*) —**cheat′er** *n.* —**cheat′ing·ly** *adv.*

**check** (chek) *n.* [OFr. *eschec,* a check at chess < ML. *scaccus* < Per. *shāh,* king] **1.** a sudden stop **2.** any restraint or control of action **3.** one that restrains or controls **4.** a supervision of accuracy, efficiency, etc. **5.** *a)* a test, comparison, etc. to see if something is as it should be *b)* a standard or sample used for this **6.** a mark (✓) to show

approval or verification or to call attention to something **7.** an identification token enabling one to re-claim an item [a hat *check*] **8.** one's bill at a restaurant or bar **9.** a written order to a bank to pay the stated amount from one's account **10.** *a)* a pattern of small squares like that of a chessboard *b)* one of these squares **11.** a fabric with such a pattern **12.** a small split or crack **13.** *Chess* the condition of a king that is in danger and must be put into a safe position **14.** *Hockey* a blocking of an opponent's play or movement —*interj.* **1.** [Colloq.] agreed! right! OK! **2.** *Chess* a call meaning the opponent's king is in check —*vt.* **1.** to make stop suddenly **2.** to hold back; restrain **3.** to rebuff, repulse, or rebuke **4.** to test, measure, verify, or control by investigation or comparison **5.** to mark with a check (✓) **6.** to mark with a pattern of squares **7.** to deposit or receive for deposit temporarily, as in a checkroom **8.** to get (esp. luggage) cleared for shipment **9.** to make chinks or cracks in **10.** *Chess* to place (an opponent's king) in check **11.** *Hockey* to block the play or movement of (an opponent) —*vi.* **1.** to agree with one another, item for item [the accounts *check*] **2.** to investigate so as to determine the condition, validity, etc. of something (often with *on*) **3.** to crack in small checks, as paint **4.** *Chess* to place an opponent's king in check —*adj.* **1.** used to check or verify **2.** having a crisscross pattern; checked —**check in 1.** to register at a hotel, convention, etc. **2.** [Colloq.] to report, as by presenting oneself [check *in* at the office] —**check off** to mark as verified, examined, etc. —**check out 1.** to settle one's bill and leave a hotel, etc. **2.** to add up the prices of (purchases) and collect the total: said of a cashier, as in a supermarket **3.** to examine and verify or approve **4.** to prove to be accurate, sound, etc. upon examination **5.** [Slang] to die —**check up on** to examine or investigate —**in check** in restraint; under control

**check·book** (-book′) *n.* a book containing detachable forms for writing checks on a bank

**checked** (chekt) *adj.* having a pattern of squares

**check·er¹** (chek′ər) *n.* [OFr. *eschekier,* a chessboard < *eschec:* see CHECK] **1.** a small square, as on a chessboard **2.** a pattern of such squares **3.** *a)* [*pl., with sing. v.*] a game played on a checkerboard by two players, each with twelve round, flat pieces to move *b)* any of these pieces —*vt.* **1.** to mark off in squares **2.** to break the uniformity of, as with varied features, changes in fortune, etc.

**check·er²** (chek′ər) *n.* **1.** a person who examines or verifies **2.** a person who checks hats, luggage, etc. **3.** a cashier, as in a supermarket

**check·er·ber·ry** (-ber′ē) *n., pl.* **-ries 1.** *same as* WINTERGREEN (sense 1) **2.** the edible, red, berrylike fruit of the wintergreen

**check·er·board** (-bôrd′) *n.* a board with 64 squares of two alternating colors, used in checkers and chess

**check·ered** (-ərd) *adj.* **1.** having a pattern of squares **2.** varied in color and shading **3.** marked by diversified features or by varied events, as a career

**checking account** a bank account against which the depositor can draw checks at any time

**check·list** (-list′) *n.* a list of things to be checked off or referred to: also **check list**

**check·mate** (-māt′) *n.* [OFr. *eschec mat,* ult. < Per. *shāh māt,* lit., the king is dead] **1.** *Chess a)* the winning move that checks the opponent's king so that it cannot be put into safety *b)* the king's position after this move **2.** complete defeat, frustration, etc. —*interj. Chess* a call indicating checkmate —*vt.* **-mat′ed, -mat′ing 1.** to place in checkmate **2.** to defeat completely

**check-off** (-ôf′) *n.* an arrangement by which dues of tradeunion members are withheld from wages and turned over to the union by the employer

**check-out** (-out′) *n.* **1.** the act or place of checking out purchases, as in a supermarket **2.** the time by which one must check out of a hotel, etc. **3.** a testing, esp. of a machine, as for accuracy Also **check′-out′**

**check·point** (-point′) *n.* a place where traffic is stopped by authorities, as for inspection

**check·rein** (-rān′) *n.* a short rein attached to the bridle to keep a horse's head up

**check·room** (-rōōm′, -room′) *n.* a room in which to check (*vt.* 7) hats, coats, parcels, etc.

**check-up** (-up′) *n.* an examination or investigation, esp. a general medical examination

**Ched·dar** (cheese) (ched′ər) [< *Cheddar,* Somersetshire, England, where orig. made] [*often* c-] a variety of hard, smooth cheese

**cheek** (chēk) *n.* [OE. *ceoke,* jaw, jawbone] **1.** either side of the face, below the eye **2.** either of two sides of a thing, as the jaws of a vise: *usually used in pl.* **3.** either of the buttocks **4.** [Colloq.] sauciness; impudence —**cheek by jowl**

close together; intimately —(with) **tongue in cheek** in a humorously ironic or insincere way

**cheek·bone** (-bōn′) *n.* the bone of the upper cheek, just below the eye

**cheek·y** (-ē) *adj.* **cheek′i·er, cheek′i·est** [CHEEK + -Y²] [Colloq.] saucy; impudent; insolent —**cheek′i·ly** *adv.* —**cheek′i·ness** *n.*

**cheep** (chēp) *n.* [echoic] the short, faint, shrill sound of a young bird; peep —*vt., vi.* to make, or utter with, such a sound —**cheep′er** *n.*

**cheer** (chir) *n.* [< OFr. *chiere* < LL. *cara,* the head < Gr. *kara*] **1.** state of mind or of feeling; spirit: now in **be of good cheer, with good cheer,** etc. **2.** gladness; joy **3.** festive food or entertainment **4.** encouragement **5.** *a)* a shout of welcome, approval, encouragement, etc. *b)* a jingle, etc. shouted in unison in rooting for a team —*vt.* **1.** to fill with joy and hope; gladden; comfort (often with *up*) **2.** to urge on or encourage by cheers **3.** to greet or applaud with cheers —*vi.* **1.** to be or become cheerful; feel encouraged (usually with *up*) **2.** to shout cheers

**cheer·ful** (-fəl) *adj.* **1.** full of cheer; joyful **2.** filling with cheer; bright and attractive *[a cheerful room]* **3.** willing; ready *[a cheerful helper]* —**cheer′ful·ly** *adv.* —**cheer′ful·ness** *n.*

**cheer·i·o** (-ē ō′) *interj., n., pl.* **-os′** [Brit. Colloq.] **1.** goodbye **2.** good health: a toast

**cheer·lead·er** (-lē′dər) *n.* one who leads others in cheering for a football team, etc.

**cheer·less** (-lis) *adj.* not cheerful; dismal —**cheer′less·ly** *adv.* —**cheer′less·ness** *n.*

**cheers** (chirz) *interj.* [Chiefly Brit.] good health: a toast

**cheer·y** (chir′ē) *adj.* **cheer′i·er, cheer′i·est** cheerful —**cheer′i·ly** *adv.* —**cheer′i·ness** *n.*

**cheese¹** (chēz) *n.* [OE. *cyse,* akin to L. *caseus*] **1.** a food made from curds of soured milk pressed together to form a solid, variously hardened, ripened, etc. **2.** a shaped mass of this

**cheese²** (chēz) *n.* [Hindi *chīz* (< Per. *čiz*), thing] [Slang] an important person or thing

**cheese·burg·er** (chēz′bʉr′gər) *n.* [CHEESE¹ + -BURGER] a hamburger topped with melted cheese

**cheese·cake** (-kāk′) *n.* **1.** a kind of cake made of cottage cheese or cream cheese, eggs, sugar, etc., usually baked with a bottom crust of crumbs **2.** [Slang] display of the figure, esp. the legs, of a pretty girl, as in photographs

**cheese·cloth** (-klôth′) *n.* [from use as cheese wrapping] a thin cotton cloth with a loose weave

**cheese·par·ing** (-per′iŋ) *n.* **1.** anything as worthless as a paring of cheese rind **2.** miserly handling of money —*adj.* stingy; miserly

**chees·y** (-ē) *adj.* **chees′i·er, chees′i·est** **1.** like cheese **2.** [Slang] inferior; poor —**chees′i·ness** *n.*

**chee·tah** (chēt′ə) *n.* [Hindi *chītā* < Sans. *citra,* spotted] a swift, leopardlike animal of Africa and S Asia, with a small head, long legs, and a black-spotted, tawny coat: it can be trained to hunt

**chef** (shef) *n.* [Fr. < *chef de cuisine,* lit., head of the kitchen: see CHIEF] **1.** a head cook, as in a restaurant **2.** any cook

**‡chef-d'oeu·vre** (she dĕ′vr′) *n., pl.* **chefs-d'oeu′vre** (she dĕ′vr′) [Fr., principal work] a masterpiece, as in art or literature

**Che·khov** (chek′ôf; *Russ.* chekh′ôf), **An·ton (Pavlovich)** (än tôn′) 1860–1904; Russ. dramatist & short-story writer: also sp. **Chekov**

**che·la** (kē′lə) *n., pl.* **-lae** (-lē) [ModL. < Gr. *chēlē,* claw] a pincerlike claw of a crab, lobster, scorpion, etc.

**che·late** (kē′lāt) *adj.* resembling or having chelae —*n. Chem.* a compound in which a central atom (usually a metal ion) is attached to at least two other atoms by bonds so as to form a ring structure —*vt.* **-lat·ed, -lat·ing** to cause (a metal ion) to react with another molecule to form a chelate —**che·la′tion** *n.*

**che·lic·er·a** (kə lis′ə rə) *n., pl.* **-er·ae′** (-ə rē′) [ModL. < Gr. *chēlē,* claw + *keras,* horn] either of the first pair of appendages of spiders and other arachnids, used for grasping and crushing

**che·lo·ni·an** (ki lō′nē ən) *adj.* [< ModL. *Chelonia* < Gr. *chelōnē*] of, like, or being a turtle or tortoise —*n.* a turtle or tortoise

**Chel·ya·binsk** (chi lyä′binsk) city in the SW R.S.F.S.R., in the S Urals: pop. 851,000

**chem. 1.** chemical(s) **2.** chemist **3.** chemistry

**chem·ic** (kem′ik) *adj.* [Now Poet.] chemical

**chem·i·cal** (kem′i k'l) *adj.* **1.** of or having to do with chemistry **2.** involving the use of chemicals —*n.* any substance used in or obtained by a chemical process —**chem′i·cal·ly** *adv.*

**chemical engineering** the science or profession of applying chemistry to industrial uses

**chemical warfare** warfare using poisonous gases, flame throwers, incendiary bombs, etc.

**chem·i·lu·mi·nes·cence** (kem′i lōō′mə nes′'ns) *n.* visible light chemically produced without heat

**che·mise** (shə mēz′) *n.* [OFr. < VL. *camisia,* shirt < Gaul.] **1.** a woman's undergarment somewhat like a loose, short slip **2.** a straight, loose dress

**chem·ist** (kem′ist) *n.* [< (AL)CHEMIST] **1.** an expert or specialist in chemistry **2.** [Brit.] a pharmacist, or druggist

**chem·is·try** (kem′is trē) *n., pl.* **-tries** [prec. + -RY] **1.** the science dealing with the composition and properties of substances, and with the reactions by which substances are produced or converted into other substances **2.** the application of this to a specified subject or field of activity **3.** the chemical properties, composition, reactions, and uses of a substance **4.** any process of synthesis or analysis similar to that used in chemistry *[the chemistry of wit]*

**chem·o-** *a combining form meaning* of, with, or by chemicals or chemistry *[chemotherapy]*

**chem·o·re·cep·tor** (kem′ō ri sep′tər, kē′mō-) *n.* a nerve ending or sense organ responsive to chemical stimuli, as a taste bud —**chem′o·re·cep′tion** *n.*

**chem·o·sur·ger·y** (-sʉr′jər ē) *n.* the removal of diseased tissue or abnormal growths by using chemicals

**chem·o·ther·a·py** (-ther′ə pē) *n.* the prevention or treatment of infection or disease by doses of chemical drugs: also **chem′o·ther′a·peu′tics** (-ther′ə pyōōt′iks) —**chem′o·ther′a·peu′tic** *adj.* —**chem′o·ther′a·peu′ti·cal·ly** *adv.* —**chem′o·ther′a·pist** *n.*

**chem·ur·gy** (kem′ər jē) *n.* [CHEM(O)- + -URGY] the branch of chemistry dealing with the industrial use of organic products, esp. from farms (e.g., the use of soybeans as a base for plastics) —**chem·ur′gic** (kem ʉr′jik) *adj.*

**Cheng·tu** (chuŋ′dōō′) city in SC China: pop. 1,135,000

**che·nille** (shi nēl′) *n.* [Fr., lit., hairy caterpillar < L. *canicula,* little dog] **1.** a tufted, velvety yarn used for trimming, embroidery, etc. **2.** a fabric filled or woven with this, as for rugs

**che·nin blanc** (shə nan blän′, shen′in blänk′) [*also* **C- B-**] [Fr.] a light, dry or semisweet white wine

**che·ong·sam, che·ong-sam** (chē ôŋ′säm′) *n.* [Chin.] a high-necked, closefitting Chinese dress with the skirt slit part way up the sides

**Che·ops** (kē′äps) *Gr. name of* KHUFU

**cheque** (chek) *n. Brit. sp. of* CHECK (*n.* 9)

**cheq·uer** (chek′ər) *n., vt. Brit. sp. of* CHECKER¹

**Cher·bourg** (sher′boorg; *Fr.* sher bōōr′) seaport in NW France, on the English Channel: pop. 37,000

**cher·ish** (cher′ish) *vt.* [< OFr. < *cher,* dear < L. *carus*] **1.** to hold dear; feel or show love for **2.** to take good care of; protect; foster *[to cherish one's rights]* **3.** to cling to the idea of

**Cher·o·kee** (cher′ə kē′) *n.* [prob. < Choctaw *chiluk-ki,* "cave people"] **1.** *pl.* **-kees′, -kee′** a member of a tribe of Iroquoian Indians, most of whom were moved from the SE U.S. to Oklahoma **2.** their Iroquoian language

**Cherokee rose** an evergreen climbing rose with fragrant, large, white flowers and glossy leaves, native to China but now growing wild in the S U.S.

**che·root** (shə rōōt′) *n.* [< Tamil *churuttu,* a roll] a cigar with both ends cut square

**cher·ry** (cher′ē) *n., pl.* **-ries** [Anglo-Fr. *cherise* < OFr. < VL. < Gr. *kerasion* < *kerasos,* cherry tree] **1.** a small, fleshy fruit, yellow to dark red, with a smooth, hard pit **2.** any tree of the rose family which bears this fruit, or its wood **3.** the bright-red color of certain cherries —*adj.* **1.** bright-red **2.** of cherry wood **3.** made with cherries

**cherry bomb** a round, red, powerful firecracker

**cher·ry·stone** (-stōn′) *n.* a small quahog, a variety of clam: also **cherrystone clam**

**chert** (chʉrt) *n.* [< ?] a very fine-grained, tough rock composed mainly of silica —**chert′y** (-ē) *adj.*

**cher·ub** (cher′əb) *n., pl.* **-ubs**; for 1–3 usually **-u·bim** (-ə bim, -yoo bim) or (KJV) **-u·bims** [< LL. < Heb. *kerūbh*] **1.** *Bible* one of certain winged heavenly beings: Ezek. 10 **2.** *Christian Theol.* any of the second order of angels, just below the seraphim **3.** a representation of a cherub, now usually as a chubby, rosy-faced child with wings **4.** a person, esp. a child, with a sweet, innocent face —**che·ru·bic** (chə rōō′bik) *adj.* —**che·ru′bi·cal·ly** *adv.*

**cher·vil** (chʉr′vəl) *n.* [< OE. < L. < Gr. < *chairein,* to rejoice + *phyllon,* leaf] a plant of the parsley family, with leaves used to flavor soups, etc.

**Ches·a·peake** (ches′ə pēk′) [see ff.] city in SE Va., at the base of Chesapeake Bay: pop. 114,000

**Chesapeake Bay** [*Chesapeake* < Algonquian, lit., country on a big river] arm of the Atlantic, extending north into Va. and Md.

**Chesh·ire cat** (chesh′ir, -ər) a proverbial grinning cat from Cheshire, a county of W England, esp. one described in Lewis Carroll's *Alice's Adventures in Wonderland*

**Chesh·van** (khesh′vän) *n. same as* HESHVAN

**chess** (ches) *n.* [< OFr. *esches,* pl. of *eschec:* see CHECK] a game for two, each with 16 pieces moved variously on a chessboard in alternation, the object being to checkmate the opponent's king

**chess·board** (-bôrd′) *n.* a board with 64 squares of two alternating colors, for chess and checkers

**chess·man** (-man′, -mən) *n., pl.* **-men′** (-men′, -mən) any of the pieces used in chess

**chess pie** [< ?] a dessert made of a custard-like mixture of butter, sugar, eggs, etc., baked in a pie shell

**chest** (chest) *n.* [< OE. < L. < Gr. *kistē,* a box] **1.** a box with a lid and, often, a lock, for storing or shipping things **2.** a public fund *[community chest]* **3.** *same as* CHEST OF DRAWERS **4.** a cabinet for medicines, toiletries, etc. **5.** *a)* the part of the body enclosed by the ribs; thorax *b)* the outside front of this —**get (something) off one's chest** [Colloq.] to unburden oneself of (some trouble, etc.) by talking about it

**chest·ed** (-id) *adj.* having a (specified kind of) chest, or thorax *[hollow-chested]*

**Ches·ter** (ches′tər) [< OE. < L. *castra,* a camp] **1.** a masculine name **2.** [after *Chester,* city in W England] seaport in SE Pa., on the Delaware River: pop. 46,000

**Ches·ter·field** (ches′tər fēld′), 4th Earl of (*Philip Dormer Stanhope*) 1694-1773; Eng. statesman & writer: called *Lord Chesterfield*

**ches·ter·field** (ches′tər fēld′) *n.* [after a 19th-c. Earl of *Chesterfield*] **1.** a single-breasted topcoat, usually with a velvet collar **2.** a sofa with upright ends

**Chester White** [after *Chester* County, Pa.] a variety of large, white hog

**chest·nut** (ches′nut′, -nət) *n.* [< OFr. < L. < Gr. *kastaneia*] **1.** the smooth-shelled, sweet, edible nut of certain trees of the beech family **2.** one of these trees, or the wood **3.** *same as* HORSE CHESTNUT **4.** reddish brown **5.** a reddish-brown horse **6.** [Colloq.] *a)* an old, stale joke or phrase; cliché *b)* a familiar story, piece of music, etc., repeated too often —*adj.* reddish-brown

**chest of drawers** a set of drawers within a frame, as for keeping clothing in a bedroom; bureau

**chest·y** (ches′tē) *adj.* **chest′i·er, chest′i·est** [Colloq.] **1.** having a large chest, or thorax **2.** bosomy **3.** boastful

**che·val glass** (shə val′) [Fr. *cheval,* horse, support + GLASS] a full-length mirror on swivels in a frame

**chev·a·lier** (shev′ə lir′; *for 1, often* shə val′yā′) *n.* [see CAVALIER] **1.** a member of the lowest rank of the French Legion of Honor **2.** a cavalier; gallant

**Chev·i·ot** (chev′ē ət; *also, and for 2 always,* shev′-) *n.* [after the *Cheviot Hills,* between England and Scotland] **1.** any of a breed of sheep with short, dense wool **2.** *[usually* c-] *a)* a rough wool fabric in a twill weave *b)* a cotton cloth resembling this

**chev·ron** (shev′rən) *n.* [< OFr., rafter (from its shape), ult. < L. *capra,* she-goat] a V-shaped bar or bars worn on the sleeve, as of a military uniform, to show rank or service

**chev·y** (chev′ē) *n., pl.* **chev′ies** [< hunting cry *chivy,* in the ballad of *Chevy Chase*] [Brit.] a hunt; chase —*vt., vi.* **chev′ied, chev′y·ing 1.** [Brit.] to hunt; chase; run about **2.** to worry; fret; chivy

**chew** (chōō) *vt.* [< OE. *ceowan*] **1.** to bite and crush with the teeth **2.** *a)* to think over *b)* to discuss **3.** [Slang] to rebuke severely (often with *out*) —*vi.* **1.** to do chewing **2.** [Colloq.] to chew tobacco —*n.* **1.** a chewing **2.** something chewed or for chewing, as a portion of tobacco —**chew the rag** (or **fat**) [Slang] to converse idly —**chew′er** *n.*

**chew·ing gum** (chōō′iŋ) chicle or other gummy substance, flavored and sweetened for chewing

**che·wink** (chi wiŋk′) *n.* [echoic of its note] the eastern towhee of N. America, with the iris of the eye bright red

**chew·y** (chōō′ē) *adj.* **chew′i·er, chew′i·est** needing much chewing —**chew′i·ness** *n.*

**Chey·enne**[1] (shī en′, -an′) *n.* [Dakota *shaiyena* < *shaia,* to speak unintelligibly] **1.** *pl.* **-ennes′, -enne′** a member of a tribe of Algonquian Indians now of Montana and Oklahoma but originally of Minnesota **2.** their language

**Chey·enne**[2] (shī an′, -en′) [< prec.] capital of Wyo., in the SE part: pop. 47,000

**‡chez** (shā) *prep.* [Fr.] by; at; at the home of

**chg.** *pl.* **chgs.** charge

**chgd.** charged

**chi** (kī) *n.* [Gr.] the 22d letter of the Greek alphabet (X, ξ)

**Chiang Kai-shek** (chaŋ′kī shek′; *Chin.* jyäŋ′-) (born *Chiang Chung-chen*) 1888-1975; Chin. generalissimo & head of government on Taiwan (1950-75)

**Chi·an·ti** (kē än′tē, -an′-) *n.* [It.] a dry, red wine, orig. made in Tuscany

**chi·a·ro·scu·ro** (kē är′ə skyoor′ō) *n., pl.* **-ros** [It. < L. *clarus,* clear + *obscurus,* dark] **1.** the treatment of light and shade in a painting, drawing, etc., as to produce an illusion of depth **2.** a style or a painting, etc. emphasizing this

**chic** (shēk) *n.* [Fr. < MLowG. *schick,* order, skill] smart elegance of style and manner —*adj.* **chic·quer** (shēk′ər), **chic′quest** (-ist) smartly stylish

**Chi·ca·go** (shə kä′gō, -kô′-) [< Fr. < Algonquian, lit., place of the wild onion] city in NE Ill., on Lake Michigan: pop. 3,005,000 (met. area 7,058,000) —**Chi·ca′go·an** *n.*

**chi·cane** (shi kān′, chi-) *n.* [Fr. < *chicaner,* to quibble < MLowG. *schikken,* to arrange] *same as* CHICANERY —*vi.* **-caned′, -can′ing** to use chicanery —*vt.* **1.** to trick **2.** to get by chicanery

**chi·can·er·y** (-ər ē) *n., pl.* **-er·ies 1.** the use of clever but tricky talk or action to deceive, evade, etc. **2.** an instance of this

**Chi·ca·no** (chi kä′nō) *n., pl.* **-nos** [altered < AmSp. (*Mé*)*jicano,* a Mexican) [*also* c-] [Southwest] a U.S. citizen or inhabitant of Mexican descent

**chi·chi, chi-chi** (shē′shē, chē′chē) *adj.* [Fr.] extremely chic; very elegant or sophisticated, esp. in an affected or showy way —*n.* anything chichi

**chick** (chik) *n.* [< CHICKEN] **1.** a young chicken **2.** any young bird **3.** a child: term of endearment **4.** [Slang] a young woman

**chick·a·dee** (chik′ə dē′) *n.* [echoic of its note] any of various small birds closely related to the titmice, with black, gray, and white feathers

**chick·a·ree** (chik′ə rē′) *n.* [echoic of its cry] a reddish squirrel of the W U.S.

**Chick·a·saw** (chik′ə sô′) *n.* **1.** *pl.* **-saws′, -saw′** a member of a tribe of Muskogean Indians now of Oklahoma but formerly of Mississippi and Tennessee **2.** their dialect

**chick·en** (chik′ən) *n.* [< OE. *cycen,* lit., little cock] **1.** a common farm bird raised for its edible eggs or flesh; hen or rooster, esp. a young one **2.** its flesh **3.** any young bird **4.** a young or inexperienced person **5.** [Slang] a timid or cowardly person —*adj.* **1.** of chicken **2.** small and tender *[a chicken lobster]* **3.** [Slang] timid or cowardly —*vi.* [Slang] to lose courage and abandon a plan, action, etc. (usually with *out*) —**count one's chickens before they are hatched** to count on something that may not materialize

**chicken feed** [Slang] a petty sum of money

**chick·en-fried** (-frīd′) *adj.* coated with seasoned flour or batter and fried *[chicken-fried steak]*

**chicken hawk** a hawk preying on barnyard fowl

**chick·en-heart·ed** (-här′tid) *adj.* timid; cowardly: also **chick′en-liv′ered**

**chicken pox** an acute, contagious virus disease, usually of young children, with fever and a series of skin eruptions

**chicken wire** light, pliable wire fencing, used esp. for enclosing chicken coops

**chick·pea** (chik′pē′) *n.* [for *chich pea,* ult. < L. *cicer,* pea] **1.** a bushy annual plant of the legume family, with short, hairy pods containing usually two seeds **2.** the edible seed

**chick·weed** (-wēd′) *n.* any of several low-growing plants of the pink family, often found as weeds

**chic·le** (chik′'l) *n.* [AmSp. < Nahuatl *chictli*] a gumlike substance made from the milky juice of the sapodilla tree, used in making chewing gum

**Chic·o·pee** (chik′ə pē) [< AmInd., lit., swift river] city in SW Mass.: pop. 55,000

**chic·o·ry** (chik′ə rē) *n., pl.* **-ries** [< OFr. < L. < Gr. *kichora*] **1.** a weedy plant of the composite family, with blue flowers: the leaves are used for salad **2.** its root, roasted and ground for mixing with coffee or for use as a coffee substitute

**chide** (chīd) *vt., vi.* **chid·ed** or **chid** (chid), **chid′ed** or **chid** or **chid·den** (chid′'n), **chid′ing** [OE. *cidan*] to scold; now, usually, to reprove mildly —**chid′er** *n.* —**chid′ing·ly** *adv.*

**chief** (chēf) *n.* [< OFr. < L. *caput,* the head] **1.** the head or leader of a group, organization, etc. **2.** [Archaic] the main part **3.** *Heraldry* the upper third of a shield —*adj.* **1.** highest in rank, office, etc. **2.** main; principal —*adv.* [Archaic] chiefly —**in chief** in the chief position; of highest title or authority

**Chief Executive** the President of the U.S.

**chief justice** the presiding judge of a court made up of several judges

**chief·ly** (-lē) *adv.* **1.** most of all; above all **2.** mainly; mostly —*adj.* of or like a chief

**chief·tain** (-tən) *n.* [< OFr. < LL. < L. *caput,* the head] a leader, esp. of a clan or tribe —**chief′tain·cy,** *pl.* **-cies, chief′tain·ship** *n.*

**chif·fon** (shi fän′, shif′än) *n.* [Fr.], dim. of *chiffe,* a rag] **1.** a sheer, lightweight fabric of silk, nylon, etc. **2.** [*pl.*] rib-

CHEVRON

bons, laces, etc. used as accessories to a woman's dress
—*adj.* **1.** made of chiffon **2.** *Cooking* made light and
porous as by adding beaten egg whites

**chif·fo·nier, chif·fon·ier** (shif′ə nir′) *n.* [Fr., orig., rag-
picker < prec.] a narrow, high bureau or chest of drawers,
often with a mirror

**chig·ger** (chig′ər) *n.* [of Afr. origin] **1.** the tiny, red larva
of certain mites, whose bite causes severe itching **2.** *same
as* CHIGOE

**chi·gnon** (shēn′yän) *n.* [Fr. < OFr. < L. *catena*, a chain]
a knot or coil of hair sometimes worn at the back of the
neck by women

**chig·oe** (chig′ō) *n., pl.* **-oes** (-ōz) [? via Fr. *chique* < WInd.
native name] **1.** a flea of tropical S. America and Africa:
the female burrows into the skin, causing painful sores
**2.** *same as* CHIGGER

**Chi·hua·hua** (chi wä′wä) city in NC Mexico: pop. 247,000
—*n.* any of an ancient Mexican breed of very small dog
with large, pointed ears

**chil·blain** (chil′blān′) *n.* [CHIL(L) + BLAIN] a painful
swelling or sore on the foot or hand, caused by exposure to
cold —**chil′blained′** *adj.*

**child** (chīld) *n., pl.* **chil·dren** [< OE. *cild*, pl. *cildru*] **1.** an
infant; baby **2.** an unborn offspring **3.** a boy or girl in
the period before puberty **4.** a son or daughter **5.** a descendant **6.** a person like a child; immature or childish
adult **7.** a person or thing viewed as produced by a certain
place, time, source, etc. *[a child of the Renaissance]* —**with
child** pregnant —**child′less** *adj.* —**child′less·ness** *n.*

**child·bear·ing** (-ber′iŋ) *n.* the act of giving birth to children; parturition

**child·bed** (-bed′) *n.* the condition of a woman giving birth
to a child

**child·birth** (-burth′) *n.* the act of giving birth to a child;
parturition

**child·hood** (-hood′) *n.* the time or state of being a child;
period from infancy to puberty

**child·ish** (-ish) *adj.* **1.** of or like a child **2.** not fit for an
adult; immature; silly —**child′ish·ly** *adv.* —**child′ish-
ness** *n.*

**child·like** (-līk′) *adj.* like a child, esp. in being innocent,
trusting, etc. —**child′like′ness** *n.*

**chil·dren** (chil′drən) *n. pl. of* CHILD

**child's play** (chīldz) anything simple to do

**Chil·e** (chil′ē; *Sp.* chē′le) country on the SW coast of
S. America: 286,397 sq. mi.; pop. 9,566,000; cap. Santiago
—**Chil′e·an** *adj., n.*

**chil·e** (chil′ē) *n. same as* CHILI

**chil·e con car·ne** (chil′ē kən kär′nē, kän′) *same as* CHILI
CON CARNE

**Chile saltpeter** native sodium nitrate

**chil·i** (chil′ē) *n., pl.* **chil′ies** [MexSp. < Nahuatl *chilli*]
**1.** the dried pod of red pepper, a very hot seasoning **2.** the
tropical American plant, of the nightshade family, that
bears this pod **3.** *same as* CHILI CON CARNE

**chil·i con car·ne** (chil′ē kən kär′nē, kän′) [< MexSp., lit.,
red pepper with meat] a highly seasoned dish with beef
ground or in bits, chilies or chili powder, beans, and often
tomatoes

**chili powder** a powder of dried chili pods, herbs, etc.

**chili sauce** a spiced sauce of chopped tomatoes, green and
red sweet peppers, onions, etc.

**chill** (chil) *n.* [OE. *ciele*] **1.** a feeling of coldness that
makes one shiver **2.** a moderate coldness **3.** a discourag-
ing influence **4.** a feeling of sudden fear **5.** unfriendliness —*adj. same as* CHILLY —*vi.* **1.** to become cool or cold
**2.** to shiver from cold, fear, etc. —*vt.* **1.** to make cool or
cold **2.** to cause a chill in **3.** to check (enthusiasm, etc.)
**4.** to depress; dispirit **5.** *Metallurgy* to harden (metal) on
the surface by rapid cooling —**chill′er** *n.* —**chill′ing·ly** *adv.*
—**chill′ness** *n.*

**chill factor** the combined effect of low temperature and
high winds on loss of body heat

**chil·li** (chil′ē) *n., pl.* **-lies** *same as* CHILI

**chill·y** (chil′ē) *adj.* **chill′i·er, chill′i·est** **1.** moderately
cold; uncomfortably cool **2.** chilling **3.** cool in manner;
unfriendly **4.** depressing; dispiriting —**chill′i·ly** *adv.*
—**chill′i·ness** *n.*

**Chi·mae·ra** (ki mir′ə, kī-) *same as* CHIMERA —*n.* [c-] a
chimera

**chime¹** (chīm) *n.* [< OFr. < L. *cymbalum*, CYMBAL]
**1.** [*usually pl.*] *a)* a tuned set of bells or metal tubes *b)*
the sounds produced by these **2.** a single bell in a clock,
etc. **3.** harmony; agreement —*vi.* **chimed, chim′ing** **1.**
to sound as a chime **2.** to sound in harmony, as bells
**3.** to harmonize; agree —*vt.* **1.** to ring (a chime or chimes)
**2.** to indicate (time) by chiming —**chime in** **1.** to join in
or interrupt, as talk **2.** to agree —**chim′er** *n.*

**chime²** (chīm) *n.* [ME. *chimb* < OE. *cimb*- (only in compounds)] the extended rim at each end of a cask or barrel

**Chi·me·ra** (ki mir′ə, kī-) *n.* [< OFr. < L. < Gr. *chimaira*,
she-goat] *Gr. Myth.* a fire-breathing monster with a

lion's head, goat's body, and serpent's tail —*n.* [c-] **1.** any
similar unreal monster **2.** an impossible or foolish fancy

**chi·mer·i·cal** (ki mir′i k'l, -mer′-; kī-) *adj.* [see prec.]
**1.** imaginary; unreal **2.** absurd; impossible **3.** visionary
Also **chi·mer′ic** —**chi·mer′i·cal·ly** *adv.*

**chim·ney** (chim′nē) *n., pl.* **-neys** [< OFr. < LL. *caminata*,
fireplace < L. *caminus* < Gr. *kaminos*, oven] **1.** the passage through which smoke escapes from a fire; flue **2.** a
structure containing a flue and extending above the roof
**3.** a glass tube around the flame of a lamp, etc. **4.** a fissure
or vent, as in a cliff or volcano

**chimney pot** a short pipe on a chimney top to carry the
smoke off and increase the draft

**chimney swallow** **1.** *same as* CHIMNEY SWIFT **2.** the
European barn swallow

**chimney sweep** a person whose work is cleaning the soot
from chimneys

**chimney swift** a sooty-brown N. American bird resembling
the swallow: so called from its habit of making a nest in an
unused chimney

**chimp** (chimp) *n.* [Colloq.] a chimpanzee

**chim·pan·zee** (chim′pan zē′, chim pan′zē) *n.* [< Fr. <
Bantu *kampenzi*] an anthropoid ape
of Africa, with black hair and large
ears: it is smaller than a gorilla and is
noted for its intelligence

**chin** (chin) *n.* [OE. *cin*] the part of
the face below the lower lip; projecting part of the lower jaw —*vt.*
**chinned, chin′ning** to pull (oneself)
up, while hanging by the hands from a
horizontal bar, until the chin is just
above the level of the bar —*vi.* **1.** to
chin oneself **2.** [Slang] to chat, gossip, etc. —**keep one's chin up** to bear
up bravely —**take it on the chin**
[Slang] to suffer defeat, hardship, etc.

CHIMPANZEE
(35–60 in. high)

**Chin.** **1.** China **2.** Chinese

**Chi·na** (chī′na) country in E Asia,
south and east of the U.S.S.R.: 3,691,000 sq. mi.; pop.
732,000,000; cap. Peking: see also TAIWAN

**chi·na** (chī′nə) *n.* **1.** *a)* porcelain, orig. from China
*b)* vitrified ceramic ware like porcelain **2.** dishes, etc. of
this **3.** any earthenware dishes or crockery

**chi·na·ber·ry** (-ber′ē) *n., pl.* **-ries** **1.** a tree, orig. of tropical Asia, bearing yellow, beadlike fruit **2.** a tree of Mexico
and the SW U.S. with an orange-brown fruit formerly used
as soap **3.** either fruit

**Chi·na·town** (-toun′) *n.* the Chinese quarter of a city, as in
San Francisco

**chi·na·ware** (-wer′) *n. same as* CHINA

**chin·ca·pin** (chiŋ′kə pin) *n. same as* CHINQUAPIN

**chinch** (chinch) *n.* [Sp. *chinche* < L. *cimex*, bug] *same as:*
**1.** BEDBUG **2.** CHINCH BUG

**chinch bug** a small, white-winged, black bug that damages
grain plants

**chin·chil·la** (chin chil′ə) *n.* [Sp., prob. dim. of *chinche:* see
CHINCH] **1.** a small rodent of the Andes, bred extensively
for its fur **2.** its expensive, soft, pale-gray fur **3.** a heavy,
nubby wool cloth

**chine** (chīn) *n.* [< OFr. *eschine* < Frank. *skina*, small bone,
shin bone] **1.** the backbone; spine **2.** a cut of meat containing part of the backbone **3.** a ridge —*vt.* **chined,
chin′ing** to cut along or across the backbone of (a meat
carcass)

**Chi·nese** (chī nēz′, -nēs′; *for adj., often* chī′nēz′) **1.** *pl.*
**-nese′** a native of China or a person of Chinese descent **2.** the standard language of the Chinese; Mandarin
**3.** any Chinese language —*adj.* of China, its people, etc.

**Chinese cabbage** any of several vegetables of the mustard
family, with long, narrow leaves in loose, cylindrical heads
and a cabbagelike taste

**Chinese checkers** [< ?] a game like checkers for two to
six players, using marbles on a board with holes in a star-
shaped pattern

**Chinese lantern** a lantern of brightly colored paper, made
so that it can be folded up

**Chin·ese-lan·tern plant** (-lan′tərn) a perennial herb of
the nightshade family, with a bladderlike red calyx

**Chinese puzzle** any intricate puzzle

**Chinese red** a brilliant orange-red

**chink¹** (chiŋk) *n.* [OE. *cine*] a crack; fissure —*vt.* to close
up the chinks in

**chink²** (chiŋk) *n.* [echoic] a sharp, clinking sound, as of
coins striking together —*vi., vt.* to make or cause to make a
sharp, clinking sound

**chin·ka·pin** (chiŋ′kə pin) *n. same as* CHINQUAPIN

**chi·no** (chē′nō, shē′-) *n.* **1.** a strong, twilled cotton
cloth **2.** [*pl.*] pants of chino

**chin·oise·rie** (shin′wäz rē′) *n.* [Fr. < *Chinois*, Chinese +
*-erie*, -ERY] **1.** an ornate decorative style based on Chinese
motifs **2.** articles, designs, etc. in this style

**Chi·nook** (chi nŏŏk', -nŏŏk'; *for 4, usually* shi-) *n.* **1.** *pl.* **-nooks', -nook'** any of a family of Indian tribes, formerly of the Columbia River valley **2.** their language **3.** *same as* CHINOOK JARGON **4.** [*usually* c-] a warm, moist SW wind blowing from the sea onto the coast of the NW U.S. and SW Canada in winter and spring; also, a dry wind blowing down the E slope of the Rocky Mountains: in full, **chinook wind** —**Chi·nook'an** (-ən) *adj., n.*

**Chinook jargon** a former pidgin language made up of simple Chinook mixed with English and French

**chinook salmon** the largest Pacific salmon

**chin·qua·pin** (chiŋ'kə pin') *n.* [of Algonquian origin] **1.** the dwarf chestnut tree **2.** a related evergreen tree of the beech family **3.** the edible nut of either of these trees

**chintz** (chints) *n.* [earlier a pl. form < Hindi *chhīnt* < Sans. *citra*, spotted, bright] a cotton cloth printed in colors and usually glazed

**chintz·y** (-ē) *adj.* **chintz'i·er, chintz'i·est 1.** like chintz **2.** [Colloq.] cheap, stingy, etc.

**chip** (chip) *vt.* **chipped, chip'ping** [< OE. hyp. *cippian*] **1.** *a)* to break or cut a small piece or thin slice from *b)* to break or cut off (a small piece or pieces) **2.** to shape by cutting or chopping —*vi.* to break off into small pieces —*n.* **1.** a small, thin piece of wood, etc. cut or broken off **2.** a place where a small piece has been chipped off **3.** wood, palm leaf, or straw split and woven into hats, etc. **4.** a fragment of dried animal dung, sometimes used for fuel **5.** a worthless thing **6.** a small, round disk used in poker, etc. as a money token; counter **7.** a thin slice or shaving of food [potato *chips*] **8.** *Electronics a)* a semiconductor body for an integrated circuit *b) same as* INTEGRATED CIRCUIT —**chip in** [Colloq.] **1.** to share in giving money or help **2.** to add one's comments —**chip off the old block** a person much like his father —**chip on one's shoulder** [Colloq.] an inclination to fight —**in the chips** [Slang] rich; wealthy —**let the chips fall where they may** whatever the consequences —**when the chips are down** when something is really at stake

**chip·munk** (-muŋk') *n.* [of Algonquian origin] a small, striped N. American squirrel: it lives mainly on the ground

**chipped beef** shavings of dried or smoked beef

**Chip·pen·dale** (chip''n dāl') *adj.* [after T. *Chippendale* (1718?-79), Eng. cabinetmaker] designating or of an 18th-cent. Eng. style of furniture with graceful lines and, often, rococo ornamentation

**chip·per** (chip'ər) *adj.* [< N Brit. *kipper*] [Colloq.] in good spirits; lively

**Chip·pe·wa** (chip'ə wô', -wä', -wə, -wā') *n., pl.* **-was, -wa** *var. of* OJIBWA: also **Chip'pe·way'** (-wā')

**chi·ro-** [< Gr. *cheir*, the hand] *a combining form meaning* hand [*chiromancy*]

**chi·rog·ra·phy** (kī räg'rə fē) *n.* [CHIRO- + -GRAPHY] handwriting; penmanship —**chi·rog'ra·pher** *n.* —**chi·ro·graph·ic** (kī'rə graf'ik), **chi'ro·graph'i·cal** *adj.*

**chi·ro·man·cy** (kī'rə man'sē) *n.* [CHIRO- + -MANCY] *same as* PALMISTRY —**chi'ro·man'cer** *n.*

**chi·rop·o·dy** (kə räp'ə dē, kī-) *n.* [CHIRO- + -POD + -Y³] *same as* PODIATRY —**chi·rop'o·dist** *n.*

**chi·ro·prac·tic** (kī'rə prak'tik, kī'rə prak'tik) *n.* [< CHIRO- & Gr. *praktikos*, practical] a method of treating disease by manipulation of the body joints, esp. of the spine —**chi'ro·prac'tor** *n.*

**chirp** (churp) *vi.* [echoic] **1.** to make the short, shrill sound of some birds or insects **2.** to speak in a lively, shrill way —*vt.* to utter in a sharp, shrill tone —*n.* a short, shrill sound —**chirp'er** *n.*

**chirr** (chur) *n.* [echoic] a shrill, trilled sound, as of some insects or birds —*vi.* to make such a sound

**chir·rup** (chur'əp, chir'-) *vi.* [var. of CHIRP] to chirp repeatedly —*n.* a chirruping sound

**chis·el** (chiz''l) *n.* [ONormFr. < VL. < L. pp. of *caedere*, to cut] a sharp-edged tool for cutting or shaping wood, stone, or metal —*vi., vt.* **-eled** or **-elled, -el·ing** or **-el·ling 1.** to cut or shape with a chisel **2.** [Colloq.] to take advantage of (someone) or get (something) by cheating, sponging, etc. —**chisel in** [Colloq.] to force oneself, uninvited, upon others —**chis'el·er, chis'el·ler** *n.*

**chi-square** (kī'skwer') *n.* a statistical method used to test whether the classification of data can be ascribed to chance or to some underlying law

**chit¹** (chit) *n.* [ME. *chitte*, prob. var. of *kitte*, for kitten] **1.** a child **2.** an immature or childish girl

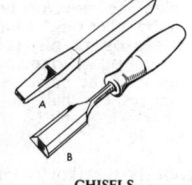

CHISELS
(A, cold;
B, wood)

**chit²** (chit) *n.* [< Hindi < Sans. *citra*, spotted] **1.** [Chiefly Brit.] a memorandum **2.** a voucher of a small sum owed for drink, food, etc.

**chit·chat** (chit'chat') *n.* [< CHAT] **1.** light, familiar, informal talk; small talk **2.** gossip

**chi·tin** (kīt''n) *n.* [Fr. *chitine* < Gr.: see CHITON] a tough, horny substance forming the outer covering of insects, crustaceans, etc. —**chi'tin·ous** *adj.*

**chit·lins, chit·lings** (chit'lənz) *n.pl. dial. var. of* CHITTERLINGS

**chi·ton** (kīt''n, kī'tän) *n.* [Gr. *chitōn*, garment, tunic < Sem.] a loose garment similar to a tunic, worn by both men and women in ancient Greece

**chit·ter·lings** (chit'lənz; *now chiefly Brit.* chit'ər liŋz) *n.pl.* [ME. *chiterling* < Gmc. base] the small intestines of pigs, used for food

**chiv·al·ric** (shi val'rik, shiv''l rik) *adj.* **1.** of chivalry **2.** *same as* CHIVALROUS

**chiv·al·rous** (shiv''l rəs) *adj.* **1.** having the attributes of an ideal knight; gallant, courteous, honorable, etc. **2.** of chivalry; chivalric —**chiv'al·rous·ly** *adv.* —**chiv'al·rous·ness** *n.*

**chiv·al·ry** (shiv''l rē) *n.* [< OFr. *chivalerie* < *chevaler*, a knight: doublet of CAVALRY] **1.** a group of knights or gallant gentlemen **2.** the medieval system of knighthood **3.** the noble qualities a knight was supposed to have, such as courage, honor, and a readiness to help the weak and protect women **4.** the demonstration of any of these qualities

**chives** (chīvz) *n.pl.* [< OFr. < L. *cepa*, onion] [*often with sing. v.*] a plant of the lily family, with small, hollow leaves having a mild onion odor: used to flavor soups, stews, etc.

**chiv·y, chiv·vy** (chiv'ē) *n., pl.* **chiv'ies** or **chiv'vies** *same as* CHEVY —*vt., vi.* **chiv'ied** or **chiv'vied, chiv'y·ing** or **chiv'vy·ing 1.** to fret; worry; nag **2.** to manipulate **3.** *same as* CHEVY

**chlo·ral** (klôr'əl) *n.* [CHLOR(O)- + AL(COHOL)] **1.** a thin, oily, colorless liquid, CCl₃CHO, with a pungent odor, prepared by the action of chlorine on alcohol **2.** *same as* CHLORAL HYDRATE

**chloral hydrate** a colorless, crystalline compound, CCl₃·CH(OH)₂, used chiefly as a sedative

**chlor·am·phen·i·col** (klôr'am fen'ə kôl', -kōl') *n.* [CHLOR(O)- + AM(IDE) + PHE(NO)- + NI(TRO)- + (GLY)COL] an antibiotic drug, C₁₁H₁₂Cl₂N₂O₅, used against a wide variety of bacterial and rickettsial diseases and against some viruses

**chlo·rate** (klôr'āt, -it) *n.* a salt of chloric acid

**chlor·dane** (klôr'dān) *n.* [CHLOR(O)- + (in)dane, a coal-tar derivative] a poisonous, volatile oil, C₁₀H₆Cl₈, used as an insecticide: also **chlor'dan** (-dan)

**chlo·ric** (klôr'ik) *adj.* **1.** of or containing chlorine with a higher valence than in corresponding chlorous compounds **2.** designating or of a colorless acid, HClO₃, whose salts are chlorates

**chlo·ride** (-īd) *n.* a compound in which chlorine is combined with another element or radical (e.g., a salt of hydrochloric acid)

**chloride of lime** a white powder, CaOCl₂, obtained by treating slaked lime with chlorine and used for disinfecting and bleaching

**chlo·ri·nate** (klôr'ə nāt') *vt.* **-nat'ed, -nat'ing** to treat or combine (a substance) with chlorine; esp., to pass chlorine into (water or sewage) for purification —**chlo'ri·na'tion** *n.* —**chlo'ri·na'tor** *n.*

**chlo·rine** (klôr'ēn, -in) *n.* [CHLOR(O)- + -INE⁴] a greenish-yellow, poisonous, gaseous chemical element with a disagreeable odor, used in bleaching, water purification, etc.: symbol, Cl; at. wt., 35.453; at. no., 17

**chlo·rite** (-īt) *n.* a salt of chlorous acid

**chlo·ro-** [< Gr. *chlōros*, pale green] *a combining form meaning:* **1.** green [*chlorophyll*] **2.** having chlorine in the molecule [*chloroform*] Also, before a vowel, **chlor-**

**chlo·ro·form** (klôr'ə fôrm') *n.* [see CHLORO- & FORMYL] a sweetish, colorless, volatile liquid, CHCl₃, used as a general anesthetic and as a solvent —*vt.* **1.** to anesthetize with chloroform **2.** to kill with chloroform

**Chlo·ro·my·ce·tin** (klôr'ə mī sēt''n) [CHLORO- + -MYCET(E) + -IN¹] *a trademark for* CHLORAMPHENICOL

**chlo·ro·phyll, chlo·ro·phyl** (klôr'ə fil') *n.* [< Fr. < Gr. *chlōros*, green + *phyllon*, a leaf] the green pigment of plants: it is involved in the photosynthetic process —**chlo'ro·phyl'lose** (-ōs), **chlo'ro·phyl'lous** (-əs) *adj.*

**chlo·ro·plast** (klôr'ə plast') *n.* [CHLORO- + Gr. *plastos*, formed] an oval, chlorophyll-bearing body found in the cytoplasm in cells of green plants

**chlo·rous** (klôr'əs) *adj.* **1.** of or containing chlorine with a lower valence than in corresponding chloric compounds

**2.** designating or of an unstable acid, $HClO_2$, a strong oxidizing agent whose salts are chlorites

**chlor·prom·a·zine** (klôr präm'ə zēn') *n.* a synthetic drug, $C_{17}H_{19}N_2SCl$, used as a tranquilizer

**chlor·tet·ra·cy·cline** (-tet'rə sī'klēn, -klin) *n.* a yellow antibiotic, $C_{22}H_{23}ClN_2O_8$, used against a wide variety of bacterial and rickettsial infections and certain viruses

**chm., chmn.** chairman

**chock** (chäk) *n.* [ONormFr. *choque*, a block] **1.** a block or wedge placed under a wheel, barrel, etc. to prevent motion **2.** *Naut.* a block with two hornlike projections curving inward, through which a rope may be run —*vt.* to provide or wedge fast as with chocks —*adv.* as close or tight as can be

**chock·a·block** (-ə bläk') *adj.* **1.** pulled so tight as to have the blocks touching: said of a hoisting tackle **2.** crowded — *adv.* tightly together

**chock-full** (chäk'fool', chuk'-) *adj.* as full as possible; filled to capacity

**choc·o·late** (chôk'lət, chäk'-; -ə lət) *n.* [< Fr. < Sp. < Nahuatl *chocolatl*] **1.** a paste, powder, etc. made from cacao seeds that have been roasted and ground **2.** a drink made of chocolate, hot milk or water, and sugar **3.** a candy made of or coated with chocolate **4.** reddish brown —*adj.* **1.** made of or with chocolate **2.** reddish-brown

**Choc·taw** (chäk'tô) *n.* [< tribal name *Chata* < ?] **1.** *pl.* **-taws, -taw** a member of a tribe of Muskogean Indians originally of the Southeast now living in Oklahoma **2.** their Muskogean dialect

**choice** (chois) *n.* [< OFr. < *choisir*, to choose < Goth. *kausjan*, to taste] **1.** a choosing; selection **2.** the right or power to choose; option **3.** a person or thing chosen **4.** the best part **5.** a variety from which to choose **6.** a supply well chosen **7.** an alternative **8.** care in choosing —*adj.* **choic'er, choic'est 1.** of special excellence **2.** carefully chosen —**of choice** that is preferred —**choice'ly** *adv.* — **choice'ness** *n.*

**choir** (kwīr) *n.* [< OFr. *cuer* < ML. *chorus*, choir < L.; see CHORUS] **1.** a group of singers trained to sing together, esp. in a church **2.** the part of a church they occupy **3.** an instrumental section of an orchestra **4.** any organized group

**choke** (chōk) *vt.* **choked, chok'ing** [< OE. *aceocian*] **1.** to prevent from breathing by stopping the windpipe; strangle; suffocate **2.** to block up; obstruct by clogging **3.** to hinder the growth or action of **4.** to fill up **5.** to cut off some air from the carburetor of (a gasoline engine) so as to make a richer gasoline mixture **6.** to hold (a bat, golf club, etc.) toward the middle of the handle —*vi.* **1.** to be suffocated **2.** to be blocked up; be obstructed —*n.* **1.** the act or sound of choking **2.** the valve that chokes a carburetor —**choke back** to hold back (feelings, sobs, etc.) —**choke down** to swallow with difficulty —**choke off** to bring to an end; end the growth of —**choke up 1.** to block up; clog **2.** to fill too full **3.** [Colloq.] to be unable to speak, act efficiently, etc., as because of fear, tension, etc.

**choke·bore** (-bôr') *n.* **1.** a shotgun bore that tapers toward the muzzle to keep the shot closely bunched **2.** a gun with such a bore

**choke·cher·ry** (-cher'ē) *n., pl.* **-ries 1.** a N. American wild cherry tree **2.** its astringent fruit

**choke·damp** (chōk'damp') *n. same as* BLACKDAMP

**choke-full** (chōk'fool') *adj. same as* CHOCK-FULL

**chok·er** (chōk'ər) *n.* **1.** a person or thing that chokes **2.** a closely fitting necklace

**chok·y** (-ē) *adj.* **chok'i·er, chok'i·est 1.** inclined to choke **2.** suffocating; stifling Also sp. **chok'ey**

**chol·e-** *same as* CHOLO-: also, before a vowel, **chol-**

**chol·er** (käl'ər) *n.* [< OFr. < L. *cholera*: see ff.] **1.** [Obs.] bile: in medieval times yellow bile was considered the source of anger and irritability **2.** [Now Rare] anger or ill humor

**chol·er·a** (käl'ər ə) *n.* [L., jaundice < Gr. *cholera*, nausea < *cholē*, bile] any of several intestinal diseases; esp., ASIATIC CHOLERA —**chol'e·ra'ic** (-ə rā'ik) *adj.*

**chol·er·ic** (käl'ər ik, kə ler'ik) *adj.* [see CHOLER] showing a quick temper or irascible nature

**cho·les·ter·ol** (kə les'tə rōl', -rôl') *n.* [< CHOLE- + Gr. *stereos*, solid + -OL[1]] a crystalline fatty alcohol, $C_{27}H_{46}OH$, found esp. in animal fats, blood, and bile

**cho·line** (kō'lēn, käl'ēn) *n.* [CHOL(O)- + -INE[4]] a viscous liquid, $C_5H_{15}O_2N$, found in many animal and vegetable tissues: a vitamin of the B complex

**chol·o-** [< Gr. *cholē*, bile] *a combining form meaning* bile

**chomp** (chämp) *vt., vi.* [dial. var. of CHAMP[1]] **1.** to chew hard and noisily **2.** to bite down (*on*) repeatedly and restlessly —*n.* the act or sound of chomping —**chomp'er** *n.*

**chon** (chän) *n., pl.* **chon** [Korean, orig., a unit of weight] *see* MONETARY UNITS, table (Korea)

**choose** (chōōz) *vt.* **chose, cho'sen** or obs. **chose, choos'ing** [OE. *ceosan*] **1.** to pick out; take as a choice; select **2.** to decide or prefer [to *choose* to remain] —*vi.* **1.** to make

one's selection **2.** to have the desire or wish —**cannot choose but** cannot do otherwise than —**choose up** [Colloq.] to decide on the opposing players, as for a ball game — **choos'er** *n.*

**choos·y, choos·ey** (chōō'zē) *adj.* **choos'i·er, choos'i·est** [Colloq.] very careful or fussy

**chop[1]** (chäp) *vt.* **chopped, chop'ping** [ME. *choppen*, prob. < OFr. *c(h)oper*, to cut] **1.** to cut by blows with an ax or other sharp tool **2.** to cut into small bits **3.** to say in an abrupt way **4.** to hit with a short, sharp stroke —*vi.* **1.** to make quick, cutting strokes with a sharp tool **2.** to act with a quick, jerky motion —*n.* **1.** the act of chopping **2.** a short, sharp blow or stroke **3.** a piece chopped off **4.** a slice of lamb, pork, veal, etc. cut from the rib, loin, or shoulder **5.** a short, broken movement of waves

**chop[2]** (chäp) *n.* [var. of CHAP[1]] **1.** a jaw **2.** a cheek See CHOPS

**chop[3]** (chäp) *vi.* **chopped, chop'ping** [OE. *ceapian*, to bargain] to shift or veer suddenly, as the wind; change direction —**chop logic** to argue

**chop·fall·en** (-fô'lən) *adj. same as* CHAPFALLEN

**chop·house** (-hous') *n.* a restaurant that specializes in chops and steaks

**Cho·pin** (shō'pan; *Fr.* shô pan'), **Fré·dé·ric Fran·çois** (frā dā rēk' frän swä') 1810–49; Pol. composer & pianist, in France after 1831

**chop·per** (chäp'ər) *n.* **1.** a person or thing that chops **2.** [*pl.*] [Slang] a set of teeth, esp. false teeth **3.** [Colloq.] a helicopter

**chop·py[1]** (-ē) *adj.* **-pi·er, -pi·est** [< CHOP[3] + -Y[2]] shifting constantly and abruptly, as the wind —**chop'pi·ness** *n.*

**chop·py[2]** (-ē) *adj.* **-pi·er, -pi·est** [< CHOP[1] + -Y[2]] **1.** rough with short, broken waves, as the sea **2.** making abrupt starts and stops; jerky —**chop'pi·ly** *adv.* —**chop'pi·ness** *n.*

**chops** (chäps) *n.pl.* [see CHAP[1]] **1.** the jaws **2.** the mouth and lower cheeks **3.** [Slang] technical skill, esp. of a jazz or rock musician

**chop·sticks** (chäp'stiks') *n.pl.* [PidE. for Chin. *k'wai-tsze*, the quick ones] two small sticks held together in one hand and used in some Asian countries to lift food to the mouth

**chop su·ey** (chäp' sōō'ē) [altered < Chin. *tsa-sui*, lit., various pieces] a Chinese-American dish of meat, bean sprouts, celery, mushrooms, etc. cooked together in a sauce and served with rice

**cho·ral** (kôr'əl) *adj.* [Fr.] of, for, sung by, or recited by a choir or chorus —**cho'ral·ly** *adv.*

**cho·rale, cho·ral** (kə ral', kô-) *n.* [< G. *choral* (*gesang*), choral (song)] **1.** a hymn tune **2.** a choral composition based on such a tune **3.** a group of singers; choir

**chord[1]** (kôrd) *n.* [altered (after L. *chorda*) < CORD] **1.** a feeling or emotion thought of as being played on like the string of a harp [to strike a sympathetic *chord*] **2.** *Anat.* same as CORD (sense 5) **3.** *Engineering* a principal horizontal member in a rigid framework, as of a bridge **4.** *Geom.* a straight line joining any two points on an arc, curve, or circumference

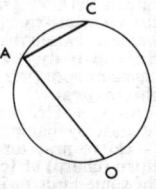

**chord[2]** (kôrd) *n.* [< *cord*, aphetic < ACCORD] *Music* a combination of three or more tones sounded together in harmony —*vi., vt.* **1.** to harmonize **2.** to play chords on —**chord'al** *adj.*

CHORDS (AC, AO)

**chore** (chôr) *n.* [< OE. *cierr*: see CHARE] **1.** a small routine task; odd job: *often used in pl.* **2.** a hard or unpleasant task

**cho·re·a** (kô rē'ə) *n.* [ModL. < L. < Gr. *choreia*, choral dance] a nervous disorder characterized by jerking movements caused by involuntary muscular contractions; Saint Vitus' dance

**chor·e·o·graph** (kôr'ē ə graf') *vt., vi.* [< ff.] to design or plan the movements of (a dance, esp. a ballet) —**chor'e·og'ra·pher** (-äg'rə fər) *n.*

**chor·e·og·ra·phy** (kôr'ē äg'rə fē) *n.* [Gr. *choreia*, dance + -GRAPHY] **1.** dancing, esp. ballet dancing **2.** the arrangement of the movements of a dance **3.** the art of devising dances, esp. ballets —**chor'e·o·graph'ic** (-ə graf'ik) *adj.* — **chor'e·o·graph'i·cal·ly** *adv.*

**cho·ric** (kôr'ik) *adj.* of, for, or like a chorus, esp. in an ancient Greek play

**chor·is·ter** (kôr'is tər) *n.* [< OFr. *cueristre*: see CHOIR] a member of a choir, esp. a boy singer

**C-horizon** *n. see* ABC SOIL

**cho·roid** (kôr'oid) *adj.* [< Gr. < *chorion*, leather + *eidos*, form] designating of or certain vascular membranes —*n.* the dark, vascular membrane between the sclera and retina of the eye Also **cho'ri·oid'** (-ē oid')

**chor·tle** (chôr't'l) *vi., vt.* **-tled, -tling** [coined by Lewis Carroll, prob. < CHUCKLE + SNORT] to make, or utter with,

a gleeful chuckling or snorting sound —*n.* such a sound —**chor′tler** *n.*
**cho·rus** (kôr′əs) *n.* [L. < Gr. *choros,* a dance, chorus] **1.** in ancient Greek drama, a group whose singing, dancing, and narration supplement the main action **2.** a group of dancers and singers performing together as in an opera **3.** the part of a drama, song, etc. performed by a chorus **4.** a group trained to sing or speak something together simultaneously **5.** a simultaneous utterance by many [*a chorus* of protest] **6.** music written for group singing **7.** *a)* the refrain of a song following each verse *b)* the main tune, as of a jazz piece, following the introduction —*vt., vi.* to sing, speak, or say in unison —**in chorus** in unison
**chorus girl** (or **boy**) a woman (or man) singing or dancing in the chorus of a musical show
**chose** (chōz) *pt. & obs. pp. of* CHOOSE
**Cho·sen** (chō′sen′) *Jap. name of* KOREA
**cho·sen** (chō′z′n) *pp. of* CHOOSE —*adj.* picked out by preference; selected
**Chou** (jō) a Chinese dynasty (1122? to 256? B.C.)
**chow** (chou) *n.* [< Chin. dial. form akin to Cantonese *kaú,* a dog] **1.** any of a breed of medium-sized dog, originally from China, with a compact, muscular body and thick coat of brown or black: official name **chow chow 2.** [Slang] food
**chow·chow** (chou′chou′) *n.* [PidE. < Chin.] chopped pickles in a highly seasoned mustard sauce
**chow·der** (chou′dər) *n.* [Fr. *chaudière,* a pot < LL. *caldaria:* see CALDRON] a thick soup of onions, potatoes, and salt pork, sometimes corn, tomatoes, etc. and often, specif., clams and milk
**chow mein** (chou mān′) [Chin. *ch'ao,* to fry + *mien,* flour] a Chinese-American dish consisting of a thick stew of meat, celery, bean sprouts, etc., served with fried noodles and usually soy sauce
**Chr. 1.** Christ **2.** Christian **3.** Chronicles
**chrism** (kriz′m) *n.* [< OE. < LL. < Gr. *chrisma* < *chriein,* to anoint] consecrated oil used in baptism and other sacraments —**chris′mal** *adj.*
**Christ** (krīst) *n.* [< LL. < Gr. *christos,* the anointed (in NT., MESSIAH) < *chriein,* to anoint] Jesus of Nazareth, regarded by Christians as the Messiah prophesied in the Old Testament
**Christ·church** (krīst′church′) city on the E coast of South Island, New Zealand: pop. (of urban area) 256,000
**chris·ten** (kris′'n) *vt.* [OE. *cristnian*] **1.** to take into a Christian church by baptism; baptize **2.** to give a name to at baptism **3.** to give a name to (a ship being launched, etc.) **4.** [Colloq.] to make use of for the first time —**chris′ten·ing** *n.*
**Chris·ten·dom** (-dəm) *n.* **1.** Christians collectively **2.** those parts of the world where most of the inhabitants profess Christianity
**Chris·tian** (kris′chən) a masculine name —*n.* [OE. *cristen,* ult. < Gr. *christos:* see CHRIST] **1.** a person professing belief in Jesus as the Christ, or in the religion based on the teachings of Jesus **2.** [Colloq.] a decent, respectable person —*adj.* **1.** of Jesus Christ or his teachings **2.** of or professing the religion based on these teachings **3.** having the qualities demonstrated and taught by Jesus Christ, as love, kindness, etc. **4.** of or representing Christians or Christianity **5.** [Colloq.] humane, decent, etc. —**Chris′tian·ly** *adj., adv.*
**Christian Era** the era beginning with the year formerly thought to be that of the birth of Jesus Christ (born probably c. 8–4 B.C.)
**Chris·ti·a·ni·a** (kris′chē an′ē ə, -tē än′-) former name of OSLO —*n.* [*also* c-] *same as* CHRISTIE
**Chris·ti·an·i·ty** (kris′chē an′ə tē) *n.* **1.** Christians collectively **2.** the Christian religion **3.** a particular Christian religious system **4.** the state of being a Christian
**Chris·tian·ize** (kris′chə nīz′) *vt.* -ized′, -iz′ing **1.** to convert to Christianity **2.** to cause to conform with Christian character or precepts —**Chris′tian·i·za′tion** *n.* —**Chris′tian·iz′er** *n.*
**Christian name** the baptismal name or given name, as distinguished from the surname or family name
**Christian Science** a religion and system of healing founded by Mary Baker Eddy c. 1866: official name, CHURCH OF CHRIST, SCIENTIST —**Christian Scientist**
**chris·tie, chris·ty** (kris′tē) *n., pl.* -ties [< CHRISTIANIA] Skiing any of various high-speed turns to change direction, stop, etc., made by shifting weight, with skis usually kept parallel
**Chris·tine** (kris tēn′) [< LL. fem. of CHRISTIAN] a feminine name: var. *Christina*
**Christ·like** (krīst′līk′) *adj.* like Jesus Christ, esp. in character or spirit —**Christ′like′ness** *n.*

**Christ·ly** (-lē) *adj.* of Jesus Christ; Christlike —**Christ′liness** *n.*
**Christ·mas** (kris′məs) *n.* [OE. *Cristesmæsse:* see CHRIST & MASS] **1.** a holiday on Dec. 25 celebrating the birth of Jesus Christ: also **Christmas Day 2.** *same as* CHRISTMASTIDE
**Christmas Eve** the evening before Christmas Day
**Christ·mas·tide** (-tīd′) *n.* Christmas time, from Christmas Eve through New Year's Day or to Epiphany (Jan. 6)
**Chris·to·pher** (kris′tə fər) [< LL. < Gr. *Christophoros,* lit., bearing Christ] **1.** a masculine name: dim. *Chris* **2.** Saint, 3d cent. A.D.?; patron saint of travelers
**chro·mate** (krō′māt) *n.* a salt of chromic acid
**chro·mat·ic** (krō mat′ik) *adj.* [< LL. < Gr. < *chrōma,* color] **1.** of or having color or colors **2.** highly colored **3.** *Music a)* using or progressing by semitones [*a chromatic scale*] *b)* using tones not in the key of a work —*n.* Music a tone modified by an accidental —**chro·mat′i·cal·ly** *adv.* —**chro·mat′i·cism** (-ə siz′m) *n.*
**chro·mat·ics** (krō mat′iks) *n.pl.* [*with sing. v.*] the scientific study of colors
**chromatic scale** the musical scale made up of thirteen successive semitones to the octave
**chro·ma·tin** (krō′mə tin) *n.* [< Gr. *chrōma* (gen. *chrōmatos*), color + -IN[1]] a protoplasmic substance in the nucleus of living cells that readily takes a deep stain: chromatin forms the chromosomes
**chro·ma·to-** [< Gr. *chrōma:* see prec.] *a combining form meaning:* **1.** color or pigmentation **2.** chromatin Also, before a vowel, **chromat-**
**chrome** (krōm) *n.* [Fr. < Gr. *chrōma,* color] **1.** chromium or chromium alloy, esp. as plating **2.** any of certain salts of chromium, used in dyeing and tanning **3.** a chromium pigment —*vt.* **chromed, chrom′ing 1.** to plate with chromium **2.** to treat with a salt of chromium, as in dyeing
**-chrome** (krōm) [< Gr. *chrōma,* color] *a suffix meaning:* **1.** color or coloring agent **2.** chromium
**chro·mic** (krō′mik) *adj.* designating or of compounds containing trivalent chromium
**chromic acid** an acid, $H_2CrO_4$, existing only in solution or known in the form of its salts
**chro·mi·um** (krō′mē əm) *n.* [CHROM(E) + -IUM] a very hard, metallic chemical element with a high resistance to corrosion: symbol, Cr; at. wt., 51.996; at. no., 24
**chromium steel** a very strong, hard alloy steel containing chromium: also **chrome steel**
**chro·mo** (krō′mō) *n., pl.* -mos a chromolithograph
**chro·mo-** [< Gr. *chrōma,* color] *a combining form meaning* color or pigment [*chromosome*]: also, before a vowel, **chrom-**
**chro·mo·lith·o·graph** (krō′mō lith′ə graf′) *n.* a colored picture printed by the lithographic process from a series of stone or metal plates
**chro·mo·some** (krō′mə sōm′) *n.* [CHROMO- + -SOME[3]] any of the microscopic rod-shaped bodies into which the chromatin of a cell nucleus separates during mitosis: they carry the genes, which convey hereditary characters, and are constant in number for each species —**chro′mo·so′mal** *adj.*
**chro·mo·sphere** (-sfir′) *n.* [CHROMO- + -SPHERE] the reddish layer of gases around the sun between the photosphere and the corona —**chro′mo·spher′ic** (-sfir′ik, -sfer′-) *adj.*
**chro·mous** (krō′məs) *adj.* designating or of compounds containing bivalent chromium
**Chron.** Chronicles
**chron. 1.** chronological **2.** chronology
**chron·ic** (krän′ik) *adj.* [< Fr. < L. < Gr. < *chronos,* time] **1.** lasting a long time or recurring often: said of a disease, and distinguished from ACUTE **2.** having had an ailment for a long time **3.** perpetual; constant [*a chronic worry*] **4.** habitual —*n.* a chronic patient —**chron′i·cal·ly** *adv.*
**chron·i·cle** (krän′i k'l) *n.* [< Anglo-Fr. < OFr. < L. < Gr. *chronika,* annals: see prec.] **1.** a historical record of events in the order in which they happened **2.** a narrative; history —*vt.* -cled, -cling to tell or write the history of; put into a chronicle —**chron′i·cler** (-klər) *n.*
**Chron·i·cles** (-k'lz) either of two books of the Bible, I and II Chronicles
**chro·no-** [Gr. < *chronos,* time] *a combining form meaning* time: also, before a vowel, **chron-**
**chron·o·graph** (krän′ə graf′, krō′nə-) *n.* [CHRONO- + -GRAPH] an instrument for measuring brief, precisely spaced intervals of time, as a stopwatch
**chron·o·log·i·cal** (krän′ə läj′i k'l) *adj.* **1.** arranged in the order of occurrence **2.** relating to a narrative or history Also **chron′o·log′ic** —**chron′o·log′i·cal·ly** *adv.*
**chro·nol·o·gy** (krə näl′ə jē) *n., pl.* -gies [CHRONO- + -LOGY] **1.** the science of measuring time and of dating

events in proper order 2. an arrangement or list of events, dates, etc. in the order of occurrence —**chro·nol'o·gist, chro·nol'o·ger** *n.*

**chro·nom·e·ter** (-näm'ə tər) *n.* [CHRONO- + -METER] an instrument for measuring time precisely; highly accurate kind of clock or watch —**chron·o·met·ric** (krän'ə met'rik, krō'nə-), **chron'o·met'ri·cal** *adj.* —**chron'o·met'ri·cal·ly** *adv.*

**chro·nom·e·try** (krə näm'ə trē) *n.* the scientific measurement of time

**-chro·ous** (krō əs) [Gr. *chrōs, chroos,* color] *a terminal combining form meaning* colored

**chrys·a·lid** (kris''l id) *n. same as* CHRYSALIS —*adj.* of a chrysalis

**chrys·a·lis** (kris''l əs) *n., pl.* **chry·sal·i·des** (kri sal'ə dēz'), **chrys'a·lis·es** [< L. < Gr. *chrysallis,* golden-colored chrysalis < *chrysos,* gold] **1.** the pupa of a butterfly, when it is in a case or cocoon **2.** the case or cocoon **3.** anything in a formative or undeveloped stage

**chrys·an·the·mum** (kri san'thə məm) *n.* [L. < Gr. < *chrysos,* gold + *anthemon,* a flower] **1.** any of a genus of late-blooming plants of the composite family, cultivated for their showy flowers, in a wide variety of colors **2.** the flower

**chrys·o·lite** (kris'ə līt') *n.* [< OFr. < L. < Gr. < *chrysos,* gold + *lithos,* stone] *same as* OLIVINE

**chrys·o·prase** (-prāz') *n.* [< OFr. < L. < Gr. < *chrysos,* gold + *prason,* leek] a light-green variety of chalcedony sometimes used as a semiprecious stone

**chub** (chub) *n., pl.* **chubs, chub:** see PLURAL, II, D, 1 [ME. *chubbe*] any of several small, freshwater fishes related to the minnows and carp

**chub·by** (chub'ē) *adj.* **-bi·er, -bi·est** [< prec.] round and plump —**chub'bi·ness** *n.*

**chuck¹** (chuk) *vt.* [< ? Fr. *choquer,* to strike against] **1.** to tap or pat gently, esp. under the chin, as a playful gesture **2.** to throw with a quick, short movement; toss **3.** [Slang] *a)* to discard; get rid of *b)* to quit *c)* to vomit (often with *up*) —*n.* **1.** a light tap or squeeze under the chin **2.** a toss **3.** [Chiefly Western] food

**chuck²** (chuk) *n.* [prob. var. of CHOCK] **1.** a cut of beef including the parts around the neck and the shoulder blade **2.** a clamplike device, as on a lathe, by which the tool or work is held

**chuck-a-luck** (chuk'ə luk') *n.* [< CHUCK¹ + LUCK] a gambling game using three dice: also called **chuck'-luck'**

**chuck-full** (chuk'fool') *adj. same as* CHOCK-FULL

**chuck·hole** (chuk'hōl') *n.* [< dial. *chock,* a bump + HOLE] a rough hole in a road, made by wear and weathering

**chuck·le** (chuk''l) *vi.* **-led, -ling** [prob. < *chuck,* to cluck] **1.** to laugh softly in a low tone, as in mild amusement **2.** to cluck, as a hen —*n.* a soft, low-toned laugh —**chuck'ler** *n.*

**chuck·le·head** (-hed') *n.* [Colloq.] a stupid person

CHUCK (of a drill)

**chuck wagon** [CHUCK¹, *n.* 3 + WAGON] [Slang] a wagon equipped as a kitchen for feeding cowboys or other outdoor workers

**chuff** (chuf) *vi., n.* [echoic] *same as* CHUG

**chug** (chug) *n.* [echoic] any of a series of abrupt, puffing or explosive sounds, as of a locomotive —*vi.* **chugged, chug'ging** to make, or move with, such sounds

**chuk·ka** (boot) (chuk'ə) [< CHUKKER] a man's ankle-high bootlike shoe, often fleece-lined

**chuk·ker, chuk·kar** (chuk'ər) *n.* [Hindi *chakar* < Sans. *cakra,* wheel] any of the periods of play, 7 1/2 minutes each, of a polo match

**Chu·la Vis·ta** (chōō'lə vis'tə) [AmSp., lit., beautiful view] city in SW Calif.: suburb of San Diego: pop. 84,000

**chum** (chum) *n.* [17th-c. slang; prob. < *chamber* in *chamber mate*] [Colloq.] a close friend —*vi.* **chummed, chum'ming** [Colloq.] to be close friends

**chum·my** (chum'ē) *adj.* **-mi·er, -mi·est** [Colloq.] intimate; friendly —**chum'mi·ly** *adv.* —**chum'mi·ness** *n.*

**chump** (chump) *n.* [< ? CHUCK² or CHUNK + LUMP¹] **1.** a heavy block of wood **2.** a thick, blunt end **3.** [Colloq.] a foolish, stupid, or gullible person

**Chung·king** (choon'kin'; *Chin.* joon'chin') city in SC China, on the Yangtze: pop. 4,070,000

**chunk** (chunk) *n.* [< ? CHUCK²] **1.** a short, thick piece, as of meat, wood, etc. **2.** a considerable portion **3.** a stocky animal, esp. a horse

**chunk·y** (chun'kē) *adj.* **chunk'i·er, chunk'i·est** **1.** short and thick **2.** stocky; thickset **3.** containing chunks —**chunk'i·ness** *n.*

**church** (church) *n.* [< OE. *cirice,* ult. < Gr. *kyriakē (oikia),* Lord's (house) < *kyros,* supreme power] **1.** a building for public worship, esp. one for Christian worship **2.** public worship; religious service **3.** [*usually* C-] *a)* all Christians collectively *b)* a particular sect or denomination of Chris-

tians **4.** ecclesiastical government, or its power, as opposed to secular government **5.** the profession of the clergy **6.** a group of worshipers —*adj.* of a church or of organized Christian worship —**church'less** *adj.*

**church·go·er** (-gō'ər) *n.* a person who attends church, esp. regularly —**church'go'ing** *n., adj.*

**Church·ill** (chur'chil), **Sir Winston (Leonard Spencer)** 1874–1965; Brit. statesman & writer; prime minister (1940–45; 1951–55)

**church·ly** (church'lē) *adj.* of, fit for, or belonging to, a church —**church'li·ness** *n.*

**church·man** (-mən) *n., pl.* **-men 1.** a clergyman **2.** a member of a church

**Church of Christ, Scientist** *see* CHRISTIAN SCIENCE

**Church of England** the episcopal church of England; Anglican Church: it is an established church with the sovereign as its head

**Church of Jesus Christ of Latter-day Saints** *see* MORMON

**church·ward·en** (-wôr'd'n) *n.* a lay officer chosen annually in every parish of the Church of England or of the Protestant Episcopal Church to attend to certain secular matters

**church·wom·an** (-woom'ən) *n., pl.* **-wom'en** (-wim'in) a woman member of a church

**church·yard** (-yärd') *n.* the yard adjoining a church, often used as a place of burial

**churl** (churl) *n.* [OE. *ceorl,* freeman] **1.** a peasant **2.** a surly, ill-bred, or miserly person —**churl'ish** *adj.* —**churl'ish·ly** *adv.* —**churl'ish·ness** *n.*

**churn** (churn) *n.* [OE. *cyrne*] **1.** a container or contrivance in which milk or cream is beaten and shaken to form butter **2.** unusually strong agitation —*vt.* **1.** to beat and shake (milk or cream) in a churn **2.** to make (butter) in a churn **3.** to stir up vigorously **4.** to make (foam, etc.) by stirring vigorously —*vi.* **1.** to use a churn in making butter **2.** to move as if in a churn; seethe

**churr** (chur) *n.* a low, trilled or whirring sound made by some birds —*vi.* to make such a sound

**chute¹** (shoot) *n.* [Fr., a fall, ult. < L. *cadere,* to fall] **1.** a waterfall or rapids in a river **2.** an inclined or vertical trough or passage down which something may slide or be slid or dropped

**chute²** (shoot) *n. colloq. clipped form of* PARACHUTE —**chut'ist** *n.*

**chut·ney** (chut'nē) *n., pl.* **-neys** [Hindi *chatni*] a relish made of fruits, spices, and herbs: also sp. **chut'nee**

**chutz·pah, chutz·pa** (hoots'pə, khoots'-; -pä) *n.* [Heb.] [Colloq.] shameless audacity; impudence; brass

**chyle** (kīl) *n.* [< LL. < Gr. *chylos* < *cheein,* to pour] a milky fluid composed of lymph and emulsified fats: it is formed from chyme in the small intestine and is passed into the blood through the thoracic duct —**chy·la·ceous** (kī lā'shəs), **chy'lous** *adj.*

**chyme** (kīm) *n.* [< LL. < Gr. *chymos,* juice < *cheein,* to pour] the semifluid mass resulting from gastric digestion of food: see CHYLE —**chy'mous** *adj.*

**CIA, C.I.A.** Central Intelligence Agency

‡**ciao** (chou) *interj.* [It.] an informal expression of greeting or farewell

**ci·bo·ri·um** (si bôr'ē əm) *n., pl.* **-ri·a** (-ə) [ML. < L., a cup < Gr. *kibōrion,* seed vessel of the Egyptian waterlily, hence, a cup] **1.** a canopy covering an altar **2.** a covered cup for holding the consecrated wafers of the Eucharist

**ci·ca·da** (si kā'də, -kä'-) *n., pl.* **-das, -dae** (-dē) [L.] a large flylike insect with transparent wings: the male makes a loud, shrill sound by vibrating a special organ on its underside

**cic·a·trix** (sik'ə triks) *n., pl.* **ci·cat·ri·ces** (si kat'rə sēz', sik'ə trī'sēz) [L.] **1.** *Med.* the contracted fibrous tissue at the place where a wound has healed; scar **2.** *Bot.* the scar left where a branch, leaf, seed, etc. was once attached or where a wound has healed Also **cic'a·trice** (-tris) —**cic'a·tri'cial** (-trish'əl) *adj.*

**cic·a·trize** (-trīz') *vt., vi.* **-trized', -triz'ing** to heal with the formation of a scar —**cic'a·tri·za'tion** *n.*

**Cic·er·o** (sis'ə rō') [after ff.] city in NE Ill.: suburb of Chicago: pop. 61,000

**Cic·er·o** (sis'ə rō'), **(Marcus Tullius)** 106–43 B.C.; Rom. statesman & orator —**Cic'e·ro'ni·an** *adj.*

**ci·ce·ro·ne** (sis'ə rō'nē, *It.* chē che rō'ne) *n., pl.* **-nes;** *It.* **-ni** (-nē) [It. < L. *Cicero,* the orator] a well-informed guide for sightseers

**Cid** (sid; *Sp.* thēth), **the** [Sp. < Ar. *sayyid,* a lord] (born *Rodrigo,* or *Ruy, Díaz de Bivar*) 1040?–99; Sp. hero and soldier of fortune

**-cide** (sīd) [< Fr. *-cide* or L. *-cida* < L. *caedere,* to kill] *a suffix meaning:* **1.** killer [*pesticide*] **2.** killing [*genocide*]

**ci·der** (sī'dər) *n.* [< OFr. < LL. < Gr. *sikera* < Heb. *shēkār,* strong drink] the juice pressed from apples, used as a beverage or for making vinegar: **sweet cider** is unfermented, **hard cider** is fermented

**C.I.F., c.i.f.** cost, insurance, and freight

**ci·gar** (si gär′) *n.* [Sp. *cigarro,* prob. < Maya *sicar,* to smoke < *sīc,* tobacco] a compact roll of tobacco leaves for smoking

**cig·a·rette, cig·a·ret** (sig′ə ret′, sig′ə ret′) *n.* [Fr., dim. of *cigare,* cigar] a small roll of finely cut tobacco wrapped in thin paper for smoking

**cig·a·ril·lo** (sig′ə ril′ō) *n., pl.* **-los** [Sp., dim. of *cigarro,* CIGAR] a small, thin cigar

**cil·i·a** (sil′ē ə) *n.pl., sing.* **-i·um** (-əm) [L.] **1.** the eyelashes **2.** *Bot.* small hairlike processes, as on the edges of some leaves **3.** *Zool.* hairlike outgrowths of certain cells, capable of rhythmic beating that can produce locomotion, as in protozoans or small worms —**cil′i·ate** (-it, -āt′), **cil′i·at′ed** *adj.*

**cil·i·ar·y** (sil′ē er′ē) *adj.* of, like, or having cilia

**cim·ba·lom, cym·ba·lom** (sim′bə ləm) *n.* [< Hung. < L. *cymbalum,* cymbal] a type of large dulcimer associated with Hungarian folk music

**Cim·me·ri·an** (si mir′ē ən) *n. Class. Myth.* any of a people living in a land of perpetual mist and darkness —*adj.* dark; gloomy

**cinch** (sinch) *n.* [< Sp. < L. *cingulum,* a girdle < *cingere,* to encircle] **1.** a saddle or pack girth **2.** [Colloq.] a firm grip **3.** [Slang] a sure or easy thing —*vt.* **1.** to gird with a cinch **2.** [Slang] *a)* to get a firm hold on *b)* to make sure of

**cin·cho·na** (sin kō′nə, siŋ-) *n.* [ModL., after the Countess del *Chinchón,* wife of a 17th-c. Peruv. viceroy, who was treated with the bark] **1.** a tropical S. American tree from the bark of which quinine is obtained **2.** the bitter bark of this tree —**cin·chon′ic** (-kän′ik) *adj.*

**cin·cho·nize** (sin′kə nīz′) *vt.* **-nized′, -niz′ing** to treat with cinchona, quinine, etc.

**Cin·cin·nat·i** (sin′sə nat′ē, -ə) [ult. after *Cincinnatus,* Rom. general of 5th c. B.C.] city in SW Ohio, on the Ohio River: pop. 385,000 (met. area 1,392,000)

**cinc·ture** (siŋk′chər) *n.* [L. *cinctura,* a girdle < *cingere:* see CINCH] **1.** an encircling or girding **2.** anything that encircles, as a belt or girdle —*vt.* **-tured, -tur·ing** to encircle with or as with a cincture

**cin·der** (sin′dər) *n.* [OE. *sinder*] **1.** slag, as from the smelting of ores **2.** any matter, as coal or wood, burned but not reduced to ashes **3.** a minute piece of such matter **4.** a coal that is still burning but not flaming **5.** [*pl.*] ashes from coal or wood —**cin′der·y** *adj.*

**cinder block** a building block, usually hollow, made of concrete and fine cinders

**Cin·der·el·la** (sin′də rel′ə) the title character of a fairy tale, a household drudge who, with the help of a fairy godmother, marries a prince

**cin·e·ma** (sin′ə mə) *n.* [< CINEMA(TOGRAPH)] [Chiefly Brit.] **1.** a motion picture **2.** a motion-picture theater —**the cinema 1.** the art or business of making motion pictures **2.** motion pictures; the movies —**cin′e·mat′ic** (-mat′ik) *adj.* —**cin′e·mat′i·cal·ly** *adv.*

**cin·e·mat·o·graph** (sin′ə mat′ə graf′) *n.* [< Fr. < Gr. *kinēma,* motion + *graphein,* to write] [Chiefly Brit.] a motion-picture projector, camera, theater, etc. —*adj.* [Chiefly Brit.] motion-picture

**cin·e·ma·tog·ra·pher** (sin′ə mə täg′rə fər) *n.* [Chiefly Brit.] a motion-picture cameraman

**cin·e·ma·tog·ra·phy** (-fē) *n.* the art of photography in making motion pictures —**cin′e·mat′o·graph′ic** (-mat′ə graf′ik), **cin′e·mat′o·graph′i·cal** *adj.* —**cin′e·mat′o·graph′i·cal·ly** *adv.*

‡**cin·é·ma vér·i·té** (sē nä mä′ vā rē tā′) [Fr., lit., truth cinema] a form of documentary film in which a small camera and unobtrusive techniques are used to record scenes as naturally as possible

**cin·e·rar·i·a** (sin′ə rer′ē ə) *n.* [ModL. < L. < *cinis,* ashes: the leaves have an ash-colored down] a common hothouse plant of the composite family, with heart-shaped leaves and colorful flowers

**cin·e·rar·i·um** (-ē əm) *n., pl.* **-rar′i·a** (-ə) [L. < *cinis,* ashes] a place to keep the ashes of cremated bodies —**cin′e·rar′y** *adj.*

**cin·er·a·tor** (sin′ə rāt′ər) *n.* [< CINERARIUM] a furnace for cremation; crematory

**cin·na·bar** (sin′ə bär′) *n.* [< L. < Gr. *kinnabari* < ? Per. *šangarf*] **1.** mercuric sulfide, HgS, a heavy, bright-red mineral, the principal ore of mercury **2.** artificial mercuric sulfide, used as a red pigment **3.** brilliant red; vermilion

**cin·na·mon** (sin′ə mən) *n.* [< OFr. < L. < Gr. < Heb. *qinnāmōn*] **1.** the yellowish-brown spice made from the dried inner bark of a laurel tree or shrub native to the East Indies and SE Asia **2.** this bark **3.** any tree or shrub from which it is obtained **4.** yellowish brown —*adj.* **1.** yellowish-brown **2.** made or flavored with cinnamon

**cinque·foil** (siŋk′foil′) *n.* [< OFr. < It. < L. < *quinque,* five + *folium,* leaf] **1.** a plant of the rose family with a fruit like a dry strawberry: some species have compound leaves with five leaflets **2.** *Archit.* a circular design of five converging arcs

**CIO, C.I.O.** Congress of Industrial Organizations: see AFL-CIO

**ci·on** (sī′ən) *n. same as* SCION (sense 1)

**Ci·pan·go** (si paŋ′gō) *old name for* JAPAN

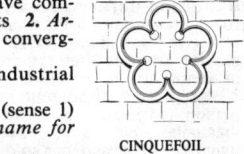

CINQUEFOIL

**ci·pher** (sī′fər) *n.* [< OFr. < ML. < Ar. *sifr,* nothing < *safare,* to be empty] **1.** the symbol 0, indicating a value of naught; zero **2.** a person or thing of no importance or value; nonentity **3.** *a)* a system of secret writing based on a key *b)* a message in such writing *c)* the key to such a system See also CODE **4.** a monogram **5.** an Arabic numeral —*vt., vi.* **1.** [Now Rare] to do, or solve by, arithmetic **2.** to write in cipher, or secret writing

**cir., circ. 1.** circa **2.** circulation **3.** circumference

**cir·ca** (sur′kə) *prep.* [L.] about: used before an approximate date, figure, etc. [*circa* 1650]

**cir·ca·di·an** (sər kā′dē ən) *adj.* [coined < L. *circa,* about + acc. sing. of *dies,* day] designating or of certain biological rhythms associated with the 24-hour daily cycles, as, in man, the regular metabolic, glandular, and sleep rhythms

**Cir·cas·si·a** (sər kash′ə, -kash′ē ə) region of the U.S.S.R., in the NW Caucasus —**Cir·cas′si·an** *adj., n.*

**Cir·ce** (sur′sē) in Homer's *Odyssey,* an enchantress who turned men into swine —**Cir·ce·an** (sər sē′ən, sur′sē ən) *adj.*

**cir·cle** (sur′k'l) *n.* [< OFr. < L. *circulus,* dim. of *circus:* see CIRCUS] **1.** a plane figure bounded by a single curved line every point of which is equally distant from the point at the center **2.** the line bounding such a figure; circumference **3.** anything shaped like a circle, as a ring, crown, etc. **4.** the orbit of a heavenly body **5.** a section of seats in a theater, as in a balcony [the dress *circle*] **6.** a complete or recurring series, usually ending as it began; cycle; period **7.** a group of people bound together by common interests; group; coterie **8.** range or extent, as of influence or interest; scope —*vt.* **-cled, -cling 1.** to form a circle around; encompass; surround **2.** to move around, as in a circle —*vi.* to go around in a circle; revolve —**come full circle** to return to an original position or state after going through a series or cycle —**cir′cler** *n.*

**cir·clet** (sur′klit) *n.* **1.** a small circle **2.** a circular band worn as an ornament, esp. on the head

**cir·cuit** (sur′kit) *n.* [OFr. < L. *circuitus < circum,* around + *ire,* to go] **1.** the line or the length of the line forming the boundaries of an area **2.** the area bounded **3.** a going around something; course or journey around **4.** *a)* the regular journey through a fixed district of a person performing his duties, as of a circuit court judge *b)* such a district **5.** a chain or group of theaters, resorts, etc. at which plays, movies, entertainers, etc. appear in turn **6.** *Elec. a)* a complete or partial path over which current may flow *b)* a hookup that is connected into this path —*vi.* to go in a circuit —*vt.* to make a circuit about —**cir′cuit·al** *adj.*

**circuit breaker** a device that automatically interrupts the flow of an electric current

**circuit court** a State court having original jurisdiction in several counties or a district

**cir·cu·i·tous** (sər kyōō′i təs) *adj.* [see CIRCUIT] roundabout; indirect; devious —**cir·cu′i·tous·ly** *adv.* —**cir·cu′i·tous·ness, cir·cu′i·ty** *n., pl.* **-ties**

**circuit rider** a minister who travels from place to place in his circuit to preach

**cir·cuit·ry** (sur′kə trē) *n.* the scheme, system, or components of an electric circuit

**cir·cu·lar** (sur′kyə lər) *adj.* [L. *circularis*] **1.** in the shape of a circle; round **2.** relating to a circle **3.** moving in a circle or spiral **4.** roundabout; circuitous **5.** intended for circulation among a number of people —*n.* a circular advertisement, letter, etc. —**cir′cu·lar′i·ty** (-ler′ə tē) *n.* —**cir′cu·lar·ly** *adv.*

**cir·cu·lar·ize** (-lə rīz′) *vt.* **-ized′, -iz′ing 1.** to make circular **2.** to send circulars to **3.** to canvass —**cir′cu·lar·i·za′tion** *n.* —**cir′cu·lar·iz′er** *n.*

**circular saw** a saw in the form of a disk with a toothed edge, rotated at high speed by a motor

**cir·cu·late** (sur′kyə lāt′) *vi.* **-lat′ed, -lat′ing** [< L. pp. of *circulari,* to form a circle] **1.** to move in a circle or circuit and return to the same point, as the blood **2.** to go from person to person or from place to place; specif., *a)* to move about freely, as air *b)* to move about in society, at a party, meeting, etc. *c)* to be made widely known or felt *d)* to be distributed to a mass of readers —*vt.* to cause to circulate —**cir′cu·la′tor** *n.* —**cir′cu·la·to′ry** (-lə tôr′ē), **cir′cu·la′tive** (-lā′tiv) *adj.*

**circulating library** a library from which books can be borrowed, sometimes for a small daily fee

**cir·cu·la·tion** (sur′kyə lā′shən) *n.* **1.** a circulating or moving around, often specif. in a complete circuit, as of air in ventilating or of blood through the arteries and veins **2.** the passing of something, as money, news, etc., from person to person **3.** *a)* the distribution of newspapers, magazines, etc. *b)* the average number of copies of a magazine or newspaper sold in a given period

**cir·cum-** [< L. *circum*, around, about] *a prefix meaning* around, about, surrounding, on all sides

**cir·cum·am·bi·ent** (sur′kəm am′bē ənt) *adj.* [CIRCUM- + AMBIENT] extending all around; surrounding —**cir′cum·am′bi·ence, cir′cum·am′bi·en·cy** *n.*

**cir·cum·cise** (sur′kəm sīz′) *vt.* -**cised′**, -**cis′ing** [< OFr. < L. pp. of *circumcidere* < *circum-*, around + *caedere*, to cut] to cut off all or part of the foreskin of —**cir′cum·ci′sion** (-sizh′ən) *n.*

**cir·cum·fer·ence** (sər kum′fər əns, -frəns) *n.* [< L. prp. of *circumferre* < *circum-*, around + *ferre*, to carry] **1.** the line bounding a circle or other rounded surface or area **2.** the distance measured by this line —**cir·cum′fer·en′tial** (-fə ren′shəl) *adj.* —**cir·cum′fer·en′tial·ly** *adv.*

**cir·cum·flex** (sur′kəm fleks′) *n.* [< L. pp. of *circumflectere* < *circum-*, around + *flectere*, to bend] a mark (∧, ⌒, ~) used over certain vowels in some languages to indicate a specific sound, or as a diacritical mark in some pronunciation systems: also **circumflex accent** —*adj.* **1.** of or marked by a circumflex **2.** bending around; curved —*vt.* **1.** to bend around; curve **2.** to write with a circumflex —**cir′cum·flex′ion** *n.*

**cir·cum·flu·ent** (sər kum′floo wənt) *adj.* [< L. prp. of *circumfluere* < *circum-*, around + *fluere*, to flow] flowing around; surrounding: also **cir·cum′flu·ous**

**cir·cum·fuse** (sur′kəm fyooz′) *vt.* -**fused′**, -**fus′ing** [< L. pp. of *circumfundere* < *circum-*, around + *fundere*, to pour] **1.** to pour or spread (a fluid) around; diffuse **2.** to surround (*with* a fluid); suffuse (*in*) —**cir′cum·fu′sion** *n.*

**cir·cum·lo·cu·tion** (-lō kyoo′shən) *n.* [< L.: see CIRCUM- & LOCUTION] a roundabout, indirect, or lengthy way of expressing something —**cir′cum·loc′u·to′ry** (-läk′yə tôr′ē) *adj.*

**cir·cum·nav·i·gate** (-nav′ə gāt′) *vt.* -**gat′ed**, -**gat′ing** [< L. pp. of *circumnavigare*: see CIRCUM- & NAVIGATE] to sail or fly around (the earth, an island, etc.) —**cir′cum·nav′i·ga′tion** *n.* —**cir′cum·nav′i·ga′tor** *n.*

**cir·cum·scribe** (sur′kəm skrīb′, sur′kəm skrīb′) *vt.* -**scribed′**, -**scrib′ing** [< L. < *circum-*, around + *scribere*, to write] **1.** to trace a line around; encircle **2.** *a)* to limit; confine *b)* to restrict **3.** *Geom. a)* to draw a figure around (another figure) so as to touch it at as many points as possible *b)* to be thus drawn around —**cir′cum·scrib′a·ble** *adj.* —**cir′cum·scrib′er** *n.* —**cir′cum·scrip′tion** (-skrip′shən) *n.*

**cir·cum·spect** (sur′kəm spekt′) *adj.* [< L. pp. of *circumspicere* < *circum-*, around + *specere*, to look] careful to consider all related circumstances before acting, deciding, etc.; cautious —**cir′cum·spec′tion** *n.* —**cir′cum·spect′ly** *adv.*

**cir·cum·stance** (-stans′, -stəns) *n.* [< OFr. < L. < *circum-*, around + *stare*, to stand] **1.** a fact or event, esp. one accompanying another, either incidentally or as a determining factor **2.** [*pl.*] conditions affecting a person, esp. financial conditions **3.** chance; luck **4.** ceremony; show [*pomp and circumstance*] **5.** *a)* surrounding detail *b)* fullness of detail —*vt.* -**stanced′**, -**stanc′ing** to place in certain circumstances —**under no circumstances** under no conditions; never —**under the circumstances** conditions being what they are or were —**cir′cum·stanced′** *adj.*

**cir·cum·stan·tial** (sur′kəm stan′shəl) *adj.* **1.** having to do with, or depending on, circumstances **2.** incidental **3.** full or complete in detail **4.** ceremonial —**cir′cum·stan′ti·al′i·ty** (-shē al′ə tē) *n., pl.* -**ties** —**cir′cum·stan′tial·ly** *adv.*

**circumstantial evidence** *Law* evidence offered to prove certain circumstances from which the existence of the fact at issue may be inferred

**cir·cum·stan·ti·ate** (-stan′shē āt′) *vt.* -**at′ed**, -**at′ing** to give detailed proof or support of —**cir′cum·stan′ti·a′tion** *n.*

**cir·cum·val·late** (-val′āt) *vt.* -**lat·ed**, -**lat·ing** [< *circumvallare* < *circum-*, around + *vallare*, to wall] to surround with or as with a wall or trench —*adj.* surrounded by a wall, trench, etc. —**cir′cum·val·la′tion** *n.*

**cir·cum·vent** (sur′kəm vent′) *vt.* [< L. pp. of *circumvenire* < *circum-*, around + *venire*, to come] **1.** to surround or circle around **2.** to surround with evils, enmity, etc.; entrap **3.** to get the better of or prevent from happening by craft or ingenuity —**cir′cum·ven′tion** *n.*

**cir·cus** (sur′kəs) *n.* [L. < or akin to Gr. *kirkos*, a circle] **1.** in ancient Rome, an oval or oblong arena with tiers of seats around it, used for games, races, etc. **2.** a similar arena for a traveling show of acrobats, trained animals, clowns, etc. **3.** such a show or the performance of such a show **4.** [Colloq.] any riotously entertaining person, event, etc.

**ci·ré** (sə rā′) *adj.* [Fr., lit., waxed, ult. < Gr. *kēros*, wax] having a smooth, glossy finish as by treatment with wax —*n.* a ciré silk, straw, etc.

**cir·rho·sis** (sə rō′sis) *n.* [ModL. < Gr. *kirrhos*, tawny + -OSIS: after the yellowish color of the diseased liver] a degenerative disease in a bodily organ, esp. the liver, marked by excess formation of connective tissue and the subsequent contraction of the organ —**cir·rhot′ic** (-rät′ik) *adj.*

**cir·ri-** [< L. *cirrus*] *a combining form meaning* curl, ringlet: also **cir′ro-, cir′rho-**

**cir·ro·cu·mu·lus** (sir′ō kyoo′myə ləs) *n.* a high formation of clouds in small, white puffs, flakes, or streaks

**cir·ro·stra·tus** (-strāt′əs, -strat′-) *n.* a high formation of clouds in a thin, whitish veil

**cir·rus** (sir′əs) *n., pl.,* for 1 -**ri** (-ī); for 2 -**rus** [L., a curl] **1.** *a)* a plant tendril *b)* a flexible, threadlike appendage, as a feeler in certain organisms *c)* a cluster of fused cilia as in some infusorians **2.** a high formation of clouds in wispy filaments or feathery tufts

**cis-** [< L. *cis*, on this side] *a prefix meaning:* **1.** on this side of **2.** subsequent to

**cis·al·pine** (sis al′pīn, -pin) *adj.* on this (the Roman, or southern) side of the Alps

**cis·co** (sis′kō) *n., pl.* -**co, -coes, -cos**: see PLURAL, II, D, 2 [< CanadFr. < Algonquian] a fish related to the whitefish, found in the colder lakes of the NE U.S. and of Canada

**cis·lu·nar** (sis loo′nər) *adj.* on this side of the moon, between the moon and the earth

**Cis·ter·cian** (sis tur′shən) *adj.* [< OFr. < ML. *Cistercium* (now *Citeaux*, France)] designating or of a monastic order following the Benedictine rule strictly —*n.* a Cistercian monk or nun

**cis·tern** (sis′tərn) *n.* [< OFr. < L. < *cista*, CHEST] **1.** a large receptacle, usually underground, for storing water, esp. rain water **2.** *Anat.* a sac or cavity containing a natural body fluid

**cit·a·del** (sit′ə d′l, -del′) *n.* [< Fr. < It. dim. of *cittade*, city < L. *civitas*, CITY] **1.** a fortress on a commanding height for defense of a city **2.** a fortified place; stronghold **3.** a place of safety; refuge

**ci·ta·tion** (sī tā′shən) *n.* [< OFr. < L. pp. of *citare*: see ff.] **1.** a summons to appear before a court of law **2.** a citing; quoting **3.** a passage cited; quotation **4.** a reference to a legal statute, a previous law case, etc. **5.** *a)* official honorable mention for meritorious service in the armed forces *b)* a formal statement honoring a person —**ci′ta·tor** *n.* —**ci·ta·to·ry** (sīt′ə tôr′ē) *adj.*

**cite** (sīt) *vt.* **cit′ed, cit′ing** [< OFr. < L. *citare*, to summon < *ciere*, to rouse] **1.** to summon to appear before a court of law **2.** to quote (a passage, book, writer, etc.) **3.** to refer to or mention by way of example, proof, etc. **4.** to mention in a citation (sense 5) —**cit′a·ble, cite′a·ble** *adj.*

**cith·a·ra** (sith′ə rə) *n.* [L. < Gr. *kithara*] an ancient musical instrument somewhat like a lyre

**cith·er** (sith′ər) *n.* [< Fr. < prec.] *same as* CITTERN: also **cith′ern** (-ərn)

**cit·i·fied** (sit′i fīd′) *adj.* having the manners, dress, etc. attributed to city people

**cit·i·zen** (sit′ə zən) *n.* [Anglo-Fr. *citizein* < OFr. < *cite*: see CITY] **1.** formerly, an inhabitant of a town or city **2.** a member of a state or nation who owes allegiance to it by birth or naturalization and is entitled to full civil rights **3.** a civilian, as distinguished from a soldier, policeman, etc.

**cit·i·zen·ry** (-rē) *n.* all citizens as a group

**citizens' band** either of two bands of shortwave radio frequencies for local use at low power by private persons

**cit·i·zen·ship** (-ship′) *n.* **1.** the status or condition of a citizen, or his duties, rights, and privileges **2.** one's conduct as a citizen

**cit·rate** (si′trāt, sī′-) *n.* [CITR(US) + -ATE²] a salt or ester of citric acid

**cit·ric** (si′trik) *adj.* [CITR(US) + -IC] **1.** of or from lemons, oranges, or similar fruits **2.** designating or of an acid, $C_6H_8O_7$, obtained from such fruits, used in making dyes, citrates, etc.

**cit·ri·cul·ture** (-trə kul′chər) *n.* the cultivation of citrus fruits

**cit·rine** (-trin, -trēn, -trīn) *adj.* [< OFr. < ML. < L. *citrus*, CITRUS] of the yellow color of a lemon —*n.* **1.** lemon yellow **2.** a yellow quartz

**cit·ron** (-trən) *n.* [Fr., lemon < It. *citrone* < L. *citrus*, CITRUS] **1.** a yellow, thick-skinned fruit resembling a lemon but larger and less acid **2.** the semitropical tree bearing this fruit **3.** the candied rind of this fruit, used in fruitcake, etc.

**cit·ron·el·la** (si′trə nel′ə) *n.* [ModL. < prec.] **1.** a volatile, sharp-smelling oil used in perfume, soap, insect repellents, etc.: also **citronella oil 2.** a grass of S Asia from which it is derived

**cit·rus** (si′trəs) *n.* [L., citron tree (whence Gr. *kitron*)] **1.** any of a genus of trees and shrubs that bear oranges, lemons, limes, or other such fruit **2.** any such fruit —*adj.* of these trees or shrubs: also **cit′rous** (-trəs)

**cit·tern** (sit′ərn) *n.* [< CITHER, prob. infl. by ME. *giterne,* GITTERN] a stringed instrument of the guitar family, popular in the 16th & 17th cent.

**cit·y** (sit′ē) *n., pl.* **cit′ies** [< OFr. *cite* < L. *civitas,* orig. citizenship < *civis,* citizen] **1.** a center of population larger or more important than a town or village **2.** in the U.S., an incorporated municipality whose boundaries and powers of self-government are defined by a charter from its State **3.** in Canada, a large urban municipality within a province **4.** all the people of a city —*adj.* of or in a city

**city chicken** skewered pieces of pork or veal breaded and cooked by braising or baking

**city fathers** the important officials of a city

**cit·y·fied** (sit′i fīd′) *adj. same as* CITIFIED

**city hall 1.** a building housing the offices of a municipal government **2.** a municipal government —**fight city hall** to fight futilely against petty or impersonal bureaucracy

**city manager** a chief municipal administrator appointed by a city council on a professional basis, with tenure free from public elections

**cit·y·scape** (sit′ē skāp′) *n.* [CITY + (LAND)SCAPE] **1.** a painting, photograph, etc. of a section of a city **2.** a view of a section of a city, esp. of buildings silhouetted against the horizon

**cit·y-state** (-stāt′) *n.* a state made up of an independent city and the territory directly controlled by it, as in ancient Greece

**Ciu·dad Juá·rez** (syōō thä′th hwä′res) city in N Mexico, on the Rio Grande: pop. 522,000

**civ. 1.** civil **2.** civilian

**civ·et** (siv′it) *n.* [< Fr. < It. *zibetto* < Ar. *zabād*] **1.** a yellowish substance with a musklike scent, secreted by a gland of the civet cat and used in making some perfumes **2.** the civet cat or its fur

**civet cat** a catlike, flesh-eating mammal of Africa and S Asia, with spotted, yellowish fur

**civ·ic** (siv′ik) *adj.* [L. *civicus* < *civis:* see CITY] **1.** of a city **2.** of citizens or citizenship —**civ′i·cal·ly** *adv.*

**civ·ics** (siv′iks) *n.pl.* [*with sing. v.*] the branch of political science dealing with civic affairs and the duties and rights of citizenship

**civ·ies** (siv′ēz) *n.pl.* [Colloq.] *same as* CIVVIES

**civ·il** (siv′'l) *adj.* [OFr. < L. *civilis* < *civis:* see CITY] **1.** of a citizen or citizens [*civil rights*] **2.** of a community of citizens, their government, or their interrelations **3.** civilized **4.** polite or courteous, esp. in a merely formal way **5.** not military or religious [*civil marriage*] **6.** *Law* relating to private rights and legal actions involving these

**civil defense** a system of warning devices, air-raid or fallout shelters, etc. for defense of a population against enemy attack

**civil disobedience** nonviolent opposition to a government policy or law by refusing to comply with it, on the grounds of conscience: see also NONCOOPERATION, PASSIVE RESISTANCE

**civil engineering** the branch of engineering dealing with the design and construction of highways, bridges, harbors, etc. —**civil engineer**

**ci·vil·ian** (sə vil′yən) *n.* [< OFr. < L.: see CIVIL] a person not an active member of the armed forces or of an official force having police power —*adj.* of or for civilians; nonmilitary

**ci·vil·i·ty** (-ə tē) *n., pl.* **-ties 1.** politeness, esp. in a merely formal kind **2.** a civil act or utterance

**civ·i·li·za·tion** (siv′ə lə zā′shən) *n.* **1.** a civilizing or becoming civilized **2.** the condition of being civilized; social organization of a high order **3.** the total culture of a people, nation, period, etc. **4.** the countries and peoples considered to have reached a high stage of social and cultural development **5.** intellectual and cultural refinement **6.** the comforts of civilized life

**civ·i·lize** (siv′ə līz′) *vt.* **-lized′, -liz′ing** [< Fr. < L.: see CIVIL & -IZE] **1.** to bring out of a primitive or savage condition and into a state of civilization **2.** to improve in habits or manners; refine —**civ′i·liz′a·ble** *adj.* —**civ′i·lized′** *adj.*

**civil law 1.** the body of codified law developed from Roman law **2.** the body of law that an individual nation or state has established for itself **3.** the body of law concerning private rights

**civil liberties** liberties guaranteed to the individual by law and custom; rights of thinking, speaking, and acting as one likes without hindrance except in the interests of the public welfare

**civ·il·ly** (siv′'l ē) *adv.* **1.** with civility; politely **2.** in relation to civil law, civil rights, etc.

**civil marriage** a marriage performed by a public official, not by a clergyman

**civil rights** those rights guaranteed to the individual by the 13th, 14th, 15th, and 19th Amendments to the Constitution

**civil service 1.** all those employed in government work except those in the armed forces **2.** any government service in which a position is secured through competitive public examination —**civil servant**

**civil war** war between different sections or factions of the same nation —**the Civil War** the war between the North (the Union) and the South (the Confederacy) in the U.S. (1861–1865)

**civ·vies** (siv′ēz) *n.pl.* [Colloq.] civilian clothes, as distinguished from a military uniform; mufti

**ck.** *pl.* **cks. 1.** cask **2.** check

**Cl** *Chem.* chlorine

**cl. 1.** centiliter(s) **2.** claim **3.** class **4.** clause

**clab·ber** (klab′ər) *n.* [Ir. *clabar*] [Dial.] thickly curdled sour milk —*vi., vt.* [Dial.] to curdle

**clack** (klak) *vi.* [prob. < ON. *klaka,* of echoic origin] **1.** to make a sudden, sharp sound [high heels *clacking*] **2.** to chatter —*vt.* to cause to make a sudden, sharp sound —*n.* **1.** a clacking sound **2.** chatter —**clack′er** *n.*

**clad** (klad) *alt. pt. & pp. of* CLOTHE —*adj.* **1.** clothed; dressed **2.** having a layer of another metal or of an alloy bonded to it [*clad* steel]

**clad·ding** (-iŋ) *n.* [see prec.] **1.** a layer of some metal or alloy bonded to another **2.** the process of bonding such materials

**claim** (klām) *vt.* [< OFr. < L. *clamare,* to cry out] **1.** to demand as rightfully belonging to one; assert one's right to (a title, etc. that should be recognized) **2.** to call for; require; deserve [problems *claiming* our attention] **3.** to assert; maintain —*n.* **1.** a demand for something rightfully due **2.** a right or title to something **3.** something claimed, as land staked out by a settler **4.** an assertion —**claim′a·ble** *adj.* —**claim′er** *n.*

**claim·ant** (klā′mənt) *n.* one who makes a claim

**Claire** (kler) [Fr., equiv. of CLARA] a feminine name

**clair·voy·ance** (kler voi′əns) *n.* [Fr. < ff.] **1.** the supposed ability to perceive things that are not in sight or that cannot be seen **2.** keen perception or insight

**clair·voy·ant** (-ənt) *adj.* [Fr. < *clair,* clear + prp. of *voir,* to see] **1.** of or apparently having clairvoyance **2.** having keen insight —*n.* a clairvoyant person —**clair·voy′ant·ly** *adv.*

**clam** (klam) *n., pl.* **clams, clam:** see PLURAL, II, D, 1 [< OE. *clamm,* fetter, in reference to the action of the shells] **1.** any of certain hard-shelled, bivalve mollusks living in the shallows of the sea or in fresh water **2.** the soft, edible part of these mollusks **3.** *same as* CLAMSHELL (sense 2) —*vi.* to dig, or go digging, for clams —**clam up** [Colloq.] to refuse to talk

**clam·bake** (-bāk′) *n.* a picnic at which steamed or baked clams and other foods are served

**clam·ber** (klam′bər) *vi., vt.* [ME. *clambren*] to climb clumsily or with effort, using both hands and feet —*n.* a hard or clumsy climb —**clam′ber·er** *n.*

**clam·my** (klam′ē) *adj.* **-mi·er, -mi·est** [prob. < OE. *clam,* clay] unpleasantly moist, cold, and sticky —**clam′mi·ly** *adv.* —**clam′mi·ness** *n.*

**clam·or** (klam′ər) *n.* [< OFr. < L. *clamare,* to cry out] **1.** a loud outcry; uproar **2.** a strong, insistent public demand or complaint **3.** a loud, sustained noise —*vi.* to make a clamor; cry out, demand, or complain noisily —*vt.* to express with clamor Also, Brit. sp., **clam′our** —**clam′or·er** *n.*

**clam·or·ous** (-əs) *adj.* **1.** loud and confused; noisy **2.** loudly demanding or complaining —**clam′or·ous·ly** *adv.* —**clam′or·ous·ness** *n.*

**clamp** (klamp) *n.* [< MDu. *klampe*] a device for clasping or fastening things together; esp., an appliance with two parts brought together to grip something —*vt.* **1.** to grip, fasten, or brace with a clamp **2.** to impose forcefully —**clamp down (on)** to become more strict (with)

**clam·shell** (klam′shel′) *n.* **1.** the shell of a clam **2.** a dredging bucket, hinged like the shell of a clam

**clan** (klan) *n.* [Gael. & Ir. *clann,* offspring < L. *planta,* offshoot] **1.** a social group, as in the Scottish Highlands, composed of several fami-

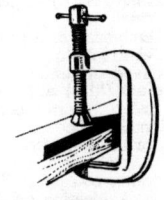

CLAMP

lies descended from a common ancestor **2.** a group of people with interests in common **3.** [Colloq.] family (sense 3)

**clan·des·tine** (klan des′t'n) *adj.* [< Fr. < L. *clandestinus* < *clam*, secret] kept secret or hidden, esp. for some illicit purpose; surreptitious —**clan·des′tine·ly** *adv.*

**clang** (klaŋ) *vi., vt.* [echoic] to make or cause to make a loud, sharp, ringing sound, as by striking metal —*n.* a clanging sound or cry

**clan·gor** (klaŋ′ər) *n.* [L. < *clangere*, to clang] a clanging sound, esp. a continued clanging —*vi.* to make a clangor Also, Brit. sp., **clan′gour** —**clan′gor·ous** *adj.* —**clan′gor·ous·ly** *adv.*

**clank** (klaŋk) *n.* [echoic] a sharp, metallic sound, not so resonant as a clang —*vi.* to make, or move with, a clank —*vt.* to cause to clank

**clan·nish** (klan′ish) *adj.* **1.** of a clan **2.** tending to associate closely and to avoid others —**clan′nish·ly** *adv.* —**clan′nish·ness** *n.*

**clans·man** (klanz′mən) *n., pl.* -**men** a member of a clan —**clans′wom′an** *n.fem., pl.* -**wom′en**

**clap** (klap) *vi.* **clapped** or archaic **clapt, clap′ping** [OE. *clæppan*, to beat] **1.** to make a sudden, explosive sound, as of two flat surfaces being struck together **2.** to strike the hands together, as in applauding —*vt.* **1.** to strike together briskly and loudly **2.** to strike with an open hand **3.** to put, move, etc. swiftly [*clapped* into jail] **4.** to put together hastily —*n.* **1.** the sound of clapping **2.** the act of striking the hands together **3.** a sharp slap, as in hearty greeting —**clap eyes on** [Colloq.] to catch sight of; see

**clap·board** (klab′ərd, klap′bôrd′) *n.* [partial transl. of MDu. *klapholt* < *klappen*, to fit + *holt*, wood] a thin board with one edge thicker than the other, used as siding —*vt.* to cover with clapboards

**clap·per** (klap′ər) *n.* **1.** a person who claps **2.** a thing that makes a clapping noise, as the tongue of a bell or, facetiously, that of a person

**clap·trap** (-trap′) *n.* [CLAP + TRAP¹] showy, insincere, empty talk, etc. intended only to get applause or attention —*adj.* showy and cheap

**claque** (klak) *n.* [Fr. < *claquer*, to clap] **1.** a group of people paid to go to a play, opera, etc. and applaud **2.** a group of fawning followers

**Clar·a** (klar′ə) [< L. fem. of *clarus*, bright] a feminine name: var. *Clare, Clarice, Clarissa*

**Clar·ence** (klar′əns) [< name of Eng. dukedom of *Clarence*] a masculine name

**clar·et** (klar′it) *n.* [< OFr. dim. of *cler* < L. *clarus*, clear] **1.** a dry red wine, esp. red Bordeaux **2.** purplish red: also **claret red** —*adj.* purplish-red

**clar·i·fy** (klar′ə fī′) *vt., vi.* **-fied′, -fy′ing** [< OFr. < L. < *clarus*, clear + *facere*, to make] **1.** to make or become clear and free from impurities: said esp. of liquids **2.** to make or become easier to understand [*clarify* your meaning] —**clar′i·fi·ca′tion** *n.* —**clar′i·fi′er** *n.*

**clar·i·net** (klar′ə net′, klar′ə nit) *n.* [Fr. *clarinette*, dim. of *clarine*, little bell < ML. *clario:* see ff.] a single-reed, woodwind instrument with a long wooden or metal tube and a flaring bell, played by means of holes and keys — **clar′i·net′ist, clar′i·net′tist** *n.*

**clar·i·on** (klar′ē ən) *n.* [OFr. < ML. *clario* < L. *clarus*, clear] **1.** a trumpet of the Middle Ages producing clear, sharp, shrill tones **2.** [Poet.] a sound of or like a clarion —*adj.* clear, sharp, and ringing [a *clarion* call] —*vt.* to announce forcefully or loudly

**clar·i·ty** (klar′ə tē) *n.* [OFr. *clarte* < L. *claritas* < *clarus*, clear] a being clear; clearness

**Clark** (klärk) [< OFr. & OE.: see CLERK] **1.** a masculine name **2. William,** 1770–1838; Am. explorer: see Meriwether LEWIS

**clash** (klash) *vi.* [echoic] **1.** to collide with a loud, harsh, metallic noise **2.** *a*) to conflict; disagree *b*) to fail to harmonize —*vt.* to strike together, shut, etc. with a loud, harsh noise —*n.* **1.** the sound of clashing **2.** *a*) conflict *b*) lack of harmony —**clash′er** *n.*

**clasp** (klasp) *n.* [ME. *claspe*] **1.** a fastening, as a hook or catch, to hold two things or parts together **2.** a grasping; embrace **3.** a grip of the hand —*vt.* **1.** to fasten with a clasp **2.** to grasp firmly; embrace **3.** to grip with the hand **4.** to cling to —**clasp′er** *n.*

**class** (klas) *n.* [< Fr. < L. *classis*, prob. akin to *calare*, to call] **1.** a number of people or things grouped together because of certain likenesses; kind; sort **2.** a group of people of the same social or economic status [the middle *class*] **3.** high social rank or caste **4.** the division of society into ranks or castes **5.** *a*) a group of students taught together *b*) a meeting of such a group *c*) a group of students graduating together **6.** grade or quality [travel first *class*] **7.** [Slang] excellence, as of style **8.** *Biol.* a group of animals or plants ranking below a phylum and above an order —*vt.* to put in a class; classify —*vi.* to be classed —**in a class by itself** (or **oneself**) unique

**class. 1.** classic; **2.** classical; **3.** classification; **4.** classified

**class consciousness** an awareness of belonging to a certain economic class in the social order —**class′-con′scious** *adj.*

**clas·sic** (klas′ik) *adj.* [L. *classicus*, superior < *classis*, CLASS] **1.** of the highest class; being a model of its kind; standard **2.** *a*) of the art, literature, and culture of the ancient Greeks or Romans, or their writers, artists, etc. *b*) derived from their literary and artistic standards **3.** balanced, formal, objective, restrained, regular, etc. **4.** famous as traditional or typical **5.** [Colloq.] simple in style and continuing in fashion: said of an article of apparel —*n.* **1.** a writer, artist, etc., or a literary or artistic work, recognized as excellent, authoritative, etc. **2.** a famous traditional event **3.** [Colloq.] a suit, dress, etc. that is classic (sense 5) **4.** [Colloq.] an automobile of the period 1925–42 —**the classics** literature regarded as classic (senses 1, 2)

**clas·si·cal** (-i k'l) *adj.* **1.** *same as* CLASSIC (senses 1, 2, 3) **2.** versed in and devoted to Greek and Roman culture, literature, etc. **3.** designating or of music that conforms to certain established standards of form, complexity, musical literacy, etc.: distinguished from POPULAR, ROMANTIC **4.** standard and traditionally authoritative, not new and experimental [*classical* economics] —**clas′si·cal′i·ty** (-kal′ə tē), **clas′si·cal·ness,** *n.* —**clas′si·cal·ly** *adv.*

**clas·si·cism** (klas′ə siz'm) *n.* **1.** the aesthetic principles or qualities of ancient Greece and Rome: generally contrasted with ROMANTICISM **2.** adherence to such principles **3.** knowledge of the literature and art of ancient Greece and Rome **4.** a Greek or Latin idiom or expression Also **clas′si·cal·ism** —**clas′si·cist** *n.*

**clas·si·cize** (-sīz′) *vt.* **-cized′, -ciz′ing** to make classic —*vi.* to use a classic style

**clas·si·fi·ca·tion** (klas′ə fi kā′shən) *n.* **1.** an arrangement according to some systematic division into classes or groups **2.** such a class or group **3.** *Biol. same as* TAXONOMY —**clas·si·fi·ca·to·ry** (klas′ə fi kā′tər ē, -kə tôr′ē) *adj.*

**classified advertising** advertising, as in newspaper columns, under such listings as *help wanted, for sale,* etc.

**clas·si·fy** (klas′ə fī′) *vt.* **-fied′, -fy′ing 1.** to arrange in classes according to some system or principle **2.** to place in a category **3.** to designate (government documents, etc.) as secret or confidential —**clas′si·fi′a·ble** *adj.* —**clas′si·fi′er** *n.*

**class·less** (klas′lis) *adj.* having no distinct class or economic classes [a *classless* society]

**class·mate** (-māt′) *n.* a member of the same class at a school or college

**class·room** (-rōōm′) *n.* a room in a school or college in which classes are taught

**class·y** (-ē) *adj.* **class′i·er, class′i·est** [Slang] first-class, esp. in style or manner —**class′i·ness** *n.*

**clat·ter** (klat′ər) *vi.* [ME. *clateren*] **1.** to make, or move with, a rapid succession of loud, sharp noises, as dishes rattling **2.** to chatter noisily —*vt.* to cause to clatter —*n.* **1.** a rapid succession of loud, sharp noises **2.** a tumult; hubbub **3.** noisy chatter —**clat′ter·er** *n.* —**clat′ter·ing·ly** *adv.*

**Claude** (klôd) [Fr. < L. *Claudius*, name of a Roman gens] a masculine name

**Clau·di·a** (klô′dē ə) [L., fem. of prec.] a feminine name

**clause** (klôz) *n.* [OFr. < ML. *clausa* < L. pp. of *claudere*, to close] **1.** a group of words containing a subject and verb, usually forming part of a compound or complex sentence: cf. MAIN CLAUSE, SUBORDINATE CLAUSE **2.** a particular article, stipulation, or provision in a formal or legal document —**claus′al** *adj.*

**claus·tro·pho·bi·a** (klôs′trə fō′bē ə) *n.* [< L. *claustrum* (see CLOISTER) + -PHOBIA] an abnormal fear of being in an enclosed or confined place —**claus′tro·pho′bic** *adj.*

**cla·vate** (klā′vāt) *adj.* [< L. *clava*, a club + -ATE¹] club-shaped —**cla′vate·ly** *adv.* —**cla·va′tion** *n.*

**clave** (klāv) *archaic pt. of* CLEAVE¹ & CLEAVE²

**clav·i·chord** (klav′ə kôrd′) *n.* [< ML. < L. *clavis*, a key + *chorda*, a string] a stringed musical instrument with a keyboard, predecessor of the piano

**clav·i·cle** (klav′ə k'l) *n.* [< Fr. < L. *clavicula*, dim. of *clavis*, a key] a bone connecting the breastbone with the shoulder blade; collarbone —**cla·vic·u·lar** (klə vik′yoo lər) *adj.*

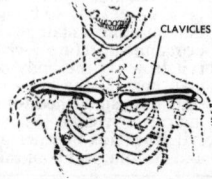
CLAVICLES

**cla·vi·er** (klə vir′; *for 1, also* klav′ē ər) *n.* [Fr., keyboard < L. *clavis*, a key] **1.** the keyboard of an organ, piano, etc. **2.** any stringed instrument that has a keyboard

**claw** (klô) *n.* [OE. *clawu*] **1.** a sharp, hooked nail on the foot of a bird and of many reptiles and mammals **2.** a foot with such nails **3.** a pincer, or chela, of a lobster, crab, etc. **4.** anything regarded as or resembling a claw, as a hammer (**claw hammer**) with one end forked and curved, used to pull nails —*vt., vi.* to scratch, clutch, pull, dig, or tear with or as with claws —**clawed** *adj.*

**clay** (klā) *n.* [OE. *clæg*] **1.** a firm, plastic earth, used in the manufacture of bricks, pottery, etc. **2.** *a)* earth *b)* the human body —**clay′ey** *adj.* **clay′i·er, clay′i·est** —**clay′ish** *adj.*

**Clay** (klā), **Henry** 1777–1852; U.S. statesman

**clay·more** (klā′môr′) *n.* [Gael. *claidheamhmor*, great sword] **1.** a large, two-edged broadsword formerly used by Scottish Highlanders **2.** a broadsword with a basket hilt worn by Highland regiments

**clay pigeon** a disk as of baked clay, tossed into the air from a trap as a target in trapshooting

**clean** (klēn) *adj.* [OE. *clæne*] **1.** free from dirt or impurities; unsoiled; unstained **2.** producing little immediate fallout: said of nuclear weapons **3.** recently laundered; fresh **4.** *a)* morally pure *b)* not obscene or indecent **5.** sportsmanlike **6.** keeping oneself or one's surroundings neat and tidy **7.** shapely or trim [*clean* lines] **8.** skillful; deft [*a clean* stroke] **9.** having no obstructions or flaws; clear **10.** complete; thorough **11.** empty —*adv.* **1.** in a clean manner **2.** completely —*vt.* **1.** to make clean **2.** to remove (dirt, impurities, etc.) **3.** to empty or clear **4.** to prepare (fish, fowl, etc.) for cooking **5.** [Slang] to take away or use up the money, etc. of (often with *out*) —*vi.* to undergo or perform the act of cleaning —**clean out 1.** to empty so as to make clean **2.** to empty —**clean up 1.** to make clean or neat **2.** to get washed, combed, etc. **3.** [Colloq.] to finish **4.** [Slang] to make much profit —**clean up on** [Slang] to defeat; beat —**come clean** [Slang] to confess; tell the truth —**clean′a·ble** *adj.* —**clean′ness** *n.*

**clean-cut** (-kut′) *adj.* **1.** clearly and sharply outlined **2.** well-formed **3.** distinct; clear **4.** good-looking, trim, neat, etc.

**clean·er** (-ər) *n.* a person or thing that cleans; specif., *a)* one who dry-cleans *b)* a preparation for removing dirt, stains, etc. —**take to the cleaners** [Slang] to take all the money of, as in gambling

**clean·ly¹** (klēn′lē) *adj.* **-li·er, -li·est 1.** keeping oneself or one's surroundings clean **2.** always kept clean —**clean′li·ly** *adv.* —**clean′li·ness** *n.*

**clean·ly²** (klēn′lē) *adv.* in a clean manner

**cleanse** (klenz) *vt.* **cleansed, cleans′ing** [OE. *clænsian*] to make clean, pure, etc.; purge

**cleans·er** (klen′zər) *n.* a preparation for cleansing, esp. a powder for scouring pots, sinks, etc.

**clean·up** (klēn′up′) *n.* **1.** a cleaning up **2.** elimination of crime, vice, etc. **3.** [Slang] profit; gain —*adj. Baseball* designating the fourth batter in a team's lineup

**clear** (klir) *adj.* [< OFr. < L. *clarus*] **1.** free from clouds or mist; bright; light **2.** transparent; not turbid **3.** having no blemishes [*a clear* skin] **4.** easily seen; sharply defined; distinct **5.** perceiving acutely; keen **6.** serene and calm **7.** not obscure; easily understood **8.** obvious **9.** certain; positive **10.** free from guilt; innocent **11.** free from charges or deductions; net **12.** free from debt or encumbrance **13.** absolute; complete **14.** free from obstruction; open **15.** emptied of freight or cargo —*adv.* **1.** in a clear manner **2.** all the way; completely [it sank *clear* to the bottom] —*vt.* **1.** to make clear or bright **2.** to free from impurities, muddiness, blemishes, etc. **3.** *a)* to make intelligible or lucid *b)* to decode or decipher **4.** to rid of obstructions; open **5.** to get rid of; remove **6.** to empty or unload **7.** to free (a person or thing) *of* or *from* something **8.** to free from guilt or blame **9.** to pass over, under, by, etc. with space to spare **10.** to discharge (a debt) by paying it **11.** to give or get clearance for **12.** to be passed or approved by **13.** to make (a given amount) as profit; net **14.** *Banking* to pass (a check, etc.) through a clearinghouse —*vi.* **1.** to become clear, unclouded, etc. **2.** to pass away; vanish **3.** to get clearance, as a ship leaving port **4.** *Banking* to exchange checks, etc., and balance accounts, through a clearinghouse —*n.* a clear space —**clear away 1.** to take away so as to leave a cleared space **2.** to go away —**clear off 1.** to clear away **2.** to remove things from (a surface) —**clear out 1.** to clear by emptying **2.** [Colloq.] to depart —**clear the air** (or **atmosphere**) to get rid of emotional tensions, etc. —**clear up 1.** to make or become clear **2.** to make orderly **3.** to explain **4.** to cure or become cured —**in the clear 1.** in the open **2.** [Colloq.] free from suspicion, guilt, etc. —**clear′a·ble** *adj.* —**clear′er** *n.* —**clear′ly** *adv.* —**clear′ness** *n.*

**clear·ance** (-əns) *n.* **1.** a making clear **2.** the clear space between things, or between a moving object and that which it passes by, through, over, under, etc. **3.** official authorization to see classified documents, work on secret projects,

etc. **4.** *Banking* the adjustment of accounts in a clearinghouse **5.** *Naut.* a certificate authorizing a ship to enter or leave port: also called **clearance papers**

**clear-cut** (-kut′) *adj.* **1.** clearly and sharply outlined **2.** distinct; definite; certain

**clear·head·ed** (-hed′id) *adj.* having or indicating a clear mind; lucid; unconfused —**clear′head′ed·ly** *adv.* —**clear′-head′ed·ness** *n.*

**clear·ing** (klir′iŋ) *n.* **1.** a making clear or being cleared **2.** an area of land cleared of trees **3.** *Banking a)* same as CLEARANCE *b)* [*pl.*] the amount of the balances settled in clearance

**clear·ing·house** (-hous′) *n.* **1.** an office maintained by a group of banks as a center for exchanging checks, balancing accounts, etc. **2.** a central office for getting and giving information, etc.

**clear·sight·ed** (klir′sīt′id) *adj.* **1.** seeing clearly **2.** understanding or thinking clearly —**clear′sight′ed·ly** *adv.* —**clear′sight′ed·ness** *n.*

**clear·sto·ry** (-stôr′ē) *n., pl.* **-ries** *same as* CLERESTORY

**Clear·wa·ter** (klir′wôt′ər, -wät′-) city in WC Fla., on the Gulf of Mexico: suburb of St. Petersburg: pop. 85,000

**cleat** (klēt) *n.* [< OE. hyp. *cleat*, a lump] **1.** a piece of wood or metal, often wedge-shaped, fastened to something to strengthen it or give secure footing **2.** *Naut.* a small piece of wood or metal with projecting ends on which a rope can be fastened —*vt.* to fasten to or with a cleat

**cleav·age** (klē′vij) *n.* **1.** a cleaving, splitting, or dividing **2.** the manner in which a thing splits **3.** a cleft; fissure **4.** the hollow between a woman's breasts, as exposed by a low-cut neckline **5.** *Biol.* cell division that transforms the fertilized ovum into the earliest embryonic stage

**cleave¹** (klēv) *vt.* **cleaved** or **cleft** or **clove, cleaved** or **cleft** or **clo′ven, cleav′ing** [OE. *cleofan*] **1.** to divide by a blow, as with an ax; split **2.** to pierce **3.** to sever; disunite —*vi.* **1.** to split; separate **2.** to make one's way by or as by cutting —**cleav′a·ble** *adj.*

**cleave²** (klēv) *vi.* **cleaved, cleav′ing** [OE. *cleofian*] **1.** to adhere; cling (*to*) **2.** to be faithful (*to*)

**cleav·er** (-ər) *n.* a heavy cleaving tool with a broad blade, used by butchers

**cleav·ers** (-ərz) *n., pl.* **-ers** [< CLEAVE²] a plant of the madder family, with stalkless leaves, clusters of small flowers, and prickly stems

**clef** (klef) *n.* [Fr. < L. *clavis*, a key] a symbol used in music to indicate the pitch of the notes on the staff: there are three clefs: G (treble), F (bass), and C (tenor or alto)

G CLEF    F CLEF

**cleft¹** (kleft) *n.* [< OE. hyp. *clyft < cleofan*, CLEAVE¹] **1.** an opening made by or as by cleaving; crack; crevice **2.** a hollow between two parts

**cleft²** *alt. pt. & pp. of* CLEAVE¹ —*adj.* split; divided

**clem·a·tis** (klem′ə tis, klə mat′is) *n.* [L. < Gr. < *klēma*, vine, twig] a perennial plant or woody vine of the buttercup family, with bright-colored flowers

**Cle·men·ceau** (klā män sō′; E. klem′ən sō′), **Georges (Benjamin Eugéne)** (zhôrzh) 1841–1929; Fr. statesman; premier of France (1906–09; 1917–20)

C CLEFS
TYPES OF CLEF

**clem·en·cy** (klem′ən sē) *n., pl.* **-cies** [< L. < *clemens*, merciful] **1.** forbearance, leniency, or mercy **2.** mildness, as of weather

**Clem·ens** (klem′ənz), **Samuel Lang·horne** (laŋ′hôrn) (pseud. *Mark Twain*) 1835–1910; U.S. writer & humorist

**Clem·ent** (klem′ənt) [L. < *clemens*, mild, gentle] a masculine name: dim. *Clem*

**clem·ent** (klem′ənt) *adj.* [L. *clemens*] **1.** lenient; merciful **2.** mild, as weather —**clem′ent·ly** *adv.*

**Clem·en·tine** (klem′ən tīn′, -tēn′) [Fr. < L. fem. of CLEMENT] a feminine name

**clench** (klench) *vt.* [< OE. -*clencan* (in *beclencan*), lit., to make cling] **1.** to clinch, as a nail **2.** to bring together tightly; close (the teeth or fist) firmly **3.** to grip tightly —*n.* **1.** a firm grip **2.** a device that clenches —**clench′er** *n.*

**Cle·o·pa·tra** (klē′ə pat′rə, -pā′trə, -pä′trə) 69?–30 B.C.; queen of Egypt (51–49; 48–30)

**clep·sy·dra** (klep′si drə) *n., pl.* **-dras** or **-drae′** (-drē′) [L. < Gr. < *kleptein*, to steal + *hydōr*, water] *same as* WATER CLOCK

**clep·to·ma·ni·a** (klep′tə mā′nē ə) *n. same as* KLEPTOMANIA

**clere·sto·ry** (klir′stôr′ē) *n., pl.* **-ries** [< ME. < *cler*, clear

+ **storie,** STORY²] **1.** the wall of a church rising above the roofs of the flanking aisles and containing windows for lighting the central part of the structure **2.** any similar windowed wall

**cler·gy** (klur'jē) *n., pl.* **-gies** [< OFr. < LL. *clericus:* see CLERK] ministers, priests, rabbis, etc. collectively

**cler·gy·man** (-mən) *n., pl.* **-men** a member of the clergy; minister, priest, rabbi, etc.

**cler·ic** (kler'ik) *n.* [LL. *clericus:* see CLERK] a clergyman —*adj.* of a clergyman or the clergy

**cler·i·cal** (kler'i k'l) *adj.* [LL. *clericalis* < *clericus:* see CLERK] **1.** relating to a clergyman or the clergy **2.** relating to office clerks or their work **3.** favoring clericalism —*n.* **1.** a clergyman **2.** [*pl.*] clergymen's garments **3.** one who favors clericalism —**cler'i·cal·ly** *adv.*

**clerical collar** a stiff, white collar buttoned at the back, worn by certain clergymen

**cler·i·cal·ism** (-iz'm) *n.* political influence or power of the clergy —**cler'i·cal·ist** *n.*

**clerk** (klurk; *Brit.* klärk) *n.* [< OFr. & OE. < LL. *clericus* < Gr. *klērikos,* priest] **1.** a layman who has minor duties in a church **2.** an office worker who keeps records, types letters, does filing, etc. **3.** an official in charge of records, etc. of a court, town, etc. **4.** a hotel employee who keeps the register, assigns guests to rooms, etc. **5.** one who sells in a store; salesclerk **6.** [Archaic] *a)* a clergyman *b)* a scholar —*vi.* to work as a clerk, esp. a salesclerk —**clerk'ly** *adj., adv.* —**clerk'ship** *n.*

**Cleve·land** (klēv'lənd) [after M. *Cleaveland,* 18th-c. Conn. surveyor] city in NE Ohio, on Lake Erie: pop. 574,000 (met. area 1,896,000)

**Cleve·land** (klēv'lənd), (**Stephen**) **Gro·ver** (grō'vər) 1837–1908; 22d and 24th president of the U.S. (1885–89; 1893–97)

**Cleveland Heights** city in NE Ohio: suburb of Cleveland: pop. 56,000

**clev·er** (klev'ər) *adj.* [prob. < EFris. *klüfer* or Norw. *klöver,* skillful] **1.** skillful in doing something; adroit; dexterous **2.** intelligent, quick-witted, witty, facile, etc. **3.** showing quick, sometimes superficial, intelligence [a *clever* book] —**clev'er·ly** *adv.* —**clev'er·ness** *n.*

**clev·is** (klev'is) *n.* [ult. akin to CLEAVE²] a U-shaped piece of iron with holes in the ends through which a pin is run to attach one thing to another

**clew** (kloo) *n.* [< OE. *cliwen*] **1.** a ball of thread or yarn **2.** something that leads out of a maze or perplexity or helps to solve a problem: usually sp. **clue 3.** *Naut. a)* a lower corner of a square sail *b)* the lower corner aft of a fore-and-aft sail *c)* a metal loop in the corner of a sail —*vt.* **1.** to wind (*up*) into a ball **2.** *same as* CLUE —**clew down** (or **up**) to lower (or raise) a sail by the clews

**cli·ché** (klē shā') *n.* [Fr. < *clicher,* to stereotype] a trite expression or idea

**cli·chéd** (klē shād') *adj.* **1.** full of clichés [a dull, *cliched* style] **2.** trite; stereotyped [a *clichéd* theme]

**click** (klik) *n.* [echoic] **1.** a slight, sharp sound like that of a door latch snapping into place **2.** a mechanical device, as a catch or pawl, that clicks into position **3.** *Phonet.* a sound made by drawing the breath into the mouth and clicking the tongue —*vi.* **1.** to make a click **2.** [Colloq.] *a)* to be suddenly comprehensible *b)* to work or get along together successfully *c)* to be a success —*vt.* to cause to click —**click'er** *n.*

**cli·ent** (klī'ənt) *n.* [OFr. < L. *cliens,* follower] **1.** a person or company for whom a lawyer, accountant, etc. is acting **2.** a customer —**cli·en·tal** (klī en't'l) *adj.*

**cli·en·tele** (klī'ən tel'; *also, chiefly Brit.,* klē'än-) *n.* [< Fr. < L. *clientela*] all one's clients or customers, collectively: also **cli·ent·age** (klī'ən tij)

**cliff** (klif) *n.* [OE. *clif*] a high, steep face of rock, esp. one on a coast; precipice —**cliff'y** *adj.*

**cliff·hang·er, cliff-hang·er** (-haŋ'ər) *n.* any highly suspenseful story, situation, etc. as in an early type of serialized movie with an episode in which the hero is hanging from a cliff —**cliff'hang'ing, cliff'-hang'ing** *adj.*

**Clif·ton** (klif'tən) [< CLIFF + *-ton,* town] **1.** a masculine name **2.** [< its location at the foot of a mountain] city in NE N.J.: pop. 74,000

**cli·mac·ter·ic** (klī mak'tər ik, klī'mak ter'ik) *n.* [< L. < Gr. < *klimax,* ladder] **1.** a period in a person's life when an important physiological change occurs, esp. the menopause **2.** any crucial period —*adj.* of or resembling a climacteric: also **cli'mac·ter'i·cal**

**cli·mac·tic** (klī mak'tik) *adj.* of or constituting a climax: also **cli·mac'ti·cal** —**cli·mac'ti·cal·ly** *adv.*

**cli·mate** (klī'mət) *n.* [< OFr. < L. < Gr. *klima,* region] **1.** the prevailing weather conditions of a place, as determined by the temperature and meteorological changes over a period of years **2.** any prevailing conditions affecting life, activity, etc. **3.** a region with certain prevailing weather conditions [move to a warm *climate*] —**cli·mat·ic** (klī mat'ik) *adj.* —**cli·mat'i·cal·ly** *adv.*

**cli·ma·tol·o·gy** (klī'mə täl'ə jē) *n.* the science dealing with climate and climate phenomena —**cli'ma·to·log'i·cal** (-tə läj'i k'l) *adj.* —**cli'ma·tol'o·gist** *n.*

**cli·max** (klī'maks) *n.* [L. < Gr. *klimax,* ladder] **1.** formerly, an arrangement of ideas, images, etc. with the most forceful last **2.** the final, culminating element or event in a series; highest point, as of interest, excitement, etc.; specif. *a)* the decisive turning point of the action, as in drama *b)* an orgasm **3.** *Ecol.* a final, self-perpetuating, local community of plants or animals —*vi., vt.* to reach, or bring to, a climax

**climb** (klīm) *vi., vt.* **climbed** or archaic **clomb, climb'ing** [OE. *climban*] **1.** to go up by using the feet and often the hands **2.** to rise or ascend gradually; mount **3.** to move (*down, over, along,* etc.) using the hands and feet **4.** *Bot.* to grow upward on by winding around or adhering with tendrils —*n.* **1.** a climbing; rise; ascent **2.** a thing or place to be climbed —**climb'a·ble** *adj.*

**climb·er** (-ər) *n.* **1.** one that climbs **2.** *same as* LINEMEN'S CLIMBER: also **climbing iron 3.** [Colloq.] one who constantly tries to advance himself socially or in business **4.** *Bot.* a climbing plant or vine

**clime** (klīm) *n.* [L. *clima:* see CLIMATE] [Poet.] a region, esp. with reference to its climate

**clinch** (klinch) *vt.* [var. of CLENCH] **1.** to fasten (a nail, bolt, etc. driven through something) by bending or flattening the projecting end **2.** to fasten together by this means **3.** *a)* to settle (an argument, deal, etc.) definitely *b)* to win conclusively —*vi.* **1.** *Boxing* to grip the opponent's body with the arms **2.** [Slang] to embrace —*n.* **1.** *a)* a clinching, as with a nail *b)* a clinched nail, bolt, etc. *c)* the part clinched **2.** *Boxing* an act of clinching **3.** [Slang] an embrace

**clinch·er** (-ər) *n.* **1.** a tool for clinching nails **2.** a decisive point, argument, act, etc.

**cling** (kliŋ) *vi.* **clung, cling'ing** [OE. *clingan*] **1.** to hold fast by or·as by embracing, entwining, or sticking; adhere **2.** *a)* to be or stay near *b)* to be emotionally attached —**cling'er** *n.* —**cling'ing·ly** *adv.* —**cling'y** *adj.*

**cling·stone** (-stōn') *adj.* having a stone that clings to the fleshy part: said of some peaches —*n.* a peach of this sort

**clin·ic** (klin'ik) *n.* [L. *clinicus,* physician who attends bedridden persons < Gr. *klinikos,* of a bed < *klinē,* a bed] **1.** the teaching of medicine by examining and treating patients in the presence of students **2.** a class so taught **3.** a place where patients are treated by specialist physicians practicing as a group **4.** a department of a hospital or medical school where outpatients are treated, sometimes free or for a small fee **5.** an organization that offers some kind of advice, treatment, or instruction **6.** a brief, intensive session of group instruction in a specific skill, field of knowledge, etc. [a basketball *clinic*]

**clin·i·cal** (-i k'l) *adj.* **1.** of or connected with a clinic **2.** having to do with the treatment and observation of patients, as distinguished from experimental or laboratory study **3.** scientifically impersonal **4.** austere, antiseptic, etc., like a medical clinic —**clin'i·cal·ly** *adv.*

**clinical thermometer** a thermometer with which the body temperature is measured

**cli·ni·cian** (kli nish'ən) *n.* an expert in or practitioner of clinical medicine, psychology, etc.

**clink** (kliŋk) *vi., vt.* [< MDu. *klinken:* echoic] to make or cause to make a slight, sharp sound, as of glasses striking together —*n.* **1.** such a sound **2.** [< name of an 18th-c. London prison] [Colloq.] a jail; prison

**clink·er** (-ər) *n.* [Du. *klinker,* vitrified brick < *klinken,* to ring] **1.** a hard mass of fused stony matter formed in a furnace, as from impurities in the coal **2.** [Slang] *a)* a mistake; error *b)* a total failure —*vi.* to form clinkers in burning

**cli·nom·e·ter** (klī näm'ə tər) *n.* [< Gr. < *klinein,* to slope + -METER] an instrument for measuring angles of slope or inclination —**cli'no·met'ric** (klī'nə met'rik), **cli'no·met'ri·cal** *adj.* —**cli·nom'e·try** (-ə trē) *n.*

**Clin·ton** (klin't'n) [Eng. place name < ? ME. *clint,* cliff + *tun,* village] a masculine name

**Cli·o** (klī'ō) [L. < Gr. < *kleos,* fame] *Gr. Myth.* the Muse of history

**cli·o·met·rics** (klī'ō met'riks) *n.pl.* [*with sing. v.*] [< prec. + Gr. *metron,* measure] the use of mathematical and statistical methods, and often of computers, in analyzing historical data —**cli'o·met'ric** *adj.* —**cli'o·me·tri'cian** (-mə trish'ən) *n.*

**clip¹** (klip) *vt.* **clipped, clip'ping** [< ON. *klippa*] **1.** to cut or cut off as with shears **2.** to cut (an item) out of (a newspaper, etc.) **3.** *a)* to cut short *b)* to shorten by omitting syllables, etc. **4.** to cut the hair of **5.** [Colloq.] to hit with a quick, sharp blow **6.** [Slang] to cheat, esp. by overcharging —*vi.* **1.** to clip something **2.** to move rapidly —*n.* **1.** the act of clipping **2.** a thing clipped; specif., *a)* the amount of wool clipped from sheep at one time *b)* a sequence clipped from a movie film **3.** a rapid pace **4.** [Colloq.] a quick, sharp blow **5.** *same as* CLIPPED FORM

**clip²** (klip) *vi.*, *vt.* **clipped, clip′ping** [OE. *clyppan*, to embrace] **1.** to grip tightly; fasten **2.** *Football* to block (an opponent who is not carrying the ball) from behind: an illegal act —*n.* **1.** any device that clips or fastens things together **2.** *same as* CARTRIDGE CLIP **3.** *Football* a clipping

**clip·board** (-bôrd′) *n.* a portable writing board with a hinged clip at the top to hold papers

**clipped form** (or **word**) a shortened form of a word, as *pike* (for *turnpike*) or *fan* (for *fanatic*)

**clip·per** (klip′ər) *n.* [ME. < *clippen*, CLIP¹] **1.** a person who cuts, trims, etc. **2.** [*usually pl.*] a tool for cutting or trimming **3.** [for sense, cf. CUTTER] a sharp-bowed, narrow-beamed sailing ship built for great speed

**clip·ping** (-iŋ) *n.* **1.** something cut out or trimmed off **2.** an item clipped from a newspaper, magazine, etc.

CLIPPER SHIP

**clique** (klēk, klik) *n.* [Fr. < *cliquer*, to make a noise] a small, exclusive circle of people; snobbish or narrow coterie —**cliqu′ish, cliqu′ey, cliqu′y** *adj.* —**cliqu′ish·ly** *adv.* —**cliqu′ish·ness** *n.*

**clit·o·ris** (klit′ər əs, klīt′-) *n.* [ModL. < Gr. < *kleitys*, hill] a small, sensitive, erectile organ at the upper end of the vulva: it corresponds to the penis in the male —**clit′o·ral** (-ər əl), **cli·tor·ic** (klī tôr′ik) *adj.*

**Clive** (klīv) [< the surname] **1.** a masculine name **2. Robert,** Baron Clive of Plassey, 1725–74; Brit. soldier & statesman in India

**clk.** clerk

**clo·a·ca** (klō ā′kə) *n.*, *pl.* **-cae** (-sē, -kē), **-cas** [L. < *cluere*, to cleanse] **1.** a sewer or cesspool **2.** *Zool.* the cavity into which the intestinal and genitourinary tracts empty in reptiles, birds, amphibians, and many fishes —**clo·a′cal** *adj.*

**cloak** (klōk) *n.* [< OFr. < ML. *clocca* (see CLOCK¹), a bell, cloak: so called from its bell-like appearance] **1.** a loose, usually sleeveless outer garment **2.** something that covers or conceals —*vt.* **1.** to cover as with a cloak **2.** to conceal; hide

**cloak-and-dag·ger** (-ən dag′ər) *adj.* dealing in a melodramatic way with spies and spying

**cloak·room** (-rōōm′) *n.* a room where hats, coats, umbrellas, etc. can be left temporarily

**clob·ber** (kläb′ər) *vt.* [< ?] [Slang] **1.** to beat or hit repeatedly; maul **2.** to defeat decisively

**cloche** (klōsh) *n.* [Fr. < ML. *clocca*: see ff.] a closefitting, bell-shaped hat for women

**clock¹** (kläk) *n.* [ME. *clokke*, orig., clock with bells < ML. *clocca*, bell < Celt.] **1.** a device for measuring and indicating time, as by pointers moving over a dial: clocks, unlike watches, are not carried on one's person **2.** *same as* TIME CLOCK —*vt.* **1.** to measure or record the time of (a race, runner, etc.) with a stopwatch, etc. **2.** to register (an amount, etc.) on a meter —**around the clock** day and night, without stopping

**clock²** (kläk) *n.* [< ? prec., because orig. bell-shaped] a woven or embroidered ornament on the side of a sock or stocking, going up from the ankle —**clocked** *adj.*

**clock·like** (-līk′) *adj.* as precise or regular as a clock

**clock radio** a radio with a built-in clock that can be set to turn the radio on or off

**clock·wise** (-wīz′) *adv.*, *adj.* in the direction in which the hands of a clock rotate

**clock·work** (-wurk′) *n.* **1.** the mechanism of a clock **2.** any similar mechanism, consisting of springs and geared wheels, as in some mechanical toys —**like clockwork** very regularly and precisely

**clod** (kläd) *n.* [OE.] **1.** a lump, esp. of earth, clay, loam, etc. **2.** earth; soil **3.** a dull, stupid fellow; dolt —**clod′·dish** *adj.* —**clod′dish·ly** *adv.* —**clod′dish·ness** *n.* —**clod′dy** *adj.*

**clod·hop·per** (-häp′ər) *n.* [CLOD + HOPPER] **1.** a plowman **2.** a clumsy, stupid fellow; lout **3.** a coarse, heavy shoe

**clog** (kläg) *n.* [ME. *clogge*, a lump of wood] **1.** a weight fastened to an animal's leg to hinder motion **2.** anything that hinders or obstructs **3.** a shoe with a thick, usually wooden sole: light clogs are used in clog dancing **4.** *same as* CLOG DANCE —*vt.* **clogged, clog′ging 1.** to hinder; impede **2.** to fill with obstructions or with thick, sticky matter; stop up —*vi.* **1.** to become stopped up **2.** to do a clog dance —**clog′gi·ness** *n.* —**clog′gy** *adj.*

**clog dance** a dance in which clogs are worn to beat out the rhythm —**clog dancer** —**clog dancing**

**cloi·son·né** (kloi′zə nā′) *adj.* [Fr., lit., partitioned] denoting a kind of enamel work in which the surface decora-

tion is set in hollows formed by thin strips of wire welded to a metal plate in a complex pattern —*n.* cloisonné enamel

**clois·ter** (klois′tər) *n.* [< OFr. < L. *claustrum*, bolt, place shut in < pp. of *claudere*, to close] **1.** a place of religious seclusion; monastery or convent **2.** monastic life **3.** any place where one may lead a secluded life **4.** a covered walk along the inside walls of a monastery, convent, etc., with a columned opening along one side —*vt.* **1.** to seclude or confine as in a cloister **2.** to furnish with a cloister —**clois′tered** *adj.* —**clois′tral** *adj.*

**clomb** (klōm) *archaic pt. & pp. of* CLIMB

**clomp** (klämp) *vi.* to walk heavily or noisily; clump

**clone** (klōn) *n.* [< Gr. *klōn*, a twig] *Biol.* all the descendants derived asexually from a single individual: also **clon** (klōn, klän)

**clonk** (kläŋk) *n.*, *vi.*, *vt. same as* CLUNK

**clo·nus** (klō′nəs) *n.* [ModL. < Gr. *klonos*, turmoil] a series of muscle spasms —**clon·ic** (klän′ik) *adj.* —**clo·nic·i·ty** (klə nis′ə tē) *n.* —**clo′nism** *n.*

**clop** (kläp) *n.* [echoic] a sharp, clattering sound, like hoofbeats on a pavement —*vi.* **clopped, clop′ping** to make, or move with, such a sound

**close¹** (klōs) *adj.* **clos′er, clos′est** [< OFr. *clos*, pp. of *clore*: see ff.] **1.** shut; not open **2.** enclosed or enclosing; shut in **3.** confined or confining [*close* quarters] **4.** carefully guarded [*close* custody] **5.** hidden; secluded **6.** secretive; reserved **7.** miserly; stingy **8.** restricted, as in membership **9.** oppressively warm and stuffy, as stale air **10.** not readily available [credit is *close*] **11.** with little space between; near together **12.** compact; dense [a *close* weave] **13.** fitting tightly **14.** *a)* down or near to the surface [a *close* shave] *b)* nearby [a *close* neighbor] **15.** very near in interests, affection, etc.; intimate [a *close* friend] **16.** varying little from the original [a *close* translation] **17.** strict; thorough; careful [*close* attention] **18.** *a)* concise *b)* accurate; precise **19.** nearly equal or alike [*close* in age] **20.** nearly even [a *close* contest] —*adv.* in a close manner —**close to the wind** *Naut.* heading as closely as possible in the direction from which the wind blows —**close′ly** *adv.* —**close′ness** *n.*

**close²** (klōz) *vt.* **closed, clos′ing** [< OFr. < *clore* < L. *claudere*, to close] **1.** to shut **2.** to block up or stop (an opening, passage, etc.) **3.** to bring together; unite [*close* forces] **4.** to bring to an end; finish **5.** to stop or suspend the operation of (a school, business, etc.) **6.** to complete or make final (a sale, agreement, etc.) —*vi.* **1.** to undergo shutting **2.** to come to an end **3.** to end or suspend operations; specif., in the stock exchange, to show an indicated price level at day's end **4.** to become joined together **5.** to come together **6.** to take hold **7.** to throng closely **8.** to lessen an intervening distance **9.** to come close in order to fight —*n.* **1.** a closing or being closed **2.** the final part; end —**close down 1.** to shut or stop entirely **2.** to settle down (*on*), as darkness or fog —**close in** to surround, cutting off escape —**close out** to sell out (goods), as in ending a business —**close up 1.** to draw nearer together **2.** to shut or stop up entirely **3.** to heal, as a wound does —**clos′er** *n.*

**close³** (klōs) *n.* [< OFr. *clos* < L. *clausum*, neut. pp. of *claudere*: see prec.] [Chiefly Brit.] **1.** an enclosed place **2.** enclosed grounds around or beside a building [a cathedral *close*] **3.** a narrow street or passageway

**close call** (klōs) [Colloq.] a narrow escape from danger: also **close shave**

**closed** (klōzd) *adj.* **1.** not open; shut **2.** covered over or enclosed **3.** functioning independently **4.** not open to new ideas, discussion, etc. **5.** restricted; exclusive **6.** *Math. a)* of a curve whose ends are joined *b)* of a surface whose plane sections are closed curves **7.** *Phonet.* ending in a consonant sound [a *closed* syllable]

**closed chain** the structural form of certain molecules, graphically represented as a ring of atoms

**closed circuit** a system of television transmission by cables to a limited number of receivers on a circuit —**closed′-cir′cuit** *adj.*

**closed-end** (-end′) *adj.* of an investment company with a fixed number of shares traded on the open market

**closed primary** *see* DIRECT PRIMARY ELECTION

**closed shop** a factory, business, etc. operating under a contract with a labor union by which only members of the union may be employed

**close·fist·ed** (klōs′fis′tid) *adj.* stingy; miserly

**close·fit·ting** (-fit′iŋ) *adj.* fitting tightly, esp. so as to show the contours of the body

**close-hauled** (-hôld′) *adj.* with the sails set for heading as nearly as possible into the wind

**close·mouthed** (-mouthd′, -mouth′) *adj.* not talking much; taciturn: also **close′lipped** (-lipt′)

**close punctuation** punctuation characterized by the use of many commas and other marks

**clos·et** (kläz'it) *n.* [OFr., dim. of *clos:* see CLOSE[3]] **1.** a small room or cupboard for clothes, supplies, etc. **2.** a small, private room for reading, consultation, etc. **3.** *same as* WATER CLOSET —*adj.* private or secret —*vt.* to shut up in a private room for confidential discussion

**closet drama** drama written mainly to be read, not staged

**close-up** (klōs'up') *n.* a photograph, or a movie or TV shot, made at very close range

**clo·sure** (klō'zhər) *n.* [OFr. < L. *clausura* < pp. of *claudere*, CLOSE[2]] **1.** a closing or being closed **2.** a finish; end; conclusion **3.** anything that closes **4.** *same as* CLOTURE —*vt.* -sured, -sur·ing *same as* CLOTURE

**clot** (klät) *n.* [OE. *clott*] a soft, thickened area or lump formed on or within a liquid [a blood *clot*] —*vt., vi.* clot'-ted, clot'ting to thicken or form into a clot or clots; coagulate

**cloth** (klôth, kläth) *n., pl.* **cloths** (klôthz, kläthz; *also* klôths, kläths *for "kinds of cloth"*) [OE. *clath*] **1.** a woven, knitted, or pressed fabric of fibrous material, as cotton, wool, silk, hair, synthetic fibers, etc. **2.** a piece of such fabric for a special use [*tablecloth, washcloth*] —*adj.* made of cloth —the cloth **1.** the identifying dress of a profession **2.** the clergy collectively

**clothe** (klōth) *vt.* **clothed** or **clad, cloth'ing** [OE. *clathian* < prec.] **1.** to put clothes on; dress **2.** to provide with clothes **3.** to cover over as if with a garment

**clothes** (klōz, klōthz) *n.pl.* [OE. *clathas*, pl. of *clath*, CLOTH] **1.** articles, usually of cloth, to cover the body; apparel; garments **2.** *same as* BEDCLOTHES

**clothes·horse** (-hôrs') *n.* **1.** a frame on which to hang clothes, etc. for airing or drying **2.** [Slang] one who pays too much attention to his clothes

**clothes·line** (-līn') *n.* a rope or wire on which clothes, etc. are hung for airing or drying

**clothes·pin** (-pin') *n.* a small clip, as of wood or plastic, for fastening clothes on a line

**clothes·press** (-pres') *n.* a closet, wardrobe, or chest in which to keep clothes

**clothes tree** an upright pole with branching hooks or pegs near the top to hold coats and hats

**cloth·ier** (klōth'yər, klō'thē ər) *n.* **1.** a person who makes or sells clothes **2.** a dealer in cloth

**cloth·ing** (klō'thiŋ) *n.* **1.** wearing apparel; clothes; garments **2.** a covering

**Clo·tho** (klō'thō) *Gr. & Rom. Myth.* one of the three Fates, spinner of the thread of human life

**clo·ture** (klō'chər) *n.* [Fr. < OFr. < ML. < L. *clausura:* see CLOSURE] the parliamentary procedure by which debate is closed and the measure put to an immediate vote —*vt.* -tured, -tur·ing to apply cloture to (a debate, bill, etc.)

**cloud** (kloud) *n.* [OE. *clud*, mass of rock] **1.** a visible mass of condensed water vapor suspended in the atmosphere **2.** a mass of smoke, dust, steam, etc. **3.** a great number of moving things close together [a *cloud* of locusts] **4.** a murkiness or dimness, as in a liquid **5.** a dark marking, as in marble **6.** anything that darkens, obscures, or makes gloomy —*vt.* **1.** to cover with clouds **2.** to make muddy or foggy **3.** to darken; obscure **4.** to make gloomy or troubled **5.** to sully (a reputation, etc.) —*vi.* **1.** to become cloudy **2.** to become gloomy or troubled —in the clouds **1.** high up in the sky **2.** fanciful; impractical **3.** in a reverie or daydream —under a cloud **1.** under suspicion of wrongdoing **2.** troubled; depressed —cloud'less *adj.* —cloud'less·ly *adv.* —cloud'less·ness *n.*

**cloud·burst** (-bʉrst') *n.* a sudden, very heavy rain

**cloud nine** [Slang] a state of euphoria

**cloud·y** (-ē) *adj.* cloud'i·er, cloud'i·est **1.** covered with clouds; overcast **2.** of or like clouds **3.** streaked, as marble **4.** opaque, muddy, or foggy [a *cloudy* liquid] **5.** obscure; vague **6.** troubled; gloomy —cloud'i·ly *adv.* —cloud'i·ness *n.*

**clout** (klout) *n.* [OE. *clut*] **1.** [Archaic] a piece of cloth **2.** a blow, as with the hand; rap **3.** [Colloq.] *a)* a long hit in baseball *b)* power or influence; esp., political power —*vt.* **1.** [Colloq.] to strike, as with the hand **2.** [Slang] to hit (a ball) a far distance

**clove**[1] (klōv) *n.* [OFr. *clou* < L. *clavus*, nail: from its shape] **1.** the dried flower bud of a tropical evergreen tree of the myrtle family: it is used as a pungent, fragrant spice **2.** the tree

**clove**[2] (klōv) *n.* [OE. *clufu*, akin to *cleofan*, CLEAVE[1]] a segment of a bulb, as of garlic

**clove**[3] (klōv) *alt. pt. of* CLEAVE[1]

**clo·ven** (klō'v'n) *alt. pp. of* CLEAVE[1] —*adj.* divided; split

**cloven foot** (or **hoof**) a foot divided by a cleft, as in the ox, deer, and sheep: used as a symbol of the Devil, usually pictured with such hoofs —clo'ven-foot'ed, clo'ven-hoofed' *adj.*

**clo·ver** (klō'vər) *n.* [< OE. *clafre*] **1.** any of a genus of low-growing herbs of the legume family, with leaves of three leaflets and small flowers in dense heads **2.** any similar plant: cf. SWEET CLOVER —in clover living in ease and luxury

**clo·ver·leaf** (-lēf') *n., pl.* -leafs' a multiple highway interchange in the form of a four-leaf clover, which, by means of an overpass with curving ramps, permits traffic to move or turn in any of four directions with little interference —*adj.* in the shape of a leaf of clover

**clown** (kloun) *n.* [altered < ? Fr. *colon*, farmer < L. *colonus:* see COLONY] **1.** orig., a peasant; rustic **2.** a clumsy, boorish person **3.** a performer who entertains, as in a circus, by antics, jokes, tricks, etc. **4.** a buffoon —*vi.* **1.** to perform as a clown **2.** to play practical jokes, act silly, etc. —clown'er·y *n.* —clown'ish *adj.* —clown'ish·ly *adv.* —clown'ish·ness *n.*

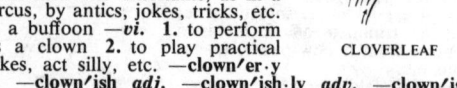

CLOVERLEAF

**cloy** (kloi) *vt., vi.* [< OFr. *encloyer*, to fasten with a nail, hinder < *clou:* see CLOVE[1]] to surfeit by too much of something, esp. something sweet, rich, etc. —cloy'ing·ly *adv.*

**club** (klub) *n.* [< ON. *klumba*, mass of something, clump] **1.** *a)* a heavy stick, usually thinner at one end, used as a weapon *b)* anything used to threaten **2.** any stick or bat used to strike a ball in a game [a golf *club*] **3.** *same as* INDIAN CLUB **4.** a group of people associated for a common purpose **5.** the room, building, etc. used by such a group **6.** *same as* NIGHTCLUB **7.** *a)* [pl.] a suit of playing cards marked with a black cloverleaf figure (♣) *b)* a card of this suit —*vt.* **clubbed, club'bing 1.** to strike as with a club **2.** to unite for a common purpose **3.** to pool (resources, etc.) —*vi.* to unite or combine for a common purpose

**club car** a railroad lounge car, usually with a bar

**club·foot** (-foot') *n.* **1.** a congenital deformity of the foot, often with a clublike appearance; talipes **2.** *pl.* -feet' a foot so deformed —club'foot'ed *adj.*

**club·house** (-hous') *n.* **1.** a building occupied by a club **2.** a locker room for an athletic team

**club·man** (-mən, -man') *n., pl.* -men (-mən, -men') a man who is a member of, or spends much time at, a private club or clubs —club'wom'an *n.fem., pl.* -wom'en

**club sandwich** a sandwich of several layers, often toasted, containing chicken, bacon, lettuce, etc.

**club soda** *same as* SODA WATER

**cluck** (kluk) *vi.* [< OE. *cloccian:* orig. echoic] to make a low, sharp, clicking sound, as of a hen calling her chickens —*vt.* to utter with such a sound —*n.* **1.** the sound of clucking **2.** [Slang] a dull, stupid person; dolt

**clue** (klōō) *n.* a clew; esp., a fact, object, etc. that helps solve a mystery or problem —*vt.* clued, clu'ing **1.** to indicate by or as by a clue **2.** [Colloq.] to provide with necessary information (often with *in*)

**Cluj** (klōōzh) city in NW Romania: pop. 191,000

**clump** (klump) *n.* [< Du. *klomp* or LowG. *klump*] **1.** a lump; mass **2.** a cluster, as of trees **3.** the sound of heavy footsteps —*vi.* **1.** to tramp heavily **2.** to form clumps —*vt.* **1.** to group together in a cluster **2.** to cause to form clumps —clump'ish *adj.* —clump'y *adj.* clump'i·er, clump'i·est

**clum·sy** (klum'zē) *adj.* -si·er, -si·est [ME. *clumsid*, numb with cold < ON. base] **1.** lacking grace or skill; awkward **2.** awkwardly shaped or made; ill-constructed **3.** inelegant [a *clumsy* style] —clum'si·ly *adv.* —clum'si·ness *n.*

**clung** (klʉŋ) *pt. & pp. of* CLING

**clunk** (klʉŋk) *n.* [echoic] **1.** a dull, metallic sound **2.** [Colloq.] a heavy blow **3.** [Slang] a dull or stupid person —*vi., vt.* to move or strike with a clunk or clunks

**clunk·er** (-ər) *n.* [Slang] an old machine or automobile in poor repair

**clus·ter** (klus'tər) *n.* [OE. *clyster*] **1.** a number of things of the same sort gathered or growing together; bunch **2.** a number of persons or animals grouped together **3.** *Linguis.* two or more consecutive consonants —*vi., vt.* to gather or grow in a cluster or clusters —clus'ter·y *adj.*

**clutch**[1] (kluch) *vt.* [OE. *clyccan*, to clench] **1.** to grasp or snatch with a hand or claw **2.** to grasp or hold eagerly or tightly —*vi.* to snatch or seize (*at*) —*n.* **1.** a claw or hand in the act of seizing **2.** [*usually pl.*] power; control **3.** *a) a* clutching *b)* a grasp; grip **4.** *a)* a mechanical device, as in an automobile, for engaging or disengaging the motor *b)* the lever or pedal that operates this **5.** a device for gripping **6.** a woman's small handbag with no handle or strap: also **clutch bag 7.** [Colloq.] an emergency

**clutch**[2] (kluch) *n.* [< ME. *clekken* (< ON. *klekja*), to hatch] **1.** a nest of eggs **2.** a brood of chicks **3.** a cluster of persons, animals, or things

**clut·ter** (klut'ər) *n.* [< CLOT] **1.** a number of things scattered in disorder; jumble **2.** *dial. var. of* CLATTER **3.** the interfering traces on a radarscope caused by hills, buildings, etc. —*vt.* to put into disorder; jumble (often with *up*) —*vi.* [Dial.] to make a clatter —**clut′ter·y** *adj.*

**Clyde** (klīd) [< ?] a masculine name

**Clydes·dale** (klīdz′dāl′) *n.* [orig. from *Clydesdale*, Scotland] any of a breed of strong draft horse

**clyp·e·ate** (klip′ē it, -āt′) *adj.* [< L. < *clypeus*, a shield] *Biol.* **1.** shaped like a round shield **2.** having a shieldlike process Also **clyp′e·at′ed**

**clys·ter** (klis′tər) *n.* [< L. < Gr. *klystēr* < *klyzein*, to wash] *same as* ENEMA

**Cly·tem·nes·tra, Cly·taem·nes·tra** (klīt′əm nes′trə) *Gr. Myth.* the wife of Agamemnon: see ELECTRA

**Cm** *Chem.* curium

**cm, cm.** centimeter; centimeters

**cmdg.** commanding

**cml.** commercial

**Cnos·sus** (näs′əs) ancient city in N Crete: center of ancient Minoan civilization

**C-note** (sē′nōt′) *n.* [for CENTURY-note] [Slang] a one-hundred-dollar bill

**co-** **1.** *a prefix shortened from* COM- *meaning:* *a)* together with [*cooperation*] *b)* joint [*co-owner*] *c)* equally [*coextensive*] **2.** *a prefix meaning* complement of [*cosine*]

**Co** *Chem.* cobalt

**CO** Colorado

**Co., co.** *pl.* **Cos., cos.** **1.** company **2.** county

**C/O, co.** **1.** care of **2.** carried over

**C.O., CO** **1.** Commanding Officer **2.** conscientious objector

**coach** (kōch) *n.* [< Fr. < G. < Hung. *kocsi (szekér)*, (carriage of) *Kócs*, village in Hungary] **1.** a large, covered, four-wheeled carriage with an open, raised seat in front for the driver; stagecoach **2.** a railroad passenger car with the lowest-priced seating accommodations **3.** the lowest-priced class of accommodations on some airlines **4.** a bus **5.** an enclosed automobile, usually a two-door sedan **6.** a private tutor who prepares a student as for an examination **7.** an instructor or trainer, as of athletes, singers, etc. **8.** *Sports* a person in charge of a team or of some aspect of team play or practice —*vt.* **1.** to instruct by private tutoring **2.** to instruct and train (athletes, actors, etc.) —*vi.* to act as a coach

**coach dog** *same as* DALMATIAN

**coach·man** (-mən) *n., pl.* **-men** the driver of a coach or carriage

**co·ad·ju·tor** (kō aj′ə tər; *also, and for* 2 *usually,* kō′ə-jōōt′ər) *n.* [< OFr. < L. < *co-*, together + *adjuvare*, to help] **1.** an assistant; helper **2.** a bishop appointed to assist a bishop

**co·ag·u·la·ble** (kō ag′yōo lə b′l) *adj.* that can be coagulated —**co·ag′u·la·bil′i·ty** *n.*

**co·ag·u·late** (kō ag′yoo lāt′) *vt.* **-lat′ed, -lat′ing** [< L. pp. of *coagulare* < *coagulum*, coagulating agent < *cogere*, to curdle: see COGENT] to cause (a liquid) to become a soft, semisolid mass; curdle; clot —*vi.* to become coagulated —**co·ag′u·lant** *n.* —**co·ag′u·la′tion** *n.* —**co·ag′u·la′tive** *adj.* —**co·ag′u·la′tor** *n.*

**coal** (kōl) *n.* [OE. *col*, a live coal, charcoal] **1.** a black, combustible, mineral solid resulting from the partial decomposition of vegetable matter away from air and under high heat and great pressure over millions of years: used as a fuel and in the production of coke and many coal-tar compounds **2.** a piece or, collectively, pieces of this substance **3.** an ember **4.** charcoal —*vt.* to provide with coal —*vi.* to take in a supply of coal —**haul (or rake, drag, call) over the coals** to criticize sharply; censure —**heap coals of fire on (someone's) head** to cause (someone) to feel remorse by returning good for his evil —**coal′y** *adj.*

**coal·er** (-ər) *n.* a ship, railroad freight car (also **coal car**), etc. that transports or supplies coal

**co·a·lesce** (kō′ə les′) *vi.* **-lesced′, -lesc′ing** [< L. *coalescere* < *co-*, together + *alescere*, to grow up] **1.** to grow together **2.** to unite or merge into a single body, group, or mass —**co′a·les′cence** *n.* —**co′a·les′cent** *adj.*

**coal gas** **1.** a gas produced by the distillation of bituminous coal: used for lighting and heating **2.** a poisonous gas given off by burning coal

**co·a·li·tion** (kō′ə lish′ən) *n.* [< ML. < LL., orig. pp. of *coalescere*: see COALESCE] **1.** a combination; union **2.** a temporary alliance of political parties, nations, etc. for some specific purpose —**co′a·li′tion·ist** *n.*

**coal measures** coal beds or strata

**coal oil** **1.** kerosene **2.** crude petroleum

**coal tar** a black, thick, opaque liquid obtained by the distillation of bituminous coal: many synthetic compounds have been developed from it, including dyes, medicines, explosives, and perfumes

**coam·ing** (kō′miŋ) *n.* [< ?] a raised border around a hatchway, etc. to keep out water

**coarse** (kôrs) *adj.* [var. of COURSE in sense of "ordinary or usual order," as in *of course*] **1.** of inferior or poor quality; common **2.** consisting of rather large particles [*coarse* sand] **3.** not fine in texture, form, etc.; rough [*coarse* cloth] **4.** for rough work or results [a *coarse* file] **5.** lacking in refinement; vulgar [a *coarse* joke] —**coarse′ly** *adv.* —**coarse′ness** *n.*

**coarse-grained** (-grānd′) *adj.* **1.** having a coarse texture **2.** lacking in refinement; crude

**coars·en** (-'n) *vt., vi.* to make or become coarse

**coast** (kōst) *n.* [< OFr. < L. *costa*, a rib, side] **1.** land alongside the sea; seashore **2.** [< CanadFr., hillside, slope] an incline down which a slide is taken **3.** a slide or ride down, as on a sled —*vi.* **1.** to sail near or along a coast **2.** to go down an incline on a sled **3.** to continue in motion on momentum after propelling power has stopped **4.** to let one's past efforts carry one along —*vt.* to sail along or near the coast of —**the Coast** [Colloq.] in the U.S., the Pacific coast —**the coast is clear** there is no apparent danger or hindrance

**coast·al** (-'l) *adj.* of, at, near, or along a coast

**coast·er** (kōs′tər) *n.* **1.** a person or thing that coasts **2.** a ship that travels from port to port along a coast **3.** a sled or wagon for coasting **4.** a small tray, mat, disk, etc. placed under a glass or bottle to protect a table or other surface

**coaster brake** a brake in the hub of the rear wheel of a bicycle, worked by reverse pressure on the pedals: it also permits free coasting

**coast guard** **1.** a governmental force employed to defend a nation's coasts, prevent smuggling, aid vessels in distress, etc.; specif., [C- G-] such a branch of the U.S. armed forces, normally under the control of the Department of Transportation **2.** a member of a coast guard —**coast guards′-man, coast guard′man,** *pl.* **-men**

**coast·land** (kōst′land′) *n.* land along a coast

**coast·line** (-līn′) *n.* the outline of a coast

**coast·ward** (-wərd) *adj., adv.* toward the coast: also **coast′wards** *adv.*

**coast·wise** (-wīz′) *adv., adj.* along the coast: also **coast′ways′** (-wāz′) *adv.*

**coat** (kōt) *n.* [< OFr. < ML. *cot(t)a*, a tunic < Frank. hyp. *kotta*, coarse cloth] **1.** a sleeved outer garment opening down the front, as a suit jacket or an overcoat **2.** the natural covering of an animal, as of skin, fur, wool, etc. **3.** any outer covering, as of a plant **4.** a layer of some substance, as paint, over a surface —*vt.* **1.** to provide or cover with a coat **2.** to cover with a layer of something —**coat′ed** *adj.* —**coat′less** *adj.*

**co·a·ti** (kō ät′ē) *n., pl.* **-tis** [Tupi < *cua*, a cincture + *tim*, the nose] a small, flesh-eating, tree-dwelling mammal of Mexico and Central and South America, like the raccoon but with a long, flexible snout Also **co·a′ti-mun′di, co·a′ti-mon′di** (-mon′dē)

**coat·ing** (kōt′iŋ) *n.* **1.** a coat or layer over a surface **2.** cloth for making coats

**coat of arms** [after Fr. *cotte d'armes*, light garment worn over armor, and blazoned with one's heraldic arms] a group of emblems and figures (heraldic bearings) usually arranged on and around a shield and used as the insignia of a family, etc.

**coat of mail** *pl.* **coats of mail** a suit of armor made of linked metal rings or overlapping plates

**coat·tail** (-tāl′) *n.* the back part of a coat below the waist; esp., either half of this part when divided —**ride** (or **hang,** etc.) **on (someone's) coattails** to have one's success dependent on that of someone else

**co·au·thor** (kō ô′thər) *n.* a joint author

**coax** (kōks) *vt.* [< obs. slang *coax, cokes,* a fool] **1.** to persuade or urge by soothing words, flattery, etc.; wheedle **2.** to get by coaxing —*vi.* to use gentle persuasion, urging, etc. —**coax′er** *n.* —**coax′ing** *adj., n.* —**coax′ing·ly** *adv.*

**co·ax·i·al** (kō ak′sē əl) *adj.* [CO- + AXIAL] **1.** having a common axis: also **co·ax′al** **2.** designating a compound loudspeaker consisting of a smaller unit mounted within and connected with a larger one on a common axis **3.** designating a high-frequency transmission cable or line for telephone, telegraph, television, etc.: its outer conductor tube surrounds an insulated, solid or stranded central conductor

**cob** (käb) *n.* [prob. < LowG.] **1.** [Brit. Dial.] *a)* a lump *b)* a leader; chief **2.** a corncob **3.** a male swan **4.** a short, thickset horse

**co·balt** (kō′bôlt) *n.* [G. *kobalt* < *kobold*, goblin, demon of the mines] a hard, lustrous, steel-gray, ductile metallic chemical element, used in alloys, inks, paints, etc.: symbol

Co; at. wt., 58.9332; at. no., 27: a radioactive isotope (**cobalt 60**) is used in the treatment of cancer, in research, etc. —**co·bal′tic** *adj.* —**co·bal′tous** *adj.*

**cobalt blue** **1.** a dark blue pigment made from cobalt and aluminum oxides **2.** dark blue

**cob·ble¹** (käb′'l) *vt.* -**bled, -bling** [prob. akin to COB] **1.** to mend (shoes, etc.) **2.** to mend or put together clumsily or crudely

**cob·ble²** (käb′'l) *n.* [prob. < COB] *same as* COBBLESTONE —*vt.* -**bled, -bling** to pave with cobblestones

**cob·bler¹** (-lər) *n.* [of U.S. orig. < ?] **1.** an iced drink of wine, whiskey, or rum, an orange or lemon slice, sugar, etc. **2.** a deep-dish fruit pie

**cob·bler²** (-lər) *n.* **1.** a person whose work is mending shoes **2.** [Archaic] a clumsy workman

**cob·ble·stone** (käb′'l stōn′) *n.* [COBBLE² + STONE] a rounded stone of a kind formerly much used for paving streets

**cob coal** coal in large, rounded lumps

**co·bel·lig·er·ent** (kō′bə lij′ər ənt) *n.* a nation associated but not formally allied with another or others in waging war

**co·bi·a** (kō′bē ə) *n.* [< ?] a large, voracious game fish of warm seas

**co·bra** (kō′brə) *n.* [< Port. *cobra* (*de capello*), serpent (of the hood)] a very poisonous snake of Asia and Africa: loose skin around the neck expands into a hood when the snake is excited

**cob·web** (käb′web′) *n.* [< ME. *coppe*, spider + WEB] **1.** a web spun by a spider **2.** a single thread of such a web **3.** anything flimsy, gauzy, or ensnaring, like a spider's web —*vt.* -**webbed′**, -**web′bing** to cover as with cobwebs —**cob′web′by** *adj.*

**co·ca** (kō′kə) *n.* [Quechuan *cuca*] **1.** any of certain S. American shrubs, esp. a species whose dried leaves are the source of cocaine and some other alkaloids **2.** these dried leaves

INDIAN COBRA
(to 6 ft. long)

**co·caine, co·cain** (kō kān′, kō′kān) *n.* [COCA + -INE⁴] a crystalline alkaloid, $C_{17}H_{21}NO_4$, obtained from dried coca leaves: it is a narcotic and local anesthetic

**-coc·cal** (käk′'l) *a combining form meaning* of or produced by a (specified kind of) coccus [*staphylococcal*]: also **-coc′cic** (-sik)

**coc·cus** (käk′əs) *n., pl.* **coc·ci** (käk′sī) [ModL. < Gr. *kokkos*, a berry] a bacterium of a spherical shape —**coc′coid** (-oid) *adj.*

**-coc·cus** (käk′əs) *a combining form meaning* coccus: used in names of various bacteria [*gonococcus*]

**coc·cyx** (käk′siks) *n., pl.* **coc·cy·ges** (käk sī′jēz) [L. < Gr. *kokkyx*, cuckoo: from its shape like a cuckoo's beak] a small, triangular bone at the lower end of the vertebral column —**coc·cyg′e·al** (-sij′ē əl) *adj.*

**Co·chin** (kō′chin′, käch′in) *n.* [< ff.] [*also* c-] a large domestic fowl with thickly feathered legs: also **Cochin China**

**Cochin China, Cochin-China** region < former Fr. colony in S Indochina: now part of South Vietnam

**coch·i·neal** (käch′ə nēl′, käch′ə nēl′) *n.* [< Fr. < It. < L. *coccinus*, scarlet-colored < *coccum*, a berry] a red dye made from the dried bodies of female cochineal insects: used, esp. formerly, in coloring foods and cosmetics and as a dye

**cochineal insect** a scale insect having a brilliant red body fluid and feeding on cactus: found chiefly in Mexico and a source of cochineal

**coch·le·a** (käk′lē ə) *n., pl.* -**le·ae′** (-ē′), -**le·as** [L. < Gr. *kochlias*, snail] the spiral-shaped part of the internal ear, containing the auditory nerve endings —**coch′le·ar** *adj.*

**coch·le·ate** (-it, -āt′) *adj.* [< L.: see prec.] shaped like a snail shell: also **coch′le·at′ed**

**cock¹** (käk) *n.* [OE. *coc*] **1.** *a)* the male of the chicken; rooster *b)* the male of certain other birds **2.** a weathercock **3.** a leader or chief **4.** a faucet or valve for regulating the flow of liquid or gas **5.** the hammer of a firearm, or the position of the hammer set for firing **6.** a jaunty, erect position [the *cock* of a hat] —*vt.* **1.** to set (a hat, etc.) jauntily on one side **2.** to raise up; erect [a dog *cocks* his ears] **3.** to turn (the eye or ear) toward something **4.** *a)* to set the hammer of (a gun) in firing position *b)* to set (a tripping device, as for a camera shutter) **5.** to draw back (one's fist, etc.) ready to strike —*vi.* to assume an upright or tilted position

**cock²** (käk) *n.* [ME. *cokke*] a small, cone-shaped pile, as of hay —*vt.* to pile in cocks

**cock·ade** (kä kād′) *n.* [Fr. *cocarde* < *coq*, a cock] a rosette, knot of ribbon, etc. worn on the hat as a badge —**cock·ad′ed** *adj.*

**cock·a·lo·rum** (käk′ə lôr′əm) *n.* [pseudo L. extension of COCK¹] **1.** a little man with an exaggerated idea of his own importance **2.** boastful talk

**cock·a·ma·mie** (käk′ə mā′mē) *adj.* [alteration of DECALCOMANIA] [Slang] of poor quality; inferior

**cock-and-bull story** (käk′'n bool′) [< Fr. *coq à l'âne*] an absurd, improbable story

**cock·a·teel, cock·a·tiel** (käk′ə tēl′) *n.* [< Du. dim. of *kaketoe*: see ff.] a small, crested, Australian parrot with a long tail and yellow head

**cock·a·too** (käk′ə tōō′, käk′ə tōō′) *n., pl.* -**toos′** [Du. *kaketoe* < Malay *kakatua*; prob. echoic] a crested parrot of Australia and the East Indies, with white plumage tinged with yellow or pink

**cock·a·trice** (käk′ə tris′) *n.* [< OFr. < L. *calcare*, to tread < *calx*, the heel] a legendary serpent supposedly hatched from a cock's egg and having power to kill by a look

**cock·boat** (käk′bōt′) *n.* [< ME. < *cok*, ship's boat + *bote*, BOAT] a small boat, esp. one used as a ship's tender

**cock·chaf·er** (-chāf′ər) *n.* [COCK¹ (? because of size) + CHAFER] a large European beetle whose grubs feed on the roots of plants

**cock·crow** (-krō′) *n.* the time when roosters begin to crow; dawn: also **cock′crow′ing**

**cocked hat** **1.** a three-cornered hat with a turned-up brim **2.** a peaked hat pointed in front and in back —**knock into a cocked hat** [Slang] to damage or spoil completely; ruin

**cock·er·el** (käk′ər əl, käk′rəl) *n.* [dim. of COCK¹] a young rooster, less than a year old

**cock·er (spaniel)** (käk′ər) [from its use in hunting woodcock] a small spaniel with a compact body, long, silky hair, and long, drooping ears

**cock·eye** (käk′ī′) *n.* [COCK¹, *vi.* + EYE] a squinting eye

**cock·eyed** (-īd′) *adj.* **1.** cross-eyed **2.** [Slang] *a)* tilted; crooked; awry *b)* silly; foolish *c)* drunk

**cock·fight** (-fīt′) *n.* a fight between gamecocks, usually wearing metal spurs —**cock′fight′ing** *n.*

**cock·horse** (-hôrs′) *n.* [16th c., toy horse] *same as* ROCKING HORSE or HOBBYHORSE (sense 1)

**cock·le¹** (käk′'l) *n.* [< OFr. *coquille*, a shell < L. < Gr. < *konchē*, CONCH] **1.** an edible shellfish with two heart-shaped, radially ridged shells **2.** a cockleshell **3.** a wrinkle; pucker —*vi., vt.* -**led, -ling** to wrinkle; pucker —**cockles of one's heart** one's deepest feelings or emotions

**cock·le²** (käk′'l) *n.* [< OE. *coccel*, tares] any of various weeds that grow in grainfields

**cock·le·bur** (-bur′) *n.* a coarse plant of the composite family, bearing burs, that grows as a weed

**cock·le·shell** (-shel′) *n.* **1.** the shell of a cockle **2.** loosely, a scallop shell, etc. **3.** a small boat

**cock·ney** (käk′nē) *n., pl.* -**neys** [ME. *cokenei*, spoiled child; understood as *coken-ey*, lit., cock's egg; ? infl. by Fr. *acoquiné*, idle < *coquin*, rascal] [*often* C-] **1.** a native of the East End of London, England, speaking a dialect characterized by loss of initial *h*, use of an intrusive *r*, etc. **2.** this dialect: also **cock′ney·ese′** (-ēz′) [*often* C-] or like cockneys or their dialect —**cock′ney·ish** *adj.* —**cock′ney·ism** *n.*

**cock·pit** (käk′pit′) *n.* **1.** an enclosed space for cockfighting **2.** in small decked vessels, a sunken space toward the stern used by the steersman, etc. **3.** the space in a small airplane for the pilot and, sometimes, passengers, or in a large airplane for the pilot and copilot or crew

**cock·roach** (-rōch′) *n.* [Sp. *cucaracha*, altered after COCK¹ + ROACH] an insect with long feelers, and a flat, soft body: a common household pest

**cocks·comb** (käks′kōm′) *n.* **1.** the red, fleshy growth on the head of a rooster **2.** *same as* COXCOMB **3.** a plant related to the amaranth, with red or yellow flower heads

**cock·sure** (käk′shoor′, -shur′) *adj.* [COCK¹ (cf. COCKY) + SURE] **1.** absolutely sure **2.** self-confident and overbearing —**cock′sure′ness** *n.*

**cock·swain** (käk′s'n, -swān′) *n. same as* COXSWAIN

**cock·tail** (-tāl′) *n.* [< ?] **1.** an alcoholic drink, usually iced, made of a distilled liquor mixed with a wine, fruit juice, etc. **2.** an appetizer, as fruit juice, diced fruits, or seafood

**cock·y** (käk′ē) *adj.* **cock′i·er, cock′i·est** [COCK¹ + -Y²] [Colloq.] jauntily conceited; self-confident in an aggressive or swaggering way —**cock′i·ly** *adv.* —**cock′i·ness** *n.*

**co·co** (kō′kō) *n., pl.* -**cos** [Sp. & Port. < L. *coccum*, a seed > Gr. *kokkos*, a berry] **1.** *same as* COCONUT PALM **2.** its fruit; coconut —*adj.* made of the fiber from coconut husks

**co·coa** (kō′kō) *n.* [Sp. & Port. *cacao* < Nahuatl *cacauatl*] **1.** powder made from cacao seeds that have been roasted and ground **2.** a drink made by adding sugar and hot water or milk to this powder **3.** a reddish-yellow brown

**cocoa butter** a yellowish fat prepared from cacao seeds: used in pharmacy and cosmetics

**co·co·nut, co·coa·nut** (kō′kə nut′) *n.* the fruit of the coconut palm, a thick, brown, oval husk enclosing a layer of edible white meat: the hollow center is filled with a sweet, milky fluid called **coconut milk**

**coconut oil** oil obtained from the dried meat of coconuts, used for making soap, etc.

**coconut palm** (or **tree**) a tall tropical palm tree that bears coconuts: also **coco palm**

**co·coon** (kə kōōn′) *n.* [< Fr. < Pr. *coucoun*, egg shell, ult. < ML. *coco*, shell] **1.** the silky case which the larvae of certain insects spin about themselves for shelter during the pupa stage **2.** any protective cover like this

**cod** (käd) *n.*, *pl.* **cod, cods:** see PLURAL, II, D, 2 [ME.] an important food fish, with firm flesh and soft fins, found in northern seas

**C.O.D., c.o.d.** cash (or collect) on delivery

**Cod** (käd), **Cape** peninsula in E Mass.

**co·da** (kō′də) *n.* [It. < L. *cauda*, a tail] *Music* a passage formally ending a composition or section

**cod·dle** (käd′'l) *vt.* **-dled, -dling** [prob. < CAUDLE] **1.** to cook (esp. eggs) gently in water not quite boiling **2.** to treat tenderly; pamper

**code** (kōd) *n.* [< OFr. < L. *codex*, wooden tablet for writing, orig., tree trunk] **1.** a body of laws of a nation, city, etc. arranged systematically for easy reference **2.** any set of principles *[a moral code]* **3.** *a)* a set of signals for sending messages, as by telegraph, flags, etc. *b)* any set of signals, as that (**genetic code**) in the chromosomes determining the pattern of growth, etc. **4.** *a)* a system of secret writing, information processing, etc., in which letters, figures, etc. are given certain meanings *b)* the symbols used —*vt.* **cod′ed, cod′ing** to put in the form or symbols of a code —**cod′er** *n.*

**co·deine** (kō′dēn, -dē in) *n.* [< Gr. *kōdeia*, poppy head + -INE[4]] an alkaloid, $C_{18}H_{21}O_3N \cdot H_2O$, derived from opium and resembling morphine: used for the relief of pain and in cough medicines: also **co′dein, co·de·ia** (kō dē′ə)

**co·dex** (kō′deks) *n.*, *pl.* **co·di·ces** (kō′də sēz′, käd′ə-) [L.: see CODE] **1.** orig., a code, or body of laws **2.** a manuscript volume, esp. of the Scriptures or of a classic text

**cod·fish** (käd′fish′) *n.*, *pl.* **-fish′, -fish′es:** see FISH *same as* COD

**codg·er** (käj′ər) *n.* [prob. var. of CADGER] [Colloq.] an eccentric, esp. elderly, fellow

**cod·i·cil** (käd′i s′l, -sil′) *n.* [< L. dim. of *codex:* see CODE] **1.** *Law* an addition to a will to change, revoke, or add provisions **2.** an appendix or supplement —**cod′i·cil′la·ry** *adj.*

**cod·i·fy** (käd′ə fī′, kō′də-) *vt.* **-fied′, -fy′ing** [see CODE & -FY] to arrange (laws, etc.) systematically —**cod′i·fi·ca′-tion** *n.* —**cod′i·fi′er** *n.*

**cod·ling[1]** (käd′liŋ) *n.*, *pl.* **-ling, -lings:** see PLURAL, II, D, 2 a young cod

**cod·ling[2]** (käd′liŋ) *n.* [ult. < Fr. *coeur de lion*, lit., heart of lion] **1.** a variety of elongated apple **2.** a small, unripe apple   Also **cod′lin**

**codling** (or **codlin**) **moth** a small moth whose larva destroys apples, pears, quinces, etc.

**cod-liv·er oil** (käd′liv′ər) oil obtained from the liver of the cod and related fishes: it is rich in vitamins A and D

**Co·dy** (kō′dē), **William Frederick** 1846–1917; U.S. plainsman & showman: called *Buffalo Bill*

**co·ed, co-ed** (kō′ed′) *n.* [Colloq.] a girl attending a coeducational college or university —*adj.* [Colloq.] **1.** coeducational **2.** of a coed

**co·ed·u·ca·tion** (kō′ej ə kā′shən) *n.* [CO- + EDUCATION] the educational system in which students of both sexes attend classes together —**co′ed·u·ca′tion·al** *adj.* —**co′ed·u·ca′tion·al·ly** *adv.*

**co·ef·fi·cient** (kō′ə fish′ənt) *n.* [CO- + EFFICIENT] **1.** a factor that contributes to produce a result **2.** *Math.* a number, symbol, etc. used as a multiplier **3.** *Physics* a number, constant for a given substance, used as a multiplier in measuring the change in some property of the substance under given conditions

**coe·la·canth** (sē′lə kanth′) *n.* [ModL. < Gr. *koilos* (see ff.) + *akantha*, point] any of a group of primitive, almost entirely extinct fishes that were possibly ancestors to land animals

**-coele, -coel** (sēl) [< Gr. *koilia*, body cavity < *koilos*, hollow] *a combining form meaning* cavity, chamber of the body

**coe·len·ter·ate** (si len′tə rāt′, -tər it) *n.* [ult. < Gr. *koilos* (see prec.) + *enteron*, intestine] any of a large group of marine animals, as the hydroids, jellyfishes, corals, etc., in which the characteristic structure is a large central cavity with a single opening

**coe·li·ac** (sē′lē ak′) *adj. same as* CELIAC

**coe·lom** (sē′ləm) *n.* [< Gr. < *koilos:* see -COELE] the main body cavity of most higher animals, in which the visceral organs are suspended

**coe·no-** [< Gr. *koinos*, common] *a combining form meaning* common: also, before a vowel, **coen-**

**coe·no·bite** (sē′nə bīt′, sen′ə-) *n. same as* CENOBITE

**co·e·qual** (kō ē′kwəl) *adj.*, *n.* equal —**co′e·qual′i·ty** (-i-kwäl′ə tē) *n.* —**co·e′qual·ly** *adv.*

**co·erce** (kō urs′) *vt.* **-erced′, -erc′ing** [< OFr. < L. *coercere* < *co-*, together + *arcere*, to confine] **1.** to restrain or constrain by force; curb **2.** to force; compel **3.** to enforce —**co·erc′er** *n.* —**co·er′ci·ble** *adj.* —**co·er′ci·bly** *adv.*

**co·er·cion** (kō ur′shən, -zhən) *n.* **1.** the act or power of coercing **2.** government by force

**co·er·cive** (-siv) *adj.* of coercion or tending to coerce —**co·er′cive·ly** *adv.* —**co·er′cive·ness** *n.*

**co·e·val** (kō ē′v'l) *adj.* [< LL. < L. *co-*, together + *aevum*, age + -AL] of the same age or period; contemporary —*n.* a contemporary —**co·e′val·ly** *adv.*

**co·ex·ec·u·tor** (kō′ig zek′yōō tər) *n.* a person acting as executor jointly with another

**co·ex·ist** (-ig zist′) *vi.* **1.** to exist together, at the same time, or in the same place **2.** to live together without hostility or conflict despite differences, as in political systems —**co′ex·ist′ence** *n.* —**co′ex·ist′ent** *adj.*

**co·ex·tend** (-ik stend′) *vt.*, *vi.* to extend equally in space or time —**co′ex·ten′sion** *n.* —**co′ex·ten′sive** *adj.* —**co′ex·ten′sive·ly** *adv.*

**C. of C.** Chamber of Commerce

**cof·fee** (kôf′ē, käf′ē) *n.* see PLURAL, II, D, 3 [< It. < Turk. *qahwe* < Ar. *qahwa*, orig., wine] **1.** a dark-brown, aromatic drink made by brewing in water the roasted and ground beanlike seeds of a tall tropical shrub of the madder family **2.** these seeds: also **coffee beans 3.** the shrub **4.** the color of coffee with milk or cream in it; brown

**coffee break** a brief respite from work when coffee or other refreshment may be taken

**cof·fee·cake** (-kāk′) *n.* a kind of cake or roll, often nut-filled, coated with icing, etc., to be eaten with coffee or the like

**cof·fee·house** (-hous′) *n.* a place where coffee and other refreshments are served and people gather for conversation, entertainment, etc.

**coffee klatch** (or **klatsch**) *same as* KAFFEEKLATSCH

**cof·fee·pot** (-pät′) *n.* a container with a lid and spout, for making and serving coffee

**coffee shop** an informal restaurant, as in a hotel, where light refreshments or meals are served

**coffee table** a low table, usually in a living room, for serving refreshments

**cof·fer** (kôf′ər, käf′-) *n.* [< OFr. < L. *cophinus:* see COFFIN] **1.** a chest or strongbox for keeping valuables **2.** [*pl.*] a treasury; funds **3.** a decorative sunken panel in a vault, dome, etc. **4.** a cofferdam **5.** a lock in a canal —*vt.* **1.** to enclose in a coffer **2.** to furnish with coffers (*n.* 3)

**cof·fer·dam** (-dam′) *n.* [prec. + DAM[1]] **1.** a watertight temporary structure in a river, lake, etc. to keep the water from an enclosed area that has been pumped dry so that dams, etc. may be constructed **2.** a watertight box attached to the side of a ship so that repairs can be made below the waterline

**cof·fin** (kôf′in, käf′-) *n.* [< OFr. < L. *cophinus* < Gr. *kophinos*, basket] the case or box in which a dead person is buried

**coffin nail** [Old Slang] a cigarette

**cog[1]** (käg) *n.* [< Scand.] **1.** *a)* any of a series of teeth on the rim of a wheel, for transmitting or receiving motion by fitting between the teeth of another wheel; gear tooth *b)* a cogwheel **2.** [Colloq.] a person thought of as one small part in the working of a business, etc. —**cogged** *adj.*

**cog[2]** (käg) *n.* [altered (after prec.) < earlier *cock*, to secure] a projection on a beam that fits into a corresponding groove or notch in another beam, making a joint —*vt.*, *vi.* **cogged, cog′ging** to join by a cog or cogs

**co·gent** (kō′jənt) *adj.* [< L. prp. of *cogere*, to collect < *co-*, together + *agere*, to drive] forceful and to the point, as a reason or argument; compelling —**co′gen·cy** *n.* —**co′gent·ly** *adv.*

**cog·i·tate** (käj′ə tāt′) *vi.*, *vt.* **-tat′ed, -tat′ing** [< L. pp. of *cogitare*, to ponder] to think seriously and deeply (about); ponder; consider —**cog′i·ta·ble** *adj.* —**cog′i·ta′tion** *n.* —**cog′i·ta′tive** *adj.* —**cog′i·ta′tor** *n.*

**co·gnac** (kōn′yak, kän′-, kôn′-) *n.* [Fr.] **1.** a French brandy distilled from wine near Cognac, France **2.** loosely, any brandy

**cog·nate** (käg′nāt) *adj.* [L. *cognatus* < *co-*, together + pp. of (g)*nasci*, to be born] **1.** related by family **2.** derived from a common original form *[French and Italian are cognate languages]* **3.** having the same nature or quality —*n.* **1.** a person related to another through common ancestry **2.** a cognate word, language, or thing —**cog·na′tion** *n.*

**cog·ni·tion** (käg nish′ən) *n.* [L. *cognitio*, knowledge < pp. of *cognoscere* < *co-*, together + (g)*noscere*, to know] **1.**

the process of knowing in the broadest sense, including perception, memory, judgment, etc. 2. the result of such a process; perception, etc. —**cog·ni′tion·al** *adj.* —**cog′ni·tive** *adj.*

**cog·ni·za·ble** (käg′ni zə b'l, käg nī′-; *occas.* kän′ə-) *adj.* 1. that can be known or perceived 2. *Law* within the jurisdiction of a court

**cog·ni·zance** (käg′nə zəns, kän′ə-) *n.* [< OFr. *conoissance*, knowledge < L. *cognoscere:* see COGNITION] 1. perception or knowledge; esp., the range of knowledge possible through observation 2. official observation 3. *Heraldry* a distinguishing crest or mark 4. *Law a*) a court hearing *b*) the right or power of dealing with a matter judicially —**take cognizance of** to notice or recognize **cog·ni·zant** (-zənt) *adj.* having cognizance; aware or informed (*of* something)

**cog·no·men** (käg nō′mən) *n., pl.* **-no′mens, -nom′i·na** (-näm′i nə) [L. < *co-*, with + *nomen*, name] 1. the third or family name of an ancient Roman 2. any family name; surname 3. any name; esp., a nickname —**cog·nom′i·nal** (-näm′i n'l) *adj.*

**cog·wheel** (käg′hwēl′) *n.* a wheel with a rim notched into teeth which mesh with those of another wheel or of a rack to transmit or receive motion

**co·hab·it** (kō hab′it) *vi.* [< LL. < L. *co-*, together + *habitare*, to dwell] 1. to live together as husband and wife, esp. when not legally married 2. [Archaic] to live together —**co·hab′it·ant** *n.* —**co·hab′i·ta′tion** *n.*

COGWHEELS

**co·heir** (kō′er′) *n.* a person who inherits jointly with another or others —**co′heir′ess** *n.fem.*

**co·here** (kō hir′) *vi.* **-hered′, -her′ing** [< L. < *co-*, together + *haerere*, to stick] 1. to stick together, as parts of a mass 2. to be connected naturally or logically 3. to be in accord

**co·her·ence** (kō hir′əns) *n.* 1. the condition of cohering 2. the quality of being logically consistent and intelligible Also **co·her′en·cy**

**co·her·ent** (-ənt) *adj.* 1. sticking together; having cohesion 2. showing logical consistency or intelligibility —**co·her′ent·ly** *adv.*

**co·he·sion** (kō hē′zhən) *n.* 1. the act or condition of cohering; tendency to stick together 2. *Bot.* the union of like flower parts 3. *Physics* the force by which the molecules of a substance are held together: distinguished from ADHESION —**co·he′sive** (-hēs′iv) *adj.* —**co·he′sive·ly** *adv.* —**co·he′sive·ness** *n.*

**co·ho** (kō′hō) *n., pl.* **-ho, -hos:** see PLURAL, II, D, 2 [< ?] a small Pacific salmon, now a freshwater game fish in N U.S.: also **coho salmon**

**co·hort** (kō′hôrt) *n.* [< L. *cohors*, enclosure, crowd] 1. an ancient Roman military unit, one tenth of a legion 2. a band of soldiers 3. any group or band 4. an associate, colleague, or supporter

**coif** (koif; *for n. 2 & vt. 2, usually* kwäf) *n.* [< OFr. < LL. *cofea*, a cap, hood] 1. a cap that fits the head closely, as that once worn under a hood of mail 2. [< COIFFURE] a style of arranging the hair —*vt.* **coifed, coif′ing;** also, and for 2 usually, **coiffed, coif′fing** 1. to cover as with a coif 2. *a*) to style (the hair) *b*) to give a coiffure to

**coif·feur** (kwä fur′; *Fr.* kwä fër′) *n.* [Fr. < *coiffer*, to dress the hair < prec.] a male hairdresser

**coif·fure** (kwä fyoor′, -fyʉr′; *Fr.* kwà für′) *n.* [Fr. < *coiffe*, coif] 1. a headdress 2. a style of arranging the hair —*vt.* **-fured′, -fur′ing** to coif (sense 2)

**coign of vantage** (koin) [archaic var. of *coin* (QUOIN)] an advantageous position

**coil** (koil) *vt.* [< OFr. < L. *colligere:* see COLLECT²] to wind or gather (rope, etc.) into a circular or spiral form —*vi.* 1. to wind around and around 2. to move in a winding course —*n.* 1. anything wound into a series of rings or a spiral 2. such a series of rings or a spiral 3. a single turn of a coiled figure 4. a series of connected pipes in rows or coils 5. *Elec.* a spiral of wire, etc. used as an inductor, heating element, etc.

**coin** (koin) *n.* [< OFr. < L. *cuneus*, a wedge] 1. *archaic var. of* QUOIN 2. *a*) a piece of metal with a distinctive stamp, issued by a government as money *b*) such pieces collectively 3. [Slang] money —*vt.* 1. *a*) to make (coins) by stamping metal *b*) to make (metal) into coins 2. to invent (a new word or phrase) rapidly —**coin money** [Colloq.] to earn money rapidly —**coin′er** *n.*

**coin·age** (koi′nij) *n.* 1. the act or process of coining 2. metal money 3. a system of metal currency 4. an invented word or expression

**co·in·cide** (kō′in sīd′) *vi.* **-cid′ed, -cid′ing** [< Fr. < ML. < L. *co-*, together + *incidere*, to fall upon] 1. to take up the same place in space 2. to occur at the same time 3. to hold equivalent positions, as on a scale 4. to be identical; correspond exactly 5. to be in accord; agree

**co·in·ci·dence** (kō in′sə dəns) *n.* 1. the fact or condition of coinciding 2. an accidental and remarkable occurrence of events, ideas, etc. at the same time, with no apparent causal relationship

**co·in·ci·dent** (-dənt) *adj.* 1. occurring at the same time 2. in the same position in space at the same time 3. in agreement; identical [*desire coincident* with need] —**co·in′ci·dent·ly** *adv.*

**co·in·ci·den·tal** (kō in′sə den′t'l) *adj.* characterized by coincidence —**co·in′ci·den′tal·ly** *adv.*

**coir** (koir) *n.* [< Port., ult. < Tamil *kayaru*, to be twisted] the prepared fiber of the husks of coconuts, used to make rope, etc.

**co·i·tus** (kō′it əs, kō ēt′əs) *n.* [L. < *co-*, together + *ire*, to go] sexual intercourse: also **co·i·tion** (kō ish′ən) —**co′i·tal** *adj.*

**coke** (kōk) *n.* [< ME. *colke*, core, charcoal] coal from which most of the gases have been removed by heating: it burns with intense heat and little smoke, and is used as an industrial fuel —*vt., vi.* **coked, cok′ing** to change into coke

**Col.** 1. Colombia 2. Colonel 3. Colorado: also **Colo.** 4. Colossians

**col.** 1. collected 2. collector 3. college 4. colony 5. color(ed) 6. column

**co·la** (kō′lə) *n.* [< WAfr. name] 1. an African tree whose nuts yield an extract with caffeine, used in soft drinks and medicine 2. a sweet, carbonated soft drink flavored with this extract

**col·an·der** (kul′ən dər, käl′-) *n.* [prob. ult. < L. *colare*, to strain < *colum*, strainer] a pan with a perforated bottom to drain off liquids

**col·chi·cine** (käl′chə sēn′, -ki sin) *n.* [< ff. + -INE⁴] a poisonous alkaloid, $C_{22}H_{25}O_6N$, extracted from colchicum, used to treat gout and to produce chromosome doubling in plants

COLANDER

**col·chi·cum** (-kəm) *n.* [L. < Gr. *kolchikon*, plant with a poisonous root] 1. a plant of the lily family, with crocuslike flowers usually blooming in the fall 2. its dried seeds or corm

**cold** (kōld) *adj.* [OE. *cald*] 1. of a temperature much lower than that of the human body; very chilly; frigid 2. without the proper heat or warmth [*this soup is cold*] 3. dead 4. feeling chilled 5. without warmth of feeling; not cordial [*a cold personality*] 6. sexually frigid 7. depressing or saddening [*the cold truth*] 8. not involving one's feelings; detached [*cold logic*] 9. designating or having colors that suggest cold, as tones of blue, green, or gray 10. faint or stale [*a cold scent*] 11. [Colloq.] with little or no preparation [*to enter a game cold*] 12. [Slang] completely mastered [*the actor had his lines down cold*] 13. [Slang] unconscious [*knocked cold*] —*n.* 1. *a*) absence of heat; lack of warmth: often thought of as an active force *b*) a low temperature; esp., one below freezing 2. the sensation produced by a loss or absence of heat 3. cold weather 4. an acute inflammation of the mucous membranes of the nose and throat, thought to be caused by a virus and characterized by nasal discharge, malaise, etc. —**catch** (or **take**) **cold** to become ill with a cold —**cold comfort** little or no comfort —**have** (or **get**) **cold feet** [Colloq.] to be (or become) timid or fearful —**in the cold** ignored; neglected —**throw cold water on** to discourage —**cold′ly** *adv.* —**cold′ness** *n.*

**cold·blood·ed** (-blud′id) *adj.* 1. having a body temperature approximating that of the surrounding air, land, or water, as fishes and reptiles 2. easily affected by cold 3. without pity; cruel —**cold′blood′ed·ly** *adv.* —**cold′blood′ed·ness** *n.*

**cold chisel** a hardened and tempered steel chisel for cutting or chipping cold metal

**cold cream** a creamy, soothing preparation for softening and cleansing the skin

**cold cuts** slices of cold meats and, often, cheeses

**cold duck** [transl. of G. *kalte ente* < ?] a drink made from equal parts of sparkling burgundy and champagne

**cold frame** an unheated, boxlike, glass-covered structure for protecting young plants

**cold front** *Meteorol.* the forward edge of a cold air mass advancing into a warmer air mass

**cold·heart·ed** (-här′tid) *adj.* lacking sympathy or kindness; unfeeling —**cold′heart′ed·ly** *adv.* —**cold′heart′ed·ness** *n.*

**cold pack** a process of canning foodstuffs in which the raw products are placed in jars first and then subjected to heat —**cold′-pack′** *vt.*

**cold shoulder** [Colloq.] deliberate indifference; slight or snub: often with *the* —**cold′-shoul′der** *vt.*

**cold sore** *same as* HERPES SIMPLEX

**cold turkey** [Slang] 1. the abrupt, total withdrawal of drugs from an addict 2. in a frank, blunt way [to talk *cold* *turkey]* **3.** without preparation *[take a test cold turkey]* —**cold′·tur′key** *adj.*

**cold war** sharp conflict in diplomacy, economics, etc. between states, without actual warfare

**cold wave** **1.** a period of weather colder than is normal **2.** a permanent wave in which the hair is set with a liquid preparation instead of heat

**cole** (kōl) *n.* [OE. *cal* < L. *caulis, colis,* a cabbage] any of various plants of the mustard family, to which cabbage belongs; esp., rape

**co·le·op·ter·an** (kō′lē äp′tər ən, käl′ē-) *n.* [< Gr. *koleos,* sheath + *pteron,* wing] any of a large group of insects, including beetles and weevils, with the front wings forming a horny covering for the membranous hind wings —**co′le·op′ter·ous** *adj.*

**Cole·ridge** (kōl′rij, -ər ij), **Samuel Taylor** 1772–1834; Eng. poet & critic

**cole·slaw** (kōl′slô′) *n.* [< Du. *kool,* cabbage (akin to COLE) + *sla,* for *salade,* salad] a salad made of shredded raw cabbage: also **cole slaw**

**co·le·us** (kō′lē əs) *n.* [ModL. < Gr. *koleos,* a sheath] a plant of the mint family, with showy, bright-colored leaves

**cole·wort** (kōl′wurt′) *n.* [COLE + WORT²] any cabbage whose leaves do not form a compact head

**col·ic** (käl′ik) *n.* [< OFr. < L. < Gr. < *kolon,* colon] acute abdominal pain caused by various abnormal conditions in the bowels —*adj.* **1.** of colic **2.** of the colon —**col′·ick·y** *adj.*

**co·li·form** (kō′lə fôrm′, käl′ə-) *adj.* designating, of, or like the aerobic bacillus normally found in the colon: a coliform count is an indicator of fecal contamination of water supplies

**Co·lin** (kō′lin, käl′in) [prob. < L. *columba,* a dove] a masculine name

**col·i·se·um** (käl′ə sē′əm) [see COLOSSEUM] [C-] *same as* COLOSSEUM —*n.* a large building or stadium for sports events, shows, etc.

**co·li·tis** (kō līt′is) *n.* [ModL. < Gr. *kolon,* colon + -ITIS] inflammation of the large intestine

**coll.** **1.** collect **2.** collection **3.** college

**col·lab·o·rate** (kə lab′ə rāt′) *vi.* **-rat′ed, -rat′ing** [< L. pp. of *collaborare* < *com-,* with + *laborare,* to work] **1.** to work together, esp. in some literary, artistic, or scientific undertaking **2.** to cooperate with an enemy invader —**col·lab′o·ra′tion** *n.* —**col·lab′o·ra′tive** *adj.* —**col·lab′o·ra′tor** *n.*

**col·lab·o·ra·tion·ist** (kə lab′ə rā′shən ist) *n.* a person who cooperates with an enemy invader

**col·lage** (kə läzh′) *n.* [Fr. < *colle,* paste < Gr. *kolla*] **1.** an art form in which bits of objects, as newspaper, cloth, leaves, etc., are pasted together on a surface **2.** a composition so made

**col·la·gen** (käl′ə jen′) *n.* [< Gr. *kolla,* glue + -GEN] a fibrous protein found in connective tissue, bone, and cartilage —**col′la·gen′ic** *adj.*

**col·lapse** (kə laps′) *vi.* **-lapsed′, -laps′ing** [< L. pp. of *collabi* < *com-,* together + *labi,* to fall] **1.** to fall down or fall to pieces; cave in **2.** to break down suddenly; fail; give way **3.** *a)* to break down suddenly in health *b)* to fall down, as from a blow or exhaustion *c)* to fall or drop drastically, as in value, force, etc. **4.** to fold or come together compactly —*vt.* to cause to collapse —*n.* the act of collapsing; a falling in or together; failure or breakdown, as in business, health, etc. —**col·laps′i·bil′i·ty** *n.* —**col·laps′i·ble** *adj.*

**col·lar** (käl′ər) *n.* [< OFr. < L. < *collum,* the neck] **1.** the part of a garment that encircles the neck **2.** a cloth band attached to the neck of a garment **3.** a band of leather or metal for the neck of a dog, cat, etc. **4.** the part of the harness that fits over the neck of a horse **5.** a ring or flange, as on rods or pipes, to prevent sideward motion, connect parts, etc. **6.** a band of contrasting color, etc. on an animal's neck —*vt.* **1.** to put a collar on **2.** to seize by or as by the collar

**col·lar·bone** (-bōn′) *n.* a slender bone joining the breastbone to the shoulder blade; clavicle

**col·lard** (käl′ərd) *n.* [contr. < COLEWORT] a kind of kale whose coarse leaves are borne in tufts

**collat.** collateral

**col·late** (kä lāt′, kə-; käl′āt) *vt.* **-lat′ed, -lat′ing** [< L. *collatus,* pp. of *conferre* < *com-,* together + *ferre,* to bring] **1.** to compare (texts, data, etc.) critically **2.** *a)* to gather (the sections of a book) together in proper order for binding *b)* to examine (such sections) to see that all pages are present and in proper order —**col·la′tor** *n.*

**col·lat·er·al** (kə lat′ər əl) *adj.* [< ML. *collateralis* < L. *com-,* together + *lateralis,* LATERAL] **1.** side by side; parallel **2.** accompanying the main thing in a subordinate or

corroborative way **3.** of the same ancestors but in a different line **4.** *a)* designating or of security given as a pledge for the fulfillment of an obligation *b)* secured by stocks, bonds, etc. *[a collateral loan]* —*n.* **1.** a collateral relative **2.** stocks, bonds, etc. used for collateral security —**col·lat′er·al·ly** *adv.*

**col·la·tion** (kä lā′shən, kə-) *n.* **1.** the act, process, or result of collating **2.** a light meal

**col·league** (käl′ēg) *n.* [< Fr. < L. *collega* < *com-,* with + *legare,* to appoint as deputy] a fellow worker in the same profession; associate in office

**col·lect¹** (kə lekt′) *vt.* [< OFr. < L. *collectus:* see ff.] **1.** to gather together; assemble **2.** to gather (stamps, books, etc.) for a hobby **3.** to call for and receive (money) for (rent, a fund, taxes, bills, etc.) **4.** to regain control of (oneself or one's wits) —*vi.* **1.** to gather; assemble *[a crowd collected]* **2.** to accumulate *[water collects in the basement]* **3.** to collect payments, etc. —*adj., adv.* with payment to be made by the receiver *[to telephone collect]*

**col·lect²** (käl′ekt) *n.* [< OFr., ult. < L. *collectus,* pp. of *colligere* < *com-,* together + *legere,* to gather] *[also C-]* a short prayer used in certain church services

**col·lect·ed** (kə lek′tid) *adj.* **1.** gathered together; assembled **2.** in control of oneself; calm —**col·lect′ed·ly** *adv.* —**col·lect′ed·ness** *n.*

**col·lect·i·ble, col·lect·a·ble** (-tə b'l) *adj.* **1.** that can be collected **2.** suitable as a collectible —*n.* any of a class of old things, but not antiques, that people collect as a hobby, usually things of no great intrinsic value

**col·lec·tion** (-shən) *n.* **1.** the act or process of collecting **2.** things collected *[a collection of stamps]* **3.** a mass or pile; accumulation **4.** money collected, as during a church service

**col·lec·tive** (-tiv) *adj.* **1.** formed by collecting; gathered into a whole **2.** of or as a group; of or by the individuals in a group acting together *[the collective effort of the students]* **3.** designating or of any enterprise in which people work together as a group, esp. under a system of collectivism *[a collective farm]* **4.** *Gram.* designating a noun which is singular in form but denotes a collection of individuals (e.g., *army, crowd*) —*n.* **1.** *a)* any collective enterprise; specif., a collective farm *b)* the people involved **2.** *Gram.* a collective noun —**col·lec′tive·ly** *adv.* —**col·lec′tiv′i·ty** *n.*

**collective bargaining** negotiation between organized workers and their employer or employers concerning wages, hours, and working conditions

**col·lec·tiv·ism** (kə lek′tə viz′m) *n.* the ownership and control of the means of production and distribution by the people collectively —**col·lec′tiv·ist** *n., adj.* —**col·lec′tiv·is′tic** *adj.*

**col·lec·tiv·ize** (-tə vīz′) *vt.* **-ized′, -iz′ing** to establish or organize under a system of collectivism —**col·lec′ti·vi·za′tion** *n.*

**col·lec·tor** (kə lek′tər) *n.* a person or thing that collects; specif., *a)* a person whose work is collecting taxes, overdue bills, etc. *b)* a person who collects stamps, books, coins, etc. as a hobby

**Col·leen** (käl′ēn, kə lēn′) [see ff.] a feminine name

**col·leen** (käl′ēn, kə lēn′) *n.* [< Ir., dim. of *caile,* girl] [Irish] a girl

**col·lege** (käl′ij) *n.* [< OFr. < L. *collegium,* a society, guild < *collega,* COLLEAGUE] **1.** an association of individuals having certain powers, duties, etc. *[the electoral college]* **2.** an institution of higher education that grants degrees; specif., *a)* any of the schools of a university granting degrees in any of several specialized courses of study *b)* the undergraduate division of a university, which offers a general four-year course leading to the bachelor's degree **3.** a school offering specialized instruction in some occupation *[a secretarial college]* **4.** the buildings, students, faculty, or administrators of a college

**College of Cardinals** the cardinals of the Roman Catholic Church, serving as a privy council to the Pope and electing his successor

**col·le·gi·al** (kə lē′jē əl) *adj.* **1.** with authority shared equally among colleagues **2.** *same as* COLLEGIATE

**col·le·gi·al·i·ty** (kə lē′jē al′ə tē) *n.* **1.** the sharing of authority among colleagues **2.** *R. C. Ch.* the principle that authority is shared by the Pope and the bishops

**col·le·gian** (kə lē′jən) *n.* a college student

**col·le·giate** (-jət, -jē ət) *adj.* of or like a college or college students

**collegiate church** a church with a chapter of canons although it is not a bishop's see

**col·lide** (kə līd′) *vi.* **-lid′ed, -lid′ing** [L. *collidere* < *com-,* together + *laedere,* to strike] **1.** to come into violent contact; strike violently against each other; crash **2.** to come into conflict; clash

**col·lie** (käl′ē) *n.* [< ? *coaly*, from black coat of earlier collies] a large, long-haired dog with a long, narrow head: first bred in Scotland to herd sheep

**col·lier** (käl′yər) *n.* [see COAL & -IER] [Chiefly Brit.] **1.** a coal miner **2.** a ship for carrying coal

**col·lier·y** (-ē) *n., pl.* **-lier·ies** [Chiefly Brit.] a coal mine and its buildings, equipment, etc.

**col·li·mate** (käl′ə māt′) *vt.* **-mat′ed, -mat′ing** [< false reading of L. *collineare* < *com-*, with + *lineare*, to make straight < *linea*, a line] **1.** to make (light rays, etc.) parallel **2.** to adjust the line of sight of (a telescope, etc.) —**col′li·ma′tion** *n.*

COLLIE
(24–26 in. high at shoulder)

**col·li·ma·tor** (-māt′ər) *n.* [see prec.] a small telescope with cross hairs at its focus, fixed to another telescope, surveying instrument, etc. for adjusting the line of sight

**Col·lins** (käl′inz) *n.* an iced drink made with gin (*Tom Collins*), or vodka, rum, whiskey, etc., mixed with soda water, lime or lemon juice, and sugar

**col·li·sion** (kə lizh′ən) *n.* **1.** a colliding, or coming together with sudden, violent force **2.** a clash or conflict of opinions, interests, etc.

**col·lo·cate** (käl′ə kāt′) *vt.* **-cat′ed, -cat′ing** [< L. pp. of *collocare*: see LOCATE] to arrange or place together, esp. side by side —**col′lo·ca′tion** *n.*

**col·lo·di·on** (kə lō′dē ən) *n.* [< Gr. < *kolla*, glue + *eidos*, form] a highly flammable solution of nitrated cellulose that dries quickly, forming a tough, elastic film: used to protect wounds, in photographic films, etc.

**col·logue** (kə lōg′) *vi.* **-logued′, -lo′guing** [< Fr. < L.: see COLLOQUY] **1.** to confer privately **2.** [Dial.] to conspire

**col·loid** (käl′oid) *n.* [< Gr. *kolla*, glue + -OID] a solid, liquid, or gaseous substance made up of insoluble, non-diffusible particles (as single large molecules or masses of smaller molecules) that remain suspended in a medium of different matter —**col·loi′dal** *adj.*

**colloq. 1.** colloquial(ly) **2.** colloquialism

**col·lo·qui·al** (kə lō′kwē əl) *adj.* [see COLLOQUY] **1.** having to do with or like conversation **2.** designating or of the words, phrases, and idioms characteristic of informal speech and writing; informal: the label [Colloq.] is used throughout this dictionary in this sense, and does not indicate substandard or illiterate usage —**col·lo′qui·al·ly** *adv.* —**col·lo′qui·al·ness** *n.*

**col·lo·qui·al·ism** (-iz′m) *n.* **1.** colloquial quality, style, or usage **2.** a colloquial word or expression

**col·lo·qui·um** (kə lō′kwē əm) *n., pl.* **-qui·a** (-ə), **-qui·ums** [L.: see ff.] an organized conference or seminar on some subject, involving a number of scholars or experts

**col·lo·quy** (käl′ə kwē) *n., pl.* **-quies** [L. *colloquium*, conversation < *com-*, together + *loqui*, to speak] a conversation, esp. a formal discussion; conference —**col′lo·quist** *n.*

**col·lude** (kə lōōd′) *vi.* **-lud′ed, -lud′ing** [< L. < *com-*, with + *ludere*, to play] to act in collusion

**col·lu·sion** (kə lōō′zhən) *n.* [see prec.] a secret agreement for fraudulent or illegal purpose; conspiracy —**col·lu′sive** (-siv) *adj.* —**col·lu′sive·ly** *adv.*

**Colo.** Colorado

**Co·logne** (kə lōn′) city in W West Germany, on the Rhine: pop. 854,000

**co·logne** (kə lōn′) *n.* same as EAU DE COLOGNE

**Co·lom·bi·a** (kə lum′bē ə; *Sp.* kô lôm′byä) country in NW S. America: 455,335 sq. mi.; pop. 20,463,000; cap. Bogotá —**Co·lom′bi·an** *adj., n.*

**Co·lom·bo** (kə lum′bō) capital of Ceylon: seaport on the W coast: pop. 512,000

**Co·lón** (kə lōn′) seaport in Panama, at the Caribbean entrance to the Panama Canal: pop. 64,000

**co·lon¹** (kō′lən) *n.* [L. < Gr. *kōlon*, member, limb] a mark of punctuation (:) used before a long quotation, example, series, etc., and after the salutation of a formal letter

**co·lon²** (kō′lən) *n., pl.* **-lons, -la** (-lə) [L. < Gr. *kolon*] that part of the large intestine extending from the cecum to the rectum —**co·lon·ic** (kə län′ik) *adj.*

**co·lon³** (kə lōn′; *Sp.* kô lôn′) *n., pl.* **-lons′**, *Sp.* **-lon′es** (-lō′nes) [AmSp. *colón* < *Sp. Colón*, COLUMBUS] *see* MONETARY UNITS, table (Costa Rica, El Salvador)

**colo·nel** (kur′n'l) *n.* [earlier *coronel* < Fr. < It. < *colonna*, (military) column < L. *columna*] **1.** a military officer ranking above a lieutenant colonel **2.** an honorary, nonmilitary title in some southern or western States —**colo′nel·cy** (-sē) *n., pl.* **-cies**

**co·lo·ni·al** (kə lō′nē əl) *adj.* **1.** of or living in a colony or colonies **2.** [*often* C-] of or characteristic of the thirteen British colonies that became the U.S., or of their period **3.** made up of or having colonies —*n.* an inhabitant of a colony —**co·lo′ni·al·ly** *adv.*

**co·lo·ni·al·ism** (-iz′m) *n.* the system or policy by which a country maintains foreign colonies, esp. in order to exploit them economically —**co·lo′ni·al·ist** *n., adj.*

**col·o·nist** (käl′ə nist) *n.* **1.** any of the original settlers of a colony **2.** an inhabitant of a colony

**col·o·nize** (käl′ə nīz′) *vt., vi.* **-nized′, -niz′ing 1.** to found or establish a colony or colonies (in) **2.** to settle in a colony —**col′o·ni·za′tion** *n.* —**col′o·niz′er** *n.*

**col·on·nade** (käl′ə nād′) *n.* [Fr. < It. < L. *columna*, column] *Archit.* a series of columns set at regular intervals, usually supporting a roof or series of arches —**col′on·nad′ed** *adj.*

**col·o·ny** (käl′ə nē) *n., pl.* **-nies** [< L. < *colonus*, farmer < *colere*, to cultivate] **1.** *a)* a group of people who settle in a distant land but under the jurisdiction of their native land *b)* the region thus settled **2.** a territory distant from the state having jurisdiction over it **3.** [C-] [*pl.*] the thirteen British colonies in N. America that became the U.S. **4.** a community of people of the same nationality or pursuits concentrated in a particular place [an artists' *colony*] **5.** *Bacteriology* a group of similar bacteria growing in a culture medium **6.** *Biol.* a group of similar plants or animals living or growing together **7.** *Zool.* a compound organism of incompletely separated individuals, as in corals

COLONNADE

**col·o·phon** (käl′ə fän′, -fən) *n.* [LL. < Gr. *kolophōn*, summit, top, end] **1.** a note in a book giving facts about its production **2.** the distinctive emblem of the publisher

**col·or** (kul′ər) *n.* [< OFr. < L. < OL. *colos*, orig., a covering] **1.** the sensation resulting from stimulation of the retina of the eye by light waves **2.** the property of reflecting light of a particular wavelength: the distinct colors of the spectrum are red, orange, yellow, green, blue, indigo, and violet; the *primary colors* of the spectrum are red, green, and blue **3.** any coloring matter; dye; pigment; paint: the *primary colors* (red, yellow, and blue) and *secondary colors* formed from these (green, orange, purple, etc.) are sometimes distinguished from black, white, and gray (*achromatic colors*) **4.** color of the face; esp., a healthy rosiness or a blush **5.** the color of the skin of a Negro or other person not Caucasoid **6.** [*pl.*] a colored badge, costume, etc. that identifies the wearer **7.** [*pl.*] *a)* a flag of a country, regiment, etc. *b)* the armed forces of a country, symbolized by the flag [to serve with the *colors*] **8.** [*pl.*] one's position or opinion [stick to your *colors*] **9.** outward appearance or semblance; plausibility **10.** appearance of truth; justification [the news lent *color* to the rumor] **11.** general nature; character [the *color* of his mind] **12.** vivid quality, as in a personality, literary work, etc. **13.** *Art* the way of using color —*adj. TV, Radio* designating or of a sports commentator who supplies details and analysis between play-by-play accounts of the action —*vt.* **1.** to give color to; paint; stain; dye **2.** to change the color of **3.** to alter or influence, as by distortion [prejudice *colored* his views] —*vi.* **1.** to become colored **2.** to change in color **3.** to blush or flush —**call to the colors 1.** call or order to serve in the armed forces **2.** *Mil.* a bugle call for the daily flag-raising and flag-lowering ceremonies —**change color 1.** to become pale **2.** to blush or flush —**lose color** to become pale —**under color of** under the pretext of —**col′or·er** *n.*

**col·or·a·ble** (-ə b'l) *adj.* **1.** capable of being colored **2.** apparently plausible, but actually specious; deceptive

**Col·o·ra·do** (käl′ə rad′ō, -rä′dō) **1.** [after the river] Mountain State of the U.S.: 104,247 sq. mi.; pop. 2,889,000; cap. Denver: abbrev. **Colo., CO 2.** [< *Sp. Rio Colorado*, Red River] river flowing from N Colo. southwest into the Gulf of California —**Col′o·rad′an, Col′o·rad′o·an** *adj., n.*

**col·o·ra·do** (käl′ə rad′ō, -rä′dō) *adj.* [Sp., red] of medium strength and color: said of cigars

**Colorado beetle** a widely distributed black-and-yellow beetle that is a destructive pest of potatoes and other plants

**Colorado Springs** city in C Colo.: pop. 215,000

**col·or·ant** (kul′ər ənt) *n.* [Fr. < prp. of *colorer*, to color] anything used to give color to something; pigment, dye, etc.

**col·or·a·tion** (kul′ə rā′shən) *n.* **1.** a being colored **2.** the way a thing is colored **3.** the technique of using colors

**col·o·ra·tu·ra** (kul′ər ə toor′ə, -tyoor′-) *n.* [It. < L. pp. of *colorare*, to color] **1.** brilliant runs, trills, etc., used to display a singer's skill **2.** music containing such ornamentation **3.** a soprano who sings such music: in full, **coloratura soprano**

**col·or·blind** (kul′ər blīnd′) *adj.* unable to perceive colors or to distinguish between certain colors, as red and green —**col′or·blind′ness** *n.*

**col·or·cast** (-kast′) *n.* [COLOR + (TELE)CAST] a television broadcast in color —*vt., vi.* **-cast′** or **-cast′ed, -cast′ing** to televise in color

**col·ored** (kul′ərd) *adj.* **1.** having color **2.** of a (specified) color **3.** of a group of mankind other than the Caucasoid; specif., Negro **4.** [C-] in South Africa, of racially mixed parentage: usually **Coloured 5.** of or having to do with colored persons **6.** altered, distorted, or exaggerated —**the colored** colored persons

**col·or·fast** (kul′ər fast′) *adj.* that will keep its color without fading or running —**col′or·fast′ness** *n.*

**col·or·ful** (-fəl) *adj.* **1.** full of vivid colors **2.** full of interest or variety; picturesque; vivid —**col′or·ful·ly** *adv.* —**col′or·ful·ness** *n.*

**color guard** persons escorting the colors (flag)

**col·or·ing** (kul′ər iŋ) *n.* **1.** the act or art of applying colors **2.** anything applied to impart color; pigment, dye, stain, etc. **3.** *same as* COLORATION **4.** skin color **5.** specious or false appearance **6.** alteration or influence

**col·or·ist** (-ist) *n.* **1.** a person who uses colors **2.** an artist skillful in using colors

**col·or·less** (-lis) *adj.* **1.** without color **2.** dull in color; gray or pallid **3.** lacking interest; dull —**col′or·less·ly** *adv.* —**col′or·less·ness** *n.*

**color line** the barrier of social, political, and economic restrictions imposed on Negroes or other nonwhites

**Co·los·sae** (kə läs′ē) city in ancient Phrygia, SW Asia Minor —**Co·los′sian** (-läsh′ən) *adj., n.*

**co·los·sal** (kə läs′'l) *adj.* **1.** like a colossus in size; huge; gigantic **2.** [Colloq.] extraordinary [a colossal fool] —**co·los′sal·ly** *adv.*

**Col·os·se·um** (käl′ə sē′əm) [L., neut. of colosseus, gigantic: see COLOSSUS] an amphitheater in Rome, built c. 75–80 A.D.: much of it is still standing —n. [c-] *same as* COLISEUM

**Co·los·sians** (kə läsh′ənz) a book of the New Testament: an epistle from the Apostle Paul to the Christians of Colossae

**co·los·sus** (kə läs′əs) *n., pl.* **-los′si** (-ī) **-los′sus·es** [L. < Gr. kolossos] **1.** a gigantic statue; esp., [C-] that of Apollo set at the entrance to the harbor of Rhodes c. 280 B.C. **2.** any huge or important person or thing

**col·our** (kul′ər) *n., vt., vi. Brit. sp. of* COLOR

**-co·lous** (kə ləs) [< base of L. colere, to inhabit + -OUS] a combining form meaning growing (or living) in or among

**colt** (kōlt) *n.* [OE.] **1.** a young horse, donkey, zebra, etc.; specif., a male racehorse four years of age or under **2.** a young, inexperienced person

**col·ter** (kōl′tər) *n.* [< OFr. or OE., both < L. culter, plowshare] a blade or disk on a plow, for making vertical cuts in the soil

**colt·ish** (kōl′tish) *adj.* of or like a colt; esp., frisky, frolicsome, etc. —**colt′ish·ly** *adv.*

**colts·foot** (kōlts′foot′) *n., pl.* **-foots′** a plant of the composite family, with yellow flowers and large leaves suggesting the print of a colt's foot

**Co·lum·bi·a** (kə lum′bē ə, -byə) [after Christopher COLUMBUS] **1.** [Poet.] the U.S. personified as a woman **2.** capital of S.C.: pop. 99,000 **3.** city in C Mo.: pop. 62,000 **4.** river flowing from SE British Columbia, through Wash., into the Pacific —**Co·lum′bi·an** *adj.*

**col·um·bine** (käl′əm bīn′) *n.* [OFr. < ML. < L. columbinus, dovelike < columba, dove] a plant of the buttercup family, with showy, spurred flowers of various colors

**Co·lum·bus** (kə lum′bəs) [after ff.] **1.** capital of Ohio, in the C part: pop. 565,000 (met. area 1,089,000) **2.** city in W Ga.: pop. 169,000

**Co·lum·bus** (kə lum′bəs), **Christopher** (It. name *Cristoforo Colombo*; Sp. name *Cristóbal Colón*) 1451?–1506; It. explorer in the service of Spain: discovered America (1492)

**Columbus Day** a legal holiday in the U.S. commemorating the discovery of America by Columbus in 1492, observed on the second Monday in October

**col·umn** (käl′əm) *n.* [< OFr. < L. columna] **1.** a slender upright structure, generally a cylindrical shaft with a base and a capital; pillar: it is usually a supporting or ornamental member in a building **2.** anything like a column in shape or function [the spinal column] **3.** a formation of troops, ships, etc. in a file **4.** any of the vertical sections of printed matter lying side by side on a page and separated by a rule or blank space **5.** a series of feature articles under a fixed title in a newspaper or magazine, written by a special writer or devoted to a certain subject —**co·lum′nar** (kə lum′nər), **col′umned** *adj.*

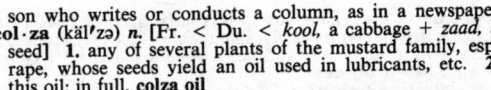

CAPITAL

SHAFT

BASE

COLUMN

**co·lum·ni·a·tion** (kə lum′nē ā′shən) *n.* the architectural use or arrangement of columns

**col·um·nist** (käl′əm nist, -ə mist) *n.* a per-son who writes or conducts a column, as in a newspaper

**col·za** (käl′zə) *n.* [Fr. < Du. < kool, a cabbage + zaad, a seed] **1.** any of several plants of the mustard family, esp. rape, whose seeds yield an oil used in lubricants, etc. **2.** this oil: in full, **colza oil**

**com-** [L. com- < OL. com (L. cum), with] a prefix meaning with or together [combine] : also used as an intensive [command] : assimilated to **col-** before *l;* **cor-** before *r;* **con-** before *c, d, g, j, n, q, s, t,* and *v;* and **co-** before *h, w,* and all vowels

**COM** computer-output microfilm (or microfiche)

**Com. 1.** Commander **2.** Commission(er) **3.** Committee

**com. 1.** commerce **2.** commercial **3.** common **4.** communication

**co·ma¹** (kō′mə) *n.* [ModL. < Gr. koma, deep sleep] **1.** a state of deep and prolonged unconsciousness caused by injury or disease **2.** a condition of stupor or lethargy

**co·ma²** (kō′mə) *n., pl.* **-mae** (-mē) [L. < Gr. komē, hair] **1.** Astron. a globular, cloudlike mass around the nucleus of a comet **2.** *a)* a bunch of branches, as on the top of some palms *b)* a tuft of hairs at the end of certain seeds —**co′mate** (-māt) *adj.*

**co·make** (kō′māk′) *vt.* **-made′, -mak′ing** *same as* COSIGN —**co′mak′er** *n.*

**Co·man·che** (kə man′chē) *n.* [MexSp. < Ute komanchi, stranger] **1.** *pl.* **-ches, -che** any member of a tribe of Uto-Aztecan Indians who ranged from the Platte River to the Mexican border and now live in Oklahoma **2.** their Shoshonean dialect of Uto-Aztecan

**co·ma·tose** (kō′mə tōs′, käm′ə-) *adj.* **1.** of, like, or in a coma or stupor **2.** as if in a coma; torpid

**comb** (kōm) *n.* [OE. camb] **1.** a thin strip of hard rubber, plastic, metal, etc. with teeth, passed through the hair to arrange or clean it, or set in the hair to hold it in place **2.** anything like a comb in form or function; specif., *a)* a currycomb *b)* a tool for cleaning and straightening wool, flax, etc. *c)* a red, fleshy outgrowth on the top of the head, as of a rooster *d)* a thing like a rooster's comb in position or appearance, as a helmet crest **3.** a honeycomb —*vt.* **1.** to clean or arrange with a comb **2.** to remove with or as with a comb; separate (often with *out*) **3.** to search thoroughly; look everywhere in —*vi.* to roll over; break: said of waves

**com·bat** (*for v.,* kəm bat′, käm′bat; *for n. & adj.,* käm′bat, kum′-) *vi.* **-bat′ed** *or* **-bat′ted, -bat′ing** *or* **-bat′ting** [< Fr. < VL. < L. com-, with + battuere, to beat] to fight, contend, or struggle —*vt.* to fight or struggle against; oppose; resist, or seek to get rid of —*n.* **1.** armed fighting; battle **2.** any struggle or conflict; strife —*adj. Mil.* of or for combat

**com·bat·ant** (käm′bə tənt, kəm bat′'nt) *adj.* **1.** fighting **2.** ready or prepared to fight —*n.* a person who engages in combat; fighter

**combat fatigue** a neurotic condition characterized by anxiety, irritability, depression, etc., often occurring after prolonged combat in warfare

**com·bat·ive** (kəm bat′iv, käm′bə tiv) *adj.* ready or eager to fight; pugnacious —**com·bat′ive·ly** *adv.* —**com·bat′ive·ness** *n.*

**comb·er** (kō′mər) *n.* **1.** one that combs wool, flax, etc. **2.** a large wave that breaks as on a beach

**com·bi·na·tion** (käm bə nā′shən) *n.* **1.** a combining or being combined **2.** a thing formed by combining **3.** an association of persons, firms, political parties, etc. for a common purpose **4.** the series of numbers or letters used in opening a combination lock **5.** a one-piece undergarment combining an undershirt and drawers **6.** Math. any of the various groupings, or subsets, into which a number, or set, of units may be arranged without regard to order —**com′bi·na′tion·al, com′bi·na′tive** *adj.*

**combination lock** a lock operated by a dial that is turned to a set series of numbers or letters to work the mechanism that opens it

**com·bine** (kəm bīn′; *for n. & v. 3,* käm′bīn) *vt., vi.* **-bined′, -bin′ing** [< OFr. < LL. combinare < L. com-, together + bini, two by two: see BI-] **1.** to come or bring into union; act or mix together; unite; join **2.** to unite to form a chemical compound **3.** to harvest and thresh with a combine —*n.* **1.** a machine for harvesting and threshing grain **2.** an association of persons, corporations, etc. for commercial or political, often unethical, purposes —**com·bin′a·ble** *adj.* —**com·bin′er** *n.*

**comb·ings** (kō′miŋz) *n.pl.* loose hair, wool, etc. removed in combing

**combining form** a word form that occurs only in compounds or derivatives, and that can combine with other such forms or with affixes to form a word (Ex.: cardio- and -graph in cardiograph)

**com·bo** (käm′bō) *n., pl.* **-bos** [Colloq.] a combination; specif., a small jazz ensemble

**com·bus·ti·ble** (kəm bus′tə b'l) *adj.* [see ff.] **1.** that catches fire and burns easily; flammable **2.** easily aroused; fiery —*n.* a flammable substance —**com·bus′ti·bil′i·ty** *n.* —**com·bus′ti·bly** *adv.*

**com·bus·tion** (-chən) *n.* [< OFr. < LL. < L. pp. of *comburere* < *com-*, intens. + *urere*, to burn] **1.** the act or process of burning **2.** rapid oxidation accompanied by heat and, usually, light **3.** slow oxidation accompanied by relatively little heat and no light **4.** violent excitement; tumult —**com·bus′tive** (-tiv) *adj.*

**com·bus·tor** (-tər) *n.* the chamber in a jet engine, gas turbine, etc. in which combustion occurs

**Comdr.** Commander

**Comdt.** Commandant

**come** (kum) *vi.* **came, come, com′ing** [OE. *cuman*] **1.** to move from a place thought of as "there" to a place thought of as "here" **2.** to approach by moving toward **3.** to arrive or appear [help will *come*] **4.** to extend; reach **5.** to take place; happen [*success came* to him] **6.** to take form in the mind [her name *came* to him] **7.** to occur in a certain place or order [after 9 *comes* 10] **8.** to become actual; evolve; develop [will peace *come*?] **9.** *a*) to be derived or descended *b*) to be a resident or former resident (with *from*) **10.** to be caused; result **11.** to be due or owed (*to*): used in the participle [to get what is *coming* to one] **12.** to pass as by inheritance **13.** to get to be; become [it *came* loose] **14.** to be available [this dress *comes* in four sizes] **15.** to amount; add up [to] —*interj.* look! see here! stop! —**come about 1.** to happen; occur **2.** to turn about —**come across 1.** to find by chance **2.** [Colloq.] to be effective, etc. **3.** [Slang] to give, do, or say what is wanted —**come again?** [Colloq.] what did you say? —**come and get it!** [Colloq.] the meal is ready! —**come around** (or **round**) **1.** to revive; recover **2.** to make a turn **3.** to concede or yield —**come at 1.** to reach; attain **2.** to approach angrily or swiftly —**come back 1.** to return **2.** [Colloq.] to make a comeback —**come between** to estrange; divide —**come by 1.** to get; gain **2.** to pay a visit —**come down** to suffer loss in status, wealth, etc. —**come down on** (or **upon**) to scold; criticize harshly —**come in 1.** to enter **2.** to come into fashion **3.** to finish in a contest [he *came in* fifth] —**come in for** [Colloq.] to get; acquire —**come into 1.** to enter into **2.** to inherit —**come off 1.** to become detached **2.** to occur **3.** [Colloq.] to prove successful, etc. —**come on 1.** to make progress **2.** to find **3.** to appear, make an entrance, etc. —**come on!** [Colloq.] **1.** get started! hurry! **2.** stop behaving like that! —**come one's way** to yield or become agreeable —**come out 1.** to be disclosed **2.** to be offered for public sale, etc. **3.** to make a debut **4.** to end up; turn out —**come out for** to support; endorse —**come out with 1.** to disclose **2.** to say; publish **3.** to offer for public sale, etc. —**come through 1.** to complete or endure something successfully **2.** [Slang] to do or give what is wanted —**come to 1.** to recover consciousness **2.** to anchor —**come up 1.** to arise, as in discussion **2.** to rise, as in status **3.** to be put forward, as for a vote —**come upon** to find —**come up to 1.** to reach to **2.** to equal —**come up with** to propose, produce, find, etc. —**how come?** [Colloq.] how is it that? why?

**come·back** (kum′bak′) *n.* [Colloq.] **1.** a return to a previous state or position, as of success **2.** a witty answer **3.** ground for complaint

**co·me·di·an** (kə mē′dē ən) *n.* **1.** an actor who plays comic parts **2.** an entertainer who tells jokes, sings comic songs, etc. **3.** a person who amuses others by behaving in a comic way

**co·me·di·enne** (kə mē′dē en′) *n.* a woman comedian

**com·e·do** (käm′ə dō′) *n., pl.* **com′e·do′nes** (-dō′nēz), **com′e·dos′** [< L. < *comedere:* see COMESTIBLE] *same as* BLACKHEAD (sense 2)

**come·down** (kum′doun′) *n.* a fall to a lower status or position, as of power, wealth, etc.

**com·e·dy** (käm′ə dē) *n., pl.* **-dies** [< OFr. < L. < Gr. *kō-mōidia* < *kōmōs*, festival + *aeidein*, to sing] **1.** orig., a drama or narrative with a happy ending or nontragic theme **2.** *a*) any of various types of play or motion picture with a humorous treatment of characters and situation and a happy ending *b*) the branch of drama having to do with such plays **3.** a novel or any narrative having a comic theme, tone, etc. **4.** the comic element in a literary work, or in life —**cut the comedy** [Slang] to stop joking —**co·me·dic** (kə-mē′dik, -med′ik) *adj.*

**comedy of manners** a type of comedy satirizing the manners and customs of fashionable society

**come-hith·er** (kum′hith′ər) *adj.* [Colloq.] flirtatious or inviting [a *come-hither* look]

**come·ly** (kum′lē) *adj.* **-li·er, -li·est** [OE. *cymlic* < *cyme*, delicate, orig., feeble] **1.** pleasant to look at; attractive **2.** [Archaic] seemly; proper —**come′li·ness** *n.*

**come-on** (kum′än′) *n.* [Slang] **1.** an inviting look or gesture **2.** an inducement **3.** a swindler

**com·er** (-ər) *n.* **1.** a person who comes [a contest open to all *comers*] **2.** [Colloq.] a person or thing that shows promise of being a success

**co·mes·ti·ble** (kə mes′tə b'l) *adj.* [Fr. < L. pp. of *comedere* < *com-*, intens. + *edere*, to eat] [Rare] eatable; edible —*n.* [usually pl.] food

**com·et** (käm′ət) *n.* [< OE. < L. *cometa* < Gr. < *komē*, hair] a heavenly body having a starlike nucleus with a luminous mass (*coma*) around it, and, usually, a long, luminous tail: comets move in orbits around the sun —**com′et·ar′y** (-ə ter′ē), **co·met·ic** (kä met′ik) *adj.*

**come·up·pance** (kum′up′′ns) *n.* [< COME + UP¹ + -ANCE] [Colloq.] deserved punishment; retribution

**com·fit** (kum′fit, käm′-) *n.* [< OFr. < L. *conficere:* see CONFECT] a candy or sweetmeat, as a candied fruit

**com·fort** (kum′fərt) *vt.* [< OFr. < LL. < L. *com-*, intens. + *fortis*, strong] **1.** to soothe in distress or sorrow; console **2.** to give a sense of ease to **3.** *Law* to help; aid —*n.* **1.** aid; encouragement: now only in **aid and comfort 2.** relief from distress, grief, etc. **3.** a person or thing that comforts **4.** a state of, or thing that provides, ease and quiet enjoyment **5.** a quilted bed covering —**com′fort·ing** *adj.* —**com′fort·ing·ly** *adv.* —**com′fort·less** *adj.*

**com·fort·a·ble** (kumf′tər b'l, kum′fər tə b'l) *adj.* **1.** providing comfort [*comfortable* shoes] **2.** at ease in body or mind; contented **3.** [Colloq.] sufficient to satisfy [a *comfortable* salary] —**com′fort·a·ble·ness** *n.* —**com′fort·a·bly** *adv.*

**com·fort·er** (kum′fər tər, -fə tər) *n.* **1.** a person or thing that comforts **2.** a quilted bed covering —**the Comforter** *Bible* the Holy Spirit: John 14:26

**comfort station** a public toilet or restroom

**com·fy** (kum′fē) *adj.* **-fi·er, -fi·est** [contr. < COMFORTABLE] [Colloq.] comfortable

**com·ic** (käm′ik) *adj.* [< L. < Gr. *kōmikos*] **1.** of or having to do with comedy **2.** amusing; humorous; funny **3.** of comic strips or cartoons —*n.* **1.** a comedian **2.** the humorous element in art or life **3.** *a*) *same as* COMIC STRIP or COMIC BOOK *b*) [pl.] a section of comic strips, as in a newspaper

**com·i·cal** (käm′i k'l) *adj.* causing amusement; humorous; funny; droll —**com′i·cal′i·ty** (-kal′ə tē), **com′i·cal·ness** *n.* —**com′i·cal·ly** *adv.*

**comic book** a paper booklet of extended comic strips, sometimes sensational or violent

**comic opera** opera with humorous situations, a story that ends happily, and some spoken dialogue

**comic strip** a series of cartoons, as in a newspaper, telling a humorous or adventurous story

**Com·in·form** (käm′in fôrm′) *n.* [< Com(munist) Inform(ation)] the Communist Information Bureau, an association of various European Communist parties (1947-56)

**com·ing** (kum′iŋ) *adj.* **1.** approaching; next [this *coming* Tuesday] **2.** showing promise of being successful, etc. [the *coming* thing] —*n.* arrival; advent

**Com·in·tern** (käm′in turn′) *n.* [< Com(munist) Intern(ational)] the international organization (*Third International*) of Communist parties (1919-43)

**com·i·ty** (käm′ə tē) *n., pl.* **-ties** [< L. *comitas* < *comis*, polite, kind] **1.** courteous behavior; politeness **2.** agreement among Christian denominations to avoid duplication of churches, missions, etc. in specific areas

**comity of nations** the respect of peaceful nations for each other's laws and institutions

**comm. 1.** commander **2.** commission **3.** committee **4.** commonwealth

**com·ma** (käm′ə) *n.* [L. < Gr. *komma*, clause, that which is cut off < *koptein*, to cut off] **1.** a mark of punctuation (,) used to indicate a slight separation of sentence elements, as in setting off nonrestrictive or parenthetical elements, quotations, items in a series, etc. **2.** a slight pause

**comma bacillus** the bacillus causing Asiatic cholera

**com·mand** (kə mand′) *vt.* [< OFr. < VL. < L. *com-*, intens. + *mandare:* see MANDATE] **1.** to give an order to; direct with authority **2.** to have authority over; control **3.** to have ready for use [to *command* a large vocabulary] **4.** to deserve and get; require as due [to *command* respect] **5.** to control or overlook from a higher position —*vi.* to exercise authority; be in control; act as commander —*n.* **1.** an order; direction; mandate **2.** authority to command **3.** power to control by position **4.** range of view **5.** ability to use; mastery **6.** *a*) a military or naval force, organization, or district, under a specified authority *b*) *same as* AIR COMMAND **7.** the post where the person in command is stationed

**com·man·dant** (käm′ən dant′, -dänt′) *n.* a commanding officer of a fort, service school, etc.

**com·man·deer** (käm′ən dir′) *vt.* [< Du. or Afrik. < Fr. *commander*, to command] **1.** to force into military service **2.** to seize (property) for military or governmental use **3.** [Colloq.] to take forcibly

**com·mand·er** (kə man′dər) *n.* **1.** a person who commands; leader **2.** *same as* COMMANDING OFFICER **3.** *U.S. Navy* an officer ranking above a lieutenant commander —**com·mand′er·ship′** *n.*

**commander in chief** *pl.* **commanders in chief 1.** the supreme commander of the armed forces of a nation, as, in the U.S., the President **2.** an officer in command of all armed forces in a certain theater of war

**commanding officer** the officer in command of any of certain military units or installations

**com·mand·ment** (kə mand′mənt) *n.* an authoritative command or order; mandate; precept; specif., any of the Ten Commandments

**com·man·do** (kə man′dō) *n., pl.* **-dos, -does** [Afrik. < Port., lit., party commanded] **1.** orig., in South Africa, a force of Boer troops **2.** *a)* a small raiding force trained to operate inside enemy territory *b)* a member of such a group

**command post** the field headquarters of a military unit, where the commander directs operations

**com·me·dia del·l'ar·te** (kôm mä′dyä del lär′te) [It., lit., comedy of art] a type of Italian comedy of the 16th century, having a stereotyped plot, improvised dialogue, and stock characters

‡**comme il faut** (kô mēl fō′) [Fr.] as it should be; proper; fitting

**com·mem·o·rate** (kə mem′ə rāt′) *vt.* **-rat′ed, -rat′ing** [< L. pp. of *commemorare* < *com-*, intens. + *memorare*, to remind] **1.** to honor the memory of, as by a ceremony **2.** to serve as a memorial to —**com·mem′o·ra′tion** *n.* —**com·mem′o·ra·tive** (-ər ə tiv, -ə rāt′iv), **com·mem′o·ra·to′ry** *adj.* —**com·mem′o·ra·tive·ly** *adv.* —**com·mem′o·ra′tor** *n.*

**com·mence** (kə mens′) *vi., vt.* **-menced′, -menc′ing** [< OFr. < L. *com-*, together + *initiare*, to INITIATE] to begin; start; originate —**com·menc′er** *n.*

**com·mence·ment** (-mənt) *n.* **1.** the act or time of commencing; beginning; start **2.** the ceremonies at which degrees or diplomas are conferred at a school or college **3.** the day this takes place

**com·mend** (kə mend′) *vt.* [< L. *commendare*: see COMMAND] **1.** to put in the care of another; entrust **2.** to mention as worthy; recommend **3.** to express approval of; praise —**com·mend′a·ble** *adj.* —**com·mend′a·bly** *adv.*

**com·men·da·tion** (käm′ən dā′shən) *n.* a commending; esp., recommendation or praise

**com·mend·a·to·ry** (kə men′də tôr′ē) *adj.* **1.** expressing praise or approval **2.** recommending

**com·men·su·ra·ble** (kə men′shər ə b′l, -sər-) *adj.* [LL. *commensurabilis* < L. *com-*, together + *mensurare*: see ff.] measurable by the same standard or measure —**com·men′su·ra·bil′i·ty** *n.* —**com·men′su·ra·bly** *adv.*

**com·men·su·rate** (-shər it, -sər-) *adj.* [< LL. < *com-*, with + pp. of *mensurare*, to measure < L. *mensura*, MEASURE] **1.** equal in measure or size; coextensive **2.** corresponding in extent or degree; proportionate **3.** commensurable —**com·men′su·rate·ly** *adv.* —**com·men·su·ra′tion** (-ā′shən) *n.*

**com·ment** (käm′ent) *n.* [OFr. < L. < pp. of *comminisci*, to contrive < *com-*, intens. + base of *meminisse*, to remember] **1.** a note or notes in explanation or criticism of something written or said; annotation **2.** a remark or observation made as in criticism **3.** talk; gossip —*vi.* [< OFr. < L. *commentari*, to consider thoroughly] to make a comment or comments (*on* or *upon*); make remarks

**com·men·tar·y** (käm′ən ter′ē) *n., pl.* **-tar′ies 1.** a series of explanatory notes or annotations **2.** a series of remarks or observations **3.** something having the force of a comment or remark **4.** [*usually pl.*] a memoir —**com′men·tar′i·al** *adj.*

**com·men·tate** (-tāt′) *vt.* **-tat′ed, -tat′ing** [back-formation from ff.] to give a commentary on —*vi.* to perform as a commentator (sense 2)

**com·men·ta·tor** (-ər) *n.* **1.** a person who gives a commentary **2.** a person who reports and analyzes news events, trends, etc., as on radio and TV

**com·merce** (käm′ərs) *n.* [Fr. < L. *commercium* < *com-*, together + *merx* (gen. *mercis*), merchandise] **1.** the buying and selling of goods, as between cities, states, or countries; trade **2.** social intercourse **3.** [Rare] sexual intercourse

**com·mer·cial** (kə mur′shəl) *adj.* **1.** of or connected with commerce or trade **2.** of or having to do with stores, office buildings, etc. **3.** of a lower grade, or for use in large quantities in industry **4.** *a)* made or done primarily for profit *b)* designed to have wide popular appeal **5.** offering training in business skills, etc. **6.** *Radio & TV* paid for by sponsors —*n.* *Radio & TV* a paid advertisement —**com·mer′cial·ly** *adv.*

**commercial bank** a bank that accepts demand deposits, used as checking accounts

**com·mer·cial·ism** (-iz′m) *n.* the practices and spirit of commerce or business, esp. in seeking profits —**com·mer′-cial·ist** *n.* —**com·mer′cial·is′tic** *adj.*

**com·mer·cial·ize** (-īz′) *vt.* **-ized′, -iz′ing 1.** to apply commercial or business methods to **2.** to make use of or do mainly for profit **3.** to imbue with commercialism —**com·mer′cial·i·za′tion** *n.*

**commercial paper** negotiable instruments, such as promissory notes and bills of exchange

**commercial traveler** *same as* TRAVELING SALESMAN

**Com·mie** (käm′ē) *adj., n.* [*sometimes* c-] [Colloq.] Communist

**com·min·gle** (kə miŋ′g'l) *vt., vi.* **-gled, -gling** to mingle together; intermix; blend

**com·mi·nute** (käm′ə nōōt′, -nyōōt′) *vt.* **-nut′ed, -nut′ing** [< L. pp. of *comminuere* < *com-*, intens. + *minuere*, to make small] to reduce to powder or minute particles; pulverize —**com′mi·nu′tion** *n.*

**com·mis·er·ate** (kə miz′ə rāt′) *vt.* **-at′ed, -at′ing** [< L. pp. of *commiserari* < *com-*, intens. + *miserari*, to pity] to feel or show sorrow or pity for —*vi.* to condole or sympathize (*with*) —**com·mis′er·a′tion** *n.* —**com·mis′er·a·tive** (-ə rāt′iv, -ər ə tiv) *adj.* —**com·mis′er·a·tive·ly** *adv.*

**com·mis·sar** (käm′ə sär′) *n.* [< Russ. < ML. *commissarius*: see COMMISSARY] the head of a commissariat (sense 2): since 1946, called *minister*

**com·mis·sar·i·at** (käm′ə ser′ē ət) *n.* **1.** the branch of an army which provides food and supplies for the troops **2.** formerly, a government department in the U.S.S.R.: since 1946, called *ministry*

**com·mis·sar·y** (käm′ə ser′ē) *n., pl.* **-sar′ies** [ML. *commissarius* < L. pp. of *committere*: see COMMIT] **1.** a deputy assigned to some duty **2.** formerly, an army officer in charge of providing food and supplies **3.** a store in a lumber camp, army camp, etc. handling food and supplies **4.** a restaurant in a movie or TV studio —**com′mis·sar′i·al** *adj.*

**com·mis·sion** (kə mish′ən) *n.* [OFr. < ML. < L. pp. of *committere*: see COMMIT] **1.** an authorization to perform certain duties or to take on certain powers **2.** a document giving such authorization **3.** the state of being so authorized **4.** authority to act for another **5.** that which one is authorized to do for another **6.** a committing or perpetration, as of a crime **7.** *a)* a group of people officially appointed to perform specified duties *b)* an administrative agency of the government **8.** a percentage of the money taken in on sales, allotted to the salesclerk or agent **9.** *Mil. a)* an official certificate conferring a rank of officer *b)* the rank conferred —*vt.* **1.** to give a commission to **2.** to authorize; empower **3.** to give an order to make or do **4.** *Naut.* to put (a vessel) into service —**in** (or **out of**) **commission 1.** in (or not in) use **2.** in (or not in) working order

**commissioned officer** an officer in the armed forces holding rank by a commission

**com·mis·sion·er** (-ə nər) *n.* **1.** a member of a commission (sense 7) **2.** an official in charge of a certain government bureau, commission, etc. **3.** an official appointed to administer a territory, province, etc.: usually **high commissioner 4.** a man selected to regulate and control a professional sport

**com·mit** (kə mit′) *vt.* **-mit′ted, -mit′ting** [L. *committere* < *com-*, together + *mittere*, to send] **1.** to give in charge or trust; consign [*we commit his fame to posterity*] **2.** to put officially in custody or confinement [*committed to prison*] **3.** to set apart for some purpose **4.** to do or perpetrate (an offense or crime) **5.** to bind as by a promise; pledge [*committed to the struggle*] **6.** to make known the opinions or views of [*to commit oneself on an issue*] **7.** to refer (a bill, etc.) to a committee to be considered —**commit to memory** to learn by heart; memorize —**commit to paper** (or **writing**) to write down —**com·mit′ta·ble** *adj.*

**com·mit·ment** (-mənt) *n.* **1.** a committing or being committed **2.** official consignment by court order of a person to prison, to a mental hospital, etc. **3.** a pledge or promise Also **com·mit′tal**

**com·mit·tee** (kə mit′ē) *n.* [< Anglo-Fr. < L. *committere*: see COMMIT] **1.** a group of people chosen, as in a legislature or club, to consider or act on some matter **2.** a group of people organized to support some cause —**in committee** under consideration by a committee, as a resolution or bill

**com·mit·tee·man** (-mən) *n., pl.* **-men 1.** a member of a committee **2.** a ward or precinct political party leader —**com·mit′tee·wom′an** *n.fem., pl.* **-wom′en**

**com·mode** (kə mōd′) *n.* [Fr. < L. *commodus*, suitable: see COM- & MODE] **1.** a chest of drawers **2.** a small, low table with drawers or cabinet space: also **commode table 3.** a movable washstand **4.** a chair enclosing a chamber pot **5.** a toilet

**com·mo·di·ous** (kə mō′dē əs) *adj.* [ME., convenient: see prec.] spacious; roomy —**com·mo′di·ous·ly** *adv.* —**com·mo′di·ous·ness** *n.*

**com·mod·i·ty** (kə mäd′ə tē) *n., pl.* **-ties** [< OFr. < L. < *commodus*: see COMMODE] **1.** any useful thing **2.** anything bought and sold, as in commerce

**com·mo·dore** (käm′ə dôr′) *n.* [prob. via Du. *kommandeur* < Fr. *commandeur*: see COMMAND] **1.** *U.S. Navy* formerly, an officer ranking above a captain: the rank was temporarily restored in World War II **2.** *Brit. Navy* a title for a captain temporarily heading a squadron or division of a fleet **3.** a courtesy title, as of the president of a yacht club

**com·mon** (käm′ən) *adj.* [< OFr. < L. *communis*, shared by all or many] **1.** belonging equally to, or shared by all **2.** belonging or relating to the community at large; public **3.** widely existing; general; prevalent **4.** notorious [a *common criminal*] **5.** familiar; usual **6.** not of the upper classes; of the masses [the *common people*] **7.** having no rank [a *common soldier*] **8.** below ordinary; inferior **9.** vulgar; low; coarse **10.** *Gram. a)* designating a noun that refers to any of a group or class, as *book, apple, street: b)* opposed to PROPER *b)* either masculine or feminine [the word *child* is of *common* gender] **11.** *Math.* belonging equally to two or more quantities [a *common* denominator] —*n.* [sometimes *pl.*] land owned or used by all the inhabitants of a place —**in common** equally with, or shared by, another or all concerned —**com′mon·ly** *adv.* —**com′mon·ness** *n.*

**com·mon·al·i·ty** (käm′ə nal′ə tē) *n.* **1.** the common people **2.** a sharing of common features, etc.

**com·mon·al·ty** (käm′ən əl tē) *n., pl.* **-ties** **1.** the common people **2.** a general body or group **3.** a corporation or its membership

**common carrier** a person or company in the business of transporting people or goods for a fee

**common cold** same as COLD (*n.* 4)

**com·mon·er** (-ər) *n.* one of the common people

**Common Era** same as CHRISTIAN ERA

**common fraction** a fraction whose numerator and denominator are both whole numbers

**common law** the law of a country or state based on custom, usage, and the decisions of law courts: separate from STATUTE LAW and now largely codified

**com·mon-law marriage** (käm′ən lô′) *Law* a marriage not solemnized by religious or civil ceremony but effected by agreement to live together as husband and wife and by the fact of such cohabitation

**common market** an association of countries formed to effect a closer economic union; specif., [C- M-] the European Economic Community

**com·mon·place** (-plās′) *n.* **1.** a trite or obvious remark; truism; platitude **2.** anything common or ordinary —*adj.* neither new nor interesting; obvious or ordinary —**com′·mon·place′ness** *n.*

**common pleas** *Law* in some States, a court having general and original jurisdiction over civil and criminal trials

**com·mons** (käm′ənz) *n.pl.* **1.** the common people **2.** [*often with sing. v.*] [C-] same as HOUSE OF COMMONS **3.** [*often with sing. v.*] food provided for meals in common for a whole group, or a dining room where such food is served, as at a college

**common sense** ordinary good sense or sound practical judgment —**com′mon-sense′**, **com′mon-sen′si·cal** (-sen′si k'l) *adj.*

**common stock** ordinary capital stock in a company without a definite dividend rate or the privileges of preferred stock

**common time** *Music* a meter of four beats to the measure; 4/4 time: also **common measure**

**com·mon·weal** (käm′ən wēl′) *n.* the public good; the general welfare

**com·mon·wealth** (-welth′) *n.* **1.** the people of a nation or state **2.** *a)* a democracy or republic *b)* a federation of states **3.** loosely, any State of the U.S.; strictly, Ky., Mass., Pa., or Va. **4.** a group of people united by common interests —**the Commonwealth 1.** the government in England under the Cromwells and Parliament (1649–1660) **2.** same as BRITISH COMMONWEALTH (OF NATIONS)

**com·mo·tion** (kə mō′shən) *n.* [< L. pp. of *commovere* < *com-*, together + *movere*, to move] **1.** violent motion; turbulence **2.** confusion; bustle

**com·mu·nal** (käm′yoon 'l, kə myoon′'l) *adj.* **1.** of a commune or communes **2.** of or belonging to the community; public **3.** designating of or social or economic organization in which there is common ownership of property —**com·mu′nal·ly** *adv.*

**com·mu·nal·ism** (-iz'm) *n.* **1.** a theory or system of government in which communes or local communities have virtual autonomy in a federated state **2.** communal organization; loosely, socialism —**com·mu′nal·ist** *n., adj.* —**com·mu′nal·is′tic** *adj.*

**com·mu·nal·ize** (-īz′) *vt.* **-ized′**, **-iz′ing** to make communal —**com·mu′nal·i·za′tion** *n.*

**com·mune¹** (kə myoon′; *for n.* käm′yoon) *vi.* **-muned′**, **-mun′ing** [< OFr. *comuner*, to share < *comun* (see COMMON)] **1.** *a)* to talk together intimately *b)* to be in close rapport [to *commune* with nature] **2.** to receive Holy Communion —*n.* [Poet.] intimate conversation —**commune with oneself** to ponder

**com·mune²** (käm′yoon) *n.* [< OFr., ult. < L. *communis*, COMMON] **1.** a community; specif., the smallest administrative district of local government in France, Belgium, and some other European countries **2.** a collective farm, as in China **3.** a small group of people living communally and sharing in work, earnings, etc. —**the Commune** the revolutionary government of Paris from 1792 to 1794 or in 1871

**com·mu·ni·ca·ble** (kə myoo′ni kə b'l) *adj.* **1.** that can be communicated, as an idea **2.** that can be transmitted, as a disease —**com·mu′ni·ca·bil′i·ty** *n.* —**com·mu′ni·ca·bly** *adv.*

**com·mu·ni·cant** (-kənt) *n.* a person who receives Holy Communion or belongs to a church celebrating this sacrament

**com·mu·ni·cate** (-kāt′) *vt.* **-cat′ed**, **-cat′ing** [< L. pp. of *communicare* < *communis*, COMMON] **1.** to pass along; impart; transmit **2.** to make known; give (information, etc.) —*vi.* **1.** to receive Holy Communion **2.** *a)* to give or exchange information, etc., as by talk, writing, etc. *b)* to have a sympathetic personal relationship **3.** to be connected [*communicating* rooms] —**com·mu′ni·ca′tor** *n.*

**com·mu·ni·ca·tion** (kə myoo′nə kā′shən) *n.* **1.** *a)* transmitting **2.** *a)* a giving or exchanging of information, etc. by talk, writing, etc. *b)* the information so given **3.** close, sympathetic relationship **4.** a means of communicating; specif., *a)* [*pl.*] a system for sending and receiving messages, as by telephone or radio *b)* [*pl.*] a system for moving troops and materiel *c)* a passage for getting from one place to another **5.** [*often pl., with sing. v.*] *a)* the art of expressing ideas *b)* the science of transmitting information

**com·mu·ni·ca·tive** (kə myoo′nə kāt′iv, -ni kə tiv) *adj.* **1.** giving information readily; talkative **2.** of communication —**com·mu′ni·ca′tive·ly** *adv.*

**com·mun·ion** (kə myoon′yən) *n.* [OFr. < L. < *communis*, COMMON] **1.** a sharing; possession in common **2.** a sharing of one's thoughts and emotions **3.** an intimate relationship with deep understanding **4.** a Christian denomination **5.** [C-] a sharing in, or celebrating, of, Holy Communion

**com·mu·ni·qué** (kə myoo′nə kā′; kə myoo′nə kā′) *n.* [Fr.] an official communication or bulletin

**com·mu·nism** (käm′yə niz'm) *n.* [< Fr.: see COMMON & -ISM] **1.** a theory or system based on the ownership of all property by the community as a whole **2.** [*often* C-] *a)* a hypothetical stage of socialism, as formulated by Marx, Engels, Lenin, etc., to be characterized by a classless and stateless society and the equal distribution of economic goods *b)* the form of government in the U.S.S.R., China, etc., professing to be working toward this stage **3.** [*often* C-] *a)* a political movement for establishing a Communist system *b)* the doctrines, methods, etc. of the Communist parties **4.** loosely, communalism See also SOCIALISM

**com·mu·nist** (-nist) *n.* **1.** an advocate or supporter of communism **2.** [C-] a member of a Communist Party —*adj.* **1.** of, characteristic of, or like communism or communists **2.** advocating or supporting communism **3.** [C-] designating or of a political party advocating Communism —**com′mu·nis′tic** *adj.* —**com′mu·nis′ti·cal·ly** *adv.*

**com·mu·ni·ty** (kə myoo′nə tē) *n., pl.* **-ties** [< OFr. < L. *communitas* < *communis*, COMMON] **1.** *a)* all the people living in a particular district, city, etc. *b)* the district, city, etc. where they live **2.** a group of people living together as a smaller social unit within a larger one, and having interests, work, etc. in common [a college *community*] **3.** a group of nations associated because of common traditions or for mutual advantage **4.** society; the public **5.** ownership or participation in common **6.** similarity; likeness [a *community* of tastes] **7.** friendly association **8.** *Ecology* a group of animals and plants living together and having close interactions

**community center** a meeting place in a community for cultural, recreational, or social activities

**community chest** (or **fund**) a fund collected annually in many cities and towns by private contributions for certain local welfare agencies

**community college** a junior college serving a certain community and supported by it in part

**com·mu·nize** (käm′yə nīz′) *vt.* **-nized′**, **-niz′ing** **1.** to subject to communal ownership and control **2.** to make communistic —**com′mu·ni·za′tion** *n.*

**com·mu·tate** (käm′yə tāt′) *vt.* **-tat′ed**, **-tat′ing** [back-formation < ff.] to change the direction of (an electric current); esp., to change (alternating current) to direct current

**com·mu·ta·tion** (käm′yə tā′shən) *n.* [< OFr. < L. < pp. of *commutare*, COMMUTE] **1.** an exchange; substitution **2.** the substitution of one kind of payment for another **3.** the act of traveling as a commuter **4.** *Elec.* change of the direction of a current by a commutator **5.** *Law* a change of a punishment to one that is less severe —**com·mu·ta·tive** (käm′yə tāt′iv, kə myōōt′ə tiv) *adj.*

**com·mu·ta·tor** (käm′yə tāt′ər) *n.* **1.** a device for commutating an electric current **2.** in a dynamo or motor, a revolving part that collects the current from, or distributes it to, the brushes

**com·mute** (kə myōōt′) *vt.* **-mut′ed, -mut′ing** [< L. *commutare* < *com-*, intens. + *mutare*, to change] **1.** to exchange; substitute **2.** to change (an obligation, punishment, etc.) to one that is less severe —*vi.* **1.** to be a substitute **2.** to travel as a commuter —**com·mut′a·ble** *adj.*

**com·mut·er** (-ər) *n.* a person who travels regularly, esp. by train, bus, etc., between two points at some distance

**Com·o·ros** (käm′ə rōs′) country on a group of islands in the Indian Ocean, between Mozambique and Madagascar: formerly a Fr. territory: 700 sq. mi.; pop. 292,000

**comp¹** (kämp) *vi.* [< ACCOMPANY] [Colloq.] *Jazz* to play an accompaniment: said of a pianist, guitarist, etc.

**comp²** (kämp) *n.* [< COMPLIMENTARY] [Slang] a free theater ticket, book, etc. given usually for promotional purposes

**comp.** **1.** comparative **2.** compare **3.** compiled **4.** composition **5.** compositor **6.** compound

**com·pact** (kəm pakt′; *also for adj., and for n. always,* käm′pakt) *adj.* [< L. pp. of *compingere* < *com-*, together + *pangere*, to fasten] **1.** closely and firmly packed; dense **2.** taking little space **3.** not wordy; terse **4.** composed (*of*) **5.** designating or of a small, economical model of automobile —*vt.* **1.** to pack or join firmly together **2.** to make by putting together **3.** to condense —*n.* **1.** a small cosmetic case, usually containing face powder and a mirror **2.** a compact automobile **3.** [< L. pp. of *compacisci*, to agree together] an agreement —**com·pact′ly** *adv.* —**com·pact′ness** *n.*

**com·pac·tor** (-pak′tər) *n.* a device that compresses trash into small bundles for easy disposal

**com·pan·ion¹** (kəm pan′yən) *n.* [< OFr. < hyp. VL. *companio*, messmate < L. *com-*, with + *panis*, bread] **1.** one who associates with or accompanies another or others; associate; comrade **2.** a person employed to live or travel with another **3.** a thing that matches another in sort, color, etc. —*vt.* to accompany —**com·pan′ion·ship′** *n.*

**com·pan·ion²** (kəm pan′yən) *n.* [< Du. < OFr. < It. (*camera della*) *compagna*, (room of the) company, crew] *Naut.* **1.** the covering at the head of a companionway **2.** a companionway

**com·pan·ion·a·ble** (-ə b'l) *adj.* having the qualities of a good companion; sociable —**com·pan′ion·a·bil′i·ty** *n.*

**com·pan·ion·ate** (-it) *adj.* of or characteristic of companions

**com·pan·ion·way** (-wā′) *n.* a stairway leading from the deck of a ship to the cabins or space below

**com·pa·ny** (kum′pə nē) *n., pl.* **-nies** [< OFr. < VL. hyp. *compania*, lit., group sharing bread: see COMPANION¹] **1.** companionship; society **2.** a group of people; specif., *a)* a group gathered for social purposes *b)* a group associated for some purpose [a business *company*] **3.** the partners who are not named in the title of a firm [John Smith and *Company*] **4.** a guest or guests **5.** one's habitual associates **6.** *Mil.* a body of troops, as of infantry, normally composed of two or more platoons **7.** *Naut.* the whole crew of a ship: in full, **ship's company** —**keep (a person) company** to stay with (a person) and provide companionship —**keep company 1.** to associate (*with*) **2.** to go together, as a couple intending to marry —**part company 1.** to stop associating (*with*) **2.** to separate and go in different directions

**compar.** **1.** comparative **2.** comparison

**com·pa·ra·ble** (käm′pər ə b'l; *occas.* kəm par′ə b'l) *adj.* **1.** that can be compared **2.** worthy of comparison —**com′pa·ra·bil′i·ty, com′pa·ra·ble·ness** *n.* —**com′pa·ra·bly** *adv.*

**com·par·a·tive** (kəm par′ə tiv) *adj.* **1.** that compares; involving comparison as a method [*comparative* linguistics] **2.** relative [*comparative* joy] **3.** *Gram.* designating or of the second degree of comparison of adjectives and adverbs: usually indicated by the suffix *-er* (*harder*) or by the use of *more* (*more beautiful*) —*n. Gram.* **1.** the comparative degree **2.** a word or form in this degree —**com·par′a·tive·ly** *adv.*

**com·pare** (kəm per′) *vt.* **-pared′, -par′ing** [< OFr. < L. *comparare* < *com-*, with + *par*, equal] **1.** to regard as similar; liken (*to*) **2.** to examine in order to observe similarities or differences (often followed by *with*) **3.** *Gram.* to form the positive, comparative, and superlative degrees of (an adjective or adverb) —*vi.* **1.** to be worthy of comparison (*with*) **2.** to be regarded as similar —*n.* [Poet.] comparison —**beyond** (or **past** or **without**) **compare** without equal

**com·par·i·son** (kəm par′ə s'n) *n.* **1.** a comparing or being compared; estimation of similarities and differences **2.** likeness; similarity [no *comparison* between the two] **3.** *Gram.* change in an adjective or adverb to show the positive, comparative, and superlative degrees (Ex.: *long, longer, longest; good, better, best; slowly, more slowly, most slowly*) —**in comparison with** compared with

**com·part·ment** (kəm pärt′mənt) *n.* [< Fr. < It. < LL. < L. *com-*, intens. + *partiri*, to divide < *pars*, a part] **1.** any of the divisions into which a space is partitioned off **2.** a separate section, part, division, or category —*vt. same as* COMPARTMENTALIZE —**com·part′men′tal** (-men′t'l) *adj.* —**com·part′ment·ed** *adj.*

**com·part·men·tal·ize** (kəm pärt′men′tə līz′) *vt.* **-ized′, -iz′ing** to put or separate into detached compartments, divisions, or categories —**com·part′men′tal·i·za′tion** *n.*

**com·pass** (kum′pəs) *vt.* [< OFr., ult. < L. *com-*, together +

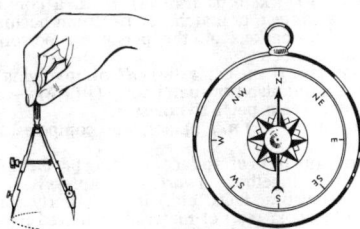

DRAWING COMPASS　　DIRECTIONAL COMPASS

*passus*, a step] **1.** to go round **2.** to surround; encircle **3.** to understand; comprehend **4.** to achieve; accomplish **5.** to plot or contrive (something harmful) —*n.* **1.** [*often pl.*] an instrument consisting of two pivoted legs, used for drawing arcs or circles or for taking measurements: also called **pair of compasses 2.** a boundary; circumference **3.** an enclosed area **4.** full extent or range; reach; scope; specif., range of tones, as of a voice **5.** an instrument for showing direction, esp. one consisting of a magnetic needle swinging freely on a pivot and pointing to the magnetic north —*adj.* round; circular or semicircular

**compass card** the circular card mounted on a free pivot inside a compass and marked with points of direction and, often, the degrees of the circle

**com·pas·sion** (kəm pash′ən) *n.* [OFr. < LL. *compassio*, ult. < L. *com-*, together + *pati*, to suffer] sorrow for the sufferings or trouble of another, with the urge to help; pity

**com·pas·sion·ate** (-it; *for v.* -āt′) *adj.* feeling or showing compassion; sympathizing deeply —*vt.* **-at′ed, -at′ing** to pity —**com·pas′sion·ate·ly** *adv.*

**com·pat·i·ble** (kəm pat′ə b'l) *adj.* [Fr. < LL.: see COMPASSION] **1.** capable of living together harmoniously or getting along well together; in agreement **2.** that can be mixed without adverse effects: said of drugs, etc. **3.** *TV* designating or of a system of color transmission producing satisfactory black and white pictures —**com·pat′i·bil′i·ty, com·pat′i·ble·ness** *n.* —**com·pat′i·bly** *adv.*

**com·pa·tri·ot** (kəm pā′trē ət; *chiefly Brit.* -pat′rē-) *n.* [< Fr. < LL. *compatriota*: see COM- & PATRIOT] **1.** a fellow countryman **2.** a colleague —*adj.* of the same country

**com·peer** (käm′pir, kəm pir′) *n.* [< OFr. < L. < *com-*, with + *par*, equal] **1.** an equal; peer **2.** a companion; comrade

**com·pel** (kəm pel′) *vt.* **-pelled′, -pel′ling** [< OFr. < L. *compellere* < *com-*, together + *pellere*, to drive] **1.** to force or constrain, as to do something **2.** to get or bring about by force —**com·pel′ler** *n.* —**com·pel′ling·ly** *adv.*

**com·pen·di·ous** (kəm pen′dē əs) *adj.* [L. *compendiosus*: see ff.] containing all the essentials in a brief form; concise but comprehensive —**com·pen′di·ous·ly** *adv.* —**com·pen′di·ous·ness** *n.*

**com·pen·di·um** (-əm) *n., pl.* **-di·ums, -di·a** (-ə) [L., an abridgment < *com-*, together + *pendere*, to weigh] a summary containing the essential information in a brief form; concise but comprehensive treatise

**com·pen·sa·ble** (kəm pen′sə b'l) *adj.* entitling to compensation

**com·pen·sate** (käm′pən sāt′) *vt.* **-sat′ed, -sat′ing** [< L. pp. of *compensare* < *com-*, with + *pensare*, freq. of *pendere*, to weigh] **1.** to make up for; counterbalance in weight, force, etc. **2.** to make equivalent return to; recompense —*vi.* to make or serve as compensation or amends (*for*) —**com·pen·sa·tive** (käm′pən sāt′iv, kəm pen′sə tiv) *adj.* —**com′pen·sa′tor** *n.* —**com·pen·sa·to·ry** (kəm pen′sə tôr′ē) *adj.*

**com·pen·sa·tion** (käm′pən sā′shən) *n.* **1.** a compensating or being compensated **2.** *a)* anything given as an equivalent, or to make amends for a loss, etc. *b)* payment for services; esp., wages **3.** the counterbalancing of a defect by a greater activity or development of some other part, quality, etc. —**com′pen·sa′tion·al** *adj.*

**com·pete** (kəm pēt′) *vi.* -**pet′ed,** -**pet′ing** [< L. *competere* < *com-*, together + *petere,* to seek] to enter into or be in rivalry; contend; vie (*in* a contest, etc.)

**com·pe·tence** (käm′pə təns) *n.* [< Fr. < L. < prp. of *competere:* see prec.] **1.** sufficient means for one's needs **2.** ability; fitness; specif., legal capability, power, or jurisdiction Also **com′pe·ten·cy**

**com·pe·tent** (-tənt) *adj.* [< OFr. < L. prp. of *competere:* see COMPETE] **1.** well qualified; capable; fit **2.** sufficient; adequate **3.** *Law* legally qualified or fit —**com′pe·tent·ly** *adv.*

**com·pe·ti·tion** (käm′pə tish′ən) *n.* **1.** a competing; rivalry **2.** a contest, or match **3.** rivalry in business, as for customers or markets **4.** the person or persons against whom one competes

**com·pet·i·tive** (kəm pet′ə tiv) *adj.* of, involving, or based on competition: also **com·pet′i·to·ry** (-tôr′ē) —**com·pet′i·tive·ly** *adv.* —**com·pet′i·tive·ness** *n.*

**com·pet·i·tor** (-tər) *n.* a person who competes, as a business rival

**com·pile** (kəm pīl′) *vt.* -**piled′,** -**pil′ing** [< OFr. < L. *compilare* < *com-*, together + *pilare,* to compress] **1.** to gather together (statistics, facts, etc.) in an orderly form **2.** to compose (a book, etc.) of materials gathered from various sources —**com·pi·la·tion** (käm′pə lā′shən) *n.* —**com·pil′er** *n.*

**com·pla·cen·cy** (kəm plās′'n sē) *n.* [< LL. < L.: see ff.] quiet satisfaction; contentment; often, self-satisfaction, or smugness: also **com·pla′cence**

**com·pla·cent** (-'nt) *adj.* [< L. prp. of *complacere* < *com-*, intens. + *placere,* please] **1.** self-satisfied; smug **2.** affable; complaisant —**com·pla′cent·ly** *adv.*

**com·plain** (kəm plān′) *vi.* [< OFr. < VL. *complangere* < L. *com-*, intens. + *plangere,* to strike (the breast)] **1.** to express pain, displeasure, etc. **2.** to find fault **3.** to make an accusation or a formal charge —**com·plain′er** *n.* —**com·plain′ing·ly** *adv.*

**com·plain·ant** (-ənt) *n. Law* one who files a charge or makes the complaint in court; plaintiff

**com·plaint** (kəm plānt′) *n.* **1.** a complaining; utterance of pain, displeasure, annoyance, etc. **2.** a subject or cause for complaining **3.** an illness; ailment **4.** *Law* a formal charge

**com·plai·sant** (kəm plā′z'nt, -s'nt) *adj.* [< Fr. < prp. of *complaire* < L. *complacere:* see COMPLACENT] willing to please; affably agreeable; obliging —**com·plai′sance** *n.* —**com·plai′sant·ly** *adv.*

**com·plect·ed** (kəm plek′tid) *adj.* [altered < COMPLEXIONED] [Dial. or Colloq.] *same as* COMPLEXIONED

**com·ple·ment** (käm′plə mənt; *for v.* -ment′) *n.* [L. *complementum* < *complere:* see COMPLETE] **1.** that which completes or brings to perfection **2.** the amount needed to fill or complete **3.** a complete set; entirety **4.** either of two parts that complete each other **5.** *Gram.* a word or words that complete the meaning of the predicate (Ex.: *foreman* in *make him foreman, paid* in *he expects to get paid*) **6.** *Math.* the number of degrees added to an angle or arc to make it equal 90 degrees —*vt.* to make complete; be a complement to

**com·ple·men·ta·ry** (käm′plə men′tər ē) *adj.* **1.** acting as a complement; completing **2.** mutually making up what is lacking Also **com′ple·men′tal** —**com′ple·men·tar′i·ty** (-ter′ə tē) *n.*

**complementary angle** either of two angles that together form a 90° angle

**complementary colors** any two colors of the spectrum that combine to form white light

**com·plete** (kəm plēt′) *adj.* [< OFr. < L. pp. of *complere* < *com-*, intens. + *plere,* to fill] **1.** lacking no component part; entire **2.** ended; finished **3.** thorough; absolute —*vt.* -**plet′ed,** -**plet′ing 1.** to end; finish **2.** to make whole, full, or perfect —**com·plete′ly** *adv.* —**com·plete′-ness** *n.*

COMPLEMENT
(arc YM, complement of arc WY; angle YXM, complement of angle WXY)

**com·ple·tion** (kəm plē′shən) *n.* **1.** a completing, or finishing **2.** the state of being completed

**com·plex** (kəm pleks′; *also, and for n. always,* käm′pleks) *adj.* [< L. pp. of *complecti* < *com-*, with + *plectere,* to weave] **1.** consisting of two or more related parts **2.** not simple; complicated —*n.* **1.** a group of related ideas, activities, things, etc. that form, or are viewed as forming, a single whole **2.** *Psychoanalysis a)* a group of largely unconscious impulses, ideas, and emotions related to a particular object, activity, etc., strongly influencing the individual's behavior *b)* popularly, an exaggerated dislike or fear —**com·plex′ly** *adv.* —**com·plex′ness** *n.*

**complex fraction** a fraction with a fraction in its numerator or denominator, or in both

**com·plex·ion** (kəm plek′shən) *n.* [OFr. < L. < *complexus:* see COMPLEX] **1.** one's temperament or disposition **2.** the color, texture, etc. of the skin, esp. of the face **3.** general appearance or nature; character; aspect —**com·plex′ion·al** *adj.*

**com·plex·ioned** (-shənd) *adj.* having a (specified) complexion [*light-complexioned*]

**com·plex·i·ty** (kəm plek′sə tē) *n.* **1.** a complex condition or quality **2.** *pl.* -**ties** anything complex or intricate; complication

**complex sentence** a sentence consisting of a main clause and one or more subordinate clauses

**com·pli·ance** (kəm plī′əns) *n.* **1.** a complying, or giving in to a request, demand, etc. **2.** a tendency to give in readily to others Also **com·pli′an·cy** —**in compliance with** complying with

**com·pli·ant** (-ənt) *adj.* complying; yielding; submissive —**com·pli′ant·ly** *adv.*

**com·pli·cate** (käm′plə kāt′) *vt.,* *vi.* -**cat′ed,** -**cat′ing** [< L. pp. of *complicare* < *com-*, together + *plicare,* to fold] to make or become intricate, difficult, or involved

**com·pli·cat·ed** (-kāt′id) *adj.* intricately involved; hard to untangle, solve, analyze, etc. —**com′pli·cat′ed·ly** *adv.* —**com′pli·cat′ed·ness** *n.*

**com·pli·ca·tion** (käm′plə kā′shən) *n.* **1.** a complicating **2.** a complicated condition or structure **3.** a complicating factor, as in the plot of a story **4.** *Med.* a second disease or abnormal condition occurring during the course of a primary disease

**com·plic·i·ty** (kəm plis′ə tē) *n., pl.* -**ties** [< Fr. < L. *complex* (gen. *complicis*): see COMPLEX] the fact or state of being an accomplice in wrongdoing

**com·pli·ment** (käm′plə mənt; *for v.* -ment′) *n.* [Fr. < It., ult. < L. *complere,* to COMPLETE] **1.** a formal act of courtesy **2.** something said in praise **3.** [*pl.*] respects —*vt.* **1.** to pay a compliment to **2.** to present something to (a person) to show respect

**com·pli·men·ta·ry** (käm′plə men′tər ē) *adj.* **1.** paying or containing a compliment **2.** given free as a courtesy [a *complimentary* ticket] —**com′pli·men·tar′i·ly** (-men ter′ə lē, -men′tər ə lē) *adv.*

**com·pline, com·plin** (käm′plən) *n.* [< OFr. < L. *completus:* see COMPLETE] *Eccles.* [often C-] the last of the seven canonical hours: also **com′plines, com′plins** (-plənz)

**com·ply** (kəm plī′) *vi.* -**plied′,** -**ply′ing** [< OFr. < L. *complere:* see COMPLETE] to act in accordance (*with* a request, order, rule, etc.) —**com·pli′er** *n.*

**com·po·nent** (kəm pō′nənt) *adj.* [< L. prp. of *componere:* see COMPOSITE] serving as one of the parts of a whole —*n.* **1.** an element or ingredient **2.** a main constituent part, as of a hi-fi set

**com·port** (kəm pôrt′) *vt.* [< OFr. < L. *comportare* < *com-*, together + *portare,* to bring] to behave (oneself) in a specified manner —*vi.* to agree or accord (*with*) —**com·port′-ment** *n.*

**com·pose** (kəm pōz′) *vt.* -**posed′,** -**pos′ing** [< OFr. *composer* < *com-*, with + *poser,* to place] **1.** to make up; constitute **2.** to put in proper order or form **3.** to create (a musical or literary work) **4.** to adjust or settle [*to compose* differences] **5.** to calm (oneself, one's mind, etc.); allay **6.** *Printing* to set (type) —*vi.* **1.** to create musical or literary works **2.** to set type

**com·posed** (-pōzd′) *adj.* calm; tranquil; self-possessed —**com·pos′ed·ly** (-pō′zid lē) *adv.* —**com·pos′ed·ness** *n.*

**com·pos·er** (-pō′zər) *n.* a person who composes, esp. one who composes music

**com·pos·ite** (kəm päz′it) *adj.* [< L. pp. of *componere* < *com-*, together + *ponere,* to put] **1.** formed of distinct parts; compound **2.** designating a large family of plants, as the daisy, chrysanthemum, etc., having flower heads composed of dense clusters of small flowers **3.** [C-] *Archit.* designating the classic order which combines features of the Ionic and Corinthian capitals —*n.* **1.** a thing of distinct parts **2.** a composite plant —**com·pos′ite·ly** *adv.*

**composite photograph** a photograph made by superimposing one or more photographs on another

**com·po·si·tion** (käm′pə zish′ən) *n.* **1.** a composing; specif., *a)* the art of writing *b)* the creation of musical works **2.** the makeup of a thing or person; constitution **3.** that which is composed; specif., *a)* a mixture of several parts or ingredients *b)* a work of music, literature, or art *c)* an exercise in writing done as schoolwork **4.** an aesthetically unified arrangement of parts **5.** an agreement, or settlement, often by compromise **6.** *Printing* the work of setting type —**com′po·si′tion·al** *adj.*

**com·pos·i·tor** (kəm päz′ə tər) *n.* a person who sets type; typesetter

**com·pos men·tis** (käm′pəs men′tis) [L.] *Law* of sound mind; sane

**com·post** (käm′pōst) *n.* [< OFr. < L.: see COMPOSITE] **1.** a compound **2.** a mixture of decomposing vegetation, manure, etc. for fertilizing soil

**com·po·sure** (kəm pō′zhər) *n.* [COMPOS(E) + -URE] calmness; tranquillity; self-possession

**com·pote** (käm′pōt) *n.* [Fr.: see COMPOST] **1.** a dish of fruits stewed in a syrup **2.** a long-stemmed dish for serving candy, fruit, etc.

**com·pound**[1] (käm pound′, kəm-; *for n. and, usually, for adj.,* käm′pound) *vt.* [< OFr. < L. *componere:* see COMPOSITE] **1.** to mix or combine **2.** to make by combining parts **3.** to settle by mutual agreement **4.** to settle (a debt) by compromise payment **5.** to intensify by adding new elements [to *compound* a problem] **6.** to compute (interest) as compound interest —*vi.* to agree or compromise —*adj.* made up of two or more separate parts or elements —*n.* **1.** a thing formed by the combination of parts **2.** a substance containing two or more elements chemically combined in fixed proportions: distinguished from MIXTURE in that a compound has characteristics different from those of its constituents **3.** a word composed of two or more base morphemes —**compound a felony** (or **crime**) to agree, for payment, not to inform about or prosecute for a felony (or crime)

**com·pound**[2] (käm′pound) *n.* [Anglo-Ind. < Malay *kampong*] **1.** in the Orient, an enclosed space with a building or group of buildings in it, esp. if occupied by foreigners **2.** any similar space

**compound eye** an eye made up of numerous simple eyes functioning collectively, as in insects

**compound fraction** *same as* COMPLEX FRACTION

**compound fracture** a bone fracture in which broken ends of bone have pierced the skin

**compound interest** interest paid on both the principal and the accumulated unpaid interest

**compound leaf** a leaf divided into two or more leaflets with a common leafstalk

**compound number** a quantity expressed in two or more sorts of related units (Ex.: 4 ft., 7 in.)

**compound sentence** a sentence consisting of two or more independent, coordinate clauses

**com·pre·hend** (käm′prə hend′) *vt.* [< L. *comprehendere* < *com-*, with + *prehendere*, to seize] **1.** to grasp mentally; understand **2.** to include; comprise —**com′pre·hend′ing·ly** *adv.*

**com·pre·hen·si·ble** (-hen′sə b′l) *adj.* that can be comprehended; intelligible —**com′pre·hen′si·bil′i·ty** *n.* —**com′pre·hen′si·bly** *adv.*

**com·pre·hen·sion** (-hen′shən) *n.* **1.** the fact of including or comprising; inclusiveness **2.** the act of or capacity for understanding

**com·pre·hen·sive** (-hen′siv) *adj.* **1.** including much; inclusive **2.** able to comprehend fully —**com′pre·hen′sive·ly** *adv.* —**com′pre·hen′sive·ness** *n.*

**com·press** (kəm pres′; *for n.* käm′pres) *vt.* [< OFr. < LL. < L. pp. of *comprimere* < *com-*, together + *premere*, to press] to press together; make more compact as by pressure —*n.* **1.** a pad of folded cloth, often medicated or wet, for applying pressure, heat, cold, etc. to a part of the body **2.** a machine for compressing cotton bales —**compressed′** *adj.* —**com·pres′si·bil′i·ty** *n.* —**com·pres′si·ble** *adj.* —**com·pres′sive·ly** *adv.*

**compressed air** air held under pressure in a container: its expansive force can operate machines

**com·pres·sion** (kəm presh′ən) *n.* **1.** a compressing or being compressed **2.** the compressing of a working fluid in an engine, as of the mixture in an internal-combustion engine just before ignition

**com·pres·sor** (-pres′ər) *n.* **1.** one that compresses **2.** a muscle that compresses a part **3.** a machine for compressing air, gas, etc.

**com·prise** (-prīz′) *vt.* **-prised′, -pris′ing** [< OFr. pp. of *comprendre:* see COMPREHEND] **1.** to include; contain **2.** to consist of [a nation *comprising* fifty States] **3.** to make up; form [a nation *comprised* of fifty States]: in this sense regarded by some as a loose usage —**com·pris′a·ble** *adj.* —**com·pris′al** *n.*

**com·pro·mise** (käm′prə mīz′) *n.* [< OFr. < LL. < L. pp. of *compromittere* < *com-*, together + *promittere*, to PROMISE] **1.** a settlement in which each side makes concessions **2.** the result of such a settlement **3.** something midway between two other things **4.** *a)* exposure, as of one's reputation, to danger, suspicion, or disrepute *b)* a weakening, as of one's principles —*vt.* **-mised′, -mis′ing 1.** to settle by concessions on both sides **2.** to lay open to danger, suspicion, or disrepute **3.** to weaken (one's principles, etc.) —*vi.* to make a compromise —**com′pro·mis′er** *n.*

**Comp·ton** (kämp′tən) [after G. *Compton*, a founder of the U. of S Cal.] city in SW Calif.: suburb of Los Angeles: pop. 81,000

**comp·trol·ler** (kən trō′lər) *n.* [altered (after Fr. *compte*, an account) < CONTROLLER] *same as* CONTROLLER (sense 1) —**comp·trol′ler·ship′** *n.*

**com·pul·sion** (kəm pul′shən) *n.* [< LL. < L. pp. of *compellere*] **1.** a compelling or being compelled; coercion **2.** a driving force **3.** *Psychol.* an irresistible, repeated, irrational impulse to perform some act

**com·pul·sive** (-siv) *adj.* of, having to do with, or resulting from compulsion —**com·pul′sive·ly** *adv.* —**com·pul′sive·ness** *n.*

**com·pul·so·ry** (-sər ē) *adj.* **1.** obligatory; required **2.** compelling; coercive —**com·pul′so·ri·ly** *adv.* —**com·pul′so·ri·ness** *n.*

**com·punc·tion** (kəm puŋk′shən) *n.* [< OFr. < LL. *compunctio*, a pricking (of conscience) < L. *com-*, intens. + *pungere*, to prick] **1.** a sharp feeling of uneasiness brought on by a sense of guilt; remorse **2.** a feeling of slight regret for something done —**com·punc′tious** *adj.* —**com·punc′tious·ly** *adv.*

**com·pu·ta·tion** (käm′pyoo tā′shən) *n.* **1.** a computing; calculation **2.** a method of computing **3.** a computed amount —**com′pu·ta′tion·al** *adj.*

**com·pute** (kəm pyoot′) *vt., vi.* **-put′ed, -put′ing** [ L. *computare* < *com-*, with + *putare*, to reckon] to determine (an amount, etc.) by reckoning; calculate —**com·put′a·bil′i·ty** *n.* —**com·put′a·ble** *adj.*

**com·put·er** (kəm pyoot′ər) *n.* a person or thing that computes; specif., an electronic machine that performs rapid, often complex calculations or compiles, correlates, and selects data: see also ANALOG COMPUTER, DIGITAL COMPUTER

**com·put·er·ize** (-īz′) *vt.* **-ized′, -iz′ing** to equip with, or operate, produce, control, etc. by or as if by means of, an electronic computer —**com·put′er·i·za′tion** *n.*

**com·rade** (käm′rad, -rəd) *n.* [< Fr. < Sp. *camarada*, chamber mate < L. *camera:* see CAMERA] **1.** a friend; close companion **2.** one who shares interests and activities in common with others; associate **3.** [C-] [Colloq.] a Communist —**com′rade·ly** *adj.* —**com′rade·ship′** *n.*

**comrade in arms** a fellow soldier

**com·rade·ry** (-rē) *n. same as* CAMARADERIE

‡**comte** (kōnt) *n.* [Fr.] *same as* COUNT[2] —**com·tesse** (kōn·tes′) *n.fem.*

**Comte** (kōnt; *E.* kōmt), (Isidore) Au·guste (ô güst′) 1798–1857; Fr. philosopher: founder of positivism —**Com·ti·an, Com·te·an** (käm′tē ən, kōm′-) *adj.*

**con**[1] (kän) *adv.* [contr. < L. *contra*, against] against; in opposition [to argue pro and *con*] —*n.* a reason, vote, position, etc. in opposition

**con**[2] (kän) *vt.* **conned, con′ning** [ME. *connen*, to be able: see CAN[1]] to peruse or learn carefully

**con**[3] (kän) *vt., n. same as* CONN

**con**[4] (kän) *adj.* [Slang] confidence [a *con* man] —*vt.* **conned, con′ning** [Slang] **1.** to swindle (a victim) by first gaining his confidence **2.** to trick or fool, esp. by glib, persuasive talk

**con**[5] (kän) *n.* [Slang] a convict

**con.** **1.** concerto **2.** conclusion **3.** consolidated

**Con·a·kry** (kän′ə krē′) capital of Guinea; seaport on the Atlantic: pop. 120,000

**con a·mo·re** (kän′ə môr′e; *It.* kôn′ä mô′re) [It.] with love; tenderly: a direction in music

**con bri·o** (kän brē′ō, kōn) [It.] with spirit; spiritedly: a direction in music

**con·cat·e·nate** (kän kat′′n āt′, kən-) *adj.* [< LL. pp. of *concatenare* < L. < *com-*, together + *catenare* < *catena*, a chain] linked together; connected —*vt.* **-nat′ed, -nat′ing** to link or join, as in a chain

**con·cat·e·na·tion** (kän kat′′n ā′shən, kən-) *n.* **1.** a linking together or being linked together **2.** a series of things or events regarded as causally connected

**con·cave** (kän kāv′; *also, and for n. usually,* kän′kāv) *adj.* [< OFr. < L. < *com-*, intens. + *cavus*, hollow] hollow and curved like the inside half of a hollow ball —*n.* a concave surface, line, object, etc. —*vt.* **-caved′, -cav′ing** to make concave —**con·cave′ly** *adv.* —**con·cave′ness** *n.*

**con·cav·i·ty** (kän kav′ə tē) n. 1. the quality or condition of being concave 2. pl. -ties a concave surface, line, etc.

**con·ca·vo-con·cave** (kän kā′vō kän kāv′) adj. concave on both sides, as some lenses

**con·ca·vo-con·vex** (-kän veks′) adj. concave on one side and convex on the other

**con·ceal** (kən sēl′) vt. [< OFr. < L. concelare < com-, together + celare, to hide] 1. to put out of sight; hide 2. to keep from another's knowledge; keep secret [to conceal one's amusement] —con·ceal′ment n.

**con·cede** (kən sēd′) vt. -ced′ed, -ced′ing [L. concedere < com-, with + cedere, to cede] 1. to admit as true; acknowledge 2. to admit as certain 3. to grant as a right —vi. 1. to make a concession 2. to acknowledge defeat in an election —con·ced′er n.

**con·ceit** (kən sēt′) n. [see CONCEIVE] 1. orig., an idea 2. an exaggerated opinion of oneself, one's merits, etc.; vanity 3. a fanciful or witty expression or notion; often, specif., a strained or bizarre figure of speech 4. a flight of imagination; fancy

**con·ceit·ed** (-id) adj. having an exaggerated opinion of oneself, one's merits, etc.; vain —con·ceit′ed·ly adv. —con·ceit′ed·ness n.

**con·ceiv·a·ble** (kən sē′və b'l) adj. that can be conceived, understood, imagined, or believed —con·ceiv′a·bil′i·ty n. —con·ceiv′a·bly adv.

**con·ceive** (kən sēv′) vt. -ceived′, -ceiv′ing [< OFr. < L. concipere, to receive < com-, together + capere, to take] 1. to become pregnant with 2. to form in the mind 3. to think; imagine 4. to understand 5. to express in words —vi. 1. to become pregnant 2. to form an idea (of)

**con·cel·e·brate** (kän sel′ə brāt′) vt. -brat′ed, -brat′ing [< L. pp. of concelebrare: see COM- & CELEBRATE] to celebrate (the Eucharistic liturgy) jointly: said of two or more priests —con′cel·e·bra′tion n.

**con·cen·ter** (kən sen′tər) vt., vi. [< Fr. < L. com-, together + centrum, CENTER] to bring or come to a common center; concentrate or converge

**con·cen·trate** (kän′sən trāt′) vt. -trat′ed, -trat′ing [< prec. + -ATE¹] 1. to bring to a common center 2. to focus (one's thoughts, efforts, etc.) 3. to increase the strength, density, or intensity of —vi. 1. to come to a common center 2. to fix one's attention (on or upon) —n. a substance that has been concentrated —adj. concentrated —con′cen·tra′tive adj. —con′cen·tra′tor n.

**con·cen·tra·tion** (kän′sən trā′shən) n. 1. a concentrating or being concentrated 2. close or fixed attention 3. strength or density, as of a solution

**concentration camp** a prison camp in which political dissidents, members of minority ethnic groups, etc. are confined

**con·cen·tric** (kən sen′trik) adj. [< OFr. < ML. < L. com-, together + centrum, CENTER] having a center in common [concentric circles]: also con·cen′tri·cal —con·cen′tri·cal·ly adv. —con·cen·tric·i·ty (kän′sen tris′ə tē) n.

**Con·cep·ción** (kən sep′sē ōn′; Sp. kōn sep′syōn′) seaport on a river in SC Chile: pop. 202,000

**con·cept** (kän′sept) n. [< L. pp. of concipere: see CONCEIVE] an idea or thought, esp. a generalized idea of a class of objects; abstract notion

**con·cep·tion** (kən sep′shən) n. 1. a conceiving or being conceived in the womb 2. an embryo or fetus 3. the beginning of some process, etc. 4. the formulation of ideas 5. a mental impression; concept 6. an original idea, design, plan, etc. —con·cep′tion·al adj. —con·cep′tive adj.

**con·cep·tu·al** (kən sep′choo wəl) adj. of conception or concepts —con·cep′tu·al·ly adv.

**con·cep·tu·al·ize** (-īz′) vt. -ized′, -iz′ing to form a concept or idea of; conceive —con·cep′tu·al·i·za′tion n.

**con·cern** (kən surn′) vt. [< ML. < LL. concernere < L. com-, with + cernere, to sift] 1. to have a relation to; deal with 2. to engage or involve; be a proper affair of 3. to make uneasy or anxious —n. 1. a matter of interest or importance to one; affair 2. interest in or regard for a person or thing 3. relation; reference 4. worry; anxiety 5. a business firm —as concerns in regard to —concern oneself 1. to busy oneself (with, about, over, in something) 2. to be worried, anxious, or uneasy

**con·cerned** (-surnd′) adj. 1. involved or interested (often with in) 2. uneasy or anxious

**con·cern·ing** (-sur′niŋ) prep. relating to; having to do with; in regard to; about

**con·cern·ment** (-surn′mənt) n. [Rare] concern; specif., a) an affair; matter b) importance c) worry

**con·cert** (kən surt′; for n. & adj. kän′sərt) vt., vi. [Fr. < It. < L. concertare < com-, with + certare, to strive] to arrange by mutual understanding; plan together; devise —n. 1. mutual agreement; concord 2. musical consonance 3. a program of vocal or instrumental music —adj. of or for concerts —in concert in unison; together

**con·cert·ed** (kən sur′tid) adj. 1. mutually arranged or agreed upon; done together 2. Music arranged in parts —con·cert′ed·ly adv.

**con·cer·ti·na** (kän′sər tē′nə) n. [CONCERT + -INA: a coinage] a small musical instrument similar to an accordion, with buttons instead of a keyboard

**con·cert·ize** (kän′sər tīz′) vi. -ized′, -iz′ing to perform as a soloist in concerts

**con·cert·mas·ter** (kän′sərt mas′tər) n. [transl. of G. konzertmeister] the leader of the first violins of a symphony orchestra, often an assistant to the conductor: also con′cert·meis′ter (-mīs′-)

CONCERTINA

**con·cer·to** (kən cher′tō) n., pl. -tos, -ti (-tē) [It.: see CONCERT] a composition, usually in three movements in symphonic form, for one or more solo instruments and an orchestra

**con·ces·sion** (kən sesh′ən) n. 1. a conceding 2. a thing conceded; acknowledgment, as of an argument 3. a privilege granted by a government, company, etc.; esp., a) the right to use land b) the right to sell food, parking space, etc. on the lessor's premises —con·ces′sive (-ses′iv) adj.

**con·ces·sion·aire** (kən sesh′ə ner′) n. [Fr. concessionnaire] the holder of a concession granted by a government, company, etc.: also con·ces′sion·er

**con·ces·sion·ar·y** (kən sesh′ə ner′ē) adj. of a concession —n., pl. -ar′ies a concessionaire

**conch** (käŋk, känch) n., pl. conchs (käŋks), conch·es (kän′chəz) [< L. < Gr. konchē] 1. the spiral, one-piece shell of various sea mollusks 2. such a mollusk, often edible

**con·chol·o·gy** (käŋ käl′ə jē) n. [see prec. & -LOGY] the branch of zoology that deals with mollusks and shells —con·chol′o·gist n.

**con·ci·erge** (kän′sē urzh′; Fr. kōn syerzh′) n. [Fr.] 1. a doorkeeper 2. a custodian or head porter

**con·cil·i·ar** (kən sil′ē ər) adj. [< L. concilium, COUNCIL] of, from, or by means of a council

**con·cil·i·ate** (-āt′) vt. -at′ed, -at′ing [< L. pp. of conciliare < concilium, COUNCIL] 1. to win over; make friendly; placate 2. to gain (regard, good will, etc.) by friendly acts 3. [Archaic] to reconcile; make consistent —con·cil′i·a·ble adj. —con·cil′i·a′tion n. —con·cil′i·a′tor n.

**con·cil·i·a·to·ry** (-ə tôr′ē) adj. tending to conciliate or reconcile: also con·cil′i·a′tive (-āt′iv)

**con·cise** (kən sīs′) adj. [< L. pp. of concidere < com-, intens. + caedere, to cut] brief and to the point; short and clear —con·cise′ly adv. —con·cise′ness, con·ci′sion (-sizh′ən) n.

**con·clave** (kän′klāv, käŋ′-) n. [OFr. < L., a room, closet < com-, with + clavis, a key] 1. R.C.Ch. a) the private meeting of the cardinals to elect a pope b) the cardinals collectively 2. any private or secret meeting

**con·clude** (kən klood′) vt. -clud′ed, -clud′ing [< L. concludere < com-, together + claudere, to shut] 1. to bring to a close; end; finish 2. to decide by reasoning; infer; deduce 3. to decide (to do something); determine 4. to settle; come to an agreement about —vi. 1. to come to a close; end; finish 2. to come to an agreement

**con·clu·sion** (kən kloo′zhən) n. 1. the end or last part; as, a) the last division of a discourse b) the last step in a reasoning process; judgment or opinion formed after thought c) the last of a chain of events; outcome 2. a concluding; final arrangement (of a pact, treaty, etc.) —in conclusion lastly; in closing

**con·clu·sive** (-siv) adj. that settles a question; final; decisive —con·clu′sive·ly adv. —con·clu′sive·ness n.

**con·coct** (kən käkt′, kän-) vt. [< L. pp. of concoquere < com-, together + coquere, to cook] 1. to make by combining ingredients 2. to devise; plan —con·coct′er n. —con·coc′tion n. —con·coc′tive adj.

**con·com·i·tance** (kən käm′ə təns) n. the fact of being concomitant: also con·com′i·tan·cy

**con·com·i·tant** (-käm′ə tənt) adj. [< L. prp. of concomitari < com-, together + comitari, to accompany < comes, companion] accompanying; attendant —n. an accompanying or attendant condition, circumstance, or thing —con·com′i·tant·ly adv.

**Con·cord** (käŋ′kôrd; for 2 & 3 & n. kän′kərd) [< ?] 1. city in W Calif., near Oakland: pop. 103,000 2. capital of N.H., in the SC part: pop. 30,000 3. town in E Mass., near Boston: site of one of the 1st battles of the Revolutionary War: pop. 16,000 —n. 1. a large, dark-blue grape: in full, Concord grape 2. a wine made from it

**con·cord** (kän′kôrd, käŋ′-) n. [< OFr. < L. < concors (gen. concordis), of the same mind < com-, together + cor, heart] 1. agreement; harmony 2. a) peaceful relations, as between nations b) a treaty establishing this 3. Gram. same as AGREEMENT 4. musical consonance

**con·cord·ance** (kən kôr′d'ns, kän-) n. [see CONCORD]

**1.** agreement; harmony **2.** an alphabetical list of the important words of a book or author, with references to the passages in which they occur

**con·cord·ant** (-d'nt) *adj.* agreeing; consonant; harmonious —**con·cord′ant·ly** *adv.*

**con·cor·dat** (-dat) *n.* [Fr. < ML. < L. pp. of *concordare*, to agree < *concors*: see CONCORD] **1.** a compact; formal agreement **2.** an agreement between a pope and a government concerning church affairs

**con·course** (kän′kôrs, käŋ′-) *n.* [< OFr. < L. < *concurrere*: see CONCUR] **1.** a coming or flowing together **2.** a crowd; throng **3.** a large open space where crowds gather, as in a park or airport terminal **4.** a broad boulevard

**con·crete** (kän krēt′; *also, and for n. & vt. 2 usually,* kän′-krēt) *adj.* [< L. pp. of *concrescere* < *com-*, together + *crescere*, to grow] **1.** formed into a solid mass; coalesced **2.** having a material, perceptible existence; real; actual **3.** specific, not general or abstract **4.** made of concrete **5.** *Gram.* designating a thing or class of things that can be perceived by the senses; not abstract —*n.* **1.** a concrete thing, idea, etc. **2.** a building material of sand and gravel bonded with cement into a hard substance: used in making bridges, road surfaces, etc. —*vt.* **-cret′ed, -cret′ing 1.** to form into a mass; solidify **2.** to cover with concrete —*vi.* to solidify —**con·crete′ly** *adv.* —**con·crete′ness** *n.*

**con·cre·tion** (kän krē′shən) *n.* [see prec.] **1.** a solidifying or being solidified **2.** a solidified mass

**con·cre·tize** (kän′krə tīz′, kän′-) *vt.* **-tized′, -tiz′ing** to make (something) concrete; make specific

**con·cu·bine** (käŋ′kyə bīn′, kän′-) *n.* [< OFr. < L. < *concumbere* < *com-*, with + *cubare*, to lie down] **1.** a woman who cohabits with a man although not legally married to him **2.** in certain polygamous societies, a secondary wife, of inferior social and legal status —**con·cu·bi·nage** (kän kyōō′bə nij) *n.*

**con·cu·pis·cence** (kän kyōōp′ə s'ns) *n.* [OFr. < LL. < L. prp. of *concupiscere* < *com-*, intens. + *cupere*, to desire] strong or abnormal desire or appetite, esp. sexual desire; lust —**con·cu′pis·cent** *adj.*

**con·cur** (kən kur′) *vi.* **-curred′, -cur′ring** [< L. *concurrere* < *com-*, together + *currere*, to run] **1.** to occur at the same time; coincide **2.** to act together **3.** to agree (*with*); be in accord (*in* an opinion, etc.)

**con·cur·rence** (-əns) *n.* **1.** a coming or happening together **2.** a combining to bring about something **3.** agreement; accord Also **con·cur′ren·cy**

**con·cur·rent** (-ənt) *adj.* **1.** occurring or existing at the same time **2.** meeting in the same point **3.** acting together **4.** in agreement **5.** *Law* exercised equally over the same area *[concurrent* jurisdiction] —**con·cur′rent·ly** *adv.*

**concurrent resolution** a resolution passed by one legislative branch and concurred in by the other, without the force of law: cf. JOINT RESOLUTION

**con·cuss** (kən kus′) *vt.* to give a concussion to

**con·cus·sion** (kən kush′ən) *n.* [L. *concussio* < pp. of *cutere* < *com-*, together + *quatere*, to shake] **1.** a violent shaking; agitation; shock, as from impact **2.** *Med.* a condition of impaired functioning, esp. of the brain, as a result of a violent blow or impact —**con·cus′sive** (-kus′iv) *adj.*

**con·demn** (kən dem′) *vt.* [< OFr. < L. *condemnare* < *com-*, intens. + *damnare*, to harm, condemn] **1.** to disapprove of strongly; censure **2.** *a*) to declare guilty of wrongdoing; convict *b*) to inflict a penalty upon *c*) to doom **3.** to declare (property) legally appropriated for public use **4.** to declare unfit for use or service —**con·dem′na·ble** (-dem′nə b'l, -ə b'l) *adj.* —**con·demn′er** *n.*

**con·dem·na·tion** (kän′dem nā′shən, -dəm-) *n.* **1.** a condemning or being condemned **2.** a cause for condemning —**con·dem·na·to·ry** (kən dem′nə tôr′ē) *adj.*

**con·den·sa·tion** (kän′dən sā′shən) *n.* **1.** a condensing or being condensed **2.** anything condensed

**con·dense** (kən dens′) *vt.* **-densed′, -dens′ing** [< Fr. < L. < *com-*, intens. + *densus*, dense] **1.** to make more dense or compact; compress **2.** to express in fewer words; make concise; abridge **3.** to change (a substance) to a denser form, as from a gas to a liquid —*vi.* to become condensed —**con·dens′a·bil′i·ty, con·dens′i·bil′i·ty** *n.* —**con·dens′a·ble, con·dens′i·ble** *adj.*

**condensed milk** a thick milk made by evaporating part of the water from cow's milk and adding sugar

**con·dens·er** (kən den′sər) *n.* a person or thing that condenses; specif., *a*) an apparatus for liquefying gases or vapors *b*) a lens or series of lenses for concentrating light rays on an area *c*) *Elec.* same as CAPACITOR

**con·de·scend** (kän′də send′) *vi.* [< OFr. < LL. *condescendere* < L. *com-*, together + *descendere*, DESCEND] **1.** to descend voluntarily to the level, regarded as lower, of the person that one is dealing with; deign **2.** to deal with others in a patronizing manner —**con′de·scend′ing** *adj.* —**con′de·scen′sion** (-sen′shən), **con′de·scend′ence** *n.*

**con·dign** (kən dīn′) *adj.* [< OFr. < L. *condignus* < *com-*, intens. + *dignus*, worthy] deserved; suitable: said esp. of punishment —**con·dign′ly** *adv.*

**con·di·ment** (kän′də mənt) *n.* [< OFr. < L. *condimentum*, a spice < *condire*, to pickle] a seasoning or relish for food, as pepper, mustard, sauces, etc.

**con·di·tion** (kən dish′ən) *n.* [< OFr. < L. *condicio*, agreement < *com-*, together + *dicere*, to speak] **1.** anything required before the performance or completion of something else; provision; stipulation **2.** prerequisite **3.** anything that modifies the nature of something else *[good business conditions]* **4.** manner or state of being **5.** *a*) state of health *[the patient's condition]* *b*) [Colloq.] an illness; ailment *[a lung condition]* **6.** a proper or healthy state *[athletes out of condition]* **7.** social position; rank; station **8.** the requirement that a student make up deficiencies in a subject in order to pass it **9.** *Law* a clause in a contract, will, etc. that revokes or modifies a stipulation on certain contingencies —*vt.* **1.** to set as a requirement; stipulate **2.** to impose a condition or conditions on **3.** to be a condition of; determine **4.** to affect, modify, or influence **5.** to bring into a proper or desired condition **6.** *Psychol. a*) to develop a conditioned reflex or behavior pattern in *b*) to cause to become accustomed (*to*) —**on condition that** provided that —**con·di′tion·er** *n.*

**con·di·tion·al** (-'l) *adj.* **1.** containing or dependent on a condition; qualified *[a conditional award]* **2.** expressing a condition *[a conditional clause]* —*n. Gram.* the mood expressing a condition —**con·di′tion·al′i·ty** (-al′ə tē) *n.* —**con·di′tion·al·ly** *adv.*

**conditioned reflex** (or **response**) a reflex (e.g., secretion of saliva in a dog) is occasioned by a secondary stimulus (e.g., the ringing of a bell) repeatedly associated with the primary stimulus (e.g., the sight of meat)

**con·do** (kän′dō) *n., pl.* **-dos, -does** *clipped form of* CONDOMINIUM (sense 2)

**con·dole** (kən dōl′) *vi.* **-doled′, -dol′ing** [< LL. *condolere* < L. *com-*, with + *dolere*, to grieve] to express sympathy; mourn in sympathy —**con·do′la·to′ry** (-dō′lə tôr′ē) *adj.*

**con·do·lence** (kən dō′ləns) *n.* expression of sympathy with another in grief: also **con·dole′ment**

**con·dom** (kun′dəm, kän′-) *n.* [supposedly after a 17th-c. Brit. colonel] a thin leather sheath, esp. of rubber, for the penis, used to prevent venereal disease or as a contraceptive

**con·do·min·i·um** (kän′də min′ē əm) *n.* [ModL. < L. *com-*, together + *dominium*, dominion] **1.** joint rule by two or more states **2.** *pl.* **-i·ums, -i·a** (-ə) an apartment building or multiple-unit dwelling in which each tenant holds full title to his unit and joint ownership in the common grounds

**con·done** (kən dōn′) *vt.* **-doned′, -don′ing** [< L. *condonare* < *com-*, intens. + *donare*, to give] to forgive, pardon, or overlook (an offense) —**con·don′a·ble** *adj.* —**con·do·na·tion** (kän′dō nā′shən, -də-) *n.* —**con·don′er** *n.*

**con·dor** (kän′dər) *n.* [Sp. < Quechua *cuntur*] **1.** a very large vulture of the S. American Andes, with a bare head and a neck ruff of downy white feathers **2.** a similar vulture of S Calif. **3.** *pl.* **con·dor·es** (kən dô′res) any of various S. American gold coins

**con·duce** (kən dōōs′, -dyōōs′) *vi.* **-duced′, -duc′ing** [< L. *conducere* < *com-*, together + *ducere*, to lead] to tend or lead (*to* an effect); contribute

**con·du·cive** (-dōō′siv, -dyōō′-) *adj.* conducing; tending or leading (*to*) —**con·du′cive·ness** *n.*

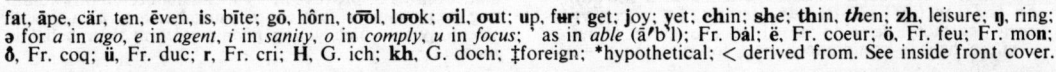

CONDOR
(wingspread to 12 ft.)

**con·duct** (kän′dukt′; *for v.* kən dukt′) *n.* [< L. pp. of *conducere*: see CONDUCE] **1.** management; handling **2.** the way that one acts; behavior —*vt.* **1.** to lead; guide; escort **2.** to manage, control, or direct **3.** to direct (an orchestra, choir, etc.) **4.** to behave (oneself) **5.** to be able to transmit *[copper conducts electricity]* —*vi.* to act as a conductor —**con·duct′i·bil′i·ty** *n.* —**con·duct′i·ble** *adj.*

**con·duct·ance** (kən duk′təns) *n.* the ability of a component to conduct electricity, measured by the ratio of the current to applied electromotive force

**con·duc·tion** (kən duk′shən) *n.* **1.** a conveying, as of liquid through a channel **2.** the transmission of nerve impulses **3.** *Physics a)* transmission (*of* electricity, heat, etc.) by the passage of energy from particle to particle *b) same as* CONDUCTIVITY: see also CONVECTION, RADIATION
**con·duc·tive** (-tiv) *adj.* having conductivity
**con·duc·tiv·i·ty** (kän′duk tiv′ə tē) *n.* the property of conducting heat, electricity, etc.
**con·duc·tor** (kən duk′tər) *n.* **1.** a person who conducts; leader; guide **2.** the director of an orchestra, choir, etc. **3.** one who has charge of the passengers and collects fares on a train, streetcar, or bus **4.** a thing that conducts electricity, heat, etc. —**con·duc·to·ri·al** (kən duk′tôr′ē əl) *adj.* —**con·duc′tor·ship′** *n.* —**con·duc′tress** *n.fem.*
**con·duit** (kän′dit, -doo wit) *n.* [< OFr. < L. pp. of *conducere*: see CONDUCE] **1.** a pipe or channel for conveying fluids **2.** a tube or protected trough for electric wires
**con·dyle** (kän′dīl, -dil) *n.* [Fr. < L. < Gr. *kondylos*, knuckle] a rounded process at the end of a bone — **con′dy·lar** (-də lər) *adj.* —**con′dy·loid** (-də loid) *adj.*
**cone** (kōn) *n.* [< L. < Gr. *kōnos*] **1.** *a)* a solid with a circle for its base and a curved surface tapering evenly to a point *b)* a surface described by a moving straight line passing through a fixed point and tracing a fixed curve, as a circle or ellipse, at another point **2.** any object shaped like a cone, as a shell of pastry for holding ice cream, the peak of a volcano, etc. **3.** a reproductive structure of certain lower plants, with an elongated central axis bearing overlapping scales, bracts, etc. which produce pollen, spores, or ovules **4.** *Zool.* any of the flask-shaped cells in the retina, sensitive to light and color —*vt.* **coned, con′ing** to shape like a cone

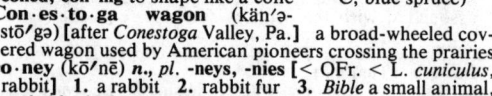

CONES
(A, longleaf pine;
B, piñon,
C, blue spruce)

**Con·es·to·ga wagon** (kän′ə-stō′gə) [after *Conestoga* Valley, Pa.] a broad-wheeled covered wagon used by American pioneers crossing the prairies
**co·ney** (kō′nē) *n., pl.* -neys, -nies [< OFr. < L. *cuniculus*, rabbit] **1.** a rabbit **2.** rabbit fur **3.** *Bible* a small animal, probably the hyrax **4.** *same as* PIKA
**Co·ney Island** (kō′nē) [< Du. *Konynen Eyland*, rabbit island] beach & amusement park in Brooklyn, N.Y., at the SW end of Long Island
**conf. 1.** conference **2.** confessor
**con·fab** (kän′fab′; *for v., usually* kən fab′) *n.* [Colloq.] a confabulation —*vi.* -**fabbed′**, -**fab′bing** [Colloq.] to confabulate
**con·fab·u·late** (kən fab′yə lāt′) *vi.* -**lat′ed**, -**lat′ing** [< L. pp. of *confabulari* < *com-*, together + *fabulari*, to talk: see FABLE] **1.** to talk together informally; chat **2.** to recount fictitious events as if they really occurred —**con·fab′u·la′tion** *n.*
**con·fect** (kən fekt′) *vt.* [< L. pp. of *conficere* < *com-*, with + *facere*, to make, do] to prepare or make, esp. by mixing or combining
**con·fec·tion** (kən fek′shən) *n.* **1.** a confecting **2.** any candy or other sweet preparation, as ice cream **3.** a frivolous piece of work **4.** a fancy article of women's clothing —**con·fec′tion·ar′y** *adj.*
**con·fec·tion·er** (-ər) *n.* one whose work or business is making or selling confectionery
**confectioners' sugar** very fine powdered sugar
**con·fec·tion·er·y** (-er′ē) *n., pl.* -**er′ies 1.** confections or candy, collectively **2.** the business, work, or shop of a confectioner
**con·fed·er·a·cy** (kən fed′ər ə sē) *n., pl.* -**cies** [see ff.] **1.** people, nations, etc. united for some common purpose **2.** a league or alliance formed by such a union; federation **3.** a conspiracy —**the Confederacy** the league of Southern States that seceded from the U.S. in 1860 & 1861: official name **Confederate States of America**
**con·fed·er·ate** (kən fed′ər it; *for v.* -ə rāt′) *adj.* [< LL. pp. of *confoederare*, to unite by a league < *foedus*, a league] **1.** united in a confederacy or league **2.** [C-] of the Confederacy —*n.* **1.** a person, group, or state united with another or others for a common purpose; ally **2.** an associate in crime; accomplice **3.** [C-] any Southern supporter of the Confederacy —*vt., vi.* -**at′ed**, -**at′ing** to unite in a confederacy; ally
**con·fed·er·a·tion** (kən fed′ə rā′shən) *n.* **1.** a uniting or being united in a league or alliance **2.** nations or states joined in a league, as for common defense —**the Confederation** the United States of America (1781–1789) under the **Articles of Confederation**, the constitution of the 13 original States —**con·fed′er·al** *adj.* —**con·fed′er·a′tive** *adj.*
**con·fer** (kən fur′) *vt.* -**ferred′**, -**fer′ring** [< L. *conferre* < *com-*, together + *ferre*, to BEAR¹] to give, grant, or bestow —*vi.* to have a conference; meet for discussion —**con-**

**fer′ment, con·fer′ral** *n.* —**con·fer′ra·ble** *adj.* —**con·fer′rer** *n.*
**con·fer·ee** (kän′fə rē′) *n.* **1.** a participant in a conference **2.** a person on whom an honor, degree, favor, etc. is conferred
**con·fer·ence** (kän′fər əns, -frəns) *n.* **1.** a conversing or consulting on a serious matter **2.** a formal meeting of a group for discussion or consultation, as of committees of legislative branches to reconcile differences between their bills **3.** [*often* C-] the governing body of some churches **4.** an association, as of colleges or athletic teams —**con·fer·en·tial** (kän′fə ren′shəl) *adj.*
**con·fess** (kən fes′) *vt.* [< OFr. < L. pp. of *confiteri* < *com-*, together + *fateri*, to acknowledge] **1.** *a)* to admit (a fault, crime, etc.) *b)* to acknowledge (an opinion, etc.) **2.** to declare one's faith in **3.** *Eccles. a)* to tell (one's sins) to God, in worship service or in private *b)* to hear the confession of (a person): said of a priest —*vi.* **1.** to admit a fault or crime **2.** *a)* to make one's confession *b)* to hear confessions: said of a priest —**confess to** to admit or admit having —**stand confessed as** to be revealed as
**con·fess·ed·ly** (-id lē) *adv.* admittedly
**con·fes·sion** (kən fesh′ən) *n.* **1.** a confessing; admission of guilt or sin; specif., a confessing of sins in the sacrament of penance **2.** something confessed **3.** *a)* a statement of religious beliefs: in full, **confession of faith** *b)* a church having such a confession; communion
**con·fes·sion·al** (-'l) *n.* a small, enclosed place in a church, where a priest hears confessions —*adj.* of or for a confession
**con·fes·sor** (kən fes′ər) *n.* **1.** one who confesses **2.** *R.C.Ch.* a male saint who was not a martyr **3.** a priest authorized to hear confessions
**con·fet·ti** (kən fet′ē) *n.pl.* [with *sing. v.*] [It., pl. of *confetto*, sweetmeat: candies were formerly so scattered] bits of colored paper scattered about at carnivals and other celebrations
**con·fi·dant** (kän′fə dant′, -dänt′; kän′fə dant′, -dänt′) *n.* a close, trusted friend to whom one confides personal secrets —**con′fi·dante′** *n.*
**con·fide** (kən fīd′) *vi.* -**fid′ed**, -**fid′ing** [L. *confidere* < *com-*, intens. + *fidere*, to trust] to trust (*in* someone), esp. by sharing secrets or discussing private affairs —*vt.* **1.** to tell or talk about as a secret [*to confide* one's troubles to a friend] **2.** to entrust (a duty, person, etc.) *to* someone —**con·fid′er** *n.*
**con·fi·dence** (kän′fə dəns) *n.* **1.** firm belief; trust; reliance **2.** certainty; assurance **3.** belief in one's own abilities; self-confidence **4.** a relationship as confidant [*take me into your confidence*] **5.** the belief that another will keep a secret [*told in strict confidence*] **6.** something told as a secret —*adj.* swindling or used to swindle
**confidence game** a swindle effected by one (**confidence man**) who first gains the confidence of his victim
**con·fi·dent** (-dənt) *adj.* full of confidence; specif., *a)* assured; certain [*confident* of victory] *b)* sure of oneself; self-confident; bold [*a confident* boy] —*n. same as* CONFIDANT —**con′fi·dent·ly** *adv.*
**con·fi·den·tial** (kän′fə den′shəl) *adj.* **1.** told in confidence; secret **2.** of or showing confidence **3.** entrusted with private or secret matters [*a confidential* agent] —**con′fi·den′tial·ly** *adv.*
**con·fid·ing** (kən fīd′iŋ) *adj.* trustful or inclined to trust —**con·fid′ing·ly** *adv.*
**con·fig·u·ra·tion** (kən fig′yə rā′shən) *n.* [< L. *configurare* < *com-*, together + *figurare*: see FIGURE] **1.** arrangement of parts **2.** form, contour, or structure as determined by the arrangement of parts —**con·fig′u·ra′tion·al** *adj.* —**con·fig′u·ra′tive** *adj.*
**con·fine** (kən fīn′; *for n.* kän′fīn′) *n.* [< OFr. < L. *confinium*, boundary < *com-*, with + *finis*, an end, limit] [*usually pl.*] a boundary or bounded region; border; limit —*vt.* -**fined′**, -**fin′ing 1.** to keep within limits; restrict [*to confine* a talk to ten minutes] **2.** to keep shut up, as in prison, in bed because of illness, indoors, etc. —**be confined** to be undergoing childbirth —**con·fin′a·ble, con·fine′a·ble** *adj.*
**con·fine·ment** (kən fīn′mənt) *n.* a confining or being confined; specif., *a)* imprisonment *b)* restriction; restraint *c)* childbirth; lying-in
**con·firm** (kən furm′) *vt.* [< OFr. < L. *confirmare* < *com-*, intens. + *firmare* < *firmus*, firm] **1.** to make firm; strengthen; establish **2.** to make valid by formal approval; ratify **3.** to prove the truth or validity of; verify **4.** to cause to undergo religious confirmation —**con·firm′a·ble** *adj.*
**con·fir·ma·tion** (kän′fər mā′shən) *n.* **1.** a confirming or being confirmed; ratification; verification **2.** something that confirms or proves **3.** *a)* a Christian ceremony admitting a person to full church membership *b)* a Jewish ceremony in which young people reaffirm their belief in Judaism

con·firm·a·to·ry (kən fur′mə tôr′ē) *adj.* confirming or tending to confirm: also con·firm′a·tive

con·firmed (-furmd′) *adj.* 1. firmly established, as in a habit or condition [a confirmed liar] 2. chronic, as a disease 3. corroborated 4. having accepted religious confirmation —con·firm′ed·ly *adv.*

con·fis·cate (kän′fə skāt′) *vt.* -cat′ed, -cat′ing [< L. pp. of confiscare, to lay up in a chest < com-, together + fiscus, money chest, treasury] 1. to seize (private property) for the public treasury, usually as a penalty 2. to seize as by authority; appropriate —con′fis·ca′tion *n.* —con′fis·ca′tor *n.*

con·fis·ca·to·ry (kən fis′kə tôr′ē) *adj.* 1. of, constituting, or effecting confiscation [a confiscatory tax] 2. confiscating

con·fit·e·or (kən fit′ē ôr′) *n.* [< LL., I confess] a formal prayer in which sins are confessed

con·fla·gra·tion (kän′flə grā′shən) *n.* [< L. < pp. of conflagrare < com-, intens. + flagrare, to burn] a big, destructive fire

con·flict (kən flikt′; for n. kän′flikt) *vi.* [< L. pp. of confligere < com-, together + fligere, to strike] 1. orig., to fight 2. to be antagonistic, incompatible, or contradictory; clash —n. 1. a fight or struggle 2. sharp disagreement or opposition, as of interests or ideas 3. emotional disturbance resulting from opposing impulses —con·flic′tion *n.* —con·flic′tive *adj.*

conflict of interest a conflict between one's obligation to the public and one's self-interest, as in the case of an elected official who owns stock in a company seeking government contracts

con·flu·ence (kän′floo əns) *n.* [OFr. < LL. < L. prp. of confluere < com-, together + fluere, to flow] 1. a flowing together, esp. of two or more streams 2. the place where they join, or a stream formed in this way 3. a coming together as of people; crowd; throng —con′flu·ent *adj.*

con·form (kən fôrm′) *vt.* [< OFr. < L. conformare < com-, together + formare, to FORM] 1. to make the same or similar 2. to bring into harmony or agreement; adapt —vi. 1. to be or become the same or similar 2. to be in accord or agreement 3. to accept without question customs, traditions, prevailing opinion, etc. —con·form′er *n.* —con·form′ism *n.* —con·form′ist *n.*

con·form·a·ble (-fôr′mə b'l) *adj.* 1. that conforms; specif., a) similar b) in harmony or agreement c) suited; adapted 2. quick to conform; obedient; submissive —con·form′a·bil′i·ty *n.* —con·form′a·bly *adv.*

con·for·mal (-fôr′m'l) *adj.* [< LL. < L.: see CONFORM] designating or of a map projection in which shapes at any point are true, but areas become increasingly exaggerated

con·form·ance (-fôr′məns) *n. same as* CONFORMITY

con·for·ma·tion (kän′fôr mā′shən) *n.* 1. a symmetrical formation and arrangement of the parts of a thing 2. the structure or form of a thing as determined by the arrangement of its parts

con·form·i·ty (kən fôr′mə tē) *n., pl.* -ties 1. the condition or fact of being in harmony or agreement; correspondence; similarity 2. action in accordance with customs, rules, popular opinion, etc.

con·found (kän found′, kän-; for 3, usually kän′-) *vt.* [< OFr. < L. confundere < com-, together + fundere, to pour] 1. to mix up or lump together indiscriminately; confuse 2. to make feel confused; bewilder 3. to damn: used as a mild oath 4. [Archaic] to defeat or destroy

con·found·ed (-id) *adj.* 1. confused; bewildered 2. damned: a mild oath —con·found′ed·ly *adv.*

con·fra·ter·ni·ty (kän′frə tur′nə tē) *n., pl.* -ties [< ML.: see COM- & FRATERNITY] 1. brotherhood 2. a group of men associated for some purpose, often religious

con·frere (kän′frer, kōn′-) *n.* [OFr. confrère] a fellow member or worker; colleague

con·front (kən frunt′) *vt.* [Fr. < ML. confrontare < L. com-, together + frons, forehead, front] 1. to stand or meet face to face 2. to face or oppose boldly or defiantly 3. to bring face to face (with) [to confront one with the facts] —con·fron·ta·tion (kän′frən tā′shən), con·front′al *n.*

Con·fu·cian·ism (kən fyōo′shən iz'm) *n.* the ethical teachings of Confucius, emphasizing devotion to parents, ancestor worship, and the maintenance of justice and peace —Con·fu′cian·ist *n., adj.*

Con·fu·cius (kən fyōo′shəs) (L. name of K'ung Fu-tse) 551?–479? B.C.; Chin. philosopher & teacher —Con·fu′cian (-shən) *adj. n.*

con·fuse (kən fyōoz′) *vt.* -fused′, -fus′ing [< OFr. < L. pp. of confundere: see CONFOUND] 1. to mix up; jumble together; put into disorder 2. to mix up mentally; specif., a) to bewilder; perplex b) to embarrass; discon-

cert c) to fail to distinguish between; mistake the identity of —con·fus′ed·ly (-fyōoz′id lē) *adv.* —con·fus′edness *n.* —con·fus′ing *adj.* —con·fus′ing·ly *adv.*

con·fu·sion (kən fyōo′zhən) *n.* a confusing or being confused; specif., a) state of disorder b) bewilderment c) embarrassment d) failure to distinguish between things —covered with confusion greatly embarrassed —con·fu′sion·al *adj.*

con·fute (kən fyōot′) *vt.* -fut′ed, -fut′ing [L. confutare] to prove (a person, statement, etc.) to be in error or false; overcome by argument or proof —con·fu·ta·tion (kän′fyoo tā′shən) *n.* —con·fu′ta·tive *adj.* —con·fut′er *n.*

**Cong.** 1. Congress 2. Congressional

con·ga (kän′gə) *n.* [AmSp., ult. < CONGO] 1. a Latin American dance in which the dancers form a winding line 2. music for this dance, in 4/4 syncopated time —vi. to dance the conga

con·gé (kän′zhā, -jā′; Fr. kōn zhā′) *n.* [Fr. < OFr. < L. < com-, intens. + meare, to go] 1. a dismissal 2. permission to leave 3. a formal farewell

con·geal (kən jēl′) *vt., vi.* [< OFr. < L. congelare < com-, together + gelare, to freeze] 1. to solidify or thicken by cooling or freezing 2. to thicken; coagulate; jell —congeal′a·ble *adj.* —con·geal′ment *n.*

con·gen·er (kän′jə nər) *n.* [L. < com-, together + genus (gen. generis), race, kind] a person or thing of the same kind, class, genus, etc. —con′ge·ner′ic (-ner′ik), con·gen·er·ous (kən jen′ər əs) *adj.*

con·gen·ial (kən jēn′yəl) *adj.* [see COM- & GENIAL] 1. kindred; compatible 2. having the same tastes and temperament; sympathetic [congenial friends] 3. suited to one's needs or disposition; agreeable [congenial work] —con·ge′ni·al′i·ty (-jēn′ē al′ə tē) *n.* —con·gen′ial·ly *adv.*

con·gen·i·tal (kän jen′ə t'l) *adj.* [< L.: see COM- & GENITAL] 1. existing as such at birth; resulting from one's prenatal environment [a congenital disease] 2. existing as if inborn; inherent [a congenital cheerfulness] —con·gen′i·tal·ly *adv.*

con·ger (eel) (käŋ′gər) [< OFr. < L. < Gr. gongros] a large, edible saltwater eel

con·ge·ries (kän′jə rēz′, kän jir′ēz) *n., pl.* con′ge·ries′ [see ff.] a collection of things or parts massed together; heap; pile

con·gest (kən jest′) *vt.* [< L. pp. of congerere, to pile up < com-, together + gerere, to carry] 1. to cause too much blood to accumulate in the vessels of (a part of the body) 2. to fill to excess; overcrowd; clog [a congested highway] —vi. to become congested —con·ges′tion (-jes′chən) *n.* —con·ges′tive (-tiv) *adj.*

con·glom·er·ate (kən gläm′ə rāt′; for adj. & n. -ər it) *vt., vi.* -at′ed, -at′ing [< L. pp. of conglomerare < com-, together + glomerare < glomus, a ball] to form or collect into a rounded or compact mass —adj. 1. formed into a rounded or compact mass; clustered 2. made up of separate substances collected into a single mass 3. Geol. made up of rock fragments or pebbles cemented together by clay, silica, etc.: also con·glom′er·at′ic (-ə rat′ik), con·glom′er·it′ic (-ə rit′ik) —n. 1. a conglomerate mass; cluster 2. a large corporation formed by merging many diverse companies 3. Geol. a conglomerate rock —con·glom′er·a′tion *n.*

CONGLOMERATE ROCK

Con·go (käŋ′gō) 1. river in C Africa, flowing through Zaire into the Atlantic 2. country in WC Africa, west of Zaire: 132,046 sq. mi.; pop. 826,000; cap. Brazzaville 3. former name of ZAIRE —Con′go·lese′ (-gə lēz′) *adj., n.*

congo eel (or snake) an eellike amphibious animal with two pairs of small, weak legs, of the SE U.S.

con·grat·u·late (kən grach′ə lāt′) *vt.* -lat′ed, -lat′ing [< L. pp. of congratulari < com-, together + gratulari, to wish joy < gratus, agreeable] to express to (a person) one's pleasure at his good fortune, success, etc. —con·grat′u·la′tor *n.* —con·grat′u·la·to′ry (-lə tôr′ē) *adj.*

con·grat·u·la·tion (kən grach′ə lā′shən) *n.* 1. a congratulating 2. [pl.] expressions of pleasure and good wishes at another's fortune or success

con·gre·gate (käŋ′grə gāt′; for adj. -git) *vt., vi.* -gat′ed, -gat′ing [< L. pp. of congregare < com-, together + gregare, to gather < grex, a flock] to gather into a mass or crowd; collect; assemble —adj. 1. assembled; collected 2. collective —con′gre·ga′tive *adj.* —con′gre·ga′tor *n.*

con·gre·ga·tion (käŋ′grə gā′shən) *n.* 1. a congregating or being congregated 2. a gathering of people or things; assemblage 3. an assembly of people for religious worship

**4.** the members of a particular place of worship **5.** *R.C.Ch.* a religious community not necessarily under solemn vows but bound by a common rule

**con·gre·ga·tion·al** (-'l) *adj.* **1.** of or like a congregation **2.** [C-] of Congregationalism or Congregationalists

**con·gre·ga·tion·al·ism** (-'l iz'm) *n.* **1.** a form of church organization in which each local congregation is self-governing **2.** [C-] the faith and form of organization of a Protestant denomination in which each member church is self-governing —**Con'gre·ga'tion·al·ist** *n., adj.*

**con·gress** (käŋ'grəs) *n.* [< L. pp. of *congredi* < *com-*, together + *gradi*, to walk < *gradus*, a step] **1.** a coming together; meeting **2.** an association or society **3.** an assembly or conference **4.** any of various legislatures, esp. the national legislature of a republic **5.** [C-] *a)* the legislature of the U.S., consisting of the Senate and the House of Representatives *b)* its session *c)* the body of Senators and Representatives during any of the two-year terms of Representatives

**con·gres·sion·al** (kən gresh'ən 'l) *adj.* **1.** of a congress **2.** [C-] of Congress —**con·gres'sion·al·ly** *adv.*

**Congressional district** any of the districts into which a State is divided for electing Congressmen

**con·gress·man** (käŋ'grəs mən) *n., pl.* -**men** [*often* C-] a member of Congress, esp. of the House of Representatives —**con'gress·wom'an** *n.fem.* (a former usage)

**Con·greve** (kän'grēv, käŋ'-), **William** 1670–1729; Eng. Restoration playwright

**con·gru·ence** (käŋ'grōō wəns, kən grōō'əns) *n.* [see ff.] **1.** the state or quality of being in agreement; harmony **2.** *Math.* the relation between two numbers each of which, when divided by a third, leaves the same remainder Also **con'gru·en·cy**

**con·gru·ent** (-wənt, -ənt) *adj.* [< L. prp. of *congruere*, to come together, agree] **1.** in agreement; harmonious **2.** *Geom.* of the same shape and size **3.** *Math.* in congruence [*congruent* numbers] —**con'gru·ent·ly** *adv.*

**con·gru·i·ty** (kən grōō'ə tē) *n., pl.* -**ties 1.** the condition or fact of being congruous or congruent; specif., *a)* agreement; harmony *b)* appropriateness *c) Geom.* exact coincidence (of two or more figures) **2.** an instance of agreement

**con·gru·ous** (käŋ'grōō wəs) *adj.* **1.** *same as* CONGRUENT **2.** corresponding to what is right, proper, or reasonable; fitting; suitable; appropriate —**con'gru·ous·ly** *adv.* —**con'gru·ous·ness** *n.*

**con·ic** (kän'ik) *adj. same as* CONICAL —*n. same as* CONIC SECTION

**con·i·cal** (-i k'l) *adj.* **1.** of a cone **2.** resembling or shaped like a cone —**con'i·cal·ly** *adv.*

**conic section** a curve, as an ellipse, circle, parabola, or hyperbola, produced by the intersection of a plane with a right circular cone

**co·nid·i·um** (kə nid'ē əm) *n., pl.* -**i·a** (-ə) [ModL. < Gr. *konis*, dust] a small asexual spore of certain fungi —**co·nid'i·al, co·nid'i·an** *adj.*

**co·ni·fer** (kän'ə fər, kō'nə-) *n.* [L. < *conus*, a cone + *ferre*, to BEAR[1]] any of an order of cone-bearing trees and shrubs, mostly evergreens, as the pine, spruce, fir, cedar, yew, etc. —**co·nif·er·ous** (kə nif'ər əs) *adj.*

**conj. 1.** conjugation **2.** conjunction

**con·jec·tur·al** (kən jek'chər əl) *adj.* based on or involving conjecture —**con·jec'tur·al·ly** *adv.*

**con·jec·ture** (kən jek'chər) *n.* [< L. *conjectura* < pp. of *conjicere*, to guess < *com-*, together + *jacere*, to throw] **1.** an inferring, theorizing, or predicting from incomplete evidence; guesswork **2.** an inference, theory, or prediction based on guesswork; guess —*vt., vi.* -**tured**, -**tur·ing** to arrive at or propose (something) by conjecture; guess —**con·jec'tur·a·ble** *adj.* —**con·jec'tur·er** *n.*

**con·join** (kən join') *vt., vi.* [< OFr. < L. *conjungere* < *com-*, together + *jungere*, to join] to join together; unite; combine —**con·join'er** *n.*

**con·joint** (-joint') *adj.* [see prec.] **1.** joined together; united; combined **2.** of or involving two or more in association; joint —**con·joint'ly** *adv.*

**con·ju·gal** (kän'jə gəl, kən jōō'-) *adj.* [< L. < *conjunx*, spouse < *com-*, together + base akin to *jugum*, yoke] of marriage or the relation between husband and wife; matrimonial —**con'ju·gal'i·ty** (-jə gal'ə tē) *n.* —**con'ju·gal·ly** *adv.*

**con·ju·gate** (kän'jə gət; *also, and for v. always,* -gāt') *adj.* [< L. pp. of *conjugare* < *com-*, together + *jugare*, to join < *jugum*, a yoke] **1.** joined together, esp. in a pair; coupled **2.** *Gram.* derived from the same base and, usually, related in meaning —*n.* a conjugate word —*vt.* -**gat'ed**, -**gat'ing 1.** [Archaic] to join together; couple **2.** *Gram.* to inflect (a verb) systematically, according to voice, mood, tense, number, and person —*vi. Gram.* **1.** to conjugate a verb **2.** to be conjugated —**con'ju·ga'tive** *adj.* —**con'ju·ga'tor** *n.*

**con·ju·ga·tion** (kän'jə gā'shən) *n.* **1.** a conjugating or being conjugated; union **2.** *Gram. a)* a methodical present-

ation or arrangement of the inflectional forms of a verb *b)* a class of verbs with similar inflectional forms —**con'ju·ga'tion·al** *adj.* —**con'ju·ga'tion·al·ly** *adv.*

**con·junc·tion** (kən juŋk'shən) *n.* [see CONJOIN] **1.** a joining together or being joined together; union; combination **2.** coincidence **3.** *Astrol., Astron. a)* the apparent closeness of two or more heavenly bodies *b)* the condition of being in the same celestial longitude [planets in *conjunction*] **4.** *Gram.* an uninflected word used to connect words, phrases, clauses, or sentences; connective: conjunctions may be coordinating (e.g., *and, but, or*), subordinating (e.g., *if, when, as, because, though*), or correlative (e.g., *either . . . or, both . . . and*) —**con·junc'tion·al** *adj.* —**con·junc'tion·al·ly** *adv.*

**con·junc·ti·va** (kän'jəŋk tī'və, kən juŋk'ti və) *n., pl.* -**vas**, -**vae** (-vē) [< ModL. (*membrana*) *conjunctiva*, connecting (membrane)] the mucous membrane lining the inner surface of the eyelids and covering the front part of the eyeball —**con'junc·ti'val** *adj.*

**con·junc·tive** (kən juŋk'tiv) *adj.* **1.** serving to join together; connective **2.** united; combined; joint **3.** *Gram.* used as a conjunction [a *conjunctive* adverb] —*n. Gram.* a conjunctive word; esp., a conjunction —**con·junc'tive·ly** *adv.*

**con·junc·ti·vi·tis** (kən juŋk'tə vīt'is) *n.* [see -ITIS] inflammation of the conjunctiva

**con·junc·ture** (kən juŋk'chər) *n.* [< ML.: see CONJOIN] **1.** [Rare] a joining or being joined together **2.** a combination of events or circumstances, esp. one creating a critical situation; crisis

**con·ju·ra·tion** (kän'jə rā'shən) *n.* **1.** a conjuring; invocation **2.** a magic spell; incantation

**con·jure** (kän'jər, kun'-; *for vt. 1* kən joor') *vi.* -**jured**, -**jur·ing** [< OFr. < L. *conjurare* < *com-*, together + *jurare*, to swear] **1.** to summon a demon, spirit, etc. by a magic spell **2.** to practice magic —*vt.* **1.** to appeal to or entreat solemnly **2.** to summon (a devil, etc.) by a magic spell —**conjure away** to cause to go away as by magic —**conjure up 1.** to cause to appear as by magic **2.** to call to mind [the music *conjured up* memories]

**con·jur·er, con·ju·ror** (kän'jər ər, kun'-; *for 1* kən joor'ər) *n.* **1.** one who solemnly entreats someone **2.** a magician **3.** one skilled in legerdemain

**conk** (käŋk, kôŋk) *n.* [< CONCH] [Slang] a blow on the head —*vt.* [Slang] to hit on the head —**conk out** [Slang] **1.** to fail suddenly in operation **2.** to become very tired and, usually, fall asleep

**con man** [Slang] *same as* CONFIDENCE MAN

**conn** (kän) *vt.* **conned, con'ning** [< OFr. < L. *conducere:* see CONDUCE] *Naut.* to direct the course of (a vessel) —*n.* the act of conning

**Conn.** Connecticut

**con·nect** (kə nekt') *vt.* [< L. *connectere* < *com-*, together + *nectere*, to fasten] **1.** to join (two things together, or one thing *with* or *to* another); link; couple **2.** to show or think of as related; associate **3.** to plug into an electrical circuit —*vi.* **1.** to be joined or be related **2.** to meet so that passengers can change to another bus, airplane, etc. **3.** [Colloq.] *Sports* to hit a ball, target, etc. solidly —**con·nec'tor, con·nect'er** *n.*

**Con·nect·i·cut** (kə net'ə kət) [< Algonquian, lit., place of the long river] New England State of the U.S.: 5,009 sq. mi.; pop. 3,108,000; cap. Hartford: abbrev. **Conn., CT**

**connecting rod** a rod connecting by reciprocating motion two or more moving parts of a machine, as the crankshaft and a piston of an automobile

**con·nec·tion** (kə nek'shən) *n.* **1.** a joining or being joined; coupling; union **2.** a thing that joins; means of joining **3.** a relation; association; coherence **4.** *a)* a relative, esp. by marriage *b)* a business associate, friend, etc., esp. an influential one: *usually used in pl.* **5.** [*usually pl.*] the act or means of transferring from one bus, airplane, etc. to another **6.** a group of people associated in politics, business, etc. **7.** *Elec.* a circuit —**in connection with 1.** together with; in conjunction with **2.** with reference to —**con·nec'tion·al** *adj.*

**con·nec·tive** (kə nek'tiv) *adj.* connecting or serving to connect —*n.* something that connects, esp. a word that connects words, phrases, or clauses, as a conjunction or relative pronoun —**con·nec'tive·ly** *adv.* —**con·nec·tiv·i·ty** (kän'ek tiv'ə tē) *n.*

**connective tissue** body tissue that connects and supports other tissues and organs in the body

**conn·ing tower** (kän'iŋ) [prp. of CONN] **1.** an armored pilothouse on the deck of a warship **2.** on submarines, a low observation tower serving also as an entrance to the interior

**con·nip·tion (fit)** (kə nip'shən) [pseudo-Latin] [Colloq.] [*often pl.*] a fit of anger, hysteria, etc.

**con·niv·ance** (kə nī'vəns) *n.* a conniving; esp., passive cooperation, as by consent or pretended ignorance, esp. in wrongdoing

**con·nive** (kə nīv') *vi.* **-nived', -niv'ing** [< L. *conivere*, to wink, connive] **1.** to pretend not to see or look (*at* something wrong or evil), thus giving tacit consent or cooperation **2.** *a*) to cooperate secretly (*with* someone), esp. in wrongdoing *b*) to scheme underhandedly —**con·niv'er** *n.*

**con·nois·seur** (kän'ə sur', -soor') *n.* [< Fr. < OFr. < L. *cognoscere*, to know: see COGNITION] one who has expert knowledge and keen discrimination in some field, esp. in the fine arts

**con·no·ta·tion** (kän'ə tā'shən) *n.* **1.** the act or process of connoting **2.** an idea suggested by or associated with a word, phrase, etc. in addition to its explicit meaning —**con·no·ta·tive** (kän'ə tāt'iv, kə nōt'ə tiv), **con'no·ta'tion·al** *adj.* —**con'no·ta'tive·ly** *adv.*

**con·note** (kə nōt') *vt.* **-not'ed, -not'ing** [< ML. *connotare* < L. *com-*, together + *notare*, to mark: see NOTE] **1.** to suggest or convey (associations, overtones, etc.) in addition to the explicit, or denoted, meaning **2.** to imply or involve

**con·nu·bi·al** (kə nōō'bē əl, -nyōō'-) *adj.* [< L. < *conubium*, marriage < *com-*, together + *nubere*, to marry] of marriage or the state of being married; conjugal —**con·nu'bi·al'i·ty** (-bē al'ə tē) *n.* —**con·nu'bi·al·ly** *adv.*

**co·noid** (kō'noid) *adj.* cone-shaped: also **co·noi'dal**

**con·quer** (käŋ'kər) *vt.* [< OFr. < VL. *conquarere* < L. *com-*, intens. + *quaerere*, to seek] **1.** to get possession or control of by or as by winning a war **2.** to overcome by physical, mental, or moral force; defeat —*vi.* to be victorious; win —**con'quer·a·ble** *adj.* —**con'quer·or** *n.*

**con·quest** (käŋ'kwest, kän'-) *n.* [< OFr. < ML. < L. pp. of *conquirere*, to procure] **1.** the act of conquering **2.** something conquered **3.** *a*) a winning of someone's love *b*) one whose love has been won

**con·quis·ta·dor** (kän kwis'tə dôr', -kēs'-; käŋ-) *n., pl.* **-dors', -dores'** [Sp., conqueror] any of the Spanish conquerors of Mexico, Peru, or other parts of America in the 16th century

**Con·rad** (kän'rad) [< G. or Fr. < OHG. < *kuon*, bold, wise + *rat*, counsel] **1.** a masculine name **2. Joseph,** (born *Józef Teodor Naellecz Korzeniowski*) 1857-1924; Eng. novelist, born in Poland

**cons. 1.** consolidated **2.** consonant **3.** consulting

**cons., Cons. 1.** constitution **2.** consul

**con·san·guin·e·ous** (kän'saŋ gwin'ē əs, -san-) *adj.* [see COM- & SANGUINE] having the same ancestor; closely related: also **con·san'guine** (-saŋ'gwin) —**con'san·guin'e·ous·ly** *adv.* —**con'san·guin'i·ty** *n.*

**con·science** (kän'shəns) *n.* [OFr. < L. < prp. of *conscire* < *com-*, with + *scire*, to know] a knowledge or sense of right and wrong, with a compulsion to do right; moral judgment that keeps one from violating one's ethical principles —**in (all) conscience** in fairness —**on one's conscience** causing one to feel guilty —**con'science·less** *adj.*

**conscience money** money one pays to relieve one's conscience, as for some former dishonesty

**con·sci·en·tious** (kän'shē en'shəs, -chəs) *adj.* [see CONSCIENCE] **1.** governed by, or done according to, what one knows is right; scrupulous **2.** showing care; painstaking —**con'sci·en'tious·ly** *adv.* —**con'sci·en'tious·ness** *n.*

**conscientious objector** a person who for reasons of conscience refuses to take part in warfare

**con·scious** (kän'shəs) *adj.* [< L. *conscius* < *conscire*: see CONSCIENCE] **1.** having a feeling or knowledge (with *of* or *that*); aware; cognizant **2.** able to feel and think; in the normal waking state **3.** aware of oneself as a thinking being **4.** *same as* SELF-CONSCIOUS **5.** intentional [*conscious* humor] **6.** known to or felt by oneself [*conscious* guilt] —**con'scious·ly** *adv.*

**con·scious·ness** (-nis) *n.* **1.** the state of being conscious; awareness of one's own feelings, what is happening around one, etc. **2.** the totality of one's thoughts, feelings, and impressions; conscious mind

**con·script** (kən skript'; *for adj. & n.* kän'skript) *vt.* [< the *adj.*] **1.** to enroll for compulsory service in the armed forces; draft **2.** to force (labor, capital, etc.) into service for the government —*adj.* [< L. pp. of *conscribere*, enroll < *com-*, with + *scribere*, to write] conscripted —*n.* a conscripted person; draftee —**con·scrip'tion** *n.*

**con·se·crate** (kän'sə krāt') *vt.* **-crat'ed, -crat'ing** [< L. pp. of *consecrare* < *com-*, together + *sacrare*, to make holy < *sacer*, sacred] **1.** to set apart as holy; make or declare sacred for religious use **2.** to devote entirely; dedicate [to *consecrate* one's life to art] **3.** to cause to be revered; hallow [ground *consecrated* by their martyrdom] —**con'se·cra'tion** *n.* —**con'se·cra'tor** *n.*

**con·sec·u·tive** (kən sek'yə tiv) *adj.* [< Fr. < ML. < pp. of L. *consequi*: see CONSEQUENCE] **1.** following in order,

without interruption; successive **2.** proceeding from one part or idea to the next in logical order —**con·sec'u·tive·ly** *adv.* —**con·sec'u·tive·ness** *n.*

**con·sen·sus** (kən sen'səs) *n.* [L. < pp. of *consentire*: see ff.] **1.** an opinion held by all or most **2.** general agreement

**con·sent** (kən sent') *vi.* [< OFr. < L. *consentire* < *com-*, with + *sentire*, to feel] **1.** to agree (*to* do something) **2.** to give permission or approval (*to* something) —*n.* **1.** permission, approval, or assent **2.** agreement [by common *consent*] —**con·sent'er** *n.*

**con·sen·tu·al** (kən sen'choo wəl) *adj.* involving consent, esp. mutual consent [*consentual* divorce]

**con·se·quence** (kän'sə kwens', -kwəns) *n.* [OFr. < L. < prp. of *consequi* < *com-*, with + *sequi*, to follow] **1.** a result of an action, process, etc.; effect **2.** a logical result or conclusion; inference **3.** importance as a cause [a matter of slight *consequence*] **4.** importance in rank [a person of *consequence*] —**in consequence (of)** as a result (of) —**take the consequences** to accept the results of one's actions

**con·se·quent** (-kwent', -kwənt) *adj.* **1.** following as a result; resulting **2.** proceeding in logical sequence —*n.* anything that follows —**consequent on** (or **upon**) **1.** following as a result of **2.** inferred from

**con·se·quen·tial** (kän'sə kwen'shəl) *adj.* **1.** following as an effect **2.** important —**con'se·quen'ti·al'i·ty** (-shē al'ə tē) *n.* —**con'se·quen'tial·ly** *adv.*

**con·se·quent·ly** (kän'sə kwent'lē, -kwənt-) *adv.* as a result; by logical inference; therefore

**con·ser·van·cy** (kən sur'vən sē) *n.* conservation of natural resources —*adj.* set apart for the protection of natural resources, as a State district

**con·ser·va·tion** (kän'sər vā'shən) *n.* **1.** a conserving; protection from loss, waste, etc. **2.** the official care and protection of natural resources, as forests —**con'ser·va'tion·al** *adj.* —**con'ser·va'tion·ist** *n.*

**conservation of energy** the principle that energy is never consumed but only changes form, and that the total energy in the universe remains fixed

**conservation of matter** (or **mass**) the principle that matter is neither created nor destroyed during any physical or chemical change

**con·ser·va·tism** (kən sur'və tiz'm) *n.* the principles and practices of a conservative person or party

**con·ser·va·tive** (-tiv) *adj.* **1.** conserving or tending to conserve; preservative **2.** tending to preserve established institutions or methods and to resist or oppose any changes in these **3.** [C-] designating or of the major right-wing political party of Great Britain or of Canada **4.** [C-] designating or of a movement in Judaism moderately adapting religious ritual, etc. to modern conditions **5.** moderate; cautious; safe —*n.* **1.** a conservative person **2.** [C-] a member of a Conservative party —**con·ser'va·tive·ly** *adv.* —**con·ser'va·tive·ness** *n.*

**con·ser·va·toire** (kən sur'və twär', -sur'və twär') *n.* [Fr.] *same as* CONSERVATORY (*n.* 2)

**con·ser·va·tor** (kän'sər vāt'ər, kən sur'və tər) *n.* [see CONSERVE] a protector, guardian, or custodian

**con·ser·va·to·ry** (kən sur'və tôr'ē) *n., pl.* **-ries** [see ff.] **1.** a room enclosed in glass, for growing and showing plants **2.** a school, or academy, of music, art, etc.

**con·serve** (kən surv'; *for n., usually* kän'sərv) *vt.* **-served', -serv'ing** [< OFr. < L. *conservare* < *com-*, with + *servare*, to guard] **1.** to keep from being damaged, lost, or wasted **2.** to make (fruit) into preserves —*n.* [*often pl.*] a preserve of two or more fruits —**con·serv'a·ble** *adj.* —**con·serv'er** *n.*

**con·sid·er** (kən sid'ər) *vt.* [< OFr. < L. *considerare*, to observe < *com-*, with + *sidus*, a star] **1.** to think about in order to understand or decide; ponder **2.** to keep in mind; take into account **3.** to be thoughtful of (others, their feelings, etc.) **4.** to regard as; think to be [I *consider* him an expert] —*vi.* to think carefully; reflect

**con·sid·er·a·ble** (-ə b'l) *adj.* **1.** worth considering; important **2.** much or large —**con·sid'er·a·bly** *adv.*

**con·sid·er·ate** (-it) *adj.* [see CONSIDER] having or showing regard for others and their feelings; thoughtful —**con·sid'er·ate·ly** *adv.* —**con·sid'er·ate·ness** *n.*

**con·sid·er·a·tion** (kən sid'ə rā'shən) *n.* **1.** the act of considering; deliberation **2.** *a*) thoughtful or sympathetic regard for others *b*) esteem **3.** something considered in making a decision **4.** a thought or opinion produced by considering **5.** a recompense, as for a service rendered; fee; compensation —**in consideration of 1.** because of **2.** in return for —**take into consideration** to keep in mind; take into account —**under consideration** being thought over

**con·sid·ered** (kən sid'ərd) *adj.* arrived at after careful thought

**con·sid·er·ing** (-ər iŋ) *prep.* in view of; taking into account —*adv.* [Colloq.] all things considered

**con·sign** (kən sīn') *vt.* [L. *consignare*, to seal < *com-*, together + *signare* < *signum*, a sign] 1. to hand over; deliver 2. to put in the care of another; entrust 3. to assign to an undesirable position or place; relegate 4. to send or deliver (goods) —**con·sign'a·ble** *adj.* —**con·sign·ee** (kän'sī nē', kən sī'nē') *n.* —**consign'or**, **con·sign'er** *n.*

**con·sign·ment** (-mənt) *n.* 1. a consigning or being consigned 2. something consigned; esp., a shipment of goods sent to an agent for sale or safekeeping

**con·sist** (kən sist') *vi.* [L. *consistere* < *com-*, together + *sistere*, to stand] 1. to be formed or composed (*of*) 2. to be contained or inherent (*in*) as a cause, characteristic, etc. 3. to exist in harmony (*with*)

**con·sis·ten·cy** (-ən sē) *n., pl.* -**cies** 1. *a*) firmness or thickness, as of a liquid *b*) degree of this 2. agreement; harmony 3. conformity with previous practice or principle Also **con·sis'tence**

**con·sis·tent** (-ənt) *adj.* [see CONSIST] 1. [Rare] firm; solid 2. in agreement or harmony; compatible 3. holding always to the same principles or practice —**con·sis'tent·ly** *adv.*

**con·sis·to·ry** (kən sis'tər ē) *n., pl.* -**ries** [< OFr. < L. *consistorium*, place of assembly < *consistere*: see CONSIST] 1. a church council or court, as the papal senate 2. a session of such a body —**con·sis·to·ri·al** (kän'sis tôr'ē əl) *adj.*

**con·so·la·tion** (kän'sə lā'shən) *n.* 1. a consoling or being consoled; solace 2. a person or thing that consoles

**consolation prize** a prize given to a contestant who does well but does not win

**con·sol·a·to·ry** (kən sōl'ə tôr'ē, -säl'-) *adj.* consoling or tending to console; comforting

**con·sole¹** (kən sōl') *vt.* -**soled'**, -**sol'ing** [< Fr. < L. *consolari* < *com-*, with + *solari*, to solace] to make feel less sad or disappointed; comfort —**con·sol'a·ble** *adj.* —**con·sol'ing·ly** *adv.*

**con·sole²** (kän'sōl) *n.* [Fr.] 1. an ornamental bracket for supporting a shelf, bust, cornice, etc. 2. same as CONSOLE TABLE 3. the desklike frame containing the keys, stops, pedals, etc. of an organ 4. a radio, television, or phonograph cabinet designed to stand on the floor 5. an instrument panel or unit, containing the controls for operating aircraft, computers, etc.

**console table** a small table with legs resembling consoles, placed against a wall

CONSOLE (of an organ)

**con·sol·i·date** (kən säl'ə dāt') *vt., vi.* -**dat'ed**, -**dat'ing** [< L. pp. of *consolidare* < *com-*, together + *solidare* < *solidus*, solid] 1. to combine into a single whole; merge; unite 2. to make or become strong, stable, etc. [the troops *consolidated* their position] 3. to make or become solid or compact —**con·sol'i·da'tion** *n.* —**con·sol'i·da'tor** *n.*

**con·sols** (kən sälz', kän'sälz) *n.pl.* [< *consolidated annuities*] British government bonds

**con·som·mé** (kän'sə mā') *n.* [Fr., orig. pp. of *consommer*, CONSUMMATE, confused with *consumer*, CONSUME] a clear soup made by boiling meat, and sometimes vegetables, in water and straining

**con·so·nance** (kän'sə nəns) *n.* [OFr. < L. < prp. of *consonare* < *com-*, with + *sonare*, to sound < *sonus*, a sound] 1. harmony or agreement of elements or parts; accord 2. harmony of musical tones Also **con'so·nan·cy**

**con·so·nant** (kän'sə nənt) *adj.* [see prec.] 1. in harmony or agreement; in accord 2. harmonious in tone: opposed to DISSONANT 3. consonantal —*n.* 1. any speech sound produced by obstructing the breath stream in any of various ways, as the sounds of p, t, k, m, l, f, etc. 2. a letter or symbol representing such a sound —**con'so·nant·ly** *adv.*

**con·so·nan·tal** (kän'sə nant''l) *adj.* of, being, or having a consonant or consonants

**con·sort** (kän'sôrt; *for v.* kən sôrt') *n.* [< OFr. < L. *consors* (gen. *consortis*) < *com-*, with + *sors*, a share] 1. orig., a partner; companion 2. a wife or husband; spouse, esp. of a reigning king or queen 3. a ship that travels along with another —*vi.* 1. to keep company; associate 2. to agree; be in accord —*vt.* to associate; join

**con·sor·ti·um** (kən sôr'shē əm) *n., pl.* -**ti·a** (-ə) [L., community of goods: see prec.] 1. an alliance, as of two or more business firms in one venture 2. an international banking agreement or association

**con·spec·tus** (kən spek'təs) *n.* [L., a view, pp. of *conspicere*: see ff.] 1. a general view; survey 2. a summary; synopsis; digest

**con·spic·u·ous** (kən spik'yoo wəs) *adj.* [< L. < *conspicere*, to look at < *com-*, intens. + *specere*, to see] 1. easy to see or perceive; obvious 2. attracting attention by being outstanding; striking [*conspicuous* bravery, *conspicuous* folly] —**con·spic'u·ous·ly** *adv.* —**con·spic'u·ous·ness** *n.*

**con·spir·a·cy** (kən spir'ə sē) *n., pl.* -**cies** 1. a conspiring, esp. in an unlawful or harmful plot 2. such a plot 3. the group taking part in such a plot 4. a combining or working together [the *conspiracy* of events]

**con·spir·a·tor** (-tər) *n.* a person who takes part in a conspiracy —**con·spir·a·to·ri·al** (kən spir'ə tôr'ē əl) *adj.* —**con·spir'a·to'ri·al·ly** *adv.*

**con·spire** (kən spīr') *vi.* -**spired'**, -**spir'ing** [< OFr. < L. *conspirare* < *com-*, together + *spirare*, to breathe] 1. to plan and act together secretly, esp. in order to commit a crime 2. to combine or work together for any purpose or effect [events *conspired* to ruin him]

**con spi·ri·to** (kän spir'i tō') [It.] *Music* with spirit; with vigor

**con·sta·ble** (kän'stə b'l, kun'-) *n.* [< OFr. < LL. *comes stabuli*, lit., count of the stable] 1. in the Middle Ages, the highest ranking official of a royal household, court, etc. 2. a peace officer in a town or village 3. [Chiefly Brit.] a policeman

**Con·sta·ble** (kun'stə b'l, kän'-), **John** 1776–1837; Eng. landscape painter

**con·stab·u·lar·y** (kən stab'yə ler'ē) *n., pl.* -**ies** 1. constables, collectively, as of a district 2. a police force characterized by a military organization —*adj.* of constables or a constabulary: also **con·stab'u·lar** (-lər)

**Con·stance** (kän'stəns) [Fr. < L. *Constantia*, lit., constancy] a feminine name

**con·stant** (kän'stənt) *adj.* [< OFr. < L. prp. of *constare* < *com-*, together + *stare*, to stand] 1. not changing; remaining the same; specif., *a*) remaining firm in purpose; resolute *b*) loyal; faithful *c*) regular; stable; unvarying 2. going on all the time; continual; persistent [*constant* interruptions] —*n.* 1. anything that does not change or vary 2. *Math., Physics a*) a quantity that always has the same value *b*) a quantity or factor assumed to have one value throughout a particular discussion or investigation: symbol, c (or k): opposed to VARIABLE —**con'stan·cy** *n.* —**con'stant·ly** *adv.*

**Con·stan·tine I** (kän'stən tēn', -tīn') 280?–337 A.D.; emperor of Rome (306–337): called *the Great*

**Con·stan·ti·no·ple** (kän'stan tə nō'p'l) *former name* (330 A.D.–1930) *of* ISTANBUL

**con·stel·late** (kän'stə lāt') *vi., vt.* -**lat'ed**, -**lat'ing** to unite in a constellation; cluster

**con·stel·la·tion** (kän'stə lā'shən) *n.* [< OFr. < LL. < L. *com-*, with + pp. of *stellare*, to shine < *stella*, a star] 1. *a*) an arbitrary group of fixed stars, usually named after some object, animal, or mythological being that they supposedly suggest in outline *b*) the part of the heavens occupied by such a group 2. any brilliant cluster, gathering, or collection 3. a group of related ideas, feelings, etc. —**con·stel·la·to·ry** (kən stel'ə tôr'ē) *adj.*

**con·ster·nate** (kän'stər nāt') *vt.* -**nat'ed**, -**nat'ing** to overcome with consternation; dismay

**con·ster·na·tion** (kän'stər nā'shən) *n.* [< L. < *consternare*, to terrify] great fear or shock that makes one feel helpless or bewildered

**con·sti·pate** (kän'stə pāt') *vt.* -**pat'ed**, -**pat'ing** [< L. pp. of *constipare* < *com-*, together + *stipare*, to cram] to cause constipation in

**con·sti·pa·tion** (kän'stə pā'shən) *n.* [see prec.] a condition in which the feces are hard and elimination from the bowels is infrequent and difficult

**con·stit·u·en·cy** (kən stich'oo wən sē) *n., pl.* -**cies** [< CONSTITUENT + -CY] 1. all the people, esp. voters, served by a particular elected official 2. the district of such a group of voters, etc.

**con·stit·u·ent** (-oo wənt) *adj.* [< L. prp. of *constituere*: see ff.] 1. necessary in forming a whole; component [a *constituent* part] 2. that can appoint or elect 3. authorized to make or revise a constitution or establish a government [a *constituent* assembly] —*n.* 1. a person who appoints another as his representative 2. a member of a constituency 3. a necessary part or element; component

**con·sti·tute** (kän'stə tōōt', -tyōōt') *vt.* -**tut'ed**, -**tut'ing** [< L. pp. of *constituere* < *com-*, together + *statuere*, to set] 1. to establish (a law, government, institution, etc.) 2. to set up (an assembly, proceeding, etc.) in a legal form 3. to give a certain office or function to [we *constitute* you our spokesman] 4. to make up; form; compose

**con·sti·tu·tion** (kän'stə tōō'shən, -tyōō'-) *n.* 1. a constituting; establishment; appointment, or formation 2. structure; organization; makeup 3. the physical makeup of a person 4. *a*) the system of fundamental laws and principles of a government, state, society, etc. *b*) a document in which these are written down; specif., [C-] such a document of the U.S.: it consists of seven articles and twenty-five amendments, and has been the supreme law of the nation since its adoption in 1789

**con·sti·tu·tion·al** (-əl) *adj.* **1.** of or in the constitution of a person or thing; basic; essential **2.** for improving a person's constitution **3.** of or in accordance with the constitution of a nation, society, etc. *[constitutional* rights] **4.** upholding the constitution —*n.* a walk or other exercise taken for one's health —**con′sti·tu′tion·al′i·ty** (-shə-nal′ə tē) *n.* —**con′sti·tu′tion·al·ly** *adv.*

**con·sti·tu·tive** (kän′stə tōōt′iv, -tyōōt′-) *adj.* **1.** having power to establish, appoint, or enact **2.** making a thing what it is; basic **3.** forming a part (*of*); constituent —**con′sti·tu′tive·ly** *adv.*

**constr. 1.** construction **2.** construed

**con·strain** (kən strān′) *vt.* [< OFr. < L. *constringere* < *com-,* together + *stringere,* to draw tight] **1.** to force into, or hold in, close bounds; confine **2.** to hold back or in by force or strain; restrain **3.** to compel *[constrained* to agree] —**con·strained′** *adj.* —**con·strain′ed·ly** (-strā′nid lē) *adv.*

**con·straint** (-strānt′) *n.* **1.** a constraining or being constrained; specif., *a)* confinement or restriction *b)* compulsion or coercion **2.** forced, unnatural manner

**con·strict** (kən strikt′) *vt.* [< L. pp. of *constringere:* see CONSTRAIN] **1.** to make smaller or narrower by binding, squeezing, etc.; contract **2.** to hold in; limit —**con·stric′tive** *adj.*

**con·stric·tion** (-strik′shən) *n.* **1.** a constricting or being constricted **2.** a feeling of tightness or pressure, as in the chest **3.** something that constricts **4.** a constricted part

**con·stric·tor** (-strik′tər) *n.* that which constricts; specif., *a)* a muscle that contracts an opening or compresses an organ *b)* a snake that kills by coiling around its prey and squeezing

**con·struct** (kən strukt′; *for n.* kän′strukt) *vt.* [< L. pp. of *construere* < *com-,* together + *struere,* to pile up] **1.** to build, form, or devise by fitting parts or elements together systematically **2.** *Geom.* to draw (a figure) so as to meet the specified requirements —*n.* something built or put together systematically —**con·struc′tor, con·struct′er** *n.*

**con·struc·tion** (kən struk′shən) *n.* **1.** the act or process of constructing **2.** the way in which something is constructed **3.** something constructed; structure; building **4.** an explanation or interpretation, as of a statement **5.** the arrangement and relation of words in a phrase, clause, or sentence **6.** a three-dimensional work of art of various materials —**con·struc′tion·al** *adj.* —**con·struc′tion·al·ly** *adv.*

**con·struc·tion·ist** (-ist) *n.* [see prec., sense 4] a person who interprets a law, document, etc. in a specified way

**con·struc·tive** (kən struk′tiv) *adj.* **1.** helping to construct; leading to improvements *[constructive* criticism] **2.** of construction or structure **3.** inferred or implied by legal or judicial interpretation —**con·struc′tive·ly** *adv.* —**con·struc′tive·ness** *n.*

**con·strue** (kən strōō′) *vt.* **-strued′, -stru′ing** [< L. *con-struere:* see CONSTRUCT] **1.** to analyze (a sentence, clause, etc.) so as to show its syntactical construction and meaning **2.** to translate **3.** to explain or deduce the meaning of; interpret *[her silence was construed* as agreement] **4.** *Gram.* to combine in syntax *[*the verb "let," unlike "permit," is *construed* with an infinitive omitting the "to"]

**con·sul** (kän′s'l) *n.* [< OFr. < L. < *consulere,* to deliberate] **1.** either of the two chief magistrates of the ancient Roman republic **2.** any of the three highest officials of the French republic from 1799 to 1804 **3.** a government official appointed to live in a foreign city and serve his country's citizens and business interests there —**con′sul·ar** (-ər) *adj.* —**con′sul·ship′** *n.*

**con·sul·ate** (-it) *n.* **1.** the position, powers, and duties of a consul **2.** the office or residence of a consul **3.** the term of office of a consul **4.** government by consuls; specif., [C-] the government of France from 1799 to 1804

**consul general** *pl.* **consuls general, consul generals** a consul in a principal commercial city, who supervises other consuls within his district

**con·sult** (kən sult′) *vi.* [L. *consultare* < pp. of *consulere,* to deliberate] to talk things over in order to decide something; confer —*vt.* **1.** *a)* to ask the advice of *b)* to refer to, esp. for information **2.** to show regard for; consider *[consult* your own wishes in the matter] —**con·sult′er** *n.*

**con·sult·ant** (kən sul′t'nt) *n.* **1.** a person who consults with another **2.** an expert called on for professional or technical advice or opinions

**con·sul·ta·tion** (kän′s'l tā′shən) *n.* **1.** the act of consulting **2.** a meeting to discuss, decide, or plan something —**con·sul·ta·tive** (kən sul′tə tiv, kän′s'l tā′-), **con·sul′-ta·to′ry** (-tôr′ē) *adj.*

**con·sume** (kən sōōm′, -syōōm′) *vt.* **-sumed′, -sum′ing** [< OFr. < L. *consumere* < *com-,* together + *sumere,* to take < *sub-,* under + *emere,* to buy] **1.** to destroy, as by fire **2.** to use up; spend or waste (time, energy, money, etc.) **3.** to eat or drink up; devour **4.** to engross or obsess *[consumed* with envy] —**con·sum′a·ble** *adj.*

**con·sum·ed·ly** (-id lē) *adv.* extremely or excessively

**con·sum·er** (kən sōō′mər, -syōō′-) *n.* a person or thing that consumes; specif., a person who buys goods or services for his own needs and not for resale or to use in the production of other goods for resale: opposed to PRODUCER

**con·sum·er·ism** (-iz'm) *n.* **1.** the movement for consumer protection in connection with defective and unsafe products, misleading business practices, etc. **2.** the consumption of goods and services

**con·sum·mate** (kən sum′it; *for v.* kän′sə māt′) *adj.* [< L. pp. of *consummare,* to sum up < *com-,* together + *summa,* a sum] **1.** complete or perfect **2.** highly expert *[a consummate* liar] —*vt.* **-mat′ed, -mat′ing 1.** to bring to completion or fulfillment; finish **2.** to make (a marriage) actual by sexual intercourse —**con·sum′mate·ly** *adv.* —**con·sum·ma·tive** (kän′sə māt′iv), **con·sum′ma·to′ry** (-ə tôr′ē) *adj.* —**con′sum·ma′tor** *n.*

**con·sum·ma·tion** (kän′sə mā′shən) *n.* **1.** a consummating or being consummated **2.** an end; outcome

**con·sump·tion** (kən sump′shən) *n.* **1.** *a)* a consuming or being consumed; specif., the using up of goods or services *b)* the amount consumed **2.** a disease causing wasting away of the body; esp., tuberculosis of the lungs

**con·sump·tive** (-tiv) *adj.* **1.** consuming or tending to consume; destructive; wasteful **2.** *Med.* of, having, or relating to tuberculosis of the lungs —*n.* a person who has tuberculosis of the lungs —**con·sump′tive·ly** *adv.*

**cont. 1.** containing **2.** contents **3.** continent **4.** continue **5.** continued **6.** contra

**con·tact** (kän′takt) *n.* [< L. pp. of *contingere* < *com-,* together + *tangere,* to touch] **1.** the act of touching or meeting **2.** the state or fact of being in touch, communication, or association (*with*) **3.** *a)* an acquaintance, esp. one who is influential *b)* a connection with such a person **4.** *Elec. a)* a connection between two conductors in a circuit *b)* a device for opening and closing such a connection —*vt.* **1.** to place in contact **2.** to get in touch with —*vi.* to be in or come into contact —*adj.* of, involving, or relating to contact

**contact lens** a tiny, thin correctional lens of glass or plastic placed in the fluid over the cornea of the eye

**con·ta·gion** (kən tā′jən) *n.* [L. *contagio,* a touching < *contingere:* see CONTACT] **1.** the spreading of disease by contact **2.** a contagious disease **3.** the causative agent of a communicable disease **4.** *a)* the spreading of an emotion, idea, etc. from person to person *b)* the emotion, idea, etc. so spread

**con·ta·gious** (-jəs) *adj.* [< OFr. < LL. *contagiosus*] **1.** spread by contact: said of diseases **2.** carrying the causative agent of such a disease **3.** spreading from person to person —**con·ta′gious·ly** *adv.* —**con·ta′gious·ness** *n.*

**con·tain** (kən tān′) *vt.* [< OFr. < L. *continere* < *com-,* together + *tenere,* to hold] **1.** to have in it; hold, enclose, or include **2.** to have the capacity for holding **3.** to hold back or within fixed limits; specif., *a)* to restrain (one's feelings, oneself, etc.) *b)* to check the power or expansion of **4.** to be divisible by, esp. without a remainder *[10 contains* 5 and 2] —**con·tain′a·ble** *adj.*

**con·tain·er** (-ər) *n.* a thing for containing something; box, can, jar, etc.

**con·tain·er·ize** (-īz′) *vt.* **-ized′, -iz′ing** to pack (general cargo) in large, standardized containers for more efficient shipment —**con·tain′er·i·za′tion** *n.*

**con·tain·ment** (-mənt) *n.* the policy of attempting to prevent the influence of an opposing nation or political system from spreading

**con·tam·i·nant** (kən tam′ə nənt) *n.* a substance that contaminates another substance, the air, water, etc.

**con·tam·i·nate** (-ə nāt′) *vt.* **-nat′ed, -nat′ing** [< L. pp. of *contaminare,* to defile < *contamen,* contact < *com-,* together + base of *tangere,* to touch] to make impure, infected, corrupt, radioactive, etc. by contact with or addition of something; pollute; defile; sully; taint —**con·tam′i·na′tion** *n.* —**con·tam′i·na′tive** *adj.* —**con·tam′i·na′tor** *n.*

**contd.** continued

**con·temn** (kən tem′) *vt.* [< OFr. < L. *contemnere* < *com-,* intens. + *temnere,* to scorn] to treat with contempt; scorn —**con·temn′er, con·tem′nor** (-tem′ər, -tem′nər) *n.*

**con·tem·plate** (kän′təm plāt′) *vt.* **-plat′ed, -plat′ing** [< L. pp. of *contemplari,* to observe (orig., in augury, to mark out a space for observation) < *com-,* intens. + *templum,* TEMPLE[1]] **1.** to look at intently; gaze at **2.** to think about

---

fat, āpe, cär; ten, ēven; is, bīte; gō, hôrn, tōōl, look; oil, out; up, fur; get; joy; yet; chin; she; thin, then; zh, leisure; ŋ, ring; ə for *a* in *ago, e* in *agent, i* in *sanity, o* in *comply, u* in *focus;* ' as in *able* (ā′b'l); Fr. bal; ë, Fr. coeur; ö, Fr. feu; Fr. mon; ô, Fr. coq; ü, Fr. duc; r, Fr. cri; H, G. ich; kh, G. doch; ‡foreign; *hypothetical; < derived from. See inside front cover.

intently; study carefully; consider **3.** to expect or intend —*vi.* to meditate or muse —**con′tem·pla′tion** *n.* —**con′-tem·pla′tor** *n.*

**con·tem·pla·tive** (kən tem′plə tiv, kän′təm plāt′iv) *adj.* of or inclined to contemplation; thoughtful; meditative —*n.* a member of a religious order dedicated to contemplation —**com·tem′pla·tive·ly** *adv.* —**con·tem′pla·tive·ness** *n.*

**con·tem·po·ra·ne·ous** (kən tem′pə rā′nē əs) *adj.* [< L. < *com-*, with + *tempus* (gen. *temporis*), time] existing or happening in the same period of time —**con·tem′po·ra·ne′i·ty** (-pər ə nē′ə tē), **con·tem′po·ra′ne·ous·ness** *n.* —**con·tem′po·ra′ne·ous·ly** *adv.*

**con·tem·po·rar·y** (kən tem′pə rer′ē) *adj.* [< L. *com-*, with + *temporarius* < *tempus*, time] **1.** living or happening in the same period **2.** of about the same age **3.** of or in the style of the present or recent times; modern —*n., pl.* **-ies** a person or thing of the same period or about the same age as another or others

**con·tem·po·rize** (kən tem′pə rīz′) *vt., vi.* **-rized′, -riz′ing** to make or become contemporary

**con·tempt** (kən tempt′) *n.* [OFr. < L. pp. of *contemnere:* see CONTEMN] **1.** the feeling of a person toward someone or something he considers worthless or beneath notice; scorn **2.** the condition of being despised or scorned **3.** *Law* a showing disrespect for the dignity of a court (or legislature): in full, **contempt of court** (or **congress,** etc.)

**con·tempt·i·ble** (kən temp′tə b′l) *adj.* deserving contempt or scorn; despicable —**con·temp′ti·bil′i·ty, con·temp′ti·ble·ness** *n.* —**con·temp′ti·bly** *adv.*

**con·temp·tu·ous** (kən temp′chōo wəs) *adj.* full of contempt; scornful; disdainful —**con·temp′tu·ous·ly** *adv.* —**con·temp′tu·ous·ness** *n.*

**con·tend** (kən tend′) *vi.* [< L. *contendere* < *com-*, together + *tendere,* to stretch] **1.** to strive in combat; fight **2.** to strive in debate; argue **3.** to strive in competition; compete; vie —*vt.* to hold to be a fact; assert —**con·tend′er** *n.*

**con·tent**[1] (kən tent′) *adj.* [< OFr. < L. pp. of *continere:* see CONTAIN] **1.** happy enough with what one has or is; satisfied **2.** willing; assenting —*vt.* to make content; satisfy —*n.* contentment

**con·tent**[2] (kän′tent) *n.* [< L. pp. of *continere:* see CONTAIN] **1.** [*usually pl.*] *a)* all that is contained in something *b)* all that is dealt with in a writing or speech [a table of *contents*] **2.** *a)* all that is dealt with in an area of study, work of art, discussion, etc. *b)* meaning; substance **3.** the amount contained [iron with a high carbon *content*]

**con·tent·ed** (kən ten′tid) *adj.* having or showing no desire for something more or different; satisfied —**con·tent′ed·ly** *adv.* —**con·tent′ed·ness** *n.*

**con·ten·tion** (kən ten′shən) *n.* [see CONTEND] **1.** the act of contending; strife, struggle, controversy, dispute, quarrel, etc. **2.** a statement or point that one argues for as true or valid

**con·ten·tious** (-ten′shəs) *adj.* **1.** quarrelsome **2.** of or characterized by contention —**con·ten′tious·ly** *adv.* —**con·ten′tious·ness** *n.*

**con·tent·ment** (kən tent′mənt) *n.* the state, quality, or fact of being contented

**con·ter·mi·nous** (kən tur′mə nəs, kän-) *adj.* [< L. < *com-*, together + *terminus,* an end] **1.** having a common boundary; contiguous **2.** contained within the same boundaries or limits —**con·ter′mi·nous·ly** *adv.*

**con·tes·sa** (kôn tes′sä) *n.* [It.] *same as* COUNTESS

**con·test** (kən test′; *for n.* kän′test) *vt.* [< Fr. < L. *contestari* < *com-*, together + *testari,* to bear witness < *testis,* a witness] **1.** to try to disprove or invalidate (something); dispute [to *contest* a will] **2.** to fight for; struggle to win or keep —*vi.* to struggle (*with* or *against*); contend —*n.* **1.** a fight, struggle, or controversy **2.** any race, game, etc. in which individuals or teams compete to determine the winner —**con·test′a·ble** *adj.* —**con·test′er** *n.*

**con·test·ant** (kən tes′tənt) *n.* [Fr.] **1.** one that competes in a contest **2.** one who contests a claim, decision, etc.

**con·text** (kän′tekst) *n.* [< L. pp. of *contexere* < *com-*, together + *texere,* to weave] the parts of a sentence, paragraph, etc. next to or surrounding a word or passage and determining its exact meaning —**con·tex·tu·al** (kən teks′chōo wəl) *adj.* —**con·tex′tu·al·ly** *adv.*

**con·ti·gu·i·ty** (kän′tə gyōo′ə tē) *n., pl.* **-ties** the state of being contiguous; nearness or contact

**con·tig·u·ous** (kən tig′yōo wəs) *adj.* [< L. *contiguus* < base of *contingere:* see CONTACT] **1.** in physical contact; touching along all or most of one side **2.** near, next, or adjacent —**con·tig′u·ous·ly** *adv.* —**con·tig′u·ous·ness** *n.*

**con·ti·nence** (känt′′n əns) *n.* [see ff.] **1.** self-restraint; moderation **2.** self-restraint in sexual activity; esp., total abstinence

**con·ti·nent** (-ənt) *adj.* [< OFr. < L. prp. of *continere:* see CONTAIN] **1.** self-restrained; temperate **2.** characterized by self-restraint, esp. by total abstinence, in sexual activity —*n.* any of the main large land areas of the earth (Africa, Asia, Australia, Europe, N. America, S. America, and, some-

times, Antarctica) —**the Continent** all of Europe except the British Isles —**con′ti·nent·ly** *adv.*

**con·ti·nen·tal** (känt′′n en′t′l) *adj.* **1.** of a continent **2.** [*sometimes* C-] European **3.** [C-] of the American colonies at the time of the American Revolution —*n.* **1.** [*usually* C-] a European **2.** [C-] a soldier of the American army during the Revolution **3.** a piece of paper money issued by the Continental Congress: it became almost worthless before the end of the war, hence the phrases **not care** (or **give**), or **not worth, a continental** —**con′ti·nen′tal·ly** *adv.*

**continental breakfast** [*also* C- b-] a light breakfast, usually of rolls and coffee or tea

**Continental Congress** either of the two assemblies of representatives from the American colonies during the Revolutionary period: the second issued the Declaration of Independence (1776)

**continental drift** the hypothetical drifting of continents due to currents in the earth's mantle

**continental shelf** the submerged, gradually sloping shelf of land that borders a continent and ends in a steep descent (**continental slope**) to the deep ocean

**con·tin·gen·cy** (kən tin′jən sē) *n., pl.* **-cies 1.** a contingent quality or condition; esp., dependence on chance or uncertain conditions **2.** a possible, unforeseen, or accidental occurrence **3.** some thing or event which depends on or is incidental to another Also **con·tin′gence**

**con·tin·gent** (-jənt) *adj.* [< L. prp. of *contingere:* see CONTACT] **1.** that may or may not happen; possible **2.** happening by chance; accidental **3.** unpredictable because dependent on chance **4.** dependent (*on* or *upon* an uncertainty); conditional —*n.* **1.** a chance happening **2.** a share or quota, as of troops, laborers, etc. **3.** a group forming part of a larger group —**con·tin′gent·ly** *adv.*

**con·tin·u·al** (kən tin′yōo wəl) *adj.* **1.** repeated often; going on in rapid succession **2.** going on uninterruptedly; continuous —**con·tin′u·al·ly** *adv.*

**con·tin·u·ance** (kən tin′yōo wəns) *n.* **1.** the act or process of continuing **2.** the time during which an action or state lasts; duration **3.** the fact of remaining (*in* a place or condition); stay **4.** an unbroken succession **5.** [Rare] a sequel **6.** *Law* postponement or adjournment to a later date

**con·tin·u·a·tion** (kən tin′yōo wā′shən) *n.* **1.** a keeping up or going on without stopping **2.** a beginning again after an interruption; resumption **3.** a part or thing by which something is continued; extension, sequel, etc.

**con·tin·ue** (kən tin′yōō, -yoo) *vi.* **-ued, -u·ing** [< OFr. < L. *continuare,* to join < *continere:* see CONTAIN] **1.** to last; endure **2.** to go on in a specified course of action or condition; persist **3.** to go on or extend **4.** to stay **5.** to go on again after an interruption; resume —*vt.* **1.** to go on with; carry on; keep up **2.** to extend **3.** to resume **4.** to cause to remain; retain **5.** *Law* to postpone or adjourn to a later date —**con·tin′u·a·ble** *adj.* —**con·tin′u·er** *n.*

**con·ti·nu·i·ty** (känt′ə nōō′ə tē, -nyōō′-) *n., pl.* **-ties 1.** a continuous state or quality **2.** an unbroken, coherent whole **3.** continuous duration **4.** the script or scenario for a motion picture, radio or television program, etc. **5.** a series of comments connecting the parts of a radio or television program

**con·tin·u·ous** (kən tin′yōo wəs) *adj.* [L. *continuus:* see CONTINUE] going on or extending without interruption or break; unbroken; connected —**con·tin′u·ous·ly** *adv.*

**con·tin·u·um** (-yōo wəm) *n., pl.* **-u·a** (-wə), **-u·ums** [L.] a continuous whole, quantity, or series

**con·tort** (kən tôrt′) *vt., vi.* [< L. pp. of *contorquere* < *com-*, together + *torquere,* to twist] to twist or wrench out of its usual form into one that is grotesque; distort violently —**con·tor′tion** *n.* —**con·tor′tive** *adj.*

**con·tor·tion·ist** (kən tôr′shən ist) *n.* a person who can twist his body into unnatural positions

**con·tour** (kän′toor) *n.* [Fr. < It. < LL. *contornare* < L. *com-*, intens. + *tornare,* to turn: see TURN] the outline of a figure, land, etc. —*vt.* **1.** to represent in contour **2.** to shape or mold to the contour of something —*adj.* **1.** made so as to conform to the shape or outline of something **2.** characterized by the making of furrows along the natural contour lines so as to avoid erosion, as on a hillside [*contour* farming]

**contour map** a map with lines (**contour lines**) connecting all points of the same elevation

**contr. 1.** contract **2.** contraction **3.** contrary

**con·tra-** [< L. *contra,* against] *a prefix meaning:* **1.** against, opposite, opposed to **2.** lower in musical pitch [*contrabassoon*]

**con·tra·band** (kän′trə band′) *n.* [< Sp. < It. < *contra-*, against + *bando* < VL. *bannum* (akin to BAN[1])] **1.** unlawful or prohibited trade **2.** smuggled goods, illegally imported or

CONTOUR MAP

exported **3.** *same as* CONTRABAND OF WAR —*adj.* forbidden by law to be imported or exported —**con'tra·band'ist** *n.*

**contraband of war** war materiel which, by international law, may be seized by a belligerent when shipped to the other one by a neutral

**con·tra·bass** (kän'trə bās') *adj.* [see CONTRA- & BASS¹] having its pitch an octave lower than the normal bass —*n.* *same as* DOUBLE BASS —**con'tra·bass'ist** *n.*

**con·tra·bas·soon** (kän'trə bə sōōn') *n.* the double bassoon, which is larger than the ordinary bassoon and an octave lower in pitch

**con·tra·cep·tion** (kän'trə sep'shən) *n.* [CONTRA- + (CON)CEPTION] intentional prevention of the fertilization of the human ovum, as by special devices, drugs, etc. —**con'tra·cep'tive** *adj., n.*

**con·tract** (kän'trakt *for n. & usually for vt. 1 & vi. 1;* kən trakt' *for v. generally*) *n.* [OFr. < L. pp. of *contrahere* < *com-,* together + *trahere,* to draw] **1.** an agreement to do something, esp. a written one enforceable by law **2.** a formal agreement of marriage or betrothal **3.** a document containing the terms of an agreement **4.** *Bridge a)* the number of tricks bid by the highest bidder *b) same as* CONTRACT BRIDGE —*vt.* **1.** to enter upon, or undertake, by contract **2.** to get, acquire, or incur **3.** to reduce in size; draw together; shrink **4.** to narrow in scope; restrict **5.** *Gram.* to shorten (a word or phrase) by the omission of a letter or sound (*I'm, e'er*) —*vi.* **1.** to make a contract **2.** to become reduced in size or bulk —**contract out** to assign (a job) by contract —**con·tract'i·bil'i·ty** *n.* —**con·tract'i·ble** *adj.*

**con·tract bridge** (kän'trakt) a form of auction bridge: only the tricks bid may be counted toward a game

**con·trac·tile** (kən trak't'l) *adj.* **1.** having the power of contracting **2.** producing contraction —**con·trac·til·i·ty** (kän'trak til'ə tē) *n.*

**con·trac·tion** (-shən) *n.* **1.** a contracting or being contracted **2.** the drawing up and thickening of a muscle in action **3.** *Gram. a)* the shortening of a word or phrase *b)* a word form resulting from this (Ex.: *aren't* for *are not*) —**con·trac'tion·al** *adj.* —**con·trac'tive** (-tiv) *adj.*

**con·trac·tor** (kän'trak tər, kən trak'-) *n.* **1.** one of the parties to a contract **2.** one, esp. one in the building trades, who contracts to supply certain materials or do certain work for a stipulated sum **3.** a muscle that contracts

**con·trac·tu·al** (kən trak'choo wəl) *adj.* of, or having the nature of, a contract —**con·trac'tu·al·ly** *adv.*

**con·tra·dance** (kän'trə dans') *n. same as* CONTREDANSE

**con·tra·dict** (kän'trə dikt') *vt.* [< L. pp. of *contradicere* < *contra-,* against + *dicere,* to speak] **1.** *a)* to assert the opposite of (a statement) *b)* to deny the statement of (a person) **2.** to be contrary to everyone; to go against —**con'tra·dict'a·ble** *adj.* —**con'tra·dic'tor, con'tra·dict'er** *n.*

**con·tra·dic·tion** (-dik'shən) *n.* **1.** a contradicting or being contradicted **2.** a statement in opposition to another; denial **3.** a condition in which things tend to be contrary to each other; inconsistency; discrepancy

**con·tra·dic·to·ry** (-dik'tər ē) *adj.* **1.** involving a contradiction; inconsistent **2.** inclined to contradict or deny Also **con'tra·dic'tive** —**con'tra·dic'to·ri·ly** *adv.* —**con'tra·dic'to·ri·ness** *n.*

**con·tra·dis·tinc·tion** (-dis tiŋk'shən) *n.* distinction by contrast —**con'tra·dis·tinc'tive** *adj.*

**con·tral·to** (kən tral'tō) *n., pl.* -tos, -ti (-tē) [It.: see CONTRA- & ALTO] **1.** the range of the lowest female voice **2.** a voice or singer with such range **3.** a part for this voice —*adj.* of or for a contralto

**con·trap·tion** (kən trap'shən) *n.* [< ?] [Colloq.] a contrivance or gadget

**con·tra·pun·tal** (kän'trə pun't'l) *adj.* [< It. *contrappunto* (see COUNTERPOINT) + -AL] **1.** of or characterized by counterpoint **2.** according to the principles of counterpoint —**con'tra·pun'tal·ly** *adv.* —**con'tra·pun'tist** *n.*

**con·tra·ri·e·ty** (kän'trə rī'ə tē) *n.* **1.** the condition or quality of being contrary **2.** *pl.* -ties anything that is contrary; inconsistency

**con·trar·i·wise** (kän'trer ē wīz'; *for 3, often* kən trer'-) *adv.* **1.** on the contrary; from the opposite point of view **2.** in the opposite way, order, direction, etc. **3.** perversely

**con·trar·y** (kän'trer ē; *for adj. 4, often* kən trer'ē) *adj.* [< OFr. < L. *contrarius* < *contra,* against] **1.** in opposition **2.** opposite in nature, order, direction, etc.; altogether different **3.** unfavorable *(contrary winds)* **4.** inclined to oppose stubbornly; perverse —*n., pl.* -trar·ies the opposite; thing that is the opposite of another —*adv.* in a contrary way —**on the contrary** as opposed to what has been said —**to the contrary** to the opposite effect —**con'trar·i·ly** *adv.* —**con'trar·i·ness** *n.*

**con·trast** (kən trast'; *for n.* kän'trast) *vt.* [< Fr. < It. & VL. < L. *contra,* against + *stare,* to stand] to compare so as to point out the differences; set off against one another —*vi.* to show differences when compared —*n.* **1.** a contrasting or being contrasted **2.** a difference, esp. a striking difference, between things being compared **3.** a person or thing showing differences when compared with another —**con·trast'a·ble** *adj.* —**con·trast'ive** *adj.*

**con·tra·vene** (kän'trə vēn') *vt.* -vened', -ven'ing [< Fr. < LL. < L. *contra,* against + *venire,* to come] **1.** to go against; oppose; violate **2.** to disagree with; contradict —**con'tra·ven'er** *n.* —**con'tra·ven'tion** (-ven'shən) *n.*

**con·tre·danse** (kän'trə dans', kôn'trə däns') *n.* [Fr., altered (after *contre,* opposite) < COUNTRY-DANCE] a folk dance with the partners in two facing lines

**con·tre·temps** (kôn trə tän') *n., pl.* -temps' (-tän') [Fr., ult. < OFr. prp. of *contrester,* CONTRAST] an inopportune happening causing embarrassment

**con·trib·ute** (kən trib'yōōt, -yoot) *vt., vi.* -ut·ed, -ut·ing [< L. pp. of *contribuere;* see COM- & TRIBUTE] **1.** to give jointly with others to a common fund **2.** to write (an article, poem, etc.) for a magazine, newspaper, etc. **3.** to furnish (ideas, etc.) —**contribute to** to have a share in bringing about —**con·trib'u·tive** *adj.* —**con·trib'u·tor** *n.*

**con·tri·bu·tion** (kän'trə byōō'shən) *n.* **1.** a contributing **2.** something contributed **3.** [Archaic] a special levy or tax

**con·trib·u·to·ry** (kən trib'yoo tôr'ē) *adj.* **1.** contributing **2.** involving a contribution —*n., pl.* -ries a person or thing that contributes

**con·trite** (kən trīt', kän'trīt) *adj.* [OFr. < LL. < L. pp. of *conterere,* to grind < *com-,* together + *terere,* to rub] **1.** feeling deep sorrow or remorse for having sinned or done wrong **2.** resulting from remorse or guilt —**con·trite'ly** *adv.* —**con·trite'ness, con·tri'tion** (-trish'ən) *n.*

**con·triv·ance** (kən trī'vəns) *n.* **1.** the act, way, or power of contriving **2.** something contrived, as an invention, mechanical device, plan, etc.

**con·trive** (kən trīv') *vt.* -trived', -triv'ing [< OFr. *controver,* to find out < VL. *contropare,* to compare] **1.** to devise; plan **2.** to construct skillfully or ingeniously; fabricate **3.** to bring about, as by a scheme —*vi.* to form plans; scheme —**con·triv'a·ble** *adj.* —**con·triv'er** *n.*

**con·trived** (-trīvd') *adj.* not spontaneous

**con·trol** (kən trōl') *vt.* -trolled', -trol'ling [< Anglo-Fr. < Fr. < ML. *contrarotulus,* a register < L. *contra,* against + *rotulus:* see ROLL] **1.** to regulate (financial affairs) **2.** to exercise authority over; direct; command **3.** to curb; restrain —*n.* **1.** power to direct or regulate **2.** the condition of being directed; restraint **3.** a means of controlling; check **4.** a standard of comparison for checking the findings of an experiment **5.** [*usually pl.*] an apparatus to regulate a mechanism —**con·trol'la·bil'i·ty** *n.* —**con·trol'la·ble** *adj.*

**control experiment** an experiment in which one factor after another is varied while the other factors are controlled

**con·trol·ler** (kən trōl'ər) *n.* **1.** a person in charge of expenditures or finances, as in a business, government (usually sp. *comptroller*), etc. **2.** a person or device that controls —**con·trol'ler·ship'** *n.*

**control tower** a tower at an airport, from which air traffic is directed

**con·tro·ver·sial** (kän'trə vur'shəl) *adj.* of, subject to, or stirring up controversy; debatable —**con'tro·ver'sial·ist** *n.* —**con'tro·ver'sial·ly** *adv.*

**con·tro·ver·sy** (kän'trə vur'sē) *n., pl.* -sies [< L. < *contra,* against + pp. of *vertere,* to turn] **1.** a discussion of a question in which opposing opinions clash; debate **2.** a quarrel or dispute

**con·tro·vert** (kän'trə vurt', kän'trə vurt') *vt.* [backformation < prec.] **1.** to argue or reason against; dispute **2.** to argue about; debate —**con'tro·vert'i·ble** *adj.* —**con'tro·vert'i·bly** *adv.*

**con·tu·ma·cious** (kän'too mā'shəs, -tyoo-) *adj.* [< ff.] obstinately resisting authority; disobedient

**con·tu·ma·cy** (kän'too mə sē, -tyoo-; kən too'-) *n., pl.* -cies [< L. < *contumax,* stubborn < *com-,* intens. + *tumere,* to swell up] stubborn refusal to submit to authority; disobedience

**con·tu·me·ly** (kän'too mə lē, -mē'-, -tyoo-; kən too'-) *n., pl.* -lies [< OFr. < L. *contumelia,* reproach, prob. akin to prec.] **1.** haughty rudeness; humiliating treatment **2.** a scornful insult —**con'tu·me'li·ous** (-mē'lē əs) *adj.*

**con·tuse** (kən tooz', -tyooz') *vt.* -tused', -tus'ing [< L. pp. of *contundere* < *com-,* intens. + *tundere,* to beat] to bruise without breaking the skin

**con·tu·sion** (-tōō'zhən, -tyōō'-) *n.* a bruise

**co·nun·drum** (kə nun′drəm) *n.* [16th-c. Oxford University L. slang] **1.** a riddle whose answer contains a pun **2.** any puzzling question or problem

**con·ur·ba·tion** (kän′ər bā′shən) *n.* [< CON- + L. *urbs,* city + -ATION] a densely populated urban area, including suburbs and towns around a large city

**con·va·lesce** (kän′və les′) *vi.* -lesced′, -lesc′ing [< L. *convalescere* < *com-,* intens. + *valescere* < *valere,* to be strong] to recover gradually from illness; regain health

**con·va·les·cence** (-les′'ns) *n.* [see prec.] **1.** a gradual recovery of health after illness **2.** the period of such recovery —**con′va·les′cent** *adj., n.*

**con·vec·tion** (kən vek′shən) *n.* [< L. < pp. of *convehere* < *com-,* together + *vehere,* to carry] **1.** a transmitting or conveying **2.** *a)* the movement of parts of a fluid within the fluid because of differences in the density, temperature, etc. of the parts *b)* the transference of heat by such movement —**con·vec′tion·al** *adj.* —**con·vec′tive** *adj.* —**con·vec′tive·ly** *adv.* —**con·vec′tor** *n.*

**con·vene** (kən vēn′) *vi., vt.* -vened′, -ven′ing [< OFr. < L. *convenire* < *com-,* together + *venire,* to come] to assemble for a meeting —**con·ven′er** *n.*

**con·ven·ience** (kən vēn′yəns) *n.* [< L. < *convenire,* CONVENE] **1.** the quality or condition of being convenient **2.** personal comfort **3.** anything that adds to one's comfort or saves work —**at one's convenience** at a time, place, etc. that suits one

**con·ven·ient** (-yənt) *adj.* **1.** favorable to one's comfort; easy to do, use, or get to; handy **2.** [Colloq.] easily accessible (*to*); near (*to*) —**con·ven′ient·ly** *adv.*

**con·vent** (kän′vənt, -vent) *n.* [< OFr. < L. *conventus,* assembly, orig. pp. of *convenire,* CONVENE] **1.** a community of nuns or, sometimes, monks, living under strict religious vows **2.** the building or buildings in which they live

**con·ven·ti·cle** (kən ven′ti k'l) *n.* [< OFr. < L. dim. of prec.] **1.** a religious assembly, esp. an illegal or secret one **2.** a place where such an assembly meets

**con·ven·tion** (kən ven′shən) *n.* **1.** an assembly, often periodical, or the delegates to it [a political *convention,* lawyers' *convention*] **2.** *a)* an agreement between persons, nations, etc. *b)* general agreement on the usages and practices of social life **3.** a customary practice, rule, etc.

**con·ven·tion·al** (-'l) *adj.* **1.** having to do with a convention **2.** of, sanctioned by, or growing out of custom or usage; customary **3.** *a)* conforming to accepted rules or standards; formal; not natural, original, or spontaneous *b)* not unusual; ordinary **4.** stylized; conventionalized **5.** nonnuclear [*conventional* weapons] —**con·ven′tion·al·ism** *n.* —**con·ven′tion·al·ist** *n.* —**con·ven′tion·al·ly** *adv.*

**con·ven·tion·al·i·ty** (kən ven′shə nal′ə tē) *n., pl.* -ties **1.** a being conventional **2.** conventional behavior or act **3.** a conventional form, usage, or rule

**con·ven·tion·al·ize** (kən ven′shən 'l īz′) *vt.* -ized′, -iz′ing **1.** to make conventional **2.** *Art* to treat in a conventional manner —**con·ven′tion·al·i·za′tion** *n.*

**conventional wisdom** the generally accepted belief with regard to some matter, or the set of beliefs held by most people

**con·ven·tu·al** (kən ven′choō wəl) *adj.* of or like a convent —*n.* a member of a convent

**con·verge** (kən vurj′) *vi.* -verged′, -verg′ing [< LL. *convergere* < L. *com-,* together + *vergere,* to turn] to come together or tend to come together at a point —*vt.* to cause to converge

**con·ver·gence** (-vur′jəns) *n.* **1.** the act, fact, or condition of converging **2.** the point at which things converge Also **con·ver′gen·cy,** *pl.* -cies —**con·ver′gent** *adj.*

**con·vers·a·ble** (kən vur′sə b'l) *adj.* **1.** easy to talk to; affable **2.** liking to converse or talk

**con·ver·sant** (kən vur′s'nt, kän′vər-) *adj.* [see CONVERSE¹] familiar or acquainted (*with*), esp. as a result of study or experience; versed (*in*) —**con·ver′sance, con·ver′san·cy** *n.* —**con·ver′sant·ly** *adv.*

**con·ver·sa·tion** (kän′vər sā′shən) *n.* [see CONVERSE¹] a talking together; specif., *a)* familiar talk; verbal exchange of ideas, opinions, etc. *b)* an informal conference by representatives of governments, factions, etc.

**con·ver·sa·tion·al** (-'l) *adj.* **1.** of, like, or for conversation **2.** given to conversation; liking to converse —**con′ver·sa′tion·al·ist, con′ver·sa′tion·ist** *n.*

**conversation piece** an unusual article of furniture, bric-a-brac, etc. that attracts attention or invites comment

**con·verse¹** (kən vurs′; *for n.* kän′vərs) *vi.* -versed′, -vers′ing [< OFr. < L. *conversari,* to live with, ult. < *convertere:* see CONVERT] to hold a conversation; talk —*n.* informal talk; conversation —**con·vers′er** *n.*

**con·verse²** (kän′vərs; *also, for adj.,* kən vurs′) *adj.* [< L. pp. of *convertere:* see CONVERT] reversed in position, order, etc.; opposite; contrary —*n.* a thing related in a converse way; the opposite —**con·verse′ly** *adv.*

**con·ver·sion** (kən vur′zhən, -shən) *n.* a converting or being converted; specif., a change from lack of faith to religious belief or from one religion to another —**con·ver′sion·al, con·ver′sion·ar′y** *adj.*

**con·vert** (kən vurt′; *for n.* kän′vərt) *vt.* [< OFr. < L. *convertere* < *com-,* together + *vertere,* to turn] **1.** to change from one form or use to another; transform [*convert* grain into flour] **2.** to cause to change from one belief, religion, etc. to another **3.** to exchange for something equal in value **4.** *Finance* to change (a security, currency, etc.) into an equivalent of another form **5.** *Law* to take and use (another's property) unlawfully —*vi.* **1.** to be converted **2.** *Bowling* to knock down all of the standing pins on the second bowl, scoring a spare **3.** *Football* to score the extra point or points after a touchdown —*n.* a person converted, as to a religion

**con·vert·er** (kən vur′tər) *n.* a person or thing that converts; specif., *a)* a furnace for converting pig iron into steel *b)* *Elec.* a device for converting alternating current into direct current: cf. INVERTER *c)* *Radio & TV* any device for adapting a receiver to added frequencies or modulations Also sp. **con·ver′tor**

**converter reactor** a nuclear reactor that produces less fissionable material than it consumes

**con·vert·i·ble** (kən vur′tə b'l) *adj.* that can be converted —*n.* **1.** a thing that can be converted **2.** an automobile with a top that can be folded back —**con·vert′i·bil′i·ty** *n.*

**con·vex** (kän veks′, kən-; *also, & for n. usually,* kän′veks) *adj.* [< L. *convexus,* pp. of *convehere* < *com-,* together + *vehere,* to bring] curving outward like the surface of a sphere —*n.* a convex surface, line, object, etc. —**con·vex′i·ty** *n., pl.* -ties —**con·vex′ly** *adv.*

**con·vex·o-con·cave** (kən vek′sō kän kāv′) *adj.* convex on one side and concave on the other

**con·vex·o-con·vex** (-kän veks′) *adj.* convex on both sides, as some lenses

CONVEX LENSES (A, plano-convex; B, convexo-concave; C, convexo-convex)

**con·vey** (kən vā′) *vt.* [< Anglo-Fr. *conveier,* to escort < L. *com-,* together + *via,* way] **1.** to take from one place to another; transport; carry **2.** to serve as a channel or medium for; transmit **3.** to make known; communicate **4.** to transfer, as title to property, to another person —**con·vey′a·ble** *adj.*

**con·vey·ance** (-əns) *n.* **1.** a conveying **2.** a means of conveying, esp. a vehicle **3.** *a)* the transfer of the ownership of real property from one person to another *b)* a deed —**con·vey′anc·er** *n.*

**con·vey·or, con·vey·er** (-ər) *n.* one that conveys; esp., a mechanical contrivance, as a continuous chain or belt (**conveyor belt**)

**con·vict** (kən vikt′; *for n.* kän′vikt) *vt.* [< L. pp. of *convincere:* see CONVINCE] **1.** to prove (a person) guilty [*convicted* by the evidence] **2.** to judge and find guilty of an offense charged —*n.* **1.** one found guilty of a crime and sentenced by a court **2.** one serving a sentence in prison

**con·vic·tion** (kən vik′shən) *n.* **1.** a convicting or being convicted **2.** the state or appearance of being convinced, as of the truth of a belief [to speak with *conviction*] **3.** a strong belief —**con·vic′tive** *adj.* —**con·vic′tive·ly** *adv.*

**con·vince** (kən vins′) *vt.* -vinced′, -vinc′ing [L. *convincere* < *com-,* intens. + *vincere,* to conquer] to overcome the doubts of; persuade by argument or evidence; make feel sure —**con·vinc′er** *n.* —**con·vinc′ing·ly** *adv.*

**con·viv·i·al** (kən viv′ē əl) *adj.* [< L. < *convivium,* a feast < *com-,* together + *vivere,* to live] **1.** having to do with a feast or festive activity **2.** fond of eating, drinking, and good company; sociable; jovial —**con·viv′i·al·ist** *n.* —**con·viv′i·al′i·ty** *n.* —**con·viv′i·al·ly** *adv.*

**con·vo·ca·tion** (kän′və kā′shən) *n.* **1.** a convoking **2.** a group that has been convoked; esp., an ecclesiastical or academic assembly —**con′vo·ca′tion·al** *adj.*

**con·voke** (kən vōk′) *vt.* -voked′, -vok′ing [< Fr. < L. *convocare* < *com-,* together + *vocare,* to call] to call together; summon to assemble; convene —**con·vok′er** *n.*

**con·vo·lute** (kän′və loot′) *adj.* [< L. pp. of *convolvere:* see CONVOLVE] rolled up in a spiral with the coils falling one upon the other; coiled —*vt., vi.* -lut′ed, -lut′ing to wind around; coil —**con′vo·lute′ly** *adv.*

**con·vo·lut·ed** (-id) *adj.* **1.** having convolutions; coiled **2.** involved; intricate; complicated

**con·vo·lu·tion** (kän′və loo′shən) *n.* **1.** a twisting, coiling, or winding together **2.** a convoluted condition **3.** a fold, twist, or coil of something convoluted; specif., any of the irregular folds or ridges on the surface of the brain

**con·volve** (kən välv′) *vt., vi.* -volved′, -volv′ing [< L. *convolvere* < *com-,* together + *volvere,* to roll] to roll, coil, or twist together

**con·vol·vu·lus** (kən väl′vyə ləs) *n., pl.* **-lus·es, -li′** (-lī′) [L., bindweed: see prec.] any of a genus of trailing or twining plants related to the morning glory

**con·voy** (kän′voi; *also for v.* kən voi′) *vt.* [< OFr. *convoier,* CONVEY] to go along with as an escort, esp. in order to protect —*n.* **1.** the act of convoying **2.** a protecting escort, as for ships or troops **3.** a group of ships, vehicles, etc. traveling together for mutual protection

**con·vulse** (kən vuls′) *vt.* **-vulsed′, -vuls′ing** [< L. *convulsus,* pp. of *convellere* < com-, together + *vellere,* to pluck] **1.** to shake or disturb violently; agitate **2.** to cause convulsions, or spasms, in **3.** to cause to shake with laughter, rage, grief, etc. —**con·vul′sive** *adj.* —**con·vul′sive·ly** *adv.*

**con·vul·sion** (-vul′shən) *n.* **1.** a violent, involuntary contraction or spasm of the muscles: *often used in pl.* **2.** a violent fit of laughter **3.** any violent disturbance

**co·ny** (kō′nē) *n., pl.* **-nies** *same as* CONEY

**coo** (kō̄o) *vi.* [echoic] **1.** to make the soft, murmuring sound of pigeons or doves or a sound like this **2.** to speak gently and lovingly: see BILL², *vi.* **2** —*vt.* to express lovingly, as with a coo —*n.* a cooing sound —**coo′ing·ly** *adv.*

**cook** (kook) *n.* [OE. *coc* < L. < *coquere,* to cook] a person who prepares food for eating —*vt.* **1.** to prepare (food) for eating by boiling, baking, frying, etc. **2.** to subject to heat or a treatment suggestive of this **3.** [Slang] to spoil —*vi.* **1.** to act as a cook **2.** to undergo cooking —**cook up** [Colloq.] to concoct; devise —**what's cooking?** [Slang] what's happening? —**cook′er** *n.*

**Cook** (kook), **James** 1728–79; Eng. naval officer & explorer: explored Australia, New Zealand, etc.

**cook·book** (-book′) *n.* a book with recipes and other information about preparing food

**cook·er·y** (-ər ē) *n.* [Chiefly Brit.] the art, practice, or work of cooking

**cook·ie, cook·y** (-ē) *n., pl.* **-ies** [prob. Du. *koekje,* dim. of *koek,* a cake] **1.** a small, sweet cake, usually flat **2.** [Slang] a person, esp. one qualified as "tough, smart, etc."

**cook·out** (-out′) *n.* a meal prepared on an outdoor grill, etc. and eaten outdoors

**cool** (kool) *adj.* [OE. *col*] **1.** moderately cold; neither warm nor very cold **2.** tending to reduce discomfort in hot weather *[cool drinks]* **3.** *a)* not excited; calm; composed *b)* restrained *[cool jazz]* *c)* [Slang] emotionally uninvolved; dispassionate **4.** showing dislike or indifference **5.** calmly impudent or bold **6.** not suggesting warmth: said of blue-green colors **7.** [Colloq.] without exaggeration *[a cool thousand dollars]* **8.** [Slang] pleasing; excellent —*adv.* in a cool manner —*n.* **1.** a cool place, time, thing, etc. **2.** [Slang] cool, dispassionate attitude or manner —*vt., vi.* to make or become cool —**cool off 1.** to calm down **2.** to lose interest or zeal —**play it cool** [Slang] to stay aloof —**cool′ish** *adj.* —**cool′ly** *adv.* —**cool′ness** *n.*

**cool·ant** (-ənt) *n.* a substance, usually a fluid, used to remove heat as from a nuclear reactor, molten metal, an internal-combustion engine, etc.

**cool·er** (-ər) *n.* **1.** a device, container, or room for cooling things or keeping them cool **2.** anything that cools **3.** [Slang] a jail

**Coo·lidge** (kool′lij), **(John) Calvin** 1872–1933; 30th president of the U.S. (1923–29)

**coo·lie** (kool′lē) *n.* [Hindi *qūlī,* hired servant] **1.** an unskilled native laborer, esp. formerly, in China, India, etc. **2.** any person doing heavy labor for little pay

**coon** (kōon) *n. clipped form of* RACCOON

**coon·skin** (-skin′) *n.* the skin of a raccoon, used as a fur

**coop** (kōop) *n.* [ult. < L. *cupa,* tub, cask] **1.** a small cage, pen, or building for poultry, etc. **2.** any place of confinement; specif., [Slang] a jail —*vt.* to confine in or as in a coop —**fly the coop** [Slang] to escape, as from a jail

**co-op** (kō′äp) *n.* [Colloq.] a cooperative

**co-op., coop.** cooperative

**coop·er** (kōop′ər, koop′-) *n.* [< MDu. < LL. *cuparius* < L. *cupa,* a cask] a person whose work is making or repairing barrels and casks —*vt., vi.* to make or repair (barrels and casks)

**Coop·er** (kōop′ər, koop′-), **James Fen·i·more** (fen′ə môr′) 1789–1851; U.S. novelist

**coop·er·age** (-ij) *n.* **1.** the work or workshop of a cooper: also **coop′er·y,** *pl.* **-ies 2.** the price for such work

**co·op·er·ate, co-op·er·ate** (kō äp′ə rāt′) *vi.* **-at′ed, -at′ing** [< LL. pp. of *cooperari* < L. *co-,* with + *operari,* to work < *opus,* work] to act or work together with another or others: also **co·öp′er·ate′** —**co·op′er·a′tor** *n.*

**co·op·er·a·tion, co-op·er·a·tion** (kō äp′ə rā′shən) *n.* **1.** a cooperating; joint effort or operation **2.** the association

of a number of people in an enterprise for mutual benefits or profits Also **co·öp′er·a′tion** —**co·op′er·a′tion·ist,** **co-op′er·a′tion·ist** *n.*

**co·op·er·a·tive, co-op·er·a·tive** (kō äp′ər ə tiv, -ə rāt′iv; -äp′rə tiv) *adj.* **1.** cooperating or inclined to cooperate **2.** designating or of an organization (as for the production or marketing of goods), an apartment house, store, etc. owned collectively by members who share in its benefits —*n.* a cooperative society, store, etc. Also **co·öp′er·a·tive** —**co·op′er·a·tive·ly, co-op′er·a·tive·ly** *adv.* —**co·op′er·a·tive·ness, co-op′er·a·tive·ness** *n.*

**co-opt** (kō äpt′) *vt.* [< L. < *co-,* with + *optare,* to choose] **1.** to elect or appoint as an associate **2.** to get (an opponent) to join one's group, accept one's views, etc. Also **co·öpt′** —**co′-op·ta′tion, co-op′tion** *n.* —**co-op′ta·tive, co-op′tive** *adj.*

**co·or·di·nate, co-or·di·nate** (kō ôr′d'n it; *also for v.* always, -də nāt′) *adj.* [< ML. pp. of *coordinare* < L. *co-,* with + *ordinare,* to arrange < *ordo* (gen. *ordinis*), order] **1.** of equal order or importance **2.** of or involving coordination or coordinates **3.** *Gram.* being of equal structural rank *[coordinate clauses]* —*n.* **1.** a coordinate person or thing **2.** *Math.* any of two or more magnitudes used to define the position of a point, line, curve, or plane —*vt.* **-nat′ed, -nat′ing 1.** to make coordinate **2.** to bring into proper order or relation; adjust —*vi.* to become coordinate; function harmoniously Also **co·ör′di·nate** —**co·or′di·nate·ly, co-or′di·nate·ly** *adv.* —**co·or′di·na·tive, co-or′di·na·tive** (-nə tiv, -nāt′iv) *adj.* —**co·or′di·na′tor, co-or′di·na′tor** *n.*

**coordinating conjunction** a conjunction that connects coordinate words, phrases, or clauses (Ex.: *and, but, for, or, nor, yet*)

**co·or·di·na·tion, co-or·di·na·tion** (kō ôr′d'n ā′shən) *n.* **1.** a coordinating or being coordinated **2.** harmonious action, as of muscles Also **co·ör′di·na′tion**

**coot** (kōot) *n., pl.* **coots:** also for 1 & 2 **coot:** see PLURAL, II, D, 1 [< ? MDu. *koet*] **1.** a ducklike, freshwater bird of the rail family with unwebbed toes **2.** *same as* SCOTER **3.** [Colloq.] a foolish, stupid, or senile person

**coot·ie** (-ē) *n.* [Slang] a louse

**cop** (käp) *vt.* **copped, cop′ping** [< obs. *cap,* to seize; ? ult. < L. *capere,* to take] [Slang] to seize, capture, win, steal, etc. —*n.* [Slang] a policeman —**cop out** [Slang] **1.** to confess to the police **2.** to back down; renege *b)* to give up; quit

**co·pal** (kō′pəl, -pal) *n.* [Sp. < Nahuatl *copalli,* resin] a hard resin from tropical trees

**co·part·ner** (kō pärt′nər) *n.* a partner, or associate —**co·part′ner·ship′** *n.*

**cope¹** (kōp) *vi.* **coped, cop′ing** [OFr. *couper,* to strike < *coup,* COUP] **1.** to fight or contend (*with*) successfully or on equal terms **2.** to deal with problems, troubles, etc.

**cope²** (kōp) *n.* [< ML. *capa,* var. of *cappa:* see CAP] **1.** a large, capelike vestment worn by priests at certain ceremonies **2.** anything that covers like a cope, as a canopy —*vt.* **coped, cop′ing** to cover with a cope or coping

**cope³** (kōp) *vt.* **coped, cop′ing** [< COPING] to cut so as to fit against a coping or molding with curves, angles, etc.

**Co·pen·hag·en** (kō′pən hā′gən, -hä′-) capital of Denmark, on the E coast of Zealand & on an adjacent island: pop. 874,000 (met. area 1,378,000)

**Copernican system** the theory of Copernicus that the planets revolve around the sun and that the earth rotates

**Co·per·ni·cus** (kō pur′ni kəs), **Nic·o·la·us** (nik′ə lā′əs) (L. form of *Mikollaj Kopernik*) 1473–1543; Pol. astronomer —**Co·per′ni·can** *adj., n.*

**cope·stone** (kōp′stōn′) *n.* **1.** the top stone of a wall; stone in a coping **2.** a finishing touch

**cop·i·er** (käp′ē ər) *n.* **1.** one who copies; imitator, transcriber, etc. **2.** a duplicating machine

**co·pi·lot** (kō′pi′lət) *n.* the assistant pilot of an aircraft, who aids or relieves the pilot

**cop·ing** (kō′piŋ) *n.* [< fig. use of COPE²] the top layer of a masonry wall, usually sloped

**coping saw** a saw with a narrow blade in a U-shaped frame, esp. for cutting curved outlines

**co·pi·ous** (kō′pē əs) *adj.* [< L. < *copia,* abundance] **1.** plentiful; abundant **2.** wordy; profuse or diffuse **3.** full of information —**co′pi·ous·ly** *adv.* —**co′pi·ous·ness** *n.*

**Cop·land** (kōp′lənd), **Aaron** 1900– ; U.S. composer

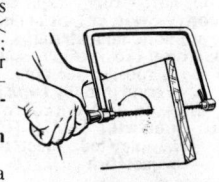

COPING SAW

**cop-out** (käp′out′) *n.* [Slang] a copping out, as by confessing, backing down, quitting, etc.

---

fat, āpe, cär, ten, ēven, is, bīte; gō, hôrn, tool, look; oil, out; up, fur; get; joy; yet; chin; she; thin, then; zh, leisure; ŋ, ring; ə for *a* in *ago, e* in *agent, i* in *sanity, o* in *comply, u* in *focus;* ′ as in *able* (ā′b'l); Fr. bal; ë, Fr. coeur; ö, Fr. feu; Fr. mon; b, Fr. coq; ü, Fr. duc; r, Fr. cri; H, G. ich; kh, G. doch; ‡foreign; *hypothetical; < derived from. See inside front cover.

**cop·per¹** (käp′ər) *n.* see PLURAL, II, D, 3 [OE. *coper* < LL. *cuprum*, contr. < *Cyprium* (*aes*), Cyprian (metal) < Gr. *Kyprios*, Cyprus, noted for its copper mines] **1.** a reddish-brown, malleable, ductile, metallic element that is an excellent conductor of electricity and heat: symbol, Cu; at. wt., 63.546; at. no., 29 **2.** [Now chiefly Brit.] a copper coin, as a penny **3.** the color of copper; reddish brown —*adj.* **1.** of copper **2.** reddish-brown —*vt.* to coat with copper —**cop′per·y** *adj.*

**cop·per²** (käp′ər) *n.* [prob. < COP] [Slang] a policeman

**cop·per·as** (-əs) *n.* [< OFr. < ML. (*aqua*) *cuprosa*, lit., copper (water)] ferrous sulfate, FeSO₄·7H₂O, a green, crystalline compound used in dyeing, the making of ink, etc.

**cop·per·head** (-hed′) *n.* **1.** a poisonous N. American pit viper with a copper-colored head **2.** [C-] a Northerner who sympathized with the South during the Civil War: so called in the North

**cop·per·plate** (-plāt′) *n.* **1.** a sheet of copper etched or engraved for printing **2.** a print made from this **3.** copperplate printing or engraving

**cop·per·smith** (-smith′) *n.* a person whose work is making utensils, etc. out of copper

**copper sulfate** a blue, crystalline substance, CuSO₄·5H₂O: used in making pigments, batteries, etc.

**cop·pice** (käp′is) *n.* [< OFr. *copeis* < *couper*, to cut: see COUP] *same as* COPSE

**co·pra** (kō′prə, käp′rə) *n.* [Port. < Malayalam < Hindi *khoprā*] dried coconut meat, the source of coconut oil

**copse** (käps) *n.* [< COPPICE] a thicket of small trees or shrubs; coppice

**Copt** (käpt) *n.* **1.** a native of Egypt descended from the ancient inhabitants of that country **2.** a member of the Coptic Church

**cop·ter** (käp′tər) *n. shortened form of* HELICOPTER

**Cop·tic** (käp′tik) *adj.* [< ModL. < Ar. *Quft*, the Copts < Gr. *Aigyptios*, Egyptian] **1.** of the Copts, their language, etc. **2.** of the Coptic Church —*n.* the Afro-Asiatic language of the Copts, derived from ancient Egyptian

**Coptic Church** the native Christian church of Egypt and of Ethiopia

**cop·u·la** (käp′yə lə) *n., pl.* -las [L., a link < *co-*, together + OL. *apere*, to join] something that connects or links together; specif., *same as* LINKING VERB —**cop′u·lar** *adj.*

**cop·u·late** (-lāt′) *vi.* -lat′ed, -lat′ing [< L. pp. of *copulare*, to couple < *copula*: see prec.] to have sexual intercourse —**cop′u·la′tion** *n.* —**cop′u·la·to′ry** (-lə tôr′ē) *adj.*

**cop·u·la·tive** (-lāt′iv, -lə tiv) *adj.* **1.** coupling **2.** *Gram.* *a)* connecting coordinate words, phrases, or clauses *b)* involving connected words or clauses *c)* being a copula [*a copulative* verb] **3.** of or for copulating —*n.* a copulative word —**cop′u·la′tive·ly** *adv.*

**cop·y** (käp′ē) *n., pl.* -ies [< OFr. < ML. *copia*, copious transcript < L. *copia*, plenty] **1.** a thing made just like another; imitation **2.** any of a number of books, magazines, engravings, etc. having the same printed matter **3.** a manuscript or illustration to be set in type or printed **4.** subject matter for a writer **5.** the words of an advertisement —*vt., vi.* cop′ied, cop′y·ing **1.** to make a copy or copies of; reproduce **2.** to imitate

**cop·y·book** (-book′) *n.* a book with models of handwriting, formerly used in teaching penmanship —*adj.* ordinary; trite [*copybook* maxims]

**cop·y·cat** (-kat′) *n.* a person who habitually imitates or mimics: a child's term

**copy desk** the desk in a newspaper office where copy is edited and headlines are written

**cop·y·ist** (-ist) *n.* **1.** a person who makes written copies; transcriber **2.** a person who imitates

**cop·y·read·er** (-rē′dər) *n.* a person whose work is editing articles or other copy for publication

**cop·y·right** (-rīt′) *n.* [COPY + RIGHT] the exclusive right to the publication, production, or sale of a literary, musical, or artistic work, granted by law for a specified period of time to an author, composer, etc. —*vt.* to protect (a book, etc.) by copyright —*adj.* protected by copyright —**cop′y·right′a·ble** *adj.* —**cop′y·right′er** *n.*

**cop·y·writ·er** (-rīt′ər) *n.* a writer of copy for advertising or promotional material

**co·quet** (kō ket′) *vi.* -quet′ted, -quet′ting [< Fr. < dim. of *coq*, a rooster: see COCK¹] **1.** to behave as a coquette; flirt **2.** to trifle or dally (*with* an idea, offer, etc.) —*adj.* coquettish —**co·quet′ry** (kōk′ə trē, kō ket′rē) *n., pl.* -ries

**co·quette** (kō ket′) *n.* [Fr.: see prec.] a girl or woman flirt —*vi.* -quet′ted, -quet′ting to behave as a coquette; flirt —**co·quet′tish** *adj.* —**co·quet′tish·ly** *adv.* —**co·quet′tish·ness** *n.*

**co·qui·na** (kō kē′nə) *n.* [Sp., shellfish < L. *concha*: see CONCH] **1.** a soft, whitish limestone made up of broken seashells and corals **2.** a small saltwater clam

**Cor.** **1.** Corinthians **2.** Coroner

**cor.** **1.** corner **2.** cornet **3.** correct **4.** correction **5.** correlative **6.** correspondence

**Cor·a** (kôr′ə) [L. < Gr. *Korē*, lit., maiden] a feminine name

**cor·a·cle** (kôr′ə k'l, kär′-) *n.* [< W. < *corwg*, orig., leather-covered boat] a small boat of waterproof material stretched over a wooden frame

**cor·a·coid** (kôr′ə koid′, kär′-) *adj.* [< Gr. < *korax*, raven + *eidos*, form] designating or of a bony process extending from the shoulder blade toward the breastbone —*n.* this bony process

**cor·al** (kôr′əl, kär′-) *n.* [OFr. < L. < Gr. *korallion* < ? Heb. *gōral*, pebble] **1.** the hard, stony skeleton of some marine polyps, often in masses forming reefs and atolls in tropical seas **2.** any of such polyps, living singly or in large colonies **3.** a piece of coral **4.** yellowish red or yellowish pink: also **coral red** or **coral pink** —*adj.* **1.** made of coral **2.** coral-red or coral-pink

**coral reef** a reef made up chiefly of coral

**cor·al·root** (-rōōt′, -root′) *n.* a brownish orchid with corallike rootstocks and no leaves

CORAL
(A, organ-pipe; B, reef; C, mushroom; D, Bermuda)

**Coral Sea** part of the S Pacific, northeast of Australia & south of the Solomon Islands

**coral snake** a small, poisonous snake with coral-red, yellow, and black bands around its body, found in the southern U.S.

**cor·bel** (kôr′bəl) *n.* [OFr. < L. *corvus*, raven] a bracket of stone, wood, etc. projecting from a wall to support a cornice, etc. —*vt.* -beled or -belled, -bel·ing or -bel·ling to provide or support with a corbel or corbels

**cor·bie** (kôr′bē) *n., pl.* -bies [see prec.] [Scot.] a crow or raven

**Corbusier, Le** see LE CORBUSIER

**cord** (kôrd) *n.* [< OFr. < L. < Gr. *chordē*] **1.** (a) thick string or thin rope **2.** any force acting as a tie or bond **3.** [from cord used in measuring] a measure of wood cut for fuel (128 cubic feet) **4.** *a)* a rib on the surface of a fabric *b)* corduroy *c)* [*pl.*] corduroy trousers **5.** *Anat.* any part like a cord [the spinal *cord*]: also CHORD **6.** *Elec.* a slender, insulated cable fitted with a plug or plugs —*vt.* **1.** to fasten or provide with a cord or cords **2.** to stack (wood) in cords

**cord·age** (-ij) *n.* **1.** cords and ropes collectively, esp. the ropes in a ship's rigging **2.** the amount of wood, in cords, in a given area

**cor·date** (kôr′dāt) *adj.* [< ModL. < L. *cor* (gen. *cordis*), heart] heart-shaped —**cor′date·ly** *adv.*

**cord·ed** (kôr′did) *adj.* **1.** fastened with cords **2.** made of cords **3.** that looks like a tight cord, as a muscle **4.** having a ribbed surface, as corduroy **5.** stacked in cords, as wood

**Cor·del·ia** (kôr dēl′yə) [prob. ult. < Celt. *Creiryddlydd*, lit., daughter of the sea] a feminine name

**cor·dial** (kôr′jəl) *adj.* [< ML. < L. *cor* (gen. *cordis*), heart] **1.** [Rare] invigorating **2.** warm and friendly; hearty; sincere —*n.* **1.** [Rare] a stimulating medicine, food, or drink **2.** an aromatic, alcoholic drink; liqueur —**cor′dial·ly** *adv.* —**cor′dial·ness** *n.*

**cor·di·al·i·ty** (kôr′jē al′ə tē, kôr jal′-) *n.* **1.** a cordial quality; warm, friendly feeling **2.** *pl.* -ties a cordial act or remark

**cor·dil·le·ra** (kôr′dil yer′ə, kôr dil′ər ə) *n.* [Sp. < dim. of *cuerda*, rope < L. *chorda*, CORD] a chain of mountains; esp., the principal mountain range of a continent —**cor′dil·le′ran** *adj.*

**cord·ing** (kôr′diŋ) *n.* the ribbed surface of corded cloth

**cord·ite** (-dīt) *n.* [CORD + -ITE: from its stringiness] a smokeless explosive made of nitroglycerin, guncotton, petroleum jelly, and acetone

**cord·less** (kôrd′lis) *adj.* operated by batteries rather than by current from an outlet

**Cor·do·ba** (kôr′də bə, -və; *Sp.* kôr′thô bä) **1.** city in NC Argentina: pop. 589,000 **2.** city in S Spain: pop. 220,000

**cor·do·ba** (kôr′də bə) *n.* [after F. F. de *Córdoba*, 16th-cent. Sp. explorer] *see* MONETARY UNITS, table (Nicaragua)

**cor·don** (kôr′d'n) *n.* [Fr., dim. of *corde*: see CORD] **1.** a line or circle of police, ships, etc. stationed around an area to guard it **2.** a cord, ribbon, or braid worn as a decoration or badge —*vt.* to encircle or shut (*off*) with a cordon

**cor·do·van** (kôr′də vən) *adj.* [< Sp. < CÓRDOBA] made of cordovan —*n.* **1.** a fine-grained, colored leather, usually of split horsehide **2.** [*pl.*] shoes made of this leather

**cor·du·roy** (kôr′də roi′) *n.* [prob. < CORD + obs. *duroy*, a coarse fabric] **1.** a heavy cotton fabric with a velvety surface, ribbed vertically **2.** [*pl.*] trousers made of this —*adj.* **1.** made of, or ribbed like, corduroy **2.** made of logs laid crosswise [a *corduroy* road]

**cord·wood** (kôrd′wood′) *n.* wood stacked or sold in cords

**core** (kôr) *n.* [< OFr., prob. < L. *cor*, heart] **1.** the central part of an apple, pear, etc., containing the seeds **2.** the central part of anything **3.** the most important part; essence; pith **4.** in foundry work, that part of a mold forming the interior of a hollow casting **5.** a sample section of the earth's strata from underground, obtained with a hollow drill **6.** the center of a nuclear reactor that contains the fissionable fuel **7.** *Chem.* the nucleus of an atom with its electron shells **8.** *Elec.* a mass of iron inside a wire coil: it increases the magnetic field —*vt.* **cored, cor′ing** to remove the core of —**cor′er** *n.*

**CORE** (kôr) Congress of Racial Equality

**co·re·li·gion·ist** (kō′ri lij′ə nist) *n.* a person of the same religion or religious denomination

**co·re·op·sis** (kôr′ē äp′sis) *n.* [ModL. < Gr. *koris*, bug + *opsis*, appearance: from the shape of the fruit] a plant of the composite family, with showy flowers of yellow, crimson, or maroon

**co·re·spond·ent** (kō′ri spän′dənt) *n.* [CO- + RESPONDENT] *Law* a person charged with having committed adultery with the wife or husband from whom a divorce is being sought —**co′re·spond′en·cy** *n.*

**cor·gi** (kôr′gē) *n. same as* WELSH CORGI

**co·ri·an·der** (kôr′ē an′dər) *n.* [< OFr. < L. < Gr. *koriandron*] **1.** a European herb of the parsley family **2.** its strong-smelling, seedlike fruit, used in flavoring food and liqueurs

**Cor·inth** (kôr′inth, kär′-) ancient city in the NE Peloponnesus, Greece: noted for its riches

**Co·rin·thi·an** (kə rin′thē ən) *adj.* **1.** of Corinth, its people, or culture **2.** dissolute and loving luxury, as the people of Corinth were said to be **3.** designating or of the most elaborate of the three orders of Greek architecture, distinguished by a bell-shaped capital with a design of acanthus leaves: cf. DORIC, IONIC —*n.* a native or inhabitant of Corinth

**Co·rin·thi·ans** (-ənz) either of two books of the New Testament, epistles from the Apostle Paul to the Christians of Corinth

CORINTHIAN CAPITAL

**Cor·i·o·lis force** (kô′rē ō′lis) [after G. de *Coriolis*, 19th-c. Fr. mathematician] the apparent force, caused by the earth's rotation, that produces the deflection (**Coriolis effect**) of a moving body to the right in the Northern Hemisphere and to the left in the Southern

**Cork** (kôrk) seaport in S Ireland: pop. 122,000

**cork** (kôrk) *n.* [< Sp. *corcho*, ult. (via ? Ar.) < L. *quercus*, oak] **1.** the light, thick, elastic outer bark of an oak tree, the **cork oak**, of the Mediterranean area **2.** a piece of cork; esp., a stopper for a bottle, cask, etc. **3.** any stopper, as one of rubber, etc. **4.** the outer bark of the stems of woody plants —*adj.* made of cork —*vt.* **1.** to stop with a cork **2.** to restrain; check **3.** to blacken with burnt cork

**cork·er** (kôr′kər) *n.* **1.** a worker or device that corks bottles **2.** [Slang] *a)* a remarkable person or thing *b)* a preposterous lie

**cork·ing** (-kiŋ) *adj., adv., interj.* [Chiefly Brit. Slang] very good; excellent

**cork·screw** (kôrk′skrōō′) *n.* a spiral-shaped device for pulling corks out of bottles —*adj.* shaped like a corkscrew —*vi., vt.* to move in a spiral; twist

**cork·y** (kôr′kē) *adj.* **cork′i·er, cork′i·est** **1.** of or like cork **2.** tasting of the cork: said of wine

**corm** (kôrm) *n.* [< Gr. *kormos*, a lopped tree trunk < *keirein*, to cut off] the fleshy, scaly, underground stem of certain plants, as the gladiolus

**cor·mo·rant** (kôr′mə rənt) *n.* [< OFr. < L. < *corvus*, raven + *marinus*, MARINE] **1.** a large, voracious, diving bird with webbed toes: used by fishermen in the Orient to catch fish **2.** a greedy person

**corn¹** (kôrn) *n.* see PLURAL, II, D, 3 [OE.] **1.** a small, hard seed, esp. a seed or grain of a cereal grass; kernel: chiefly in compounds [*peppercorn*] **2.** *a)* a cultivated American cereal plant, with the grain borne on cobs enclosed in husks; maize; Indian corn *b)* its ears or kernels **3.** [Brit.] the seeds of all cereal grasses; grain **4.** the leading cereal crop, as wheat in England or oats in Scotland and Ireland **5.** [Colloq.] corn whiskey **6.** [Slang] ideas, music, etc. considered old-fashioned, trite, sentimental, etc. —*vt.* to preserve or pickle (meat, etc.) with salt granules or in brine —**corned** *adj.*

**corn²** (kôrn) *n.* [< OFr. < L. *cornu*, a horn] a hard, thick, painful growth of skin, esp. on a toe

**corn·ball** (-bôl′) *adj.* [CORN¹, *n.* 6 + (SCREW)BALL] [Slang] unsophisticated; corny —*n.* [Slang] a person or thing that is corny

**Corn Belt** NC plains region of the Middle West where much corn and cornfed livestock are raised

**corn borer** a moth larva that feeds on corn, sorghum, etc.

**corn bread** a bread made with cornmeal

**corn·cob** (-käb′) *n.* **1.** the woody core of an ear of corn **2.** a tobacco pipe with a bowl made of a hollowed, dried piece of such a core: in full, **corncob pipe**

**corn cockle** a tall weed of the pink family, with pink flowers, often found in grainfields

**cor·ne·a** (kôr′nē ə) *n.* [< ML. < L. *cornea* (*tela*), horny (tissue) < *cornu*, a horn] the transparent outer coat of the eyeball, covering the iris and pupil —**cor′ne·al** *adj.*

**Cor·neille** (kôr nā′y′), **Pierre** 1606–84; Fr. dramatist

**cor·nel** (kôr′n′l, -nel) *n.* [< OFr. < VL. < L. *cornus*] any of a genus of shrubs and small trees with very hard wood, including the dogwoods

**cor·nel·ian** (kôr nēl′yən) *n.* [< OFr. *corneola*, prob. < VL. *cornea*: see CORNEL] *same as* CARNELIAN

**cor·ner** (kôr′nər) *n.* [< OFr. < ML. < *cornu*, a horn] **1.** the point or place where lines or surfaces join and form an angle **2.** the space within the angle formed at the joining of lines or surfaces **3.** the tip of any angle formed at a street intersection **4.** something used to form, mark, protect, or decorate a corner **5.** a remote or secluded spot **6.** region; quarter [*every corner of America*] **7.** an awkward position from which escape is difficult **8.** a monopoly acquired on a stock or commodity to raise the price —*vt.* **1.** to force into a corner or awkward position, so that escape is difficult **2.** to get a monopoly on (a stock or commodity) —*vi.* **1.** to meet at or abut (*on*) said of buildings, etc. **2.** to turn corners: said of a vehicle —*adj.* **1.** at or on a corner **2.** used in a corner —**around the corner** very near or imminent —**cut corners** **1.** to take a direct route by going across corners **2.** to cut down expenses, time, labor, etc. —**cor′nered** *adj.*

**cor·ner·back** (-bak′) *n. Football* a player of the defensive backfield between the line of scrimmage and the safety men

**cor·ner·stone** (-stōn′) *n.* **1.** a stone laid in the corner of a building, esp. at a ceremony for beginning a building **2.** the basic part; foundation

**cor·ner·wise** (-wiz′) *adv.* **1.** with the corner to the front **2.** from one corner to its opposite; diagonally Also **cor′ner·ways′**

**cor·net** (kôr net′) *n.* [< OFr. < L. *cornu*, a horn] **1.** a brass-wind musical instrument of the trumpet class **2.** *a)* a cone-shaped paper for holding candy, etc. *b)* a cone-shaped pastry —**cor·net′ist, cor·net′tist** *n.*

**corn·flakes** (kôrn′flāks′) *n.pl.* a breakfast cereal of crisp flakes made from hulled corn

**corn·flow·er** (-flou′ər) *n.* a plant of the composite family, with white, pink, or blue flowers

**corn·husk·ing** (-hus′kiŋ) *n.* a gathering of people for husking corn —**corn′husk′er** *n.*

**cor·nice** (kôr′nis) *n.* [Fr. < It. < L. < Gr. *korōnis*, a wreath] **1.** a horizontal molding projecting along the top of a wall, building, etc. **2.** the top part of an entablature **3.** a decorative strip above a window for hiding a curtain rod —*vt.* **-niced, -nic·ing** to top as with a cornice

**Cor·nish** (kôr′nish) *adj.* of Cornwall, its people, or culture —*n.* **1.** the Brythonic Celtic language spoken in Cornwall until c. 1800 **2.** *pl.* **Cor′nish** *a)* a British breed of chicken *b)* a breed of chicken crossbred from these and Plymouth Rocks: also **Cornish hen** or **Rock Cornish (hen)**

**corn·meal** (kôrn′mēl′) *n.* meal made from corn (maize)

**corn pone** [Chiefly Southern] a kind of corn bread baked in small, oval loaves (*pones*)

**corn·row** (kôrn′rō′) *n.* an African hairstyle in which the hair is arranged in an intricate pattern of tight braids separated by wide parts —*vt.* to arrange in a cornrow

**corn silk** the long, silky fibers that hang in a tuft from the husk of an ear of corn

**corn·stalk** (-stôk′) *n.* a stalk of corn (maize)

**corn·starch** (-stärch′) *n.* a starch made from corn and used in cooking and to make corn syrup, etc.

**corn syrup** a sweet syrup made from cornstarch

**cor·nu·co·pi·a** (kôr′nə kō′pē ə, -nyōō-) *n.* [L. *cornu copiae*, horn of plenty] **1.** a representation in painting, sculpture, etc. of a horn overflowing with fruits, flowers, and grain; horn of plenty **2.** an abundance **3.** any cone-shaped container

**Corn·wall** (kôrn′wôl; *chiefly Brit.* -wəl) county at the SW tip of England: 1,357 sq. mi.

**Corn·wal·lis** (kôrn wôl′is, -wäl′-), **Charles**, 1st Marquis Cornwallis, 1738–1805; Eng. general: a commander of Brit. forces in the Am. Revolution

**corn whiskey** whiskey made from corn (maize)

CORNUCOPIA

**corn·y** (kôr′nē) *adj.* **corn′i·er, corn′i·est 1.** of corn **2.** [Colloq.] unsophisticated, old-fashioned, trite, sentimental, etc. —**corn′i·ness** *n.*

**corol., coroll.** corollary

**co·rol·la** (kə räl′ə, -rōl′ə) *n.* [L., dim. of *corona,* CROWN] the petals, or inner floral leaves, of a flower —**cor·ol·late** (kôr′ə lāt′, kär′-), **cor′ol·lat′ed** *adj.*

**cor·ol·lar·y** (kôr′ə ler′ē, kär′-) *n., pl.* **-lar′ies** [< LL. *corollarium,* a deduction < L., a gift < *corolla:* see prec.] **1.** a proposition that follows from another that has been proved **2.** an inference or deduction **3.** anything that follows as a normal result

**co·ro·na** (kə rō′nə) *n., pl.* **-nas, -nae** (-nē) [L., CROWN] **1.** a crown or something like a crown **2.** a long cigar with blunt ends **3.** *Anat.* the upper part of a tooth, of a skull, etc. **4.** *Astron. a)* the outermost part of the sun's atmosphere, seen during a total eclipse *b)* a ring of colored light seen around a luminous body, as the sun or moon, as a result of diffraction by mist, dust, etc. **5.** *Bot.* the cuplike part on the inner side of the corolla of certain flowers, as the daffodil **6.** *Elec.* a sometimes visible electric discharge around a conductor at high potential —**cor·o′nal** *adj.*

**Co·ro·na·do** (kôr′ə nä′dō; *Sp.* kō′rō nä′thō), **Fran·cis·co Vás·quez de** (frän thēs′kō väs′keth the) 1510?–54?; Sp. explorer in SW N. America

**cor·o·nar·y** (kôr′ə ner′ē, kär′-) *adj.* [see CORONA] **1.** of, or in the form of, a crown **2.** *Anat.* designating or of either of two arteries branching from the aorta and supplying blood directly to the heart muscle —*n., pl.* **-nar′ies** *same as* CORO-NARY THROMBOSIS

**coronary insufficiency** inability of the coronary arteries to supply enough blood to the myocardium

**coronary thrombosis** the formation of an obstructing clot in a coronary artery: also **coronary occlusion**

**cor·o·na·tion** (kôr′ə nä′shən, kär′-) *n.* [< OFr. < L. pp. of *coronare* < *corona,* CROWN] the act or ceremony of crowning a sovereign

**cor·o·ner** (kôr′ə nər, kär′-) *n.* [ME., officer of the crown < Anglo-Fr. < L. *corona,* CROWN] a public officer whose chief duty is to determine by inquest before a jury the causes of any deaths not obviously due to natural causes

**cor·o·net** (kôr′ə net′, kär′-) *n.* [< OFr. dim. of *corone,* CROWN] **1.** a small crown worn by princes and others of high rank **2.** an ornamental band, as of gold, jewels, or flowers, worn around the head —**cor′o·net′ed, cor′o·net′-ted** *adj.*

**Co·rot** (kə rō′; *Fr.* kô rō′), **Jean Bap·tiste Ca·mille** (zhän bá tēst′ ká mē′y) 1796–1875; Fr. painter

**corp., corpn.** corporation

**cor·po·ral¹** (kôr′pər əl) *n.* [< Fr. < It. < *capo,* chief < L. *caput,* the head: sp. infl. by *corps* or ff.] the lowest-ranking noncommissioned officer, just below a sergeant; specif., an enlisted man or woman in the fourth grade in the U.S. Army and Marine Corps: abbrev. **Corp., Cpl** —**cor′po·ral·cy,** *pl.* **-cies, cor′po·ral·ship′** *n.*

**cor·po·ral²** (kôr′pər əl) *adj.* [< L. *corporalis* < *corpus,* body] of the body; bodily —**cor′po·ral′i·ty** (-pə ral′ə tē) *n.* —**cor′po·ral·ly** *adv.*

**cor·po·ral³** (kôr′pə rəl) *n.* [OFr. < ML. *corporalis* (*palla*), body (cloth): see prec.] *Eccles.* a small, linen altar cloth on which the bread and chalice are placed for the Eucharist

**corporal punishment** punishment inflicted directly on the body, as flogging

**cor·po·rate** (kôr′pər it) *adj.* [< L. pp. of *corporare,* to make into a body < *corpus,* body] **1.** incorporated **2.** of a corporation **3.** shared by all in a group *[corporate blame]* —**cor′po·rate·ly** *adv.*

**cor·po·ra·tion** (kôr′pə rā′shən) *n.* **1.** a group of people who get a charter granting them as a body certain of the legal powers, rights, and liabilities of an individual **2.** a group of people, as the mayor and aldermen of an incorporated town, legally authorized to act as an individual —**cor′po·ra·tive** *adj.* —**cor′po·ra′tor** *n.*

**cor·po·re·al** (kôr pôr′ē əl) *adj.* [< L. < *corpus* (gen. *corporis*), body] **1.** of or for the body; bodily **2.** material; physical; tangible —**cor·po′re·al′i·ty** (-al′ə tē) *n.* —**cor·po′re·al·ly** *adv.*

**corps** (kôr) *n., pl.* **corps** (kôrz) [< OFr. *corps, cors* < L. *corpus,* body] **1.** a body of people associated in some work, organization, etc. **2.** *Mil. a)* a branch of the armed forces with some specialized function *[Signal Corps] b)* a tactical subdivision of an army, normally composed of two or more divisions

**corpse** (kôrps) *n.* [var. of CORPS] **1.** a dead body, esp. of a person **2.** something lifeless and of no use

**corps·man** (kôr′mən) *n., pl.* **-men** *same as* AIDMAN

**cor·pu·lence** (kôr′pyoo ləns) *n.* [OFr. < L. < *corpus,* body] fatness or stoutness of body; obesity: also **cor′pu·len·cy** —**cor′pu·lent** *adj.* —**cor′pu·lent·ly** *adv.*

**cor·pus** (kôr′pəs) *n., pl.* **cor′po·ra** (-pər ə) [L.] **1.** a human or animal body; esp., a dead one: now mainly a facetious usage **2.** a complete or comprehensive collection, as of

laws or writings of a specified type **3.** the main body or substance of anything

**Corpus Christ·i** (kris′tē) [L., Body of Christ] **1.** *R.C.Ch.* a festival celebrated on the Thursday after Trinity Sunday, in honor of the Eucharist **2.** city in SE Tex., on the Gulf of Mexico: pop. 232,000

**cor·pus·cle** (kôr′pəs 'l, -pus′'l) *n.* [< L. dim. of *corpus,* body] **1.** a very small particle **2.** *Anat.* a protoplasmic particle with a special function; esp., any of the erythrocytes (**red corpuscles**) or leukocytes (**white corpuscles**) that float in the blood, lymph, etc. of vertebrates: also **cor·pus·cule** (kôr pus′kyool) —**cor·pus′cu·lar** (-kyoo lər) *adj.*

**corpus de·lic·ti** (di lik′tī) [ModL., lit., body of the crime] **1.** the facts constituting or proving a crime **2.** loosely, the body of a murder victim

**corpus ju·ris** (joor′is) [L., body of law] a collection of all the laws of a nation or district

**corpus lu·te·um** (lōō′tē əm) *pl.* **cor·po·ra lu·te·a** (kôr′pər ə lōō′tē ə) [ModL., lit., yellow body] a mass of yellow tissue, formed in the ovary after ovulation, that secretes progesterone if fertilization occurs

**corr. 1.** corrected **2.** correspondence

**cor·ral** (kə ral′) *n.* [Sp. < *corro,* a circle < L. *currere,* to run] an enclosure for holding or capturing horses, cattle, etc.; pen —*vt.* **-ralled′, -ral′ling 1.** to drive into or confine in a corral **2.** to surround or capture; round up

**cor·rect** (kə rekt′) *vt.* [< L. pp. of *corrigere* < *com-,* together + *regere,* to lead straight] **1.** to make right; change from wrong to right **2.** to mark the errors or faults of **3.** to make conform to a standard **4.** to scold or punish so as to cause to rectify faults **5.** to cure or counteract (a fault, disease, etc.) —*vi.* to make corrections or an adjustment to compensate (*for* an error, etc.) —*adj.* **1.** conforming to an established standard; proper **2.** conforming to fact or logic; true; accurate; right **3.** equal to the required number, amount, etc. —**cor·rect′a·ble** *adj.* —**cor·rect′ly** *adv.* —**cor·rect′ness** *n.* —**cor·rec′tor** *n.*

**cor·rec·tion** (kə rek′shən) *n.* **1.** a correcting or being corrected **2.** a change that corrects a mistake; rectification **3.** punishment or scolding to correct faults —**cor·rec′tion·al** *adj.*

**cor·rec·tive** (-tiv) *adj.* tending or meant to correct or improve; remedial —*n.* something corrective; remedy —**cor·rec′tive·ly** *adv.*

**Cor·reg·gio** (kə rej′ō), (**Antonio Allegri da**) 1494?–1534; It. painter

**cor·re·late** (kôr′ə lāt′, kär′-) *n.* [*cor-* (see COM-) + L. *relatus:* see RELATE] either of two interrelated things —*adj.* closely and naturally related —*vi.* **-lat′ed, -lat′ing** to be mutually related (*to* or *with*) —*vt.* to bring (a thing) into mutual relation (*with* another); calculate or show the relation between

**cor·re·la·tion** (kôr′ə lā′shən, kär′-) *n.* [see prec.] **1.** a mutual relationship or connection **2.** the degree of relative correspondence between two sets of data **3.** a correlating or being correlated —**cor′re·la′tion·al** *adj.*

**cor·rel·a·tive** (kə rel′ə tiv) *adj.* **1.** having a mutual relationship; reciprocally dependent **2.** *Gram.* expressing mutual relation and used in pairs *[neither . . . nor* are *correlative* conjunctions*] —n.* **1.** a thing closely related to something else **2.** a correlative word —**cor·rel′a·tive·ly** *adv.* —**cor·rel′a·tiv′i·ty** *n.*

**cor·re·spond** (kôr′ə spänd′, kär′-) *vi.* [< Fr. < ML. *corresponder* < L. *com-,* together + *respondere,* to answer] **1.** to be in agreement (*with* something); conform (*to* something); match **2.** to be similar, analogous, or equal (*to* something) **3.** to communicate (*with* someone) by letters —**cor′re·spond′ing·ly** *adv.*

**cor·re·spond·ence** (-spän′dəns) *n.* [see prec.] **1.** agreement; conformity **2.** similarity; analogy **3.** *a)* communication by exchange of letters *b)* the letters written or received

**correspondence school** a school that gives courses of instruction (**correspondence courses**) by mail

**cor·re·spond·ent** (kôr′ə spän′dənt, kär′-) *adj.* corresponding —*n.* **1.** a thing that corresponds **2.** a person who exchanges letters with, or writes a letter to, another **3.** a person hired as by a newspaper to send news regularly from a distant place

**cor·ri·dor** (kôr′ə dər, kär′-; -dôr′) *n.* [Fr. < It. < L. *currere,* to run] **1.** a long passageway or hall **2.** a strip of land providing passage through foreign-held land, as from a country to its seaport

**cor·ri·gen·dum** (kôr′ə jen′dəm, kär′-) *n., pl.* **-da** (-də) [L., gerundive of *corrigere:* see CORRECT] an error to be corrected in a printed work, or [*pl.*] a list of such errors inserted in the work

**cor·ri·gi·ble** (kôr′i jə b'l, kär′-) *adj.* [< OFr. < ML. < L. *corrigere:* see CORRECT] capable of being corrected, improved, or reformed —**cor′ri·gi·bil′i·ty** *n.* —**cor′ri·gi·bly** *adv.*

**cor·rob·o·rate** (kə räb′ə rāt′) *vt.* **-rat′ed, -rat′ing** [< L. pp. of *corroborare* < *com-,* intens. + *roborare* < *robur,* strength] to confirm; bolster; support —**cor·rob′o·ra′tion** *n.* —**cor·rob′o·ra′tor** *n.*

**cor·rob·o·ra·tive** (kə räb′ə rāt′iv, -ər ə tiv) *adj.* corroborating; confirmatory: also **cor·rob′o·ra·to′ry** (-ər ə-tôr′ē) —**cor·rob′o·ra′tive·ly** *adv.*

**cor·rode** (kə rōd′) *vt.* **-rod′ed, -rod′ing** [< OFr. < L. *corrodere* < *com-*, intens. + *rodere*, to gnaw] to eat into or wear away gradually, as by rusting or by the action of chemicals —*vi.* to become corroded —**cor·rod′i·ble** *adj.*

**cor·ro·sion** (kə rō′zhən) *n.* **1.** a corroding or being corroded **2.** a substance formed by corroding

**cor·ro·sive** (kə rōs′iv) *adj.* [< OFr. < ML. *corrosivus*] causing corrosion —*n.* something causing corrosion —**cor·ro′sive·ly** *adv.* —**cor·ro′sive·ness** *n.*

**corrosive sublimate** *same as* MERCURIC CHLORIDE

**cor·ru·gate** (kôr′ə gāt′, kär′-; -yoo-) *vt., vi.* **-gat′ed, -gat′ing** [< L. pp. of *corrugare* < *com-*, intens. + *rugare*, to wrinkle] to shape into parallel grooves and ridges; make wrinkles in; furrow [*corrugated* iron, *corrugated* paper]

CORRUGATED SURFACE

**cor·ru·ga·tion** (kôr′ə gā′shən, kär′-; -yoo-) *n.* **1.** a corrugating or being corrugated **2.** any ridge or groove of a corrugated surface

**cor·rupt** (kə rupt′) *adj.* [< L. pp. of *corrumpere*, to ruin < *com-*, together + *rumpere*, to break] **1.** orig., spoiled; rotten **2.** morally debased; evil; depraved **3.** taking bribes **4.** containing alterations, foreign admixtures, or errors [a *corrupt* text] —*vt., vi.* to make or become corrupt —**corrupt′er, cor·rup′tor** *n.* —**cor·rup′tive** *adj.* —**cor·rupt′ly** *adv.* —**cor·rupt′ness** *n.*

**cor·rupt·i·ble** (kə rup′tə b′l) *adj.* that can be corrupted, esp. morally —**cor·rupt′i·bil′i·ty** *n.* —**cor·rupt′i·bly** *adv.*

**cor·rup·tion** (kə rup′shən) *n.* **1.** a making, becoming, or being corrupt **2.** depravity **3.** bribery **4.** decay; rottenness **5.** something corrupted

**cor·sage** (kôr säzh′, -säj′) *n.* [Fr.: see CORPS & -AGE] **1.** the bodice of a dress **2.** a small bouquet for a woman to wear, as at the waist or shoulder

**cor·sair** (kôr′ser) *n.* [< Fr. < Pr. < It. < L. *cursus*, a COURSE] **1.** a privateer **2.** a pirate **3.** a pirate ship

**corse** (kôrs) *n.* [Archaic or Poet.] a corpse

**corse·let** (kôrs′lət; *for 2* kôr′sə let′) *n.* [see ff.] **1.** a medieval piece of body armor: also sp. **cors′let 2.** a woman's lightweight corset: also sp. **cor′se·lette′**

**cor·set** (kôr′sit) *n.* [OFr., dim. of *cors*: see CORPS] [*sometimes pl.*] a closefitting undergarment, often reinforced with stays, worn, chiefly by women, to give support to or shape the torso —*vt.* to dress in, or fit with, a corset

**Cor·si·ca** (kôr′si kə) Fr. island in the Mediterranean, north of Sardinia: 3,367 sq. mi.; pop. 270,000; cap. Ajaccio: Fr. name Corse (kôrs) —**Cor′si·can** *adj., n.*

**cor·tege, cor·tège** (kôr tezh′, -tāzh′) *n.* [Fr. < It. *corteggio*, retinue < L. *cohors*: see COURT] **1.** a group of attendants; retinue **2.** a ceremonial procession, as at a funeral

**Cor·tés** (kôr tez′; *Sp.* kôr tes′), **Her·nan·do** (hər nan′dō) or **Her·nán** (er nän′) 1485–1547; Sp. explorer: conqueror of Mexico: also sp. **Cortez**

**cor·tex** (kôr′teks) *n., pl.* **-ti·ces** (-tə sēz′) [L., bark of a tree] *a)* the outer part of an internal organ, as of the kidney *b)* the outer layer of gray matter over most of the brain **2.** a layer of tissue under the epidermis in plant roots and stems **3.** the bark or rind of a plant —**cor′ti·cal** (-ti k'l) *adj.* —**cor′ti·cal·ly** *adv.*

**cor·ti·cate** (kôr′ti kit, -kāt′) *adj.* [L. *corticatus* < *cortex*] covered with bark: also **cor′ti·cat′ed, cor′ti·cose′** (-kōs′)

**cor·ti·sone** (kôrt′ə sōn′, -zōn′) *n.* [< *corticosterone*, a hormone] an adrenal-gland hormone, $C_{21}H_{28}O_5$, used in treating adrenal insufficiency and various inflammatory and allergic diseases

**co·run·dum** (kə run′dəm) *n.* [Tamil *kuruvindam* < Sans. *kuruvinda*, ruby] a hard mineral, aluminum oxide, $Al_2O_3$, used for grinding and polishing: the ruby, sapphire, etc. are precious varieties

**cor·us·cate** (kôr′əs kāt′, kär′-) *vt.* **-cat′ed, -cat′ing** [< L. pp. of *coruscare* < *coruscus*, vibrating] to emit flashes of light; glitter; sparkle —**co·rus·cant** (kə rus′kənt) *adj.* —**cor′us·ca′tion** *n.*

**cor·vette** (kôr vet′) *n.* [Fr., prob. ult. < L. *corbita (navis)*, cargo (ship) < *corbis*, basket] **1.** formerly, a sailing warship smaller than a frigate **2.** a small, fast British warship used for antisubmarine and convoy duty

**cor·vine** (kôr′vīn, -vin) *adj.* [< L. *corvus*, a raven] of or like a crow or raven

**Cor·y·bant** (kôr′ə bant′) *n., pl.* **-bants′, Cor′y·ban′tes** (-ban′tēz) **1.** *a)* Gr. Myth. an attendant of the god-

dess Cybele at her orgiastic revelries *b)* a priest of Cybele **2.** [c-] a reveler —**Cor′y·ban′tic, Cor′y·ban′tian** (-ban′-shən) *adj.*

**cor·ymb** (kôr′im, -imb; kär′-) *n.* [< Fr. < L. *corymbus*, flower cluster < Gr. *korymbos*] a broad, flat cluster of flowers in which the outer stems are long and those toward the center progressively shorter —**co·rym·bose** (kə rim′-bōs), **co·rym′bous** *adj.* —**co·rym′bose·ly** *adv.*

**co·ry·za** (kə rī′zə) *n.* [ModL. < LL. < Gr. *koryza*, catarrh] a cold in the head; acute nasal congestion

**cos** cosine

**Cos., cos. 1.** companies **2.** counties

**cosec** cosecant

**co·se·cant** (kō sē′kənt, -kant) *n. Trigonometry* the ratio between the hypotenuse and the side opposite a given acute angle in a right triangle

**co·sey, co·sie** (kō′zē) *adj., n. same as* COZY

**co·sign** (kō′sīn′) *vt., vi.* **1.** to sign (a promissory note) in addition to the maker, thus becoming responsible for the obligation if the maker should default **2.** to sign jointly —**co′sign′er** *n.*

**co·sig·na·to·ry** (kō sig′nə tôr′ē) *adj.* signing jointly —*n., pl.* **-ries** one of two or more joint signers

**co·sine** (kō′sīn) *n. Trigonometry* the ratio between the side adjacent to a given acute angle in a right triangle and the hypotenuse

**cos·met·ic** (käz met′ik) *adj.* [< Gr. *kosmētikos*, skilled in arranging < *kosmos*, order] **1.** designed to beautify the complexion, hair, etc. **2.** for improving the appearance by correcting deformities, esp. of the face —*n.* any cosmetic preparation for the skin, hair, etc. —**cos·met′i·cal·ly** *adv.*

**cos·me·tol·o·gy** (käz′mə täl′ə jē) *n.* the work of applying cosmetics to women, as in a beauty shop —**cos′me·tol′o·gist** *n.*

**cos·mic** (käz′mik) *adj.* [Gr. *kosmikos* < *kosmos*, order] **1.** of the cosmos; relating to the universe as a whole **2.** vast —**cos′mi·cal·ly** *adv.*

**cosmic dust** small particles falling from interstellar space to the earth

**cosmic rays** streams of highly penetrating charged particles that bombard the earth from outer space

**cos·mo-** [see COSMOS] *a combining form meaning* world, universe *[cosmology]*

**cos·mog·o·ny** (käz mäg′ə nē) *n.* [< Gr. < *kosmos*, universe + *gignesthai*, to produce] **1.** the origin of the universe **2.** *pl.* **-nies** a theory or account of this —**cos·mo·gon′ic** (-mə gän′ik), **cos′mo·gon′i·cal, cos·mog′o·nal** *adj.* —**cos·mog′o·nist** *n.*

**cos·mog·ra·phy** (käz mäg′rə fē) *n.* [< LL. < Gr.: see COSMO- & -GRAPHY] the science dealing with the structure of the universe as a whole —**cos·mog′ra·pher** *n.* —**cos·mo·graph′ic** (-mə graf′ik), **cos′mo·graph′i·cal** *adj.* —**cos′mo·graph′i·cal·ly** *adv.*

**cos·mol·o·gy** (käz mäl′ə jē) *n.* [COSMO- + -LOGY] the study of the universe as a whole and of its form, nature, etc. as a physical system —**cos′mo·log′i·cal** (-mə läj′ə k'l) *adj.* —**cos′mo·log′i·cal·ly** *adv.* —**cos·mol′o·gist** *n.*

**cos·mo·naut** (käz′mə nôt′, -nät′) *n.* [Russ. *kosmonaut* < *kosmo-*, COSMO- + *-naut* < Gr. *nautēs*, sailor (see NAUTICAL)] *same as* ASTRONAUT

**cos·mo·pol·i·tan** (käz′mə päl′ə t'n) *adj.* [COSMOPOLIT(E) + -AN] **1.** representative of all or many parts of the world **2.** not bound by local or national prejudices; at home in all countries or places —*n.* a cosmopolitan person —**cos′mo·pol′i·tan·ism** *n.*

**cos·mop·o·lite** (käz mäp′ə līt′) *n.* [< Gr. < *kosmos*, world + *politēs*, citizen < *polis*, city] **1.** a cosmopolitan person **2.** a plant or animal common to all or most parts of the world

**cos·mos** (käz′məs; *for 1 & 2 also* -mōs) *n.* [Gr. *kosmos*, universe, harmony] **1.** the universe considered as a harmonious and orderly system **2.** any complete and orderly system **3.** *pl.* **cos′mos** a tropical American plant of the composite family, with white, pink, or purple flower heads

**co·spon·sor** (kō′spän′sər) *n.* a joint sponsor, as of a proposed piece of legislation —*vt.* to be a cosponsor of —**co′spon′sor·ship′** *n.*

**Cos·sack** (käs′ak, -ək; kô′sak) *n.* [Russ. *kozak* < Turk.] a member of a people of southern Russia, famous as horsemen —*adj.* of the Cossacks

**cos·set** (käs′it) *n.* [< ? OE. *cot-sæta*, cot dweller] a pet lamb, or any small pet —*vt.* to make a pet of; pamper

**cost** (kôst) *vt.* **cost** or, *for 2,* **cost′ed, cost′ing** [< OFr. < ML. *costare* < L. < *com-*, together + *stare*, to stand] **1.** *a)* to be obtained or obtainable for (a certain price) *b)* to require the expenditure, loss, or experience of **2.** *Business* to estimate the cost of producing (often with *out*) —*n.* **1.** *a)* the amount asked or paid for a thing *b)* the amount spent in producing a commodity **2.** *a)* the amount of money, effort, etc. required to achieve an end *b)* loss; sacrifice **3.** [*pl.*] *Law* court expenses of a lawsuit —**at all costs** by any means required: also **at any cost**

**cos·tal** (käs′t′l) *adj.* [Fr. < ML. < L. *costa,* a rib] of or near a rib or the ribs

**Cos·ta Me·sa** (kōs′tə mā′sə) [Sp., lit., coast plateau] city in SW Calif., near Long Beach: pop. 82,000

**Cos·ta Ri·ca** (käs′tə rē′kə, kôs′-) country in Central America: 19,575 sq. mi.; pop. 1,685,000; cap. San José —**Cos′ta Ri′can**

**cos·ter·mon·ger** (käs′tər muŋ′gər, kôs′-) *n.* [< *costard,* a kind of apple + MONGER] [Brit.] a person who sells fruit or vegetables from a cart or street stand: also **cos′ter**

**cos·tive** (käs′tiv, kôs′-) *adj.* [< OFr. pp. of *costever* < L. *constipare:* see CONSTIPATE] constipated or constipating —**cos′tive·ly** *adv.* —**cos′tive·ness** *n.*

**cost·ly** (kôst′lē) *adj.* **-li·er, -li·est 1.** *a)* costing much; expensive; dear *b)* at the cost of great effort, damage, etc. **2.** magnificent; sumptuous —**cost′li·ness** *n.*

**cost of living** the average cost of the necessities of life, as food, shelter, and clothes

**cost-plus** (kôst′plus′) *adj.* with the price for goods or services set at the cost of materials, labor, etc. plus a specified amount of profit

**cos·tume** (käs′tōōm, -tyōōm) *n.* [< Fr. < It. < L. *consuetudo,* CUSTOM] **1.** *a)* the style of dress typical of a certain period, people, etc. *b)* a set of such clothes as worn in a play or at a masquerade **2.** a set of outer clothes for some occasion, esp. one worn by a woman —*vt.* **-tumed, -tum·ing** to provide with a costume

**costume jewelry** relatively inexpensive jewelry

**cos·tum·er** (-ər) *n.* one who makes, sells, or rents costumes, as for masquerades, theaters, etc.: also **cos·tum·ier** (käs tōōm′yər, -tyōōm′-)

**co·sy** (kō′zē) *adj.* **-si·er, -si·est** & *n., pl.* **-sies** same as COZY —**co′si·ly** *adv.* —**co′si·ness** *n.*

**cot**[1] (kät) *n.* [Anglo-Ind. < Hindi *khāṭ* < Sans.] a narrow, collapsible bed, as one made of canvas on a folding frame

**cot**[2] (kät) *n.* [OE.] **1.** [Poet.] a cottage **2.** a cote **3.** a sheath, as for a hurt finger

**cot** cotangent

**co·tan·gent** (kō tan′jənt) *n. Trigonometry* the ratio between the side adjacent to a given acute angle in a right triangle and the side opposite

**cote** (kōt) *n.* [ME., COT[2]] **1.** a small shelter for sheep, doves, etc. **2.** [Dial.] a cottage

**co·ten·ant** (kō ten′ənt) *n.* one of two or more tenants who share a place —**co·ten′an·cy** *n.*

**co·te·rie** (kōt′ər ē) *n.* [Fr., orig., organization of feudal tenants < OFr. *cotier,* COTTER[1]] a close circle of friends with common interests

**co·ter·mi·nous** (kō tur′mə nəs) *adj.* same as CONTERMINOUS: also **co·ter′mi·nal** —**co·ter′mi·nous·ly** *adv.*

**co·til·lion** (kō til′yən, kə-) *n.* [Fr. *cotillon,* orig., petticoat < OFr. *cotte,* a COAT] **1.** a dance with many intricate figures and the continual changing of partners **2.** a formal ball, esp. one at which debutantes are presented Also sp. **co·til′lon**

**cot·tage** (kät′ij) *n.* [< ML. *cotagium* < OFr. *cote* or ME. *cot,* hut] a small house, now often a summer home or any of the separate dwelling units for small groups in certain institutions, etc.

**cottage cheese** a soft, white cheese made by straining and seasoning the curds of sour milk

**cottage pudding** cake covered with a sweet sauce

**cot·tag·er** (-ər) *n.* **1.** a person who lives in a cottage **2.** [Brit.] a farm laborer

**cot·ter**[1], **cot·tar** (kät′ər) *n.* [< OFr. *cotier* < OE. *cot,* COT[2]] **1.** a cottager **2.** [Scot.] a tenant farmer

**cot·ter**[2] (kät′ər) *n.* [< ?] **1.** a bolt or wedge put through a slot to hold together parts of machinery **2.** same as COTTER PIN

**cotter pin** a split pin used as a cotter, fastened in place by spreading apart its ends after it is inserted

**cot·ton** (kät′'n) *n.* [< OFr. < Ar. *quṭun*] **1.** the soft, white seed hairs filling the seedpods of various shrubby plants of the mallow family **2.** a plant or plants producing this material **3.** the crop of such plants **4.** thread or cloth made of cotton —*adj.* of cotton —**cotton to** [Colloq.] **1.** to take a liking to **2.** to become aware of (a situation) —**cotton up to** [Colloq.] to try to make friends with —**cot′ton·y** *adj.*

COTTER PIN

**cotton batting** thin, pressed layers of fluffy, absorbent cotton, used for surgical dressing, etc.

**Cotton Belt** region in S and SE U.S. where much cotton is grown

**cotton candy** a cottony candy consisting of fibers of melted sugar spun into a fluffy mass around a paper cone

**cotton flannel** a soft, fleecy cotton cloth

**cotton gin** [see GIN[2]] a machine for separating cotton fibers from the seeds

**cotton-mouth** (-mouth′) *n.* [from its whitish mouth] *same as* WATER MOCCASIN

**cot·ton-pick·ing** (-pik′'n) *adj.* [Slang] worthless, damned, hateful, etc.

**cot·ton·seed** (-sēd′) *n.* the seed of the cotton plant, from which an oil (**cottonseed oil**) is pressed for use in margarine, cooking oil, etc.

**cot·ton·tail** (-tāl′) *n.* a common American rabbit with a short, fluffy tail

**cot·ton·wood** (-wood′) *n.* **1.** a poplar that has seeds covered with cottony hairs **2.** its wood

**cotton wool** raw cotton or cotton batting

**cot·y·le·don** (kät′'l ēd′'n) *n.* [L. < Gr. < *kotylē,* a cavity] the first single leaf or either of the first pair of leaves produced by the embryo of a flowering plant —**cot′y·le′don·al** *adj.*

**couch** (kouch) *n.* [< OFr.: see the *v.*] **1.** an article of furniture on which one may sit or lie down; sofa **2.** any resting place —*vt.* [< OFr. *coucher,* to lie down < L. *collocare* < *com-,* together + *locare,* to place] **1.** to lay as on a couch: now usually used reflexively or in the passive voice **2.** to bring down; esp., to lower (a spear, etc.) to an attacking position **3.** to put in words; express —*vi.* **1.** to lie down on a bed; recline **2.** to lie in hiding or ambush

**couch·ant** (-ənt) *adj.* [see prec.] *Heraldry* lying down

**couch grass** (kouch) [var. of QUITCH] a weedy grass that spreads rapidly by its underground stems

**cou·gar** (kōō′gər, -gär) *n., pl.* **-gars, -gar:** see PLURAL, II, D, 1 [< Fr. < Port. *çuçuarana* < Tupi < *suusú,* deer + *rana,* false] a large, tawny-brown animal of the cat family, with a long, slender body

**cough** (kôf) *vi.* [ME. *coughen*] to expel air suddenly and noisily from the lungs through the glottis —*vt.* to expel by coughing —*n.* **1.** a coughing **2.** a condition, as of the lungs or throat, causing frequent coughing —**cough up 1.** to bring up (phlegm, etc.) by coughing **2.** [Slang] to hand over (money, etc.) —**cough′er** *n.*

**cough drop** a small, flavored, medicated tablet for the relief of coughs, hoarseness, etc.

**could** (kood) *v.* [< OE. *cuthe,* pt. of *cunnan:* see CAN[1]] **1.** *pt. of* CAN[1] **2.** an auxiliary in verbal phrases with present or future sense, generally equivalent to *can* in meaning and use, expressing esp. a shade of doubt or a smaller degree of possibility [it *could* be so]

**could·n't** (-'nt) could not

**couldst** (koodst) *archaic or poetic 2d pers. sing., past indic., of* CAN[1]: *used with* thou

**cou·lee** (kōō′lē) *n.* [Fr. < *couler,* to flow < L. < *colum,* a strainer] **1.** a stream or sheet of lava **2.** [Northwest] a deep gulch or ravine, usually dry in summer

**cou·lomb** (kōō läm′, kōō′läm) *n.* [after C. A. de *Coulomb* (1736–1806), Fr. physicist] the meter-kilogram-second unit of electric charge; charge transported through a conductor by a current of one ampere flowing for one second

**coul·ter** (kōl′tər) *n. same as* COLTER

**coun·cil** (koun′s'l) *n.* [< OFr. < L. *concilium,* meeting < *com-,* with + *calere,* to call] **1.** a group of people called together for consultation, advice, etc. **2.** a group of people chosen as an administrative or legislative assembly **3.** the legislative body of a city or town **4.** a church assembly to discuss points of doctrine, etc. **5.** any of various organizations or societies

**Council Bluffs** [scene of councils with Indians by LEWIS & CLARK] city in SW Iowa: pop. 56,000

**coun·cil·man** (-mən) *n., pl.* **-men** a member of a council, esp. of a city or town —**coun′cil·man′ic** (-man′ik) *adj.*

**coun·ci·lor** (koun′sə lər) *n.* [< COUNSELOR] a member of a council: also [Chiefly Brit.] **coun′cil·lor** —**coun′cil·lor·ship′** *n.*

**coun·sel** (koun′s'l) *n.* [< OFr. < L. *consilium*] **1.** a mutual exchange of ideas, opinions, etc.; discussion **2.** *a)* advice resulting from such an exchange *b)* any advice **3.** *a)* a lawyer or group of lawyers giving legal advice or acting for clients *b)* a consultant —*vt.* **-seled** or **-selled, -sel·ing** or **-sel·ling 1.** to give advice to; advise **2.** to urge the acceptance of (a plan, etc.) —*vi.* to give or take advice —**keep one's own counsel** to keep one's thoughts, plans, etc. to oneself —**take counsel** to consult; exchange advice, opinions, etc.

**coun·se·lor, coun·sel·lor** (-ər) *n.* **1.** a person who counsels; adviser **2.** a lawyer, esp. one who conducts cases in court: in full, **counselor-at-law 3.** a group worker in a children's camp —**coun′se·lor·ship′, coun′sel·lor·ship′** *n.*

**count**[1] (kount) *vt.* [< OFr. < L. *computare,* COMPUTE] **1.** to name numbers in regular order to (a certain number) [to *count* five] **2.** to add up, one by one, by units or groups, so as to get a total **3.** to check by numbering off; inventory **4.** to take account of; include [ten, *counting* you] **5.** to believe to be; consider [to *count* oneself fortunate] —*vi.* **1.** to name numbers or add up items in order **2.** to be taken into account; have importance, value, etc. **3.** to have a specified value (often with *for*) **4.** to rely or depend (*on* or *upon*) —*n.* **1.** a counting, or adding up **2.** the number or a total reached by counting **3.** a reckoning or accounting **4.** *Baseball* the number of balls and strikes that have been pitched to the batter **5.** *Boxing* ten seconds counted to give a fallen boxer time to rise before he loses the match **6.** *Law* any of the charges in an indictment, each of which is sufficient for prosecution —**count in** to include —**count off** to separate into equal divisions by counting —**count out** **1.** to disregard; omit **2.** *Boxing* to declare (a boxer) defeated when he has remained down for a count of ten —**count′a·ble** *adj.*

**count²** (kount) *n.* [< OFr. < L. *comes* (gen. *comitis*), companion < *com-,* with + *ire,* to go] a European nobleman equal in rank to an English earl

**count·down** (-doun′) *n.* the schedule of operations just before the firing of a rocket, etc.; also, the counting off, in reverse order, of units of time in such a schedule

**coun·te·nance** (koun′tə nəns) *n.* [< OFr. < L. *continentia,* bearing < *continere,* CONTAIN] **1.** the look on a person's face that shows his nature or feelings **2.** the face; facial features **3.** *a)* a look of approval *b)* approval; support **4.** calm control; composure —*vt.* **-nanced, -nanc·ing** to give support to; approve —**in countenance** calm; composed —**put out of countenance** to disconcert

**count·er¹** (koun′tər) *n.* [see COUNT¹] **1.** a person or thing that counts or keeps count **2.** a small piece of metal, wood, etc., used in some games, esp. for keeping score **3.** an imitation coin, or token **4.** a long table, board, etc., as in a store or kitchen for the display of goods, serving of food, etc. —**over the counter** sold directly, not through a stock exchange —**under the counter** in a surreptitious manner: said of illegal sales

**coun·ter²** (koun′tər) *adv.* [< Fr. < L. *contra,* against] in a contrary direction, manner, etc.; opposite —*adj.* acting in opposition or in an opposite direction —*n.* **1.** the opposite; contrary **2.** an opposing action **3.** a stiff leather piece around the heel of a shoe **4.** the part of a ship's stern between the waterline and the curved part **5.** *Boxing a)* a blow given while parrying an opponent's blow *b)* a giving of such a blow —*vt., vi.* **1.** to oppose or check (a person or thing) **2.** to say or do (something) in reply or retaliation **3.** *Boxing* to strike one's opponent while parrying (his blow)

**coun·ter-** [< Fr. < L. *contra-,* against] *a combining form meaning:* **1.** opposite, contrary to [*counterclockwise*] **2.** in retaliation or return [*counterplot*] **3.** complementary [*counterpart*]

**coun·ter·act** (koun′tər akt′) *vt.* to act against; neutralize the effect of with opposing action —**coun′ter·ac′tion** *n.* —**coun′ter·ac′tive** *adj., n.*

**coun·ter·at·tack** (koun′tər ə tak′; *for v.,* usually koun′tər ə tak′) *n.* an attack made in opposition to another attack —*vt., vi.* to attack so as to offset the enemy's attack

**coun·ter·bal·ance** (koun′tər bal′əns; *for v.,* usually koun′tər bal′əns) *n.* **1.** a weight used to balance another weight **2.** any force or influence that balances or offsets another —*vt.* **-anced, -anc·ing** to be a counterbalance to; offset

**coun·ter·check** (koun′tər chek′; *for v.,* usually koun′tər chek′) *n.* **1.** anything that checks, restrains, etc. **2.** a double-check to be sure —*vt.* **1.** to check or counteract **2.** to check again to be sure

**counter check** a check obtained at a bank by a depositor making a withdrawal

**coun·ter·claim** (koun′tər klām′; *for v.,* usually koun′tər klām′) *n.* an opposing claim to offset another —*vt., vi.* to make a counterclaim (of) —**coun′ter·claim′ant** *n.*

**coun·ter·clock·wise** (koun′tər kläk′wīz) *adj., adv.* in a direction opposite to that in which the hands of a clock move

**coun·ter·cul·ture** (koun′tər kul′chər) *n.* the culture of the young people of the 1960's and 1970's with a life style opposed to the prevailing culture

**coun·ter·es·pi·on·age** (coun′tər es′pē ə näzh′, -näj′, -nij) *n.* actions to prevent or thwart enemy espionage

**coun·ter·feit** (koun′tər fit) *adj.* [< OFr. pp. of *contrefaire,* to imitate < *contre-,* counter- + *faire* (< L. *facere*), to make] **1.** made in imitation of something genuine so as to defraud; forged [*counterfeit* money] **2.** pretended; sham; feigned —*n.* **1.** an imitation made to deceive **2.** something so much like something else as to mislead —*vt., vi.* **1.** to make an imitation of (money, pictures, etc.) in order to defraud **2.** to pretend **3.** to resemble (something) closely —**coun′ter·feit′er** *n.*

**coun·ter·foil** (-foil′) *n.* [COUNTER- + FOIL²] the stub of a check, receipt, etc. kept by the issuer as a record

**coun·ter·in·sur·gen·cy** (koun′tər in sur′jən sē) *n.* military and political action carried on to defeat an insurgency

**coun·ter·in·tel·li·gence** (-in tel′ə jəns) *n.* actions to counter enemy intelligence or espionage activity, prevent sabotage, etc.

**coun·ter·ir·ri·tant** (-ir′ə tənt) *n.* anything used to produce a slight irritation to relieve more serious inflammation elsewhere

**count·er·man** (koun′tər man′, -mən) *n., pl.* **-men′** (-men′, -mən) a man whose work is serving customers at a counter as of a lunchroom

**coun·ter·mand** (koun′tər mand′; *also, and for n. always,* koun′tər mand′) *vt.* [< OFr. < L. *contra,* against + *mandare:* see MANDATE] **1.** to cancel or revoke (a command or order) **2.** to call back or order back by a contrary order —*n.* a command or order canceling another

**coun·ter·march** (koun′tər märch′; *for v.,* also koun′tər märch′) *n.* a march back or in the opposite direction —*vi., vt.* to march back

**coun·ter·move** (koun′tər moov′; *for v.,* also koun′tər moov′) *n.* a move made in opposition or retaliation —*vi., vt.* **-moved′, -mov′ing** to move in opposition or retaliation

**coun·ter·of·fen·sive** (koun′tər ə fen′siv) *n.* an attack in force by troops who have been defending a position

**coun·ter·pane** (koun′tər pān′) *n.* [altered < ME. *countrepoint,* quilt < OFr. < L. *culcita puncta,* pricked (i.e., embroidered) quilt] a bedspread

**coun·ter·part** (-pärt′) *n.* **1.** a person or thing that corresponds to or closely resembles another **2.** a thing that completes or complements another **3.** a copy or duplicate, as of a lease

**coun·ter·plot** (koun′tər plät′; *for v.,* also koun′tər plät′) *n.* a plot to defeat another plot —*vt., vi.* **-plot′ted, -plot′ting** to plot against (a plot); defeat (a plot) with another

**coun·ter·point** (-point′) *n.* [< Fr. < It. *contrappunto,* lit., pointed against: see COUNTER- & POINT, n.] **1.** a melody accompanying another melody note for note **2.** *a)* the art of adding related but independent melodies to a basic melody, in accordance with the fixed rules of harmony *b)* this kind of composition

**coun·ter·poise** (-poiz′) *n.* [< ONormFr.: see COUNTER² & POISE] **1.** same as COUNTERBALANCE **2.** a state of balance or equilibrium —*vt.* **-poised′, -pois′ing** same as COUNTERBALANCE

**coun·ter·pro·po·sal** (-prə pō′z'l) *n.* a proposal in response to one regarded as unsatisfactory

**Counter-Reformation** the reform movement in the Roman Catholic Church in the 16th cent., following in reaction to the Protestant Reformation

**coun·ter·rev·o·lu·tion** (koun′tər rev′ə loo′shən) *n.* **1.** a political movement or revolution against a government or social system set up by a previous revolution **2.** a movement to combat revolutionary tendencies —**coun′ter·rev′o·lu′tion·ar′y** *adj., n.* —**coun′ter·rev′o·lu′tion·ist** *n.*

**coun·ter·shaft** (koun′tər shaft′) *n.* an intermediate shaft that transmits motion from the main shaft of a machine to a working part

**coun·ter·sign** (koun′tər sīn′; *for v.,* also koun′tər sīn′) *n.* **1.** a signature added to a previously signed document for confirmation **2.** *Mil.* a secret word or signal which must be given to a sentry by someone wishing to pass —*vt.* to confirm (a previously signed document) by signing —**coun′ter·sig′na·ture** (-sig′nə chər) *n.*

**coun·ter·sink** (koun′tər sink′; *for v.,* also koun′tər sink′) *vt.* **-sunk′, -sink′ing** **1.** to enlarge the top part of (a hole in metal, wood, etc.) to make the head of a bolt, screw, etc. fit into it **2.** to sink (a bolt, screw, etc.) into such a hole —*n.* **1.** a tool for countersinking holes **2.** a countersunk hole

**coun·ter·spy** (-spī′) *n.* a spy in counterespionage

**coun·ter·ten·or** (-ten′ər) *n.* **1.** the range of the highest mature male voice, above tenor **2.** a voice, singer, or part with such a range

**coun·ter·vail** (koun′tər vāl′) *vt.* [< OFr. < *contre* (see COUNTER²) + *valoir,* to avail < L. *valere,* to be strong] **1.** to make up for; compensate **2.** to counteract; avail against —*vi.* to avail (*against*)

**coun·ter·weigh** (-wā′) *vt. same as* COUNTERBALANCE —**coun′ter·weight′** *n.*

**counter word** any word freely used as a general term of approval or disapproval without reference to its more exact meaning, as *nice* or *terrible*

**count·ess** (koun′tis) *n.* **1.** the wife or widow of a count or earl **2.** a noblewoman whose rank is equal to that of a count or earl

**count·ing·house** (koun′tiŋ hous′) *n.* [Now Rare] an office where a firm keeps accounts, etc.

**count·less** (kount′lis) *adj.* too many to count; innumerable; myriad

**coun·tri·fied** (kun′tri fīd′) *adj.* 1. rural; rustic 2. having the appearance, actions, etc. attributed to country people Also sp. **coun′try·fied′**

**coun·try** (kun′trē) *n., pl.* **-tries** [< OFr. < VL. *contrata*, that which is beyond < L. *contra*, opposite] 1. an area of land; region [wooded *country*] 2. the whole territory of a nation 3. the people of a nation 4. the land of a person's birth or citizenship 5. land with farms and small towns; rural region —*adj.* 1. of, in, or from a rural district 2. like that of the country; rustic

**country club** a social club in the outskirts of a city, equipped with a clubhouse, golf course, etc.

**coun·try-dance** (-dans′) *n.* an English folk dance, esp. one in which partners form two facing lines

**coun·try·man** (-mən) *n., pl.* **-men** 1. a man who lives in the country; rustic 2. a man of one's own country; compatriot —**coun′try·wom′an** *n.fem., pl.* **-wom′en**

**country music** rural folk music, esp. a commercialized variety deriving from the folk music of the Southern highlands and backwoods

**coun·try·seat** (-sēt′) *n.* a rural mansion or estate

**coun·try·side** (-sīd′) *n.* a rural region or its inhabitants

**coun·ty** (koun′tē) *n., pl.* **-ties** [< OFr. < ML. *comitatus*, jurisdiction of a count < L. *comes:* see COUNT²] 1. a small administrative district; esp., *a)* the largest local administrative subdivision of most States *b)* any of the chief administrative and judicial districts into which Great Britain and Ireland are divided 2. the people in a county

**county agent** a government-employed specialist assigned to inform farmers in a county of improved practices in agriculture

**county commissioner** a member of an elected governing board in the counties of certain States

**county seat** a town or city that is the seat of government of a county

**coup** (ko͞o) *n., pl.* **coups** (ko͞oz; *Fr.* ko͞o) [Fr. < VL. < L. *colaphus*, a blow < Gr. *kolaphos*] 1. literally, a blow 2. a sudden, successful move or action; brilliant stroke 3. *same as* COUP D'ÉTAT

‡**coup de grâce** (ko͞o də gräs′) [Fr., lit., stroke of mercy] 1. the blow, shot, etc. that brings death to a sufferer 2. a finishing stroke

‡**coup de main** (man′) [Fr., lit., stroke of hand] a surprise attack or movement, as in war

‡**coup d'é·tat** (dā tä′) [Fr., lit., stroke of state] a sudden, forceful stroke in politics, esp. the sudden, forcible overthrow of a government

**coupe** (ko͞op; *orig., but now rarely,* ko͞o pā′) *n.* [see ff.] a closed, two-door automobile with a body smaller than that of a sedan

**cou·pé** (ko͞o pā′) *n.* [Fr., pp. of *couper*, to cut] 1. a closed carriage seating two passengers, with a seat outside for the driver 2. *same as* COUPE

**cou·ple** (kup′'l) *n.* [< OFr. < L. *copula:* see COPULA] 1. anything joining two things together; bond; link 2. two things or persons of the same sort that are somehow associated 3. a man and a woman who are engaged, married, or partners in a dance, etc. 4. [Colloq.] a few; several: now often used with adjectival force [a *couple* ideas] —*vt.* **-pled, -pling** to join together; link; connect —*vi.* 1. to come together; unite 2. to copulate

**cou·pler** (kup′lər) *n.* a person or thing that couples; specif., a pneumatic device for coupling two railroad cars

**cou·plet** (kup′lit) *n.* [Fr. dim.: see COUPLE] 1. two successive lines of poetry, esp. two of the same length that rhyme 2. [Rare] a couple

**cou·pling** (kup′liŋ) *n.* 1. a joining together 2. a mechanical device for joining parts together 3. a device for joining railroad cars 4. a method or device for joining two electric circuits to transfer energy from one to the other

COUPLING

**cou·pon** (ko͞o′pän, kyo͞o′-) *n.* [Fr. < *couper*, to cut] 1. a detachable printed statement on a bond, specifying the interest due at a given time 2. a certificate or ticket entitling the holder to a specified right, as reduced purchase price 3. a part of a printed advertisement for use in ordering goods, etc.

**cour·age** (kur′ij) *n.* [< OFr. < L. *cor*, heart] a willingness to face and deal with danger, trouble, or pain; fearlessness; bravery; valor —**the courage of one's convictions** the courage to do what one thinks is right

**cou·ra·geous** (kə rā′jəs) *adj.* having or showing courage; brave —**cou·ra′geous·ly** *adv.* —**cou·ra′geous·ness** *n.*

**Cour·bet** (ko͞or be′), **Gus·tave** (güs täv′) 1819–77; Fr. painter

**cou·ri·er** (ko͞or′ē ər, kur′-) *n.* [< OFr., ult. < L. *currere*, to run] a messenger sent in haste or on a regular schedule with important or urgent messages

**course** (kôrs) *n.* [< OFr. *cours* < L. pp. of *currere*, to run] 1. an onward movement; progress 2. a way, path, or channel of movement; specif., *same as: a)* [Brit.] RACECOURSE *b)* GOLF COURSE 3. the direction taken, as by a ship or plane [a *course* due south] 4. *a)* a regular manner of procedure [the law must take its *course*] *b)* a way of behaving; mode of conduct 5. *a)* a series of like things in some regular order *b)* a particular succession of events or actions 6. natural development [the *course* of true love] 7. a part of a meal served at one time 8. a horizontal layer, as of bricks, in the face of a building 9. *Educ. a)* a complete series of studies leading to graduation, a degree, etc. *b)* any of the separate units of instruction in a subject —*vt.* **coursed, cours′ing** 1. to pursue 2. to cause (esp. hunting hounds) to chase 3. to traverse —*vi.* 1. to run or race 2. to hunt with hounds —**in due course** in the usual or proper sequence (of events) —**in the course of** in the process of; during —**of course** 1. as is or was to be expected; naturally 2. certainly —**on** (or **off**) **course** moving (or not moving) in the intended direction

**cours·er** (kôr′sər) *n.* [see prec.] [Poet.] a graceful, spirited, or swift horse

**court** (kôrt) *n.* [OFr. < LL. < L. *cohors:* see COHORT] 1. an uncovered space wholly or partly surrounded by buildings or walls 2. a short street, often closed at one end 3. *a)* an area for playing any of several ball games *b)* a part of such an area 4. a motel: in full, **motor court** 5. *a)* the palace of a sovereign *b)* the family, advisers, etc. of a sovereign, as a group *c)* a sovereign and his councilors as a governing body *d)* any formal gathering held by a sovereign 6. attention paid to someone in order to get something 7. courtship; wooing 8. *a)* a person or persons appointed to try law cases, make investigations, etc.; judge or judges *b)* a place where trials are held, investigations made, etc. *c)* a judicial assembly; also, a regular session of such an assembly —*vt.* 1. to pay attention to (a person) in order to get something 2. to try to get the love of; woo 3. to try to get; seek [to *court* favor] 4. to make oneself open to [to *court* insults] —*vi.* to woo —*adj.* of or fit for a court —**out of court** without a trial —**pay court to** to court, as for favor or love —**court′er** *n.*

**cour·te·ous** (kur′tē əs) *adj.* [< OFr. *courteis* < *court:* see COURT & -EOUS] polite and gracious; considerate of others; well-mannered —**cour′te·ous·ly** *adv.* —**cour′te·ous·ness** *n.*

**cour·te·san** (kôr′tə z'n, kur′-) *n.* [< Fr. < It. *cortigiana*, court lady < *corte*, COURT] a prostitute; esp., formerly, a mistress of a king, nobleman, etc.: also **cour′te·zan**

**cour·te·sy** (kur′tə sē) *n., pl.* **-sies** [< OFr. *curteisie:* see COURTEOUS] 1. courteous behavior; gracious politeness 2. a polite or considerate act or remark 3. an act or usage intended to honor or compliment [a title of *courtesy*]

**courtesy card** a card entitling the bearer to special privileges, as at a hotel, bank, etc.

**court·house** (kôrt′hous′) *n.* 1. a building in which law courts are held 2. a building that houses the offices of a county government

**cour·ti·er** (kôr′tē ər, -tyər) *n.* 1. an attendant at a royal court 2. a person who courts favor by flattery, etc.

**court·ly** (kôrt′lē) *adj.* **-li·er, -li·est** 1. suitable for a king's court; dignified, elegant, etc. 2. flattering, esp. in an obsequious or humble way —*adv.* in a courtly manner —**court′li·ness** *n.*

**court-mar·tial** (-mär′shəl) *n., pl.* **courts′-mar′tial;** for 2, now more often **court′-mar′tials** 1. a court of personnel in the armed forces to try offenses against military law 2. a trial by a court-martial —*vt.* **-tialed** or **-tialled, -tial·ing** or **-tial·ling** to try by a court-martial

**court of appeals** [*often* C- A-] 1. a State court to which appeals are taken from the trial courts 2. any of the Federal appellate courts, between the U.S. district courts and the Supreme Court

**Court of St. James** [< *St. James Palace*, former royal residence] the British royal court

**court plaster** [from former use by court ladies for beauty spots] cloth covered with an adhesive material, formerly used to protect minor skin wounds

**court·room** (kôrt′ro͞om′) *n.* a room in which a law court is held

**court·ship** (-ship′) *n.* the act, process, or period of courting, or wooing

**court tennis** *see* TENNIS

**court·yard** (-yärd′) *n.* a space enclosed by walls, adjoining or in a large building

**cous·cous** (ko͞os′ko͞os, ko͞os ko͞os′) *n.* [Fr. < Berber < Ar. < *kaskasa*, to grind] a N African dish of crushed grain, usually steamed and served with meat

**cous·in** (kuz′'n) *n.* [< OFr. < L. < *com-*, with + *sobrinus*, maternal cousin < *soror*, sister] 1. the son or daughter of one's uncle or aunt: also **cous′in-ger′man**, **first** (or **full**) **cousin** 2. loosely, any relative by blood or marriage 3. a person thought of as related to another 4. a title of address used by one sovereign to another or to a nobleman —**cous′in·ly** *adj., adv.* —**cous′in·ship′** *n.*

**cou·ture** (kōō tōōr′) *n.* [Fr., sewing < L. pp. of *consuere* < *com*-, together + *suere*, to sew] the work or business of designing new fashions in women's clothes

‡**cou·tu·rier** (kōō tü ryā′; *E.* kōō tŏŏr′ē ā′) *n.* [Fr.] a man engaged in couture —**cou·tu·rière** (-tü ryer′; *E.* -tŏŏr′ē er′) *n.fem.*

**co·va·lence** (kō vā′ləns) *n.* the number of pairs of electrons an atom can share with neighboring atoms —**co·va′lent** *adj.*

**cove** (kōv) *n.* [< OE. *cofa*, cave, cell] 1. a sheltered nook or recess, as in cliffs 2. a small bay or inlet 3. a small valley 4. a concave molding 5. a trough for concealed lighting on a wall near a ceiling —*vt., vi.* **coved**, **cov′ing** to curve concavely

**cov·en** (kuv′ən, kō′vən) *n.* [< OFr. < L. *convenire*, CONVENE] a gathering or meeting, esp. of witches

**cov·e·nant** (kuv′ə nənt) *n.* [OFr. < L. *convenire*, CONVENE] 1. a binding agreement made by two or more individuals, parties, etc. to do or keep from doing a specified thing; compact 2. *Law* a formal, sealed contract 3. *Theol.* the promises made by God to man, as recorded in the Bible —*vt., vi.* to promise by or in a covenant —**cov′e·nan′tal** (-nan′t'l) *adj.* —**cov′e·nant·er**, **cov′e·nan·tor** (-nan-tər) *n.*

**Cov·en·try** (kuv′ən trē, käv′-) city in C England: pop. 335,000 —*n.* ostracism [to send someone to *Coventry*]

**cov·er** (kuv′ər) *vt.* [< OFr. < L. < *co-*, intens. + *operire*, to hide] 1. to place something on, over, or in front of 2. to extend over; overlay 3. to mate with (a mare): said of a stallion 4. to clothe 5. to coat, sprinkle, etc. thickly 6. to sit on (eggs); brood 7. to conceal by hiding or screening 8. to protect as by shielding 9. to take into account 10. *a)* to protect against financial loss, or make up for (a loss, etc.), as by insurance *b)* to be sufficient for payment of (a debt, etc.) *c)* to buy stock to replace (shares borrowed from a broker to effect a short sale) 11. to accept (a bet) 12. to travel over [to *cover* a distance] 13. to be responsible for (an area or range of activity) 14. to deal with [to *cover* a subject] 15. to point a firearm at 16. *Journalism* to get news, pictures, etc. of [to *cover* a train wreck] 17. *Sports* to guard or obstruct (an opponent, position, etc.) —*vi.* 1. to spread over a surface, as a liquid 2. to put on a cap, hat, etc. 3. to provide an alibi or excuse (*for* another) —*n.* 1. anything that covers, as a binding, lid, top, etc. 2. a protective shelter or a hiding place 3. a tablecloth and a place setting for one person 4. *same as* COVER-UP 5. an envelope, wrapping, etc. for mail —**break cover** to come out of protective shelter —**cover up** 1. to cover entirely 2. to keep blunders, crimes, etc. from being known —**take cover** to seek protective shelter —**under cover** in secrecy or concealment —**cov′er·er** *n.*

**cov·er·age** (-ij) *n.* 1. the amount, extent, etc. covered by something 2. *Insurance* all the risks covered by an insurance policy

**cov·er·all** (-ôl′) *n.* [*usually pl.*] a one-piece garment with sleeves and legs, worn like overalls

**cover charge** a fixed charge added to the cost of food and drink, as at a nightclub or restaurant

**cover crop** a crop, as vetch or clover, grown to protect soil from erosion and to keep it fertile

**Cov·er·dale** (kuv′ər dāl′), **Miles** 1488–1568; Eng. clergyman & translator of the Bible (1535)

**covered wagon** a large wagon with an arched cover of canvas, used by American pioneers

**cover girl** [Colloq.] a girl model whose picture is often put on magazine covers, etc.

**cov·er·ing** (kuv′ər iŋ) *n.* anything that covers

**cov·er·let** (kuv′ər lit) *n.* [< Anglo-Fr. < OFr. *covrir*, COVER + *lit*, a bed < L. *lectus*] 1. a bedspread 2. any covering Also [Dial.] **cov′er·lid**

**cov·ert** (kuv′ərt, kō′vərt) *adj.* [OFr., pp. of *covrir*, COVER] concealed, hidden, or disguised —*n.* 1. a covered or protected place; shelter 2. a hiding place for game 3. any of the small feathers covering the bases of the larger feathers of a bird's wing and tail —**cov′ert·ly** *adv.* —**cov′ert·ness** *n.*

**covert** (cloth) a smooth, twilled, lightweight cloth, usually of wool, used for suits, topcoats, etc.

**cov·er·ture** (kuv′ər chər) *n.* 1. a covering 2. a refuge 3. a concealment or disguise

**cov·er-up** (kuv′ər up′) *n.* something used for hiding one's real activities, intentions, etc.

**cov·et** (kuv′it) *vt., vi.* [< OFr. < L. *cupiditas*: see CUPIDITY] to want ardently (esp., something that another has) —**cov′et·a·ble** *adj.* —**cov′et·er** *n.*

**cov·et·ous** (-əs) *adj.* greedy; avaricious —**cov′et·ous·ly** *adv.* —**cov′et·ous·ness** *n.*

**cov·ey** (kuv′ē) *n., pl.* **-eys** [< OFr. < *cover*, to hatch < L. *cubare*, to lie down] 1. a small flock of birds, esp. partridges or quail 2. a small group of people or, sometimes, things

**Cov·ing·ton** (kuv′iŋ tən) [after Gen. L. *Covington*, 1768–1813] city in N Ky.: pop. 53,000

**cow¹** (kou) *n., pl.* **cows**; archaic **kine** (kīn) [OE. *cu*] 1. the mature female of domestic cattle, valued for its milk, or of certain other animals, as the buffalo, elephant, etc.: the male of such animals is called a *bull* 2. [Western] any domestic bovine animal, whether a steer, bull, cow, or calf

**cow²** (kou) *vt.* [< ON. *kūga*, to subdue] to make timid and submissive by filling with fear or awe

**cow·ard** (kou′ərd) *n.* [< OFr. < *coe* < L. *cauda*, tail] one who lacks courage or suffers from cowardice —*adj.* cowardly

**cow·ard·ice** (-is) *n.* lack of courage; esp., shamefully excessive fear of danger, difficulty, etc.

**cow·ard·ly** (-lē) *adj.* of or typical of a coward; shamefully fearful —*adv.* in the manner of a coward —**cow′ard·li·ness** *n.*

**cow·bell** (kou′bel′) *n.* a bell hung from a cow's neck so she can be found by its clanking

**cow·ber·ry** (-ber′ē) *n., pl.* **-ries** 1. a low creeping shrub with white or pink flowers and dark-red, acid berries 2. its berry

**cow·bird** (-burd′) *n.* a small American blackbird often seen near cattle

**cow·boy** (-boi′) *n.* 1. a ranch worker who rides horseback on his job of herding cattle: also **cow′hand′** 2. a performer in a rodeo —**cow′girl′** *n.fem.*

**cow·catch·er** (-kach′ər, -kech′ər) *n.* a metal frame on the front of a locomotive or streetcar to remove obstructions from the tracks

**cow·er** (kou′ər) *vi.* [ME. *couren*, prob. < ON.] 1. to crouch or huddle up, as from fear 2. to shrink and tremble, as from someone's anger, threats, or blows; cringe —**cow′er·ing·ly** *adv.*

**cow·herd** (kou′hurd′) *n.* a tender of grazing cattle

**cow·hide** (-hīd′) *n.* 1. the hide of a cow 2. leather made from it 3. a whip made of this —*vt.* **-hid′ed**, **-hid′ing** to flog with a cowhide

**cow killer** a large, wingless, antlike wasp of the S U.S. that has a vicious sting

**cowl** (koul) *n.* [< OE. < LL. < L. *cucullus*, hood] 1. *a)* a monk's hood *b)* a monk's cloak with a hood 2. something shaped like a cowl; esp., *a)* a cover for the top of a chimney, to increase the draft *b)* the top front part of an automobile body, to which the windshield and dashboard are fastened *c)* a cowling —*vt.* to cover as with a cowl —**cowled** *adj.*

**cow·lick** (kou′lik) *n.* [< the notion that it looks as if it has been licked by a cow] a tuft of hair on the head that cannot easily be combed flat

**cowl·ing** (koul′iŋ) *n.* [see COWL] a detachable metal covering for an airplane engine, etc.

**cow·man** (kou′mən) *n., pl.* **-men** 1. the owner or operator of a cattle ranch 2. a cowherd

**co-work·er** (kō′wur′kər) *n.* a fellow worker

**cow·pea** (kou′pē′) *n.* 1. a bushlike annual forage plant of the legume family, with seeds in slender pods 2. its edible seed

**Cow·per** (kōō′pər, koop′ər; *now occas.* kou′pər), **William** 1731–1800; Eng. poet

**cow·poke** (kou′pōk′) *n.* [cf. COWPUNCHER] [Colloq.] a cowboy

**cow pony** a pony used in herding cattle

**cow·pox** (kou′päks′) *n.* a contagious disease of cows that causes pustules on the udders: smallpox vaccine is made from the virus

**cow·punch·er** (-pun′chər) *n.* [from the prodding of animals in herding] [Colloq.] a cowboy

**cow·rie, cow·ry** (kou′rē) *n., pl.* **-ries** [< Hindi < Sans. *kaparda*] 1. any of certain gastropods of warm seas, with brightly colored shells 2. the shell of such a mollusk, esp. of the **money cowrie**, formerly used as currency in parts of Africa and S Asia

**cow·shed** (kou′shed′) *n.* a shelter for cows

**cow·slip** (-slip′) *n.* [< OE., lit., cow dung < *cu*, cow + *slyppe*, paste] 1. a European primrose with yellow or purple flowers 2. *same as:* *a)* MARSH MARIGOLD *b)* VIRGINIA COWSLIP

**cox** (käks) *n., pl.* **cox′es** [Colloq.] a coxswain —*vt., vi.* to be coxswain for (a boat or crew)

**cox·a** (käk′sə) *n., pl.* **cox′ae** (-sē) [L.] 1. the hip or hip joint 2. the basal segment of an arthropod leg —**cox′al** *adj.*

**cox·al·gi·a** (käk sal′jē ə, -jə) *n.* [see prec. & -ALGIA] pain in, or disease of, the hip or hip joint: also **cox·al′gy** (-jē) —**cox·al′gic** *adj.*

**cox·comb** (käks′kōm′) *n.* [for *cock's comb*] **1.** a cap topped with a notched strip of red cloth like a cock's comb, formerly worn by jesters **2.** a silly, vain, foppish fellow; dandy —**cox·comb·i·cal** (käks kō′mi k'l, -käm′i-) *adj.* —**cox′comb′i·cal·ly** *adv.* —**cox′comb′ry** (-kōm′rē) *n., pl.* **-ries**

**cox·swain** (käk′s'n, -swān′) *n.* [< COCK(BOAT) + SWAIN] **1.** a person in charge of a ship's boat and acting as its steersman **2.** the steersman of a racing shell, calling out the stroke rhythm

**coy** (koi) *adj.* [< OFr. < LL. < L. *quietus:* see QUIET] **1.** bashful; shy **2.** affecting innocence or shyness, esp. playfully or coquettishly **3.** reticent in making a commitment —**coy′ly** *adv.* —**coy′ness** *n.*

**coy·o·te** (kī ōt′ē, kī′ōt) *n., pl.* **coy·o′tes, coy·o′te:** see PLURAL, II, D, 1 [AmSp. < Nahuatl *coyotl*] a small wolf of western N. American prairies

**coy·pu** (koi′pōō) *n., pl.* **-pus, -pu:** see PLURAL, II, D, 1 [< AmSp. < native name] *same as* NUTRIA

**coz** (kuz) *n.* [Colloq.] cousin

**coz·en** (kuz′'n) *vt., vi.* [< ME. *cosin,* fraud < ?] to cheat, defraud, or deceive —**coz′en·age** *n.*

**co·zy** (kō′zē) *adj.* **-zi·er, -zi·est** [Scot., prob. < Scand.] warm and comfortable; snug —*n., pl.* **-zies** a knitted or padded cover to keep a teapot hot —**cozy up to** [Colloq.] to try to ingratiate oneself with —**play it cozy** [Slang] to act cautiously —**co′zi·ly** *adv.* —**co′zi·ness** *n.*

COYOTE
(to 4 ft. long, including tail)

**CP** Command Post

**cp, c.p.** candlepower

**C.P. 1.** Common Pleas **2.** Common Prayer

**c.p.** chemically pure

**CPA, C.P.A.** Certified Public Accountant

**cpd.** compound

**Cpl, Cpl.** Corporal

**cpm, c.p.m.** cycles per minute

**CPO, C.P.O.** Chief Petty Officer

**cps, c.p.s.** cycles per second

**cpt.** counterpoint

**CQ** amateur radio operators' signal inviting a reply

**Cr** *Chem.* chromium

**cr. 1.** credit **2.** creditor **3.** crown

**C.R.** Costa Rica

**crab¹** (krab) *n.* [< OE. *crabba*] **1.** any of various crustaceans with four pairs of legs, one pair of pincers, a flattish shell, and a short, broad abdomen folded under its thorax **2.** any of several similar animals **3.** *same as* CRAB LOUSE **4.** a machine for hoisting heavy weights —[-C-] Cancer, the constellation and zodiac sign —*vi.* **crabbed, crab′bing** to fish for or catch crabs —**catch a crab** *Rowing* to unbalance the boat by a faulty stroke —**crab′ber** *n.*

**crab²** (krab) *n.* [akin ? to Scot. *scrabbe,* Sw. dial. *scrabba,* wild apple] **1.** *same as* CRAB APPLE **2.** a sour-tempered person —*adj.* of a crab apple —*vi.* **crabbed, crab′bing** [Colloq.] to complain peevishly —**crab one's act (the deal,** etc.) [Colloq.] to spoil one's scheme (the deal, etc.) —**crab′ber** *n.*

**crab apple 1.** a small, very sour apple, used for jellies, etc. **2.** a tree bearing crab apples: also **crab tree**

**crab·bed** (krab′id) *adj.* [< CRAB (APPLE)] **1.** peevish; cross **2.** hard to understand; intricate **3.** hard to read; illegible —**crab′bed·ly** *adv.* —**crab′bed·ness** *n.*

**crab·by** (-ē) *adj.* **-bi·er, -bi·est** [see prec.] peevish; cross —**crab′bi·ly** *adv.* —**crab′bi·ness** *n.*

**crab grass** a coarse, weedy annual grass that spreads rapidly because of its freely rooting stems

**crab louse** a louse, somewhat crablike in shape, infesting the pubic regions, armpits, etc.

**crack** (krak) *vi.* [< OE. *cracian,* to resound] **1.** to make a sudden, sharp breaking noise **2.** to break or split, usually without complete separation of parts **3.** to become rasping or change pitch suddenly, as the voice **4.** [Colloq.] to break down [to *crack* under the strain] —*vt.* **1.** to cause to make a sharp, sudden noise **2.** to cause to break or split **3.** to destroy or impair **4.** to subject (as petroleum) to cracking: see CRACKING **5.** to hit or strike with a sudden, sharp blow or impact **6.** to manage to solve [to *crack* a code] **7.** [Colloq.] to break open or into **8.** [Slang] to make (a joke) —*n.* **1.** a sudden, sharp noise **2.** *a)* a break, usually partial *b)* a flaw *b)* a chink; fissure **4.** an abrupt, erratic shift of vocal tone **5.** a moment; instant [the *crack* of dawn] **6.** [Colloq.] a sudden, sharp blow or impact **7.** [Colloq.] an attempt; try **8.** [Slang] a joke or gibe —*adj.* [Colloq.] excelling in skill; first-rate [*crack*

troops] —**crack a smile** [Slang] to relax or unbend enough to smile —**crack down (on)** to become strict or stricter (with) —**cracked up to be** [Colloq.] alleged or believed to be —**crack up 1.** to crash, as (in) an airplane **2.** [Colloq.] *a)* to break down physically or mentally *b)* to break into a fit of laughter or tears

**crack·a·jack** (krak′ə jak′) *adj., n.* [Slang] *same as* CRACKERJACK

**crack·brain** (-brān′) *n.* a crazy person

**crack·brained** (-brānd′) *adj.* crazy

**crack·down** (-doun′) *n.* a resorting to strict or stricter measures of discipline or punishment

**cracked** (krakt) *adj.* **1.** broken, usually without complete separation of parts **2.** harsh [a *cracked* voice] **3.** [Colloq.] crazy

**cracked wheat** coarsely milled wheat particles

**crack·er** (krak′ər) *n.* **1.** one that cracks **2.** a firecracker **3.** a little paper roll used as a party favor: it contains candy, etc. and pops open when the ends are pulled **4.** a thin, crisp wafer **5.** *same as* POOR WHITE: contemptuous term

**crack·er-bar·rel** (-bar′əl) *adj.* [< the large barrel of soda crackers formerly found in general stores] [Colloq.] designating or typical of informal discussions by persons gathered at a country store

**crack·er·jack** (krak′ər jak′) *adj.* [extension of CRACK, *adj.* + JACK (nickname)] [Slang] excellent —*n.* [Slang] an excellent person or thing

**crack·ers** (krak′ərz) *adj.* [altered < CRACKED] [Chiefly Brit. Slang] crazy

**crack·ing¹** (krak′iŋ) *adj.* [Colloq.] excellent; fine —*adv.* [Colloq.] very

**crack·ing²** (krak′iŋ) *n.* the process of breaking down heavier hydrocarbons, as by heat and pressure, into lighter hydrocarbons, as in producing gasoline

**crack·le** (krak′'l) *vi.* **-led, -ling** [freq. of CRACK] **1.** to make slight, sharp popping sounds, as of dry wood burning **2.** to be bursting with vivacity, etc. **3.** to develop a finely cracked surface —*vt.* **1.** to crush or break with crackling sounds **2.** to produce a finely cracked surface on —*n.* **1.** crackling sounds **2.** fine, irregular surface cracks, as on old oil paintings **3.** crackleware

**crack·le·ware** (krak′'l wer′) *n.* pottery, porcelain, etc. with a finely cracked surface

**crack·ling** (krak′liŋ; *for 2 usually* -lin) *n.* **1.** the production of slight, sharp popping sounds **2.** *a)* the browned, crisp rind of roast pork *b)* [*pl.*] crisp bits left when hog fat is rendered

**crack·ly** (-lē) *adj.* that crackles; crackling

**crack·pot** (-pät′) *n.* [Colloq.] a crazy or eccentric person —*adj.* [Colloq.] crazy or eccentric

**crack·up** (krak′up′) *n.* **1.** a crash, as of an airplane **2.** [Colloq.] a mental or physical collapse

**-cra·cy** (krə sē) [< Fr. < ML. < Gr. *-kratia < kratos,* rule] *a combining form meaning* a (specified) type of government; rule by [*autocracy*]

**cra·dle** (krā′d'l) *n.* [OE. *cradol*] **1.** a baby's small bed, usually on rockers **2.** infancy **3.** the place of a thing's beginning **4.** anything cradlelike; specif., *a)* a framework to hold or lift a boat, etc. being built or repaired *b)* the support for the handset of a telephone (**cradle telephone**) *c)* *Agric.* a frame on a scythe (**cradle scythe**) for laying the grain evenly as it is cut *d)* *Mining* a boxlike device on rockers for washing out gold —*vt.* **-dled, -dling 1.** to place, rock, or hold in or as in a cradle **2.** *Mining* to wash (sand) in a cradle

**cra·dle·song** (-sôŋ′) *n.* a lullaby

**craft** (kraft) *n.* [OE. *cræft,* strength, power] **1.** a special skill or art **2.** an occupation requiring this; esp., any manual art **3.** the members of a skilled trade **4.** skill in deceiving; guile **5.** *pl.* **craft** a boat, ship, or aircraft —*vt.* to make with skill or artistry: usually in pp.

**-craft** (kraft) [< prec.] *a combining form meaning* the work, skill, or practice of [*handicraft*]

**crafts·man** (krafts′mən) *n., pl.* **-men 1.** a skilled workman **2.** a skillful artist or one having only technical skill —**crafts′man·ship′** *n.*

**craft union** a labor union to which only workers in a certain trade, craft, or occupation can belong: distinguished from INDUSTRIAL UNION

**craft·y** (kraf′tē) *adj.* **craft′i·er, craft′i·est** sly; cunning —**craft′i·ly** *adv.* —**craft′i·ness** *n.*

**crag** (krag) *n.* [< Celt.] a steep, rugged rock rising above others or projecting from a rock mass

**crag·gy** (-ē) *adj.* **-gi·er, -gi·est** having many crags: also **crag′ged** (-id) —**crag′gi·ness** *n.*

**crake** (krāk) *n., pl.* **crakes, crake:** see PLURAL, II, D, 1 [< ON. *kraka,* crow] any of several rails with long legs and a short bill

**cram** (kram) *vt.* **crammed, cram′ming** [OE. *crammian,* to stuff] **1.** to pack full or too full **2.** to stuff; force **3.** to feed to excess **4.** to prepare (a student) or review (a subject) for an examination in a hurried, intensive way —*vi*

**1.** to eat too much or too quickly **2.** to study a subject in a hurried, intensive way, for an examination —*n.* **1.** a crowded condition **2.** a cramming —**cram'mer** *n.*

**cramp¹** (kramp) *n.* [< OFr. *crampe*, bent, twisted < Frank.] **1.** a sudden, painful, involuntary contraction of a muscle from chill, strain, etc. **2.** partial local paralysis, as from excessive use of muscles **3.** [*usually pl.*] abdominal spasms and pain —*vt.* to cause a cramp in

**cramp²** (kramp) *n.* [MDu. *krampe*, lit., bent in] **1.** a metal bar bent at each end at a right angle, for holding together timbers, etc.: also **cramp iron 2.** a clamp **3.** anything that confines or hampers —*vt.* **1.** to fasten as with a cramp **2.** to confine or hamper **3.** to turn (the wheels of a car, etc.) sharply —*adj.* same as CRAMPED —**cramp one's style** [Slang] to hamper one's usual skill, confidence, etc. in doing something

**cramped** (krampt) *adj.* **1.** confined; restricted **2.** irregular and crowded, as some handwriting

**cramp·fish** (kramp'fish') *n., pl.* **-fish'**, **-fish'es**: see FISH *same as* ELECTRIC RAY

**cram·pon** (kram'pän, -pən) *n.* [Fr., akin to CRAMP²] **1.** either of a pair of iron hooks for raising heavy weights **2.** either of a pair of spiked iron plates fastened on shoes to prevent slipping Also **cram·poon** (kram pōōn')

**cran·ber·ry** (kran'ber'ē, -bər ē) *n., pl.* **-ries** [< Du. *kranebere*, LowG. *kraanbere*, lit., crane berry] **1.** a firm, sour, edible, red berry of an evergreen shrub of the heath family **2.** this shrub

**crane** (krān) *n.* [OE. *cran*] **1.** *pl.* **cranes, crane:** see PLURAL, II, D, 1 *a*) a large wading bird with very long legs and neck, and a long, straight bill *b*) popularly, any of various herons or storks **2.** a machine for lifting or moving heavy weights by means of a movable projecting arm or a horizontal traveling beam **3.** any device with a swinging arm fixed on a vertical axis, as to hold a kettle —*vt., vi.* **craned, cran'ing 1.** to raise or move as by a crane **2.** to stretch (the neck) in trying to see over something

**Crane** (krān) **1. (Harold) Hart,** 1899–1932; U.S. poet **2. Stephen,** 1871–1900; U.S. writer

**crane fly** any of various two-winged, slender flies with very long legs

**cranes·bill, crane's-bill** (krānz'bil') *n. a popular name for* GERANIUM (sense 1)

**cra·ni·al** (krā'nē əl) *adj.* of or from the cranium

**cranial nerve** any of the pairs of nerves, twelve in man, connected directly with the brain

**cra·ni·ate** (krā'nē it, -āt') *adj.* having a cranium, as mammals —*n.* a craniate animal

**cra·ni·o-** [Gr. *kranio-* < *kranion*, skull] *a combining form meaning* of the head, cranial

**cra·ni·ol·o·gy** (krā'nē äl'ə jē) *n.* the scientific study of skulls, esp. human skulls

**cra·ni·om·e·try** (-äm'ə trē) *n.* the science of measuring skulls; cranial measurement

**cra·ni·ot·o·my** (-ät'ə mē) *n., pl.* **-mies** the surgical operation of opening the skull

**cra·ni·um** (krā'nē əm) *n., pl.* **-ni·ums, -ni·a** (-ə) [ML. < Gr. *kranion*] **1.** the skull **2.** the bones forming the enclosure of the brain

**crank** (kraŋk) *n.* [< OE. *cranc-*, as in *crancstæf*, yarn comb] **1.** a handle or arm at right angles to a shaft of a machine, to transmit or change motion **2.** [Colloq.] *a*) an eccentric person *b*) an irritable, complaining person —*vt.* to start or operate by a crank —*vi.* to turn a crank

**crank·case** (kraŋk'kās') *n.* the metal casing of the crankshaft of an internal-combustion engine

**crank·pin** (-pin') *n.* a cylindrical bar or pin, as part of a crankshaft, to which a connecting rod is attached: also **crank pin**

**crank·shaft** (-shaft') *n.* a shaft having one or more cranks for transmitting motion

**crank·y** (kraŋ'kē) *adj.* **crank'i·er, crank'i·est 1.** out of order; loose **2.** irritable; cross **3.** queer; eccentric —**crank'i·ly** *adv.* —**crank'i·ness** *n.*

**Cran·mer** (kran'mər), **Thomas** 1489–1556; Eng. churchman; archbishop of Canterbury

**cran·ny** (kran'ē) *n., pl.* **-nies** [OFr. *cran* < OIt. < LL. *crena*, a notch] a small, narrow opening; crevice —**cran'nied** (-ēd) *adj.*

**Cran·ston** (kran'stən) [after S. *Cranston*, 18th-c. colonial governor] city in EC R.I.: pop. 72,000

**crap¹** (krap) *n.* [see CRAPS] **1.** *same as* CRAPS **2.** a losing throw at craps —**crap out 1.** to make a losing throw at craps **2.** [Slang] to fail, give up, etc. because of exhaustion, etc.

**crap²** (krap) *n.* [< OFr., ordure] [Vulgar Slang] **1.** nonsense, insincerity, etc. **2.** trash; junk —**crap'py** *adj.* **-pi·er, -pi·est**

**crape** (krāp) *n.* [Fr. *crêpe:* see CREPE] **1.** *same as* CREPE (sense 1) **2.** a piece of black crepe as a sign of mourning

**crape·hang·er** (-haŋ'ər) *n.* [Slang] a pessimist

**crap·pie** (krap'ē) *n., pl.* **-pies, -pie:** see PLURAL, II, D, 1 [< ?] a small sunfish of the E and C U.S.

**craps** (kraps) *n.pl.* [*with sing. v.*] [Fr. *crabs, craps* < obs. E. *crabs,* lowest throw at hazard, two aces] a gambling game played with two dice, in which, for example, a first throw of seven or eleven wins

**crap·shoot·er** (krap'shōōt'ər) *n.* a gambler at craps —**crap'shoot'ing** *n.*

**crap·u·lence** (krap'yoo ləns) *n.* [see ff.] **1.** sickness from excess in drinking or eating **2.** gross intemperance, esp. in drinking —**crap'u·lent** *adj.*

**crap·u·lous** (-ləs) *adj.* [< LL. < L. *crapula,* drunkenness < Gr. *kraipalē,* drunken headache] **1.** intemperate, esp. in drinking **2.** sick from such intemperance

**crash¹** (krash) *vi.* [ME. *crashen,* prob. echoic var. of *craken,* CRACK] **1.** to fall, collide, or break with force and with a loud, smashing noise **2.** *a*) to make this noise *b*) to move with such a noise **3.** to fall and be damaged or destroyed: said of aircraft **4.** to collapse, as a business —*vt.* **1.** to break into pieces; smash **2.** to cause to crash **3.** to force or impel with a crashing noise (with *in, out,* etc.) **4.** [Colloq.] to get into (a party, etc.) without an invitation, etc. —*n.* **1.** a loud, smashing noise **2.** a crashing **3.** a sudden collapse —*adj.* [Colloq.] using all possible resources, effort, and speed /a *crash* program/

**crash²** (krash) *n.* [prob. < Russ. *krashenina,* colored linen] a coarse cloth of plain, loose weave

**crash dive** a sudden submergence of a submarine to escape from attack —**crash'-dive'** *vi.* **-dived', -div'ing**

**crash helmet** a thickly padded, protective helmet worn by motorcyclists, aviators, etc.

**crash·ing** (-iŋ) *adj.* [Colloq.] thorough; complete /a *crashing* bore/

**crash-land** (krash'land') *vt., vi.* to bring (an airplane) down in a forced landing, with some damage —**crash landing**

**crass** (kras) *adj.* [L. *crassus,* gross] **1.** grossly stupid, dull, or obtuse **2.** tasteless, insensitive, materialistic, etc. —**crass'ly** *adv.* —**crass'ness, cras'si·tude'** (-ə tōōd', -ə tyōōd') *n.*

**-crat** (krat) [< Fr. < Gr. *-kratēs* < *kratos,* rule] *a combining form meaning* participant in or supporter of (a specified kind of) government or ruling body /democrat, aristocrat/

**crate** (krāt) *n.* [L. *cratis,* wickerwork] **1.** a box or case made of wood slats, for shipping or storing things **2.** [Slang] an old, decrepit automobile or airplane —*vt.* **crat'ed, crat'ing** to pack in a crate —**crat'er** *n.*

**cra·ter** (krāt'ər) *n.* [< Gr. *kratēr*] **1.** in ancient Greece, a kind of bowl or jar **2.** a bowl-shaped cavity, as at the mouth of a volcano or on the moon **3.** any pit like this, as one made by an exploding bomb

**craunch** (krônch, kränch) *vt., vi., n. same as* CRUNCH

**cra·vat** (krə vat') *n.* [< Fr. < *Cravate,* Croat: referring to scarves worn by Croatian soldiers] **1.** a neckerchief or scarf **2.** a necktie

**crave** (krāv) *vt.* **craved, crav'ing** [OE. *crafian*] **1.** to ask for earnestly; beg **2.** to long for; desire strongly **3.** to need greatly —*vi.* to have a longing or strong desire (*for*) —**crav'er** *n.*

**cra·ven** (krā'vən) *adj.* [< OFr. < L. *crepare,* to creak] very cowardly —*n.* a thorough coward —**cra'ven·ly** *adv.* —**cra'ven·ness** *n.*

**crav·ing** (krā'viŋ) *n.* an intense desire or longing, as for affection or a food, drug, etc.

**craw** (krô) *n.* [ME. *craue*] **1.** the crop of a bird or insect **2.** the stomach of any animal —**to stick in the** (or **one's**) **craw** to be unacceptable

**craw·fish** (krô'fish') *n., pl.* **-fish'**, **-fish'es:** see FISH *same as* CRAYFISH —*vi.* [Colloq.] to withdraw from a position; back down

**crawl¹** (krôl) *vi.* [< ON. *krafla*] **1.** to move slowly by drawing the body along the ground, as a worm **2.** to go on hands and knees **3.** to move slowly **4.** to act abjectly servile **5.** to swarm (*with* crawling things) **6.** to feel as if insects were crawling on the skin —*n.* **1.** a crawling; slow movement **2.** an overarm swimming stroke, face downward —**crawl'er** *n.*

**crawl²** (krôl) *n.* [WIndDu. *kraal* < Sp. *corral:* see CORRAL] an enclosure made in shallow water for confining fish, turtles, etc.

**crawl space** a narrow space, as under a roof or floor, allowing access to wiring, plumbing, etc.

**crawl·y** (krôl'ē) *adj.* **crawl'i·er, crawl'i·est** *same as* CREEPY

**cray·fish** (krā'fish') *n., pl.* **-fish'**, **-fish'es** see FISH [< OFr. *crevice* < OHG.] **1.** any of certain small, lobster-shaped freshwater crustaceans **2.** *same as* SPINY LOBSTER

---

**cray·on** (krā′ən, -än′) *n.* [Fr. < *craie*, chalk < L. *creta*] **1.** a small stick of chalk, charcoal, or colored wax, used for drawing, coloring, or writing **2.** a crayon drawing —*vt.* to draw or color with crayons —**cray′on·ist** *n.*

**craze** (krāz) *vt.* **crazed, craz′ing** [ME. *crasen*, to crack < Scand.] **1.** to make mentally ill or insane **2.** to produce small cracks in the surface or glaze of (pottery, etc.) —*vi.* to become finely cracked, as pottery glaze —*n.* **1.** a mania **2.** a fad **3.** a crack in the glaze of pottery, etc.

**cra·zy** (krā′zē) *adj.* **-zi·er, -zi·est** [< CRAZE] **1.** flawed, cracked, or rickety **2.** mentally unbalanced or insane **3.** [Colloq.] foolish, wild, fantastic, etc. **4.** [Colloq.] very enthusiastic or eager **5.** [Slang] excellent, thrilling, etc. —**cra′zi·ly** *adv.* —**cra′zi·ness** *n.*

**crazy bone** *same as* FUNNY BONE

**crazy quilt** a quilt made of pieces of cloth of various colors, patterns, shapes, and sizes

**cra·zy·weed** (-wēd′) *n. same as* LOCOWEED

**creak** (krēk) *vi., vt.* [ME. *creken*, akin to CROAK] to make, cause to make, or move with a harsh, shrill, grating, or squeaking sound, as rusted hinges —*n.* such a sound

**creak·y** (-ē) *adj.* **creak′i·er, creak′i·est** creaking —**creak′i·ly** *adv.* —**creak′i·ness** *n.*

**cream** (krēm) *n.* [OFr. *cresme*, prob. a blend of LL. *chrisma* (see CHRISM) & VL. *crama*, cream] **1.** the oily, yellowish part of milk **2.** any food made of cream or having a creamy consistency **3.** a creamy cosmetic or emulsion **4.** the best part **5.** yellowish white —*adj.* of, with, or like cream; creamy, cream-colored, etc. —*vi.* to form cream or a creamy foam —*vt.* **1.** to take cream from **2.** to add cream to **3.** to cook with cream or a cream sauce **4.** to make creamy by beating, etc. **5.** [Slang] to beat soundly —**cream of** creamed purée of [*cream of* tomato soup]

**cream cheese** a soft, white cheese made of cream or of milk enriched with cream

**cream·er** (-ər) *n.* **1.** a small pitcher for cream **2.** a device for separating cream from milk

**cream·er·y** (-ər ē) *n., pl.* **-er·ies 1.** a place where milk and cream are pasteurized, separated, and bottled, and butter and cheese are made **2.** a shop where dairy products are sold

**cream of tartar** a white, acid, crystalline substance, $KHC_4H_4O_6$, used in baking powder

**cream puff** a round shell of pastry filled with whipped cream or custard

**cream sauce** a sauce made of butter and flour cooked together with milk or cream

**cream soda** soda pop, usually colorless, that is flavored with vanilla

**cream·y** (-ē) *adj.* **cream′i·er, cream′i·est 1.** full of cream **2.** like cream in consistency or color —**cream′i·ness** *n.*

**crease¹** (krēs) *n.* [earlier *creaste*, lit., ridge < ME. *creste*, crest < OFr. *creste*: see CREST] **1.** a line, mark, or ridge made by folding and pressing cloth, paper, etc. **2.** a fold or wrinkle [*creases* in a jowl] —*vt.* **1.** to make a crease in **2.** to graze with a bullet —*vi.* to become creased —**creas′er** *n.* —**creas′y** *adj.*

**crease²** (krēs) *n. same as* KRIS

**cre·ate** (krē āt′) *vt.* **-at′ed, -at′ing** [< L. pp. of *creare*] **1.** to bring into being; originate, design, invent, etc. **2.** to bring about; cause **3.** to invest with a new rank, function, etc. **4.** *Theater* to be the first to portray (a role)

**cre·a·tion** (-ā′shən) *n.* **1.** a creating or being created **2.** the whole universe **3.** anything created; esp., an original design, etc. —**the Creation** *Theol.* God's creating of the world

**cre·a·tive** (-āt′iv) *adj.* **1.** creating or able to create **2.** productive (*of*) **3.** imaginative and inventive **4.** stimulating the inventive powers —**cre·a′tive·ly** *adv.* —**cre·a′tive·ness** *n.* —**cre·a·tiv·i·ty** (krē′ā tiv′ə tē) *n.*

**cre·a·tor** (-āt′ər) *n.* **1.** one who creates **2.** [C-] God

**crea·ture** (krē′chər) *n.* [< OFr. < L. *creatura*] **1.** anything created, animate or inanimate **2.** a living being; esp., *a*) a domestic animal *b*) a human being: often used patronizingly or contemptuously **3.** one completely dominated by or dependent on another —**crea′tur·al, crea′ture·ly** *adj.*

**crèche** (kresh, krāsh) *n.* [Fr. < Frank. hyp. *kripja*, crib] **1.** a display of a stable with figures, representing a scene at the birth of Jesus **2.** an institution for foundlings **3.** [Chiefly Brit.] a day nursery

**cre·dal** (krēd′'l) *adj.* of a creed

**cre·dence** (krēd′'ns) *n.* [< OFr. < ML. < L. prp. of *credere:* see CREED] **1.** belief, esp. in another's reports or testimony **2.** credentials: now only in **letter of credence 3.** *Eccles.* a small side table for the Eucharistic wine, etc.

**cre·den·tial** (kri den′shəl, -chəl) *n.* **1.** that which entitles to credit, confidence, etc. **2.** [*usually pl.*] a letter or certificate showing that one has a right to a certain position or authority

**cre·den·za** (kri den′zə) *n.* [It.] a type of buffet, or sideboard

**cred·i·ble** (kred′ə b'l) *adj.* [< L. < *credere:* see CREED] that can be believed; believable —**cred′i·bil′i·ty, cred′i·ble·ness** *n.* —**cred′i·bly** *adv.*

**cred·it** (kred′it) *n.* [< Fr. < It. < L. pp. of *credere:* see CREED] **1.** belief or trust; confidence **2.** *a*) good reputation *b*) one's influence based on one's reputation **3.** praise to which one is entitled **4.** a source of approval or honor [a *credit* to the team] **5.** acknowledgment of work done or help given; specif., [*pl.*] a list of such acknowledgments in a movie, TV show, etc. **6.** *a*) the amount in a bank account, etc. *b*) a sum made available by a bank for withdrawal by someone specified **7.** *Accounting a*) acknowledgment of a payment by entry of the amount in an account *b*) the right-hand side of an account, for such entries *c*) an entry, or the sum of entries, there *d*) a deduction from a debt or an addition (as to a bank account) in making an adjustment **8.** *Business a*) trust in one's ability to make payments when due *b*) time allowed for payment **9.** *Educ. a*) certification of a successfully completed unit or course of study *b*) a unit so certified —*vt.* **1.** to believe in the truth, reliability, etc. of; trust **2.** to give credit to or deserved commendation for **3.** to give credit in a bank account, etc. **4.** *Accounting* to enter on the credit side **5.** *Educ.* to enter credits on the record of (a student) —**credit one with** to ascribe to one —**do credit to** to bring approval or honor to —**give credit to 1.** to trust **2.** to commend —**give one credit for 1.** to commend one for **2.** to believe or recognize that one has —**on credit** with agreement on future payment —**to one's credit** bringing approval or honor to one

**cred·it·a·ble** (-ə b'l) *adj.* **1.** praiseworthy **2.** ascribable (*to*) —**cred′it·a·bil′i·ty, cred′it·a·ble·ness** *n.* —**cred′it·a·bly** *adv.*

**credit bureau** an agency supplying information on the credit rating of individuals or firms

**credit card** a card allowing a person to charge bills at certain restaurants, gas stations, etc.

**cred·i·tor** (-ər) *n.* a person who extends credit or to whom money is owed

**credit rating** the rating of an individual or firm as a credit risk, based on past records of debt repayment, financial status, etc.

**credit union** a cooperative association for pooling savings of members and making loans to them at a low rate of interest

**cre·do** (krē′dō, krā′dō) *n., pl.* **-dos** [L., I believe: see CREED] **1.** *same as* CREED **2.** [*usually* C-] the Apostles' Creed or the Nicene Creed

**cre·du·li·ty** (krə dōō′lə tē, -dyōō′-) *n.* a tendency to believe too readily

**cred·u·lous** (krej′oo ləs) *adj.* [L. *credulus* < *credere:* see CREED] **1.** tending to believe too readily **2.** resulting from or indicating credulity —**cred′u·lous·ly** *adv.* —**cred′u·lous·ness** *n.*

**Cree** (krē) *n.* [< AmInd.] **1.** *pl.* **Crees, Cree** a member of a tribe of Algonquian Indians of C Canada **2.** the Algonquian language of this tribe

**creed** (krēd) *n.* [< OE. < L. *credo*, lit., I believe < *credere*, to trust] **1.** a brief statement of religious belief, esp. as accepted by a church **2.** any statement of belief, opinions, etc. —**creed′al** *adj.*

**Creek** (krēk) *n.* [from the many creeks in their territory] **1.** *pl.* **Creeks, Creek** an American Indian of any of several tribes, mainly Muskogean, orig. in SE U.S., now in Oklahoma **2.** their language

**creek** (krēk, krik) *n.* [ME. *creke* < ON. *-kriki*, a winding] **1.** a small stream, somewhat larger than a brook **2.** [Now chiefly Brit.] a narrow inlet or bay —**up the creek** [Slang] in trouble

**creel** (krēl) *n.* [< OFr. *grail:* see GRIDDLE] a wicker basket for fishermen to carry fish caught

**creep** (krēp) *vi.* **crept, creep′ing** [OE. *creopan*] **1.** to move along with the body close to the ground, as on hands and knees **2.** to come on or move slowly, gradually, stealthily, etc. **3.** to grow along the ground, etc., as some plants **4.** to change position or shape slightly —*n.* **1.** a creeping **2.** [Slang] a person regarded as very annoying, etc. —**make one's flesh** (or **skin**) **creep** to make one fearful, cold, etc., as if insects were creeping on one's skin —**the creeps** [Colloq.] a feeling of fear, repugnance, etc.

CREEL

**creep·age** (-ij) *n.* a gradual creeping movement

**creep·er** (-ər) *n.* **1.** a person, animal, or thing that creeps **2.** a plant whose stem puts out tendrils or rootlets for creeping along a surface **3.** [*pl.*] a baby's one-piece garment, of pants and shirt

**creep·y** (krēp′ē) *adj.* **creep′i·er, creep′i·est 1.** creeping; moving slowly **2.** having or causing fear or disgust, as if insects were creeping on one's skin —**creep′i·ly** *adv.* —**creep′i·ness** *n.*

**creese** (krēs) *n. same as* KRIS

**cre·mate** (krē′māt, kri māt′) *vt.* **-mat·ed, -mat·ing** [< L. pp. of *cremare*, to burn] to burn up; esp., to burn (a dead body) to ashes —**cre·ma′tion** *n.* —**cre′ma·tor** *n.*

**cre·ma·to·ry** (krē′mə tôr′ē; *chiefly Brit.* krem′ə-) *n., pl.* **-ries 1.** a furnace for cremating **2.** a building with such a furnace in it Also **cre′ma·to′ri·um** (-ē əm), *pl.* **-ri·ums, -ri·a** (-ə) —*adj.* of or for cremation: also **cre′ma·to′ri·al**

**crème** (krem, krēm) *n.* [Fr.] **1.** cream **2.** a thick liqueur

**crème de ca·ca·o** (də kä′ō, -kā′ō; də kō′kō) [Fr.] a sweet, chocolate-flavored liqueur

**crème de menthe** (də mänt′, menth′, mint′) [Fr.] a sweet, mint-flavored liqueur, green or colorless

**Cre·mo·na** (kri mō′nə) *n.* any famous violin formerly made in Cremona, Italy, as by Stradivari

**cre·nate** (krē′nāt) *adj.* [< ModL. < VL. *crena*, a notch] having a scalloped edge, as certain leaves: also **cre′nat·ed** —**cre′nate·ly** *adv.* —**cre·na′tion** *n.*

**cren·el** (kren′'l) *n.* [OFr. < VL. *crena*, a notch ] an indentation in the top of a battlement or wall: also **cre·nelle** (kri·nel′) —*vt.* **-eled** or **-elled, -el·ing** or **-el·ling** to crenelate

**cren·el·ate, cren·el·late** (kren′'l āt′) *vt.* **-el·at′ed** or **-lat′ed, -el·at′ing** or **-el·lat′ing** to furnish with crenels or with squared notches —**cren′el·a′tion, cren′el·la′tion** *n.*

**Cre·ole, cre·ole** (krē′ōl) *n.* [< Fr. < Sp. *criollo* < Port. < *criar*, to rear < L. *creare*, to create] **1.** orig., a person of European parentage born in Latin America or the Gulf States **2.** *a)* a descendant of such persons, esp. of French settlers in Louisiana or of Spanish settlers in the Gulf States *b)* a person of mixed Creole and Negro descent **3.** French as spoken by Creoles —*adj.* **1.** of Creoles or their languages **2.** [*usually* c-] made with sautéed tomatoes, green peppers, onions, etc.

**cre·o·sol** (krē′ə sōl′, -sôl′) *n.* [CREOS(OTE) + -OL¹] a colorless, oily, antiseptic liquid, C₈H₁₀O₂, obtained esp. from beech tar

**cre·o·sote** (krē′ə sōt′) *n.* [< Gr. *kreas*, flesh + *sōzein*, to save] a transparent, pungent, oily liquid distilled from wood tar or coal tar: used as an antiseptic and a wood preservative —*vt.* **-sot′ed, -sot′ing** to treat with creosote

**crepe, crêpe** (krāp; *for* 3, *also* krep) *n.* [Fr. *crêpe* < L. *crispus:* see CRISP] **1.** a thin, crinkled cloth, as of silk or wool; crape **2.** *same as: a)* CRAPE (sense 2) *b)* CREPE PAPER *c)* CREPE RUBBER **3.** a very thin pancake, generally rolled up or folded with a filling: usually **crêpe**

**crepe paper** thin paper crinkled like crepe

**crepe rubber** soft rubber in sheets with a wrinkled surface, used for some shoe soles

**crêpes su·zette** (krāp′ sōo zet′; *Fr.* krɛp sü-) [Fr.] crêpes in a hot, orange-flavored sauce, usually served in flaming brandy

**crep·i·tate** (krep′ə tāt′) *vi.* **-tat′ed, -tat′ing** [< L. pp. of *crepitare*, freq. of *crepare*, to creak] to crackle —**crep′i·tant** *adj.* —**crep′i·ta′tion** *n.*

**crept** (krept) *pt. & pp.* of CREEP

**cre·pus·cu·lar** (kri pus′kyoo lər) *adj.* [< L. *crepusculum*, twilight < *creper*, dark] of, like, or active at, twilight

**cre·scen·do** (krə shen′dō) *adj., adv.* [It. < L. *crescere:* see ff.] *Music* gradually getting louder: symbol < —*n., pl.* **-dos 1.** a gradual increase in loudness or intensity **2.** a passage played crescendo —*vi.* **-doed, -do·ing** to get louder

**cres·cent** (kres′'nt) *n.* [< OFr. < L. *crescere*, to grow] **1.** the moon in its first or last quarter, when it appears concavo-convex **2.** a figure of or like this **3.** anything of similar shape, as a curved roll **4.** [*also* C-] [< the Turkish crescent emblem] Turkish or Moslem power —*adj.* **1.** [Poet.] increasing; growing **2.** shaped like a crescent —**cres·cen′tic** (krə sen′tik) *adj.*

**cre·sol** (krē′sōl, -sôl) *n.* [< CREOSOTE + -OL¹] any of three colorless, oily liquids or solids, C₇H₈O, distilled from coal tar: used in disinfectants, etc.

**cress** (kres) *n.* [OE. *cressa*, lit., ? *creeper*] a plant of the mustard family, as watercress, with pungent leaves used in salads and as garnishes

**cres·set** (kres′it) *n.* [< OFr.] a metal container for burning oil, wood, etc., used as a torch or lantern

**crest** (krest) *n.* [< OFr. < L. *crista*] **1.** a comb, tuft, etc. on the heads of some animals or birds **2.** a plume or emblem on a helmet **3.** a helmet **4.** a heraldic device above the shield in a coat of arms or used on silverware, note paper, etc. **5.** top; ridge **6.** the highest point or level —*vt.* **1.** to provide with a crest **2.** to reach the top of —*vi.* to form or reach a crest —**crest′ed** *adj.*

**crest·fall·en** (krest′fôl′ən) *adj.* **1.** with drooping crest or bowed head **2.** dejected or humbled

**cre·ta·ceous** (kri tā′shəs) *adj.* [< L. < *creta:* see CRAYON] **1.** of, like, or containing chalk **2.** [C-] designating or of the third geological period of the Mesozoic Era —**the Cretaceous** the Cretaceous Period or its rocks: see GEOLOGY, chart

**Crete** (krēt) Greek island in the E Mediterranean: 3,218 sq. mi.; pop. 483,000 —**Cre′tan** *adj., n.*

**cre·tin** (krēt′'n) *n.* [< Fr. dial. form of *chrétien*, Christian, hence human being] a person suffering from cretinism —**cre′ti·nous** *adj.*

**cre·tin·ism** (-iz'm) *n.* [see prec.] a congenital thyroid deficiency with resulting deformity and idiocy

**cre·tonne** (krē′tän, kri tän′) *n.* [Fr. < *Creton*, village in Normandy] a heavy, unglazed, printed cotton or linen cloth, for curtains, etc.

**cre·vasse** (kri vas′) *n.* [Fr. < OFr. *crevace*, CREVICE] **1.** a deep crack or fissure, esp. in a glacier **2.** a break in a levee, as of a river —*vt.* **-vassed′, -vas′sing** to make crevasses in

**crev·ice** (krev′is) *n.* [< OFr. < L. *crepare*, to creak] a narrow opening caused by a crack or split; fissure; cleft —**crev′iced** *adj.*

**crew¹** (krōo) *n.* [OFr. *creue*, growth < L. *crescere*, to grow] **1.** a group of people associating or working together or classed together; company, set, gang, etc. **2.** the personnel of a ship, usually excepting the officers, or of an aircraft **3.** a rowing team —*vt., vi.* to serve (on) as a crew member —**crew′man** (-mən) *n., pl.* **-men**

**crew²** (krōo) *alt. pt.* of CROW² (sense 1)

**crew cut** a man's style of close-cropped haircut

**crew·el** (krōo′əl) *n.* [LME. *crule* < ?] a fine worsted yarn used in fancywork and embroidery —**crew′el·work′** *n.*

**crew neck** a round, closefitting neckline

**crib** (krib) *n.* [OE.] **1.** a rack, trough, or box for fodder; manger **2.** a small, crude house or room **3.** a small bed with high sides, for a baby **4.** a framework of bars for support or strengthening **5.** a framework or enclosure for storage **6.** a structure anchored under water, serving as a pier, water intake, etc. **7.** [Colloq.] *a)* a petty theft *b)* plagiarism *c)* a translation or other aid used, often dishonestly, in doing schoolwork —*vt.* **cribbed, crib′bing 1.** to confine **2.** to provide with a crib **3.** [Colloq.] *a)* to steal *b)* to plagiarize —*vi.* [Colloq.] to do schoolwork dishonestly, as by using a crib —**crib′ber** *n.*

**crib·bage** (krib′ij) *n.* [< prec. + -AGE] a card game in which the object is to form various combinations that count for points: score is kept on a pegboard

**crib biting** a habit some horses have of biting the feeding trough and swallowing air —**crib′-bite′** *vi.* **-bit′, -bit′ten** or **-bit′, -bit′ing**

**crick¹** (krik) *n.* [< ? ON.] a painful cramp in the neck, back, etc. —*vt.* to cause a crick in

**crick²** (krik) *n.* [Dial.] *same as* CREEK (sense 1)

**crick·et¹** (krik′it) *n.* [< OFr. < *criquer*, to creak] **1.** a leaping insect, usually with long antennae, related to the locusts and grasshoppers: the males make a chirping noise with their forewings **2.** a small toy or device pressed to make a clicking sound

**crick·et²** (krik′it) *n.* [< OFr.; prob. < MDu. *cricke*, a stick] **1.** an outdoor game played by two teams of eleven men each, in which a ball, bats, and wickets are used **2.** [Colloq.] fair play; sportsmanship —*vi.* to play cricket —**crick′et·er** *n.*

**crick·et³** (krik′it) *n.* [< ?] a wooden footstool

**cried** (krīd) *pt. & pp.* of CRY

**cri·er** (krī′ər) *n.* **1.** a person who cries **2.** a person who shouts out news, proclamations, etc.

**crime** (krīm) *n.* [OFr. < L. *crimen*, verdict, offense] **1.** an act committed or omitted in violation of a law; specif., any felony or misdemeanor except a petty violation of a local ordinance **2.** an offense against morality; sin **3.** criminal acts, collectively **4.** [Colloq.] something deplorable; shame

**Cri·me·a** (krī mē′ə, krə-) peninsula in SW U.S.S.R., extending into the Black Sea —**Cri·me′an** *adj.*

**crim·i·nal** (krim′ə n'l) *adj.* **1.** having the nature of crime; being a crime **2.** relating to or dealing with crime **3.** guilty of crime **4.** [Colloq.] deplorable —*n.* a person guilty of, or convicted of, a crime —**crim′i·nal′i·ty** (-ə nal′ə tē) *n., pl.* **-ties** —**crim′i·nal·ly** *adv.*

**criminal conversation** *Law* adultery

**criminal law** law dealing with crime

**crim·i·nate** (krim′ə nāt′) *vt.* **-nat′ed, -nat′ing** [< L. pp. of *criminari* < *crimen:* see CRIME] **1.** to accuse of a crime **2.** to incriminate —**crim′i·na′tion** *n.* —**crim′i·na′tive, crim′i·na·to·ry** (-nə tôr′ē) *adj.* —**crim′i·na′tor** *n.*

**crim·i·nol·o·gy** (krim'ə näl'ə jē) *n.* [< L. *crimen* (gen. *criminis*): see CRIME & -LOGY] the scientific study and investigation of crime —**crim'i·no·log'i·cal** (-nə läj'i k'l) *adj.* —**crim'i·no·log'i·cal·ly** *adv.* —**crim'i·nol'o·gist** *n.*

**crimp¹** (krimp) *vt.* [< OE. (*ge*)*crympan*, to curl & MDu. *crimpen*, to wrinkle] **1.** to press into narrow, regular folds; pleat **2.** to make (hair, etc.) wavy or curly **3.** to pinch together **4.** [Colloq.] to hamper —*n.* **1.** a crimping **2.** anything crimped or crimpy **3.** crimpy condition —**put a crimp in** [Colloq.] to hamper —**crimp'er** *n.*

**crimp²** (krimp) *n.* [< prec.] a person who gets men by force or trickery to serve as sailors or soldiers —*vt.* to get (men) thus into such service

**crimp·y** (krim'pē) *adj.* **crimp'i·er, crimp'i·est** [< CRIMP¹] curly; wavy; frizzly —**crimp'i·ness** *n.*

**crim·son** (krim'z'n) *n.* [< ML., ult. < Ar. *qirmiz*: see CARMINE] **1.** deep red **2.** deep-red coloring matter —*adj.* **1.** deep-red **2.** bloody —*vt., vi.* to make or become crimson

**cringe** (krinj) *vi.* **cringed, cring'ing** [OE. *cringan*, to fall (in battle)] **1.** to draw back, crouch, etc., as when afraid; cower **2.** to act servilely; fawn —*n.* a cringing —**cring'er** *n.*

**crin·gle** (kriŋ'g'l) *n.* [< ON. *kringla*, circle, or MDu. *kringel*, ring] a small ring or loop of rope or metal on the edge of a sail, for inserting a rope

**crin·kle** (kriŋ'k'l) *vi., vt.* **-kled, -kling** [OE. *crincan*, var. of *cringan*: see CRINGE] **1.** to be or make full of wrinkles or ripples **2.** to rustle, as paper when crushed —*n.* **1.** a wrinkle, twist, or ripple **2.** a rustling sound —**crin'kly** *adj.* **-kli·er, -kli·est**

**cri·noid** (krī'noid, krin'oid) *adj.* [< Gr. < *krinon*, lily + *-eidēs*, -OID] **1.** lily-shaped **2.** designating or of a class of marine animals that are flowerlike and anchored by a stalk or that are free-swimming —*n.* such an animal

**crin·o·line** (krin''l in) *n.* [Fr. < It. < L. *crinis*, hair + *linum*, thread] **1.** a coarse, stiff, heavily sized cloth, orig. of horsehair and linen, used as lining to stiffen garments **2.** a petticoat of this, to puff out a skirt **3.** *same as* HOOP SKIRT

**crip·ple** (krip''l) *n.* [< OE. < base of *creopan*, to creep] a person or animal that is lame or disabled in a way preventing normal movement —*vt.* **-pled, -pling** to lame or disable —**crip'pler** *n.*

**cri·sis** (krī'sis) *n., pl.* **-ses** (-sēz) [L. < Gr. < *krinein*, to separate] **1.** the turning point in a disease, indicating either imminent recovery or death **2.** a turning point in the course of anything **3.** a time of great danger or trouble

**crisp** (krisp) *adj.* [OE. < L. *crispus*, curly] **1.** easily broken or crumbled; brittle **2.** fresh and firm, as celery **3.** fresh and tidy, as a uniform **4.** sharp and clear [*a crisp analysis*] **5.** lively, as talk **6.** invigorating [*crisp air*] **7.** closely curled and wiry **8.** rippled; wavy —*n.* something crisp —*vt., vi.* to make or become crisp —**crisp'ly** *adv.* —**crisp'ness** *n.*

**crisp·y** (kris'pē) *adj.* **crisp'i·er, crisp'i·est** *same as* CRISP —**crisp'i·ness** *n.*

**criss·cross** (kris'krôs') *n.* [earlier Christ's cross, for the symbol *X*, abbrev. of Christ] **1.** a mark made of two crossed lines (X) **2.** a pattern of crossed lines **3.** a being confused —*adj.* marked with or moving in crossing lines —*vt., vi.* **1.** to mark with crossing lines **2.** to cross back and forth —*adv.* **1.** crosswise **2.** awry

**cri·ter·i·on** (krī tir'ē ən) *n., pl.* **-i·a** (-ē ə), **-i·ons** [< Gr. < *kritēs*, judge: see ff.] a standard, rule, or test by which something can be judged

**crit·ic** (krit'ik) *n.* [< L. < Gr. *kritikos*, orig., able to discern, akin to *krinein*: see CRISIS] **1.** a person who forms and expresses judgments of people or things; specif., one who writes judgments of books, plays, music, etc. professionally **2.** a person given to faultfinding and censure

**crit·i·cal** (krit'i k'l) *adj.* **1.** tending to find fault; censorious **2.** characterized by careful analysis **3.** of critics or criticism **4.** of or forming a crisis; decisive **5.** dangerous or risky **6.** designating or of supplies subject to increased production and restricted distribution, as in wartime **7.** designating or of the point at which a change of character, property, or condition is effected, or at which a nuclear chain reaction becomes self-sustaining —**crit'i·cal'i·ty** (-kal'ə tē), **crit'i·cal·ness** *n.* —**crit'i·cal·ly** *adv.*

**crit·i·cise** (krit'ə sīz') *vi., vt.* **-cised', -cis'ing** *Brit. sp. of* CRITICIZE—**crit'i·cis'er** *n.*

**crit·i·cism** (krit'ə siz'm) *n.* **1.** the act, art, or principles of criticizing, esp. of criticizing literary or artistic work **2.** a comment, review, article, etc. expressing this **3.** faultfinding; disapproval

**crit·i·cize** (-sīz') *vi., vt.* **-cized', -ciz'ing** **1.** to analyze and judge as a critic **2.** to find fault (with) —**crit'i·ciz'a·ble** *adj.* —**crit'i·ciz'er** *n.*

**cri·tique** (kri tēk') *n.* [Fr.] **1.** a critical analysis or evaluation **2.** the art of criticizing

**crit·ter, crit·tur** (krit'ər) *n. dial. var. of* CREATURE

**croak** (krōk) *vi.* [< OE. < *cræcettan*, of echoic origin] **1.** to make a deep, hoarse sound, as that of a frog **2.** to talk dismally; grumble **3.** [Slang] to die —*vt.* **1.** to utter in deep, hoarse tones **2.** [Slang] to kill —*n.* a croaking sound —**croak'y** (-ē) *adj.* **croak'i·er, croak'i·est**

**croak·er** (-ər) *n.* **1.** an animal or fish that makes croaking sounds **2.** a foreteller of evil; grumbler

**Cro·at** (krō'at, -ət; krōt) *n.* **1.** a native or inhabitant of Croatia **2.** *same as* CROATIAN (*n.* 2) —*adj. same as* CROATIAN

**Cro·a·tia** (krō ā'shə) republic of Yugoslavia, in the NW part: 21,830 sq. mi.; cap. Zagreb

**Cro·a·tian** (-shən) *adj.* of Croatia, its people, language, etc. —*n.* **1.** a Croat **2.** the South Slavic language of the Croats: see SERBO-CROATION

**cro·chet** (krō shā') *n.* [Fr., small hook: see CROTCHET] needlework in which loops of thread or yarn are interwoven with a hooked needle (**crochet hook**) —*vi., vt.* **-cheted'** (-shād'), **-chet'ing** to do crochet or make by crochet —**cro·chet'er** *n.*

**crock¹** (kräk) *n.* [OE. *crocca*] **1.** an earthenware pot or jar **2.** [Slang] something absurd; nonsense

**crock²** (kräk) *n.* [< ON. *kraki*, bent object] [Slang] anyone or anything worthless or useless, as from age

**crocked** (kräkt) *adj.* [Slang] drunk; intoxicated

**crock·er·y** (kräk'ər ē) *n.* [CROCK¹ + -ERY (sense 5)] earthenware pots, jars, dishes, etc.

**Crock·ett** (kräk'it), **David** (called *Davy Crockett*) 1786-1836; Am. frontiersman & politician

**croc·o·dile** (kräk'ə dīl') *n.* [< OFr. < ML. < L. < Gr. *krokodilos* < ? *kroke*, pebble + *drilos*, worm] **1.** a large, flesheating, lizardlike reptile of tropical streams, with a thick, horny skin, long tail, and long, narrow head with massive jaws **2.** leather made from a crocodile's hide

**crocodile tears** insincere tears or a hypocritical show of grief

**croc·o·dil·i·an** (kräk'ə dil'ē ən) *adj.* **1.** of or like a crocodile **2.** of a group of reptiles including the crocodile, alligator, cayman, and gavial —*n.* any reptile of this group

CROCODILE
(to 20 ft. long)

**cro·cus** (krō'kəs) *n., pl.* **cro'cus·es, cro'ci** (-sī) [L. < Gr *krokos*, saffron, via Sem. ult. < Sans.] any of a genus of spring-blooming plants with fleshy corms and a yellow, purple, or white flower

**Croe·sus** (krē'səs) fl. 6th cent. B.C.; last king of Lydia (560-546), noted for his great wealth —*n.* a very rich man

**croft** (krôft) *n.* [OE.] [Brit.] **1.** a small enclosed field **2.** a small farm, esp. one worked by a renter —**croft'er** *n.*

**crois·sant** (krə sänt') *n.* [Fr., lit., CRESCENT] a rich, flaky bread roll in the shape of a crescent

**†croix de guerre** (krwä də ger') [Fr., cross of war] a French military decoration for bravery

**Cro·Ma·gnon** (krō mag'nən, -man'yən) *adj.* [after the Cro-Magnon cave in SW France, where remains were found] belonging to a prehistoric, Caucasoid type of man, tall and erect, who lived on the European continent —*n.* a member of this group

**crom·lech** (kräm'lek) *n.* [W. < *crom*, bent + *llech*, flat stone] **1.** *same as* DOLMEN **2.** an ancient monument of monoliths, arranged in a circle around a mound or dolmen

**Crom·well** (kräm'wel, -wəl) **1.** Oliver, 1599-1658; Eng revolutionary leader & Protector of the Commonwealth (1653-58) **2.** Richard, 1626-1712; Protector of the Commonwealth (1658-59): son of *prec.*

**crone** (krōn) *n.* [< Anglo-Fr. *carogne* (cf. CARRION) or via MDu. *kronje*, old ewe] an ugly, withered old woman; hag

**Cro·nus** (krō'nəs) Gr. Myth. a Titan who overthrew his father, Uranus, and was himself overthrown by his son Zeus: identified with the Roman Saturn

**cro·ny** (krō'nē) *n., pl.* **-nies** [Brit. university slang < ? Gr *chronios*, long-continued (hence "old friend")] a close companion

**crook** (krook) *n.* [< ON. *krōkr*, hook] **1.** a hooked, bent or curved thing or part; hook **2.** *a)* a shepherd's staff *b* a crosier **3.** a bend or curve **4.** [Colloq.] a swindler o thief —*vt., vi.* **crooked** (krookt), **crook'ing** to bend or curve

**crook·ed** (krookt; *for* 2 & 3 krook'id) *adj.* **1.** having a crook or hook **2.** not straight; bent; curved **3.** dishonest; swindling —**crook'ed·ly** *adv.* —**crook'ed·ness** *n.*

**crook·neck** (krook'nek') *n.* a squash with a long, tapering curved neck

**croon** (kroon) *vi., vt.* [< MDu. *cronen*, to growl] **1.** to sing or hum in a low, gentle tone **2.** to sing (popular songs) in a soft, sentimental manner —*n.* a low, gentle singing or humming —**croon'er** *n.*

**crop** (kräp) *n.* [OE. *croppa*, cluster, flower, crop of bird] **1.** a saclike enlargement of a bird's gullet, in which food i stored before digestion; craw **2.** any agricultural product growing or harvested, as wheat, fruit, etc. **3.** the yield of any product in one season or place **4.** a group or collection **5.** the handle or butt of a whip **6.** a short whip with a looped lash, used in horseback riding **7.** hair cut close to the head **8.** an earmark on an animal, made by clipping —*vt.* **cropped, crop′ping 1.** to cut off or bite off the tops or ends of **2.** to grow or harvest as a crop **3.** to cut short —*vi.* **1.** to plant, grow, or bear crops **2.** to feed by grazing —**crop out** (or **up**) **1.** to appear unexpectedly **2.** to appear at the surface, as a rock formation

**crop-dust·ing** (-dust′iŋ) *n.* the spraying of growing crops with pesticides from an airplane —**crop′-dust′** *vi., vt.* —**crop′-dust′er** *n.*

**crop·per** (-ər) *n.* **1.** a person or thing that crops **2.** a sharecropper —**come a cropper** [Colloq.] **1.** to fall heavily or headlong **2.** to fail

**crop·pie** (kräp′ē) *n., pl.* **-pies, -pie:** see PLURAL, II, D, 1 *same as* CRAPPIE

**crop rotation** a system of growing successive crops that have different food requirements, to prevent soil depletion, break up a disease cycle, etc.

**cropt** (kräpt) *occas. pt. & pp. of* CROP

**cro·quet** (krō kā′) *n.* [Fr., dial. form of *crochet:* see CROTCHET] an outdoor game in which the players use mallets to drive a wooden ball through a series of hoops placed in the ground

**cro·quette** (krō ket′) *n.* [Fr. < *croquer,* to crunch] a small mass of chopped meat, fish, etc., coated with crumbs and fried in deep fat

**cro·sier** (krō′zhər) *n.* [< OFr. < *croce* < ML. *crocia* < Frank. hyp. *krukja,* crutch] a staff with a crook at the top, carried by or before a bishop or abbot as a symbol of his office

**cross** (krôs) *n.* [< OE. *cros* & ON. *kross,* both < OIr. *cros* < L. *crux* (gen. *crucis*), a cross] **1.** an upright post with a bar across it near the top, on which the ancient Romans fastened convicted persons to die **2.** a representation of a cross, used as a badge, crossroad marker, etc. **3.** a representation of a cross as a symbol of the crucifixion of Jesus, and hence of the Christian religion **4.** any trouble or affliction that one has to bear or that thwarts one **5.** any mark made by intersecting lines or surfaces **6.** such a mark (X) made as a signature by one who cannot write **7.** *a)* a crossing of varieties or breeds; hybridization *b)* the result of such mixing; hybrid **8.** something that combines the qualities of two different things or types **9.** [Slang] a double-cross —*vt.* **1.** to make the sign of the cross over or upon **2.** to place across or crosswise [*cross* your fingers] **3.** to lie or cut across; intersect **4.** to draw a line or lines across **5.** to pass over; go across **6.** to carry or lead across **7.** to extend across [the bridge *crosses* a river] **8.** to bring into contact, causing electrical interference [the wires were *crossed*] **9.** to thwart; oppose **10.** to interbreed (animals or plants); hybridize —*vi.* **1.** to intersect **2.** to go or extend from one side to the other **3.** to pass each other while moving in opposite directions **4.** to interbreed —*adj.* **1.** lying or passing across; crossing; transverse **2.** going counter; contrary; opposed **3.** ill-tempered; cranky; irritable **4.** involving reciprocation **5.** of mixed variety or breed; hybrid —*adv.* crosswise —**cross off** (or **out**) to cancel by or as by drawing lines across —**cross one's mind** to come suddenly or briefly to one's mind —**cross one's palm** to pay one money, esp. as a bribe —**cross one's path** to meet one —**cross up 1.** to confuse or disorder **2.** to deceive or double-cross —**the Cross 1.** the cross on which Jesus was put to death **2.** the suffering and death or Atonement of Jesus **3.** Christianity or Christendom —**cross′a·ble** *adj.* —**cross′ly** *adv.* —**cross′ness** *n.*

**cross·bar** (krôs′bär′) *n.* a bar, line, or stripe placed crosswise —*vt.* **-barred′, -bar′ring** to furnish with crossbars

**cross·beam** (-bēm′) *n.* a beam placed across another or from one wall to another

**cross·bill** (-bil′) *n.* a finch having a bill with curving points that cross

**cross·bones** (-bōnz′) *n. see* SKULL AND CROSSBONES

**cross·bow** (-bō′) *n.* a medieval weapon consisting of a bow set transversely on a wooden stock: the stock was grooved to direct an arrow or stone —**cross′bow′man** *n., pl.* **-men**

**cross·bred** (-bred′, -bred′) *adj.* produced by the interbreeding of different varieties or breeds —*n.* a hybrid; mongrel

**cross·breed** (-brēd′, -brēd′) *vt., vi.* **-bred** (-bred′, -bred′), **-breed′ing** *same as* HYBRIDIZE —*n. same as* HYBRID (sense 1)

**cross-coun·try** (-kun′trē) *adj., adv.* **1.** across open country or fields, not by roads **2.** across a country —*n.* cross-country footracing

**cross·cur·rent** (-kur′ənt) *n.* **1.** a current flowing at an angle to the main current **2.** an opposing opinion, influence, or tendency

**cross·cut** (-kut′) *adj.* **1.** made or used for cutting across [a *crosscut* saw] **2.** cut across —*n.* **1.** a cut across **2.** something that cuts across **3.** *Mining* a cutting made across a vein —*vt.* **-cut′, -cut′ting** to cut across

**crosse** (krôs) *n.* [Fr.: see CROSIER] the pouched racket used in playing lacrosse

**cross-ex·am·ine** (krôs′ig zam′in) *vt., vi.* **-ined, -in·ing 1.** to question closely **2.** *Law* to question (a witness already questioned by the opposing side) to determine the validity of his testimony —**cross′-ex·am′i·na′tion** *n.* —**cross′-ex·am′in·er** *n.*

**cross-eye** (krôs′ī′) *n.* an abnormal condition in which the eyes are turned toward each other; convergent strabismus —**cross′-eyed′** (-īd′) *adj.*

**cross-fer·ti·lize** (-furt′'l īz′) *vt., vi.* **-lized′, -liz′ing** to fertilize or be fertilized by pollen from another plant or variety of plant —**cross′-fer′ti·li·za′tion** *n.*

**cross fire 1.** *Mil.* a firing at an objective from two or more positions so that the lines of fire cross **2.** any complex of opposing forces, opinions, etc.

**cross-grained** (-grānd′) *adj.* **1.** having an irregular or transverse grain: said of wood **2.** contrary; perverse; cantankerous

**cross·hatch** (-hach′) *vt., vi.* to shade with two sets of crossing parallel lines

**cross·ing** (-iŋ) *n.* **1.** the act of passing across, thwarting, interbreeding, etc. **2.** an intersection, as of lines, streets, etc. **3.** a place where a street, river, etc. may be crossed

**cross-leg·ged** (-leg′id, -legd′) *adj., adv.* with ankles crossed, or with one leg crossed over the other

**cross·patch** (-pach′) *n.* [CROSS + dial. *patch,* fool] [Colloq.] a cross, bad-tempered person

**cross·piece** (-pēs′) *n.* a piece lying across another

**cross·pol·li·nate** (krôs′päl′ə nāt′) *vt., vi.* **-nat′ed, -nat′ing** to transfer pollen from the anther of (one flower) to the stigma of (another) —**cross′-pol′li·na′tion** *n.*

**cross-pur·pose** (krôs′pur′pəs) *n.* a contrary or conflicting purpose —**at cross-purposes** having a misunderstanding as to each other's purposes

**cross-ques·tion** (-kwes′chən) *vt.* to cross-examine —*n.* a question asked in cross-examination

**cross-re·fer** (-ri fur′) *vt., vi.* **-ferred′, -fer′ring** to refer from one part to another

**cross-ref·er·ence** (-ref′ər əns, -ref′rəns) *n.* a reference from one part of a book, catalog, index, etc. to another part —*vt., vi.* **-enced, -enc·ing 1.** to provide (an index, reference book, etc.) with systematic cross-references **2.** *same as* CROSS-REFER

**cross·road** (-rōd′) *n.* **1.** a road that crosses another **2.** a road that connects main roads **3.** [*usually pl.*] *a)* the place where roads intersect *b)* any center of congregation, activity, etc. for a wide area —**at the crossroads** at the point where one must choose between different courses of action

**cross·ruff** (-ruf′) *n. Card Games* a sequence of plays in which each of two partners in turn leads a card which the other can trump

**cross section 1.** *a)* a cutting through something, esp. at right angles to its axis *b)* a piece so cut off *c)* a drawing of a plane surface as exposed by such a cutting **2.** a sample with enough of each kind to show what the whole is like —**cross′-sec′tion** *vt.* —**cross′-sec′tion·al** *adj.*

**cross-stitch** (-stich′) *n.* **1.** a stitch made by crossing two stitches diagonally in the form of an X **2.** needlework made with this stitch —*vt., vi.* to sew or embroider with this stitch

**cross·tie** (-tī′) *n.* a beam, rod, etc. placed crosswise to give support; specif., any of the transverse timbers supporting a railroad track

**cross-town** (-toun′) *adj.* going across the main avenues or transportation lines of a city

**cross·trees** (-trēz′) *n.pl.* two short, horizontal bars across a ship's masthead, which spread the rigging that supports the mast

**cross·walk** (-wôk′) *n.* a lane marked off for pedestrians to use in crossing a street

**cross·way** (-wā′) *n. same as* CROSSROAD

**cross·wise** (-wīz′) *adv.* so as to cross; across: also **cross′-ways′** (-wāz′)

**cross·word puzzle** (-wurd′) an arrangement of numbered squares to be filled in with words, a letter to each square:

**CROSSES**
(A, Greek; B, Maltese; C, Latin; D, Patriarchal)

numbered synonyms, definitions, etc. are given as clues for the words

**crotch** (kräch) *n.* [ME. *croche,* var. of *crucche,* CRUTCH] **1.** a pole forked on top **2.** a forked place, as where a tree trunk divides into two branches **3.** the place where the legs fork from the human body **4.** the place where the legs of a pair of pants, etc. meet —**crotched** *adj.*

**crotch·et** (kräch'it) *n.* [OFr. *crochet,* dim. < *croc,* hook] **1.** a peculiar whim or stubborn notion **2.** [Brit.] *same as* QUARTER NOTE

**crotch·et·y** (-ē) *adj.* full of peculiar whims or stubborn notions —**crotch'et·i·ness** *n.*

**cro·ton** (krōt''n) *n.* [ModL. < Gr. *kroton*] any of a large, mostly tropical genus of shrubs and trees of the spurge family: one species yields an oil (**croton oil**) formerly used in medicine

**Croton bug** [< *Croton* Aqueduct in New York City] a small cockroach

**crouch** (krouch) *vi.* [< OFr. *crochir* < *croc,* a hook] **1.** to stoop low with the limbs close to the body, as an animal ready to pounce or cowering **2.** to cringe or bow in a servile manner —*n.* the act or position of crouching

**croup**[1] (krōōp) *n.* [< obs. or dial. *croup,* to speak hoarsely, of echoic origin] an inflammation of the respiratory passages, with labored breathing and hoarse coughing —**croup'y** *adj.*

**croup**[2] (krōōp) *n.* [OFr. *croupe* < Frank.] the rump of a horse, etc.

**crou·pi·er** (krōō'pē ā', -ər) *n.* [Fr., orig., one who rides on the croup: see prec.] a person in charge of a gambling table, who rakes in and pays out the money

**crou·ton** (krōō'tän, krōō tän') *n.* [< Fr. < *croûte* < L. *crusta:* see CRUST] a small piece of toasted or fried bread, often served in soup or salads

**Crow** (krō) *n.* [transl., via Fr., of their native name, *Absaroke,* crow people] **1.** *pl.* **Crows, Crow** a member of a tribe of Siouan Indians living near the Yellowstone River **2.** their Siouan language

**crow**[1] (krō) *n.* [OE. *crawa*] a large bird with glossy black plumage and a typical harsh call: the raven, rook, and jackdaw are crows —**as the crow flies** in a direct line —**eat crow** [Colloq.] to undergo the humiliation of admitting an error, etc.

**crow**[2] (krō) *vi.* **crowed** or, for 1, chiefly Brit., **crew** (krōō), **crowed, crow'ing** [OE. *crawan*] **1.** to make the shrill cry of a rooster **2.** to boast in triumph; exult **3.** to make a sound expressive of well-being or pleasure, as a baby does —*n.* a crowing sound

**crow·bar** (krō'bär') *n.* a long metal bar, chisellike at one end, used as a lever for prying, etc.

**crowd**[1] (kroud) *vi.* [OE. *crudan*] **1.** to press, push, or squeeze **2.** to push one's way (*forward, into,* etc.) **3.** to throng —*vt.* **1.** to press, push, or shove **2.** to press closely together; cram **3.** to fill too full **4.** to be or press very near to **5.** [Colloq.] to put (a person) under pressure, as by dunning —*n.* **1.** a large number of people or things gathered closely together **2.** the common people; the masses **3.** [Colloq.] a set or clique —**crowd out** to exclude because of insufficient space or time —**crowd'ed** *adj.*

**crowd**[2] (kroud) *n.* [W. *crwth*] an obsolete Celtic musical instrument somewhat like a violin but with a shallow, broad body

**crow·foot** (krō'foot') *n., pl.* **-foots'** a plant of the buttercup family, with leaves somewhat resembling a crow's foot

**crown** (kroun) *n.* [< OFr. < L. *corona,* a garland < Gr. *korōnē,* wreath] **1.** a garland or wreath worn on the head as a sign of honor, victory, etc. **2.** a reward or honor given for merit; specif., a sports championship **3.** the emblematic headdress of a monarch **4.** [often C-] *a*) the power or dominion of a monarch *b*) the monarch as head of the state **5.** anything serving to adorn or honor like a crown **6.** a thing like a crown in shape, position, etc., as the top of the head, of a hat, etc. **7.** *a*) orig., any coin bearing the figure of a crown *b*) a British coin equal to five shillings **8.** the highest point, as of an arch **9.** the highest quality, state, etc. of anything **10.** *a*) the part of a tooth projecting beyond the gum line *b*) an artificial substitute for this **11.** the lowest point of an anchor, between the arms —*vt.* **1.** *a*) to put a crown on the head of *b*) to enthrone **2.** to honor or reward as with a crown **3.** to be the crown or highest part of **4.** to put the finishing touch on **5.** to cover (a tooth) with an artificial crown **6.** [Slang] to hit on the head **7.** *Checkers* to make a king of —**crown'er** *n.*

**crown colony** a British colony directly under the control of the home government in London

**crown glass** a very clear optical glass

**crown prince** the male heir apparent to a throne

**crown princess 1.** the wife of a crown prince **2.** a female heir presumptive to a throne

**crow's-foot** (krōz'foot') *n., pl.* **-feet'** any of the wrinkles that often develop at the outer corners of the eyes: *usually used in pl.*

**crow's-nest** (-nest') *n.* **1.** a small, partly enclosed platform close to the top of a ship's mast, used by the lookout **2.** any platform like this

**cro·zier** (krō'zhər) *n. same as* CROSIER

**cru·ces** (krōō'sēz) *n. alt. pl. of* CRUX

**cru·cial** (krōō'shəl) *adj.* [Fr. < L. *crux,* CROSS] **1.** of supreme importance; decisive; critical **2.** extremely trying; severe —**cru'cial·ly** *adv.*

**cru·ci·ble** (krōō'sə b'l) *n.* [< ML. *crucibulum,* lamp] **1.** a container made of a heat-resistant substance, as graphite, for melting ores, metals, etc. **2.** a severe test or trial

**cru·ci·fix** (krōō'sə fiks') *n.* [< OFr. or ML., orig. pp. of LL. *crucifigere,* CRUCIFY] **1.** a representation of a cross with the figure of Jesus crucified on it **2.** the cross as a Christian symbol

CROW'S-NEST

**cru·ci·fix·ion** (krōō'sə fik'shən) *n.* **1.** a crucifying or being crucified **2.** [C-] the crucifying of Jesus, or a representation of this in painting, statuary, etc.

**cru·ci·form** (krōō'sə fôrm') *adj.* [< L. *crux,* CROSS + -FORM] cross-shaped —**cru'ci·form'ly** *adv.*

**cru·ci·fy** (krōō'sə fī') *vt.* **-fied', -fy'ing** [< OFr. < L. *crucificare,* for *crucifigere* < L. *crux,* CROSS + *figere,* FIX] **1.** to execute by nailing or binding to a cross and leaving to die of exposure **2.** to torment; torture —**cru'ci·fi'er** *n.*

**crud**[1] (krud) *vt., vi.* **crud'ded, crud'ding** [ME. *crud:* see CURD] [Dial.] to curdle —*n.* [Slang] **1.** any coagulated substance, caked deposit, dregs, filth, etc. **2.** a worthless, disgusting, or contemptible person or thing —**crud'dy** *adj.* **-di·er, -di·est**

**crud**[2] (krud) *n.* [< ? W. *cryd,* plague] [Slang] an imaginary or vaguely identified disease or ailment

**crude** (krōōd) *adj.* [L. *crudus,* raw, rough] **1.** in a raw or natural condition; not refined or processed **2.** lacking grace, taste, etc.; uncultured [a *crude* remark] **3.** not carefully made or done; rough **4.** stark [*crude* reality] —**crude'ly** *adv.* —**crude'ness** *n.*

**cru·di·tés** (krōō'də tā; *Fr.* krü dē tā') *n.pl.* [Fr., lit., something raw] raw vegetables cut up and served as appetizers, usually with a dip

**cru·di·ty** (krōō'də tē) *n.* **1.** a crude condition or quality **2.** *pl.* **-ties** a crude remark, etc.

**cru·el** (krōō'əl) *adj.* [OFr. < L. *crudelis* < *crudus:* see CRUDE] **1.** enjoying others' suffering; merciless **2.** causing, or of a kind to cause, pain, distress, etc. —**cru'el·ly** *adv.* —**cru'el·ness** *n.*

**cru·el·ty** (-tē) *n.* **1.** the quality of being cruel; inhumanity; hardheartedness **2.** *pl.* **-ties** a cruel action, remark, etc. **3.** *Law* willful mistreatment harmful to life or to health

**cru·et** (krōō'it) *n.* [< Anglo-Fr. dim. of OFr. *crue,* earthen pot < Gmc.] a small glass bottle, as for holding vinegar, oil, etc., for the table

**cruise** (krōōz) *vi.* **cruised, cruis'ing** [< Du. *kruisen,* to cross < *kruis* < L. *crux,* CROSS] **1.** to sail from place to place, as for pleasure or in search of something **2.** to go or drive about in a similar manner, as a taxi **3.** to move at the most efficient speed for sustained travel —*vt.* to sail, journey, or move over or about —*n.* the action of cruising; esp., a cruising voyage

**cruis·er** (-ər) *n.* **1.** one that cruises, as an airplane, squad car, etc. **2.** a fast warship somewhat smaller than a battleship and having less armor and fire power **3.** *same as* CABIN CRUISER

**crul·ler** (krul'ər) *n.* [Du. < *krullen,* to curl] a kind of twisted doughnut made with a rich dough

**crumb** (krum) *n.* [OE. *cruma*] **1.** a small piece broken off something, as of bread or cake **2.** any bit or scrap [*crumbs* of knowledge] **3.** the soft, inner part of bread **4.** [Slang] a worthless or despicable person: also **crum'bum'** —*vt.* **1.** to clear (a table, etc.) of crumbs **2.** *Cooking* to cover or thicken with crumbs

**crum·ble** (krum'b'l) *vt.* **-bled, -bling** [freq. of prec.] to break into crumbs or small pieces —*vi.* to fall to pieces; decay

**crum·bly** (-blē) *adj.* **-bli·er, -bli·est** apt to crumble; easily crumbled —**crum'bli·ness** *n.*

**crumb·y** (krum'ē) *adj.* **crumb'i·er, crumb'i·est 1.** full of crumbs **2.** soft, as the inner part of bread **3.** [Slang] *same as* CRUMMY —**crumb'i·ness** *n.*

**crum·my** (krum'ē) *adj.* **-mi·er, -mi·est** [< CRUM(B) + -Y[2]] [Slang] **1.** dirty, cheap, etc. **2.** inferior, worthless, contemptible, etc. —**crum'mi·ness** *n.*

**crum·pet** (krum'pit) *n.* [prob. < ME. *crompid* < OE. *crompeht,* flat cake] a batter cake baked on a griddle: it is usually toasted before serving

**crum·ple** (krum'p'l) *vt., vi.* **-pled, -pling** [ME. *crumplen,* var. of *crimplen,* to wrinkle, freq. of *crimpen,* CRIMP[1]] **1.** to crush or become crushed together into wrinkles **2.** to break down; collapse —*n.* a crease or wrinkle —**crum'ply** *adj.*

**crunch** (krunch) *vi., vt.* [of echoic origin] **1.** to chew with a noisy, crackling sound **2.** to press, grind, tread, etc. with a noisy, crushing sound —*n.* **1.** the act or sound of crunching **2.** [Slang] *a)* a showdown *b)* a tight situation

**crunch·y** (-ē) *adj.* **crunch′i·er, crunch′i·est** making a crunching sound —**crunch′i·ness** *n.*

**crup·per** (krup′ər, kroop′-) *n.* [< OFr. *cropiere* < *crope,* rump] **1.** a leather strap attached to a saddle or harness and passed under the horse's tail **2.** a horse's rump; croup

**cru·sade** (krōo sād′) *n.* [< Sp. *cruzada* & Fr. *croisade,* both < ML. pp. of *cruciare,* to mark with a cross < L. *crux,* CROSS] **1.** [*sometimes* C-] any of the military expeditions which Christians undertook from the 11th to the 13th cent. to recover the Holy Land from the Moslems **2.** any church-sanctioned war or expedition like this **3.** vigorous, concerted action for some cause or against some abuse —*vi.* -**sad′ed,** -**sad′ing** to engage in a crusade —**cru·sad′er** *n.*

**cruse** (krōoz, krōos) *n.* [OE. *cruse*] a small container for water, oil, honey, etc.

**crush** (krush) *vt.* [< OFr. *croisir,* to break < Frank. *krostjan,* to gnash] **1.** to press between opposing forces so as to break or put out of shape; crumple **2.** to grind or pound into small particles **3.** to subdue; overwhelm **4.** to oppress **5.** to extract by pressing or squeezing —*vi.* **1.** to be or become crushed **2.** to crowd (*into,* etc.) —*n.* **1.** a crushing; severe pressure **2.** a crowded mass of people **3.** a drink with fruit juice **4.** [Colloq.] an infatuation —**crush′a·ble** *adj.* —**crush′er** *n.*

**Cru·soe** (krōo′sō), **Robinson** *see* ROBINSON CRUSOE

**crust** (krust) *n.* [< OFr. *crouste* or < L. *crusta*] **1.** *a)* the hard, outer part of bread *b)* a piece of this *c)* any dry, hard piece of bread **2.** the pastry shell of a pie **3.** any hard surface layer, as of snow, soil, etc. **4.** *same as* SCAB (*n.* 1) **5.** [Slang] audacity; insolence **6.** *Geol.* the solid outer shell of the earth —*vt., vi.* **1.** to cover or become covered with a crust **2.** to harden into a crust —**crus·tal** (krus′t'l) *adj.* —**crust′ed** *adj.*

**crus·ta·cean** (krus tā′shən) *n.* [< ModL. < *crustaceus,* having a crust < L. *crusta,* crust] any of a class of arthropods, including shrimps, crabs, barnacles, and lobsters, that usually live in water and breathe through gills: they have a hard outer shell and jointed appendages and bodies —*adj.* of crustaceans: also **crus·ta′ceous**

**crust·y** (krus′tē) *adj.* **crust′i·er, crust′i·est** **1.** having, forming, or resembling a crust **2.** rudely abrupt or surly; bad-tempered —**crust′i·ly** *adv.* —**crust′i·ness** *n.*

**crutch** (kruch) *n.* [OE. *crycce,* staff] **1.** a staff with a hand grip and a crosspiece on top that fits under the armpit, used by lame people as an aid in walking **2.** anything relied on for support; prop **3.** any device that resembles a crutch —*vt.* to support with or as with a crutch; prop up

**crux** (kruks) *n., pl.* **crux′es, cru·ces** (krōo′sēz) [L., CROSS] **1.** a difficult problem **2.** the essential or deciding point

**cru·zei·ro** (krōo zā′rō; *Port.* krōo zā′roo) *n., pl.* **-ros** [Port. < *cruz,* a cross < L. *crux,* CROSS] *see* MONETARY UNITS, table (Brazil)

**cry** (krī) *vi.* **cried, cry′ing** [OFr. *crier* < L. *quiritare,* to wail] **1.** to make a loud vocal sound or utterance, as for help **2.** to sob and shed tears in expressing sorrow, pain, etc.; weep **3.** *a)* to plead or clamor (*for*) *b)* to show a great need (*for*) [problems *crying* for solution] **4.** to utter its characteristic call: said of an animal —*vt.* **1.** to plead or beg [to *cry* quarter] **2.** to utter loudly; shout **3.** to call out (wares for sale, etc.) —*n., pl.* **cries** **1.** a loud vocal sound expressing pain, anger, etc. **2.** any loud utterance; shout **3.** an announcement called out publicly **4.** an urgent appeal; plea **5.** popular report; rumor; rallying call **6.** the current opinion or fashion **7.** public outcry **8.** a slogan **9.** a fit of weeping **10.** the characteristic vocal sound of an animal **11.** the baying of hounds in the chase —**a far cry** a great distance or difference —**cry down** to belittle; disparage —**cry one's eyes out** to weep much and bitterly —**cry out** **1.** to shout; yell **2.** to complain loudly —**cry up** to praise highly —**in full cry** in eager pursuit

**cry·ba·by** (-bā′bē) *n., pl.* **-bies** **1.** a child who cries often or with little cause **2.** a person who complains when he fails to win or get his own way

**cry·ing** (-iŋ) *adj.* **1.** that cries **2.** demanding immediate notice —**for crying out loud** [Slang] an exclamation of annoyance, surprise, etc.

**cry·o-** [< Gr. *kryos,* cold] *a combining form meaning* cold or freezing [*cryolite*]

**cry·o·gen** (krī′ō jən) *n.* [CRYO- + -GEN] a refrigerant

**cry·o·gen·ics** (krī′ə jen′iks) *n.pl.* [*with sing. v.*] [CRYOGEN + -ICS] the science that deals with the effects of very low temperatures on the properties of matter

**cry·o·lite** (krī′ə līt′) *n.* [CRYO- + -LITE] a fluoride of sodium and aluminum, $Na_3AlF_6$, a source of aluminum

**cry·on·ics** (krī än′iks) *n.pl.* [*with sing. v.*] [CRYO- + -*n-* + -ICS] the practice of freezing a body just after death to preserve it for possible resuscitation, as when a cure is found for the disease that caused death —**cry·on′ic** *adj.*

**cry·o·sur·ger·y** (krī′ə sur′jə rē) *n.* [CRYO- + SURGERY] surgery in which tissues are destroyed by freezing

**crypt** (kript) *n.* [< L. < Gr. < *kryptein,* to hide] an underground chamber; esp., a vault under the main floor of a church, used as a burial place

**cryp·tic** (krip′tik) *adj.* [< LL. < Gr.: see prec.] **1.** having a hidden meaning; mysterious **2.** obscure and curt Also **cryp′ti·cal** —**cryp′ti·cal·ly** *adv.*

**cryp·to-** *a combining forming meaning:* **1.** secret or hidden **2.** being such secretly Also, before a vowel, **crypt-**

**cryp·to·gam** (krip′tə gam′) *n.* [< Fr. < Gr. *kryptos,* hidden + *gamos,* marriage] a plant that bears no flowers or seeds but propagates by means of spores, as algae, mosses, ferns, etc. —**cryp′to·gam′ic, cryp·tog′a·mous** (-täg′ə məs) *adj.*

**cryp·to·gram** (krip′tə gram′) *n.* [CRYPTO- + -GRAM] something written in code or cipher: also **cryp′to·graph′** (-graf′) —**cryp′to·gram′mic** *adj.*

**cryp·tog·ra·phy** (krip täg′rə fē) *n.* [CRYPTO- + -GRAPHY] **1.** the art of writing or deciphering messages in code **2.** a code system —**cryp′to·gra′pher, cryp·tog′ra·phist** *n.* —**cryp·to·graph·ic** (krip′tə graf′ik) *adj.* —**cryp′to·graph′i·cal·ly** *adv.*

**cryst. 1.** crystalline **2.** crystallized

**crys·tal** (kris′t'l) *n.* [< OE. & OFr. < L. < Gr. *krystallos,* ice < *kryos,* frost] **1.** *a)* a clear, transparent quartz *b)* a piece of this cut in the form of an ornament **2.** *a)* a very clear, brilliant glass *b)* an article or articles made of such glass, as goblets, bowls, etc. **3.** the transparent covering over the face of a watch **4.** anything clear and transparent like crystal **5.** a solidified form of a substance made up of plane faces in three dimensions in a symmetrical arrangement **6.** *Radio* a piezoelectric material, as quartz, used to produce and control very precisely a desired frequency, as in transmitters, etc. —*adj.* **1.** of or composed of crystal **2.** like crystal; transparent **3.** *Radio* using a crystal

CRYSTALS (A, isometric; B, monoclinic; C, triclinic)

**crystal detector** *Radio* a semiconductor rectifier used for demodulation

**crystal gazing** the practice of gazing into a large glass ball (**crystal ball**) and professing to see images, esp. of future events —**crystal gazer**

**crys·tal·line** (kris′tə lin) *adj.* **1.** consisting of or made of crystal or crystals **2.** like crystal; clear and transparent **3.** having the character or structure of a crystal

**crystalline lens** the lens of the eye, serving to focus light on the retina

**crys·tal·lize** (kris′tə līz′) *vt.* -**lized′,** -**liz′ing** **1.** to cause to form crystals **2.** to give a definite form to **3.** to coat with sugar —*vi.* **1.** to become crystalline in form **2.** to take on a definite form —**crys′tal·liz′a·ble** *adj.* —**crys′tal·li·za′tion** *n.*

**crys·tal·lo-** [< Gr. *krystallos,* CRYSTAL] *a combining form meaning* crystal Also **crys·tall-**

**crys·tal·log·ra·phy** (kris′tə läg′rə fē) *n.* [prec. + -GRAPHY] the science of the form, structure, properties, and classification of crystals —**crys′tal·lo·graph′ic** (-lə graf′ik), **crys′·tal·lo·graph′i·cal** *adj.*

**crys·tal·loid** (kris′tə loid′) *adj.* **1.** like a crystal **2.** having the nature of a crystalloid —*n.* a substance, usually crystallizable, which, when in solution, readily passes through vegetable and animal membranes —**crys′tal·loi′dal** *adj.*

**crystal pickup** a piezoelectric vibration pickup, often used on electric phonographs

**crystal set** an early type of radio receiver with a crystal, instead of an electron tube, detector

**Cs** *Chem.* cesium

**cs.** case; cases

**C.S.** Christian Science

**C.S., c.s. 1.** capital stock **2.** civil service

**CSC** Civil Service Commission

**csc** cosecant

**CST, C.S.T.** Central Standard Time

**CT** Connecticut

**ct.′ 1.** *pl.* **cts.** cent **2.** court

**ctn. 1.** carton: also **ctn. 2.** cotangent

**ctr.** center

**cts. 1.** centimes **2.** cents

**Cu** [L. *cuprum*] *Chem.* copper

**cu.** cubic

**cub** (kub) *n.* [< ? OIr. *cuib*, whelp] **1.** the young of certain mammals, as the fox, bear, lion, whale, etc. **2.** an inexperienced or callow person, esp. a novice reporter —**cub′bish** *adj.* —**cub′bish·ness** *n.*

**Cu·ba** (kyōō′bə; *Sp.* kōō′bä) island country in the West Indies, south of Fla.: 44,218 sq. mi.; pop. 8,074,000; cap. Havana —**Cu′ban** *adj., n.*

**cub·by·hole** (kub′ē hōl′) *n.* [< Brit. dial. *cub*, little shed + HOLE] **1.** a small, enclosed space or room **2.** a pigeon-hole

**cube** (kyōōb) *n.* [Fr. < L. < Gr. *kybos*, a cube, die] **1.** a solid with six equal, square sides **2.** anything having more or less this shape *[an ice cube]* **3.** the product obtained by multiplying a given number or quantity by its square; third power *[the cube of 3 is 27 (3x3x3)]* —*vt.* **cubed, cub′ing** **1.** to raise to the third power **2.** to cut or shape into cubes —**cub′er** *n.*

**cu·beb** (kyōō′beb) *n.* [< Fr. < ML. < Ar. *kabāba*] the spicy berry of an East Indian vine, formerly used medicinally in cigarettes

**cube root** the number or quantity of which a given number or quantity is the cube *[the cube root of 8 is 2]*

**cu·bic** (kyōō′bik) *adj.* **1.** having the shape of a cube **2.** having three dimensions, or having the volume of a cube whose length, width, and depth each measure the given unit *[a cubic foot]* **3.** relating to the cubes of numbers or quantities —**cu′bi·cal** (-bi k'l) *adj.* —**cu′bi·cal·ly** *adv.*

**cu·bi·cle** (kyōō′bi k'l) *n.* [L. *cubiculum* < *cubare*, to lie down] **1.** a small sleeping compartment, as in a dormitory **2.** any small compartment

**cubic measure** a system of measuring volume in cubic units, esp. that in which 1,728 cubic inches = 1 cubic foot and 1,000 cubic millimeters = 1 cubic centimeter: see TABLE OF WEIGHTS AND MEASURES in Supplements

**cu·bi·form** (kyōō′bə fôrm′) *adj.* cube-shaped

**cub·ism** (kyōō′biz'm) *n.* a movement in art, esp. of the early 20th century, characterized by the use of cubes and other geometric forms in abstract arrangements rather than by a realistic representation of nature —**cub′ist** *n., adj.* —**cu·bis′tic** *adj.*

**cu·bit** (kyōō′bit) *n.* [< OE. < L. *cubitum*, the elbow, cubit] an ancient measure of length, about 18–22 inches; orig., the length of the arm from the end of the middle finger to the elbow

**cu·boid** (kyōō′boid) *adj.* cube-shaped: also **cu·boi′dal** —*n.* a six-sided figure with all faces rectangular

**Cub Scout** a member of a division of the Boy Scouts for boys eight through ten years old

**cuck·old** (kuk′'ld) *n.* [< OFr. *cucuault* < *cucu*: see ff.] a man whose wife has committed adultery —*vt.* to make a cuckold of —**cuck′old·ry** (-rē) *n.*

**cuck·oo** (kōō′kōō′, kook′ōō) *n., pl.* **cuck′oos** [< OFr. *coucou, cucu*, echoic of its cry] **1.** any of a family of grayish-brown birds with a long, slender body: the European species lays eggs in the nests of other birds, but the American varieties hatch their own young **2.** the call of a cuckoo, which sounds somewhat like its name **3.** an imitation of this **4.** [Slang] a crazy or foolish person —*vi.* to utter the call of a cuckoo —*vt.* to repeat continually —*adj.* [Slang] crazy; silly

**cuckoo clock** a clock with a toy bird that pops out and cuckoos to mark intervals of time

**cuckoo spit** (or **spittle**) a froth produced on plants by the nymphs of certain insects

**cu·cul·late** (kyōō′kə lāt′, kyoo kul′it) *adj.* [< L. *cucullus*, hood] shaped like a hood, as the leaves of violets: also **cu′cul·lat′ed**

**cu·cum·ber** (kyōō′kum bər) *n.* [< OFr. < L. *cucumis* (gen. *cucumeris*)] **1.** an annual vine of the gourd family, grown for its edible fruit **2.** the long fruit, with a green rind and firm, white flesh, used in salads or preserved as pickles —**cool as a cucumber 1.** comfortably cool **2.** calm and self-possessed

**cud** (kud) *n.* [OE. *cudu*] a mouthful of swallowed food regurgitated from the first stomach of cattle and other ruminants and chewed slowly a second time —**chew the cud** to ruminate; ponder

**cud·dle** (kud′'l) *vt.* **-dled, -dling** [? < ME. hyp. *couthelen* < *couth*, known, hence comfortable with + *-le*, freq. suffix] to hold lovingly and gently in one's arms; embrace and fondle —*vi.* to lie close and snug; nestle —*n.* **1.** a cuddling **2.** an embrace; hug —**cud′dle·some** (-səm), **cud′dly** *adj.* **-dli·er, -dli·est**

**cud·dy** (kud′ē) *n., pl.* **-dies** [< ?] **1.** a small cabin on a ship **2.** the cook's galley on a small ship

**cudg·el** (kuj′əl) *n.* [OE. *cycgel*] a short, thick stick or club —*vt.* **-eled** or **-elled, -el·ing** or **-el·ling** to beat with a cudgel —**cudgel one's brains** to think hard —**take up the cudgels (for)** to come to the defense (of)

**cue¹** (kyōō) *n.* [< *q, Q* (? for L. *quando*, when) found in 16th-c. plays to mark actors' entrances] **1.** a bit of dialogue, action, or music that is a signal for an actor's entrance or speech, or for lights, sound effects, etc. **2.** anything serving as a signal to do something **3.** an indirect suggestion; hint —*vt.* **cued, cu′ing** or **cue′ing** to give a cue to

**cue²** (kyōō) *n.* [var. of QUEUE] **1.** *same as* QUEUE **2.** a long, tapering rod used in billiards, pool, etc. to strike the cue ball **3.** a long, shovellike stick used in shuffleboard to push the disks —*vt.* **cued, cu′ing** or **cue′ing** **1.** to braid (hair, etc.) **2.** to strike (a cue ball, etc.) with a cue

**cue ball** the ball, usually white, that a player strikes with his cue in billiards or pool

**cuff¹** (kuf) *n.* [< ME. *cuffe*, glove] **1.** a fixed or detachable band or fold at the end of a sleeve **2.** a turned-up fold at the bottom of a trouser leg **3.** a handcuff —*vt.* to put a cuff on —**off the cuff** [Slang] in an offhand manner —**on the cuff** [Slang] on credit

**cuff²** (kuf) *vt.* [< ? CUFF¹ (in orig. sense "glove")] to strike, esp. with the open hand; slap —*n.* a slap or blow

**cuff link** a pair of linked buttons or any similar small device for keeping a shirt cuff closed

‡**cui bo·no** (kwē bō′nō) [L., to whom for a good] **1.** for whose benefit? **2.** to what purpose?

**cui·rass** (kwi ras′) *n.* [< Fr. < It. < L. (*vestis*) *coriacea*, leather (clothing) < *corium*, leather] **1.** a piece of closefitting armor for protecting the breast and back **2.** the breastplate of such armor —*vt.* to cover as with a cuirass

**cui·ras·sier** (kwi′rə sir′) *n.* [Fr.] a cavalryman wearing a cuirass

**cui·sine** (kwi zēn′) *n.* [Fr. < LL. *coquina*, kitchen < L. *coquere*, to cook] **1.** style of cooking or preparing food **2.** the food prepared, as at a restaurant

**cuisse** (kwis) *n.* [< OFr. < L. *coxa*, hip] a piece of armor to protect the thigh: also **cuish** (kwish)

**cul-de-sac** (kul′də sak′, kool′-; *Fr.* küt säk′) *n., pl.* **cul-de-sacs**; *Fr.* **culs-de-sac** (küt säk′) [Fr., lit., bottom of a sack] a passage or position with one outlet; blind alley

**-cule** (kyōōl, kyool) [< Fr. or L.] *a suffix meaning* small

**cu·lex** (kyōō′leks) *n.* [L., a gnat] any of a large genus of mosquitoes including many of the most common species found in N. America and Europe

**cu·li·nar·y** (kyōō′lə ner′ē, kul′ə-) *adj.* [< LL. < L. *culina*, kitchen] of the kitchen or of cooking

**cull** (kul) *vt.* [< OFr. < L. *colligere*: see COLLECT²] **1.** to pick out; select and gather **2.** to pick over —*n.* something picked out; esp., something rejected as not being up to standard

**culm¹** (kulm) *n.* [< ME. *colme* < ? OE. *col*, coal] waste material from coal screenings or washings

**culm²** (kulm) *n.* [L. *culmus*, a stem] the jointed stem of various grasses, usually hollow —*vi.* to grow or develop into a culm

**cul·mi·nate** (kul′mə nāt′) *vi.* **-nat′ed, -nat′ing** [< ML. pp. of *culminare* < L. *culmen* (gen. *culminis*), peak] to reach its highest point or climax —*vt.* to bring to its climax —**cul′mi·nant** *adj.*

**cul·mi·na·tion** (kul′mə nā′shən) *n.* **1.** a culminating **2.** the highest point; climax

**cu·lotte** (kōō lät′, kyōō-) *n.* [Fr. < *cul*, posterior < L. *culus*] *[often pl.]* trousers made full in the legs to resemble a skirt, worn by women and girls

**cul·pa·ble** (kul′pə b'l) *adj.* [< OFr. < L. < *culpa*, fault, blame] deserving blame; blameworthy —**cul′pa·bil′i·ty** *n.* —**cul′pa·bly** *adv.*

**cul·prit** (kul′prit) *n.* [< Anglo-Fr. *cul.*, contr. for *culpable*, guilty + *prit*, ready (i.e., to prove guilt)] **1.** a person accused of a crime or offense, as in a court **2.** a person guilty of a crime or offense; offender

**cult** (kult) *n.* [< L. *cultus*, care, orig. pp. of *colere*, to till] **1.** a system of religious worship or ritual **2.** *a)* devoted attachment to, or admiration for, a person, principle, etc. *b)* the object of such attachment **3.** a group of followers; sect —**cult′ic** *adj.* —**cult′ism** *n.* —**cult′ist** *n.*

**cul·ti·va·ble** (kul′tə və b'l) *adj.* that can be cultivated: also **cul′ti·vat′a·ble** (-vāt′ə b'l) —**cul′ti·va·bil′i·ty** *n.*

**cul·ti·vate** (kul′tə vāt′) *vt.* **-vat′ed, -vat′ing** [< ML. < LL. *cultivus*, tilled < L. *cultus*: see CULT] **1.** to prepare and use (land) for growing crops; till **2.** to break up the surface soil around (plants) in order to aerate it, destroy weeds, etc. **3.** to grow (plants or crops) **4.** to develop (plants) by various horticultural techniques **5.** to develop or improve by care, training, etc.; refine *[to cultivate one's mind]* **6.** to seek to become familiar with —**cul′ti·vat′ed** *adj.*

**cul·ti·va·tion** (kul′tə vā′shən) *n.* **1.** the act of cultivating (in various senses) **2.** refinement, or culture

**cul·ti·va·tor** (kul′tə vāt′ər) *n.* **1.** one who cultivates **2.** a tool or machine for loosening the earth and destroying weeds around growing plants

**cul·tur·al** (kul′chər əl) *adj.* **1.** of culture **2.** obtained by breeding —**cul′tur·al·ly** *adv.*

**cul·ture** (kul′chər) *n.* [< L. *cultura* < *colere*: see CULT] **1.** cultivation of the soil **2.** development or improvement of a particular plant or animal **3.** a growth of bacteria, etc.

in a specially prepared nourishing substance (**culture medium**) 4. *a*) development, improvement, or refinement of the mind, manners, taste, etc. *b*) the result of this 5. development or improvement of physical qualities by special training or care *[body culture]* 6. the ideas, customs, skills, arts, etc. of a given people in a given period; civilization —*vt.* **-tured, -tur·ing** to cultivate —**cul′tur·ist** *n.*

**cul·tured** (-chərd) *adj.* 1. produced by cultivation 2. refined in speech, behavior, etc.

**cul·tus** (kul′təs) *n.* [L.] a religious cult

**cul·ver·in** (kul′vər in) *n.* [< Fr. < L. *colubra*, a snake] 1. a musket used in the Middle Ages 2. a long cannon of the 16th and 17th centuries

**cul·vert** (kul′vərt) *n.* [< ?] a conduit, esp. a drain, under a road, through an embankment, etc.

**cum·ber** (kum′bər) *vt.* [< OFr. *en-combrer* < *en-* (see EN¹-) + *combre*, obstruction] 1. to hinder by obstruction or interference; hamper 2. to burden in a troublesome way

CULVERT

**Cum·ber·land** (kum′bər lənd) [after the Duke of *Cumberland* (1721–65), Eng. general] river in S Ky. & N Tenn., flowing west into the Ohio

**Cumberland Gap** pass in the W Appalachians, at the juncture of the Va., Ky., & Tenn. borders

**cum·ber·some** (kum′bər səm) *adj.* burdensome; unwieldy; clumsy —**cum′ber·some·ly** *adv.* —**cum′ber·some·ness** *n.*

**cum·brance** (kum′brəns) *n.* a troublesome burden

**cum·brous** (-brəs) *adj. same as* CUMBERSOME —**cum′brous·ly** *adv.* —**cum′brous·ness** *n.*

**cum·in** (kum′in) *n.* [< OFr. < L. < Gr. < Sem., as in Heb. *kammōn*, Ar. *kammūn*] 1. a small plant of the parsley family 2. its aromatic fruits, used for flavoring pickles, soups, etc. Also sp. **cum′min**

‡**cum lau·de** (koom lou′de, kum lô′dē) [L.] with praise: phrase used to signify graduation with honors from a college or university

**cum·mer·bund** (kum′ər bund′) *n.* [Hindi & Per. *kamarband*, loin band] a wide sash worn as a waistband, esp. with men's formal dress

**cum·quat** (kum′kwät) *n. same as* KUMQUAT

**cu·mu·late** (kyōōm′yə lāt′) *vt., vi.* **-lat′ed, -lat′ing** [< L. pp. of *cumulare*, to heap up < *cumulus*, a heap] *same as* ACCUMULATE —**cu′mu·la′tion** *n.*

**cu·mu·la·tive** (kyōōm′yə lāt′iv, -lə tiv) *adj.* [see prec.] increasing in effect, size, quantity, etc. by successive additions; accumulated *[cumulative* interest is interest added to the principal and drawing additional interest*]* —**cu′mu·la′tive·ly** *adv.*

**cu·mu·lo·nim·bus** (kyōōm′yoo lō nim′bəs) *n.* a towering cloud type, usually producing heavy rain

**cu·mu·lus** (-yə ləs) *n., pl.* **-li′** (-lī′) [L., a heap] 2. a thick cloud type with a dark, horizontal base and upper parts resembling domes —**cu′mu·lous** *adj.*

**cu·ne·ate** (kyōō′nē it, -āt′) *adj.* [< L. < *cuneus*, a wedge] wedge-shaped; tapering, as some leaves: also **cu′ne·al, cu′ne·at′ed** (-āt′id), **cu′ne·at′ic** (-at′ik)

**cu·ne·i·form** (kyōō nē′ə fôrm′, kyōō′nē ə-) *adj.* [< L. *cuneus* (see prec.) + -FORM] wedge-shaped; esp., designating the characters used in ancient Assyrian, Babylonian, and Persian inscriptions, or such inscriptions —*n.* cuneiform characters or inscriptions

**cun·ning** (kun′iŋ) *adj.* [ME. < prp. of *cunnen*, to know: see CAN¹] 1. [Now Rare] skillful or clever 2. skillful in deception; sly; crafty 3. made or done with skill or ingenuity 4. pretty in a delicate way; cute —*n.* 1. [Now Rare] skill 2. skill in deception; slyness; craftiness —**cun′ning·ly** *adv.* —**cun′ning·ness** *n.*

**cup** (kup) *n.* [OE. *cuppe* < LL. *cuppa* < L. *cupa*, tub] 1. a small, bowl-shaped container for beverages, often with a handle 2. the bowl part of a drinking vessel 3. a cup and its contents 4. the amount a cup holds; cupful: see CUPFUL 5. anything shaped like a cup 6. an ornamental cup given as a prize 7. the wine chalice at Communion; also, the wine 8. one's portion or allotment 9. something served in a cup 10. *Golf* the hole in each putting green —*vt.* **cupped, cup′ping** 1. to shape like a cup 2. to take in or put into a cup 3. *Med.* to subject to cupping —**in one's cups** drunk —**cup′like′** *adj.*

**cup·bear·er** (-ber′ər) *n.* a person who fills and serves the wine cups, as in a king's palace

**cup·board** (kub′ərd) *n.* a closet or cabinet with shelves for holding cups, plates, food, etc.

**cup·cake** (kup′kāk′) *n.* a little cake for one person, baked in a cup-shaped mold

**cup·ful** (kup′fool′) *n., pl.* **-fuls′** as much as a cup will hold: a standard measuring cup holds eight ounces

**Cu·pid** (kyōō′pid) [< C⁻r. < L. < *cupido*, desire] the Roman god of love, son of Venus: identified with the Greek god Eros —*n.* [c-] a representation of Cupid as a naked, winged cherub with bow and arrow

**cu·pid·i·ty** (kyōō pid′ə tē) *n.* [< Anglo-Fr. < L. < *cupere*, to desire] strong desire for wealth; greed

**cup of tea** [Colloq.] a favorite thing, activity, etc. *[golf isn't his cup of tea]*

**cu·po·la** (kyōō′pə lə) *n.* [It. < L. dim. of *cupa*, a tub] 1. a rounded roof or ceiling 2. a small dome or similar structure on a roof —**cu′po·laed** (-ləd) *adj.*

**cup·ping** (kup′iŋ) *n.* the use of a glass cup (**cupping glass**) from which the air has been exhausted, to draw blood to the surface of the skin: used, esp. formerly, in medicine —**cup′per** *n.*

**cu·pre·ous** (kyōō′prē əs) *adj.* [< L.: see COPPER¹] of, like, or containing copper

**cu·pric** (kyōō′prik) *adj.* [CUPR(O)- + -IC] *Chem.* of or containing copper with a valence of two

**cu·pro-** [< L. *cuprum*: see COPPER¹] *a combining form meaning* copper (and): also **cu·pri-, cupr-**

**cu·pro·nick·el** (kyōō′prō nik′'l) *n.* an alloy of copper and nickel, used in condenser tubes, some coins, etc.

**cu·prous** (kyōō′prəs) *adj.* [CUPR(O)- + -OUS] *Chem.* of or containing copper with a valence of one

**cur** (kur) *n.* [prob. < ON. *kurra* or MLowG. *korren*, to growl] 1. a dog of mixed breed; mongrel 2. a mean, contemptible, or cowardly person

**cur.** 1. currency 2. current

**cur·a·ble** (kyoor′ə b'l) *adj.* that can be cured —**cur′a·bil′i·ty** *n.*

**Cu·ra·çao** (kyoor′ə sô′, kyoor′ə sou′) largest island of the Netherlands Antilles, off the N coast of Venezuela —*n.* [c-] a liqueur flavored with orange peel

**cu·ra·cy** (kyoor′ə sē) *n., pl.* **-cies** the position, office, or work of a curate

**cu·ra·re, cu·ra·ri** (kyoo rä′rē, koo-) *n.* [< Port. or Sp. < native (Tupi) name] 1. a black, resinous substance prepared from the juices of certain S. American plants, used as an arrow poison by some Indians and in medicine to relax muscles 2. any of the plants from which this is prepared

**cu·rate** (kyoor′it) *n.* [< ML. < L. pp. of *curare*: see CURATOR] a clergyman who assists a vicar or rector

**cur·a·tive** (kyoor′ə tiv) *adj.* curing or having the power to cure —*n.* a thing that cures; remedy

**cu·ra·tor** (kyoo rāt′ər; kyoor′āt′ər, -ə tər) *n.* [L. < *curare*, take care of < *cura*, care] a person in charge of a museum, library, etc. —**cu·ra·to·ri·al** (kyoor′ə tôr′ē əl) *adj.* —**cu·ra′tor·ship′** *n.*

**curb** (kurb) *n.* [< OFr. < L. *curvus*, bent] 1. a chain or strap passed around a horse's lower jaw and attached to the bit, used to check the horse 2. anything that checks, restrains, or subdues 3. a raised margin along an edge, to strengthen or confine 4. the stone or concrete edging forming a gutter along a street 5. a market dealing in stocks and bonds not listed on the stock exchange —*vt.* 1. to restrain; check; control 2. to lead (a dog) to the curb to pass its waste matter 3. to provide with a curb

**curb bit** a horse's bit with a curb

**curb·ing** (-iŋ) *n.* 1. material for a curb 2. a curb (sense 4)

**curb roof** *same as* MANSARD ROOF *or* GAMBREL ROOF

**curb·stone** (-stōn′) *n.* any of the stones, or a row of stones, making up a curb

**cur·cu·li·o** (kər kyōō′lē ō′) *n., pl.* **-li·os′** [L., weevil] any of a family of weevils with long snouts: some are harmful to fruit

**curd** (kurd) *n.* [< ME. *crud*, orig., any coagulated substance] *[often pl.]* the coagulated part of milk, from which cheese is made: it is formed when milk sours and is distinguished from whey, the watery part —*vt., vi.* to curdle —**curd′y** *adj.*

**cur·dle** (kur′d'l) *vt., vi.* **-dled, -dling** [< CURD + -LE, freq. suffix] to form into curd; coagulate; congeal —**curdle one's blood** to horrify or terrify one

**cure** (kyoor) *n.* [OFr. < L. *cura*, care] 1. a healing or being healed 2. a medicine or treatment for restoring health; remedy 3. a method or course of treating a disease, ailment, etc. 4. *same as* CURACY 5. a process for curing meat, fish, tobacco, etc. —*vt.* **cured, cur′ing** 1. to restore to health or a sound condition; heal 2. to get rid of (an ailment, evil, etc.) 3. to get rid of an undesirable condition in (with *of*) *[cured* him of lying*]* 4. *a*) to preserve (meat, fish, etc.), as by salting or smoking *b*) to process (tobacco, leather, etc.), as by drying or aging —*vi.* 1. to bring about a cure  **2.** to undergo curing, preserving, or processing —**cure′less** *adj.* —**cur′er** *n.*

**cu·ré** (kyōō rā′) *n.* [Fr.]  in France, a parish priest

**cure-all** (kyōōr′ôl′) *n.* something supposed to cure all ailments or evils; panacea

**cu·ret, cu·rette** (kyōō ret′) *n.* [Fr. < *curer,* to cleanse] a spoon-shaped surgical instrument for the removal of tissue from the walls of body cavities —*vt.* **-ret′ted, -ret′ting** to clean or scrape with a curet

**cu·ret·tage** (kyōōr′ə täzh′, kyōō ret′ij) *n.* [Fr.: see prec.] the process of curetting

**cur·few** (kur′fyōō) *n.* [< OFr. *covrefeu* < *covrir,* to COVER + *feu,* fire < L. *focus,* fireplace] **1.** *a)* in the Middle Ages, the ringing of a bell every evening as a signal for people to cover fires, put out lights, and retire  *b)* the bell  *c)* the time at which it was rung  **2.** *a)* a time in the evening set as a deadline beyond which children, etc. may not appear on the streets  *b)* the regulation establishing this time

**cu·ri·a** (kyōōr′ē ə) *n., pl.* **-ri·ae′** (-ē′) [L.]  **1.** a medieval judicial court held in the king's name  **2.** [C-] the administrative body of the Roman Catholic Church, consisting of various departments, courts, officials, etc. functioning under the authority of the Pope: in full, **Curia Ro·ma·na** (rō-mä′nə, -mā′-) —**cu′ri·al** *adj.*

**Cu·rie** (kyōō rē′, kyōōr′ē; *Fr.* kü rē′), **Marie** (born *Marie Sklodowska*) 1867–1934; Pol. chemist & physicist in France: discoverer, with her husband **Pierre** (1859–1906), of polonium & radium

**cu·rie** (kyōōr′ē, kyōō rē′) *n.* [after Marie CURIE]  the unit used in measuring radioactivity

**cu·ri·o** (kyōōr′ē ō′) *n., pl.* **-os′** [contr. of CURIOSITY]  any unusual or rare article

**cu·ri·os·i·ty** (kyōōr′ē äs′ə tē) *n., pl.* **-ties** [< OFr. < L. *curiositas* < *curiosus:* see CURIOUS]  **1.** a desire to learn or know  **2.** a desire to learn about things that do not properly concern one  **3.** anything curious, rare, or novel

**cu·ri·ous** (kyōōr′ē əs) *adj.* [OFr. < L. *curiosus,* careful] **1.** eager to learn or know  **2.** unnecessarily inquisitive; prying  **3.** arousing attention or interest because unusual or strange —**cu′ri·ous·ly** *adv.* —**cu′ri·ous·ness** *n.*

**cu·ri·um** (kyōōr′ē əm) *n.* [ModL., after Marie & Pierre CURIE] a radioactive chemical element of the actinide series: symbol, Cm; at. wt., 247 (?); at. no., 96

**curl** (kurl) *vt.* [ME. *curlen* < *crul,* curly] **1.** to wind (esp. hair) into ringlets or coils  **2.** to cause to bend around  **3.** to raise the upper corner of (the lip), as in showing scorn —*vi.* **1.** to become curled  **2.** to form, or move in, a spiral or curve  **3.** to play the game of curling —*n.* **1.** a ringlet of hair  **2.** anything with a curled shape; coil  **3.** a curling or being curled —**curl up 1.** to gather into spirals or curls  **2.** to sit or lie with the legs drawn up —**in curl** curled —**curl′er** *n.*

**cur·lew** (kur′lōō, -lyōō) *n., pl.* **-lews, -lew:** see PLURAL, II, D, 1 [< OFr. *corlieu,* of echoic origin] a large, brownish wading bird with long legs

**curl·i·cue** (kur′li kyōō′) *n.* [< CURLY + CUE²] a fancy curve, flourish, etc., as in a design

**curl·ing** (kur′liŋ) *n.* a game played on ice by sliding a heavy disk (**curling stone**) toward a target circle

**curling iron** (or **irons**) a metal rod heated for curling or waving hair rolled around it

CURLEW (length to 19 in.; wingspread to 33 in.)

**curl·y** (kur′lē) *adj.* **curl′i·er, curl′i·est 1.** curling or tending to curl  **2.** having curls  **3.** having a wavy grain, as certain woods —**curl′i·ness** *n.*

**cur·mudg·eon** (kər muj′ən) *n.* [< ?] a surly, ill-mannered person; cantankerous fellow

**cur·rant** (kur′ənt) *n.* [< Anglo-Fr. (*raisins de*) *Corauntz,* lit., (raisins of) Corinth] **1.** a small, seedless raisin from the Mediterranean region  **2.** *a)* the sour, red, white, or black berry of several species of hardy shrubs, used for jellies and jams  *b)* a shrub bearing this fruit

**cur·ren·cy** (kur′ən sē) *n., pl.* **-cies** [< L. *currens:* see ff.] **1.** a continual passing from hand to hand; circulation  **2.** the money in circulation in any country  **3.** common acceptance or use; prevalence

**cur·rent** (kur′ənt) *adj.* [< OFr. < L. *currere,* to run] **1.** *a)* now in progress [his *current* job] *b)* contemporary [*current* fashions] *c)* of most recent date [the *current* edition] **2.** passing from person to person; circulating  **3.** commonly used or accepted; prevalent —*n.* **1.** a flow of water or air in a definite direction  **2.** a general tendency or drift; course  **3.** *Elec.* the flow or rate of flow of electric charge in a conductor —**cur′rent·ly** *adv.*

**cur·ri·cle** (kur′i k'l) *n.* [< L.: see ff.] a two-wheeled carriage drawn by two horses abreast

**cur·ric·u·lum** (kə rik′yə ləm) *n., pl.* **-u·la** (-lə), **-u·lums** [L., a course, race < *currere,* to run] **1.** a series of studies

required, as for graduation  **2.** all of the courses, collectively, offered in a school, college, etc., or in a particular subject —**cur·ric′u·lar** *adj.*

**cur·rish** (kur′ish) *adj.* like a cur; mean; ill-bred —**cur′rish·ly** *adv.*

**cur·ry¹** (kur′ē) *vt.* **-ried, -ry·ing** [< OFr. *correier,* to put in order] **1.** to rub down and clean the coat of (a horse, etc.) with a currycomb or brush  **2.** to prepare (tanned leather) by soaking, cleaning, beating, etc. —**curry favor** to try to win favor by flattery, fawning, etc. —**cur′ri·er** *n.*

**cur·ry²** (kur′ē) *n., pl.* **-ries** [Tamil *kari,* sauce] **1.** *same as* CURRY POWDER  **2.** a sauce made with curry powder  **3.** a kind of stew prepared with curry —*vt.* **-ried, -ry·ing** to prepare with curry powder

**cur·ry·comb** (kur′ē kōm′) *n.* a comb with teeth or ridges, to curry a horse —*vt.* to curry with this

**curry powder** a seasoning prepared from turmeric and various spices and herbs

**curse** (kurs) *n.* [Late OE. *curs,* n., *cursian,* v.] **1.** a calling on God or the gods to send evil or injury to some person or thing  **2.** a profane or blasphemous oath, imprecation, etc. **3.** a thing cursed  **4.** evil or injury that seems to come in answer to a curse  **5.** any cause of evil or injury —*vt.* **cursed** or **curst, curs′ing 1.** to call evil or injury down on; damn  **2.** to swear at  **3.** to bring evil or injury on; afflict —*vi.* to swear; blaspheme —**be cursed with** to suffer from —**curs′er** *n.*

CURRYCOMB

**curs·ed** (kur′sid, kurst) *adj.* **1.** under a curse  **2.** deserving to be cursed; specif., *a)* evil; wicked *b)* hateful —**curs′ed·ly** *adv.* —**curs′ed·ness** *n.*

**cur·sive** (kur′siv) *adj.* [ML. *cursivus* < L. *cursus:* see COURSE] designating or of writing in which the letters are joined in each word —*n.* **1.** a cursive character  **2.** *Printing* a typeface that looks like handwriting —**cur′sive·ly** *adv.* —**cur′sive·ness** *n.*

**cur·so·ry** (kur′sər ē) *adj.* [< L. < *cursor,* runner < *cursus:* see COURSE] hastily, often superficially, done; performed rapidly with little attention to detail —**cur′so·ri·ly** *adv.* —**cur′so·ri·ness** *n.*

**curt** (kurt) *adj.* [L. *curtus*] **1.** orig., short or shortened **2.** so brief as to be rude; terse; brusque [a *curt* reply] —**curt′ly** *adv.* —**curt′ness** *n.*

**cur·tail** (kər tāl′) *vt.* [< OFr. *curtald,* shortened < L. *curtus,* short] to cut short; reduce; abridge —**cur·tail′er** *n.* —**cur·tail′ment** *n.*

**cur·tain** (kur′t'n) *n.* [< OFr. < LL. *cortina,* circle of a theater < L. *cohors,* a COURT] **1.** a piece of cloth, etc., often one that can be drawn up or sideways, hung, as at a window, to decorate, cover, or conceal  **2.** anything that covers, conceals, or shuts off  **3.** *Theater a)* the drape at the front of the stage, which is drawn up or aside to reveal the stage  *b)* the opening or the closing of the curtain for a play, act, or scene  **4.** [*pl.*] [Slang] death; the end —*vt.* to provide or shut off as with a curtain —**draw (or drop) the curtain on 1.** to end  **2.** to conceal —**lift (or raise) the curtain on 1.** to begin  **2.** to reveal

**curtain call 1.** a call, usually by continued applause, for the performers to return to the stage  **2.** such a return, acknowledging the applause

**curtain raiser 1.** a short play or skit presented before a longer production  **2.** any brief preliminary event

**curtain wall** an independently supported outer wall bearing only its own weight

**Cur·tis** (kur′tis) [< ONormFr. *curteis,* courteous] a masculine name

**curt·sy** (kurt′sē) *n., pl.* **-sies** [var. of COURTESY] a gesture of greeting, respect, etc. made, esp. formerly, by girls and women and characterized by a bending of the knees and a slight lowering of the body —*vi.* **-sied, -sy·ing** to make a curtsy Also sp. **curt′sey**

**cur·va·ceous** (kər vā′shəs) *adj.* [CURV(E) + -ACEOUS] [Colloq.] having a full, shapely figure: said of a woman

**cur·va·ture** (kur′və chər) *n.* **1.** a curving or being curved **2.** a curve; curved part of anything

**curve** (kurv) *n.* [L. *curvus,* bent] **1.** a line having no straight part; bend with no angles  **2.** a thing or part with the shape of a curve  **3.** a curving, or the extent of this **4.** a curved line indicating variations, as in prices  **5.** *Baseball* a pitched ball thrown so that it curves before crossing the plate  **6.** *Math.* a one-dimensional continuum of points in a space of two or more dimensions —*vt., vi.* **curved, curv′ing 1.** to form a curve by bending  **2.** to move in a curve

**cur·vet** (kur′vit; *for v.,* usually kər vet′) *n.* [< It. dim. < *corvo* < L. *curvus,* bent] an upward leap by a horse, raising its hind legs just before its forelegs come down again —*vi.* **-vet′ted** or **-vet′ed, -vet′ting** or **-vet′ing 1.** to make a curvet  **2.** to leap; frolic —*vt.* to cause to curvet

**cur·vi·lin·e·ar** (kur′və lin′ē ər) *adj.* consisting of or enclosed by a curved line or lines: also **cur′vi·lin′e·al**

**curv·y** (kur′vē) *adj.* **curv′i·er, curv′i·est** 1. having curves or a curve 2. [Colloq.] curvaceous

**cush·ion** (koosh′ən) *n.* [< OFr. *coissin* < ML. *coxinum* (infl. by L. *coxa*, hip) < L. *culcita*] 1. a pillow or pad for sitting or kneeling on, or reclining against 2. a thing like this in shape or use 3. anything serving to absorb shock, as air or steam in some machines, the elastic inner rim of a billiard table, or a soft, padded insole 4. anything that relieves distress, provides comfort, etc. —*vt.* 1. to provide with a cushion 2. to seat or set on a cushion 3. to absorb (shock or noise) 4. to act as a cushion as in protecting from injury, relieving distress, etc.

**Cush·it·ic** (kush it′ik, koosh-) *adj.* [< *Cush*, son of HAM] designating of a group of languages spoken in Ethiopia and E Africa —*n.* this group of languages

**cush·y** (koosh′ē) *adj.* **cush′i·er, cush′i·est** [orig. Brit. army slang < Hindi *khush*, pleasant < Per.] [Slang] easy; comfortable [a *cushy* job] —**cush′i·ly** *adv.* —**cush′i·ness** *n.*

**cusp** (kusp) *n.* [L. *cuspis*, a point] 1. a pointed end; peak 2. any of the elevations on the chewing surface of a tooth 3. any triangular fold of a heart valve 4. either horn of a crescent, as of the moon 5. *Geom.* a corner point formed by two tangent branches of a curve

**cus·pid** (kus′pid) *n.* a canine tooth: see CANINE

**cus·pi·date** (kus′pə dāt′) *adj.* 1. having a cusp or cusps 2. having a short, abrupt point, as some leaves Also **cus′-pi·dat′ed**

**cus·pi·dor** (kus′pə dôr′) *n.* [< Port. < *cuspir*, to spit < L. < *com-*, intens. + *spuere*, to spit out] *same as* SPITTOON

**cuss** (kus) *n.* [< CURSE] [Colloq.] 1. a curse 2. a person or animal regarded as queer or annoying —*vt., vi.* [Colloq.] to curse —**cuss′ed** (-id) *adj.* —**cuss′ed·ly** *adv.* —**cuss′ed·ness** *n.* —**cuss′er** *n.*

**cus·tard** (kus′tərd) *n.* [< L. *crusta*, a crust] 1. a mixture of eggs, milk, flavoring, and, often, sugar, either boiled or baked 2. a similar mixture frozen like ice cream: in full, **frozen custard**

**cus·tard-ap·ple** (-ap′'l) *n.* 1. any of several tropical trees with edible, heart-shaped fruits 2. the fruit

**Cus·ter** (kus′tər), **George Armstrong** 1839–76; U.S. army officer: killed in a battle with Sioux Indians

**cus·to·di·an** (kəs tō′dē ən) *n.* 1. one who has the custody or care of something; keeper 2. a janitor —**cus·to′-di·an·ship′** *n.*

**cus·to·dy** (kus′tə dē) *n., pl.* **-dies** [< L. < *custos*, a guard] a guarding or keeping safe; care —**in custody** in the keeping of the police; under arrest —**take into custody** to arrest —**cus·to′di·al** (-tō′dē əl) *adj.*

**cus·tom** (kus′təm) *n.* [< OFr. < L. *consuetudo* < *com-*, intens. + *suere*, to be accustomed] 1. a usual practice or habitual way of behaving; habit 2. *a)* a social convention carried on by tradition *b)* such practices, collectively 3. [*pl.*] *a)* duties or taxes imposed by a government on imported and, occasionally, exported goods *b)* [*with sing. v.*] the agency in charge of collecting these duties 4. the regular patronage of a business establishment 5. *Law* such usage as by common consent and long-established practice has taken on the force of law —*adj.* 1. made or done to order or as if to order 2. making things to order, or dealing in such things

**cus·tom·ar·y** (kus′tə mer′ē) *adj.* 1. in keeping with custom, or usage; usual; habitual 2. *Law* holding or held by custom —**cus′tom·ar′i·ly** *adv.* —**cus′tom·ar′i·ness** *n.*

**cus·tom-built** (kus′təm bilt′) *adj.* built to order, according to the customer's specifications

**cus·tom·er** (kus′tə mər) *n.* [see CUSTOM] 1. a person who buys, esp. one who patronizes an establishment regularly 2. [Colloq.] any person with whom one has dealings [a rough *customer*]

**cus·tom·house** (kus′təm hous′) *n.* a building or office where customs or duties are paid, and ships cleared for entering or leaving: also **cus′toms·house′**

**cus·tom·ize** (-īz′) *vt., vi.* **-ized′, -iz′ing** [CUSTOM + -IZE] to make or build according to individual specifications —**cus′tom·iz′er** *n.*

**cus·tom-made** (-mād′) *adj.* made to order, according to the customer's specifications

**cut** (kut) *vt.* **cut, cut′ting** [ME. *cutten*] 1. to make an opening in as with a sharp-edged instrument; pierce; gash 2. to pierce sharply so as to hurt 3. to hurt the feelings of 4. to grow (a new tooth making its way through the gum) 5. to divide into parts with a sharp-edged instrument; sever 6. to carve (meat) 7. to fell; hew 8. to mow or reap 9. to pass through or across; intersect [the path *cuts* the meadow] 10. to divide (a pack of cards) at random before dealing 11. to stop photographing (a motion-picture

scene) 12. to reduce; lessen; curtail [to *cut* salaries] 13. to make shorter by trimming (hair, branches, etc.) 14. to dilute (alcohol, etc.) 15. to dissolve the fat globules of [lye *cuts* grease] 16. to make or do by or as by cutting; specif., *a)* to make (an opening, clearing, channel, etc.) *b)* to type or otherwise mark (a stencil) for mimeographing *c)* to cut cloth so as to form (a garment) *d)* to perform [to *cut* a caper] *e)* to hit, drive, or throw (a ball) so that it spins or is deflected *f)* to cause (a wheel) to turn sharply *g)* to edit (movie film) as by deleting scenes *h)* to make a recording of (a speech, music, etc.) on (a phonograph record) 17. [Colloq.] to pretend not to see or know (a person) 18. [Colloq.] to stay away from (a school class, etc.) without being excused 19. [Slang] to stop; discontinue —*vi.* 1. to do the work of a sharp-edged instrument; pierce; sever, gash, etc. 2. to work as a cutter 3. to take cutting [pine *cuts* easily] 4. to use an instrument that cuts 5. to cause pain by sharp, piercing strokes [the wind *cut* through his coat] 6. to swing a bat, etc. (*at* a ball) 7. to move swiftly 8. to make a sudden shift to another scene, as in a movie —*adj.* 1. that has been cut 2. made or formed by cutting 3. reduced; lessened —*n.* 1. a cutting or being cut 2. a stroke or blow with a sharp-edged instrument, whip, etc. 3. a stroke taken at a ball 4. an opening, wound, etc. made by a sharp-edged instrument 5. the omission of a part 6. a piece or part cut off or out, as from a meat animal 7. *a)* the amount cut *b)* a reduction; decrease 8. the shortest way across: usually **short cut** 9. a passage or channel cut out or worn away 10. the style in which a thing is cut; fashion [a stylish *cut*] 11. an act, remark, etc. that hurts one's feelings 12. a block or plate engraved for printing, or the impression made from it 13. [Colloq.] the act of snubbing or ignoring 14. [Colloq.] an unauthorized absence from school, etc. 15. [Slang] a share, as of profits or loot —**a cut above** [Colloq.] somewhat better than —**cut across** to take a shorter course by going straight across —**cut a figure** to attract attention or make a (certain) impression —**cut and dried** 1. arranged beforehand 2. lifeless; dull; boring —**cut back** 1. to make shorter by cutting off the end 2. to reduce or discontinue (production, etc.) 3. to go back to earlier narrative events, as in a novel 4. to change direction suddenly, as a runner in football —**cut dead** [Colloq.] to snub completely —**cut down** 1. to make fall by cutting 2. to kill 3. to reduce; lessen —**cut in** 1. to move in suddenly 2. to interrupt 3. to interrupt a couple dancing in order to dance with one of them 4. to make a connection, as in an electrical circuit 5. to give a share to —**cut it fine** [Colloq.] to make exact calculations or distinctions —**cut it out** [Colloq.] to stop what one is doing —**cut loose** [Colloq.] to act without restraint —**cut no ice** [Colloq.] to make no impression —**cut off** 1. to sever 2. to stop abruptly 3. to shut off 4. to interrupt 5. to intercept 6. to disinherit —**cut out** 1. to remove by cutting 2. to remove; omit 3. to eliminate and take the place of (a rival) 4. to make or form as by cutting 5. [Colloq.] to discontinue; stop 6. [Slang] to leave abruptly —**cut out for** suited for —**cut short** to stop abruptly before the end —**cut up** 1. to cut into pieces 2. to inflict cuts on 3. [Colloq.] *a)* to criticize harshly *b)* to cause to be dejected 4. [Slang] to clown, joke, etc. to attract attention

**cu·ta·ne·ous** (kyoo tā′nē əs) *adj.* [< ML. < L. *cutis*, the skin] of, on, or affecting the skin

**cut·a·way** (kut′ə wā′) *n.* a man's formal daytime coat with the front of the skirt cut so as to curve back to the tails: also **cutaway coat** —*adj.* designating of or a diagram or model having outer parts cut away so as to show the inside

**cut·back** (kut′bak′) *n.* a cutting back; specif., a reduction, as of production, personnel, etc.

**cute** (kyoot) *adj.* **cut′er, cut′est** [< ACUTE] [Colloq.] 1. clever; sharp; shrewd 2. pretty, esp. in a dainty way 3. straining for effect; artificial —**cute′ly** *adv.* —**cute′-ness** *n.*

**cut glass** glass, esp. flint glass, shaped or ornamented by grinding and polishing —**cut′-glass′** *adj.*

**cut·i·cle** (kyoot′i k'l) *n.* [L. *cuticula*, skin, dim. < *cutis*, skin] 1. *same as* EPIDERMIS 2. hardened skin accumulating at the base and sides of a fingernail or toenail 3. *Zool.* the tough, nonliving outer structure secreted by the epidermis in many invertebrates

**cu·tin·i·za·tion** (kyoot′'n ə zā′shən) *n.* [< L. *cutis*, skin] a process in which the outermost plant cells become thickened and covered with a varnishlike material (**cutin**), making them waterproof —**cu′tin·ize′** (-īz′) *vi., vt.* **-ized′, -iz′ing**

**cu·tis** (kyoot′is) *n.* [L.] 1. the vertebrate skin, including both of its layers, the dermis and the epidermis 2. the dermis only

**cut·lass, cut·las** (kut'ləs) *n.* [< Fr. < It. < L. < *culter*, a knife] a short, thick, curved sword with a single cutting edge, formerly used esp. by sailors

**cut·ler** (kut'lər) *n.* [< Anglo-Fr. < OFr. < ML. < L. < *culter*, a knife] a person who makes, sells, or repairs knives and other cutting tools

**cut·ler·y** (kut'lər ē) *n.* 1. the work or business of a cutler 2. cutting instruments, such as knives and scissors; often, specif., such implements used in preparing food

**cut·let** (kut'lit) *n.* [< Fr. *côtelette* < OFr. dim. of *coste*, a rib < L. *costa*] 1. a small slice of meat from the ribs or leg, often breaded and fried, etc. 2. a small, flat croquette of chopped meat or fish

**cut·off** (kut'ôf') *n.* 1. the act of cutting off; esp., the limit set for a process, activity, etc. 2. a road or passage that is a short cut 3. the act of stopping steam, etc. from entering the cylinder of an engine 4. any device for cutting off the flow of a fluid, a connection, etc.

**cut·out** (-out') *n.* 1. a device for breaking or closing an electric circuit 2. a device for letting the exhaust gases of an internal-combustion engine pass directly into the air instead of through a muffler 3. a design to be cut out

**cut·o·ver** (-ō'vər) *adj.* cleared of trees

**cut·purse** (-purs') *n.* 1. orig., a thief who cut purses from belts 2. a pickpocket

**cut-rate** (-rāt') *adj.* 1. available at a lower price 2. offering cut-rate goods or services

**cut·ter** (kut'ər) *n.* 1. a device for cutting 2. a person whose work is cutting, as the sections of a garment 3. a small, swift vessel; specif., *a*) a boat carried by large ships as a communications tender: also **ship's cutter** *b*) an armed sailing vessel, formerly used to pursue smugglers, etc.: also **revenue cutter** *c*) a small, armed, engine-powered ship, used by the Coast Guard: also **Coast Guard cutter** *d*) a single-masted sailboat with two headsails 4. a small, light sleigh, usually drawn by one horse

**cut·throat** (kut'thrōt') *n.* a murderer —*adj.* 1. murderous 2. merciless; ruthless

**cut·ting** (kut'iŋ) *n.* 1. the act of one that cuts 2. a piece cut off 3. [Brit.] a newspaper clipping 4. a shoot cut away from a plant for rooting or grafting —*adj.* 1. that cuts; sharp 2. chilling or piercing 3. sarcastic; harsh —**cut'ting·ly** *adv.*

**cut·tle·bone** (kut''l bōn') *n.* the internal shell of cuttlefish, used as food for caged birds and, when powdered, as a polishing agent

**cut·tle·fish** (-fish') *n., pl.* -**fish'**, -**fish'es**: see FISH [OE. *cudele*] a squidlike sea mollusk with ten sucker-bearing arms and a hard internal shell: when in danger, some cuttlefish eject an inky fluid: also **cuttle**

**cut·up** (kut'up') *n.* [Colloq.] a person who clowns, plays practical jokes, etc. to attract attention

**cut·wa·ter** (-wôt'ər, -wät'ər) *n.* the fore part of a ship's stem

**cut·worm** (-wurm') *n.* any of a number of caterpillars that feed on young plants of cabbage, corn, etc., cutting them off at ground level

**Cuy·a·ho·ga Falls** (kī'ə hō'gə, -hô'-) [< Iroquois name] city in NE Ohio: suburb of Akron: pop. 50,000

**Cuz·co** (kōōs'kō) city in S Peru: capital of the former Inca empire: pop. 93,000

**CWO** Chief Warrant Officer

**C.W.O., c.w.o.** cash with order

**cwt.** hundredweight

**-cy** (sē, si) [< OFr. -*cie*, L. -*cia*, Gr. -*kia*] *a suffix meaning:* 1. quality, condition, state, or fact of being [*hesitancy*] 2. position, rank, or office of [*curacy*]

**cy·a·nate** (sī'ə nāt') *n.* a salt of cyanic acid

**cy·an·ic** (sī an'ik) *adj.* 1. of or containing cyanogen 2. blue

**cyanic acid** a colorless, poisonous acid, HOCN

**cy·a·nide** (sī'ə nīd', -nid) *n.* a compound containing the cyanogen radical, —CN; esp., potassium cyanide, KCN, or sodium cyanide, NaCN, highly poisonous compounds with many industrial uses

**cy·an·o·gen** (sī an'ə jən) *n.* [< Gr. *kyanos*, blue + -GEN] 1. a colorless, poisonous, flammable gas, $C_2N_2$ 2. the univalent radical —CN, in cyanides

**cy·a·no·sis** (sī'ə nō'sis) *n.* [ModL. < Gr. *kyanos*, blue] a bluish coloration of the skin caused by lack of oxygen in the blood —**cy'a·not'ic** (-nät'ik) *adj.*

**Cyb·e·le** (sib'ə lē) a nature goddess of ancient Asia Minor: identified with the Greek goddess Rhea

**cy·ber·na·tion** (sī'bər nā'shən) *n.* [CYBERN(ETICS) + -ATION] the use of computers in connection with automation —**cy'ber·nate'** *vt.* -**nat'ed, -nat'ing**

**cy·ber·net·ics** (sī'bər net'iks) *n.pl.* [*with sing. v.*] [< Gr. *kybernētēs*, helmsman + -ICS] a science dealing with the comparative study of the operations of complex electronic computers and the human nervous system —**cy'ber·net'ic** *adj.*

**cyc.** 1. cyclopedia 2. cyclopedic

**cy·cad** (sī'kad) *n.* [ModL. *Cycas* < Gr. *kykas*, erroneous pl. of *koīx*, a palm] any of an order of tropical shrubs and trees resembling thick-stemmed palms, with crowns of leathery, fernlike leaves

**Cyc·la·des** (sik'lə dēz') group of Greek islands in the S Aegean: 995 sq. mi.

**cy·cla·mate** (sī'klə māt', sik'lə-) *n.* a complex organic compound with an extremely sweet taste

**cyc·la·men** (sī'klə mən, sik'lə-) *n., pl.* -**mens** [< L. < Gr. *kyklaminos*] a plant of the primrose family, having heart-shaped leaves and white, pink, or red flowers with reflexed petals

**cy·cle** (sī'k'l) *n.* [< LL. *cyclus* < Gr. *kyklos*, a circle] 1. *a*) a period of time within which a round of regularly recurring events is completed *b*) a complete set or series of such events 2. a very long period of time; an age 3. all the traditional poems, songs, etc. connected with a hero or an event 4. a series of poems or songs on the same theme 5. a bicycle, tricycle, or motorcycle 6. *Elec.* one complete period of the reversal of an alternating current —*vi.* -**cled, -cling** 1. to occur in cycles; pass through a cycle 2. to ride a bicycle, tricycle, or motorcycle

**cy·clic** (sī'klik, sik'lik) *adj.* 1. of, or having the nature of, a cycle; moving or occurring in cycles 2. *Chem.* arranged in a ring or closed-chain structure: said of atoms Also **cy'cli·cal** —**cy'cli·cal·ly** *adv.*

**cy·clist** (sī'klist) *n.* a person who rides a bicycle, motorcycle, etc.

**cy·cli·zine** (sī'klə zēn') *n.* an antihistamine, $C_{18}H_{22}N_2$, used to treat nausea and motion sickness

**cy·clo-** [< Gr. *kyklos*, a circle] *a combining form meaning* of a circle or wheel, circular: also, before a vowel, **cycl-**

**cy·cloid** (sī'kloid) *adj.* [< Gr. < *kyklos*, a circle + *eidos*, form] circular: also **cy·cloi·dal** (sī kloi'd'l)

**cy·clom·e·ter** (sī kläm'ə tər) *n.* [CYCLO- + -METER] an instrument that records the revolutions of a wheel, for measuring distance traveled

**cy·clone** (sī'klōn) *n.* [< Gr. *kykloein*, to whirl < *kyklos*, a circle] 1. loosely, a violent, whirling windstorm; tornado or hurricane 2. *Meteorol.* a storm with strong winds rotating about a moving center of low atmospheric pressure —**cy·clon·ic** (sī klän'ik) *adj.* —**cy·clon'i·cal·ly** *adv.*

**Cy·clo·pe·an** (sī'klə pē'ən) *adj.* 1. of the Cyclopes 2. [c-] huge; gigantic; enormous

**cy·clo·pe·di·a, cy·clo·pae·di·a** (sī'klə pē'dē ə) *n.* same as ENCYCLOPEDIA —**cy'clo·pe'dic, cy'clo·pae'dic** *adj.* —**cy'clo·pe'dist, cy'clo·pae'dist** *n.*

**Cy·clops** (sī'kläps) *n., pl.* **Cy·clo·pes** (sī klō'pēz) [L. < Gr. < *kyklos*, a circle + *ōps*, an eye] *Gr. Myth.* any of a race of giants who had only one eye, centered in the forehead

**cy·clo·ra·ma** (sī'klə ram'ə) *n.* [CYCLO- + Gr. *horama*, sight] 1. a series of large pictures, as of a landscape, put on the wall of a circular room so as to suggest natural perspective to a viewer 2. a large, curved curtain or screen used as a background for stage sets —**cy'clo·ram'ic** *adj.*

**cy·clo·tron** (sī'klə trän') *n.* [CYCLO- + (ELEC)TRON] an apparatus for giving high energy to particles, usually protons and deuterons, so as to produce transmutations or radioactivity in a target element

**cyg·net** (sig'nət) *n.* [dim. < Fr. *cygne*, swan < VL. < L. *kyknos*, swan] a young swan

**cyl.** 1. cylinder 2. cylindrical

**cyl·in·der** (sil'ən dər) *n.* [< Fr. < L. < Gr. < *kylindein*, to roll] 1. *Geom.* a solid figure described by the edge of a rectangle rotated around the parallel edge as axis: the ends of a cylinder are parallel and equal circles 2. anything, hollow or solid, with the shape of a cylinder; specif., *a*) the turning part of a revolver, containing chambers for cartridges *b*) the chamber in which the piston moves in a reciprocating engine *c*) the barrel of a pump

**cy·lin·dri·cal** (sə lin'dri k'l) *adj.* 1. having the shape of a cylinder 2. of a cylinder Also **cy·lin'dric** —**cy·lin'dri·cal'i·ty** (-kal'ə tē) *n.* —**cy·lin'dri·cal·ly** *adv.*

**Cym.** Cymric

**cym·bal** (sim'b'l) *n.* [< OFr. & OE. < L. < Gr. < *kymbē*, hollow of a vessel] a circular, slightly concave brass plate used as a percussion instrument: it is struck with a drumstick, brush, etc. or used in pairs which are struck together to produce a crashing, ringing sound —**cym'bal·ist** *n.*

**cym·bid·i·um** (sim bid'ē əm) *n., pl.* -**i·ums, -i·a** (-ə) [ModL. < L. *cymba*, a boat < Gr. *kymbē* < ModL. -*idium*, dim. suffix] any of various tropical Asiatic orchids with sprays of white, pink, yellow, or maroon flowers

CYMBALS

**cyme** (sīm) *n.* [< L. < Gr. *kyma*, swelling < *kyein*, to be pregnant] a flat-topped flower cluster in which the central flower blooms first, followed by the outer ones —**cy·mose** (sī′mōs, sī mōs′) *adj.*

**Cym·ric** (kim′rik; *occas.* sim′-) *adj.* [< W. < *Cymru*, Wales] **1.** of the Celtic people of Wales **2.** of their language —*n.* Brythonic: see CELTIC

**Cym·ry** (-rē) *n.pl.* the Cymric Celts; the Welsh

**cyn·ic** (sin′ik) *n.* [see ff.] **1.** [C-] a member of a school of ancient Greek philosophers who held virtue to be the only good, and stressed independence from worldly needs and pleasures: they became critical of materialistic social values **2.** a cynical person —*adj.* **1.** [C-] of or like the Cynics or their doctrines **2.** *same as* CYNICAL

**cyn·i·cal** (sin′i k'l) *adj.* [< L. < Gr. *kynikos*, canine < *kyōn*, dog] **1.** denying the sincerity of people's motives and actions, or the value of living **2.** sarcastic, sneering, etc. **3.** [C-] *same as* CYNIC —**cyn′i·cal·ly** *adv.* —**cyn′i·cal·ness** *n.*

**cyn·i·cism** (sin′ə siz'm) *n.* **1.** [C-] the philosophy of the Cynics **2.** the attitude or beliefs of a cynical person **3.** a cynical remark, idea, or action

**cy·no·sure** (sī′nə shoor′, sin′ə-) [L. < Gr. *kynosoura*, dog's tail] [C-] *an old name for:* **1.** URSA MINOR **2.** NORTH STAR —*n.* any person or thing that is a center of attention or interest

**Cyn·thi·a** (sin′thē ə) [L. < Gr. *Kynthia*, epithet of Artemis] **1.** a feminine name **2.** Artemis, goddess of the moon **3.** the moon personified

**cy·pher** (sī′fər) *n., vt., vi.* Brit. *var. of* CIPHER

**cy·press** (sī′prəs) *n.* [< OFr. < L. *cupressus* < Gr. *kyparissos*] **1.** any of a group of dark-foliaged, cone-bearing evergreens, native to N. America, Europe, and Asia **2.** any of a number of related trees **3.** the wood of any of these **4.** cypress branches used as a symbol of mourning

**cyp·ri·noid** (sip′rə noid′) *adj.* [< Gr. *kyprinos*, carp + -OID] of or like the fishes of the carp family —*n.* any of a family of freshwater fishes, including the carps, minnows, dace, etc. Also **cyp′ri·nid** (-nid)

**cyp·ri·pe·di·um** (sip′rə pē′dē əm) *n., pl.* **-di·ums, -di·a** (-ə) [ModL. < Gr. *Kypris*, Venus + *podion*, slipper] *same as* LADY-SLIPPER

**Cy·prus** (sī′prəs) country on an island at the E end of the Mediterranean: a member of the Commonwealth: 3,572 sq. mi.; pop. 630,000; cap. Nicosia —**Cyp·ri·ot** (sip′-rē ət) *adj., n.*

**Cyr·il** (sir′əl) [< Gr. < *kyrios*, lord] a masculine name

**Cyr·il·lic** (sə ril′ik) *adj.* designating or of the Slavic alphabet attributed to Saint Cyril, 9th-cent. apostle to the Slavs: it is used in Russia, Bulgaria, and other Slavic countries

**Cy·rus** (sī′rəs) [L. < Gr. < OPer. *Kūrush*] **1.** a masculine name **2.** ?-529 B.C.; king of the Medes & Persians: founded Persian Empire: called *the Great*

**cyst** (sist) *n.* [ModL. *cystis* < Gr. *kystis*, sac] **1.** any of certain saclike structures in plants or animals; specif., such a structure when abnormal and filled with fluid or diseased matter **2.** a protective membrane surrounding certain organisms in a resting stage —**cyst′ic** *adj.* —**cyst′oid** *adj., n.*

**-cyst** (sist) [see prec.] *a suffix meaning* sac, pouch, bladder [*encyst*]

**cys·ti·cer·cus** (sis′tə sur′kəs) *n., pl.* **-cer′ci** (-sī) [ModL. < CYSTI- (see CYSTO-) + Gr. *kerkos*, tail] the larva of certain tapeworms having the head and neck partly enclosed in a cyst

**cystic fibrosis** a congenital disease of children, characterized by fibrosis and malfunctioning of the pancreas, and frequent respiratory infections

**cys·ti·tis** (sis tīt′is) *n.* [CYST- + -ITIS] an inflammation of the urinary bladder

**cys·to-** [see CYST] *a combining form meaning* of or like a bladder or sac: also **cyst-, cysti-**

**cys·to·scope** (sis′tə skōp′) *n.* [CYSTO- + -SCOPE] an instrument for visually examining the interior of the urinary bladder —*vt.* **-scoped′, -scop′ing** to examine with a cystoscope —**cys′to·scop′ic** (-skäp′ik) *adj.* —**cys·tos′co·py** (-täs′kə pē) *n.*

**-cyte** (sīt) [< Gr. *kytos*, a hollow] *a combining form meaning* a cell [*lymphocyte*]

**Cyth·e·re·a** (sith′ə rē′ə) *same as* APHRODITE —**Cyth′e·re′an** *adj.*

**cy·to-** [see -CYTE] *a combining form meaning* of a cell or cells: also, before a vowel, **cyt-**

**cy·to·ge·net·ics** (sīt′ō jə net′iks) *n.pl.* [with sing. *v.*] the science correlating cytology and genetics with regard to heredity and variation —**cy′to·ge·net′ic, cy′to·ge·net′i·cal** *adj.* —**cy′to·ge·net′i·cal·ly** *adv.* —**cy′to·ge·net′i·cist** *n.*

**cy·tol·o·gy** (sī täl′ə jē) *n.* [CYTO- + -LOGY] the branch of biology dealing with the structure, function, pathology, and life history of cells —**cy·to·log·ic** (sī′tə läj′ik), **cy′to·log′i·cal** *adj.* —**cy′to·log′i·cal·ly** *adv.* —**cy·tol′o·gist** *n.*

**cy·to·plasm** (sīt′ə plaz′m) *n.* [CYTO- + -PLASM] the protoplasm of a cell, exclusive of the nucleus: also **cy′to·plast′** —**cy′to·plas′mic** *adj.*

**cy·to·sine** (sīt′ə sēn′) *n.* [G. *zytosin*] a nitrogenous base, $C_4H_5N_3O$, a constituent of various nucleic acids

**C.Z., CZ** Canal Zone

**czar** (zär) *n.* [< Russ. < OSlav. via Goth. < L. *Caesar*] **1.** an emperor: title of any of the former emperors of Russia **2.** an absolute ruler; despot —**czar′dom** *n.* —**czar′ism** *n.* —**czar′ist** *adj., n.*

**czar·das** (chär′dəsh, -däsh) *n.* [Hung. *csárdás*] **1.** a Hungarian dance with fast and slow sections **2.** music for this dance

**czar·e·vitch** (zär′ə vich′) *n.* [< Russ.] the eldest son of a czar of Russia

**cza·ri·na** (zä rē′nə) *n.* [< G. < Russ. *tsaritsa*] the wife of a czar; empress of Russia: also **cza·rit′za** (-rit′sə)

**Czech** (chek) *n.* **1.** a Bohemian, Moravian, or Silesian Slav of Czechoslovakia **2.** the West Slavic language of the Czechs —*adj.* of Czechoslovakia, its people, or their language: also **Czech′ish**

**Czech·o·slo·vak** (chek′ə slō′väk) *adj.* of Czechoslovakia or its people —*n.* a Czech or Slovak living in Czechoslovakia Also **Czech′o·slo·vak′i·an** (-slō vä′kē ən)

**Czech·o·slo·va·ki·a** (chek′ə slō vä′kē ə) country in C Europe, east of Germany: 49,367 sq. mi.; pop. 14,445,000; cap. Prague

# D

**D, d** (dē) *n., pl.* **D's, d's** **1.** the fourth letter of the English alphabet **2.** the sound of *D* or *d* **3.** *a symbol for the* fourth in a sequence or group

**D** (dē) *n.* **1.** a Roman numeral for 500 **2.** *Chem.* deuterium **3.** *Educ.* a grade indicating below-average work, or merely passing **4.** *Music* a) the second tone in the ascending scale of C major b) the scale having this tone as the keynote **5.** *Physics the symbol for* density

**D.** **1.** December **2.** Democrat(ic) **3.** Dutch

**d.** **1.** daughter **2.** day(s) **3.** dead **4.** delete **5.** diameter **6.** died **7.** dose **8.** dyne **9.** [L. *denarius*, pl. *denarii*] penny; pence

**'d** **1.** *contracted auxiliary form of* had or would [*I'd, they'd*] **2.** *contraction of* -ed [*foster'd*]

**D.A.** District Attorney

**dab¹** (dab) *vt., vi.* **dabbed, dab′bing** [ME. *dabben*, to strike] **1.** to touch lightly and quickly **2.** to pat with something

soft or moist **3.** to put on (paint, etc.) with light, quick strokes —*n.* **1.** a light, quick stroke; tap; pat **2.** a bit, esp. of a soft or moist thing [*a dab of rouge*] —**dab′ber** *n.*

**dab²** (dab) *n.* [ME. *dabbe* < ?] **1.** any of several flounders of coastal waters **2.** any small flatfish

**dab·ble** (dab′'l) *vt.* **-bled, -bling** [Du. *dabbelen*, freq. of *dabben*, to strike, DAB¹] **1.** to dip lightly in and out of a liquid **2.** to spatter or splash —*vi.* **1.** to play in water, as with the hands **2.** to do something superficially (with *in* or *at*) [*to dabble in art*] —**dab′bler** *n.*

**dab·chick** (dab′chik′) *n.* [DAB¹ + CHICK] either of two small grebes of Europe and the Americas

**‡da ca·po** (dä kä′pō) [It.] *Music* from the beginning: a direction to repeat

**Dac·ca** (dak′ə, däk′ə) capital of Bangladesh, in the EC part: pop. 557,000

**dace** (dās) *n., pl.* **dace, dac′es:** see PLURAL, II, D, 2 [< OFr.

dars < VL. *darsus*] a small freshwater fish of the carp family
‡da·cha (dä′chə) *n.* [Russ.] a country house or cottage used as a summer home
Da·chau (dä′khou) city in S Germany: site of a Nazi concentration camp & extermination center
dachs·hund (däks′hoond, -hoont; dash′hund) *n.* [G. *dachs*, a badger + *hund*, a dog] a small dog of German breed, with a long body and short legs
Da·cron (dā′krän, dak′rän) [arbitrary coinage, after (NYL)ON] *a trademark for* a synthetic polyester fiber or a washable, wrinkle-resistant fabric made from it —*n.* [*also* d-] this fiber or fabric

DACHSHUND (8–10 in. high at shoulder)

dac·tyl (dak′t′l) *n.* [< L. < Gr. *dak-tylos*, a finger or (by analogy with a finger's three joints) a dactyl] a metrical foot of three syllables, the first accented and the others unaccented, as in English verse (Ex.: "táke hĕr ŭp/ téndĕrlў") —dac·tyl′ic *adj.*
dad (dad) *n.* [< child's cry *dada*] [Colloq.] father: also dad·dy (dad′ē), *pl.* -dies
da·da (dä′dä, -də) *n.* [Fr., lit., hobbyhorse < baby talk] [*also* D-] a cult (1916–22) in art and literature characterized by fantastic, abstract, or incongruous creations and by nihilistic satire: also da′da·ism —da′da·ist *adj., n.* —da′da·is′tic *adj.*
dad·dy-long·legs (dad′ē lôŋ′legz′) *n., pl.* -long′legs′ same as: 1. HARVESTMAN (sense 2) 2. CRANE FLY
da·do (dā′dō) *n., pl.* -does [< It. < L. *datum*, a die] 1. the part of a pedestal between the cap and the base 2. the lower part of the wall of a room if decorated differently from the upper part 3. *a*) a rectangular groove cut in the side of one board so that another board may be fitted into it *b*) the joint thus made: in full, dado joint —*vt.* -doed, -do·ing 1. to furnish with a dado 2. to fit into a dado groove
Daed·a·lus (ded′′l əs, dēd′-) *Gr. Myth.* the builder of the Labyrinth in Crete from which, by means of wings he fabricated, he and his son Icarus escaped —Dae·da·li·an, Dae·da·le·an (di dāl′yan, -ē ən) *adj.*
dae·mon (dē′mən) *n.* [L. < Gr. *daimōn*] 1. *Gr. Myth.* any of the secondary divinities ranking below the gods 2. a guardian spirit 3. *same as* DEMON —dae·mon·ic (di män′ik) *adj.*
daf·fa·down·dil·ly, daf·fy·down·dil·ly (daf′ə doun dil′ē) *n., pl.* -lies [Dial.] a daffodil: also daf′fo·dil′ly, daf′-fa·dil′ly, *pl.* -lies
daf·fo·dil (daf′ə dil′) *n.* [< ML. < L. < Gr. *asphodelos*] 1. any of several hardy kinds of narcissus, typically having a single, yellow flower and a large, trumpetlike central crown 2. the flower
daf·fy (daf′ē) *adj.* -fi·er, -fi·est [see ff.] [Colloq.] 1. crazy; foolish; silly 2. frolicsome in a giddy way —daf′fi·ness *n.*
daft (daft) *adj.* [< OE. (*ge*)*dæfte*, mild, gentle] 1. silly; foolish 2. insane; crazy —daft′ly *adv.* —daft′ness *n.*
da Gam·a (də gam′ə; *Port.* dä gä′mä), Vas·co (väs′kō) 1469?–1524; Port. navigator
dag·ger (dag′ər) *n.* [< ML. *daggarius*] 1. a weapon with a short, pointed blade, used for stabbing 2. *Printing* a reference mark (†) —*vt.* 1. to stab with a dagger 2. to mark with a dagger —look daggers at to look at with anger or hatred
Da·gon (dā′gän) [< LL. < LGr. < Heb.] the main god of the ancient Philistines, represented as half man and half fish
da·guerre·o·type (də ger′ə tīp′) *n.* [after L. J. M. *Daguerre* (1789–1851), Fr. inventor] 1. a photograph made by an early method on a plate of chemically treated metal or glass 2. this method —*vt.* -typed′, -typ′ing to photograph by this method —da·guerre′o·typ′y *n.*
Dag·wood (sandwich) (dag′wood′) [after a character in a comic strip by Chic Young (1901–73)] a tall sandwich with a wide variety of ingredients
dahl·ia (dal′yə, *chiefly Brit.* däl′-) *n.* [after A. *Dahl*, 18th-c. Swed. botanist] 1. a perennial plant of the composite family, with tuberous roots and large, showy flowers 2. the flower
Da·ho·mey (də hō′mē) *former name of* BENIN
Dail Eir·eann (dôl′er′ən) [Ir. *dáil*, assembly + *Éireann*, gen. of *Éire*, Ireland] the lower house of the legislature of Ireland
dai·ly (dā′lē) *adj.* 1. relating to, done, happening, or published every day or every weekday 2. calculated by the day [*daily rate*] —*n., pl.* -lies a daily newspaper —*adv.* every day; day after day
daily double a betting procedure or bet, the success of which depends on choosing both winners in two specified races on the same program
daily dozen [Colloq.] gymnastic setting-up exercises (originally twelve) done daily

dain·ty (dān′tē) *n., pl.* -ties [< OFr. *deinté*, worth, delicacy < L. *dignitas*, worth, dignity] a choice food; delicacy —*adj.* 1. delicious and choice 2. delicately pretty or lovely 3. *a*) of or showing delicate and refined taste *b*) overly fastidious; squeamish —dain′ti·ly *adv.* —dain′ti·ness *n.*
dai·qui·ri (dak′ər ē, dīk′-) *n.* [after *Daiquirī*, village in Cuba] a cocktail made of rum, sugar, and lime or lemon juice
dair·y (der′ē) *n., pl.* dair′ies [ME. *daierie* < *daie*, dairymaid < OE. *dæge*, breadmaker] 1. a room, building, etc. where milk and cream are kept and butter, cheese, etc. are made 2. a farm (dairy farm) in the business of producing milk and milk products 3. *a*) a commercial establishment that processes and distributes milk and milk products *b*) a retail store where these are sold —*adj.* of milk, cream, butter, cheese, etc.
dairy cattle cows raised mainly for their milk
dair·y·ing (-iŋ) *n.* the business of producing or selling dairy products
dair·y·maid (-mād′) *n.* a girl or woman who milks cows or works in a dairy
dair·y·man (-mən) *n., pl.* -men a man who works in or for a dairy or who owns a dairy
da·is (dā′is, dī′-) *n., pl.* da′is·es [< OFr. < ML. *discus*, table < L. *discus*, DISCUS] a platform raised above the floor at one end of a hall or room, as for a speaker's stand, seats of honor, etc.
Dai·sy (dā′zē) [< ff.] a feminine name
dai·sy (dā′zē) *n., pl.* -sies [< OE. *dæges eage*, lit., day's eye] 1. a plant of the composite family, bearing flowers with white rays around a yellow disk 2. any similar member of the composite family 3. the flower of any of these plants —push up (the) daisies [Slang] to be dead and buried
Da·kar (dä kär′, dak′är) capital of Senegal, at the western-most point of Africa: pop. 474,000
Da·ko·ta¹ (də kō′tə) *n.* [< Dakota *dakóta*, allies] 1. *pl.* -tas, -ta a member of a group of Indian tribes (also called Sioux) of the northern plains of the U.S. and adjacent S Canada 2. their Siouan language —*adj.* 1. of the Dakota Indians or their language 2. of North Dakota, South Dakota, or both —the Dakotas North Dakota and South Dakota —Da·ko′tan *adj., n.*
Da·ko·ta² (də kō′tə) [< prec.] former U.S. territory from which N.Dak. & S.Dak. were formed in 1889
Da·lai La·ma (dä lī′ lä′mə) [Mongol. *dalai*, ocean + *blama*: see LAMA] the traditional high priest of the Lamaist religion: see LAMAISM
da·la·si (dä′la sē) *n., pl.* -si [native term, lit., complete] *see* MONETARY UNITS, table (Gambia)
dale (dāl) *n.* [OE. *dæl*] a valley
d'A·lem·bert (dä län ber′), Jean le Rond (zhän lə rōn′) 1717–83; Fr. philosopher & encyclopedist
Da·li (dä′lē), Sal·va·dor (sal′və dôr′) 1904– ; Sp. surrealist painter
Dal·las (dal′əs) [after G. *Dallas* (1792–1864), U.S. vice president (1845–49)] city in NE Tex: pop. 904,000 (met. area, with Fort Worth, 2,964,000)
dal·li·ance (dal′ē əns) *n.* the act of dallying; flirting, toying, trifling, etc.
dal·ly (dal′ē) *vi.* -lied, -ly·ing [< OFr. *dalier*, to converse, trifle] 1. to make love in a playful way 2. to deal lightly or carelessly (*with*); trifle; toy 3. to waste time; loiter —dally away to waste (time) in trifling activities
Dal·ma·tia (dal mā′shə) region along the Adriatic coast of Yugoslavia: part of Croatia
Dal·ma·tian (-shən) *adj.* of Dalmatia or its people —*n.* a large, short-haired dog with dark spots on a white coat
‡dal se·gno (däl se′nyō) [It.] *Music* from the sign: a direction to return and repeat from the sign (𝄋)
Da·ly City (dā′lē) [after a prominent citizen, J. *Daly*] city in W Calif.: suburb of San Francisco: pop. 79,000
dam¹ (dam) *n.* [< Gmc. base seen in ON. *dammr*, to stop up] 1. a barrier built to hold back flowing water 2. the water thus kept back 3. any barrier like a dam —*vt.* dammed, dam′ming 1. to build a dam in 2. to keep back or confine as by a dam (usually with *up*)
dam² (dam) *n.* [ME., var. of *dame*, DAME] 1. the female parent of any four-legged animal 2. [Archaic] a mother
dam·age (dam′ij) *n.* [OFr. < L. *damnum*, loss, injury] 1. injury or harm resulting in a loss in soundness, value, etc. 2. [*pl.*] *Law* money claimed by, or ordered paid to, a person to compensate for injury, loss, etc. that is another's fault 3. [Colloq.] cost or expense —*vt.* -aged, -ag·ing to do damage to —*vi.* to incur damage —dam′age·a·ble *adj.*
Dam·a·scene (dam′ə sēn′, dam′ə sēn′) *adj.* [L. *Damas-cenus*, of Damascus] 1. of Damascus, its people, etc. 2. [d-] of damascening or damask —*n.* 1. a native or inhabitant of Damascus 2. [d-] damascened work —*vt.* -scened′, -scen′ing [d-] to decorate (steel, etc.) with wavy markings or with inlaid patterns of gold or silver
Da·mas·cus (də mas′kəs) capital of Syria, a very ancient city in the SC part: pop. 530,000

**Damascus steel** a hard, flexible steel decorated with wavy lines, orig. made in Damascus and used for sword blades: also **damask steel**

**dam·ask** (dam'əsk) *n.* [< It. < L. *Damascus* (the city)] 1. a durable, lustrous, reversible fabric as of silk or linen, in figured weave, used for table linen, upholstery, etc. 2. *a*) *same as* DAMASCUS STEEL *b*) the wavy markings of such steel 3. deep pink or rose —*adj.* 1. orig., of or from Damascus 2. made of damask 3. like damask 4. deep-pink or rose —*vt.* 1. to ornament with flowered designs or wavy lines 2. to make deep-pink or rose

**damask rose** a very fragrant rose important as a source of attar of roses

**dame** (dām) *n.* [OFr. < L. *domina,* lady, fem. of *dominus,* a lord] 1. orig., a title given to the mistress of a household 2. a lady 3. an elderly woman 4. [D-] in Great Britain *a*) the legal title of the wife of a knight or baronet *b*) the title of a woman who has received an order of knighthood 5. [Slang] a woman or girl

**damn** (dam) *vt.* **damned, damn'ing** [< OFr. < L. *damnare,* to condemn < *damnum,* loss] 1. *a*) to condemn to an unhappy fate; doom *b*) *Theol.* to condemn to endless punishment 2. to condemn as bad, inferior, etc. 3. to criticize adversely 4. to cause the ruin of; make fail 5. to swear at by saying "damn" —*vi.* to swear or curse; say "damn," etc. —*n.* the saying of "damn" as a curse —*adj., adv.* [Colloq.] *clipped form of* DAMNED —*interj.* an expression of anger, annoyance, disappointment, etc. —**damn with faint praise** to condemn by praising mildly —**not give (or care) a damn** [Colloq.] not care at all —**not worth a damn** [Colloq.] worthless

**dam·na·ble** (dam'nə b'l) *adj.* deserving to be damned; outrageous; execrable —**dam'na·bly** *adv.*

**dam·na·tion** (dam nā'shən) *n.* a damning or being damned —*interj.* an expression of anger, annoyance, etc.

**dam·na·to·ry** (dam'nə tôr'ē) *adj.* 1. threatening with damnation; damning 2. condemning [*damnatory* evidence]

**damned** (damd; *occas.* dam'nid) *adj.* 1. condemned or deserving condemnation 2. [Colloq.] deserving cursing; outrageous: now often a mere intensive [*a damned* shame] —*adv.* [Colloq.] very [*a damned* good job] —**do (or try) one's damnedest (or damndest)** [Colloq.] to do or try one's utmost —**the damned** *Theol.* souls doomed to eternal punishment

**Dam·o·cles** (dam'ə klēz') a courtier of ancient Syracuse who, according to legend, was given a lesson in the perils to a ruler's life when the king seated him at a feast under a sword hanging by a hair —**sword of Damocles** any imminent danger

**dam·oi·selle, dam·o·sel, dam·o·zel** (dam'ə zel') *n.* [Archaic or Poet.] a damsel

**Da·mon and Pyth·i·as** (dā'mən ən pith'ē əs) *Classical Legend* friends so devoted to each other that when Pythias, who had been condemned to death, wanted time to arrange his affairs, Damon pledged his life that his friend would return

**damp** (damp) *n.* [MDu., vapor] 1. a slight wetness; moisture 2. any harmful gas in a mine; firedamp, blackdamp, etc. —*adj.* somewhat moist or wet; humid —*vt.* 1. to make damp; moisten 2. to reduce or check (energy, action, etc., as fire in a furnace or the vibration of a piano string) —**damp'ish** *adj.* —**damp'ly** *adv.* —**damp'ness** *n.*

**damp-dry** (-drī') *vt.* **-dried', -dry'ing** to dry (laundry) so that some moisture is retained —*adj.* designating or of laundry so treated

**damp·en** (dam'pən) *vt.* 1. to make damp; moisten 2. to deaden, depress, reduce, or lessen —*vi.* to become damp

**damp·er** (-pər) *n.* [see DAMP] 1. anything that deadens or depresses 2. a movable plate or valve in the flue of a stove or furnace, for controlling the draft 3. a device to check vibration in the strings of a piano, etc. 4. a device for lessening the oscillation of a magnetic needle, a moving coil, etc.

**dam·sel** (dam'z'l) *n.* [< OFr. *dameisele* < L. *domina:* see DAME] [Archaic or Poet.] a girl; maiden

**dam·son** (dam'z'n, -s'n) *n.* [< OFr. < L. *Damascenus,* (plum) of Damascus] 1. a variety of small, purple plum 2. the tree on which it grows

DAMPER

**Dan** (dan) 1. *Bible a*) the fifth son of Jacob *b*) the tribe of Israel descended from him 2. village in NE Israel: site of an ancient town at the northernmost extremity of Israelite territory

**Dan.** 1. Daniel 2. Danish

**Da·na·i·des, Da·na·ï·des** (də nā'ə dēz') *n.pl., sing.* **Dan·a·id, Dan·a·ïd** (dan'ē id) *Gr. Myth.* the fifty daughters of Danaus, a king of Argos: forty-nine murdered their husbands at their father's command and were condemned in Hades to keep drawing water with a sieve

**Dan·a·us** (dan'ē əs) *see* DANAIDES

**Dan·bur·y** (dan'ber'ē, -bər ē) [after *Danbury,* town in England] city in SW Conn., near Bridgeport: pop. 60,000

**dance** (dans) *vi.* **danced, danc'ing** [< OFr. *danser*] 1. to move the body and feet in rhythm, ordinarily to music 2. to move lightly, rapidly, or gaily about, as leaves in a wind 3. to bob up and down —*vt.* 1. to take part in or perform (a dance) 2. to cause to dance —*n.* 1. rhythmic movement of the body and feet, ordinarily to music 2. a particular kind of dance, as the waltz, tango, etc. 3. the art of dancing 4. one round of a dance 5. a party to which people come to dance 6. a piece of music for dancing 7. rapid, lively movement —**dance attendance** to be always near so as to lavish attentions on —**dance to another tune** to alter one's actions or opinions as a result of changed conditions —**danc'er** *n.*

**D and C** dilatation (of the cervix) and curettage (of the uterus)

**dan·de·li·on** (dan'də lī'ən, -dē-) *n.* [< OFr. *dent de lion* < L. *dens* (gen. *dentis*), tooth + *de,* of + *leo,* lion] a common weed with jagged leaves, often used as greens, and yellow flowers

**dan·der** (dan'dər) *n.* [< ?] [Colloq.] anger or temper —**get one's dander up** [Colloq.] to become or make angry; lose, or make lose, one's temper

**dan·di·fy** (dan'də fī') *vt.* **-fied', -fy'ing** to dress up like a dandy —**dan'di·fi·ca'tion** *n.*

**dan·dle** (dan'd'l) *vt.* **-dled, -dling** [< ? OIt. *dandolare,* to dally] 1. to dance (a child) up and down on the knee or in the arms 2. to fondle; pet

**dan·druff** (dan'drəf) *n.* [< earlier *dandro* (< ?) + dial. *hurf,* scab] little scales or flakes of dead skin formed on the scalp —**dan'druff·y** *adj.*

**dan·dy** (dan'dē) *n., pl.* **-dies** [Scot. var. of *Andy* < *Andrew* (see MERRY-ANDREW)] 1. a man overly attentive to his clothes and appearance; fop 2. [Colloq.] something very good or first-rate —*adj.* **-di·er, -di·est** [Colloq.] very good; first-rate —**dan'dy·ish** *adj.* —**dan'dy·ism** *n.*

**Dane** (dān) *n.* a native or inhabitant of Denmark

**Dane·law, Dane·lagh** (-lô') *n.* the law code enforced in NE England by Danish invaders in the 9th and 10th cent. A.D.; also, this part of England

**dan·ger** (dān'jər) *n.* [< OFr. < L. < *dominus,* a master] 1. liability to injury, damage, loss, or pain 2. a thing that may cause injury, pain, etc.

**dan·ger·ous** (-əs) *adj.* full of danger; unsafe; perilous —**dan'ger·ous·ly** *adv.* —**dan'ger·ous·ness** *n.*

**dan·gle** (daŋ'g'l) *vi.* **-gled, -gling** [< Scand.] 1. to hang swinging loosely 2. to be a hanger-on; follow (*after*) 3. *Gram.* to lack clear connection, as one sentence element modifying another [*a dangling* participle] —*vt.* to cause to dangle —**dan'gler** *n.*

**Dan·iel** (dan'yəl) [Heb. *dānī'ēl,* lit., God is my judge] 1. a masculine name: dim. *Dan* 2. *Bible a*) a Hebrew prophet whose faith saved him in the lions' den *b*) the book containing his story

**Dan·ish** (dā'nish) *adj.* of Denmark, the Danes, or their language —*n.* 1. the language of the Danes 2. [also d-] clipped form of DANISH PASTRY

**Danish pastry** [also d- p-] a rich, flaky pastry of raised dough filled with fruit, cheese, etc. and usually topped with icing

**dank** (daŋk) *adj.* [ME., akin to ON.] disagreeably damp; moist and chilly —**dank'ly** *adv.* —**dank'ness** *n.*

**dan·seuse** (dän sooz'; *Fr.* dän söz') *n., pl.* **-seus'es** (-sooz'əz; *Fr.* -söz') [Fr.] a girl or woman dancer, esp. a ballet dancer

**Dan·te (Alighieri)** (dän'tä, -tē; dan'tē; *It.* dän'te) 1265–1321; It. poet: wrote *The Divine Comedy* —**Dan'te·an** *adj., n.* —**Dan·tesque'** (-tesk') *adj.*

**Dan·ube** (dan'yoob) river in S Europe, flowing from SW Germany eastward into the Black Sea: c. 1,770 mi. —**Da·nu'bi·an** *adj.*

**Dan·zig** (dan'sig; *G.* dän'tsiH) German name of GDAŃSK

**Daph·ne** (daf'nē) [L. < Gr. *daphnē,* the laurel tree] 1. a feminine name 2. *Gr. Myth.* a nymph who escaped from Apollo by becoming a laurel tree

**dap·per** (dap'ər) *adj.* [< ? MDu. *dapper,* nimble] 1. small and active 2. trim, neat, or smart in appearance —**dap'per·ly** *adv.* —**dap'per·ness** *n.*

**dap·ple** (dap''l) *adj.* [< ON. *depill,* a spot < *dapi,* a pool] marked or variegated with spots; mottled: also **dap'pled** —*n.* 1. a spotted condition 2. an animal with skin that is spotted —*vt.*, *vi.* **-pled, -pling** to cover or become covered with spots

**dap·ple-gray** (-grā′) *adj.* gray spotted with darker gray —*n.* a dapple-gray horse

**DAR, D.A.R.** Daughters of the American Revolution

**Dar·by and Joan** (där′bē ən jōn′) [< an 18th-cent. song] an old married couple devoted to each other

**Dar·da·nelles** (där′də nelz′) strait between the Aegean Sea & the Sea of Marmara

**dare** (der, dar) *vi.* **dared** or archaic **durst** (dʉrst), **dared, dar′ing;** 3d pers. sing., pres. indic., **dare** or **dares** [< OE. *dear*, 1st pers. sing. of *durran*, to dare] to have enough courage or audacity for some act; be fearless —*vt.* 1. to have courage for; venture upon 2. to oppose and defy [he *dared* the wrath of the tyrant] 3. to test the courage of (someone) with a dare —*n.* a challenge to do a hard, dangerous, or rash thing as a test of courage —**dare say** to think likely or probable; suppose [I *dare say* you're right] —**dar′er** *n.*

**dare·dev·il** (-dev′'l) *adj.* bold and reckless —*n.* a bold, reckless person —**dare′dev′il·ry, dare′dev′il·try** *n.*

**Dar es Sa·laam** (där′ es sə läm′) capital of Tanzania, on the Indian Ocean: pop. 373,000

**dar·ing** (der′iŋ, dar′-) *adj.* having or showing a bold willingness to take risks, etc.; fearless —*n.* bold courage —**dar′ing·ly** *adv.*

**Da·ri·us I** (də rī′əs) 550?–486? B.C.; king of Persia (521–486?): called *the Great*

**Dar·jee·ling** (där jē′liŋ) *n.* a fine variety of tea from Darjeeling, a district in NE India

**dark** (därk) *adj.* [< OE. *deorc*] 1. entirely or partly without light 2. neither giving nor receiving light 3. giving no performance [this theater is *dark* tonight] 4. *a)* almost black *b)* not light in color; deep in shade 5. not fair in complexion; brunet 6. hidden; secret 7. not easily understood 8. gloomy; dismal 9. angry or sullen 10. evil; sinister 11. ignorant; unenlightened —*n.* 1. the state of being dark 2. night; nightfall 3. a dark color or shade —**in the dark** uninformed; ignorant —**keep dark** to keep secret or hidden —**dark′ish** *adj.* —**dark′ly** *adv.* —**dark′ness** *n.*

**Dark Ages, dark ages** the Middle Ages; esp., the early part from 476 A.D. to the late 10th cent.

**dark·en** (där′kən) *vt.*, *vi.* to make or become dark or darker —**not darken one's door** (or **doorway**) not come to one's home —**dark′en·er** *n.*

**dark horse** [Colloq.] 1. an unexpected, almost unknown winner, as in a horse race 2. *Politics* a person who gets or may get the nomination unexpectedly, often by a compromise

**dark lantern** a lantern with a shutter that can hide the light

**dark·ling** (där′kliŋ) *adv.* [DARK + -LING²] [Poet.] in the dark —*adj.* [Poet.] dark, dim, obscure, etc.

**dark·room** (där′rōōm′) *n.* a room from which all actinic rays are excluded, where photographs can be developed

**dark·some** (-səm) *adj.* [Poet.] 1. dark; darkish 2. dismal; gloomy

**Dar·ling** (där′liŋ) river in SE Australia, flowing southwest into the Murray River

**dar·ling** (där′liŋ) *n.* [OE. *deorling*, dim. of *deore*, DEAR] 1. a person much loved by another 2. a favorite or a lovable person —*adj.* 1. very dear; beloved 2. [Colloq.] cute; attractive [a *darling* dress]

**darn¹** (därn) *vt.*, *vi.* [< MFr. dial. *darner*, to mend] to mend (cloth, etc.) or repair (a hole in cloth) by sewing a network of stitches across the gap —*n.* a darned place in fabric —**darn′er** *n.*

**darn²** (därn) *vt.*, *vi.*, *n.*, *adj.*, *adv.*, *interj.* [Colloq.] a euphemism for DAMN (the curse) —**darned** *adj.*, *adv.*

**dar·nel** (där′n'l) *n.* [< Fr. dial. *darnelle*] a weedy rye grass often found in grainfields: a certain fungus can make the seeds poisonous

**darn·ing** (där′niŋ) *n.* 1. a mending with interlaced stitches 2. things to be darned

**darning needle** 1. a large needle for darning 2. *same as* DRAGONFLY

**Dar·row** (dar′ō), **Clarence** 1857–1938; U.S. lawyer

**dart** (därt) *n.* [< OFr.] 1. a small, pointed missile for throwing or shooting 2. anything resembling this 3. a sudden, quick movement 4. a short, tapered, stitched fold to make a garment fit more closely 5. [*pl., with sing. v.*] a game in which a number of darts (sense 1) are thrown at a target —*vt.*, *vi.* 1. to throw, shoot, send out, etc. suddenly and fast 2. to move suddenly and fast

**dart·er** (-ər) *n.* 1. a thing or animal that darts 2. a tropical diving bird with a long, pointed bill and a long neck 3. any of various small, brightly colored freshwater fishes of N. America

**dar·tle** (därt′'l) *vt.*, *vi.* **-tled, -tling** to dart about

**Dart·mouth** (därt′məth) city in S Nova Scotia, Canada, near Halifax: pop. 59,000

**Dar·von** (där′vän) *a trademark for* a pain-killing drug containing aspirin, etc.

**Dar·win** (där′win), **Charles Robert** 1809–82; Eng. naturalist —**Dar·win′i·an** (-win′ē ən) *adj.*, *n.*

**Darwinian theory** Darwin's theory of evolution, which holds that all species of plants and animals developed from earlier forms by hereditary transmission of slight variations in successive generations, those forms surviving which are best adapted to the environment (*natural selection*): also called **Dar′win·ism** —**Dar′win·ist** *adj.*, *n.*

**dash** (dash) *vt.* [< Scand., as in Sw. *daska*, to slap] 1. to throw so as to break; smash 2. to strike violently (*against*) 3. to throw, thrust, etc. (with *away, down*, etc.) 4. to splash (liquid) on (someone or something) 5. to mix with a little of another substance 6. to destroy; frustrate [to *dash* one's hopes] 7. to depress; discourage 8. to put to shame; abash 9. [Colloq.] *a euphemism for* DAMN —*vi.* 1. to strike violently (*against* or on) 2. to move swiftly; rush —*n.* 1. the sound of smashing 2. a bit of something added 3. a sudden rush 4. a short, fast run or race 5. vigor; verve 6. showy appearance 7. *short for* DASHBOARD (sense 2) 8. the mark (—), used in printing and writing to indicate a break in a sentence, a parenthetical element, an omission, etc. 9. *Telegraphy* a long sound or signal, as in Morse code: cf. DOT —**dash off** 1. to do, write, etc. hastily 2. to rush away —**dash′er** *n.*

**dash·board** (-bôrd′) *n.* 1. a screen at the front or side of a carriage, boat, etc., for protection against splashing 2. a panel with instruments and gauges on it, as in an automobile

**dash·ing** (-iŋ) *adj.* 1. full of dash or spirit; lively 2. showy; stylish —**dash′ing·ly** *adv.*

**dash light** a light to illuminate a dashboard (sense 2)

**das·tard** (das′tərd) *n.* [ME., prob. < Scand. base] a sneaky, cowardly evildoer

**das·tard·ly** (-lē) *adj.* [see prec.] mean, sneaky, cowardly, etc. —**das′tard·li·ness** *n.*

**das·y·ure** (das′ē yoor′) *n.* [< Gr. *dasys*, hairy + *oura*, tail] a small tree-dwelling marsupial of Australia

**dat.** dative

**da·ta** (dāt′ə, dat′ə) *n.pl.* [*often with sing. v.*] [L., things given < pp. of *dare*, to give] things known or assumed; facts or figures from which conclusions can be inferred; information: the sing. form is **datum**

**data base** (or **bank**) a large collection of data in a computer organized so that it can be expanded, updated, and retrieved rapidly for various uses: also **da′ta·base′, da′ta·bank′** *n.*

**data processing** the recording and handling of information by means of mechanical or electronic equipment

**date¹** (dāt) *n.* [< OFr. < L. *data*, as in *data Romae*, etc., lit., given at Rome, etc., formula used in letters for place and date] 1. a statement on a writing, coin, etc. of when it was made 2. the time at which a thing happens or is done 3. the time that anything lasts 4. the day of the month 5. *a)* an appointment for a set time; specif., a social engagement with a person of the opposite sex *b)* the person with whom one has such an engagement —*vt.* **dat′ed, dat′ing** 1. to mark (a letter, etc.) with a date 2. to find out or give the date of 3. to assign a date to 4. *a)* to show or reveal as typical of a certain period or age *b)* to make seem old-fashioned or out of date 5. to reckon by dates 6. to have a social engagement with —*vi.* to belong to, or have origin in, a definite period in the past (usually with *from*) —**out of date** no longer in use; old-fashioned —**to date** until now; as yet —**up to date** in or into agreement with the latest facts, ideas, styles, etc. —**dat′a·ble, date′a·ble** *adj.* —**dat′er** *n.*

**date²** (dāt) *n.* [< OFr. < L. < Gr. *daktylos*, a date, lit., a finger] 1. the sweet, fleshy fruit of a cultivated palm (**date palm**) 2. the tree itself

**date·less** (-lis) *adj.* 1. without a date 2. without limit or end 3. too old for its date to be fixed 4. still good or interesting though old

**date·line** (-līn′) *n.* 1. the date and place of writing or issue, as given in a line in a newspaper, a dispatch, etc. 2. *same as* DATE LINE —*vt.* **-lined′, -lin′ing** to furnish with a dateline

**date line** an imaginary line drawn north and south through the Pacific Ocean, largely along the 180th meridian: at this line, by international agreement, each calendar day begins at midnight, so that when it is Sunday just west of the line, it is Saturday just east of it

**da·tive** (dāt′iv) *adj.* [L. *dativus*, of giving < *datus*, pp. of *dare*, to give] designating, of, or in that case of a noun, pronoun, or adjective which expresses the indirect object of a verb and, in many languages, approach toward something —*n.* 1. the dative case: in English, the dative is expressed by *to* or by word order (Ex.: I gave the book *to him*, I gave *him* the book) 2. a word or phrase in the dative case —**da·ti·val** (dā tī′v'l) *adj.* —**da′tive·ly** *adv.*

**da·tum** (dāt′əm, dat′-) *n. sing. of* DATA

**dau.** daughter

**daub** (dôb) *vt.*, *vi.* [< OFr. < L. *dealbare*, to whitewash < *de-*, intens. + *albus*, white] 1. to cover or smear with sticky, soft matter, such as plaster, grease, etc. 2. to smear on (grease, etc.) **3.** to paint coarsely and unskillfully —*n.* **1.** anything daubed on **2.** a daubing stroke or splash **3.** a poorly painted picture —**daub'er** *n.*

**Dau·det** (dō dā'), **Al·phonse** (ál fōns') 1840–97; Fr. novelist

**daugh·ter** (dôt'ər) *n.* [< OE. *dohtor*] **1.** a girl or woman as she is related to either or both parents: sometimes also used of animals **2.** a female descendant **3.** *a*) a daughter-in-law *b*) a stepdaughter **4.** a female thought of as if in the relation of child to parent [a *daughter* of France] **5.** anything thought of as like a daughter in relation to its origin —**daugh'ter·li·ness** *n.* —**daugh'ter·ly** *adj.*

**daugh·ter-in-law** (-in lô') *n., pl.* **daugh'ters-in-law'** the wife of one's son

**Dau·mier** (dō myā'), **Ho·no·ré** (ô nô rā') 1809–79; Fr. painter & caricaturist

**daunt** (dônt, dänt) *vt.* [< OFr. < L. < *domare,* to tame] to make afraid or discouraged; intimidate; dishearten

**daunt·less** (-lis) *adj.* that cannot be daunted or discouraged; fearless —**daunt'less·ly** *adv.* —**daunt'less·ness** *n.*

**dau·phin** (dô'fin; *Fr.* dō faŋ') *n.* [Fr., lit., DOLPHIN: orig. a proper name] the eldest son of the king of France: a title used from 1349 to 1830

**Dav·en·port** (dav'ən pôrt') [after Col. G. *Davenport,* 19th-c. fur trader] city in E Iowa, on the Mississippi: pop. 103,000

**dav·en·port** (dav'ən pôrt') *n.* [< ?] a large sofa, sometimes one convertible into a bed

**Da·vid** (dā'vid) [Heb. *dāvīd,* lit., beloved] **1.** a masculine name: dim. **Dave, Davy 2.** *Bible* the second king of Israel, succeeded by his son Solomon **3.** (dà vēd'), **Jacques Louis** (zhàk lwē), 1748–1825; Fr. painter

**da Vin·ci** (də vin'chē; *It.* dä vēn'chē), **Le·o·nar·do** (lē'ə när'dō; *It.* le'ô när'dô) 1452–1519; It. painter, sculptor, architect, & scientist

**Da·vis** (dā'vis), **Jefferson** 1808–89; U.S. statesman; president of the Confederacy (1861–65)

**dav·it** (dav'it) *n.* [< OFr. dim. of *David*] either of a pair of uprights projecting over the side of a ship for suspending, lowering, or raising a boat

**Da·vy** (dā'vē), **Sir Humphry** 1778–1829; Eng. chemist

**Da·vy Jones** (dā'vē jōnz') the spirit of the sea: humorous name given by sailors

**Davy Jones's locker** (jōn'ziz, jōnz) the bottom of the sea; grave of those drowned or buried at sea

**daw** (dô) *n.* [ME. *dawe*] same as JACKDAW

**daw·dle** (dôd''l) *vi., vt.* **-dled, -dling** [< ?] to waste (time) in trifling or by being slow; loiter (often with *away*) —**daw'dler** *n.*

DAVITS

**dawn** (dôn) *vi.* [< OE. < *dagian,* to become day < *dæg,* DAY] **1.** to begin to be day; grow light **2.** to begin to appear, develop, etc. **3.** to begin to be understood or felt (usually with *on* or *upon*) [the meaning *dawned* on me] —*n.* **1.** daybreak **2.** the beginning (*of* something)

**day** (dā) *n.* [< OE. *dæg*] **1.** *a*) the period of light between sunrise and sunset *b*) daylight *c*) sunshine **2.** *a*) the time (24 hours) that it takes the earth to revolve once on its axis: the civil day is from midnight to midnight *b*) *Astron.* the time that it takes any celestial body to revolve once on its axis **3.** [*often* D-] a particular or specified day [Memorial *Day*] **4.** [*also pl.*] a period of time; era [the best writer of his *day,* in *days* of old] **5.** a time of power, glory, success, etc. [he has had his *day*] **6.** the time one works each day [an eight-hour *day*] **7.** [*pl.*] one's lifetime [to spend one's *days* in study] —**call it a day** [Colloq.] to stop working for the day **—day after day** every day —**day by day** each day —**day in, day out** every day —**from day to day 1.** from one day to the next **2.** without particular concern about the future

**Day·ak** (dī'ak) *n.* same as DYAK

**day·bed** (dā'bed') *n.* a couch that can also be used as a bed

**day·book** (-book') *n.* **1.** a diary or journal **2.** *Bookkeeping* a book used for recording the transactions of each day as they occur

**day·break** (-brāk') *n.* the time in the morning when light first appears; dawn

**day care** daytime care given to preschool children, as at a day nursery, or to the elderly, as at a social agency or nursing home —**day'-care'** *adj.*

**day·dream** (-drēm') *n.* **1.** a pleasant, dreamlike thinking or wishing; reverie **2.** a pleasing but visionary notion —*vi.* to have daydreams —**day'dream'er** *n.*

**day laborer** an unskilled worker paid by the day

**day letter** a telegram with a minimum charge for fifty words or fewer, sent in the daytime: it is cheaper but slower than a regular telegram

**Day-Lew·is** (dā'lōō'is), **C(ecil)** 1904–72; Brit. poet & novelist, born in Ireland

**day·light** (-līt') *n.* **1.** the light of day; sunlight **2.** dawn; daybreak **3.** daytime **4.** full understanding or knowledge of something hidden or obscure **5.** the approaching end of a task, etc. [to see *daylight*] **6.** [*pl.*] [Slang] orig., the eyes; hence, consciousness: often used hyperbolically, as in scare (or beat, knock, etc.) **the daylights out of**

**day·light-sav·ing time** (-sā'viŋ) standard time that is one hour later than the standard time for a given zone based on Greenwich time: it is used to give an hour more of daylight at the end of the usual working day

**day·long** (dā'lôŋ') *adj., adv.* during the whole day

**day nursery** a nursery school for the daytime care and training of preschool children, as of working mothers

**Day of Atonement** *same as* YOM KIPPUR

**day room** a room for recreation, reading, etc., as in a barracks, institution, or the like

**days** (dāz) *adv.* on every day or most days

**day school 1.** a school that has classes only in the daytime **2.** a private school whose students live at home and attend classes daily

**day·time** (dā'tīm') *n.* the period of daylight

**day-to-day** (dā'tə dā') *adj.* everyday; daily

**Day·ton** (dāt''n) [after Gen. E. *Dayton* (1737–1807)] city in SW Ohio: pop. 244,000 (met. area 827,000)

**day·work** (dā'wurk') *n.* work done (esp. by a domestic worker) and paid for on a daily basis

**daze** (dāz) *vt.* **dazed, daz'ing** [< ON. *dasast,* to become weary < *dasi,* tired] **1.** to stun or bewilder, as by a shock or blow **2.** to dazzle —*n.* a dazed condition; bewilderment —**daz'ed·ly** *adv.*

**daz·zle** (daz''l) *vt.* **daz'zled, daz'zling** [freq. of DAZE] **1.** to overpower or dim the vision of with very bright light or moving lights **2.** to surprise or overpower with brilliant qualities, display, etc. —*vi.* **1.** to be overpowered by glare **2.** to arouse admiration by brilliant display —*n.* **1.** a dazzling **2.** something that dazzles —**daz'zle·ment** *n.* —**daz'zler** *n.* —**daz'zling·ly** *adv.*

**db** decibel; decibels

**dbl.** double

**DC, D.C., d.c.** direct current

**D.C., DC** District of Columbia

**dd., d/d** delivered

**D.D. 1.** demand draft: also **D/D 2.** [L. *Divinitatis Doctor*] Doctor of Divinity

**D-day** (dē'dā') *n.* the day for beginning a military operation; specif., June 6, 1944, the day Allied forces invaded W Europe in World War II

**DDD** a colorless, crystalline insecticide related to DDT but considered to be less toxic to animals

**D.D.S.** Doctor of Dental Surgery

**DDT** a powerful insecticide effective upon contact

**de-** [< Fr. *dé-* or L. *de* < L. *dis-:* see DIS-] *a prefix meaning:* **1.** away from, off [*derail*] **2.** down [*decline*] **3.** wholly, entirely [*defunct*] **4.** reverse the action of; undo [*defrost, decode*]

**dea·con** (dēk''n) *n.* [OE. < LL. < Gr. *diakonos,* servant] **1.** a cleric ranking just below a priest in the Roman Catholic and Anglican churches **2.** in certain other Christian churches, a church officer who helps the minister, esp. in secular matters

**dea·con·ess** (dēk''n is) *n.* a woman appointed as an assistant in a church, as for helping with the care of the sick and poor of a parish

**de·ac·ti·vate** (dē ak'tə vāt') *vt.* **-vat'ed, -vat'ing 1.** to make (an explosive, chemical, etc.) inactive or inoperative **2.** *Mil.* to place (troops, etc.) on nonactive status —**de·ac'ti·va'tion** *n.*

**dead** (ded) *adj.* [OE.] **1.** no longer living; having died **2.** without life; inanimate [*dead* stones] **3.** deathlike **4.** lacking vitality, interest, variety, warmth, brilliance, etc. **5.** without feeling, motion, or power **6.** *a*) extinguished *b*) extinct [a *dead* volcano] **7.** slack, stagnant, etc. **8.** no longer resilient **9.** no longer used or significant; obsolete [*dead* languages] **10.** barren or unprofitable [*dead* soil] **11.** unerring; sure [a *dead* shot] **12.** exact; precise [*dead* center] **13.** complete; absolute [a *dead* stop] **14.** [Colloq.] very tired; exhausted **15.** *Elec. a*) without current [a *dead* line] *b*) uncharged [a *dead* battery] **16.** *Sports* no longer in play [a *dead* ball] —*n.* the time of greatest darkness, most intense cold, etc. [the *dead* of night, the *dead* of winter] —*adv.* **1.** completely; absolutely [*dead* right] **2.** directly; straight [*dead* ahead] —**the dead** those who have died —**dead'ness** *n.*

---

fat, āpe, cär, ten, ēven, is, bīte, gō, hôrn, tōol, look; oil, out; up, fur; get; joy; yet; chin; she; thin, then; zh, leisure; ŋ, ring; ə for *a* in *ago, e* in *agent, i* in *sanity, o* in *comply, u* in *focus;* ' as in *able* (ā'b'l); Fr. bàl; ë, Fr. coeur; ö, Fr. feu; Fr. mon; ô, Fr. coq; ü, Fr. duc; r, Fr. cri; H, G. ich; kh, G. doch; ‡foreign; *hypothetical; < derived from. See inside front cover.

**dead·beat** (-bēt′) *n.* [Slang] **1.** a person who evades paying his debts, etc. **2.** a lazy, idle person

**dead·en** (ded′'n) *vt.* **1.** to lessen the vigor or intensity of **2.** to make numb **3.** to make soundproof —*vi.* to become as if dead; lose vigor, etc.

**dead-end** (-end′) *adj.* **1.** having only one outlet [a *dead-end* street] **2.** giving no opportunity for progress [a *dead-end* plan] **3.** [Colloq.] [< *Dead End*, a play (1935) by S. Kingsley] of or characteristic of slums or slum life

**dead end** **1.** an end of a street, etc. that has no regular exit **2.** an impasse

**dead·eye** (-ī′) *n.* **1.** a round, flat wooden block with three holes in it for the lanyard, used on a ship to fasten the shrouds **2.** [Slang] an accurate marksman

**dead·fall** (-fôl′) *n.* a trap arranged so that a heavy weight is dropped on the prey

**dead·head** (-hed′) *n.* **1.** a person using a free ticket as to get into a show **2.** a vehicle traveling without cargo or passengers **3.** [Slang] a boring person —*vt., vi.* to drive (a vehicle) or travel as a deadhead —*adv.* without passengers or cargo

**dead heat** a race in which two or more contestants reach the finish line at exactly the same time; tie

**dead letter** **1.** a law, practice, etc. no longer enforced or operative but not formally done away with **2.** a letter that cannot be delivered or returned, as because incorrectly addressed

**dead·line** (-līn′) *n.* **1.** a boundary which it is forbidden to cross **2.** the latest time by which something must be done or completed

**dead·lock** (-läk′) *n.* **1.** a standstill resulting from the action of equal and opposed forces **2.** a tie between opponents —*vt., vi.* to bring or come to a deadlock

**dead·ly** (-lē) *adj.* **-li·er, -li·est** **1.** causing or likely to cause death **2.** to the death; mortal [*deadly* combat] **3.** typical of death [*deadly* pallor] **4.** very harmful **5.** extreme or excessive [*deadly* silence] **6.** oppressively tiresome [a *deadly* bore] **7.** perfectly accurate [*deadly* aim] **8.** *Theol.* causing spiritual death [*deadly* sins] —*adv.* **1.** as if dead [to lie *deadly* still] **2.** extremely or excessively [*deadly* serious] —**dead′li·ness** *n.*

**deadly nightshade** *same as* BELLADONNA (sense 1)

**dead march** funeral music in slow march tempo

**dead·pan** (-pan′) *n.* [Slang] an expressionless face, or a person with such a face —*adj., adv.* [Slang] without expression

**dead reckoning** [< ? *ded* (for *deduced*) *reckoning*] the finding of a ship's position by an estimate based on data recorded in the log, such as the time spent on a specified course, speed, etc., rather than by taking astronomical observations

**Dead Sea** inland body of salt water between Israel and Jordan: c. 1,290 ft. below sea level

**Dead Sea Scrolls** scrolls dating from 100? B.C.–70? A.D. discovered since 1947 in caves near the Dead Sea: they contain Jewish Scriptural writings, etc.

**dead soldier** [Slang] an emptied bottle, as of liquor

**dead weight** **1.** the weight of an inert person or thing **2.** the weight of a vehicle without a load

**dead·wood** (-wood′) *n.* **1.** dead wood on trees **2.** a useless or burdensome person or thing

**deaf** (def) *adj.* [OE.] **1.** totally or partially unable to hear **2.** unwilling to hear or listen [*deaf* to her pleas] —**deaf′ly** *adv.* —**deaf′ness** *n.*

**deaf-and-dumb** (-'n dum′) *adj.* **1.** deaf-mute **2.** of or for deaf-mutes Now opprobrious

**deaf·en** (-'n) *vt.* **1.** to make deaf **2.** to overwhelm with noise **3.** to soundproof with insulation —**deaf′en·ing** *adj., n.* —**deaf′en·ing·ly** *adv.*

**deaf-mute** (-myōōt′) *n.* a person who is deaf, esp. from birth, and unable to speak: most deaf-mutes, having the necessary vocal organs, can be taught to speak —*adj.* of or being a deaf-mute

**deal**[1] (dēl) *vt.* **dealt, deal′ing** [OE. *dælan*] **1.** to portion out or distribute **2.** to give or administer (a blow) —*vi.* **1.** to have to do (*with*) [books *dealing* with fish] **2.** to act or conduct oneself (followed by *with*) [*deal* fairly with others] **3.** to consider or attend to; cope (*with*) [to *deal* with a problem] **4.** to do business; trade (*with* or *in*) [to *deal* in hardware] **5.** to distribute playing cards to the players —*n.* **1.** *a)* the act of distributing playing cards *b)* cards dealt *c)* a player's turn to deal *d)* the playing of one deal of cards **2.** a business transaction **3.** a bargain or agreement, esp. when secret or underhanded **4.** *a)* [Colloq.] behavior or conduct toward another; treatment [a square *deal*] *b)* a particular plan, policy, etc. [the New *Deal*] —**big deal** [Colloq.] a very important or impressive thing —**deal′er** *n.*

**deal**[2] (dēl) *n.* [OE. *dæl*, a part] an indefinite or considerable amount [a *deal* of trouble] —**a good** (or **great**) **deal** **1.** a large amount **2.** very much

**deal**[3] (dēl) *n.* [MDu. *dele*] **1.** a fir or pine board **2.** fir or pine wood —*adj.* made of deal

**deal·er·ship** (dēl′ər ship′) *n.* a franchise to market a product in an area, or a distributor holding this

**deal·ing** (dēl′iŋ) *n.* **1.** distribution **2.** way of acting toward others **3.** [*usually pl.*] transactions or relations, usually of business

**dealt** (delt) *pt. and pp. of* DEAL[1]

**dean** (dēn) *n.* [< OFr. < LL. *decanus*, head of ten soldiers or monks < L. *decem*, ten] **1.** *a)* the presiding official of a cathedral or collegiate church *b)* R.C.Ch. a priest chosen by his bishop to supervise a number of parishes within the diocese **2.** a college or university official in charge of a school or faculty, or of the students **3.** the senior or preeminent member of a particular group [the *dean* of American poets] —**dean′ship′** *n.*

**dean·er·y** (dēn′ər ē) *n., pl.* **-er·ies** **1.** the rank or authority of a dean **2.** the residence of a dean

**dean's list** a list of students with the highest grades, issued periodically at certain colleges

**dear** (dir) *adj.* [OE. *deore*] **1.** much loved; beloved **2.** much valued; esteemed: a polite form of address [*Dear* Sir] **3.** *a)* high-priced *b)* charging high prices **4.** earnest [our *dearest* wish] —*adv.* **1.** with deep affection **2.** at a high cost —*n.* a loved or endearing person —*interj.* an expression of surprise, pity, etc. —**dear′ly** *adv.* —**dear′ness** *n.*

**Dear·born** (dir′bərn, -bôrn′) [after Gen. H. *Dearborn*, U.S. Secretary of War (1801–09)] city in SE Mich.: suburb of Detroit: pop. 91,000

**Dearborn Heights** city in SE Mich.: suburb of Detroit: pop. 68,000

**dearth** (durth) *n.* [see DEAR & -TH[1]] **1.** scarcity of food; famine **2.** any scarcity or lack

**dear·y, dear·ie** (dir′ē) *n., pl.* **-ies** [Colloq.] dear; darling: now often ironic or humorous

**death** (deth) *n.* [OE.] **1.** the act or fact of dying; permanent ending of life **2.** [D-] the personification of death, usually as a skeleton holding a scythe **3.** the state of being dead **4.** any end resembling dying [the *death* of fascism] **5.** any experience thought of as like dying or being dead **6.** the cause of death **7.** murder or bloodshed —**at death's door** nearly dead —**put to death** to kill; execute —**to death** very much [worried *to death*] —**to the death** **1.** to the very end of (a struggle, etc.) **2.** always —**death′like′** *adj.*

**death·bed** (-bed′) *n.* the bed on which a person dies or spends his last hours of life —*adj.* done or made in one's last hours of life [a *deathbed* wish]

**death·blow** (-blō′) *n.* **1.** a blow that kills **2.** a thing destructive or fatal (*to* something)

**death cup** a deadly mushroom with a white cap and a cuplike structure around the base of the stalk

**death duty** [Brit.] *same as* INHERITANCE TAX

**death house** a cell block or place where prisoners condemned to die are kept until their execution

**death·less** (-lis) *adj.* that cannot die; immortal —**death′less·ly** *adv.* —**death′less·ness** *n.*

**death·ly** (-lē) *adj.* **1.** causing death; deadly **2.** like or characteristic of death —*adv.* **1.** in a deathlike way **2.** extremely [*deathly* ill]

**death mask** a cast of a dead person's face

**death rate** the number of deaths per year per thousand of population: sometimes other units of time or population are used

**death row** *same as* DEATH HOUSE

**death's-head** (deths′hed′) *n.* a human skull or a representation of it, symbolizing death

**death tax** *same as* INHERITANCE TAX

**death·trap** (deth′trap′) *n.* **1.** an unsafe building, vehicle, etc. **2.** any very dangerous place or situation

**Death Valley** dry, hot desert basin in E Calif. & S Nev.: 282 ft. below sea level

**death warrant** **1.** an official order to put a person to death **2.** anything that makes inevitable the destruction or end of a person or thing

**death·watch** (-wäch′, -wôch′) *n.* **1.** a vigil kept beside a dead or dying person **2.** a guard set over a person soon to be executed

**deb** (deb) *n.* [Colloq.] *short for* DEBUTANTE

**deb.** debenture

**de·ba·cle** (di bäk′'l, -bak′-; dā-) *n.* [< Fr. < *débâcler*, to break up] **1.** a breaking up of ice in a river, etc. **2.** a rush of debris-filled waters **3.** an overwhelming defeat or rout **4.** a total, often ludicrous, collapse or failure

**de·bar** (dē bär′) *vt.* **-barred′, -bar′ring** [< Anglo-Fr.: see DE- & BAR[1]] **1.** to exclude (*from* something); bar **2.** to prevent or prohibit —**de·bar′ment** *n.*

**de·bark** (di bärk′) *vt., vi.* [< Fr.: see DE- & BARK[3]] to unload from or leave a ship or aircraft —**de·bar·ka·tion** (dē′bär kā′shən) *n.*

**de·base** (di bās′) *vt.* **-based′, -bas′ing** [DE- + (A)BASE] to make lower in value, quality, character, dignity, etc.; cheapen —**de·base′ment** *n.* —**de·bas′er** *n.*

**de·bate** (di bāt′) *vi.* **-bat′ed, -bat′ing** [< OFr. *debatre*, to fight: see DE- & BATTER[1]] **1.** to discuss opposing reasons;

argue **2.** to take part in a formal discussion or a debate (*n.* 2) —*vt.* **1.** to dispute about, esp. in a meeting or legislature **2.** to argue (a question) or argue with (a person) formally **3.** to consider reasons for and against (*with* oneself or *in* one's own mind) —*n.* **1.** discussion of opposing reasons; argument **2.** a formal contest of skill in reasoned argument, with two teams taking opposite sides of a specified question **3.** the art or study of formal debate —de·bat′a·ble *adj.* —de·bat′er *n.*

de·bauch (di bôch′) *vt.* [< Fr. < OFr. *desbaucher,* to seduce] to lead astray morally; corrupt —*vi.* to indulge in debauchery; dissipate —*n.* **1.** debauchery **2.** an orgy —de·bauch′ed·ly (-id lē) *adv.* —de·bauch′er *n.* —de·bauch′ment *n.*

deb·au·chee (di bôch′ē′; deb′ô chē′, -shē′) *n.* one who indulges in debauchery; dissipated person

de·bauch·er·y (di bôch′ər ē) *n., pl.* -er·ies **1.** extreme indulgence of one's appetites; dissipation **2.** [*pl.*] orgies **3.** a leading astray morally

de·ben·ture (di ben′chər) *n.* [< ML. < L. *debentur,* there are owing < *debere:* see DEBT] **1.** a voucher acknowledging that a debt is owed by the signer **2.** an interest-bearing bond issued by a corporation or governmental unit, often without security

de·bil·i·tate (di bil′ə tāt′) *vt.* -tat′ed, -tat′ing [< L. pp. of *debilitare,* to weaken < *debilis,* weak] to make weak; enervate —de·bil′i·ta′tion *n.*

de·bil·i·ty (-tē) *n., pl.* -ties [< OFr. < L. *debilitas* < *debilis,* weak] bodily weakness; feebleness

deb·it (deb′it) *n.* [< OFr. < L. *debitum,* what is owing; neut. pp. of *debere:* see DEBT] **1.** an entry on the left-hand side of an account, giving rise to an increase in an asset account or decrease in a liability or net worth account **2.** the total of such entries —*vt.* to enter as a debit or debits

deb·o·nair, deb·o·naire (deb′ə ner′) *adj.* [< OFr. < *de bon aire,* lit., of good breed] **1.** friendly in a cheerful way; genial; affable **2.** carefree in manner; jaunty; sprightly —deb′o·nair′ly *adv.*

Deb·o·rah (deb′ə rə, deb′rə) [Heb. *deborāh,* lit., a bee] **1.** a feminine name: dim. *Debby* **2.** *Bible* a prophetess and judge of Israel: Judg. 4 & 5

de·bouch (di boosh′) *vi.* [< Fr. < *dé-,* DE- + *bouche,* the mouth < L. *bucca,* cheek] **1.** *Mil.* to come forth from a narrow or shut-in place into open country **2.** to come forth; emerge —de·bouch′ment *n.*

de·brief (dē brēf′) *vt.* [DE- + BRIEF] to question and instruct (a pilot, emissary, etc.) following a flight or mission —de·brief′ing *n.*

de·bris, dé·bris (də brē′; *also, esp. Brit. & Canad.,* de′brē, dā′-) *n.* [Fr. < OFr. *desbrisier,* to break apart] **1.** broken pieces of stone, wood, etc., as after destruction; rubble **2.** bits of rubbish; litter **3.** a heap of rock fragments, as from a glacier

Debs (debz), **Eugene Victor** 1855–1926; U.S. labor leader & Socialist candidate for president

debt (det) *n.* [< OFr. < L. *debitum,* neut. pp. of *debere,* to owe < *de-,* from + *habere,* to have] **1.** something owed by one person to another **2.** an obligation or liability to pay or return something **3.** the condition of owing /to be in *debt*/ **4.** *Theol.* a sin

**debt of honor** a gambling or betting debt

debt·or (-ər) *n.* one that owes a debt

de·bug (dē bug′) *vt.* -bugged′, -bug′ging [DE- + BUG] **1.** to remove insects from **2.** [Slang] to find and correct defects, faults, etc. in **3.** [Slang] to find and remove hidden electronic listening devices from (a room, etc.)

de·bunk (di buŋk′) *vt.* [DE- + BUNK²] [Colloq.] to expose the false or exaggerated claims, pretensions, glamour, etc. of —de·bunk′er *n.*

De·bus·sy (də bü sē′; *E.* deb′yoo sē′, də byoo′sē), (**Achille**) **Claude** 1862–1918; Fr. composer

de·but, dé·but (di byoo′, dā-; dā′byoo) *n.* [Fr. < *débuter,* to lead off < (*jouer de but,* (to play) for the mark] **1.** the first appearance before the public, as of an actor **2.** the formal introduction of a girl into society **3.** the beginning of a career, course, etc.

deb·u·tante (deb′yoo tänt′, deb′yoo tänt′) *n.* [< Fr. *débutant,* prp. of *débuter,* to make a DEBUT] a girl making a debut, esp. into society

**Dec.** December

**dec. 1.** deceased **2.** decimeter **3.** declension **4.** declination **5.** decrease

dec·a- [< Gr. *deka,* ten] *a combining form meaning* ten *[decagon, decameter]* : also, before a vowel, **dec-**

dec·ade (dek′ād) *n.* [< OFr. < L. < Gr. < *deka,* ten] **1.** a group of ten **2.** a period of ten years

dec·a·dence (dek′ə dəns, di kā′d'ns) *n.* [< Fr. < ML. < prp. of VL. *decadere* < L. *de-,* from + *cadere,* to fall] a process, condition, or period of decline, as in morals, art, literature, etc.; deterioration; decay

dec·a·dent (-dənt) *adj.* in a state of decline; characterized by decadence —*n.* a decadent person, esp. a decadent writer or artist —dec′a·dent·ly *adv.*

dec·a·gon (dek′ə gän′) *n.* [see DECA- & -GON] a plane figure with ten sides and ten angles —de·cag·o·nal (di kag′ə nəl) *adj.*

dec·a·gram (-gram′) *n.* [see DECA- & GRAM] a measure of weight, equal to 10 grams: also, chiefly Brit., **dec′a·gramme′** (-gram′)

dec·a·he·dron (dek′ə hē′drən) *n., pl.* -drons, -dra (-drə) [see DECA- & -HEDRON] a solid figure with ten plane surfaces —dec′a·he′dral (-drəl) *adj.*

de·cal (di kal′, dē′kal) *n. same as* DECALCOMANIA

de·cal·ci·fy (dē kal′sə fī′) *vt.* -fied′, -fy′ing to remove calcium or lime from (bones, etc.) —de·cal′ci·fi·ca′tion *n.* —de·cal′ci·fi′er *n.*

de·cal·co·ma·ni·a (di kal′kə mā′nē ə) *n.* [< Fr. < *dé-,* DE- + *calquer,* to copy + *manie,* mania] **1.** the process of transferring decorative pictures or designs from specially prepared paper onto glass, wood, etc. **2.** a picture or design of this kind

dec·a·li·ter (dek′ə lēt′ər) *n.* [see DECA- & LITER] a measure of capacity, equal to 10 liters: also, chiefly Brit., **dec′a·li′tre** (-lēt′ər)

Dec·a·logue, Dec·a·log (dek′ə lôg′, -läg′) *n.* [< LL. < Gr. *dekalogos:* see DECA- & -LOGUE] [*sometimes* d-] *same as* TEN COMMANDMENTS

dec·a·me·ter (dek′ə mēt′ər) *n.* [see DECA- & METER¹] a measure of length, equal to 10 meters: also, chiefly Brit., **dec′a·me′tre** (-mēt′ər)

de·camp (di kamp′) *vi.* [< Fr.: see DE- & CAMP] **1.** to break or leave camp **2.** to go away suddenly and secretly; run away —de·camp′ment *n.*

de·cant (di kant′) *vt.* [< Fr. < ML. < L. *de-,* from + *canthus,* rim, edge] to pour off (a liquid) gently without stirring up the sediment —de·can·ta·tion (dē′kan tā′shən) *n.*

de·cant·er (-ər) *n.* a decorative glass bottle, used for serving wine, etc.

de·cap·i·tate (di kap′ə tāt′) *vi.* -tat′ed, -tat′ing [< Fr. < ML. pp. of *decapitare* < L. *de-,* off + *caput,* the head] to cut off the head of; behead —de·cap′i·ta′tion *n.* —de·cap′i·ta′tor *n.*

dec·a·pod (dek′ə päd′) *adj.* [see DECA- & -POD] ten-legged —*n.* **1.** any crustacean with ten legs, as a lobster, shrimp, crab, etc. **2.** any cephalopod with ten arms, as a squid —de·cap·o·dal (di kap′ə d'l), de·cap′o·dous (-dəs) *adj.* —de·cap′o·dan (-dən) *adj., n.*

DECANTER

de·car·bon·ate (dē kär′bə nāt′) *vt.* -at′ed, -at′ing to remove carbon dioxide or carbonic acid from —de·car′bon·a′tion *n.*

de·car·bon·ize (-nīz′) *vt.* -ized′, -iz′ing to remove carbon from: also de·car′bu·rize′ (-bə rīz′, -byoo-) -rized′, -riz′ing —de·car′bon·i·za′tion *n.*

dec·a·syl·la·ble (dek′ə sil′ə b'l) *n.* a line of verse with ten syllables —dec′a·syl·lab′ic (-si lab′ik) *adj.*

de·cath·lon (di kath′län, -lən) *n.* [DEC(A)- + Gr. *athlon,* a contest] an athletic contest consisting of ten events in track and field sports: the contestant receiving the highest total of points wins

De·ca·tur (di kāt′ər) [after ff.] city in C Ill.: pop. 94,000

De·ca·tur (di kāt′ər), **Stephen** 1779–1820; U.S. naval officer

de·cay (di kā′) *vi.* [< Anglo-Fr. & OFr. < VL. *decadere:* see DECADENCE] **1.** to lose strength, soundness, prosperity, etc. gradually; deteriorate **2.** to rot —*vt.* to cause to decay —*n.* **1.** a gradual decline; deterioration **2.** a rotting **3.** *a)* rottenness *b)* rotted matter **4.** *a)* the spontaneous disintegration of radioactive atoms with a resulting decrease in their number *b)* the spontaneous disintegration of a particle or nucleus, as a meson, with the formation of a more stable state

de·cease (di sēs′) *n.* [< OFr. < L. *decessus,* pp. of *decedere* < *de-,* from + *cedere,* to go] death —*vi.* -ceased′, -ceas′ing to die

de·ceased (di sēst′) *adj.* dead —the deceased the dead person or persons

de·ce·dent (di sēd′nt) *n. Law* a deceased person

de·ceit (di sēt′) *n.* [< OFr. pp. of *deceivir*] **1.** the act of deceiving or lying **2.** a dishonest action or trick; lie **3.** the quality of being deceitful

de·ceit·ful (-fəl) *adj.* **1.** tending to deceive; apt to lie or cheat **2.** intended to deceive; deceptive; false —de·ceit′ful·ly *adv.* —de·ceit′ful·ness *n.*

de·ceive (di sēv′) vt. -ceived′, -ceiv′ing [< OFr. deceveir < L. decipere, to ensnare < de-, from < capere, to take] to make (a person) believe what is not true; mislead —vi. to use deceit —de·ceiv′a·ble adj. —de·ceiv′er n. —de·ceiv′ing·ly adv.

de·cel·er·ate (dē sel′ə rāt′) vt., vi. -at′ed, -at′ing [DE- + (AC)CELERATE] to slow down —de·cel·er·a′tion n. —de·cel′er·a′tor n.

De·cem·ber (di sem′bər) n. [< OFr. < L. < decem, ten: the early Romans reckoned from March] the twelfth and last month of the year, having 31 days: abbrev. Dec., D.

de·cem·vir (di sem′vər) n., pl. -virs, -vir·i′ (-və rī′) [L. < decem, ten + vir, a man] a member of a council of ten magistrates in ancient Rome

de·cen·cy (dē′s'n sē) n., pl. -cies 1. a being decent; propriety; proper behavior, modesty, good taste, etc. 2. [pl.] socially proper actions 3. [pl.] things needed for a proper standard of living

de·cen·ni·al (di sen′ē əl) adj. [< L. decem, ten + annus, year + -AL] 1. of or lasting ten years 2. occurring every ten years —n. a tenth anniversary —de·cen′ni·al·ly adv.

de·cent (dē′s'nt) adj. [< L. prp. of decere, to befit] 1. proper and fitting 2. not immodest; not obscene 3. conforming to approved social standards; respectable 4. reasonably good; adequate [decent wages] 5. fair and kind 6. [Colloq.] adequately clothed for propriety —de′cent·ly adv.

de·cen·tral·ize (dē sen′trə līz′) vt. -ized′, -iz′ing to break up a concentration of (governmental authority, etc.) in a main center and distribute more widely —de·cen′tral·i·za′tion n.

de·cep·tion (di sep′shən) n. [< OFr. < L. pp. of decipere] 1. a deceiving or being deceived 2. something that deceives, as an illusion, or is meant to deceive, as a fraud

de·cep·tive (-tiv) adj. deceiving or meant to deceive —de·cep′tive·ly adv. —de·cep′tive·ness n.

dec·i- [Fr. < L. < decem, ten] a combining form meaning one tenth [decigram]

dec·i·bel (des′ə bel′, -b'l) n. [DECI- + bel (after A. G. Bell)] a numerical expression of the relative loudness of a sound or of the relative power level of an electrical signal

de·cide (di sīd′) vt. -cid′ed, -cid′ing [< L. decidere < de-, off + caedere, to cut] 1. to end (a contest, dispute, etc.) by giving one side the victory 2. to reach a decision about 3. to cause to reach a decision —vi. to arrive at a judgment or decision —de·cid′a·ble adj. —de·cid′er n.

de·cid·ed (di sīd′id) adj. 1. definite; clear-cut 2. unhesitating; determined —de·cid′ed·ly adv.

de·cid·u·ous (di sij′oo wəs) adj. [L. deciduus < de-, off + cadere, to fall] 1. falling off at a certain season or stage of growth, as some leaves, antlers, etc. 2. shedding leaves annually: opposed to EVERGREEN —de·cid′u·ous·ly adv. —de·cid′u·ous·ness n.

dec·i·gram (des′ə gram′) n. [see DECI- & GRAM] a metric weight, equal to 1/10 gram: also, chiefly Brit., dec′i·gramme′

dec·i·li·ter (des′ə lēt′ər) n. [see DECI- & LITER] a metric measure of volume, equal to 1/10 liter: also, chiefly Brit., dec′i·li′tre

de·cil·lion (di sil′yən) n. [DECI- + (M)ILLION] 1. in the U.S. and France, the number written as 1 followed by 33 zeros 2. in England and Germany, the number written as 1 followed by 60 zeros —adj. amounting to one decillion in number

dec·i·mal (des′ə m'l) adj. [OFr. < ML. decimalis < L. decem, ten] of or based on the number 10; progressing by tens —n. a fraction with an unwritten denominator of 10 or some power of ten, indicated by a point (decimal point) before the numerator (Ex.: .5 = 5/10): in full, decimal fraction —dec′i·mal·ly adv.

decimal classification a library system of classifying books by use of numbers with decimals

dec·i·mate (des′ə māt′) vt. -mat′ed, -mat′ing [< L. pp. of decimare < decem, ten] 1. orig., to select by lot and kill every tenth one of 2. to destroy or kill a large part of —dec′i·ma′tion n. —dec′i·ma′tor n.

dec·i·me·ter (des′ə mēt′ər) n. [see DECI- & METER¹] a metric measure of length, equal to 1/10 meter: also, chiefly Brit., dec′i·me′tre

de·ci·pher (di sī′fər) vt. [DE- + CIPHER] 1. to translate (a message in cipher or code) into ordinary language; decode 2. to make out the meaning of (ancient inscriptions, a scrawl, etc.) —de·ci′pher·a·ble adj. —de·ci′pher·ment n.

de·ci·sion (di sizh′ən) n. 1. the act of deciding something 2. a judgment or conclusion reached or given 3. determination; firmness of mind [a man of decision] 4. Boxing a victory on points instead of by a knockout —de·ci′sion·al adj.

de·ci·sive (di sī′siv) adj. 1. that settles a dispute, question, etc.; conclusive 2. critically important; crucial 3. showing decision or determination —de·ci′sive·ly adv. —de·ci′sive·ness n.

dec·i·stere (des′ə stir′) n. [see DECI- & STERE] a metric measure of volume, 1/10 cubic meter

deck¹ (dek) n. [prob. < MLowG. verdeck (< ver-, prefix + decken, to cover)] 1. a roof over a section of a ship's hold, serving as a floor 2. any platform or floor like a ship's deck 3. a pack of playing cards —vt. [Slang] to knock down —clear the decks to get ready for action —hit the deck [Slang] 1. to get out of bed 2. to get ready for action 3. to throw oneself to the ground, as to avoid injury 4. to be knocked down —on deck [Colloq.] ready; on hand

deck² (dek) vt. [MDu. decken, to cover] 1. to cover with finery or ornaments; adorn 2. to furnish (a ship, etc.) with a deck

deck chair a folding chair, usually with a leg rest

-deck·er (dek′ər) a combining form meaning having (a specified number of) decks, layers, etc.

deck·hand (dek′hand′) n. a common sailor

deck·le edge (dek′'l) [G. dim. of decke, a cover] a rough, irregular edge sometimes given to a sheet of paper

de·claim (di klām′) vi., vt. [< L. < de-, intens. + clamare, to shout] 1. to recite (a speech, poem, etc.) with artificial eloquence 2. to speak or utter in a pompous way 3. to deliver a tirade (against) —de·claim′er n.

dec·la·ma·tion (dek′lə mā′shən) n. [< L. declamatio < pp. of prec.] 1. the act or art of declaiming 2. a speech, poem, etc. that is or can be declaimed —de·clam·a·to·ry (di klam′ə tôr′ē) adj.

de·clar·a·ble (di klar′ə b'l, -kler′-) adj. that can be or must be declared for taxation

dec·la·ra·tion (dek′lə rā′shən) n. 1. the act of declaring; announcement 2. a thing declared 3. a formal statement 4. a statement of taxable goods 5. the winning bid in a game of bridge

Declaration of Independence a formal statement adopted July 4, 1776, by the Second Continental Congress, declaring the thirteen American colonies free and independent of Great Britain

de·clar·a·tive (di klar′ə tiv, -kler′-) adj. making a statement or assertion: also de·clar′a·to·ry (-ə tôr′ē) —de·clar′a·tive·ly adv.

de·clare (di kler′) vt. -clared′, -clar′ing [< OFr. < L. < de-, intens. + clarare < clarus, clear] 1. to make clearly known; announce openly, formally, etc. 2. to show or reveal 3. to say emphatically 4. to make a statement of (taxable goods), as at customs 5. to authorize payment of (a dividend, etc.) 6. Card Games to establish (trump or no-trump) by a successful bid —vi. 1. to make a declaration 2. to state openly a choice, opinion, etc. (for or against) —declare oneself 1. to state strongly one's opinion 2. to reveal one's true character, etc. —I declare! I am surprised, startled, etc. —de·clar′er n.

de·clas·si·fy (dē klas′ə fī′) vt. -fied′, -fy′ing to remove (governmental documents, reports, etc.) from secret or restricted classifications and make available to the public

de·clen·sion (di klen′shən) n. [< OFr. < L. < pp. of declinare: see DECLINE] 1. a sloping; descent 2. a declining; deterioration 3. Gram. a) a class of nouns, pronouns, or adjectives having the same or a similar system of inflections to show case b) their inflection —de·clen′sion·al adj.

dec·li·na·tion (dek′lə nā′shən) n. 1. a bending or slop-ing downward 2. an oblique variation from a definite direction 3. the angle formed by a magnetic needle with the line pointing to true north 4. a polite refusal 5. Astron. the angular distance of a heavenly body north or south from the celestial equator

de·cline (di klīn′) vi. -clined′, -clin′ing [< OFr. < L. < de-, from + -clinare, to bend] 1. to bend or slope downward or aside 2. to sink, as the setting sun 3. to approach the end; wane 4. to deteriorate; decay 5. to descend to base or immoral behavior 6. to refuse to do something —vt. 1. to cause to bend or slope downward or aside 2. to refuse, esp. politely 3. Gram. to give the inflected forms of (a noun, pronoun, or adjective) —n. 1. a declining; deterioration; decay 2. a failing of health, etc. 3. a period of decline 4. the last part 5. a wasting disease, esp. tuberculosis of the lungs 6. a downward slope —de·clin′a·ble adj. —de·clin′er n.

de·cliv·i·tous (di kliv′ə təs) adj. fairly steep

de·cliv·i·ty (-tē) n., pl. -ties [< L. < de-, down + clivus, a slope] a downward slope of the ground

de·coct (di käkt′) vt. [< L. pp. of decoquere < de-, down + coquere, to cook] to extract the essence, flavor, etc. of by boiling —de·coc′tion n.

DECLINATION
(CP, celestial poles;
CE, celestial equator; O, observer, or
center of earth; DS,
or angle DOS, declination of star S)

**de·code** (dē kōd′) *vt.* **-cod′ed, -cod′ing** to translate (a coded message) into ordinary, understandable language —**de·cod′er** *n.*

**dé·col·le·té** (dā kal′ə tā′; *Fr.* dā kôl tā′) *adj.* [Fr., ult. < L. *de*, from + *collum,* the neck] **1.** cut low so as to bare the neck and shoulders **2.** wearing a décolleté dress, etc.

**de·col·o·ni·za·tion** (dē käl′ə nə zā′shən) *n.* a freeing or being freed from colonialism or colonial status —**de·col′o·nize′** (-nīz′) *vt., vi.* **-nized′, -niz′ing**

**de·com·pose** (dē′kəm pōz′) *vt., vi.* **-posed′, -pos′ing** [< Fr.: see DE- & COMPOSE] **1.** to break up into basic components or parts **2.** to rot —**de′com·pos′a·ble** *adj.* —**de′com·po·si′tion** (-käm pə zish′ən) *n.*

**de·com·press** (dē′kəm pres′) *vt.* to free from pressure —**de′com·pres′sion** *n.*

**decompression sickness** a condition caused by the formation of nitrogen bubbles in the blood or body tissues as a result of a sudden lowering of air pressure, resulting in collapse in severe cases

**de·con·gest·ant** (dē′kən jes′tənt) *n.* a medication that relieves congestion, as in the nasal passages

**de·con·tam·i·nate** (-tam′ə nāt′) *vt.* **-nat′ed, -nat′ing** to rid of a harmful substance, as radioactive products —**de′con·tam′i·na′tion** *n.*

**de·con·trol** (-trōl′) *vt.* **-trolled′, -trol′ling** to free from controls —*n.* withdrawal of controls

**dé·cor, de·cor** (dā kôr′, dā′kôr) *n.* [Fr. < L. < *decere,* to befit] the decorative scheme of a room, stage set, etc.

**dec·o·rate** (dek′ə rāt′) *vt.* **-rat′ed, -rat′ing** [< L. pp. of *decorare* < *decus,* an ornament] **1.** to adorn; ornament **2.** to plan and arrange the colors, furnishings, etc. of **3.** to paint or wallpaper **4.** to give a medal or similar token of honor to —**dec·o·ra·tive** (dek′ər ə tiv, -ə rāt′iv; dek′rə-) *adj.* —**dec′o·ra·tive·ly** *adv.* —**dec′o·ra·tive·ness** *n.* —**dec′o·ra′tor** *n.*

**dec·o·ra·tion** (dek′ə rā′shən) *n.* **1.** the act of decorating **2.** anything used for decorating; ornament **3.** a medal, badge, or similar token of honor

**Decoration Day** *same as* MEMORIAL DAY

**dec·or·ous** (dek′ər əs, di kôr′əs) *adj.* [L. *decorus,* becoming < *decor:* see DÉCOR] characterized by or showing decorum, good taste, etc. —**dec′o·rous·ly** *adv.*

**de·co·rum** (di kôr′əm) *n.* [L., neut. of *decorus:* see prec.] **1.** whatever is suitable or proper; propriety **2.** propriety and good taste in behavior, speech, dress, etc. **3.** an act or requirement of polite behavior: *often used in pl.*

**de·cou·page, dé·cou·page** (dā′kōō päzh′) *n.* [Fr., a cutting up] the mounting of decorative paper cutouts on a surface

**de·coy** (di koi′; *for n. also* dē′koi) *n.* [< Du. *de kooi,* the cage < L. *cavea,* CAGE] **1.** a place into which wild ducks, etc. are lured for capture **2.** an artificial or trained bird or animal used to lure game to a place where it can be shot **3.** a thing or person used to lure into a trap —*vt., vi.* to lure or be lured into a trap, danger, etc.

DECOY

**de·crease** (di krēs′; *also, & for n. usually,* dē′krēs) *vi., vt.* **-creased′, -creas′ing** [< OFr. < L. < *de-,* from + *crescere,* to grow] to become or cause to become gradually less, smaller, etc.; diminish —*n.* **1.** a decreasing; lessening **2.** amount of decreasing —**on the decrease** decreasing —**de·creas′ing·ly** *adv.*

**de·cree** (di krē′) *n.* [< OFr. < L. *decretum* < *de-,* from + *cernere,* to see, judge] **1.** an official order or decision, as of a government **2.** something that is or seems to be foreordained —*vt.* **-creed′, -cree′ing** to order, decide, or appoint by decree —*vi.* to issue a decree

**de·crep·it** (di krep′it) *adj.* [< OFr. < L. < *de-,* intens. + pp. of *crepare,* to creak] broken down or worn out by old age, illness, or long use —**de·crep′it·ly** *adv.*

**de·crep·i·tude** (di krep′ə tōōd′, -tyōōd′) *n.* a decrepit condition; feebleness or infirmity

**de·cre·scen·do** (dē′krə shen′dō, dā′-) *adj., adv.* [It.] *Music* with a gradual decrease in loudness —*n., pl.* **-dos** *Music* **1.** a gradual decrease in loudness: symbol > **2.** a decrescendo passage

**de·cre·tal** (di krēt′'l) *adj.* [< LL. *decretalis*] of or containing a decree —*n.* **1.** a decree **2.** *R.C.Ch.* a decree issued by the Pope on some matter of ecclesiastical discipline

**de·crim·i·nal·ize** (dē krim′ə n'l īz′) *vt.* **-ized′, -iz′ing** to eliminate or reduce the legal penalties for (a specified crime) [*to decriminalize* the use of marijuana]

**de·cry** (di krī′) *vt.* **-cried′, -cry′ing** [< Fr. < OFr. *descrier:*

see DE- & CRY] **1.** to speak out against strongly and openly; denounce **2.** to depreciate (money, etc.) officially —**de·cri′al** *n.* —**de·cri′er** *n.*

**de·cum·bent** (di kum′bənt) *adj.* [< L. prp. of *decumbere* < *de-,* down + *-cumbere, cubare,* to recline] **1.** lying down **2.** *Bot.* trailing on the ground and rising at the tip, as some stems —**de·cum′ben·cy** *n.*

**ded·i·cate** (ded′ə kāt′) *vt.* **-cat′ed, -cat′ing** [< L. pp. of *dedicare* < *de-,* intens. + *dicare,* to proclaim < *dicere,* to speak] **1.** to devote to a sacred purpose **2.** to devote to some work, duty, etc. **3.** to address (a book, artistic performance, etc.) to someone as a sign of honor or affection —**ded′i·ca′tor** *n.*

**ded·i·ca·tion** (ded′ə kā′shən) *n.* **1.** a dedicating or being dedicated **2.** an inscription, as in a book, dedicating it to someone **3.** wholehearted devotion —**ded′i·ca·to′ry, ded′i·ca′tive** *adj.*

**de·duce** (di dōōs′, -dyōōs′) *vt.* **-duced′, -duc′ing** [< L. < *de-,* down + *ducere,* to lead] **1.** to trace the course or derivation of **2.** to infer by logical reasoning; conclude from known facts or general principles —**de·duc′i·ble** *adj.*

**de·duct** (di dukt′) *vt.* [L. *deductus,* pp. of *deducere:* see prec.] to take away or subtract (a quantity)

**de·duct·i·ble** (-ə b'l) *adj.* **1.** that can be deducted **2.** that is allowed as a deduction in computing income tax —**de·duct′i·bil′i·ty** *n.*

**de·duc·tion** (di duk′shən) *n.* **1.** a deducting or being deducted; subtraction **2.** the amount deducted **3.** *Logic* reasoning from the general to the specific, or from a premise to a logical conclusion; also, a conclusion so deduced: opposed to INDUCTION —**de·duc′tive** *adj.* —**de·duc′tive·ly** *adv.*

**deed** (dēd) *n.* [OE. *ded, dæd*] **1.** a thing done; act **2.** a feat of courage, skill, etc. **3.** action; actual performance **4.** *Law* a document under seal which, when delivered, transfers a present interest in property —*vt.* to transfer (property) by such a document —**in deed** in fact; really

**deem** (dēm) *vt., vi.* [OE. *deman,* to judge < base of *dom,* DOOM] to think, believe, or judge

**de·em·pha·size** (dē em′fə sīz′) *vt.* **-sized′, -siz′ing** to lessen the importance or prominence of —**de·em′pha·sis** (-sis) *n.*

**deep** (dēp) *adj.* [OE. *deop*] **1.** extending far downward from the top, inward from the surface, or backward from the front **2.** extending down, back, or in a specified distance [two feet *deep*] **3.** *a)* located far down or back *b)* coming from or going far down or back **4.** hard to understand; abstruse **5.** extremely grave or serious [in *deep* trouble] **6.** strongly felt **7.** intellectually profound **8.** *a)* tricky and sly *b)* carefully guarded [a *deep* secret] **9.** dark and rich [a *deep* red] **10.** absorbed by [*deep* in thought] **11.** *a)* intense *b)* heavy and unbroken [a *deep* sleep] **12.** of low pitch [a *deep* voice] —*n.* **1.** a deep place **2.** the middle part; part that is darkest, etc. [the *deep* of the night] —*adv.* in a deep way; far down, far back, far on, etc. —**go off the deep end** [Colloq.] to become angry or excited —**in deep water** in trouble or difficulty —**the deep** [Poet.] the sea or ocean —**deep′ly** *adv.* —**deep′ness** *n.*

**deep-dish pie** (-dish′) a pie baked in a deep dish and having only a top crust

**deep·en** (-'n) *vt., vi.* to make or become deep or deeper

**Deep·freeze** (-frēz′) *a trademark for* a deep freezer —*n.* [d-] **1.** storage in a deep freezer **2.** a condition of suspended activity —*vt.* [d-] **-froze′** *or* **-freezed′, -fro′zen** *or* **-freezed′, -freez′ing 1.** to subject (foods) to sudden freezing so as to preserve and store **2.** to store in a deep freezer

**deep-fry** (-frī′) *vt.* **-fried′, -fry′ing** to fry in a deep pan of boiling fat or oil

**deep-root·ed** (-rōōt′id, -root′id) *adj.* **1.** having deep roots **2.** firmly fixed; hard to remove

**deep-seat·ed** (-sēt′id) *adj.* **1.** placed or originating far beneath the surface **2.** firmly fixed

**deep-set** (-set′) *adj.* **1.** deeply set **2.** firmly fixed

**deer** (dir) *n., pl.* **deer,** *occas.* **deers** [OE. *deor,* wild animal] any of a family of hoofed, cud-chewing animals, including the moose, reindeer, caribou, etc., the males of which usually bear antlers that are shed annually

**deer·skin** (-skin′) *n.* **1.** the hide of a deer **2.** leather or a garment made from this

**de·es·ca·late** (dē es′kə lāt′) *vi., vt.* **-lat′ed, -lat′ing** to lessen in scope, magnitude, etc. —**de·es′ca·la′tion** *n.*

**def.** **1.** defendant **2.** deferred **3.** definite **4.** definition

**de·face** (di fās′) *vt.* **-faced′, -fac′ing** [< OFr. *desfacier:* see DE- & FACE] to spoil or mar the surface or appearance of —**de·face′ment** *n.* —**de·fac′er** *n.*

**de fac·to** (di fak′tō, dā′) [L.] existing in actual fact though not by official recognition, etc. [a *de facto* government]: cf. DE JURE

**de·fal·cate** (di fal'kāt, -fôl'-) *vi.* **-cat·ed, -cat·ing** [< ML. pp. of *defalcare*, to cut off < L. *de-*, from + *falx* (gen. *falcis*), sickle] to steal or misuse funds entrusted to one's care; embezzle —**de·fal·ca·tion** (dē'fal kā'shən, -fôl-) *n.* —**de·fal'ca·tor** *n.*

**de·fame** (di fām') *vt.* **-famed', -fam'ing** [< OFr. or ML. < L. < *dis-*, from + *fama*, FAME] to attack the reputation of; slander or libel —**def·a·ma·tion** (def'ə mā'shən) *n.* —**de·fam·a·to·ry** (di fam'ə tôr'ē) *adj.* —**de·fam'er** *n.*

**de·fault** (di fôlt') *n.* [< OFr. *defaute* < L. *de-*, away + *fallere*, to fail, deceive] failure to do or appear as required; specif., *a*) failure to pay money due *b*) failure to appear in court to defend or prosecute a case *c*) failure to take part in or finish a contest —*vi.* **1.** to fail to do or appear as required; specif., *a*) failure to make payment when due *b*) to fail to appear in court *c*) to fail to take part in or finish a contest **2.** to lose by default —*vt.* **1.** to fail to do, pay, finish, etc. (something) when required **2.** to lose (a contest, etc.) by default —**de·fault'er** *n.*

**de·feat** (di fēt') *vt.* [< OFr. < ML. < L. *dis-*, from + *facere*, to do] **1.** to win victory over; overcome; beat **2.** to bring to nothing; frustrate **3.** to make null and void —*n.* a defeating or being defeated

**de·feat·ist** (-ist) *n.* a person who too readily accepts or expects defeat —*adj.* of or like a defeatist —**de·feat'ism** *n.*

**def·e·cate** (def'ə kāt') *vt.* **-cat·ed, -cat·ing** [< L. pp. of *defaecare* < *de-*, from + *faex* (gen. *faecis*), dregs] to remove impurities from; refine —*vi.* **1.** to become free from impurities **2.** to excrete waste matter from the bowels —**def'e·ca'tion** *n.* —**def'e·ca'tor** *n.*

**de·fect** (dē'fekt; *also, and for v. always*, di fekt') *n.* [< L. pp. of *deficere*, to fail < *de-*, from + *facere*, to do] **1.** lack of something necessary for completeness; shortcoming **2.** an imperfection; fault; blemish —*vi.* to forsake a party, cause, etc.; desert —**de·fec'tor** *n.*

**de·fec·tion** (di fek'shən) *n.* **1.** abandonment of loyalty, duty, etc.; desertion **2.** a failure

**de·fec·tive** (-tiv) *adj.* **1.** having a defect or defects; faulty **2.** *Gram.* lacking some of the usual grammatical forms **3.** subnormal in intelligence —*n.* a person with some bodily or mental defect —**de·fec'tive·ly** *adv.* —**de·fec'tive·ness** *n.*

**de·fence** (di fens') *n. Brit. sp.* of DEFENSE

**de·fend** (di fend') *vt.* [< OFr. < L. *defendere* < *de-*, away + *fendere*, to strike] **1.** to guard from attack; protect **2.** to support, maintain, or justify **3.** *Law a*) to oppose (an action, etc.) *b*) to act as lawyer for (an accused) —*vi.* to make a defense —**de·fend'a·ble** *adj.* —**de·fend'er** *n.*

**de·fend·ant** (di fen'dənt) *adj.* defending —*n. Law* the person sued or accused: opposed to PLAINTIFF

**de·fense** (di fens', dē'fens) *n.* [OFr. < LL. < L. pp. of *defendere*] **1.** a defending against attack or danger **2.** a being defended **3.** means of protection **4.** justification or support by speech or writing **5.** self-protection, as by boxing **6.** the side that is defending in any contest **7.** *a*) the arguments of the defendant in contesting a case *b*) the defendant and his lawyer or lawyers, collectively —**de·fense'less** *adj.* —**de·fense'less·ly** *adv.* —**de·fense'less·ness** *n.*

**defense mechanism** *Psychiatry* any behavior unconsciously used by an individual to protect himself against painful feelings, impulses, etc.

**de·fen·si·ble** (di fen'sə b'l) *adj.* that can be defended or justified —**de·fen'si·bil'i·ty, de·fen'si·ble·ness** *n.* —**de·fen'si·bly** *adv.*

**de·fen·sive** (-siv) *adj.* **1.** defending **2.** of or for defense **3.** *Psychol.* feeling under attack and hence quick to justify one's actions —*n.* a position of defense: chiefly in the phrase **on the defensive**, in a position that makes defense necessary —**de·fen'sive·ly** *adv.* —**de·fen'sive·ness** *n.*

**de·fer¹** (di fur') *vt., vi.* **-ferred', -fer'ring** [< OFr. *differer*: see DIFFER] **1.** to put off; postpone; delay **2.** to postpone the induction of (a person) into compulsory military service —**de·fer'ment, de·fer'ral** *n.* —**de·fer'rer** *n.*

**de·fer²** (di fur') *vi.* **-ferred', -fer'ring** [< OFr. < L. *de-*, down + *ferre*, to bear] to give in or yield to the wish or judgment of another

**def·er·ence** (def'ər əns) *n.* **1.** a yielding in opinion, judgment, etc. **2.** courteous regard or respect —**in deference to** out of regard for (a person, his wishes, etc.)

**def·er·en·tial** (def'ə ren'shəl) *adj.* showing deference; very respectful: also **def·er·ent** (def'ər ənt) —**def'er·en'tial·ly** *adv.*

**de·fi·ance** (di fī'əns) *n.* **1.** a defying; open, bold resistance to authority or opposition **2.** a challenge —**bid defiance to** to defy —**in defiance of** in spite of —**de·fi'ant** *adj.* —**de·fi'ant·ly** *adv.*

**de·fib·ril·late** (di fib'rə lāt') *vt.* **-lat·ed, -lat'ing** to stop fibrillation of the heart, as by electric current —**de·fib'ril·la'tion** *n.* —**de·fib'ril·la'tor** *n.*

**de·fi·cien·cy** (di fish'ən sē) *n.* **1.** the quality or state of

being deficient; absence of an essential; incompleteness **2.** *pl.* **-cies** *a*) a shortage *b*) the amount of shortage; deficit

**deficiency disease** a disease, as rickets, caused by lack of vitamins, minerals, etc. in the diet

**de·fi·cient** (di fish'ənt) *adj.* [< L. *deficiens*, prp. of *deficere*: see DEFECT] **1.** lacking in some essential; incomplete; defective **2.** inadequate in amount, quality, degree, etc. —*n.* a deficient person or thing —**de·fi'cient·ly** *adv.*

**def·i·cit** (def'ə sit) *n.* [L., it is lacking < *deficere*, to lack] the amount by which a sum of money is less than the required amount, as an excess of expenditure over income

**de·fi·er** (di fī'ər) *n.* a person who defies

**de·file¹** (di fīl') *vt.* **-filed', -fil'ing** [< OFr. *defouler*, to tread underfoot (infl. by OE. *fylan*, make foul)] **1.** to make filthy; pollute **2.** to corrupt **3.** to profane or sully (a person's name, etc.) **4.** [Archaic] to violate the chastity of —**de·file'ment** *n.* —**de·fil'er** *n.*

**de·file²** (di fīl', dē'fīl) *vi.* **-filed', -fil'ing** [< Fr. < *dé-* (L. *de*), from + *filer*, to form a line] to march in single file or by files —*n.* **1.** a narrow passage through which troops must defile **2.** any narrow valley or mountain pass

**de·fine** (di fīn') *vt.* **-fined', -fin'ing** [< OFr. < L. *definire*, to limit < *de-*, from + *finis*, boundary] **1.** to determine the boundaries of **2.** to determine the extent and nature of **3.** to state the meaning or meanings of (a word, etc.) —*vi.* to prepare definitions —**de·fin'a·ble** *adj.* —**de·fin'er** *n.*

**def·i·nite** (def'ə nit) *adj.* [< L. pp. of *definire*: see prec.] **1.** having exact limits **2.** precise and clear in meaning; explicit **3.** certain; positive **4.** *Gram.* limiting or specifying ["the" is the *definite* article] —**def'i·nite·ly** *adv.* —**def'i·nite·ness** *n.*

**def·i·ni·tion** (def'ə nish'ən) *n.* **1.** a defining or being defined **2.** a statement of the meaning of a word, phrase, etc. **3.** *a*) a putting or being in clear, sharp outline *b*) a making or being definite or explicit **4.** the power of a lens to show (an object) in clear, sharp outline **5.** *Radio & TV* the clearness with which sounds or images are reproduced —**def'i·ni'tion·al** *adj.*

**de·fin·i·tive** (di fin'ə tiv) *adj.* **1.** decisive; conclusive **2.** most nearly complete and accurate **3.** serving to define precisely **4.** *Biol.* fully developed —**de·fin'i·tive·ly** *adv.* —**de·fin'i·tive·ness** *n.*

**de·flate** (di flāt') *vt., vi.* **-flat·ed, -flat'ing** [DE- + (IN)FLATE] **1.** to collapse by letting out air or gas **2.** to make or become smaller or less important **3.** to cause deflation of (currency, prices, etc.) Opposed to INFLATE —**de·fla'tor** *n.*

**de·fla·tion** (di flā'shən) *n.* **1.** a deflating or being deflated **2.** a lessening of the amount of money in circulation, causing a rise in its value and a fall in prices —**de·fla'tion·ar'y** *adj.*

**de·flect** (di flekt') *vt., vi.* [< L. < *de-*, from + *flectere*, to bend] to bend or turn to one side; swerve —**de·flec'tion** or Brit. **de·flex'ion** *n.* —**de·flec'tive** *adj.* —**de·flec'tor** *n.*

**de·flow·er** (di flou'ər) *vt.* [see DE- & FLOWER] **1.** to make (a woman) no longer a virgin **2.** to ravage or spoil **3.** to remove flowers from (a plant) —**def·lo·ra·tion** (def'lə rā'shən) *n.*

**De·foe** (di fō'), **Daniel** 1660?–1731; Eng. writer

**de·fo·li·ant** (dē fō'lē ənt) *n.* a chemical spray that strips growing plants of their leaves

**de·fo·li·ate** (-āt') *vt.* **-at·ed, -at'ing** [< LL. pp. of *defoliare* < L. *de-*, from + *folium*, a leaf] **1.** to strip (trees, etc.) of leaves **2.** to use defoliants on —**de·fo'li·a'tion** *n.* —**de·fo'li·a'tor** *n.*

**de·for·est** (dē fôr'ist, -fär'-) *vt.* to clear (land) of forests or trees —**de·for'est·a'tion** *n.*

**De For·est** (di fôr'ist, fär'-), **Lee** 1873–1961; U.S. inventor

**de·form** (di fôrm') *vt.* [< OFr. < L. < *de-*, from + *forma*, form] **1.** to impair the form or shape of **2.** to make ugly; disfigure **3.** *Physics* to change the shape of by pressure or stress —*vi.* to become deformed —**de·form'a·ble** *adj.* —**de·for·ma·tion** (dē'fôr mā'shən, def'ər-) *n.*

**de·formed** (di fôrmd') *adj.* changed as in form or shape, esp. so as to be misshapen, ugly, etc.

**de·form·i·ty** (di fôr'mə tē) *n., pl.* **-ties** **1.** the condition of being deformed **2.** a deformed or disfigured part of the body **3.** ugliness or depravity **4.** anything deformed or disfigured

**de·fraud** (di frôd') *vt.* [< OFr. < L. *defraudare* < *de-*, from + *fraus*, FRAUD] to take or hold back property, rights, etc. from by fraud; cheat —**de·frau·da·tion** (dē'frô dā'shən) *n.*

**de·fray** (di frā') *vt.* [< Fr. < OFr., prob. < L. *de*, from + *fractum*, neut. pp. of *frangere*, to break] to pay (the cost or expenses) —**de·fray'a·ble** *adj.* —**de·fray'al, de·fray'ment** *n.*

**de·frost** (di frôst') *vt.* **1.** to remove frost or ice from by thawing **2.** to cause (frozen foods) to become unfrozen —*vi.* to become defrosted

**de·frost·er** (-ər) *n.* a device for melting ice and frost, as on a windshield

**deft** (deft) *adj.* [see DAFT] skillful in a quick, sure, and easy way —**deft′ly** *adv.* —**deft′ness** *n.*

**de·funct** (di fuŋkt′) *adj.* [< L. *defunctus,* pp. of *defungi,* to finish, die < *de-,* from, off + *fungi,* to perform] no longer living or existing; dead or extinct

**de·fuse** (dē fyoōz′) *vt.* -**fused′,** -**fus′ing** 1. to remove the fuse from (a bomb or the like) 2. to render harmless

**de·fy** (di fī′; *also for n.* dē′fī) *vt.* -**fied′,** -**fy′ing** [< OFr. *defier* < L. *dis-,* from + *fidus,* faithful] 1. to resist or oppose boldly or openly 2. to resist completely in a baffling way 3. to dare (someone) to do or prove something —*n., pl.* -**fies** [Colloq.] a defiance or challenge

**De·gas** (də gä′), (Hilaire Germain) **Ed·gar** (ed gàr′) 1834–1917; Fr. painter

**de Gaulle** (də gōl′; *Fr.* gōl′), **Charles** 1890–1970; Fr. general; president of France (1959–69)

**de·gauss** (di gous′) *vt.* [DE- + GAUSS] to demagnetize (as a ship) by passing an electric current through a coil along or around the edge in order to neutralize the surrounding magnetic field —**de·gauss′er** *n.*

**de·gen·er·a·cy** (di jen′ər ə sē) *n.* 1. the state of being degenerate 2. degenerate behavior

**de·gen·er·ate** (-ər it; *for v.* -ə rāt′) *adj.* [L. pp. of *degenerare,* ult. < *de-,* from + *genus,* race] 1. having sunk below a former or normal condition, etc.; deteriorated 2. morally corrupt; depraved —*n.* a degenerate person, esp. one who is morally depraved or sexually perverted —*vi.* -**at′ed,** -**at′ing** 1. to lose former normal or higher qualities 2. to become debased morally, culturally, etc. 3. *Biol.* to undergo degeneration —**de·gen′er·ate·ly** *adv.* —**de·gen′er·ate·ness** *n.* —**de·gen′er·a·tive** *adj.* —**de·gen′er·a·tive·ly** *adv.*

**de·gen·er·a·tion** (di jen′ə rā′shən) *n.* 1. the process of degenerating 2. a degenerate condition 3. *Biol.* deterioration or loss of a function or structure in the course of evolution 4. *Med.* deterioration in structure or function of cells, tissues, or organs, as in disease or aging

**de·grade** (di grād′) *vt.* -**grad′ed,** -**grad′ing** [< OFr. < LL. *degradare* < L. *de-,* down + *gradus:* see GRADE] 1. to lower in rank or status; demote 2. to lower or corrupt in quality, moral character, etc. 3. to bring into dishonor or contempt 4. *Chem.* to convert (an organic compound) into a simpler compound 5. *Geol.* to lower (a land surface) by erosion —**de·grad′a·ble** *adj.* —**deg·ra·da·tion** (deg′rə dā′shən) *n.* —**de·grad′er** *n.*

**de·grad·ed** (-id) *adj.* disgraced, debased, depraved, etc. —**de·grad′ed·ly** *adv.* —**de·grad′ed·ness** *n.*

**de·grad·ing** (-iŋ) *adj.* that degrades; debasing —**de·grad′ing·ly** *adv.*

**de·gree** (di grē′) *n.* [< OFr. < LL. *degradare:* see DEGRADE] 1. any of the successive steps or stages in a process or series 2. a step in the direct line of descent 3. social or official rank 4. relative condition; manner or respect 5. extent, amount, or relative intensity [hungry to a slight *degree*] 6. *Algebra* rank as determined by the sum of a term's exponents [a³c² and x⁵ are each of the fifth *degree*] 7. *Educ.* a rank given by a college or university to a student who has completed a required course of study, or to a distinguished person as an honor 8. *Gram.* a grade of comparison of adjectives and adverbs [the superlative *degree* of "good" is "best"] 9. *Law* the seriousness of a crime [murder in the first *degree*] 10. *Math., Astron., Geog.,* etc. a unit of measure for angles or arcs, 1/360 of the circumference of a circle 11. *Music a)* a line or space on the staff *b)* an interval between two such lines or spaces 12. *Physics* a unit of measure on a scale, as for temperature —**by degrees** step by step; gradually —**to a degree** somewhat

**de·hisce** (di his′) *vi.* -**hisced′,** -**hisc′ing** [< L. < *de-,* off + *hiscere,* to gape] to burst or split open, as a seedpod —**de·his′cence** *n.* —**de·his′cent** *adj.*

**de·horn** (dē hôrn′) *vt.* to remove the horns from

**de·hu·man·ize** (dē hyōō′mə nīz′) *vt.* -**ized′,** -**iz′ing** to deprive of human qualities; make inhuman or machinelike —**de·hu′man·i·za′tion** *n.*

**de·hu·mid·i·fy** (dē′hyōō mid′ə fī′) *vt.* -**fied′,** -**fy′ing** to remove moisture from (the air, etc.) —**de′hu·mid′i·fi·ca′tion** *n.* —**de′hu·mid′i·fi′er** *n.*

**de·hy·drate** (dē hī′drāt) *vt.* -**drat·ed,** -**drat·ing** to remove water from (a compound, body tissues, etc.) dry —*vi.* to lose water; become dry —**de′hy·dra′tion** *n.* —**de·hy′dra·tor** *n.*

**de·hy·dro·gen·ate** (dē hī′drə jə nāt′) *vt.* -**at′ed,** -**at′ing** to remove hydrogen from: also **de·hy′dro·gen·ize′** (-nīz′) -**ized′,** -**iz′ing** —**de·hy′dro·gen·a′tion** *n.*

**de-ice** (dē īs′) *vt.* -**iced′,** -**ic′ing** to melt ice from or keep free of ice —**de-ic′er** *n.*

**de·i·fy** (dē′ə fī′) *vt.* -**fied′,** -**fy′ing** [< OFr. < LL. < L. *deus,* god + *facere,* to make] 1. to make a god of; rank among the gods 2. to look upon or worship as a god —**de·if′ic** (-if′ik) *adj.* —**de′i·fi·ca′tion** (-ə fi kā′shən) *n.* —**de′i·fi′er** *n.*

**deign** (dān) *vi.* [< OFr. < L. *dignare* < *dignus,* worthy] to think it not beneath one's dignity (*to do* something); condescend

**de·ism** (dē′iz′m) *n.* [< Fr. < L. *deus,* god] the doctrine that God created the world and its natural laws, but takes no further part in its functioning —**de′ist** *n.* —**de·is′tic, de·is′ti·cal** *adj.* —**de·is′ti·cal·ly** *adv.*

**de·i·ty** (dē′ə tē) *n., pl.* -**ties** [< OFr. < LL. < L. *deus,* god] 1. the state of being a god; divine nature 2. a god or goddess —**the Deity** God

‡**dé·jà vu** (dā zhá vü′) [Fr., lit., already seen] *Psychol.* the illusion that one has previously experienced something actually new to one

**de·ject** (di jekt′) *vt.* [< L. pp. of *dejicere* < *de-,* down + *jacere,* to throw] to dishearten; depress

**de·ject·ed** (di jek′tid) *adj.* in low spirits; depressed; disheartened —**de·ject′ed·ly** *adv.* —**de·ject′ed·ness** *n.*

**de·jec·tion** (di jek′shən) *n.* lowness of spirits; depression

**de ju·re** (di joor′ē, dā) [L.] by right or legal establishment [*de jure* government] : cf. DE FACTO

**dek·a-** *same as* DECA-: also, before a vowel, **dek-**

**del.** 1. delegate 2. delegation 3. delete

**De·la·croix** (də lå krwä′), (Ferdinand Victor) **Eu·gène** (ö zhen′) 1798–1863; Fr. painter

**Del·a·ware** (del′ə wer′, -war′) [after Baron *De La Warr,* colonial gov. of Va. (1610–11)] 1. E State of the U.S., on the Atlantic: 2,057 sq. mi.; pop. 595,000; cap. Dover: abbrev. **Del., DE** 2. river flowing southward from S N.Y. into the Atlantic —*n.* 1. *pl.* -**wares′,** -**ware′** a member of a tribe of Indians who lived in the Delaware River valley 2. their Algonquian language —**Del′a·war′e·an** *adj., n.*

**de·lay** (di lā′) *vt.* [< OFr. < *de-,* intens. + *laier,* to leave, let < L. *laxare:* see RELAX] 1. to put off; postpone 2. to make late; detain —*vi.* to stop for a while; linger —*n.* 1. a delaying or being delayed 2. the period of time for which something is delayed —**de·lay′er** *n.*

**de·le** (dē′lē) *vt.* -**led,** -**le·ing** [L., imperative sing. of *delere:* see DELETE] *Printing* to take out (a letter, word, etc.); delete: usually in the imperative and expressed by the mark (ℛ), indicating the matter to be deleted —*n.* this mark

**de·lec·ta·ble** (di lek′tə b'l) *adj.* [< L. < *delectare:* see DELIGHT] very pleasing; delightful; now, esp., pleasing to the taste; delicious —**de·lec′ta·bil′i·ty, de·lec′ta·ble·ness** *n.* —**de·lec′ta·bly** *adv.*

**de·lec·ta·tion** (dē′lek tā′shən, di lek′-) *n.* [OFr. < L. < *delectare:* see DELIGHT] delight; entertainment

**del·e·gate** (del′ə gāt′; *also for n.* -git) *n.* [< L. pp. of *delegare* < *de-,* from + *legare,* to send] 1. a person authorized to act for others; representative, as at a convention 2. a member of a House of Delegates —*vt.* -**gat′ed,** -**gat′ing** 1. to send or appoint as a representative or deputy 2. to entrust (authority, power, etc.) to a person acting as one's representative

**del·e·ga·tion** (del′ə gā′shən) *n.* 1. a delegating or being delegated 2. a body of delegates Also **del·e·ga·cy** (del′ə gə sē) *pl.* -**cies**

**de·lete** (di lēt′) *vt.* -**let′ed,** -**let′ing** [< L. *deletus,* pp. of *delere,* to destroy] to take out (a printed or written letter, word, etc.); cross out —**de·le′tion** *n.*

**del·e·te·ri·ous** (del′ə tir′ē əs) *adj.* [Gr. *dēlētērios* < *dēleisthai,* to injure] harmful to health, well-being, etc.; injurious —**del′e·te′ri·ous·ly** *adv.* —**del′e·te′ri·ous·ness** *n.*

**delft·ware** (delft′wer′) *n.* 1. glazed earthenware, usually blue and white, which originated in Delft, a city in W Netherlands 2. any similar ware Also **delft, delf** (delf)

**Del·hi** (del′ē) city in N India: pop. 2,062,000: see also NEW DELHI

**Del·ia** (dēl′yə) [L., fem. of *Delius,* of Delos, a Greek island] a feminine name

**de·lib·er·ate** (di lib′ər it; *for v.* -āt′) *adj.* [< L. pp. of *deliberare* < *de-,* intens. + *librare,* to weigh < *libra,* a scales] 1. carefully thought out and formed, or done on purpose 2. careful in considering; not rash or hasty 3. unhurried and methodical [*deliberate* aim] —*vi.* -**at′ed,** -**at′ing** to think or consider carefully and fully; esp., to consider reasons for and against in order to make up one's mind —*vt.* to consider carefully —**de·lib′er·ate·ly** *adv.* —**de·lib′er·ate·ness** *n.* —**de·lib′er·a′tor** *n.*

**de·lib·er·a·tion** (di lib′ə rā′shən) *n.* 1. a deliberating, or considering carefully 2. [*often pl.*] consideration and discussion before reaching a decision 3. carefulness; slowness

**de·lib·er·a·tive** (di lib′ə rāt′iv, -ər ə tiv) *adj.* 1. of or for deliberating [a *deliberative* assembly] 2. characterized by deliberation —**de·lib′er·a′tive·ly** *adv.* —**de·lib′er·a′tive·ness** *n.*

**del·i·ca·cy** (del′i kə sē) *n., pl.* **-cies** 1. a delicate quality 2. graceful slightness, softness, etc.; fineness 3. weakness of constitution or health 4. a need for careful and deft handling 5. fineness of feeling or appreciation 6. fineness of touch, skill, etc. 7. a fine regard for the feelings of others 8. a sensitive distaste for what is considered improper or offensive 9. a choice food

**del·i·cate** (del′i kit) *adj.* [L. *delicatus*, delightful < OL. *delicere*: see DELIGHT] 1. pleasing in its lightness, mildness, etc. 2. beautifully fine in texture, workmanship, etc. 3. slight and subtle 4. easily damaged, disordered, spoiled, etc. 5. frail in health 6. *a*) needing careful handling, tact, etc. *[a delicate situation]* *b*) showing tact, consideration, etc. 7. finely sensitive *[a delicate gauge]* 8. finely skilled 9. having a sensitive distaste for what is considered offensive or improper —**del′i·cate·ly** *adv.* —**del′i·cate·ness** *n.*

**del·i·ca·tes·sen** (del′i kə tes′'n) *n.* [G. pl. < Fr. *délicatesse*, delicacy] 1. prepared cooked meats, smoked fish, cheeses, salads, relishes, etc., collectively 2. a shop where such foods are sold

**de·li·cious** (di lish′əs) *adj.* [< OFr. < L. < *deliciae*, delight < OL. *delicere*: see DELIGHT] 1. very enjoyable; delightful 2. very pleasing to taste or smell —*n.* [D-] a sweet, red winter apple —**de·li′cious·ly** *adv.* —**de·li′cious·ness** *n.*

**de·light** (di līt′) *vt.* [< OFr. < L. < OL. *delicere* < *de-*, from + *lacere*, to entice] to give great pleasure to —*vi.* 1. to give great pleasure 2. to be highly pleased —*n.* 1. great pleasure 2. something giving great pleasure —**de·light′ed** *adj.* —**de·light′ed·ly** *adv.* —**de·light′ed·ness** *n.*

**de·light·ful** (-fəl) *adj.* giving delight; very pleasing; charming: also [Archaic] **de·light′some** (-səm) —**de·light′ful·ly** *adv.* —**de·light′ful·ness** *n.*

**De·li·lah** (di lī′lə) [Heb. *delîlāh*, lit., delicate] *Bible* the mistress of Samson, who betrayed him to the Philistines: Judg. 16 —*n.* a seductive, treacherous woman

**de·lim·it** (di lim′it) *vt.* to set the limits or boundaries of: also **de·lim/i·tate′** -tat′ed, -tat′ing —**de·lim′i·ta′tion** *n.* —**de·lim′i·ta′tive** *adj.*

**de·lin·e·ate** (di lin′ē āt′) *vt.* **-at′ed, -at′ing** [< L. < *de-*, from + *linea*, LINE¹] 1. to trace the outline of 2. to draw; depict 3. to depict in words; describe —**de·lin′e·a′tion** *n.* —**de·lin′e·a′tive** *adj.* —**de·lin′e·a′tor** *n.*

**de·lin·quen·cy** (di liŋ′kwən sē) *n., pl.* **-cies** 1. failure or neglect to do what duty or law requires 2. an overdue debt, tax, etc. 3. a fault; misdeed 4. antisocial or illegal behavior, esp. by the young: see JUVENILE DELINQUENCY

**de·lin·quent** (-kwənt) *adj.* [< L. *delinquens*, prp. of *delinquere* < *de-*, from + *linquere*, to leave] 1. failing or neglecting to do what duty or law requires 2. overdue *[delinquent taxes]* —*n.* a delinquent person; esp., a juvenile delinquent —**de·lin′quent·ly** *adv.*

**del·i·quesce** (del′ə kwes′) *vi.* **-quesced′, -quesc′ing** [< L. *deliquescere* < *de-*, from + *liquere*, to be liquid] 1. to melt away 2. to become liquid by absorbing moisture from the air —**del′i·ques′cence** *n.* —**del′i·ques′cent** *adj.*

**de·lir·i·ous** (di lir′ē əs) *adj.* 1. in a state of delirium 2. of or caused by delirium 3. wildly excited —**de·lir′i·ous·ly** *adv.* —**de·lir′i·ous·ness** *n.*

**de·lir·i·um** (-ē əm) *n., pl.* **-i·ums, -i·a** (-ə) [L. < *delirare*, to rave, lit., to turn the furrow awry in plowing < *de-*, from + *lira*, a line] 1. a temporary state of extreme mental excitement, marked by confused speech and hallucinations: it sometimes occurs during a fever, in some forms of insanity, etc. 2. uncontrollably wild excitement

**delirium tre·mens** (trē′mənz) [ModL., lit., trembling delirium] a violent delirium resulting chiefly from excessive drinking of alcoholic liquor

**De·li·us** (dē′lē əs, dēl′yəs), **Frederick** 1862–1934; Eng. composer

**de·liv·er** (di liv′ər) *vt.* [< OFr. < VL. < L. *de-*, from + *liberare*, to free < *liber*, free] 1. to set free or save from evil, danger, etc. 2. to assist at the birth of (offspring) 3. to express in words; utter *[to deliver a speech]* 4. to hand over; transfer 5. to distribute *[deliver the mail]* 6. to strike (a blow) 7. to throw (a ball, etc.) —*vi.* to make deliveries, as of merchandise —**be delivered of** to give birth to —**deliver oneself of** to express; utter —**de·liv′er·a·ble** *adj.* —**de·liv′er·er** *n.*

**de·liv·er·ance** (-əns) *n.* 1. a freeing or being freed 2. an opinion, etc. publicly expressed

**de·liv·er·y** (-ē) *n., pl.* **-er·ies** 1. a handing over; transfer 2. a distributing, as of mail 3. a giving birth; childbirth 4. any giving forth 5. the act or manner of giving a speech, striking a blow, throwing a ball, etc. 6. something delivered

**dell** (del) *n.* [OE. *del*] a small, secluded valley or glen, usually a wooded one

**de·louse** (dē lous′, -louz′) *vt.* **-loused′, -lous′ing** to rid of lice —**de·lous′er** *n.*

**Del·phi** (del′fī) ancient city in C Greece, on the slopes of Mount Parnassus

**Del·phic** (-fik) *adj.* 1. of Delphi 2. designating or of the oracle of Apollo at Delphi in ancient times Also **Del′phi·an** (-fē ən)

**del·phin·i·um** (del fin′ē əm) *n.* [< Gr. *delphin*, dolphin: its nectary resembles a dolphin] a plant bearing spikes of spurred, irregular flowers, usually blue, on tall stalks: some are poisonous

**del·ta** (del′tə) *n.* [< Gr.] 1. the fourth letter of the Greek alphabet (Δ, δ) 2. a deposit of sand and soil, usually triangular, formed at the mouth of some rivers —**del·ta·ic** (del tā′ik) *adj.*

**delta ray** an electron ejected by the passage of a primary ionizing particle through matter

**delta wing** the triangular shape of certain kinds of jet aircraft —**del′ta-wing′, del′ta-winged′** *adj.*

**del·toid** (del′toid) *adj.* 1. shaped like a delta; triangular 2. designating or of a large, triangular muscle of the shoulder —*n.* the deltoid muscle

DELTA

**de·lude** (di lōōd′) *vt.* **-lud′ed, -lud′ing** [< L. < *de-*, from + *ludere*, to play] to mislead; deceive; trick —**de·lud′er** *n.*

**del·uge** (del′yōōj) *n.* [< OFr. < L. *diluvium* < *dis-*, off + *lavere*, to wash] 1. a great flood 2. a heavy rainfall 3. an overwhelming, floodlike rush of anything —*vt.* **-uged, -ug·ing** 1. to flood 2. to overwhelm —**the Deluge** *Bible* the great flood in Noah's time: Gen. 7

**de·lu·sion** (di lōō′zhən) *n.* 1. a deluding or being deluded 2. a false belief or opinion 3. *Psychiatry* a false, persistent belief not substantiated by sensory or objective evidence —**de·lu′sion·al** *adj.*

**de·lu·sive** (di lōōs′iv) *adj.* 1. tending to delude; misleading 2. unreal Also **de·lu′so·ry** (-lōō′sə rē) —**de·lu′sive·ly** *adv.* —**de·lu′sive·ness** *n.*

**de·luxe** (di luks′, -looks′, -lōōks′) *adj.* [Fr., lit., of luxury] of extra fine quality; luxurious; elegant —*adv.* in a deluxe manner

**delve** (delv) *vi.* **delved, delv′ing** [OE. *delfan*] 1. [Archaic] to dig with a spade 2. to investigate for information; search (*into* books, the past, etc.) —**delv′er** *n.*

**Dem.** 1. Democrat 2. Democratic

**de·mag·net·ize** (dē mag′nə tīz′) *vt.* **-ized′, -iz′ing** to deprive of magnetism —**de·mag′net·i·za′tion** *n.* —**de·mag′net·iz′er** *n.*

**dem·a·gog·ic** (dem′ə gäj′ik, -gäg′-, -gō′jik) *adj.* of, like, or characteristic of a demagogue or demagogy: also **dem′a·gog′i·cal** —**dem′a·gog′i·cal·ly** *adv.*

**dem·a·gogue, dem·a·gog** (dem′ə gäg′, -gôg′) *n.* [< Gr. < *dēmos*, the people + *agōgos*, leader < *agein*, to lead] a person who tries to stir up the people by appeals to emotion, prejudice, etc. in order to win them over quickly and so gain power —*vi.* **-gogued′** or **-goged′, -gogu′ing** or **-gog′ing** to behave as a demagogue

**dem·a·gog·y** (dem′ə gō′jē, -gäg′ē, -gôg′ē) *n.* the methods or practices of a demagogue: also **dem′a·gog′uer·y** (-gäg′ər ē, -gôg′-)

**de·mand** (di mand′) *vt.* [< OFr. < L. < *de-*, from + *mandare*, to entrust: see MANDATE] 1. to ask for boldly or urgently 2. to ask for as a right or with authority 3. to ask to know or be informed of 4. to require *[the work demands time]* —*vi.* to make a demand —*n.* 1. a demanding 2. a thing demanded 3. a strong request 4. an urgent requirement or claim 5. *a*) the desire for a commodity along with ability to pay for it *b*) the amount people are ready to buy at a certain price —**in demand** asked for —**on demand** when presented for payment —**de·mand′a·ble** *adj.* —**mand′er** *n.*

**demand deposit** *Banking* a deposit that may be withdrawn on demand, without advance notice

**de·mand·ing** (-iŋ) *adj.* making demands on one's patience, energy, etc. —**de·mand′ing·ly** *adv.*

**de·mar·cate** (di mär′kāt, dē′mär kāt′) *vt.* **-cat·ed, -cat·ing** [< ff.] 1. to mark the limits of 2. to distinguish; separate Also **de·mark′**

**de·mar·ca·tion, de·mar·ka·tion** (dē′mär kā′shən) *n.* [Sp. < *de-* (L. *de*), from + *marcar*, to mark] 1. the act of setting and marking boundaries 2. a limit or boundary 3. a separation

**dé·marche** (dā märsh′) *n.* [Fr.: see DE- & MARCH¹] a line of action; maneuver, esp. in diplomacy

**de·mean¹** (di mēn′) *vt.* [DE- + MEAN², after DEBASE] to degrade; humble *[to demean oneself by lying]*

**de·mean²** (di mēn′) *vt.* [see ff.] to behave or conduct (oneself)

**de·mean·or** (-ər) *n.* [< OFr. < *de-* (L. *de*), from + *mener*, to lead < LL. *minare*, to drive (animals) < L. *minari*, to threaten] outward behavior; conduct; deportment: also, Brit. sp., **de·mean′our**

**de·ment·ed** (di ment′id) *adj.* [< L. < *demens* (gen. *demen-*

*tis*), mad: see ff.] mentally deranged; insane —**de·ment′ed·ly** *adv.*

**de·men·tia** (di men′shə) *n.* [L. < *de-*, out from + *mens*, the mind] loss or impairment of mental powers due to organic causes: cf. AMENTIA

**dementia prae·cox** (prē′käks) [ModL.: see prec. & PRECOCIOUS] *obs. term for* SCHIZOPHRENIA

**de·mer·it** (di mer′it) *n.* [< OFr. < ML. < L. *demerere*, to deserve well, with intens. prefix *de-* mistaken as negative in ML.] **1.** a fault; defect **2.** a mark recorded against a student, trainee, etc. for poor conduct or work

**de·mesne** (di mān′, -mēn′) *n.* [OFr. *demeine* < L. *dominium*: see DOMAIN] **1.** *Law* possession (of real estate) in one's own right **2.** the land around a mansion **3.** a region or domain: also used figuratively

**De·me·ter** (di mēt′ər) *Gr. Myth.* the goddess of agriculture: identified with the Roman goddess Ceres

**dem·i-** [OFr. < L. < *dis-*, apart + *medius*, middle] *a prefix meaning:* **1.** half [*demisemiquaver*] **2.** less than usual in size, power, etc. [*demigod*]

**dem·i·god** (dem′ē gäd′) *n.* **1.** *Myth. a)* a minor deity *b)* the offspring of a human being and a god or goddess **2.** a godlike person

**dem·i·john** (-jän′) *n.* [Fr. *dame-jeanne*] a large bottle of glass or earthenware, with a narrow neck and a wicker casing and handle

**de·mil·i·ta·rize** (dē mil′ə tə rīz′) *vt.* **-rized′, -riz′ing** to free from military control or activity, or from militarism —**de·mil′i·ta·ri·za′tion** *n.*

**dem·i·mon·daine** (dem′ē män dān′) *n.* [Fr.] a woman of the demimonde

**dem·i·monde** (dem′ē mänd′, dem′ē-mänd′) *n.* [Fr. < *demi-*, DEMI- + *monde* (< L. *mundus*), world] the class of women who have lost social standing because of sexual promiscuity

DEMIJOHN

**de·mise** (di mīz′) *n.* [< Fr. fem. pp. of *démettre*, to dismiss < L. < *de-*, down + *mittere*, to send] **1.** *Law* a transfer of an estate by lease **2.** the transfer of sovereignty by death or abdication **3.** death —*vt.* **-mised′, -mis′ing 1.** to give or transfer (an estate) by lease **2.** to transfer (sovereignty) by death or abdication

**dem·i·sem·i·qua·ver** (dem′ē sem′ē kwä′vər) *n.* [Brit.] *same as* THIRTY-SECOND NOTE

**dem·i·tasse** (dem′ē tas′, -täs′) *n.* [Fr. < *demi-*, DEMI- + *tasse*, a cup] a small cup of or for after-dinner black coffee

**de·mob** (dē mäb′) *vt.* **-mobbed′, -mob′bing** [Brit. Colloq.] to demobilize

**de·mo·bi·lize** (dē mō′bə līz′) *vt.* **-lized′, -liz′ing 1.** to disband (troops) **2.** to discharge (a person) from the armed forces —**de·mo′bi·li·za′tion** *n.*

**de·moc·ra·cy** (di mäk′rə sē) *n., pl.* **-cies** [< Fr. < ML. *democratia* < Gr. < *dēmos*, the people + *kratein*, to rule] **1.** government in which the people hold the ruling power either directly or through elected representatives **2.** a country, state, etc. with such government **3.** majority rule **4.** the principle of equality of rights, opportunity, etc., or the practice of this principle

**dem·o·crat** (dem′ə krat′) *n.* **1.** a person who believes in and upholds government by the people **2.** a person who believes in and practices the principle of equality of rights, opportunity, etc. **3.** [D-] a member of the Democratic Party

**dem·o·crat·ic** (dem′ə krat′ik) *adj.* **1.** of, belonging to, or upholding (a) democracy **2.** of or for all or most people **3.** treating people of all classes in the same way **4.** [D-] of or belonging to the Democratic Party —**dem′o·crat′i·cal·ly** *adv.*

**Democratic Party** one of the two major political parties in the U.S., since about 1830

**de·moc·ra·tize** (di mäk′rə tīz′) *vt., vi.* **-tized′, -tiz′ing** to make or become democratic —**de·moc′ra·ti·za′tion** *n.*

**de·mod·u·late** (dē mäj′oo lāt′) *vt.* **-lat′ed, -lat′ing** to cause to undergo demodulation —**de·mod′u·la′tor** *n.*

**de·mod·u·la·tion** (dē mäj′oo lā′shən) *n.* Radio the recovery, at the receiver, of a signal that has been modulated on a carrier wave

**de·mog·ra·phy** (di mäg′rə fē) *n.* [< Gr. *dēmos*, the people + -GRAPHY] the statistical science dealing with the distribution, vital statistics, etc. of populations —**de·mog′ra·pher** *n.* —**de·mo·graph·ic** (dē′mə graf′ik, dem′ə-) *adj.* —**de′mo·graph′i·cal·ly** *adv.*

**dem·oi·selle** (dem′wə zel′) *n.* [Fr.] a damsel

**de·mol·ish** (di mäl′ish) *vt.* [< Fr. < L. *demoliri*, to destroy < *de-*, down + *moliri*, to build < *moles*, a mass] **1.** to tear down or smash to pieces (a building, etc.) **2.** to destroy; ruin —**de·mol′ish·er** *n.* —**de·mol′ish·ment** *n.*

**dem·o·li·tion** (dem′ə lish′ən, dē′mə-) *n.* a demolishing or being demolished; often, specif., destruction by explosives

**de·mon** (dē′mən) *n.* [L. *daemon*: see DAEMON] **1.** *same as* DAEMON **2.** a devil; evil spirit **3.** a person or thing regarded as evil, cruel, etc. **4.** a person who has great energy or skill —**de·mon·ic** (di män′ik) *adj.* —**de·mon′i·cal·ly** *adv.*

**de·mon·e·tize** (dē män′ə tīz′) *vt.* **-tized′, -tiz′ing 1.** to deprive (currency) of its standard value **2.** to stop using (silver or gold) as a monetary standard —**de·mon′e·ti·za′tion** *n.*

**de·mo·ni·ac** (di mō′nē ak′) *adj.* **1.** possessed or influenced by a demon **2.** of a demon or demons **3.** like or characteristic of a demon; fiendish Also **de·mo·ni·a·cal** (dē′mə nī′ə k'l) —*n.* a person supposedly possessed by a demon —**de′mo·ni′a·cal·ly** *adv.*

**de·mon·ism** (dē′mən iz'm) *n.* belief in the existence and powers of demons —**de′mon·ist** *n.*

**de·mon·o-** *a combining form meaning* demon: also, before a vowel, **demon-**

**de·mon·ol·a·try** (dē′mə näl′ə trē) *n.* worship of demons —**de′mon·ol′a·ter** *n.*

**de·mon·ol·o·gy** (-jē) *n.* the study of demons or of beliefs about them —**de′mon·ol′o·gist** *n.*

**de·mon·stra·ble** (di män′strə b'l, dem′ən-) *adj.* that can be demonstrated, or proved —**de·mon′stra·bil′i·ty** *n.* —**de·mon′stra·bly** *adv.*

**dem·on·strate** (dem′ən strāt′) *vt.* **-strat′ed, -strat′ing** [< L. pp. of *demonstrare* < *de-*, from + *monstrare*, to show] **1.** to show by reasoning; prove **2.** to explain by using examples, experiments, etc. **3.** to show the operation or working of **4.** to show (feelings) plainly —*vi.* **1.** to show one's feelings or views by taking part in a public meeting, parade, etc. **2.** to show military power

**dem·on·stra·tion** (dem′ən strā′shən) *n.* **1.** a making evident or proving **2.** an explanation by example, experiment, etc. **3.** a practical showing of how something works or is used **4.** a display or outward show **5.** a public show of opinion, etc., as by a mass meeting **6.** a show of military force

**de·mon·stra·tive** (di män′strə tiv) *adj.* **1.** giving convincing evidence or proof (usually with *of*) **2.** having to do with demonstration **3.** showing feelings openly and frankly **4.** *Gram.* pointing out [*"this"* is a *demonstrative* pronoun] —**de·mon′stra·tive·ly** *adv.* —**de·mon′stra·tive·ness** *n.*

**dem·on·stra·tor** (dem′ən strāt′ər) *n.* [L.] one that demonstrates; specif., a person who takes part in a public demonstration

**de·mor·al·ize** (di môr′ə līz′) *vt.* **-ized′, -iz′ing 1.** [Now Rare] to corrupt the morals of **2.** to lower the morale of **3.** to throw into confusion —**de·mor′al·i·za′tion** *n.* —**de·mor′al·iz′er** *n.*

**De·mos·the·nes** (di mäs′thə nēz′) 384?-322 B.C.; Athenian orator & statesman

**de·mote** (di mōt′) *vt.* **-mot′ed, -mot′ing** [DE- + (PRO)MOTE] to reduce to a lower grade; lower in rank —**de·mo′tion** *n.*

**de·mot·ic** (di mät′ik) *adj.* [< ML. < Gr. *dēmotes*, one of the people < *dēmos*, the people] **1.** of the people; popular; specif., vernacular (sense 2) **2.** designating or of a simplified system of ancient Egyptian writing

**de·mul·cent** (di mul′s'nt) *adj.* [< L. prp. of *demulcere* < *de-*, down + *mulcere*, to stroke] soothing —*n.* a medicine or ointment that soothes irritated mucous membrane

**de·mur** (di mur′) *vi.* **-murred′, -mur′ring** [OFr. *demorer* < L. < *de-*, from + *morari*, to delay < *mora*, a delay] **1.** to be unwilling because of doubts or objections; object **2.** *Law* to enter a demurrer —*n.* **1.** a demurring **2.** an objection raised or exception taken Also **de·mur′ral** *n.*

**de·mure** (di myoor′) *adj.* [< ME. < *de-* (prob. intens.) + *mur* < OFr. *mĕur*, ripe < L. *maturus*, mature] **1.** modest; reserved **2.** affectedly modest or shy; coy —**de·mure′ly** *adv.* —**de·mure′ness** *n.*

**de·mur·rage** (di mur′ij) *n.* [< OFr. < *demorer*: see DEMUR] **1.** the delaying of a ship, freight car, etc., as by failure to load, unload, or sail within the time allowed **2.** the compensation paid for this

**de·mur·rer** (-ər) *n.* [OFr. *demorer*, to DEMUR] **1.** a plea for the dismissal of a lawsuit on the grounds that even if the statements of the opposition are true, they do not sustain the claim **2.** an objection; demur **3.** a person who demurs

**den** (den) *n.* [OE. *denn*] **1.** the cave or other lair of a wild animal **2.** a retreat or headquarters, as of thieves **3.** a small, cozy room where a person can be alone to read, work, etc. —*vi.* **denned, den′ning** to live or hide as in a den

**Den.** Denmark

**de·nar·i·us** (di nar′ē əs, -ner′-) *n., pl.* **-nar′i·i′** (-ī′) [ < L. < *deni*, by tens < *decem*, ten] **1.** an ancient Roman silver coin, the penny of the New Testament **2.** an ancient Roman gold coin

**de·na·tion·al·ize** (dē nash′ə n′l īz′) *vt.* **-ized′, -iz′ing** **1.** to deprive of national rights or status **2.** to place (a government-controlled industry) under private ownership —**de·na′tion·al·i·za′tion** *n.*

**de·nat·u·ral·ize** (dē nach′ər ə līz′) *vt.* **-ized′, -iz′ing** **1.** to make unnatural **2.** to take citizenship away from —**de·nat′u·ral·i·za′tion** *n.*

**de·na·ture** (dē nā′chər) *vt.* **-tured, -tur·ing** **1.** to change the nature of **2.** to make (alcohol, etc.) unfit for human consumption without spoiling for other uses **3.** to change the composition of (a protein) by heat, acids, etc. —**de·na′tur·a′tion** *n.*

**den·drite** (den′drīt) *n.* [ < Gr. < *dendron:* see ff.] the branched part of a nerve cell that carries impulses toward the cell body —**den·drit′ic** (-drit′ik), **den·drit′i·cal** *adj.* —**den·drit′i·cal·ly** *adv.*

**den·dro-** [ < Gr. *dendron*, a tree] *a combining form meaning* tree: also **dendri-** or, before a vowel, **dendr-**

**den·drol·o·gy** (den dräl′ə jē) *n.* the scientific study of trees —**den′dro·log′ic** (-drə läj′ik), **den′dro·log′i·cal** *adj.* —**den·drol′o·gist** *n.*

**-den·dron** (den′drən) [see DENDRO-] *a combining form meaning* tree or treelike structure

**den·gue** (deŋ′gē, -gā) *n.* [WIndSp. < Swahili *dinga*, a cramp, infl. by Sp. *dengue*, contortion] an infectious tropical disease transmitted by mosquitoes and characterized by severe pain in the joints and back, fever, and rash

**de·ni·al** (di nī′əl) *n.* **1.** a denying; saying "no" (to a request, etc.) **2.** a statement in opposition to another **3.** a disowning; repudiation [the *denial* of one's family] **4.** a refusal to believe or accept (a doctrine, etc.) **5.** *same as* SELF-DENIAL

**de·nier¹** (den′yər) *n.* [ < OFr. < L. *denarius*, DENARIUS] a unit of weight for measuring the fineness of threads of silk, nylon, etc.

**de·ni·er²** (di nī′ər) *n.* a person who denies

**den·i·grate** (den′ə grāt′) *vt.* **-grat′ed, -grat′ing** [ < L. pp. of *denigrare* < *de-*, intens. + *nigrare*, to blacken < *niger*, black] to disparage the character of; defame —**den′i·gra′tion** *n.* —**den′i·gra′tor** *n.*

**den·im** (den′əm) *n.* [ < Fr. (*serge*) *de Nîmes*, (serge) of Nîmes, Fr. town] a coarse, twilled cotton cloth used for overalls, uniforms, etc.

**Den·is** (den′is) [Fr. < L. *Dionysius*] a masculine name: also sp. **Den′nis**

**den·i·zen** (den′i zən) *n.* [ < Anglo-Fr. < OFr. *denzein* < *denz*, within < VL. < L. *de intus*, from within] **1.** *a*) an inhabitant *b*) a frequenter of a particular place **2.** an animal, plant, etc. that has become naturalized

**Den·mark** (den′märk) country in Europe, on the peninsula of Jutland & several nearby islands: 16,615 sq. mi.; pop. 4,870,000; cap. Copenhagen

**de·nom·i·nate** (di näm′ə nāt′) *vt.* **-nat′ed, -nat′ing** [ < L. pp. of *denominare* < *de-*, intens. + *nominare:* see NOMINATE] to give a specified name to; call

**de·nom·i·na·tion** (di näm′ə nā′shən) *n.* **1.** the act of denominating **2.** a name, esp. of a class of things **3.** a class or kind with a specific name or value [coins of different *denominations*] **4.** a religious sect or body

**de·nom·i·na·tion·al** (-′l) *adj.* of, or under the control of, a religious denomination —**de·nom′i·na′tion·al·ism** *n.* —**de·nom′i·na′tion·al·ly** *adv.*

**de·nom·i·na·tive** (di näm′ə nə tiv) *adj. Gram.* formed from a noun or adjective stem

**de·nom·i·na·tor** (-nāt′ər) *n.* [ML.] the term below the line in a fraction, indicating the number of equal parts into which the whole is divided

**de·no·ta·tion** (dē′nō tā′shən) *n.* **1.** a denoting **2.** the explicit meaning or reference of a word or term: cf. CONNOTATION **3.** an indication or sign

**de·note** (di nōt′) *vt.* **-not′ed, -not′ing** [ < Fr. < L. < *de-*, down + *notare*, to mark < *nota*, NOTE] **1.** to be a sign of; indicate **2.** to signify or refer to explicitly; mean: cf. CONNOTE —**de·not′a·ble** *adj.* —**de·no·ta·tive** (dē′nō tāt′iv) *adj.*

**de·noue·ment, dé·noue·ment** (dā nōō′män; *Fr.* dā nōō mäN′) *n.* [Fr. < *dé-* (L. *dis-*), out + *nouer*, to tie < L. < *nodus:* see NODE] **1.** the outcome, solution, or unraveling of a plot in a drama, story, etc. **2.** any final revelation or outcome

**de·nounce** (di nouns′) *vt.* **-nounced′, -nounc′ing** [ < OFr. < L. *denuntiare:* see DENUNCIATION] **1.** to accuse publicly; inform against **2.** to condemn strongly as evil **3.** to give formal notice of the ending of (a treaty, armistice, etc.) —**de·nounce′ment** *n.* —**de·nounc′er** *n.*

‡**de no·vo** (dē nō′vō) [L.] once more; anew

**dense** (dens) *adj.* **dens′er, dens′est** [L. *densus*, compact] **1.** packed tightly together; compact **2.** difficult to get

through, penetrate, etc. **3.** stupid **4.** *Photog.* opaque, with good contrast in light and shade: said of a negative —**dense′ly** *adv.* —**dense′ness** *n.*

**den·si·ty** (den′sə tē) *n., pl.* **-ties** **1.** the quality or condition of being dense **2.** quantity or number per unit, as of area [the *density* of population] **3.** *Physics* the ratio of the mass of an object to its volume

**dent** (dent) *n.* [ME., var. of DINT] **1.** a slight hollow made in a surface by a blow or pressure **2.** an appreciable effect —*vt.* to make a dent in —*vi.* to become dented

**den·tal** (den′t′l) *adj.* [ModL. < L. *dens* (gen. *dentis*), a tooth] **1.** of or for the teeth or dentistry **2.** *Phonet.* formed by placing the tip of the tongue against or near the upper front teeth —*n. Phonet.* a dental consonant (th, *th*)

**dental floss** thin, strong thread for removing food particles from between the teeth

**dental hygienist** a dentist's assistant, who cleans teeth, takes dental X-rays, etc.

**den·tate** (den′tāt) *adj.* [ < L. < *dens:* see DENTAL] having teeth or toothlike projections; toothed or notched —**den′tate·ly** *adv.* —**den·ta′tion** *n.*

**den·ti-** [ < L. *dens:* see DENTAL] *a combining form meaning* tooth or teeth: also **dento-** or, before a vowel, **dent-**

**den·ti·frice** (den′tə fris) *n.* [ < L. < *dens* (see DENTAL) + *fricare*, to rub] any preparation for cleaning teeth, as a powder, paste, or liquid

**den·til** (den′til) *n.* [ < MFr. < L. *dens:* see DENTAL] *Archit.* any of a series of small rectangular blocks projecting like teeth, as from under a cornice

**den·tin** (den′tin) *n.* [ < L. *dens:* see DENTAL] the hard, calcareous tissue forming the body of a tooth, under the enamel: also **den′tine** (-tēn, -tin)

**den·tist** (den′tist) *n.* [ < Fr. < ML. < L. *dens:* see DENTAL] one whose profession is the care of teeth and surrounding tissues, the replacement of missing teeth with artificial ones, etc.

**den·tist·ry** (-rē) *n.* the profession or work of a dentist

**den·ti·tion** (den tish′ən) *n.* [ < L. < *dentire*, to cut teeth < *dens:* see DENTAL] **1.** the teething process **2.** the number and kind of teeth and their arrangement

**den·ture** (den′chər) *n.* [Fr. < L. *dens:* see DENTAL] a fitting for the mouth, with artificial teeth

**de·nu·cle·ar·ize** (dē nōō′klē ə rīz′, -nyōō′-) *vt.* **-ized′, -iz′ing** to prohibit the possession of nuclear weapons in —**de·nu′cle·ar·i·za′tion** *n.*

**de·nu·date** (di nōō′dāt, -nyōō′-; den′yoo dāt′) *vt.* **-dat·ed, -dat·ing** [ < L. pp. of *denudare* < *de-*, off + *nudare*, to strip] *same as* DENUDE —**de·nu·da·tion** (dē′nōō dā′shən, -nyōō-; den′yoo-) *n.*

**de·nude** (di nōōd′, -nyōōd′) *vt.* **-nud′ed, -nud′ing** [see prec.] **1.** to make bare; strip **2.** to destroy all life in (an area) **3.** to lay bare as by erosion

**de·nun·ci·ate** (di nun′sē āt′) *vt.* **-at′ed, -at′ing** *same as* DENOUNCE —**de·nun′ci·a′tor** *n.*

**de·nun·ci·a·tion** (di nun′sē ā′shən) *n.* [ < L. pp. of *denuntiare* < *de-*, intens. + *nuntiare:* see NUNCIO] the act of denouncing —**de·nun′ci·a·to·ry** (-ə tôr′ē), **de·nun′ci·a′tive** (-āt′iv) *adj.*

**Den·ver** (den′vər) [after J. *Denver* (1817-94), gov. of Kans.] capital of Colo., in the NC part: pop. 491,000 (met. area 1,615,000)

**de·ny** (di nī′) *vt.* **-nied′, -ny′ing** [ < OFr. < L. < *de-*, intens. + *negare*, to deny] **1.** to declare (a statement) untrue **2.** to refuse to accept as true or right **3.** to refuse to acknowledge as one's own; repudiate **4.** to refuse access to **5.** to refuse to give **6.** to refuse the request of —**deny oneself** to do without desired things

**de·o·dar** (dē′ə där′) *n.* [Hindi < Sans. *dēvadāru*, lit., tree of the gods] **1.** a Himalayan cedar with fragrant, light-red wood **2.** the wood

**de·o·dor·ant** (dē ō′dər ənt) *adj.* that prevents, destroys, or masks undesired odors —*n.* any deodorant preparation, esp. one used on the body

**de·o·dor·ize** (dē ō′də rīz′) *vt.* **-ized′, -iz′ing** to remove or mask the odor of or in —**de·o′dor·i·za′tion** *n.* —**de·o′dor·iz′er** *n.*

**de·ox·i·dize** (dē äk′sə dīz′) *vt.* **-dized′, -diz′ing** to remove oxygen, esp. chemically combined oxygen, from —**de·ox′i·diz′er** *n.*

**de·ox·y·gen·ate** (-jə nāt′) *vt.* **-at′ed, -at′ing** to remove oxygen, esp. free oxygen, from (water, air, etc.)

**dé·ox·y·ri·bo·nu·cle·ic acid** (dē äk′si rī′bō nōō klē′ik, -nyōō-) an essential component of all living matter and a basic material in the chromosomes of the cell nucleus: it contains the genetic code and transmits the hereditary pattern

**dep. 1.** department **2.** deposit **3.** deputy

**de·part** (di pärt′) *vi.* [ < OFr. *departir* < VL. < L. < *dis-*, apart + *partire*, to divide < *pars*, a PART] **1.** to go away (*from*); leave **2.** to set out; start **3.** to die **4.** to turn aside (*from* something) [to *depart* from custom] —*vt.* to leave: now only in **depart this life**, to die

**de·part·ed** (-id) *adj.* **1.** gone away; past **2.** dead —**the departed** the dead person or persons
**de·part·ment** (-mənt) *n.* [see DEPART] **1.** a separate part or division, as of a government, business, or school **2.** a field of knowledge or activity **3.** an administrative district in France or in certain Latin American countries —**de·part·men·tal** (di pärt′men′t'l, dē′pärt-) *adj.* —**de·part′men′tal·ly** *adv.*
**de·part·men·tal·ize** (di pärt′men′tə līz′, dē′pärt-) *vt.* **-ized′, -iz′ing** to organize into departments
**department store** a retail store for the sale of many kinds of goods arranged in departments
**de·par·ture** (di pär′chər) *n.* **1.** a departing, or going away **2.** a starting out, as on a trip or new course of action **3.** a deviation or turning aside (*from* something) **4.** [Archaic] death
**de·pend** (di pend′) *vi.* [< OFr. < L. < *de-*, down + *pendere*, to hang] **1.** to be influenced or determined by something else; be contingent (*on*) **2.** to be sure of; rely (*on*) **3.** to rely (*on*) for support or aid **4.** [Archaic] to hang down
**de·pend·a·ble** (di pen′də b'l) *adj.* that can be depended on; reliable —**de·pend′a·bil′i·ty** *n.* —**de·pend′a·bly** *adv.*
**de·pend·ence** (-dəns) *n.* **1.** the condition or fact of being dependent; specif., *a)* a being influenced or determined by something else *b)* reliance (*on* another) for support or aid *c)* subordination **2.** reliance; trust Also sp. **de·pend′ance**
**de·pend·en·cy** (-dən sē) *n., pl.* **-cies 1.** *same as* DEPENDENCE **2.** something dependent or subordinate **3.** a land or territory geographically distinct from the country governing it
**de·pend·ent** (-dənt) *adj.* **1.** hanging down **2.** influenced or determined by something else **3.** relying (*on* another) for support or aid **4.** subordinate —*n.* a person who depends on someone else for support, etc. Also sp., esp. for *n.,* **de·pend′ant**
**dependent clause** *same as* SUBORDINATE CLAUSE
**de·per·son·al·ize** (dē pur′s'n ə līz′) *vt.* **-ized′, -iz′ing 1.** to deprive of individuality; treat impersonally **2.** to cause to lose one's sense of personal identity —**de·per′son·al·i·za′tion** *n.*
**de·pict** (di pikt′) *vt.* [< L. pp. of *depingere* < *de-*, intens. + *pingere*, to paint] **1.** to represent in a drawing, sculpture, etc. **2.** to picture in words; describe —**de·pic′tion** *n.* —**de·pic′tor** *n.*
**dep·i·late** (dep′ə lāt′) *vt.* **-lat′ed, -lat′ing** [< L. pp. of *depilare* < *de-*, from + *pilus*, hair] to remove hair from —**dep′i·la′tion** *n.*
**de·pil·a·to·ry** (di pil′ə tôr′ē) *adj.* serving to remove unwanted hair —*n., pl.* **-ries** a depilatory agent, as in cream form
**de·plane** (dē plān′) *vi.* **-planed′, -plan′ing** to get out of an airplane after it lands
**de·plete** (di plēt′) *vt.* **-plet′ed, -plet′ing** [< L. pp. of *deplere* < *de-*, from + *plere*, to fill] **1.** to make less by gradually using up (funds, energy, etc.) **2.** to empty wholly or partly —**de·ple′tion** *n.*
**de·plor·a·ble** (di plôr′ə b'l) *adj.* **1.** that can or should be deplored; lamentable **2.** very bad; wretched —**de·plor′a·bly** *adv.*
**de·plore** (di plôr′) *vt.* **-plored′, -plor′ing** [< Fr. < L. < *de-*, intens. + *plorare*, to weep] **1.** to be regretful or sorry about; lament **2.** to regard as unfortunate or wretched
**de·ploy** (dē ploi′) *vt., vi.* [< Fr. < OFr. *desployer* < L. *dis-plicare*, to scatter, unfold: see DISPLAY] *Mil.* **1.** to spread out (troops, etc.) so as to form a wider front **2.** to station or move in accordance with a plan —**de·ploy′ment** *n.*
**de·po·lar·ize** (dē pō′lə rīz′) *vt.* **-ized′, -iz′ing** to destroy or counteract the polarization of —**de·po′lar·i·za′tion** *n.*
**de·po·nent** (di pō′nənt) *adj.* [< L. prp. of *deponere*, to set down: see DEPOSIT] *L. & Gr. Gram.* denoting a verb with a passive voice form and an active meaning —*n.* **1.** a deponent verb **2.** *Law* a person who gives written testimony under oath
**de·pop·u·late** (dē päp′yə lāt′) *vt.* **-lat′ed, -lat′ing** to reduce the population of, esp. by violence, pestilence, etc. —**de·pop′u·la′tion** *n.* —**de·pop′u·la′tor** *n.*
**de·port** (di pôrt′) *vt.* [< Fr. < L. < *de-*, from + *portare*, to carry] **1.** to behave (oneself) in a specified way **2.** to carry or send away; specif., to expel (an alien) from a country by official order
**de·por·ta·tion** (dē′pôr tā′shən) *n.* expulsion, as of an undesirable alien, from a country
**de·port·ment** (di pôrt′mənt) *n.* the manner of conducting oneself; behavior
**de·pose** (di pōz′) *vt.* **-posed′, -pos′ing** [< OFr. < *de-* < L. *de*), from + *poser* < L. *pausare*, to cease: confused with L.

*deponere:* see ff.] **1.** to remove from office or a position of power, esp. from a throne; oust **2.** *Law* to state under oath but out of court —*vi.* to bear witness —**de·pos′al** *n.*
**de·pos·it** (di päz′it) *vt.* [< L. *depositus*, pp. of *deponere*, to put down < *de-*, down + *ponere*, to put] **1.** to place or entrust, as for safekeeping [to *deposit* money in a bank] **2.** to give as a pledge or partial payment **3.** to put or set down **4.** to leave (sediment, etc.) lying —*n.* **1.** something placed for safekeeping; specif., money put in a bank **2.** a pledge or part payment **3.** a depository **4.** something left lying, as sand or clay deposited by the action of wind, water, etc. —**on deposit** placed or entrusted for safekeeping
**de·pos·i·tar·y** (di päz′ə ter′ē) *n., pl.* **-tar′ies 1.** a person, firm, etc. entrusted with something for safekeeping; trustee **2.** a storehouse; depository
**dep·o·si·tion** (dep′ə zish′ən) *n.* **1.** a deposing or being deposed, as from office **2.** a testifying **3.** a depositing or being deposited **4.** something deposited **5.** *Law* the written testimony of a witness, made under oath, to be used in court
**de·pos·i·tor** (di päz′ə tər) *n.* a person who deposits something, esp. money in a bank
**de·pos·i·to·ry** (di päz′ə tôr′ē) *n., pl.* **-ries 1.** a place where things are put for safekeeping; storehouse **2.** a trustee; depository
**de·pot** (dē′pō; *military & Brit.* dep′ō) *n.* [Fr. *dépôt*, a storehouse < L. *depositum:* see DEPOSIT] **1.** a storehouse; warehouse **2.** a railroad or bus station **3.** *Mil. a)* a storage place for supplies *b)* a station for assembling recruits or combat replacements
**de·prave** (di prāv′) *vt.* **-praved′, -prav′ing** [< OFr. < L. < *de-*, intens. + *pravus*, crooked] to make morally bad; corrupt —**dep·ra·va·tion** (dep′rə vā′shən) *n.* —**de·praved′** *adj.* —**de·prav′er** *n.*
**de·prav·i·ty** (di prav′ə tē) *n.* **1.** a depraved condition; corruption; wickedness **2.** *pl.* **-ties** a depraved act or practice
**dep·re·cate** (dep′rə kāt′) *vt.* **-cat′ed, -cat′ing** [< L. pp. of *deprecari* < *de-*, off + *precari*, PRAY] **1.** to feel and express disapproval of **2.** to depreciate; belittle —**dep′re·cat′ing·ly** *adv.* —**dep′re·ca′tion** *n.* —**dep′re·ca′tor** *n.*
**dep·re·ca·to·ry** (-kə tôr′ē) *adj.* deprecating; disapproving, belittling, etc. Also **dep′re·ca′tive** (-kāt′iv) —**dep′re·ca·to′ri·ly** *adv.*
**de·pre·ci·ate** (di prē′shē āt′) *vt.* **-at′ed, -at′ing** [< L. pp. of *depretiare* < *de-*, from + *pretiare*, to value < *pretium*, PRICE] **1.** to reduce in value or price **2.** to belittle; disparage —*vi.* to drop in value or price —**de·pre′ci·a·to′ry** (-shē ə tôr′ē, -shə tôr′ē) *adj.*
**de·pre·ci·a·tion** (di prē′shē ā′shən) *n.* **1.** a decrease in value of property through wear, deterioration, etc. **2.** a decrease in the purchasing power of money **3.** a belittling; disparagement
**dep·re·da·tion** (dep′rə dā′shən) *n.* [< LL. pp. of *depraedari* < L. *de-*, intens. + *praedari*, to plunder < *praeda*, PREY] a robbing, plundering, or laying waste
**de·press** (di pres′) *vt.* [< OFr. < L. *depressus*, pp. of *deprimere* < *de-*, down + *premere*, to PRESS¹] **1.** to press down; lower **2.** to lower in spirits; make gloomy; sadden **3.** to decrease the activity of; weaken **4.** to lower in value, price, or amount **5.** *Music* to lower the pitch of —**de·press′ing** *adj.* —**de·press′ing·ly** *adv.*
**de·pres·sant** (-ənt) *adj.* lowering the rate of muscular or nervous activity —*n.* a depressant medicine, drug, etc.; sedative
**de·pressed** (di prest′) *adj.* **1.** pressed down **2.** lowered in position, intensity, amount, etc. **3.** flattened or hollowed, as if pressed down **4.** gloomy; dejected; sad **5.** characterized by widespread unemployment, poverty, etc. [a *depressed* area] **6.** *Bot.* flattened vertically, as if from downward pressure
**de·pres·sion** (di presh′ən) *n.* **1.** a depressing or being depressed **2.** a depressed part or place; hollow or low place **3.** low spirits; dejection **4.** a decrease in force, activity, amount, etc. **5.** a period marked by slackening business activity, much unemployment, falling prices and wages, etc. **6.** *Psychol.* an emotional condition characterized by feelings of hopelessness, inadequacy, etc.
**de·pres·sive** (di pres′iv) *adj.* **1.** tending to depress **2.** characterized by psychological depression —**de·pres′sive·ly** *adv.* —**de·pres′sive·ness** *n.*
**de·pres·sor** (-ər) *n.* **1.** one that depresses **2.** a muscle that draws down a part of the body **3.** an instrument for pressing a protruding part out of the way, as during a medical examination
**dep·ri·va·tion** (dep′rə vā′shən) *n.* a depriving or being deprived

**de·prive** (di prīv′) *vt.* **-prived′, -priv′ing** [< ML. < L. *de-*, intens. + *privare*, to separate] **1.** to take something away from forcibly; dispossess **2.** to keep from having, using, or enjoying [*deprived* of his rights]

**dept. 1.** department **2.** deputy

**depth** (depth) *n.* [ME. *depthe:* see DEEP & -TH¹] **1.** *a*) the distance from the top downward, or from front to back *b*) perspective, as in a painting **2.** the condition of being deep; deepness; specif., *a*) intensity, as of colors, emotion, etc. *b*) profundity of thought *c*) lowness of pitch **3.** the middle part [the *depth* of winter] **4.** [*usually pl.*] the inmost part [the *depths* of a wood] **5.** [*usually pl.*] the deep or deepest part, as of the sea **6.** [*usually pl.*] the extreme degree, as of despair —**in depth** in a thorough way —**out of** (or **beyond**) **one's depth 1.** in water too deep for one **2.** past one's ability or understanding

**depth charge** (or **bomb**) an explosive charge that explodes under water: used esp. against submarines

**depth perception** ability to perceive perspective

**depth psychology** any system of psychology, as psychoanalysis, dealing with the unconscious

**dep·u·ta·tion** (dep′yoo tā′shən) *n.* **1.** a deputing or being deputed **2.** a group of persons, or one person, appointed to represent others; delegation

**de·pute** (di pyo͞ot′) *vt.* **-put′ed, -put′ing** [< OFr. < L. < *de-*, from + *putare,* lit., to cleanse] **1.** to give (authority, etc.) to someone else as deputy **2.** to appoint as one's substitute, agent, etc.

**dep·u·tize** (dep′yə tīz′) *vt.* **-tized′, -tiz′ing** to appoint as deputy —*vi.* to act as deputy

**dep·u·ty** (-tē) *n., pl.* **-ties** [see DEPUTE] **1.** a person appointed to substitute for, or to assist, another **2.** a member of a legislature called a Chamber of Deputies —*adj.* acting as deputy

**De Quin·cey** (də kwin′sē), **Thomas** 1785–1859; Eng. essayist & critic

**de·rac·i·nate** (di ras′ə nāt′) *vt.* **-nat′ed, -nat′ing** [< Fr. < *dé-* (L. *dis-*), from + *racine,* a root < LL. < L. *radix*] to pull up by or as by the roots; uproot; eradicate —**de·rac′i·na′-tion** *n.*

**de·rail** (di rāl′) *vi., vt.* to go or cause to go off the rails: said of a train, etc. —**de·rail′ment** *n.*

**de·range** (di rānj′) *vt.* **-ranged′, -rang′ing** [< Fr. < OFr. < *des-* (L. *dis-*), apart + *rengier:* see RANGE] **1.** to upset the order or working of **2.** to make insane —**de·ranged′** *adj.* —**de·range′ment** *n.*

**Der·by** (dur′bē; *chiefly Brit.* där′bē) city in C England: pop. 221,000 —*n., pl.* **-bies 1.** an annual race for three-year-old horses at Epsom Downs, begun by the Earl of Derby in 1780 **2.** any similar horse race, esp. the one (**Kentucky Derby**) run in Louisville, Kentucky **3.** [d-] a stiff felt hat with a round crown and curved brim

DERBY

**de·reg·u·late** (dē reg′yə lāt′) *vt.* **-lat′ed, -lat′ing** to remove regulations governing —**de·reg′u·la′tion** *n.*

**der·e·lict** (der′ə likt′) *adj.* [< L. pp. of *derelinquere* < *de-*, intens. + *relinquere:* see RELINQUISH] **1.** deserted by the owner; abandoned **2.** neglectful of duty; negligent —*n.* **1.** a property abandoned by the owner; esp., a ship deserted at sea **2.** a destitute person with no home or job

**der·e·lic·tion** (der′ə lik′shən) *n.* **1.** an abandoning or being abandoned **2.** a neglect of, or failure in, duty

**de·ride** (di rīd′) *vt.* **-rid′ed, -rid′ing** [< L. < *de-*, down + *ridere,* to laugh] to laugh at in contempt or scorn; ridicule —**de·rid′er** *n.* —**de·rid′ing·ly** *adv.*

**‡de ri·gueur** (də rē gër′) [Fr.] **1.** required by etiquette; according to good form **2.** fashionable

**de·ri·sion** (di rizh′ən) *n.* a deriding or being derided; contempt or ridicule

**de·ri·sive** (di rī′siv) *adj.* showing derision: also **de·ri′so·ry** (-sə rē) —**de·ri′sive·ly** *adv.* —**de·ri′sive·ness** *n.*

**deriv. 1.** derivation **2.** derivative **3.** derived

**der·i·va·tion** (der′ə vā′shən) *n.* **1.** a deriving or being derived **2.** something derived **3.** *a*) the source or origin of something *b*) the etymology of a word **4.** the forming of words from bases, as by adding affixes

**de·riv·a·tive** (də riv′ə tiv) *adj.* **1.** derived **2.** not original —*n.* **1.** something derived **2.** a word formed by derivation **3.** *Chem.* a substance derived from another by chemical change **4.** *Math.* the instantaneous rate of change of one variable with respect to another —**de·riv′a·tive·ly** *adv.*

**de·rive** (di rīv′) *vt.* **-rived′, -riv′ing** [< OFr. < L. *derivare,* to divert a stream < *de-*, from + *rivus,* a stream] **1.** to get or receive (*from* a source) **2.** to deduce or infer **3.** to trace from or to a source; show the derivation of **4.** *Chem.* to obtain (a compound) from another compound by replacing

one element with one or more other elements —*vi.* to come (*from* a source) —**de·riv′a·ble** *adj.*

**-derm** (durm) [see ff.] *a suffix meaning* skin or covering [*endoderm*]

**der·ma¹** (dur′mə) *n.* [ModL. < Gr. *derma,* the skin] *same as* DERMIS —**der′mal, der′mic** *adj.*

**der·ma²** (dur′mə) *n.* [< Yid. pl. of *darm,* gut, ult. < OHG. *daram*] beef casing stuffed with bread crumbs, seasoning, etc. and roasted

**der·ma·ti·tis** (dur′mə tīt′is) *n.* [ff. + -ITIS] inflammation of the skin

**der·ma·to-** [Gr. < *derma* (gen. *dermatos*)] *a combining form meaning* skin: also **dermat-, dermo-**

**der·ma·tol·o·gy** (dur′mə täl′ə jē) *n.* [DERMATO- + -LOGY] the branch of medicine dealing with the skin and its diseases —**der′ma·to·log′i·cal** (-tə läj′ə k'l) *adj.* —**der′ma·tol′o·gist** *n.*

**der·mis** (dur′mis) *n.* [ModL. < LL. *epidermis,* EPIDERMIS] the layer of skin just below the epidermis

**der·o·gate** (der′ə gāt′) *vt., vi.* **-gat′ed, -gat′ing** [< L. pp. of *derogare* < *de-*, from + *rogare,* to ask] **1.** [Archaic] to take away (*from*) so as to impair **2.** to lower (someone) in esteem; disparage —**der′o·ga′tion** *n.*

**de·rog·a·to·ry** (di räg′ə tôr′ē) *adj.* **1.** tending to lessen or impair **2.** disparaging; belittling Also **de·rog′a·tive** —**de·rog′a·to′ri·ly** *adv.*

**der·rick** (der′ik) *n.* [orig., a gallows, after T. *Derrick,* 17th-c. London hangman] **1.** a large apparatus with tackle and beams, for lifting and moving heavy objects **2.** a tall, tapering framework, as over an oil well, to support drilling machinery, etc.

**der·ri·ère** (der′ē er′) *n.* [Fr., back part < LL. < L. *de,* from + *retro,* back] the buttocks

**der·ring-do** (der′iŋ do͞o′) *n.* [ME. *der-rynge do,* daring to do] daring action; reckless courage

**der·rin·ger** (der′in jər) *n.* [after H. *Deringer,* 19th-cent. U.S. gunsmith] a small, short-barreled pistol of large caliber

DERRICK
(for oil well)

**der·vish** (dur′vish) *n.* [Turk. < Per. *darvēsh,* beggar] a member of any of various Moslem orders dedicated to poverty and chastity: some dervishes practice whirling, howling, etc. as religious acts

**de·sal·i·na·tion** (dē sal′ə nā′shən) *n.* [DE- + SALIN(E) + -ATION] the removal of salt, esp. from sea water to make it drinkable: also **de·sal′i·ni·za′tion** —**de·sal′i·nate′** *vt.*

**des·cant** (des′kant; *for vi., also* des kant′) *n.* [< Anglo-Fr. < L. *dis-*, apart + *cantus,* song] **1.** *Medieval Music a*) singing in which there is a fixed melody and a subordinate melody added above *b*) this added melody **2.** a comment; discourse —*vi.* **1.** to discourse (*on* or *upon*) **2.** to sing or play a descant **3.** to sing

**Des·cartes** (dā kärt′), **Re·né** (rə nā′) 1596–1650; Fr. philosopher & mathematician

**de·scend** (di send′) *vi.* [< OFr. < L. < *de-*, down + *scandere,* to climb] **1.** to move from a higher to a lower place; come or go down **2.** to pass from an earlier to a later time, from greater to less, etc. **3.** to slope downward **4.** to come down (*from* a source) [he is *descended* from pioneers] **5.** to pass by inheritance or heredity **6.** to stoop (*to* some act) **7.** to make a sudden visit or attack (*on* or *upon*) **8.** *Astron.* to move toward the horizon —*vt.* to move down, down along, or through —**de·scend′er** *n.* —**de·scend′i·ble** *adj.*

**de·scend·ant** (-ənt) *adj.* descending: also **de·scend′ent** —*n.* **1.** one who is an offspring, however remote, of a certain ancestor, family, group, etc. **2.** something derived from an earlier form

**de·scent** (di sent′) *n.* **1.** a descending; coming or going down **2.** lineage; ancestry **3.** one generation (in a specified lineage) **4.** a downward slope **5.** a way down **6.** a sudden attack (*on* or *upon*) **7.** a decline; fall **8.** a stooping (*to* an act) **9.** *Law* transference (of property) to heirs

**de·scribe** (di skrīb′) *vt.* **-scribed′, -scrib′ing** [< OFr. < L. < *de-*, from + *scribere,* to write] **1.** to tell or write about **2.** to picture in words **3.** to trace the outline of —**de·scrib′a·ble** *adj.*

**de·scrip·tion** (di skrip′shən) *n.* **1.** the act, process, or technique of describing **2.** a statement or passage that describes **3.** sort or variety [books of every *description*]

**de·scrip·tive** (-tiv) *adj.* of or characterized by description —**de·scrip′tive·ly** *adv.* —**de·scrip′tive·ness** *n.*

**de·scry** (di skrī′) *vt.* **-scried′, -scry′ing** [< OFr. *descrier,* to proclaim < *des-*, from + *crier*: see CRY] **1.** to catch sight of (distant or obscure objects) **2.** to detect

**Des·de·mo·na** (dez'də mō'nə) *see* OTHELLO

**des·e·crate** (des'ə krāt') *vt.* **-crat'ed, -crat'ing** [DE- + (CON)SECRATE] to violate the sacredness of; profane —**des'e·crat'er, des'e·cra'tor** *n.* —**des'e·cra'tion** *n.*

**de·seg·re·gate** (dē seg'rə gāt') *vt., vi.* **-gat'ed, -gat'ing** to abolish racial segregation in (public schools, etc.) —**de·seg're·ga'tion** *n.*

**de·sen·si·tize** (dē sen'sə tīz') *vt.* **-tized', -tiz'ing** to make insensitive or less sensitive [*desensitized* to an allergen] —**de·sen'si·ti·za'tion** *n.* —**de·sen'si·tiz'er** *n.*

**de·sert**[1] (di zurt') *vt.* [< Fr. < LL. *desertare* < L. pp. of *deserere* < *de-*, from + *serere*, to join] **1.** to forsake (someone or something that one ought not to leave); abandon **2.** to leave (one's post, etc.) without permission —*vi.* to leave one's post, etc. without permission and with no intent to return or, in war, to avoid hazardous duty —**de·sert'er** *n.*

**des·ert**[2] (dez'ərt) *n.* [< OFr. < LL. *desertum*, a desert < L. pp. of *deserere*: see prec.] **1.** an uncultivated region without inhabitants; wilderness **2.** a dry, barren, sandy region —*adj.* **1.** of a desert **2.** wild and uninhabited

**de·sert**[3] (di zurt') *n.* [< OFr. < *deservir*, DESERVE] **1.** the fact of deserving reward or punishment **2.** [*often pl.*] deserved reward or punishment

**de·ser·tion** (di zur'shən) *n.* a deserting or being deserted

**de·serve** (di zurv') *vt.* **-served', -serv'ing** [< OFr. *deservir* < L. < *de-*, intens. + *servire*, to SERVE] to be worthy of (reward, punishment, etc.); merit —*vi.* to be worthy

**de·served** (-zurvd') *adj.* rightfully earned or merited; just —**de·serv'ed·ly** (-zur'vid lē) *adv.*

**de·serv·ing** (-zur'viŋ) *adj.* having merit; worthy (*of* help, reward, etc.) —**de·serv'ing·ly** *adv.*

**de·sex** (dē seks') *vt.* **1.** to remove the sex organs of **2.** to suppress or lessen the sexual characteristics of

**des·ic·cant** (des'i kənt) *adj.* [see ff.] drying —*n.* a substance used as a drying agent

**des·ic·cate** (-kāt') *vt.* **-cat'ed, -cat'ing** [< L. pp. of *desiccare* < *de-*, intens. + *siccare* < *siccus*, dry] **1.** to dry completely **2.** to preserve (food) by drying —*vi.* to become completely dry —**des'ic·ca'tion** *n.* —**des'ic·ca'tor** *n.*

**de·sid·er·ate** (di sid'ə rāt') *vt.* **-at'ed, -at'ing** [< L. pp. of *desiderare*: see DESIRE] to want; need —**de·sid'er·a'tion** *n.*

**de·sid·er·a·tum** (di sid'ə rāt'əm, -zid'-; -rāt'-) *n., pl.* **-ta** (-ə) [L., neut. pp. of *desiderare*: see DESIRE] something needed and wanted

**de·sign** (di zīn') *vt.* [< L. < *de-*, out + *signare* < *signum*, a mark] **1.** to make preliminary sketches of; plan **2.** to form (plans, etc.) in the mind; contrive **3.** to plan and work out (something) creatively; devise **4.** to plan to do; intend **5.** to intend for some purpose —*vi.* to make original plans, patterns, etc. —*n.* **1.** a plan; scheme; project **2.** purpose; intention; aim **3.** [*pl.*] a secret, usually dishonest or selfish scheme (often with *on* or *upon*) **4.** a plan or sketch to work from; pattern **5.** the art of making designs or patterns **6.** the arrangement of parts, form, color, etc. so as to produce an artistic unit **7.** a finished artistic work or decoration —**by design** purposely

**des·ig·nate** (dez'ig nāt'; *for adj., also* -nit) *adj.* [see prec.] named for an office, etc. but not yet in it —*vt.* **-nat'ed, -nat'ing** **1.** to point out; indicate; specify **2.** to refer to by a distinguishing name, title, etc.; name **3.** to name for an office or duty —**des'ig·na'tive, des'ig·na'tor** *n.*

**designated hitter** *Baseball* a player in the regular batting order who does not play a defensive position, but has been designated to bat in place of the pitcher, whose status is otherwise unaffected

**des·ig·na·tion** (dez'ig nā'shən) *n.* **1.** a pointing out or marking out **2.** appointment to an office, post, etc. **3.** a distinguishing name, title, etc.

**de·sign·ed·ly** (di zī'nid lē) *adv.* purposely

**de·sign·er** (di zī'nər) *n.* a person who designs, or makes original sketches, patterns, etc.

**de·sign·ing** (-niŋ) *adj.* **1.** that makes or makes plans, patterns, etc. **2.** scheming; crafty —*n.* the art or work of creating designs, patterns, etc.

**de·sir·a·ble** (di zīr'ə b'l) *adj.* worth having; pleasing, excellent, etc. —**de·sir'a·bil'i·ty** *n.* —**de·sir'a·bly** *adv.*

**de·sire** (di zīr') *vt.* **-sired', -sir'ing** [< L. *desiderare* < *de-*, from + *sidus* (gen. *sideris*), a star] **1.** to wish or long for; crave **2.** to ask for; request **3.** to want sexually —*vi.* to have a desire —*n.* **1.** a strong wish or craving **2.** sexual appetite **3.** a request **4.** anything desired

**de·sir·ous** (di zīr'əs) *adj.* desiring; characterized by desire

**de·sist** (di zist') *vi.* [< OFr. < L. < *de-*, from + *sistere*, to cause to stand < *stare*, to stand] to cease (*from* an action); stop —**de·sis'tance** *n.*

**desk** (desk) *n.* [ML. *desca*, a table, ult. < L. *discus*, DISCUS] **1.** a kind of table with drawers and with a flat or sloping top for writing, etc. **2.** the place in a hotel where guests register, check out, etc.

**Des Moines** (də moin') [Fr., lit., of the monks] capital of Iowa, in the C part: pop. 191,000

**des·o·late** (des'ə lit; *for v.* -lāt') *adj.* [< L. pp. of *desolare* < *de-*, intens. + *solare*, to make lonely < *solus*, alone] **1.** lonely; solitary **2.** uninhabited; deserted **3.** made uninhabitable; laid waste **4.** forlorn; wretched —*vt.* **-lat'ed, -lat'ing** **1.** to make desolate; rid of inhabitants **2.** to make uninhabitable; lay waste; devastate **3.** to forsake; abandon **4.** to make forlorn, wretched, etc. —**des'o·late·ly** *adv.* —**des'o·late·ness** *n.*

**des·o·la·tion** (des'ə lā'shən) *n.* **1.** a making desolate **2.** a desolate condition **3.** lonely grief; misery **4.** loneliness **5.** a desolate place

**De So·to** (di sōt'ō), **Her·nan·do** (hər nan'dō) 1500?-42; Sp. explorer in America: also **de Soto**

**de·spair** (di sper') *vi.* [< OFr. < L. < *de-*, without + *sperare*, to hope < *spes*, hope] to lose hope; be without hope (usually with *of*) —*n.* **1.** a despairing; loss of hope **2.** a person or thing causing despair

**de·spair·ing** (-iŋ) *adj.* feeling or showing despair; hopeless —**de·spair'ing·ly** *adv.*

**des·patch** (di spach') *vt., n. var. sp. of* DISPATCH

**des·per·a·do** (des'pə rä'dō, -rā'-) *n., pl.* **-does, -dos** [OSp. < L. *desperare*: see DESPAIR] a dangerous, reckless criminal; bold outlaw

**des·per·ate** (des'pər it) *adj.* [< L. pp. of *desperare*: see DESPAIR] **1.** rash or violent because of despair **2.** having a very great desire, need, etc. [*desperate* for affection] **3.** causing despair; extremely dangerous or serious [a *desperate* illness] **4.** extreme; drastic [in *desperate* need] —**des'per·ate·ly** *adv.*

**des·per·a·tion** (des'pə rā'shən) *n.* **1.** the state of being desperate **2.** recklessness caused by despair

**des·pi·ca·ble** (des'pik ə b'l, di spik'-) *adj.* deserving to be despised; contemptible —**des'pi·ca·bly** *adv.*

**de·spise** (di spīz') *vt.* **-spised', -spis'ing** [< OFr. < L. *despicere* < *de*, down + *specere*, to look at] **1.** to look down on with contempt and scorn **2.** to regard with extreme dislike

**de·spite** (di spīt') *n.* [< OFr. < L. pp. of *despicere*: see prec.] **1.** malice; spite **2.** [Archaic] contempt —*prep.* in spite of; notwithstanding

**Des Plaines** (des plänz') [prob. < Miss. Valley Fr. *plaines*, sugar maples, once growing there] city in NE Ill.: suburb of Chicago: pop. 54,000

**de·spoil** (di spoil') *vt.* [< OFr. < L. < *de-*, intens. + *spoliare*, to plunder: see SPOIL] to deprive (*of* something) by force; rob; plunder —**de·spoil'er** *n.* —**de·spoil'ment** *n.*

**de·spo·li·a·tion** (di spō'lē ā'shən) *n.* a despoiling or being despoiled; pillage

**de·spond** (di spänd') *vi.* [L. *despondere*, to give up < *de*, from + *spondere*, to promise] to lose courage or hope; become disheartened —*n.* despondency: now chiefly in **slough of despond** —**de·spond'ing·ly** *adv.*

**de·spond·en·cy** (di spän'dən sē) *n.* [see prec.] loss of courage or hope; dejection: also **de·spond'ence**

**de·spond·ent** (-dənt) *adj.* filled with despondency; dejected —**de·spond'ent·ly** *adv.*

**des·pot** (des'pət, -pät) *n.* [< OFr. < Gr. *despotēs*, a master] **1.** an absolute ruler; autocrat **2.** anyone in charge who acts like a tyrant

**des·pot·ic** (des pät'ik) *adj.* of or like a despot; autocratic; tyrannical —**des·pot'i·cal·ly** *adv.*

**des·pot·ism** (des'pə tiz'm) *n.* **1.** rule by a despot; autocracy **2.** the methods of a despot; tyranny

**des·sert** (di zurt') *n.* [< OFr. < *desservir*, to clear the table < *des-* (L. *de*), from + *servir* < L. *servire*, to serve] **1.** a course of pie, cake, ice cream, etc., served at the end of a meal **2.** [Brit.] uncooked fruit and nuts served after the sweet course

**de·sta·bi·lize** (dē stā'bə līz') *vt.* **-lized', -liz'ing** to upset the stability of; unbalance

**des·ti·na·tion** (des'tə nā'shən) *n.* **1.** the end for which something or someone is destined **2.** the place toward which someone or something is going or sent

**des·tine** (des'tin) *vt.* **-tined, -tin·ing** [< OFr. < L. *destinare*, to secure, fix < *de-*, intens. + base of *stare*, to stand] **1.** to predetermine, as by fate [he seemed *destined* to succeed] **2.** to set apart for a certain purpose; intend —**destined for 1.** bound for **2.** intended for

**des·tin·y** (des'tə nē) *n., pl.* **-ies** [see prec.] **1.** the seemingly inevitable or necessary succession of events **2.** that which will necessarily happen to any person or thing; (one's) fate **3.** that which determines events

---

fat, āpe, cär, ten, ēven, is, bīte; gō, hôrn, tōol, look; oil, out; up, fur; get; joy; yet; chin; she; thin, *then*; zh, leisure; ŋ, ring; ə for *a* in *ago*, *e* in *agent*, *i* in *sanity*, *o* in *comply*, *u* in *focus*; ' as in *able* (ā'b'l); Fr. bål; ë, Fr. coeur; ö, Fr. feu; Fr. mon; ô, Fr. coq; ü, Fr. duc; r, Fr. cri; H, G. ich; kh, G. doch; ‡foreign; *hypothetical; < derived from. See inside front cover.

**des·ti·tute** (des′tə tōōt′, -tyōōt′) *adj.* [< L. pp. of *destituere*, to forsake < *de-*, down + *statuere*, to set] **1.** not having; lacking (with *of*) [*destitute* of trees] **2.** living in complete poverty

**des·ti·tu·tion** (des′tə tōō′shən, -tyōō′-) *n.* the state of being destitute; esp., abject poverty

**de·stroy** (di stroi′) *vt.* [< OFr. < L. < *de-*, down + *struere*, to build] **1.** to tear down; demolish **2.** to spoil completely; ruin **3.** to put an end to **4.** to kill **5.** to neutralize the effect of **6.** to make useless —*vi.* to bring about destruction

**de·stroy·er** (-ər) *n.* **1.** a person or thing that destroys **2.** a small, fast, heavily armed warship

**de·struct** (di strukt′, dē′strukt′) *n.* [back-formation < DESTRUCTION] the deliberate destruction of a malfunctioning missile, rocket, etc. after its launch —*vi.* to be automatically destroyed

**de·struct·i·ble** (di struk′tə b'l) *adj.* that can be destroyed —**de·struct′i·bil′i·ty** *n.*

**de·struc·tion** (di struk′shən) *n.* [< OFr. < L. pp. of *destruere:* see DESTROY] **1.** a destroying or being destroyed **2.** the cause or means of destroying

**de·struc·tive** (di struk′tiv) *adj.* **1.** tending or likely to cause destruction **2.** causing destruction; destroying **3.** merely negative; not helpful [*destructive* criticism] —**de·struc′tive·ly** *adv.* —**de·struc′tive·ness, de·struc′tiv·i·ty** *n.*

**destructive distillation** the decomposition of coal, wood, etc. by heat in the absence of air, and the recovery of the volatile products of the decomposition by condensation and other means

**des·ue·tude** (des′wi tōōd′, -tyōōd′) *n.* [< L. < pp. of *desuescere* < *de-*, from + *suescere*, to be accustomed] disuse [laws fallen into *desuetude*]

**de·sul·fur·ize** (dē sul′fə rīz′) *vt.* -ized′, -iz′ing to remove sulfur from: also **de·sul′fur**

**des·ul·to·ry** (des′'l tôr′ē) *adj.* [< L. < *desultor*, vaulter < pp. of *desilire* < *de-*, from + *salire*, to leap] **1.** passing from one thing to another in an aimless way; disconnected; not methodical **2.** lacking direct relevancy; random [a *desultory* observation] —**des′ul·to′ri·ly** *adv.* —**des′ul·to′ri·ness** *n.*

**de·tach** (di tach′) *vt.* [< Fr. < OFr. < *de-*, off + *estachier*, to ATTACH] **1.** to unfasten or separate and remove; disconnect **2.** to send (troops, ships, etc.) on a special mission —**de·tach′a·bil′i·ty** *n.* —**de·tach′a·ble** *adj.*

**de·tached** (di tacht′) *adj.* **1.** not connected; separate **2.** disinterested; impartial; aloof —**de·tach′ed·ly** (-tach′id lē) *adv.* —**de·tach′ed·ness** *n.*

**de·tach·ment** (di tach′mənt) *n.* **1.** a detaching; separation **2.** *a)* the sending of troops or ships on special service *b)* a unit of troops assigned to some special task **3.** the state of being disinterested, impartial, or aloof

**de·tail** (di tāl′, dē′tāl) *n.* [< Fr. < *dé-* (L. *de*), from + *tailler*, to cut] **1.** a dealing with things item by item **2.** a minute account [to go into *detail*] **3.** an item or particular **4.** a small part of a whole structure, design, etc. **5.** *a)* one or more soldiers, sailors, etc. chosen for a particular task *b)* the task itself —*vt.* **1.** to give the particulars of; tell, item by item **2.** to choose for a particular task [*detail* a man for sentry duty] —**in detail** item by item; with particulars —**detailed′** *adj.*

**de·tain** (di tān′) *vt.* [< OFr. < L. < *de-*, off + *tenere*, to hold] **1.** to keep in custody; confine **2.** to keep from going on; hold back —**de·tain′er** *n.* —**de·tain′ment** *n.*

**de·tect** (di tekt′) *vt.* [< L. *detectus*, pp. of *detegere* < *de-*, from + *tegere*, to cover] **1.** to catch or discover, as in a misdeed **2.** to discover (something hidden or not easily noticed) **3.** *Radio* same as DEMODULATE —**de·tect′a·ble, de·tect′i·ble** *adj.*

**de·tec·tion** (di tek′shən) *n.* **1.** a finding out or being found out **2.** *same as* DEMODULATION

**de·tec·tive** (-tiv) *adj.* **1.** of or for detection **2.** of detectives and their work —*n.* a person, usually on a police force, whose work is investigating crimes, getting secret information, etc.

**de·tec·tor** (-tər) *n.* **1.** a person or thing that detects **2.** *Radio* a device used in demodulation

**de·tent** (di tent′, dē′tent) *n.* [< Fr.] *Mech.* a part that stops or releases a movement

**dé·tente de·tente** (dā tänt′) *n.* [Fr.] a lessening of tension or hostility, esp. between nations

**de·ten·tion** (di ten′shən) *n.* a detaining or being detained; specif., *a)* a keeping in custody; confinement *b)* an enforced delay

**detention home** a place where juvenile offenders or delinquents are held in custody, esp. temporarily

**de·ter** (di tur′) *vt.* -terred′, -ter′ring [< L. < *de-*, from + *terrere*, to frighten] to keep or discourage (a person) from doing something by instilling fear, anxiety, doubt, etc. —**de·ter′ment** *n.*

**de·terge** (di turj′) *vt.* -terged′, -terg′ing [< L. < *de-*, off + *tergere*, to wipe] to cleanse, as a wound —**de·ter′gen·cy, de·ter′gence** *n.*

**de·ter·gent** (di tur′jənt) *adj.* [see prec.] cleansing —*n.* a cleansing substance that is like soap but is made synthetically and not from fats and lye

**de·te·ri·o·rate** (di tir′ē ə rāt′) *vt., vi.* -rat′ed, -rat′ing [< LL. pp. of *deteriorare* < L. *deterior*, worse] to make or become worse; depreciate —**de·te′ri·o·ra′tion** *n.* —**de·te′ri·o·ra′tive** *adj.*

**de·ter·mi·na·cy** (di tur′mi nə sē) *n.* **1.** the state or quality of being determinate **2.** the condition of being determined, as in being caused or in having predictable results

**de·ter·mi·nant** (-nənt) *adj.* determining —*n.* a thing or factor that determines

**de·ter·mi·nate** (-nit) *adj.* [see DETERMINE] **1.** having exact limits; definite; fixed **2.** settled; conclusive **3.** *Bot.* having a flower at the end of the primary axis and of each secondary axis —**de·ter′mi·nate·ly** *adv.* —**de·ter′mi·nate·ness** *n.*

**de·ter·mi·na·tion** (di tur′mə nā′shən) *n.* **1.** a determining or being determined **2.** a firm intention **3.** firmness of purpose

**de·ter·mi·na·tive** (di tur′mə nā′tiv, -nə tiv) *adj.* determining —*n.* a thing that determines —**de·ter′mi·na′tive·ly** *adv.* —**de·ter′mi·na′tive·ness** *n.*

**de·ter·mine** (di tur′mən) *vt.* -mined, -min·ing [< OFr. < L. < *de-*, from + *terminare*, to set bounds < *terminus*, an end] **1.** to set limits to; bound; define **2.** to settle conclusively; decide **3.** to reach a decision about; decide upon **4.** to establish or affect the nature, kind, or quality of [genes *determine* heredity] **5.** to find out exactly; calculate precisely **6.** to give a definite aim to; direct —*vi.* **1.** to decide; resolve **2.** *Law* to come to an end —**de·ter′mi·na·ble** *adj.* —**de·ter′min·er** *n.*

**de·ter·mined** (-mənd) *adj.* **1.** having one's mind made up; resolved **2.** resolute; unwavering —**de·ter′mined·ly** *adv.* —**de·ter′mined·ness** *n.*

**de·ter·min·ism** (-mə niz′m) *n.* the doctrine that everything, esp. one's choice of action, is determined by a sequence of causes independent of one's will —**de·ter′min·ist** *n., adj.* —**de·ter′min·is′tic** *adj.*

**de·ter·rent** (di tur′ənt) *adj.* deterring or tending to deter —*n.* anything that deters; hindrance —**de·ter′rence** *n.*

**de·test** (di test′) *vt.* [< Fr. < L. *detestari*, to curse by calling the gods to witness < *de-*, down + *testis*, a witness] to dislike intensely; hate; abhor —**de·test′er** *n.*

**de·test·a·ble** (di tes′tə b'l) *adj.* that is or should be detested; hateful; odious —**de·test′a·bil′i·ty, de·test′a·ble·ness** *n.* —**de·test′a·bly** *adv.*

**de·tes·ta·tion** (dē′tes tā′shən) *n.* **1.** intense dislike or hatred; loathing **2.** a detested person or thing

**de·throne** (dē thrōn′) *vt.* -throned′, -thron′ing to remove from a throne; depose —**de·throne′ment** *n.*

**det·o·nate** (det′'n āt′) *vi., vt.* -nat′ed, -nat′ing [< L. pp. of *detonare* < *de-*, intens. + *tonare*, to thunder] to explode noisily —**det′o·na′tion** *n.*

**det·o·na·tor** (-āt′ər) *n.* **1.** a fuse, percussion cap, etc. for setting off explosives **2.** an explosive

**de·tour** (dē′toor, di toor′) *n.* [< Fr. < *détourner*, to turn aside < OFr. < *des-* (L. *dis-*) + *tourner:* see TURN] **1.** a roundabout way **2.** a route used when the regular route is closed to traffic —*vi., vt.* to go or cause to go by way of a detour

**de·tract** (di trakt′) *vt.* [< L. pp. of *detrahere* < *de-*, from + *trahere*, to draw] to take or draw away —*vi.* to take something desirable away (*from*) [frowning *detracts* from her beauty] —**de·trac′tion** *n.* —**de·trac′tive** *adj.* —**de·trac′tor** *n.*

**de·train** (dē trān′) *vi., vt.* to get off or remove from a railroad train —**de·train′ment** *n.*

**det·ri·ment** (det′rə mənt) *n.* [OFr. < L. *detrimentum*, damage < pp. of *deterere* < *de-*, off + *terere*, to rub] **1.** damage; injury; harm **2.** anything that causes damage or injury —**det′ri·men′tal** (-men′t'l) *adj.* —**det′ri·men′tal·ly** *adv.*

**de·tri·tus** (di trīt′əs) *n.* [L., pp. of *deterere:* see prec.] fragments of rock, etc. produced by disintegration or wearing away; debris

**De·troit** (di troit′) [< Fr. *détroit*, strait] **1.** river flowing south from Lake St. Clair into Lake Erie **2.** city in SE Mich., on this river: pop. 1,203,000 (met. area 4,344,000)

**‡de trop** (də trō′) [Fr.] too much; superfluous

**deuce¹** (dōōs, dyōōs) *n.* [< OFr. < L. acc. of *duo*, two] **1.** a playing card with two spots **2.** the side of a die bearing two spots, or a throw of the dice totaling two **3.** *Tennis* a score of 40 each (or five games each) after which one side must get two successive points (or games) to win the game (or set)

**deuce²** (dōōs, dyōōs) *n., interj.* [< OFr. *dieu* & L. *deus*, God: also infl. by DEUCE¹, in reference to low score at dice] bad luck, the devil, etc.: a mild oath or exclamation of annoyance, surprise, etc.

**deu·ced** (dōō′sid, dyōō′-; dōōst, dyōōst) *adj.* **1.** devilish; confounded **2.** extreme Used in mild oaths —*adv.* extremely; very: also **deu′ced·ly**
‡**De·us** (dā′ŏos, dē′əs) [L.] God

**Deut.** Deuteronomy

**deu·te·ri·um** (dōō tir′ē əm, dyōō-) *n.* [ModL. < Gr. *deuteros,* second] the hydrogen isotope having an atomic weight of 2.0141 and boiling point of −249.7°C; heavy hydrogen: symbol, D

**deu·ter·o-, deu·ter-** [< Gr. *deuteros,* second] *a combining form meaning* second, secondary

**deu·ter·on** (dōōt′ər än′, dyōōt′-) *n.* the nucleus of an atom of deuterium

**Deu·ter·on·o·my** (dōōt′ər än′ə mē, dyōōt′-) [< LL. < Gr. < DEUTERO- + *nomos,* law] the fifth book of the Pentateuch in the Bible

**deut·sche mark** (doi′chə) *pl.* **mark,** Eng. **marks** *see* MONETARY UNITS, table (West Germany)

**Deutsch·land** (doich′länt′) [G.] *Ger. name of* GERMANY

**de·val·ue** (dē val′yōō) *vt.* **-ued, -u·ing 1.** to lessen the value of **2.** to lower the exchange value of (a currency) in relation to other currencies Also **de·val′u·ate′** (-yōō wāt′) **-at′ed, -at′ing —de·val′u·a′tion** *n.*

**dev·as·tate** (dev′ə stāt′) *vt.* **-tat′ed, -tat′ing** [< L. pp. < *de-,* intens. + *vastare,* to make empty < *vastus,* empty] **1.** to lay waste; make desolate; ravage; destroy **2.** to make helpless **—dev′as·tat′ing·ly** *adv.* **—dev′as·ta′tion** *n.* **—dev′as·ta′tor** *n.*

**de·vel·op** (di vel′əp) *vt.* [< Fr. < *dé-* (L. *dis-*), apart + OFr. *voloper,* to wrap] **1.** to cause to become gradually fuller, larger, better, stronger, etc. **2.** to bring (an idea, plan, etc.) into activity or reality **3.** to cause (a bud, etc.) to evolve gradually **4.** to make (housing, highways, etc.) more available or extensive **5.** *Music* to elaborate (a theme) **6.** *Photog.* a) to put (an exposed film, plate, or printing paper) in various chemical solutions in order to make the picture visible b) to make (a picture) thus **7.** to show or work out by degrees; make known gradually; reveal **8.** to explain more clearly —*vi.* **1.** to come into being or activity **2.** to become larger, fuller, better, etc.; make progress; grow or evolve **3.** to be disclosed **—de·vel′op·a·ble** *adj.*

**de·vel·op·er** (-ər) *n.* a person or thing that develops; esp., *Photog.* a chemical used to develop film, plates, etc.

**de·vel·op·ment** (-mənt) *n.* **1.** a developing or being developed **2.** a stage in growth, advancement, etc. **3.** an event or happening **4.** a thing that is developed, as a tract of land with newly built homes, etc. **—de·vel′op·men′tal** (-men′t'l) *adj.* **—de·vel′op·men′tal·ly** *adv.*

**de·vi·ant** (dē′vē ənt) *adj.* [< LL. prp. of *deviare:* see ff.] deviating, esp. from what is considered normal, established, etc. —*n.* a person whose behavior is deviant **—de′vi·an·cy, de′vi·ance** *n.*

**de·vi·ate** (dē′vē āt′; *for adj. & n.* -it) *vi., vt.* **-at′ed, -at′ing** [< LL. pp. of *deviare* < *de-,* from + *via,* road] to turn aside (*from* a course, direction, standard, etc.) —*adj.* same as DEVIANT —*n.* a deviant; esp., one with deviant sexual behavior **—de′vi·a′tor** *n.*

**de·vi·a·tion** (dē′vē ā′shən) *n.* **1.** a deviating or being deviant, as in behavior, political ideology, etc. **2.** *Statistics* the difference between a particular number in a set and some fixed value, usually the mean **—de′vi·a′tion·ism** *n.* **—de′vi·a′tion·ist** *adj., n.*

**de·vice** (di vīs′) *n.* [< OFr. *devis,* division < *deviser:* see DEVISE] **1.** a thing devised; esp., an underhanded scheme; trick **2.** a mechanical invention or contrivance **3.** something used for artistic effect [*rhetorical devices*] **4.** an ornamental figure or design **5.** a design or emblem on a coat of arms **6.** any motto or emblem **—leave to one's own devices** to allow to do as one wishes

**dev·il** (dev′'l) *n.* [OE. *deofol* < LL. < Gr. *diabolos,* slanderous (in N.T., devil) < *dia-,* across + *ballein,* to throw] **1.** [*often* D-] *Theol.* a) the chief evil spirit; Satan (with *the*): typically depicted as a man with horns, a tail, and cloven feet b) any demon of hell **2.** a wicked or malevolent person **3.** one who is mischievous, reckless, etc. **4.** an unlucky, unhappy person [*that poor devil*] **5.** anything hard to operate, control, etc. **6.** any machine for tearing paper, rags, etc. to bits —*vt.* **-iled** or **-illed, -il·ing** or **-il·ling 1.** to prepare (food, often finely chopped) with hot seasoning **2.** to annoy; torment; tease **—a devil of a** an extreme example of a **—between the devil and the deep (blue) sea** between equally unpleasant alternatives **—give the devil his due** to acknowledge the good qualities of even a wicked person **—go to the devil** to fall into bad habits **—play the devil with** [Colloq.] to disturb; upset **—the devil!** [Colloq.] an exclamation of anger, surprise, etc. **—the devil to pay** trouble as a consequence

**dev·il·fish** (-fish′) *n., pl.* **-fish′, -fish′es:** see FISH **1.** a large ray whose pectoral fins are hornlike when rolled up **2.** an octopus

DEVILFISH
(to 20 ft. across)

**dev·il·ish** (dev′'l ish, dev′lish) *adj.* **1.** of, like, or characteristic of a devil; diabolical **2.** mischievous; reckless **3.** [Colloq.] a) extremely bad b) extreme —*adv.* [Colloq.] extremely; very **—dev′il·ish·ly** *adv.* **—dev′il·ish·ness** *n.*

**dev·il-may-care** (dev′'l mā ker′) *adj.* reckless or careless; happy-go-lucky

**dev·il·ment** (dev′'l mənt) *n.* **1.** [Archaic] evil behavior **2.** mischief or mischievous action

**dev·il·ry** (-rē) *n., pl.* **-ries** [Chiefly Brit.] **1.** witchcraft **2.** evil behavior **3.** *same as* DEVILTRY

**devil's advocate 1.** *R.C.Ch.* an official selected to raise objections in the case of one named for beatification or canonization **2.** one who upholds the wrong side, as for argument's sake

**dev·il's-darn·ing-nee·dle** (dev′'lz där′niŋ nē′d'l) *n. same as* DRAGONFLY

**dev·il's-food cake** (dev′'lz fōōd′) a rich cake made with chocolate or cocoa and baking soda

**Devil's Island** Fr. island off the coast of French Guiana: site of a former penal colony

**dev·il·try** (dev′'l trē) *n., pl.* **-tries 1.** reckless mischief, fun, etc. **2.** *same as* DEVILRY

**de·vi·ous** (dē′vē əs) *adj.* [< L. *devius* < *de-,* off, from + *via,* road] **1.** roundabout; winding **2.** going astray **3.** not straightforward or frank; deceiving **—de′vi·ous·ly** *adv.* **—de′vi·ous·ness** *n.*

**de·vise** (di vīz′) *vt., vi.* **-vised′, -vis′ing** [< OFr. *deviser,* to distribute, direct < L. pp. of *dividere,* to divide] **1.** to work out (something) by thinking; plan; invent **2.** *Law* to bequeath (real property) by will —*n. Law* **1.** a gift of real property by will **2.** a will, or clause in a will, granting such a gift **—de·vis′a·ble** *adj.* **—de·vis′al** *n.* **—de·vis′er** *n.*

**de·vi·tal·ize** (dē vīt′'l īz′) *vt.* **-ized′, -iz′ing** to lower in vitality **—de·vi′tal·i·za′tion** *n.*

**de·void** (di void′) *adj.* [< OFr. < *des-* (L. *dis-*), from + *vuidier:* see VOID] completely without; empty (*of*)

**de·voir** (də vwär′, dev′wär) *n.* [< OFr. < L. *debere,* to owe] **1.** duty **2.** [*pl.*] acts of due respect or courtesy

**de·volve** (di välv′) *vt., vi.* **-volved′, -volv′ing** [< L. < *de-,* down + *volvere,* to roll] to pass (*on*) to another: said of duties, responsibilities, etc. **—dev·o·lu·tion** (dev′ə lōō′shən), **de·volve′ment** *n.*

**De·vo·ni·an** (di vō′nē ən) *adj.* [after *Devonshire,* county in England] *Geol.* designating or of the period after the Silurian in the Paleozoic Era **—the Devonian** the Devonian Period or its rocks: see GEOLOGY, chart

**de·vote** (di vōt′) *vt.* **-vot′ed, -vot′ing** [< L. *devotus,* pp. < *de-,* from + *vovere,* to vow] **1.** to set apart for a special use or service; dedicate **2.** to give up (oneself or one's time, energy, etc.) to some purpose, activity, or person

**de·vot·ed** (-id) *adj.* **1.** dedicated; consecrated **2.** very loving, loyal, or faithful **—de·vot′ed·ly** *adv.* **—de·vot′ed·ness** *n.*

**dev·o·tee** (dev′ə tē′, -tā′) *n.* a person strongly devoted to someone or to something, as a religion

**de·vo·tion** (di vō′shən) *n.* **1.** a devoting or being devoted **2.** piety **3.** religious worship **4.** [*pl.*] prayers **5.** loyalty or deep affection

**de·vo·tion·al** (-'l) *adj.* of or characterized by devotion —*n.* a brief worship service **—de·vo′tion·al·ly** *adv.*

**de·vour** (di vour′) *vt.* [< OFr. < L. < *de-,* intens. + *vorare,* to swallow whole] **1.** to eat (up) hungrily or voraciously **2.** to consume; destroy; devastate **3.** to take in greedily with the eyes, ears, or mind [*to devour novels*] **4.** to engross [*devoured* by curiosity] **5.** to swallow up; engulf **—de·vour′er** *n.*

**de·vout** (di vout′) *adj.* [< OFr. < L. *devotus:* see DEVOTE] **1.** very religious; pious **2.** showing reverence **3.** earnest; sincere; heartfelt **—de·vout′ly** *adv.* **—de·vout′ness** *n.*

**dew** (dōō, dyōō) *n.* [OE. *deaw*] **1.** the moisture that condenses after a warm day and appears during the night in little drops on cool surfaces **2.** anything regarded as refreshing, pure, etc., like dew **3.** any moisture in small drops —*vt.* [Poet.] to wet as with drops of dew

**dew·ber·ry** (dōō′ber′ē, dyōō-) *n., pl.* **-ries 1.** any of various trailing blackberry plants of the rose family **2.** the fruit of any of these plants

**dew·claw** (-klô′) *n.* **1.** a functionless digit on the foot of some animals, as on the inner side of a dog's leg **2.** the claw or hoof on such a digit

**dew·drop** (-dräp′) *n.* a drop of dew

**Dew·ey** (dōō′ē, dyōō′ē) **1.** George, 1837–1917; U.S. admiral in the Spanish-American War **2.** John, 1859–1952; U.S. philosopher & educator **3.** Melvil, 1851–1931; U.S. librarian: originated **Dewey Decimal System** for book classification in libraries

**dew·lap** (-lap′) *n.* [< ME. < *dew*, prob. dew + *lappe*, a fold < OE. *læppa*] **1.** a loose fold of skin hanging from the throat of cattle and certain other animals **2.** a similar loose fold under the chin of an elderly person —**dew′lapped′** (-lapt′) *adj.*

**DEW line** (dōō, dyōō) [*D*(*istant*) *E*(*arly*) *W*(*arning*)] a line of radar stations near the 70th parallel in N. America

**dew point** the temperature at which dew starts to form or vapor to condense into liquid

**dew·y** (-ē) *adj.* **dew′i·er, dew′i·est 1.** wet or damp with dew **2.** of dew **3.** [Poet.] dewlike; refreshing, etc. —**dew′i·ly** *adv.* —**dew′i·ness** *n.*

DEWLAP

**Dex·e·drine** (dek′sə drēn′, -drin) [< ff. & EPHEDRINE] *a trademark for* AMPHETAMINE

**dex·ter** (dek′stər) *adj.* [L., right] of or on the right-hand side (on a coat of arms, the left of the viewer)

**dex·ter·i·ty** (dek ster′ə tē) *n.* [< L. < *dexter:* see prec.] **1.** skill in using one's hands or body; adroitness **2.** skill in using one's mind; cleverness

**dex·ter·ous** (dek′strəs, -stər əs) *adj.* [see prec.] **1.** having or showing skill in the use of the hands or body **2.** having or showing mental skill —**dex′ter·ous·ly** *adv.* —**dex′ter·ous·ness** *n.*

**dex·tral** (dek′strəl) *adj.* [< L. *dextra*, right-hand side] **1.** on the right-hand side; right **2.** right-handed —**dex·tral′i·ty** (-stral′ə tē) *n.* —**dex′tral·ly** *adv.*

**dex·trin** (dek′strin) *n.* [< Fr. < L. *dexter*, right: it turns the plane of polarized light to the right] a soluble, gummy substance obtained from starch and used as adhesive, sizing, etc.: also **dex′trine** (-strēn, -strən)

**dex·trorse** (dek′strôrs) *adj.* [< L. < *dexter*, right + *versus*, pp. of *vertere*, to turn] *Bot.* twining upward to the right, as the stem of the hop

**dex·trose** (dek′strōs) *n.* [ult. < L. *dexter:* cf. DEXTRIN] a glucose, $C_6H_{12}O_6$, found in plants and animals

**dex·trous** (-strəs) *adj. same as* DEXTEROUS

**DF, D/F, D.F.** *Radio* direction finder

**dg.** decigram; decigrams

†**dhar·ma** (dur′mə, där′-) *n.* [Sans., law] *Hinduism, Buddhism* **1.** cosmic order or law, including the natural and moral principles that apply to all beings and things **2.** observance of this law in one's life

**dhow** (dou) *n.* [Ar. *dāwa*] a single-masted ship with a lateen sail, used along the Indian Ocean coasts

**di-¹** [Gr. *di-* < *dis*, twice] *a prefix meaning:* **1.** twice, double, twofold **2.** *Chem.* having two atoms, molecules, radicals, etc. Also **dis-**

**di-²** *same as* DIS-

**di-³** *same as* DIA-

**di., dia.** diameter

**di·a-** [< Gr.] *a prefix meaning:* **1.** through, across [*diaphragm, diagonal*] **2.** between [*diagnose*]

**di·a·be·tes** (dī′ə bēt′is, -ēz) *n.* [L. < Gr. *diabētēs*, a siphon < *dia-*, through + *bainein*, to go] any of various diseases characterized by an excessive discharge of urine; esp., DIABETES MELLITUS

**diabetes mel·li·tus** (mə līt′is) [ModL., lit., honey diabetes] a chronic form of diabetes involving an insulin deficiency and characterized by excess of sugar in the blood and urine, hunger, thirst, etc.

**di·a·bet·ic** (dī′ə bet′ik) *adj.* of or having diabetes —*n.* a person who has diabetes

**di·a·bol·ic** (dī′ə bäl′ik) *adj.* [< Fr. < LL. < Gr. *diabolos:* see DEVIL] **1.** of the Devil or devils **2.** very wicked or cruel; fiendish Also **di′a·bol′i·cal** —**di′a·bol′i·cal·ly** *adv.*

**di·ac·o·nal** (dī ak′ə n'l) *adj.* of a deacon or deacons

**di·ac·o·nate** (-nit) *n.* **1.** the rank, office, or tenure of a deacon **2.** a group of deacons

**di·a·crit·ic** (dī′ə krit′ik) *adj.* [Gr. *diakritikos* < *dia-*, across + *krinein*, to separate] *same as* DIACRITICAL —*n. same as* DIACRITICAL MARK

**di·a·crit·i·cal** (-i k'l) *adj.* **1.** serving to distinguish **2.** able to distinguish —**di′a·crit′i·cal·ly** *adv.*

**diacritical mark** a mark, as a macron or a cedilla, added to a letter or symbol to show its pronunciation or to distinguish it in some way

**di·a·dem** (dī′ə dem′, -dəm) *n.* [< OFr. < L. < Gr. *diadēma* < *dia-*, through + *dein*, to bind] **1.** a crown **2.** an ornamental cloth headband worn as a crown **3.** royal power or authority —*vt.* to crown

**di·aer·e·sis** (dī er′ə sis) *n., pl.* -ses′ (-sēz′) *same as* DIERESIS

**diag. 1.** diagonal **2.** diagram

**di·ag·nose** (dī′əg nōs′, -nōz′) *vt., vi.* -nosed′ -nos′ing to make a diagnosis of (a disease, etc.)

**di·ag·no·sis** (dī′əg nō′sis) *n., pl.* -ses (-sēz) [ModL. < Gr. < *dia-*, between + *gignōskein*, to know] **1.** the act or process of deciding the nature of a diseased condition by examination of the symptoms **2.** a careful analysis of the facts meant to explain something **3.** a decision based on such an examination or analysis —**di′ag·nos′tic** (-näs′tik) *adj.* —**di′ag·nos′ti·cal·ly** *adv.* —**di′ag·nos·ti′cian** (-näs-tish′ən) *n.*

**di·ag·o·nal** (dī ag′ə n'l) *adj.* [L. *diagonalis* < Gr. < *dia-*, through + *gōnia*, an angle] **1.** extending slantingly between opposite corners, as of a rectangle **2.** having a slanting direction or slanting markings, lines, etc. —*n.* **1.** *a*) a diagonal line or plane *b*) *same as* VIRGULE **2.** any diagonal course, row, part, etc. —**di·ag′o·nal·ly** *adv.*

DIAGONAL (AB)

**di·a·gram** (dī′ə gram′) *n.* [Gr. *diagramma* < *dia-*, across + *graphein*, to write] a drawing, plan, or chart that explains a thing, as by outlining its parts and their relationships, workings, etc. —*vt.* -**gramed′** or -**grammed′**, -**gram′ing** or -**gram′ming** to make a diagram of —**di′a·gram·mat′ic** (-grə mat′ik), **di′a·gram·mat′i·cal** *adj.* —**di′a·gram·mat′i·cal·ly** *adv.*

**di·al** (dī′əl, dīl) *n.* [< ML. *dialis*, daily < L. *dies*, day] **1.** a sundial **2.** the face of a watch or clock **3.** the face of a meter, gauge, etc. on which a pointer indicates an amount, degree, etc. **4.** a graduated disk or strip on a radio or television set, for tuning in stations or channels **5.** a rotating disk on a telephone, used in making connections automatically —*vt., vi.* -**aled** or -**alled**, -**al·ing** or -**al·ling** **1.** to measure, regulate, etc. with a dial **2.** to tune in (a radio station, television channel, program, etc.) **3.** to call on a telephone by using a dial or other automatic device

**dial. 1.** dialect(al) **2.** dialectic(al)

**di·a·lect** (dī′ə lekt′) *n.* [< L. < Gr. *dialektos*, discourse < *dia-*, between + *legein*, to talk] **1.** the sum total of local characteristics of speech **2.** any form of speech that differs from a real or imaginary standard speech **3.** the form of a spoken language peculiar to a region, community, social group, occupational group, etc. **4.** any language as a member of a group or family of languages [English is a West Germanic *dialect*] —*adj.* of or in dialect —**di′a·lec′tal** *adj.* —**di′a·lec′tal·ly** *adv.*

**di·a·lec·tic** (dī′ə lek′tik) *n.* [< OFr. < L. < Gr. < *dialektikos:* see prec.] **1.** [*often pl.*] the art or practice of examining ideas logically, often by question and answer, so as to determine their validity **2.** logical argumentation **3.** [*often pl.*] the method of logic used by Hegel and adapted by Marx to observable social and economic processes —*adj. same as* DIALECTICAL

**di·a·lec·ti·cal** (-ti k'l) *adj.* **1.** of or using dialectic or dialectics **2.** of or characteristic of a dialect; dialectal —**di′a·lec′ti·cal·ly** *adv.*

**dialectical materialism** the philosophy stemming from Marx and Engels which applies Hegel's dialectical method to observable social processes

**di·a·lec·ti·cian** (dī′ə lek tish′ən) *n.* **1.** an expert in dialectic; logician **2.** a specialist in dialects

**di·a·logue, di·a·log** (dī′ə lôg′, -läg′) *n.* [OFr. < L. < Gr. *dialogos* < *dialegein:* see DIALECT] **1.** a talking together; conversation **2.** open and frank discussion of ideas, as in seeking mutual understanding **3.** a written work in the form of a conversation **4.** the passages of talk in a play, story, etc. —*vi.* -**logued′**, -**logu′ing** to hold a conversation —*vt.* to express in dialogue —**di·al·o·gist** (dī al′ə jist, dī′ə lôg′ist) *n.*

**Dialogue Mass** *R.C.Ch.* a Low Mass at which the congregation, following an earlier custom now revived, makes the responses aloud and in unison

**dial tone** a low buzzing sound indicating to the user of a dial telephone that the line is open and a number may be dialed

**di·al·y·sis** (dī al′ə sis) *n., pl.* -ses′ (-sēz′) [L. < Gr. < *dia-*, apart + *lyein*, to loose] the separation of crystalloids from colloids in solution by the greater diffusibility of the smaller molecules through a semipermeable membrane —**di·a·lyt·ic** (dī′ə lit′ik) *adj.* —**di′a·lyt′i·cal·ly** *adv.*

**di·a·lyze** (dī′ə līz′) *vt.* -**lyzed′**, -**lyz′ing** to apply dialysis to or separate by dialysis —*vi.* to undergo dialysis —**di′a·lyz′er** *n.*

**diam.** diameter

**di·a·mag·net·ic** (dī′ə mag net′ik) *adj.* having diamagnetism —*n.* a diamagnetic substance, as bismuth or zinc: also **di′a·mag′net**

**di·a·mag·net·ism** (-mag′nə tiz′m) *n.* the property that certain substances have of being repelled by both poles of a magnet

**di·a·man·té** (dē′ə män tā′, -män′tā) *adj.* [Fr.] decorated with rhinestones or other glittering bits of material —*n.* glittering ornamentation

**di·am·e·ter** (dī am′ət ər) *n.* [< OFr. < ML. < L. < Gr. < *dia-*, through + *metron*, a measure] **1.** a straight line passing through the center of a circle, sphere, etc. from one side to the other **2.** the length of such a line

**di·a·met·ri·cal** (dī′ə met′ri k'l) *adj.* **1.** of or along a diameter **2.** designating an opposite, a difference, etc. that is wholly so [*diametrical* opposites]: also **di′a·met′ric** —**di′a·met′ri·cal·ly** *adv.*

**di·a·mond** (dī′mənd, -ə mənd) *n.* [< OFr. < ML. *diamas* (gen. *diamantis*) < L. < Gr. *adamas*, ADAMANT, diamond] **1.** a mineral consisting of nearly pure carbon in crystalline form: it is the hardest mineral known and has great brilliance: unflawed stones are cut into precious gems; less perfect forms are used for phonograph-needle tips, cutting tools, abrasives, etc. **2.** a gem cut from this mineral **3.** *a)* a lozenge-shaped plane figure (◊) *b)* a red mark like this on a suit of playing cards *c)* [*pl.*] this suit *d)* a card of this suit **4.** *Baseball a)* the infield *b)* the whole playing field —*adj.* of, like, or set with a diamond —**diamond in the rough 1.** a diamond in its natural state **2.** a person or thing of fine quality but lacking polish

**diamond anniversary** the sixtieth, or sometimes seventy-fifth, anniversary: also **diamond jubilee**

**di·a·mond·back** (-bak′) *adj.* having diamond-shaped markings on the back —*n.* **1.** a large, poisonous rattlesnake native to the S U.S. **2.** an edible turtle found in coastal salt marshes from Cape Cod to Mexico: in full, **diamondback terrapin 3.** a small, brown and white moth

**diamond wedding** a sixtieth, or sometimes seventy-fifth, wedding anniversary

**Di·an·a** (dī an′ə) [ML. < L., ult. < *divus*, divine] **1.** a feminine name: var. *Diane* **2.** *Rom. Myth.* the virgin goddess of the moon and of hunting: identified with the Greek goddess Artemis

**di·a·pa·son** (dī′ə pāz′'n, -pās′-) *n.* [< L. < Gr. contr. < *dia*, through + *pasōn*, gen. pl. of *pas*, all (notes)] **1.** *a)* the entire range of a musical instrument or voice *b)* the entire range of some activity, emotion, etc. **2.** one of the principal stops of an organ covering the instrument's complete range **3.** a swelling burst of harmony

**di·a·per** (dī′pər, dī′ə pər) *n.* [< OFr. *diapre* < ML. *diasprum*, flowered cloth] **1.** *a)* orig., cloth or fabric with a pattern of repeated small figures, such as diamonds *b)* such a pattern, as in art **2.** a soft, absorbent cloth folded and arranged between the legs and around the waist of a baby —*vt.* **1.** to give a diaper design to **2.** to put a fresh diaper on (a baby)

**di·aph·a·nous** (dī af′ə nəs) *adj.* [< ML. < Gr. < *dia-*, through + *phainein*, to show] **1.** so fine or gauzy in texture as to be transparent or translucent [*diaphanous* cloth] **2.** vague or indistinct —**di·aph′a·nous·ly** *adv.*

**di·a·pho·re·sis** (dī′ə fə rē′sis) *n.* [LL. < Gr. < *dia-*, through + *pherein*, to bear] perspiration, esp. when profuse —**di′a·pho·ret′ic** (-ret′ik) *adj., n.*

**di·a·phragm** (dī′ə fram′) *n.* [< LL. < Gr. < *dia-*, through + *phragma*, a fence < *phrassein*, enclose] **1.** the partition of muscles and tendons between the chest cavity and the abdominal cavity; midriff **2.** any separating membrane or device **3.** a device to regulate the amount of light entering a camera lens, etc. **4.** a thin, vibrating disk or cone that produces electrical signals, as in a microphone, or sound waves, as in a loudspeaker —**di′a·phrag·mat′ic** (-frag·mat′ik) *adj.* —**di′a·phrag·mat′i·cal·ly** *adv.*

**di·aph·y·sis** (dī af′ə sis) *n., pl.* **-ses′** (-sēz′) [ModL. < Gr. < *dia-*, through + *phyein*, to produce] the shaft of a long bone —**di·a·phys·e·al, di·a·phys·i·al** (dī′ə fiz′ē əl) *adj.*

**di·a·rist** (dī′ə rist) *n.* a person who keeps a diary

**di·ar·rhe·a, di·ar·rhoe·a** (dī′ə rē′ə) *n.* [< OFr. & LL. < Gr. < *dia-*, through + *rhein*, to flow] excessive frequency and looseness of bowel movements —**di′ar·rhe′al, di′ar·rhe′ic** *adj.*

**di·a·ry** (dī′ə rē) *n., pl.* **-ries** [L. *diarium* < *dies*, day] **1.** a daily written record, esp. of the writer's own experiences, thoughts, etc. **2.** a book for this

**Di·as·po·ra** (dī as′pə rə) *n.* [< Gr. < *dia-*, across + *speirein*, to sow] **1.** *a)* the dispersion of the Jews after the Babylonian exile *b)* these Jews **2.** [d-] any scattering of people with a common origin, background, beliefs, etc.

**di·a·stase** (dī′ə stās′) *n.* [Fr. < Gr. *diastasis*, separation < *dia-*, apart + *histanai*, to stand] an enzyme, occurring in the seed of grains and malt, that changes starches into maltose and later into dextrose —**di′a·stat′ic** (-stat′ik) *adj.*

**di·as·to·le** (dī as′tə lē′) *n.* [LL. < Gr. *diastolē*, expansion < *dia-*, apart + *stellein*, to put] the usual rhythmic dilatation of the heart, esp. of the ventricles, during which the chambers fill with blood —**di·a·stol·ic** (dī′ə stäl′ik) *adj.*

**di·as·tro·phism** (dī as′trə fiz′m) *n.* [< Gr. < *dia-*, aside + *strephein*, to turn + -ISM] the process by which the earth's surface is reshaped by rock movements —**di·a·stroph·ic** (dī′ə sträf′ik) *adj.*

**di·a·ther·my** (dī′ə thur′mē) *n.* [ModL. < Gr. *dia-*, through + *thermē*, heat] medical treatment in which heat is produced in the tissues beneath the skin by a high-frequency electric current —**di′a·ther′mic** *adj.*

**di·a·tom** (dī′ə täm′, -ət əm) *n.* [ModL. < Gr. < *dia-*, through + *temnein*, to cut] any of a number of related microscopic algae whose cell walls contain silica: diatoms are a source of food for marine life —**di·a·to·ma·ceous** (dī′ət·ə mā′shəs, dī at′ə-) *adj.*

**di·a·ton·ic** (dī′ə tän′ik) *adj.* [Fr. < LL. < Gr. *diatonikos*, stretched through (the notes) < *dia-*, through + *teinein*, to stretch] *Music* designating, of, or using any standard major or minor scale of eight tones without the chromatic intervals —**di′a·ton′i·cal·ly** *adv.*

**di·a·tribe** (dī′ə trīb′) *n.* [Fr. < L. < Gr. *diatribē*, a wearing away < *dia-*, through + *tribein*, to rub] a bitter, abusive criticism or denunciation

**di·bas·ic** (dī bās′ik) *adj.* denoting or of an acid with two hydrogen atoms which may be replaced by basic radicals or atoms to form a salt

**dib·ble** (dib′'l) *n.* [ME. *dibbel*, prob. < *dibben*, to dip] a pointed tool used to make holes in the soil for seeds, bulbs, or young plants: also **dib′ber** —*vt.* **-bled, -bling 1.** to make a hole in (the soil) with a dibble **2.** to plant with a dibble —*vi.* to use a dibble

**dibs** (dibz) *n.pl.* [< *dibstone*, a jack in a children's game] [Colloq.] a claim to a share of, or rights in, something wanted —*interj.* an exclamation announcing such a claim: chiefly a child's term

**dice** (dīs) *n.pl., sing.* **die** or **dice** [ME. *dis*, pl.: see DIE²] **1.** small cubes of bone, plastic, etc. marked on each side with from one to six spots and used, usually in pairs, in games of chance **2.** [*with sing. v.*] a gambling game played with dice **3.** any small cubes —*vi.* **diced, dic′ing** to play or gamble with dice —*vt.* to cut (vegetables, etc.) into small cubes —**no dice 1.** no: used in refusing a request **2.** no success, luck, etc. —**dic′er** *n.*

**di·chlo·ride** (dī klôr′īd, -id) *n.* any chemical compound in which two atoms of chlorine are combined with an element or radical

**di·chot·o·my** (dī kät′ə mē) *n., pl.* **-mies** [< Gr. < *dicha*, in two + *temnein*, to cut] **1.** division into two usually opposed parts or groups **2.** *Biol., Bot.* a dividing or branching into two parts, esp. when repeated —**di·chot′o·mize** (-mīz′) *vt.* **-mized′, -miz′ing** —**di·chot′o·mous** (-məs) *adj.*

**di·chro·mate** (dī krō′māt) *n.* any salt of dichromic acid

**di·chro·mat·ic** (dī′krō mat′ik) *adj.* [DI-¹ + CHROMATIC] **1.** having two colors **2.** *Biol.* having two varieties of coloration that are independent of sex or age —**di·chro′ma·tism** *n.*

**di·chro·mic** (dī krō′mik) *adj.* **1.** *same as* DICHROMATIC **2.** *Chem.* designating a hypothetical acid, $H_2Cr_2O_7$, from which dichromates are formed

**Dick** (dik) [< RICHARD] a masculine name —*n.* [d-] [Slang] a detective

**dick·cis·sel** (dik sis′'l) *n.* [echoic of its cry] an American bunting with a black throat and yellow breast

**dick·ens** (dik′'nz) *n., interj.* [prob. < nickname for RICHARD] [Colloq.] devil; deuce: a mild oath

**Dick·ens** (dik′'nz), **Charles** (pseud. *Boz*) 1812-70; Eng. novelist —**Dick·en·si·an** (di ken′zē ən) *adj.*

**dick·er** (dik′ər) *vi., vt.* [< *dicker*, ten, ten hides (as a unit of barter), ult. < L. *decem*, ten] to trade by bargaining, esp. on a small scale; barter; haggle —*n.* the act of bargaining or haggling

**dick·ey** (dik′ē) *n., pl.* **-eys** [< DICK] **1.** a man's detachable, or false, shirt front **2.** a woman's detachable collar or blouse front **3.** a small bird: also **dickey bird** Also sp. **dick′y,** *pl.* **dick′ies**

**Dick·in·son** (dik′in s'n), **Emily (Elizabeth)** 1830-86; U.S. poet

**di·cli·nous** (dī klī′nəs) *adj.* [< DI-¹ + Gr. *klinē*, bed + -OUS] *Bot.* having the stamens and pistils in separate flowers —**di·cli·nism** (dī′klī niz′m), **di′cli·ny** (-nē) *n.*

**di·cot·y·le·don** (dī′kät 'l ēd′'n, dī-kät′'l-) *n.* a flowering plant with two seed leaves (cotyledons) —**di′cot·y·le′don·ous** *adj.*

**di·cou·mar·in** (dī koo′mər in) *n.* [DI-¹

DIBBLE

DICKEY

+ *coumarin*, a plant extract] a chemical compound, $C_{19}H_{12}O_6$, used as an anticoagulant

**dict.** 1. dictator 2. dictionary

**dic·ta** (dik′tə) *n. alt. pl. of* DICTUM

**Dic·ta·phone** (dik′tə fōn′) [ DICTA(TE) + -PHONE] *a trademark for* a machine that records spoken words so that they can be played back later for typed transcripts, etc. —*n.* this machine

**dic·tate** (dik′tāt; *also for v.* dik tāt′) *vt., vi.* -tat·ed, -tat·ing [< L. pp. of *dictare*, freq. of *dicere*, to speak] 1. to speak or read (something) aloud for someone else to write down 2. to command expressly 3. to impose or give (orders) with authority or arbitrarily —*n.* 1. an authoritative command 2. a guiding principle [the *dictates* of conscience]

**dic·ta·tion** (dik tā′shən) *n.* 1. the dictating of words for another to write down 2. the words so spoken or read 3. the giving of authoritative orders or commands —**dic·ta′tion·al** *adj.*

**dic·ta·tor** (dik′tāt ər, dik tāt′-) *n.* 1. a ruler with absolute power and authority, esp. a tyrant or despot 2. a person who is domineering or arbitrary in giving orders, etc. 3. one who dictates words for another to write down —**dic·ta′tor·ship′** *n.*

**dic·ta·to·ri·al** (dik′tə tôr′ē əl) *adj.* of, like, or characteristic of a dictator; autocratic; tyrannical; domineering —**dic′ta·to′ri·al·ly** *adv.*

**dic·tion** (dik′shən) *n.* [< L. pp. of *dicere*, to say] 1. manner of expression in words; choice of words 2. enunciation

**dic·tion·ar·y** (dik′shə ner′ē) *n., pl.* -ar′ies [ML. *dictionarium* < LL. *dictio:* see prec.] 1. a book of alphabetically listed words in a language, with definitions, etymologies, pronunciations, etc.; lexicon 2. such a book of words in one language with their equivalents in another 3. any alphabetically arranged list of words or articles relating to a special subject [a medical *dictionary*]

**dic·tum** (dik′təm) *n., pl.* -tums, -ta (-tə) [L., neut. pp. of *dicere*, to speak] a formal statement of fact, opinion, principle, etc.; pronouncement

**Di·cu·ma·rol** (dī koo͞′mə rôl′, -kyoo͞′-) *a collective trademark for* DICOUMARIN

**did** (did) *pt. of* DO[1]

**di·dact** (dī′dakt) *n.* [< ff.] a didactic person

**di·dac·tic** (dī dak′tik) *adj.* [Gr. *didaktikos* < *didaskein*, to teach] 1. used or intended for teaching or instruction 2. morally instructive 3. too much inclined to teach others; boringly pedantic or moralistic Also **di·dac′ti·cal** —**di·dac′ti·cal·ly** *adv.* —**di·dac′ti·cism** (-tə siz′m) *n.*

**di·dac·tics** (-tiks) *n.pl.* [*usually with sing. v.*] the art or science of teaching; pedagogy

**did·dle**[1] (did′'l) *vi., vt.* -dled, -dling [Eng. dial. *duddle*, *diddle*, to totter] [Colloq.] to move back and forth jerkily; jiggle —**did′dler** *n.*

**did·dle**[2] (did′'l) *vt., vi.* -dled, -dling [ult. < OE. *dyderian*, to fool] [Colloq.] 1. to cheat or swindle 2. to waste (time) in trifling —**did′dler** *n.*

**Di·de·rot** (dē′də rō′; *Fr.* dē drō′), **Denis** 1713-84; Fr. encyclopedist & philosopher

**did·n't** (did′'nt) did not

**Di·do** (dī′dō) *Rom. Legend* queen of Carthage, who kills herself when her lover Aeneas leaves her

**di·do** (dī′dō) *n., pl.* -does, -dos [< ?] [Colloq.] a mischievous trick; prank; caper

**didst** (didst) *archaic 2d pers. sing., past indic., of* DO[1]: *used with* thou

**di·dy** (dī′dē) *n., pl.* -dies [< DIAPER] [Colloq.] a diaper (sense 2)

**di·dym·i·um** (dī dim′ē əm) *n.* [< Gr. *didymos*, twin] a mixture of two rare-earth elements, formerly considered a single element; symbol, Di

**die**[1] (dī) *vi.* died, dy′ing [ME. *dien* < ON. *deyja*] 1. to stop living; become dead 2. to suffer the agony of, or like that of, death 3. to cease existing or stop functioning; end 4. to lose force or activity 5. to fade or wither away 6. to pine away, as with desire 7. [Colloq.] to wish intensely; yearn [she's *dying* to tell] 8. *Theol.* to suffer spiritual death —**die away** (or **down**) to become weaker and cease gradually —**die back** (or **down**) to wither to the roots or woody part —**die hard** to resist to the last —**die off** to die one by one until all are gone —**die out** to go out of existence

**die**[2] (dī) *n., pl.*, for 1 **dice** (dīs); for 2 **dies** (dīz) [< OFr. *de* < L. pp. of *dare*, to give] 1. a small, marked cube used in games of chance: see also DICE 2. any of various tools or devices for molding, stamping, cutting, or shaping —*vt.* **died, die′ing** to mold, stamp, cut, or shape with a die —**the die is cast** the irrevocable decision has been made

**die casting** 1. the process of making a casting by forcing molten metal into a metallic mold, or die, under pressure 2. a casting so made —**die caster**

**dief·fen·bach·i·a** (dēf′'n bak′ē ə) *n.* [ModL. < E. *Dieffenbach* (19th-c. Ger. botanist)] a tropical plant of the arum family, with large leaves

**die-hard, die·hard** (dī′härd′) *adj.* extremely stubborn in resistance; unwilling to give in —*n.* a stubborn or resistant person, esp. an extreme conservative

**diel·drin** (dēl′drin) *n.* a highly toxic, long-lasting insecticide, $C_{12}H_8OCl_6$

**di·e·lec·tric** (dī′ə lek′trik) *n.* [< DI(A)- + ELECTRIC] a material, as rubber, glass, etc., that does not conduct electricity and that can sustain an electric field: used in capacitors, etc. —*adj.* having the properties or function of a dielectric

**di·er·e·sis** (dī er′ə sis) *n., pl* -ses′ (-sēz′) [LL. < Gr. *diairesis*, division < *dia-*, apart + *hairein*, to take] a mark (¨) placed over the second of two consecutive vowels to show that it is pronounced in a separate syllable: now usually replaced by a hyphen (*reënter, re-enter*), or simply omitted (*cooperate, naive*) The mark is also used, as in this dictionary, to show a certain pronunciation of a vowel (ä) —**di·e·ret·ic** (dī′ə ret′ik) *adj.*

**die·sel** (dē′z'l, -s'l) *n.* [after R. *Diesel* (1858-1913), Ger. inventor] [*often* D-] 1. a type of internal-combustion engine that burns fuel oil: the ignition is brought about by heat resulting from air compression, instead of by an electric spark as in a gasoline engine: also **diesel engine** (or **motor**) 2. a locomotive, truck, etc. with such an engine

**die·sink·er** (dī′siŋ′kər) *n.* a maker of dies used in stamping or shaping —**die′sink′ing** *n.*

‡**Di·es I·rae** (dē′ez ir′ā, dē′äs ir′ē) [L., Day of Wrath] a medieval Latin hymn about Judgment Day, beginning *Dies Irae*, a part of the Requiem Mass

**di·e·sis** (dī′ə sis) *n., pl.* -ses′ (-sēz′) [L. < Gr. < *diienai*, to send through] a reference mark (‡) used in printing: also called DOUBLE DAGGER

**di·et**[1] (dī′ət) *n.* [< OFr. < ML. < L. < Gr. *diaita*, way of life] 1. *a)* what a person or animal usually eats and drinks; daily fare *b)* figuratively, what a person regularly reads, listens to, does, etc. 2. a regimen of special or limited food and drink, chosen or prescribed for health or to gain or lose weight —*vi.* to eat special or limited food, esp. for losing weight —**di′et·er** *n.*

**di·et**[2] (dī′ət) *n.* [< OFr. < ML. < L. *dies*, day] 1. a formal assembly, as formerly of princes, electors, etc. of the Holy Roman Empire 2. in some countries, a national or local legislative assembly

**di·e·tar·y** (dī′ə ter′ē) *n., pl.* -ies 1. a system of diet 2. daily food allowance or ration —*adj.* 1. of diet 2. of a dietary

**di·e·tet·ic** (dī′ə tet′ik) *adj.* of, relating to, or designed for a particular diet of food and drink: also **di′e·tet′i·cal** —**di′e·tet′i·cal·ly** *adv.*

**di·e·tet·ics** (-iks) *n.pl.* [*with sing. v.*] the study of the kinds and quantities of food needed for health

**di·e·ti·tian, di·e·ti·cian** (dī′ə tish′ən) *n.* an expert in dietetics; specialist in planning meals or diets

**dif-** *same as* DIS-: used before *f*

**dif·fer** (dif′ər) *vi.* [< OFr. < L. *differre* < *dis-*, apart + *ferre*, to bear] 1. to be unlike; be not the same (often with *from*) 2. to be of opposite or unlike opinions; disagree

**dif·fer·ence** (dif′ər əns, dif′rəns) *n.* [see prec.] 1. condition or quality of being different 2. the way in which people or things are different 3. the state of holding a differing opinion; disagreement; also, the point at issue; point of disagreement 4. a dispute; quarrel 5. *Math.* the amount by which one quantity is greater or less than another —**make a difference** 1. to have an effect; matter 2. to change the situation —**split the difference** 1. to share equally what is left over 2. to make a compromise —**what's the difference?** [Colloq.] what does it matter?

**dif·fer·ent** (dif′ər ənt, dif′rənt) *adj.* [see DIFFER] 1. not alike; dissimilar (with *from*, or, esp. colloquially, *than*, and, in Brit. usage, *to*) 2. not the same; distinct; separate; other 3. various 4. unlike most others; unusual —**dif′fer·ent·ly** *adv.*

**dif·fer·en·ti·a** (dif′ə ren′shē ə, -shə) *n., pl.* -ti·ae′ (-shi-ē′) a distinguishing characteristic

**dif·fer·en·tial** (-shəl) *adj.* 1. of, showing, or depending on a difference 2. constituting a specific difference; distinguishing 3. having different effects or making use of differences [a *differential* gear] 4. *Math.* of or involving differentials —*n.* 1. a differentiating amount, degree, factor, etc. [*differentials* in salary] 2. *Math. a)* an infinitesimal difference between two consecutive values of a variable quantity *b)* the derivative of a function multiplied by the increment of the independent variable 3. *Mech. same as* DIFFERENTIAL GEAR 4. *Railroading* a difference in rates, as between different routes —**dif′fer·en′tial·ly** *adv.*

**differential calculus** the branch of higher mathematics which deals with derivatives and their applications

**differential gear** (or **gearing**) an arrangement of gears connecting two axles in the same line and allowing one axle to turn faster than the other: used in the rear axles of automobiles to permit a difference in axle speeds while turning curves

**dif·fer·en·ti·ate** (-shē āt′) *vt.* -**at′ed**, -**at′ing** 1. to constitute a difference in or between 2. to make unlike 3. to perceive or express the difference in; distinguish between 4. *Math.* to work out the differential or derivative of —*vi.* 1. to become different or differentiated 2. to perceive or express a difference —**dif′fer·en′ti·a′tion** *n.*

**dif·fi·cult** (dif′i kəlt, -kult′) *adj.* 1. hard to do, make, manage, understand, etc. 2. hard to satisfy, persuade, please, etc. —**dif′fi·cult·ly** *adv.*

**dif·fi·cul·ty** (dif′i kul′tē, -kəl-) *n., pl.* -**ties** [< OFr. < L. *difficultas* < *dis-*, not + *facilis*, easy] 1. the condition or fact of being difficult 2. something difficult; an obstacle or objection 3. trouble or distress 4. a disagreement or quarrel —**in difficulties** in distress, esp. financially

**dif·fi·dent** (dif′ə dənt) *adj.* [< L. prp. of *diffidere* < *dis-*, not + *fidere*, to trust] lacking confidence in oneself; hesitant to assert oneself; timid; shy —**dif′fi·dence** *n.* —**dif′fi·dent·ly** *adv.*

**dif·fract** (di frakt′) *vt.* [< L. pp. of *diffringere* < *dis-*, apart + *frangere*, to break] to break into parts; specif., to subject to diffraction

**dif·frac·tion** (di frak′shən) *n.* 1. the breaking up of a ray of light into dark and light bands or into the colors of the spectrum, as when it is deflected at the edge of an opaque object 2. a similar breaking up of other waves, as of sound or electricity —**dif·frac′tive** (-tiv) *adj.* —**dif·frac′tive·ly** *adv.*

**dif·fuse** (di fyōōs′; *for v.* -fyōōz′) *adj.* [< L. pp. < *dis-*, apart + *fundere*, to pour] 1. spread out; not concentrated 2. using more words than are needed —*vt., vi.* -**fused′**, -**fus′ing** 1. to pour or disperse in every direction; spread or scatter widely 2. *Physics* to mix by diffusion, as gases, liquids, etc. —**dif·fuse′ly** *adv.* —**dif·fuse′ness** *n.* —**dif·fus′er, dif·fu′sor** (-fyōō′zər) *n.* —**dif·fus′i·bil′i·ty** *n.* —**dif·fus′i·ble** *adj.*

**dif·fu·sion** (di fyōō′zhən) *n.* 1. a diffusing or being diffused; specif., *a*) a dissemination, as of news *b*) a scattering of light rays, as by reflection; also, the dispersion and softening of light, as by using frosted glass *c*) an intermingling of the molecules of liquids, gases, etc. 2. wordiness

**dif·fu·sive** (-siv) *adj.* 1. tending to diffuse 2. characterized by diffusion 3. diffuse —**dif·fu′sive·ly** *adv.* —**dif·fu′sive·ness** *n.*

**dig** (dig) *vt.* **dug** or archaic & poet. **digged, dig′ging** [< OFr. *digue*, dike < Du. *dijk*] 1. to break and turn up or remove (ground, etc.) with a spade or other tool, or with hands, claws, etc. 2. to make (a hole, cellar, etc.) as by doing this 3. to get from the ground in this way *[to dig potatoes]* 4. to find out, as by careful study; unearth (usually with *up* or *out*) *[to dig out the truth]* 5. to jab or prod 6. [Slang] *a*) to understand *b*) to approve of or like —*vi.* 1. to dig the ground 2. to make a way by or as by digging (*through, into, under*) 3. [Colloq.] to work or study hard —*n.* 1. the act of digging 2. [Colloq.] *a*) a poke, nudge, etc. *b*) a sarcastic comment 3. an archaeological excavation 4. [*pl., often with sing. v.*] [Colloq.] living quarters —**dig in** 1. to dig trenches for cover 2. to entrench oneself 3. [Colloq.] *a*) to begin to work hard *b*) to begin eating —**dig into** [Colloq.] to work hard at

**di·gest** (dī′jest; *for v.* di jest′, dī-) *n.* [< L. pp. of *digerere*, separate < *di-*, apart + *gerere*, to bear] 1. a collection of condensed, systematic information; summary or synopsis, as of legal material 2. a book, periodical, etc. consisting of such summaries —*vt.* 1. *a*) to arrange systematically, usually in condensed form *b*) to condense and summarize (a piece of writing) 2. to change (food), esp. in the stomach and intestines, so that it can be absorbed by the body 3. to aid the digestion of (food) 4. to think over and absorb 5. to soften or dissolve soluble material in, esp. with liquid —*vi.* 1. to be digested 2. to digest food —**di·gest′er** *n.*

**di·gest·i·ble** (di jes′tə b′l) *adj.* that can be digested —**di·gest′i·bil′i·ty** *n.* —**di·gest′i·bly** *adv.*

**di·ges·tion** (-chən) *n.* 1. the act or process of digesting food 2. the ability to digest food 3. the absorption of ideas 4. decomposition of sewage by bacteria

**di·ges·tive** (-tiv) *adj.* of, for, or aiding digestion —*n.* any substance or drink that aids digestion —**di·ges′tive·ly** *adv.* —**di·ges′tive·ness** *n.*

**dig·ger** (dig′ər) *n.* 1. a person or thing that digs 2. a tool or machine for digging 3. [D-] a member of any of several tribes of Indians in the W U.S. who dug roots for food 4. *same as* DIGGER WASP 5. [D-] [Slang] an Australian or New Zealander

**digger wasp** any of various wasps that dig a nest in the ground

**dig·gings** (dig′iŋz) *n.pl.* 1. materials dug out 2. [*often with sing. v.*] a place where digging or mining is carried on 3. [Slang] one's lodgings

**dight** (dīt) *vt.* **dight** or **dight′ed, dight′ing** [< OE. *dihtan*, to arrange < L. *dictare:* see DICTATE] [Archaic or Poet.] 1. to adorn 2. to equip

**dig·it** (dij′it) *n.* [L. *digitus*, a finger, toe] 1. a finger or toe 2. any numeral from 0 to 9

**dig·it·al** (-′l) *adj.* 1. of, like, or constituting a digit 2. having digits 3. performed with the finger 4. using numbers that are digits to represent all the variables involved in calculation 5. showing the time, temperature, etc. by a row of digits rather than by numbers on a dial, etc. *[a digital watch]* —*n.* 1. *Piano, etc.* 2. a key played with a finger, as on the piano —**dig′it·al·ly** *adv.*

**digital computer** a computer that uses numbers to perform calculations, usually in a binary system

**dig·i·tal·is** (dij′ə tal′is) *n.* [ModL. < L.: see DIGIT: from its flowers] 1. any of a genus of plants of the figwort family, with long spikes of thimblelike flowers 2. the dried leaves of the purple foxglove 3. a medicine made from these leaves, used as a heart stimulant

**dig·i·tate** (dij′ə tāt′) *adj.* [see DIGIT] 1. having separate fingers or toes 2. fingerlike 3. *Bot.* having fingerlike divisions, as some leaves Also **dig′i·tat′ed** —**dig′i·tate′ly** *adv.* —**dig′i·ta′tion** *n.*

**dig·ni·fied** (dig′nə fīd′) *adj.* having or showing dignity or stateliness —**dig′ni·fied′ly** *adv.*

**dig·ni·fy** (dig′nə fī′) *vt.* -**fied′**, -**fy′ing** [< OFr. < ML. < L. *dignus*, worthy + *facere*, to make] to give dignity to; make worthy of esteem; honor; exalt

**dig·ni·tar·y** (-ter′ē) *n., pl.* -**tar′ies** [< L. *dignitas*, dignity + -ARY] a person holding a high, dignified position or office

**dig·ni·ty** (-tē) *n., pl.* -**ties** [< OFr. < L. < *dignus*, worthy] 1. the quality of being worthy of esteem or honor 2. high repute; honor 3. the degree of worth, repute, or honor 4. a high position, rank, or title 5. loftiness of appearance or manner; stateliness 6. proper pride and self-respect

**di·graph** (dī′graf) *n.* [DI-¹ + -GRAPH] a combination of two letters to express a simple sound (Ex.: *read, show, graphic*) —**di·graph′ic** *adj.*

**di·gress** (dī gres′, di-) *vi.* [< L. pp. of *digredi* < *dis-*, apart + *gradi*, to go, step] to depart temporarily from the main subject in talking or writing —**di·gres′sion** (-gresh′ən) *n.*

**di·gres·sive** (-gres′iv) *adj.* given to digression —**di·gres′sive·ly** *adv.* —**di·gres′sive·ness** *n.*

**di·he·dral** (dī hē′drəl) *adj.* [< DI-¹ + Gr. *hedra*, a seat] 1. having or formed by two intersecting plane faces *[a dihedral angle]* 2. *a*) inclined to each other at a dihedral angle, as some airplane wings *b*) having such wings —*n.* a dihedral angle

DIHEDRAL ANGLE (angle formed by planes MWON and MWXY)

**Di·jon** (dē zhôn′) city in EC France: pop. 145,000

**dik-dik** (dik′dik′) *n.* [< the Ethiopian native name] any of several small antelopes found in E Africa

**dike** (dīk) *n.* [< OE. *dic* & ON. *diki*] 1. [Brit. Dial.] a ditch or watercourse 2. an embankment or dam made to prevent flooding as by the sea 3. a protective barrier 4. *Geol.* igneous rock solidified as a tabular body in a vertical fissure —*vt.* **diked, dik′ing** 1. to protect or enclose with a dike 2. to drain by a ditch —**dik′er** *n.*

**Di·lan·tin (Sodium)** (di lan′tin, dī-) *a trademark for* a drug, $C_{15}H_{11}N_2O_2Na$, used in the treatment of epileptic attacks —*n.* [d-] this substance

**di·lap·i·date** (di lap′ə dāt′) *vi., vt.* -**dat′ed, -dat′ing** [< L. pp. of *dilapidare*, to demolish < *dis-*, apart + *lapidare*, to throw stones at < *lapis*, a stone] to become or make partially ruined and in need of repairs —**di·lap′i·dat′ed** *adj.* —**di·lap′i·da′tion** *n.*

**dil·a·ta·tion** (dil′ə tā′shən, dī′lə-) *n. same as* DILATION

**di·late** (dī lāt′, di-; dī′lāt) *vt.* -**lat′ed, -lat′ing** [L. *dilatare* < *dis-*, apart + *latus*, wide] to make wider or larger; cause to expand or swell —*vi.* 1. to become wider or larger; swell 2. to speak or write in detail (*on* or *upon* a subject) —**di·lat′a·ble** *adj.* —**di·lat′ive** *adj.* —**di·la′tor** *n.*

**di·la·tion** (dī lā′shən, di-) *n.* 1. a dilating or being dilated 2. a dilated part

**dil·a·to·ry** (dil′ə tôr′ē) *adj.* [< LL. < L. *dilatus*, pp. of *differre*, DEFER¹] 1. causing or tending to cause delay 2. inclined to delay; slow; tardy —**dil′a·to′ri·ly** *adv.* —**dil′a·to′ri·ness** *n.*

**di·lem·ma** (di lem′ə) *n.* [LL. < LGr. < *di-*, two + *lēmma*, proposition] an argument or a situation in which one must choose between unpleasant alternatives —**dil·em·mat·ic** (dil′ə mat′ik) *adj.*

**dil·et·tante** (dil′ə tänt′, -tän′tē, -tan′tē; dil′ə tänt′) *n.,* *pl.* **-tantes′, -tan′ti** (-tän′tē, -tan′tē) [It. < prp. of *dilettare* < L. *delectare*, to delight] **1.** a person who loves the fine arts **2.** a person who dabbles in an art or science in a superficial way —*adj.* of or characteristic of a dilettante —**dil′et·tant′ish** *adj.* —**dil′et·tant′ism, dil′et·tan′te·ism** *n.*

**dil·i·gence**[1] (dil′ə jəns) *n.* a being diligent; constant, careful effort; perseverance; industry

**dil·i·gence**[2] (dil′ə jəns; *Fr.* dē lē zhäns′) *n.* [Fr.] a public stagecoach, esp. as formerly used in France

**dil·i·gent** (dil′ə jənt) *adj.* [OFr. < L. prp. of *diligere*, to esteem highly < *di-*, apart + *legere*, to choose] **1.** persevering and careful in work; industrious **2.** done with careful, steady effort; painstaking —**dil′i·gent·ly** *adv.*

**dill** (dil) *n.* [OE. *dile*] **1.** a plant of the parsley family, with bitter seeds and aromatic leaves, used to flavor pickles, etc. **2.** the seeds or leaves

**dill pickle** a cucumber pickle flavored with dill

**dil·ly** (dil′ē) *n.,* *pl.* **-lies** [< ? DEL(IGHTFUL) + -Y[1]] [Slang] a surprising or remarkable person or thing

**dil·ly·dal·ly** (dil′ē dal′ē) *vi.* **-lied, -ly·ing** [redupl. form of DALLY] to waste time in hesitation; loiter or dawdle

**di·lute** (di lōōt′, dī-) *vt.* **-lut′ed, -lut′ing** [< L. pp. of *diluere* < *dis-*, off + *-luere* < *lavare*, to wash] **1.** to thin down or weaken by mixing with water or other liquid **2.** to change or weaken (in brilliance, force, effect, etc.) by mixing with something else —*vi.* to become diluted —*adj.* diluted —**di·lute′ness** *n.* —**di·lut′er, di·lu′tor** *n.*

DILL

**di·lu·tion** (-lōō′shən) *n.* **1.** a diluting or being diluted **2.** something diluted

**di·lu·vi·al** (di lōō′vē əl) *adj.* [< LL. < L. *diluvium*, a deluge] of or caused by a flood, esp. the Deluge Also **di·lu′vi·an**

**dim** (dim) *adj.* **dim′mer, dim′mest** [OE. *dimm*] **1.** not bright; somewhat dark; dull **2.** not clear or distinct; lacking definition, strength, etc. **3.** not clearly seen, heard, or understood; vague **4.** not clearly seeing, hearing, or understanding **5.** not likely to turn out well [dim prospects] —*vt., vi.* dimmed, dim′ming to make or grow dim —*n.* **1.** [Poet.] dim light; dusk **2.** a dim headlight on an automobile —**take a dim view of** to view skeptically, etc. —**dim′ly** *adv.* —**dim′ness** *n.*

**dim., dimin. 1.** diminuendo **2.** diminutive

**dime** (dīm) *n.* [< OFr. < L. *decimus*, a tenth < *decem*, ten] a coin of the U.S. and of Canada equal to ten cents; tenth of a dollar —**a dime a dozen** [Colloq.] very abundant or cheap

**di·men·hy·dri·nate** (dī′men hī′drə nāt′) *n.* a white, crystalline solid, $C_{24}H_{28}ClN_5O_3$, used to control nausea and vomiting, as in motion sickness

**dime novel** a very cheap, melodramatic novel

**di·men·sion** (də men′shən) *n.* [L. *dimensio* < pp. of *dimetiri* < *dis-*, off + *metiri*, to MEASURE] **1.** any measurable extent, as length, width, depth, etc.: see also FOURTH DIMENSION **2.** [*pl.*] measurements in length and width, and often depth **3.** [*often pl.*] *a)* extent or size *b)* scope or importance —**di·men′sion·al** *adj.* —**di·men′sion·al·ly** *adv.*

**dime store** *same as* FIVE-AND-TEN-CENT STORE

**di·min·ish** (də min′ish) *vt.* [a blend of ME. *diminuen* (ult. < L. *deminuere*, to make smaller) & *minishen* (ult. < L. *minutus*, MINUTE[2])] **1.** to make, or make seem, smaller; reduce in size, degree, importance, etc. **2.** *Music* to reduce (a minor interval) by a semitone —*vi.* to become smaller or less —**di·min′ish·a·ble** *adj.* —**di·min′ished** *adj.*

**di·min·u·en·do** (də min′yoo wen′dō) *adj., adv., n., pl.* **-dos** [It. < L. *diminuere*, make smaller] *same as* DECRESCENDO

**dim·i·nu·tion** (dim′ə nyoo′shən, -noo′-) *n.* a diminishing or being diminished; lessening; decrease

**di·min·u·tive** (də min′yoo tiv) *adj.* **1.** very small; tiny **2.** *Gram.* expressing smallness or diminution [a diminutive suffix] —*n.* **1.** a very small person or thing **2.** *a)* a word or name formed from another by the addition of a suffix expressing smallness and, sometimes, endearment or condescension, as *ringlet, Jackie, sonny b)* such a suffix —**di·min′u·tive·ly** *adv.* —**di·min′u·tive·ness** *n.*

**dim·i·ty** (dim′ə tē) *n., pl.* **-ties** [< ML. < MGr. *dimitos*, double-threaded < *dis-*, two + *mitos*, a thread] a thin, often corded or patterned cotton cloth, used for curtains, dresses, etc.

**dim·mer** (dim′ər) *n.* **1.** a person that dims **2.** a device for dimming an electric light, as in automobile headlights or theater stage lights

**dim·out** (-out′) *n.* a dimming or reduction of the night lighting in a city, etc., to make it less easily visible, as to enemy aircraft

**dim·ple** (dim′p′l) *n.* [ME. *dimpel*] **1.** a small, natural hollow spot, as on the cheek or chin **2.** any little hollow, as on water —*vt.* **-pled, -pling** to make dimples in —*vi.* to show or form dimples

**dim·wit** (dim′wit′) *n.* [Slang] a stupid person; simpleton —**dim′wit′ted** *adj.* —**dim′wit′ted·ly** *adv.* —**dim′wit′ted·ness** *n.*

**din** (din) *n.* [OE. *dyne*] a loud, continuous noise; confused clamor or uproar —*vt.* **dinned, din′ning 1.** to beset with a din **2.** to repeat insistently or noisily [to din an idea into one's ears] —*vi.* to make a din

**Di·nah** (dī′nə) [Heb. *dīnāh*, lit., judged] a feminine name

**di·nar** (di när′) *n.* [< Ar. < L. *denarius:* see DENARIUS] the monetary unit of Algeria, Iraq, Jordan, Libya, Tunisia, etc., and a coin of Iran: see MONETARY UNITS, table

**dine** (dīn) *vi.* **dined, din′ing** [< OFr. *disner*, ult. < L. *dis-*, away + *jejunus*, fasting] to eat dinner —*vt.* to provide a dinner for, or entertain at dinner —**dine out** to dine away from home

**din·er** (dī′nər) *n.* **1.** a person eating dinner **2.** *same as* DINING CAR **3.** a small restaurant built to look like a dining car

**di·nette** (dī net′) *n.* **1.** an alcove or small, partitioned space used as a dining room **2.** a set of tables and chairs for such a space [a 5-piece *dinette*]

**ding** (diŋ) *vi.* [< Scand. (as in ON. *dengja*, to hammer)] **1.** to make a sound like that of a bell; ring **2.** [Colloq.] to speak repetitiously and tiresomely —*vt.* [Colloq.] to repeat insistently or tiresomely; din —*n.* the sound of a bell

**ding-a-ling, ding·a·ling** (diŋ′ə liŋ′) *n.* [Slang] a person who seems crazy, silly, eccentric, etc.

**ding-dong** (-dôŋ′, -däŋ′) *n.* [echoic] the sound of a bell struck repeatedly —*adj.* [Colloq.] vigorously contested —*vi.* to sound with a ding-dong

**din·ghy** (diŋ′gē, diŋ′ē) *n., pl.* **-ghies** [Hindi *ḍiṅgī*] **1.** orig., a rowboat used on the rivers of India **2.** any small boat used as a tender to a yacht, etc. **3.** a small, undecked, single-masted racing boat **4.** an inflatable life raft Also sp. **din′gey**

**din·go** (diŋ′gō) *n., pl.* **-goes** [native name] the Australian wild dog

**din·gus** (diŋ′əs) *n.* [Du. *dinges* (or G. *dings*), orig. gen. of *ding*, thing] [Colloq.] any device; contrivance; gadget: humorous substitute for a name not known or temporarily forgotten

**din·gy** (din′jē) *adj.* **-gi·er, -gi·est** [orig. dial. var. of DUNGY] **1.** dirty-colored; not bright or clean **2.** dismal; shabby —**din′gi·ly** *adv.* —**din′gi·ness** *n.*

**dining car** a railroad car equipped to serve meals to passengers

**dining room** a room where meals are eaten

**din·key** (diŋ′kē) *n., pl.* **-keys** [prob. < ff.] [Colloq.] **1.** a small locomotive for hauling cars, etc. in a railroad yard **2.** a small trolley car

**din·ky** (diŋ′kē) *adj.* **-ki·er, -ki·est** [< Scot. *dink*, trim + -Y[2]] [Colloq.] small and unimportant; of no consequence —*n., pl.* **-kies** *same as* DINKEY

**din·ner** (din′ər) *n.* [< OFr. *disner*, inf. used as n.: see DINE] **1.** the chief meal of the day, whether eaten in the evening or about noon **2.** a banquet in honor of some person or event **3.** a complete meal at a set price with no course omitted; table d'hôte

**dinner jacket** a tuxedo jacket

**din·ner·ware** (-wer′) *n.* **1.** plates, cups, saucers, etc., collectively **2.** a set of such dishes

**di·no·saur** (dī′nə sôr′) *n.* [< Gr. *deinos*, terrible + *sauros*, lizard] any of a large group of extinct, four-limbed reptiles of the Mesozoic Era, including some almost 100 ft. long —**di′no·sau′ri·an** *adj.*

**dint** (dint) *n.* [OE. *dynt*, a blow] **1.** force; exertion: now chiefly in **by dint of 2.** a dent —*vt.* **1.** to dent **2.** to drive in with force

**dioc. 1.** diocesan **2.** diocese

**di·oc·e·san** (dī äs′ə s′n) *adj.* of a diocese —*n.* the bishop of a diocese

**di·o·cese** (dī′ə sis, -sēs′) *n.* [< OFr. < L. < Gr. *dioikēsis*, administration < *dioikein*, to keep house < *dia-*, through + *oikos*, a house] the district under a bishop's jurisdiction

**di·ode** (dī′ōd) *n.* [DI-[1] + -ODE] an electron tube or semiconductor device having two terminals and conducting electricity in only one direction

**di·oe·cious** (dī ē′shəs) *adj.* [< DI-[1] + Gr. *oikos*, a house + -OUS] *Biol.* having the male reproductive organs in one individual and the female organs in another —**di·oe′cious·ly** *adv.* —**di·oe′cism** (-siz′m) *n.*

**Di·og·e·nes** (dī äj′ə nēz′) 412?–323? B.C.; Gr. Cynic philosopher

**Di·o·ny·sian** (dī′ə nish′ən, -nis′ē ən, -nī′sē ən) *adj.* [< DIONYSUS] wild, frenzied, and sensuous

**Di·o·ny·si·us** (dī'ə nish'əs, -nis'ē əs, -nī'sē əs) 430?-367 B.C.; Gr. tyrant of ancient Syracuse

**Di·o·ny·sus, Di·o·ny·sos** (dī'ə nī'səs) *Gr. Myth.* the god of wine and revelry; Bacchus

**di·op·ter, di·op·tre** (dī äp'tər) *n.* [< L. < Gr. *dioptra*, leveling instrument < *dia-*, through + base of *opsis*, sight] a unit of measure of the refractive power of a lens, equal to the power of a lens with a focal distance of one meter —**di·op'tral** *adj.*

**di·o·ra·ma** (dī'ə ram'ə) *n.* [DI(A)- + (PAN)ORAMA] 1. a picture painted on a set of transparent curtains and looked at through a small opening 2. a miniature scene depicting three-dimensional figures in a naturalistic setting 3. a museum display of a preserved or reconstructed specimen, as of wildlife in a simulated habitat

**di·ox·ide** (dī äk'sīd) *n.* an oxide containing two atoms of oxygen per molecule

**dip** (dip) *vt.* **dipped** or, occas., **dipt, dip'ping** [OE. *dyppan*] 1. to put into liquid for a moment and then quickly take out 2. to dye in this way 3. to baptize by immersion 4. to bathe and clean (sheep or hogs) in disinfectant 5. to make (a candle) by putting a wick repeatedly in melted tallow or wax 6. to take out as by scooping up with a container, the hand, etc. 7. to lower and immediately raise again *[dip the flag in salute]* —*vi.* 1. to plunge into a liquid and quickly come out 2. to sink or seem to sink suddenly *[the sun dips into the ocean]* 3. to undergo a slight decline *[sales dipped in May]* 4. to slope down 5. to lower a container, the hand, etc. into liquid, a receptacle, etc., esp. in order to take something out: often figurative *[to dip into one's savings]* 6. to read or study casually or superficially (with *into*) *[to dip into a book]* 7. *Aeron.* to drop suddenly before climbing —*n.* 1. a dipping or being dipped 2. *a)* a brief plunge into a liquid *b)* a brief swim 3. a liquid into which something is dipped, as for dyeing 4. whatever is removed by dipping 5. a candle made by dipping 6. *a)* a downward slope or inclination or a deviation *b)* the amount of this 7. a slight hollow 8. a short downward plunge, as of an airplane 9. *a)* a sweet liquid sauce for desserts *b)* a thick, creamy sauce into which one dips crackers or other appetizers 10. [Slang] a pickpocket

**diph·the·ri·a** (dif thir'ē ə, dip-) *n.* [ModL. < Fr. < Gr. *diphthera*, leather < *dephein*, to tan hides] an acute infectious disease caused by a bacterium and characterized by weakness, high fever, and the formation in the air passages of a membrane-like obstruction to breathing —**diph·the'ri·al** *adj.* —**diph·the·rit'ic** (-thə rit'ik), **diph·ther'ic** *adj.*

**diph·thong** (dif'thôŋ, dip'-) *n.* [< LL. < Gr. < *di-*, two + *phthongos*, sound] *Phonet.* a complex vowel sound made by gliding continuously from the position for one vowel to that for another within the same syllable, as (ou) in *down*, (oi) in *boy* —**diph·thon'gal** (-thôŋ'g'l) *adj.*

**diph·thong·ize** (-īz') *vt.* **-ized', -iz'ing** to pronounce (a simple vowel) as a diphthong —*vi.* to become a diphthong —**diph'thong·i·za'tion** *n.*

**dip·loid** (dip'loid) *adj.* [< Gr. *diploos*, double + -OID] 1. twofold or double 2. *Biol.* having twice the number of chromosomes normally occurring in a mature germ cell: most somatic cells are diploid: see HAPLOID—**dip·loi'dy** (-loi'dē) *n.*

**di·plo·ma** (di plō'mə) *n.* [L. < Gr. *diplōma*, folded letter < *diploos*, double] 1. a certificate conferring honors, privileges, etc. 2. a certificate recording the graduation of a student from a school, college, or university, or conferring a degree

**di·plo·ma·cy** (di plō'mə sē) *n., pl.* **-cies** [< Fr.: see ff.] 1. (skill in) conducting relations between nations 2. tact in dealing with people

**dip·lo·mat** (dip'lə mat') *n.* [< Fr., ult. < L. *diploma*, DI-PLOMA] 1. a representative of a government who conducts relations with another government in the interests of his own country 2. a tactful person Also **di·plo·ma·tist** (di plō'mə tist)

**dip·lo·mat·ic** (dip' lə mat'ik) *n.* 1. of or connected with diplomacy 2. tactful and adroit in dealing with people — **dip'lo·mat'i·cal·ly** *adv.*

**diplomatic immunity** exemption from local taxes, court action, etc. in a foreign country, granted to all members of a diplomatic service

**di·pole** (dī'pōl') *n.* 1. *Physics* any system having two equal but opposite electric charges or magnetic poles separated by a small distance 2. an antenna usually separated at the center by an insulator and fed by a balanced transmission line: in full, **dipole antenna** —**di·po'lar** *adj.*

**dip·per** (dip'ər) *n.* 1. a person whose work is dipping something in liquid 2. a container for dipping; esp., a long-handled cup 3. [D-] either of two groups of stars in the shape of a dipper: see BIG DIPPER, LITTLE DIPPER

4. any of a genus of songbirds, as the water ouzel, which wade and submerge in streams in search of insects, etc. —**dip'per·ful'** *n., pl.* **-fuls'**

**dip·so·ma·ni·a** (dip'sə mā'nē ə, -nyə) *n.* [ModL. < Gr. *dipsa*, thirst + -MANIA] an abnormal and insatiable craving for alcoholic drink —**dip'so·ma'ni·ac'** (-ak') *n.* —**dip'so·ma·ni'a·cal** (-mə nī'ə k'l) *adj.*

**dip·stick** (dip'stik') *n.* a graduated rod for measuring the depth of a substance in its container

**dipt** (dipt) *occas. pt. & pp. of* DIP

**dip·ter·an** (dip'tər ən) *n.* [see ff.] any of a large order of insects, including the housefly, gnat, etc., having two pair of wings, one pair usually vestigial

**dip·ter·ous** (-əs) *adj.* [<ModL. < Gr. < *di-*, two + *pteron*, a wing] 1. having two wings or two winglike appendages 2. of the dipterans

**dip·tych** (dip'tik) *n.* [< LL. < Gr. < *di-*, twice + *ptychē*, a fold] 1. an ancient writing tablet made up of a hinged pair of wooden or ivory pieces 2. a picture painted or carved on two hinged tablets

**dire** (dīr) *adj.* **dir'er, dir'est** [L. *dirus*] 1. arousing terror; dreadful 2. urgent *[a dire need]* —**dire'ly** *adv.* —**dire'ness** *n.*

**di·rect** (di rekt', dī-) *adj.* [< L. pp. of *dirigere*, to lay straight < *dis-*, apart + *regere*, to rule] 1. by the shortest way; not roundabout; straight *[a direct route]* 2. honest and straightforward; frank 3. with nothing or no one between; immediate *[direct contact]* 4. in an unbroken line of descent; lineal 5. exact; complete *[the direct opposite]* 6. in the exact words of the speaker *[a direct quotation]* 7. by action of the people through popular vote instead of through representatives —*vt.* 1. to manage the affairs or action of; guide; conduct 2. to order or command with authority 3. to turn or point (a person or thing) toward an object or goal; aim; head 4. to tell (a person) the way to a place 5. to address (words, etc.) to a specific person or persons 6. to write the name and address on (a letter, etc.) 7. *a)* to plan and supervise the action of (a play, motion picture, etc.) or of (the actors, etc.) *b)* to rehearse and conduct the performance of (a choir, band, etc.) —*vi.* 1. to give directions 2. to be a director —*adv.* directly —**di·rect'ness** *n.*

**direct current** an electric current flowing in one direction

**di·rec·tion** (də rek'shən, dī-) *n.* 1. the act of directing; management; supervision 2. [*usually pl.*] instructions for doing, using, etc. 3. an authoritative order or command 4. the point toward which one faces or line along which one moves or lies 5. an aspect, way, trend, etc. *[research in new directions]*

**di·rec·tion·al** (-'l) *adj.* 1. of, aimed at, or indicating (a specific) direction 2. designed for radiating or receiving radio signals most effectively in one or more particular directions *[a directional antenna]* 3. designed to pick up or send out sound most efficiently in one direction —**di·rec'tion·al'i·ty** *n.* —**di·rec'tion·al·ly** *adv.*

**direction finder** a device for finding out the direction from which radio waves or signals are coming

**di·rec·tive** (də rek'tiv, dī-) *adj.* 1. directing 2. indicating direction —*n.* a general instruction or order issued authoritatively

**di·rect·ly** (-rekt'lē) *adv.* 1. in a direct way or line; straight 2. with nothing coming between *[directly responsible]* 3. exactly *[directly opposite]* 4. right away —*conj.* [Chiefly Brit.] as soon as

**direct mail** mail sent directly to a large number of individuals, promoting a product, institution, etc., and soliciting orders, donations, etc.

**direct object** the word or words denoting the thing or person that receives the action of a transitive verb (Ex.: *ball* in *he hit the ball*)

**di·rec·tor** (di rek'tər) *n.* a person or thing that directs; specif., *a)* the supervisor of a bureau, school, etc. *b)* a member of a board chosen to direct the affairs of a corporation or institution *c)* a person who directs the production of a play, motion picture, etc. *d)* *Music* a conductor —**di·rec·to·ri·al** (də rek'tôr'ē əl, dī-) *adj.* —**di·rec'tor·ship'** *n.* —**di·rec'tress** (-tris) *n.fem.*

**di·rec·tor·ate** (-it) *n.* 1. the position of director 2. a board of directors

**di·rec·to·ry** (də rek'tə rē, dī-) *adj.* directing or advising —*n., pl.* **-ries** 1. a book of directions 2. a book listing the names, addresses, etc. of a specific group of persons 3. a directorate

**direct primary election** a preliminary election at which candidates for public office are chosen by direct vote of the people instead of by delegates at a convention: in **closed primary elections** voters may vote only for candidates of their party

---

fat, āpe, cär; ten, ēven; is, bīte; gō, hôrn, tōōl, look; oil, out; up, fur; get; joy; yet; chin; she; thin, then; zh, leisure; ŋ, ring; ə for *a* in *ago*, *e* in *agent*, *i* in *sanity*, *o* in *comply*, *u* in *focus*; ' as in *able* (ā'b'l); Fr. bal; ë, Fr. coeur; ö, Fr. feu; Fr. mon; ô, Fr. coq; ü, Fr. duc; r, Fr. cri; H, G. ich; kh, G. doch; ‡foreign; *hypothetical; < derived from. See inside front cover.

**direct tax** a tax levied directly on the person who is to pay it, as an income tax or property tax

**dire·ful** (dir′fəl) *adj.* dreadful; terrible —**dire′ful·ly** *adv.*

**dirge** (durj) *n.* [< L. *dirige* (imper. of *dirigere*, to direct), first word of an antiphon in the Office of the Dead] **1.** a funeral hymn **2.** a slow, sad song, poem, etc. expressing grief or mourning

**dir·ham** (dir ham′) *n.* [Ar. < L. *drachma*, DRACHMA] *see* MONETARY UNITS, table (Morocco, Qatar, United Arab Emirates)

**dir·i·gi·ble** (dir′i jə b′l, də rij′ə-) *adj.* [ML. *dirigibilis:* see DIRECT & -IBLE] that can be directed or steered —*n. same as* AIRSHIP

**dirk** (durk) *n.* [earlier *dork*, *durk* < ?] a short, straight dagger —*vt.* to stab with a dirk

**dirn·dl** (durn′d′l) *n.* [G., dial. dim. of *dirne*, girl] **1.** a kind of dress with a full skirt, gathered waist, and closefitting bodice **2.** the skirt of such a dress: also **dirndl skirt**

**dirt** (durt) *n.* [ME. < *drit* < ON. *dritr*, excrement] **1.** any unclean matter, as mud, trash, etc.; filth **2.** earth or garden soil **3.** dirtiness, corruption, etc. **4.** obscene writing, speech, etc. **5.** malicious talk or gossip **6.** *Gold Mining* the gravel, soil, etc. from which gold is separated by washing or panning —*adj.* surfaced with compacted earth *[a dirt road]* —**do one dirt** [Slang] to harm one —**hit the dirt** [Slang] to drop to the ground

**dirt-cheap** (-chēp′) *adj.* [Colloq.] as cheap as dirt; very inexpensive

**dirt farmer** [Colloq.] a farmer who works his own land

**dirt·y** (-ē) *adj.* **dirt′i·er, dirt′i·est** **1.** soiled or soiling with dirt; unclean **2.** muddy or clouded *[a dirty green]* **3.** obscene; pornographic *[dirty jokes]* **4.** mean; nasty; vile *[a dirty coward]* **5.** unfair; dishonest *[a dirty player]* **6.** producing much fallout: said of nuclear weapons **7.** *Naut.* squally; rough *[dirty weather]* —*vt., vi.* **dirt′ied, dirt′y·ing** to make or become dirty; soil; stain —**a dirty shame** a very unfortunate circumstance —**dirty linen** (or **wash**) private matters that could cause gossip —**dirty pool** [Slang] unfair or dishonest tactics —**dirt′i·ly** *adv.* —**dirt′i·ness** *n.*

**Dis** (dis) *Rom. Myth.* **1.** the god of the lower world: identified with the Greek Pluto **2.** Hades

**dis-** [< OFr. or L.; OFr. *des-* < L. *dis-:* cf. DE-] **1.** a *v.-forming prefix meaning:* a) away, apart *[dismiss]* b) deprive of, expel from *[disbar]* c) cause to be the opposite of *[disable]* d) fail, cease, refuse to *[dissatisfy]* or do the opposite of *[disjoin]* **2.** *an adj.-forming prefix meaning* not, un-, the opposite of *[dishonest]* **3.** *a n.-forming prefix meaning* opposite of, lack of *[disunion]*

**dis·a·bil·i·ty** (dis′ə bil′ə tē) *n., pl.* **-ties** **1.** a disabled condition **2.** that which disables, as an illness or injury **3.** a legal disqualification **4.** a limitation or disadvantage

**dis·a·ble** (dis ā′b′l) *vt.* **-bled, -bling** **1.** to make unable, unfit, or ineffective; cripple; incapacitate **2.** to disqualify legally —**dis·a′ble·ment** *n.*

**dis·a·buse** (dis′ə byōōz′) *vt.* **-bused′, -bus′ing** to rid of false ideas; undeceive

**dis·ad·van·tage** (-əd van′tij) *n.* **1.** an unfavorable situation or circumstance; drawback; handicap **2.** harm or detriment to one's interests —*vt.* **-taged, -tag·ing** to act to the disadvantage of —**at a disadvantage** in an unfavorable situation

**dis·ad·van·taged** (-tijd) *adj.* deprived of a decent standard of living, education, etc. by poverty and a lack of opportunity; underprivileged

**dis·ad·van·ta·geous** (dis ad′vən tā′jəs) *adj.* causing disadvantage; unfavorable; adverse —**dis·ad′van·ta′geous·ly** *adv.*

**dis·af·fect** (dis′ə fekt′) *vt.* to make unfriendly, discontented, or disloyal, as toward the government —**dis′af·fect′ed** *adj.* —**dis′af·fec′tion** *n.*

**dis·af·fil·i·ate** (-ə fil′ē āt′) *vt., vi.* **-at′ed, -at′ing** to end an affiliation (with) —**dis′af·fil′i·a′tion** *n.*

**dis·a·gree** (-ə grē′) *vi.* **-greed′, -gree′ing** **1.** to fail to agree; differ **2.** to differ in opinion; often, specif., to quarrel or dispute **3.** to give distress *[corn disagrees with me]*

**dis·a·gree·a·ble** (-ə b′l) *adj.* **1.** not to one's taste; unpleasant; offensive **2.** hard to get along with; quarrelsome —**dis′a·gree′a·ble·ness** *n.* —**dis′a·gree′a·bly** *adv.*

**dis·a·gree·ment** (-mənt) *n.* **1.** refusal to agree **2.** failure to agree; difference; discrepancy **3.** difference of opinion **4.** a quarrel or dispute

**dis·al·low** (dis′ə lou′) *vt.* to refuse to allow; reject as invalid or illegal —**dis′al·low′ance** *n.*

**dis·ap·pear** (-ə pir′) *vi.* **1.** to cease to be seen; go out of sight **2.** to cease being; become lost or extinct —**dis′ap·pear′ance** *n.*

**dis·ap·point** (-ə point′) *vt.* **1.** to fail to satisfy the hopes or expectations of; leave unsatisfied **2.** to frustrate (hopes, etc.) —**dis′ap·point′ing·ly** *adv.*

**dis·ap·point·ment** (-mənt) *n.* **1.** a disappointing or being disappointed **2.** a person or thing that disappoints

**dis·ap·pro·ba·tion** (-ap′rə bā′shən) *n.* disapproval

**dis·ap·prov·al** (-ə prōōv′'l) *n.* **1.** failure or refusal to approve **2.** unfavorable opinion

**dis·ap·prove** (-ə prōōv′) *vt.* **-proved′, -prov′ing** **1.** to have or express an unfavorable opinion of **2.** to refuse to approve; reject —*vi.* to feel or express disapproval (*of*) —**dis′ap·prov′ing·ly** *adv.*

**dis·arm** (dis ärm′) *vt.* **1.** to take away weapons or armaments from **2.** to make harmless **3.** to overcome the hostility of —*vi.* **1.** to lay down arms **2.** to reduce or do away with armed forces and armaments

**dis·ar·ma·ment** (-är′mə mənt) *n.* **1.** the act of disarming **2.** the reduction of armed forces and armaments, as to a limitation set by treaty

**dis·arm·ing** (-är′miŋ) *adj.* removing suspicions, fears, or hostility —**dis·arm′ing·ly** *adv.*

**dis·ar·range** (dis′ə rānj′) *vt.* **-ranged′, -rang′ing** to upset the order or arrangement of; make less neat; disorder —**dis′ar·range′ment** *n.*

**dis·ar·ray** (-ə rā′) *vt.* **1.** to throw into disorder or confusion; upset **2.** [Archaic] to undress —*n.* **1.** disorder; confusion **2.** a state of disorderly or insufficient dress

**dis·as·sem·ble** (-ə sem′b′l) *vt.* **-bled, -bling** to take apart —**dis′as·sem′bly** *n.*

**dis·as·so·ci·ate** (-ə sō′shē āt′, -sē-) *vt.* **-at′ed, -at′ing** to sever association with; separate; dissociate —**dis′as·so′ci·a′tion** *n.*

**dis·as·ter** (di zas′tər) *n.* [< OFr. < It. < L. *dis-* + *astrum* < Gr. *astron*, a star: cf. ILL-STARRED] any happening that causes great harm or damage; serious or sudden misfortune; calamity

**dis·as·trous** (-trəs) *adj.* of the nature of a disaster; causing great harm, damage, grief, etc.; calamitous —**dis·as′trous·ly** *adv.*

**dis·a·vow** (dis′ə vou′) *vt.* to deny any knowledge or approval of, or responsibility for; disclaim; disown —**dis′a·vow′al** *n.*

**dis·band** (dis band′) *vt.* **1.** to break up (an association or organization) **2.** to dismiss (a military force) from service —*vi.* to cease to exist as an organization; scatter; disperse —**dis·band′ment** *n.*

**dis·bar** (-bär′) *vt.* **-barred′, -bar′ring** to expel (a lawyer) from the bar; deprive of the right to practice law —**dis·bar′ment** *n.*

**dis·be·lief** (dis′bə lēf′) *n.* refusal to believe; absence of belief

**dis·be·lieve** (-lēv′) *vt.* **-lieved′, -liev′ing** to reject as untrue —*vi.* to refuse to believe (*in*) —**dis′be·liev′er** *n.*

**dis·bur·den** (dis bur′d'n) *vt.* to relieve of a burden or of anything burdensome

**dis·burse** (-burs′) *vt.* **-bursed′, -burs′ing** [< OFr. *desbourser*: see DIS- & BOURSE] to pay out; expend —**dis·burs′a·ble** *adj.* —**dis·burse′ment** *n.* —**dis·burs′er** *n.*

**disc** (disk) *n.* **1.** *same as* DISK **2.** a) a phonograph record b) a thin, flat, circular plate coated with ferromagnetic particles, on which computer data can be stored **3.** any of the sharp, circular blades on a disc harrow **4.** *Biol.* any disc-shaped part or structure: cf. DISK

**disc. 1.** discount **2.** discovered

**dis·card** (dis kärd′; *for n.* dis′kärd) *vt.* [< OFr.: see DIS- & CARD[1]] **1.** *Card Games* a) to remove (a card or cards) from the hand dealt b) to play (a card not a trump and not in the suit led) **2.** to get rid of as no longer valuable or useful —*vi. Card Games* to make a discard —*n.* **1.** a discarding or being discarded **2.** something discarded **3.** *Card Games* the card or cards discarded

**disc brake** a brake, as on an automobile, that causes two friction pads to press on either side of a disc rotating along with the wheel

**dis·cern** (di surn′, -zurn′) *vt.* [< OFr. < L. < *dis-*, apart + *cernere*, to separate] **1.** to recognize as separate or different **2.** to perceive or recognize; make out clearly —*vi.* to perceive or recognize the difference —**dis·cern′i·ble** *adj.* —**dis·cern′i·bly** *adv.*

**dis·cern·ing** (-iŋ) *adj.* having or showing good judgment or understanding —**dis·cern′ing·ly** *adv.*

**dis·cern·ment** (-mənt) *n.* **1.** a discerning **2.** keen perception or judgment; insight; acumen

**dis·charge** (dis chärj′; *for n. usually* dis′chärj) *vt.* **-charged′, -charg′ing** [< OFr. < L. *dis-*, from + *carrus*, wagon, CAR] **1.** to relieve of or release from something that burdens or confines; specif., a) to remove the cargo of (a ship) b) to release the charge of (a gun) c) to release (a soldier, jury, etc.) from duty d) to dismiss from employment e) to release (a prisoner) from jail, (a defendant) from suspicion, (a debtor or bankrupt) from obligations, etc. **2.** to release or remove (that by which one is burdened or confined); specif., a) to unload (a cargo) b) to shoot (a projectile) **3.** to relieve oneself or itself of (a burden, load, etc.); specif., a) to throw off; emit *[to discharge pus]* b) to pay (a debt) or perform (a duty) **4.** *Elec.* to remove stored energy from (a battery or capacitor) —*vi.* **1.** to get rid of a burden, load, etc. **2.** to be released or thrown off **3.** to go off: said of a gun, etc. **4.** to emit waste matter: said of a wound, etc. —*n.* **1.** a discharging or being discharged **2.** that which discharges, as a legal order for release, a certificate of dismissal from military service, etc. **3.** that which is discharged, as pus from a sore **4.** a flow of electric current across a gap, as in a spark or arc —**dis·charge′a·ble** *adj.* —**dis·charg′er** *n.*

**discharge tube** a device in which a gas or metal vapor conducting an electric discharge is the source of light

**disc harrow** a harrow with sharp, revolving circular blades used to break up the soil for sowing

**dis·ci·ple** (di sī′p'l) *n.* [ < OFr. & OE., both < L. *discipulus*, pupil < *dis-*, apart + *capere*, to hold] **1.** a pupil or follower of any teacher or school **2.** an early follower of Jesus, esp. one of the Apostles —**dis·ci′ple·ship′** *n.*

**dis·ci·pli·nar·i·an** (dis′ə pli ner′ē ən) *n.* one who believes in or enforces strict discipline

**dis·ci·pli·nar·y** (dis′ə pli ner′ē) *adj.* **1.** of or having to do with discipline **2.** that enforces discipline by punishing or correcting

DISC HARROW

**dis·ci·pline** (dis′ə plin) *n.* [ < OFr. < L. *disciplina* < *discipulus*: see DISCIPLE] **1.** a branch of knowledge or learning **2.** *a)* training that develops self-control or orderliness and efficiency *b)* strict control to enforce obedience **3.** the result of such training or control; orderly conduct, obedience, etc. **4.** a system of rules, as for a monastic order **5.** treatment that corrects or punishes —*vt.* **-plined, -plin·ing 1.** to subject to discipline; train; control **2.** to punish —**dis′ci·plin·a·ble** *adj.* —**dis′ci·plin·er** *n.*

**disc jockey** a person who conducts a radio program of recorded music or plays recorded music at a disco

**dis·claim** (dis klām′) *vt.* **1.** to give up any claim to or connection with **2.** to refuse to acknowledge or admit; repudiate —*vi.* to make a disclaimer —**dis·cla·ma·tion** (dis′klə mā′shən) *n.*

**dis·claim·er** (-ər) *n.* **1.** a disclaiming or renunciation, as of a claim, title, etc. **2.** a disavowing

**dis·close** (-klōz′) *vt.* **-closed′, -clos′ing 1.** to bring into view; uncover **2.** to reveal; make known —**dis·clos′er** *n.*

**dis·clos·ure** (-klō′zhər) *n.* **1.** a disclosing or being disclosed **2.** a thing disclosed; revelation

**dis·co** (dis′kō) *n., pl.* **-cos** [DISCO(THÈQUE)] **1.** a public place for dancing to music played by a disc jockey **2.** such music, with a strong beat and simple lyrics

**dis·cob·o·lus** (dis käb′ə ləs) *n.* [L. < Gr. < *diskos*, discus + *ballein*, to throw] a discus thrower

**dis·cog·ra·phy** (dis käg′rə fē) *n., pl.* **-phies** [ < L. *discus*, a disk + (BIBLIO)GRAPHY] **1.** the systematic cataloging of phonograph records **2.** a list of the recordings of a particular performer, composer, etc. —**dis·cog′ra·pher** *n.*

**dis·coid** (dis′koid) *adj.* [ < LL. < Gr. < *diskos*, a disk + *eidos*, form] shaped like a disk: also **dis·coi′dal** —*n.* anything shaped like a disk

**dis·col·or** (dis kul′ər) *vt., vi.* to change in color by fading, streaking, or staining —**dis·col′or·a′tion** *n.*

**dis·com·bob·u·late** (dis′kəm bäb′yoo lāt′) *vt.* **-lat′ed, -lat′ing** [prob. whimsical alteration of ff.] [Colloq.] to upset the composure of; disconcert

**dis·com·fit** (dis kum′fit) *vt.* [ < OFr. < L. *dis-* + *conficere*: see CONFECT] **1.** orig., to defeat **2.** to frustrate the plans or expectations of **3.** to make uneasy; disconcert —**dis·com′fi·ture** (-fi chər) *n.*

**dis·com·fort** (dis kum′fərt) *n.* **1.** lack of comfort; uneasiness; inconvenience **2.** anything causing this —*vt.* to cause discomfort to; distress

**dis·com·mode** (dis′kə mōd′) *vt.* **-mod′ed, -mod′ing** [ < DIS- + L. *commodare*, to make suitable] to cause bother to; inconvenience

**dis·com·pose** (-kəm pōz′) *vt.* **-posed′, -pos′ing 1.** to disturb the calm or poise of; fluster; disconcert **2.** [Now Rare] to disturb the order of; disarrange —**dis·com·po′sure** (-pō′zhər) *n.*

**dis·con·cert** (-kən sʉrt′) *vt.* **1.** to upset or frustrate (plans, etc.) **2.** to upset the composure of —**dis′con·cert′ing** *adj.* —**dis′con·cert′ing·ly** *adv.*

**dis·con·nect** (-kə nekt′) *vt.* to break or undo the connection of; separate, detach, unplug, etc. —**dis′con·nec′tion** *n.*

**dis·con·nect·ed** (-nek′tid) *adj.* **1.** separated, detached, etc. **2.** broken up into unrelated parts; incoherent —**dis′con·nect′ed·ly** *adv.* —**dis′con·nect′ed·ness** *n.*

**dis·con·so·late** (dis kän′sə lit) *adj.* [ < ML. < L.: see DIS- & CONSOLE¹] **1.** so unhappy that nothing will console;

dejected **2.** causing dejection; cheerless —**dis·con′so·late·ly** *adv.* —**dis·con′so·late·ness, dis·con·so·la′tion** (-lā′shən) *n.*

**dis·con·tent** (dis′kən tent′) *adj. same as* DISCONTENTED —*n.* lack of contentment; dissatisfaction: also **dis′con·tent′ment** —*vt.* to make discontented

**dis·con·tent·ed** (-id) *adj.* not contented; wanting something more or different —**dis′con·tent′ed·ly** *adv.* —**dis′con·tent′ed·ness** *n.*

**dis·con·tin·ue** (dis′kən tin′yōō) *vt.* **-ued, -u·ing 1.** to stop using, doing, etc.; cease; give up **2.** *Law* to stop (a suit) prior to trial —*vi.* to stop; end —**dis′con·tin′u·ance** (-yōō wəns), **dis′con·tin′u·a′tion** (-yoo wā′shən) *n.*

**dis·con·tin·u·ous** (-yōō wəs) *adj.* not continuous; broken; intermittent —**dis·con·ti·nu·i·ty** (dis kän′tə nōō′ə tē, dis′kän-; -nyōō′-) *n.* —**dis′con·tin′u·ous·ly** *adv.*

**dis·co·phile** (dis′kə fīl′) *n.* [ < L. *discus*, disk + -PHILE] an expert on, or collector of, phonograph records

**dis·cord** (dis′kôrd; *for v., usually* dis kôrd′) *n.* [ < OFr. < L. < *discors* (gen. *discordis*), discordant < *dis-*, apart + *cor*, heart] **1.** lack of concord; disagreement **2.** a harsh or confused noise, as the sound of battle **3.** *Music* a lack of harmony in tones sounded together; dissonance —*vi.* to disagree; clash

**dis·cord·ant** (dis kôr′d'nt) *adj.* **1.** not in accord; disagreeing; conflicting **2.** not in harmony; dissonant; clashing —**dis·cord′ance, dis·cord′an·cy** *n.* —**dis·cord′ant·ly** *adv.*

**dis·co·thèque** (dis′kə tek) *n.* [Fr. < *disque*, record + *bibliothèque*, library] *the full name for* DISCO (*n.* 1.)

**dis·count** (dis′kount; *for v., also* dis kount′) *n.* [ < OFr. < ML. *discomputare*: see DIS- & COMPUTE] **1.** *a)* a reduction from a usual or list price *b)* a deduction from a debt, allowed for prompt or cash payment **2.** the interest deducted in advance by one who lends money on a promissory note, etc. **3.** the rate of interest (**discount rate**) charged for this **4.** a discounting —*vt.* **1.** to pay or receive the value of (a promissory note, etc.), minus the discount (sense 2) **2.** to deduct an amount or percent from (a bill, price, etc.) **3.** to sell at less than the regular price **4.** *a)* to take (a story, etc.) at less than face value, allowing for exaggeration, bias, etc. *b)* to disbelieve or disregard entirely **5.** to reckon with in advance —**at a discount 1.** below the regular price **2.** worth little —**dis′count·a·ble** *adj.*

**dis·coun·te·nance** (dis koun′tə nəns) *vt.* **-nanced, -nanc·ing 1.** to make ashamed or embarrassed; disconcert **2.** to refuse approval or support to

**discount house** (or **store**) a retail store that sells goods for less than regular or list prices

**dis·cour·age** (dis kʉr′ij) *vt.* **-aged, -ag·ing** [OFr. *descoragier*] **1.** to deprive of courage; dishearten **2.** to advise or persuade (a person) to refrain **3.** to prevent or try to prevent by disapproving —*vi.* to become discouraged —**dis·cour′age·ment** *n.* —**dis·cour′ag·ing** *adj.* —**dis·cour′ag·ing·ly** *adv.*

**dis·course** (dis′kôrs; *also, and for v. usually,* dis kôrs′) *n.* [ < OFr. < L. pp. < *dis-*, from + *currere*, to run] **1.** communication of ideas, information, etc., esp. by talking; conversation **2.** a formal treatment of a subject, in speech or writing **3.** [Archaic] ability to reason —*vi.* **-coursed′, -cours′ing 1.** to converse; talk **2.** to speak or write (*on* or *upon* a subject) formally —*vt.* [Archaic] to utter or tell —**dis·cours′er** *n.*

**dis·cour·te·ous** (dis kʉr′tē əs) *adj.* not courteous; impolite; ill-mannered —**dis·cour′te·ous·ly** *adv.* —**dis·cour′te·ous·ness** *n.*

**dis·cour·te·sy** (-tə sē) *n.* **1.** lack of courtesy; impoliteness; rudeness **2.** *pl.* **-sies** a rude or impolite act or remark

**dis·cov·er** (dis kuv′ər) *vt.* [ < OFr. < LL. *discooperire*: see DIS- & COVER] **1.** to be the first to find, see, or know about **2.** to be the first non-native person to come to or see **3.** to find out; realize **4.** [Archaic] *a)* to reveal *b)* to uncover —**dis·cov′er·a·ble** *adj.* —**dis·cov′er·er** *n.*

**dis·cov·er·y** (-ər ē) *n., pl.* **-er·ies 1.** a discovering **2.** anything discovered **3.** [Archaic] a revealing **4.** *Law* any disclosure that a defendant is compelled to make

**Discovery Day** *same as* COLUMBUS DAY

**dis·cred·it** (dis kred′it) *vt.* **1.** to reject as untrue **2.** to cast doubt on **3.** to damage the reputation of; disgrace —*n.* **1.** loss of belief or trust; doubt **2.** damage to one's reputation; disgrace **3.** something that causes disgrace —**dis·cred′it·a·ble** *adj.* —**dis·cred′it·a·bly** *adv.*

**dis·creet** (dis krēt′) *adj.* [ < OFr. < L. pp. of *discernere*: see DISCERN] careful about what one says or does; prudent; esp., preserving confidences when necessary —**dis·creet′ly** *adv.* —**dis·creet′ness** *n.*

**dis·crep·an·cy** (dis krep′ən sē) *n., pl.* **-cies** [ < OFr. < L. < prp. of *discrepare*, to sound differently < *dis-*, from + *crepare*, to rattle] lack of agreement, or an instance of this;

difference; inconsistency —**dis·crep′ant** *adj.* —**dis·crep′-ant·ly** *adv.*

**dis·crete** (dis krēt′) *adj.* [< L.: see DISCREET] 1. separate and distinct; not attached to others; unrelated 2. made up of distinct parts; discontinuous —**dis·crete′ly** *adv.* —**dis·crete′ness** *n.*

**dis·cre·tion** (dis kresh′ən) *n.* 1. the freedom or authority to make decisions and choices 2. the quality of being discreet; prudence —**at one's discretion** as one wishes

**dis·cre·tion·ar·y** (-er′ē) *adj.* left to one's discretion: also **dis·cre′tion·al**

**dis·crim·i·na·ble** (dis krim′ə nə b'l) *adj.* that can be discriminated or distinguished

**dis·crim·i·nate** (dis krim′ə nāt′; *for adj.* -nit) *vt.* **-nat′ed, -nat′ing** [< L. pp. of *discriminare* < *discrimen*, division < *discernere:* see DISCERN] 1. to constitute a difference between; differentiate 2. to recognize the difference between; distinguish —*vi.* 1. to see the difference (*between* things); distinguish 2. to be discerning 3. to show partiality (*in favor of*) or prejudice (*against*) —*adj.* distinguishing carefully —**dis·crim′i·nat′ing** *adj.* —**dis·crim′i·na′tive** (-nāt′iv, -nə tiv) *adj.* —**dis·crim′i·na′tor** *n.*

**dis·crim·i·na·tion** (dis krim′ə nā′shən) *n.* 1. the act of discriminating, or distinguishing differences 2. the ability to do this 3. a showing of partiality or prejudice in treatment; specif., policies directed against the welfare of minority groups

**dis·crim·i·na·to·ry** (-krim′ə nə tôr′ē) *adj.* 1. practicing discrimination, or showing prejudice 2. discriminating, or distinguishing

**dis·cur·sive** (dis kur′siv) *adj.* [< ML. < L.: see DISCOURSE] 1. wandering from one topic to another; rambling; digressive 2. *Philos.* going from premises to conclusions in a series of logical steps —**dis·cur′sive·ly** *adv.* —**dis·cur′sive·ness** *n.*

**dis·cus** (dis′kəs) *n., pl.* **dis′cus·es, dis·ci** (dis′ī) [L. < Gr. *diskos*] 1. a heavy disk of metal and wood, orig. often of stone, thrown for distance in competition 2. such a contest: in full, **discus throw**

DISCUS THROWER

**dis·cuss** (dis kus′) *vt.* [< L. pp. of *discutire* < *dis-*, apart + *quatere*, to shake] to talk or write about; consider and argue the pros and cons of —**dis·cuss′a·ble, dis·cuss′i·ble** *adj.* —**dis·cuss′ant, dis·cuss′er** *n.*

**dis·cus·sion** (dis kush′ən) *n.* talk or writing in which the pros and cons or various aspects of a subject are considered —**under discussion** being discussed

**dis·dain** (dis dān′) *vt.* [< OFr. < L. *dis-*, not + *dignari*, DEIGN] to regard as beneath one's dignity; specif., to refuse or reject with aloof contempt or scorn —*n.* aloof contempt or scorn —**dis·dain′ful** *adj.* —**dis·dain′ful·ly** *adv.* —**dis·dain′ful·ness** *n.*

**dis·ease** (di zēz′) *n.* [OFr. *desaise* < *des-*, DIS- + *aise*, EASE] 1. any departure from health; illness in general 2. a particular destructive process in an organ or organism; specific illness 3. a harmful condition, as of society —*vt.* **-eased′, -eas′ing** to cause disease in; infect —**dis·eased′** *adj.*

**dis·em·bark** (dis′im bärk′) *vt.* to unload (passengers or goods) from a ship, aircraft, etc. —*vi.* to go ashore from a ship or leave an aircraft, etc. —**dis·em·bar·ka·tion** (dis′-em bär kā′shən) *n.*

**dis·em·bar·rass** (-im bar′əs) *vt.* to rid or relieve of something embarrassing, annoying, entangling, perplexing, or burdensome

**dis·em·bod·y** (-im bäd′ē) *vt.* **-bod′ied, -bod′y·ing** to free from bodily existence; make incorporeal —**dis′em·bod′ied** *adj.* —**dis′em·bod′i·ment** *n.*

**dis·em·bow·el** (-im bou′əl) *vt.* **-eled** *or* **-elled, -el·ing** *or* **-el·ling** to take out the bowels, or entrails, of; eviscerate —**dis′em·bow′el·ment** *n.*

**dis·em·ployed** (-im ploid′) *adj.* out of work, esp. because of lack of training or education, rather than because work is unavailable —**dis′em·ploy′ment** *n.*

**dis·en·chant** (-in chant′) *vt.* to set free from an enchantment or illusion —**dis′en·chant′ment** *n.*

**dis·en·cum·ber** (-in kum′bər) *vt.* to relieve of a burden; free from a hindrance or annoyance

**dis·en·fran·chise** (-in fran′chīz) *vt.* **-chised, -chis·ing** *same as* DISFRANCHISE —**dis′en·fran′chise·ment** *n.*

**dis·en·gage** (-in gāj′) *vt.* **-gaged′, -gag′ing** to release or loosen from something that binds, holds, entangles, etc.; unfasten; detach —*vi.* to release oneself or itself —**dis′en·gage′ment** *n.*

**dis·en·tan·gle** (-in taŋ′g'l) *vt.* **-gled, -gling** 1. to free from something that entangles, confuses, etc.; extricate 2. to straighten out (anything tangled, confused, etc.);

untangle —*vi.* to get free from a tangle —**dis′en·tan·gle·ment** *n.*

**dis·e·qui·lib·ri·um** (dis ē′kwə lib′rē əm) *n., pl.* **-ri·ums, -ri·a** (-ə) lack or destruction of equilibrium, esp. in the economy

**dis·es·tab·lish** (dis′ə stab′lish) *vt.* 1. to deprive of the status of being established 2. to deprive (a state church) of official sanction and support by the government —**dis′es·tab′lish·ment** *n.*

**dis·es·teem** (-ə stēm′) *vt.* to hold in low esteem; dislike; slight —*n.* lack of esteem; disfavor

**dis·fa·vor** (dis fā′vər) *n.* 1. an unfavorable opinion; dislike; disapproval 2. the state of being disliked or disapproved of 3. an unkind act; disservice —*vt.* to regard or treat unfavorably; slight

**dis·fig·ure** (-fig′yər) *vt.* **-ured, -ur·ing** to hurt the appearance or attractiveness of; deface; mar —**dis·fig′ure·ment, dis·fig′u·ra′tion** *n.*

**dis·fran·chise** (-fran′chīz) *vt.* **-chised, -chis·ing** 1. to deprive of the rights of citizenship, esp. of the right to vote 2. to deprive of a privilege, right, or power —**dis·fran′-chise·ment** *n.*

**dis·gorge** (-gôrj′) *vt., vi.* **-gorged′, -gorg′ing** [< OFr.: see DIS- & GORGE] 1. to vomit 2. to give up (something) against one's will 3. to pour forth (its contents)

**dis·grace** (-grās′) *n.* [< Fr. < It. < *dis-* (L. *dis-*), not + *grazia*, favor < L. *gratia:* see GRACE] 1. a being in disfavor as because of bad conduct 2. loss of respect; public dishonor; shame 3. a person or thing that brings shame (*to* one) —*vt.* **-graced′, -grac′ing** to bring shame or dishonor upon; be a discredit to —**dis·grac′er** *n.*

**dis·grace·ful** (-fəl) *adj.* causing or characterized by disgrace; shameful —**dis·grace′ful·ly** *adv.* —**dis·grace′ful·ness** *n.*

**dis·grun·tle** (-grun′t'l) *vt.* **-tled, -tling** [DIS- + obs. *gruntle*, freq. of GRUNT] to make peevishly discontented —**dis·grun′tle·ment** *n.*

**dis·guise** (-gīz′) *vt.* **-guised′, -guis·ing** [< OFr.: see DIS- & GUISE] 1. to make appear, sound, etc. different from usual so as to be unrecognizable 2. to hide the real nature of —*n.* 1. any clothes, equipment, manner, etc. used for disguising 2. the state of being disguised 3. the act or practice of disguising —**dis·guis′ed·ly** *adv.* —**dis·guis′er** *n.*

**dis·gust** (-gust′) *n.* [< MFr. < *des-* (see DIS-) + L. *gustus*, taste] a sickening distaste or dislike; deep aversion; repugnance —*vt.* to cause to feel disgust; be sickening or repulsive to —**dis·gust′ed** *adj.* —**dis·gust′ed·ly** *adv.* —**dis·gust′ing** *adj.* —**dis·gust′ing·ly** *adv.*

**dish** (dish) *n.* [OE. *disc*, dish, ult. < L. *discus*, DISCUS] 1. *a)* any container, generally shallow and concave, for food *b)* [*pl.*] plates, bowls, cups, etc., collectively 2. *a)* the food in a dish *b)* a particular kind of food 3. a dishful 4. a dish-shaped object or concavity 5. [Slang] *a)* a pretty girl or woman *b)* a favorite thing: also **dish of tea** —*vt.* 1. to serve (food) in a dish (usually with *up* or *out*) 2. to make concave —*vi.* to be or become dish-shaped; cave in —**dish it out** [Slang] to scold, harass, etc.

**dis·ha·bille** (dis′ə bēl′) *n.* [< Fr. < *dés-* (see DIS-) + *habiller*, to dress] the state of being dressed only partially or in night clothes

**dish antenna** a radio transmitting or receiving antenna with a dish-shaped reflector

**dis·har·mo·ny** (dis här′mə nē) *n.* lack of harmony; discord —**dis′har·mo′ni·ous** (-mō′nē əs) *adj.*

**dish·cloth** (dish′klôth′, -kläth′) *n.* a cloth for washing dishes

**dis·heart·en** (dis härt′'n) *vt.* to discourage; depress —**dis·heart′en·ing** *adj.* —**dis·heart′en·ing·ly** *adv.* —**dis·heart′en·ment** *n.*

**di·shev·el** (di shev′'l) *vt.* **-eled** *or* **-elled, -el·ing** *or* **-el·ling** [< OFr. < *des-*, DIS- + *chevel*, hair < L. *capillus*] 1. to cause (hair, clothing, etc.) to become disarranged and untidy; rumple 2. to cause the hair or clothes of (a person) to become disarranged —**di·shev′eled, di·shev′elled** *adj.* —**di·shev′el·ment** *n.*

**dish·ful** (dish′fool′) *n., pl.* **-fuls′** as much as a dish holds

**dis·hon·est** (dis än′ist) *adj.* not honest; lying, cheating, etc. —**dis·hon′est·ly** *adv.*

**dis·hon·es·ty** (-ist ē) *n.* 1. the quality of being dishonest 2. *-ties* a dishonest act or statement; fraud, lie, etc.

**dis·hon·or** (dis än′ər) *n.* 1. *a)* loss of honor, respect, etc. *b)* state of shame; disgrace 2. a cause of dishonor; discredit 3. a refusal or failure to pay a check, draft, etc. —*vt.* 1. to treat disrespectfully 2. to disgrace 3. to refuse or fail to pay (a check, draft, etc.)

**dis·hon·or·a·ble** (-ə b'l) *adj.* causing or deserving dishonor; shameful; disgraceful —**dis·hon′or·a·ble·ness** *n.* —**dis·hon′or·a·bly** *adv.*

**dish·pan** (dish′pan′) *n.* a pan in which dishes, cooking utensils, etc. are washed

**dish·rag** (-rag′) *n. same as* DISHCLOTH

**dish towel** a towel for drying dishes

**dis·il·lu·sion** (dis′i l$\overline{oo}$′zhən) *vt.* **1.** to free from illusion or false ideas **2.** to take away the idealism of and make disappointed, bitter, etc. —*n.* a disillusioning or being disillusioned: also **dis′il·lu′sion·ment**

**dis·in·cli·na·tion** (dis in′klə nā′shən) *n.* a dislike or unwillingness; aversion; reluctance

**dis·in·cline** (dis′in klīn′) *vt.* **-clined′, -clin′ing** to make unwilling

**dis·in·fect** (-in fekt′) *vt.* to destroy the harmful bacteria, viruses, etc. in or on —**dis′in·fec′tion** *n.*

**dis·in·fect·ant** (-ənt) *adj.* disinfecting —*n.* anything that disinfects

**dis·in·fla·tion** (-in flā′shən) *n. Econ.* a reduction of price levels, planned to increase purchasing power but control deflation —**dis′in·fla′tion·ar′y** *adj.*

**dis·in·gen·u·ous** (-in jen′yoo wəs) *adj.* not straightforward; not candid; insincere —**dis′in·gen′u·ous·ly** *adv.* —**dis′in·gen′u·ous·ness** *n.*

**dis·in·her·it** (-in her′it) *vt.* **1.** to deprive of an inheritance or the right to inherit **2.** to deprive of any right or privilege —**dis′in·her′it·ance** *n.*

**dis·in·te·grate** (-in′tə grāt′) *vt., vi.* **-grat′ed, -grat′ing 1.** to separate into parts or fragments; break up **2.** to undergo or cause to undergo a nuclear transformation —**dis·in′te·gra′tion** *n.* —**dis·in′te·gra′tive** *adj.* —**dis·in′te·gra′tor** *n.*

**dis·in·ter** (dis′in tur′) *vt.* **-terred′, -ter′ring 1.** to remove from a grave, tomb, etc.; dig up; exhume **2.** to bring to light —**dis′in·ter′ment** *n.*

**dis·in·ter·est** (dis in′trist, -tər ist) *n.* **1.** lack of personal or selfish interest **2.** lack of interest

**dis·in·ter·est·ed** (-id) *adj.* **1.** not influenced by personal interest or selfish motives; impartial **2.** uninterested: a revival of an obsolete meaning —**dis·in′ter·est·ed·ly** *adv.* —**dis·in′ter·est·ed·ness** *n.*

**dis·join** (-join′) *vt.* to separate or detach

**dis·joint** (-joint′) *vt.* **1.** to put out of joint; dislocate **2.** to dismember **3.** to destroy the unity, connections, or orderliness of —*vi.* to come apart at the joints —**dis·joint′ed** *adj.* —**dis·joint′ed·ly** *adv.* —**dis·joint′ed·ness** *n.*

**dis·junc·tion** (-juŋk′shən) *n.* **1.** a disjoining or being disjoined; separation: also **dis·junc′ture** (-chər) **2.** *a)* the relation between alternatives of a disjunctive proposition *b)* a disjunctive proposition

**dis·junc·tive** (-tiv) *adj.* **1.** disjoining; separating or causing to separate **2.** *Gram.* indicating a contrast or an alternative between words, clauses, etc. ["or" and "but" are *disjunctive* conjunctions] **3.** *Logic* presenting alternatives [a *disjunctive* proposition] —*n.* **1.** *Gram.* a disjunctive conjunction **2.** *Logic* a disjunctive proposition —**dis·junc′tive·ly** *adv.*

**disk** (disk) *n.* [< L. *discus*, DISCUS] **1.** any thin, flat, circular thing **2.** anything like this in form [the moon's *disk*] **3.** same as DISC; specif., *a)* the disk-shaped center of certain composite flowers *b)* a layer of fibrous connective tissue, with some cartilage, occurring between vertebrae

**disk flower** any of the tubular flowers in the central disk of the flower head of a composite plant

**disk harrow** same as DISC HARROW

**disk jockey** same as DISC JOCKEY

**dis·like** (dis līk′) *vt.* **-liked′, -lik′ing** to have a feeling of not liking; feel aversion to —*n.* a feeling of not liking; distaste; aversion —**dis·lik′a·ble, dis·like′a·ble** *adj.*

**dis·lo·cate** (dis′lō kāt′, dis lō′kāt) *vt.* **-cat′ed, -cat′ing 1.** to put out of place; specif., to displace (a bone) from its proper position at a joint **2.** to disarrange; disrupt —**dis′lo·ca′tion** *n.*

**dis·lodge** (dis läj′) *vt., vi.* **-lodged′, -lodg′ing** to force or be forced from a position or place where lodged, hiding, etc. —**dis·lodg′ment** *n.*

**dis·loy·al** (-loi′əl) *adj.* not loyal or faithful; faithless —**dis·loy′al·ly** *adv.*

**dis·loy·al·ty** (-tē) *n.* **1.** the quality of being disloyal **2.** *pl.* **-ties** a disloyal act

**dis·mal** (diz′m'l) *adj.* [ME., orig. n., evil days < OFr. < ML. *dies mali*] **1.** causing gloom or misery **2.** dark and gloomy; bleak; dreary **3.** depressed; miserable —**dis′mal·ly** *adv.*

**dis·man·tle** (dis man′t'l) *vt.* **-tled, -tling** [< OFr. *desmanteller*: see DIS- & MANTLE] **1.** to strip of covering **2.** to strip (a house, ship, etc.) of furniture, equipment, etc. **3.** to take apart; disassemble —**dis·man′tle·ment** *n.*

**dis·may** (-mā′) *vt.* [< Anglo-Fr. < OFr. *des-*, intens. + *es-mayer*, to deprive of power] to make discouraged at the prospect of trouble; fill with alarm; daunt —*n.* a loss of courage at the prospect of trouble

**dis·mem·ber** (-mem′bər) *vt.* [< OFr.: see DIS- & MEMBER] **1.** to remove the limbs of by cutting or tearing **2.** to pull or cut to pieces; divide up or mutilate —**dis·mem′ber·ment** *n.*

**dis·miss** (-mis′) *vt.* [< ML. pp. of *dismittere*, for L. *dimittere* < *dis-*, from + *mittere*, to send] **1.** to send away; cause or allow to leave **2.** to remove or discharge from an office, employment, etc. **3.** to put out of one's mind **4.** *Law* to reject (a claim or action) —**dis·miss′al** *n.* —**dis·miss′i·ble** *adj.*

**dis·mount** (-mount′) *vi.* to get off, as from a horse or bicycle —*vt.* **1.** to remove (a thing) from its mounting or setting **2.** to cause to dismount **3.** to take apart —*n.* a dismounting

**dis·o·be·di·ence** (dis′ə bē′dē əns) *n.* refusal to obey; failure to follow commands; insubordination —**dis′o·be′di·ent** *adj.* —**dis′o·be′di·ent·ly** *adv.*

**dis·o·bey** (dis′ə bā′) *vt., vi.* to refuse or fail to obey

**dis·o·blige** (-ə blīj′) *vt.* **-bliged′, -blig′ing 1.** to refuse to oblige, or do a favor for **2.** to slight; offend —**dis′o·blig′-ing** *adj.* —**dis′o·blig′ing·ly** *adv.*

**dis·or·der** (dis ôr′dər) *n.* **1.** a lack of order; confusion **2.** a breach of public peace; riot **3.** a disregard of system; irregularity **4.** an upset of normal function; ailment —*vt.* **1.** to throw into disorder; disarrange **2.** to upset the normal functions or health of —**dis·or′dered** *adj.*

**dis·or·der·ly** (-lē) *adj.* **1.** not orderly; untidy; unsystematic **2.** unruly; riotous **3.** *Law* violating public peace, safety, or order —**dis·or′der·li·ness** *n.*

**dis·or·gan·ize** (dis ôr′gə nīz′) *vt.* **-ized′, -iz′ing** to break up the order, arrangement, or system of; throw into disorder —**dis·or′gan·i·za′tion** *n.*

**dis·o·ri·ent** (-ôr′ē ent′) *vt.* **1.** to cause to lose one's bearings **2.** to confuse mentally Also **dis·o′ri·en·tate′** (-ən tāt′) **-tat′ed, -tat′ing** —**dis·o′ri·en·ta′tion** *n.*

**dis·own** (-ōn′) *vt.* to refuse to acknowledge as one's own; repudiate; cast off

**dis·par·age** (-par′ij) *vt.* **-aged, -ag·ing** [< OFr. *desparagi-er*, to marry one of inferior rank < *des-* (see DIS-) + *parage*, rank < *per*, PEER¹] **1.** to lower in esteem; discredit **2.** to speak slightingly of; belittle —**dis·par′age·ment** *n.* —**dis·par′ag·ing** *adj.* —**dis·par′ag·ing·ly** *adv.*

**dis·pa·rate** (dis′pər it) *adj.* [< L. pp. of *disparare* < *dis-*, apart, not + *parare*, to make equal < *par*, equal] distinct or different in kind; unequal —**dis′pa·rate·ly** *adv.* —**dis′-pa·rate·ness** *n.*

**dis·par·i·ty** (dis par′ə tē) *n., pl.* **-ties 1.** inequality or difference, as in quality **2.** incongruity

**dis·pas·sion·ate** (-pash′ən it) *adj.* free from passion, emotion, or bias; calm; impartial —**dis·pas′sion** *n.* —**dis·pas′sion·ate·ly** *adv.*

**dis·patch** (-pach′) *vt.* [< Sp. & It. < OFr. *despeechier*, ult. < L. *dis-*, not + LL. *impedicare*, to entangle < L. < *pes*, a foot] **1.** to send off or out promptly on a specific errand or official business; specif., to send out (trains, buses, etc.) according to a schedule **2.** to kill **3.** to finish quickly or promptly —*n.* **1.** a sending out or off **2.** a killing **3.** efficient speed; promptness **4.** a message, esp. an official message **5.** a news story sent to a newspaper, TV station, etc., as by a special reporter or news agency —**dis·patch′-er** *n.*

**dis·pel** (-pel′) *vt.* **-pelled′, -pel′ling** [< L. *dispellere* < *dis-*, away + *pellere*, to drive] to scatter and drive away; disperse

**dis·pen·sa·ble** (-pen′sə b'l) *adj.* **1.** that can be dispensed or dealt out **2.** that can be dispensed with —**dis·pen′sa·bil′i·ty** *n.*

**dis·pen·sa·ry** (-sə rē) *n., pl.* **-ries** a room or place, as in a school or factory, where medicines and first aid are available

**dis·pen·sa·tion** (dis′pən sā′shən, -pen-) *n.* **1.** a dispensing; distribution **2.** anything distributed **3.** an administrative system; management **4.** a release from an obligation **5.** *R.C.Ch.* an exemption from a specific church law **6.** *Theol. a)* the ordering of events under divine authority *b)* any religious system —**dis′pen·sa′tion·al** *adj.*

**dis·pen·sa·to·ry** (dis pen′sə tôr′ē) *n., pl.* **-ries** a handbook on medicines; pharmacopeia

**dis·pense** (-pens′) *vt.* **-pensed′, -pens′ing** [< OFr. < L. *dispensare* < pp. of *dispendere* < *dis-*, out + *pendere*, to weigh] **1.** to give or deal out; distribute **2.** to prepare and give out (medicines, prescriptions, etc.) **3.** to administer [to *dispense* the law] **4.** to exempt; excuse —**dispense with 1.** to get rid of **2.** to do without

**dis·pen·ser** (-pen′sər) *n.* one that dispenses, as a container designed to dispense its contents in handy units or portions

**dis·perse** (-purs′) *vt.* **-persed′, -pers′ing** [< L. pp. of *dispergere* < *dis-*, out + *spargere*, to strew] **1.** to break up and scatter in all directions; distribute widely **2.** to dispel (mist, etc.) **3.** to break up (light) into its component colored rays —*vi.* to move in different directions —**dis·per′sal** *n.* —**dis·pers′er** *n.* —**dis·pers′i·ble** *adj.* —**dis·per′sive** (-pur′siv) *adj.*

**dis·per·sion** (dis pur′zhən, -shən) *n.* **1.** a dispersing or being dispersed **2.** the breaking up of light into component colored rays, as by a prism **3.** a colloidal system with its dispersed particles and the medium in which these are suspended

**dis·pir·it** (di spir′it) *vt.* to depress; deject —**dis·pir′it·ed** *adj.* —**dis·pir′it·ed·ly** *adv.*

**dis·place** (dis plās′) *vt.* **-placed′, -plac′ing 1.** to move from its usual or proper place **2.** to discharge **3.** to replace [a ship *displaces* a certain amount of water]

**displaced person** a person forced from his country, esp. in war, and left homeless elsewhere

**dis·place·ment** (-mənt) *n.* **1.** a displacing or being displaced **2.** *a)* the weight or volume of a fluid displaced by a floating object; specif., the weight of water displaced by a ship *b)* the volume displaced by a piston

**dis·play** (-plā′) *vt.* [< OFr. < L. *displicare* < *dis-*, apart + *plicare*, to fold] **1.** to unfold; spread out **2.** to put or spread out to be seen; exhibit **3.** to disclose; reveal —*n.* **1.** a displaying; exhibition **2.** anything displayed; exhibit **3.** showy exhibition; ostentation **4.** *a)* a manifestation [a *display* of courage] *b)* a mere show; sham [a *display* of pity] —*adj.* designating printing types used for headings, advertisements, etc. —**dis·play′er** *n.*

**dis·please** (-plēz′) *vt., vi.* **-pleased′, -pleas′ing** to fail to please; annoy; offend

**dis·pleas·ure** (-plezh′ər) *n.* **1.** the fact or feeling of being displeased; dissatisfaction, annoyance, etc. **2.** [Archaic] discomfort, trouble, etc.

**dis·port** (-pôrt′) *vi.* [< OFr. < *des-* (see DIS-) + *porter* < L. *portare*, to carry] to play; frolic —*vt.* to amuse or divert (oneself)

**dis·pos·a·ble** (-pō′zə b'l) *adj.* **1.** that can be discarded **2.** that can be disposed as one wishes

**dis·pos·al** (-pō′z'l) *n.* **1.** a disposing; specif., *a)* arrangement in a particular order *b)* a dealing with matters; settling of affairs *c)* a giving away; transfer *d)* a getting rid of **2.** the power to dispose **3.** *same as* DISPOSER (sense 2) —**at one's disposal** available to be used as one wishes

**dis·pose** (-pōz′) *vt.* **-posed′, -pos′ing** [< OFr. < L. pp. of *disponere:* see DIS- & POSITION] **1.** to place in a certain order; arrange **2.** to arrange (matters); settle (affairs) **3.** to make willing **4.** to make susceptible or liable —*vi.* to have the power to arrange or settle affairs —**dispose of 1.** to deal with; settle **2.** to give away or sell **3.** to throw away **4.** to eat or drink up

**dis·pos·er** (-pō′zər) *n.* **1.** one that disposes **2.** a device installed in a sink drain to grind up garbage that is then flushed away

**dis·po·si·tion** (dis′pə zish′ən) *n.* **1.** proper or orderly arrangement **2.** management or settlement of affairs **3.** a selling, giving away, etc. of something **4.** the power to dispose; control **5.** an inclination or tendency **6.** one's nature or temperament

**dis·pos·sess** (-pə zes′) *vt.* to deprive of the possession of land, a house, etc.; oust —**dis′pos·ses′sion** (-zesh′ən) *n.* —**dis′pos·ses′sor** *n.*

**dis·praise** (dis prāz′) *vt.* **-praised′, -prais′ing** to speak of with disapproval; disparage; censure —*n.* a dispraising; blame —**dis·prais′ing·ly** *adv.*

**dis·proof** (-proof′) *n.* **1.** a disproving; refutation **2.** evidence that disproves

**dis·pro·por·tion** (dis′prə pôr′shən) *n.* lack of proportion; lack of symmetry —*vt.* to cause to be disproportionate —**dis′pro·por′tion·al** *adj.* —**dis′pro·por′tion·al·ly** *adv.*

**dis·pro·por·tion·ate** (-it) *adj.* not proportionate; not in proportion —**dis′pro·por′tion·ate·ly** *adv.*

**dis·prove** (dis proov′) *vt.* **-proved′, -prov′ing** to prove to be false or in error —**dis·prov′a·ble** *adj.*

**dis·pu·ta·ble** (dis pyoot′ə b'l, dis′pyoot-) *adj.* that can be disputed; debatable —**dis·pu′ta·bil′i·ty** *n.* —**dis·pu′ta·bly** *adv.*

**dis·pu·tant** (dis pyoot′'nt, dis′pyoo tənt) *adj.* disputing —*n.* one who disputes, or debates

**dis·pu·ta·tion** (dis′pyoo tā′shən) *n.* **1.** a disputing; dispute **2.** a debatelike discussion

**dis·pu·ta·tious** (-shəs) *adj.* inclined to dispute; fond of arguing: also **dis·pu·ta·tive** (dis pyoot′ə tiv) —**dis′pu·ta′tious·ly** *adv.* —**dis′pu·ta′tious·ness** *n.*

**dis·pute** (dis pyoot′) *vi.* **-put′ed, -put′ing** [< OFr. < L. *disputare* < *dis-*, apart + *putare*, to think] **1.** to argue; debate **2.** to quarrel —*vt.* **1.** to argue or debate (a question) **2.** to question the truth of; doubt **3.** to oppose in any way; resist **4.** to fight for; contest —*n.* **1.** a disputing; argument; debate **2.** a quarrel —**beyond dispute 1.** not open to dispute; settled **2.** indisputably —**in dispute** not settled —**dis·put′er** *n.*

**dis·qual·i·fy** (-kwäl′ə fī′) *vt.* **-fied′, -fy′ing 1.** to make unfit or unqualified **2.** to make or declare ineligible, as to

participate further in a sport, for breaking rules —**dis·qual′i·fi·ca′tion** (-fi kā′shən) *n.*

**dis·qui·et** (-kwī′ət) *vt.* to make anxious or restless; disturb —*n.* restlessness; anxiety —**dis·qui′et·ing** *adj.* —**dis·qui′et·ing·ly** *adv.*

**dis·qui·e·tude** (-kwī′ə tood′, -tyood′) *n.* a disturbed or uneasy condition; restlessness; anxiety

**dis·qui·si·tion** (dis′kwə zish′ən) *n.* [< L. < pp. of *disquirere* < *dis-*, apart + *quaerere*, to seek] a formal discussion of some subject; treatise

**Dis·rae·li** (diz rā′lē), **Benjamin,** 1st Earl of Beaconsfield, 1804–81; Eng. prime minister

**dis·re·gard** (dis′ri gärd′) *vt.* **1.** to pay little or no attention to **2.** to treat without due respect; slight —*n.* **1.** lack of attention **2.** lack of due regard or respect —**dis′re·gard′ful** *adj.*

**dis·re·mem·ber** (-ri mem′bər) *vt.* [Dial. or Colloq.] to forget; be unable to remember

**dis·re·pair** (-ri per′) *n.* the condition of needing repairs; state of neglect; dilapidation

**dis·rep·u·ta·ble** (dis rep′yoo tə b'l) *adj.* **1.** not reputable; having or causing a bad reputation **2.** not fit to be seen; shabby, dirty, etc. —**dis·rep′u·ta·bly** *adv.*

**dis·re·pute** (dis′ri pyoot′) *n.* lack or loss of repute; bad reputation; disgrace; disfavor

**dis·re·spect** (-ri spekt′) *n.* lack of respect or esteem; discourtesy —*vt.* to have or show a lack of respect for —**dis′re·spect′ful** *adj.* —**dis′re·spect′ful·ly** *adv.* —**dis′re·spect′ful·ness** *n.*

**dis·robe** (dis rōb′) *vt., vi.* **-robed′, -rob′ing** to undress —**dis·rob′er** *n.*

**dis·rupt** (-rupt′) *vt., vi.* [< L. pp. of *disrumpere* < *dis-*, apart + *rumpere*, to break] **1.** to break apart; rend asunder **2.** to interrupt the orderly course of (a meeting, etc.) —**dis·rupt′er, dis·rup′tor** *n.* —**dis·rup′tion** *n.* —**dis·rup′tive** *adj.*

**dis·sat·is·fac·tion** (dis sat′is fak′shən) *n.* the condition of being dissatisfied; discontent

**dis·sat·is·fac·to·ry** (-tə rē) *adj.* not satisfactory

**dis·sat·is·fy** (dis sat′is fī′) *vt.* **-fied′, -fy′ing** to fail to satisfy; discontent; displease

**dis·sect** (di sekt′, dī-) *vt.* [< L. pp. of *dissecare* < *dis-*, apart + *secare*, to cut] **1.** to cut apart piece by piece; separate into parts, as a body for purposes of study **2.** to examine or analyze closely —**dis·sec′tion** *n.* —**dis·sec′tor** *n.*

**dis·sect·ed** (-id) *adj.* **1.** cut up into parts **2.** *Bot.* consisting of many lobes and segments, as some leaves **3.** *Geol.* cut by erosion into valleys and hills

**dis·sem·ble** (di sem′b'l) *vt.* **-bled, -bling** [< OFr. < *des-*, DIS- + *sembler* < L. *simulare*, SIMULATE] **1.** to conceal under a false appearance [to *dissemble* fear by smiling] **2.** to make a false show of; feign [to *dissemble* innocence] —*vi.* to conceal the truth, or one's true feelings, motives, etc., by pretense —**dis·sem′blance** *n.* —**dis·sem′bler** *n.*

**dis·sem·i·nate** (di sem′ə nāt′) *vt.* **-nat′ed, -nat′ing** [< L. pp. of *disseminare* < *dis-*, apart + *seminare*, to sow < *semen*, seed] to scatter far and wide; spread abroad; promulgate widely —**dis·sem′i·na′tion** *n.* —**dis·sem′i·na′tive** *adj.* —**dis·sem′i·na′tor** *n.*

**dis·sen·sion** (di sen′shən) *n.* a dissenting in opinion; disagreement or, esp., violent quarreling or wrangling

**dis·sent** (di sent′) *vi.* [< L. *dissentire* < *dis-*, apart + *sentire*, to feel] **1.** to differ in belief or opinion; disagree **2.** to reject the doctrines and forms of an established church —*n.* a dissenting; specif., *a)* a minority opinion in the decision of a law case *b)* religious nonconformity —**dis·sent′er** *n.* —**dis·sent′ing** *adj.*

**dis·sen·tient** (di sen′shənt) *adj.* dissenting, esp. from the majority opinion —*n.* one who dissents

**dis·ser·ta·tion** (dis′ər tā′shən) *n.* [< L. < pp. of *dissertare*, to discuss, freq. of *disserere* < *dis-*, apart + *serere*, to join] a formal and lengthy discourse or treatise; thesis

**dis·serv·ice** (dis sur′vis) *n.* harmful action; injury

**dis·sev·er** (di sev′ər) *vt.* **1.** to sever; separate **2.** to divide into parts —*vi.* to separate; disunite —**dis·sev′er·ance, dis·sev′er·ment** *n.*

**dis·si·dence** (dis′ə dəns) *n.* [< L. < prp. of *dissidere* < *dis-*, apart + *sidere*, to sit] disagreement; dissent —**dis′si·dent** *adj., n.* —**dis′si·dent·ly** *adv.*

**dis·sim·i·lar** (di sim′ə lər) *adj.* not similar or alike; different —**dis·sim′i·lar′i·ty** *n., pl.* **-ties** —**dis·sim′i·lar·ly** *adv.*

**dis·sim·i·la·tion** (di sim′ə lā′shən) *n.* **1.** a making or becoming dissimilar **2.** the replacement or disappearance of a phoneme when it recurs in the same word (Ex.: Eng. marble < OFr. ma*r*bre)

**dis·si·mil·i·tude** (dis′si mil′ə tood′, -tyood′) *n.* dissimilarity; difference

**dis·sim·u·late** (di sim′yə lāt′) *vt., vi.* **-lat′ed, -lat′ing** [< L. pp. of *dissimulare:* see DIS- & SIMULATE] to hide (one's feelings, motives, etc.) by pretense; dissemble —**dis·sim′u·la′tion** *n.* —**dis·sim′u·la′tor** *n.*

**dis·si·pate** (dis′ə pāt′) *vt.* **-pat′ed, -pat′ing** [< L. pp. of *dissipare < dis-*, apart + *supare*, to throw] **1.** to scatter; disperse **2.** to drive completely away; make disappear **3.** to waste or squander —*vi.* **1.** to be dispelled; vanish **2.** to indulge in pleasure to the point of harming oneself —**dis'si·pat'er, dis'si·pa'tor** *n.* —**dis'si·pa'tive** *adj.*

**dis·si·pat·ed** (-id) *adj.* **1.** scattered **2.** squandered or wasted **3.** dissolute; debauched

**dis·si·pa·tion** (dis'ə pā'shən) *n.* a dissipating or being dissipated; dispersion, squandering, dissoluteness, etc.

**dis·so·ci·ate** (di sō'shē āt', -sē-) *vt.* **-at'ed, -at'ing** [< L. pp. of *dissociare < dis-*, apart + *sociare*, to join < *socius*, companion] **1.** to break the ties between; sever association with; separate; disunite **2.** to cause to undergo dissociation —*vi.* **1.** to stop associating **2.** to undergo dissociation —**dissociate oneself from** to repudiate any connection with

**dis·so·ci·a·tion** (di sō'sē ā'shən, -shē-) *n.* **1.** a dissociating or being dissociated **2.** *Chem.* the breaking up of a compound into simpler components **3.** *Psychol.* a split in the individual consciousness in which a group of mental activities functions as a separate unit —**dis'so'ci·a'tive** *adj.*

**dis·sol·u·ble** (di säl'yoo b'l) *adj.* that can be dissolved —**dis·sol'u·bil'i·ty** *n.*

**dis·so·lute** (dis'ə loot') *adj.* [< L. pp. of *dissolvere:* see DISSOLVE] dissipated and immoral; debauched —**dis'so·lute'ly** *adv.* —**dis'so·lute'ness** *n.*

**dis·so·lu·tion** (dis'ə loo'shən) *n.* a dissolving or being dissolved; specif., *a)* a breaking up or into parts; disintegration *b)* the termination, as of a business or union *c)* death *d)* the dismissal of an assembly or adjournment of a meeting

**dis·solve** (di zälv', -zôlv') *vt., vi.* **-solved', -solv'ing** [< L. *dissolvere < dis-*, apart + *solvere*, to loosen: see SOLVE] **1.** to make or become liquid; melt **2.** to merge with a liquid; pass or make pass into solution **3.** to break up; decompose **4.** to end as by breaking up; terminate **5.** to disappear or make disappear **6.** *Motion Pictures & TV* to fade or be faded out by means of a lap dissolve —*n. Motion Pictures & TV same as* LAP DISSOLVE —**dissolved in tears** weeping —**dis·solv'a·ble** *adj.* —**dis·solv'er** *n.*

**dis·so·nance** (dis'ə nəns) *n.* [< LL. < L. prp. of *dissonare < dis-*, apart + *sonare*, to SOUND¹] **1.** an inharmonious combination of sounds; discord **2.** any lack of harmony or agreement; incongruity **3.** *Music* a chord that sounds harsh and incomplete

**dis·so·nant** (-nənt) *adj.* **1.** characterized by or constituting a dissonance **2.** opposing in opinion, temperament, etc.; incompatible —**dis'so·nant·ly** *adv.*

**dis·suade** (di swād') *vt.* **-suad'ed, -suad'ing** [L. *dissuadere < dis-*, away + *suadere*, to persuade] to turn (a person) aside (*from* a course, etc.) by persuasion or advice —**dis·suad'er** *n.* —**dis·sua'sion** *n.* —**dis·sua'sive** *adj.* —**dis·sua'sive·ly** *adv.*

**dis·syl·la·ble** (dis'sil'ə b'l) *n. same as* DISYLLABLE —**dis·syl·lab·ic** (dis'si lab'ik) *adj.*

**dist. 1.** distance **2.** distinguish **3.** district

**dis·taff** (dis'taf) *n.* [< OE. < *dis-*, flax + *stæf*, a staff] **1.** a staff on which flax, wool, etc. is wound for use in spinning **2.** woman's work or concerns **3.** woman, or women in general —*adj.* female, or designating the maternal side of a family

DISTAFF

**dis·tal** (dis't'l) *adj.* [DIST(ANT) + -AL] *Anat.* farthest from the center or the point of attachment or origin —**dis'tal·ly** *adv.*

**dis·tance** (dis'təns) *n.* [< OFr. < L. < prp. of *distare < dis-*, apart + *stare*, to stand] **1.** the fact or condition of being separated in space or time; remoteness **2.** a space between two points **3.** an interval between two points in time **4.** the length of a line between two points **5.** a remoteness in relationship or in behavior **6.** a remote point in space or time —*vt.* **-tanced, -tanc·ing** to leave behind; outdistance —**go the distance** to last through an activity —**keep at a distance** to treat aloofly —**keep one's distance** to be aloof

**dis·tant** (-tənt) *adj.* **1.** having a space between; separated **2.** widely separated; far apart in space or time **3.** away [ten miles *distant*] **4.** far apart in relationship [a *distant* cousin] **5.** cool in manner; aloof **6.** from or at a distance **7.** faraway or dreamy [a *distant* look] —**dis'tant·ly** *adv.*

**dis·taste** (dis tāst') *n.* dislike or aversion (*for*)

**dis·taste·ful** (-fəl) *adj.* **1.** unpleasant to taste **2.** causing distaste; unpleasant; disagreeable —**dis·taste'ful·ly** *adv.* —**dis·taste'ful·ness** *n.*

**dis·tem·per¹** (dis tem'pər) *vt.* [< OFr. < ML. *distemperare*, to disorder < L. *dis-*, apart + *temperare*, to mix in proportion] to upset the functions of; derange; disorder —*n.* **1.** a mental or physical disorder; disease **2.** an infectious virus disease of young dogs **3.** civil disorder

**dis·tem·per²** (dis tem'pər) *n.* [< OFr. < ML. < L. *dis-*, intens. + *temperare*: see prec.] [Chiefly Brit.] any of various water-based paints, as for walls, etc.

**dis·tend** (dis tend') *vt., vi.* [< L. *distendere < dis-*, apart + *tendere*, to stretch] **1.** to stretch out **2.** to expand; make or become swollen —**dis·ten'si·ble** *adj.* —**dis·ten'tion, dis·ten'sion** *n.*

**dis·tich** (dis'tik) *n.* [< L. < Gr. < *di-*, two + *stichos*, a row] two successive lines of verse regarded as a unit; couplet

**dis·till, dis·til** (dis til') *vi.* **-tilled', -till'ing** [< OFr. < L. *destillare < de-*, down + *stillare*, to drip < *stilla*, a drop] **1.** to fall in drops; drip **2.** to undergo distillation **3.** to be produced as the essence of something —*vt.* **1.** to let fall in drops **2.** to subject to distillation **3.** to remove, extract, etc. by distillation **4.** to purify, refine, or concentrate as by distillation

**dis·til·late** (dis'tə lāt', -t'l it) *n.* **1.** a liquid obtained by distilling **2.** the essence of anything

**dis·til·la·tion** (dis'tə lā'shən) *n.* **1.** a distilling **2.** the process of heating a mixture to separate the more volatile from the less volatile parts, and condensing the resulting vapor to produce a more nearly pure substance **3.** a distillate

**dis·till·er** (dis til'ər) *n.* **1.** a person or apparatus that distills **2.** a person, company, etc. in the business of distilling alcoholic liquors

**dis·till·er·y** (-til'ər ē) *n., pl.* **-er·ies** a place where distilling is carried on

**dis·tinct** (-tiŋkt') *adj.* [OFr. < L. pp. of *distinguere:* see DISTINGUISH] **1.** not alike; different **2.** separate; individual **3.** clearly marked off; plain **4.** well-defined; unmistakable —**dis·tinct'ly** *adv.* —**dis·tinct'ness** *n.*

**dis·tinc·tion** (-tiŋk'shən) *n.* **1.** the act of making or keeping distinct **2.** the condition of being different **3.** a quality, mark, or feature that differentiates **4.** fame; eminence **5.** the quality that makes one seem superior **6.** a mark or sign of honor

**dis·tinc·tive** (-tiŋk'tiv) *adj.* distinguishing from others; characteristic —**dis·tinc'tive·ly** *adv.* —**dis·tinc'tive·ness** *n.*

**dis·tin·gué** (dis taŋ gā') *adj.* [Fr.] having an air of distinction; distinguished: also, sometimes, **dis·tin·guée'** *fem.*

**dis·tin·guish** (dis tiŋ'gwish) *vt.* [< L. *distinguere < dis-*, apart + *-stinguere*, to prick, pierce] **1.** to perceive or show the difference in; differentiate **2.** to characterize **3.** to recognize plainly by any of the senses **4.** to separate and classify **5.** to make famous or eminent —*vi.* to make a distinction (*between* or *among*) —**dis·tin'guish·a·ble** *adj.* —**dis·tin'guish·a·bly** *adv.*

**dis·tin·guished** (-gwisht) *adj.* **1.** celebrated; famous **2.** having an air of distinction

**dis·tort** (dis tôrt') *vt.* [< L. pp. of *distorquere < dis-*, intens. + *torquere*, to twist] **1.** to twist out of the usual shape, form, or appearance **2.** to misrepresent; pervert **3.** to modify (a sound, etc.) so as to produce an unfaithful reproduction —**dis·tort'er** *n.* —**dis·tor'tion** *n.*

**distr. 1.** distributed **2.** distribution

**dis·tract** (dis trakt') *vt.* [< L. pp. of *distrahere < dis-*, apart + *trahere*, to draw] **1.** to draw (the mind, etc.) away in another direction; divert **2.** to create conflict and confusion in —**dis·tract'ed** *adj.* —**dis·tract'ed·ly** *adv.* —**dis·tract'i·ble** *adj.* —**dis·tract'ing** *adj.* —**dis·tract'ing·ly** *adv.*

**dis·trac·tion** (-trak'shən) *n.* **1.** a distracting or being distracted; confusion **2.** anything that distracts; specif., *a)* a cause of mental confusion *b)* anything that gives mental relaxation **3.** great mental distress —**dis·trac'tive** *adj.*

**dis·train** (dis trān') *vt., vi.* [< OFr. < ML. *distringere* < L. < *dis-*, apart + *stringere*, to stretch] *Law* to seize and hold (property) as security or indemnity for a debt —**dis·train'a·ble** *adj.* —**dis·train'er, dis·trai'nor** *n.* —**dis·traint'** *n.*

**dis·trait** (-trā') *adj.* [< OFr. < L. *distrahere:* see DISTRACT] absent-minded; inattentive

**dis·traught** (-trôt') *adj.* [var. of prec.] **1.** very troubled or confused **2.** driven mad; crazed

**dis·tress** (dis tres') *vt.* [< OFr. < ML. < L. pp. of *distringere:* see DISTRAIN] **1.** to cause sorrow, misery, or suffering to; pain; trouble **2.** to weaken with strain —*n.* **1.** the state of being distressed; pain, suffering, etc. **2.** anything that distresses; affliction **3.** a state of danger or trouble **4.** *Law a)* a distraint *b)* the property distrained —**dis·tress'ful** *adj.* —**dis·tress'ful·ly** *adv.* —**dis·tress'ing** *adj.* —**dis·tress'ing·ly** *adv.*

**dis·tressed** (-trest') *adj.* **1.** full of distress; troubled, etc. **2.** given an antique appearance, as by having the finish

---

fat, āpe, cär; ten, ēven; is, bīte; gō, hôrn, tōol, look; oil, out; up, fur; get; joy; yet; chin; she; thin, then; zh, leisure; ŋ, ring; ə for *a* in *ago*, *e* in *agent*, *i* in *sanity*, *o* in *comply*, *u* in *focus*; ' as in *able* (ā'b'l); Fr. bal; ë, Fr. coeur; ö, Fr. feu; Fr. mon; ô, Fr. coq; ü, Fr. duc; r, Fr. cri; H, G. ich; kh, G. doch; ‡foreign; *hypothetical; < derived from. See inside front cover.

marred *[distressed* walnut*]* **3.** designating an area in which there is much poverty, unemployment, etc. **4.** designating repossessed goods sold at low prices

**dis·trib·ute** (dis trib'yŏŏt) *vt.* **-ut·ed, -ut·ing** [< L. pp. of *distribuere* < *dis-*, apart + *tribuere*, to allot] **1.** to divide and give out in shares; allot **2.** to scatter or spread out, as over a surface **3.** to classify **4.** to put (things) in various distinct places —**dis·trib'ut·a·ble** *adj.*

**dis·tri·bu·tion** (dis'trə byōō'shən) *n.* **1.** a distributing or being distributed; specif., *a)* apportionment by law (*of* funds, etc.) *b)* the process by which commodities get to consumers *c)* frequency of occurrence or extent of existence **2.** anything distributed; portion; share **3.** *Statistics* the arrangement of a set of numbers classified according to some property, as frequency, or to some other criterion, as time or location —**dis'tri·bu'tion·al** *adj.*

**dis·trib·u·tive** (dis trib'yoo tiv) *adj.* **1.** distributing or tending to distribute **2.** relating to distribution **3.** *Gram.* referring to each member of a group regarded individually *["each"* is a *distributive* word] **4.** *Math.* of the principle in multiplication that allows the multiplier to be used separately with each term of the multiplicand —*n.* a distributive word —**dis·trib'u·tive·ly** *adv.*

**dis·trib·u·tor** (-tər) *n.* a person or thing that distributes; specif., *a)* an agent or business firm that distributes goods to consumers or dealers *b)* a device for distributing electric current to spark plugs —**dis·trib'u·tor·ship'** *n.*

**dis·trict** (dis'trikt) *n.* [Fr. < ML. < L. pp. of *distringere:* see DISTRAIN] **1.** a geographical or political division made for a specific purpose *[a* school *district]* **2.** any region; part of a country, city, etc. —*vt.* to divide into districts

**district attorney** a lawyer serving in a specified judicial district as a prosecutor for the State or Federal government in criminal cases

**district court 1.** the Federal trial court sitting in each district of the U.S. **2.** in some States, the court of general jurisdiction in each judicial district

**District of Columbia** [after Christopher COLUMBUS] Federal district of the U.S., on the Potomac: 69 sq. mi.; pop. 638,000; coextensive with the city of Washington: abbrev. **D.C., DC**

**dis·trust** (dis trust') *n.* a lack of trust or of confidence; doubt; suspicion —*vt.* to have no trust or confidence in; doubt; suspect

**dis·trust·ful** (-fəl) *adj.* distrusting; doubting —**distrustful of** suspicious of —**dis·trust'ful·ly** *adv.*

**dis·turb** (dis turb') *vt.* [< OFr. < L. *disturbare* < *dis-*, intens. + *turbare*, to disorder < *turba*, a mob] **1.** to break up the quiet or calm of; agitate **2.** to make uneasy or anxious **3.** to break up the settled order of **4.** to break in on; interrupt **5.** to inconvenience —**dis·turb'er** *n.*

**dis·turb·ance** (-əns) *n.* **1.** *a)* a disturbing or being disturbed *b)* any departure from normal **2.** anything that disturbs **3.** commotion; disorder

**di·sul·fide** (dī sul'fīd) *n.* a chemical compound of two sulfur atoms united with a single radical or with a single atom of an element

**dis·un·ion** (dis yōōn'yən) *n.* **1.** the ending of union; separation **2.** lack of unity; discord

**dis·u·nite** (dis'yoo nīt') *vt.* **-nit'ed, -nit'ing** to destroy the unity of; separate —*vi.* to become separated or divided —**dis·u'ni·ty** (-yōō'nə tē) *n.*

**dis·use** (dis yōōz'; *for n.* -yōōs') *vt.* **-used', -us'ing** to stop using —*n.* lack of use

**di·syl·la·ble** (dī sil'ə b'l, di-; dī'sil'-) *n.* [< Fr. < L. < Gr. < *di-*, two + *syllabē*, SYLLABLE] a word of two syllables —**di·syl·lab·ic** (dī'si lab'ik, di'-) *adj.*

**ditch** (dich) *n.* [OE. *dic*] a long, narrow channel dug into the earth, as a trough for drainage or irrigation —*vt.* **1.** to make a ditch in **2.** to cause (a car, etc.) to go into a ditch **3.** to set (a disabled aircraft) down on water and abandon it **4.** [Slang] to get rid of or get away from —*vi.* **1.** to dig a ditch **2.** to ditch a disabled plane

**dith·er** (dith'ər) *vi.* [prob. akin to ME. *daderen*, DODDER] to be nervously excited or confused —*n.* a nervously excited or confused condition

**dith·y·ramb** (dith'ə ram', -ramb') *n.* [< L. < Gr. *dithyrambos*] **1.** in ancient Greece, a wild choric hymn in honor of Dionysus **2.** any wildly emotional speech or writing —**dith'y·ram'bic** *adj., n.*

**dit·to** (dit'ō) *n., pl.* **-tos** [It. < L. *dictum*, a saying: see DICTUM] **1.** the same (as something stated above or before) **2.** a duplicate **3.** *same as* DITTO MARK —*adv.* as said before; likewise —*vt.* **-toed, -to·ing 1.** to duplicate **2.** to indicate repetition by ditto marks **3.** to repeat

**ditto mark** a mark (") used in lists or tables to show that the item above is to be repeated

**dit·ty** (dit'ē) *n., pl.* **-ties** [< OFr. < L. pp. of *dictare:* see DICTATE] a short, simple song

**ditty bag** (or **box**) [< ? obs. *dutty*, coarse calico, orig. Anglo-Ind.] a small bag (or box) used as by sailors for carrying sewing equipment, toilet articles, etc.

**di·u·ret·ic** (dī'yoo ret'ik) *adj.* [< LL. < Gr. < *dia-*, through + *ourein*, to urinate] increasing the secretion and flow of urine —*n.* a diuretic drug or other substance —**di'u·ret'i·cal·ly** *adv.*

**di·ur·nal** (dī ur'n'l) *adj.* [< L. < *diurnus* < *dies*, day] **1.** happening each day; daily **2.** of or in the daytime: opposed to NOCTURNAL —**di·ur'nal·ly** *adv.*

**div. 1.** dividend **2.** division **3.** divorced

**di·va** (dē'və) *n., pl.* **-vas;** It. **-ve** (-ve) [It. < L., goddess] a prima donna in grand opera

**di·va·gate** (dī'və gāt') *vi.* **-gat'ed, -gat'ing** [< LL. < L. *dis-*, from + *vagari*, to wander] **1.** to wander about **2.** to digress —**di'va·ga'tion** *n.*

**di·va·lent** (dī vā'lənt) *adj. Chem. same as* BIVALENT

**di·van** (dī'van, di van') *n.* [< Turk. *dīwān* < Per.] a large, low couch or sofa, usually without armrests or back

**dive** (dīv) *vi.* **dived** or **dove, dived, div'ing** [OE. *dyfan*] **1.** to plunge headfirst into water **2.** to go under water; submerge, as a submarine **3.** to plunge the hand or body suddenly into something *[to dive* into a foxhole*]* **4.** to bring oneself zestfully into something *[to dive* into one's work*]* **5.** to make a steep, sudden descent, as an airplane —*vt.* to cause to dive; specif., to send (one's airplane) into a dive —*n.* **1.** a plunge into water **2.** any sudden plunge **3.** a sharp descent, as of an airplane **4.** [Colloq.] a cheap, disreputable bar, nightclub, etc. —**take a dive** [Slang] to lose a prizefight purposely by pretending to get knocked out

**dive bomber** an airplane designed to release bombs while diving at a target —**dive'bomb'** *vt., vi.*

**div·er** (dīv'ər) *n.* one that dives; specif., *a)* one who works or explores under water *b)* any of several diving water birds, esp. the loon

**di·verge** (də vurj', dī-) *vi.* **-verged', -verg'ing** [ML. *divergere* < L. *dis-*, apart + *vergere*, to turn] **1.** to branch off or go in different directions from a common point or from each other **2.** to take on gradually a different form *[customs diverge]* **3.** to depart from a given viewpoint, practice; etc.; differ —*vt.* to make diverge

**di·ver·gence** (-vur'jəns) *n.* **1.** a diverging, or branching off **2.** a becoming different in form or kind **3.** departure from a particular viewpoint, practice, etc. **4.** difference of opinion; disagreement Also **di·ver'gen·cy,** *pl.* **-cies** —**di·ver'gent** *adj.* —**di·ver'gent·ly** *adv.*

**di·vers** (dī'vərz) *adj.* [OFr.: see ff.] several; various

**di·verse** (dī vurs', də-; dī'vurs) *adj.* [OFr. < L. pp. of *divertere* < *dis-*, apart + *vertere*, to turn] **1.** different; dissimilar **2.** varied —**di·verse'ly** *adv.* —**di·verse'ness** *n.*

**di·ver·si·fy** (də vur'sə fī') *vt.* **-fied', -fy'ing** [see prec. & -FY] **1.** to make diverse; give variety to; vary **2.** to divide up (investments, liabilities, etc.) among different companies, securities, etc. **3.** to expand (a business, etc.) by adding different products to the line, etc. —*vi.* to multiply business operations —**di·ver'si·fi·ca'tion** *n.*

**di·ver·sion** (də vur'zhən, dī-) *n.* **1.** a diverting, or turning aside **2.** distraction of attention **3.** a pastime

**di·ver·sion·ar·y** (-er'ē) *adj.* serving to divert or distract *[diversionary* military tactics*]*

**di·ver·si·ty** (də vur'sə tē, dī-) *n., pl.* **-ties 1.** a being diverse; difference **2.** variety

**di·vert** (-vurt') *vt.* [< OFr. < L. *divertere:* see DIVERSE] **1.** to turn aside (*from* a course, direction, etc.); deflect **2.** to amuse; entertain

**di·ver·tic·u·li·tis** (dī'vər tik'yoo līt'əs) *n.* [see -ITIS] inflammation of a diverticulum

**di·ver·tic·u·lum** (dī'vər tik'yoo ləm) *n., pl.* **-la** (-lə) [L. < *devertere* < *de-*, from + *vertere*, to turn] *Anat.* a normal or abnormal pouch or sac opening out from a tubular organ or main cavity

**di·vert·ing** (də vurt'iŋ, dī-) *adj.* that diverts; esp., amusing or entertaining —**di·vert'ing·ly** *adv.*

‡**di·ver·tisse·ment** (dē ver tēs män'; E. di vurt'is mənt) *n.* [Fr.] **1.** a diversion; amusement **2.** a short ballet, etc. as an entr'acte

**di·vest** (də vest', dī-) *vt.* [altered < earlier *devest*, ult. < L. *devestire* < *dis-*, from + *vestire*, to dress] **1.** to strip (*of* clothing, etc.) **2.** to deprive or dispossess (*of* rank, rights, etc.) **3.** to rid (*of* something) —**di·vest'i·ture** (-ə chər), **di·vest'ment, di·ves'ture** *n.*

**di·vide** (də vīd') *vt.* **-vid'ed, -vid'ing** [< L. *dividere*] **1.** to separate into parts; split up **2.** to separate into groups; classify **3.** to make or keep separate as by a partition **4.** to give out in shares; apportion **5.** to cause to disagree; alienate **6.** *Math.* to separate into equal parts by a divisor **7.** *Mech.* to mark off the divisions of; graduate —*vi.* **1.** to be or become separate; part **2.** to disagree **3.** to separate into groups in voting on a question **4.** to share **5.** *Math.* to do division —*n.* a ridge that divides two drainage areas; watershed —**di·vid'a·ble** *adj.*

**di·vid·ed** (-id) *adj.* **1.** *a)* separated into parts *b)* having a median strip separating traffic *[a divided* highway*] c)* having indentations reaching to the base or midrib, as some leaves **2.** disagreeing

**div·i·dend** (div′ə dend′) *n.* [< L.] **1.** the number or quantity to be divided **2.** *a)* a sum of money to be divided among stockholders, creditors, etc. *b)* a single share of this **3.** a bonus

**di·vid·er** (də vīd′ər) *n.* a person or thing that divides; specif., *a)* [pl.] an instrument for dividing lines, etc.; compasses *b)* a set of shelves, etc. used to separate a room into distinct areas

**div·i·na·tion** (div′ə nā′shən) *n.* [< L. < pp. of *divinare:* see ff.] **1.** the act or practice of trying to foretell the future or the unknown by occult means **2.** a prophecy; augury **3.** a successful guess —**di·vin·a·to·ry** (də vin′ə tôr′ē) *adj.*

**di·vine** (də vīn′) *adj.* [< OFr. < L. *divinus* < *divus,* a god] **1.** of or like God or a god **2.** given or inspired by God; holy; sacred **3.** devoted to God; religious **4.** supremely great, good, etc. **5.** [Colloq.] very pleasing, attractive, etc. —*n.* **1.** a clergyman **2.** a theologian —*vt.* **-vined′, -vin′ing 1.** to prophesy **2.** to guess; conjecture **3.** to find out by intuition —*vi.* **1.** to engage in divination **2.** to use a divining rod — **di·vine′ly** *adv.* —**di·vin′er** *n.*

**Divine Comedy** a long narrative poem in Italian, written (c. 1307–1321) by Dante Alighieri

**Divine Office** the prayers for the canonical hours

**divine right of kings** the God-given right of kings to rule, as formerly believed

**div·ing bell** (dīv′in) a large, hollow, air-filled apparatus in which divers can work under water

**diving board** a springboard projecting over a swimming pool, lake, etc., for use in diving

**diving suit** a heavy, waterproof garment worn by divers working under water: it has a detachable helmet into which air is pumped through a hose

**divining rod** a forked stick alleged to reveal hidden water or minerals by dipping downward

**di·vin·i·ty** (də vin′ə tē) *n., pl.* **-ties 1.** the quality or condition of being divine **2.** a god; deity **3.** the study of religion; theology —**the Divinity** God

**di·vis·i·ble** (də viz′ə b'l) *adj.* that can be divided, esp. without leaving a remainder —**di·vis′i·bil′i·ty** *n.*

**di·vi·sion** (də vizh′ən) *n.* **1.** a dividing or being divided **2.** a sharing or distribution **3.** a difference of opinion; disagreement **4.** a separation into groups in voting **5.** anything that divides; partition; boundary **6.** anything separated or distinguished from the larger unit of which it is a part; a section, group, rank, segment, etc. **7.** the process of finding how many times a number (the *divisor*) is contained in another (the *dividend*): the answer is the *quotient* **8.** *Mil.* a major tactical or administrative unit under one command; specif., an army unit larger than a regiment and smaller than a corps —**di·vi′sion·al** *adj.*

**division sign** (or **mark**) the symbol (÷), indicating that the preceding number is to be divided by the following number (Ex.: 8 ÷ 4 = 2)

**di·vi·sive** (də vī′siv, -vis′iv) *adj.* causing disagreement or dissension —**di·vi′sive·ly** *adv.* —**di·vi′sive·ness** *n.*

**di·vi·sor** (də vī′zər) *n.* [L.] the number or quantity by which the dividend is divided to produce the quotient

**di·vorce** (də vôrs′) *n.* [OFr. < L. *divortium* < *divertere:* see DIVERSE] **1.** legal dissolution of a marriage **2.** any complete separation or disunion —*vt.* **-vorced′, -vorc′ing 1.** to dissolve legally a marriage between **2.** to separate from (one's spouse) by divorce **3.** to separate; disunite —*vi.* to get a divorce —**di·vorce′ment** *n.*

**di·vor·cé** (də vôr′sā′, -sē′; -vôr′sā, -sē) *n.* [Fr.] a divorced man

**di·vor·cée, di·vor·cee** (-vôr′sā′, -sē′; -vôr′sā, -sē) *n.* [Fr.] a divorced woman

**div·ot** (div′ət) *n.* [Scot. dial. < ?] *Golf* a lump of turf dislodged in making a stroke

**di·vulge** (də vulj′) *vt.* **-vulged′, -vulg′ing** [< L. *divulgare* < *dis-,* apart + *vulgare,* to make public < *vulgus,* the common people] to make known; disclose; reveal —**di·vul′gence** (-vul′jəns), **di·vulge′ment** *n.* —**di·vulg′er** *n.*

**div·vy** (div′ē) *vt., vi.* **-vied, -vy·ing** [< DIVIDE] [Slang] to share; divide (*up*) —*n.* [Slang] a division

**Dix·ie** (dik′sē) *n.* [< title of song (1859) by D.D. Emmett, ult. < proper name] the Southern States of the U.S., collectively

**Dix·ie·land** (-land′) *adj.* in, of, or like a style of jazz modified by white New Orleans musicians, with a fast, ragtime tempo —*n.* **1.** the South; Dixie: also **Dixie Land 2.** Dixieland jazz

**diz·en** (diz′'n, dī′z'n) *vt.* [MDu. *disen,* to put flax on a distaff < LowG. *diesse,* bunch of flax] [Archaic or Poet.] *same as* BEDIZEN

**diz·zy** (diz′ē) *adj.* **-zi·er, -zi·est** [OE. *dysig,* foolish] **1.** feel-ing giddy or unsteady **2.** causing or likely to cause giddiness [*dizzy* heights] **3.** confused; bewildered **4.** [Colloq.] silly —*vt.* **-zied, -zy·ing** to make dizzy —**diz′zi·ly** *adv.* — **diz′zi·ness** *n.*

**D.J., DJ** disc jockey

**Dji·bou·ti** (ji boot′ē) country in E Africa, on the Gulf of Aden: 8,500 sq. mi.; pop. 180,000

**dkg.** decagram; decagrams

**dkl.** decaliter; decaliters

**dkm.** decameter; decameters

**dl, dl.** deciliter; deciliters

**D layer** the lowest layer of the ionosphere

**DM, Dm** deutsche mark

**dm.** decimeter; decimeters

**DMZ** demilitarized zone

**DNA** deoxyribonucleic acid

**Dne·pr** (nē′pər; *Russ.* dnye′pər) river in W U.S.S.R., flowing south & southwest into the Black Sea

**Dne·pro·pe·trovsk** (dnye′prə pye trôfsk′) city in the Ukrainian S.S.R., on the Dnepr: pop. 837,000

**Dnes·tr** (nēs′tər; *Russ.* dnyes′tər) river in SW U.S.S.R., flowing southeast into the Black Sea

**do¹** (dōō) *vt.* **did, done, do′ing** [OE. *don*] **1.** *a)* to perform (an action, etc.) [*do* great deeds] *b)* to carry out **2.** to bring to completion; finish [dinner has been *done* for an hour] **3.** to bring about; cause [it *does* no harm] **4.** to exert (efforts, etc.) [*do* your best] **5.** to deal with as is required; attend to [*do* the ironing] **6.** to have as one's occupation; work at **7.** to work out; solve [*do* a problem] **8.** to produce (a play, etc.) [we *did* Hamlet] **9.** to play the role of [she *did* Juliet] **10.** to write (a book), compose (a musical score), etc. **11.** *a)* to cover (distance) [*do* a mile in four minutes] *b)* to move along at a speed of [to *do* 60 miles an hour] **12.** to give; render [*do* honor to the dead] **13.** to be convenient to; suit [this will *do* me very well] **14.** [Colloq.] to cheat; swindle [you've been *done*] **15.** [Colloq.] to serve (a jail term) **16.** [Slang] to take; ingest; use [to *do* drugs] —*vi.* **1.** to behave [he *does* well when praised] **2.** to be active; work [*do;* don't talk] **3.** to get along; fare [the patient is *doing* well] **4.** to be adequate or suitable [that necktie will *do*] **5.** to take place [anything *doing* tonight?] Auxiliary uses of *do:* **1.** to give emphasis [please *do* stay] **2.** to ask a question [*did* you write?] **3.** to help express negation [*do* not go] **4.** to serve as a substitute verb [love me as I *do* (love) you] **5.** to form inverted constructions after some adverbs [little *did* he realize] —*n., pl.* **do's** or **dos 1.** [Colloq.] a party or social event **2.** something to be done — **do by** to act toward or for —**do for** [Colloq.] to ruin; destroy —**do in** [Slang] to kill —**do over** [Colloq.] to redecorate —**do up** [Colloq.] **1.** to clean and prepare (laundry, etc.) **2.** to wrap up; tie up **3.** to arrange (the hair) off the neck and shoulders —**do without** to get along without —**have to do with 1.** to be related to **2.** to deal with —**make do** to get along with what is available

**do²** (dō) *n.* [It.: used instead of earlier *ut:* see GAMUT] *Music* a syllable representing the first or last tone of the diatonic scale

**do.** ditto

**D.O.** Doctor of Osteopathy

**do·a·ble** (dōō′ə b'l) *adj.* that can be done

**dob·bin** (däb′in) *n.* [< *Dobbin,* nickname for ROBERT (sense 1)] a horse, esp. a plodding, patient one

**Do·ber·man pin·scher** (dō′bər mən pin′shər) [< G.] a breed of large dog, with smooth, dark hair and tan markings

**dob·son·fly** (däb′s'n flī′) *n., pl.* **-flies′** a large insect whose larvae live in water: some males develop huge mandibles

**doc** (däk) *n.* [Slang] doctor: often used as a general term of address like Mac, Bud, Jack, etc.

**doc.** document

**doc·ile** (däs′'l) *adj.* [Fr. < L. *docilis* < *docere,* to teach] **1.** [Now Rare] easy to teach **2.** easy to manage or discipline; tractable —**doc′ile·ly** *adv.* —**do·cil·i·ty** (dä sil′ə tē) *n.*

**dock¹** (däk) *n.* [< MDu. *docke,* channel < It. *doccia:* see DOUCHE] **1.** a large excavated basin with floodgates, for receiving ships between voyages **2.** *a)* a landing pier; wharf *b)* the water between two piers **3.** a platform at which trucks or freight cars are loaded and unloaded **4.** a building or area for servicing aircraft —*vt.* **1.** to pilot (a ship) to a dock **2.** to join (vehicles) together in outer space —*vi.* **1.** to come into a dock **2.** to join up with another vehicle in outer space

**dock²** (däk) *n.* [< Fl. *dok,* cage] the place where the accused stands or sits in court

**dock³** (däk) *n.* [OE. *docce*] a coarse weed of the buckwheat family, with large leaves

fat, āpe, cär, ten, ēven, is, bīte; gō, hôrn, tool, look; oil, out; up, fur; get; joy; yet; chin; she; thin, *then;* zh, leisure; ŋ, ring; ə for a in ago, e in agent, i in sanity, o in comply, u in focus; ' as in able (ā′b'l); Fr. bal; ë, Fr. coeur; ö, Fr. feu; Fr. mon; ô, Fr. coq; ü, Fr. duc; r, Fr. cri; H, G. ich; kh, G. doch; ‡foreign; *hypothetical; < derived from. See inside front cover.

**dock**⁴ (däk) *n.* [< OE. *-docca* or ON. *dockr*] **1.** the solid part of an animal's tail **2.** an animal's bobbed tail —*vt.* **1.** to cut off the end of (a tail); bob **2.** to bob the tail of **3.** to deduct from (wages, etc.) **4.** to deduct from the wages of **5.** to remove part of —**dock′er** *n.*

**dock·age**¹ (däk′ij) *n.* **1.** docking accommodations **2.** the fee for this **3.** the docking of ships

**dock·age**² (däk′ij) *n.* a docking, or cutting off

**dock·et** (däk′it) *n.* [earlier *doggette*, register] **1.** a summary, as of legal decisions **2.** a list of cases to be tried by a law court **3.** any list of things to be done; agenda **4.** a label listing the contents of a package, directions, etc. —*vt.* **1.** to enter in a docket **2.** to put a docket on; label

**dock·side** (däk′sīd′) *n.* the area alongside a dock

**dock·yard** (-yärd′) *n.* a place with docks, machinery, etc. for repairing or building ships

**doc·tor** (däk′tər) *n.* [< OFr. or < L. *doctor*, teacher < pp. of *docere*, to teach] **1.** orig., a teacher or learned man **2.** a person on whom a university or college has conferred any of several high degrees [*Doctor of Philosophy*] **3.** a physician or surgeon (M.D.) **4.** a person licensed to practice any of the healing arts, as an osteopath, dentist, veterinarian, etc. **5.** a witch doctor or medicine man —*vt.* [Colloq.] **1.** to try to heal; apply medicine to **2.** to repair; mend **3.** to tamper with —*vi.* [Colloq.] **1.** to practice medicine **2.** to undergo medical treatment, take medicine, etc. —**doc′tor·al** (-əl) *adj.*

**doc·tor·ate** (-it) *n.* the degree or status of doctor conferred by a university or college

**doc·tri·naire** (däk′trə ner′) *n.* [Fr.] a person who dogmatically tries to apply theories regardless of the practical problems involved —*adj.* adhering to a doctrine or theory in an unyielding, dogmatic way —**doc′tri·nair′ism** *n.*

**doc·trine** (däk′trən) *n.* [< L. *doctrina* < *doctor*: see DOCTOR] **1.** something taught; teachings **2.** something taught as the principles of a religion, political party, etc.; tenet or tenets; dogma **3.** a principle of law **4.** a statement of basic policy [the Monroe *Doctrine*] —**doc′tri·nal** *adj.* —**doc′tri·nal·ly** *adv.*

**doc·u·ment** (däk′yə mənt; *for v.* -ment′) *n.* [OFr. < L. *documentum*, lesson, proof < *docere*, to teach] **1.** anything printed, written, etc., relied upon to record or prove something **2.** any proof —*vt.* **1.** to provide (a book, etc.) with documents or supporting references **2.** to prove or support by reference to documents —**doc′u·men′tal** *adj.*

**doc·u·men·ta·ry** (däk′yə men′tə rē) *adj.* **1.** of, in, supported by, or serving as a document or documents **2.** dramatically showing or analyzing news events, social conditions, etc., with little or no fictionalization —*n.*, *pl.* -ries a documentary film, television show, etc.

**doc·u·men·ta·tion** (-mən tā′shən, -men-) *n.* **1.** the supplying of documents or supporting references **2.** the documents or references supplied **3.** the collecting, abstracting, and coding of printed or written information for future reference

**dod·der** (däd′ər) *vi.* [ME. *daderen*] **1.** to shake or tremble, as from old age **2.** to totter —**dod′der·ing** *adj.*

**do·dec·a-** [< Gr. *dōdeka*, twelve] *a prefix meaning* twelve: also, before a vowel, **do·dec-**

**do·dec·a·gon** (dō dek′ə gän′) *n.* [< Gr.: see DODECA- & -GON] a plane figure with twelve angles and twelve sides

**do·dec·a·he·dron** (dō′dek ə hē′drən) *n.*, *pl.* -drons, -dra (-drə) [< Gr.: see DODECA- & -HEDRON] a solid figure with twelve plane faces —**do′dec·a·he′dral** *adj.*

**Do·dec·a·nese** (dō dek′ə nēz′, -nēs′) group of Greek islands in the Aegean

**dodge** (däj) *vi.* dodged, dodg′ing [? akin to Scot. *dod*, to jog] **1.** to move or twist quickly aside, as to avoid a blow **2.** to use tricks or evasions —*vt.* **1.** to avoid by moving quickly aside **2.** to evade by trickery, cleverness, etc. **3.** to avoid meeting —*n.* **1.** a dodging **2.** a trick used in evading or cheating —**dodg′y** *adj.* dodg′i·er, dodg′i·est

**dodg·er** (-ər) *n.* **1.** a person who dodges **2.** a tricky, dishonest person **3.** a small handbill

**do·do** (dō′dō) *n.*, *pl.* -dos, -does [Port. *doudo*, lit., foolish, stupid] **1.** a large bird, now extinct, that had rudimentary wings useless for flying: formerly found on Mauritius **2.** an old-fashioned person; fogy

**Doe** a name (*John Doe*) used in legal papers, etc. to refer to any person whose name is unknown

**doe** (dō) *n.*, *pl.* does, doe: see PLURAL, II, D, 1 [OE. *da*] the female of the deer, or of the antelope, rabbit, or almost any other animal the male of which is called a buck

**do·er** (dōō′ər) *n.* **1.** a person who does something **2.** a person who gets things done

**does** (duz) *3d pers. sing., pres. indic., of* DO¹

DODO
(2 ft. high)

**doe·skin** (dō′skin′) *n.* **1.** the skin of a female deer **2.** leather made from this or, now usually, from lambskin **3.** a fine, soft, smooth woolen cloth

**does·n't** (duz′'nt) does not

**do·est** (dōō′ist) *archaic 2d pers. sing., pres. indic., of* DO¹: *used with* thou

**do·eth** (-ith) *archaic 3d pers. sing., pres. indic., of* DO¹: *used with* thou

**doff** (däf, dôf) *vt.* [ME. *doffen* < *don of*: see DO¹ & OFF] **1.** to take off (clothes, etc.); esp., to remove or raise (one's hat) **2.** to put aside or discard

**dog** (dôg, däg) *n.*, *pl.* dogs, dog: see PLURAL, II, D, 1 [OE. *docga*] **1.** any of a large group of domesticated animals belonging to the same family as the fox, wolf, jackal, etc. **2.** the male of any of these **3.** a mean, contemptible fellow **4.** a prairie dog, dogfish, or other animal thought to resemble a dog **5.** an andiron **6.** [Colloq.] a boy or man [lucky *dog*] **7.** [*pl.*] [Slang] feet **8.** [Slang] *a)* an unattractive or unpopular person *b)* an unsatisfactory thing or unsuccessful venture **9.** [D-] *Astron.* either of the constellations Great Dog or Little Dog **10.** *Mech.* a device for holding or grappling —*vt.* dogged, dog′ging to follow or hunt like a dog —*adv.* very; completely [*dog*-tired] —a **dog's age** [Colloq.] a long time —**a dog's life** a wretched existence —**dog eat dog** ruthless competition —**dog in the manger** a person who keeps others from using something which he cannot or will not use —**go to the dogs** [Colloq.] to deteriorate; degenerate —**put on the dog** [Slang] to make a show of being very elegant, wealthy, etc.

**dog biscuit** a hard biscuit containing ground bones, meat, etc., for feeding dogs

**dog·cart** (-kärt′) *n.* **1.** a small, light cart drawn by dogs **2.** a small, light, open carriage having two seats arranged back to back

**dog·catch·er** (-kach′ər) *n.* a local official whose work is catching and impounding stray animals

**dog days** the hot, humid days in July and August

**doge** (dōj) *n.* [It. < L. *dux*, leader] the chief magistrate of either of the former republics of Venice and Genoa

**dog-ear** (dôg′ir′, däg′-) *n.* a turned-down corner of the leaf of a book —*vt.* to turn down the corner or corners of (a leaf in a book) —**dog′eared′** *adj.*

**dog-face** (-fās′) *n.* [Slang] an enlisted man in the army, esp. an infantryman

**dog·fight** (-fīt′) *n.* a rough, violent fight, as between dogs; specif., *Mil.* combat as between fighter planes at close quarters

**dog·fish** (-fish′) *n.*, *pl.* -fish′, -fish′es: see FISH **1.** any of various small sharks **2.** any of several other fishes, as the bowfin

**dog·ged** (dôg′id, däg′-) *adj.* [see DOG] not giving in readily; persistent; stubborn —**dog′ged·ly** *adv.* —**dog′ged·ness** *n.*

**dog·ger·el** (-ər əl) *n.* [prob. < It. *doga*, barrel stave] trivial, poorly constructed verse, usually of a comic sort; jingle —*adj.* designating or of such verse Also **dog′grel** (-rəl)

**dog·gie bag** (dôg′ē, däg′-) a bag supplied to a patron of a restaurant, in which he may place leftovers as to take to his dog

**dog·gish** (-ish) *adj.* of or like a dog —**dog′gish·ly** *adv.* —**dog′gish·ness** *n.*

**dog·gone** (dôg′gôn′, däg′gän′) *interj.* damn! darn! —*vt.* -goned′, -gon′ing [Colloq.] to damn —*n.* [Colloq.] a damn —*adj.* [Colloq.] damned: also **dog′goned′**

**dog·gy, dog·gie** (-ē) *n.*, *pl.* -gies a little dog: a child's word —*adj.* -gi·er, -gi·est **1.** of or like a dog **2.** [Colloq.] stylish and showy

**dog·house** (-hous′) *n.* a dog's shelter; kennel —**in the doghouse** [Slang] in disfavor

**do·gie, do·gy** (dō′gē) *n.* [< ?] in the western U.S., a stray or motherless calf

**dog·leg** (dôg′leg′, däg′-) *n.* a sharp angle or bend like that formed by a dog's hind leg, as in a golf fairway

**dog·ma** (dôg′mə, däg′-) *n.*, *pl.* -mas, -ma·ta (-mə tə) [L. < Gr. < *dokein*, to think] **1.** a doctrine; tenet; belief **2.** doctrines, tenets, or beliefs, collectively **3.** a positive, arrogant assertion of opinion **4.** *Theol.* a doctrine or body of doctrines formally and authoritatively affirmed

**dog·mat·ic** (dôg mat′ik, däg-) *adj.* **1.** of or like dogma **2.** asserted without proof **3.** stating opinion in a positive or arrogant manner: also **dog·mat′i·cal** —**dog·mat′i·cal·ly** *adv.*

**dog·ma·tism** (dôg′mə tiz′m, däg′-) *n.* dogmatic assertion of opinion, usually without reference to evidence —**dog′ma·tist** *n.*

**dog·ma·tize** (-tīz′) *vi.* -tized′, -tiz′ing to speak or write dogmatically —*vt.* to formulate or express as dogma —**dog′ma·tiz′er** *n.*

**dog·nap** (-nap′) *vt.* -napped′ or -naped′, -nap′ping or -nap′ing [DOG + (KID)NAP] to steal (a dog), esp. in order to sell it to a medical research laboratory —**dog′nap′per, dog′nap′er** *n.*

**do·good·er** (dōō′good′ər) *n.* [Colloq.] a person who seeks to correct social ills in an idealistic, but usually impractical way —**do′·good′, do′·good′ing** *adj.* —**do′·good′ism** *n.*

**dog rose** a European wild rose with single, pink flowers and hooked spines

**dog sled** (or **sledge**) a sled (or sledge) drawn by dogs

**Dog Star 1.** the brightest star in the constellation Canis Major; Sirius **2.** Procyon

**dog tag 1.** an identification tag or license tag for a dog **2.** [Slang] a military identification tag worn about the neck

**dog·tooth** (dôg′tōōth′, däg′-) *n., pl.* **-teeth** a canine tooth

**dogtooth violet 1.** a small American plant of the lily family, with a yellow or white flower **2.** a European plant with a purple or rose flower Also **dog's-tooth violet**

**dog·trot** (-trät′) *n.* a slow, easy trot

**dog·watch** (-wäch′, -wôch′) *n. Naut.* a duty period, either from 4 to 6 P.M. or from 6 to 8 P.M.

**dog·wood** (-wood′) *n.* **1.** a small tree of eastern U.S., with groups of small flowers surrounded by four large white or pink bracts **2.** its hard wood

**doi·ly** (doi′lē) *n., pl.* **-lies** [after name of a 17th-c. London draper] a small mat, as of lace or paper, used to protect or decorate a surface

**do·ings** (dōō′inz) *n.pl.* things done; actions, events, etc.

**do-it-your·self** (dōō′it yoor self′) *n.* the practice of constructing, repairing, redecorating, etc. by oneself instead of hiring another to do it —*adj.* of, used for, or engaged in do-it-yourself

**dol.** *pl.* **dols.** dollar

**dol·drums** (däl′drəmz, dōl′-) *n.pl.* [< ? ME. *dul*, DULL] **1.** low spirits; dull, listless feeling **2.** sluggishness; stagnation **3.** equatorial ocean regions noted for dead calms and light, fluctuating winds

**dole**[1] (dōl) *n.* [OE. *dal*] **1.** a giving out of money or food to those in need **2.** that which is thus given out **3.** anything given out sparingly **4.** a form of payment by a government to the unemployed —*vt.* **doled, dol′ing** to give sparingly or as a dole —**on the dole** receiving a dole (sense 4)

**dole**[2] (dōl) *n.* [see ff.] [Archaic] sorrow

**dole·ful** (dōl′fəl) *adj.* [< OFr. < VL. < L. *dolere*, to suffer + *-ful*, -FUL] full of sorrow or sadness; mournful —**dole′·ful·ly** *adv.* —**dole′ful·ness** *n.*

**dol·i·cho·ce·phal·ic** (däl′i kō′sə fal′ik) *adj.* [< Gr. *dolichos*, long + -CEPHALIC] having a relatively long head: also **dol′i·cho·ceph′a·lous** (-sef′ə ləs) : see CEPHALIC INDEX — **dol′i·cho·ceph′a·ly** (-ə lē) *n.*

**doll** (däl) *n.* [< *Doll*, nickname for DOROTHY] **1.** a child's toy made to resemble a human being **2.** a pretty but silly young woman **3.** a pretty child **4.** [Slang] *a)* any young woman *b)* any lovable person —*vt., vi.* [Colloq.] to dress stylishly or showily (with *up*)

**dol·lar** (däl′ər) *n.* [< LowG. & Early ModDu. < G. *thaler*, contr. < *Joachimsthaler*, coin made at *Joachimstal*, Bohemia] **1.** the monetary unit of the U.S., equal to 100 cents: symbol, $ **2.** the monetary unit of various other countries, as of Canada, Australia, Ethiopia, etc.: see MONETARY UNITS, table **3.** a monetary unit used only in trade, as the British Hong Kong dollar **4.** a coin or paper bill of the value of a dollar

**dollar diplomacy** the use of the economic power of a government to promote in other countries the business interests of its corporations, etc.

**dollar sign** (or **mark**) a symbol, $, for dollar(s)

**dol·lop** (däl′əp) *n.* [< ?] **1.** a soft mass, as of some food **2.** a splash, jigger, etc. of liquid **3.** a small amount

**dol·ly** (däl′ē) *n., pl.* **-lies 1.** a doll: child's word **2.** any of several kinds of low, flat, wheeled frames or platforms for moving heavy objects —*vi.* **-lied, -ly·ing** to move a camera on a dolly (*in, out,* etc.) as in televising —*vt.* to move on a dolly

**dol·man sleeve** (däl′mən, dōl′-) [< Fr. < Turk. *dolama*, long robe] a kind of sleeve for a woman's coat or dress, tapering from a wide opening at the armhole to a narrow one at the wrist

**dol·men** (däl′mən, dōl′-) *n.* [Fr. < Bret. *taol*, a table + *men*, stone] a prehistoric monument formed by a large, flat stone laid across upright stones

**do·lo·mite** (dō′lə mīt′, däl′ə-) *n.* [after the Fr. geologist *Dolomieu* (1750–1801)] a common rock-forming mineral, CaMg(CO₃)₂

**do·lor** (dō′lər) *n.* [< OFr. < L. *dolor* < *dolere*, to suffer] [Poet.] sorrow; grief

**Do·lor·es** (də lôr′əs) [Sp. < *María de los Dolores*, lit., Mary of the sorrows] a feminine name

**do·lor·ous** (dō′lər əs, däl′ər-) *adj.* **1.** sorrowful or sad; mournful **2.** painful —**do′lor·ous·ly** *adv.*

**dol·phin** (däl′fən, dôl′-) *n.* [< OFr. < L. < Gr. *delphis* (gen. *delphinos*)] **1.** any of several water-dwelling mammals, with numerous teeth and often a beaklike snout **2.** either of two swift marine game fishes that change to bright colors out of water

**dolt** (dōlt) *n.* [prob. < ME. pp. of *dullen*, to dull] a stupid, slow-witted person; blockhead —**dolt′ish** *adj.* —**dolt′ish·ly** *adv.* —**dolt′ish·ness** *n.*

**-dom** (dəm) [OE. *dom*, state] *a suffix meaning:* **1.** the rank, position, or dominion of [*kingdom*] **2.** fact or state of being [*martyrdom*] **3.** a total of all who are [*officialdom*]

BOTTLE-NOSED
DOLPHIN
(70–160 in. long)

**dom. 1.** domestic **2.** dominion

**do·main** (dō mān′, də-) *n.* [< MFr. < L. < *dominus*, a lord] **1.** territory under one government or ruler **2.** land belonging to one person; estate **3.** field of activity or influence

**dome** (dōm) *n.* [< Fr. < Pr. < LL. < Gr. *dōma*, housetop, house] **1.** a hemispherical roof or one formed by a series of rounded arches or vaults on a round or many-sided base **2.** any dome-shaped structure **3.** [Slang] the head —*vt.* **domed, dom′ing 1.** to cover as with a dome **2.** to form into a dome —*vi.* to swell out like a dome

**do·mes·tic** (də mes′tik) *adj.* [< OFr. < L. *domesticus* < *domus*, house] **1.** of the home or family [*domestic joys*] **2.** of one's own country or the country referred to **3.** made in the home country; native **4.** domesticated; tame: said of animals **5.** devoted to home and family life —*n.* a servant for the home, as a maid —**do·mes′ti·cal·ly** *adv.*

**do·mes·ti·cate** (də mes′tə kāt′) *vt.* **-cat′ed, -cat′ing 1.** to accustom to home life; make domestic **2.** *a)* to tame (wild animals) *b)* to adapt (wild plants) to home cultivation **3.** to naturalize (a custom, word, etc.) from another country —*vi.* to become domestic —**do·mes′ti·ca′tion** *n.*

**do·mes·tic·i·ty** (dō′mes tis′ə tē) *n., pl.* **-ties 1.** home life; family life **2.** devotion to home and family life **3.** [*pl.*] household affairs

**domestic science** *same as* HOME ECONOMICS

**dom·i·cile** (däm′ə sil′, -sil; dō′mə-) *n.* [OFr. < L. < *domus*, house] a customary dwelling place; home; residence —*vt.* **-ciled′, -cil′ing** to establish (oneself or another) in a domicile —**dom′i·cil′i·ar′y** (-sil′ē er′ē) *adj.*

**dom·i·nance** (däm′ə nəns) *n.* a dominating; being dominant; control; authority: also **dom′i·nan·cy**

**dom·i·nant** (-nənt) *adj.* **1.** dominating; ruling; prevailing **2.** *Genetics* designating or of that one of any pair of allelic characters which, when both are present in the germ plasm, dominates over the other and appears in the organism: opposed to RECESSIVE **3.** *Music* of or based upon the fifth note of a diatonic scale —*n. Music* the fifth note of a diatonic scale —**dom′i·nant·ly** *adv.*

**dom·i·nate** (-nāt′) *vt., vi.* **-nat′ed, -nat′ing** [< L. pp. of *dominari*, to rule < *dominus*, a master] **1.** to rule or control by superior power or influence **2.** to tower over; rise high above (the surroundings, etc.) —**dom′i·na′tion** *n.* —**dom′i·na′tive** (-nāt′iv) *adj.* —**dom′i·na′tor** *n.*

**dom·i·neer** (däm′ə nir′) *vt., vi.* [< Du. < Fr. < L.: see prec.] to rule (*over*) in a harsh or arrogant way; tyrannize

**dom·i·neer·ing** (-iŋ) *adj.* overbearing; tyrannical

**Dom·i·nic** (däm′ə nik) [L. *Dominicus*, lit., belonging to a lord < *dominus*, a master] **1.** a masculine name **2.** Saint, 1170–1221; Sp. priest; founder of the Dominican order

**Dom·i·ni·ca** (däm′ə nē′kə, də min′i kə) a country that is an island in the Windward group of the West Indies: 290 sq. mi.; pop. 80,000

**Do·min·i·can** (də min′i kən) *adj.* **1.** of Saint Dominic or of a mendicant order founded by him **2.** of the Dominican Republic —*n.* **1.** a friar or nun of one of the Dominican orders **2.** a native or inhabitant of the Dominican Republic

**Dominican Republic** country occupying the E part of Hispaniola, in the West Indies: 18,816 sq. mi.; pop. 4,012,000; cap. Santo Domingo

**dom·i·nie** (däm′ə nē) *n.* [< vocative case (*domine*) of L. *dominus*, a master] **1.** in Scotland, a schoolmaster **2.** [Colloq.] a clergyman

**do·min·ion** (də min′yən) *n.* [< ML. *dominio* < L. *dominus*, a lord] **1.** rule or power to rule; sovereignty **2.** a governed territory or country **3.** [D-] formerly, any of certain self-governing member nations of the British Commonwealth of Nations

**Dominion Day** in Canada, July 1, a legal holiday, the anni-

fat, āpe, cär, ten, ēven, is, bīte; gō, hôrn, tōōl, look; oil, out; up, fur; get; joy; yet; chin; she; thin, *then*; zh, leisure; ŋ, ring; ə for *a* in *ago*, *e* in *agent*, *i* in *sanity*, *o* in *comply*, *u* in *focus*; as in *able* (ā′b'l); Fr. bäl; ë, Fr. coeur; ö, Fr. feu; Fr. mon; ô, Fr. coq; ü, Fr. duc; r, Fr. cri; H, G. ich; kh, G. doch; ‡foreign; *hypothetical; < derived from. See inside front cover.

versary of the proclamation in 1867 of the establishment of the Dominion of Canada

**dom·i·no** (däm'ə nō') *n., pl.* **-noes'**, **-nos'** [Fr. & It. < dat. of L. *dominus,* a lord] **1.** a loose cloak with wide sleeves, hood, and mask, worn at masquerades **2.** a small mask for the eyes; half mask **3.** one dressed in such a cloak or mask **4.** a small, oblong piece of wood, etc. marked with dots **5.** [*pl., with sing. v.*] a game played with such pieces

**DOMINOES**

**domino theory** the theory that a certain result (**domino effect**) will follow a certain cause like a row of upright dominoes falling if only one is pushed; specif., the theory that if a nation becomes Communist, the nations nearby will also become Communist

**Don** (dän; *Russ.* dôn) river of the C European R.S.F.S.R., flowing south into the Sea of Azov

**don¹** (dän) *n.* [Sp. < L. *dominus,* master] **1.** [D-] Sir; Mr.: a Spanish title of respect **2.** a Spanish nobleman or gentleman **3.** a distinguished man **4.** [Colloq.] a head, tutor, or fellow of any college of Oxford or Cambridge

**don²** (dän) *vt.* **donned, don'ning** [contr. of *do on*] to put on (a garment, etc.)

**‡Do·ña** (dô′nyä) *n.* [Sp. < L. *domina,* mistress] **1.** Lady; Madam: a Spanish title of respect **2.** [d-] a Spanish lady

**Don·ald** (dän′ld) [Ir. *Donghal,* lit., brown stranger (or ? Gael. *Domhnall,* lit., world ruler)] a masculine name: dim. **Don**

**do·nate** (dō′nāt, dō nāt′) *vt., vi.* **-nat·ed, -nat·ing** [prob. back-formation < DONATION] to give or contribute, as to some cause —**do′na·tor** *n.*

**Do·na·tel·lo** (dän′ə tel′ō) (born *Donato di Niccolò di Betto Bardi*) 1386?-1466; It. sculptor

**do·na·tion** (dō nā′shən) *n.* [< L. < pp. of *donare* < *donum,* gift] **1.** the act of donating **2.** a gift or contribution

**done** (dun) *pp.* of DO¹ —*adj.* **1.** completed **2.** sufficiently cooked **3.** socially acceptable —**done (for)** [Colloq.] dead, ruined, finished, etc. —**done in** [Colloq.] exhausted

**do·nee** (dō nē′) *n.* one who receives a donation

**Do·nets** (də nets′; *Russ.* dô nyets′) river in SW European U.S.S.R., flowing into the Don

**Do·netsk** (dô nyetsk′) city in SE Ukrainian S.S.R., in the Donets River valley: pop. 855,000

**dong¹** (dôŋ, däŋ) *n.* [echoic] a sound of, or like that of, a large bell

**dong²** (däŋ) *n. see* MONETARY UNITS, table (Vietnam)

**Don·i·zet·ti** (dän′ə zet′ē), **Ga·e·ta·no** (gä e tä′nō) 1797-1848; It. composer of operas

**don·jon** (dun′jən, dän′-) *n.* [old sp. of DUNGEON] the heavily fortified inner tower of a castle

**Don Ju·an** (dän′ jōō′ən, dän′ wän′; *Sp.* dôn Hwän′) **1.** *Sp. Legend* a dissolute nobleman and seducer of women **2.** any man who seduces women; libertine

**don·key** (dän′kē, dôn′-, duŋ′-) *n., pl.* **-keys** [< ? DUNCAN or < ? DUN¹] **1.** a domesticated ass **2.** a stupid or stubborn person **3.** a small steam engine: in full, **donkey engine**

**Don·na** (dän′ə) [It. < L. *domina,* mistress] a feminine name —*n.* (*It.* dôn′nä) **1.** Lady; Madam: an Italian title of respect **2.** [d-] an Italian lady

**Donne** (dun), **John** 1573-1631; Eng. poet

**don·nish** (dän′ish) *adj.* of or like a university don —**don′nish·ly** *adv.* —**don′nish·ness** *n.*

**don·ny·brook** (dän′ē brook′) *n.* [< a fair formerly held at *Donnybrook,* Ireland: scene of many fights] [Colloq.] a rough, rowdy fight or free-for-all

**do·nor** (dō′nər) *n.* [< Anglo-Fr. < L. *donator*] **1.** one who donates; giver **2.** one from whom blood for transfusion, tissue for grafting, etc. is taken

**Don Qui·xo·te** (dän′ kē hōt′ē, dän kwik′sət; *Sp.* dôn′kē Hō′te) **1.** a satirical romance by Cervantes **2.** the chivalrous, unrealistic hero of this romance

**don't** (dōnt) **1.** do not **2.** does not: in this sense now generally considered substandard

**do·nut** (dō′nut′) *n. informal sp. for* DOUGHNUT

**doo·dad** (dōō′dad′) *n.* [fanciful extension of DO¹] [Colloq.] **1.** a trinket **2.** any small object or device whose name does not readily occur to one

**doo·dle** (dōōd′'l) *vi.* **-dled, -dling** [G. *dudeln,* to play (the bagpipe), hence to trifle] to scribble or draw aimlessly, esp. when the attention is elsewhere —*n.* a mark, design, etc. made in doodling —**doo′dler** *n.*

**doo·hick·ey** (dōō′hik′ē) *n.* [fanciful extension of DO¹] [Colloq.] any small object or device whose name is not known or temporarily forgotten

**doom** (dōōm) *n.* [OE. *dom*] **1.** a judgment; esp., a sentence of condemnation **2.** destiny; fate **3.** tragic fate; ruin or death —*vt.* **1.** to pass judgment on; condemn **2.** to destine to a tragic fate **3.** to ordain as a penalty

**dooms·day** (dōōmz′dā′) *n.* **1.** *same as* JUDGMENT DAY **2.** any day of judgment

**door** (dôr) *n.* [OE. *dor, duru*] **1.** a movable structure for opening or closing an entrance, as to a building, room, closet, etc.: most doors turn on hinges, slide in grooves, or revolve on an axis **2.** the room or building to which a particular door belongs /*two doors down the hall*/ **3.** *same as* DOORWAY —**lay at the door of** to blame (a person) for —**out of doors** outdoors —**show (someone) the door** to command (someone) to leave

**door·bell** (dôr′bel′) *n.* a bell rung by someone wishing to enter a building or room

**door·jamb** (-jam′) *n.* a vertical piece of wood, etc. forming the side of a doorway: also **door′post′** (-pōst′)

**door·keep·er** (-kēp′ər) *n.* a person guarding the entrance of a house, hotel, etc.; porter

**door·knob** (-näb′) *n.* a small knob or lever on a door, usually for releasing the latch

**door·man** (-man′, -mən) *n., pl.* **-men** (-men′, -mən) a man whose work is opening the door of a building for those who enter or leave, hailing taxicabs, etc.

**door·mat** (-mat′) *n.* a mat to wipe the shoes on before entering a house, room, etc.

**door·nail** (-nāl′) *n.* a large-headed nail used in studding some doors —**dead as a doornail** dead beyond a doubt

**door·plate** (-plāt′) *n.* a plate on an entrance door, bearing the number, a name, etc.

**door prize** a prize given by lottery to one or more of those attending some gathering

**door·sill** (-sil′) *n.* a length of wood, masonry, etc. placed beneath a door; threshold

**door·step** (-step′) *n.* a step that leads from an outer door to a path, lawn, etc.

**door·stop** (-stäp′) *n.* any device for controlling or stopping the closing of a door

**door-to-door** (-tə dôr′) *adj., adv.* from one home to the next, calling on each in turn

**door·way** (-wā′) *n.* **1.** an opening in a wall that can be closed by a door **2.** any means of access

**door·yard** (-yärd′) *n.* a yard onto which a door of a house opens

**doo·zy** (dōō′zē) *n., pl.* **-zies** [< ?] [Slang] anything outstanding of its kind

**dope** (dōp) *n.* [Du. *doop,* sauce < *doopen,* to dip] **1.** any thick liquid or paste used as a lubricant or absorbent **2.** a varnish or filler, as for protecting the cloth covering of airplane wings **3.** any additive, as a food preservative **4.** [Slang] any drug or narcotic, or such drugs collectively **5.** [Slang] a slow-witted or stupid person **6.** [Slang] information, esp. as used for predicting —*vt.* **doped, dop′ing 1.** to give dope to **2.** to drug or stupefy **3.** to introduce an adulterant or additive into —**dope out** [Colloq.] to figure out or work out —**dop′er** *n.*

**dope·ster** (dōp′stər) *n.* [Colloq.] an analyzer or predictor of trends in politics, sports, etc.

**dop·ey, dop·y** (dō′pē) *adj.* **dop′i·er, dop′i·est** [Slang] **1.** under the influence of a narcotic **2.** lethargic or stupid —**dop′i·ness** *n.*

**Dor·a** (dôr′ə) [dim. of DOROTHEA] a feminine name

**Do·ré** (dô rā′), **(Paul) Gus·tave** (güs tàv′) 1832?-83; Fr. artist

**Dor·ic** (dôr′ik, där′-) *adj.* [< L. < Gr. *Dorikos,* of *Dōris:* see ff. etym.] designating or of the simplest of the classic orders of architecture, distinguished by fluted, heavy columns with simple capitals: cf. CORINTHIAN, IONIC

**Dor·is** (-is) [L. < Gr. *Dōris,* an ancient region of Greece] a feminine name

**dorm** (dôrm) *n.* [Colloq.] *same as* DORMITORY

**dor·mant** (dôr′mənt) *adj.* [OFr. prp. of *dormir* < L. *dormire,* to sleep] **1.** sleeping **2.** as if asleep; quiet; still **3.** inactive, as some animals or plants in winter —**dor′man·cy** (-mən sē) *n.*

DORIC CAPITAL

**dor·mer** (dôr′mər) *n.* [< OFr. < L. *dormitorium:* see ff.] **1.** a window set upright in a sloping roof **2.** the roofed projection in which this window is set Also **dormer window**

**dor·mi·to·ry** (dôr′mə tôr′ē) *n., pl.* **-ries** [L. *dormitorium* < pp. of *dormire,* to sleep] **1.** a room with sleeping accommodations for a number of people **2.** a building with many rooms that provide sleeping and living accommodations for a number of people, as at a college

**dor·mouse** (dôr′mous′) *n., pl.* **-mice** (-mīs′) [ME. *dormous* ? altered by folk etym. (after *mous,* MOUSE) < OFr.

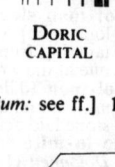

**DORMER**

*dormeuse,* sleepy < *dormir:* see DORMANT] a small, old-world rodent that resembles a squirrel

**Dor·o·the·a** (dôr′ə thē′ə, där′-) [L. < Gr. *Dōrothea,* lit., gift of God < *dōron,* gift + *theos,* God] a feminine name: dim. *Dolly, Dora, Dotty*

**Dor·o·thy** (dôr′ə thē, där′-) [var. of prec.] a feminine name

**dor·sal** (dôr′s'l) *adj.* [< ML. < L. < *dorsum,* the back] of, on, or near the back —**dor′sal·ly** *adv.*

**Dort·mund** (dôrt′moont; *E.* dôrt′mənd) city in W West Germany: pop. 648,000

**do·ry** (dôr′ē) *n., pl.* **-ries** [AmInd. (Central America) *dori,* a dugout] a small, flat-bottomed fishing boat with high sides

**dos·age** (dōs′ij) *n.* 1. a dosing or being dosed 2. the system to be followed in taking doses, as of medicine 3. the amount used in a dose

**dose** (dōs) *n.* [OFr. < ML. < Gr. *dosis,* orig., a giving < *didonai,* to give] 1. an amount of medicine to be taken at one time or at stated intervals 2. amount of a punishment or other unpleasant experience undergone at one time 3. the amount of ionizing radiation delivered to a specified area or body part —*vt.* **dosed, dos′ing** to give doses of medicine to —*vi.* to take a dose of medicine

**do·sim·e·ter** (dō sim′ə tər) *n.* [see DOSE & -METER] a device for measuring radiation a person has absorbed

**dos·si·er** (däs′ē ā′, dôs′-) *n.* [Fr. < *dos,* the back: so named because labeled on the back] a collection of documents about some person or matter

**dost** (dust) *archaic 2d pers. sing., pres. indic., of* DO¹: used *with* thou (chiefly as an auxiliary)

**Dos·to·ev·ski** (dôs′tô yef′skē), **Feo·dor** (Mikhailovich) (fyô′dôr) 1821–81; Russ. novelist

**dot¹** (dät) *n.* [OE. *dott,* head of boil] 1. a tiny spot, speck, or mark; point; as, *a)* the mark placed above an *i* or *j b) Music* a point after a note, increasing its time value by one half; also, a point above or below a note to show it is staccato 2. any small, round spot 3. a short sound or click in Morse code —*vt.* **dot′ted, dot′ting** 1. to mark with a dot or dots 2. to cover as with dots *[trees dotted the landscape]* —*vi.* to make a dot or dots —**dot one's i's and cross one's t's** to be minutely correct —**on the dot** [Colloq.] at the exact time —**dot′ter** *n.*

**dot²** (dät) *n.* [Fr. < L. *dos* (gen. *dotis*) < *dare,* to give] a woman's marriage dowry —**do·tal** (dōt′'l) *adj.*

**dot·age** (dōt′ij) *n.* [ME. < *doten,* DOTE] 1. feeble and childish state due to old age; senility 2. a doting; foolish or excessive affection

**dot·ard** (-ərd) *n.* [ME. < *doten,* DOTE] a foolish and doddering old person

**dote** (dōt) *vi.* **dot′ed, dot′ing** [ME. *doten*] 1. to be foolish or weak-minded, esp. because of old age 2. to be excessively or foolishly fond (with *on* or *upon*) —**dot′er** *n.* —**dot′ing** *adj.* —**dot′ing·ly** *adv.*

**doth** (duth) *archaic 3d pers. sing., pres. indic., of* DO¹ (chiefly in auxiliary uses)

**dot·ter·el** (dät′ər əl) *n., pl.* **-els, -el:** see PLURAL, II, D, 1 [< DOTE, because easy to catch] a European and Asian plover with a short bill

**dot·tle, dot·tel** (dät′'l) *n.* [< ME. var. of *dosel,* a plug] the tobacco plug left in the bowl of a pipe after it has been smoked

**dot·ty** (dät′ē) *adj.* **-ti·er, -ti·est** 1. covered with dots; dotted 2. [Colloq.] feeble; unsteady 3. [Colloq.] feeble-minded or crazy

**Dou·ay Bible** (dōō ā′) [< *Douai,* in France, where it was published in part (1609–10)] an English translation of the Bible from the Vulgate, for Roman Catholics: also **Douay Version**

**dou·ble** (dub′'l) *adj.* [OFr. < L. *duplus,* lit., twofold] 1. twofold; duplex 2. having two layers; folded in two 3. having two of one kind; repeated *[a double consonant]* 4. being of two kinds; dual *[a double standard]* 5. having two meanings; ambiguous 6. twice as much, as many, as large, etc. 7. of extra size, value, strength, etc. 8. made for two *[a double bed]* 9. two-faced; deceiving 10. having a tone an octave lower *[double bass]* 11. *Bot.* having more than one set of petals —*adv.* 1. twofold 2. two together; in pairs —*n.* 1. anything twice as much, as many, or as large as normal 2. a person or thing looking very much like another; duplicate; counterpart 3. a stand-in, as in motion pictures 4. a fold; second ply 5. a sharp shift of direction 6. a trick; shift 7. *[pl.]* a game of tennis, handball, etc. with two players on each side 8. *Baseball* a hit on which the batter reaches second base 9. *Bridge a)* the doubling of an opponent's bid *b)* a hand that makes this possible —*vt.* **-bled, -bling** 1. to make twice as much or many 2. to fold 3. to repeat or duplicate 4. to be the double of 5. *Baseball a)* to put out (the second runner) in executing a double

play *b)* to advance (a runner) by hitting a double 6. *Bridge* to increase the point value or penalty of (an opponent's bid) 7. *Naut.* to sail around *[they doubled Cape Horn]* —*vi.* 1. to become double 2. to turn sharply backward *[the animal doubled on its tracks]* 3. to serve as a double 4. to serve an additional purpose or function 5. [Colloq.] to double-date 6. *Baseball* to hit a double —**double back** 1. to fold back 2. to turn back in the direction from which one came —**double up** 1. to fold completely; clench (one's fist) 2. to bend over, as in laughter or pain 3. to share a room, etc. with someone —**on** (or **at**) **the double** [Colloq.] 1. in double time 2. quickly —**dou′bler** *n.*

**double agent** a spy who infiltrates an enemy espionage organization in order to betray it

**dou·ble-bar·reled** (-bar′əld) *adj.* 1. having two barrels, as a kind of shotgun 2. having a double purpose or meaning

**double bass** (bās) the largest and deepest-toned instrument of the violin family (orig. of the viol family), with a range of approximately three octaves

**double bassoon** *same as* CONTRABASSOON

**double boiler** a utensil consisting of two pans, one of which fits over the other: food is cooked in the upper one by water boiling in the lower

**dou·ble-breast·ed** (-bres′tid) *adj.* overlapping across the breast and having a double row of buttons, as a coat

**dou·ble-check** (-chek′) *vt., vi.* to check again; verify —*n.* the act of double-checking

**double chin** a fold of flesh beneath the chin

**dou·ble-cross** (-krôs′) *vt.* [Colloq.] to betray (a person) by doing the opposite of, or intentionally failing to do, what one has promised —**dou′ble-cross′er** *n.*

**double cross** [Colloq.] a double-crossing; treachery

**double dagger** a mark (‡) used in printing and writing to indicate a note or cross-reference

**dou·ble-date** (-dāt′) *vi., vt.* **-dat′ed, -dat′ing** [Colloq.] to go out on a double date (*with*)

**double date** [Colloq.] a social engagement shared by two couples

**dou·ble-deal·ing** (-dēl′iŋ) *n.* the act of doing the opposite of what one pretends to do; duplicity —**dou′ble-deal′er** *n.*

**dou·ble-deck·er** (-dek′ər) *n.* 1. any structure or vehicle with two levels 2. [Colloq.] a sandwich with two layers of filling

**dou·ble-dig·it** (-dij′it) *adj.* amounting to ten percent or more *[double-digit inflation]*

**dou·ble-edged** (-ejd′) *adj.* 1. having two cutting edges 2. applicable both ways, as an argument

**dou·ble-en·ten·dre** (dōō′blän tän′drə, dub′'l än-) *n.* [Fr. (now obs.), double meaning] a word or phrase with two meanings, esp. when one of them is risqué or indecorous

**double entry** a system of bookkeeping in which each transaction is entered as a debit and a credit

**double exposure** *Photog.* 1. the making of two exposures on one film or plate 2. a photograph resulting from this

**dou·ble-faced** (dub′'l fāst′) *adj.* 1. having two faces or aspects 2. hypocritical; insincere

**double feature** two full-length motion pictures on the same program

**dou·ble-head·er** (-hed′ər) *n.* two games played in succession on the same day

**double indemnity** a clause in some insurance policies providing for the payment of twice the face value of the contract for accidental death

**double jeopardy** *Law* the jeopardy in which a defendant is placed by a second prosecution for the same offense: prohibited by the U.S. Constitution

**dou·ble-joint·ed** (-join′tid) *adj.* having joints that permit limbs, fingers, etc. to bend at other than the usual angles

**dou·ble-knit** (-nit′) *adj.* knit with a double stitch, which gives extra thickness to the fabric

**dou·ble-park** (-pärk′) *vt., vi.* to park (a vehicle) parallel to another parked alongside a curb

**double play** *Baseball* a play in which two players are put out

**double pneumonia** pneumonia of both lungs

**dou·ble-quick** (-kwik′) *adj.* very quick —*n.* a very quick marching pace; specif., *same as* DOUBLE TIME (sense 2) —*vi., vt.* to march at such a pace —*adv.* at this pace

**dou·ble-reed** (-rēd′) *adj.* designating or of a group of woodwind instruments, as the oboe or bassoon, having two

DOUBLE BASS

reeds separated by a narrow opening —*n.* a double-reed instrument

**dou·ble-space** (-spās′) *vt., vi.* **-spaced′, -spac′ing** to type (copy) so as to leave a full space between lines

**double standard** a system, code, etc. applied unequally; specif., one that is stricter for women than for men, esp. in matters of sex

**dou·blet** (dub′lit) *n.* [OFr. dim. of *double*, orig., something folded] **1.** a man's short, closefitting jacket of the 14th to the 16th cent. **2.** either of a pair of similar things **3.** a pair; couple **4.** either of two words that derive ultimately from the same source but have changed in form (e.g., *card*, *chart*)

**double take** a delayed reaction to some remark, situation, etc., in which there is first unthinking acceptance and then startled surprise or a second glance as the real meaning strikes one

**double talk** **1.** ambiguous and deceptive talk **2.** deliberately confusing talk made up of a mixture of real words and meaningless syllables

**double time** **1.** a rate of payment twice as high as usual, as for overtime on Sundays **2.** a marching cadence of 180 three-foot steps a minute

**dou·ble·tree** (dub′'l trē′) *n.* [DOUBLE + (SINGLE)TREE] a crossbar on a wagon, plow, etc.

**dou·bloon** (du blōōn′) *n.* [< Fr. < Sp. < L. *duplus*, double] an obsolete Spanish gold coin

**dou·bly** (dub′lē) *adv.* **1.** twice **2.** two at a time

**doubt** (dout) *vi.* [< OFr. < L. *dubitare*] to be uncertain in opinion or belief; be undecided —*vt.* **1.** to be uncertain about; question **2.** to be inclined to disbelieve **3.** [Archaic] to be fearful of —*n.* **1.** *a)* a lack of conviction; uncertainty *b)* lack of trust **2.** a condition of uncertainty **3.** an unsettled point or matter; difficulty —**beyond** (or **without**) **doubt** certainly —**no doubt 1.** certainly **2.** probably —**doubt′a·ble** *adj.* —**doubt′er** *n.* —**doubt′ing·ly** *adv.*

**doubt·ful** (-fəl) *adj.* **1.** in doubt; not definite **2.** uncertain **3.** giving rise to doubt; questionable, as in reputation **4.** feeling doubt; unsettled —**doubt′ful·ly** *adv.* —**doubt′ful·ness** *n.*

**doubt·less** (-lis) *adj.* [Rare] free from doubt —*adv.* **1.** without doubt; certainly **2.** probably —**doubt′less·ly** *adv.* —**doubt′less·ness** *n.*

**douche** (dōōsh) *n.* [Fr. < It. *doccia*, shower, orig., conduit, ult. < L. *ductus*, pp. of *ducere*, to lead] **1.** a jet of liquid applied externally or internally to some part of the body **2.** a bath or treatment of this kind **3.** a device for douching —*vt., vi.* **douched, douch′ing** to apply a douche (to)

**dough** (dō) *n.* [OE. *dag*] **1.** a mixture of flour, liquid, and other ingredients, worked into a soft, thick mass for baking into bread, etc. **2.** any pasty mass like this **3.** [Slang] money

**dough·boy** (-boi′) *n.* [Colloq.] a U.S. infantryman, esp. of World War I

**dough·nut** (-nut′) *n.* a small, usually ring-shaped cake, fried in deep fat

**dough·ty** (dout′ē) *adj.* **-ti·er, -ti·est** [< OE. < *dugan*, to avail] valiant; brave: now used with a consciously archaic flavor —**dough′ti·ly** *adv.* —**dough′ti·ness** *n.*

**dough·y** (dō′ē) *adj.* **dough′i·er, dough′i·est** of or like dough; soft, pasty, etc. —**dough′i·ness** *n.*

**Doug·las** (dug′ləs) [< Gael., lit., black stream] **1.** a masculine name: dim. **Doug 2. Stephen A(rnold),** 1813–61; U.S. politician

**Douglas fir** (or **spruce, pine, hemlock**) [after David *Douglas,* 19th-c. Scot. botanist in U.S.] a tall evergreen tree of the pine family, found in W N. America and valued for its wood

**Doug·lass** (dug′ləs), **Frederick** 1817?–95; U.S. Negro leader, journalist, & statesman

**dour** (door, dōōr, dour) *adj.* [< L. *durus*, hard] **1.** [Scot.] stern; severe **2.** [Scot.] obstinate **3.** sullen; gloomy —**dour′ly** *adv.* —**dour′ness** *n.*

**douse¹** (dous) *vt.* **doused, dous′ing** [< ?] **1.** *Naut.* to lower (sails) quickly **2.** [Colloq.] to put out (a light or fire) quickly

**douse²** (dous) *vt.* **doused, dous′ing** [< ? prec.] **1.** to plunge or thrust suddenly into liquid **2.** to drench; pour liquid over —*vi.* to get immersed or drenched —*n.* an immersion or drenching

**douse³** (douz) *vi.* **doused, dous′ing** same as DOWSE²

**dove¹** (duv) *n.* [< ? ON. *dūfa*] **1.** a bird of the pigeon family, with a full-breasted body and short legs: a symbol of peace **2.** an advocate of the use of peaceful measures to solve international conflicts **3.** a person regarded as gentle or innocent —**dov′ish** *adj.*

**dove²** (dōv) *alt. pt. of* DIVE

**dove·cote** (duv′kōt′, -kät′) *n.* [DOVE¹ + COTE] a small house or box with compartments for nesting pigeons: also **dove′cot′** (-kät′)

**Do·ver** (dō′vər) **1.** seaport in SE England, on the Strait of Dover: pop. 36,000 **2.** capital of Del.: pop. 24,000 **3.**

**Strait** (or **Straits**) **of,** strait between France and England

**dove·tail** (duv′tāl′) *n.* **1.** a thing shaped like a dove's tail; specif., a projecting, wedge-shaped part that fits into a corresponding indentation to form a joint **2.** a joint thus formed —*vt.* **1.** to join together by means of dovetails **2.** to piece together (facts, etc.) —*vi.* to fit together closely or logically

**dow·a·ger** (dou′ə jər) *n.* [< OFr. < *douage*, dowry, ult. < L. *dos*: see DOT²] **1.** a widow with a title or property derived from her dead husband **2.** an elderly woman of wealth and dignity

**dow·dy** (dou′dē) *adj.* **-di·er, -di·est** [< ME. *doude*, unattractive woman] not neat or fashionable in dress; shabby —*n., pl.* **-dies** a dowdy woman —**dow′di·ly** *adv.* —**dow′di·ness** *n.* —**dow′dy·ish** *adj.*

DOVETAIL

**dow·el** (dou′əl) *n.* [ME. *doule*] a peg or pin of wood, metal, etc., usually fitted into corresponding holes in two pieces to fasten them together —*vt.* **-eled** or **-elled, -el·ing** or **-el·ling** to fasten with dowels

**dow·er** (dou′ər) *n.* [< OFr. < ML. *dotarium* < L. *dos*: see DOT²] **1.** that part of a man's property which his widow inherits for life **2.** a dowry **3.** a natural talent, or endowment —*vt.* **1.** to give a dower to **2.** to endow (*with*)

DOWEL

**dow·er·y** (-ē) *n., pl.* **-er·ies** same as DOWRY

**down¹** (doun) *adv.* [< OE. *adune*, from the hill < *a-*, off + *dune*, hill] **1.** from a higher to a lower place **2.** in or on a lower position or level **3.** *a)* in or to a place thought of as lower; often, specif., southward *b)* out of one's hands [put it *down*] **4.** below the horizon **5.** from an earlier to a later period or person **6.** into a low physical or emotional condition **7.** in an inferior position or condition **8.** to a lower amount or bulk **9.** into a tranquil or quiet state **10.** seriously; earnestly [get *down* to work] **11.** completely [loaded *down*] **12.** in cash or when bought [$5 *down*] **13.** in writing; on record [take *down* his name] —*adj.* **1.** directed toward a lower position **2.** in a lower place **3.** gone, brought, pulled, etc. down **4.** dejected; discouraged **5.** prostrate; ill **6.** completed [four *down*, six to go] **7.** in cash, as part of the purchase price [a *down* payment] **8.** *Sports a)* no longer in play: said of a football *b)* trailing an opponent by a specified number of points, strokes, etc. *c) Baseball* put out —*prep.* down toward, along, through, into, or upon —*vt.* **1.** *a)* to put, bring, get, throw, or knock down *b)* to defeat, as in a game **2.** to gulp or eat rapidly —*n.* **1.** a downward movement or depressed condition; *phr.* UPS AND DOWNS at UP **2.** *Football a)* one of four consecutive plays in which a team, in order to keep possession of the ball, must either score or advance the ball at least ten yards *b)* the declaring of the ball as down, or no longer in play —**down and out 1.** *Boxing* knocked out **2.** penniless, friendless, ill, etc. —**down on** [Colloq.] hostile to; angry or annoyed with —**down to the ground** thoroughly; completely —**down with!** do away with!

**down²** (doun) *n.* [< ON. *dūnn*] **1.** soft, fine feathers **2.** soft, fine hair or hairy growth

**down³** (doun) *n.* [OE. *dun*, a hill] **1.** an expanse of open, high, grassy land: *usually used in pl.* **2.** [confused with *dune*] [Archaic] a sandy mound formed by the wind

**down·beat** (-bēt′) *n. Music* a downward stroke made by a conductor to show the first beat of each measure

**down·cast** (-kast′) *adj.* **1.** directed downward **2.** very unhappy or discouraged; dejected

**Down East** [Colloq.] New England, esp. Maine: also **down east** —**down′-east′** *adj.* —**down′-east′er** *n.*

**down·er** (-ər) *n.* [Slang] **1.** any depressant or sedative, as a barbiturate, tranquilizer, etc. **2.** something depressing; esp., a depressing experience

**Dow·ney** (dou′nē) [after J. *Downey,* gov. of Calif., 1860–62] city in SW Calif.: suburb of Los Angeles: pop. 83,000

**down·fall** (doun′fôl′) *n.* **1.** *a)* a sudden fall, as from prosperity or power *b)* the cause of such a fall **2.** a sudden, heavy fall, as of snow

**down·grade** (-grād′) *n.* a downward slope, esp. in a road —*adv., adj.* downhill; downward —*vt.* **-grad′ed, -grad′ing** **1.** to demote to a less skilled job at lower pay **2.** to lower in importance, value, etc. **3.** to belittle —**on the downgrade** losing status, influence, health, etc.; declining

**down·heart·ed** (-här′tid) *adj.* discouraged; dejected —**down′heart′ed·ly** *adv.*

**down·hill** (-hil′) *adv.* **1.** toward the bottom of a hill **2.** to a poorer condition, status, etc. —*adj.* **1.** sloping or going downward **2.** of or relating to skiing downhill

**Down·ing Street** (doun′iŋ) [after Sir G. *Downing* (1623–

84), who owned property there] **1.** street in the West End of London, location of some important government offices **2.** the British government

**down·pour** (doun′pôr′) *n.* a heavy rain

**down·range** (-rānj′) *adv., adj.* along the course away from the launching site

**down·right** (-rīt′) *adv.* thoroughly; utterly —*adj.* **1.** absolute; thoroughgoing; utter **2.** straightforward; plain; frank

**down·spout** (-spout′) *n.* a vertical pipe for carrying rain water from a roof gutter to ground level

**Down's syndrome** (dounz) [after J.L.H. *Down* (1828–96), Eng. physician] a congenital disease in which there is mental deficiency and a characteristic broad face, with slanting eyes, etc.

**down·stairs** (doun′sterz′) *adv.* **1.** down the stairs **2.** on or to a lower floor —*adj.* situated on a lower floor —*n.* a lower floor or floors

**down·state** (-stāt′) *n.* that part of a State farther to the south —*adj., adv.* in, to, or from downstate

**down·stream** (-strēm′) *adv., adj.* in the direction of the current of a stream

**down·swing** (-swiŋ′) *n.* a downward trend, as in business: also **down′turn′** (-turn′)

**down-to-earth** (-tə urth′) *adj.* realistic or practical

**down·town** (-toun′) *adj., adv.* of, in, like, to, or toward the lower part or main business section of a city or town —*n.* the downtown section

**down·trod·den** (-träd′'n) *adj.* **1.** trampled on or down **2.** oppressed; tyrannized over

**down under** [Colloq.] Australia or New Zealand

**down·ward** (-wərd) *adv., adj.* **1.** toward a lower place, state, etc. **2.** from an earlier to a later time Also **down′wards** *adv.* —**down′ward·ly** *adv.*

**down·wind** (-wind′) *adv., adj.* in the direction in which the wind is blowing or usually blows

**down·y** (-ē) *adj.* **down′i·er, down′i·est 1.** of or covered with soft, fine feathers or hair **2.** soft and fluffy, like down —**down′i·ness** *n.*

**dow·ry** (dou′rē) *n., pl.* **-ries** [see DOWER] **1.** the property that a woman brings to her husband at marriage **2.** a natural talent, gift, etc.

**dowse**[1] (dous) *vt.* **dowsed, dows′ing** same as DOUSE[1]

**dowse**[2] (douz) *vi.* **dowsed, dows′ing** [< ? ME. *dushen,* to push down] to search for a source of water or minerals with a divining rod (**dowsing rod**) —**dows′er** *n.*

**dox·ol·o·gy** (däk säl′ə jē) *n., pl.* **-gies** [ML. *doxologia* < Gr. < *doxa,* praise + *-logia,* -LOGY] a hymn of praise to God; specif., *a)* the **greater doxology,** which begins "Glory to God in the highest" *b)* the **lesser doxology,** which begins "Glory to the Father" *c)* a hymn beginning "Praise God from whom all blessings flow"

**Doyle** (doil), Sir **Arthur Co·nan** (kō′nən) 1859–1930; Eng. writer of *Sherlock Holmes* stories

**doz.** dozen; dozens

**doze** (dōz) *vi.* **dozed, doz′ing** [prob. < Scand.] to sleep lightly or fitfully; be half asleep —*vt.* to spend (time) in dozing —*n.* a light sleep; nap —**doze off** to fall into a light sleep —**doz′er** *n.*

**doz·en** (duz′'n) *n., pl.* **-ens** or, esp. after a number, **-en** [< OFr. < *douze,* twelve < L. < *duo,* two + *decem,* ten] a set of twelve —**doz′enth** *adj.*

**doz·y** (dō′zē) *adj.* **doz′i·er, doz′i·est** sleepy; drowsy —**doz′i·ly** *adv.* —**doz′i·ness** *n.*

**DP, D.P.** displaced person

**dpt.** **1.** department **2.** deponent

**Dr. 1.** Doctor **2.** Drive

**dr. 1.** debit **2.** debtor **3.** drachma(s) **4.** dram(s)

**drab**[1] (drab) *n.* [< Fr. *drap,* cloth < VL. *drappus*] a dull yellowish brown —*adj.* **drab′ber, drab′best 1.** of a dull yellowish-brown color **2.** dull; monotonous —**drab′ly** *adv.* —**drab′ness** *n.*

**drab**[2] (drab) *n.* [< Celt. as in Ir. *drabog,* slattern] **1.** a slovenly woman **2.** a prostitute —*vi.* **drabbed, drab′bing** to fornicate with prostitutes

**drachm** (dram) *n. same as:* **1.** DRACHMA **2.** DRAM

**drach·ma** (drak′mə) *n., pl.* **-mas, -mae** (-mē), **-mai** (-mī) [L. < Gr. *drachmē,* lit., a handful < *drassesthai,* to grasp] **1.** an ancient Greek silver coin **2.** the monetary unit of modern Greece: see MONETARY UNITS, table

**draft** (draft) *n.* [ME. *draught,* a drawing < OE. *dragan,* DRAW] **1.** *a)* a drawing, as of a vehicle or load *b)* the thing, quantity, or load pulled **2.** *a)* a drawing in of a fish net *b)* the amount of fish caught in one draw **3.** *a)* a drinking *b)* the amount taken at one drink **4.** *a)* a drink; specif., a dose of medicine *b)* [Colloq.] a portion of beer, ale, etc. drawn from a cask **5.** *a)* a drawing into the lungs, as of air *b)* the amount of air, etc. drawn in **6.** a rough sketch of a writing **7.** a plan or drawing of a work to be

done **8.** a current of air, as in a room **9.** a device for regulating the current of air in a heating system **10.** a written order from one person, firm, etc., directing the payment of money to another; check **11.** a demand or drain made on something **12.** *a)* the taking of persons for a special purpose, esp. compulsory military service *b)* those so taken **13.** *Naut.* the depth of water that a ship displaces, esp. when loaded **14.** *Sports* a system of allotting to each team in a professional league exclusive rights to certain new players —*vt.* **1.** to take, as for compulsory military service, by drawing from a group **2.** to draw off or away **3.** to make a preliminary sketch of or working plans for —*adj.* **1.** used for pulling loads *[draft* animals*]* **2.** drawn from a cask on order *[draft* beer*]* **3.** in a preliminary or rough form —**on draft** ready to be drawn directly from the cask —**draft′a·ble** *adj.* —**draft′er** *n.*

**draft·ee** (draf tē′) *n.* a person drafted, esp. for service in the armed forces

**drafts·man** (drafts′mən) *n., pl.* **-men 1.** a person who draws plans of structures or machinery **2.** a person who draws up legal documents, speeches, etc. **3.** an artist skillful in drawing —**drafts′man·ship′** *n.*

**draft·y** (draf′tē) *adj.* **draft′i·er, draft′i·est** letting in, having, or exposed to a draft or drafts of air —**draft′i·ly** *adv.* —**draft′i·ness** *n.*

**drag** (drag) *vt.* **dragged, drag′ging** [< OE. *dragan* or ON. *draga:* see DRAW] **1.** to pull, draw, or move with effort, esp. along the ground; haul **2.** to force into some action, etc. **3.** to pull a grapnel, net, etc. over the bottom of (a river, etc.) in searching for something; dredge **4.** to draw a harrow over (land) **5.** to draw (something) out over a period of time —*vi.* **1.** to be dragged; trail **2.** to lag behind **3.** to move or pass too slowly **4.** to search a body of water with a grapnel, net, etc. **5.** [Slang] to draw (*on*) a cigarette, etc. **6.** [Slang] to participate in a drag race —*n.* **1.** something dragged along the ground; specif., *a)* a harrow *b)* a heavy sledge or sled **2.** a grapnel, dragnet, etc. **3.** anything that hinders **4.** a dragging **5.** [Slang] influence **6.** [Slang] a puff of a cigarette, etc. **7.** [Slang] street; road *[the main drag]* **8.** [Slang] a dull or boring person, situation, etc. **9.** [Slang] clothing of the opposite sex **10.** *Aeron.* a resisting force exerted on an aircraft, tending to retard its motion —**drag on** (or **out**) to prolong or be prolonged tediously —**drag one's feet** (or **heels**) [Slang] to be uncooperative —**drag′ger** *n.* —**drag′gy** *adj.* **-gi·er, -gi·est**

**drag·gle** (drag′'l) *vt., vi.* **-gled, -gling** [freq. of DRAG] to make or become wet or dirty by dragging in mud or water

**drag·net** (-net′) *n.* **1.** net dragged along the bottom of a river, lake, etc. for catching fish **2.** a net for catching small game **3.** an organized system or network for catching criminals, etc.

**drag·o·man** (drag′ə mən) *n., pl.* **-mans, -men** [< OFr. < It. < MGr. *dragomanos* < Ar. *tarǧumān*] in the Near East, an interpreter or guide

**drag·on** (drag′ən) *n.* [< OFr. < L. < Gr. *drakōn < derkesthai,* to see] **1.** a mythical monster, usually represented as a large reptile with wings and claws, breathing out fire and smoke **2.** a fierce person, esp. a strict chaperon

**drag·on·fly** (-flī′) *n., pl.* **-flies′** a large, harmless insect having narrow, transparent, net-veined wings: it feeds mostly on flies, etc.

**dra·goon** (drə goon′) *n.* [Fr. *dragon:* see DRAGON] a heavily armed cavalryman —*vt.* **1.** to harass or persecute by dragoons **2.** to force (*into* doing)

**drag race** a race between automobiles to test their rates of acceleration from a complete stop, specif. between hot-rod cars (**dragsters**) on a short, straight course (**drag strip**) —**drag′-race′** *vi.* **-raced′, -rac′ing**

**drain** (drān) *vt.* [< OE. *dreahnian* < base of *dryge,* DRY] **1.** to draw off (liquid) gradually **2.** to draw liquid from gradually *[to drain* a swamp*]* **3.** to receive the waters of **4.** to drink all the liquid from (a cup, etc.) **5.** to exhaust (strength, emotions, or resources) gradually —*vi.* **1.** to flow off gradually **2.** to become dry by the drawing or flowing off of liquid **3.** to disappear gradually **4.** to discharge its waters *[central Europe drains into the Danube]* —*n.* **1.** a channel, pipe, tube, etc. for carrying off water, sewage, pus, etc. **2.** a draining **3.** that which gradually exhausts strength, etc. —**down the drain** lost in a wasteful, heedless way —**drain′er** *n.*

**drain·age** (-ij) *n.* **1.** the act, process, or method of draining **2.** a system of pipes, etc. for carrying off waste matter **3.** that which is drained off **4.** an area drained, as by a river

**drainage basin** the land drained by a river system

**drain·pipe** (-pīp′) *n.* a large pipe used to carry off water, sewage, etc.

**drake** (drāk) *n.* [< WGmc. hyp. *drako*, male] a male duck
**Drake** (drāk), Sir **Francis** 1540?-96; Eng. admiral, navigator, & buccaneer
**dram** (dram) *n.* [< OFr. < ML. < L. *drachma*: see DRACHMA] **1.** *Apothecaries' Weight* a unit equal to 1/8 ounce **2.** *Avoirdupois Weight* a unit equal to 1/16 ounce **3.** *same as* FLUID DRAM **4.** a small drink of alcoholic liquor **5.** a small amount of anything
**dra·ma** (drä'mə, dram'ə) *n.* [LL. < Gr., a deed, drama < *dran*, to do] **1.** a literary composition that tells a story by means of dialogue and action, to be performed by actors; play **2.** the art or profession of writing, acting, or producing plays (often with *the*) **3.** plays collectively **4.** a series of events as interesting, vivid, etc. as a play **5.** the quality of being dramatic
**Dram·a·mine** (dram'ə mēn') *a trademark for* DIMENHYDRINATE —*n.* [d-] this substance
**dra·mat·ic** (drə mat'ik) *adj.* **1.** of or connected with drama **2.** *a)* like a play *b)* full of action; vivid, striking, exciting, etc. —**dra·mat'i·cal·ly** *adv.*
**dra·mat·ics** (-iks) *n.pl.* **1.** [*usually with sing. v.*] the art of performing or producing plays **2.** plays presented by amateurs **3.** dramatic effect
**dram·a·tis per·so·nae** (dram'ə tis pər sō'nē) [ModL.] the characters in a play
**dram·a·tist** (dram'ə tist) *n.* a playwright
**dram·a·tize** (dram'ə tīz') *vt.* **-tized'**, **-tiz'ing** **1.** to make into a drama; adapt for performance on the stage, screen, etc. **2.** to regard or present in a dramatic manner —*vi.* **1.** to be capable of being dramatized **2.** to dramatize oneself —**dram'a·ti·za'tion** *n.* —**dram'a·tiz'er** *n.*
**dram·a·tur·gy** (-tur'jē) *n.* [< G. < Gr. *dramatourgia* < *drama*, DRAMA + *ergon*, work] the art of writing or producing plays —**dram'a·tur'gic, dram'a·tur'gi·cal** *adj.* —**dram'a·tur'gi·cal·ly** *adv.* —**dram'a·tur'gist, dram'a·turge'** *n.*
**drank** (draŋk) *pt. & often colloq. pp. of* DRINK
**drape** (drāp) *vt.* **draped**, **drap'ing** [< OFr. < *drap*, cloth: see DRAB¹] **1.** to cover, hang, or decorate as with cloth or clothes in loose folds **2.** to arrange (a garment, cloth, etc.) artistically in folds or hangings —*vi.* to hang or fall in folds —*n.* cloth hanging in loose folds; esp., a drapery: *usually used in pl.*
**drap·er** (drā'pər) *n.* [Brit.] a dealer in dry goods
**drap·er·y** (drā'pər ē) *n.*, *pl.* **-er·ies** **1.** *a)* hangings, etc. arranged in loose folds *b)* an artistic arrangement of such hangings **2.** [*pl.*] curtains of heavy material
**dras·tic** (dras'tik) *adj.* [Gr. *drastikos*, active < *dran*, to do] acting with force; having a violent effect; severe; harsh —**dras'ti·cal·ly** *adv.*
**draught** (draft) *n.*, *vt.*, *adj.* now chiefly Brit. sp. of DRAFT
**draughts** (drafts) *n.pl.* [Brit.] the game of checkers
**draughts·man** (-mən) *n.*, *pl.* **-men** Brit. sp. of DRAFTSMAN —**draughts'man·ship'** *n.*
**draught·y** (draf'tē) *adj.* **draught'i·er, draught'i·est** Brit. sp. of DRAFTY —**draught'i·ness** *n.*
**Dra·vid·i·an** (drə vid'ē ən) *n.* **1.** any of a group of intermixed races chiefly in S India and N Ceylon **2.** the family of non-Indo-European languages spoken by these races, including Tamil, Malayalam, etc. —*adj.* of the Dravidians or their languages: also **Dra·vid'ic**
**draw** (drô) *vt.* **drew, drawn, draw'ing** [< OE. *dragan*] **1.** to make move toward one or along with one; pull; drag **2.** to pull up, down, in, across, back, etc. **3.** to need (a specified depth of water) to float in: said of a ship **4.** to attract; charm **5.** to breathe in; inhale **6.** to bring forth; elicit *[his challenge drew no reply]* **7.** to bring on; provoke *[to draw enemy fire]* **8.** to pull out; extract (a cork, sword, etc.) **9.** *a)* to remove (liquid) by sucking, draining, etc. *b)* to bring up, as water from a well *c)* to cause (liquid) to flow *[to draw a bath, draw blood]* **10.** to disembowel **11.** *a)* to get from some source *[to draw a salary]* *b)* to get or pick at random **12.** to withdraw (money) held in an account **13.** to have accruing to it *[savings draw interest]* **14.** to write (a check or draft) **15.** to reach (a conclusion, etc.): deduce **16.** to bring (a game or contest) to a tie **17.** to stretch tautly or to full length **18.** to distort **19.** to flatten or shape (metal) by die stamping, hammering, etc. **20.** to make (metal) into wire by pulling it through holes **21.** to make (lines, pictures, etc.) as with a pencil, pen, brush, etc. **22.** to describe or formulate in words —*vi.* **1.** to draw something (in various senses of the *vt.*) **2.** to be drawn or have a drawing effect **3.** to come; move *[to draw near]* **4.** to shrink; contract **5.** to allow a draft, as of smoke, to move through **6.** to attract audiences —*n.* **1.** a drawing or being drawn (in various senses) **2.** the result of drawing **3.** a thing drawn **4.** the cards dealt as replacement in draw poker **5.** a tie; stalemate **6.** a thing that attracts interest, audiences, etc. **7.** the movable part of a drawbridge **8.** a gully or ravine that water drains into —**draw away** to move away or ahead —**draw on** (or **nigh**) to approach —**draw out**

**1.** to extend **2.** to take out; extract **3.** to get (a person) to talk —**draw up** **1.** to arrange in order **2.** to compose (a document) in proper form **3.** to stop
**draw·back** (-bak') *n.* anything that prevents or lessens full satisfaction; shortcoming
**draw·bridge** (-brij') *n.* a bridge that can be raised, lowered, or drawn aside
**draw·ee** (drô'ē') *n.* the party that the drawer directs, by a draft, etc., to pay money over to a third party (called *payee*)
**draw·er** (drô'ər; *for 4* drôr) *n.* **1.** a person or thing that draws **2.** one who draws an order for the payment of money **3.** a draftsman **4.** a sliding box in a table, chest, bureau, etc., that can be drawn out and then pushed back into place
**drawers** (drôrz) *n.pl. same as* UNDERPANTS
**draw·ing** (drô'iŋ) *n.* **1.** the act of one that draws; specif., the art of representing something by lines made on a surface with a pencil, pen, etc. **2.** a picture, design, etc. thus made **3.** a lottery
**drawing card** an entertainer, speaker, show, etc. that normally draws a large audience
**drawing room** [< earlier *withdrawing room*, to which guests withdrew after dinner] **1.** a room where guests are received or entertained; parlor **2.** a private compartment on a railroad sleeping car
**draw·knife** (drô'nīf') *n.*, *pl.* **-knives'** (-nīvz') a knife with a handle at each end; the user draws it toward him in shaving a surface: also **drawing knife, draw'shave'** (-shāv')
**drawl** (drôl) *vt.*, *vi.* [prob. freq. of DRAW] to speak slowly, prolonging the vowels —*n.* a slow manner of speech in which vowels are prolonged —**drawl'er** *n.* —**drawl'ing·ly** *adv.*
**drawn** (drôn) *pp. of* DRAW —*adj.* **1.** pulled out of the sheath **2.** even; tied **3.** eviscerated **4.** tense; haggard
**drawn butter** melted butter, sometimes thickened and seasoned, used as a sauce
**drawn·work** (-wurk') *n.* ornamental work done on textiles by pulling out threads to produce a lacelike design
**draw poker** a form of poker in which each player is dealt five cards face down, and may be dealt replacements for unwanted cards (usually three or fewer)
**draw·string** (drô'striŋ') *n.* a string that tightens or closes an opening, as of a bag, when drawn
**dray** (drā) *n.* [< OE. *dræge*, something drawn < *dragan*, to draw] a low cart with detachable sides, for carrying heavy loads —*vt.* to carry on a dray —*vi.* to drive a dray
**dray·age** (-ij) *n.* **1.** the hauling of a load by dray **2.** the charge made for this
**dray·man** (-mən) *n.*, *pl.* **-men** the driver of a dray
**dread** (dred) *vt.* [OE. *drædan*] to anticipate with great fear, misgiving, or distaste —*n.* **1.** intense fear, esp. of something which may happen **2.** fear mixed with awe **3.** something dreaded —*adj.* **1.** dreaded or dreadful **2.** inspiring awe
**dread·ful** (-fəl) *adj.* **1.** inspiring dread; terrible or awesome **2.** [Colloq.] very bad, offensive, disagreeable, etc. —**dread'ful·ness** *n.*
**dread·ful·ly** (-fəl ē) *adv.* **1.** in a dreadful manner **2.** [Colloq.] very; extremely *[dreadfully tired]*
**dread·nought, dread·naught** (-nôt', -nät') *n.* a large, heavily armored battleship with big guns
**dream** (drēm) *n.* [form < OE. *dream*, joy, music; sense < ON. *draumr*, a dream] **1.** a sequence of sensations, images, thoughts, etc. passing through a sleeping person's mind **2.** a fanciful vision of the conscious mind; daydream; reverie **3.** the state in which such a daydream occurs **4.** a fond hope or aspiration **5.** anything so lovely, transitory, etc. as to seem dreamlike —*vi.* **dreamed** (drēmd, dremt) or **dreamt** (dremt), **dream'ing** **1.** to have dreams **2.** to have daydreams **3.** to think (*of*) as at all possible, etc. —*vt.* **1.** *a)* to have (a dream or dreams) *b)* to have a dream of **2.** to spend in dreaming (with *away* or *out*) **3.** to imagine as possible —*adj.* ideal *[her dream house]* —**dream up** [Colloq.] to conceive of or devise —**dream'er** *n.* —**dream'ful** *adj.* —**dream'less** *adj.* —**dream'like'** *adj.*
**dream·y** (drē'mē) *adj.* **dream'i·er, dream'i·est** **1.** filled with dreams **2.** visionary; impractical **3.** like something in a dream; misty, vague, etc. **4.** lulling; soothing *[dreamy music]* **5.** [Slang] delightful —**dream'i·ly** *adv.* —**dream'i·ness** *n.*
**drear** (drir) *adj.* [Poet.] dreary; melancholy
**drear·y** (-ē) *adj.* **drear'i·er, drear'i·est** [< OE. *dreorig*, sad, orig., bloody, gory] gloomy; cheerless; depressing; dismal; dull —**drear'i·ly** *adv.* —**drear'i·ness** *n.*
**dredge¹** (drej) *n.* [prob. < MDu. *dregge*] **1.** a net attached to a frame, dragged along the bottom of a river, bay, etc. to gather shellfish, etc. **2.** an apparatus for scooping or sucking up mud, sand, etc., as in deepening or clearing channels, harbors, etc. **3.** a barge or other boat with a dredge on it —*vt.* **dredged**, **dredg'ing** **1.** to gather (*up*) with or as with a dredge **2.** to enlarge or clean out (a river channel,

harbor, etc.) with a dredge —*vi.* **1.** to use a dredge **2.** to search as with a dredge —**dredg′er** *n.*

**dredge**² (drej) *vt.* **dredged, dredg′ing** [< ME. *dragge,* sweetmeat, ult. < Gr. *tragēma,* dessert] **1.** to coat (food) with flour or the like, as by sprinkling **2.** to sprinkle (flour, etc.) —**dredg′er** *n.*

**dregs** (dregz) *n.pl.* [< ON. *dregg*] **1.** the particles that settle at the bottom of a liquid; lees **2.** the most worthless part [*dregs of society*] —**dreg′gi·ness** *n.* —**dreg′gy** *adj.* **-gi·er, -gi·est**

**Drei·ser** (drī′sər, -zər), **Theodore (Herman Albert)** 1871–1945; U.S. novelist

**drench** (drench) *vt.* [< OE. *drencan,* caus. of *drincan,* to drink] **1.** to make (a horse, cow, etc.) swallow a medicinal liquid **2.** to make wet all over; soak or saturate —*n.* **1.** a large liquid dose, esp. for a sick animal **2.** a drenching; soaking **3.** a solution for soaking

**Dres·den** (drez′dən) city in SC East Germany, on the Elbe: pop. 500,000 —*n.* a fine porcelain or chinaware made near Dresden —*adj.* designating or of such porcelain or chinaware

**dress** (dres) *vt.* **dressed** or **drest, dress′ing** [< OFr. *drecier,* to arrange < L. *directus:* see DIRECT] **1.** to put clothes on; clothe **2.** to provide with clothing **3.** to decorate; trim; adorn **4.** to arrange a display in [to *dress* a store window] **5.** to arrange or do up (the hair) **6.** to arrange (troops, etc.) in straight lines **7.** to apply medicines and bandages to (a wound, etc.) **8.** to treat in preparing for use, grooming, etc.; esp., *a)* to clean and draw (a fowl, etc.) *b)* to cultivate (fields or plants) *c)* to smooth or finish (leather, stone, etc.) —*vi.* **1.** to put on or wear clothes **2.** to dress in formal clothes **3.** to get into a straight line —*n.* **1.** clothes; clothing; apparel **2.** the usual outer garment of women, generally of one piece with a skirt **3.** formal clothes **4.** external covering or appearance —*adj.* **1.** of or for dresses [*dress* material] **2.** worn on formal occasions [a *dress* suit] **3.** requiring formal clothes [a *dress* occasion] —**dress down** to scold severely; reprimand —**dress up** to dress in formal clothes, or in clothes more elegant, showy, etc. than usual

**dres·sage** (drə säzh′) *n.* [Fr., training] exhibition horsemanship in which the horse is controlled by very slight movements of the rider

**dress circle** a section of seats in a theater or concert hall, usually a mezzanine, where formal dress was orig. customary

**dress·er**¹ (dres′ər) *n.* **1.** a person who dresses people, as actors in their costumes, or things, as store windows, leather, wounds, etc. **2.** one who dresses elegantly or in a certain way [a fancy *dresser*]

**dress·er**² (dres′ər) *n.* [< OFr. *dreceur*] **1.** formerly, a table on which food was prepared for serving **2.** a kitchen cupboard **3.** a chest of drawers for clothes, usually with a mirror; bureau

**dress·ing** (-iŋ) *n.* **1.** the act of one that dresses **2.** that which is used to dress something (as manure applied to soil, bandages applied to a wound, etc.) **3.** a sauce for salads, etc. **4.** a stuffing, as of bread and seasoning, for fowl, etc.

**dress·ing-down** (-doun′) *n.* a sound scolding

**dressing gown** a loose robe for wear when one is undressed or lounging

**dressing room** a room for getting dressed in, esp. backstage in a theater

**dressing table** a low table with a mirror, for use while putting on cosmetics, grooming the hair, etc.

**dress·mak·er** (dres′māk·ər) *n.* one who makes women's dresses, suits, etc. to order —*adj.* designating a woman's suit, coat, etc. not cut on severe, mannish lines: cf. TAILORED —**dress′mak′ing** *n.*

**dress parade** a military parade in dress uniform

**dress rehearsal** a final rehearsal, as of a play, performed exactly as it is to take place

**dress suit** a man's formal suit for evening wear

**dress·y** (-ē) *adj.* **dress′i·er, dress′i·est** **1.** showy in dress or appearance **2.** stylish, elegant, etc. —**dress′i·ly** *adv.* —**dress′i·ness** *n.*

**drew** (droō) *pt.* of DRAW

**Drey·fus** (drā′fəs, drī′-; *Fr.* dre füs′), **Alfred** 1859–1935; Fr. army officer convicted of treason and imprisoned but later exonerated when proved to be the victim of anti-Semitism and conspiracy

**drib** (drib) *vi., vt.* **dribbed, drib′bing** [< DRIP] [Obs.] to fall, or let fall, in driblets —**dribs and drabs** small amounts

**drib·ble** (-'l) *vi., vt.* **-bled, -bling** [freq. of DRIB] **1.** to flow, or let flow, in drops or driblets; trickle **2.** to come forth or let out a little at a time **3.** to slaver; drool **4.** in certain games, to move (the ball or puck) along by rapid, repeated bounces, short kicks, or light taps —*n.* **1.** a small drop, or

a flowing in small drops **2.** a very small amount **3.** the act of dribbling a ball or puck **4.** a drizzling rain —**drib′bler** *n.*

**drib·let** (-lit) *n.* [dim. of prec.] a small amount

**dried** (drīd) *pt. & pp.* of DRY

**dri·er** (drī′ər) *n.* **1.** a substance added to paint, varnish, etc. to make it dry fast **2.** *same as* DRYER —*adj. compar. of* DRY

**dri·est** (-ist) *adj. superl.* of DRY

**drift** (drift) *n.* [< OE. *drifan,* to drive] **1.** a being driven or carried along, as by a current of air or water or by circumstances **2.** the course on which something is directed **3.** the deviation of a ship or aircraft from its course, caused by side currents or winds **4.** *a)* a slow ocean current *b)* a gradual shifting *c)* a random course, variation, etc. **5.** a tendency or trend **6.** general meaning; tenor **7.** *a)* something driven, as rain or snow before the wind *b)* a heap of snow, sand, etc. piled up by the wind, or floating matter washed ashore **8.** *Geol.* gravel, boulders, etc. moved and deposited by a glacier or water **9.** *Mining* a horizontal passageway, as along the path of a vein —*vi.* **1.** to be carried along as by a current **2.** to go along aimlessly **3.** to wander about from place to place, etc. **4.** to pile up in heaps by force of wind or water **5.** to move gradually away from a set position —*vt.* **1.** to cause to drift **2.** to cover with drifts —**drift′er** *n.*

**drift·age** (-ij) *n.* **1.** a drifting **2.** deviation caused by drifting **3.** that which has drifted

**drift·wood** (-wood′) *n.* wood drifting in the water, or that has been washed ashore

**drill**¹ (dril) *n.* [Du. *dril* < *drillen,* to bore] **1.** a tool or apparatus for boring holes in wood, metal, etc. **2.** a snail that bores into the shells of oysters and kills them **3.** military or physical training, esp. of a group, as in marching, the manual of arms, or gymnastic exercises **4.** the process of training or teaching by the repetition of an exercise **5.** a single exercise in drilling —*vt.* **1.** to bore (a hole) in (something) with or as with a drill **2.** to train in military or physical exercises **3.** to teach by having do repeated exercises **4.** to instill (ideas, etc. into) by repetition **5.** [Colloq.] to cause to move swiftly and directly [he *drilled* the ball past me] **6.** [Slang] to penetrate with bullets —*vi.* **1.** to bore a hole or holes **2.** to engage in military, physical, or mental exercises —**drill′er** *n.*

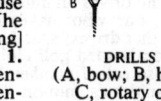

DRILLS
(A, bow; B, hand;
C, rotary oil)

**drill**² (dril) *n.* [< ? prec.] **1.** a furrow in which seeds are planted **2.** a row of planted seeds **3.** a machine for making holes or furrows, dropping seeds into them, and covering them —*vt.* **1.** to sow (seeds) in rows **2.** to plant (a field) in drills

**drill**³ (dril) *n.* [< earlier *drilling,* ult. < L. < *tri-,* TRI- + *licium,* a thread] a coarse linen or cotton twill, used for work clothes, linings, etc.

**drill**⁴ (dril) *n.* [< ? Fr. *drill,* a soldier] a bright-cheeked monkey native to W Africa

**drill·mas·ter** (-mas′tər) *n.* **1.** an instructor in military drill **2.** one who teaches by drilling

**drill press** a machine tool for drilling holes

**dri·ly** (drī′lē) *adv. same as* DRYLY

**drink** (driŋk) *vt.* **drank** or archaic **drunk, drunk** or now colloq. **drank** or archaic **drunk′en, drink′ing** [OE. *drincan*] **1.** to swallow (liquid) **2.** to absorb (liquid or moisture) **3.** to swallow the contents of **4.** to join in (a toast) **5.** to bring (oneself) into a specified condition by drinking **6.** to use (*up*) or spend by drinking alcoholic liquor —*vi.* **1.** to swallow liquid **2.** to absorb anything as if in drinking **3.** to drink alcoholic liquor, etc. to excess —*n.* **1.** any liquid for drinking; beverage **2.** alcoholic liquor **3.** habitual or excessive use of alcoholic liquor —**drink in** to take in eagerly with the senses or with the mind —**drink to** to drink a toast to —**the drink** [Colloq.] a body of water, esp. the ocean —**drink′a·ble** *adj.* —**drink′er** *n.*

**drinking fountain** a device for providing a jet or flow of drinking water, as in a public place

**drip** (drip) *vi.* **dripped** or **dript, drip′ping** [OE. *dryppan*] **1.** to fall in drops **2.** to let drops of liquid fall —*vt.* to let fall in drops —*n.* **1.** a falling in drops **2.** liquid falling in drops, or the sound made by this **3.** a projecting part of a sill, etc. that sheds rain water **4.** [Slang] a person regarded as dull, insipid, etc.

**drip-dry** (-drī′) *adj.* designating or of fabrics or garments that dry quickly when hung soaking wet and require little or no ironing —*vi.* -dried′, -dry′ing to launder as a drip-dry fabric does

**drip·pings** (drip′iŋz) *n.* the fat and juices that drip from roasting meat

**drip·py** (-ē) *adj.* -pi·er, -pi·est 1. characterized by dripping water, rain, etc. 2. [Slang] overly sentimental, stupid, etc.

**drive** (drīv) *vt.* drove, driv′en, driv′ing [OE. *drifan*] 1. to force to go; push forward 2. to force into or from a state or act *[he drove her mad]* 3. to force to work, usually to excess 4. *a)* to force as by a blow *b)* to hit or cast (a ball) hard and swiftly 5. to make penetrate 6. to produce by penetrating *[to drive a hole through metal]* 7. to control the movement of (a vehicle) 8. to transport in a vehicle 9. to cause to function 10. to push (a bargain, etc.) through —*vi.* 1. to advance violently; dash 2. to work or try hard 3. to drive a blow, ball, etc. 4. to be driven; operate: said of a motor vehicle 5. to be conveyed in a vehicle 6. to operate a motor vehicle —*n.* 1. a driving 2. a trip in a vehicle 3. *a)* a road for automobiles, etc. *b)* a driveway 4. *a)* a rounding up of animals as for branding *b)* the animals rounded up 5. a hard, swift blow, thrust, etc. 6. an organized movement to achieve some purpose; campaign 7. aggressive vigor; energy; push 8. that which is urgent, as a basic biological impulse 9. a collection of logs floating down a river 10. *a)* the propelling mechanism of a motor vehicle, machine, etc. *b)* that arrangement in an automatic transmission of a motor vehicle allowing forward speeds —**drive at** 1. to aim at 2. to mean; intend —**drive in** 1. to force in, as by a blow 2. *Baseball* to cause (a runner) to score or (a run) to be scored, as by getting a hit —**let drive** to hit or aim

**drive-in** (-in′) *adj.* designating or of a restaurant, movie theater, etc. that renders its services to persons who drive up and remain seated in their cars —*n.* such a restaurant, theater, etc.

**driv·el** (driv′l) *vi.* -eled or -elled, -el·ing or -el·ling [< OE. *dreflian*] 1. to let saliva flow from one's mouth; slobber 2. to speak in a silly or stupid manner —*vt.* to say in a silly, stupid, or nonsensical manner —*n.* silly, stupid talk; childish nonsense —**driv′el·er**, **driv′el·ler** *n.*

**driv·en** (driv′n) *pp.* of DRIVE —*adj.* moved along and piled up by the wind *[driven snow]*

**driv·er** (drī′vər) *n.* 1. a person who drives; specif., *a)* one who drives an automobile, etc. *b)* one who herds cattle *c)* one who makes his subordinates work hard 2. a thing that drives; specif., *a)* a mallet, hammer, etc. *b)* a wooden-headed golf club used in hitting the ball from the tee: also called **number 1 wood** *c)* any machine part that communicates motion —**the driver's seat** the position of control or dominance

**drive·way** (drīv′wā′) *n.* a path for cars, leading from a street to a garage, house, etc.

**driz·zle** (driz′l) *vi., vt.* -zled, -zling [prob. freq. of ME. hyp. *drisnen*, to fall as dew] to rain or let fall in fine, mistlike drops —*n.* a fine, mistlike rain —**driz′zly** *adj.*

**drogue** (drōg) *n.* [prob. < Scot. *drug*, DRAG] 1. *same as* SEA ANCHOR 2. a funnel-shaped device towed behind an aircraft for its drag effect (also **drogue parachute**), or as a target, etc.

**droll** (drōl) *adj.* [< Fr. < MDu. *drol*, short, stout fellow] amusing in an odd or wry way —**droll′ness** *n.* —**droll′ly** *adv.*

**droll·er·y** (-ər ē) *n., pl.* -er·ies 1. a droll act, remark, picture, story, etc. 2. the act of joking 3. quaint or wry humor

**-drome** (drōm) [< Gr. *dromos*, a running] *a suffix meaning* running, racecourse *[hippodrome]*

**drom·e·dar·y** (dräm′ə der′ē) *n., pl.* -dar·ies [< OFr. < LL. < L. < Gr. < *dramein*, to run] the one-humped camel, found from N Africa to India and trained for fast riding

**drone**[1] (drōn) *n.* [< OE. *dran*] 1. a male honeybee, having only a reproductive function and no sting 2. an idle parasite or loafer 3. a pilotless airplane directed by remote control —*vi.* **droned**, **dron′ing** to live in idleness; loaf

**drone**[2] (drōn) *vi.* **droned**, **dron′ing** [LME. *dronen* < prec.] 1. to make a continuous humming sound 2. to talk on and on in a monotonous way —*vt.* to utter in a dull, monotonous tone —*n.* 1. a continuous humming sound 2. *a)* a bagpipe *b)* any of the pipes of fixed tone in a bagpipe

**drool** (drōōl) *vi.* [< DRIVEL] 1. to let saliva flow from one's mouth; drivel 2. to flow from the mouth, as saliva 3. [Slang] to speak in a silly or stupid way 4. [Slang] to be overly enthusiastic, etc. —*vt.* to let drivel from the mouth —*n.* saliva running from the mouth

**droop** (drōōp) *vi.* [< ON. *drūpa*] 1. to sink, hang, or bend down 2. to lose vitality or strength 3. to become dejected —*vt.* to let sink or hang down —*n.* a drooping

**droop·y** (-ē) *adj.* **droop′i·er**, **droop′i·est** 1. tending to droop 2. [Colloq.] tired or dejected —**droop′i·ly** *adv.* —**droop′i·ness** *n.*

**drop** (dräp) *n.* [OE. *dropa*] 1. a small quantity of liquid that is somewhat spherical, as when falling 2. a very small quantity of liquid 3. *[pl.]* liquid medicine taken in drops 4. a very small quantity of anything 5. a thing like a drop in shape, size, etc. 6. a dropping; sudden fall, descent, slump, etc. 7. *same as* AIRDROP 8. anything that drops or is used for dropping, as a drop curtain, a trapdoor, a slot for depositing letters, etc. 9. the distance between a higher and lower level —*vi.* **dropped** or, occas., **dropt**, **drop′ping** 1. to fall in drops 2. to fall; come down 3. to fall exhausted, wounded, or dead 4. to pass into a specified state *[to drop off to sleep]* 5. to come to an end *[let the matter drop]* 6. to become lower or less, as prices, etc. 7. to move down with a current of water or air —*vt.* 1. to let or make fall; release hold of 2. to give birth to: said of animals 3. to utter (a hint, etc.) casually 4. to send (a letter) 5. to cause to fall, as by wounding, killing, etc. 6. *a)* to stop or have done with *b)* to dismiss 7. to lower or lessen 8. to make (the voice) less loud 9. *same as* AIRDROP 10. to omit (a letter or sound) in a word 11. [Colloq.] to leave (a person or thing) at a specified place 12. [Slang] to lose (money or a game) —**at the drop of a hat** immediately —**drop back** 1. to move back; retreat 2. to be outdistanced: also **drop behind** —**drop in** (or **over, by,** etc.) to pay a casual or unexpected visit —**drop off** 1. to decline; decrease 2. [Colloq.] to fall asleep —**drop out** to stop being a member or participant

**drop cookie** a cookie made from batter dropped onto a baking sheet as by teaspoonfuls

**drop curtain** a theater curtain that is lowered and raised rather than drawn

**drop-forge** (-fôrj′) *vt.* -forged′, -forg′ing to pound (heated metal) between dies with a drop hammer or a press —**drop′-forg′er** *n.*

**drop forging** a product made by drop-forging

**drop hammer** 1. a machine for pounding metal into shape, with a heavy weight that is raised and then dropped on the metal 2. this weight

**drop kick** *Football* a kick in which the ball is dropped to the ground and kicked just as it rebounds —**drop′-kick′** *vt., vi.* —**drop′-kick′er** *n.*

**drop·let** (-lit) *n.* a very small drop

**drop·out** (-out′) *n.* a person who withdraws from school, esp. high school, before graduating

**drop·per** (-ər) *n.* 1. a person or thing that drops 2. a small tube of glass, plastic, etc. with a hollow rubber bulb at one end, used to release a liquid in drops

**drop press** *same as* DROP HAMMER

**drop·sy** (dräp′sē) *n.* [< OFr. < L. < Gr. *hydrōps* < *hydōr*, water] *an earlier term for* EDEMA —**drop′si·cal** (-si k′l), **drop′sied** *adj.* —**drop′si·cal·ly** *adv.*

**dropt** (dräpt) *occas. pt. & pp.* of DROP

**drosh·ky** (dräsh′kē, drôsh′-) *n., pl.* -kies [Russ. *drozhki*] a low, open, four-wheeled Russian carriage: also **dros′ky** (dräs′-, drôs′-) *pl.* -kies

**dro·soph·i·la** (drə säf′ə lə, drō-) *n., pl.* -lae′ (-lē′) [ModL. < Gr. *drosos*, dew + fem. of *philos*, loving] a tiny fly used in laboratory experiments in heredity; fruit fly

**dross** (drôs, dräs) *n.* [OE. *dros*, dregs] 1. a scum formed on the surface of molten metal 2. waste matter; rubbish —**dross′i·ness** *n.* —**dross′y** *adj.* **dross′i·est**

**drought** (drout, drouth) *n.* [OE. *drugoth*, dryness < *drugian*, to dry up] 1. prolonged dry weather; lack of rain 2. a serious deficiency —**drought′y** *adj.* **drought′i·er**, **drought′i·est**

**drouth** (drouth, drout) *n. same as* DROUGHT

**drove**[1] (drōv) *n.* [OE. *draf* < *drifan*, DRIVE] 1. a number of cattle, sheep, etc. driven or moving as a group; flock; herd 2. a moving crowd of people

**drove**[2] (drōv) *pt.* of DRIVE

**drov·er** (drō′vər) *n.* a person who herds droves of animals, esp. to market

**drown** (droun) *vi.* [prob. < var. of ON. *drukna*] to die by suffocation in water or other liquid —*vt.* 1. to kill by such suffocation 2. *a)* to cover with water; flood *b)* to overwhelm 3. to be so loud as to overcome (another sound): usually with *out* 4. to get rid of *[to drown one's sorrow in drink]*

**drowse** (drouz) *vi.* **drowsed**, **drows′ing** [< OE. *drusian*, to become sluggish] to sleep lightly; doze —*vt.* to spend (time) in drowsing —*n.* the act or an instance of drowsing; doze

**drow·sy** (drou′zē) *adj.* -si·er, -si·est 1. *a)* sleepy or half asleep *b)* making sleepy 2. brought on by sleepiness 3. peacefully quiet or inactive —**drow′si·ly** *adv.* —**drow′si·ness** *n.*

**drub** (drub) *vt.* **drubbed**, **drub′bing** [< ? Turk. *durb* < Ar. *darb*, a beating] 1. to beat as with a stick; cudgel 2. to defeat soundly in a fight, contest, etc. —*vi.* to drum or tap —*n.* a blow as with a club —**drub′ber** *n.*

**drub·bing** (drub′iŋ) *n.* a thorough beating or defeat
**drudge** (druj) *n.* [prob. < OE. *dreogan*, to suffer] a person who does hard, menial, or tedious work —*vi.* **drudged, drudg′ing** to do such work
**drudg·er·y** (druj′ər ē) *n., pl.* **-er·ies** work that is hard, menial, or tiresome
**drug** (drug) *n.* [< OFr. *drogue*] **1.** any substance used as or in a medicine **2.** a narcotic, hallucinogen, etc., esp. a habit-forming one —*vt.* **drugged, drug′ging 1.** to put a harmful drug in (a drink, etc.) **2.** to administer a drug to **3.** to stupefy as with a drug —**drug on the market** something for which there is a plentiful supply but little demand
**drug addict** a habitual user of narcotics
**drug·gist** (-ist) *n.* **1.** a dealer in drugs, medical equipment, etc. **2.** a person authorized to fill prescriptions; pharmacist **3.** an owner or manager of a drugstore
**drug·store** (-stôr′) *n.* a store where drugs and medical supplies are sold: most drugstores also sell a wide variety of merchandise
**dru·id** (droo′id) *n.* [< Fr. < L. *druides*, pl. < Celt.] [*often* D-] a member of a Celtic religious order in ancient Britain, Ireland, and France —**dru·id′ic, dru·id′i·cal** *adj.* —**dru′id·ism** *n.*
**drum** (drum) *n.* [< Du. *trom*] **1.** a percussion instrument consisting of a hollow cylinder or hemisphere with a membrane stretched tightly over the end or ends **2.** the sound produced by beating a drum, or any sound like this **3.** any drumlike cylindrical object; specif., *a*) a metal cylinder around which cable, etc. is wound in a machine *b*) a barrellike metal container for oil, etc. **4.** any of various fishes that make a drumming sound **5.** *Anat. same as: a*) MIDDLE EAR *b*) EARDRUM —*vi.* **drummed, drum′ming 1.** to beat a drum **2.** to beat or tap continually, as with the fingers —*vt.* **1.** to beat out (a tune, etc.) as on a drum **2.** to beat or tap continually **3.** to assemble by beating a drum **4.** to instill (ideas, facts, etc. *into*) by continued repetition —**beat the drum for** [Colloq.] to try to arouse enthusiasm for —**drum out of** to expel from in disgrace —**drum up 1.** to summon as by beating a drum **2.** to get (business) by soliciting
**drum·beat** (-bēt′) *n.* a sound made by beating a drum
**drum·fish** (-fish′) *n., pl.* **-fish′, -fish′es** see FISH *same as* DRUM (*n.* 4)
**drum·head** (-hed′) *n.* the membrane stretched over the open end or ends of a drum
**drum·lin** (-lin) *n.* [< Ir. *druim*, a ridge + *-lin*, dim. suffix] a long ridge formed by glacial drift
**drum major** a person who leads or precedes a marching band, often twirling a baton and prancing —**drum majorette** *fem.*
**drum·mer** (-ər) *n.* **1.** a drum player **2.** an animal that makes a drumming sound **3.** [see DRUM, phr. *drum up*] [Colloq.] a traveling salesman
**drum·stick** (-stik′) *n.* **1.** a stick for beating a drum **2.** the lower half of the leg of a cooked fowl
**drunk** (druŋk) *pp. & archaic pt. of* DRINK —*adj.* [*usually used in the predicate*] **1.** overcome by alcoholic liquor; intoxicated **2.** overcome by any powerful emotion **3.** [Colloq.] *same as* DRUNKEN (sense 2) —*n.* [Slang] **1.** a drunken person **2.** a drinking spree
**drunk·ard** (druŋ′kərd) *n.* a person who often gets drunk; inebriate
**drunk·en** (-kən) *archaic pp. of* DRINK —*adj.* [*used before the noun*] **1.** intoxicated or habitually intoxicated **2.** caused by or occurring during intoxication —**drunk′en·ly** *adv.* —**drunk′en·ness** *n.*
**drupe** (droop) *n.* [< ModL. *drupa* < L. *drupa* (*oliva*), overripe (olive) < Gr. *dryppa*, olive] any fruit with a soft, fleshy part around an inner stone that contains the seed, as an apricot, cherry, plum, etc. —**dru·pa·ceous** (droo pā′shəs) *adj.*
**drupe·let** (-lit) *n.* a small drupe: a single blackberry consists of many drupelets
**druth·ers** (druth′ərz) *n.* [contr. < *I'd rather*, with sound infl. by OTHER] [Dial. or Colloq.] a choice or preference (if I had my *druthers*]
**dry** (drī) *adj.* **dri′er, dri′est** [OE. *dryge*] **1.** not under water [*dry* land] **2.** having no moisture; not wet or damp **3.** not shedding tears **4.** lacking rain [a *dry* summer] **5.** *a*) having lost water or moisture; arid, withered, dehydrated, etc. *b*) empty of water or other liquid **6.** thirsty **7.** not yielding milk [a *dry* cow] **8.** without butter, jam, etc. [*dry* toast] **9.** solid; not liquid **10.** not sweet [*dry* wine]

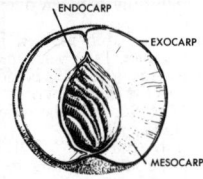
ENDOCARP
EXOCARP
MESOCARP

DRUPE (of peach)

**11.** having no mucous or watery discharge [a *dry* cough] **12.** prohibiting or opposed to the sale of alcoholic liquors [a *dry* town] **13.** plain or sober [*dry* facts] **14.** funny in a quiet but sharp way [*dry* wit] **15.** not productive **16.** dull or boring —*n., pl.* **drys** [Colloq.] a prohibitionist —*vt., vi.* **dried, dry′ing** to make or become dry —**dry up 1.** to make or become thoroughly dry **2.** to make or become unproductive, uncreative, etc. **3.** [Slang] to stop talking —**not dry behind the ears** [Colloq.] immature; inexperienced
**dry·ad** (drī′əd, -ad) *n., pl.* **-ads, -ad·es′** (-ə dēz′) [L. *dryas* (gen. *dryadis*) < Gr. < *drys*, an oak, tree] [*also* D-] *Gr. & Rom. Myth.* any nymph living in a tree; wood nymph
**dry battery 1.** an electric battery made up of several connected dry cells **2.** a dry cell
**dry cell** a voltaic cell containing an absorbent so that its contents cannot spill
**dry-clean** (drī′klēn′) *vt.* to clean (garments, etc.) with some solvent other than water, as naphtha, gasoline, etc. —**dry cleaner** —**dry cleaning**
**Dry·den** (drīd′n), **John** 1631–1700; Eng. poet, critic, & playwright
**dry-dock** (drī′däk′) *vt., vi.* to place or go into a dry dock
**dry dock** a dock from which the water can be emptied, used for building and repairing ships
**dry·er** (-ər) *n.* **1.** a person or thing that dries; specif., an apparatus for drying by heating or blowing air, esp. an appliance for drying clothes **2.** *same as* DRIER
**dry-eyed** (-īd′) *adj.* shedding no tears
**dry farming** farming in an almost rainless region without irrigation: done by conserving the soil moisture and planting drought-resistant crops —**dry′-farm′** *vt., vi.* —**dry farmer**
**dry goods** cloth, cloth products, thread, etc.
**dry ice** carbon dioxide solidified and compressed into snowlike cakes, used as a refrigerant
**dry·ly** (-lē) *adv.* in a dry manner; matter-of-factly
**dry measure** a system of measuring the volume of dry things, as grain, vegetables, etc.; esp., the system in which 2 pints = 1 quart, 8 quarts = 1 peck, and 4 pecks = 1 bushel: SEE TABLE OF WEIGHTS AND MEASURES in Supplements
**dry·ness** (-nis) *n.* the quality or state of being dry
**dry point 1.** a needle for engraving lines on a copper plate without using acid **2.** a print from such a plate **3.** this way of engraving
**dry rot 1.** a fungous decay causing seasoned timber to crumble to powder **2.** a similar fungous disease of plants, fruits, etc. —**dry′-rot′** *vi., vt.* **-rot′ted, -rot′ting**
**dry run 1.** [Mil. Slang] practice in firing without using live ammunition **2.** [Slang] a rehearsal
**dry wall 1.** a wall of rocks or stones with no mortar **2.** a wall constructed of wallboard, plasterboard, etc. without using wet plaster —**dry′wall′** *adj.*
**D.S., d.s.** [It. *dal segno*] (repeat) from this sign
**D.S., D.Sc.** Doctor of Science
**D.S.C., DSC** Distinguished Service Cross
**D.S.M., DSM** Distinguished Service Medal
**D.S.O., DSO** Distinguished Service Order
**D.S.T., DST** Daylight Saving Time
**D.T.'s, d.t.'s** (dē′tēz′) [Slang] *same as* DELIRIUM TREMENS
**Du. 1.** Duke **2.** Dutch
**du·al** (doo′əl, dyoo′-) *adj.* [L. *dualis* < *duo*, two] **1.** of two **2.** having or composed of two parts or kinds, like or unlike; double; twofold —*n. Linguis.* **1.** *same as* DUAL NUMBER **2.** a word having dual number —**du·al′i·ty** (-al′ə tē) *n.* —**du′al·ly** *adv.*
**du·al·ism** (-iz′m) *n.* **1.** the state of being dual; duality **2.** any theory or doctrine based on a twofold distinction, as the theory that the world is ultimately composed of mind and matter —**du′al·ist** *n.* —**du′al·is′tic** *adj.* —**du′al·is′ti·cal·ly** *adv.*
**du·al·ize** (-īz′) *vt.* **-ized′, -iz′ing** to make, or consider as, dual
**dual number** in some languages, a grammatical number indicating *two, a pair:* distinguished from *singular* and *plural*
**dub¹** (dub) *vt.* **dubbed, dub′bing** [< OE. *dubbian*, to strike] **1.** to confer knighthood on by tapping on the shoulder with a sword **2.** to confer a title, name, or nickname upon **3.** to make smooth, as by hammering, scraping, or rubbing **4.** [Slang] to bungle (a golf stroke, etc.) —*n.* [Slang] a clumsy, unskillful person —**dub′ber** *n.*
**dub²** (dub) *vt.* **dubbed, dub′bing** [contr. < DOUBLE] to insert (dialogue, music, etc.) in a film or recording (often with *in*) —*n.* dialogue, music, etc. so inserted —**dub′ber** *n.*
**du Bar·ry** (doo bar′ē; Fr. dü bà rē′) comtesse (born *Marie Jeanne Bécu*) 1743?–93; mistress of Louis XV of France
**du·bi·e·ty** (doo bī′ə tē, dyoo-) *n.* [LL. *dubietas*] **1.** a being dubious **2.** *pl.* **-ties** a doubtful thing

**du·bi·ous** (dōō′bē əs, dyōō′-) *adj.* [< L. < *dubius,* uncertain] **1.** causing doubt; ambiguous **2.** feeling doubt; skeptical **3.** uncertain *[dubious battle]* **4.** questionable *[a dubious character]* —**du′bi·ous·ly** *adv.* —**du′bi·ous·ness** *n.*

**Dub·lin** (dub′lən) capital of Ireland; seaport on the Irish Sea: pop. 569,000

**Du Bois** (dōō bois′), **William Edward Burghardt** 1868–1963; U.S. historian & Negro leader

**Du·buque** (də byōōk′) [after J. *Dubuque,* early lead miner] city in E Iowa, on the Mississippi: pop. 62,000

**du·cal** (dōō′k'l, dyōō′-) *adj.* [see DUKE] of a duke or dukedom —**du′cal·ly** *adv.*

**duc·at** (duk′ət) *n.* [OFr. < It. *ducato,* coin with image of a duke < LL. *ducatus:* see DUCHY] **1.** any of several former European coins of gold or silver **2.** [Slang] a ticket

**du·ce** (dōō′che) *n.* [It. < L. *dux,* leader] chief; leader: title *(Il Duce)* assumed by Benito Mussolini

**Du·champ** (dü shän′), **Marcel** 1887–1968; U.S. painter, born in France

**duch·ess** (duch′is) *n.* **1.** the wife or widow of a duke **2.** a woman who, like a duke, rules a duchy

**duch·y** (-ē) *n., pl.* **duch′ies** [< OFr. < LL. *ducatus,* military command < L. *dux:* see DUKE] the territory ruled by a duke or duchess; dukedom

**duck¹** (duk) *n.* [< OE. *duce,* lit., diver < base of ff.] **1.** *pl.* **ducks, duck:** see PLURAL, II, D, 1 a swimming bird with a flat bill, short neck and legs, and webbed feet **2.** a female duck: opposed to DRAKE **3.** the flesh of a duck as food **4.** [Slang] a person *[an odd duck]* —**like water off a duck's back** with no effect or reaction

**duck²** (duk) *vt., vi.* [ME. *douken* < hyp. OE. *ducan,* to dive] **1.** to plunge or dip under water for a moment **2.** to lower or move (the head, body, etc.) suddenly, as in avoiding a blow or in hiding **3.** [Colloq.] to avoid (a task, person, etc.) **4.** [Slang] to run (*in* or *out*) —*n.* a ducking

**duck³** (duk) *n.* [Du. *doek*] **1.** a cotton or linen cloth like canvas but finer and lighter in weight **2.** [*pl.*] [Colloq.] trousers made of this cloth

**duck⁴** (duk) *n.* [altered (after DUCK¹) < *DUKW,* code name] [Mil. Slang] an amphibious motor vehicle

**duck·bill** (duk′bil′) *n.* same as PLATYPUS

**duck·ling** (-liŋ) *n.* a young duck

**duck·pins** (-pinz′) *n.pl.* **1.** [*with sing. v.*] a game like bowling or tenpins, played with smaller pins and balls **2.** the pins used

**duck soup** [Slang] something that is easy to do

**duck·weed** (-wēd′) *n.* a minute flowering plant that floats on ponds and sluggish streams

**duck·y** (-ē) *adj.* **duck′i·er, duck′i·est** [Slang] pleasing, delightful, darling, etc.

**duct** (dukt) *n.* [< ML. < L. *ductus,* pp. of *ducere,* to lead] **1.** a tube or channel through which a fluid moves **2.** a tube in the body for the passage of excretions or secretions *[a bile duct]* **3.** a tubule in plant tissues, conducting resin, etc. **4.** a pipe or conduit enclosing wires —**duct′less** *adj.*

**duc·tile** (duk′t'l) *adj.* [see prec.] **1.** that can be stretched, drawn, or hammered thin without breaking: said of metals **2.** easily molded; pliant **3.** easily led; tractable —**duc·til′i·ty** (-til′ə tē) *n.*

**ductless gland** an endocrine gland

**dud** (dud) *n.* [prob. < Du. *dood,* dead] [Colloq.] **1.** a bomb or shell that fails to explode **2.** a person or thing that fails —*adj.* [Colloq.] worthless

**dude** (dōōd) *n.* [< ?] **1.** a dandy; fop **2.** [Western Slang] a city fellow or tourist, esp. an Easterner —**dud′ish** *adj.* —**dud′ish·ly** *adv.*

**dude ranch** a ranch or farm operated as a vacation resort, with horseback riding, etc.

**dudg·eon** (duj′ən) *n.* [prob. < Anglo-Fr. *en digeon,* at the dagger hilt] anger or resentment: now chiefly in **in high dudgeon,** very angry, offended, or resentful

**duds** (dudz) *n.pl.* [prob. < ON. < *dutha,* to wrap up, swathe] [Colloq.] **1.** clothes **2.** belongings

**due** (dōō) *adj.* [< OFr. *deu,* pp. of *devoir,* to owe < L. *debere:* see DEBT] **1.** owed or owing as a debt, right, etc.; payable **2.** suitable; proper *[due respect]* **3.** enough; adequate *[due care]* **4.** expected or scheduled to arrive or be ready *[the plane is due now]* —*adv.* exactly; directly *[due west]* —*n.* anything due; specif., *a)* deserved recognition *b)* [*pl.*] fees, taxes, or other charges *[membership dues]* —**become** (or **fall**) **due** to become payable as previously arranged —**due to 1.** caused by; resulting from *[deaths due to cancer]* **2.** [Colloq.] because of *[due to his help, we won the game]*

**du·el** (dōō′əl, dyōō′-) *n.* [< ML. < OL. *duellum* (L. *bellum,* war] **1.** a formal, prearranged fight between two persons armed with deadly weapons **2.** any contest suggesting such a fight *[a verbal duel]* —*vi., vt.* **-eled** or **-elled, -el·ing** or **-el·ling** to fight a duel (with) —**du′el·ist** or **du′el·list, du′el·er** or **du′el·ler** *n.*

**du·en·na** (dōō en′ə, dyōō-) *n.* [Sp. *dueña* < L. *domina,*

mistress] **1.** an elderly woman who has charge of the young unmarried women of a Spanish or Portuguese family **2.** a chaperon or governess

**due process** (of law) the course of legal proceedings established to protect individual rights

**du·et** (dōō et′, dyōō-) *n.* [< It. < L. *duo,* two] *Music* **1.** a composition for two voices or instruments **2.** the two performers of such a composition

**duff** (duf) *n.* [dial. var. of DOUGH] a thick flour pudding boiled in a cloth bag

**duf·fel, duf·fle** (duf′'l) *n.* [Du. < *Duffel,* town in N Belgium] **1.** a coarse woolen cloth **2.** clothing and equipment carried by a camper, soldier, etc. **3.** same as DUFFEL BAG

**duffel** (or **duffle**) **bag** a large, cylindrical cloth bag for carrying clothing and personal belongings

**duf·fer** (duf′ər) *n.* [< thieves' slang *duff,* to fake] [Slang] an incompetent or stupid person; specif., a relatively unskilled golfer

**Du·fy** (dü fē′), **Ra·oul** (**Ernest Joseph**) (rä ōōl′) 1877–1953; Fr. painter

**dug¹** (dug) *pt. & pp. of* DIG

**dug²** (dug) *n.* [< same base as Dan. *dægge,* to suckle] a nipple, teat, or udder

**du·gong** (dōō′gôŋ, -gän) *n.* [Malay *dūyung*] a large, whalelike mammal of tropical seas

**dug·out** (dug′out′) *n.* **1.** a boat or canoe hollowed out of a log **2.** a shelter, as in warfare, dug in the ground or in a hillside **3.** a covered shelter near a baseball diamond for the players to sit in

**dui·ker** (dīk′ər) *n., pl.* **-kers, -ker:** see PLURAL, II, D, 1 [Slang] any of several small, African antelopes

**Duis·burg** (düs′bōōrk) city in W West Germany, on the Rhine: pop. 469,000

**duke** (dōōk, dyōōk) *n.* [< OFr. < L. *dux,* leader < *ducere,* to lead] **1.** the ruler of an independent duchy **2.** a nobleman of the highest hereditary rank below that of a prince —**duke′dom** *n.*

**dukes** (dōōks, dyōōks) *n.pl.* [< *duke,* short for *Duke of York,* used in 19th-c. E. rhyming slang for *fork,* fingers] [Slang] the fists or hands

**dul·cet** (dul′sit) *adj.* [< OFr. < L. *dulcis,* sweet] soothing or pleasant to hear; melodious

**dul·ci·mer** (dul′sə mər) *n.* [< OFr. < Sp. < L. < *dulce,* sweet + *melos* < Gr. *melos,* a song] **1.** a musical instrument with metal strings, which are struck with two small hammers by the player **2.** a violin-shaped stringed instrument of the southern Appalachians, plucked with a plectrum or a goose quill: also **dul′ci·more′** (-môr′, -mər)

**dull** (dul) *adj.* [OE. *dol,* stupid] **1.** mentally slow; stupid **2.** lacking sensitivity; unfeeling **3.** physically slow; sluggish **4.** lacking spirit; listless **5.** not active; slack **6.** causing boredom; tedious **7.** not sharp; blunt **8.** not felt keenly *[a dull headache]* **9.** not vivid **10.** not glossy **11.** not distinct; muffled *[a dull thud]* **12.** gloomy; cloudy —*vt., vi.* to make or become dull —**dull′ish** *adj.* —**dull′ness, dul′ness** *n.* —**dul′ly** *adv.*

DULCIMER

**dull·ard** (-ərd) *n.* a stupid person

**dulse** (duls) *n.* [Ir. & Gael. *duileasq*] any of several edible marine algae with large, red fronds

**Du·luth** (də lōōth′) [after D. *Du Lhut,* 17th-c. Fr. explorer] city in NE Minn.: pop. 93,000

**du·ly** (dōō′lē, dyōō′-) *adv.* in due manner; specif., *a)* as due; rightfully *b)* when due; at the right time *c)* as required; sufficiently

**Du·ma** (dōō′mä) *n.* [Russ. < Gmc., as in OE. *dom,* judgment] the parliament of czarist Russia (1905–17)

**Du·mas** (dü mä′; E. dōō′mä) **1. Alexandre,** 1802–70; Fr. novelist & playwright: called *Dumas père* **2. Alexandre,** 1824–95; Fr. playwright & novelist: son of *prec.:* called *Dumas fils*

**dumb** (dum) *adj.* [OE.] **1.** lacking the power of speech; mute **2.** unwilling to talk; silent **3.** not accompanied by speech **4.** temporarily speechless, as from fear **5.** [G. *dumm*] [Colloq.] stupid; moronic —**dumb′ly** *adv.* —**dumb′ness** *n.*

**dumb·bell** (dum′bel′) *n.* **1.** a device usually used in pairs for muscular exercise: each pair has round weights joined by a short bar **2.** [Slang] a dumb or stupid person

**dumb·found, dum·found** (dum′found′) *vt.* [DUMB + (CON)FOUND] to make speechless by shocking

**dumb show 1.** formerly, a part of a play done in pantomime **2.** gestures without speech

**dumb·wait·er** (dum′wāt′ər) *n.* **1.** a small, portable stand for serving food **2.** a small elevator for sending food, trash, etc. from one floor to another

**dum·dum (bullet)** (dum′dum′) [< *Dumdum,* arsenal near

Calcutta, India] a soft-nosed bullet that expands when it hits, inflicting a large wound

**dum·my** (dum'ē) *n., pl.* **-mies** **1.** a person unable to talk: a vulgar usage **2.** a figure made in human form, as for displaying clothing, practicing tackling in football, etc. **3.** an imitation or sham **4.** a person secretly acting for another while apparently representing his own interests **5.** [Slang] a stupid person **6.** *Bridge, Whist,* etc. *a)* the declarer's partner, whose hand is exposed on the board and played by the declarer *b)* such a hand **7.** the skeleton copy, as of a book, upon which the format is laid out —*adj.* **1.** imitation; sham **2.** secretly acting as a front for another **3.** *Bridge,* etc. played with a dummy —**dummy up, -mied, -my·ing** [Slang] to refuse to talk

**dump¹** (dump) *vt.* [prob. < ON.] **1.** to empty out or unload as in a heap or mass **2.** *a)* to throw away (rubbish, etc.) esp. in or at a dump *b)* to get rid of abruptly or roughly **3.** to sell (a commodity) in a large quantity at a low price, esp. abroad —*vi.* **1.** to fall in a heap or mass **2.** to unload rubbish **3.** to dump commodities —*n.* **1.** a rubbish pile or a place for dumping **2.** *Mil.* a temporary storage center, as for ammunition **3.** [Slang] a place that is unpleasant, ugly, etc. —**dump'er** *n.*

**dump²** (dump) *n.* [< ? Du. *domp,* haze] [Obs.] a sad song —**in the dumps** in low spirits; depressed

**dump·ling** (-liŋ) *n.* [< Brit. *dump,* lump + -LING¹] **1.** a small piece of dough, steamed or boiled and served with meat or soup **2.** a crust of dough filled with fruit and steamed or baked

**dump truck** a truck that is unloaded by tilting the truck bed backward with the tailgate open

**dump·y¹** (dum'pē) *adj.* **dump'i·er, dump'i·est** **1.** short and thick; squat **2.** [Slang] ugly, rundown, etc. —**dump'i·ly** *adv.* —**dump'i·ness** *n.*

**dump·y²** (dum'pē) *adj.* **dump'i·er, dump'i·est** [see DUMP²] melancholy; depressed

**dun¹** (dun) *adj.* [OE.] dull grayish-brown —*n.* **1.** a dull grayish brown **2.** a dun horse

**dun²** (dun) *vt., vi.* dunned, dun'ning [? dial. var. of DIN] to ask (a debtor) repeatedly for payment —*n.* an insistent demand for payment of a debt

**Dun·can** (duŋ'kən) [Gael. *Donnchadh,* lit., brown warrior] a masculine name

**dunce** (duns) *n.* [< *Dunsmen* or *Dunces,* followers of DUNS SCOTUS, who were considered foes of new ideas] **1.** a dull, ignorant person **2.** a person slow at learning

**dunce cap** a cone-shaped hat which children slow at learning were formerly forced to wear in school

**Dun·dee** (dun dē') seaport in E Scotland, on the North Sea: pop. 182,000

**dun·der·head** (dun'dər hed') *n.* [< Du. *donder,* thunder, infl. by BLUNDER] a stupid person; dunce

**dune** (dōōn, dyōōn) *n.* [Fr. < ODu. *duna*] a rounded hill or ridge of sand heaped up by the wind

**dune buggy** [from orig. use on sand dunes] a small, light automobile made from a standard, compact chassis and a prefabricated body

**Dun·e·din** (də nē'd'n) city on the SE coast of South Island, New Zealand: pop. 110,000

**dung** (duŋ) *n.* [OE.] **1.** animal excrement; manure **2.** filth —*vt.* to spread with dung, as in fertilizing —**dung'y** *adj.* **dung'i·er, dung'i·est**

**dun·ga·ree** (duŋ'gə rē') *n.* [Hindi *dungrī*] **1.** a coarse cotton cloth; specif., blue denim **2.** [*pl.*] work trousers or overalls of this cloth

**dun·geon** (dun'jən) *n.* [< OFr. *donjon*] **1.** same as DONJON **2.** a dark, underground cell or prison

**dung·hill** (duŋ'hil') *n.* **1.** a heap of dung **2.** anything vile or filthy

**dunk** (duŋk) *vt.* [G. *tunken,* to dip < OHG. *dunchôn*] **1.** to dip (bread, cake, etc.) into coffee or other liquid before eating it **2.** to immerse in liquid for a short time

**Dun·kirk** (dun'kərk) seaport in N France: scene of the evacuation of Allied troops under fire (1940): Fr. name **Dun·kerque** (dön kerk')

**dun·lin** (dun'lin) *n., pl.* **-lins, -lin:** see PLURAL, II, D, 1 [< DUN¹ + -LING¹] a small sandpiper with a reddish back and a black patch on its belly

**dun·nage** (dun'ij) *n.* [< ML. *dennagium* < ?] **1.** a loose packing of any bulky material put around cargo for protection **2.** personal baggage or belongings

**Duns Sco·tus** (dunz skōt'əs), **John** 1265?-1308; Scot. scholastic philosopher & theologian

**du·o** (dōō'ō, dyōō'ō) *n., pl.* **du'os, du'i** (-ē) [It.] **1.** same as DUET (esp. sense 2) **2.** a pair; couple

**du·o-** [< L. *duo,* two] a combining form meaning two, double [*duologue*]

**du·o·dec·i·mal** (dōō'ə des'ə m'l, dyōō'-) *adj.* [< L. <

---

*duo,* two + *decem,* ten + -AL] **1.** relating to twelve or twelfths **2.** consisting of or counting by twelves —*n.* **1.** one twelfth **2.** [*pl.*] *Math.* a system of numeration with twelve as its base

**du·o·dec·i·mo** (-mō') *n., pl.* **-mos'** [< L. *in duodecimo,* in twelve] **1.** a page size (about 5 by 7 1/2 in.), 1/12 of a printer's sheet **2.** a book with pages of this size Also called *twelvemo,* and written *12mo* or *12°* —*adj.* with pages of this size

**du·o·de·num** (dōō'ə dē'nəm, dyōō'-; dōō äd''n əm) *n., pl.* **-de'na** (-nə), **-de'nums** [< ML. < L. *duodeni,* twelve each: its length is about twelve fingers' breadth] the first section of the small intestine, between the stomach and the jejunum —**du'o·de'nal** *adj.*

**du·o·logue** (dōō'ə lôg', -läg'; dyōō'-) *n.* [DUO- + (MONO)LOGUE] a conversation between two people

**du·op·o·ly** (dōō äp'ə lē, dyōō-) *n.* [DUO- + (MONO)POLY] control of a commodity or service by only two producers or suppliers

**dup.** duplicate

**dupe** (dōōp, dyōōp) *n.* [Fr. < OFr. < L. *upupa,* hoopoe, stupid bird] a person easily tricked or fooled —*vt.* **duped, dup'ing** to deceive or cheat —**dup'a·ble** *adj.* —**dup'er** *n.* —**dup'er·y** *n., pl.* **-er·ies**

**du·ple** (dōō'p'l, dyōō'-) *adj.* [L. *duplus:* see DOUBLE] **1.** double; twofold **2.** *Music* having two (or a multiple of two) beats to the measure [*duple time*]

**du·plex** (dōō'pleks, dyōō'-) *adj.* [L. < *duo,* two + *-plex,* -fold, akin to *plaga,* area] **1.** double; twofold **2.** having two units operating in the same way or simultaneously —*n.* same as DUPLEX HOUSE or DUPLEX APARTMENT —**du·plex'i·ty** *n.*

**duplex apartment** an apartment with rooms on two floors and a private inner stairway

**duplex house** a house consisting of two separate family units

**du·pli·cate** (dōō'plə kit, dyōō'-; *for v.* -kāt') *adj.* [< L. pp. of *duplicare,* to double: see DUPLEX] **1.** double **2.** having two similar parts **3.** corresponding exactly **4.** designating a game of bridge, etc. in which the same hands are played off again by other players to compare scores —*n.* **1.** an exact copy; replica; facsimile **2.** a counterpart or double **3.** a duplicate game of bridge, etc. —*vt.* **-cat'ed, -cat'ing** **1.** to make double or twofold **2.** to make an exact copy of **3.** to make, do, or cause to happen again —**in duplicate** in two precisely similar forms —**du'pli·ca·ble, du'pli·cat'a·ble** *adj.* —**du'pli·ca'tion** *n.* —**du'pli·ca'tive** *adj.*

**duplicating machine** a machine for making exact copies of a letter, photograph, drawing, etc.: also **du'pli·ca'tor** *n.*

**du·plic·i·ty** (dōō plis'ə tē, dyōō-) *n., pl.* **-ties** [< OFr. < LL. *duplicitas:* see DUPLEX] hypocritical cunning or deception; double-dealing

**du Pont** (dōō pänt', dyōō' pänt; dyōō) name of a family prominent as U.S. industrialists since 1802

**dur·a·ble** (door'ə b'l, dyoor'-) *adj.* [OFr. < L. < *durare,* to last, harden < *durus,* hard] **1.** lasting in spite of hard wear or frequent use **2.** continuing to exist; stable —*n.* [*pl.*] same as DURABLE GOODS —**du'ra·bil'i·ty** *n.* —**du'ra·bly** *adv.*

**durable goods** goods usable for a relatively long time, as machinery, cars, or home appliances

**du·ral·u·min** (doo ral'yoo m'n, dyoo-) *n.* [DUR(ABLE) + ALUMIN(UM)] a strong, lightweight alloy of aluminum with copper, manganese, magnesium, and silicon

**du·ra ma·ter** (door'ə māt'ər, dyoor'-) [ML., lit., hard mother < an Ar. term] the outermost and toughest of the three membranes covering the brain and spinal cord: also **du'ra** *n.* —**du'ral** *adj.*

**du·ra·men** (doo rā'mən, dyoo-) *n.* [L. < *durare:* see DURABLE] same as HEARTWOOD

**dur·ance** (door'əns, dyoor'-) *n.* [< OFr. < L. *durans,* prp. of *durare:* see DURABLE] imprisonment: mainly in phrase **in durance vile**

**du·ra·tion** (doo rā'shən, dyoo-) *n.* [< ML. < pp. of L. *durare:* see DURABLE] **1.** continuance in time **2.** the time that a thing continues or lasts

**Dur·ban** (dur'bən) seaport in Natal, on the E coast of South Africa: pop. 663,000

**dur·bar** (dur'bär) *n.* [Hindi < Per. < *dar,* portal + *bār,* court] **1.** formerly in India or Africa, a reception or audience held by a native prince or British governor **2.** the place where this was held

**Dü·rer** (dü'rər; *E.* dyoor'ər), **Al·brecht** (äl'breHt) 1471-1528; Ger. painter & wood engraver

**du·ress** (doo res', dyoo-; door'is, dyoor'-) *n.* [< OFr. < L. *duritia,* hardness < *durus,* hard] **1.** imprisonment **2.** the use of force or threats [signed under *duress*]

---

**Dur·ham** (dʉr′əm) [after *Durham* County, England] city in NC N.C.: pop. 101,000 —*n.* one of a breed of short-horned beef cattle, orig. bred in Durham County, England

**dur·ing** (door′iŋ, dyoor′-) *prep.* [see DURABLE] **1.** throughout the entire time of **2.** at some point in the entire time of; in the course of

**Du·roc-Jer·sey** (door′äk jʉr′zē, dyoor′-) *n.* any of a breed of large, red hog: also **Du′roc**

**dur·ra** (door′ə) *n.* [Ar. *dhurah*] a kind of grain sorghum

**durst** (dʉrst) *archaic pt. of* DARE

**du·rum** (**wheat**) (door′əm, dyoor′-) [L., neut. of *durus*, hard] a hard wheat that yields flour and semolina used in macaroni, spaghetti, etc.

**Du·shan·be** (dōō shän′be) capital of the Tadzhik S.S.R., in the W part: pop. 345,000

**dusk** (dusk) *adj.* [by metathesis < OE. *dox*, dark-colored] [Poet.] dark in color; dusky —*n.* **1.** the dim part of twilight **2.** gloom; dusky quality —*vt.*, *vi.* to make or become dusky or shadowy

**dusk·y** (dus′kē) *adj.* **dusk′i·er**, **dusk′i·est 1.** somewhat dark in color; esp., swarthy **2.** lacking light; dim **3.** gloomy —**dusk′i·ly** *adv.* —**dusk′i·ness** *n.*

**Düs·sel·dorf** (düs′əl dôrf′) city in W West Germany, on the Rhine: pop. 689,000

**dust** (dust) *n.* [OE.] **1.** powdery earth or any finely powdered matter **2.** a cloud of such matter **3.** confusion; turmoil **4.** *a)* earth *b)* disintegrated mortal remains **5.** a humble or abject condition **6.** anything worthless **7.** *same as* GOLD DUST —*vt.* **1.** to sprinkle with dust, powder, etc. **2.** to sprinkle (powder, etc.) on **3.** to rid of dust, as by brushing or wiping —*vi.* to remove dust, as from furniture —**bite the dust** to be killed, esp. in battle —**dust off** [Slang] to pitch a baseball deliberately close to (the batter) —**shake the dust off one's feet** to leave with disdain —**throw dust in (someone's) eyes** to deceive (someone) —**dust′less** *adj.*

**dust·bin** (-bin′) *n.* [Brit.] a container for rubbish

**dust bowl** a region where eroded topsoil is blown away by winds during droughts

**dust·er** (-ər) *n.* **1.** a person or thing that dusts; specif., *a)* a brush or cloth for removing dust from furniture, etc. *b)* a device for sprinkling on a powder **2.** a short, loose, lightweight housecoat

**dust jacket** a detachable paper cover for protecting the binding of a book

**dust·man** (-mən) *n.*, *pl.* **-men** [Brit.] a man whose work is removing rubbish, ashes, garbage, etc.

**dust·pan** (-pan′) *n.* a shovellike receptacle into which dust or debris is swept from a floor

**dust storm** a windstorm that sweeps up clouds of dust when passing over an arid region

**dust·y** (-ē) *adj.* **dust′i·er**, **dust′i·est 1.** covered with or full of dust **2.** like dust; powdery **3.** of the color of dust —**dust′i·ly** *adv.* —**dust′i·ness** *n.*

**Dutch** (duch) *adj.* [< MDu. *Duutsch*, Dutch, German] **1.** of the Netherlands, its people, language, or culture **2.** of the Pennsylvania Dutch **3.** [Slang] German —*n.* **1.** the language of the Netherlands **2.** [Slang] German —**beat the Dutch** [Colloq.] to be very unusual —**go Dutch** [Colloq.] to have each pay his own expenses —**in Dutch** [Colloq.] in trouble or disfavor —**the Dutch 1.** the people of the Netherlands **2.** the Pennsylvania Dutch

**Dutch bob** a haircut with bangs and a straight, even bob that covers the ears

**Dutch courage** [Colloq.] courage stimulated by drinking alcoholic liquor

**Dutch door** a door with upper and lower halves that can be opened separately

**Dutch East Indies** *same as* NETHERLANDS (EAST) INDIES

**Dutch elm disease** [from its first appearance in the Netherlands] a widespread fungous disease of elms that causes the tree to die

**Dutch Guiana** *former name of* SURINAME

**Dutch·man** (-mən) *n.*, *pl.* **-men 1.** a native or inhabitant of the Netherlands **2.** a Dutch ship **3.** [Slang] a German

**Dutch·man's-breech·es** (-mənz brich′iz) *n.*, *pl.* **-breech′es** a spring wildflower with pink-ish flowers, found in E U.S.

DUTCH DOOR

**Dutch oven 1.** a heavy metal pot with a high, arched lid, for cooking pot roasts, etc. **2.** a metal container for roasting meats, etc., with an open side placed toward the fire

**Dutch treat** [Colloq.] any entertainment, etc. at which each participant pays his own expenses

**Dutch uncle** [Colloq.] a person who bluntly and sternly lectures or scolds someone else

**Dutch West Indies** *former name of* NETHERLANDS ANTILLES

**du·te·ous** (dōōt′ē əs, dyōōt′-) *adj.* dutiful; obedient —**du′te·ous·ly** *adv.* —**du′te·ous·ness** *n.*

**du·ti·a·ble** (dōōt′ē ə b'l, dyōōt′-) *adj.* necessitating payment of a duty or tax, as imported goods

**du·ti·ful** (-ə fəl) *adj.* **1.** showing, or resulting from, a sense of duty **2.** obedient —**du′ti·ful·ly** *adv.*

**du·ty** (dōōt′ē, dyōōt′ē) *n.*, *pl.* **-ties** [< Anglo-Fr. *dueté*, what is due: see DUE & -TY¹] **1.** obedience or respect to parents, older people, etc. **2.** conduct based on moral or legal obligation **3.** any action required by one's occupation or position **4.** a sense of obligation **5.** service, esp. military service **6.** a payment due to the government, esp. a tax imposed on imports, exports, etc. **7.** service or use: see HEAVY-DUTY —**on** (or **off**) **duty** at (or having time off from) one's work or duty

**du·ty-free** (-frē′) *adj.*, *adv.* with no payment of a duty or tax required

**du·um·vir** (dōō um′vər, dyōō-) *n.*, *pl.* **-virs**, **-vi·ri′** (-və rī′) [L. < *duo*, two + *vir*, a man] either of two magistrates in ancient Rome who held office jointly

**du·um·vi·rate** (-və rit) *n.* **1.** governmental position held jointly by two men **2.** two such men

**du·ve·tyne**, **du·ve·tyn** (dōō′və tēn′) *n.* [< Fr. < *duvet*, eiderdown] a soft, velvetlike textile, originally made of cotton and silk

**D.V.M.** Doctor of Veterinary Medicine

**Dvo·řák** (dvôr′zhäk, -zhak), **An·ton** (än′tôn) 1841–1904; Czech composer

**dwarf** (dwôrf) *n.*, *pl.* **dwarfs**, **dwarves** (dwôrvz) [OE. *dweorg*] **1.** a person, animal, or plant much smaller than usual for its species **2.** Folklore an ugly little being with supposed magic powers **3.** a star of relatively small mass and low luminosity: in full, **dwarf star** —*vt.* **1.** to stunt the growth of **2.** to make small or insignificant **3.** to make seem small by comparison —*adj.* undersized; stunted —**dwarf′ish** *adj.* —**dwarf′ish·ness** *n.* —**dwarf′ism** *n.*

**dwell** (dwel) *vi.* **dwelt** or **dwelled**, **dwell′ing** [OE. *dwellan*, to lead astray, hinder] to make one's home; reside —**dwell on** (or **upon**) to linger over in thought or speech —**dwell′er** *n.*

**dwell·ing** (-iŋ) *n.* a place to live in; residence; house; abode: also **dwelling place**

**DWI**, **D.W.I.** driving while intoxicated

**Dwight** (dwīt) [a surname < ?] a masculine name

**dwin·dle** (dwin′d'l) *vi.*, *vt.* **-dled**, **-dling** [freq. of ME. *dwinen* < OE. *dwinan*, to wither] to become or make smaller or less; diminish; shrink

**dwt.** [*d(enarius)* *w(eigh)t*] pennyweight(s)

**DX**, **D.X.** *Radio* **1.** distance **2.** distant

**Dy** *Chem.* dysprosium

**Dy·ak** (dī′ak) *n.* [Malay *dayak*, savage] **1.** a member of an aboriginal people of Borneo **2.** their Indonesian language

**dyb·buk** (dib′ək) *n.* [Heb. *dibbūq* < *dābhaq*, to cleave] *Jewish Folklore* the spirit of a dead person that enters and possesses the body of a living person

**dye** (dī) *n.* [OE. *deag*] **1.** color produced in fabric, hair, etc. by saturating it with a coloring agent; tint; hue **2.** any such coloring agent or a solution containing it —*vt.* **dyed**, **dye′ing** to color as with a dye —*vi.* to take on color in dyeing —**of** (**the**) **deepest dye** of the worst sort —**dy′er** *n.*

**dyed-in-the-wool** (dīd′n *th*ə wool′) *adj.* **1.** dyed before being woven **2.** thoroughgoing; unchanging

**dye·ing** (dī′iŋ) *n.* the process or work of coloring fabrics, hair, etc. with dyes

**dye·stuff** (dī′stuf′) *n.* any substance yielding a dye

**dy·ing** (dī′iŋ) *prp. of* DIE¹ —*adj.* **1.** about to die or come to an end **2.** of or at the time of death —*n.* a ceasing to live or exist; death

**dyke** (dīk) *n.*, *vt. same as* DIKE

**dy·nam·ic** (dī nam′ik) *adj.* [< Fr. < Gr. < *dynamis*, power < *dynasthai*, to be able] **1.** relating to energy or physical force in motion: opposed to STATIC **2.** relating to dynamics **3.** energetic; vigorous; forceful **4.** relating to change Also **dy·nam′i·cal** —*n. same as* DYNAMICS (sense 2a) —**dy·nam′i·cal·ly** *adv.*

**dy·nam·ics** (-iks) *n.pl.* [*with sing. v. for 1, 2c, & 3*] **1.** the branch of mechanics dealing with the motions of material bodies under the action of given forces; kinetics **2.** *a)* the various forces, physical, moral, economic, etc., operating in any field *b)* the way such forces operate mutually *c)* the study of such forces **3.** the effect of varying degrees of loudness in musical performance

**dy·na·mism** (dī′nə miz′m) *n.* **1.** the theory that force or energy is the basic universal principle **2.** a dynamic quality —**dy′na·mis′tic** *adj.*

**dy·na·mite** (dī′nə mīt′) *n.* [coined (1866–67) by A. NOBEL < Gr. *dynamis*: see DYNAMIC] a powerful explosive made of some absorbent soaked with nitroglycerin —*vt.* **-mit′ed**, **-mit′ing** to blow up with dynamite —*adj.* [Slang] outstanding; very exciting, effective, etc. —**dy′na·mit′er** *n.*

**dy·na·mo** (-mō′) *n.*, *pl.* **-mos′** [< *dynamoelectric machine*] **1.** a machine that generates electricity: see GENERATOR **2.** a forceful, dynamic person

**dy·na·mo-** [< Gr. *dynamis*: see DYNAMIC] *a combining form meaning* power [*dynamoelectric*]

**dy·na·mo·e·lec·tric** (dī′nə mō i lek′trik) *adj.* having to do with production of electrical energy from mechanical energy, or the reverse process: also **dy′na·mo·e·lec′tri·cal**

**dy·na·mom·e·ter** (-mäm′ə tər) *n.* an apparatus for measuring force or power, esp. mechanical power —**dy′na·mo·met′ric** (-mō met′rik) *adj.* —**dy′na·mom′e·try** *n.*

**dy·na·mo·tor** (dī′nə mōt′ər) *n.* an electrical machine combining generator and motor, for transforming current from one voltage to another

**dy·nast** (dī′nast, -nast) *n.* [< L. < Gr. < *dynasthai*, to be strong] a ruler, esp. a hereditary ruler

**dy·nas·ty** (dī′nəs tē) *n., pl.* **-ties** [see prec.] 1. a succession of rulers who are members of the same family 2. the period during which a certain family reigns —**dy·nas·tic** (dī nas′tik), **dy·nas′ti·cal** *adj.* —**dy·nas′ti·cal·ly** *adv.*

**dyne** (dīn) *n.* [Fr. < Gr. *dynamis*, power] the amount of force that imparts to a mass of one gram an acceleration of one centimeter per second per second

**Dy·nel** (dī nel′) *a trademark for* a synthetic fiber —*n.* [d-] this fiber or a furlike fabric made from it

**dys-** [Gr.] *a prefix meaning* bad, ill, abnormal, impaired, difficult, etc. [*dysfunction*]

**dys·en·ter·y** (dis′′n ter′ē) *n.* [< OFr. < L. < Gr. < *dys-*, bad + *entera*, bowels] a painful intestinal inflammation characterized by diarrhea with bloody, mucous feces —**dys′en·ter′ic** *adj.*

**dys·func·tion** (dis funk′shən) *n.* abnormal, impaired, or incomplete functioning, as of a body organ or part —**dys·func′tion·al** *adj.*

**dys·lex·i·a** (dis lek′sē ə) *n.* [ModL. < Gr. *dys-*, bad + *lexis*, speech < *legein*, to speak] impairment of the ability to read, often from brain injury or genetic defect —**dys·lex′ic** *adj.*

**dys·pep·si·a** (dis pep′shə, -sē ə) *n.* [L. < Gr. < *dys-*, bad + *pepsis*, cooking < *peptein*, to digest] impaired digestion; indigestion: also [Dial.] **dys·pep′sy**

**dys·pep·tic** (-tik) *adj.* 1. of, causing, or having dyspepsia 2. gloomy; grouchy —*n.* a person who has dyspepsia —**dys·pep′ti·cal·ly** *adv.*

**dysp·ne·a** (disp′nē ə, disp nē′ə) *n.* [< L. < Gr. < *dys-*, hard + *pnoē* < *pnein*, to breathe] difficult or painful breathing —**dysp·ne′al, dysp·ne′ic** *adj.*

**dys·pro·si·um** (dis prō′sē əm, -zē-, -shē-) *n.* [< Gr. *dysprositos*, difficult of access] a chemical element of the rare-earth group: symbol, Dy; at. wt., 162.50; at. no., 66: it is one of the most magnetic of all known substances

**dys·tro·phy** (dis′trə fē) *n.* [ModL. *dystrophia*: see DYS- & -TROPHY] 1. faulty nutrition 2. faulty development, or degeneration: cf. MUSCULAR DYSTROPHY —**dys·tro′phic** (-träf′ik, -trō′fik) *adj.*

**dz.** dozen; dozens

# E

**E, e** (ē) *n., pl.* **E's, e's** 1. the fifth letter of the English alphabet 2. a sound of *E* or *e*

**E** (ē) *n.* 1. *Educ. a)* a grade indicating below-average work *b)* occas., a grade indicating excellence 2. *Music a)* the third tone in the ascending scale of C major *b)* the scale having this tone as the keynote

**e** 1. *Physics* erg 2. *Math.* the number used as the base of a system of logarithms, approximately 2.71828: written *e*

**e-** *a prefix meaning* out, from, etc.: see EX-

**E, E., e, e.** 1. east 2. eastern

**E.** 1. Earl 2. Easter 3. English

**E., e.** 1. earth 2. engineer(ing) 3. *Baseball* errors

**ea.** each

**each** (ēch) *adj., pron.* [< OE. *ælc*] every one of two or more considered separately —*adv.* apiece [ten cents *each*] —**each other** each one the other; one another: some use *each other* only of two and *one another* of more than two, but in common use no distinction is made [help *each other*]

**ea·ger** (ē′gər) *adj.* [< OFr. *aigre* < L. *acer*, sharp, keen] feeling or showing keen desire; impatient or anxious to do or get —**ea′ger·ly** *adv.* —**ea′ger·ness** *n.*

**ea·gle** (ē′g'l) *n.* [< OFr. *aigle* < L. *aquila*] 1. a large, strong, flesh-eating bird of prey having sharp vision and powerful wings 2. a representation of the eagle as a symbol of a nation, etc.; esp., the national emblem of the U.S. 3. a former U.S. gold coin worth $10 4. *Golf* a score of two below par on any hole

**ea·gle-eyed** (-īd′) *adj.* having keen vision

**ea·glet** (ē′glit) *n.* a young eagle

**-e·an** (ē′ən) [< L. & Gr.] *a suffix meaning* of, belonging to, like [*European*]

**ear**[1] (ir) *n.* [OE. *eare*] 1. the part of the body that perceives sound; organ of hearing 2. the visible, external part of the ear 3. the sense of hearing 4. the ability to recognize slight differences in sound, esp. in musical tones 5. anything shaped or placed like an ear —**be all ears** to listen attentively or eagerly —**bend someone's ear** [Slang] to talk excessively to someone —**fall on deaf ears** to be ignored or unheeded —**have (or keep) an ear to the ground** to pay attention to the trends of public opinion —**play by ear** to play

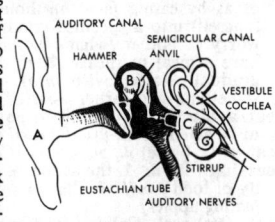

AUDITORY CANAL
SEMICIRCULAR CANAL
HAMMER
ANVIL
VESTIBULE
COCHLEA
STIRRUP
EUSTACHIAN TUBE
AUDITORY NERVES

HUMAN EAR
(A, external ear;
B, middle ear;
C, inner ear)

(a musical instrument or piece) without the use of notation —**play it by ear** [Colloq.] to act as the situation demands —**turn a deaf ear** to be unwilling to listen or heed

**ear**[2] (ir) *n.* [< OE. *ær*] the grain-bearing spike of a cereal plant [an *ear* of corn] —*vi.* to sprout ears

**ear·ache** (ir′āk′) *n.* an ache or pain in the ear

**ear·drum** (-drum′) *n. same as:* 1. TYMPANIC MEMBRANE 2. MIDDLE EAR

**ear·ful** (-fool′) *n.* [Colloq.] talk listened to that is especially gossipy, scolding, tedious, etc.

**Earl, Earle** (url) [see ff.] a masculine name

**earl** (url) *n.* [OE. *eorl*, warrior, nobleman] a British nobleman ranking above a viscount and below a marquess —**earl′dom** *n.*

**ear·lap** (ir′lap′) *n.* 1. the ear lobe 2. the external ear

**ear·ly** (ur′lē) *adv., adj.* -li·er, -li·est [< OE. < *ær*, before (see ERE) + *-lice* (see -LY²)] 1. near the beginning of a given period of time or of a series, as of events 2. before the expected or usual time 3. in the far distant past 4. in the near future; before long —**ear′li·ness** *n.*

**early bird** [Colloq.] a person who arrives early or gets up early in the morning

**Early Modern English** English as spoken and written from about 1450 to about 1750

**ear·mark** (ir′märk′) *n.* 1. an identification mark put on the ear of an animal to show ownership 2. an identifying mark or feature; sign —*vt.* 1. to mark the ears of (livestock) for identification 2. to set a distinctive mark upon; identify 3. to reserve or set aside for a special purpose

**ear·muffs** (-mufs′) *n.pl.* cloth or fur coverings for the ears in cold weather

**earn** (urn) *vt.* [OE. *earnian*, to gain, lit., to harvest] 1. to receive (salary, wages, etc.) for one's labor or service 2. to get or deserve as a result of something done 3. to gain (interest, etc.) as profit 4. *Baseball* to score (a run not a result of an error) against a pitcher —**earn′er** *n.*

**Ear·nest** (ur′nist) [var. of ERNEST] a masculine name

**ear·nest**[1] (ur′nist) *adj.* [OE. *eornoste*] 1. serious and intense; not joking; zealous and sincere 2. not petty; important —**in earnest** 1. serious 2. in a determined manner —**ear′nest·ly** *adv.* —**ear′nest·ness** *n.*

**ear·nest**[2] (ur′nist) *n.* [< OFr. *erres* < L. *arrae*, pl. < Gr. *arrabōn* < Heb. *'ērābōn*] 1. money given as a part payment and pledge in binding a bargain: in full, **earnest money** 2. something given or done as an indication of what is to come; token

**earn·ings** (ur′ninz) *n.pl.* 1. wages or other recompense 2. profits, interest, dividends, etc.

**ear·phone** (ir′fōn′) *n.* a receiver for radio, telephone, etc. held to or put into the ear

**ear·plug** (-plug′) *n.* a plug inserted in the outer ear, as to keep out sound or water

**ear·ring** (-riŋ′) *n.* a ring or other small ornament for the lobe of the ear

**ear·shot** (-shät′) *n.* the distance within which a sound, esp. that of the unaided human voice, can be heard

**earth** (urth) *n.* [OE. *eorthe*] **1.** the planet that we live on: it is the fifth largest planet of the solar system and the third in distance from the sun: diameter, 7,927 mi. **2.** this world, as distinguished from heaven and hell **3.** all the people on the earth **4.** land, as distinguished from sea or sky **5.** soil; ground **6.** [Poet.] *a)* the human body *b)* worldly matters **7.** the hole of a burrowing animal **8.** *Chem.* any of the metallic oxides which are reduced with difficulty, as alumina **9.** *Elec.* [Brit.] *same as* GROUND¹ —*vt.* to cover (*up*) with soil for protection, as seeds or plants —**come back** (or **down**) **to earth** to return to reality —**down to earth** practical; realistic —**on earth** of all things: an intensive /*what on earth* is that?/ —**run to earth 1.** to hunt down **2.** to find by search

**earth·bound** (-bound′) *adj.* **1.** confined to or by the earth or earthly things **2.** headed for the earth

**earth·en** (ur′thən) *adj.* **1.** made of earth or of baked clay **2.** earthly

**earth·en·ware** (-wer′) *n.* the coarser sort of containers, tableware, etc. made of baked clay

**earth·ly** (urth′lē) *adj.* **1.** of the earth; specif., *a)* terrestrial *b)* worldly *c)* temporal or secular **2.** conceivable; possible —**earth′li·ness** *n.*

**earth·man** (-man′) *n., pl.* **-men′** (-men′) a person on or from the planet earth, as in science fiction

**earth·nut** (-nut′) *n.* the root, tuber, or underground pod of various plants, as the peanut

**earth·quake** (-kwāk′) *n.* a shaking of the crust of the earth, caused by underground volcanic forces or by shifting of rock

**earth·ward** (-wərd) *adv., adj.* toward the earth: also **earth′-wards** *adv.*

**earth·work** (-wurk′) *n.* **1.** a defensive embankment made by piling up earth **2.** *Engineering* the work of excavating or building embankments

**earth·worm** (-wurm′) *n.* a round, segmented worm that burrows in the soil

**earth·y** (ur′thē) *adj.* **earth′i·er, earth′i·est 1.** of or like earth or soil **2.** *a)* coarse; unrefined *b)* simple and natural —**earth′i·ness** *n.*

**ear trumpet** a trumpet-shaped tube formerly used as a hearing aid by the partially deaf

**ear·wax** (ir′waks′) *n.* the yellowish, waxlike secretion in the canal of the outer ear; cerumen

**ear·wig** (-wig′) *n.* [< OE. < *eare*, EAR¹ + *wicga*, beetle, worm] any of an order of insects with short, horny forewings and a pair of forceps at the tail end

**ease** (ēz) *n.* [< OFr. *aise* < L. *adjacens*, lying nearby: see ADJACENT] **1.** freedom from pain or trouble; comfort **2.** natural, unstrained manner; poise **3.** freedom from difficulty; facility **4.** freedom from poverty; affluence **5.** leisure; relaxation —*vt.* **eased, eas′ing 1.** to free from pain or trouble; comfort **2.** to lessen (pain, anxiety, etc.) **3.** to make easier; facilitate **4.** to reduce the strain or pressure of **5.** to move by careful shifting, etc. —*vi.* **1.** to move or be moved by careful shifting, etc. **2.** to lessen in tension, speed, pain, etc. —**at ease 1.** without pain, anxiety, etc. **2.** *Mil.* relaxed, but keeping silent and standing in place —**take one's ease** to relax in comfort —**ease′ful** *adj.*

**ea·sel** (ē′z'l) *n.* [< Du. *ezel* (G. *esel*), ass, ult. < L. *asinus*, ASS] an upright frame or tripod to hold an artist's canvas, a picture on display, etc.

**ease·ment** (ēz′mənt) *n.* **1.** an easing or being eased **2.** a comfort, relief, or convenience **3.** *Law* a right that one may have in another's land, as a right of way

**eas·i·ly** (ē′z'l ē) *adv.* **1.** in an easy way **2.** by far /*easily* the best/ **3.** very likely /it may *easily* rain/

**eas·i·ness** (ē′zē nis) *n.* the quality or state of being easy to do or get, or of being at ease

**east** (ēst) *n.* [OE. *east*] **1.** the direction to the right of a person facing north; direction in which sunrise occurs (90° on the compass, opposite west) **2.** a region or district in or toward this direction **3.** [E-] Asia and the nearby islands; the Orient —*adj.* **1.** in, of, to, or toward the east **2.** from the east **3.** [E-] designating the eastern part of a country, etc. —*adv.* in or toward the east —**the East** the eastern part of the U.S., esp. from Maine through Maryland

**East Berlin** E section of Berlin; capital of East Germany: pop. 1,084,000: cf. BERLIN

**east·bound** (-bound′) *adj.* going eastward

**East China Sea** part of the Pacific Ocean east of China and west of Kyushu, Japan

**East·er** (ēs′tər) *n.* [< OE. < *Eastre*, dawn goddess] **1.** an annual Christian festival celebrating the resurrection of Jesus, held on the first Sunday after the first full moon on or after March 21 **2.** this Sunday: also **Easter Sunday**

**Easter egg** a colored egg or an egg-shaped candy, etc., used as an Easter gift or ornament

**Easter Island** [discovered *Easter* day, 1722] Chilean island in the South Pacific, c. 2,000 mi. west of Chile: 64 sq. mi.

**east·er·ly** (ēs′tər lē) *adj., adv.* **1.** toward the east **2.** from the east

**east·ern** (-tərn) *adj.* **1.** in, of, or toward the east **2.** from the east **3.** [E-] of or characteristic of the East —**east′ern·most′** (-mōst′) *adj.*

**Eastern Church 1.** *a)* orig., the Christian Church in E Europe, W Asia, and Egypt *b)* those Churches descended from this Church and in union with Rome but having their own rite (**Eastern Rite**) **2.** *same as* ORTHODOX EASTERN CHURCH

**east·ern·er** (-ər) *n.* a native or inhabitant of the east, specif. [E-] of the eastern part of the U.S.

**Eastern Hemisphere** that half of the earth that includes Europe, Africa, Asia, and Australia

**Eastern Orthodox Church** *same as* ORTHODOX EASTERN CHURCH

**Eastern Roman Empire** Byzantine Empire, esp. so called until 476 A.D.: cf. WESTERN ROMAN EMPIRE

**Eastern Standard Time** *see* STANDARD TIME

**East·er·tide** (ēs′tər tīd′) *n.* the period after Easter, extending in various churches to Ascension Day, Whitsunday, or Trinity Sunday

**East Germany** E section of Germany, constituting a country in NC Europe: 41,800 sq. mi.; pop. 17,084,000; cap. East Berlin: cf. GERMANY

**East Indies 1.** Malay Archipelago; esp., the islands of Indonesia **2.** formerly, India, the Indochinese peninsula, the Malay Peninsula, and the Malay Archipelago —**East Indian**

**east-north·east** (ēst′nôrth′ēst′; *nautical* -nôr′-) *n.* the direction halfway between due east and northeast; 22°30′ north of due east —*adj., adv.* **1.** in or toward this direction **2.** from this direction

**East Orange** city in NE N.J., adjoining Newark: pop. 77,000

**East Prussia** former province of NE Germany, on the Baltic Sea: since 1945, in Poland & the U.S.S.R.

**East River** strait in SE N.Y., separating Manhattan Island from Long Island

**east-south·east** (ēst′south′ēst′; *nautical* -sou′-) *n.* the direction halfway between due east and southeast; 22°30′ south of due east —*adj., adv.* **1.** in or toward this direction **2.** from this direction

**East St. Louis** city in SW Ill., on the Mississippi, opposite St. Louis: pop. 55,000

**east·ward** (ēst′wərd) *adj., adv.* toward the east: also **east′-wards** *adv.* —*n.* an eastward direction, point, or region

**east·ward·ly** (-lē) *adv., adj.* **1.** toward the east **2.** from the east

**eas·y** (ē′zē) *adj.* **eas′i·er, eas′i·est** [< OFr. *aisé* < *aise*: see EASE] **1.** that can be done, got, etc. with ease; not difficult **2.** free from trouble, anxiety, pain, etc. **3.** providing comfort or rest **4.** fond of comfort or ease **5.** not stiff or awkward **6.** not strict; lenient **7.** compliant or credulous **8.** *a)* unhurried *b)* gradual —*adv.* [Colloq.] **1.** easily **2.** slowly and carefully —**easy does it** be careful —**go easy on** [Colloq.] **1.** to use with restraint **2.** to deal with leniently —**on easy street** well-to-do —**take it easy** [Colloq.] **1.** to refrain from anger, haste, violence, etc. **2.** to refrain from hard work; relax; rest

**easy chair** a stuffed or padded armchair

**eas·y·go·ing** (-gō′iŋ) *adj.* **1.** not hurried or agitated **2.** lenient or lackadaisical

**eat** (ēt) *vt.* **ate** (āt; *Brit.* et) or archaic & dial. **eat** (et, ēt), **eat·en** (ēt′'n) or archaic **eat** (et, ēt), **eat′ing** [OE. *etan*] **1.** to chew and swallow (food) **2.** to use up or destroy as by eating; consume or ravage (usually with *away* or *up*) **3.** to penetrate and destroy, as acid does; corrode **4.** to make by or as by eating /acid *ate* holes in the cloth/ **5.** to bring (oneself) into a specified condition by eating **6.** [Slang] to worry or bother /what's *eating* him?/ —*vi.* **1.** to eat food; have a meal or meals **2.** to destroy or use up something gradually (often with *into*) —**eat one's words** to retract something said earlier —**eat′er** *n.*

**eat·a·ble** (-ə b'l) *adj.* fit to be eaten; edible —*n.* a thing fit to be eaten; food: *usually used in pl.*

**eat·er·y** (-ər ē) *n., pl.* **-er·ies** [Colloq.] a restaurant

**eat·ing** (-iŋ) *n.* **1.** the action of one that eats **2.** edible quality of food —*adj.* **1.** that eats **2.** good for eating uncooked /*eating* apples/

**eats** (ēts) *n.pl.* [Colloq.] food; meals

**eau de Co·logne** (ō′də kə lōn′) [Fr., lit., water of Cologne] a perfumed toilet water made of alcohol and aromatic oils: usually clipped to *cologne*

**eaves** (ēvz) *n.pl., sing.* **eave** [orig. sing., OE. *efes*] the lower edge or edges of a roof, usually projecting beyond the sides of a building

**eaves·drop** (-dräp′) *vi.* **-dropped′, -drop′ping** [prob. back-formation < *eavesdropper*, lit., one who stands under the eaves to listen] to listen secretly to a private conversation —**eaves′drop′per** *n.*

**ebb** (eb) *n.* [OE. *ebba*] **1.** the flow of water back toward the sea, as the tide falls **2.** a weakening or lessening; decline —*vi.* **1.** to flow back; recede, as the tide **2.** to weaken or lessen; decline

**ebb tide** the outgoing or falling tide

**eb·on** (eb′ən) *adj., n.* [< L. *ebenus* < Gr. *ebenos* < Egypt. *hbnj* (Heb. *hobnim*)] [Poet.] *same as* EBONY

**eb·on·ite** (-īt′) *n. same as* VULCANITE

**eb·on·ize** (-īz′) *vt.* **-ized′, -iz′ing** to give a finish to (wood, etc.) like that of ebony

**eb·on·y** (-ē) *n., pl.* **-on·ies** [< LL. *ebenius* < *ebenus*: see EBON] **1.** the hard, heavy, dark, durable wood of certain tropical trees, used in decorative woodwork, etc. **2.** such a tree —*adj.* **1.** made of ebony **2.** like ebony, esp. in color; dark; black

**e·bul·lient** (i bool′yənt, -bul′-) *adj.* [< L. prp. of *ebullire* < *e-*, out + *bullire*, to BOIL¹] **1.** bubbling; boiling **2.** overflowing with enthusiasm, etc.; exuberant —**e·bul′·lience, e·bul′lien·cy** *n.* —**e·bul′lient·ly** *adv.*

**e·bul·li·tion** (eb′ə lish′ən) *n.* **1.** a boiling or bubbling up **2.** a sudden outburst, as of emotion

**ec·cen·tric** (ik sen′trik) *adj.* [< ML. < LL. < Gr. < *ek-*, out of + *kentron*, CENTER] **1.** not having the same center, as two circles: opposed to CONCENTRIC **2.** not having the axis exactly in the center; off center **3.** not exactly circular in shape or motion **4.** deviating from the norm, as in conduct; odd; unconventional —*n.* **1.** a disk set off center on a shaft in an apparatus for converting circular motion into back-and-forth motion **2.** an eccentric person —**ec·cen′·tri·cal·ly** *adv.*

**ec·cen·tric·i·ty** (ek′sen tris′ə tē, -sən-) *n., pl.* **-ties 1.** the state, quality, or amount of being eccentric **2.** deviation from the norm; oddity

**eccl., eccles.** ecclesiastical

**Eccles., Eccl.** Ecclesiastes

**Ec·cle·si·as·tes** (i klē′zē as′tēz) [LL. < Gr. (see ff.): transl. of Heb. *qōheleth*, speaker before an assembly] a book of the Bible, written as though by Solomon

**ec·cle·si·as·tic** (-tik) *adj.* [< LL. < Gr. < *ekklēsia*, assembly, ult. < *ek-*, out + *kalein*, to call] *same as* ECCLESIASTICAL —*n.* a clergyman

**ec·cle·si·as·ti·cal** (-ti k′l) *adj.* of the church or the clergy —**ec·cle′si·as′ti·cal·ly** *adv.*

**Ec·cle·si·as·ti·cus** (-ti kəs) [LL.] a book of proverbs in the Apocrypha: abbrev. **Ecclus.**

**ECG** electrocardiogram

**ech·e·lon** (esh′ə län′) *n.* [< Fr. < OFr. *eschelle* < L. *scala*, ladder] **1.** a steplike formation of ships, aircraft, or troops **2.** a functional or positional military subdivision **3.** *a)* an organizational level, as of responsibility *b)* persons at such a level —*vt., vi.* to assemble in echelon

**e·chid·na** (i kid′nə) *n.* [ModL. < Gr. *echidna*, adder] a small, egg-laying, ant-eating Australasian mammal with a long snout and a spiny coat

**e·chi·no·derm** (i kī′nə derm′, ek′ə-) *n.* [< ModL. < Gr. *echinos*, sea urchin, hedgehog + *derma*, skin] any of a group of marine animals with a hard, spiny skeleton and radial body, as a starfish

**ech·o** (ek′ō) *n., pl.* **-oes** [< L. < Gr. *ēchō*] **1.** *a)* the repetition of a sound by reflection of sound waves from a surface *b)* a sound so made **2.** *a)* any repetition or imitation of the words, ideas, etc. of another *b)* a person doing this **3.** sympathetic response **4.** a radar wave reflected from an object, appearing as a spot of light on a radarscope —[E-] *Gr. Myth.* a nymph who pined away for Narcissus until only her voice remained —*vi.* **-oed, -o·ing 1.** to resound with an echo **2.** to be repeated as an echo —*vt.* **1.** to repeat (the words, ideas, etc.) of (another) **2.** to repeat or reflect (sound) from a surface

**e·cho·ic** (e kō′ik) *adj.* **1.** having the nature of an echo **2.** imitative in sound; onomatopoeic, as a word formed in approximate imitation of some sound (e.g., *clash*) —**ech′o·ism** *n.*

**ech·o·lo·ca·tion** (ek′ō lō kā′shən) *n.* the determination, as by a bat, of an object's position by emission of sound waves which are reflected back to the sender —**ech′o·lo′·cate** *vt.* **-cat·ed, -cat·ing**

**echo sounding** determination of water depth or of underwater distances by a device (**echo sounder**) that measures the time it takes for a sound wave to be reflected

**é·clair** (ā kler′, ē-, i-) *n.* [Fr., lit., lightning] a small, oblong pastry shell filled with flavored custard or whipped cream and covered with frosting

**é·clat** (ā klä′, i-) *n.* [Fr. < *éclater*, to burst (out)] **1.** brilliant success **2.** dazzling display **3.** approval; acclaim **4.** fame; renown

**ec·lec·tic** (i klek′tik, e-) *adj.* [< Gr. < *ek-*, out + *legein*, to pick] **1.** selecting from various systems, doctrines, or sources **2.** composed of material selected thus —*n.* one who uses eclectic methods —**ec·lec′ti·cal·ly** *adv.* —**ec·lec′ti·cism** (-siz′m) *n.*

**e·clipse** (i klips′, ē-) *n.* [< OFr. < L. < Gr. *ekleipsis* < *ek-*, out + *leipein*, to leave] **1.** a partial or total obscuring of the sun when the moon comes between it and the earth (**solar eclipse**), or of the moon when the earth's shadow is cast upon it (**lunar eclipse**) **2.** a dimming or extinction, as of fame or glory —*vt.* **e·clipsed′, e·clips′ing 1.** to cause an eclipse of **2.** to overshadow or surpass

**e·clip·tic** (i klip′tik, ē-) *n.* **1.** the apparent annual path of the sun on the celestial sphere **2.** a great circle on the celestial sphere formed by the intersection of an infinite plane through the earth's orbit with the celestial sphere —*adj.* of eclipses or the ecliptic

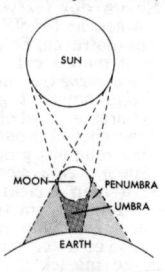

SUN

MOON — PENUMBRA

UMBRA

EARTH

ECLIPSE
(of the sun)

**ec·logue** (ek′lôg, -läg) *n.* [< Fr. < L. < Gr. < *eklegein*: see ECLECTIC] a short pastoral poem, usually a dialogue between two shepherds

**e·co-** [< LL. < Gr. < *oikos*, house] *a combining form meaning* environment or habitat [*ecosystem*]

**ecol. 1.** ecological **2.** ecology

**e·col·o·gy** (ē käl′ə jē) *n.* [< G. < Gr. *oikos*, house + *-logia*, -LOGY] the interrelationship of organisms and their environment, or the study of this —**ec·o·log·i·cal** (ek′ə läj′i k′l, ē′kə-), **ec′o·log′ic** *adj.* —**ec′o·log′i·cal·ly** *adv.* —**e·col′o·gist** *n.*

**econ. 1.** economic **2.** economics **3.** economy

**e·con·o·met·rics** (i kän′ə met′riks) *n.pl.* [*with sing. v.*] [< ECONOMY + METER² + -ICS] the use of mathematical and statistical methods to verify and develop economic theories —**e·con′o·met′ric** *adj.* —**e·con′o·me·tri′cian** (-mə·trish′ən) *n.*

**e·co·nom·ic** (ē′kə näm′ik, ek′ə-) *adj.* **1.** of the management of the income, expenditures, etc. of a business, community, etc. **2.** of the production, distribution, and consumption of wealth **3.** of economics **4.** of the satisfaction of the material needs of people

**e·co·nom·i·cal** (-i k′l) *adj.* **1.** not wasting money, time, material, etc.; thrifty or efficient **2.** expressed or done with economy **3.** of economics —**e′co·nom′i·cal·ly** *adv.*

**e·co·nom·ics** (-iks) *n.pl.* [*with sing. v.*] **1.** the science dealing with the production, distribution, and consumption of wealth and with the various related problems of labor, finance, taxation, etc. **2.** economic factors

**e·con·o·mist** (i kän′ə mist) *n.* a specialist in economics

**e·con·o·mize** (-mīz′) *vi.* **-mized′, -miz′ing** to avoid waste or reduce expenses —*vt.* to manage or use with thrift —**e·con′o·miz′er** *n.*

**e·con·o·my** (-mē) *n., pl.* **-mies** [< L. < Gr. < *oikonomos*, manager < *oikos*, house + *nomos*, managing < *nemein*, to distribute] **1.** management of income, expenditures, etc. **2.** *a)* careful management of wealth, resources, etc.; thrift *b)* restrained or efficient use of one's materials, techniques, etc., as in the arts *c)* an instance of such management or use **3.** an orderly arrangement or management of parts **4.** an economic system of a specified kind, place, era, or condition

**e·co·sys·tem** (ē′kō sis′təm, ek′ō-) *n.* [ECO- + SYSTEM] a given community of animals, plants, and bacteria and its interrelated physical and chemical environment

**ec·ru** (ek′roo, ā′kroo) *adj., n.* [Fr. *écru*, unbleached < OFr. < *es-* (L. *ex-*), intens. + *cru*, raw < L. *crudus*] light tan; beige

**ec·sta·sy** (ek′stə sē) *n., pl.* **-sies** [< OFr. < LL. < Gr. *ekstasis*, distraction < *ek-*, out + *histanai*, to place] **1.** an overpowering feeling of joy or delight; state of rapture **2.** a trance, as of a religious mystic

**ec·stat·ic** (ik stat′ik, ek-) *adj.* of, feeling, causing, or caused by ecstasy —**ec·stat′i·cal·ly** *adv.*

**ec·to-** [ModL. < Gr. *ektos*, outside] *a combining form meaning* outside, external: also, before a vowel, **ect-**

**ec·to·derm** (ek′tə derm′) *n.* [ECTO- + -DERM] the outer layer of cells of an embryo, from which the skin, hair, etc. develop —**ec′to·der′mal, ec′to·der′mic** *adj.*

**ec·to·mor·phic** (ek′tə môr′fik) *adj.* [ECTO- + -MORPHIC] designating or of the slender type of human body, in which the structures developed from the ectoderm predominate —**ec′to·morph′** *n.*

**-ec·to·my** (ek′tə mē) [< Gr. < *ek-*, out + *temnein*, to cut] *combining form meaning* a surgical excision of *[appendectomy]*

**ec·to·plasm** (ek′tə plaz′m) *n.* [ECTO- + -PLASM] **1.** the outer cytoplasm of a cell **2.** a vaporous, luminous substance believed by spiritualists to emanate from the medium in a trance —**ec′to·plas′mic** *adj.*

**Ec·ua·dor** (ek′wə dôr′) country on the NW coast of S. America: 104,506 sq. mi.; pop. 5,840,000; cap. Quito —**Ec′ua·do′re·an, Ec′ua·do′ri·an, Ec′ua·dor′an** *adj., n.*

**ec·u·men·i·cal** (ek′yoo men′i k′l) *adj.* [< LL. < Gr. < *oikoumenē* (*gē*), the inhabited (world) < *oikein*, to inhabit < *oikos*, house] **1.** general, or universal; esp., of the Christian church as a whole **2.** *a*) furthering the unity of Christian churches *b*) promoting better understanding among differing religious groups Also **ec′u·men′ic** —**ec′u·men′i·cal·ism** *n.* —**ec′u·men′i·cal·ly** *adv.*

**ec·u·men·i·cism** (-i siz′m) *n. same as* ECUMENISM

**ec·u·men·ism** (ek′yoo mə niz′m, e kyōō′-) *n.* **1.** any ecumenical movement **2.** ecumenical principles or practice Also **ec′u·me·nic′i·ty** (-nis′ə tē) —**ec′u·men·ist** *n.*

**ec·ze·ma** (ek′sə mə, eg′zə-; ig zē′mə) *n.* [ModL. < Gr. < *ek-*, out of + *zein*, to boil] a disorder of the skin in which it becomes inflamed, scaly, and very itchy —**ec·zem·a·tous** (ig zem′ə təs, -zē′mə-) *adj.*

**-ed** (id, əd; d, t) [< OE.] **1.** *a suffix used: a*) to form the past tense and past participle of weak verbs *[wanted] b*) to form adjectives from nouns or verbs *[cultured]* or from adjectives ending in *-ate [serrated]* **2.** *a suffix added to nouns, meaning* having *[bearded]*

**ed.** **1.** edited **2.** *pl.* **eds.** *a*) edition *b*) editor **3.** education

**E·dam** (cheese) (ē′dəm, -dam) [orig. made in the Du. town of *Edam*] a round, mild, yellow cheese, usually coated with red paraffin

**Ed.B.** Bachelor of Education

**Ed.D.** Doctor of Education

**Ed·da** (ed′ə) [ON.] either of two early Icelandic literary works: *a*) the **Prose**, or **Younger, Edda** (c. 1230), a summary of Norse mythology *b*) the **Poetic**, or **Elder, Edda** (c. 1200), a collection of Old Norse poetry —**Ed·dic** (ed′ik), **Ed·da·ic** (i dā′ik) *adj.*

**ed·dy** (ed′ē) *n., pl.* **-dies** [prob. < ON. *itha*] **1.** a current of air, water, etc. moving with a circular motion against the main current; little whirlpool or whirlwind **2.** a contrary movement —*vi.* **-died, -dy·ing** to move in an eddy; whirl

**Ed·dy** (ed′ē), **Mary Baker** 1821-1910; U.S. founder of Christian Science

**e·del·weiss** (ā′d′l vīs′) *n.* [G. < *edel*, noble + *weiss*, white] a small plant of the composite family, native to the high mountains of Europe and C Asia, esp. the Alps, with white, woolly leaves and bracts

**e·de·ma** (i dē′mə) *n., pl.* **-mas, -ma·ta** (-mə tə) [ModL. < Gr. *oidēma*, a swelling] **1.** an abnormal accumulation of fluid in tissues or cavities of the body, causing swelling **2.** a similar swelling in plants —**e·dem·a·tous** (i dem′ə təs, i dē′mə-) *adj.*

**E·den** (ē′d′n) [LL. < Heb. *'ēdhen*, lit., delight] *Bible* the garden where Adam and Eve first lived; Paradise —*n.* any delightful place or state

**e·den·tate** (ē den′tāt) *adj.* [< L. pp. of *edentare*, to make toothless < *e-*, out + *dens*, tooth] **1.** without teeth **2.** of the edentates —*n.* any of an order of mammals with molars only or no teeth at all, as sloths and anteaters

**Ed·gar** (ed′gər) [< OE. < *ead*, riches + *gar*, a spear] a masculine name: dim. **Ed**

**edge** (ej) *n.* [OE. *ecg*] **1.** the sharp, cutting part of a blade **2.** sharpness; keenness **3.** a projecting ledge, as of a cliff **4.** the line or part where something begins or ends; border; margin **5.** the line at which two surfaces of a solid meet **6.** the verge or brink, as of a condition **7.** [Colloq.] advantage *[you have the edge on me]* —*vt.* **edged, edg′ing** **1.** *a*) to put an edge on *b*) to trim the edge of **2.** to make (one's way) sideways **3.** to move gradually or cautiously **4.** [Colloq.] to defeat narrowly (often with *out*) —*vi.* to move sideways or gradually or cautiously —**on edge** irritable or impatient —**set one's teeth on edge** **1.** to give a sensation of tingling discomfort **2.** to irritate; provoke —**take the edge off** to dull the intensity or pleasure (of) —**edg′er** *n.*

**edge·ways** (-wāz′) *adv.* with the edge foremost; on, by, or toward the edge: also **edge′wise′** (-wīz′) —**get a word in edgeways** to manage to say something in a conversation monopolized by others

**edg·ing** (ej′in) *n.* something forming an edge

**edg·y** (-ē) *adj.* **edg′i·er, edg′i·est** **1.** having an edge; sharp **2.** irritable; on edge —**edg′i·ly** *adv.* —**edg′i·ness** *n.*

**ed·i·ble** (ed′ə b′l) *adj.* [LL. *edibilis* < L. *edere*, to eat] fit to be eaten —*n.* anything fit to be eaten —**ed′i·bil′i·ty** (-bil′ə tē), **ed′i·ble·ness** *n.*

**e·dict** (ē′dikt) *n.* [< L. pp. of *edicere*, to proclaim < *e-*, out + *dicere*, to say] an official public proclamation issued by authority; decree

**ed·i·fice** (ed′ə fis) *n.* [< OFr. < L. *aedificium*, a building < *aedificare:* see ff.] **1.** a building, esp. a large, imposing one **2.** any complicated organization

**ed·i·fy** (ed′ə fī′) *vt.* **-fied′, -fy′ing** [< OFr. < L. *aedificare* to build < *aedes*, a house + *-ficare* < *facere*, to make] to instruct so as to improve morally or spiritually —**ed′i·fi- ca′tion** (-fi kā′shən) *n.* —**ed′i·fi′er** *n.*

**Ed·in·burgh** (ed′'n bur′ə, -o) capital of Scotland, on the Firth of Forth: pop. 468,000

**Ed·i·son** (ed′ə s'n), **Thomas Al·va** (al′və) 1847-1931; U.S. inventor

**ed·it** (ed′it) *vt., vi.* [back-formation < EDITOR] **1.** to prepare (an author's works, a manuscript, etc.) for publication by selecting, arranging, revising, etc. **2.** to govern the policy for (a newspaper or periodical) **3.** to prepare (a movie film, video tape, or recording) for presentation by cutting, rearranging, etc. —**edit out** to delete in editing

**edit.** **1.** edited **2.** edition **3.** editor

**E·dith** (ē′dith) [< OE. < *ead*, riches + *guth*, battle] a feminine name

**e·di·tion** (i dish′ən) *n.* [< L. *editio*, a publishing < *edere:* see ff.] **1.** the size, style, or form in which a book, etc. is published **2.** *a*) the total number of copies of a book, etc. published at the same time *b*) one of these copies

**ed·i·tor** (ed′i tər) *n.* [< L. pp. of *edere*, to publish < *e-*, out + *dare*, to give] **1.** a person who edits **2.** the head of a department of a newspaper, magazine, etc. **3.** a device used to edit (sense 3) —**ed′i·tor·ship′** *n.*

**ed·i·to·ri·al** (ed′ə tôr′ē əl) *adj.* of, by, or characteristic of an editor or editors —*n.* a statement of opinion in a newspaper, etc. or on radio or TV by an editor, publisher, etc. —**ed′i·to′ri·al·ly** *adv.*

**ed·i·to·ri·al·ist** (-ist) *n.* an editorial writer

**ed·i·to·ri·al·ize** (-īz′) *vt., vi.* **-ized′, -iz′ing** **1.** to express editorial opinions about (something) **2.** to express editorial opinions in (an article, etc.) —**ed′i·to′ri·al·i·za′tion** *n.* —**ed′i·to′ri·al·iz′er** *n.*

**editor in chief** *pl.* **editors in chief** the editor who heads the editorial staff of a publication

**Ed·mon·ton** (ed′mən tən) capital of Alberta, Canada, in the C part: pop. 461,000

**Ed·mund, Ed·mond** (ed′mənd) [< OE. < *ead*, riches + *mund*, protection] a masculine name

**Ed·na** (ed′nə) [Gr. < Heb. *'ednāh*, rejuvenation] a feminine name

**E·dom** (ē′dəm) ancient kingdom in SW Asia, south of the Dead Sea —**E′dom·ite′** (-īt′) *n.*

**EDP** electronic data processing

**ed·u·ca·ble** (ej′ə kə b′l) *adj.* that can be educated or trained —**ed′u·ca·bil′i·ty** *n.*

**ed·u·cate** (ej′ə kāt′) *vt.* **-cat′ed, -cat′ing** [< L. pp. of *educare*, to train < *educere* < *e-*, out + *ducere*, to lead] **1.** to train, teach, instruct, or develop, esp. by formal schooling **2.** to pay for the schooling of (a person)

**ed·u·cat·ed** (-kāt′id) *adj.* **1.** having, or indicating, education **2.** based on knowledge or experience

**ed·u·ca·tion** (ej′ə kā′shən) *n.* **1.** an educating or a being educated **2.** knowledge, ability, etc. thus developed **3.** type of formal schooling **4.** study of the methods of teaching and learning —**ed′u·ca′tion·al, ed′u·ca′tive** *adj.* —**ed′u·ca′tion·al·ly** *adv.*

**ed·u·ca·tion·ist** (-ist) *n.* an educator; esp., an authority on educational theory: often a disparaging term: also **ed′u·ca′tion·al·ist**

**ed·u·ca·tor** (ej′ə kāt′ər) *n.* **1.** a person whose work is to educate others; teacher **2.** a specialist in educational methods, theories, etc.

**e·duce** (i dōōs′, ē-; -dyōōs′) *vt.* '-duced′, -duc′ing** [L. *educere:* see EDUCATE] **1.** to draw out; elicit **2.** to deduce —**e·duc′i·ble** *adj.* —**e·duc·tion** (i duk′shən, ē-) *n.*

**Ed·ward** (ed′wərd) [< OE. < *ead*, riches + *weard*, guardian] **1.** a masculine name **2.** name of eight kings of England in the 13th-16th cent. & in the 20th cent.; specif., **Edward VII** 1841-1910; king (1901-10); son of Queen VicTORIA

**Ed·ward·i·an** (ed wär′dē ən, -wôr′-) *adj.* designating or of the reign of any of the English kings named Edward; specif. of Edward VII

**Ed·wards** (ed′wərdz), **Jonathan** 1703-58; Am. theologian

**Edward the Confessor** 1004?-66; king of England (1042-66)

**Ed·win** (ed′win) [< OE. < *ead*, riches + *wine*, friend] a masculine name

**-ee** (ē) [< OFr. *-é*, orig. masc. ending of pp. of verbs in *-er*] *n.-forming suffix designating:* **1.** the recipient of a specific action or benefit *[appointee, mortgagee]* **2.** a person in a specified condition *[absentee, employee]* **3.** a person or thing associated in some way with another *[goatee]*

**E.E.C.** European Economic Community

**EEG** electroencephalogram

**eel** (ēl) *n., pl.* **eels, eel**: see PLURAL, II, D, 1 [OE. æl] a snakelike fish with a long, slippery body and no pelvic fins —**eel′like′, eel′y** *adj.*

**eel·grass** (-gras′) *n.* an underwater flowering plant with long, grasslike leaves

**eel·pout** (-pout′) *n., pl.* **-pout′, -pouts′**: see PLURAL, II, D, 2 [OE. ælepute] **1.** a saltwater fish resembling the blenny **2.** *same as* BURBOT

**eel·worm** (-wurm′) *n.* any of various nematode worms, either free-living or parasitic on plants

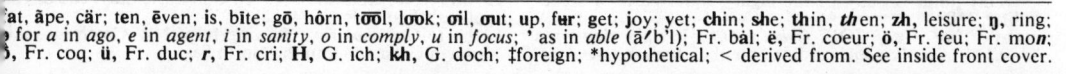

EEL
(to 5 ft. long)

**e′en** (ēn) *adv.* [Poet.] even —*n.* [Poet. or Dial.] even(ing)

**e′er** (er, ar) *adv.* [Poet.] ever

**-eer** (ir) [Fr. *-ier* < L. *-arius*] *a suffix used to form:* **1.** *nouns meaning* one that has to do with [*mountaineer*] or one that writes, makes, etc. [*pamphleteer*] **2.** *verbs meaning* to have to do with [*electioneer*]

**ee·rie, ee·ry** (ir′ē) *adj.* **-ri·er, -ri·est** [prob. ult. < OE. *earg*, timid] weird or uncanny, esp. in a frightening way —**ee′ri·ly** *adv.* —**ee′ri·ness** *n.*

**ef·face** (i fās′, e-) *vt.* **-faced′, -fac′ing** [Fr. *effacer* < e- (L. *ex*, out) + *face*: see FACE] **1.** to rub out or wipe out; erase [to efface a memory] **2.** to make (oneself) inconspicuous —**ef·face′a·ble** *adj.* —**ef·face′ment** *n.* —**ef·fac′er** *n.*

**ef·fect** (ə fekt′, i-) *n.* [< OFr. (& L.) < L. pp. of *efficere* < *ex-*, out + *facere*, to do] **1.** anything brought about by a cause or agent; result **2.** the power to produce results; efficacy **3.** influence or action [a cathartic effect] **4.** general meaning; purport [he spoke to this effect] **5.** *a)* the impression produced, as by artistic design, a way of speaking, acting, etc. [done for effect] *b)* something that makes such an impression [cloud effects] **6.** the condition or fact of being in force [a law now in effect] **7.** [pl.] belongings; property [personal effects] —*vt.* to bring about; cause; accomplish —**in effect 1.** in result; actually **2.** in essence; virtually —**take effect** to begin to produce results; become operative —**ef·fect′er** *n.*

**ef·fec·tive** (ə fek′tiv, i-) *adj.* **1.** having an effect **2.** producing a desired effect **3.** in effect; operative **4.** actual, not merely theoretical **5.** making a striking impression **6.** equipped and ready for combat —*n.* a combat-ready soldier, unit, etc. —**ef·fec′tive·ly** *adv.* —**ef·fec′tive·ness** *n.*

**ef·fec·tu·al** (ə fek′choo wəl, i-) *adj.* **1.** producing, or able to produce, the desired effect **2.** having legal force; valid —**ef·fec′tu·al′i·ty** (-wal′ə tē) *n.* —**ef·fec′tu·al·ly** *adv.*

**ef·fec·tu·ate** (-wāt′) *vt.* **-at′ed, -at′ing** to bring about; effect —**ef·fec′tu·a′tion** *n.*

**ef·fem·i·nate** (i fem′ə nit) *adj.* [< L. pp. of *effeminare* < *ex-*, out + *femina*, woman] having or showing qualities generally attributed to women, as weakness, delicacy, etc.; unmanly —**ef·fem′i·na·cy** (-nə sē) *n.* —**ef·fem′i·nate·ly** *adv.*

**ef·fen·di** (i fen′dē) *n., pl.* **-dis** [< Turk. < ModGr. < Gr. *authentēs*, a master] Sir; Master: former Turkish title of respect

**ef·fer·ent** (ef′ər ənt) *adj.* [< L. prp. of *efferre* < *ex-*, out + *ferre*, to bear] *Physiol.* carrying away from a central part; specif., designating nerves that carry impulses away from a nerve center: opposed to AFFERENT

**ef·fer·vesce** (ef′ər ves′) *vi.* **-vesced′, -vesc′ing** [< L. < *ex-*, out + *fervescere*, to begin to boil < *fervere*, to boil] **1.** to give off gas bubbles, as soda water; bubble **2.** to be lively —**ef′fer·ves′cence** *n.* —**ef′fer·ves′cent** *adj.* —**ef′fer·ves′cent·ly** *adv.*

**ef·fete** (e fēt′, i-) *adj.* [L. *effetus*, exhausted by bearing < *ex-*, out + *fetus*, productive] **1.** no longer able to produce; spent and sterile **2.** decadent, soft, etc. —**ef·fete′ly** *adv.* —**ef·fete′ness** *n.*

**ef·fi·ca·cious** (ef′ə kā′shəs) *adj.* [L. *efficax* < *efficere* (see EFFECT) + *-OUS*] producing or capable of producing the desired effect; effective —**ef′fi·ca′cious·ly** *adv.* —**ef′fi·ca′·cious·ness** *n.*

**ef·fi·ca·cy** (ef′i kə sē) *n., pl.* **-cies** [see prec.] power to produce intended results; effectiveness

**ef·fi·cien·cy** (ə fish′ən sē, i-) *n., pl.* **-cies 1.** ability to produce a desired effect with the least effort or waste; a being efficient **2.** the ratio of effective work to energy used in producing it: said of a machine, etc. **3.** *same as* EFFICIENCY APARTMENT

**efficiency apartment** a one-room apartment having a kitchenette and a bathroom

**ef·fi·cient** (-ənt) *adj.* [< L. prp. of *efficere*: see EFFECT] **1.** directly producing an effect or result; effective **2.** pro-

ducing a desired effect with the least effort or waste —**ef·fi′cient·ly** *adv.*

**ef·fi·gy** (ef′ə jē) *n., pl.* **-gies** [< Fr. < L. *effigies* < *ex-*, out + *fingere*, to form] a statue or other likeness; often, a crude representation of a despised person —**burn** ( or **hang**) **in effigy** to burn (or hang) a despised person's effigy in public protest

**ef·flo·resce** (ef′lô res′, -lə-) *vi.* **-resced′, -resc′ing** [< L. < *ex-*, out + *florescere*, to blossom < *flos*, a flower] **1.** to blossom out; flower **2.** *Chem.* *a)* to change from crystals to a powder through loss of the water of crystallization *b)* to develop a powdery crust by evaporation or chemical change

**ef·flo·res·cence** (-res′'ns) *n.* **1.** a flowering **2.** the time of flowering **3.** *Chem.* *a)* an efflorescing *b)* the resulting powder or crust **4.** *Med.* an eruption on the skin; rash —**ef′flo·res′cent** *adj.*

**ef·flu·ence** (ef′loo wəns) *n.* [< L. prp. of *effluere* < *ex-*, out + *fluere*, to flow] **1.** a flowing out or forth **2.** a thing that flows out or forth; emanation —**ef′flu·ent** *adj., n.*

**ef·flu·vi·um** (e floo′vē əm, i-) *n., pl.* **-vi·a** (-ə), **-vi·ums** [L., a flowing out: see prec.] a vaporous or invisible emanation; esp., a disagreeable or foul vapor or odor —**ef·flu′vi·al** *adj.*

**ef·fort** (ef′ərt) *n.* [Fr. < OFr. < *esforcier*, to make an effort, ult. < L. *ex-*, intens. + *fortis*, strong] **1.** use of energy to do something; physical or mental exertion **2.** a try; attempt **3.** a result of working or trying; achievement —**ef′fort·less** *adj.* —**ef′fort·less·ly** *adv.* —**ef′fort·less·ness** *n.*

**ef·fron·ter·y** (e frun′tər ē, i-) *n., pl.* **-ter·ies** [< Fr. < L. *effrons*, shameless, barefaced < *ex-*, from + *frons*, forehead] unashamed boldness; impudence

**ef·ful·gence** (e ful′jəns, i-) *n.* [< L. prp. of *effulgere* < *ex-*, forth + *fulgere*, to shine] great brightness; radiance —**ef·ful′gent** *adj.*

**ef·fuse** (e fyooz′, i-) *vt., vi.* **-fused′, -fus′ing** [< L. pp. of *effundere* < *ex-*, out + *fundere*, to pour] to pour, or spread, out or forth

**ef·fu·sion** (e fyoo′zhən, i-) *n.* [see prec.] **1.** a pouring forth **2.** unrestrained expression in words

**ef·fu·sive** (-siv) *adj.* too demonstrative; gushy —**ef·fu′·sive·ly** *adv.* —**ef·fu′sive·ness** *n.*

**eft** (eft) *n.* [OE. *efeta*] *same as* NEWT

**eft·soon** (eft soon′) *adv.* [OE. < *eft*, again + *sona*, soon] [Archaic] soon after: also **eft·soons′** (-soonz′)

**Eg. 1.** Egypt **2.** Egyptian **3.** Egyptology

**e.g.** [L. *exempli gratia*] for example

**e·gad** (i gad′, ē-) *interj.* [prob. < *oh God*] a softened or euphemistic oath

**e·gal·i·tar·i·an** (i gal′ə ter′ē ən, ē-) *adj.* [< Fr. < *égalité*, equality + *-IAN*] of or for equal rights for all —*n.* an advocate of equal rights —**e·gal′i·tar′i·an·ism** *n.*

**egg**[1] (eg) *n.* [ON.] **1.** an oval or round body laid by a female bird, fish, insect, etc. containing within a shell or membrane the germ of a new individual and food for its development **2.** a female reproductive cell; ovum: also called **egg cell 3.** a hen's egg, raw or cooked **4.** something egglike, esp. in shape **5.** [Slang] a person —**lay an egg** [Slang] to fail, as a performance

**egg**[2] (eg) *vt.* [< ON. *eggja*, lit., to give edge to < *egg*, edge] to urge or incite (with *on*)

**egg·beat·er** (-bēt′ər) *n.* **1.** a kitchen utensil for beating eggs, etc. **2.** [Slang] a helicopter

**egg·head** (-hed′) *n.* [Slang] an intellectual

**egg·nog** (-näg′) *n.* [EGG[1] + NOG] a drink of beaten eggs, milk, sugar, and nutmeg, often with alcoholic liquor

**egg·plant** (-plant′) *n.* **1.** a plant of the nightshade family, with a large, ovoid, usually purple-skinned fruit eaten as a vegetable **2.** the fruit

**egg·shell** (-shel′) *n.* the shell of an egg; esp., the hard, brittle covering of a bird's egg —*adj.* **1.** fragile and thin, like an eggshell **2.** yellowish-white

**eg·lan·tine** (eg′lən tīn′, -tēn′) *n.* [< Fr. < OFr. *aiglent* < L. *aculeus*, a sting, dim. of *acus*, a point] a European rose with hooked spines, sweet-scented leaves, and usually pink flowers

**e·go** (ē′gō; chiefly Brit. eg′ō) *n., pl.* **e′gos** [L., I] **1.** the self; the individual as aware of himself **2.** egotism; conceit **3.** *Psychoanalysis* the part of the psyche resolving conflicts

HEN'S EGG
(A, yolk; B, air space; C, white; D, outer shell membrane; E, inner shell membrane; F, chalaza-bearing membrane; G, chalaza; H, shell)

at, āpe, cär; ten, ēven; is, bīte; gō, hôrn, tool, look; oil, out; up, fur; get; joy; yet; chin; she; thin, then; zh, leisure; ŋ, ring; ə for *a* in *ago*, *e* in *agent*, *i* in *sanity*, *o* in *comply*, *u* in *focus*; ′ as in *able* (ā′b'l); Fr. bàl; ë, Fr. coeur; ö, Fr. feu; Fr. mon; , Fr. coq; ü, Fr. duc; r, Fr. cri; H, G. ich; kh, G. doch; ‡foreign; *hypothetical; < derived from. See inside front cover.

between the impulses of the id, the demands of the environment, and the standards of the superego

**e·go·cen·tric** (ē'gō sen'trik; *chiefly Brit.* eg'ō-) *adj.* self-centered —*n.* an egocentric person —**e'go·cen'tri·cal·ly** *adv.* —**e'go·cen·tric'i·ty** (-tris'ə tē) *n.* —**e'go·cen'trism** *n.*

**e·go·ism** (ē'gō iz'm; *chiefly Brit.* eg'ō-) *n.* 1. the tendency to be self-centered 2. self-conceit; egotism 3. the doctrine that self-interest is the proper goal of all human actions: opposed to ALTRUISM —**e'go·ist** *n.* —**e'go·is'tic, e'go·is'ti·cal** *adj.* —**e'go·is'ti·cal·ly** *adv.*

**e·go·ma·ni·a** (ē'gō mā'nē ə, -mān'yə) *n.* abnormally excessive egotism —**e'go·ma'ni·ac'** (-ak') *n.* —**e'go·ma·ni'a·cal** (-mə nī'ə k'l) *adj.*

**e·go·tism** (ē'gə tiz'm; *chiefly Brit.* eg'ə-) *n.* 1. constant, excessive reference to oneself in speaking or writing 2. self-conceit 3. selfishness *Egotism* is generally considered a more opprobrious term than *egoism* —**e'go·tist** *n.* —**e'go·tis'tic, e'go·tis'ti·cal** *adj.* —**e'go·tis'ti·cal·ly** *adv.*

**e·gre·gious** (i grē'jəs, -jē əs) *adj.* [L. *egregius*, apart from the herd, outstanding < *e*-, out + *grex*, a herd] remarkably bad; flagrant [an *egregious* error] —**e·gre'gious·ly** *adv.* —**e·gre'gious·ness** *n.*

**e·gress** (ē'gres) *n.* [< L. pp. of *egredi* < *e*-, out + *gradi*, to step, go] 1. a going out; emergence: also **e·gres·sion** (i gresh'ən) 2. the right to go out 3. a way out; exit

**e·gret** (ē'grit, eg'rit) *n.* [< OFr. *aigrette* < Pr. < *aigron*, a heron < Frank.] 1. *pl.* **-grets, -gret**: see PLURAL, II, D, 1 a heronlike wading bird, usually with long, white plumes, esp. the **American egret** of temperate and tropical America 2. an aigrette (sense 1)

**E·gypt** (ē'jipt) country in NE Africa, on the Mediterranean and Red seas: c. 386,000 sq. mi.; pop. 32,501,000; cap. Cairo

**Egypt.** Egyptian

**E·gyp·tian** (i jip'shən, ē-) *adj.* of Egypt, its people, etc. —*n.* 1. a native or inhabitant of Egypt 2. the language of the ancient Egyptians

**E·gyp·tol·o·gy** (ē'jip täl'ə jē) *n.* the study of ancient Egyptian culture, language, architecture, etc. —**E'gyp·tol'o·gist** *n.*

**eh** (ā, e, en) *interj.* a sound expressing: 1. surprise 2. doubt or inquiry

**EHF** extremely high frequency

**Ehr·lich** (er'lik; *G.* er'liH), **Paul** 1854–1915; Ger. bacteriologist & immunologist

**ei·der** (ī'dər) *n.* [ult. < ON. gen. of *æthr*] 1. *pl.* **-ders, -der:** see PLURAL, II, D, 1 a large sea duck of northern regions: often **eider duck** 2. *same as* EIDERDOWN

**ei·der·down** (-doun') *n.* 1. the soft, fine breast feathers, or down, of the eider duck, used to stuff quilts, pillows, etc. 2. a quilt so stuffed

**ei·det·ic** (ī det'ik) *adj.* [< Gr. < *eidos*, what is seen] designating or of unusually vivid or lifelike mental images —**ei·det'i·cal·ly** *adv.*

**Eif·fel Tower** (ī'f'l) [after A. G. *Eiffel* (1832–93), Fr. engineer] tower of iron framework in Paris, built for the 1889 Exposition: 984 ft. high

**eight** (āt) *adj.* [OE. *eahta*] totaling one more than seven —*n.* 1. the cardinal number between seven and nine; 8; VIII 2. anything having eight units or members, or numbered eight, or shaped like 8; specif., an eight-cylinder engine or automobile

**eight ball** a black ball with the number eight on it, used in playing pool —**behind the eight ball** [Slang] in a very unfavorable position

**eight·een** (ā'tēn') *adj.* [OE. *eahtatiene*] eight more than ten —*n.* the cardinal number between seventeen and nineteen; 18; XVIII

**eight·eenth** (ā'tēnth') *adj.* 1. preceded by seventeen others in a series; 18th 2. designating any of the eighteen equal parts of something —*n.* 1. the one following the seventeenth 2. any of the eighteen equal parts of something; 1/18

**eight·fold** (āt'fōld') *adj.* [see -FOLD] 1. having eight parts 2. having eight times as much or as many —*adv.* eight times as much or as many

**eighth** (ātth, āth) *adj.* 1. preceded by seven others in a series; 8th 2. designating any of the eight equal parts of something —*n.* 1. the one following the seventh 2. any of the eight equal parts of something; 1/8 3. *Music* the interval of an octave

**eighth note** *Music* a note having one eighth the duration of a whole note: see NOTE, illus.

**eight·i·eth** (āt'ē ith) *adj.* 1. preceded by seventy-nine others in a series; 80th 2. designating any of the eighty equal parts of something —*n.* 1. the one following the seventy-ninth 2. any of the eighty equal parts of something; 1/80

**eight·y** (āt'ē) *adj.* [OE. *(hund)eahtatig*] eight times ten —*n., pl.* **eight'ies** the cardinal number between seventy-

nine and eighty-one; 80; LXXX —**the eighties** the numbers or years, as of a century, from eighty through eighty-nine

**ei·kon** (ī'kän) *n. same as* ICON

**Ei·leen** (ī lēn', ā-) [Ir. *Eibhlin*] a feminine name

**Eind·ho·ven** (īnt'hō'vən) city in S Netherlands: pop. 185,000

**Ein·stein** (īn'stīn), **Albert** 1879–1955; U.S. physicist, born in Germany: formulated theory of relativity —**Ein·stein'i·an** (-stī'nē ən) *adj.*

**ein·stein·i·um** (īn stī'nē əm) *n.* [after prec.] a radioactive chemical element produced by irradiating plutonium with neutrons: symbol, Es; at. wt., 252(?); at. no., 99

**Eir·e** (er'ə) *Gaelic name of* IRELAND (sense 2)

**Ei·sen·how·er** (ī'z'n hou'ər), **Dwight David** 1890–1969; U.S. general & 34th president of the U.S. (1953–61)

**ei·ther** (ē'thər, ī'-) *adj.* [OE. *æghwæther* < *a* (æ), always (see AYE¹) + *gehwæther*, each of two (cf. WHETHER)] 1. one or the other (of two) [use *either* hand] 2. each (of two) [doors open at *either* end of the room] —*pron.* one or the other (of two) —*conj.* a correlative used with *or*, implying a choice of alternatives [either go or stay] —*adv.* 1. any more than the other; also (after negatives) [if he won't, she won't *either*] 2. [Colloq.] an intensifier in a negative statement ["It's his. It isn't *either*!"]

**e·jac·u·late** (i jak'yə lāt') *vt., vi.* -lat'ed, -lat'ing [< L. pp. of *ejaculari* < *e*-, out + *jaculari*, to throw < *jaculum*, a dart < *jacere*, to throw] 1. to eject or discharge (esp. semen) 2. to utter suddenly and vehemently; exclaim —**e·jac'u·la'tion** *n.* —**e·jac'u·la'tor** *n.* —**e·jac'u·la·to'ry** *adj.*

**e·ject** (i jekt', ē-) *vt.* [< L. pp. of *ejicere* < *e*-, out + *jacere* to throw] 1. to throw out; expel; discharge 2. to drive out; evict —**e·ject'a·ble** *adj.* —**e·jec'tion** *n.* —**e·jec'tive** *adj.* —**e·jec'tor** *n.*

**eke¹** (ēk) *vt.* eked, ek'ing [OE. *eacan* & *eacian*] [Archaic or Dial.] to increase —**eke out** 1. to supplement [to *eke out* one's income with a second job] 2. to make (a living) with difficulty 3. to use (a supply) frugally

**eke²** (ēk) *adv., conj.* [OE. *eac*] [Archaic] also

**EKG** electrocardiogram

**el** (el) *n.* 1. *same as* ELL¹ 2. [< *el(evated)*] [Colloq.] an elevated railway

**e·lab·o·rate** (i lab'ər it; *for v.* -ə rāt') *adj.* [< L. pp. of *elaborare* < *e*-, out + *laborare* < *labor*, LABOR] 1. developed in great detail 2. complicated 3. painstaking —*vt.* -rat'ed, -rat'ing 1. to produce by effort 2. to work out in careful detail 3. to change (food or substances in the body) into compounds that can be assimilated, etc. —*vi.* to state something in detail or add more details (usually with *on* or *upon*) —**e·lab'o·rate·ly** *adv.* —**e·lab'o·rate·ness** *n.* —**e·lab'o·ra'tion** *n.* —**e·lab'o·ra'tive** *adj.* —**e·lab'o·ra'tor** *n.*

**E·laine** (i lān', ē-) [OFr., equiv. of HELEN] a feminine name

**E·lam** (ē'ləm) ancient kingdom of SW Asia, on the Persian Gulf —**E'lam·ite'** (-īt') *adj., n.*

**é·lan** (ā län'; *Fr.* -län') *n.* [Fr. < *élancer*, to dart] spirited self-assurance; verve; dash

**e·land** (ē'lənd) *n., pl.* **e'land, e'lands:** see PLURAL, II, D, 2 [Afrik. < Du., elk] either of two large, oxlike African antelopes with spirally twisted horns

**e·lapse** (i laps') *vi.* **e·lapsed', e·laps'ing** [< L. pp. of *elab < e*-, out + *labi*, to glide] to slip by; pass: said of time

**e·las·mo·branch** (i laz'mə braŋk', -las'-) *adj.* [< ModL. < Gr. *elasmos*, beaten metal + L. *branchia*, gills] of a class of fishes with cartilaginous skeletons, horny scales, and no air bladders —*n.* any fish of this class, as the shark, ray, etc.

**e·las·tic** (i las'tik) *adj.* [< ModL. < LGr. *elastikos* < Gr *elaunein*, to drive] 1. having the property of immediately returning to its original size, shape, or position after being stretched, squeezed, etc.; springy 2. able to recover easily from dejection, fatigue, etc.; buoyant 3. readily adaptable to circumstances —*n.* 1. *a)* an elastic fabric loosely woven with strands of rubber, etc. running through it *b)* a band garter, etc. made of this 2. a rubber band —**e·las'ti·cal·ly** *adv.* —**e·las·tic·i·ty** (i las'tis'ə tē, ē'las-) *n., pl.* **-ties**

**e·las·ti·cize** (i las'tə sīz') *vt.* -cized', -ciz'ing to make (fabric) elastic

**e·las·to·mer** (i las'tə mər) *n.* [< ELAST(IC) + (POLY)MER] a rubberlike synthetic polymer, as silicone rubber —**e·las'to·mer'ic** (-mer'ik) *adj.*

**e·late** (i lāt', ē-) *vt.* -lat'ed, -lat'ing [< L. *elatus*, pp. of *efferre* < *ex*-, out + *ferre*, to bear] to raise the spirits of make very proud, happy, joyful, etc. —**e·lat'ed·ly** *adv* —**e·lat'ed·ness** *n.*

**e·la·tion** (i lā'shən, ē-) *n.* high spirits

**E layer** a layer of the ionosphere at an altitude of about 6( miles that can reflect radio waves

**El·ba** (el'bə) It. island between Corsica & Italy: site of Na poleon's first exile (1814–15)

**El·be** (el'bə, elb) river flowing from NW Czechoslovakia through Germany into the North Sea

**el·bow** (el'bō) n. [OE. *elboga*] **1.** the joint between the upper and lower arm; esp., the outer part of the angle made by a bent arm **2.** anything bent like an elbow, as a pipe fitting —vt., vi. **1.** to shove or jostle with the elbow **2.** to push (one's way) thus —**out at (the) elbows** shabby or poor

**elbow grease** [Colloq.] vigorous physical effort

**el·bow·room** (-rōm', -room') n. room enough to move or work in; sufficient space

ELBOW (sense 2)

**El·brus** (el'broos, -broōz), **Mount** mountain of the Caucasus range, in the Georgian S.S.R.: highest peak in Europe, 18,481 ft.: also sp. **El'brus**

**El·burz Mountains** (el boorz') mountain range in N Iran, along the Caspian Sea

**El Ca·jon** (el kə hōn') [Sp., the box] city in S Calif.: suburb of San Diego: pop. 74,000

**eld** (eld) n. [< OE. < base of *ald*, OLD] [Archaic] **1.** old age **2.** ancient times; days of yore

**eld·er**[1] (el'dər) adj. [OE. *eldra*, compar. < base of *ald*, OLD] **1.** born or brought forth earlier than another or others; senior; older **2.** of superior rank, validity, etc. **3.** earlier; former —n. **1.** an older person, esp. one with authority in a tribe or community **2.** an ancestor **3.** an officer in an early Christian church **4.** in some Protestant churches, a minister; also, a member of the ruling body —**eld'er·ship'** n.

**el·der**[2] (el'dər) n. [OE. *ellern*] a shrub or tree with flat-topped clusters of small white flowers and red or purple berries

**el·der·ber·ry** (-ber'ē) n., pl. -ries **1.** same as ELDER[2] **2.** its berry, or drupe, used in wines, etc.

**eld·er·ly** (-lē) adj. somewhat old; approaching old age —**eld'er·li·ness** n.

**eld·est** (el'dist) adj. [OE. superl. of *ald*, old] oldest; esp., first-born or oldest surviving

**El Do·ra·do, El·do·ra·do** (el'də rä'dō, -rā'dō, -rad'ō) pl. -dos [Sp., the gilded] **1.** a legendary country in S. America, supposed to be rich in gold and jewels **2.** any place that is, or is supposed to be, rich in gold, opportunity, etc.

**El·ea·nor** (el'ə nər, -nôr') [var. of HELEN] a feminine name

**elec., elect. 1.** electric **2.** electrical **3.** electricity

**e·lect** (i lekt') adj. [< L. pp. of *eligere* < *e-*, out + *legere*, to choose] **1.** chosen; given preference **2.** elected but not yet installed in office [the mayor-*elect*] **3.** *Theol.* chosen by God for salvation and eternal life —n. a person who is elect —vt. **1.** to select for some office by voting **2.** to choose; select —vi. to make a choice; choose —**the elect 1.** persons belonging to a specially privileged group **2.** *Theol.* those who are elect

**e·lec·tion** (i lek'shən) n. **1.** a choosing or choice **2.** a choosing or being chosen for office by vote **3.** *Theol.* the selection by God of certain people for salvation and eternal life

**e·lec·tion·eer** (i lek'shə nir') vi. to canvass votes for a candidate, party, etc. in an election —**e·lec'tion·eer'er** n. —**e·lec'tion·eer'ing** n.

**e·lec·tive** (i lek'tiv) adj. **1.** a) filled by election [an elective office] b) chosen by election **2.** of or based on election **3.** having the power to choose **4.** that may be chosen but is not required; optional —n. an optional course in a school or college curriculum —**e·lec'tive·ly** adv.

**e·lec·tor** (-tər) n. **1.** one who elects; specif., a qualified voter **2.** a member of the electoral college **3.** [usually E-] any of the German princes of the Holy Roman Empire who took part in the election of the emperor —**e·lec'tor·al** adj.

**electoral college** an assembly elected by the voters to perform the formal duty of electing the president and the vice-president of the United States

**e·lec·tor·ate** (-tər it) n. all those qualified to vote in an election

**E·lec·tra** (i lek'trə) *Gr. Myth.* a daughter of Agamemnon and Clytemnestra: she encouraged her brother, Orestes, to kill their mother and their mother's lover, to avenge Agamemnon's murder

**e·lec·tric** (i lek'trik) adj. [ModL. *electricus*, orig., produced from amber by rubbing < ML. < L. *electrum*, amber < Gr. *ēlektron*] **1.** of, charged with, or conducting electricity [an electric wire] **2.** producing, or produced by, electricity [an electric generator] **3.** operated by electricity [an electric iron] **4.** very tense or exciting; electrifying —n. a train, car, etc. operated by electricity

**e·lec·tri·cal** (-tri k'l) adj. **1.** same as ELECTRIC **2.** connected with the science or use of electricity [an electrical engineer] —**e·lec'tri·cal·ly** adv.

**electric chair 1.** an apparatus in the form of a chair, used in electrocuting persons sentenced to death **2.** the death sentence by electrocution

**electric eel** a large, eel-shaped fish of N S. America, with special organs that can give electric shocks

**electric eye** same as PHOTOELECTRIC CELL

**electric field** a region at every point within which there is a force on an electric charge

**electric guitar** a guitar whose tones are transmitted to an amplifier and loudspeaker through an electrical pickup attached to the instrument

**e·lec·tri·cian** (i lek'trish'ən, ē'lek-) n. a person whose work is the construction, repair, or installation of electric apparatus

**e·lec·tric·i·ty** (-tris'ə tē) n. **1.** a property of certain fundamental particles of all matter, as electrons (negative charges) and protons or positrons (positive charges) that have a force field associated with them and that can be separated by the expenditure of energy: electrical charge can be generated by friction, induction, or chemical change **2.** a) an electric current: see CURRENT (n. 3) b) an electric charge: see CHARGE (n. 2) **3.** the branch of physics dealing with electricity **4.** electric current as a public utility for lighting, heating, etc. **5.** strong emotional tension, excitement, etc.

**electric needle** a slender, pointed electrode used in surgery to cut and cauterize tissue, etc.

**electric ray** a cartilaginous fish with electric organs that can stun enemies or prey

**e·lec·tri·fy** (i lek'trə fī') vt. -fied', -fy'ing **1.** to charge with electricity **2.** to give an electric shock to **3.** to give a shock of excitement to; thrill **4.** to equip for the use of electricity; provide with electric power —**e·lec'tri·fi'a·ble** adj. —**e·lec'tri·fi·ca'tion** n. —**e·lec'tri·fi'er** n.

**e·lec·tro** (i lek'trō) n., pl. -tros short for: **1.** ELECTROTYPE **2.** ELECTROPLATE

**e·lec·tro-** a combining form meaning: **1.** electric [electromagnet] **2.** electrically [electrocute] **3.** electricity [electrostatics]

**e·lec·tro·car·di·o·gram** (i lek'trō kär'dē ə gram') n. a tracing showing the changes in electric potential produced by contractions of the heart

**e·lec·tro·car·di·o·graph** (-kär'dē ə graf') n. an instrument for making an electrocardiogram —**e·lec'tro·car'di·o·graph'ic** adj. —**e·lec'tro·car'di·og'ra·phy** (-äg'rə fē) n.

**e·lec·tro·chem·is·try** (-kem'is trē) n. the science dealing with the use of electrical energy to bring about a chemical reaction or with the generation of electrical energy by chemical action —**e·lec'tro·chem'i·cal** adj. —**e·lec'tro·chem'i·cal·ly** adv.

**e·lec·tro·con·vul·sive therapy** (-kən vul'siv) see SHOCK THERAPY

**e·lec·tro·cute** (i lek'trə kyoot') vt. -cut'ed, -cut'ing [ELECTRO- + (EXE)CUTE] to kill with a charge of electricity; specif., to execute in the electric chair —**e·lec'tro·cu'tion** n.

**e·lec·trode** (i lek'trōd) n. [ELECTR(O-) + -ODE] any terminal that conducts an electric current into or away from various conducting substances in a circuit, as the anode or cathode in a battery, or that emits, collects, or controls the flow of electrons in an electron tube, as the cathode, plate, or grid

**e·lec·tro·dy·nam·ics** (i lek'trō dī nam'iks) n.pl. [with sing. v.] the branch of physics dealing with the phenomena of electric currents and associated magnetic forces —**e·lec'tro·dy·nam'ic** adj.

**e·lec·tro·en·ceph·a·lo·gram** (-en sef'ə lə gram') n. a tracing showing the changes in electric potential produced by the brain

**e·lec·tro·en·ceph·a·lo·graph** (-en sef'ə lə graf') n. an instrument for making electroencephalograms —**e·lec'tro·en·ceph'a·lo·graph'ic** adj. —**e·lec'tro·en·ceph'a·log'ra·phy** (-ə läg'rə fē) n.

**e·lec·trol·y·sis** (i lek'träl'ə sis) n. [ELECTRO- + -LYSIS] **1.** the decomposition of an electrolyte by the action of an electric current passing through it **2.** the removal of unwanted hair from the body by destroying the hair roots with an electrified needle

**e·lec·tro·lyte** (i lek'trə līt') n. [ELECTRO- + -LYTE] any substance which in solution can conduct an electric current by the movement of its dissociated positive and negative ions to the electrodes of opposite charge, where the ions are deposited as a coating, liberated as a gas, etc. —**e·lec'tro·lyt'ic** (-lit'ik) adj. —**e·lec'tro·lyt'i·cal·ly** adv.

**e·lec·tro·lyze** (i lek'trə līz') vt. -lyzed', -lyz'ing to subject to electrolysis

**e·lec·tro·mag·net** (i lek'trō mag'nit) n. a soft iron core surrounded by a coil of wire, that temporarily becomes a magnet when an electric current flows through the wire

**e·lec·tro·mag·net·ic** (-mag net′ik) *adj.* of, produced by, or having to do with electromagnetism or an electromagnet —**e·lec′tro·mag·net′i·cal·**ly *adv.*

**electromagnetic wave** a wave propagated through space or matter by the oscillating electric and magnetic field generated by an oscillating electric charge

**e·lec·tro·mag·net·ism** (-mag′nə tiz'm) *n.* **1.** magnetism produced by an electric current **2.** the branch of physics dealing with the relations between electricity and magnetism

**e·lec·trom·e·ter** (i lek′träm′ə tər, ē′lek-) *n.* a device for detecting or measuring differences of potential by means of electrostatic or mechanical forces

**e·lec·tro·mo·tive** (i lek′trə mōt′iv) *adj.* **1.** producing an electric current through differences in potential **2.** relating to electromotive force

**electromotive force** the force that causes or tends to cause a current to flow in a circuit, equivalent to the potential difference between the terminals and commonly measured in volts

**e·lec·tron** (i lek′trän) *n.* [arbitrary coinage < ELECTR(IC) + -ON] any of the negatively charged particles that form a part of all atoms: the number of electrons circulating around a nucleus is equal to the number of positive charges on the nucleus

**e·lec·tro·neg·a·tive** (i lek′trō neg′ə tiv) *adj.* **1.** having a negative electrical charge; tending to move to the positive electrode, or anode, in electrolysis **2.** able to attract electrons, esp. in forming a chemical bond

**e·lec·tron·ic** (i lek′trän′ik, ē′lek-) *adj.* **1.** of electrons **2.** operating, produced, or done by the action of electrons or by devices dependent on such action —**e·lec′tron′i·cal·**ly *adv.*

**electronic data processing** data processing by means of electronic equipment, esp. computers

**electronic music** music in which the sounds are originated or altered by electronic devices, and arranged and recorded on tape for presentation

**electronic organ** a musical instrument with a console like that of a pipe organ, but producing tones by means of electronic devices instead of pipes

**e·lec·tron·ics** (-iks) *n.pl.* [*with sing. v.*] the science that deals with the behavior and control of electrons in vacuums and gases, and with the use of electron tubes, transistors, etc.

**electron microscope** an instrument for focusing a beam of electrons, using electric or magnetic fields, to form an enlarged image of an object on a fluorescent screen or photographic plate: it is much more powerful than any optical microscope

**electron tube** a sealed glass or metal tube completely evacuated or filled with gas at low pressure and having two or more electrodes, used to control the flow of electrons

**e·lec·tron-volt** (-vōlt′) *n.* a unit of energy equal to that attained by an electron falling unimpeded through a potential difference of one volt

**e·lec·tro·pho·re·sis** (i lek′trō fə rē′sis) *n.* [ModL. < ELECTRO- + Gr. *phorēsis* < *pherein*, BEAR¹] the migration of colloidal particles in an electric field

**e·lec·troph·o·rus** (i lek′träf′ər əs) *n., pl.* -**ri**′ (-ī′) [ModL. < ELECTRO- + Gr. *-phoros* < *pherein*, BEAR¹] an apparatus consisting of a resin disk and a metal plate, for generating static electricity by induction

**e·lec·tro·plate** (i lek′trə plāt′) *vt.* -**plat′ed**, -**plat′ing** to deposit a coating of metal on by electrolysis —*n.* anything so plated

**e·lec·tro·pos·i·tive** (i lek′trə päz′ə tiv) *adj.* **1.** having a positive electrical charge; tending to move to the negative electrode, or cathode, in electrolysis **2.** able to give up electrons, esp. in forming a chemical bond

**e·lec·tro·scope** (i lek′trə skōp′) *n.* [ELECTRO- + -SCOPE] an instrument for detecting very small charges of electricity, as by the divergence of electrically charged strips of gold leaf —**e·lec′tro·scop′ic** (-skäp′ik) *adj.*

**e·lec·tro·shock therapy** (-shäk′) *see* SHOCK THERAPY

**e·lec·tro·stat·ics** (i lek′trə stat′iks) *n.pl.* [*with sing. v.*] the branch of physics dealing with the phenomena accompanying electric charges at rest, or static electricity —**e·lec′tro·stat′ic** *adj.* —**e·lec′tro·stat′i·cal·**ly *adv.*

GOLD LEAF

ELECTROSCOPE

**e·lec·tro·ther·a·py** (-ther′ə pē) *n.* the treatment of disease by means of electricity, as by diathermy —**e·lec′tro·ther′a·pist** *n.*

**e·lec·tro·type** (i lek′trə tīp′) *n. Printing* **1.** a facsimile plate made by electroplating a wax or plastic impression of the surface to be reproduced **2.** a print made from such a plate **3.** *same as* ELECTROTYPY —*vt., vi.* -**typed**′, -**typ′ing** to make an electrotype or electrotypes (of) —**e·lec′tro·typ′er** *n.*

**e·lec·tro·typ·y** (-tīp′ē) *n.* the process of making electrotypes

**e·lec·trum** (i lek′trəm) *n.* [L. < Gr. *ēlektron*: see ELECTRIC] a light-yellow alloy of gold and silver

**e·lec·tu·ar·y** (i lek′chōō wer′ē) *n., pl.* -**ar′ies** [< LL. < Gr. < *ek-*, out + *leichein*, to lick] a medicine mixed with honey or syrup to form a paste

**el·ee·mos·y·nar·y** (el′i mäs′ə ner′ē, el′ē ə-) *adj.* [< ML. < LL. < Gr. *eleēmosynē*, pity (in NT., alms) < *eleos*, mercy] **1.** of or for charity; charitable **2.** supported by or dependent on charity **3.** given as charity; free

**el·e·gance** (el′ə gəns) *n.* **1.** the quality of being elegant; specif., *a*) dignified richness and grace *b*) polished fastidiousness or refined grace **2.** anything elegant Also, esp. for sense 2, **el′e·gan·cy,** *pl.* -**cies**

**el·e·gant** (-gənt) *adj.* [< Fr. < L. *elegans* < *e-*, out + hyp. *legare*, var. of *legere*, to choose] **1.** characterized by dignified richness and grace, as of design, dress, style, etc.; tastefully luxurious **2.** impressively fastidious or refined in manners and tastes **3.** [Colloq.] excellent; fine —**el·e·gant·**ly *adv.*

**el·e·gi·ac** (el′ə jī′ak, i lē′jē ak′) *adj.* **1.** *Gr. & Rom. Prosody* of or composed in dactylic hexameter couplets, the second line having only an accented syllable in the third and sixth feet: the form was used for elegies, etc. **2.** of, like, or fit for an elegy **3.** sad; mournful Also **el′e·gi′a·cal** —*n.* **1.** an elegiac couplet **2.** [*pl.*] a poem or poems written in such couplets

**el·e·gize** (el′ə jīz′) *vi.* -**gized**′, -**giz′ing** to write elegies —*vt.* to lament as in an elegy

**el·e·gy** (-jē) *n., pl.* -**gies** [< Fr. < L. < Gr. *elegeia* < *elegos*, a lament] **1.** a poem or song of lament and praise for the dead **2.** any poem in elegiac verse **3.** a poem, song, etc. in a mournfully contemplative tone —**el′e·gist** *n.*

**elem.** **1.** element(s) **2.** elementary

**el·e·ment** (el′ə mənt) *n.* [OFr. < L. *elementum*] **1.** any of the four substances—earth, air, fire, water—formerly believed to constitute all physical matter **2.** the natural or suitable environment, situation, etc. for a person or thing **3.** *a*) a component part or quality, often one that is basic or essential *b*) a constituent group of a specified kind [the criminal *element*] **4.** *Chem.* any substance that cannot be separated into different substances by ordinary chemical methods: all matter is composed of such substances **5.** [*pl.*] *Eccles.* the bread and wine of Communion **6.** *Elec.* the wire coil, etc. that becomes glowing hot, as in an electric oven —**the elements** **1.** the first or basic principles; rudiments **2.** wind, rain, etc.; forces of the atmosphere See table of CHEMICAL ELEMENTS on next page

**el·e·men·tal** (el′ə men′t'l) *adj.* **1.** of the four elements (sense 1) **2.** of or like the forces of nature **3.** basic and powerful; primal [hunger is an *elemental* drive] **4.** *same as* ELEMENTARY (sense 2 *a*) **5.** being an essential part or parts **6.** being a chemical element in uncombined form —*n.* a basic principle: *usually used in pl.* —**el′e·men′tal·**ly *adv.*

**el·e·men·ta·ry** (-tər ē, -trē) *adj.* **1.** *same as* ELEMENTAL **2.** *a*) of first principles or fundamentals; introductory; basic *b*) of or having to do with the formal instruction of children in basic subjects —**el′e·men′ta·ri·**ly *adv.* —**el′e·men′ta·ri·ness** *n.*

**elementary particle** a subatomic particle that is capable of independent existence, as a neutron, proton, etc.

**elementary school** a school of the first six grades (sometimes, first eight grades), where basic subjects are taught

**el·e·phant** (el′ə fənt) *n., pl.* -**phants, -phant:** see PLURAL, II, D, 1 [< L. < Gr. *elephas* (gen. *elephantos*), elephant, ivory] a huge, thick-skinned mammal, the largest of extant four-footed animals, with a long, flexible snout (called a *trunk*) and, usually, two ivory tusks: the **African elephant** has a flatter head and larger ears than the **Asian** (or **Indian**) **elephant**

**el·e·phan·ti·a·sis** (el′ə fən-tī′ə sis) *n.* a chronic disease of the skin characterized by the enlargement of the legs or other parts, and by the hardening of the skin: it is caused by obstruction of the lymphatic vessels, esp. by filarial worms

**el·e·phan·tine** (el′ə fan′tēn, -tin, -tin) *adj.* **1.** of an elephant or elephants **2.** like an elephant in size or gait; huge, heavy, slow, clumsy, etc.

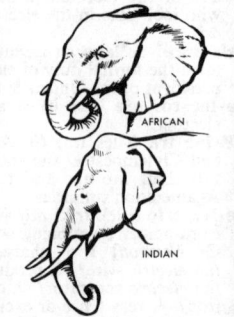

AFRICAN

INDIAN

ELEPHANTS
(shoulder height:
African, 10–13 ft.;
Indian, 8½–10 ft.)

**El·eu·sin·i·an** (el′yōō sin′ē ən) *adj.* [after *Eleusis,* ancient Gr. city near Athens, where celebrated] of the secret

# CHEMICAL ELEMENTS
With International Atomic Weights. Carbon at 12 is the standard.

| | Symbol | Atomic Number | Atomic Weight | | Symbol | Atomic Number | Atomic Weight |
|---|---|---|---|---|---|---|---|
| actinium............. | Ac | 89 | 227(?) | mercury.............. | Hg | 80 | 200.59 |
| aluminum............ | Al | 13 | 26.9815 | molybdenum.......... | Mo | 42 | 95.94 |
| americium............ | Am | 95 | 243.13 | neodymium........... | Nd | 60 | 144.24 |
| antimony............. | Sb | 51 | 121.75 | neon................. | Ne | 10 | 20.183 |
| argon................ | Ar | 18 | 39.948 | neptunium........... | Np | 93 | 237.00 |
| arsenic.............. | As | 33 | 74.9216 | nickel............... | Ni | 28 | 58.71 |
| astatine............. | At | 85 | 210(?) | niobium............. | Nb | 41 | 92.906 |
| barium.............. | Ba | 56 | 137.34 | nitrogen............. | N | 7 | 14.0067 |
| berkelium............ | Bk | 97 | 248(?) | nobelium............ | No | 102 | 255(?) |
| beryllium............ | Be | 4 | 9.0122 | osmium.............. | Os | 76 | 190.2 |
| bismuth............. | Bi | 83 | 208.980 | oxygen.............. | O | 8 | 15.9994 |
| boron............... | B | 5 | 10.811 | palladium............ | Pd | 46 | 106.4 |
| bromine............. | Br | 35 | 79.909 | phosphorus.......... | P | 15 | 30.9738 |
| cadmium............ | Cd | 48 | 112.40 | platinum............. | Pt | 78 | 195.09 |
| calcium.............. | Ca | 20 | 40.08 | plutonium........... | Pu | 94 | 239.05 |
| californium........... | Cf | 98 | 251(?) | polonium............ | Po | 84 | 210.05 |
| carbon.............. | C | 6 | 12.01115 | potassium........... | K | 19 | 39.102 |
| cerium.............. | Ce | 58 | 140.12 | praseodymium........ | Pr | 59 | 140.907 |
| cesium.............. | Cs | 55 | 132.905 | promethium.......... | Pm | 61 | 145(?) |
| chlorine............. | Cl | 17 | 35.453 | protactinium......... | Pa | 91 | 231.10 |
| chromium........... | Cr | 24 | 51.996 | radium.............. | Ra | 88 | 226.00 |
| cobalt............... | Co | 27 | 58.9332 | radon............... | Rn | 86 | 222.00 |
| copper.............. | Cu | 29 | 63.546 | rhenium............. | Re | 75 | 186.2 |
| curium.............. | Cm | 96 | 247(?) | rhodium............. | Rh | 45 | 102.905 |
| dysprosium.......... | Dy | 66 | 162.50 | • rubidium............. | Rb | 37 | 85.47 |
| einsteinium.......... | Es | 99 | 252(?) | ruthenium........... | Ru | 44 | 101.07 |
| erbium.............. | Er | 68 | 167.28 | samarium............ | Sm | 62 | 150.35 |
| europium............ | Eu | 63 | 151.96 | scandium............ | Sc | 21 | 44.956 |
| fermium............. | Fm | 100 | 257(?) | selenium............. | Se | 34 | 78.96 |
| fluorine............. | F | 9 | 18.9984 | silicon............... | Si | 14 | 28.086 |
| francium ............ | Fr | 87 | 223(?) | silver................ | Ag | 47 | 107.868 |
| gadolinium........... | Gd | 64 | 157.25 | sodium.............. | Na | 11 | 22.9898 |
| gallium.............. | Ga | 31 | 69.72 | strontium............ | Sr | 38 | 87.62 |
| germanium........... | Ge | 32 | 72.59 | sulfur............... | S | 16 | 32.064 |
| gold................. | Au | 79 | 196.967 | tantalum............. | Ta | 73 | 180.948 |
| hafnium............. | Hf | 72 | 178.49 | technetium........... | Tc | 43 | 97(?) |
| helium.............. | He | 2 | 4.0026 | tellurium............. | Te | 52 | 127.60 |
| holmium............. | Ho | 67 | 164.930 | terbium............. | Tb | 65 | 158.924 |
| hydrogen............ | H | 1 | 1.00797 | thallium............. | Tl | 81 | 204.37 |
| indium.............. | In | 49 | 114.82 | thorium............. | Th | 90 | 232.038 |
| iodine............... | I | 53 | 126.9044 | thulium............. | Tm | 69 | 168.934 |
| iridium.............. | Ir | 77 | 192.2 | tin.................. | Sn | 50 | 118.69 |
| iron................. | Fe | 26 | 55.847 | titanium............. | Ti | 22 | 47.90 |
| krypton............. | Kr | 36 | 83.80 | tungsten............. | W | 74 | 183.85 |
| lanthanum........... | La | 57 | 138.91 | uranium............. | U | 92 | 238.03 |
| lawrencium.......... | Lr | 103 | 256(?) | vanadium............ | V | 23 | 50.942 |
| lead................. | Pb | 82 | 207.19 | xenon............... | Xe | 54 | 131.30 |
| lithium.............. | Li | 3 | 6.939 | ytterbium........... | Yb | 70 | 173.04 |
| lutetium............. | Lu | 71 | 174.97 | yttrium............. | Y | 39 | 88.905 |
| magnesium........... | Mg | 12 | 24.312 | zinc................. | Zn | 30 | 65.37 |
| manganese........... | Mn | 25 | 54.9380 | zirconium............ | Zr | 40 | 91.22 |
| mendelevium......... | Md | 101 | 258(?) | | | | |

fat, āpe, cär; ten, ēven; is, bīte; gō, hôrn, to͞ol, lo͝ok; oil, out; up, fûr; get; joy; yet; chin; she; thin, then; zh, leisure; ŋ, ring; ə for a in ago, e in agent, i in sanity, o in comply, u in focus; ' as in able (ā′b'l); Fr. bàl; ë, Fr. coeur; ö, Fr. feu; Fr. mon; ô, Fr. coq; ü, Fr. duc; r, Fr. cri; H, G. ich; kh, G. doch; ‡foreign; *hypothetical; < derived from. See inside front cover.

religious rites (**Eleusinian mysteries**) anciently celebrated in honor of Demeter and Persephone

**elev.** elevation

**el·e·vate** (el'ə vāt') *vt.* **-vat'ed, -vat'ing** [< L. pp. of *elevare* < *e-*, out + *levare*, to lift < *levis*, light] **1.** to lift up; raise **2.** to raise in rank or position **3.** to raise to a higher intellectual or moral level **4.** to raise the spirits of; elate

**el·e·vat·ed** (-vāt'id) *adj.* **1.** lifted up; raised; high **2.** exalted; dignified; lofty **3.** high-spirited; exhilarated —*n.* a railway elevated above street level: in full, **elevated railway**

**el·e·va·tion** (el'ə vā'shən) *n.* **1.** an elevating or being elevated **2.** a high place or position **3.** height above the surface of the earth **4.** dignity; loftiness **5.** a flat scale drawing of the front, rear, or side of a building, etc. **6.** *Astron.* altitude **7.** *Geog.* height above sea level

**el·e·va·tor** (el'ə vāt'ər) *n.* **1.** a person or thing that raises or lifts up **2.** a cage or car for hoisting or lowering people or things, attached by cables to a machine that moves it in a shaft **3.** a machine, usually consisting of buckets or scoops fastened to an endless belt, for hoisting grain, etc. **4.** a warehouse for storing, hoisting, and discharging grain **5.** a movable airfoil like a horizontal rudder, for making an aircraft go up or down

**e·lev·en** (i lev'ən) *adj.* [OE. *endleofan*, lit., one left over (ten)] totaling one more than ten —*n.* **1.** the cardinal number between ten and twelve; 11; XI **2.** a football or cricket team

**e·lev·enth** (-ənth) *adj.* **1.** preceded by ten others in a series; 11th **2.** designating any of the eleven equal parts of something —*n.* **1.** the one following the tenth **2.** any of the eleven equal parts of something; 1/11 —**at the eleventh hour** at the last possible time

**elf** (elf) *n., pl.* **elves** (elvz) [OE. *ælf*] **1.** *Folklore* a tiny, often prankish fairy **2.** a mischievous, small child or being —**elf'ish** *adj.* —**elf'ish·ly** *adv.* —**elf'ish·ness** *n.* —**elf'like'** *adj.*

**elf·in** (el'fin) *adj.* of, appropriate to, or like an elf; fairylike —*n.* an elf

**elf·lock** (elf'läk') *n.* a tangled, matted lock of hair

**El·gar** (el'gər, -gär), Sir **Edward** (**William**) 1857–1934; Eng. composer

**El·gin** (el'jən) [after *Elgin*, city in Scotland] city in NE Ill., near Chicago: pop. 64,000

**El Grec·o** (el grek'ō) (born *Domenikos Theotokopoulos* 1541?–1614?; painter in Italy & Spain, born in Crete

**E·li** (ē'lī) [Heb. *ēlī*, lit., high] a masculine name

**e·lic·it** (i lis'it) *vt.* [< L. pp. of *elicere* < *e-*, out + *lacere*, to entice] **1.** to draw forth; evoke [to *elicit* a reply] **2.** to cause to be revealed [to *elicit* facts] —**e·lic'i·ta'tion** *n.* —**e·lic'i·tor** *n.*

**e·lide** (i līd') *vt.* **e·lid'ed, e·lid'ing** [< L. *elidere* < *e-*, out + *laedere*, to strike] **1.** to leave out; suppress; omit **2.** to leave out or slur over (a vowel, syllable, etc.) in pronunciation —**e·lid'i·ble** *adj.*

**el·i·gi·ble** (el'i jə b'l) *adj.* [< ML. < L. *eligere:* see ELECT] **1.** fit to be chosen; qualified **2.** desirable, esp. for marriage —*n.* an eligible person —**el'i·gi·bil'i·ty** *n.* —**el'i·gi·bly** *adv.*

**E·li·jah** (i lī'jə) [Heb. *ēlīyāhū*, lit., Jehovah is God] **1.** a masculine name **2.** a prophet of Israel in the 9th century B.C.: I Kings 17–19; II Kings 2:1–11 Also **E·li·as** (i lī'əs)

**e·lim·i·nate** (i lim'ə nāt') *vt.* **-nat'ed, -nat'ing** [< L. pp. of *eliminare* < *e-*, out + *limen*, threshold] **1.** to take out; get rid of **2.** to leave out of consideration; reject; omit **3.** to drop (a person, team, etc. losing a round or match) from further competition **4.** *Algebra* to get rid of (an unknown quantity) by combining equations **5.** *Physiol.* to excrete —**e·lim'i·na'tion** *n.* —**e·lim'i·na'tive** *adj.* —**e·lim'i·na'tor** *n.* —**e·lim'i·na·to'ry** *adj.*

**el·int** (el'int) *n.* [*el(ectronic) int(elligence)*] the gathering of intelligence by monitoring with electronic equipment from airplanes, ships, satellites, etc.

**El·i·ot** (el'ē ət, el'yət) [dim. of ELLIS] **1.** a masculine name **2.** **George**, (pseud. of *Mary Ann Evans*) 1819–80; Eng. novelist **3.** **T**(**homas**) **S**(**tearns**), 1888–1965; Brit. poet & critic, born in the U.S.

**E·li·sha** (i lī'shə) [Heb. *elīshā'*, lit., God is salvation] **1.** a masculine name **2.** *Bible* a prophet of Israel, who succeeded Elijah: II Kings 2

**e·li·sion** (i lizh'ən) *n.* **1.** the eliding of a vowel, syllable, etc. in pronunciation (Ex.: it's, they'd, we've) **2.** any leaving out of parts

**e·lite, é·lite** (i lēt', ā-) *n.* [< Fr., ult. < L. *eligere:* see ELECT] **1.** [*also used with pl. v.*] the group or part of a group selected or regarded as the finest, best, most powerful, etc. **2.** a size of type for typewriters, measuring 12 characters to the inch —*adj.* of, forming, or for an elite

**e·lit·ism** (-iz'm) *n.* government or control by an elite, or advocacy of such control —**e·lit'ist** *adj., n.*

**e·lix·ir** (i lik'sər) *n.* [< ML. < Ar. *al-iksīr*, prob. < Gr. *xērion*, powder for drying wounds < *xēros*, dry] **1.** a hypothetical substance sought for by medieval alchemists to

change base metals into gold or (in full, **elixir of life**) to prolong life indefinitely **2.** [Rare] the quintessence **3.** a cure-all **4.** a medicine made of drugs in alcoholic solution, usually sweetened

**E·liz·a·beth¹** (i liz'ə bəth) [< LL. < Gr. < Heb. *elīsheba'*, lit., God is (my) oath] **1.** a feminine name: dim. *Elsie;* var. *Elisabeth, Eliza* **2.** **Elizabeth I** 1533–1603: queen of England (1558–1603): daughter of HENRY VIII **3.** **Elizabeth II** 1926– ; queen of Great Britain & Northern Ireland (1952– ): daughter of GEORGE VI

**E·liz·a·beth²** (i liz'ə bəth) [after wife of Sir G. Carteret, proprietor] city in NE N.J., adjacent to Newark: pop. 106,000

**E·liz·a·be·than** (i liz'ə bē'thən, -beth'ən) *adj.* of or characteristic of the time when Elizabeth I was queen of England —*n.* an English person, esp. a writer, of the time of Queen Elizabeth I

**Elizabethan sonnet** *same as* SHAKESPEAREAN SONNET

**elk** (elk) *n., pl.* **elk, elks:** see PLURAL, II, D, 2 [OE. *eolh*] **1.** a large, mooselike deer of N Europe and Asia, with broad antlers **2.** *same as* WAPITI

**ell¹** (el) *n.* something L-shaped; specif., an extension or wing at right angles to the main structure

**ell²** (el) *n.* [OE. *eln*] a former English measure of length, mainly for cloth, equal to 45 in.

**El·la** (el'ə) [dim. of ELEANOR] a feminine name

**El·len** (el'ən) [var. of HELEN] a feminine name

**el·lipse** (i lips', ə-) *n., pl.* **-lip'ses** (-lip'siz) [< ModL. < Gr. < *elleipein*, to fall short (of a perfect circle)] *Geom.* the path of a point that moves so that the sum of its distances from two fixed points (called *foci*) is constant

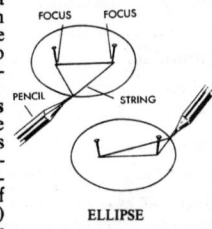

ELLIPSE

**el·lip·sis** (i lip'sis, ə-) *n., pl.* **-ses** (-sēz) [see prec.] **1.** *Gram.* the omission of a word or words necessary for complete grammatical construction but understood in the context (Ex.: "if possible" for "if it is possible") **2.** *Writing & Printing a*) a mark ( . . . or formerly ***) indicating an intentional omission of words or letters, a lapse of time, etc. *b*) the use of such marks

**el·lip·soid** (-soid) *n. Geom.* a solid whose plane sections are all ellipses or circles —*adj.* shaped like an ellipsoid: also **el·lip'soi'dal**

**el·lip·ti·cal** (i lip'ti k'l, ə-) *adj.* **1.** of, or having the form of, an ellipse **2.** of or characterized by ellipsis; with a word or words omitted; with incomplete constructions, etc. Also **el·lip'tic** —**el·lip'ti·cal·ly** *adv.*

**El·lis** (el'is) [var. of ELISHA] **1.** a masculine name **2.** (**Henry**) **Have·lock** (hav'läk, -lək), 1859–1939; Eng. psychologist & writer

**Ellis Island** [after S. *Ellis,* former owner] small island in New York Bay: former examination center for immigrants seeking to enter the U.S.

**elm** (elm) *n.* [OE.] **1.** a tall, hardy shade tree growing largely in the North Temperate Zone **2.** the hard, heavy wood of this tree

**El·mer** (el'mər) [< ? OE. < *æthel*, noble or *egil-* (< *ege*, awe) + *mære*, famous] a masculine name

**Elm·hurst** (elm'hurst') [after *elm* + *hurst*, grove] city in NE Ill.: suburb of Chicago: pop. 51,000

**El Mon·te** (el män'tē) [Sp., lit., the thicket] city in SW Calif.: suburb of Los Angeles: pop. 79,000

**el·o·cu·tion** (el'ə kyoo'shən) *n.* [< L. < pp. of *eloqui:* see ELOQUENT] **1.** style or manner of speaking or reading in public **2.** the art of public speaking or declaiming —**el'o·cu'tion·ar'y** *adj.* —**el'o·cu'tion·ist** *n.*

**El·o·ise** (el'ə wēz', el'ə wēz') [var. of LOUISE] a feminine name

**e·lon·gate** (i lôn'gāt) *vt., vi.* **-gat·ed, -gat·ing** [< LL. pp. of *elongare*, to prolong < L. *e-*, out + *longus*, long] to make or become longer; stretch —*adj.* **1.** lengthened; stretched **2.** *Bot.* long and narrow —**e·lon·ga·tion** (i lôn'gā'shən, ē'lôn-) *n.*

**e·lope** (i lōp', ə-) *vi.* **e·loped', e·lop'ing** [Anglo-Fr. *aloper*, prob. < ME. < OE. < *a-*, away + *hleapan*, to run] **1.** to run away secretly, esp. in order to get married **2.** to run away; escape —**e·lope'ment** *n.* —**e·lop'er** *n.*

**el·o·quence** (el'ə kwəns) *n.* **1.** speech or writing that is forceful, fluent, etc. **2.** the art or manner of such speech or writing **3.** persuasive power

**el·o·quent** (-kwənt) *adj.* [OFr. < L. prp. of *eloqui* < *e-*, out + *loqui*, to speak] **1.** having or characterized by, eloquence; fluent, forceful, and persuasive **2.** vividly expressive —**el'o·quent·ly** *adv.*

**El Pas·o** (el pas'ō) [Sp., the ford] city in westernmost Tex., on the Rio Grande: pop. 425,000

**El·sa** (el'sə) [G. < ?] a feminine name

**El Sal·va·dor** (el sal'və dôr'; *Sp.* säl'vä *thôr'*) country in Central America, on the Pacific: 8,260 sq. mi.; pop. 3,390,000; cap. San Salvador

**else** (els) *adj.* [OE. *elles*, adv. gen. of n. base *el-*, other] **1.** different; other *[somebody else]* **2.** in addition; more *[is there anything else?] —adv.* **1.** in a different or additional time, place, or manner; otherwise *[where else can I go?]* **2.** if not *[study, (or) else you will fail]*

**else·where** (-hwer', -wer') *adv.* in or to some other place; somewhere else

**El·sie** (el'sē) [dim. of ELIZABETH¹] a feminine name

**e·lu·ci·date** (i loo'sə dāt', ə-) *vt., vi.* -dat'ed, -dat'ing [< LL. pp. of *elucidare* < L. *e-*, out + *lucidus*, clear < *lux*, light] to make clear (esp. something abstruse); explain —e·lu'ci·da'tion —e·lu'ci·da'tive *adj.* —e·lu'ci·da'tor *n.*

**e·lude** (i lood') *vt.* e·lud'ed, e·lud'ing [< L. *eludere* < *e-*, out + *ludere*, to play] **1.** to avoid or escape from by quickness, cunning, etc.; evade **2.** to escape detection, notice, or understanding by —e·lud'er *n.* —e·lu·sion (i loo'zhən, ə-) *n.*

**El·ul** (el'ool) *n.* [Heb.] the twelfth month of the Jewish year: see JEWISH CALENDAR

**e·lu·sive** (i loo'siv) *adj.* **1.** tending to elude **2.** hard to grasp or retain mentally; baffling —e·lu'sive·ly *adv.* —e·lu'sive·ness *n.*

**el·ver** (el'vər) *n.* [for *eelfare*, migration of eels] a young eel

**elves** (elvz) *n. pl. of* ELF

**El·vi·ra** (el vī'rə, -vir'ə) [Sp., prob. < Goth.] a feminine name

**elv·ish** (el'vish) *adj.* of or like an elf —elv'ish·ly *adv.*

**E·lyr·i·a** (i lir'ē ə, ə-) [after J. *Ely*, proprietor, & Ma*ria*, his wife] city in N Ohio, near Cleveland: pop. 58,000

**E·ly·si·um** (i lizh'ē əm, -liz'-) [L. < Gr.] *Gr. Myth.* the dwelling place of virtuous people after death —*n.* any place or condition of ideal bliss or complete happiness; paradise Also Elysian Fields —E·ly·sian (i lizh'ən, -ē ən) *adj.*

**em** (em) *n.* **1.** the letter M, m **2.** *Printing* a square of any type body, used as a unit of measure, as of column width; esp., an em pica, about 1/6 in.

**'em** (əm, 'm) *pron.* [Colloq.] them

**e·ma·ci·ate** (i mā'shē āt', -sē-) *vt.* -at'ed, -at'ing [< L. pp. of *emaciare* < *e-*, out + *macies*, leanness < *macer*, lean] to cause to become abnormally lean; cause to lose much flesh or weight, as by starvation or disease —e·ma'ci·a'tion *n.*

**em·a·nate** (em'ə nāt') *vi.* -nat'ed, -nat'ing [< L. pp. of *emanare* < *e-*, out + *manare*, to flow] to come forth; issue, as from a source —*vt.* [Rare] to send forth; emit

**em·a·na·tion** (em'ə nā'shən) *n.* **1.** an emanating **2.** something that comes forth from a source **3.** *Chem. a)* same as RADON *b)* a gas given off by several radioactive substances —em'a·na'tive *adj.*

**e·man·ci·pate** (i man'sə pāt') *vt.* -pat'ed, -pat'ing [< L. pp. of *emancipare* < *e-*, out + *mancipare*, to deliver up as property, ult. < *manus*, the hand + *capere*, to take] **1.** to set free (a slave, etc.); release from bondage or serfdom **2.** to free from restraint or influence —e·man'ci·pa'tion *n.* —e·man'ci·pa·tive, e·man'ci·pa·to'ry (-pə tôr'ē) *adj.* —e·man'ci·pa'tor *n.*

**e·mas·cu·late** (i mas'kyə lāt') *vt.* -lat'ed, -lat'ing [< L. pp. of *emasculare* < *e-*, out + *masculus*, MASCULINE] **1.** to deprive (a male) of the power to reproduce, as by removing the testicles; castrate **2.** to destroy the strength or force of; weaken —e·mas'cu·la'tive, e·mas'cu·la'tive, e·mas'cu·la·to'ry (-lə tôr'ē) *adj.* —e·mas'cu·la'tor *n.*

**em·balm** (im bäm') *vt.* [< OFr. *embaumer*: see EN- & BALM] **1.** to treat (a dead body) with various chemicals to keep it from decaying rapidly **2.** to preserve in memory **3.** to make fragrant; perfume —em·balm'er *n.* —em·balm'ment *n.*

**em·bank** (im baŋk') *vt.* to protect, support, or enclose with a bank of earth, rubble, etc.

**em·bank·ment** (-mənt) *n.* **1.** the act or process of embanking **2.** a bank of earth, rubble, etc. used to keep back water, hold up a roadway, etc.

**em·bar·ca·de·ro** (em bär'kə der'ō) *n., pl.* -der'os [Sp. < pp. of *embarcar*, EMBARK] a wharf, dock, or pier

**em·bar·go** (im bär'gō) *n., pl.* -goes [Sp., ult. < L. *in-*, in, on + ML. *barra*, BAR¹] **1.** a government order prohibiting the entry or departure of commercial ships at its ports **2.** any restriction, restraint, or prohibition, esp. one imposed on commerce by law —*vt.* -goed, -go·ing to put an embargo on

**em·bark** (im bärk') *vt.* [< Fr. < Sp. or OPr. < *em-* (L. *in-*) + L. *barca*, BARK³] to put or take (passengers or goods) aboard a ship, airplane, etc. —*vi.* **1.** to go aboard a ship,

airplane, etc. **2.** to begin a journey **3.** to get started in an enterprise —em·bar·ka·tion (em'bär kā'shən), em·bark'·ment *n.*

**em·bar·rass** (im ber'əs) *vt.* [< Fr. < Sp. < It. < *imbarrare*, to impede < *in-* (L. *in-*) + *barra*, BAR¹] **1.** to cause to feel self-conscious; disconcert **2.** to cause difficulties to; hinder **3.** to cause to be in debt; cause financial difficulties to **4.** to complicate —em·bar'rass·ing *adj.* —em·bar'rass·ing·ly *adv.* —em·bar'rass·ment *n.*

**em·bas·sy** (em'bə sē) *n., pl.* -sies [< MFr. < OIt. < Pr. < hyp. *ambaissa*: see AMBASSADOR] **1.** the position or functions of an ambassador **2.** the official residence or offices of an ambassador **3.** an ambassador and his staff **4.** a person or group sent on an official mission to a foreign government **5.** any important or official mission

**em·bat·tle¹** (im bat''l) *vt.* -tled, -tling to provide with battlements; build battlements on

**em·bat·tle²** (im bat''l) *vt.* -tled, -tling [Rare, except in pp.] to prepare or set in line for battle

**em·bay** (im bā') *vt.* to shut in; enclose or surround, as in a bay —em·bay'ment *n.*

**em·bed** (im bed') *vt.* -bed'ded, -bed'ding **1.** to set or fix firmly in a surrounding mass *[to embed tiles in cement]* **2.** to fix in the mind, memory, etc. —em·bed'ment *n.*

**em·bel·lish** (im bel'ish) *vt.* [< OFr. *embelir* < *em-* (L. *in*) + *bel* < L. *bellus*, beautiful] **1.** to decorate; ornament; adorn **2.** to improve (a story, etc.) by adding details, often of a fictitious kind; touch up —em·bel'lish·ment *n.*

**em·ber¹** (em'bər) *n.* [< OE. *æmerge*] **1.** a glowing piece of coal, wood, etc. from a fire **2.** [*pl.*] the smoldering remains of a fire

**em·ber²** (em'bər) *adj.* [< OE. < *ymbryne* < *ymb*, round + *ryne*, a running] [*often* E-] designating or of three days (Wednesday, Friday, and Saturday) set aside for prayer and, sometimes, fasting in a specified week of each season of the year: observed in the Roman Catholic Church and certain other churches

**em·bez·zle** (im bez''l) *vt.* -zled, -zling [< Anglo-Fr. < OFr. < *en-* (see EN-) + *besillier*, to destroy] to steal (money, etc. entrusted to one's care); take by fraud for one's own use —em·bez'zle·ment *n.* —em·bez'zler *n.*

**em·bit·ter** (-bit'ər) *vt.* to cause to have bitter or more bitter feelings —em·bit'ter·ment *n.*

**em·bla·zon** (im blā'z'n) *vt.* [see BLAZON] **1.** to decorate (*with* coats of arms, etc.) **2.** to display brilliantly; decorate with bright colors **3.** to praise; celebrate —em·bla'zon·ment *n.*

**em·blem** (em'bləm) *n.* [orig., inlaid work < L. < Gr. *emblēma*, insertion < *en-*, in + *ballein*, to throw] **1.** a visible symbol of a thing, idea, etc.; object that stands for or suggests something else *[the cross is an emblem of Christianity]* **2.** a sign, badge, or device

**em·blem·at·ic** (em'blə mat'ik) *adj.* of, containing, or serving as an emblem; symbolic: also **em'blem·at'i·cal** —em'·blem·at'i·cal·ly *adv.*

**em·bod·i·ment** (im bäd'ē mənt) *n.* **1.** an embodying or being embodied **2.** that in which some idea, quality, etc. is embodied *[she is the embodiment of virtue]*

**em·bod·y** (-bäd'ē) *vt.* -bod'ied, -bod'y·ing **1.** to give bodily form to; incarnate **2.** to give definite or visible form to **3.** to bring together into, or make part of, an organized whole; incorporate *[the latest findings embodied in the new book]*

**em·bold·en** (-bōl'd'n) *vt.* to give courage to; cause to be bold or bolder

**em·bo·lism** (em'bə liz'm) *n. Med.* the obstruction of a blood vessel by an embolus

**em·bo·lus** (-ləs) *n., pl.* -li' (-lī') [ModL. < Gr. < *en-*, in + *ballein*, to throw] any foreign matter, as a blood clot or air bubble, carried in the bloodstream —em·bol'ic (-bäl'ik) *adj.*

**em·bos·om** (im booz'əm, -boo'zəm) *vt.* **1.** to embrace; cherish **2.** to enclose; surround; shelter

**em·boss** (-bôs', -bäs') *vt.* [< OFr.: see EN- & BOSS²] **1.** to decorate with designs, etc. raised above the surface **2.** to raise (a design, etc.) in relief —em·boss'er *n.* —em·boss'·ment *n.*

**em·bou·chure** (äm'boo shoor', äm'boo shoor') *n.* [Fr. < *emboucher*, to put into the mouth < L. *in*, in + *bucca*, the cheek] **1.** the mouth of a river **2.** *Music a)* the mouthpiece of a wind instrument *b)* the method of applying the lips and tongue to the mouthpiece of a wind instrument

**em·bow·er** (im bou'ər) *vt.* to enclose or shelter in or as in a bower

**em·brace** (-brās') *vt.* -braced', -brac'ing [< OFr. < L. *im-*, in + *brachium*, an arm] **1.** to clasp in the arms lovingly or affectionately; hug **2.** to accept readily *[to embrace an opportunity]* **3.** to take up or adopt, esp. eagerly or seriously [to *embrace* a new profession] **4.** to encircle; surround **5.** to include; contain —*vi.* to clasp each other in the arms —*n.* an embracing; hug —**em·brace′a·ble** *adj.* —**em·brace′ment** *n.* —**em·brac′er** *n.*

**em·bra·sure** (im brā′zhər) *n.* [Fr. < obs. *embraser*, to widen an opening] **1.** an opening (for a door, window, etc.) with the sides slanted so that it is wider on the inside than on the outside **2.** an opening, as in a parapet, with the sides slanting outward to increase the angle of fire of a gun

**em·bro·cate** (em′brō kāt′, -brə-) *vt.* **-cat′ed, -cat′ing** [< LL. pp. of *embrocare*, to foment < L. < Gr. < *en-*, in + *brechein*, to wet] to moisten and rub (a part of the body) with an oil, liniment, etc. —**em′bro·ca′tion** *n.*

**em·broi·der** (im broi′dər) *vt.* [< OFr. < *en-*, in + *brosder*, to embroider] **1.** to ornament (fabric) with a design in needlework **2.** to make (a design, etc.) on fabric with needlework **3.** to embellish (a story, etc.); exaggerate —*vi.* **1.** to do embroidery **2.** to exaggerate —**em·broi′der·er** *n.*

**em·broi·der·y** (-ē) *n., pl.* **-der·ies** **1.** the art or work of ornamenting fabric with needlework **2.** embroidered work or fabric **3.** embellishment, as of a story **4.** an unnecessary but attractive addition

**em·broil** (im broil′) *vt.* [< Fr.: see EN- & BROIL²] **1.** to confuse (affairs, etc.); mix up; muddle **2.** to draw into a conflict or fight; involve in trouble —**em·broil′ment** *n.*

**em·bry·o** (em′brē ō′) *n., pl.* **-os′** [ML. < Gr. *embryon* < *en-*, in + *bryein*, to swell] **1.** an animal in the earliest stages of its development in the uterus: the human organism up to the third month after conception is called an *embryo*, thereafter a *fetus* **2.** *a)* an early or undeveloped stage of something *b)* anything in such a stage **3.** the rudimentary plant contained in a seed —*adj.* embryonic

**em·bry·o-** *a combining form meaning* embryo, embryonic [*embryology*]

**em·bry·ol·o·gy** (em′brē äl′ə jē) *n.* [EMBRYO- + -LOGY] the branch of biology dealing with the formation and development of embryos —**em′bry·o·log′ic** (-ə läj′ik), **em′bry·o·log′i·cal** *adj.* —**em′bry·o·log′i·cal·ly** *adv.* —**em′bry·ol′o·gist** *n.*

**em·bry·on·ic** (-än′ik) *adj.* **1.** of or like an embryo **2.** in an early stage; rudimentary

**em·cee** (em′sē′) *vt., vi.* **-ceed′, -cee′ing** [< M.C., sense 1] [Colloq.] to act as master of ceremonies (for) —*n.* [Colloq.] a master of ceremonies

**e·meer** (ə mir′) *n. same as* EMIR —**e·meer′ate** *n.*

**e·mend** (i mend′) *vt.* [L. *emendare*, to correct < *e-*, out + *mendum*, a fault] to make scholarly corrections or improvements in (a text)

**e·men·date** (ē′mən dāt′) *vt.* **-dat′ed, -dat′ing** *same as* EMEND —**e·men·da·tion** (ē′mən dā′shən, em′ən-) *n.* —**e′men·da′tor** *n.* —**e·mend·a·to·ry** (i men′də tôr′ē) *adj.*

**em·er·ald** (em′ər əld, em′rəld) *n.* [< OFr. < VL. *smaraldus* < L. < Gr. *smaragdos*] **1.** a bright-green, transparent precious stone; green variety of beryl **2.** a similar variety of corundum **3.** bright green —*adj.* **1.** bright-green **2.** made of or with an emerald or emeralds **3.** designating or of a cut of gem in a rectangular style used esp. with emeralds

**Emerald Isle** [< its green landscape] Ireland

**e·merge** (i murj′) *vi.* **e·merged′, e·merg′ing** [L. *emergere* < *e-*, out + *mergere*, to dip] **1.** to rise as from a fluid **2.** *a)* to come forth into view; become visible *b)* to become apparent or known **3.** to develop as something new, improved, etc. [a strong breed *emerged*] —**e·mer′gence** *n.* —**e·mer′gent** *adj.*

**e·mer·gen·cy** (i mur′jən sē) *n., pl.* **-cies** [orig. sense, an emerging] a sudden, generally unexpected occurrence or set of circumstances demanding immediate action —*adj.* for use in case of sudden necessity [an *emergency* exit]

**e·mer·i·tus** (i mer′ə təs) *adj.* [L., pp. of *emereri* < *e-*, out + *mereri*, to serve] retired from active service, usually for age, but retaining one's rank or title [professor *emeritus*]

**e·mer·sion** (ē mur′zhən, -shən) *n.* an emerging

**Em·er·son** (em′ər sən), **Ralph Waldo** 1803–82; U.S. essayist, philosopher, & poet

**em·er·y** (em′ər ē, em′rē) *n.* [< Fr. < OFr. < It. < MGr. *smeri*, for Gr. *smyris*, emery] a dark, impure variety of corundum used in solid, crushed, or powdered form for grinding, polishing, etc.

**e·met·ic** (i met′ik) *adj.* [< L. < Gr. *emetikos < emein*, to vomit] causing vomiting —*n.* an emetic medicine or other substance

**E.M.F., e.m.f., EMF, emf** electromotive force

**-e·mi·a** (ēm′ē ə, ēm′yə) [ModL. < Gr. < *haima*, blood] *a suffix meaning* a (specified) condition or disease of the blood [*leukemia*]

**em·i·grant** (em′ə grənt) *adj.* **1.** emigrating **2.** of emigrants or emigration —*n.* one who emigrates

**em·i·grate** (-grāt′) *vi.* **-grat′ed, -grat′ing** [< L. pp. of *emigrare* < *e-*, out + *migrare*, to move] to leave one country or region to settle in another —**em′i·gra′tion** *n.*

**é·mi·gré, e·mi·gré** (em′ə grā′, ā′mə grā′) *n.* [Fr.] **1.** an emigrant **2.** a person forced to flee his country for political reasons

**E·mil** (ā′m′l, ē′-; em′l′) [G. < Fr. < L. *aemulus:* see EMULATE] a masculine name

**Em·i·ly** (em′′l ē) [fem. of EMIL] a feminine name: var. *Emilia*

**em·i·nence** (em′ə nəns) *n.* [< OFr. < L. < prp. of *eminere*, to stand out] **1.** a high or lofty place, thing, etc., as a hill **2.** *a)* superiority in rank, position, etc.; greatness *b)* a person of eminence **3.** [E-] *R.C.Ch.* a title of honor used in speaking to or of a cardinal, preceded by *His* or *Your*

**em·i·nent** (-nənt) *adj.* [< L.: see prec.] **1.** rising high above others; high; lofty **2.** projecting; prominent **3.** standing high by comparison with others; exalted; distinguished **4.** outstanding; noteworthy —**em′i·nent·ly** *adv.*

**eminent domain** *Law* the right of a government to take private property for public use, just compensation usually being given to the owner

**e·mir** (i mir′) *n.* [Ar. *amir*, commander] **1.** in certain Moslem countries, a ruler, prince, or commander **2.** a title given Mohammed's descendants through his daughter Fatima —**e·mir′ate** (-it, -āt) *n.*

**em·is·sar·y** (em′ə ser′ē) *n., pl.* **-sar′ies** [< L. < pp. of *emittere:* see EMIT] a person or agent, esp. a secret agent, sent on a specific mission —*adj.* of, or serving as, an emissary or emissaries

**e·mis·sion** (i mish′ən) *n.* **1.** an emitting; issuance **2.** something emitted; discharge —**e·mis′sive** *adj.*

**e·mit** (i mit′) *vt.* **e·mit′ted, e·mit′ting** [< L. *emittere* < *e-*, out + *mittere*, to send] **1.** to send out; give forth **2.** to utter (sounds, etc.) **3.** to transmit (a signal) as by radio waves **4.** to give off (electrons) under the influence of heat, etc. —**e·mit′ter** *n.*

**Em·ma** (em′ə) [G. < *Erma* < names beginning with *Erm-:* see IRMA] a feminine name

**Em·man·u·el** (i man′yōō wəl) [< Gr. < Heb. *'immānūēl*, lit., God with us] **1.** a masculine name: var. *Emanuel* **2.** the Messiah: see IMMANUEL

**Em·my** (em′ē) *n., pl.* **-mys** [altered < *Immy*, slang for a kind of TV camera] [Slang] any of the statuettes awarded annually in the U.S. for special achievement in television programming, acting, etc.

**EmnE., EMnE.** Early Modern English

**e·mol·li·ent** (i mäl′yənt) *adj.* [< L. prp. of *emollire* < *e-*, out + *mollire*, to soften < *mollis*, soft] softening; soothing —*n.* an emollient preparation, esp. for the surface tissues of the body

**e·mol·u·ment** (i mäl′yōō mənt) *n.* [< L. < *emolere* < *e-*, out + *molere*, to grind] gain from employment or position; salary, wages, fees, etc.

**e·mote** (i mōt′) *vi.* **e·mot′ed, e·mot′ing** [< ff., by analogy with DEVOTE] [Colloq.] to express emotion in a showy or theatrical manner

**e·mo·tion** (i mō′shən) *n.* [Fr. (prob. after *motion*) < L. *emovere* < *e-*, out + *movere*, to move] **1.** strong feeling; excitement **2.** any specific feeling, as love, hate, fear, anger, etc.

**e·mo·tion·al** (-′l) *adj.* **1.** of emotion or the emotions **2.** showing emotion, esp. strong emotion **3.** easily aroused to emotion **4.** appealing to or arousing the emotions —**e·mo′tion·al·ly** *adv.*

**e·mo·tion·al·ism** (-′l iz′m) *n.* **1.** the tendency to be emotional **2.** display of emotion **3.** an appeal to emotion, esp. to sway an audience

**e·mo·tion·al·ize** (-′l īz′) *vt.* **-ized′, -iz′ing** to treat, present, or interpret in an emotional way —**e·mo′tion·al·i·za′tion** *n.*

**e·mo·tive** (i mōt′iv) *adj.* **1.** expressing or producing emotion **2.** relating to the emotions

**Emp.** **1.** Emperor **2.** Empire **3.** Empress

**em·pan·el** (im pan′′l) *vt.* **-eled** or **-elled, -el·ing** or **-el·ling** *same as* IMPANEL

**em·pa·thy** (em′pə thē) *n.* [< Gr. < *en-*, in + *pathos*, feeling] intellectual or emotional identification with another —**em·path·ic** (im path′ik), **em·pa·thet·ic** (em′pə thet′ik) *adj.*

**Em·ped·o·cles** (em ped′ə klēz′) 495?–435? B.C.; philosopher

**em·per·or** (em′pər ər) *n.* [< OFr. < L. *imperator* < pp. of *imperare*, to command < *in-*, in + *parare*, to set in order] the supreme ruler of an empire

**em·pha·sis** (em′fə sis) *n., pl.* **-ses′** (-sēz′) [L. < Gr. < *emphainein*, to indicate < *en-*, in + *phainein*, to show] **1** force of expression, feeling, action, etc. **2.** special stress given to a syllable, word, phrase, etc. in speaking **3.** special attention given to something so as to make it stand out in importance; stress

**em·pha·size** (-sīz′) *vt.* **-sized′, -siz′ing** to give emphasis or special force, to; stress

**em·phat·ic** (im fat′ik) *adj.* **1.** expressed, felt, or done with emphasis **2.** using emphasis in speaking, expressing etc. **3.** very striking; forcible; definite [an *emphatic* defeat] **4.** *Gram.* designating or of a present tense or past tense in which a form of *do* is used as an auxiliary for emphasis (Ex.: I *do* care) —**em·phat′i·cal·ly** *adv.*

**em·phy·se·ma** (em′fə sē′mə) *n.* [Gr. < *en*-, in + *physaein*, to blow] abnormal distention of the alveoli, or air cells, of the lungs, accompanied by loss of elasticity in the tissues and impairment in breathing

**em·pire** (em′pīr; *for adj. usually* äm pir′) *n.* [< OFr. < L. < *imperare:* see EMPEROR] **1.** supreme rule; absolute power or authority **2.** government by an emperor or empress **3.** *a)* a group of states or territories under the sovereignty of an emperor or empress *b)* a state uniting many territories and peoples under one ruler **4.** an extensive social or economic organization under the control of a single person, family, or corporation —*adj.* [E-] of or characteristic of the first French Empire (1804–15) under Napoleon [*Empire* furniture]

**em·pir·ic** (em pir′ik) *n.* [< L. < Gr. < *empeiria*, experience < *en*-, in + *peira*, a trial] a person who relies solely on practical experience rather than on scientific principles —*adj.* empirical

**em·pir·i·cal** (-i k'l) *adj.* [see prec.] **1.** relying or based solely on experiment and observation rather than theory [the *empirical* method] **2.** relying or based on practical experience without reference to scientific principles [an *empirical* remedy] —**em·pir′i·cal·ly** *adv.*

**em·pir·i·cism** (-ə siz′m) *n.* **1.** experimental method; search for knowledge by observation and experiment **2.** *a)* a disregarding of scientific methods and relying solely on experience *b)* quackery **3.** *Philos.* the theory that experience is the only source of knowledge —**em·pir′i·cist** *n.*

**em·place** (im plās′) *vt.* **-placed′, -plac′ing** to place in position

**em·place·ment** (-mənt) *n.* **1.** an emplacing; placement **2.** the position in which something is placed; specif., *Mil.* the prepared position from which a heavy gun or guns are fired

**em·plane** (em plān′) *vi.* **-planed′, -plan′ing** same as ENPLANE

**em·ploy** (im ploi′) *vt.* [< OFr. < L. *implicare*, to enfold: see IMPLY] **1.** to make use of; use **2.** to keep busy or occupied; devote **3.** to provide work and pay for **4.** to engage the services or labor of for pay; hire —*n.* the state of being employed; paid service; employment —**em·ploy′a·ble** *adj.*

**em·ploy·ee, em·ploy·e** (im ploi′ē, em′ploi ē′) *n.* a person hired by another, or by a business firm, etc., to work for wages or salary

**em·ploy·er** (im ploi′ər) *n.* one who employs; esp., a person, business firm, etc. that hires one or more persons to work for wages or salary

**em·ploy·ment** (-mənt) *n.* **1.** an employing or being employed **2.** the thing at which one is employed; work; occupation; job **3.** the number or percentage of persons gainfully employed

**em·po·ri·um** (em pôr′ē əm) *n., pl.* **-ri·ums, -ri·a** (-ə) [L. < Gr. < *emporos*, traveler < *en*-, in + *poros*, way] **1.** a place of commerce; trading center; marketplace **2.** a large store with a wide variety of things for sale

**em·pow·er** (im pou′ər) *vt.* **1.** to give power to; authorize **2.** to enable; permit —**em·pow′er·ment** *n.*

**em·press** (em′pris) *n.* **1.** the wife of an emperor **2.** a woman ruler of an empire

**emp·ty** (emp′tē) *adj.* **-ti·er, -ti·est** [< OE. *æmettig*, unoccupied < *æmetta*, leisure + -*ig*, -*y*²] **1.** containing nothing; having nothing in it **2.** having no one in it; unoccupied [an *empty* house] **3.** worthless; unsatisfying [*empty* pleasures] **4.** meaningless; insincere; vain [*empty* promises] **5.** [Colloq.] hungry —*vt.* **-tied, -ty·ing 1.** to make empty **2.** to pour out or remove (the contents) of something **3.** to unburden or discharge (oneself or itself) —*vi.* **1.** to become empty **2.** to pour out; discharge —*n., pl.* **-ties** an empty freight car, truck, bottle, etc. —**empty of** lacking; without; devoid of —**emp′ti·ly** *adv.* —**emp′ti·ness** *n.*

**emp·ty-hand·ed** (-han′did) *adj.* bringing or carrying away nothing

**emp·ty-head·ed** (-hed′id) *adj.* silly and ignorant

**em·pur·ple** (im pur′p'l) *vt., vi.* **-pled, -pling** to make or become purple

**em·pyr·e·al** (em pir′ē əl; em′pī rē′əl, -pə-) *adj.* [< L. < Gr. *empyrios*, fiery < *en*-, in + *pyr*, a fire] of the empyrean; heavenly; celestial

**em·py·re·an** (em′pī rē′ən, -pə-; em pir′ē ən) *n.* [see prec. & -AN] **1.** the highest heaven: among the ancients, the sphere of pure light or fire **2.** the sky; the firmament —*adj.* same as EMPYREAL

**e·mu** (ē′myoo) *n.* [prob. < Port. *ema*, a crane] a large, nonflying Australian bird, similar to the ostrich but somewhat smaller

**E.M.U., e.m.u., emu** electromagnetic units

**em·u·late** (em′yə lāt′) *vt.* **-lat′ed, -lat′ing** [< L. pp. of *aemulari* < *aemulus*, trying to equal] **1.** to try to equal or surpass **2.** to imitate (a person or thing admired) **3.** to rival successfully —**em′u·la′tion** *n.* —**em′u·la′tive** *adj.* —**em′u·la′tor** *n.*

**em·u·lous** (em′yə ləs) *adj.* **1.** desirous of equaling or surpassing **2.** characterized or caused by emulation —**em′u·lous·ly** *adv.* —**em′u·lous·ness** *n.*

EMU
(to 5 ft. high)

**e·mul·si·fy** (i mul′sə fī′) *vt., vi.* **-fied′, -fy′ing** to form into an emulsion —**e·mul′si·fi′a·ble** *adj.* —**e·mul′si·fi·ca′tion** *n.* —**e·mul′si·fi′er** *n.*

**e·mul·sion** (i mul′shən) *n.* [< ModL. < L. pp. of *emulgere* < *e*-, out + *mulgere*, to milk] a fluid, as milk, formed by the suspension of one liquid in another; specif., *a) Pharmacy* a preparation of an oily substance held in suspension in a watery liquid *b) Photog.* a suspension of a salt of silver in gelatin or collodion, used to coat plates and film —**e·mul′sive** *adj.*

**en** (en) *n.* **1.** the letter N, n **2.** *Printing* a space half the width of an em

**en-** (in, en) [OFr. < L. *in*- < *in*, IN] **1.** *a prefix meaning: a)* to put or get into or on [*entrain*] *b)* to cover with [*enrobe*] *c)* to make, cause to be [*endanger, enfeeble*] *d)* in or into [*enclose*] **2.** *a prefix used as an intensifier* [*enliven*] It is assimilated to *em*- before *p, b, m* Many words with *en*- are also spelled *in*- (Ex.: enquire, inquire)

**-en** (ən, 'n) [< OE. suffixes *-nian, -an, -en*] *any of several suffixes:* **1.** *meaning: a)* to become or cause to be [*darken, weaken*] *b)* to come to have, cause to have [*strengthen*] **2.** *meaning* made of [*woolen*] **3.** *used to form the pp. of strong verbs* [*risen*] **4.** *used to form plurals* [*children*] **5.** *used to form diminutives* [*chicken*]

**en·a·ble** (in ā′b'l) *vt.* **-bled, -bling 1.** to make able; provide with means, opportunity, power, or authority (*to* do something) **2.** to make possible

**en·act** (in akt′) *vt.* **1.** to make (a bill, etc.) into a law; pass (a law); decree; ordain **2.** to represent or perform in or as in a play; act out —**en·ac′tive** *adj.* —**en·ac′tor** *n.*

**en·act·ment** (-mənt) *n.* **1.** an enacting or being enacted **2.** something enacted, as a law

**en·am·el** (i nam′'l) *n.* [see the *v.*] **1.** a glassy, colored, opaque substance fused to surfaces, as of metals, as an ornamental or protective coating **2.** any smooth, hard, glossy coating like enamel **3.** the hard, white, glossy coating of the crown of a tooth **4.** anything enameled **5.** paint or varnish with a smooth, hard, glossy surface when it dries —*vt.* **-eled or -elled, -el·ing or -el·ling** [< Anglo-Fr. < *en*- (see EN-) + *amayl* < OFr. *esmail*, enamel] **1.** to inlay or cover with enamel **2.** to decorate in various colors, as if with enamel **3.** to form an enamellike surface on —**en·am′el·er, en·am′el·ler, en·am′el·ist, en·am′el·list** *n.*

**en·am·el·ware** (-wər′) *n.* kitchen utensils, etc. made of enameled metal

**en·am·or** (in am′ər) *vt.* [< OFr. < *en*-, in + *amour* < L. *amor*, love] to fill with love and desire; charm; captivate: now mainly in the passive voice, with *of* [much *enamored* of her]

**en bloc** (en bläk′; *Fr.* än blôk′) [Fr., lit., in a block] in one lump; as a whole; all together

**enc., encl.** enclosure

**en·camp** (in kamp′) *vi.* to set up a camp —*vt.* **1.** to put in a camp **2.** to form into a camp

**en·camp·ment** (-mənt) *n.* **1.** an encamping or being encamped **2.** a camp or campsite

**en·cap·su·late** (in kap′sə lāt′, -syoo-) *vt.* **-lat′ed, -lat′ing 1.** to enclose in or as if in a capsule **2.** to condense; abridge Also **en·cap′sule** (-s'l, -syool) **-suled, -sul·ing** —**en·cap′su·la′tion** *n.*

**en·case** (in kās′) *vt.* **-cased′, -cas′ing 1.** to cover completely; enclose **2.** to put into a case or cases —**en·case′·ment** *n.*

**en·cas·se·role** (en kas′ə rōl′; *Fr.* än kàs rôl′) [Fr.] (baked and served) in a casserole

**en·caus·tic** (en kôs′tik) *adj.* [< L. < Gr. < *en*-, in + *kaiein*, to burn] done by a process of burning in or applying heat [*encaustic* tile] —*n.* a method of painting in which colors in wax are fused to a surface with hot irons —**en·caus′ti·cal·ly** *adv.*

fat, āpe, cär; ten, ēven; is, bīte; gō, hôrn, tool, look; oil, out; up, fur; get; joy; yet; chin; she; thin, then; zh, leisure; ŋ, ring; ə for *a* in *ago*, *e* in *agent*, *i* in *sanity*, *o* in *comply*, *u* in *focus*; ' as in *able* (ā′b'l); Fr. bal; ë, Fr. coeur; ö, Fr. feu; Fr. mon; ô, Fr. coq; ü, Fr. duc; r, Fr. cri; H, G. ich; kh, G. doch; ‡foreign; *hypothetical; < derived from. See inside front cover.

**-ence** (əns, 'ns) [< OFr. *-ence* & L. *-entia* (see -ENT + -IA)] *a suffix meaning* act, fact, quality, state, result, or degree *[conference, excellence]*

‡**en·ceinte** (än sant′; *E.* än sänt′) *adj.* [Fr., ult. < L. *in-*, not + pp. of *cingere*, to gird] pregnant

**en·ceph·a·li·tis** (en sef′ə līt′is, en′sef-) *n.* [< ff. + -ITIS] inflammation of the brain —**en·ceph′a·lit′ic** (-lit′ik) *adj.*

**en·ceph·a·lo-** [< Gr. *enkephalos*, the brain] *a combining form meaning* of the brain: also **en·ceph′al-**

**en·ceph·a·lo·gram** (en sef′ə lō gram′) *n. clipped form of:* 1. ELECTROENCEPHALOGRAM 2. PNEUMOENCEPHALOGRAM

**en·ceph·a·lon** (-län′) *n., pl.* **-la** (-lə) [ModL. < Gr. < *en-*, in + *kephalē*, the head] *Anat.* the brain —**en·ce·phal·ic** (en′sə fal′ik) *adj.*

**en·chain** (in chān′) *vt.* 1. to bind with chains; fetter 2. to captivate —**en·chain′ment** *n.*

**en·chant** (in chant′) *vt.* [< OFr. < L. *incantare*, to bewitch: see INCANTATION] 1. to cast a spell over, as by magic; bewitch 2. to charm greatly; delight —**en·chant′er** *n.* —**en·chant′ress** *n.fem.*

**en·chant·ing** (-iŋ) *adj.* 1. charming; delightful 2. bewitching; fascinating —**en·chant′ing·ly** *adv.*

**en·chant·ment** (-mənt) *n.* 1. an enchanting or being enchanted 2. a magic spell or charm 3. something that charms greatly 4. great delight

**en·chase** (in chās′) *vt.* **-chased′, -chas′ing** [< OFr. *enchasser*: see CHASE³] 1. to put in a setting 2. to ornament by engraving, inlaying with gems, etc. 3. to carve (designs, etc.)

**en·chi·la·da** (en′chə lä′də) *n.* [AmSp.] a tortilla rolled with meat inside and served with a chili-flavored sauce

**en·cir·cle** (in sur′k′l) *vt.* **-cled, -cling** 1. to make a circle around; surround 2. to move in a circle around —**en·cir′cle·ment** *n.*

**en·clave** (en′klāv) *n.* [Fr. < OFr. < L. *in*, in + *clavis*, a key] 1. a territory surrounded by the territory of a foreign country 2. a minority culture group that exists within a larger group

**en·clit·ic** (en klit′ik) *adj.* [< LL. < Gr. < *enklinein*, to lean toward] *Gram.* dependent for its stress on the preceding word, often one with which it has combined (Ex.: *man* in *layman*) —*n.* any such word or particle

**en·close** (in klōz′) *vt.* **-closed′, -clos′ing** 1. to shut in all around; surround 2. to insert in an envelope, wrapper, etc., often along with something else 3. to contain

**en·clo·sure** (-klō′zhər) *n.* 1. an enclosing or being enclosed 2. something that encloses 3. something enclosed; specif., *a*) an enclosed place *b*) a document, money, etc. enclosed as with a letter

**en·code** (in kōd′) *vt.* **-cod′ed, -cod′ing** to put (information, etc.) into code —**en·cod′er** *n.*

**en·co·mi·ast** (en kō′mē ast′) *n.* [< Gr. < *enkōmiazein*, to praise] a person who speaks or writes encomiums; eulogist —**en·co′mi·as′tic** *adj.*

**en·co·mi·um** (en kō′mē əm) *n., pl.* **-mi·ums, -mi·a** (-ə) [L. < Gr. *enkōmion*, song of praise < *en-*, in + *kōmos*, a revel] a formal expression of high praise; eulogy; panegyric

**en·com·pass** (in kum′pəs) *vt.* 1. to shut in all around; surround 2. to contain; include 3. to compass or achieve — **en·com′pass·ment** *n.*

**en·core** (äŋ′kôr, än kôr′) *interj.* [Fr., yet, again] again; once more —*n.* 1. a demand by the audience, shown by applause, for further performance 2. the performance or piece performed in answer to such a demand —*vt.* **-cored, -cor·ing** to demand further performance of or by

**en·coun·ter** (in koun′tər) *vt.* [< OFr. < L. *in*, in + *contra*, against] 1. to meet unexpectedly; come upon 2. to meet in conflict or battle 3. to face (difficulties, trouble, etc.) —*vi.* to meet accidentally or in opposition —*n.* 1. a direct meeting, as in conflict or battle 2. an unexpected meeting —*adj.* designating or of a small group meeting to explore personal relationships through an open exchange of intimate feelings, release of inhibitions, etc.

**en·cour·age** (in kur′ij) *vt.* **-aged, -ag·ing** 1. to give courage, hope, or confidence to; hearten 2. to give support to; foster; help —**en·cour′ag·ing** *adj.* —**en·cour′ag·ing·ly** *adv.*

**en·cour·age·ment** (-mənt) *n.* 1. an encouraging or being encouraged 2. something that encourages

**en·croach** (in krōch′) *vi.* [< OFr. *encrochier*, to seize upon < *en-*, in + *croc*, a hook] 1. to trespass or intrude (on or upon the rights, property, etc. of another) 2. to advance beyond the proper, original, or customary limits —**en·croach′ment** *n.*

**en·crust** (in krust′) *vt., vi. same as* INCRUST —**en′crus·ta′tion** *n.*

**en·cum·ber** (in kum′bər) *vt.* [< OFr.: see EN- & CUMBER] 1. to hold back the motion or action of, as with a burden; hinder 2. to fill so as to obstruct; block up 3. to load or weigh down; burden

**en·cum·brance** (-brəns) *n.* 1. something that encumbers; hindrance; burden 2. *Law same as* INCUMBRANCE

**-en·cy** (ən sē, 'n sē) [L. *-entia*] *a suffix meaning* act, fact, quality, state, result, or degree *[dependency, efficiency]*

**ency., encyc., encycl.** encyclopedia

**en·cyc·li·cal** (in sik′li k′l, -sī′kli-) *adj.* [LL. *encyclicus* < Gr. < *en-*, in + *kyklos*, a circle] for general circulation: also **en·cyc′lic** —*n. R.C.Ch.* a letter from the Pope to the bishops, usually dealing with doctrinal matters

**en·cy·clo·pe·di·a, en·cy·clo·pae·di·a** (in sī′klə pē′dē ə) *n.* [ModL. < Gr. *enkyklopaideia* < *enkyklios*, general + *paideia*, education] a book or set of books giving information on all or many branches of knowledge, or on one of these, generally in articles alphabetically arranged —**en·cy′clo·pe′dic, en·cy′clo·pae′dic** *adj.* —**en·cy′clo·pe′di·cal·ly, en·cy′clo·pae′di·cal·ly** *adv.* —**en·cy′clo·pe′dist, en·cy′clo·pae′dist** *n.*

**en·cyst** (en sist′) *vt., vi.* to enclose or become enclosed in a cyst, capsule, or sac —**en·cyst′ment, en′cys·ta′tion** (-sis tā′shən) *n.*

**end** (end) *n.* [OE. *ende*] 1. a limit or limiting part; boundary 2. the last part of anything; final point; finish; conclusion 3. a ceasing to exist; death or destruction 4. the part at or near either extremity of anything; tip 5. a purpose; intention; object 6. an outcome; result; consequence 7. a piece left over; remnant *[odds and ends]* 8. the reason for being 9. *Football a)* a player at either end of the line *b*) his position —*vt.* 1. to bring to an end; finish; stop 2. to form the end of —*vi.* 1. to come to an end; terminate: often with *up* 2. to die —*adj.* at the end; final *[end* product*]* —**ends of the earth** remote regions —**make an end of** 1. to finish; stop 2. to do away with —**make (both) ends meet** to keep one's expenses within one's income —**no end** [Colloq.] extremely —**on end** 1. in an upright position 2. without interruption *[for days on end]* —**put an end to** 1. to stop 2. to do away with

**en·da·moe·ba** (en′də mē′bə) *n.* [see ENDO- & AMOEBA] any of a genus of parasitic amoebas, including the species that causes amoebic dysentery in man: also sp. **en′da·me′ba** — **en′da·moe′bic** *adj.*

**en·dan·ger** (in dān′jər) *vt.* to expose to danger, harm, or loss; imperil —**en·dan′ger·ment** *n.*

**en·dan·gered species** (-jərd) a species of animal or plant in danger of becoming extinct

**en·dear** (in dir′) *vt.* to make dear or beloved

**en·dear·ing** (-iŋ) *adj.* 1. that makes dear or well liked 2. expressing affection *[endearing* tones*]*

**en·dear·ment** (-mənt) *n.* 1. warm liking; affection 2. a word or act expressing affection

**en·deav·or** (in dev′ər) *vi.* [< *en-* + OFr. *deveir*, duty < L. *debere*, to owe] to make an earnest attempt —*vt.* 1. [Archaic] to try to achieve 2. to try (*to* do something) —*n.* an earnest attempt or effort Also, Brit. sp., **en·deav′our**

**en·dem·ic** (en dem′ik) *adj.* [Fr. < Gr. < *en-*, in + *dēmos*, the people] 1. native to a particular country, region, etc.: said of plants and animals 2. restricted to and present in a particular country or locality: said of a disease: also **en·dem′i·cal** —*n.* 1. an endemic plant or animal 2. an endemic disease —**en·dem′i·cal·ly** *adv.* —**en·de·mic·i·ty** (en′də mis′ə tē), **en·dem′ism** *n.*

**end·ing** (en′diŋ) *n.* 1. *a)* the last part; finish *b*) death 2. *Gram.* the final letter or letters added to a word base to make a derivative or an inflectional form *[-ed* is the *ending* in *wanted]*

**en·dive** (en′dīv, än′dēv) *n.* [OFr. < ML. < MGr. < L. *intibus* < Gr. *entybon*] 1. *a)* a cultivated plant of the composite family, with curled, narrow leaves used in salads *b*) another form of this with wide, smooth leaves 2. the young leaves of chicory (sense 1) blanched for salads

**end·less** (end′lis) *adj.* 1. having no end; going on forever; eternal; infinite 2. lasting too long *[an endless* speech*]* 3. continual *[endless* interruptions*]* 4. with the ends joined to form a closed unit that can move continuously over wheels, etc. *[an endless* belt*]* —**end′less·ly** *adv.* —**end′less·ness** *n.*

**end·most** (-mōst′) *adj.* at the end; farthest; last

**en·do-** [< Gr. *edon*, within] *a combining form meaning* within, inner *[endoderm]* : also, before a vowel, **end-**

**en·do·blast** (en′də blast′) *n. same as* ENDODERM

**en·do·car·di·tis** (en′dō kär dīt′is) *n.* [ModL. < ENDO- + Gr. *kardia*, heart + -ITIS] inflammation of the thin membrane lining the heart cavities

**en·do·carp** (en′də kärp′) *n.* the inner layer of the wall of a ripened ovary or fruit, as the pit around the seed of a plum

**en·do·crine** (en′də krin, -krīn′, -krēn′) *adj.* [ENDO- + Gr. *krinein*, to separate] 1. designating or of any gland producing one or more internal secretions that, introduced into the bloodstream, are carried to other parts of the body whose functions they regulate 2. designating or of such a secretion —*n.* any such gland or its secretion, as the thyroid, adrenal, and pituitary glands

**en·do·cri·nol·o·gy** (en'dō kri näl'ə jē, -krī-) *n.* the branch of medicine dealing with the endocrine glands and the internal secretions of the body —**en'do·cri'no·log'i·cal** (-nə läj'ə k'l) *adj.* —**en'do·cri·nol'o·gist** *n.*

**en·do·derm** (en'də dʉrm') *n.* the inner layer of cells of the embryo, from which is formed the lining of the digestive tract, of other internal organs, and of certain glands —**en'do·der'mal, en'do·der'mic** *adj.*

**en·dog·a·my** (en däg'ə mē) *n.* [ENDO- + -GAMY] 1. the custom of marrying only within one's own tribe, clan, etc.; inbreeding 2. cross-pollination among flowers of the same plant —**en·dog'a·mous, en·do·gam·ic** (en'də gam'ik) *adj.*

**en·dog·e·nous** (en däj'ə nəs) *adj.* 1. developing from within; originating internally 2. *Biol.* growing or developing from or on the inside —**en·dog'e·nous·ly** *adv.*

**en·do·mor·phic** (en'də môr'fik) *adj.* [ENDO- + -MORPHIC] designating or of the fleshy or heavy type of human body, in which the structures developed from the endoderm predominate —**en'do·morph'** *n.*

**en·do·plasm** (en'də plaz'm) *n.* the inner part of the cytoplasm of a cell —**en'do·plas'mic** *adj.*

**end organ** any structure at the end of a nerve fibre that either receives a sensation or sends an impulse to a muscle

**en·dorse** (in dôrs') *vt.* -dorsed', -dors'ing [< OFr. < ML. < L. *in*, on + *dorsum*, the back] 1. to write on the back of (a document); specif., to sign (one's name) as payee on the back of (a check, etc.) 2. to give approval to; support; sanction —**en·dors'a·ble** *adj.* —**en·dor·see** (in dôr'sē', en'dôr sē') *n.* —**en·dors'er** *n.*

**en·dorse·ment** (-mənt) *n.* 1. an endorsing 2. something written in endorsing; specif., *a*) the signature of a payee on the back of a check, etc. *b*) a statement endorsing a person, product, etc.

**en·do·skel·e·ton** (en'də skel'ə t'n) *n.* the internal bony, supporting structure in vertebrates

**en·do·sperm** (en'də spʉrm') *n.* [ENDO- + SPERM¹] a tissue which surrounds the developing embryo of a seed and provides food for its growth; albumen —**en'do·sper'mic** *adj.*

**en·dow** (in dou') *vt.* [< Anglo-Fr. < OFr. < *en*-, in + *dou·er* < L. *dotare*, to endow] 1. to provide with some talent, quality, etc. [*endowed* with courage] 2. to think of as having some quality or characteristic [to *endow* gods with human traits] 3. to give money or property so as to provide an income for the support of (a college, hospital, etc.)

**en·dow·ment** (-mənt) *n.* 1. an endowing 2. that with which something is endowed; bequest 3. a gift of nature; talent, ability, etc.

**endowment policy** an insurance policy by which a stated amount is paid to the insured after the period of time specified in the contract

**end product** the final result of any series of changes, processes, or chemical reactions

**end table** a small table placed beside a chair, etc.

**en·due** (in dōō', -dyōō') *vt.* -dued', -du'ing [< OFr. < L. *inducere*: see INDUCE] to provide (*with* something); specif., to endow (*with* qualities, talents, etc.)

**en·dur·ance** (in door'əns, -dyoor'-) *n.* 1. an enduring 2. ability to last, continue, or remain 3. ability to stand pain, distress, fatigue, etc.; fortitude 4. duration

**en·dure** (in door', -dyoor') *vt.* -dured', -dur'ing [< OFr. < L. < L. < *in*-, in + *durare*, to harden < *durus*, hard] 1. to hold up under (pain, fatigue, etc.); bear 2. to put up with; tolerate —*vi.* 1. to continue in existence; last; remain 2. to bear pain, etc. without flinching; hold out —**en·dur'a·ble** *adj.* —**en·dur'a·bly** *adv.*

**en·dur·ing** (-iŋ) *adj.* lasting; permanent; durable —**en·dur'ing·ly** *adv.* —**en·dur'ing·ness** *n.*

**end·ways** (end'wāz') *adv.* 1. on end; upright 2. with the end foremost 3. lengthwise 4. end to end Also **end'wise'** (-wīz')

**end zone** *Football* the area between the goal line and the end boundary (**end line**) ten yards behind it, at each end of the playing field

**-ene** (ēn) [after L. *-enus*, Gr. *-ēnos*, adj. suffix] *a suffix used:* 1. *Chem.* to form names for some hydrocarbons [*propylene, benzene*] 2. to form some commercial names

**ENE, E.N.E., e.n.e.** east-northeast

**en·e·ma** (en'ə mə) *n.* [LL. < Gr. < *en*-, in + *hienai*, to send] 1. a liquid injected into the colon through the anus, as a purgative, medicine, etc. 2. such an injection

**en·e·my** (en'ə mē) *n., pl.* -mies [< OFr. < L. *inimicus* < *in*-, not + *amicus*, friend] 1. a person who hates another, and wishes or tries to injure him; foe 2. *a*) a nation or force hostile to another *b*) troops, fleet, ship, member, etc. of a hostile nation 3. a person hostile to an idea, cause, etc. 4. anything injurious or harmful —*adj.* of an enemy

energy; vigorous; forceful —**en'er·get'i·cal·ly** *adv.*

**en·er·gize** (en'ər jīz') *vt.* -gized', -giz'ing 1. to give energy to; invigorate 2. *Elec.* to apply a source of voltage or current to (a circuit, etc.) —**en'er·giz'er** *n.*

**en·er·gy** (en'ər jē) *n., pl.* -gies [< LL. < Gr. *energeia* < *en*-, in + *ergon*, work] 1. force of expression 2. potential forces; capacity for action 3. effective power 4. *Physics* the capacity for doing work and overcoming resistance

**en·er·vate** (en'ər vāt') *vt.* -vat·ed, -vat'ing [< L. pp. of *enervare* < *e*-, out + *nervus*, a nerve, sinew] to deprive of strength, force, vigor, etc.; debilitate —*adj.* enervated; weakened —**en'er·va'tion** *n.* —**en'er·va'tor** *n.*

**‡en fa·mille** (än fà mē'y') [Fr.] 1. with one's family; at home 2. in an informal way

**‡en·fant ter·ri·ble** (än fän te rē'bl') [Fr.] 1. an unmanageable, mischievous child 2. a person who causes trouble or embarrassment by his imprudent remarks or actions

**en·fee·ble** (in fē'b'l) *vt.* -bled, -bling to make feeble —**en·fee'ble·ment** *n.*

**en·fi·lade** (en'fə lād', en'fə lād') *n.* [Fr. < *enfiler*, to thread < *en*- (L. *in*), in + *fil* (L. *filum*), a thread] 1. gunfire directed from either flank along the length of a line of troops 2. a placement of troops that makes them vulnerable to such fire —*vt.* -lad'ed, -lad'ing to direct such gunfire at (a column, etc.)

**en·fold** (in fōld') *vt.* 1. to wrap in folds; envelop 2. to embrace —**en·fold'ment** *n.*

**en·force** (in fôrs') *vt.* -forced', -forc'ing 1. to give force to [to *enforce* an argument by analogies] 2. to bring about or impose by force [to *enforce* one's will on a child] 3. to compel observance of (a law, etc.) —**en·force'a·ble** *adj.* —**en·force'ment** *n.* —**en·forc'er** *n.*

**en·fran·chise** (in fran'chīz) *vt.* -chised, -chis·ing 1. to free from slavery, bondage, etc. 2. to give a franchise to; specif., to admit to citizenship, esp. to the right to vote —**en·fran'chise·ment** (-chiz mənt, -chīz-) *n.* —**en·fran'chis·er** *n.*

**Eng.** 1. England 2. English

**eng.** 1. engineer(ing) 2. engraved 3. engraving

**en·gage** (in gāj') *vt.* -gaged', -gag'ing [< OFr. *engagier*: see EN- & GAGE¹] 1. to bind (oneself) by a promise; pledge; specif. (now only in the passive), to bind by a promise of marriage; betroth 2. to hire; employ 3. to arrange for the use of; reserve [to *engage* a hotel room] 4. to draw into; involve, as in conversation 5. to attract and hold (the attention, etc.) 6. to keep busy; occupy 7. to enter into conflict with (the enemy) 8. to interlock with; mesh together [*engage* the gears] —*vi.* 1. to pledge oneself; promise; undertake 2. to involve oneself; be active [to *engage* in dramatics] 3. to enter into conflict 4. to interlock; mesh

**en·gaged** (-gājd') *adj.* 1. pledged; esp., pledged in marriage; betrothed 2. occupied or busy 3. involved in combat, as troops 4. attached to or partly set into a wall, etc. [*engaged* columns] 5. in gear; interlocked; meshed

**en·gage·ment** (-gāj'mənt) *n.* 1. an engaging or being engaged; specif., *a*) a betrothal *b*) an appointment or commitment *c*) employment or period of employment, esp. in the performing arts *d*) a conflict; battle *e*) [*usually pl.*] financial obligations *f*) state of being in gear 2. something that engages

**en·gag·ing** (-gāj'iŋ) *adj.* attractive; winning; charming —**en·gag'ing·ly** *adv.*

**‡en garde** (än gàrd') [Fr.] *Fencing* on guard: the opening position in which the fencer is prepared either to attack or defend

**En·gels** (eŋ'əls), **Frie·drich** (frē'driH) 1820–95; Ger. socialist theoretician (with Karl Marx)

**en·gen·der** (in jen'dər) *vt.* [< OFr. < L. < *in*-, in + *generare*, GENERATE] to bring into being; cause; produce [*militarism engenders* war]

**engin.** 1. engineer 2. engineering

**en·gine** (en'jən) *n.* [< OFr. < L. *ingenium*, genius < *in*-, in & base of *gignere*, to produce] 1. any machine that uses energy to develop mechanical power; esp., a machine for starting motion in some other machine 2. a railroad locomotive 3. any instrument or machine; apparatus [*engines* of torture] 4. *same as* FIRE ENGINE

**en·gi·neer** (en'jə nir') *n.* 1. a person skilled in some branch of engineering [a mechanical *engineer*] 2. *a*) an operator of engines or technical equipment [a locomotive *engineer*, radio *engineer*] *b*) a specialist in planning or directing operations in some technical field 3. a skillful or clever manager 4. *Mil.* a member of that branch of the armed forces concerned with the construction and demolition of bridges, roads, etc. —*vt.* 1. to plan, construct, or manage as an engineer 2. to plan and direct skillfully [to *engineer* a business merger]

**en·gi·neer·ing** (-iŋ) *n.* **1.** *a)* the science concerned with putting scientific knowledge to practical uses, divided into different branches, as civil, electrical, mechanical, or chemical engineering *b)* the planning, designing, construction, or management of machinery, roads, bridges, buildings, waterways, etc. **2.** a maneuvering or managing

**Eng·land** (iŋ′glənd) **1.** division of the United Kingdom, occupying most of the S part of Great Britain: 50,331 sq. mi.; pop. 47,023,000; cap. London **2.** *same as* UNITED KINGDOM

**Eng·lish** (iŋ′glish) *adj.* [OE. *Englisc*, lit., of the Angles] **1.** of England, its people, their culture, etc. **2.** of their language —*n.* **1.** the language of the people of England, the official language of the British Commonwealth, the U.S., Liberia, etc. **2.** the English language of a specific period: see OLD ENGLISH, MIDDLE ENGLISH, MODERN ENGLISH **3.** [*sometimes* e-] *Billiards, Bowling*, etc. a spinning motion given to a ball, as by striking it on one side —*vt.* **1.** to translate into English **2.** to Anglicize (a foreign word) —**the English** the people of England

**English Channel** arm of the Atlantic, between England & France: 21-150 mi. wide

**English horn** a double-reed instrument of the woodwind family, similar to the oboe but larger and a fifth lower in pitch

**English ivy** *same as* IVY (sense 1)

**Eng·lish·man** (-mən) *n., pl.* **-men** a native or inhabitant of England, esp. a man —**Eng′lish·wom′an** *n.fem., pl.* **-wom′en**

**English muffin** a large, flat yeast roll, often baked on a griddle, and served split and toasted

**English setter** any of a breed of setter with a white, long-haired coat with black, yellow, or orange spots

**English sonnet** *same as* SHAKESPEAREAN SONNET

**English sparrow** the common sparrow, a small brownish-gray, finchlike bird of European origin

ENGLISH HORN

**English walnut** **1.** an Asiatic walnut tree now grown in Europe and N. America **2.** its nut

**en·gorge** (in gôrj′) *vt., vi.* **-gorged′, -gorg′ing** **1.** to eat gluttonously; gorge; glut **2.** *Med.* to congest with blood or other fluid —**en·gorge′ment** *n.*

**engr.** **1.** engineer **2.** engraved **3.** engraver

**en·graft** (in graft′) *vt.* **1.** to graft (a shoot, etc.) from one plant onto another **2.** to establish firmly; implant —**en·graft′ment** *n.*

**en·grave** (in grāv′) *vt.* **-graved′, -grav′ing** [< Fr. < *en-*, in + *graver*, to incise, ult. < Gr. *graphein*, to write] **1.** to cut or etch (letters, designs, etc.) in or on (a surface) or into a metal plate, wooden block, etc. for printing **2.** to print by means of such a plate, block, etc. **3.** to impress deeply on the mind or memory —**en·grav′er** *n.*

**en·grav·ing** (-iŋ) *n.* **1.** the act, process, or art of one who engraves **2.** an engraved plate, design, etc. **3.** a print made from an engraved surface

**en·gross** (in grōs′) *vt.* [< OFr.: see EN- & GROSS] **1.** *a)* to write in the large letters once used for legal documents *b)* to make a final fair copy of (a document) **2.** to express formally or in legal form **3.** to take the entire attention of; occupy wholly; absorb —**en·gross′er** *n.* —**en·gross′ing** *adj., n.* —**en·gross′ment** *n.*

**en·gulf** (in gulf′) *vt.* **1.** to swallow up; overwhelm **2.** to plunge, as into a gulf —**en·gulf′ment** *n.*

**en·hance** (-hans′) *vt.* **-hanced′, -hanc′ing** [< Anglo-Fr. < OFr. *enhaucier*, ult. < L. *in*, in + *altus*, high] to make greater, as in value, attractiveness, etc.; heighten —*vi.* to increase, as in value or price —**en·hance′ment** *n.* —**en·hanc′er** *n.*

**e·nig·ma** (ə nig′mə) *n., pl.* **-mas** [< L. < Gr. *ainigma* < *ainissesthai*, to speak in riddles < *ainos*, tale] **1.** a perplexing, usually ambiguous, statement; riddle **2.** a perplexing or baffling matter, person, etc. —**e·nig·mat·ic** (en′ig-mat′ik, ē′nig-), **e′nig·mat′i·cal** *adj.* —**e′nig·mat′i·cal·ly** *adv.*

**en·join** (in join′) *vt.* [< OFr. < L. < *in-*, in + *jungere*, to join] **1.** to order; enforce [*to enjoin* silence] **2.** to prohibit, esp. by legal injunction; forbid **3.** to order (someone) to do something, esp. by legal injunction

**en·joy** (in joi′) *vt.* [< OFr. *enjoir* < *en-*, in + *joir* < L. *gaudere*, to be glad] **1.** to have or experience with joy; get pleasure from; relish **2.** to have the use or benefit of —**enjoy oneself** to have a good time —**en·joy′a·ble** *adj.* —**en·joy′a·ble·ness** *n.* —**en·joy′a·bly** *adv.*

**en·joy·ment** (-mənt) *n.* **1.** an enjoying **2.** something enjoyed **3.** pleasure; gratification; joy

**en·kin·dle** (en kin′d'l) *vt.* **-dled, -dling** **1.** to set on fire; make blaze up **2.** to stir up; arouse

**enl.** **1.** enlarge **2.** enlisted

**en·lace** (in lās′) *vt.* **-laced′, -lac′ing** **1.** to wind about as with a lace; encircle; enfold **2.** to entangle; interlace —**en·lace′ment** *n.*

**en·large** (in lärj′) *vt.* **-larged′, -larg′ing** **1.** to make larger; increase in size, volume, extent, etc.; expand **2.** *Photog.* to reproduce on a larger scale —*vi.* **1.** to become larger; increase **2.** to discuss at greater length or in greater detail (with *on* or *upon*) —**en·large′ment** *n.* —**en·larg′er** *n.*

**en·light·en** (in līt′'n) *vt.* **1.** to give the light of knowledge to; free from ignorance, prejudice, or superstition **2.** to give clarification to (a person) as to meanings, intentions, etc.; inform —**en·light′en·er** *n.*

**en·light·en·ment** (-mənt) *n.* an enlightening or being enlightened —**the Enlightenment** an 18th-cent. European philosophical and social movement characterized by rationalism

**en·list** (in list′) *vt.* **1.** to enroll in some branch of the armed forces **2.** to win the support of **3.** to get (another's help, support, etc.) —*vi.* **1.** to join some branch of the armed forces **2.** to join or support a cause or movement (with *in*) —**en·list′ee′** *n.*

**enlisted man** any man in the armed forces who is not a commissioned officer or warrant officer

**en·list·ment** (-mənt) *n.* **1.** an enlisting or being enlisted **2.** the period for which one enlists

**en·liv·en** (in līv′n) *vt.* to make active, vivacious, interesting, or cheerful; liven up or brighten —**en·liv′en·er** *n.* —**en·liv′en·ment** *n.*

**en masse** (en mas′; *Fr.* än màs′) [Fr., lit., in mass] in a group; as a whole; all together

**en·mesh** (en mesh′) *vt.* to catch in or as in the meshes of a net; entangle

**en·mi·ty** (en′mə tē) *n., pl.* **-ties** [< OFr. < L. *inimicus*, ENEMY] the bitter attitude or feelings of an enemy or mutual enemies; hostility

**en·no·ble** (i nō′b'l) *vt.* **-bled, -bling** **1.** to raise to the rank of nobleman **2.** to give a noble quality to; dignify —**en·no′ble·ment** *n.* —**en·no′bler** *n.*

**en·nui** (än′wē; *Fr.* än nwē′) *n.* [Fr.: see ANNOY] weariness and dissatisfaction resulting from inactivity or lack of interest; boredom

**e·nor·mi·ty** (i nôr′mə tē) *n., pl.* **-ties** [< Fr. < L. < *enormis*, irregular, immense < *e-*, out + *norma*, rule] **1.** great wickedness *[the enormity* of a crime] **2.** a very wicked crime **3.** enormous size or extent: generally considered a loose usage

**e·nor·mous** (i nôr′məs) *adj.* [see prec.] **1.** very much exceeding the usual size, number, or degree; huge; vast **2.** [Archaic] very wicked; outrageous —**e·nor′mous·ly** *adv.* —**e·nor′mous·ness** *n.*

**e·nough** (i nuf′) *adj.* [OE. *genoh*] as much or as many as necessary, desirable, or tolerable; sufficient —*n.* the amount or number needed, desired, or allowed —*adv.* **1.** as much or as often as necessary; sufficiently **2.** fully; quite *[oddly enough]* **3.** just adequately; tolerably; fairly *[he played well enough]*

**e·now** (i nou′) *adj., n., adv.* [Archaic] enough

**en·plane** (en plān′) *vi.* **-planed′, -plan′ing** to board an airplane

**en·quire** (in kwīr′) *vt., vi.* **-quired′, -quir′ing** *same as* INQUIRE —**en·quir′y** *n., pl.* **-quir′ies**

**en·rage** (in rāj′) *vt.* **-raged′, -rag′ing** to put into a rage; infuriate —**en·rage′ment** *n.*

‡**en rap·port** (än rà pôr′) [Fr.] in harmony; in sympathy; in accord

**en·rapt** (in rapt′) *adj.* enraptured; rapt

**en·rap·ture** (-rap′chər) *vt.* **-tured, -tur·ing** to fill with great pleasure or delight: also **en·rav′ish**

**en·rich** (in rich′) *vt.* to make rich or richer; specif., *a)* to give more wealth to *b)* to give greater value or effectiveness to *[to enrich* a curriculum] *c)* to decorate; adorn *d)* to fertilize (soil) *e)* to add vitamins, minerals, etc. to (bread, etc.) for more food value —**en·rich′ment** *n.*

**en·roll, en·rol** (in rōl′) *vt.* **-rolled′, -roll′ing** **1.** to record in a list **2.** to enlist **3.** to accept as a member —*vi.* to enroll oneself or become enrolled; register; become a member —**en·roll′ee′** *n.*

**en·roll·ment, en·rol·ment** (-mənt) *n.* **1.** an enrolling or being enrolled **2.** a list of those enrolled **3.** the number of those enrolled

**en route** (än rōōt′, en) [Fr.] on or along the way

**Ens.** Ensign

**en·sconce** (in skäns′) *vt.* **-sconced′, -sconc′ing** [EN- + SCONCE²] **1.** [Now Rare] to hide; conceal; shelter **2.** to place or settle snugly

**en·sem·ble** (än säm′b'l) *n.* [Fr. < OFr. < L. < *in-*, in + *simul*, at the same time] **1.** all the parts considered as a whole; total effect **2.** a whole costume, esp. of matching or complementary articles of dress **3.** a company of actors, dancers, etc. **4.** *Music a)* a small group of musicians performing together *b)* their instruments or voices *c)* the performance together of such a group, or of an orchestra, chorus, etc.

**en·shrine** (in shrīn′) *vt.* **-shrined′, -shrin′ing 1.** to enclose in or as in a shrine **2.** to hold as sacred; cherish —**en·shrine′ment** *n.*

**en·shroud** (-shroud′) *vt.* to cover as if with a shroud; hide; veil; obscure

**en·sign** (en′sīn; *also, and for 4 always,* -s′n) *n.* [< OFr. < L. < *insignia:* see INSIGNIA] **1.** a badge, symbol, or token of office or authority **2.** a flag or banner; specif., a national flag **3.** *Brit. Army* formerly, a commissioned officer who served as standard-bearer **4.** *U.S. Navy* a commissioned officer of the lowest rank, ranking below a lieutenant junior grade —**en′sign·ship′, en′sign·cy** *n.*

**en·si·lage** (en′s′l ij) *n.* [Fr.] **1.** the preserving of green fodder by storage in a silo **2.** green fodder so preserved; silage

**en·slave** (in slāv′) *vt.* **-slaved′, -slav′ing 1.** to put into slavery; make a slave of **2.** to dominate; subjugate —**en·slave′ment** *n.* —**en·slav′er** *n.*

**en·snare** (-sner′) *vt.* **-snared′, -snar′ing** to catch in or as in a snare; trap —**en·snare′ment** *n.*

**en·snarl** (-snärl′) *vt.* to draw into a snarl or tangle

**en·sue** (in sōō′, -syōō′) *vi.* **-sued′, -su′ing** [< OFr., ult. < L. *insequi* < *in-,* in + *sequi,* to follow] **1.** to come afterward; follow immediately **2.** to happen as a consequence; result

**en·sure** (in shoor′) *vt.* **-sured′, -sur′ing** [< Anglo-Fr. *enseurer:* see EN- & SURE] **1.** to make sure; guarantee **2.** to make safe; protect

**-ent** (ənt, ′nt) [< OFr. *-ent,* L. *-ens* (gen. *entis*), stem ending of certain present participles] **1.** *a suffix meaning* that has, shows, or does *[insistent]* **2.** *a suffix meaning* a person or thing that *[superintendent, solvent]*

**en·tab·la·ture** (en tab′lə chər) *n.* [MFr. < It. *intavolatura* < *in-,* in + *tavola* < L. *tabula,* TABLE] *Archit.* **1.** a horizontal superstructure supported by columns and composed of architrave, frieze, and cornice **2.** any structure like this

**en·tail** (in tāl′) *vt.* [< ME. < *en-,* in + *taile,* an agreement < OFr. < *taillier,* to cut: see TAILOR] **1.** *Law* to limit the inheritance of (real property) to a specific line or class of heirs **2.** to cause or require as a necessary consequence; necessitate *[the plan entails work]* —*n.* **1.** an entailing or being entailed **2.** an entailed inheritance **3.** the order of descent for an entailed inheritance —**en·tail′ment** *n.*

**en·tan·gle** (in taŋ′g′l) *vt.* **-gled, -gling 1.** to involve in a tangle; ensnare **2.** to involve in difficulty **3.** to confuse; perplex **4.** to cause to be tangled; complicate —**en·tan′gle·ment** *n.*

**en·tente** (än tänt′) *n.* [Fr. < OFr. < *entendre,* to understand] **1.** an understanding or agreement, as between nations **2.** the parties to this

**en·ter** (en′tər) *vt.* [< OFr. *entrer* < L. *intrare* < *intra,* within] **1.** to come or go in or into **2.** to force a way into; penetrate **3.** to put into; insert **4.** to write down in a record, list, etc. **5.** to become a participant in (a contest) **6.** to join; become a member of (a school, club, etc.) **7.** to get (someone) admitted **8.** to start upon; begin (a career, etc.) **9.** to submit *[to enter a protest]* **10.** to register (a ship or cargo) at a customhouse **11.** *Law* to place on record before a court —*vi.* **1.** to come or go into some place **2.** to pierce; penetrate —**enter into 1.** to engage in; take part in **2.** to form a part or component of **3.** to deal with; discuss —**enter on** (or **upon**) **1.** to begin; start **2.** to begin to possess or enjoy

**en·ter·ic** (en ter′ik) *adj.* [see ff.] intestinal: also **en·ter·al** (en′tər əl)

**en·ter·o-** [< Gr. *enteron,* intestine] *a combining form meaning* intestine: also **enter-**

**en·ter·prise** (en′tər prīz′) *n.* [< OFr. < *entreprendre,* to undertake < *entre-* (L. *inter*), in + *prendre* (L. *prehendere*), to take] **1.** an undertaking; project; specif., *a)* a bold, difficult, dangerous, or important undertaking *b)* a business venture or company **2.** willingness to undertake new or risky projects; energy and initiative **3.** active participation in projects —**en′ter·pris′er** *n.*

**en·ter·pris·ing** (-prī′ziŋ) *adj.* showing enterprise; full of energy and initiative; venturesome —**en′ter·pris′ing·ly** *adv.*

**en·ter·tain** (en′tər tān′) *vt.* [< OFr. *entre* (< L. *inter*), between + *tenir* (L. *tenere*), to hold] **1.** to hold the interest of and give pleasure to; divert; amuse **2.** to give hospitality to; have as a guest **3.** to have in mind; consider, as an idea —*vi.* to have guests

**en·ter·tain·er** (-ər) *n.* a person who entertains; esp., a popular singer, dancer, comedian, etc.

**en·ter·tain·ing** (-iŋ) *adj.* interesting and pleasurable; amusing —**en′ter·tain′ing·ly** *adv.*

**en·ter·tain·ment** (-mənt) *n.* **1.** an entertaining or being entertained **2.** something that entertains; interesting, diverting, or amusing thing; esp., a show or performance

**en·thrall, en·thral** (in thrôl′) *vt.* **-thralled′, -thrall′ing** [see EN- & THRALL] **1.** [Now Rare] to enslave **2.** to hold as if in a spell; captivate; fascinate —**en·thrall′ment, en·thral′ment** *n.*

**en·throne** (-thrōn′) *vt.* **-throned′, -thron′ing 1.** to place on a throne; make a king, etc. of **2.** to accord the highest place to; exalt —**en·throne′ment** *n.*

**en·thuse** (-thōōz′, -thyōōz′) *vi.* **-thused′, -thus′ing** [backformation < ff.] [Colloq.] to express enthusiasm —*vt.* [Colloq.] to make enthusiastic

**en·thu·si·asm** (in thōō′zē az′m, -thyōō′-) *n.* [< Gr. < *enthous,* possessed by a god, inspired < *en-,* in + *theos,* god] **1.** intense or eager interest; zeal; fervor **2.** something arousing this

**en·thu·si·ast** (-ast′) *n.* a person full of enthusiasm; an ardent supporter, a devotee, etc.

**en·thu·si·as·tic** (in thōō′zē as′tik, -thyōō′-) *adj.* of, having, or showing enthusiasm; ardent —**en·thu′si·as′ti·cal·ly** *adv.*

**en·tice** (in tīs′) *vt.* **-ticed′, -tic′ing** [< OFr. *enticier,* to set afire, excite, prob. ult. < L. *in,* in + *titio,* a firebrand] to attract by offering hope of reward or pleasure; tempt —**en·tice′ment** *n.* —**en·tic′er** *n.* —**en·tic′ing·ly** *adv.*

**en·tire** (in tīr′) *adj.* [< OFr. *entier* < L. *integer,* untouched, whole] **1.** *a)* not lacking any of the parts; whole *b)* complete; absolute **2.** unbroken; intact **3.** being wholly of one piece **4.** not castrated **5.** *Bot.* having an unbroken margin, as some leaves —**en·tire′ly** *adv.* —**en·tire′ness** *n.*

**en·tire·ty** (-tē) *n., pl.* **-ties 1.** the state or fact of being entire; wholeness; completeness **2.** an entire thing; whole —**in its entirety** as a whole

**en·ti·tle** (in tīt′′l) *vt.* **-tled, -tling 1.** to give a title or name to **2.** to honor or dignify by a title **3.** to give a right or legal title to

**en·ti·ty** (en′tə tē) *n., pl.* **-ties** [< Fr. or < ML. *entitas* < L. prp. of *esse,* to be] **1.** being; existence **2.** a thing that has definite, individual existence in reality or in the mind

**en·to-** [ModL. < Gr. *entos,* within] *a combining form meaning* within or inner

**entom., entomol.** entomology

**en·tomb** (in tōōm′) *vt.* to place in a tomb or grave; bury —**en·tomb′ment** *n.*

**en·to·mo-** [Fr. < Gr. *entoma* (*zōa*), lit., notched animals: cf. INSECT] *a combining form meaning* insect or insects

**en·to·mol·o·gy** (en′tə mäl′ə jē) *n.* [see prec. & -LOGY] the branch of zoology that deals with insects —**en′to·mo·log′i·cal** (-mə läj′i k′l), **en′to·mo·log′ic** *adj.* —**en′to·mo·log′i·cal·ly** *adv.* —**en′to·mol′o·gist** *n.*

**en·tou·rage** (än′tōō räzh′) *n.* [Fr. < *entourer,* to surround] a group of accompanying attendants, assistants, or associates; retinue

**en·tr'acte** (än trakt′, än′trakt) *n.* [Fr. < *entre-,* between + *acte,* an act] **1.** the interval between two acts of a play, opera, etc.; intermission **2.** music, a dance, etc. performed during this interval

**en·trails** (en′trālz, -trəlz) *n.pl.* [< OFr. < ML. *intralia* < L. < *interaneus,* internal < *inter,* between] **1.** the inner organs of men or animals; specif., the intestines; viscera; guts **2.** the inner parts of a thing

**en·train** (in trān′) *vt.* to put aboard a train —*vi.* to go aboard a train —**en·train′ment** *n.*

**en·trance¹** (en′trəns) *n.* **1.** the act or point of entering **2.** a place for entering; door, gate, etc. **3.** permission or right to enter; admission

**en·trance²** (in trans′) *vt.* **-tranced′, -tranc′ing 1.** to put into a trance **2.** to enchant; charm; enrapture —**en·trance′ment** *n.* —**en·tranc′ing·ly** *adv.*

**en·trant** (en′trənt) *n.* a person who enters

**en·trap** (in trap′) *vt.* **-trapped′, -trap′ping 1.** to catch as in a trap **2.** to trick into difficulty, as into incriminating oneself —**en·trap′ment** *n.*

**en·treat** (-trēt′) *vt.* [< Anglo-Fr. < OFr. < *en-,* in + *traiter:* see TREAT] **1.** to ask earnestly; beg; beseech; implore —*vi.* to make an earnest appeal; plead —**en·treat′ing·ly** *adv.* —**en·treat′ment** *n.*

**en·treat·y** (-ē) *n., pl.* **-treat′ies** an earnest request; plea

**en·tree, en·trée** (än′trā; *Fr.* än trā′) *n.* [< Fr. < OFr. *entrer,* ENTER] **1.** *a)* the act of entering *b)* the right or freedom to enter, participate, etc.; access **2.** *a)* the main course of a meal *b)* formerly, and still in some countries, a dish served before the roast or between the main courses

**en·trench** (in trench′) *vt.* **1.** to surround or fortify with a trench or trenches **2.** to establish securely *[entrenched in office]* —**en·trench′ment** *n.*

**en·tre·pre·neur** (än′trə prə nur′, -noor′, -nyoor′) *n.* [Fr. < OFr. *entreprendre:* see ENTERPRISE] a person who organizes and manages a business undertaking, assuming the risk for the sake of profit

**en·tro·py** (en′trə pē) *n.* [G. *entropie,* arbitrary use of Gr. *entropē,* a turning toward] a measure of the amount of energy unavailable for work in a thermodynamic system: entropy keeps increasing and available energy diminishing in a closed system, as the universe

**en·trust** (in trust′) *vt.* **1.** to charge with a trust or duty **2.** to assign the care of; turn over for safekeeping

**en·try** (en′trē) *n., pl.* **-tries** [< OFr. < *entrer,* ENTER] **1.** *a)* the act of entering; entrance *b)* the right or freedom to enter; entree **2.** a way or passage by which to enter; door, hall, etc. **3.** *a)* the recording of an item or note in a list, journal, etc. *b)* an item thus recorded **4.** the registration of a ship or cargo at a customhouse **5.** one entered in a race, competition, etc. **6.** *Law* the taking possession of buildings, land, etc. by entering them

**en·twine** (in twīn′) *vt., vi.* **-twined′, -twin′ing** to twine or twist together or around

**e·nu·mer·ate** (i nŏŏ′mə rāt′, -nyŏŏ′-) *vt.* **-at′ed, -at′ing** [< L. pp. of *enumerare* < *e-,* out + *numerare,* to count < *numerus,* a number] **1.** to determine the number of; count **2.** to name one by one; specify, as in a list —**e·nu′mer·a′-tion** *n.* —**e·nu′mer·a′tive** *adj.* —**e·nu′mer·a′tor** *n.*

**e·nun·ci·ate** (i nun′sē āt′, -shē-) *vt.* **-at′ed, -at′ing** [< L. pp. of *enuntiare* < *e-,* out + *nuntiare,* ANNOUNCE] **1.** to state definitely **2.** to announce; proclaim **3.** to pronounce (words) —*vi.* to pronounce words, esp. clearly; articulate — **e·nun′ci·a′tion** *n.* —**e·nun′ci·a′tor** *n.*

**en·u·re·sis** (en′yŏŏ rē′sis) *n.* [ModL. < Gr. *enourein,* to urinate in] inability to control urination; esp., bed-wetting —**en′u·ret′ic** (-ret′ik) *adj.*

**en·vel·op** (in vel′əp) *vt.* [< OFr. *envoluper:* see EN- & DEVELOP] **1.** to wrap up; cover completely **2.** to surround **3.** to conceal; hide —**en·vel′op·ment** *n.*

**en·ve·lope** (en′və lōp′, än′-) *n.* [< Fr. < OFr.: see prec.] **1.** a thing that envelops; wrapper; covering **2.** a folded paper container for letters, etc., usually with a gummed flap **3.** the bag that contains the gas in a dirigible or balloon **4.** any enclosing membrane, skin, etc.

**en·ven·om** (in ven′əm) *vt.* **1.** to put venom or poison on or into **2.** to fill with hate; embitter

**en·vi·a·ble** (en′vē ə b'l) *adj.* worthy to be envied or desired —**en′vi·a·ble·ness** *n.* —**en′vi·a·bly** *adv.*

**en·vi·ous** (-əs) *adj.* [< OFr. < L. < *invidia,* ENVY] feeling, showing, or resulting from envy —**en′vi·ous·ly** *adv.*

**en·vi·ron** (in vī′rən) *vt.* [< OFr. < *environ,* about: see ENVIRONS] to surround; encircle

**en·vi·ron·ment** (in vī′rən mənt, -ərn mənt) *n.* [prec. + -MENT] **1.** surroundings **2.** all the conditions, circumstances, and influences surrounding, and affecting the development of, an organism or group of organisms —**en·vi′-ron·men′tal** (-men′t'l) *adj.* —**en·vi′ron·men′tal·ly** *adv.*

**en·vi·ron·men·tal·ist** (in vī′rən men′t'l ist) *n.* a person working to solve environmental problems, such as air and water pollution, the careless use of natural resources, uncontrolled population growth, etc.

**en·vi·rons** (in vī′rəns, -ərnz; en′vər ənz) *n.pl.* [< OFr. *en-,* in + *viron,* a circuit < *virer,* to turn] **1.** the districts surrounding a city; suburbs or outskirts **2.** vicinity

**en·vis·age** (en viz′ij) *vt.* **-aged, -ag·ing** [< Fr.: see EN- & VISAGE] to form an image of in the mind

**en·vi·sion** (en vizh′ən) *vt.* to imagine (something not yet in existence)

**en·voi** (en′voi, än′-) *n.* [Fr.] **1.** *same as* ENVOY[2] **2.** a remark made in farewell or conclusion

**en·voy**[1] (en′voi, än′-) *n.* [< Fr. < *envoyer,* to send < OFr. < *en-* (L. *in*), in + *voie* (L. *via*), way] **1.** a messenger; agent **2.** an agent sent by a government or ruler to transact diplomatic business: an envoy extraordinary ranks just below an ambassador

**en·voy**[2] (en′voi, än′-) *n.* [< OFr. *envoy,* lit., a sending: see prec.] a postscript to a poem, essay, or book, containing a dedication, explanation, etc.

**en·vy** (en′vē) *n., pl.* **-vies** [< OFr. < L. *invidia* < *invidere,* to look askance at < *in-,* upon + *videre,* to look] **1.** a feeling of discontent and ill will because of another's advantages, possessions, etc. **2.** desire for some advantage, quality, etc. that another has **3.** an object of envious feeling —*vt.* **-vied, -vy·ing** to feel envy toward, at, or because of —**en′vi·er** *n.* —**en′vy·ing·ly** *adv.*

**en·wrap** (en rap′) *vt.* **-wrapped′, -wrap′ping** to wrap; envelop

**en·wreathe** (-rēth′) *vt.* **-wreathed′, -wreath′ing** to encircle with or as with a wreath

**en·zyme** (en′zīm) *n.* [< G. < LGr. *enzymos,* leavened < Gr. *en-,* in + *zymē,* leaven] a proteinlike substance, formed in plant and animal cells, that acts as an organic catalyst in initiating or speeding up specific chemical reactions —**en′zy·mat′ic** (-zī mat′ik, -zi-), **en·zy′mic** *adj.*

**e·o-** [< Gr. *ēōs,* dawn] *a prefix meaning* early, early part of a period *[Eocene]*

**E·o·cene** (ē′ə sēn′) *adj.* [EO- + Gr. *kainos,* new] designating or of the second and longest epoch of the Tertiary Period in the Cenozoic Era —**the Eocene** the Eocene Epoch or its rocks: see GEOLOGY, chart

**E·o·li·an** (ē ō′lē ən) *adj., n. same as* AEOLIAN

**e·o·lith·ic** (ē′ə lith′ik) *adj.* [EO- + -LITHIC] designating or of the early part of the Stone Age, during which crude stone tools were first used

**e·on** (ē′ən, ē′än) *n.* [LL. < Gr. *aiōn,* an age, lifetime] an extremely long, indefinite period of time

**E·os** (ē′äs) [see EO-] *Gr. Myth.* the goddess of dawn: identified with the Roman goddess Aurora

**e·o·sin** (ē′ə sin) *n.* [< Gr. *ēōs,* dawn + -IN[1]] a rosecolored dye, $C_{20}H_8O_5Br_4$, used as an industrial pigment and biological stain: also **e′o·sine** (-sin, -sēn′) —**e′o·sin′ic** *adj.*

**-e·ous** (ē əs) [< L. *-eus* + -OUS] *a suffix meaning* having the nature of, like *[beauteous]*

**EPA** Environmental Protection Agency

**ep·au·let, ep·au·lette** (ep′ə let′) *n.* [< Fr. < OFr. < L. *spatula:* see SPATULA] a shoulder ornament, as on military uniforms

**e·pee, é·pée** (e pā′, ā-) *n.* [Fr. < OFr. < L. < Gr. *spathē,* blade] a sword, esp. a thin, pointed sword without a cutting edge, used in fencing —**e·pee′ist, é·pée′ist** *n.*

**Eph.** Ephesians: also **Ephes.**

**e·phah, e·pha** (ē′fə) *n.* [< LL. < Heb. *'ēphāh*] an ancient Hebrew dry measure, estimated at from 1/3 bushel to a little over one bushel

EPAULETS

**e·phed·rine** (i fed′rin) *n.* [< ModL. *Ephedra,* genus name of the plants < L. < Gr. *ephedra,* the horsetail] an alkaloid, $C_{10}H_{15}NO$, derived from certain Asiatic plants or synthesized, used to relieve nasal congestion and asthma

**e·phem·er·al** (i fem′ər əl) *adj.* [< Gr. < *epi-,* upon + *hēmera,* a day + -AL] **1.** lasting only one day **2.** short-lived; transitory —*n.* an ephemeral thing —**e·phem′er·al·ly** *adv.*

**e·phem·er·id** (-id) *n.* [see prec. & -ID] *same as* MAYFLY

**e·phem·er·is** (-is) *n., pl.* **eph·e·mer·i·des** (ef′ə mer′ə dēz′) [see EPHEMERAL] a table giving the daily positions of a heavenly body for a given period

**E·phe·sians** (i fē′zhənz) a book of the New Testament: an epistle of the Apostle Paul to the Christians of Ephesus

**Eph·e·sus** (ef′ə səs) ancient Greek city in W Asia Minor — **E·phe·sian** (i fē′zhən) *adj., n.*

**eph·od** (ef′äd, -əd) *n.* [< LL. < Heb. *āphad,* to put on] an outer vestment worn by ancient Jewish priests

**eph·or** (ef′ôr, -ər) *n., pl.* **-ors, -or·i′** (-ə rī′) [< L. < Gr. < *epi-,* over + *horan,* to see] any of a body of five magistrates of ancient Sparta

**E·phra·im** (ē′frē əm) [LL. < Gr. < Heb. *ephrayim,* lit., very fruitful] **1.** a masculine name **2.** *Bible a)* the younger son of Joseph *b)* the tribe of Israel descended from this son *c)* the kingdom of Israel

**ep·i-** [< Gr. *epi,* at, on, upon, etc.] *a prefix meaning* on, upon, over, on the outside, anterior, beside *[epiglottis, epidemic, epidermis]* : also **ep-** (before a vowel) and **eph-** (in an aspirated word, as *ephemeral)*

**ep·ic** (ep′ik) *n.* [< L. < Gr. < *epos,* a word, song] **1.** a long narrative poem with a dignified style and certain formalities of structure, about the deeds of a traditional or historical hero or heroes, as the *Iliad* and *Odyssey* **2.** a prose narrative, play, etc. regarded as having the qualities of an epic **3.** a series of events regarded as a proper subject for an epic —*adj.* of, or having the nature of, an epic; heroic; grand; majestic: also **ep′i·cal** —**ep′i·cal·ly** *adv.*

**ep·i·ca·lyx** (ep′ə kā′liks, -kal′iks) *n., pl.* **-lyx·es, -ly·ces′** (-lə sēz′) [EPI- + CALYX] a ring of small leaves (called *bracts)* at the base of certain flowers, resembling an extra outer calyx

**ep·i·can·thus** (-kan′thəs) *n.* [EPI- + CANTHUS] a small fold of skin sometimes covering the inner corner of the eye —**ep′i·can′thic** *adj.*

EPICALYX

**ep·i·car·di·um** (-kär′dē əm) *n., pl.* **-di·a** (-ə) [ModL. < EPI- + Gr. *kardia,* heart] the innermost layer of the pericardium —**ep′i·car′di·al** *adj.*

**ep·i·carp** (ep′ə kärp′) *n.* [EPI- + -CARP] *same as* EXOCARP

**ep·i·cene** (ep'ə sēn') *adj.* [< L. < Gr. < *epi-*, to + *koinos*, common] belonging to one sex but having characteristics of the other, or of neither —*n.* an epicene person

**ep·i·cen·ter** (-sen'tər) *n.* **1.** the area of the earth's surface directly above the place of origin, or focus, of an earthquake: also **ep'i·cen'trum** (-trəm), *pl.* **-tra** (-trə) **2.** a focal or central point —**ep'i·cen'tral** *adj.*

**ep·i·cure** (ep'i kyoor') *n.* [< L. < Gr.: see EPICURUS] **1.** a person who enjoys and has a discriminating taste for fine foods and drinks **2.** [Archaic] a person who is especially fond of luxury and sensuous pleasure —**ep'i·cur·ism** *n.*

**Ep·i·cu·re·an** (ep'i kyoo rē'ən, -kyoor'ē ən) *adj.* **1.** of Epicurus or his philosophy **2.** [e-] *a)* fond of luxury and sensuous pleasure, esp. that of eating and drinking *b)* suited to or characteristic of an epicure —*n.* **1.** a follower of Epicurus or his philosophy **2.** [e-] an epicure —**Ep'i·cu·re'an·ism, ep'i·cu·re'an·ism** *n.*

**Ep·i·cu·rus** (ep'ə kyoor'əs) 341?-270 B.C.; Gr. philosopher: he held that the goal of man should be a life of calm pleasure regulated by morality, temperance, serenity, and cultural development

**ep·i·dem·ic** (ep'ə dem'ik) *adj.* [< Fr. < épidémie < ML. < Gr. < epi-, among + dēmos, people] prevalent and spreading rapidly among many individuals in a community at the same time, as a contagious disease: also **ep'i·dem'i·cal** —*n.* **1.** an epidemic disease **2.** the epidemic spreading of a disease **3.** the rapid, widespread occurrence of a fad, fashion, etc. —**ep'i·dem'i·cal·ly** *adv.*

**ep·i·der·mis** (ep'ə dur'mis) *n.* [LL. < Gr. < epi-, upon + derma, the skin] **1.** the outermost layer of skin in vertebrates **2.** the outermost layer of cells covering seed plants and ferns **3.** any of various other integuments —**ep'i·der'mal, ep'i·der'mic** *adj.*

**ep·i·der·moid** (-dur'moid) *adj.* like epidermis: also **ep'i·der·moi'dal**

**ep·i·glot·tis** (ep'ə glät'is) *n.* [see EPI- & GLOTTIS] the thin, triangular, lidlike piece of cartilage that folds back over the opening of the windpipe during swallowing, thus preventing food, etc. from entering the lungs —**ep'i·glot'tal, ep'i·glot'tic** *adj.*

**ep·i·gram** (ep'ə gram') *n.* [< OFr. < L. < Gr. epigramma < epi-, upon + graphein, to write] **1.** a short poem with a witty or satirical point **2.** any terse, witty, pointed statement, often with a clever twist in thought (Ex.: "Experience is the name everyone gives to his mistakes") —**ep·i·gram·mat·ic** (ep'i grə mat'ik), **ep'i·gram·mat'i·cal** *adj.* —**ep'i·gram·mat'i·cal·ly** *adv.* —**ep'i·gram'ma·tist** *n.*

**ep·i·gram·ma·tize** (ep'ə gram'ə tīz') *vt., vi.* **-tized', -tiz'ing** to express (something) epigrammatically; make epigrams (about)

**ep·i·graph** (ep'ə graf') *n.* [Gr. epigraphē, inscription < epigraphein: see EPIGRAM] **1.** an inscription on a building, monument, etc. **2.** a motto or quotation at the beginning of a book, chapter, etc.

**ep·i·graph·ic** (ep'ə graf'ik) *adj.* of an epigraph or epigraphy: also **ep'i·graph'i·cal** —**ep'i·graph'i·cal·ly** *adv.*

**e·pig·ra·phy** (i pig'rə fē) *n.* [see EPIGRAPH] **1.** inscriptions collectively **2.** the study that deals with deciphering, interpreting, and classifying inscriptions —**e·pig'ra·phist, e·pig'ra·pher** *n.*

**ep·i·lep·sy** (ep'ə lep'sē) *n.* [< OFr. < LL. < Gr. epilēpsia < epi-, upon + lambanein, to seize] a chronic disease of the nervous system, characterized by convulsions and, often, unconsciousness

**ep·i·lep·tic** (ep'ə lep'tik) *adj.* of or having epilepsy —*n.* a person who has epilepsy

**ep·i·logue, ep·i·log** (ep'ə lôg', -läg') *n.* [< OFr. < L. < Gr. epilogos, conclusion < epi-, upon + legein, to say] **1.** a closing section of a novel, play, etc., providing further comment **2.** a short speech or poem spoken to the audience by one of the actors at the end of a play **3.** the actor speaking this

**ep·i·neph·rine** (ep'ə nef'rin, -rēn) *n.* [EPI- + NEPHR- + -INE⁴] a hormone secreted by the adrenal gland, that stimulates the heart, increases muscular strength, etc.: it is extracted from animal adrenals or prepared synthetically for therapeutic use

**E·piph·a·ny** (i pif'ə nē) *n., pl.* **-nies** [< OFr. < LL. < Gr. epiphaneia, appearance < epi-, upon + phainein, to show] in many Christian churches, a yearly festival (January 6) commemorating both the revealing of Jesus as the Christ to the Gentiles in the persons of the Magi and the baptism of Jesus

**ep·i·phyte** (ep'ə fīt') *n.* [EPI- + -PHYTE] a nonparasitic plant that grows on another plant, producing its own food by photosynthesis, as certain orchids, mosses, and lichens; air plant —**ep'i·phyt'ic** (-fīt'ik) *adj.* —**ep'i·phyt'i·cal·ly** *adv.*

**E·pi·rus** (i pī'rəs) ancient kingdom on the Ionian Sea, in what is now S Albania & NW Greece

**Epis.** Epistle

**Epis., Episc.** **1.** Episcopal **2.** Episcopalian

**e·pis·co·pa·cy** (i pis'kə pə sē) *n., pl.* **-cies** [< LL. < episcopus, BISHOP] **1.** church government by bishops **2.** same as EPISCOPATE

**e·pis·co·pal** (-kə pəl) *adj.* [see prec.] **1.** of or governed by bishops **2.** [E-] designating or of any of various churches governed by bishops, as the Protestant Episcopal or the Anglican Church —**e·pis'co·pal·ly** *adv.*

**E·pis·co·pa·li·an** (i pis'kə pāl'yən, -pā'lē ən) *adj.* same as EPISCOPAL —*n.* a member of the Protestant Episcopal Church —**E·pis'co·pa'li·an·ism** *n.*

**e·pis·co·pate** (i pis'kə pit, -pāt') *n.* **1.** the position, rank, or term of office of a bishop **2.** a bishop's see **3.** bishops collectively

**ep·i·sode** (ep'ə sōd') *n.* [< Gr. < epeisodios, following upon the entrance < epi-, upon + eis-, into + hodos, a way] **1.** any part of a novel, poem, musical composition, etc. that is complete in itself; incident **2.** any event or series of events complete in itself but forming part of a larger one **3.** any installment of a serialized story or drama

**ep·i·sod·ic** (ep'ə säd'ik) *adj.* **1.** of the nature of an episode; incidental **2.** made up of episodes, often not well integrated Also **ep'i·sod'i·cal** —**ep'i·sod'i·cal·ly** *adv.*

**e·pis·te·mol·o·gy** (i pis'tə mäl'ə jē) *n., pl.* **-gies** [< Gr. epistēmē, knowledge + -LOGY] the study or theory of the origin, nature, methods, and limits of knowledge —**e·pis'te·mo·log'i·cal** (-mə läj'i k'l) *adj.* —**e·pis'te·mo·log'i·cal·ly** *adv.* —**e·pis'te·mol'o·gist** *n.*

**e·pis·tle** (i pis''l) *n.* [< OFr. < L. < Gr. epistolē < epi-, to + stellein, to send] **1.** a letter, esp. a long, formal, instructive letter: now used humorously **2.** [E-] *a)* any of the letters of the Apostles in the New Testament *b)* a selection from these Epistles, read as part of Mass, Communion, etc. in various churches —**e·pis'tler** *n.*

**e·pis·to·lar·y** (-tə ler'ē) *adj.* [see prec.] **1.** of or suitable to letters or letter writing **2.** contained in, conducted by, or made up of letters

**ep·i·taph** (ep'ə taf') *n.* [< OFr. < L. epitaphium, eulogy < Gr. < epi-, upon + taphos, tomb] an inscription, as on a tomb, in memory of the person buried there —**ep'i·taph'ic, ep'i·taph'i·al** *adj.*

**ep·i·the·li·um** (ep'ə thē'lē əm) *n., pl.* **-li·ums, -li·a** (-ə) [ModL. < Gr. epi-, upon + thēlē, nipple] cellular tissue covering surfaces, forming glands, and lining most cavities of the body —**ep'i·the'li·al** *adj.*

**ep·i·thet** (ep'ə thet', -thət) *n.* [< L. < Gr. epitheton < epi-, on + tithenai, to put] **1.** a word or phrase used to characterize some person or thing, often specif. a disparaging one (Ex.: "egghead" for an intellectual) **2.** a descriptive name or title (Ex.: Philip the Fair) —**ep'i·thet'i·cal, ep'i·thet'ic** *adj.*

**e·pit·o·me** (i pit'ə mē) *n., pl.* **-mes** [L. < Gr. epitomē, abridgment < epi-, upon + temnein, to cut] **1.** a short statement of the main points of a book, report, etc.; abstract; summary **2.** a person or thing that is representative of the characteristics of a whole class

**e·pit·o·mize** (-mīz') *vt.* **-mized', -miz'ing** to make or be an epitome of —**e·pit'o·miz'er** *n.*

**ep·i·zo·ot·ic** (ep'ə zō ät'ik) *adj.* [< Fr. < Gr. epi-, upon + zōion, animal] epidemic among animals —*n.* an epizootic disease

**‡e plu·ri·bus u·num** (ē' ploor'ə bəs yōo'nəm) [L.] out of many, one: a motto of the U.S.

**ep·och** (ep'ək; Brit. & Canad., usually ē'päk) *n.* [< ML. < Gr. epochē, a pause < epi-, upon + echein, to hold] **1.** the beginning of a new and important period in the history of anything [the first earth satellite marked a new epoch in man's study of the universe] **2.** a period of time considered in terms of noteworthy events, developments, persons, etc. [an epoch of social revolution] **3.** Astron. the time at which observations are made, as of the positions of planets or stars **4.** Geol. a subdivision of a geologic period [the Eocene Epoch] —**ep'och·al** *adj.* —**ep'och·al·ly** *adv.*

**ep·ode** (ep'ōd) *n.* [MFr. < L. < Gr. epōidos, aftersong < epi-, upon + aeidein, to sing] the final stanza in certain lyric odes, following the strophe and antistrophe

**ep·o·nym** (ep'ə nim') *n.* [< Gr. < epi-, upon + onyma, a name] **1.** a real or mythical person from whose name the name of a nation, race, etc. is derived [William *Penn* is the *eponym* of *Pennsylvania*] 2. a person whose name has become identified with some period, movement, theory, etc. —**e·pon·y·mous** (i pän'ə məs), **ep'o·nym'ic** (-nim'ik) *adj.*

**ep·ox·y** (e päk'sē) *adj.* [EP(I)- + OXY(GEN)] designating or of a compound in which an oxygen atom is joined to two carbon atoms in a chain to form a bridge; specif., designating a tough resin formed by polymerization, used in glues, etc. —*n., pl.* **-ox·ies** an epoxy resin

**ep·si·lon** (ep'sə län', -lən) *n.* [Gr.] the fifth letter of the Greek alphabet (E, ε)

**Ep·som** (ep'səm) town in England, near London: site of **Epsom Downs**, where the Derby is run

**Epsom salts** (or **salt**) [< prec.] a white, crystalline salt, magnesium sulfate, $MgSO_4 \cdot 7H_2O$, used as a cathartic

**Ep·stein** (ep'stīn), Sir **Jacob** 1880–1959; Brit. sculptor, born in the U.S.

**eq.** 1. equal 2. equation 3. equivalent

**eq·ua·ble** (ek'wə b'l, ē'kwə-) *adj.* [< L. < *aequare*, to make equal < *aequus*: see ff.] 1. not varying or fluctuating much; steady; uniform [an *equable* temperature] 2. even; serene [an *equable* temperament] —**eq'ua·bil'i·ty** *n.* —**eq'ua·bly** *adv.*

**e·qual** (ē'kwəl) *adj.* [< L. < *aequus*, plain, even, flat] 1. of the same quantity, size, number, value, degree, etc. 2. having the same rights, ability, rank, etc. 3. evenly proportioned; being balanced or uniform 4. having the necessary ability, power, courage, etc. (*to*) [*equal* to the challenge] 5. [Archaic] fair; just —*n.* any thing or person that is equal [to be the *equal* of another] —*vt.* **e'qualed** or **e'qualled**, **e'qual·ing** or **e'qual·ling** 1. to be equal to; match in value 2. to do or make something equal to [to *equal* a record]

**e·qual·i·tar·i·an** (i kwäl'ə ter'ē ən, -kwôl'-) *adj., n. same as* EGALITARIAN —**e·qual'i·tar'i·an·ism** *n.*

**e·qual·i·ty** (i kwäl'ə tē, -kwôl'-) *n., pl.* **-ties** state or instance of being equal

**e·qual·ize** (ē'kwə līz') *vt.* **-ized'**, **-iz'ing** 1. to make equal 2. to make uniform —**e'qual·i·za'tion** *n.* —**e'qual·iz'er** *n.*

**e·qual·ly** (ē'kwə lē) *adv.* in an equal manner; to an equal degree; uniformly, impartially, etc.

**equal sign** (or **mark**) the arithmetical sign (=), indicating equality (Ex.: $2 + 2 = 4$)

**e·qua·nim·i·ty** (ek'wə nim'ə tē, ē'kwə-) *n.* [< L. < *aequus* + *animus*, the mind] calmness of mind; evenness of temper; composure

**e·quate** (i kwāt') *vt.* **e·quat'ed**, **e·quat'ing** [< L. pp. of *aequare*, to make equal < *aequus*, plain, even] 1. *a)* to make equal or equivalent *b)* to treat, regard, or express as equal, equivalent, or closely related 2. *Math.* to state the equality of; put in the form of an equation —**e·quat'a·ble** *adj.*

**e·qua·tion** (i kwā'zhən) *n.* 1. an equating or being equated 2. a complex whole 3. a statement of equality between two quantities, as shown by the equal sign (=) [a quadratic *equation*] 4. an expression in which symbols and formulas are used to represent a chemical reaction (Ex.: $H_2SO_4 + 2NaCl = 2HCl + Na_2SO_4$) —**e·qua'tion·al** *adj.*

**e·qua·tor** (i kwāt'ər) *n.* [< ML. < LL. *aequator* < L. *aequare*: see EQUATE] 1. an imaginary circle around the earth, equally distant from the North Pole and the South Pole: it divides the earth into the Northern Hemisphere and the Southern Hemisphere 2. any circle that divides a sphere, etc. into two equal parts 3. *same as* CELESTIAL EQUATOR

**e·qua·to·ri·al** (ē'kwə tôr'ē əl, ek'wə-) *adj.* 1. of or near the earth's equator 2. of any equator 3. like or characteristic of conditions near the earth's equator [*equatorial* heat]

**Equatorial Guinea** country in C Africa, including a mainland section & two islands in the Atlantic: 10,832 sq. mi.; pop. 286,000

**eq·uer·ry** (ek'wər ē; *also, esp. Brit.*, i kwer'ī) *n., pl.* **-ries** [altered (after L. *equus*, horse) < Fr. < OFr. *escuerie*, status of a squire] 1. formerly, an officer in charge of the horses of a royal or noble household 2. an officer who is a personal attendant on some member of a royal family

**e·ques·tri·an** (i kwes'trē ən) *adj.* [< L. *equestris* < *eques*, horseman < *equus*, a horse] 1. of horses, horsemen, or horsemanship 2. on horseback [an *equestrian* statue] —*n.* a rider on horseback, as in a circus —**e·ques'tri·an·ism** *n.* —**e·ques'tri·enne'** (-trē en') *n.fem.*

**e·qui-** [< L. *aequus*, equal] *a combining form meaning* equal, equally [*equidistant*]

**e·qui·an·gu·lar** (ē'kwə aŋ'gyə lər) *adj.* having all angles equal

**e·qui·dis·tant** (-dis'tənt) *adj.* equally distant —**e'qui·dis'tance** *n.* —**e'qui·dis'tant·ly** *adv.*

**e·qui·lat·er·al** (-lat'ər əl) *adj.* [< LL. < L. *aequus*, equal + *latus*, side] having all sides equal [an *equilateral* trian-

gle] —*n.* 1. a figure having equal sides 2. a side exactly equal to another

**e·quil·i·brant** (i kwil'ə brənt) *n.* [< Fr. < L. *aequilibrium*, EQUILIBRIUM] *Physics* a force or combination of forces that can balance another

**e·quil·i·brate** (i kwil'ə brāt', ē'kwə lī'brāt) *vt., vi.* **-brat'ed**, **-brat'ing** to bring into or be in equilibrium; balance or counterbalance —**e·quil'i·bra'tion** *n.* —**e·quil'i·bra'tor** *n.*

**e·qui·lib·ri·um** (ē'kwə lib'rē əm) *n., pl.* **-ri·ums**, **-ri·a** (-ə) [L. *aequilibrium* < *aequus*, equal + *libra*, a balance] 1. a state of balance or equality between opposing forces 2. a state of balance or adjustment of conflicting desires, interests, etc. 3. *a)* bodily stability or balance *b)* mental or emotional stability

**e·quine** (ē'kwīn, ek'wīn) *adj.* [< L. < *equus*, a horse] of, like, or characteristic of a horse —*n.* a horse

**e·qui·noc·tial** (ē'kwə näk'shəl) *adj.* 1. relating to either of the equinoxes 2. occurring at about the time of an equinox [an *equinoctial* storm] 3. equatorial —*n.* 1. *same as* CELESTIAL EQUATOR 2. an equinoctial storm

**equinoctial circle** (or **line**) *same as* CELESTIAL EQUATOR

**e·qui·nox** (ē'kwə näks') *n.* [< OFr. < ML. < L. < *aequus*, equal + *nox*, night] 1. the time when the sun crosses the equator, making night and day of equal length in all parts of the earth: the **vernal equinox** occurs about March 21, the **autumnal equinox** about September 22 2. either of the two points on the celestial equator where the sun crosses it on these dates: also **equinoctial point**

**e·quip** (i kwip') *vt.* **e·quipped'**, **e·quip'ping** [< Fr. < OFr. *esquiper*, embark, prob. < OE. < *scip*, a ship; or < ? ON. *skipa*, to arrange] 1. to provide with what is needed; outfit 2. to prepare by training, instruction, etc. —**e·quip'per** *n.*

**eq·ui·page** (ek'wə pij) *n.* 1. the equipment of a ship, army, expedition, etc. 2. a carriage, esp. one with horses and liveried servants

**e·quip·ment** (i kwip'mənt) *n.* 1. an equipping or being equipped 2. whatever one is equipped with; supplies, furnishings, apparatus, etc. 3. one's abilities, knowledge, etc.

**eq·ui·poise** (ek'wə poiz', ē'kwə-) *n.* [EQUI- + POISE] 1. equal distribution of weight; state of balance 2. a weight or force that balances another

**eq·ui·se·tum** (ek'wə sēt'əm) *n., pl.* **-tums**, **-ta** (-tə) [ModL. < L. < *equus*, horse + *saeta*, bristle] *same as* HORSETAIL (sense 2)

**eq·ui·ta·ble** (ek'wit ə b'l) *adj.* 1. characterized by equity; fair; just 2. *Law a)* having to do with equity, as distinguished from common or statute law *b)* valid in equity —**eq'ui·ta·ble·ness** *n.* —**eq'ui·ta·bly** *adv.*

**eq·ui·ta·tion** (ek'wə tā'shən) *n.* [< L. < pp. of *equitare*, to ride < *eques*, horseman] the art of riding on horseback; horsemanship

**eq·ui·ty** (ek'wət ē) *n., pl.* **-ties** [< OFr. < L. *aequitas*, equality < *aequus*, equal] 1. fairness; impartiality; justice 2. anything that is fair or equitable 3. the value of property beyond the total amount owed on it in mortgages, liens, etc. 4. *Law a)* a system of rules and doctrines, as in the U.S., supplementing common and statute law and superseding such law when it proves inadequate for just settlement *b)* a right or claim recognized in a court of equity

**equity capital** 1. funds contributed by the owners of a business 2. assets minus liabilities; net worth

**equiv.** equivalent

**e·quiv·a·lence** (i kwiv'ə ləns) *n.* the condition of being equivalent; equality of quantity, value, meaning, etc.: also **e·quiv'a·len·cy**

**e·quiv·a·lent** (-lənt) *adj.* [< OFr. < LL. < L. *aequus*, equal + *valere*, to be strong] 1. equal in quantity, value, force, meaning, etc. 2. *Chem.* having the same valence 3. *Geom.* equal in area or volume but not of the same shape —*n.* 1. an equivalent thing 2. *Chem.* the quantity by weight (of a substance) that combines with one gram of hydrogen or eight grams of oxygen —**e·quiv'a·lent·ly** *adv.*

**e·quiv·o·cal** (i kwiv'ə k'l) *adj.* [< LL. *aequivocus* (see ff.) + -AL] 1. having two or more meanings; purposely vague or ambiguous [an *equivocal* reply] 2. uncertain; doubtful [an *equivocal* outcome] 3. suspicious; questionable [*equivocal* conduct] —**e·quiv'o·cal'i·ty** (-kal'ə tē), **e·quiv'o·cal·ness** *n.* —**e·quiv'o·cal·ly** *adv.*

**e·quiv·o·cate** (-kāt') *vi.* **-cat'ed**, **-cat'ing** [< LL. *aequivocus*, of like sound < L. *aequus*, equal + *vox*, voice] to use equivocal terms in order to deceive, mislead, hedge, etc. —**e·quiv'o·ca'tion** *n.* —**e·quiv'o·ca'tor** *n.*

**er** (*variously* u, ə, ä, *etc.*; ʉr, ər *are spelling pronunciations*) *interj.* a conventionalized representation of a sound often made by a speaker when hesitating briefly

**-er** (ər) *a suffix of various origins and meanings:* 1. [OE. *-ere*] *a)* a person having to do with [*hatter*]: see also -IER, -YER *b)* a person living in [*New Yorker*] *c)* a thing or action connected with [*diner*] *d)* a person or thing that [*sprayer, roller*] 2. [OE. *-ra*] more: *added to many adjectives and adverbs to form the comparative degree* [*greater,* *later]* **3.** [< Anglo-Fr. inf. suffix] the action of ——ing: *used in legal language [demurrer, waiver]* **4.** [OE. *-rian*, freq. suffix] repeatedly *[flicker]*

**Er** *Chem.* erbium

**e·ra** (ir'ə; *now often* er'ə) *n.* [LL. *aera*, era, earlier sense, "counters" < pl. of L. *aes*, brass] **1.** a system of reckoning time by numbering the years from some given date *[the Christian Era]* **2.** an event or date that marks the beginning of a new period in the history of something **3.** a period of time measured from some important occurrence or date **4.** a period of time considered in terms of noteworthy and characteristic events, men, etc. *[an era of progress]* **5.** any of the five main divisions of geologic time *[the Paleozoic Era]* : see also EPOCH, PERIOD, AGE

**ERA** Equal Rights Amendment

**e·ra·di·ate** (ē rā'dē āt') *vi., vt.* -**at'ed**, -**at'ing** *same as* RADIATE —**e·ra'di·a'tion** *n.*

**e·rad·i·cate** (i rad'ə kāt') *vt.* -**cat'ed**, -**cat'ing** [< L. pp. of *eradicare*, to root out < *e-*, out + *radix*, a root] **1.** to tear out by the roots; uproot **2.** to wipe out; destroy —**e·rad'i·ca·ble** (-kə b'l) *adj.* —**e·rad'i·ca'tion** *n.* —**e·rad'i·ca'tive** *adj.* —**e·rad'i·ca'tor** *n.*

**e·rase** (i rās') *vt.* **e·rased'**, **e·ras'ing** [< L. pp. of *eradere* < *e-*, out + *radere*, to scrape] **1.** to rub, scrape, or wipe out (esp. writing or printing); efface **2.** to remove (something recorded) from (magnetic tape) **3.** to remove any sign of; obliterate, as from the mind **4.** [Slang] to kill —**e·ras'a·ble** *adj.*

**e·ras·er** (i rā'sər) *n.* a thing that erases; specif., a device made of rubber for erasing ink or pencil marks, or a pad of felt or cloth for removing chalk marks from a blackboard

**E·ras·mus** (i raz'məs), **Des·i·der·i·us** (des'ə dir'ē əs) (born *Gerhard Gerhards*) 1466?–1536; Du. humanist & scholar —**E·ras'mi·an** (-mē ən) *adj., n.*

**e·ra·sure** (i rā'shər; *chiefly Brit.* -zhər) *n.* **1.** an erasing **2.** an erased word, mark, etc. **3.** the place where something has been erased

**Er·a·to** (er'ə tō') *Gr. Myth.* the Muse of love poetry

**er·bi·um** (ʉr'bē əm) *n.* [ModL. < (*Ytt*)*erby*, Sw. town where first found] a metallic chemical element of the rare-earth group: symbol, Er; at. wt., 167.28; at. no., 68

**ere** (er) *prep.* [< OE. *ær*] [Archaic or Poet.] before (in time) —*conj.* [Archaic or Poet.] **1.** before **2.** rather than

**Er·e·bus** (er'ə bəs) *Gr. Myth.* the dark place under the earth through which the dead passed before entering Hades

**e·rect** (i rekt') *adj.* [< L. *erectus*, pp. of *erigere* < *e-*, up + *regere*, to make straight] **1.** upright; vertical **2.** sticking out or up; bristling; stiff —*vt.* **1.** to raise or construct (a building, etc.) **2.** to set up; cause to arise *[to erect social barriers]* **3.** to set in an upright position; raise **4.** to put together; assemble **5.** [Archaic] to establish; found **6.** *Geom.* to construct or draw (a perpendicular, figure, etc.) upon a base line —**e·rec'tion** *n.* —**e·rect'ly** *adv.* —**e·rect'ness** *n.* —**e·rec'tor** *n.*

**e·rec·tile** (i rek't'l; *chiefly Brit.* -tīl') *adj.* that can become erect: used esp. of tissue that becomes swollen and rigid when filled with blood —**e·rec'til'i·ty** (-til'ə tē) *n.*

**ere·long** (er'lôŋ') *adv.* [Archaic or Poet.] before long; soon

**er·e·mite** (er'ə mīt') *n.* [< OFr. or LL.: see HERMIT] a religious recluse; hermit —**er'e·mit'ic** (-mit'ik), **er'e·mit'i·cal** *adj.*

**e·rep·sin** (i rep'sin) *n.* [G. < L. pp. of *eripere* < *e-*, out + *rapere*, to snatch + G. *pepsin*, PEPSIN] an enzyme mixture secreted by the intestine and involved in the breaking down of proteins into their component amino acids

**Er·furt** (er'foort) city in SW East Germany: pop. 193,000

**erg** (ʉrg) *n.* [< Gr. *ergon*, work] *Physics* the unit of work or energy in the cgs (metric) system, being the work done by one dyne acting through a distance of one centimeter

**er·go** (ʉr'gō, er'-) *conj., adv.* [L.] therefore

**er·go·nom·ics** (ʉr'gə näm'iks) *n.pl.* [*with sing. v.*] [ERG + (EC)ONOMICS] the study of the problems of people in adjusting to their environment; esp., the science that seeks to adapt work or working conditions to suit the worker —**er'go·nom'i·cal** *adj.*

**er·gos·ter·ol** (ər gäs'tə rōl') *n.* [< ff. + STEROL] an alcohol, $C_{28}H_{44}O$, formerly prepared from ergot but now chiefly from yeast: when exposed to ultraviolet rays it produces a vitamin ($D_2$) used to prevent or cure rickets

**er·got** (ʉr'gət) *n.* [Fr. < OFr. *argot*, a rooster's spur: from the shape of the growth] **1.** a fungous growth that invades the kernels of rye, or of other cereal plants **2.** the disease in which this occurs **3.** an extract of the dried rye fungus, used as a drug to contract blood vessels and smooth muscle tissue

**Er·ic** (er'ik) [Scand. < ON. *Eirîkr*, lit., honorable ruler] a masculine name

**Er·ics·son** (er'ik sən), **Leif** (lāf) fl. 1000; Norw. explorer:

discovered what is now believed to be part of N. America: son of *ff.* Also sp. **Ericson**

**Eric the Red** fl. 10th cent.; Norw. explorer: discovered & colonized Greenland

**Er·ie**[1] (ir'ē) *n., pl.* **Er'ies**, **Er'ie** [AmFr. < Huron *yĕňresh*, wildcat + *-'e*, at the place of] a member of a tribe of Iroquoian Indians who lived in an area east and southeast of Lake Erie

**Er·ie**[2] (ir'ē) [after prec.] **1.** port on Lake Erie, in NW Pa.: pop. 119,000 **2. Lake,** one of the Great Lakes, between Lake Huron & Lake Ontario: 9,914 sq. mi.; 241 mi. long

**Erie Canal** barge canal between Buffalo, on Lake Erie, and Albany, on the Hudson: completed 1825: now part of the New York State Barge Canal

**Er·in** (er'in) [OIr.] *poet. name for* IRELAND

**E·rin·y·es** (i rin'ē ēz') *n.pl., sing.* **E·rin·ys** (i rin'is, -rī'nis) *Gr. Myth. same as* FURIES

**E·ris** (ir'is, er'-) *Gr. Myth.* the goddess of strife and discord

**ERISA** Employee Retirement Income Security Act

**Er·i·tre·a** (er'ə trē'ə) province of Ethiopia, on the Red Sea: 45,000 sq. mi. —**Er'i·tre'an** *adj., n.*

**er·mine** (ʉr'mən) *n., pl.* **-mines**, **-mine**: see PLURAL, II, D, 1 [OFr.; prob. < MHG. < OHG. *harmo*, weasel] **1.** a weasel of northern regions whose fur is brown in summer but white with a black-tipped tail in winter **2.** the soft, white fur of this animal **3.** the position, rank, or functions of some European judges or peers, whose state robe is trimmed with ermine —**er'mined** *adj.*

ERMINE
(body 5–10 in. long;
tail 1–6 in. long)

**erne, ern** (ʉrn) *n.* [OE. *earn*] the European white-tailed eagle, which lives near the sea

**Er·nest** (ʉr'nəst) [< G. < OHG. *Ernust*, lit., resolute < *ernust*, seriousness] a masculine name

**Er·nes·tine** (ʉr'nəs tēn') [G., fem. < prec.] a feminine name

**e·rode** (i rōd') *vt.* **e·rod'ed**, **e·rod'ing** [< Fr. < L. < *e-*, out, off + *rodere*, to gnaw] **1.** to eat into; wear away; disintegrate *[acid erodes metal]* **2.** to form by wearing away gradually *[the stream eroded a gully]* **3.** to cause to deteriorate, decay, or vanish —*vi.* to become eroded

**e·rog·e·nous** (i räj'ə nəs) *adj.* [< Gr. *erōs*, love + -GENOUS] *same as* EROTOGENIC

**E·ros** (er'äs, ir'-) *Gr. Myth.* the god of love, son of Aphrodite: identified with the Roman god Cupid

**e·ro·sion** (i rō'zhən) *n.* an eroding or being eroded —**e·ro'sion·al** *adj.* —**e·ro'sive** *adj.*

**e·rot·ic** (i rät'ik) *adj.* [Gr. *erōtikos* < *erōs* (gen. *erōtos*), love] of, having, or arousing sexual feelings or desires; having to do with sexual love —**e·rot'i·cal·ly** *adv.*

**e·rot·i·ca** (-i kə) *n.pl.* [*often with sing. v.*] erotic books, pictures, etc.

**e·rot·i·cism** (-ə siz'm) *n.* **1.** erotic quality or character **2.** sexual excitement or behavior **3.** preoccupation with sex Also, and for 2 now usually, **er·o·tism** (er'ə tiz'm)

**e·ro·to·gen·ic** (i rät'ə jen'ik; er'ə tə-) *adj.* [*eroto-* (< Gr.), sexual desire + -GENIC] designating or of those areas of the body that are highly sensitive to sexual stimulation

**err** (ʉr, er) *vi.* [< OFr. *errer* < L. *errare*, to wander] **1.** to be wrong or mistaken; fall into error **2.** to deviate from the established moral code; do wrong

**er·rand** (er'ənd) *n.* [OE. *ærende*, message] **1.** a short trip to do a definite thing, often for someone else **2.** the thing for which one goes or is sent on a trip

**er·rant** (er'ənt) *adj.* [OFr., prp. of *errer*, to travel, ult. < L. *iter*, a journey] **1.** roving or wandering, esp. in search of adventure *[a knight-errant]* **2.** *a)* [see ERR] erring *b)* shifting about *[an errant wind]* —**er'rant·ry** *n.*

**er·rat·ic** (i rat'ik) *adj.* [< OFr. < L. *erraticus* < pp. of *errare*, to wander] **1.** having no fixed course; irregular; random **2.** eccentric; queer —**er·rat'i·cal·ly** *adv.*

**er·ra·tum** (e rät'əm, -rāt'-, -rat'-) *n., pl.* **-ta** (-ə) [L., neut. pp. of *errare*, to wander] an error in printing or writing

**er·ro·ne·ous** (ə rō'nē əs, e-) *adj.* containing or based on error; mistaken; wrong —**er·ro'ne·ous·ly** *adv.*

**er·ror** (er'ər) *n.* [< OFr. < L. *error* < *errare*, to wander] **1.** the state of believing what is untrue or incorrect **2.** a wrong belief; incorrect opinion **3.** something incorrect or wrong; inaccuracy; mistake **4.** transgression; wrongdoing; sin **5.** the amount by which something deviates from what is required or correct **6.** *Baseball* any misplay in fielding a ball which results in a player being safe who should have been out or which permits a runner to advance —**er'ror·less** *adj.*

**er·satz** (ʉr'zäts, er'-) *n., adj.* [G.] substitute or synthetic: the word usually suggests inferior quality

**Erse** (ʉrs) *adj., n.* [ME. *Erish*, var. of *Irisc*, Irish] *same as* GAELIC, *adj.* 2, *n.* 2

**erst** (ʉrst) *adv.* [OE. *ærest*, superl. of *ær*, ere] [Archaic] formerly —*adj.* [Obs.] first

**erst·while** (-hwīl′) *adv.* [Archaic] some time ago; formerly —*adj.* former

**e·ruct** (i rukt′) *vt., vi.* [< L. *eructare* < *e-*, out + *ructare*, to belch] to belch: also **e·ruc′tate** (-tāt) **-tat·ed, -tat·ing** — **e·ruc·ta·tion** (i ruk′tā′shən, ē′ruk-) *n.*

**er·u·dite** (er′yoo dīt′, -ōō-) *adj.* [< L. pp. of *erudire*, to instruct < *e-*, out + *rudis*, RUDE] learned; scholarly —**er′u·dite′ly** *adv.*

**er·u·di·tion** (er′yoo dish′ən, -ōō-) *n.* learning acquired by reading and study; scholarship

**e·rupt** (i rupt′) *vi.* [< L. *eruptus*, pp. of *erumpere* < *e-*, out + *rumpere*, to break] **1.** to burst forth or out, as from some restraint [the lava *erupted*, a riot *erupted*] **2.** to throw forth lava, water, steam, etc., as a volcano **3.** to break out in a rash **4.** to break through the gums, as a new tooth —*vt.* to cause to burst forth —**e·rupt′i·ble** *adj.*

**e·rup·tion** (i rup′shən) *n.* **1.** a bursting forth or out **2.** a throwing forth of lava, water, steam, etc. **3.** *Med. a)* a breaking out in a rash *b)* a rash —**e·rup′tive** *adj.* —**e·rup′tive·ly** *adv.*

**Er·win** (ʉr′win) [G. < OHG. *hari*, host + *wini*, friend] a masculine name

**-er·y** (ər ē) [< OFr. *-erie* < LL. *-aria*, or < OFr. *-ier* + *-ie* (L. *-ia*)] *a suffix meaning:* **1.** a place to [*tannery*] **2.** a place for [*nunnery*] **3.** the practice, act, or occupation of [*surgery*] **4.** the product or goods of [*pottery*] **5.** a collection of [*crockery*] **6.** the state or condition of [*drudgery*] **7.** the behavior or qualities of [*tomfoolery*]

**er·y·sip·e·las** (er′ə sip′ʼl əs, ir′-) *n.* [< L. < Gr. < *erythros*, red + *-pelas* (L. *pellis*), skin] an acute infectious disease of the skin or mucous membranes caused by a streptococcus and characterized by local inflammation and fever

**e·ryth·ro-** [< Gr. *erythros*, red] *a combining form meaning:* **1.** red [*erythrocyte*] **2.** erythrocyte

**e·ryth·ro·cyte** (i rith′rə sīt′) *n.* [prec. + -CYTE] a red blood corpuscle: it is a very small, circular disk and contains hemoglobin, which carries oxygen to the body tissues —**e·ryth′ro·cyt′ic** (-sit′ik) *adj.*

**e·ryth·ro·my·cin** (i rith′rə mī′sin) *n.* [< ERYTHRO- + Gr. *mykēs*, fungus + -INⁱ] an antibiotic derived from a soil bacterium, used to treat various bacterial diseases

**Es** *Chem.* einsteinium

**-es** (iz, əz, z) [variously < OE. *-as, -s*] *a suffix used:* **1.** to form the plural of some nouns, as in *fishes:* see PLURAL **2.** to form the third person singular, present indicative, of verbs, as in (he) *kisses:* cf. -s

**E·sau** (ē′sô) [L. < Gr. < Heb. '*ēsāw*, lit., hairy] *Bible* the son of Isaac and Rebekah, who sold his birthright to his younger twin brother, Jacob: Gen. 25:21–34, 27

**es·ca·drille** (es′kə dril′; *Fr.* es kà drē′y′) *n.* [Fr. < Sp. < *escuadra*, squad] a squadron of airplanes, as in the French armed forces of World War I

**es·ca·lade** (es′kə lād′, es′kə lād′) *n.* [< Fr. < It. < *scalare*, to climb < L. *scala*, ladder] the act of climbing the walls of a fortified place by ladders —*vt.* **-lad′ed, -lad′ing** to climb (a wall, etc.) or enter (a fortified place) by ladders

**es·ca·late** (es′kə lāt′) *vi.* **-lat′ed, -lat′ing** [back-formation < ff.] **1.** to rise as on an escalator **2.** to expand, as from a limited conflict into a general war **3.** to increase rapidly, as prices —*vt.* to cause to escalate —**es′ca·la′tion** *n.*

**es·ca·la·tor** (-ər) *n.* [< ESCALA(DE) + -*tor*, as in (ELEVA)TOR] a moving stairway consisting of treads linked in an endless belt

**escalator clause** a clause in a contract by which wages, etc. are adjusted to cost of living, etc.

**es·cal·lop, es·cal·op** (e skäl′əp, -skal′-) *n., vt.* [< OFr.: see SCALLOP] *same as* SCALLOP

**es·ca·pade** (es′kə pād′) *n.* [Fr., ult. < ff.] a reckless adventure or prank

**es·cape** (ə skāp′, e-) *vi.* **-caped′, -cap′ing** [< ONormFr. < L. *ex-*, out of + *cappa*, cloak (i.e., leave one's cloak)] **1.** to get free; get away **2.** to avoid an illness, accident, pain, etc. **3.** to flow, drain, or leak away [gas *escaping* from a pipe] **4.** to slip away; disappear —*vt.* **1.** to get away from; flee from **2.** to manage to keep away from; avoid [to escape punishment] **3.** to come from involuntarily [a scream *escaped* her lips] **4.** to slip away from; be missed or forgotten by [his name *escapes* me] —*n.* **1.** an escaping or the state of having escaped **2.** a means of escape **3.** an outward flow or leakage **4.** a temporary mental release from reality —*adj.* **1.** giving temporary mental release from reality **2.** *a)* making escape possible [an escape hatch] *b)* giving a basis for evading a claim, responsibility, etc. [an escape clause] —**es·cap′a·ble** *adj.* —**es·cap′er** *n.*

**es·cap·ee** (ə skā′pē′, e-) *n.* a person who has escaped, esp. from confinement

**es·cape·ment** (ə skāp′mənt, e-) *n.* **1.** [Rare] a means of escape **2.** the part in a clock or watch that controls the speed and regularity of the balance wheel or pendulum, by means of a notched wheel (**escape wheel**), one tooth of which is allowed to escape from the detaining catch at a time **3.** a ratchet mechanism, esp. on a typewriter to regulate the horizontal movement of the carriage

ESCAPEMENT

**escape velocity** the minimum speed required for a particle, space vehicle, etc. to escape permanently from the gravitational field of a planet, star, etc.

**es·cap·ism** (ə skāp′iz′m, e-) *n.* a tendency to escape from reality, the responsibilities of real life, etc., esp. by unrealistic imaginative activity —**es·cap′ist** *adj., n.*

**es·ca·role** (es′kə rōl′) *n.* [Fr. < ML. < L. < *esca*, food] *same as* ENDIVE (sense 1)

**es·carp·ment** (e skärp′mənt) *n.* [< Fr.: see SCARP] **1.** a steep slope or cliff formed by erosion or by faulting **2.** ground formed into a steep slope on the exterior of a fortification See also SCARP

**-es·cence** (es′ʼns) *a n.-forming suffix corresponding to the adjective suffix* -ESCENT [*obsolescence*]

**-es·cent** (es′ʼnt) [< L. *-escens, -escentis*, prp. ending] *an adj.-forming suffix meaning:* **1.** starting to be; being or becoming [*convalescent*] **2.** giving off or reflecting light, or exhibiting a play of color [*phosphorescent*]

**es·cheat** (es chēt′) *n.* [< OFr. < pp. of *escheoir*, to fall to one's share < VL. < L. *ex-*, out + *cadere*, to fall] *Law* **1.** the reverting of property to the lord of the manor, to the crown, or to the government when there are no legal heirs **2.** property so reverting —*vt., vi.* to confiscate or revert by escheat —**es·cheat′a·ble** *adj.*

**es·chew** (es chōō′) *vt.* [< Anglo-Fr. < OFr. < OHG. *sciuhan*, to fear] to keep away from (something harmful or disliked); shun —**es·chew′al** *n.*

**es·cort** (es′kôrt; *for v.* ə skôrt′) *n.* [< Fr. < It. < *scorta* < *scorgere*, to lead < L. *ex-*, out + *corrigere*, to CORRECT] **1.** one or more persons (or cars, ships, airplanes, etc.) accompanying another or others to give protection or show honor **2.** a man or boy accompanying a woman or girl, as to a party **3.** accompaniment by an escort —*vt.* to go with as an escort

**es·cri·toire** (es′krə twär′) *n.* [< OFr. < LL. < pp. of L. *scribere*, to write] a writing desk or table; secretary

**es·crow** (es′krō; *chiefly Brit.* es krō′) *n.* [OFr. *escroue*, scroll] *Law* a written agreement, as a bond or deed, put in the care of a third party until certain conditions are fulfilled —**in escrow** *Law* so put in the care of a third party

**es·cu·do** (es kōō′dō) *n., pl.* **-dos** [Sp., a shield < L. *scutum*] **1.** any of several obsolete coins of Spain and Portugal **2.** the monetary unit of Portugal, Cape Verde, and Mozambique: see MONETARY UNITS, table

**es·cu·lent** (es′kyoo lənt) *adj.* [< L. < *esca*, food] fit for food; eatable; edible —*n.* something fit for food, esp. a vegetable

**es·cutch·eon** (i skuch′ən) *n.* [ONormFr. < L. *scutum*, shield] a shield or shield-shaped surface on which a coat of arms is displayed —**a blot on one's escutcheon** a stain on one's honor

**Es·dras** (ez′drəs) *Douay Bible* name for EZRA

**-ese** (ēz, ēs) [< OFr. & It. < L. *-ensis*] *a suffix meaning:* **1.** (a native or inhabitant) of [*Javanese*] **2.** (in) the language or dialect of [*Cantonese*] **3.** (in) the style of [*journalese*]

**ESE, E.S.E., e.s.e.** east-southeast

**Es·fa·hán** (es′fä hän′) city in WC Iran: pop. 575,000

**Es·ki·mo** (es′kə mō′) *n.* [< Fr. < Algonquian: lit., eater of raw flesh] **1.** *pl.* **-mos′, -mo′** a member of a group of native N. American people living in Greenland, N Canada and Alaska, and the NE tip of Asia **2.** either of the two languages of the Eskimos —*adj.* of the Eskimos, their language, or their culture —**Es′ki·mo′an** *adj.*

**Eskimo dog** a strong breed of dog with grayish, shaggy fur, used by the Eskimos to pull sleds

**e·soph·a·gus** (i säf′ə gəs) *n., pl.* **-gi** (-jī′) [< OFr. < ML. < Gr. *oisophagos* < *oisein*, fut. inf. of *pherein*, to carry + *phagein*, to eat] the tube through which food passes from the pharynx to the stomach: see EPIGLOTTIS, illus. —**e·soph·a·ge·al** (i säf′ə jē′əl) *adj.*

**es·o·ter·ic** (es′ə ter′ik) *adj.* [< Gr. < *esōteros*, inner, compar. of *esō*, within] **1.** *a)* understood by only a chosen few, as an inner group of disciples or initiates *b)* beyond the understanding or knowledge of most people; abstruse **2.** confidential; private —**es′o·ter′i·cal·ly** *adv.*

**ESP** extrasensory perception

**esp., espec.** especially

**es·pa·drille** (es′pə dril′) *n.* [Fr. < Sp. *esparto*, ESPARTO] a shoe for casual wear, with a canvas upper and a sole of twisted rope or of rubber, etc.

**es·pal·ier** (es pal′yər) *n.* [Fr. < It. *spalliera*, support < *spalla*, the shoulder < L. *spatula*: see SPATULA] **1.** a lattice or trellis on which trees and shrubs are trained to grow flat **2.** a plant, tree, etc. so trained —*vt.* **1.** to train as or on an espalier **2.** to provide with an espalier

**Es·pa·ña** (es pä′nyä) *Sp. name of* SPAIN

**es·par·to** (es pär′tō) *n.* [Sp. < L. *spartum* < Gr. *sparton*] a long, coarse grass of Spain and N Africa, used to make rope, shoes, etc.: also **esparto grass**

**es·pe·cial** (ə spesh′əl, es pesh′-) *adj.* special; particular; exceptional —**es·pe′cial·ly** *adv.*

ESPALIER

**Es·pe·ran·to** (es′pə rän′tō, -ran′-) *n.* [after pseudonym of Dr. L. L. Zamenhof (1859–1917), its inventor] an artificial language for international (chiefly European) use, based on word bases common to the main European languages

**es·pi·al** (ə spī′əl, es pī′-) *n.* **1.** an espying or being espied; observation **2.** discovery

**es·pi·o·nage** (es′pē ə näzh′, -nij′) *n.* [< Fr. < *espion*, a spy < It. *spione* < *spia*, a spy] **1.** the act of spying **2.** the use of spies by a government to learn the military secrets of other nations

**es·pla·nade** (es′plə näd′, -näd′) *n.* [Fr. < It. < *spianare* < L. *explanare*, to level: see EXPLAIN] a level, open space of ground; esp., a public walk or roadway, often along a shore; promenade

**es·pous·al** (i spou′z'l) *n.* **1.** [*often pl.*] *a)* a betrothal ceremony *b)* a wedding **2.** an espousing (of some cause, idea, etc.); advocacy

**es·pouse** (i spouz′) *vt.* **-poused′, -pous′ing** [< OFr. < LL. *sponsare* < L. *sponsus*: see SPOUSE] **1.** to marry, esp. to take as a wife **2.** to take up, support, or advocate (some cause, idea, etc.) —**es·pous′er** *n.*

**es·pres·so** (es pres′ō) *n.,* pl. **-sos** [It. (*caffè*) *espresso,* pressed-out (coffee)] coffee prepared in a special machine by forcing steam through finely ground coffee beans

**es·prit** (es prē′) *n.* [Fr.] **1.** spirit **2.** lively intelligence or wit

**es·prit de corps** (es prē′ də kôr′) [Fr.] group spirit; sense of pride, honor, etc. shared by those in the same group or undertaking

**es·py** (ə spī′, es pī′) *vt.* **-pied′, -py′ing** [< OFr. *espier*: see SPY] to catch sight of; spy

**Esq., Esqr.** Esquire

**-esque** (esk) [Fr. < It. *-esco*] *a suffix meaning:* **1.** in the manner or style of [*Romanesque*] **2.** having the quality of [*picturesque*]

**Es·qui·mau** (es′kə mō′) *n.,* pl. **-maux′** (-mō′, -mōz′), **-mau′** [Fr.] *same as* ESKIMO

**es·quire** (əˈkwīr, ə skwīr′) *n.* [< OFr. < LL. *scutarius,* a shield-bearer < L. *scutum,* a shield] **1.** formerly, a candidate for knighthood, acting as attendant for a knight **2.** in England, a member of the gentry ranking just below a knight **3.** [E-] a title of courtesy, usually abbrev. *Esq., Esqr.,* placed after a man's surname

**ess** (es) *n.,* pl. **ess′es 1.** the letter S, s **2.** something shaped like an S

**-ess** (is, əs; *occas.* es) [< OFr. < LL. *-issa* < Gr.] *a suffix meaning* female [*lioness*]: as applied to persons (*poetess,* etc.), now often avoided as discriminating

**es·say** (e sā′; *for n. 1 usually, and for n. 2 always,* es′ā) *vt.* [< OFr. < LL. < L. *exagium,* a weighing < *ex-,* out of + *agere,* to do] to try; attempt —*n.* **1.** an attempt; trial **2.** a short, personal literary composition of an analytical or interpretive kind —**es·say′er** *n.*

**es·say·ist** (es′ā ist) *n.* a writer of essays

**Es·sen** (es′'n) city in W West Germany, in the Ruhr valley: pop. 705,000

**es·sence** (es′'ns) *n.* [< OFr. & < L. *essentia* < *esse,* to be] **1.** an entity **2.** that which makes something what it is; fundamental nature or most important quality (of something) **3.** *a)* a substance that keeps, in concentrated form, the flavor, fragrance, etc. of the plant, drug, food, etc. from which it is extracted *b)* a solution of such a substance in alcohol *c)* a perfume **4.** *Philos. a)* inward nature; true substance *b)* indispensable conceptual characteristics and relations

**Es·sene** (es′ēn, ə sēn′) *n.* [< L. < Gr. *Essēnoi*] a member of a mystical Jewish sect, existing from the 2d century B.C. to the 2d century A.D.

**es·sen·tial** (ə sen′shəl) *adj.* **1.** of or constituting the essence of something; basic; inherent **2.** absolute; perfect **3.** absolutely necessary; indispensable —*n.* something necessary, fundamental, or indispensable —**es·sen·ti·al-**

**i·ty** (i sen′shē al′ə tē) *n.* —**es·sen′tial·ly** *adv.* —**es·sen′tial·ness** *n.*

**es·sen·tial·ism** (-iz′m) *n. Philos.* a theory which stresses essence as opposed to existence

**essential oil** any volatile oil that gives distinctive odor, flavor, etc. to a plant, flower, or fruit

**Es·sex** (es′iks), 2d Earl of (*Robert Devereux*) 1566–1601; Eng. soldier & courtier

**-est** (ist, əst) [< OE. *-est, -ost, -ast*] *a suffix used to form:* **1.** the superlative degree of adjectives and adverbs [*greatest, soonest*] **2.** the archaic 2d pers. sing., pres. indic., of verbs [*goest*]

**EST, E.S.T.** Eastern Standard Time

**est. 1.** established **2.** estimate **3.** estimated

**es·tab·lish** (ə stab′lish) *vt.* [< OFr. *establir* < L. < *stabilis,* STABLE¹] **1.** to make stable; settle **2.** to order, ordain, or enact (a law, statute, etc.) permanently **3.** to set up (a nation, business, etc.); found **4.** to cause to be; bring about [*to establish* good relations] **5.** to settle in an office, or set up in business or a profession **6.** to make a state institution of (a church) **7.** to cause (a precedent, theory, etc.) to be accepted or recognized **8.** to prove; demonstrate (a case at law) —**es·tab′lish·er** *n.*

**established church** the church given exclusive recognition and official support by a government; specif., [E- C-] the Church of England

**es·tab·lish·ment** (-mənt) *n.* **1.** an establishing or being established **2.** a thing established, as a business, military organization, household, etc. —**the Establishment** the ruling inner circle of any nation, institution, etc.

**es·tate** (ə stāt′) *n.* [< OFr. *estat,* STATE] **1.** *a)* a condition or stage of life [*to come to man's estate*] *b)* status or rank **2.** formerly, any of the three social classes having specific political powers: the clergy (**first estate**), the nobility (**second estate**), and the commons, or bourgeoisie (**third estate**) **3.** property; possessions **4.** landed property; individually owned piece of land containing a residence **5.** *Law a)* the degree, nature, and extent of ownership that one has in land or other property *b)* all the property, real or personal, owned by one

**es·teem** (ə stēm′) *vt.* [< OFr. < L. *aestimare,* to value, estimate] **1.** to have great regard for; value highly; respect **2.** to hold to be; consider —*n.* favorable opinion; high regard

**Es·tel·la** (e stel′ə) [Sp. < L. *Stella,* lit., star] a feminine name: var. *Estelle*

**es·ter** (es′tər) *n.* [G., contr. < *essig,* vinegar + *äther,* ETHER] an organic compound, comparable to an inorganic salt, formed by the reaction of an acid and an alcohol, or a phenol: the organic radical of the alcohol or phenol replaces the acid hydrogen of the acid

**Es·ther** (es′tər) [< LL. < Gr. < Heb. *estēr,* prob. < Bab. *Ishtar,* Ishtar] **1.** a feminine name **2.** *Bible a)* the Jewish wife of a Persian king: she saved her people from slaughter *b)* the book telling her story: abbrev. *Esth.*

**es·thete** (es′thēt′) *n. same as* AESTHETE —**es·thet′ic** (-thet′ik) *adj.* —**es·thet′i·cal·ly** *adv.* —**es·thet′i·cism** (-ə siz′m) *n.*

**es·thet·ics** (es thet′iks) *n.pl. same as* AESTHETICS

**es·ti·ma·ble** (es′tə mə b'l) *adj.* worthy of esteem —**es′ti·ma·ble·ness** *n.* —**es′ti·ma·bly** *adv.*

**es·ti·mate** (es′tə māt′; *for n.* -mit) *vt.* **-mat′ed, -mat′ing** [< L. pp. of *aestimare:* see ESTEEM] **1.** to form an opinion about **2.** to determine generally but carefully (size, value, cost, etc.); calculate approximately —*vi.* to make an estimate —*n.* **1.** a general calculation of size, value, etc.; esp., an approximate computation of the probable cost of a piece of work made by a person undertaking to do the work **2.** an opinion or judgment —**es′ti·ma′tive** *adj.* —**es′ti·ma′tor** *n.*

**es·ti·ma·tion** (es′tə mā′shən) *n.* **1.** an estimating **2.** an opinion or judgment **3.** esteem; regard

**es·ti·val** (es′tə v'l, es tī′-) *adj.* [< L. < *aestivus < aestas,* summer] of or for summer

**es·ti·vate** (es′tə vāt′) *vi.* **-vat′ed, -vat′ing** [< L. pp. of *aestivare < aestas,* summer] **1.** to spend the summer **2.** to pass the summer in a dormant state, as snails —**es′ti·va′tion** *n.*

**Es·to·ni·a** (es tō′nē ə) republic of the U.S.S.R., in NE Europe, on the Baltic Sea: 17,410 sq. mi.; pop. 1,300,000; cap. Tallinn: in full, **Estonian Soviet Socialist Republic** —**Es·to′ni·an** *adj., n.*

**es·top** (e stäp′) *vt.* **-topped′, -top′ping** [< Anglo-Fr. & OFr. < L. *stuppa,* oakum] *Law* to stop or prevent (a person) from contradicting a previous statement

**es·trange** (ə strānj′) *vt.* **-tranged′, -trang′ing** [OFr. *estranger* < ML. < L. *extraneus,* STRANGE] **1.** to remove; keep apart or away **2.** to turn (a person) from an affec-

fat, āpe, cär; ten, ēven; is, bīte; gō, hôrn, tōol, look; oil, out; up, fur; get; joy; yet; chin; she; thin, *th*en; zh, leisure; ŋ, ring; ə for *a* in ago, *e* in agent, *i* in sanity, *o* in comply, *u* in focus; ′ as in able (ā′b'l); Fr. bal; ë, Fr. coeur; ö, Fr. feu; Fr. mon; ô, Fr. coq; ü, Fr. duc; r, Fr. cri; H, G. ich; kh, G. doch; ‡foreign; *hypothetical; < derived from. See inside front cover.

tionate or friendly attitude to an indifferent, unfriendly, or hostile one; alienate the affections of —**es·trange′ment** *n.*

**es·tro·gen** (es′trə jən) *n.* [< ESTRUS + -GEN] any of several female sex hormones or similar synthetic compounds —**es′tro·gen′ic** (-jen′ik) *adj.*

**estrous cycle** the regular female reproductive cycle of most placental mammals that is under hormonal control and includes a period of heat

**es·trus** (es′trəs, ēs′-) *n.* [ModL. < L. *oestrus* < Gr. *oistros,* frenzy] the periodic sexual excitement, or heat, of most female placental mammals, or the period of this Also **es′·trum** (-trəm) —**es′trous** *adj.*

**es·tu·ar·y** (es′choo wer′ē) *n., pl.* **-ar′ies** [< L. < *aestus,* the tide] an inlet or arm of the sea; esp., the wide mouth of a river, where the tide meets the current —**es′tu·ar′i·al, es′tu·ar·ine** (-in, -īn′) *adj.*

**-et** (it, ət) [< OFr. *-et,* masc., *-ete* (Fr. *-ette*), fem.] *a suffix added to nouns, meaning* little *[islet]*

**e·ta** (āt′ə, ēt′ə) *n.* the seventh letter of the Greek alphabet (Η, η): it is shown as *ē* in the etymologies of this dictionary

**‡é·ta·gère** (ā tä zher′) *n.* [Fr.] a stand with open shelves like a whatnot, for displaying small art objects, ornaments, etc.

**et al.** 1. [L. *et alibi*] and elsewhere 2. [L. *et alii*] and others

**etc.** et cetera

**et·cet·er·a** (et set′ər ə, set′rə) [L.] and others; and the like; and the rest; and so forth

**et·cet·er·as** (-əz, -rəz) *n.pl.* additional things or persons; customary extras

**etch** (ech) *vt.* [< Du. < G. < MHG. *etzen,* to cause to eat] 1. to make (a drawing, design, etc.) on metal, glass, etc. by the action of an acid, esp. by coating the surface with wax and letting the acid eat into lines and areas laid bare with a needle 2. to engrave (a metal plate, glass, etc.) in this way for use in printing such drawings, etc. 3. to depict or impress sharply and distinctly —*vi.* to make etchings —**etch′·er** *n.*

**etch·ing** (-iŋ) *n.* 1. an etched plate, drawing, or design 2. a print made from an etched plate 3. the art of making such drawings, etc.

**e·ter·nal** (i tur′n'l) *adj.* [< OFr. < LL. *aeternalis* < L. < *aevum,* an age] 1. without beginning or end; everlasting 2. of eternity 3. forever the same; unchanging *[eternal truths]* 4. never stopping or ending; perpetual *[eternal rest]* 5. seeming never to stop; continual *[eternal bickering]* 6. timeless —**the Eternal God** —**e·ter′nal·ly** *adv.* —**e·ter′nal·ness** *n.*

**e·ter·ni·ty** (i tur′nə tē) *n., pl.* **-ties** 1. the quality, state, or fact of being eternal; continuance without end 2. infinite time; time without beginning or end 3. a long period of time that seems endless 4. the endless time after death

**e·ter·nize** (-nīz) *vt.* **-nized, -niz·ing** 1. to make eternal 2. to make famous forever; immortalize Also **e·ter′nal·ize′ -ized′, -iz′ing** —**e·ter′ni·za′tion** *n.*

**-eth¹** (əth, ith) *same as* -TH² *[fortieth, sixtieth, etc.]*

**-eth²** (ith, əth) [< OE. *-(a)th*] archaic ending of the third person singular, present indicative, of verbs *[asketh, bringeth]:* see also -TH³

**Eth.** 1. Ethiopia 2. Ethiopian 3. Ethiopic

**E·than** (ē′thən) [LL. < Heb. *ēthān,* strength] a masculine name

**eth·ane** (eth′ān) *n.* [ETH(YL) + -ANE] an odorless, colorless, gaseous hydrocarbon, $C_2H_6$: it is found in natural gas and used as a fuel, etc.

**eth·a·nol** (eth′ə nōl′, -nōl′) *n.* [ETHAN(E) + -OL¹] *same as* ALCOHOL (sense 1)

**Eth·el** (eth′əl) [< OE. < *æthel,* noble] a feminine name

**Eth·el·red II** (eth′əl red′) 968-1016; king of England (978-1016): called *the Unready*

**eth·ene** (eth′ēn) *n. same as* ETHYLENE

**e·ther** (ē′thər) *n.* [< L. < Gr. *aithēr* < *aithein,* to kindle, burn] 1. the upper regions of space; clear sky 2. *Chem.* a volatile, colorless, highly flammable liquid, $(C_2H_5)_2O$: it is used as an anesthetic and a solvent for resins and fats 3. *Physics* an invisible substance postulated (in older theory) as pervading space and serving as the medium for the transmission of radiant energy, as light waves

**e·the·re·al** (i thir′ē əl) *adj.* 1. of or like the ether, or upper regions of space 2. very light; airy; delicate 3. heavenly —**e·the′re·al′i·ty** (-al′ə tē), **e·the′re·al·ness** *n.* —**e·the′re·al·ly** *adv.*

**e·the·re·al·ize** (-ə līz′) *vt.* **-ized′, -iz′ing** to make, or treat as being, ethereal —**e·the′re·al·i·za′tion** *n.*

**e·ther·ize** (ē′thər īz′) *vt.* **-ized′, -iz′ing** to anesthetize as by causing to inhale ether fumes —**e′ther·i·za′tion** *n.*

**eth·ic** (eth′ik) *n.* [see ff.] 1. ethics or a system of ethics *[the humanist ethic]* 2. any single element in a system of ethics —*adj. same as* ETHICAL

**eth·i·cal** (-i k'l) *adj.* [< L. < Gr. *ēthikos* < *ēthos,* character, custom + -AL] 1. having to do with ethics or morality; of or conforming to moral standards 2. conforming to

professional standards of conduct 3. designating or of a drug available only on a doctor's prescription —**eth′i·cal′i·ty** (-kal′ə tē), **eth′i·cal·ness** *n.* —**eth′i·cal·ly** *adv.*

**eth·ics** (eth′iks) *n.pl.* [with sing. v. in 1 & 2, and occas. 3] [see prec.] 1. the study of standards of conduct and moral judgment 2. a treatise on this study 3. the system or code of morals of a particular person, religion, group, profession, etc.

**E·thi·o·pi·a** (ē′thē ō′pē ə) 1. ancient kingdom in NE Africa, corresponding to modern Sudan & N Ethiopia (sense 2) 2. country in E Africa, on the Red Sea: 457,000 sq. mi.; pop. 24,769,000; cap. Addis Ababa —**E′thi·o′pi·an** *adj., n.*

**E·thi·op·ic** (-äp′ik, -ō′pik) *adj.* 1. *same as* ETHIOPIAN 2. of the Semitic languages of the Ethiopians —*n.* 1. the classical Semitic language of Ethiopia, used in the liturgy of the Christian church in Ethiopia 2. the group of languages spoken by Ethiopians, belonging to the Semitic branch of the Afro-Asiatic language family

**eth·nic** (eth′nik) *adj.* [< LL. < Gr. *ethnikos,* national < *ethnos,* nation] designating or of any of the basic groups or divisions of mankind or of a heterogeneous population, as distinguished by customs, characteristics, language, etc.; ethnological Also **eth′ni·cal** —*n.* a member of an ethnic group, esp. a member of a minority or nationality group that is part of a larger community —**eth′ni·cal·ly** *adv.*

**eth·no-** [< Gr. *ethnos,* nation] *a combining form meaning* ethnic group or division; people or peoples *[ethnology]*

**eth·no·cen·trism** (eth′nə sen′triz'm) *n.* the emotional attitude that one's own ethnic group, nation, or culture is superior to all others —**eth′no·cen′tric** *adj.* —**eth′no·cen′tri·cal·ly** *adv.*

**eth·nog·ra·phy** (eth näg′rə fē) *n.* the branch of anthropology that deals descriptively with specific cultures, esp. those of nonliterate peoples —**eth·nog′ra·pher** *n.* —**eth′no·graph′ic** (-nə graf′ik), **eth′no·graph′i·cal** *adj.*

**eth·nol·o·gy** (eth näl′ə jē) *n.* the branch of anthropology that deals with the comparative cultures of various peoples, including their distribution, characteristics, folkways, etc. —**eth·no·log′i·cal** (eth′nə läj′i k'l), **eth′no·log′ic** *adj.* —**eth′no·log′i·cal·ly** *adv.* —**eth·nol′o·gist** *n.*

**e·thol·o·gy** (e thäl′ə jē, ē-) *n.* [L. *ethologia,* character portrayal < Gr.: see ETHOS & -LOGY] *Biol.* the scientific study of the characteristic behavior patterns of animals —**e·tho·log·i·cal** (eth′ə läj′i k'l, ē′thə-) *adj.* —**e·thol′o·gist** *n.*

**e·thos** (ē′thäs) *n.* [Gr. *ēthos,* character] the characteristic attitudes, habits, beliefs, etc. of an individual or group

**eth·yl** (eth′'l) *n.* [ETH(ER) + -YL] the monovalent hydrocarbon radical, $C_2H_5$, which forms the base of common alcohol, ether, and many other compounds

**ethyl alcohol** *same as* ALCOHOL (sense 1)

**eth·yl·ene** (eth′ə lēn′) *n.* [ETHYL + -ENE] a colorless, flammable, gaseous hydrocarbon, $C_2H_4$, used as a fuel and anesthetic, in hastening the ripening of fruits, and to form polyethylene

**ethylene glycol** a colorless, viscous alcohol, $C_2H_6O_2$, used as an antifreeze, solvent, in resins, etc.

**e·ti·ol·o·gy** (ēt′ē äl′ə jē) *n., pl.* **-gies** [< LL. < Gr. < *aitia,* cause + -LOGY] 1. the assignment of a cause, or the cause assigned *[the etiology of a folkway]* 2. the science of causes or origins 3. *Med.* the causes of a disease —**e′ti·o·log′ic** (-ə läj′ik), **e′ti·o·log′i·cal** *adj.* —**e′ti·o·log′i·cal·ly** *adv.*

**et·i·quette** (et′i kət, -ket′) *n.* [Fr. *étiquette,* a ticket] the forms, manners, and ceremonies established by convention as acceptable or required in social relations

**Et·na** (et′nə) volcanic mountain in E Sicily

**E·ton** (ēt′'n) town in SC England, near London: site of a private preparatory school for boys **(Eton College)** —**E·to·ni·an** (ē tō′nē ən) *adj., n.*

**Eton collar** a broad, white linen collar worn with an Eton jacket, or a collar like this

**Eton jacket** (or **coat**) a black waist-length jacket with broad lapels, left open in front, as that worn by students at Eton

**E·tru·ri·a** (i troor′ē ə) ancient country in what is now WC Italy

**E·trus·can** (i trus′kən) *adj.* of Etruria, its people, their language, or culture —*n.* 1. a native or inhabitant of Etruria 2. the language of the ancient Etruscans Also **E·tru·ri·an** (i troor′ē ən)

**et seq.** 1. [L. *et sequens*] and the following 2. [L. *et sequentes* or *et sequentia*] and those that follow

**Et·ta** (et′ə) [dim. of HENRIETTA] a feminine name

**-ette** (et) [Fr.: see -ET] *a suffix meaning:* 1. little *[statuette]* 2. female *[majorette]* 3. a substitute for *[leatherette]*

**é·tude** (ā′tood, -tyood; *Fr.* ā tüd′) *n.* [Fr., STUDY] a musical composition for a solo instrument, designed to give practice in some special point of technique

**ETV** educational television

ety., etym., etymol. 1. etymological 2. etymology

et·y·mol·o·gy (et'ə mäl'ə jē) n., pl. -gies [< OFr. < L. < Gr. < *etymon*, literal sense of a word, neut. of *etymos*, true + -LOGY] the origin and development of a word, affix, phrase, etc.; the tracing of a word or words back as far as possible, or the branch of linguistics dealing with this —et'·y·mo·log'i·cal (-mə läj'ə k'l) adj. —et'y·mol'o·gist n. —et'y·mol'o·gize' (-jīz') vt., vi. -gized', -giz'ing

eu- [Fr. < Gr.] a prefix meaning good, well [euphemism, eugenic] : opposed to DYS-, CACO-

Eu Chem. europium

eu·ca·lyp·tus (yōō'kə lip'təs) n., pl. -tus·es, -ti (-tī) [ModL. < EU- + Gr. *kalyptos*, covered (from the covering of the buds) < *kalyptein*, to cover] any of a genus of tall, chiefly Australian evergreen trees of the myrtle family, valued for their timber, gum, and oil: also eu'·ca·lypt'

eucalyptus oil an essential oil from eucalyptus leaves, used as an antiseptic and expectorant

EUCALYPTUS (tree and leaves)

Eu·cha·rist (yōō'kə rist) n. [< OFr. < LL. < Gr. *eucharistia*, gratitude < *eu-*, well + *charis*, favor] 1. same as HOLY COMMUNION 2. the consecrated bread and wine used in Holy Communion —Eu'cha·ris'tic adj.

eu·chre (yōō'kər) n. [earlier *yuker*, *uker* < ?] 1. a card game for two, three, or four players, played with thirty-two cards 2. a euchring or being euchred —vt. -chred, -chring 1. to prevent (the trump-declaring opponent at euchre) from taking the required three tricks 2. [Colloq.] to outwit

Eu·clid¹ (yōō'klid) fl. 300 B.C.; Gr. mathematician: author of a basic work in geometry —Eu·clid'e·an, Eu·clid'i·an (-ē ən) adj.

Eu·clid² (yōō'klid) [so named (after prec.) by its surveyors] city in NE Ohio: suburb of Cleveland: pop. 60,000

Eu·gene (yōō'jēn; also, & for sense 2 always, yōō jēn') [< Fr. < L. < Gr. < *eugenēs*, well-born] 1. a masculine name 2. [after *Eugene* Skinner, early settler] city in W Oreg.: pop. 106,000

Eu·ge·ni·a (yōō jē'nē ə, -jēn'yə) [L., fem. of prec.] a feminine name

eu·gen·ic (yōō jen'ik) adj. [< Gr.: see EU- & GENESIS] 1. relating to the bearing of sound offspring 2. of, relating to, or improved by eugenics —eu·gen'i·cal·ly adv.

eu·gen·i·cist (-ə sist) n. a specialist in or advocate of eugenics: also eu·gen·ist (yōō'jə nist, yōō jen'ist)

eu·gen·ics (yōō jen'iks) n.pl. [with sing. v.] the movement devoted to improving the human species by control of hereditary factors in mating

eu·lo·gis·tic (yōō'lə jis'tik) adj. of or expressing eulogy; praising highly —eu'lo·gis'ti·cal·ly adv.

eu·lo·gize (yōō'lə jīz') vt. -gized', -giz'ing to praise as in a eulogy —eu'lo·gist, eu'lo·giz'er n.

eu·lo·gy (-jē) n., pl. -gies [< ML. < Gr. < *eulegein*, to speak well of] 1. speech or writing in praise of a person, event, or thing; esp., a funeral oration 2. high praise

Eu·men·i·des (yōō men'ə dēz') n.pl. [L. < Gr. *Eumenidēs*, lit., the gracious ones: a propitiatory euphemism] same as FURIES

Eu·nice (yōō'nis) [LL. < Gr. *Eunikē* < *eu-*, well + *nikē*, victory] a feminine name

eu·nuch (yōō'nək) n. [< L. < Gr. *eunouchos*, bed guardian < *eunē*, bed + *echein*, to keep] a castrated man; esp., one in charge of a harem or employed as a chamberlain in an Oriental palace

eu·pep·si·a (yōō pep'shə, -sē ə) n. [ModL. < Gr. *eupepsia*, digestibility] good digestion —eu·pep'tic adj. —eu·pep'ti·cal·ly adv.

eu·phe·mism (yōō'fə miz'm) n. [< Gr. < *eu-*, good + *phēmē*, voice < *phanai*, to speak] 1. the use of a less expressive or direct word or phrase for one considered distasteful or offensive 2. a word or phrase so substituted (Ex.: *remains* for *corpse*) —eu'phe·mist n. —eu'phe·mis'tic, eu'phe·mis'ti·cal adj. —eu'phe·mis'ti·cal·ly adv.

eu·phe·mize (-mīz') vt., vi. -mized', -miz'ing to speak or write (of) euphemistically

eu·phon·ic (yōō fän'ik) adj. 1. of euphony 2. same as EUPHONIOUS Also eu·phon'i·cal —eu·phon'i·cal·ly adv.

eu·pho·ni·ous (yōō fō'nē əs) adj. characterized by euphony; having a pleasant sound; harmonious —eu·pho'ni·ous·ly adv. —eu·pho'ni·ous·ness n.

eu·pho·ni·um (-əm) n. a brass-wind instrument like the baritone but having a more mellow tone

eu·pho·ny (yōō'fə nē) n., pl. -nies [< LL. < Gr. < *eu-*, well + *phōnē*, voice] the quality of having a pleasing sound; pleasant combination of agreeable sounds in spoken words

eu·phor·bi·a (yōō fôr'bē ə) n. [< L. < *Euphorbus*, physician of 1st cent. A.D.] same as SPURGE

eu·pho·ri·a (yōō fôr'ē ə) n. [ModL. < Gr. < *eu-*, well + *pherein*, to bear] a feeling of well-being or high spirits, specif. *Psychol.* one that seems exaggerated and without cause —eu·phor'ic adj.

eu·pho·tic (yōō fōt'ik) adj. [< EU- + Gr. *phōs* (gen. *phōtos*), a light + -IC] *Ecol.* of or pertaining to the upper portion of a body of water receiving enough light for photosynthesis and plant growth

Eu·phra·tes (yōō frät'ēz) river flowing from EC Turkey through Syria & Iraq, joining the Tigris to form the Shatt-al-Arab

eu·phu·ism (yōō'fyoo wiz'm) n. [< *Euphues*, fictitious character in two works by J. LYLY < Gr. *euphyēs*, graceful < *eu-*, well + *phyē*, growth] 1. an artificial, affected, high-flown style of speaking or writing, esp. such a style of the late 16th cent., characterized by alliteration, balanced sentences, farfetched figures of speech, etc. 2. an instance of this —eu'phu·ist n. —eu'phu·is'tic, eu'phu·is'ti·cal adj.

Eur. 1. Europe 2. European

Eur·a·sia (yōō rā'zhə; chiefly Brit. -shə) land mass made up of the continents of Europe & Asia

Eur·a·sian (-zhən; chiefly Brit. -shən) adj. 1. of Eurasia 2. of mixed European and Asian descent —n. a person with one European parent and one Asian parent, or of mixed European and Asian descent

Eur·a·tom (yoor'ə täm') European Atomic Energy Community, an agency of the European Economic Community

eu·re·ka (yoo rē'kə) interj. [Gr. *heurēka*] I have found (it): an exclamation of triumphant achievement

eu·rhyth·mics (yoo rith'miks) n.pl. same as EURYTHMICS —eu·rhyth'mic adj. —eu·rhyth'my n.

Eu·rip·i·des (yoo rip'ə dēz') 479?–406? B.C.; Gr. writer of tragedies —Eu·rip'i·de'an (-dē'ən) adj.

Eu·ro- a combining form meaning Europe, European [*Eurodollars*, *Euromart*]

Eu·ro·com·mu·nism (yoor'ə käm'yə niz'm) n. a form of Communism in Europe stressing the independence of national Communist parties from Soviet Communism, their support of democratic political procedures, etc. —Eu'ro·com'mu·nist adj., n.

Eu·ro·mart (yoor'ə märt') n. same as EUROPEAN ECONOMIC COMMUNITY: also Eu'ro·mar'ket (-mär'kit)

Eu·ro·pa (yoo rō'pə) Gr. Myth. a Phoenician princess loved by Zeus: disguised as a bull, he carried her off to Crete

Eu·rope (yoor'əp) continent between Asia (or the Ural Mountains) & the Atlantic Ocean: c.3,750,000 sq. mi.; pop. c.637,366,000 —Eu'ro·pe'an (-ə pē'ən) adj., n.

European Economic Community the European common market formed in 1958 by Belgium, France, West Germany, Italy, Luxembourg, and the Netherlands: also European Community

European plan a system of hotel operation in which the charge to guests covers rooms and service but not meals: distinguished from AMERICAN PLAN

eu·ro·pi·um (yoo rō'pē əm) n. [ModL. < EUROPE] a chemical element of the rare-earth group: symbol, Eu; at. wt., 151.96; at. no., 63

Eu·ryd·i·ce (yoo rid'ə sē') Gr. Myth. the wife of Orpheus: see ORPHEUS

eu·ryth·mics (yoo rith'miks) n.pl. [with sing. v.] [< L. < Gr. < *eu-*, well + *rhythmos*, RHYTHM] the art of performing various bodily movements in rhythm, usually to musical accompaniment —eu·ryth'mic, eu·ryth'mi·cal adj.

Eu·sta·chi·an tube (yoo stā'shən, -shē ən, -kē ən) [after B. *Eustachio* (1520–1574), It. anatomist] a slender tube between the middle ear and the pharynx, which serves to equalize air pressure on both sides of the eardrum

Eu·ter·pe (yoo tur'pē) Gr. Myth. the Muse of music and lyric poetry

eu·tha·na·si·a (yōō'thə nā'zhə, -zhē ə) n. [< Gr. < *eu-*, well + *thanatos*, death] 1. an easy and painless death 2. act or method of causing death painlessly to end suffering

eu·then·ics (yoo then'iks) n.pl. [with sing. v.] [< Gr. *euthenein*, to flourish + -ICS] the movement devoted to improving species and breeds, esp. the human species, by control of environmental factors

eu·troph·ic (-träf'ik, -trō'fik) adj. [< EU- + Gr. *trophikos* < *trophē*, food] designating or of a lake, pond, etc. rich in mineral and plant nutrients but often deficient in oxygen —eu'troph·i·ca'tion n.

Eux·ine Sea (yōōk'sən, -sīn) ancient name of the BLACK SEA

ev, EV electron-volt

E·va (ē'və, ev'ə) [var. of EVE] a feminine name

fat, āpe, cär, ten, ēven, is, bīte; gō, hôrn, tōōl, look; oil, out; up, fur; get; joy; yet; chin; she; thin, then; zh, leisure; ŋ, ring; ə for a in ago, e in agent, i in sanity, o in comply, u in focus; ' as in able (ā'b'l); Fr. bál; ë, Fr. coeur; ö, Fr. feu; Fr. mon; ô, Fr. coq; ü, Fr. duc; r, Fr. cri; H, G. ich; kh, G. doch; ‡foreign; *hypothetical; < derived from. See inside front cover.

**e·vac·u·ate** (i vak′yoo wāt′) *vt.* **-at′ed, -at′ing** [< L. pp. of *evacuare* < *e-*, out + *vacuare*, to make empty < *vacuus*, empty] **1.** to make empty; remove the contents of; specif., to remove the air from **2.** to discharge (bodily waste, esp. feces) **3.** to remove (inhabitants, troops, etc.) from (a place or area), as for protective purposes —*vi.* **1.** to withdraw, as from a danger area **2.** to discharge bodily waste —e·vac′u·a′tion *n.* —e·vac′u·a′tive *adj.* —e·vac′u·a′tor *n.* —e·vac′u·ee′ *n.*

**e·vade** (i vād′) *vi.* e·vad′ed, e·vad′ing [< Fr. < L. < *e-*, out, from + *vadere*, to go] to be deceitful or clever in avoiding or escaping something —*vt.* **1.** to avoid or escape from by deceit or cleverness **2.** to avoid doing or answering directly [to *evade* tax payment] —e·vad′er *n.*

**e·val·u·ate** (i val′yoo wāt′) *vt.* **-at′ed, -at′ing** [< Fr. < *é-* (L. *ex-*), out + *valuer*, to VALUE] **1.** to find the value or amount of **2.** to judge or determine the worth or quality of; appraise —e·val′u·a′tion *n.* —e·val′u·a′tive *adj.*

**Ev·an** (ev′ən) [W., var. of JOHN] a masculine name

**ev·a·nesce** (ev′ə nes′) *vi.* **-nesced′, -nesc′ing** [< L. < *e-*, out + *vanescere*, to vanish < *vanus*, empty] to fade from sight like mist or smoke; vanish

**ev·a·nes·cent** (-nes′′nt) *adj.* tending to fade away; vanishing; fleeting —ev′a·nes′cence *n.* —ev′a·nes′cent·ly *adv.*

**e·van·gel** (i van′jəl) *n.* [< OFr. < LL. < L. < Gr. *euangelos*, bringing good news < *eu-*, well + *angelos*, messenger] **1.** the gospel **2.** [E-] any of the four Gospels **3.** an evangelist

**e·van·gel·i·cal** (ē′van jel′i k′l, ev′ən-) *adj.* **1.** in, of, or according to the Gospels or the New Testament **2.** of those Protestant churches, as the Methodist and Baptist, that emphasize salvation by faith in the atonement of Jesus **3.** *same as* EVANGELISTIC Also e′van·gel′ic —*n.* a member of an evangelical church —e′van·gel′i·cal·ism *n.* —e′van·gel′i·cal·ly *adv.*

**e·van·gel·ism** (i van′jə liz′m) *n.* **1.** a preaching of, or zealous effort to spread, the gospel, as in revival meetings **2.** any zealous effort in propagandizing for a cause —e·van′gel·is′tic *adj.* —e·van′gel·is′ti·cal·ly *adv.*

**e·van·gel·ist** (-list) *n.* **1.** [E-] any of the four writers of the Gospels: Matthew, Mark, Luke, or John **2.** anyone who evangelizes; esp., a traveling preacher; revivalist

**e·van·gel·ize** (-līz′) *vt.* **-ized′, -iz′ing 1.** to preach the gospel to **2.** to convert to Christianity —*vi.* to preach the gospel —e·van′gel·i·za′tion *n.*

**Ev·ans·ton** (ev′ən stən) [after Dr. J. *Evans*, local philanthropist] city in NE Ill.: suburb of Chicago: pop. 74,000

**Ev·ans·ville** (ev′ənz vil′) [after Gen. R. *Evans*, who served in the War of 1812] city in SW Ind., on the Ohio River: pop. 130,000

**e·vap·o·rate** (i vap′ə rāt′) *vt.* **-rat′ed, -rat′ing** [< L. pp. of *evaporare* < *e-*, out + *vapor*, vapor] **1.** to change (a liquid or solid) into vapor **2.** to remove moisture from (milk, vegetables, etc.), as by heating, so as to get a concentrated product —*vi.* **1.** to become vapor **2.** to give off vapor **3.** to disappear; vanish —e·vap′o·ra·bil′i·ty *n.* —e·vap′o·ra′ble *adj.* —e·vap′o·ra′tion *n.* —e·vap′o·ra′tive *adj.* —e·vap′o·ra′tor *n.*

**evaporated milk** unsweetened milk thickened by evaporation to about half its weight, and then canned: cf. CONDENSED MILK

**e·va·sion** (i vā′zhən) *n.* **1.** an evading; specif., an avoiding of a duty, question, etc. by deceit or cleverness **2.** a way of doing this; subterfuge

**e·va·sive** (-siv) *adj.* **1.** tending or seeking to evade; not straightforward; tricky **2.** hard to catch, grasp, etc.; elusive —e·va′sive·ly *adv.* —e·va′sive·ness *n.*

**Eve** (ēv) [< LL. < Heb. *ḥawwāh*, lit., ? life] **1.** a feminine name **2.** *Bible* Adam's wife, the first woman: Gen. 3:20

**eve** (ēv) *n.* [ME., var. of *even* < OE. *æfen*, EVENING] **1.** [Poet.] evening **2.** [*often* E-] the evening or day before a holiday [Christmas *Eve*] **3.** the period immediately before some event

**Ev·e·line** (ev′ə līn′, -lin′) [ONormFr. < *Aveline*, prob. ult. < Gmc.] a feminine name: var. *Evelina*

**Ev·e·lyn** (ev′ə lin′; *Brit. usually* ēv′lin) [see prec.] a feminine and masculine name

**e·ven¹** (ē′vən, -v′n) *adj.* [OE. *efne, efen*] **1.** flat; level; smooth [*even* country] **2.** not varying; constant [an *even* tempo] **3.** calm; tranquil [an *even* disposition] **4.** in the same plane or line [*even* with the rim] **5.** equally balanced **6.** *a)* owing and being owed nothing *b)* with neither a profit nor a loss **7.** revenged for a wrong, insult, etc. **8.** just; fair [an *even* exchange] **9.** equal or identical in number, quantity, etc. **10.** exactly divisible by two: said of numbers **11.** exact [an *even* mile] —*adv.* **1.** moreover; however improbable; indeed; fully [*even* a fool could do it] **2.** exactly; just [it happened *even* as I expected] **3.** just as; while [*even* as he spoke, she entered] **4.** comparatively; still; yet [an *even* worse mistake] —*vt., vi.* to make, become, or be even; level (*off*) —**break even** [Colloq.] to finish as neither a winner

nor a loser —**even if** despite the fact that; though —e′ven·ly *adv.* —e′ven·ness *n.*

**e·ven²** (ē′vən) *n.* [see EVE] [Poet.] evening

**e·ven·fall** (-fôl′) *n.* [Poet.] twilight; dusk

**e·ven·hand·ed** (-han′did) *adj.* impartial; fair —e′ven·hand′ed·ly *adv.* —e′ven·hand′ed·ness *n.*

**eve·ning** (ēv′niŋ) *n.* [< OE. < *æfnian*, to become evening < *æfen*, evening] **1.** the last part of the day and early part of night **2.** in some parts of the South, the period from noon through sunset **3.** the last period, as of life, a career, etc. —*adj.* in, for, or of the evening

**evening primrose** a plant having yellow flowers that open in the evening

**eve·nings** (-niŋz) *adv.* during every evening or most evenings

**evening star** a bright planet, esp. Venus, seen in the western sky soon after sunset

**e·ven·song** (ē′vən sôŋ′) *n.* **1.** *R.C.Ch.* vespers (see VESPER, sense 2*a*) **2.** *Anglican Ch.* the worship service assigned to the evening

**e·ven·ste·ven, e·ven·ste·phen** (ē′v′n stē′v′n) *adj.* [rhyming slang < EVEN¹ + STEVEN] [Colloq.] [*often* S-] *same as* EVEN¹ (senses 4-9): also **even steven, even stephen**

**e·vent** (i vent′) *n.* [OFr. < L. pp. of *evenire*, to happen < *e-*, out + *venire*, to come] **1.** a happening or occurrence, esp. when important **2.** a result; outcome **3.** a particular contest or item in a program of sports —**in any event** no matter what happens; anyhow: also **at all events** —**in the event of** in case of —**in the event that** if it should happen that

**e·ven-tem·pered** (ē′vən tem′pərd) *adj.* not quickly angered or excited; placid; calm

**e·vent·ful** (i vent′fəl) *adj.* **1.** full of outstanding events **2.** having an important outcome —e·vent′ful·ly *adv.* —e·vent′ful·ness *n.*

**e·ven·tide** (ē′vən tīd′) *n.* [Archaic] evening

**e·ven·tu·al** (i ven′choo wəl) *adj.* **1.** [Archaic] depending on events; contingent **2.** happening in the end; ultimate —e·ven′tu·al·ly *adv.*

**e·ven·tu·al·i·ty** (i ven′choo wal′ə tē) *n., pl.* **-ties** a possible event, outcome, or condition; contingency

**e·ven·tu·ate** (i ven′choo wāt′) *vi.* **-at′ed, -at′ing** to happen in the end; result (often with *in*)

**ev·er** (ev′ər) *adv.* [< OE. *æfre*] **1.** at all times; always [lived happily *ever* after] **2.** at any time [have you *ever* seen her?] **3.** at all; by any chance; in any way [how can I *ever* repay you?] **4.** [Colloq.] truly; indeed [was she *ever* tired!] —**ever so** [Colloq.] very —**for ever and a day** always: also **for ever and ever**

**Ev·er·est** (ev′ər ist, ev′rist), **Mount** peak of the Himalayas, on the border of Nepal & Tibet: highest known mountain in the world: 29,028 ft.

**Ev·er·ett** (ev′ər it, ev′rit) [< Du. < OFr. < OHG. < *ebur*, wild boar + *harto*, strong] **1.** a masculine name **2.** [after *Everett* Colby, son of a founder] port in NW Wash., near Seattle: pop. 54,000

**ev·er·glade** (ev′ər glād′) *n.* swampland —**the Everglades** large tract of swampland in S & SE Fla.

**ev·er·green** (ev′ər grēn′) *adj.* having green leaves throughout the year: opposed to DECIDUOUS —*n.* **1.** an evergreen plant or tree **2.** [*pl.*] the branches and twigs of evergreens, used for decoration

**ev·er·last·ing** (ev′ər las′tiŋ) *adj.* **1.** lasting forever; eternal **2.** going on for a long time **3.** going on too long; seeming never to stop —*n.* **1.** eternity **2.** *a)* any of various plants whose blossoms keep their color and shape when dried; esp., an annual with pink, lilac, or white flowers *b)* the blossom of such a plant —**the Everlasting God** —ev′er·last′ing·ly *adv.*

**ev·er·more** (-môr′) *adv.* **1.** forever; constantly **2.** [Poet.] for all future time —**for evermore** forever

**e·ver·sion** (ē vur′zhən, -shən) *n.* an everting or being everted —e·ver′si·ble (-sə b'l) *adj.*

**e·vert** (ē vurt′) *vt.* [L. *evertere* < *e-*, out + *vertere*, to turn] to turn outward or inside out, as an eyelid

**ev·er·y** (ev′rē; *occas.* -ər ē) *adj.* [< OE. *æfre ælc*, lit., ever each] **1.** each, individually and separately [*every* man among you] **2.** the fullest possible; all that there could be [he was given *every* chance] **3.** each group or interval of (a specified number or time) [a pill *every* three hours] —**every now and then** from time to time: also [Colloq.] **every so often** —**every other** each alternate, as the first, third, fifth, etc. —**every which way** [Colloq.] in complete disorder

**ev·er·y·bod·y** (-bäd′ē, -bud′ē) *pron.* every person; everyone

**ev·er·y·day** (-dā′) *adj.* **1.** daily [one's *everyday* routine] **2.** suitable for ordinary days [*everyday* shoes] **3.** usual; common [an *everyday* occurrence]

**ev·er·y·one** (-wən, -wun′) *pron.* everybody

**every one** every person or thing of those named [remind *every one* of the students]

**ev·er·y·thing** (-thiŋ′) *pron.* **1.** every thing; all **2.** all things pertinent to a specified matter **3.** the most important thing [*money isn't everything*]

**ev·er·y·where** (-hwer′, -wer′) *adv.* in or to every place

**e·vict** (i vikt′) *vt.* [< L. *evictus*, pp. of *evincere*: see EVINCE] to remove (a tenant) from leased premises by legal procedure, as for failure to pay rent —**e·vic′tion** *n.*

**ev·i·dence** (ev′ə dəns) *n.* **1.** the condition of being evident **2.** something that makes another thing evident; indication; sign **3.** something that tends to prove **4.** *Law* something presented before a court, as a statement of a witness, an object, etc., which bears on or establishes the point in question —*vt.* **-denced, -denc·ing 1.** to make evident; indicate; show **2.** to bear witness to; attest —**in evidence** plainly visible or perceptible

**ev·i·dent** (-dənt, -dent′) *adj.* [< OFr. < L. *evidens*, clear < *e-*, from + prp. of *videre*, to see] easy to see or perceive; clear; obvious; plain —**ev′i·dent·ly** *adv.*

**ev·i·den·tial** (ev′ə den′shəl) *adj.* of, serving as, or providing evidence —**ev′i·den′tial·ly** *adv.*

**e·vil** (ē′v'l) *adj.* [OE. *yfel*] **1.** *a*) morally bad or wrong; wicked; depraved *b*) resulting from conduct regarded as immoral [*an evil reputation*] **2.** harmful; injurious **3.** offensive **4.** unlucky; disastrous —*n.* **1.** wickedness; depravity; sin **2.** anything that causes harm, pain, disaster, etc. —**the Evil One** the Devil —**e′vil·ly** *adv.* —**e′vil·ness** *n.*

**e·vil·do·er** (-dōō′ər) *n.* a person who does evil, esp. habitually —**e′vil·do′ing** *n.*

**evil eye** a look which, in superstitious belief, is able to harm or bewitch the one stared at; also, the supposed power to cast such a look: with *the*

**e·vil-mind·ed** (-mīn′did) *adj.* having an evil mind or disposition; specif., *a*) malicious or wicked *b*) inclined to view everything in an evil or obscene way —**e′vil-mind′ed·ly** *adv.* —**e′vil-mind′ed·ness** *n.*

**e·vince** (i vins′) *vt.* **e·vinced′, e·vinc′ing** [< L. < *e-*, intens. + *vincere*, to conquer] to show plainly; make manifest; esp., to show that one has (a specified quality, feeling, etc.) —**e·vin′ci·ble** *adj.* —**e·vin′cive** *adj.*

**e·vis·cer·ate** (i vis′ə rāt′) *vt.* **-at·ed, -at·ing** [< L. pp. of *eviscerare* < *e-*, out + *viscera*, VISCERA] **1.** to remove the entrails from **2.** to deprive of an essential part —**e·vis′cer·a′tion** *n.*

**ev·o·ca·ble** (ev′ə kə b'l, i vō′kə b'l) *adj.* that can be evoked

**ev·o·ca·tion** (ev′ə kā′shən, ē′vō-) *n.* an evoking —**e·voc·a·tive** (i väk′ə tiv) *adj.* —**e·voc′a·tive·ly** *adv.* —**e·voc′a·tive·ness** *n.* —**ev′o·ca′tor** *n.*

**e·voke** (i vōk′) *vt.* **e·voked′, e·vok′ing** [< Fr. < L. < *e-*, out + *vocare*, to call < *vox*, the voice] **1.** to conjure up (a spirit, etc.) **2.** to draw forth or elicit (a particular mental image, reaction, etc.) —**e·vok′er** *n.*

**ev·o·lu·tion** (ev′ə lōō′shən) *n.* [< L. pp. of *evolvere*: see EVOLVE] **1.** an unfolding, opening out, or working out; process of development **2.** a result of this; thing evolved **3.** a movement that is part of a series or pattern **4.** a setting free or giving off, as of gas in a chemical reaction **5.** *Biol.* *a*) the development of a species, organism, or organ from its original to its present state *b*) a theory that all species of plants and animals developed from earlier forms: see DARWINIAN THEORY **6.** *Math.* the extracting of a root **7.** *Mil.* any of various maneuvers by which troops, ships, etc. change formation —**ev′o·lu′tion·al** *adj.* —**ev′o·lu′tion·al·ly** *adv.* —**ev′o·lu′tion·ar′y** *adj.*

**ev·o·lu·tion·ist** (-ist) *n.* a person who accepts the principles of evolution, esp. in biology —*adj.* **1.** of the theory of evolution **2.** of evolutionists —**ev′o·lu′tion·ism** *n.* —**ev′o·lu′tion·is′tic** *adj.* —**ev′o·lu′tion·is′ti·cal·ly** *adv.*

**e·volve** (i välv′) *vt.* **e·volved′, e·volv′ing** [< L. < *e-*, out + *volvere*, to roll] **1.** to develop by gradual changes; unfold **2.** to set free or give off (gas, heat, etc.) **3.** to produce or change by evolution —*vi.* **1.** to develop gradually by a process of growth and change **2.** to become disclosed; unfold —**e·volve′ment** *n.*

**Ev·voi·a** (ev′ē ə) large Greek island in the Aegean Sea, off the E coast of Greece

**ewe** (yōō; *dial.* yō) *n.* [OE. *eowu*] a female sheep

**ew·er** (yōō′ər) *n.* [< Anglo-Fr. < OFr. *evier*, ult. < L. *aquarius*: see AQUARIUM] a large water pitcher with a wide mouth

EWER

**ex** (eks) *prep.* [L.] without; exclusive of [*ex interest*] —*n., pl.* **ex′es** [Colloq.] one's divorced husband or wife

**ex-** [< OFr. or L., akin to Gr. *ex-, exō-*] **1.** *a prefix meaning:* *a*) from, out [*expel*] *b*) beyond [*excess*] *c*) out of [*expatriate*] *d*) thoroughly [*exterminate*] *e*) upward [*exalt*] It is assimilated to *ef-* before *f; e-* before *b, d, g, l, m, n, r,* and *v;* and, often,

---

*ec-* before *c* or *s* **2.** *a prefix meaning* former, previously [*ex-president*]

**Ex.** Exodus

**ex. 1.** examined **2.** example **3.** except(ed) **4.** express **5.** extra

**ex·ac·er·bate** (ig zas′ər bāt′) *vt.* **-bat·ed, -bat·ing** [< L. pp. of *exacerbare* < *ex-*, intens. + *acerbus*, harsh, sour] **1.** to make more intense or sharp; aggravate (disease, pain, feelings, etc.) **2.** to irritate —**ex·ac′er·ba′tion** *n.*

**ex·act** (ig zakt′) *adj.* [< L. pp. of *exigere*, to measure < *ex-*, out + *agere*, to do] **1.** characterized by, requiring, or capable of accuracy of detail; methodical; correct **2.** without variation; precise [an *exact* replica] **3.** being the very (one specified or understood) **4.** strict; severe; rigorous —*vt.* **1.** to extort (with *from* or *of*) **2.** to demand and get by authority or force (with *from* or *of*) **3.** to make necessary; require —**ex·act′a·ble** *adj.* —**ex·act′ness** *n.* —**ex·ac′tor, ex·act′er** *n.*

**ex·act·ing** (-iŋ) *adj.* **1.** making severe demands; not easily satisfied; strict **2.** demanding great care, effort, etc.; arduous —**ex·act′ing·ly** *adv.* —**ex·act′ing·ness** *n.*

**ex·ac·tion** (ig zak′shən) *n.* **1.** an exacting **2.** an extortion **3.** an exacted fee, tax, etc.

**ex·ac·ti·tude** (ig zak′tə tōōd′, -tyōōd′) *n.* the quality of being exact; precision; accuracy

**ex·act·ly** (ig zakt′lē) *adv.* in an exact manner; accurately; precisely: also used as an affirmative reply, equivalent to "I agree," "quite true"

**ex·ag·ger·ate** (ig zaj′ə rāt′) *vt.* **-at·ed, -at·ing** [< L. pp. of *exaggerare* < *ex-*, out + *aggerare*, to heap up < *agger*, a heap] **1.** to think, speak, or write of as greater than is really so; overstate **2.** to increase or enlarge to an abnormal degree —*vi.* to give an exaggerated account —**ex·ag′ger·at′ed·ly** *adv.* —**ex·ag′ger·a′tion** *n.* —**ex·ag′ger·a′tive** *adj.* —**ex·ag′ger·a′tor** *n.*

**ex·alt** (ig zôlt′) *vt.* [< OFr. < LL. *exaltare* < *ex-*, out, up + *altus*, high] to lift up; specif., *a*) to raise in status, dignity, power, wealth, etc. *b*) to praise; glorify; extol *c*) to fill with joy, pride, etc.; elate: used in the passive or in participial form *d*) to heighten or intensify the action or effect of —**ex·alt′ed·ly** *adv.* —**ex·alt′er** *n.*

**ex·al·ta·tion** (eg′zôl tā′shən) *n.* **1.** an exalting or being exalted **2.** elation; rapture

**ex·am** (ig zam′) *n.* [Colloq.] examination

**ex·am·i·na·tion** (ig zam′ə nā′shən) *n.* **1.** an examining or being examined; investigation; inquiry **2.** means or method of examining **3.** a set of questions asked in testing; test —**ex·am′i·na′tion·al** *adj.* —**ex·am′i·na·to′ri·al** (-nə tôr′ē əl) *adj.*

**ex·am·ine** (ig zam′ən) *vt.* **-ined, -in·ing** [< OFr. < L. < *examen*, tongue of a balance, examination] **1.** to look at or into critically or methodically to find out the facts, condition, etc. of; investigate; inspect **2.** to test by questioning to find out the knowledge, skill, etc. of —**ex·am′i·na·ble** *adj.* —**ex·am′i·nee′** *n.* —**ex·am′in·er, ex·am′i·nant** *n.*

**ex·am·ple** (ig zam′p'l) *n.* [< OFr. < L. *exemplum* < *eximere*, to take out < *ex-*, out + *emere*, to buy] **1.** something selected to show the nature or character of the rest; sample **2.** a case that serves as a warning or caution **3.** a person or thing to be imitated; model **4.** a problem, as in mathematics, that illustrates a principle or method —*vt.* **-pled, -pling** [Obs. except in the passive] to exemplify —**set an example** to behave so as to be a pattern or model for others —**without example** having no precedent

**ex·as·per·ate** (ig zas′pə rāt′) *vt.* **-at·ed, -at·ing** [< L. pp. of *exasperare* < *ex-*, out + *asperare*, to roughen < *asper*, rough] to irritate or annoy very much; vex —**ex·as′per·at′ing·ly** *adv.* —**ex·as′per·a′tion** *n.*

**Ex·cal·i·bur** (eks kal′ə bər) *n. Arthurian Legend* King Arthur's sword

**ex ca·the·dra** (eks′ kə thē′drə, kath′i drə) [ModL., lit., from the chair] with the authority that comes from one's rank or office: often used of certain authoritative papal pronouncements on faith or morals

**ex·ca·vate** (eks′kə vāt′) *vt.* **-vat·ed, -vat·ing** [< L. pp. of *excavare* < *ex-*, out + *cavare*, to make hollow < *cavus*, hollow] **1.** to make a hole or cavity in, as by digging; hollow out **2.** to form by hollowing out [to *excavate* a tunnel] **3.** to uncover by digging; unearth **4.** to dig out (earth, soil, etc.) —**ex′ca·va′tion** *n.* —**ex′ca·va′tor** *n.*

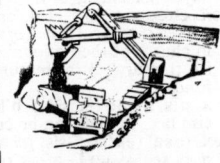
EXCAVATION

**ex·ceed** (ik sēd′) *vt.* [< OFr. < L. < *ex-*, out + *cedere*, to go] **1.** to go or be beyond (a limit, measure, etc.) **2.** to be more

---

than or greater than; surpass —*vi.* to surpass others, as in quality or quantity

**ex·ceed·ing** (-iŋ) *adj.* surpassing; extraordinary; extreme —*adv.* [Archaic] extremely —**ex·ceed′ing·ly** *adv.*

**ex·cel** (ik sel′) *vi., vt.* **-celled′, -cel′ling** [< OFr. < L. < *ex-*, out of + *-cellere*, to rise] to be better or greater than (another or others)

**ex·cel·lence** (ek′s'l əns) *n.* **1.** the fact or condition of excelling; superiority **2.** something in which a person or thing excels **3.** [E-] *same as* EXCELLENCY

**ex·cel·len·cy** (-ən sē) *n., pl.* **-cies 1.** [E-] a title of honor applied to various persons of high position, as an ambassador, bishop, etc. **2.** *same as* EXCELLENCE

**ex·cel·lent** (-ənt) *adj.* outstandingly good of its kind; of exceptional merit, virtue, etc. —**ex′cel·lent·ly** *adv.*

**ex·cel·si·or** (ek sel′sē ôr′; *for n.* ik sel′sē ər) *adj., interj.* [L., compar. of *excelsus*, high < *excellere*, EXCEL] higher; always upward —*n.* long, thin wood shavings used for packing or as stuffing

**ex·cept** (ik sept′) *vt.* [< Fr. < L. < pp. of *excipere* < *ex-*, out + *capere*, to take] to leave out or take out; exclude; omit —*vi.* to take exception; object —*prep.* leaving out; other than; but [to everyone *except* me] —*conj.* **1.** [Archaic] unless **2.** [Colloq.] were it not that [I'd quit *except* I need the money] —**except for** if it were not for

**ex·cept·ing** (-iŋ) *prep., conj. same as* EXCEPT

**ex·cep·tion** (ik sep′shən) *n.* **1.** an excepting or being excepted; exclusion **2.** anything that is excepted; specif., *a)* a case to which a rule, principle, etc. does not apply *b)* a person or thing different from others of the same class **3.** an objection —**take exception 1.** to object **2.** to resent; feel offended —**ex·cep′tion·less** *adj.*

**ex·cep·tion·a·ble** (-ə b'l) *adj.* liable or open to exception —**ex·cep′tion·a·bly** *adv.*

**ex·cep·tion·al** (-əl) *adj.* **1.** being an exception; not ordinary or average; esp., much above average in quality, ability, etc. **2.** *Educ.* needing special attention because mentally gifted or, esp., because mentally or physically handicapped —**ex·cep′tion·al·ly** *adv.*

**ex·cerpt** (ik surpt′; *also, and for n. always,* ek′surpt′) *vt.* [< L. pp. of *excerpere* < *ex-*, out + *carpere*, to pick] to select or quote (passages from a book, etc.); extract —*n.* a passage selected or quoted from a book, etc.; extract —**ex·cerp′tion** *n.*

**ex·cess** (ik ses′; *also, and for adj. usually,* ek′ses′) *n.* [< OFr. < L. pp. of *excedere:* see EXCEED] **1.** action or conduct that goes beyond the usual, reasonable, or lawful limit **2.** intemperance; overindulgence **3.** an amount or quantity greater than is necessary, desirable, etc. **4.** the amount or degree by which one thing exceeds another; surplus —*adj.* extra or surplus —**in excess of** more than —**to excess** too much

**ex·ces·sive** (ik ses′iv) *adj.* characterized by excess; being too much; immoderate —**ex·ces′sive·ly** *adv.* —**ex·ces′sive·ness** *n.*

**ex·change** (iks chānj′) *vt.* **-changed′, -chang′ing** [< OFr. < VL. hyp. *excambiare:* see EX- & CHANGE] **1.** *a)* to give or transfer (for another thing in return) *b)* to receive or give another thing for (something returned) **2.** to interchange (gifts, etc.) **3.** to give up for a substitute or alternative [to *exchange* honor for wealth] —*vi.* **1.** to make an exchange; barter **2.** *Finance* to pass in exchange —*n.* **1.** a giving or taking of one thing for another; barter **2.** a giving to one another of similar things **3.** the substituting of one thing for another **4.** a thing given or received in exchange **5.** a place for exchanging; esp., a place where trade is carried on by brokers, merchants, etc. [a stock *exchange*] **6.** a central office in a telephone system, serving a certain area **7.** *Commerce, Finance a)* the payment of debts by negotiable drafts or bills of exchange *b)* a bill of exchange *c)* a fee paid for settling accounts or collecting a draft, bill of exchange, etc. *d)* an exchanging of a sum of money of one country for the equivalent in the money of another country *e)* the rate of exchange; value of one currency in terms of the other —*adj.* **1.** exchanged **2.** having to do with an exchange —**ex·change′a·bil′i·ty** *n.* —**ex·change′a·ble** *adj.* —**ex·chang′er** *n.*

**ex·cheq·uer** (iks chek′ər, eks′chek ər) *n.* [< OFr. *escheki-er:* see CHECKER[1]] **1.** [often E-] the British state department in charge of the national revenue **2.** the funds in the British treasury **3.** a treasury **4.** money in one's possession; funds

**ex·cis·a·ble** (ik sī′zə b'l, ek′sī-) *adj.* **1.** subject to an excise tax **2.** that can be cut out

**ex·cise**[1] (ek′sīz, -sīs; *for v.* ik sīz′) *n.* [< MDu. < OFr. *assise:* see ASSIZE] a tax on the manufacture, sale, or consumption of various commodities within a country, as liquor, tobacco, etc.: also **excise tax** —*vt.* **-cised′, -cis′ing** to put an excise on

**ex·cise**[2] (ik sīz′) *vt.* **-cised′, -cis′ing** [< L. pp. of *excidere* < *ex-*, out + *caedere*, to cut] to remove (a tumor, etc.) by cutting out or away —**ex·ci′sion** (-sizh′ən) *n.*

**ex·cise·man** (ik sīz′mən) *n., pl.* **-men** (-mən) in Great Britain, an official who collects excises

**ex·cit·a·ble** (ik sīt′ə b'l) *adj.* that is easily excited —**ex·cit′a·bil′i·ty** *n.* —**ex·cit′a·bly** *adv.*

**ex·ci·ta·tion** (ek′sī tā′shən, -si-) *n.* an exciting or being excited (esp. in senses 4, 5, 6)

**ex·cite** (ik sīt′) *vt.* **-cit′ed, -cit′ing** [< OFr. < L. *excitare* < *ex-*, out + pp. of *ciere*, to call] **1.** to put into motion or activity; stir up **2.** to arouse; provoke [to *excite* pity] **3.** to arouse the feelings and passions of **4.** *Elec.* to supply electric current to, as to produce a magnetic field **5.** *Physics* to raise (a nucleus, atom, etc.) to a higher energy state **6.** *Physiol.* to produce the response of (an organ, tissue, etc.) to a proper stimulus —**ex·cit′a·tive** (-ə tiv), **ex·cit′a·to′ry** (-ə tôr′ē) *adj.* —**ex·cit′er, ex·ci′tor** *n.*

**ex·cit·ed** (-id) *adj.* emotionally aroused; stirred up —**ex·cit′ed·ly** *adv.*

**ex·cite·ment** (-mənt) *n.* **1.** an exciting or being excited; agitation **2.** something that excites

**ex·cit·ing** (-iŋ) *adj.* causing excitement; stirring, thrilling, etc. —**ex·cit′ing·ly** *adv.*

**ex·claim** (iks klām′) *vi., vt.* [< Fr. < L. *exclamare* < *ex-*, out + *clamare*, to shout] to cry out; speak or say suddenly and excitedly, as in surprise, anger, etc. —**ex·claim′er** *n.*

**ex·cla·ma·tion** (eks′klə mā′shən) *n.* **1.** the act of exclaiming **2.** something exclaimed; interjection —**ex·clam·a·to·ry** (iks klam′ə tôr′ē) *adj.*

**exclamation mark** (or **point**) a mark (!) used after a word or sentence in writing or printing to express surprise, strong feeling, etc.

**ex·clude** (iks klood′) *vt.* **-clud′ed, -clud′ing** [< L. *excludere* < *ex-*, out + *claudere*, CLOSE[2]] **1.** to refuse to admit, consider, include, etc.; shut out; reject; bar **2.** to put out; force out; expel —**ex·clud′a·ble** *adj.* —**ex·clud′er** *n.*

**ex·clu·sion** (-kloo′zhən) *n.* **1.** an excluding or being excluded **2.** a thing excluded —**to the exclusion of** so as to keep out, bar, etc. —**ex·clu′sion·ar′y** *adj.*

**ex·clu·sive** (-kloo′siv) *adj.* **1.** excluding all others; shutting out other considerations, happenings, etc. [an *exclusive* interest] **2.** excluding all but what is specified **3.** not shared or divided; sole [an *exclusive* right] **4.** *a)* excluding certain people or groups, as for social or economic reasons *b)* snobbish; undemocratic **5.** dealing only in costly items [an *exclusive* shop] —**exclusive of** not including or allowing for —**ex·clu′sive·ly** *adv.* —**ex·clu′sive·ness** *n.*

**ex·clu·siv·i·ty** (eks′kloo siv′ə tē) *n.* the condition or practice of being exclusive; esp., clannishness or isolationism: also **ex·clu′siv·ism** —**ex·clu′siv·ist** *n., adj.* —**ex·clu′siv·is′tic** *adj.*

**ex·com·mu·ni·cate** (eks′kə myoo′nə kāt′; *for adj. and n., usually* -kit) *vt.* **-cat′ed, -cat′ing** to exclude, by ecclesiastical authority, from the sacraments, privileges, etc. of a church; censure by cutting off from communion with a church —*adj.* excommunicated —*n.* an excommunicated person —**ex′com·mu·ni·ca′tion** *n.* —**ex′com·mu′ni·ca·tive** *adj.* —**ex′com·mu′ni·ca′tor** *n.* —**ex′com·mu′ni·ca·to′ry** (-kə tôr′ē) *adj.*

**ex·co·ri·ate** (ik skôr′ē āt′) *vt.* **-at′ed, -at′ing** [< L. pp. of *excoriare* < *ex-*, off + *corium*, the skin] **1.** to strip, scratch, or rub off the skin of **2.** to denounce harshly —**ex·co′ri·a′tion** *n.*

**ex·cre·ment** (eks′krə mənt) *n.* [< Fr. < L. < *excretus:* see EXCRETE] waste matter from the bowels; feces —**ex′cre·men′tal** (-men′t'l) *adj.*

**ex·cres·cence** (iks kres′'ns) *n.* [< OFr. < L. < *ex-*, out + *crescere*, to grow] **1.** [Now Rare] a normal outgrowth, as a fingernail **2.** an abnormal or disfiguring outgrowth, as a bunion —**ex·cres′cent** *adj.*

**ex·cres·cen·cy** (-'n sē) *n.* **1.** the condition of being excrescent **2.** *pl.* **-cies** *same as* EXCRESCENCE

**ex·cre·ta** (eks krēt′ə) *n.pl.* waste matter excreted from the body, esp. sweat or urine —**ex·cre′tal** *adj.*

**ex·crete** (iks krēt′) *vt., vi.* **-cret′ed, -cret′ing** [< L. *excretus*, pp. of *excernere* < *ex-*, out of + *cernere*, to sift] to separate (waste matter) from the blood or tissue and eliminate from the body —**ex·cre′tion** *n.* —**ex·cre′tive** *adj.*

**ex·cre·to·ry** (eks′krə tôr′ē) *adj.* of or for excreting —*n., pl.* **-ries** an excretory organ

**ex·cru·ci·ate** (iks kroo′shē āt′) *vt.* **-at′ed, -at′ing** [< L. pp. of *excruciare* < *ex-*, intens. + *cruciare*, to crucify < *crux* (gen. *crucis*), a cross] **1.** to cause intense bodily pain to; torture **2.** to subject to mental anguish; torment —**ex·cru′ci·a′tion** *n.*

**ex·cru·ci·at·ing** (-āt′iŋ) *adj.* **1.** causing intense physical or mental pain **2.** intense or extreme [*excruciating* care] —**ex·cru′ci·at′ing·ly** *adv.*

**ex·cul·pate** (eks′kəl pāt′, ik skul′pāt) *vt.* **-pat′ed, -pat′ing** [< L. *ex*, out + pp. of *culpare*, to blame < *culpa*, fault] to free from blame; declare or prove guiltless —**ex·cul·pa·ble** (ik skul′pə b'l) *adj.* —**ex′cul·pa′tion** *n.* —**ex·cul·pa·to′ry** *adj.*

**ex·cur·sion** (ik skur′zhən) *n.* [< L. < pp. of *excurrere* <

*ex-*, out + *currere*, to run] **1.** a short trip or journey, as for pleasure **2.** a round trip (on a train, bus, etc.) at special reduced rates **3.** a group taking such a trip **4.** a deviation or digression **5.** [Obs.] a military sortie; raid —*adj.* of or for an excursion —**ex·cur′sion·ist** *n.*

**ex·cur·sive** (-siv) *adj.* rambling; desultory; digressive —**ex·cur′sive·ly** *adv.* —**ex·cur′sive·ness** *n.*

**ex·cuse** (ik skyōoz′; *for n.* -skyōos′) *vt.* **-cused′, -cus′ing** [< OFr. < L. *excusare* < *ex-*, from + *causa*, a charge] **1.** to try to free (a person) of blame **2.** to try to minimize (a fault); apologize or give reasons for **3.** to disregard (an offense or fault); overlook [*excuse* my rudeness] **4.** to release from an obligation, promise, etc. **5.** to permit to leave **6.** to serve as an explanation or justification for; justify; absolve —*n.* **1.** a plea in defense of some action; apology **2.** a release from obligation, duty, etc. **3.** something that excuses; justifying factor **4.** a pretended reason; pretext —**a poor** (or **bad**, etc.) **excuse for** a very inferior example of —**excuse oneself 1.** to apologize. **2.** to ask for permission to leave —**ex·cus′a·ble** *adj.* —**ex·cus′a·bly** *adv.* —**ex·cus′er** *n.*

**ex·ec** (ig zek′) *n.* [Colloq.] an executive officer

**exec. 1.** executive **2.** executor

**ex·e·cra·ble** (ek′si krə b'l) *adj.* [L. *execrabilis*] abominable; detestable —**ex′e·cra·bly** *adv.*

**ex·e·crate** (-krāt′) *vt.* **-crat′ed, -crat′ing** [< L. pp. of *exe-crare*, to curse < *ex-*, out + *sacrare*, to consecrate < *sacer*, sacred] **1.** orig., to call down evil upon; curse **2.** to denounce scathingly **3.** to loathe; detest; abhor —*vi.* to curse —**ex′e·cra′tion** *n.* —**ex′e·cra′tive, ex′e·cra·to′ry** (-krə tôr′ē) *adj.* —**ex′e·cra′tor** *n.*

**ex·e·cute** (ek′sə kyōot′) *vt.* **-cut′ed, -cut′ing** [< OFr. < L. pp. of *ex*(*s*)*equi* < *ex-*, intens. + *sequi*, to follow] **1.** to carry out; do; perform; fulfill **2.** to carry into effect; administer (laws, etc.) **3.** to put to death in accordance with a legally imposed sentence **4.** to create in accordance with an idea, plan, etc. **5.** to perform (a piece of music, etc.) **6.** *Law* to make valid (a deed, contract, etc.) as by signing, sealing, and delivering —**ex′e·cut′a·ble** *adj.* —**ex′e·cut′er** *n.*

**ex·e·cu·tion** (ek′sə kyōo′shən) *n.* **1.** the act of executing; specif., *a)* a carrying out, doing, etc. *b)* a putting to death in accordance with a legally imposed sentence **2.** the manner of doing or producing something, as of performing a piece of music **3.** *Law* a writ, issued by a court, giving authority to put a judgment into effect

**ex·e·cu·tion·er** (-ər) *n.* a person who carries out the death penalty imposed by a court

**ex·ec·u·tive** (ig zek′yə tiv) *adj.* **1.** of, capable of, or concerned with, carrying out duties, functions, etc., as in a business **2.** empowered and required to administer (laws, government affairs, etc.) **3.** of managerial personnel or functions —*n.* **1.** a person, group, or branch of government empowered and required to administer the laws and affairs of a nation **2.** a person whose function is to administer or manage affairs, as of a corporation

**Executive Mansion 1.** the White House (in Washington, D.C.), official home of the President of the U.S. **2.** the official home of the governor of a State

**executive officer** *Mil.* an officer who is chief assistant to the commanding officer

**ex·ec·u·tor** (ek′sə kyōot′ər; *for 2* ig zek′yə tər) *n.* **1.** a person who gets something done or produced **2.** a person appointed by a testator to carry out the provisions in his will —**ex·ec·u′to′ri·al** (-tôr′ē əl), **ex·ec′u·tor·y** (-ē) —**ex·ec′u·trix** (-triks) *n.fem.*, *pl.* **-trix·es, -tri′ces** (-trī′sēz)

**ex·e·ge·sis** (ek′sə jē′sis) *n.*, *pl.* **-ge′ses** (-sēz) [< Gr. < *ex-*, out + *hēgeisthai*, to guide] analysis or interpretation of a word, literary passage, etc., esp. of the Bible —**ex′e·get′ic** (-jet′ik),′ **ex′e·get′i·cal** *adj.* —**ex′e·get′i·cal·ly** *adv.*

**ex·e·gete** (ek′sə jēt′) *n.* an expert in exegesis

**ex·em·plar** (ig zem′plär, -plər) *n.* [< OFr. < LL. *ex-emplum*, EXAMPLE] **1.** one that is considered worthy of imitation; model **2.** a typical specimen or example

**ex·em·pla·ry** (-plə rē) *adj.* **1.** serving as a model or example; worth imitating [*exemplary* behavior] **2.** serving as a warning [*exemplary* punishment] **3.** serving as a sample; illustrative —**ex·em·pla·ri·ly** (eg′zəm pler′ə lē) *adv.* —**ex·em′pla·ri·ness** *n.*

**exemplary damages** *Law* damages beyond the actual loss, imposed as a punishment

**ex·em·pli·fy** (ig zem′plə fī′) *vt.* **-fied′, -fy′ing** [< OFr. < ML. < L. *exemplum*, an example + *facere*, to make] **1.** to show by example; serve as an example of **2.** to make a certified copy of (a document, etc.) under seal —**ex·em′pli·fi·ca′tion** *n.*

**ex·empt** (ig zempt′) *vt.* [< Anglo-Fr. < L. pp. of *eximere*:

see EXAMPLE] to free from a rule or obligation which applies to others; excuse; release —*adj.* not subject to or bound by a rule, obligation, etc. applying to others —*n.* an exempted person —**ex·empt′i·ble** *adj.* —**ex·emp′tion** *n.*

**ex·er·cise** (ek′sər sīz′) *n.* [< OFr. < L. < pp. of *exercere*, to drive out (farm animals to work) < *ex-*, out + *arcere*, to enclose] **1.** active use or operation [the *exercise* of wit] **2.** performance (of duties, etc.) **3.** activity for training or developing the body or mind; esp., bodily exertion for the sake of health **4.** a series of movements to strengthen or develop some part of the body **5.** a problem or task to be worked out for developing some technical skill, as in mathematics **6.** [*pl.*] a set program of formal speeches, etc., as at a graduation —*vt.* **-cised′, -cis′ing 1.** to use; employ [to *exercise* self-control] **2.** to put (the body, mind, etc.) into use so as to develop or train **3.** to drill (troops) **4.** to engage the attention and energy of, esp. so as to worry, perplex, or harass **5.** to exert or have (influence, control, etc.) —*vi.* to take exercise; do exercises —**ex′er·cis′a·ble** *adj.* —**ex′er·cis′er** *n.*

**ex·ert** (ig zurt′) *vt.* [< L. < *exserere*, to stretch out < *ex-*, out + *serere*, to join] **1.** to put into action or use [*exert* your will] **2.** to apply (oneself) with great energy or effort —**ex·er′tive** *adj.*

**ex·er·tion** (ig zur′shən) *n.* **1.** the act, fact, or process of exerting **2.** energetic activity; effort

**ex·e·unt** (ek′sē ənt, -oont) [L.] they (two or more characters) leave the stage: a stage direction

**exeunt om·nes** (äm′nēz) [L.] all (of the characters who are on stage) leave: a stage direction

**ex·fo·li·ate** (eks fō′lē āt′) *vt., vi.* **-at′ed, -at′ing** [< LL. pp. of *exfoliare*, to strip of leaves < *ex-*, out + *folium*, a leaf] to cast or come off in flakes, scales, or layers, as skin, bark, etc. —**ex·fo′li·a′tion** *n.* —**ex·fo′li·a′tive** *adj.*

**ex·hale** (eks hāl′, ek sāl′) *vi.* **-haled′, -hal′ing** [< Fr. < L. *exhalare* < *ex-*, out + *halare*, to breathe] **1.** to breathe forth air **2.** to rise into the air as vapor; evaporate —*vt.* **1.** to breathe forth (air) **2.** to give off (vapor, fumes, etc.) —**ex·ha·la·tion** (eks′hə lā′shən, ek′sə-) *n.*

**ex·haust** (ig zôst′) *vt.* [< L. pp. of *exhaurire* < *ex-*, out + *haurire*, to draw] **1.** to draw off or let out completely (air, gas, etc.), as from a container **2.** to use up; expend completely **3.** to empty completely; drain [to *exhaust* a well] **4.** to drain of power, resources, etc. **5.** to tire out; weaken **6.** to deal with or study completely and thoroughly [to *exhaust* a subject] —*vi.* to be let out, as gas or steam from an engine —*n.* **1.** the withdrawing of air, gas, etc. from a container or enclosure, as by means of a fan or pump **2.** *a)* the discharge of used steam, gas, etc. from the cylinders of an engine at the end of every working stroke of the pistons *b)* the pipe through which such steam, gas, etc. is released **3.** something given off, as fumes from a gasoline engine —**ex·haust′i·bil′i·ty** *n.* —**ex·haust′i·ble** *adj.* —**ex·haust′less** *adj.*

**ex·haus·tion** (ig zôs′chən) *n.* **1.** an exhausting **2.** the state of being exhausted; esp., *a)* great fatigue or weariness *b)* complete consumption

**ex·haus·tive** (ig zôs′tiv) *adj.* **1.** exhausting or tending to exhaust **2.** leaving nothing out; covering every detail —**ex·haus′tive·ly** *adv.* —**ex·haus′tive·ness** *n.*

**ex·hib·it** (ig zib′it) *vt.* [< L. pp. of *exhibere* < *ex-*, out + *habere*, to hold, have] **1.** to show; display **2.** to present to public view **3.** *Law* to present (evidence, etc.) officially to a court —*vi.* to put pictures, wares, etc. on public display —*n.* **1.** a show; display **2.** an object or objects displayed publicly **3.** *Law* an object produced as evidence in a court —**ex·hib′i·tor, ex·hib′it·er** *n.*

**ex·hi·bi·tion** (ek′sə bish′ən) *n.* **1.** the act or fact of exhibiting **2.** the thing or things exhibited **3.** a public show or display, as of art

**ex·hi·bi·tion·ism** (-iz'm) *n.* **1.** a tendency to call attention to oneself or show off one's talents, skill, etc. **2.** *Psychol.* a tendency to expose parts of the body that are conventionally concealed —**ex′hi·bi′tion·ist** *n.* —**ex′-hi·bi′tion·is′tic** *adj.*

**ex·hib·i·tive** (ig zib′ə tiv) *adj.* serving or tending to exhibit (usually with *of*)

**ex·hil·a·rate** (ig zil′ə rāt′) *vt.* **-rat′ed, -rat′ing** [< L. pp. of *exhilarare* < *ex-*, intens. + *hilarare*, to gladden < *hilaris*, glad] **1.** to make merry or lively **2.** to stimulate —**ex·hil′a·ra′tive** *adj.* —**ex·hil′a·ra′tion** *n.*

**ex·hort** (ig zôrt′) *vt., vi.* [< L. *exhortari* < *ex-*, out + *hortari*, to urge] to urge earnestly by advice, warning, etc.; entreat —**ex·hor·ta·tion** (eg′zôr tā′shən, ek′sər-) *n.* —**ex·hor′ta·to′ry** (-tə tôr′ē), **ex·hor′ta·tive** *adj.* —**ex·hort′-er** *n.*

**ex·hume** (ig zyōom′, iks hyōom′) *vt.* **-humed′, -hum′ing** [< ML. *exhumare* < L. *ex*, out + *humus*, the ground] **1.** to dig out of the earth; disinter **2.** to reveal —**ex·hu·ma·tion** (eks'hyoo mā'shən) *n.*

**ex·i·gen·cy** (ek'sə jən sē) *n., pl.* **-cies** [see ff.] **1.** urgency **2.** a situation calling for immediate action or attention **3.** [*pl.*] pressing needs; demands [the *exigencies* of a situation] Also **ex'i·gence**

**ex·i·gent** (ek'sə jənt) *adj.* [< L. prp. of *exigere*: see EXACT] **1.** calling for immediate action or attention; urgent **2.** requiring more than is reasonable; demanding; exacting —**ex'i·gent·ly** *adv.*

**ex·ig·u·ous** (eg zig'yoo wəs) *adj.* [< L. < *exigere*: see EXACT] scanty; little; small; meager —**ex·i·gu·i·ty** (ek'sə-gyoo'ə tē) *n.*

**ex·ile** (eg'zīl, ek'sīl) *n.* [< OFr. < L. *exilium* < *exul*, an exile] **1.** a prolonged, often enforced, living away from one's country, community, etc.; banishment, sometimes self-imposed **2.** a person in exile —*vt.* **-iled, -il·ing** to force (a person) to leave his country, community, etc.; banish —**ex·il·ic** (ig zil'ik, ik sil'ik) *adj.*

**ex·ist** (ig zist') *vi.* [< Fr. < L. *existere* < *ex-*, forth + *sistere*, to cause to stand] **1.** to have reality or actual being; be **2.** to occur or be present (*in*) **3.** to continue being; live —**ex·ist'ent** *adj.*

**ex·ist·ence** (-əns) *n.* **1.** the act of existing; state or fact of being **2.** continuance of being; life; living **3.** occurrence **4.** a manner of existing **5.** a being; entity; thing that exists

**ex·is·ten·tial** (eg'zis ten'shəl, ek'sis-) *adj.* **1.** of, based on, or expressing existence **2.** of, relating to, or as conceived of in, existentialism

**ex·is·ten·tial·ism** (-shəl iz'm) *n.* a philosophical and literary movement which holds that man is totally free and responsible for his acts, and that this responsibility causes man's dread and anguish —**ex'is·ten'tial·ist** *n.*

**ex·it** (eg'zit, ek'sit) *n.* [L. *exitus*, orig. pp. of *exire* < *ex-*, out + *ire*, to go] **1.** an actor's departure from the stage **2.** a going out; departure **3.** a way out **4.** [L., 3d pers. sing., pres. indic., of *exire*] he (or she) leaves: a stage direction —*vi.* to leave a place; depart

**‡ex li·bris** (eks lē'bris, lī'-) [L.] **1.** from the library of: an inscription on bookplates **2.** a bookplate

**ex·o-** [< Gr. *exō*, without] *a prefix meaning* outside, outer, outer part

**ex·o·bi·ol·o·gy** (ek'sō bī äl'ə jē) *n.* [EXO- + BIOLOGY] the study of the possible existence of living organisms elsewhere in the universe than on earth —**ex'o·bi'o·log'i·cal** *adj.* —**ex'o·bi·ol'o·gist** *n.*

**ex·o·carp** (ek'sō kärp') *n.* [EXO- + -CARP] the outer layer of a ripened ovary or fruit; peel

**ex·o·crine** (ek'sə krin, -krīn', -krēn') *adj.* [EXO- + (ENDO)CRINE] designating or of a gland secreting externally, either directly or through a duct —*n.* any such gland, as a sweat gland, or its secretion

**Exod. Exodus**

**ex·o·dus** (ek'sə dəs) *n.* [< LL. < Gr. < *ex-*, out + *hodos*, way] a going out or forth, esp. in a large group —[E-] **1.** the departure of the Israelites from Egypt (with *the*) **2.** the second book of the Pentateuch, which describes this

**ex of·fi·ci·o** (eks' ə fish'ē ō') [L., lit., from office] by virtue of one's office, or position

**ex·og·a·my** (ek säg'ə mē) *n.* [EXO- + -GAMY] the custom of marrying only outside one's own tribe, clan, etc.; outbreeding —**ex·og'a·mous, ex·o·gam·ic** (ek'sə gam'ik) *adj.*

**ex·og·e·nous** (ek säj'ə nəs) *adj.* [EXO- + -GENOUS] **1.** developing from without; originating externally **2.** *Biol.* of or relating to external factors, as food, light, etc., that have an effect on an organism —**ex·og'e·nous·ly** *adv.*

**ex·on·er·ate** (ig zän'ə rāt') *vt.* **-at·ed, -at·ing** [< L. pp. of *exonerare* < *ex-*, out + *onerare*, to load < *onus*, a burden] to free from a charge of guilt; declare or prove blameless —**ex·on'er·a'tion** *n.* —**ex·on'er·a'tive** *adj.* —**ex·on'er·a'tor** *n.*

**ex·oph·thal·mos** (ek'säf thal'məs) *n.* [< Gr. < *ex-*, out + *ophthalmos*, an eye] abnormal bulging out of the eyeball, caused by disease: also **ex'oph·thal'mus, ex'oph·thal'-mi·a** (-mē ə) —**ex'oph·thal'mic** *adj.*

**ex·or·bi·tant** (ig zôr'bə tənt) *adj.* [< L. prp. of *exorbitare* < *ex-*, out + *orbita*, a track, ORBIT] going beyond what is reasonable, fair, usual, etc., as a price; excessive; extravagant —**ex·or'bi·tance, ex·or'bi·tan·cy** *n.* —**ex·or'bi·tant·ly** *adv.*

**ex·or·cise, ex·or·cize** (ek'sôr sīz') *vt.* **-cised' or -cized', -cis'ing or -ciz'ing** [< LL. < Gr. < *ex-*, out + *horkizein*, to make one swear < *horkos*, an oath] **1.** to drive (an evil spirit) out or away by ritual prayers, incantations, etc. **2.** to free from such a spirit —**ex'or·cis'er, ex'or·ciz'er** *n.*

**ex·or·cism** (-siz'm) *n.* **1.** the act of exorcising **2.** a formula or ritual used in exorcising —**ex'or·cist** *n.*

**ex·or·di·um** (ig zôr'dē əm) *n., pl.* **-di·ums, -di·a** (-ə) [< L. < *ex-*, from + *ordiri*, to begin] **1.** a beginning **2.** the opening part of a speech, treatise, etc.

**ex·o·skel·e·ton** (ek'sō skel'ə t'n) *n. Zool.* any hard, ex-

ternal supporting structure, as the shell of crustaceans —**ex'o·skel'e·tal** *adj.*

**ex·ot·ic** (ig zät'ik) *adj.* [< L. < Gr. *exōtikos* < *exō*, outside] **1.** foreign; not native **2.** strangely beautiful, enticing, etc. —*n.* **1.** a foreign or imported thing **2.** a plant that is not native —**ex·ot'i·cal·ly** *adv.* —**ex·ot'i·cism** (-ə siz'm) *n.*

**exotic dancer** a belly dancer, stripteaser, or the like

**exp. 1.** expenses **2.** export **3.** express

**ex·pand** (ik spand') *vt.* [< L. < *ex-*, out + *pandere*, to spread] **1.** to spread out; open out; stretch out; unfold **2.** to make greater in size, scope, etc.; enlarge; dilate **3.** to enlarge upon (a topic, idea, etc.); develop in detail or fully —*vi.* to spread out, unfold, enlarge, etc. —**ex·pand'er** *n.*

**expanded metal** sheet metal stretched out in latticelike strips, used as lath for plastering, etc.

**ex·panse** (ik spans') *n.* a large, open area or unbroken surface; wide extent; great breadth

**ex·pan·si·ble** (ik span'sə b'l) *adj.* that can be expanded: also **ex·pand'a·ble** —**ex·pan'si·bil'i·ty** *n.*

**ex·pan·sion** (ik span'shən) *n.* **1.** an expanding or being expanded; enlargement **2.** an expanded thing or part **3.** the extent or degree of expansion **4.** a development or full treatment, as of a topic

**ex·pan·sion·ar·y** (-er'ē) *adj.* directed toward expansion

**ex·pan·sion·ism** (-iz'm) *n.* the policy of expanding a nation's territory or its sphere of influence, often at the expense of other nations —**ex·pan'sion·ist** *adj., n.* —**ex·pan'sion·is'tic** *adj.*

**ex·pan·sive** (ik span'siv) *adj.* **1.** tending or being able to expand **2.** of, or working by means of, expansion **3.** broad; extensive; comprehensive **4.** sympathetic; demonstrative [an *expansive* person] —**ex·pan'sive·ly** *adv.* —**ex·pan'sive·ness** *n.*

**ex·pa·ti·ate** (ik spā'shē āt') *vi.* **-at·ed, -at·ing** [< L. pp. of *expatiari*, to wander < *ex-*, out + *spatiari*, to walk < *spatium*, space] to speak or write in great detail (*on* or *upon*) —**ex·pa'ti·a'tion** *n.*

**ex·pa·tri·ate** (eks pā'trē āt'; *for adj. & n., usually* -it) *vt.* **-at·ed, -at·ing** [< ML. pp. of *expatriare* < L. *ex*, out of + *patria*, fatherland < *pater*, father] **1.** to exile or banish **2.** to withdraw (oneself) from one's native land —*adj.* expatriated —*n.* an expatriated person —**ex·pa'tri·a'tion** *n.*

**ex·pect** (ik spekt') *vt.* [< L. < *ex-*, out + *spectare*, to look] **1.** to look for as likely to occur or appear; look forward to; anticipate **2.** to look for as due, proper, or necessary [to *expect* a reward] **3.** [Colloq.] to suppose; presume; guess —**be expecting** [Colloq.] to be pregnant —**ex·pect'a·ble** *adj.*

**ex·pect·an·cy** (ik spek'tən sē) *n., pl.* **-cies 1.** an expecting or being expected; expectation **2.** that which is expected, esp. on a statistical basis [life *expectancy*] Also **ex·pect'ance**

**ex·pect·ant** (-tənt) *adj.* expecting; specif., *a*) having or showing expectation *b*) waiting, as for a position, the birth of a child, etc. —*n.* a person who expects something —**ex·pect'ant·ly** *adv.*

**ex·pec·ta·tion** (ek'spek tā'shən) *n.* **1.** a looking forward to; anticipation **2.** a looking for as due, proper, or necessary **3.** a thing looked forward to **4.** [*also pl.*] prospect of future success, prosperity, etc. —**in expectation** in the state of being looked for —**ex·pec·ta·tive** (ik spek'tə tiv) *adj.*

**ex·pec·to·rant** (ik spek'tər ənt) *adj.* causing or easing the bringing up of phlegm, mucus, etc. from the respiratory tract —*n.* an expectorant medicine

**ex·pec·to·rate** (-tə rāt') *vt., vi.* **-rat·ed, -rat·ing** [< L. pp. of *expectorare* < *ex-*, out + *pectus* (gen. *pectoris*), breast] **1.** to cough up and spit out (phlegm, mucus, etc.) **2.** to spit —**ex·pec'to·ra'tion** *n.*

**ex·pe·di·en·cy** (ik spē'dē ən sē) *n., pl.* **-cies 1.** the quality or state of being expedient; suitability for a given purpose **2.** the doing or consideration of what is of use or advantage rather than what is right or just; self-interest **3.** an expedient Also **ex·pe'di·ence**

**ex·pe·di·ent** (-ənt) *adj.* [< OFr. < L. prp. of *expedire*: see ff.] **1.** useful for effecting a desired result; suited to the circumstances; convenient **2.** based on what is of use or advantage rather than what is right or just; guided by self-interest —*n.* an expedient thing —**ex·pe'di·ent·ly** *adv.*

**ex·pe·dite** (ek'spə dīt') *vt.* **-dit·ed, -dit·ing** [< L. pp. of *expedire*, lit., to free one caught by the feet < *ex-*, out + *pes* (gen. *pedis*), foot] **1.** to speed up or make easy the progress or action of; facilitate **2.** to do quickly

**ex·pe·dit·er** (-ər) *n.* a person who expedites; esp., one employed, as in industry, to expedite urgent or involved projects

**ex·pe·di·tion** (ek'spə dish'ən) *n.* [< OFr. < L. < pp. of *expedire*: see EXPEDITE] **1.** *a*) a journey, voyage, etc., as for exploration or battle *b*) the people, ships, etc. on such a journey **2.** efficient speed; dispatch —**ex'pe·di'tion·ar'y** *adj.*

**ex·pe·di·tious** (ek'spə dish'əs) *adj.* efficient and speedy; prompt —**ex'pe·di'tious·ly** *adv.*

**ex·pel** (ik spel') *vt.* **-pelled'**, **-pel'ling** [< L. *expellere* < *ex-*, out + *pellere*, to thrust] **1.** to drive out by force; force out; eject **2.** to dismiss or send away by authority —**expel'la·ble** *adj.* —**ex·pel·lee** (ek'spel ē') *n.* —**ex·pel'ler** *n.*

**ex·pend** (ik spend') *vt.* [< L. *expendere*, to pay out < *ex-*, out + *pendere*, to weigh] **1.** to spend **2.** to consume by using; use up —**ex·pend'er** *n.*

**ex·pend·a·ble** (ik spen'də b'l) *adj.* **1.** that can be expended **2.** *Mil.* designating equipment (and hence, men) expected to be used up (or sacrificed) in service —*n.* a person or thing considered expendable —**ex·pend'a·bil'i·ty** *n.* —**ex·pend'a·bly** *adv.*

**ex·pend·i·ture** (-də chər) *n.* **1.** an expending; a spending or using up of money, time, etc. **2.** the amount of money, time, etc. expended

**ex·pense** (ik spens') *n.* [< Anglo-Fr. < LL. *expensa* (*pecunia*), paid out (money) < L. pp. of *expendere*: see EXPEND] **1.** financial cost; fee **2.** any cost or sacrifice **3.** [*pl.*] *a*) charges met with in doing one's work, etc. *b*) money to pay for these charges **4.** a cause of spending —**at the expense of** with the payment, loss, etc. borne by

**expense account** **1.** an arrangement whereby certain expenses of an employee related to his work are paid for by his employer **2.** a record of these

**ex·pen·sive** (ik spen'siv) *adj.* requiring or involving much expense; high-priced; dear —**ex·pen'sive·ly** *adv.* —**ex·pen'sive·ness** *n.*

**ex·pe·ri·ence** (ik spir'ē əns) *n.* [< OFr. < L. < prp. of *experiri*, to try < *ex-*, out + base as in *peritus*, experienced] **1.** the act of living through an event or events **2.** anything or everything observed or lived through **3.** effect on one of anything or everything that has happened to him **4.** *a*) activity that includes training and personal participation *b*) the period of such activity *c*) knowledge, skill, or practice resulting from this —*vt.* **-enced, -enc·ing** to have experience of; undergo

**ex·pe·ri·enced** (-ənst) *adj.* **1.** having had much experience **2.** having learned from experience; made wise, competent, etc. by experience

**ex·pe·ri·en·tial** (ik spir'ē en'shəl) *adj.* of or based on experience —**ex·pe'ri·en'tial·ly** *adv.*

**ex·per·i·ment** (ik sper'ə mənt, -spir'-; *for v.*, *also* -ment') *n.* [< OFr. < L. *experimentum* < *experiri*: see EXPERIENCE] **1.** any action or process undertaken to discover something not yet known or to demonstrate or test something known **2.** the conducting of such tests or trials —*vi.* to make an experiment —**ex·per'i·ment'er** *n.*

**ex·per·i·men·tal** (ik sper'ə men't'l, -spir'-) *adj.* **1.** of or based on experience rather than on theory or authority **2.** based on, tested by, or having the nature of, experiment **3.** of or used for experiments —**ex·per'i·men·tal·ism** *n.* —**ex·per'i·men·tal·ist** *n., adj.* —**ex·per'i·men'tal·ly** *adv.*

**ex·per·i·men·ta·tion** (ik sper'ə mən tā'shən, -men-) *n.* the conducting of experiments

**ex·pert** (ek'spərt; *also, for adj.*, ik spurt') *adj.* [< OFr. < L. pp. of *experiri*: see EXPERIENCE] **1.** very skillful; having much training and knowledge in some special field **2.** of or from an expert [an *expert* opinion] —*n.* a person who is very skillful or highly trained and informed in some special field —**ex'pert·ly** *adv.* —**ex'pert·ness** *n.*

**ex·pert·ise** (ek'spər tēz') *n.* [Fr.] the skill, knowledge, judgment, etc. of an expert

**ex·pi·ate** (ek'spē āt') *vt.* **-at'ed, -at'ing** [< L. pp. of *expiare* < *ex-*, out + *piare*, to appease < *pius*, devout] **1.** to make amends for (wrongdoing or guilt); atone for **2.** to suffer for —**ex'pi·a·ble** (-ə b'l) *adj.* —**ex'pi·a'tion** *n.* —**ex'pi·a'tor** *n.*

**ex·pi·a·to·ry** (ek'spē ə tôr'ē) *adj.* that expiates or is meant to expiate

**ex·pi·ra·tion** (ek'spə rā'shən) *n.* **1.** a breathing out, as of air from the lungs **2.** something breathed out **3.** a breathing one's last; dying **4.** a coming to an end; close —**ex·pir·a·to·ry** (ik spir'ə tôr'ē) *adj.*

**ex·pire** (ik spir') *vt.* **-pired', -pir'ing** [< L. *exspirare* < *ex-*, out + *spirare*, to breathe] to breathe out (air from the lungs) —*vi.* **1.** to breathe out air **2.** to breathe one's last breath; die **3.** to come to an end; terminate

**ex·plain** (ik splān') *vt.* [< L. < *ex-*, out + *planare*, to make level < *planus*, level] **1.** to make plain or understandable **2.** to give the meaning or interpretation of; expound **3.** to account for; state reasons for —*vi.* to give an explanation —**explain away** to state reasons for so as to justify —**explain oneself 1.** to make clear what one means **2.** to give reasons justifying one's conduct —**ex·plain'a·ble** *adj.* —**ex·plain'er** *n.*

**ex·pla·na·tion** (eks'plə nā'shən) *n.* **1.** an explaining **2.** something that explains **3.** the interpretation, meaning, etc. given in explaining

**ex·plan·a·to·ry** (ik splan'ə tôr'ē) *adj.* explaining or intended to explain: also **ex·plan'a·tive** (-ə tiv) —**ex·plan'a·to'ri·ly** *adv.*

**ex·ple·tive** (eks'plə tiv) *n.* [< LL. < L. pp. of *explere* < *ex-*, out + *plere*, to fill] **1.** an oath or exclamation **2.** a word, phrase, etc. used merely to fill out a sentence or metrical line —*adj.* used to fill out a sentence, line, etc.: also **ex'ple·to'ry** (-tôr'ē)

**ex·pli·ca·ble** (eks'pli kə b'l, iks plik'ə b'l) *adj.* that can be explained

**ex·pli·cate** (eks'pli kāt') *vt.* **-cat'ed, -cat'ing** [< L. pp. of *explicare* < *ex-*, out + *plicare*, to fold] to make clear or explicit (something obscure or implied); explain fully —**ex'pli·ca'tion** *n.* —**ex'pli·ca'tive** (-kāt'iv, ik splik'ə-tiv), **ex'pli·ca·to'ry** (-kə tôr'ē, ik splik'ə-) *adj.* —**ex'pli·ca'tor** *n.*

**ex·plic·it** (ik splis'it) *adj.* [< ML. < L. pp. of *explicare*: see prec.] **1.** clearly stated or expressed, with nothing implied; definite **2.** saying what is meant, without reservation; outspoken **3.** plain to see —**ex·plic'it·ly** *adv.* —**ex·plic'it·ness** *n.*

**ex·plode** (ik splōd') *vt.* **-plod'ed, -plod'ing** [orig., to drive off the stage by hooting < L. *explodere* < *ex-*, off + *plaudere*, to applaud] **1.** to expose as false; discredit [to *explode* a theory] **2.** to make burst with a loud noise **3.** to cause a rapid, violent change in by chemical reaction or by nuclear fission or fusion —*vi.* **1.** to burst noisily and violently **2.** to break forth noisily [to *explode* with anger] **3.** to increase very rapidly [an *exploding* population] —**explod'a·ble** *adj.* —**ex·plod'er** *n.*

**ex·ploit** (eks'ploit; *also, and for v. usually*, ik sploit') *n.* [< OFr. < L. pp. of *explicare*: see EXPLICATE] an act remarkable for brilliance or daring; bold deed —*vt.* **1.** to make use of; utilize productively **2.** to make use of or profit from the labor of (others) in an unethical way **3.** to promote or further the sales of (a product, etc.) —**ex·ploit'a·ble** *adj.* —**ex'ploi·ta'tion** *n.* —**ex·ploit'a·tive, ex·ploi'tive** *adj.* —**ex·ploit'er** *n.*

**ex·plo·ra·tion** (eks'plə rā'shən, -plō-) *n.* an exploring or being explored —**ex·plor·a·to·ry** (ik splôr'ə tôr'ē), **ex·plor'a·tive** (-tiv) *adj.*

**ex·plore** (ik splôr') *vt.* **-plored', -plor'ing** [L. *explorare*, to search out < *ex-*, out + *plorare*, to cry out] **1.** to look into closely; investigate **2.** to travel in (a region previously unknown or little known) for discovery **3.** *Med.* to examine (an organ, etc.) by operation, probing, etc., as in order to make a diagnosis —*vi.* to explore new regions, etc. —**ex·plor'er** *n.*

**ex·plo·sion** (ik splō'zhən) *n.* **1.** an exploding; esp., a blowing up; detonation **2.** the noise made by exploding **3.** a noisy outburst **4.** a sudden, rapid, and widespread increase

**ex·plo·sive** (-siv) *adj.* **1.** of, causing, or having the nature of, an explosion **2.** tending to explode; esp., tending to burst forth noisily **3.** *same as* PLOSIVE —*n.* **1.** a substance that can explode, as gunpowder **2.** *same as* PLOSIVE —**explo'sive·ly** *adv.* —**ex·plo'sive·ness** *n.*

**ex·po·nent** (ik spō'nənt; *for n. 3, usually* ek'spō'nənt) *adj.* [< L. prp. of *exponere*: see EXPOUND] explaining, interpreting, or expounding —*n.* **1.** a person who expounds or promotes (principles, methods, etc.) **2.** a person or thing that is an example or symbol (*of* something) **3.** *Algebra* a small figure or symbol placed at the upper right of another figure or symbol to show how many times the latter is to be multiplied by itself (Ex.: $b^2 = b \times b$) —**ex·po·nen·tial** (eks'-pō nen'shəl) *adj.* —**ex'po·nen'tial·ly** *adv.*

**ex·port** (ik spôrt'; *also, and for n. & adj. always*, eks'pôrt) *vt.* [< L. < *ex-*, out + *portare*, to carry] **1.** to carry or send (goods, etc.) to other countries, esp. for purposes of sale **2.** to carry or send (ideas, culture, etc.) from one place to another —*n.* **1.** something exported **2.** an exporting Also **ex'por·ta'tion** —*adj.* of or for exporting or exports —**ex·port'a·ble** *adj.* —**ex·port'er** *n.*

**ex·pose** (ik spōz') *vt.* **-posed', -pos'ing** [< OFr. < L. pp. or *exponere*: see EXPOUND] **1.** *a*) to lay open (*to* danger, attack, ridicule, etc.) *b*) to leave unprotected **2.** to make accessible or subject (*to* an influence or action) **2.** to leave out in the open, as to die **3.** to allow to be seen; reveal; display **4.** *a*) to make (a crime, fraud, etc.) known *b*) to make known the crimes, etc. of **5.** *Photog.* to subject (a sensitized film or plate) to radiation as of light rays —**ex·pos'-er** *n.*

**ex·po·sé** (eks'pō zā') *n.* [Fr., pp. of *exposer*, to expose] a public disclosure of a scandal, crime, etc.

**ex·po·si·tion** (eks'pə zish'ən) *n.* [< OFr. < L. pp. of *ex-*

*ponere:* see EXPOUND] **1.** a setting forth of facts, ideas, etc.; detailed explanation **2.** writing or speaking that sets forth or explains **3.** a large public exhibition or show **4.** the first section of certain musical forms, introducing the main theme or themes

**ex·pos·i·tor** (ik späz'ə tər) *n.* one that expounds or explains

**ex·pos·i·to·ry** (-ə tôr'ē) *adj.* of, like, or containing exposition; explanatory: also **ex·pos'i·tive** (-ə tiv)

**ex post fac·to** (eks pōst fak'tō) [L., from (the thing) done afterward] done or made afterward, esp. when having retroactive effect

**ex·pos·tu·late** (ik späs'chə lāt') *vi.* -lat'ed, -lat'ing [< L. pp. of *expostulare* < *ex-*, intens. + *postulare*, to demand] to reason with a person earnestly, objecting to his actions or intentions; remonstrate (*with*) —**ex·pos'tu·la'tion** *n.* —**ex·pos'tu·la'tor** *n.* —**ex·pos'tu·la·to·ry** (-lə tôr'ē) *adj.*

**ex·po·sure** (ik spō'zhər) *n.* **1.** an exposing or being exposed **2.** a location, as of a house, in relation to the sun, winds, etc. [an eastern *exposure*] **3.** appearance before the public, as on TV, etc. **4.** a being exposed, when helpless, to the elements **5.** *Photog.* *a)* the subjection of a film or plate to light, etc. *b)* a film section for making one picture *c)* the time during which film is exposed

**ex·pound** (ik spound') *vt.* [< OFr. < L. < *ex-*, out + *ponere*, to put] **1.** to set forth; state in detail **2.** to explain or interpret —**ex·pound'er** *n.*

**ex·press** (ik spres') *vt.* [< ML. < L. *expressus*, pp. of *exprimere* < *ex-*, out + *premere*: see PRESS¹] **1.** to press out or squeeze out (juice, etc.) **2.** to put into words; state **3.** to make known; show [his face *expressed* joy] **4.** to represent in art, music, etc. **5.** to show by a sign; symbolize **6.** to send by express —*adj.* **1.** *a)* expressed and not implied; explicit [an *express* warranty] *b)* specific [his *express* reason for going] **2.** exact [the *express* image of her aunt] **3.** fast, direct, and making few stops [an *express* train] **4.** *a)* for fast driving [an *express* highway] *b)* having to do with express (*n.* 2) —*adv.* by express —*n.* **1.** an express train, bus, elevator, etc. **2.** *a)* a method or service for transporting goods rapidly: express is usually more expensive than freight *b)* the things sent by express **3.** any method or means of swift transmission —**express oneself 1.** to state one's thoughts **2.** to give expression to one's feelings, imagination, talents, etc. —**ex·press'er** *n.* —**ex·press'i·ble** *adj.*

**ex·press·age** (-ij) *n.* **1.** the carrying of packages, etc. by express **2.** the charge for this

**ex·pres·sion** (ik spresh'ən) *n.* **1.** a pressing out or squeezing out, as of juice **2.** a putting into words **3.** a representing in art, music, etc. **4.** a manner of expressing; esp., eloquence in speaking, etc. **5.** a particular word or phrase [a trite *expression*] **6.** a showing of feeling, character, etc. [laughter is an *expression* of joy] **7.** a look, intonation, etc. that conveys meaning or feeling [a quizzical *expression*] **8.** a symbol or set of symbols expressing some mathematical fact **9.** a showing by a symbol, sign, figures, etc. —**ex·pres'sion·less** *adj.* —**ex·pres'sion·less·ly** *adv.*

**ex·pres·sion·ism** (-iz'm) *n.* an early 20th-cent. movement in art, drama, etc., characterized by distortion of reality and the use of symbols, stylization, etc. to give objective expression to inner experience —**ex·pres'sion·ist** *adj., n.* —**ex·pres'sion·is'tic** *adj.* —**ex·pres'sion·is'ti·cal·ly** *adv.*

**ex·pres·sive** (ik spres'iv) *adj.* **1.** of or characterized by expression **2.** that expresses; indicative (*of*) [a song *expressive* of joy] **3.** full of meaning or feeling [an *expressive* nod] —**ex·pres'sive·ly** *adv.* —**ex·pres'sive·ness**, **ex'pres·siv'i·ty** *n.*

**ex·press·ly** (-lē) *adv.* **1.** plainly; definitely; explicitly **2.** especially; particularly

**ex·press·man** (-mən) *n., pl.* -men a person employed by an express company; esp., a driver of an express truck, who collects and delivers packages

**ex·pres·so** (ek spres'ō) *n. same as* ESPRESSO

**ex·press·way** (ik spres'wā) *n.* a divided highway for through traffic, with controlled access and generally with overpasses or underpasses at intersections

**ex·pro·pri·ate** (eks prō'prē āt') *vt.* -at'ed, -at'ing [< ML. pp. of *expropriare* < L. *ex-*, out + *proprius*, one's own] to take (land, property, etc.) from its owner, esp. for public use —**ex·pro'pri·a'tion** *n.* —**ex·pro'pri·a'tor** *n.*

**ex·pul·sion** (ik spul'shən) *n.* an expelling, or forcing out, or the condition of being expelled —**ex·pul'sive** (-siv) *adj.*

**ex·punge** (ik spunj') *vt.* -punged', -pung'ing [L. *expungere* < *ex-*, out + *pungere*, to prick] to erase or remove completely; blot out or strike out; delete —**ex·punc'tion** (-spuŋk'shən) *n.*

**ex·pur·gate** (eks'pər gāt') *vt.* -gat'ed, -gat'ing [< L. pp. of *expurgare* < *ex-*, out + *purgare*, PURGE] to remove passages considered obscene or otherwise objectionable from (a book, etc.) —**ex'pur·ga'tion** *n.* —**ex'pur·ga'tor** *n.* —**ex·pur·ga·to·ry** *adj.*

**ex·qui·site** (eks'kwi zit, ik skwiz'it) *adj.* [< L. pp. of *exquirere*, to search out < *ex-*, out + *quaerere*, to ask] **1.** carefully done or elaborately made **2.** very beautiful, esp. in a delicate or carefully wrought way **3.** of highest quality; consummate **4.** highly sensitive; keenly discriminating [an *exquisite* ear for music] **5.** sharply intense; keen [*exquisite* pain] —*n.* one who makes a great show of being refined and fastidious in his tastes, etc. —**ex'qui·site·ly** *adv.* —**ex'qui·site·ness** *n.*

**ext. 1.** extension **2.** exterior **3.** external **4.** extinct **5.** extra **6.** extract

**ex·tant** (ek'stənt, ik stant') *adj.* [< L. prp. of *exstare* < *ex-*, out + *stare*, to stand] still existing

**ex·tem·po·ra·ne·ous** (ik stem'pə rā'nē əs) *adj.* [< LL.: see EXTEMPORE] **1.** made, done, or spoken without any preparation; offhand **2.** spoken with some preparation but not written out or memorized: cf. IMPROMPTU **3.** speaking without preparation **4.** improvised; makeshift —**ex·tem'po·ra'ne·ous·ly** *adv.*

**ex·tem·po·rar·y** (ik stem'pə rer'ē) *adj. same as* EXTEMPORANEOUS —**ex·tem'po·rar'i·ly** *adv.* —**ex·tem'po·rar'i·ness** *n.*

**ex·tem·po·re** (-pə rē) *adv., adj.* [L. < *ex*, out of + *tempore*, abl. of *tempus*, time] without preparation; offhand [to speak *extempore*]

**ex·tem·po·rize** (-rīz') *vi., vt.* -rized', -riz'ing **1.** to speak, perform, or compose extempore; improvise **2.** to contrive as a makeshift —**ex·tem'po·ri·za'tion** *n.* —**ex·tem'po·riz'er** *n.*

**ex·tend** (ik stend') *vt.* [L. *extendere* < *ex-*, out + *tendere*, to stretch] **1.** *a)* to stretch out or draw out *b)* to draw out or lengthen in time or space; prolong **2.** to enlarge in area, scope, influence, etc.; expand; spread **3.** to stretch forth; hold out **4.** to offer; accord; grant **5.** to straighten out (a flexed limb of the body) **6.** to make (oneself) work or try hard **7.** to increase the bulk of (a substance) by adding another, usually cheaper or inferior, substance —*vi.* **1.** to be extended **2.** to reach or stretch out —**ex·tend'ed** *adj.* —**ex·tend'er** *n.*

**ex·ten·si·ble** (ik sten'sə b'l) *adj.* that can be extended: also **ex·tend'i·ble** —**ex·ten·si·bil'i·ty** *n.*

**ex·ten·sion** (ik sten'shən) *n.* **1.** an extending or being extended **2.** range; extent **3.** a part that forms a continuation or addition **4.** an extra period of time allowed a debtor for making payment **5.** a branch of a university away from the university proper **6.** an extra telephone on the same line as the main telephone **7.** *Physics* that property of a body by which it occupies space —*adj.* designating a device that extends or can extend something else [*extension* ladder, *extension* cord] —**ex·ten'sion·al** *adj.*

**ex·ten·sive** (-siv) *adj.* **1.** of great extent, or area, amount, length, etc.; vast **2.** broad in scope, influence, etc.; far-reaching —**ex·ten'sive·ly** *adv.* —**ex·ten'sive·ness** *n.*

**ex·ten·sor** (-sər) *n.* a muscle that extends or straightens some part of the body, esp. a flexed arm or leg

**ex·tent** (ik stent') *n.* **1.** the space, amount, or degree to which a thing extends; size; length; breadth **2.** range or limits; scope; coverage **3.** an extended space; vast area

EXTENSOR

**ex·ten·u·ate** (ik sten'yoo wāt') *vt.* -at'ed, -at'ing [< L. pp. of *extenuare* < *ex-*, out + *tenuare*, to make thin < *tenuis*, thin] to lessen or seem to lessen the seriousness of (an offense, guilt, etc.) by giving excuses or serving as an excuse [*extenuating* circumstances] —**ex·ten'u·a'tion** *n.* —**ex·ten'u·a·to·ry**, **ex·ten'u·a'tive** *adj.*

**ex·te·ri·or** (ik stir'ē ər) *adj.* [L., compar. of *exter(us)*, on the outside: see EXTERNAL] **1.** *a)* on the outside; outer; outermost *b)* for use on the outside [*exterior* paint] **2.** acting or coming from without [*exterior* forces] —*n.* **1.** an outside or outside surface **2.** an outward appearance **3.** a picture, view, setting, etc. of an outdoor scene —**ex·te'ri·or·ly** *adv.*

**exterior angle** any of the four angles formed on the outside of two straight lines by a straight line cutting across them

**ex·te·ri·or·ize** (-ə rīz') *vt.* -ized', -iz'ing **1.** to give or attribute an external form or objective character to (states of mind, etc.) **2.** *same as* EXTERNALIZE —**ex·te'ri·or·i·za'tion** *n.*

**ex·ter·mi·nate** (ik stur'mə nāt') *vt.* -nat'ed, -nat'ing [< L. pp. of *exterminare*, to drive out, destroy < *ex-*, out + *terminus*, a boundary] to destroy or get rid of entirely, as by killing; wipe out; annihilate —**ex·ter'mi·na'tion** *n.* —**ex·ter'mi·na·to·ry**, **ex·ter'mi·na'tive** *adj.*

EXTERIOR ANGLES
(CEL, LER, ADT, TDF)

**ex·ter·mi·na·tor** (-nāt′ər) *n.* a person or thing that exterminates; specif., *a)* one whose work is exterminating rats, cockroaches, and other vermin *b)* any preparation for exterminating vermin

**ex·ter·nal** (ik stur′n'l) *adj.* [< L. *externus* < *exter(us)*, on the outside, compar. form < *ex*, out of (see EX-) + -AL] **1.** on the outside; outer; exterior **2.** on, or for use on, the outside of the body *[a medicine for external use only]* **3.** *a)* outwardly visible *b)* existing apart from the mind; material **4.** acting or coming from without **5.** *a)* for outward appearance or show; superficial *b)* not basic or essential **6.** having to do with foreign countries —*n.* **1.** an outside or outward surface or part **2.** *[pl.]* outward appearance or behavior —**ex·ter·nal·i·ty** (eks′tər nal′ə tē) *n., pl.* **-ties** —**ex·ter′nal·ly** *adv.*

**ex·ter·nal·ize** (-īz′) *vt.* **-ized′, -iz′ing 1.** to make external; embody **2.** *same as* EXTERIORIZE —**ex·ter′nal·i·za′tion** *n.*

**ex·tinct** (ik stiŋkt′) *adj.* [< L. pp. of *exstinguere:* see EXTINGUISH] **1.** having died down or burned out **2.** no longer active *[an extinct volcano]* **3.** no longer in existence *[an extinct species]*

**ex·tinc·tion** (ik stiŋk′shən) *n.* **1.** a putting out or being put out, as of a fire **2.** a destroying or being destroyed **3.** the fact or state of being or becoming extinct

**ex·tin·guish** (ik stiŋ′gwish) *vt.* [< L. *exstinguere* < *ex-*, out + *stinguere*, to extinguish] **1.** to put out (a fire, etc.); quench **2.** to put an end to; destroy **3.** to eclipse; obscure —**ex·tin′guish·a·ble** *adj.* —**ex·tin′guish·er** *n.* —**ex·tin′guish·ment** *n.*

**ex·tir·pate** (ek′stər pāt′, ik stur′pāt) *vt.* **-pat′ed, -pat′ing** [< L. pp. of *ex(s)tirpare* < *ex-*, out + *stirps*, root] **1.** to pull up by the roots **2.** to destroy completely; abolish —**ex′tir·pa′tion** *n.* —**ex′tir·pa′tive** *adj.* —**ex′tir·pa′tor** *n.*

**ex·tol, ex·toll** (ik stōl′) *vt.* **-tolled′, -tol′ling** [< L. *extollere* < *ex-*, up + *tollere*, to raise] to praise highly; laud —**ex·tol′ler** *n.* —**ex·tol′ment, ex·toll′ment** *n.*

**ex·tort** (ik stôrt′) *vt.* [< L. pp. of *extorquere* < *ex-*, out + *torquere*, to twist] to get (money, etc.) by violence, threats, misuse of authority, etc.; exact *(from)* —**ex·tort′er** *n.* —**ex·tor′tive** *adj.*

**ex·tor·tion** (ik stôr′shən) *n.* **1.** an extorting: sometimes applied to the exaction of too high a price **2.** *Law* the offense of an official who extorts **3.** something extorted —**ex·tor′tion·ate, ex·tor′tion·ar′y** *adj.*

**ex·tor·tion·er** (-ər) *n.* a person guilty of extortion: also **ex·tor′tion·ist**

**ex·tra** (eks′trə) *adj.* [contr. < EXTRAORDINARY; also < L. < *extra, adv.*, more than, outside: see ff.] **1.** more, larger, or better than is normal, expected, necessary, etc.; additional **2.** to be paid for by an added charge —*n.* an extra person or thing; specif., *a)* an additional charge *b)* formerly, a special newspaper edition for important news *c)* an extra benefit or feature *d)* a spare copy *e)* an extra worker *f)* *Motion Pictures* an actor hired by the day to play a minor part —*adv.* more than usually *[extra hot]*

**ex·tra-** [L. < *exter(us)*: see EXTERNAL] *a prefix meaning* outside, outside the scope of, beyond, as in the following list:

| | |
|---|---|
| extrafamilial | extramarital |
| extragovernmental | extraofficial |
| extrajudicial | extraterrestrial |

**ex·tract** (ik strakt′; *for n.* eks′trakt) *vt.* [< L. pp. of *extrahere* < *ex-*, out + *trahere*, to draw] **1.** to draw out by effort; pull out *[to extract teeth, to extract a promise]* **2.** to separate (metal) from ore **3.** to obtain by pressing, distilling, using a solvent, etc. *[to extract juice from fruit]* **4.** to deduce, derive, or elicit **5.** to copy out or quote (a passage from a book, etc.) **6.** *Math.* to compute (the root of a quantity) —*n.* something extracted; specif., *a)* a concentrated form of a food, flavoring, etc. *b)* a quotation from a book, etc. —**ex·tract′a·ble, ex·tract′i·ble** *adj.* —**ex·trac′tive** *adj.* —**ex·trac′tor** *n.*

**ex·trac·tion** (ik strak′shən) *n.* **1.** an extracting; specif., the extracting of a tooth **2.** origin; lineage; descent **3.** a thing extracted; extract

**ex·tra·cur·ric·u·lar** (eks′trə kə rik′yə lər) *adj.* not part of the required curriculum but under the supervision of the school, as athletics

**ex·tra·dite** (eks′trə dīt′) *vt.* **-dit′ed, -dit′ing** [back-formation < ff.] **1.** to turn over (an alleged criminal, fugitive, etc.) to the jurisdiction of another country, State, etc. **2.** to obtain the extradition of —**ex′tra·dit′a·ble** *adj.*

**ex·tra·di·tion** (eks′trə dish′ən) *n.* [Fr. < L. *ex*, out + *traditio*, a surrender: see TRADITION] the turning over of an alleged criminal, fugitive, etc. by one country, State, etc. to another

**ex·tra·dos** (eks′trə däs′, -dōs′; ik strä′däs) *n.* [Fr. < L. *extra*, beyond + Fr. *dos* < L. *dorsum*, back] *Archit.* the outside curved surface of an arch

EXTRADOS

**ex·tra·le·gal** (eks′trə lē′g'l) *adj.* outside of legal control or authority —**ex′tra·le′gal·ly** *adv.*

**ex·tra·mu·ral** (-myoor′əl) *adj.* [EXTRA- + MURAL] outside the limits of a city, school, university, etc.

**ex·tra·ne·ous** (ik strā′nē əs) *adj.* [< L. *extraneus* < *extra:* see EXTRA-] **1.** coming from outside; foreign **2.** not essential **3.** not pertinent —**ex·tra′ne·ous·ly** *adv.* —**ex·tra′ne·ous·ness** *n.*

**ex·traor·di·nar·y** (ik strôr′d'n er′ē; *for 3* eks′trə ôr′-) *adj.* [< L. < *extra ordinem*, out of the usual order] **1.** not according to the usual custom or regular plan **2.** very unusual; exceptional; remarkable **3.** outside of the regular staff; sent on a special errand *[an envoy extraordinary]* —**ex·traor′di·nar′i·ly** *adv.* —**ex·traor′di·nar′i·ness** *n.*

**ex·trap·o·late** (ik strap′ə lāt′) *vt., vi.* **-lat′ed, -lat′ing** [L. *extra* (see EXTRA-) + (INTER)POLATE] **1.** to estimate (a value, quantity, etc. beyond the known range) on the basis of certain known variables **2.** to arrive at (conclusions) by speculating on the basis of (known facts) —**ex·trap′o·la′tion** *n.* —**ex·trap′o·la′tive** *adj.* —**ex·trap′o·la′tor** *n.*

**ex·tra·sen·so·ry** (eks′trə sen′sər ē) *adj.* designating or of perception that seems to occur apart from the normal function of the senses

**ex·tra·ter·ri·to·ri·al** (-ter′ə tôr′ē əl) *adj.* **1.** outside the territorial limits or jurisdiction of the country, State, etc. **2.** of extraterritoriality —**ex′tra·ter′ri·to′ri·al·ly** *adv.*

**ex·tra·ter·ri·to·ri·al·i·ty** (-tôr′ē al′ə tē) *n.* **1.** freedom from the jurisdiction of a country: a privilege of foreign diplomats, etc. **2.** jurisdiction of a country over its citizens in foreign lands

**ex·trav·a·gance** (ik strav′ə gəns) *n.* **1.** a going beyond reasonable or proper limits; excess **2.** a spending of more than is reasonable or necessary **3.** an instance of excess in spending, behavior, or speech Also **ex·trav′a·gan·cy,** *pl.* **-cies**

**ex·trav·a·gant** (-gənt) *adj.* [< Anglo-Fr. < ML. prp. of *extravagari* < L. *extra*, beyond + *vagari*, to wander] **1.** going beyond reasonable limits; excessive or unrestrained **2.** too ornate or showy **3.** costing or spending too much —**ex·trav′a·gant·ly** *adv.*

**ex·trav·a·gan·za** (ik strav′ə gan′zə) *n.* [< It. *estravaganza*, extravagance] **1.** a literary, musical, or dramatic fantasy characterized by a loose structure and farce **2.** a spectacular, elaborate theatrical show, as some musicals

**ex·trav·a·sate** (ik strav′ə sāt′) *vi., vt.* **-sat′ed, -sat′ing** [L. *extra* (see EXTRA-) + *vas*, a vessel + -ATE¹] to escape or force to flow into surrounding tissue, as blood, lymph, etc. —**ex·trav′a·sa′tion** *n.*

**ex·tra·ve·hic·u·lar** (eks′trə vē hik′yoo lər) *adj.* designating of or activity by an astronaut outside a vehicle in space

**ex·treme** (ik strēm′) *adj.* [OFr. < L. *extremus*, superl. of *exterus*, outer: see EXTERNAL] **1.** at the end or outermost point; farthest away **2.** to the greatest or an excessive degree **3.** very unconventional **4.** deviating furthest from a central or moderate view; specif., furthest to the right or left in politics **5.** very severe; drastic —*n.* **1.** either of two things that are as different or as far as possible from each other **2.** an extreme degree **3.** an extreme act, expedient, etc. **4.** an extreme state **5.** *Math.* the first or last term of a proportion —**go to extremes** to be immoderate in speech or action —**in the extreme** to the utmost degree —**ex·treme′ly** *adv.* —**ex·treme′ness** *n.*

**extreme unction** *same as* ANOINTING OF THE SICK

**ex·trem·ism** (ik strēm′iz'm) *n.* a being extreme, esp. in politics —**ex·trem′ist** *adj., n.*

**ex·trem·i·ty** (ik strem′ə tē) *n., pl.* **-ties 1.** the outermost or utmost point or part; end **2.** the greatest degree **3.** a state of extreme necessity, danger, etc. **4.** the end of life; dying **5.** an extreme measure; strong action: *usually used in pl.* **6.** *a)* a body limb *b)* *[pl.]* the hands and feet

**ex·tri·cate** (eks′trə kāt′) *vt.* **-cat′ed, -cat′ing** [< L. pp. of *extricare* < *ex-*, out + *tricae*, hindrances, vexations] to set free; disentangle *(from* a net, difficulty, embarrassment, etc.) —**ex′tri·ca·bil′i·ty** *n.* —**ex′tri·ca·ble** (-kə b'l) *adj.* —**ex′tri·ca′tion** *n.*

**ex·trin·sic** (eks strin′sik) *adj.* [< Fr. < L. *extrinsecus*, from without < *exter*, without + *secus*, following] **1.** not belonging to the real nature of a thing; not inherent **2.** being, coming, or acting from the outside; extraneous —**ex·trin′si·cal·ly** *adv.*

**ex·tro·ver·sion** (eks'trə vur'zhən, -shən) *n.* [< G. < L. *extra-* (see EXTRA-) + ML. *versio,* a turning: see VERSION] *Psychol.* an attitude in which a person directs his interest to things outside himself rather than to his own experiences and feelings: opposed to INTROVERSION

**ex·tro·vert** (eks'trə vurt') *n. Psychol.* a person characterized by extroversion; one who is active and expressive: opposed to INTROVERT —*adj.* characterized by extroversion: usually **ex'tro·vert'ed**

**ex·trude** (ik strood') *vt.* **-trud'ed, -trud'ing** [L. *extrudere* < *ex-,* out + *trudere,* to thrust] **1.** to push or force out **2.** to force (metal, plastic, etc.) through a die or very small holes to give it a certain shape —*vi.* to be extruded; esp., to protrude —**ex·trud'er** *n.* —**ex·tru'sion** (-stroo'zhən) *n.* —**ex·tru'sive** *adj.*

**ex·u·ber·ance** (ig zoo'bər əns, -zyoo'-) *n.* [< Fr. < L. < prp. of *exuberare* < *ex-,* intens. + *uberare,* to bear abundantly < *uber,* udder] **1.** the state or quality of being exuberant; great abundance **2.** an instance of this; esp., action or speech showing high spirits Also **ex·u'ber·an·cy,** *pl.* **-cies**

**ex·u·ber·ant** (-ənt) *adj.* **1.** growing profusely; luxuriant **2.** full of life, vitality, or high spirits **3.** overly elaborate **4.** very great; extreme —**ex·u'ber·ant·ly** *adv.*

**ex·ude** (ig zood', -zyood') *vt., vi.* **-ud'ed, -ud'ing** [< L. < *ex-,* out + *sudare,* to sweat < *sudor,* sweat] **1.** to pass out in drops through pores, an incision, etc.; ooze **2.** to diffuse or seem to radiate [to *exude* joy] —**ex·u·da·tion** (eks'yə dā'shən) *n.*

**ex·ult** (ig zult') *vi.* [< Fr. < L. *ex(s)ultare,* to leap for joy < *ex-,* intens. + *saltare,* freq. of *salire,* to leap] to rejoice greatly; be jubilant; glory —**ex'ul·ta'tion** *n.*

**ex·ult·ant** (-'nt) *adj.* exulting; triumphant; jubilant —**ex·ult'ant·ly** *adv.*

**ex·ur·bi·a** (eks ur'bē ə) *n.* [EX- + (SUB)URBIA] the small, semirural communities beyond the suburbs, lived in by upper-income people working in the city —**ex·ur'ban** (-bən) *adj.* —**ex·ur'ban·ite'** (-bə nīt') *n., adj.*

**ex·u·vi·ate** (ig zoo'vē āt') *vt., vi.* **-at'ed, -at'ing** [< L. *exuere,* to strip off + -ATE¹] to cast off (a skin, shell, etc.); molt —**ex·u'vi·a'tion** *n.*

**-ey** (ē, i) *same as* -Y²: used esp. after words ending in *y* [*clayey*]

**eye** (i) *n.* [OE. *eage*] **1.** the organ of sight in man and animals **2.** *a)* the eyeball *b)* the iris **3.** the area around the eye [a black *eye*] **4.** [*often pl.*] sight; vision [weak *eyes*] **5.** a look; glance **6.** attention; observation **7.** the power of judging, estimating, etc. by eyesight [a good *eye* for distances] **8.** [*often pl.*] judgment; opinion [in the *eyes* of the law] **9.** a thing like an eye in shape or function, as a bud of a potato, the hole of a needle, a loop of metal, any primitive, light-sensitive organ, etc. **10.** [Slang] a detective: esp. in *private eye* **11.** *Meteorol.* the calm, low-pressure center (of a hurricane), around which the winds whirl —*vt.* **eyed, eye'ing** or **ey'ing** to look at; observe —**all eyes** extremely attentive —**an eye for an eye** punishment or retaliation equivalent to the injury suffered —**catch one's eye** to attract one's attention —**easy on the eyes** [Slang] attractive —**feast one's eyes on** to look at with pleasure —**have an eye for** to have a keen appreciation of —**have eyes for** [Colloq.] to be interested in and want —**in the public eye** often brought to public attention —**keep an eye on** to look after; watch —**keep an eye out for** to be watchful for —**keep one's eyes open** (or **peeled** or **skinned**) to be watchful —**lay** (or **set** or **clap**) **eyes on** to see; look at —**make eyes at** to look at flirtatiously; ogle —**my eye!** [Slang] an exclamation of contradiction, astonishment, etc. —**open one's eyes** to make one aware of the facts —**run one's eye over** to glance over —**see eye to eye** to agree completely —**shut one's eyes to** to refuse to see or think about —**with an eye to** paying attention to

**eye·ball** (-bôl') *n.* the ball-shaped part of the eye, enclosed by the socket and eyelids —*vt., vi.* [Slang] to examine or observe (something)

**eye·brow** (-brou') *n.* **1.** the bony arch over each eye **2.** the arch of hair growing on this —**raise** (or **lift**) **an eyebrow** to appear skeptical, etc.

**eye-catch·er** (-kach'ər) *n.* something that especially attracts one's attention —**eye'-catch'ing** *adj.*

**eye·cup** (-kup') *n.* a small cup used in applying medicine to the eyes or washing them

**eyed** (īd) *adj.* having eyes (of a specified kind) [*blue-eyed*]

**eye·drop·per** (ī'dräp'ər) *n. same as* DROPPER (*n.* 2)

**eye·ful** (-fool') *n.* **1.** a quantity of something in the eye **2.** a full look at something **3.** [Slang] a person or thing that looks striking or unusual

**eye·glass** (-glas') *n.* **1.** a lens to help faulty vision; monocle **2.** [*pl.*] a pair of such lenses, usually in a frame; glasses **3.** *same as* EYEPIECE

**eye·hole** (-hōl') *n.* **1.** the socket for the eyeball **2.** a peephole **3.** *same as* EYELET (sense 1)

**eye·lash** (-lash') *n.* **1.** any of the hairs on the edge of the eyelid **2.** a fringe of these hairs

**eye·less** (-lis) *adj.* without eyes; blind

**eye·let** (-lit) *n.* [< OFr. dim. of *oeil* < L. *oculus,* eye] **1.** a small hole for receiving a cord, hook, etc. **2.** a metal ring or short tube for lining such a hole **3.** a small hole edged by stitching in embroidered work **4.** a peephole or loophole —*vt.* to provide with eyelets

**eye·lid** (-lid') *n.* either of the two folds of skin that cover and uncover the front of the eyeball

**eye liner** a cosmetic preparation applied in a thin line on the eyelid at the base of the eyelashes

**eye-o·pen·er** (-ō'p'n ər) *n.* **1.** a surprising piece of news, sudden realization, etc. **2.** [Colloq.] an alcoholic drink, esp. one taken early in the day

**eye·piece** (-pēs') *n.* in a telescope, microscope, etc., the lens or lenses nearest the viewer's eye

**eye shadow** a cosmetic preparation, usually green or blue, applied to the upper eyelids

**eye·shot** (-shät') *n.* range of vision

**eye·sight** (-sīt') *n.* **1.** the power of seeing; sight; vision **2.** the range of vision

**eye·sore** (-sôr') *n.* a thing that is unpleasant to look at

**eye·spot** (-spät') *n.* a small spot of pigment sensitive to light, found in many invertebrates

**eye·strain** (-strān') *n.* a tired or strained condition of the eye muscles, caused by too much use or an incorrect use of the eyes

**eye·tooth** (-tooth') *n., pl.* **-teeth'** a canine tooth of the upper jaw —**cut one's eyeteeth** to become experienced or sophisticated

**eye·wash** (-wôsh', -wäsh') *n.* **1.** a lotion for the eyes **2.** [Slang] *a)* nonsense *b)* flattery *c)* something done only to impress an observer

**eye·wink** (-wiŋk') *n.* **1.** a wink of the eye **2.** an instant

**eye·wit·ness** (-wit'nis) *n.* **1.** a person who sees something happen, as an accident, crime, etc. **2.** a person who testifies to what he has seen

**ey·rie, ey·ry** (er'ē, ir'-) *n., pl.* **-ries** *same as* AERIE

**ey·rir** (ā'rir) *n., pl.* **au·rar** (ou'rär) [Ice. <ON., a coin, unit of weight <L. *aureus,* a gold coin, orig. adj., golden: see AUREATE] *see* MONETARY UNITS, table (Iceland)

**E·zek·i·el** (i zē'kē əl, -kyəl) [< LL. < Gr. < Heb. *yehez-q'ēl,* lit., God strengthens] **1.** a masculine name **2.** *Bible a)* a Hebrew prophet of the 6th cent. B.C. *b)* the book containing his prophetic writings: abbrev. Ezek.

**Ez·ra** (ez'rə) [LL. < Heb. *ezrā,* lit., help] **1.** a masculine name **2.** *Bible a)* a Hebrew scribe, prophet, and religious reformer of the 5th cent. B.C. *b)* the book telling of his life and teachings: abbrev. Ez., Ezr.

# F

**F, f** (ef) *n., pl.* **F's, f's** **1.** the sixth letter of the English alphabet **2.** the sound of *F* or *f*
**F** (ef) *n.* **1.** *Chem.* fluorine **2.** *Educ. a)* a grade indicating failing work *b)* sometimes, a grade indicating fair work **3.** *Music a)* the fourth tone in the ascending scale of C major *b)* the scale having this tone as the keynote
**F** **1.** Fahrenheit **2.** farad **3.** fathom
**F/, f/, f:, f.** f-number
**F-** fighter (plane)

**F.** **1.** Fahrenheit **2.** February **3.** Fellow **4.** France **5.** French **6.** Friday
**F., f.** **1.** farad **2.** farthing **3.** fathom **4.** feminine **5.** fluid **6.** folio(s) **7.** following **8.** *Music* forte **9.** franc(s)

**fa** (fä) *n.* [< ML. < *fa(muli):* see GAMUT] *Music* a syllable representing the fourth tone of the diatonic scale
**Fa·bi·an** (fā'bē ən) *adj.* [< L. < *Fabius,* Roman general in 2d Punic War] **1.** using a cautious strategy of delay and

avoidance of battle **2.** designating or of an English social-ist organization (**Fabian Society**) advocating gradual re-forms —*n.* a member of the Fabian Society —**Fa′bi·an·ism** *n.*

**fa·ble** (fā′b'l) *n.* [< OFr. < L. *fabula*, a story < *fari*, to speak] **1.** a fictitious story meant to teach a moral lesson: the characters are usually talking animals **2.** a myth or leg-end **3.** a falsehood or fiction —*vi., vt.* **-bled, -bling** to write or tell (fables, legends, or falsehoods) —**fa′bler** *n.*

**fa·bled** (-b'ld) *adj.* **1.** legendary **2.** fictitious

**fab·ric** (fab′rik) *n.* [< MFr. < L. *fabrica*, a workshop < *faber*, a workman] **1.** *a)* anything made of parts put together *b)* the basic structure of anything **2.** the style or plan of construction **3.** any woven, knitted, or felted material

**fab·ri·cate** (fab′rə kāt′) *vt.* **-cat′ed, -cat′ing** [< L. pp. of *fabricari*, to build < *fabrica*: see prec.] **1.** to make, build, construct, etc., esp. by assembling parts; manufacture **2.** to make up (a story, lie, etc.) —**fab′ri·ca′tion** *n.* —**fab′ri·ca′tor** *n.*

**Fab·ri·koid** (-koid′) [see FABRIC & -OID] *a trademark for* a fabric made to resemble leather

**fab·u·list** (fab′yoo list) *n.* **1.** a person who writes or tells fables **2.** a liar

**fab·u·lous** (-ləs) *adj.* [< L. < *fabula*: see FABLE] **1.** of or like a fable; imaginary; fictitious; legendary **2.** incredible; astounding **3.** [Colloq.] wonderful —**fab′u·lous·ly** *adv.* —**fab′u·lous·ness** *n.*

**fa·çade, fa·cade** (fə säd′) *n.* [Fr. < It. < VL. *facia*: see ff.] **1.** the front of a building **2.** an im-posing appearance concealing something shoddy

**face** (fās) *n.* [< OFr. < VL. *facia* < L. *facies*, the face] **1.** the front of the head; countenance **2.** the ex-pression of the countenance **3.** a surface of a thing; esp., *a)* the main surface or side *b)* the front, upper, or outer surface *c)* any of the sur-faces of a crystal **4.** the side or sur-face that is marked or intended to be seen, as of a clock, playing card, etc. **5.** the appearance; outward aspect **6.** [< Chin. idiom] dignity; self-respect: in **lose** (or **save**) **face 7.** the topography (of an area) **8.** the functional or striking surface (of a tool, etc.) **9.** [Colloq.] effrontery; audacity **10.** *Typography a)* the printing surface of a letter or plate *b)* the design of type —*vt.* **faced, fac′ing 1.** to turn, or have the face turned, toward [the house *faces* the park] **2.** to meet face to face **3.** to confront with bold-ness, courage, etc. **4.** to put another material on the sur-face of **5.** to sew a facing to (a collar, etc.) **6.** to put a smooth surface on (a stone, tool, etc.) **7.** to turn (a card, etc.) with the face up —*vi.* **1.** to turn, or have the face turned, toward a specified thing or in a specified direction **2.** *Mil.* to pivot in a specified direction [right *face!*] —**face off** *Hockey* to start play with a face-off —**face to face 1.** confronting one another **2.** in the presence of: followed by *with* —**face up to 1.** to confront and resist **2.** to realize and be ready to meet —**in the face of 1.** in the presence of **2.** in spite of —**make a face** to distort the face; grimace —**on the face of it** apparently —**pull** (or **wear**) **a long face** to look sad, glum, disapproving, etc. —**faced** *adj.* —**face′less** *adj.*

FAÇADE

**face card** any king, queen, or jack in a deck of cards

**face lifting 1.** plastic surgery for removing wrinkles, sag-ging flesh, etc. from the face **2.** an altering, cleaning, etc., as of the exterior of a building Also **face lift** —**face′-lift′** *vt.*

**face-off** (-ôf′) *n. Hockey* the starting of play by the referee's dropping the puck between two opposing players

**face powder** a cosmetic powder, as of flesh-colored talc, ap-plied to the face

**face-sav·ing** (-sā′viŋ) *adj.* preserving or intended to preserve one's dignity or self-respect

**fac·et** (fas′it) *n.* [< Fr. dim. of *face*: see FACE] **1.** any of the small, polished plane surfaces of a cut gem **2.** any of the sides or aspects, as of a personality —*vt.* **-et·ed** or **-et·ted, -et·ing** or **-et·ting** to cut or make facets on

**fa·ce·tious** (fə sē′shəs) *adj.* [< Fr. < L. < *facetus*, witty] joking or trying to be jocular, esp. at an inappropriate time —**fa·ce′tious·ly** *adv.* —**fa·ce′tious·ness** *n.*

**face value 1.** the value printed or written on a bill, bond, etc. **2.** the seeming value [to take a promise at *face value*]

**fa·cial** (fā′shəl) *adj.* of or for the face —*n.* a cosmetic treat-ment intended to improve facial appearance —**fa′cial·ly** *adv.*

**-fa·cient** (fā′shənt) [< L. prp. of *facere*, to make] *a suffix meaning* making or causing to become [liquefacient]

**fa·ci·es** (fā′shē ēz′) *n., pl* **fa′ci·es′** [L., face] **1.** the general appearance of anything **2.** *Geol.* the characteristics of a rock body, part of a rock body, etc. that differentiate it from others **3.** *Med. a)* the appearance of the face *b)* a sur-face

**fac·ile** (fas′'l) *adj.* [Fr. < L. *facilis* < *facere*, to make, do] **1.** not hard to do; easy **2.** acting, working, or done quickly and smoothly; fluent; ready **3.** not sincere or profound; superficial —**fac′ile·ly** *adv.* —**fac′ile·ness** *n.*

**fa·cil·i·tate** (fə sil′ə tāt′) *vt.* **-tat′ed, -tat′ing** [< Fr. < It. < L. *facilis* (see prec.) + -ATE¹] to make easy or easier —**fa·cil′i·ta′tion** *n.* —**fa·cil′i·ta′tive** *adj.*

**fa·cil·i·ty** (fə sil′ə tē) *n., pl* **-ties** [< OFr. < L. < *facilis*, FACILE] **1.** ease; absence of difficulty **2.** a ready ability; skill; fluency **3.** [*usually pl.*] the means by which something can be done **4.** a building, room, etc. for some activity

**fac·ing** (fās′iŋ) *n.* **1.** a lining, often decorative, sewn on a collar, cuff, etc. **2.** any material used for this **3.** a covering of contrasting material, as for decorating or protecting a building

**fac·sim·i·le** (fak sim′ə lē) *n.* [L. *fac*, imper. of *facere*, to make + *simile*, like] **1.** (an) exact reproduction or copy **2.** the transmission and reproduction of graphic matter by electrical means, as radio or wire —*adj.* of or like a fac-simile —*vt.* **-led, -le·ing** to make a facsimile of

**fact** (fakt) *n.* [L. *factum*, deed < *facere*, to do] **1.** a deed; act: now esp. "a criminal deed" in **before** (or **after**) **the fact** [an accessory *after the fact*] **2.** a thing that has actually happened or is true **3.** the state of things as they are; real-ity; truth **4.** something said to have occurred or supposed to be true [check your *facts*] —**as a matter of fact** in reality; really: also **in fact, in point of fact** —**the facts of life 1.** basic information about life, esp. about sexual reproduc-tion **2.** the harsh, unpleasant facts one must face in life

**fac·tion** (fak′shən) *n.* [< Fr. < L. *factio*, a making < pp. of *facere*, to do, act] **1.** a group of people in a political party, club, etc. working in a common cause against the main body; clique **2.** partisan conflict within an organization or country; dissension —**fac′tion·al** *adj.* —**fac′tion·al·ism** *n.* —**fac′tion·al·ist** *n., adj.* —**fac′tion·al·ly** *adv.*

**fac·tious** (fak′shəs) *adj.* **1.** producing or tending to produce faction, or dissension **2.** produced or character-ized by faction —**fac′tious·ly** *adv.* —**fac′tious·ness** *n.*

**fac·ti·tious** (fak tish′əs) *adj.* [< L. < pp. of *facere*, to do] not genuine or spontaneous; forced or artificial —**fac·ti′-tious·ly** *adv.* —**fac·ti′tious·ness** *n.*

**fac·tor** (fak′tər) *n.* [< OFr. < L. < pp. of *facere*, to do, make] **1.** a person who carries on business transactions for another; commission merchant **2.** any of the circum-stances, conditions, etc. that bring about a result **3.** *Biol. same as* GENE **4.** *Math.* any of two or more quantities which form a product when multiplied together —*vt. Math.* to resolve into factors: also **fac′tor·ize′** (-tə rīz′) **-ized′, -iz′ing** —*vi.* to act as a factor (sense 1) —**fac′tor·a·ble** *adj.* —**fac′tor·ship′** *n.*

**fac·tor·age** (-ij) *n.* **1.** the business of a factor **2.** a factor's commission

**fac·to·ri·al** (fak tôr′ē əl) *n. Math.* the product of a given series of consecutive whole numbers beginning with 1 [the *factorial* of 4 is 1 × 2 × 3 × 4, or 24]

**fac·to·ry** (fak′tə rē, -trē) *n., pl.* **-ries** [see FACTOR] a building or buildings in which things are manufactured; manufac-turing plant

**fac·to·tum** (fak tōt′əm) *n.* [ModL. < L. *fac*, imper. of *facere*, to do + *totum*, all] a person hired to do all sorts of work; handyman

**fac·tu·al** (fak′choo wəl) *adj.* [FACT + (ACT)UAL] **1.** of or containing facts **2.** having the nature of fact; real; actual —**fac′tu·al·ly** *adv.*

**fac·ul·ty** (fak′'l tē) *n., pl.* **-ties** [< OFr. < L. < *facilis*: see FACILE] **1.** formerly, the ability to perform an action **2.** any natural or specialized power of a living organism [the *faculty* of speech] **3.** special aptitude or skill; knack **4.** all the teachers of a school, college, or university or of one of its divisions **5.** all the members of any profession **6.** an au-thorization **7.** *Psychol.* any of the powers formerly thought of as composing the mind, such as will, reason, etc.

**fad** (fad) *n.* [< Brit. Midland dial.] a custom, style, etc. that many people are interested in for a short time; craze —**fad′dish** *adj.* —**fad′dish·ly** *adv.* —**fad′dish·ness** *n.* —**fad′-dism** *n.* —**fad′dist** *n.*

**fade** (fād) *vi.* **fad′ed, fad′ing** [< OFr. *fader* < *fade*, pale] **1.** to become less distinct; lose color, brilliance, intensity, etc. **2.** to lose freshness or strength; wither; wane **3.** to disap-pear slowly; die out **4.** to lose braking power: said of brakes —*vt.* to cause to fade —**fade in** (or **out**) *Motion Pic-*

tures, *Radio & TV* to appear (or disappear) gradually or cause to do so; become or make more (or less) distinct

**fade-in** (-in′) *n. Motion Pictures, Radio & TV* a fading in of a scene or sound

**fade-out** (-out′) *n. Motion Pictures, Radio & TV* a fading out of a scene or sound

**fae·ces** (fē′sēz) *n.pl. same as* FECES **—fae′cal** (-k′l) *adj.*

**fa·er·ie, fa·er·y** (fer′ē; *also, for 1,* fā′ər ē) *n.* [Archaic] **1.** fairyland **2.** *pl.* **-ies** a fairy **—***adj.* [Archaic] fairy Also written **faërie, faëry**

**Faer·oe Islands** (fer′ō) group of Danish islands in the N Atlantic, north of the British Isles

**fag**[1] (fag) *vi.* **fagged, fag′ging** [< ?] **1.** to work hard and become very tired **2.** [Brit. Colloq.] to serve as a fag or servant **—***vt.* to make tired by hard work **—***n.* **1.** [Brit. Colloq.] *a)* drudgery *b)* a boy in an English public school who acts as a servant for another boy in a higher form **2.** [Slang] a male homosexual: also **fag′got** (-ət)

**fag**[2] (fag) *n.* [< ff.] [Old Slang] a cigarette

**fag end** [< ME. *fagge*, broken thread] **1.** *a)* the last part or coarse end of a piece of cloth *b)* the frayed, untwisted end of a rope **2.** the last and worst part of anything

**fag·ot, fag·got** (fag′ət) *n.* [< OFr., ult. < Gr. *phakelos*, a bundle] **1.** a bundle of sticks or twigs, esp. for use as fuel **2.** *Metallurgy* a stack of iron or steel pieces to be welded into bars **—***vt.* **1.** to form a fagot of **2.** to decorate with fagoting

**fag·ot·ing, fag·got·ing** (-iŋ) *n.* **1.** a kind of drawnwork or hemstitch with wide spaces **2.** openwork decoration in which the thread is drawn in crisscross or barlike stitches across the open seam

**Fah., Fahr.** Fahrenheit

**Fahr·en·heit** (fer′ən hīt′, fär′-) *adj.* [after G. D. *Fahrenheit*, 18th-c. G. physicist] designating or of a thermometer on which 32° is the freezing point and 212° the boiling point of water: abbrev. F

FAGOTING
(A, bar; B, crisscross)

**fa·ience** (fī äns′, fā-) *n.* [Fr. < *Faenza*, Italy] earthenware having a colorful, opaque glaze

**fail** (fāl) *vi.* [< OFr. < L. *fallere*, to deceive] **1.** to be lacking or insufficient; fall short; default **2.** to lose power or strength; weaken; die away **3.** to stop functioning **4.** to be unsuccessful in obtaining a desired end **5.** to become bankrupt **6.** *Educ.* to get a grade of failure **—***vt.* **1.** to be of no help to; disappoint **2.** to leave; abandon /his courage *failed* him/ **3.** to miss, neglect, or omit /to *fail* to go/ **4.** *Educ. a)* to give a grade of failure to *b)* to get a grade of failure in **—***n.* failure: now only in **without fail,** without failing (to occur, do, etc.) **—fail of** to fail to achieve

**fail·ing** (-iŋ) *n.* **1.** a failure **2.** a slight fault or defect; weakness **—***prep.* without; lacking

**faille** (fīl, fāl) *n.* [Fr.] a ribbed, soft fabric of silk or rayon

**fail-safe** (fāl′sāf′) *adj.* [FAIL, *v.* + SAFE, *adj.*] designating an intricate procedure designed to prevent malfunctioning or accidental operation, as of nuclear-armed aircraft

**fail·ure** (fāl′yər) *n.* [see FAIL] **1.** the act or fact of failing, or falling short, losing strength, breaking down, going bankrupt, not doing or succeeding, etc. **2.** a person or thing that fails **3.** *Educ. a)* a failing to pass *b)* a grade or mark (usually F) indicating a failing to pass

**fain** (fān) *adj.* [OE. *fægen*, glad] [Archaic] **1.** glad; ready **2.** reluctantly willing **3.** eager **—***adv.* [Archaic] gladly or willingly /he would *fain* stay/

**faint** (fānt) *adj.* [< OFr., orig. pp. of *feindre:* see FEIGN] **1.** without strength; weak; feeble **2.** without courage; timid **3.** done without vigor or enthusiasm **4.** feeling weak and dizzy, as if about to swoon **5.** dim; indistinct **6.** slight /a *faint* hope/ **—***n.* a condition of temporary loss of consciousness **—***vi.* to fall into a faint; swoon **—faint′ish** *adj.* **—faint′ly** *adv.* **—faint′ness** *n.*

**faint·heart·ed** (-här′tid) *adj.* cowardly; timid **—faint′-heart′ed·ly** *adv.* **—faint′heart′ed·ness** *n.*

**fair**[1] (fer) *adj.* [OE. *fæger*] **1.** beautiful /a *fair* maiden/ **2.** unblemished; clean /a *fair* name/ **3.** light in color; blond /*fair* hair/ **4.** clear and sunny **5.** easy to read; clear /a *fair* hand/ **6.** just and honest; impartial; specif., free from discrimination based on race, religion, sex, etc. /*fair* housing/ **7.** according to the rules /a *fair* blow/ **8.** likely; promising /in a *fair* way to benefit/ **9.** pleasant and courteous, often deceptively **10.** favorable; helpful /a *fair* wind/ **11.** of moderately good size **12.** neither very bad nor very good; average **—***adv.* **1.** in a fair manner /play *fair*/ **2.** squarely /struck *fair* in the face/ **—fair and square** [Colloq.] with justice and honesty **—fair to middling** [Colloq.] moderately good **—fair′ish** *adj.* **—fair′ness** *n.*

**fair**[2] (fer) *n.* [< OFr. < ML. < LL. < L. *feriae, pl.,* festivals] **1.** orig., a gathering of people at regular intervals for barter and sale of goods **2.** a carnival where there is

entertainment and things are sold, often for charity; bazaar **3.** an exhibition, often regionally competitive (**county fair, state fair**), of farm, household, and manufactured products, or of international displays (**world's fair**), with amusement facilities and educational displays; exposition

**fair ball** *Baseball* a batted ball that first strikes the ground inside the foul line and does not pass the foul line before first or third base

**fair game 1.** game that may lawfully be hunted **2.** any legitimate object of attack or pursuit

**fair·ground** (fer′ground′) *n.* [*often pl.*] an open space where fairs are held

**fair-haired** (-herd′) *adj.* **1.** having blond hair **2.** [Colloq.] favorite /mother's *fair-haired* boy/

**fair·ly** (-lē) *adv.* **1.** justly; equitably **2.** moderately; somewhat **3.** clearly; distinctly **4.** completely or really /his voice *fairly* rang/

**fair-mind·ed** (-mīn′did) *adj.* just; impartial **—fair′-mind′-ed·ly** *adv.* **—fair′-mind′ed·ness** *n.*

**fair play** an abiding by the rules or by decency and honor in sports, business, etc.

**fair sex** women collectively: used with *the*

**fair-spo·ken** (-spō′kən) *adj.* speaking or spoken civilly and pleasantly or smoothly and plausibly

**fair-trade** (-trād′) *adj.* designating or of an agreement whereby a seller is to charge no less than the minimum price set by the manufacturer **—***vt.* **-trad′ed, -trad′ing** to sell (a commodity) under a fair-trade agreement

**fair·way** (-wā′) *n.* **1.** a navigable channel in a river, harbor, etc. **2.** the mowed part of a golf course between a tee and a green

**fair-weath·er** (-weth′ər) *adj.* **1.** suitable only for fair weather **2.** dependable only in easy circumstances /*fair-weather* friends/

**fair·y** (fer′ē) *n., pl.* **fair′ies** [< OFr. *faerie < fée:* see FAY] **1.** a tiny, graceful imaginary being in human form, supposed to have magic powers **2.** [Slang] a male homosexual **—***adj.* **1.** of fairies **2.** like a fairy; graceful; delicate

**fair·y·land** (-land′) *n.* **1.** the imaginary land where the fairies live **2.** a lovely, enchanting place

**fairy tale 1.** a story about fairies, magic deeds, etc. **2.** an unbelievable or untrue story; lie

‡**fait ac·com·pli** (fe tá kōn plē′) [Fr., lit., an accomplished fact] a thing already done, so that opposition or argument is useless

**Faith** (fāth) [see ff.] a feminine name

**faith** (fāth) *n.* [< OFr. < L. *fides < fidere,* to trust] **1.** unquestioning belief **2.** unquestioning belief in God, religious tenets, etc. **3.** a particular religion **4.** anything believed **5.** complete trust or confidence **6.** loyalty **—***interj.* indeed **—bad faith** insincerity; duplicity **—good faith** sincerity; honesty **—in faith** indeed; really

**faith cure** a trying to cure disease by religious faith, praying, etc.: also **faith healing**

**faith·ful** (-fəl) *adj.* **1.** keeping faith; loyal **2.** responsible; conscientious **3.** accurate; exact **—the faithful** the true believers or loyal followers **—faith′ful·ly** *adv.* **—faith′ful·ness** *n.*

**faith·less** (-lis) *adj.* **1.** not keeping faith; dishonest; disloyal **2.** unreliable; undependable **—faith′less·ly** *adv.* **—faith′-less·ness** *n.*

**fake** (fāk) *vt., vi.* **faked, fak′ing** [< ? G. *fegen,* to clean, sweep] to practice deception by giving a false indication or appearance of (something); feign **—***n.* anything or anyone not genuine; fraud **—***adj.* fraudulent; sham; false **—fak′er** *n.* **—fak′er·y** *n., pl.* **-er·ies**

**fa·kir** (fə kir′) *n.* [Ar. *faqīr,* lit., poor] **1.** a member of a Moslem holy sect who lives by begging **2.** a Hindu ascetic Also sp. **fa·keer′**

**fa·la·fel** (fə läf′'l) *n., pl.* **-fel** [Ar. *falāfil*] a patty of ground chickpeas and other vegetables and spices, deep-fried and, usually, served in a pita

**Fa·lange** (fā′lanj) *n.* [Sp., lit., phalanx] a fascist organization that became the only official political party of Spain under Franco **—Fa·lang′ist** *n.*

**fal·cate** (fal′kāt) *adj.* [< L. < *falx* (gen. *falcis*), a sickle] sickle-shaped; curved; hooked

**fal·chion** (fôl′chən, -shən) *n.* [< OFr. < L. *falx:* see prec.] **1.** a medieval sword with a short, broad, slightly curved blade **2.** [Poet.] any sword

**fal·con** (fal′kən, fôl′-, fô′-) *n.* [< OFr. < LL. *falco* (gen. *falconis*), derived by folk etym. < L. *falx:* see FALCATE] **1.** any hawk trained to hunt and kill small game **2.** a hawklike bird with long, pointed wings and a short, curved, notched beak

**fal·con·ry** (-rē) *n.* **1.** the art of training falcons to hunt game **2.** the sport of hunting with falcons **—fal′con·er** *n.*

**fal·de·ral** (fôl′də rôl′, fal′də ral′) *n.* [nonsense syllables] **1.** a showy but worthless trinket **2.** mere nonsense **3.** a refrain in some old songs

**Falk·land Islands** (fôk′lənd) group of Brit. islands, east of the S tip of S. America

**fall** (fôl) *vi.* **fell, fall'en, fall'ing** [OE. *feallan*] **1.** to come down by the force of gravity, as when detached, pushed, dropped, etc. [apples *fall* from the tree] **2.** to come down suddenly from a standing or sitting position; tumble **3.** to be wounded or killed in battle **4.** to collapse **5.** to hang down [hair *falling* about her shoulders] **6.** to strike; hit [to *fall* wide of the mark] **7.** to take a downward direction [land *falling* away to the sea] **8.** to become lower in amount, degree, etc.; drop; abate [prices *fell*] **9.** to lose power [the government *fell*] **10.** to lose status, reputation, dignity, etc. **11.** *a)* to do wrong; sin *b)* to lose chastity **12.** to be captured or conquered **13.** to take on a dejected look [his face *fell*] **14.** to become lower in pitch or volume [her voice *fell*] **15.** to take place; occur [the meeting *fell* on a Friday] **16.** to come by lot, inheritance, etc. [the estate *falls* to the son] **17.** to pass into a specified condition; become [to *fall* ill] **18.** to come at a specified place [the accent *falls* on the third syllable] **19.** to be directed by chance [his eye *fell* on us] **20.** to be spoken involuntarily [an oath *fell* from his lips] **21.** to be divided (*into*) [to *fall* into two classes] —*n.* **1.** a dropping; descending **2.** a coming down suddenly from a standing or sitting position **3.** a hanging down, or a part hanging down **4.** a downward direction or slope **5.** a becoming lower or less; reduction in value, price, etc. **6.** a capture; overthrow; ruin **7.** a loss of status, reputation, etc. **8.** something that has fallen [a *fall* of leaves] **9.** autumn **10.** the amount of what has fallen [a six-inch *fall* of snow] **11.** the distance that something falls **12.** [*usually pl., often with sing. v.*] water falling over a cliff, etc.; cascade **13.** a long tress of hair, often synthetic, used by women to fill out their coiffure **14.** *a)* the throwing of an opponent in wrestling on his back so that both shoulders touch the floor *b)* a division of a wrestling match —*adj.* of, for, or in the autumn —**fall (all) over oneself** [Colloq.] to behave in too eager or zealous a manner —**fall away 1.** to take away friendship, support, etc.; desert **2.** to become less in size, strength, etc.; *specif.,* to grow thin and weak —**fall back** to withdraw; give way; retreat —**fall back on** (or **upon**) to turn, or return, to for help —**fall flat** to fail to have the desired effect —**fall for** [Colloq.] **1.** to fall in love with **2.** to be tricked by —**fall in 1.** to agree **2.** *Mil.* to line up in proper formation —**fall off** to become smaller, less, worse, etc. —**fall on** (or **upon**) **1.** to attack **2.** to be the duty of —**fall out 1.** to quarrel **2.** to happen; result **3.** *Mil.* to leave one's place in a formation —**fall through** to come to nothing; fail —**fall to 1.** to begin; start **2.** to start attacking **3.** to start eating —**fall under 1.** to come under (an influence, etc.) **2.** to be classified as —**ride for a fall** to behave in a manner likely to cause one trouble or injury —**the Fall (of Man)** *Christian Theol.* Adam's sin of yielding to temptation in eating the forbidden fruit

**fal·la·cious** (fə lā'shəs) *adj.* [see ff.] **1.** containing a fallacy **2.** misleading, deceptive, or delusive —**fal·la'cious·ly** *adv.* —**fal·la'cious·ness** *n.*

**fal·la·cy** (fal'ə sē) *n., pl.* **-cies** [< OFr. < L. < *fallax* (gen. *fallacis*) < *fallere*, to deceive] **1.** aptness to mislead **2.** a false or mistaken idea, opinion, etc.; error **3.** an error in reasoning; *specif., Logic* an argument based on incorrect demonstration, as a vicious circle

**fall·en** (fôl'ən) *adj.* **1.** having come down; dropped **2.** on the ground; prostrate **3.** degraded **4.** captured; overthrown **5.** ruined **6.** dead

**fall guy** [Slang] a person left to face the consequences, as of a scheme that has miscarried

**fal·li·ble** (fal'ə b'l) *adj.* [< ML. < L. *fallere*, to deceive] **1.** liable to be mistaken or deceived **2.** liable to be erroneous or inaccurate —**fal'li·bil'i·ty** *n.* —**fal'li·bly** *adv.*

**fall·ing-out** (fôl'iŋ out') *n.* a quarrel

**falling sickness** *former name for* EPILEPSY

**falling star** *same as* METEOR (sense 1)

**fall-off** (fôl'ôf') *n.* the act or an instance of becoming less or worse; decline

**Fal·lo·pi·an tube** (fə lō'pē ən) [after G. *Fallopio*, It. anatomist (1523–62)] either of two slender tubes that carry ova from the ovaries to the uterus

**fall·out** (fôl'out') *n.* **1.** the descent to earth of radioactive particles, as after a nuclear explosion **2.** these particles **3.** an incidental consequence

**fal·low¹** (fal'ō) *n.* [< OE. *fealh*] **1.** land plowed but not seeded for one or more seasons, to kill weeds, enrich the soil, etc. **2.** the plowing of land to be left idle thus —*adj.* **1.** left uncultivated or unplanted **2.** untrained; inactive: said esp. of the mind —*vt.* to leave (land) unplanted after plowing —**lie fallow** to remain uncultivated, unused, etc. for a time —**fal'low·ness** *n.*

**fal·low²** (fal'ō) *adj.* [< OE. *fealo*] pale-yellow

**fallow deer** a small European deer having a yellowish coat spotted with white in summer

**Fall River** [transl. of Algonquian name of local river] seaport in SE Mass.: pop. 93,000

**false** (fôls) *adj.* **fals'er, fals'est** [ < OFr. < L. pp. of *fallere*, to deceive] **1.** not true; in error; incorrect; wrong **2.** untruthful; lying **3.** disloyal; unfaithful **4.** deceiving; misleading [a *false* scent] **5.** not real; artificial; counterfeit [*false* teeth] **6.** not properly so named [*false* jasmine] **7.** based on mistaken ideas [*false* pride] **8.** temporary, nonessential, or added on for protection, disguise, etc. [a *false* drawer] **9.** *Music* pitched inaccurately —*adv.* in a false manner —**play** (a person) **false** to deceive or betray (a person) —**false'ly** *adv.* —**false'ness** *n.*

**false arrest** *Law* any forceful and unlawful restraint of a person by another

**false·heart·ed** (-här'tid) *adj.* disloyal; deceitful

**false·hood** (-hood') *n.* **1.** lack of accuracy or truth; falsity **2.** the telling of lies; lying **3.** a false statement; lie **4.** a false belief, theory, idea, etc.

**false imprisonment** *Law* the unlawful arrest or detention of another person

**false ribs** the five lower ribs on each side of the body: so called because not directly attached to the breastbone

**false step 1.** a misstep **2.** a social blunder

**fal·set·to** (fôl set'ō) *n., pl.* **-tos** [It. dim. < L.: see FALSE] **1.** *a)* an artificial way of singing or speaking, in which the voice is placed in a register much higher than that of the natural voice *b)* this voice **2.** a person using falsetto: also **fal·set'tist** —*adj.* of or singing in falsetto —*adv.* in falsetto

**fal·si·fy** (fôl'sə fī') *vt.* **-fied', -fy'ing** [ < OFr. < ML. < L. *falsus*, FALSE + *facere*, to make] **1.** to make false; *specif., a)* to give an untrue account of *b)* to alter (a record, etc.) fraudulently **2.** to prove to be unfounded —*vi.* to tell falsehoods; lie —**fal'si·fi·ca'tion** *n.* —**fal'si·fi'er** *n.*

**fal·si·ty** (-tē) *n., pl.* **-ties 1.** the condition or quality of being false; *specif., a)* incorrectness *b)* dishonesty *c)* deceitfulness *d)* disloyalty **2.** something false; *esp.,* a lie

**Fal·staff, Sir John** (fôl'staf, -stäf) a fat, jovial, witty knight that is a character in some of Shakespeare's plays —**Fal·staff'i·an** *adj.*

**fal·ter** (fôl'tər) *vi.* [ME. *faltren*, prob. < ON.] **1.** to move uncertainly or unsteadily; stumble **2.** to stumble in speech; stammer **3.** to act hesitantly; show uncertainty; waver **4.** to lose strength; weaken [the economy *faltered*] —*vt.* to say hesitatingly or timidly —*n.* **1.** a faltering **2.** a faltering sound —**fal'ter·er** *n.* —**fal'ter·ing·ly** *adv.*

**fame** (fām) *n.* [ < OFr. < L. *fama*, fame, akin to *fari*, to speak] **1.** [Archaic] public report; rumor **2.** reputation, esp. for good **3.** the state of being well known or much talked about; renown —*vt.* **famed, fam'ing** [Archaic] to tell about widely; make famous

**famed** (fāmd) *adj.* much talked about or widely known; famous; renowned (*for* something)

**fa·mil·ial** (fə mil'yəl) *adj.* of, involving, or common to a family

**fa·mil·iar** (fə mil'yər) *adj.* [ < OFr. < L. < *familia*, FAMILY] **1.** friendly, informal, or intimate **2.** too friendly; unduly intimate or bold **3.** closely acquainted (*with*) [*familiar* with the Bible] **4.** well-known; common [a *familiar* sight] —*n.* **1.** a close friend **2.** in superstitious belief, a spirit acting as servant to a witch —**fa·mil'iar·ly** *adv.*

**fa·mil·i·ar·i·ty** (fə mil'yar'ə tē, -mil'ē ar'-) *n., pl.* **-ties 1.** intimacy **2.** free and intimate behavior **3.** intimacy that is too bold or unwelcome **4.** a highly intimate act, remark, etc.; *specif.,* a caress **5.** close acquaintance (*with* something)

**fa·mil·iar·ize** (fə mil'yə rīz') *vt.* **-ized', -iz'ing 1.** to make commonly known **2.** to make (another or oneself) accustomed or fully acquainted [*familiarize* yourself with the job] —**fa·mil'iar·i·za'tion** *n.*

**fam·i·ly** (fam'ə lē, fam'lē) *n., pl.* **-lies** [L. *familia*, household < *famulus*, servant] **1.** orig., all the people living in the same house; household **2.** *a)* a social unit consisting of parents and their children *b)* the children of the same parents **3.** a group of people related by ancestry or marriage; relatives **4.** all those claiming descent from a common ancestor; tribe or clan; lineage **5.** a group of things having a common source or similar features; *specif., a) Biol.* a taxonomic category, ranking above a genus and below an order *b) Linguis.* a group of languages having a common ancestral language *c) Math.* a set of curves, etc. with some shared property —*adj.* of or for a family —**in a family way** [Colloq.] pregnant

**family name** a surname

**family planning** *same as* BIRTH CONTROL

**family style** a way of serving food so that each person at the table helps himself from large dishes

**family tree 1.** all the ancestors and descendants in a family **2.** a chart showing their relationship

**fam·ine** (fam′ən) *n*. [< OFr., ult. < L. *fames*, hunger] **1.** an acute and general shortage of food, or a period of this **2.** any acute and general shortage **3.** [Archaic] starvation; great hunger

**fam·ish** (-ish) *vt.*, *vi*. [< OFr. < L. *ad*, to + *fames*, hunger] **1.** to make or be very hungry; make or become weak from hunger **2.** [Obs.] to starve to death

**fa·mous** (fā′məs) *adj*. [< L. < *fama*, FAME] **1.** having fame, or celebrity; renowned **2.** [Colloq.] excellent; first-rate —**fa′mous·ly** *adv*.

**fan¹** (fan) *n*. [OE. *fann* < L. *vannus*, basket for winnowing grain] **1.** orig., a device for winnowing grain **2.** any device used to set up a current of air for ventilating or cooling; specif., *a*) any flat surface moved by hand *b*) a folding device of paper, cloth, etc. that opens as a sector of a circle *c*) a motor-driven device with revolving blades **3.** anything in the shape of a fan (sense 2 *b*) —*vt.* **fanned**, **fan′ning 1.** to move or agitate (air) as with a fan **2.** to direct a current of air toward with or as with a fan; blow on **3.** to stir up; excite **4.** to blow or drive away with a fan **5.** to spread out into the shape of a fan (*n.* 2 *b*) **6.** to separate (grain) from chaff **7.** [Slang] to fire (a pistol) several times quickly in succession by slapping the hammer back between shots **8.** *Baseball* to strike (a batter) out —*vi. Baseball* to strike out —**fan out** to scatter or spread out like an open fan —**fan the air** to strike at but fail to hit something —**fan′like′** *adj*.

**fan²** (fan) *n*. [contr. < ff.] [Colloq.] a person enthusiastic about a specified sport, pastime, or performer; devotee [a baseball *fan*]

**fa·nat·ic** (fə nat′ik) *adj*. [< L. < *fanum*, a temple] unreasonably enthusiastic; overly zealous: also **fa·nat′i·cal** —*n*. a person whose extreme zeal, piety, etc. goes beyond what is reasonable; zealot —**fa·nat′i·cal·ly** *adv*.

**fa·nat·i·cism** (-ə siz′m) *n*. excessive and unreasonable zeal —**fa·nat′i·cize′** (-sīz′) *vt.*, *vi*. **-cized′**, **-ciz′ing**

**fan·cied** (fan′sēd) *adj*. imaginary; imagined

**fan·ci·er** (fan′sē ər) *n*. a person with a special interest in and knowledge of something, particularly plant or animal breeding [a dog *fancier*]

**fan·ci·ful** (fan′si fəl) *adj*. **1.** full of fancy; having or showing a playful imagination [*fanciful* costumes] **2.** not real, practical, etc.; imaginary [a *fanciful* tale] —**fan′ci·ful·ly** *adv*. —**fan′ci·ful·ness** *n*.

**fan·cy** (fan′sē) *n.*, *pl.* **-cies** [contr. < FANTASY] **1.** imagination, now esp. light, whimsical, or capricious imagination **2.** a mental image **3.** an arbitrary idea; notion; caprice; whim **4.** an inclination, liking, or fondness, often temporary [to take a *fancy* to someone] —*adj.* **-ci·er**, **-ci·est 1.** capricious; whimsical; fanciful **2.** extravagant [a *fancy* price] **3.** not plain; decorated, elaborate, ornamental, etc. [a *fancy* necktie] **4.** of superior skill [*fancy* diving] **5.** of superior quality and therefore more expensive **6.** bred for some special feature —*vt.* **-cied**, **-cy·ing 1.** to form an idea of; imagine **2.** to have a liking for **3.** to think or suppose —**fancy** (that)! can you imagine (that)! —**fan′ci·less** *adj*. —**fan′ci·ly** *adv*. —**fan′ci·ness** *n*.

**fan·cy-free** (-frē′) *adj*. **1.** free to fall in love; not married, engaged, etc. **2.** carefree

**fan·cy·work** (-wurk′) *n*. embroidery, crocheting, and other ornamental needlework

**fan·dan·go** (fan daŋ′gō) *n.*, *pl.* **-gos** [Sp.] **1.** a lively Spanish dance in rhythm varying from slow to quick 3/4 time **2.** music for this

**fane** (fān) *n*. [L. *fanum*] [Archaic] a temple or church

**fan·fare** (fan′fer′) *n*. [Fr., prob. < *fanfaron*, braggart] **1.** a loud flourish of trumpets **2.** noisy or showy display

**fang** (faŋ) *n*. [OE. < base of *fon*, to seize] **1.** *a*) one of the long, pointed teeth with which meat-eating animals seize and tear their prey *b*) one of the long, hollow or grooved teeth through which poisonous snakes inject their venom **2.** the pointed part of something —**fanged** (faŋd) *adj*.

FANGS

**fan·light** (fan′līt′) *n*. a semicircular window, often with sash bars in a fanlike arrangement, over a door or larger window

**fan mail** letters of praise or adulation from fans

**Fan·nie, Fan·ny** (fan′ē) [dim. of FRANCES] a feminine name

**fan·tail** (fan′tāl′) *n*. **1.** a part, tail, or end spread out like an opened fan **2.** *Naut*. the part of the main deck at the stern **3.** *Zool*. a variety of domestic pigeon, a breed of goldfish, etc. with a fanlike tail

**fan-tan** (fan′tan′) *n*. [< Chin. *fan*, number of times + *t'an*, apportion] **1.** a Chinese gambling game **2.** a card game in which the players seek to discard all their cards in proper sequence Also **fan tan**

**fan·ta·si·a** (fan tā′zhə, -zē ə; fan′tə zē′ə) *n*. [It. < L.: see FANTASY] **1.** a musical composition of no fixed form **2.** a medley of familiar tunes

**fan·ta·size** (fan′tə sīz′) *vt.*, *vi*. **-sized′**, **-siz′ing** [FANTAS(Y) + -IZE] to create or imagine (something) in a fantasy; have daydreams (about) —**fan′ta·sist** *n*.

**fan·tas·tic** (fan tas′tik) *adj*. [< OFr. < ML. < LL. < Gr. *phantastikos*, able to present to the mind < *phainein*, to show] **1.** imaginary; unreal [*fantastic* terrors] **2.** grotesque; odd; quaint [*fantastic* designs] **3.** extravagant; capricious; eccentric [a *fantastic* plan] **4.** seemingly impossible; incredible [*fantastic* progress] Also **fan·tas′ti·cal** —**fan·tas′ti·cal·ly** *adv*. —**fan·tas′ti·cal·ness** *n*.

**fan·ta·sy** (fan′tə sē, -zē) *n.*, *pl.* **-sies** [OE. < L. < Gr. *phantasia*, appearance < *phainein*, to show] **1.** imagination or fancy; esp., wild, visionary fancy **2.** an unnatural or bizarre mental image **3.** an odd notion; whim; caprice **4.** a highly imaginative poem, play, etc. **5.** *same as* FANTASIA **6.** a daydream or daydreaming, esp. about an unfulfilled desire —*vt.* **-sied**, **-sy·ing** to form fantasies about —*vi.* to indulge in fantasies, as by daydreaming

**FAO** Food and Agriculture Organization (of the UN)

**far** (fär) *adj*. **far′ther**, **far′thest** [OE. *feorr*] **1.** distant in space or time; not near **2.** extending a long way [a far journey] **3.** more distant [the far side of the room] **4.** very different in quality or nature [far from poor] —*adv.* **1.** very distant in space, time, or degree **2.** to or from a great distance in time or position **3.** very much [far better] **4.** to a certain distance or degree [how far did you go?] —*n.* a distant place [to come from far] —**as far as 1.** to the distance, extent, or degree that **2.** [Colloq.] with reference to; as for —**by far** very much: also **far and away** —**far and near** (or **wide**) everywhere —**far be it from me** I would not presume or wish —**far gone** in an advanced state of deterioration —**far out** *same as* FAR-OUT (see below) —**few and far between** scarce; rare —**go far 1.** to cover much extent; last long **2.** to have a strong tendency **3.** to accomplish much —**in so far as** to the extent or degree that —**so far** up to this place, time, or degree —**so far as** to the extent or point that —**so far, so good** up to this point everything is all right —**far′ness** *n*.

**far·ad** (far′ad, -əd) *n*. [after ff.] a unit of capacitance, equal to the amount that permits the storing of one coulomb of charge for each volt of applied potential

**Far·a·day** (far′ə dā′), Michael 1791-1867; Eng. scientist: noted esp. for his work in electricity

**far·a·way** (fär′ə wā′) *adj*. **1.** distant in time or place **2.** dreamy; abstracted [a faraway look]

**farce** (färs) *n*. [Fr. < L. *farcire*, to stuff: early farces were used to fill interludes between acts] **1.** an exaggerated comedy based on broadly humorous, highly unlikely situations **2.** broad humor of the kind found in such plays **3.** a ridiculous display, pretense, etc.

**far·ci·cal** (fär′si k'l) *adj*. of, or having the nature of, a farce; absurd, ridiculous, etc. —**far′ci·cal′i·ty** (-kal′ə tē) *n*. —**far′ci·cal·ly** *adv*.

**far·del** (fär′d'l) *n*. [OFr.] [Archaic] a burden

**fare** (fer) *vi*. **fared**, **far′ing** [OE. *faran*, to go, wander] **1.** [Poet.] to travel; go **2.** to happen; result [how did it fare with him?] **3.** to be in a specified condition; get on [she *fared* well on his trip] **4.** to eat or be given food —*n.* **1.** money paid for a trip in a train, taxi, plane, etc. **2.** a passenger who pays a fare **3.** *a*) food *b*) the usual diet

**Far East** E Asia, including China, Japan, Korea, & Mongolia, &, sometimes, Indochina & Malaya

**fare-thee-well** (fer′*the* wel′) *n*. the highest or ultimate degree: usually in the phrase **to a fare-thee-well**

**fare·well** (fer′wel′; *for adj.* -wel′) *interj*. [FARE (imperative) + WELL²] goodbye —*n.* **1.** parting words; good wishes at parting **2.** a leaving or going away —*adj.* parting; last; final [a farewell gesture]

**far·fel** (fär′f'l) *n*. [Yid. *farfal* < MHG.] noodle dough chopped into small grains, served as in soup

**far-fetched** (fär′fecht′) *adj*. resulting or introduced in a forced, or unnatural, way; strained

**far-flung** (-fluŋ′) *adj*. extending over a wide area

**Far·go** (fär′gō) [after W. *Fargo* of Wells, Fargo & Co., shippers] city in E N.Dak.: pop. 61,000

**fa·ri·na** (fə rē′nə) *n*. [L. < *far*, kind of grain] flour or meal made from cereal grains (esp. whole wheat), potatoes, nuts, etc., eaten as a cooked cereal

**far·i·na·ceous** (far′ə nā′shəs) *adj*. [see prec.] **1.** containing, consisting of, or made from flour or meal **2.** like meal **3.** containing starch

**far·kle·ber·ry** (fär′k'l ber′ē) *n.*, *pl.* **-ries** [< ?] a shrub or small tree of the southern U.S., with black, inedible berries

**farm** (färm) *n*. [< OFr. < ML. *firma*, fixed payment < *firmare*, to lease < L. *firmus*, steadfast] **1.** the letting out, for a fixed amount, of the privilege to collect and keep taxes **2.** a piece of land (with house, barns, etc.) on which crops or animals are raised; orig., such land let out to tenants **3.** any place where certain things are raised [a tract of water for raising fish is a fish *farm*] **4.** *Baseball* a minor-league team owned by or associated with a major-league team: also **farm club** —*vt.* **1.** to cultivate (land) **2.** to collect (taxes) for a fixed amount **3.** to turn over to another for a fee —*vi.* to work on or operate a farm; raise crops or animals on a farm —**farm out** 1. to rent (land, a business, etc.) for a fixed payment 2. to send (work) from a shop, office, etc. to workers on the outside 3. to let out the labor of (a convict, etc.) for a fixed amount 4. *Baseball* to assign to a farm

**farm·er** (fär′mər) *n.* 1. a person who earns his living by farming; esp., one who manages or operates a farm 2. a person who pays for a right, as, formerly, to collect and keep taxes 3. a person who contracts to do something for a fixed price

**farm·hand** (färm′hand′) *n.* a hired farm laborer

**farm·house** (-hous′) *n.* a house on a farm; esp., the main dwelling house on a farm

**farm·ing** (fär′miŋ) *adj.* of or for agriculture —*n.* 1. the business of operating a farm 2. the letting out to farm of land, revenue, etc.

**farm·stead** (färm′sted′) *n.* the land and buildings of a farm

**farm·yard** (-yärd′) *n.* the yard surrounding or enclosed by the farm buildings

**far·o** (fer′ō) *n.* [Fr. *pharaon* < ? *Pharaoh*] a gambling game in which players bet on the cards to be turned up from the top of the dealer's pack

**far-off** (fär′ôf′) *adj.* distant; remote

**fa·rouche** (fa rōōsh′) *adj.* [Fr. < OFr., ult. < L. *foras*, out-of-doors] 1. wild; savage 2. lacking social grace

**far-out** (fär′out′) *adj.* [Colloq.] very advanced, experimental, or nonconformist; esp., avant-garde

**Far·quhar** (fär′kwər, -kər), **George** 1678–1707; Brit. playwright, born in Ireland

**far·ra·go** (fa rä′gō, -rä′-) *n., pl.* **-goes** [L., mixed fodder, mixture < *far:* see FARINA] a confused mixture; jumble —**far·rag′i·nous** (-raj′ə nəs) *adj.*

**Far·ra·gut** (far′ə gət), **David Glasgow** (born *James Glasgow Farragut*) 1801–70; U.S. admiral

**far-reach·ing** (fär′rēch′iŋ) *adj.* having a wide range, extent, influence, or effect

**far·ri·er** (far′ē ər) *n.* [< OFr. < ML. < L. *ferrum*, iron] [Brit.] a blacksmith who shoes horses; also, sometimes, one who treats their diseases —**far′ri·er·y** *n., pl.* **-er·ies**

**far·row** (far′ō) *n.* [< OE. *fearh*, young pig] a litter of pigs —*vt., vi.* to give birth to (a litter of pigs)

**far·see·ing** (fär′sē′iŋ) *adj.* same as FARSIGHTED (senses 1 & 2)

**far·sight·ed** (-sīt′id) *adj.* 1. capable of seeing far 2. prudent in judgment and foresight 3. having better vision for distant objects than for near ones —**far′sight′ed·ly** *adv.* —**far′sight′ed·ness** *n.*

**far·ther** (fär′thər) *adj. compar. of* FAR [ME. *ferther*, var. of *further*, FURTHER] 1. more distant 2. additional; further —*adv. compar. of* FAR 1. at or to a greater distance or more remote point 2. to a greater degree; further 3. in addition; further In sense 2 of the *adj.* and senses 2 and 3 of the *adv.*, FURTHER is more commonly used

**far·ther·most** (-mōst′) *adj.* most distant; farthest

**far·thest** (fär′thist) *adj. superl. of* FAR [ME. *ferthest:* see FARTHER] most distant —*adv. superl. of* FAR 1. at or to the greatest distance or most remote point 2. to the greatest degree

**far·thing** (fär′thiŋ) *n.* [OE. *feorthing*, dim. of *feortha*, fourth] 1. a former small British coin, equal to one fourth of a penny 2. a thing of little value; the least amount

**far·thin·gale** (fär′thiŋ gāl′) *n.* [OFr. *verdugalle* < Sp. < *verdugo*, tree shoot, rod < *verde* < L. *viridis*, green] a hoop skirt worn by women in the 16th and 17th centuries

**fas·ces** (fas′ēz) *n.pl.* [L., pl. of *fascis*, a bundle] a bundle of rods bound about an ax, carried before ancient Roman magistrates as a symbol of authority: later the symbol of Italian fascism

**fas·ci·a** (fash′ē ə, fash′ə) *n., pl.* **-ci·ae′** (-ē′), **-ci·as** [L., a band] 1. a flat strip; band 2. *Anat.* a thin layer of connective tissue —**fas′ci·al** *adj.*

**fas·ci·cle** (fas′i k'l) *n.* [< OFr. < L. dim. of *fascis:* see FASCES] 1. a single section of a book published in installments 2. a small bundle or cluster, as of leaves, stems, etc. —**fas′ci·cled** *adj.*

**fas·cic·u·late** (fə sik′yoo lit, -lāt′) *adj.* [see prec.] formed of, or growing in, bundles or clusters: also **fas·cic′u·lat′ed** (-lāt′id), **fas·cic′u·lar**

**fas·ci·nate** (fas′ə nāt′) *vt.* **-nat′ed, -nat′ing** [< L. pp. of *fascinare*, to bewitch < *fascinum*, an enchanting] 1. orig., to put under a spell 2. to hold motionless, as by inspiring terror 3. to hold the attention of by being very interesting or delightful; charm —**fas′ci·nat′ing·ly** *adv.*

**fas·ci·na·tion** (fas′ə nā′shən) *n.* 1. a fascinating or being fascinated 2. charm; allure

**fas·ci·na·tor** (fas′ə nāt′ər) *n.* 1. a person who fascinates 2. a woman's light scarf, knitted or crocheted: an old-fashioned term

**fas·cism** (fash′iz'm) *n.* [It. *fascismo* < L. *fascis:* see FASCES] 1. [F-] the doctrines, methods, or movement of the Fascisti 2. a system of government characterized by dictatorship, belligerent nationalism, racism, militarism, etc.: first instituted in Italy in 1922 3. fascist behavior

**fas·cist** (-ist) *n.* 1. [F-] *a)* a member of the Fascisti *b)* a member of some similar party; Nazi, Falangist, etc. 2. an adherent of fascism —*adj.* 1. [F-] of Fascists or Fascism 2. of, believing in, or practicing fascism —**fa·scis′tic** (fa shis′tik) *adj.* —**fa·scis′ti·cal·ly** *adv.*

**Fa·scis·ti** (fa shis′tē) *n.pl.* [It., pl. of *fascista*, a Fascist < L. *fascis:* see FASCES] an Italian political organization which seized power and set up a fascist dictatorship (1922-43) under Mussolini

**fash·ion** (fash′ən) *n.* [< OFr. *faceon* < L. *factio:* see FACTION] 1. the make, form, or shape of a thing 2. [Now Rare] kind; sort 3. way; manner 4. the current style of dress, conduct, etc. 5. something in the current style 6. fashionable people [a man of *fashion*] —*vt.* 1. to make or form in a certain way; shape 2. to fit, accommodate (*to*) 3. [Archaic] to contrive —**after** (or **in**) **a fashion** to some extent, but not very well —**fash′ion·er** *n.*

**fash·ion·a·ble** (-ə b'l) *adj.* 1. in fashion; stylish 2. of, characteristic of, or used by people who follow fashion —*n.* a fashionable person —**fash′ion·a·ble·ness** *n.* —**fash′ion·a·bly** *adv.*

**fashion plate** 1. a picture showing a current style in dress 2. a fashionably dressed person

**fast¹** (fast) *adj.* [OE. *fæst*] 1. firm, fixed, or stuck 2. firmly fastened or shut 3. loyal; devoted 4. that will not fade [*fast* colors] 5. swift; quick; speedy 6. permitting swift movement [a *fast* highway] 7. lasting a short time [a *fast* lunch] 8. showing a time that is ahead of the correct time [his watch is *fast*] 9. *a)* reckless; wild [a *fast* crowd] *b)* sexually promiscuous 10. [Colloq.] glib and deceptive [a *fast* talker] 11. [Slang] acting, gotten, done, etc. quickly and often dishonestly [out for a *fast* buck] 12. *Photog.* adapted to very short exposure time 13. [Dial.] complete; sound [a *fast* sleep] —*adv.* 1. firmly; fixedly 2. thoroughly; soundly [*fast* asleep] 3. rapidly; swiftly 4. ahead of time 5. in a reckless, dissipated way; wildly 6. [Obs.] close; near [*fast* by the river] —**a fast one** [Slang] a deceptive act [to pull *a fast one*] —**play fast and loose** to behave with duplicity or insincerity

**fast²** (fast) *vi.* [OE. *fæstan*] 1. to abstain from all or certain foods, as in observing a holy day 2. to eat very little or nothing —*n.* 1. the act of fasting 2. a period of fasting —**break one's fast** to eat food for the first time after fasting

**fast·back** (-bak′) *n.* an automobile contour with an unbroken curve from windshield to rear bumper

**fast day** a holy day, etc. observed by fasting

**fas·ten** (fas′'n) *vt.* [OE. *fæstnian* < base of *fæst*, FAST¹] 1. to join (one thing to another); attach 2. to make secure, as by locking, buttoning, etc. 3. to hold or direct (the attention, etc.) steadily (*on*) 4. to cause to be attributed; impute [to *fasten* a crime on someone] 5. to force (oneself *on* or *upon* another) in an annoying way —*vi.* 1. to become attached or joined 2. to take a firm hold (*on* or *upon*); seize 3. to concentrate (*on* or *upon*) —**fas′ten·er** *n.*

**fas·ten·ing** (-iŋ) *n.* anything used to fasten; bolt, clasp, hook, lock, button, etc.

**fas·tid·i·ous** (fas tid′ē əs, fəs-) *adj.* [< L. < *fastidium*, a loathing < *fastus*, disdain + *taedium:* see TEDIUM] 1. not easy to please; very critical 2. daintily refined; easily disgusted —**fas·tid′i·ous·ly** *adv.* —**fas·tid′i·ous·ness** *n.*

**fast·ness** (fast′nis) *n.* 1. the quality or condition of being fast 2. a secure place; stronghold

**fast time** same as DAYLIGHT-SAVING TIME

**fat** (fat) *adj.* **fat′ter, fat′test** [OE. *fætt*, pp. of *fætan*, to fatten] 1. containing or full of fat; oily; greasy 2. *a)* fleshy; plump *b)* too plump; obese 3. thick; broad 4. fertile; productive [*fat* land] 5. profitable; lucrative [a *fat* job] 6. prosperous 7. plentiful; ample 8. stupid; dull 9. [Slang] large or important [a *fat* role in a play] —*n.* 1. any of various solid or semisolid oily or greasy materials found in animal tissue and in plant seeds 2. fleshiness; corpulence 3. the richest part of anything 4. anything unnecessary that can be trimmed away 5. *Chem.* a class of glyceryl esters of fatty acids, insoluble in water —*vt., vi.* **fat′ted, fat′ting** to make or become fat: now usually FATTEN —**a fat chance** [Slang] very little or no chance —**chew the fat** [Slang] to talk together; chat —**the fat of the land** the best obtainable; great luxury —**fat′ly** *adv.* —**fat′ness** *n.*

**fa·tal** (fāt′'l) *adj.* [OFr. < L. *fatalis* < *fatum*, FATE] 1. fateful; decisive [the *fatal* day arrived] 2. resulting in death **3.** very destructive; most unfortunate —**fa′tal·ly** *adv.* —**fa′tal·ness** *n.*

**fa·tal·ism** (-iz′m) *n.* **1.** the belief that all events are determined by fate and are hence inevitable **2.** acceptance of every event as inevitable —**fa′tal·ist** *n.* —**fa′tal·is′tic** *adj.* —**fa′tal·is′ti·cal·ly** *adv.*

**fa·tal·i·ty** (fə tal′ə tē, fā-) *n., pl.* -**ties 1.** fate or necessity; subjection to fate **2.** something caused by fate **3.** an inevitable liability to disaster **4.** a fatal quality; deadliness *[the fatality of a disease]* **5.** a death caused by a disaster, as in an accident, war, etc.

**fat·back** (fat′bak′) *n.* **1.** fat from a hog's back, usually dried and salted in strips **2.** same as MENHADEN

**fat cat** [Slang] a wealthy, influential person

**fate** (fāt) *n.* [< L. *fatum*, oracle < neut. pp. of *fari*, to speak] **1.** the power or agency supposed to determine the outcome of events; destiny **2.** *a)* something supposedly determined by this power *b)* a person's lot or fortune **3.** final outcome **4.** death; destruction —*vt.* **fat′ed, fat′ing** to destine: now usually in the passive —**the Fates** *Gr. & Rom. Myth.* the three goddesses who control human destiny and life: see CLOTHO, LACHESIS, and ATROPOS

**fat·ed** (fāt′id) *adj.* **1.** destined **2.** doomed

**fate·ful** (-fəl) *adj.* **1.** prophetic **2.** having important consequences; decisive **3.** controlled as if by fate **4.** bringing death or destruction —**fate′ful·ly** *adv.* —**fate′ful·ness** *n.*

**fat·head** (fat′hed′) *n.* [Slang] a stupid person —**fat′head′ed** *adj.*

**fa·ther** (fä′thər) *n.* [OE. *fæder*] **1.** a male parent; esp., a man as he is related to his child **2.** *a)* a stepfather *b)* father-in-law **3.** a guardian or protector **4.** [F-] God, or God as the first person of the Trinity **5.** a forefather; ancestor **6.** an originator; founder; inventor **7.** any of the leaders of a city, assembly, etc.: *usually used in the pl.* **8.** [*often* F-] *a)* any of the important early Christian religious writers *b)* a Christian priest: used esp. as a title —*vt.* **1.** to be the father of; beget **2.** to care for as a father does; protect, rear, etc. **3.** to found, originate, or invent —**fa′ther·hood′** *n.* —**fa′ther·less** *adj.*

**father confessor 1.** a priest who hears confessions **2.** a person in whom one habitually confides

**father image** (or **figure**) a person substituted in one's mind for one's father

**fa·ther-in-law** (-ən lô′) *n., pl.* **fa′thers-in-law′** the father of one's wife or husband

**fa·ther·land** (-land′) *n.* a person's native land or, sometimes, the land of his ancestors

**fa·ther·ly** (-lē) *adj.* of or like a father; kindly; protective —*adv.* [Archaic] in a fatherly manner —**fa′ther·li·ness** *n.*

**Father's Day** the third Sunday in June, a day set aside (in the U.S.) in honor of fathers

**Father Time** time personified as a very old man carrying a scythe and an hourglass

**fath·om** (fath′əm) *n.* [OE. *fæthm*, the two arms outstretched to measure, etc.)] a nautical unit of depth or length, equal to 6 feet —*vt.* **1.** to measure the depth of; sound **2.** to understand thoroughly —**fath′om·a·ble** *adj.* —**fath′om·less** *adj.* —**fath′om·less·ness** *n.*

**Fa·thom·e·ter** (fath äm′ə tər) *a trademark for* a sonar device used to measure depth of oceans, etc. —*n.* [f-] such a device

**fa·tigue** (fə tēg′) *n.* [Fr. < L. *fatigare*, to weary] **1.** physical or mental exhaustion; weariness **2.** *a)* manual labor or menial duty, other than drill or instruction, assigned to soldiers: in full, **fatigue duty** *b)* [*pl.*] sturdy work clothing worn on fatigue duty: also **fatigue clothes** (or **clothing**) **3.** the tendency of a metal or other material to crack under repeated stress —*vt.*, *vi.* -**tigued′**, -**tigu′ing 1.** to make or become tired; weary **2.** to subject to or undergo fatigue —**fat′i·ga·bil′i·ty** *n.* —**fat′i·ga·ble** (fat′i gə b′l) *adj.*

**Fat·i·ma** (fat′i mə, fät′-; fə tē′mə) 606?-632 A.D.; daughter of Mohammed

**fat·ling** (fat′liŋ) *n.* a calf, lamb, kid, or young pig fattened before being slaughtered

**fat·ten** (fat′'n) *vt.*, *vi.* to make or become fat —**fat′ten·er** *n.*

**fat·tish** (-ish) *adj.* somewhat fat

**fat·ty** (-ē) *adj.* -**ti·er**, -**ti·est 1.** of or containing fat **2.** very plump **3.** resembling fat; greasy; oily —*n.* [Colloq.] a fat person —**fat′ti·ness** *n.*

**fatty acid 1.** any of a series of saturated organic acids having the general formula $C_nH_{2n+1}COOH$ **2.** any of a number of saturated or unsaturated organic acids usually having an even number of carbon atoms

**fa·tu·i·ty** (fə tōō′ə tē, -tyōō′-; fa-) *n., pl.* -**ties 1.** complacent stupidity; smug foolishness **2.** a fatuous remark, act, etc. —**fa·tu′i·tous** *adj.*

**fat·u·ous** (fach′oo wəs) *adj.* [L. *fatuus*, foolish] **1.** complacently stupid; foolish **2.** [Archaic] illusory —**fat′u·ous·ly** *adv.* —**fat′u·ous·ness** *n.*

**fau·ces** (fô′sēz) *n.pl.* [L., throat] the passage leading from the back of the mouth into the pharynx —**fau′cal** (-kəl), **fau′cial** (-shəl) *adj.*

**fau·cet** (fô′sit) *n.* [< OFr., prob. < *faulser*, to breach, falsify < LL. < L. *falsus*, FALSE] a device with a valve for regulating the flow of a liquid from a pipe, etc.; cock; tap

**Faulk′ner** (fôk′nər), **William** 1897-1962; U.S. novelist

**fault** (fôlt) *n.* [< OFr. *faulte*, ult. < L. *falsus*, FALSE] **1.** something that mars; flaw; defect **2.** *a)* a misdeed; offense *b)* an error; mistake **3.** responsibility for something wrong; blame *[it's my fault that he's late]* **4.** *Geol.* a fracture or zone of fractures in rock strata along with displacement of the strata **5.** *Tennis, Squash,* etc. an error in service —*vt.* **1.** to find fault with; blame **2.** *Geol.* to cause a fault in —*vi.* **1.** to commit a fault in tennis, etc. **2.** *Geol.* to develop a fault —**at fault** guilty of error; deserving blame —**find fault (with)** to seek and point out faults (of) —**to a fault** excessively

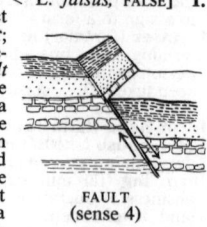
FAULT
(sense 4)

**fault·find·ing** (-fīn′diŋ) *n., adj.* finding fault; calling attention to defects —**fault′find′er** *n.*

**fault·less** (-lis) *adj.* without any fault; perfect —**fault′less·ly** *adv.* —**fault′less·ness** *n.*

**fault·y** (-ē) *adj.* **fault′i·er, fault′i·est** having a fault or faults; imperfect —**fault′i·ly** *adv.* —**fault′i·ness** *n.*

**faun** (fôn) *n.* [< L. < *Faunus,* a Roman nature god] any of a class of minor Roman deities, usually represented as having the body of a man, but the horns, ears, tail, and hind legs of a goat

**fau·na** (fô′nə) *n., pl.* -**nas, -nae** (-nē) [ModL. < LL. *Fauna,* Roman goddess] the animals of a specified region or time —**fau′nal** *adj.*

**Fau·ré** (fô rā′), **Gabriel** 1845-1924; Fr. composer

**Faust** (foust) the hero of a medieval legend, and later literary and operatic works, who sells his soul to the devil to gain knowledge and power: also **Faus′tus** (fôs′təs, fous′-) —**Faust′i·an** *adj.*

**fau·vism** (fō′viz m) *n.* [< Fr. < *fauve,* wild beast] [*often* F-] a French form of expressionist painting characterized by bold distortions and strong, pure color —**fauve** (fōv), **fau′vist** *n., adj.*

**faux pas** (fō′ pä′) *pl.* **faux pas** (fō′ päz′) [Fr., lit., false step] a social blunder; error in etiquette

**fa·vor** (fā′vər) *n.* [< OFr. < L. < *favere,* to favor] **1.** friendly regard; good will **2.** unfair partiality; favoritism **3.** a kind or obliging act **4.** a small gift, souvenir, or token —*vt.* **1.** to regard with favor; approve or like **2.** to be partial to; prefer unfairly **3.** to support; advocate **4.** to make easier; help *[rain favored his escape]* **5.** to do a kindness for **6.** to look like; resemble *[to favor one's mother]* **7.** to use gently; spare *[to favor an injured leg]* —**find favor** to be pleasing —**in favor of 1.** approving; supporting **2.** to the advantage of **3.** payable to, as a check —**in one's favor** to one's advantage —**fa′vor·er** *n.*

**fa·vor·a·ble** (-ə b'l) *adj.* **1.** approving or commending **2.** helpful or advantageous **3.** pleasing or desirable *[a favorable impression]* —**fa′vor·a·ble·ness** *n.* —**fa′vor·a·bly** *adv.*

**fa·vored** (fā′vərd) *adj.* **1.** treated with favor; specially privileged **2.** having (specified) features *[ill-favored]*

**fa·vor·ite** (fā′vər it, fāv′rit) *n.* **1.** a person or thing regarded with special liking; specif., a person granted special privileges, as by a king, etc. **2.** a contestant regarded as most likely to win —*adj.* held in special regard; best liked; preferred

**fa·vor·it·ism** (-iz′m) *n.* **1.** the act of being unfairly partial **2.** the condition of being a favorite

**fa·vour** (fā′vər) *n., vt. Brit. var. of* FAVOR

**Fawkes** (fôks), **Guy** 1570-1606; Eng. conspirator in a plot to blow up the king & Parliament

**fawn¹** (fôn) *vi.* [< OE. *fagnian* < *fagen,* var. of *fægen,* fain] **1.** to show friendliness by licking hands, wagging its tail, etc.: said of a dog **2.** to cringe and flatter —**fawn′er** *n.* —**fawn′ing·ly** *adv.*

**fawn²** (fôn) *n.* [< OFr. *faon,* ult. < L. *fetus,* FETUS] **1.** a young deer less than one year old **2.** a pale, yellowish brown —*adj.* of this color —*vi., vt.* to bring forth (young): said of deer

**Fay, Faye** (fā) [< ? ME. *faie,* FAY or ? ME. *fei,* faith] a feminine name

**fay** (fā) *n.* [< OFr. < VL. < L. *fatum,* FATE] a fairy

**Fay·ette·ville** (fā′ət vil′) [after Marquis de (La)FAYETTE] city in SC N.C.: pop. 60,000

**faze** (fāz) *vt.* **fazed, faz′ing** [< OE. *fesan,* to drive] [Colloq.] to disturb; disconcert

**FBI, F.B.I.** Federal Bureau of Investigation

**FCC, F.C.C.** Federal Communications Commission

**F clef** *same as* BASS CLEF

**FDA, F.D.A.** Food and Drug Administration

**FDIC, F.D.I.C.** Federal Deposit Insurance Corporation

**Fe** [L. *ferrum*] *Chem.* iron

**F.E.A., FEA** Federal Energy Administration

**fe·al·ty** (fē′əl tē) *n., pl.* **-ties** [< OFr. *feauté* < L. *fidelitas,* FIDELITY] **1.** the loyalty owed by a vassal to his feudal lord **2.** [Archaic] loyalty

**fear** (fir) *n.* [OE. *fær,* danger] **1.** anxiety and agitation caused by the presence of danger, evil, pain, etc.; fright **2.** awe; reverence **3.** a feeling of uneasiness or apprehension; concern **4.** a cause for fear —*vt.* **1.** to be afraid of **2.** to feel reverence or awe for **3.** to expect with misgiving [*I fear* I am late] **4.** [Obs.] to frighten —*vi.* **1.** to feel fear **2.** to be uneasy or anxious —**for fear of** in order to avoid or prevent —**fear′less** *adj.* —**fear′less·ly** *adv.* —**fear′less·ness** *n.*

**fear·ful** (-fəl) *adj.* **1.** causing fear; dreadful **2.** feeling fear; afraid **3.** showing fear [*a fearful* look] **4.** [Colloq.] very bad, great, etc. [*a fearful* liar] —**fear′ful·ly** *adv.* —**fear′ful·ness** *n.*

**fear·some** (-səm) *adj.* **1.** causing fear; frightful **2.** frightened; timid —**fear′some·ly** *adv.* —**fear′some·ness** *n.*

**fea·si·ble** (fē′zə b'l) *adj.* [< OFr. < *faire,* to make, do < L. *facere*] **1.** capable of being done or carried out; practicable; possible **2.** within reason; likely; probable **3.** capable of being used successfully; suitable —**fea′si·bil′i·ty** *pl.* **-ties, fea′si·ble·ness** *n.* —**fea′si·bly** *adv.*

**feast** (fēst) *n.* [< OFr. < VL. *festa* < pl. of L. *festum* < *festus,* festal] **1.** a festival; esp., a religious festival **2.** a rich and elaborate meal; banquet **3.** anything that gives pleasure by its abundance or richness —*vi.* **1.** to eat a rich, elaborate meal **2.** to have a special treat —*vt.* **1.** to entertain at a feast or banquet **2.** to delight or gratify [*to feast* one's eyes on a sight] —**feast′er** *n.*

**feat** (fēt) *n.* [< Anglo-Fr. < OFr. < L. *factum,* a deed < pp. of *facere,* to do] an act or deed showing unusual daring, skill, etc.

**feath·er** (feth′ər) *n.* [OE. *fether*] **1.** *Zool.* any of the growths covering the body of a bird and making up a large part of the wing surface **2.** anything like a feather in appearance, lightness, etc. **3.** [*pl.*] *a)* plumage *b)* attire **4.** class; kind [*birds of a feather*] —*vt.* **1.** to provide or adorn as with feathers **2.** to give a featheredge to **3.** to join by inserting a wedge-shaped part into a groove **4.** to turn the edge of (the blade of an oar or propeller) toward the line of movement —*vi.* **1.** to grow feathers **2.** to move, grow, or look like feathers **3.** to feather an oar or propeller —**feather in one's cap** an achievement worthy of pride —**feather one's nest** to provide for one's own comfort or security —**in feather** feathered —**in fine** (or **high** or **good**) **feather** in very good humor, health, or form —**feath′ered** *adj.* —**feath′er·ing** *n.* —**feath′er·less** *adj.*

**feather bed** a strong cloth container thickly filled with feathers or down, used as a mattress

**feath·er·bed·ding** (-bed′iŋ) *n.* the practice of limiting output or requiring extra workers, as by union contract, in order to provide more jobs —**feath′er·bed′** *adj., vi., vt.* **-bed′ded, -bed′ding**

**feath·er·brain** (-brān′) *n.* a silly, foolish, or frivolous person —**feath′er·brained′** *adj.*

**feath·er·edge** (-ej′) *n.* a very thin edge, easily broken or curled —*vt.* **-edged′, -edg′ing** to give such an edge to

**feath·er·stitch** (-stich′) *n.* an embroidery stitch forming a zigzag line —*vt., vi.* to embroider with such a stitch

**feath·er·weight** (-wāt′) *n.* **1.** any person or thing of light weight or small size **2.** a boxer who weighs over 118 but not over 126 pounds **3.** a wrestler who weighs over 123 but not over 134 pounds —*adj.* **1.** of featherweights **2.** light or trivial

**feath·er·y** (-ē) *adj.* **1.** covered with or as with feathers **2.** resembling feathers; soft, light, etc. —**feath′er·i·ness** *n.*

**fea·ture** (fē′chər) *n.* [< OFr. < L. *factura,* a making < pp. of *facere,* to make] **1.** orig., the make, form, or appearance of a person or thing. *a)* [*pl.*] the form or look of the face *b)* any of the parts of the face, as the eyes, nose, mouth, etc. **3.** a distinct or outstanding part or quality of something **4.** a prominently displayed or publicized attraction at an entertainment, sale, etc. **5.** a special story, article, etc. in a newspaper or magazine **6.** a full-length motion picture —*vt.* **-tured, -tur·ing** **1.** to give prominence to; make a feature of **2.** to sketch or show the features of **3.** to be a feature of **4.** [Slang] to conceive of —*vi.* to have a prominent part —**fea′ture·less** *adj.*

FEATHER-STITCH

**fea·tured** (-chərd) *adj.* **1.** having (a specified kind of) facial features [*broad-featured*] **2.** given special prominence as a main attraction

**feaze** (fēz, fāz) *vt.* **feazed, feaz′ing** *var. of* FAZE

**Feb.** February

**feb·ri-** [< L. *febris*] *a combining form meaning* fever [*febrifuge*]

**feb·ri·fuge** (feb′rə fyo͞oj′) *n.* [< Fr.: see FEBRI- & -FUGE] any substance for reducing fever; antipyretic —*adj.* reducing fever

**fe·brile** (fē′brəl, feb′rəl) *adj.* [< Fr. < L. *febris,* fever] of or characterized by fever; feverish

**Feb·ru·ar·y** (feb′roo wer′ē, feb′yoo wer′ē) *n.* [L. *Februarius* < *februa,* Roman festival of purification held Feb. 15] the second month of the year, having 28 days (or 29 days in leap years): abbrev. **Feb., F.**

**fe·cal** (fē′kəl) *adj.* of or consisting of feces

**fe·ces** (fē′sēz) *n.pl.* [< L. *faeces,* dregs] waste matter expelled from the bowels; excrement

**feck·less** (fek′lis) *adj.* [Scot. < *feck* (< EFFECT) + -LESS] **1.** weak; ineffective **2.** careless; irresponsible —**feck′less·ly** *adv.* —**feck′less·ness** *n.*

**fe·cund** (fē′kənd, fek′ənd) *adj.* [< OFr. < L. *fecundus,* fruitful] fruitful or fertile; productive —**fe·cun·di·ty** (fi-kun′də tē) *n.*

**fe·cun·date** (fē′kən dāt′, fek′ən-) *vt.* **-dat′ed, -dat′ing** [< L. pp. of *fecundare* < *fecundus:* see prec.] **1.** to make fecund **2.** to fertilize; impregnate; pollinate —**fe′cun·da′tion** *n.*

**fed¹** (fed) *pt. & pp. of* FEED —**fed up** [Colloq.] having had enough to become disgusted, bored, etc.

**fed²** (fed) *n.* [*often* F-] [Slang] a Federal agent or officer

**Fed.** **1.** Federal. **2.** Federated. **3.** Federation

**fed·a·yeen** (fed′ä yēn′) *n.pl.* [Ar., lit., those who sacrifice themselves] Arab irregulars or guerrillas in the Middle East

**fed·er·al** (fed′ər əl, fed′rəl) *adj.* [< L. *foedus* (gen. *foederis*), a league] **1.** of or formed by a compact; specif., designating or of a union of states, groups, etc. in which each member subordinates its governmental power to a central authority in certain common affairs **2.** designating or of a central government in such a union; specif., [*usually* F-] of the central government of the U.S. **3.** [F-] of the Federalist Party **4.** [F-] of or supporting the U.S. government in the Civil War; Union —*n.* **1.** [F-] a Federalist **2.** [F-] a supporter or soldier of the U.S. government in the Civil War **3.** [F-] a Federal agent or officer —**fed′er·al·ly** *adv.*

**Federal Bureau of Investigation** a branch of the U.S. Department of Justice whose duty is to investigate violations of Federal laws

**Federal Communications Commission** a Federal agency which regulates communication by wire and radio, including licensing of radio and TV stations

**fed·er·al·ism** (-iz′m) *n.* **1.** the federal principle of government or organization **2.** [F-] the principles of the Federalist Party

**fed·er·al·ist** (-ist) *n.* **1.** one who believes in or supports federalism **2.** [F-] a member or supporter of the Federalist Party —*adj.* **1.** of or supporting federalism **2.** [F-] of or supporting the Federalist Party or its principles Also **fed′er·al·is′tic**

**Federalist** (or **Federal**) **Party** a political party in the U.S. (1789–1816) which advocated the adoption of the Constitution and the establishment of a strong, centralized government

**fed·er·al·ize** (fed′ər ə līz′, fed′rə-) *vt.* **-ized′, -iz′ing** **1.** to unite (states, etc.) in a federal union **2.** to put under the authority of a federal government —**fed′er·al·i·za′tion** *n.*

**Federal Reserve Bank** any of the twelve district banks of the Federal Reserve System

**Federal Reserve note** any piece of U.S. paper currency issued by the individual Federal Reserve Banks

**Federal Reserve System** a centralized banking system in the U.S., with supervisory powers over Federal Reserve Banks and about 6,000 member banks

**Federal Trade Commission** a Federal agency whose duty is to investigate and stop unfair methods of competition in business, fraudulent advertising, etc.

**fed·er·ate** (fed′ər it; *for v.* -ə rāt′) *adj.* [< L. pp. of *foederare* < *foedus:* see FEDERAL] united by common agreement under a central government or authority —*vt.,* *vi.* **-at′ed, -at′ing** to unite in a federation

**fed·er·a·tion** (fed′ə rā′shən) *n.* **1.** the act of uniting or of forming a union of states, groups, etc. by agreement of each member to subordinate its power to a central authority in common affairs **2.** an organization formed thus; a federal union, as of states —**fed′er·a′tive** *adj.* —**fed′er·a′tive·ly** *adv.*

**fe·do·ra** (fə dôr′ə) *n.* [Fr. < *Fédora* (1882), play by V. Sardou, Fr. dramatist] a soft felt hat with the crown creased lengthwise and a curved brim

**fee** (fē) *n.* [< Anglo-Fr. *fee* & < OE. *feoh*, cattle, property] **1.** orig., a fief **2.** payment asked or given for professional services, licenses, tuition, etc.; charge **3.** *Law* an inheritance in land: an estate can be held with unrestricted rights of disposition (**fee simple**) or with restrictions as to a specified class of heirs (**fee tail**)

**fee·ble** (fē'b'l) *adj.* **-bler, -blest** [< OFr. < L. *flebilis*, to be wept over < *flere*, to weep] weak; not strong; specif., *a)* infirm [a *feeble* old man] *b)* without force or effectiveness [a *feeble* light] *c)* easily broken; frail [a *feeble* barrier] —**fee'ble·ness** *n.* —**fee'bly** *adv.*

**fee·ble·mind·ed** (-mīn'did) *adj.* mentally retarded: term no longer used in psychology —**fee'ble·mind'ed·ly** *adv.* —**fee'ble·mind'ed·ness** *n.*

**feed** (fēd) *vt.* **fed, feed'ing** [< OE. *fedan* < base of *foda*, food] **1.** to give food to; provide food for **2.** *a)* to provide as food [to *feed* oats to horses] *b)* to serve as food for **3.** to provide something necessary for the growth or existence of; nourish [to *feed* one's anger] **4.** to provide (material to be used up, processed, etc.) [to *feed* coal into a stove] **5.** to provide with material [*feed* the stove] **6.** to provide satisfaction for; gratify [to *feed* one's vanity] —*vi.* **1.** to eat: said chiefly of animals **2.** to flow steadily, as into a machine for use, processing, etc. —*n.* **1.** *a)* food given to animals; fodder *b)* the amount of fodder given at one time **2.** *a)* the material fed into a machine *b)* the part of the machine supplying this material *c)* the supplying of this material **3.** [Colloq.] a meal —**off one's feed** [Slang] lacking appetite; somewhat sick —**feed'er** *n.*

**feed·back** (-bak') *n.* **1.** *Elec.* the transfer of part of the output back to the input: it may be an unwanted effect or one desired, as to reduce distortion **2.** a process in which the result modifies the factors producing the result

**feed bag** a bag filled with grain, fastened over a horse's muzzle for feeding

**feed·stock** (-stäk') *n.* raw material for industrial processing, as petroleum products for making petrochemicals

**feel** (fēl) *vt.* **felt, feel'ing** [OE. *felan*] **1.** to touch; examine by touching or handling **2.** to be aware of through physical sensation [to *feel* rain on the face] **3.** *a)* to experience (an emotion or condition) *b)* to be emotionally moved by **4.** to be aware of mentally **5.** to think or believe, often for emotional reasons —*vi.* **1.** to have physical sensation **2.** to appear to the senses, esp. to the sense of touch [the water *feels* warm] **3.** to have the indicated effect [it *feels* good to be home] **4.** to search by touching; grope (*for*) **5.** to be aware of being [to *feel* sad] **6.** to be moved to sympathy, pity, etc. (*for*) —*n.* **1.** the act of feeling **2.** the sense of touch **3.** the nature of a thing perceived through touch **4.** an emotional sensation **5.** instinctive ability or appreciation [a *feel* for design] —**feel (a person) out** to try cautiously to find out the opinions of (a person) —**feel like** [Colloq.] to have a desire for —**feel one's way** to move cautiously —**feel up to** [Colloq.] to feel capable of

**feel·er** (-ər) *n.* **1.** a person or thing that feels **2.** a specialized organ of touch in an animal or insect, as an antenna **3.** a remark, question, offer, etc. made to feel out another

**feel·ing** (-iŋ) *adj.* sensitive and sympathetic —*n.* **1.** the sense of touch, by which sensations of contact, pressure, temperature, and pain are transmitted through the skin **2.** the ability to experience physical sensation **3.** an awareness; sensation [a *feeling* of pain] **4.** an emotion **5.** [*pl.*] sensitivities; sensibilities [to hurt one's *feelings*] **6.** sympathy or pity **7.** *a)* an opinion or sentiment *b)* a premonition [a *feeling* of doom] **8.** air; atmosphere [the lonely *feeling* of the city] **9.** a natural ability or sensitive appreciation **10.** the emotional quality in a work of art —**feel'ing·ly** *adv.*

**feet** (fēt) *n. pl. of* FOOT —**have one's feet on the ground** to be practical, realistic, etc. —**on one's feet** firmly established —**sit at the feet of** to be an admiring disciple or pupil of —**stand on one's own feet** to be independent —**sweep (or carry) off one's feet 1.** to fill with enthusiasm **2.** to impress deeply

**feign** (fān) *vt.* [< OFr. *feindre* < L. *fingere*, to shape] **1.** to make up (a story, excuse, etc.); fabricate **2.** to make a false show of; pretend —*vi.* to pretend; dissemble —**feigned** *adj.* —**feign'er** *n.* —**feign'ing·ly** *adv.*

**Fei·ning·er** (fī'niŋ ər), **Ly·o·nel** (**Charles Adrian**) (lī'ə n'l) 1871–1956; U.S. painter

**feint** (fānt) *n.* [< Fr. pp. of *feindre*: see FEIGN] **1.** a false show; sham **2.** a pretended blow or attack intended to take the opponent off his guard, as in boxing or fencing —*vi., vt.* to deliver (such a blow or attack)

**feist·y** (fīs'tē) *adj.* **feist'i·er, feist'i·est** [< ME. *fist*, a breaking of wind + -Y²] [Colloq. or Dial.] **1.** lively; energetic **2.** quarrelsome; belligerent

**feld·spar** (feld'spär', fel'-) *n.* [< G. < *feld*, field + *spat(h)*, spar] any of several hard, crystalline minerals made up of aluminum silicates with sodium, potassium, or calcium —**feld·spath'ic** (-spa'thik), **feld·spath'ose** (-späth'ōs) *adj.*

**Fe·li·ci·a** (fə lish'ē ə) [fem. of FELIX] a feminine name

**fe·lic·i·tate** (fə lis'ə tāt') *vt.* **-tat'ed, -tat'ing** [< L. pp. of *felicitare* < *felix*, happy] to wish happiness to —**fe·lic'i·ta'tion** *n.* —**fe·lic'i·ta'tor** *n.*

**fe·lic·i·tous** (-təs) *adj.* [< ff. + -OUS] **1.** used or expressed in a way suitable to the occasion; appropriate **2.** having the knack of appropriate and pleasing expression —**fe·lic'i·tous·ly** *adv.* —**fe·lic'i·tous·ness** *n.*

**fe·lic·i·ty** (-tē) *n., pl.* **-ties** [< OFr. < L. < *felix* (gen. *felicis*), happy] **1.** happiness; bliss **2.** anything producing happiness **3.** a quality of appropriate and pleasing expression in writing, speaking, etc. **4.** an apt expression or thought

**fe·line** (fē'līn) *adj.* [< L. < *felis*, cat] **1.** of a cat or the cat family **2.** catlike; esp., *a)* sly, stealthy, etc. *b)* sleekly graceful —*n.* any animal of the cat family, including the cat, lion, panther, tiger, etc. —**fe'line·ly** *adv.* —**fe'line·ness, fe·lin·i·ty** (fi lin'ə tē) *n.*

**Fe·lix** (fē'liks) [L., lit., happy] a masculine name

**fell¹** (fel) *pt. of* FALL

**fell²** (fel) *vt.* [OE. *fellan*] **1.** to make fall; knock down **2.** to cut down (a tree) **3.** to turn over (the rough edge of a seam) and sew down flat on the underside —*n.* **1.** the trees cut down in one season **2.** a felled seam —**fell'a·ble** *adj.* —**fell'er** *n.*

**fell³** (fel) *adj.* [< OFr. < ML. *fello:* see FELON¹] **1.** fierce; terrible; cruel **2.** [Archaic] causing death; deadly [a *fell* plague] —**fell'ness** *n.*

**fell⁴** (fel) *n.* [OE. *fel*] an animal's hide or skin

**fell⁵** (fel) *n.* [< Scand.] [Brit.] a moor; down

**fel·lah** (fel'ə) *n., pl.* **fel'lahs;** Ar. **fel·la·heen, fel·la·hin** (fel'ə hēn') [< Ar. < *falāha*, to plow] a peasant or farm laborer in Egypt or some other countries where Arabic is spoken

**fel·loe** (fel'ō) *n. same as* FELLY

**fel·low** (fel'ō, -ə) *n.* [< Late OE. *feolaga*, partner < *feoh* (see FEE) + *laga*, a laying down] **1.** a companion; associate **2.** one of the same class or rank; equal **3.** either of a pair of corresponding things; mate **4.** a graduate student holding a fellowship in a university or college **5.** a member of a learned society **6.** at some British and U.S. universities, a member of the governing body **7.** [Colloq.] *a)* a man or boy *b)* a person; one [a *fellow* must eat] **8.** [Colloq.] a suitor; beau —*adj.* having the same ideas, position, work, etc.; associated [*fellow* workers]

**fel·low·ship** (-ship') *n.* **1.** companionship; friendly association **2.** a mutual sharing, as of activity, etc. **3.** a group of people with the same interests **4.** an endowment, or a sum of money paid from it, for the support of a graduate student, scholar, etc. doing advanced study **5.** the rank or position of a fellow in a university or college

**fellow traveler** a person who espouses the cause of a party without being a member

**fel·ly** (fel'ē) *n., pl.* **-lies** [OE. *felg*] the rim of a spoked wheel, or a segment of the rim

**fel·on¹** (fel'ən) *n.* [< OFr. < ML. *felo*, earlier *fello* < ?] *Law* a person guilty of a major crime; criminal —*adj.* [Poet.] wicked; base

**fel·on²** (fel'ən) *n.* [< ? same base as prec.] a painful, pus-producing infection near the nail of a finger or toe

**fe·lo·ni·ous** (fə lō'nē əs) *adj.* **1.** [Poet.] wicked; base **2.** *Law* of, like, or constituting a felony —**fe·lo'ni·ous·ly** *adv.* —**fe·lo'ni·ous·ness** *n.*

**fel·o·ny** (fel'ə nē) *n., pl.* **-nies** [< OFr. < ML. < *felo*, FELON¹] a major crime, as murder, arson, rape, etc., for which statute provides a greater punishment than for a misdemeanor

**fel·spar** (fel'spär') *n. same as* FELDSPAR

**felt¹** (felt) *n.* [OE.] **1.** a fabric of wool, often mixed with fur, cotton, rayon, etc., the fibers being worked together by pressure, heat, chemical action, etc.: also **felt'ing 2.** anything like felt, with a fuzzy, springy surface **3.** anything made of felt —*adj.* made of felt —*vt.* **1.** *a)* to make into felt *b)* to cover with felt **2.** to mat (fibers) together —*vi.* to become matted together

**felt²** (felt) *pt. and pp. of* FEEL

**fe·luc·ca** (fə luk'ə, -loo'kə) *n.* [< It. *feluca*, prob. < Ar.] a small, narrow ship propelled by oars or lateen sails, used esp. in the Mediterranean

**fem.** feminine

**fe·male** (fē'māl) *adj.* [< OFr. < L. dim. of *femina*, a woman] **1.** designating or of the sex that produces ova and bears offspring **2.** of, like, or suitable to members of this sex; feminine **3.** of women or girls **4.** having a hollow part shaped to receive a corresponding inserted part (called *male*): said of electric sockets, etc. **5.** *Bot.* having a pistil and no stamen —*n.* a female person, animal, or plant —**fe'male·ness** *n.*

**fem·i·nine** (fem'ə nin) *adj.* [< OFr. < L. < *femina*, woman] **1.** of women or girls **2.** having qualities regarded as characteristic of women and girls, as delicacy, etc. **3.** suitable to or characteristic of a woman **4.** effeminate: said of a man **5.** *Gram.* designating or of the gender of words referring to females or things orig. regarded as female **6.** *Prosody* designating or of a rhyme of two or three syllables with only the first stressed (Ex.: danger, stranger) —*n. Gram.* **1.** the feminine gender **2.** a word or form in this gender —**fem′i·nine·ly** *adv.* —**fem′i·nin′i·ty, fem′i·nine·ness** *n.*

**fem·i·nism** (fem′ə niz'm) *n.* **1.** the principle that women should have political, economic, and social rights equal to those of men **2.** the movement to win these rights —**fem′-i·nist** *n., adj.* —**fem′i·nis′tic** *adj.*

**fem·i·nize** (fem′ə niz′) *vt., vi.* **-nized′, -niz′ing** to make or become feminine or effeminate —**fem′i·ni·za′tion** *n.*

**femme** (fem; *Fr.* fàm) *n., pl.* **femmes** (femz; *Fr.* fàm) [Fr.] [Slang] a woman or wife

**fe·mur** (fē′mər) *n., pl.* **fe′murs, fem·o·ra** (fem′ər ə) [ModL. < L., thigh] *same as* THIGHBONE —**fem′o·ral** *adj.*

**fen¹** (fen) *n.* [OE.] an area of low, flat, marshy land; swamp; bog —**fen′ny** *adj.*

**fen²** (fen) *n. see* MONETARY UNITS, table (China)

**fe·na·gle** (fə nā′g'l) *vi., vt.* **-gled, -gling** *same as* FINAGLE —**fe·na′gler** *n.*

**fence** (fens) *n.* [ME. *fens*, short for *defens*, DEFENSE] **1.** a barrier of posts, wire, rails, etc., used as a boundary or means of protection or confinement **2.** the art of self-defense with foil, saber, etc.; fencing **3.** *a)* one who buys and sells stolen goods *b)* a place for such dealings —*vt.* **fenced, fenc′ing 1.** to enclose, restrict, etc. with a fence (with *in, off,* etc.) **2.** to keep (*out*) by or as by a fence —*vi.* **1.** to practice the art of fencing **2.** to avoid giving a direct reply; be evasive (*with*) **3.** to buy or sell stolen goods —**mend** (one's) **fences** to engage in politicking: said esp. of a legislator —**on the fence** not taking one side or the other; uncommitted —**fence′less** *adj.* —**fenc′er** *n.*

**fenc·ing** (fen′siŋ) *n.* **1.** the art of fighting with a foil or other sword **2.** *a)* material for making fences *b)* a system of fences

**fend** (fend) *vt.* [ME. *fenden*, short for *defenden*, DEFEND] [Archaic] to defend —*vi.* to resist; parry —**fend for oneself** to get along without help from others —**fend off** to ward off; turn aside

**fend·er** (fen′dər) *n.* anything that fends off or protects something else; specif., *a)* any of the metal frames over the wheels of an automobile or other vehicle to protect against splashing mud, etc. *b)* a device on the front of a streetcar or locomotive to catch or push aside anything on the track *c)* a screen or guard placed in front of a fireplace

**fen·es·tra·tion** (fen′ə strā′shən) *n.* [ult. < L. *fenestra*, window] **1.** the arrangement of windows and doors in a building **2.** the surgical operation of making an opening into the inner ear in certain cases of otosclerosis

**Fe·ni·an** (fē′nē ən, fēn′yən) *n.* [< pl. of Ir. Gael. *Fiann*, the old militia of Ireland] a member of a secret Irish revolutionary group formed in New York about 1858 to free Ireland from English rule —*adj.* of the Fenians —**Fe′ni·an·ism** *n.*

**fen·nel** (fen′'l) *n.* [< OE. < L. *feniculum*, dim. of *fenum*, hay] a tall herb of the parsley family, with yellow flowers: its aromatic seeds are used as a seasoning and in medicine

**feoff** (fef, fēf) *vt.* [< Anglo-Fr. < OFr. < *fieu*, fief] to give or sell a fief to —*n.* a fief —**feoff′ment** *n.* —**feof′for, feoff′-er** *n.*

**FEP** Fair Employment Practice(s)

**-fer** (fər) [< Fr. or L. < *ferre*, BEAR¹] *a suffix meaning* bearer, producer [*conifer*]

**fe·ral** (fir′əl) *adj.* [< L. < *ferus*, fierce + -AL] **1.** untamed; wild **2.** savage; brutal

**fer-de-lance** (fer′də läns′) *n.* [Fr., iron tip of a lance] a large, poisonous pit viper, related to the rattlesnake, found in tropical America

**Fer·di·nand** (fur′d'n and′) [Fr., prob. < Gmc. bases meaning "bold in peace"] **1.** a masculine name **2. Ferdinand V** 1452-1516; king of Castile (1474-1504): husband of ISABELLA I

**fer·ma·ta** (fer mät′ə) *n.* [It. < *fermare*, to stop] **1.** the holding of a tone or rest beyond its written value, at the performer's discretion **2.** the sign (⌒) or (⌣) indicating this

**fer·ment** (fur′ment; *for v.* fər ment′) *n.* [< OFr. < L. *fermentum* < *fervere*, to boil] **1.** a substance or organism causing fermentation, as yeast, bacteria, etc. **2.** *same as* FERMENTATION **3.** a state of excitement or agitation —*vt.* **1.** to cause fermentation in **2.** to excite; agitate —*vi.* **1.** to be in the process of fermentation **2.** to be excited or agitated —**fer·ment′a·ble** *adj.*

**fer·men·ta·tion** (fur′mən tā′shən, -men-) *n.* **1.** the breakdown of complex molecules in organic compounds, caused by a ferment [bacteria curdle milk by *fermentation*]

**2.** excitement; agitation —**fer·ment·a·tive** (fər men′tə tiv) *adj.*

**Fer·mi** (fer′mē), **En·ri·co** (en rē′kō) 1901-54; It. nuclear physicist, in the U.S. after 1938

**fer·mi·um** (fer′mē əm) *n.* [after prec.] a radioactive chemical element: symbol, Fm; at. wt., 257(?); at. no., 100

**fern** (furn) *n.* [OE. *fearn*] any of a widespread class of nonflowering plants having roots, stems, and fronds, and reproducing by spores instead of by seeds —**fern′y** *adj.*

**fern·er·y** (fur′nər ē) *n., pl.* **-er·ies** a place where ferns are grown; collection of growing ferns

**fe·ro·cious** (fə rō′shəs) *adj.* [< L. *ferox* (gen. *ferocis*) < *ferus*, fierce + -OUS] **1.** fierce; savage; violently cruel **2.** [Colloq.] very great [a *ferocious* appetite] —**fe·ro′cious·ly** *adv.* —**fe·ro′cious·ness** *n.*

**fe·roc·i·ty** (fə räs′ə tē) *n., pl.* **-ties** wild force or cruelty; ferociousness

**-fer·ous** (fər əs) [L. *-fer* < *ferre*, BEAR¹ + -OUS] *a suffix meaning* bearing, producing [*coniferous*]

**fer·ret** (fer′it) *n.* [< OFr. < LL. dim. of *furo* < L. *fur*, thief] a small, weasellike animal, easily tamed and used for hunting rabbits, rats, etc. —*vt.* **1.** to force out of hiding as with a ferret **2.** to search for persistently and discover (facts, etc.); search (*out*) —*vi.* **1.** to hunt with ferrets **2.** to search around —**fer′ret·er** *n.*

**fer·ri-** *a combining form meaning* containing ferric iron: see FERRO-

**fer·ric** (fer′ik) *adj.* [FERR(O)- + -IC] **1.** of, containing, or derived from iron **2.** *Chem.* designating or of iron with a valence of three, or compounds containing such iron

**Fer·ris wheel** (fer′is) [after G. Ferris (1859-1896), U.S. engineer who invented it] a large, upright wheel revolving on a fixed axle and having seats hanging from the frame: used as an amusement ride

**fer·ro-** [< L. *ferrum*, iron] *a combining form meaning:* **1.** iron [*ferromagnetic*] **2.** iron and [*ferromanganese*] **3.** containing ferrous iron

**fer·ro·con·crete** (fer′ō kän′krēt, -kän krēt′) *n. same as* REINFORCED CONCRETE

**fer·ro·mag·net·ic** (-mag net′ik) *adj.* designating a material, as iron, nickel, or cobalt, having a high magnetic permeability —**fer′ro·mag′net·ism** *n.*

**fer·ro·man·ga·nese** (-maŋ′gə nēs′, -nēz′) *n.* an alloy of iron and manganese, used for making hard steel

**fer·rous** (fer′əs) *adj.* [< L. *ferrum*, iron + -OUS] **1.** of, containing, or derived from iron **2.** *Chem.* designating or of iron with a valence of two, or compounds containing it

**fer·ru·gi·nous** (fə rōō′ji nəs) *adj.* [< L. < *ferrugo*, iron rust < *ferrum*, iron] **1.** of, containing, or having the nature of, iron **2.** having the color of iron rust; reddish-brown

**fer·rule** (fer′əl, -ool) *n.* [< OFr. < L. *viriola*, dim. of *viriae*, bracelets] a metal ring or cap put around the end of a cane, tool handle, etc. to give added strength —*vt.* **-ruled, -rul·ing** to furnish with a ferrule

**fer·ry** (fer′ē) *vt.* **-ried, -ry·ing** [OE. *ferian*, to carry] **1.** to take across a river, etc. in a boat **2.** to cross (a river, etc.) on a ferry **3.** to deliver (airplanes) by flying to the destination —*vi.* to cross a river, etc. by ferry —*n., pl.* **-ries 1.** a system for carrying people, cars, etc. across a river, etc. by boat **2.** a boat [*fer′ry·boat′*] used for this, or the place where it docks on either shore **3.** the delivery of airplanes to their destination by flying them —**fer′ry·man** *n., pl.* **-men**

**fer·tile** (fur′t'l; *chiefly Brit.* -tīl) *adj.* [< OFr. < L. *fertilis* < stem of *ferre*, BEAR¹] **1.** producing abundantly; rich in resources or invention; fruitful **2.** able to produce young, seeds, fruit, etc. **3.** capable of developing into a new individual; fertilized —**fer′tile·ly** *adv.* —**fer′tile·ness** *n.*

**fer·til·i·ty** (fər til′ə tē) *n.* the quality, state, or degree of being fertile; fecundity

**fer·til·ize** (fur′t'l īz′) *vt.* **-ized′, -iz′ing 1.** to make fertile; make fruitful or productive **2.** to spread fertilizer on **3.** to make (the female reproductive cell or female individual) fruitful by introducing the male germ cell; impregnate —**fer′til·iz′a·ble** *adj.* —**fer′til·i·za′tion** *n.*

**fer·til·iz·er** (-ī′zər) *n.* one that fertilizes; specif., manure, chemicals, etc. put in soil to improve the quality or quantity of plant growth

**fer·ule** (fer′əl, -ool) *n.* [L. *ferula*, rod] a flat stick or ruler used for punishing children —*vt.* **-uled, -ul·ing** to strike with a ferule

**fer·vent** (fur′vənt) *adj.* [< L. prp. of *fervere*, to glow, boil] **1.** hot; burning; glowing **2.** having or showing great warmth of feeling; intensely earnest —**fer′ven·cy** (-vən sē) *n.* —**fer′vent·ly** *adv.*

**fer·vid** (fur′vəd) *adj.* [< L. < *fervere*: see prec.] **1.** hot; glowing **2.** impassioned; fervent; ardent —**fer′vid·ly** *adv.* —**fer′vid·ness** *n.*

**fer·vor** (fur′vər) *n.* [< OFr. < L. < *fervere*: see FERVENT] 1. intense heat 2. great warmth of emotion; ardor; zeal Brit. sp. **fer′vour**

**fes·cue** (fes′kyōō) *n.* [< OFr. < L. *festuca*, a straw] a tough grass used for pasture or lawns

**fess, fesse** (fes) *n.* [< OFr. < L. *fascia*, a band] *Heraldry* a horizontal band forming the middle third of an escutcheon

**-fest** (fest) [< G. *fest*, a celebration < L. *festum*, feast] *an informal combining form meaning* an occasion of much [*funfest*]

**fes·tal** (fes′t'l) *adj.* [< L. *festum*, feast] of or like a joyous celebration; festive —**fes′tal·ly** *adv.*

**fes·ter** (fes′tər) *n.* [< OFr. < L. *fistula*, ulcer] a small sore filled with pus —*vi.* 1. to form pus 2. to cause irritation; rankle 3. to decay —*vt.* 1. to cause pus to form in 2. to make rankle

**fes·ti·val** (fes′tə v'l) *n.* [< OFr. < ML. < L. *festivus*: see ff.] 1. a time or day of feasting or celebration 2. a celebration or series of performances of a certain kind [a Bach *festival*] 3. merrymaking; festivity —*adj.* of, for, or fit for a festival

**fes·tive** (fes′tiv) *adj.* [< L. *festivus* < *festum*, feast] of or for a feast or festival; merry; joyous —**fes′tive·ly** *adv.* —**fes′tive·ness** *n.*

**fes·tiv·i·ty** (fes tiv′ə tē) *n., pl.* **-ties** 1. merrymaking; gaiety 2. *a*) a festival *b*) [*pl.*] festive proceedings; things done in celebration

**fes·toon** (fes tōōn′) *n.* [< Fr. < It. *festone* < *festa*, feast] 1. a garland of flowers, leaves, etc. hanging in a loop or curve 2. any molding or decoration like this —*vt.* to adorn with, form into, or join by festoons —**fes·toon′er·y** *n.*

**fet·a** (cheese) (fet′ə) [< ModGr. < It. *fetta*, a slice, ult. < L. *offa*, a piece] a white, soft cheese made in Greece from ewe's milk or goat's milk

**fe·tal** (fēt′'l) *adj.* of or like a fetus

**fetch** (fech) *vt.* [OE. *feccan*] 1. to go after and come back with; bring; get 2. to cause to come; produce 3. to draw (a breath) or heave (a sigh, groan, etc.) 4. to bring as a price; sell for 5. [Colloq.] to attract; charm 6. [Colloq.] to deliver or deal (a blow, etc.) —*vi.* to go after things and bring them back —*n.* 1. a fetching 2. a trick; dodge —**fetch up** 1. [Colloq.] to reach; stop 2. [Dial.] to raise (a child, pet, etc.)

**fetch·ing** (-iŋ) *adj.* attractive; charming —**fetch′ing·ly** *adv.*

**fete, fête** (fāt) *n.* [Fr. < OFr.: see FEAST] a festival; entertainment, esp. one held outdoors —*vt.* **fet′ed** or **fêt′ed,** **fet′ing** or **fêt′ing** to celebrate or honor with a fete; entertain

**fet·id** (fet′id, fēt′-) *adj.* [< L. *f(o)etidus* < *f(o)etere,* to stink] having a bad smell, as of decay; stinking —**fet′id·ly** *adv.* —**fet′id·ness** *n.*

**fet·ish** (fet′ish, fēt′-) *n.* [< Fr. < Port. *feitiço,* a charm < L. *facticius,* FACTITIOUS] 1. any object believed by superstitious people to have magical power 2. any thing or activity to which one is irrationally devoted 3. *Psychiatry* any nonsexual object that evokes fetishism Also sp. **fet′ich**

**fet·ish·ism** (-iz′m) *n.* 1. worship of or belief in fetishes 2. *Psychiatry* an abnormal condition in which erotic feelings are excited by a nonsexual object, as a foot, glove, etc. Also sp. **fet′ich·ism** —**fet′ish·ist** *n.* —**fet′ish·is′tic** *adj.*

**fet·lock** (fet′läk′) *n.* [ME. *fitlok* < MDu. or MLowG.] 1. a tuft of hair on the back of the leg of a horse, donkey, etc., just above the hoof 2. the joint or projection bearing this tuft

**fet·ter** (fet′ər) *n.* [OE. *feter* < base of *fot,* foot] 1. a shackle or chain for the feet 2. anything that holds in check; restraint —*vt.* 1. to bind with fetters; shackle; chain 2. to hold in check; restrain

**fet·tle** (fet′'l) *vt.* **-tled, -tling** [ME. *fetlen,* to make ready, prob. < OE. *fetel,* belt] [Dial.] to arrange —*n.* condition of body and mind [in fine *fettle*]

**fe·tus** (fēt′əs) *n., pl.* **-tus·es** [L., a bringing forth] the unborn young of an animal while still in the uterus or egg, esp. in its later stages: cf. EMBRYO

**feud**[1] (fyōōd) *n.* [OFr. *faide* < Frank. *faida*] a bitter, long-continued, and deadly quarrel, esp. between clans or families —*vi.* to carry on a feud; quarrel —**feu′dal** *adj.* —**feud′ist** *n.*

**feud**[2] (fyōōd) *n.* [< ML. *feodum* < OHG. *feho,* cattle + *od,* wealth] land held from a feudal lord in return for service; fief

**feu·dal** (fyōōd′'l) *adj.* 1. of a feud (land) 2. of or like feudalism —**feu′dal·ly** *adv.*

**feu·dal·ism** (-iz′m) *n.* the economic, political, and social system (**feudal system**) in medieval Europe, in which land, worked by serfs who were bound to it, was held by vassals in exchange for military and other services given to overlords —**feu′dal·ist** *n.* —**feu′dal·is′tic** *adj.*

**feu·da·to·ry** (fyōō′də tôr′ē) *n., pl.* **-ries** 1. a feudal vassal 2. a feudal estate; fief —*adj.* 1. of the feudal relationship between vassal and lord 2. owing feudal allegiance (*to*)

**fe·ver** (fē′vər) *n.* [< OE. *fefer* & OFr. *fievre,* both < L. *febris*] 1. a state of abnormally increased body temperature, often accompanied by a quickened pulse, delirium, etc. 2. any of various diseases characterized by a high fever 3. a condition of nervousness —*vt.* to cause fever in —**fe′vered** *adj.*

**fever blister** (or **sore**) *same as* HERPES SIMPLEX

**fe·ver·few** (-fyōō′) *n.* [< OE., ult. < L. *febris,* fever + *fugia* < *fugare,* to drive away] a bushy plant of the composite family, with small, white heads of flowers

**fe·ver·ish** (-ish) *adj.* 1. having fever, esp. slight fever 2. of, like, or caused by fever 3. causing fever 4. greatly excited or agitated Also **fe′ver·ous** —**fe′ver·ish·ly** *adv.* —**fe′ver·ish·ness** *n.*

**few** (fyōō) *adj.* [OE. *feawe, pl.*] not many; a small number of —*pron., n.* not many; a small number —**quite a few** [Colloq.] a rather large number —**the few** a small select group —**few′ness** *n.*

**fey** (fā) *adj.* [OE. *fæge,* fated] 1. [Archaic or Scot.] *a*) fated to die *b*) highly excited 2. strange, as in being eccentric, puckish, visionary, etc.

**fez** (fez) *n., pl.* **fez′zes** [Fr. < Turk. < *Fez,* city in Morocco] a conical felt hat, usually red, with a black tassel hanging from its flat crown: formerly the Turkish national headdress of men

**ff.** 1. folios 2. following (pages, lines, entry, etc.) 3. fortissimo

**FHA** Federal Housing Administration

**fi·an·cé** (fē′än sā′, fē än′sā) *n.* [Fr., pp. of *fiancer* < OFr. *fiance,* a promise] the man to whom a woman is engaged to be married

**fi·an·cée** (fē′än sā′, fē än′sā) *n.* [Fr., fem. pp. of *fiancer:* see prec.] the woman to whom a man is engaged to be married

FEZ

**fi·as·co** (fē as′kō) *n., pl.* **-coes, -cos** [Fr. < It. (*far*) *fiasco,* to fail < *fiasco,* bottle] a complete failure; esp., an ambitious project that ends as a ridiculous failure

**fi·at** (fī′at, -ət) *n.* [L., let it be done] 1. an order issued by legal authority; decree 2. a sanction; authorization 3. any arbitrary order

**fiat money** paper currency made legal tender by law or fiat, although not backed by gold or silver and not necessarily redeemable in coin

**fib** (fib) *n.* [? ult. < *fable*] a lie about something unimportant —*vi.* **fibbed, fib′bing** to tell such a lie or lies —**fib′ber** *n.*

**fi·ber, fi·bre** (fī′bər) *n.* [< L. *fibra*] 1. *a*) a slender, threadlike structure that combines with others to form animal or vegetable tissue *b*) the tissue so formed [muscle *fiber*] 2. *a*) any substance that can be separated into threadlike structures for weaving, etc. *b*) such a threadlike structure 3. a threadlike root 4. the texture of something 5. character or nature [a man of strong moral *fiber*] —**fi′ber·like′** *adj.*

**fi·ber·board** (-bôrd′) *n.* a flexible boardlike material made from pressed fibers of wood, etc., used in building

**Fi·ber·glas** (-glas′) *a trademark for* finespun filaments of glass made into textiles, used as insulation, etc. —*n.* [f-] this substance: usually **fiberglass, fiber glass,** or **fiber-glass**

**fi·bril** (fī′brəl) *n.* 1. a small fiber 2. a root hair —**fi′bril·lar** (-brə lər), **fi′bril·lar′y** (-brə ler′ē) *adj.* —**fi′bril·lose′** (-brə lōs′) *adj.*

**fi·bril·la·tion** (fib′rə lā′shən, fī′brə-) *n.* [< FIBRIL + -ATION] a rapid series of contractions of the heart, causing weak and irregular heartbeats

**fi·brin** (fī′brən) *n.* [FIBR(E) + -IN¹] an elastic, threadlike, insoluble protein formed in the clotting of blood —**fi′brin·ous** *adj.*

**fi·bro-** [< L. *fibra,* fiber] *a combining form meaning* of fibrous matter or tissue: also, before a vowel, **fibr-**

**fi·broid** (fī′broid) *adj.* [FIBR(O)- + -OID] like, composed of, or forming fibrous tissue [*fibroid* tumors]

**fi·bro·sis** (fī brō′sis) *n.* [FIBR(O)- + -OSIS] an abnormal increase in the amount of fibrous connective tissue in an organ or tissue —**fi·brot′ic** (-brät′ik) *adj.*

**fi·brous** (fī′brəs) *adj.* 1. containing or composed of fibers 2. like fiber

**fib·u·la** (fib′yoo lə) *n., pl.* **-lae′** (-lē′), **-las** [L., a clasp] 1. the long, thin, outer bone of the human leg below the knee 2. a similar bone in the hind leg of other animals —**fib′u·lar** *adj.*

**-fic** (fik) [< Fr. < *-fique* < L. *-ficus* < *facere,* to make] *a suffix meaning* making, creating [*terrific*]

**FICA** Federal Insurance Contributions Act

**-fi·ca·tion** (fi kā′shən) [< Fr. & L., ult. < L. *facere,* to make] *a suffix meaning* a making, creating, causing [*glorification*]

**fich·u** (fish′ōō) *n.* [Fr.] a three-cornered lace or muslin cape for women, worn with the ends fastened or crossed in front

**fick·le** (fik′'l) *adj.* [OE. *ficol*] changeable or unstable in affection, interest, etc. —**fick′le·ness** *n.*

**fic·tion** (fik'shən) *n.* [< OFr. < L. *fictio*, a making < pp. of *fingere*, to form, mold] **1.** anything made up or imagined, as a statement, story, etc. **2.** *a)* any literary work portraying imaginary characters and events, as a novel, story, or play *b)* such works collectively **3.** *Law* something accepted as fact for convenience, although not necessarily true —**fic'tion·al, fic'tive** *adj.* —**fic'tion·al·ly** *adv.*

**fic·tion·al·ize** (-'l īz') *vt.* **-ized', -iz'ing** to deal with (historical events, etc.) as fiction: also **fic'tion·ize'** —**fic'tion·al·i·za'tion** *n.*

**fic·ti·tious** (fik tish'əs) *adj.* **1.** of or like fiction; imaginary **2.** not real; pretended **3.** assumed for disguise or deception [a *fictitious* name] —**fic·ti'tious·ly** *adv.* —**fic·ti'tious·ness** *n.*

**fid** (fid) *n.* [< ?] **1.** a hard, tapering pin for separating the strands of rope in splicing **2.** a bar or pin for supporting something; specif., a square bar for supporting a topmast

**-fid** (fid) [< L. < *findere*, to cleave] *a combining form meaning* split or separated into parts

**fid·dle** (fid''l) *n.* [OE. *fithele*] any stringed instrument played with a bow, esp. the violin —*vt.* **-dled, -dling** [Colloq.] to play (a tune) on a fiddle —*vi.* **1.** [Colloq.] to play on a fiddle **2.** to tamper or tinker (*with*), esp. in a nervous way —**fiddle around** [Colloq.] to pass time aimlessly —**fiddle away** to waste (time) —**fit as a fiddle** in excellent health —**fid'dler** *n.*

**fiddler (crab)** a small, burrowing crab, the male of which has one claw much larger than the other

**fid·dle·stick** (fid''l stik') *n.* **1.** the bow for a fiddle **2.** a trifle; mere nothing

**fid·dle·sticks** (-stiks') *interj.* nonsense!

**fi·del·i·ty** (fə del'ə tē, fī-) *n., pl.* **-ties** [< OFr. < L. < *fides*, FAITH] **1.** faithful devotion to duty, obligations, or vows **2.** accuracy of a description, translation, sound reproduction, etc.

FIDDLER CRAB
(width to 1 2/3 in.; length to 1 in.)

**fidg·et** (fij'it) *n.* [< ? ON. *fikja*] **1.** a being restless, nervous, or uneasy **2.** a fidgety person —*vi.* to move about in a restless, nervous, or uneasy way —*vt.* to make restless or uneasy —**the fidgets** restless, uneasy feelings or movements —**fidg'et·i·ness** *n.* —**fidg'et·y** *adj.*

**fi·du·ci·ar·y** (fi dōō'shē er'ē, -shə rē) *adj.* [< L. < *fiducia*, trust < *fidere*: see FAITH] **1.** designating or of one who holds something in trust for another [a *fiduciary* guardian for a child] **2.** held in trust [*fiduciary* property] **3.** valuable only because of public confidence: said of certain paper money —*n., pl.* **-ar'ies** a trustee

**fie** (fī) *interj.* [< OFr., of echoic origin] for shame!: now often used in mock reproach

**fief** (fēf) *n.* [Fr.: see FEE] **1.** under feudalism, heritable land held from a lord in return for service **2.** the right to hold such land

**field** (fēld) *n.* [OE. *feld*] **1.** a wide stretch of open land; plain **2.** a piece of cleared land for raising crops or pasturing livestock **3.** a piece of land for some particular purpose [a landing *field*] **4.** an area of land producing some natural resource [a gold *field*] **5.** any wide, unbroken expanse [a *field* of ice] **6.** *a)* a battlefield *b)* a battle **7.** an area of military operations **8.** *a)* an area where practical work is done, away from the central office, laboratory, etc. *b)* a realm of knowledge or of special work [the *field* of electronics] **9.** an area of observation, as in a microscope **10.** the background, as on a flag or coin **11.** *a)* an area where athletic events are held *b)* the part of such an area, usually inside a closed racing track, where contests in jumping, shot put, pole vault, etc. are held *c)* in baseball, the outfield *d)* all the entrants in a contest **12.** *Physics* a space within which magnetic or electrical lines of force are active: in full, **field of force** —*adj.* **1.** of, operating in, or held on the field or fields **2.** living or growing in fields —*vt. Baseball*, etc. **1.** to stop or catch or to catch and throw (a ball) in play **2.** to put (a player) into a field position —*vi. Baseball*, etc. to play as a fielder —**play the field** to explore every opportunity —**take** (or **leave**) **the field** to begin (or withdraw from) activity in a game, military operation, etc.

**field artillery** movable artillery capable of accompanying an army into battle

**field corn** corn (maize) grown to feed livestock

**field day 1.** a day of military exercises and display, or of athletic events **2.** a day of enjoyably exciting events or highly satisfactory activity

**field·er** (-ər) *n. Baseball*, etc. a player in the field

**field event** any of the contests held on the field in a track meet, as the high jump, shot put, etc.

**field glass** a small, portable, binocular telescope: *usually used in pl.* (**field glasses**)

**field goal 1.** *Basketball* a basket toss made from play, scoring two points **2.** *Football* a goal kicked from the field, scoring three points

**field hand** a hired farm laborer

**field hockey** *same as* HOCKEY (sense 2)

**field house 1.** a building near an athletic field, with lockers, showers, etc. for the athletes' use **2.** a large building for indoor sports events

**Field·ing** (fēl'diŋ), **Henry** 1707–54; Eng. novelist

**field magnet** the magnet used to create and maintain the magnetic field in a motor or generator

**field marshal** in some armies, an officer of the highest rank

**field officer** a colonel, lieutenant colonel, or major in the army

**field·piece** (fēld'pēs') *n.* a mobile artillery piece

**field-test** (-test') *vt.* to test (a device, method, etc.) under actual operating conditions

**field·work** (-wʉrk') *n.* **1.** any temporary fortification made by troops in the field **2.** the work of collecting scientific data in the field —**field'work'er** *n.*

**fiend** (fēnd) *n.* [OE. *feond*] **1.** an evil spirit; devil **2.** an inhumanly wicked or cruel person **3.** [Colloq.] *a)* a person addicted to some activity, habit, etc. [a fresh-air *fiend*] *b)* one who is excellent at some activity [a *fiend* at tennis] —**the Fiend** the Devil —**fiend'like'** *adj.*

**fiend·ish** (-ish) *adj.* **1.** of or like a fiend; devilish; inhumanly wicked or cruel **2.** extremely vexatious or difficult —**fiend'ish·ly** *adv.* —**fiend'ish·ness** *n.*

**fierce** (firs) *adj.* **fierc'er, fierc'est** [< OFr. < L. *ferus*, wild] **1.** of a violently cruel nature; savage [a *fierce* dog] **2.** violent; uncontrolled [a *fierce* storm] **3.** intensely eager; ardent [a *fierce* effort] **4.** [Colloq.] very distasteful, bad, etc. —**fierce'ly** *adv.* —**fierce'ness** *n.*

**fi·er·y** (fī'ər ē) *adj.* **-er·i·er, -er·i·est** [ME. *firi*] **1.** containing or consisting of fire **2.** like fire; glaring, hot, etc. **3.** characterized by strong emotion; ardent **4.** easily stirred up; excitable [a *fiery* nature] **5.** inflamed [a *fiery* sore] —**fi'er·i·ly** *adv.* —**fi'er·i·ness** *n.*

**fi·es·ta** (fē es'tə) *n.* [Sp. < VL. *festa:* see FEAST] **1.** a religious festival; esp., a saint's day **2.** any gala celebration; holiday

**fife** (fīf) *n.* [< G. < MHG. < OHG. *pfifa*] a small, shrill-toned musical instrument resembling a flute —*vt., vi.* **fifed, fif'ing** to play on a fife —**fif'er** *n.*

**fif·teen** (fif'tēn') *adj.* [OE. *fiftene*] five more than ten —*n.* the cardinal number between fourteen and sixteen; 15; XV

**fif·teenth** (-tēnth') *adj.* **1.** preceded by fourteen others in a series; 15th **2.** designating any of the fifteen equal parts of something —*n.* **1.** the one following the fourteenth **2.** any of the fifteen equal parts of something; 1/15

**fifth** (fifth) *adj.* [< OE. < *fif*, five] **1.** preceded by four others in a series; 5th **2.** designating any of the five equal parts of something —*n.* **1.** the one following the fourth **2.** any of the five equal parts of something; 1/5 **3.** a fifth of a gallon **4.** *Music a)* the fifth tone of an ascending diatonic scale, or a tone four degrees above or below a given tone *b)* the interval between two such tones, or a combination of them —**fifth'ly** *adv.*

**Fifth Amendment** the fifth amendment to the U.S. Constitution; specif., the clause protecting a person from being compelled to be a witness against himself

**fifth column** [orig. (1936) applied to Franco sympathizers inside Madrid, then besieged by four of his columns on the outside] a group of people who give aid and support to the enemy from within their own country —**fifth columnist**

**fifth wheel** any superfluous person or thing

**fif·ti·eth** (fif'tē ith) *adj.* **1.** preceded by forty-nine others in a series; 50th **2.** designating any of the fifty equal parts of something —*n.* **1.** the one following the forty-ninth **2.** any of fifty equal parts of something; 1/50

**fif·ty** (fif'tē) *adj.* [OE. *fiftig*] five times ten —*n., pl.* **-ties** the cardinal number between forty-nine and fifty-one; 50; L —**the fifties** the numbers or years, as of a century, from fifty through fifty-nine

**fif·ty-fif·ty** (fif'tē fif'tē) *adj.* [Colloq.] equal; even —*adv.* [Colloq.] equally

**fig** (fig) *n.* [< OFr., ult. < L. *ficus*] **1.** a small, hollow, pear-shaped fruit with sweet, seed-filled flesh **2.** a tree bearing this fruit **3.** a trifle [not worth a *fig*]

**fig. 1.** figurative(ly) **2.** figure(s)

**fig·eat·er** (-ēt'ər) *n.* a large, green beetle that feeds on ripe fruit: the June bug of the southeastern U.S.

**fight** (fīt) *vi.* **fought, fight'ing** [OE. *feohtan*] **1.** to take part in a physical struggle or battle, specif. in a boxing match **2.** to struggle or work hard in trying to overcome; contend —*vt.* **1.** to oppose physically, as with fists in boxing or in

battle with weapons, etc. **2.** to struggle against or contend with, as by argument **3.** to engage in or carry on (a war, conflict, etc.) **4.** to gain by struggle *[he fought his way up]* **5.** to cause to fight; manage (a boxer, etc.) —*n.* **1.** a physical struggle; battle; combat **2.** any struggle, contest, or quarrel **3.** power or readiness to fight —**fight it out** to fight until one side is defeated —**fight off** to struggle to avoid
**fight·er** (-ər) *n.* **1.** one that fights or is inclined to fight **2.** a boxer; prizefighter **3.** a small, fast, highly maneuverable airplane for aerial combat
**fig·ment** (fig′mənt) *n.* [< L. *figmentum* < *fingere*, to make, devise] something merely imagined or made up in the mind
**fig·u·ra·tion** (fig′yə rā′shən) *n.* **1.** a forming; shaping **2.** form; appearance **3.** a representing by or ornamenting with figures —**fig′u·ra′tion·al** *adj.*
**fig·u·ra·tive** (fig′yər ə tiv) *adj.* **1.** representing by means of a figure or symbol **2.** not in its usual, literal, or exact sense or reference; metaphorical **3.** containing or using figures of speech —**fig′u·ra·tive·ly** *adv.* —**fig′u·ra·tive·ness** *n.*
**fig·ure** (fig′yər; *chiefly Brit.* fig′ər) *n.* [< OFr. < L. *figura* < *fingere*, to form] **1.** the outline or shape of something; form **2.** the human form **3.** a person seen or thought of in a specified way *[a great social figure]* **4.** a likeness of a person or thing **5.** an illustration; diagram; picture **6.** an artistic design in fabrics, etc.; pattern **7.** *a)* the symbol for a number *[the figure 5]* *b)* [pl.] arithmetic **8.** a sum of money **9.** *Dancing & Skating* a series or pattern of steps or movements **10.** *Geom.* a surface or space bounded on all sides by lines or planes **11.** *Music* a series of consecutive tones or chords forming a distinct group **12.** *Rhetoric* same as FIGURE OF SPEECH —*vt.* **-ured, -ur·ing** **1.** to represent in definite form **2.** to represent mentally; imagine **3.** to ornament with a design **4.** to compute with figures **5.** [Colloq.] to believe, think, decide, etc. —*vi.* **1.** to appear prominently; be conspicuous **2.** to do arithmetic **3.** [Colloq.] to be as expected —**figure in** to add in; include —**figure on** to plan or depend on —**figure out** **1.** to solve; compute **2.** to understand; reason out —**figure up** to add; total —**fig′ur·er** *n.*
**fig·ured** (-yərd) *adj.* **1.** shaped; formed **2.** having a design or pattern **3.** *Music* with numbers to indicate accompanying chords: said of the bass
**fig·ure·head** (fig′yər hed′) *n.* **1.** a carved figure on the bow of a ship **2.** a person holding a high position but having no real power or authority
**figure of speech** an expression, as a metaphor or simile, using words in a nonliteral or unusual sense to add vividness, etc. to what is said
**figure skating** ice skating in which the performer traces various elaborate figures on the ice
**fig·u·rine** (fig′yə rēn′) *n.* [Fr. < It. *figurina*] a small sculptured or molded figure; statuette
**fig·wort** (fig′wurt′) *adj.* designating a large family of plants including the foxglove, snapdragon, etc. —*n.* any of a genus of plants of the figwort family, with square stems and small flowers
**Fi·ji** (fē′jē) country on a group of islands (**Fiji Islands**) in the SW Pacific, north of New Zealand: a member of the Commonwealth: c.7,000 sq. mi.; pop. 512,000 —**Fi′ji·an** *adj., n.*
**fil·a·gree** (fil′ə grē′) *n., adj., vt.* **-greed′, -gree′ing** same as FILIGREE
**fil·a·ment** (fil′ə mənt) *n.* [Fr. < ML. < VL. < L. *filum*, a thread] **1.** a very slender thread or threadlike part; specif., *a)* the fine metal wire in a light bulb which is made incandescent by an electric current *b)* the wire cathode of a thermionic tube **2.** *Bot.* the stalk of a stamen bearing the anther —**fil′a·men′ta·ry** (-men′tər ē) *adj.* —**fil′a·men′tous** *adj.*
**fi·lar·i·a** (fi ler′ē ə) *n., pl.* **fi·lar′i·ae′** (-ē ē′) [ModL. < L. *filum*, a thread] any of several kinds of threadlike parasitic worms that live in the blood and tissues of vertebrate animals —**fi·lar′i·al, fi·lar′i·an** *adj.*
**fil·a·ri·a·sis** (fil′ə rī′ə sis) *n.* [see prec.] a disease caused by filarial worms transmitted by mosquitoes: the worms cause swelling, esp. in the lower parts of the body
**fil·bert** (fil′bərt) *n.* [ult. < St. *Philibert*, whose feast came in the nutting season] **1.** the edible nut of a cultivated European hazel tree **2.** a tree bearing this nut **3.** same as HAZELNUT
**filch** (filch) *vt.* [ME. *filchen*] to steal (esp. something small or petty); pilfer —**filch′er** *n.*
**file¹** (fil) *vt.* **filed, fil′ing** [Fr. < OFr. *filer*, to string papers on a thread < VL. *filare*, to spin < L. *filum*, a thread] **1.** to arrange (papers, etc.) in order for future reference **2.** to dispatch (a news story) to a newspaper office **3.** to register (an application, etc.) **4.** to put (a legal document) on public record **5.** to initiate (a legal action) —*vi.* **1.** to move in a line **2.** to register or apply *(for)* —*n.* **1.** a folder, cabinet, etc. for keeping papers in order **2.** an orderly arrangement of papers, cards, etc., as for reference **3.** a line of persons or things, one behind another —**on file** kept as in a file for reference —**file′a·ble** *adj.* —**fil′er** *n.*
**file²** (fil) *n.* [OE. *feol*] a steel tool with a rough, ridged surface for smoothing or grinding down something —*vt.* **filed, fil′ing** to smooth or grind down with a file —**fil′er** *n.*
**file·fish** (fil′fish′) *n., pl.* **-fish′, -fish′es:** see FISH a fish with very small, rough scales
**fi·let** (fi lā′, fil′ā) *n.* [see FILLET] **1.** a net or lace with a simple pattern on a square mesh background **2.** same as FILLET (*n.* 3) —*vt.* **-leted** (-lād′), **-let′ing** (-lā′iŋ) same as FILLET (*vt.* 2)
**fi·let mi·gnon** (fi lā′ min yōn′, -yän′; *Fr.* fē le mē·nyōn′) [Fr., lit., tiny fillet] a thick, round cut of lean beef tenderloin broiled, usually with mushrooms and bacon
**fil·i·al** (fil′ē əl, fil′yəl) *adj.* [< LL. < L. *filius*, son, *filia*, daughter] **1.** of, suitable to, or due from a son or daughter *[filial devotion]* **2.** *Genetics* of the indicated generation (i.e., F₁, F₂, etc.) following the parental —**fil′i·al·ly** *adv.*
**fil·i·bus·ter** (fil′ə bus′tər) *n.* [< Sp. < MDu. *vrijbuiter*, freebooter] **1.** an adventurer who engages in unauthorized warfare against another country; freebooter **2.** a member of a legislative body who obstructs the passage of a bill by making long speeches, introducing irrelevant issues, etc.: also **fil′i·bus′ter·er** **3.** the use of such methods to obstruct a bill —*vi.* **1.** to engage in unauthorized warfare as a freebooter **2.** to engage in a filibuster —*vt.* to obstruct the passage of (a bill) by a filibuster
**fil·i·gree** (fil′ə grē′) *n.* [< earlier *filigrain* < Fr. < It. < L. *filum*, a thread + *granum*, grain] **1.** lacelike ornamental work of intertwined wire of gold, silver, etc. **2.** any delicate work or design like this —*adj.* like, made of, or made into filigree —*vt.* **-greed′, -gree′ing** to ornament with filigree
**fil·ing** (fil′iŋ) *n.* a small piece, as of metal, scraped off with a file: *usually used in pl.*
**Fil·i·pine** (fil′ə pēn′) *adj.* same as PHILIPPINE
**Fil·i·pi·no** (fil′ə pē′nō) *n.* [Sp.] **1.** *pl.* **-nos** a native or citizen of the Philippines **2.** *see also* PILIPINO —*adj.* Philippine
**fill** (fil) *vt.* [OE. *fyllan* < base of *full,* FULL¹] **1.** *a)* to put as much as possible into; make full *b)* to put a great amount of something into **2.** *a)* to take up or occupy all or nearly all the capacity or extent of *[the crowd filled the room]* *b)* to spread throughout **3.** *a)* to occupy (an office, position, etc.) *b)* to put a person into (an office, position, etc.) **4.** to fulfill (an engagement to perform, etc.) **5.** *a)* to supply the things called for in (an order, prescription, etc.) *b)* to satisfy (a need, requirement, etc.) **6.** to close or plug (holes, cracks, etc.) **7.** to satisfy the hunger or desire of —*vi.* to become full —*n.* **1.** all that is needed to make full **2.** all that is needed to satisfy **3.** anything that fills; esp., earth, gravel, etc. used for filling holes, etc. —**fill in** **1.** to fill with some substance **2.** to complete by supplying (something) **3.** to be a substitute —**fill one in on** [Colloq.] to provide one with additional details about —**fill out** **1.** to make or become rounder, shapelier, etc. **2.** to complete (a document, etc.) by inserting information —**fill up** to make or become completely full
**fill·er** (fil′ər) *n.* a person or thing that fills; specif., *a)* matter added to increase bulk, solidity, etc. *b)* a preparation used to fill in cracks, etc. *c)* the tobacco inside a cigar *d)* a short, space-filling item in a newspaper *e)* the paper for a loose-leaf notebook
**fil·lér** (fēl′er) *n., pl.* **-lér, -lérs** see MONETARY UNITS, table (Hungary)
**fil·let** (fil′it; *for n.* 3 & *vt.* 2, *usually* fil′ā, fi lā′) *n.* [< OFr. dim. of *fil* < L. *filum*, a thread] **1.** a narrow band worn around the head as to hold the hair in place **2.** a thin strip or band **3.** a boneless, lean piece of meat or fish —*vt.* **1.** to bind or decorate with a band, molding, etc. **2.** to bone and slice (meat or fish)
**fill·ing** (fil′iŋ) *n.* **1.** a thing used to fill something else; specif., *a)* the metal, plastic, etc. inserted by a dentist into a prepared cavity in a tooth *b)* the foodstuff used in a pastry shell, etc. **2.** the woof in a woven fabric
**filling station** same as SERVICE STATION
**fil·lip** (fil′əp) *n.* [echoic extension of FLIP¹] **1.** the snap made by a finger held down by the thumb and then suddenly released **2.** a light tap given in this way **3.** anything that stimulates or livens up —*vt.* **1.** to strike or snap with a fillip **2.** to stimulate or liven up —*vi.* to make a fillip
**Fill·more** (fil′môr), **Mill·ard** (mil′ərd) 1800–74; 13th president of the U.S. (1850–53)

FILLIP

**fil·ly** (fil′ē) *n., pl.* **-lies** [ON. *fylja*] **1.** a young female horse, specif. one under five years of age **2.** [Colloq.] a vivacious girl
**film** (film) *n.* [OE. *filmen*] **1.** a fine, thin skin or coating

**2.** a flexible cellulose material covered with a substance sensitive to light and used in taking photographs or making motion pictures **3.** a haze or blur, as over the eyes **4.** a motion picture or motion pictures **5.** a gauzy web —*vt.* **1.** to cover as with a film **2.** to take a photograph of **3.** to make a motion picture of —*vi.* **1.** to become covered with a film **2.** *a)* to make a motion picture *b)* to be filmed or suitable for filming —**film′er** *n.*

**film·ic** (fil′mik) *adj.* of motion pictures or the art of making them

**film·strip** (film′strip′) *n.* a length of film containing still photographs arranged in sequence for projection separately and used in teaching, etc.

**film·y** (fil′mē) *adj.* **film′i·er, film′i·est 1.** of or like a film; hazy, gauzy, etc. **2.** covered as with a film —**film′i·ly** *adv.* —**film′i·ness** *n.*

**fils** (fēls, fils) *n., pl.* **fils** [< Ar. < LGr. *phollis,* a small coin] *see* MONETARY UNITS, table (Bahrain, Iraq, Jordan, Kuwait, United Arab Emirates, Yemen)

**fil·ter** (fil′tər) *n.* [< OFr. < ML. *filtrum, feltrum,* felt (used for filters)] **1.** a device for passing a fluid through a porous substance so as to strain out solid particles, impurities, etc. **2.** any porous substance so used, as sand, charcoal, etc. **3.** *a)* a device that passes electric currents of certain frequencies only *b)* a substance that absorbs certain light rays *[a color filter for a camera lens]* —*vt.* **1.** to pass (a fluid) through a filter **2.** to remove (solid particles, etc.) from a fluid with a filter **3.** to act as a filter for —*vi.* **1.** to pass through or as if through a filter **2.** to pass slowly *[the news filtered through town]*

**fil·ter·a·ble** (-ə b′l) *adj.* that can be filtered: also **fil′tra·ble** (-trə b′l) —**fil′ter·a·bil′i·ty** *n.*

**filterable virus** any virus: so called because most viruses can pass through fine filters that bacteria cannot pass through

**filter paper** porous paper for filtering liquids

**filth** (filth) *n.* [OE. *fylthe* < base of *ful,* FOUL + -TH¹] **1.** disgustingly offensive dirt, garbage, etc. **2.** anything considered grossly indecent or obscene **3.** gross moral corruption

**filth·y** (fil′thē) *adj.* **filth′i·er, filth′i·est 1.** full of filth; disgustingly foul **2.** grossly obscene **3.** morally corrupt —**filth′i·ly** *adv.* —**filth′i·ness** *n.*

**fil·trate** (fil′trāt) *vt.* **-trat·ed, -trat·ing** to filter —*n.* a filtered liquid —**fil·tra′tion** *n.*

**fin¹** (fin) *n.* [OE. *finn*] **1.** any of several winglike, membranous organs on the body of a fish, dolphin, etc., used in swimming and balancing **2.** anything like a fin in shape or use, as on an aircraft or boat

**fin²** (fin) *n.* [< Yid. < MHG. < OHG. *fimf,* five] [Slang] a five-dollar bill

**fin. 1.** finance **2.** financial **3.** finis

**fi·na·gle** (fə nā′g′l) *vt.* **-gled, -gling** [< ?] to get or arrange by cleverness, persuasion, etc., or esp. by craftiness or trickery —*vi.* to use craftiness or trickery —**fi·na′gler** *n.*

**fi·nal** (fī′n′l) *adj.* [< OFr. < L. *finalis* < *finis,* end] **1.** of or coming at the end; last; concluding **2.** deciding; conclusive *[a final decree]* **3.** having to do with the ultimate purpose or end *[a final cause]* —*n.* **1.** anything final **2.** *[pl.]* the last of a series of contests **3.** a final examination

**fi·na·le** (fə nä′lē, -nal′ē) *n.* [It.] **1.** the concluding part of a musical composition or an entertainment **2.** the conclusion; end

**fi·nal·ist** (fī′n′l ist) *n.* a contestant who participates in the final, deciding contest of a series

**fi·nal·i·ty** (fī nal′ə tē) *n.* **1.** the quality or condition of being final, settled, or complete; conclusiveness **2.** *pl.* **-ties** anything final

**fi·nal·ize** (fī′n′l īz′) *vt.* **-ized′, -iz′ing** [FINAL + -IZE] to make final —**fi′nal·i·za′tion** *n.*

**fi·nal·ly** (-ē) *adv.* **1.** at the end; in conclusion **2.** decisively; conclusively

**fi·nance** (fə nans′, fī′nans) *n.* [< OFr. < *finer,* to end, settle accounts < *fin* < L. *finis,* an end] **1.** *[pl.]* the money resources, income, etc. of a nation, organization, or person **2.** the managing or science of managing money matters —*vt.* **-nanced′, -nanc′ing** to supply or obtain money or credit for

**fi·nan·cial** (fə nan′shəl, fī-) *adj.* of finance, finances, or financiers —**fi·nan′cial·ly** *adv.*

**fin·an·cier** (fin′ən sir′) *n.* [Fr.] **1.** a person skilled in finance **2.** a person who engages in financial operations on a large scale

**fin·back** (fin′bak′) *n.* a large whalebone whale of the eastern coast of the U.S., with a large dorsal fin

**finch** (finch) *n.* [OE. *finc*] any of a large group of small songbirds with short beaks, including the bunting, canary, cardinal, and sparrow

**find** (fīnd) *vt.* **found, find′ing** [OE. *findan*] **1.** to happen on; discover by chance **2.** to get by searching **3.** to get sight or knowledge of; perceive; learn **4.** to experience or feel **5.** *a)* to recover (something lost) *b)* to recover the use of **6.** to consider; think *[he finds TV boring]* **7.** to get to; reach *[the arrow found its mark]* **8.** to declare after deliberation *[to find him guilty]* **9.** to supply; furnish —*vi.* **1.** to announce a decision *[the jury found for the accused]* —*n.* **1.** a finding **2.** something found, esp. something valuable —**find oneself 1.** to learn what one's real talents are and begin to apply them **2.** to become aware of being *[to find oneself tired]* —**find out 1.** to discover; learn **2.** to learn the true character or identity of

**find·er** (fīn′dər) *n.* **1.** a person or thing that finds **2.** a camera device that shows what will appear in the photograph **3.** a small telescope attached to, and used to locate objects for closer view with, a larger, more powerful one

‡**fin de siè·cle** (fant sye′kl) [Fr., end of the century] of or like the last years of the 19th century

**find·ing** (fīn′diŋ) *n.* **1.** the act of one who finds; discovery **2.** something found or discovered **3.** *[often pl.]* the conclusion reached after consideration of facts, as by a judge, scholar, etc.

**fine¹** (fīn) *adj.* **fin′er, fin′est** [< OFr. < ML. *finus,* for L. *finis,* an end] **1.** orig., perfected **2.** superior in quality, character, ability, etc.; excellent **3.** with no impurities; refined **4.** containing a specified proportion of pure metal: said of gold or silver **5.** clear and bright: said of the weather **6.** not heavy, gross, or coarse *[fine sand]* **7.** *a)* very thin *[fine thread]* *b)* very small *[fine print]* **8.** sharp; keen *[a knife with a fine edge]* **9.** discriminating; subtle *[fine distinctions]* **10.** having a delicate quality *[fine china]* **11.** involving precision *[a fine adjustment]* **12.** too elegant; showy *[fine writing]* —*adv.* **1.** same as FINELY **2.** [Colloq.] very well —*vt., vi.* **fined, fin′ing** to make or become fine or finer —**fine′ly** *adv.* —**fine′ness** *n.*

**fine²** (fīn) *n.* [< OFr. *fin* < L. *finis,* an end] a sum of money required to be paid as punishment for an offense —*vt.* **fined, fin′ing** to order to pay a fine —**in fine 1.** in conclusion **2.** in brief

**fine art** any of the art forms that include drawing, painting, sculpture, and ceramics, or, occasionally, architecture, literature, music, dramatic art, or dancing: *usually used in pl.*

**fine-drawn** (fīn′drôn′) *adj.* **1.** drawn out until very fine, as wire **2.** very subtle: said of reasoning, arguments, etc.

**fine-grained** (-grānd′) *adj.* having a fine, smooth grain, as some wood, leather, etc.

**fin·er·y** (fīn′ər ē) *n., pl.* **-er·ies** showy, gay, elaborate decoration, esp. clothes, jewelry, etc.

**fine·spun** (fīn′spun′) *adj.* **1.** delicate; fragile **2.** extremely or overly subtle

**fi·nesse** (fi nes′) *n.* [Fr. < OFr. *fin,* FINE¹] **1.** adroitness and delicacy of performance **2.** the ability to handle delicate and difficult situations diplomatically **3.** cunning; skill **4.** *Bridge* an attempt to take a trick with a lower card while holding a higher card not in sequence with it —*vt., vi.* **-nessed′, -ness′ing 1.** to manage by or use finesse **2.** *Bridge* to make a finesse with (a card)

**fine-toothed comb** (fīn′tōōtht′) a comb with fine, closely set teeth: also **fine-tooth comb** —**go over with a fine-toothed comb** to examine very thoroughly

**fin·ger** (fiŋ′gər) *n.* [OE.] **1.** any of the five parts at the end of the hand, esp. any of these other than the thumb **2.** the part of a glove covering a finger **3.** anything like a finger in shape or use **4.** a unit of measurement based on the breadth of a finger (about 3/4 inch) or the length of a finger (about 4 1/2 inches) —*vt.* **1.** to touch or handle with the fingers **2.** to play (an instrument) by using the fingers on strings, keys, etc. —*vi.* to be fingered, as a violin —**have a finger in the pie** to participate —**put one's finger on** to indicate or ascertain exactly

**fin·ger·board** (-bôrd′) *n.* a strip of hard wood in the neck of a violin, cello, etc., against which the strings are pressed with the fingers to produce the desired tones

**fin·gered** (fiŋ′gərd) *adj.* having fingers (of a specified kind or number) *[thick-fingered]*

**fin·ger·ing** (fiŋ′gər iŋ) *n.* **1.** a touching with the fingers **2.** *Music a)* technique of using the fingers on the strings, keys, etc. to produce tones *b)* directions on a score for using the fingers

**fin·ger·ling** (-liŋ) *n.* **1.** any small object **2.** a small fish about the length of a finger

**fin·ger·nail** (-nāl′) *n.* the horny substance on the upper part of the end joint of a finger

**finger painting** the process of painting by using the fingers or hand to spread paints (**finger paints**) made of starch, glycerin, and pigments on moistened paper —**fin′ger-paint′** (-pānt′) *vi., vt.*

---

fat, āpe, cär, ten, ēven, is, bīte; gō, hôrn, tōōl, look; oil, out; up, fur; get; joy; yet; chin; she; thin, *then;* zh, leisure; ŋ, ring; ə for *a* in *ago,* e in *agent, i* in *sanity, o* in *comply, u* in *focus;* ′ as in *able* (ā′b′l); Fr. bäl; ĕ, Fr. coeur; ö, Fr. feu; Fr. mon; ô, Fr. coq; ü, Fr. duc; r, Fr. cri; H, G. ich; kh, G. doch; ‡foreign; *hypothetical; < derived from. See inside front cover.

**fin·ger·print** (-print′) *n.* an impression of the lines and whorls on the inner surface of the end joint of the finger, used to identify a person —*vt.* to take the fingerprints of

**finger tip** the tip of a finger —**have at one's finger tips 1.** to have available for instant use **2.** to be completely familiar with —**to one's (or the ) finger tips** entirely; altogether

**fin·i·al** (fin′ē əl) *n.* [ME., orig. adj., FINAL] a decorative part at the tip of a spire, lamp shade support, etc., or projecting upward from the top of a cabinet, etc.

**fin·i·cal** (fin′i k'l) *adj.* [< FINE¹] *same as* FINICKY —**fin′i·cal·ly** *adv.*

**fin·ick·y** (fin′i kē′) *adj.* [see prec.] too particular; overly fastidious; fussy: also **fin′ick·ing, fin′nick·y** —**fin′ick·i·ness** *n.*

**fi·nis** (fin′is, fī′nis) *n., pl.* **-nis·es** [L.] the end, as of a book; conclusion

**fin·ish** (fin′ish) *vt.* [< OFr. < L. *finire* < *finis,* an end] **1.** *a)* to bring to an end; complete  *b)* to come to the end of **2.** to use up; consume entirely **3.** to give final touches to **4.** to give (cloth, wood, etc.) a desired surface effect **5.** *a)* to cause the defeat, death, etc. of  *b)* to render worthless, useless, etc. —*vi.* **1.** to come to an end **2.** to complete something being done —*n.* **1.** the last part; end **2.** anything used to give a desired surface effect, as varnish, wax, etc. **3.** completeness; perfection **4.** the manner or method of completion **5.** the way in which the surface, as of furniture, is finished **6.** refinement in manners, speech, etc. **7.** defeat, collapse, etc. or that which brings it about **8.** finishing joiner work, as doors, moldings, panels, etc. —**finish off 1.** to end or complete **2.** to kill or destroy —**finish up 1.** to end or complete **2.** to consume all of —**finish with 1.** to end or complete **2.** to end relations with—**fin′ished** *adj.* —**fin′ish·er** *n.*

**finishing school** a private school for girls that specializes in imparting social poise and polish

**fi·nite** (fī′nīt) *adj.* [< L. *finitus,* pp. of *finire,* FINISH] **1.** having definable limits; not infinite **2.** *Gram.* having limits of person, number, and tense: said of a verb that can be used in a predicate —**fi′nite·ly** *adv.* —**fi′nite·ness** *n.*

**fin·i·tude** (fin′ə tōōd′, fī′nə-; -tyōōd′) *n.* the state or quality of being finite

**fink** (fiŋk) *n.* [< ?] [Slang] **1.** an informer or strikebreaker **2.** a person regarded as obnoxious

**Fin·land** (fin′lənd) **1.** country in N Europe, northeast of the Baltic Sea: 130,119 sq. mi.; pop. 4,696,000; cap. Helsinki **2. Gulf of,** arm of the Baltic Sea, between Finland & the U.S.S.R.

**Finn** (fin) *n.* a native or inhabitant of Finland

**Finn.** Finnish

**fin·nan had·die** (fin′ən had′ē) [prob. < Findhorn (Scot. fishing port) *haddock*] smoked haddock: also **finnan haddock**

**Finn·ish** (fin′ish) *adj.* **1.** of Finland **2.** of the Finns, their language, or culture —*n.* the Finno-Ugric language of the Finns

**Fin·no-** *a combining form meaning* Finn, Finnish

**Fin·no-U·gric** (fin′ō ōō′grik, -yōō′-) *adj.* designating or of a subfamily of the Uralic languages spoken in NE Europe, W Siberia, and Hungary: it includes Finnish, Estonian, Hungarian, etc. —*n.* this subfamily of languages Also **Fin′no-U′gri·an** (-grē ən)

**fin·ny** (fin′ē) *adj.* **1.** *a)* having fins  *b)* like a fin **2.** of or being fish

**fiord** (fyôrd) *n.* [< Norw. < ON. *fjörthr*] a narrow inlet of the sea bordered by steep cliffs, esp. in Norway

**fip·ple flute** (fip′'l) [< ?] any of a class of vertical flutes, as the recorder, in which a plug (fipple) near the mouthpiece diverts the breath in producing the tones

**fir** (fur) *n.* [< OE. *fyrh*] **1.** a cone-bearing evergreen tree of the pine family **2.** its wood

**fire** (fir) *n.* [OE. *fyr*] **1.** the heat and light of combustion **2.** something burning, as fuel in a furnace **3.** a destructive burning [a forest *fire*] **4.** anything like fire in heat, brilliance, etc. **5.** torture by burning **6.** extreme distress; tribulation **7.** fever or inflammation **8.** strong feeling; fervor **9.** vivid imagination **10.** *a)* a discharge of firearms or artillery  *b)* anything like this in speed and continuity [a fire of criticism] —*vt.* **fired, fir′ing 1.** to make burn; ignite **2.** to supply with fuel [to *fire* a furnace] **3.** to bake (bricks, pottery, etc.) in a kiln **4.** to dry by heat **5.** to animate, inspire, excite, etc. **6.** to shoot or discharge (a gun, bullet, etc.) **7.** to hurl or direct with force [to *fire* questions]

FINGERPRINT

FIORD

**8.** to dismiss from a job; discharge —*vi.* **1.** to start burning; flame **2.** to tend a fire **3.** to become excited or aroused **4.** to shoot a firearm **5.** to discharge a projectile —**between two fires** shot at, criticized, etc. from both sides —**catch (on) fire** to begin burning —**fire up** to start a fire, as in a furnace —**miss fire 1.** to fail to fire, as a gun **2.** to fail in an attempt —**on fire 1.** burning **2.** greatly excited —**open fire 1.** to begin to shoot **2.** to begin; start —**play with fire** to do something risky —**set fire to** to make burn; ignite —**take fire 1.** to begin to burn **2.** to become excited —**under fire 1.** under attack, as by gunfire **2.** subjected to criticism, etc. —**fir′er** *n.*

**fire·arm** (-ärm′) *n.* any weapon from which a shot is fired by explosive force; esp., such a weapon small enough to be carried, as a rifle

**fire·boat** (-bōt′) *n.* a boat equipped with firefighting equipment, used along waterfronts

**fire·bomb** (-bäm′) *n.* a bomb intended to start a fire; incendiary bomb —*vt.* to attack with a firebomb or firebombs

**fire·box** (-bäks′) *n.* the place for the fire in a furnace, etc.

**fire·brand** (-brand′) *n.* **1.** a piece of burning wood **2.** a person who stirs up strife, etc.

**fire·break** (-brāk′) *n.* a strip of land cleared to stop the spread of fire, as in a forest

**fire·brick** (-brik′) *n.* a brick made to withstand great heat, used to line furnaces, etc.

**fire·bug** (-bug′) *n.* [Colloq.] a person who deliberately sets fire to buildings, etc.; pyromaniac

**fire·clay** (-klā′) *n.* a clay that can resist intense heat, used to make firebricks, furnace linings, etc.

**fire·crack·er** (-krak′ər) *n.* a roll of paper that contains an explosive and an attached fuse, set off as a noisemaker at celebrations, etc.

**fire·damp** (-damp′) *n.* a gas, largely methane, formed in coal mines, which is explosive when mixed with a certain proportion of air

**fire·dog** (-dôg′) *n. same as* ANDIRON

**fire door** a door of metal or other fire-resistant material designed to keep a fire from spreading

**fire·eat·er** (-ēt′ər) *n.* **1.** an entertainer who pretends to eat fire **2.** a belligerent person

**fire engine** **1.** a motor truck equipped to spray water, chemicals, etc. on fires to put them out **2.** loosely, any motor truck for carrying firemen and equipment to a fire

**fire escape** a stairway, ladder, etc. down an outside wall, for escape from a burning building

**fire extinguisher** a portable device containing chemicals for spraying on a fire to put it out

**fire·fight·er** (-fīt′ər) *n. same as* FIREMAN (sense 1)

**fire·fly** (-flī′) *n., pl.* **-flies′** a winged beetle whose abdomen glows with a luminescent light

**fire insurance** insurance against loss or damage resulting from fire

**fire·light** (-līt′) *n.* light from an open fire

**fire·man** (-mən) *n., pl.* **-men 1.** a man whose work is fighting fires **2.** a man who tends a fire in a furnace, locomotive engine, etc. **3.** *U.S. Navy* a nonrated enlisted man whose duties are concerned with the ship's engines, etc. **4.** [Slang] *Baseball* a relief pitcher

**Fi·ren·ze** (fē ren′dze) *It.* name of FLORENCE, Italy

**fire·place** (fir′plās′) *n.* a place for a fire, esp. an open place built in a wall, at a chimney base

**fire·plug** (-plug′) *n.* a street hydrant to which a hose can be attached for fighting fires

**fire·pow·er** (-pou′ər) *n. Mil.* **1.** the effectiveness of a weapon in terms of the accuracy and volume of its fire **2.** the capacity of a given unit to deliver fire

**fire·proof** (-prōōf′) *adj.* that does not burn or is not easily destroyed by fire —*vt.* to make fireproof

**fire sale** a sale of goods damaged in a fire

**fire·side** (-sīd′) *n.* **1.** the part of a room near a fireplace; hearth **2.** home or home life

**fire station** the place where fire engines are kept and where firemen stay when on duty: also **fire′house′** (-hous′) *n.*

**fire·storm** (-stôrm′) *n.* an intense fire over a large area, as one caused by an atomic explosion

**fire·trap** (-trap′) *n.* a building unsafe in case of fire, as because it lacks adequate exits

**fire·wa·ter** (-wôt′ər, -wät′ər) *n.* [prob. transl. of AmInd. term] alcoholic liquor: now humorous

**fire·weed** (-wēd′) *n.* any of various plants that grow readily on cleared or burned-over land

**fire·works** (-wurks′) *n.pl.* **1.** firecrackers, rockets, etc. used, as in celebrations, to produce loud noises or brilliant lighting effects: *sometimes used in sing.* **2.** a display of or as of fireworks

**firing line** **1.** the line from which gunfire is directed against the enemy **2.** the front position in any kind of activity

**fir·kin** (fur′kin) *n.* [< MDu. dim. of *vierdel,* a fourth] **1.** a small wooden tub for butter, lard, etc. **2.** a measure of capacity equal to 1/4 barrel

**firm**[1] (fₑrm) *adj.* [< OFr. < L. *firmus*] **1.** not yielding easily under pressure; solid **2.** not moved or shaken easily; fixed; stable **3.** remaining the same; steady *[a firm market]* **4.** resolute; constant *[a firm faith]* **5.** showing determination, strength, etc. *[a firm command]* **6.** formally concluded; definite; final *[a firm contract]* —*vt., vi.* to make or become firm: often with *up* —**firm′ly** *adv.* —**firm′ness** *n.*

**firm**[2] (fₑrm) *n.* [It. *firma*, signature < L. < *firmus*, FIRM[1]] a business company or partnership

**fir·ma·ment** (fₑr′mə mənt) *n.* [< OFr. < LL. < L. *firmare*, to strengthen < *firmus*, FIRM[1]] the sky, viewed poetically as a solid arch or vault

**first** (fₑrst) *adj.* [< OE. *fyrst*] **1.** before any others; 1st: used as the ordinal of ONE **2.** happening or acting before all others; earliest **3.** foremost in rank, quality, importance, etc. **4.** *Music* playing or singing the part highest in pitch or the leading part —*adv.* **1.** *a)* before any other person or thing *b)* before doing anything else **2.** as the first point **3.** for the first time **4.** sooner; preferably —*n.* **1.** the first person, thing, class, place, etc. **2.** the first day of the month **3.** the beginning; start **4.** a first happening or thing of its kind **5.** [*pl.*] the best quality of merchandise **6.** the winning place, as in a race **7.** the first or lowest forward gear ratio of a motor vehicle

**first aid** emergency treatment for injury or sudden illness, before regular medical care is available —**first′-aid′** *adj.*

**first base** *Baseball* the base on the pitcher's left, the first of the four bases a runner must touch in succession to score a run —**get to first base** [Slang] get the first stage done

**first·born** (-bôrn′) *adj.* born first in a family; oldest —*n.* the firstborn child

**first-class** (-klas′) *adj.* **1.** of the highest class, rank, quality, etc.; excellent **2.** designating or of the most expensive accommodations, as on a ship **3.** designating or of a class of mail consisting of sealed matter and carrying the highest regular postage rates —*adv.* **1.** with the most expensive accommodations **2.** as or by first-class mail

**first cousin** the son or daughter of one's aunt or uncle

**first finger** the finger next to the thumb

**first·hand** (-hand′) *adj., adv.* from the original producer or source; direct

**first lady** [*often* F- L-] the wife of the U.S. president

**first lieutenant** a U.S. military officer ranking above a second lieutenant

**first·ling** (-liŋ) *n.* **1.** the first of a kind **2.** the first fruit, produce, offspring, etc.

**first·ly** (-lē) *adv.* in the first place; first

**first mate** a merchant ship's officer next in rank below the captain: also **first officer**

**first mortgage** a mortgage having priority over all other liens on the same property

**first offender** a person convicted for the first time of an offense against the law

**first person** that form of a pronoun (as *I* or *we*) or verb (as *do*) which refers to the speaker or speakers

**first-rate** (-rāt′) *adj.* of the highest class, rank, or quality; excellent —*adv.* [Colloq.] very well

**first sergeant** *U.S. Army & Marine Corps* the noncommissioned officer, usually a master sergeant, serving as chief assistant to the commander of a company, battery, etc.

**first-string** (-striŋ′) *adj.* [Colloq.] **1.** *Sports* that is the first choice for regular play at a specified position **2.** first-class; excellent

**first water** the best quality and purest luster: said of gems, but also used figuratively

**firth** (fₑrth) *n.* [< ON. *fjörthr*] a narrow arm of the sea; estuary

**fis·cal** (fis′kəl) *adj.* [Fr. < LL. < L. *fiscus*, money basket] **1.** having to do with the public treasury or revenues **2.** financial —**fis′cal·ly** *adv.*

**fiscal year** the twelve-month period between settlements of financial accounts: the U.S. government fiscal year legally ends June 30

**fish** (fish) *n.,* *pl.* **fish**; in referring to different species, **fish′es:** see PLURAL, II, D, 2 [OE. *fisc*] **1.** any of a large group of cold-blooded animals living in water and having backbones, gills for breathing, fins, and, usually, scales **2.** loosely, any animal living in water only, as a crab, oyster, etc. **3.** the flesh of a fish used as food **4.**

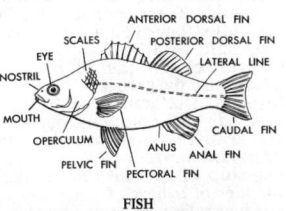

ANTERIOR DORSAL FIN
POSTERIOR DORSAL FIN
SCALES
EYE
LATERAL LINE
NOSTRIL
MOUTH
OPERCULUM
CAUDAL FIN
ANUS
PELVIC FIN
ANAL FIN
PECTORAL FIN

FISH

[Colloq.] a person thought of as like a fish in being easily lured, lacking emotion, etc. —[**F-** ] the constellation Pisces —*vi.* **1.** to catch or try to catch fish **2.** to try to get something indirectly or by cunning (often with *for*) —*vt.* **1.** to fish in (a stream, lake, etc.) **2.** to grope for, find, and bring to view *[he fished a coin out of his pocket]* —*adj.* **1.** of fish or fishing **2.** selling fish —**drink like a fish** to drink heavily, esp. alcoholic liquor —**like a fish out of water** in surroundings not suited to one —**neither fish, flesh, nor fowl** not anything definite or recognizable —**other fish to fry** other, more important things to attend to —**fish′a·ble** *adj.* —**fish′like** *adj.*

**Fish** (fish), **Hamilton** 1808–93; U.S. statesman

**fish and chips** [Chiefly Brit.] fried fillets of fish served with French fried potatoes

**fish·er** (fish′ər) *n.* **1.** a fisherman **2.** *pl.* **-ers, -er:** see PLURAL, II, D, 1 a flesh-eating animal of the marten family, like a weasel but larger

**fish·er·man** (-mən) *n.,* *pl.* **-men** **1.** a person who fishes for sport or for a living **2.** a ship used in fishing

**fish·er·y** (-ē) *n.,* *pl.* **-er·ies** **1.** the business of catching fish **2.** a place where fish are caught **3.** the legal right to catch fish in certain waters or at certain times **4.** a place where fish are bred

**fish-eye lens** (fish′ī′) a camera lens designed to record a 180-degree field of vision

**fish hawk** *same as* OSPREY

**fish·hook** (-hook′) *n.* a hook, usually barbed, for catching fish

**fish·ing** (-iŋ) *n.* the catching of fish for sport or for a living

**fishing pole** a simple device for fishing, consisting of a pole, line, and hook

**fishing rod** a slender pole with an attached line, hook, and usually a reel, used in fishing

**fish joint** a joint, as of two railroad rails, held together by fishplates along the sides

**fish meal** ground, dried fish, used as fertilizer or fodder

**fish·mon·ger** (-muŋ′gər, -mäŋ′-) *n.* a dealer in fish

**fish·plate** (-plāt′) *n.* [prob. < Fr. *fiche*, means of fixing] either of a pair of steel plates bolting two rails together lengthwise, as on a railroad

**fish story** [Colloq.] an exaggerated story

**fish·wife** (-wīf′) *n.,* *pl.* **-wives′** (-wīvz′) **1.** a woman who sells fish **2.** a coarse, scolding woman

**fish·y** (-ē) *adj.* **fish′i·er, fish′i·est** **1.** of or full of fish **2.** like a fish in odor, taste, etc. **3.** dull or expressionless *[a fishy stare]* **4.** [Colloq.] questionable; odd *[a fishy story]* —**fish′i·ly** *adv.* —**fish′i·ness** *n.*

**fis·sile** (fis′l) *adj.* [< L. < *fissus*, pp. of *findere*, to split] **1.** that can be split **2.** that can undergo fission; fissionable —**fis·sil·i·ty** (fi sil′ə tē) *n.*

**fis·sion** (fish′ən) *n.* [< L. < *fissus:* see prec.] **1.** a splitting apart; division into parts **2.** *same as* NUCLEAR FISSION **3.** *Biol.* a form of asexual reproduction in which the parent organism divides into two or more parts, each becoming an independent individual —*vi., vt.* to undergo or cause to undergo nuclear fission —**fis′sion·a·ble** *adj.*

**fis·sure** (fish′ər) *n.* [< OFr. < L. *fissura* < *fissus:* see FISSILE] **1.** a long, narrow, deep cleft or crack **2.** a dividing or breaking into parts —*vt., vi.* **-sured, -sur·ing** to crack or split apart

**fist** (fist) *n.* [< OE. *fyst*] **1.** a hand with the fingers closed tightly into the palm **2.** [Colloq.] *a)* a hand *b)* the grasp **3.** *Printing* the sign (☞), used to direct special attention to something

**fist·ic** (fis′tik) *adj.* having to do with boxing; fought with the fists; pugilistic

**fist·i·cuffs** (fis′ti kufs′) *n.pl.* [< FIST + CUFF[2]] **1.** a fight with the fists **2.** the science of boxing

**fis·tu·la** (fis′choo lə) *n.,* *pl.* **-las, -lae′** (-lē′) [< OFr. < L., a pipe, ulcer] an abnormal passage from an abscess, cavity, or hollow organ to the skin or to another abscess, cavity, or organ —**fis′tu·lous, fis′tu·lar** *adj.*

**fit**[1] (fit) *vt.* **fit′ted** or **fit, fit′ted, fit′ting** [ME. *fitten* < ? ON. *fitja*, to knit, tie] **1.** to be suitable or adapted to **2.** to be the proper size, shape, etc. for **3.** *a)* to make or alter so as to fit *b)* to measure (a person) for something that must be fitted **4.** to make suitable or qualified **5.** *a)* to insert, as into a receptacle *b)* to make a place for (with *in* or *into*) **6.** to equip; outfit (often with *out*) —*vi.* **1.** to be suitable or proper **2.** to be in accord or harmony (often with *in* or *into*) **3.** to have the proper size or shape for a particular figure, space, etc. *[his coat fits well]* —*adj.* **fit′ter, fit′test** **1.** adapted, qualified, or suited to some purpose, function, etc. **2.** proper; right **3.** in good physical condition; healthy —*n.* **1.** a fitting or being fitted **2.** the manner of fitting *[a tight fit]* **3.** anything that fits —**fit to be tied** [Colloq.] frustrated or angry —**fit′ly** *adv.* —**fit′ness** *n.*

---

fat, āpe, cär, ten, ēven, is, bīte; gō, hôrn, tōol, look; oil, out; up, fɑr; get; joy; yet; chin; she; thin, *then*; zh, leisure; ŋ, ring; ə for *a* in *ago, e* in *agent, i* in *sanity, o* in *comply, u* in *focus;* ′ as in *able* (ā′b'l); Fr. bâl; ë, Fr. coeur; ö, Fr. feu; Fr. mon; ô, Fr. coq; ü, Fr. duc; *r,* Fr. cri; H, G. ich; kh, G. doch; ‡foreign; *hypothetical; < derived from. See inside front cover.

**fit²** (fit) *n.* [OE. *fitt*, conflict] **1.** any sudden, uncontrollable attack [a *fit* of coughing] **2.** a sharp, brief display of feeling [a *fit* of anger] **3.** a temporary burst of activity **4.** *Med.* a seizure in which one loses consciousness or has convulsions or both —**by fits and starts** in an irregular way —**have** (or **throw**) **a fit** [Colloq.] to become very angry or upset

**fitch** (fich) *n.* [< OFr. < MDu. *vitsche*] *same as* POLECAT (sense 1): also **fitch′et** (-it), **fitch′ew** (-ōō)

**fit·ful** (fit′fəl) *adj.* characterized by intermittent activity, impulses, etc.; spasmodic —**fit′ful·ly** *adv.* —**fit′ful·ness** *n.*

**fit·ted** (fit′id) *adj.* designed to conform to the contours of that which it covers

**fit·ter** (-ər) *n.* **1.** a person who alters or adjusts garments to fit **2.** a person who installs or adjusts machinery, pipes, etc.

**fit·ting** (-iŋ) *adj.* suitable; proper; appropriate —*n.* **1.** an adjustment or trying on of clothes, etc. for fit **2.** a part used to join, adjust, or adapt other parts, as in a system of pipes **3.** [*pl.*] the fixtures, furnishings, or decorations of a house, automobile, office, etc. —**fit′ting·ly** *adv.* —**fit′ting·ness** *n.*

**Fitz·Ger·ald** (fits jer′əld), **Edward** (born *Edward Purcell*) 1809–83; Eng. poet & translator of *The Rubáiyát*, a long poem written by OMAR KHAYYÁM: also **Fitzgerald**

**Fitz·ger·ald** (fits jer′əld), **F(rancis) Scott** (Key) 1896–1940; U.S. author

**Fiu·me** (fyōō′me) *former* (*It.*) name of RIJEKA

**five** (fīv) *adj.* [< OE. *fif*] totaling one more than four —*n.* **1.** the cardinal number between four and six; 5; V **2.** anything having five units or members, or numbered five; specif., *a*) a basketball team *b*) [Colloq.] a five-dollar bill

**five-and-ten-cent store** (-′n ten′sent′) a store that sells a wide variety of inexpensive merchandise: also **five′-and-ten′, five′-and-dime′**

**five·fold** (-fōld′) *adj.* [see -FOLD] **1.** having five parts **2.** having five times as much or as many —*adv.* five times as much or as many

**Five Nations** a confederation of Iroquoian Indians, including the Mohawks, Oneidas, Onondagas, Cayugas, and Senecas

**fix** (fiks) *vt.* [< L. *fixus*, pp. of *figere*, to fasten] **1.** *a*) to make firm, stable, or secure *b*) to fasten firmly **2.** to set firmly in the mind **3.** to direct steadily [to *fix* the eyes on a spot] **4.** to make rigid **5.** to make permanent or lasting **6.** to establish definitely; set or determine **7.** to set in order; adjust **8.** to repair, mend, etc. **9.** to prepare (food or meals) **10.** [Colloq.] to influence the result or action of (a race, election, etc) by bribery, trickery, etc. **11.** [Colloq.] to revenge oneself on; punish **12.** [Colloq.] to spay or castrate **13.** *Chem.* *a*) to make solid or nonvolatile *b*) to combine (atmospheric nitrogen) in the form of useful compounds, as nitrates, ammonia, etc. **14.** *Photog.* to make (a film, print, etc.) permanent by washing in a chemical solution —*vi.* **1.** to become fixed, firm, or stable **2.** [Colloq. or Dial.] to prepare or intend [I'm *fixing* to go] —*n.* **1.** the position of a ship or aircraft determined as from the bearings of two or more known points **2.** [Colloq.] a difficult or awkward situation; predicament **3.** [Slang] *a*) the fixing of the outcome of a contest, situation, etc. *b*) a contest, situation, etc. that has been fixed **4.** [Slang] an injection of a narcotic, as heroin —**fix on** (or **upon**) to choose —**fix up** [Colloq.] **1.** to repair, mend, etc. **2.** to set in order **3.** to make arrangements for —**fix′a·ble** *adj.* —**fix′er** *n.*

**fix·ate** (fik′sāt) *vt., vi.* -at·ed, -at·ing **1.** to make or become fixed **2.** *Psychoanalysis* to subject to or undergo fixation

**fix·a·tion** (fik sā′shən) *n.* **1.** a fixing or being fixed, as in chemistry, photography, etc. **2.** popularly, an exaggerated preoccupation; obsession **3.** *Psychoanalysis* attachment to objects of an earlier stage of psychosexual development [a father *fixation*]

**fix·a·tive** (fik′sə tiv) *adj.* that is able or tends to make permanent, prevent fading, etc. —*n.* a fixative substance, as a mordant

**fixed** (fikst) *adj.* **1.** firmly placed or attached; not movable **2.** established; set **3.** steady; resolute **4.** obsessive [a *fixed* idea] **5.** [Colloq.] supplied with something, specif. money [comfortably *fixed* for life] **6.** [Slang] with the outcome dishonestly prearranged **7.** *Chem.* *a*) nonvolatile [*fixed* oils] *b*) incorporated into a stable compound from its free state, as atmospheric nitrogen —**fix·ed·ly** (fik′sid-lē) *adv.* —**fix′ed·ness** *n.*

**fixed star** a star that appears to keep the same position in relation to other stars

**fix·ings** (fik′siŋz) *n.pl.* [Colloq.] accessories or trimmings [roast turkey and all the *fixings*]

**fix·i·ty** (-sə tē) *n.* **1.** the quality or state of being fixed; steadiness or permanence **2.** *pl.* -ties anything fixed

**fixt** (fikst) *poet. pt. and pp. of* FIX

**fix·ture** (fiks′chər) *n.* [< LL. *fixura* < L. *fixus* (see FIX):

form infl. by MIXTURE] **1.** anything firmly in place **2.** any of the firmly attached fittings of a house, store, etc. [bathroom *fixtures*] **3.** a person or thing long-established in a place or job

**fizz** (fiz) *n.* [echoic] **1.** a hissing, sputtering sound, as of an effervescent drink **2.** an effervescent drink —*vi.* **1.** to make a hissing or bubbling sound **2.** to give off gas bubbles; effervesce

**fiz·zle** (fiz′'l) *vi.* -zled, -zling [ME. *fesilen*, to break wind silently] **1.** to make a hissing or sputtering sound **2.** [Colloq.] to fail, esp. after a successful beginning —*n.* **1.** a hissing or sputtering sound **2.** [Colloq.] a failure

**fizz·y** (fiz′ē) *adj.* fizz′i·er, fizz′i·est fizzing; effervescent

**fjord** (fyôrd) *n. same as* FIORD

**FL** Florida

**Fl.** **1.** Flanders **2.** Flemish

**fl.** **1.** [L. *floruit*] (he or she) flourished **2.** fluid

**Fla.** Florida

**flab** (flab) *n.* [back-formation < FLABBY] [Colloq.] soft, sagging flesh

**flab·ber·gast** (flab′ər gast′) *vt.* [< ? ff. + AGHAST] to dumbfound; amaze

**flab·by** (flab′ē) *adj.* -bi·er, -bi·est [var. of *flappy* < FLAP] **1.** lacking firmness; limp and soft [*flabby* muscles] **2.** lacking force; weak —**flab′bi·ly** *adv.* —**flab′bi·ness** *n.*

**flac·cid** (flak′sid, flas′id) *adj.* [L. *flaccidus* < *flaccus*, flabby] **1.** soft and limp; flabby **2.** weak; feeble —**flac·cid′i·ty** *n.* —**flac′cid·ly** *adv.*

‡**fla·con** (flá kōn′; E. flak′'n) *n.* [Fr.: see FLAGON] a small bottle with a stopper, as for perfume

**flag¹** (flag) *n.* [< ? FLAG⁴, in obs. sense "to flutter"] **1.** a piece of cloth with colors, patterns, or devices, used as a national or state symbol or as a signal; banner, standard **2.** the tail of a deer **3.** the bushy tail of certain dogs, as setters **4.** *Music* any of the lines extending from a stem, indicating whether the note is an eighth, sixteenth, etc. —*vt.* **flagged, flag′ging 1.** to decorate or mark with flags **2.** to signal with or as with a flag; esp., to signal to stop (often with *down*) —**flag′ger** *n.*

**flag²** (flag) *n.* [ON. *flaga*, slab of stone] *same as* FLAGSTONE —*vt.* **flagged, flag′ging** to pave with flagstones

**flag³** (flag) *n.* [ME. *flagge*, akin ? to ff.] **1.** any of various irises, with flowers of blue, purple, white, yellow, etc. **2.** *same as* SWEET FLAG

**flag⁴** (flag) *vi.* **flagged, flag′ging** [< ? ON. *flakka*, to flutter] to lose strength; grow weak or tired

**Flag Day** June 14, anniversary of the day in 1777 when the U.S. flag was adopted

**flag·el·lant** (flaj′ə lənt) *n.* [see ff.] a person who whips; specif., one who whips himself or has himself whipped as for religious discipline —*adj.* engaging in flagellation

**flag·el·late** (flaj′ə lāt′) *vt.* -lat·ed, -lat·ing [< L. < *flagellare*, to whip < *flagellum*, a whip] to whip; flog —*adj.* **1.** having a flagellum or flagella: also **flag′el·lat′ed 2.** shaped like a flagellum —**flag′el·la′tion** *n.* —**flag′el·la′tor** *n.*

**fla·gel·lum** (flə jel′əm) *n., pl.* -la (-ə), -lums [L.: see prec.] **1.** *Biol.* a whiplike part serving as an organ of locomotion in certain cells, bacteria, protozoans, etc. **2.** *Bot.* a threadlike shoot or runner

**flag·eo·let** (flaj′ə let′) *n.* [Fr., dim. of OFr. *flageol*, a flute < L. *flare*, to blow] a small fipple flute similar to the recorder

**flag·ging¹** (flag′iŋ) *adj.* [prp. of FLAG⁴] weakening or drooping —**flag′ging·ly** *adv.*

**flag·ging²** (flag′iŋ) *n.* flagstones or a pavement made of flagstones

**fla·gi·tious** (flə jish′əs) *adj.* [< L. < *flagitium*, shameful act < *flagitare*, to demand] shamefully wicked; vile and scandalous —**fla·gi′tious·ly** *adv.* —**fla·gi′tious·ness** *n.*

**flag·man** (flag′mən) *n., pl.* -men a person whose work is signaling with a flag or lantern

**flag officer** *U.S. Navy* any officer above the rank of captain

**flag·on** (flag′ən) *n.* [< OFr. *flacon* < LL. < *flasca*, flask] **1.** a container for liquids, with a handle, a spout, and, often, a lid **2.** the contents of a flagon

**flag·pole** (flag′pōl′) *n.* a pole on which a flag is flown: also **flag′staff′** (-staf′)

**fla·gran·cy** (flā′grən sē) *n.* the quality or state of being flagrant: also **fla′grance**

**fla·grant** (flā′grənt) *adj.* [< L. prp. of *flagrare*, to blaze] glaringly bad; notorious; outrageous —**fla′grant·ly** *adv.*

‡**fla·gran·te de·lic·to** (flə gran′tē di lik′tō) [L.] *same as* IN FLAGRANTE DELICTO

**flag·ship** (flag′ship′) *n.* **1.** the ship carrying the commander of a fleet or squadron and displaying his flag **2.** the finest, largest, or newest ship of a steamship line

**flag·stone** (flag′stōn′) *n.* **1.** any hard stone that splits into flat pieces used to pave walks, terraces, etc. **2.** a piece of such stone

**flag-wav·ing** (flag′wā′viŋ) *n.* an emotional appeal calculated to arouse intense patriotic feelings

**flail** (flāl) *n.* [OFr. *flaiel* < L. *flagellum*, a whip] a farm tool having a free-swinging stick attached to a long handle, used to thresh grain by hand —*vt., vi.* **1.** to thresh with a flail **2.** to beat as with a flail **3.** to move (one's arms) about like flails

**flair** (fler) *n.* [< OFr. < *flairer*, ult. < L. *fragrare*, to smell] **1.** keen, natural discernment **2.** an aptitude; knack **3.** [Colloq.] smartness in style; dash

**flak** (flak) *n.* [G. < *Fl(ieger)-a(bwehr)k(anone)*, antiaircraft gun] the fire of antiaircraft guns

**flake** (flāk) *n.* [< Scand., as in Norw. *flak*, ice floe, ON. *flackna*, to flake off] **1.** a small, thin mass [a *flake* of snow] **2.** a thin piece or layer split or peeled off from anything; chip —*vt., vi.* **flaked, flak′ing** **1.** to form into flakes **2.** to chip or peel off in flakes **3.** to make or become spotted with flakes —**flak′er** *n.*

**flak·y** (flāk′ē) *adj.* **flak′i·er, flak′i·est** **1.** containing or made up of flakes **2.** breaking easily into flakes **3.** [Slang] very eccentric —**flak′i·ly** *adv.* —**flak′i·ness** *n.*

**‡flam·bé** (flän bā′) *adj.* [Fr., lit., flaming] served with a flaming sauce containing brandy, rum, etc.

**flam·beau** (flam′bō) *n., pl.* **-beaux** (-bōz), **-beaus** [Fr., dim. of OFr. *flambe*, FLAME] a lighted torch

**flam·boy·ant** (flam boi′ənt) *adj.* [Fr. < OFr. < *flambe*, FLAME] **1.** characterized by flamelike tracery of windows and florid decoration, as late French Gothic architecture **2.** flamelike or brilliant **3.** too showy or ornate —**flamboy′ance, flam·boy′an·cy** *n.* —**flam·boy′ant·ly** *adv.*

**flame** (flām) *n.* [< OFr. < L. < *flamma* < *flagrare*, to burn] **1.** the burning gas of a fire, seen as a flickering light; blaze **2.** a tongue of light rising from a fire **3.** the state of burning with a blaze of light **4.** a thing like a flame in heat, etc. **5.** an intense emotion **6.** a sweetheart: now usually humorous —*vi.* **flamed, flam′ing** **1.** to burst into flame; blaze **2.** to grow red or hot **3.** to become very excited —*vt.* to treat with flame —**flame up** (or **out**) to burst out in or as in flame

**fla·men·co** (flə meŋ′kō) *n.* [Sp., Flemish < DuFl. *Flaming*, a Fleming] **1.** the energetic, emotional style of dance or music of Spanish gypsies **2.** *pl.* **-cos** a song or dance in this style

**flame·out** (flām′out′) *n.* the ceasing of combustion in a jet engine, due to an abnormal flight condition

**flame thrower** a military weapon for shooting a stream of flaming gasoline, oil, etc.

**flam·ing** (flā′miŋ) *adj.* **1.** burning with flames; blazing **2.** like a flame in brilliance or heat **3.** ardent; passionate —**flam′ing·ly** *adv.*

**fla·min·go** (flə miŋ′gō) *n., pl.* **-gos, -goes** [Port. < Sp. *flamenco*, lit., Flemish: infl. by *flama*, FLAME] a tropical wading bird with long legs, a long neck, and bright pink or red feathers

**flam·ma·ble** (flam′ə b'l) *adj.* easily set on fire: term now preferred to INFLAMMABLE in commerce, industry, etc. — **flam′ma·bil′i·ty** *n.*

**Flan·ders** (flan′dərz) region in NW Europe, on the North Sea, including W Belgium & a part of NW France & a part of SW Netherlands

**flange** (flanj) *n.* [< ? ME. *flaunch*, an outer edge of a coat of arms] a projecting rim or collar on a wheel, pipe, etc., to hold it in place, give it strength, or attach it to something else —*vt.* **flanged, flang′ing** to put a flange on

**flank** (flaŋk) *n.* [< OFr. *flanc*] **1.** the fleshy side of a person or animal between the ribs and the hip **2.** a cut of beef from this part **3.** the side of anything **4.** *Mil.* the right or left side of a formation or force —*adj.* of or having to do with the flank —*vt.* **1.** to be at the side of **2.** to place at the side, or on either side, of **3.** *a)* to attack the side of (an enemy unit) *b)* to pass around the side of (an enemy unit) —*vi.* to be located at the side (with *on* or *upon*)

**flank·er** (-ər) *n.* one that flanks; specif., *Football* an offensive back who takes a position closer to the sidelines than the rest of the team

**flan·nel** (flan′'l) *n.* [< W. *gwlanen* < *gwlan*, wool] **1.** a soft, lightweight, loosely woven woolen cloth **2.** *same as* COTTON FLANNEL **3.** [*pl.*] *a)* trousers, etc. made of light flannel *b)* heavy woolen underwear —**flan′nel·ly** *adj.*

**flan·nel·ette, flan·nel·et** (flan′ə let′) *n.* a soft cotton cloth like cotton flannel but lighter

**flap** (flap) *n.* [ME. *flappe* < v. *flappen*: prob. echoic] **1.** anything flat and broad that is attached at one end and

FLAIL

hangs loose or covers an opening **2.** the motion or slapping sound of a swinging flap **3.** a hinged section of an airplane wing, used in landing and taking off **4.** [Slang] a commotion; fuss —*vt.* **flapped, flap′ping** **1.** to slap with something flat and broad **2.** to move back and forth or up and down [the bird *flapped* its wings] **3.** to throw, slam, etc. abruptly or noisily —*vi.* **1.** to move back and forth or up and down, as in the wind; flutter **2.** to fly or try to fly by flapping the wings **3.** [Slang] to become excited or confused —**flap′less** *adj.* —**flap′py** *adj.*

**flap·jack** (flap′jak′) *n.* a pancake or griddlecake

**flap·per** (flap′ər) *n.* **1.** one that flaps **2.** [Colloq.] in the 1920's, a young woman considered bold or unconventional in actions and dress

**flare** (fler) *vi.* **flared, flar′ing** [ME. *fleare* < ?] **1.** to blaze up brightly or burn unsteadily **2.** to burst out suddenly in anger, etc. (often with *up* or *out*) **3.** to curve or spread outward, as the bell of a trumpet —*vt.* to make flare —*n.* **1.** a bright, brief, unsteady blaze of light **2.** a very bright light used as a distress signal, etc. **3.** a sudden, brief outburst, as of emotion or sound **4.** *a)* a curving outward, as of a skirt *b)* a part that curves or spreads outward **5.** a short-lived outburst of brightness on the sun

**flare-up** (-up′) *n.* a sudden outburst of flame or of anger, trouble, etc.

**flar·ing** (fler′iŋ) *adj.* **1.** blazing brightly for a little while **2.** curving or spreading outward —**flar′ing·ly** *adv.*

**flash** (flash) *vi.* [ME. *flaschen*, to splash: echoic] **1.** to send out a sudden, brief light, esp. at intervals **2.** to sparkle or gleam **3.** to speak abruptly, esp. in anger (usually with *out*) **4.** to come or pass swiftly and suddenly —*vt.* **1.** to send out (light, etc.) in sudden, brief spurts **2.** to cause to flash **3.** to signal with light **4.** to send (news, etc.) swiftly or suddenly **5.** [Colloq.] to show briefly or ostentatiously [to *flash* a roll of money] —*n.* **1.** *a)* a sudden, brief light *b)* a sudden burst of flame or heat **2.** a brief time; moment **3.** a sudden, brief display [a *flash* of wit] **4.** a brief item of news sent by telegraph or radio **5.** a gaudy display **6.** anything that flashes; specif., [Colloq.] a person adept at something —*adj.* **1.** happening swiftly or suddenly [a *flash* flood] **2.** working along with a flash of light [a *flash* camera] —**flash in the pan** [orig. of priming in pan of a flintlock] **1.** a sudden, apparently brilliant effort that fails **2.** one that fails after such an effort —**flash′er** *n.* —**flash′-ing·ly** *adv.*

**flash·back** (-bak′) *n.* **1.** an interruption in the continuity of a story, play, etc. by the presentation of some earlier episode **2.** such an episode

**flash·bulb** (-bulb′) *n. Photog.* an electric light bulb giving a brief, dazzling light

**flash·card** (-kärd′) *n.* any of a set of cards with words, numbers, etc. on them, flashed one by one before a class in a drill

**flash·cube** (-kyōōb′) *n.* a small, rotating cube containing a flashbulb in each of four sides

**flash·ing** (-iŋ) *n.* sheets of metal, etc. used to weatherproof joints, edges, etc., esp. of a roof

**flash·light** (-līt′) *n.* **1.** a portable electric light, usually operated by batteries **2.** a brief, dazzling light for taking photographs at night or indoors

**flash point** the lowest temperature at which the vapor of a volatile oil will ignite with a flash

**flash·y** (-ē) *adj.* **flash′i·er, flash′i·est** **1.** dazzling or bright for a little while **2.** gaudy; showy —**flash′i·ly** *adv.* —**flash′i·ness** *n.*

**flask** (flask) *n.* [< ML. *flasco* & OE. *flasce* < LL. < *flasca*] **1.** any small bottle with a narrow neck, used in laboratories, etc. **2.** a small, flat pocket container for liquor, etc.

**flat¹** (flat) *adj.* **flat′ter, flat′test** [< ON. *flatr*] **1.** having a smooth, level surface **2.** *a)* lying extended at full length *b)* spread out smooth and level **3.** *a)* broad, even, and thin *b)* having a flat heel or no heel [*flat* shoes] **4.** almost straight or level [a *flat* trajectory or flight] **5.** absolute; positive [a *flat* denial] **6.** not fluctuating [a *flat* rate] **7.** having little or no sparkle or taste **8.** monotonous; dull **9.** not clear or full [a *flat* sound] **10.** emptied of air [a *flat* tire] **11.** without gloss [*flat* paint] **12.** *Art a)* lacking relief or perspective *b)* uniform in tint **13.** *Music a)* below the true or proper pitch *b)* lower in pitch by a half step [D-*flat*] **14.** *Phonet.* designating the vowel *a* sounded with the tongue in a relatively level position, as in *can* — *adv.* **1.** in a flat manner **2.** in a flat position **3.** *a)* exactly; precisely [ten seconds *flat*] *b)* bluntly; abruptly [she left him *flat*] **4.** *Music* below the true or proper pitch —*n.* **1.** a flat surface or part [the *flat* of the hand] **2.** an expanse of level land **3.** a low-lying marsh **4.** a shallow; shoal **5.** a shallow box, as for growing seedlings **6.** a piece of theatrical scenery on a flat frame **7.** a deflated tire

**8.** [*pl.*] flat-heeled shoes  **9.** *Music* *a*) a note or tone one half step below another  *b*) the symbol (♭) indicating such a note —*vt.*, *vi.* **flat′ted, flat′ting** to make or become flat —**fall flat** to arouse no response —**flat′ly** *adv.* —**flat′ness** *n.* —**flat′tish** *adj.*

**flat²** (flat) *n.* [altered < Scot. dial. *flet* (OE. *flet*), a floor of a dwelling]  an apartment or suite of rooms on one floor of a building

**flat·bed, flat-bed** (-bed′) *adj.* designating or of a truck, trailer, etc. having a bed or platform without sides or stakes —*n.* a flatbed truck, trailer, etc.

**flat·boat** (-bōt′) *n.* a flat-bottomed boat for carrying freight in shallow waters or on rivers

**flat·car** (-kär′) *n.* a railroad car without sides or a roof, for carrying certain freight

**flat·fish** (-fish′) *n.*, *pl.* **-fish′, -fish′es:** see FISH  a fish with a flat body and both eyes on the uppermost side, as the flounder, halibut, etc.

**flat·foot** (-foot′) *n.*  **1.** a condition in which the instep arch of the foot has been flattened  **2.** [Slang] a policeman

**flat-foot·ed** (-foot′id) *adj.* **1.** having flatfoot  **2.** [Colloq.] downright and firm —**catch flat-footed** [Colloq.] to take by surprise; catch unprepared —**flat′-foot′ed·ly** *adv.* —**flat′-foot′ed·ness** *n.*

**flat·i·ron** (-ī′ərn) *n.* an iron for pressing clothes

**flat silver** silver knives, forks, spoons, etc.

**flat·ten** (-'n) *vt.*, *vi.*  **1.** to make or become flat or flatter  **2.** to make or become prostrate —**flat′ten·er** *n.*

**flat·ter** (flat′ər) *vt.* [< OFr. *flater*, to smooth < Frank. *flat*] **1.** to praise too much or insincerely, as to win favor  **2.** to try to please, or get the favor of, as by praise  **3.** to make seem more attractive than is so [his portrait *flatters* him]  **4.** to make feel pleased or honored —*vi.* to use flattery —**flatter oneself** to be smug or deluded in thinking (*that*) —**flat′ter·er** *n.* —**flat′ter·ing·ly** *adv.*

**flat·ter·y** (flat′ər ē) *n.*, *pl.* **-ter·ies**  **1.** a flattering  **2.** excessive or insincere praise

**flat·top** (-täp′) *n.* [Slang] something with a flat or level surface, as an aircraft carrier

**flat·u·lent** (flach′ə lənt, -yoo-) *adj.* [Fr. < ModL. < L. < *flare*, to blow]  **1.** of, having, or producing gas in the stomach or intestines  **2.** windy or empty in speech; pompous; pretentious —**flat′u·lence, flat′u·len·cy** *n.* —**flat′u·lent·ly** *adv.*

**flat·ware** (flat′wer′) *n.* relatively flat tableware; specif., knives, forks, and spoons

**flat·work** (-wurk′) *n.* sheets, napkins, and other flat pieces that can be pressed in a mangle

**flat·worm** (-wurm′) *n.* same as PLATYHELMINTH

**Flau·bert** (flō ber′), **Gus·tave** (güs täv′) 1821–80; Fr. novelist

**flaunt** (flônt) *vi.* [prob. < dial. *flant*, to strut coquettishly] **1.** to make a gaudy or impudent display  **2.** to flutter freely —*vt.* to show off proudly or impudently —**flaunt′ing·ly** *adv.*

**flau·tist** (flôt′ist, flout′-) *n.* [It. *flautista* < *flauto*, flute] *same as* FLUTIST

**fla·vin** (flā′vin, flav′in) *n.* [< L. *flavus*, yellow + -IN¹] **1.** a complex ketone, $C_{10}H_6N_4O_2$  **2.** a natural or synthetic yellow pigment  Also **fla′vine** (-vēn, -ēn)

**fla·vone** (flā′vōn, flav′ōn) *n.* [G. *flavon* < L. *flavus*, yellow] **1.** a colorless crystalline compound, $C_{15}H_{10}O_2$: a base for some yellow dyes  **2.** any derivative of this

**fla·vor** (flā′vər) *n.* [< OFr. *flaur* < L. *flatare*, freq. of *flare*, to blow]  **1.** *a*) the combined taste and smell of something  *b*) taste in general  **2.** *same as* FLAVORING  **3.** characteristic quality —*vt.* to give flavor to —**fla′vor·less** *adj.*

**fla·vor·ful** (-fəl) *adj.* full of flavor; tasty: also **fla′vor·some** (-səm), **fla′vor·ous** (-əs), **fla′vor·y** (-ē) —**fla′vor·ful·ly** *adv.*

**fla·vor·ing** (-iŋ) *n.* an essence, extract, etc. added to a food or drink to give it a certain taste

**fla·vour** (flā′vər) *n.*, *vt. Brit. sp. of* FLAVOR

**flaw¹** (flô) *n.* [prob. < Scand.: see FLAKE]  **1.** a break, scratch, crack, etc. that spoils something; blemish  **2.** a defect; fault; error —*vt.*, *vi.* to make or become faulty —**flaw′less** *adj.* —**flaw′less·ly** *adv.* —**flaw′less·ness** *n.*

**flaw²** (flô) *n.* [prob. < ON. *flaga*, sudden onset] a sudden, brief gust of wind; squall

**flax** (flaks) *n.* [OE. *fleax*]  **1.** any of a certain genus of plants; esp., a slender, erect annual with delicate blue flowers and narrow leaves: the seed (**flax′seed′**) yields linseed oil, and the fibers of the stem are spun into linen thread  **2.** these fibers

**flax·en** (-'n) *adj.*  **1.** of or made of flax  **2.** like flax in color; pale-yellow: also **flax′y**

**flay** (flā) *vt.* [OE. *flean*]  **1.** to strip off the skin or hide of, as by whipping  **2.** to criticize or scold mercilessly  **3.** to rob; pillage —**flay′er** *n.*

**F layer** the highest regular layer of the ionosphere, reflecting high-frequency radio waves

**fl. dr.** fluid dram; fluid drams

**flea** (flē) *n.* [< OE. *fleah*]  a small, wingless jumping insect that is parasitic and sucks blood

**flea·bag** (-bag′) *n.* [Slang] a very cheap hotel

**flea-bit·ten** (-bit′'n) *adj.*  **1.** bitten by or infested with fleas  **2.** wretched; shabby

**flea market** an outdoor bazaar dealing mainly in cheap, secondhand goods

**fleck** (flek) *n.* [ON. *flekkr*]  **1.** a spot or small patch of color, etc.; speck  **2.** a particle; flake —*vt.* to cover or sprinkle with flecks; speckle

**flec·tion** (flek′shən) *n.* [< L. pp. of *flectere*, to bend]  **1.** a bending; flexing  **2.** a bent part  **3.** *Anat. same as* FLEXION —**flec′tion·al** *adj.*

**fled** (fled) *pt. & pp. of* FLEE

**fledge** (flej) *vi.* **fledged, fledg′ing** [< OE. (*un*)*flycge*, (un)fledged]  to grow the feathers needed for flying —*vt.* **1.** to rear (a young bird) until it can fly  **2.** to supply with feathers

**fledg·ling** (flej′liŋ) *n.*  **1.** a young bird just fledged  **2.** a young, inexperienced person  Also, chiefly Brit., **fledge′ling**

**flee** (flē) *vi.* **fled, flee′ing** [OE. *fleon*]  **1.** to run away or escape from danger, pursuit, etc.  **2.** to pass away swiftly; vanish  **3.** to go swiftly —*vt.* to run away from; shun —**fle′er** *n.*

**fleece** (flēs) *n.* [OE. *fleos*]  **1.** the wool covering a sheep or similar animal  **2.** the amount of wool cut from a sheep in one shearing  **3.** a covering like a sheep's  **4.** a soft, warm napped fabric —*vt.* **fleeced, fleec′ing**  **1.** to shear fleece from  **2.** to steal from by fraud; swindle —**fleec′er** *n.*

**fleec·y** (-ē) *adj.* **fleec′i·er, fleec′i·est** made of, covered with, or like fleece —**fleec′i·ly** *adv.* —**fleec′i·ness** *n.*

**fleer** (flir) *vi.*, *vt.* [prob. < Scand.]  to laugh derisively (at); sneer or jeer (at) —*n.* a derisive grimace, laugh, etc. —**fleer′ing·ly** *adv.*

**fleet¹** (flēt) *n.* [OE. *fleot* < *fleotan*, to float]  **1.** *a*) a number of warships under one command  *b*) an entire navy  **2.** any group of ships, trucks, buses, airplanes, etc. under one control

**fleet²** (flēt) *vi.* [OE. *fleotan:* see prec.]  to move swiftly; fly —*adj.* swift; rapid —**fleet′ly** *adv.* —**fleet′ness** *n.*

**fleet admiral** *U.S. Navy* an admiral of the highest rank, having the insignia of five stars

**fleet·ing** (flēt′iŋ) *adj.* passing swiftly; not lasting —**fleet′ing·ly** *adv.* —**fleet′ing·ness** *n.*

**Flem·ing** (flem′iŋ) *n.* [< MDu. *Vlaming*]  **1.** a native of Flanders  **2.** a Flemish-speaking Belgian

**Flem·ing** (flem′iŋ), **Sir Alexander** 1881–1955; Brit. bacteriologist: codiscoverer of penicillin

**Flem·ish** (-ish) *adj.* of Flanders, the Flemings, or their language —*n.* the West Germanic language of the Flemings —**the Flemish** the people of Flanders

**flense** (flens) *vt.* **flensed, flens′ing** [< Du. *vlensen* or Dan. *flense*]  to cut blubber or skin from (a whale, seal, etc.): also **flench** (flench)

**flesh** (flesh) *n.* [OE. *flæsc*]  **1.** *a*) the soft substance of the body (of a person or animal); esp., the muscular tissue  *b*) the skin of the body  **2.** meat; esp., meat other than fish or fowl  **3.** the pulpy or edible part of fruits and vegetables  **4.** the human body, as distinguished from the soul  **5.** human nature, esp. in its sensual aspect  **6.** all living beings, esp. all mankind  **7.** kindred: now mainly in **one's (own) flesh and blood**, one's close relatives  **8.** the typical color of a white person's skin; yellowish pink —*vt.* **1.** to incite to bloodshed, etc. by a foretaste  **2.** to fatten  **3.** to fill out by adding details, etc. (usually with *out*) —*vi.* to grow fat (usually with *out* or *up*) —**flesh and blood** the human body —**in the flesh**  **1.** alive  **2.** in person

**flesh-col·ored** (-kul′ərd) *adj.* yellowish-pink

**flesh·ly** (-lē) *adj.* **-li·er, -li·est**  **1.** of the body  **2.** sensual  **3.** *same as* FLESHY —**flesh′li·ness** *n.*

**flesh·pot** (-pät′) *n.*  **1.** a pot for cooking meat  **2.** [*pl.*] *a*) bodily comfort and pleasures; luxuries  *b*) a place where such pleasures are provided

**flesh·y** (-ē) *adj.* **flesh′i·er, flesh′i·est**  **1.** having much flesh; plump  **2.** of or like flesh  **3.** having a firm pulp: said of some fruits —**flesh′i·ness** *n.*

**fleur-de-lis** (flur′də lē′, -lēs′) *n.*, *pl.* **fleurs-de-lis** (flur′də-lēz′) [< OFr. *flor de lis*, lit., flower of the lily]  **1.** *same as* IRIS (senses 3 & 4)  **2.** the coat of arms of the former French royal family  **3.** *Heraldry* a lilylike emblem  Also sp. **fleur-de-lys**

**flew** (floo) *pt. of* FLY¹

**flex** (fleks) *vt.*, *vi.* [< L. *flexus*, pp. of *flectere*, to bend]  **1.** to bend (an arm, knee, etc.)  **2.** to contract (a muscle)

**flex·i·ble** (flek′sə b'l) *adj.* [< OFr. < L. < *flexus:* see prec.]  **1.** able to bend without breaking  **2.** easily persuaded or influenced  **3.** adjustable to change — **flex′i·bil′i·ty** *n.* —**flex′i·bly** *adv.*

**flex·ion** (flek′shən) *n.*  **1.** *same as* FLECTION  **2.** *Anat.* the

FLEUR-DE-LIS

bending of a joint or limb by means of the flexor muscles —**flex′ion·al** *adj.*

**flex·i·time** (fleks′ə tīm′) *n.* a system allowing individual employees some flexibility in choosing the time of their working hours: also **flex′time′** (fleks′-)

**flex·or** (flek′sər) *n.* [ModL. < L.: see FLEX] a muscle that bends a limb or other part of the body

**flex·u·ous** (-shoo wəs) *adj.* winding or wavering —**flex′u·os′i·ty** (-wäs′ə tē) *n., pl.* **-ties**

**flex·ure** (-shər) *n.* **1.** a bending; curving; flexing **2.** a bend; curve; fold —**flex′ur·al** *adj.*

**flib·ber·ti·gib·bet** (flib′ər tē jib′it) *n.* [< ?] an irresponsible, flighty person

**flick**[1] (flik) *n.* [echoic, but infl. by FLICKER[1]] **1.** a light, quick stroke, jerk, or snap **2.** a light, snapping sound **3.** a fleck; speck —*vt.* **1.** to strike, remove, etc. with a light, quick stroke **2.** to make such a stroke with (a whip, etc.) —*vi.* to flutter

**flick**[2] (flik) *n.* [< ff.] [Slang] *same as* MOVIE —**the flicks** [Slang] the movies (see MOVIE)

**flick·er**[1] (flik′ər) *vi.* [OE. *flicorian*] **1.** to move with a quick, light, wavering motion **2.** to burn or shine unsteadily, as a candle flame —*vt.* to make flicker —*n.* **1.** a flickering **2.** a flame or light that flickers **3.** a quick, passing look or feeling —**flick′er·y** *adj.*

**flick·er**[2] (flik′ər) *n.* [echoic of its cry] any of several N. American woodpeckers, esp. one with wings of a golden color on the underside

**flied** (flīd) *pt. & pp.* of FLY[1] (*vi.* 8)

**fli·er** (flī′ər) *n.* **1.** a thing that flies **2.** an aviator **3.** a bus, train, etc. on a fast schedule **4.** a small handbill **5.** [Colloq.] a reckless gamble or speculation Also, esp. for 2, 3, & 5, **fly′er**

**flight**[1] (flīt) *n.* [OE. *flyht*] **1.** the act, manner, or power of flying or moving through space **2.** distance flown at one time, as by an airplane, bird, etc. **3.** a group of birds, arrows, etc. flying together **4.** *a)* a formation of military airplanes in flight *b)* U.S. Air Force the smallest tactical unit, a subdivision of a squadron **5.** an airplane scheduled to fly a certain trip **6.** a trip by airplane **7.** a soaring above the ordinary [a *flight* of fancy] **8.** a set of stairs, as between floors

**flight**[2] (flīt) *n.* [< OE. < base of *fleon*, to flee] a fleeing, as from danger —**put to flight** to force to flee —**take (to) flight** to run away; flee

**flight·less** (-lis) *adj.* not able to fly

**flight·y** (-ē) *adj.* **flight′i·er, flight′i·est 1.** frivolous or irresponsible **2.** foolish; silly —**flight′i·ly** *adv.* —**flight′i·ness** *n.*

**flim·flam** (flim′flam′) *n.* [< ?] **1.** nonsense **2.** a sly trick or deception —*vt.* **-flammed′, -flam′ming** [Colloq.] to trick —**flim′flam′mer·y** *n.*

**flim·sy** (flim′zē) *adj.* **-si·er, -si·est** [< ?] **1.** thin and easily broken or damaged; fragile **2.** weak or inadequate [a *flimsy* excuse] —*n.* **1.** a sheet of thin paper **2.** copy written on such paper, as by a reporter —**flim′si·ly** *adv.* —**flim′si·ness** *n.*

**flinch** (flinch) *vi.* [< OFr. *flenchir*] **1.** to draw back, as from a blow, difficulty, etc. **2.** to wince, as because of pain —*n.* a flinching

**flin·ders** (flin′dərz) *n.pl.* [< Scand., as in Norw. *flindra*, splinter] splinters or fragments: chiefly in **break** (or **fly**) **into flinders**

**fling** (fliŋ) *vt.* **flung, fling′ing** [ME. *flingen*, to rush < ON. *flengja*, to whip] **1.** to throw, esp. with force; hurl **2.** to put abruptly or violently [to be *flung* into confusion] **3.** to move (one's limbs, head, etc.) suddenly or impulsively **4.** to throw (oneself) spiritedly (*into* a task, etc.) **5.** to cast aside —*vi.* to move suddenly and violently; rush —*n.* **1.** a flinging **2.** a brief time of self-indulgence **3.** a spirited dance [the Highland *fling*] **4.** [Colloq.] a trial effort; try

**Flint** (flint) [after nearby Flint River, so called from the flint stones in it] city in SE Mich.: pop. 160,000 (met. area 522,000)

**flint** (flint) *n.* [OE.] **1.** a fine-grained, very hard, siliceous rock that makes sparks when struck with steel **2.** a piece of this stone, used to start a fire, for primitive tools, etc. **3.** anything like flint in hardness, use, etc. [a heart of *flint*, a lighter *flint* of iron-cerium alloy]

**flint glass** a hard, bright lead-oxide glass, used for lenses, crystal, etc.

**flint·lock** (-läk′) *n.* **1.** a gunlock using a flint in the hammer to strike sparks to ignite the powder **2.** an old-fashioned gun with such a lock

**flint·y** (flin′tē) *adj.* **flint′i·er, flint′i·est 1.** of or containing flint **2.** like flint; very hard or firm —**flint′i·ness** *n.*

**flip**[1] (flip) *vt.* **flipped, flip′ping** [echoic] **1.** to move with a quick jerk **2.** to snap (a coin) into the air with the thumb,

as in betting on which side will land uppermost **3.** to turn (a card, etc.) over quickly —*vi.* **1.** to make a quick, light stroke or move; snap **2.** to flip a coin **3.** to do a flip **4.** [Slang] to lose self-control from excitement, anger, etc.: also **flip one's lid** (or **wig**) —*n.* **1.** a flipping; snap, toss, etc. **2.** a somersault in the air

**flip**[2] (flip) *n.* [prob. < prec.] a sweetened mixed drink of wine or liquor with egg, spices, etc.

**flip**[3] (flip) *adj.* **flip′per, flip′pest** [contr. < FLIPPANT] [Colloq.] flippant; saucy; impertinent

**flip-flop** (flip′fläp′) *n.* **1.** an acrobatic spring backward from feet to hands to feet **2.** an abrupt change, as to the opposite opinion **3.** a flapping noise **4.** *Electronics* a circuit with two stable states, switching from one to the other on signal —*vi.* **-flopped′, -flop′ping** to do a flip-flop

**flip·pan·cy** (flip′ən sē) *n.* **1.** a being flippant **2.** *pl.* **-cies** a flippant act or remark

**flip·pant** (-ənt) *adj.* [Early ModE., nimble, prob. < FLIP[1]] frivolous and disrespectful; saucy —**flip′pant·ly** *adv.*

**flip·per** (-ər) *n.* [< FLIP[1]] **1.** a broad, flat limb, as of a seal, adapted for swimming **2.** a paddlelike rubber piece worn on each foot as a help in swimming and skin diving **3.** [Slang] a hand

**flip side** [Colloq.] the reverse side (of a phonograph recording), esp. the less important side

**flirt** (flurt) *vt.* [< ? OFr. *fleureter*, lit., move from flower to flower < *fleur*, FLOWER] to move quickly back and forth —*vi.* **1.** to move jerkily **2.** to woo someone lightly or frivolously **3.** to toy, as with an idea —*n.* **1.** a flirting movement **2.** a person who plays at love —**flirt′y** *adj.*

**flir·ta·tion** (flər tā′shən) *n.* a flirting, or playing at love

**flir·ta·tious** (-shəs) *adj.* flirting or inclined to flirt —**flirta′tious·ly** *adv.* —**flir·ta′tious·ness** *n.*

**flit** (flit) *vi.* **flit′ted, flit′ting** [< ON. *flytja*] to pass or fly lightly and rapidly; dart; flutter —*n.* a flitting —**flit′ter** *n.*

**flitch** (flich) *n.* [OE. *flicce*] the cured and salted side of a hog; side of bacon —*vt.* to cut into flitches

**flit·ter** (flit′ər) *vi., vt.* [freq. of FLIT] [Chiefly Dial.] *same as* FLUTTER

**fliv·ver** (fliv′ər) *n.* [< ?] [Old Slang] a small, cheap automobile, esp. an old one

**float** (flōt) *n.* [OE. *flota* < *fleotan*, to float] **1.** anything staying, or making something else stay, on or at a liquid's surface; specif., *a)* a fishing-line cork *b)* a floating, valve-controlling ball, etc. that regulates liquid level, as in a tank *c)* a buoyant device on an aircraft for landing on water **2.** a platform on wheels that carries a display or exhibit in a parade **3.** a cold beverage with ice cream floating in it —*vi.* **1.** to stay on or at a liquid's surface **2.** to drift gently on water, in air, etc. **3.** to move about vaguely and without purpose —*vt.* **1.** to make float **2.** to flood **3.** *a)* to put into circulation [*float* a bond issue] *b)* to establish or start (a business, etc.) **4.** to arrange for (a loan)

**float·a·tion** (flō tā′shən) *n. same as* FLOTATION

**float·er** (flōt′ər) *n.* **1.** one that floats **2.** a person who illegally votes at several polling places **3.** a person who changes his place of residence or work frequently **4.** an insurance policy covering movable property wherever it is at the time of loss

**float·ing** (-iŋ) *adj.* **1.** that floats **2.** not fixed; moving about **3.** *Finance a)* designating an unfunded, short-time debt *b)* not permanently invested [*floating* capital] **4.** *Mech.* designating or of suspension that reduces vibration **5.** *Med.* displaced and more movable [a *floating* kidney]

**floating ribs** the eleventh and twelfth pairs of ribs, not attached to the breastbone or to other ribs but only to the vertebrae

**floc·cu·late** (fläk′yoo lāt′) *vt., vi.* **-lat′ed, -lat′ing** to collect (clouds, precipitates, etc.) into small, flocculent masses —**floc′cu·la′tion** *n.*

**floc·cu·lent** (-lənt) *adj.* [< L. *floccus*, flock of wool + -ULENT] woolly; fluffy —**floc′cu·lence** *n.*

**flock**[1] (fläk) *n.* [OE. *flocc*, a troop] **1.** a group of certain animals, as goats or sheep, or of birds, living, feeding, etc. together **2.** any group, esp. a large one, as of church members —*vi.* to assemble or travel in a flock

**flock**[2] (fläk) *n.* [< OFr. < L. *floccus*] **1.** a small tuft of wool, cotton, etc. **2.** wool or cotton waste used to stuff furniture, etc. **3.** tiny fibers put on wallpaper, etc. to form a velvety surface or design Also sp. **floc** —**flock′y** *adj.*

**flock·ing** (-iŋ) *n.* **1.** *same as* FLOCK[2] (sense 3) **2.** a material or surface with flock on it

**floe** (flō) *n.* [prob. < Norw. *flo*, layer] *same as* ICE FLOE

**flog** (fläg, flôg) *vt.* **flogged, flog′ging** [? cant abbrev. of L. *flagellare*, to whip] **1.** to beat with a stick, whip, etc. **2.** [Brit. Slang] to sell, esp. illegally —**flog′ger** *n.*

**flood** (flud) *n.* [OE. *flod*] **1.** an overflowing of water on an area normally dry; deluge **2.** the flowing in of water from the sea as the tide rises **3.** a great flow or outpouring, as of words **4.** [Archaic] a large body of water —*vt.* **1.** to cover or fill with or as with a flood; inundate /rain *flooded* the earth, music *flooded* the room/ **2.** to put much or too much liquid on or in —*vi.* **1.** to rise, flow, or gush out in or as in a flood **2.** to become flooded —**the Flood** *Bible* the great flood in Noah's time: Gen. 7

**flood·gate** (-gāt') *n.* **1.** a gate in a stream or canal, to control water height and flow **2.** anything like this in controlling an outburst

**flood·light** (-līt') *n.* **1.** a lamp that casts a broad beam of bright light **2.** such light —*vt.* **-light'ed** or **-lit'**, **-light'ing** to illuminate by a floodlight

**flood tide** the incoming or rising tide

**floor** (flôr) *n.* [OE. *flor*] **1.** the inside bottom surface of a room **2.** any bottom surface /the ocean *floor*/ **3.** the platform of a bridge, pier, etc. **4.** a level or story in a building **5.** *a)* the part of a legislative chamber, stock exchange, etc. occupied by members *b)* the members as a group **6.** the right to speak in an assembly **7.** a lower limit set on anything —*vt.* **1.** to cover or furnish with a floor **2.** to knock down **3.** [Colloq.] *a)* to defeat *b)* to make unable to act, as by shocking, amazing, confusing, etc. **4.** [Colloq.] to press (a car accelerator) to the floor

**floor·age** (-ij) *n.* the area of a floor: also **floor space**

**floor·board** (-bôrd') *n.* **1.** a board in a floor **2.** the floor of an automobile, etc.

**floor exercise** *Gymnastics* any of several exercises, as cart wheels, performed without apparatus

**floor·ing** (-iŋ) *n.* **1.** a floor **2.** floors collectively **3.** material for making a floor

**floor leader** a member of a legislature chosen by his political party to direct its actions on the floor

**floor plan** a scale drawing of the layout of rooms, halls, etc. on one floor of a building

**floor show** a show presenting singers, dancers, etc. in a restaurant, nightclub, etc.

**floor·walk·er** (-wôk'ər) *n.* formerly, a department store employee supervising sales, etc.: now usually **floor (or sales) manager**

**floo·zy, floo·zie** (floo'zē) *n., pl.* **-zies** [Slang] a loose, disreputable woman: also sp. **floo'sy, floo'sie**

**flop** (fläp) *vt.* **flopped**, **flop'ping** [var. of FLAP] to flap or throw noisily and clumsily —*vi.* **1.** *a)* to move or flap around loosely or clumsily *b)* to fall or drop thus **2.** [Colloq.] to be a failure —*n.* **1.** the act or sound of flopping **2.** [Colloq.] a failure —*adv.* with a flop —**flop'per** *n.*

**flop·house** (-hous') *n.* [Colloq.] a very cheap hotel frequented chiefly by vagrants

**flop·py** (-ē) *adj.* **-pi·er**, **-pi·est** [Colloq.] tending to flop —**flop'pi·ly** *adv.* —**flop'pi·ness** *n.*

**floppy disk** (or **disc**) a small, flexible, relatively inexpensive computer disc for storing data

**Flo·ra** (flôr'ə) *n.* [< *flos*, a FLOWER] **1.** a feminine name **2.** *Rom. Myth.* the goddess of flowers —*n.* [f-] *pl.* **-ras, -rae** (-ē) the plants of a specified region or time

**flo·ral** (flôr'əl) *adj.* of, made of, or like flowers

**Flor·ence** (flôr'əns, flär'-) [Fr. < L. *Florentia*, lit., a blooming < *flos*, a FLOWER] **1.** a feminine name **2.** city in Tuscany, C Italy: pop. 455,000

**Flor·en·tine** (flôr'ən tēn') *adj.* of Florence, Italy, or its people, art, etc. —*n.* a native or inhabitant of Florence

**flo·res·cence** (flô res''ns, flə-) *n.* [< L. prp. of *florescere* < *florere*, to bloom < *flos*, FLOWER] a blooming or flowering —**flo·res'cent** *adj.*

**flo·ret** (flôr'it) *n.* [< OFr. dim. of *flor* < L. *flos*, FLOWER] **1.** a small flower **2.** any of the small flowers making up the head of a composite plant

**flo·ri·cul·ture** (flôr'ə kul'chər) *n.* the cultivation of flowers —**flo'ri·cul'tur·al** *adj.* —**flo'ri·cul'tur·ist** *n.*

**flor·id** (flôr'id, flär'-) *adj.* [L. *floridus* < *flos*, FLOWER] **1.** flushed with red: said of the complexion **2.** showy; ornate —**flo·rid·i·ty** (flô rid'ə tē, flə-), **flor'id·ness** *n.* —**flor'id·ly** *adv.*

**Flor·i·da** (flôr'ə də, flär'-) [Sp. < L. < *flos*, FLOWER] **1.** SE State of the U.S., mostly on a peninsula between the Atlantic & the Gulf of Mexico: 58,560 sq. mi.; pop. 9,740,000; cap. Tallahassee: abbrev. **Fla., FL 2. Straits of,** strait between the S tip of Fla. & Cuba —**Flo·rid'i·an** (flô rid'ē ən), **Flor'i·dan** *adj., n.*

**flor·in** (flôr'in, flär'-) *n.* [< OFr. < It. < L. *flos*, FLOWER: the figure of a lily was stamped on the original coins] **1.** a gold coin of medieval Florence **2.** any of various European or South African silver or gold coins

**Flo·ris·sant** (flôr'ə sənt) [Fr., flourishing] city in E Mo.: suburb of St. Louis: pop. 55,000

**flo·rist** (flôr'ist, flär'-) *n.* [< L. *flos*, FLOWER] a person who cultivates or sells flowers

**flo·ris·tic** (flô ris'tik) *adj.* of flowers or flora

**floss** (flôs, fläs) *n.* [prob. < Fr. < L. *floccus*, FLOCK²] **1.** the rough silk covering a silkworm's cocoon **2.** short, downy waste fibers of silk **3.** a soft thread or yarn, as of silk (**floss**

silk) or linen (**linen floss**), used in embroidery **4.** a soft, silky substance resembling floss, as in milkweed pods **5.** *same as* DENTAL FLOSS —*vt., vi.* to clean (the teeth) with dental floss

**floss·y** (-ē) *adj.* **floss'i·er**, **floss'i·est 1.** of or like floss; downy; fluffy **2.** [Slang] elegant and showy

**flo·ta·tion** (flō tā'shən) *n.* a floating; specif., the starting or financing of a business, etc., as by selling an entire issue of bonds

**flo·til·la** (flō til'ə) *n.* [Sp., dim. of *flota*, a fleet] **1.** a small fleet, or a fleet of small ships **2.** *U.S. Navy* a unit consisting of two or more squadrons

**flot·sam** (flät'səm) *n.* [< OFr. < MDu. *vloten* (or OE. *flotian*), to float] the wreckage of a ship or its cargo floating at sea: chiefly in **flotsam and jetsam,** *a* ) such wreckage or cargo either floating or washed ashore *b*) miscellaneous trifles *c*) transient, unemployed people

**flounce¹** (flouns) *vi.* **flounced, flounc'ing** [prob. < Scand.] to move with quick, flinging motions of the body, as in anger —*n.* the act of flouncing

**flounce²** (flouns) *n.* [earlier *frounce* < OFr. < *froncir*, to wrinkle] a wide, ornamental ruffle, as on a skirt —*vt.* **flounced, flounc'ing** to trim with a flounce or flounces —**flounc'y** *adj.*

**floun·der¹** (floun'dər) *vi.* [? var. of FOUNDER¹] **1.** to struggle or plunge about awkwardly, as in deep mud **2.** to speak or act in an awkward, confused way —*n.* a floundering

**floun·der²** (floun'dər) *n., pl.* **-ders, -der:** see PLURAL, II, D, 1 [< Scand.] any of a large group of flatfishes caught for food, as the halibut

**flour** (flour) *n.* [var. of FLOWER, after Fr. *fleur de farine*, lit., flower (i.e., best) of meal] **1.** a fine, powdery substance produced by grinding and sifting grain or certain roots, etc. **2.** any finely powdered substance —*vt.* **1.** to put flour on or in **2.** to make into flour —**flour'y** *adj.*

**flour·ish** (flur'ish) *vi.* [< OFr. *florir*, to blossom, ult. < L. *flos*, FLOWER] **1.** to grow vigorously; thrive; prosper **2.** to be at the peak of development, activity, etc. **3.** to make showy, wavy motions **4.** [Now Rare] to perform a fanfare —*vt.* to brandish (a sword, hat, etc.) —*n.* **1.** anything done in a showy way **2.** a brandishing **3.** a decorative line or lines in writing **4.** a fanfare —**flour'ish·er** *n.* —**flour'ishing** *adj.* —**flour'ish·ing·ly** *adv.*

**flout** (flout) *vt., vi.* [prob. < ME. *flouten*, to play the flute] to show scorn or contempt (for) —*n.* a flouting —**flout'er** *n.* —**flout'ing·ly** *adv.*

**flow** (flō) *vi.* [OE. *flowan*] **1.** to move as a liquid does **2.** to stream **3.** to move gently and smoothly; glide **4.** to pour out **5.** to be derived; proceed **6.** to hang loose or in waves [*flowing* hair] **7.** to rise, as the tide **8.** to be plentiful —*vt.* to flood —*n.* **1.** a flowing, or the manner or rate of this **2.** anything that flows; stream or current **3.** a continuous production

**flow chart** a diagram showing the progress of work through a sequence of operations

**flow·er** (flou'ər, flour) *n.* [< OFr. < L. *flos* (gen. *floris*), a flower] **1.** *a)* the structure of many plants that produces seeds, typically with brightly colored petals and leaflike sepals; blossom; bloom *b)* the reproductive structure of any plant **2.** a plant cultivated for its blossoms **3.** the best or finest part or example **4.** the best period of a person or thing **5.** something decorative: esp., a figure of speech **6.** [*pl.*] *Chem.* a powder made from condensed vapors —*vi.* **1.** to produce flowers or blossoms; bloom **2.** to reach the best period —*vt.* to decorate with flowers or floral patterns —**in flower** in a state of flowering —**flow'er·less** *adj.* —**flow'er·like'** *adj.*

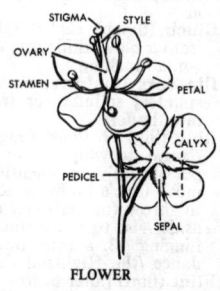

STIGMA  STYLE
OVARY
STAMEN  PETAL
CALYX
PEDICEL
SEPAL
FLOWER

**flow·ered** (flou'ərd) *adj.* **1.** bearing or containing flowers **2.** having a floral design

**flow·er·et** (-ər it) *n. same as* FLORET

**flow·er·ing** (-ər iŋ) *adj.* **1.** having flowers; in bloom **2.** bearing showy or profuse flowers

**flowering crab** a small apple tree bearing many large, rosered to light-pink flowers

**flow·er·pot** (-pät') *n.* a container, usually made of porous clay, in which to grow plants

**flow·er·y** (-ē) *adj.* **-er·i·er**, **-er·i·est 1.** covered or decorated with flowers **2.** of or like flowers **3.** full of figurative and ornate expressions and fine words —**flow'er·i·ly** *adv.* —**flow'er·i·ness** *n.*

**flown** (flōn) *pp. of* FLY¹

**Floyd** (floid) [var. of LLOYD] a masculine name

**fl. oz.** fluid ounce; fluid ounces

**flt.** flight

**flu** (floo) *n.* 1. *a shortened form for* INFLUENZA 2. popularly, any of various respiratory or intestinal infections caused by a virus

**flub** (flub) *vt., vi.* **flubbed, flub′bing** [? < FL(OP) + (D)UB¹] [Colloq.] to botch (a job, chance, etc.); bungle —*n.* [Colloq.] a mistake or blunder

**fluc·tu·ate** (fluk′choo wāt′) *vi.* **-at′ed, -at′ing** [< L. pp. of *fluctuare < fluctus*, a wave] 1. to move back and forth or up and down 2. to vary irregularly —*vt.* 1. to cause to fluctuate —**fluc′tu·ant** *adj.* —**fluc′tu·a′tion** *n.*

**flue** (floo) *n.* [< ? OFr. *fluie*, a flowing] 1. a tube or shaft for the passage of smoke, hot air, etc., as in a chimney 2. *a) same as* FLUE PIPE *b)* the opening for air in a flue pipe

**flu·ent** (floo′ənt) *adj.* [< L. prp. of *fluere*, to flow] 1. flowing smoothly and easily 2. able to write or speak easily, smoothly, and expressively —**flu′en·cy** *n.* —**flu′ent·ly** *adv.*

**flue pipe** an organ pipe whose tone is produced by an air current striking a narrow side opening

**fluff** (fluf) *n.* [? blend of *flue*, downy mass + PUFF] 1. soft, light down 2. a loose, soft, downy mass, as of dust 3. any light or trivial matter or talk 4. *Theater, Radio, TV* an error in speaking a line —*vt.* 1. to shake or pat until loose, soft, and light 2. *Theater, Radio, TV* to make an error in speaking (one's lines, etc.) 3. to botch; bungle —*vi.* 1. to become fluffy 2. to make an error

**fluff·y** (-ē) *adj.* **fluff′i·er, fluff′i·est** 1. soft and light like fluff; feathery 2. covered with fluff —**fluff′i·ness** *n.*

**flu·id** (floo′id) *adj.* [L. *fluidus < fluere*, to flow] 1. that can flow; not solid 2. of a fluid 3. not settled or fixed *[fluid plans]* 4. moving gracefully; flowing 5. available for investment or as cash *[fluid assets]* —*n.* any substance that can flow; liquid or gas —**flu·id·ic** (floo wid′ik) *adj.* —**flu·id′i·ty, flu′id·ness** *n.* —**flu′id·ly** *adv.*

**fluid dram** (or **drachm**) a liquid measure equal to 1/8 fluid ounce

**fluid ounce** a liquid measure equal to 1/16 pint, or 29.57 ml.: also **flu′id·ounce′** *n.*

**fluke¹** (flook) *n.* [OE. *floc*] 1. any of several flatfishes, esp. flounders 2. a flatworm parasitic in internal organs of vertebrates

**fluke²** (flook) *n.* [prob. < prec.] 1. the triangular, pointed end of an anchor arm, by which the anchor catches in the ground 2. a barb or barbed head of an arrow, harpoon, etc. 3. either of the two lobes of a whale's tail

**fluke³** (flook) *n.* [< ?] 1. [Old Slang] a lucky stroke in billiards, etc. 2. [Colloq.] a lucky or unlucky outcome —*vt.* **fluked, fluk′ing** [Colloq.] to hit or get by a fluke

**fluk·y** (floo′kē) *adj.* **fluk′i·er, fluk′i·est** [< prec.] [Colloq.] 1. resulting from chance 2. uncertain —**fluk′i·ness** *n.*

**flume** (floom) *n.* [< OFr. < L. *flumen*, river < *fluere*, to flow] 1. an inclined chute or trough for carrying water to furnish power, transport logs, etc. 2. a narrow gorge with a stream running through it —*vt.* **flumed, flum′ing** to send (logs, etc.) down a flume

**flum·mer·y** (flum′ər ē) *n., pl.* **-mer·ies** [W. *llymru*, soured oatmeal] 1. any soft, easily eaten food, as custard 2. meaningless flattery or silly talk

**flung** (fluŋ) *pt. & pp. of* FLING

**flunk** (fluŋk) *vt.* [19th-c. college slang < ?] [Colloq.] 1. to fail in (schoolwork) 2. to give a grade of *failure* to (a student) —*vi.* [Colloq.] to fail, esp. in schoolwork —*n.* [Colloq.] a grade of *failure* —**flunk out** [Colloq.] to send or be sent away from school or college because of failure

**flun·ky** (fluŋ′kē) *n., pl.* **-kies** [orig. Scot. < ? Fr. *flanquer*, to flank] 1. one who obeys superiors in a servile way 2. one having minor or menial tasks Also sp. **flun′key** —**flun′ky·ism** *n.*

**flu·or** (floo′ər, -ôr) *n.* [ModL. < L. *flux < fluere*, to flow] *same as* FLUORITE

**flu·o·resce** (floo′ə res′; floo res′, flô-) *vi.* **-resced′, -resc′ing** to show or undergo fluorescence

**flu·o·res·cence** (-′ns) *n.* [< FLUOR (SPAR) + -ESCENCE] 1. the property of a substance, as fluorite, of producing light when acted upon by radiant energy, as ultraviolet rays or X-rays 2. production of such light 3. light so produced —**flu′o·res′cent** *adj.*

**fluorescent lamp** (or **tube**) a glass tube coated inside with a fluorescent substance giving off light (**fluorescent light**) when mercury vapor in the tube is acted upon by electrons from the cathode

**fluor·i·date** (flôr′ə dāt′, floor′-) *vt.* **-dat′ed, -dat′ing** to add fluorides to (a water supply) so as to reduce the incidence of tooth decay —**fluor′i·da′tion** *n.*

**flu·o·ride** (floor′īd, flôr′-; floo′ə rīd′) *n.* a compound of fluorine and another element or radical

**fluor·i·nate** (flôr′ə nāt′, floor′-) *vt.* **-nat′ed, -nat′ing** 1. to treat, or cause to combine, with fluorine 2. *same as* FLUORIDATE —**fluor′i·na′tion** *n.*

**flu·o·rine** (floor′ēn, flôr′-; floo′ə rēn′, -rin) *n.* [< FLUOR + -INE⁴] a corrosive, poisonous, pale greenish-yellow, gaseous chemical element, the most reactive nonmetallic element known, forming fluorides with almost all elements: symbol, F; at. wt., 18.9984; at. no., 9

**flu·o·rite** (floor′īt, flôr′-; floo′ə rīt′) *n.* [< FLUOR(O)- + -ITE] calcium fluoride, $CaF_2$, a transparent, crystalline mineral of various colors: it is the principal source of fluorine and is used as a flux, in glassmaking, etc.

**flu·o·ro-** *a combining form meaning:* 1. fluorine 2. fluorescence Also, before a vowel, **flu·or-**

**flu·o·ro·car·bon** (floor′ə kär′bən, flôr′-; floo′ər ə-, -ə rō′-) *n.* any of a class of inert organic compounds containing carbon, fluorine, and sometimes hydrogen: used as lubricants, plastics, etc.

**flu·o·rom·e·ter** (floo räm′ə tər, floo′ə-) *n.* an instrument for measuring the wavelength and intensity of fluorescence —**flu·o·ro·met·ric** (floor′ə met′rik, floo′ər ə-) *adj.* —**flu·o·rom′e·try** *n.*

**fluor·o·scope** (floor′ə skōp′, flôr′-) *n.* [FLUORO- + -SCOPE] a machine for examining internal structures by viewing the shadows cast on a fluorescent screen by objects through which X-rays are directed —*vt.* **-scoped′, -scop′ing** to examine with a fluoroscope —**fluor′o·scop′ic** (-skäp′ik) *adj.* —**fluor′o·scop′i·cal·ly** *adv.*

**flu·o·ros·co·py** (floo räs′kə pē, floo′ə-) *n.* examination by fluoroscope —**flu·o·ros′co·pist** *n.*

**fluor spar** *same as* FLUORITE: also **flu′or·spar′** *n.*

**flur·ry** (flur′ē) *n., pl.* **-ries** [< ?] 1. a sudden, brief rush of wind or fall of snow 2. a sudden confusion or commotion 3. a spurt of increased trading and price fluctuation in the stock market —*vt.* **-ried, -ry·ing** to confuse; agitate —*vi.* to move in a quick, flustered way

**flush¹** (flush) *vi.* [blend of FLASH & ME. *flusschen*, to fly up suddenly] 1. to flow and spread suddenly 2. to blush or glow 3. to become cleaned or emptied with a sudden flow of water, etc. 4. to start up from cover: said of birds —*vt.* 1. to make flow 2. to clean or empty with a sudden flow of water, etc. 3. to make blush or glow 4. to excite; exhilarate *[flushed with victory]* 5. to drive (game birds) from cover 6. to make level or even —*n.* 1. a sudden, rapid flow, as of water 2. a sudden, vigorous growth *[the first flush of youth]* 3. sudden excitement or exhilaration 4. a blush or glow 5. a sudden feeling of heat, as in a fever —*adj.* 1. well supplied, esp. with money 2. abundant 3. ruddy 4. *a)* making an even line or plane *b)* even with a margin or edge 5. direct; full *[a blow flush in the face]* —*adv.* 1. so as to be level or in alignment 2. directly; squarely

**flush²** (flush) *n.* [Fr. *flux:* see FLUX] a hand of cards all in the same suit

**flus·ter** (flus′tər) *vt., vi.* [prob. < Scand.] to get confused or nervous —*n.* a flustered state

**flute** (floot) *n.* [< OFr. < Pr. *flaüt < ?*] 1. *a)* a high-pitched wind instrument consisting of a long, slender tube with finger holes and keys, played by blowing across a hole near one end *b)* any similar instrument, as the recorder 2. an ornamental groove —*vt., vi.* **flut′ed, flut′ing** 1. to sing, speak, etc. in a flutelike tone 2. to play on the flute 3. to make ornamental grooves (in)

**flut·ing** (-iŋ) *n.* 1. a series of ornamental grooves, as in a column 2. the act of one that flutes

**flut·ist** (-ist) *n.* a flute player; flautist

**flut·ter** (flut′ər) *vi.* [OE. *flotorian*, freq. of *flotian* < base of *fleotan*, to float] 1. to flap the wings rapidly 2. to wave or vibrate rapidly and irregularly *[a flag fluttering in the wind]* 3. to move with quick vibrations, flaps, etc. 4. to tremble; quiver 5. to move about in a restless, fussy way —*vt.* 1. to make flutter 2. to excite or confuse —*n.* 1. a fluttering 2. a state of excitement or confusion —**flut′ter·er** *n.* —**flut′ter·y** *adj*

**flut·y** (floot′ē) *adj.* flutelike in tone; soft, clear, and high-pitched

**flu·vi·al** (floo′vē əl) *adj.* [< L. *fluvius*, a river < *fluere*, to flow] of, found in, or produced by a river

**flux** (fluks) *n.* [OFr. < L. *fluxus* < pp. of *fluere*, to flow] 1. a flowing or flow 2. a coming in of the tide 3. continual change 4. any abnormal discharge of fluid matter from the body 5. *a)* a substance used to help fuse metals together, as in soldering *b)* a substance used, as in smelting, to fuse with undesired matter in forming a more fluid slag 6. *Physics* the rate of flow of energy, fluids, etc. over a surface —*vt.* 1. to make fluid 2. to fuse (metals)

**fly¹** (flī) *vi.* **flew, flown, fly′ing** [OE. *fleogan*] 1. to move through the air by using wings, as a bird 2. to travel through the air in an aircraft 3. to be propelled through the air or through space, as a missile **4.** to operate an air-craft **5.** to wave or float in the air, as a flag or kite **6.** to move or go swiftly **7.** to flee **8. flied, fly′ing** Baseball to hit a fly —*vt.* **1.** *a*) to cause to float in the air *b*) to display (a flag) as from a pole **2.** to operate (an aircraft) **3.** to travel over in an aircraft **4.** to carry in an aircraft **5.** to flee from or avoid —*n., pl.* **flies 1.** a flap concealing the zipper, buttons, etc. in a garment **2.** a flap serving as a tent door **3.** the length of a flag from the staff outward **4.** *same as: a*) FLYWHEEL *b*) FLYLEAF **5.** Baseball a ball batted high, esp. within the foul lines **6.** [*pl.*] Theater the space behind and above the proscenium arch —**fly at** to attack by or as by springing toward —**fly out** Baseball to be put out by hitting a fly that is caught —**let fly (at) 1.** to shoot or throw (at) **2.** to unleash a verbal attack (at) —**on the fly 1.** while in flight **2.** [Colloq.] while in a hurry

**fly²** (flī) *n., pl.* **flies** [OE. *fleoge*] **1.** *a*) *same as* HOUSEFLY *b*) any of a large group of insects with two transparent wings, as the housefly and gnat *c*) any of several four-winged insects, as the mayfly **2.** a hooked lure for fishing, made to resemble an insect

**fly·a·ble** (-ə b'l) *adj.* suitable or ready for flying [*flyable* weather, a *flyable* airplane]

**fly ash** airborne bits of unburnable ash

**fly·blown** (-blōn′) *adj.* **1.** full of flies' eggs or larvae **2.** spoiled; tainted **3.** [Colloq.] shabby; dingy

**fly·by, fly-by** (-bī′) *n., pl.* **-bies′** a flight past a given point by an aircraft or spacecraft

**fly-by-night** (-bī nīt′) *adj.* not trustworthy, esp. financially —*n.* a fly-by-night person

**fly·cast** (-kast′) *vi.* **-cast′, -cast′ing** to fish by casting artificial flies

**fly·catch·er** (-kach′ər) *n.* any of various small birds, as the pewee, that catch insects in flight

**fly·er** (-ər) *n. same as* FLIER

**fly·ing** (-iŋ) *adj.* **1.** that flies or can fly **2.** moving as if flying; fast **3.** hasty and brief **4.** of or for aircraft or aviators **5.** organized to act quickly —*n.* the action of one that flies

**flying boat** an airplane with a hull that permits it to land on and take off from water

**flying bridge** Naut. a small structure over the main bridge, from which a vessel may be conned

**flying buttress** a buttress connected with a wall by an arch, serving to resist outward pressure

**flying colors 1.** flags flying in the air **2.** notable victory or success

**flying fish** any of a number of chiefly warm-water sea fishes with winglike pectoral fins that enable them to glide through the air

**flying gurnard** a marine fish with winglike pectoral fins for gliding short distances in the air

**flying jib** a small, triangular sail in front of the jib

**flying saucer** *same as* UFO

**flying squirrel** any of a number of squirrels with winglike folds of skin attached to the legs and body that enable them to make gliding leaps

FLYING
BUTTRESS

**fly·leaf** (flī′lēf′) *n., pl.* **-leaves′** (-lēvz′) a blank leaf at the beginning or end of a book

**fly·pa·per** (-pā′pər) *n.* a sticky or poisonous paper set out to catch or kill flies

**fly·speck** (-spek′) *n.* **1.** a speck of fly excrement **2.** any tiny spot **3.** a petty or insignificant error or flaw —*vt.* to make flyspecks on

**fly·trap** (-trap′) *n.* **1.** any device for catching flies **2.** a plant that catches insects

**fly·way** (-wā′) *n.* a flying route of migratory birds

**fly·weight** (-wāt′) *n.* a boxer who weighs 112 pounds or less —*adj.* of flyweights

**fly·wheel** (-hwēl′) *n.* a heavy wheel attached to a machine so as to regulate its speed and motion

**Fm** Chem. fermium

**FM** frequency modulation

**fm. 1.** fathom **2.** from

**f-num·ber** (ef′num′bər) *n.* Photog. the ratio of a lens diameter to its focal length: the lower the f-number, the shorter the exposure required

**fo.** folio

**foal** (fōl) *n.* [OE. *fola*] a young horse, mule, donkey, etc.; colt or filly —*vt., vi.* to give birth to (a foal)

**foam** (fōm) *n.* [OE. *fam*] **1.** the whitish mass of bubbles formed on or in liquids by agitation, fermentation, etc. **2.** something like foam, as frothy saliva **3.** a rigid or spongy cellular mass made by gas bubbles dispersed in liquid rubber, plastic, etc. —*vi.* to produce foam; froth —*vt.* to cause to foam —**foam at the mouth** to be very angry; rage —**foam′less** *adj.*

**foam rubber** rubber treated to form a firm, spongy foam, used in seats, mattresses, etc.

**foam·y** (-ē) *adj.* **foam′i·er, foam′i·est 1.** foaming or covered with foam **2.** of or like foam —**foam′i·ly** *adv.* —**foam′i·ness** *n.*

**fob¹** (fäb) *n.* [prob. < dial. G. *fuppe*, a pocket] **1.** a watch pocket in the front of a man's trousers **2.** a short ribbon or chain hanging from a watch in such a pocket, often with an ornament at the end **3.** such an ornament

**fob²** (fäb) *vt.* **fobbed, fob′bing** [< ME. *fobben*, to cheat] [Obs.] to cheat or deceive —**fob off 1.** to trick or put off (a person) with second-rate articles, lies, excuses, etc. **2.** to get rid of (something worthless) by deceit or trickery

**F.O.B., f.o.b.** free on board

**fo·cal** (fō′k'l) *adj.* of or at a focus —**fo′cal·ly** *adv.*

**fo·cal·ize** (fō′kə līz′) *vt., vi.* **-ized′, -iz′ing** to adjust or come to a focus —**fo′cal·i·za′tion** *n.*

**focal length** the distance from the optical center of a lens to the point where the light rays converge; length of the focus: also **focal distance**

**fo·c's'le** (fōk′s'l) *n. phonetic spelling of* FORECASTLE

**fo·cus** (fō′kəs) *n., pl.* **fo′cus·es, fo′ci** (-sī) [ModL. < L., hearth] **1.** the point where rays of light, heat, etc. or waves of sound come together, or from which they spread or seem to spread; specif., the point where rays of light reflected by a mirror or refracted by a lens meet **2.** *same as* FOCAL LENGTH **3.** adjustment of focal length to make a clear image **4.** any center of activity, attention, etc. **5.** a part of the body where an infection is most active **6.** Math. *a*) either of the two fixed points used in determining an ellipse *b*) any analogous point for a parabola or hyperbola —*vt.* **-cused** or **-cussed, -cus·ing** or **-cus·sing 1.** to bring into focus **2.** to adjust the focal length of (the eye, a lens, etc.) so as to make a clear image **3.** to concentrate [*focus* one's attention] —*vi.* to come to a focus —**in focus** clear; distinct —**out of focus** indistinct; blurred —**fo′cus·er** *n.*

**fod·der** (fäd′ər) *n.* [OE. *fodor* < *foda*, food] coarse food for cattle, horses, etc., as cornstalks, hay, and straw —*vt.* to feed with fodder

**foe** (fō) *n.* [OE. *fah*, hostile, (*ge*)*fah*, enemy] *same as* ENEMY (in all senses)

**foe·man** (fō′mən) *n., pl.* **-men** [Archaic] a foe

**foe·tid** (fet′id, fēt′-) *adj. same as* FETID

**foe·tus** (fēt′əs) *n. same as* FETUS —**foe′tal** *adj.*

**fog** (fôg, fäg) *n.* [prob. < Scand.] **1.** a large mass of water vapor condensed to fine particles, just above the earth's surface **2.** a similar mass of smoke, dust, etc. obscuring the atmosphere **3.** a vaporized liquid, as insecticide, widely dispersed **4.** a state of mental confusion **5.** a blur on a photograph or film —*vi.* **fogged, fog′ging 1.** to become covered by fog **2.** to be or become blurred or dimmed —*vt.* **1.** to cover with fog **2.** to blur or dim **3.** to confuse

**fog bank** a dense mass of fog

**fog·gy** (-ē) *adj.* **-gi·er, -gi·est 1.** full of fog **2.** dim; blurred **3.** confused; perplexed —**fog′gi·ly** *adv.* —**fog′gi·ness** *n.*

**fog·horn** (-hôrn′) *n.* a horn blown to give warning to ships in a fog

**fo·gy** (fō′gē) *n., pl.* **-gies** [< ?] a person who is old-fashioned or highly conservative: also **fo′gey,** *pl.* **-geys** —**fo′gy·ish** *adj.* —**fo′gy·ism** *n.*

**foi·ble** (foi′b'l) *n.* [obs. form of Fr. *faible*, FEEBLE] a small weakness in character; frailty

**foil¹** (foil) *vt.* [< OFr. *fuler*, to trample on] to keep from being successful; thwart; frustrate

**foil²** (foil) *n.* [< OFr. < VL. < L. *folium*, a leaf] **1.** a leaf-like, rounded space or design, as in windows, etc. in Gothic architecture **2.** a very thin sheet, leaf, or coating of metal **3.** a thin leaf of polished metal put under an inferior or artificial gem to give it brilliance **4.** one that sets off or enhances another by contrast **5.** [etym. unc.] *a*) a long, thin fencing sword with a button on the point to prevent injury *b*) [*pl.*] the art or sport of fencing with foils —*vt.* **1.** to cover or back with foil **2.** to decorate (windows, etc.) with foils

**foist** (foist) *vt.* [prob. < dial. Du. *vuisten*, to hide in the hand < *vuist*, a fist] **1.** to put in slyly or surreptitiously **2.** to impose by fraud; palm off

**fol. 1.** folio **2.** following

**fold¹** (fōld) *vt.* [OE. *faldan*] **1.** to bend or press (something) so that one part is over another **2.** to draw together and intertwine [to *fold* the arms] **3.** to draw (wings) close to the body **4.** to clasp in the arms; embrace **5.** to wrap up; envelop —*vi.* **1.** to be or become folded **2.** [Colloq.] *a*) to fail; be forced to close, as a business *b*) to succumb, as to exhaustion —*n.* **1.** a folded part or layer **2.** a mark, hollow, or crease made by folding **3.** Geol. a rock layer folded by pressure —**fold in** Cooking to blend (an ingredient) into a mixture, using gentle, cutting strokes

**fold²** (fōld) *n.* [OE. *fald*] **1.** a pen in which to keep sheep **2.** a flock of sheep **3.** a group or organization with common aims, faith, etc., as a church —*vt.* to keep or confine in a pen

**-fold** (fōld) [OE. *-feald*] *a suffix meaning:* **1.** having (a specified number of) parts [*tenfold*] **2.** (a specified number of) times as many or as much

**fold·a·way** (fōld′ə wā′) *adj.* that can be folded for easy storage [*a foldaway cot*]

**fold·er** (fōl′dər) *n.* **1.** a person or thing that folds **2.** a sheet of heavy paper folded as a holder for papers **3.** an unstitched, folded booklet

**fol·de·rol** (fäl′də räl′, fōl′də rōl′) *n.* same as FALDERAL

**folding door** a door with hinged leaves or accordion pleats that can be folded back

**fo·li·a·ceous** (fō′lē ā′shəs) *adj.* [< L. < *folium,* a leaf] **1.** of or like the leaf of a plant **2.** having leaves **3.** consisting of thin layers

**fo·li·age** (fō′lē ij) *n.* [< OFr. < VL. *folia* < L. *folium,* a leaf] **1.** leaves, as of a plant or tree **2.** a decoration consisting of a representation of leaves, branches, flowers, etc.

**fo·li·ate** (fō′lē āt′; *for adj., usually* -it) *vt.* **-at′ed, -at′ing** [L. *foliatus,* leafy < *folium,* a leaf] to divide into thin layers — *vi.* **1.** to separate into layers **2.** to send out leaves — *adj.* having or covered with leaves

**fo·li·a·tion** (fō′lē ā′shən) *n.* **1.** a growing of or developing into a leaf or leaves **2.** the state of being in leaf **3.** the way leaves are arranged in the bud **4.** the act of beating metal into layers **5.** a leaflike decoration

**fo·lic acid** (fō′lik) [< L. *folium,* a leaf + -IC] a crystalline substance, $C_{19}H_{19}N_7O_6$, one of the vitamin B group, found in green leaves, etc. and used esp. in treating certain anemias

**fo·li·o** (fō′lē ō′) *n., pl.* **-li·os′** [L. abl. of *folium,* a leaf] **1.** a large sheet of paper folded once, so that it forms two leaves, or four pages, of a book, etc. **2.** a book (the largest regular size), now often 12 by 15 inches, made of sheets so folded **3.** a leaf of a book, etc. numbered on only one side **4.** the number of a page in a book, etc. — *adj.* of the size of a folio — **in folio** in the form of a folio

**folk** (fōk) *n., pl.* **folk, folks** [OE. *folc*] **1.** *a)* a people; nation; ethnic group *b)* the common people of such a group: with *the* **2.** [*pl.*] people in general; persons [*folks* don't agree] — *adj.* of or having to do with the common people — (one's) **folks** [Colloq.] (one's) family

**folk dance** **1.** a traditional dance of the common people of a country **2.** music for this

**folk etymology** the change that occurs in the form of a word so as to give it an apparent connection with some other word, as *coleslaw* becomes *cold slaw*

**folk·lore** (fōk′lôr′) *n.* **1.** the traditional beliefs, legends, sayings, etc. of a people **2.** the study of these — **folk′lor′ic** *adj.* — **folk′lor′ist** *n.*

**folk medicine** the treatment of disease, including the use of herbs, as practiced by the common people over many years

**folk music** music made and handed down among the common people

**folk-rock** (-räk′) *n.* music with a rock-and-roll beat combined with words in a folk-song style

**folk song** **1.** a song made and handed down among the common people **2.** a song composed in imitation of such a song — **folk singer**

**folk·sy** (-sē) *adj.* **-si·er, -si·est** [Colloq.] friendly or sociable in a simple and direct or overly familiar manner — **folk′si·ly** *adv.* — **folk′si·ness** *n.*

**folk tale** (or **story**) a story, often legendary, made and handed down orally among the common people

**folk·way** (-wā′) *n.* any way of thinking, behaving, etc. characteristic of a certain social group

**fol·li·cle** (fäl′i k'l) *n.* [ModL. *folliculus* < L., a small bag, dim. of *follis,* bellows] **1.** *Anat.* any small sac, cavity, or gland for excretion or secretion [a hair *follicle*] **2.** *Bot.* a dry, one-celled seed capsule, opening along one side, as a milkweed pod — **fol·li·cu·lar** (fə lik′yoo lər) *adj.* — **fol·lic′u·late** (-lit, -lāt′), **fol·lic′u·lat′ed** *adj.*

**follicle-stimulating hormone** a pituitary hormone that stimulates growth of ova and sperm

**fol·low** (fäl′ō) *vt.* [< OE. *folgian*] **1.** to come or go after **2.** to chase; pursue **3.** to go along [*follow* the road] **4.** to come after in time, in a series, etc. **5.** to take the place of in rank, position, etc. **6.** to take up; engage in (a trade, etc.) **7.** to result from **8.** to take as a model; imitate **9.** to accept the authority of; obey **10.** to listen to, watch, or observe closely **11.** to understand the continuity or logic of — *vi.* **1.** to come, go, or happen after something else in place, sequence, or time **2.** to result — *n.* the act of following — **follow out** to carry out fully — **follow through** to continue and complete a stroke or action — **follow up** **1.** to follow closely and persistently **2.** to carry out fully **3.** to make more effective by doing something more

**fol·low·er** (fäl′ə wər) *n.* one that follows; specif., *a)* a person who follows another's belief or teachings; disciple *b)* a servant or attendant

**fol·low·ing** (-ə win) *adj.* that follows; next after — *n.* a group of followers or adherents — *prep.* after [*following* dinner he went home] — **the following** **1.** the one or ones to be mentioned immediately **2.** what follows

**fol·low-through** (-ō thrōō′) *n.* **1.** the act or manner of continuing the swing or stroke of a club, racket, etc. after striking or releasing the ball, etc. **2.** the completing of an undertaking

**fol·low-up** (-up′) *adj.* following as a review, addition, etc. — *n.* **1.** a follow-up thing or event **2.** a following up, as with follow-up letters, visits, etc.

**fol·ly** (fäl′ē) *n., pl.* **-lies** [< OFr. < *fol:* see FOOL] **1.** a lack of sense or rational conduct; foolishness **2.** any foolish action or belief **3.** any foolish but expensive undertaking

**fo·ment** (fō ment′) *vt.* [< OFr. < LL. *fomentare* < L. < *fovere,* to keep warm] **1.** to treat with warm water, medicated lotions, etc. **2.** to stir up; incite [to *foment* a riot] — **fo′men·ta′tion** *n.*

**fond** (fänd) *adj.* [< ME. *fonned,* pp. of *fonnen,* to be foolish] **1.** [Now Rare] foolishly naive **2.** tender and affectionate, sometimes in a foolish way **3.** greatly cherished — **fond of** having a liking for — **fond′ly** *adv.* — **fond′ness** *n.*

**fon·dant** (fän′dənt) *n.* [Fr. < prp. of *fondre,* to melt] a soft, creamy candy made of sugar, used esp. as a filling for other candies

**fon·dle** (fän′d'l) *vt.* **-dled, -dling** [freq. of obs. *fond, v.*] to stroke lovingly; caress — **fon′dler** *n.*

**fon·due, fon·du** (fän dōō′, fän′dōō) *n.* [Fr. < pp. of *fondre,* to melt] **1.** cheese melted in wine, used as a dip for cubes of bread **2.** any of various dishes, as hot oil into which cubes of meat are dipped for cooking **3.** cheese soufflé with bread crumbs

**font¹** (fänt) *n.* [OE. < L. *fons,* FOUNTAIN] **1.** a bowl to hold baptismal water **2.** a basin for holy water; stoup **3.** [Poet.] a fountain or spring **4.** any source — **font′al** *adj.*

**font²** (fänt) *n.* [Fr. *fonte* < OFr. *fondre:* see FOUND³] *Printing* a complete assortment of type in one size and style

**fon·ta·nel, fon·ta·nelle** (fän′tə nel′) *n.* [ME. *fontinel,* a hollow < OFr. dim. of *fontaine,* FOUNTAIN] any of the soft, boneless areas in the skull of a baby, later closed over when bone forms

FONTANELS

**food** (fōōd) *n.* [OE. *foda*] **1.** any substance taken into and assimilated by a plant or animal to keep it alive and enable it to grow; nourishment **2.** solid substances of this sort: distinguished from *drink* **3.** a specified kind of food **4.** anything that nourishes or stimulates [*food* for thought]

**food chain** *Ecol.* a sequence (as grass, rabbit, fox) in which each member feeds on the one below

**food cycle** *Ecol.* all the individual food chains in a community: also **food web**

**food poisoning** **1.** sickness from eating food contaminated by bacteria **2.** poisoning from naturally poisonous foods or from chemical contaminants in food

**food stamp** any of the Federal stamps allotted to unemployed or low-income persons for use in buying food

**food·stuff** (-stuf′) *n.* any material made into or used as food

**fool** (fōōl) *n.* [< OFr. *fol* < LL. < L. *follis,* windbag] **1.** a silly person; simpleton **2.** a man formerly kept by a nobleman or king to entertain as a clown; jester **3.** a victim of a trick; dupe — *adj.* [Colloq.] foolish — *vi.* **1.** to act like a fool; be silly **2.** to joke **3.** [Colloq.] to meddle (*with*) — *vt.* to trick; deceive; dupe — **be no** (or **nobody's**) **fool** to be shrewd and capable — **fool around** [Colloq.] to trifle — **fool away** [Colloq.] to squander — **play the fool** to clown

**fool·har·dy** (-här′dē) *adj.* **-di·er, -di·est** foolishly daring; rash — **fool′har′di·ly** *adv.* — **fool′har′di·ness** *n.*

**fool·ish** (-ish) *adj.* **1.** without good sense; silly; unwise **2.** *a)* absurd *b)* abashed; embarrassed — **fool′ish·ly** *adv.* — **fool′ish·ness** *n.*

**fool·proof** (-prōōf′) *adj.* so harmless, simple, or indestructible as not to be mishandled, damaged, etc. even by a fool

**fools·cap** (fōōlz′kap′) *n.* **1.** [from former watermark] a size of writing paper: in the U.S., 13 by 16 inches **2.** same as FOOL'S CAP

**fool's cap** a jester's cap with bells

**fool's gold** iron pyrites or copper pyrites, like gold in color

**foot** (foot) *n., pl.* **feet**: see also sense 6 [OE. *fot*] **1.** the end part of the leg, on which a person or animal stands or moves **2.** the base or bottom [the *foot* of a page] **3.** the last of a series **4.** the end, as of a bed, toward which the feet are directed **5.** the part of a stocking, etc. covering the foot **6.** a measure of length, equal to 12 inches (an average length of the human foot): symbol, ′ (e.g., 10′): abbrev. **ft.** (sing. & pl.): pl. often **foot** following a number [a six-*foot* man] **7.** [Brit.] infantry **8.** a group of syllables serving as a unit of meter in verse —*vi.* **1.** to dance **2.** to walk —*vt.* **1.** to walk, dance, or run on, over, or through **2.** to make the foot of (a stocking, etc.) **3.** to add (a column of figures) and set down a total **4.** [Colloq.] to pay (costs, etc.) [to *foot* the bill] —**foot it** [Colloq.] to dance, walk, or run —**of foot** in walking or running [swift *of foot*] —**on foot 1.** walking or running **2.** in process —**put one's best foot forward** [Colloq.] **1.** to do one's best **2.** to try to appear at one's best —**put one's foot down** [Colloq.] to act decisively —**put one's foot in it** (or **in one's mouth**) [Colloq.] to make an embarrassing blunder —**under foot 1.** on the floor, etc. **2.** in the way —**foot′less** *adj.*

**foot·age** (foot′ij) *n.* length expressed in feet

**foot-and-mouth disease** (foot′'n mouth′) an acute, contagious disease of cattle, deer, etc. characterized by fever and blisters in the mouth and around the hoofs

**foot·ball** (-bôl′) *n.* [ME. *foteballe*] **1.** any of several field games played with an inflated leather ball by two teams, the object being to get the ball across the opponents' goal: in U.S. & Canadian football, the players may kick, throw, or run with the ball, and may run ahead of it for interference, forward passes, etc.: cf. SOCCER, RUGBY **2.** the elliptical or (for soccer) round ball used in playing these games

**foot·board** (-bôrd′) *n.* **1.** a board or small platform for supporting the feet or for standing on **2.** a vertical piece across the foot of a bed

**foot·bridge** (-brij′) *n.* a narrow bridge for pedestrians

**foot·can·dle** (-kan′d'l) *n.* a unit for measuring illumination: it is equal to the amount of direct light thrown by one candle (*n.* 3) on a square foot of surface one foot away

**foot·ed** (-id) *adj.* having a foot or feet, esp. of a specified number or kind [four-*footed*]

**-foot·er** (-ər) *a combining form meaning* a person or thing (a specified number of) feet tall, high, long, etc. [six-*footer*]

**foot·fall** (-fôl′) *n.* the sound of a footstep

**foot·hill** (-hil′) *n.* a low hill at or near the foot of a mountain or mountain range

**foot·hold** (-hōld′) *n.* **1.** a place to put a foot down securely, as in climbing **2.** a secure position

**foot·ing** (-iŋ) *n.* **1.** a secure placing of the feet **2.** *a)* the condition of a surface for walking, running, etc. *b)* a secure place to put the feet **3.** a secure position or basis **4.** a basis for relationship [a friendly *footing*] **5.** *a)* the adding of a column of figures *b)* the sum obtained **6.** a projecting base under a column, wall, etc.: also **foot′er**

**foot·lights** (-līts′) *n.pl.* a row of lights along the front of a stage at the actors' foot level —**the footlights** the theater, or acting as a profession

**foot·loose** (-loos′) *adj.* free to go wherever one likes or do as one likes

**foot·man** (-mən) *n., pl.* **-men** a male servant who assists the butler in a household

**foot·note** (-nōt′) *n.* a note of comment or reference at the bottom of a page —*vt.* **-not′ed, -not′ing** to add such a note or notes to

**foot·pad** (-pad′) *n.* [see PAD³] a highway robber or holdup man who travels on foot

**foot·path** (-path′) *n.* a narrow path for pedestrians

**foot·pound** (-pound′) *n.* a unit of energy, equal to the amount of energy required to raise a weight of one pound a distance of one foot

**foot-pound-sec·ond** (-pound′sek′ənd) *adj.* designating or of a system of measurement using the foot, pound, and second as the units of length, mass, and time, respectively

**foot·print** (-print′) *n.* a mark left by a foot

**foot·race** (-rās′) *n.* a race run on foot

**foot·rest** (-rest′) *n.* a support to rest the feet on

**foot·sie** (-sē) *n., pl.* **-sies** the foot: a child's term —**play footsie (with) 1.** to touch feet or legs (with) in a caressing way, as under the table **2.** to flirt or have surreptitious dealings (with)

**foot soldier** a soldier on foot; infantryman

**foot·sore** (-sôr′) *adj.* having sore or tender feet, as from much walking

**foot·step** (-step′) *n.* **1.** the distance covered in a step **2.** the sound of a step; footfall **3.** a footprint **4.** a step in a stairway —**follow in (someone's) footsteps** to follow (someone's) example, vocation, etc.

**foot·stool** (-stool′) *n.* a low stool for supporting the feet of a seated person

**foot·wear** (-wer′) *n.* shoes, boots, slippers, etc.

**foot·work** (-wurk′) *n.* the act or manner of moving the feet, as in walking, boxing, dancing, etc.

**foo·zle** (foo′z'l) *vt., vi.* **-zled, -zling** [< ? G. *fuseln*, to bun-

gle] to make or do (something) awkwardly; esp., to bungle (a golf stroke) —*n.* the act or an instance of foozling —**foo′zler** *n.*

**fop** (fäp) *n.* [ME. *foppe*, a fool, prob. < MDu. or MLowG.] a vain, affected man who pays too much attention to his clothes, appearance, etc.; dandy —**fop′per·y** *n., pl.* **-per·ies** —**fop′pish** *adj.* —**fop′pish·ly** *adv.* —**fop′pish·ness** *n.*

**for** (fôr; *unstressed* fər) *prep.* [OE.] **1.** in place of [to use coats *for* blankets] **2.** in the interest of [his agent acted *for* him] **3.** in defense of; in favor of **4.** in honor of [to give a banquet *for* a notable] **5.** with the aim or purpose of [to carry a gun *for* protection] **6.** with the purpose of going to [to leave *for* home] **7.** in order to be, become, get, have, keep, etc. [to walk *for* exercise] **8.** in search of [looking *for* berries] **9.** meant to be received by a specified person or thing, or to be used in a specified way [flowers *for* a girl, money *for* paying bills] **10.** suitable to [a room *for* sleeping] **11.** with regard to [need *for* improvement, an ear *for* music] **12.** as being [to know *for* a fact] **13.** considering the nature of [cool *for* July] **14.** because of [to cry *for* pain] **15.** in spite of [stupid *for* all her learning] **16.** in proportion to [a dollar tax *for* every four earned] **17.** to the amount of [a bill *for* $50] **18.** at the price of [sold *for* $10] **19.** to the length, duration, etc. of; throughout [to work *for* an hour] **20.** at (a specified time) [a date *for* two o'clock] —*conj.* because; seeing that [comfort him *for* he is sad] —**for** (one) **to** that (one) will, should, must, etc. [a book *for* you to read] —**if** I wish that I had —**for** I wish that I had *[...]*

**for-** [OE., replacing *fer-*] *an Old English and Middle English prefix meaning:* **1.** away, apart, off, etc. [forbid, forget, forgo] **2.** very much [forlorn]

**for·age** (fôr′ij, fär′-) *n.* [< OFr. < Frank. *fodr*, food] **1.** food for domestic animals; fodder **2.** a search for food or provisions —*vi.* **-aged, -ag·ing 1.** to search for food or provisions **2.** to search for what one needs or wants —*vt.* **1.** to get or take food or provisions from **2.** to provide with forage; feed **3.** to get by foraging —**for′ag·er** *n.*

**fo·ra·men** (fô rā′mən, fə-) *n., pl.* **-ram′i·na** (-ram′ə nə), **-ra′mens** [L. < *forare*, to bore] a small opening, esp. in a bone or in a plant ovule —**fo·ram′i·nal** (-ram′ə n'l), **fo·ram′i·nate** (-nit) *adj.*

**fo·ra·min·i·fer** (fô rə min′ə fər, fär′-) *n., pl.* **fo·ram·i·nif·er·a** (fə ram′ə nif′ər ə) [< L. *foramen*: see prec. & -FER] any of a group of small, one-celled sea animals with calcareous shells full of tiny holes through which slender filaments project —**fo·ram′i·nif′er·al, fo·ram′i·nif′er·ous** *adj.*

**for·as·much** (fôr′əz much′) *conj.* inasmuch (as)

**for·ay** (fôr′ā) *vt., vi.* [< OFr. < *forrer*, to forage] to raid for spoils; plunder —*n.* a sudden attack or raid, as for spoils

**for·bade, for·bad** (fər bad′, fôr-) *pt. of* FORBID

**for·bear¹** (fôr ber′, fər-) *vt.* **-bore′** or archaic **-bare′, -borne′, -bear′ing** [< OE.: see FOR- & BEAR¹] to refrain from; avoid (doing, saying, etc.) —*vi.* **1.** to refrain or abstain **2.** to control oneself —**for·bear′er** *n.* —**for·bear′ing·ly** *adv.*

**for·bear²** (fôr′ber′) *n. same as* FOREBEAR

**for·bear·ance** (fôr ber′əns, fər-) *n.* **1.** the act of forbearing **2.** self-control; patient restraint

**for·bid** (fər bid′, fôr-) *vt.* **-bade′** or **-bad′, -bid′den** or archaic **-bid′, -bid′ding** [< OE.: see FOR- & BID] **1.** to rule against; prohibit **2.** to command to stay away from; bar from **3.** to make impossible; prevent —**for·bid′dance** *n.* —**for·bid′den** *adj.*

**for·bid·ding** (-iŋ) *adj.* looking dangerous, threatening, or disagreeable; repellent —**for·bid′ding·ly** *adv.*

**for·bore** (fôr bôr′, fər-) *pt. of* FORBEAR¹

**for·borne** (-bôrn′) *pp. of* FORBEAR¹

**force** (fôrs) *n.* [OFr. < LL. < L. *fortis*, strong] **1.** strength; energy; power **2.** impetus [the *force* of a blow] **3.** physical power or coercion exerted against a person or thing **4.** *a)* the power to control, persuade, etc.; effectiveness *b)* a person or thing having influence, power, etc. [a *force* for good] **5.** *a)* military, naval, or air power *b)* [pl.] the collective armed strength, as of a nation *c)* any organized group of soldiers, sailors, etc. **6.** any group of people organized for some activity [a sales *force*] **7.** *Law* binding power; validity **8.** *Physics* the cause, or agent, that puts an object at rest into motion or alters the motion of a moving object —*vt.* **forced, forc′ing 1.** to cause to do something by force; compel **2.** to rape (a woman) **3.** *a)* to break open, into, or through by force *b)* to overpower or capture in this way **4.** to take by force; wrest; extort **5.** to drive as by force; push; impel **6.** to impose as by force (with *on* or *upon*) **7.** to effect or produce as by force [to *force* a smile] **8.** to strain [to *force* one's voice] **9.** to cause (plants, fruit, etc.) to develop faster by artificial means **10.** *Baseball a)* to cause (a base runner) to be put out by a force-out: said of a batter *b)* to cause (a runner) to score or (a run) to be scored by walking the batter with the bases full (often with *in*) **11.** *Card Games* to cause (an opponent) to play (a particular card) or (one's partner) to make (a particular bid) **—in force 1.** in full strength **2.** in effect; valid **—force′a·ble** *adj.* **—force′less** *adj.* **—forc′er** *n.*

**forced** (fôrst) *adj.* **1.** done or brought about by force; compulsory *[forced* labor] **2.** produced by unusual effort; strained *[a forced* smile] **3.** due to an emergency *[a forced* landing] **4.** at a pace faster than usual *[a forced* march]

**force-feed** (fôrs′fēd′) *vt.* **-fed′, -feed′ing** to feed as by a tube through the throat to the stomach

**force·ful** (-fəl) *adj.* full of force; powerful, vigorous, effective, etc. **—force′ful·ly** *adv.* **—force′ful·ness** *n.*

**force·meat** (-mēt′) *n.* [< *farce meat* < *farce* (obs.), to stuff] meat chopped up and seasoned, usually for stuffing

**force-out** (-out′) *n. Baseball* an out that results when a base runner is forced from a base by a teammate's hit

**for·ceps** (fôr′səps) *n., pl.* **for′ceps** [L., orig., smith's tongs < *formus,* hot + *capere,* to take] small tongs or pincers for grasping, compressing, and pulling, used esp. by surgeons and dentists

**force pump** a pump with a valveless plunger for forcing a liquid through a pipe under pressure

**for·ci·ble** (fôr′sə b'l) *adj.* **1.** done or effected by force **2.** having force; forceful **—for′ci·ble·ness** *n.* **—for′ci·bly** *adv.*

FORCEPS
(A, fine bent;
B, scissors)

**ford** (fôrd) *n.* [OE.] a shallow place in a stream, river, etc. that can be crossed by wading, on horseback, in a car, etc. **—vt.** to cross (a stream) in this way **—ford′a·ble** *adj.*

**Ford** (fôrd) **1.** Gerald R(udolph), 1913– ; 38th president of the U.S. (1974–77) **2.** Henry, 1863–1947; U.S. automobile manufacturer

**for·done** (fôr dun′) *adj.* [Archaic] completely exhausted

**fore** (fôr) *adv.* [OE.] at, in, or toward the front: now only of a ship **—adj.** situated in front **—n.** the front thing or part **—interj.** *Golf* a shout warning those ahead that one is about to hit the ball **—to the fore 1.** to the front; into view **2.** available **3.** still active

**¹fore** (fôr) *prep.* [Poet.] before

**fore-** [OE.: see FORE] *a prefix meaning:* **1.** before in time, place, order, or rank *[forenoon, foreman]* **2.** the front part of *[forearm]*

**fore-and-aft** (fôr′'n aft′) *adj. Naut.* from the bow to the stern; lengthwise or set lengthwise

**fore and aft** *Naut.* **1.** from the bow to the stern; lengthwise or set lengthwise **2.** at, in, or toward both the bow and the stern

**fore·arm¹** (fôr′ärm′) *n.* the part of the arm between the elbow and the wrist

**fore·arm²** (fôr ärm′) *vt.* to arm in advance; prepare beforehand for any difficulty

**fore·bear** (fôr′ber′) *n.* [< FORE + BE + -ER] an ancestor

**fore·bode** (fôr bōd′) *vt., vi.* **-bod′ed, -bod′ing** [< OE.: see FORE- & BODE¹] **1.** to foretell; predict (esp. something bad or harmful) **2.** to have a presentiment of (something bad or harmful) **—fore·bod′er** *n.* **—fore·bod′ing** *n., adj.* **—fore·bod′ing·ly** *adv.*

**fore·brain** (fôr′brān′) *n.* the front part of the brain

**fore·cast** (fôr′kast′; *for v., also occas.* fôr kast′) *vt.* **-cast′** or **-cast′ed, -cast′ing 1.** to estimate in advance; predict (weather, etc.) **2.** to serve as a prediction or prophecy of **—vi.** to make a forecast **—n.** a prediction **—fore′cast′er** *n.*

**fore·cas·tle** (fōk′s'l; fôr′kas′'l *is a sp. pronun.*) *n.* [FORE + CASTLE] **1.** the upper deck of a ship in front of the foremast **2.** the front part of a merchant ship, where the sailors' quarters are located

**fore·close** (fôr klōz′) *vt.* **-closed′, -clos′ing** [< OFr. pp. of *forclore,* to exclude < *fors,* outside + *clore,* CLOSE²] **1.** to shut out; exclude; bar **2.** to take away the right to redeem (a mortgage, etc.) **—vi.** to foreclose a mortgage, etc. **—fore·clos′a·ble** *adj.* **—fore·clo′sure** (-klō′zhər) *n.*

**fore·doom** (fôr dōōm′) *vt.* to doom in advance; condemn beforehand

**fore·fa·ther** (fôr′fä′thər) *n.* an ancestor

**fore·fin·ger** (-fiŋ′gər) *n.* the finger nearest the thumb; index finger; first finger

**fore·foot** (-foot′) *n., pl.* **-feet′** either of the front feet of an animal with four or more feet

**fore·front** (-frunt′) *n.* **1.** the extreme front **2.** the position of most activity, importance, etc.

**fore·gath·er** (fôr gath′ər) *vi. same as* FORGATHER

**fore·go¹** (fôr gō′) *vt., vi.* **-went′, -gone′, -go′ing** [OE. *foregan*] to go before in place, time, or degree

**fore·go²** (fôr gō′) *vt. same as* FORGO

**fore·go·ing** (fôr′gō′iŋ) *adj.* previously said, written, etc. **—the foregoing 1.** the one or ones previously mentioned **2.** what has already been said or written

**fore·gone** (fôr gôn′) *adj.* **1.** that has gone before; previous **2.** *a)* previously determined *b)* inevitable or unavoidable: said of a conclusion

**fore·ground** (fôr′ground′) *n.* **1.** the part of a scene, picture, etc. nearest the viewer **2.** the most noticeable or conspicuous position

**fore·hand** (-hand′) *n.* a kind of stroke, as in tennis, made with the arm extended and the palm of the hand turned forward **—adj. 1.** foremost; front **2.** done or performed as with a forehand **—adv.** with a forehand

**fore·hand·ed** (fôr han′did) *adj.* **1.** making provision for the future; thrifty; prudent **2.** prosperous; well-off **3.** *same as* FOREHAND (*adj.* 2) **—fore·hand′ed·ly** *adv.* **—fore·hand′ed·ness** *n.*

**fore·head** (fär′id, fär′-; fôr′hed, fär′-) *n.* the part of the face between the eyebrows and the hairline

**for·eign** (fôr′in, fär′-) *adj.* [< OFr. *forain* < LL. < L. *foras,* out-of-doors] **1.** situated outside one's own country, locality, etc. **2.** of, from, or characteristic of another country *[a foreign* language] **3.** concerning the relations of one country to another *[foreign* affairs] **4.** *a)* not characteristic *b)* not pertinent **5.** not normally belonging *[foreign* matter in the eye] **—for′eign·ness** *n.*

**for·eign-born** (-bôrn′) *adj.* born in some other country **—the foreign-born** immigrants of a country

**for·eign·er** (-ər) *n.* a person from another country, thought of as an outsider; alien

**foreign office** in some countries, the office of government in charge of foreign affairs

**fore·know** (fôr nō′) *vt.* **-knew′, -known′, -know′ing** to know beforehand **—fore·know′a·ble** *adj.* **—fore·knowl·edge** (fôr′näl′ij) *n.*

**fore·land** (fôr′lənd) *n.* a headland; promontory

**fore·leg** (-leg′) *n.* either of the front legs of an animal with four or more legs

**fore·limb** (-lim′) *n.* a front limb, as an arm, foreleg, wing, or flipper

**fore·lock** (-läk′) *n.* a lock of hair growing just above the forehead

**fore·man** (-mən) *n., pl.* **-men** [orig., foremost man, leader] **1.** the chairman of a jury **2.** a man in charge of a department or group of workers in a factory, etc. **—fore′man·ship′** *n.*

**fore·mast** (fôr′mast′, -məst) *n.* the mast nearest the bow of a ship

**fore·most** (-mōst′) *adj.* [< OE. superl. of *forma,* superl. of *fore,* fore] **1.** first in place or time **2.** first in rank or importance **—adv.** first

**fore·named** (-nāmd′) *adj.* named or mentioned before

**fore·noon** (fôr′nōōn′) *n.* the time from sunrise to noon; morning **—adj.** of or in the forenoon

**fo·ren·sic** (fə ren′sik) *adj.* [< L. *forensis,* public < *forum,* marketplace] of, characteristic of, or suitable for a law court, public debate, or formal argument **—n.** [*pl.*] debate or formal argumentation **—fo·ren′si·cal·ly** *adv.*

**forensic medicine** *same as* MEDICAL JURISPRUDENCE

**fore·or·dain** (fôr′ôr dān′) *vt.* to ordain beforehand **—fore′or·di·na′tion** (-d'n ā′shən) *n.*

**fore·paw** (fôr′pô′) *n.* an animal's front paw

**fore·quar·ter** (-kwôr′tər) *n.* **1.** the front half of a side of beef or the like **2.** [*pl.*] the front quarters of a horse, etc., including the forelegs

**fore·run** (fôr run′) *vt.* **-ran′, -run′, -run′ning** [Rare] **1.** to run before; precede **2.** to be a sign of (a thing to follow) **3.** to forestall

**fore·run·ner** (fôr′run′ər, fôr run′ər) *n.* **1.** a messenger sent before or going before; herald **2.** a sign that tells or warns of something to follow **3.** *a)* a predecessor *b)* an ancestor

**fore·sail** (fôr′sāl′, -səl) *n.* **1.** the lowest sail on the foremast of a square-rigged ship **2.** the main triangular sail on the foremast of a fore-and-aft-rigged ship

**fore·see** (fôr sē′) *vt.* **-saw′, -seen′, -see′ing** to see or know beforehand **—fore·see′a·ble** *adj.* **—fore·se′er** *n.*

**fore·shad·ow** (-shad′ō) *vt.* to indicate or suggest beforehand; presage **—fore·shad′ow·er** *n.*

**fore·shank** (fôr′shaŋk′) *n.* **1.** the upper part of the front legs of cattle **2.** meat from this part

**fore·sheet** (-shēt′) *n.* **1.** one of the ropes used to trim a foresail **2.** [*pl.*] the space forward in an open boat

**fore·shock** (-shäk′) *n.* a minor earthquake preceding a greater one at or near the same place

**fore·shore** (-shôr′) *n.* the part of a shore between highwater mark and low-water mark

**fore·short·en** (fôr shôr't'n) *vt. Drawing, Painting*, etc. to represent some lines of (an object) as shorter than they actually are in order to give the illusion of proper relative size

**fore·show** (-shō') *vt.* **-showed'**, **-shown'** or **-showed'**, **-show'ing** to show or indicate beforehand

**fore·sight** (fôr'sīt') *n.* **1.** *a)* a foreseeing *b)* the power to foresee **2.** a looking forward **3.** prudent regard or provision for the future **—fore'sight'ed** *adj.* **—fore'sight'ed·ly** *adv.* **—fore'sight'ed·ness** *n.*

**fore·skin** (-skin') *n.* the fold of skin that covers the end of the penis; prepuce

**for·est** (fôr'ist, fär'-) *n.* [OFr. < ML. (*silva*) *forestis*, as if (wood) unenclosed (< L. *foris*, out-of-doors), but prob. (wood) under court control (< L. *forum*, court)] a thick growth of trees and underbrush covering an extensive tract of land; large woods **—***adj.* of or in a forest **—***vt.* to cover with trees or woods **—for'est·ed** *adj.*

FORESHORTENED ARM

**fore·stall** (fôr stôl') *vt.* [OE. *foresteall*, ambush: see FORE & STALL[2]] **1.** to prevent by doing something ahead of time **2.** to act in advance of; anticipate **—fore·stall'er** *n.* **—fore·stall'ment** *n.*

**for·est·a·tion** (fôr'is tā'shən, fär'-) *n.* the planting or care of forests

**fore·stay** (fôr'stā') *n.* a rope or cable reaching from the head of a ship's foremast to the bowsprit, for supporting the foremast

**for·est·er** (fôr'is tər, fär'-) *n.* **1.** a person trained in forestry or charged with the care of a forest **2.** a person or animal that lives in a forest

**for·est·ry** (-trē) *n.* **1.** [Rare] forest land **2.** the science of planting and taking care of forests **3.** systematic forest management for the production of timber, conservation, etc.

**fore·taste** (fôr'tāst'; *for v.* fôr tāst') *n.* a taste or sample of what can be expected **—***vt.* **-tast'ed, -tast'ing** [Rare] to taste beforehand

**fore·tell** (fôr tel') *vt.* **-told', -tell'ing** to tell or indicate beforehand; predict **—fore·tell'er** *n.*

**fore·thought** (fôr'thôt') *n.* **1.** a thinking or planning beforehand **2.** foresight; prudence **—fore'thought'ful** *adj.* **—fore'thought'ful·ly** *adv.*

**fore·to·ken** (fôr'tō'kən; *for v.* fôr tō'kən) *n.* a prophetic sign; omen **—***vt.* to foreshadow

**fore·top** (fôr'täp', -təp) *n.* the platform at the top of a ship's foremast

**fore-top·gal·lant** (fôr'täp gal'ənt, fôr'tə-) *adj.* designating or of the mast, sail, yard, etc. just above the fore-topmast

**fore-top·mast** (fôr täp'mast', -məst) *n.* the section of mast extending above the foremast

**fore-top·sail** (-sāl', -s'l) *n.* a sail set on the fore-topmast, above the foresail

**for·ev·er** (fər ev'ər, fôr-) *adv.* **1.** for eternity; for always; endlessly **2.** at all times; always Also **for·ev'er·more'** (-môr')

**fore·warn** (fôr wôrn') *vt.* to warn beforehand

**fore·wing** (fôr'wiŋ') *n.* either of the front pair of wings in most insects

**fore·word** (-wurd', -wərd) *n.* an introductory remark, preface, or prefatory note

**for·feit** (fôr'fit) *n.* [< OFr. < *forfaire*, to transgress, ult. < L. *foris*, beyond + *facere*, to do] **1.** something that one has to give up because of some crime, fault, or neglect; fine; penalty **2.** the act of forfeiting **—***adj.* lost or taken away as a forfeit **—***vt.* to lose or be deprived of as a forfeit **—for'feit·a·ble** *adj.* **—for'feit·er** *n.*

**for·fei·ture** (fôr'fə chər) *n.* **1.** a forfeiting **2.** anything forfeited; penalty or fine

**for·gath·er** (fôr gath'ər) *vi.* **1.** to come together **2.** to meet by chance **3.** to be friendly (*with*)

**for·gave** (fər gāv', fôr-) *pt. of* FORGIVE

**forge[1]** (fôrj) *n.* [< OFr. < L. *fabrica*, workshop < *faber*, workman] **1.** a furnace for heating metal to be wrought **2.** a place where metal is heated and hammered or wrought into shape; smithy **3.** a place where wrought iron is made, as from iron ore **—***vt.* **forged, forg'ing 1.** to shape (metal) by blows or pressure, usually after heating **2.** to form; shape; produce **3.** to imitate for purposes of deception or fraud; esp., to counterfeit (a check, etc.) **—***vi.* **1.** to work at a forge **2.** to commit forgery **—forg'er** *n.*

**forge[2]** (fôrj) *vt., vi.* **forged, forg'ing** [prob. altered < FORCE] **1.** to move forward steadily, as if against difficulties **2.** to move in a sudden spurt Often with *ahead*

**for·ger·y** (fôr'jər ē) *n., pl.* **-ger·ies 1.** the act or legal offense of forging documents, signatures, works of art, etc. to deceive **2.** anything forged

**for·get** (fər get', fôr-) *vt.* **-got'** or archaic **-gat'** (-gat'), **-got'ten** or **-got', -get'ting** [OE. *forgietan*] **1.** to lose

(facts, etc.) from the mind; be unable to remember **2.** to overlook or neglect, either unintentionally or intentionally **—***vi.* to forget things **—forget it** don't trouble to think about it **—forget oneself 1.** to think only of others **2.** to behave in an improper or unseemly manner **—for·get'ta·ble** *adj.* **—for·get'ter** *n.*

**for·get·ful** (-f'l) *adj.* **1.** apt to forget; having a poor memory **2.** negligent **3.** [Poet.] causing to forget **—for·get'·ful·ly** *adv.* **—for·get'ful·ness** *n.*

**for·get-me-not** (-mē nät') *n.* a marsh plant with clusters of small blue, white, or pink flowers

**for·give** (fər giv', fôr-) *vt.* **-gave', -giv'en, -giv'ing** [OE. *forgiefan*] **1.** to give up resentment against or the desire to punish; pardon **2.** to overlook (an offense) **3.** to cancel (a debt) **—***vi.* to show forgiveness **—for·giv'a·ble** *adj.* **—for·giv'er** *n.*

**for·give·ness** (-nis) *n.* **1.** a forgiving; pardon **2.** inclination to forgive

**for·giv·ing** (-iŋ) *adj.* that forgives; inclined to forgive **—for·giv'ing·ly** *adv.* **—for·giv'ing·ness** *n.*

**for·go** (fôr gō') *vt.* **-went', -gone', -go'ing** [OE. *forgan*] to do without; abstain from **—for·go'er** *n.*

**for·got** (fər gät', fôr-) *pt. & alt. pp. of* FORGET

**for·got·ten** (-'n) *pp. of* FORGET

**for·int** (fôr'int) *n. see* MONETARY UNITS, table (Hungary)

**fork** (fôrk) *n.* [OE. *forca* & Anglo-Fr. *forque*, both < L. *furca*, hayfork] **1.** an instrument with a handle and two or more prongs, used as an eating utensil or, in much larger form, for pitching hay, etc. **2.** something resembling a fork in shape: cf. TUNING FORK **3.** a division into branches; bifurcation **4.** the point where a river, road, etc. is divided into branches **5.** any of these branches **—***vi.* to divide into branches **—***vt.* **1.** to make into the form of a fork **2.** to pick up, spear, or pitch with a fork **—fork over** (or **out, up**) [Colloq.] to pay out; hand over **—fork'ful'** *n., pl.* **-fuls'**

**forked** (fôrkt) *adj.* **1.** having a fork or forks; cleft [*forked* lightning] **2.** having prongs [five-*forked*] Also **fork'y -i·er, -i·est**

**forked tongue** [prob. transl. of AmInd. expression] lying or deceitful talk [to speak with a *forked tongue*]

**fork·lift** (fôrk'lift') *n.* a device, often on a truck (**forklift truck**), for lifting, stacking, etc. heavy objects: its projecting prongs are slid under the load and raised or lowered

**for·lorn** (fər lôrn', fôr-) *adj.* [< OE. pp. of *forleosan*, to lose utterly] **1.** abandoned or deserted **2.** wretched; miserable; pitiful **3.** without hope; desperate **4.** bereft (*of*) **—for·lorn'ly** *adv.* **—for·lorn'ness** *n.*

**form** (fôrm) *n.* [< OFr. < L. *forma*] **1.** the shape, outline, or configuration of anything; structure **2.** *a)* the body or figure of a person or animal *b)* a model of a human figure used as a clothes dummy **3.** anything used to give shape to something else; mold, as for poured concrete **4.** the mode of existence a thing has or takes [water in the *form* of vapor] **5.** arrangement; esp., orderly arrangement, often of a specified kind **6.** a way of doing something [one's golf *form*] **7.** a customary way of acting or behaving; ceremony; formality **8.** a fixed order of words; formula **9.** a printed document with blank spaces to be filled in **10.** a particular kind, type, species, or variety **11.** a condition of mind or body [a boxer in good *form*] **12.** *a)* a chart giving information about horses in a race *b)* what can be expected, based on past performances [to react according to *form*] **13.** a long, wooden bench, as formerly in a schoolroom **14.** a grade or class in school in some private and British schools **15.** *Gram.* any of the different appearances of a word in changes of inflection, spelling, etc. ["am" is a *form* of "be"] **16.** *Printing* the type, plates, etc. locked in a frame for printing **—***vt.* **1.** to shape; fashion; make, as in some particular way **2.** to train; instruct **3.** to develop (habits) **4.** to think of; conceive **5.** to organize into [to *form* a club] **6.** to make up; constitute **—***vi.* **1.** to be formed **2.** to come into being; take form **3.** to take a specific form **—good** (or **bad**) **form** conduct in (or not in) accord with social custom

**-form** (fôrm) *suffix* [< Fr. < L. *-formis* < *forma*, form] *a suffix meaning:* **1.** having the form of [*cuneiform*] **2.** having (a specified number of) forms [*multiform*]

**for·mal** (fôr'məl) *adj.* [L. *formalis*] **1.** of external form or structure, rather than nature or content **2.** according to fixed customs, rules, etc. **3.** *a)* appearing to be suitable, correct, etc. but not really so *b)* stiff in manner **4.** *a)* designed for wear at ceremonies, etc. [*formal* dress] *b)* requiring such clothes [a *formal* dance] **5.** done or made in orderly, regular fashion; methodical **6.** rigidly symmetrical [a *formal* garden] **7.** done or made according to the forms that make explicit, definite, etc. [a *formal* contract] **8.** designating education in schools, colleges, etc. **9.** designating or of that level of language usage characterized by expanded vocabulary, complete syntactical constructions, complex sentences, etc.: distinguished from COLLOQUIAL **—***n.* **1.** a formal dance or ball **2.** a woman's evening dress —**go formal** [Colloq.] to go dressed in evening clothes —**for′mal·ly** *adv.*

**form·al·de·hyde** (fôr mal′də hīd′, fər-) *n.* [FORM(IC) + ALDEHYDE] a colorless, pungent gas, HCHO, used in solution as a disinfectant and preservative

**for·mal·ism** (fôr′məl iz′m) *n.* strict attention to outward forms and customs, as in art or religion —**for′mal·ist** *n.,* *adj.* —**for′mal·is′tic** *adj.*

**for·mal·i·ty** (fôr mal′ə tē) *n., pl.* **-ties 1.** a being formal; specif., *a)* an observing of prescribed customs, rules, ceremonies, etc.; propriety *b)* careful or too careful attention to order, regularity, or convention; stiffness **2.** a formal or conventional act or requirement; ceremony or form

**for·mal·ize** (fôr′mə līz′) *vt.* **-ized′, -iz′ing 1.** to give definite form to **2.** to make formal **3.** to make official, valid, etc. —**for′mal·i·za′tion** *n.*

**for·mat** (fôr′mat) *n.* [G. < L. pp. of *formare,* to form] **1.** the shape, size, and general makeup of a book, magazine, etc. **2.** general arrangement, as of a television program

**for·ma·tion** (fôr mā′shən) *n.* **1.** a forming or being formed **2.** a thing formed **3.** the way in which something is formed or arranged; structure **4.** an arrangement or positioning, as of troops, ships, a football team, etc. **5.** *Ecol.* the major unit of vegetation, as the prairie, tundra, etc. **6.** *Geol.* a rock unit having some common character, as origin

**form·a·tive** (fôr′mə tiv) *adj.* **1.** helping to shape, develop, or mold *[a formative* influence*]* **2.** of formation or development *[one's formative* years*]* **3.** *Linguis.* serving to form words, as an affix

**form class** *Linguis.* a class made up of words having a distinctive position in constructions and certain formal features in common

**for·mer**[1] (fôr′mər) *adj.* [ME. *formere,* compar. of *forme,* first < OE. *forma:* see FOREMOST] **1.** preceding in time; earlier; past **2.** first mentioned of two: opposed to LATTER: often a noun (with *the)*

**form·er**[2] (fôr′mər) *n.* a person or thing that forms

**for·mer·ly** (fôr′mər lē) *adv.* at or in a former or earlier time; in the past

**for·mic** (fôr′mik) *adj.* [< L. *formica,* an ant] **1.** of ants **2.** designating or of a colorless acid, HCOOH, found in ants, spiders, nettles, etc.

**For·mi·ca** (fôr mīk′ə) [arbitrary coinage] *a trademark for* a laminated, heat-resistant plastic used for table tops, etc.

**for·mi·da·ble** (fôr′mə də b′l) *adj.* [OFr. < L. < *formidare,* to dread] **1.** causing fear or dread **2.** hard to handle or overcome **3.** awe-inspiring in size, excellence, etc. —**for′mi·da·bil′i·ty, for′mi·da·ble·ness** *n.* —**for′mi·da·bly** *adv.*

**form·less** (fôrm′lis) *adj.* having no regular form or plan —**form′less·ly** *adv.* —**form′less·ness** *n.*

**form letter** one of a number of duplicated letters, with the date, address, etc. filled in separately

**For·mo·sa** (fôr mō′sə, -zə) *former* (*Portuguese*) *name of* TAIWAN —**For·mo′san** *adj., n.*

**for·mu·la** (fôr′myə lə) *n., pl.* **-las, -lae** (-lē′) [L., dim. of *forma,* form] **1.** a fixed form of words, esp. one that is used only as a conventional expression *[*"Very truly yours" is a *formula]* **2.** a rule or method for doing something, esp. when conventional and used or repeated without thought **3.** an exact statement of religious faith or doctrine **4.** *a)* a prescription for a medicine, a baby's food, etc. *b)* something, esp. fortified milk for a baby, prepared from a prescription **5.** a set of algebraic symbols expressing a mathematical fact, rule, etc. **6.** *Chem.* an expression of the composition, as of a compound, by a combination of symbols and figures —*adj.* designating or of any of various classes of racing car designed to conform to a particular set of specifications governing size, weight, etc.

**for·mu·lar·ize** (-lə rīz′) *vt.* **-ized′, -iz′ing** *same as* FORMULATE (sense 1)

**for·mu·lar·y** (fôr′myə ler′ē) *n., pl.* **-lar′ies 1.** a collection of formulas or prescribed forms, as of prayers **2.** a formula **3.** *Pharmacy* a list of medicines with their formulas —*adj.* of formulas

**for·mu·late** (-lāt′) *vt.* **-lat′ed, -lat′ing 1.** to express in or reduce to a formula **2.** to express (a theory, plan, etc.) in a systematic way —**for′mu·la′tion** *n.* —**for′mu·la′tor** *n.*

**for·mu·lize** (-līz′) *vt.* **-lized′, -liz′ing** *same as* FORMULATE (sense 1)

**for·ni·cate** (fôr′nə kāt′) *vi.* **-cat′ed, -cat′ing** [< LL. pp. of *fornicari* < L. *fornix* (gen. *fornicis*), a brothel] to commit fornication —**for′ni·ca′tor** *n.*

**for·ni·ca·tion** (fôr′nə kā′shən) *n.* **1.** voluntary sexual intercourse between unmarried persons **2.** *Bible* any unlawful sexual intercourse

**for·sake** (fər sāk′, fôr-) *vt.* **-sook′** (-sook′), **-sak′en, -sak′ing** [< OE. < *for-,* FOR- + *sacan,* to strive < *sacu:* see SAKE[1]] **1.** to give up; renounce (a habit, idea, etc.) **2.** to leave; abandon

**for·sak·en** (-sā′kən) *adj.* abandoned; desolate

**for·sooth** (fər sooth′, fôr-) *adv.* [OE. *forsoth*] [Archaic] in truth; no doubt; indeed

**For·ster** (fôr′stər), **E** (**dward**) **M** (**organ**) 1879–1970; Eng. novelist

**for·swear** (fôr swer′) *vt.* **-swore′** (-swôr′), **-sworn′, -swear′-ing 1.** to swear or promise earnestly to give up **2.** to deny earnestly or on oath —*vi.* to swear falsely; commit perjury —**forswear oneself** to perjure oneself

**for·syth·i·a** (fər sith′ē ə, fôr-) *n.* [ModL., after W. *Forsyth,* 18th-c. Eng. botanist] a shrub of the olive family with yellow, bell-shaped flowers, which appear in early spring before the leaves

**fort** (fôrt) *n.* [OFr. < L. *fortis,* strong] **1.** a fortified place or building for military defense **2.** a permanent army post

**For·ta·le·za** (fôr′tə lā′zə) seaport in NE Brazil, on the Atlantic: pop. 515,000

**forte**[1] (fôrt) *n.* [< OFr.: see FORT] that which one does particularly well; one's strong point

**for·te**[2] (fôr′tā, -tē) *adj., adv.* [It. < L. *fortis,* strong] *Music* loud: a direction to the performer —*n.* a forte note or passage

**Forth** (fôrth) river in SE Scotland, flowing through a long estuary (**Firth of Forth**) into the North Sea

**forth** (fôrth) *adv.* [OE.] **1.** forward; onward **2.** out into view, as from hiding —**and so forth** and so on: equivalent to *etc.*

**forth·com·ing** (fôrth′kum′iŋ) *adj.* **1.** about to appear; approaching **2.** ready when needed *[help was not forthcoming]* —*n.* a coming forth; approach

**forth·right** (-rīt′) *adj.* straightforward; direct; frank —*adv.* straight forward; directly onward —**forth′right′ly** *adv.* —**forth′right′ness** *n.*

**forth·with** (fôrth′with′, -with′) *adv.* immediately

**for·ti·eth** (fôr′tē ith) *adj.* **1.** preceded by thirty-nine others in a series; 40th **2.** designating any of the forty equal parts of something —*n.* **1.** the one following the thirty-ninth **2.** any of the forty equal parts of something; 1/40

**for·ti·fi·ca·tion** (fôr′tə fi kā′shən) *n.* **1.** the act or science of fortifying **2.** a fort or defensive earthwork, wall, etc. **3.** a fortified place

**for·ti·fy** (fôr′tə fī′) *vt.* **-fied′, -fy′ing** [< OFr. < LL. *fortificare* < L. *fortis,* strong + *facere,* to make] **1.** to strengthen physically, emotionally, etc. **2.** to strengthen against attack, as by building forts, walls, etc. **3.** to support; corroborate (an argument, etc.) **4.** to strengthen (wine, etc.) by adding alcohol **5.** to add vitamins, minerals, etc. to (milk, etc.) so as to increase the food value —*vi.* to build military fortifications —**for′ti·fi′a·ble** *adj.*

**for·tis·si·mo** (fôr tis′ə mō′) *adj., adv.* [It., superl. of *forte,* FORTE[2]] *Music* very loud: a direction to the performer —*n., pl.* **-mos′, -mi′** (-mē′) a fortissimo note or passage

**for·ti·tude** (fôr′tə tood′, -tyood′) *n.* [< L. < *fortis,* strong] patient endurance of misfortune, pain, etc.; firm courage —**for′ti·tu′di·nous** *adj.*

**Fort Knox** [see KNOXVILLE] military reservation in N Ky., near Louisville: site of U.S. gold bullion depository

**Fort Lau·der·dale** (lô′dər dāl′) [after Maj. Wm. *Lauderdale*] city on the SE coast of Fla.: pop. 153,000 (met. area 1,006,000)

**fort·night** (fôrt′nīt′) *n.* [< OE., lit., fourteen nights] [Chiefly Brit.] two weeks

**fort·night·ly** (-lē) *adv., adj.* [Chiefly Brit.] (happening or appearing) once every fortnight, or at two-week intervals —*n., pl.* **-lies** a periodical issued at two-week intervals

**for·tress** (fôr′trəs) *n.* [< OFr., ult. < L. *fortis,* strong] a fortified place; fort: often used figuratively —*vt.* to protect by a fortress

**Fort Smith** [after Gen. T. *Smith,* d. 1865] city in W Ark., on the Arkansas River: pop. 71,000

**for·tu·i·tous** (fôr too′ə təs, -tyoo′-) *adj.* [< L. < *fors* (gen. *fortis*), luck] **1.** happening by chance; accidental **2.** bringing, or happening by, good luck; fortunate —**for·tu′i·tous·ly** *adv.* —**for·tu′i·tous·ness** *n.*

**for·tu·i·ty** (-tē) *n., pl.* **-ties** [< L. (see prec.) + -ITY] **1.** a being fortuitous **2.** chance or chance occurrence

**for·tu·nate** (fôr′chə nit) *adj.* [< L. pp. of *fortunare* < *fortuna,* FORTUNE] **1.** having good luck; lucky **2.** bringing, or coming by, good luck; favorable —**for′tu·nate·ly** *adv.* —**for′tu·nate·ness** *n.*

**for·tune** (fôr′chən) *n.* [OFr. < L. *fortuna* < *fors* (gen. *fortis*), luck] **1.** the supposed power that brings good or bad to people; luck; chance; fate: often personified **2.** what happens to one; one's lot, esp. future lot, good or bad *[to tell one's fortune]* **3.** good luck; success **4.** wealth; riches —**for′tune·less** *adj.*

---

fat, āpe, cär, ten, ēven, is, bīte; gō, hôrn, tōōl, look; oil, out; up, fur; get; joy; yet; chin; she; thin, *th*en; zh, leisure; ŋ, ring; ə for *a* in *ago, e* in *agent, i* in *sanity, o* in *comply, u* in *focus;* ′ as in *able* (ā′b′l); Fr. bal; ë, Fr. coeur; ö, Fr. feu; Fr. mon; ö, Fr. coq; ü, Fr. duc; r, Fr. cri; H, G. ich; kh, G. doch; ‡foreign; *hypothetical; < derived from. See inside front cover.

**fortune cookie** a hollow Chinese cookie with a slip of paper inside predicting the future

**fortune hunter** a person who tries to become rich, esp. by marrying a rich person

**for·tune·tell·er** (-tel′ər) *n.* a person who professes to foretell events in other people's lives —**for′tune·tell′ing** *n., adj.*

**Fort Wayne** [after Anthony WAYNE] city in NE Ind.: pop. 172,000

**Fort Worth** [after Wm. *Worth* (1794–1849)] city in N Tex.: pop. 385,000: see DALLAS

**for·ty** (fôr′tē) *adj.* [OE. *feowertig*] four times ten —*n., pl.* **-ties** the cardinal number between thirty-nine and forty-one; 40; XL —**the forties** the numbers or years, as of a century, from forty through forty-nine

**for·ty-nin·er** (fôr′tē nīn′ər) *n.* [*also* F- N-] [Colloq.] a participant in the 1849 California gold rush

**forty winks** [Colloq.] a short sleep; nap

**fo·rum** (fôr′əm) *n., pl.* **-rums, -ra** (-ə) [L.] **1.** the public square or marketplace of an ancient Roman city, where legal and political business was conducted **2.** a law court; tribunal **3.** *a)* an assembly or program for the discussion of public matters *b)* an opportunity for open discussion —**the Forum** the forum of ancient Rome

**for·ward** (fôr′wərd) *adj.* [OE. *foreweard*] **1.** at, toward, or of the front **2.** advanced; specif., *a)* mentally advanced *b)* advanced socially, politically, etc. **3.** onward; advancing **4.** ready or eager; prompt **5.** too bold; presumptuous **6.** of or for the future [*forward* buying] —*adv.* **1.** toward the front; ahead **2.** toward the future [to look *forward*] **3.** into view or prominence —*n.* Basketball, Hockey, etc. any of the players in a front position —*vt.* **1.** to promote **2.** to send; transmit; dispatch **3.** to send on to another address [to *forward* mail] —**for′ward·er** *n.* —**for′ward·ly** *adv.* —**for′ward·ness** *n.*

**forward pass** *Football* a pass from behind the line of scrimmage to a teammate in a forward position

**for·wards** (-wərdz) *adv. same as* FORWARD

**for·went** (fôr went′) *pt. of* FORGO

**fos·sa** (fäs′ə) *n., pl.* **-sae** (-ē) [ModL. < L., a ditch] *Anat.* a cavity, pit, or small hollow —**fos′sate** (-āt) *adj.*

**fosse, foss** (fôs, fäs) *n.* [< OFr. < L. *fossa*, ditch] a ditch or moat, esp. in fortifications

**fos·sil** (fäs′'l, fôs′-) *n.* [< Fr. < L. *fossilis*, dug up < pp. of *fodere*, to dig up] **1.** any hardened remains or traces of plant or animal life of some previous geological age, preserved in the earth's crust **2.** anything like a fossil **3.** a person who has outmoded, fixed ideas —*adj.* **1.** of, like, or forming a fossil **2.** dug from the earth [coal is a *fossil* fuel] **3.** antiquated —**fos′sil·like′** *adj.*

**fos·sil·if·er·ous** (fäs′ə lif′ər əs, fôs′-) *adj.* [< FOSSIL + -FEROUS] containing fossils

**fos·sil·ize** (fäs′ə līz′, fôs′-) *vt.* **-ized′, -iz′ing** **1.** to change into a fossil; petrify **2.** to make out of date, rigid, or incapable of change —*vi.* to become fossilized —**fos′sil·i·za′tion** *n.*

**fos·ter** (fôs′tər, fäs′-) *vt.* [OE. *fostrian*, to nourish < base of *foda*, food] **1.** to bring up with care; rear **2.** to help to develop; promote [to *foster* discontent] **3.** to cherish [to *foster* a hope] —*adj.* **1.** having the standing of a specified member of the family but not by birth or adoption [a *foster* child] **2.** of or relating to the care of such a person [*foster* home] —**fos′ter·er** *n.*

**Fos·ter** (fôs′tər, fäs′-), **Stephen Collins** 1826–64; U.S. composer of songs

**fought** (fôt) *pt. & pp. of* FIGHT

**foul** (foul) *adj.* [OE. *ful*] **1.** stinking; loathsome [a *foul* odor] **2.** extremely dirty; disgustingly filthy **3.** full of dirt or foreign objects [a *foul* pipe] **4.** rotten: said of food **5.** not decent; obscene [*foul* language] **6.** wicked; abominable **7.** stormy; unfavorable [*foul* weather] **8.** tangled; caught [a *foul* rope] **9.** not according to the rules of a game; unfair **10.** treacherous; dishonest **11.** [Colloq.] unpleasant, disagreeable, etc. **12.** *Baseball* not fair: see FOUL BALL, FOUL LINE **13.** *Printing* marked for errors or changes [*foul* copy] —*adv.* in a foul way —*n.* anything foul; specif., *a)* a collision of boats, contestants, etc. *b)* an infraction of rules, as of a game *c)* *Baseball same as* FOUL BALL —*vt.* **1.** to make foul; dirty; soil **2.** to dishonor or disgrace **3.** to obstruct; fill up [grease *fouls* sink drains] **4.** to cover (a ship's bottom) with impeding growths **5.** to entangle; catch [a rope *fouled* in the shrouds] **6.** to collide with **7.** to make a foul against, as in a game **8.** *Baseball* to bat (the ball) so that it falls outside the foul lines —*vi.* **1.** to be or become fouled (in various senses) **2.** to break the rules of a game **3.** *Baseball* to hit a foul ball —**foul out 1.** *Baseball* to be put out by the catch of a foul ball **2.** *Basketball* to be disqualified for a certain number of personal fouls —**foul up** [Colloq.] to entangle or bungle —**run** (or **fall** or **go**) **foul of 1.** to collide with and become tangled in **2.** to get into trouble with —**foul′ly** *adv.* —**foul′ness** *n.*

**fou·lard** (fōō lärd′) *n.* [Fr.] **1.** a lightweight material of silk, rayon, or sometimes cotton **2.** a necktie, scarf, etc. of this material

**foul ball** *Baseball* a batted ball that is not a fair ball: see FAIR BALL

**foul line 1.** *Baseball* either of the lines extending from home plate through the outside corners of first base or third base and onward along the outfield **2.** *Basketball* the line from which a player makes throws granted to him when he is fouled **3.** *Tennis, Bowling,* etc. any of various lines bounding the playing area, beyond which the ball must not be hit, the player must not go, etc.

**foul play 1.** unfair play; action that breaks the rules of the game **2.** treacherous action or violence

**found¹** (found) *pt. & pp. of* FIND

**found²** (found) *vt.* [< OFr. < L. < *fundus,* bottom] **1.** to set for support; base [a statement *founded* on facts] **2.** to begin to build or organize; establish [to *found* a college] —*vi.* [Rare] to be based (*on* or *upon*)

**found³** (found) *vt.* [< OFr. < L. *fundere,* to pour] **1.** to melt and pour (metal) into a mold **2.** to make by pouring molten metal into a mold; cast

**foun·da·tion** (foun dā′shən) *n.* **1.** a founding or being founded; establishment **2.** *a)* a fund or endowment to maintain a hospital, charity, research, etc. *b)* the organization administering such a fund **3.** the base on which something rests; specif., the supporting part of a wall, house, etc. **4.** basis **5.** a woman's corset or girdle: also **foundation garment 6.** a cosmetic cream, liquid, etc. over which other makeup is applied —**foun·da′tion·al** *adj.*

**foun·der¹** (foun′dər) *vi.* [< OFr. < L. *fundus:* see FOUND²] **1.** to stumble, fall, or go lame **2.** to become stuck as in soft ground **3.** to fill with water and sink: said of a ship **4.** to break down; collapse; fail —*vt.* to cause to founder

**found·er²** (foun′dər) *n.* a person who founds, or establishes

**found·er³** (foun′dər) *n.* a person who founds metals

**found·ling** (found′liŋ) *n.* an infant of unknown parents that has been found abandoned

**found·ry** (foun′drē) *n., pl.* **-ries 1.** the act or work of founding metals; casting **2.** metal castings **3.** a place where metal is cast

**fount** (fount) *n.* [< OFr. < L. *fons,* FOUNTAIN] **1.** [Poet.] a fountain or spring **2.** a source

**foun·tain** (foun′t'n) *n.* [< OFr. < LL. *fontana* < L. < *fons* (gen. *fontis*), spring] **1.** a natural spring of water **2.** a source or origin of anything **3.** *a)* an artificial spring, jet, or flow of water *b)* the basin, pipes, etc. where this flows *c) same as* DRINKING FOUNTAIN *d) same as* SODA FOUNTAIN **4.** a container or reservoir, as for ink, oil, etc.

**foun·tain·head** (-hed′) *n.* **1.** a spring that is the source of a stream **2.** the original or main source of anything

**fountain pen** a pen which is fed ink from a supply in a reservoir or cartridge

**four** (fôr) *adj.* [OE. *feower*] totaling one more than three —*n.* **1.** the cardinal number between three and five; 4; IV **2.** anything having four units or members, or numbered four —**on all fours 1.** on all four feet **2.** on hands and knees (or feet)

**four-flush** (fôr′flush′) *vi.* **1.** *Stud Poker* to bluff when one holds four cards of the same suit (**four flush**) instead of the five in a true flush **2.** [Colloq.] to bluff —**four′-flush′er** *n.*

**four·fold** (-fōld′) *adj.* [see -FOLD] **1.** having four parts **2.** having four times as much or as many —*adv.* four times as much or as many

**four-foot·ed** (-foot′id) *adj.* having four feet

**Four-H club, 4-H club** (fôr′āch′) a rural youth organization offering instruction in scientific agriculture and home economics

**four hundred** [*also* F- H-] the exclusive social set of a particular place (preceded by *the*)

**four-in-hand** (-in hand′) *n.* **1.** *a)* a team of four horses driven by one man *b)* a coach drawn by such a team **2.** a necktie tied in a slipknot with the ends left hanging —*adj.* of a four-in-hand

**four-o'clock** (-ə kläk′) *n.* a garden plant with long-tubed, variously colored flowers that generally open in the late afternoon

**four-post·er** (-pōs′tər) *n.* a bedstead with tall corner posts often supporting a canopy or curtains

**four·score** (-skôr′) *adj., n.* four times twenty; eighty

**four·some** (-səm) *n.* **1.** a group of four people **2.** *Golf* a game involving four players

**four·square** (-skwer′) *adj.* **1.** perfectly square **2.** unyielding; firm **3.** frank; forthright —*adv.* **1.** in a square form **2.** forthrightly

**four·teen** (-tēn′) *adj.* [OE. *feowertyne*] four more than ten —*n.* the cardinal number between thirteen and fifteen; 14; XIV

**four·teenth** (-tēnth′) *adj.* **1.** preceded by thirteen others in a series; 14th **2.** designating any of the fourteen equal parts of something —*n.* **1.** the one following the thirteenth **2.** any of the fourteen equal parts of something; 1/14

**fourth** (fôrth) *adj.* [< OE.] **1.** preceded by three others in a series; 4th **2.** designating any of the four equal parts of something —*n.* **1.** the one following the third **2.** any of the four equal parts of something; 1/4 **3.** the fourth forward gear ratio of a motor vehicle **4.** *Music a)* the fourth tone of an ascending diatonic scale, or a tone three degrees above or below a given tone *b)* the interval between two such tones, or a combination of them —**fourth′ly** *adv.*

**fourth dimension** a dimension in addition to those of length, width, and depth: in the theory of relativity, time is regarded as this dimension —**fourth′-di·men′sion·al** *adj.*

**fourth estate** [cf. ESTATE (sense 2)] [*often* F- E-] journalism or journalists

**Fourth of July** *see* INDEPENDENCE DAY

**fourth world** [*often* F- W-] the poorest, most underdeveloped countries of the third world

**fowl** (foul) *n., pl.* **fowls, fowl**: see PLURAL, II, D, 1 [OE. *fugol*] **1.** any bird: used in combination [wild*fowl*] **2.** any of the larger domestic birds used as food, as the chicken, duck, turkey, etc. **3.** the flesh of any of these birds used for food —*vi.* to hunt wild birds for food or sport —**fowl′er** *n.* —**fowl′ing** *n., adj.*

**fowling piece** a shotgun for hunting wild fowl

**fox** (fäks) *n., pl.* **fox′es, fox**: see PLURAL, II, D, 1 [OE.] **1.** a small, wild, flesh-eating mammal of the dog family, with a bushy tail: thought of as sly and crafty **2.** its fur, commonly reddish-brown or gray **3.** a sly, crafty person —*vt.* **1.** to stain (book leaves, prints, etc.) with brownish discolorations **2.** to trick by slyness or craftiness **3.** to bewilder or baffle —**foxed** *adj.*

**fox fire** the luminescence of decaying wood and plant remains, caused by various fungi

FOX (average length 42 in., including tail)

**fox·glove** (fäks′gluv′) *n.* [OE. *foxes glofa*] *same as* DIGITALIS (sense 1)

**fox·hole** (-hōl′) *n.* a hole dug in the ground as a temporary protection for one or two soldiers against enemy gunfire or tanks

**fox·hound** (-hound′) *n.* a strong, swift hound with a keen scent, bred and trained to hunt foxes

**fox·tail** (-tāl′) *n.* **1.** the tail of a fox **2.** a grass having spikes bearing spikelets interspersed with stiff bristles

**fox terrier** a small, active terrier with a smooth or wire-haired coat, formerly trained to drive foxes out of hiding

**fox trot 1.** a horse gait that is a shuffling half-walk, half-trot **2.** *a)* a dance for couples in 4/4 time with a variety of steps, both fast and slow *b)* the music for such a dance —**fox′-trot′** *vi.* **-trot′ted, -trot′ting**

**fox·y** (fäk′sē) *adj.* **fox′i·er, fox′i·est 1.** foxlike; crafty; sly **2.** covered with brownish stains **3.** [Slang] attractive, stylish, etc.; specif., sexually attractive: used esp. of women —**fox′i·ly** *adv.* —**fox′i·ness** *n.*

**foy·er** (foi′ər, foi′ā, foi yā′) *n.* [Fr. < ML. < L. *focus,* hearth] an entrance hall or a lobby, as in a theater or hotel

**F.P., f.p., fp** foot-pound; foot-pounds

**f.p., fp, fp.** freezing point

**FPO** *U.S. Navy* Fleet Post Office

**fps, f.p.s. 1.** feet per second **2.** foot-pound-second

**Fr** *Chem.* francium

**Fr 1.** Father **2.** France **3.** French **4.** Friday

**fr.** franc; francs

**Fra** (frä) *n.* [It., abbrev. of *frate* < L. *frater*] brother: title given to an Italian friar or monk

**fra·cas** (frā′kəs, frak′əs) *n.* [Fr. < It. < *fracassare,* to smash] a noisy fight or loud quarrel; brawl

**frac·tion** (frak′shən) *n.* [< L. < pp. of *frangere,* to break] **1.** a small part, amount, etc.; portion; fragment **2.** *Chem.* a part separated, as by distillation, from a mixture, at its particular boiling point, etc. **3.** *Math. a)* an indicated quotient of two whole numbers, as 1/2, 13/4 *b)* any quantity expressed in terms of a numerator and denominator, as 2x/xy —**frac′tion·al** *adj.* —**frac′tion·al·ly** *adv.*

**frac·tion·ate** (-āt′) *vt.* **-at′ed, -at′ing 1.** to separate into fractions, or parts **2.** *Chem.* to separate into fractions by distillation, etc. —**frac′tion·a′tion** *n.*

**frac·tious** (frak′shəs) *adj.* [prob. < *fraction* (obs.) discord + -OUS] **1.** unruly; rebellious; refractory **2.** peevish; irritable; cross —**frac′tious·ly** *adv.* —**frac′tious·ness** *n.*

**frac·ture** (frak′chər) *n.* [< OFr. < L. *fractura* < pp. of *frangere,* to break] **1.** a breaking or being broken **2.** a break, crack, or split **3.** a break in a bone or, occasionally, a tear in a cartilage **4.** the texture of the broken surface of a mineral —*vt., vi.* **-tured, -tur·ing 1.** to break, crack, or split **2.** to disrupt —**frac′tur·al** *adj.*

**frae** (frā) *prep.* [Scot.] from

**frag·ile** (fraj′'l; *chiefly Brit. & Canad.,* -īl) *adj.* [< OFr. < L. *fragilis* < *frangere,* to break] easily broken, damaged, or destroyed; frail; delicate —**fra·gil·i·ty** (frə jil′ə tē) *n.*

**frag·ment** (frag′mənt; *for v. also* frag ment′) *n.* [< L. < *frangere,* to break] **1.** a part broken away; broken piece **2.** a detached or incomplete part [a *fragment* of a novel] —*vt., vi.* to break into fragments —**frag′ment·ed** *adj.*

**frag·men·tar·y** (frag′mən ter′ē) *adj.* consisting of fragments or bits; not complete; disconnected: also **frag·men′-tal** (-men′təl) —**frag′men·tar′i·ly** *adv.*

**frag·men·tate** (-tāt′) *vt., vi.* **-tat′ed, -tat′ing** to break into fragments —**frag′men·ta′tion** *n.*

**fra·grance** (frā′grəns) *n.* a fragrant smell; pleasant odor

**fra·grant** (frā′grənt) *adj.* [< L. prp. of *fragrare,* to emit a (sweet) smell] having a pleasant odor; sweet-smelling —**fra′grant·ly** *adv.*

**fraid·y-cat** (frā′dē kat′) *n.* [< AFRAID + CAT] [Colloq.] a person easily frightened: a child's term

**frail** (frāl) *adj.* [< OFr. < L. *fragilis,* FRAGILE] **1.** easily broken, damaged, or destroyed; fragile; delicate **2.** slender and delicate; not robust; weak **3.** easily tempted to do wrong; morally weak —*n.* [Slang] a woman or girl —**frail′ly** *adv.* —**frail′ness** *n.*

**frail·ty** (frāl′tē) *n.* **1.** the condition of being frail; weakness; esp., moral weakness **2.** *pl.* **-ties** any fault or failing arising from such weaknesses

**frame** (frām) *vt.* **framed, fram′ing** [prob. < ON. *frami,* profit, benefit; some senses < OE. *framian,* to be helpful] **1.** to shape or form according to a pattern; design [to *frame* a constitution] **2.** to put together the parts of; construct **3.** to put into words; compose; devise **4.** to adjust; fit [a tax *framed* to benefit a few] **5.** to enclose (a picture, mirror, etc.) in a border **6.** [Colloq.] to falsify evidence, testimony, etc. beforehand so as to make (an innocent person) appear guilty —*n.* **1.** *a)* formerly, anything made of parts fitted together according to a design *b)* body structure in general; build **2.** skeletal or basic, supporting structure; framework, as of a house **3.** the framework supporting the chassis of a motor vehicle **4.** the structural case or border into which a window, door, etc. is set **5.** a border, often ornamental, surrounding a picture, etc. **6.** [*pl.*] the framework for a pair of eyeglasses **7.** any of certain machines built in or on a framework **8.** the way that anything is constructed or put together; form **9.** setting or background circumstances **10.** mood; temper [a bad *frame* of mind] **11.** an established order or system **12.** [Colloq.] the act of framing (sense 6) **13.** [Colloq.] *Baseball* an inning **14.** *Bowling,* etc. any of the divisions of a game **15.** *Motion Pictures* each of the small exposures composing a strip of film **16.** *Pool same as* RACK¹ (*n.* 2) —*adj.* having a wooden framework, usually covered with boards [a *frame* house] —**fram′er** *n.*

**frame of reference 1.** *Math.* the fixed points, lines, or planes from which coordinates are measured **2.** the set of ideas, facts, or circumstances within which something exists

**frame-up** (-up′) *n.* [Colloq.] **1.** a falsifying of evidence, testimony, etc. to make an innocent person seem guilty **2.** a surreptitious, underhanded arrangement or scheme made beforehand

**frame·work** (-wurk′) *n.* **1.** a structure to hold together or to support something built or stretched over or around it [the *framework* of a house] **2.** a basic structure, arrangement, or system **3.** *same as* FRAME OF REFERENCE

**franc** (fraŋk) *n.* [Fr. < L. *Francorum rex,* king of the French, device on the coin in 1360] **1.** the monetary unit and a coin of France, Belgium, Switzerland, and Luxembourg **2.** the monetary unit of various other countries **3.** a unit of money in Morocco See MONETARY UNITS, table

**France** (frans, fräns) country in W Europe, on the Atlantic & the Mediterranean: 212,821 sq. mi.; pop. 50,620,000; cap. Paris

**France** (frans, fräns), **A·na·tole** (an′ə tōl′) (pseud. of *Jacques Anatole François Thibault*) 1844–1924; Fr. writer

**Fran·ces** (fran′sis) [< OFr. fem. of FRANCIS] a feminine name: dim. *Fran*

**fran·chise** (fran′chīz) *n.* [< OFr. < *franc,* free: see FRANK] **1.** *a)* any special right or privilege granted by a government, as to operate a public utility, etc. *b)* the jurisdiction over which this extends **2.** the right to vote; suffrage **3.** the right to market a product or provide a service in an area, as granted by a manufacturer or company —*vt.* **-chised, -chis·ing** to grant a franchise to

**Fran·cis** (fran′sis) [< OFr. < ML. *Franciscus* < LL. *Francus:* see FRANK] a masculine name

**Fran·cis·can** (fran sis′kən) *adj.* of Saint Francis of Assisi or the religious order founded by him in 1209 —*n.* any member of this order

**Francis of As·si·si** (ə sēs'ē), Saint (born *Giovanni Bernardone*) 1181?–1226; It. preacher: founder of the Franciscan Order

**fran·ci·um** (fran'sē əm) *n.* [ModL. < FRANCE] a radioactive, metallic chemical element of the alkali group: symbol, Fr; at. wt., 223(?); at. no., 87

**Franck** (fränk), **Cé·sar (Auguste)** (sā zàr') 1822–90; Fr. composer, born in Belgium

**Fran·co** (fraŋ'kō; *Sp.* frän'kð), **Fran·cis·co** (fran sis'kō; *Sp.* frän thēs'kð) 1892–1975; Sp. general & chief of state; dictator of Spain (1939–75)

**Fran·co-** [ML. < LL. *Francus,* a Frank] *a combining form meaning:* **1.** Frankish **2.** of France or the French **3.** France and; the French and *[Franco-German]*

**fran·gi·ble** (fran'jə b'l) *adj.* [< OFr. < ML. < L. *frangere,* to break] breakable; fragile —**fran'gi·bil'i·ty** *n.*

**fran·gi·pan·i** (fran'jə pan'ē, -pän'ē) *n., pl.* **-pan'i, -pan'is** [It. < Marquis *Frangipani* (16th-c. It. nobleman)] **1.** any of several tropical American shrubs and trees with large, fragrant flowers **2.** a perfume obtained from this flower **3.** a pastry made with ground almonds

**Frank** (fraŋk) [dim. of FRANCIS] a masculine name —*n.* [< OE. & OFr. < LL. *Francus:* see ff.] **1.** a member of the Germanic tribes that established the Frankish Empire, which, at its height (9th cent. A.D.), extended over what is now France, Germany, and Italy **2.** any western European: term used in the Near East

**frank** (fraŋk) *adj.* [< OFr. *franc,* free < ML. < LL. *Francus,* a Frank, hence free man] **1.** open and honest in expressing what one thinks or feels; candid **2.** free from disguise or guile; clearly evident —*vt.* **1.** to send (mail) free of postage, as by virtue of an official position **2.** to mark (mail) so that it can be sent free —*n.* **1.** the privilege of sending mail free **2.** a mark or signature on mail indicating this privilege **3.** any piece of mail sent free in this way —**frank'ly** *adv.* —**frank'ness** *n.*

**Frank.** Frankish

**Frank·en·stein** (fraŋ'kən stīn') **1.** the title character in a novel (1818) by Mary Shelley: he creates a monster that destroys him **2.** popularly, the monster —*n.* anything that becomes dangerous to its creator

**Frank·fort** (fraŋk'fərt) [after S. *Frank,* a pioneer killed there] capital of Ky.: pop. 26,000

**Frank·furt** (fraŋk'fərt; *G.* fräŋk'foort) city in C West Germany, on the Main River: pop. 662,000: also **Frankfurt am Main**

**frank·furt·er, frank·fort·er** (fraŋk'fər tər) *n.* [G., after FRANKFURT (AM MAIN)] a smoked sausage of beef or beef and pork, etc.; wiener: also [Colloq.] **frank**

**frank·in·cense** (fraŋ'kən sens') *n.* [< OFr.: see FRANK & INCENSE[1]] a gum resin from various Arabian and NE African trees, burned as incense

**Frank·ish** (fraŋ'kish) *adj.* of the Franks, their language, or culture —*n.* the West Germanic language of the Franks

**Frank·lin** (fraŋk'lin) [< Anglo-Fr. < ML. < LL. *Francus:* see FRANK] **1.** a masculine name **2. Benjamin,** 1706–90; Am. statesman, scientist, & writer

**frank·lin** (fraŋk'lin) *n.* [< Anglo-Fr. < ML. < *francus:* see FRANK] in England in the 14th and 15th cent., a landowner of free but not noble birth, ranking just below the gentry

**Franklin stove** a cast-iron heating stove, invented by Benjamin Franklin

**fran·tic** (fran'tik) *adj.* [see PHRENETIC] **1.** wild with anger, pain, worry, etc.; frenzied **2.** marked by frenzy *[frantic efforts]* —**fran'ti·cal·ly** or [Rare] **fran'tic·ly** *adv.*

**frap·pé** (fra pā') *adj.* [Fr., pp. of *frapper,* to strike] partly frozen; iced; cooled —*n.* **1.** a dessert made of partly frozen beverages, fruit juices, etc. **2.** a drink made of some beverage poured over shaved ice **3.** [Eastern] a milkshake Also, esp. for *n.* 3, **frappe** (frap)

**frat** (frat) *n.* [Colloq.] a fraternity, as at a college

FRANKLIN STOVE

**fra·ter·nal** (frə tʉr'n'l) *adj.* [< ML. < L. *fraternus < frater,* a brother] **1.** of or characteristic of brothers; brotherly **2.** of or like a fraternal order or a fraternity **3.** designating twins, of the same or different sex, developed from separately fertilized ova —**fra·ter'nal·ism** *n.* —**fra·ter'nal·ly** *adv.*

**fraternal order** (or **society, association**) a society, often secret, organized for fellowship or for work toward a common goal

**fra·ter·ni·ty** (frə tʉr'nə tē) *n., pl.* **-ties 1.** fraternal relationship or spirit; brotherliness **2.** a group of men joined together by common interests, for fellowship, etc.; specif., a Greek-letter college organization **3.** a group of people with the same beliefs, work, etc. *[the medical fraternity]*

**frat·er·nize** (frat'ər nīz') *vi.* **-nized', -niz'ing** to associate in a brotherly manner; be on friendly terms —**frat'er·ni·za'tion** *n.*

**frat·ri·cide** (frat'rə sīd') *n.* [Fr. < LL. *fratricidium* < L. < *frater,* brother + *caedere,* to kill] **1.** *a)* the act of killing one's own brother or sister *b)* the act of killing relatives or fellow-countrymen, as in a civil war **2.** a person who kills his brother or sister —**frat'ri·ci'dal** (-sīd'']) *adj.*

‡**Frau** (frou) *n., pl.* **Frau'en** (-ən) [G.] a married woman; wife: used in Germany as a title corresponding to *Mrs.*

**fraud** (frôd) *n.* [< OFr. < L. *fraus* (gen. *fraudis*)] **1.** deceit; trickery; cheating **2.** an intentional deception or dishonesty; trick **3.** a person who is not what he pretends to be

**fraud·u·lent** (frô'jə lənt) *adj.* **1.** acting with fraud; deceitful **2.** based on or characterized by fraud **3.** done or obtained by fraud —**fraud'u·lence, fraud'u·len·cy** *n.* —**fraud'u·lent·ly** *adv.*

**fraught** (frôt) *adj.* [< MDu. < *vracht,* a load] filled, charged, or loaded (*with*) *[a life fraught with hardship]*

‡**Fräu·lein** (froi'līn; *E.* froi'-, frou'-) *n., pl.* **-lein,** *E.* **-leins** [G.] an unmarried woman: used in Germany as a title corresponding to *Miss*

**fray**[1] (frā) *n.* [< AFFRAY] a noisy quarrel or fight; brawl

**fray**[2] (frā) *vt., vi.* [< OFr. < L. *fricare,* to rub] **1.** to make or become worn, ragged, etc. by rubbing **2.** to make or become weakened or strained

**fraz·zle** (fraz''l) *vt., vi.* **-zled, -zling** [Brit. dial. & U.S., prob. < dial. *fazle*] [Colloq.] **1.** to wear to tatters; fray **2.** to make or become physically or emotionally exhausted —*n.* [Colloq.] the state of being frazzled

**freak** (frēk) *n.* [< ? OE. *frician,* to dance] **1.** *a)* a sudden fancy; odd notion; whim *b)* an unusual happening **2.** any abnormal animal, person, or plant; monstrosity **3.** [Slang] *a)* a user of a specified narcotic, hallucinogen, etc. *[an acid freak] b)* a devotee or buff *[a rock freak] c) same as* HIPPIE —*adj.* oddly different from what is normal; queer —**freak (out)** [Slang] **1.** to experience in an extreme way the mental reactions, hallucinations, etc. induced by a psychedelic drug **2.** to make or become very excited, distressed, disorganized, etc. —**freak'ish, freak'y** *adj.* —**freak'ish·ly** *adv.* —**freak'ish·ness** *n.*

**freck·le** (frek''l) *n.* [< Scand.] a small, brownish spot on the skin, esp. as a result of exposure to the sun —*vt.* **-led, -ling** to cause freckles to appear on —*vi.* to become spotted with freckles —**freck'led, freck'ly** *adj.*

**Fred·er·i·ca** (fred'ə rē'kə, fred rē'kə) [fem. of ff.] a feminine name

**Fred·er·ick** (fred'rik, -ər ik) [< Fr. < G. < OHG. *Friduruh,* "peaceful ruler"] a masculine name: dim. *Fred;* var. *Frederic, Fredrick, Fredric*

**Frederick the Great** 1712–86; king of Prussia (1740–86): also **Frederick II**

**Fred·er·ic·ton** (fred'ə rik tən) capital of New Brunswick, Canada: pop. 45,000

**free** (frē) *adj.* **fre'er, fre'est** [OE. *freo*] **1.** *a)* not under the control or power of another; able to act or think without arbitrary restriction; having liberty; independent *b)* characterized by or resulting from liberty **2.** having, or existing under, a government that does not impose arbitrary restrictions on the right to speak, assemble, petition, vote, etc. **3.** able to move in any direction; not held; loose **4.** not held or confined by a court, the police, etc. **5.** not burdened by obligations, debts, discomforts, etc.; unhindered *[free from pain]* **6.** at liberty; allowed *[free to leave]* **7.** not confined to the usual rules or conventions *[free verse]* **8.** not literal; not exact *[a free translation]* **9.** not busy or in use **10.** not constrained or stilted *[a free gait]* **11.** *a)* generous; lavish *[a free spender] b)* profuse; copious **12.** frank; straightforward **13.** too frank or familiar in speech, action, etc.; forward **14.** with no charge or cost *[a free ticket]* **15.** exempt from certain impositions, as taxes or duties **16.** clear of obstructions; open *[a free road ahead]* **17.** open to all *[a free market]* **18.** not fastened *[the free end of a rope]* **19.** not united; not combined *[free oxygen]* —*adv.* **1.** without cost or payment **2.** in a free manner —*vt.* **freed, free'ing** to make free; specif., *a)* to release from bondage or arbitrary power, obligation, etc. *b)* to clear of obstruction, etc.; disengage —**free and easy** informal; unceremonious —**free from** (or **of**) lacking; without —**make free with 1.** to use freely **2.** to take liberties with —**set free** to release; liberate —**with a free hand** with generosity; lavishly —**free'ly** *adv.* —**free'ness** *n.*

**free agent** an athlete eligible to play a professional sport who is free to sign a contract with any team with which he can work out an agreement

**free·bie** (frē'bē) *n., pl.* **-bies** [Slang] something given or gotten free of charge, as a complimentary theater ticket

**free·board** (-bôrd') *n.* the height of a ship's side from the main deck or gunwale to the waterline

**free·boot·er** (-boot'ər) *n.* [< Du. < *vrij,* free + *buit,* plunder] a pirate; buccaneer —**free'boot'** *vi.*

**free·born** (-bôrn′) *adj.* **1.** born free, not in slavery **2.** of or fit for a person so born

**free city** a city that is an autonomous state

**freed·man** (frēd′mən) *n., pl.* **-men** a man legally freed from slavery or bondage

**free·dom** (frē′dəm) *n.* **1.** the state or quality of being free; esp., *a)* exemption or liberation from the control of some other person or some arbitrary power; liberty; independence *b)* exemption from arbitrary restrictions on a specified civil right; civil or political liberty [*freedom* of speech] *c)* exemption or immunity from a specified obligation, discomfort, etc. [*freedom* from want] *d)* a being able to act, move, use, etc. without hindrance *e)* ease of movement or performance; facility *f)* a being free from the usual rules, conventions, etc. *g)* frankness or easiness of manner; sometimes, an excessive frankness or familiarity **2.** a right or privilege

**free enterprise** the economic doctrine of permitting private industry to operate under freely competitive conditions with a minimum of governmental control

**free fall** the unchecked fall of a body through the air; specif., the part of a parachutist's jump before the parachute is opened

**free flight** the flight of a rocket after the fuel supply has been used up or shut off **—free′-flight′** *adj.*

**free-for-all** (frē′fər ôl′) *n.* a disorganized, general fight; brawl *—adj.* open to anyone

**free-form** (-fôrm′) *adj.* **1.** having an irregular, usually curvilinear form or outline **2.** unconventional, unrestrained, etc. in style, form, etc.

**free·hand** (-hand′) *adj.* drawn by hand without the use of instruments, measurements, etc.

**free·hand·ed** (-han′did) *adj.* generous; liberal

**free·hold** (-hōld′) *n.* **1.** an estate in land held for life or with the right to pass it on through inheritance **2.** the holding of an estate in this way *—adj.* of or held by freehold **—free′hold′er** *n.*

**free-lance** (-lans′) *adj.* of or acting as a free lance *—vi.* **-lanced′, -lanc′ing** to work as a free lance

**free lance 1.** a medieval soldier who sold his services to any state or army **2.** one who acts according to his principles and is not influenced by any group **3.** a writer, artist, etc. not under contract, who sells his services to individual buyers: also **free′-lanc′er** *n.*

**free-liv·ing** (-liv′iŋ) *adj.* **1.** freely indulging one's appetites, desires, etc. **2.** *Biol.* not parasitic or symbiotic **—free liver**

**free·load·er** (-lōd′ər) *n.* [Colloq.] a person who habitually imposes on others for free food, lodging, etc.

**free·man** (-mən) *n., pl.* **-men 1.** a person not in slavery or bondage **2.** a person who has full civil and political rights; citizen

**free market** any market where trade can be carried on without restrictions as to price, etc.

**Free·ma·son** (frē′mās″n) *n.* a member of an international secret society having as its principles brotherliness, charity, and mutual aid; Mason

**Free·ma·son·ry** (-rē) *n.* **1.** the principles, rituals, etc. of Freemasons **2.** the Freemasons **3.** [f-] a natural sympathy and understanding among persons with similar experiences

**free on board** delivered (by the seller) aboard the train, ship, etc. at the point of shipment, without charge

**free·si·a** (frē′zhē ə, -zhə, -zē ə) *n.* [ModL., after F. *Freese,* 19th-c. Ger. physician] a South African bulbous plant with fragrant, funnel-shaped flowers

**free silver** the free coinage of silver, esp. at a fixed ratio to the gold coined in the same period

**Free-Soil** (frē′soil′) *adj.* [*also* f- s-] opposed to the extension of slavery into U.S. Territories before the Civil War **—Free′-Soil′er** *n.*

**free-spo·ken** (-spō′k'n) *adj.* frank; outspoken

**free-stand·ing** (-stan′diŋ) *adj.* resting on its own support, without attachment

**free·stone** (-stōn′) *n.* **1.** a stone, esp. sandstone or limestone, that can be cut easily without splitting **2.** *a)* a peach, plum, etc. in which the pit does not cling to the pulp of the ripened fruit *b)* such a pit *—adj.* having such a pit

**free·think·er** (-thiŋ′kər) *n.* a person who forms his opinions about religion independently of tradition, authority, or established belief **—free′think′ing** *n., adj.* **—free thought**

**free trade** trade conducted without quotas on imports or exports, protective tariffs, etc.

**free verse** poetry not following regular metrical, rhyming, or stanzaic forms

**free·way** (-wā′) *n.* **1.** an expressway with interchanges for fully controlled access **2.** a highway without toll charges

**free·will** (-wil′) *adj.* voluntary; spontaneous

**free will 1.** freedom of the will to choose a course of action without external coercion; freedom of choice **2.** the doctrine that people have such freedom

**freeze** (frēz) *vi.* **froze, fro′zen, freez′ing** [OE. *freosan*] **1.** to be formed into ice; be hardened by cold **2.** to become covered or clogged with ice **3.** to be or become very cold **4.** to become attached by freezing **5.** to die or be damaged by exposure to cold **6.** to become motionless or fixed **7.** to be made momentarily unable to move, act, or speak through fright, etc. **8.** to become formal or unfriendly **9.** *Mech.* to stick or become tight as a result of expansion of parts from overheating or inadequate lubrication *—vt.* **1.** to cause to form into ice; harden or solidify by cold **2.** to cover or clog with ice **3.** to make very cold **4.** to remove sensation from, as with a local anesthetic **5.** to preserve (food) by rapid refrigeration **6.** to make fixed or attached by freezing **7.** to kill or damage by exposure to cold **8.** to make or keep motionless or stiff **9.** to discourage as by cool behavior **10.** to make formal or unfriendly **11.** *a)* to fix (prices, wages, an employee, etc.) at a given level or place by authoritative regulation *b)* to make (funds, assets, etc.) unavailable to the owners *—n.* **1.** a freezing or being frozen **2.** a period of cold, freezing weather **—freeze (on) to** [Colloq.] to hold fast to **—freeze out 1.** to die out through freezing, as plants **2.** [Colloq.] to force out by a cold manner, competition, etc. **—freeze over** to become covered with ice **—freez′a·ble** *adj.*

**freeze-dry** (frēz′drī′) *vt.* **-dried′, -dry′ing** to subject (food, vaccines, etc.) to quick-freezing followed by drying under high vacuum at a low temperature **—freeze′-dry′er** *n.*

**freez·er** (-ər) *n.* **1.** a refrigerator, compartment, or room for freezing and storing frozen foods **2.** a hand-cranked or electrically operated device for making ice cream

**freez·ing point** the temperature at which a liquid freezes: for water, it is 32°F or 0°C

**freight** (frāt) *n.* [< MDu. *vracht,* a load] **1.** a method or service for transporting goods by water, land, or air: freight is usually cheaper but slower than express **2.** the cost for such transportation **3.** the goods transported; cargo **4.** *same as* FREIGHT TRAIN **5.** any load or burden *—vt.* **1.** to load with freight **2.** to load; burden **3.** to transport as by freight

**freight·age** (-ij) *n.* **1.** the charge for transporting goods **2.** freight; cargo **3.** the transportation of goods

**freight car** a railroad car for transporting freight

**freight·er** (-ər) *n.* a ship or aircraft for carrying freight

**freight train** a railroad train of freight cars

**Fre·mont** (frē′mänt) [after J. C. *Frémont* (1813–90), U.S. politician, general, & explorer] city in W Calif.: suburb of Oakland: pop. 132,000

**French** (french) *adj.* of France, its people, their language, or culture *—n.* the Romance language of the French **—the French** the people of France **—French′man** (-mən) *n., pl.* **-men —French′wom′an** *n., pl.* **-wom′en**

**French Canadian** a Canadian of French ancestry

**French chalk** a very soft chalk used for marking lines on cloth or removing grease spots

**French Community** political union comprising France, its overseas departments & territories, & six fully independent countries that are former French colonies

**French cuff** a double cuff turned back on itself and fastened with a link

**French doors** two adjoining doors with glass panes from top to bottom, hinged at opposite sides of a doorway and opening in the middle

**French dressing** a salad dressing made of vinegar, oil, and various seasonings

**French fry** [*often* f- f-] to fry in very hot, deep fat until crisp: French fried potatoes (colloquially, **French fries** ) are first cut lengthwise into strips

**French Guiana** French possession in NE S. America

**French horn** a brass-wind instrument with a long, coiled tube ending in a wide, flaring bell

**French·i·fy** (-ə fī′) *vt., vi.* **-fied′, -fy′ing** to make or become French or like the French in customs, ideas, manners, etc.

**French leave** an unauthorized or unceremonious departure; act of leaving secretly or in haste

**French Revolution** the revolution of the people against the monarchy in France: it began in 1789, resulted in the establishment of a republic, and ended in 1799 with the Consulate

**French toast** sliced bread dipped in a batter of egg and milk and then fried

FRENCH HORN

**French windows** a pair of casement windows designed like French doors and usually extending to the floor

**fre·net·ic** (frə net′ik) *adj.* [see PHRENETIC] frantic; frenzied: also **fre·net′i·cal** —**fre·net′i·cal·ly** *adv.*

**fre·num** (frē′nəm) *n., pl.* **-nums, -na** (-nə) [L., lit., a bridle] a fold of skin or mucous membrane that checks the movements of an organ, as the fold under the tongue

**fren·zy** (fren′zē) *n., pl.* **-zies** [< OFr. < ML. < L. *phrenesis,* ult. < Gr. *phrenitis,* madness < *phrēn,* mind] wild outburst of feeling or action; brief delirium that is almost insanity —*vt.* **-zied, -zy·ing** to make frantic; drive mad —**fren′zied** *adj.* —**fren′zied·ly** *adv.*

**freq.** 1. frequent 2. frequentative

**fre·quen·cy** (frē′kwən sē) *n., pl.* **-cies** 1. frequent occurrence 2. the number of times any event, value, characteristic, etc. is repeated in a given period or group 3. *Physics* the number of periodic oscillations, vibrations, or waves per unit of time: now usually expressed in hertz

**frequency modulation** 1. the variation of the instantaneous frequency of a carrier wave in accordance with the signal to be transmitted 2. the system of radio broadcasting that uses this

**fre·quent** (frē′kwənt; *for v., usually* frē kwent′) *adj.* [< OFr. < L. *frequens,* crowded] 1. occurring often; happening repeatedly at brief intervals 2. constant; habitual —*vt.* to go to constantly; be at or in habitually —**fre′quen·ta′tion** *n.* —**fre·quent′er** *n.* —**fre′quent·ly** *adv.*

**fre·quen·ta·tive** (frē kwen′tə tiv, frē′kwən-) *adj. Gram.* expressing frequent and repeated action —*n. Gram.* a frequentative verb: *sparkle* is a frequentative of *spark*

**fres·co** (fres′kō) *n., pl.* **-coes, -cos** [It., fresh < OHG. *frisc*] 1. the art of painting with water colors on wet plaster 2. a painting or design so made —*vt.* to paint in fresco

**fresh¹** (fresh) *adj.* [< OE. *fersc,* altered after OFr. *fres, fresche*] 1. recently made, obtained, or grown [*fresh* coffee] 2. not salted, preserved, etc. 3. not spoiled or stale 4. not tired; vigorous; lively 5. not worn, soiled, etc.; bright; clean 6. youthful or healthy in appearance 7. not known before; new; recent 8. additional; further [a *fresh* start] 9. inexperienced; unaccustomed 10. having just arrived 11. original and stimulating [*fresh* ideas] 12. cool and refreshing [a *fresh* spring day] 13. brisk; strong: said of the wind 14. not salt: said of water 15. giving milk because having borne a calf: said of a cow —*adv.* in a fresh manner —**fresh out of** [Slang] having just sold or used up —**fresh′ly** *adv.* —**fresh′ness** *n.*

**fresh²** (fresh) *adj.* [< G. *frech,* bold] [Slang] saucy; impudent —**fresh′ly** *adv.* —**fresh′ness** *n.*

**fresh·en** (fresh′ən) *vt., vi.* to make or become fresh —**freshen up** to bathe oneself, change into fresh clothes, etc. —**fresh′en·er** *n.*

**fresh·et** (-it) *n.* 1. a rush of fresh water flowing into the sea 2. a flooding of a stream because of melting snow or heavy rain

**fresh·man** (-mən) *n., pl.* **-men** 1. a beginner; novice 2. a student in the ninth grade in high school, or one in the first year of college —*adj.* of or for first-year students

**fresh·wa·ter** (-wôt′ər, -wät′ər) *adj.* 1. of or living in water that is not salty 2. *a*) sailing only on inland waters, not on the sea *b*) unskilled 3. *a*) inland *b*) somewhat provincial, obscure, etc.

**Fres·no** (frez′nō) [< Sp. *fresno,* ash tree] city in C Calif.: pop. 218,000 (met. area 507,000)

**fret¹** (fret) *vt.* **fret′ted, fret′ting** [OE. *fretan,* to eat up] 1. to wear away by gnawing, rubbing, corroding, etc. 2. to make by wearing away 3. to make rough; disturb 4. to irritate; vex; worry —*vi.* 1. to gnaw (*into, on,* or *upon*) 2. to become corroded, worn, etc. 3. to become rough or disturbed 4. to be irritated, vexed, etc.; worry —*n.* irritation; worry —**fret′ter** *n.*

**fret²** (fret) *n.* [prob. merging of OFr. *frete,* interlaced work & OE. *frætwa,* ornament] an ornamental pattern of straight bars joining one another at right angles to form a design —*vt.* **fret′ted, fret′ting** to ornament with a fret

**fret³** (fret) *n.* [OFr. *frette,* a band] any of the lateral ridges across the fingerboard of a banjo, guitar, etc. to regulate the fingering —*vt.* **fret′ted, fret′ting** to furnish with frets

**fret·ful** (fret′fəl) *adj.* tending to fret; peevish —**fret′ful·ly** *adv.* —**fret′ful·ness** *n.*

**fret·work** (fret′wurk′) *n.* decorative openwork

**Freud** (froid), **Sigmund** 1856–1939; Austrian physician & neurologist: founder of psychoanalysis

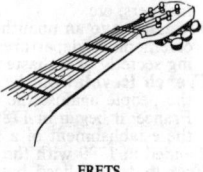

FRETS

**Freud·i·an** (froi′dē ən) *adj.* of or according to Freud or his theories —*n.* a follower of Freud or his theories of psychoanalysis —**Freud′i·an·ism** *n.*

**Fri.** Friday

**fri·a·ble** (frī′ə b'l) *adj.* [Fr. < L. *friabilis* < *friare,* to rub] easily crumbled into powder —**fri′a·bil′i·ty, fri′a·ble·ness** *n.*

**fri·ar** (frī′ər) *n.* [< OFr. *frere* < L. *frater,* brother] *R.C.Ch.* a member of any of several mendicant orders; esp., an Augustinian, Carmelite, Dominican, or Franciscan —**fri′ar·ly** *adj.*

**fri·ar·y** (-ē) *n., pl.* **-ar·ies** 1. a monastery where friars live 2. a brotherhood of friars

**fric·as·see** (frik′ə sē′, frik′ə sē′) *n.* [< Fr. < *fricasser,* to cut up and fry] meat cut into pieces, stewed or fried, and served in its own gravy —*vt.* **-seed′, -see′ing** to prepare as a fricassee

**fric·a·tive** (frik′ə tiv) *adj.* [< L. pp. of *fricare* (FRICTION) + -IVE] pronounced by forcing the breath through a narrow slit formed at some point in the mouth, as *f, v, z* —*n.* a fricative consonant

**fric·tion** (frik′shən) *n.* [Fr. < L. < pp. of *fricare,* to rub] 1. a rubbing, esp. of one object against another 2. conflict because of differences of opinion, temperament, etc. 3. the resistance to motion of moving surfaces that touch —**fric′tion·al** *adj.* —**fric′tion·al·ly** *adv.*

**friction tape** a moisture-resistant adhesive tape, esp. for insulating exposed electric wires

**Fri·day** (frī′dē, -dā) *n.* [OE. *frigedæg,* lit., day of the goddess Frig: see FRIGG] 1. the sixth day of the week 2. [after the devoted servant of ROBINSON CRUSOE] a faithful follower or efficient helper: usually **man** (or **girl**) **Friday**

**Fri·days** (-dēz, -dāz) *adv.* on or during every Friday

**fried** (frīd) *pt. & pp. of* FRY¹

**Frie·da** (frē′də) [G. < OHG. *fridu,* peace] a feminine name

**fried·cake** (frīd′kāk′) *n.* a small cake fried in deep fat; doughnut or cruller

**friend** (frend) *n.* [OE. *freond*] 1. a person whom one knows well and is fond of; close acquaintance 2. a person on the same side in a struggle; ally 3. a supporter or sympathizer [a *friend* of labor] 4. something thought of as like a friend 5. [F-] a member of the Society of Friends; Quaker —**make** (or **be**) **friends with** to become (or be) a friend of —**friend′less** *adj.* —**friend′less·ness** *n.*

**friend·ly** (-lē) *adj.* **-li·er, -li·est** 1. like, characteristic of, or suitable for a friend or friendship; kindly 2. not hostile; amicable 3. supporting; favorable [a *friendly* wind] 4. ready to be a friend —*adv.* in a friendly manner —**friend′li·ly** *adv.* —**friend′li·ness** *n.*

**friend·ship** (-ship′) *n.* 1. the state of being friends 2. friendly feeling or attitude

**fri·er** (frī′ər) *n. same as* FRYER

**frieze¹** (frēz) *n.* [< Fr. < ML. *frisium* < ? Frank.] 1. a decoration forming an ornamental band around a room, mantel, etc. 2. a horizontal band, often decorated with sculpture, between the architrave and cornice of a building

**frieze²** (frēz) *n.* [< OFr. < MDu.] a heavy wool cloth with a shaggy, uncut nap on one side

**frig·ate** (frig′it) *n.* [< Fr. < It. *fregata*] 1. a fast, medium-sized sailing warship of the 18th and early 19th cent. 2. a U.S. warship larger than a destroyer and smaller than a light cruiser

**frigate bird** a large, long-winged, tropical sea bird that robs other birds of their prey

**Frigg** (frig) [ON.] *Norse Myth.* the wife of Odin

**fright** (frīt) *n.* [OE. *fyrhto, fryhto*] 1. sudden fear or terror; alarm 2. an ugly, ridiculous, or startling person or thing —*vt.* [Rare] to frighten

**fright·en** (-'n) *vt.* 1. to cause to feel fright; make suddenly afraid; scare 2. to force (*away, out,* or *off*) or bring (*into* a specified condition) by frightening —*vi.* to become suddenly afraid —**fright′en·ing·ly** *adv.*

**fright·ful** (-fəl) *adj.* 1. causing fright; alarming 2. shocking; terrible 3. [Colloq.] *a*) unpleasant; annoying *b*) great [in a *frightful* hurry] —**fright′ful·ly** *adv.* —**fright′ful·ness** *n.*

**frig·id** (frij′id) *adj.* [< L. < *frigus,* coldness] 1. extremely cold 2. without warmth of feeling or manner; stiff and formal 3. habitually unaroused sexually: said of a woman —**fri·gid·i·ty** (frə jid′ə tē), **frig′id·ness** *n.* —**frig′id·ly** *adv.*

**Frigid Zone** either of two zones of the earth (**North Frigid Zone** & **South Frigid Zone**) between the polar circles and the poles

**fri·jol** (frē′hōl) *n., pl.* **fri·jo′les** (fri′hōlz, frē hō′lēz) [Sp. *frijol, frejol*] a bean, esp. the kidney bean, used for food in Mexico and the SW U.S.: also **fri·jo·le** (frē hō′lē)

**frill** (fril) *n.* [< ?] 1. a fringe of hair or feathers around the neck of a bird or animal 2. any unnecessary ornament; thing added only for show 3. a ruffle —*vt.* to decorate with a frill —**frill′y** *adj.* **frill′i·er, frill′i·est**

**fringe** (frinj) *n.* [< OFr. < L. *frimbria*] 1. a border or trimming of cords or threads, hanging loose or in bunches 2. anything like this [a *fringe* of whiskers] 3. an outer edge; border; margin 4. a part considered to be peripheral, extreme, or minor [the lunatic *fringe* of a political party] 5. *same as* FRINGE BENEFIT —*vt.* **fringed, fring′ing** 1.

decorate with or as with fringe **2.** to be a fringe for; line [trees *fringed* the lawn] *—adj.* **1.** at the outer edge [a *fringe* area] **2.** additional [*fringe* benefits] **3.** less important **—fring′y** *adj.* **fring′i·er, fring′i·est**

**fringe benefit** an employee's benefit other than wages or salary, such as a pension or insurance

**frip·per·y** (frip′ər ē) *n., pl.* **-per·ies** [< Fr. < OFr. < *frepe*, a rag] **1.** cheap, gaudy clothes **2.** showy display in dress, manners, speech, etc.

**Fris·bee** (friz′bē) [< "Mother *Frisbie's*" cookie jar lids] *a trademark for* a plastic disk tossed back and forth in a game *—n.* [f-] such a disk

**Fris·co** (fris′kō) [Colloq.] *nickname for* SAN FRANCISCO: not a local usage

**fri·sé** (fri zā′) *n.* [Fr. < *friser*, to curl] a type of upholstery fabric with a thick pile of loops, some of which are sometimes cut to form a design

**Fri·sian** (frizh′ən, frē′zhən) *adj.* of the Frisian Islands, N Netherlands, their people, or their language *—n.* **1.** a native or inhabitant of the Frisian Islands or N Netherlands **2.** the West Germanic language of the Frisians

**Frisian Islands** island chain in the North Sea, extending along the coast of the N Netherlands, N West Germany, & SW Denmark

**frisk** (frisk) *n.* [OFr. *frisque* < OHG. *frisc*] **1.** a frolic; gambol **2.** [Slang] the act of frisking a person *—vt.* [Slang] to search (a person) for concealed weapons, etc. by passing the hands quickly over his clothing *—vi.* to frolic; gambol

**frisk·y** (-ē) *adj.* **frisk′i·er, frisk′i·est** lively; frolicsome **—frisk′i·ly** *adv.* **—frisk′i·ness** *n.*

**frith** (frith) *n. var. of* FIRTH

**frit·il·lar·y** (frit′'l er′ē) *n., pl.* **-lar′ies** [ModL. < L. *fritillus*, dice box: from markings on the petals or wings] **1.** a plant of the lily family, with nodding, bell-shaped flowers **2.** any of a group of butterflies with spotted wings

**frit·ter¹** (frit′ər) *n.* [< ? OFr. < L. *fractura:* see FRACTURE] [Rare] a small piece *—vt.* **1.** [Rare] to break into small pieces **2.** to waste (money, time, etc.) bit by bit on petty things *—frit′ter·er n.*

**frit·ter²** (frit′ər) *n.* [< OFr., ult. < L. pp. of *frigere*, to fry] a small cake of fried batter, usually containing corn, fruit, etc.

**fri·vol·i·ty** (fri väl′ə tē) *n.* **1.** a frivolous quality **2.** *pl.* **-ties** a frivolous act or thing

**friv·o·lous** (friv′ə ləs) *adj.* [L. *frivolus*] **1.** trifling; trivial **2.** not properly serious or sensible; silly and light-minded **—friv′o·lous·ly** *adv.* **—friv′o·lous·ness** *n.*

**frizz, friz** (friz) *vt., vi.* **frizzed, friz′zing** [Fr. *friser*] to form into small, tight curls *—n.* hair, etc. that is frizzed

**friz·zle¹** (friz′'l) *vt., vi.* **-zled, -zling** [echoic alteration of FRY¹] **1.** to make or cause to make a sputtering, hissing noise, as in frying; sizzle **2.** to make or become crisp by broiling or frying

**friz·zle²** (friz′'l) *vt., vi.* **-zled, -zling** [freq. of FRIZZ] to frizz; crimp *—n.* a small, tight curl

**friz·zly** (-lē) *adj.* **-zli·er, -zli·est** full of or covered with small, tight curls: also **friz′zy, -zi·er, -zi·est**

**fro** (frō) *adv.* [< ON. *frā*] backward; back: now only in *to and fro:* see under TO *—prep.* [Scot.] from

**frock** (fräk) *n.* [OFr. *froc* (or ML. *froccus*) < OFrank.] **1.** a robe worn by friars, monks, etc. **2.** any of various other garments; specif., *a)* a smock *b)* a dress *c) same as* FROCK COAT *—vt.* **1.** to clothe in a frock **2.** to ordain as a priest

**frock coat** a man's double-breasted dress coat with a full skirt reaching to the knees, worn chiefly in the 19th cent.

**frog** (frôg, fräg) *n.* [OE. *frogga*] **1.** a tailless, leaping, four-legged amphibian with a smooth skin and webbed feet: most species, when grown, can live either in water or on land **2.** a horny pad in the sole of a horse's foot **3.** a corded or braided loop used as a fastener or decoration on clothing **4.** a device on railroad tracks for keeping cars on the proper rails at intersections or switches **5.** a device placed in a bowl, vase, etc. to hold the stems of flowers **—frog in the throat** a hoarseness due to throat irritation

**frog·gy** (-ē) *adj.* **-gi·er, -gi·est** **1.** of or like a frog **2.** full of frogs

**frog·man** (-man′) *n., pl.* **-men** (-mən) a person trained and equipped, as with scuba gear, for underwater demolition, exploration, etc.

**frog spit** (or **spittle**) **1.** *same as* CUCKOO SPIT **2.** mats of filamentous algae floating on ponds

METAMORPHOSIS OF FROG

**Frois·sart** (frwà sàr′; E. froi′särt), **Jean** (zhän) 1337?–1410?; Fr. chronicler & poet

**frol·ic** (fräl′ik) *adj.* [< MDu. *vrō,* merry] [Archaic] full of fun and pranks; merry *—n.* **1.** a playful trick; prank **2.** a lively party or game **3.** merriment; fun *—vi.* **-icked, -ick·ing 1.** to make merry; have fun **2.** to play or romp about in a happy, carefree way **—frol′ick·er** *n.*

**frol·ic·some** (-səm) *adj.* full of gaiety or high spirits; playful; merry: also **frol′ick·y**

**from** (frum, främ; *unstressed* frəm) *prep.* [OE. *from, fram*] **1.** beginning at [to walk *from* the door] **2.** starting with [*from* noon to midnight] **3.** out of [he took a comb *from* his pocket] **4.** with (a person or thing) as the maker, speaker, source, etc. [facts learned *from* reading] **5.** at a place not near to [keep away *from* me] **6.** out of the whole of or alliance with [take two *from* four] **7.** out of the possibility or use of [kept *from* going] **8.** out of the possession or control of [released *from* jail] **9.** as not being like [to tell one *from* another] **10.** by reason of; because of [to tremble *from* fear]

**frond** (fränd) *n.* [L. *frons* (gen. *frondis*), leafy branch] **1.** a leaf; specif., *a)* the leaf of a fern *b)* the leaf of a palm **2.** the leaflike part, or shoot, of a lichen, seaweed, etc. **—frond′ed** *adj.*

**front** (frunt) *n.* [< OFr. < L. *frons* (gen. *frontis*), forehead] **1.** outward, often assumed, attitude, behavior, or appearance [to put on a bold *front*] **2.** the part of something that faces forward; most important side **3.** the first part; beginning **4.** the place or position directly before a person or thing **5.** a forward or leading position or situation **6.** the first available bellhop, as in a hotel **7.** the land bordering a lake, ocean, street, etc. **8.** the advanced area of contact between opposing sides in warfare; combat zone **9.** a specified area of activity [the home *front*] **10.** a broad movement in which different groups are united for the achievement of common political or social aims **11.** a person who serves as a public representative of a business, group, etc., as because of his prestige **12.** a person or group used to cover the activity or objectives of another really in control **13.** a stiff shirt bosom, worn with formal clothes **14.** a face of a building; esp., the face with the principal entrance **15.** *Meteorol.* the boundary between two masses of air that are different, as in density *—adj.* **1.** at, to, in, on, or of the front **2.** *Phonet.* articulated toward the front of the mouth, as *i* in *bid* or *e* in *met* *—vt.* **1.** to face; be opposite to **2.** to be before in place **3.** to meet; confront **4.** to defy; oppose **5.** to supply or be a front to *—vi.* **1.** to face in a certain direction **2.** to be a front (senses 11 & 12) (with *for*) **—in front of** before; ahead of

**front·age** (-ij) *n.* **1.** the front part of a building **2.** the direction toward which this faces **3.** the land between the front edge of a building and the street **4.** *a)* the front boundary line of a lot (facing the street) *b)* the length of this line **5.** land bordering a street, river, lake, etc.

**fron·tal** (-'l) *adj.* **1.** of, in, on, at, or against the front **2.** of or for the forehead *—n.* the bone forming the forehead: in full, **frontal bone** **—fron′tal·ly** *adv.*

**fron·tier** (frun tir′) *n.* [< OFr. < *front:* see FRONT] **1.** the border between two countries **2.** that part of a settled country which lies next to an unexplored region **3.** any new or incompletely investigated field or area of learning, etc. [the *frontiers* of medicine] *—adj.* of, on, or near a frontier

**fron·tiers·man** (-tirz′mən) *n., pl.* **-men** a man who lives on the frontier

**fron·tis·piece** (frun′tis pēs′) *n.* [OFr. < LL. *frontispicium,* front view < L. *frons,* FRONT + *specere,* to look] **1.** an illustration facing the first page or title page of a book or division of a book **2.** *Archit. a)* the main façade *b)* a pediment over a door, window, etc.

**front·let** (frunt′lit) *n.* [< OFr., ult. < L. *frons,* FRONT] a phylactery worn on the forehead

**front office** the management or administration, as of a company

**front-page** (frunt′pāj′) *adj.* fit to be printed on the front page of a newspaper; important

**front-run·ner** (-run′ər) *n.* **1.** one who is leading in a race or competition **2.** one that runs best when in the lead

**frost** (frôst, fräst) *n.* [OE. < *freosan,* to freeze] **1.** a freezing or being frozen **2.** a temperature low enough to cause freezing **3.** frozen dew or vapor; hoarfrost **4.** coolness of action, feeling, manner, etc. *—vt.* **1.** to cover with frost **2.** to damage or kill by freezing **3.** to cover with frosting **4.** to give a frostlike surface to (glass)

**Frost** (frôst, fräst), **Robert (Lee)** 1874–1963; U.S. poet

**frost·bite** (-bīt′) *vt.* **-bit′, -bit′ten, -bit′ing** to injure the tissues of (a part of the body) by exposure to intense cold *—n.* tissue damage caused by such exposure

**frost·ing** (-iŋ) *n.* **1.** a mixture of sugar, butter, eggs, etc. for covering a cake; icing **2.** a dull, frostlike finish on glass, metal, etc.

**frost·y** (-ē) *adj.* **frost′i·er, frost′i·est 1.** cold enough to produce frost; freezing **2.** covered as with frost **3.** cold in manner or feeling; unfriendly **—frost′i·ly** *adv.* **—frost′i·ness** *n.*

**froth** (frôth, fräth) *n.* [ON. *frotha*] **1.** foam **2.** foaming saliva caused by disease or great excitement **3.** light, trifling, or worthless talk, ideas, etc. **—vt. 1.** to cause to foam **2.** to cover with foam **3.** to spill forth as foam **—vi.** to foam

**froth·y** (-ē) *adj.* **froth′i·er, froth′i·est 1.** foamy **2.** light; trifling; worthless **—froth′i·ly** *adv.* **—froth′i·ness** *n.*

**frou-frou** (frōō′frōō′) *n.* [Fr.; echoic] **1.** a rustling or swishing, as of a skirt **2.** [Colloq.] excessive ornateness or affected elegance

**fro·ward** (frō′ərd, -wərd) *adj.* [ME., unruly: see FRO & -WARD] not easily controlled; stubbornly willful **—fro′ward·ly** *adv.* **—fro′ward·ness** *n.*

**frown** (froun) *vi.* [< OFr. < *froigne,* sullen face < Gaul.] **1.** to contract the brows, as in displeasure or concentrated thought **2.** to show displeasure or disapproval (with *on* or *upon*) **—vt.** to express (disapproval, etc.) by frowning **—n. 1.** a contracting of the brows in sternness, thought, etc. **2.** any expression of displeasure or disapproval **—frown′er** *n.* **—frown′ing·ly** *adv.*

**frow·zy** (frou′zē) *adj.* **-zi·er, -zi·est** [< ?] **1.** [Rare] bad-smelling **2.** dirty and untidy; slovenly Also sp. **frow′sy** **—frow′zi·ly** *adv.* **—frow′zi·ness** *n.*

**froze** (frōz) *pt. of* FREEZE

**fro·zen** (-'n) *pp. of* FREEZE **—adj. 1.** turned into or covered with ice **2.** damaged or killed by freezing **3.** having heavy frosts and extreme cold *[the frozen north]* **4.** preserved by freezing, as food **5.** as if turned into ice *[frozen with terror]* **6.** without warmth or affection **7.** arbitrarily kept at a fixed level or in a fixed position **8.** not readily converted into cash *[frozen assets]*

**frozen custard** a food like ice cream, but with less butterfat content and a looser consistency

**frt.** freight

**fruc·ti·fy** (fruk′tə fī′) *vi., vt.* **-fied′, -fy′ing** [< OFr. < L. *fructificare:* see FRUIT & -FY] to bear or cause to bear fruit **—fruc′ti·fi·ca′tion** *n.*

**fruc·tose** (fruk′tōs, frook′-) *n.* [< L. *fructus,* FRUIT + -OSE[1]] a crystalline sugar, $C_6H_{12}O_6$, found in sweet fruits and in honey; fruit sugar; levulose

**fru·gal** (frōō′g'l) *adj.* [L. *frugalis* < *frugi,* fit for food < *frux* (gen. *frugis,* fruits)] **1.** not wasteful; thrifty **2.** not costly; inexpensive or meager *[a frugal meal]* **—fru·gal′i·ty** (-gal′ə tē) *n., pl.* **-ties** **—fru′gal·ly** *adv.*

**fruit** (frōōt) *n.* see PLURAL, II, D, 3 [OFr. < L. *fructus* < pp. of *frui,* to enjoy] **1.** any plant product, as grain, flax, vegetables, etc.: *usually used in pl.* **2.** a sweet and edible plant structure, consisting of a fruit (sense 5), usually eaten raw or as a dessert **3.** the result or product of any action *[the fruit of labor]* **4.** [Archaic] offspring **5.** *Bot.* the mature ovary of a flowering plant, along with its contents, as the whole peach, pea pod, etc. **—vi., vt.** to bear or cause to bear fruit

**fruit·age** (-ij) *n.* **1.** the bearing of fruit **2.** a crop of fruit **3.** a result; product; consequence

**fruit·cake** (-kāk′) *n.* a rich cake containing nuts, preserved fruit, citron, spices, etc.

**fruit fly** **1.** a small fly whose larvae feed on fruits and vegetables **2.** *same as* DROSOPHILA

**fruit·ful** (-fəl) *adj.* **1.** bearing much fruit **2.** producing much; productive; prolific **3.** producing results; profitable **—fruit′ful·ly** *adv.* **—fruit′ful·ness** *n.*

**fru·i·tion** (frōō ish′ən) *n.* [OFr. < LL. < *frui:* see FRUIT] **1.** the pleasure of using or possessing **2.** the bearing of fruit **3.** fulfillment; realization

**fruit·less** (frōōt′lis) *adj.* **1.** without results; unsuccessful; vain **2.** bearing no fruit; sterile **—fruit′less·ly** *adv.* **—fruit′less·ness** *n.*

**fruit sugar** *same as* FRUCTOSE

**fruit tree** a tree that bears edible fruit

**fruit·wood** (-wood′) *n.* the wood of any of various fruit trees, used in furniture, paneling, etc.

**fruit·y** (frōōt′ē) *adj.* **fruit′i·er, fruit′i·est 1.** like fruit in taste or smell **2.** rich or mellow in tone *[a fruity voice]* **3.** [Slang] crazy **—fruit′i·ly** *adv.* **—fruit′i·ness** *n.*

**frump** (frump) *n.* [< Du. *frompelen* < *rompelen,* to rumple] a dowdy, unattractive woman **—frump′ish** *adj.* **—frump′y** *adj.* **frump′i·er, frump′i·est**

**Frun·ze** (frōōn′ze) capital of the Kirghiz S.S.R., in the SC part: pop. 416,000

**frus·trate** (frus′trāt) *vt.* **-trat·ed, -trat·ing** [< L. pp. of *frustrare* < *frustra,* in vain] **1.** to cause to have no effect; nullify *[to frustrate plans]* **2.** to keep from an objective; foil *[to frustrate a foe]* **3.** *Psychol.* to keep from gratifying certain desires **—vi.** to become frustrated **—frus·tra′tion** *n.*

**frus·tum** (frus′təm) *n., pl.* **-tums, -ta** (-tə) [L., a piece, bit] the solid figure formed when the top of a cone or pyramid is cut off by a plane parallel to the base

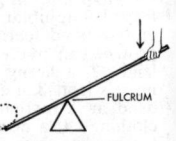
FRUSTUM

**fry**[1] (frī) *vt., vi.* **fried, fry′ing** [< OFr. < L. *frigere,* to fry] **1.** to cook or be cooked, usually in hot fat or oil, over direct heat **2.** [Slang] to electrocute or be electrocuted **—n., pl.** **fries** **1.** a fried food; esp., *[pl.]* fried potatoes **2.** a social gathering where food is fried and eaten

**fry**[2] (frī) *n., pl.* **fry** [prob. a merging of ON. *frjo,* seed, with Anglo-Fr. *frei,* spawn] **1.** young fish **2.** small adult fish, esp. in large groups **3.** offspring **—small fry 1.** children **2.** trivial people or things

**fry·er** (frī′ər) *n.* **1.** one that fries; specif., a utensil for frying foods **2.** food to be fried, esp. a young, tender chicken

**f-stop** (ef′stäp′) *n.* any of the settings for the f-number of a camera

**ft. 1.** foot; feet **2.** fort

**FTC** Federal Trade Commission

**fth., fthm.** fathom

**fuch·sia** (fyōō′shə) *n.* [ModL., after L. *Fuchs,* 16th-c. G. botanist] **1.** a shrubby plant with drooping pink, red, or purple flowers **2.** purplish red **—adj.** purplish-red

**fud·dle** (fud′'l) *vt.* **-dled, -dling** [akin ? to G. dial. *fuddeln,* to swindle] to confuse or stupefy as with alcoholic liquor **—n.** a fuddled condition

**fud·dy-dud·dy** (fud′ē dud′ē) *n., pl.* **-dies** [prob. based on dial. *fud,* buttocks] [Slang] **1.** a fussy, critical person **2.** an old-fashioned person

**fudge** (fuj) *n.* [? echoic] **1.** empty talk; nonsense **2.** [< ?] a soft candy made of butter, milk, sugar, flavoring, etc. **—vt. fudged, fudg′ing** to make dishonestly or carelessly; fake **—vi. 1.** to refuse to commit oneself **2.** to cheat

**fu·el** (fyōō′əl, fyōōl) *n.* [< OFr. *fouaille,* ult. < L. *focus,* fireplace] **1.** coal, oil, gas, wood, etc. burned to supply heat or power **2.** fissionable material, as in a nuclear reactor **3.** anything that maintains or intensifies strong feeling, etc. **—vt. -eled** or **-elled, -el·ing** or **-el·ling** to supply with fuel **—vi.** to get fuel **—fu′el·er, fu′el·ler** *n.*

**fuel cell** any of various devices that convert chemical energy directly into electrical energy

**fuel oil** any oil used for fuel

**-fuge** (fyōōj) [Fr. < L. *fugere,* to flee] *a suffix meaning* something that drives away *[vermifuge]*

**fu·gi·tive** (fyōō′jə tiv) *adj.* [< OFr. < L. pp. of *fugere,* to flee] **1.** fleeing or having fled, as from danger, justice, etc. **2.** passing quickly; fleeting; evanescent **3.** on matters of temporary interest *[fugitive essays]* **4.** roaming; shifting **—n. 1.** a person who flees or has fled from danger, justice, etc. **2.** a fleeting or elusive thing **—fu′gi·tive·ly** *adv.*

**fugue** (fyōōg) *n.* [Fr. < It. < L. < *fugere,* to flee] a musical composition in which a subject is announced by one voice and then developed contrapuntally by each of usually two or three other voices **—fu′gal** *adj.* **—fu′gist** *n.*

**‡Füh·rer, Fueh·rer** (fü′rər; *E.* fyoōr′ər) *n.* [G. < *führen,* to lead] leader: title used by A. Hitler

**Fu·ji** (fōō′jē) extinct volcano on Honshu island, Japan, near Tokyo: also **Fu′ji·ya′ma** (-yä′mə)

**-ful** (fəl, f'l; *for 4, usually* fool) [OE. < *full,* FULL[1]] *a suffix meaning:* **1.** full of, characterized by, having *[joyful]* **2.** having the qualities of *[masterful]* **3.** able or tending to *[helpful]* **4.** *pl.* **-fuls** the quantity that fills *[handful]*

**ful·crum** (fool′krəm, ful′-) *n., pl.* **-crums, -cra** (-krə) [L., akin to *fulcire,* to prop] **1.** the support or point of support on which a lever turns in raising or moving something **2.** a means of exerting influence, pressure, etc.

**ful·fill, ful·fil** (fool fil′) *vt.* **-filled′, -fill′ing** [OE. *fullfyllan*] **1.** to carry out (something promised, predicted, etc.); cause to be or happen **2.** to do (something required); obey **3.** to satisfy (a condition) **4.** to bring to an end; complete **—fulfill oneself** to realize completely one's ambitions, potentialities, etc. **—ful·fill′er** *n.* **—ful·fill′ment, ful·fil′ment** *n.*

**ful·gent** (ful′jənt, fool′-) *adj.* [< L. prp. of *fulgere,* to flash] [Now Rare] very bright; radiant

FULCRUM

**full**[1] (fool) *adj.* [OE.] **1.** having in it all there is space for; filled *[a full jar]* **2.** *a)* having eaten all that one wants *b)* having had more than one can stand *[I am full]* **3.** occupying all of a given space *[a full load]* **4.** well supplied or provided (with *of*) *[a tank full of gas]* **5.** filling the required number, measure, etc.; complete *[a full dozen]* **6.** thorough; absolute *[come to a full stop]* **7.** having reached the greatest development, size, etc. *[a full moon]* **8.** having the same parents *[full brothers]* **9.** having clearness, volume, and depth *[a full tone]* **10.** of the highest rank *[a full professor]* **11.** plump; round *[a full face]* **12.** with loose, wide folds; ample *[a full skirt]* **13.** deeply affected, engrossed, etc. —*n.* the greatest amount, extent, number, etc. —*adv.* **1.** completely *[a full-grown boy]* **2.** directly *[struck full in the face]* **3.** very *[full well]* —*vt.* to make (a skirt, etc.) with loose folds —*vi.* to become full: said of the moon —**in full 1.** to, for, or with the full amount, value, etc. **2.** not abbreviated or condensed

**full²** (fool) *vt., vi.* [< OFr., ult. < L. *fullo,* cloth fuller] to shrink and thicken (cloth, esp. of wool) with moisture, heat, and pressure

**full·back** (-bak') *n.* *Football* a member of the offensive backfield, traditionally the back farthest behind the line

**full-blood·ed** (-blud'id) *adj.* **1.** of unmixed breed or race; purebred: also **full'-blood' 2.** vigorous; lusty **3.** genuine **4.** rich and full

**full-blown** (-blōn') *adj.* **1.** in full bloom; open: said of flowers **2.** fully developed; mature

**full-bod·ied** (-bäd'ēd) *adj.* having much strength, flavor, substance, etc.

**full dress** formal clothes for important occasions; esp., formal evening clothes —**full'-dress'** *adj.*

**full·er** (fool'ər) *n.* one whose work is to full cloth

**full·er's earth** (fool'ərz) a highly absorbent clay used to remove grease from cloth in fulling, to clarify oils, etc.

**Ful·ler·ton** (fool'ər tən) [after G. *Fullerton,* a founder] city in SW Calif.: suburb of Los Angeles: pop. 102,000

**full-fash·ioned** (fool'fash'ʼnd) *adj.* knitted to conform to body contours, as hosiery or sweaters

**full-fledged** (-flejd') *adj.* completely developed or trained; of full rank or status

**full house** a poker hand containing three of a kind and a pair, as three jacks and two fives

**full moon** the phase of the moon when its entire illuminated hemisphere is seen as a full disk

**full nelson** *see* NELSON

**full·ness, ful·ness** (-nis) *n.* the quality or state of being full

**full sail 1.** with every sail set **2.** with maximum speed and energy

**full-scale** (-skāl') *adj.* **1.** according to the original or standard scale *[a full-scale drawing]* **2.** to the utmost limit, degree, etc. *[full-scale war]*

**full-time** (-tīm') *adj.* on a complete regular schedule

**full time** as a full-time employee, student, etc. *[to work full time]*

**full·y** (-ē) *adv.* **1.** to the full; completely; entirely **2.** abundantly; amply **3.** at least *[fully two hours later]*

**ful·mi·nate** (ful'mə nāt') *vi.* -nat'ed, -nat'ing [< L. pp. of *fulminare* < *fulmen,* lightning] **1.** to explode with violence; detonate **2.** to shout forth denunciations, decrees, etc. —*vt.* **1.** to cause to explode **2.** to shout forth (denunciations, etc.) —*n.* any of certain highly explosive compounds used in detonators and percussion caps —**ful'·mi·nant** *adj.* —**ful'mi·na'tion** *n.* —**ful'mi·na'tor** *n.*

**ful·some** (fool'səm, ful'-) *adj.* [ME. < *ful,* FULL¹ + *-som,* -SOME¹, but infl. by *ful,* foul] disgusting or offensive, esp. because excessive or insincere *[fulsome praise]* —**ful'·some·ly** *adv.* —**ful'some·ness** *n.*

**Ful·ton** (fool't'n), **Robert** 1765–1815; U.S. inventor & engineer: designer of the 1st commercially successful U.S. steamboat

**fum·ble** (fum'b'l) *vi., vt.* -bled, -bling [prob. < ON. *famla,* to grope] **1.** to grope clumsily **2.** to handle (a thing) clumsily; bungle **3.** to lose one's grasp on (a football, etc.) while trying to catch or hold it **4.** to make (one's way) as by groping —*n.* the act or fact of fumbling —**fum'bler** *n.* —**fum'bling·ly** *adv.*

**fume** (fyoom) *n.* [< OFr. < L. *fumus] [often pl.]* a gas, smoke, or vapor, esp. if offensive or suffocating —*vi.* **fumed, fum'ing 1.** to give off fumes **2.** to rise up or pass off in fumes **3.** to show, or give way to, anger, annoyance, etc. —*vt.* **1.** to expose to fumes **2.** to give off as fumes

**fu·mi·gant** (fyoo'mə gənt) *n.* any substance used in fumigating

**fu·mi·gate** (-gāt') *vt.* -gat'ed, -gat'ing [< L. pp. of *fumigare* < *fumus,* smoke + *agere,* to make] to expose to the action of fumes, esp. in order to disinfect or kill the vermin in —**fu'mi·ga'tion** *n.* —**fu'mi·ga'tor** *n.*

**fum·y** (fyoo'mē) *adj.* **fum'i·er, fum'i·est** full of or producing fumes; vaporous

**fun** (fun) *n.* [< ME. *fonne,* a fool, or *fonnen,* to be foolish < ?] **1.** *a)* lively, gay play or playfulness; amusement, sport, recreation, etc. *b)* enjoyment or pleasure **2.** a source of amusement; amusing person or thing —*adj.* [Colloq.] intended for pleasure and amusement *[a fun gift]* —*vi.* **funned, fun'ning** [Colloq.] to make fun; play or joke —**for** (or **in**) **fun** playfully; not seriously —**like fun** [Slang] by no means; not at all —**make fun of** to mock laughingly; ridicule

**func·tion** (funk'shən) *n.* [OFr. < L. *functio* < pp. of *fungi,* to perform] **1.** the normal or characteristic action of anything; esp., any of the specialized actions of an organ or part of an animal or plant **2.** a special duty or performance required in the course of work or activity **3.** a formal ceremony or social occasion **4.** a thing that depends on and varies with something else **5.** *Math.* a quantity whose value depends on that of another quantity or quantities —*vi.* **1.** to act in a required manner; work **2.** to have a function; be used (*as*)

**func·tion·al** (-əl) *adj.* **1.** of a function or functions **2.** *a)* performing a function *b)* intended to be useful **3.** *Med.* affecting a function of some organ without apparent structural or organic changes *[a functional disease]* —**func'tion·al·ly** *adv.*

**func·tion·al·ism** (-əl iz'm) *n.* emphasis on adapting the structure of anything to its function —**func'tion·al·ist** *n., adj.* —**func'tion·al·is'tic** *adj.*

**func·tion·ar·y** (-er'ē) *n., pl.* -ar'ies a person who performs a certain function; esp., an official

**fund** (fund) *n.* [L. *fundus,* bottom, land] **1.** a supply that can be drawn on; stock; store *[a fund of good humor]* **2.** *a)* a sum of money set aside for a particular purpose *b)* an organization to administer it *c)* *[pl.]* ready money —*vt.* **1.** to provide money to pay the interest on (a debt) **2.** to put or convert into a long-term debt that bears interest **3.** to put in a fund; accumulate **4.** to provide for with a fund

**fun·da·ment** (fun'də mənt) *n.* [< OFr. < L. < *fundus:* see prec.] **1.** the buttocks **2.** the anus

**fun·da·men·tal** (fun'də men't'l) *adj.* [< ML. < L. *fundamentum:* see prec.] **1.** of or forming a foundation or basis; basic; basic **2.** primary; original **3.** most important; chief **4.** *Music a)* designating or of the lowest, or root, tone of a chord *b)* designating or of the prime or main tone of a harmonic series —*n.* **1.** a principle, law, etc. serving as a basis; essential part **2.** *Music* the fundamental tone of a chord or harmonic series —**fun'da·men'tal·ly** *adv.*

**fun·da·men·tal·ism** (-iz'm) *n.* [*sometimes* F-] **1.** religious beliefs based on a literal interpretation of the Bible and regarded as fundamental to Christian faith **2.** among some American Protestants, the movement based on these beliefs —**fun'da·men'tal·ist** *n., adj.*

**fundamental particle** *same as* ELEMENTARY PARTICLE

**Fun·dy** (fun'dē), **Bay of** arm of the Atlantic, between New Brunswick & Nova Scotia, Canada

**fu·ner·al** (fyoo'nər əl) *adj.* [< LL. < L. *funus* (gen. *funeris),* a funeral] of or for a funeral —*n.* **1.** the ceremonies connected with burial or cremation of the dead **2.** the procession accompanying the body to the place of burial or cremation

**funeral director** the manager of a funeral home

**funeral home** (or **parlor**) a business establishment where the bodies of the dead are prepared for burial or cremation and where funeral services can be held

**fu·ne·re·al** (fyoo nir'ē əl) *adj.* suitable for a funeral; sad and solemn; gloomy —**fu·ne're·al·ly** *adv.*

**fun·gi·cide** (fun'jə sīd', fun'gə-) *n.* [< FUNGUS & -CIDE] any substance that kills fungi —**fun'gi·ci'dal** *adj.*

**fun·goid** (fun'goid) *adj.* like or characteristic of a fungus —*n.* a fungus

**fun·gous** (-gəs) *adj.* of, like, or caused by fungi

**fun·gus** (fun'gəs) *n., pl.* **fun·gi** (fun'jī, fun'gī), **fun'gus·es** [L., prob. < Gr. *spongos,* a sponge] **1.** any of a group of thallophytes, including molds, mildews, mushrooms, rusts, and smut, that lack chlorophyll, true roots, stems, and leaves and reproduce by means of spores **2.** something that grows suddenly and rapidly like a fungus —*adj.* of, like, or caused by a fungus

**fu·nic·u·lar** (fyoo nik'yoo lər) *adj.* [< L. *funiculus,* dim. of *funis,* a rope] of or worked by a rope or cable —*n.* a mountain railway on which counterbalanced cars ascend and descend by cables: also **funicular railway**

**funk¹** (funk) *n.* [< ? Fl. *fonck,* dismay] [Colloq.] **1.** a cowering through fear; panic **2.** a low, depressed mood: also **blue funk** —*vi.* [Colloq.] **1.** to be in a funk or panic —*vt.* [Colloq.] **1.** to be afraid of **2.** to shrink from in fear **3.** to frighten

**funk²** (funk) *n.* [cf. FUNKY²] **1.** a musty odor, as of moldy tobacco **2.** funky jazz

**fun·ky¹** (fun'kē) *adj.* -ki·er, -ki·est in a funk, or panic

**fun·ky²** (fun'kē) *adj.* -ki·er, -ki·est [orig. Negro argot, earthy < obs. *funk,* smell, smoke] *Jazz* having an earthy quality or style derived from early blues —**fun'ki·ness** *n.*

**fun·nel** (fun''l) *n.* [< Pr. < L. *(in)fundibulum < in-,* in + *fundere,* to pour] **1.** a slender tube with a wide, cone-shaped mouth, for pouring liquids and powders into containers with small openings **2.** anything shaped like a funnel **3.** *a)* a cylindrical smokestack, as of a steamship *b)* a chimney or flue —*vi., vt.* -neled or -nelled, -nel·ing or -nel·ling **1.** to move or pour through a funnel **2.** to move into a central channel or place

**fun·ny** (fun′ē) *adj.* -ni·er, -ni·est **1.** causing laughter; amusing; humorous **2.** [Colloq.] *a)* strange; queer *b)* deceptive or tricky —*n., pl.* -nies [Colloq.] *same as* COMIC STRIP: *usually in pl.* —**fun′ni·ly** *adv.* —**fun′ni·ness** *n.*

**funny bone** [prob. a pun on *humerus* (hence "humorous")] **1.** a place on the elbow where the ulnar nerve passes close to the surface: a sharp impact at this place causes a strange, tingling sensation in the arm **2.** inclination to laughter

**fur** (fur) *n.* [< OFr. < *fuerre*, a sheath < Frank. *fodr*] **1.** the soft, thick hair covering the body of many mammals **2.** a skin bearing such hair, processed for making garments **3.** any garment made of such skins **4.** any fuzzy coating, as diseased matter on the tongue in illness —*adj.* of fur —*vt.* **furred, fur′ring 1.** to line, cover, or trim with fur **2.** to coat with a furry deposit **3.** to make level with furring strips —*vi.* to become furred with a deposit —**make the fur fly 1.** to cause dissension or fighting **2.** to work busily

**fur·be·low** (fur′bə lō′) *n.* [var. of Fr. *falbala*] **1.** a flounce or ruffle **2.** [*usually pl.*] showy trimming —*vt.* to decorate as with furbelows

**fur·bish** (fur′bish) *vt.* [< OFr. *forbir* < WGmc.] **1.** to brighten by rubbing or scouring; burnish **2.** to make usable again; renovate —**fur′bish·er** *n.*

**fur·cate** (fur′kāt; *for adj., also* -kit) *adj.* [< ML. < L. *furca*, a fork] forked —*vi.* -cat·ed, -cat·ing to branch; fork —**fur′cate·ly** *adv.* —**fur·ca′tion** *n.*

**Fu·ries** (fyoor′ēz) *Gr. & Rom. Myth.* three female spirits who punished doers of unavenged crimes

**fu·ri·ous** (fyoor′ē əs) *adj.* [< OFr. < L. *furiosus*] **1.** full of fury or wild rage **2.** violently overpowering **3.** very great; intense [*furious* speed] —**fu′ri·ous·ly** *adv.* —**fu′ri·ous·ness** *n.*

**furl** (furl) *vt.* [< OFr. *ferlier* < *fermlier*, to tie up < *ferm*, FIRM[1] + *lier*, to tie] to roll up tightly and make secure, as a flag to a staff —*vi.* to become curled or rolled up —*n.* **1.** a roll or coil of something furled **2.** a furling or being furled

**fur·long** (fur′lôŋ) *n.* [< OE. < *furh*, a furrow + *lang*, LONG[1]] a measure of distance equal to 1/8 of a mile, or 220 yards

**fur·lough** (fur′lō) *n.* [< Du. *verlof*] a leave of absence; esp., a leave granted to military enlisted personnel —*vt.* **1.** to grant a furlough to **2.** to lay off (employees), esp. temporarily

**fur·nace** (fur′nəs) *n.* [< OFr. < L. *fornax* < *fornus*, oven] **1.** an enclosed structure in which heat is produced for heating a building, reducing ores and metals, etc. **2.** any extremely hot place

**fur·nish** (fur′nish) *vt.* [< OFr. < *furnir* < OFrank.] **1.** to equip with whatever is necessary; esp., to put furniture into (a room, apartment, etc.) **2.** to supply; provide —**fur′nish·er** *n.*

**fur·nish·ings** (-iŋz) *n.pl.* **1.** the furniture, carpets, etc. for a room, apartment, etc. **2.** articles of dress; things to wear [men's *furnishings*]

**fur·ni·ture** (fur′ni chər) *n.* [Fr. *fourniture* < *fournir*, FURNISH] **1.** the movable things in a room, etc. which equip it for living, as chairs, beds, etc. **2.** the necessary equipment of a ship, trade, etc.

**fu·ror** (fyoor′ôr) *n.* [< OFr. *fureur* < L. *furor*] **1.** fury; rage **2.** *a)* widespread enthusiasm; craze *b)* a commotion or uproar Also Fr. **fu′rore** (-ôr)

**furred** (furd) *adj.* **1.** made, trimmed, or lined with fur **2.** having fur **3.** wearing fur **4.** having a furry coating, as the tongue **5.** made level with furring strips

**fur·ri·er** (fur′ē ər) *n.* **1.** a dealer in furs **2.** one who processes furs or makes and repairs fur garments —**fur′ri·er·y** *n., pl.* -er·ies

**fur·ring** (fur′iŋ) *n.* **1.** the act of trimming, lining, etc. with fur **2.** fur so used **3.** a furry coating, as on the tongue **4.** *a)* the leveling of a floor, wall, etc. with thin strips of wood or metal before adding boards or plaster *b)* the strips (in full, **furring strips**) so used

**fur·row** (fur′ō) *n.* [OE. *furh*] **1.** a narrow groove made in the ground by a plow **2.** anything like this, as a wrinkle on the face —*vt.* to make furrows in —*vi.* **1.** to make furrows **2.** to become wrinkled

**fur·ry** (fur′ē) *adj.* -ri·er, -ri·est **1.** of, like, or made of fur **2.** covered with or wearing fur **3.** having a furlike coating —**fur′ri·ness** *n.*

**fur·ther** (fur′thər) *adj. alt. compar. of* FAR [OE. *furthra*] **1.** additional; more **2.** more distant; farther —*adv. alt. compar. of* FAR **1.** to a greater degree or extent **2.** in addition; moreover **3.** at or to a greater distance in space or time In sense 2 of the *adj.* and sense 3 of the *adv.*, FARTHER is more commonly used —*vt.* [< OE. *fyrthrian* < *furthra*] to give aid to; promote —**fur′ther·er** *n.*

**fur·ther·ance** (-əns) *n.* a furthering, or helping forward; advancement; promotion

**fur·ther·more** (-môr′) *adv.* besides; moreover; in addition

**fur·ther·most** (-mōst′) *adj.* most distant; furthest

**fur·thest** (fur′thist) *adj. alt. superl. of* FAR [ME., formed as superl. on analogy of *further*] most distant; farthest —*adv. alt. superl. of* FAR **1.** at or to the greatest distance in space or time **2.** to the greatest degree or extent; most

**fur·tive** (fur′tiv) *adj.* [< Fr. < L. *furtivus*, stolen < *fur*, thief] done or acting in a stealthy manner; sneaky —**fur′tive·ly** *adv.* —**fur′tive·ness** *n.*

**fu·ry** (fyoor′ē) *n., pl.* -ries [< OFr. < L. *furia* < *furere*, to rage] **1.** *a)* violent anger; wild rage *b)* a fit of this **2.** violence; vehemence; fierceness **3.** a violent, vengeful person **4.** [F-] any of the Furies —**like fury** [Colloq.] violently, swiftly, etc.

**furze** (furz) *n.* [OE. *fyrs*] a prickly evergreen shrub with yellow flowers, esp. on wastelands

**fuse**[1] (fyooz) *vt., vi.* **fused, fus′ing** [< L. pp. of *fundere*, to shed] **1.** to melt or to join by melting, as metals **2.** to unite or blend together

**fuse**[2] (fyooz) *n.* [< It. < L. *fusus*, hollow spindle] **1.** a tube or wick filled with combustible material for setting off an explosive charge **2.** *same as* FUZE[2] (*n.* 2) **3.** *Elec.* a strip of easily melted metal placed in a circuit as a safeguard: if the current becomes too strong, the metal melts, thus breaking the circuit —*vt.* **fused, fus′ing** to connect a fuse to —**blow a fuse 1.** to cause an electrical fuse to melt **2.** [Colloq.] to become very angry

**fu·see** (fyoo zē′) *n.* [Fr. *fusée*, rocket < ML. < L. *fusus*: see prec.] **1.** formerly, a friction match with a large head **2.** a colored flare used as a signal by railroaders, truck drivers, etc.

**fu·se·lage** (fyoo′sə läzh′, -läj′, -lij; -zə-) *n.* [Fr. < *fuselé*, tapering] the body of an airplane, exclusive of the wings, tail, and engines

**fu·sel oil** (fyoo′z'l, -s'l) [G. *fusel*, inferior liquor] an oily, acrid, poisonous liquid occurring in insufficiently distilled alcoholic products

**Fu·shun** (foo′shoon′) city in NE China: pop. 1,019,000

**fu·si·ble** (fyoo′zə b'l) *adj.* that can be fused or easily melted —**fu′si·bil′i·ty** *n.* —**fu′si·bly** *adv.*

**fu·si·form** (fyoo′zə fôrm′) *adj.* [< L. *fusus*, a spindle + -FORM] shaped like a spindle

**fu·sil** (fyoo′z'l) *n.* [Fr., orig., steel for striking sparks < ML. < L. *focus*, hearth] a light flintlock musket

**fu·sil·ier, fu·sil·eer** (fyoo′zə lir′) *n.* formerly, a soldier armed with a fusil: the term *Fusiliers* is still applied to certain British regiments

**fu·sil·lade** (fyoo′sə läd′, -läd′; -zə-) *n.* [Fr. < *fusiller*, to shoot: see FUSIL] **1.** a simultaneous discharge of many firearms **2.** something like this [a *fusillade* of questions] —*vt.* **-lad′ed, -lad′ing** to shoot down or attack with a fusillade

**fu·sion** (fyoo′zhən) *n.* **1.** a fusing or melting together **2.** a blending; coalition [a *fusion* of political parties] **3.** anything made by fusing **4.** *same as* NUCLEAR FUSION

**fu·sion·ism** (-iz′m) *n.* the promoting of coalition, esp. of political parties —**fu′sion·ist** *n., adj.*

**fuss** (fus) *n.* [prob. echoic] **1.** a flurry of nervous, excited activity; bustle **2.** nervousness, agitation, etc. **3.** [Colloq.] a quarrel **4.** [Colloq.] a showy display of delight, etc. —*vi.* **1.** to cause or make a fuss **2.** to bustle about or worry over trifles **3.** to whine or fret, as a baby —*vt.* [Colloq.] to bother unnecessarily

**fuss·budg·et** (-buj′it) *n.* [FUSS + BUDGET, prob. in sense "bag"] [Colloq.] a fussy person

**fuss·y** (fus′ē) *adj.* **fuss′i·er, fuss′i·est 1.** bustling about or worrying over trifles **2.** hard to please **3.** whining or fretting, as a baby **4.** showing or needing careful attention **5.** full of unnecessary details —**fuss′i·ly** *adv.* —**fuss′i·ness** *n.*

**fus·tian** (fus′chən) *n.* [< OFr. < ML. < L. *fustis*, wooden stick] **1.** orig., a coarse cloth of cotton and linen **2.** now, cotton corduroy or velveteen **3.** pompous, pretentious talk or writing —*adj.* **1.** made of fustian **2.** pompous; pretentious

**fus·ty** (fus′tē) *adj.* **fus′ti·er, fus′ti·est** [< *fust*, a musty smell < Early ModE., a cask < OFr., tree trunk] **1.** smelling stale or stuffy; musty; moldy **2.** old-fashioned —**fus′ti·ly** *adv.* —**fus′ti·ness** *n.*

**fut.** future

**fu·tile** (fyoot′'l; *chiefly Brit. & Canad.*, fyoo′til) *adj.* [Fr. < L. *futilis*, lit., that easily pours out, hence worthless < *fundere*, to pour] **1.** *a)* useless; vain; hopeless *b)* ineffective **2.** trifling or unimportant —**fu′tile·ly** *adv.* —**fu·til·i·ty** (fyoo til′ə tē), *pl.* -ties, **fu′tile·ness** *n.*

**fut·tock** (fut′ək) *n.* [< ? pronun. of *foot hook*] any of the curved timbers forming the ribs of a wooden ship

**fu·ture** (fyoo′chər) *adj.* [< OFr. < L. *futurus*, used as fut. part. of *esse*, to be] **1.** that is to be or come **2.** indicating time to come [the *future* tense of a verb] —*n.* **1.** the time that is to come **2.** what will happen; what is going to be **3.** prospective condition; chance to be successful [he has a great *future* in law] **4.** [*usually pl.*] a contract for a com-

modity bought or sold for delivery at a later date   **5.** *Gram.* *a)* the future tense   *b)* a verb form in this tense
**future perfect** **1.** a tense indicating an action or state as completed in relation to a specified time in the future   **2.** a verb form in this tense (Ex.: will have gone)
**future shock** a sudden awareness of one's inaccurate evaluation of the future and the resulting inability to cope with the rapid and myriad changes of modern society
**fu·tur·ism** (-iz'm) *n.* a movement in the arts shortly before World War I which opposed traditionalism and stressed the dynamic movement and violence of the machine age —**fu'·tur·ist** *n., adj.*
**fu·tur·is·tic** (fyoo'chər is'tik) *adj.* of or having to do with the future or futurism —**fu'tur·is'ti·cal·ly** *adv.*
**fu·tu·ri·ty** (fyoo toor'ə tē, -tyoor'-, -choor'-) *n., pl.* **-ties** **1.** *a)* the future   *b)* a future condition or event   **2.** the quality of being future   **3.** a horse race in which entries are made far ahead of time: in full, **futurity race**
**fuze¹** (fyooz) *vt., vi.* **fuzed, fuz'ing** *same as* FUSE¹

**fuze²** (fyooz) *n.* **1.** *same as* FUSE² (*n.* 1)   **2.** any of various devices for detonating a bomb, projectile, etc. —*vt.* **fuzed, fuz'ing** to connect a fuze to
**fu·zee** (fyoo zē') *n. same as* FUSEE
**fuzz** (fuz) *n.* [< ? Du. *voos*, or back-formation < FUZZY] very loose, light particles of down, wool, etc.; fine hairs or fibers [the *fuzz* on a peach] —*vi., vt.* **1.** to cover or become covered with fuzz   **2.** to make or become fuzzy —**the fuzz** [< ? FUSSY (sense 2)] [Slang] a policeman or the police
**fuzz·y** (-ē) *adj.* **fuzz'i·er, fuzz'i·est** [prob. < LowG. *fussig*, spongy] **1.** of, like, or covered with fuzz   **2.** not clear, distinct, or precise; blurred —**fuzz'i·ly** *adv.* —**fuzz'i·ness** *n.*
**-fy** (fī) [< OFr. *-fier* < L. *-ficare* < *facere*, to make, do] *a suffix meaning:* **1.** to make; cause to be [liquefy]   **2.** to cause to have; imbue with [glorify]   **3.** to become [putrefy]
**FYI** for your information

# G

**G, g** (jē) *n., pl.* **G's, g's** **1.** the seventh letter of the English alphabet   **2.** a sound of *G* or *g*   **3.** *Physics a)* gravity   *b)* acceleration of gravity or a unit of acceleration equal to it, used to measure the force on a body undergoing acceleration
**G** (jē) *n.* **1.** [< G(RAND), *n.* 2] [Slang] one thousand dollars   **2.** *Educ.* a grade meaning *good*   **3.** *Music a)* the fifth tone in the ascending scale of C major   *b)* the scale having this tone as the keynote
**G** general audience: a motion-picture rating meaning that the film is considered suitable for persons of all ages
**G.** German
**G., g.** (1.) *Elec.* conductance   **2.** gauge   **3.** gram(s)   **4.** guilder(s)   **5.** guinea(s)   **6.** gulf
**Ga** *Chem.* gallium
**Ga., GA** Georgia
**gab** (gab) *vi.* **gabbed, gab'bing** [< ON. *gabba*, to mock] [Colloq.] to talk much or idly; chatter —*n.* [Colloq.] idle talk; chatter —**gift of (the) gab** [Colloq.] the ability to speak glibly —**gab'ber** *n.*
**gab·ar·dine** (gab'ər dēn', gab'ər dēn') *n.* [var. of GABERDINE] **1.** a twilled cloth of wool, cotton, rayon, etc., with a fine, diagonal weave, used for suits, coats, dresses, etc.   **2.** a garment made of this cloth   **3.** *same as* GABERDINE
**gab·ble** (gab''l) *vi.* **-bled, -bling** [freq. of GAB] **1.** to talk rapidly and incoherently; jabber   **2.** to utter rapid sounds, as a goose —*vt.* to utter rapidly and incoherently —*n.* rapid, incoherent talk or meaningless utterance —**gab'bler** *n.*
**gab·by** (-ē) *adj.* **-bi·er, -bi·est** [Colloq.] inclined to chatter; talkative —**gab'bi·ness** *n.*
**gab·er·dine** (gab'ər dēn', gab'ər dēn') *n.* [< OFr. *gaverdine*, kind of cloak < ? MHG. *walvart*, pilgrimage] **1.** a loose coat of coarse cloth worn in the Middle Ages, esp. by Jews   **2.** *chiefly Brit. sp.* of GABARDINE
**gab·fest** (gab'fest') *n.* [GAB + -FEST] [Colloq.] **1.** an informal gathering of people to talk or gab   **2.** their talk
**ga·bi·on** (gā'bē ən) *n.* [Fr. < It. < *gabbia*, cage < L. *cavea*: see CAGE] **1.** a cylinder of wicker filled with earth or stones, formerly used in building fortifications   **2.** a similar cylinder of metal, used in building dams, dikes, etc.
**ga·ble** (gā'b'l) *n.* [< OFr. < Gmc., as in ON. *gafl*, gable] **1.** *a)* the triangular wall enclosed by the sloping ends of a ridged roof   *b)* popularly, the whole section formed by these   **2.** an end wall having a gable at the top   **3.** a triangular decorative feature, as over a door —*vt.* **-bled, -bling** to put gables on
**gable roof** a roof forming a gable at each end
**Ga·bon** (gá bōn') country on the W coast of Africa: 103,089 sq. mi.; pop. 480,000 —**Gab·on·ese** (gab'ə nēz') *adj., n., pl.* **-ese/ -ese/**

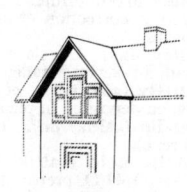

GABLE (sense 1)

**Ga·bri·el** (gā'brē əl) [Heb. *gabhrī'ēl*, lit., God is (my) strength] **1.** a masculine name: dim. *Gabe*   **2.** *Bible* an archangel, the herald of good news
**Gad** (gad) *interj.* [euphemism for GOD] [*also* **g-**] a mild oath or expression of surprise, etc.
**gad¹** (gad) *vi.* **gad'ded, gad'ding** [? a back-formation < OE. *gædeling*, companion] to wander about in a restless way, as in seeking amusement —*n.* a gadding: chiefly in **on the gad** —**gad'der** *n.*
**gad²** (gad) *n.* [ON. *gaddr*] *same as* GOAD
**gad·a·bout** (gad'ə bout') *n.* [Colloq.] a person who gads about; restless seeker after fun, excitement, etc. —*adj.* fond of gadding
**gad·fly** (-flī') *n., pl.* **-flies'** [GAD² + FLY²] **1.** a large fly that bites livestock   **2.** a person who annoys or rouses others
**gadg·et** (gaj'it) *n.* [< ?] **1.** any small mechanical contrivance   **2.** any small object
**gadg·e·teer** (gaj'ə tir') *n.* a person who contrives, or delights in, gadgets
**gadg·et·ry** (gaj'ət rē) *n.* **1.** gadgets collectively   **2.** preoccupation with mere gadgets
**gad·o·lin·i·um** (gad''l in'ē əm) *n.* [ModL., after J. *Gadolin* (1760–1852), Finn. chemist] a metallic chemical element of the rare-earth group: symbol, Gd; at. wt., 157.25; at. no., 64
**Gads·den** (gadz'dən) [after J. *Gadsden* (1788–1858), U.S. diplomat] city in NE Ala.: pop. 54,000
**gad·wall** (gad'wôl) *n., pl.* **-walls, -wall:** see PLURAL, II, D, 1 [< ?] a grayish-brown wild duck of the N freshwater regions of America
**Gae·a** (jē'ə) [Gr. *Gaia* < *gē*, earth] *Gr. Myth.* the earth personified as a goddess
**Gael** (gāl) *n.* [contr. < Gael. *Gaidheal*] a Celt of Scotland, Ireland, or the Isle of Man; esp., a Celt of the Scottish Highlands
**Gael·ic** (-ik) *adj.* **1.** of the Gaels   **2.** of the Goidelic subbranch of the Celtic family of languages; of Scottish or Irish Gaelic —*n.* one of the Goidelic languages; esp., Scottish or Irish Gaelic: abbrev. **Gael.**
**gaff** (gaf) *n.* [< OFr. < Pr. *gaf* or Sp. *gafa* < ?] **1.** a large, strong hook on a pole, or a barbed spear, for landing large fish   **2.** a sharp metal spur fastened to the leg of a gamecock   **3.** a spar or pole supporting a fore-and-aft sail   **4.** [Slang] any secret device for cheating —*vt.* to strike or land (a fish) with a gaff —**stand the gaff** [Slang] to bear up well under difficulties, punishment, etc.
**gaffe** (gaf) *n.* [Fr.] a blunder; faux pas
**gaf·fer** (gaf'ər) *n.* [altered < GODFATHER] an old man: now usually humorous
**gag** (gag) *vt.* **gagged, gag'ging** [echoic] **1.** to cause to retch or choke   **2.** to cover or stuff the mouth of, so as to keep from talking, crying out, etc.   **3.** to keep from speaking or expressing oneself freely, as by intimidation   **4.** to prevent or limit speech in (a legislative body) —*vi.* to retch or choke —*n.* **1.** something put into or over the mouth to prevent talking, etc.   **2.** any restraint of free speech   **3.** *a)* a comi-

cal remark or act, as on the stage; joke *b*) a practical joke —**gag′ger** *n.*

**gage¹** (gāj) *n.* [< OFr., a pledge, pawn < Gmc.] **1.** something pledged to insure that an obligation will be fulfilled; security **2.** a pledge to appear and fight, as a glove thrown down by a challenging knight **3.** a challenge —*vt.* **gaged, gag′ing** [Archaic] to offer as or bind by a pledge

**gage²** (gāj) *n., vt.* same as GAUGE

**gag·gle** (gag′'l) *n.* [< ME. *gagelen*, to cackle] **1.** a flock of geese **2.** any group or cluster of persons or things

**gag·man** (-man′) *n., pl.* **-men′** (-men′) a man who devises jokes, bits of comic business, etc., as for entertainers

**gai·e·ty** (gā′ə tē) *n., pl.* **-ties 1.** the state or quality of being gay; cheerfulness **2.** merrymaking; festivity **3.** finery; showy brightness

**Gail** (gāl) [dim. of ABIGAIL] a feminine name

**gai·ly** (gā′lē) *adv.* in a gay manner; specif., *a*) happily; merrily *b*) brightly; with bright display

**gain** (gān) *n.* [< OFr. < *gaaignier*, to earn] **1.** an increase; addition; specif., *a*) [*often pl.*] an increase in wealth, earnings, etc.; profit *b*) an increase in advantage; improvement **2.** the act of getting something; acquisition **3.** *Electronics a*) an increase in signal strength *b*) the ratio of output to input —*vt.* **1.** to get by labor; earn **2.** to get by effort or merit; win **3.** to attract [to *gain* one's interest] **4.** to get as an addition, profit, or advantage **5.** to make an increase in [to *gain* speed] **6.** to go faster by [my watch *gained* two minutes] **7.** to get to; reach —*vi.* **1.** to make progress; improve or advance, as in health **2.** to acquire profit **3.** to become heavier **4.** to be fast: said of a clock, etc. —**gain on 1.** to draw nearer to (an opponent in a race, etc.) **2.** to make more progress than (a competitor) —**gain over** to win over to one's side

**gain·er** (gā′nər) *n.* **1.** a person or thing that gains **2.** a fancy dive in which the diver faces forward and does a backward somersault in the air

**Gaines·ville** (gānz′vil) [after Gen. E. *Gaines* (1777–1849)] city in NC Fla.: pop. 81,000

**gain·ful** (gān′f'l) *adj.* producing gain; profitable —**gain′ful·ly** *adv.* —**gain′ful·ness** *n.*

**gain·ly** (gān′lē) *adj.* **-li·er, -li·est** [< ON. *gegn*, straight, fit] shapely and graceful —**gain′ly** *adv.*

**gain·say** (gān′sā′) *vt.* **-said′** (-sed′, -sād′), **-say′ing** [< OE. *gegn*, against + *seggan*, SAY] **1.** to deny **2.** to contradict **3.** to speak or act against; oppose —*n.* a gainsaying —**gain′-say′er** *n.*

**Gains·bor·ough** (gānz′bʉr′ō, -bər ə), **Thomas** 1727–88; Eng. painter

**'gainst, gainst** (genst, gänst) *prep. poet.* clip of AGAINST

**gait** (gāt) *n.* [< ON. *gata*, path] **1.** manner of walking or running **2.** any of various foot movements of a horse, as a trot, canter, etc. —*vt.* to train (a horse) to certain gaits —**gait′ed** *adj.*

**gai·ter** (gāt′ər) *n.* [altered (after prec.) < Fr. *guêtre*] **1.** a cloth or leather covering for the instep and ankle and, sometimes, the calf of the leg; spat or legging **2.** a shoe with elastic sides and no lacing **3.** a high overshoe with a cloth upper

**gal** (gal) *n.* [Colloq.] a girl

**Gal.** Galatians

**gal.** gallon; gallons

**ga·la** (gā′lə, gal′ə) *n.* [It. < OFr. *gale*, enjoyment] a festive occasion; festival; celebration —*adj.* festive, or suitable for a festive occasion

**ga·lac·tic** (gə lak′tik) *adj.* [Gr. *galaktikos*, milky < *gala*, milk] **1.** of or obtained from milk **2.** *Astron.* of the Milky Way or some other galaxy

**Gal·a·had** (gal′ə had′) in Arthurian legend, a knight who was successful in the quest for the Holy Grail because of his purity and noble spirit

**gal·an·tine** (gal′ən tēn′) *n.* [< OFr. < ML. *galatina*, jelly < L. pp. of *gelare*, CONGEAL] a mold of boned, seasoned, boiled white meat, as chicken or veal, chilled and served in its own jelly

**Ga·lá·pa·gos Islands** (gə lä′pə gōs′) group of islands in the Pacific on the equator, belonging to Ecuador: 3,028 sq. mi.

**Gal·a·te·a** (gal′ə tē′ə) *see* PYGMALION

**Ga·la·tia** (gə lā′shə) ancient kingdom in C Asia Minor, made a Roman province c.25 B.C. —**Ga·la′tian** *adj., n.*

**Ga·la·tians** (-shənz) the Epistle to the Galatians, a book of the New Testament written by the Apostle Paul

**gal·ax·y** (gal′ək sē) *n.* [< LL. *galaxias* < Gr. < *gala*, milk] [*often* G-] same as MILKY WAY —*n., pl.* **-ax·ies 1.** any of innumerable vast groupings of stars **2.** an assembly of illustrious people

**gale** (gāl) *n.* [< ?] **1.** a strong wind; specif., *Meteorol.* one ranging in speed from 32 to 63 miles an hour **2.** an outburst [a *gale* of laughter]

**Ga·len** (gā′lən) (L. name *Claudius Galenus*) 130?–200? A.D.; Gr. physician & writer on philosophy —**Ga·len·ic** (gə len′ik), **Ga·len′i·cal** *adj.*

**ga·le·na** (gə lē′nə) *n.* [L., lead ore] native lead sulfide, PbS, a lustrous, lead-gray mineral: it is the principal ore of lead: also **ga·le′nite** (-nīt)

**Ga·li·cia** (gə lish′ə, -ē ə) **1.** region of SE Poland & the NW Ukrainian S.S.R. **2.** region & former kingdom in NW Spain —**Ga·li′cian** *adj., n.*

**Gal·i·le·an¹** (gal′ə lē′ən) *adj.* of Galilee or its people —*n.* a native or inhabitant of Galilee —**the Galilean** Jesus

**Gal·i·le·an²** (gal′ə lē′ən) *adj.* of Galileo

**Gal·i·lee** (gal′ə lē′) **1.** region of N Israel **2. Sea of,** lake of NE Israel, on the Syria border

**Gal·i·le·o** (gal′ə lē′ō, -lā′-) (born *Galileo Galilei*) 1564–1642; It. astronomer & physicist

**gal·i·ot** (gal′ē ət) *n.* same as GALLIOT

**gall¹** (gôl) *n.* [OE. *galla*] **1.** bile, the bitter, greenish fluid secreted by the liver and stored in the gallbladder **2.** something bitter or distasteful **3.** bitter feeling **4.** [Colloq.] impudence; audacity

**gall²** (gôl) *n.* [OE. *gealla* < L. *galla:* see ff.] **1.** a sore on the skin, esp. of a horse's back, caused by chafing **2.** irritation or annoyance, or a cause of this —*vt.* **1.** to make sore by rubbing; chafe **2.** to irritate; annoy; vex

**gall³** (gôl) *n.* [< OFr. < L. *galla*, gallnut] a tumor on plant tissue caused by stimulation by fungi, insects, or bacteria: galls formed on oak trees have a high tannic acid content

**gal·lant** (gal′ənt; *for adj.* 4 & *n., usually* gə lant′; *for v., always* gə lant′) *adj.* [< OFr. prp. of *galer*, to rejoice < *gale:* see GALA] **1.** showy and gay in dress or appearance **2.** stately; imposing **3.** brave and noble **4.** polite and attentive to women —*n.* [Now Rare] **1.** a high-spirited, stylish man **2.** a man attentive and polite to women **3.** a lover —*vt., vi.* [Now Rare] to court (a woman) —**gal′lant·ly** *adv.*

**gal·lant·ry** (gal′ən trē) *n., pl.* **-ries 1.** nobility of behavior or spirit; heroic courage **2.** the courtly manner of a gallant **3.** an act or speech characteristic of a gallant **4.** amorous intrigue

**gall·blad·der** (gôl′blad′ər) *n.* a membranous sac attached to the liver, in which excess gall, or bile, is stored

**gal·le·ass** (gal′ē as′, -əs) *n.* [< Fr. < OFr. < It. < ML. *galea:* see GALLEY] a large, three-masted vessel having sails and oars and carrying heavy guns: used on the Mediterranean in the 16th and 17th cent.

**gal·le·on** (gal′ē ən) *n.* [Sp. *galeón* < ML. *galea:* see GALLEY] a large Spanish warship and trader of the 15th and 16th cent., with three or four decks at the stern

GALLEON

**gal·ler·y** (gal′ə rē) *n., pl.* **-ler·ies** [< Fr. < ML. *galeria*] **1.** *a*) a covered walk open at one side or having the roof supported by pillars *b*) [Chiefly South] a veranda or porch **2.** a long, narrow balcony on the outside of a building **3.** a platform at the stern of an early sailing ship **4.** *a*) a platform or projecting upper floor in a church, theater, etc.; esp., the highest of a series of such platforms in a theater, with the cheapest seats *b*) the people occupying these seats *c*) a group of spectators, as at a sporting event **5.** a long, narrow corridor or room **6.** a room, building, or establishment for showing or selling art works **7.** a room or establishment used as a photographer's studio, for shooting at targets, etc. **8.** an underground passage, as one used in mining —*vt.* **-ler·ied, -ler·y·ing** to furnish with a gallery —**play to the gallery** to try to win the approval of the public, esp. in a showy way

**gal·ley** (gal′ē) *n., pl.* **-leys** [< OFr. < ML. *galea*, < MGr. *galaia*, a kind of ship] **1.** a long, low, usually single-decked ship propelled by oars and sails, used in ancient and medieval times **2.** a ship's kitchen **3.** *Printing a*) a shallow, oblong tray for holding composed type to be put into a form *b*) same as GALLEY PROOF

**galley proof** printer's proof taken from type in a galley to permit correction of errors before the type is made up in pages

**galley slave 1.** a slave or convict sentenced or compelled to pull an oar on a galley **2.** a drudge

**gall·fly** (gôl′flī′) *n., pl.* **-flies′** a fly whose eggs cause galls when deposited in plant stems

**Gal·lic** (gal′ik) *adj.* **1.** of ancient Gaul or its people **2.** French

**gal·lic acid** (gal′ik) [< Fr. < *galle*, GALL³] an acid, $C_7H_6O_5 \cdot H_2O$, prepared from nutgalls, tannin, etc. and used in photography and the manufacture of inks, dyes, etc.

**Gal·li·cism, gal·li·cism** (gal′ə siz'm) *n.* a French idiom, expression, custom, trait, etc.

**Gal·li·cize, gal·li·cize** (-sīz′) *vt., vi.* **-cized′, -ciz′ing** to make or become French or like the French in thought, language, etc.

**gal·li·mau·fry** (gal′ə mô′frē) *n., pl.* **-fries** [Fr. *galimafrée*

1. orig., a hash made of meat scraps 2. a hodgepodge; jumble

**gal·li·na·cean** (gal'ə nā'shən) *adj.* same as GALLINACEOUS —*n.* any gallinaceous bird

**gal·li·na·ceous** (-shəs) *adj.* [< L. < *gallina*, hen < *gallus*, a cock] of, or having the nature of, an order of birds that nest on the ground, including poultry, pheasants, grouse, etc.

**gall·ing** (gôl'iŋ) *adj.* that galls; very annoying; vexing —**gall'ing·ly** *adv.*

**gal·li·nule** (gal'ə nyōol', -nōol') *n.* [ModL. < L. dim. of *gallina*: see GALLINACEOUS] any of various marsh birds that both swim and wade

**gal·li·ot** (gal'ē ət) *n.* [< OFr. dim. of *galie* < ML. *galea*, GALLEY] 1. a small, swift galley with sails and oars 2. a light Dutch merchant ship with a single mast

**Gal·lip·o·li Peninsula** (gə lip'ə lē) peninsula in S European Turkey, forming the NW shore of the Dardanelles

**gal·li·pot** (gal'ə pät') *n.* [see GALLEY & POT] a small pot or jar of glazed earthenware, esp. one used by druggists as a container for medicine

**gal·li·um** (gal'ē əm) *n.* [ModL. < L. *Gallia*, Gaul; also a pun on L. *gallus*, a cock, transl. of *Lecoq* (de Boisbaudran), its 19th-c. Fr. discoverer] a soft, [illegible]-white, metallic chemical element with a low melting point, used as a substitute for mercury: symbol, Ga; at. wt., 69.72; at. no., 31

**gal·li·vant** (gal'ə vant') *vi.* [arbitrary elaboration of GALLANT] 1. orig., to gad about with members of the opposite sex 2. to go about in search of amusement or excitement —**gal'li·vant'er** *n.*

**gall·nut** (gôl'nut') *n.* a nutlike gall, esp. on oaks

**Gal·lo-** (gal'ō) [L. < *Gallus*, a Gaul] *a combining form meaning:* 1. French 2. French and

**gal·lon** (gal'ən) *n.* [< ONormFr. *galon* < ML. *galo*, gallon, jug] 1. a liquid measure, equal to 4 quarts (231 cubic inches): the British imperial gallon equals 277.42 cubic inches 2. a dry measure, equal to 1/8 bushel Abbrev. **gal.**

**gal·lon·age** (-ij) *n.* amount or capacity in gallons

**gal·loon** (gə lōon') *n.* [< Fr. < *galonner*, to braid] a braid, as of cotton, silk, or metal thread, used for trimming or binding

**gal·lop** (gal'əp) *vi.* [< OFr. *galoper* < Frank.] 1. to go at a gallop 2. to move or act very fast; hurry —*vt.* to cause to gallop —*n.* 1. the fastest gait of a horse, etc., consisting of a succession of leaping strides with all the feet off the ground at one time 2. a ride on a galloping animal 3. any fast pace, speedy action, etc. —**gal'lop·er** *n.*

**gal·lows** (gal'ōz) *n., pl.* **-lows·es, -lows** [OE. *galga*] 1. an upright frame with a crossbeam and a rope, for hanging condemned persons 2. any structure like this 3. the death sentence by hanging

**gallows bird** [Colloq.] a person who deserves hanging

**gallows humor** morbid or cynical humor

**gall·stone** (gôl'stōn') *n.* a small, solid mass sometimes formed in the gallbladder or bile duct

**gal·lus·es** (gal'əs iz) *n.pl.* [< *gallus*, dial. var. of GALLOWS] [Colloq.] suspenders; braces

**gal·op** (gal'əp) *n.* [Fr.: see GALLOP] 1. a lively round dance in 2/4 time 2. music for this —*vi.* to dance a galop

**ga·lore** (gə lôr') *adv.* [Ir. *go leór*, enough] in abundance; plentifully [to attract crowds *galore*]

**ga·losh, ga·loshe** (gə läsh') *n.* [< OFr. *galoche*, prob. < LL. *gallicula*, small shoe] an overshoe, esp. a high overshoe of rubber and fabric

**Gals·wor·thy** (gôlz'wur'*th*ē, galz'-), **John** 1867-1933; Eng. novelist & playwright

**Gal·ton** (gôl't'n), Sir **Francis** 1822-1911; Eng. scientist & writer: pioneer in eugenics

**Gal·va·ni** (gal vä'nē), **Lu·i·gi** (lōo wē'jē) 1737-98; It. physiologist & physicist

**gal·van·ic** (gal van'ik) *adj.* [< ff.] 1. of, caused by, or producing an electric current, esp. from a battery 2. stimulating or stimulated as if by electric shock; startling —**gal·van'i·cal·ly** *adv.*

**gal·va·nism** (gal'və niz'm) *n.* [< Fr. < It.: after L. GALVANI] 1. electricity produced by chemical action 2. electrical current used in therapy

**gal·va·nize** (gal'və nīz') *vt.* **-nized', -niz'ing** 1. to apply an electric current to 2. to stimulate as if by electric shock; excite 3. to plate (metal) with zinc —**gal·va·ni·za'tion** *n.*

**gal·va·no-** *a combining form meaning* galvanic, galvanism

**gal·va·nom·e·ter** (gal'və näm'ə tər) *n.* an instrument for detecting and measuring a small electric current —**gal'va·no·met'ric** (-nō met'rik) *adj.* —**gal'va·nom'e·try** (-trē) *n.*

**Gal·ves·ton** (gal'vis tən) [after B. de *Gálvez*, 18th-c. gov. of La.] seaport in SE Tex.: pop. 62,000

**gam** (gam) *n.* [< dial. Fr. *gambe* < ML. *gamba* < Gr. *kampē*, a joint] [Slang] a leg; often, specif., a woman's shapely leg

**Gama, Vasco da** *see* DA GAMA

**Gam·bi·a** (gam'bē ə) country on the W coast of Africa, surrounded on three sides by Senegal: a member of the Commonwealth: c.4,000 sq. mi.; pop. 357,000

**gam·bit** (gam'bit) *n.* [Fr. < OFr. < Sp. *gambito*, a tripping < It. < ML. *gamba*: see GAM] 1. *Chess* an opening in which a pawn or other piece is sacrificed to get an advantage in position 2. a maneuver or action intended to gain an advantage

**gam·ble** (gam'b'l) *vi.* **-bled, -bling** [OE. *gamenian*, to play] 1. to play games of chance for money, etc. 2. to take a risk in order to gain some advantage —*vt.* to bet; wager —*n.* an act or undertaking involving risk of a loss —**gamble away** to squander or lose in gambling —**gam'bler** *n.*

**gam·boge** (gam bōj', -bōozh') *n.* [ModL. *gambogium* < CAMBODIA] a gum resin obtained from a tropical Asian tree, used as a yellow pigment and as a cathartic

**gam·bol** (gam'b'l) *n.* [< Fr. < Pr. < It. *gambata*, a kick < *gamba*: see GAM & GAMBIT] a jumping and skipping about in play; frolic —*vi.* **-boled** or **-bolled, -bol·ing** or **-bol·ling** to jump and skip about in play; frolic

**gam·brel** (gam'brəl) *n.* [ONormFr. < OFr. *gambe*: see GAM] 1. the hock of a horse or similar animal 2. same as GAMBREL ROOF

**gambrel roof** a roof with two slopes on each side, the lower steeper than the upper

**game¹** (gām) *n.* [OE. < *gamen*] 1. any form of play; amusement; recreation; sport 2. a) any specific amusement or sport involving competition under specific rules b) a single contest in such a competition c) a subdivision of a contest, as in a set of tennis 3. the number of points required for winning 4. a victory; win 5. a set of equipment for a competitive amusement [to sell toys and *games*] 6. a way or quality of playing [to play a good *game*] 7. any test of skill, endurance, etc. 8. a project; scheme [to see through another's *game*] 9. a) wild birds or animals hunted for sport or food b) their flesh used as food 10. any object of pursuit or attack: usually in **fair game** 11. [Colloq.] a business or vocation, esp. a risky one —*vi.* **gamed, gam'ing** to play cards, etc. for stakes; gamble —*adj.* 1. designating or of wild birds or animals hunted for sport or food 2. **gam'er, gam'est** a) plucky; courageous b) having enough spirit; ready (*for* something) —**ahead of the game** [Colloq.] in the position of winning —**make game of** to make fun of; ridicule —**off one's game** performing poorly —**play the game** [Colloq.] to follow the rules; behave as fairness or custom requires —**the game is up** failure is certain —**game'ly** *adv.* —**game'ness** *n.*

GAMBREL ROOF

**game²** (gām) *adj.* [< ?] [Colloq.] lame or injured: said esp. of a leg

**game·cock** (gām'käk') *n.* a specially bred rooster trained for cockfighting

**game fish** any fish regularly caught for sport

**game·keep·er** (-kēp'ər) *n.* a person employed to breed and take care of game birds and animals on State farms or private estates

**game laws** laws regulating hunting and fishing in order to preserve game

**games·man·ship** (gāmz'mən ship') *n.* [< GAME¹ & (SPORT)SMANSHIP] skill in using ploys to gain a victory or advantage over another person

**game·some** (gām'səm) *adj.* playful; frolicsome —**game'some·ly** *adv.* —**game'some·ness** *n.*

**game·ster** (-stər) *n.* a gambler

**gam·ete** (gam'ēt, gə mēt') *n.* [ModL. < Gr. *gametē*, a wife < *gamein*, to marry < *gamos*: see GAMO-] a reproductive cell that can unite with another gamete to form the cell (*zygote*) that develops into a new individual —**ga·met·ic** (gə met'ik) *adj.*

**game theory** a method of using mathematical analysis to select the best strategy so as to minimize one's maximum losses or maximize one's minimum winnings in a game, war, business competition, etc.

**ga·me·to-** *a combining form meaning* gamete

**ga·me·to·phyte** (gə mēt'ə fīt') *n.* in plants characterized by alternation of generations, the individual or generation that reproduces by eggs and sperms —**ga·me'to·phyt'ic** (-fit'ik) *adj.*

**gam·in** (gam'ən) *n.* [Fr.] 1. a neglected child left to roam the streets 2. a girl with a roguish, saucy charm

**gam·ing** (gā'miŋ) *n.* the practice of gambling

fat, āpe, cär; ten, ēven; is, bīte; gō, hôrn, tōol, look; oil, out; up, fur; get; joy; yet; chin; she; thin, *th*en; zh, leisure; ŋ, ring; ə for *a* in *ago*, *e* in *agent*, *i* in *sanity*, *o* in *comply*, *u* in *focus*; ' as in *able* (ā'b'l); Fr. bal; ë, Fr. coeur; ö, Fr. feu; ô, Fr. mon; ô, Fr. coq; ü, Fr. duc; r, Fr. cri; H, G. ich; kh, G. doch; ‡foreign; *hypothetical; < derived from. See inside front cover.

**gam·ma** (gam'ə) *n.* [Gr.] **1.** the third letter of the Greek alphabet (Γ, γ) **2.** the third of a group or series
**gamma globulin** that fraction of blood serum which contains most antibodies: used in the temporary prevention of measles, hepatitis, etc.
**gamma ray 1.** an electromagnetic radiation emitted by the nucleus of a radioactive substance: similar to an X-ray, but shorter in wavelength **2.** a stream of such radiation
**gam·mer** (gam'ər) *n.* [altered < GODMOTHER] an old woman: now usually contemptuous or humorous
**gam·mon¹** (gam'ən) *n.* [< ONormFr. < *gambe*: see GAM] **1.** the bottom end of a side of bacon **2.** a smoked or cured ham or side of bacon
**gam·mon²** (gam'ən) *n.* [< ME. var. of *gamen*: see GAME¹] *Backgammon* a victory in which the winner gets rid of all his men before his opponent gets rid of any —*vt.* to defeat by scoring a gammon
**gam·mon³** (gam'ən) *n., interj.* [< ?] [Brit. Colloq.] deceitful talk; humbug —*vt., vi.* [Brit. Colloq.] **1.** to talk humbug (to) **2.** to deceive
**gam·o-** [< Gr. *gamos*, marriage] *a combining form meaning:* **1.** sexually united **2.** joined or united
**gam·o·pet·al·ous** (gam'ə pet''l əs) *adj.* having the petals united so as to form a tubelike corolla
**-ga·mous** (gə məs) [< Gr. *gamos* (see GAMO-) + -OUS] *a combining form meaning* marrying, uniting sexually [*polygamous*]
**gam·ut** (gam'ət) *n.* [ML. *gamma ut* < *gamma*, GAMMA + *ut* < L. *ut*, that, in a medieval song whose phrases began on successive ascending major tones: *Ut queant laxis Resonare fibris, Mira gestorum Famuli tuorum, Sancte Iohannes*] **1.** *a)* the entire series of recognized notes in modern music *b)* any complete musical scale, esp. the major scale **2.** the entire range or extent, as of emotions
**gam·y** (gā'mē) *adj.* **gam'i·er, gam'i·est 1.** having a strong, tangy flavor like that of cooked game **2.** strong in smell or taste **3.** game; plucky **4.** risqué or racy —**gam'i·ly** *adv.* —**gam'i·ness** *n.*
**-ga·my** (gə mē) [< Gr. *gamos*: see GAMO-] *a combining form meaning* marriage, sexual union [*polygamy*]
**gan·der** (gan'dər) *n.* [OE. *gan(d)ra*] **1.** a male goose **2.** a stupid or silly fellow **3.** [Slang] a look: chiefly in the phrase **take a gander**
**Gan·dhi** (gän'dē, gan'-), **Mo·han·das K(aramchand)** (mō-hän'dəs) 1869–1948; Hindu nationalist leader & social reformer: called *Mahatma Gandhi* —**Gan'dhi·an** *adj.*
**gang¹** (gaŋ) *n.* [OE. < base of *gangan* (see ff.)] **1.** a group of people associated together in some way; specif., *a)* a group of workers directed by a foreman *b)* an organized group of criminals *c)* a group of youths from one neighborhood banded together; often, specif., a band of juvenile delinquents **2.** a set of tools, machines, etc. designed to work together —*vi.* to form, or be associated in, a gang (with *up*) —*vt.* [Colloq.] to attack as a gang —**gang up on** [Colloq.] to attack as a group
**gang²** (gaŋ) *vi.* [OE. *gangan*, to go] [Scot.] to go or walk
**Gan·ges** (gan'jēz) river in N India & Bangladesh, flowing from the Himalayas into the Bay of Bengal
**gan·gling** (gaŋ'gliŋ) *adj.* [? < dial. *gangrel*, "lanky person"] tall, thin, and awkward; of loose, lanky build: also **gan'gly**
**gan·gli·on** (gaŋ'glē ən) *n., pl.* **-gli·a** (-ə), **-gli·ons** [LL. < Gr. *ganglion*, tumor] **1.** a mass of nerve cells serving as a center from which nerve impulses are transmitted **2.** a center of force, energy, etc. —**gan'gli·on'ic** (-än'ik) *adj.*
**gang·plank** (gaŋ'plaŋk') *n.* a narrow, movable platform by which to board or leave a ship
**gan·grene** (gaŋ'grēn, gaŋ grēn') *n.* [< Fr. < L. *gangraena* < Gr. < *gran*, to gnaw] decay of tissue in a part of the body when the blood supply is obstructed by injury, disease, etc. —**gan'gre·nous** (-grə nəs) *adj.*
**gang·ster** (gaŋ'stər) *n.* a member of a gang of criminals —**gang'ster·ism** *n.*
**gang·way** (gaŋ'wā') *n.* [OE. *gangweg*] a passageway; specif., *a)* an opening in a ship's side for freight or passengers *b)* same as GANGPLANK —*interj.* make room! clear the way!
**gan·net** (gan'it) *n., pl.* **-nets, -net:** see PLURAL, II, D, 1 [OE. *ganot*] any of several large sea birds; esp., a white, goose-like, web-footed bird that breeds on cliffs along the N Atlantic coast
**gan·oid** (gan'oid) *adj.* [< Fr. < Gr. *ganos*, brightness + *-eidēs*, -OID] of a group of fishes covered by rows of hard, glossy scales or plates, including the sturgeons and gars —*n.* a ganoid fish
**gant·let¹** (gônt'lit, gant'-) *n.* [< Sw. *gatlopp*, a run down a lane < *gata*, lane + *lopp*, a run] **1.** a former military punishment in which the offender ran between two rows of men who struck him with clubs, etc. as he passed **2.** a series of troubles or difficulties Now spelled equally **gaunt'let** —**run**

**the gantlet 1.** to be punished by means of the gantlet **2.** to proceed while under attack from both sides, as by criticism or gossip
**gant·let²** (gônt'lit, gänt'-) *n.* same as GAUNTLET¹
**gan·try** (gan'trē) *n., pl.* **-tries** [< OFr. < L. *canterius*, beast of burden < Gr. < *kanthōn*] **1.** a frame for holding barrels horizontally **2.** a framework that spans a distance, as one on wheels that carries a traveling crane **3.** a wheeled framework with a crane, platforms at different levels, etc. used to position and service a rocket at its launching site
**Gan·y·mede** (gan'ə mēd) *Gr. Myth.* a beautiful youth who was cupbearer to the gods
**gaol** (jāl) *n. Brit. sp. of* JAIL —**gaol'er** *n.*
**gap** (gap) *n.* [ON. < *gapa*, to yawn, GAPE] **1.** a hole or opening made by breaking or parting; breach **2.** a mountain pass or ravine **3.** an interruption of continuity in space or time **4.** a disparity between ideas, natures, etc. **5.** same as SPARK GAP —*vi.* **gapped, gap'ping** to come apart; open
**gape** (gāp) *vi.* **gaped, gap'ing** [< ON. *gapa*] **1.** to open the mouth wide, as in yawning **2.** to stare with the mouth open, as in wonder **3.** to open wide, as a chasm —*n.* **1.** an open-mouthed stare **2.** a yawn **3.** a wide opening **4.** *Zool.* the measure of the widest possible opening of a mouth or beak —**the gapes 1.** a disease of poultry and birds, characterized by gaping **2.** a fit of yawning —**gap'er** *n.* —**gap'ing·ly** *adv.*
**gar** (gär) *n., pl.* **gar, gars:** see PLURAL, II, D, 2 [contr. < GAR-FISH] any of a group of freshwater ganoid fishes with elongated bodies, long beaklike snouts, and many sharp teeth
**G.A.R.** Grand Army of the Republic
**ga·rage** (gə räzh', -räj'; *Brit.* gar'äzh) *n.* [Fr. < *garer*, to protect] **1.** a closed shelter for automobiles **2.** a business establishment where automobiles are repaired, stored, etc. —*vt.* **-raged', -rag'ing** to put or keep in a garage
**Gar·and rifle** (gar'ənd, gə rand') [after J. C. *Garand*, U.S. inventor of it, c. 1930] a semiautomatic rapid-firing, .30-caliber rifle
**garb** (gärb) *n.* [< OFr. < It. *garbo*, elegance, prob. ult. < Gr. < *kalos*, beautiful + *poiein*, to make] **1.** clothing; manner or style of dress **2.** external form, covering, or appearance —*vt.* to clothe
**gar·bage** (gär'bij) *n.* [ME., entrails of fowls] **1.** spoiled or waste food, as from a kitchen, that is thrown away **2.** worthless or offensive matter
**gar·ble** (gär'b'l) *vt.* **-bled, -bling** [< It. < *garbello*, a sieve < Ar. < *ghirbāl* < L. dim. *cribellum*, a small sieve] **1.** to select, suppress, distort, etc. parts of (a story, etc.) in telling, so as to mislead or misrepresent **2.** to confuse or mix up (a story, etc.) unintentionally —*n.* the act or result of garbling —**gar'bler** *n.*
**‡gar·çon** (gàr sōn') *n., pl.* **-çons'** (-sōn') [Fr.] **1.** a boy or young man **2.** a waiter or servant
**gar·den** (gär'd'n) *n.* [< ONormFr. *gardin* < Frank.] **1.** a piece of ground, usually close to a house, for the growing of fruits, flowers, or vegetables **2.** an area of fertile, well-cultivated land: also **garden spot 3.** [*often pl.*] a parklike place for public enjoyment, sometimes having special displays of animals or plants —*vi.* to work in or take care of a garden, lawn, etc. —*vt.* to make a garden of —*adj.* **1.** of, for, or grown in a garden **2.** ordinary; commonplace [*a garden variety of poet*] —**lead (someone) down the garden path** to mislead or deceive (someone) —**gar'den·er** *n.*
**Garden Grove** city in SW Calif.: suburb of Los Angeles: pop. 123,000
**gar·de·ni·a** (gär dēn'yə, -dē'nē ə) *n.* [ModL., after A. *Garden*, 18th-c. Am. botanist] any of a genus of plants with glossy leaves and fragrant, white or yellow, waxy flowers
**Gar·field** (gär'fēld), **James A(bram)** 1831–81; 20th president of the U.S. (1881): assassinated
**gar·fish** (gär'fish') *n., pl.* **-fish', -fish'es:** see FISH [< ME. *gare*, spear (OE. *gar*) + *fish*, fish] same as GAR
**Gar·gan·tu·a** (gär gan'choo wə) a giant king with an enormous appetite in Rabelais' *Gargantua and Pantagruel* —**Gar·gan'tu·an, gar·gan'tu·an** *adj.*
**gar·gle** (gär'g'l) *vt., vi.* **-gled, -gling** [< Fr. < *gargouille*, throat, spout] to rinse (the throat) with a liquid kept in motion by the slow expulsion of air from the lungs —*n.* **1.** a liquid used for gargling **2.** a gargling sound
**gar·goyle** (gär'goil) *n.* [< OFr. *gargouille*: see prec.] **1.** a waterspout, usually in the form of a carved fantastic creature, projecting from the gutter of a building **2.** a person with grotesque features
**Gar·i·bal·di** (gar'ə bôl'dē; *It.* gä rē-bäl'dē), **Giu·sep·pe** (jōō zep'pe) 1807–82; It. patriot & general: leader in movement to unify Italy
**gar·ish** (ger'ish) *adj.* [prob. < ME. *gauren*, to stare] too bright or gaudy; showy —**gar'ish·ly** *adv.* —**gar'ish·ness** *n.*

GARGOYLE

**gar·land** (gär'lənd) *n.* [< OFr. *garlande*] a wreath of flowers, leaves, etc. —*vt.* to form into or decorate with garlands

**Gar·land** (gär'lənd) [after A. *Garland*, U.S. attorney general (1885–89)] city in NE Tex.: suburb of Dallas: pop. 139,000

**gar·lic** (gär'lik) *n.* [< OE. < *gar*, a spear + *leac*, a leek] 1. a bulbous plant of the lily family 2. its strong-smelling bulb, made up of small sections called cloves, used as a seasoning —**gar'lick·y** *adj.*

**gar·ment** (gär'mənt) *n.* [< OFr. *garnement* < *garnir*: see GARNISH] any article of clothing —*vt.* to clothe

**gar·ner** (gär'nər) *n.* [< OFr. < L. *granarium* < *granum*, GRAIN] 1. a granary 2. a store of something —*vt.* 1. to gather up and store 2. to get or earn 3. to collect

**gar·net** (gär'nit) *n.* [< OFr. < ML. *granatus* < *granatum*, garnet, lit., POMEGRANATE] 1. any of a group of hard silicate minerals, chiefly crystalline: red varieties are used as gems 2. a deep red

**gar·nish** (gär'nish) *vt.* [< OFr. *garnir*, to furnish, protect < Gmc.] 1. to decorate; adorn; trim 2. to decorate (food) with something that adds color or flavor 3. *Law* to bring garnishment proceedings against —*n.* 1. a decoration; ornament 2. something used to garnish food, as parsley

**gar·nish·ee** (gär'nə shē') *n. Law* a person served with a garnishment —*vt.* **-eed', -ee'ing** *Law* 1. to attach (a debtor's property, wages, etc.) by the authority of a court, so that it can be used to pay the debt 2. to serve with a garnishment

**gar·nish·ment** (gär'nish mənt) *n.* 1. a decoration; embellishment 2. *Law* a notice ordering a person not to dispose of a defendant's property or money in his possession pending settlement of the lawsuit

**gar·ni·ture** (gär'ni chər) *n.* garnish; decoration

**gar·pike** (gär'pīk') *n. same as* GAR

**gar·ret** (gar'it) *n.* [ME. *garite*, a watchtower, loft < OFr. < *garir*, to watch < Frank.] the space or rooms just below the sloping roof of a house; attic

**gar·ri·son** (gar'ə s'n) *n.* [< OFr. < *garir* (see GARRET)] 1. troops stationed in a fort 2. a military post or station —*vt.* 1. to station troops in (a fortified place) for its defense 2. to place (troops) on duty in a garrison

**Gar·ri·son** (gar'ə s'n), **William Lloyd** 1805–79; U.S. editor, lecturer, & abolitionist leader

**gar·rote** (gə rät', -rōt') *n.* [Sp., orig., a stick used to wind a cord < OFr. < Frank.] 1. *a)* a method of execution, as formerly in Spain, by strangling with an iron collar *b)* the iron collar so used 2. *a)* a cord, length of wire, etc. for strangling a person in a surprise attack *b)* a disabling by strangling in this way —*vt.* **-rot'ed** or **-rot'ted, -rot'ing** or **-rot'ting** 1. to execute or attack with a garrote or by strangling 2. to disable by strangling, as in an attack for robbery Also sp. **ga·rotte', gar·rotte'** —**gar·rot'er** *n.*

**gar·ru·lous** (gar'ə ləs, gar'yoo-) *adj.* [< L. < *garrire*, to chatter] talking much or too much, esp. about unimportant things; loquacious —**gar·ru·li·ty** (gə rōo'lə tē), **gar'ru·lous·ness** *n.* —**gar'ru·lous·ly** *adv.*

**gar·ter** (gär'tər) *n.* [< ONormFr. *gartier* < OFr. *garet*, the back of the knee < Celt.] 1. an elastic band, or a fastener suspended from a band, girdle, etc., for holding a stocking or sock in position 2. [G-] *a)* the badge of the Order of the Garter, the highest order of British knighthood *b)* the order itself —*vt.* to fasten with a garter

**garter belt** a wide belt, usually of elastic fabric, with garters suspended from it, worn by women

**garter snake** any of various small, harmless, striped snakes common in N. America

**Gar·y** (ger'ē, gar'ē) [< OE. hyp. *Garwig*, lit., spear (of) battle < *gar*, spear + *wig*, battle] 1. a masculine name 2. [after E. *Gary* (1846–1927), U.S. industrialist] city in NW Ind., on Lake Michigan: pop. 152,000 (met. area 639,000)

**gas** (gas) *n.* [ModL., coined by the Belgian chemist, Van Helmont (1577–1644), after Paracelsus' use of Gr. *chaos*, CHAOS, to mean "air"] 1. the fluid form of a substance in which it can expand indefinitely; form that is neither liquid nor solid; vapor 2. any mixture of flammable gases used for lighting, heating, or cooking 3. any gas used as an anesthetic 4. any substance dispersed through the atmosphere, as in war, to act as a poison, irritant, or asphyxiant 5. gaseous matter formed in the stomach, bowels, etc. 6. [Colloq.] *a) short for* GASOLINE *b)* the accelerator in an automobile, etc. 7. [Slang] *a)* idle or boastful talk *b)* a person or thing that is very pleasing, exciting, etc. 8. *Mining* a mixture of firedamp with air that explodes if ignited —*vt.* **gassed, gas'sing** 1. to supply with gas 2. to subject to the action of gas 3. to injure or kill by gas, as in war 4. [Slang] to thrill, delight, etc. —*vi.* [Slang] to talk idly or boastfully —*adj.* of or using gas

**gas chamber** a room in which people are put to be killed with poison gas

**Gas·con** (gas'kən) *adj.* 1. of Gascony or its people, reputed to be boastful 2. [g-] boastful —*n.* 1. a native of Gascony 2. [g-] a boaster

**gas·con·ade** (gas'kə nād') *n.* [see prec. & -ADE] boastful or blustering talk —*vi.* **-ad'ed, -ad'ing** to boast or bluster

**Gas·co·ny** (gas'kə nē) region on the SW coast of France: Fr. name, **Gas·cogne** (gås kôn'y')

**gas·e·ous** (gas'ē əs, gas'yəs) *adj.* 1. of, like, or in the form of gas 2. [Colloq.] *same as* GASSY (sense 1) —**gas'e·ous·ness** *n.*

**gas fitter** a person whose work is installing and repairing gas pipes and fixtures

**gash** (gash) *vt.* [< OFr. *garser*, ult. < Gr. *charassein*, to sharpen, cut] to make a long, deep cut in; slash —*n.* a long, deep cut

**gas·i·fy** (gas'ə fī') *vt., vi.* **-fied', -fy'ing** to change into gas —**gas'i·fi·ca'tion** *n.*

**gas jet** 1. a flame of illuminating gas 2. a nozzle or burner at the end of a gas fixture

**gas·ket** (gas'kit) *n.* [prob. < OFr. *garcette*, small cord] 1. a piece or ring of rubber, metal, etc. placed around a piston or joint to make it leakproof 2. *Naut.* a rope or cord by which a furled sail is tied to the yard

**gas·light** (gas'līt') *n.* 1. the light produced by burning illuminating gas 2. a gas jet or burner —*adj.* of or characteristic of the period of gaslight illumination [*gaslight* melodrama]

**gas mantle** a mantle (*n.* 3) for a gas burner

**gas mask** a filtering device worn over the face to protect against breathing in poisonous gases

**gas·o·hol** (gas'ə hôl) *n.* a mixture of gasoline and alcohol, usually 90 percent unleaded gasoline and 10 percent ethyl alcohol, used as a motor fuel

**gas·o·line, gas·o·lene** (gas'ə lēn', gas'ə lēn') *n.* [GAS + -OL(E) + -INE[4], -ENE] a volatile, highly flammable, colorless liquid produced by the distillation of petroleum and used chiefly as a fuel in internal-combustion engines

**gas·om·e·ter** (gas äm'ə tər) *n.* 1. a container for holding and measuring gas 2. a tank for gas

**gasp** (gasp) *vi.* [< ON. *geispa*, to yawn] to inhale suddenly, as in surprise, or breathe with effort, as in choking —*vt.* to say with gasps —*n.* a gasping; catching of the breath with difficulty

**Gas·pé Peninsula** (gas pā') peninsula in S Quebec, Canada, extending into the Gulf of St. Lawrence

**gas station** *same as* SERVICE STATION (sense 2)

**gas·sy** (gas'ē) *adj.* **-si·er, -si·est** 1. full of, containing, or producing gas; esp., flatulent 2. like gas 3. [Colloq.] full of talk —**gas'si·ness** *n.*

**gas·tric** (gas'trik) *adj.* [GASTR(O)- + -IC] of, in, or near the stomach

**gastric juice** the acid digestive fluid produced by glands in the mucous membrane lining the stomach: it contains enzymes and hydrochloric acid

**gastric ulcer** an ulcer of the stomach lining

**gas·tri·tis** (gas trīt'is) *n.* [GASTR(O)- + -ITIS] inflammation of the stomach, esp. of the stomach lining

**gas·tro-** [< Gr. *gaster*, the stomach] *a combining form meaning* the stomach (and): also **gastr-**

**gas·tro·en·ter·i·tis** (gas'trō en'tə rīt'is) *n.* [< GASTRO- + ENTER(O)- + -ITIS] an inflammation of the stomach and the intestines

**gas·tro·in·tes·ti·nal** (-in tes'tə n'l) *adj.* of the stomach and the intestines

**gas·tro·nome** (gas'trə nōm') *n.* a person who enjoys and has a discriminating taste for foods: also **gas·tron'o·mer** (-trän'ə mər), **gas·tron'o·mist**

**gas·tron·o·my** (gas trän'ə mē) *n.* [< Fr. < Gr. < *gaster*, the stomach + *nomos*, a rule] the art of good eating —**gas'tro·nom'ic** (-trə näm'ik), **gas'tro·nom'i·cal** *adj.* —**gas'tro·nom'i·cal·ly** *adv.*

**gas·tro·pod** (gas'trə päd') *n.* [< ModL. < GASTRO- + -POD] any of a large class of mollusks having a single, straight or spiral shell, as snails, limpets, etc., or no shell, as certain slugs: most gastropods move by means of a broad, muscular, ventral foot

**gas·tru·la** (gas'troo lə) *n., pl.* **-lae' (-lē')**, **-las** [ModL. dim. < Gr. *gaster*, the stomach] an embryo in an early stage of development, consisting of a sac with two layers, the ectoderm and endoderm

**gat** (gat) *archaic pt. of* GET

**gate** (gāt) *n.* [< OE. *geat*] 1. a movable structure, esp. one that swings on hinges, controlling entrance or exit through an opening in a fence or wall 2. an opening for passage through a fence or wall, with or without such a structure; gateway 3. any means of entrance or exit 4. a movable barrier, as at a railroad crossing **5.** a structure controlling the flow of water, as in a pipe, canal, etc. **6.** *a)* the total amount of admission money paid by spectators to a performance or exhibition *b)* the total number of such spectators **7.** *Electronics* a circuit that passes signals only when certain input conditions are satisfied —**get the gate** [Slang] to be dismissed or rejected —**give (someone) the gate** to dismiss or reject (someone)

**gate·fold** (gāt'fōld') *n.* a page larger than the others in a magazine or book, bound so that it can be folded out

**gate·house** (-hous') *n.* a house beside or over a gateway, used as a porter's lodge, etc.

**gate·keep·er** (-kē'pər) *n.* a person in charge of a gate to control passage through it: also **gate'man,** *pl.* **-men**

**gate·leg table** (-leg') a table with drop leaves supported by gatelike legs that swing back to let the leaves drop: also **gate'legged' table**

**gate·post** (-pōst') *n.* the post on which a gate is hung or to which it is fastened when closed

**gate·way** (-wā') *n.* **1.** an entrance in a fence, wall, etc. fitted with a gate **2.** a means of access

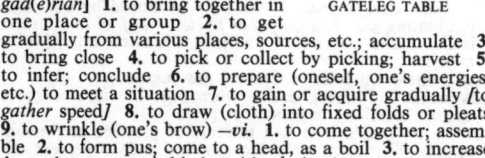

GATELEG TABLE

**gath·er** (gath'ər) *vt.* [< OE. *gad(e)rian*] **1.** to bring together in one place or group **2.** to get gradually from various places, sources, etc.; accumulate **3.** to bring close **4.** to pick or collect by picking; harvest **5.** to infer; conclude **6.** to prepare (oneself, one's energies, etc.) to meet a situation **7.** to gain or acquire gradually *[to gather speed]* **8.** to draw (cloth) into fixed folds or pleats **9.** to wrinkle (one's brow) —*vi.* **1.** to come together; assemble **2.** to form pus; come to a head, as a boil **3.** to increase **4.** to become wrinkled: said of the brow —*n.* a pleat —**gath'er·er** *n.*

**gath·er·ing** (-iŋ) *n.* **1.** the act of one that gathers **2.** what is gathered; specif., *a)* a meeting; crowd *b)* a series of pleats **3.** a boil or abscess

**Gat·ling gun** (gat'liŋ) [after R. J. *Gatling,* 19th-c. U.S. inventor] an early kind of machine gun having a rotating cluster of barrels around an axis

**gauche** (gōsh) *adj.* [Fr. < MFr. *gauchir,* to become warped, ult. < Frank.] lacking social grace; awkward; tactless —**gauche'ly** *adv.* —**gauche'ness** *n.*

**gau·che·rie** (gō'shə rē') *n.* [see prec.] **1.** awkwardness; tactlessness **2.** a gauche act or expression

**gau·cho** (gou'chō) *n., pl.* **-chos** [AmSp.] a cowboy of mixed Indian and Spanish ancestry, living on the S. American pampas

**gaud** (gôd) *n.* [ME. *gaude,* a trinket, prob. ult. < L. *gaudium,* joy] a cheap, showy ornament

**gaud·y** (gôd'ē) *adj.* **gaud'i·er, gaud'i·est** [prec. + -Y²] bright and showy, but in bad taste; cheaply ornate —**gaud'i·ly** *adv.* —**gaud'i·ness** *n.*

**gauge** (gāj) *n.* [< ONormFr. *gaugier,* to gauge] **1.** a standard measure or scale of measurement **2.** dimensions, capacity, thickness, etc. **3.** any device for measuring something, as the thickness of wire, steam pressure, etc. **4.** any means of estimating **5.** the distance between the rails of a railway: cf. STANDARD GAUGE, BROAD GAUGE, NARROW GAUGE **6.** the distance between parallel wheels at opposite ends of an axle **7.** the size of the bore of a shotgun expressed in terms of the number per pound of round lead balls of a diameter equal to that of the bore **8.** the thickness of sheet metal, diameter of wire, etc. **9.** the fineness of a machine-knitted fabric expressed in terms of the number of loops per 1½ inches —*vt.* **gauged, gaug'ing 1.** to measure accurately by means of a gauge **2.** to measure the size, amount, or capacity of **3.** to estimate; judge **4.** to make conform with a standard —**gauge'a·ble** *adj.* —**gaug'er** *n.*

WIRE GAUGE

**Gau·guin** (gō gaṅ'), (Eugène Henri) **Paul** (pôl) 1848–1903; Fr. painter, in Tahiti after 1891

**Gaul** (gôl) ancient division of the Roman Empire, including what is now mainly France & Belgium (**Transalpine Gaul**) and N Italy (**Cisalpine Gaul**) —*n.* **1.** any of the Celtic-speaking people of Gaul **2.** a Frenchman

**Gaul·ish** (-ish) *adj.* of Gaul or the Gauls —*n.* the Celtic language spoken in ancient Gaul

**gaunt** (gônt) *adj.* [ME. *gawnte, gant* < ?] **1.** thin and bony; hollow-eyed and haggard, as from great hunger or age **2.** looking grim, forbidding, or desolate —**gaunt'ly** *adv.* —**gaunt'ness** *n.*

**gaunt·let** (gônt'lit, gänt'-) *n.* [< OFr. dim. of *gant,* a glove < Frank.] **1.** a medieval glove, usually of leather covered with metal plates, worn to protect the hand in combat **2.** a long glove with a flaring cuff, or this cuff, covering the lower part of the arm —**take up the gauntlet** to

accept a challenge —**throw down the gauntlet** to challenge, as to combat —**gaunt'let·ed** *adj.*

**gaunt·let²** (gônt'lit, gänt'-) *n. same as* GANTLET¹

**gauss** (gous) *n.* [after K. *Gauss* (1777–1855), Ger. scientist] *Elec.* a cgs unit used in measuring magnetic induction or magnetic flux density

**gauze** (gôz) *n.* [Fr. *gaze,* prob. < Sp. < Ar. *kazz,* raw silk < Per.] **1.** any very thin, transparent, loosely woven material, as of cotton or silk **2.** a thin mist

**gauz·y** (gôz'ē) *adj.* **gauz'i·er, gauz'i·est** thin, light, and transparent, like gauze; diaphanous —**gauz'i·ness** *n.*

**gave** (gāv) *pt. of* GIVE

**gav·el** (gav'l) *n.* [< Scot. *gable,* a tool < OE. *gafol*] a small mallet rapped on the table by a chairman, judge, etc. to call for attention or silence

**ga·vi·al** (gā'vē əl) *n.* [Fr. < Hindi *ghaṛiyāl*] a large crocodile of India, with a very long snout

**ga·votte** (gə vät') *n.* [Fr. < Pr. *gavoto,* dance of the *Gavots,* an Alpine people] **1.** a 17th-cent. dance like the minuet, but livelier **2.** the music for this, in 4/4 time Also sp. **ga·vot'**

**Ga·wain** (gā'win, -wān) [Fr.] *Arthurian Legend* a knight of the Round Table, nephew of King Arthur

**gawk** (gôk) *n.* [prob. dial. var. of *gowk,* a simpleton] a clumsy, stupid fellow; simpleton —*vi.* to stare in a stupid way —**gawk'ish** *adj.*

**gawk·y** (gô'kē) *adj.* **gawk'i·er, gawk'i·est** [prob. < prec.] awkward; clumsy; ungainly —**gawk'i·ly** *adv.* —**gawk'i·ness** *n.*

**gay** (gā) *adj.* [< OFr.] **1.** joyous and lively; merry **2.** bright; brilliant *[gay colors]* **3.** given to social pleasures *[a gay life]* **4.** wanton; licentious *[a gay dog]* **5.** homosexual —*n.* a homosexual; esp., a male homosexual —**gay'ness** *n.*

**Gay** (gā), **John** 1685–1732; Eng. poet & playwright

**gay·e·ty** (gā'ə tē) *n., pl.* **-ties** *same as* GAIETY

**gay·ly** (gā'lē) *adv. same as* GAILY

**gaze** (gāz) *vi.* **gazed, gaz'ing** [< Scand.] to look intently and steadily; stare, as in wonder —*n.* a steady look —**gaz'er** *n.*

**ga·ze·bo** (gə zē'bō, -zā'-) *n., pl.* **-bos, -boes** [< ?] a turret, balcony, or summerhouse with an extensive view

**ga·zelle** (gə zel') *n., pl.* **-zelles', -zelle':** see PLURAL, II, D, 1 [Fr. < Ar. *ghazāl*] any of various small, swift, graceful antelopes of Africa, the Near East, and Asia, with horns that twist back in a spiral and large, lustrous eyes

**ga·zette** (gə zet') *n.* [Fr. < It. *gazzetta* < dial. *gazeta,* a small coin, price of a newspaper] **1.** a newspaper **2.** in England, any of various official publications containing announcements and bulletins —*vt.* **-zet'ted, -zet'ting** [Chiefly Brit.] to announce or list in a gazette

**gaz·et·teer** (gaz'ə tir') *n.* **1.** [Archaic] a person who writes for a gazette **2.** a dictionary or index of geographical names

**gaz·pa·cho** (gäz pä'chō) *n.* [Sp.] a Spanish soup made with tomatoes, chopped cucumbers, onions, oil, vinegar, etc. and served cold

**G.B.** Great Britain

**GCA** *Aeron.* ground control approach

**G clef** *same as* TREBLE CLEF

**GCT, G.C.T.** Greenwich civil time

**Gd** *Chem.* gadolinium

**Gdansk** (g'dänsk') seaport in N Poland, on the Baltic Sea: pop. 330,000: Ger. name, DANZIG

**Ge** *Chem.* germanium

**gear** (gir) *n.* [prob. < ON. *gervi,* preparation] **1.** clothing; apparel **2.** apparatus or equipment for some particular task, as a workman's tools, a harness, etc. **3.** *a)* a toothed wheel, disk, etc. designed to mesh with another or with the thread of a worm *b)* [*often pl.*] a system of two or more gears meshed together so that the motion of one is passed on to the others *c)* a specific adjustment of such a system: in motor-vehicle transmissions, *high gear* provides greatest speed and *low gear* greatest power *d)* any part of a mechanism performing a specific function *[the steering gear]* —*vt.* **1.** to furnish with gear; harness **2.** to adapt (one thing) so as to conform with another *[to gear production to demand]* **3.** *a)* to connect by gears *b)* to furnish with gears —*vi.* to be in, or come into, proper adjustment or working order —**in (or out of) gear 1.** (not) connected to the motor **2.** (not) in proper adjustment or working order —**shift gears 1.** to change from one gear arrangement to another **2.** to change one's method or approach

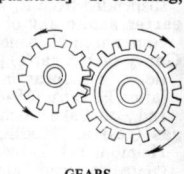

GEARS

**gear·box** (-bäks') *n.* the unit consisting of the transmission gears in a transmission system

**gear·ing** (-iŋ) *n.* **1.** the act or manner of fitting a machine with gears **2.** a system of gears or other parts for transmitting motion

**gear·shift** (-shift') *n.* a device for connecting or disconnecting any of a number of sets of transmission gears to a motor, etc.

**gear·wheel** (-hwēl′, -wēl′) *n.* a toothed wheel in a system of gears; cogwheel

**geck·o** (gek′ō) *n., pl.* **-os, -oes** [Malay *gekok*, echoic of its cry] a soft-skinned, insect-eating, tropical lizard with suction pads on its feet

**gee¹** (jē) *interj., n.* [Early ModE. < ?] a word of command to a horse, ox, etc. meaning "turn to the right!" —*vt., vi.* **geed, gee′ing** to turn to the right Opposed to HAW²

**gee²** (jē) *interj.* [euphemistic contr. < JE(SUS)] [Slang] an exclamation of surprise, wonder, etc.

**geese** (gēs) *n. pl. of* GOOSE

**gee·zer** (gē′zər) *n.* [< dial. *guiser*, a mummer < GUISE] [Slang] an eccentric old man

**Ge·hen·na** (gi hen′ə) [< Heb. *gēhinnōm*] *Bible* the valley of Hinnom, near Jerusalem, where refuse was burned: translated in the New Testament as "hell" —*n.* any place of torment

**Gei·ger counter** (gī′gər) [after H. *Geiger* (1882–1945), Ger. physicist] an instrument for detecting and counting ionizing particles: a refined version (**Geiger-Müller counter**) with an amplifying system is used for detecting and measuring radioactivity

**gei·sha** (gā′shə) *n., pl.* **-sha, -shas** [Jap.] a Japanese girl trained in singing, dancing, etc., to serve as a hired companion to men

**gel** (jel) *n.* [< ff.] a jellylike substance formed by the coagulation of a colloidal solution into a solid phase —*vi.* **gelled, gel′ling** to form a gel

**gel·a·tin, gel·a·tine** (jel′ət ′n) *n.* [< Fr. < It. < *gelata*, a jelly < pp. of L. *gelare*, to freeze] **1.** the tasteless, odorless, brittle substance extracted by boiling bones, hoofs, etc.; also, a similar vegetable substance: gelatin dissolves in hot water, forming a jellylike substance when cool, and is used in various foods, photographic film, etc. **2.** something, as a jelly, made with gelatin

**ge·lat·i·nize** (jə lat′′n īz′, jel′ət ′n īz′) *vt.* **-nized′, -niz′-ing** **1.** to change into gelatin or gelatinous matter **2.** *Photog.* to coat with gelatin —*vi.* to be changed into gelatin or gelatinous matter —**ge·lat′i·ni·za′tion** *n.*

**ge·lat·i·nous** (jə lat′′n əs) *adj.* **1.** of or containing gelatin **2.** like gelatin or jelly; viscous —**ge·lat′i·nous·ly** *adv.* —**ge·lat′i·nous·ness** *n.*

**geld** (geld) *vt.* **geld′ed** or **gelt, geld′ing** [< ON. *gelda* < *geldr*, barren] **1.** to castrate (esp. a horse) **2.** to deprive of essential vigor; weaken

**geld·ing** (gel′diŋ) *n.* a gelded animal; esp., a castrated horse

**gel·id** (jel′id) *adj.* [L. *gelidus* < *gelu*, frost] extremely cold; icy —**ge·lid·i·ty** (jə lid′ə tē) *n.*

**Gel·sen·kir·chen** (gel′zən kir′Hən) city in W West Germany, in the Ruhr valley: pop. 356,000

**gem** (jem) *n.* [< OFr. < L. *gemma*, a bud, gem] **1.** a precious or, occas., semiprecious stone, cut and polished for use as a jewel **2.** a highly valued person or thing **3.** a kind of muffin —*vt.* **gemmed, gem′-ming** to adorn or set with or as with gems

**gem·i·nate** (jem′ə nāt′) *adj.* [< L. pp. of *geminare*, to double < *geminus*, a twin] growing or combined in pairs; coupled —*vt.* **-nat′ed, -nat′ing** to arrange in pairs; double —*vi.* to become doubled or paired —**gem′i·na′tion** *n.*

CUTS OF GEM
(A, marquise; B, emerald; C, round; D, pear-shaped)

**Gem·i·ni** (jem′ə nī′, -nē′) [L., twins] **1.** a N constellation containing the stars Castor and Pollux, represented as twins seated **2.** the third sign of the zodiac: see ZODIAC, illus.

**gem·ma** (jem′ə) *n., pl.* **-mae** (-ē) [L.: cf. GEM] *Biol.* a budlike outgrowth which becomes detached and develops into a new organism

**gem·mate** (jem′āt) *adj.* [< L. pp. of *gemmare* < *gemma*, a bud] having, or reproducing by, gemmae —*vi.* **-mat·ed, -mat·ing** to have, or reproduce by, gemmae; bud —**gem·ma′tion** *n.*

**gem·mule** (jem′yool) *n. Biol.* a small gemma

**gems·bok** (gemz′bäk′) *n., pl.* **-bok′, -boks′:** see PLURAL, II, D, 2 [Afrik. < G. < *gemse* < VL. *camox*, CHAMOIS + *bock*, a buck] a large antelope of S Africa, with long, straight horns and a tufted tail

**gem·stone** (jem′stōn′) *n.* any mineral that can be used as a gem when cut and polished

**-gen** (jən, jen) [< Fr. < Gr. < base of *gignesthai*, to be born] *a suffix meaning:* **1.** something that produces [*oxygen*,

*estrogen*] **2.** something produced (in a specified way) [*zymogen*]

**Gen. 1.** General **2.** Genesis

**gen. 1.** gender **2.** general **3.** genitive

**gen·darme** (zhän′därm; *Fr.* zhän dàrm′) *n., pl.* **-darmes** (-därmz; *Fr.* -dàrm′) [Fr., ult. < L. *gens*, a people + *de*, of + *arma*, arms] **1.** in France, Belgium, etc., a soldier serving as an armed policeman **2.** any policeman: a humorous usage

**gen·dar·me·rie** (zhän där′mə rē; *Fr.* zhän dàr mə rē′) *n.* [Fr.] gendarmes collectively: also **gen·dar′mer·y**

**gen·der** (jen′dər) *n.* [< OFr. *gendre* < L. *genus*, origin, kind] **1.** *Gram. a)* the classification by which nouns, pronouns, adjectives, etc. are variously grouped and inflected as masculine, feminine, or neuter: in English, only some nouns and the third person singular pronouns are distinguished according to gender *b)* any one of such groupings **2.** [Colloq.] sex

**gene** (jēn) *n.* [< G. *gen* < *pangen* (< Gr. *pan-*, PAN- + *-gen*, -GEN)] *Genetics* any of the units occurring at specific points on the chromosomes, by which hereditary characters are transmitted and determined: see DEOXYRIBONUCLEIC ACID (DNA)

**ge·ne·al·o·gy** (jē′nē äl′ə jē, -al′ə jē) *n., pl.* **-gies** [< OFr. < LL. < Gr. < *genea*, race, stock + *-logia*, -LOGY] **1.** a chart or recorded history of the ancestry or descent of a person or family **2.** the study of family descent **3.** descent from an ancestor; pedigree; lineage —**ge′ne·a·log′i·cal** (-ə läj′i k′l, -əlōj′i k′l) *adj.* —**ge′ne·a·log′i·cal·ly** *adv.* —**ge′ne·al′o·gist** *n.*

**gen·er·a** (jen′ər ə) *n. pl. of* GENUS

**gen·er·al** (jen′ər əl, jen′rəl) *adj.* [< OFr. < L. *generalis* < *genus* (gen. *generis*), kind, class] **1.** of, for, or from the whole or all; not particular or specialized [a *general* anesthetic] **2.** of, for, or applying to a whole genus, kind, class, order, or race [the *general* classifications of matter] **3.** existing or occurring extensively; widespread [a *general* unrest] **4.** most common; usual [the *general* spelling of a word] **5.** concerned with the main or overall features; lacking in details **6.** not precise; vague [to speak in *general* terms] **7.** highest in rank [an attorney *general*] —*n.* **1.** the main or overall fact, idea, etc. **2.** the head of a religious order **3.** any of various military officers ranking above a colonel; specif., *a) U.S. Army & U.S. Air Force* an officer ranking below a GENERAL OF THE ARMY (or AIR FORCE) and above a LIEUTENANT GENERAL *b) U.S. Marine Corps* an officer of the highest rank —**in general 1.** in the main; usually **2.** without specific details —**gen′er·al·ness** *n.*

**general assembly 1.** in some States of the U.S., the legislative assembly **2.** [G- A-] the legislative assembly of the United Nations

**General Court** the legislature of New Hampshire or Massachusetts

**general election 1.** an election to choose from among candidates previously nominated **2.** a nationwide or Statewide election

**gen·er·al·is·si·mo** (jen′ər ə lis′ə mō′, jen′rə-) *n., pl.* **-mos′** [It., superl. of *generale*, GENERAL] in certain countries, **1.** the commander in chief of all the armed forces **2.** the commanding officer of several armies in the field

**gen·er·al·i·ty** (jen′ə ral′ə tē) *n., pl.* **-ties 1.** the condition or quality of being general **2.** a general or nonspecific statement, expression, etc. **3.** the bulk; main body

**gen·er·al·i·za·tion** (jen′ər ə li zā′shən, jen′rəl i-) *n.* **1.** the act or process of generalizing **2.** a general idea, statement, etc. resulting from this

**gen·er·al·ize** (jen′ər ə līz′, jen′rə-) *vt.* **-ized′, -iz′ing** to make general; esp., *a)* to state in terms of a general law *b)* to infer or derive (a general law or precept) from (particular instances) *c)* to emphasize the general character rather than specific details of *d)* to cause to be widely known or used —*vi.* **1.** to formulate general principles from particulars **2.** to talk in generalities **3.** to become general or spread throughout an area

**gen·er·al·ly** (-lē; *also* jen′ər lē) *adv.* **1.** widely; popularly; extensively **2.** in most instances; usually **3.** in a general way; not specifically

**general officer** *Mil.* any officer above a colonel in rank

**general of the army** (or **air force**) the highest rank in the U.S. Army (or U.S. Air Force), having the insignia of five stars

**general practitioner** a practicing physician who does not specialize in any particular field of medicine

**gen·er·al-pur·pose** (-pur′pəs) *adj.* having a variety of uses; suitable for general use

**gen·er·al·ship** (-ship′) *n.* **1.** *a)* the rank, tenure, or authority of a general *b)* the military skill of a general **2.** highly skillful leadership

**general staff** *Mil.* a group of officers who assist the commander in planning and supervising operations

**gen·er·ate** (jen′ə rāt′) *vt.* **-at′ed, -at′ing** [< L. pp. of *generare* < *genus*, race, kind] **1.** to produce (offspring); beget **2.** to bring into being; cause to be **3.** to originate or produce by a physical or chemical process **4.** *Math.* to trace out or form (a line, plane, figure, or solid) by the motion of a point, line, or plane

**gen·er·a·tion** (jen′ə rā′shən) *n.* **1.** the act or process of producing offspring **2.** a bringing into being; production **3.** a single stage in the succession of descent [father and son are two *generations*] **4.** the average period (about thirty years) between the birth of successive generations **5.** *a)* all the people born at about the same time *b)* a group of such people having something in common **6.** *Math.* the generating of a line, figure, etc. —**gen′er·a′tion·al** *adj.*

**gen·er·a·tive** (jen′ər ə tiv, -ə rāt′iv) *adj.* of, or having the power of, generation or production —**gen′er·a′tive·ly** *adv.* —**gen′er·a′tive·ness** *n.*

**gen·er·a·tor** (jen′ə rāt′ər) *n.* a person or thing that generates; specif., *a)* a machine for producing gas or steam *b)* a machine for changing mechanical energy into electrical energy; dynamo

**gen·er·a·trix** (jen′ə rā′triks) *n., pl.* **-er·a·tri′ces** (-ər ə-trī′sēz, -ə rā′trə sēz′) *Math.* a point, line, or plane whose motion generates a line, plane, figure, or solid

**ge·ner·ic** (jə ner′ik) *adj.* [< ML.: see GENUS & -IC] **1.** of, applied to, or referring to a whole kind, class, or group; inclusive or general **2.** that is not a trademark **3.** *Biol.* of or characteristic of a genus —**ge·ner′i·cal·ly** *adv.*

**gen·er·os·i·ty** (jen′ə räs′ə tē) *n.* **1.** the quality of being generous; specif., *a)* magnanimity *b)* unselfishness **2.** *pl.* **-ties** a generous act

**gen·er·ous** (jen′ər əs) *adj.* [L. *generosus*, of noble birth, excellent < *genus*: see GENUS] **1.** noble-minded; gracious; magnanimous **2.** willing to give or share; unselfish **3.** large; ample [*generous* portions] **4.** full-flavored and strong: said of wine —**gen′er·ous·ly** *adv.* —**gen′er·ous·ness** *n.*

**gen·e·sis** (jen′ə sis) *n., pl.* **-ses′** (-sēz′) [< OE. & LL. < L. < Gr. < *gignesthai*, to be born] a beginning; origin —[G-] the first book of the Bible, giving an account of the Creation

**-gen·e·sis** (jen′ə sis) *a combining form meaning* origination, creation, evolution (of something specified)

**gen·et** (jen′ət) *n. same as* JENNET

**ge·net·ic** (jə net′ik) *adj.* [< GENESIS] **1.** of the genesis, or origin, of something **2.** of genetics Also **ge·net′i·cal** —**ge·net′i·cal·ly** *adv.*

**genetic code** the order in which four chemical constituents are arranged in DNA molecules for transmitting genetic information to the cells

**ge·net·ics** (-iks) *n.pl.* [*with sing. v.*] [< GENETIC] the branch of biology that deals with heredity and variation in similar or related animals and plants —**ge·net′i·cist** (-ə sist) *n.*

**Ge·ne·va** (jə nē′və) **1.** city in Switzerland, on Lake Geneva: pop. 171,000 **2.** Lake (of), lake in SW Switzerland, on the border of France

**Geneva Convention** an international agreement signed at Geneva in 1864, establishing a code, later revised, for the care and protection in wartime of the sick, wounded, and prisoners of war

**Gen·e·vieve** (jen′ə vēv′) [Fr. < LL. *Genovefa* < ? Celt.] a feminine name

**Gen·ghis Khan** (geŋ′gis kän′, jeŋ′-) (born *Temuchin*) 1162?-1227; Mongol conqueror of C Asia

**ge·nial** (jēn′yəl, jē′nē əl) *adj.* [L. *genialis*, of birth < *genius*, GENIUS] **1.** promoting life and growth; warm and mild [a *genial* climate] **2.** cheerful, friendly, and sympathetic; amiable —**ge·ni·al·i·ty** (jē′nē al′ə tē, jēn yal′-) *n.* —**ge′nial·ly** *adv.*

**-gen·ic** (jen′ik) *a combining form:* **1.** *used to form adjectives corresponding to nouns ending in* -GEN *or* -GENY [*phylogenic*] **2.** *meaning* suitable to [*photogenic*]

**ge·nie** (jē′nē) *n.* [Fr. *génie*] *same as* JINNI

**gen·i·tal** (jen′ə t'l) *adj.* [< OFr. < L. *genitalis* < pp. of *genere, gignere*, to beget] **1.** of reproduction or the sexual organs **2.** *Psychoanalysis* of an early stage of psychosexual development focusing on the genital organs

**gen·i·tals** (-t'lz) *n.pl.* [< prec.] the reproductive organs; esp., the external sex organs: also **gen′i·ta′li·a** (-tāl′yə, -tā′lē ə)

**gen·i·tive** (jen′ə tiv) *adj.* [< OFr. < L. (*casus*) *genitivus*, lit., case of origin] designating, of, or in a case, as in Latin, shown by grammatical inflection or by analytical construction and typically expressing possession, source, etc. —*n.* **1.** the genitive case **2.** a word or construction in the genitive case —**gen′i·ti′val** (-tī′v′l) *adj.* —**gen′i·ti′val·ly** *adv.*

**gen·i·to·u·ri·nar·y** (jen′ə tō yoor′ə ner′ē) *adj.* designating or of the genital and urinary organs together

**ge·nius** (jēn′yəs, jē′nē əs) *n., pl.* **ge′nius·es** for 3, 4, 5; **ge·ni·i** (jē′nē ī′) for 1 & 2 [L., guardian spirit < base of *genere, gignere*, to produce] **1.** *a)* [*often* G-] the guardian spirit of a person, place, etc. *b)* either of two spirits, one good and one evil, supposed to influence one's destiny *c)* a person considered as having strong influence over another **2.** *same as* JINNI **3.** particular character or spirit of a nation, place, age, etc. **4.** a great natural ability or strong inclination (*for*) **5.** *a)* great mental and inventive ability *b)* a person having this *c)* popularly, any person with a very high intelligence quotient

**Gen·o·a** (jen′ə wə) seaport in NW Italy, on the Ligurian Sea: pop. 844,000: It. name, **Ge·no·va** (je′nō vä′) —**Gen′o·ese′** (-wēz′) *adj., n., pl.* **-ese′**

**gen·o·cide** (jen′ə sīd′) *n.* [< Gr. *genos*, race, kind + -CIDE] the systematic killing of, or a program of action intended to destroy, a whole national or ethnic group —**gen′o·ci′dal** (-sī′d′l) *adj.*

**-gen·ous** (jə nəs) [-GEN + -OUS] *a suffix meaning:* **1.** producing, generating [*nitrogenous*] **2.** produced by, generated in [*autogenous*]

**gen·re** (zhän′rə; *Fr.* zhän′r′) *n.* [Fr. < L. *genus:* see GENUS] **1.** a kind, or type, as of works of literature, art, etc. **2.** *same as* GENRE PAINTING

**genre painting** painting in which subjects from everyday life are treated realistically

**gens** (jenz) *n., pl.* **gen·tes** (jen′tēz) [L. < *gignere*, to beget] **1.** in ancient Rome, a clan united by descent through the male line from a common ancestor **2.** any tribe or clan

**gent** (jent) *n.* [Colloq.] a gentleman; man

**gen·teel** (jen tēl′) *adj.* [< Fr. *gentil* < L. *gentilis:* see GENTLE] **1.** formerly, elegant or fashionable **2.** excessively or affectedly refined, polite, etc. —**gen·teel′ly** *adv.* —**gen·teel′ness** *n.*

**gen·tian** (jen′shən) *n.* [< OFr. < L. *gentiana*] **1.** any of a large genus of plants with blue, white, red, or yellow flowers **2.** the bitter root of the yellow gentian

**gen·tile** (jen′tīl) *n.* [< Fr. *gentil* & L. *gentilis*, of the same gens, or clan] [*also* G-] **1.** any person not a Jew; specif., a Christian **2.** formerly, among Christians, a heathen or pagan **3.** among Mormons, any person not a Mormon —*adj.* [*also* G-] **1.** not Jewish **2.** heathen; pagan **3.** not Mormon

**gen·til·i·ty** (jen til′ə tē) *n., pl.* **-ties** [< OFr. < L. < *gentilis:* see ff.] **1.** the condition of belonging by birth to the upper classes **2.** the quality of being genteel

**gen·tle** (jent′'l) *adj.* **-tler, -tlest** [< OFr. < L. *gentilis*, of the same clan < *gens*, GENS] **1.** of the upper classes or polite society **2.** like or suitable to polite society; refined, courteous, etc. **3.** [Archaic] noble; chivalrous [a *gentle* knight] **4.** generous; kind **5.** easily handled; tame [a *gentle* dog] **6.** kindly; patient [a *gentle* disposition] **7.** not violent or harsh [a *gentle* tap] **8.** gradual [a *gentle* slope] —*vt.* **-tled, -tling** **1.** to tame or train (a horse) **2.** to calm as by stroking —**gen′tle·ness** *n.* —**gen′tly** *adv.*

**gen·tle·folk** (-fōk′) *n.pl.* people of high social standing: also **gen′tle·folks′**

**gen·tle·man** (-mən) *n., pl.* **-men** **1.** *a)* orig., a man born into a family of high social standing *b)* any man of independent means who does not work for a living **2.** a courteous, gracious man **3.** a valet: chiefly in **gentleman's gentleman** **4.** any man: polite term, as (chiefly in pl.) of address

**gen·tle·man-farm·er** (-fär′mər) *n., pl.* **gen′tle·men-farm′ers** a wealthy man who owns and manages a farm as an avocation

**gen·tle·man·ly** (-lē) *adj.* of, characteristic of, or fit for a gentleman; well-mannered: also **gen′tle·man·like′** —**gen′-tle·man·li·ness** *n.*

**gentlemen's (or gentleman's) agreement** an unwritten agreement secured only by the parties' pledge of honor and not legally binding

**gen·tle·wom·an** (jent′'l woom′ən) *n., pl.* **-wom′en** **1.** orig., a woman born into a family of high social standing; lady **2.** a courteous, gracious, considerate woman **3.** formerly, a woman in attendance on a lady of rank

**gen·try** (jen′trē) *n.* [< OFr. *genterise*, ult. < L. *gentilis:* see GENTLE] **1.** people of high social standing; esp., in Great Britain, the class of landowning people ranking just below the nobility **2.** people of a particular class or group

**gen·u·flect** (jen′yə flekt′) *vi.* [< ML. < L. *genu*, the knee + *flectere*, to bend] **1.** to bend the knee, as in reverence or worship **2.** to act submissively —**gen′u·flec′tion**, chiefly Brit. **gen′u·flex′ion** (-flek′shən) *n.* —**gen′u·flec′tor** *n.*

**gen·u·ine** (jen′yōo wən) *adj.* [L. *genuinus* < base of *gignere*, to be born] **1.** of the original stock; purebred **2.** really being what it is said to be; true; authentic **3.** sincere and frank; honest —**gen′u·ine·ly** *adv.* —**gen′u·ine·ness** *n.*

**ge·nus** (jē′nəs) *n., pl.* **gen·er·a** (jen′ər ə), sometimes **ge′nus·es** [L., birth, origin, race, kind] **1.** a class; kind; sort **2.** *Biol.* a classification of plants or animals with common distinguishing characteristics: a genus is the main subdivision of a family and includes one or more species; the genus name is capitalized, the species name is not (Ex.: *Homo sapiens*, modern man) **3.** *Logic* a class of things made up of subordinate classes, or species

**-gen·y** (jə nē) [< Gr.: see -GEN] *a suffix meaning* origin, production, development *[phylogeny]*

**ge·o-** [Gr. *geō-* < *gaia*, *gē*, the earth] *a combining form meaning:* **1.** earth, of the earth *[geocentric]* **2.** geographical *[geopolitics]*

**ge·o·cen·tric** (jē′ō sen′trik) *adj.* [prec. + CENTRIC] **1.** measured or viewed as from the center of the earth **2.** having or regarding the earth as a center Also **ge′o·cen′tri·cal** —**ge′o·cen′tri·cal·ly** *adv.*

**ge·o·des·ic** (jē′ə des′ik, -dē′sik) *adj.* **1.** *same as* GEODETIC (sense 1) **2.** designating the shortest line between two points on a surface, esp. a curved surface —*n.* a geodesic line

**ge·od·e·sy** (jē äd′ə sē) *n.* [< Gr. < *gē*, the earth + *daiein*, to divide] the branch of applied mathematics concerned with measuring, or determining the shape of, the earth or a large part of its surface, or with locating exactly points on its surface —**ge·od′e·sist** *n.*

**ge·o·det·ic** (jē′ō det′ik) *adj.* **1.** of or determined by geodesy **2.** *same as* GEODESIC (sense 2) Also **ge′o·det′i·cal** —**ge′o·det′i·cal·ly** *adv.*

**Geof·frey** (jef′rē) [< OFr. *Geoffroi* < Gmc.: 2d element < Gmc. hyp. *frithu*, peace] a masculine name

**geog.** **1.** geographic(al) **2.** geography

**ge·o·graph·i·cal** (jē′ə graf′i k′l) *adj.* **1.** of or according to geography **2.** with reference to the geography of a particular region Also **ge′o·graph′ic** —**ge′o·graph′i·cal·ly** *adv.*

**ge·og·ra·phy** (jē äg′rə fē) *n., pl.* **-phies** [< L. < Gr. *geō-*, GEO- + *graphein*, to write] **1.** the science dealing with the surface of the earth, its division into continents and countries, and the climate, plants, animals, natural resources, people, and industries of the various divisions **2.** the physical features of a region or place **3.** a book about geography —**ge·og′ra·pher** *n.*

**geol.** **1.** geologic(al) **2.** geologist **3.** geology

**ge·o·log·ic** (jē′ə läj′ik) *adj.* of or according to geology: also **ge′o·log′i·cal** —**ge′o·log′i·cal·ly** *adv.*

**ge·ol·o·gy** (jē äl′ə jē) *n., pl.* **-gies** [< ML.: see GEO- & -LOGY] **1.** the science dealing with the physical nature of the earth, including the structure and development of its crust and interior, types of rocks, fossil forms, etc. **2.** the structure of the earth's crust in a given region or place **3.** a book about geology —**ge·ol′o·gist** *n.*

**geom.** **1.** geometric(al) **2.** geometry

**ge·o·met·ric** (jē′ə met′rik) *adj.* **1.** of or according to geometry **2.** characterized by straight lines, triangles, circles, etc., as a pattern Also **ge′o·met′ri·cal** —**ge′o·met′ri·cal·ly** *adv.*

**geometric progression** a sequence of terms in which the ratio of each term to the preceding one is the same throughout (Ex.: 1, 2, 4, 8, etc.)

**ge·om·e·trid** (jē äm′ə trid) *n.* [< ModL. < L. < Gr. < *geōmetrein*: see ff.] any of a family of moths whose larvae move by looping the body

**ge·om·e·try** (jē äm′ə trē) *n., pl.* **-tries** [< OFr. < L. < Gr. *geōmetrein* < *gē*, earth + *metrein*, to measure] **1.** the branch of mathematics that deals with points, lines, surfaces, and solids, and examines their properties, measurement, and mutual relations in space **2.** a book about geometry —**ge·om′e·tri′cian** (-trish′ən), **ge·om′e·ter** *n.*

**ge·o·phys·ics** (jē′ō fiz′iks) *n.pl.* [*with sing. v.*] the science that deals with weather, winds, tides, etc. and their effect on the earth —**ge′o·phys′i·cal** *adj.* —**ge′o·phys′i·cist** *n.*

**ge·o·pol·i·tics** (jē′ō päl′ə tiks) *n.pl.* [*with sing. v.*] [< G. *geopolitik*] **1.** the interrelationship of politics and geography, or the study of this **2.** any program or policy, as for expansion, based on this —**ge′o·po·lit′i·cal** (-pə lit′i k′l) *adj.* —**ge′o·po·lit′i·cal·ly** *adv.* —**ge′o·pol′i·ti′cian** *n.*

**George** (jôrj) [< Fr. < LL. < Gr. < *geōrgos*, husbandman, lit., earthworker] **I.** a masculine name **2.** name of several kings of Great Britain & Ireland; specif., *a)* **George II** 1683–1760; king (1727–60) *b)* **George III** 1738–1820; king (1760–1820) *c)* **George V** 1865–1936; king (1910–36) **3. George VI** 1895–1952; king of Great Britain & Northern Ireland (1936–52) **4.** Saint, d. 303? A.D.; patron saint of England **5.** Henry, 1839–97; U.S. political economist; advocate of single tax —**by George!** an exclamation of mild surprise, determination, etc.

**geor·gette** (jôr jet′) *n.* [after *Georgette* de la Plante, Parisian modiste] a kind of thin crepe fabric, used for dresses, etc.: also **georgette crepe**

**Geor·gia** (jôr′jə) **1.** [< GEORGE] a feminine name: var. *Georgiana* **2.** [after GEORGE II] Southern State of the SE

U.S.: 58,876 sq. mi.; pop. 5,464,000; cap. Atlanta: abbrev. **Ga., GA** **3.** republic of the U.S.S.R., on the Black Sea: 26,900 sq. mi.; pop. 4,700,000; cap. Tbilisi: in full, **Georgian Soviet Socialist Republic**

**Geor·gian** (jôr′jən) *adj.* **1.** of the reigns of George I, II, III, and IV of England (1714–1830) **2.** of the Georgian S.S.R., its people, language, or culture **3.** of the State of Georgia —*n.* **1.** *a)* a native or inhabitant of the Georgian S.S.R. *b)* the South Caucasian language of the Georgians **2.** a native or inhabitant of the State of Georgia

**ge·o·stat·ics** (jē′ō stat′iks, jē′ə-) *n.pl.* [*with sing. v.*] [< GEO- + STATIC] the branch of physics dealing with the mechanics of the equilibrium of forces in rigid bodies

**ge·o·tro·pism** (jē ät′rə piz′m) *n.* [GEO- + -TROPISM] movement or growth in response to the force of gravity, either downward, as of plant roots (**positive geotropism**), or upward, as of stems (**negative geotropism**) —**ge·o·trop·ic** (jē′ə träp′ik) *adj.*

**Ger.** **1.** German **2.** Germany

**ger.** **1.** gerund **2.** gerundive

**Ger·ald** (jer′əld) [< OFr. < OHG. < *ger*, spear + base of *waldan*, to rule] a masculine name: feminine **Ger′al·dine′** (-əl dēn′, -din)

**ge·ra·ni·um** (jə rā′nē əm, -rān′yəm) *n.* [L. < Gr. *geranion*, cranesbill: its seed capsule is beaked] **1.** a plant with showy pink or purple flowers and leaves with many lobes **2.** a pelargonium

**Ger·ard** (jə rärd′) [< OFr. < OHG. < *ger*, spear + *hart*, hard] a masculine name

**ger·fal·con** (jur′fal′k′n, -fôl′-, -fô′-) *n. same as* GYRFALCON

**ger·i·at·rics** (jer′ē at′riks) *n.pl.* [*with sing. v.*] [< Gr. *gēras*, old age + -IATRICS] the branch of medicine that deals with the diseases and hygiene of old age —**ger′i·at′ric** *adj.* —**ger′i·a·tri′cian** (-ə trish′ən), **ger′i·at′rist** *n.*

**germ** (jurm) *n.* [< OFr. < L. *germen*, a sprout, bud] **1.** the rudimentary form from which a new organism is developed; seed, bud, etc. **2.** any microscopic organism, esp. one of the bacteria, that can cause disease **3.** that from which something can develop *[the germ of an idea]* —**germ′less** *adj.*

**Ger·man** (jur′mən) *adj.* [< L. *Germanus*, prob. < Celt.] of Germany, its people, language, or culture —*n.* **1.** a native or inhabitant of Germany **2.** the German language now spoken chiefly in Germany, Austria, and Switzerland, technically called *New High German* **3.** [g-] *a)* a cotillion (sense 1) *b)* a party at which the german is danced

**ger·man** (jur′mən) *adj.* [< OFr. < L. *germanus*, akin to *germen*, GERM] closely related: now chiefly in compounds, meaning: *a)* having the same parents *[a brother-german] b)* being a first cousin *[a cousin-german]*

**ger·man·der** (jər man′dər) *n.* [< OFr. < ML. *germandra*, < Gr. < *chamai*, on the ground + *drys*, tree] any of a genus of plants of the mint family, with spikes of flowers that lack an upper lip

**ger·mane** (jər mān′) *adj.* [var. of GERMAN] truly relevant; pertinent; to the point

**Ger·man·ic** (jər man′ik) *adj.* **1.** of Germany or the Germans; German **2.** designating or of the original language of the German peoples or the languages descended from it; Teutonic —*n.* **1.** the original language of the Germanic peoples: now called **Proto-Germanic 2.** a principal branch of the Indo-European family of languages, comprising this language and the languages descended from it, including Norwegian, Icelandic, Swedish, Danish (all *North Germanic*), German, Dutch, Flemish, Frisian, English (all *West Germanic*), the extinct Gothic (*East Germanic*), etc.

**ger·ma·ni·um** (jər mā′nē əm) *n.* [ModL. < L. *Germania*, Germany] a rare, grayish-white, metallic chemical element that can be a semiconductor: symbol, Ge; at. wt., 72.59; at. no., 32

**Ger·man·ize** (jur′mə nīz′) *vt., vi.* **-ized′, -iz′ing** to make or become German in character, thought, language, etc. —**Ger′man·i·za′tion** *n.*

**German measles** *same as* RUBELLA

**Ger·man·o-** *a combining form meaning* German, of Germany, or of the Germans

**German shepherd dog** a breed of dog wolflike in form and size, used in police work, as a guide for the blind, etc.: also **(German) police dog**

**German silver** *same as* NICKEL SILVER

**Ger·ma·ny** (jur′mə nē) former country in NC Europe, on the North & Baltic seas: divided (1945) into EAST GERMANY and WEST GERMANY

**germ cell** a cell from which a new organism can develop; egg or sperm cell

**ger·mi·cide** (jur′mə sīd′) *n.* [< GERM + -CIDE] anything used to destroy germs —**ger′mi·ci′dal** *adj.*

**ger·mi·nal** (jur′mə n′l) *adj.* **1.** of, like, or characteristic

# Geologic Time Chart

| ERAS | PERIODS or SYSTEMS | Epochs or Series | PRINCIPAL PHYSICAL & BIOLOGICAL FEATURES |
|---|---|---|---|
| **MAIN DIVISIONS OF GEOLOGIC TIME** | | | |
| CENOZOIC | QUATERNARY | Recent 12,000* | Glaciers restricted to Antarctica and Greenland; development and spread of modern human culture. |
| CENOZOIC | QUATERNARY | Pleistocene 600,000 | Great glaciers covered much of N North America & NW Europe; appearance of modern man late in Pleistocene. |
| CENOZOIC | TERTIARY | Pliocene 10,000,000 | W North America uplifted; continued development of mammals; first possible apelike men appeared in Africa. |
| CENOZOIC | TERTIARY | Miocene 25,000,000 | Renewed uplift of Rockies & other mountains; mammals began to acquire present-day characters; dogs, solid-hoofed horses, manlike apes appeared. |
| CENOZOIC | TERTIARY | Oligocene 35,000,000 | Many older types of mammals became extinct; mastodons, first monkeys, and apes appeared. |
| CENOZOIC | TERTIARY | Eocene 55,000,000 | Mountains raised in Rockies, Andes, Alps, & Himalayas; expansion of early mammals; primitive horses appeared. |
| CENOZOIC | TERTIARY | Paleocene 65,000,000 | Great development of primitive mammals. |
| MESOZOIC | CRETACEOUS 135,000,000 | | Rocky Mountains began to rise; dinosaurs reached maximum development & then became extinct; mammals small & very primitive. |
| MESOZOIC | JURASSIC 180,000,000 | | Sierra Nevada Mountains uplifted; conifers & cycads dominant among plants; primitive birds appeared. |
| MESOZOIC | TRIASSIC 230,000,000 | | Modern corals appeared & some insects of present-day types; great expansion of reptiles including earliest dinosaurs. |
| PALEOZOIC | PERMIAN 280,000,000 | | Trees of coal-forming forests declined; ferns abundant; conifers present; trilobites became extinct; reptiles surpassed amphibians. |
| PALEOZOIC | CARBONIFEROUS — PENNSYLVANIAN 310,000,000 | | Mountains grew along E coast of North America & in C Europe; great coal-forming swamp forests flourished in N Hemisphere; seed-bearing ferns abundant; cockroaches & first reptiles appeared. |
| PALEOZOIC | CARBONIFEROUS — MISSISSIPPIAN 345,000,000 | | Land plants became diversified; crinoids achieved greatest development; sharks of relatively modern types appeared; land animals little known. |
| PALEOZOIC | DEVONIAN 405,000,000 | | Land plants evolved rapidly, large trees appeared; brachiopods reached maximum development; many kinds of primitive fishes; first sharks, insects, & amphibians appeared. |
| PALEOZOIC | SILURIAN 425,000,000 | | Great mountains formed in NW Europe; first small land plants appeared; shelled cephalopods abundant; trilobites began decline; first jawed fish appeared. |
| PALEOZOIC | ORDOVICIAN 500,000,000 | | Much limestone deposited in shallow seas; great expansion among marine invertebrate animals; first primitive jawless fish appeared. |
| PALEOZOIC | CAMBRIAN 600,000,000 | | Shallow seas covered parts of continents; abundant record of marine life, esp. trilobites & brachiopods; other fossils rare. |
| PRECAMBRIAN | LATE PRECAMBRIAN ** 2,000,000,000 | | Metamorphosed sedimentary rocks and granite formed; first evidence of life, calcareous algae & invertebrates. |
| PRECAMBRIAN | EARLY PRECAMBRIAN ** 4,500,000,000 | | Crust formed on molten earth; crystalline rocks much disturbed; history unknown. |

*Figures indicate approximate number of years since the beginning of each division.   ** Regarded as separate eras.

of germs or germ cells **2.** in the first stage of growth or development —**ger′mi·nal·ly** *adv.*

**ger·mi·nate** (-nāt′) *vi., vt.* -**nat′ed, -nat′ing** [< L. pp. of *germinare* < *germen*, GERM] **1.** to sprout or cause to sprout, as from a seed **2.** to start developing or growing —**ger′mi·na′tion** *n.* —**ger′mi·na′tive** *adj.* —**ger′mi·na′tor** *n.*

**Ger·mis·ton** (jɐr′mis tən) city in S Transvaal, South Africa: pop. 214,000

**germ plasm** the reproductive cells of an organism, particularly that part of the cells involved in heredity

**germ warfare** the deliberate contamination of enemy territory with disease germs in warfare

**ger·on·tol·o·gy** (jer′ən täl′ə jē) *n.* [< Gr. < *gerōn*, old man + -LOGY] the scientific study of the process of aging and of the problems of aged people —**ge·ron·to·log·i·cal** (jə rän′tə läj′i k'l) *adj.* —**ger′on·tol′o·gist** *n.*

**-ger·ous** (jər əs) [L. *-ger* < *gerere*, to bear + -OUS] *a suffix meaning* producing or bearing

**ger·ry·man·der** (jer′i man′dər, ger′-) *vt.* [< E. *Gerry*, governor of Mass. when the method was employed (1812) + SALAMANDER (the shape of the redistricted Essex County)] **1.** to divide (a voting area) so as to give one political party a majority in as many districts as possible **2.** to manipulate unfairly so as to gain advantage —*vi.* to engage in gerrymandering —*n.* the act or result of gerrymandering —**ger′ry·man′der·er** *n.*

**Ger·trude** (gur′trood) [Fr. < G. < OHG. < *ger*, spear + *trut*, dear] a feminine name: dim. *Gert, Gertie*

**ger·und** (jer′ənd) *n.* [< LL. < L. *gerundus* < *gerere*, to do or carry out] *Gram.* a verbal noun ending in *-ing*, that is used like a noun but is able, like a verb, to take an object or an adverbial modifier (Ex.: *playing* in "Playing golf is his only exercise") —**ge·run·di·al** (jə run′dē əl) *adj.*

**ge·run·dive** (jə run′div) *n.* [< LL. < prec.] **1.** a Latin verbal adjective with a typical gerund stem form, used as a future passive participle expressing duty, necessity, fitness, etc. **2.** a similar form in any language —**ger·un·di·val** (jer′ən dī′vəl) *adj.*

**gest, geste** (jest) *n.* [< OFr. < L. *gesta*, deeds, pl. pp. of *gerere*, to do, act] **1.** [Archaic] an adventure; exploit **2.** a romantic story of adventure, esp. a medieval tale in verse

**Ge·stalt psychology** (gə shtält′, -stält′, -stôlt′) [G., lit. shape, form] a school of psychology, orig. German, based on the idea that the response of an individual in a given situation is a response to the whole situation, not to its components

**Ge·sta·po** (gə stä′pō; *G.* gə shtä′-) *n.* [< G. *Ge*(*heime*) *Sta*(*ats*)*po*(*lizei*), secret state police] the secret police force of the German Nazi state

**ges·tate** (jes′tāt) *vt.* -**tat′ed, -tat′ing** [< L. pp. of *gestare*, freq. of *gerere*, to bear] to carry in the uterus during pregnancy —**ges·ta′tion** *n.*

**ges·tic·u·late** (jes tik′yə lāt′) *vi.* -**lat′ed, -lat′ing** [< L. pp. of *gesticulari*, to gesture, ult. < pp. of *gerere*, to bear, do] to make or use gestures, esp. with the hands or arms, as in adding force to one's speech —*vt.* to express by gesticulating —**ges·tic′u·la′tive** *adj.* —**ges·tic′u·la′tor** *n.*

**ges·tic·u·la·tion** (jes tik′yə lā′shən) *n.* **1.** a gesticulating **2.** a gesture, esp. an energetic one —**ges·tic′u·la·to′ry** (-lə tôr′ē) *adj.*

**ges·ture** (jes′chər) *n.* [< ML. < L. pp. of *gerere*, to bear, do] **1.** a movement of the body, or of part of the body, to express or emphasize ideas, emotions, etc. **2.** anything said or done to convey a state of mind or intention, sometimes something said or done only for effect —*vi.* -**tured, -tur·ing** to make or use gestures —*vt.* to express with gestures —**ges′tur·al** *adj.* —**ges′tur·er** *n.*

**get** (get) *vt.* **got** or archaic & dial. **gat, got** or **got′ten, get′ting** [< ON. *geta*] **1.** to come into the state of having; receive, win, gain, obtain, acquire, etc. **2.** to reach; arrive at [*to get* home early] **3.** to set up communication with, as by radio [*to get* Paris] **4.** to go and bring [*get* your books] **5.** to catch; capture; gain hold of **6.** to learn; commit to memory **7.** to persuade (a person) to do something [*get* him to leave] **8.** to cause to act in a certain way [*get* the door to shut properly] **9.** to cause to be or arrive [*he got* his hands dirty, *he got* it there on time] **10.** to be sentenced to [*he got* ten years] **11.** to prepare [*to get* lunch] **12.** to give birth to; beget: usually said of animals **13.** [Colloq.] to be obliged to; feel a necessity to (with *have* or *has*) [*he's got* to pass] **14.** [Colloq.] to own; possess (with *have* or *has*) [*he's got* red hair] **15.** [Colloq.] to be or become the master of; esp., *a*) to overpower [*his* illness finally *got* him] *b*) to puzzle; baffle [*this* problem *gets* me] *c*) to take into custody, wound, or kill *d*) *Baseball*, etc. to put (an opponent) out **16.** [Colloq.] to strike; hit [*the* blow *got* him in the eye] **17.** [Colloq.] to catch the mean-

ing or import of; understand **18.** [Slang] to cause an emotional response in; irritate, please, thrill, etc. [*her* singing *gets* me] **19.** [Slang] to notice [*get* the look on his face] —*vi.* **1.** to come or arrive [*to get* to work on time] **2.** to come to be (doing something); come to be (in a situation, condition, etc.) [*he got* caught in the rain] **3.** to contrive [*to get* to do something] **4.** [Colloq.] to leave at once *Get* is used as an auxiliary for emphasis in passive construction [*we got* beaten] —*n.* **1.** the young of an animal; offspring **2.** a begetting —**get about 1.** to move from place to place **2.** to go to many social events, places, etc. **3.** to circulate widely, as news —**get across** [Colloq.] **1.** to explain convincingly **2.** to succeed, as in making oneself understood —**get after** [Colloq.] **1.** to pursue or attack **2.** to goad persistently —**get along** *see phrase under* ALONG —**get around 1.** to get about (in all senses) **2.** to circumvent. **3.** to influence or gain favor with by cajoling, flattery, etc. —**get around to 1.** to find occasion for **2.** to get started on after a delay —**get away 1.** to go away; leave **2.** to escape **3.** to start —**get away with** [Slang] to succeed in doing or taking without being discovered or punished —**get back 1.** to return **2.** to recover **3.** [Slang] to get revenge (usually with *at*) —**get by 1.** to be fairly acceptable **2.** [Colloq.] to succeed without being discovered or punished **3.** [Colloq.] to survive; manage —**get down to to** begin to consider or act on —**get in 1.** to enter; join **2.** to arrive **3.** to put in —**get off 1.** to come off, down, or out of **2.** to leave; go away **3.** to take off **4.** to escape **5.** to help to escape punishment **6.** to start, as in a race **7.** to utter (a joke, retort, etc.) **8.** to have time off —**get on 1.** to go on or into **2.** to put on **3.** to proceed **4.** to grow older **5.** to succeed **6.** to agree —**get out 1.** to go out **2.** to go away **3.** to take out **4.** to become no longer a secret **5.** to publish —**get over 1.** to recover from **2.** to forget or overlook —**get somewhere** to succeed —**get through 1.** to finish **2.** to manage to survive **3.** to push through **4.** to make oneself clear (*to*) —**get to** [Colloq.] **1.** to succeed in reaching **2.** to influence, as by bribery: also **get at** —**get together 1.** to bring or come together; assemble **2.** [Colloq.] to reach an agreement —**get up 1.** to rise (from a chair, from sleep, etc.) **2.** to contrive; organize **3.** to dress elaborately **4.** to advance; make progress —**get′ta·ble, get′a·ble** *adj.* —**get′ter** *n.*

**get·a·way** (get′ə wā′) *n.* **1.** the act of starting, as in a race **2.** the act of escaping, as from police

**Geth·sem·a·ne** (geth sem′ə nē) *Bible* a garden outside of Jerusalem, scene of the agony, betrayal, and arrest of Jesus: Matt. 26:36

**get-to·geth·er** (get′tə geth′ər) *n.* an informal social gathering or meeting

**Get·tys·burg** (get′iz burg′) [after J. *Gettys*, its 18th-c. founder] town in S Pa.: site of a crucial battle (July, 1863) of the Civil War: pop. 7,000

**get-up** (get′up′) *n.* [Colloq.] **1.** general arrangement or composition **2.** costume; outfit; dress **3.** driving ambition; energy: also **get′-up′-and-go′**

**gew·gaw** (gyōō′gô, gōō′-) *n.* [ME. *giuegoue, gugaw* < ?] something showy but useless; trinket

**gey·ser** (gī′zər, -sər; *Brit.* gā′-) *n.* [Ice. *Geysir*, a hot spring in Iceland, lit., gusher < ON. *gjosa*, to gush] a spring from which columns of boiling water and steam gush into the air at intervals

**Gha·na** (gä′nə) country in W Africa, on the Atlantic: a member of the Commonwealth: 91,843 sq. mi.; pop. 8,600,-000; cap. Accra —**Gha·na·ian** (gä′nē ən, -nä-) *adj., n.*

**ghast·ly** (gast′lē) *adj.* -**li·er, -li·est** [< OE. < *gast*, spirit, ghost] **1.** horrible; frightful **2.** ghostlike; pale **3.** [Colloq.] very unpleasant —*adv.* in a ghastly manner —**ghast′li·ness** *n.*

**ghat, ghaut** (gôt, gät) *n.* [Hindi *ghāṭ*] in India, **1.** a mountain pass **2.** a flight of steps leading down to a river landing for ritual bathers

**ghee** (gē) *n.* [Hindi *ghī*] in India, a liquid butter specially made from cow's milk or buffalo milk

**Ghent** (gent) city in NW Belgium: pop. 156,000

**gher·kin** (gur′kin) *n.* [< Du. or LowG. *gurken*, ult. < Per. *angārah*] **1.** a variety of cucumber bearing small, prickly fruit, used for pickles **2.** the immature fruit of the cucumber when pickled

**ghet·to** (get′ō) *n., pl.* -**tos, -toes** [It., lit., foundry, ult. < L. *jactare*, to cast: the former Jewish quarter on a foundry site in Venice] **1.** in certain European cities, a section to which Jews were formerly restricted **2.** any section of a city in which many members of some minority group live, or to which they are restricted by discrimination

**Ghib·el·line** (gib′ə lin, -lēn′) *n.* any member of a political party in medieval Italy that supported the authority of the German emperors in Italy

**Ghi·ber·ti** (gē ber'tē), **Lo·ren·zo** (lô ren'tsô) (born *Lorenzo di Cione di Ser Buonaccorso*) 1378-1455; Florentine sculptor, painter, & worker in metals

**ghost** (gōst) *n.* [OE. *gast*] **1.** orig., the spirit or soul: now only in **give up the ghost** (to die) and in HOLY GHOST **2.** the supposed disembodied spirit of a dead person, conceived of as appearing to the living as a pale, shadowy apparition **3.** a haunting memory **4.** a faint semblance; slight trace *[not a ghost of a chance]* **5.** [Colloq.] *same as* GHOSTWRITER **6.** *Optics & TV* an unwanted secondary image or bright spot —*vi.* [Colloq.] to work as a ghostwriter —*vt.* **1.** to haunt **2.** [Colloq.] to be the ghostwriter of —**ghost'like'** *adj.* —**ghost'li·ness** *n.* —**ghost'ly** *adj.*

**ghost town** the remains of a town that has been permanently abandoned, esp. for economic reasons

**ghost·writ·er** (-rīt'ər) *n.* a person who writes speeches, articles, etc. for another who professes to be the author —**ghost'write'** *vt., vi.* -wrote', -writ'ten, -writ'ing

**ghoul** (gōōl) *n.* [Ar. *ghūl*, demon < *ghāla*, to seize] **1.** *Oriental Folklore* an evil spirit that robs graves and feeds on the dead **2.** a robber of graves **3.** one who enjoys things that disgust or trouble most people —**ghoul'ish** *adj.* —**ghoul'ish·ly** *adv.* —**ghoul'ish·ness** *n.*

**GHQ, G.H.Q.** General Headquarters

**GI** (jē'ī') *adj.* **1.** *Mil.* government issue: designating clothing, equipment, etc. issued to military personnel **2.** [Colloq.] *a)* of or characteristic of the U.S. armed forces *[a GI haircut] b)* strict in following or enforcing military regulations *c)* of or for veterans of the U.S. armed forces —*n.,* *pl.* **GI's, GIs** [Colloq.] any member of the U.S. armed forces; esp., an enlisted soldier —*vt., vi.* **GI'd, GI'ing** [Mil. Slang] to clean up for official inspection

**GI, G.I., g.i.** gastrointestinal

**gi.** gill (unit of measure); gills

**gi·ant** (jī'ənt) *n.* [< ONormFr. < VL. < L. *gigas* < Gr.] **1.** any imaginary being of human form but of superhuman size and strength **2.** a person or thing of great size, intellect, etc. —*adj.* of great size, strength, etc. —**gi'ant·ess** *n.fem.*

**gi·ant·ism** (-iz'm) *n.* abnormally great growth of the body, due to excessive production of growth hormone by the pituitary gland

**giant panda** a large, black-and-white, bearlike mammal of China and Tibet

**giaour** (jour) *n.* [< Turk. < Per. *gabr* < Ar. *kāfir*, infidel] in Moslem usage, a non-Moslem; esp., a Christian

**gib·ber** (jib'ər) *vi., vt.* [echoic] to speak or utter rapidly and incoherently; chatter —*n.* unintelligible chatter; gibberish

**gib·ber·ish** (jib'ər ish; *Brit.* gib'-) *n.* rapid and incoherent talk; unintelligible chatter; jargon

**gib·bet** (jib'it) *n.* [< OFr. dim. < Frank. *gibb*, forked stick] **1.** a gallows **2.** a structure like a gallows, from which bodies of criminals already executed were hung and exposed to public scorn —*vt.* **1.** to execute by hanging **2.** to hang on a gibbet **3.** to expose to public scorn

GIANT PANDA
(4 ft. high at shoulder)

**gib·bon** (gib'ən) *n.* [Fr.] a small, slender, long-armed ape of India, S China, and the East Indies, that lives in trees

**Gib·bon** (gib'ən), **Edward** 1737-94; Eng. historian

**gib·bous** (gib'əs) *adj.* [< L. *gibbosus* < *gibba*, a hump] **1.** rounded and bulging **2.** designating the moon or a planet when more than half, but not all, of the disk is illuminated **3.** humpbacked —**gib·bos·i·ty** (gi bäs'ə tē) *n.* —**gib'bous·ly** *adv.*

**gibe** (jīb) *vi., vt.* **gibed, gib'ing** [< ? OFr. *giber*, to handle roughly] to jeer, or taunt; scoff (at) —*n.* a jeer; taunt; scoff —**gib'er** *n.*

**gib·let** (jib'lit) *n.* [< OFr. *gibelet*, stew made of game] any of the parts of a fowl, as the heart, gizzard, neck, etc., usually cooked separately

GIBBON (18 1/2-25 in. long, head & body)

**Gi·bral·tar** (ji brôl'tər) **1.** Brit. territory on a small peninsula at the S tip of Spain, including a port & naval base: it consists mostly of a rocky hill (**Rock of Gibraltar**) **2.** Strait **of**, strait between Spain & Morocco, joining the Mediterranean & the Atlantic —*n.* any strong fortification; unassailable fortress

**gid·dy** (gid'ē) *adj.* **-di·er, -di·est** [OE. *gydig*, insane, prob. < base of *god*, a god (i.e., "possessed by a god")] **1.** having a whirling, dazed sensation; dizzy **2.** causing such a sensation **3.** whirling **4.** *a)* inconstant; fickle *b)* frivolous;

flighty —*vt., vi.* **-died, -dy·ing** to make or become giddy —**gid'di·ly** *adv.* —**gid'di·ness** *n.*

**Gide** (zhēd), **An·dré** (**Paul Guillaume**) (än drā') 1869-1951; Fr. novelist, critic, etc.

**Gid·e·on** (gid'ē ən) [Heb. *gidh'ōn*, lit., hewer] **1.** a masculine name **2.** *Bible* a judge of Israel and a leader in the defeat of the Midianites

**gie** (gē) *vt., vi.* **gied** or **gae, gi·en** (gē'ən), **gie'ing** [Scot. & Brit. Dial.] to give

**gift** (gift) *n.* [OE., wedding gift (< *giefan*, to give) & < ON. *gipt, gift*] **1.** something given to show friendship, affection, etc.; present **2.** the act, power, or right of giving **3.** a natural ability; talent *[a gift for language]* —*vt.* to present with or as a gift

**gift·ed** (-id) *adj.* **1.** having a natural ability; talented **2.** having superior intelligence

**gift of tongues** *same as* GLOSSOLALIA

**gift-wrap** (-rap') *vt.* **-wrapped', -wrap'ping** to wrap as a gift, with decorative paper, ribbon, etc.

**gig[1]** (gig) *n.* [prob. < Scand.] **1.** a light, two-wheeled, open carriage drawn by one horse **2.** a long, light ship's boat —*vi.* **gigged, gig'ging** to travel in a gig

**gig[2]** (gig) *n.* [contr. < *fizgig* < Sp. *fisga*, kind of harpoon] a fish spear —*vt., vi.* **gigged, gig'ging** to spear or jab with or as with a gig

**gig[3]** (gig) *n.* [< ?] [Slang] a demerit —*vi.* **gigged, gig'ging** [Slang] to give a gig to

**gig[4]** (gig) *n.* [< ?] [Slang] **1.** a job to play or sing jazz, rock, etc. **2.** any stint of work

**gi·ga-** (jig'ə) [< Gr. *gigas*, giant] *a combining form meaning* one billion *[gigahertz]*

**gi·gan·tic** (jī gan'tik) *adj.* [see GIANT] **1.** of, like, or fit for a giant **2.** very big; huge; enormous; immense —**gi·gan'ti·cal·ly** *adv.*

**gi·gan·tism** (jī gan'tiz'm, jī'gan-) *n.* [see GIANT] **1.** the state of being gigantic **2.** *same as* GIANTISM

**gig·gle** (gig'l) *vi.* **-gled, -gling** [prob. < Du. *giggelen*] to laugh with uncontrollable, rapid, high-pitched sounds, suggestive of foolishness, nervousness, etc.; titter —*n.* such a laugh —**gig'gler** *n.* —**gig'gly, -gli·er, -gli·est**

**gig·o·lo** (jig'ə lō) *n., pl.* **-los** [Fr.] a man paid by a woman to be her escort

**gig·ot** (jig'ət, zhē gō') *n.* [Fr. < OFr., dim. < MHG. *giga*, a fiddle] **1.** a leg of mutton, lamb, veal, etc. **2.** a leg-of-mutton sleeve

**Gi·la monster** (hē'lə) [< the *Gila* River, Arizona] a stout, poisonous lizard covered with beadlike scales in alternating rings of black and orange: found in deserts of SW U.S. and in Mexico

**Gil·bert** (gil'bərt) [< OFr. < OHG. < *willo*, will + *beraht*, bright] **1.** a masculine name: dim. *Gil* **2.** Sir **William Schwenck** (shwenk), 1836-1911; Eng. librettist: collaborated with A. SULLIVAN in writing comic operas —**Gil·ber'ti·an** (-bər'tē ən) *adj.*

**gild[1]** (gild) *vt.* **gild'ed** or **gilt, gild'ing** [OE. *gyldan* < base of *gold*, gold] **1.** *a)* to overlay with a thin layer of gold *b)* to coat with a gold color **2.** to make appear bright and attractive **3.** to make (something) seem more attractive or valuable than it is —**gild'er** *n.*

**gild[2]** (gild) *n. same as* GUILD

**gild·ing** (gil'diŋ) *n.* **1.** the art or process of applying gold leaf or a substance like gold to a surface **2.** the substance so applied

**Gil·e·ad** (gil'ē əd) mountainous region of ancient Palestine, east of the Jordan

**gill[1]** (gil) *n.* [prob. < Anglo-N.] **1.** the organ for breathing of most animals that live in water, as fish, lobsters, clams, etc. **2.** *[pl.] a)* the wattle of a fowl *b)* the jowl of a person **3.** a thin, leaflike, radiating plate on the undersurface of a mushroom —**gilled** *adj.*

**gill[2]** (jil) *n.* [< OFr. < LL. *gillo*, cooling vessel] a liquid measure, equal to 1/4 pint

**gil·lie, gil·ly** (gil'ē) *n., pl.* **-lies** [Scot. < Gael. *gille*, boy, page] **1.** in the Scottish Highlands, a sportsman's attendant **2.** a male servant

**gil·li·flow·er** (jil'ē flou'ər) *n.* [OFr. *gilofre* < LL. < Gr. < *karyon*, nut + *phyllon*, leaf] any of several plants with clove-scented flowers, as the clove pink: also sp. **gil'ly·flow'er**

**gilt** (gilt) *alt. pt. & pp. of* GILD[1] —*adj.* overlaid with gilding —*n. same as* GILDING

**gilt-edged** (-ejd') *adj.* **1.** having gilded edges **2.** of the highest quality or value *[gilt-edged securities]* Also **gilt'-edge'**

**gim·bals** (gim'b'lz, jim'-) *n.pl.* [with sing. v.] [< L. *gemellus*, dim. of *geminus*, twin] a pair of rings pivoted in axes at right angles to each other so as to be free to swing within the other: a ship's compass will keep a horizontal position when suspended in gimbals —**gim'baled** *adj.*

**gim·crack** (jim'krak') *adj.* [altered < ME. *gibbecrak*, an ornament] showy but cheap and useless —*n.* a cheap, showy, useless thing; knickknack —**gim'crack'er·y** *n.*

**gim·let** (gim′lit) *n.* [< OFr. < MDu. dim. of *wimmel*, wimble] a small boring tool with a handle at right angles to a shaft with a spiral, pointed cutting edge —*vt.* to make a hole in as with a gimlet

**gim·let-eyed** (-īd′) *adj.* having a piercing glance

**gim·mick** (gim′ik) *n.* [< ? GIMCRACK] **1.** [Colloq.] *a)* a secret device for controlling a game of chance at a carnival, etc. *b)* any trick or secret device **2.** [Slang] *a)* an attention-getting, superficial feature for promoting a product, etc. *b)* any clever little gadget or ruse —*vt.* [Colloq.] to add gimmicks to (often with *up*) —**gim′mick·ry, gim′mick·er·y** *n.* —**gim′mick·y** *adj.*

GIMLET

**gimp**[1] (gimp) *n.* [< ? Du.] a ribbonlike braided fabric, used to trim garments, furniture, etc.

**gimp**[2] (gimp) *n.* [< ?] [Colloq.] **1.** a lame person **2.** a limp —*vi.* to limp —**gimp′y** *adj.*

**gin**[1] (jin) *n.* [< *geneva* < Du. *genever* < OFr. < L. *juniperus*, juniper] **1.** a strong alcoholic liquor distilled from grain and usually flavored with juniper berries **2.** [Slang] any alcoholic liquor

**gin**[2] (jin) *n.* [< OFr., contr. < *engin*, ENGINE] **1.** a snare or trap, as for game **2.** *same as* COTTON GIN —*vt.* **ginned, gin′ning 1.** to catch in a trap **2.** to remove seeds from (cotton) with a gin —**gin′ner** *n.*

**gin**[3] (gin) *vt., vi.* **gan, gin′ning** [ME. *ginnen* < OE. *beginnan*, to begin] [Archaic] to begin

**gin**[4] (jin) *n. same as* GIN RUMMY —*vi.* **ginned, gin′ning** to win in gin rummy with no unmatched cards left in one's hand

**gin·ger** (jin′jər) *n.* [< OE. & OFr., both < ML. < L. *zingiber* < Gr. < Pali] **1.** an Asiatic plant grown for its aromatic rootstalk, used as a spice and in medicine **2.** the rootstalk, or the spice made from it **3.** a reddish-brown color **4.** [Colloq.] vigor; spirit —**gin′ger·y** *adj.*

**ginger ale** a carbonated, sweet soft drink flavored with ginger

**ginger beer** a drink like ginger ale but with a stronger flavor

**gin·ger·bread** (-bred′) *n.* [ME. *ginge bred* < *gingebras*, preserved ginger < OFr.] **1.** a cake flavored with ginger and molasses **2.** showy ornamentation, as fancy carvings on gables, etc. —*adj.* cheap and showy: also **gin′ger·bread′y**

**gin·ger·ly** (-lē) *adv.* very carefully or cautiously —*adj.* very careful; cautious —**gin′ger·li·ness** *n.*

**gin·ger·snap** (-snap′) *n.* a crisp, spicy cookie flavored with ginger and molasses

**ging·ham** (giŋ′əm) *n.* [< Du. or Fr., ult. < Malay *ginggang*, striped (cloth)] a cotton cloth, usually woven in stripes, checks, or plaids

**gin·gi·vi·tis** (jin′jə vīt′əs) *n.* [ModL. < L. *gingiva*, the gum + -ITIS] inflammation of the gums

**gink** (giŋk) *n.* [? < dial. *gink*, a trick] [Slang] a man or boy, esp. one regarded as odd

**gink·go** (giŋ′kō) *n., pl.* **gink′goes** [Jap. *ginkyo* < Chin.] an Asiatic tree with fan-shaped leaves and yellow seeds enclosing an edible kernel: also **ging′ko**, *pl.* **ging′koes**

**gin rummy** a variety of the card game rummy: a hand which totals no more than ten points in unmatched cards and has been exposed wins unless the opponent has fewer points or an equal number

**gin·seng** (jin′seŋ) *n.* [Chin. *jen shen*] **1.** a perennial plant with a thick, forked, aromatic root: some species are found in China and N. America **2.** the root of this plant, used medicinally

**Gior·gio·ne** (jôr jô′ne), **Il** (ēl) (born *Giorgio Barbarelli*) 1478?–1510; Venetian painter

**Giot·to (di Bondone)** (jôt′tô; *E.* jät′ō) 1266?–1337; Florentine painter & architect

**gip** (jip) *n., vt., vi. same as* GYP

**gip·sy** (jip′sē) *n. same as* GYPSY

**gi·raffe** (jə raf′) *n., pl.* **-raffes′, -raffe′**: see PLURAL, II, D, 1 [Fr. < It. *giraffa* < Ar. *zarāfa*] a large, cud-chewing animal of Africa, with a very long neck and legs: the tallest of existing animals

**gird** (gurd) *vt.* **gird′ed** or **girt, gird′ing** [OE. *gyrdan*] **1.** to encircle or fasten with a belt or band **2.** to encircle; enclose **3.** to equip or endow **4.** to prepare (oneself) for action

**gird·er** (gur′dər) *n.* [prec. + -ER] a large beam of timber or steel, for supporting the joists of a floor, a framework, etc.

**gir·dle** (gur′d'l) *n.* [OE. *gyrdel*] **1.** a belt or sash for the waist **2.** anything that surrounds or encircles **3.** a woman's elasticized undergarment for supporting the waist and hips **4.** the rim of a cut gem **5.** a ring made by removing the bark around the trunk of a tree —*vt.* **-dled, -dling 1.** to surround or bind, as with a girdle **2.** to encircle **3.** to cut a ring of bark from (a tree) —**gir′dler** *n.*

**girl** (gurl) *n.* [ME. *girle, gurle*, youngster] **1.** a female child **2.** a young, unmarried woman **3.** a female servant **4.** [Colloq.] a woman of any age **5.** [Colloq.] a sweetheart —**girl′ish** *adj.* —**girl′ish·ly** *adv.* —**girl′ish·ness** *n.*

**girl·friend** (-frend′) *n.* [Colloq.] **1.** a sweetheart of a boy or man **2.** a girl who is one's friend

**girl·hood** (-hood′) *n.* **1.** the state or time of being a girl **2.** girls collectively

**girl·ie, girl·y** (gur′lē) *n., pl.* **girl′ies** [Slang] a girl or woman

**girl scout** a member of the **Girl Scouts**, a U.S. organization founded in 1912 (as **Girl Guides**) to provide character-building activities for girls

**girt**[1] (gurt) *alt. pt. & pp. of* GIRD

**girt**[2] (gurt) *vt.* [var. of GIRD] **1.** to gird; girdle **2.** to fasten with a girth

**girth** (gurth) *n.* [< ON. *gjörth*] **1.** a band put around the belly of a horse, etc. to hold a saddle or pack **2.** the circumference, as of a tree trunk or person's waist —*vt.* **1.** to encircle **2.** to bind with a girth —*vi.* to measure in girth

**gis·mo** (giz′mō) *n., pl.* **-mos** [Slang] *same as* GIZMO

**gist** (jist) *n.* [< OFr. *giste*, point at issue < *gesir*, to lie < L. *jacere*] the essence or main point, as of an article or argument

**git·tern** (git′ərn) *n.* [< OFr. *guiterne*, altered < OSp. *guittarra*: see GUITAR] an obsolete, guitarlike musical instrument with wire strings

**give** (giv) *vt.* **gave, giv′en, giv′ing** [OE. *giefan*, infl. by ON. *gefa*] **1.** to turn over the control of without cost or exchange; make a gift of **2.** to hand or pass over to be cared for [he *gave* the porter his bag] **3.** to sell (goods, services, etc.) for a price or pay (a price) for goods, services, etc. **4.** to relay [*give* my regards] **5.** to cause to have; impart **6.** to confer (a title, position, etc.) **7.** to act as host of (a party, etc.) **8.** to produce; supply [cows *give* milk] **9.** *a)* to sacrifice [he *gave* his life for his country] *b)* to devote fully [he *gives* all his time to his work] **10.** to concede; yield **11.** to show; exhibit **12.** to offer; proffer **13.** to perform [to *give* a concert] **14.** to make (a gesture, movement, etc.) [to *give* a leap] **15.** to utter (words, etc.); state [*give* a reply] **16.** to inflict (punishment, etc.) —*vi.* **1.** to make gifts **2.** to bend, sink, move, etc. from force or pressure **3.** to be resilient **4.** to provide a view of or access to [the window *gives* on the park] **5.** [Colloq.] to happen: chiefly in **what gives?** —*n.* **1.** a bending, sinking, moving, etc. under pressure **2.** resiliency —**give and take** to exchange on an even basis —**give away 1.** to make a gift of **2.** to present (the bride) ritually to the bridegroom **3.** [Colloq.] to reveal; expose —**give back** to return —**give forth** (or **off**) to send forth; emit —**give in 1.** to hand in **2.** to yield —**give it to** [Colloq.] to beat or scold —**give out 1.** to emit **2.** to make public **3.** to distribute **4.** to become worn out or used up —**give to understand** (or believe, etc.) to cause to understand (or believe, etc.) —**give up 1.** to hand over; relinquish **2.** to stop; cease **3.** to admit failure and stop trying **4.** to lose hope for **5.** to devote wholly —**giv′er** *n.*

**give-and-take** (-'n tāk′) *n.* **1.** a mutual yielding and conceding **2.** a fair and equal exchange of remarks or retorts

**give·a·way** (-ə wā′) *n.* [Colloq.] **1.** an unintentional revelation or betrayal **2.** something given free or sold cheap to attract customers, etc. **3.** the disposal of public property for private profit **4.** *Radio & TV* a program in which prizes are given to contestants

**giv·en** (giv′n) *pp. of* GIVE —*adj.* **1.** bestowed; presented **2.** accustomed; inclined [*given* to lying] **3.** stated; specified **4.** assumed; granted **5.** issued; executed [*given* under his seal as mayor]

**given name** the first name of a person, as distinguished from the surname

**Gî·za** (gē′zə) city in N Egypt, near Cairo, on the Nile: pop. 250,000

**giz·mo** (giz′mō) *n., pl.* **-mos** [< ?] [Slang] **1.** any gadget or contrivance **2.** a gimmick

**giz·zard** (giz′ərd) *n.* [< OFr. *gisier* < L. *gigeria*, pl., cooked entrails of poultry] **1.** the second stomach of a bird: it has thick, muscular walls and a tough lining for grinding food **2.** [Colloq.] the stomach: humorous usage

**Gk.** Greek

**gla·brous** (glā′brəs) *adj.* [< L. *glaber*, bald] without hair, down, or fuzz; bald —**gla′brous·ness** *n.*

**gla·cé** (gla sā′) *adj.* [Fr., pp. of *glacer*, to freeze < L. < *glacies*, ice] **1.** having a smooth, glossy surface **2.** candied or glazed, as fruits —*vt.* **-céed′, -cé′ing** to glaze (fruits, etc.)

**gla·cial** (glā′shəl) *adj.* [< L. < *glacies*, ice] **1.** of ice or glaciers **2.** of or produced by a glacial epoch **3.** freezing;

frigid **4.** cold and unfriendly **5.** as slow as the movement of a glacier **6.** having an icelike appearance —**gla′cial·ly** *adv.*

**glacial epoch** any extent of geologic time when large parts of the earth were covered with glaciers; specif., the Pleistocene Epoch, when a large part of the Northern Hemisphere was intermittently covered with glaciers; ice age

**gla·ci·ate** (glā′shē āt′, -sē-) *vt.* **-at′ed, -at′ing 1.** *a)* to cover over with ice or a glacier *b)* to form into ice; freeze **2.** to expose to or change by glacial action —**gla′ci·a′tion** *n.*

**gla·cier** (glā′shər) *n.* [Fr. < VL. < L. *glacies,* ice] a large mass of ice and snow that forms in areas where the rate of snowfall exceeds the melting rate: it moves slowly down a mountain, along a valley, etc. until it melts or breaks away

**gla·cis** (glā′sis, glas′is) *n., pl.* **-cis** (-sēz), **-cis·es** (-sis əz) [Fr. < OFr. *glacier,* to slip < *glace,* ice] **1.** a gradual slope **2.** an embankment sloping down from a fortification

**glad**[1] (glad) *adj.* **glad′der, glad′dest** [OE. *glæd*] **1.** happy; pleased **2.** causing pleasure or joy; making happy **3.** very willing [I'm *glad* to help] **4.** bright or beautiful —*vt., vi.* **glad′ded, glad′ding** [Archaic] to gladden —**glad′ly** *adv.* —**glad′ness** *n.*

**glad**[2] (glad) *n.* [Colloq.] *same as* GLADIOLUS

**glad·den** (-'n) *vt., vi.* to make or become glad

**glade** (glād) *n.* [ME., prob. < *glad,* GLAD[1]] **1.** an open space in a wood or forest **2.** an everglade

**glad hand** [Slang] a cordial, eager, or effusive welcome —**glad′-hand′** *vt., vi.* —**glad′-hand′er** *n.*

**glad·i·a·tor** (glad′ē āt′ər) *n.* [L. < *gladius,* sword] **1.** in ancient Rome, a man who fought other men or animals in an arena as a public show: gladiators were slaves, captives, or paid performers **2.** any person involved in a public controversy or fight —**glad′i·a·to′ri·al** (-ə tôr′ē əl) *adj.*

**glad·i·o·lus** (glad′ē ō′ləs; *occas.* glə dī′ə ləs) *n., pl.* **-lus·es, -li** (-lī) [ModL. < L. dim. of *gladius,* sword] a plant with swordlike leaves and tall spikes of funnel-shaped flowers in various colors: also **glad′i·o′la** (-lə)

**glad·some** (glad′səm) *adj.* joyful or cheerful —**glad′some·ly** *adv.* —**glad′some·ness** *n.*

**Glad·stone** (glad′stōn; *Brit.* -stən), **William Ew·art** (yōō′ərt) 1809–98; English prime minister

**Glad·stone (bag)** (glad′stōn; *Brit.* -stən) [after prec.] a traveling bag hinged so that it can open flat into two compartments of equal size

**Glad·ys** (glad′is) [W. *Gwladys,* prob. < L. *Claudis:* see CLAUDIA] a feminine name

**glair** (gler) *n.* [< OFr. < L. *clarus,* clear] **1.** raw white of egg, used in sizing or glazing **2.** a size or glaze made from this **3.** any sticky matter resembling raw egg white —*vt.* to cover with glair —**glair′y** *adj.*

**glaive** (glāv) *n.* [< OFr. < L. *gladius,* sword] [Archaic] a sword; esp., a broadsword

**glam·or·ize** (glam′ə rīz′) *vt.* **-ized′, -iz′ing** to make glamorous —**glam′or·i·za′tion** *n.*

**glam·or·ous, glam·our·ous** (-ər əs) *adj.* full of glamour; fascinating; alluring —**glam′or·ous·ly** *adv.*

**glam·our, glam·or** (glam′ər) *n.* [Scot. var. of *grammar* in sense of *gramarye,* magic] **1.** orig., a magic spell or charm **2.** seemingly mysterious and elusive fascination or allure, as of some person, scene, etc.; bewitching charm

**glance** (glans) *vi.* **glanced, glanc′ing** [prob. a blend < OFr. *glacier,* to slip + *guenchir,* to elude] **1.** to strike obliquely and go off at an angle **2.** to make an indirect or passing reference **3.** to flash or gleam **4.** to take a quick look —*vt.* to cause to strike (a surface) at an angle and be deflected —*n.* **1.** a glancing off; deflected impact **2.** a flash or gleam **3.** a quick look

**gland** (gland) *n.* [< Fr. < OFr. < L. *glandula,* tonsil, dim. of *glans* (gen. *glandis*), acorn] **1.** any organ that separates certain elements from the blood and secretes them in a form for the body to use (as an adrenal, a ductless gland, secretes epinephrine) or throw off (as a kidney, a gland with ducts, secretes urine) **2.** loosely, any structure like a gland in appearance, etc. [lymph *glands*]

**glan·ders** (glan′dərz) *n.pl.* [with sing. v.] [OFr. *glandres,* lit., glands] a contagious disease of horses, mules, etc. characterized by fever, swelling of glands beneath the jaw, nasal inflammation, etc.

**glan·du·lar** (glan′jə lər) *adj.* **1.** of, like, or having a gland or glands **2.** derived from or affected by glands —**glan′du·lar·ly** *adv.*

**glandular fever** *same as* INFECTIOUS MONONUCLEOSIS

**glan·dule** (glan′jool) *n.* [Fr.] a small gland

**glans** (glanz) *n., pl.* **glan·des** (glan′dēz) [L., lit., acorn] **1.** the head, or end, of the penis: in full, **glans penis 2.** the corresponding part of the clitoris

**glare**[1] (gler) *vi.* **glared, glar′ing** [ME. *glaren* < or akin to MDu. *glaren,* to gleam & OE. *glær,* amber] **1.** to shine with a steady, dazzling light **2.** to be too bright or showy **3.** to stare fiercely or angrily —*vt.* to express with a glare —*n.* **1.** a steady, dazzling light **2.** a too bright or dazzling display **3.** a fierce and angry stare

**glare**[2] (gler) *n.* [prob. < prec.] a smooth, bright, glassy surface, as of ice —*adj.* smooth, bright, and glassy

**glar·ing** (-iŋ) *adj.* **1.** dazzlingly bright **2.** too bright and showy **3.** staring fiercely **4.** flagrant [a *glaring* mistake] —**glar′ing·ly** *adv.*

**glar·y** (-ē) *adj.* **glar′i·er, glar′i·est** shining with a too bright light —**glar′i·ness** *n.*

**Glas·gow** (glas′kō, glaz′gō) seaport in SC Scotland: pop. 961,000 —**Glas·we·gi·an** (glas wē′jən, -jē ən) *adj., n.*

**glass** (glas) *n.* [OE. *glæs*] **1.** a hard, brittle substance, usually transparent, made by fusing silicates with soda or potash, lime, and, sometimes, metallic oxides **2.** *same as* GLASSWARE **3.** *a)* an article made of glass, as a drinking container, mirror, telescope, barometer, etc. *b)* [*pl.*] eyeglasses *c)* [*pl.*] binoculars **4.** the quantity contained in a drinking glass —*vt.* **1.** to put in glass jars for preserving **2.** to mirror; reflect **3.** to equip with glass; glaze **4.** to make glassy —*vi.* to become glassy —*adj.* of, made of, or like glass —**glass in** to enclose with glass panes

**glass blowing** the art or process of shaping molten glass by blowing air into a mass of it at the end of a tube —**glass blower**

**glass·ful** (-fool′) *n., pl.* **glass′fuls′** the amount that will fill a glass

**glass·house** (-hous′) *n. Brit. var. of* GREENHOUSE

**glass·ine** (gla sēn′) *n.* [GLASS + -INE[1]] a thin, tough paper used for the windows on envelopes, etc.

**glass snake** a legless lizard found in the S U.S.: so called because its tail breaks off easily

**glass·ware** (glas′wer′) *n.* articles made of glass

**glass wool** fine fibers of glass intertwined in a woolly mass, used in filters and as insulation

**glass·wort** (-wurt′) *n.* a fleshy plant of the goosefoot family, found in saline coastal or desert areas

**glass·y** (-ē) *adj.* **glass′i·er, glass′i·est 1.** like glass, as in smoothness or transparency **2.** expressionless or lifeless [a *glassy* stare] —**glass′i·ly** *adv.* —**glass′i·ness** *n.*

**glau·co·ma** (glô kō′mə, glou-) *n.* [L. < Gr. < *glaukos:* see ff. & -OMA] a disease of the eye marked by increased pressure in the eyeball: it leads to a gradual loss of sight —**glau·co′ma·tous** *adj.*

**glau·cous** (glô′kəs) *adj.* [< L. < Gr. *glaukos,* orig., gleaming] **1.** bluish-green or yellowish-green **2.** *Bot.* covered with a whitish bloom that can be rubbed off, as grapes, plums, etc.

**glaze** (glāz) *vt.* **glazed, glaz′ing** [ME. *glasen* < *glas,* GLASS] **1.** to fit (windows, etc.) with glass **2.** to give a hard, glossy finish or coating to; specif., *a)* to overlay (pottery, etc.) with a substance that gives a glassy finish when fused *b)* to cover (foods) with a coating of sugar syrup, etc. **3.** to cover with a thin layer of ice —*vi.* **1.** to become glassy or glossy **2.** to form a glaze —*n.* **1.** *a)* a glassy finish, as on pottery *b)* any substance used to form this **2.** a film or coating —**glaz′er** *n.*

**gla·zier** (glā′zhər) *n.* a person whose work is fitting glass in windows, etc. —**gla′zier·y** *n.*

**glaz·ing** (-ziŋ) *n.* **1.** the work of a glazier **2.** a glass set or to be set in frames **3.** a glaze or the application of a glaze

**gleam** (glēm) *n.* [OE. *glæm*] **1.** a flash or beam of light **2.** a faint light **3.** a reflected brightness, as from a polished surface **4.** a brief, faint manifestation, as of hope, etc. —*vi.* **1.** to shine with a gleam **2.** to be manifested briefly; appear suddenly —**gleam′y** *adj.*

**glean** (glēn) *vt., vi.* [< OFr. < VL. *glennare* < Celt.] **1.** to collect (grain left by reapers) from (a field) **2.** to collect (facts, etc.) bit by bit from (a source) —**glean′er** *n.*

**glean·ings** (-iŋz) *n.pl.* that which is gleaned

**glebe** (glēb) *n.* [< L. *gleba,* clod] **1.** church land forming part or all of a benefice **2.** [Poet.] soil; earth; land; field

**glee** (glē) *n.* [OE. *gleo*] **1.** lively joy; merriment **2.** a part song for three or more voices, usually unaccompanied

**glee club** a group formed to sing part songs

**glee·ful** (-fəl) *adj.* full of glee; merry: also **glee′some** —**glee′ful·ly** *adv.* —**glee′ful·ness** *n.*

**glen** (glen) *n.* [< ScotGael. hyp. *glenn* (now *gleann*)] a narrow, secluded valley

**Glen·dale** (glen′dāl) [GLEN + DALE] city in SW Calif.: suburb of Los Angeles: pop. 139,000

**Glen·gar·ry** (glen gar′ē) *n., pl.* **-ries** [< *Glengarry,* valley in Scotland] [*sometimes* g-] a Scottish cap for men, creased lengthwise across the top and often having short ribbons at the back: also **Glengarry bonnet** (or **cap**)

**Glenn, Glen** (glen) [Celt.: see GLEN] a masculine name

**glib** (glib) *adj.* **glib′ber, glib′best** [orig., slippery < or akin to Du. *glibberig,* slippery] **1.** done in a smooth, offhand way **2.** speaking or spoken in a smooth, fluent manner, often in a way too smooth and easy to be convincing —**glib′ly** *adv.* —**glib′ness** *n.*

**glide** (glīd) *vi.* **glid′ed, glid′ing** [OE. *glidan*] **1.** to flow or move smoothly and easily **2.** to pass gradually and almost unnoticed, as time **3.** *Aeron. a)* to fly in a glider *b)* to descend at a normal angle without engine power **4.** *Music,*

*Phonet.* to make a glide —*vt.* to cause to glide —*n.* **1.** the act of gliding **2.** a small disk or ball attached under furniture legs, etc. to allow easy sliding **3.** *Music* loosely, a slur **4.** *Phonet.* an intermediate sound made when the speech organs change from the position for one sound to another

**glid·er** (glīd′ər) *n.* **1.** a person or thing that glides **2.** an aircraft like an airplane except that it has no engine and is carried along by air currents **3.** a porch seat suspended in an upright frame so that it can glide back and forth

**glim·mer** (glim′ər) *vi.* [< base of OE. *glæm*, gleam] **1.** to give a faint, flickering light **2.** to appear or be seen faintly —*n.* **1.** a faint, flickering light **2.** a faint manifestation

**glim·mer·ing** (-iŋ) *n.* same as GLIMMER

**glimpse** (glimps) *vt.* **glimpsed, glimps′ing** [see GLIMMER] to catch a brief, quick view of, as in passing —*vi.* to look quickly; glance (*at*) —*n.* **1.** a flash **2.** a faint, fleeting appearance; slight trace **3.** a brief, quick view

**glint** (glint) *vi.* [prob. < Scand.] to gleam; flash —*n.* a gleam, flash, or glitter

**glis·sade** (gli säd′, -sād′) *n.* [Fr. < *glisser*, to slide] **1.** an intentional slide by a mountain climber down a steep, snow-covered slope. *Ballet* a gliding step —*vi.* **-sad′ed, -sad′ing** to make a glissade

**glis·san·do** (gli sän′dō) *n., pl.* **-di** (-dē), **-dos** [as if It. prp., equiv. to Fr. *glissant*, prp. of *glisser*, to slide] *Music* a sliding effect achieved by sounding a series of adjacent tones in rapid succession —*adj., adv.* (performed) with such an effect

**glis·ten** (glis′n) *vi.* [OE. *glisnian*] to shine or sparkle with reflected light, as a wet or polished surface —*n.* a glistening

**glis·ter** (glis′tər) *vi., n. archaic var. of* GLISTEN

**glit·ter** (glit′ər) *vi.* [prob. < ON. *glitra*] **1.** to shine with a sparkling light **2.** to be brilliant, showy, or attractive —*n.* **1.** a bright, sparkling light **2.** showy brilliance or attractiveness **3.** bits of glittering material —**glit′ter·y** *adj.*

**glitz·y** (glit′sē) *adj.* **glitz′i·er, glitz′i·est** [prob. via Yid. < G. *glitzern*, to glitter] [Slang] **1.** having glitter; sparkling; glittery **2.** attracting attention in an ornate or gaudy way; showy; pretentious

**gloam·ing** (glō′miŋ) *n.* [OE. *glomung* < *glom*, twilight] evening dusk; twilight

**gloat** (glōt) *vi.* [prob. < ON. *glotta*, to grin scornfully] to gaze or think with malicious pleasure —*n.* the act of gloating —**gloat′er** *n.*

**glob** (gläb) *n.* [prob. contr. < GLOBULE, after BLOB] a rounded mass or lump, as of a semisolid

**glob·al** (glō′b'l) *adj.* **1.** globe-shaped **2.** worldwide [*global war*] **3.** complete —**glob′al·ly** *adv.*

**glob·al·ism** (-iz'm) *n.* a policy, outlook, etc. that is world-wide in scope —**glob′al·ist** *n., adj.*

**globe** (glōb) *n.* [< L. *globus*, a ball] **1.** any round, ball-shaped thing; sphere; specif., *a)* the earth *b)* a spherical model of the earth **2.** anything shaped like a globe, as a rounded glass cover for a lamp —*vt., vi.* **globed, glob′ing** to form or gather into a globe —**glo·bate** (glō′bāt) *adj.*

**globe·fish** (-fish′) *n., pl.* **-fish′, -fish′es:** see FISH any of several tropical fishes that can puff themselves into a globular form

**globe-trot·ter** (-trät′ər) *n.* a person who travels widely about the world, esp. for pleasure or sightseeing

**glo·boid** (glō′boid) *adj.* shaped somewhat like a globe or ball —*n.* anything globoid

**glo·bose** (-bōs) *adj.* [L. *globosus*] same as GLOBOID: also **glo′bous** (-bəs) —**glo′bose·ly** *adv.*

**glob·u·lar** (gläb′yə lər) *adj.* **1.** shaped like a globe or ball; spherical **2.** made up of globules

**glob·ule** (-yool) *n.* [Fr. < L. dim. of *globus*, a ball] a tiny ball or globe; esp., a drop of liquid

**glob·u·lin** (-yə lin) *n.* [GLOBUL(E) + -IN¹] any of a group of proteins in animal and vegetable tissue

**glock·en·spiel** (gläk′ən spēl′, -shpēl′) *n.* [G. < *glocke*, a bell + *spiel*, play] a percussion instrument with flat metal bars set in a frame, that produce bell-like tones of the scale when struck with small hammers

**glom** (gläm) *vt.* **glommed, glom′ming** [< Scot. dial.] [Slang] **1.** to seize **2.** to steal **3.** to look over —**glom onto** [Slang] to take and hold; grasp

**glom·er·ate** (gläm′ər it) *adj.* [< L. pp. of *glomerare* < *glomus*, a ball] formed into a rounded mass; clustered —**glom′er·a′tion** *n.*

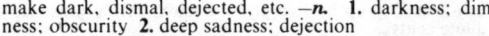

GLOCKENSPIEL

**gloom** (gloom) *vi.* [prob. < Scand.] **1.** to be or look morose or dejected **2.** to become dark, dim, or dismal —*vt.* to make dark, dismal, dejected, etc. —*n.* **1.** darkness; dimness; obscurity **2.** deep sadness; dejection

**gloom·y** (-ē) *adj.* **gloom′i·er, gloom′i·est 1.** overspread with or enveloped in darkness or dimness **2.** melancholy or sullen **3.** causing gloom; depressing —**gloom′i·ly** *adv.* —**gloom′i·ness** *n.*

**glop** (gläp) *n.* [< ? GL(UE) + (SL)OP] [Slang] any soft, gluey substance, thick liquid, etc.

**Glo·ri·a** (glôr′ē ə) [L., glory] a feminine name —*n.* **1.** either of the Latin hymns beginning *Gloria in Excelsis Deo* (glory be to God on high) or *Gloria Patri* (glory be to the Father) **2.** the music for either

**glo·ri·fy** (glôr′ə fī′) *vt.* **-fied′, -fy′ing** [< OFr. < LL. < L. *gloria*, glory + *facere*, to make] **1.** to make glorious; give glory to **2.** to exalt in worship **3.** to honor; extol **4.** to make seem better, larger, finer, etc. —**glo′ri·fi·ca′tion** *n.* —**glo′ri·fi′er** *n.*

**glo·ri·ous** (glôr′ē əs) *adj.* **1.** full of glory; illustrious **2.** giving glory **3.** receiving or deserving glory **4.** splendid; magnificent **5.** [Colloq.] very delightful or enjoyable —**glo′ri·ous·ly** *adv.* —**glo′ri·ous·ness** *n.*

**glo·ry** (glôr′ē) *n., pl.* **-ries** [< OFr. < L. *gloria*] **1.** *a)* great honor and admiration *b)* anything bringing this **2.** worshipful adoration **3.** the condition of highest achievement, prosperity, etc. **4.** splendor; magnificence **5.** heaven or the bliss of heaven **6.** same as HALO (*n.* 1 & 2) —*vi.* **-ried, -ry·ing** to be very proud; exult (with *in*) —**gone to glory** dead — **in one's glory** at one's best, happiest, etc.

**gloss¹** (glôs, gläs) *n.* [prob. < Scand.] **1.** the luster of a smooth, polished surface; sheen **2.** a deceptively pleasant outward appearance, as in manners or speech —*vt.* **1.** to make lustrous **2.** to cover up (an error, fault, etc.) by minimizing (often with *over*) —*vi.* to become shiny

**gloss²** (glôs, gläs) *n.* [< OFr. or < ML. < L. < Gr. *glôssa*, the tongue] **1.** a translation inserted between the lines of a text **2.** a note of comment or explanation, as in a footnote **3.** a glossary —*vt.* **1.** to furnish (a text) with glosses **2.** to interpret falsely —*vi.* to annotate —**gloss′er** *n.*

**glos·sa·ry** (gläs′ə rē, glôs′-) *n., pl.* **-ries** [< L. < *glossa* < Gr. *glôssa*, the tongue] a list of difficult, technical, or foreign terms with definitions or translations, as for a particular author, subject, book, etc. —**glos·sar·i·al** (glä ser′ē əl) *adj.* —**glos′sar·ist** *n.*

**glos·so·la·li·a** (gläs′ə lā′lē ə, glôs′-) *n.* [ModL., ult. < Gr. *glôssa*, tongue + *lalein*, to speak] an ecstatic utterance of unintelligible speechlike sounds, regarded as caused by religious ecstasy

**gloss·y** (glôs′ē, gläs′-) *adj.* **gloss′i·er, gloss′i·est 1.** having a smooth, shiny appearance or finish **2.** specious —*n., pl.* **gloss′ies 1.** a photographic print with a glossy surface **2.** [Colloq.] a magazine printed on glossy paper —**gloss′i·ly** *adv.* —**gloss′i·ness** *n.*

**glot·tal** (glät′'l) *adj.* of or produced in or at the glottis

**glot·tis** (glät′is) *n., pl.* **-tis·es, -ti·des′** (-ə dēz′) [ModL. < Gr. < *glôtta*, var. of *glôssa*, the tongue] the opening between the vocal cords in the larynx

**glove** (gluv) *n.* [< OE. *glof* & ON. *glofi*] **1.** a covering for the hand, with a separate sheath for each finger and the thumb **2.** *Sports a)* a baseball player's mitt *b)* a padded mitten worn by boxers: usually **boxing glove** —*vt.* **gloved, glov′ing 1.** to supply with gloves **2.** to cover as with a glove **3.** *Baseball* to catch (a ball) with a glove

**glov·er** (-ər) *n.* one who makes or sells gloves

**glow** (glō) *vi.* [OE. *glowan*] **1.** to give off a bright light as a result of great heat; be incandescent or red-hot **2.** to give out a steady, even light without flame **3.** to be or feel hot **4.** to radiate health **5.** to be elated or enlivened by emotion **6.** to be bright with color —*n.* **1.** a light given off as the result of great heat **2.** steady, even light without flame or blaze **3.** brilliance of color **4.** brightness of skin color; flush **5.** a sensation of warmth and well-being **6.** warmth of emotion —**glow′ing** *adj.* —**glow′ing·ly** *adv.*

**glow·er** (glou′ər) *vi.* [prob. < ON.] to stare with sullen anger; scowl —*n.* a sullen, angry stare; scowl —**glow′er·ing** *adj.* —**glow′er·ing·ly** *adv.*

**glow·worm** (glō′wurm′) *n.* a wingless insect or insect larva that gives off a luminescent light; esp., the wingless female or the larva of the firefly

**glox·in·i·a** (gläk sin′ē ə) *n.* [ModL., after B. P. *Gloxin*, 18th-c. Ger. botanist] a cultivated tropical plant with bell-shaped flowers of various colors

**gloze** (glōz) *vt.* **glozed, gloz′ing** [< OFr. < *glose:* see GLOSS²] to explain away; gloss (often with *over*)

**glu·cose** (gloo′kōs) *n.* [Fr. < Gr. *gleúkos*, sweet wine, sweetness] a crystalline sugar, $C_6H_{12}O_6$, occurring naturally in fruits, honey, etc.: the commercial form is prepared as a sweet syrup by hydrolyzing starch in the presence of dilute acids

**glu·co·side** (gloo′kə sīd′) *n.* [GLUCOS(E) + -IDE] any glycoside having glucose as its sugar constituent —**glu′co·sid′ic** (-sid′ik) *adj.*

**glue** (gloo) *n.* [< OFr. *glu*, birdlime < LL. *glus*, glue] 1. a sticky, viscous substance made from animal skins, bones, hoofs, etc. by boiling, etc. and used to stick things together 2. any similar adhesive made from casein, resin, etc. —*vt.* **glued, glu′ing** to make stick as with glue —**glu′er** *n.*

**glue·y** (-ē) *adj.* **glu′i·er, glu′i·est** 1. like glue; sticky 2. covered with or full of glue

**glum** (glum) *adj.* **glum′mer, glum′mest** [prob. < ME. var. of *gloum(b)en*, to look morose] gloomy; sullen; morose —**glum′ly** *adv.* —**glum′ness** *n.*

**glume** (gloom) *n.* [ModL. *gluma* < L., husk] either of the two empty bracts at the base of a grass spikelet, etc.

**glut** (glut) *vi.* **glut′ted, glut′ting** [< OFr. *gloter*, to swallow < L. *gluttire*] to eat like a glutton —*vt.* 1. to feed, fill, etc. to excess; surfeit 2. to flood (the market) with certain goods so that the supply is greater than the demand —*n.* 1. a glutting or being glutted 2. a supply of certain goods that is greater than the demand

**glu·ten** (gloot′'n) *n.* [L., glue] a gray, sticky substance found in wheat and other grain, the protein part of flour and bread —**glu′ten·ous** *adj.*

**glu·te·us** (gloo tē′əs, gloot′ē-) *n., pl.* **-te′i** (-ī) [ModL. < Gr. *gloutos*, rump] any of the three muscles forming each of the buttocks —**glu·te′al** *adj.*

**glu·ti·nous** (gloot′'n əs) *adj.* [< L. < *gluten*, glue] gluey; sticky —**glu′ti·nous·ly** *adv.*

**glut·ton** (glut′'n) *n.* [< OFr. < L. *gluto* < *glutire*, to devour] 1. a person who greedily eats too much 2. a person with a great capacity for something 3. a furry, northern animal related to the marten: the American variety is the WOLVERINE —**glut′ton·ize** *vt., vi.* **-ized′, -iz′ing**

**glut·ton·ous** (-əs) *adj.* inclined to eat too much and greedily —**glut′ton·ous·ly** *adv.*

**glut·ton·y** (-ē) *n., pl.* **-ton·ies** the habit or act of eating too much

**glyc·er·ide** (glis′ər īd′) *n.* an ester of glycerol

**glyc·er·in** (glis′ər in, glis′rin) *n.* [< Fr. < Gr. *glykeros*, sweet] *popular and commercial term for* GLYCEROL: also sp. **glyc′er·ine**

**glyc·er·ol** (glis′ər ōl′, -ôl′) *n.* [< prec. + -OL¹] an odorless, colorless, syrupy liquid, $C_3H_8O_3$, prepared by the hydrolysis of fats and oils: used as a solvent, skin lotion, etc., and in explosives, etc.

**gly·co-** [< Gr. < *glykys*, sweet] *a combining form meaning* glycerol, sugar, glycogen: also, before a vowel, **glyc-**

**gly·co·gen** (glī′kə jən) *n.* [prec. + -GEN] a partially soluble, starchlike substance, $(C_6H_{10}O_5)x$, produced in animal tissues, esp. in the liver and muscles, and changed into a simple sugar as the body needs it —**gly′co·gen′ic** (-jen′ik) *adj.*

**gly·col** (glī′kôl, -kōl) *n.* [GLYC(ERIN) + -OL¹] 1. *same as* ETHYLENE GLYCOL 2. any of a group of alcohols of which ethylene glycol is the type

**gly·co·side** (glī′kə sīd′) *n.* [Fr. < *glycose* (for GLUCOSE) + -ide, -IDE] any of a group of sugar derivatives, widely distributed in plants, which on hydrolysis yield a sugar and one or more other substances —**gly′co·sid′ic** (-sid′ik) *adj.*

**gm.** gram(s)

**G-man** (jē′man′) *n., pl.* **G′-men′** (-men′) [associated with g(*overnment*) man, but prob. < G division of the Dublin Police] [Colloq.] an agent of the Federal Bureau of Investigation

**Gmc.** Germanic

**gnarl** (närl) *n.* [back-formation < ff.] a knot on the trunk or branch of a tree —*vt., vi.* to make or become knotted or twisted

**gnarled** (närld) *adj.* [ult.< ME. *knur*, a knot] knotty and twisted [a *gnarled* tree, *gnarled* hands]: also **gnarl′y**

**gnash** (nash) *vt., vi.* [ME. *gnasten*, prob. < ON.] to grind or strike (the teeth) together, as in anger or pain —*n.* the act of gnashing

**gnat** (nat) *n.* [OE. *gnæt*] 1. any of a number of small, two-winged insects some of which can bite or sting 2. [Brit.] a mosquito —**gnat′ty** *adj.*

**gnaw** (nô) *vt.* **gnawed, gnawed** or, rarely, **gnawn, gnaw′ing** [OE. *gnagen*] 1. to bite and wear away bit by bit 2. to make by gnawing 3. to consume; corrode 4. to torment, as by constant pain, fear, etc. —*vi.* 1. to bite repeatedly (*on, at*, etc.) 2. to have a gnawing effect

**gnaw·ing** (-iŋ) *n.* 1. a sensation of dull, constant pain or suffering 2. [pl.] pangs, as of hunger

**gneiss** (nīs) *n.* [< G. < OHG. *gneisto*, a spark] a coarse-grained, granitelike rock formed of layers of feldspar, quartz, mica, etc. —**gneiss′ic** *adj.*

**gnome** (nōm) *n.* [Fr., ult. < Gr. *gnōmē*, thought] *Folklore* a dwarf supposed to dwell in the earth and guard its treasures —**gnom′ish** *adj.*

**gno·mic** (nō′mik) *adj.* [< Gr. *gnōmikos* < *gnōmē*, thought] wise and pithy; full of aphorisms

**gno·mon** (nō′män) *n.* [L. < Gr. < base of *gignōskein*, to know] a column, pin on a sundial, etc. that casts a shadow indicating the time of day

**-gnomy** [Gr. *-gnōmia* < *gnōmē*, thought] *a combining form meaning* art of judging or determining [*physiognomy*]

**-gnosis** [see ff.] *a combining form meaning* knowledge, recognition [*diagnosis*]

**gnos·tic** (näs′tik) *adj.* [< Gr. *gnōstikos* < *gnōsis*, knowledge] 1. of or having knowledge 2. [G-] of the Gnostics or Gnosticism —*n.* [G-] a believer in Gnosticism

**Gnos·ti·cism** (näs′tə siz′m) *n.* a system of belief combining ideas derived from Greek philosophy, Oriental mysticism, and, ultimately, Christianity

**GNP** gross national product

**gnu** (noo, nyoo) *n., pl.* **gnus, gnu:** see PLURAL, II, D, 1 [< the native (Bushman) name] a large African antelope with an oxlike head and horns and a horselike mane and tail; wildebeest

GNU (40–50 in. high at shoulder)

**go** (gō) *vi.* **went, gone, go′ing** [OE. *gan*] 1. to move along; travel; proceed 2. to be in operation; work [the clock won't *go*] 3. to gesture, act, or make sounds as specified or shown 4. to take a particular course, line of action, etc.; proceed 5. to result; turn out [the war *went* badly] 6. to pass: said of time 7. to pass from person to person, as a rumor 8. to be in a certain state [he *goes* in rags] 9. to become; turn [to *go* mad] 10. to be expressed, sung, etc. [as the saying *goes*] 11. to be in harmony; fit in 12. to put oneself [to *go* to some trouble] 13. to tend; help [facts that *go* to prove a case] 14. to have force, acceptance, etc. 15. to leave; depart 16. to pass away [the pain is *gone*] 17. to die 18. to be removed or eliminated 19. to break away [the mast *went* in the storm] 20. to fail; give way [his eyesight is *going*] 21. to be given [the prize *goes* to you] 22. to be sold [it *went* for $10] 23. to extend to or along a specified place or time; reach 24. to turn to, enter, or participate in a certain activity, occupation, etc. [to *go* to college] 25. to pass (*through*), fit (*into*), etc. 26. to be a divisor (*into*) 27. to endure; last 28. to continue (unpunished, unrewarded, etc.) 29. to have a regular place [pencils *go* on the desk] —*vt.* 1. to travel or proceed along [he's *going* my way] 2. to bet 3. [Colloq.] to tolerate [I can't *go* him] 4. [Colloq.] to furnish (bail) 5. [Colloq.] to be willing to pay, bid, etc. (a specified sum) —*n., pl.* **goes** 1. the act of going 2. a success 3. [Colloq.] animation; energy 4. [Colloq.] a state of affairs 5. [Colloq.] an agreement, or bargain [is it a *go*?] 6. [Colloq.] a try; attempt —*adj.* [Slang: orig. astronaut's jargon] functioning properly or ready to go —**as people** (or **things**) **go** in comparison with how other people (or things) are —**go about** 1. to be busy at; do 2. to circulate 3. *Naut.* to tack; change direction —**go after** [Colloq.] to try to catch or get —**go against** to be or act in opposition to —**go along** 1. to continue 2. to agree 3. to accompany —**go around** 1. to surround 2. to be enough to provide a share for each 3. to circulate —**go at** to attack or work at —**go back on** [Colloq.] 1. to betray 2. to break (a promise, etc.) —**go beyond** to exceed —**go by** 1. to pass 2. to be guided by 3. to be known or referred to by (the name of) —**go down** 1. to sink; set 2. to suffer defeat 3. to be perpetuated, as in history —**go for** 1. to be taken as 2. to try to get 3. to support 4. [Colloq.] to attack 5. [Colloq.] to be attracted by —**go hard with** to cause trouble to —**go in for** [Colloq.] to engage or indulge in —**go into** 1. to inquire into 2. to take up as a study or occupation —**go in with** to share obligations with; join —**go it** [Colloq.] to carry on; proceed [to *go it* alone] —**go off** 1. to leave, esp. suddenly 2. to explode 3. to happen —**go on** 1. to continue 2. to behave 3. to happen —**go out** 1. to be extinguished, become outdated, etc. 2. to attend social affairs, the theater, etc. 3. to go on strike 4. to try out (*for*) —**go over** 1. to examine thoroughly 2. to do again 3. to review 4. [Colloq.] to be successful —**go some** [Colloq.] to do or achieve quite a lot —**go through** 1. to perform thoroughly 2. to endure; experience 3. to search 4. to get acceptance 5. to spend —**go through with** to complete —**go together** 1. to harmonize 2. [Colloq.] to be sweethearts —**go under** to fail, as in business —**go up** to rise in price, etc.; increase —**go with** [Colloq.] to be a sweetheart of —**go without** to do without —**let go** 1. to let escape 2. to release one's hold 3. to give up; abandon 4. to dismiss from a job —**let oneself go** to be unrestrained in emotion, action, etc. —**no go** [Colloq.] not possible; no use —**on the go** [Colloq.] in constant motion or action —**to go** [Colloq.] 1. to be taken out: said of food in a restaurant **2.** left to complete, etc. —**what goes?** [Slang] what's happening?

**goad** (gōd) *n.* [OE. *gad*] **1.** a sharp-pointed stick for driving oxen **2.** any driving impulse; spur —*vt.* to drive as with a goad; prod into action

**go·a·head** (gō′ə hed′) *n.* permission or a signal to proceed: usually with *the*

**goal** (gōl) *n.* [ME. *gol*, boundary] **1.** the place where a race, trip, etc. is ended **2.** an end that one strives to attain; aim **3.** in certain games, *a)* the line, net, etc. over or into which the ball or puck must go to score *b)* the act of so scoring *c)* the score made

**goal·keep·er** (-kēp′ər) *n.* in certain games, a player stationed at a goal to prevent the ball or puck from crossing or entering it: also **goal′ie** (-ē), **goal′tend′er**

**goat** (gōt) *n.* [OE. *gat*] **1.** *pl.* **goats, goat:** see PLURAL, II, D, 1 *a)* a cud-chewing mammal with hollow horns, related to the sheep *b)* same as ROCKY MOUNTAIN GOAT **2.** a lecherous man **3.** [Colloq.] a scapegoat —[G-] the constellation Capricorn —**get one's goat** [Colloq.] to annoy or anger one —**goat′ish** *adj.* —**goat′ish·ly** *adv.*

**goat·ee** (gō tē′) *n.* a pointed beard on a man's chin

**goat·herd** (gōt′hurd′) *n.* one who herds goats

**goat·skin** (-skin′) *n.* **1.** the skin of a goat **2.** leather made from this **3.** a container for wine, water, etc., made of this leather

**goat·suck·er** (-suk′ər) *n.* a large-mouthed, nocturnal bird that feeds on insects, as the whippoorwill

**gob¹** (gäb) *n.* [< OFr. *gobe*, prob. < *gobet:* see GOBBET] **1.** a lump or mass, as of something soft **2.** [*pl.*] [Colloq.] a large quantity or amount

**gob²** (gäb) *n.* [< ?] [Slang] a sailor in the U.S. Navy

**gob·bet** (gäb′it) *n.* [OFr. *gobet*, mouthful, prob. < Gaul.] [Archaic] **1.** a fragment or bit, esp. of raw flesh **2.** a lump; chunk **3.** a mouthful

**gob·ble¹** (gäb′'l) *n.* [echoic, var. of GABBLE] the characteristic throaty sound made by a male turkey —*vi.* **-bled, -bling** to make this sound

**gob·ble²** (gäb′'l) *vt., vi.* **-bled, -bling** [prob. < OFr. *gober*, to swallow < *gobe*, mouthful, GOB¹] **1.** to eat quickly and greedily **2.** to snatch (*up*)

**gob·ble·dy·gook** (gäb′'l dē gook′) *n.* [Slang] pompous and wordy talk or writing: also **gob′ble·de·gook′**

**gob·bler** (gäb′lər) *n.* a male turkey

**Gob·e·lin** (gäb′ə lin, gō′bə-; *Fr.* gô blan′) *adj.* of or like a kind of tapestry made at the Gobelin works in Paris —*n.* Gobelin tapestry

**go·be·tween** (gō′bi twēn′) *n.* one who deals with each of two sides in making arrangements between them; intermediary

**Go·bi** (gō′bē) large desert plateau in E Asia, chiefly in Mongolia

**gob·let** (gäb′lit) *n.* [< OFr. < *gobel* < ? Bret. *gob*] **1.** orig., a cup without handles **2.** a drinking glass with a base and stem

**gob·lin** (gäb′lin) *n.* [< OFr. < ML. *gobelinus*, ult. < ? Gr. *kobalos*, sprite] *Folklore* an evil or mischievous sprite, ugly or misshapen in form

**go·by** (gō′bē) *n., pl.* **-bies, -by:** see PLURAL, II, D, 1 [L. *gobio*, gudgeon < Gr. *kōbios*] any of a group of small, spiny-finned fishes: the ventral fins are sometimes modified into a suction disk

**go-by** (gō′bī′) *n.* [Colloq.] a passing by; esp., an intentional disregard or slight: chiefly in **give** (or **get**) **the go-by,** to slight (or be slighted)

**go-cart** (-kärt′) *n.* **1.** a framework on casters, to support a child learning to walk **2.** a small, low baby carriage **3.** same as KART (sense 2)

**god** (gäd, gôd) *n.* [OE.] **1.** any of various beings conceived of as supernatural, immortal, and having power over people and nature; deity, esp. a male one **2.** an idol **3.** a person or thing deified or excessively honored —[G-] in monotheistic religions, the creator and ruler of the universe, eternal, infinite, all-powerful, and all-knowing

**god·child** (gäd′chīld′) *n., pl.* **-chil′dren** the person for whom a godparent is sponsor

**god·daugh·ter** (gäd′dôt′ər) *n.* a female godchild

**god·dess** (gäd′is) *n.* **1.** a female god **2.** a woman greatly admired, as for her beauty

**god·fa·ther** (gäd′fä′thər) *n.* a male godparent

**God-fear·ing** (-fir′iŋ) *adj.* [*occas.* g-] **1.** fearing God **2.** devout; pious

**God·for·sak·en** (-fər sā′kən) *adj.* [*occas.* g-] **1.** depraved; wicked **2.** desolate; forlorn

**God·frey** (gäd′frē) [< OHG. < *god*, God + *fridu*, peace, lit., peace (of) God] a masculine name

**God-giv·en** (gäd′giv′ən) *adj.* [*occas.* g-] **1.** given by God **2.** very welcome; opportune

**god·head** (-hed′) *n.* **1.** godhood **2.** [G-] God

**god·hood** (-hood′) *n.* the state or quality of being a god; divinity

**Go·di·va** (gə dī′və) a legendary 11th-cent. noblewoman of Coventry who, on the dare of her husband, rode naked through the streets on horseback so that he would abolish a heavy tax

**god·less** (gäd′lis) *adj.* **1.** denying the existence of God or a god; irreligious **2.** impious; wicked —**god′less·ness** *n.*

**god·like** (-līk′) *adj.* like or suitable to God or a god; divine

**god·ly** (-lē) *adj.* **-li·er, -li·est 1.** divine **2.** pious; devout; religious —**god′li·ness** *n.*

**god·moth·er** (-muth′ər) *n.* a female godparent

**god·par·ent** (gäd′per′ənt, -par′-) *n.* a person who sponsors a child, as at baptism, and assumes responsibility for its faith; godmother or godfather

**god·send** (gäd′send′) *n.* anything unexpected and needed that comes at the opportune moment, as if sent by God

**god·son** (-sun′) *n.* a male godchild

**God·speed** (-spēd′) *n.* [contr. of *God speed you*] success; good fortune: a wish for a person starting on a trip

**God·win Austen** (gäd′win) mountain in N Jammu & Kashmir, near the Chinese border: second highest mountain in the world: 28,250 ft.

**god·wit** (gäd′wit) *n.* [? echoic] a brownish wading bird, with a long bill that curves up

**go·er** (gō′ər) *n.* one that goes

**Goe·the** (gö′tə; *also Anglicized to* gur′tə, gät′ə), **Jo·hann Wolf·gang von** (yō′hän vôlf′gäŋ fôn) 1749–1832; Ger. poet & dramatist

**go·fer, go-fer** (gō′fər) *n.* [from being asked to go *for* whatever is needed] [Slang] an employee who performs minor or menial tasks such as running errands

**go-get·ter** (gō′get′ər) *n.* [Colloq.] an enterprising and aggressive person

**gog·gle** (gäg′'l) *vi.* **-gled, -gling** [ME. *gogelen*] **1.** *a)* to stare with bulging eyes *b)* to roll the eyes **2.** *a)* to bulge in a stare *b)* to roll: said of the eyes —*n.* **1.** a staring with bulging eyes **2.** [*pl.*] large spectacles, esp. those fitted with side guards to protect the eyes from wind, etc. —*adj.* bulging: said of the eyes —**gog′gle-eyed′** (-īd′) *adj.*

**Gogh, Vincent van** *see* VAN GOGH

**go-go** (gō′gō′) *adj.* [< Fr. *à gogo,* in plenty, ad lib.] **1.** of rock-and-roll dancing or cafés, etc. featuring it **2.** [Slang] lively, energetic, etc.

**Go·gol** (gō′gôl; *E.* gō′gəl), **Ni·ko·lai Va·sil·ie·vich** (nē′kô lī′ vä sēl′yə vich) 1809–52; Russ. novelist & dramatist

**Goi·del·ic** (goi del′ik) *adj.* [< OIr. *Góidel*] **1.** of the Gaels **2.** designating or of their languages —*n.* the subbranch of Celtic languages that includes Irish Gaelic, Scottish Gaelic, and Manx

**go·ing** (gō′iŋ) *n.* **1.** the act of one who goes **2.** a departure **3.** the condition of the ground or land as it affects traveling **4.** circumstances affecting progress —*adj.* **1.** moving; running; working **2.** operating successfully [a *going* concern] **3.** in existence or available [the best bet *going*] **4.** current [the *going* rate] —**be going to** to be intending to; will or shall —**get going** [Colloq.] to start —**get one going** [Slang] to make one excited, angry, etc. —**going on** [Colloq.] nearing or nearly (a specified age or time)

**go·ing-o·ver** (-ō′vər) *n.* [Colloq.] **1.** an inspection, esp. a thorough one **2.** a severe scolding or beating

**go·ings-on** (gō′iŋz än′) *n.pl.* [Colloq.] actions or events, esp. when regarded with disapproval

**goi·ter, goi·tre** (goit′ər) *n.* [< Fr., ult. < L. *guttur*, throat] an enlarged thyroid gland, often visible as a swelling in the front of the neck —**goi·trous** (goi′trəs) *adj.*

**gold** (gōld) *n.* [OE.] **1.** a heavy, yellow, metallic chemical element that is highly ductile and malleable: it is a precious metal and is used in coins, jewelry, alloys, etc.: symbol, Au; at. wt., 196.967; at. no., 79 **2.** *a)* gold coin *b)* money; riches **3.** the bright yellow color of gold **4.** a thing regarded as having the value, brilliance, etc. of gold —*adj.* **1.** of, made of, or like gold **2.** having the color of gold

**gold·brick** (-brik′) *n.* **1.** [Colloq.] anything worthless passed off as genuine or valuable **2.** [Mil. Slang] one who avoids work; shirker: also **gold′brick′er** —*vi.* [Mil. Slang] to shirk; loaf

**gold digger** [Slang] a woman who tries to get money and gifts from her men friends

**gold dust** gold in very small bits or as a powder

**gold·en** (gōl′d'n) *adj.* **1.** of, containing, or yielding gold **2.** bright-yellow, like gold **3.** precious; excellent **4.**

prosperous and joyful  **5.** auspicious  **6.** richly mellow, as a voice  **7.** marking the 50th anniversary [a *golden* jubilee] —**gold′en·ly** *adv.* —**gold′en·ness** *n.*

**Golden Age  1.** *Gr. & Rom. Myth.* an early age in which people were ideally happy, innocent, etc.  **2.** [g- a-] a period of great progress, culture, etc.  **3.** [*also* g- a-] of or for golden agers

**golden ag·er** (āj′ər) [Colloq.] [*also* G- A-] an elderly person, esp. one 65 or older and retired

**gold·en·eye** (gōl′d'n ī′) *n., pl.* **-eyes′, -eye′**: see PLURAL, II, D, 1  a swift, diving wild duck of N. America and the Old World, with yellow eyes and a dark-green back

**Golden Fleece** *Gr. Myth.* the fleece of gold guarded by a dragon until captured by Jason

**Golden Gate** strait between San Francisco Bay & the Pacific

**golden mean** the safe, prudent way between extremes; moderation

**golden retriever** any of a breed of hunting dog with a thick, golden coat

**gold·en·rod** (-räd′) *n.* a N. American plant of the composite family, typically with long, branching stalks bearing clusters of small, yellow flower heads through late summer and fall

**golden rule** the precept that one should behave toward others as he would want others to behave toward him: see Matt. 7:12; Luke 6:31

**golden wedding** a 50th wedding anniversary

**gold-filled** (gōld′fild′) *adj.* made of a base metal overlaid with gold

**gold·finch** (-finch′) *n.* [OE. *goldfinc*]  **1.** a European songbird with yellow-streaked wings  **2.** any of several small American finches, esp. one the male of which has a yellow body and black markings on the wings

**gold·fish** (-fish′) *n., pl.* **-fish′, -fish′es**: see FISH  a small, golden-yellow or orange fish of the carp family, often kept in fishbowls

**gold foil** gold beaten into thin sheets slightly thicker than gold leaf —**gold′-foil′** *adj.*

**gold leaf** gold beaten into very thin sheets, used for gilding —**gold′-leaf′** *adj.*

**gold plate** tableware made of gold

**gold rush** a rush of people to territory where gold has recently been discovered

**gold·smith** (-smith′) *n.* a skilled worker who makes articles of gold

**Gold·smith** (gōld′smith′), **Oliver** 1728–74; Brit. poet, playwright, & novelist, born in Ireland

**gold standard** a monetary standard in which the basic currency unit is made equal to and redeemable by a specified quantity of gold

**golf** (gôlf, gälf) *n.* [< ? Scot. *gowf*, to strike]  an outdoor game played on a golf course with a small, hard ball and a set of clubs, the object being to hit the ball into each of 9 or 18 holes in turn, with the fewest possible strokes —*vi.* to play golf —**golf′er** *n.*

**golf club  1.** any of a set of clubs used in golf: each has a wooden or metal head and a long, slender shaft  **2.** an organization operating a golf course, clubhouse, etc.

**golf course** (or **links**) a tract of land for playing golf, with tees, fairways, greens, etc.

**Gol·go·tha** (gäl′gə thə) [see CALVARY]  the place where Jesus was crucified; Calvary

**Go·li·ath** (gə lī′əth) *Bible* the Philistine giant killed by David with a stone from a sling

**gol·ly** (gäl′ē) *interj.* an exclamation of surprise, etc.: a euphemism for *God*

**go·losh, go·loshe** (gə läsh′) *n. Brit. var. of* GALOSH

**Go·mor·rah, Go·mor·rha** (gə môr′ə) *see* SODOM

**Gom·pers** (gäm′pərz), **Samuel** 1850–1924; U.S. labor leader, born in England

**-gon** (gän, gən) [< Gr. < *gōnia*, an angle]  *a combining form meaning* a figure having (a specified number of) angles [*pentagon*]

**go·nad** (gō′nad; *occas.* gän′ad) *n.* [< ModL. < Gr. *gonē*, a seed]  an animal organ producing reproductive cells; ovary or testis —**go·nad′al** *adj.*

**gon·do·la** (gän′də lə, gän dō′lə) *n.* [It. (Venetian) < ?]  **1.** a long, narrow boat with a high, pointed prow and stern, propelled by a pole or one oar on the canals of Venice  **2.** a flat-bottomed river barge  **3.** a railroad freight car with low sides and no top: also **gondola car  4.** the car of an airship or balloon  **5.** a car suspended from and moved along a cable, for holding passengers

**gon·do·lier** (gän′də lir′) *n.* a man who rows or poles a gondola

GONDOLA

**gone** (gôn, gän) *pp. of* GO —*adj.*  **1.** moved away  **2.** ruined  **3.** lost  **4.** dead  **5.** faint; weak  **6.** used up; consumed  **7.** ago; past  **8.** [Slang] *a)* excellent *b)* enraptured *c)* pregnant —**far gone  1.** deeply involved  **2.** very tired —**gone on** [Colloq.] in love with

**gon·er** (gôn′ər, gän′-) *n.* [Colloq.] one beyond help or seemingly sure to die soon, be ruined, etc.

**gon·fa·lon** (gän′fə lən, -län′) *n.* [Fr. < OFr. < Frank. < *gund*, a battle + *fano*, banner]  a flag hanging from a crosspiece instead of on an upright staff, usually ending in streamers

**gong** (gôŋ, gäŋ) *n.* [Malay *guṅ*: echoic]  **1.** a slightly convex metallic disk that gives a loud, resonant tone when struck  **2.** a saucer-shaped bell with such a tone

**-go·ni·um** (gō′nē əm) [ModL. < Gr. *gonos*, seed]  *a combining form meaning* a cell or structure in which reproductive cells are formed [*sporogonium*]

**gon·o·coc·cus** (gän′ə käk′əs) *n., pl.* **-coc′ci** (-käk′sī) [ModL. < Gr. *gonos*, a seed + COCCUS]  the microorganism that causes gonorrhea

**gon·or·rhe·a, gon·or·rhoe·a** (-rē′ə) *n.* [< LL. < Gr. < *gonos*, a seed, semen + *rheein*, to flow]  a venereal disease marked by inflammation of the mucous membrane of the genitourinary tract and a discharge of mucus and pus —**gon′or·rhe′al, gon′or·rhoe′al** *adj.*

**-go·ny** (gə nē) [< L. < Gr. < base of *gignesthai*, to be born]  *a combining form meaning* something generated, produced, descended, etc. [*cosmogony*]

**goo** (gōō) *n.* [Slang]  **1.** anything sticky, as glue  **2.** anything sticky and sweet  **3.** sentimentality

**goo·ber** (gōō′bər) *n.* [< native Afr. name *nguba*]  [Chiefly South]  a peanut

**good** (good) *adj.* **bet′ter, best** [OE. *gōd*]  **1.** *a)* suitable to a purpose; efficient [a *good* lamp] *b)* beneficial [*good* exercise]  **2.** unspoiled [*good* eggs]  **3.** valid; genuine; real [*good* money]  **4.** healthy [*good* eyesight]  **5.** financially sound [a *good* investment]  **6.** honorable; worthy [one's *good* name]  **7.** enjoyable, happy, etc. [a *good* life]  **8.** dependable; reliable [*good* advice]  **9.** thorough [did a *good* job]  **10.** *a)* above average [a *good* novel] *b)* not for everyday use; best [her *good* china]  **11.** adequate; satisfying [a *good* meal]  **12.** morally sound or excellent; specif., *a)* virtuous *b)* pious *c)* kind, generous, etc. *d)* well-behaved; dutiful  **13.** proper; correct [*good* manners]  **14.** able; skilled [a *good* swimmer]  **15.** loyal or conforming [a *good* Democrat]  **16.** considerable [a *good* many]  **17.** full; complete [a *good* six hours] —*n.* something good; specif., *a)* worth; virtue; merit [the *good* in a man] *b)* benefit; advantage [for the *good* of all] *c)* something desirable or desired  See also GOODS —*interj.* an exclamation of satisfaction, pleasure, etc. —*adv.* well, fully, etc.: variously regarded as substandard, dialectal, or colloquial —**as good as** virtually; nearly —**for good (and all)** for always; permanently —**good and** [Colloq.] very or altogether —**good for  1.** able to endure or be used for (a period of time)  **2.** worth  **3.** able to pay or give  **4.** sure to result in [*good for* a laugh] —**make good  1.** to repay or replace  **2.** to fulfill  **3.** to succeed in doing; accomplish  **4.** to be successful  **5.** to prove —**no good** useless or worthless —**the good  1.** those who are good  **2.** what is morally good —**to the good** as a profit or advantage

**Good Book** the Bible (usually with *the*)

**good·bye, good-bye** (good′bī′) *interj., n., pl.* **-byes′** [contr. of *God be with ye*]  farewell: term used in parting: also **good′by′, good′-by′**

**good day** a salutation of greeting or farewell

**good-for-nothing** (good′fər nuth′iŋ) *adj.* useless or worthless —*n.* such a person

**Good Friday** the Friday before Easter Sunday, commemorating the crucifixion of Jesus

**good-heart·ed** (-här′tid) *adj.* kind and generous —**good′-heart′ed·ly** *adv.* —**good′-heart′ed·ness** *n.*

**Good Hope, Cape of  1.** cape at the SW tip of Africa  **2.** province of South Africa, in the southernmost part

**good humor** a cheerful, agreeable, or pleasant mood —**good′-hu′mored** *adj.* —**good′-hu′mored·ly** *adv.*

**good·ish** (-ish) *adj.* fairly good or fairly large

**good looks** attractive appearance; esp., pleasing facial features —**good′-look′ing** *adj.*

**good·ly** (-lē) *adj.* **-li·er, -li·est  1.** of attractive appearance  **2.** of good quality; fine  **3.** rather large; ample —**good′li·ness** *n.*

**good·man** (-mən) *n., pl.* **-men** [Archaic]  **1.** a husband or master of a household  **2.** a title like *Mr.*, for a man ranking below a gentleman

**good morning** a salutation of greeting or farewell used in the morning

**good nature** a pleasant, agreeable, or kindly disposition —**good′-na′tured** *adj.* —**good′-na′tured·ly** *adv.*

**good·ness** (-nis) *n.*  **1.** the state or quality of being good; specif., *a)* virtue; excellence *b)* kindness; generosity  **2.** the best part —*interj.* an exclamation of surprise

**good night** a salutation of parting or farewell used at night

**goods** (goodz) *n.pl.* **1.** movable personal property **2.** merchandise; wares **3.** fabric; cloth **4.** [Brit.] freight —**deliver the goods** [Colloq.] to do or produce the thing required —**get (or have) the goods on** [Slang] to discover (or know) something incriminating about —**the goods** [Slang] what is required or genuine

**good Samaritan** one who pities and unselfishly helps another or others: Luke 10:30–37

**Good Shepherd** an epithet for JESUS: John 10:11

**good-sized** (good'sīzd') *adj.* big or fairly big

**good-tem·pered** (-tem'pərd) *adj.* not easily angered or annoyed —**good'-tem'pered·ly** *adv.*

**good turn** a good deed; friendly, helpful act

**good·wife** (-wīf') *n., pl.* **-wives'** (-wīvz') [Archaic] **1.** a wife or mistress of a household **2.** a title like *Mrs.*, for a woman ranking below a lady

**good will 1.** a friendly or kindly attitude **2.** cheerful consent; willingness **3.** the value of a business in patronage, reputation, etc., over and beyond its tangible assets Also **good'will'** *n.*

**good·y**[1] (-ē) *n., pl.* **good·ies** [Colloq.] **1.** something good to eat, as a candy **2.** *same as* GOODY-GOODY —*adj.* [Colloq.] *same as* GOODY-GOODY —*interj.* a child's exclamation of delight

**good·y**[2] (-ē) *n., pl.* **good·ies** [< GOODWIFE] [Archaic] a woman, esp. an old woman or a housewife, of lowly social status: used as a title with the surname

**Good·year** (good'yir'), **Charles** 1800–60; U.S. inventor of the process of vulcanizing rubber

**good·y-good·y** (good'ē good'ē) *adj.* [Colloq.] moral or pious in a smug, showy way —*n.* [Colloq.] a goody-goody person

**goo·ey** (goo'ē) *adj.* **goo'i·er, goo'i·est** [Slang] **1.** sticky **2.** sticky and sweet **3.** sentimental

**goof** (goof) *n.* [prob. ult. < It. *goffo*, clumsy] [Slang] **1.** a stupid or silly person **2.** a mistake; blunder —*vi.* [Slang] **1.** to err, blunder, fail, etc. **2.** to waste time, shirk duty, etc. (with *off*)

**goof·y** (-ē) *adj.* **goof'i·er, goof'i·est** [Slang] like or characteristic of a goof; stupid or silly —**goof'i·ly** *adv.* —**goof'i·ness** *n.*

**gook** (gook, gook) *n.* [GOO + (GUN)K] [Slang] any sticky, greasy, or slimy substance

**goon** (goon) *n.* [Slang] **1.** [< ? GUN] a ruffian or thug **2.** [after a comic-strip character of E.C. Segar, 20th-c. U.S. cartoonist] a person who is awkward, grotesque, stupid, etc.

**goo·ney bird** (goo'nē) [< *gooney*, sailors' name for the albatross] an albatross of a black-footed species: also **goo'-ny bird**

**goop** (goop) *n.* [GOO + (SOU)P] [Slang] any sticky, semiliquid substance —**goop'y** *adj.* **-i·er, -i·est**

**goose** (goos) *n., pl.* **geese**; for 4 & 5 **goos'es** [OE. *gos*] **1.** a long-necked, web-footed, wild or domestic bird that is like a duck but larger, esp. the female **2.** its flesh, used for food **3.** a silly person **4.** a tailor's pressing iron, with a long, curved handle **5.** [Slang] a sudden, playful prod in the backside —*vt.* **goosed, goos'ing** [Slang] **1.** to prod suddenly and playfully in the backside so as to startle **2.** to feed gasoline to (an engine) in irregular spurts **3.** to prod or stir into action —**cook one's goose** [Colloq.] to spoil one's chances, hopes, etc.

**goose·ber·ry** (goos'ber'ē, -bə rē; gooz'-) *n., pl.* **-ries 1.** a small, round, sour berry used in preserves, etc. **2.** the shrub it grows on

**goose egg** [Slang] **1.** a zero **2.** a large swelling or lump, esp. one caused by a blow

**goose flesh** a roughened condition of the skin in which the papillae are raised, caused by cold, fear, etc.: also **goose bumps (or pimples or skin)**

**goose·foot** (goos'foot') *adj.* designating a family of plants including spinach and beets —*n., pl.* **-foots'** any of a genus of plants of this family, with small, green flowers and, often, fleshy foliage

**goose·neck** (-nek') *n.* any of various mechanical devices shaped like a goose's neck, as a flexible rod for supporting a desk lamp

**goose step** a parade marching step in which the legs are raised high and kept rigidly unbent —**goose'-step'** *vi.* **-stepped', -step'ping**

**GOP, G.O.P.** Grand Old Party (Republican Party)

**go·pher** (gō'fər) *n.* [< Fr. *gaufre*, honeycomb: from its burrowing] **1.** a burrowing rodent, about the size of a large rat, with wide cheek pouches: also **pocket gopher 2.** a striped ground squirrel of N. American prairies, related to the chipmunk

**Gor·di·an knot** (gôr'dē ən) *Gr. Legend* a knot tied by King Gordius of Phrygia, to be undone only by the future master of Asia: Alexander the Great, failing to untie it, cut the knot with his sword —**cut the Gordian knot** to find a quick, bold solution for a problem

**Gor·don** (gôr'd'n) [Scot. < surname *Gordon*] **1.** a masculine name **2. Charles George,** 1833–85; Brit. general in China, Egypt, & Sudan

**gore**[1] (gôr) *n.* [OE. *gor*, dung, filth] blood shed from a wound; esp., clotted blood

**gore**[2] (gôr) *vt.* **gored, gor'ing** [< OE. *gar*, a spear] to pierce as with a horn or tusk

**gore**[3] (gôr) *n.* [OE. *gara*, corner < base of *gar*, a spear] a tapering piece of cloth in a skirt, sail, etc. to give it fullness —*vt.* **gored, gor'ing** to make or insert a gore or gores in

**gorge** (gôrj) *n.* [< OFr., throat, ult. < L. *gurges*, whirlpool] **1.** the throat or gullet **2.** the maw or stomach, or food filling it **3.** a deep, narrow pass between steep heights **4.** a mass, as of ice, blocking a passage —*vi., vt.* **gorged, gorg'ing** to stuff (oneself) with food; glut —**make one's gorge rise** to make one disgusted, angry, etc.

**gor·geous** (gôr'jəs) *adj.* [< OFr. *gorgias*, beautiful] **1.** brilliantly colored; resplendent **2.** [Slang] beautiful, wonderful, delightful, etc. —**gor'geous·ly** *adv.* —**gor'geous·ness** *n.*

**gor·get** (gôr'jit) *n.* [< OFr. < *gorge*: see GORGE] **1.** a piece of armor to protect the throat **2.** a collar **3.** a patch of color on a bird's throat

**Gor·gon** (gôr'gən) *n.* **1.** *Gr. Myth.* any of three sisters with snakes for hair, so horrible that the beholder was turned to stone **2.** [g-] any ugly, terrifying, or repulsive woman

**Gor·gon·zo·la** (gôr'gən zō'lə) *n.* [< *Gorgonzola*, town in Italy] a white Italian pressed cheese with veins of blue-green mold and a strong flavor

**go·ril·la** (gə ril'ə) *n.* [< Gr. *gorillai* < an ancient W. African name] **1.** the largest and most powerful manlike ape, native to the jungles of equatorial Africa **2.** [Slang] *a)* a person regarded as like a gorilla in appearance, strength, etc. *b)* a gangster; thug

**Gor·ki, Gor·kiy (Gor·ky)** (gôr'kē) city in E European R.S.F.S.R., on the Volga: pop. 1,139,000

**Gor·ki** (gôr'kē), **Max·im** (mak'sim) (pseud. of *Aleksei Maximovich Peshkov*) 1868–1936; Russ. novelist & playwright: also sp. **Gorky**

**gor·mand** (gôr'mənd) *n. same as* GOURMAND

**gor·mand·ize** (gôr'mən dīz') *vi., vt.* **-ized', -iz'ing** [< Fr. *gourmandise*, gluttony] to eat or devour like a glutton —**gor'mand·iz'er** *n.*

**gorse** (gôrs) *n.* [OE. *gorst*] furze —**gors'y** *adj.*

**gor·y** (gôr'ē) *adj.* **gor'i·er, gor'i·est 1.** covered with gore; bloody **2.** full of bloodshed or killing —**gor'i·ly** *adv.* —**gor'i·ness** *n.*

**gosh** (gäsh) *interj.* an exclamation of surprise, wonder, etc.: a euphemism for *God*

**gos·hawk** (gäs'hôk') *n.* [< OE.: see GOOSE & HAWK[1]] a large, swift hawk with short wings

**Go·shen** (gō'shən) *Bible* the fertile land assigned to the Israelites in Egypt: Gen. 45:10 —*n.* a land of plenty

**gos·ling** (gäz'liŋ) *n.* [< ON.] a young goose

**gos·pel** (gäs'p'l) *n.* [OE. *godspel*, lit., good news] **1.** [often G-] *a)* the teachings of Jesus and the Apostles *b)* the history of the life and teachings of Jesus **2.** [G-] *a)* any of the first four books of the New Testament (*Matthew, Mark, Luke, or John*) *b)* an excerpt from any of these, read in a religious service **3.** anything regarded as the absolute truth: also **gospel truth 4.** any doctrine or rule widely or ardently maintained **5.** a style of folk singing originally associated with evangelistic revival meetings —*adj.* of (the) gospel or evangelism

**gos·sa·mer** (gäs'ə mər) *n.* [ME. *gosesomer*, lit., goose summer: the period in fall when geese are in season] **1.** a filmy cobweb in the air or on bushes or grass **2.** a very thin, soft, filmy cloth **3.** anything like gossamer —*adj.* light, thin, and filmy: also **gos'sa·mer·y** (-mər ē)

**gos·sip** (gäs'əp) *n.* [< Late OE. *godsibbe*, godparent: see GOD & SIB] **1.** [Obs. or Dial.] *a)* a godparent *b)* a close friend **2.** one who chatters or repeats idle talk and rumors, esp. about others' private affairs **3.** *a)* such talk or rumors *b)* chatter —*vi.* to indulge in idle talk or rumors about others —**gos'sip·er** *n.* —**gos'sip·y** *adj.*

**got** (gät) *pt. & alt. pp.* of GET

**Gö·te·borg** (yö'tə bôr'y') seaport in SW Sweden, on the Kattegat: pop. 445,000

---

fat, āpe, cär; ten, ēven; is, bīte; gō, hôrn, tōōl, look; oil, out; up, fur; get; joy; yet; chin; she; thin, then; zh, leisure; ŋ, ring; ə for a in ago, e in agent, i in sanity, o in comply, u in focus; ' as in able (ā'b'l); Fr. bal; ë, Fr. coeur; ö, Fr. feu; Fr. mon; ô, Fr. coq; ü, Fr. duc; r, Fr. cri; H, G. ich; kh, G. doch; ‡foreign; *hypothetical; < derived from. See inside front cover.

**Goth** (gäth, gôth) *n.* [< LL. < Gr. *Gothoi,* pl.] **1.** a member of a Germanic people that invaded and conquered most of the Roman Empire in the 3d–5th cent. A.D. **2.** an uncouth, uncivilized person

**Goth., goth.** Gothic

**Goth·am** (gäth′əm, gō′thəm; *for 1,* Brit. gät′-) **1.** a village near Nottingham, England, whose inhabitants were, according to legend, very foolish **2.** *nickname for* NEW YORK CITY —**Goth′am·ite′** (-īt′) *n.*

**Goth·ic** (gäth′ik) *adj.* **1.** of the Goths or their language **2.** designating or of a style of architecture developed in W Europe from the 12th to 16th cent., characterized by flying buttresses, pointed arches, etc. **3.** [*sometimes* g-] *a*) medieval *b*) not classical *c*) barbarous **4.** of a style of literature using a medieval or macabre setting, atmosphere, etc., to suggest horror and mystery —*n.* **1.** the East Germanic language of the Goths **2.** Gothic style, esp. in architecture **3.** *Printing* [*often* g-] a plain type with straight lines of uniform width and no serifs —**Goth′i·cal·ly** *adv.*

**Gothic arch** a pointed arch

**Got·land** (gät′lənd; *Sw.* gôt′-) Swed. island in the Baltic, off the SE coast of Sweden

**got·ten** (gät′'n) *alt. pp. of* GET

**gouache** (gwäsh) *n.* [Fr. < It. *guazzo,* water color < L. < *aqua,* water] **1.** a way of painting with opaque water colors mixed with gum **2.** such a pigment **3.** a painting made with such pigments

**Gou·da (cheese)** (gou′də, gōō′-) [< *Gouda,* city in Netherlands] a mild, semisoft to hard cheese, usually coated with red wax

**gouge** (gouj) *n.* [< OFr. < VL. *gubia,* for LL. *gulbia* < Celt.] **1.** a chisel with a curved, hollowed blade, for cutting grooves or holes in wood **2.** *a*) a gouging *b*) the groove or hole **3.** [Colloq.] extortion or swindle —*vt.* **gouged, goug′ing 1.** to make grooves or holes in as with a gouge **2.** to scoop or dig out **3.** in fighting, to push one's thumb into the eye of **4.** [Colloq.] to cheat out of money, etc.; also, to overcharge —**goug′er** *n.*

**gou·lash** (gōō′läsh, -lash) *n.* [< G. < Hung. *gulyás,* herdsman, hence herdsman's food] a stew of beef or veal and vegetables, seasoned with paprika, etc.: also **Hungarian goulash**

**Gould** (gōōld), **Jay** 1836–92; U.S. financier

**Gou·nod** (gōō nō′; *E.* gōō′nō), **Charles (François)** (shàrl) 1818–93; Fr. composer

**gou·ra·mi** (goor′ə mē, goo rä′mē) *n., pl.* **-mis, -mi:** see PLURAL, II, D, 1 [Malay *gurami*] **1.** a food fish of SE Asia, that builds a nest **2.** any of a number of related fishes, mostly brightly colored, that are often kept in aquariums

**gourd** (gôrd, goord) *adj.* [< OFr. < L. *cucurbita*] designating a family of plants that includes the squash, melon, pumpkin, etc. —*n.* **1.** any trailing or climbing plant of this family **2.** *a*) *same as* CALABASH (sense 2a) *b*) the ornamental, inedible fruit of certain related plants **3.** the dried, hollowed-out shell of such a fruit, used as a drinking cup, dipper, etc.

**gourde** (goord) *n.* [Fr. < L. *gurdus,* heavy] *see* MONETARY UNITS, table (Haiti)

**gour·mand** (goor′mənd, goor mänd′) *n.* [< OFr.] **1.** a person who likes to indulge in good food and drink, sometimes to excess **2.** *same as* GOURMET

**gour·met** (goor′mā; *Fr.* gōōr me′) *n.* [Fr. < OFr. *gourmet,* wine taster] a person who likes and is an excellent judge of fine foods and drinks; epicure

**gout** (gout) *n.* [< OFr. < L. *gutta,* a drop] **1.** a disease marked by deposits of uric acid salts in tissues and joints, esp. of the feet and hands, with swelling and great pain, esp. in the big toe **2.** a spurt, splash, etc. —**gout′i·ly** *adv.* —**gout′i·ness** *n.* —**gout′y** *adj.* **gout′i·er, gout′i·est**

**gov., Gov. 1.** government **2.** governor

**gov·ern** (guv′ərn) *vt.* [< OFr. < L. *gubernare* < Gr. *kybernan,* to steer] **1.** to exercise authority over; rule, control, manage, etc. **2.** to influence the action or conduct of; guide **3.** to hold in check; curb **4.** to regulate the speed of **5.** to be a rule or law for **6.** *Gram. a*) to require (a word) to be in a particular case or mood *b*) to require (a particular case or mood) —*vi.* to govern someone or something; rule —**gov′ern·a·ble** *adj.*

**gov·ern·ance** (-ər nəns) *n.* control or rule

**gov·ern·ess** (-ər nəs) *n.* a woman employed in a private home to train and teach the children

**gov·ern·ment** (guv′ər mənt, -ərn mənt) *n.* **1.** *a*) the exercise of authority over a state, district, group, etc.; control; rule *b*) the right, function, or power of governing **2.** *a*) a system of ruling, controlling, etc. *b*) an established system of political administration by which a nation, state, etc. is governed *c*) the study of such systems **3.** all the people that administer the affairs of a nation, state, institution, etc. **4.** [*often* G-] the executive or administrative branch of government of a particular nation **5.** *Gram.* the influence of a word over the case or mood of another —**gov′ern·men′tal** *adj.* —**gov′ern·men′tal·ly** *adv.*

**gov·er·nor** (guv′ə nər, -ər nər) *n.* **1.** a person who governs; esp., *a*) one appointed to govern a dependency, province, etc. *b*) the elected head of any State of the U.S. *c*) one of the group directing an organization or institution **2.** a device automatically controlling the speed of an engine or motor as by regulating fuel intake **3.** [Brit. Colloq.] a person with authority; esp., one's father or employer —**gov′er·nor·ship′** *n.*

**governor general** *pl.* **governors general, governor generals** a governor with deputy governors under him, as in the British Commonwealth: also, Brit., **gov′er·nor-gen′er·al** *n., pl.* **gov′er·nors-gen′er·al**

**govt., Govt.** government

**gown** (goun) *n.* [< OFr. < LL. *gunna*] **1.** a woman's long, usually formal dress **2.** a dressing gown **3.** a nightgown, nightshirt, etc. **4.** a surgeon's smock **5.** a long, flowing robe worn traditionally by certain officials, clergymen, professors, etc. **6.** the members of a college, etc. collectively —*vt.* to dress in a gown

**Goy·a (y Lucientes)** (gô′yä), **Fran·cis·co Jo·sé de** (frän thēs′kô hô se′ *the*) 1746–1828; Sp. painter

**G.P., g.p.** general practitioner

**GPO, G.P.O.** Government Printing Office

**Gr. 1.** Grecian **2.** Greece **3.** Greek

**gr. 1.** grade **2.** grain(s) **3.** gram(s) **4.** gravity **5.** great **6.** gross

**grab** (grab) *vt.* **grabbed, grab′bing** [prob. < MDu., MLowG. *grabben*] **1.** to seize or snatch suddenly **2.** to get possession of by unscrupulous methods **3.** [Slang] to impress (one) greatly —*vi.* to grab or try to grab something (often with *for, at,* etc.) —*n.* **1.** a grabbing **2.** something grabbed **3.** a device for clutching something to be hoisted —**up for grabs** [Slang] available to the highest bidder, the most aggressive person, etc. —**grab′ber** *n.*

**grab bag** a container holding wrapped or bagged articles sold unseen at a fixed price

**grab·by** (-ē) *adj.* **-bi·er, -bi·est** avaricious

**Grace** (grās) [see ff.] a feminine name

**grace** (grās) *n.* [< OFr. < L. *gratia,* pleasing quality < *gratus,* pleasing] **1.** beauty or charm of form, movement, or expression **2.** an attractive quality, feature, manner, etc. **3.** *a*) a sense of what is right and proper; decency *b*) thoughtfulness toward others **4.** good will; favor **5.** [Archaic] mercy **6.** a delay granted beyond the date set for the performance or payment of an obligation **7.** a short prayer of blessing or thanks for a meal **8.** [G-] a title of respect in speaking to or of an archbishop, duke, or duchess **9.** *Music* [*pl.*] ornamental notes or effects, collectively **10.** *Theol. a*) the unmerited love and favor of God toward man *b*) divine influence acting in man to make him pure and good *c*) the condition of a person thus influenced *d*) a special virtue given to a person by God —*vt.* **graced, grac′ing 1.** to give or add grace or graces to **2.** to honor; dignify **3.** *Music* to add a grace note or notes to —**in the good** (or **bad**) **graces of** in favor (or disfavor) with —**with good** (or **bad**) **grace** in a willing (or unwilling) way

**grace·ful** (-f'l) *adj.* having grace (sense 1) —**grace′ful·ly** *adv.* —**grace′ful·ness** *n.*

**grace·less** (-lis) *adj.* **1.** lacking any sense of what is right or proper **2.** clumsy or inelegant —**grace′less·ly** *adv.* —**grace′less·ness** *n.*

**grace note** *Music* a merely ornamental note

**Grac·es** (grā′siz) *Gr. Myth.* three sister goddesses who controlled pleasure, charm, elegance, and beauty in human life and in nature

**gra·cious** (grā′shəs) *adj.* **1.** having or showing kindness, courtesy, charm, etc. **2.** merciful; compassionate **3.** polite to those held to be inferiors **4.** marked by the taste, ease, etc. associated with prosperity, education, etc. [*gracious living*] —*interj.* an expression of surprise —**gra′cious·ly** *adv.* —**gra′cious·ness** *n.*

**grack·le** (grak′'l) *n.* [L. *graculus,* jackdaw] any of several American blackbirds that are somewhat smaller than a crow

**grad** (grad) *n.* [Colloq.] a graduate

**grad. 1.** graduate **2.** graduated

**gra·date** (grā′dāt) *vt., vi.* **-dat·ed, -dat·ing** [back-formation < ff.] to change, etc. by gradation; shade into one another, as colors

**gra·da·tion** (grā dā′shən) *n.* [Fr. < L. *gradatio* < *gradus:* see ff.] **1.** a forming or arranging in grades, stages, or steps **2.** a gradual change by steps or stages **3.** a shading of one tone or color into another **4.** a step, stage, or degree in a graded series **5.** *same as* ABLAUT —**gra·da′tion·al** *adj.* —**gra·da′tion·al·ly** *adv.*

**grade** (grād) *n.* [Fr. < L. *gradus,* a step < *gradi,* to step] **1.** any of the stages in a systematic progression **2.** *a*) a degree in a scale of quality, rank, etc. *b*) any of the official ranks or ratings of officers or enlisted men *c*) an accepted standard or level [*up to grade*] *d*) a group of the same rank, merit, etc. **3.** *a*) the degree of rise or descent of a slope, as of a road *b*) the slope itself **4.** a division in a school curriculum, usually equal to one year **5.** a mark or

rating on an examination, in a school course, etc. —*vt.*
**grad′ed, grad′ing 1.** to classify by grades of quality, rank, etc.; sort **2.** to give a grade (sense 5) to **3.** to gradate **4.** to make (ground) level or slope (ground) evenly for a roadway, etc. —*vi.* **1.** to be of a certain grade **2.** to change by gradation —**make the grade 1.** to get to the top of a steep incline **2.** to overcome obstacles and succeed
**-grade** (grād) [< L. *gradi,* to walk] *a combining form meaning* walking or moving *[plantigrade]*
**grade crossing** a place where two railroads or a railroad and roadway intersect on the same level
**grad·er** (grā′dər) *n.* **1.** a person or thing that grades **2.** a pupil in a specified grade at school
**grade school** *same as* ELEMENTARY SCHOOL
**gra·di·ent** (grā′dē ənt, -dyənt) *adj.* [< L. prp. of *gradi,* to step] ascending or descending with a uniform slope —*n.* **1.** *a)* a slope, as of a road *b)* the degree of such slope **2.** *Physics* the rate of change of temperature, pressure, etc.
**grad·u·al** (graj′ōō wəl) *adj.* [< ML. < L. *gradus:* see GRADE] taking place little by little, not sharply or suddenly —*n. Eccles.* **1.** a set of verses, esp. from the Psalms, following the Epistle at Mass **2.** a book containing these and other sung parts of the Mass —**grad′u·al·ly** *adv.* —**grad′u·al·ness** *n.*
**grad·u·al·ism** (-iz′m) *n.* the principle of seeking only gradual social or political change —**grad′u·al·ist** *n., adj.* —**grad′u·al·is′tic** *adj.*
**grad·u·ate** (graj′ōō wit; *for v., and occas. for n.,* -wāt′) *n.* [< ML. pp. of *graduare,* to graduate < L. *gradus:* see GRADE] **1.** a person who has completed a course of study at a school or college and has received a degree or diploma **2.** a container marked off for measuring the contents —*vt.* **-at′ed, -at′ing 1.** to give a degree or diploma to upon completion of a course of study **2.** to mark with degrees for measuring **3.** to grade by size, quality, etc. —*vi.* **1.** to become a graduate of a school, etc. **2.** to change, esp. advance, by degrees —*adj.* **1.** graduated from a school, college, etc. **2.** of or for studies leading to degrees above the bachelor's —**grad′u·a′tor** *n.*
**grad·u·a·tion** (graj′ōō wā′shən) *n.* **1.** *a)* a graduating or being graduated from a school or college *b)* the ceremony connected with this; commencement **2.** *a)* a marking with degrees for measuring *b)* a degree or the degrees marked **3.** a grading by size, quality, etc.
**Grae·cism** (grē′siz′m) *n. same as* GRECISM
**Grae·co-** *same as* GRECO-
**graf·fi·to** (grə fēt′ō) *n., pl.* **-fi′ti** (-ē) [It., a scribbling] an inscription or drawing scratched or scribbled on a wall, etc. in a public place
**graft** (graft) *n.* [< OFr. *graffe* < L. < Gr. *grapheion,* stylus: from resemblance of the scion to a pointed pencil] **1.** *a)* a shoot or bud of a plant or tree inserted into the stem or trunk of another for continued growth as a permanent part *b)* the inserting of such a shoot, etc. or the place of insertion *c)* a tree or plant with such an insertion **2.** a joining of one thing to another as if by grafting **3.** *a)* a taking advantage of one's position to gain money, etc. dishonestly, as in politics *b)* anything so gained **4.** *Surgery a)* a piece of skin, bone, etc. transplanted from one body, or place on a body, to another, where it grows permanently *b)* such a transplanting —*vt.* **1.** *a)* to insert (a shoot or bud) as a graft *b)* to insert a graft of (one plant) in another *c)* to produce (a fruit, flower, etc.) by a graft **2.** to join as if by grafting **3.** *Surgery* to transplant as a graft —*vi.* **1.** to be grafted **2.** to make a graft **3.** to obtain money, etc. by graft —**graft′age** *n.* —**graft′er** *n.*
**gra·ham** (grā′əm) *adj.* [after S. Graham (1794–1851), U.S. dietary reformer] designating or made of finely ground whole-wheat flour *[graham crackers]*
**Grail** (grāl) [< OFr. *graal* < ML. *gradalis,* cup < ?] *Medieval Legend* the cup or platter used by Jesus at the Last Supper and the receptacle of drops of blood from Jesus' body at the Crucifixion: also called **Holy Grail**
**grain** (grān) *n.* [< OFr. < L. *granum*] **1.** a small, hard seed or seedlike fruit, esp. of a cereal plant, as wheat, rice, corn, etc. **2.** cereal seeds or cereal plants **3.** a tiny, solid particle, as of salt or sand **4.** a tiny bit *[a grain of sense]* **5.** the smallest unit in the system of weights of the U.S. and Great Britain, equal to 0.0648 gram **6.** *a)* the arrangement of fibers, layers, or particles of wood, leather, etc. *b)* the markings or texture due to this **7.** the side of leather from which the hair has been removed **8.** disposition; nature —*vt.* **1.** to form into grains; granulate **2.** to paint or finish in imitation of the grain of wood, marble, etc. **3.** to put a finish on the grain surface of (leather) —*vi.* to form grains —**against the** (or **one's**) **grain** contrary to one's feelings, nature, etc.

**grain alcohol** ethyl alcohol, esp. when made from grain
**grain·y** (-ē) *adj.* **grain′i·er, grain′i·est 1.** having a well-defined grain, as wood **2.** coarsely textured; granular —**grain′i·ness** *n.*
**gram** (gram) *n.* [< Fr. < LL. < Gr. *gramma,* a small weight, lit., what is written < *graphein,* to write] the basic unit of weight in the metric system, about 1/28 oz.
**-gram** (gram) [< Gr.: see prec.] *a combining form meaning:* **1.** something written or recorded *[telegram]* **2.** grams or part of a gram *[kilogram, milligram]*
**gram. 1.** grammar **2.** grammatical
**gram·mar** (gram′ər) *n.* [< OFr. < L. < Gr. *grammatikē (technē),* (art) of grammar, learning < *gramma:* see GRAM] **1.** language study dealing with word forms *(morphology),* word order in sentences *(syntax),* and now often language sounds *(phonology)* **2.** the system of word forms and word order of a given language at a given time **3.** a body of rules for speaking or writing a given language **4.** a book or treatise on grammar **5.** one's manner of speaking or writing as judged by how it conforms to the rules of grammar
**gram·mar·i·an** (grə mer′ē ən) *n.* a specialist or expert in grammar
**grammar school 1.** *earlier name for* ELEMENTARY SCHOOL **2.** in England, a secondary school
**gram·mat·i·cal** (grə mat′i k'l) *adj.* **1.** of or according to grammar **2.** conforming to the rules of grammar —**gram·mat′i·cal·ly** *adv.* —**gram·mat′i·cal·ness** *n.*
**gramme** (gram) *n. alt. sp. of* GRAM
**gram molecule** *same as* MOLE⁴: also **gram-mo·lec·u·lar weight** (gram′mə lek′yoo lər)
**Gram·my** (gram′ē) *n., pl.* **-mys, -mies** [< ff.] any of the annual awards in the U.S. for special achievement in the recording industry, as for the best recordings
**gram·o·phone** (gram′ə fōn′) *n.* [arbitrary inversion of PHONOGRAM] [Chiefly Brit.] a phonograph
**gram·pus** (gram′pəs) *n., pl.* **-pus·es** [< OFr. *graspeis* < L. *crassus,* fat + *piscis,* fish] any of a genus of small, black, fierce whales related to the dolphins
**Gra·na·da** (grə nä′də; *Sp.* grä nä′thä) **1.** former Moorish kingdom in S Spain **2.** city in S Spain: pop. 164,000
**gran·a·ry** (gran′ər ē, grā′nər ē) *n., pl.* **-ries** [< L. < *granum,* grain] **1.** a building for storing threshed grain **2.** a region producing much grain
**grand** (grand) *adj.* [OFr. < L. *grandis,* large] **1.** higher in rank or status than others with the same title **2.** most important; main *[the grand ballroom]* **3.** imposing in size, beauty, and extent **4.** marked by splendor and display **5.** distinguished; illustrious **6.** self-important; pretentious **7.** lofty and dignified, as in style **8.** overall *[the grand total]* **9.** [Colloq.] excellent, delightful, etc. —*n.* **1.** a grand piano **2.** [Slang] a thousand dollars —**grand′ly** *adv.* —**grand′ness** *n.*
**grand-** *a combining form meaning* of the generation older (or younger) than *[grandfather, grandson]*
**gran·dam** (gran′dam, -dəm) *n.* [< Anglo-Fr.: see GRAND & DAME] [Archaic] **1.** a grandmother **2.** an old woman Also sp. **gran′dame**
**Grand Army of the Republic** an association (1866–1949) of Union veterans of the Civil War
**grand·aunt** (grand′ant′) *n. same as* GREAT-AUNT
**Grand Banks** (or **Bank**) large shoal in the Atlantic, southeast of Newfoundland: noted fishing grounds
**Grand Canyon** deep gorge of the Colorado River, in NW Ariz.: over 200 mi. long; 1 mi. deep
**grand·child** (gran′chīld′) *n., pl.* **-chil′dren** a child of one's son or daughter
**Grand Cou·lee** (kōō′lē) dam on the Columbia River, NE Wash.: 500 ft. high
**grand·dad, grand-dad** (gran′dad′) *n.* [Colloq.] grandfather
**grand·daugh·ter** (-dôt′ər) *n.* a daughter of one's son or daughter
**grand duchess 1.** the wife or widow of a grand duke **2.** a woman who has the rank of a grand duke and rules a grand duchy **3.** in czarist Russia, a royal princess
**grand duchy** the territory or a country ruled by a grand duke or a grand duchess
**grand duke 1.** the sovereign ruler of a grand duchy, ranking just below a king **2.** in czarist Russia, a royal prince
**grande dame** (gränd däm) [Fr., great lady] a woman, esp. an older one, of great dignity or prestige
**gran·dee** (gran dē′) *n.* [Sp. & Port. *grande:* see GRAND] **1.** a Spanish or Portuguese nobleman of the highest rank **2.** a man of high rank
**gran·deur** (gran′jər, -joor) *n.* [Fr. < *grand:* see GRAND] **1.** splendor; magnificence **2.** moral and intellectual greatness; nobility

---

**grand·fa·ther** (gran′fä′thər, grand′-) *n.* **1.** the father of one's father or mother **2.** a forefather

**grand·fa·ther·ly** (-lē) *adj.* **1.** of a grandfather **2.** having the conventional characteristics of a grandfather; kindly, indulgent, etc.

**gran·dil·o·quent** (gran dil′ə kwənt) *adj.* [< L. < *grandis*, grand + *loqui*, to speak] using high-flown, pompous, bombastic words and expressions —**gran·dil′o·quence** *n.* —**gran·dil′o·quent·ly** *adv.*

**gran·di·ose** (gran′dē ōs′) *adj.* [Fr. < It. < L. *grandis*, great] **1.** having grandeur; imposing; impressive **2.** pompous and showy —**gran′di·ose′ly** *adv.* —**gran′di·os′i·ty** (-äs′ə tē) *n.*

**grand jury** a jury that investigates accusations against persons charged with crime and indicts them for trial if there is sufficient evidence

**Grand Lama** *same as* DALAI LAMA

**grand larceny** *see* LARCENY

**grand·ma** (gran′mä, gra′mä) *n.* [Colloq.] grandmother

**grand·moth·er** (gran′muth′ər, grand′-, gra′-) *n.* **1.** the mother of one's father or mother **2.** a female ancestor; ancestress

**grand·moth·er·ly** (-lē) *adj.* **1.** of a grandmother **2.** having the conventional characteristics of a grandmother; kindly, indulgent, etc.

**grand·neph·ew** (gran′nef′yōō, grand′-; *chiefly Brit.* -nev′yōō) *n.* the grandson of one's brother or sister

**grand·niece** (-nēs′) *n.* the granddaughter of one's brother or sister

**grand opera** opera, generally on a serious theme, in which the whole text is set to music

**grand·pa** (gran′pä, grand′-, gram′-) *n.* [Colloq.] grandfather

**grand·par·ent** (-per′ənt) *n.* a grandfather or grandmother

**grand piano** a large piano with strings set horizontally in a harp-shaped case

**Grand Prairie** city in NE Tex.: suburb of Dallas: pop. 71,000

**Grand Rapids** [after the *rapids* on the *Grand* River] city in SW Mich.: pop. 182,000 (met. area 601,000)

**grand·sire** (gran′sīr′, grand′-) *n.* [Archaic] **1.** a grandfather **2.** a male ancestor **3.** an old man

**grand slam 1.** *Baseball* (designating) a home run hit when the bases are loaded: also **grand′-slam′mer** *n.* **2.** *Bridge* the winning of all the tricks in a deal

**grand·son** (gran′sun′, grand′-) *n.* a son of one's son or daughter

**grand·stand** (-stand′) *n.* the main seating structure for spectators at a sporting event, etc. —*vi.* [Colloq.] to make an unnecessarily showy play (**grandstand play**), as in baseball, to get applause

**grand tour** a tour of continental Europe

**grand·un·cle** (grand′un′k'l) *n. same as* GREAT-UNCLE

**grange** (grānj) *n.* [< Anglo-Fr. < ML. *granica* < L. *granum*, grain] **1.** a farm with its dwelling house, barns, etc. **2.** [G-] *a)* the Patrons of Husbandry, an association of farmers organized in the U.S. in 1867 for mutual welfare and advancement *b)* any of its local lodges

**grang·er** (-ər) *n.* **1.** a farmer **2.** [G-] a member of the Grange —**grang′er·ism** *n.*

**gran·ite** (gran′it) *n.* [< It. *granito*, grained, ult. < L. *granum*, grain] a very hard, crystalline, plutonic rock consisting chiefly of feldspar and quartz —**gra·nit·ic** (grə nit′ik, grə-) *adj.*

**gran·ite·ware** (-wer′) *n.* a variety of ironware coated with a hard, grained enamel

**gran·ny, gran·nie** (gran′ē) *n., pl.* **-nies** [Colloq.] **1.** a grandmother **2.** an old woman **3.** a fussy, exacting person **4.** *same as* GRANNY KNOT

**granny knot** a knot like a square knot but with the ends crossed the wrong way, forming an awkward, insecure knot: also **granny's knot**

**grant** (grant) *vt.* [< OFr. *craanter*, to promise, ult. < L. *prp.* of *credere*, to believe] **1.** to give (what is requested, as permission, etc.); assent to **2.** *a)* to give formally or according to legal procedure *b)* to transfer (property) by a deed **3.** to admit as true without proof; concede —*n.* **1.** a granting **2.** something granted, as property, a right, money, etc. —**take for granted** to accept as a matter of course —**grant′a·ble** *adj.* —**grant′er,** *Law* **grant′or** *n.*

**Grant** (grant), **Ulysses Simp·son** (simp′sən) (born *Hiram Ulysses Grant*) 1822–85; 18th president of the U.S. (1869–77); commander of Union forces in the Civil War

**grant·ee** (grant ē′) *n. Law* a person to whom a grant is made

**grant-in-aid** (grant′in ād′) *n., pl.* **grants′-in-aid′** a grant of funds, as by a foundation, to support a specific program or project

**gran·u·lar** (gran′yə lər) *adj.* **1.** containing or consisting of grains or granules **2.** like grains or granules **3.** having a grainy surface —**gran′u·lar′i·ty** (-ler′ə tē) *n.* —**gran′u·lar·ly** *adv.*

**gran·u·late** (-lāt′) *vt., vi.* **-lat′ed, -lat′ing 1.** to form into

grains or granules **2.** to make or become rough on the surface by the development of granules —**gran′u·la′tion** *n.* —**gran′u·la′tive** *adj.* —**gran′u·la′tor, gran′u·lat′er** *n.*

**gran·ule** (gran′yool) *n.* [< LL. *granulum*, dim. of L. *granum*, a grain] **1.** a small grain **2.** a small, grainlike particle or spot

**grape** (grāp) *n.* [< OFr. *grape*, bunch of grapes < *graper*, to gather with a hook < Frank. *krappo*, hook] **1.** a small, round, smooth-skinned, juicy berry, growing in clusters on woody vines and eaten raw, used to make wine or dried to make raisins **2.** a grapevine **3.** a dark purplish red **4.** *same as* GRAPESHOT

**grape·fruit** (-frōōt′) *n.* **1.** a large, round, edible citrus fruit with a pale-yellow rind and a somewhat sour, juicy pulp **2.** the tree it grows on

**grape·shot** (-shät′) *n.* a cluster of small iron balls formerly fired as a cannon charge

**grape sugar** *same as* DEXTROSE

**grape·vine** (-vīn′) *n.* **1.** a woody vine bearing grapes **2.** a secret means of spreading information: in full, **grapevine telegraph 3.** a rumor

**graph** (graf) *n.* [short for *graphic formula*] **1.** a diagram, or a visual representation, as a broken line, that shows the relationship between certain sets of numbers **2.** *Math. a)* a picture showing the values taken on by a function *b)* a diagram consisting of nodes and links and representing logical relationships or sequences of events —*vt.* to represent by a graph

GRAPH

**-graph** (graf) [Gr. *-graphos* < *graphein*, to write] *a combining form meaning:* **1.** something that writes or records [*telegraph*] **2.** something written [*monograph*]

**-gra·pher** (grə fər) *a combining form meaning* a person who writes, records, makes copies, etc. [*telegrapher, stenographer*]

**graph·ic** (graf′ik) *adj.* [< L. < Gr. *graphikos* < *graphein*, to write] **1.** described in realistic detail; vivid **2.** of the GRAPHIC ARTS **3.** *a)* of or expressed in handwriting *b)* written or inscribed **4.** shown by graphs or diagrams Also **graph′i·cal** —**graph′i·cal·ly** *adv.* —**graph′ic·ness** *n.*

**-graph·ic** (graf′ik) *a combining form* used to form adjectives corresponding to nouns ending in -GRAPH: also **-graph′i·cal**

**graphic arts 1.** any form of visual artistic representation, esp. painting, drawing, etc. **2.** those arts in which impressions are printed from various kinds of blocks, plates, etc., as etching, lithography, offset, etc.

**graph·ite** (graf′īt) *n.* [G. *graphit* < Gr. *graphein*, to write] a soft, black, lustrous form of carbon found in nature and used for lead in pencils, for lubricants, electrodes, etc. —**gra·phit·ic** (grə fit′ik) *adj.*

**graph·ol·o·gy** (gra fäl′ə jē) *n.* [< Fr. < Gr. *graphein*, to write + -LOGY] the study of handwriting, esp. as a clue to character, aptitudes, etc. —**graph·ol′o·gist** *n.*

**graph paper** paper with small ruled squares on which to make graphs, diagrams, etc.

**-gra·phy** (grə fē) [< L. < Gr. < *graphein*, to write] *a combining form meaning:* **1.** a process or method of writing, or graphically representing [*lithography*] **2.** a descriptive science [*geography*]

**grap·nel** (grap′n'l) *n.* [< OFr. *grapil* < Pr. < *grapa* < Frank. *krappo*: see GRAPE] **1.** a small anchor with several flukes **2.** an iron bar with claws at one end for grasping and holding things

**grap·ple** (grap′'l) *n.* [OFr. *grapil*: see prec.] **1.** *same as* GRAPNEL (sense 2) **2.** a device consisting of two or more hinged, movable iron prongs for grasping and moving heavy objects **3.** a coming to grips —*vt.* **grap′pled, grap′pling** to grip and hold; seize —*vi.* **1.** to use a grapnel (sense 2) **2.** to struggle in hand-to-hand combat **3.** to struggle or try to cope (*with*) —**grap′pler** *n.*

GRAPNEL

**grappling iron** (or **hook**) *same as* GRAPNEL (sense 2): also **grap′pling** *n.*

**grap·y** (grā′pē) *adj.* of or like grapes

**grasp** (grasp) *vt.* [ME. *graspen*, prob. < MLowG.] **1.** to take hold of firmly as with the hand; grip **2.** to take hold of eagerly; seize **3.** to understand; comprehend —*vi.* **1.** to try to seize (with *at*) **2.** to accept eagerly (with *at*) —*n.* **1.** the act of grasping **2.** control; possession **3.** the power to hold or seize **4.** comprehension —**grasp′a·ble** *adj.* —**grasp′er** *n.*

**grasp·ing** (-iŋ) *adj.* **1.** that grasps **2.** eager for gain; avaricious —**grasp′ing·ly** *adv.*

**grass** (gras) *n.* [OE. *gærs, græs*] **1.** any of a family of plants with long, narrow leaves, jointed stems, and seedlike fruit, as wheat, rye, oats, sugar cane, etc. **2.** any of various green plants with long, narrow leaves that are eaten by grazing animals **3.** ground covered with grass; pasture land or lawn **4.** [Slang] marijuana —*vt.* **1.** to put (animals) out to pasture or graze **2.** to grow grass over **3.** to lay (textiles, etc.) on the grass for bleaching —*vi.* to become covered with grass —**grass′like′** *adj.*

**grass·hop·per** (-häp′ər) *n.* **1.** any of a group of plant-eating insects with two pairs of wings and powerful hind legs adapted for jumping **2.** *Mil. Slang* a small, light airplane for scouting, etc.

**grass·land** (-land′) *n.* **1.** land with grass growing on it, used for grazing; pasture land **2.** prairie

**grass roots** [Colloq.] **1.** the common people, thought of in relation to their attitudes on political issues **2.** the basic source or support, as of a movement —**grass′-roots′** *adj.*

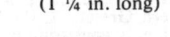

GRASSHOPPER
(1 ¼ in. long)

**grass widow** a woman divorced or otherwise separated from her husband —**grass widower**

**grass·y** (-ē) *adj.* **grass′i·er, grass′i·est** **1.** of or consisting of grass **2.** covered with grass **3.** green like growing grass —**grass′i·ness** *n.*

**grate¹** (grāt) *vt.* **grat′ed, grat′ing** [< OFr. *grater* < Frank.] **1.** to grind into particles by scraping **2.** to rub against (an object) with a harsh, scraping sound **3.** to grind (the teeth) together with a rasping sound **4.** to irritate; annoy —*vi.* **1.** to grind or rub with a rasping sound **2.** to make a harsh or rasping sound **3.** to cause irritation or annoyance — **grat′er** *n.*

**grate²** (grāt) *n.* [< ML. < L. *cratis,* a hurdle] **1.** *same as* GRATING¹ **2.** a frame of metal bars for holding fuel in a fireplace, etc. **3.** a fireplace —*vt.* **grat′ed, grat′ing** to provide with a grate or grates

**grate·ful** (grāt′fəl) *adj.* [obs. *grate* (< L. *gratus*), pleasing + -FUL] **1.** feeling or expressing gratitude; thankful **2.** causing gratitude; welcome —**grate′ful·ly** *adv.* —**grate′-ful·ness** *n.*

**grat·i·fy** (grat′ə fī′) *vt.* **-fied′, -fy′ing** [< Fr. < L. *gratificare* < *gratus,* pleasing + *-ficare,* -FY] **1.** to give pleasure or satisfaction to **2.** to indulge; humor —**grat′i·fi·ca′tion** *n.* —**grat′i·fi′er** *n.*

**grat·ing¹** (grāt′iŋ) *n.* a framework of parallel or latticed bars set in a window, door, etc.

**grat·ing²** (grāt′iŋ) *adj.* **1.** harsh and rasping **2.** irritating or annoying —**grat′ing·ly** *adv.*

**gra·tis** (grat′is, grāt′-) *adv., adj.* [L. < *gratia,* a favor] without charge or payment; free

**grat·i·tude** (grat′ə tōōd′, -tyōōd′) *n.* [Fr. < ML. < L. *gratus,* thankful] a feeling of thankful appreciation for favors received; thankfulness

**gra·tu·i·tous** (grə tōō′ə təs, -tyōō′-) *adj.* [< L. < *gratus,* pleasing] **1.** *a)* given or received without charge; free *b)* granted without obligation **2.** without cause or justification; uncalled-for —**gra·tu′i·tous·ly** *adv.* —**gra·tu′i·tous·ness** *n.*

**gra·tu·i·ty** (grə tōō′ə tē, -tyōō′-) *n., pl.* **-ties** [see prec.] a gift of money, etc., esp. one given for a service rendered; tip

**gra·va·men** (grə vā′men) *n., pl.* **-mens, gra·vam′i·na** (-vam′ə nə) [LL. < L. < *gravis,* heavy] **1.** a grievance **2.** *Law* the gist of an accusation

**grave¹** (grāv) *adj.* [Fr. < L. *gravis,* heavy] **1.** important; weighty **2.** threatening; ominous [*a grave illness*] **3.** solemn or sedate **4.** somber; dull **5.** low or deep in pitch —*n. same as* GRAVE ACCENT —**grave′ly** *adv.* —**grave′ness** *n.*

**grave²** (grāv) *n.* [OE. *græf* < *grafan,* to dig] **1.** *a)* a hole in the ground in which to bury a dead body *b)* any place of burial; tomb **2.** final end or death —*vt.* **graved, grav′en** or **graved, grav′ing** **1.** to carve out; sculpture **2.** [Archaic] to engrave; incise **3.** to impress or fix sharply and clearly —**grav′er** *n.*

**grave accent** a mark (`) used to indicate: **1.** in French, the quality of an open *e* (è), as in *chère* **2.** full pronunciation of a syllable normally elided, as in *lovèd* **3.** secondary stress, as in *týpewrìter*

**grave·clothes** (grāv′klōz′, -klōthz′) *n.pl.* the clothes in which a dead body is buried

**grave·dig·ger** (-dig′ər) *n.* a person whose work is digging graves

**grav·el** (grav′'l) *n.* [< OFr. dim. of *grave,* coarse sand, beach] **1.** a loose mixture of pebbles and rock fragments coarser than sand **2.** *Med.* a deposit of small concretions in the kidneys, gallbladder, or urinary bladder —*vt.* **-eled** or **-elled, -el·ing** or **-el·ling** **1.** to cover (a walk, etc.) with gravel **2.** to perplex **3.** [Colloq.] to annoy

**grav·el·ly** (-ē) *adj.* **1.** full of, like, or consisting of gravel **2.** sounding harsh [*a gravelly voice*]

**grav·en** (grāv′n) *alt. pp. of* GRAVE²

**graven image** an idol made from stone, wood, etc.

**grave·side** (grāv′sīd′) *n.* the area alongside a grave —*adj.* being, or taking place, beside a grave

**grave·stone** (-stōn′) *n.* an engraved stone marking a grave; tombstone

**grave·yard** (-yärd′) *n.* a burial ground; cemetery

**graveyard shift** [Colloq.] a work shift that starts during the night, usually at midnight

**grav·i·tate** (grav′ə tāt′) *vi.* **-tat′ed, -tat′ing** **1.** to move or tend to move in accordance with the force of gravity **2.** to be attracted or tend to move (*toward*) —**grav′i·ta′tive** *adj.*

**grav·i·ta·tion** (grav′ə tā′shən) *n.* **1.** the act, process, or fact of gravitating **2.** *Physics a)* the force by which every mass or particle of matter attracts and is attracted by every other mass or particle of matter *b)* the tendency of these masses or particles to move toward each other —**grav′i·ta′tion·al** *adj.* —**grav′i·ta′tion·al·ly** *adv.*

**grav·i·ty** (grav′ə tē) *n., pl.* **-ties** [< L. < *gravis,* heavy] **1.** the state or condition of being grave; esp., *a)* solemnity or sedateness; earnestness *b)* danger or threat *c)* seriousness **2.** weight; heaviness [specific *gravity*] **3.** lowness of musical pitch **4.** gravitation; esp., the force that tends to draw all bodies in the earth's sphere toward the center of the earth

**gra·vure** (grə vyoor′, grā′vyoor) *n.* [Fr. < *graver,* to carve < Frank.] **1.** *a)* any process that makes or uses intaglio printing plates *b)* a plate or print so made **2.** clipped form of: *a)* PHOTOGRAVURE *b)* ROTOGRAVURE

**gra·vy** (grā′vē) *n., pl.* **-vies** [? a misreading of OFr. *grané* < ? *grain,* cooking ingredients] **1.** the juice given off by meat in cooking **2.** a sauce made with this juice and flour, seasoning, etc. **3.** [Slang] *a)* money easily obtained *b)* any extra benefit

**gravy boat** a boat-shaped dish for serving gravy

**gray** (grā) *adj.* [< OE. *græg*] **1.** of the color gray **2.** *a)* darkish; dull *b)* dreary; dismal **3.** *a)* having hair that is gray *b)* old **4.** dressed in gray **5.** designating a vague, intermediate area, as between morality and immorality —*n.* **1.** a color made by mixing black and white **2.** a gray animal or thing **3.** [*often* G-] a person dressed in a gray uniform —*vt., vi.* to make or become gray —**gray′ly** *adv.* —**gray′ness** *n.*

**Gray** (grā), **Thomas** 1716–71; Eng. poet

**gray·beard** (-bird′) *n.* an old man

**gray·hound** (-hound′) *n. same as* GREYHOUND

**gray·ish** (-ish) *adj.* somewhat gray

**gray·lag** (-lag′) *n.* [short for *gray lag goose:* from its color and its late migration] the European wild gray goose

**gray·ling** (-liŋ) *n., pl.* **-ling, -lings:** see PLURAL, II, D, 2 [GRAY + -LING¹: from the color] **1.** a freshwater game fish related to the salmon **2.** any of several varieties of gray or brown butterfly

**gray matter 1.** grayish nerve tissue of the brain and spinal cord, consisting of nerve cells and some nerve fibers **2.** [Colloq.] intelligence

**gray squirrel** a large, gray squirrel with a bushy tail, native to E N. America

**gray wolf** a large, gray wolf that hunts in packs and was formerly common in the northern part of the Northern Hemisphere

**Graz** (gräts) city in SE Austria: pop. 237,000

**graze¹** (grāz) *vt.* **grazed, graz′ing** [OE. *grasian* < *græs,* grass] **1.** to feed on (growing grass, herbage, etc.) **2.** to put livestock to feed on (a pasture, etc.) **3.** to cause (livestock) to graze **4.** to be pasture for —*vi.* to feed on growing grass, etc. —**graz′er** *n.*

**graze²** (grāz) *vt.* **grazed, graz′ing** [prob. < prec. in sense "to come close to the grass"] **1.** to touch or rub lightly in passing **2.** to scrape or scratch in passing [*the shot grazed him*] —*vi.* to scrape, touch, or rub lightly against something in passing —*n.* a grazing, or a scratch or scrape caused by it

**gra·zier** (grā′zhər; *Brit.* -zyər) *n.* [Chiefly Brit.] a person who grazes beef cattle for sale

**graz·ing** (grā′ziŋ) *n.* land to graze on; pasture

**Gr. Brit., Gr. Br.** Great Britain

**grease** (grēs; *for v. also* grēz) *n.* [< OFr., ult. < L. *crassus,* fat] **1.** melted animal fat **2.** any thick, oily substance or lubricant —*vt.* **greased, greas′ing** **1.** to smear or lubricate with grease **2.** to bribe or tip: chiefly in **grease the palm** (or **hand**) of —**greas′er** *n.*

**grease·paint** (-pānt′) *n.* a mixture of grease and coloring matter used by performers in making up

**grease·wood** (-wood′) *n.* a thorny plant of desert regions in the W U.S., with fleshy leaves

**greas·y** (grē′sē, -zē) *adj.* **greas′i·er, greas′i·est** **1.** smeared or soiled with grease **2.** containing grease, esp. much grease **3.** like grease; oily; slippery —**greas′i·ly** *adv.* —**greas′i·ness** *n.*

**great** (grāt) *adj.* [OE. *great*] **1.** of much more than ordinary size, extent, number, etc. [the *Great* Lakes, a *great* company] **2.** much above the ordinary or average in some quality or degree; esp., *a*) existing in a high degree; intense [great pain] *b*) very much of a [a *great* reader] *c*) eminent; distinguished; superior [a *great* playwright] *d*) very impressive or imposing [great ceremony] *e*) having or showing nobility of mind, purpose, etc. [a *great* man] **3.** of most importance; main; chief [the *great* seal] **4.** designating a relationship one generation removed [great-grandmother] **5.** [Colloq.] clever; skillful [great at tennis] **6.** [Colloq.] excellent, splendid, fine, etc. —*adv.* [Colloq.] very well —*n.* a great or distinguished person: *usually used in pl.* —**great on** [Colloq.] enthusiastic about —**great′ly** *adv.* —**great′ness** *n.*

**great-aunt** (-ant′) *n.* a sister of any of one's grandparents; grandaunt

**Great Barrier Reef** coral reef off the NE coast of Queensland, Australia

**Great Bear** the constellation URSA MAJOR

**Great Bear Lake** lake in Northwest Territories, NW Canada

**Great Britain 1.** principal island of the United Kingdom, including England, Scotland, & Wales **2.** popularly, the United Kingdom

**great calorie** *same as* CALORIE (sense 2)

**great circle** any circle described on the surface of the earth or other sphere by a plane which passes through the center of the sphere: the shortest course between any two points on the earth's surface lies along a great circle passing through these points

**great·coat** (grāt′kōt′) *n.* a heavy overcoat

**Great Dane** any of a breed of large, powerful dog with short, smooth hair

**Great Divide** a principal mountain watershed; specif., the main ridge of the Rocky Mountains

**great·en** (grāt′'n) *vt., vi.* to make or become great or greater

**Greater Antilles** group of islands in the West Indies, made up of the N & W Antilles, including Cuba, Jamaica, Hispaniola, & Puerto Rico

**Great Falls** city in WC Mont., on the Missouri River: pop. 57,000

**great-grand·child** (grāt′gran′chīld′) *n., pl.* **-chil′dren** a child of any of one's grandchildren —**great′-grand′daugh′-ter** *n.* —**great′-grand′son′** *n.*

**great-grand·par·ent** (-gran′per′ənt) *n.* a parent of any of one's grandparents —**great′-grand′fa′ther** *n.* —**great′-grand′moth′er** *n.*

**great-great-** *a combining form used with nouns of relationship to indicate* two degrees of removal [great-great-grandparent]

**great gross** twelve gross

**great·heart·ed** (-här′tid) *adj.* **1.** brave; fearless; courageous **2.** generous; unselfish

**Great Lakes** chain of freshwater lakes in EC N. America; Lakes Superior, Michigan, Huron, Erie, & Ontario

**Great Mogul 1.** the title of the ruler of the Mongol empire in India in the 16th cent. **2.** [g- m-] a person of importance

**great-neph·ew** (-nef′yōō; *chiefly Brit.* -nev′-) *n.* a grandson of one's brother or sister; grandnephew —**great′-niece′** (-nēs′) *n.fem.*

**Great Plains** sloping region of valleys & plains in WC N. America, east of the base of the Rockies

**Great Salt Lake** shallow saltwater lake in NW Utah

**great seal** the chief seal of a nation, state, etc., with which official papers are stamped

**Great Slave Lake** lake in Northwest Territories, NW Canada

**Great Smoky Mountains** mountain range of the Appalachians, along the Tenn.-N.C. border

**great-un·cle** (-uŋ′k'l) *n.* a brother of any of one's grandparents; granduncle

**Great Wall of China** stone & earth wall across N China: built (3d cent. B.C.) as a defense against invaders

**greaves** (grēvz) *n.pl.* [< OFr. pl. of *greve,* shin] armor for the legs from the ankle to the knee

**grebe** (grēb) *n., pl.* **grebes, grebe:** see PLURAL, II, D, 1 [Fr. *grèbe*] any of a family of diving and swimming birds related to the loons, with partially webbed feet, and legs set far back on the body

**Gre·cian** (grē′shən) *adj. same as* GREEK (sense 1) —*n.* a Greek

**Gre·cism** (grē′siz'm) *n.* **1.** an idiom of the Greek language **2.** the spirit of Greek culture **3.** imitation of Greek style in the arts

**Gre·cize** (grē′sīz) *vt.* **-cized, -ciz·ing** to make Greek; give a

Greek form to —*vi.* to imitate the Greeks in language, manner, etc.

**Greco,El** *see* EL GRECO

**Gre·co-** *a combining form meaning:* **1.** Greek or Greeks **2.** Greek and or Greece and

**Gre·co-Ro·man** (grē′kō rō′mən) *adj.* of or influenced by both Greece and Rome

**Greece** (grēs) country in the S Balkan Peninsula, including islands in the Aegean, Ionian, & Mediterranean seas: 50,534 sq. mi.; pop. 8,835,000; cap. Athens: in ancient times, the region was comprised of many small monarchies & republics

**greed** (grēd) *n.* [back-formation < ff.] excessive desire for getting or having, esp. wealth; avarice

**greed·y** (-ē) *adj.* **greed′i·er, greed′i·est** [OE. *grædig*] **1.** wanting or taking all that one can get; desiring more than one needs or deserves; avaricious **2.** having too strong a desire for food and drink; gluttonous **3.** intensely eager —**greed′i·ly** *adv.* —**greed′i·ness** *n.*

**Greek** (grēk) *n.* **1.** a native or inhabitant of ancient or modern Greece **2.** the branch of the Indo-European language family consisting of the dialects of Greece, ancient or modern —*adj.* **1.** of ancient or modern Greece, its people, language, or culture **2.** designating, of, or using the rite of the Orthodox Eastern Church —**be Greek to one** to be incomprehensible to one

**Greek fire** an incendiary material used in ancient warfare, described as able to burn in water

**Greek (Orthodox) Church 1.** the established church of Greece, an autonomous part of the Orthodox Eastern Church **2.** *popular name for* ORTHODOX EASTERN CHURCH Also **Greek Church**

**Gree·ley** (grē′lē), **Horace** 1811–72; U.S. journalist & political leader

**green** (grēn) *adj.* [OE. *grene*] **1.** of the color that is characteristic of growing grass **2.** overspread with green foliage [a green field] **3.** keeping the green grass of summer; snowless [a green December] **4.** sickly or bilious, as from illness, fear, etc. **5.** not mature; unripe **6.** not trained; inexperienced **7.** easily led or deceived; naive **8.** not dried, seasoned, or cured **9.** fresh; new **10.** flourishing; vigorous **11.** [Colloq.] jealous —*n.* **1.** the color of growing grass; color between blue and yellow in the spectrum **2.** any green pigment or dye **3.** anything colored green, as clothing **4.** [*pl.*] green leaves, branches, etc., used for ornamentation **5.** [*pl.*] green leafy plants or vegetables, as spinach, lettuce, etc. **6.** an area of smooth turf set aside for special purposes [a village green] **7.** *Golf* a putting green —*vt., vi.* to make or become green —**green with envy** very envious —**the Green** Ireland's national color —**green′ish** *adj.* —**green′ly** *adv.* —**green′ness** *n.*

**green·back** (-bak′) *n.* any piece of U.S. paper money printed in green ink on the back

**Green Bay** [transl. of Fr. *Baie Verte,* Green Bay, arm of Lake Michigan on which city is located] city in NE Wis.: pop. 88,000

**green bean** the edible, immature green pod of the kidney bean

**green·bri·er** (-brī′ər) *n. same as* CAT BRIER

**green corn** young ears of sweet corn, in the milky stage, roasted or boiled for eating

**green·er·y** (grēn′ər ē) *n., pl.* **-er·ies 1.** green vegetation; verdure **2.** greens: see GREEN (*n.* 4) **3.** a greenhouse

**green-eyed** (-īd′) *adj.* **1.** having green eyes **2.** very jealous

**green·gage** (-gāj′) *n.* [after Sir William *Gage,* who introduced it into England, c. 1725] a large plum with golden-green skin and flesh

**green·gro·cer** (-grō′sər) *n.* [Brit.] a retail dealer in fresh vegetables and fruit —**green′gro′cer·y** *n.*

**green·horn** (-hôrn′) *n.* [orig. with reference to a young animal with immature horns] an inexperienced person; beginner; novice

**green·house** (-hous′) *n.* a building made mainly of glass, with heat and humidity regulated for growing plants; hothouse

**green·ing** (-iŋ) *n.* any of various apples having greenish-yellow skins when ripe

**Green·land** (grēn′lənd) [< ON.: orig. so called to attract settlers] self-governing island northeast of N. America, under Danish protection: the world's largest island: 840,000 sq. mi.; pop. 40,000

**green light** [after the green ("go") signal of a traffic light] [Colloq.] permission or authorization to proceed with some undertaking: usually in **give** (or **get**) **the green light**

**Green Mountains** range of the Appalachians, extending the length of Vermont

**green onion** an immature onion with a long stalk and green leaves, eaten raw; scallion

**green pepper** the green, immature fruit of the sweet red pepper, eaten as a vegetable

**green·room** (-rōōm′, -room′) *n.* a waiting room in some theaters, for use by performers when they are offstage

**Greens·bor·o** (grēnz′bur′ō) [after N. *Greene,* Am. general in Revolutionary War] city in north central N.C.: pop. 156,000

**green-stick fracture** (grēn′stik′) a partial fracture in which the bone is broken on only one side

**green·sward** (-swôrd′) *n.* green, grassy ground

**green tea** tea prepared from leaves not fermented before drying

**green turtle** a large, edible sea turtle with an olive-colored shell

**Green·ville** (grēn′vil) [see GREENSBORO] city in NW S.C.: pop. 58,000

**Green·wich (mean) time** (gren′ich; *chiefly Brit.* grin′ij) mean solar time of the prime meridian, which passes through Greenwich, a borough of London: used as the basis for standard time

**Green·wich Village** (gren′ich) section of New York City: noted as a center for artists, writers, etc.

**green·wood** (grēn′wood′) *n.* a forest in leaf

**greet** (grēt) *vt.* [OE. *gretan*] 1. to address with expressions of friendliness, respect, etc., as in meeting or by letter; hail; welcome 2. to meet, receive, or acknowledge (a person, event, etc.) in a specified way *[he was greeted by a rifle shot]* 3. to come or appear to; meet *[a roaring sound greeted his ears]* —**greet′er** *n.*

**greet·ing** (grēt′iŋ) *n.* 1. the act or words of a person who greets; salutation; welcome 2. *[often pl.]* a message of regards from someone absent

**greeting card** a decorated card bearing a greeting for some occasion, as a birthday

**gre·gar·i·ous** (grə ger′ē əs) *adj.* [< L. < *grex* (gen. *gregis*), a flock] 1. living in herds or flocks 2. fond of the company of others; sociable 3. having to do with a herd, flock, or crowd 4. *Bot.* growing in clusters —**gre·gar′i·ous·ly** *adv.* —**gre·gar′i·ous·ness** *n.*

**Gre·go·ri·an** (grə gôr′ē ən) *adj.* of or relating to Pope Gregory I or Pope Gregory XIII

**Gregorian calendar** a corrected form of the Julian calendar, introduced by Pope Gregory XIII in 1582 and now used in most countries of the world

**Gregorian chant** the ritual plainsong of the Roman Catholic Church, introduced under Pope Gregory I: it is unaccompanied and not divided into measures

**Greg·o·ry** (greg′ər ē) [< LL. < Gr. *Grēgorios,* lit., vigilant, hence, watchman] 1. a masculine name: dim. **Greg** 2. **Gregory I, Saint** 540?-604 A.D.; Pope (590-604): called *the Great* 3. **Gregory XIII** 1502-85; Pope (1572-85): see GREGORIAN CALENDAR

**greige** (grāzh) *n.* [Fr. *grège,* raw (silk)] a color blending gray and beige —*adj.* grayish-beige

**grem·lin** (grem′lən) *n.* [prob. < Dan. hyp. *græmling,* imp, dim. of obs. *gram,* a devil] an imaginary small creature humorously blamed when things fail to work

**Gre·na·da** (grə nä′də) country consisting of the southernmost island of the Windward group of the West Indies, and a chain of nearby islands: 133 sq. mi.; pop. 95,000

**gre·nade** (grə nād′) *n.* [Fr. < OFr., pomegranate, ult. < L. *granatus,* having seeds < *granum,* a seed] 1. a small bomb detonated by a fuse and thrown by hand or fired from a rifle 2. a glass container thrown to break on impact and disperse chemicals inside: used to spread tear gas, etc.

**gren·a·dier** (gren′ə dir′) *n.* [Fr. < *grenade*] 1. orig., an infantryman who threw grenades 2. a member of a special regiment or corps, as the British Grenadier Guards

**gren·a·dine**[1] (gren′ə dēn′, gren′ə dēn′) *n.* [Fr. < *grenade,* pomegranate] a syrup made from pomegranate juice, used for flavoring drinks, etc.

**gren·a·dine**[2] (gren′ə dēn′, gren′ə dēn′) *n.* [Fr.] a thin, loosely woven cloth, used for dresses, etc.

**Gre·no·ble** (grə nō′b'l; *Fr.* grə nô′bl') city in SE France, in the Alps: pop. 162,000

**Gret·na Green** (gret′nə) 1. border village in S Scotland, where, formerly, many eloping English couples went to be married 2. any similar village

**grew** (grōō) *pt. of* GROW

**grey** (grā) *adj., n., vt., vi. Brit. sp. of* GRAY

**grey·hound** (grā′hound′) *n.* [OE. *grighund*] any of a breed of tall, slender, swift hound with a narrow, pointed head and a smooth coat

**grid** (grid) *n.* [short for GRIDIRON] 1. a framework of parallel bars; gridiron; grating 2. a network of crossing parallel lines, as on graph paper 3. a metallic plate in a storage cell for conducting the electric current 4. an electrode, usually a wire spiral or

GREYHOUND (28 in. high at shoulder)

mesh, for controlling the passage of electrons or ions in an electron tube —*adj.* [Slang] of football

**grid·der** (grid′ər) *n.* [< GRID, *adj.* & GRIDIRON] [Slang] a football player

**grid·dle** (grid′'l) *n.* [< Anglo-Fr. *gridil* < OFr. *graïl* < L. < *craticula,* gridiron < *cratis,* wickerwork] a flat, metal plate or pan for cooking pancakes, etc. —*vt.* **-dled, -dling** to cook on a griddle

**grid·dle·cake** (-kāk′) *n.* a thin, flat batter cake cooked on a griddle; pancake

**grid·i·ron** (grid′ī′ərn) *n.* [ME. *gredirne,* folk etym. on *irne* (see IRON) < *gredire,* var. of *gredil:* see GRIDDLE] 1. a framework of metal bars or wires on which to broil meat or fish; grill 2. any framework resembling a gridiron 3. a football field

**grief** (grēf) *n.* [< OFr. < *grever:* see GRIEVE] 1. intense emotional suffering caused by loss, disaster, etc.; acute sorrow; deep sadness 2. a cause or the subject of such suffering —**come to grief** to fail or be ruined

**grief-strick·en** (-strik′'n) *adj.* stricken with grief; keenly distressed; sorrowful

**Grieg** (grēg; *Norw.* grig), **Ed·vard (Hagerup)** (ed′värd; *Norw.* ed′värt) 1843-1907; Norw. composer

**griev·ance** (grē′vəns) *n.* 1. a circumstance thought to be unjust or injurious and ground for complaint or resentment 2. complaint or resentment, or a statement expressing this, against a real or imagined wrong

**grieve** (grēv) *vt.* **grieved, griev′ing** [OFr. *grever* < L. *gravare,* to burden < *gravis,* heavy] to cause to feel grief; afflict with deep sorrow or distress —*vi.* to feel deep sorrow or distress; mourn; lament —**griev′er** *n.*

**griev·ous** (grē′vəs) *adj.* 1. causing grief 2. showing or full of grief 3. causing suffering; severe 4. deplorable; atrocious *[a grievous crime]* —**griev′ous·ly** *adv.* —**griev′ous·ness** *n.*

**grif·fin** (grif′ən) *n.* [< OFr. < OHG. or It. *grifo,* both < L. *gryphus* < Gr. < *grypos,* hooked] a mythical animal, part eagle and part lion: also sp. **griffon**

**Grif·fith** (grif′ith) [W. *Gruffydd*] 1. a masculine name 2. **D(avid) (Lewelyn) W(ark),** 1875-1948; U.S. motion-picture director

**grift·er** (grif′tər) *n.* [prob. altered < *grafter*] [Slang] a petty swindler, as an operator of a dishonest gambling device at a carnival —**grift** *vi., vt., n.*

**grill**[1] (gril) *n.* [Fr. *gril* < OFr. *graïl:* see GRIDDLE] 1. a gridiron (sense 1) 2. a large griddle 3. grilled food 4. *short for* GRILLROOM —*vt.* 1. to cook on a grill 2. to torture by applying heat 3. to question relentlessly —*vi.* to be subjected to grilling —**grilled** *adj.* —**grill′er** *n.*

**grill**[2] (gril) *n. same as* GRILLE

**grille** (gril) *n.* [Fr. < OFr. *graïlle:* see GRIDDLE] an open grating of wrought iron, wood, etc., forming a screen to a door, window, or other opening, or used as a divider —**grilled** *adj.*

**grill·room** (gril′rōōm′) *n.* a restaurant that makes a specialty of grilled foods

**grill·work** (-wurk′) *n.* a grille, or something worked into the form of a grille

**grilse** (grils) *n., pl.* **grilse, grils′es:** see PLURAL, II, D, 2 [<? OFr. dim. of *gris,* gray] a young salmon on its first return from the sea to fresh water

**grim** (grim) *adj.* **grim′mer, grim′mest** [OE. *grimm*] 1. fierce; cruel; savage 2. hard and unyielding; relentless; stern 3. appearing stern, forbidding, harsh, etc. 4. repellent; uninviting; ghastly —**grim′ly** *adv.* —**grim′ness** *n.*

**gri·mace** (gri mās′, grim′əs) *n.* [Fr. < OFr. *grimuche,* prob. < Frank.] a distortion of the face, as in expressing pain, contempt, etc., or a wry look —*vi.* **-maced′, -mac′ing** to make grimaces —**gri·mac′er** *n.*

**gri·mal·kin** (gri mal′kin, -môl′-) *n.* [earlier *gray malkin* (cat)] 1. a cat; esp., an old female cat 2. a malicious old woman

**grime** (grīm) *n.* [prob. < Fl. *grijm*] sooty dirt rubbed into or covering a surface, as of the skin —*vt.* **grimed, grim′ing** to make very dirty or grimy

**Grimm** (grim), **Ja·kob (Ludwig Karl)** (yä′kôp), 1785-1863 & **Wil·helm (Karl)** (vil′helm), 1786-1859; Ger. brother philologists & collaborators in the collection of fairy tales

**grim·y** (grī′mē) *adj.* **grim′i·er, grim′i·est** covered with grime; very dirty —**grim′i·ly** *adv.* —**grim′i·ness** *n.*

**grin** (grin) *vi.* **grinned, grin′ning** [OE. *grennian*] 1. to smile broadly 2. to draw back the lips and show the teeth in pain, scorn, etc. —*vt.* to express by grinning —*n.* the act or look of one who grins —**grin′ner** *n.* —**grin′ning·ly** *adv.*

**grind** (grīnd) *vt.* **ground, grind′ing** [OE. *grindan*] 1. to crush into bits or fine particles between two hard surfaces; pulverize 2. to afflict with cruelty, hardship, etc.; oppress 3. to sharpen, shape, or smooth by friction 4. to press down or rub together harshly or gratingly [to grind one's teeth] **5.** to operate by turning the crank of [to grind a coffee mill] **6.** to produce as by grinding —*vi.* **1.** to perform the act of grinding something **2.** to undergo grinding **3.** to grate **4.** [Colloq.] to work or study hard and steadily —*n.* **1.** a grinding **2.** the degree of fineness of something ground into particles **3.** long, difficult work or study **4.** [Colloq.] a student who studies very hard —**grind out** to produce by steady or laborious effort —**grind′ing·ly** *adv.*

**grind·er** (grīn′dər) *n.* **1.** a person or thing that grinds; specif., *a)* any of various machines for crushing or sharpening *b)* a molar tooth *c)* [*pl.*] [Colloq.] the teeth **2.** *same as* HERO SANDWICH

**grind·stone** (grīnd′stōn′) *n.* a revolving stone disk for sharpening tools or shaping and polishing things —**keep (or have** or **put) one's nose to the grindstone** to work hard and steadily

**grip** (grip) *n.* [< OE. *gripa*, handful < *gripan*, to seize] **1.** a secure grasp; firm hold, as with the hand, teeth, etc. **2.** any special manner of clasping hands, as between members of a secret society **3.** the power of grasping firmly **4.** mental grasp **5.** firm control; mastery **6.** a mechanical contrivance for clutching or grasping **7.** the part by which something is grasped; handle **8.** a small traveling bag or satchel **9.** *Sports* the manner of holding a bat, golf club, etc. —*vt.* **gripped** or **gript, grip′ping 1.** to take firmly and hold fast with the hand, teeth, etc. **2.** to give a grip (*n.* 2) to **3.** to fasten or join firmly (*vt.* 4. *a)* to get and hold the attention of *b)* to have a strong emotional impact on —*vi.* **1.** to get a grip —**come to grips** to struggle or try to cope (*with*) —**grip′per** *n.*

**gripe** (grip) *vt.* **griped, grip′ing** [OE. *gripan*, to seize] **1.** formerly, *a)* to grasp; clutch *b)* to distress; afflict **2.** to cause sudden, sharp pain in the bowels of **3.** [Slang] to annoy; irritate —*vi.* **1.** to feel sharp pains in the bowels **2.** [Slang] to complain —*n.* **1.** distress, affliction **2.** a sudden, sharp pain in the bowels: *usually used in pl.* **3.** [Slang] a complaint **4.** [Archaic] *a)* a grasping *b)* control —**grip′er** *n.*

**grippe** (grip) *n.* [Fr., lit., a seizure < *gripper* < Frank.] *earlier term for* INFLUENZA

**gript** (gript) *alt. pt. & pp. of* GRIP

**Gri·sel·da** (gri zel′də, -sel′-) *Medieval Tales* a heroine famous for her patience

**gri·sette** (gri zet′) *n.* [Fr., orig., gray woolen dress cloth < *gris*, gray] a French working girl

**gris·ly** (griz′lē) *adj.* **-li·er, -li·est** [OE. *grislic*] terrifying; ghastly —**gris′li·ness** *n.*

**grist** (grist) *n.* [OE.] grain that is to be or has been ground; esp., a batch of such grain —**grist to (or for) one's mill** anything one can use profitably

**gris·tle** (gris′'l) *n.* [OE.] cartilage, now esp. as found in meat —**gris′tli·ness** *n.* —**gris·tly** (gris′lē) *adj.*

**grist·mill** (grist′mil′) *n.* a mill for grinding grain, esp. for individual customers

**grit** (grit) *n.* [OE. *greot*] **1.** rough, hard particles of sand, stone, etc. **2.** a sandstone with sharp grains **3.** stubborn courage; pluck —*vt.* **grit′ted, grit′ting** to grind (the teeth) in anger or determination —*vi.* to make a grating sound

**grits** (grits) *n.pl.* [< OE. *grytte*] wheat or corn coarsely ground; esp., [South] fine hominy

**grit·ty** (grit′ē) *adj.* **-ti·er, -ti·est 1.** of, like, or containing grit; sandy **2.** brave; plucky —**grit′ti·ly** *adv.* —**grit′ti·ness** *n.*

**griz·zle** (griz′'l) *n.* [< OFr. < *gris*, gray] **1.** [Archaic] gray hair **2.** gray —*vt., vi.* **-zled, -zling** to make or become gray —*adj.* [Archaic] gray

**griz·zled** (griz′'ld) *adj.* **1.** gray or streaked with gray **2.** having gray hair

**griz·zly** (-lē) *adj.* **-zli·er, -zli·est** grayish; grizzled —*n., pl.* **-zlies** *short for* GRIZZLY BEAR

**grizzly bear** a large, ferocious bear of western N. America, with brown, gray, or yellow fur

**groan** (grōn) *vi.* [OE. *granian*] **1.** to utter a deep sound expressing pain, distress, or disapproval **2.** to make a creaking sound, as from great strain **3.** to be so weighed down as to groan —*vt.* to utter with a groan or groans —*n.* a sound made in groaning —**groan′er** *n.* —**groan′ing·ly** *adv.*

**groat** (grōt) *n.* [< MDu. or < MLowG. *grote*] **1.** an obsolete English silver coin worth fourpence **2.** a trifling sum

**groats** (grōts) *n.pl.* [< OE. *grotan*, pl.] any grain that is hulled, or hulled and coarsely cracked

**gro·cer** (grō′sər) *n.* [< OFr. *grossier* < *gros*, GROSS] a storekeeper who sells food and various household supplies

**gro·cer·y** (grō′sər ē) *n., pl.* **-cer·ies 1.** a grocer's store **2.** [*pl.*] the food and supplies sold by a grocer

**grog** (gräg) *n.* [after *Old Grog*, nickname of E. Vernon (1684–1757), Brit. admiral] any alcoholic liquor, as rum, esp. when diluted with water

**grog·gy** (-ē) *adj.* **-gi·er, -gi·est** [< GROG + -Y²] **1.** orig., drunk; intoxicated **2.** shaky or dizzy —**grog′gi·ly** *adv.* —**grog′gi·ness** *n.*

**groin** (groin) *n.* [prob. < OE. *grynde*, abyss] **1.** the hollow or fold where the abdomen joins either thigh **2.** *Archit.* the sharp, curved edge at the junction of two intersecting vaults, or the rib covering it —*vt.* to build with a groin

GROIN

**grok** (gräk) *vt., vi.* **grokked, grok′king** [coined 1961 by R. A. Heinlein] [Slang] to have empathy (*with*)

**grom·met** (gräm′it, grum′-) *n.* [< obs. Fr. *gromette*, a curb] **1.** a ring of rope or metal used to fasten the edge of a sail to its stay, hold an oar in place, etc. **2.** an eyelet of metal, plastic, etc.

**Gro·ning·en** (grō′niŋ ən; *Du.* khrō′niŋ ən) city in the N Netherlands: pop. 157,000

**groom** (grōom, grŏom) *n.* [ME. *grom*, boy < ?] **1.** a man or boy whose work is tending horses **2.** any of various officials of the British Royal household **3.** *same as* BRIDE-GROOM **4.** [Archaic] a manservant —*vt.* **1.** to clean and curry (a horse, dog, etc.) **2.** to make neat and tidy **3.** to train for a particular purpose [to *groom* a man for political office]

**grooms·man** (grōomz′mən, grŏomz′-) *n., pl.* **-men** a man who attends a bridegroom at the wedding

**groove** (grōov) *n.* [< ON. *grof*, a pit] **1.** a long, narrow furrow cut in a surface with a tool **2.** any channel or rut cut or worn in a surface **3.** a habitual way of doing something; settled routine **4.** [Slang] an exciting or stimulating person, place, experience, etc. —*vt.* **grooved, groov′ing** to make a groove or grooves in —*vi.* [Slang] to have understanding, appreciation, enjoyment, etc. in a relaxed, unthinking way (usually with *on* or *with*) —**in the groove** [Slang] performing or performed with smooth, effortless skill: orig. of jazz

**groov·y** (grōov′ē) *adj.* **groov′i·er, groov′i·est** [< phrase *in the groove*: see prec.] [Slang] very pleasing

**grope** (grōp) *vi.* **groped, grop′ing** [OE. *grapian*, to seize] to feel or search about blindly or uncertainly —*vt.* to seek or find (one's way) by groping —*n.* a groping —**grop′er** *n.* —**grop′ing·ly** *adv.*

**Gro·pi·us** (grō′pē əs), **Walter** 1883–1969; Ger. architect, in the U.S. after 1937

**gros·beak** (grōs′bēk′) *n.* [< Fr.: see GROSS & BEAK] any of various finchlike birds, with a thick, strong, conical bill

**gro·schen** (grō′shən) *n., pl.* **-schen** [G., ult. < ML. (*denarius*) *grossus*, lit., thick (denarius)] *see* MONETARY UNITS, table (Austria)

**gros·grain** (grō′grān′) *n.* [Fr. < OFr. *gros*, coarse + *grain*, GRAIN] a closely woven silk or rayon fabric with crosswise ribbing, used for ribbons, etc.

**gross** (grōs) *adj.* [< OFr. < LL. *grossus*, thick] **1.** big or fat and coarse-looking; corpulent **2.** flagrant; very bad **3.** dense; thick **4.** *a)* lacking fineness, as in texture *b)* lacking specific details **5.** insensitive or unrefined **6.** vulgar; obscene [gross language] **7.** total; entire; with no deductions: opposed to NET² [gross income] —*n.* **1.** *pl.* **gross′es** overall total, as of income, before deductions **2.** *pl.* **gross** twelve dozen —*vt., vi.* [Colloq.] to earn (a specified total amount) before expenses are deducted —**in the gross 1.** in bulk; as a whole **2.** wholesale: also **by the gross** —**gross′ly** *adv.* —**gross′ness** *n.*

**gross national product** the total value of a nation's annual output of goods and services

**gross ton** a unit of weight, equal to 2,240 pounds

**gross weight** the total weight of a commodity, including the packaging or container

**grosz** (grōsh) *n., pl.* **grosz′y** (-ē) [Pol.] *see* MONETARY UNITS, table (Poland)

**gro·tesque** (grō tesk′) *adj.* [Fr. < It. < *grotta*, a grotto: from designs in Roman caves] **1.** in or of a style of painting, sculpture, etc. in which forms of persons and animals are intermingled with foliage, etc. in a fantastic or bizarre design **2.** characterized by distortions or incongruities in appearance, shape, etc.; bizarre **3.** ludicrously eccentric; absurd —*n.* **1.** a grotesque painting, sculpture, design, etc. **2.** a grotesque thing or quality —**gro·tesque′ly** *adv.* —**gro·tesque′ness** *n.*

**grot·to** (grät′ō) *n., pl.* **-toes, -tos** [< It. < ML. *grupta* < VL. < L. *crypta*, crypt] **1.** a cave **2.** a cavelike summerhouse, shrine, etc.

**grouch** (grouch) *vi.* [< ME. *grucchen:* see GRUDGE] to grumble or complain in a sulky way —*n.* **1.** a person who grouches continually **2.** a grumbling or sulky mood **3.** a complaint

**grouch·y** (-ē) *adj.* **grouch′i·er, grouch′i·est** in a grouch; grumbling; sulky —**grouch′i·ly** *adv.* —**grouch′i·ness** *n.*

**ground¹** (ground) *n.* [OE. *grund*, bottom] **1.** *a)* orig., the lowest part or bottom of anything *b)* the bottom of a body of water **2.** the solid surface of the earth **3.** the soil of the earth; earth; land **4.** *a)* a particular piece of land *[a hunting ground]* *b)* [pl.] land surrounding or attached to a building; esp., the lawns, gardens, etc. of an estate **5.** any particular area of reference, discussion, etc.; subject *[arguments covering the same ground]* **6.** *[often pl.]* basis; foundation **7.** *[often pl.]* the logical basis of a conclusion, action, etc.; valid reason or cause **8.** the underlying, often primed, surface of a painting, colored pattern, etc. **9.** [pl.] the particles that settle to the bottom of a liquid; dregs *[coffee grounds]* **10.** *Elec.* the connection of an electrical conductor with the ground —*adj.* **1.** of, on, or near the ground **2.** growing or living in or on the ground —*vt.* **1.** to set on, or cause to touch, the ground **2.** to cause (a ship, etc.) to run aground **3.** to found on a firm basis; establish **4.** to base (a claim, argument, etc.) on something specified **5.** to instruct (a person) in the elements or first principles of **6.** to provide with a background **7.** to keep (an aircraft or pilot) from flying **8.** *Élec.* to connect (a conductor) with the ground —*vi.* **1.** to strike the bottom or run ashore: said of a ship **2.** *Baseball a)* to hit a grounder *b)* to be put out on a grounder (usually with *out*) —**break ground 1.** to dig; excavate **2.** to plow **3.** to start any undertaking —**cover ground 1.** to move or traverse a certain distance **2.** to make a certain amount of progress —**cut the ground from under one (or one's feet)** to deprive one of effective defense or argument —**from the ground up** completely; thoroughly —**gain ground 1.** to move forward **2.** to make progress **3.** to gain in strength, popularity, etc. —**get off the ground** to get (something) started; begin to make progress —**give ground** to withdraw under attack; yield —**hold (or stand) one's ground** to keep one's position against opposition —**lose ground 1.** to drop back; fall behind **2.** to lose in strength, popularity, etc. —**run into the ground** [Colloq.] to overdo (a thing) —**shift one's ground** to change one's argument or defense

**ground²** (ground) *pt. & pp. of* GRIND

**ground control** personnel, electronic equipment, etc. on the ground for guiding aircraft or spacecraft in takeoff, flight, and landing operations

**ground cover** ivy, myrtle, etc. used instead of grass for covering the ground

**ground crew** a group of people in charge of the maintenance and repair of aircraft

**ground·er** (groun'dər) *n. Baseball*, etc. a batted ball that strikes the ground almost immediately and rolls or bounces along: also **ground ball**

**ground floor** that floor of a building which is on or near the ground level; first floor —**in on the ground floor** [Colloq.] in at the beginning of an enterprise and thus in an advantageous position

**ground glass 1.** glass whose surface has been ground so that it diffuses light and is not transparent **2.** glass ground into fine particles

**ground·hog** (ground'hôg', -häg') *n.* [prob. transl. of Du. *aardvark*, AARDVARK] *same as* WOODCHUCK

**Groundhog Day** February 2, when, according to legend, if the groundhog sees his shadow, he returns to his hole for six more weeks of winter weather

**ground·less** (-lis) *adj.* without reason or cause —**ground'less·ly** *adv.* —**ground'less·ness** *n.*

**ground·ling** (-liŋ) *n.* **1.** *a)* a fish that lives close to the bottom of the water *b)* an animal that lives on or in the ground *c)* a plant that grows close to the ground **2.** [orig. of spectators in a theater pit] a person lacking critical taste

**ground·nut** (-nut') *n.* **1.** any of various plants with edible tubers or tuberlike parts, as the peanut **2.** the edible tuber or tuberlike part

**ground plan 1.** *same as* FLOOR PLAN **2.** a first or basic plan

**ground rule 1.** *Baseball* any of a set of rules adapted to playing conditions in a specific ballpark **2.** any of a set of rules governing a specific activity

**ground·sel** (ground's'l, groun'-) *n.* [< OE., ? < *gund*, pus + *swelgan*, to swallow: from use in poultices] any of a group of plants of the composite family, with usually yellow, rayed flower heads

**ground·sill** (ground'sil) *n.* the bottom horizontal timber in a framework: also **ground'sel** (-s'l)

**grounds·keep·er** (groundz'kē'pər) *n.* a person who tends the grounds of a playing field, estate, cemetery, etc.: also **ground'keep'er**

**ground squirrel** any of various small, burrowing animals related to tree squirrels and chipmunks

**ground·swell** (ground'swel') *n.* **1.** a violent swelling or rolling of the ocean, caused by a distant storm or earth-

quake **2.** a rapidly growing wave of public opinion, etc. Also **ground swell**

**ground water** water found underground in porous rock strata and soils, as in a spring

**ground wire** a wire acting as a conductor from an electric circuit, antenna, etc. to the ground

**ground·work** (-wurk') *n.* a foundation; basis

**ground zero** the surface area directly below or above the point of detonation of a nuclear bomb

**group** (grσσp) *n.* [< Fr. < It. *gruppo*] **1.** a number of persons or things gathered together and forming a unit; cluster; band **2.** a collection of objects or figures forming a design, as in a work of art **3.** a number of persons or things classified together because of common characteristics, interests, etc. **4.** *Chem. same as* RADICAL **5.** *U.S. Air Force* a unit under the command of a colonel **6.** *U.S. Mil.* a unit made up of two or more battalions or squadrons —*vt., vi.* to form into a group or groups —*adj.* of or involving a group

**group·er** (grσσp'ər) *n., pl.* **-ers, -er:** see PLURAL, II, D, 1 [Port. *garoupa*] any of several large fishes found in warm seas

**group·ie** (grσσp'ē) *n.* [Colloq.] a girl fan of rock groups or other popular personalities, who follows them about, often in the hope of achieving sexual intimacy

**group work** social work in which the worker helps individuals develop through cultural and recreational group activities —**group worker**

**grouse¹** (grous) *n., pl.* **grouse** [Early ModE. < ?] any of a number of game birds with a round, plump body, as the ruffed grouse, sage hen, etc.

**grouse²** (grous) *vi.* **groused, grous'ing** [orig. Brit. army slang < ?] [Colloq.] to complain; grumble —*n.* [Colloq.] a complaint —**grous'er** *n.*

**grout** (grout) *n.* [OE. *grut*] **1.** a thin mortar used to fill chinks, as between tiles **2.** a fine plaster for finishing surfaces —*vt.* to fill or finish with grout —**grout'er** *n.*

**grove** (grōv) *n.* [< OE. *graf*] **1.** a small wood or group of trees without undergrowth **2.** a group of trees planted to bear fruit, nuts, etc.; orchard

**grov·el** (gruv''l, gräv'-) *vi.* **-eled** or **-elled, -el·ing** or **-el·ling** [< earlier *grovelling, adv.*, face downward < ON.] **1.** to lie prone or crawl in a prostrate position, esp. abjectly **2.** to behave humbly or abjectly **3.** to wallow in what is low or contemptible —**grov'el·er, grov'el·ler** *n.*

**grow** (grō) *vi.* **grew, grown, grow'ing** [OE. *growan*] **1.** to come into being or be produced naturally; spring up **2.** to exist as living vegetation; thrive *[cactus grows in sand]* **3.** to increase in size and develop toward maturity **4.** to increase in size, quantity, or degree **5.** to come to be; become *[to grow weary]* **6.** to become attached or united by growth —*vt.* **1.** to cause to grow; raise; cultivate **2.** to cover with a growth: used in the passive **3.** to allow to grow *[to grow a beard]* **4.** to cause to be or to exist; develop —**grow into** to grow or develop so as to be or to fit *[a boy grows into a man; he grew into his job]* —**grow on** to become gradually more acceptable, likable, etc. —**grow out of 1.** to develop from **2.** to outgrow —**grow up** to reach maturity; become adult —**grow'er** *n.*

**growl** (groul) *vi.* [< ? OFr. < MDu. *grollen*, to be noisy] **1.** to make a low, rumbling, menacing sound in the throat, as a dog does **2.** to complain angrily —*vt.* to express by growling —*n.* the act or sound of growling —**growl'er** *n.* —**growl'ing·ly** *adv.*

**grown** (grōn) *pp. of* GROW —*adj.* **1.** having completed its growth; mature **2.** covered with a growth **3.** cultivated as specified *[home-grown]*

**grown-up** (grōn'up'; *for n.* -up') *adj.* **1.** adult **2.** of or for adults —*n.* an adult: also **grown'up'**

**growth** (grōth) *n.* **1.** a growing or developing **2.** degree or extent of increase in size, weight, power, etc. **3.** something that grows or has grown *[a thick growth of grass]* **4.** an outgrowth or offshoot **5.** a tumor or other abnormal mass of tissue in or on the body

**grub** (grub) *vi.* **grubbed, grub'bing** [ME. *grubben*] **1.** to dig in the ground **2.** to work hard, esp. at menial or tedious jobs; drudge —*vt.* **1.** to clear (ground) of roots and stumps by digging them up **2.** to dig up as by the roots; uproot —*n.* **1.** the short, fat, wormlike larva of an insect, esp. of a beetle **2.** a drudge **3.** [Slang] food —**grub'ber** *n.*

**grub·by** (-ē) *adj.* **-bi·er, -bi·est 1.** infested with grubs **2.** dirty; messy; untidy **3.** inferior, mean, etc. —**grub'bi·ly** *adv.* —**grub'bi·ness** *n.*

**grub·stake** (-stāk') *n.* [GRUB, *n.* 3 + STAKE] [Colloq.] **1.** money or supplies advanced to a prospector in return for a share in his findings **2.** money advanced for any enterprise —*vt.* [Colloq.] **-staked', -stak'ing** to provide with a grubstake —**grub'stak'er** *n.*

**grudge** (gruj) *vt.* **grudged, grudg′ing** [OFr. *grouchier*] **1.** to envy (someone) because of his possession or enjoyment of (something) **2.** to give with reluctance —*n.* a strong feeling of hostility or ill will against someone over a grievance —**grudg′er** *n.* —**grudg′ing·ly** *adv.*

**gru·el** (grōō′əl, grōōl) *n.* [OFr., coarse meal] thin, easily digested broth made by cooking meal in water or milk

**gru·el·ing, gru·el·ling** (-iŋ) *adj.* [prp. of obs. v. *gruel*, to punish] extremely trying; exhausting

**grue·some** (grōō′səm) *adj.* [< dial. *grue*, to shudder + -SOME¹] causing horror or loathing; grisly —**grue′some·ly** *adv.* —**grue′some·ness** *n.*

**gruff** (gruf) *adj.* [< Early ModDu. *grof*] **1.** rough or surly in manner or speech; rude **2.** harsh and throaty; hoarse —**gruff′ly** *adv.* —**gruff′ness** *n.*

**grum·ble** (grum′b'l) *vi.* **-bled, -bling** [prob. < Du. *grommelen*] **1.** to make low, unintelligible sounds in the throat **2.** to mutter or complain in a surly way **3.** to rumble —*vt.* to express by grumbling —*n.* a grumbling, esp. in complaint —**grum′bler** *n.* —**grum′bling·ly** *adv.* —**grum′bly** *adj.*

**grump** (grump) *n.* [prob. echoic] **1.** [*often pl.*] a fit of bad humor **2.** a grumpy person —*vi.* to complain and grumble

**grump·y** (grum′pē) *adj.* **grump′i·er, grump′i·est** [prec. + -Y²] grouchy; peevish; bad-tempered: also **grump′ish** —**grump′i·ly** *adv.* —**grump′i·ness** *n.*

**Grun·dy, Mrs.** (grun′dē) [a prudish busybody referred to in an 18th-c. play] a personification of conventional social disapproval, prudishness, narrow-mindedness, etc. —**Grun′dy·ism** *n.*

**grun·ion** (grun′yən) *n., pl.* **-ion, -ions:** see PLURAL, II, D, 2 [prob. < Sp.] a sardine-shaped fish of the California coast

**grunt** (grunt) *vi.* [OE. *grunnettan*, freq. of *grunian*, to grunt] **1.** to make the short, deep, hoarse sound of a hog **2.** to make a sound like this, as in annoyance —*vt.* to express by grunting —*n.* **1.** the sound of grunting **2.** a saltwater fish that grunts when removed from water **3.** [Slang] a U.S. infantryman in Vietnam —**grunt′er** *n.*

**Gru·yère (cheese)** (grōō yer′, grē-) [< *Gruyère*, Switzerland] a light-yellow Swiss cheese, rich in butterfat, or an American cheese like this

**gr. wt.** gross weight

**gryph·on** (grif′ən) *n. same as* GRIFFIN

**G.S., g.s.** **1.** general secretary **2.** ground speed

**GSA, G.S.A.** **1.** General Services Administration **2.** Girl Scouts of America

**G-string** (jē′striŋ′) *n.* **1.** a narrow loincloth **2.** a similar band, worn by striptease dancers

**G-suit** (-sōōt′) *n.* [G for *gravity*] a garment for pilots or astronauts, pressurized to counteract the effects of rapid acceleration or deceleration

**GT** gross ton

**gt.** **1.** [L. *gutta*] *pl.* **gtt.** *Pharmacy* a drop **2.** great

**Gt. Brit., Gt. Br.** Great Britain

**gtd.** guaranteed

**GU, g.u.** genitourinary

**gua·ca·mo·le** (gwä′kə mō′lā) *n.* [AmSp. < Nahuatl] a thick sauce or dip of seasoned, puréed avocados

**Gua·da·la·ja·ra** (gwä′d'l ə här′ə; *Sp.* gwä′*th*ä lä hä′rä) city in W Mexico: pop. 1,352,000

**Gua·de·loupe** (gwä′də lōōp′) French possession consisting of two large islands and five smaller ones in the Leeward group of the West Indies

**guai·a·cum** (gwī′ə kəm) *n.* [ModL. < genus name] **1.** *a)* any of several tropical American trees with purplish flowers and hard, durable wood *b)* this wood **2.** a greenish-brown resin from certain of these trees, used in medicine, in varnishes, etc.

**Guam** (gwäm) largest of the Mariana Islands, in the W Pacific: a possession of the U.S.: 209 sq. mi.; pop. 87,000; cap. Agaña

**gua·na·co** (gwə nä′kō) *n., pl.* **-cos, -co:** see PLURAL, II, D, 1 [Sp. < Quechua *huanacu*] a woolly, reddish-brown, wild animal of the Andes, related to the camel and llama

**gua·nine** (gwä′nēn) *n.* [< *ff.* + -INE⁴] an organic base, C₅H₅N₅O, that is in deoxyribonucleic acid and is found in all plant and animal tissues

**gua·no** (gwä′nō) *n., pl.* **-nos** [Sp. < Quechua *huanu*, dung] **1.** the manure of sea birds, found especially on islands off the coast of Peru: it is used as a fertilizer **2.** any fertilizer resembling this

**guar.** guaranteed

**Gua·ra·ní** (gwä′rä nē′) *n.* [*Guaraní*, lit., warrior] **1.** *pl.* **-nís′, -ní′** a member of a tribe of S. American Indians who lived east of the Paraguay River **2.** their language **3.** [g-] *pl.* **-nís′** *see* MONETARY UNITS, table (Paraguay)

**guar·an·tee** (gar′ən tē′, gär′-) *n.* [altered < GUARANTY] **1.** *same as* GUARANTY (*n.* 1 & 3) **2.** *a)* a pledge that something will be replaced if it is not as represented *b)* a posi-

GUANACO
(4 ft. high
at shoulder)

tive assurance that something will be done in the manner specified **3.** a guarantor **4.** one who receives a guaranty **5.** something that promises the happening of some event [the dark clouds were a *guarantee* of rain] —*vt.* **-teed′, -tee′ing** **1.** to give a guarantee or guaranty for **2.** to promise [I *guarantee* to be there]

**guar·an·tor** (gar′ən tôr′, -tər; gär′-) *n.* one who makes or gives a guaranty or guarantee

**guar·an·ty** (-tē) *n., pl.* **-ties** [< OFr. < *garant*, a warrant < Frank.] **1.** a pledge by which a person promises to pay another's debt or fulfill another's obligation if the other fails to do so **2.** an agreement that secures the existence or maintenance of something **3.** something given or held as security **4.** a guarantor —*vt.* **-tied, -ty·ing** *same as* GUARANTEE

**guard** (gärd) *vt.* [< the *n.*] **1.** to watch over and protect; defend; shield **2.** *a)* to keep from escape or trouble *b)* to hold in check; control; restrain *c)* *Sports* to keep (an opponent) from making a gain or scoring; also, to cover (a goal or area) in defensive play —*vi.* **1.** to keep watch (*against*) **2.** to act as a guard —*n.* [< OFr. < *garder*, to protect < Gmc.] **1.** the act or duty of guarding; defense; protection **2.** a posture of defense, as in boxing, fencing, etc. **3.** any device that protects against injury or loss **4.** a person or group that guards; specif., *a)* a sentinel or sentry *b)* a railway brakeman or gateman *c)* a person who guards prisoners *d)* [*pl.*] a special unit of troops assigned to the British royal household *e)* a military unit with a ceremonial function [a color *guard*] **5.** *Basketball* either of the two players whose function is to set up offensive plays **6.** *Football* either of two players on offense, left and right of the center —**mount guard** to go on sentry duty —**off (one's) guard** not alert for defense —**on (one's) guard** alert for defense —**stand guard** to do sentry duty —**guard′er** *n.*

**guard·ed** (-id) *adj.* **1.** kept safe; watched over and protected; defended **2.** held in check; supervised **3.** cautious; noncommittal —**guard′ed·ly** *adv.* —**guard′ed·ness** *n.*

**guard·house** (-hous′) *n. Mil.* **1.** a building used by the members of a guard when not walking a post **2.** a building where personnel are confined for minor offenses or while awaiting court-martial

**guard·i·an** (-ē ən) *n.* **1.** a person who guards or takes care of another person, property, etc. **2.** a person legally placed in charge of the affairs of a minor or of someone incapable of managing his own affairs —*adj.* protecting —**guard′i·an·ship′** *n.*

**guard·room** (-rōōm′) *n. Mil.* a room used by the members of a guard when not walking a post

**guards·man** (gärdz′mən) *n., pl.* **-men** a member of a National Guard or of any military guard

**Gua·te·ma·la** (gwä′tə mä′lə) **1.** country in Central America, south & east of Mexico: 42,042 sq. mi.; pop. 5,014,000 **2.** its capital: pop. 577,000: also **Guatemala City** —**Gua′te·ma′lan** *adj., n.*

**gua·va** (gwä′və) *n.* [Sp. *guayaba* < native name in Brazil] **1.** any of several tropical American plants, esp. a tree bearing a yellowish, edible fruit **2.** the fruit, used for jelly, preserves, etc.

**Guay·a·quil** (gwī′ä kēl′) seaport in W Ecuador: pop. 680,000

**Guay·na·bo** (gwī nä′bô, -vô) city in NE Puerto Rico, near San Juan: pop. 54,000

**gua·yu·le** (gwä yōō′lē) *n.* [AmSp. < Nahuatl *quauhitl*, plant + *olli*, gum] **1.** a small shrub of N Mexico, Texas, etc. **2.** rubber (**guayule rubber**) obtained from it

**gu·ber·na·to·ri·al** (gōō′bər nə tôr′ē əl) *adj.* [L. *gubernator*, governor < *gubernare*, to steer] of a governor or his office

**gudg·eon** (guj′ən) *n.* [< OFr. < L. *gobio* < Gr. *kōbios*] **1.** a small, European freshwater fish, easily caught, and used for bait **2.** a goby or killifish **3.** a person easily cheated or tricked; dupe —*vt.* to cheat; trick; dupe

**Guelph¹, Guelf** (gwelf) *n.* any member of a political party in medieval Italy supporting the Pope

**Guelph²** (gwelf) city in SE Ontario, Canada: pop. 51,000

**guer·don** (gur′d'n) *n., vt.* [< OFr., ult. < OHG. *widar*, back + *lōn*, reward] [Archaic] reward

**Guern·sey** (gurn′zē) one of the Channel Islands —*n., pl.* **-seys** any of a breed of dairy cattle, originally from this island, usually fawn-colored with white markings

**guer·ril·la, gue·ril·la** (gə ril′ə) *n.* [Sp. dim. of *guerra*, war < OHG.] any member of a small defensive force of irregular soldiers, usually volunteers, making surprise raids, esp. behind the lines of an invading enemy army —*adj.* of or by guerrillas

**guess** (ges) *vt., vi.* [prob. < MDu. *gessen*] **1.** to form a judgment or estimate of (something) without actual knowledge or enough facts for certainty; conjecture; surmise **2.** to judge correctly by doing this **3.** to think or suppose [I *guess* I can do it] —*n.* **1.** a guessing **2.** something guessed; conjecture; surmise —**guess′er** *n.*

**guess·work** (-wʉrk′) *n.* **1.** the act of guessing **2.** a judgment, result, etc. arrived at by guessing

**guest** (gest) *n.* [ON. *gestr*] **1.** *a*) a person entertained at the home of another; visitor *b*) a person entertained by another acting as host at a restaurant, theater, etc. **2.** any paying customer of a hotel, restaurant, etc. **3.** a person receiving the hospitality of a club, institution, etc. of which he is not a member **4.** a person who appears on a program by special invitation **5.** an organism, as an insect, that lives on or in the abode of another —*adj.* **1.** for guests **2.** performing by special invitation *[a guest artist]* —*vt.* to entertain as a guest —*vi.* to be, or perform as, a guest

**guff** (guf) *n.* [echoic] [Slang] **1.** foolish talk; nonsense **2.** brash or insolent talk

**guf·faw** (gə fô′) *n.* [echoic] a loud, coarse burst of laughter —*vi.* to laugh in this way

**Gui·a·na** (gē an′ə, -än′ə) region in N S. America, including Guyana, Surinam, & French Guiana

**guid·ance** (gīd′'ns) *n.* **1.** the act of guiding; direction; leadership **2.** something that guides **3.** advice or assistance, as that given to students by counselors **4.** the process of directing the course of a spacecraft, missile, etc.

**guide** (gīd) *vt.* **guid′ed, guid′ing** [OFr. *guider*, var. of *guier* < Frank.] **1.** to point out the way for; conduct; lead **2.** to direct the course of (a vehicle, implement, etc.) **3.** to direct in (policies, actions, work, etc.); manage; regulate —*vi.* to act as a guide —*n.* a person or thing that guides; specif., *a*) one who leads others on a trip or tour *b*) one who directs, or serves as the model for, another in his conduct, career, etc. *c*) a part that controls the motion of other parts *d*) a guidebook *e*) a book of basic instruction in some subject; handbook *[a guide to mathematics]* —**guid′a·ble** *adj.*

**guide·book** (-book′) *n.* a book containing directions and information for tourists

**guided missile** a military missile whose course is controlled by radio signals, radar devices, etc.

**guide dog** a dog trained to lead a blind person

**guide·line** (-līn′) *n.* a standard or principle by which to determine a policy or action: also **guide line**

**guide·post** (-pōst′) *n.* **1.** a post, as at a roadside, with a sign and directions for travelers **2.** anything that serves as a guide, standard, etc.

**gui·don** (gīd′'n, gī′dän) *n.* [Fr. < It. *guidone*] **1.** the identification flag of a military unit **2.** the soldier carrying it

**guild** (gild) *n.* [< OE. *gyld* and ON. *gildi*, both < base seen in OE. *gieldan*, to pay] **1.** in medieval times, a union of men in the same craft or trade to uphold standards and protect the members **2.** any association for mutual aid and the promotion of common interests

**guil·der** (gil′dər) *n.* [< ME. < MDu.: see GULDEN] **1.** the monetary unit and a coin of the Netherlands and Surinam: see MONETARY UNITS, table

**guild·hall** (gild′hôl′) *n.* **1.** a hall where a guild meets **2.** a town hall

**guilds·man** (gildz′mən) *n., pl.* **-men** (-mən) a member of a guild

**guile** (gīl) *n.* [OFr. *guile*, prob. < Frank. *wigila*, guile] slyness and cunning in dealing with others; craftiness —**guile′less** *adj.* —**guile′less·ly** *adv.* —**guile′less·ness** *n.*

**guile·ful** (-fəl) *adj.* full of guile; deceitful; tricky —**guile′ful·ly** *adv.* —**guile′ful·ness** *n.*

**guil·le·mot** (gil′ə mät′) *n.* [Fr., dim. of *Guillaume*, William] any of various narrow-billed, northern diving birds

**guil·lo·tine** (gil′ə tēn′; *for v.* gil′ə tēn′) *n.* [Fr., after J. I. *Guillotin* (1738–1814), who advocated its use] an instrument for beheading by means of a heavy blade dropped between two grooved uprights —*vt.* **-tined′, -tin′ing** to behead with a guillotine

**guilt** (gilt) *n.* [OE. *gylt*, a sin] **1.** *a*) the act or state of having done a wrong or committed an offense *b*) a feeling of self-reproach resulting from a belief that one has done something wrong or immoral **2.** conduct involving guilt; crime; sin

**guilt·less** (-lis) *adj.* **1.** free from guilt; innocent **2.** having no knowledge or experience (with *of*) —**guilt′less·ly** *adv.* —**guilt′less·ness** *n.*

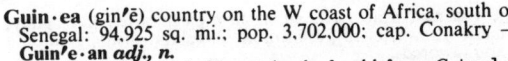

GUILLOTINE

**guilt·y** (gil′tē) *adj.* **guilt′i·er, guilt′i·est** **1.** having guilt; deserving blame or punishment **2.** having one's guilt proved **3.** showing or conscious of guilt *[a guilty look]* **4.** of or involving guilt or a sense of guilt *[a guilty conscience]* —**guilt′i·ly** *adv.* —**guilt′i·ness** *n.*

**Guin·ea** (gin′ē) country on the W coast of Africa, south of Senegal: 94,925 sq. mi.; pop. 3,702,000; cap. Conakry — **Guin′e·an** *adj., n.*

**guin·ea** (gin′ē) *n.* **1.** [first coined of gold from *Guinea*] a former English gold coin, last minted in 1813, equal to 21 shillings **2.** the sum of 21 English shillings

**Guin·ea-Bis·sau** (-bi sou′) country in W Africa, on the coast between Guinea & Senegal: formerly a Port. territory: 15,505 sq. mi.; pop. 487,000

**guinea fowl** [orig. imported from *Guinea*] a domestic fowl with a featherless head, rounded body, and dark feathers spotted with white

**guinea hen 1.** a female guinea fowl **2.** any guinea fowl

**guinea pig** [prob. orig. brought to England by ships plying between England, *Guinea*, and S. America] **1.** a small, fat mammal of the rat family, with short ears and no external tail, used in biological experiments **2.** any person or thing used in an experiment or test

**Guin·e·vere** (gwin′ə vir′) *Arthurian Legend* the wife of King Arthur and mistress of Sir Lancelot Also **Guin′e·ver′** (-vir′, -vər)

**guise** (gīz) *n.* [OFr. < OHG. *wisa*, manner] **1.** manner of dress; garb **2.** outward aspect; semblance **3.** a false appearance; pretense *[under the guise of friendship]*

**gui·tar** (gi tär′) *n.* [< Fr. < Sp. *guitarra* < Ar. < Gr. *kithara*, lyre] a musical instrument related to the lute but having a flat back and usually six strings that are plucked or strummed with the fingers or a plectrum —**gui·tar′ist** *n.*

**gulch** (gulch) *n.* [prob. < dial. *gulch*, to swallow greedily] a steep-walled valley cut by a swift stream; narrow ravine

**gul·den** (gool′dən) *n., pl.* **-dens, -den** [MDu. *gulden (florijn)*, golden (florin)] *same as* GUILDER

**gulf** (gulf) *n.* [< OFr. < It. *golfo*: ult. < Gr. *kolpos*, bosom] **1.** a large area of ocean, larger than a bay, reaching into land **2.** a wide, deep chasm or abyss **3.** a wide or impassable gap or separation —*vt.* to swallow up; engulf

**Gulf States** States on the Gulf of Mexico: Fla., Ala., Miss., La., & Tex.

**Gulf Stream** warm ocean current flowing from the Gulf of Mexico along the E coast of the U.S., turning east at the Grand Banks toward Europe

**gull¹** (gul) *n., pl.* **gulls, gull**: see PLURAL, II, D, 1 [< Celt.] a water bird with large wings, webbed feet, and white and gray feathers

**gull²** (gul) *n.* [prob. < ME. *golle*, silly fellow, lit., unfledged bird < ?] a person easily tricked; dupe —*vt.* to cheat; trick

**Gul·lah** (gul′ə) *n.* [< ? *Gola (Gula)* or < ? *Ngola*, tribal groups in Africa] **1.** any of a group of Negroes living in coastal S. Carolina and Georgia and esp. on the nearby sea islands **2.** their English dialect

**gul·let** (gul′ət) *n.* [OFr. *goulet* < L. *gula*, throat] **1.** the tube leading from the mouth to the stomach; esophagus **2.** the throat or neck

**gul·li·ble** (gul′ə b'l) *adj.* easily tricked; credulous —**gul′li·bil′i·ty** *n.* —**gul′li·bly** *adv.*

**gul·ly** (gul′ē) *n., pl.* **-lies** [altered < ME. *golet*, water channel, orig., gullet: see GULLET] a channel worn by running water; small, narrow ravine —*vt.* **-lied, -ly·ing** to make a gully in

**gulp** (gulp) *vt.* [prob. < Du. *gulpen*, to gulp] **1.** to swallow hastily, greedily, or in large amounts **2.** to choke back as if swallowing —*vi.* to catch the breath as in swallowing —*n.* **1.** the act of gulping **2.** the amount swallowed at one time —**gulp′er** *n.* —**gulp′ing·ly** *adv.*

**gum¹** (gum) *n.* [< OFr. < L. *gumma* < Egypt. *kemai*] **1.** a sticky, colloidal carbohydrate found in certain trees and plants, which dries into a brittle mass that dissolves or swells in water **2.** any similar plant secretion, as resin **3.** any plant gum processed for use in industry, art, etc. **4.** *a*) an adhesive, as on the back of a postage stamp *b*) any of various sticky substances or deposits **5.** *same as:* GUM TREE *b*) GUMWOOD **6.** *same as* CHEWING GUM —*vt.* **gummed, gum′ming** to coat, unite, or stiffen with gum —*vi.* **1.** to secrete or form gum **2.** to become sticky or clogged — **gum up** [Slang] to put out of working order

**gum²** (gum) *n.* [OE. *goma*] [*often pl.*] the firm flesh surrounding the base of the teeth —*vt.* **gummed, gum′ming** to chew with toothless gums

**gum ammoniac** *same as* AMMONIAC

**gum arabic** a gum obtained from several African acacias, used in medicine and candy, for stabilizing emulsions, etc.

**gum·bo** (gum′bō) *n.* [< Bantu name for okra] **1.** *same as* OKRA **2.** a soup thickened with unripe okra pods **3.** a fine, silty soil of the Western prairies, which becomes sticky and nonporous when wet: also **gumbo soil**

**gum·boil** (gum′boil′) *n.* an abscess on the gum

---

fat, āpe, cär, ten, ēven, is, bīte; gō, hôrn, tool, look; oil, out; up, fʉr; get; joy; yet; chin; she; thin, then; zh, leisure; ŋ, ring; ə for *a* in *ago*, *e* in *agent*, *i* in *sanity*, *o* in *comply*, *u* in *focus*; ' as in *able* (ā′b'l); Fr. bäl; ë, Fr. coeur; ö, Fr. feu; Fr. mon; ô, Fr. coq; ü, Fr. duc; r, Fr. cri; H, G. ich; kh, G. doch; ‡foreign; *hypothetical; < derived from. See inside front cover.

**gum·drop** (-dräp′) *n.* a small, firm piece of jellylike candy, made of sweetened gum arabic or gelatin, usually colored and flavored

**gum·my** (gum′ē) *adj.* **-mi·er, -mi·est** **1.** having the nature of gum; sticky **2.** covered with or containing gum **3.** yielding gum —**gum′mi·ness** *n.*

**gump·tion** (gump′shən) *n.* [< Scot. dial.] [Colloq.] **1.** orig., common sense **2.** courage and initiative; enterprise and boldness: the current sense

**gum resin** a mixture of gum and resin, given off by certain trees and plants

**gum·shoe** (gum′shōō′) *n.* **1.** orig., *a)* a rubber overshoe *b)* [*pl.*] sneakers **2.** [Slang] a detective

**gum tree** any of various trees that yield gum, as the sour gum, sweet gum, eucalyptus, etc.

**gum·wood** (-wōōd′) *n.* the wood of a gum tree

**gun** (gun) *n.* [< ON. *Gunnhildr*, fem. name (< *gunnr*, war + *hildr*, battle)] **1.** a weapon consisting of a metal tube from which a projectile is discharged by the force of an explosive: specif., *a)* technically, a heavy weapon, as a cannon, etc. *b)* a rifle *c)* popularly, a pistol or revolver **2.** any similar device not discharged by an explosive [an air *gun*] **3.** a discharge of a gun in signaling or saluting **4.** anything like a gun in shape or use **5.** [Slang] *same as* GUNMAN (sense 1) —*vi.* **gunned, gun′ning** to shoot or hunt with a gun —*vt.* **1.** [Colloq.] to shoot (a person) **2.** [Slang] to advance the throttle of (an engine) so as to increase the speed —**give it the gun** [Slang] to cause something to start or gain speed —**gun for** **1.** to hunt for with a gun **2.** [Slang] to seek —**jump the gun** [Slang] to begin before the signal to start, or before the proper time —**stick to one's guns** to be firm under attack

**gun·boat** (-bōt′) *n.* a small armed ship of shallow draft, used to patrol rivers, etc.

**gun·cot·ton** (-kät′'n) *n.* nitrocellulose in a highly nitrated form, used as an explosive

**gun·fight** (-fīt′) *n.* a fight between persons using pistols or revolvers —**gun′fight′er** *n.*

**gun·fire** (-fīr′) *n.* the firing of a gun or guns

**gung-ho** (guŋ′hō′) *adj.* [Chin., lit., work together] overly enthusiastic, enterprising, etc.

**gunk** (guŋk) *n.* [< ? G(OO) + (J)UNK¹] [Slang] any oily or thick, messy substance —**gunk/y** *adj.*

**gun·lock** (gun′läk′) *n.* in some guns, the mechanism by which the charge is set off

**gun·man** (-mən) *n., pl.* **-men** **1.** a man armed with a gun, esp. an armed gangster or hired killer **2.** a man skilled in the use of a gun

**gun·met·al** (-met′'l) *n.* **1.** a kind of bronze formerly used for making cannons; also, any metal or alloy treated to resemble this **2.** the dark gray color (**gunmetal gray**) of tarnished gunmetal —*adj.* dark gray

**gun·nel¹** (gun′'l) *n.* [< ?] a small, slimy fish resembling the blenny, found in the N Atlantic

**gun·nel²** (gun′'l) *n. same as* GUNWALE

**gun·ner** (gun′ər) *n.* **1.** a soldier, sailor, etc. who helps fire artillery **2.** a naval warrant officer in charge of a ship's guns **3.** a hunter with a gun

**gun·ner·y** (-ē) *n.* **1.** heavy guns **2.** the science of making and using heavy guns and projectiles

**gunnery sergeant** a noncommissioned Marine Corps officer ranking above a staff sergeant

**gun·ny** (gun′ē) *n., pl.* **-nies** [< Hindi < Sans. *gōṇī*, a sack] **1.** a coarse, heavy fabric of jute or hemp, used for sacks **2.** *same as* GUNNYSACK

**gun·ny·sack** (-sak′) *n.* a sack made of gunny

**gun·play** (gun′plā′) *n.* an exchange of gunshots, as between gunmen and police

**gun·point** (-point′) *n.* the muzzle of a gun —**at gunpoint** under threat of being shot with a gun

**gun·pow·der** (-pou′dər) *n.* an explosive powder, esp. a mixture of sulfur, saltpeter, and charcoal, used in cartridges, shells, etc., for blasting, etc.

**gun·run·ning** (-run′iŋ) *n.* the smuggling of guns and ammunition into a country —**gun′run′ner** *n.*

**gun·shot** (-shät′) *n.* **1.** shot fired from a gun **2.** the range of a gun —*adj.* caused by a shot from a gun

**gun·smith** (-smith′) *n.* a person who makes or repairs small guns

**gun·stock** (-stäk′) *n.* the wooden handle or butt to which the barrel of a gun is attached

**gun·wale** (gun′'l) *n.* [first applied to bulwarks supporting a ship's guns] the upper edge of the side of a ship or boat

**gup·py** (gup′ē) *n., pl.* **-pies** [after R. *Guppy*, of Trinidad] a tiny, brightly colored tropical fish

**gur·gle** (gur′g'l) *vi.* **-gled, -gling** [prob. echoic] **1.** to flow with a bubbling or rippling sound **2.** to make such a sound in the throat —*vt.* to utter with a gurgle —*n.* the act or sound of gurgling

**gur·nard** (gur′nərd) *n., pl.* **-nards, -nard**: SEE PLURAL, II, D, 1 [< OFr. < *grogner*, to grunt] *same as* FLYING GURNARD

**gu·ru** (goor′ōō, goo rōō′) *n.* [Hindi < Sans. *guru-ḥ*,

venerable] **1.** in Hinduism, one's spiritual adviser **2.** a leader with devoted followers

**gush** (gush) *vi.* [prob. akin to ON. *gjosa*, to gush] **1.** to flow out suddenly and plentifully **2.** to have a sudden, plentiful flow of blood, tears, etc. **3.** to express exaggerated enthusiasm or feeling —*vt.* to cause to flow out suddenly and plentifully —*n.* **1.** a sudden, plentiful outflow **2.** gushing talk or writing —**gush′ing·ly** *adv.*

**gush·er** (-ər) *n.* **1.** a person who gushes **2.** an oil well from which oil spouts without being pumped

**gush·y** (-ē) *adj.* **gush′i·er, gush′i·est** characterized by gush (*n.* 2) —**gush′i·ly** *adv.* —**gush′i·ness** *n.*

**gus·set** (gus′it) *n.* [< OFr. *gousset*] **1.** a triangular or diamond-shaped piece inserted in a garment, glove, etc. to make it stronger or roomier **2.** a triangular metal brace for reinforcing a corner or angle —*vt.* to furnish with a gusset

GUSSET

**gus·sie, gus·sy** (gus′ē) *vt., vi.* **-sied, -sy·ing** [< *Gussie*, nickname for AUGUSTA] [Slang] to dress (*up*) or decorate in a fine or showy way

**gust** (gust) *n.* [< ON. *gustr* < *gjosa*, to gush] **1.** a sudden, strong rush of air or wind **2.** a sudden outburst of rain, laughter, rage, etc. —*vi.* to blow in gusts

**gus·ta·to·ry** (gus′tə tôr′ē) *adj.* of or having to do with tasting or the sense of taste: also **gus′ta·tive**

**gus·to** (gus′tō) *n.* [It. & Sp. < L. *gustus*, taste] **1.** taste; liking **2.** zest; relish **3.** great vigor

**gust·y** (gus′tē) *adj.* **gust′i·er, gust′i·est** characterized by gusts of air or wind, or by sudden outbursts —**gust′i·ly** *adv.* —**gust′i·ness** *n.*

**gut** (gut) *n.* [OE. *guttas*, pl. < base of *geotan*, to pour] **1.** *a)* [*pl.*] the bowels; entrails *b)* the stomach or belly Regarded as an indelicate usage **2.** all or part of the alimentary canal, esp. the intestine **3.** tough cord made from animal intestines, used for violin strings, surgical sutures, etc. **4.** a narrow passage or gully **5.** [*pl.*] [Colloq.] the basic or inner parts **6.** [*pl.*] [Slang] *a)* daring, courage, etc. *b)* impudence; effrontery *c)* power or force —*vt.* **gut′ted, gut′ting** **1.** to remove the intestines from; eviscerate **2.** to destroy the interior of, as by fire —*adj.* [Slang] **1.** urgent and basic [*gut* issues in politics] **2.** easy; simple [a *gut* course in college]

**Gu·ten·berg** (gōōt′'n burg′), **Jo·hann** (yō′hän) (born *Johannes Gensfleisch*) 1400?–68; Ger. printer: reputedly the first European to print with movable type

**gut·less** (gut′lis) *adj.* [Slang] lacking courage

**guts·y** (gut′sē) *adj.* **guts′i·er, guts′i·est** [Slang] full of guts; courageous, forceful, etc.

**gut·ta-per·cha** (gut′ə pur′chə) *n.* [< Malay < *gĕtah*, gum + *pĕrchah*, tree from which it is obtained] a rubberlike gum produced from the latex of various SE Asian trees, used in insulation, dentistry, etc.

**gut·ter** (gut′ər) *n.* [< OFr. < L. *gutta*, a drop] **1.** a trough along or under the eaves of a roof, to carry off rain water **2.** any narrow channel, as along the side of a road or street to carry off water **3.** the adjoining inner margins of two facing pages in a book, etc. —*vt.* to furnish with gutters —*vi.* **1.** to flow in a stream **2.** to melt rapidly so that the wax runs down in channels: said of a candle

**gut·ter·snipe** (-snīp′) *n.* a child living in the slums, for the most part in the streets: contemptuous term

**gut·tur·al** (gut′ər əl) *adj.* [< L. *guttur*, throat] **1.** of the throat **2.** loosely, produced in the throat; harsh, rasping, etc.: said of sounds **3.** formed with the back of the tongue close to or against the soft palate, as the *k* in *keen* —*n.* a guttural sound —**gut′tur·al·ly** *adv.* —**gut′tur·al·ness** *n.*

**Guy** (gī) [Fr., lit., leader] a masculine name

**guy¹** (gī) *n.* [< OFr. < *guier*, to GUIDE] a rope, chain, etc. attached to something to steady or guide it —*vt.* to guide or steady with a guy

**guy²** (gī) *n.* [after Guy FAWKES] **1.** a person who looks odd **2.** [Slang] *a)* a man or boy; fellow *b)* any person —*vt.* to make fun of; ridicule

**Guy·a·na** (gī an′ə, -än′ə) country in NE S. America, on the Atlantic: a member of the Commonwealth: 83,000 sq. mi.; pop. 763,000 —**Guy′a·nese′** (-ə nēz′) *adj., n., pl.* **-nese′**

**guz·zle** (guz′'l) *vi., vt.* **-zled, -zling** [< ? OFr. < *gosier*, throat] to drink greedily or immoderately —**guz′zler** *n.*

**Gwen·do·len, Gwen·do·line, Gwen·do·lyn** (gwen′d'l ən) [< Celt.; first element prob. W. *gwen*, white] a feminine name: dim. **Gwen**

**gybe** (jīb) *n., vi., vt.* **gybed, gyb′ing** *same as* JIBE¹

**gym** (jim) *n.* [Colloq.] *same as:* **1.** GYMNASIUM **2.** PHYSICAL EDUCATION

**gym·na·si·um** (jim nā′zē əm) *n., pl.* **-si·ums, -si·a** (-ə) [L. < Gr. *gymnasion*, ult. < *gymnos*, naked] **1.** a room or building equipped for physical training and athletic sports **2.** [G-] (gim nä′zē oom) in Germany and some other European countries, a secondary school for students preparing to enter a university

**gym·nast** (jim′nast) *n.* an expert in gymnastics

**gym·nas·tic** (jim nas′tik) *adj.* [< L. < Gr.: see GYMNASIUM] of or having to do with gymnastics: also **gym·nas′ti·cal** —**gym·nas′ti·cal·ly** *adv.*

**gym·nas·tics** (-tiks) *n.pl.* exercises that develop and train the body and the muscles

**gym·no-** [< Gr. *gymnos*, naked] *a combining form meaning* naked, stripped, bare: also **gymn-**

**gym·no·sperm** (jim′nə spurm′) *n.* [< ModL. < Gr.: see prec. & -SPERM] any of a large class of seed plants having the ovules borne on open scales, usually in cones, as pines and cedars —**gym′no·sper′mous** (-spur′məs) *adj.* —**gym′no·sper′my** (-spur′mē) *n.*

**gym shoe** same as SNEAKER (sense 2)

**gyn·e·co-** [< Gr. < *gynē*, a woman] *a combining form meaning* woman, female: also **gynec-**

**gyn·e·col·o·gy** (gī′nə käl′ə jē, jin′ə-, jī′nə-) *n.* [prec. + -LOGY] the branch of medicine dealing with the specific functions, diseases, etc. of women —**gyn′e·co·log′ic** (-kəläj′ik), **gyn′e·co·log′i·cal** *adj.* —**gyn′e·col′o·gist** *n.*

**gy·noe·ci·um** (ji nē′sē əm, jī-, gī-) *n., pl.* **-ci·a** (-ə) [ModL. < L., ult. < Gr. *gynē*, a woman + *oikos*, house] the female organ or organs of a flower; pistil or pistils: also sp. **gyn·ae·ce·um** (jī′nə sē′əm) *pl.* **-ce′a** (-ə) or **gyne′ci·um**, *pl.* **-ci·a** (-ə)

**gyn·o·phore** (jin′ə fôr′, jī′nə-, gī′nə-) *n.* [< Gr. *gynē*, woman + -PHORE] a stalk bearing the gynoecium above the petals and stamens

**-gyn·ous** (ji nəs) [< ModL. < Gr. < *gynē*, a woman] *a combining form meaning:* **1.** woman or female [*polygynous*] **2.** having female organs or pistils as specified [*androgynous*]

**-gyn·y** (ji nē) *a combining form used to form nouns from adjectives ending in* -GYNOUS

**gyp** (jip) *n.* [prob. < GYPSY] [Colloq.] **1.** an act of cheating; swindle **2.** a swindler: also **gyp′per, gyp′ster** —*vt., vi.* **gypped, gyp′ping** [Colloq.] to swindle; cheat

**gyp·soph·i·la** (jip säf′ə lə) *n.* [ModL.: see GYPSUM & -PHIL(E)] any of a genus of plants of the pink family, bearing clusters of small white or pink flowers with a delicate fragrance, as baby's breath

**gyp·sum** (jip′səm) *n.* [L. < Gr. *gypsos*, chalk < Sem.] a hydrated sulfate of calcium, $CaSO_4 \cdot 2H_2O$, occurring naturally in sedimentary rocks and used for making plaster of Paris, in treating soil, etc.

**Gyp·sy** (jip′sē) *n., pl.* **-sies** [< *Egipcien*, Egyptian: orig. thought to have come from Egypt] **1.** [*also* g-] a member of a wandering Caucasoid people with dark skin and black hair, believed to have originated in India: they are known throughout the world as musicians, fortunetellers, etc. **2.** *same as* ROMANY (sense 2) **3.** [g-] a person whose appearance or habits are like those of a Gypsy —*adj.* of or like a Gypsy or Gypsies

**gypsy moth** a European moth, brownish or white, now common in the E U.S.: its larvae feed on leaves, damaging trees and plants

**gy·rate** (jī′rāt) *vi.* **-rat·ed, -rat·ing** [< L. pp. of *gyrare*, to turn, ult. < Gr. *gyros*, a circle] to move in a circular or spiral path; rotate or revolve on an axis; whirl —*adj.* spiral, coiled, or circular —**gy·ra′tion** *n.* —**gy′ra·tor** *n.*

**gyre** (jīr) *n.* [< L. < Gr. *gyros*, a circle] [Chiefly Poet.] **1.** a circular or spiral motion; whirl **2.** a circular or spiral form; ring or vortex —*vi., vt.* **gyred, gyr′ing** [Chiefly Poet.] to whirl

**gyr·fal·con** (jur′fal′kən, -fôl′-, -fô′-) *n.* [< OFr. *girfaucon* < Frank.] a large, fierce, strong falcon of the Arctic

**gy·ro** (jī′rō) *n., pl.* **-ros** *short for:* **1.** GYROSCOPE **2.** GYRO-COMPASS

**gy·ro-** [< Gr. *gyros*, a circle] *a combining form meaning:* **1.** gyrating [*gyroscope*] **2.** gyroscope [*gyrocompass*] Also, before a vowel, **gyr-**

**gy·ro·com·pass** (-kum′pəs) *n.* a compass consisting of a motor-operated gyroscope whose rotating axis points to the geographic north pole instead of to the magnetic pole

**gy·ro·scope** (-skōp′) *n.* [GYRO- + -SCOPE] a wheel mounted in a ring so that its axis is free to turn in any direction: when the wheel is spun rapidly, it will keep its original plane of rotation no matter which way the ring is turned —**gy′ro·scop′ic** (-skäp′ik) *adj.* —**gy′ro·scop′i·cal·ly** *adv.*

GYROSCOPE

**gy·ro·sta·bi·liz·er** (jī′rō stā′bə lī′zər) *n.* a device consisting of a gyroscope spinning in a vertical plane, used to stabilize the side-to-side rolling of a ship

**gyve** (jīv) *n., vt.* **gyved, gyv′ing** [< Anglo-Fr. *gyves*, pl.] [Archaic or Poet.] fetter; shackle

# H

**H, h** (āch) *n., pl.* **H's, h's** **1.** the eighth letter of the English alphabet **2.** the sound of *H* or *h*

**H** (āch) *n.* **1.** *Chem.* the symbol for hydrogen **2.** *Physics* the symbol for henry **3.** [Slang] heroin —*adj.* shaped like *H*

**H., h.** **1.** harbor **2.** hard(ness) **3.** height **4.** high **5.** *Baseball* hits **6.** hour(s) **7.** husband

**ha** (hä) *interj.* [echoic] an exclamation variously expressing surprise, anger, triumph, etc. —*n.* the sound of this exclamation or of a laugh

**Haar·lem** (här′ləm) city in NW Netherlands: pop. 173,000

**Ha·bak·kuk** (hab′ə kuk, hə bak′ək) *Bible* **1.** a Hebrew prophet of the 7th cent. B.C. **2.** the book containing his prophecies: abbrev. **Hab.** Also, in the Douay Bible, **Ha′ba·cuc**

**Ha·ba·na** (ä bä′nä), **(La)** *Sp. name of* HAVANA

**ha·be·as cor·pus** (hā′bē əs kôr′pəs) [L., (that) you have the body] *Law* a writ requiring that a detained person be brought before a court to decide the legality of his detention or imprisonment

**hab·er·dash·er** (hab′ər dash′ər, hab′ə-) *n.* [prob. < Anglo-Fr. *hapertas*, kind of cloth] **1.** a person who sells men's furnishings, such as hats, shirts, gloves, etc. **2.** [Brit.] a dealer in various small articles, such as ribbons, thread, etc.

**hab·er·dash·er·y** (-ē) *n., pl.* **-er·ies** **1.** things sold by a haberdasher **2.** a haberdasher's shop

**hab·er·geon** (hab′ər jən) *n.* [OFr. *haubergeon*, dim. of

*hauberc*, hauberk] **1.** a short, high-necked jacket of mail **2.** *same as* HAUBERK

**ha·bil·i·ment** (hə bil′ə mənt) *n.* [< MFr. < *habiller*, to clothe] **1.** [*usually pl.*] clothing; dress **2.** [*pl.*] furnishings or equipment; trappings

**ha·bil·i·tate** (-tāt′) *vt.* **-tat·ed, -tat·ing** [< ML. pp. of *habilitare*, to make suitable] **1.** to clothe; equip; outfit **2.** to educate or train (the handicapped, the disadvantaged, etc.) to function better in society —**ha·bil′i·ta′tion** *n.* —**ha·bil′i·ta′tive** *adj.*

**hab·it** (hab′it) *n.* [OFr. < L. *habitus* < pp. of *habere*, to have] **1.** a distinctive religious costume **2.** a costume for certain occasions [a riding *habit*] **3.** characteristic or usual way of being, doing, growing, etc.; character, tendency, disposition, etc. **4.** *a)* a thing done often and, hence, easily; practice; custom *b)* an acquired pattern of action that is automatic and thus difficult to break **5.** an addiction, esp. to narcotics —*vt.* to dress

**hab·it·a·ble** (-ə b'l) *adj.* fit to be lived in —**hab′it·a·bil′i·ty** *n.* —**hab′it·a·bly** *adv.*

**hab·it·ant** (-ənt) *n.* [Fr. < L. prp. of *habitare*, to inhabit] an inhabitant; resident

**hab·i·tat** (hab′ə tat′) *n.* [L., it inhabits] **1.** native environment **2.** the place where a person or thing is ordinarily found

**hab·i·ta·tion** (hab′ə tā′shən) *n.* **1.** an inhabiting; occupancy **2.** a place in which to live; dwelling; home **3.** a colony or settlement

**hab·it-form·ing** (hab′it fôr′miŋ) *adj.* resulting in the formation of a habit or in addiction

**ha·bit·u·al** (hə bich′ōō wəl) *adj.* **1.** done by habit or fixed as a habit; customary **2.** being or doing a certain thing by habit; steady *[a habitual* smoker*]* **3.** much seen, done, or used; usual; frequent —**ha·bit′u·al·ly** *adv.* —**ha·bit′u·al·ness** *n.*

**ha·bit·u·ate** (-ōō wāt′) *vt.* **-at′ed, -at′ing** [< LL., ult. < L. *habitus:* see HABIT] to make used (*to*); accustom; familiarize —**ha·bit′u·a′tion** *n.*

**hab·i·tude** (hab′ə tōōd′, -tyōōd′) *n.* **1.** habitual condition of mind or body; disposition **2.** custom

**ha·bit·u·é** (hə bich′ōō wā′) *n.* [Fr.] a person who frequents a certain place or places

**Habs·burg** (häps′bōōrkh) *same as* HAPSBURG

**ha·ci·en·da** (hä′sē en′də, has′ē-) *n.* [Sp. < L. *facienda,* things to be done < *facere,* to do] in Spanish America. **1.** a large estate, ranch, etc. **2.** the main dwelling on any of these

**hack¹** (hak) *vt.* [OE. *haccian*] **1.** *a)* to chop or cut roughly or irregularly *b)* to shape, trim, etc. thus **2.** to break up (land) with a hoe, etc. **3.** [Slang] to deal with successfully —*vi.* **1.** to make rough or irregular cuts **2.** to give harsh, dry coughs —*n.* **1.** a tool for hacking; ax, hoe, etc. **2.** a slash, gash, or notch **3.** a harsh, dry cough —**hack it** [Slang] to make a success of some undertaking, deal with a situation, etc. —**hack′er** *n.*

**hack²** (hak) *n.* [contr. < HACKNEY] **1.** a horse for hire **2.** a saddle horse **3.** an old, worn-out horse **4.** a person hired to do routine writing **5.** a devoted, unquestioning worker for a political party **6.** a carriage or coach for hire **7.** [Colloq.] *a)* a taxicab *b)* a cabdriver —*vt.* **1.** to employ as a hack **2.** to hire out (a horse, etc.) **3.** to wear out by constant use —*vi.* [Colloq.] to drive a taxicab —*adj.* **1.** employed as a hack **2.** done by a hack **3.** stale; trite

**hack·a·more** (hak′ə môr′) *n.* [altered < Sp. *jaquima,* halter < Ar. *shakīma*] [Western] a rope or rawhide halter, used in breaking horses

**hack·ber·ry** (hak′ber′ē) *n., pl.* **-ries** [< Scand.] **1.** an American tree with a small fruit resembling a cherry **2.** its fruit or its wood

**hack·le¹** (hak′'l) *n.* [ME. *hechele,* prob. infl. by dial. *hackle,* bird's plumage < OE. *hacele*] **1.** a comb for separating the fibers of flax, hemp, etc. **2.** any of the long, slender feathers at the neck of a rooster, pigeon, etc. **3.** *Fishing a)* a tuft of feathers from a rooster's neck, used in making artificial flies *b)* such a fly **4.** [*pl.*] the bristling hairs on a dog's neck and back —*vt.* **-led, -ling** to separate the fibers of (flax, hemp, etc.) with a hackle —**get one's hackles up** to become tense with anger; bristle

**hack·le²** (hak′'l) *vt., vi.* **-led, -ling** [freq. of HACK¹] to cut roughly; hack; mangle

**hack·ma·tack** (hak′mə tak′) *n.* [AmInd. (Algonquian)] *same as* TAMARACK

**hack·ney** (hak′nē) *n., pl.* **-neys** [< ME. < *Hackeney* (now *Hackney*), an English village] **1.** a horse for ordinary driving or riding **2.** a carriage for hire

**hack·neyed** (-nēd′) *adj.* made trite by overuse

**hack·saw** (hak′sô′) *n.* a saw for cutting metal, consisting of a narrow, fine-toothed blade held in a frame: also **hack saw**

**had** (had; *unstressed* had, əd) *pt. & pp. of* HAVE: also used to indicate preference or necessity, with certain words and phrases, such as *rather, better, as well* (Ex.: I *had* better leave)

HACKSAW

**had·dock** (had′ək) *n., pl.* **-dock, -docks:** see PLURAL, II, D, 2 [< ? OFr. *hadot*] a food fish related to the cod, found off the coasts of Europe and N. America

**Ha·des** (hā′dēz) **1.** *Gr. Myth. a)* the home of the dead, beneath the earth *b)* the ruler of the underworld **2.** the resting place of the dead: used in some New Testament translations —*n.* [*often* h-] [Colloq.] hell: a euphemism

**had·n't** (had′'nt) had not

**Ha·dri·an** (hā′drē ən) (L. name *Publius Aelius Hadrianus*) 76–138 A.D.; Roman emperor (117–138)

**hadst** (hadst) *archaic 2d pers. sing., past indic.,* of HAVE: *used with* thou

**Haeck·el** (hek′əl), **Ernst Hein·rich** (ernst hīn′riH) 1834–1919; Ger. biologist & philosopher

**haemat-, haemato-, haemo-** *see* HEMATO-, HEMO-

**hae·mo·glo·bin** (hē′mə glō′bin, hem′ə-) *n. same as* HEMOGLOBIN

**haf·ni·um** (haf′nē əm) *n.* [ModL. < L. *Hafnia,* Roman name of Copenhagen] a metallic chemical element found with zirconium and somewhat resembling it: symbol, Hf; at. wt., 178.49; at. no., 72

**haft** (haft) *n.* [OE. *hæft*] a handle or hilt of a knife, ax, etc.

**hag** (hag) *n.* [< OE. *hægtes* < *haga,* a hedge] **1.** a witch **2.** an ugly, often vicious old woman —**hag′gish** *adj.*

**Hag.** Haggai

**Ha·gar** (hā′gər) *Bible* a concubine of Abraham and slave of his wife Sarah

**Ha·gen** (hä′gən) city in W West Germany, in the Ruhr valley: pop. 200,000

**hag·fish** (hag′fish′) *n., pl.* **-fish′, -fish′es:** see FISH [HAG + FISH] a small, eellike saltwater fish with a round, sucking mouth and horny teeth, with which it bores into other fish and devours them

**Hag·ga·da, Hag·ga·dah** (hä gä dä′; *E.* hə gä′də) *n., pl.* **-ga·dot′** (-dôt′) [Heb. *haggādāh* < *higgid,* to tell] **1.** *a)* [*often* h-] in the *Talmud,* an anecdote that explains some point of law *b)* the part of the Talmud devoted to such narratives **2.** the narrative of the Exodus read at the Seder during Passover —**hag·gad·ic** (hə gad′ik, -gä′dik) *adj.*

**Hag·ga·i** (hag′ē ī′, hag′ī) *Bible* **1.** a Hebrew prophet who lived c. 500 B.C. **2.** the book attributed to him

**hag·gard** (hag′ərd) *adj.* [MFr. *hagard,* untamed] having a wild, wasted, worn look, as from grief or illness —**hag′gard·ly** *adv.* —**hag′gard·ness** *n.*

**hag·gis** (hag′is) *n.* [ME. *hagas,* kind of pudding] a Scottish dish made of the lungs, heart, etc. of a sheep or calf, mixed with suet, seasoning, and oatmeal and boiled in the animal's stomach

**hag·gle** (hag′'l) *vt.* **-gled, -gling** [freq. of Scot. *hag,* to chop, cut] to hack; mangle —*vi.* **1.** to argue about terms, price, etc.; wrangle —*n.* a haggling —**hag′gler** *n.*

**hag·i·o-** [< Gr. *hagios,* holy] *a prefix meaning* saintly, sacred: also, before a vowel, *hag-*

**hag·i·ol·o·gy** (hag′ē äl′ə jē, hā′jē-) *n., pl.* **-gies** [prec. + -LOGY] **1.** literature about saints' lives and legends, sacred writings, etc. **2.** a list of saints —**hag′i·o·log′ic** (-ə läj′ik), **hag′i·o·log′i·cal** *adj.* —**hag′i·ol′o·gist** *n.*

**hag·rid·den** (hag′rid′'n) *adj.* obsessed or harassed, as by fears

**Hague** (hāg), **The** city in W Netherlands; seat of the government (cf. AMSTERDAM): pop. 576,000

**hah** (hä) *interj., n. same as* HA

**Hai·fa** (hī′fə) seaport in NW Israel: pop. 210,000

**hai·ku** (hī′kōō) *n.* [Jap.] **1.** a Japanese verse form of three unrhymed lines of 5, 7, and 5 syllables respectively, usually on some subject in nature **2.** *pl.* **-ku** a poem in this form

**hail¹** (hāl) *vt.* [< ON. < *heill,* whole, sound] **1.** to welcome, greet, etc. as with cheers; acclaim **2.** to salute as *[they hailed* him their leader*]* **3.** to call out to, as in summoning *[to hail a taxi]* —*vi. Naut.* to call out or signal to a ship —*n.* **1.** a hailing or greeting **2.** the distance that a shout will carry *[within hail]* —*interj.* an exclamation of tribute, greeting, etc. —**hail fellow well met** very friendly to everyone —**hail from** to come from (one's birthplace, etc.)

**hail²** (hāl) *n.* [OE. *hægel*] **1.** small, rounded pieces of ice that sometimes fall during thunderstorms; hailstones **2.** a falling, showering, etc. of or like hail *[a hail of bullets]* —*vi.* to pour down hail *[it is hailing]* —*vt.* to shower, hurl, etc. violently like hail (often with *on* or *upon*) *[to hail curses on someone]*

**Hai·le Se·las·sie** (hī′lē sə las′ē, -läs′ē) (born *Tafari Makonnen*) 1891–1975; emperor of Ethiopia (1930–74)

**hail·stone** (hāl′stōn′) *n.* a pellet of hail

**hail·storm** (-stôrm′) *n.* a storm with hail

**Hai·phong** (hī′fäŋ′) seaport in N Vietnam: pop. 369,000

**hair** (her) *n.* [OE. *hær*] **1.** any of the fine, threadlike outgrowths from the skin of an animal or human being **2.** a growth of these; esp., the growth covering the human head or the skin of most mammals **3.** an extremely small space, degree, etc. **4.** a threadlike growth on a plant —*adj.* **1.** made of or with hair **2.** for the care of the hair *[hair* tonic*]* —**get in one's hair** [Slang] to annoy one —**let one's hair down** [Slang] to be very informal, relaxed, etc. —**make one's hair stand on end** to horrify one —**split hairs** to make petty distinctions; quibble —**to a hair** exactly; perfectly —**hair′less** *adj.* —**hair′less·ness** *n.* —**hair′like′** *adj.*

**hair·breadth** (-bredth′) *n.* an extremely small space or amount —*adj.* very narrow; close Also **hairs′breadth′**

**hair·cloth** (-klôth′) *n.* cloth woven from horsehair, camel's hair, etc.: used esp. for upholstery

**hair·cut** (-kut′) *n.* **1.** a cutting of the hair of the head **2.** the style in which the hair is cut —**hair′cut′ter** *n.*

**hair·do** (-dōō′) *n., pl.* **-dos′** the style in which (a woman's) hair is arranged; coiffure

**hair·dress·er** (-dres′ər) *n.* a person whose work is dressing (women's) hair —**hair′dress′ing** *n., adj.*

**hair·line** (-līn′) *n.* **1.** a very thin line or stripe **2.** the outline of the hair on the head, esp. above the forehead

**hair·net** (-net′) *n.* a net or fine-meshed cap for keeping the hair in place

**hair·piece** (-pēs′) *n.* a toupee or wig

**hair·pin** (-pin′) *n.* a small, usually U-shaped, piece of wire, shell, etc., for keeping the hair in place —*adj.* U-shaped [a *hairpin* turn]

**hair-rais·ing** (-rā′ziŋ) *adj.* [Colloq.] causing the hair to stand on end; terrifying —**hair′-rais′er** *n.*

**hair shirt** a shirt or girdle of haircloth, worn for self-punishment by religious ascetics

**hair·split·ting** (-split′iŋ) *adj., n.* making petty distinctions; quibbling —**hair′split′ter** *n.*

**hair·spring** (-spriŋ′) *n.* a very slender, hairlike coil that controls the regular movement of the balance wheel in a watch or clock

**hair trigger** a trigger so delicately adjusted that slight pressure on it discharges the firearm

**hair·y** (-ē) *adj.* **hair′i·er, hair′i·est** 1. covered with hair 2. of or like hair 3. [Slang] difficult, distressing, etc. —**hair′i·ness** *n.*

**Hai·ti** (hāt′ē) country occupying the W portion of the island of Hispaniola, West Indies: 10,714 sq. mi.; pop. 4,768,000; cap. Port-au-Prince —**Hai·tian** (hā′shən, hāt′ē ən) *adj., n.*

**hajj** (haj) *n.* [Ar. *ḥajj* < *ḥajji*, to go on a pilgrimage] the pilgrimage to Mecca that every Moslem is expected to make at least once

**haj·ji, haj·i** (haj′ē) *n.* [< Ar., pilgrim: see prec.] a Moslem who has made a pilgrimage to Mecca

**hake** (hāk) *n., pl.* **hake, hakes**: see PLURAL, II, D, 2 [prob. < ON. *haki*, a hook (from shape of the jaw)] any of various marine food fishes related to the cod, as the **silver hake**

**ha·kim**[1] (hä kēm′) *n.* [Ar. *ḥakīm*, wise, learned] in Moslem regions, a doctor; physician

**ha·kim**[2] (hä′kēm, -kim) *n.* [Ar. *ḥākim*, governor] in Moslem regions, a ruler, judge, or governor

**Hak·luyt** (hak′lōōt), **Richard** 1552?–1616; Eng. geographer & chronicler of explorations & discoveries

**hal·berd** (hal′bərd) *n.* [ult. < MHG. *helmbarte* < *helm*, handle + *barte*, an ax] a combination spear and battle-ax used in the 15th and 16th cent.: also **hal′bert** (-bərt) —**hal′berd·ier′** (-bər dir′) *n.*

**hal·cy·on** (hal′sē ən) *n.* [< L. < Gr. *alkyōn*, kingfisher] a legendary bird, identified with the kingfisher, supposed to have a peaceful, calming influence on the sea at the time of the winter solstice —*adj.* 1. of the halcyon 2. tranquil, happy, idyllic, etc.: esp. in phrase **halcyon days**

**hale**[1] (hāl) *adj.* **hal′er, hal′est** [OE. *hal*] strong and healthy

**hale**[2] (hāl) *vt.* **haled, hal′ing** [< OFr. *haler*, prob. < ODu. *halen*: see HAUL] to force (one) to go [*haled* him into court]

**Hale** (hāl), **Nathan** 1755–76; Am. soldier in the Revolutionary War: hanged by the British as a spy

**hal·er** (hä′lər) *n., pl.* **-er·u′** (-ə rōō′), **-ers** [Czech, ult. < MHG. *Haller* (*pfenninc*), (penny of) Hall, a Ger. coin made at Hall, Swabia] *see* MONETARY UNITS, table (Czechoslovakia)

**half** (haf) *n., pl.* **halves** [OE. *healf*] 1. either of the two equal, or almost equal, parts of something 2. a half hour [*half* past one] 3. *Basketball, Football,* etc. either of the two equal periods of the game, between which the players rest —*adj.* 1. *a)* being either of the two equal parts *b)* being about a half of the amount, length, etc. 2. incomplete; partial —*adv.* 1. to an extent approximately or exactly fifty percent of the whole 2. [Colloq.] to some extent [to be *half* convinced] 3. [Colloq.] by any means; at all: used with *not* [not *half* bad] —**by half** considerably; very much —**in half** into halves —**not the half of** only a small part of

**half-and-half** (haf′'n haf′) *n.* something that is half one thing and half another; esp., *a)* a mixture of equal parts of milk and cream *b)* [Chiefly Brit.] a mixture of equal parts of porter and ale, beer and stout, etc. —*adj.* combining two things equally —*adv.* in two equal parts

**half·back** (-bak′) *n. Football* either of two players whose position is behind the line of scrimmage together with the fullback and the quarterback

**half-baked** (-bākt′) *adj.* 1. only partly baked 2. not completely planned or thought out 3. having or showing little intelligence and experience

**half-blood** (-blud′) *n.* 1. a person related to another through one parent only 2. *same as* HALF-BREED —*adj. same as* HALF-BLOODED

**half blood** 1. kinship through one parent only [sisters of the *half blood*] 2. *same as* HALF-BLOODED

**half-blood·ed** (-blud′id) *adj.* 1. related through one parent only 2. born of parents of different races

**half boot** a boot reaching halfway up the lower leg

**half-breed** (-brēd′) *n.* a person whose parents are of different races —*adj. same as* HALF-BLOODED Sometimes regarded as a contemptuous term

**half brother** a brother through one parent only

**half-caste** (-kast′) *n.* a half-breed; esp., an offspring of one European parent and one Asiatic parent —*adj.* of a half-caste

**half cock** the halfway position of the hammer of a firearm, when the trigger is locked —**go off half-cocked** 1. to go off too soon: said of a firearm 2. to speak or act thoughtlessly or too hastily: also **go off at half cock** —**half′-cocked′** *adj.*

**half dollar** a coin of the U.S. and Canada, worth 50 cents

**half gainer** a fancy dive in which the diver, facing forward, does a back flip in the air so as to enter the water headfirst, facing the board

**half·heart·ed** (-här′tid) *adj.* with little enthusiasm, determination, interest, etc. —**half′heart′ed·ly** *adv.*

**half hitch** a knot made by passing the end of the rope around the rope and then through the loop thus made

**half-hour** (-our′) *n.* 1. half of an hour; thirty minutes 2. the point thirty minutes after any given hour —*adj.* 1. lasting for thirty minutes 2. occurring every thirty minutes —**half′-hour′ly** *adj., adv.*

**half-life** (-līf′) *n.* the period required for the disintegration of half of the atoms in a sample of some radioactive substance: also **half life**

**half-mast** (-mast′) *n.* the position of a flag lowered about halfway down its staff, as in public mourning —*vt.* to hang (a flag) at half-mast

**half-moon** (-mōōn′) *n.* 1. the moon when only half its disk is clearly seen 2. anything shaped like a half-moon or crescent

**half nelson** *see* NELSON

**half note** *Music* a note having one half the duration of a whole note: see NOTE, illus.

**half·pen·ny** (hā′pə nē, hāp′nē) *n., pl.* **-pence** (-pens), **-pen·nies** a former British coin equal to half a penny —*adj.* worth a halfpenny, or very little

**half pint** 1. a liquid or dry measure equal to 1/4 quart 2. [Slang] a small person

**half sister** a sister through one parent only

**half size** any of a series of sizes in women's garments for short-waisted, mature figures

**half-sole** (haf′sōl′) *vt.* **-soled′, -sol′ing** to repair (shoes or boots) by attaching new half soles

**half sole** a sole (of a shoe or boot) from the arch to the toe

**half step** 1. *Mil.* a short marching step of fifteen inches (in double time, eighteen inches) 2. *Music same as* SEMITONE

**half-tim·bered** (-tim′bərd) *adj. Archit.* made of a wooden framework having the spaces filled with plaster, brick, etc.

**half time** the rest period between halves of a football game, basketball game, etc.

**half·tone** (-tōn′) *n.* 1. *Art* a tone or shading between light and dark 2. *Music same as* SEMITONE 3. *Photoengraving a)* a technique of shadings by dots produced by photographing the object from behind a fine screen *b)* a photoengraving so made

**half·track** (-trak′) *n.* an army truck, armored vehicle, etc. with tractor treads instead of rear wheels, but with a pair of wheels in front

**half·way** (-wā′) *adj.* 1. equally distant between two points, states, etc. 2. incomplete; partial —*adv.* 1. half the distance; to the midway point 2. incompletely; partially —**meet halfway** to be willing to compromise with

**halfway house** a place where persons are aided in readjusting to society following imprisonment, hospitalization, etc.

**half-wit** (-wit′) *n.* a stupid, silly, or imbecilic person; fool; dolt —**half′-wit′ted** *adj.*

**hal·i·but** (hal′ə bət) *n., pl.* **-but, -buts**: see PLURAL, II, D, 2 [< ME. < *hali*, holy + *butt*, a flounder: because eaten on holidays] a large, edible flatfish found in northern seas, esp. the **Atlantic halibut**: they sometimes weigh hundreds of pounds

**Hal·i·car·nas·sus** (hal′ə kär nas′əs) ancient city in SW Asia Minor, on the Aegean

**hal·ide** (hal′īd, hā′līd) *n.* [HAL(OGEN) + -IDE] *Chem.* a compound of a halogen with another element or a radical —*adj. same as* HALOID

**Hal·i·fax** (hal′ə faks′) capital of Nova Scotia; seaport on the Atlantic; pop. 118,000

**hal·ite** (hal′īt, hā′līt) *n.* [< Gr. *hals*, salt + -ITE] native sodium chloride; rock salt

**hal·i·to·sis** (hal′ə tō′sis) *n.* [ModL. < L. *halitus*, breath + -OSIS] bad-smelling breath

**hall** (hôl) *n.* [OE. *heall* < base of *helan*, to cover] 1. the dwelling of a baron, squire, etc. 2. [*sometimes* H-] a building containing public offices or the headquarters of an organization 3. a large public or semipublic room or auditorium for gatherings, entertainments, etc. 4. [*sometimes*

H-] a college dormitory, classroom building, etc. **5.** a passageway or room between the entrance and the interior of a building **6.** a passageway or corridor onto which rooms open

**Hal·le** (hál'ə; *E.* hal'ē) city in SC East Germany: pop. 266,000

**hal·le·lu·jah, hal·le·lu·iah** (hal'ə lōō'yə) *interj.* [ < LL. < Gr. < Heb. < *hallelū,* praise + *yāh,* Jehovah] praise (ye) the Lord! —*n.* an exclamation or hymn of praise to God

**Hal·ley's comet** (hal'ēz) a comet, last seen in 1910, whose periodic reappearance (c. 75 years) was predicted by Edmund Halley (1656–1742), Eng. astronomer

**hal·liard** (hal'yərd) *n. same as* HALYARD

**hall·mark** (hôl'märk') *n.* **1.** an official mark stamped on British gold and silver articles orig. at Goldsmiths' Hall in London, as a guarantee of genuineness **2.** any mark or symbol of genuineness or high quality —*vt.* to put a hallmark on

**hal·lo, hal·loa** (hə lō') *interj., n., vi., same as* HALLOO

**hal·loo** (hə lōō') *vi., vt.* **-looed', -loo'ing 1.** to call out in order to attract the attention of (a person) **2.** to urge on (hounds) by shouting **3.** to shout —*interj., n.* a shout or call

**hal·low** (hal'ō) *vt.* [OE. *halgian* < *halig,* holy] **1.** to make holy or sacred; consecrate **2.** to regard as holy; honor as sacred

**hal·lowed** (*in poetry or liturgy, often* hal'ə wid) *adj.* **1.** made holy or sacred **2.** honored as holy

**Hal·low·een, Hal·low·e'en** (hal'ə wēn', häl'-) *n.* [contr. < *all hallow even*] the evening of October 31, which is followed by All Saints' Day

**hall tree** a clothes tree, esp. one in an entrance hall

**hal·lu·ci·nate** (hə lōō'sə nāt') *vi., vt.* **-nat'ed, -nat'ing** [ < L. pp. of *hallucinari,* to wander mentally] to have or cause to have hallucinations

**hal·lu·ci·na·tion** (hə lōō'sə nā'shən) *n.* **1.** the apparent perception of sights, sounds, etc. that are not actually present **2.** the imaginary thing apparently seen, heard, etc. —**hal·lu'ci·na'tive, hal·lu'ci·na·to'ry** (-nə tôr'ē) *adj.*

**hal·lu·ci·no·gen** (hə lōō'sə nə jen, hal'yoo sin'ə jen) *n.* a drug or other substance that produces hallucinations —**hal·lu'ci·no·gen'ic** *adj.*

**hall·way** (hôl'wā') *n.* **1.** a passageway or room between the entrance and the interior of a building **2.** a passageway; corridor; hall

**ha·lo** (hā'lō) *n., pl.* **-los, -loes** [ < L. < Gr. *halōs,* circular threshing floor, halo around the sun < *halein,* to grind] **1.** a ring of light that seems to encircle the sun, moon, etc. **2.** a symbolic ring or disk of light shown around the head of a saint, etc. **3.** the glory with which a famed, revered, or idealized person or thing is invested —*vt.* **-loed, -lo·ing** to encircle with a halo

**hal·o·gen** (hal'ə jən) *n.* [ < Gr. *hals* (gen. *halos*), salt + -GEN] any of the five very active, nonmetallic chemical elements, fluorine, chlorine, bromine, astatine, and iodine —**ha·log·e·nous** (hə läj'ə nəs) *adj.*

**hal·o·gen·ate** (-jə nāt') *vt.* **-at'ed, -at'ing** to treat or combine with a halogen —**hal'o·gen·a'tion** *n.*

**hal·oid** (hal'oid, hā'loid) *adj.* [ < Gr. *hals,* salt + -OID] of or like a halide —*n. same as* HALIDE

**Hals** (häls), **Frans** (fräns) 1580?–1666; Du. painter

**halt**[1] (hôlt) *n.* [ < Fr. < G. < *halten,* to hold] a stop, esp. a temporary one, as in marching —*vi., vt.* to come or bring to a halt —**call a halt** to order a stop

**halt**[2] (hôlt) *vi.* [ < OE. *healtian* < *healt,* adj.] **1.** [Archaic] to limp **2.** to be uncertain; hesitate [to halt in one's speech] **3.** to have defects in flow, as of rhythm or logic —*adj.* limping; lame —*n.* [Archaic] a lameness —**the halt** those who are lame —**halt'ing·ly** *adv.*

**hal·ter** (hôl'tər) *n.* [OE. *hælftre*] **1.** a rope, strap, etc. for tying or leading an animal **2.** a rope for hanging a person; noose **3.** a woman's garment for covering the breast, held up by a loop around the neck —*vt.* to put a halter on (an animal)

**hal·vah, hal·va** (häl vä') *n.* [Turk. *helwa* < Ar. *ḥalwa*] a Turkish confection made of ground sesame seeds and nuts mixed with honey, etc.

**halve** (hav) *vt.* **halved, halv'ing 1.** to divide into two equal parts **2.** to share equally (*with* someone) **3.** to reduce to half **4.** *Golf* to play (a hole, match, etc.) in the same number of strokes as one's opponent

**halves** (havz) *n. pl. of* HALF —**by halves 1.** halfway; imperfectly **2.** halfheartedly —**go halves** to share expenses, etc. equally

**hal·yard** (hal'yərd) *n.* [ < ME. *halier* < *halien* (see HALE[2])] a rope or tackle for raising or lowering a flag, sail, etc.

**Ham** (ham) *Bible* Noah's second son

**ham** (ham) *n.* [OE. *hamm*] **1.** the part of the leg behind the knee. **2.** *a)* the back of the thigh *b)* the thigh and the buttock together **3.** the hock or hind leg of a four-legged animal **4.** the upper part of a hog's hind leg, salted, smoked,

etc. **5.** [Colloq.] an amateur radio operator **6.** [Slang] an incompetent actor or performer, esp. one who overacts —*vi., vt.* **hammed, ham'ming** [Slang] to act with exaggeration; overact: often in **ham it up**

**Ha·man** (hā'mən) *Bible* a Persian official who sought the destruction of the Jews but was hanged from his own gallows: Esth. 7

**Ham·burg** (ham'bərg; *G.* häm'boorkh) seaport in N West Germany, on the Elbe: pop. 1,833,000

**ham·burg·er** (ham'bur'gər) *n.* [earlier *Hamburg steak,* after HAMBURG] **1.** ground beef **2.** a fried, broiled, or baked patty of such meat, often eaten as a sandwich in a round bun Also **ham'burg**

**hame** (hām) *n.* [ < MDu., horse collar] either of the two rigid pieces along the sides of a horse's collar, to which the traces are attached

**Ham·il·ton** (ham'əl t'n) **1.** city & port in SE Ontario, Canada, on Lake Ontario: pop. 312,000 **2.** [after A. HAMILTON] city in SW Ohio: pop. 63,000 **3.** capital of Bermuda: pop. 3,000

**Ham·il·ton** (ham'əl t'n), **Alexander** 1757–1804; Am. statesman; 1st secretary of the U.S. treasury (1789–95) —**Ham·il'to·ni·an** (-tō'nē ən) *adj., n.*

**Ham·ite** (ham'īt) *n.* **1.** a person regarded as descended from Ham **2.** a member of any of several usually dark-skinned peoples of N and E Africa, including the Egyptians, Berbers, etc.

**Ham·it·ic** (ha mit'ik, hə-) *adj.* **1.** of Ham or the Hamites **2.** designating or of a group of African languages, including ancient Egyptian, Berber, and Cushitic

**Ham·let** (ham'lit) **1.** a famous tragedy by Shakespeare (c. 1602) **2.** the hero of this play

**ham·let** (ham'lit) *n.* [ < OFr. dim. of *hamel,* itself dim. of LowG. *hamm,* enclosed area] a very small village

**ham·mer** (ham'ər) *n.* [OE. *hamor*] **1.** a tool for pounding, usually consisting of a metal head and a handle **2.** a thing like this tool in shape or use; specif., *a)* the mechanism that strikes the firing pin or cap in a firearm *b)* any of the felted mallets that strike against the strings of a piano *c)* a power tool for pounding **3.** the malleus, one of the bones of the middle ear **4.** an auctioneer's gavel **5.** *Sports* a heavy metal ball attached to a wire and thrown for distance in a field event (**hammer throw**) —*vt.* **1.** to strike repeatedly as with a hammer **2.** to make or fasten with a hammer **3.** to drive, force, or shape as with hammer blows —*vi.* to strike repeated blows as with a hammer —**hammer** (away) at **1.** to work energetically at **2.** to keep emphasizing —**hammer out 1.** to shape or flatten by hammering **2.** to take out by hammering **3.** to develop or work out by careful thought or repeated effort —**ham'mer·er** *n.* —**ham'mer·like'** *adj.*

CLAW HAMMER

BALL PEEN HAMMER

TYPES OF HAMMER

**ham·mer·head** (-hed') *n.* a medium-sized shark that has a mallet-shaped head

**ham·mer·lock** (-läk') *n.* a wrestling hold in which one arm of the opponent is twisted upward behind his back

**ham·mer·toe** (-tō') *n.* **1.** a condition in which the first joint of a toe is permanently bent downward, resulting in a clawlike deformity **2.** such a toe

**ham·mock** (ham'ək) *n.* [Sp. *hamaca* < native WInd. name] a length of netting, canvas, etc. swung from ropes at both ends and used as a bed or couch

**Ham·mond** (ham'ənd) [after G. *Hammond,* local meatpacker] city in NW Ind., near Chicago: pop. 94,000

**Ham·mu·ra·bi** (hä'moo rä'bē, ham'ə-) fl. 18th cent. B.C.; king of Babylon: a famous code of laws is attributed to him

**ham·my** (ham'ē) *adj.* **-mi·er, -mi·est** [Slang] like or characteristic of a ham (actor); overacting

**ham·per**[1] (ham'pər) *vt.* [ME. *hampren*] to hinder; impede; encumber

**ham·per**[2] (ham'pər) *n.* [ < OFr. < *hanap,* a cup < Frank.] a large basket, usually with a cover

**Hamp·ton** (hamp'tən) [after a town in England] seaport in SE Va., on Hampton Roads: pop. 123,000

**Hampton Roads** [see prec. & ROAD (sense 4)] channel in SE Va., linking the James River estuary with Chesapeake Bay

**ham·ster** (ham'stər) *n.* [G.] a ratlike animal with large cheek pouches: it is often used in scientific experiments or kept as a pet

**ham·string** (ham'striŋ') *n.* **1.** one of the tendons at the back of the human knee **2.** the great tendon at the back of the hock in a four-legged animal —*vt.* **-strung', -string'ing 1.** to disable by cutting a hamstring **2.** to make powerless or ineffective

**Han·cock** (han'käk), **John** 1737–93; Am. statesman; 1st signer of the Declaration of Independence

**hand** (hand) *n.* [OE.] **1.** the part of the human arm below the wrist, used for grasping **2.** the corresponding part in apes, monkeys, etc. **3.** a side, direction, or position indicated by a hand [at one's right *hand*] **4.** possession or care [the papers are in my *hands*] **5.** control; power [to strengthen one's *hand*] **6.** an active part; share [take a *hand* in this work] **7.** *a)* a handshake, as a pledge *b)* a promise to marry **8.** skill; ability [a master's *hand*] **9.** *a)* handwriting *b)* a signature **10.** a clapping of hands; applause [they gave the singer a *hand*] **11.** assistance; help [to lend a *hand*] **12.** a person whose chief work is with his hands, as a sailor, farm laborer, etc. **13.** a person regarded as having some special skill [quite a *hand* at sewing] **14.** a person (or, sometimes, thing) from or through which something comes; source [to get a story at second *hand*] **15.** anything like a hand, as the pointer on a clock **16.** the breadth of a hand, about 4 inches **17.** *Card Games a)* the cards held by a player at one time *b)* a player *c)* a round of play —*adj.* of, for, made by, or controlled by the hand —*vt.* **1.** to give as with the hand; transfer **2.** to help, conduct, steady, etc. with the hand [to *hand* a lady into her car] —**(at) first hand** from the original source —**at hand 1.** near; close by **2.** immediately available —**(at) second hand 1.** not from the original source **2.** previously used —**at the hand (or hands) of** through the action of —**by hand** not by machines but with the hands —**change hands** to pass from one owner to another —**from hand to mouth** with just enough for immediate needs —**hand down 1.** to bequeath **2.** to announce (a verdict, etc.) —**hand in** to give; submit —**hand in hand 1.** holding one another's hand **2.** together —**hand it to** [Slang] to give deserved credit to —**hand on** to pass along; transmit —**hand out** to distribute —**hand over** to give up; deliver —**hand over fist** [Colloq.] easily and in large amounts —**hands down** without effort; easily —**hands off!** don't touch! don't interfere! —**hand to hand** at close quarters: said of fighting —**have one's hands full** to be extremely busy —**in hand 1.** in order or control **2.** in possession **3.** in process —**lay hands on 1.** to attack physically **2.** to seize; take **3.** to touch with the hands in blessing, etc. —**off one's hands** no longer in one's care —**on every hand** on all sides —**on hand 1.** near **2.** available **3.** present —**on one's hands** in one's care —**on the one hand** from one point of view —**on the other hand** from the opposed point of view —**out of hand 1.** out of control **2.** immediately **3.** over and done with —**show (or tip) one's hand** to disclose one's intentions —**take in hand 1.** to take control of **2.** to handle; treat **3.** to try; attempt —**to hand 1.** near; accessible **2.** in one's possession —**turn (or put) one's hand to** to undertake; work at —**wash one's hands of** to refuse to go on with or take responsibility for —**with a high hand** with arrogance —**with clean hands** without guilt —**hand′less** *adj.*

**hand-** *a combining form meaning* of, with, by, or for a hand or hands [handclasp, handcuff]

**hand·bag** (hand′bag′) *n.* **1.** a small container for money, toilet articles, keys, etc., carried by women; purse **2.** a small suitcase or valise

**hand·ball** (-bôl′) *n.* **1.** a game in which players bat a small ball against a wall or walls with the hand **2.** the small rubber ball

**hand·bar·row** (-bar′ō) *n.* a frame carried by two people, each holding a pair of handles attached at either end

**hand·bill** (-bil′) *n.* a small printed notice, advertisement, etc. to be passed out by hand

**hand·book** (-book′) *n.* **1.** a compact reference book on some subject; manual **2.** a guidebook

**hand·breadth** (-bredth′, -bretth′) *n.* the breadth of the human palm, about 4 inches

**hand·cart** (-kärt′) *n.* a small cart, often with only two wheels, pulled or pushed by hand

**hand·clasp** (-klasp′) *n.* a clasping of each other's hand in greeting, farewell, etc.

**hand·craft** (-kraft′) *n. same as* HANDICRAFT —*vt.* to make by hand with skill —**hand′craft′ed** *adj.*

**hand·cuff** (-kuf′) *n.* either of a pair of connected metal rings that can be locked about the wrists, as in fastening a prisoner to a policeman: *usually used in pl.* —*vt.* **1.** to put handcuffs on; manacle **2.** to hinder the activities of

**hand·ed** (han′did) *adj.* **1.** having, or for use by one having, a specified handedness [right-*handed*] **2.** having or using a specified number of hands [two-*handed*] **3.** involving (a specified number of) players [three-*handed* pinochle]

**hand·ed·ness** (-nis) *n.* ability in using one hand more skillfully than the other

**Han·del** (han′d'l), **George Frederick** (born *Georg Friedrich Händel*) 1685-1759; Eng. composer, born in Germany

**hand·ful** (hand′fool′) *n., pl.* -**fuls′ 1.** as much or as many as the hand will hold **2.** a few; not many **3.** [Colloq.] someone or something hard to manage

**hand·gun** (-gun′) *n.* any firearm that is held and fired with one hand, as a pistol

**hand·i·cap** (han′dē kap′) *n.* [orig. a game in which forfeits were drawn from a cap < *hand in cap*] **1.** *a)* a race or other competition in which difficulties are imposed on the superior contestants, or advantages given to the inferior, to make their chances of winning equal *b)* such a difficulty or advantage **2.** something that hampers one; disadvantage —*vt.* -**capped**, -**cap′ping 1.** to give a handicap to **2.** to cause to be at a disadvantage; hinder —**the handicapped** those who are physically disabled or mentally retarded —**hand′i·cap′per** *n.*

**hand·i·craft** (han′dē kraft′) *n.* [OE. *handcræft*] **1.** skill with the hands **2.** an occupation or art calling for such skill, as weaving —**hand′i·crafts′man** *n., pl.* -**men**

**hand·i·work** (-wurk′) *n.* **1.** *same as* HANDWORK **2.** anything made or done by a particular person

**hand·ker·chief** (haŋ′kər chif, -chēf′) *n., pl.* -**chiefs** (-chifs, -chēfs′, -chivz, -chēvz′) **1.** a small, square piece of cloth for wiping the nose, eyes, or face, or worn for ornament **2.** a kerchief

**han·dle** (han′d'l) *n.* [OE. < *hand*, HAND] **1.** that part of a utensil, tool, etc. which is to be held, turned, etc. with the hand **2.** a thing like a handle **3.** [Colloq.] a person's name, nickname, or title —*vt.* -**dled**, -**dling 1.** to touch, lift, etc. with the hand or hands **2.** to operate or use with the hands **3.** to manage, control, etc. **4.** to deal with [to *handle* a problem tactfully] **5.** to sell or deal in **6.** to behave toward; treat —*vi.* to respond to control [the car *handles* well] —**fly off the handle** [Colloq.] to become violently angry or excited —**get a handle on** [Colloq.] to find a means of dealing with, understanding, etc.

**han·dle·bar** (-bär′) *n.* **1.** [*often pl.*] a curved metal bar with handles on the ends, for steering a bicycle, etc. **2.** [Colloq.] a mustache with long curved ends: in full, **handlebar mustache**

**han·dler** (han′dlər) *n.* a person or thing that handles; specif., *a)* a boxer's trainer and second *b)* a person who trains and manages an animal

**hand·made** (hand′mād′) *adj.* made by hand, not by machine

**hand·maid·en** (-mād′'n) *n.* **1.** [Archaic] a woman or girl servant **2.** that which accompanies in a useful but subordinate capacity Also **hand′maid′**

**hand-me-down** (-mē doun′) *n.* [Colloq.] a used article of clothing, etc. which is passed along to someone else —*adj.* [Colloq.] **1.** used; secondhand **2.** ready-made and cheap

**hand organ** a barrel organ played by turning a crank by hand

**hand·out** (hand′out′) *n.* **1.** a gift of food, clothing, etc., as to a beggar or tramp **2.** a leaflet, statement, etc. handed out as for publicity

**hand·pick** (-pik′) *vt.* **1.** to pick (fruit or vegetables) by hand **2.** to choose with care or for a special purpose —**hand′picked′** *adj.*

**hand·rail** (-rāl′) *n.* a rail serving as a guard or hand support, as along a stairway

**hand·saw** (-sô′) *n.* a saw used with one hand

**hand's-breadth** (handz′bredth′, -bretth′) *n. same as* HAND-BREADTH

**hand·sel** (han′s'l, hant′-) *n.* [< ON. *handsal*, sealing of a bargain by a handclasp] a present for good luck, as at the new year or on the launching of a new business —*vt.* -**seled** or -**selled**, -**sel·ing** or -**sel·ling** to give a handsel to

**hand·set** (hand′set′) *n.* a telephone mouthpiece and receiver in a single unit, held in one hand

**hand·shake** (-shāk′) *n.* a gripping of each other's hand in greeting, agreement, etc.

**hand·some** (han′səm) *adj.* [orig., easily handled < ME.: see HAND & -SOME¹] **1.** large; considerable [a *handsome* sum] **2.** generous; gracious [a *handsome* gesture] **3.** good-looking; of pleasing appearance, esp. in a manly or dignified way —**hand′some·ly** *adv.* —**hand′some·ness** *n.*

**hand·spring** (hand′spriŋ′) *n.* a tumbling feat in which the performer turns over in midair with one or both hands touching the ground

HANDSET

**hand-to-hand** (han′tə hand′) *adj.* in close contact; at close quarters: said of fighting

**hand-to-mouth** (-mouth′) *adj.* barely subsisting

**hand·work** (hand′wɵrk′) *n.* work done or made by hand, not by machine —**hand′worked′** *adj.*

**hand·writ·ing** (-rīt′iŋ) *n.* **1.** writing done by hand, with pen, pencil, chalk, etc. **2.** a style or form of such writing — **hand′writ′ten** (-rit′'n) *adj.*

**hand·y** (han′dē) *adj.* **hand′i·er, hand′i·est 1.** close at hand; easily reached **2.** easily used; convenient **3.** clever with the hands; deft —**hand′i·ly** *adv.* —**hand′i·ness** *n.*

**han·dy·man** (-man′) *n., pl.* -**men′** a man who does odd jobs

**hang** (haŋ) *vt.* **hung, hang′ing;** for *vt.* 3 & *vi.* 4 **hanged** is preferred pt. & pp. [OE. *hangian*] **1.** to attach to something above with no support from below; suspend **2.** to attach so as to permit free motion *[to hang a door on its hinges]* **3.** to put to death by suspending from a rope about the neck **4.** to fasten (pictures, etc.) to a wall **5.** to ornament or cover *[to hang a room with pictures]* **6.** to paste (wallpaper) to walls **7.** to deadlock (a jury) by one's vote **8.** to fix (something) *on* a person or thing —*vi.* **1.** to be suspended **2.** to swing, as on a hinge **3.** to drape, as cloth, a coat, etc. **4.** to die by hanging **5.** to droop; bend **6.** to be doubtful; hesitate **7.** to have one's pictures exhibited at a museum, etc. —*n.* the way that a thing hangs —**get** (or **have**) **the hang of 1.** to learn (or have) the knack of **2.** to understand the significance or idea of —**hang around** (or **about**) **1.** to cluster around **2.** [Colloq.] to loiter around —**hang back** (or **off**) to be reluctant to advance —**hang fire** to be unsettled or undecided —**hang on 1.** to keep hold **2.** to persevere **3.** to depend on **4.** to listen attentively to —**hang out 1.** to lean out **2.** to display, as by suspending **3.** [Slang] to spend much time —**hang over** to project, hover, or loom over —**hang together 1.** to stick together **2.** to make sense, as a story —**hang up 1.** to put on a hanger, hook, etc. **2.** to end a telephone conversation by replacing the receiver **3.** to delay or suspend the progress of —**not care** (or **give**) **a hang** about to not care the least bit about

**hang·ar** (haŋ′ər) *n.* [Fr., a shed] a repair shed or shelter for aircraft

**Hang·chow** (haŋ′chou′; *Chin.* hän′jō′) river & canal port in E China: pop. 784,000

**hang·dog** (haŋ′dôg′) *adj.* **1.** contemptible, sneaking, or abject **2.** ashamed and cringing *[a hangdog expression]*

**hang·er** (haŋ′ər) *n.* **1.** a person who hangs things *[a paperhanger]* **2.** a thing that hangs **3.** a thing on which objects, as garments, are hung

**hang·er-on** (-än′) *n., pl.* **hang′ers-on′** a follower or dependent; specif., *a)* one who attaches himself to another, to some group, etc. although not wanted *b)* a sycophant

**hang gliding** the sport of gliding through the air while hanging suspended by a harness from a large type of kite (**hang glider**)

**hang·ing** (haŋ′iŋ) *adj.* **1.** suspended **2.** leaning over **3.** located on a steep slope **4.** deserving or imposing the death penalty —*n.* **1.** a suspending or being suspended **2.** a putting to death by hanging **3.** something hung, as a drapery, tapestry, etc.

**hang·man** (-mən) *n., pl.* -**men** an executioner who hangs convicted criminals

**hang·nail** (-nāl′) *n.* [altered < ME. *angnail* < OE. *angnægl*, a corn] a bit of torn skin hanging at the side or base of a fingernail

**hang·out** (-out′) *n.* [Slang] a place frequented by some person or group

**hang·o·ver** (-ō′vər) *n.* **1.** something remaining from a previous time or state; a survival **2.** headache, nausea, etc. occurring as an aftereffect of drinking much alcoholic liquor

**hang-up** (-up′) *n.* [Slang] an emotional problem that cannot easily be resolved

**hank** (haŋk) *n.* [prob. < Scand.] **1.** a loop or coil of something flexible **2.** a standard length of coiled thread or yarn

**hank·er** (haŋ′kər) *vi.* [prob. < Du. or LowG.] to crave or long (followed by *after, for,* or an infinitive) —**hank′er·er** *n.* —**hank′er·ing** *n.*

**han·kie, han·ky** (haŋ′kē) *n., pl.* -**kies** [Colloq.] a handkerchief

**han·ky-pan·ky** (haŋ′kē paŋ′kē) *n.* [altered < HOCUS-POCUS] [Colloq.] trickery or deception

**Han·nah, Han·na** (han′ə) [var. of ANNA] a feminine name

**Han·ni·bal** (han′ə b'l) 247?–183? B.C.; Carthaginian general: crossed the Alps to invade Italy in 218 B.C.

**Ha·noi** (hä noi′, ha-) capital of Vietnam, in the N part: pop. 644,000

**Han·o·ver**[1] (han′ō vər) ruling family of England (1714–1901): founded by George I, orig. Elector of a territory which included the city of Hanover —**Han′o·ve′ri·an** (-vir′ē ən) *adj., n.*

**Han·o·ver**[2] (han′ō vər) city in N West Germany: pop. 527,000 Ger. name **Ha·no·ver** (hä nō′vər, -fər)

**hanse** (hans) *n.* [ult. < OHG. *hansa*, band of men] a medieval guild of merchants: also **han·sa** (han′sə) —**the Hanse** a

medieval league of free towns in N Germany and adjoining countries, for economic advancement and protection: also **Hanseatic League**

**Han·se·at·ic** (han′sē at′ik) *adj.* of the Hanse

**han·sel** (han′s'l) *n. same as* HANDSEL

**Han·sen's disease** (han′s'nz, hän′-) [after A. *Hansen* (1841–1912), Norw. physician] *same as* LEPROSY

**han·som (cab)** (han′səm) [after J. A. *Hansom* (1803–1882), Eng. inventor] a two-wheeled covered carriage for two passengers, pulled by one horse: the driver's seat is above and behind the cab

**Ha·nu·ka** (khä′nōō kä′, -kə; hä′-) *n.* [Heb. *hanŭkkāh*, dedication] a Jewish festival in early winter commemorating the rededication of the Temple by the Maccabees in 165 B.C.: also **Ha′nuk·kah′, Ha′nuk·ka′**

**hap** (hap) *n.* [< ON. *happ*] chance; luck —*vi.* **happed, hap′ping** to occur by chance; happen

**hap·haz·ard** (hap′haz′ərd) *n.* [prec. + HAZARD] mere chance; accident —*adj.* not planned; casual —*adv.* by chance —**hap′haz′ard·ly** *adv.* —**hap′haz′ard·ness** *n.*

**hap·less** (hap′lis) *adj.* unfortunate; unlucky —**hap′less·ly** *adv.* —**hap′less·ness** *n.*

**hap·loid** (hap′loid) *adj.* [< Gr. *haploos*, single + -OID] *Biol.* having the full number of chromosomes normally occurring in the mature germ cell: see DIPLOID —**hap′loi′dy** (-loi′dē) *n.*

**hap·ly** (hap′lē) *adv.* [Archaic] by chance

**hap·pen** (hap′'n) *vi.* [ME. *happenen:* see HAP & -EN] **1.** to take place; occur **2.** to be or occur by chance **3.** to have the luck or occasion; chance *[I happened to see it]* **4.** to come by chance (*along, by, in,* etc.) —**happen on** (or **upon**) to meet or find by chance —**happen to** to be done to or be the fate of; befall

**hap·pen·ing** (-iŋ) *n.* something that happens; occurrence; incident; event

**hap·pen·stance** (-stans′) *n.* [HAPPEN + (CIRCUM)STANCE] [Colloq.] chance occurrence

**hap·py** (hap′ē) *adj.* -**pi·er, -pi·est** [ME. *happi* < HAP] **1.** favored by circumstances; lucky; fortunate **2.** having, showing, or causing a feeling of pleasure, joy, etc. **3.** suitable and clever; apt; felicitous *[a happy suggestion]* —**hap′pi·ly** *adv.* —**hap′pi·ness** *n.*

**hap·py-go-luck·y** (-gō luk′ē) *adj.* easygoing; trusting to luck —*adv.* haphazardly; by chance

**Haps·burg** (haps′bɵrg′; *G.* häps′bōōrkh) ruling family of Austria, Austria-Hungary, Spain, & the Holy Roman Empire at various times from 1278 to 1918

**ha·ra-ki·ri** (hä′rə kir′ē, har′ə-; *popularly* her′ē ker′ē) *n.* [Jap. *hara*, belly + *kiri*, a cutting] ritual suicide by disembowelment: it was practiced by high-ranking Japanese to avoid facing disgrace

**ha·rangue** (hə raŋ′) *n.* [< OFr. *arenge* < OIt. < *aringo*, site for public assemblies < Goth.] a long, blustering or scolding speech; tirade —*vi., vt.* -**rangued′, -rangu′ing** to speak or address in a harangue —**ha·rangu′er** *n.*

**har·ass** (hə ras′, har′əs) *vt.* [Fr. *harasser* < OFr. *harer,* to set a dog on < Frank.] **1.** to trouble, worry, or torment, as with cares, debts, etc. **2.** to trouble by repeated raids or attacks, etc.; harry —**har·ass′er** *n.* —**har·ass′ment** *n.*

**Har·bin** (här′bin) city in NE China: pop. 1,552,000

**har·bin·ger** (här′bin jər) *n.* [OFr. *herbergeor,* provider of lodging < *herberge,* a shelter < Frank.] a person or thing that comes before to announce or indicate what follows

**har·bor** (här′bər) *n.* [< OE. < *here,* army + *beorg,* a shelter] **1.** a place of refuge, safety, etc.; shelter **2.** a protected inlet of a sea, lake, etc., for anchoring ships; port —*vt.* **1.** to serve as, or provide, a place of protection to; shelter or house **2.** to hold in the mind; cling to *[to harbor a grudge]* —*vi.* to take shelter, as in a harbor —**har′bor·er** *n.*

**har·bor·age** (-ij) *n.* a shelter for ships

**harbor master** the official in charge of enforcing the regulations governing the use of a harbor

**har·bour** (här′bər) *n., vt., vi. Brit. sp. of* HARBOR

**hard** (härd) *adj.* [OE. *heard*] **1.** not easily pierced or crushed; firm to the touch; solid and compact **2.** having firm muscles; vigorous and robust **3.** powerful; violent *[a hard blow]* **4.** demanding great effort or labor; difficult; specif., *a)* difficult to do *[hard work]* *b)* difficult to understand or explain *[a hard question]* *c)* firmly fastened or tied *[a hard knot]* **5.** not easily moved; unfeeling *[a hard heart]* **6.** practical and shrewd *[a hard customer]* **7.** *a)* firm or definite, esp. in an aggressive way *[a hard line in foreign policy]* *b)* undeniable or actual *[hard facts]* **8.** causing pain or discomfort; specif., *a)* difficult to endure *[a hard life]* *b)* harsh; severe; stern *[a hard master]* **9.** sharp or too sharp *[hard outlines, a hard red]* **10.** having in solution mineral salts that interfere with the lathering of soap: said of water **11.** energetic and persistent *[a hard worker]* **12.** *a)* alcoholic *[hard cider]* *b)* strongly alcoholic *[hard liquor]* **13.** [Colloq.] designating any drug, as heroin, that is addictive and potentially very damaging to the body or mind **14.** popularly, designating the letter *c* sounded as in *can* or the letter *g* sounded as in *gun* **15.** *Commerce* high and stable: said of a market, prices, etc. —*adv.* **1.** energetically and persistently *[work hard]* **2.** with strength, violence, or severity *[hit hard]* **3.** with difficulty *[hard-earned]* **4.** so as to withstand much wear, use, etc. *[hard-wearing clothes]* **5.** firmly; tightly *[hold on hard]* **6.** close; near *[we live hard by]* **7.** so as to be or make firm or solid *[to freeze hard]* **8.** with vigor and to the fullest extent *[turn hard right]* —**be hard on 1.** to treat severely **2.** to be difficult or unpleasant for —**hard and fast** invariable; strict —**hard of hearing** partially deaf —**hard put to it** having considerable difficulty —**hard up** [Colloq.] in great need of something, esp. money —**hard′ness** *n.*

**hard·back** (-bak′) *n.* a hard-cover book
**hard-bit·ten** (-bit′'n) *adj.* stubborn; tough; enduring; dogged *[hard-bitten soldiers]*
**hard·board** (-bôrd′) *n.* a boardlike material made in sheets by subjecting fibers from wood chips to pressure and heat
**hard-boiled** (-boild′) *adj.* **1.** cooked in boiling water until both the white and the yolk solidify: said of an egg **2.** [Colloq.] not affected by sentiment, pity, etc.; callous
**hard coal** *same as* ANTHRACITE
**hard-core** (-kôr′) *adj.* **1.** constituting or of a hard core **2.** absolute; complete; thorough
**hard core** the firm, unyielding, or unchanging central part or group
**hard-cov·er** (-kuv′ər) *adj.* designating any book bound in a relatively stiff cover: also **hard′-bound′** (-bound′) See also PAPERBACK
**hard·en** (här′d'n) *vt., vi.* to make or become hard (in various senses) —**hard′en·er** *n.*
**hard·ened** (-d′nd) *adj.* **1.** made hard or harder **2.** confirmed or inveterate in a callous way
**hard·fist·ed** (härd′fis′tid) *adj.* stingy; miserly
**hard·goods** (-goodz′) *n.pl.* durable goods, such as automobiles, furniture, etc.: also **hard goods**
**hard hat 1.** a protective helmet worn by construction workers, etc. **2.** [Slang] such a worker
**hard·head·ed** (-hed′id) *adj.* **1.** shrewd and unsentimental; practical **2.** stubborn —**hard′head′ed·ly** *adv.* —**hard′head′ed·ness** *n.*
**hard·heart·ed** (-här′tid) *adj.* unfeeling; pitiless —**hard′heart′ed·ly** *adv.* —**hard′heart′ed·ness** *n.*
**har·di·hood** (här′dē hood′) *n.* boldness, daring, fortitude, vigor, etc.
**Har·ding** (här′diŋ), **Warren Ga·ma·li·el** (gə mā′lē əl) 1865–1923; 29th president of the U.S. (1921–23)
**hard landing** a landing, as of a rocket on the moon, made at such a high speed as to destroy the equipment
**hard·ly** (härd′lē) *adv.* **1.** with difficulty **2.** severely; harshly **3.** only just; scarcely: often used ironically to mean "not at all" *[hardly the person to ask]* **4.** probably not; not likely
**hard maple** *same as* SUGAR MAPLE
**hard-nosed** (-nōzd′) *adj.* [Slang] **1.** tough; stubborn **2.** shrewd and practical —**hard′nose′** *n.*
**hard palate** the bony part of the roof of the mouth
**hard·pan** (-pan′) *n.* **1.** a layer of hard, clayey soil **2.** solid, unplowed ground **3.** the hard, underlying part of anything; solid foundation
**hard sauce** a creamy mixture of butter, sugar, and flavoring, served with plum pudding, etc.
**hard sell** high-pressure salesmanship —**hard′-sell′** *adj.*
**hard-shell** (-shel′) *adj.* **1.** having a hard shell: also **hard′-shelled′ 2.** [Colloq.] strict; strait-laced; uncompromising, esp. in religious matters
**hard·ship** (-ship′) *n.* **1.** hard circumstances of life **2.** a thing hard to bear
**hard·tack** (-tak′) *n.* [HARD + *tack* (food)] unleavened bread made in very hard, large wafers: traditionally a part of army and navy rations
**hard·top** (-täp′) *n.* an automobile like a convertible in having no post between the front and rear windows, but with a metal top that cannot fold back
**hard·ware** (-wer′) *n.* **1.** articles made of metal, as tools, nails, fittings, utensils, etc. **2.** heavy military equipment or its parts **3.** *a)* apparatus used for controlling spacecraft, etc. *b)* the mechanical, magnetic, and electronic design, structure, and devices of a computer: cf. SOFTWARE
**hard·wood** (-wood′) *n.* **1.** any tough, heavy timber with a compact texture. *Forestry* wood other than that from a needle-bearing conifer **3.** a tree yielding hardwood
**har·dy** (här′dē) *adj.* **-di·er, -di·est** [< OFr. pp. of *hardir*, to make bold < Frank.] **1.** bold and resolute; daring **2.** too bold; rash **3.** able to withstand fatigue, privation, etc.;

vigorous **4.** able to survive the winter without special care: said of plants —**har′di·ly** *adv.* —**har′di·ness** *n.*
**Har·dy** (här′dē), **Thomas** 1840–1928; Eng. novelist & poet
**hare** (her) *n., pl.* **hares, hare:** see PLURAL, II, D, 1 [OE. *hara*] a swift mammal related to the rabbit, with long ears, soft fur, a cleft upper lip, a short tail, and long, powerful hind legs; specif., one whose young are furry at birth
**hare·bell** (-bel′) *n.* a slender, delicate perennial, with clusters of blue, bell-shaped flowers
**hare·brained** (-brānd′) *adj.* having or showing little sense; reckless, flighty, giddy, rash, etc.
**Ha·re Krishna** (hä′rē) [< Hindi *Hari*, a name for Vishnu + KRISHNA] a cult based on some Vedic beliefs and devoted to Vishnu, founded (1966) in the U.S. **2.** a member of this cult
**hare·lip** (-lip′) *n.* **1.** a congenital deformity consisting of a harelike cleft of the lip **2.** a lip with such a deformity —**hare′lipped′** *adj.*
**ha·rem** (her′əm, har′-) *n.* [Ar. *ḥarīm*, lit., prohibited (place)] **1.** that part of a Moslem's household in which the women live **2.** the wives, concubines, women servants, etc. in a harem **3.** a number of female animals, as of fur seals, who mate and lodge with one male Also **ha·reem** (hä rēm′)
**har·i·cot** (har′ə kō′) *n.* [Fr., ult. < ? Nahuatl *ayecotli*, bean] [Chiefly Brit.] **1.** *same as* KIDNEY BEAN **2.** the pod or seed of other edible beans
**ha·ri·ka·ri** (her′ē ker′ē, hä′rē kä′rē) *n. same as* HARA-KIRI
**hark** (härk) *vi.* [< ? OE. *heorcnian*, to hearken] to listen carefully: usually in the imperative —**hark back** to go back; revert
**hark·en** (här′k'n) *vi., vt. same as* HEARKEN
**Har·lem** (här′ləm) [var. of HAARLEM] section of New York City, in N Manhattan
**Har·le·quin** (här′lə kwin, -kin) [< Fr. < OFr. *hierlekin*, demon] a traditional comic character in pantomime, who wears a mask and gay, spangled, diamond-patterned tights of many colors —*n.* [h-] a clown; buffoon —*adj.* [h-] **1.** comic; ludicrous **2.** of many colors; colorful

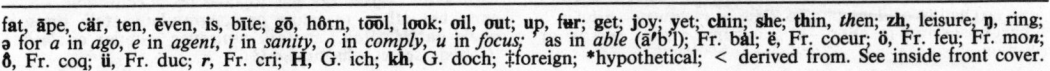

HARLEQUIN

**har·lot** (här′lət) *n.* [OFr., rogue] a prostitute
**har·lot·ry** (-rē) *n.* **1.** prostitution **2.** prostitutes, collectively
**harm** (härm) *n.* [OE. *hearm*] **1.** hurt; injury; damage **2.** moral wrong; evil —*vt.* to do harm to; hurt, damage, etc. —**harm′er** *n.*
**harm·ful** (-fəl) *adj.* causing or able to cause harm; hurtful —**harm′ful·ly** *adv.* —**harm′ful·ness** *n.*
**harm·less** (-lis) *adj.* causing no harm; inoffensive —**harm′less·ly** *adv.* —**harm′less·ness** *n.*
**har·mon·ic** (här män′ik) *adj.* **1.** harmonious in feeling or effect; agreeing **2.** *Music a)* of or in harmony *b)* pertaining to an overtone —*n.* **1.** *same as* OVERTONE (sense 1) **2.** *Elec.* an alternating-current voltage or current or a component of this, whose frequency is some integral multiple of a fundamental frequency —**har·mon′i·cal·ly** *adv.*
**har·mon·i·ca** (-i kə) *n.* [L.: see HARMONY] a small wind instrument played with the mouth; mouth organ: it has a series of graduated metal reeds that vibrate and produce tones when air is blown or sucked across them
**har·mon·ics** (-iks) *n.pl.* [with *sing. v.*] the physical science dealing with musical sounds
**har·mo·ni·ous** (här mō′nē əs) *adj.* [< Fr.: see HARMONY] **1.** having parts combined in a proportionate, orderly, or pleasing way **2.** having similar feelings, ideas, interests, etc. **3.** having musical tones combined for a pleasing effect —**har·mo′ni·ous·ly** *adv.* —**har·mo′ni·ous·ness** *n.*
**har·mo·nist** (här′mə nist) *n.* a musician expert in harmony
**har·mo·ni·um** (här mō′nē əm) *n.* [< Fr.: see HARMONY] a small kind of reed organ
**har·mo·nize** (här′mə nīz′) *vi.* **-nized′, -niz′ing 1.** to be in harmony; accord; agree **2.** to sing in harmony —*vt.* **1.** to make harmonious; bring into agreement **2.** to add chords to (a melody) so as to form a harmony —**har′mo·ni·za′tion** *n.* —**har′mo·niz′er** *n.*
**har·mo·ny** (här′mə nē) *n., pl.* **-nies** [< OFr. < L. < Gr. *harmonia* < *harmos*, a fitting] **1.** a combination of parts into a pleasing or orderly whole **2.** agreement in feeling, action, ideas, etc.; peaceable or friendly relations **3.** a state of agreement or orderly arrangement as to color, shape, etc. **4.** agreeable sounds; music **5.** *Music a)* the sounding together of two or more tones, esp. when satisfying to the ear *b)* structure in terms of the arrangement, modulation, etc. of chords *c)* the study of this structure

---

**har·ness** (här′nis) *n.* [< OFr. *harneis*, armor < ON.] **1.** orig., armor for a man or horse **2.** the leather straps and metal pieces by which a horse, mule, etc. is fastened to a vehicle, plow, or load **3.** any trappings or gear similar to this —*vt.* **1.** to put harness on (a horse, etc.) **2.** to control so as to use the power of *[to harness one's energy]* —**in harness** in or at one's routine work

**harness race** a horse race between either trotters or pacers, each pulling a sulky and driver

**Har·old** (har′əld) [OE. *Hereweald & Harald* < ON. *Haraldr*, lit., leader of the army] **1.** a masculine name **2.** Harold II 1022?–66; 1st Saxon king of England (1066): killed in the Battle of Hastings

**harp** (härp) *n.* [OE. *hearpe*] **1.** a musical instrument with strings stretched across an open, triangular frame, held upright and played by plucking with the fingers **2.** a harpshaped object or implement —*vi.* **1.** to play a harp **2.** to persist in talking or writing tediously or continuously (*on* or *upon* something) —**harp′er** *n.*

**harp·ist** (här′pist) *n.* a harp player

**har·poon** (här pōōn′) *n.* [< MDu. < MFr. < *harper*, to claw < ON. *harpa*, to squeeze] a barbed spear with a line attached to it, used for spearing whales or other large sea animals —*vt.* to strike or kill with a harpoon —**har·poon′er** *n.*

**harp·si·chord** (härp′si kôrd′) *n.* [< obs. Fr. or < It.: see HARP & CORD] a stringed musical instrument with a keyboard, predecessor of the piano: the strings are plucked by leather or quill points by pressing the keys —**harp′si·chord′ist** *n.*

**Har·py** (här′pē) *n.,* pl. **-pies** [< MFr. < L. < Gr. < *harpazein*, to seize] **1.** *Gr. Myth.* any of several hideous, winged monsters with the head and trunk of a woman and the tail, legs, and talons of a bird **2.** [h-] a greedy or grasping person

**har·que·bus** (här′kwi bəs) *n.* [< Fr., ult. < Du. *haak*, hook + *bus*, a gun] an early type of portable gun

**har·ri·dan** (har′i d'n) *n.* [prob. < Fr. *haridelle*, worn-out horse] a disreputable, shrewish old woman

**har·ri·er¹** (har′ē ər) *n.* [< HARE + -IER] **1.** a dog like the English foxhound, used for hunting hares and rabbits **2.** a cross-country runner

**har·ri·er²** (har′ē ər) *n.* **1.** one who harries **2.** a hawk that preys on small mammals, reptiles, etc.

**Har·ri·et** (har′ē it) [fem. dim. of HARRY] a feminine name: var. *Harriot*

**Har·ris** (har′is), Joel Chan·dler (chan′dlər) 1848–1908; U.S. writer, esp. of the *Uncle Remus* stories

**Har·ris·burg** (har′is burg′) [after John *Harris,* Jr., the founder] capital of Pa., on the Susquehanna: pop. 53,000

**Har·ri·son** (har′ə s'n) **1. Benjamin,** 1833–1901; 23d president of the U.S. (1889–93): grandson of *ff.* **2. William Henry,** 1773–1841; 9th president of the U.S. (1841)

**har·row** (har′ō) *n.* [prob. < ON. *harfr*] a heavy frame with spikes or sharp-edged disks, drawn by a horse or tractor and used for breaking up and leveling plowed ground, covering seeds, etc. —*vt.* **1.** to draw a harrow over (land) **2.** to cause mental distress to; torment; vex —*vi.* to take harrowing *[ground that harrows well]* —**har′row·er** *n.* —**har′row·ing** *adj.* —**har′row·ing·ly** *adv.*

**har·rumph** (hə rumpf′: *conventionalized pronun.*) *vi.* [echoic] **1.** to clear one's throat, esp. in a studied, pompous way **2.** to protest in a pompous or self-righteous way —*n.* a harrumphing

**Har·ry** (har′ē) [< HENRY] a masculine name

**har·ry** (har′ē) *vt.* **-ried, -ry·ing** [< OE. *hergian* < base of *here,* army] **1.** to raid and ravage or rob; plunder **2.** to torment; harass **3.** to force along

**harsh** (härsh) *adj.* [ME. *harsk*] **1.** unpleasantly sharp or rough to the ear, eye, taste, or touch; grating, glaring, bitter, coarse, etc. **2.** unpleasantly crude or abrupt **3.** rough, crude, or forbidding in appearance **4.** excessively severe; cruel or unfeeling —**harsh′ly** *adv.* —**harsh′ness** *n.*

**hart** (härt) *n.,* pl. **harts, hart:** see PLURAL, II, D, 1 [OE. *heorot*] a male of the European red deer, esp. after its fifth year; stag

**Harte** (härt), **Bret** (bret) (born *Francis Brett Hart*) 1836–1902; U.S. writer, esp. of short stories

**har·te·beest** (här′tə bēst′, härt′bēst′) *n.,* pl. **-beests′, -beest′:** see PLURAL, II, D, 1 [obs. Afrik. < *harte,* hart + *beest,* beast] a large, swift South African antelope having long horns curved backward at the tips

**Hart·ford** (härt′fərd) [after *Hertford*shire, county in England] capital of Conn., in the C part: pop. 136,000 (met. area 726,000)

**harts·horn** (härts′hôrn′) *n.* **1.** a hart's horn **2.** [Now Rare] ammonium carbonate, used in smelling salts: orig. obtained from deer's antlers

**har·um-scar·um** (her′əm sker′əm) *adj.* [< ? HARE + SCARE + 'EM] acting or done in a reckless or rash way —*adv.* in a harum-scarum manner —*n.* a harum-scarum person or action

**ha·rus·pex** (hə rus′peks, har′əs peks) *n.,* pl. **-rus′pi·ces′** (-pə sēz′) [L.] a soothsayer in ancient Rome who professed to foretell the future by interpreting the entrails of sacrificial animals —**ha·rus′pi·cal** (-pi k'l) *adj.*

**har·vest** (här′vist) *n.* [OE. *hærfest*] **1.** the time of the year when grain, fruit, vegetables, etc. are reaped and gathered in **2.** a season's yield of grain, fruit, etc.; crop **3.** the gathering in of a crop **4.** the outcome of any effort —*vt., vi.* **1.** to gather in (a crop, etc.) **2.** to gather the crop from (a field) **3.** to get (something) as the result of an action or effort —**har′vest·a·ble** *adj.*

**har·vest·er** (-ər) *n.* **1.** a person who gathers in a crop of grain, fruit, etc. **2.** any of various farm machines for harvesting crops

**har·vest·man** (-mən) *n.,* pl. **-men 1.** a man who harvests **2.** a spiderlike animal with long, thin legs and a short, broad, segmented abdomen

**harvest moon** the full moon at or about the time of the autumnal equinox, September 22 or 23

**Har·vey** (här′vē) [< Fr. < OHG. *Herewig*, lit., army battle] **1.** a masculine name **2. William,** 1578–1657; Eng. physician: discovered the circulation of the blood

**Harz (Mountains)** (härts) mountain range in C Germany: highest peak, 3,747 ft.

**has** (haz; *unstressed* həz, əz) *3d pers. sing., pres. indic.,* of HAVE

**has-been** (haz′bin′) *n.* [Colloq.] a person or thing whose popularity or effectiveness is past

**ha·sen·pfef·fer** (häs′'n fef′ər) *n.* [G. < *hase,* rabbit + *pfeffer,* pepper] a German dish of rabbit meat marinated in vinegar and stewed in the marinade

**hash¹** (hash) *vt.* [Fr. *hacher,* to chop] **1.** to chop (meat or vegetables) into small pieces for cooking **2.** [Colloq.] to make a mess of; bungle —*n.* **1.** a chopped mixture of cooked meat and vegetables, usually baked or browned **2.** a mixture or rehash **3.** a hodgepodge; muddle —**hash out** [Colloq.] to settle by prolonged discussion —**hash over** [Colloq.] to discuss at length —**settle one's hash** [Colloq.] to overcome or subdue one

**hash²** (hash) *n.* [Slang] hashish

**hash house** [Slang] a cheap restaurant

**hash·ish** (hash′ēsh, -ish) *n.* [Ar. *ḥashīsh,* dried hemp] a drug formed from the resin contained in the flowering tops of Indian hemp, chewed or smoked for its intoxicating or euphoric effects: also **hash′eesh** (-ēsh)

**hash mark** [Mil. Slang] *same as* SERVICE STRIPE

**Has·i·dim** (has′i dim; *Heb.* khä sē′dim) *n.pl., sing.* **Has·id** (has′id; *Heb.* khä′sid) [< Heb. *ḥāsid,* a pious person] a sect of Jewish mystics, orig. in 18th-cent. Poland, that emphasizes joyful worship —**Ha·sid·ic** (ha sid′ik) *adj.*

**has·n't** (haz′'nt) has not

**hasp** (hasp) *n.* [OE. *hæpse*] a hinged metal fastening for a door, window, lid, etc.; esp., a metal piece fitted over a staple and fastened by a bolt or padlock

**has·sle** (has′'l) *n.* [< ?] [Colloq.] **1.** a heated argument; squabble **2.** a troublesome situation —*vi.* **-sled, -sling** [Colloq.] to have a heated argument —*vt.* [Colloq.] to cause trouble or difficulty for; harass

**has·sock** (has′ək) *n.* [OE. *hassuc*] **1.** [Now Rare] a thick clump or tuft of grass **2.** a firmly stuffed cushion used as a footstool or seat

HASP

**hast** (hast; *unstressed* həst, əst) *archaic 2d pers. sing., pres. indic.,* of HAVE: used with thou

**has·tate** (has′tāt) *adj.* [< L. < *hasta,* a spear] having a triangular shape, as some leaves

**haste** (hāst) *n.* [OFr. *haste* < Frank.] **1.** quickness of motion; hurrying **2.** careless or reckless hurrying *[haste makes waste]* **3.** necessity for hurrying; urgency —*vt., vi.* **hast′ed, hast′ing** [Rare] *same as* HASTEN —**in haste 1.** in a hurry **2.** in too great a hurry —**make haste** to hasten

**has·ten** (hās′'n) *vt.* to cause to be or come faster; speed up —*vi.* to move swiftly; hurry

**Has·tings** (hās′tiŋz) city in SE England, on the English Channel: nearby is the site of the decisive battle of the Norman Conquest

**hast·y** (hās′tē) *adj.* **hast′i·er, hast′i·est 1.** done or made with haste; hurried **2.** done or made too quickly and with too little thought; rash *[a hasty decision]* **3.** short-tempered or impetuous **4.** showing irritation or impatience *[hasty words]* —**hast′i·ly** *adv.* —**hast′i·ness** *n.*

**hasty pudding 1.** mush made of cornmeal **2.** [Brit.] mush made of flour or oatmeal

**hat** (hat) *n.* [OE. *hætt*] a covering for the head, usually with a brim and crown —*vt.* **hat′ted, hat′ting** to cover or provide with a hat —**pass the hat** to take up a collection —**take one's hat off to** to salute or congratulate —**talk through one's hat** [Colloq.] to talk nonsense —**under one's hat** [Colloq.] secret —**hat′less** *adj.*

**hat·band** (-band′) *n.* a band of cloth around the crown of a hat, just above the brim

**hat·box** (-bäks′) *n.* a box or case for carrying or storing a hat or hats

**hatch¹** (hach) *vt.* [ME. *hacchen*] **1.** *a)* to bring forth (young) from an egg or eggs by applying warmth *b)* to bring forth young from (an egg or eggs) **2.** to bring (a plan, idea, etc.) into existence; esp., to plot —*vi.* **1.** to bring forth young: said of eggs **2.** to come forth from the egg —*n.* **1.** the process of hatching **2.** the brood hatched —**hatch′er** *n.*

**hatch²** (hach) *n.* [OE. *hæcc*, a grating] **1.** the lower half of a door, gate, etc. that has two separately movable halves **2.** *same as* HATCHWAY **3.** a covering for a ship's hatchway, or a lid or trapdoor for a hatchway in a building

**hatch³** (hach) *vt.* [< OFr. < *hache*, an ax] to mark or engrave with fine, crossed or parallel lines so as to indicate shading —*n.* any of these lines

**hatch·back** (-bak′) *n.* [HATCH² + BACK] an automobile body with a rear that swings up, providing a wide opening into a storage area

**hatch·el** (hach′əl) *n., vt.* -eled *or* -elled, -el·ing *or* -el·ling *same as* HACKLE¹

**hatch·er·y** (hach′ər ē) *n., pl.* -er·ies a place for hatching eggs, esp. those of fish or poultry

**hatch·et** (hach′it) *n.* [< OFr. dim. of *hache*, an ax] **1.** a small ax with a short handle, for use with one hand **2.** *same as* TOMAHAWK —**bury the hatchet** to stop fighting; make peace

**hatchet man** [Colloq.] **1.** a man hired to commit murder **2.** any person assigned by another to carry out disagreeable or unscrupulous tasks

**hatch·ing** (hach′iŋ) *n.* [HATCH³ + -ING] **1.** the drawing or engraving of fine, parallel or crossed lines to show shading **2.** such lines

**hatch·way** (-wā′) *n.* **1.** a covered opening in a ship's deck **2.** a similar opening in the floor or roof of a building

**hate** (hāt) *vt.* hat′ed, hat′ing [OE. *hatian*] **1.** to have strong dislike or ill will for; despise **2.** to dislike or wish to avoid; shrink from [to *hate* arguments] —*vi.* to feel hatred —*n.* **1.** a strong feeling of dislike or ill will; hatred **2.** a person or thing hated —**hate′a·ble, hat′a·ble** *adj.* —**hat′er** *n.*

**hate·ful** (-fəl) *adj.* **1.** [Now Rare] feeling or showing hate; malevolent **2.** causing or deserving hate; odious —**hate′-ful·ly** *adv.* —**hate′ful·ness** *n.*

**hate·mon·ger** (-muŋ′gər, -mäŋ′-) *n.* a propagandist who seeks to provoke hatred and prejudice

**hath** (hath) *archaic 3d pers. sing., pres. indic., of* HAVE

**hat·rack** (hat′rak′) *n.* a rack, set of pegs or hooks, etc. to hold hats

**ha·tred** (hā′trid) *n.* [ME. < *hate*, hate + *-red* < OE. *ræden*, state] strong dislike or ill will

**hat·ter** (hat′ər) *n.* one who makes or sells hats

**Hat·ter·as** (hat′ər əs), **Cape** [< AmInd. tribal name] cape on an island of N.C., in the Atlantic

**hau·ber·geon** (hô′bər jən) *n. obs. var. of* HABERGEON

**hau·berk** (hô′bərk) *n.* [< OFr., ult. < Frank. *hals*, the neck + *bergan*, to protect] a medieval coat of armor, usually of chain mail

**haugh·ty** (hôt′ē) *adj.* -ti·er, -ti·est [< OFr. *haut*, high < L. *altus*, high + -Y²] **1.** having or showing great pride in oneself and contempt or scorn for others **2.** [Archaic] lofty; noble —**haugh′ti·ly** *adv.* —**haugh′ti·ness** *n.*

**haul** (hôl) *vt.* [< OFr. *haler*, to draw < ODu. *halen*, to fetch] **1.** to move by pulling or drawing; tug; drag **2.** to transport by wagon, truck, etc. [to *haul* coal] **3.** *same as* HALE² **4.** *Naut.* to change the course of (a ship) by setting the sails —*vi.* **1.** to pull; tug **2.** to shift direction: said of the wind **3.** *Naut.* to change the course of a ship by trimming sail —*n.* **1.** the act of hauling; pull; tug **2.** *a)* the amount of fish taken in a single pull of a net *b)* [Colloq.] the amount gained, won, earned, etc. at one time **3.** the distance or route covered in transporting or traveling **4.** a load transported —**haul off** [Colloq.] to draw the arm back before hitting —**haul up 1.** to sail nearer the direction of the wind **2.** to come to rest; stop —**in** (or **over**) **the long haul** over a long period of time —**haul′er** *n.*

**haul·age** (-ij) *n.* **1.** the act or process of hauling **2.** the charge made for hauling, as by a railroad

**haunch** (hônch, hänch) *n.* [< OFr. *hanche* < Gmc.] **1.** the part of the body including the hip, buttock, and thickest part of the thigh; hindquarter **2.** an animal's loin and leg together

**haunt** (hônt, hänt; *for n. 2, usually* hant) *vt.* [< OFr. *hanter*, to frequent] **1.** to visit (a place) often or continually **2.** to seek the company or companionship of; run after **3.** to recur repeatedly to [memories *haunted* her] **4.** to fill the atmosphere of; pervade [a house *haunted* by sorrow] —*n.* **1.** a place often visited or frequented [to make the library one's haunt] **2.** [Dial.] a ghost

**haunt·ed** (-id) *adj.* supposedly frequented by ghosts

**haunt·ing** (-iŋ) *adj.* often recurring to the mind [a *haunting* melody] —**haunt′ing·ly** *adv.*

**haut·boy** (hō′boi′, ō′-) *n.* [< Fr. < *haut*, high + *bois*, wood] *earlier name for* OBOE

**‡haute cou·ture** (ōt kōō tür′) [Fr., lit., high sewing] the leading designers and creators of new fashions in women's clothing, or their creations

**hau·teur** (hō tur′; *Fr.* ō tër′) *n.* [Fr. < *haut*, high, proud] disdainful pride; haughtiness; snobbery

**‡haut monde** (ō mōnd′) [Fr.] high society

**Ha·van·a** (hə van′ə) capital of Cuba, on the Gulf of Mexico: pop. 788,000 —*n.* **1.** a cigar made in Cuba or of Cuban tobacco **2.** Cuban tobacco

**have** (hav; həv, əv; *before* "to" haf) *vt.* had, hav′ing [OE. *habban*] **1.** to hold; own; possess [to *have* wealth] **2.** to possess as a part, characteristic, etc. [the week *has* seven days] **3.** to be afflicted with [to *have* a cold] **4.** to experience; undergo [*have* a good time] **5.** to understand or know [to *have* a little Spanish] **6.** to hold or keep in the mind [to *have* an idea] **7.** to declare or state [so gossip has it] **8.** *a)* to get, take, or obtain [*have* a look at it] *b)* to eat or drink [*have* some tea] **9.** to bear or beget (offspring) **10.** to perform; engage in [to *have* an argument] **11.** *a)* to cause to [*have* him sing] *b)* to cause to be [*have* it fixed] **12.** to be in a certain relation to [to *have* a wife] **13.** to feel and show [*have* pity on her] **14.** to permit; tolerate [I won't *have* this nuisance] **15.** [Colloq.] *a)* to hold at a disadvantage [I *had* my opponent now] *b)* to deceive; cheat [they were *had* in that business deal] *Have* is used as an auxiliary to form phrases expressing completed action, as in the perfect tenses (Ex.: I *had* left), and with infinitives to express obligation or necessity (Ex.: we *have* to go) *Have got* often replaces *have Have* is conjugated in the present indicative: (I) *have*, (he, she, it) *has*, (we, you, they) *have*; in the past indicative (I, he, she, it, we, you, they) *had* Archaic forms are: (thou) *hast, hadst*, (he, she, it) *hath* —*n.* a person or nation with relatively much wealth or rich resources —**have at** to attack; strike —**have done** to stop; finish —**have had it** [Slang] to be defeated, disgusted, etc. or no longer popular, useful, etc. —**have it good** [Colloq.] to be well-off —**have it out** to settle a disagreement by fighting or discussion —**have on** to be wearing —**have to be** [Colloq.] to be unquestionably

**ha·ven** (hā′vən) *n.* [OE. *hæfen*] **1.** a port; harbor **2.** any sheltered, safe place; refuge —*vt.* to provide a haven for

**have-not** (hav′nät′) *n.* a person or nation with little or no wealth or resources

**have·n't** (hav′′nt) have not

**hav·er·sack** (hav′ər sak′) *n.* [< Fr. < G. *habersack*, lit., sack of oats] a canvas bag for rations, worn over one shoulder, as by soldiers and hikers

**hav·oc** (hav′ək) *n.* [< Anglo-Fr. < OFr. *havot*, plunder] great destruction and devastation —**cry havoc 1.** orig., to give (an army) the signal for pillaging **2.** to warn of great danger —**play havoc with** to devastate; destroy; ruin

**Havre, Le** *see* LE HAVRE

**haw¹** (hô) *n.* [OE. *haga*] **1.** the berry of the hawthorn **2.** *same as* HAWTHORN

**haw²** (hô) *interj., n.* [< ?] a word of command to a horse, ox, etc., meaning "turn to the left!" —*vt., vi.* to turn to the left Opposed to GEE¹

**haw³** (hô) *vi.* [echoic] to hesitate in speaking; falter: usually in HEM AND HAW (see HEM²) —*n.* a conventionalized expression of sound often made by a speaker when hesitating briefly

**Haw.** Hawaiian

**Ha·wai·i** (hə wä′ē, -yē, -yə) [Haw. < ?] **1.** a State of the U.S., consisting of a group of islands (**Hawaiian Islands**) in the North Pacific: 6,424 sq. mi.; pop. 965,000; cap. Honolulu: abbrev. **HI 2.** largest of the islands of Hawaii

**Ha·wai·ian** (-yən) *adj.* of Hawaii, its people, language, etc. —*n.* **1.** a native or inhabitant of Hawaii; specif., a native of Polynesian descent **2.** the Polynesian language of the Hawaiians

**hawk¹** (hôk) *n.* [OE. *hafoc*] **1.** any of a group of birds of prey characterized by short, rounded wings, a long tail and legs, and a hooked beak and claws: hawks include the falcons, buzzards, harriers, kites, and caracaras, but not vultures and eagles **2.** an advocate of all-out war or of the provocation of open hostilities —*vi.* to hunt birds with the help of hawks —*vt.* to prey on as a hawk does —**hawk′er** *n.* —**hawk′ing** *n.* —**hawk′ish** *adj.* —**hawk′like′** *adj.*

SHINGLING HATCHET

CLAW HATCHET

TYPES OF HATCHET

fat, āpe, cär, ten, ēven, is, bīte; gō, hôrn, tōōl, look; oil, out; up, fur; get; joy; yet; chin; she; thin, *then*; zh, leisure; ŋ, ring; ə for *a* in *ago*, *e* in *agent*, *i* in *sanity*, *o* in *comply*, *u* in *focus*; ´ as in *able* (ā′b'l); Fr. bal; ë, Fr. coeur; ö, Fr. feu; Fr. mon; ö, Fr. coq; ü, Fr. duc; r, Fr. cri; H, G. ich; kh, G. doch; ‡foreign; *hypothetical; < derived from. See inside front cover.

**hawk²** (hôk) *vt., vi.* [< HAWKER] to advertise or peddle (goods) in the street by shouting

**hawk³** (hôk) *vi.* [echoic] to clear the throat audibly —*vt.* to bring up (phlegm) by coughing —*n.* an audible clearing of the throat

**hawk·er** (hôk′ər) *n.* [ult. < MLowG. *hoken,* to peddle] a person who hawks goods in the street

**hawk-eyed** (-īd′) *adj.* keen-sighted like a hawk

**hawk·moth** (-môth′) *n.* a moth with a thick, tapering body, slender wings, and a long feeding tube used for sucking the nectar of flowers

**hawks·bill (turtle)** (hôks′bil′) a medium-sized turtle of warm seas, having a hawklike beak and a shell from which tortoise shell is obtained

**hawk·weed** (hôk′wēd′) *n.* a plant of the composite family, with yellow or scarlet ray flowers

**hawse** (hôz) *n.* [< ON. *hals,* the neck] 1. that part of the bow of a ship containing the hawseholes 2. *same as* HAWSE-HOLE 3. the space between the bow of a ship and the anchors

**hawse·hole** (-hōl′) *n.* any of the holes in a ship's bow through which a hawser or cable is passed

**haw·ser** (hô′zər) *n.* [< Anglo-Fr. < OFr. *haucier,* ult. < L. *altus,* high] a large rope or small cable, by which a ship is anchored, moored, or towed

**haw·thorn** (hô′thôrn′) *n.* [< OE. < *haga,* hedge + *thorn*] a thorny shrub or small tree of the rose family, with flowers of white, pink, or red, and small, red fruits (*haws*) resembling miniature apples

**Haw·thorne** (hô′thôrn′) [after ff.] city in SW Calif.: suburb of Los Angeles: pop. 56,000

**Haw·thorne** (hô′thôrn′), **Nathaniel** 1804–64; U.S. novelist & short-story writer

**hay** (hā) *n.* [OE. *hieg*] 1. grass, alfalfa, clover, etc. cut and dried for use as fodder 2. [Slang] bed —*vi.* to mow grass, alfalfa, etc. and spread it out to dry —**hit the hay** [Slang] to go to bed to sleep —**make hay while the sun shines** to make the most of an opportunity

**hay·cock** (-käk′) *n.* a small, conical heap of hay drying in a field

**Hay·dn** (hīd′'n), **Franz Jo·seph** (fränts yō′zef) 1732–1809; Austrian composer

**Hayes** (hāz), **Ruth·er·ford B(irchard)** (ruth′ər fərd) 1822–93; 19th president of the U.S. (1877–81)

**hay fever** an acute inflammation of the eyes and upper respiratory tract: it is an allergic reaction, caused by the pollen of some grasses and trees

**hay·field** (hā′fēld′) *n.* a field of grass, alfalfa, etc. to be made into hay

**hay·loft** (-lôft′) *n.* a loft, or upper story, in a barn or stable, for storing hay

**hay·mak·er** (-mā′kər) *n.* 1. a person who cuts hay and spreads it out to dry 2. [Slang] a powerful blow with the fist

**hay·mow** (-mou′) *n.* 1. a pile of hay in a barn 2. *same as* HAYLOFT

**hay·ride** (-rīd′) *n.* a pleasure ride taken by a group in a wagon partly filled with hay

**hay·seed** (-sēd′) *n.* 1. grass seed shaken from mown hay 2. [Old Slang] a rustic; yokel

**hay·stack** (-stak′) *n.* a large heap of hay piled up outdoors: also **hay′rick′** (-rik′)

**Hay·ward** (hā′wərd) [after W. *Hayward,* local postmaster] city in W Calif.: suburb of Oakland: pop. 94,000

**hay·wire** (hā′wīr′) *n.* wire for tying up bales of hay —*adj.* [Slang] 1. out of order; confused 2. crazy: usually in **go haywire,** to become crazy

**haz·ard** (haz′ərd) *n.* [OFr. *hasard,* game of dice < Ar. *az-zahr*] 1. an early game of chance played with dice 2. chance 3. risk; peril; danger 4. an obstacle on a golf course —*vt.* to risk or venture

**haz·ard·ous** (-əs) *adj.* risky; dangerous —**haz′ard·ous·ly** *adv.* —**haz′ard·ous·ness** *n.*

**haze¹** (hāz) *n.* [prob. < HAZY] 1. a thin vapor of fog, smoke, dust, etc. in the air 2. slight confusion or vagueness of mind —*vi., vt.* **hazed, haz′ing** to make or become hazy (often with *over*)

**haze²** (hāz) *vt.* **hazed, haz′ing** [< ? OFr. *haser,* to irritate] to initiate or discipline (fellow students) by forcing to do humiliating or painful things

**Ha·zel** (hā′z'l) [Heb. *ḥazā′ēl,* lit., God sees] a feminine name

**ha·zel** (hā′z'l) *n.* [OE. *hæsel*] 1. a shrub or tree related to the birch, bearing edible nuts 2. *same as* HAZELNUT 3. a light brown —*adj.* 1. of the hazel tree 2. light-brown: hazel eyes are usually flecked with green or gray —**ha′zel·ly** *adj.*

**ha·zel·nut** (-nut′) *n.* the small, edible, roundish nut of the hazel; filbert

**Haz·litt** (haz′lit), **William** 1778–1830; Eng. essayist

**ha·zy** (hā′zē) *adj.* **-zi·er, -zi·est** [prob. < OE. *hasu,* dusky] 1. characterized by haze; somewhat foggy or smoky 2. vague, obscure, or indefinite [*hazy* thinking] —**ha′zi·ly** *adv.* —**ha′zi·ness** *n.*

**Hb** *the symbol for* hemoglobin

**hb** *Football* halfback

**H-bomb** (āch′bäm′) *n. same as* HYDROGEN BOMB

**hd.** head

**hdqrs.** headquarters

**he** (hē; *unstressed* hi, ē, i) *pron. for pl. see* THEY [OE.] 1. the man, boy, or male animal previously mentioned 2. the person; the one; anyone [*he* who laughs last laughs best] *He* is the nominative case form of the masculine third personal pronoun —*n., pl.* **hes** a man, boy, or male animal

**He** *Chem.* helium

**head** (hed) *n.* [OE. *heafod*] 1. the top part of the body in man, the apes, etc., or the front part in most other animals: in higher animals it is a bony structure containing the brain, and including the eyes, ears, nose, and mouth 2. the head as the seat of reason, memory, and imagination; mind; intelligence [to use one's *head*] 3. a person [dinner at five dollars a *head*] 4. *pl.* **head** the head as a unit of counting [fifty *head* of cattle] 5. the obverse of a coin, usually showing a head: often **heads** 6. the highest or uppermost part or thing; top; specif., *a*) the top of a page, column, etc. *b*) a topic of a section, chapter, etc. *c*) a headline *d*) froth floating on newly poured effervescent beverages *e*) that end of a cask or barrel which is uppermost 7. the foremost part of a thing; front; specif., *a*) a part associated with the human head [the *head* of a bed] *b*) the front part of a ship; bow *c*) *Naut.* a toilet, or lavatory *d*) the front position, as of a column of marching men *e*) either end of something 8. the projecting part of something; specif., *a*) the part designed for holding, striking, etc. [the *head* of a pin/ *b*) a headland *c*) a projecting place, as in a boil, where pus is about to break through *d*) the part of a tape recorder that records or plays back the magnetic signals on the tape 9. the membrane stretched across the end of a drum, tambourine, etc. 10. the source of a river, stream, etc. 11. a source of water kept at some height to supply a mill, etc. 12. the pressure in an enclosed fluid, as steam 13. a position of leadership or honor [the *head* of the class] 14. the person in charge; leader, ruler, director, etc. 15. a headmaster 16. *Bot. a)* a dense, flattened cluster of flowers, as in the dandelion *b*) a large, compact bud [a *head* of cabbage] 17. *Music* the rounded part of a note, at the end of the stem 18. [Slang] a habitual user of marijuana, LSD, etc. —*adj.* 1. of or having to do with the head 2. most important; principal; first 3. to be found at the top or front 4. striking against the front [*head* current] —*vt.* 1. to be chief of or in charge of 2. to lead; precede 3. to supply (a pin, etc.) with a head 4. [Rare] to behead 5. to trim the higher part from (a tree or plant); poll 6. to cause to go in a specified direction —*vi.* 1. to grow or come to a head 2. to set out; travel [to *head* eastward] —**by a head** by a small margin —**come to a head** 1. to be about to suppurate, as a boil 2. to culminate —**give one his head** to let one do as he likes —**go to one's head** 1. to confuse or intoxicate one 2. to make one vain —**hang** (or **hide**) **one's head** to lower one's head or conceal one's face as in shame —**head off** to get ahead of and intercept —**head over heels** 1. deeply; completely 2. hurriedly; recklessly —**heads up!** [Colloq.] look out! be careful! —**keep** (or **lose**) **one's head** to keep (or lose) one's poise, self-control, etc. —**make head** to go forward; advance —**make head or tail of** to understand: usually in the negative —**on** (or **upon**) **one's head** as one's responsibility or misfortune —**out of** (or **off**) **one's head** [Colloq.] 1. crazy 2. delirious; raving —**over one's head** 1. too difficult to understand 2. to a higher authority —**put** (or **lay**) **heads together** to consult or scheme together —**take it into one's head** to conceive the notion, plan, or intention —**turn one's head** 1. to make one dizzy 2. to make one vain or overconfident

**-head** (hed) *same as* -HOOD [godhead]

**head·ache** (hed′āk′) *n.* 1. a continuous pain in the head 2. [Colloq.] a cause of worry, trouble, etc.

**head·board** (-bôrd′) *n.* a board or frame that forms the head of a bed, etc.

**head·cheese** (-chēz′) *n.* a loaf of jellied, seasoned meat made from the head and feet of hogs

**head·dress** (-dres′) *n.* 1. a covering or decoration for the head 2. a style of arranging the hair

**head·ed** (-id) *adj.* 1. formed into a head, as cabbage 2. having a heading

**-head·ed** (-id) *a combining form meaning:* 1. having a (specified kind of) head [clearheaded] 2. having a (specified number of) heads [two-headed]

**head·er** (-ər) *n.* 1. a person or device that puts heads on pins, nails, rivets, etc. 2. a machine that takes off the heads of grain and loads them into a truck 3. [Colloq.] a headlong fall or dive 4. a wooden beam placed between two long beams with the ends of short beams resting against it 5. a brick or stone laid against the thickness of a wall with the short end exposed in the wall face

**head·first** (-fûrst′) *adv.* 1. with the head in front; headlong 2. in a reckless way; rashly; impetuously Also **head′fore′-most′** (-fôr′mōst′)

**head·gear** (-gir′) *n.* 1. a covering for the head; hat, cap, etc. 2. the harness for the head of a horse, mule, etc.

**head·hunt·er** (-hun′tər) *n.* a member of any of certain primitive tribes who remove the heads of slain enemies and preserve them as trophies —**head′hunt′ing** *n.*

**head·ing** (-iŋ) *n.* 1. something forming or used to form the head, top, edge, or front; specif., an inscription at the top of a chapter, page, etc., giving the title, topic, etc. 2. a topic or category 3. the direction in which a ship, plane, etc. is moving: usually expressed as a compass reading

**head·land** (-lənd) *n.* a point of land reaching out into the water; cape, a promontory

**head·less** (-lis) *adj.* 1. without a head 2. without a leader 3. stupid; foolish

**head·light** (-līt′) *n.* a light with a reflector and lens, at the front of an automobile, locomotive, etc.: also **head′lamp′**

**head·line** (-līn′) *n.* 1. a line at the top of a page, giving the running title, page number, etc. 2. a line or lines at the top of a newspaper article, giving its topic 3. an important news item —*vt.* **-lined′, -lin′ing** 1. to provide with a headline 2. to give featured billing to

**head·lin·er** (-lī′nər) *n.* a featured entertainer

**head·long** (-lôŋ′) *adv.* [< ME. *hedelinge(s)* < *hede,* head + *-linge,* adv. suffix] 1. with the head first; headfirst 2. with uncontrolled speed and force 3. recklessly; rashly; impetuously —*adj.* 1. having the head first 2. moving with uncontrolled speed and force 3. reckless; impetuous

**head·man** (hed′mən, -man′) *n., pl.* **-men** (-mən, -men′) a leader, chief, or overseer

**head·mas·ter** (-mas′tər) *n.* in some, esp. private, schools, the man who is the principal —**head′mas′ter·ship′** *n.* — **head′mis′tress** (-mis′tris) *n.*

**head·most** (-mōst′) *adj.* in the lead; foremost

**head-on** (-än′) *adj., adv.* 1. with the head or front foremost [a head-on collision] 2. directly or in direct opposition [meet problems head-on]

**head·phone** (-fōn′) *n.* a telephone or radio receiver held to the ear by a band over the head

**head·piece** (-pēs′) *n.* 1. a protective covering for the head, as a helmet 2. the mind; intellect

**head·pin** (-pin′) *n.* the pin at the front of a triangle of bowling pins

**head·quar·ters** (-kwôr′tərz) *n.pl.* [often with sing. v.] 1. the main office, or center of operations, of one in command, as in an army or police force 2. the main office in any organization —**head′quar′ter** *vt.*

**head·rest** (-rest′) *n.* a support for the head, as on a dentist's chair

**head·room** (-rōōm′) *n.* space or clearance overhead, as in a doorway or tunnel

**head·set** (-set′) *n.* an earphone or earphones, often with a mouthpiece transmitter attached

**head·ship** (-ship′) *n.* the position or authority of a chief or leader; leadership; command

**heads·man** (hedz′mən) *n., pl.* **-men** an executioner who beheads those condemned to die

**head·stall** (hed′stôl′) *n.* the part of a bridle or halter that fits over a horse's head

**head start** an early start or other advantage given to or taken by a contestant or competitor

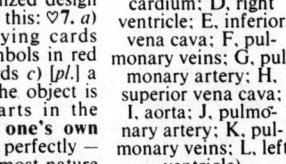

HEADSET

**head·stock** (-stäk′) *n.* the part of a lathe supporting the spindle

**head·stone** (-stōn′) *n.* 1. [Rare] a cornerstone 2. a stone marker placed at the head of a grave

**head·stream** (-strēm′) *n.* a stream forming the source of another and larger stream

**head·strong** (-strôŋ′) *adj.* 1. determined not to follow orders, advice, etc. but to do as one pleases; self-willed 2. showing such determination [headstrong desire]

**head·wait·er** (-wāt′ər) *n.* a supervisor of waiters, often in charge of table reservations

**head·wa·ters** (-wôt′ərz, -wät′-) *n.pl.* the small streams that are the sources of a river

**head·way** (-wā′) *n.* 1. forward motion 2. progress in work, etc. 3. same as HEADROOM 4. the difference in time or miles between two vehicles traveling the same route

**head wind** a wind blowing in the direction directly opposite the course of a ship or aircraft

**head·work** (hed′wurk′) *n.* mental effort; thought

**head·y** (-ē) *adj.* **head′i·er, head′i·est** 1. impetuous; rash; willful 2. tending to affect the senses; intoxicating —**head′-i·ly** *adv.* —**head′i·ness** *n.*

**heal** (hēl) *vt.* [OE. *hælan* < *hal,* sound, healthy] 1. to make well or healthy again 2. a) to cure (a disease) b) to cause (a wound, sore, etc.) to become closed or scarred 3. to free from grief, troubles, evil, etc. 4. to remedy (grief, troubles, etc.) —*vi.* 1. to become well or healthy again; be cured 2. to become closed or scarred: said of a wound —**heal′er** *n.*

**health** (helth) *n.* [OE. *hælth* < *hal,* sound, healthy + -TH¹] 1. physical and mental well-being; freedom from disease, etc. 2. condition of body or mind [good health] 3. a wish for a person's health and happiness, as in drinking a toast 4. soundness or vitality, as of a society or culture

**health food** food considered to be especially healthful; often, specif., such food when organically grown and free of chemical additives

**health·ful** (-fəl) *adj.* 1. helping to produce or maintain health; wholesome 2. [Rare] same as HEALTHY —**health′-ful·ly** *adv.* —**health′ful·ness** *n.*

**health·y** (hel′thē) *adj.* **health′i·er, health′i·est** 1. having good health 2. showing or resulting from good health [a healthy appetite] 3. same as HEALTHFUL 4. [Colloq.] large, vigorous, etc. [a healthy yell] —**health′i·ly** *adv.* —**health′i·ness** *n.*

**heap** (hēp) *n.* [OE. *heap,* a troop, band] 1. a pile or mass of things jumbled together 2. [Colloq.] a large amount 3. [Slang] an old automobile —*vt.* 1. to make a heap of 2. to give in large amounts [to heap gifts on one] 3. to fill (a plate, etc.) full or to overflowing —*vi.* to accumulate or rise in a heap or pile

**hear** (hir) *vt.* **heard** (hurd), **hear′ing** [OE. *hieran*] 1. to perceive or sense (sounds) by the ear 2. to listen to and consider; specif., a) to listen to carefully or officially [to hear a child's lesson] b) to conduct a hearing of (a law case, etc.); try c) to consent to; grant [hear my plea] 3. to be informed of; be told —*vi.* 1. to be able to hear sounds 2. to listen 3. to be told (of or about) —**hear from** to get a letter, telegram, etc. from —**hear! hear!** well said! —**not hear of** to forbid or refuse to consider —**hear′er** *n.*

**hear·ing** (-iŋ) *n.* 1. the act or process of perceiving sounds 2. the sense by which sounds are perceived 3. opportunity to speak, sing, etc.; audience 4. a court appearance before a judge, other than a trial 5. a formal meeting of an official body for hearing and gathering testimony, etc. 6. the distance a sound will carry [within hearing]

**hearing aid** a small, battery-powered electronic device worn to compensate for hearing loss

**heark·en** (här′kən) *vi.* [OE. *heorcnian* < *hieran,* to hear] to pay careful attention; listen carefully

**hear·say** (hir′sā′) *n.* something one has heard but does not know to be true; rumor; gossip —*adj.* based on hearsay

**hearse** (hurs) *n.* [< OFr. < L. *hirpex,* a harrow] a vehicle used in a funeral for carrying the corpse

**heart** (härt) *n.* [OE. *heorte*] 1. the hollow, muscular organ that circulates the blood by alternate dilation and contraction 2. any place or part centrally located like the heart [hearts of celery, the heart of the city] 3. the central, vital, or main part; essence; core 4. the human heart considered as the center of emotions, personality attributes, etc.; specif., a) innermost thought and feeling [to know in one's heart] b) one's emotional nature; disposition [to have a kind heart] c) any of various humane feelings; love, sympathy, etc. d) mood; feeling [to have a heavy heart] e) spirit or courage [to lose heart] 5. a loved one 6. a conventionalized design of a heart, shaped like this: ♡ 7. a) any of a suit of playing cards marked with such symbols in red b) [pl.] this suit of cards c) [pl.] a card game in which the object is to avoid getting hearts in the tricks taken —**after one's own heart** that pleases one perfectly — **at heart** in one's innermost nature —**break one's heart** to overwhelm one with grief or disappointment —**change of heart** a change of mind, affections, etc. —**eat one's heart out** to brood over some frustra-

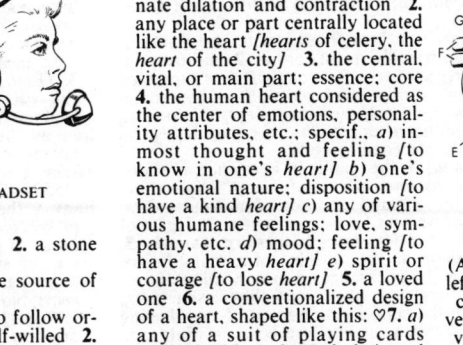

HUMAN HEART
(A, right atrium; B, left atrium; C, myocardium; D, right ventricle; E, inferior vena cava; F, pulmonary veins; G, pulmonary artery; H, superior vena cava; I, aorta; J, pulmonary artery; K, pulmonary veins; L, left ventricle)

—**by heart** by or from memorization

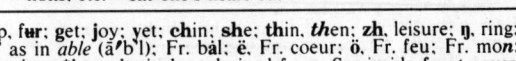

tion or in regret —**have one's heart in one's mouth** (or **boots**) to be full of fear or nervous anticipation —**have one's heart in the right place** to be well-meaning —**heart and soul** with all one's effort, enthusiasm, etc. —**lose one's heart (to)** to fall in love (with) —**set one's heart on** to have a fixed desire for —**take heart** to cheer up —**take to heart 1.** to consider seriously **2.** to be troubled by —**to one's heart's content** as much as one desires —**wear one's heart on one's sleeve** to show one's feelings plainly —**with all one's heart** with complete sincerity, devotion, etc.

**heart·ache** (-āk′) *n.* sorrow or grief

**heart·beat** (-bēt′) *n.* one pulsation, or full contraction and dilation, of the heart

**heart block** defective transmission of impulses regulating the heartbeat

**heart·break** (-brāk′) *n.* overwhelming sorrow, grief, or disappointment —**heart′break′ing** *adj.* —**heart′bro′ken** *adj.*

**heart·burn** (-burn′) *n.* a burning sensation beneath the breastbone resulting from a spastic backflow of acid stomach contents into the esophagus

**heart·ed** (-id) *adj.* having a (specified kind of) heart: used in compounds *[stouthearted]*

**heart·en** (-′n) *vt.* to cheer up; encourage

**heart failure** the inability of the heart to pump enough blood through the body

**heart·felt** (-felt′) *adj.* with or expressive of deep feeling; sincere

**hearth** (härth) *n.* [OE. *heorth*] **1.** the stone or brick floor of a fireplace **2.** *a)* the fireside *b)* the home **3.** the lowest part of a blast furnace, where the molten metal settles, or the floor of a furnace on which the ore or metal rests for exposure to the flame

**hearth·stone** (-stōn′) *n.* **1.** the stone forming a hearth **2.** the home, or home life

**heart·i·ly** (härt′′l ē) *adv.* **1.** in a sincere, cordial way **2.** with enthusiasm **3.** with zestful appetite **4.** completely; very

**heart·i·ness** (-ē nis) *n.* a being hearty

**heart·less** (-lis) *adj.* lacking kindness; hard and pitiless —**heart′less·ly** *adv.* —**heart′less·ness** *n.*

**heart-rend·ing** (-ren′din) *adj.* causing much grief or mental anguish —**heart′-rend′ing·ly** *adv.*

**hearts·ease, heart′s-ease** (härts′ēz′) *n.* **1.** peace of mind **2.** *same as* WILD PANSY

**heart·sick** (härt′sik′) *adj.* sick at heart; extremely unhappy or despondent: also **heart′sore′** (-sôr′)

**heart-strick·en** (-strik′′n) *adj.* deeply grieved or greatly dismayed: also **heart′-struck′** (-struk′)

**heart·strings** (-strinz′) *n.pl.* [orig. tendons or nerves formerly believed to brace and sustain the heart] deepest feelings or affections

**heart·throb** (-thräb′) *n.* **1.** *same as* HEARTBEAT **2.** [Old Slang] one's sweetheart

**heart-to-heart** (-tə härt′) *adj.* intimate and candid

**heart·warm·ing** (-wôr′min) *adj.* such as to kindle a warm glow of genial feelings

**heart·wood** (-wood′) *n.* the hard wood at the core of a tree trunk: cf. SAPWOOD

**heart·y** (-ē) *adj.* **heart′i·er, heart′i·est** [SEE HEART & -Y2] **1.** extremely warm and friendly; most cordial **2.** enthusiastic; wholehearted *[hearty support]* **3.** strongly felt or expressed *[a hearty dislike]* **4.** strong and healthy **5.** *a)* nourishing and plentiful *[a hearty meal]* *b)* liking plenty of food *[a hearty eater]* —*n., pl.* **heart′ies** [Archaic] a comrade; esp., a fellow sailor (usually preceded by *my*)

**heat** (hēt) *n.* [OE. *hætu*] **1.** the quality of being hot; hotness: in physics, heat is considered a form of energy whose effect is produced by the accelerated vibration of molecules **2.** *a)* much hotness; great warmth *b) same as* FEVER **3.** degree of hotness or warmth **4.** a feeling of hotness or warmth **5.** hot weather or climate **6.** the warming of a room, house, etc., as by a furnace **7.** appearance as an indication of hotness *[blue heat in metals]* **8.** *a)* strong feeling; excitement, ardor, anger, etc. *b)* the period or condition of such feeling *[in the heat of battle]* **9.** a single effort, bout, or trial; esp., a preliminary round of a race, etc. **10.** *a)* sexual excitement *b)* the period of this in animals; esp., the estrus of females **11.** *Metallurgy* a single heating, as of metal, in a furnace or forge **12.** [Slang] *a)* coercion *b)* great pressure, as in criminal investigation —*vt., vi.* **1.** to make or become warm or hot **2.** to make or become excited

**heat·ed** (hēt′id) *adj.* **1.** hot **2.** vehement, impassioned, or angry —**heat′ed·ly** *adv.*

**heat·er** (-ər) *n.* a stove, furnace, radiator, etc. for heating a room, car, water, etc.

**heat exchanger** any device for transferring heat to a cooler medium from a warmer one

**heat exhaustion** a mild form of heatstroke, characterized by faintness, dizziness, heavy sweating, etc.

**heath** (hēth) *n.* [OE. *hæth*] **1.** a tract of open wasteland, esp.

in the British Isles, covered with heather, low shrubs, etc. **2.** any of various shrubs and plants that grow on heaths, as heather —*adj.* designating a family of woody plants, including the blueberry, cranberry, azalea, etc.

**heath·bird** (-burd′) *n. same as* BLACK GROUSE

**hea·then** (hē′thən) *n., pl.* **-thens, -then** [OE. *hæthen*] orig., a member of any people not worshiping the God of Israel **2.** anyone not a Jew, Christian, or Moslem **3.** a person regarded as uncivilized, irreligious, etc. —*adj.* **1.** of heathens; pagan **2.** irreligious, uncivilized, etc. —**hea′then·dom** *n.* —**hea′then·ish** *adj.* —**hea′then·ism** *n.*

**hea·then·ize** (-īz′) *vt., vi.* **-ized′, -iz′ing** to make or become heathen

**heath·er** (heth′ər) *n.* [altered (after HEATH) < ME. *haddyr*] a low-growing plant of the heath family, common in the British Isles, with stalks of small, bell-shaped, purplish-pink flowers —*adj.* like heather in color or appearance —**heath′er·y** *adj.*

**heat lightning** lightning without thunder, seen near the horizon, esp. on hot summer evenings

**heat prostration** *same as* HEAT EXHAUSTION

**heat pump** a device for cooling an enclosed space by pumping hot air out, and for warming it by extracting heat from outdoor air or some other source and pumping it in

**heat rash** *same as* PRICKLY HEAT

**heat·stroke** (hēt′strōk′) *n.* a condition resulting from excessive exposure to intense heat, characterized by high fever and collapse

HEATHER

**heat wave 1.** unusually hot weather, resulting from a slowly moving air mass of relatively high temperature **2.** a period of such weather

**heaume** (hōm) *n.* [Fr. < OFr. *helme*; see HELMET] a heavy helmet worn in the Middle Ages

**heave** (hēv) *vt.* **heaved** or (esp. *Naut.*) **hove, heav′ing** [< OE. *hebban*] **1.** to raise or lift, esp. with effort **2.** to lift in this way and throw **3.** to make rise or swell **4.** to utter (a sigh, etc.) with great effort **5.** *Naut. a)* to raise, haul, etc. by pulling with a rope or cable *b)* to move (a ship) in a specified manner or direction —*vi.* **1.** to swell up; bulge out **2.** to rise and fall rhythmically **3.** *a)* to retch or vomit *b)* to pant; breathe hard; gasp **4.** *Naut. a)* to tug or haul (on or at a cable, rope, etc.) *b)* to proceed; move *[a ship hove into sight]* —*n.* the act or effort of heaving —**heave ho!** pull hard! —**heave to 1.** *Naut.* to stop forward movement **2.** to stop —**heav′er** *n.*

**heav·en** (hev′'n) *n.* [OE. *heofon*] **1.** [*usually pl.*] the space surrounding the earth; firmament **2.** *Theol. a)* [*often H-*] the place where God is and where the blessed go after death *b)* [H-] God; Providence **3.** *a)* any place of great beauty and pleasure *b)* a state of great happiness —**move heaven and earth** to do all that can be done

**heav·en·ly** (-lē) *adj.* **1.** of or in the heavens *[the sun is a heavenly body]* **2.** *a)* causing or marked by great happiness, beauty, etc. *b)* [Colloq.] very pleasing, attractive, etc. **3.** *Theol.* of or in heaven; holy; divine —**heav′en·li·ness** *n.*

**heav·en·ward** (-wərd) *adv., adj.* toward heaven: also **heav′en·wards** *adv.*

**heaves** (hēvz) *n.pl.* [*with sing. v.*] a respiratory disease of horses, marked by coughing, heaving of the flanks, etc.

**Heav·i·side layer** (hev′ē sīd′) [after O. *Heaviside* (1850-1925), Eng. physicist] *same as* E LAYER

**heav·y** (hev′ē) *adj.* **heav′i·er, heav′i·est** [OE. *hefig* < base of *hebban*, to heave + *-ig*, -Y2] **1.** hard to lift or move because of great weight; weighty **2.** of concentrated weight for the size **3.** above the usual or a defined weight **4.** larger, greater, rougher, more intense, etc. than usual *[a heavy blow, a heavy vote, a heavy thunder, heavy features]* **5.** being such to an unusual extent *[a heavy drinker]* **6.** serious; grave *[a heavy responsibility]* **7.** hard to endure *[heavy demands]* **8.** hard to do or manage *[heavy work]* **9.** hard to bear *[heavy sorrow]* **10.** sorrowful *[a heavy heart]* **11.** burdened with sleep or fatigue *[heavy eyelids]* **12.** hard to digest *[a heavy meal]* **13.** not leavened properly *[a heavy cake]* **14.** clinging; penetrating *[a heavy odor]* **15.** cloudy; gloomy *[a heavy sky]* **16.** tedious; dull **17.** clumsy; awkward *[a heavy gait]* **18.** steeply inclined *[a heavy grade]* **19.** designating any large, basic industry that uses massive machinery **20.** heavily armed **21.** *Chem.* designating an isotope of greater atomic weight than the normal or most abundant isotope **22.** *Theater* serious, tragic, or villainous —*adv.* heavily *[heavy-laden]* —*n., pl.* **heav′ies 1.** something heavy **2.** *Theater a)* a serious, tragic, or villainous role *b)* an actor who plays such roles —**hang heavy** ( **on one's hands** ) to pass slowly; drag: said of time

—**heavy with child** pregnant —**heav′i·ly** adv. —**heav′i·ness** n.

**heav·y·du·ty** (-dōōt′ē, -dyōōt′ē) adj. made to withstand great strain, bad weather, etc.

**heav·y·hand·ed** (-han′did) adj. **1.** clumsy or tactless **2.** cruel; tyrannical —**heav′y-hand′ed·ly** adv. —**heav′y-hand′ed·ness** n.

**heav·y·heart·ed** (-här′tid) adj. sad; depressed —**heav′y-heart′ed·ly** adv. —**heav′y-heart′ed·ness** n.

**heavy hydrogen** same as DEUTERIUM

**heav·y·set** (-set′) adj. stout or stocky in build

**heavy spar** same as BARITE

**heavy water** water composed of isotopes of hydrogen of atomic weight greater than one or of oxygen greater than 16, or of both; esp., deuterium oxide

**heav·y·weight** (-wāt′) n. **1.** a person or animal weighing much more than average **2.** a boxer or wrestler who weighs over 175 pounds **3.** [Colloq.] a very intelligent or important person

**Heb. 1.** Hebrew **2.** Hebrews

**heb·dom·a·dal** (heb däm′ə dəl) adj. [< L. < Gr. hebdomas, seven (days) < hepta, seven] weekly —**heb·dom′a·dal·ly** adv.

**He·be** (hē′bē) Gr. Myth. the goddess of youth: she was a cupbearer to the gods

**He·bra·ic** (hi brā′ik) adj. of or characteristic of the Hebrews, their language, culture, etc.; Hebrew —**He·bra′i·cal·ly** adv.

**He·bra·ism** (hē′bri iz′m, -brā-) n. **1.** a Hebrew idiom, custom, etc. **2.** the characteristic ethical system, moral attitude, etc. of the Hebrews —**He′bra·ist** n. —**He′bra·is′tic** adj.

**He·brew** (hē′brōō) n. [< OFr., ult. < Heb. 'ibhri, lit., one from across (the river)] **1.** any member of a group of Semitic peoples tracing descent from Abraham, Isaac, and Jacob; specif., an Israelite: in modern, but not recent, usage interchangeable with Jew **a)** the ancient Semitic language of the Israelites, in which most of the Old Testament was written **b)** its modern form, the official language of Israel —adj. **1.** of Hebrew or the Hebrews **2.** same as JEWISH

**Hebrew calendar** same as JEWISH CALENDAR

**He·brews** (-brōōz) Bible the Epistle to the Hebrews, a book of the New Testament

**Heb·ri·des** (heb′rə dēz′) Scottish island group off W Scotland —**Heb′ri·de′an** (-dē′ən) adj., n.

**Hec·a·te** (hek′ə tē; occas. hek′it) Gr. Myth. a goddess of the moon, earth, and underworld, later regarded as the goddess of sorcery

**hec·a·tomb** (hek′ə tōm′, -tōōm′) n. [< L. < Gr. < hekaton, a hundred + bous, ox] **1.** in ancient Greece, the mass slaughter of 100 cattle as an offering to the gods **2.** any large-scale slaughter

**heck** (hek) interj., n. [Colloq.] a euphemism for HELL

**heck·le** (hek′′l) vt. -led, -ling [ME. < hechele: see HACKLE¹] to annoy or harass (a speaker, etc.) by interrupting with questions or taunts —**heck′ler** n.

**hec·tare** (hek′ter) n. [Fr.: see HECTO- & ARE²] a metric measure of surface, equal to 10,000 square meters (100 ares or 2.471 acres)

**hec·tic** (hek′tik) adj. [< OFr. < LL. < Gr. hektikos, habitual] **1.** of or characteristic of a wasting disease, as tuberculosis, or the fever accompanying this **2.** feverish or flushed **3.** full of confusion, rush, excitement, etc. —**hec′ti·cal·ly** adv.

**hec·to-** [Fr. < Gr. hekaton, a hundred] a combining form meaning a hundred

**hec·to·gram** (hek′tə gram′) n. [< Fr.: see prec. & GRAM] a metric measure of weight, equal to 100 grams (3.527 ounces)

**hec·to·graph** (-graf′) n. [< G. < hekto-, HECTO- + -graph, -GRAPH] a duplicating device by which written or typed matter is transferred to a sheet of gelatin, from which many copies can be taken —vt. to duplicate by means of a hectograph

**Hec·tor** (hek′tər) Gr. Myth. a Trojan hero killed by Achilles: he was Priam's son

**hec·tor** (hek′tər) n. [< prec.] a swaggering fellow; bully —vt., vi. to browbeat; bully

**Hec·u·ba** (hek′yōō bə) Gr. Myth. wife of Priam and mother of Hector, Paris, and Cassandra

**he'd** (hēd) **1.** he had **2.** he would

**hedge** (hej) n. [OE. hecg] **1.** a row of closely planted shrubs, bushes, etc. forming a boundary or fence **2.** any fence or barrier **3.** the act of hedging —adj. **1.** of, in, or near a hedge **2.** low, disreputable, etc. —vt. **hedged, hedg′ing 1.** to place a hedge around or along **2.** to hinder or guard as with a barrier; hem in **3.** to try to avoid

loss in (a bet, risk, etc.) by making counterbalancing bets, etc. —vi. to refuse to commit oneself; avoid direct answers —**hedg′er** n.

**hedge·hog** (hej′hôg′, -häg′) n. **1.** a small, insect-eating, old-world mammal, with sharp spines on the back, which bristle and form a defense when the animal curls up **2.** the American porcupine

**hedge·hop** (-häp′) vi. **-hopped′, -hop′ping** [Colloq.] to fly an airplane very close to the ground, as for spraying insecticide —**hedge′hop′per** n.

**hedge·row** (-rō′) n. a row of shrubs, bushes, etc., forming a hedge

**he·do·nism** (hēd′′n iz'm) n. [< Gr. hēdonē, pleasure] **1.** the doctrine that pleasure or happiness is the principal good and the proper aim of action **2.** pleasure-seeking as a way of life —**he′do·nist** n. —**he′do·nis′tic** adj. —**he′do·nis′ti·cal·ly** adv.

**-he·dral** (hē′drəl) a combining form used to form adjectives from nouns ending in -HEDRON

**-he·dron** (hē′drən) [< Gr. < hedra, a side, base] a combining form meaning a geometric figure or crystal with (a specified number of) surfaces

**heed** (hēd) vt., vi. [OE. hedan] to pay close attention (to); take careful notice (of) —n. close attention; careful notice —**heed′ful** adj. —**heed′ful·ly** adv.

**heed·less** (-lis) adj. not taking heed; careless; unmindful —**heed′less·ly** adv. —**heed′less·ness** n.

**hee·haw** (hē′hô′) n., vi. [echoic] same as BRAY

**heel¹** (hēl) n. [OE. hela] **1.** the back part of the human foot, under the ankle **2.** the corresponding part of the hind foot of an animal **3.** that part of a stocking, etc. which covers the heel **4.** the built-up part of a shoe, supporting the heel **5.** anything like the human heel in location, shape, or function, as the end of a loaf of bread **6.** [Colloq.] a despicable person; cad —vt. **1.** to furnish with a heel **2.** to follow closely at the rear of **3.** to touch or drive forward as with the heel **4.** [Colloq.] to provide (a person) with money —vi. to follow along at the heels of someone —**at heel** just behind —**cool one's heels** [Colloq.] to be kept waiting for some time —**down at the heel(s) 1.** with the heels of one's shoes worn down **2.** shabby; seedy —**kick up one's heels** to have fun —**on** (or **upon**) **the heels of** close behind —**out at the heel(s) 1.** having holes in the heels of one's shoes or socks **2.** shabby; seedy —**take to one's heels** to run away: also **show one's heels** —**to heel 1.** just behind **2.** under control —**turn on one's heel** to turn around abruptly —**heel′less** adj.

**heel²** (hēl) vi. [OE. hieldan] to lean to one side; list: said esp. of a ship —vt. to make (a ship) list —n. the act or extent of heeling

**heeled** (hēld) adj. [Colloq.] **1.** having money **2.** armed, esp. with a gun

**heel·er** (hē′lər) n. **1.** one that heels **2.** [Colloq.] same as WARD HEELER

**heel·tap** (hēl′tap′) n. **1.** a layer of leather, etc. serving as a lift in the heel of a shoe **2.** a bit of liquor left in a glass after drinking

**heft** (heft) n. [< base of HEAVE] [Colloq.] **1.** weight; heaviness **2.** importance; influence —vt. [Colloq.] **1.** to lift or heave **2.** to estimate the weight of by lifting —vi. [Colloq.] to weigh

**heft·y** (hef′tē) adj. **heft′i·er, heft′i·est** [Colloq.] **1.** weighty; heavy **2.** large and powerful **3.** big or fairly big —**heft′i·ly** adv. —**heft′i·ness** n.

**He·gel** (hā′gəl), **Ge·org Wil·helm Frie·drich** (gā ôrkh′vil′helm frē′driH) 1770-1831; Ger. philosopher —**He·ge′li·an** (-gā′lē ən, hi jē′-) adj., n. —**He·ge′li·an·ism** n.

**he·gem·o·ny** (hi jem′ə nē; hej′ə mō′nē) n., pl. **-nies** [< Gr. < hēgemōn, leader] leadership or dominance, esp. of one nation over others

**he·gi·ra** (hi jī′rə, hej′ər ə) n. [ML. < Ar. hijrah, lit., flight] **1.** [often H-] the forced journey of Mohammed from Mecca to Medina in 622 A.D.: the Moslem era dates from this event **2.** any journey for safety or as an escape; flight

**Hei·del·berg** (hīd′'l burg′; G. hī′dəl berkh′) city in SW West Germany: site of a famous university (founded 1386): pop. 122,000

**heif·er** (hef′ər) n. [OE. heahfore] a young cow that has not borne a calf

**heigh** (hī, hā) interj. an exclamation to attract notice, show pleasure, express surprise, etc.

**heigh-ho** (-hō′) interj. an exclamation of mild surprise, boredom, fatigue, etc.

**height** (hīt, occas. colloq. hīth) n. [OE. heihthu < heah, high] **1.** the topmost point of anything **2.** the highest limit or degree; extreme **3.** the distance from the bottom to the top **4.** elevation or distance above a given level, as above the surface of the earth or sea; altitude **5.** a relatively great distance above a given level or from bottom to top **6.** [*often pl.*] a high place; eminence

**height·en** (hīt'ʼn) *vt., vi.* **1.** to bring or come to a higher position **2.** to make or become larger, greater, etc.; increase —**height'en·er** *n.*

**Hei·ne** (hī'nə), **Hein·rich** (hīn'riH) 1797–1856; Ger. poet & essayist

**hei·nous** (hā'nəs) *adj.* [< OFr. < *haine*, hatred < Frank.] outrageously evil or wicked; abominable —**hei'nous·ly** *adv.* —**hei'nous·ness** *n.*

**heir** (er) *n.* [< OFr. < L. *heres*] **1.** a person who inherits or is entitled to inherit another's property or title upon the other's death **2.** a person who appears to get some trait from a predecessor or to carry on in his tradition —**heir'dom, heir'ship'** *n.*

**heir apparent** *pl.* **heirs apparent** the heir whose right to a certain property or title cannot be denied if he outlives the ancestor

**heir·ess** (-is) *n.* a woman or girl who is an heir, esp. to great wealth

**heir·loom** (-lōōm') *n.* [HEIR + LOOM¹] **1.** a piece of personal property that goes to an heir **2.** any treasured possession handed down from generation to generation

**heir presumptive** *pl.* **heirs presumptive** an heir whose right to a certain property or title will be lost if someone more closely related is born before the ancestor dies

**heist** (hīst) *n.* [< HOIST] [Slang] a robbery or holdup —*vt.* [Slang] to rob or steal **2.** *dial. var. of* HOIST —**heist'er** *n.*

**He·jaz** (he jaz', hē-; -jäz') district of NW Saudi Arabia: formerly a kingdom: c. 150,000 sq. mi.

**he·ji·ra** (hi jī'rə, hej'ər ə) *n. same as* HEGIRA

**Hek·a·te** (hek'ə tē) *same as* HECATE

**hek·to-** *same as* HECTO-

**held** (held) *pt. & pp. of* HOLD¹

**Hel·en** (hel'ən) [< OFr. < L. < Gr. *Helenē*, lit., torch] a feminine name

**Hel·e·na** (hel'i nə; *also, for 1,* hə lē'nə) **1.** [var. of prec.] a feminine name **2.** [prob. ult. after *Helena* (?–338 A.D.), mother of CONSTANTINE I] capital of Mont.: pop. 24,000

**Helen of Troy** *Gr. Legend* the beautiful wife of Menelaus, king of Sparta: the Trojan War was started because Paris abducted her and took her to Troy

**hel·i·cal** (hel'i kəl, hē'lə-) *adj.* of, or having the form of, a helix; spiral —**hel'i·cal·ly** *adv.*

**hel·i·ces** (hel'ə sēz', hē'lə-) *n. alt. pl. of* HELIX

**hel·i·coid** (hel'ə koid', hē'lə-) *adj.* [< Gr. < *helix*, a spiral + *eidos*, form] shaped like a spiral; coiled: also **hel'i·coi'dal** —*n. Geom.* a spiral or screw-shaped surface

**Hel·i·con** (hel'ə kän', -kən) mountain group in SC Greece: in Greek mythology, the home of the Muses —*n.* [prob. < Gr. *helix*, a spiral: from the shape] [h-] a brass-wind instrument, similar to a bass tuba

**hel·i·cop·ter** (hel'ə käp'tər, hē'lə-) *n.* [< Fr. < Gr. *helix*, a spiral + *pteron*, wing] a kind of aircraft moved in any direction, or kept hovering, by large, rotary blades (*rotors*) mounted horizontally —*vi., vt.* to travel or convey by helicopter

**he·li·o-** [L. < Gr. < *hēlios*, the sun] *a combining form meaning* the sun, bright, radiant: also **heli-**

**he·li·o·cen·tric** (hē'lē ō sen'trik) *adj.* [HELIO- + -CENTRIC] **1.** calculated from, or viewed as from, the center of the sun **2.** having or regarding the sun as the center

**he·li·o·graph** (hē'lē ə graf') *n.* [HELIO- + -GRAPH] a device for sending a message (**heliogram**) or signaling by flashing the sun's rays from a mirror —*vt., vi.* to signal or communicate by heliograph —**he'li·og'ra·pher** (-äg'rə fər) *n.* —**he'li·o·graph'ic** *adj.* —**he'li·og'ra·phy** *n.*

**He·li·os** (hē'lē äs') *Gr. Myth.* the sun god

**he·li·o·trope** (hē'lē ə trōp', hēl'yə-) *n.* [< Fr. < L. < Gr. < *hēlios* (see HELIO-) + *trepein*, to turn] **1.** formerly, a sunflower **2.** a plant with fragrant clusters of small, white or reddish-purple flowers **3.** reddish purple **4.** *same as* BLOODSTONE —*adj.* reddish-purple

**he·li·ot·ro·pism** (hē'lē ät'rə piz'm) *n.* the tendency of certain plants or other organisms to turn toward or from light, esp. sunlight —**he'li·o·trop'ic** (-ə träp'ik) *adj.* —**he'li·o·trop'i·cal·ly** *adv.*

**hel·i·port** (hel'ə pôrt') *n.* [HELI(COPTER) + (AIR)PORT] a flat place where helicopters land and take off

**he·li·um** (hē'lē əm) *n.* [ModL. < Gr. *hēlios*, the sun] one of the chemical elements, a very light, inert, colorless gas: it is used for inflating balloons, etc.: symbol, He; at. wt., 4.0026; at. no., 2

**he·lix** (hē'liks) *n., pl.* **-lix·es, -li·ces'** (hel'ə sēz', hē'lə-) [L. < Gr., a spiral < *helissein*, to turn around] **1.** any spiral, either lying in a single plane or, esp., moving around a cone, cylinder, etc. as a screw thread does **2.** the folded rim of cartilage around the outer ear **3.** *Archit.* an ornamental spiral

**hell** (hel) *n.* [OE. *hel* < base of *helan*, to hide] **1.** *Bible* the place where the spirits of the dead are **2.** [*often* H-] *a*) *Christianity* the place to which sinners and unbelievers go

after death for punishment *b*) those in hell *c*) the powers of evil or darkness **3.** any place or condition of evil, pain, cruelty, etc. **4.** [Colloq.] *a*) any very disagreeable experience *b*) devilishness [*full of hell*] —*vi.* [Slang] to live or act in a reckless or dissolute way (often with *around*) —*interj.* an exclamation of irritation, anger, emphasis, etc.: regarded as profanity —**be hell on** [Slang] **1.** to be very difficult or painful for **2.** to be very strict with **3.** to be very damaging to —**catch** (or **get**) **hell** [Slang] to receive a severe scolding, punishment, etc. —**for the hell of it** [Slang] for no serious reason

**he'll** (hēl; *unstressed* hil, il) **1.** he will **2.** he shall

**hell·bend·er** (hel'ben'dər) *n.* a large, edible salamander, found esp. in the Ohio valley

**hell·bent** (-bent') *adj.* [Slang] **1.** firmly or recklessly determined **2.** moving fast or recklessly

**hell·cat** (-kat') *n.* **1.** a witch **2.** an evil, spiteful, bad-tempered woman

**hell·div·er** (-dī'vər) *n.* the American dabchick

**hel·le·bore** (hel'ə bôr') *n.* [< OFr. < L. < Gr. *helleboros*, orig. prob. "plant eaten by fawns"] **1.** any of a group of winter-blooming plants of the buttercup family, with flowers shaped like buttercups but of various colors **2.** any of a group of plants of the lily family **3.** the poisonous rhizomes of certain of these plants that have been used in medicine

**Hel·lene** (hel'ēn) *n.* [< Gr.] a Greek

**Hel·len·ic** (hə len'ik, he-) *adj.* **1.** of the Hellenes; Greek **2.** of the history, language, or culture of the ancient Greeks from the late 8th century B.C. to the death of Alexander the Great (323 B.C.) —*n.* the language of ancient Greece

**Hel·len·ism** (hel'ən iz'm) *n.* **1.** a Greek phrase, idiom, or custom **2.** the character, thought, culture, or ethics of ancient Greece **3.** adoption of the Greek language, customs, etc. —**Hel'len·ist** *n.*

**Hel·len·is·tic** (hel'ə nis'tik) *adj.* **1.** of or characteristic of Hellenism **2.** of Greek history, culture, etc. after the death of Alexander the Great (323 B.C.) —**Hel'len·is'ti·cal·ly** *adv.*

**Hel·len·ize** (hel'ə nīz') *vt., vi.* **-ized', -iz'ing** to make or become Greek, as in customs, ideals, etc. —**Hel'len·i·za'tion** *n.* —**Hel'len·iz'er** *n.*

**Hel·les·pont** (hel'əs pänt') *ancient name of the* DARDANELLES

**hell·fire** (hel'fīr') *n.* the fire or torment of hell

**hel·lion** (hel'yən) *n.* [Colloq.] a person fond of deviltry; mischievous troublemaker

**hell·ish** (hel'ish) *adj.* **1.** of, from, or like hell **2.** devilish; fiendish **3.** [Colloq.] very unpleasant; detestable —**hell'ish·ly** *adv.* —**hell'ish·ness** *n.*

**hel·lo** (he lō', hə lō', hel'ō) *interj.* [var. of HOLLO] an exclamation *a*) of greeting or of response, as in telephoning *b*) to attract attention *c*) of surprise —*n., pl.* **-los** a saying of "hello" —*vi., vt.* **-loed', -lo'ing** to say "hello" (to)

**helm¹** (helm) *n., or* [OE.] *archaic var. of* HELMET

**helm²** (helm) *n.* [OE. *helma*] **1.** the wheel or tiller or, with the rudder, etc., all the gear by which a ship is steered **2.** the control or leadership, as of an organization —*vt.* to guide; steer

**hel·met** (hel'mət) *n.* [OFr., dim. of *helme*, helmet < Frank.] **1.** a hard, protective head covering, variously designed for use in combat, certain sports, diving, etc. **2.** something like such a head covering in appearance or function —*vt.* to equip with a helmet —**hel'met·ed** *adj.*

**hel·minth** (hel'minth) *n.* [Gr. *helmins* (gen. *helminthos*)] a worm or wormlike animal; esp., a parasite of the intestine, as the tapeworm, hookworm, or roundworm —**hel·min·thic** (hel min'thik) *adj.*

**helms·man** (helmz'mən) *n., pl.* **-men** the man at the helm; person who steers a ship

**Hé·lo·ïse** (ā lô ēz'; E. hel'ə wēz') 1101?–64?; mistress and, later, wife of her teacher, Pierre ABÉLARD

**Hel·ot** (hel'ət, hē'lət) *n.* [< L. < Gr. *Heilōtes*, serfs] a member of the lowest class of serfs in ancient Sparta **2.** [h-] any serf or slave —**hel'ot·ism** *n.* —**hel'ot·ry** *n.*

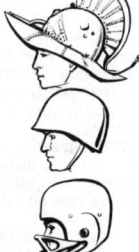

HELMETS

**help** (help) *vt.* [OE. *helpan*] **1.** to make things easier or better for (a person); aid; assist; specif., *a*) to give (one in need) relief, money, etc. *b*) to share the labor of [*help* us lift this] *c*) to aid in getting (*up, down, in, to, into, out of,* etc.) **2.** to make it easier for (something) to exist, happen, improve, etc.; promote **3.** to remedy; relieve [this will *help* your cough] **4.** *a*) to keep from; avoid [she can't *help* crying] *b*) to stop, prevent, change, etc. [faults that can't be *helped*] **5.** to serve or wait on (a customer), etc.) —*vi.* **1.** to give assistance; be useful or beneficial **2.** to act as a waiter, clerk, etc. —*n.* **1.** a helping; aid; assistance **2.** relief; remedy **3.** *a)* a hired helper, as a servant, farmhand, etc. *b)* hired helpers; employees —**cannot help but** to be compelled or obliged to —**cannot help oneself** to be the victim of circumstances, a habit, etc. —**help oneself to 1.** to serve oneself with (food, etc.) **2.** to steal —**help out** to help in getting or doing something —**so help me** (God) as God is my witness: used in oaths —**help′er** *n.*

**help·ful** (-fəl) *adj.* giving help; useful —**help′ful·ly** *adv.* —**help′ful·ness** *n.*

**help·ing** (-iŋ) *n.* **1.** a giving of aid; assisting **2.** a portion of food served to one person

**help·less** (-lis) *adj.* **1.** not able to help oneself; weak **2.** lacking help or protection **3.** incompetent; ineffective —**help′less·ly** *adv.* —**help′less·ness** *n.*

**help·mate** (-māt′) *n.* [altered < ff.] a helpful companion; specif., a wife or husband

**help·meet** (-mēt′) *n.* [misreading of "an *help meet* for him" (Gen. 2:18)] *same as* HELPMATE

**Hel·sin·ki** (hel′siŋ kē) capital of Finland; seaport on the Gulf of Finland; pop. 527,000

**hel·ter-skel·ter** (hel′tər skel′tər) *adv.* [arbitrary formation] in haste and confusion; in a disorderly, hurried manner —*adj.* hurried and confused; disorderly —*n.* anything helter-skelter

**helve** (helv) *n.* [OE. *helfe*] the handle of a tool, esp. of an ax or hatchet —*vt.* **helved, helv′ing** to put a helve on

**Hel·ve·tia** (hel vē′shə) *Latin name of* SWITZERLAND —**Helve′tian** *adj., n.*

**hem¹** (hem) *n.* [OE.] **1.** the border on a garment or piece of cloth, usually made by folding the edge and sewing it down **2.** any border or edge —*vt.* **hemmed, hem′ming** to fold back the edge of and sew down —**hem in** (or **around** or **about**) **1.** to encircle; surround **2.** to confine or restrain —**hem′mer** *n.*

**hem²** (hem; *conventionalized pronun.*) *interj., n.* the sound made in clearing the throat —*vi.* **hemmed, hem′ming 1.** to make this sound, as to get attention or show doubt **2.** to grope about in speech, seeking the right words: usually in **hem and haw**

**he-man** (hē′man′) *n.* [Colloq.] a strong, virile man

**hem·a·tite** (hem′ə tīt′, hē′mə-) *n.* [< L. < Gr. *haimatitēs*, bloodlike < *haima*, blood] native ferric oxide, Fe₂O₃, an important iron ore, brownish red or black —**hem′a·tit′ic** (-tit′ik) *adj.*

**hem·a·to-** [< Gr. *haima* (gen. *haimatos*), blood] *a combining form meaning* blood: also **hemat-**

**hem·a·to·crit** (hi mat′ə krit′) *n.* [< HEMATO- + Gr. *kritēs*, a judge] **1.** a centrifuge for measuring the relative volumes of blood cells and fluid in blood **2.** the proportion of blood cells to a volume of blood so measured: also **hematocrit reading**

**he·ma·tol·o·gy** (hē′mə täl′ə jē, hem′ə-) *n.* the study of blood and its diseases —**he′ma·to·log′ic** (-tə läj′ik), **he′ma·to·log′i·cal** *adj.* —**he′ma·tol′o·gist** *n.*

**he·ma·to·ma** (-tō′mə) *n., pl.* **-mas, -ma·ta** (-tə) [ModL.: see HEMAT(O)- & -OMA] a local swelling or tumor filled with bloody fluid

**hem·er·a·lo·pi·a** (hem′ər ə lō′pē ə) *n.* [ModL. < Gr. < *hēmera*, day + *alaos*, blind + *ōps*, eye + -IA] an eye defect in which vision is reduced in bright light —**hem′er·a·lop′ic** (-läp′ik) *adj.*

**hem·i-** [Gr. *hēmi-*] *a prefix meaning* half

**hem·i·dem·i·sem·i·qua·ver** (hem′ē dem′ē sem′ē-kwä′vər) *n.* [Brit.] *same as* SIXTY-FOURTH NOTE

**Hem·ing·way** (hem′iŋ wā′), **Ernest** (**Miller**) 1899–1961; U.S. novelist & short-story writer

**he·mip·ter·an** (hi mip′tər ən) *n.* [< ModL.: see HEMI- & PTERO-] any of a group of insects, including bedbugs, lice, aphids, etc., with piercing and sucking mouthparts —**hemip′ter·ous** *adj.*

**hem·i·sphere** (hem′ə sfir′) *n.* [< L. < Gr.: see HEMI- & SPHERE] **1.** half of a sphere or globe **2.** *a)* one of the halves of the earth: the Northern, Southern, Eastern, or Western Hemisphere *b)* a model or map of any of these halves —**hem′i·spher′i·cal** (-sfer′i kəl), **hem′i·spher′ic** *adj.* —**hem′i·spher′i·cal·ly** *adv.*

**hem·i·stich** (hem′i stik′) *n.* [< L. < Gr. < *hēmi-*, half + *stichos*, a line] **1.** half a line of verse, esp. as divided by the caesura **2.** a metrically short line of verse

**hem·line** (hem′līn′) *n.* the bottom edge of a dress, coat, etc., where the edge meets the leg

**hem·lock** (hem′läk′) *n.* [OE. *hymlic*] **1.** *a)* a poisonous European plant of the parsley family, with small white flowers: also **poison hemlock** *b)* a poison made from this plant **2.** *a)* an evergreen tree of the pine family, with short, flat needles: the bark is used in tanning *b)* the wood of this tree

**he·mo-** [< Gr. < *haima*, blood] *a combining form meaning* blood [*hemoglobin*]: also **hem-**

**he·mo·cy·tom·e·ter** (hē′mō sī täm′ə tər, hem′ō-) *n.* [HEMO- + CYTO- + -METER] a device for counting the number of cells in a sample of blood

**he·mo·glo·bin** (hē′mə glō′bin, hem′ə-; hē′mə glō′bin, hem′ə-) *n.* [contr. < *haematoglobulin*: see HEMATO- & GLOBULIN] the red coloring matter of the red blood corpuscles: it carries oxygen from the lungs to the tissues, and carbon dioxide from the tissues to the lungs —**he′mo·glo′bin·ous** *adj.*

**he·mol·y·sis** (hi mäl′ə sis) *n.* [HEMO- + -LYSIS] the destruction of red corpuscles with liberation of hemoglobin into the surrounding fluid —**he·mo·lyt·ic** (hē′mə lit′ik, hem′ə-) *adj.*

**he·mo·phil·i·a** (hē′mə fil′ē ə, hem′ə-; -fil′yə) *n.* [ModL.: see HEMO-, -PHILE, & -IA] a hereditary condition in which one of the normal blood-clotting factors is absent, causing prolonged bleeding from even minor cuts —**he′mo·phil′i·ac** (-fil′ē ak, -fil′yak) *n.*

**hem·or·rhage** (hem′ər ij, hem′rij) *n.* [< Fr. < L. < Gr. < *haima*, blood + *rhēgnynai*, to break] the escape of large quantities of blood from a blood vessel; heavy bleeding —*vi.* **-rhaged, -rhag·ing** to have a hemorrhage —**hem′or·rhag′ic** (-ə raj′ik) *adj.*

**hem·or·rhoid** (hem′ə roid′, hem′roid) *n.* [< L. < Gr. < *haima*, blood + *rhein*, to flow] a painful swelling of a vein in the region of the anus, often with bleeding: *usually used in pl.* —**hem′or·rhoid′al** *adj.*

**he·mo·stat** (hē′mə stat′, hem′ə-) *n.* [HEMO- + -STAT] anything used to stop bleeding; specif., a clamplike instrument used in surgery

**hemp** (hemp) *n.* [OE. *hænep*] **1.** *a)* a tall Asiatic plant having tough fiber in its stem *b)* the fiber, used to make rope, sailcloth, etc. *c)* a substance, such as marijuana, hashish, etc., made from the leaves and flowers of this plant **2.** *a)* any of various plants yielding a hemplike fiber, as sisal *b)* this fiber —**hemp′en** *adj.*

**hem·stitch** (hem′stich′) *n.* **1.** an ornamental stitch, used esp. at a hem, made by pulling out several parallel threads and tying the cross threads into small bunches **2.** decorative needlework done with this stitch —*vt.* to put hemstitches on —**hem′stitch′er** *n.* —**hem′stitch′ing** *n.*

**hen** (hen) *n.* [< OE. *henn*, fem. of *hana*, rooster] **1.** the female of the chicken (the domestic fowl) **2.** the female of various other birds

HEMSTITCH

**hen·bane** (-bān′) *n.* a coarse, hairy, foul-smelling, poisonous plant of the nightshade family, used in medicine

**hence** (hens) *adv.* [< OE. *heonan*, from here + -(e)s, adv. gen. suffix] **1.** from this place; away [go *hence*] **2.** *a)* from this time [a year *hence*] *b)* thereafter; subsequently **3.** from this life **4.** for this reason; therefore —*interj.* [Archaic] go away! —**hence with** [Archaic] away with!

**hence·forth** (-fôrth′) *adv.* from this time on: also **hence′for′ward**

**hench·man** (hench′mən) *n., pl.* **-men** [OE. *hengest*, male horse + -*man*: orig. sense prob. "groom"] **1.** a trusted helper or follower **2.** a political underling who seeks to advance himself **3.** any of the followers of a criminal gang leader

**hen·e·quen** (hen′ə kin) *n.* [< Sp. < native Yucatan name] **1.** a tropical American agave, cultivated for the hard fiber of the leaves **2.** the fiber, similar to the related sisal, used for rope, twine, rugs, etc.

**hen·house** (hen′hous′) *n.* a shelter for poultry

**hen·na** (hen′ə) *n.* [Ar. *ḥinnā'*] **1.** *a)* an old-world plant with white or red flowers *b)* a dye extracted from its leaves, often used to tint the hair auburn **2.** reddish brown —*adj.* reddish-brown —*vt.* **-naed, -na·ing** to tint with henna

**hen·ner·y** (hen′ər ē) *n., pl.* **-ner·ies** a place where poultry is kept or raised

**hen·peck** (hen′pek′) *vt.* to nag and domineer over (one's husband) —**hen′pecked′** *adj.*

**Hen·ri·et·ta** (hen′rē et′ə) [< Fr. fem. dim. of *Henri*, HENRY] a feminine name

**Hen·ry** (hen′rē) [< Fr. < G. < OHG. *Haganrih*, lit., ruler of an enclosure & *Heimerich*, lit., home ruler] **1.** a masculine name **2. Henry IV** *a)* 1367–1413; king of England (1399–1413); 1st Lancastrian king *b)* 1553–1610; king of France (1589–1610); 1st Bourbon king **3. Henry V** 1387–1422; king of England (1413–22) **4. Henry VI** 1421–71; king of England (1422–61; 1470–71) **5. Henry VIII** 1491–

---

fat, āpe, cär; ten, ēven; is, bīte; gō, hôrn, tōol, look; oil, out; up, fur; get; joy; yet; chin; she; thin, then; zh, leisure; ŋ, ring; ə for *a* in *ago*, *e* in *agent*, *i* in *sanity*, *o* in *comply*, *u* in *focus*; ' as in *able* (ā′b'l); Fr. bal; ë, Fr. coeur; ö, Fr. feu; Fr. mon; ô, Fr. coq; ü, Fr. duc; r, Fr. cri; H, G. ich; kh, G. doch; ‡foreign; *hypothetical; < derived from. See inside front cover.

1547; king of England (1509–47): established the Church of England **6. O.,** (pseud. of *William Sydney Porter*) 1862–1910; U.S. short-story writer **7. Patrick,** 1736–99; Am. patriot, statesman, & orator

**hen·ry** (hen′rē) *n., pl.* **-rys, -ries** [after J. *Henry* (1797–1878), U.S. physicist] *Elec.* the unit of inductance, equal to the inductance of a circuit in which the variation of current at the rate of one ampere per second induces an electromotive force of one volt

**hep** (hep) *adj.* [< ?] [Slang] *earlier form of* HIP³

**he·pat·ic** (hi pat′ik) *adj.* [< L. < Gr. < *hēpar*, the liver] **1.** of or affecting the liver **2.** like the liver in color or shape

**he·pat·i·ca** (-i kə) *n.* [ModL. (see prec.): it has liver-shaped leaves] a small plant of the buttercup family, with spring flowers of white, pink, or purple

**hep·a·ti·tis** (hep′ə tīt′is) *n.* [ModL. < Gr. *hēpar* (gen. *hepatos*), liver + -ITIS] inflammation of the liver

**He·phaes·tus** (hi fes′təs) *Gr. Myth.* the god of fire and forge: identified with the Roman god Vulcan

**Hep·ple·white** (hep′′l hwīt′) *adj.* [after G. *Hepplewhite* (?–1786), Eng. cabinetmaker] designating or of a style of furniture with graceful curves

**hep·ta-** [< Gr. *hepta*, seven] *a combining form meaning* seven: also, before a vowel, **hept-**

**hep·ta·chlor** (hep′tə klôr′) *n.* an insecticide, C₁₀H₇Cl₇, similar to chlordane

**hep·ta·gon** (hep′tə gän′) *n.* [< Gr.: see HEPTA- & -GON] a plane figure with seven angles and seven sides —**hep·tag′o·nal** (-tag′ə n′l) *adj.*

**hep·tam·e·ter** (hep tam′ə tər) *n.* [HEPTA- + -METER] a line of verse with seven metrical feet

**hep·tane** (hep′tān) *n.* [HEPT(A)- + -ANE] a flammable, colorless liquid, C₇H₁₆, used as a standard in octane rating, etc.

**hep·tar·chy** (hep′tär kē) *n., pl.* **-chies 1.** government by seven rulers **2.** a group of seven allied kingdoms, specif. [**the H-**] in Anglo-Saxon England before the 9th century

**her** (hur; *unstressed* ər) *pron.* [OE. *hire*] *objective case of* SHE: also used colloquially as a predicate complement with a linking verb (Ex.: that's *her*) —*possessive pronominal adj.* of, belonging to, made, or done by her

**her.** heraldry

**He·ra** (hir′ə) *Gr. Myth.* the wife of Zeus, queen of the gods, and goddess of marriage: identified with the Roman goddess Juno

**Her·a·cli·tus** (her′ə klīt′əs) fl. about 500 B.C.; Gr. philosopher

**Her·a·kles, Her·a·cles** (her′ə klēz′) *same as* HERCULES

**her·ald** (her′əld) *n.* [< OFr. *heralt* < Frank.] **1.** formerly, an official who made proclamations, carried state messages, took charge of tournaments, etc. **2.** in England, an official in charge of genealogies, heraldic arms, etc. **3.** a person who announces significant news **4.** a person or thing that presages what is to follow; forerunner; harbinger —*vt.* **1.** to announce, foretell, etc. **2.** to publicize

**he·ral·dic** (he ral′dik) *adj.* of heraldry or heralds

**her·ald·ry** (her′əl drē) *n., pl.* **-ries 1.** the art or science having to do with coats of arms, genealogies, etc. **2.** heraldic arms, etc. **3.** heraldic ceremony or pomp

**herb** (urb, hurb) *n.* [< OFr. < L. *herba*] **1.** any seed plant whose stem withers away annually, as distinguished from a tree or shrub whose woody stem lives from year to year **2.** any plant used as a medicine, seasoning, or flavoring, as mint, thyme, basil, or sage **3.** grass; herbage —**herb′like′** *adj.* —**herb′y** *adj.*

**her·ba·ceous** (hər bā′shəs, ər-) *adj.* **1.** of or like an herb **2.** like a green leaf in texture, color, etc.

**herb·age** (ur′bij, hur′-) *n.* **1.** herbs collectively, esp. those used as pasturage; grass **2.** the green foliage and juicy stems of herbs

**herb·al** (hur′b′l, ur′-) *adj.* of herbs —*n.* formerly, a book about herbs or plants

**herb·al·ist** (-ist) *n.* **1.** orig., a botanist **2.** a person who grows, collects, or deals in herbs

**her·bar·i·um** (hər ber′ē əm, ər-) *n., pl.* **-i·ums, -i·a** (-ə) [LL. < L. *herba*, herb] **1.** a collection of dried plants used for botanical study **2.** a room, building, etc. for keeping such a collection

**Her·bert** (hur′bərt) [OE. *Herebeorht*, lit., bright army] **1.** a masculine name: dim. *Herb* **2. George,** 1593–1633; Eng. poet **3. Victor,** 1859–1924; U.S. composer & conductor, born in Ireland

**her·bi·cide** (hur′bə sīd′, ur′-) *n.* [< L. *herba*, herb + -CIDE] any chemical substance used to destroy plants, esp. weeds —**her′bi·ci′dal** *adj.*

**her·bi·vore** (-vôr′) *n.* [Fr.] a herbivorous animal

**her·biv·o·rous** (hər biv′ər əs) *adj.* [< L. *herba*, herb + -VOROUS] feeding chiefly on grass or other plants

**Her·ce·go·vi·na** (hert′sə gō vē′nə) former independent duchy: now, with Bosnia, a republic of Yugoslavia: see BOSNIA AND HERCEGOVINA

**Her·cu·le·an** (hur′kyə lē′ən, hər kyōō′lē ən) *adj.* **1.** of

Hercules **2.** [*usually* **h-**] *a)* having the great size and strength of Hercules *b)* calling for great strength, size, or courage, as a task

**Her·cu·les** (hur′kyə lēz′) **1.** *Class. Myth.* a son of Zeus, renowned for feats of strength, esp. twelve labors imposed on him **2.** a large N constellation —*n.* [**h-**] any very large, strong man

**herd¹** (hurd) *n.* [OE. *heord*] **1.** a number of cattle or other large animals feeding, living, or being driven together **2.** a crowd **3.** the common people; masses: contemptuous term —*vt., vi.* to form into or move as a herd, group, crowd, etc.

**herd²** (hurd) *n.* [OE. *hierde*] a herdsman: now chiefly in combination [*cowherd*] —*vt.* to tend or drive as a herdsman —**ride herd on 1.** to control a moving herd of (cattle) from horseback **2.** to keep a close watch or control over —**herd′er** n.

**herds·man** (hurdz′mən) *n., pl.* **-men** a person who keeps or tends a herd

**here** (hir) *adv.* [OE. *her*] **1.** at or in this place: often used as an intensive [John *here* is a good player] **2.** toward, to, or into this place [come *here*] **3.** at this point in action, speech, etc.; now **4.** in earthly life —*interj.* an exclamation used to call attention, answer a roll call, etc. —*n.* this place or point —**here and there** in, at, or to various places —**here goes!** an exclamation used when the speaker is about to do something daring, disagreeable, etc. —**neither here nor there** beside the point; irrelevant

**here·a·bout** (hir′ə bout′) *adv.* in this general vicinity: about or near here: also **here′a·bouts′**

**here·af·ter** (hir af′tər) *adv.* **1.** from now on; in the future **2.** following this, as in a writing **3.** in the state or life after death —*n.* **1.** the future **2.** the state or life after death

**here·at** (hir at′) *adv.* **1.** at this time; when this occurred **2.** at this; for this reason

**here·by** (hir′bī′) *adv.* by this means

**he·red·i·ta·ble** (hə red′i tə b′l) *adj. same as* HERITABLE —**he·red′i·ta·bil′i·ty** n.

**he·red·i·tar·y** (hə red′ə ter′ē) *adj.* [< L. < *hereditas:* see ff.] **1.** *a)* of, or passed down by, inheritance from an ancestor *b)* having title, etc. by inheritance **2.** of, or passed down by, heredity **3.** being such because of attitudes, beliefs, etc. passed down through generations —**he·red′i·tar′i·ly** *adv.* —**he·red′i·tar′i·ness** n.

**he·red·i·ty** (hə red′ə tē) *n., pl.* **-ties** [< Fr. < L. *hereditas,* heirship < *heres,* heir] **1.** the transmission of characteristics from parents to offspring by means of genes in the chromosomes **2.** all the characteristics that one inherits genetically

**Her·e·ford** (hur′fərd, her′ə-) *n.* [orig. bred in *Hereford-shire,* England] any of a breed of beef cattle having a white face and a red body with white markings

**here·in** (hir in′) *adv.* **1.** in here **2.** in this writing **3.** in this matter, detail, etc.

**here·in·a·bove** (hir′in ə buv′) *adv.* in the preceding part (of this document, speech, etc.): also **here′in·be·fore′**

**here·in·af·ter** (-af′tər) *adv.* in the following part (of this document, speech, etc.): also **here′in·be·low′**

**here·in·to** (hir in′tōō) *adv.* **1.** into this place **2.** into this matter, condition, etc.

**here·of** (-uv′) *adv.* **1.** of this **2.** concerning this

**here·on** (-än′) *adv. same as* HEREUPON

**here's** (hirz) here is

**here's to!** here's a toast to! I wish joy, etc. to!

**her·e·sy** (her′ə sē) *n., pl.* **-sies** [< OFr. < L. < Gr. *hairesis,* a selection, sect < *hairein,* to take] **1.** *a)* a religious belief opposed to the orthodox doctrines of a church; esp., such a belief denounced by the church *b)* rejection of a belief that is part of church dogma **2.** any opinion opposed to established views or doctrines **3.** the holding of any such belief or opinion

**her·e·tic** (her′ə tik) *n.* a person who professes a heresy; esp., a church member who holds beliefs opposed to church dogma —*adj. same as* HERETICAL

**he·ret·i·cal** (hə ret′i k′l) *adj.* **1.** of heresy or heretics **2.** characterized by, or having the nature of, heresy —**he·ret′i·cal·ly** *adv.*

**here·to** (hir tōō′) *adv.* to this (document, etc.) [attached *hereto*]: also **here·un′to**

**here·to·fore** (hir′tə fôr′, hir′tə fôr′) *adv.* up to now; until the present; before this

**here·un·der** (hir un′dər) *adv.* **1.** under or below this (in a document, etc.) **2.** under the terms stated here

**here·up·on** (hir′ə pän′, hir′ə pän′) *adv.* **1.** immediately following this **2.** concerning this

**here·with** (hir with′, -with′) *adv.* **1.** along with this **2.** by this method or means

**her·it·a·ble** (her′it ə b′l) *adj.* **1.** that can be inherited **2.** that can inherit —**her′it·a·bil′i·ty** n.

**her·it·age** (her′ət ij) *n.* [OFr. < LL. < L. *hereditas:* see HEREDITY] **1.** property that is or can be inherited **2.** *a)*

something handed down from one's ancestors or the past, as a characteristic, a culture, tradition, etc. *b*) birthright
**Her·man** (hur′mən) [< G. < OHG. *Hariman* < *heri*, army + *man*, man] a masculine name
**her·maph·ro·dite** (hər maf′rə dīt′) *n.* [< L. < Gr. < *Hermaphroditos*, son of Hermes and Aphrodite, united in a single body with a nymph] **1.** a person or animal with the sexual organs of both the male and the female **2.** a plant having stamens and pistils in the same flower **3.** *short for* HERMAPHRODITE BRIG —**her·maph′ro·dit′ism**, **her·maph′ro·dism** *n.*
**hermaphrodite brig** a ship with a square-rigged foremast and a fore-and-aft-rigged mainmast
**her·maph·ro·dit·ic** (-dit′ik) *adj.* of or like a hermaphrodite: also **her·maph′ro·dit′i·cal** —**her·maph′ro·dit′i·cal·ly** *adv.*
**Her·mes** (hur′mēz) *Gr. Myth.* a god who served as messenger of the other gods: identified with the Roman god Mercury and pictured with winged shoes and hat, carrying a caduceus
**her·met·ic** (hər met′ik) *adj.* [< ModL. < L. < Gr. *Hermēs* (reputed founder of alchemy)] airtight: also **her·met′i·cal** —**her·met′i·cal·ly** *adv.*
**her·mit** (hur′mit) *n.* [< OFr. < LL. < LGr. < Gr. *erēmitēs* < *erēmos*, solitary] a person who lives by himself in a secluded spot, often from religious motives; recluse —**her·mit′ic**, **her·mit′i·cal** *adj.* —**her·mit′i·cal·ly** *adv.* —**her′mit·like′** *adj.*
**her·mit·age** (-ij) *n.* **1.** the place where a hermit lives **2.** a place where a person can live away from other people; secluded retreat
**hermit crab** any of various soft-bellied crabs that live in the empty shells of certain mollusks, as snails
**her·ni·a** (hur′nē ə) *n., pl.* **-ni·as**, **-ni·ae′** (-ē′) [L.] the protrusion of all or part of an organ, esp. a part of the intestine, through a tear in the wall of the surrounding structure; rupture —**her′ni·al** *adj.*
**He·ro** (hir′ō) *Gr. Legend* a priestess of Aphrodite: her lover, Leander, swam the Hellespont every night to be with her
**he·ro** (hir′ō, hē′rō) *n., pl.* **-roes** [< L. < Gr. *hērōs*] **1.** *Myth. & Legend* a man of great strength and courage, favored by the gods and in part descended from them **2.** any man admired for his courage, nobility, or exploits **3.** any man regarded as an ideal or model **4.** the central, usually sympathetic, male character in a novel, play, poem, etc. **5.** a central figure who played an admirable role in any important event or period **6.** *same as* HERO SANDWICH
**Her·od** (her′əd) Edomite family of ancient Palestine, including, esp., **1.** **Herod (the Great)** 73?–4 B.C.; king of Judea (37–4) **2.** **Herod A·grip·pa (I)** (ə grip′ə) 10? B.C.–44 A.D.; king of Judea (37–44): grandson of *prec.* **3.** **Herod Agrippa (II)** 27?–100? A.D.; king of Judea (53–100): son of *prec.* **4.** **Herod An·ti·pas** (an′ti pas′) ?–40? A.D.; ruler of Galilee (4? B.C.–39 A.D.): son of *Herod the Great*
**He·rod·o·tus** (hə räd′ə təs) 485?–425? B.C.; Gr. historian: called the *Father of History*
**he·ro·ic** (hi rō′ik) *adj.* **1.** like or characteristic of a hero or his deeds [*heroic* conduct] **2.** of, about, or characterized by heroes and their deeds; epic [a *heroic* poem] **3.** exalted; eloquent [*heroic* words] **4.** exceptionally daring and risky [*heroic* measures] **5.** *Art* somewhat larger than life-size [a *heroic* statue] Also **he·ro′i·cal** —*n.* **1.** *a*) a heroic poem *b*) [*pl.*] *same as* HEROIC VERSE **2.** [*pl.*] extravagant or melodramatic talk or action, meant to seem heroic —**he·ro′i·cal·ly** *adv.*
**heroic couplet** a pair of rhymed lines in iambic pentameter
**heroic verse** the verse form in which epic poetry is traditionally written, as iambic pentameter
**her·o·in** (her′ə win) *n.* [G., orig. a trademark] a very powerful, habit-forming narcotic, a derivative of morphine
**her·o·ine** (her′ə win) *n.* a girl or woman hero in life or literature
**her·o·ism** (-wiz′m) *n.* the qualities and actions of a hero or heroine; great bravery, nobility, etc.
**her·on** (her′ən) *n., pl.* **-ons**, **-on:** see PLURAL, II, D, 1 [< OFr. *hairon* < Frank.] any of a group of wading birds with a long neck, long legs, and a long, tapered bill
**her·on·ry** (-rē) *n., pl.* **-ries** a place where many herons gather to breed
**hero sandwich** a large roll sliced lengthwise and filled with cold meats, cheese, vegetables, etc.
**hero worship** great or exaggerated admiration for heroes —**he′ro-wor′ship** *vt.* —**he′ro-wor′ship·er** *n.*
**her·pes** (hur′pēz) *n.* [L. < Gr. < *herpein*, to creep] a virus disease characterized by the eruption of small blisters on the skin and mucous membranes —**her·pet′ic** (hər pet′ik) *adj.*
**herpes simplex** a form of herpes principally involving the mouth, lips, and face

**herpes zos·ter** (zäs′tər) [Gr. *zōstēr*, a girdle] a viral infection of certain sensory nerves, causing pain and an eruption of blisters along the course of the affected nerve; shingles
**her·pe·tol·o·gy** (hur′pə täl′ə jē) *n.* [< Gr. *herpeton*, reptile + -LOGY] the branch of zoology having to do with the study of reptiles and amphibians —**her′pe·to·log′ic** (-tə·läj′ik), **her′pe·to·log′i·cal** *adj.* —**her′pe·tol′o·gist** *n.*
**‡Herr** (her) *n., pl.* **Her′ren** (-ən) in Germany, a man; gentleman: also used as a title corresponding to *Mr.* or *Sir*
**Her·rick** (her′ik), **Robert** 1591–1674; Eng. poet
**her·ring** (her′in) *n., pl.* **-rings**, **-ring:** see PLURAL, II, D, 1 [OE. *hæring*] **1.** a small food fish of the N Atlantic: eaten cooked, dried, salted, or smoked: the young are canned as sardines **2.** loosely, the sprat, pilchard, etc.
**her·ring·bone** (-bōn′) *n.* **1.** the spine of a herring, with the ribs extending from opposite sides in rows of parallel, slanting lines **2.** a pattern with such a design or anything having such a pattern —*adj.* having the pattern of a herringbone —*vi., vt.* **-boned′**, **-bon′ing** to stitch, weave, arrange, etc. in a herringbone pattern
**hers** (hurz) *pron.* that or those belonging to her: used without a following noun [that book is *hers*, *hers* are better]: also used after *of* to indicate possession [a friend of *hers*]
**Her·schel** (hur′shəl) **1.** **Sir John Frederick William**, 1792–1871; Eng. astronomer & physicist: son of *ff.* **2.** **Sir William**, (born *Friedrich Wilhelm Herschel*) 1738–1822; Eng. astronomer, born in Germany
**her·self** (hər self′) *pron.* a form of the 3d pers. sing., fem. pronoun, used: *a*) as an intensive [she went *herself*] *b*) as a reflexive [she hurt *herself*] *c*) as a quasi-noun meaning "her real or true self" [she is not *herself* today]
**hertz** (hurts) *n., pl.* **hertz** [see ff.] the international unit of frequency, equal to one cycle per second
**Hertz·i·an waves** (hurt′sē ən, hert′-) [after H. R. *Hertz* (1857–1894), Ger. physicist] [*sometimes* **h**-] radio waves or other electromagnetic radiation resulting from the oscillations of electricity in a conductor
**Herzegovina** *same as* HERCEGOVINA
**he's** (hēz) **1.** he is **2.** he has
**Hesh·van** (khesh vän′; *E.* hesh′vən) *n.* [Heb.] the second month of the Jewish year: see JEWISH CALENDAR
**hes·i·tan·cy** (hez′ə tən sē) *n., pl.* **-cies** hesitation or indecision; doubt: also **hes′i·tance**
**hes·i·tant** (-tənt) *adj.* hesitating or undecided; doubtful —**hes′i·tant·ly** *adv.*
**hes·i·tate** (-tāt′) *vi.* **-tat′ed**, **-tat′ing** [< L. pp. of *haesitare*, intens. of *haerere*, to stick] **1.** to stop in indecision; pause or delay in acting or deciding **2.** to pause; stop momentarily **3.** to be reluctant [I *hesitate* to ask] **4.** to pause continually in speaking; stammer —**hes′i·tat′er**, **hes′i·ta′tor** *n.* —**hes′i·tat′ing·ly** *adv.*
**hes·i·ta·tion** (hez′ə tā′shən) *n.* a hesitating; specif., *a*) indecision *b*) reluctance *c*) halting speech *d*) a pausing —**hes′i·ta′tive** *adj.* —**hes′i·ta′tive·ly** *adv.*
**Hes·per·i·des** (hes per′ə dēz′) *n.pl.* **1.** *sing.* **Hes·per·id** (hes′pər id) *Gr. Myth.* the nymphs who guarded the golden apples given as a wedding gift by Gaea to Hera **2.** the garden where the apples grew
**Hes·per·us** (hes′pər əs) *n.* [L.] the evening star, esp. Venus: also **Hes′per**
**Hesse** (hes, hes′i) former region in WC Germany, now a state of West Germany
**Hes·sian** (hesh′ən) *adj.* of Hesse or its people —*n.* **1.** a native or inhabitant of Hesse **2.** any of the Hessian mercenaries who fought for the British in the Revolutionary War
**Hessian fly** a small, two-winged fly whose larvae destroy wheat crops
**hest** (hest) *n.* [< OE. *hæs*, command < *hatan*, to call] [Archaic] behest; order
**Hes·ter**, **Hes·ther** (hes′tər) [var. of ESTHER] a feminine name
**he·tae·ra** (hi tir′ə) *n., pl.* **-rae** (-ē), **-ras** [< Gr. < *hetairos*, companion] in ancient Greece, a courtesan: also **he·tai′ra** (-tī′rə), *pl.* **-rai** (-ī′)
**het·er·o-** [< Gr. < *heteros*, the other (of two)] *a combining form meaning* other, another, different [*heterosexual*]: opposed to HOMO-: also **heter-**
**het·er·o·cy·clic** (het′ər ō sī′klik, -sik′lik) *adj.* designating or of a cyclic molecular arrangement of atoms of carbon and other elements
**het·er·o·dox** (het′ər ə däks′) *adj.* [< Gr. < *hetero-*, HETERO- + *doxa*, opinion] departing from or opposed to the usual beliefs or established doctrines, esp. in religion; unorthodox
**het·er·o·dox·y** (-däk′sē) *n., pl.* **-dox′ies** **1.** the quality or fact of being heterodox **2.** a heterodox belief or doctrine
**het·er·o·dyne** (-dīn′) *adj.* [HETERO- + DYNE] designating or of the combination of two different radio frequencies to

produce beats with new frequencies —*vi.* -dyned', -dyn'ing to combine two different frequencies so as to produce such beats

**het·er·o·ge·ne·ous** (het'ər ə jē'nē əs, het'rə-; -jēn'yəs) *adj.* [< ML. < Gr. < *hetero-,* HETERO- + *genos,* a kind] **1.** differing or opposite in structure, quality, etc.; dissimilar **2.** composed of unrelated or unlike elements or parts; varied; miscellaneous —**het'er·o·ge·ne'i·ty** (-jə nē'ə tē) *n., pl.* -ties —**het'er·o·ge'ne·ous·ly** *adv.* —**het'er·o·ge'ne·ous·ness** *n.*

**het·er·o·nym** (het'ər ə nim') *n.* [< Gr. < *hetero-,* HETERO- + *onyma,* name] a word with the same spelling as another but with a different meaning and pronunciation (Ex.: *tear,* a drop from the eye; *tear,* to rip) —**het'er·on'y·mous** (-än'ə məs) *adj.*

**het·er·o·sex·u·al** (het'ər ə sek'shoo wəl) *adj.* **1.** of or characterized by sexual desire for those of the opposite sex **2.** *Biol.* of different sexes —*n.* a heterosexual individual —**het'er·o·sex'u·al'i·ty** (-wal'ə tē) *n.*

**het·man** (het'mən) *n., pl.* -mans [Pol. < G. < *haupt,* head + *mann,* man] a Cossack chief

**het up** (het) [*het,* dial. pt. & pp. of *heat*] [Slang] excited or angry

**HEW** (Dept. of) Health, Education, and Welfare

**hew** (hyōō) *vt.* **hewed, hewed** or **hewn, hew'ing** [OE. *heawan*] **1.** to chop or cut with an ax, knife, etc. **2.** to make or shape by or as by cutting or chopping with an ax, etc. **3.** to chop *down* (a tree) with an ax —*vi.* **1.** to make cutting or chopping blows with an ax, knife, etc. **2.** to adhere (*to* a line, principle, etc.) —**hew'er** *n.*

**hex** (heks) *n.* [< G. *hexe* < OHG.] **1.** [Dial.] a witch or sorcerer **2.** *a)* a sign, spell, etc. supposed to bring bad luck *b)* a jinx —*vt.* to cause to have bad luck; jinx

**hex·a-** [< Gr. *hex,* six] *a combining form meaning* six [*hexagram*] : also, before a vowel, **hex-**

**hex·a·chlo·ro·phene** (hek'sə klôr'ə fēn') *n.* [< HEXA- + CHLORO- + PHENOL] a white powder, $C_{13}Cl_6H_6O_2$, used, esp. formerly, in deodorants, soaps, etc. to kill bacteria

**hex·a·gon** (hek'sə gän') *n.* [< L. < Gr. < *hex,* six + *gōnia,* a corner, angle] a plane figure with six angles and six sides —**hex·ag'o·nal** (-sag'ə n'l) *adj.* —**hex·ag'o·nal·ly** *adv.*

**hex·a·gram** (hek'sə gram') *n.* [HEXA- + -GRAM] a six-pointed star formed by extending all sides of a regular hexagon to points of intersection

**hex·a·he·dron** (hek'sə hē'drən) *n., pl.* -drons, -dra (-drə) [see HEXA- &-HEDRON] a solid figure with six plane surfaces —**hex'a·he'dral** *adj.*

**hex·am·e·ter** (hek sam'ə tər) *n.* [< L. < Gr.: see HEXA- & METER[1]] **1.** a line of verse containing six metrical feet **2.** verse consisting of hexameters —*adj.* having six metrical feet

**hex·a·pod** (hek'sə päd') *n.* [see HEXA- & -POD] an insect (sense 1) —*adj.* having six legs, as a true insect: also **hex·ap·o·dous** (hek sap'ə dəs)

**hey** (hā) *interj.* [ME. *hei,* echoic formation] an exclamation used to attract attention, express surprise, etc., or in asking a question

**hey·day** (hā'dā') *n.* the time of greatest health, vigor, success, prosperity, etc.; prime

**Hez·e·ki·ah** (hez'ə kī'ə) *Bible* a king of Judah: II Kings 18–20

**Hf** *Chem.* hafnium

**HF, H.F., hf, h.f.** high frequency

**hf.** half

**Hg** [L. *hydrargyrum*] *Chem.* mercury

**HG., H.G.** High German

**hg.** hectogram; hectograms

**hgt.** height

**H.H.** **1.** His (or Her) Highness **2.** His Holiness

**hhd.** hogshead

**HI** Hawaii

**hi** (hī) *interj.* [ME. *hy,* var. of *hei,* HEY] an exclamation of greeting

**Hi·a·le·ah** (hī'ə lē'ə) [< ? Seminole-Creek *haiyakpo hili,* lit., pretty prairie] city in SE Fla.: suburb of Miami: pop. 145,000

**hi·a·tus** (hī āt'əs) *n., pl.* -tus·es, -tus [L., pp. of *hiare,* to gape] **1.** a break or gap where a part is missing or lost **2.** any gap **3.** a slight pause in pronunciation between two successive vowel sounds, as between the *e's* in *reentry*

**Hi·a·wa·tha** (hī'ə wô'thə, hē'-; -wä'-) the Indian hero of *The Song of Hiawatha,* a long narrative poem (1855) by Longfellow

**hi·ba·chi** (hi bä'chē) *n., pl.* -chis [Jap. < *hi,* fire + *bachi,* bowl] a charcoal-burning brazier and grill of Japanese design

**hi·ber·nal** (hī bur'nəl) *adj.* [< L. < *hibernus:* see ff.] of winter; wintry

**hi·ber·nate** (hī'bər nāt') *vi.* -nat'ed, -nat'ing [< L. pp. of *hibernare* < *hibernus,* wintry] to spend the winter in a dormant state —**hi'ber·na'tion** *n.* —**hi'ber·na'tor** *n.*

**Hi·ber·ni·a** (hī bur'nē ə) [L.] *poet.* name of IRELAND —**Hi·ber'ni·an** *adj., n.*

**hi·bis·cus** (hī bis'kəs, hi-) *n.* [< L. *hibiscus*] a plant, shrub, or small tree related to the mallow, with large, colorful flowers

**hic·cup** (hik'əp) *n.* [altered < Early ModE. *hikop, hicket,* of echoic orig.: sp. infl. by association with COUGH] **1.** a sudden, involuntary contraction of the diaphragm that closes the glottis at the moment of breathing, making a sharp, quick sound **2.** [*pl.*] a condition of repeated contractions of this kind —*vi.* -cuped or -cupped, -cup·ing or -cup·ping to make a hiccup —*vt.* to utter with a hiccup Also **hic·cough** (hik'əp)

‡**hic ja·cet** (hik' jā'sit) [L.] **1.** here lies: inscribed on tombstones **2.** an epitaph

**hick** (hik) *n.* [altered < RICHARD] [Colloq.] an awkward, unsophisticated person regarded as typical of rural areas: somewhat contemptuous term —*adj.* [Colloq.] of or like a hick

**hick·o·ry** (hik'ər ē, hik'rē) *n., pl.* -ries [< AmInd. *pawcohiccora,* product made from the nuts] **1.** a N. American tree related to the walnut, with smooth-shelled, edible nuts **2.** its hard, tough wood **3.** its nut: also **hickory nut**

**hi·dal·go** (hi dal'gō) *n., pl.* -gos [Sp., contr. of *hijo de algo,* son of something] a Spanish nobleman of secondary rank, below that of a grandee

**hid·den** (hid''n) *alt. pp. of* HIDE[1] —*adj.* concealed; secret

HICKORY
(leaf, nut & tree)

**hide[1]** (hīd) *vt.* **hid, hid'den** or **hid, hid'ing** [OE. *hydan*] **1.** to put or keep out of sight; secrete; conceal **2.** to keep secret **3.** to keep from being seen by covering up, obscuring, etc. **4.** to turn away [to *hide* one's head in shame] —*vi.* **1.** to be concealed **2.** to conceal oneself —**hid'er** *n.*

**hide[2]** (hīd) *n.* [OE. *hid*] **1.** an animal skin or pelt, either raw or tanned **2.** [Colloq.] the skin of a person —*vt.* **hid'ed, hid'ing** [Colloq.] to beat; flog —**neither hide nor hair** nothing whatsoever

**hide-and-seek** (hīd''n sēk') *n.* a children's game in which one player tries to find the other players, who have hidden: also **hide'-and-go-seek'**

**hide·a·way** (hīd'ə wā') *n.* [Colloq.] a place where one can hide, be secluded, etc.

**hide·bound** (-bound') *adj.* **1.** having the hide tight over the body structure, as an emaciated cow **2.** obstinately conservative and narrow-minded

**hid·e·ous** (hid'ē əs) *adj.* [< Anglo-Fr. < OFr. < *hide,* fright] horrible; very ugly or revolting; dreadful —**hid'e·ous·ly** *adv.* —**hid'e·ous·ness** *n.*

**hide-out** (hīd'out') *n.* [Colloq.] a hiding place

**hid·ing[1]** (hīd'iŋ) *n.* **1.** *a)* the act of one that hides *b)* the condition of being hidden: usually in the phrase **in hiding** **2.** a place to hide

**hid·ing[2]** (hīd'iŋ) *n.* [Colloq.] a severe beating

**hie** (hī) *vi., vt.* **hied, hie'ing** or **hy'ing** [OE. *higian*] to hurry or hasten: usually reflexive

**hi·er·arch** (hī'ə rärk', hī'rärk) *n.* [< ML. < Gr. < *hieros,* sacred + *archos,* ruler] a chief priest

**hi·er·ar·chy** (hī'ə -rär'kē) *n., pl.* -chies [< OFr. < ML.: see prec.] **1.** a system of church government by priests or other clergy in graded ranks **2.** the group of officials in such a system **3.** a group of persons or things arranged in order of rank, grade, etc. —**hi'er·ar'chi·cal, hi'er·ar'chic,** **hi'er·ar'chal** *adj.* —**hi'er·ar'chi·cal·ly** *adv.*

**hi·er·at·ic** (hī'ə rat'ik) *adj.* [< L. < Gr. *hieratikos* < *hieros,* sacred] **1.** of or used by priests; priestly **2.** designating or of the abridged form of cursive hieroglyphic writing once used by Egyptian priests Also **hi'er·at'i·cal** —**hi'er·at'i·cal·ly** *adv.*

**hi·er·o·glyph** (hī'ər ə glif', hī'rə-) *n. same as* HIEROGLYPHIC

**hi·er·o·glyph·ic** (hī'ər ə glif'ik, hī'rə-) *adj.* [< Fr. < LL. < Gr. < *hieros,* sacred + *glyphein,* to carve] **1.** of, like, or written in hieroglyphics **2.** hard to read or understand Also **hi'er·o·glyph'i·cal** —*n.* **1.** a picture or symbol representing a word, syllable, or sound, used by the ancient Egyptians and others **2.** [*usually pl.*] a method of writing using hieroglyphics **3.** a symbol, sign, etc. hard to understand **4.** [*pl.*] writing hard to decipher —**hi'er·o·glyph'i·cal·ly** *adv.*

**hi-fi** (hī'fī') *n.* **1.** *same as* HIGH FIDELITY **2.** a radio, phonograph, etc. having high fidelity —*adj.* of or having high fidelity of sound reproduction

**hig·gle** (hig''l) *vi.* -gled, -gling *same as* HAGGLE —**hig'gler** *n.*

**hig·gle·dy-pig·gle·dy** (hig''l dē pig''l dē) *adv.* [redupl., prob. after PIG] in disorder; in jumbled confusion —*adj.* disorderly; jumbled; confused

**high** (hī) *adj.* [OE. *heah*] **1.** of more than normal height;

lofty; tall: not used of persons **2.** extending upward a (specified) distance **3.** situated far above the ground or other level **4.** reaching to or done from a height *[a high jump, a high dive]* **5.** above others in rank, position, quality, character, etc.; superior **6.** grave; very serious *[high treason]* **7.** greatly developed; complex: usually in the comparative *[higher mathematics]* **8.** main; principal; chief *[a high priest]* **9.** greater in size, amount, degree, power, etc. than usual *[high prices]* **10.** advanced to its acme or fullness *[high noon]* **11.** expensive; costly **12.** luxurious and extravagant *[high living]* **13.** haughty; overbearing **14.** raised or acute in pitch; sharp; shrill **15.** slightly tainted; strong-smelling: said of meat, esp. game **16.** extremely formal in matters of ceremony, doctrine, etc. **17.** excited; elated *[high spirits]* **18.** far from the equator *[a high latitude]* **19.** designating or of that gear ratio of a motor vehicle transmission which produces the highest speed **20.** [Slang] *a)* drunk; intoxicated *b)* under the influence of a drug **21.** *Phonet.* produced with the tongue held in a relatively elevated position: said of a vowel, as (ē) —*adv.* **1.** in a high manner **2.** in or to a high level, degree, rank, etc. —*n.* **1.** a high level, place, etc. **2.** an area of high barometric pressure **3.** high gear (see *adj.* 19) **4.** [Slang] a condition of euphoria induced as by drugs —**high and dry** stranded —**high and low** everywhere —**high and mighty** [Colloq.] arrogant; haughty —**high on** [Colloq.] enthusiastic about —**on high 1.** high above **2.** in heaven

**high·ball** (-bôl′) *n.* **1.** liquor, usually whiskey, served with water, soda water, ginger ale, etc. and ice **2.** a railroad signal meaning "go ahead" —*vi.* [Slang] to go very fast

**high·born** (-bôrn′) *adj.* of noble birth

**high·boy** (-boi′) *n.* a high chest of drawers mounted on legs

**high·bred** (-bred′) *adj.* showing good breeding; cultivated

**high·brow** (-brou′) *n.* [Colloq.] a person who is or tries to be intellectual —*adj.* [Colloq.] of or for a highbrow

**High Church** that party of the Anglican Church which emphasizes the importance of the priesthood and of traditional rituals and doctrines —**High′-Church′** *adj.* —**High′-Church′man** *n., pl.* -men

**high comedy** comedy reflecting the life of the upper social classes, characterized by a witty, sardonic treatment

**high commissioner 1.** the chief representative of the British government to one of the Commonwealth countries or from one of these countries to the British government **2.** the chief officer of a commission

**high·er-up** (hī′ər up′) *n.* [Colloq.] a person of higher rank or position

**high·fa·lu·tin, high·fa·lu·ting** (hī′fə lōōt′'n) *adj.* [Colloq.] ridiculously pretentious or pompous

**high fidelity** in radio, sound recording, etc., a nearly exact reproduction of a wide range of sound frequencies, from about 20 to 20,000 hertz

**high·fli·er, high·fly·er** (-flī′ər) *n.* **1.** a person or thing that flies high **2.** a person who acts or talks in an extravagant manner —**high′fly′ing** *adj.*

**high-flown** (-flōn′) *adj.* **1.** extravagantly ambitious **2.** high-sounding but meaningless; bombastic

**high frequency** any radio frequency between 3 and 30 megahertz

**High German 1.** the West Germanic dialects spoken in C and S Germany: distinguished from LOW GERMAN **2.** the official and literary form of the German language, technically called *New High German:* see also OLD HIGH GERMAN, MIDDLE HIGH GERMAN

**high-grade** (-grād′) *adj.* of superior quality

**high·hand·ed** (-han′did) *adj.* acting or done in an overbearing or arbitrary manner —**high′hand′ed·ly** *adv.* —**high′hand′ed·ness** *n.*

**high-hat** (-hat′) *adj.* [Slang] snobbish and aloof —*n.* [Slang] a snob —*vt.* **-hat′ted, -hat′ting** [Slang] to snub

**High Holidays** the period encompassing Rosh Hashana and Yom Kippur in the Jewish calendar

**high·jack** (-jak′) *vt.* [Colloq.] *same as* HIJACK

**high jump** a track and field event in which the contestants jump for height over a horizontal bar

**high·land** (-lənd) *n.* a region higher than adjacent land and containing many hills or mountains —*adj.* of, in, or from such a region —**the Highlands** mountainous region occupying nearly all of N Scotland —**high′land·er, High′land·er** *n.*

**Highland fling** a lively dance of the Highlands

**high life** the luxurious way of life of fashionable society

**high·light** (-līt′) *n.* **1.** *a)* a part on which light is brightest *b)* a part of a painting, etc. on which light is represented as brightest *c)* the representation or effect of such light in a painting, etc. Also **high light 2.** the most important or interesting part, scene, etc. —*vt.* **1.** to give a highlight or highlights to **2.** to give prominence to **3.** to be the most outstanding in

**high·ly** (-lē) *adv.* **1.** in a high office or rank **2.** very much **3.** favorably **4.** at a high wage, salary, etc.

**High Mass** *R.C.Ch.* a sung Mass, usually celebrated with the complete ritual, at which the celebrant is assisted by a deacon and subdeacon: also **Solemn (High) Mass**

**high-mind·ed** (-mīn′did) *adj.* **1.** [Obs.] haughty **2.** having or showing high ideals, principles, etc. —**high′-mind′ed·ly** *adv.* —**high′-mind′ed·ness** *n.*

**high·ness** (-nis) *n.* **1.** the quality or state of being high; height **2.** [H-] a title used in speaking to or of a member of a royal family (with *His, Her,* or *Your*)

**high-pitched** (-picht′) *adj.* **1.** high in pitch; shrill **2.** exalted **3.** agitated **4.** steep in slope

**High Point** [after its location, the highest point on the N.C. Railroad] city in C N.C.: pop. 64,000

**high-pow·ered** (-pou′ərd) *adj.* very powerful

**high-pres·sure** (-presh′ər) *adj.* **1.** *a)* having, using, or withstanding relatively high pressure *b)* having a high barometric pressure **2.** using forcefully persuasive or insistent methods or arguments —*vt.* **-sured, -sur·ing** [Colloq.] to urge with such methods or arguments

**high priest** a chief priest; specif., the chief priest of the ancient Jewish priesthood

**high-proof** (-prōōf′) *adj.* high in alcohol content

**high-rise** (-rīz′) *adj.* designating or of a tall apartment house, office building, etc. of many stories —*n.* a high-rise building

**high·road** (-rōd′) *n.* **1.** [Chiefly Brit.] a main road; highway **2.** an easy or direct way

**high roller** [from rolling the dice in gambling] [Slang] **1.** a person who gambles for very high stakes **2.** a person who spends or invests money freely or recklessly

**high school** a secondary school that usually includes grades 10, 11, and 12, and sometimes grade 9 —**high′-school′** *adj.*

**high seas** open ocean waters outside the territorial limits of any single nation

**high-sound·ing** (-soun′diŋ) *adj.* sounding pretentious or impressive

**high-spir·it·ed** (-spir′i tid) *adj.* **1.** having or showing a courageous or noble spirit **2.** spirited; fiery **3.** gay; lively

**high-strung** (-struŋ′) *adj.* nervous and tense

**high-tech·nol·o·gy** (-tek näl′ə jē) *adj.* of or involving industries and businesses engaged in highly specialized, complex technology, as in electronics

**high-ten·sion** (hī′ten′shən) *adj.* having, carrying, or operating under a high voltage

**high-test** (-test′) *adj.* **1.** passing severe tests **2.** vaporizing at a low temperature: said of gasoline

**high tide 1.** the highest level to which the tide rises **2.** the time when the tide is at this level **3.** any culminating point or time

**high time 1.** none too soon **2.** [Slang] a gay, exciting time: also **high old time**

**high-toned** (-tōnd′) *adj.* **1.** [Now Rare] high in tone or pitch **2.** characterized by dignity, high principles, etc. **3.** [Colloq.] of or imitating the manners, attitudes, etc. of the upper classes

**high treason** treason against the ruler or government

**high water 1.** *same as* HIGH TIDE **2.** the highest level reached by a body of water

**high-wa·ter mark** (hī′wôt′ər, -wät′ər) **1.** the highest level reached by a body of water **2.** the mark left after high water has receded **3.** a culminating point; highest point

**high·way** (-wā′) *n.* **1.** a public road **2.** a main road; thoroughfare **3.** a direct way

**high·way·man** (-wā mən) *n., pl.* -men formerly, a man who robbed travelers on a highway

**hi·jack** (hī′jak′) *vt.* [prob. *hi* (for HIGH) + JACK, *v.*] [Colloq.] **1.** to steal (goods in transit, a truck and its contents, etc.) from (a person) by force **2.** to swindle, as by the use of force **3.** to force the pilot of (an aircraft) to fly to a nonscheduled landing point —**hi′jack′er** *n.*

**hike** (hīk) *vi.* **hiked, hik′ing** [< dial. *heik*] **1.** to take a long, vigorous walk; tramp or march **2.** to move up out of place —*vt.* [Colloq.] **1.** to pull up; hoist **2.** to raise (prices, etc.) —*n.* **1.** a long, vigorous walk **2.** [Colloq.] a moving upward; rise —**hik′er** *n.*

**hi·lar·i·ous** (hi ler′ē əs, hī-; -lar′-) *adj.* [< L. < Gr. *hilaros,* cheerful] **1.** noisily merry; boisterous and gay **2.** provoking laughter; funny —**hi·lar′i·ous·ly** *adv.*

**hi·lar·i·ty** (-ə tē) *n.* the state or quality of being hilarious

HIGHBOY

**Hil·da** (hil′də) [G. < Gmc. hyp. *hild-*, war] a feminine name

**hill** (hil) *n.* [OE. *hyll*] **1.** a natural raised part of the earth's surface, often rounded, smaller than a mountain **2.** a small pile, heap, or mound [an *anthill*] **3.** *a)* a small mound of soil heaped over and around plant roots *b)* the plant or plants rooted in such a mound —*vt.* **1.** to shape into or like a hill **2.** to cover with a hill (sense 3*a*) —**over the hill** [Colloq.] **1.** absent without permission; AWOL **2.** in one's decline —**hill′er** *n.*

**hill·bil·ly** (hil′bil′ē) *n., pl.* **-lies** [HILL + *Billy*, dim. of WILLIAM] [Colloq.] a person who lives in or comes from the mountains or backwoods, esp. of the South: somewhat contemptuous term —*adj.* [Colloq.] of or characteristic of hillbillies

**Hil·lel** (hil′el, -əl) 60? B.C.–10? A.D.; Jewish rabbi & scholar in Jerusalem

**hill·ock** (hil′ək) *n.* a small hill; mound —**hill′ock·y** *adj.*

**hill·side** (hil′sīd′) *n.* the side or slope of a hill

**hill·top** (-täp′) *n.* the top of a hill

**hill·y** (-ē) *adj.* **hill′i·er, hill′i·est** **1.** full of hills **2.** like a hill; steep —**hill′i·ness** *n.*

**hilt** (hilt) *n.* [OE.] the handle of a sword, dagger, tool, etc. —(**up**) **to the hilt** thoroughly; entirely

**hi·lum** (hī′ləm) *n., pl.* **hi′la** (-lə) [ModL. < L., little thing] *Bot.* a scar on a seed, marking the place where it was attached to the seed stalk

**him** (him; *unstressed* im, əm) *pron.* [OE.] objective case of HE: also used colloquially as a predicate complement with a linking verb (Ex.: that's *him*)

**Hi·ma·la·yas** (him′ə lā′əz, hi mäl′-yəz) mountain system in SC Asia, along the India-Tibet border: highest peak, Mt. Everest: also **Himalaya Mountains** —**Hi′ma·la′yan** *adj., n.*

**him·self** (him self′) *pron.* a form of the 3d pers. sing., masc. pronoun, used: *a)* as an intensive [he went *himself*] *b)* as a reflexive [he hurt *himself*] *c)* as a quasi-noun meaning "his real or true self" [he is not *himself* today] *d)* [Irish] as a subject [*himself* will have his tea now]

**hind¹** (hīnd) *adj.* **hind′er, hind′most** or **hind′er·most′** [prob. < HINDER²] back; rear; posterior

**hind²** (hīnd) *n., pl.* **hinds, hind:** see PLURAL, II, D, 1 [OE.] the female of the red deer, in and after its third year

**hind³** (hīnd) *n.* [OE. *hina, higna*] **1.** in N England and Scotland, a skilled farm worker or servant **2.** [Archaic] a simple peasant; rustic

**hind·brain** (-brān′) *n.* the hindmost of the three primary divisions of the vertebrate brain

**Hin·de·mith** (hin′də məth; *G.* -mit), **Paul** 1895–1963; U.S. composer, born in Germany

**hin·der¹** (hin′dər) *vt.* [OE. *hindrian*] **1.** to keep back; restrain; prevent; stop **2.** to make difficult for; thwart; frustrate —*vi.* to be a hindrance

**hind·er²** (hīn′dər) *adj.* [OE. *hinder, adv.*, behind: now felt as compar. of HIND¹] hind; rear; posterior

**Hin·di** (hin′dē) *adj.* [Hindi *hindī* < *Hind:* see HINDU] of or associated with northern India —*n.* an Indo-Iranian language, the main, now official, language of India

**hind·most** (hīnd′mōst′) *adj. superl. of* HIND¹; farthest back; last: also **hind′er·most′** (hīn′dər-)

**Hin·doo** (hin′doo) *adj., n., pl.* **-doos** *same as* HINDU

**hind·quar·ter** (hīnd′kwôr′tər) *n.* **1.** a hind leg and loin of a carcass of veal, beef, lamb, etc. **2.** [*pl.*] the hind part of a four-legged animal

**hin·drance** (hin′drəns) *n.* **1.** the act of hindering **2.** any person or thing that hinders; obstacle

**hind·sight** (hīnd′sīt′) *n.* an understanding, after the event, of what should have been done

**Hin·du** (hin′doo) *n.* [< Per. < *Hind,* India, ult. < Sans. *sindhu,* river, the Indus] **1.** any of the peoples of India that speak an Indic language **2.** a follower of Hinduism **3.** popularly, any native of India —*adj.* **1.** of the Hindus, their language, etc. **2.** of Hinduism

**Hin·du·ism** (hin′doo wiz′m) *n.* the religion and social system of the Hindus

**Hindu Kush** (koosh) mountain range in SW Asia, mostly in Afghanistan: highest peak, 25,230 ft.

**Hin·du·stan** (hin′doo stan′, -stän′) **1.** region in N India, where Hindi is spoken **2.** the entire Indian peninsula **3.** the republic of India

**Hin·du·sta·ni** (-stan′ē, -stä′nē) *n.* the most important dialect of Western Hindi, used as a trade language in N India —*adj.* **1.** of Hindustan or its people **2.** of Hindustani

**hinge** (hinj) *n.* [< ME. *hengen,* to hang] **1.** a joint, etc. on which a door, gate, lid, etc. swings **2.** a natural joint, as of the bivalve shell of a clam or oyster **3.** anything on which matters turn or depend —*vt.* **hinged, hing′ing** to equip with or attach by a hinge —*vi.* to be contingent; depend (*on*)

**hin·ny** (hin′ē) *n., pl.* **-nies** [L. *hinnus* < Gr. *innos*] the offspring of a male horse and a female donkey: cf. MULE¹

**hint** (hint) *n.* [< OE. *henten,* to seize] **1.** a slight indication of a fact, wish, etc.; indirect suggestion or reference **2.** a very small amount or degree; trace —*vt., vi.* to give a hint (of) —**hint at** to suggest indirectly; intimate —**take a hint** to perceive and act on a hint —**hint′er** *n.*

**hin·ter·land** (hin′tər land′) *n.* [G. < *hinter,* back + *land,* land] **1.** the land or district behind that bordering on a coast or river **2.** an area far from big cities and towns; back country

**hip¹** (hip) *n.* [OE. *hype*] **1.** *a)* the part of the body surrounding and including the joint formed by each thighbone and pelvis *b) same as* HIP JOINT **2.** the angle formed by the meeting of two sloping sides of a roof —*vt.* **hipped, hip′ping** to make (a roof) with such an angle

**hip²** (hip) *n.* [OE. *heope*] the fleshy fruit of the rose: it is rich in vitamin C

**hip³** (hip) *adj.* **hip′per, hip′pest** [< ? *hep*] [Slang] **1.** *a)* sophisticated; knowing; aware *b)* fashionable; stylish **2.** of or associated with hipsters or hippies —**get** (or **be**) **hip to** [Slang] to become (or be) informed or knowledgeable about —**hip′ness** *n.*

**hip·bone** (hip′bōn′) *n.* **1.** *same as: a)* INNOMINATE BONE *b)* ILIUM **2.** the neck of the femur

**hip joint** the junction between the thighbone and its socket in the pelvis

**hipped¹** (hipt) *adj.* **1.** having hips of a specified kind [*broad-hipped*] **2.** *Archit.* having a hip or hips [a *hipped* roof]

**hipped²** (hipt) *adj.* [< HYP(OCHONDRIA)] [Colloq.] having a great interest; obsessed (with *on*)

**hip·pie** (hip′ē) *n.* [< HIP³ + -IE] [Slang] a young person alienated from conventional society, who has turned to mysticism, drugs, communal living, etc.

**hip·po** (hip′ō) *n., pl.* **-pos** [Colloq.] a hippopotamus

**Hip·poc·ra·tes** (hi päk′rə tēz′) 460?-370? B.C.; Gr. physician: called the *Father of Medicine* —**Hip·po·crat·ic** (hip′ə krat′ik) *adj.*

**Hippocratic oath** the oath, attributed to Hippocrates, generally taken by medical graduates: it sets forth an ethical code for the medical profession

**hip·po·drome** (hip′ə drōm′) *n.* [< Fr. < L. < Gr. < *hippos,* a horse + *dromos,* a course] **1.** in ancient Greece and Rome, an oval course for horse races and chariot races, surrounded by tiers of seats **2.** an arena or building for a circus, etc.

**hip·po·pot·a·mus** (hip′ə pät′ə məs) *n., pl.* **-mus·es, -mi** (-mī′), **-mus:** see PLURAL, II, D, 1 [L. < Gr. < *hippos,* a horse + *potamos,* river] a large, plant-eating mammal with a heavy, thick-skinned, almost hairless body and short legs: it lives chiefly in or near rivers in Africa

**hip·py¹** (hip′ē) *n., pl.* **-pies** [Slang] *same as* HIPPIE

**hip·py²** (hip′ē) *adj.* [Colloq.] having large hips [she has a tendency to be *hippy*]

**hip roof** a roof with sloping ends and sides

**hip·ster** (hip′stər) *n.* [Slang] **1.** a hip person **2.** a beatnik: term of the 1950's and early 1960's

**Hi·ram** (hī′rəm) [Heb. *ḥīrām,* prob. < *'aḥīrām,* exalted brother] a masculine name: dim. *Hi*

**hir·cine** (hur′sin, -sin) *adj.* [< L. < *hircus,* goat] of or like a goat, esp. in odor

**hire** (hīr) *n.* [OE. *hyr*] **1.** the amount paid for the services of a person or the use of a thing **2.** a hiring or being hired —*vt.* **hired, hir′ing** **1.** to get the services of (a person) or the use of (a thing) in return for payment; employ or engage **2.** to give the use of (a thing) or the services of (oneself or another) for payment (often with *out*) —**for hire** available for work or use, for payment: also **on hire** —**hire out** to work for payment —**hir′a·ble, hire′a·ble** *adj.* —**hir′er** *n.*

**hire·ling** (-liŋ) *n.* [see HIRE & -LING¹] a person who will follow anyone's orders for pay; mercenary

**Hi·ro·hi·to** (hir′ō hē′tō) 1901– ; emperor of Japan (1926– )

**Hi·ro·shi·ma** (hir′ə shē′mə) seaport in SW Honshu, Japan: largely destroyed (Aug. 6, 1945) by a U.S. atomic bomb, the first ever used in warfare: pop. 504,000

**hir·sute** (hur′soot, hir′-; hər soot′) *adj.* [L. *hirsutus*] hairy; shaggy; bristly —**hir′sute·ness** *n.*

**his** (hiz) *pron.* [OE.] that or those belonging to him: used without a following noun [that book is *his, his* are better]: also used after *of* to indicate possession [a friend of *his*] —*possessive pronominal adj.* of, belonging to, or done by him

**His·pa·ni·a** (his pä′nē ə, -pā′-) **1.** *Latin name of the* IBERIAN PENINSULA **2.** *poet. name of* SPAIN

**His·pan·ic** (his pan′ik) *adj.* Spanish or Spanish and Portuguese —**His·pan′i·cism** (-ə siz′m) *n.*

**His·pan·io·la** (his′pən yō′lə) island in the West Indies, between Cuba & Puerto Rico, divided between Haiti & the Dominican Republic

**hiss** (his) *vi.* [echoic] **1.** to make a sound like that of a prolonged *s,* as of a goose, snake, escaping steam, etc. **2.** to show dislike or disapproval by hissing —*vt.* **1.** to say or indicate by hissing **2.** to condemn, force, or drive by hissing —*n.* the act or sound of hissing —**hiss'er** *n.*

**hist** (st; hist) *interj.* be quiet! listen!

**hist. 1.** historian **2.** historical **3.** history

**his·ta·mine** (his'tə mēn', -mən) *n.* [see HISTO- & AMINE] an amine, $C_5H_9N_3$, released by the tissues in allergic reactions: it dilates blood vessels, stimulates gastric secretion, etc. —**his'ta·min'ic** (-min'ik) *adj.*

**his·to-** [< Gr. *histos*, a loom, web] *a combining form meaning* tissue *[histology]* : also **hist-**

**his·tol·o·gy** (his täl'ə jē) *n.* [prec. + -LOGY] the branch of biology concerned with the microscopic study of the structure of tissues —**his·to·log·ic** (his'tə läj'ik), **his'to·log'i·cal** *adj.* —**his'to·log'i·cal·ly** *adv.* —**his·tol'o·gist** *n.*

**his·to·ri·an** (his tôr'ē ən) *n.* **1.** a writer of history **2.** an authority on or specialist in history

**his·tor·ic** (his tôr'ik, -tär'-) *adj.* historical; esp., famous in history

**his·tor·i·cal** (-i k'l) *adj.* **1.** of or concerned with history as a science *[the historical* method] **2.** providing evidence for a fact of history *[a historical* document] **3.** based on people or events of the past *[a historical* novel] **4.** established by history; factual **5.** in chronological order **6.** famous in history: now usually HISTORIC —**his·tor'i·cal·ly** *adv.* —**his·tor'i·cal·ness** *n.*

**historical present** the present tense used in telling about past events: also **historic present**

**his·to·ric·i·ty** (his'tə ris'ə tē) *n.* the condition of having actually occurred in history

**his·to·ri·og·ra·pher** (his tôr'ē äg'rə fər) *n.* [< LL. < Gr. < *historia*, history + *graphein*, to write] a historian; esp., one appointed to write the history of some institution, country, etc. —**his·to'ri·o·graph'ic** (-ə graf'ik), **his·to'ri·o·graph'i·cal** *adj.* —**his·to'ri·og'ra·phy** *n.*

**his·to·ry** (his'tə rē, his'trē) *n.*, *pl.* **-ries** [< L. < Gr. *historia* < *histōr*, learned] **1.** an account of what has happened; narrative. *a)* what has happened in the life of a people, country, institution, etc. *b)* a systematic account of this **3.** all recorded events of the past **4.** the branch of knowledge that deals systematically with the recording, analyzing, and correlating of past events **5.** a known or recorded past *[this coat has a history]* —**make history** to be or do something important enough to be recorded

**his·tri·on·ic** (his'trē än'ik) *adj.* [< LL. < L. *histrio*, actor] **1.** of, or having the nature of, acting or actors **2.** overacted or overacting; artificial —**his'tri·on'i·cal·ly** *adv.*

**his·tri·on·ics** (-iks) *n.pl.* [*sometimes with sing. v.*] **1.** theatricals; dramatics **2.** an artificial or affected manner, display of emotion, etc.

**hit** (hit) *vt.* **hit**, **hit'ting** [OE. *hittan* < ON. *hitta*, to meet with] **1.** to come against, usually with force; strike *[the car hit the tree]* **2.** to give a blow to; strike **3.** to strike by throwing or shooting a missile *[to hit the target]* **4.** to cause to bump or strike, as in falling, moving, etc. **5.** to affect strongly or adversely *[a town hit hard by floods]* **6.** to come upon by accident or after search *[to hit the right answer]* **7.** to reach; attain *[stocks hit a new high]* **8.** *same as* STRIKE, *vt.* 9, 10, 11 **9.** [Slang] to apply oneself to steadily or frequently *[to hit the books]* **10.** [Slang] to demand or require of *[he hit me for a loan]* **11.** *Baseball* to get (a specified base hit) —*vi.* **1.** to give a blow or blows; strike **2.** to attack suddenly **3.** to knock, bump, or strike **4.** to come by accident or after search (with *on* or *upon*) **5.** to ignite the combustible mixture in its cylinders: said of an internal-combustion engine **6.** *Baseball* to get a base hit —*n.* **1.** a blow that strikes its mark **2.** a collision **3.** an effectively witty or sarcastic remark **4.** a stroke of good fortune **5.** a successful and popular song, book, play, etc. **6.** *Baseball same as* BASE HIT —**hit it off** to get along well together —**hit or miss** in a haphazard or aimless way —**hit the road** [Slang] to leave; go away —**hit'ter** *n.*

**hit-and-run** (-'n run') *adj.* hitting and then fleeing *[a hit-and-run* driver]

**hitch** (hich) *vi.* [ME. *hicchen*, to move jerkily < ?] **1.** to move jerkily; limp; hobble **2.** to become fastened or caught **3.** [Slang] to hitchhike —*vt.* **1.** to move, pull, or shift with jerks **2.** to fasten with a hook, knot, etc. **3.** [Colloq.] to marry: usually in the passive **4.** [Slang] to hitchhike —*n.* **1.** a short, sudden movement or pull; tug; jerk **2.** a hobble; limp **3.** a hindrance; obstacle **4.** a catching or fastening; catch **5.** [Slang] a period of time served, as of military service **6.** *Naut.* a kind of knot easy to undo —**without a hitch** smoothly and successfully

**hitch·hike** (-hīk') *vi.* **-hiked'**, **-hik'ing** to travel by asking for rides from motorists along the way —*vt.* to get (a ride) or make (one's way) by hitchhiking —**hitch'hik'er** *n.*

**hith·er** (hith'ər) *adv.* [OE. *hider*] to this place; here —*adj.* on or toward this side; nearer

**hith·er·most** (-mōst') *adj.* nearest

**hith·er·to** (-tōō', hith'ər tōō') *adv.* until this time; to now

**Hit·ler** (hit'lər), **Adolf** 1889-1945; Nazi dictator of Germany (1933-45), born in Austria

**Hit·ler·ism** (-iz'm) *n.* the fascist program, ideas, and methods of Hitler and the Nazis —**Hit'ler·ite'** (-īt') *n.*, *adj.*

**hit man** [< underworld slang *hit*, murder] [Slang] a man paid to kill someone; hired murderer

**hit-skip** (hit'skip') *adj. same as* HIT-AND-RUN

**Hit·tite** (hit'īt) *n.* **1.** any of an ancient people of Asia Minor and Syria (fl. 1700-700 B.C.) **2.** the language of the Hittites —*adj.* of the Hittites, their language, or culture

**hive** (hīv) *n.* [OE. *hyf*] **1.** a box or other shelter for a colony of domestic bees; beehive **2.** a colony of bees living in a hive **3.** a crowd of busy, active people **4.** a place with many busy people —*vt.* **hived**, **hiv'ing** **1.** to gather (bees) into a hive **2.** to store up (honey) in a hive —*vi.* **1.** to enter a hive **2.** to live together as in a hive —**hive'like'** *adj.*

**hives** (hīvz) *n.* [orig. Scot. dial.] an allergic skin condition characterized by the appearance of intensely itching wheals

**H.M. 1.** Her Majesty **2.** His Majesty

**H.M.S. 1.** His (or Her) Majesty's Service **2.** His (or Her) Majesty's Ship or Steamer

**ho** (hō) *interj.* an exclamation of surprise, derision, etc.: also used to get attention *[land ho!]*

**Ho** *Chem.* holmium

**hoar** (hôr) *adj.* [OE. *har*] *same as* HOARY

**hoard** (hôrd) *n.* [OE. *hord*] a supply stored up and hidden or kept in reserve —*vi.* to store away money, goods, etc. —*vt.* to accumulate and store away —**hoard'er** *n.* —**hoard'ing** *n.*

**hoard·ing** (hôr'diŋ) *n.* [< OFr. < Frank. *hurda*, a pen, fold] [Brit.] **1.** a temporary wooden fence around a site of building construction or repair **2.** a billboard

**hoar·frost** (hôr'frôst') *n.* white, frozen dew on the ground, leaves, etc.; rime

**hoar·hound** (-hound') *n. same as* HOREHOUND

**hoarse** (hôrs) *adj.* **hoars'er**, **hoars'est** [OE. *has*] **1.** sounding harsh and grating, rough and husky, etc. **2.** having a rough, husky voice —**hoarse'ly** *adv.* —**hoarse'ness** *n.*

**hoars·en** (-'n) *vt.*, *vi.* to make or become hoarse

**hoar·y** (hôr'ē) *adj.* **hoar'i·er**, **hoar'i·est** **1.** white, gray, or grayish-white **2.** having white or gray hair because very old **3.** very old; ancient —**hoar'i·ly** *adv.* —**hoar'i·ness** *n.*

**hoax** (hōks) *n.* [< ? HOCUS] a trick or fraud, esp. one meant as a practical joke —*vt.* to deceive with a hoax —**hoax'er** *n.*

**hob¹** (häb) *n.* [? var. of HUB] **1.** a projecting ledge at the back or side of a fireplace, for keeping a kettle, pan, etc. warm **2.** a peg used as a target in quoits, etc.

**hob²** (häb) *n.* [old form of *Rob*, for *Robin* Goodfellow, elf of English folklore] an elf; goblin —**play** (or **raise**) **hob with** to make trouble for

**Ho·bart** (hō'bərt, -bärt) capital of Tasmania, on the SE coast; pop. 53,000 (with suburbs, 119,000)

**Hobbes** (häbz), **Thomas** 1588-1679; Eng. social philosopher

**hob·ble** (häb''l) *vi.* **-bled**, **-bling** [ME. *hobelen* < base of *hoppen*, HOP¹ + freq. suffix] **1.** to go unsteadily, haltingly, etc. **2.** to walk lamely; limp —*vt.* **1.** to cause to limp **2.** to hamper the movement of (a horse, etc.) by tying two legs together **3.** to hinder —*n.* **1.** a halting walk; limp **2.** a rope, strap, etc. used to hobble a horse —**hob'bler** *n.*

**hob·by** (häb'ē) *n.*, *pl.* **-bies** [ME. *hoby* < ? Du. *hobben*, to move back and forth] **1.** a hobbyhorse **2.** something that a person likes to work at, collect, etc. in his spare time —**hob'by·ist** *n.*

**hob·by·horse** (-hôrs') *n.* **1.** a toy consisting of a horse's head on a stick that one pretends to ride **2.** *same as* ROCKING HORSE

**hob·gob·lin** (häb'gäb'lin) *n.* [HOB² + GOBLIN] **1.** an elf; goblin **2.** a bogy; bugbear

**hob·nail** (-nāl') *n.* [HOB¹, sense 2 + NAIL] a short nail with a broad head, put on the soles of heavy shoes to prevent wear or slipping —*vt.* to put hobnails on —**hob'-nailed'** *adj.*

**hob·nob** (-näb') *vi.* **-nobbed'**, **-nob'bing** [< ME. *habben*, to have + *nabben*, not to have, esp. with reference to alternation in drinking] to be on close terms (*with*); associate in a familiar way

**ho·bo** (hō'bō) *n.*, *pl.* **-bos**, **-boes** **1.** esp. formerly, a migratory worker **2.** a vagrant; tramp

**Hob·son's choice** (häb'sənz) [after T. *Hobson* (1544?-1631), Eng. liveryman,

HOBNAILS

who let horses in strict order according to their position near the door] a choice of taking what is offered or nothing

**Ho Chi Minh** (hō′ chē′ min′) 1890?–1969; president of North Vietnam (1954–69)

**hock**[1] (häk) *n*. [OE. *hoh*, the heel] the joint bending backward in the hind leg of a horse, ox, etc., but corresponding to the human ankle —*vt*. to disable by cutting the tendons of the hock

**hock**[2] (häk) *n*. [< *Hochheimer* < *Hochheim*, Germany] [Chiefly Brit.] a white Rhine wine

**hock**[3] (häk) *vt.*, *n*. [< Du. *hok*, prison, (slang) debt] [Slang] *same as* PAWN[1]

**hock·ey** (häk′ē) *n*. [prob. < OFr. *hoquet*, bent stick] 1. a team game played on ice, in which the players, using curved sticks (**hockey sticks**) and wearing skates, try to drive a rubber disk (*puck*) into their opponents' goal 2. a similar game played on foot on a field with a small ball instead of a puck

**hock·shop** (häk′shäp′) *n*. [Slang] a pawnshop

**ho·cus** (hō′kəs) *vt.* **-cused** or **-cussed**, **-cus·ing** or **-cus·sing** [contr. < ff.] 1. to play a trick on; dupe 2. to drug 3. to put drugs in (a drink)

**ho·cus-po·cus** (-pō′kəs) *n*. [imitation L.] 1. meaningless words used as a formula by conjurers 2. sleight of hand; legerdemain 3. trickery; deception —*vt.*, *vi.* **-cused** or **-cussed**, **-cus·ing** or **-cus·sing** [Colloq.] to trick; dupe

**hod** (häd) *n*. [prob. < MDu. *hodde*] 1. a long-handled wooden trough, used for carrying bricks, mortar, etc. on the shoulder 2. a coal scuttle

**hodge·podge** (häj′päj′) *n*. [< OFr. *hochepot*, stew < *hocher*, to shake + *pot*, POT] any jumbled mixture; mess

**Hodg·kin's disease** (häj′kinz) [after Dr. T. *Hodgkin* (1798–1866)] a disease characterized by progressive enlargement of the lymph nodes

**hoe** (hō) *n*. [< OFr. *houe* < OHG. < *houwan*, to hew] a tool with a thin, flat blade set across the end of a long handle, used for weeding, loosening soil, etc. —*vt.*, *vi.* **hoed**, **hoe′ing** to dig, cultivate, weed, etc. with a hoe —**ho′er** *n*.

**hoe·down** (-doun) *n*. [infl. by BREAK-DOWN, sense 2] 1. a lively dance, often a square dance 2. music for this 3. a party at which hoedowns are danced

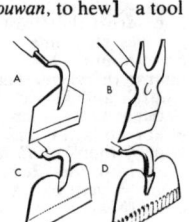

TYPES OF HOE
(A, nursery; B, weeding; C, garden; D, serrated)

**hog** (hôg, häg) *n.*, *pl.* **hogs**, **hog**: see PLURAL, II, D, 1 [OE. *hogg*] 1. a pig; esp., a full-grown pig of more than 120 lbs. raised for its meat 2. [Colloq.] a selfish, greedy, or filthy person —*vt.* **hogged**, **hog′ging** [Slang] to take all of or an unfair share of —**go (the) whole hog** [Slang] to go all the way —**high on (or off) the hog** [Colloq.] in a luxurious or costly way

**ho·gan** (hō′gôn, -gän) *n*. [Navaho *qoghan*, house] the typical dwelling of the Navaho Indians, built of earth walls supported by timbers

**Ho·garth** (hō′gärth), **William** 1697–1764; Eng. painter & engraver

**hog·back** (hôg′bak, häg′-) *n*. a ridge with a sharp crest and abruptly sloping sides

**hog·gish** (hôg′ish, häg′-) *adj*. like a hog; very selfish, greedy, coarse, or filthy —**hog′gish·ly** *adv*. —**hog′gish·ness** *n*.

**hog·nose snake** (hôg′nōz′, häg′-) any of several small, harmless N. American snakes with a flat snout: also **hog′nosed′ snake**

**hogs·head** (hôgz′hed′, hägz′-) *n*. [ME. *hoggeshede*, lit., hog's head] 1. a large barrel or cask holding from 63 to 140 gallons 2. any of various liquid measures, esp. one equal to 63 gallons

**hog·tie** (hôg′tī′, häg′-) *vt.* **-tied′**, **-ty′ing** or **-tie′ing** 1. to tie the four feet or the hands and feet of 2. [Colloq.] to make incapable of effective action

**hog·wash** (-wôsh′, -wäsh′) *n*. 1. refuse fed to hogs; swill 2. useless or insincere talk, writing, etc.

**Hoh·en·zol·lern** (hō′ən tsôl′ərn; *E.* -zäl′ərn) ruling family of Prussia (1701–1918) & of Germany (1871–1918)

**hoi pol·loi** (hoi′ pə loi′) [Gr., the many] the common people; the masses: usually patronizing

**hoist** (hoist) *vt.* [< earlier *hyce* < Du. *hijschen* & LowG. *hissen*] to raise aloft; lift, esp. by means of a pulley, crane, etc. —*n*. 1. a hoisting 2. an apparatus for raising heavy things

**hoi·ty-toi·ty** (hoit′ē toit′ē) *adj*. [< obs. *hoit*, to be noisily mirthful] haughty or petulant

**hoke** (hōk) *vt.* **hoked**, **hok′ing** [< HOKUM] [Slang] to treat in an overly sentimental or showily or falsely contrived way: usually with *up* —*n*. [Slang] *same as* HOKUM —**hok′ey** *adj.*

**Hok·kai·do** (hō kī′dō) one of the four main islands of Japan, north of Honshu: 30,364 sq. mi.

**ho·kum** (hōk′əm) *n*. [altered < HOCUS(-POCUS)] [Slang] 1. crudely comic or mawkishly sentimental elements in a play, story, etc., used to gain an immediate emotional response 2. nonsense; humbug

**Hol·bein** (hōl′bīn), **Hans** (häns) 1. 1460?–1524; Ger. painter: called *the Elder* 2. 1497?–1543; Ger. painter in England: son of *prec.*: called *the Younger*

**hold**[1] (hōld) *vt.* **held**, **hold′ing**; archaic pp. **hold′en** [OE. *haldan*] 1. to take and keep with the hands, arms, or other means; grasp; clutch 2. to keep from going away; not let escape [to *hold* a prisoner] 3. to keep in a certain position or condition [*hold* your head up] 4. to restrain or control; specif., *a*) to keep from falling; support *b*) to keep from acting [*hold* your tongue] *c*) to get and keep control of [to *hold* our attention] *d*) to maintain [to *hold* a course] *e*) to keep (a room, etc.) for use later 5. to have and keep as one's own; own; occupy [he *holds* the office of mayor] 6. to have or conduct together; specif., to carry on (a meeting, conversation, etc.) 7. to have room for; contain [this can *holds* a pint] 8. to have or keep in the mind 9. to regard; consider [to *hold* a statement to be untrue] 10. *Law a*) to decide; decree *b*) to possess by legal title [to *hold* a mortgage] 11. *Music* to prolong (a tone or rest) —*vi.* 1. to retain a hold, firm contact, etc. [*hold* tight] 2. to go on being firm, loyal, etc. [he *held* to his resolve] 3. to remain unbroken or unyielding [the rope *held*] 4. to be true or valid [a rule which still *holds*] 5. to keep up; continue [the wind *held* steady] 6. to halt: usually in the imperative —*n*. 1. a grasping or seizing; grip; specif., a way of gripping an opponent in wrestling 2. a thing to hold on by 3. a controlling force; restraining authority [to have a *hold* over someone] 4. an order to make a temporary halt or delay 5. an order reserving something 6. [Archaic] a stronghold 7. *Music same as* FERMATA —**catch hold of** to seize; grasp —**get hold of** 1. to seize; grasp 2. to acquire —**hold back** 1. to restrain 2. to refrain 3. to retain —**hold down** 1. to restrain 2. [Colloq.] to have and keep (a job) —**hold forth** 1. to preach; lecture 2. to offer —**hold in** 1. to keep in or back 2. to control oneself —**hold off** 1. to keep at a distance 2. to keep from attacking or doing something —**hold on** 1. to retain one's hold 2. to persist 3. [Colloq.] stop! wait! —**hold one's own** to persist in spite of obstacles —**hold out** 1. to last; endure 2. to stand firm 3. to offer 4. [Colloq.] to refuse to give (what is to be given) —**hold out for** [Colloq.] to stand firm in demanding —**hold over** 1. to postpone consideration of or action on 2. to keep or stay for an additional period —**hold up** 1. to prop up 2. to show 3. to last; endure 4. to stop; delay 5. to stop forcibly and rob —**hold with** 1. to agree with 2. to approve of —**lay (or take) hold of** 1. to seize; grasp 2. to get control of

**hold**[2] (hōld) *n*. [altered < HOLE or < MDu. < *hol*] an area below the decks, as in a ship, for carrying cargo

**hold·er** (hōld′ər) *n*. 1. a person who holds; specif., one who is legally entitled to payment of a bill, note, or check 2. a device for holding something

**hold·fast** (-fast′) *n*. a specialized organ or part by which certain animals and plants attach themselves to an object

**hold·ing** (-iŋ) *n*. 1. land, esp. a farm, rented from another 2. [usually pl.] property owned, esp. stocks or bonds

**holding company** a corporation organized to hold bonds or stocks of other corporations, which it usually controls

**hold·out** (-out′) *n*. a player in a professional sport who delays signing his contract because he wants better terms

**hold·o·ver** (-ō′vər) *n*. [Colloq.] a person or thing staying on from a previous period

**hold·up** (-up′) *n*. 1. a stoppage; delay 2. the act of stopping forcibly and robbing

**hole** (hōl) *n*. [OE. *hol*] 1. a hollow place; cavity [a hole in the ground, a swimming *hole*] 2. an animal's burrow or lair; den 3. a small, dingy, squalid place 4. *a*) an opening in or through anything; gap *b*) a tear or rent, as in a garment 5. a flaw; fault; defect [*holes* in an argument] 6. [Colloq.] an embarrassing situation; predicament 7. *Golf a*) a cylindrical cup sunk into a green, into which the ball is to be hit *b*) any of the sections of a course, including the tee, fairway, and green 8. *Physics* an energy state in which a particle is missing, esp. when the energy levels above and below are occupied —*vt.* **holed**, **hol′ing** to put or drive into a hole —**hole in one** *Golf* the act of getting the ball into the hole on the shot from the tee —**hole up** [Colloq.] 1. to hibernate, usually in a hole 2. to shut oneself in —**in the hole** [Colloq.] financially embarrassed or behind —**pick holes in** to pick out errors or flaws in —**hol′ey** *adj.*

**hol·i·day** (häl′ə dā′) *n*. 1. a religious festival: see HOLY DAY 2. a day of freedom from labor; day for leisure and recreation 3. [often pl.] [Chiefly Brit.] a vacation 4. a day set aside, as by law, for the suspension of business, in commemoration of some event —*adj.* of or suited to a holiday; joyous; gay

**ho·li·er-than-thou** (hō′lē ər *thən* thou′) *adj.* annoyingly sanctimonious or self-righteous

**ho·li·ly** (hō′lə lē) *adv.* in a holy manner

**ho·li·ness** (-lē nis) *n.* 1. a being holy 2. [H-] a title of the Pope (with *His* or *Your*)

**Hol·ins·hed** (häl′inz hed′, -in shed′), **Raphael** ?–1580?; Eng. chronicler

**Hol·land** (häl′ənd) *same as the* NETHERLANDS —**Hol′land·er** *n.*

**hol·land** (häl′ənd) *n.* [< prec., where first made] a linen or cotton cloth used for clothing, window shades, etc.

**hol·lan·daise sauce** (häl′ən dāz′) [Fr., of Holland] a creamy sauce, as for vegetables, made of butter, egg yolks, lemon juice, etc.

**hol·ler** (häl′ər) *vi., vt., n.* [altered < HOLLO] [Colloq.] shout or yell

**hol·lo** (häl′ō, hə lō′) *interj., n., pl.* **-los** 1. a shout or call, as to attract a person's attention or to urge on hounds in hunting 2. a shout of greeting or surprise —*vi., vt.* **-loed, -lo·ing** 1. to shout (at) so as to attract attention 2. to urge on (hounds) by calling out ″hollo″ 3. to shout, in greeting or surprise

**hol·low** (häl′ō) *adj.* [OE. *holh*] 1. having a cavity within it; not solid 2. shaped like a cup or bowl; concave 3. deeply set; sunken *[hollow cheeks]* 4. empty or worthless *[hollow praise]* 5. hungry 6. deep-toned and muffled, as though resounding from something hollow —*adv.* in a hollow manner —*n.* 1. a hollow place; cavity; hole 2. a valley —*vt., vi.* to make or become hollow —**beat all hollow** [Colloq.] to outdo or surpass by far —**hollow out** to make by hollowing —**hol′low·ly** *adv.* —**hol′low·ness** *n.*

**hol·lo·ware** (häl′ō wer′) *n.* serving pieces and table accessories, esp. of silver, that are relatively hollow or concave: also **hol′low-ware′**

**hol·ly** (häl′ē) *n., pl.* **-lies** [OE. *holegn*] 1. a small tree or shrub with glossy, sharp-pointed leaves and bright-red berries 2. the leaves and berries, used as Christmas ornaments

**hol·ly·hock** (häl′ē häk′) *n.* [< OE. *halig*, holy + *hoc*, mallow] 1. a tall, biennial plant of the mallow family, with a hairy stem and large, showy flowers of various colors 2. its flower

**Hol·ly·wood** (häl′ē wood′) [HOLLY + WOOD] 1. section of Los Angeles, once the site of many U.S. motion-picture studios; hence, the U.S. motion-picture industry or its life, etc. 2. city on the SE coast of Fla., near Miami: pop. 117,000

**Hollywood bed** a bed consisting of a mattress on a box spring that rests on a metal frame or has attached legs: it sometimes has a headboard

HOLLYHOCK

**holm** (hōm) *n. same as* HOLM OAK

**Holmes** (hōmz, hōlmz), **Oliver Wendell** 1. 1809–94; U.S. writer & physician 2. 1841–1935; associate justice, U.S. Supreme Court (1902–32): son of *prec.*

**hol·mi·um** (hōl′mē əm) *n.* [ModL. < *Holmia*, Latinized form of *Stockholm*] a metallic chemical element of the rare-earth group: symbol, Ho; at. wt., 164.930; at. no., 67

**holm oak** [< OE. *holegn*, holly] 1. a south European evergreen oak with hollylike leaves 2. its wood

**hol·o-** [Fr. < L. < Gr. *holos*, whole] a combining form meaning whole, entire *[holography]*

**hol·o·caust** (häl′ə kôst′, hō′lə-) *n.* [< OFr. < LL. < Gr. < *holos*, whole + *kaustos*, burnt: see CAUSTIC] great destruction of life, esp. by fire —**the Holocaust** the destruction of millions of Jews by the Nazis

**hol·o·gram** (-gram′) *n.* a photographic plate containing the record of the interference pattern produced by means of holography

**hol·o·graph** (-graf′) *adj.* [< Fr. < LL. < LGr. < Gr. *holos*, whole + *graphein*, to write] written entirely in the handwriting of the person under whose name it appears —*n.* a holograph document, letter, etc. —**hol′o·graph′ic** *adj.*

**ho·log·ra·phy** (hə läg′rə fē) *n.* [HOLO- + -GRAPHY] a method used to produce three-dimensional images by laser light and to record on a photographic plate the interference patterns from which an image can be reconstructed

**holp** (hōlp) *archaic pt. & obs. pp. of* HELP

**Hol·stein** (hōl′stēn, -stīn) *n.* [after SCHLESWIG-HOLSTEIN, where orig. bred] any of a breed of large, black-and-white dairy cattle: also **Hol′stein-Frie′sian** (-frē′zhən)

**hol·ster** (hōl′stər) *n.* [Du.] a pistol case, usually of leather and attached to a belt or saddle

**ho·ly** (hō′lē) *adj.* **-li·er, -li·est** [OE. *halig* < base of *hal*, sound, whole] *[often H-]* 1. dedicated to religious use; consecrated; sacred 2. spiritually pure; sinless; saintly 3. regarded with or deserving deep respect or reverence 4. [Slang] very much of a *[a holy terror]* —*n., pl.* **-lies** a holy thing or place

**Holy Communion** any of various Christian rites in which bread and wine are consecrated and received as the body and blood of Jesus or as symbols of them

**holy day** a day consecrated to religious observances or to a religious festival

**Holy Father** a title of the Pope

**Holy Ghost** the third person of the Trinity

**Holy Grail** *see* GRAIL

**Holy Land** *same as* PALESTINE (sense 1)

**Holy Mother** Mary, mother of Jesus

**holy of holies** 1. the innermost part of the Jewish tabernacle and Temple, where the ark of the covenant was kept 2. any most sacred place

**Hol·yoke** (hōl′yōk) [after E. *Holyoke*, 18th-c. pres. of Harvard U.] city in SW Mass.: pop. 50,000

**holy orders** 1. the sacrament or rite of ordination 2. the position of being an ordained Christian minister or priest 3. ranks or grades of the Christian ministry; specif., *a)* R.C.Ch. *same as* MAJOR ORDERS or, sometimes, MINOR ORDERS *b)* Anglican Ch. bishops, priests, and deacons

**Holy Roman Empire** empire of WC Europe, comprising the German-speaking peoples & N Italy: begun in 800 A.D. or, in another view, in 962, it lasted until 1806

**Holy Scripture** (or **Scriptures**) *see* BIBLE

**Holy See** the position, authority, or court of the Pope; Apostolic See

**Holy Spirit** the spirit of God; specif., third person of the Trinity

**ho·ly·stone** (hō′lē stōn′) *n.* [< ?] a flat piece of sandstone for scouring a ship's wooden decks —*vt.* **-stoned′, -ston′ing** to scour with a holystone

**Holy Synod** the administrative council of any branch of the Orthodox Eastern Church

**Holy Week** the week before Easter

**Holy Writ** the Bible

**hom·age** (häm′ij, äm′-) *n.* [< OFr. < ML. *hominaticum* < L. *homo*, a man] 1. orig., *a)* a public avowal of allegiance by a vassal to his lord *b)* an act done or thing given to show the relationship between lord and vassal 2. anything given or done to show reverence, honor, etc.: usually with *do* or *pay* *[to pay homage to a hero]*

**hom·bre** (äm′brā, -brē) *n.* [Sp. < L. *homo*, a man] [Slang] a man; fellow

**hom·burg** (häm′bərg) *n.* [< *Homburg*, Prussia] a man's felt hat with a crown dented front to back and a stiff, slightly curved brim

**home** (hōm) *n.* [OE. *ham*] 1. the place where a person (or family) lives; one's dwelling place 2. the city, state, or country where one was born or reared 3. a place where one likes to be; restful or congenial place 4. the members of a family as a unit; a household and its affairs 5. an institution for the care of orphans, the aged, etc. 6. the natural environment of an animal, plant, etc. 7. the place of origin, development, etc. *[Paris is the home of fashion]* 8. in many games, the base or goal; esp., the home plate in baseball —*adj.* 1. of one's home or country; domestic 2. of or at the center of operations *[home office]* 3. played in the city, at the school, etc. where the team originates —*adv.* 1. at, to, or in the direction of home 2. to the point aimed at 3. to the heart of a matter; closely —*vi.* **homed, hom′ing** 1. to go to one's home 2. to have a home —**at home** 1. in one's own house, city, or country 2. as if in one's own home; comfortable; at ease 3. willing to receive visitors —**bring (something) home to** to impress upon or make clear to —**home (in)** on to be directed as by radar to (a destination) —**home′less** *adj.* —**home′like′** *adj.*

**home·bod·y** (-bäd′ē) *n., pl.* **-bod′ies** a person whose interests and activities focus on the home

**home-brew** (-brōō′) *n.* an alcoholic beverage, esp. beer, made at home

**home·com·ing** (-kum′iŋ) *n.* in many colleges, an annual celebration attended by alumni

**home economics** the science and art of homemaking, including nutrition, budgeting, etc.

**home·land** (-land′) *n.* the country in which one was born or makes one's home

**home·ly** (-lē) *adj.* **-li·er, -li·est** 1. characteristic of or suitable for home or home life; plain or simple *[homely virtues]* 2. not elegant; crude 3. not good-looking; plain or unattractive —**home′li·ness** *n.*

**home·made** (-mād′) *adj.* 1. made at home 2. as if made at home; esp., plain, simple, or crude

**home·mak·er** (-māk′ər) *n.* a person who manages a home; esp., a housewife —**home′mak′ing** *n.*

**ho·me·o-** [Gr. *homoio-* < *homos*, same] *a combining form meaning* like, the same, similar

**ho·me·op·a·thy** (hō′mē äp′ə thē) *n.* [< G.: see prec. & -PATHY] a system of medical treatment based on the theory that certain diseases can be cured with small doses of drugs which in a healthy person and in large doses would produce symptoms like those of the disease: opposed to ALLOPATHY —**ho′me·o·path′** (-ə path′), **ho′me·op′a·thist** *n.* —**ho′me·o·path′ic** (-ə path′ik) *adj.*

**ho·me·o·sta·sis** (hō′mē ō stā′sis) *n.* [ModL.: see HOMEO- & STASIS] the tendency to maintain, or the maintenance of, stability or equilibrium within an organism, social group, etc. —**ho′me·o·stat′ic** (-stat′ik) *adj.*

**home·own·er** (hōm′ō′nər) *n.* a person who owns the house he lives in

**home plate** *Baseball* the slab that the batter stands beside, across which the pitcher must throw the ball for a strike

**Ho·mer** (hō′mər) [< L. < Gr. < *homēros*, a pledge, hostage, one led, hence blind] **1.** a masculine name **2.** c. 8th cent. B.C.; semilegendary Gr. epic poet: reputed author of the *Iliad* & the *Odyssey* **3. Wins·low** (winz′lō), 1836–1910; U.S. painter

**hom·er** (hō′mər) *n.* [Colloq.] *same as* HOME RUN —*vi.* [Colloq.] to hit a home run

**Ho·mer·ic** (hō mer′ik) *adj.* of, like, or characteristic of the poet Homer, his poems, or the Greek civilization that they describe (c. 1200–800 B.C.)

**home·room** (hōm′rōōm′) *n.* the room where a class in school meets daily to be checked for attendance, receive school bulletins, etc.: also **home room**

**home rule** the administration of the affairs of a country, colony, city, etc. granted to the citizens who live in it by a superior governing authority

**home run** *Baseball* a safe hit that allows the batter to touch all bases and score a run

**home·sick** (-sik′) *adj.* longing for home —**home′sick′ness** *n.*

**home·spun** (-spun′) *n.* **1.** cloth made of yarn spun at home **2.** coarse, loosely woven cloth like this —*adj.* **1.** spun at home **2.** made of homespun **3.** plain; homely [*homespun virtues*]

**home·stead** (-sted′) *n.* **1.** a place where a family makes its home, including the land, house, and outbuildings **2.** a 160-acre tract of public land granted by the U.S. government to a settler to develop as a farm —*vi.* to become a settler on a homestead —**home′stead′er** *n.*

**home·stretch** (-strech′) *n.* **1.** the part of a race track between the last turn and the finish line **2.** the final part of any undertaking

**home·ward** (hōm′wərd) *adv., adj.* toward home: also **home′wards** *adv.*

**home·work** (-wurk′) *n.* **1.** work done at home **2.** schoolwork to be done outside the classroom **3.** study or research in preparation for some project, activity, etc.: usually in **do one's homework**

**home·y** (-ē) *adj.* **hom′i·er, hom′i·est** having qualities usually associated with home; comfortable, familiar, etc.

**hom·i·cide** (häm′ə sīd′, hō′mə-) *n.* [< OFr. < LL. < L. < *homo*, a man + *caedere*, to cut, kill] **1.** any killing of one human being by another **2.** a person who kills another — **hom′i·ci′dal** *adj.*

**hom·i·let·ics** (häm′ə let′iks) *n.pl.* [with sing. *v.*] [< LL. < Gr. < *homilein*, to converse < *homilos*: see ff.] the art of writing and preaching sermons —**hom′i·let′ic** *adj.*

**hom·i·ly** (häm′ə lē) *n., pl.* **-lies** [< OFr. < LL. *homilia* < Gr. < *homilos*, assembly, prob. < *homou*, together + *ilē*, a crowd] **1.** a sermon, esp. one about something in the Bible **2.** a solemn, moralizing talk or writing —**hom′i·list** *n.*

**hom·ing** (hō′min) *adj.* **1.** homeward bound **2.** having to do with guidance to a goal, target, etc.

**homing pigeon** a pigeon trained to find its way home from distant places

**hom·i·nid** (häm′ə nid) *n.* [< ModL. *Hominidae* (family name)] any form of man, extinct or living

**hom·i·noid** (-noid′) *n.* [< ModL. *Hominoidea* (superfamily name)] any form of man or the great apes, extinct or living —*adj.* manlike

**hom·i·ny** (häm′ə nē) *n.* [contr. < *rockahominy* < Algonquian] dry corn with the hull and germ removed and often coarsely ground (**hominy grits**): it is boiled for food

**ho·mo** (hō′mō) *n., pl.* **hom·in·es** (häm′ə nēz′) [L., a man] any of a genus of primates including modern man (*Homo sapiens*) and extinct species of man

**ho·mo-** [< Gr. < *homos*, same] *a combining form meaning* same, equal, like

**ho·mo·ge·ne·ous** (hō′mə jē′nē əs, häm′ə-) *adj.* [< ML. < Gr. < *homos*, same + *genos*, a race, kind] **1.** the same in structure, quality, etc.; similar or identical **2.** composed of similar or identical parts; uniform —**ho′mo·ge·ne′i·ty** (-jə nē′ə tē) *n.* —**ho′mo·ge′ne·ous·ly** *adv.*

**ho·mog·e·nize** (hə mäj′ə nīz′) *vt.* **-nized′, -niz′ing 1.** to make homogeneous **2.** to make more uniform throughout; specif., to process (milk) so that the fat particles are so finely divided and emulsified that the cream does not separate on standing —**ho·mog′e·ni·za′tion** *n.*

**hom·o·graph** (häm′ə graf′, hō′mə-) *n.* [HOMO- + -GRAPH] a word with the same spelling as another but with a different meaning and origin (Ex.: *bow*, the front part of a ship, *bow*, to bend) —**hom′o·graph′ic** *adj.*

**ho·mol·o·gize** (hō mäl′ə gīz′, hə-) *vt.* **-gized′, -giz′ing 1.** to make homologous **2.** to demonstrate homology in —*vi.* to be homologous

**ho·mol·o·gous** (-ə gəs) *adj.* [< Gr. < *homos*, same + *legein*, to say] **1.** matching in structure, position, character, etc. **2.** *Biol.* corresponding in structure and origin, as the wing of a bat and the foreleg of a mouse

**ho·mol·o·gy** (hō mäl′ə jē, hə-) *n., pl.* **-gies 1.** the quality or state of being homologous **2.** a homologous correspondence or relationship

**ho·mol·o·sine projection** (hə mäl′ə sin, hō-; -sīn′) [< Gr. *homalos*, even, level + SINE] a map of the earth's surface with the land areas shown in their proper relative size and form, with a minimum of distortion

**ho·mo·mor·phism** (hō′mə môr′fiz′m, häm′ə-) *n.* [HOMO- + -MORPH + -ISM] **1.** similarity in form **2.** *Biol.* resemblance or similarity, without actual relationship, in structure or origin Also **ho′mo·mor′phy** —**ho′mo·mor′phic, ho′mo·mor′phous** *adj.*

**hom·o·nym** (häm′ə nim, hō′mə-) *n.* [< Fr. < L. < Gr. < *homos*, same + *onyma*, name] a word with the same pronunciation as another but with a different meaning, origin, and, usually, spelling (Ex.: *bore* and *boar*) —**ho·mon′y·mous** (hō män′ə məs), **hom′o·nym′ic** *adj.*

**hom·o·phone** (häm′ə fōn′) *n.* [< Gr. < *homos*, same + *phōnē*, a sound] **1.** any of two or more letters or groups of letters having the same pronunciation (Ex.: *c* in *civil* and *s* in *song*) **2.** *same as* HOMONYM

**hom·o·phon·ic** (häm′ə fän′ik, hō′mə-) *adj.* [< Gr.: see prec.] **1.** *Music* having a single part, or voice, carrying the melody **2.** of, or having the nature of, a homonym —**ho·moph′o·ny** (hō mäf′ə nē) *n., pl.* **-nies**

**ho·mop·ter·ous** (hō mäp′tər əs) *adj.* [HOMO- + -PTEROUS] belonging to an order of insects with sucking mouthparts and two pairs of membranous wings of uniform thickness throughout, as aphids, cicadas, etc.

**Ho·mo sa·pi·ens** (hō′mō sā′pē enz′, hō′mō sap′ē ənz) [ModL.: see HOMO & SAPIENT] modern man; mankind; human being: the only living species of the genus *Homo*

**ho·mo·sex·u·al** (hō′mə sek′shoo wəl) *adj.* of or having sexual desire for those of the same sex as oneself —*n.* a homosexual person —**ho′mo·sex′u·al′i·ty** (-wal′ə tē) *n.* —**ho′mo·sex′u·al·ly** *adv.*

**ho·mun·cu·lus** (hō mun′kyoo ləs) *n., pl.* **-li′** (-lī′) [L., dim. of *homo*, man] a little man; dwarf

**hom·y** (hō′mē) *adj.* **hom′i·er, hom′i·est** *same as* HOMEY

**Hon., hon.** **1.** honorable **2.** honorary

**Hon·du·ras** (hän door′əs, -dyoor′-) country in Central America, north of Nicaragua: 43,227 sq. mi.; pop. 2,495,000; cap. Tegucigalpa —**Hon·du′ran** *adj., n.*

**hone** (hōn) *n.* [< OE. *han*, a stone] a whetstone used to sharpen cutting tools, esp. razors —*vt.* **honed, hon′ing** to sharpen as with a hone

**hon·est** (än′əst) *adj.* [< OFr. < L. *honestus* < *honor*, honor] **1.** that will not lie, cheat, or steal; trustworthy; truthful **2.** *a)* showing fairness and sincerity [an *honest* effort] *b)* gained by fair methods [an *honest* living] **3.** being what it seems; genuine [to give *honest* measure] **4.** frank and open [an *honest* face] **5.** [Archaic] chaste —*adv.* [Colloq.] honestly; truly: an intensive

**hon·est·ly** (-lē) *adv.* **1.** in an honest manner **2.** truly; really: an intensive [*honestly*, it is so]

**hon·es·ty** (än′əs tē) *n.* the state or quality of being honest; specif., *a)* being truthful, trustworthy, or upright *b)* sincerity; straightforwardness

**hon·ey** (hun′ē) *n., pl.* **-eys** [OE. *hunig*] **1.** a thick, sweet, syrupy substance that bees make as food from the nectar of flowers **2.** sweet quality; sweetness **3.** sweet one; darling **4.** [Colloq.] something pleasing or excellent of its kind — *adj.* **1.** of or like honey **2.** sweet; dear —*vt.* **-eyed** or **-ied, -ey·ing 1.** to make sweet as with honey **2.** to flatter

**hon·ey·bee** (-bē′) *n.* a bee that makes honey

**hon·ey·comb** (-kōm′) *n.* **1.** the structure of six-sided wax cells made by bees to hold their honey, eggs, etc. **2.** anything like this —*vt.* **1.** to fill with holes like a honeycomb; riddle **2.** to permeate or undermine *[honeycombed* with intrigue*]* —*adj.* of, like, or patterned after a honeycomb: also **hon′ey·combed′**

**hon·ey·dew** (-dōō′, -dyōō′) *n.* **1.** a sweet fluid exuded from various plants **2.** a sweet substance secreted by some juice-sucking plant insects **3.** *short for* HONEYDEW MELON

**honeydew melon** a variety of melon with a smooth, whitish rind and sweet, greenish flesh

**hon·eyed** (hun′ēd) *adj.* **1.** sweetened, covered, or filled with honey **2.** sweet as honey; flattering or affectionate *[honeyed* words*]*

**honey locust** a N. American tree of the legume family, with strong, thorny branches, featherlike foliage, and large, twisted pods

**hon·ey·moon** (hun′ē mōōn′) *n.* [as if < HONEY + MOON, but ? folk-etym. for ON. *hjūnōttsmānathr,* lit., wedding-night month] **1.** formerly, the first month of marriage **2.** the vacation spent together by a newly married couple **3.** a brief period of apparent agreement —*vi.* to have or spend a honeymoon —**hon′ey·moon′er** *n.*

**hon·ey·suck·le** (-suk′'l) *n.* **1.** any of a genus of largely woody plants with small, fragrant flowers of red, yellow, or white **2.** any of several similar plants

**Hong Kong** (häŋ′ käŋ′, hôŋ′ kôŋ′) Brit. crown colony consisting of a small area on the SE coast of China & several offshore islands: also **Hong′kong′**

**hon·ied** (hun′ēd) *adj. same as* HONEYED

**honk** (hôŋk, häŋk) *n.* [echoic] **1.** the call of a wild goose **2.** any similar sound, as of an automobile horn —*vi., vt.* to make or cause to make such a sound —**honk′er** *n.*

**hon·ky-tonk** (hôŋ′kē tôŋk′, häŋ′kē täŋk′) *n.* [ < ?] [Slang] a cheap, disreputable cabaret or nightclub

**Hon·o·lu·lu** (hän′ə lōō′lōō, hō′nə-) [Haw., lit., sheltered bay] capital of Hawaii; seaport on Oahu: pop. 365,000 (met. area 763,000)

**hon·or** (än′ər) *n.* [ < OFr. < L. *honor, honos*] **1.** high regard or great respect given or received; esp., *a)* glory; fame; renown *b)* good reputation; credit **2.** a keen sense of right and wrong; adherence to principles considered right *[to* behave with *honor]* **3.** chastity; purity **4.** high rank or position; distinction *[the* great *honor* of the presidency*]* **5.** [H-] a title given to certain officials, as judges (preceded by *His, Her,* or *Your*) **6.** something done or given as a token of respect; specif., *a)* a social courtesy *[may* I have the *honor* of this dance?*]* *b)* [pl.] public ceremonies of respect *[funeral honors]* *c)* [pl.] special distinction given to students for high academic achievement; also, an advanced course of study for exceptional students **7.** one that brings respect and fame to a school, country, etc. **8.** *Bridge a)* any of the five highest cards in a suit *b)* [pl.] the four or five highest cards of the trump suit *c)* [pl.] in a no-trump hand, the aces **9.** *Golf* the privilege of driving first from the tee —*vt.* **1.** to respect greatly; regard highly **2.** to treat with deference and courtesy **3.** to worship (a deity) **4.** to do something in honor of **5.** to accept and pay when due *[to* honor a check*]* —*adj.* of or showing honor *[honor* roll*]* —**do honor to 1.** to show great respect for **2.** to bring honor to —**do the honors** to act as host or hostess, esp. by making introductions, serving at table, etc. —**on** (or **upon**) **one's honor** staking one's good name on one's truthfulness or reliability

**hon·or·a·ble** (-ə b'l) *adj.* **1.** worthy of being honored; specif., *a)* of, or having a position of, high rank or worth: used as a title of courtesy *b)* noble; illustrious *c)* of good reputation; respectable **2.** having or showing a sense of right and wrong; upright **3.** bringing honor *[honorable* mention*]* **4.** accompanied with marks of respect *[an* honorable burial*]* —**hon′or·a·bly** *adv.*

**honorable mention** a citation of honor, esp. to one who was not a winner, as in a competition

**hon·o·ra·ri·um** (än′ə rer′ē əm) *n., pl.* **-ri·ums, -ri·a** (-ə) [L. *honorarium* (*donum*), honorary (gift)] a payment as to a professional person for services on which no fee is set

**hon·or·ar·y** (än′ə rer′ē) *adj.* [L. *honorarius,* of or conferring honor] **1.** given as an honor only *[an* honorary degree*]* **2.** *a)* designating an office held as an honor only, without service or pay *b)* holding such an office —**hon′or·ar′i·ly** *adv.*

**hon·or·if·ic** (än′ə rif′ik) *adj.* [ < L. < *honor + facere,* to make] conferring honor; showing respect *[an* honorific title*]* —**hon′or·if′i·cal·ly** *adv.*

**honor system** in some schools, prisons, etc., a system whereby individuals are trusted to obey rules, do their work, take tests, etc. without direct supervision

**hon·our** (än′ər) *n., vt., adj. Brit. var. of* HONOR

**Hon·shu** (hän′shōō′) largest of the islands forming Japan: 88,946 sq. mi.

**hooch** (hōōch) *n.* [ < Alaskan Ind. *hoochinoo,* crude alcoholic liquor] [Slang] alcoholic liquor, esp. when made or obtained surreptitiously

**hood**[1] (hood) *n.* [OE. *hod*] **1.** a covering for the head and neck, worn separately or as part of a robe or cloak **2.** anything like a hood in shape or use; specif., *a)* the metal cover over the engine of an automobile *b)* *Falconry* the covering for a falcon's head when it is not chasing game —*vt.* to cover as with a hood —**hood′ed** *adj.* —**hood′less** *adj.*

**hood**[2] (hood, hŏod) *n.* [Slang] *short for* HOODLUM

**-hood** (hood) [ < OE. *had,* order, condition, rank] *a suffix meaning:* **1.** state, quality, condition *[childhood]* **2.** the whole group of (a specified class, profession, etc.) *[priesthood]*

**Hood, Robin** *see* ROBIN HOOD

**hood·lum** (hōōd′ləm) *n.* [prob. < G. dial. *hudilump,* wretch] a wild, lawless person, often a member of a gang of criminals —**hood′lum·ism** *n.*

**hoo·doo** (hōō′dōō) *n., pl.* **-doos** [var. of VOODOO] **1.** *same as* VOODOO **2.** [Colloq.] *a)* a person or thing that causes bad luck *b)* bad luck —*vt.* [Colloq.] to bring bad luck to

**hood·wink** (hood′wiŋk′) *vt.* [HOOD[1] + WINK] **1.** orig., to blindfold **2.** to deceive; trick; dupe

**hoo·ey** (hōō′ē) *interj., n.* [echoic] [Slang] nonsense; bunk

**hoof** (hoof, hŏof) *n., pl.* **hoofs, hooves** (hoovz, hŏovz) [OE. *hof]* the horny covering on the feet of cattle, deer, horses, etc., or the entire foot —*vt., vi.* [Colloq.] to walk (often with *it*) —**on the hoof** not butchered; alive —**hoofed** *adj.* —**hoof′less** *adj.*

**hoof-and-mouth disease** (-'n mouth′) *same as* FOOT-AND-MOUTH DISEASE

**hoof·beat** (-bēt′) *n.* the sound made by the hoof of an animal when it runs, walks, etc.

**hoof·er** (hoof′ər, hŏof′-) *n.* [Slang] a professional dancer, esp. a tap dancer, soft-shoe dancer, etc.

**hook** (hook) *n.* [ < OE. *hoc*] **1.** a curved or bent piece of metal, wood, etc. used to catch, hold, or pull something; specif., *a)* a curved piece of wire with a barbed end, for catching fish *b)* a curved piece used to hang things on, etc. *[a* coat *hook]* *c)* a small metal catch inserted in a loop, or eye, to fasten clothes together **2.** a curved metal implement for cutting grain, etc. **3.** something shaped like a hook, as a curving headland or cape **4.** *a)* the path of a hit or thrown ball that curves away to the left from a right-handed player or to the right from a left-handed player *b)* a ball that follows such a path **5.** *Boxing* a short blow delivered with the arm bent at the elbow **6.** *Music same as* FLAG[1] (sense 4) —*vt.* **1.** to fasten as with a hook **2.** to take hold of or catch as with a hook **3.** to shape into a hook **4.** to make (a rug) by drawing strips of cloth or yarn through a canvas or burlap backing with a hook **5.** to hit or throw (a ball) in a hook (*n.* 4a) **6.** [Colloq.] to steal; snatch **7.** *Boxing* to hit with a hook —*vi.* **1.** to curve as a hook does **2.** to be fastened with a hook or hooks **3.** to be caught by a hook —**by hook or by crook** by any means, honest or dishonest —**hook up 1.** to connect or attach with a hook or hooks **2.** to arrange and connect the parts of (a radio, etc.) —**off the hook** [Colloq.] out of trouble, freed from an obligation, etc. —**on one's own hook** [Colloq.] by oneself, without help from others

**hook·ah, hook·a** (hook′ə) *n.* [Ar. *huqqah*] an Oriental tobacco pipe with a long, flexible tube by means of which the smoke is drawn through water in a vase or bowl and cooled

**hooked** (hookt) *adj.* **1.** curved like a hook **2.** having a hook or hooks **3.** made with a hook *[a* hooked rug*]* **4.** [Slang] addicted as to the use of a drug (often with *on*) **5.** [Slang] married

**hook·er** (hook′ər) *n.* **1.** one that hooks **2.** [Slang] a drink of whiskey **3.** [Slang] a prostitute

**hook·up** (-up′) *n.* **1.** the arrangement and connection of parts, circuits, etc., as in (a) radio **2.** [Colloq.] a connection or alliance

HOOKAH

**hook·worm** (-wurm′) *n.* any of a number of small, parasitic roundworms with hooks around the mouth, infesting the small intestine and causing a disorder (**hookworm disease**) characterized by anemia, weakness, and abdominal pain

**hook·y** (hook′ē) *n. see* PLAY HOOKY

**hoo·li·gan** (hōō′li gən) *n.* [ < *? Hooligan* (or *Houlihan*), an Irish family in London] [Slang] a hoodlum, esp. a young one —**hoo′li·gan·ism** *n.*

**hoop** (hōōp) *n.* [OE. *hop*] **1.** a circular band or ring for holding together the staves of a barrel, cask, etc. **2.** anything like a hoop; specif., *a)* any of the rings forming the framework of a hoop skirt  *b) Basketball* the metal rim of the basket  *c) Croquet same as* WICKET

**hoop·la** (hōōp′lä) *n.* [Colloq.] **1.** great excitement **2.** showy publicity; ballyhoo

**hoo·poe** (hōō′pōō) *n.* [< Fr. *huppe* < L. *upupa*, prob. echoic] a European bird with a long, curved bill and an erectile crest

**hoop skirt** a skirt worn over a framework of hoops, or rings, to make it spread out

**hoo·ray** (hoo rā′, hə-, hōō-) *interj., n., vi., vt. same as* HURRAH

**hoose·gow, hoos·gow** (hōōs′gou) *n.* [< Sp. *juzgado*, court of justice, ult. < L. *judex*, JUDGE] [Slang] a jail

**Hoo·sier** (hōō′zhər) *n.* [prob. < dial. *hoozer*, something big] [Colloq.] a native or inhabitant of Indiana

**hoot** (hōōt) *vi.* [orig. echoic] **1.** to utter its characteristic hollow sound: said of an owl **2.** to utter a sound like this **3.** to shout, esp. in scorn or disapproval —*vt.* **1.** to express (scorn, disapproval, etc.) by hooting **2.** to express scorn or disapproval of by hooting **3.** to chase away by hooting [to *hoot* an actor off the stage] —*n.* **1.** the sound that an owl makes **2.** any sound like this **3.** a shout of scorn or disapproval **4.** the least bit; whit [not worth a *hoot*] —**hoot′er** *n.*

**hoot·en·an·ny** (hōōt′'n an′ē) *n., pl.* **-nies** [a fanciful coinage] a meeting of folk singers, as for public entertainment

**Hoo·ver** (hōō′vər) **1. Herbert Clark,** 1874–1964; 31st president of the U.S. (1929–33) **2. J(ohn) Edgar,** 1895–1972; director of the FBI (1924–72)

**Hoover Dam** [after Pres. HOOVER] dam on the Colorado River, on the Ariz.-Nev. border

**hooves** (hoovz, hōōvz) *n. alt. pl. of* HOOF

**hop¹** (häp) *vi.* **hopped, hop′ping** [OE. *hoppian*] **1.** to make a short leap or leaps on one foot **2.** to move by leaping or springing on both (or all) feet at once, as a frog, bird, etc. **3.** [Colloq.] *a)* to go or move briskly *b)* to take a short, quick trip (with *up, down,* or *over*) —*vt.* **1.** to jump over [to *hop* a fence] **2.** to get aboard [to *hop* a train] —*n.* **1.** a hopping **2.** a bounce, as of a baseball **3.** [Colloq.] a dance, esp. an informal one **4.** [Colloq.] a short flight in an airplane —**hop on** (or **all over**) [Slang] to scold; reprimand

**hop²** (häp) *n.* [< MDu. *hoppe*] **1.** a twining vine with the female flowers borne in small cones **2.** [*pl.*] the dried ripe cones, used for flavoring beer, ale, etc. —*vt.* **hopped, hop′ping** to flavor with hops —**hop up** [Slang] **1.** to stimulate by or as by a drug **2.** to supercharge (an automobile engine, etc.)

**Hope** (hōp) [< ff.] a feminine name

**hope** (hōp) *n.* [OE. *hopa*] **1.** a feeling that what is wanted will happen **2.** the thing that one has a hope for **3.** a reason for hope **4.** a person or thing on which one may base some hope **5.** [Archaic] trust; reliance —*vt.* **hoped, hop′ing 1.** to want and expect **2.** to want very much —*vi.* **1.** to have hope (*for*) **2.** [Archaic] to trust or rely —**hope against hope** to continue having hope though it seems baseless —**hop′er** *n.*

**hope chest** a chest in which a young woman hoping to get married collects linen, clothing, etc.

**hope·ful** (-fəl) *adj.* **1.** feeling or showing hope **2.** inspiring or giving hope —*n.* a person who hopes, or seems likely, to succeed —**hope′ful·ness** *n.*

**hope·ful·ly** (-ē) *adv.* **1.** in a hopeful manner **2.** it is to be hoped (that) [*hopefully* we will win]: regarded by some as a loose usage

**hope·less** (-lis) *adj.* **1.** without hope **2.** allowing no hope [a *hopeless* situation] **3.** impossible to solve, deal with, etc. —**hope′less·ly** *adv.* —**hope′less·ness** *n.*

**Ho·pi** (hō′pē) *n.* [Hopi *Hópitu,* lit., good] **1.** *pl.* **-pis, -pi** a member of a Pueblo tribe of Indians in NE Arizona **2.** their language

**hop·lite** (häp′līt) *n.* [< Gr. < *hoplon,* a tool] a heavily armed foot soldier of ancient Greece

**hop·per** (häp′ər) *n.* **1.** a person or thing that hops **2.** any hopping insect **3.** a container from which the contents can be emptied slowly and evenly [the *hopper* of an automatic coal stoker]

**hop·sack·ing** (häp′sak·iŋ) *n.* [lit., sacking for hops] **1.** a coarse material for bags **2.** a fabric somewhat simulating this, used for suits, etc. Also **hop′sack′**

**hop·scotch** (häp′skäch′) *n.* [HOP¹ + SCOTCH] a children's game in which each player hops from one compartment to another of a figure drawn on the ground

**Hor·ace** (hôr′is, här′-) [< L.: see ff.] **1.** a masculine name **2.** (L. name *Quintus Horatius Flaccus*) 65–8 B.C.; Roman poet: known for his odes —**Ho·ra·tian** (hə-rā′shən, hô-) *adj.*

**Ho·ra·ti·o** (hə rā′shō, -shē ō; hô-) [< L. *Horatius,* name of a Roman gens] a masculine name

**horde** (hôrd) *n.* [< Fr. < G. < Pol. *horda* < Turk. *ordū*] **1.** a nomadic tribe or clan of Mongols **2.** a large, moving crowd; swarm —*vi.* **hord′ed, hord′ing** to form or gather in a horde

**hore·hound** (hôr′hound′) *n.* [< OE. < *har,* white + *hune,* horehound] **1.** a bitter plant of the mint family, with white, downy leaves **2.** a bitter juice extracted from its leaves **3.** cough medicine or candy made with this juice

**ho·ri·zon** (hə rī′z'n) *n.* [< OFr. < L. < Gr. *horizōn (kyklos),* the bounding (circle)] **1.** the line where the sky seems to meet the earth: called **visible** or **apparent horizon 2.** [*usually pl.*] the limit of one's experience, interest, knowledge, etc.

**hor·i·zon·tal** (hôr′ə zän′t'l, här′-) *adj.* **1.** *a)* parallel to the plane of the horizon; not vertical *b)* placed or acting in a horizontal direction **2.** flat and even; level **3.** at, or made up of elements at, the same level or status [a *horizontal* union] —*n.* a horizontal line, plane, etc. —**hor′i·zon·tal′i·ty** (-tal′ə tē) *n.* —**hor′i·zon′tal·ly** *adv.*

**horizontal union** *same as* CRAFT UNION

**hor·mone** (hôr′mōn) *n.* [< Gr. < *horman,* to excite < *hormē,* impulse] **1.** a substance formed in some organ of the body, as the adrenal glands, pituitary, etc., and carried to another organ or tissue, where it has a specific effect: often prepared synthetically **2.** a similar substance in plants —**hor·mo′nal** (-mō′n'l), **hor·mon·ic** (-män′ik) *adj.*

**horn** (hôrn) *n.* [OE.] **1.** *a)* a hard, permanent projection of bone or keratin, that grows on the head of cattle, sheep, etc. *b)* the antler of a deer, shed annually **2.** anything that protrudes from the head of an animal, as a tentacle of a snail **3.** the substance that horns are made of **4.** a container made by hollowing out a horn **5.** a cornucopia **6.** anything shaped like a horn; specif., *a)* a peninsula or cape *b)* either end of a crescent *c)* a projection above the pommel of a cowboy's saddle **7.** *a)* an instrument made of horn and sounded by blowing *b)* any brass-wind instrument; specif., the French horn; also, *Jazz* any wind instrument *c)* a device sounded to give a warning [a *foghorn*] *d)* a horn-shaped loudspeaker —*vt.* **1.** to strike or gore with the horns **2.** to furnish with horns —*adj.* made of horn —**blow one's own horn** [Colloq.] to boast —**horn in (on)** [Colloq.] to meddle (in) —**lock horns** to have a conflict —**pull** (or **draw** or **haul**) **in one's horns 1.** to hold oneself back **2.** to withdraw; recant —**horned** *adj.* —**horn′less** *adj.* —**horn′like′** *adj.*

**Horn, Cape** southernmost point of S. America, on an island (**Horn Island**) in Tierra del Fuego, Chile

**horn·bill** (-bil′) *n.* any of a family of large, tropical, old-world birds with a huge, curved bill

**horn·blende** (-blend′) *n.* [G.: see HORN & BLENDE] a black, rock-forming mineral, a type of amphibole common in some granitic rocks

**horn·book** (-book′) *n.* **1.** a parchment sheet with the alphabet, numbers, etc. on it, mounted on a small board under a thin, clear plate of horn: formerly a child's primer **2.** an elementary treatise

**horned pout** *same as* BULLHEAD: also **horn′pout′** *n.*

**horned toad** any of several small, scaly lizards of the New World that eat insects and have short tails and hornlike spines

**horned viper** a poisonous N African snake with a hornlike spine above each eye

**hor·net** (hôr′nit) *n.* [OE. *hyrnet*] any of several large, yellow-and-black social wasps

**horn of plenty** *same as* CORNUCOPIA

**horn·pipe** (hôrn′pīp′) *n.* **1.** an obsolete wind instrument with a bell and mouthpiece made of horn **2.** a lively dance formerly popular with sailors **3.** music for this

**horn·y** (hôr′nē) *adj.* **horn′i·er, horn′i·est 1.** of, like, or made of horn **2.** having horns **3.** toughened and calloused **4.** [Slang] lustful —**horn′i·ness** *n.*

**ho·ro·loge** (hôr′ə lōj′, här′-) *n.* [< OFr. < L. < Gr. < *hōra,* hour + *legein,* to tell] a timepiece; clock, hourglass, sundial, etc.

**ho·rol·o·gist** (hô räl′ə jist) *n.* an expert in horology; maker of or dealer in timepieces: also **ho·rol′o·ger**

**ho·rol·o·gy** (hô räl′ə jē) *n.* [< Gr. *hōra,* hour + -LOGY] the science or art of measuring time or making timepieces —**hor·o·log·ic** (hôr′ə läj′ik, här′-), **hor′o·log′i·cal** *adj.*

**hor·o·scope** (hôr′ə skōp′, här′-) *n.* [Fr. < L. < Gr. < *hōra,* hour + *skopos,* watcher] **1.** the position of the planets and stars with relation to one another at a given time, esp. at a person's birth, regarded in astrology as determining his destiny **2.** a chart of the zodiacal signs and the positions of the planets, etc. by which astrologers profess to tell a person's future —**hor′o·scop′ic** (-skäp′ik) *adj.* —**ho·ros·co·py** (hô räs′kə pē) *n.*

**hor·ren·dous** (hô ren′dəs, hə-) *adj.* [L. *horrendus* < prp. of *horrere,* to bristle] horrible; frightful —**hor·ren′dous·ly** *adv.*

**hor·ri·ble** (hôr′ə b'l, här′-) *adj.* [< OFr. < L. < *horrere:* see prec.] **1.** causing a feeling of horror; terrible; dreadful **2.** [Colloq.] very bad, ugly, unpleasant, etc. —**hor′ri·bly** *adv.*

**hor·rid** (hôr′id, här′-) *adj.* **1.** causing a feeling of horror; terrible; revolting **2.** very bad, ugly, unpleasant, etc. —**hor′rid·ly** *adv.* —**hor′rid·ness** *n.*

**hor·ri·fy** (hôr′ə fī′, här′-) *vt.* **-fied′, -fy′ing 1.** to cause to feel horror **2.** [Colloq.] to shock or disgust —**hor′ri·fi·ca′tion** *n.*

**hor·ror** (hôr′ər, här′-) *n.* [< OFr. < L. *horror* < *horrere*, to bristle, be afraid] **1.** the strong feeling caused by something frightful or shocking; terror and repugnance **2.** strong dislike or aversion **3.** the quality of causing horror **4.** something that causes horror **5.** [Colloq.] something very bad, ugly, disagreeable, etc. —*adj.* intended to cause horror *[horror movies]* —**the horrors** [Colloq.] a fit of extreme nervousness, panic, etc.

‡**hors de com·bat** (ôr′ də kōn bä′) [Fr., out of combat] put out of action; disabled

**hors d'oeu·vre** (ôr′dúrv′, -duv′; *Fr.* ôr dö′vr′) *pl.* **hors′ d'oeuvres** (dúrvz′, duvz′); *Fr.* **hors d'oeu′vre** [Fr., lit., outside of work] an appetizer, as olives, anchovies, canapés, etc., served usually at the beginning of a meal

**horse** (hôrs) *n., pl.* **hors′es, horse:** see PLURAL, II, D, 1 [OE. *hors*] **1.** a large, strong animal with four legs, solid hoofs, and flowing mane and tail, long ago domesticated for drawing loads, carrying riders, etc. **2.** the full-grown male of the horse **3.** a frame on legs to support something *[a sawhorse]* **4.** *slang for:* a) HORSEPOWER b) HEROIN **5.** *Gym.* a padded block on legs, used for jumping or vaulting **6.** *Mil.* [*with pl. v.*] mounted troops; cavalry —*vt.* **horsed, hors′ing 1.** to supply with a horse or horses; put on horseback **2.** [Colloq.] to shove; push **3.** [Slang] to subject to horseplay —*vi.* to mount or go on horseback —*adj.* **1.** of a horse or horses **2.** mounted on horses **3.** large, strong, or coarse of its kind *[horseradish]* —**from the horse's mouth** [Colloq.] from the original or authoritative source of information —**hold one's horses** [Slang] to curb one's impatience —**horse around** [Slang] to engage in horseplay —**horse of another** (or **a different**) **color** an entirely different matter —**on one's high horse** [Colloq.] acting in an arrogant or disdainful manner —**to horse!** mount your horse!

HORSE (sense 5)

**horse·back** (-bak′) *n.* the back of a horse —*adv.* on horseback

**horse·car** (-kär′) *n.* **1.** a streetcar drawn by horses **2.** a car for transporting horses

**horse chestnut** *a)* a tree with large, palmately compound leaves, clusters of white flowers, and glossy brown seeds *b)* its seed **2.** any of various related shrubs or trees —**horse′-chest′nut** *adj.*

**horse·flesh** (-flesh′) *n.* **1.** the flesh of the horse, esp. as food **2.** horses collectively

**horse·fly** (-flī′) *n., pl.* **-flies′** any of various large flies, the female of which sucks the blood of horses, cattle, etc.

**horse·hair** (-her′) *n.* **1.** hair from the mane or tail of a horse **2.** a stiff fabric made from this hair; haircloth —*adj.* **1.** of horsehair **2.** covered or stuffed with horsehair

**horse·hide** (-hīd′) *n.* **1.** the hide of a horse **2.** leather made from this

**horse latitudes** either of two belts of calms, light winds, and high barometric pressure, at c. 30°–35° N. and S. latitude

**horse·laugh** (-laf′) *n.* a loud, boisterous, usually derisive laugh; guffaw

**horse·less** (-lis) *adj.* **1.** without a horse **2.** self-propelled *[a horseless carriage]*

**horse·man** (-mən) *n., pl.* **-men 1.** a man who rides on horseback **2.** a man skilled in the riding or care of horses —**horse′man·ship′** *n.*

**horse opera** [Slang] a motion picture or play about cowboys, rustlers, etc., esp. in the W U.S.

**horse pistol** a large pistol formerly carried by horsemen

**horse·play** (-plā′) *n.* rough, boisterous fun

**horse·pow·er** (-pou′ər) *n.* a unit for measuring the power of motors or engines, equal to 746 watts or to a rate of 33,000 foot-pounds per minute

**horse·rad·ish** (-rad′ish) *n.* **1.** a plant of the mustard family, grown for its pungent, white root **2.** a relish made by grating this root

**horse sense** [Colloq.] ordinary common sense

**horse·shoe** (hôr′shoo̅′, hôrs′-) *n.* **1.** a flat, U-shaped, protective metal plate nailed to a horse's hoof **2.** anything shaped like this **3.** *[pl.]* a game in which the players toss horseshoes in an attempt to encircle a stake or come as close

to it as possible —*vt.* **-shoed′, -shoe′ing** to fit with a horseshoe or horseshoes —**horse′sho′er** *n.*

**horseshoe crab** a sea arthropod shaped like the base of a horse's foot and having a long, spinelike tail

**horse·tail** (hôrs′tāl′) *n.* **1.** a horse's tail **2.** a rushlike plant with hollow, jointed stems and scalelike leaves

**horse trade** any bargaining marked by shrewd calculation —**horse′-trade′** *vi.* **-trad′ed, -trad′ing** —**horse′-trad′er** *n.*

**horse·whip** (-hwip′, -wip′) *n.* a whip for driving or managing horses —*vt.* **-whipped′, -whip′ping** to lash with a horsewhip

**horse·wom·an** (-woom′ən) *n., pl.* **-wom′en 1.** a woman who rides on horseback **2.** a woman skilled in the riding or care of horses

**hors·y** (hôr′sē) *adj.* **hors′i·er, hors′i·est 1.** of, like, or suggesting a horse; esp., having large features and a big body that looks strong but awkward **2.** of, like, or characteristic of people who are fond of horses, fox hunting, or horse racing Also **hors′ey** —**hors′i·ly** *adv.* —**hors′i·ness** *n.*

**hort. 1.** horticultural **2.** horticulture

**hor·ta·to·ry** (hôr′tə tôr′ē) *adj.* [< LL. < L. pp. of *hortari*, freq. of *horiri*, to urge] **1.** encouraging or urging to good deeds **2.** exhorting; giving advice Also **hor′ta·tive**

**Hor·tense** (hôr tens′, hôr′tens) [Fr. < L. < *hortensius*, of a garden] a feminine name

**hor·ti·cul·ture** (hôr′tə kul′chər) *n.* [< L. *hortus*, a garden + *cultura*, culture] the art or science of growing flowers, fruits, vegetables, etc. —**hor′ti·cul′tur·al** *adj.* —**hor′ti·cul′tur·ist** *n.*

**Hos.** Hosea

**ho·san·na** (hō zan′ə) *n., interj.* [< OE. < LL. < Gr. *hōsanna* < Heb. *hōshī′ah nnā*, lit., save, we pray] an exclamation of praise to God

**hose** (hōz) *n., pl.* **hose** or, for 3, usually **hos′es** [OE. *hosa*] **1.** orig., a man's tightfitting outer garment covering the hips, legs, and feet **2.** *[pl.]* a) stockings b) socks **3.** [prob. infl. by Du. *hoos*, water pipe] a flexible pipe or tube, used to convey fluids, esp. water from a hydrant —*vt.* **hosed, hos′ing 1.** to water with a hose **2.** [Slang] to beat as with a hose

**Ho·se·a** (hō zā′ə, -zē′ə) *Bible* **1.** a Hebrew prophet of the 8th cent. B.C. **2.** the book containing his writings

**ho·sen** (hō′z'n) *n. archaic pl. of* HOSE (n. 1 & 2)

**ho·sier** (hō′zhər) *n.* [Chiefly Brit.] a person who makes or sells hosiery

**ho·sier·y** (-ē) *n.* **1.** hose; stockings and socks **2.** [Chiefly Brit.] similar knitted or woven goods

**hos·pice** (häs′pis) *n.* [Fr. < L. < *hospes*, host, guest] a place of shelter for travelers, esp. such a shelter maintained by monks

**hos·pi·ta·ble** (häs′pi tə b'l, häs pit′ə-) *adj.* [MFr. < ML. < L. < *hospes*: see prec.] **1.** showing or characterized by friendliness, kindness, and solicitude toward guests **2.** favoring health, growth, etc. *[a hospitable climate]* **3.** receptive or open, as to new ideas —**hos′pi·ta·bly** *adv.*

**hos·pi·tal** (häs′pi t'l) *n.* [< OFr. < LL. *hospitale*, inn < L. < *hospes*: see HOSPICE] an institution where the ill or injured may receive medical or surgical treatment, nursing care, lodging, etc.

**hos·pi·tal·i·ty** (häs′pə tal′ə tē) *n., pl.* **-ties** the act, practice, or quality of being hospitable

**hospitalization insurance** insurance providing hospitalization for the subscriber and, usually, members of his immediate family

**hos·pi·tal·ize** (häs′pi t'l īz′) *vt.* **-ized′, -iz′ing** to send to, put in, or admit to a hospital —**hos′pi·tal·i·za′tion** *n.*

**host¹** (hōst) *n.* [< OFr. < ML. < L. *hostia*, animal sacrificed] a wafer of the Eucharist; esp., [H-] a consecrated wafer

**host²** (hōst) *n.* [< OFr. < L. *hospes*: see HOSPICE] **1.** a man who entertains guests in his own home or at his own expense **2.** a man who keeps an inn or hotel **3.** any organism on or in which another (called a *parasite*) lives —*vi., vt.* to act as host or hostess (to)

**host³** (hōst) *n.* [< OFr. < ML. < L. *hostis*, army] **1.** an army **2.** a multitude; great number

**hos·tage** (häs′tij) *n.* [< OFr. < L. *hoste:* see HOST²] a person given as a pledge, or taken prisoner as by an enemy, until certain conditions are met

**hos·tel** (häs′t'l) *n.* [< HOSPITAL] an inn; hostelry; specif., *same as* YOUTH HOSTEL

**hos·tel·er** (-ər) *n.* **1.** [Archaic] an innkeeper **2.** a traveler who stops at youth hostels

**hos·tel·ry** (-rē) *n., pl.* **-ries** an inn; hotel

**host·ess** (hōs′tis) *n.* **1.** a woman who entertains guests in her own home or at her own expense; often, the wife of a host **2.** a) a stewardess, as on an airplane b) a woman employed in a restaurant to supervise waitresses, seating, etc. *c)* a woman who serves as paid partner at a public dance hall

**hos·tile** (häs't'l; *chiefly Brit.* -tīl) *adj.* [< L. < *hostis*, enemy] **1.** of or characteristic of an enemy **2.** unfriendly; antagonistic **3.** not hospitable; adverse —**hos'tile·ly** *adv.*

**hos·til·i·ty** (häs til'ə tē) *n., pl.* -**ties** **1.** a feeling of enmity, ill will, unfriendliness, etc. **2.** *a)* an expression of enmity and ill will; hostile act *b)* [*pl.*] acts of war; warfare

**hos·tler** (häs'lər, äs'-) *n.* [contr. of HOSTELER] one who takes care of horses at an inn, stable, etc.

**hot** (hät) *adj.* **hot'ter, hot'test** [OE. *hat*] **1.** *a)* having a high temperature, esp. one that is higher than that of the human body *b)* having a relatively or abnormally high temperature **2.** producing a burning sensation [*hot* pepper] **3.** full of or characterized by any intense feeling or activity, as *a)* impetuous; excitable [a *hot* temper] *b)* violent; angry [*hot* words] *c)* full of enthusiasm; eagerly intent *d)* lustful *e)* very controversial **4.** following closely [*hot* pursuit] **5.** as if heated by friction; specif., *a)* electrically charged [a *hot* wire] *b)* highly radioactive **6.** designating or of a color that suggests heat, as intense red **7.** [Colloq.] that has not yet lost heat, freshness, etc.; specif., *a)* recent; new [*hot* news] *b)* clear; strong [a *hot* scent] *c)* recent and from an inside source [a *hot* tip] **8.** [Slang] *a)* recently stolen *b)* sought by the police **9.** [Slang] excellent, good, etc. **10.** *Jazz* designating or of music or playing having exciting rhythmic and tonal effects, improvisation, etc. —*adv.* in a hot manner —**hot up** [Slang] to heat or warm up —**make it hot for** [Colloq.] to make things uncomfortable for —**hot'ly** *adv.* —**hot'ness** *n.*

**hot air** [Slang] empty or pretentious talk

**hot·bed** (-bed') *n.* **1.** a bed of earth covered with glass and heated by manure, for forcing plants **2.** any place that fosters rapid growth

**hot-blood·ed** (-blud'id) *adj.* easily excited; excitable, ardent, passionate, reckless, etc.

**hot·box** (-bäks') *n.* an overheated bearing on an axle or shaft

**hot cake** *same as* GRIDDLECAKE —**sell like hot cakes** [Colloq.] to be sold rapidly in large quantities

**hot cell** a shielded enclosure used in handling radioactive materials by remote control

**hot cross bun** a bun marked with a cross of frosting, eaten esp. during Lent

**hot dog** [Colloq.] a wiener, esp. one served in a soft roll

**ho·tel** (hō tel') *n.* [< Fr. < OFr. *hostel*, HOSTEL] an establishment providing lodging, and often meals, for travelers, semipermanent guests, etc.

**ho·tel·ier** (hō'tel yā', -tə lir') *n.* [Fr.] an owner or manager of a hotel

**hot·foot** (hät'foot') *adv.* [Colloq.] in great haste —*vi.* [Colloq.] to hurry; hasten —*n., pl.* -**foots'** the prank of secretly inserting and lighting a match between the sole and upper of a victim's shoe

**hot·head** (-hed') *n.* a hotheaded person

**hot·head·ed** (-hed'id) *adj.* **1.** quick-tempered **2.** hasty; impetuous —**hot'head'ed·ly** *adv.* —**hot'head'ed·ness** *n.*

**hot·house** (-hous') *n.* a heated building for growing plants; greenhouse —*adj.* **1.** grown in a hothouse **2.** needing careful treatment; delicate

**hot line** a telephone or telegraph line for direct, instant communication as in a crisis, esp. between heads of state

**hot pepper** any of various pungent peppers

**hot plate** a small gas or electric stove for cooking

**hot rod** [Slang] **1.** an old automobile adjusted or rebuilt for quick acceleration and high speed **2.** a driver of hot rods: also **hot rod·der** (räd'ər)

**hot spring** a spring whose water is above 98° F. (36.7° C)

**hot-tem·pered** (-tem'pərd) *adj.* having a fiery temper; easily made angry

**Hot·ten·tot** (hät''n tät') *n.* [Afrik.: echoic origin] **1.** a member of a nomadic pastoral people of SW Africa **2.** their language —*adj.* of the Hottentots or their language

**hot war** actual warfare: opposed to COLD WAR

**hot water** [Colloq.] trouble: preceded by *in* or *into*

**Hou·din·i** (hōō dē'nē), **Harry** (born *Ehrich Weiss*) 1874–1926; U.S. stage magician

**hound** (hound) *n.* [OE. *hund*, a dog] **1.** any of several breeds of hunting dogs with long, drooping ears and short hair **2.** any dog **3.** a contemptible person **4.** [Slang] a devotee or fan —*vt.* **1.** to hunt or chase with or as with hounds [to *hound* a debtor] **2.** to urge on; incite to pursuit —**follow the** (or **ride to**) **hounds** to hunt (a fox, etc.) on horseback with hounds

**hounds·tooth check** (houndz'tōōth') a pattern of irregular broken checks, used in woven material

**hour** (our) *n.* [< OFr. < L. < Gr. *hōra*, hour, time] **1.** a division of time, one of the twenty-four parts of a day; sixty minutes **2.** a point or period of time; specif., *a)* a

fixed point or period of time for a particular activity, etc. [the dinner *hour*] *b)* [*pl.*] a period fixed for work, etc. [office *hours*] *c)* [*pl.*] the usual times for getting up or going to bed [to keep late *hours*] **3.** the time of day as indicated by a timepiece **4.** a measure of distance set by the time it takes to travel it **5.** *Astron.* 1/24 of a SIDEREAL DAY **6.** *Eccles. a) same as* CANONICAL HOUR *b)* the prayers said at a canonical hour **7.** *Educ.* a class session of about an hour: regarded as a unit of academic credit —**after hours** after the regular hours for business, school, etc. —**hour after hour** every hour —**of the hour** prominent at this time —**the small** (or **wee**) **hours** the hours just after midnight

**hour·glass** (-glas') *n.* an instrument for measuring time by the trickling of sand, mercury, etc. from one glass bulb to another below it: the shift of contents takes one hour

**hou·ri** (hoor'ē, hou'rē) *n., pl.* -**ris** [Fr. < Per. *hūri* < Ar., ult. < *hawira*, to be dark-eyed] a beautiful nymph of the Moslem Paradise

**hour·ly** (our'lē) *adj.* **1.** done or happening every hour or during an hour **2.** reckoned by the hour [*hourly* wage] **3.** continual —*adv.* **1.** at or during every hour **2.** at any hour **3.** continually

**house** (hous; *for v.* houz) *n., pl.* **hous·es** (hou'ziz) [OE. *hus*] **1.** a building for human beings to live in; specif., *a)* the building or part of a building occupied by one family *b)* a building where a group of people live as a unit [a fraternity *house*] **2.** the people who live in a house; family; household **3.** a family as including kin, ancestors, and descendants, esp. a royal family [the *House* of Tudor] **4.** something regarded as a house, in providing shelter; specif., *a)* the habitation of an animal, as the shell of a mollusk *b)* a building where things are kept or stored **5.** *a)* a theater *b)* the audience in a theater **6.** *a)* a place of business *b)* a business firm **7.** the management of a gambling establishment **8.** [*often* H-] *a)* the building or rooms where a legislative assembly meets *b)* a legislative assembly **9.** *Astrol.* any of the twelve parts into which the heavens are divided —*vt.* **housed** (houzd). **hous'ing** **1.** to provide a house or lodgings for **2.** to store in a house **3.** to cover, shelter, etc. as if by putting in a house —*vi.* **1.** to take shelter **2.** to reside; live —**keep house** to take care of the affairs of a home —**on the house** given free, at the expense of the establishment —**set** (or **put**) **one's house in order** to put one's affairs in order

HOURGLASS

**house·boat** (-bōt') *n.* a large, flat-bottomed boat designed for use as a dwelling place

**house·break** (-brāk') *vt.* -**broke'**, -**bro'ken**, -**break'ing** to make housebroken

**house·break·ing** (-brāk'iŋ) *n.* the act of breaking into another's house to commit theft or some other felony —**house'break'er** *n.*

**house·bro·ken** (-brōk'ən) *adj.* trained to live in a house (i.e., to void outdoors or in a special place): said of a dog, cat, etc.

**house·clean·ing** (-klēn'iŋ) *n.* **1.** the cleaning of the furniture, floors, etc. of a house **2.** a getting rid of unwanted things —**house'clean'** *vi., vt.*

**house·coat** (-kōt') *n.* a woman's long, loose garment for casual wear at home

**house·dress** (-dres') *n.* any fairly cheap dress, as of printed cotton, worn at home for housework

**house·fly** (-flī') *n., pl.* -**flies'** a two-winged fly found in and around houses: it feeds on garbage, manure, and food

**house·ful** (-fool') *n.* as much or as many as a house will hold or provide room for [a *houseful* of guests]

**house·hold** (-hōld') *n.* **1.** all those living in one house; family, or family and servants **2.** the home and its affairs —*adj.* **1.** of a household **2.** ordinary

**house·hold·er** (-hōl'dər) *n.* **1.** one who owns or maintains a house **2.** the head of a household

**household word** a very familiar word or saying

**house·keep·er** (-kēp'ər) *n.* a woman who manages a home, esp. one hired to do so —**house'keep'ing** *n.*

**house·lights** (-līts') *n.pl.* lights that illuminate the part of a theater where the audience sits

**house·maid** (-mād') *n.* a girl or woman servant who does housework

**housemaid's knee** an inflammation of the saclike cavity covering the kneecap

**house·moth·er** (-muth'ər) *n.* a woman in charge of a dormitory, sorority house, etc., often as housekeeper

**House of Burgesses** the lower branch of the colonial legislature of Virginia

**house of cards** any flimsy structure, plan, etc.

**House of Commons** the lower branch of the legislature of Great Britain or Canada

**house of correction** a place of short-term confinement for persons convicted of minor offenses

**House of Delegates** the lower branch of the legislature of Maryland, Virginia, or West Virginia

**House of Lords** the upper branch of the legislature of Great Britain, made up of the nobility and high-ranking clergy

**House of Representatives** the lower branch of the legislature of the U.S., certain other countries, and most of the States of the U.S.

**house organ** a periodical published by a business firm for its employees, affiliates, etc.

**house party** the entertainment of guests overnight or over a period of a few days in a home

**house physician** a resident physician of a hospital, hotel, etc.: also **house doctor**

**house·rais·ing** (-rā′ziŋ) *n.* a gathering of the members of a rural community to help a neighbor build his house or its framework

**house·top** (-täp′) *n.* the top of a house; roof —**from the housetops** publicly and widely

**house·warm·ing** (-wôr′miŋ) *n.* a party given by or for someone moving into a new home

**house·wife** (-wīf′; *for 2, usually* huz′if) *n., pl.* **-wives′** (-wīvz′; *for 2, usually* huz′ivz) **1.** a woman, esp. a married woman, who manages a household **2.** a small sewing kit —**house′wife′ly** *adj., adv.* —**house′wif′er·y** *n.*

**house·work** (-wurk′) *n.* the work involved in housekeeping, such as cleaning, cooking, etc.

**hous·ing**[1] (hou′ziŋ) *n.* **1.** the act of providing shelter or lodging **2.** shelter or lodging, as in houses, apartments, etc. **3.** houses collectively **4.** a shelter; covering **5.** *Mech.* a frame, box, etc. for containing some part

**hous·ing**[2] (hou′ziŋ) *n.* [< OFr. *houce* < Frank.] an ornamental covering draped over a horse

**Hous·man** (hous′mən), **A(lfred) E(dward)** 1859–1936; Eng. poet & classical scholar

**Hous·ton** (hyōōs′tən) [after ff.] city in SE Tex.: pop. 1,594,000 (met. area 2,891,000)

**Hous·ton** (hyōōs′tən), **Samuel** 1793–1863; U.S. general & statesman; president of the Republic of Texas (1836–38; 1841–44)

**hove** (hōv) *alt. pt. & pp. of* HEAVE

**hov·el** (huv′'l, häv′-) *n.* [ME. < ?] **1.** a low, open shed for sheltering animals, storing equipment, etc. **2.** any small, miserable dwelling; hut —*vt.* **-eled** or **-elled, -el·ing** or **-el·ling** to shelter in a hovel

**hov·er** (huv′ər, häv′-) *vi.* [< ME. freq. of *hoven*, to stay] **1.** to stay suspended or flutter in the air near one place **2.** to linger or wait close by, esp. in a protective way **3.** to be in an uncertain condition; waver —*n.* a hovering —**hov′er·er** *n.*

**how** (hou) *adv.* [OE. *hu*] **1.** in what manner or way **2.** in what state or condition **3.** for what reason; why **4.** by what name **5.** with what meaning **6.** to what extent, degree, amount, etc. **7.** at what price **8.** [Colloq.] what: usually a request to repeat something said *How* is also used in exclamations and as an intensive —*n.* the way of doing; manner; method —**how about** what is your thought concerning? —**how now?** what is the meaning of this? —**how so?** how is it so?

**How·ard** (hou′ərd) [< the surname *Howard*] a masculine name

**how·be·it** (hou bē′it) *adv.* [Archaic] however it may be; nevertheless

**how·dah** (hou′də) *n.* [Anglo-Ind. < Hindi < Ar. *haudaj*] a canopied seat for riding on the back of an elephant or camel

**how·dy** (hou′dē) *interj.* [contr. < *how do you (do)?*] [Dial. or Colloq.] an expression of greeting

**Howe** (hou), **E·li·as** (i lī′əs) 1819–67; U.S. inventor of a sewing machine

**How·ells** (hou′əlz), **William Dean** (dēn) 1837–1920; U.S. novelist, critic, & editor

**how·ev·er** (hou ev′ər) *adv.* **1.** no matter how; in whatever manner **2.** to whatever degree or extent **3.** by what means: intensive of HOW **4.** nevertheless; yet: often used as a conjunctive adverb Also [Poet.] **how·e′er′** (-er′)

**how·itz·er** (hou′it sər) *n.* [< Du. < Early ModG. < Czech *haufnice*, orig., a sling] a short cannon, firing shells in a relatively high trajectory

**howl** (houl) *vi.* [ME. *houlen* < echoic base] **1.** to utter the long, wailing cry of wolves, dogs, etc. **2.** to utter a similar cry of pain, anger, etc. **3.** to make a sound like this [the wind *howls*] **4.** to shout or laugh in scorn, mirth, etc. —*vt.* **1.** to utter with a howl **2.** to drive or effect by howling —*n.* **1.** the long, wailing cry of a wolf, dog, etc. **2.** any similar sound **3.** [Colloq.] something hilarious —**howl down** to drown out with shouts of scorn, etc.

**howl·er** (houl′ər) *n.* **1.** a person or thing that howls **2.** [Colloq.] a ludicrous blunder

**howl·ing** (-iŋ) *adj.* **1.** that howls **2.** mournful; dreary **3.** [Slang] great [a howling success] —**howl′ing·ly** *adv.*

**How·rah** (hou′rə) city in NE India, in the Ganges delta, near Calcutta: pop. 513,000

**how·so·ev·er** (hou′sō ev′ər) *adv.* **1.** to whatever degree or extent **2.** by whatever means

**hoy·den** (hoid′'n) *n.* [< ? Du. *heiden*, heathen] a bold, boisterous girl; tomboy —*adj.* bold and boisterous; tomboyish —*vi.* to behave like a hoyden —**hoy′den·ish** *adj.*

**Hoyle** (hoil) *n.* a book of rules and instructions for card games, orig. compiled by Edmond Hoyle (1672–1769) —**according to Hoyle** according to the rules and regulations; in a fair way

**HP, H.P., hp, h.p.** **1.** high pressure **2.** horsepower

**HQ, H.Q., hq, h.q.** headquarters

**hr.** *pl.* **hrs.** hour; hours

**H.R.** House of Representatives

**h.r., hr, HR** home run

**H.R.H.** His (or Her) Royal Highness

**H.S., h.s.** high school

**HT** high tension

**ht.** **1.** heat **2.** *pl.* **hts.** height

**hua·ra·ches** (hə rä′chēz) *n.pl.* [MexSp.] flat sandals with straps or woven strips for uppers

**hub** (hub) *n.* [? akin to HOB[1]] **1.** the center part of a wheel, etc. **2.** a center of interest, importance, or activity —**the Hub** Boston

**hub·bub** (hub′ub′) *n.* [prob. < Celt.] a confused sound of many voices; tumult

**hub·by** (hub′ē) *n., pl.* **-bies** [Colloq.] a husband

**hub·cap** (hub′kap′) *n.* a tightfitting metal cap for the hub of a wheel, esp. of a car

**Hu·bert** (hyōō′bərt) [Fr. < OHG. < *hugu*, mind, spirit + *beraht*, bright] a masculine name

**hu·bris** (hyōō′bris) *n.* [Gr. *hybris*] wanton insolence or arrogance resulting from excessive pride or from passion —**hubris′tic** *adj.*

**huck·a·back** (huk′ə bak′) *n.* [< ?] a coarse linen or cotton cloth with a rough surface, used for toweling: also **huck**

**huck·le·ber·ry** (huk′'l ber′ē) *n., pl.* **-ries** [prob. altered < *hurtleberry,* WHORTLEBERRY] **1.** a shrub of the heath family having dark-blue berries with ten large seeds **2.** the fruit of this shrub

**huck·ster** (huk′stər) *n.* [< MDu. *hoekster* < *hoeken*, to peddle] **1.** a peddler, esp. of fruits, vegetables, etc. **2.** an aggressive or haggling merchant **3.** [Colloq.] a person engaged in advertising or promotion —*vt.* to sell or advertise, esp. in an aggressive way —**huck′ster·ism** *n.*

**HUD** (Dept. of) Housing and Urban Development

**hud·dle** (hud′'l) *vi.* **-dled, -dling** [? var. of ME. *hoderen,* to cover up] **1.** to crowd close together, as cows do in a storm **2.** to draw or hunch oneself up, as from cold **3.** [Colloq.] to hold a private, informal conference **4.** *Football* to gather in a huddle —*vt.* **1.** to crowd close together **2.** to hunch or draw (oneself) up **3.** to do, put, or make hastily and carelessly **4.** to push in a hurried manner —*n.* **1.** a confused crowd or heap **2.** confusion; jumble **3.** [Colloq.] a private, informal conference **4.** *Football* a grouping of a team behind the line of scrimmage to receive signals before a play

**Hud·son** (hud′s'n) [after ff.] river in E N.Y., flowing southward into the Atlantic at New York City

**Hud·son** (hud′s'n), **Henry** ?–1611; Eng. explorer, esp. of the waters about NE N. America

**Hudson Bay** inland sea in NE Canada; arm of the Atlantic

**Hudson seal** muskrat fur treated to resemble seal

**hue**[1] (hyōō) *n.* [OE. *heow*] **1.** color; esp., the distinctive characteristics of a given color **2.** a particular shade or tint of a given color —**hued** *adj.*

**hue**[2] (hyōō) *n.* [< OFr. *hu,* a warning cry] a shouting; outcry: now only in **hue and cry,** meaning: *a*) orig., a loud shout or cry by those pursuing a felon *b*) any loud outcry or clamor

**huff** (huf) *vt.* [prob. echoic] to make angry; offend —*vi.* **1.** to blow; puff **2.** to become angry —*n.* a condition of smoldering anger or resentment

**huff·y** (-ē) *adj.* **huff′i·er, huff′i·est** **1.** easily offended; touchy **2.** angered or offended —**huff′i·ly** *adv.* —**huff′i·ness** *n.*

**hug** (hug) *vt.* **hugged, hug′ging** [prob. < ON. *hugga,* to comfort] **1.** to put the arms around and hold closely, esp. affectionately **2.** to squeeze tightly with the forelegs, as a bear does **3.** to cling to (a belief, opinion, etc.) **4.** to keep close to [the bus *hugged* the curb] —*vi.* to embrace one another closely —*n.* **1.** a close, fond embrace **2.** a tight hold with the arms, as in wrestling **3.** a bear's squeeze

---

fat, āpe, cär, ten, ēven, is, bīte; gō, hôrn, tōōl, look; oil, out; up, fur; get; joy; yet; chin; she; thin, *then*; zh, leisure; ŋ, ring; ə for *a* in *ago, e* in *agent, i* in *sanity, o* in *comply, u* in *focus;*  as in *able* (ā′b'l); Fr. bål; ë, Fr. coeur; ö, Fr. feu; Fr. mon; o͝, Fr. coq; ü, Fr. duc; r, Fr. cri; H, G. ich; kh, G. doch; ‡foreign; *hypothetical; < derived from. See inside front cover.

**huge** (hyōōj, yōōj) *adj.* [OFr. *ahuge*] very large; gigantic; immense —**huge′ly** *adv.* —**huge′ness** *n.*

**hug·ger·mug·ger** (hug′ər mug′ər) *n.* [prob. based on ME. *mokeren*, to conceal] a confusion; muddle; jumble —*adj.* confused; muddled —*adv.* in a confused or jumbled manner

**Hugh** (hyōō) [< OFr. < OHG. *Hugo*, prob. < *hugu*, heart, mind] a masculine name

**Hughes** (hyōōz), **Charles Ev·ans** (ev′ənz) 1862–1948; U.S. jurist; chief justice of the U.S. (1930–41)

**Hu·go** (hyōō′gō) 1. [var. of HUGH] a masculine name 2. (*also Fr.* ü gō′) **Vic·tor Ma·rie** (vēk tôr′ má rē′) 1802–85; Fr. poet, novelist, & playwright

**Hu·gue·not** (hyōō′gə nät′) *n.* [MFr. < G. *eidgenosse*, confederate] any French Protestant of the 16th or 17th century

**huh** (hu, hun) *interj.* an exclamation used to express contempt, surprise, etc., or to ask a question

**hu·la** (hōō′lə) *n.* [Haw.] a native Hawaiian dance marked by flowing gestures: also **hu′la-hu′la**

**hulk** (hulk) *n.* [OE. *hulc*] 1. a big, unwieldy ship 2. the body of a ship, esp. if old and dismantled 3. a deserted wreck or ruins 4. a big, clumsy person or thing —*vi.* to loom bulkily

**hulk·ing** (hul′kiŋ) *adj.* large, heavy, and often unwieldy or clumsy: also **hulk′y** (-kē)

**Hull** (hul) 1. seaport in NE England: pop. 295,000: officially *Kingston upon Hull* 2. city in SW Quebec, Canada, near Ottawa: pop. 60,000

**hull¹** (hul) *n.* [OE. *hulu*] 1. the outer covering of a seed or fruit, as the husk of grain, shell of nuts, etc. 2. the calyx of some fruits, as the strawberry 3. any outer covering —*vt.* to take the hull or hulls off —**hull′er** *n.*

**hull²** (hul) *n.* [special use of prec., prob. infl. by Du. *hol*, ship's hold] 1. the frame or body of a ship, excluding the masts, sails, rigging, superstructure, etc. 2. *a)* the main body of an airship *b)* the frame or main body of a flying boat, amphibian, hydrofoil, etc. —*vt.* to pierce the hull of (a ship) with a torpedo, etc.

**hul·la·ba·loo** (hul′ə bə lōō′) *n.* [echoic, based on ff.] a clamor or hubbub

**hul·lo** (hə lō′) *interj., n., vt., vi. same as:* 1. HOLLO 2. HELLO

**hum¹** (hum) *vi.* **hummed, hum′ming** [echoic] 1. to make the low, murmuring sound of a bee, a motor, etc. 2. to sing with the lips closed, not producing words 3. to give forth a confused, droning sound [*the room* hummed *with voices*] 4. [Colloq.] to be full of activity —*vt.* 1. to sing (a tune, etc.) with the lips closed 2. to produce an effect on by humming [*to* hum *a child to sleep*] —*n.* the act or sound of humming —**hum′mer** *n.*

**hum²** (hom: *conventionalized pronun.*) *interj., n. same as:* 1. HEM² 2. HUMPH —*vi.* **hummed, hum′ming** *same as* HEM²

**hu·man** (hyōō′mən, yōō′-) *adj.* [< OFr. < L. *humanus*] 1. of, belonging to, or typical of mankind [*the* human *race*] 2. consisting of or produced by men [*human* society] 3. having or showing qualities characteristic of people [*human* values] —*n.* a person: the phrase **human being** is still preferred by some —**hu′man·ness** *n.*

**hu·mane** (hyōō mān′, hyoo-, yōō-) *adj.* [earlier var. of prec.] 1. kind, tender, merciful, sympathetic, etc. 2. civilizing; humanizing [*humane* learning] —**hu·mane′ly** *adv.* —**hu·mane′ness** *n.*

**hu·man·ism** (hyōō′mə niz′m, yōō′-) *n.* 1. the quality of being human; human nature 2. any system of thought or action based on the nature, dignity, and ideals of man; specif., a rationalist movement that holds that man can be ethical, find self-fulfillment, etc. without recourse to supernaturalism 3. the study of the humanities 4. [H-] the intellectual and cultural secular movement that stemmed from the study of classical Greek and Roman culture in the Middle Ages and helped give rise to the Renaissance —**hu′man·ist** *n., adj.* —**hu′man·is′tic** *adj.* —**hu′man·is′ti·cal·ly** *adv.*

**hu·man·i·tar·i·an** (hyōō man′ə ter′ē ən, hyoo-, yōō-) *n.* a person devoted to promoting the welfare of humanity; philanthropist —*adj.* helping humanity —**hu·man′i·tar′i·an·ism** *n.*

**hu·man·i·ty** (hyōō man′ə tē, hyoo-, yōō-) *n., pl.* **-ties** 1. the fact or quality of being human; human nature 2. the human race; mankind; people 3. the fact or quality of being humane; kindness, mercy, sympathy, etc. —**the humanities** 1. languages and literature, esp. classical Greek and Latin 2. the branches of learning concerned with human thought and relations; esp., literature, philosophy, the fine arts, history, etc.

**hu·man·ize** (hyōō′mə nīz′, yōō′-) *vt., vi.* **-ized′, -iz′ing** 1. to make or become human 2. to make or become humane —**hu′man·i·za′tion** *n.* —**hu′man·iz′er** *n.*

**hu·man·kind** (hyōō′mən kīnd′, yōō′-) *n.* the human race; mankind; people

**hu·man·ly** (-lē) *adv.* 1. in a human manner 2. by human means 3. from a human viewpoint

**hu·man·oid** (-oid′) *adj.* nearly human —*n.* a nearly human creature; specif., *a)* any of the earliest ancestors of modern man *b)* in science fiction, a reasoning creature of another planet

**hum·ble** (hum′b'l, um′-) *adj.* **-bler, -blest** [OFr. < L. *humilis*, low, akin to *humus*, earth] 1. having or showing a consciousness of one's defects or shortcomings; not proud 2. low in condition or rank; lowly; unpretentious —*vt.* **-bled, -bling** 1. to lower in condition or rank; abase 2. to make modest or humble in mind —**hum′ble·ness** *n.* —**hum′bler** *n.* —**hum′bly** *adv.*

**humble pie** [< *umbles*, entrails of a deer < OFr. *nombles* < L. < *lumbus*, loin] formerly, a pie made of the inner parts of a deer, served to the servants after a hunt —**eat humble pie** to undergo humiliation, as by admitting one's error

**hum·bug** (hum′bug′) *n.* [< ?] 1. *a)* a fraud; sham *b)* misleading or empty talk 2. a person who is not what he claims to be 3. a spirit of trickery, deception, etc. —*vt.* **-bugged′, -bug′ging** to dupe; deceive; hoax —*interj.* nonsense! —**hum′bug′ger** *n.* —**hum′bug′ger·y** *n.*

**hum·ding·er** (hum′diŋ′ər) *n.* [Slang] a person or thing considered excellent of its kind

**hum·drum** (hum′drum′) *adj.* lacking variety; dull; monotonous —*n.* humdrum talk, routine, etc.

**Hume** (hyōōm), **David** 1711–76; Scot. philosopher & historian

**hu·mec·tant** (hyōō mek′tənt) *n.* [< L. prp. of *humectare*, ult. < *umere*, to be moist] a substance, as glycerol, added or applied to another to help it retain moisture

**hu·mer·us** (hyōō′mər əs) *n., pl.* **-mer·i′** (-ī′) [L. *humerus, umerus*, the upper arm] the bone of the upper arm or forelimb, from the shoulder to the elbow —**hu′mer·al** *adj.*

**hu·mid** (hyōō′mid, yōō′-) *adj.* [< Fr. < L. *humidus*, ult. < *umere*, to be moist] full of water vapor; damp; moist —**hu′mid·ly** *adv.*

**hu·mid·i·fy** (hyōō mid′ə fī′, yōō-) *vt.* **-fied′, -fy′ing** to make humid; moisten; dampen —**hu·mid′i·fi·ca′tion** *n.* —**hu·mid′i·fi′er** *n.*

**hu·mid·i·ty** (-tē) *n., pl.* **-ties** 1. moistness; dampness 2. the amount of moisture in the air —**relative humidity** the ratio of the amount of moisture in the air to the maximum amount that the air could contain at the same temperature, stated as a percentage

**hu·mi·dor** (hyōō′mə dôr′, yōō′-) *n.* a jar, case, etc. with a device for keeping tobacco, etc. moist

**hu·mil·i·ate** (hyōō mil′ē āt′, hyoo-, yōō-) *vt.* **-at′ed, -at′ing** [< L. pp. of *humiliare* < L. *humilis*, HUMBLE] to hurt the pride or dignity of by causing to seem foolish, etc.; mortify —**hu·mil′i·a′tion** *n.*

**hu·mil·i·ty** (hyōō mil′ə tē) *n.* [< OFr. < L. *humilitas*] the state or quality of being humble; absence of pride

**hum·ming·bird** (hum′iŋ bʉrd′) *n.* any of a family of very small, brightly colored birds with a long, slender bill and narrow wings that vibrate rapidly, with a humming sound

**hum·mock** (hum′ək) *n.* [orig. naut. < ?] 1. a low, rounded hill; knoll 2. a ridge or rise in an ice field 3. a tract of wooded land, higher than a surrounding marshy area

**hu·mon·gous** (hyōō mäŋ′gəs, -muŋ′-) *adj.* [? blend of HUGE, MONSTROUS, & TREMENDOUS] [Slang] very large or great

**hu·mor** (hyōō′mər, yōō′-) *n.* [< OFr. < L. *humor, umor*, moisture, fluid] 1. formerly, any of the four fluids (**cardinal humors**) considered responsible for one's health and disposition; blood, phlegm, choler (yellow bile), or melancholy (black bile) 2. *a)* a person's temperament *b)* a mood; state of mind 3. whim; fancy; caprice 4. comic or amusing quality 5. *a)* the ability to appreciate or express what is funny, amusing, or ludicrous *b)* the expression of this in speech, writing, or action 6. any fluid or fluidlike substance of the body [*the aqueous* humor] —*vt.* 1. to comply with the mood or whim of (another); indulge 2. to adapt oneself to —**out of humor** cross; disagreeable —**hu′mor·less** *adj.*

**hu·mor·esque** (hyōō′mə resk′) *n.* [G. *humoreske*] a light, fanciful or playful musical composition

**hu·mor·ist** (hyōō′mər ist, yōō′-) *n.* 1. a person with a good sense of humor 2. a professional writer or teller of amusing stories, jokes, etc.

**hu·mor·ous** (-əs) *adj.* having or expressing humor; funny; amusing; comical —**hu′mor·ous·ly** *adv.*

**hu·mour** (hyōō′mər, yōō′-) *n., vt. Brit. sp. of* HUMOR

**hump** (hump) *n.* [< or akin to LowG. *humpe*, thick piece] 1. a rounded, protruding lump, as the fleshy mass on the back of a camel: in man, a hump is caused by a deformity of the spine 2. a hummock; mound —*vt.* to hunch; arch [*the cat* humped *its back*] —*vi.* [Slang] 1. to exert oneself 2. to hurry —**over the hump** [Colloq.] over the worst part —**humped** *adj.* —**hump′y** *adj.* **-i·er, -i·est**

**hump·back** (-bak′) *n.* 1. a humped, deformed back 2. a person having a humped back; hunchback 3. a large whale having long flippers and a dorsal fin resembling a hump-back —**hump′backed′** *adj.*

**humph** (humf: *conventionalized pronun.*) *interj., n.* a snorting or grunting sound expressing doubt, surprise, disdain, disgust, etc.

**Hum·phrey** (hum′frē) [OE. *Hunfrith,* lit., strength in peace] a masculine name: also sp. **Hum′phry**

**Hump·ty Dump·ty** (hump′tē dump′tē) the personification of an egg in an old nursery rhyme

**hu·mus** (hyōō′məs, yōō′-) *n.* [L., earth] the brown or black organic part of the soil, resulting from the partial decay of plant and animal matter

**Hun** (hun) *n.* **1.** a member of a warlike Asiatic people who invaded eastern and central Europe in the 4th and 5th centuries A.D. **2.** [*often* h-] any savage or destructive person; vandal

**hunch** (hunch) *vt.* [< ?] to draw (one's body, etc.) up so as to form a hump —*vi.* **1.** to push oneself forward jerkily **2.** to sit or stand with the back arched —*n.* **1.** a hump **2.** a chunk; hunk **3.** [Colloq.] a premonition or suspicion

**hunch·back** (-bak′) *n.* same as HUMPBACK (senses 1, 2) —**hunch′backed′** *adj.*

**hun·dred** (hun′drid, -dərd) *n.* [OE.] **1.** the cardinal number next above ninety-nine; ten times ten; 100; C **2.** a division of an English county —*adj.* ten times ten

**hun·dred·fold** (-fōld′) *adj.* [see -FOLD] having a hundred times as much or as many —*adv.* a hundred times as much or as many

**hun·dredth** (hun′dridth) *adj.* **1.** preceded by ninety-nine others in a series; 100th **2.** designating any of the hundred equal parts of something —*n.* **1.** the one following the ninety-ninth **2.** any of the hundred equal parts of something; 1/100

**hun·dred·weight** (hun′drid wāt′, -dərd-) *n.* a unit of weight equal to 100 pounds in the U.S. and 112 pounds in England: abbrev. **cwt.**

**hung** (huŋ) *pt. & pp. of* HANG —**hung up (on)** [Slang] **1.** emotionally disturbed (by) **2.** baffled, frustrated, etc. (by) **3.** addicted (to); obsessed (to)

**Hung. 1.** Hungarian **2.** Hungary

**Hun·gar·i·an** (huŋ ger′ē ən) *adj.* of Hungary, its people, their language, or culture —*n.* **1.** a native or inhabitant of Hungary **2.** the Finno-Ugric language of the Hungarians; Magyar

**Hun·ga·ry** (huŋ′gər ē) country in SC Europe: 35,919 sq. mi.; pop. 10,331,000; cap. Budapest

**hun·ger** (huŋ′gər) *n.* [OE. *hungor*] **1.** *a)* the discomfort, pain, or weakness caused by a need for food *b)* famine; starvation **2.** a need or appetite for food **3.** any strong desire; craving —*vi.* **1.** to be hungry **2.** to crave; long (with *for* or *after*)

**hunger strike** a refusal, as of a prisoner, to eat until certain demands are granted

**hun·gry** (huŋ′grē) *adj.* **-gri·er, -gri·est 1.** feeling or showing hunger; specif., *a)* wanting or needing food *b)* craving; eager [*hungry* for praise] **2.** not fertile; barren: said of soil —**hun′gri·ly** *adv.* —**hun′gri·ness** *n.*

**hunk** (huŋk) *n.* [Fl. *hunke,* hunk] [Colloq.] a large piece, lump, or slice of bread, meat, etc.

**hun·ker** (huŋ′kər) *vi.* [prob. < or akin to ON. *hokra,* to creep] to settle down on one's haunches; squat or crouch —*n.* [*pl.*] haunches

**hun·ky-do·ry** (huŋ′kē dôr′ē) *adj.* [Slang] all right; satisfactory; fine

**hunt** (hunt) *vt.* [OE. *huntian*] **1.** to go out to kill or catch (game) for food or sport **2.** to search carefully for; try to find **3.** *a)* to chase; drive *b)* to hound; harry **4.** *a)* to go through (a woods, etc.) in pursuit of game *b)* to search (a place) carefully **5.** to use (dogs or horses) in chasing game —*vi.* **1.** to go out after game **2.** to search; seek —*n.* **1.** a hunting **2.** a group of people who hunt together **3.** a district covered in hunting **4.** a search

**Hunt** (hunt) **1.** (James Henry) Leigh (lē), 1784-1859; Eng. poet, critic, & essayist **2.** (William) Hol·man (hōl′mən), 1827-1910; Eng. painter

**hunt·er** (-ər) *n.* **1.** a person who hunts **2.** a horse or dog trained for hunting

**hunt·ing** (-iŋ) *n.* the act of a person or animal that hunts —*adj.* of or for hunting

**Hun·ting·ton** (hun′tiŋ tən) [after C.P. *Huntington* (1821-1900), its founder] city in W W.Va., on the Ohio: pop. 64,000

**Huntington Beach** [after H. *Huntington,* U.S. railroad executive] city in SW Calif.: suburb of Los Angeles: pop. 171,000

**hunt·ress** (hun′tris) *n.* a woman who hunts

**hunts·man** (hunts′mən) *n., pl.* **-men 1.** a hunter **2.** the manager of a hunt

**Hunts·ville** (hunts′vil′) [after J. *Hunt,* its 1st settler (1805)] city in N Ala.: pop. 143,000

**hur·dle** (hur′d'l) *n.* [OE. *hyrdel*] **1.** [Brit.] a portable frame of interlaced twigs, etc., used as a temporary fence **2.** any of a series of framelike barriers over which horses or runners must leap in a race (the **hurdles**) **3.** a difficulty to be overcome —*vt.* **-dled, -dling 1.** to fence off with hurdles **2.** to jump over (a barrier), as in a race **3.** to overcome (an obstacle) —**hur′dler** *n.*

**hur·dy-gur·dy** (hur′dē gur′dē) *n., pl.* **-gur′dies** [prob. echoic] **1.** an early, lutelike instrument played by turning a crank **2.** same as BARREL ORGAN

**hurl** (hurl) *vt.* [prob. < ON.] **1.** to throw with force or violence **2.** to cast down; overthrow **3.** to utter vehemently **4.** [Colloq.] *Baseball* to pitch —*vi.* **1.** to throw or fling something **2.** to rush —*n.* a violent throw —**hurl′er** *n.*

HURDLES

**hurl·y-burl·y** (hur′lē bur′lē) *n., pl.* **-burl′ies** a turmoil; uproar —*adj.* disorderly and confused

**Hu·ron** (hyoor′ən, -än) *n.* [Fr., ruffian] **1.** *pl.* **-rons, -ron** a member of a confederation of Indian tribes that lived east of Lake Huron and now live in Oklahoma and Quebec **2.** their Iroquoian language

**Huron, Lake** second largest of the Great Lakes, between Mich. & Ontario, Canada: 24,328 sq. mi.; 247 mi. long

**hur·rah** (hə rô′, -rä′) *interj.* [ult. echoic] a shout of joy, approval, etc. —*n.* **1.** a shouting of "hurrah" **2.** excitement, commotion, etc. —*vi., vt.* to cheer; shout "hurrah" (for) Also **hur·ray′** (-rā′)

**hur·ri·cane** (hur′ə kān′, -kən) *n.* [< Sp. < WInd. *huracan*] a violent tropical cyclone with winds of 73 or more miles per hour, often with torrential rains, and originating usually in the West Indies

**hurricane lamp 1.** an oil lamp or candlestick with a tall glass chimney to keep the flame from being blown out **2.** an electric lamp in imitation of this

**hur·ried** (hur′ēd) *adj.* in a hurry; rushed or rushing —**hur′ried·ly** *adv.* —**hur′ried·ness** *n.*

**hur·ry** (hur′ē) *vt.* **-ried, -ry·ing** [prob. akin to HURL] **1.** to move, send, or carry with haste **2.** to cause to occur or be done more rapidly or too rapidly **3.** to urge or cause to act soon or too soon —*vi.* to move or act with haste —*n.* **1.** a rush; urgency **2.** eagerness to do, act, go, etc. quickly —**hur′ri·er** *n.*

**hur·ry-scur·ry, hur·ry-skur·ry** (-skur′ē) *n.* a disorderly confusion —*vi.* **-ried, -ry·ing** to hurry and scurry about —*adj.* hurried and confused —*adv.* in a hurried, confused manner

**hurt** (hurt) *vt.* **hurt, hurt′ing** [OFr. *hurter,* to push, hit. prob. < Frank.] **1.** to cause pain or injury to; wound **2.** to harm or damage in any way **3.** to offend or distress —*vi.* **1.** to cause injury, damage, or pain **2.** to give or have the sensation of pain; be sore —*n.* **1.** a pain or injury **2.** harm or damage **3.** something that wounds the feelings —*adj.* damaged [*hurt* books] —**hurt′er** *n.*

**hurt·ful** (-fəl) *adj.* causing hurt; harmful —**hurt′ful·ly** *adv.* —**hurt′ful·ness** *n.*

**hur·tle** (hurt′'l) *vi.* **-tled, -tling** [< freq. of ME. *hurten,* HURT] **1.** orig., to crash; collide **2.** to move swiftly and with great force —*vt.* to throw, shoot, or fling with great force; hurl

**hus·band** (huz′bənd) *n.* [Late OE. *husbonda* < ON. < *hūs,* house + *bondi,* freeholder] a married man —*vt.* to manage economically; conserve

**hus·band·man** (-mən) *n., pl.* **-men** [Archaic] a farmer

**hus·band·ry** (huz′bən drē) *n.* **1.** orig., management of domestic affairs, resources, etc. **2.** careful, thrifty management **3.** farming

**hush** (hush) *vt.* [< ME. < *huscht,* quiet] **1.** to make quiet or silent **2.** to soothe; lull —*vi.* to be or become quiet or silent —*n.* quiet; silence —*interj.* an exclamation calling for silence —**hush up 1.** to keep quiet **2.** to keep secret; suppress

**hush-hush** (hush′hush′) *adj.* [Colloq.] very secret; most confidential

**hush money** money paid to a person to keep him from telling something

**hush puppy** [< ?] in the southern U.S., a small, fried ball of cornmeal dough

**husk** (husk) *n.* [prob. < MDu. *huuskijn,* dim. of *huus,* a house] **1.** the dry outer covering of various fruits or seeds, as of an ear of corn **2.** the dry, rough, or useless outside covering of anything —*vt.* to remove the husk from —**husk′er** *n.*

**husk·ing (bee)** (hus′kiŋ) same as CORNHUSKING

**hus·ky¹** (hus'kē) *n., pl.* **-kies** [altered < ? Eskimo] [*sometimes* H-] a hardy dog used for pulling sleds in the Arctic²

**husk·y²** (hus'kē) *adj.* **husk'i·er, husk'i·est 1.** *a)* full of or consisting of husks *b)* like a husk **2.** sounding deep and hoarse **3.** big and strong; robust —*n., pl.* **husk'ies** a husky person —**husk'i·ly** *adv.* —**husk'i·ness** *n.*

**Huss** (hus), **John** 1369?-1415; Bohemian religious reformer & martyr, burned as a heretic: Czech name **Jan Hus** (yän hoos) —**Huss'ite** (-īt) *n., adj.*

**hus·sar** (hoo zär', hə-) *n.* [< Hung. < Serb. *husar* < L. *cursus:* see CORSAIR] a member of any European regiment of light-armed cavalry, usually with brilliant dress uniforms

**hus·sy** (huz'ē, hus'-) *n., pl.* **-sies** [contr. < ME. *huswife,* housewife] **1.** a woman, esp. one of low morals **2.** a bold, saucy girl; minx

**hus·tings** (hus'tiŋz) *n.pl.* [*usually with sing. v.*] [OE. < ON. < *hūs,* a house + *thing,* assembly] **1.** the proceedings at an election **2.** the route followed by a political campaigner

**hus·tle** (hus''l) *vt.* **-tled, -tling** [Du. *hutseln,* to shake up] **1.** to push about; jostle in a rude, rough manner **2.** to force in a rough, hurried manner *[he hustled* them into the bus*]* **3.** [Colloq.] to hurry (a person, a job, etc.) **4.** [Slang] to get, victimize, etc. by aggressive tactics —*vi.* **1.** to move hurriedly **2.** [Colloq.] to work or act rapidly or energetically **3.** [Slang] *a)* to obtain money by aggressive or dishonest means *b)* to work as a prostitute —*n.* **1.** a hustling **2.** [Colloq.] energetic action; drive —**hus'tler** *n.*

**hut** (hut) *n.* [< Fr. < MHG. < OHG. *hutta*] a little house or cabin of the plainest or crudest kind —*vt., vi.* **hut'ted, hut'ting** to shelter or be sheltered in or as in a hut

**hutch** (huch) *n.* [OFr. *huche,* bin < ML. *hutica,* a chest] **1.** a bin, chest, or box for storage **2.** a china cabinet with open shelves on top **3.** a pen or coop for small animals **4.** a hut

**Hux·ley** (huks'lē) **1.** **Al·dous (Leonard)** (ôl'dəs), 1894-1963; Eng. novelist & essayist **2.** **Sir Julian (Sorrell),** 1887-1975; Eng. biologist & writer: brother of *prec.* **3.** **Thomas Henry,** 1825-95; Eng. biologist & writer: grandfather of *Aldous & Julian*

**huz·zah, huz·za** (hə zä') *interj., n., vi., vt.* [echoic] *former var. of* HURRAH

**H.V., HV, h.v., hv** high voltage

**Hwang Ho** (hwän' hō') river in N China, flowing from Tibet into the Yellow Sea: c. 2,900 mi.

**hwy.** highway

**hy·a·cinth** (hī'ə sinth') *n.* [< L. < Gr. *hyakinthos*] **1.** *a)* among the ancients, a blue gem *b)* a reddish-orange or brownish gem **2.** a plant of the lily family, with spikes of fragrant, bell-shaped flowers **3.** a bluish purple —**hy'a·cin'thine** (-sin'thin, -thīn) *adj.*

**hy·ae·na** (hī ē'nə) *n. same as* HYENA

**hy·a·line** (hī'ə lin, -līn') *adj.* [< LL. < Gr. < *hyalos,* glass] transparent as glass; glassy: also **hy'a·loid'** (-loid') —*n.* anything transparent or glassy

**hy·a·lite** (hī'ə līt') *n.* [< Gr. *hyalos,* glass + -ITE] a colorless variety of opal

**hy·brid** (hī'brid) *n.* [L. *hybrida,* offspring of mixed parentage] **1.** the offspring of two animals or plants of different species, etc. **2.** anything of mixed origin, unlike parts, etc. **3.** *Linguis.* a word made up of elements from different languages —*adj.* of, or having the nature of, a hybrid —**hy'brid·ism, hy·brid'i·ty** *n.*

**hy·brid·ize** (hī'brə dīz') *vi., vt.* **-ized', -iz'ing** to produce or cause to produce hybrids; crossbreed —**hy'brid·i·za'tion** *n.* —**hy'brid·iz'er** *n.*

**Hyde Park** (hīd) **1.** public park in London **2.** village in SE N.Y.: site of the estate & burial place of F.D. Roosevelt

**Hy·der·a·bad** (hī'dər ə bad', -bäd'; hī'drə-) city in SC India: pop. 1,119,000

**hydr-** *same as* HYDRO-: used before vowels

**Hy·dra** (hī'drə) [< OFr. *ydre* < L. < Gr. *hydra,* water serpent] *Gr. Myth.* the nine-headed serpent slain by Hercules: each head grew back double when cut off —*n., pl.* **-dras, -drae** (-drē) [h-] **1.** any persistent or ever-increasing evil **2.** a small freshwater polyp with a soft, tubelike body and a mouth surrounded by tentacles

**hy·dran·ge·a** (hī drān'jə, -dran'-; -jē ə) *n.* [ModL. < HYDR- + Gr. *angeion,* vessel] a shrubby plant, with opposite leaves and large, showy clusters of white, blue, or pink flowers

**hy·drant** (hī'drənt) *n.* [< Gr. *hydōr,* water] **1.** a large discharge pipe with a valve for drawing water from a water main; fireplug **2.** [Dial.] a faucet

**hy·drate** (hī'drāt) *n.* [HYDR- + -ATE¹] a compound formed by the chemical combination of water and some other substance *[*plaster of Paris, $2CaSO_4 \cdot H_2O$, is a *hydrate]* —*vi., vt.* **-drat·ed, -drat·ing 1.** to become or cause to become a hydrate **2.** to combine with water —**hy·dra'tion** *n.,* —**hy'dra·tor** *n.*

**hy·drau·lic** (hī drô'lik, -drä'-) *adj.* [< Fr. < L. < Gr. *hydraulikos;* ult. < *hydōr,* water + *aulos,* tube] **1.** of hydraulics **2.** operated by the movement and pressure of liquid, esp. of a liquid forced through an aperture, etc. *[hydraulic* brakes*]* **3.** setting or hardening under water *[hydraulic* mortar*]* —**hy·drau'li·cal·ly** *adv.*

**hydraulic ram** a device to move a flowing liquid up by using the momentum of the flowing liquid

**hy·drau·lics** (-liks) *n.pl.* [*with sing. v.*] the branch of physics having to do with the mechanical properties of water and other liquids in motion and their application in engineering

HYDRAULIC PRESS

**hy·dra·zine** (hī'drə zēn', -zin) *n.* [HYDR- + AZ(O) + -INE⁴] a colorless liquid base, $NH_2NH_2$, used as a jet and rocket fuel

**hy·dric** (hī'drik) *adj.* [HYDR- + -IC] of or containing hydrogen

**hy·dride** (hī'drīd) *n.* [HYDR- + -IDE] a compound of hydrogen with another element or a radical

**hy·dro-** [< Gr. *hydōr,* water] *a combining form meaning:* **1.** water *[hydrometer]* **2.** containing hydrogen *[hydrocyanic]*

**hy·dro·car·bon** (hī'drə kär'bən) *n.* any compound, as benzene, containing only hydrogen and carbon

**hy·dro·ceph·a·lus** (hī'drə sef'ə ləs) *n.* [ModL. < Gr. < *hydōr,* water + *kephalē,* head] a condition characterized by an abnormal amount of fluid in the cranium, causing enlargement of the head: also **hy'dro·ceph'a·ly** (-lē) —**hy'dro·ce·phal'ic** (-sə fal'ik) *adj., n.* —**hy'dro·ceph'a·lous** *adj.*

**hy·dro·chlo·ric acid** (hī'drə klôr'ik) [HYDRO- + CHLORIC] a strong, corrosive acid, HCl, that is a solution of the gas hydrogen chloride in water

**hy·dro·cy·an·ic acid** (-sī an'ik) [HYDRO- + CYANIC] a weak, highly poisonous acid, HCN, a colorless liquid with the odor of bitter almonds

**hy·dro·dy·nam·ics** (-dī nam'iks) *n.pl.* [*with sing. v.*] the branch of physics dealing with the motion and action of water and other liquids —**hy'dro·dy·nam'ic** *adj.* —**hy'dro·dy·nam'i·cal·ly** *adv.*

**hy·dro·e·lec·tric** (-i lek'trik) *adj.* producing, or relating to the production of, electricity by water power —**hy'dro·e·lec'tric'i·ty** *n.*

**hy·dro·fluor·ic acid** (hī'drə flôr'ik, -floor'-) [HYDRO- + FLUOR(INE) + -IC] an acid, HF, existing as a colorless, fuming, corrosive liquid: it is used in etching glass

**hy·dro·foil** (hī'drə foil') *n.* [HYDRO- + (AIR)FOIL] **1.** a winglike structure on the hull of some watercraft: at high speeds the craft skims along on the hydrofoils **2.** a craft with hydrofoils

**hy·dro·gen** (hī'drə jən) *n.* [< Fr.: see HYDRO- & -GEN] a flammable, colorless, odorless, gaseous chemical element, the lightest of all known substances: symbol, H; at. wt., 1.00797; at. no., 1 —**hy·drog'e·nous** (hī dräj'ə nəs) *adj.*

**hy·dro·gen·ate** (hī'drə jə nāt', hī dräj'ə-) *vt.* **-at'ed, -at'ing** to combine or treat with hydrogen, as in making a solid fat of oil —**hy'dro·gen·a'tion** *n.*

**hydrogen bomb** a highly destructive nuclear bomb, in which the atoms of heavy isotopes of hydrogen are fused by explosion of a nuclear-fission unit in the bomb

**hydrogen ion** the positively charged ion in all acids: symbol, H+

**hydrogen peroxide** an unstable liquid, $H_2O_2$, often used, diluted, as a bleach or disinfectant, and in more concentrated form as a rocket fuel

**hydrogen sulfide** a gaseous compound, $H_2S$, with the characteristic odor of rotten eggs

**hy·drog·ra·phy** (hī dräg'rə fē) *n.* [< Fr.: see HYDRO- & -GRAPHY] the study, description, and mapping of oceans, lakes, and rivers —**hy·drog'ra·pher** *n.* —**hy·dro·graph·ic** (hī'drə graf'ik), **hy·dro·graph'i·cal** *adj.*

**hy·droid** (hī'droid) *adj.* [HYDR(A) + -OID] **1.** like a hydra or polyp **2.** of or related to the group of hydrozoans of which the hydra is a member —*n.* any member of a group of hydrozoans, mostly marine, typically consisting of polyps

**hy·drol·y·sis** (hī dräl'ə sis) *n., pl.* **-ses'** (-sēz') [HYDRO- + -LYSIS] the breaking up of a substance, often in the presence of a catalyst, into other substances by reaction with water, as a starch into glucose, natural fats into glycerol and fatty acids, etc. —**hy·dro·lyt·ic** (hī'drə lit'ik) *adj.*

**hy·dro·lyte** (hī'drə līt') *n.* any substance undergoing hydrolysis

**hy·dro·lyze** (-līz') *vt., vi.* **-lyzed', -lyz'ing** to undergo or cause to undergo hydrolysis —**hy'dro·lyz'a·ble** *adj.*

**hy·drom·e·ter** (hī dräm'ə tər) *n.* [HYDRO- + -METER] an instrument consisting of a graduated, weighted tube, used for measuring the specific gravity of liquids —**hy·dro·met·ric** (hī′drə met′rik), **hy′dro·met′ri·cal** *adj.* —**hy·drom′e·try** *n.*

**hy·drop·a·thy** (hī dräp′ə thē) *n.* [HYDRO- + -PATHY] a system of treating all diseases by the external or internal use of water —**hy·dro·path·ic** (hī′drə path′ik) *adj.* —**hy′drop′a·thist** *n.*

**hy·dro·pho·bi·a** (hī′drə fō′bē ə) *n.* [LL. < Gr.: see HYDRO- & -PHOBIA] **1.** an abnormal fear of water **2.** [from the symptomatic inability to swallow liquids] *same as* RA-BIES —**hy′dro·pho′bic** *adj.*

**hy·dro·phyte** (hī′drə fīt′) *n.* [HYDRO- + -PHYTE] any plant growing only in water or very wet earth —**hy′dro·phyt′ic** (-fit′ik) *adj.*

**hy·dro·plane** (-plān′) *n.* [HYDRO- + PLANE⁴] **1.** a small, light motorboat with hydrofoils or with a flat bottom that can skim along the water at high speeds **2.** *same as* SEA-PLANE —*vi.* **-planed′, -plan′ing** to drive or ride in a hydro-plane

**hy·dro·pon·ics** (hī′drə pän′iks) *n.pl.* [*with sing. v.*] [< HYDRO- + Gr. *ponos,* labor + -ICS] the cultivation of plants in solutions, or moist inert material, containing minerals, instead of in soil —**hy′dro·pon′ic** *adj.* —**hy′dro·pon′i·cal·ly** *adv.*

**hy·dro·pow·er** (hī′drə pou′ər) *n.* hydroelectric power

**hy·dro·sphere** (-sfir′) *n.* [HYDRO- + -SPHERE] **1.** all the water on the surface of the earth **2.** the moisture in the atmosphere surrounding the earth

**hy·dro·stat·ics** (hī′drə stat′iks) *n.pl.* [*with sing. v.*] [< Fr.: see HYDRO- & STATIC] the branch of physics having to do with the pressure and equilibrium of water and other liquids —**hy′dro·stat′ic, hy′dro·stat′i·cal** *adj.* —**hy′dro·stat′i·cal·ly** *adv.*

**hy·dro·ther·a·peu·tics** (hī′drō ther′ə pyōōt′iks) *n.pl.* [*with sing. v.*] *same as* HYDROTHERAPY —**hy′dro·ther′a·peu′·tic** *adj.*

**hy·dro·ther·a·py** (-ther′ə pē) *n.* [HYDRO- + THERAPY] the treatment of disease, esp. in physical therapy, by the use of baths, compresses, etc.

**hy·drot·ro·pism** (hī drät′rə piz′m) *n.* [HYDRO- + -TROPISM] movement or growth, as of a plant root, in response to the stimulus of moisture —**hy·dro·trop·ic** (hī′drə träp′ik) *adj.*

**hy·drous** (hī′drəs) *adj.* [HYDR- + -OUS] containing water, as certain chemical compounds

**hy·drox·ide** (hī dräk′sīd) *n.* [HYDR- + OXIDE] a compound consisting of an element or radical combined with the hydroxyl radical (OH)

**hy·drox·yl** (-sil) *n.* the monovalent radical OH, present in all hydroxides

**hy·dro·zo·an** (hī′drə zō′ən) *adj.* [< HYDRA + ZO(O)- + -AN] of a class of coelenterate animals having a saclike body and a mouth that opens directly into the body cavity —*n.* any animal of this class, as a hydra, hydroid, etc.

**hy·e·na** (hī ē′nə) *n.* [< L. < Gr. *hyaina* < *hys,* a hog] a wolflike animal of Africa and Asia, with a characteristic shrill cry: hyenas feed on carrion and are thought of as cowardly

**Hy·ge·ia** (hī jē′ə) *Gr. Myth.* the goddess of health

**hy·giene** (hī′jēn) *n.* [< Fr. < Gr. *hygieinē* < *hygiēs,* healthy] **1.** the science of health and its maintenance; system of principles for preserving health and preventing disease **2.** hygienic practices

**hy·gi·en·ic** (hī′jē en′ik, -jē′nik, -jen′ik) *adj.* **1.** of hygiene or health **2.** promoting health; sanitary —**hy′gi·en′i·cal·ly** *adv.*

**hy·gi·en·ics** (-iks) *n.pl.* [*with sing. v.*] the science of health; hygiene

**hy·gi·en·ist** (hī′jē ə nist, -jē nist; hī jē′nist) *n.* an expert in hygiene

**hy·gro-** [< Gr. *hygros,* wet] *a combining form meaning* wet, moisture: also, before a vowel, **hygr-**

**hy·grom·e·ter** (hī gräm′ə tər) *n.* [< Fr.: see prec. & -METER] any of various instruments for measuring moisture in the air —**hy·gro·met·ric** (hī′grə met′rik) *adj.* —**hy·grom′e·try** (-trē) *n.*

**hy·gro·scope** (hī′grə skōp′) *n.* [HYGRO- + -SCOPE] an instrument that indicates, without actually measuring, changes in atmospheric humidity

**hy·gro·scop·ic** (hī′grə skäp′ik) *adj.* **1.** *a)* absorbing moisture from the air *b)* changed by the absorption of moisture **2.** of or according to a hygroscope —**hy′gro·scop′i·cal·ly** *adv.*

**hy·ing** (hī′ig) *alt. prp. of* HIE

**hy·la** (hī′lə) *n.* [< Gr. *hylē,* wood] *same as* TREE FROG

**Hy·men** (hī′mən) *Gr. Myth.* the god of marriage —*n.* [h-] [Poet.] **1.** marriage **2.** a wedding song

**hy·men** (hī′mən) *n.* [Gr. *hymēn,* membrane] the thin

membrane that usually closes part of the opening of the vagina in a virgin —**hy′men·al** *adj.*

**hy·me·ne·al** (hī′mə nē′əl) *adj.* [see HYMEN] of marriage —*n.* [Poet.] a wedding song

**hy·me·nop·ter·an** (hī′mə näp′tər ən) *n.* [< Gr. < *hymēn,* membrane + *pteron,* a wing + -AN] any of a large order of insects, including wasps, bees, ants, etc., which have a sucking mouth and four membranous wings —**hy′me·nop′ter·ous** *adj.*

**hymn** (him) *n.* [< OE. & OFr. < LL. < Gr. *hymnos*] **1.** a song in praise or honor of God, a god, or gods **2.** any song of praise —*vt.* to praise in a hymn —*vi.* to sing a hymn —**hymn′ist** (-nist) *n.*

**hym·nal** (him′nəl) *n.* a collection of religious hymns: also **hymn′book′** —*adj.* of hymns

**hym·no·dy** (-nə dē) *n.* [< ML. < Gr.: see HYMN & ODE] **1.** the singing of hymns **2.** hymns collectively **3.** *same as* HYMNOLOGY —**hym′no·dist** *n.*

**hym·nol·o·gy** (him näl′ə jē) *n.* [< ML. < Gr.: see HYMN & -LOGY] **1.** the study of hymns, their history, use, etc. **2.** the composition of hymns **3.** *same as* HYMNODY (sense 2) —**hym·nol′o·gist** *n.*

**hy·oid** (hī′oid) *adj.* [< Fr. < ModL. < Gr. *hyoeidēs,* shaped like the letter *v* (upsilon) < *hy,* upsilon + *eidos,* form] designating or of a U-shaped bone at the base of the tongue —*n.* a hyoid bone

**hyp. 1.** hypotenuse **2.** hypothesis **3.** hypothetical

**hype** (hīp) *vt.* **hyped, hyp′ing** [< HYPODERMIC] [Slang] to stimulate, excite, etc. artificially by or as by the injection of a drug: usually with *up*

**hy·per-** [Gr. < *hyper,* over, above] *a prefix meaning* over, above, more than normal, excessive [*hypercritical*]

**hy·per·a·cid·i·ty** (hī′pər ə sid′ə tē) *n.* excessive acidity, as of the gastric juice —**hy′per·ac′id** (-as′id) *adj.*

**hy·per·ac·tive** (-ak′tiv) *adj.* extremely or abnormally active —**hy′per·ac·tiv′i·ty** (-tiv′ə tē) *n.*

**hy·per·bo·la** (hī pur′bə lə) *n., pl.* **-las,** *occas.* **-lae′** (-lē′) [ModL. < Gr. *hyperbolē* < *hyper-,* over + *ballein,* to throw] a curve formed by the section of a cone cut by a plane more steeply inclined to the base than to the side of the cone

**hy·per·bo·le** (-bə lē) *n.* [L. < Gr.: see prec.] exaggeration for effect, not meant to be taken literally (Ex.: He's as strong as an ox)

HYPERBOLA

**hy·per·bol·ic** (hī′pər bäl′ik) *adj.* **1.** of, having the nature of, or using hyperbole; exaggerated or exaggerating **2.** of, or having the form of, a hyperbola Also **hy′per·bol′i·cal** —**hy′per·bol′i·cal·ly** *adv.*

**hy·per·bo·lize** (hī pur′bə līz′) *vt., vi.* **-lized′, -liz′ing** to express with or use hyperbole

**hy·per·bo·re·an** (hī′pər bôr′ē ən, -bə rē′ən) *adj.* [< LL. < L. < Gr. *hyperboreos,* beyond the north wind] **1.** of the far north **2.** very cold —*n.* [H-] *Gr. Myth.* an inhabitant of a region of sunshine and eternal spring, beyond the north wind

**hy·per·crit·i·cal** (-krit′i k′l) *adj.* too critical —**hy′per·crit′i·cal·ly** *adv.*

**hy·per·gly·ce·mi·a** (-glī sē′mē ə) *n.* [ModL. < HYPER- + Gr. *glykys,* sweet + -EMIA] an abnormally high concentration of sugar in the blood

**Hy·pe·ri·on** (hī pir′ē ən) *Gr. Myth.* **1.** a Titan, father of the sun god Helios **2.** Helios himself

**hy·per·me·tro·pi·a** (hī′pər mi trō′pē ə) *n.* [ModL. < Gr. *hypermetros,* excessive + -ōpia, -OPIA] farsightedness; abnormal vision in which distant objects are seen more clearly than near ones —**hy′per·me·trop′ic** (-träp′ik) *adj.*

**hy·per·o·pi·a** (-ō′pē ə) *n. same as* HYPERMETROPIA —**hy′per·op′ic** (-äp′ik) *adj.*

**hy·per·sen·si·tive** (-sen′sə tiv) *adj.* abnormally or excessively sensitive —**hy′per·sen′si·tiv′i·ty** *n.*

**hy·per·son·ic** (-sän′ik) *adj.* designating, of, or moving at a speed equal to about five times the speed of sound or greater: see SONIC

**hy·per·ten·sion** (-ten′shən) *n.* abnormally high blood pressure, or a disease of which this is the chief sign —**hy′per·ten′sive** *adj., n.*

**hy·per·thy·roid·ism** (-thī′roid iz′m) *n.* **1.** excessive activity of the thyroid gland **2.** the disorder caused by this, characterized by nervousness, a rapid pulse, etc. —**hy′per·thy′roid** *adj., n.*

**hy·per·tro·phy** (hī pur′trə fē) *n.* [ModL.: see HYPER- & -TROPHY] an abnormal increase in the size of an organ or tissue —*vi., vt.* **-phied, -phy·ing** to undergo or cause to undergo hypertrophy —**hy′per·troph·ic** (hī′pər träf′ik) *adj.*

**hy·per·ven·ti·la·tion** (hī′pər ven′t'l ā′shən) *n.* very rapid or deep breathing that overoxygenates the blood, causing dizziness, fainting, etc. —**hy′per·ven′ti·late′** *vi.*, *vt.* **-lat′ed, -lat′ing**

**hy·pha** (hī′fə) *n.*, *pl.* **-phae** (-fē) [ModL. < Gr. *hyphē*, a web] any of the threadlike parts making up the mycelium of a fungus —**hy′phal** *adj.*

**hy·phen** (hī′f'n) *n.* [LL. < Gr. < *hypo-*, under + *hen*, neut. acc. of *heis*, one] a mark (-) used between the parts of a compound word or the syllables of a divided word, as at the end of a line —*vt. same as* HYPHENATE

**hy·phen·ate** (-āt′) *vt.* **-at′ed, -at′ing 1.** to connect by a hyphen **2.** to write or print with a hyphen —*adj.* hyphenated —**hy′phen·a′tion** *n.*

**hyp·no-** [< Gr. *hypnos*, sleep] *a combining form meaning:* **1.** sleep **2.** hypnotism

**hyp·noid** (hip′noid) *adj.* resembling sleep or hypnosis: also **hyp·noid′al**

**hyp·nol·o·gy** (hip näl′ə jē) *n.* [HYPNO- + -LOGY] the science dealing with sleep and hypnotism

**hyp·no·sis** (hip nō′sis) *n.*, *pl.* **-ses** (-sēz) [ModL.: see HYPNO- & -OSIS] **1.** a sleeplike condition psychically induced, usually by another person, in which the subject is in a state of altered consciousness and responds, with certain limitations, to the suggestions of the hypnotist **2.** *same as* HYPNOTISM

**hyp·not·ic** (hip nät′ik) *adj.* [< Fr. < LL. < Gr. *hypnōtikos*, tending to sleep < *hypnos*, sleep] **1.** causing sleep; soporific **2.** of, like, or inducing hypnosis **3.** easily hypnotized —*n.* **1.** any agent causing sleep **2.** a hypnotized person or one easily hypnotized —**hyp·not′i·cal·ly** *adv.*

**hyp·no·tism** (hip′nə tiz'm) *n.* **1.** the act or practice of inducing hypnosis **2.** the science of hypnosis —**hyp′no·tist** *n.*

**hyp·no·tize** (-tīz′) *vt.* **-tized′, -tiz′ing 1.** to induce hypnosis in **2.** to spellbind by or as if by hypnotism —**hyp′no·tiz′a·ble** *adj.*

**hy·po¹** (hī′pō) *n.*, *pl.* **-pos** (-pōz) *short for:* **1.** HYPODERMIC **2.** HYPOCHONDRIA

**hy·po²** (hī′pō) *n.* [contr. < HYPOSULFITE] *same as* SODIUM THIOSULFATE

**hy·po-** [Gr. < *hypo*, less than] *a prefix meaning:* **1.** under, beneath [*hypodermic*] **2.** less than, deficient in [*hypothyroid*] **3.** *Chem.* having a lower state of oxidation

**hy·po·chlo·rite** (hī′pə klôr′īt) *n.* any salt of hypochlorous acid

**hy·po·chlo·rous acid** (-klôr′əs) [HYPO- + CHLOROUS] an unstable acid, HClO, known only in solution and used as a bleach and oxidizer

**hy·po·chon·dri·a** (hī′pə kän′drē ə) *n.* [ModL. < LL., pl., abdomen (supposed seat of this condition) < Gr. < *hypo-*, under + *chondros*, cartilage of the sternum] abnormal anxiety over one's health, often with imaginary illnesses and severe melancholy

**hy·po·chon·dri·ac** (-ak′) *adj.* of or having hypochondria: also **hy′po·chon·dri′a·cal** (-kən drī′ə k'l) —*n.* a person who has hypochondria —**hy′po·chon·dri′a·cal·ly** *adv.*

**hy·po·chon·dri·a·sis** (-kən drī′ə sis) *n. same as* HYPOCHONDRIA: term preferred in medicine

**hy·po·cot·yl** (hī′pə kät′'l) *n.* [HYPO- + COTYL(EDON)] the part of the axis, or stem, below the cotyledons in the embryo of a plant —**hy′po·cot′y·lous** *adj.*

**hy·poc·ri·sy** (hi päk′rə sē) *n.*, *pl.* **-sies** [< OFr. < L. < Gr. *hypokrisis*, acting a part, ult. < *hypo-*, under + *krinesthai*, to dispute] a pretending to be what one is not, or to feel what one does not feel; esp., a pretense of virtue, piety, etc.

**hyp·o·crite** (hip′ə krit) *n.* [< OFr. < L. *hypocrita*, an actor: see prec.] a person who pretends to be better than he really is, or to be pious, virtuous, etc. without really being so —**hyp′o·crit′i·cal** (-krit′i k'l) *adj.* —**hyp′o·crit′i·cal·ly** *adv.*

**hy·po·der·mic** (hī′pə dur′mik) *adj.* [HYPO- + DERM(A)¹ + -IC] **1.** of the parts under the skin **2.** injected under the skin —*n. same as:* **1.** HYPODERMIC INJECTION **2.** HYPODERMIC SYRINGE —**hy′po·der′mi·cal·ly** *adv.*

**hypodermic injection** the injection of a medicine or drug under the skin

**hypodermic syringe** a piston syringe as of glass, attached to a hollow metal needle (**hypodermic needle**), used for giving hypodermic injections

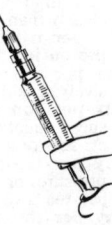

HYPODERMIC
SYRINGE

**hy·po·der·mis** (-mis) *n.* [ModL.: see HYPO- & DERMIS] **1.** *Bot.* a specialized layer of cells, as for support or water storage, just beneath the epidermis of a plant **2.** *Zool.* an epidermis secreting an overlying cuticle, as in arthropods and annelids

**hy·po·phos·phate** (hī′pə fäs′fāt) *n.* a salt or ester of hypophosphoric acid

**hy·po·phos·phite** (-fäs′fīt) *n.* a salt or ester of hypophosphorous acid

**hy·po·phos·phor·ic acid** (-fäs fôr′ik) an acid, $H_4P_2O_6$, obtained when phosphorus is slowly oxidized in moist air

**hy·po·phos·pho·rous acid** (-fäs′fər əs, -fäs fôr′əs) a monobasic acid of phosphorus, $H_3PO_2$: it is a strong reducing agent

**hy·poph·y·sis** (hī päf′ə sis) *n.*, *pl.* **-ses′** (-sēz′) [Gr., undergrowth] *same as* PITUITARY GLAND

**hy·po·sul·fite** (hī′pə sul′fīt) *n.* **1.** any salt of hyposulfurous acid **2.** *a popular but erroneous var. of* SODIUM THIOSULFATE

**hy·po·sul·fu·rous acid** (-səl fyoor′əs) an unstable acid, $H_2S_2O_4$, which has strong reducing properties

**hy·po·ten·sion** (-ten′shən) *n.* abnormally low blood pressure —**hy′po·ten′sive** *adj.*

**hy·pot·e·nuse** (hī pät′'n oos′, -yoos′) *n.* [< L. < Gr. *hypoteinousa*, lit., subtending < *hypo-*, under + *teinein*, to stretch] the side of a right-angled triangle opposite the right angle: also **hy·poth′e·nuse** (-hīpäth′-)

**hy·po·thal·a·mus** (hī′pə thal′ə məs) *n.*, *pl.* **-mi′** (-mī′) [ModL.: see HYPO- & THALAMUS] the part of the brain that forms the floor of the third ventricle and regulates many body functions, as temperature —**hy′po·tha·lam′ic** (-thə lam′ik) *adj.*

**hy·poth·e·cate** (hī päth′ə kāt′) *vt.* **-cat′ed, -cat′ing** [< ML. pp. of *hypothecare*, ult. < Gr. *hypotithenai*, to pledge] **1.** to pledge (property) to another as security; mortgage **2.** *same as* HYPOTHESIZE —**hy·poth′e·ca′tion** *n.* —**hy·poth′e·ca′tor** *n.*

**hy·poth·e·sis** (hī päth′ə sis, hi-) *n.*, *pl.* **-ses′** (-sēz′) [Gr. < *hypo-*, under + *tithenai*, to place] an unproved theory, proposition, etc. tentatively accepted to explain certain facts or (**working hypothesis**) to provide a basis for further investigation, argument, etc.

**hy·poth·e·size** (-sīz′) *vi.* **-sized′, -siz′ing** to make a hypothesis —*vt.* to assume; suppose

**hy·po·thet·i·cal** (hī′pə thet′i k'l) *adj.* **1.** based on or involving a hypothesis; assumed; supposed **2.** given to the use of hypotheses [*a hypothetical* mind] **3.** *Logic* conditional [*a hypothetical* proposition] Also **hy′po·thet′ic** —**hy′po·thet′i·cal·ly** *adv.*

**hy·po·thy·roid·ism** (hī′pō thī′roid iz'm) *n.* **1.** deficient activity of the thyroid gland **2.** the disorder resulting from this, characterized by a retarded rate of metabolism, sluggishness, puffiness, etc. —**hy′po·thy′roid** *adj., n.*

**hy·rax** (hī′raks) *n.*, *pl.* **-rax·es, -ra·ces′** (-rə sēz′) [Gr., shrew mouse] a small, hoofed mammal of Africa and SW Asia, that feeds on plants

**hys·sop** (his′əp) *n.* [< OFr. < L. < Gr. *hyssōpos* < Heb. *ēzōbh*] **1.** a fragrant, blue-flowered plant of the mint family, used in folk medicine as a tonic, stimulant, etc. **2.** *Bible* a plant whose twigs were used for sprinkling in certain ancient Jewish rites

**hys·ter·ec·to·my** (his′tə rek′tə mē) *n.*, *pl.* **-mies** [< Gr. *hystera*, uterus + -ECTOMY] surgical removal of all or part of the uterus

**hys·ter·e·sis** (his′tə rē′sis) *n.* [Gr., a deficiency] *Physics* a lag of effect, as in magnetization, when the forces acting on a body are changed

**hys·te·ri·a** (his tir′ē ə, -ter′-) *n.* [ModL. < ff. + -IA] **1.** a psychiatric condition characterized by excitability, sensory and motor disturbances, or the unconscious simulation of organic disorders **2.** any outbreak of wild, uncontrolled excitement, such as fits of laughing and crying

**hys·ter·ic** (his ter′ik) *adj.* [< L. < Gr. *hysterikos*, suffering in the womb < *hystera*, uterus: the ancients thought of hysteria as a woman's disorder caused by disturbances of the uterus] *same as* HYSTERICAL —*n.* **1.** [*usually pl., occas. with sing. v.*] a hysterical fit **2.** a person subject to hysteria

**hys·ter·i·cal** (-i k'l) *adj.* [prec. + -AL] **1.** of, like, or characteristic of hysteria **2.** extremely comical **3.** having or subject to hysteria

**Hz, hz** hertz

# I

**I, i** (ī) *n., pl.* **I's, i's 1.** the ninth letter of the English alphabet **2.** a sound of *I* or *i*
**I¹** (ī) *n.* **1.** a Roman numeral for 1 **2.** *Chem.* iodine —*adj.* shaped like *I*
**I²** (ī) *pron. for pl. see* WE [OE. *ic*] the person speaking or writing: *I* is the nominative case form of the first personal singular pronoun —*n., pl.* **I's** the ego
**i** (ī) *n.* **1.** a Roman numeral for 1 [page *iii*] **2.** *Math. the symbol for* √−1, the square root of −1
**I., i. 1.** island(s) **2.** isle(s)
**-i·a** (ē ə, yə) [L. & Gr.] *a suffix used in:* **1.** names of certain diseases [*pneumonia*] **2.** names of some plants and animals [*zinnia*]
**Ia., IA** Iowa
**I·a·go** (ē ä′gō) the villain in Shakespeare's *Othello*
**-i·al** (ē əl, yəl, əl) [L. *-ialis, -iale*] *same as* -AL (senses 1, 2) [*racial, centennial*]
**i·amb** (ī′amb, -am) *n.* [< Fr. < L. < Gr. *iambos*] a metrical foot of two syllables, the first unaccented and the other accented, as in English verse (Ex.: "Tŏ bé,|ŏr nót|tŏ bé")
**i·am·bic** (ī am′bik) *adj.* of or made up of iambs —*n.* **1.** an iamb **2.** an iambic verse
**i·am·bus** (-bəs) *n., pl.* **-bus·es, -bi** (-bī) [L.] *same as* IAMB
**-i·an** (ē ən, yən, ən) [< L. *-ianus*] *same as* -AN [*Indian, reptilian, Grecian*]
**-i·an·a** (ē an′ə) *same as* -ANA
**-i·a·sis** (ī′ə sis) [< Gr. *-iasis*] *a combining form meaning* diseased condition [*psoriasis*]
**-i·at·rics** (ē at′riks) [< Gr. < *iatros*, physician] *a combining form meaning* treatment of disease [*pediatrics*]
**i·at·ro·gen·ic** (ī at′rə jen′ik) *adj.* [< Gr. *iatros*, physician + -GENIC] caused by a physician's words or actions: said esp. of imagined symptoms
**-i·a·try** (ī′ə trē) [< Gr. *iatreia*, healing] *a combining form meaning* medical treatment [*psychiatry*]
**I·ba·dan** (ē bä′dän) city in SW Nigeria: pop. 600,000
**I·be·ri·a** (ī bir′ē ə) peninsula in SW Europe, comprising Spain & Portugal: often called **Iberian Peninsula** —**I·be′ri·an** *adj., n.*
**i·bex** (ī′beks) *n., pl.* **i′bex·es, i·bi·ces** (ib′ə sēz′, ī′bə-), **i′bex:** see PLURAL, II, D, 1 [L.] any of certain wild goats of Europe, Asia, or Africa: the male has large, backward-curved horns
**ibid.** [L. *ibidem*] in the same place: used in citing again the book, page, etc. cited just before
**-i·bil·i·ty** (ə bil′ə tē) *pl.* **-ties** [< L. *-ibilitas*] *a suffix used to form nouns from adjectives ending in* -IBLE [*sensibility*]
**i·bis** (ī′bis) *n., pl.* **i′bis·es, i′bis:** see PLURAL, II, D, 1 [L. < Gr. < Egypt. *hīb*] a large wading bird related to the herons, with long legs and a long, curved bill, as the sacred ibis of the Nile
**-i·ble** (i b′l, ə b′l) [L. *-ibilis*] *same as* -ABLE [*legible*]
**Ib·sen** (ib′s'n), **Hen·rik** (hen′rik) 1828–1906; Norw. playwright & poet
**-ic** (ik) [< Fr. *-ique* or L. *-icus* or Gr. *-ikos*] **1.** *a suffix forming adjectives, meaning:* a) of, having to do with [*volcanic*] b) like, having the nature of [*angelic*] c) produced by, caused by [*photographic*] d) producing, causing [*psychedelic*] e) consisting of, containing [*dactylic*] f) having, affected by [*lethargic*] g) *Chem.* of or derived from [*citric*]; also, of a higher valence than the compound ending in *-ous* [*nitric*] **2.** *a suffix forming nouns, meaning* a person or thing having the nature of, affected by, belonging to, producing, etc. [*paraplegic, cynic, hypnotic*]
**-i·cal** (i k′l, ə k′l) [< LL. < *-icus*, -IC + *-alis*, -AL] *same as* -IC: adjectives formed with *-ical* sometimes have differentiated meanings (e.g., *historical, economical*) beyond those of the corresponding *-ic* forms
**Ic·a·rus** (ik′ə rəs) *Gr. Myth.* the son of Daedalus: using wings made by Daedalus, Icarus flew so high that the sun's heat melted the wax in them and he fell to his death
**-i·car·i·an** (i ker′ē ən, i-) *adj.*
**ICBM** intercontinental ballistic missile
**ICC, I.C.C.** Interstate Commerce Commission
**ice** (īs) *n.* [OE. *is*] **1.** water frozen solid by cold **2.** a

piece, layer, or sheet of this **3.** anything like frozen water in appearance, etc. **4.** coldness in manner or attitude **5.** a frozen dessert, usually of water, fruit juice, and sugar **6.** icing **7.** [Slang] diamonds —*vt.* **iced, ic′ing 1.** to change into ice; freeze **2.** to cover with ice **3.** to cool by putting ice on, in, or around **4.** to cover with icing —*vi.* to freeze (often with *up* or *over*) —**break the ice 1.** to make a start by getting over initial difficulties **2.** to make a start toward getting better acquainted —**cut no ice** [Colloq.] to have no effect —**on ice** [Slang] **1.** in readiness or reserve **2.** in abeyance **3.** with success assured —**on thin ice** [Colloq.] in a risky situation
**-ice** (is, əs) [< OFr. *-ice* < L. *-itius*] *a suffix meaning* condition or quality of [*justice*]
**Ice. 1.** Iceland **2.** Icelandic
**ice age** *same as* GLACIAL EPOCH
**ice bag** a bag, of rubber, for holding ice, applied to the body to reduce a swelling, ease pain, etc.
**ice·berg** (īs′bʉrg′) *n.* [prob. via Du. *ijsberg*, lit., ice mountain < Scand.] a great mass of ice broken off from a glacier and floating in the sea
**iceberg lettuce** a variety of lettuce with crisp leaves tightly folded into a round, compact head
**ice·boat** (-bōt′) *n.* **1.** a light, boatlike frame, often triangular, equipped with runners and driven over ice by a sail, propeller, or jet engine **2.** *same as* ICEBREAKER (sense 1)
**ice·bound** (-bound′) *adj.* **1.** held fast by ice, as a boat **2.** made inaccessible by ice, as a port
**ice·box** (-bäks′) *n.* a cabinet with ice in it for keeping foods, etc. cold; also, any refrigerator
**ice·break·er** (-brā′kər) *n.* **1.** a sturdy ship for breaking a channel through ice **2.** anything lessening formality
**ice·cap** (-kap′) *n.* a mass of glacial ice that spreads slowly out from a center
**ice-cold** (īs′kōld′) *adj.* very cold
**ice cream** [orig., *iced cream*] a sweet, creamy frozen food made from variously flavored cream and milk products and often containing gelatin, eggs, fruits, etc. —**ice′-cream′** *adj.*
**ice field 1.** *same as* ICECAP **2.** an extensive area of floating sea ice
**ice floe 1.** *same as* ICE FIELD (sense 2) **2.** a single piece, large or small, of floating sea ice
**ice hockey** *same as* HOCKEY (sense 1)
**Ice·land** (īs′lənd) island country in the North Atlantic, southeast of Greenland: 39,768 sq. mi.; pop. 204,000; cap. Reykjavik —**Ice′land·er** *n.*
**Ice·lan·dic** (īs lan′dik) *adj.* of Iceland, its people, their language, or culture —*n.* the N. Germanic language of the Icelanders
**ice·man** (īs′man′, -mən) *n., pl.* **-men′** (-men′, -mən) a person who sells or delivers ice
**ice milk** a frozen dessert like ice cream, but with a lower butterfat content
**ice pack 1.** a large, floating expanse of ice masses frozen together **2.** an ice bag, folded cloth, etc. filled with crushed ice and applied to the body, as to reduce a swelling or ease pain
**ice pick** a sharply pointed metal tool used to chop ice into small pieces
**ice sheet** a thick layer of ice covering an extensive area for a long period, as in the ice age
**ice shelf** a thick mass of glacial ice along a polar shore, often protruding out to sea for many miles
**ice skate** a skate for skating on ice: see SKATE¹ (sense 1) —**ice′-skate′** *vi.* **-skat′ed, -skat′ing** —**ice skater**
**ich·neu·mon** (ik nyōo′mən, -nōō′-) *n.* [L. < Gr. *ichneumōn*, lit., tracker < *ichnos*, a track] **1.** the Egyptian species of mongoose **2.** *same as* ICHNEUMON FLY
**ichneumon fly** a hymenopteran insect whose larvae live as parasites in or on other insect larvae: also **ichneumon wasp**
**i·chor** (ī′kôr, -kər) *n.* [Gr. *ichōr*] **1.** *Gr. Myth.* the fluid flowing instead of blood in the veins of the gods **2.** a watery discharge from a wound or sore —**i′chor·ous** (-kər əs) *adj.*

**ich·thy·o-** [< Gr. < *ichthys*, a fish] *a combining form meaning* fish, like a fish: also **ichthy-**

**ich·thy·ol·o·gy** (ik'thē äl'ə jē) *n.* [< ModL.: see ICHTHYO- & -LOGY] the branch of zoology dealing with fishes —**ich'thy·o·log'i·cal** (-ə läj'i k'l), **ich'thy·o·log'ic** *adj.* —**ich'·thy·ol'o·gist** *n.*

**ich·thy·o·saur** (ik'thē ə sôr') *n.* [< ModL. < ICHTHYO- + Gr. *sauros*, lizard] a prehistoric marine reptile, now extinct, which had a fishlike body, four paddle-shaped flippers, and a dolphinlike head —**ich'thy·o·sau'ri·an** (-sôr'ē ən) *adj.*

**-i·cian** (ish'ən) [< Fr.: see -IC & -IAN] *a suffix meaning* a person engaged in, practicing, or specializing in *[mortician]*

**i·ci·cle** (ī'si k'l) *n.* [< OE. < *is*, ice + *gicel*, piece of ice] a hanging piece of ice, formed by the freezing of dripping water —**i'ci·cled** *adj.*

**ic·ing** (ī'siŋ) *n.* a mixture, as of sugar, butter, flavoring, etc., for covering a cake or pastries; frosting

**ick·y** (ik'ē) *adj.* **ick'i·er, ick'i·est** [baby talk for STICKY] [Slang] **1.** unpleasantly sticky **2.** cloyingly sentimental **3.** very distasteful; disgusting —**ick'i·ness** *n.*

**i·con** (ī'kän) *n.* [L. < Gr. *eikōn*, an image] **1.** an image **2.** *Orthodox Eastern Ch.* an image or picture of Jesus, Mary, a saint, etc., venerated as sacred —**i·con·ic** (ī kän'ik) *adj.*

**i·con·o-** [< Gr. *eikōn*, an image] *a combining form meaning* image, figure: also **icon-**

**i·con·o·clast** (ī kän'ə klast') *n.* [< ML. < MGr. < Gr. *eikōn*, an image + *klaein*, to break] **1.** anyone opposed to the religious use of images **2.** a person who attacks or ridicules traditional or venerated institutions or ideas —**i·con'·o·clasm** *n.* —**i·con'o·clas'tic** *adj.* —**i·con'o·clas'ti·cal·ly** *adv.*

**i·con·o·scope** (-skōp') *n.* [ICONO- + -SCOPE] an early form of television camera tube

**-ics** (iks) [-IC + -s (*pl.*)] *a pl. suffix meaning:* **1.** [*usually with sing. v.*] *a)* art, science, study [*economics*] *b)* arrangement, system [*statistics*] **2.** [*usually with pl. v.*] *a)* activities, practices [*histrionics*] *b)* qualities, properties [*atmospherics*]

**ic·tus** (ik'təs) *n., pl.* **-tus·es, -tus** [< L. < pp. of *icere*, to hit] **1.** rhythmical or metrical stress, or accent **2.** *Med.* a stroke or sudden attack

**i·cy** (ī'sē) *adj.* **i'ci·er, i'ci·est 1.** having much ice; full of or covered with ice **2.** of ice **3.** like ice; slippery or very cold **4.** cold in manner; unfriendly —**i'ci·ly** *adv.* —**i'ci·ness** *n.*

**id** (id) *n.* [ModL. < L., it] *Psychoanalysis* that part of the psyche which is the reservoir of the instinctual drives, dominated by the pleasure principle and irrational wishing

**-id** (id, əd) [ult. < L. or Gr.] *a suffix meaning:* **1.** a thing belonging to or connected with [*Aeneid, arachnid*] **2.** *Chem.* same as -IDE

**ID, I.D.** identification —*n.* (ī'dē'), *pl.* **ID's, I.D.'s** a card (**ID card**) or document that identifies a person, proves his age, etc.

**id.** [L. *idem*] the same

**I'd** (īd) **1.** I had **2.** I would **3.** I should

**I·da** (ī'də) [ML. < OHG.: akin ? to ON. *Ithunn*, goddess of youth] a feminine name

**Ida.** Idaho

**-i·dae** (i dē') [ModL.] *a suffix used to form the name of* a zoological family [*Canidae* (the dog family)]

**I·da·ho** (ī'də hō') [< AmInd. tribal name] Mountain State of the NW U.S.: 83,557 sq. mi.; pop. 944,000; cap. Boise: abbrev. **Ida., ID** —**I'da·ho'an** *adj., n.*

**-ide** (īd; *occas.* id) [< (OX)IDE] *a suffix added to part of the name of* the nonmetallic or electronegative element or radical in a binary compound [*sodium chloride*] *or used in forming the name of* a class of compounds [*glycoside*]

**i·de·a** (ī dē'ə) *n.* [L. < Gr. *idea*, appearance of a thing] **1.** a thought; mental conception or image; notion **2.** an opinion or belief **3.** a plan; scheme; intention **4.** a hazy perception; vague impression; inkling **5.** meaning or significance **6.** *Philos.* according to Plato, a model or archetype of which all real things are but imperfect imitations

**i·de·al** (ī dē'əl; *also, esp. for adj.* 2 & 4 *and for n.,* ī dēl') *adj.* [< Fr. < LL. < L. *idea:* see prec.] **1.** existing as an idea; being a model or archetype **2.** thought of as perfect; exactly as one would wish **3.** identifying or illustrating an idea or conception **4.** existing only in the mind as an image or concept; imaginary **5.** *Philos.* of idealism —*n.* **1.** a conception of something in its most excellent form **2.** a perfect model or standard **3.** a goal or principle

**i·de·al·ism** (ī dē'əl iz'm) *n.* **1.** behavior or thought based on a conception of things as one thinks they should be **2.** the representation of idealized persons or things in art or literature **3.** a striving to achieve one's ideals **4.** *Philos.* any theory which holds that things exist only as ideas in the mind or that things are really imperfect imitations of unchanging models or forms having independent existence apart from the material world: cf. MATERIALISM

**i·de·al·ist** (-ist) *n.* **1.** *a)* a person whose behavior or thought is based on ideals *b)* a visionary or impractical dreamer **2.** an adherent or practitioner of idealism in art, literature, or philosophy —*adj.* same as IDEALISTIC

**i·de·al·is·tic** (ī'dē ə lis'tik, ī dē'ə-) *adj.* **1.** of or characteristic of an idealist **2.** of, characterized by, or based on idealism —**i'de·al·is'ti·cal·ly** *adv.*

**i·de·al·ize** (ī dē'ə līz') *vt.* **-ized', -iz'ing** to make ideal; regard or show as perfect or more nearly perfect than is true —*vi.* to represent things in the manner of an idealist —**i·de'al·i·za'tion** *n.* —**i·de'al·iz'er** *n.*

**i·de·al·ly** (ī dē'əl ē) *adv.* **1.** in an ideal manner; perfectly **2.** in theory

**i·de·ate** (ī'dē āt', ī dē'āt) *vt., vi.* **-at'ed, -at'ing** to form an idea (of) —**i'de·a'tion** *n.* —**i'de·a'tion·al** *adj.* —**i'de·a'·tion·al·ly** *adv.*

**‡i·dée fixe** (ē dā fēks') [Fr.] a fixed idea; obsession

**‡i·dem** (ī'dem, ē'-) *pron.* [L.] the same as that previously mentioned

**i·den·ti·cal** (ī den'ti k'l) *adj.* [< ML. < LL. *identitas* (see IDENTITY) + -AL] **1.** the very same **2.** exactly alike **3.** designating twins, always of the same sex, developed from a single fertilized ovum and very much alike in appearance —**i·den'ti·cal·ly** *adv.*

**i·den·ti·fi·ca·tion** (ī den'tə fi kā'shən, i-) *n.* **1.** an identifying or being identified **2.** anything by which a person or thing can be identified **3.** *Psychoanalysis* a mainly unconscious process by which a person thinks, feels, and acts in a way which resembles his image of another person important to him

**i·den·ti·fy** (ī den'tə fī', i-) *vt.* **-fied', -fy'ing 1.** to make identical; treat as the same **2.** to show to be the very person or thing known, described, or claimed **3.** to connect or associate closely **4.** *Psychoanalysis* to make identification of (oneself) with someone else —*vi.* to understand and share another's feelings; sympathize (*with*) —**i·den'ti·fi'a·ble** *adj.* —**i·den'ti·fi'er** *n.*

**i·den·ti·ty** (ī den'tə tē) *n., pl.* **-ties** [< Fr. < LL. *identitas* < L. *idem*, the same] **1.** the condition or fact of being the same or exactly alike; sameness **2.** *a)* the condition or fact of being a specific person or thing; individuality *b)* the condition of being the same as a person or thing described or claimed

**identity crisis** [coined by E. Erikson (1902- ), U.S. psychoanalyst] the condition of being uncertain of one's feelings about oneself, esp. with regard to character, goals, and origins, occurring esp. in adolescence

**id·e·o-** [< Fr. *ideo-* or < Gr. *idea*] *a combining form meaning* idea [*ideology*]

**id·e·o·gram** (id'ē ə gram', ī'dē-) *n.* [prec. + -GRAM] **1.** a graphic symbol representing an object or idea without expressing the sounds that form its name **2.** a symbol representing an idea rather than a word (Ex.: 5, +, ÷) Also **id'·e·o·graph'**

**id·e·o·graph·ic** (id'ē ə graf'ik) *adj.* of, or having the nature of, an ideogram: also **id'e·o·graph'i·cal** —**id'e·o·graph'i·cal·ly** *adv.*

**i·de·o·log·i·cal** (ī'dē ə läj'i k'l, id'ē ə-) *adj.* of or concerned with ideology: also **i'de·o·log'ic** —**i'de·o·log'i·cal·ly** *adv.*

**i·de·ol·o·gy** (ī'dē äl'ə jē, id'ē-) *n., pl.* **-gies** [< Fr.: see IDEO- & -LOGY] **1.** the study of ideas, their nature and source **2.** thinking of an idealistic, abstract, or impractical nature **3.** the doctrines, opinions, or way of thinking of an individual, class, etc.; specif., the ideas on which a political, economic, or social system is based —**i'de·ol'o·gist** *n.*

**ides** (īdz) *n.pl.* [*often with sing. v.*] [Fr. < L. *idus*] in the ancient Roman calendar, the 15th day of March, May, July, or October, or the 13th of the other months

**‡id est** (id est) [L.] that is (to say)

**id·i·o·cy** (id'ē ə sē) *n., pl.* **-cies 1.** the state of being an idiot **2.** great foolishness or stupidity

**id·i·om** (id'ē əm) *n.* [< Fr. & LL. < Gr. *idios*, one's own] **1.** the language or dialect of a people, region, etc. **2.** the usual way in which the words of a particular language are joined together to express thought **3.** an accepted phrase or expression having a meaning different from the literal **4.** the style of expression characteristic of an individual **5.** a characteristic style, as in art or music

**id·i·o·mat·ic** (id'ē ō mat'ik) *adj.* **1.** characteristic of a particular language **2.** using or having many idioms **3.** of, or having the nature of, an idiom or idioms —**id'i·o·mat'i·cal·ly** *adv.*

**id·i·o·syn·cra·sy** (id'ē ə siŋ'krə sē, -sin'-) *n., pl.* **-sies** [< Gr. < *idio-*, one's own + *synkrasis*, mixture < *syn-*, together + *kerannynai*, to mix] **1.** the temperament peculiar to a person or group **2.** any personal peculiarity, mannerism, reaction, etc. —**id'i·o·syn·crat'ic** (-sin krat'ik) *adj.* —**id'i·o·syn·crat'i·cal·ly** *adv.*

**id·i·ot** (id'ē ət) *n.* [OFr. < L. < Gr. *idiōtēs*, ignorant person < *idios*, one's own] **1.** a person having severe mental retardation: an obsolescent term: see MENTAL RETARDATION **2.** a very foolish or stupid person

**id·i·ot·ic** (id'ē ät'ik) *adj.* of or like an idiot; very foolish or stupid —**id'i·ot'i·cal·ly** *adv.*

**i·dle** (ī'd'l) *adj.* **i'dler, i'dlest** [OE. *idel*, empty] **1.** a) worthless; useless [*idle* talk] *b*) futile; pointless [an *idle* wish] **2.** baseless; unfounded [*idle* rumors] **3.** *a*) unemployed [*idle* men] *b*) not in use [*idle* machines] **4.** lazy —*vi.* **i′dled, i′dling 1.** to move slowly or aimlessly **2.** to be unemployed or inactive **3.** to operate without transmitting any power, esp. with disengaged gears —*vt.* **1.** to waste; squander [*idling* away one's youth] **2.** to make (a motor, etc.) idle **3.** to make inactive or unemployed — **i′dle·ness** *n.* —**i′dly** *adv.*

**i·dler** (īd′lər) *n.* **1.** one who loafs **2.** *a*) a gearwheel placed between two others to transfer motion from one to the other without changing their direction or speed: also **idler gear** (or **wheel**), **idle wheel** *b*) a pulley guiding a belt or taking up slack: also **idler pulley**

**i·dol** (ī′d'l) *n.* [< OFr. < L. < Gr. *eidolon*, an image < *eidos*, form] **1.** an image of a god, used as an object of worship **2.** an object of excessive devotion or admiration

IDLE WHEEL

**i·dol·a·ter** (ī däl′ə tər) *n.* [< OFr. < LL. < LGr. < *eidōlon* (see prec.) + *latris*, servant] **1.** a worshiper of idols **2.** a devoted admirer; adorer —**i·dol′a·tress** (-tris) *n.fem.*

**i·dol·a·trize** (-trīz′) *vt., vi.* **-trized′, -triz′ing** to worship as an idolater

**i·dol·a·trous** (-trəs) *adj.* **1.** of, or having the nature of, idolatry **2.** worshiping idols **3.** having or showing excessive admiration or devotion —**i·dol′a·trous·ly** *adv.* —**i·dol′a·trous·ness** *n.*

**i·dol·a·try** (-trē) *n., pl.* **-tries 1.** worship of idols **2.** excessive devotion or reverence

**i·dol·ize** (ī′d'l īz′) *vt.* **-ized′, -iz′ing 1.** to make an idol of **2.** to love or admire excessively —*vi.* to worship idols — **i′dol·i·za′tion** *n.* —**i′dol·iz′er** *n.*

**i·dyll, i·dyl** (ī′d'l; *Brit. often* id′'l) *n.* [< L. < Gr. dim. of *eidos*, a form, image] **1.** a short poem or prose work describing a simple, pleasant scene of rural or pastoral life **2.** a scene or incident suitable for such a work —**i·dyl′lic** *adj.* —**i·dyl′li·cal·ly** *adv.* —**i′dyll·ist** *n.*

**-ie** (ē) [earlier form of -Y¹] *a suffix meaning:* **1.** small, little [*doggie*]: often used to express affection **2.** one that is as specified [*softie*]

**IE, I.E.** Indo-European

**i.e.** [L. *id est*] that is (to say)

**-i·er** (ir, ər, ē′ər, yər) [< OFr. < L. *-arius*] *a suffix meaning* a person concerned with (a specified action or thing) [*bombardier, furrier*]

**if** (if) *conj.* [OE. *gif*] **1.** on condition that; in case that [*if* I come, I'll see him] **2.** granting that [*if* he was there, I didn't see him] **3.** whether [ask him *if* he knows her] *If* is also used in exclamations expressing: *a*) a wish [*if* I had only known!] *b*) surprise, annoyance, etc. [*if* that isn't the limit!] —*n.* **1.** a supposition **2.** a condition [an idea filled with *ifs*] —**as if** as the situation would be if; as though

**if·fy** (if′ē) *adj.* [Colloq.] full of uncertainty

**IFR** Instrument Flight Rules

**ig·loo** (ig′lōō) *n., pl.* **-loos** [Esk. *igdlu*, snow house] an Eskimo house or hut, usually dome-shaped and built of blocks of packed snow

**Ig·na·tius (of) Loy·o·la** (ig nā′shəs loi ō′lə), Saint (born *Iñigo López de Recalde*) 1491-1556; Sp. priest: founder of the Jesuit order

**ig·ne·ous** (ig′nē əs) *adj.* [< L. < *ignis*, a fire] **1.** of, like, or containing fire **2.** formed by volcanic action or intense heat [*igneous* rock]

**ig·nis fat·u·us** (ig′nis fach′ōō wəs) *pl.* **ig·nes fat·u·i** (ig′nēz fach′ōō wī′) [ML. < L. *ignis*, a fire + *fatuus*, foolish] **1.** a light seen at night moving over swamps, etc., probably caused by a combustion of marsh gas: popularly called *will-o′-the-wisp, jack-o′-lantern* **2.** a deceptive hope, goal, or influence; delusion

**ig·nite** (ig nīt′) *vt., vi.* **-nit′ed, -nit′ing** [< L. pp. of *ignire* < *ignis*, a fire] **1.** to start burning **2.** to get excited —**ig·nit′a·ble, ig·nit′i·ble** *adj.* —**ig·nit′er, ig·ni′tor** *n.*

**ig·ni·tion** (ig nish′ən) *n.* **1.** an igniting or means of igniting **2.** in an internal-combustion engine, *a*) the igniting of the explosive mixture in the cylinder *b*) the device or system for doing this

**ig·no·ble** (ig nō′b'l) *adj.* [MFr. < L. < *in-*, not + *nobilis*, known] not noble in character or quality; dishonorable; base; mean —**ig·no′ble·ness** *n.* —**ig·no′bly** *adv.*

**ig·no·min·i·ous** (ig′nə min′ē əs) *adj.* **1.** shameful; disgraceful **2.** despicable **3.** degrading —**ig′no·min′i·ous·ly** *adv.* —**ig′no·min′i·ous·ness** *n.*

**ig·no·min·y** (ig′nə min′ē) *n., pl.* **-min′ies** [< Fr. < L. *ig-nominia* < *in-*, without + *nomen*, name] **1.** loss of one's

reputation; shame and dishonor **2.** disgraceful or shameful quality or action

**ig·no·ra·mus** (ig′nə rā′məs, -ram′əs) *n., pl.* **-mus·es** [< the name of a lawyer in a 17th-c. play; L., lit., we ignore (a legal term)] an ignorant person

**ig·no·rance** (ig′nər əns) *n.* the condition or quality of being ignorant; lack of knowledge

**ig·no·rant** (-ənt) *adj.* [< OFr. < L. prp. of *ignorare*: see ff.] **1.** lacking knowledge, education, or experience **2.** caused by or showing lack of these **3.** unaware (*of*) —**ig′-no·rant·ly** *adv.*

**ig·nore** (ig nôr′) *vt.* **-nored′, -nor′ing** [< Fr. < L. *ignorare* < *in-*, not + base of *gnarus*, knowing] to disregard deliberately; pay no attention to; refuse to consider —**ig·nor′er** *n.*

**I·go·rot** (ig′ə rōt′, ē′gə-) *n.* **1.** *pl.* **-rots′, -rot′** a member of a Malayan people of Luzon, in the Philippines **2.** their Indonesian language

**i·gua·na** (i gwä′nə) *n.* [Sp. < S. AmInd. *iuana*] a large, harmless, tropical American lizard with spines from neck to tail

**IHP, I.H.P., ihp., i.h.p.** indicated horsepower

**IHS** a contraction misread from the Greek word IHΣΟΥΣ, Jesus, used as a symbol or monogram

**IJs·sel·meer** (ī′səl mer′) freshwater lake in N & C Netherlands: formerly part of the Zuider Zee

LAND IGUANA
(to 5 ft. long)

**i·kon** (ī′kän) *n. var. of* ICON

**il-** *see* IN-¹, IN-²

**IL** Illinois

**-ile** (il, əl, 'l; *also, chiefly Brit.* īl) [< Fr. *-il, -ile* < L. *-ilis*] *a suffix meaning* of, having to do with, that can be, like, suitable for [*docile, missile*]: sometimes -il [*civil*]

**il·e·i·tis** (il′ē īt′is) *n.* inflammation of the ileum

**il·e·um** (il′ē əm) *n., pl.* **il′e·a** (-ə) [ModL. < L., flank, groin (var. of *ilium*)] the lowest part of the small intestine —**il′e·ac′** (-ak′), **il′e·al** (-əl) *adj.*

**i·lex** (ī′leks) *n.* [L.] *same as:* **1.** HOLLY **2.** HOLM OAK

**Il·i·ad** (il′ē əd) [< L. < Gr. < *Ilios*, Troy] a long Greek epic poem, ascribed to Homer, about the final part of the Trojan War

**-il·i·ty** (il′ə tē) *pl.* **-ties** *a suffix used in nouns formed from adjectives ending in* -ILE, -IL [*imbecility, civility*]

**Il·i·um** (il′ē əm) Latin name for TROY (sense 1)

**il·i·um** (il′ē əm) *n., pl.* **il′i·a** (-ə) [ModL. < *same as* ILEUM] the flat, uppermost section of the innominate bone —**il′i·ac′** (-ak′) *adj.*

**ilk** (ilk) *adj.* [Scot. dial. < OE. *ilca*, same] [Obs.] same; like —*n.* kind; sort: only in **of that** (or **his, her**, etc.) **ilk**: a misunderstanding of the orig. Scottish phrase meaning "of the same name"

**ill** (il) *adj.* **worse, worst** [< ON. *illr*] **1.** *a*) morally bad [*ill* repute] *b*) adverse [*ill* fortune] *c*) not kind or friendly [*ill* will] *d*) unfavorable [an *ill* omen] **2.** not healthy, normal, or well; sick **3.** faulty; improper —*n.* anything causing harm, trouble, pain, etc.; evil —*adv.* **worse, worst 1.** in an ill way; specif., *a*) badly *b*) unkindly **2.** with difficulty; scarcely [he can *ill* afford it] —**ill at ease** uneasy; uncomfortable

**I'll** (īl) **1.** I shall **2.** I will

**Ill.** Illinois

**ill.** **1.** illustrated **2.** illustration

**ill-ad·vised** (il′əd vīzd′) *adj.* showing or resulting from a lack of sound advice or proper consideration; unwise — **ill′-ad·vis′ed·ly** (-vī′zid lē) *adv.*

**ill-bred** (-bred′) *adj.* badly brought up; rude

**ill-con·sid·ered** (-kən sid′ərd) *adj.* not properly considered; not suitable or wise

**ill-dis·posed** (-dis pōzd′) *adj.* **1.** having a bad disposition; malicious or malevolent **2.** unfriendly or unfavorable (*toward*)

**il·le·gal** (i lē′gəl) *adj.* not lawful; against the law or against the rules —**il·le·gal·i·ty** (il′ē gal′ə tē) *n., pl.* **-ties** —**il·le′gal·ly** *adv.*

**il·leg·i·ble** (i lej′ə b'l) *adj.* difficult or impossible to read because badly written or printed, faded, etc. —**il·leg′i·bil′i·ty** *n.* —**il·leg′i·bly** *adv.*

**il·le·git·i·mate** (il′ə jit′ə mit) *adj.* **1.** born of parents not married to each other **2.** incorrectly deduced **3.** not lawful **4.** unsanctioned —**il′le·git′i·ma·cy** (-mə sē) *n., pl.* **-cies** —**il′le·git′i·mate·ly** *adv.*

**ill-fat·ed** (il′fāt′id) *adj.* **1.** having or sure to have an evil fate or unlucky end **2.** unlucky

**ill-fa·vored** (-fā′vərd) *adj.* **1.** unpleasant or ugly in appearance **2.** offensive

**ill·found·ed** (-foun'did) *adj.* not supported by facts or sound reasons

**ill·got·ten** (-gät'n) *adj.* obtained by evil, unlawful, or dishonest means *[ill-gotten* gains*]*

**ill humor** a disagreeable, cross, or sullen mood or state of mind —**ill'-hu'mored** *adj.* —**ill'-hu'mored·ly** *adv.*

**il·lib·er·al** (i lib'ər əl) *adj.* 1. [Archaic] without culture; unrefined 2. intolerant; narrow-minded 3. miserly; stingy —**il·lib'er·al'i·ty** (-ə ral'ə tē) *n.* —**il·lib'er·al·ly** *adv.*

**il·lic·it** (i lis'it) *adj.* not allowed by law, custom, etc.; unlawful —**il·lic'it·ly** *adv.* —**il·lic'it·ness** *n.*

**il·lim·it·a·ble** (i lim'it ə b'l) *adj.* without limit or bounds —**il·lim'it·a·bil'i·ty**, il·lim'it·a·ble·ness *n.* —**il·lim'it·a·bly** *adv.*

**Il·li·nois¹** (il'ə noi'; *occas.* -noiz') *n.* [Fr. < Illinois *ileniwe,* man] 1. *pl.* **-nois'** a member of a tribe or confederacy of Indians who lived in N Illinois, S Wisconsin, and parts of Iowa and Missouri 2. their Algonquian dialect

**Il·li·nois²** (il'ə noi'; *occas.* -noiz') [< *prec.*] Middle Western State of the U.S.: 56,400 sq. mi.; pop. 11,418,000; cap. Springfield: abbrev. Ill., IL —**Il'li·nois'an** (-noi'ən, -noiz'ən) *adj., n.*

**il·lit·er·a·cy** (i lit'ər ə sē) *n.* 1. the state of being illiterate 2. *pl.* **-cies** a mistake (in writing or speaking) suggesting poor education

**il·lit·er·ate** (-it) *adj.* 1. ignorant; uneducated; esp., not knowing how to read or write 2. having or showing limited knowledge, experience, or culture 3. violating accepted usage in language —*n.* an illiterate person —**il·lit'er·ate·ly** *adv.*

**ill-man·nered** (il'man'ərd) *adj.* rude; impolite

**ill nature** an unpleasant, disagreeable disposition —**ill'-na'tured** *adj.* —**ill'-na'tured·ly** *adv.*

**ill·ness** (-nis) *n.* the condition of being ill; sickness; disease

**il·log·ic** (i läj'ik) *n.* lack of logic

**il·log·i·cal** (-i k'l) *adj.* not logical; using or based on faulty reasoning —**il·log'i·cal'i·ty** (-i kal'ə tē), il·log'i·cal·ness *n.* —**il·log'i·cal·ly** *adv.*

**ill-spent** (il'spent') *adj.* misspent; wasted

**ill-starred** (-stärd') *adj.* unlucky; doomed

**ill-tem·pered** (-tem'pərd) *adj.* bad-tempered

**ill-timed** (-tīmd') *adj.* coming or done at the wrong time; inopportune

**ill-treat** (il'trēt') *vt.* to treat unkindly, cruelly, or unfairly; abuse —**ill'-treat'ment** *n.*

**il·lu·mi·nance** (i lōō'mə nəns) *n. same as* ILLUMINATION (sense 2)

**il·lu·mi·nant** (-nənt) *adj.* giving light; illuminating —*n.* something that gives light

**il·lu·mi·nate** (-nāt') *vt.* **-nat'ed, -nat'ing** [< L. pp. of *illuminare* < *in-,* in + *luminare,* to light < *lumen,* a light] 1. *a)* to give light to; light up *b)* to brighten; animate 2. *a)* to make clear; explain *b)* to inform; enlighten 3. to make famous 4. to decorate with lights 5. to decorate (an initial letter, a page border, etc.) with designs of gold, bright colors, etc. —**il·lu'mi·na·ble** *adj.* —**il·lu'mi·na'tive** *adj.* —**il·lu'mi·na'tor** *n.*

**il·lu·mi·na·tion** (i lōō'mə nā'shən) *n.* 1. an illuminating or being illuminated 2. the intensity of light per unit of area 3. the designs used in illuminating manuscripts

**il·lu·mine** (i lōō'min) *vt.* **-mined, -min·ing** *same as* ILLUMINATE —**il·lu'mi·na·ble** *adj.*

**illus., illust.** 1. illustrated 2. illustration

**ill-us·age** (il'yōō'sij, -zij) *n.* unfair, unkind, or cruel treatment; abuse: also **ill usage**

**ill-use** (-yōōz'; *for n.* -yōōs') *vt.* **-used', -us'ing** to subject to ill-usage —*n. same as* ILL-USAGE

**il·lu·sion** (i lōō'zhən) *n.* [< OFr. < L. < pp. of *illudere,* to mock] 1. a false idea or conception 2. an unreal or misleading appearance or image 3. a false perception or interpretation of what one sees 4. a hallucination —**il·lu'sion·al,** il·lu'sion·ar'y *adj.*

**il·lu·sion·ist** (-ist) *n.* an entertainer who performs sleight-of-hand tricks

**il·lu·sive** (i lōō'siv) *adj.* illusory; unreal —**il·lu'sive·ly** *adv.* —**il·lu'sive·ness** *n.*

**il·lu·so·ry** (-sər ē) *adj.* producing, based on, or having the nature of, illusion; deceptive; unreal —**il·lu'so·ri·ly** *adv.* —**il·lu'so·ri·ness** *n.*

**il·lus·trate** (il'ə strāt', i lus'trāt) *vt.* **-trat'ed, -trat'ing** [< L. pp. of *illustrare* < *in-,* in + *lustrare,* to illuminate] 1. to make clear or explain, as by examples or comparisons 2. *a)* to furnish (books, etc.) with explanatory or decorative drawings, pictures, etc. *b)* to explain or decorate: said of pictures, etc. —*vi.* to illustrate something —**il'lus·tra'tor** *n.*

**il·lus·tra·tion** (il'ə strā'shən) *n.* 1. an illustrating or being illustrated 2. an explanatory example, story, etc. 3. an explanatory or decorative picture, diagram, etc. —**il'lus·tra'tion·al** *adj.*

**il·lus·tra·tive** (i lus'trə tiv, il'ə strāt'iv) *adj.* serving to illustrate —**il·lus'tra·tive·ly** *adv.*

**il·lus·tri·ous** (i lus'trē əs) *adj.* [< L. *illustris,* bright] very distinguished; famous; eminent —**il·lus'tri·ous·ly** *adv.* —**il·lus'tri·ous·ness** *n.*

**ill will** unfriendly feeling; hostility; hate

**il·ly** (il'lē) *adv.* [Now Dial.] badly; ill

**Il·lyr·i·a** (i lir'ē ə) ancient region along the E coast of the Adriatic —**Il·lyr'i·an** *adj., n.*

**ILO, I.L.O.** International Labor Organization

**ILS** instrument landing system

**I'm** (īm) I am

**im-** *see* IN-¹, IN-²

**im·age** (im'ij) *n.* [OFr. < L. < *imago* < base of *imitari,* to imitate] 1. a representation of a person or thing, drawn, painted, etc.; esp., a statue 2. the visual impression of something produced by a mirror, lens, etc. 3. a copy; counterpart; likeness 4. *a)* a mental picture of something; conception *b)* the public conception of a person, product, etc., often created by publicity 5. a type; embodiment *[the image of laziness]* 6. a figure of speech, esp. a metaphor or simile —*vt.* **-aged, -ag·ing** 1. to portray; delineate 2. to reflect; mirror 3. to picture in the mind 4. to typify 5. to describe vividly

**im·age·ry** (im'ij rē, -ər ē) *n., pl.* **-ries** 1. mental images 2. descriptions and figures of speech

**i·mag·i·na·ble** (i maj'ə nə b'l) *adj.* that can be imagined —**i·mag'i·na·bly** *adv.*

**i·mag·i·nar·y** (i maj'ə ner'ē) *adj.* existing only in the imagination; unreal —**i·mag'i·nar'i·ly** *adv.* —**i·mag'i·nar'i·ness** *n.*

**i·mag·i·na·tion** (i maj'ə nā'shən) *n.* 1. *a)* the act or power of forming mental images of what is not actually present *b)* the act or power of creating mental images of what has never been actually experienced, or of creating new images or ideas by combining previous experiences 2. anything imagined 3. a foolish notion 4. responsiveness to the imaginative creations of others 5. resourcefulness in dealing with new or unusual experiences

**i·mag·i·na·tive** (i maj'ə nə tiv, -nāt'iv) *adj.* 1. having, using, or showing imagination 2. given to imagining 3. of or resulting from imagination —**i·mag'i·na·tive·ly** *adv.* —**i·mag'i·na·tive·ness** *n.*

**i·mag·ine** (i maj'in) *vt., vi.* **-ined, -in·ing** [< OFr. < L. *imaginari* < *imago,* an IMAGE] 1. to make a mental image (of); conceive in the mind 2. to suppose; guess; think —*interj.* an exclamation of surprise

**im·ag·ism** (im'ə jiz'm) *n.* a movement in modern poetry (c. 1909–1917) using precise, concrete images, free verse, and suggestion —**im'ag·ist** *n., adj.* —**im'ag·is'tic** *adj.*

**i·ma·go** (i mā'gō) *n., pl.* **-goes, -gos,** i·mag·i·nes (i maj'ə nēz') [ModL. < L., an IMAGE] an insect in its final, adult, reproductive stage

**i·mam** (i mäm') *n.* [Ar. *imām*] 1. the prayer leader in a Moslem mosque 2. [*often* I-] title for a Moslem ruler

**im·bal·ance** (im bal'əns) *n.* lack of balance

**im·be·cile** (im'bə s'l) *n.* [< Fr. < L. *imbecilis,* feeble] 1. a person having moderate mental retardation: obsolescent term: see MENTAL RETARDATION 2. a very foolish or stupid person —*adj.* very foolish or stupid: also **im'be·cil'ic** (-sil'ik)

**im·be·cil·i·ty** (im'bə sil'ə tē) *n., pl.* **-ties** 1. the state of being an imbecile 2. great foolishness or stupidity 3. an imbecile act or remark

**im·bed** (im bed') *vt. same as* EMBED

**im·bibe** (im bīb') *vt.* **-bibed', -bib'ing** [< L. *imbibere* < *in-,* in + *bibere,* to drink] 1. *a)* to drink (esp. alcoholic liquor) *b)* to take in with the senses or mind; drink in 2. to absorb (moisture) —*vi.* to drink, esp. alcoholic liquor —**im·bib'er** *n.*

**im·bri·cate** (im'brə kit; *also, and for v. always,* -kāt') *adj.* [< LL. pp. of *imbricare,* to cover with tiles < L. *imbrex,* gutter tile < *imber,* rain] 1. overlapping evenly, as tiles or fish scales 2. ornamented as with overlapping scales —*vt., vi.* **-cat'ed, -cat'ing** to make or be imbricate —**im'bri·cate·ly** *adv.* —**im'bri·ca'tion** *n.*

**im·bro·glio** (im brōl'yō) *n., pl.* **-glios** [It. < *imbrogliare,* to embroil] 1. an involved and confusing situation 2. a confused misunderstanding or disagreement

**im·brue** (im brōō') *vt.* **-brued', -bru'ing** [< OFr., ult. < L. *imbibere:* see IMBIBE] to wet, soak, or stain, esp. with blood —**im·brue'ment** *n.*

**im·bue** (im byōō') *vt.* **-bued', -bu'ing** [< L. *imbuere*] 1. [Rare] to saturate 2. to fill with color; dye 3. to permeate or inspire (*with* principles, ideas, emotions, etc.)

**imit.** 1. imitation 2. imitative

**im·i·tate** (im'ə tāt') *vt.* **-tat'ed, -tat'ing** [< L. pp. of *imitari,* to imitate] 1. to follow the example of 2. to act the same as; mimic 3. to copy the form, color, etc. of 4. to be like in appearance; resemble —**im'i·ta·ble** (-tə b'l) *adj.* —**im'i·ta'tor** *n.*

**im·i·ta·tion** (im'ə tā'shən) *n.* 1. an imitating 2. the result or product of imitating —*adj.* made to resemble something that is usually superior or genuine *[imitation* leather*]*

**im·i·ta·tive** (im′ə tāt′iv) *adj.* **1.** formed from a model **2.** given to imitating **3.** not genuine **4.** sounding like the thing signified, as the word *clang* —**im′i·ta′tive·ly** *adv.* —**im′i·ta′tive·ness** *n.*

**im·mac·u·late** (i mak′yə lit) *adj.* [< L. < *in-*, not + pp. of *maculare*, to soil < *macula*, a spot] **1.** perfectly clean; spotless **2.** without flaw **3.** pure; innocent; sinless —**im·mac′u·late·ly** *adv.* —**im·mac′u·late·ness, im·mac′u·la·cy** (-lə sē) *n.*

**Immaculate Conception** *R.C.Ch.* the doctrine that the Virgin Mary was from the moment of conception free from original sin

**im·ma·nent** (im′ə nənt) *adj.* [< LL. prp. of *immanere* < *in-*, in + *manere*, to remain] **1.** living, remaining, or operating within; inherent **2.** present throughout the universe: said of God —**im′ma·nence, im′ma·nen·cy** *n.* —**im′ma·nent·ly** *adv.*

**Im·man·u·el** (i man′yoo wəl) **1.** [var. of EMMANUEL] a masculine name **2.** a name given by Isaiah to the Messiah of his prophecy (Isa. 7:14), often applied to Jesus (Matt. 1:23)

**im·ma·te·ri·al** (im′ə tir′ē əl) *adj.* **1.** not consisting of matter; spiritual **2.** that does not matter; not pertinent; unimportant —**im′ma·te′ri·al′i·ty** (-al′ə tē) *n.*, *pl.* **-ties** —**im′ma·te′ri·al·ly** *adv.*

**im·ma·ture** (im′ə toor′, -choor′, -tyoor′) *adj.* **1.** not mature or ripe; not completely grown or developed **2.** not finished or perfected —**im′ma·ture′ly** *adv.* —**im′ma·tu′ri·ty, im′ma·ture′ness** *n.*

**im·meas·ur·a·ble** (i mezh′ər ə b′l) *adj.* not measurable; boundless —**im·meas′ur·a·bil′i·ty, im·meas′ur·a·ble·ness** *n.* —**im·meas′ur·a·bly** *adv.*

**im·me·di·a·cy** (i mē′dē ə sē) *n.* the quality or condition of being immediate

**im·me·di·ate** (i mē′dē it) *adj.* [< LL.: see IN-² & MEDIATE] having nothing coming between; with no intermediary; specif., *a)* not separated in space; in direct contact; closest; also, close by *b)* not separated in time; without delay *c)* of the present *d)* next in order, succession, etc.; also, directly or closely related *e)* directly affecting; direct

**im·me·di·ate·ly** (-lē) *adv.* in an immediate manner; specif., *a)* without intervening agency or cause *b)* without delay; at once —*conj.* [Chiefly Brit.] as soon as *[go immediately]* he comes

**im·me·mo·ri·al** (im′ə môr′ē əl) *adj.* back beyond memory or record —**im′me·mo′ri·al·ly** *adv.*

**im·mense** (i mens′) *adj.* [Fr. < L. < *in-*, not + pp. of *metiri*, to measure] **1.** very large; vast; huge **2.** [Slang] very good; excellent —**im·mense′ly** *adv.* —**im·mense′ness** *n.*

**im·men·si·ty** (i men′sə tē) *n.*, *pl.* **-ties** **1.** great size or extent **2.** infinite space or being

**im·merge** (i murj′) *vi.* **-merged′, -merg′ing** [see ff.] to plunge, as into a liquid

**im·merse** (i murs′) *vt.* **-mersed′, -mers′ing** [< L. pp. of *immergere*, to plunge: see IN-¹ & MERGE] **1.** to plunge or dip into or as if into a liquid **2.** to baptize by dipping under water **3.** to absorb deeply; engross —**im·mers′i·ble** *adj.* —**im·mer′sion** *n.*

**immersion heater** an electric coil or rod that heats water while directly immersed in it

**im·mi·grant** (im′ə grənt) *n.* one that immigrates —*adj.* immigrating

**im·mi·grate** (-grāt′) *vi.* **-grat′ed, -grat′ing** [< L. pp. of *immigrare*: see IN-¹ & MIGRATE] to come into a new country or region, esp. in order to settle there: opposed to EMIGRATE —**im′mi·gra′tion** *n.*

**im·mi·nence** (im′ə nəns) *n.* **1.** a being imminent: also **im′mi·nen·cy** **2.** something imminent

**im·mi·nent** (-nənt) *adj.* [< L. prp. of *imminere* < *in-*, in + *minere*, to project] likely to happen soon: said of danger, evil, etc. —**im′mi·nent·ly** *adv.*

**im·mis·ci·ble** (i mis′ə b′l) *adj.* [< IN-² + MISCIBLE] that cannot be mixed, as oil and water —**im·mis′ci·bil′i·ty** *n.*

**im·mo·bile** (i mō′b′l, -bēl, -bil) *adj.* not movable or moving; stable; motionless —**im′mo·bil′i·ty** *n.*

**im·mo·bi·lize** (i mō′bə līz′) *vt.* **-lized′, -liz′ing** **1.** to make immobile **2.** to prevent the movement of (a limb or joint) with splints or a cast —**im·mo′bi·li·za′tion** *n.*

**im·mod·er·ate** (i mäd′ər it) *adj.* not moderate; without restraint; excessive —**im·mod′er·ate·ly** *adv.* —**im·mod′er·a′tion, im·mod′er·ate·ness, im·mod′er·a·cy** (-ə sē) *n.*

**im·mod·est** (i mäd′ist) *adj.* not modest; specif., *a)* indecent; improper *b)* bold; forward —**im·mod′est·ly** *adv.* —**im·mod′es·ty** *n.*

**im·mo·late** (im′ə lāt′) *vt.* **-lat′ed, -lat′ing** [< L. pp. of *immolare*, to sprinkle with sacrificial meal < *in-*, on + *mola*, meal] to sacrifice; esp., to kill as a sacrifice —**im′mo·la′tion** *n.* —**im′mo·la′tor** *n.*

**im·mor·al** (i môr′əl, -mär′-) *adj.* not in conformity with accepted principles of right behavior; wicked; sometimes, specif., unchaste; lewd —**im·mor′al·ly** *adv.*

**im·mo·ral·i·ty** (im′ə ral′ə tē, im′ô-) *n.* **1.** the state or quality of being immoral **2.** immoral behavior **3.** *pl.* **-ties** an immoral act or practice

**im·mor·tal** (i môr′t′l) *adj.* **1.** not mortal; living or lasting forever **2.** of immortal beings or immortality **3.** lasting a long time; enduring **4.** having lasting fame —*n.* an immortal being; specif., *a)* [*pl.*] the ancient Greek or Roman gods *b)* a person of lasting fame —**im′mor·tal′i·ty** (-tal′ə tē) *n.* —**im·mor′tal·ly** *adv.*

**im·mor·tal·ize** (i môr′tə līz′) *vt.* **-ized′, -iz′ing** to make immortal; esp., to give lasting fame to —**im·mor′tal·i·za′tion** *n.* —**im·mor′tal·iz′er** *n.*

**im·mor·telle** (im′ôr tel′) *n.* [Fr. fem. of *immortel*, undying] *same as* EVERLASTING (*n.* 2)

**im·mov·a·ble** (i moov′ə b′l) *adj.* **1.** that cannot be moved; firmly fixed **2.** motionless; stationary **3.** unyielding; steadfast **4.** unemotional; impassive —*n.* [*pl.*] *Law* immovable objects or property, as land, buildings, etc. —**im·mov′a·bil′i·ty, im·mov′a·ble·ness** *n.* —**im·mov′a·bly** *adv.*

**im·mune** (i myoon′) *adj.* [< L. *immunis*, exempt < *in-*, without + *munia*, duties] having immunity; specif., *a)* exempt from or protected against something disagreeable or harmful *b)* not susceptible to a specified disease because having the specific antibodies

**immune body** *same as* ANTIBODY

**im·mu·ni·ty** (i myoon′ə tē) *n.*, *pl.* **-ties** **1.** exemption or freedom from something burdensome or otherwise unpleasant **2.** resistance to or protection against a specified disease

**im·mu·nize** (im′yə nīz′) *vt.* **-nized′, -niz′ing** to give immunity to —**im′mu·ni·za′tion** *n.*

**im·mu·no·gen·ic** (im′yoo nō jen′ik) *adj.* producing immunity —**im′mu·no·gen′i·cal·ly** *adv.*

**im·mu·nol·o·gy** (im′yoo näl′ə jē) *n.* the branch of medicine dealing with immunity to disease or with allergic reactions, etc. —**im′mu·no·log′i·cal** (-nə läj′i k′l), **im′mu·no·log′ic** *adj.* —**im′mu·no·log′i·cal·ly** *adv.* —**im′mu·nol′o·gist** *n.*

**im·mure** (i myoor′) *vt.* **-mured′, -mur′ing** [< OFr. < ML. *immurare* < L. *im-*, in + *murus*, a wall] to shut up as within walls —**im·mure′ment** *n.*

**im·mu·ta·ble** (i myoot′ə b′l) *adj.* never changing or varying; unchangeable —**im·mu′ta·bil′i·ty, im·mu′ta·ble·ness** *n.* —**im·mu′ta·bly** *adv.*

**imp** (imp) *n.* [< OE., ult. < Gr. *emphyta*, scion < *em-*, in + *phyton*, a plant] **1.** a young demon **2.** a mischievous child

**imp. 1.** imperative **2.** imperfect **3.** imperial **4.** impersonal **5.** import **6.** importer **7.** imprimatur

**im·pact** (im pakt′; *for n.* im′pakt) *vt.* [< L. pp. of *impingere*, to press firmly together] to force tightly together; wedge —*n.* **1.** a striking together; collision **2.** the force of a collision; shock **3.** the power of an event, idea, etc. to produce changes, move feelings, etc. —**im·pac′tion** *n.*

**im·pact·ed** (im pak′tid) *adj.* **1.** firmly lodged in the jaw: said of a tooth unable to erupt **2.** densely populated

**im·pair** (im per′) *vt.* [< OFr., ult. < L. *in-*, intens. + *pejor*, worse] to make worse, less, weaker, etc.; damage; reduce —**im·pair′ment** *n.*

**im·pa·la** (im pä′lə, -pal′ə) *n.*, *pl.* **-la, -las**: see PLURAL, II, D, 2 [Zulu] a medium-sized, reddish antelope of C and S Africa

**im·pale** (im pāl′) *vt.* **-paled′, -pal′ing** [< Fr. < ML. *impalare* < L. *in-*, on + *palus*, a pole] **1.** to pierce through with, or fix on, something pointed **2.** to torture by fixing on a stake **3.** to make helpless, as if fixed on a stake *[impaled by her glance]* —**im·pale′ment** *n.*

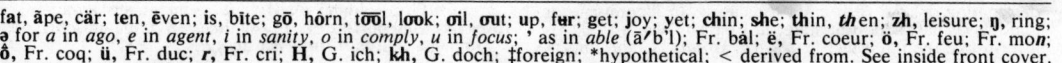

IMPACTED TOOTH

**im·pal·pa·ble** (im pal′pə b′l) *adj.* **1.** not perceptible to the touch **2.** too slight or subtle to be grasped easily by the mind —**im·pal′pa·bil′i·ty** *n.* —**im·pal′pa·bly** *adv.*

**im·pan·el** (im pan′′l) *vt.* **-eled** or **-elled, -el·ing** or **-el·ling 1.** to enter the name or names of on a jury list **2.** to choose (a jury) from such a list —**im·pan′el·ment** *n.*

**im·part** (im pärt′) *vt.* [< OFr. < L. *impartire*: see IN-¹ & PART] **1.** to give a share or portion of; give **2.** to tell; reveal —**im·part′a·ble** *adj.* —**im′par·ta′tion** *n.* —**im·part′er** *n.*

**im·par·tial** (im pär′shəl) *adj.* favoring no one side or party more than another; fair —**im·par′ti·al′i·ty** (-shē al′ə tē) *n.* —**im·par′tial·ly** *adv.*

**im·pass·a·ble** (im pas′ə b′l) *adj.* that cannot be passed, crossed, or traveled over —**im·pass′a·bil′i·ty** *n.* —**im·pass′a·bly** *adv.*

**im·passe** (im′pas, im pas′) *n.* [Fr.] **1.** a passage open only at one end; blind alley **2.** a situation offering no escape; deadlock

**im·pas·si·ble** (im pas′ə b′l) *adj.* [< OFr. < LL. < L. *im-*, not + *passibilis* < *pati*, to suffer] **1.** that cannot feel pain **2.** that cannot be injured **3.** that cannot be moved emotionally —**im·pas′si·bil′i·ty** *n.* —**im·pas′si·bly** *adv.*

**im·pas·sioned** (im pash′ənd) *adj.* filled with passion; passionate; fiery; ardent —**im·pas′sioned·ly** *adv.*

**im·pas·sive** (im pas′iv) *adj.* **1.** not feeling pain; insensible **2.** not feeling or showing emotion; placid; calm —**im·pas′sive·ly** *adv.* —**im·pas·siv·i·ty** (im′pə siv′ə tē) *n.*

**im·pas·to** (im päs′tō) *n.* [< It. *impastare*, to paste over] painting with the paint laid on thickly

**im·pa·tience** (im pā′shəns) *n.* lack of patience; specif., *a)* annoyance because of delay, opposition, etc. *b)* restless eagerness to do something, etc.

**im·pa·ti·ens** (im pā′shē enz′, -shənz) *n.* [ModL. < L.: see ff.] a plant with spurred flowers and pods that burst and scatter their seeds when ripe

**im·pa·tient** (im pā′shənt) *adj.* feeling or showing impatience —**im·pa′tient·ly** *adv.*

**im·peach** (im pēch′) *vt.* [< OFr. < LL. *impedicare*, to entangle < L. *in-*, in + *pedica*, a fetter < *pes*, foot] **1.** to challenge or discredit (a person's honor, etc.) **2.** to challenge the practices or honesty of; esp., to bring (a public official) before the proper tribunal on a charge of wrongdoing —**im·peach′a·bil′i·ty** *n.* —**im·peach′a·ble** *adj.* —**im·peach′ment** *n.*

**im·pec·ca·ble** (im pek′ə b′l) *adj.* [< L. < *in-*, not + *peccare*, to sin] **1.** not liable to sin or wrongdoing **2.** without defect or error; flawless —**im·pec′ca·bil′i·ty** *n.* —**im·pec′ca·bly** *adv.*

**im·pe·cu·ni·ous** (im′pi kyōō′nē əs) *adj.* [< IN-² + obs. *pecunious*, wealthy < OFr. < L. < *pecunia*, money] having no money; penniless —**im′pe·cu′ni·os′i·ty** (-äs′ə tē), **im′pe·cu′ni·ous·ness** *n.* —**im′pe·cu′ni·ous·ly** *adv.*

**im·ped·ance** (im pēd′′ns) *n.* [IMPED(E) + -ANCE] the total opposition (a combination of resistance and reactance) offered by an electric circuit to the flow of an alternating current of a single frequency: it is measured in ohms

**im·pede** (im pēd′) *vt.* **-ped′ed, -ped′ing** [< L. *impedire* < *in-*, in + *pes* (gen. *pedis*), foot] to bar or hinder the progress of; obstruct or delay —**im·ped′er** *n.*

**im·ped·i·ment** (im ped′ə mənt) *n.* [< L. *impedimentum*, hindrance] anything that impedes; specif., a speech defect; lisp, stammer, etc.

**im·ped·i·men·ta** (im ped′ə men′tə) *n.pl.* [L., pl.: see prec.] things hindering progress, as on a trip; esp., baggage, supplies, etc.

**im·pel** (im pel′) *vt.* **-pelled′, -pel′ling** [L. *impellere* < *in-*, on + *pellere*, to drive] **1.** to push, drive, or move forward; propel **2.** to force, compel, or urge —**im·pel′lent** *adj., n.*

**im·pend** (im pend′) *vi.* [L. *impendere* < *in-*, in + *pendere*, to hang] to be about to happen; threaten

**im·pen·e·tra·ble** (im pen′i trə b′l) *adj.* **1.** that cannot be penetrated or passed through **2.** that cannot be solved or understood; unfathomable **3.** unreceptive to ideas, influences, etc. —**im·pen′e·tra·bil′i·ty** *n.* —**im·pen′e·tra·bly** *adv.*

**im·pen·i·tent** (im pen′ə tənt) *adj.* without regret, shame, or remorse; unrepentant —*n.* an impenitent person —**im·pen′i·tence, im·pen′i·ten·cy** *n.* —**im·pen′i·tent·ly** *adv.*

**imper.** imperative

**im·per·a·tive** (im per′ə tiv) *adj.* [< LL. < pp. of L. *imperare*, to order] **1.** of or indicating power or authority; commanding [an *imperative* gesture] **2.** absolutely necessary; urgent **3.** *Gram.* designating or of a verb mood expressing a command, request, etc. —*n.* **1.** a compelling rule, duty, etc. **2.** a command **3.** *Gram. a)* the imperative mood *b)* a verb in this mood —**im·per′a·tive·ly** *adv.* —**im·per′a·tive·ness** *n.*

**im·pe·ra·tor** (im′pə rät′ər, -rät′-; -ôr) *n.* [L. < pp. of *imperare*, to command] in ancient Rome, a title of honor for generals and, later, emperors —**im·per·a·to·ri·al** (im·pir′ə tôr′ē əl) *adj.*

**im·per·cep·ti·ble** (im′pər sep′tə b′l) *adj.* not easily perceived by the senses or mind; very slight, gradual, subtle, etc. —**im′per·cep′ti·bil′i·ty** *n.* —**im′per·cep′ti·bly** *adv.*

**im·per·cep·tive** (-tiv) *adj.* not perceiving; lacking perception: also **im′per·cip′i·ent** (-sip′ē ənt) —**im′per·cep′tive·ness** *n.*

**imperf.** **1.** imperfect **2.** imperforate

**im·per·fect** (im pur′fikt) *adj.* **1.** not finished or complete; lacking in something **2.** not perfect; having a defect or error **3.** in the grammar of certain inflected languages, designating or of a verb tense indicating an incomplete or continuous past action or state: in English, "was writing" is a form like the imperfect tense —*n. Gram.* **1.** the imperfect tense **2.** a verb in this tense —**im·per′fect·ly** *adv.* —**im·per′fect·ness** *n.*

**im·per·fec·tion** (im′pər fek′shən) *n.* **1.** a being imperfect **2.** a shortcoming; defect; blemish

**im·per·fo·rate** (im pur′fər it, -fə rāt′) *adj.* **1.** having no holes or openings **2.** having a straight edge without perforations: said of a postage stamp Also **im·per′fo·rat′ed** —*n.* an imperforate stamp —**im·per′fo·ra′tion** *n.*

**im·pe·ri·al** (im pir′ē əl) *adj.* [< OFr. < L. < *imperium*, empire] **1.** of an empire **2.** of a country having control over other countries or colonies **3.** of, or having the rank of, an emperor or empress **4.** having supreme authority **5.** majestic; august **6.** of great size or superior quality **7.** *a)* of the British Commonwealth *b)* of a system of weights and measures, formerly official in Great Britain, in which the gallon equals 277.42 cubic inches —*n.* **1.** a size of writing paper (23 x 31 in.) **2.** a pointed tuft of beard on the lower lip and chin —**im·pe′ri·al·ly** *adv.*

**im·pe·ri·al·ism** (-iz′m) *n.* **1.** imperial state, authority, or government **2.** the policy and practice of forming and maintaining an empire by conquest, colonization, economic or political domination, etc. —**im·pe′ri·al·ist** *n., adj.* —**im·pe′ri·al·is′tic** *adj.* —**im·pe′ri·al·is′ti·cal·ly** *adv.*

**Imperial Valley** irrigated agricultural region in S Calif. & NW Mexico, reclaimed from the desert

**im·per·il** (im per′əl) *vt.* **-iled** or **-illed, -il·ing** or **-il·ling** to put in peril —**im·per′il·ment** *n.*

**im·pe·ri·ous** (im pir′ē əs) *adj.* [< L. < *imperium*, empire] **1.** arrogant; domineering **2.** urgent —**im·pe′ri·ous·ly** *adv.* —**im·pe′ri·ous·ness** *n.*

**im·per·ish·a·ble** (im per′ish ə b′l) *adj.* that will not die or decay; indestructible; immortal —**im·per′ish·a·bil′i·ty** *n.* —**im·per′ish·a·bly** *adv.*

**im·per·ma·nent** (im pur′mə nənt) *adj.* not permanent; not lasting; temporary —**im·per′ma·nence, im·per′ma·nen·cy** *n.* —**im·per′ma·nent·ly** *adv.*

**im·per·me·a·ble** (im pur′mē ə b′l) *adj.* not permeable; not permitting passage, esp. of fluids —**im·per′me·a·bil′i·ty** *n.* —**im·per′me·a·bly** *adv.*

**im·per·son·al** (im pur′s′n əl) *adj.* **1.** not personal; specif., *a)* without reference to any particular person [an *impersonal* comment] *b)* not existing as a person [an *impersonal* force] **2.** *Gram. a)* designating or of a verb occurring only in the third person singular (Ex.: "it is snowing") *b)* indefinite: said of a pronoun —*n.* an impersonal verb or pronoun —**im·per′son·al′i·ty** (-al′ə tē) *n.* —**im·per′son·al·ly** *adv.*

**im·per·son·al·ize** (-ə līz′) *vt.* **-ized′, -iz′ing** to make impersonal

**im·per·son·ate** (im pur′sə nāt′) *vt.* **-at′ed, -at′ing** **1.** [Now Rare] to personify; embody **2.** to act the part of **3.** *a)* to mimic (a person) for purposes of entertainment *b)* to pretend to be (an officer, etc.) with fraudulent intent —**im·per′son·a′tion** *n.* —**im·per′son·a′tor** *n.*

**im·per·ti·nence** (im pur′t′n əns) *n.* **1.** the quality or fact of being impertinent; specif., *a)* irrelevance *b)* insolence **2.** an impertinent act, remark, etc. Also **im·per′ti·nen·cy**, *pl.* **-cies**

**im·per·ti·nent** (-ənt) *adj.* **1.** not pertinent; irrelevant **2.** insolent —**im·per′ti·nent·ly** *adv.*

**im·per·turb·a·ble** (im′pər tur′bə b′l) *adj.* that cannot be perturbed or excited; impassive —**im′per·turb·a·bil′i·ty** *n.* —**im′per·turb′a·bly** *adv.*

**im·per·vi·ous** (im pur′vē əs) *adj.* **1.** not pervious; impermeable **2.** not affected by (with *to*) —**im·per′vi·ous·ly** *adv.* —**im·per′vi·ous·ness** *n.*

**im·pe·ti·go** (im′pə tī′gō) *n.* [L. < *impetere:* see IMPETUS] a skin disease with eruption of pustules; esp., a contagious disease of this kind

**im·pet·u·os·i·ty** (im pech′ŏŏ wäs′ə tē, im′pech-) *n.* **1.** the quality of being impetuous **2.** *pl.* **-ties** an impetuous action or feeling

**im·pet·u·ous** (im pech′ŏŏ wəs) *adj.* [< OFr. < LL. < L. *impetus:* see ff.] **1.** moving with great force or violence; rushing **2.** acting or done suddenly with little thought; rash; impulsive —**im·pet′u·ous·ly** *adv.* —**im·pet′u·ous·ness** *n.*

**im·pe·tus** (im′pə təs) *n., pl.* **-tus·es** [L. < *impetere*, to attack < *in-*, in + *petere*, to rush at] **1.** the force with which a body moves against resistance, resulting from its mass and initial velocity **2.** a stimulus to action; incentive

**im·pi·e·ty** (im pī′ə tē) *n.* **1.** lack of piety, esp. toward God **2.** *pl.* **-ties** an impious act or remark

**im·pinge** (im pinj′) *vi.* **-pinged′, -ping′ing** [L. *impingere* < *in-*, in + *pangere*, to strike] **1.** *a)* to strike or hit (*on, upon, or against*) *b)* to touch (*on or upon*) **2.** to make inroads or encroach (*on or upon*) —**im·pinge′ment** *n.* —**im·ping′er** *n.*

**im·pi·ous** (im′pē əs) *adj.* not pious; specif., lacking reverence for God —**im′pi·ous·ly** *adv.* —**im′pi·ous·ness** *n.*

**imp·ish** (im′pish) *adj.* of or like an imp; mischievous —**imp′ish·ly** *adv.* —**imp′ish·ness** *n.*

**im·plac·a·ble** (im plak′ə b′l, -plā′kə-) *adj.* not placable; that cannot be appeased or pacified —**im·plac′a·bil′i·ty** *n.* —**im·plac′a·bly** *adv.*

**im·plant** (im plant′; *for n.* im′plant′) *vt.* **1.** to plant firmly; embed **2.** to fix firmly in the mind; instill **3.** *Med.* to insert (an organ, tissue, etc.) within the body —*n. Med.* an implanted organ, etc. —**im′plan·ta′tion** (-plan tā′-shən) *n.*

**im·plau·si·ble** (im plô′zə b′l) *adj.* not plausible —**im·plau′si·bil′i·ty** *n.*, *pl.* **-ties** —**im·plau′si·bly** *adv.*

**im·ple·ment** (im′plə mənt; *for v.* -ment′) *n.* [< LL. *implementum*, a filling up < L. *implere* < *in-*, in + *plere*, to fill] **1.** any tool, instrument, utensil, etc. used or needed in a given activity **2.** a means to an end —*vt.* **1.** to carry into effect **2.** to provide the means for accomplishing **3.** to provide with implements —**im′ple·men′tal** *adj.* —**im′ple·men·ta′tion** (-mən tā′shən) *n.*

**im·pli·cate** (im′plə kāt′) *vt.* **-cat′ed, -cat′ing** [< L. pp. of *implicare*: see IMPLY] **1.** to cause to be involved in or associated with a crime, fault, etc. **2.** to imply —**im′pli·ca′tion** *n.* —**im′pli·ca′tive** *adj.* —**im′pli·ca′tive·ly** *adv.*

**im·plic·it** (im plis′it) *adj.* [< L. pp. of *implicare*: see IMPLY] **1.** suggested or to be understood though not plainly expressed; implied: distinguished from EXPLICIT **2.** necessarily or naturally involved though not plainly apparent or expressed; inherent **3.** without reservation or doubt; absolute —**im·plic′it·ly** *adv.* —**im·plic′it·ness** *n.*

**im·plied** (im plīd′) *adj.* involved, suggested, or understood without being directly expressed

**im·plode** (im plōd′) *vt., vi.* **-plod′ed, -plod′ing** [< IN-¹ + (EX)PLODE] to burst inward —**im·plo′sion** (-plō′zhən) *n.*

**im·plore** (im plôr′) *vt.* **-plored′, -plor′ing** [< L. *implorare* < *in-*, intens. + *plorare*, to cry out] **1.** to ask earnestly for; beseech **2.** to beg (a person) to do something —**im·plor′ing·ly** *adv.*

**im·ply** (im plī′) *vt.* **-plied′, -ply′ing** [< OFr. < L. *implicare*, to involve < *in-*, in + *plicare*, to fold] **1.** to have as a necessary part, condition, or effect [*war implies killing*] **2.** to indicate indirectly; hint; suggest [*he implied that we cheat*]

**im·po·lite** (im′pə līt′) *adj.* not polite; discourteous; rude —**im′po·lite′ly** *adv.* —**im′po·lite′ness** *n.*

**im·pol·i·tic** (im päl′ə tik) *adj.* not politic; unwise; injudicious —**im·pol′i·tic·ly** *adv.*

**im·pon·der·a·ble** (im pän′dər ə b′l) *adj.* [< LL.: see IN-² & PONDER] **1.** that cannot be weighed or measured **2.** that cannot be conclusively determined or explained —*n.* anything imponderable —**im·pon′der·a·bil′i·ty** *n.* —**im·pon′der·a·bly** *adv.*

**im·port** (im pôrt′; *also, and for n. always,* im′pôrt) *vt.* [< L. *importare* < *in-*, in + *portare*, to carry] **1.** *a)* to bring in from the outside *b)* to bring (goods) from another country, esp. for selling **2.** to mean; signify —*vi.* to be of importance; matter —*n.* **1.** the importing of goods **2.** something imported **3.** meaning **4.** importance —**im·port′a·ble** *adj.* —**im·port′er** *n.*

**im·por·tance** (im pôr′t′ns) *n.* the state or quality of being important; significance; consequence

**im·por·tant** (-t′nt) *adj.* [Fr. < OIt. < ML. prp. of *importare*: see IMPORT] **1.** meaning a great deal; having much significance or consequence **2.** having, or acting as if having, power, authority, high position, etc. —**im·por′tant·ly** *adv.*

**im·por·ta·tion** (im′pôr tā′shən) *n.* **1.** an importing or being imported **2.** something imported

**im·por·tu·nate** (im pôr′chə nit) *adj.* urgent or annoyingly persistent in asking or demanding —**im·por′tu·nate·ly** *adv.* —**im·por′tu·nate·ness** *n.*

**im·por·tune** (im′pôr tōōn′, -tyōōn′; im pôr′chən) *vt.* **-tuned′, -tun′ing** [< Fr. < OFr. < L. *importunus*, troublesome < *in-*, not + (*op*)*portunus*: see OPPORTUNE] to trouble with requests or demands; entreat persistently —*vi.* to be importunate —**im′por·tune′ly** *adv.* —**im′por·tun′er** *n.*

**im·por·tu·ni·ty** (-tōōn′ə tē, -tyōōn′-) *n.*, *pl.* **-ties** an importuning or being importunate

**im·pose** (im pōz′) *vt.* **-posed′, -pos′ing** [< Fr. < L. *imponere* < *in-*, on + *ponere*, to place] **1.** to place (a burden, tax, etc. *on* or *upon*) **2.** to force (oneself) on another **3.** to pass off by deception; foist **4.** to arrange (pages of type) in a frame for printing —**impose on** (or **upon**) **1.** to put to some trouble or use unfairly for one's own benefit **2.** to cheat or defraud —**im·pos′er** *n.*

**im·pos·ing** (im pō′ziŋ) *adj.* impressive in size, dignity, etc. —**im·pos′ing·ly** *adv.*

**im·po·si·tion** (im′pə zish′ən) *n.* **1.** an imposing or imposing on; specif., a taking advantage of friendship, etc. **2.** something imposed; specif., *a)* a tax, fine, etc.

*b)* an unjust burden or requirement *c)* a deception; fraud

**im·pos·si·bil·i·ty** (im päs′ə bil′ə tē) *n.* **1.** the fact or quality of being impossible **2.** *pl.* **-ties** something that is impossible

**im·pos·si·ble** (im päs′ə b′l) *adj.* not possible; specif,, *a)* not capable of being, being done, or happening *b)* not capable of being endured, used, agreed to, etc. because disagreeable or unsuitable —**im·pos′si·bly** *adv.*

**im·post¹** (im′pōst) *n.* [OFr. < ML. < L. *impositus*, pp. of *imponere*: see IMPOSE] **1.** a tax; esp., a duty on imported goods **2.** the weight assigned to a horse in a handicap race

**im·post²** (im′pōst) *n.* [ult. < L.: see prec.] the top part of a pillar, pier, etc. supporting an arch

**im·pos·tor** (im päs′tər) *n.* [see IMPOSE] a person who deceives or cheats others, esp. by pretending to be someone or something that he is not

**im·pos·ture** (-chər) *n.* the act or practice of an impostor; fraud; deception

**im·po·tence** (im′pə təns) *n.* the quality or condition of being impotent: also **im′po·ten·cy**

**im·po·tent** (-tənt) *adj.* [see IN-² & POTENT] **1.** lacking physical strength **2.** ineffective, powerless, or helpless **3.** unable to engage in sexual intercourse, esp. because of an inability to have an erection —**im′po·tent·ly** *adv.*

**im·pound** (im pound′) *vt.* **1.** to shut up (an animal) in a pound **2.** to take and hold (evidence, etc.) in legal custody **3.** to gather and enclose (water) for irrigation, etc. —**im·pound′ment** *n.*

**im·pov·er·ish** (im päv′ər ish, -päv′rish) *vt.* [< OFr. < *em-* (< L. *in-*, in) + *povre* (< L. *pauper*, poor)] **1.** to make poor **2.** to deprive of strength, resources, etc. —**im·pov′er·ish·ment** *n.*

**im·prac·ti·ca·ble** (im prak′ti kə b′l) *adj.* **1.** not capable of being carried out in practice [*an impracticable plan*] **2.** not capable of being used [*an impracticable road*] —**im·prac′ti·ca·bil′i·ty, im·prac′ti·ca·ble·ness** *n.* —**im·prac′ti·ca·bly** *adv.*

**im·prac·ti·cal** (im prak′tə k′l) *adj.* not practical; specif., *a)* not workable or useful *b)* not handling practical matters well *c)* idealistic —**im·prac′ti·cal′i·ty, im·prac′ti·cal·ness** *n.*

**im·pre·cate** (im′prə kāt′) *vt.* **-cat′ed, -cat′ing** [< L. pp. of *imprecari* < *in-*, on + *precari*, to PRAY] to pray for or invoke (evil, a curse, etc.) —**im′pre·ca′tion** *n.* —**im′pre·ca′tor** *n.* —**im′pre·ca·to′ry** *adj.*

**im·pre·cise** (im′pri sīs′) *adj.* not precise or definite —**im′pre·cise′ly** *adv.* —**im′pre·ci′sion** *n.*

**im·preg·na·ble¹** (im preg′nə b′l) *adj.* [< OFr.: see IN-² & PREGNABLE] **1.** not capable of being captured or entered by force **2.** unshakable; firm —**im·preg′na·bil′i·ty** *n.* —**im·preg′na·bly** *adv.*

**im·preg·na·ble²** (im preg′nə b′l) *adj.* [IMPREGN(ATE) + -ABLE] that can be impregnated

**im·preg·nate** (im preg′nāt; *for adj.* -nit) *vt.* **-nat·ed, -nat·ing** [< LL. pp. of *impraegnare*, to make pregnant < L. *in-*, in + *praegnans*, PREGNANT] **1.** to fertilize **2.** to make pregnant **3.** to fill or saturate **4.** to imbue (*with* ideas, feelings, etc.) —*adj.* impregnated —**im′preg·na′tion** *n.* —**im′preg′na·tor** *n.*

**im·pre·sa·ri·o** (im′prə sär′ē ō, -ser′-) *n.*, *pl.* **-ri·os** [It. < *impresa*, enterprise, ult. < L. *in-*, in + *prehendere*, to take, grasp] the organizer or manager of an opera company, concert series, etc.

**im·pre·scrip·ti·ble** (im′pri skrip′tə b′l) *adj.* that cannot rightfully be taken away or revoked; inviolable —**im′pre·scrip′ti·bly** *adv.*

**im·press¹** (im pres′) *vt.* [< IN-¹ + PRESS²] **1.** to force (men) into public service, esp. into a navy **2.** to levy or seize for public use —**im·press′ment** *n.*

**im·press²** (im pres′; *for n.* im′pres) *vt.* [< L. pp. of *imprimere*: see IN-¹ & PRESS¹] **1.** to use pressure on so as to leave a mark **2.** to mark by using pressure; stamp; imprint **3.** *a)* to affect strongly the mind or emotions of *b)* to arouse the interest or approval of **4.** to fix in the memory —*n.* **1.** an impressing **2.** any mark, imprint, etc.; stamp **3.** a quality or effect produced by some strong influence —**im·press′i·bil′i·ty** *n.* —**im·press′i·ble** *adj.* —**im·press′i·bly** *adv.*

**im·pres·sion** (im presh′ən) *n.* **1.** an impressing **2.** *a)* a mark, imprint, etc. made by physical pressure *b)* an effect produced on the mind or senses *c)* the effect produced by any effort or activity [*cleaning made no impression on the stain*] **3.** a vague notion **4.** an amusing impersonation **5.** *Printing a)* a printed copy *b)* all the copies printed at one time from a set of type or plates —**im·pres′sion·al** *adj.*

**im·pres·sion·a·ble** (-ə b′l) *adj.* easily affected by impressions; capable of being influenced; sensitive —**im·pres′sion·a·bil′i·ty** *n.* —**im·pres′sion·a·bly** *adv.*

**im·pres·sion·ism** (-iz'm) *n.* a theory and school of art whose chief aim is to capture an impression of a subject, esp. to reproduce the play of light on surfaces: the term has been extended to literature and music which seeks to convey moods and impressions —**im·pres'sion·ist** *n., adj.* —**im·pres'sion·is'tic** *adj.* —**im·pres'sion·is'ti·cal·ly** *adv.*

**im·pres·sive** (im pres'iv) *adj.* impressing or tending to impress the mind or emotions; striking, imposing, etc. —**im·pres'sive·ly** *adv.*

**im·pri·ma·tur** (im'pri mät'ər, -māt'-) *n.* [ModL., let it be printed (see ff.)] **1.** license or permission to publish or print a book, article, etc.; specif., *R.C.Ch.* such permission granted by an ecclesiastical censor **2.** any sanction or approval

**im·print** (im print'; *for n.* im'print) *vt.* [< OFr. < L. *imprimere* < *in-,* on + *premere,* to PRESS[1]] **1.** to mark by pressing or stamping; impress **2.** to press [*to imprint a kiss on the cheek*] **3.** to fix in the memory —*n.* **1.** a mark made by imprinting **2.** a lasting effect or characteristic result **3.** a publisher's note, as on the title page of a book, giving his name, the place of publication, etc.

**im·print·ing** (im print'iŋ) *n. Psychol.* a learning mechanism of very young animals by which an initial stimulus establishes an irreversible behavior pattern with reference to the same stimulus in the future

**im·pris·on** (im priz''n) *vt.* **1.** to put or keep in prison; jail **2.** to restrict, limit, or confine in any way —**im·pris'on·ment** *n.*

**im·prob·a·ble** (im präb'ə b'l) *adj.* not probable; unlikely to happen or be true —**im'prob·a·bil'i·ty** *n., pl.* **-ties** —**im·prob'a·bly** *adv.*

**im·promp·tu** (im prämp'tōō, -tyōō) *adj., adv.* [Fr. < L. *in promptu,* in readiness: see PROMPT] without preparation or advance thought; offhand —*n.* an impromptu speech, performance, etc.

**im·prop·er** (im präp'ər) *adj.* **1.** not proper or suitable; poorly adapted; unfit **2.** not in accordance with the truth, fact, etc.; incorrect **3.** not in good taste; indecent; indecorous **4.** not normal or regular —**im·prop'er·ly** *adv.* —**im·prop'er·ness** *n.*

**improper fraction** a fraction in which the denominator is less than the numerator (Ex.: 5/3)

**im·pro·pri·e·ty** (im'prə prī'ə tē) *n., pl.* **-ties 1.** the quality of being improper **2.** improper action or behavior **3.** an improper use of a word (Ex.: "borrow" for "lend")

**im·prove** (im prōōv') *vt.* -proved', -prov'ing [< Anglo-Fr. < *en-,* in + *prou,* gain < LL. < L. *prodesse,* to be of advantage] **1.** to use (time, etc.) profitably **2.** to make better **3.** to make (land or structures) more valuable by cultivation, construction, etc. —*vi.* to become better —**improve on** (or **upon**) to do or make better than —**im·prov'a·bil'i·ty** *n.* —**im·prov'a·ble** *adj.* —**im·prov'er** *n.*

**im·prove·ment** (-mənt) *n.* **1.** an improving or being improved; esp., *a)* betterment *b)* an increase in value *c)* profitable use **2.** *a)* an addition or change that improves something or adds to its value *b)* a person or thing representing a higher degree of excellence

**im·prov·i·dent** (im präv'ə dənt) *adj.* failing to provide for the future; lacking foresight or thrift —**im·prov'i·dence** *n.* —**im·prov'i·dent·ly** *adv.*

**im·pro·vise** (im'prə vīz') *vt., vi.* -vised', -vis'ing [< Fr. < It. < *improvviso,* unprepared < L. < *in-,* not + pp. of *providere,* to foresee, PROVIDE] **1.** to compose and simultaneously perform without any preparation; extemporize **2.** to make, provide, or do with whatever is at hand —**im·prov·i·sa·tion** (im präv'ə zā'shən, im'prə vi-) *n.* —**im·prov'i·sa'tion·al** *adj.* —**im'pro·vis'er, im'pro·vi'sor, im·prov'i·sa'tor** *n.*

**im·pru·dent** (im prōōd''nt) *adj.* not prudent; without thought of the consequences; rash; indiscreet —**im·pru'dence** *n.* —**im·pru'dent·ly** *adv.*

**im·pu·dence** (im'pyoo dəns) *n.* **1.** the quality of being impudent **2.** impudent speech or behavior: also **im'pu·den·cy,** *pl.* **-cies**

**im·pu·dent** (-dənt) *adj.* [< Fr. < L. < *in-,* not + prp. of *pudere,* to feel shame] **1.** orig., immodest; shameless **2.** shamelessly bold; disrespectful; insolent —**im'pu·dent·ly** *adv.*

**im·pugn** (im pyōōn') *vt.* [< OFr. < L. < *in-,* against + *pugnare,* to fight] to attack by argument or criticism; oppose or challenge as false or questionable —**im·pugn'a·ble** *adj.* —**im·pug·na·tion** (im'pəg nā'shən) *n.* —**im·pugn'er** *n.*

**im·pulse** (im'puls) *n.* [< L. pp. of *impellere,* IMPEL] **1.** *a)* an impelling, or driving forward with sudden force *b)* an impelling force; push; impetus *c)* the motion or effect caused by such a force **2.** *a)* incitement to action arising from a state of mind or an external stimulus *b)* a sudden inclination to act, without conscious thought **3.** *Elec.* a momentary surge in one direction of voltage or current **4.** *Physiol.* a stimulus transmitted in a muscle or nerve, which causes or inhibits activity

**im·pul·sion** (im pul'shən) *n.* **1.** an impelling or being impelled **2.** an impelling force; impetus

**im·pul·sive** (-siv) *adj.* **1.** impelling; driving forward **2.** *a)* acting or likely to act on impulse *b)* resulting from impulse [*an impulsive remark*] —**im·pul'sive·ly** *adv.* —**im·pul'sive·ness** *n.*

**im·pu·ni·ty** (im pyōō'nə tē) *n.* [< Fr. < L. < *impunis* < *in-,* without + *poena,* punishment] exemption from punishment, penalty, or harm

**im·pure** (im pyoor') *adj.* not pure; specif., *a)* unclean; dirty *b)* unclean according to religious ritual *c)* immoral; obscene *d)* mixed with foreign matter; adulterated *e)* mixed so as to lack purity in color, style, etc. *f)* not idiomatic or grammatical —**im·pure'ly** *adv.* —**im·pure'ness** *n.*

**im·pu·ri·ty** (-pyoor'ə tē) *n.* **1.** a being impure **2.** *pl.* **-ties** an impure thing or element

**im·pute** (im pyōōt') *vt.* -put'ed, -put'ing [< OFr. < L. < *in-,* to + *putare,* to estimate, think] to attribute (esp. a fault or misconduct) to another; charge with; ascribe —**im·put'a·bil/i·ty** *n.* —**im·put'a·ble** *adj.* —**im'pu·ta'tion** *n.* —**im·put'a·tive** *adj.*

**in** (in, ən, 'n) *prep.* [OE.] **1.** contained or enclosed by; inside [*in the room*] **2.** wearing [*a lady in red*] **3.** during the course of [*done in a day*] **4.** at or near the end of [*return in an hour*] **5.** perceptible to (one of the senses) [*in sight*] **6.** out of a group of [*one in ten*] **7.** amidst; surrounded by [*in a storm*] **8.** affected by; having [*in trouble*] **9.** employed at or occupied by [*in business, in a search for truth*] **10.** with regard to; as concerns [*weak in faith, in my opinion*] **11.** with; by; using [*to paint in oil, speak in French*] **12.** made of [*done in wood*] **13.** because of; for [*to cry in pain*] **14.** by way of [*in recompense*] **15.** belonging to [*not in his nature*] **16.** into [*come in the house*] *In* expresses inclusion with relation to space, place, time, state, circumstances, manner, quality, a class, etc. —*adv.* **1.** from a point outside to one inside **2.** so as to be contained by a certain space, condition, or position **3.** so as to be agreeing or involved [*he fell in with our plans*] **4.** so as to form a part [*mix in the cream*] —*adj.* **1.** that is successful or in power [*the in group*] **2.** inner; inside **3.** ingoing [*the in door*] **4.** gathered, counted, etc. [*the votes are in*] **5.** [Colloq.] currently smart, popular, etc. [*an in joke*] —*n.* **1.** a person, group, etc. in power, office, etc.: *usually used in pl.* **2.** [Colloq.] special influence, favor, etc. —**have it in for** [Colloq.] to hold a grudge against —**in for** certain to have or get (usually an unpleasant experience) —**in on** having a share or part of —**ins and outs** all the parts, details, and intricacies —**in that** because; since —**in with** associated with as a friend, partner, etc.

**in-**[1] [< the prep. IN; also < OE. & MFr. *in-* or OFr. *en-* < L. *in-* < in] *a prefix meaning* in, into, within, on, toward [*inbreed, induct*]: also used as an intensive in some words of Latin origin [*inflame*] and assimilated to *il-* before *l* [*illuminate*], *ir-* before *r* [*irrigate*], and *im-* before *m, p,* and *b*

**in-**[2] [< OFr. & ML. < L. *in-*] *a prefix meaning* no, not, without, non- [*inhumane*]: assimilated to *il-* before *l* [*illegal*], *ir-* before *r* [*irregular*], and *im-* before *m, p,* and *b*

**-in**[1] (in) [see -INE[4]] *a suffix used in forming the names of* various compounds [*albumin, streptomycin*]

**-in**[2] (in) *a combining form used in terms formed by analogy* with SIT-IN [*teach-in*]

**In** *Chem.* indium

**IN** Indiana

**in.** inch; inches

**-i·na** (ē'nə) [L.] *a suffix used to form* feminine names, titles, etc. [*Christina, czarina*]

**in·a·bil·i·ty** (in'ə bil'ə tē) *n.* a being unable; lack of ability, capacity, means, or power

**in ab·sen·ti·a** (in əb sen'shə, ab sen'shē ə) [L., lit., in absence] although not present

**in·ac·ces·si·ble** (in'ək ses'ə b'l) *adj.* not accessible; specif., *a)* impossible to reach or enter *b)* that cannot be seen, talked to, etc. *c)* not obtainable —**in'ac·ces'si·bil'i·ty** *n.* —**in'ac·ces'si·bly** *adv.*

**in·ac·cu·ra·cy** (in ak'yər ə sē) *n.* **1.** lack of accuracy **2.** *pl.* **-cies** an error; mistake

**in·ac·cu·rate** (-yər it) *adj.* not accurate; not correct; not exact; in error —**in·ac'cu·rate·ly** *adv.*

**in·ac·tion** (in ak'shən) *n.* absence of action or motion; inertness or idleness

**in·ac·ti·vate** (-tə vāt') *vt.* -vat'ed, -vat'ing **1.** to make inactive **2.** *Chem.* to destroy the activity of (a substance), as by heat —**in·ac'ti·va'tion** *n.*

**in·ac·tive** (-tiv) *adj.* **1.** not active or moving; inert **2.** idle; sluggish **3.** not functioning **4.** not in active service in the armed forces —**in·ac'tive·ly** *adv.* —**in'ac·tiv'i·ty** *n.*

**in·ad·e·quate** (in ad'ə kwət) *adj.* not adequate; not sufficient —**in·ad'e·qua·cy** *pl.* **-cies, in·ad'e·quate·ness** *n.* —**in·ad'e·quate·ly** *adv.*

**in·ad·mis·si·ble** (in'əd mis'ə b'l) *adj.* not admissible;

not to be allowed, granted, etc. —**in′ad·mis′si·bil′i·ty** *n.* —**in′ad·mis′si·bly** *adv.*

**in·ad·vert·ence** (in′əd vur′təns) *n.* **1.** a being inadvertent **2.** an instance of this; oversight; mistake Also **in′ad·vert′en·cy**, *pl.* **-cies**

**in·ad·vert·ent** (-tənt) *adj.* **1.** not attentive or observant **2.** due to oversight; unintentional —**in′ad·vert′ent·ly** *adv.*

**in·ad·vis·a·ble** (in′əd vi′zə b′l) *adj.* not advisable; not wise or prudent —**in′ad·vis′a·bil′i·ty** *n.*

**in·al·ien·a·ble** (in āl′yən ə b′l) *adj.* that may not be taken away or transferred *[inalienable* rights*]* —**in·al′ien·a·bil′i·ty** *n.* —**in·al′ien·a·bly** *adv.*

**in·am·o·ra·ta** (in am′ə rät′ə, in′am-) *n.* [It. < *innamorare,* to fall in love] a woman in relation to the man who is her lover; sweetheart or mistress

**in·ane** (in ān′) *adj.* [L. *inanis*] **1.** empty **2.** lacking sense; silly; foolish —**in·ane′ly** *adv.*

**in·an·i·mate** (in an′ə mit) *adj.* **1.** not animate; without life **2.** not animated; dull —**in·an′i·mate·ly** *adv.* —**in·an′i·mate·ness** *n.*

**in·an·i·ty** (in an′ə tē) *n.* **1.** a being inane; specif., *a)* emptiness *b)* silliness **2.** *pl.* **-ties** something inane; senseless or silly act, remark, etc.

**in·ap·pli·ca·ble** (in ap′li kə b′l) *adj.* not applicable; not suitable; inappropriate —**in′ap·pli·ca·bil′i·ty** *n.* —**in·ap′pli·ca·bly** *adv.*

**in·ap·po·site** (in ap′ə zit) *adj.* not apposite; irrelevant —**in·ap′po·site·ly** *adv.*

**in·ap·pre·ci·a·ble** (in′ə prē′shə b′l, -shē ə-) *adj.* too small to be observed or have any value; negligible —**in′ap·pre′ci·a·bly** *adv.*

**in·ap·pro·pri·ate** (in′ə prō′prē it) *adj.* not appropriate; not suitable, fitting, or proper —**in′ap·pro′pri·ate·ly** *adv.* —**in′ap·pro′pri·ate·ness** *n.*

**in·apt** (in apt′) *adj.* **1.** not apt; inappropriate **2.** lacking skill or aptitude; inept —**in·apt′i·tude′** (-ap′tə tood′, -tyood′) *n.* —**in·apt′ly** *adv.* —**in·apt′ness** *n.*

**in·ar·tic·u·late** (in′är tik′yə lit) *adj.* **1.** produced without the articulation of normal speech *[an inarticulate* cry*]* **2.** *a)* unable to speak; mute *b)* not able to speak coherently or effectively **3.** *Zool.* without joints, hinges, etc. —**in′ar·tic′u·late·ly** *adv.* —**in′ar·tic′u·late·ness** *n.*

**in·ar·tis·tic** (in′är tis′tik) *adj.* not artistic; lacking artistic taste —**in′ar·tis′ti·cal·ly** *adv.*

**in·as·much as** (in′əz much′əz) **1.** seeing that; since; because **2.** to the extent that

**in·at·ten·tion** (in′ə ten′shən) *n.* failure to pay attention; heedlessness; negligence

**in·at·ten·tive** (-tiv) *adj.* not attentive; heedless —**in′at·ten′tive·ly** *adv.* —**in′at·ten′tive·ness** *n.*

**in·au·di·ble** (in ô′də b′l) *adj.* not audible; that cannot be heard —**in·au·di·bil′i·ty** *n.* —**in·au′di·bly** *adv.*

**in·au·gu·ral** (in ô′gyə rəl, -gə rəl) *adj.* [Fr.] **1.** of an inauguration, or ceremonial induction into office **2.** that begins a series —*n.* an inaugural ceremony or address

**in·au·gu·rate** (-rāt′) *vt.* **-rat′ed, -rat′ing** [< L. pp. of *inaugurare,* to practice augury] **1.** to induct into office with a formal ceremony **2.** to make a formal beginning of **3.** to celebrate formally the first public use of —**in·au′gu·ra′tion** *n.* —**in·au′gu·ra′tor** *n.*

**in·aus·pi·cious** (in′ô spish′əs) *adj.* not auspicious; unfavorable; unlucky; ill-omened —**in′aus·pi′cious·ly** *adv.* —**in′aus·pi′cious·ness** *n.*

**in·board** (in′bôrd′) *adv., adj.* [< *in board:* see BOARD] **1.** inside the hull or bulwarks of a ship or boat **2.** close or closer to the fuselage or hull of an aircraft —*n.* **1.** a marine motor mounted inboard **2.** a boat with such a motor

**in·board-out·board** (-out′bôrd′) *adj.* designating or of a power unit for small watercraft that has an inboard motor connected by a drive shaft to a propeller at the stern —*n.* a boat thus powered

**in·born** (in′bôrn′) *adj.* present in the organism at birth; innate; natural

**in·bound** (in′bound′) *adj.* traveling or going inward

**in·bred** (in′bred′) *adj.* **1.** innate or deeply instilled **2.** resulting from inbreeding

**in·breed** (in′brēd′) *vt.* **-bred′, -breed′ing** to breed by continual mating of individuals of the same or closely related stocks —*vi.* **1.** to engage in such breeding **2.** to become too refined, effete, etc. from moving in too narrow a social range

**inc.** **1.** inclosure **2.** including **3.** inclusive **4.** incorporated **5.** increase

**In·ca** (iŋ′kə) *n.* any member of a group of Indian tribes that dominated ancient Peru until the Spanish conquest: the Incas had a highly developed civilization —**In′can** *adj.*

**in·cal·cu·la·ble** (in kal′kyə lə b′l) *adj.* **1.** that cannot be calculated; too great or too many to be counted **2.** un-

predictable; uncertain —**in·cal′cu·la·bil′i·ty** *n.* —**in·cal′cu·la·bly** *adv.*

**in·can·desce** (in′kən des′) *vi., vt.* **-desced′, -desc′ing** to become or make incandescent

**in·can·des·cent** (-des′′nt) *adj.* [< L.: see IN-[1] & CANDESCENT] **1.** glowing with intense heat; red-hot or, esp., white-hot **2.** very bright; shining brilliantly —**in′can·des′cence** *n.* —**in′can·des′cent·ly** *adv.*

**incandescent lamp** a lamp in which the light is produced by a filament contained in a vacuum and heated to incandescence by an electric current

**in·can·ta·tion** (in′kan tā′shən) *n.* [OFr. < LL. < L. pp. of *incantare,* enchant < *in-,* IN-[1] + *cantare,* to chant] **1.** the chanting of special words or a formula in magic spells or rites **2.** words or a formula so chanted —**in′can·ta′tion·al** *adj.* —**in·can′ta·to′ry** (-kan′tə tôr′ē) *adj.*

**in·ca·pa·ble** (in kā′pə b′l) *adj.* not capable; lacking the necessary ability, competence, qualifications, etc. —**incapable of 1.** not allowing or admitting; not able to accept or experience *[incapable* of change*]* **2.** lacking the ability or fitness for **3.** not legally qualified for —**in′ca·pa·bil′i·ty, in·ca′pa·ble·ness** *n.* —**in·ca′pa·bly** *adv.*

**in·ca·pac·i·tate** (in′kə pas′ə tāt′) *vt.* **-tat′ed, -tat′ing** **1.** to make unable or unfit; esp., to make incapable of normal activity; disable **2.** *Law* to disqualify —**in′ca·pac′i·ta′tion** *n.*

**in·ca·pac·i·ty** (in′kə pas′ə tē) *n., pl.* **-ties** **1.** lack of capacity, power, or fitness; disability **2.** legal ineligibility

**in·car·cer·ate** (in kär′sə rāt′) *vt.* **-at′ed, -at′ing** [< ML. pp. of *incarcerare* < L. *in,* in + *carcer,* prison] **1.** to imprison; jail **2.** to confine —**in·car′cer·a′tion** *n.* —**in·car′cer·a′tor** *n.*

**in·car·na·dine** (in kär′nə dīn′, -din, -dēn′) *adj.* [< Fr. < It. *incarnatino* < LL. *incarnatus:* see ff.] **1.** flesh-colored; pink **2.** red; esp., blood-red —*n.* the color of either flesh or blood —*vt.* **-dined′, -din′ing** to make incarnadine

**in·car·nate** (in kär′nit; *also, and for v. always,* -nāt) *adj.* [< LL. *incarnatus,* pp. of *incarnari,* to become flesh < L. *in-,* in + *caro,* flesh] endowed with a human body; personified *[evil incarnate*] —*vt.* **-nat′ed, -nat′ing** **1.** to give bodily form to; embody **2.** to give actual form to; make real **3.** to be the type or embodiment of

**in·car·na·tion** (in′kär nā′shən) *n.* [see prec.] **1.** endowment with a human body **2.** [I-] the taking on of human form and nature by Jesus as the Son of God **3.** any person or animal serving as the embodiment of a god or spirit **4.** any person or thing serving as the embodiment of a quality or concept

**in·case** (in kās′) *vt.* **-cased′, -cas′ing** *same as* ENCASE —**in·case′ment** *n.*

**in·cau·tion** (in kô′shən) *n.* lack of caution

**in·cau·tious** (-shəs) *adj.* not cautious; not careful or prudent; reckless; rash —**in·cau′tious·ly** *adv.* —**in·cau′tious·ness** *n.*

**in·cen·di·ar·y** (in sen′dē er′ē) *adj.* [< L. < *incendium,* a fire < *incendere:* see ff.] **1.** relating to the willful destruction of property by fire **2.** designed to cause fires, as certain bombs **3.** willfully stirring up strife, riot, etc. —*n., pl.* **-ar′ies** **1.** a person who willfully destroys property by fire **2.** a person who willfully stirs up strife, riot, etc. **3.** an incendiary bomb, substance, etc. —**in·cen′di·a·rism** (-ə riz′m) *n.*

**in·cense**[1] (in′sens) *n.* [< OFr. < LL. < L. pp. of *incendere,* to inflame < *in-,* in + *candere,* to burn] **1.** *a)* any substance burned for its pleasant odor *b)* the odor or smoke so produced **2.** any pleasant odor **3.** pleasing attention or praise —*vt.* **-censed, -cens·ing** **1.** to make fragrant with incense **2.** to burn or offer incense to —*vi.* to burn incense

**in·cense**[2] (in sens′) *vt.* **-censed′, -cens′ing** [< OFr. < L. pp. of *incendere:* see prec.] to make very angry; enrage —**in·cense′ment** *n.*

**in·cen·tive** (in sen′tiv) *adj.* [< LL. *incentivum* < L. < *in-,* on + *canere,* to sing] stimulating to action; encouraging; motivating —*n.* a stimulus; motive

**in·cep·tion** (in sep′shən) *n.* [< L. < pp. of *incipere:* see INCIPIENT] a beginning; start; commencement

**in·cep·tive** (-tiv) *adj.* [< OFr. < LL. < L. pp. of *incipere:* see INCIPIENT] **1.** beginning; introductory **2.** *Gram.* expressing the beginning of an action —*n.* an inceptive verb —**in·cep′tive·ly** *adv.*

**in·cer·ti·tude** (in sur′tə tood′, -tyood′) *n.* [Fr. < ML.:

INCANDESCENT LAMP
(A, inert gas filling; B, coiled tungsten wire filament; C, glass envelope; D, glass support; E, metal base)

see IN-² + CERTITUDE] **1.** an uncertain state of mind; doubt **2.** insecurity

**in·ces·sant** (in ses′′nt) *adj.* [< LL. < L. *in-*, not + prp. of *cessare*, to CEASE] never ceasing; continuing or repeated endlessly; constant —**in·ces′san·cy** *n.* —**in·ces′sant·ly** *adv.*

**in·cest** (in′sest) *n.* [< L. < *in-*, not + *castus*, chaste] sexual intercourse between persons too closely related to marry legally

**in·ces·tu·ous** (in ses′ch∞ wəs) *adj.* **1.** guilty of incest **2.** of, or having the nature of, incest —**in·ces′tu·ous·ly** *adv.* —**in·ces′tu·ous·ness** *n.*

**inch** (inch) *n.* [OE. *ynce* < L. *uncia*, a twelfth, OUNCE¹] **1.** a measure of length equal to 1/12 foot: symbol, " (e.g., 10"): abbrev. **in.** (sing. & pl.) **2.** a fall (of rain, snow, etc.) that would cover a surface to the depth of one inch **3.** a very small amount, degree, or distance —*vt., vi.* to move by degrees; move very slowly —**every inch** in all respects; thoroughly —**inch by inch** gradually; slowly: also **by inches** —**within an inch of** very close to; almost to —**within an inch of one's life** almost to one's death

**inch·meal** (inch′mēl′) *adv.* [prec. + MEAL¹] gradually; inch by inch: also **by inchmeal**

**in·cho·ate** (in kō′it) *adj.* [< L. pp. of *inchoare, incohare*, to begin, orig. "hitch up" < *in-*, in + *cohum*, a strap from plow to yoke] **1.** just begun; in the early stages **2.** not yet clearly formed; disordered —**in·cho′ate·ly** *adv.* —**in·cho′ate·ness** *n.* —**in·cho·a′tion** (-ā′shən) *n.*

**in·cho·a·tive** (-ə tiv) *adj., n. Gram.* same as INCEPTIVE

**inch·worm** (inch′wurm′) *n.* same as MEASURING WORM

**in·ci·dence** (in′si dəns) *n.* **1.** the act, fact, or manner of falling upon or influencing **2.** the degree or range of occurrence or effect; extent of influence See also ANGLE OF INCIDENCE

**in·ci·dent** (-dənt) *adj.* [< OFr. < ML. < prp. of L. *incidere* < *in-*, on + *cadere*, to fall] **1.** likely to happen in connection with; incidental (*to*) [the cares *incident* to parenthood] **2.** falling upon or affecting [*incident* rays] —*n.* **1.** something that happens; occurrence **2.** a minor event or episode, esp. one in a novel, play, etc. **3.** an apparently minor conflict, etc. that may have serious results

**in·ci·den·tal** (in′si den′t'l) *adj.* **1.** happening or likely to happen in connection with something more important; casual **2.** secondary or minor —*n.* **1.** something incidental **2.** [*pl.*] miscellaneous items

**in·ci·den·tal·ly** (-dent′lē, den′t'l ē) *adv.* **1.** in an incidental manner **2.** by the way

**in·cin·er·ate** (in sin′ə rāt′) *vt., vi.* -**at′ed**, -**at′ing** [< ML. pp. of *incinerare* < L. *in*, to + *cinis*, ashes] to burn to ashes; burn up —**in·cin′er·a′tion** *n.*

**in·cin·er·a·tor** (-rāt′ər) *n.* a furnace or other device for incinerating trash

**in·cip·i·ent** (in sip′ē ənt) *adj.* [< L. prp. of *incipere*, to begin < *in-*, on + *capere*, to take] just beginning to exist or to come to notice [an *incipient* illness] —**in·cip′i·ence, in·cip′i·en·cy** *n.* —**in·cip′i·ent·ly** *adv.*

**in·cise** (in sīz′) *vt.* -**cised′**, -**cis′ing** [< Fr. < L. pp. of *incidere* < *in-*, into + *caedere*, to cut] to cut into with a sharp tool; specif., to engrave or carve —**in·cised′** *adj.*

**in·ci·sion** (-sizh′ən) *n.* **1.** the act or result of incising; cut **2.** incisive quality **3.** *Surgery* a cut made into a tissue or organ

**in·ci·sive** (in sī′siv) *adj.* **1.** cutting into **2.** sharp; keen; penetrating; acute [an *incisive* mind] —**in·ci′sive·ly** *adv.* —**in·ci′sive·ness** *n.*

**in·ci·sor** (in sī′zər) *n.* any of the front cutting teeth between the canines in either jaw

**in·cite** (in sīt′) *vt.* -**cit′ed**, -**cit′ing** [< OFr. < L. < *in-*, in, on + *citare*, to arouse] to urge to action; stir up; rouse —**in·cite′ment, in·ci·ta·tion** (in′sī tā′shən, -si-) *n.* —**in·cit′er** *n.*

**in·ci·vil·i·ty** (in′sə vil′ə tē) *n.* [see IN-² & CIVIL] **1.** a lack of courtesy or politeness; rudeness **2.** *pl.* -**ties** a rude or discourteous act

**incl. 1.** inclosure **2.** including **3.** inclusive

**in·clem·ent** (in klem′ənt) *adj.* [< L.: see IN-² & CLEMENT] **1.** rough; severe; stormy **2.** lacking mercy or leniency; harsh —**in·clem′en·cy** *n., pl.* -**cies** —**in·clem′ent·ly** *adv.*

**in·cli·na·tion** (in′klə nā′shən) *n.* **1.** an inclining, leaning, bowing, etc. **2.** a slope; slant **3.** the extent or degree of incline from the horizontal or vertical **4.** the angle made by two lines or planes **5.** *a)* a particular bent of mind; tendency *b)* a liking or preference —**in′cli·na′tion·al** *adj.*

**in·cline** (in klīn′; *for n., usually* in′klīn) *vi.* -**clined′**, -**clin′ing** [< OFr. < L. < *in-*, on + *clinare*, to lean] **1.** to lean; slope; slant **2.** to bow the body or head **3.** to have a tendency **4.** to have a preference or liking —*vt.* **1.** to cause to lean, slope, etc. **2.** to bend or bow (the body or head) **3.** to make willing; influence —*n.* an inclined plane or surface; slope; grade —**incline one's ear** to listen willingly —**in·clin′a·ble** *adj.* —**in·clined′** *adj.* —**in·clin′er** *n.*

**inclined plane** a plane surface set at any angle other than a right angle against a horizontal surface

INCLINED PLANE

**in·cli·nom·e·ter** (in′klə näm′ə tər) *n.* [< INCLINE + -METER] **1.** same as CLINOMETER **2.** an instrument that measures the inclination of an axis of an aircraft or ship in relation to the horizontal

**in·close** (in klōz′) *vt.* -**closed′**, -**clos′ing** same as ENCLOSE —**in·clo′sure** (-klō′zhər) *n.*

**in·clude** (in kl∞d′) *vt.* -**clud′ed**, -**clud′ing** [< L. < *in-*, + *claudere*, to close] **1.** to shut up or in; enclose **2.** to have as part of a whole; contain; comprise **3.** to take into account; put in a total, category, etc. —**in·clud′a·ble, in·clud′i·ble** *adj.*

**in·clu·sion** (in kl∞′zhən) *n.* **1.** an including or being included **2.** something included

**in·clu·sive** (in kl∞′siv) *adj.* **1.** including or tending to include; esp., taking everything into account **2.** including the terms, limits, or extremes mentioned [the first to the tenth *inclusive*] —**inclusive of** including —**in·clu′sive·ly** *adv.* —**in·clu′sive·ness** *n.*

**incog.** incognito

**in·cog·ni·to** (in′käg nēt′ō, in käg′ni tō) *adv., adj.* [It. < L. < *in-*, not + pp. of *cognoscere*, to know] with true identity unrevealed or disguised; under an assumed name, rank, etc. —*n., pl.* -**tos 1.** a person who is incognito **2.** *a)* the state of being incognito *b)* the disguise assumed —**in′cog·ni′ta** (-ə, -tə) *adj., n.fem., pl.* -**tas**

**in·co·her·ence** (in′kō hēr′əns) *n.* **1.** a being incoherent **2.** incoherent speech, thought, etc. Also **in′co·her′en·cy**, *pl.* -**cies**

**in·co·her·ent** (-ənt) *adj.* not coherent; specif., *a)* lacking cohesion; not sticking together *b)* not logically connected; disjointed *c)* characterized by incoherent speech, thought, etc. —**in′co·her′ent·ly** *adv.*

**in·com·bus·ti·ble** (in′kəm bus′tə b'l) *adj.* not combustible; that cannot be burned —*n.* an incombustible substance —**in′com·bus′ti·bil′i·ty** *n.*

**in·come** (in′kum′) *n.* the money or other gain received, esp. in a given period, by an individual, corporation, etc. for labor or services, or from property, investments, etc.

**income tax** a tax on net income or on that part of income which exceeds a certain amount

**in·com·ing** (in′kum′iŋ) *adj.* coming in or about to come in —*n.* a coming in

**in·com·men·su·ra·ble** (in′kə men′shər ə b'l, -sər-) *adj.* **1.** that cannot be measured or compared by the same standard or measure **2.** not worthy of comparison **3.** having no common divisor —*n.* an incommensurable thing, quantity, etc. —**in′com·men′su·ra·bil′i·ty** *n.* —**in′com·men′su·ra·bly** *adv.*

**in·com·men·su·rate** (-it) *adj.* not commensurate; specif., *a)* not proportionate; not adequate *b)* same as INCOMMENSURABLE (sense 1) —**in′com·men′su·rate·ly** *adv.*

**in·com·mode** (in′kə mōd′) *vt.* -**mod′ed**, -**mod′ing** [< Fr. < L. < *in-*, not + *commodus*, convenient] to inconvenience; put to some trouble; bother

**in·com·mo·di·ous** (-mō′dē əs) *adj.* **1.** causing inconvenience; uncomfortable **2.** inconveniently small, narrow, etc. —**in′com·mo′di·ous·ly** *adv.* —**in′com·mo′di·ous·ness** *n.*

**in·com·mu·ni·ca·ble** (in′kə my∞′ni kə b'l) *adj.* that cannot be communicated or told —**in′com·mu′ni·ca·bil′i·ty** *n.* —**in′com·mu′ni·ca·bly** *adv.*

**in·com·mu·ni·ca·do** (in′kə my∞′nə kä′dō) *adj.* [Sp.] unable or not allowed to communicate

**in·com·pa·ra·ble** (in käm′pər ə b'l; *occas.* in′kəm par′ə b'l) *adj.* that cannot be compared; specif., *a)* having no basis of comparison; incommensurable *b)* beyond comparison; unequaled; matchless [*incomparable* skill] —**in·com′pa·ra·bil′i·ty** *n.* —**in·com′pa·ra·bly** *adv.*

**in·com·pat·i·ble** (in′kəm pat′ə b'l) *adj.* **1.** not compatible; not able to exist in harmony; not going, or getting along, well together **2.** logically contradictory **3.** not suitable for being used together: said of certain drugs or medicines —*n.* an incompatible person or thing —**in′com·pat′i·bil′i·ty** *n., pl.* -**ties** —**in′com·pat′i·bly** *adv.*

**in·com·pe·tent** (in käm′pə tənt) *adj.* **1.** without adequate ability, knowledge, fitness, etc. **2.** not legally qualified —*n.* an incompetent person; esp., one who is mentally retarded —**in·com′pe·tence, in·com′pe·ten·cy** *n.* —**in·com′pe·tent·ly** *adv.*

**in·com·plete** (in′kəm plēt′) *adj.* **1.** lacking a part or parts **2.** unfinished; not concluded **3.** not perfect; not thorough —**in′com·plete′ly** *adv.* —**in′com·plete′ness, in·com·ple′tion** *n.*

**in·com·pre·hen·si·ble** (in′käm pri hen′sə b'l, in käm′-) *adj.* not comprehensible; that cannot be understood —**in′com·pre·hen′si·bil′i·ty** *n.* —**in′com·pre·hen′si·bly** *adv.*

**in·com·press·i·ble** (in'kəm pres'ə b'l) *adj.* that cannot be compressed —**in'com·press'i·bil'i·ty** *n.*

**in·con·ceiv·a·ble** (in'kən sē'və b'l) *adj.* that cannot be conceived; that cannot be thought of, imagined, etc. —**in'con·ceiv'a·bil'i·ty, in'con·ceiv'a·ble·ness** *n.* —**in'con·ceiv'a·bly** *adv.*

**in·con·clu·sive** (in'kən klōō'siv) *adj.* not conclusive or final; not leading to a definite result —**in'con·clu'sive·ly** *adv.* —**in'con·clu'sive·ness** *n.*

**in·con·gru·i·ty** (in'kən grōō'ə tē) *n.* **1.** a being incongruous; specif., *a*) lack of harmony or agreement *b*) lack of fitness or appropriateness **2.** *pl.* **-ties** something incongruous

**in·con·gru·ous** (in kāŋ'grōō wəs) *adj.* not congruous; specif., *a*) lacking harmony or agreement *b*) having inharmonious parts, elements, etc. *c*) unsuitable; inappropriate —**in·con'gru·ous·ly** *adv.* —**in·con'gru·ous·ness** *n.*

**in·con·se·quent** (in kän'sə kwent', -kwənt) *adj.* not consequent; specif., *a*) not following as a result *b*) not following as a logical inference; irrelevant *c*) not proceeding in logical sequence —**in·con'se·quence'** *n.* —**in·con'se·quent'ly** *adv.*

**in·con·se·quen·tial** (in kän'sə kwen'shəl) *adj.* **1.** inconsequent; illogical **2.** of no consequence; unimportant —*n.* something inconsequential —**in'con·se·quen'ti·al'i·ty** (-shē al'ə tē) *n.* —**in·con'se·quen'tial·ly** *adv.*

**in·con·sid·er·a·ble** (in'kən sid'ər ə b'l) *adj.* not worth consideration; trivial; small —**in'con·sid'er·a·ble·ness** *n.* —**in'con·sid'er·a·bly** *adv.*

**in·con·sid·er·ate** (-it) *adj.* without thought or consideration for others; thoughtless —**in'con·sid'er·ate·ly** *adv.* —**in'con·sid'er·ate·ness, in'con·sid'er·a'tion** (-ə rā'shən) *n.*

**in·con·sis·ten·cy** (in'kən sis'tən sē) *n.* **1.** a being inconsistent **2.** *pl.* **-cies** an inconsistent act, remark, etc. Also **in'con·sis'tence**

**in·con·sis·tent** (-tənt) *adj.* not consistent; specif., *a*) not in agreement or harmony; incompatible *b*) not uniform; self-contradictory [*inconsistent* testimony] *c*) not holding to the same principles or practice; changeable —**in'con·sis'tent·ly** *adv.*

**in·con·sol·a·ble** (in'kən sōl'ə b'l) *adj.* that cannot be consoled —**in'con·sol'a·bil'i·ty, in'con·sol'a·ble·ness** *n.* —**in'con·sol'a·bly** *adv.*

**in·con·so·nant** (in kän'sə nənt) *adj.* not consonant; not in harmony or agreement —**in·con'so·nance** *n.* —**in·con'so·nant·ly** *adv.*

**in·con·spic·u·ous** (in'kən spik'yōō wəs) *adj.* not conspicuous; attracting little attention —**in'con·spic'u·ous·ly** *adv.* —**in'con·spic'u·ous·ness** *n.*

**in·con·stant** (in kän'stənt) *adj.* not constant; changeable; specif., *a*) not remaining firm in mind or purpose *b*) fickle *c*) not uniform; irregular —**in·con'stan·cy** *n.* —**in·con'stant·ly** *adv.*

**in·con·test·a·ble** (in'kən tes'tə b'l) *adj.* not to be contested; unquestionable —**in'con·test'a·bil'i·ty** *n.* —**in'con·test'a·bly** *adv.*

**in·con·ti·nent** (in känt''n ənt) *adj.* [< OFr. < L.: see IN-[2] & CONTINENT] **1.** *a*) without self-restraint, esp. in regard to sexual activity *b*) unrestrained **2.** incapable of containing, holding, etc. **3.** unable to restrain a natural discharge, as of urine —**in·con'ti·nence** *n.* —**in·con'ti·nent·ly** *adv.*

**in·con·tro·vert·i·ble** (in'kän trə vʉr'tə b'l, in·kän'-) *adj.* that cannot be controverted; not disputable or debatable; undeniable —**in'con·tro·vert'i·bil'i·ty** *n.* —**in'con·tro·vert'i·bly** *adv.*

**in·con·ven·ience** (in'kən vēn'yəns) *n.* **1.** a being inconvenient; lack of comfort, ease, etc. **2.** anything inconvenient Also **in'con·ven'ien·cy,** *pl.* **-cies** —*vt.* **-ienced, -iencing** to cause inconvenience to; trouble; bother

**in·con·ven·ient** (-yənt) *adj.* not convenient; not favorable to one's comfort; causing trouble, bother, etc. —**in'con·ven'ient·ly** *adv.*

**in·con·vert·i·ble** (in'kən vʉr'tə b'l) *adj.* that cannot be converted; that cannot be changed or exchanged —**in'con·vert'i·bil'i·ty** *n.*

**in·cor·po·rate** (in kôr'pər it; *for v.* -pə rāt') *adj.* [< LL.: see IN-[1] & CORPORATE] combined, merged, or incorporated —*vt.* **-rat'ed, -rat'ing** **1.** to combine with something already formed; embody **2.** to bring together into a single whole; merge **3.** to admit into association as a member **4.** to form into a corporation **5.** to give material form to —*vi.* **1.** to unite or combine into a single whole **2.** to form a corporation —**in·cor'po·ra'tion** *n.* —**in·cor'po·ra'tive** *adj.* —**in·cor'po·ra'tor** *n.*

**in·cor·po·re·al** (in'kôr pôr'ē əl) *adj.* not corporeal; without material body or substance —**in'cor·po're·al·ly** *adv.*

**in·cor·rect** (in'kə rekt') *adj.* not correct; specif., *a*) im-

proper *b*) untrue; inaccurate; wrong; faulty —**in'cor·rect'ly** *adv.* —**in'cor·rect'ness** *n.*

**in·cor·ri·gi·ble** (in kôr'i jə b'l, -kär'-) *adj.* not corrigible; that cannot be corrected, improved, or reformed, esp. because firmly set, as a habit, or because set in bad habits, as a child —*n.* an incorrigible person —**in·cor'ri·gi·bil'i·ty, in·cor'ri·gi·ble·ness** *n.* —**in·cor'ri·gi·bly** *adv.*

**in·cor·rupt** (in'kə rupt') *adj.* not corrupt; sound, pure, upright, honest, etc. —**in'cor·rupt'ly** *adv.* —**in'cor·rupt'ness** *n.*

**in·cor·rupt·i·ble** (-rup'tə b'l) *adj.* that cannot be corrupted, esp. morally —**in'cor·rupt'i·bil'i·ty** *n.* —**in'cor·rupt'i·bly** *adv.*

**incr. 1.** increase **2.** increased **3.** increasing

**in·crease** (in krēs'; *also, and for n. always,* in'krēs) *vi.* **-creased', -creas'ing** [< OFr. < L. < *in-,* in + *crescere,* to grow] **1.** to become greater in size, amount, etc.; grow **2.** to become greater in numbers by producing offspring; multiply —*vt.* to cause to become greater in size, amount, etc. —*n.* **1.** an increasing or becoming increased **2.** the result or amount of an increasing —**on the increase** increasing —**in·creas'a·ble** *adj.* —**in·creas'er** *n.*

**in·creas·ing·ly** (in krēs'iŋ lē) *adv.* more and more; to an ever-increasing degree

**in·cred·i·ble** (in kred'ə b'l) *adj.* **1.** not credible; unbelievable **2.** so great, unusual, etc. as to seem impossible —**in·cred'i·bil'i·ty** *n.* —**in·cred'i·bly** *adv.*

**in·cre·du·li·ty** (in'krə dōō'lə tē, -dyōō'-) *n.* unwillingness or inability to believe; doubt

**in·cred·u·lous** (in krej'oo ləs) *adj.* **1.** unwilling or unable to believe; doubting **2.** showing doubt or disbelief —**in·cred'u·lous·ly** *adv.*

**in·cre·ment** (in'krə mənt, iŋ'-) *n.* **1.** a becoming greater or larger; increase; gain **2.** amount of increase [an annual *increment* of $300 in salary] —**in'cre·men'tal** (-men't'l) *adj.*

**in·crim·i·nate** (in krim'ə nāt') *vt.* **-nat'ed, -nat'ing** [< ML.: see IN-[1] & CRIMINATE] **1.** to charge with a crime; accuse **2.** to involve in, or make appear guilty of, a crime or fault —**in·crim'i·na'tion** *n.* —**in·crim'i·na·to'ry** *adj.*

**in·crust** (in krust') *vt.* **1.** to cover as with a crust **2.** to decorate, as with gems —*vi.* to form a crust —**in·crus·ta'tion** *n.*

**in·cu·bate** (iŋ'kyə bāt', in-) *vt.* **-bat'ed, -bat'ing** [< L. pp. of *incubare* < *in-,* on + *cubare,* to lie] **1.** to sit on and hatch (eggs) **2.** to keep (eggs, embryos, etc.) in a favorable environment for hatching or developing **3.** to develop, as by thought or planning —*vi.* to undergo incubation

**in·cu·ba·tion** (iŋ'kyə bā'shən, in'-) *n.* **1.** an incubating or being incubated **2.** the phase in the development of a disease between the infection and the first appearance of symptoms —**in'cu·ba'tion·al** *adj.* —**in'cu·ba'tive** *adj.*

**in·cu·ba·tor** (iŋ'kyə bāt'ər, in'-) *n.* a person or thing that incubates; specif., *a*) an artificially heated container for hatching eggs *b*) a similar apparatus in which premature babies are kept for a period *c*) an apparatus for developing bacterial cultures

**in·cu·bus** (iŋ'kyə bəs, in'-) *n., pl.* **-bus·es, -bi** (-bī') [< LL., nightmare (in ML., a demon) < L. *incubare:* see INCUBATE] **1.** a spirit or demon thought in medieval times to lie on sleeping women **2.** a nightmare **3.** an oppressive burden

**in·cul·cate** (in kul'kāt, in'kul kāt') *vt.* **-cat·ed, -cat·ing** [< L. pp. of *inculcare* < *in-,* in + *calcare,* to trample underfoot < *calx,* a heel] to impress upon the mind by repetition or persistent urging —**in·cul·ca'tion** *n.* —**in·cul'ca·tor** *n.*

**in·cul·pate** (in kul'pāt, in'kul pāt') *vt.* **-pat·ed, -pat·ing** [< ML. pp. of *inculpare* < L. *in,* on + *culpa,* a fault, blame] *same as* INCRIMINATE —**in'cul·pa'tion** *n.* —**in·cul'pa·to'ry** *adj.*

**in·cum·ben·cy** (in kum'bən sē) *n., pl.* **-cies** **1.** a duty or obligation **2.** *a*) the holding and administering of a position *b*) tenure of office

**in·cum·bent** (-bənt) *adj.* [< L. prp. of *incumbere* < *in-,* on + *cubare,* to lie down] **1.** lying, resting, or pressing with its weight on something else **2.** currently in office —*n.* the holder of an office or benefice —**incumbent on** (or **upon**) resting upon as a duty or obligation

**in·cum·ber** (in kum'bər) *vt. same as* ENCUMBER

**in·cum·brance** (-brəns) *n.* **1.** *Law* a lien, claim, mortgage, etc. on property **2.** *same as* ENCUMBRANCE

**in·cu·nab·u·la** (in'kyoo nab'yə lə) *n.pl., sing.* **-u·lum** (-ləm) [< L. < *in-,* in + *cunabula,* neut. pl., a cradle] **1.** the very first stages of anything; beginnings **2.** early printed books; esp., books printed before 1500 —**in'cu·nab'u·lar** *adj.*

**in·cur** (in kʉr′) *vt.* **-curred′, -cur′ring** [< L. < *in-*, in + *currere*, to run] **1.** to acquire (something undesirable) [to *incur* a debt] **2.** to bring upon oneself through one's own actions

**in·cur·a·ble** (in kyoor′ə b'l) *adj.* not curable; that cannot be remedied or corrected —*n.* a person having an incurable disease —in·cur′a·bil′i·ty *n.* —in·cur′a·bly *adv.*

**in·cu·ri·ous** (in kyoor′ē əs) *adj.* not curious; uninterested; indifferent —in·cu·ri·os·i·ty (in′kyoor ē äs′ə tē), in·cu′ri·ous·ness *n.* —in·cu′ri·ous·ly *adv.*

**in·cur·sion** (in kʉr′zhən; *chiefly Brit.* -shən) *n.* [< L. *incursio* < *incurrere*: see INCUR] **1.** a running in; inroad **2.** a sudden, brief invasion or raid —in·cur′sive *adj.*

**in·curve** (in kʉrv′; *for n.* in′kʉrv′) *vt., vi.* **-curved′, -curv′ing** to curve inward —*n. Baseball* same as SCREWBALL

**in·cus** (iŋ′kəs) *n., pl.* **in·cu·des** (in kyōō′dēz) [ModL. < L., anvil] the central one of the three small bones in the middle ear: also called *anvil*

**Ind.** **1.** India **2.** Indian **3.** Indiana **4.** Indies

**ind.** **1.** independent **2.** index **3.** industrial

**in·debt·ed** (in det′id) *adj.* **1.** in debt **2.** obliged; owing gratitude

**in·debt·ed·ness** (-nis) *n.* **1.** a being indebted **2.** the amount owed; all one's debts

**in·de·cen·cy** (in dē′s'n sē) *n.* **1.** a being indecent **2.** *pl.* **-cies** an indecent act, statement, etc.

**in·de·cent** (-s'nt) *adj.* not decent; specif., *a)* not proper and fitting; unseemly *b)* morally offensive; obscene —in·de′cent·ly *adv.*

**in·de·ci·pher·a·ble** (in′di sī′fər ə b'l) *adj.* that cannot be deciphered; illegible —in′de·ci′pher·a·bil′i·ty *n.*

**in·de·ci·sion** (in′di sizh′ən) *n.* inability to decide or a tendency to change the mind frequently

**in·de·ci·sive** (-sī′siv) *adj.* **1.** not decisive **2.** showing indecision; hesitating or vacillating —in′de·ci′sive·ly *adv.* —in′de·ci′sive·ness *n.*

**in·de·clin·a·ble** (in′di klīn′ə b'l) *adj. Gram.* having no case inflections; not declinable

**in·dec·o·rous** (in dek′ər əs; *occas.* in′di kôr′əs) *adj.* lacking decorum, good taste, etc. —in·dec′o·rous·ly *adv.* —in·dec′o·rous·ness *n.*

**in·de·co·rum** (in′di kôr′əm) *n.* **1.** lack of decorum **2.** indecorous conduct, speech, etc.

**in·deed** (in dēd′) *adv.* [see IN, *prep.* & DEED] certainly; truly; admittedly —*interj.* an exclamation of surprise, doubt, sarcasm, etc.

**indef.** indefinite

**in·de·fat·i·ga·ble** (in′di fat′i gə b'l) *adj.* [< MFr. < L. < *in-*, not + *defatigare*, to tire out: see DE- & FATIGUE] that cannot be tired out; untiring —in′de·fat′i·ga·bil′i·ty *n.* —in′de·fat′i·ga·bly *adv.*

**in·de·fea·si·ble** (in′di fē′zə b'l) *adj.* that cannot be undone or made void —in′de·fea′si·bil′i·ty *n.* —in′de·fea′si·bly *adv.*

**in·de·fen·si·ble** (in′di fen′sə b'l) *adj.* **1.** that cannot be defended **2.** that cannot be justified —in′de·fen′si·bil′i·ty *n.* —in′de·fen′si·bly *adv.*

**in·de·fin·a·ble** (-fīn′ə b'l) *adj.* that cannot be defined —in′de·fin′a·bil′i·ty *n.* —in′de·fin′a·bly *adv.*

**in·def·i·nite** (in def′ə nit) *adj.* not definite; specif., *a)* having no exact limits *b)* not precise in meaning; vague *c)* not clear in outline; blurred *d)* not sure; uncertain *e) Gram.* not limiting or specifying [*a* and *an* are *indefinite* articles, *any* is an *indefinite* pronoun] —in·def′i·nite·ly *adv.* —in·def′i·nite·ness *n.*

**in·de·his·cent** (in′di his′'nt) *adj.* not dehiscent; not opening at maturity to discharge its seeds —in′de·his′cence *n.*

**in·del·i·ble** (in del′ə b'l) *adj.* [< L., ult. < *in-*, not + *delere*, to destroy] **1.** that cannot be erased, blotted out, eliminated, etc.; permanent **2.** leaving an indelible mark [*indelible* ink] —in·del′i·bil′i·ty *n.* —in·del′i·bly *adv.*

**in·del·i·ca·cy** (in del′i kə sē) *n.* **1.** a being indelicate **2.** *pl.* **-cies** something indelicate

**in·del·i·cate** (-kit) *adj.* not delicate; coarse; esp., lacking propriety or modesty —in·del′i·cate·ly *adv.* —in·del′i·cate·ness *n.*

**in·dem·ni·fy** (in dem′nə fī′) *vt.* **-fied′, -fy′ing** [< L. *indemnis*, unhurt < *in-*, not + *damnum*, hurt + -FY] **1.** to protect against loss, damage, etc.; insure **2.** *a)* to repay for loss or damage *b)* to make good (a loss) —in·dem′ni·fi·ca′tion *n.* —in·dem′ni·fi′er *n.*

**in·dem·ni·ty** (-tē) *n., pl.* **-ties** **1.** protection or insurance against loss, damage, etc. **2.** legal exemption from penalties incurred by one's actions **3.** repayment for loss, damage, etc.

**in·dent¹** (in dent′; *for n., usually* in′dent) *vt.* [< OFr. < ML. < L. *in*, in + *dens*, tooth] **1.** *a)* to cut toothlike points into (an edge or border); notch; also, to join by mating notches *b)* to make jagged in outline **2.** to bind (a servant or apprentice) by indenture **3.** to space (the first line of a paragraph, etc.) in from the regular margin —*vi.* **1.** to form or be marked by notches, points, or a jagged border

**2.** to space in from the margin —*n.* **1.** a notch or cut in an edge **2.** an indenture **3.** an indented line, paragraph, etc.

**in·dent²** (in dent′; *for n., usually* in′dent) *vt.* [IN-¹ + DENT] **1.** to make a dent in **2.** to press (a mark, etc.) in —*n.* a dent, or slight hollow

**in·den·ta·tion** (in′den tā′shən) *n.* **1.** an indenting or being indented **2.** a notch, cut, or inlet on a coastline, etc. **3.** a dent, or slight hollow **4.** an indention; space in from a margin

**in·den·tion** (in den′shən) *n.* **1.** a spacing in from the margin **2.** an empty or blank space left by this **3.** *a)* a dent *b)* the making of a dent

**in·den·ture** (in den′chər) *n.* [< INDENT¹: orig., duplicates of a contract had correspondingly jagged edges for identification] **1.** a written contract or agreement **2.** [*often pl.*] a contract binding a person to work for another, as an apprentice to a master —*vt.* **-tured, -tur·ing** to bind by indenture

**In·de·pend·ence** (in′di pen′dəns) [after A. JACKSON, alluding to his *independence* of character] city in W Mo.: suburb of Kansas City: pop. 112,000

**in·de·pend·ence** (in′di pen′dəns) *n.* a being independent; freedom from the control of another

**Independence Day** the Fourth of July, the anniversary of the adoption of the Declaration of Independence on July 4, 1776

**in·de·pend·en·cy** (-dən sē) *n., pl.* **-cies** **1.** *same as* INDEPENDENCE **2.** an independent nation, etc.

**in·de·pend·ent** (-dənt) *adj.* **1.** free from the influence or control of others; specif., *a)* free from the rule of another; self-governing *b)* free from persuasion or bias; objective *c)* self-confident; self-reliant *d)* not adhering to any political party [an *independent* voter] *e)* not connected with others; separate [an *independent* grocer] **2.** *a)* not depending on another, esp. for financial support *b)* designating, of, or having an income large enough to enable one to live without working **3.** [I-] of or having to do with Independents —*n.* a person who is independent in thinking, action, etc.; specif., [*often* I-] a voter not an adherent of any political party —**independent** of apart from; regardless of —in′de·pend′ent·ly *adv.*

**independent clause** *Gram. same as* MAIN CLAUSE

**independent variable** *Math.* a quantity whose value may be determined freely without reference to other variables

**in-depth** (in′depth′) *adj.* carefully worked out, detailed, thorough, etc. [an *in-depth* study]

**in·de·scrib·a·ble** (in′di skrī′bə b'l) *adj.* that cannot be described; beyond the power of description —in′de·scrib′a·bil′i·ty *n.* —in′de·scrib′a·bly *adv.*

**in·de·struct·i·ble** (in′di struk′tə b'l) *adj.* that cannot be destroyed —in′de·struct′i·bil′i·ty *n.* —in′de·struct′i·bly *adv.*

**in·de·ter·mi·na·ble** (in′di tʉr′mi nə b'l) *adj.* not determinable; specif., *a)* that cannot be decided *b)* that cannot be ascertained —in′de·ter′mi·na·ble·ness *n.* —in′de·ter′mi·na·bly *adv.*

**in·de·ter·mi·nate** (-nit) *adj.* not determinate; specif., *a)* inexact in its limits, nature, etc.; indefinite; vague *b)* not yet settled; inconclusive —in′de·ter′mi·na·cy, in′de·ter′mi·nate·ness *n.* —in′de·ter′mi·nate·ly *adv.*

**in·de·ter·mi·na·tion** (in′di tʉr′mə nā′shən) *n.* **1.** lack of determination **2.** the state or quality of being indeterminate

**in·dex** (in′deks) *n., pl.* **-dex·es, -di·ces′** (-də sēz′) [L. < *indicare*, INDICATE] **1.** *short for* INDEX FINGER **2.** a pointer, as the needle on a dial **3.** an indication or sign [performance is an *index* of ability] **4.** *a)* an alphabetical list of names, subjects, etc. together with the page numbers where they appear in the text, usually placed at the end of a publication *b) short for* THUMB INDEX *c)* a catalog [a library *index*] **5.** *a)* the relation or ratio of one amount or dimension to another, or the formula expressing this relation *b)* a number used to measure changes in prices, wages, etc.: it shows percentage variation from an arbitrary standard: in full, **index number** **6.** [I-] *R.C.Ch.* formerly, a list of books forbidden to be read **7.** *Math. a)* an exponent (sense 3) *b)* a number or symbol placed above and to the left of a radical **8.** *Printing* a sign (☞) calling special attention to certain information —*vt.* **1.** *a)* to make an index of or for *b)* to include in an index *c)* to supply with a thumb index **2.** to indicate —in′dex·er *n.* —in·dex′i·cal *adj.*

**index finger** the finger next to the thumb

**In·di·a** (in′dē ə) **1.** region in S Asia, south of the Himalayas, including a large peninsula between the Arabian Sea & the Bay of Bengal **2.** republic in C & S India: member of the Commonwealth: 1,177,000 sq. mi.; pop. 536,984,000; cap. New Delhi

**India ink** **1.** a black pigment of lampblack mixed with a gelatinous substance and dried into cakes or sticks **2.** a liquid ink made from this

**In·di·an** (in'dē ən) *adj.* **1.** of India or the East Indies, their people, or culture **2.** of any of the aboriginal peoples (**American Indians**) of N. America, S. America, or the West Indies, or of their cultures **3.** of a type used or made by Indians —*n.* **1.** a native of India or the East Indies **2.** a member of any of the aboriginal peoples of N. America, S. America, or the West Indies **3.** popularly, any of the languages spoken by American Indians

**In·di·an·a** (in'dē an'ə) [ModL., "land of the Indians"] Middle Western State of the U.S.: 36,291 sq. mi.; pop. 5,490,000; cap. Indianapolis: abbrev. **Ind., IN** —**In'di·an'·i·an** *adj., n.*

**Indian agent** a U.S. or Canadian official representing the government in dealings with American Indians, as on reservations

**In·di·an·ap·o·lis** (in'dē ə nap'ə lis) [INDIANA + Gr. *polis,* city] capital of Indiana, in the C part: pop. 701,000 (met. area 1,162,000)

**Indian club** a club of wood, metal, etc. shaped like a tenpin and swung in the hand for exercise

**Indian corn** *same as* CORN[1] (sense 2)

**Indian file** *same as* SINGLE FILE

**Indian giver** [Colloq.] a person who gives something and then asks for it back

**Indian meal** meal made from corn (maize); cornmeal

**Indian Ocean** ocean south of Asia, between Africa & Australia

**Indian pipe** a leafless, fleshy, white plant of the heath family, native to N Hemisphere forests, bearing a single, nodding, white flower

**Indian pudding** a cornmeal pudding made with INDIAN milk, molasses, etc.

**Indian summer** a period of mild, warm, hazy CLUB weather following the first frosts of late autumn

**Indian tobacco** a poisonous annual plant, common in the E U.S., with light blue flowers in spikes

**India paper** a thin, strong, opaque printing paper, used for some Bibles, dictionaries, etc.

**India** (or **india**) **rubber** crude, natural rubber obtained from latex —**In'di·a-rub'ber** *adj.*

**In·dic** (in'dik) *adj.* **1.** of India **2.** designating or of a subgroup of the Indo-Iranian branch of the Indo-European language family, including many of the languages of India, Pakistan, etc.

**indic.** indicative

**in·di·cate** (in'də kāt') *vt.* **-cat'ed, -cat'ing** [< L. pp. of *indicare* < *in-,* in + *dicare,* to declare] **1.** to direct attention to; point out **2.** to be or give a sign of; signify [*fever indicates* illness] **3.** to show the need for; call for; make necessary **4.** to show or point out as a cause, treatment, or outcome: said of a disease, etc. **5.** to state briefly

**in·di·ca·tion** (in'də kā'shən) *n.* **1.** an indicating **2.** something that indicates, or shows; sign **3.** something that is indicated as necessary **4.** the amount or degree registered by an indicator

**in·dic·a·tive** (in dik'ə tiv) *adj.* **1.** giving an indication or intimation; signifying: also **in·dic·a·to·ry** (in dik'ə tôr'ē, in'dik-) **2.** designating or of that mood of a verb used to express an act, state, or occurrence as actual, or to ask a question of fact —*n.* **1.** the indicative mood **2.** a verb in this mood —**in·dic'a·tive·ly** *adv.*

**in·di·ca·tor** (in'də kāt'ər) *n.* **1.** a person or thing that indicates; specif., any device, as a gauge, dial, register, or pointer, that measures something **2.** any substance used to indicate acidity or alkalinity, the beginning or end of a chemical reaction, etc., by changes in color

**in·di·ces** (in'də sēz') *n. alt. pl. of* INDEX

**in·di·ci·a** (in dish'ē ə, -dish'ə) *n.pl.* [L., ult. < *index:* see INDEX] marks or tokens; esp., printed markings on mail in place of stamps or cancellations

**in·dict** (in dīt') *vt.* [< Anglo-L. *indictare,* ult. < L. *in,* against + *dictare:* see DICTATE] to charge with the commission of a crime; esp., to make formal accusation against on the basis of positive legal evidence —**in·dict'a·ble** *adj.* —**in·dict'er,** or **in·dict'or** *n.*

**in·dict·ment** (in dīt'mənt) *n.* **1.** an indicting or being indicted **2.** a charge; specif., a formal accusation charging someone with a crime, presented by a grand jury to the court

**In·dies** (in'dēz) **1.** *same as:* a) EAST INDIES (sense 1) b) WEST INDIES **2.** formerly, *same as* EAST INDIES

**in·dif·fer·ence** (in dif'ər əns, in dif'rəns) *n.* a being indifferent; specif., a) lack of concern or interest b) lack of importance or meaning

**in·dif·fer·ent** (-ənt, -rənt) *adj.* **1.** having or showing no preference; neutral **2.** having or showing no interest, concern, etc.; uninterested or unmoved **3.** of no importance **4.** not particularly good or bad, large or small, etc.; average **5.** not really good **6.** neutral in quality, as a chemical or magnet; inactive —**in·dif'fer·ent·ly** *adv.*

**in·di·gence** (in'di jəns) *n.* the condition of being indigent: also **in'di·gen·cy**

**in·dig·e·nous** (in dij'ə nəs) *adj.* [< LL. < L. *indigena* < OL. *indu,* in + *gignere,* to be born] **1.** existing, growing, or produced naturally in a region or country; native (*to*) **2.** innate; inborn —**in·dig'e·nous·ly** *adv.* —**in·dig'e·nous·ness** *n.*

**in·di·gent** (in'di jənt) *adj.* [OFr. < L. prp. of *indigere,* to be in need < OL. *indu,* in + *egere,* to need] poor; needy —*n.* an indigent person —**in'di·gent·ly** *adv.*

**in·di·gest·i·ble** (in'di jes'tə b'l, -dī-) *adj.* not digestible; not easily digested —**in'di·gest'i·bil'i·ty** *n.*

**in·di·ges·tion** (-jes'chən, -jesh'-) *n.* **1.** inability to digest, or difficulty in digesting, food **2.** the discomfort caused by this

**in·dig·nant** (in dig'nənt) *adj.* [< L. prp. of *indignari,* to consider unworthy, ult. < *in-,* not + *dignus,* worthy] feeling or expressing indignation —**in·dig'nant·ly** *adv.*

**in·dig·na·tion** (in'dig nā'shən) *n.* anger or scorn that is a reaction to injustice or meanness

**in·dig·ni·ty** (in dig'nə tē) *n., pl.* **-ties** something that humiliates, insults, or injures the dignity or self-respect; affront

**in·di·go** (in'di gō') *n., pl.* **-gos', -goes'** [Sp. < L. *indicum* < Gr. < *Indikos,* Indian < *India,* India] **1.** a blue dye obtained from certain plants or made synthetically **2.** a plant of the legume family that yields indigo **3.** a deep violet blue: also **indigo blue** —*adj.* of a deep violet-blue: also **in'di·go'blue'**

**indigo bunting** (or **bird**) a small finch of the E U.S.: the male is indigo, the female brown

**in·di·rect** (in'di rekt', -dī-) *adj.* not direct; specif., a) not straight; roundabout b) not straight to the point or object [an *indirect* reply] c) not straightforward; dishonest [*indirect* dealing] d) not immediate; secondary [an *indirect* result] —**in'di·rect'ly** *adv.* —**in'di·rect'ness** *n.*

**indirect discourse** statement of the speaker but not in his exact words (Ex.: she said that she would go)

**in·di·rec·tion** (-rek'shən) *n.* **1.** roundabout act, procedure, or means **2.** deceit; dishonesty **3.** lack of direction or purpose

**indirect lighting** lighting reflected, as from a ceiling, wall panel, etc., or diffused so as to avoid glare

**indirect object** *Gram.* the person or thing indirectly affected by the action of the verb, i.e., the one to which something is given or for which something is done (Ex.: *him* in "do *him* a favor")

**indirect tax** a tax on manufactured goods, imports, etc. paid indirectly when included in the price

**in·dis·cern·i·ble** (in'di sur'nə b'l, -zur'-) *adj.* that cannot be discerned; imperceptible —**in'dis·cern'i·bly** *adv.*

**in·dis·creet** (in'dis krēt') *adj.* not discreet; lacking prudence; unwise —**in'dis·creet'ly** *adv.* —**in'dis·creet'ness** *n.*

**in·dis·cre·tion** (in'dis kresh'ən) *n.* **1.** lack of discretion **2.** an indiscreet act or remark

**in·dis·crim·i·nate** (in'dis krim'ə nit) *adj.* **1.** not based on careful selection; random or promiscuous **2.** not discriminating; not making careful choices or distinctions —**in'dis·crim'i·nate·ly** *adv.* —**in'dis·crim'i·nate·ness, in'dis·crim'i·na'tion** *n.*

**in·dis·pen·sa·ble** (in'dis pen'sə b'l) *adj.* **1.** that cannot be dispensed with or neglected **2.** absolutely necessary or required —*n.* an indispensable person or thing —**in'dis·pen'sa·bil'i·ty** *n.* —**in'dis·pen'sa·bly** *adv.*

**in·dis·pose** (in'dis pōz') *vt.* **-posed', -pos'ing 1.** to make unfit or unable **2.** to make unwilling or disinclined **3.** to make slightly ill

**in·dis·posed** (-pōzd') *adj.* **1.** slightly ill **2.** unwilling; disinclined

**in·dis·po·si·tion** (in'dis pə zish'ən) *n.* **1.** a slight illness **2.** unwillingness; disinclination

**in·dis·pu·ta·ble** (in'dis pyōōt'ə b'l, in dis'pyōō tə-) *adj.* that cannot be disputed; unquestionable —**in'dis·pu'ta·bil'i·ty** *n.* —**in'dis·pu'ta·bly** *adv.*

**in·dis·sol·u·ble** (in'di säl'yoo b'l) *adj.* that cannot be dissolved, decomposed, or destroyed; firm; lasting —**in'dis·sol'u·bil'i·ty** *n.* —**in'dis·sol'u·bly** *adv.*

**in·dis·tinct** (in'dis tiŋkt') *adj.* not distinct; specif., a) not seen, heard, or perceived clearly; obscure b) not separate or separable; not plainly defined —**in'dis·tinct'ly** *adv.* —**in'dis·tinct'ness** *n.*

**in·dis·tin·guish·a·ble** (-tiŋ'gwish ə b'l) *adj.* that cannot be distinguished or recognized as different or separate —**in'dis·tin'guish·a·bly** *adv.*

**in·dite** (in dīt') *vt.* **-dit'ed, -dit'ing** [< OFr., ult. < L.: see

INDICT] to put in writing; compose and write —**in·dite′·ment** *n.* —**in·dit′er** *n.*

**in·di·um** (in′dē əm) *n.* [ModL. < L. *indicum*, indigo: from its spectrum] a rare metallic chemical element, soft, ductile, and silver-white: symbol, In; at. wt., 114.82; at. no., 49

**in·di·vid·u·al** (in′di vij′ōo wəl, -vij′əl) *adj.* [< ML. < L. *individuus*, not divisible] **1.** existing as a separate thing or being; single; particular **2.** of, for, or by a single person or thing **3.** of or characteristic of a single person or thing **4.** unique or striking [an *individual* style] —*n.* **1.** a single thing, being, or organism, esp. as a member of a class, etc. **2.** a person

**in·di·vid·u·al·ism** (-iz′m) *n.* **1.** individual character; individuality **2.** the doctrine of unrestricted individual freedom in economic enterprise **3.** the doctrine that the state exists to serve the individual **4.** the doctrine that self-interest is the proper goal of all human actions; egoism **5.** *a)* action based on any such doctrine *b)* the leading of one's life in one's own way without conforming to conventions —**in′di·vid′u·al·ist** *n., adj.* —**in′di·vid′u·al·is′tic** *adj.*

**in·di·vid·u·al·i·ty** (in′di vij′ōo wal′ə tē) *n., pl.* **-ties** **1.** *a)* the sum of the characteristics that set one person or thing apart; individual character *b)* personal identity; personality **2.** separate existence **3.** an individual

**in·di·vid·u·al·ize** (-vij′ōo wə līz′, -vij′ōo līz′) *vt.* **-ized′, -iz′ing** **1.** to make individual; mark as different from others **2.** to make suitable for a particular individual **3.** to consider individually —**in′di·vid′u·al·i·za′tion** *n.*

**in·di·vid·u·al·ly** (-vij′ōo wəl ē, -vij′əl ē) *adv.* **1.** one at a time; separately **2.** as an individual; personally **3.** in a way showing individual characteristics; distinctively

**in·di·vis·i·ble** (in′di viz′ə b'l) *adj.* **1.** that cannot be divided **2.** *Math.* that cannot be divided without leaving a remainder —*n.* anything indivisible —**in′di·vis′i·bil′i·ty** *n.* —**in′di·vis′i·bly** *adv.*

**In·do·chi·na** (in′dō chī′nə) **1.** large peninsula south of China, including Burma, Thailand, Indochina (sense 2), & Malaya **2.** E part of this peninsula, consisting of Laos, Cambodia, & Vietnam Also sp. **Indo-China, Indo China**

**In·do·chi·nese, In·do-Chi·nese** (-chī nēz′) *adj.* of Indochina, its Mongoloid people, their language, or their culture —*n., pl.* **-nese′** a native or inhabitant of Indochina

**in·doc·tri·nate** (in däk′trə nāt′) *vt.* **-nat′ed, -nat′ing** [prob. < OFr. *endoctriner*: see IN-[1] & DOCTRINE] **1.** to instruct in doctrines, theories, or beliefs, as of a sect **2.** to instruct; teach —**in·doc′tri·na′tion** *n.* —**in·doc′tri·na′tor** *n.*

**In·do-Eu·ro·pe·an** (in′dō yoor′ə pē′ən) *adj.* designating or of a family of languages that includes most of those spoken in Europe and many of those spoken in southwestern Asia and India —*n.* **1.** this family of languages, including the Indo-Iranian, Greek, Italic, Germanic, and Slavic languages **2.** the hypothetical language from which these languages are thought to have descended

**In·do-I·ra·ni·an** (-i rā′nē ən) *adj.* designating or of a subfamily of the Indo-European language family that includes Indic and Iranian

**in·do·lent** (in′də lənt) *adj.* [< LL. < L. *in-*, not + prp. of *dolere*, to feel pain] disliking or avoiding work; idle; lazy —**in′do·lence** *n.* —**in′do·lent·ly** *adv.*

**in·dom·i·ta·ble** (in däm′it ə b'l) *adj.* [< LL. < L. < *in-*, not + pp. of *domitare*, intens. < *domare*, to tame] not easily discouraged or defeated; unyielding —**in·dom′i·ta·bil′i·ty, in·dom′i·ta·ble·ness** *n.* —**in·dom′i·ta·bly** *adv.*

**In·do·ne·sia** (in′də nē′zhə, -shə) republic in the Malay Archipelago, consisting of Java, Sumatra, most of Borneo, Celebes, West Irian, & many smaller islands: 736,510 sq. mi.; pop. 113,721,000; cap. Jakarta

**In·do·ne·sian** (-zhən, -shən) *adj.* **1.** of Indonesia, its people, etc. **2.** designating or of a large group of Malayo-Polynesian languages spoken in Indonesia, the Philippines, Java, etc. —*n.* **1.** a member of a light-brown people of Indonesia, the Philippines, Java, etc. **2.** an inhabitant of Indonesia **3.** the Indonesian languages **4.** the official Malay language of Indonesia

**in·door** (in′dôr′) *adj.* **1.** of the inside of a house or building **2.** living, belonging, or carried on within a house or building

**in·doors** (in′dôrz′) *adv.* in or into a house or other building

**in·dorse** (in dôrs′) *vt.* **-dorsed′, -dors′ing** *same as* ENDORSE

**In·dra** (in′drə) [Sans.] the chief god of the early Hindu religion, a god associated with rain and thunder

**in·du·bi·ta·ble** (in dōō′bi tə b'l, -dyōō′-) *adj.* that cannot be doubted; unquestionable —**in·du′bi·ta·bly** *adv.*

**in·duce** (in dōōs′, -dyōōs′) *vt.* **-duced′, -duc′ing** [< L. *inducere* < *in-*, in + *ducere*, to lead] **1.** to lead on to some action, condition, etc.; persuade **2.** to bring on; cause [to *induce* vomiting with an emetic] **3.** to draw (a general rule or conclusion) from particular facts **4.** *Physics* to bring about (an electric or magnetic effect) in a body by exposing it to the influence of a field of force —**in·duc′er** *n.* —**in·duc′i·ble** *adj.*

**in·duce·ment** (-mənt) *n.* **1.** an inducing or being induced **2.** anything that induces; motive

**in·duct** (in dukt′) *vt.* [< L. pp. of *inducere*: see INDUCE] **1.** formerly, to bring or lead in **2.** to place formally in an official position **3.** *a)* to initiate into a society *b)* to provide with knowledge of something not open to all *c)* to enroll (esp. a draftee) into the armed forces

**in·duct·ance** (-duk′təns) *n.* the property of an electric circuit by which a varying current in it induces voltages in the same circuit or in one nearby

**in·duct·ee** (in duk′tē′) *n.* a person inducted or being inducted, esp. into the armed forces

**in·duc·tile** (in duk′t'l) *adj.* not ductile, malleable, or pliant —**in′duc·til′i·ty** (-til′ə tē) *n.*

**in·duc·tion** (in duk′shən) *n.* **1.** an inducting or being inducted; installation **2.** a bringing forward of separate facts or instances, esp. so as to prove a general statement **3.** *Logic* reasoning from particular facts to a general conclusion; also, a conclusion so reached: opposed to DEDUCTION **4.** *Physics* the act or process by which an electric or magnetic effect is produced in an electrical conductor or magnetizable body when it is exposed to the influence of a field of force

**induction coil** an apparatus made up of two magnetically coupled coils in a circuit in which interruptions of the direct-current supply to one coil produce an alternating current of high potential in the other

**induction heating** the heating of a conducting material by means of electric current induced by an alternating magnetic field

**in·duc·tive** (in duk′tiv) *adj.* **1.** of or using logical induction [*inductive* reasoning] **2.** produced by induction **3.** of inductance or electrical or magnetic induction —**in·duc′tive·ly** *adv.*

**in·duc·tor** (-tər) *n.* a person or thing that inducts; specif., a device designed to introduce inductance into an electric circuit

**in·due** (in dōō′, -dyōō′) *vt.* **-dued′, -du′ing** *same as* ENDUE

**in·dulge** (in dulj′) *vt.* **-dulged′, -dulg′ing** [L. *indulgere*, to be kind to] **1.** to yield to or satisfy (a desire); give oneself up to [to *indulge* a craving for sweets] **2.** to gratify the wishes of; humor —*vi.* to give way to one's own desires; indulge oneself (*in* something) —**in·dulg′er** *n.*

**in·dul·gence** (in dul′jəns) *n.* **1.** an indulging or being indulgent **2.** a thing indulged in **3.** a giving way to one's desires **4.** a favor or privilege **5.** *R.C.Ch.* a remission of temporal or purgatorial punishment still due for a sin after the guilt has been forgiven

**in·dul·gent** (-jənt) *adj.* indulging or inclined to indulge; kind or lenient, often to excess —**in·dul′gent·ly** *adv.*

**in·du·rate** (in′dōo rāt′, -dyoo-) *vt.* **-rat′ed, -rat′ing** [< L. pp. of *indurare* < *in-*, in + *durare*, to harden] **1.** to make hard; harden **2.** to make callous or unfeeling **3.** to cause to be firmly established —*vi.* to become indurated —*adj.* **1.** hardened **2.** callous or unfeeling —**in′du·ra′tion** *n.* —**in′du·ra′tive** *adj.*

**In·dus** (in′dəs) river in S Asia, flowing from SW Tibet into the Arabian Sea: c.1,900 mi.

**in·dus·tri·al** (in dus′trē əl) *adj.* **1.** having the nature of or characterized by industries **2.** of, connected with, or resulting from industries **3.** working in industries **4.** of or concerned with people working in industries **5.** for use by industries: said of products —**in·dus′tri·al·ly** *adv.*

**industrial arts** the mechanical and technical skills used in industry, esp. as taught in schools

**in·dus·tri·al·ism** (in dus′trē əl iz′m) *n.* social and economic organization characterized by large industries, machine production, concentration of workers in cities, etc.

**in·dus·tri·al·ist** (-əl ist) *n.* a person who owns or manages an industrial enterprise

**in·dus·tri·al·ize** (-ə līz′) *vt.* **-ized′, -iz′ing** **1.** to develop industrialism in **2.** to organize as an industry —*vi.* to become industrial —**in·dus′tri·al·i·za′tion** *n.*

**industrial park** an area zoned for industrial and business use, usually on the outskirts of a city

**industrial relations** relations between industrial employers and their employees

**Industrial Revolution** [*often* i- r-] the great social and economic changes due to the introduction of machine and power tools and large-scale industrial production: it began in England about 1760

**industrial union** a labor union to which all workers in a given industry may belong, regardless of occupation or trade: cf. CRAFT UNION

**in·dus·tri·ous** (in dus′trē əs) *adj.* characterized by earnest, steady effort; hard-working —**in·dus′tri·ous·ly** *adv.* —**in·dus′tri·ous·ness** *n.*

**in·dus·try** (in′dəs trē) *n., pl.* **-tries** [< MFr. < L. *industria* < *industrius*, active] **1.** earnest, steady effort; diligence in work **2.** systematic work **3.** *a)* any particular branch of productive, esp. manufacturing, enterprise [the paper *industry*]; also, all such enterprises collectively *b)* any large-scale business activity [the TV *industry*] **4.** the owners and managers of industry

**in·dwell** (in dwel′) *vi., vt.* **-dwelt′, -dwell′ing** to dwell (in); reside (within) —**in′dwell′er** *n.*

**-ine**[1] (īn, in, ēn, ən) [< Fr. < L. *-inus*] *a suffix meaning* of, having the nature of, like [*divine, marine, crystalline*]

**-ine**[2] (in, ən, īn, ēn) [< L. < Gr. *-inē*] *a suffix used to form feminine nouns* [*heroine*]

**-ine**[3] (in, ən) [Fr. < L. *-ina*] *a suffix used to form certain abstract nouns* [*medicine, doctrine*]

**-ine**[4] (ēn, in, īn, ən) [arbitrary use of L. *-inus*] *a suffix used to form certain commercial names* [*Vaseline*] or the chemical names of *a*) halogens [*iodine*] *b*) alkaloids or nitrogen bases [*morphine*]

**in·e·bri·ate** (in ē′brē āt′; *for adj. & n., usually* -it) *vt.* **-at′ed, -at′ing** [< L. pp. of *inebriare*, ult. < *in-*, intens. + *ebrius*, drunk] **1.** to make drunk; intoxicate **2.** to excite; exhilarate —*adj.* drunk; intoxicated —*n.* a drunken person, esp. a drunkard —**in·e′bri·at′ed** *adj.* —**in·e′bri·a′tion** *n.*

**in·e·bri·e·ty** (in′ē brī′ə tē) *n.* drunkenness

**in·ed·i·ble** (in ed′ə b'l) *adj.* not edible; not fit to be eaten —**in′ed·i·bil′i·ty** *n.*

**in·ed·u·ca·ble** (in ej′ə kə b'l) *adj.* thought to be incapable of being educated

**in·ef·fa·ble** (in ef′ə b'l) *adj.* [< MFr. < L. < *in-*, not + *effabilis*, utterable < *ex-*, out + *fari*, to speak] **1.** too overwhelming to be expressed in words **2.** too sacred to be spoken —**in′ef·fa·bil′i·ty, in·ef′fa·ble·ness** *n.* —**in·ef′fa·bly** *adv.*

**in·ef·face·a·ble** (in′i fās′ə b'l) *adj.* that cannot be effaced; impossible to wipe out —**in′ef·face′a·bil′i·ty** *n.* —**in′ef·face′a·bly** *adv.*

**in·ef·fec·tive** (in′i fek′tiv) *adj.* **1.** not effective; not producing the desired effect **2.** not capable of performing satisfactorily; incompetent; inefficient —**in′ef·fec′tive·ly** *adv.* —**in′ef·fec′tive·ness** *n.*

**in·ef·fec·tu·al** (-chōō wəl) *adj.* not effectual; not producing or not able to produce the desired effect —**in′ef·fec′tu·al′i·ty** (-wal′ə tē), **in′ef·fec′tu·al·ness** *n.* —**in′ef·fec′tu·al·ly** *adv.*

**in·ef·fi·ca·cious** (in′ef ə kā′shəs) *adj.* not efficacious; unable to produce the desired effect [an *inefficacious* medicine] —**in′ef·fi·ca′cious·ly** *adv.* —**in′ef·fi·ca′cious·ness** *n.*

**in·ef·fi·ca·cy** (in ef′i kə sē) *n.* lack of efficacy; inability to produce the desired effect

**in·ef·fi·cient** (in′ə fish′ənt) *adj.* not efficient; specif., *a*) not producing the desired effect with a minimum use of energy, time, etc. *b*) lacking the necessary ability; incapable —**in′ef·fi′cien·cy** *n.* —**in′ef·fi′cient·ly** *adv.*

**in·e·las·tic** (in′i las′tik) *adj.* not elastic; inflexible, rigid, unyielding, unadaptable, etc. —**in′e·las·tic′i·ty** (-las tis′ə tē) *n.*

**in·el·e·gance** (in el′ə gəns) *n.* **1.** lack of elegance **2.** something inelegant Also **in·el′e·gan·cy,** *pl.* **-cies**

**in·el·e·gant** (-gənt) *adj.* not elegant; lacking refinement, good taste, grace, etc.; coarse; crude —**in·el′e·gant·ly** *adv.*

**in·el·i·gi·ble** (in el′i jə b'l) *adj.* not eligible; not qualified under the rules —*n.* an ineligible person —**in·el′i·gi·bil′i·ty** *n.* —**in·el′i·gi·bly** *adv.*

**in·e·luc·ta·ble** (in′i luk′tə b'l) *adj.* [< L. < *in-*, not + *eluctari*, resistible < *eluctari*, to struggle] not to be avoided or escaped; inevitable —**in′e·luc′ta·bil′i·ty** *n.* —**in′e·luc′ta·bly** *adv.*

**in·ept** (in ept′) *adj.* [< Fr. < L. < *in-*, not + *aptus*, fit] **1.** unsuitable; unfit **2.** wrong in a foolish and awkward way [*inept praise*] **3.** clumsy or bungling; inefficient —**in·ept′ly** *adv.* —**in·ept′ness** *n.*

**in·ep·ti·tude** (in ep′tə tōōd′, -tyōōd′) *n.* **1.** the quality or condition of being inept **2.** an inept act, remark, etc.

**in·e·qual·i·ty** (in′i kwäl′ə tē, -kwôl′-) *n., pl.* **-ties** **1.** a being unequal; lack of equality **2.** an instance of this; specif., *a*) a difference in size, amount, quality, rank, etc. *b*) an unevenness in surface *c*) a lack of proper proportion; unequal distribution **3.** *Math.* *a*) the relation between two unequal quantities *b*) an expression of this

**in·eq·ui·ta·ble** (in ek′wit ə b'l) *adj.* not equitable; unfair; unjust —**in·eq′ui·ta·bly** *adv.*

**in·eq·ui·ty** (in ek′wət ē) *n.* **1.** lack of justice; unfairness **2.** *pl.* **-ties** an instance of this

**in·e·rad·i·ca·ble** (in′i rad′ə kə b'l) *adj.* that cannot be eradicated —**in′e·rad′i·ca·bly** *adv.*

**in·ert** (in ʉrt′) *adj.* [< L. < *in-*, not + *ars*, ART[1]] **1.** without power to move or act **2.** inactive; dull; slow **3.** having few or no active properties [an *inert* gas] —**in·ert′ly** *adv.* —**in·ert′ness** *n.*

**in·er·tia** (in ʉr′shə) *n.* [see prec.] **1.** *Physics* the tendency of matter to remain at rest (or to keep moving in the same

direction) unless affected by an outside force **2.** a tendency to remain fixed, inactive, unchanging, etc. —**in·er′tial** *adj.*

**inertial guidance** (or **navigation**) the guidance (or navigation) of an aircraft, spacecraft, etc. along a preassigned course by means of self-contained, automatic instruments that utilize the laws of inertia

**in·es·cap·a·ble** (in′ə skāp′ə b'l) *adj.* that cannot be escaped or avoided; inevitable —**in′es·cap′a·bly** *adv.*

**in·es·ti·ma·ble** (in es′tə mə b'l) *adj.* too great or valuable to be properly measured or estimated —**in·es′ti·ma·bly** *adv.*

**in·ev·i·ta·ble** (in ev′ə tə b'l) *adj.* [< L. < *in-*, not + *evitabilis*, avoidable] that cannot be avoided; certain to happen —**in·ev′i·ta·bil′i·ty** *n.* —**in·ev′i·ta·bly** *adv.*

**in·ex·act** (in′ig zakt′) *adj.* not exact; not accurate —**in′ex·act′ly** *adv.* —**in′ex·act′ness** *n.*

**in·ex·cus·a·ble** (in′ik skyōō′zə b'l) *adj.* that cannot or should not be excused; unjustifiable —**in′ex·cus′a·bil′i·ty** *n.* —**in′ex·cus′a·bly** *adv.*

**in·ex·haust·i·ble** (in′ig zôs′tə b'l) *adj.* that cannot be exhausted; specif., *a*) that cannot be used up or emptied *b*) tireless —**in′ex·haust′i·bil′i·ty** *n.* —**in′ex·haust′i·bly** *adv.*

**in·ex·o·ra·ble** (in ek′sər ə b'l) *adj.* [< L. < *in-*, not + *exorare*, to move by entreaty] **1.** that cannot be influenced by entreaty; unrelenting **2.** that cannot be altered, checked, etc. [*inexorable* fate] —**in·ex′o·ra·bil′i·ty** *n.* —**in·ex′o·ra·bly** *adv.*

**in·ex·pe·di·ent** (in′ik spē′dē ənt) *adj.* not expedient; not suitable or practicable; unwise —**in′ex·pe′di·en·cy, in′ex·pe′di·ence** *n.* —**in′ex·pe′di·ent·ly** *adv.*

**in·ex·pen·sive** (in′ik spen′siv) *adj.* not expensive; costing relatively little; cheap —**in′ex·pen′sive·ly** *adv.* —**in′ex·pen′sive·ness** *n.*

**in·ex·pe·ri·ence** (in′ik spir′ē əns) *n.* lack of experience or of the knowledge or skill resulting from experience —**in′ex·pe′ri·enced** *adj.*

**in·ex·pert** (in ek′spʉrt, in′ik spʉrt′) *adj.* not expert; unskillful; amateurish —**in·ex′pert·ly** *adv.* —**in·ex′pert·ness** *n.*

**in·ex·pi·a·ble** (in ek′spē ə b'l) *adj.* that cannot be expiated or atoned for [an *inexpiable* sin]

**in·ex·pli·ca·ble** (in eks′pli kə b'l, in′iks plik′ə b'l) *adj.* not explicable; that cannot be explained or understood —**in·ex′pli·ca·bil′i·ty** *n.* —**in·ex′pli·ca·bly** *adv.*

**in·ex·press·i·ble** (in′ik spres′ə b'l) *adj.* that cannot be expressed; indescribable or unutterable —**in′ex·press′i·bil′i·ty** *n.* —**in′ex·press′i·bly** *adv.*

**in·ex·pres·sive** (in′ik spres′iv) *adj.* not expressive; lacking meaning or expression —**in′ex·pres′sive·ly** *adv.*

‡**in ex·ten·so** (in ik sten′sō) [L.] at full length

**in·ex·tin·guish·a·ble** (in′ik stiŋ′gwish ə b'l) *adj.* not extinguishable; that cannot be put out or stopped —**in′ex·tin′guish·a·bly** *adv.*

‡**in ex·tre·mis** (in′ ik strē′mis) [L., in extremity] at the point of death

**in·ex·tri·ca·ble** (in eks′tri kə b'l, in′ik strik′ə b'l) *adj.* **1.** that one cannot extricate himself from **2.** that cannot be disentangled or untied **3.** insolvable —**in·ex′tri·ca·bil′i·ty** *n.* —**in·ex′tri·ca·bly** *adv.*

**I·nez** (ī′niz, ī′nez′, ī nez′) [Sp. *Iñez*] a feminine name

**inf.** **1.** [L. *infra*] below **2.** infantry: also **Inf. 3.** infinitive **4.** information

**in·fal·li·ble** (in fal′ə b'l) *adj.* [< ML.: see IN-[2] & FALLIBLE] **1.** incapable of error; never wrong **2.** not liable to fail, go wrong, etc.; reliable **3.** *R.C.Ch.* incapable of error in setting forth doctrine on faith and morals —**in·fal′li·bil′i·ty** *n.* —**in·fal′li·bly** *adv.*

**in·fa·mous** (in′fə məs) *adj.* **1.** having a very bad reputation; notorious **2.** causing or deserving a bad reputation —**in′fa·mous·ly** *adv.*

**in·fa·my** (-mē) *n., pl.* **-mies** [< OFr. < L.: see IN-[2] & FAMOUS] **1.** very bad reputation; disgrace; dishonor **2.** the quality of being infamous; great wickedness **3.** an infamous act

**in·fan·cy** (in′fən sē) *n., pl.* **-cies** **1.** the state or period of being an infant; babyhood **2.** the beginning or earliest stage of anything **3.** *Law* the state of being a minor; period before the age of legal majority, usually twenty-one

**in·fant** (in′fənt) *n.* [< OFr. < L., ult. < *in-*, not + prp. of *fari*, to speak] **1.** a very young child; baby **2.** *Law* a minor —*adj.* **1.** of or for infants or infancy **2.** in a very early stage

**in·fan·ta** (in fan′tə, -fän′-) *n.* [Sp. & Port., fem. of *infante*: see ff.] **1.** any daughter of a king of Spain or Portugal **2.** the wife of an infante

**in·fan·te** (-tā) *n.* [Sp. & Port. < L.: see INFANT] any son of a king of Spain or Portugal, except the heir to the throne

---

fat, āpe, cär; ten, ēven; is, bīte; gō, hôrn, tōol, look; oil, out; up, fʉr; get; joy; yet; chin; she; thin, then; zh, leisure; ŋ, ring; ə for *a* in *ago*, *e* in *agent*, *i* in *sanity*, *o* in *comply*, *u* in *focus*; ′ as in *able* (ā′b'l); Fr. bal; ë, Fr. coeur; ö, Fr. feu; Fr. mon; ô, Fr. coq; ü, Fr. duc; r, Fr. cri; H, G. ich; kh, G. doch; ‡foreign; *hypothetical; < derived from. See inside front cover.

**in·fan·ti·cide** (in fan′tə sīd′) *n.* [Fr. < LL.: see INFANT & -CIDE] **1.** the murder of a baby **2.** a person guilty of this
**in·fan·tile** (in′fən til′, -til) *adj.* **1.** of infants or infancy **2.** like or characteristic of an infant; babyish **3.** in the earliest stage of development
**infantile paralysis** *same as* POLIOMYELITIS
**in·fan·ti·lism** (in′fən t′l iz′m, in fan′-) *n.* immature or childish behavior; specif., *Psychol.* an abnormal state in which such behavior persists into adult life
**in·fan·tine** (in′fən tīn′, -tin) *adj.* infantile
**in·fan·try** (in′fən trē) *n., pl.* **-tries** [< Fr. < It. < *infante*, child, knight's page, foot soldier] **1.** foot soldiers collectively; esp., that branch of an army consisting of soldiers trained and equipped to fight chiefly on foot **2.** [I-] a (designated) infantry regiment
**in·fan·try·man** (-mən) *n., pl.* **-men** (-mən) a soldier in the infantry
**in·fat·u·ate** (in fach′ᵒᵒ wāt′) *vt.* **-at′ed, -at′ing** [< L. pp. of *infatuare* < L. intens. + *fatuus*, foolish] **1.** to make foolish **2.** to inspire with foolish or shallow love —*adj.* infatuated —*n.* a person who is infatuated —in·fat′u·a′·tion *n.*
**in·fat·u·at·ed** (-id) *adj.* **1.** foolish **2.** completely carried away by foolish or shallow love
**in·fect** (in fekt′) *vt.* [< MFr. < L. pp. of *inficere*, to stain < *in-*, in + *facere*, to make] **1.** to contaminate with a disease-producing organism **2.** to cause to become diseased by bringing into contact with such an organism **3.** to invade (an individual, organ, tissue, etc.) **4.** to imbue with one's feelings or beliefs —in·fec′tor *n.*
**in·fec·tion** (in fek′shən) *n.* **1.** an infecting; specif., *a)* a causing to become diseased *b)* an affecting with one's feelings or beliefs **2.** a being infected, esp. by bacteria, viruses, etc. **3.** something that results from infecting or being infected; specif., a disease resulting from infection (sense 2) **4.** anything that infects
**in·fec·tious** (-shəs) *adj.* **1.** likely to cause infection **2.** designating a disease that can be communicated by infection (sense 2) **3.** tending to spread to others [an *infectious* laugh] —in·fec′tious·ly *adv.* —in·fec′tious·ness *n.*
**infectious hepatitis** a viral disease causing inflammation of the liver
**infectious mononucleosis** an acute disease, esp. of young people, characterized by fever, swollen lymph nodes, etc.
**in·fec·tive** (in fek′tiv) *adj.* likely to cause infection —in·fec′tive·ness, in′fec·tiv′i·ty *n.*
**in·fe·lic·i·tous** (in′fə lis′ə təs) *adj.* not felicitous; unfortunate or unsuitable —in′fe·lic′i·tous·ly *adv.*
**in·fe·lic·i·ty** (-tē) *n.* **1.** a being infelicitous **2.** *pl.* **-ties** something infelicitous; unsuitable or inapt remark, action, etc.
**in·fer** (in fur′) *vt.* **-ferred′, -fer′ring** [< L. *inferre* < *in-*, in + *ferre*, to bring] **1.** to conclude by reasoning from something known or assumed **2.** *a)* to lead to as a conclusion; indicate *b)* to indicate indirectly; imply: sometimes regarded as a loose usage —*vi.* to draw inferences —in·fer′a·ble *adj.* —in·fer′a·bly *adv.* —in·fer′rer *n.*
**in·fer·ence** (in′fər əns) *n.* **1.** an inferring; specif., the deriving of a conclusion by induction or deduction **2.** something inferred; conclusion
**in·fer·en·tial** (in′fə ren′shəl) *adj.* of or based on inference —in′fer·en′tial·ly *adv.*
**in·fe·ri·or** (in fir′ē ər) *adj.* [L., compar. of *inferus*, low] **1.** lower in space; placed lower down **2.** lower in order, status, rank, etc. **3.** lower in quality or value than (with *to*) **4.** poor in quality; below average —*n.* an inferior person or thing —in·fe′ri·or′i·ty (-ôr′ə tē, -är′-) *n.*
**inferiority complex** **1.** *Psychol.* a neurotic condition resulting from various feelings of inferiority or inadequacy, often manifested through overcompensation in excessive aggressiveness, etc. **2.** popularly, any feeling of inferiority, inadequacy, etc.
**in·fer·nal** (in fur′n′l) *adj.* [< OFr. < LL. *infernalis*, ult. < L. *inferus*: see INFERIOR] **1.** *a)* of the ancient mythological world of the dead *b)* of hell **2.** hellish; fiendish **3.** [Colloq.] hateful; outrageous —in·fer′nal·ly *adv.*
**infernal machine** *earlier name for* a booby trap or time bomb
**in·fer·no** (in fur′nō) *n., pl.* **-nos** [It. < L.: see INFERNAL] hell or any place suggesting hell
**in·fer·tile** (in fur′t′l) *adj.* not fertile; barren; sterile —in·fer·til·i·ty (in′fər til′ə tē) *n.*
**in·fest** (in fest′) *vt.* [< Fr. < L. *infestus*, hostile] **1.** to overrun or swarm about in large numbers, usually so as to be harmful or bothersome **2.** to be parasitic in or on —in′fes·ta′tion *n.*
**in·fi·del** (in′fə d′l) *n.* [< MFr. < L. < *in-*, not + *fidelis*, faithful] **1.** a person who does not believe in a particular, esp. the prevailing, religion **2.** a person who holds no religious belief —*adj.* **1.** that is an infidel; unbelieving **2.** of infidels
**in·fi·del·i·ty** (in′fə del′ə tē) *n., pl.* **-ties** **1.** the fact or

state of being an infidel **2.** unfaithfulness or disloyalty to another; esp., sexual unfaithfulness of a husband or wife; adultery **3.** an unfaithful or disloyal act
**in·field** (in′fēld′) *n.* **1.** *a)* the area enclosed by the four base lines on a baseball field *b)* the infielders collectively, or the area they cover **2.** the area inside a race track or running track
**in·field·er** (-ər) *n. Baseball* a player whose position is in the infield; shortstop, first baseman, second baseman, or third baseman
**in·fight·ing** (in′fīt′iŋ) *n.* **1.** fighting, esp. boxing, at close range **2.** intense competition or conflict, often personal, as between political opponents or within an organization —in′fight′er *n.*
**in·fil·trate** (in fil′trāt, in′fil trāt′) *vi., vt.* **-trat·ed, -trat·ing** **1.** to pass into or through (a substance), as in filtering **2.** to pass, or cause (individual troops) to pass, through weak places in the enemy's lines **3.** to penetrate, or cause to penetrate, (a region or group) gradually or stealthily, so as to gain influence or control —*n.* something that infiltrates —in′fil·tra′tion *n.* —in′fil·tra′tive *adj.* —in′fil·tra′tor *n.*
**infin.** infinitive
**in·fi·nite** (in′fə nit) *adj.* [< L.: see IN-² & FINITE] **1.** lacking limits or bounds; extending beyond measure or comprehension; endless **2.** very great; vast; immense **3.** *Math.* indefinitely large; greater than any finite number —*n.* something infinite —**the Infinite (Being)** God —in′fi·nite·ly *adv.* —in′fi·nite·ness *n.*
**in·fin·i·tes·i·mal** (in′fin ə tes′ə məl, in fin′-) *adj.* [< ModL. < L. *infinitus*, infinite (patterned after *centesimus*, hundredth)] too small to be measured; infinitely small —*n.* an infinitesimal quantity —in′fin·i·tes′i·mal·ly *adv.*
**in·fin·i·tive** (in fin′ə tiv) *adj.* [< LL. < L. *infinitus* (*modus*), lit., unlimited (mood)] *Gram.* of or connected with an infinitive —*n. Gram.* the form of the verb which expresses existence or action without reference to person, number, or tense: usually following the marker *to* (*to go*) or another verb form (*let him try*) —in·fin′i·ti′val (-tī′vəl) *adj.*
**in·fin·i·tude** (in fin′ə tōōd′, -tyōōd′) *n.* **1.** a being infinite **2.** an infinite quantity or extent
**in·fin·i·ty** (-tē) *n., pl.* **-ties** **1.** the quality of being infinite **2.** endless or unlimited space, time, distance, etc. **3.** an indefinitely large number or amount
**in·firm** (in furm′) *adj.* **1.** not firm or strong physically; weak; feeble **2.** not firm in mind or purpose; vacillating **3.** not stable; frail; shaky, as a structure **4.** not secure or valid —in·firm′ly *adv.* —in·firm′ness *n.*
**in·fir·ma·ry** (in fur′mə rē) *n., pl.* **-ries** a place for the care of the sick, injured, or infirm; esp., a building or room, as in a school, that serves as a hospital or dispensary
**in·fir·mi·ty** (-mə tē) *n.* **1.** a being infirm; feebleness; weakness **2.** *pl.* **-ties** *a)* a physical weakness or defect *b)* a moral weakness
**in·fix** (in fiks′; *also, and for n. always,* in′fiks′) *vt.* **1.** to fasten or set firmly in or on **2.** to fix firmly in the mind; instill **3.** to place (an infix) within the body of a word —*n. Linguis.* a bound morpheme added within a word that has no affixes or within that part of a word to which affixes are added
**†in fla·gran·te de·lic·to** (in flə gran′tē di lik′tō) [L.] in the very act of committing the offense
**in·flame** (in flām′) *vt.* **-flamed′, -flam′ing** [< OFr. < L.: see IN-¹ & FLAME] **1.** to set on fire **2.** to arouse passion, desire, or violence in; excite intensely **3.** to increase the intensity of (passion, desire, etc.) **4.** to cause inflammation in (some organ or tissue) —*vi.* **1.** to become roused, excited, etc. **2.** to catch fire **3.** to become hot, feverish, sore, etc. —in·flam′er *n.*
**in·flam·ma·ble** (in flam′ə b′l) *adj.* **1.** *same as* FLAMMABLE **2.** easily excited —*n.* anything flammable —in·flam′ma·bil′i·ty *n.* —in·flam′ma·bly *adv.*
**in·flam·ma·tion** (in′flə mā′shən) *n.* **1.** an inflaming or being inflamed **2.** a condition of some part of the body in reaction to injury, infection, etc., characterized by redness, pain, heat, and swelling
**in·flam·ma·to·ry** (in flam′ə tôr′ē) *adj.* **1.** rousing or likely to rouse excitement, anger, violence, etc. **2.** *Med.* of or characterized by inflammation
**in·flate** (in flāt′) *vt.* **-flat′ed, -flat′ing** [< L. pp. of *inflare* < *in-*, in + *flare*, to blow] **1.** to blow full or swell out as with air or gas **2.** to raise in spirits; make proud **3.** to increase or raise beyond what is normal; specif., to cause inflation of (money, credit, etc.) —*vi.* to become inflated —in·flat′a·ble *adj.* —in·flat′er, in·fla′tor *n.*
**in·fla·tion** (in flā′shən) *n.* **1.** an inflating or being inflated **2.** an increase in the amount of money in circulation, resulting in a fall in its value and a rise in prices —in·fla′tion·ar′y *adj.*
**in·fla·tion·ism** (-iz′m) *n.* advocacy or promotion of monetary inflation —in·fla′tion·ist *adj., n.*

**in·flect** (in flekt′) *vt.* [< L. *inflectere* < *in-*, in + *flectere*, to bend] **1.** to turn, bend, or curve **2.** to vary the tone or pitch of (the voice) **3.** *Gram.* to change the form of (a word) by inflection, as in conjugating or declining —*vi.* to be changed by inflection —**in·flec′tive** *adj.*

**in·flec·tion** (in flek′shən) *n.* **1.** a turn, bend, or curve **2.** a change in tone or pitch of the voice **3.** *Gram. a)* the change of form by which some words indicate certain grammatical relationships, as number, case, gender, tense, etc. *b)* an inflected form *c)* an inflectional element

**in·flec·tion·al** (-'l) *adj.* of, having, or showing grammatical inflection —**in·flec′tion·al·ly** *adv.*

**in·flex·i·ble** (in flek′sə b'l) *adj.* not flexible; specif., *a)* that cannot be bent or curved; rigid *b)* firm in mind or purpose; stubborn *c)* that cannot be changed; unalterable —**in·flex′·i·bil′i·ty, in·flex′i·ble·ness** *n.* —**in·flex′i·bly** *adv.*

**in·flict** (in flikt′) *vt.* [< L. pp. of *infligere* < *in-*, against + *fligere*, to strike] **1.** to cause (pain, wounds, etc.) as by striking **2.** to impose (a punishment, disagreeable task, etc. on or upon) —**in·flict′er, in·flic′tor** *n.* —**in·flic′tive** *adj.*

**in·flic·tion** (in flik′shən) *n.* **1.** an inflicting **2.** something inflicted, as punishment

**in-flight** (in′flīt′) *adj.* done, occurring, shown, etc. while an aircraft is in flight

**in·flo·res·cence** (in′flô res′'ns, -flə-) *n.* [< ModL. < LL.: see IN-¹ & FLORESCENCE] *Bot.* **1.** the producing of blossoms; flowering **2.** the arrangement of flowers on a stem or axis **3.** a flower cluster on a common axis **4.** flowers collectively —**in′flo·res′cent** *adj.*

**in·flow** (in′flō′) *n.* **1.** a flowing in or into **2.** anything that flows in

**in·flu·ence** (in′floo wəns) *n.* [< OFr. < ML. < L. prp. of *influere* < *in-*, in + *fluere*, to flow] **1.** *a)* the power of persons or things to affect others *b)* the effect of such power **2.** the ability to produce effects indirectly by means of power based on wealth, high position, etc. **3.** one that has influence —*vt.* **-enced, -enc·ing** to have influence on; affect the nature, behavior, or thought of

TYPES OF INFLORESCENCE
(A, spike; B, catkin; C, raceme; D, spadix; E, head with disk flowers and ray flowers; F, umbel; G, compound umbel)

**in·flu·en·tial** (in′floo wen′shəl) *adj.* having or exerting influence, esp. great influence; powerful —**in′flu·en′tial·ly** *adv.*

**in·flu·en·za** (in′floo wen′zə) *n.* [It., lit., an influence (because attributed to astrological influences)] an acute, contagious, infectious disease, caused by a virus and characterized by inflammation of the respiratory tract, fever, and muscular pain —**in′flu·en′zal** *adj.*

**in·flux** (in′fluks′) *n.* [Fr. < LL. pp. of *influere:* see INFLUENCE] **1.** a flowing in or continual coming in; inflow **2.** the point where a river joins another body of water

**in·fold** (in fōld′) *vt. same as* ENFOLD

**in·form** (in fôrm′) *vt.* [< OFr. < L.: see IN-¹ & FORM] **1.** *a)* to give character to *b)* to inspire; animate **2.** to give knowledge of something to; tell —*vi.* **1.** to give information **2.** to give information laying blame or accusation upon another

**in·for·mal** (in fôr′məl) *adj.* not formal; specif., *a)* not according to fixed customs, rules, etc. *b)* casual, easy, unceremonious, or relaxed *c)* for everyday use or casual wear *d)* not requiring formal dress *e) same as* COLLOQUIAL —**in·for′mal·ly** *adv.*

**in·for·mal·i·ty** (in′fôr mal′ə tē) *n.* **1.** a being informal **2.** *pl.* **-ties** an informal act

**in·form·ant** (in fôr′mənt) *n.* a person who gives, or serves as a source of, information

**in·for·ma·tion** (in′fər mā′shən) *n.* **1.** an informing or being informed; esp., a telling or being told **2.** news; word **3.** knowledge acquired in any manner; facts; data **4.** a person or agency answering questions as a service to others **5.** any data stored in a computer **6.** *Law* an accusation of a criminal offense made by a public officer, rather than by a grand jury indictment —**in′for·ma′tion·al** *adj.*

**in·form·a·tive** (in fôr′mə tiv) *adj.* giving information; instructive —**in·form′a·tive·ly** *adv.*

**in·formed** (in fôrmd′) *adj.* having much information, knowledge, or education

**in·form·er** (in fôr′mər) *n.* a person who informs; esp., one who secretly accuses, or gives evidence against, another, often for a reward

**in·fra-** [< L. *infra*, below] *a prefix meaning* below, beneath [*infrared*]

**in·frac·tion** (in frak′shən) *n.* [< L. < pp. of *infringere*: see INFRINGE] a violation of a law, pact, etc.

**in·fra dig** (in′frə dig′) [< L. *infra dig(nitatem)*] [Colloq.] beneath one's dignity

**in·fran·gi·ble** (in fran′jə b'l) *adj.* **1.** that cannot be broken or separated **2.** that cannot be violated or infringed —**in·fran′gi·bil′i·ty, in·fran′gi·ble·ness** *n.* —**in·fran′gi·bly** *adv.*

**in·fra·red** (in′frə red′) *adj.* designating or of those invisible rays just beyond the red of the visible spectrum: their waves are longer than those of the spectrum colors and give off penetrating heat

**in·fra·son·ic** (-sän′ik) *adj.* designating or of a frequency of sound below the range audible to the human ear

**in·fra·struc·ture** (in′frə struk′chər) *n.* the basic facilities on which a city, state, etc. depends, as roads or schools —**in′fra·struc′tur·al** *adj.*

**in·fre·quent** (in frē′kwənt) *adj.* not frequent; happening seldom; rare —**in·fre′quen·cy, in·fre′quence** *n.* —**in·fre′quent·ly** *adv.*

**in·fringe** (in frinj′) *vt.* **-fringed′, -fring′ing** [L. *infringere* < *in-*, in + *frangere*, to break] to break (a law or agreement); violate —**infringe on** (or **upon**) to break in on; encroach on (the rights, etc. of others) —**in·fringe′ment** *n.* —**in·fring′er** *n.*

**in·fu·ri·ate** (in fyoor′ē āt′) *vt.* **-at′ed, -at′ing** [< ML. pp. of *infuriare* < L. *in-*, in + *furia*, rage] to cause to become very angry; enrage —**in·fu′ri·at′ing·ly** *adv.* —**in·fu′ri·a′tion** *n.*

**in·fuse** (in fyooz′) *vt.* **-fused′, -fus′ing** [< L. pp. of *infundere* < *in-*, in + *fundere*, to pour] **1.** to instill or impart (qualities, etc.) **2.** to imbue or inspire (*with* a quality, feeling, etc.) **3.** to steep or soak (tea leaves, etc.) so as to extract flavor or other qualities —**in·fus′er** *n.*

**in·fu·si·ble** (in fyoo′zə b'l) *adj.* that cannot be fused or melted —**in·fu′si·bil′i·ty, in·fu′si·ble·ness** *n.*

**in·fu·sion** (in fyoo′zhən) *n.* **1.** an infusing **2.** something infused **3.** the liquid extract that results from steeping a substance in water

**in·fu·so·ri·an** (in′fyoo sôr′ē ən) *n.* [< ModL.: from their occurrence in infusions] any of certain protozoans having cilia that permit free movement —*adj.* of these protozoans: also **in′fu·so′ri·al**

**-ing** (iŋ) **1.** [< OE. *-ende*] *a suffix used to form the present participle* [*hearing*] **2.** [< OE. *-ung*] *a suffix used to form verbal nouns meaning: a)* the act or an instance of [*talking*] *b)* something produced by the action of [*painting*] *c)* something that does the action of [*a head covering*] *d)* material used for [*carpeting*] **3.** [< OE.] *a suffix, sometimes with diminutive force, meaning* one of a specified kind [*farthing*]

**in·gen·ious** (in jēn′yəs) *adj.* [< MFr. < L. < *ingenium*, ability < *in-*, in + *gignere*, to produce] **1.** clever, resourceful, and inventive **2.** cleverly or originally made or done —**in·gen′ious·ly** *adv.* —**in·gen′ious·ness** *n.*

**in·gé·nue** (an′zhə nü′) *n., pl.* **-nues′** (-nooz′; *Fr.* -nü′) [< Fr. < L. *ingenuus,* INGENUOUS] **1.** an innocent, inexperienced, unworldly young woman **2.** *Theater a)* the role of such a character *b)* an actress playing such a role

**in·ge·nu·i·ty** (in′jə noo′ə tē, -nyoo′-) *n.* [< L. < *ingenuus* (see ff.): associated with INGENIOUS] a being ingenious; cleverness, originality, etc.

**in·gen·u·ous** (in jen′yoo wəs) *adj.* [< L. *ingenuus* < *in-*, in + *gignere*, to produce] **1.** frank; open; candid **2.** simple; artless; naive —**in·gen′u·ous·ly** *adv.* —**in·gen′u·ous·ness** *n.*

**in·gest** (in jest′) *vt.* [< L. pp. of *ingerere* < *in-*, into + *gerere*, to carry] to take (food, drugs, etc.) into the body, as by swallowing or absorbing —**in·ges′tion** *n.* —**in·ges′tive** *adj.*

**in·gle** (iŋ′g'l) *n.* [Scot. < Gael. *aingeal*, fire] [Brit. Dial.] **1.** a fire or blaze **2.** a fireplace

**in·gle·nook** (-nook′) *n.* [Chiefly Brit.] a corner by a fireplace: also **ingle nook**

**In·gle·wood** (iŋ′g'l wood′) [after the home town in Canada of the owner of the site] city in SW Calif.: suburb of Los Angeles: pop. 94,000

**in·glo·ri·ous** (in glôr′ē əs) *adj.* **1.** not giving or deserving glory; shameful; disgraceful **2.** [Now Rare] without glory; not famous —**in·glo′ri·ous·ly** *adv.* —**in·glo′ri·ous·ness** *n.*

**in·go·ing** (in′gō′iŋ) *adj.* going in; entering

**in·got** (iŋ′gət) *n.* [< MFr. *lingot* (with faulty separation of *l-*) < OPr.] a mass of metal cast into a bar or other convenient shape

**in·graft** (in graft′) *vt. same as* ENGRAFT

**in·grained** (in grānd′, in′grānd) *adj.* **1.** worked into the fiber; firmly fixed or established **2.** inveterate; thoroughgoing [an ingrained liar]

**in·grate** (in′grāt) *n.* [< OFr. < L. < *in-*, not + *gratus*, grateful] an ungrateful person

**in·gra·ti·ate** (in grā′shē āt′) *vt.* -at′ed, -at′ing [< L. < *in*, in + *gratia*, favor] to bring (oneself) into another's favor or good graces —**in·gra′ti·at′ing·ly** *adv.* —**in·gra′ti·a′tion** *n.*

**in·grat·i·tude** (in grat′ə tōōd′, -tyōōd′) *n.* lack of gratitude; ungratefulness

**in·gre·di·ent** (in grē′dē ənt) *n.* [< L. prp. of *ingredi:* see INGRESS] **1.** any of the things that a mixture is made of **2.** a component part of anything

**In·gres** (aṅ′gr′), **Jean Au·guste Do·mi·nique** (zhäṅ ō·güst′dō mē nēk′) 1780–1867; Fr. painter

**in·gress** (in′gres) *n.* [< L. pp. of *ingredi,* to enter < *in-*, into + *gradi,* to go] **1.** the act of entering: also **in·gres′sion** (-gresh′ən) **2.** the right to enter **3.** an entrance —**in·gres′sive** *adj.*

**Ing·rid** (iŋ′grid) [< Scand.; ult. < ON. *Ingvi,* name of a Gmc. god + *rida,* ride] a feminine name

**in·grow·ing** (in′grō′iŋ) *adj.* growing within, inward, or into; esp., growing into the flesh

**in·grown** (-grōn′) *adj.* grown within, inward, or into; esp., grown into the flesh, as a toenail

**in·gui·nal** (iŋ′gwə n′l) *adj.* [< L. *inguen,* the groin] of or near the groin

**in·gulf** (in gulf′) *vt. same as* ENGULF

**in·hab·it** (in hab′it) *vt.* [< OFr. < L. *inhabitare* < *in-*, in + *habitare,* to dwell] to live in (a region, house, etc.); occupy —**in·hab′it·a·bil′i·ty** *n.* —**in·hab′it·a·ble** *adj.* —**in·hab′i·ta′tion** *n.* —**in·hab′it·er** *n.*

**in·hab·it·ant** (-i tənt) *n.* a person or animal that inhabits some specified region, house, etc.

**in·hal·ant** (in hāl′ənt) *adj.* used in inhalation —*n.* a medicine to be inhaled as a vapor

**in·ha·la·tor** (in′hə lāt′ər) *n.* **1.** an apparatus for administering medicinal vapors in inhalation **2.** *same as* RESPIRATOR (sense 2)

**in·hale** (in hāl′) *vt., vi.* -haled′, -hal′ing [L. *inhalare* < *in-*, in + *halare,* to breathe] to breathe in; draw (air, vapor, smoke, etc.) into the lungs —**in·ha·la·tion** (in′hə lā′shən) *n.*

**in·hal·er** (-ər) *n.* **1.** a person who inhales **2.** *same as:* a) RESPIRATOR (sense 1) b) INHALATOR (sense 1)

**in·har·mon·ic** (in′här män′ik) *adj.* not harmonic; discordant

**in·har·mo·ni·ous** (-mō′nē əs) *adj.* not harmonious; discordant, in conflict, etc. —**in′har·mo′ni·ous·ly** *adv.* —**in′har·mo′ni·ous·ness** *n.*

**in·here** (in hir′) *vi.* -hered′, -her′ing [< L. < *in-*, in + *haerere,* to stick] to be inherent; exist as a quality, characteristic, or right (*in*)

**in·her·ent** (in hir′ənt) *adj.* [see prec.] existing in someone or something as a natural and inseparable quality or right; inborn —**in·her′ence, in·her′en·cy** *n., pl.* -**cies** —**in·her′ent·ly** *adv.*

**in·her·it** (in her′it) *vt.* [< OFr. < LL., ult. < L. *in,* in + *heres,* heir] **1.** to receive (property, etc.) by or as if by inheritance or bequest from a predecessor **2.** to have (certain characteristics) by heredity —*vi.* to receive an inheritance —**in·her′i·tor** *n.* —**in·her′i·tress** (-i tris) *n.fem.*

**in·her·it·a·ble** (-ə b′l) *adj.* **1.** capable of inheriting; having the rights of an heir **2.** that can be inherited —**in·her′it·a·bil′i·ty, in·her′it·a·ble·ness** *n.*

**in·her·it·ance** (-əns) *n.* **1.** the action of inheriting **2.** something inherited or to be inherited; legacy; bequest **3.** right to inherit **4.** anything received as if by inheritance **5.** any characteristic passed on by heredity

**inheritance tax** a tax on inherited property

**in·hib·it** (in hib′it) *vt.* [< L. pp. of *inhibere,* to curb < *in-*, in + *habere,* to hold] to hold back or keep from some action, feeling, etc. —**in·hib′i·tive, in·hib′i·to·ry** (-i tôr′ē) *adj.* —**in·hib′i·tor, in·hib′it·er** *n.*

**in·hi·bi·tion** (in′hi bish′ən, in′ə-) *n.* **1.** an inhibiting or being inhibited **2.** a mental or psychological process that restrains an action, emotion, or thought

**in·hos·pi·ta·ble** (in häs′pi tə b′l, in′häs pit′ə b′l) *adj.* **1.** not hospitable **2.** not offering protection, shelter, etc.; barren; forbidding —**in·hos′pi·ta·ble·ness** *n.* —**in·hos′pi·ta·bly** *adv.*

**in·hos·pi·tal·i·ty** (in′häs pi tal′ə tē, in häs′-) *n.* lack of hospitality; inhospitable treatment

**in·hu·man** (in hyōō′mən, -yōō′-) *adj.* not human; esp., not having normal human characteristics; unfeeling, cruel, etc. —**in·hu′man·ly** *adv.*

**in·hu·mane** (in′hyōō mān′, -yōō-) *adj.* not humane; unmoved by the suffering of others; cruel, brutal, unkind, etc. —**in′hu·mane′ly** *adv.*

**in·hu·man·i·ty** (-man′ə tē) *n.* **1.** a being inhuman or inhumane **2.** *pl.* -**ties** an inhuman or inhumane act or remark

**in·im·i·cal** (in im′i k′l) *adj.* [< LL. < L. *inimicus,* ENEMY] **1.** hostile; unfriendly **2.** in opposition; adverse —**in·im′i·cal·ly** *adv.*

**in·im·i·ta·ble** (in im′ə tə b′l) *adj.* that cannot be imitated or matched; too good to be equaled or copied —**in·im′i·ta·bil′i·ty, in·im′i·ta·ble·ness** *n.* —**in·im′i·ta·bly** *adv.*

**in·iq·ui·tous** (in ik′wə təs) *adj.* showing iniquity; wicked; unjust —**in·iq′ui·tous·ly** *adv.* —**in·iq′ui·tous·ness** *n.*

**in·iq·ui·ty** (-wə tē) *n.* [< OFr. < L. < *iniquus,* unequal < *in-*, not + *aequus,* equal] **1.** lack of righteousness or justice; wickedness **2.** *pl.* -**ties** a wicked, unjust, or unrighteous act

**in·i·tial** (i nish′əl) *adj.* [< Fr. < L. *initialis,* ult. < *in-*, in + *ire,* to go] having to do with or occurring at the beginning —*n.* a capital, or upper-case, letter; specif., the first letter of a name —*vt.* -**tialed** or -**tialled**, -**tial·ing** or -**tial·ling** to mark or sign with an initial or initials

**in·i·tial·ly** (-ē) *adv.* at the beginning; first

**in·i·ti·ate** (i nish′ē āt′; *for adj. & n., usually* -it) *vt.* -at′ed, -at′ing [< L. pp. of *initiare:* see INITIAL] **1.** to bring into practice or use **2.** to teach the fundamentals of some subject to **3.** to admit as a member into a fraternity, club, etc., esp. with a special or secret ceremony —*adj.* initiated —*n.* a person who has recently been, or is about to be, initiated —**in·i′ti·a′tor** *n.*

**in·i·ti·a·tion** (i nish′ē ā′shən) *n.* **1.** an initiating or being initiated **2.** the ceremony by which one is initiated into a fraternity, etc.

**in·i·ti·a·tive** (i nish′ē ə tiv, -nish′ə-) *adj.* of, or having the nature of, initiation —*n.* **1.** the action of taking the first step or move **2.** the characteristic of originating new ideas or methods **3.** *a)* the right of a legislature to introduce new legislation *b)* the right of a group of citizens to introduce a matter for legislation to the legislature or directly to the voters *c)* the procedure for this

**in·i·ti·a·to·ry** (-tôr′ē) *adj.* **1.** beginning; introductory **2.** of or used in an initiation

**in·ject** (in jekt′) *vt.* [< L. pp. of *injicere* < *in-*, in + *jacere,* to throw] **1.** to force or drive (a fluid) into some passage or cavity or into some part of the body by means of a syringe, etc. **2.** to fill by injection **3.** to introduce (a missing quality, etc.) **4.** to interject (a remark, etc.) —**in·ject′a·ble** *adj.* —**in·jec′tion** *n.* —**in·jec′tor** *n.*

**in·ju·di·cious** (in′jōō dish′əs) *adj.* not judicious; showing poor judgment; not discreet or wise —**in′ju·di′cious·ly** *adv.* —**in′ju·di′cious·ness** *n.*

**in·junc·tion** (in juŋk′shən) *n.* [< LL. < pp. of *injungere,* ENJOIN] **1.** an enjoining; command **2.** an order **3.** a writ or order from a court prohibiting a person or group from carrying out a given action, or ordering a given action to be done —**in·junc′tive** *adj.*

**in·jure** (in′jər) *vt.* -jured, -jur·ing [see INJURY] **1.** to do physical harm to; hurt **2.** to offend (one's feelings, etc.) **3.** to weaken (a reputation, etc.) **4.** to be unjust to —**in′jur·er** *n.*

**in·ju·ri·ous** (in joor′ē əs) *adj.* **1.** injuring or likely to injure; harmful **2.** offensive or abusive —**in·ju′ri·ous·ly** *adv.* —**in·ju′ri·ous·ness** *n.*

**in·ju·ry** (in′jər ē) *n., pl.* -**ries** [< L. *injuria,* ult. < *in-*, not + *jus* (gen. *juris*), right] **1.** physical harm to a person, etc. **2.** an injurious act; injustice, as in injuring a person's feelings or rights, a reputation, etc.

**in·jus·tice** (in jus′tis) *n.* **1.** the quality of being unjust or unfair **2.** an unjust act; injury

**ink** (iŋk) *n.* [OFr. *enque* < LL. < Gr. *enkauston,* red ink < *enkaiein,* to burn in] **1.** a colored liquid used for writing, etc. **2.** a sticky, colored paste used in printing **3.** a dark, liquid secretion squirted out by cuttlefish, etc. for protection —*vt.* **1.** to cover with ink **2.** to mark or color with ink (often with *in*) —**ink′er** *n.* —**ink′like′** *adj.*

**ink·blot** (-blät′) *n.* any of a group of irregular blots of ink, used as in the Rorschach test

**ink·horn** (-hôrn′) *n.* a small container made of horn, etc., formerly used to hold ink

**ink·ling** (iŋk′liŋ) *n.* **1.** an indirect suggestion; hint **2.** a vague idea or notion

**ink·stand** (iŋk′stand′) *n.* **1.** a small stand holding an inkwell, pens, etc. **2.** *same as* INKWELL

**ink·well** (iŋk′wel) *n.* a container for holding ink, usually set in a desk, inkstand, etc.

**ink·y** (iŋ′kē) *adj.* **ink′i·er, ink′i·est 1.** like ink in color; dark; black **2.** colored, marked, or covered with ink —**ink′i·ness** *n.*

**in·laid** (in'lād', in lād') *adj.* **1.** set in pieces into a surface of another material so as to form a smooth surface **2.** decorated with such a surface

**in·land** (in'lənd; *for n. & adv., usually* -land') *adj.* **1.** of, located in, or confined to the interior of a country or region; away from the coast or border **2.** [Brit.] within a country; domestic —*n.* inland areas —*adv.* into or toward the interior

**in-law** (in'lô') *n.* [< (MOTHER-)IN-LAW, etc.] [Colloq.] a relative by marriage

INLAID WOOD

**in·lay** (in'lā'; *for v., also* in lā') *vt.* -laid', -lay'ing **1.** *a)* to set (pieces of wood, metal, etc.) into, and level with, a surface to make a design *b)* to decorate thus **2.** to add extra silverplating to —*n., pl.* -lays' **1.** inlaid decoration or material **2.** a filling for a tooth made from a mold and cemented into the cavity —in'lay'er *n.*

**in·let** (in'let, -lit) *n.* **1.** *a)* a narrow strip of water extending into a body of land from a river, lake, ocean, etc. *b)* a narrow strip of water between islands **2.** an entrance, as to a culvert

‡**in lo·co pa·ren·tis** (in lō'kō pə ren'tis) [L.] in the place of a parent

**in·ly** (in'lē) *adv.* [Poet.] **1.** inwardly **2.** intimately

**in·mate** (in'māt') *n.* [IN-¹ + MATE¹] a person living with others in the same building, now esp. one confined with others in a prison, etc.

‡**in me·di·as res** (in mā'dē äs rās') [L., lit., into the midst of things] in the middle of the action

**in me·mo·ri·am** (in mə môr'ē əm) [L.] in memory (of)

**in-mi·grant** (in'mi'grənt) *adj.* coming in from another region of the country —*n.* an in-migrant person

**in·most** (in'mōst') *adj.* **1.** located farthest within **2.** most intimate or secret [*inmost* thoughts]

**inn** (in) *n.* [OE.] **1.** an establishment providing food and lodging for travelers; hotel **2.** a restaurant or tavern Now chiefly in the names of such places

**in·nards** (in'ərdz) *n.pl.* [< INWARD(S)] [Dial. or Colloq.] the internal organs of the body; viscera

**in·nate** (i nāt', in'āt) *adj.* [< L. pp. of *innasci* < *in-*, in + *nasci*, to be born] **1.** existing naturally rather than acquired [*innate* talent] **2.** existing as an inherent attribute [the *innate* humor of a situation] —in·nate'ly *adv.* —in·nate'ness *n.*

**in·ner** (in'ər) *adj.* **1.** located farther within; interior **2.** of the mind or spirit **3.** more intimate or secret [the *inner* emotions]

**inner city** the sections of a large city in or near its center, esp. when crowded or blighted

**Inner Mongolia** region in NE China, south & southeast of the Mongolian People's Republic

**in·ner·most** (in'ər mōst') *adj.* **1.** located farthest within **2.** most intimate or secret

**In·ness** (in'is), **George** 1825–94; U.S. painter

**in·ning** (in'iŋ) *n.* [OE. *innung*, a getting in] **1.** *Baseball & (pl.) Cricket a)* the period of play in which a team has a turn at bat *b)* a numbered round of play in which both teams have a turn at bat **2.** [*often pl.*] the period of, or opportunity for, action, exercise of authority, etc.

**inn·keep·er** (in'kē'pər) *n.* the proprietor of an inn

**in·no·cence** (in'ə səns) *n.* **1.** a being innocent; specif., *a)* freedom from sin or guilt *b)* guilelessness; simplicity *c)* naiveté *d)* harmlessness *e)* ignorance: also **in'no·cen·cy 2.** *same as* BLUET

**In·no·cent** (in'ə sənt) any of 13 popes, including **1. Innocent I, Saint** ?–417 A.D.; Pope (401–417) **2. Innocent III** 1161?–1216; Pope (1198–1216) **3. Innocent IV** ?–1254; Pope (1243–54) **4. Innocent XI** 1611–89; Pope (1676–89)

**in·no·cent** (in'ə sənt) *adj.* [< OFr. < L. < *in-*, not + prp. of *nocere*, to do wrong to] **1.** free from sin, evil, or guilt; specif., *a)* doing or thinking nothing morally wrong; pure *b)* not guilty of a specific crime or offense *c)* free from harmful effect or cause **2.** *a)* knowing no evil *b)* without guile or cunning; artless *c)* naive *d)* ignorant **3.** totally lacking (with *of*) —*n.* **1.** a person knowing no evil or sin, as a child **2.** a very naive person —in'no·cent·ly *adv.*

**in·noc·u·ous** (i näk'yoo wəs) *adj.* [< L. < *in-*, not + *nocuus*, harmful < *nocere*, to harm] **1.** that does not injure or harm; harmless **2.** not controversial or offensive; dull and uninspiring —in·noc'u·ous·ly *adv.*

**in·nom·i·nate bone** (i näm'ə nit) [< LL. *innominatus*, unnamed + BONE] either of two large, irregular bones of the pelvis, each formed of the ilium, ischium, and pubis; hipbone

**in·no·vate** (in'ə vāt') *vi.* -vat'ed, -vat'ing [< L. pp. of *innovare* < *in-*, in + *novare*, to alter < *novus*, new] to introduce new methods, devices, etc. —*vt.* to bring in as an innovation —in'no·va'tive *adj.* —in'no·va'tor *n.*

**in·no·va·tion** (in'ə vā'shən) *n.* **1.** an innovating **2.** something newly introduced; new method, practice, device, etc. —in'no·va'tion·al *adj.*

**in·nu·en·do** (in'yoo wen'dō) *n., pl.* -does, -dos [L., abl. of gerund of *innuere*, to nod to, hint] an indirect remark, gesture, or reference, usually implying something derogatory; insinuation

**in·nu·mer·a·ble** (i nōō'mər ə b'l, -nyōō'-) *adj.* too numerous to be counted; countless —in·nu'mer·a·bil'i·ty, in·nu'mer·a·ble·ness *n.* —in·nu'mer·a·bly *adv.*

**in·oc·u·late** (i näk'yoo lāt') *vt.* -lat'ed, -lat'ing [< L. pp. of *inoculare*, to engraft a bud < *in-*, in + *oculus*, an eye, bud] **1.** to inject a serum, vaccine, etc. into (a living organism), esp. in order to create immunity **2.** to implant microorganisms into (soil, a culture medium, etc.) to develop a culture, fix nitrogen, etc. **3.** to imbue with ideas, etc. —in·oc'u·la·bil'i·ty, in·oc'u·la·ble *adj.* —in·oc'u·la'tion *n.* —in·oc'u·la'tive *adj.* —in·oc'u·la'tor *n.*

**in·of·fen·sive** (in'ə fen'siv) *adj.* not offensive; unobjectionable; causing no harm or annoyance —in'of·fen'sive·ly *adv.* —in'of·fen'sive·ness *n.*

**in·op·er·a·ble** (in äp'ər ə b'l) *adj.* not operable; specif., *a)* not practicable *b)* that will not practicably allow of surgical operation

**in·op·er·a·tive** (-ər ə tiv, -ə rāt'iv) *adj.* not operative; without effect —in·op'er·a·tive·ness *n.*

**in·op·por·tune** (in äp'ər tōōn', -tyōōn') *adj.* not opportune; coming or happening at a poor time; not appropriate —in·op'por·tune'ly *adv.* —in·op'por·tune'ness *n.*

**in·or·di·nate** (in ôr'd'n it) *adj.* [< L.: see IN-² & ORDINATE] **1.** disordered; not regulated **2.** lacking restraint or moderation; excessive —in·or'di·nate·ly *adv.* —in·or'di·nate·ness *n.*

**in·or·gan·ic** (in'ôr gan'ik) *adj.* not organic; specif., *a)* designating or composed of matter that is not animal or vegetable; not living *b)* not like an organism in structure *c)* designating or of any chemical compound not organic *d)* designating or of the branch of chemistry dealing with these compounds —in'or·gan'i·cal·ly *adv.*

**in·o·si·tol** (i nō'sə tōl', -tôl') *n.* [< Gr. *is* (gen. *inos*), muscle + -IT(E) + -OL¹] a sweet crystalline alcohol, $C_6H_6(OH)_6$, esp. the form found in the vitamin B complex that apparently promotes growth: also **in·o·site** (in'ə sit')

‡**in per·pe·tu·um** (in' pər pech'oo wəm) [L.] forever

**in·put** (in'poot) *n.* what is put in; specif., *a)* the amount of money, material, effort, etc. put into a project or process *b)* electric current or power put into a circuit, machine, etc. *c)* information fed into a computer, etc.

**in·quest** (in'kwest) *n.* [< OFr. < VL. pp. of hyp. *inquaerere*: see INQUIRE] **1.** a judicial inquiry, as a coroner's investigation of a death **2.** the jury or group holding such an inquiry **3.** the verdict of such an inquiry

**in·qui·e·tude** (in kwi'ə tōōd', -tyōōd') *n.* restlessness; uneasiness

**in·quire** (in kwīr') *vi.* -quired', -quir'ing [< OFr. < LL. hyp. *inquaerere*, for L. *inquirere* < *in*, into + *quaerere*, to seek] **1.** to ask a question or questions **2.** to carry out an examination or investigation (usually with *into*) —*vt.* to seek information about [to inquire the way] —inquire after to pay respects by asking about the health of —in·quir'er *n.* —in·quir'ing·ly *adv.*

**in·quir·y** (in'kwə rē, -kwī'-; in kwīr'ē) *n., pl.* -quir·ies **1.** the act of inquiring **2.** an investigation or examination **3.** a question; query

**in·qui·si·tion** (in'kwə zish'ən) *n.* **1.** an inquiring; investigation **2.** [I-] *R.C.Ch. a)* formerly, the general tribunal established to discover and suppress heresy and heretics *b)* the activities of this tribunal **3.** *a)* any harsh or arbitrary suppression of dissent or nonconformity *b)* any relentless questioning *Law* an inquest or any judicial inquiry —in'qui·si'tion·al *adj.*

**in·quis·i·tive** (in kwiz'ə tiv) *adj.* **1.** inclined to ask many questions or seek information **2.** unnecessarily curious; meddlesome; prying —in·quis'i·tive·ly *adv.* —in·quis'i·tive·ness *n.*

**in·quis·i·tor** (-tər) *n.* **1.** an official whose work is making an inquisition **2.** any harsh or prying questioner **3.** [I-] an official of the Inquisition

**in·quis·i·to·ri·al** (in kwiz'ə tôr'ē əl) *adj.* **1.** of, or having the nature of, an inquisitor or an inquisition **2.** inquisitive —in·quis'i·to'ri·al·ly *adv.*

**in re** (in rē, rā) [L.] in the matter (of); concerning

**I.N.R.I.** [L. *Iesus Nazarenus, Rex Iudaeorum*] Jesus of Nazareth, King of the Jews

---

**in·road** (in′rōd′) *n.* **1.** a sudden invasion or raid **2.** [*usually pl.*] any injurious encroachment

**in·rush** (-rush′) *n.* a rushing in; inflow; influx

**ins. 1.** inches **2.** insulated **3.** insurance

**in·sane** (in sān′) *adj.* **1.** not sane; mentally ill or deranged; mad: cf. INSANITY **2.** of or for insane people [*an insane asylum*] **3.** very foolish; senseless —**in·sane′ly** *adv.*

**in·san·i·tar·y** (in san′ə ter′ē) *adj.* not sanitary; unhealthful

**in·san·i·ty** (in san′ə tē) *n., pl.* **-ties 1.** the state of being insane; mental illness or derangement: a term used formally in law but not in psychiatry **2.** great folly; extreme senselessness

**in·sa·ti·a·ble** (in sā′shə b′l, -shē ə-) *adj.* constantly wanting more; that cannot be satisfied; very greedy —**in·sa′ti·a·bil′i·ty** *n.* —**in·sa′ti·a·bly** *adv.*

**in·sa·ti·ate** (-shē it) *adj.* not satiated; insatiable —**in·sa′ti·ate·ly** *adv.* —**in·sa′ti·ate·ness** *n.*

**in·scribe** (in skrīb′) *vt.* **-scribed′, -scrib′ing** [< L.: see IN-¹ & SCRIBE] **1.** *a)* to mark or engrave (words, symbols, etc.) on some surface *b)* to write on, mark, or engrave (a surface) **2.** to add the name of (someone) to a list; enroll **3.** *a)* to dedicate (a book, etc.) informally *b)* to write a short, signed message in (a book, etc. one is presenting as a gift) **4.** to fix or impress deeply in the mind, memory, etc. **5.** *Geom.* to draw (a figure) inside another figure so that their boundaries touch at as many points as possible —**in·scrib′a·ble** *adj.* —**in·scrib′er** *n.*

**in·scrip·tion** (in skrip′shən) *n.* **1.** an inscribing **2.** something inscribed or engraved, as on a coin or monument **3.** *a)* an informal dedication in a book, etc. *b)* a short, signed message written in a book, etc. one is presenting as a gift —**in·scrip′tive, in·scrip′tion·al** *adj.*

**in·scru·ta·ble** (in skrōōt′ə b′l) *adj.* [< LL. < L. *in-*, not + *scrutari*, to examine] that cannot be easily understood; completely obscure or mysterious; enigmatic —**in·scru′ta·bil′i·ty, in·scru′ta·ble·ness** *n.* —**in·scru′ta·bly** *adv.*

**in·seam** (in′sēm′) *n.* the inner seam from the crotch to the bottom of a trouser leg

**in·sect** (in′sekt) *n.* [< L. *insectum (animale)*, lit., notched (animal): from the segmented bodies] **1.** any of a large class of small arthropod animals, including beetles, bees, flies, wasps, etc., having, in the adult state, a head, thorax, and abdomen, three pairs of legs, and, usually, two pairs of membranous wings **2.** popularly, any of a group of small animals, usually wingless, including spiders, centipedes, ticks, mites, etc.

**in·sec·ti·cide** (in sek′tə sīd′) *n.* any substance used to kill insects —**in·sec′ti·ci′dal** *adj.*

**in·sec·ti·vore** (in sek′tə vôr′) *n.* [< ModL.: see INSECT & -VOROUS] **1.** any of an order of insect-eating mammals, including moles, shrews, hedgehogs, etc. **2.** any animal or plant that feeds on insects —**in·sec·tiv·o·rous** (in′sek·tiv′ər əs) *adj.*

**in·se·cure** (in′si kyoor′) *adj.* not secure; specif., *a)* not safe from danger *b)* not confident; filled with anxieties *c)* not firm or dependable —**in′se·cure′ly** *adv.* —**in′se·cu′ri·ty** *n., pl.* **-ties**

**in·sem·i·nate** (in sem′ə nāt′) *vt.* **-nat′ed, -nat′ing** [< L. pp. of *inseminare* < *in-*, in + *seminare*, to sow < *semen*, seed] **1.** to sow seeds in; esp., to impregnate with semen **2.** to implant (ideas, etc.) in (the mind, etc.) —**in·sem′i·na′tion** *n.*

**in·sen·sate** (in sen′sāt, -sit) *adj.* **1.** lacking sensation; inanimate **2.** without sense or reason; stupid **3.** without feeling for others; insensitive —**in·sen′sate·ly** *adv.*

**in·sen·si·ble** (in sen′sə b′l) *adj.* **1.** lacking sensation; unable to perceive with the senses **2.** having lost sensation; unconscious **3.** not recognizing or realizing; unaware; indifferent **4.** so small or slight as to be virtually imperceptible —**in·sen′si·bil′i·ty** *n.* —**in·sen′si·bly** *adv.*

**in·sen·si·tive** (-tiv) *adj.* not sensitive; having little or no reaction (*to*) —**in·sen′si·tive·ly** *adv.* —**in·sen′si·tiv′i·ty, in·sen′si·tive·ness** *n.*

**in·sen·ti·ent** (in sen′shē ənt, -shənt) *adj.* not sentient; without life, consciousness, or perception —**in·sen′ti·ence** *n.*

**in·sep·a·ra·ble** (in sep′ər ə b′l) *adj.* that cannot be separated or parted —*n.* [*pl.*] inseparable persons or things —**in·sep′a·ra·bil′i·ty, in·sep′a·ra·ble·ness** *n.* —**in·sep′a·ra·bly** *adv.*

**in·sert** (in surt′; *for n.* in′sərt) *vt.* [< L. pp. of *inserere* < *in-*, in + *serere*, to join] to put or fit (something) into something else; set in —*n.* anything inserted or for insertion; esp., an extra leaf or section inserted in a newspaper, etc. —**in·sert′er** *n.*

**in·ser·tion** (in sur′shən) *n.* **1.** an inserting or being inserted **2.** something inserted; specif., *a)* a piece of lace or embroidery that can be set into a piece of cloth for ornamentation *b)* a single placement of an advertisement, as in a newspaper

**in·ser·vice** (in′sur′vis) *adj.* designating or of training given to employees in connection with their work to help them develop skills, etc.

**in·set** (in set′; *also, and for n. always,* in′set) *vt.* **-set′, -set′ting** to set into something; insert —*n.* something set in; insert

**in·shore** (in′shôr′, in shôr′) *adv., adj.* **1.** in toward the shore **2.** near the shore —**inshore of** nearer than (something else) to the shore

**in·side** (in′sīd′, -sīd′; *for prep. & adv., usually* in′sīd′) *n.* **1.** the part within; inner side, surface, or part **2.** the part closest to something implied, as the part of a sidewalk closest to the buildings **3.** [*pl.*] [Colloq.] the internal organs of the body; viscera —*adj.* **1.** on or in the inside; internal **2.** working or used indoors **3.** known only to insiders; secret or private [*the inside story*] —*adv.* **1.** on or to the inside; within **2.** indoors —*prep.* inside of; in; within —**inside of** within the space or time of —**inside out 1.** with the inside where the outside should be; reversed **2.** [Colloq.] thoroughly; completely —**on the inside 1.** in a position of confidence, special advantage or favor, etc. **2.** in one's inner thoughts or feelings

**inside job** [Colloq.] a crime committed by, or with the aid of, a person employed or trusted by the victim

**in·sid·er** (in sī′dər) *n.* **1.** a person inside a given place or group **2.** a person having or likely to have secret or confidential information

**in·sid·i·ous** (in sid′ē əs) *adj.* [< L. < *insidiae*, an ambush < *in-*, in + *sedere*, to sit] **1.** characterized by treachery or slyness; crafty **2.** more dangerous than seems evident [*an insidious disease*] —**in·sid′i·ous·ly** *adv.* —**in·sid′i·ous·ness** *n.*

**in·sight** (in′sīt′) *n.* **1.** the ability to see and understand clearly the inner nature of things, esp. by intuition **2.** a clear understanding of the inner nature of some specific thing —**in′sight′ful** *adj.*

**in·sig·ni·a** (in sig′nē ə) *n.pl.* (*in sense 1*), *n.sing.* (*in sense 2*) [< L., pl. of *insigne*, ult. < *in-*, in + *signum*, a mark] **1.** *sing.* **in·sig′ne** (-nē) badges, emblems, etc., as of rank or membership **2.** *pl.* **in·sig′ni·as** such a badge, emblem, etc.

**in·sig·nif·i·cant** (in′sig nif′ə kənt) *adj.* **1.** having little or no meaning **2.** having little or no importance; trivial **3.** small; unimposing **4.** low in position, character, etc. —**in′sig·nif′i·cance, in′sig·nif′i·can·cy** *n.* —**in′sig·nif′i·cant·ly** *adv.*

**in·sin·cere** (in′sin sir′) *adj.* not sincere; deceptive or hypocritical —**in′sin·cere′ly** *adv.*

**in·sin·cer·i·ty** (-ser′ə tē) *n.* **1.** a being insincere **2.** *pl.* **-ties** an insincere act, remark, etc.

**in·sin·u·ate** (in sin′yoo wāt′) *vt.* **-at′ed, -at′ing** [< L. pp. of *insinuare* < *in-*, in + *sinus*, curved surface] **1.** to introduce or work into gradually, indirectly, and artfully **2.** to hint indirectly; imply —*vi.* to make insinuations —**in·sin′u·at′ing·ly** *adv.* —**in·sin′u·a′tive** *adj.* —**in·sin′u·a′tor** *n.*

**in·sin·u·a·tion** (in sin′yoo wā′shən) *n.* **1.** an insinuating **2.** something insinuated; specif., *a)* a sly hint *b)* an act or remark intended to win favor

**in·sip·id** (in sip′id) *adj.* [< Fr. < LL. < L. *in-*, not + *sapidus*, savory < *sapere*, to taste] **1.** without flavor; tasteless **2.** not exciting; dull; lifeless —**in′si·pid′i·ty, in·sip′id·ness** *n.* —**in·sip′id·ly** *adv.*

**in·sist** (in sist′) *vi.* [< MFr. < L. *insistere* < *in-*, in + *sistere*, to stand] to take and maintain a stand or make a firm demand (often with *on* or *upon*) —*vt.* **1.** to demand strongly **2.** to declare firmly —**in·sist′er** *n.* —**in·sist′ing·ly** *adv.*

**in·sist·ent** (in sis′tənt) *adj.* **1.** insisting or demanding; persistent in demands or assertions **2.** compelling the attention [*an insistent rhythm*] —**in·sist′ence, in·sist′en·cy** *n.* —**in·sist′ent·ly** *adv.*

**‡in si·tu** (in sī′tōō) [L.] in position

**in·snare** (in sner′) *vt.* **-snared′, -snar′ing** same as ENSNARE

**in·so·bri·e·ty** (in′sə brī′ə tē, -sō-) *n.* lack of sobriety; intemperance, esp. in drinking

**in·so·far** (in′sə fär′, -sō-) *adv.* to such a degree or extent (usually with *as*)

**in·sole** (in′sōl′) *n.* **1.** the inside sole of a shoe **2.** an extra, removable inside sole for comfort

**in·so·lent** (in′sə lənt) *adj.* [< L. < *in-*, not + prp. of *solere*, to be accustomed] **1.** boldly disrespectful in speech or behavior; impertinent; impudent **2.** [Now Rare] overbearing —**in′so·lence** *n.* —**in′so·lent·ly** *adv.*

INSOLE

**in·sol·u·ble** (in säl′yoo b′l) *adj.* **1.** that cannot be solved; unsolvable **2.** that cannot be dissolved; not soluble —**in·sol′u·bil′i·ty, in·sol′u·ble·ness** *n.* —**in·sol′u·bly** *adv.*

**in·solv·a·ble** (in säl′və b′l) *adj.* not solvable

**in·sol·vent** (in säl′vənt) *adj.* **1.** not solvent; unable to pay debts; bankrupt **2.** not enough to pay all debts **3.** of insolvents —*n.* an insolvent person —**in·sol′ven·cy** *n., pl.* **-cies**

**in·som·ni·a** (in säm′nē ə) *n.* [< L. < *in-*, without + *somnus*, sleep] abnormally prolonged inability to sleep, esp. when chronic —**in·som′ni·ac′** (-ak′) *n., adj.*

**in·so·much** (in′sō much′, -sə-) *adv.* **1.** to such a degree or extent; so (with *that*) **2.** inasmuch (*as*)

**in·sou·ci·ant** (in sōō′sē ənt) *adj.* [Fr.] calm and unbothered; carefree; indifferent —**in·sou′ci·ance** (-əns) *n.* —**in·sou′ci·ant·ly** *adv.*

**in·spect** (in spekt′) *vt.* [< L. pp. of *inspicere* < *in-*, at + *specere*, to look] **1.** to look at carefully; examine critically **2.** to examine or review (troops, etc.) officially —**in·spec′tive** *adj.*

**in·spec·tion** (in spek′shən) *n.* **1.** careful examination **2.** official examination, as of troops

**in·spec·tor** (in spek′tər) *n.* **1.** one who inspects; official examiner **2.** an officer on a police force, ranking next below a superintendent or police chief —**in·spec′to·ral, in′spec·to′ri·al** (-tôr′ē əl) *adj.* —**in·spec′tor·ship′** *n.*

**in·spi·ra·tion** (in′spə rā′shən) *n.* **1.** a breathing in; inhaling **2.** an inspiring or being inspired mentally or emotionally **3.** *a)* any stimulus to creative thought or action *b)* an inspired idea, action, etc. **4.** a prompting of something written or said **5.** *Theol.* a divine influence upon human beings —**in′spi·ra′tion·al** *adj.* —**in′spi·ra′tion·al·ly** *adv.*

**in·spire** (in spīr′) *vt.* **-spired′, -spir′ing** [< OFr. < L. *inspirare* < *in-*, in + *spirare*, to breathe] **1.** to draw (air) into the lungs; inhale **2.** to influence, stimulate, or impel, as to some creative or effective effort **3.** to guide or motivate by divine influence **4.** to arouse (a thought or feeling) [*kindness inspires* love] **5.** to affect with a specified feeling [praise *inspires* us with confidence] **6.** to cause to be written or said —*vi.* **1.** to inhale **2.** to give inspiration —**in·spir′a·ble** *adj.* —**in·spir′ing·ly** *adv.*

**in·spir·it** (in spir′it) *vt.* to put spirit into; cheer; hearten

**in·spis·sate** (in spis′āt, in′spə sāt′) *vt., vi.* **-sat·ed, -sat·ing** [< LL., ult. < L. *in-*, in + *spissus*, thick] to thicken by evaporation; condense —**in′spis·sa′tion** *n.* —**in′spis·sa′tor** *n.*

**Inst. 1.** Institute **2.** Institution

**inst. 1.** instant (*adj.* 2) **2.** instrumental

**in·sta·bil·i·ty** (in′stə bil′ə tē) *n.* unstable condition; lack of firmness, steadiness, etc.

**in·sta·ble** (in stā′b'l) *adj. same as* UNSTABLE

**in·stall, in·stal** (in stôl′) *vt.* **-stalled′, -stall′ing** [< ML. < *in-*, in + *stallum* < OHG. *stal*, a place] **1.** to place in an office, rank, etc. with formality **2.** to establish in a place or condition [to *install* oneself in a seat] **3.** to fix in position for use [to *install* new fixtures] —**in·stall′er** *n.*

**in·stal·la·tion** (in′stə lā′shən) *n.* **1.** an installing or being installed **2.** apparatus, etc. installed [a heating *installation*] **3.** any military post, camp, base, etc.

**in·stall·ment, in·stal·ment¹** (in stôl′mənt) *n.* [< earlier *estall*, to arrange payments for < OFr. < OHG. *stal*: see INSTALL] **1.** any of the parts of a debt or other sum of money to be paid at regular times over a specified period **2.** any of several parts, as of a serial story, appearing at intervals

**in·stall·ment, in·stal·ment²** (in stôl′mənt) *n.* an installing or being installed; installation

**installment plan** a system by which debts, as for purchased articles, are paid in installments

**in·stance** (in′stəns) *n.* [OFr. < L. *instantia*, a being present < *instans*: see ff.] **1.** an example; case; illustration **2.** a step in proceeding; occasion [in the first *instance*] —*vt.* **-stanced, -stanc·ing 1.** to exemplify **2.** to use as an example; cite —**at the instance of** at the suggestion of —**for instance** as an example

**in·stant** (in′stənt) *adj.* [< MFr. < L. *instans*, prp. of *instare* < *in-*, upon + *stare*, to stand] **1.** urgent; pressing **2.** of the current month [your letter of the 13th *instant*] **3.** soon to happen; imminent **4.** without delay; immediate **5.** designating a food or beverage in readily soluble, concentrated, or precooked form, that can be prepared quickly —*adv.* [Poet.] at once —*n.* **1.** a moment **2.** a particular moment —**the instant** as soon as

**in·stan·ta·ne·ous** (in′stən tā′nē əs, -tān′yəs) *adj.* **1.** done, made, or happening in an instant **2.** done or made without delay; immediate —**in′stan·ta′ne·ous·ly** *adv.* —**in′stan·ta′ne·ous·ness** *n.*

**in·stan·ter** (in stan′tər) *adv.* [L., pressingly] immediately

**in·stant·ly** (in′stənt lē) *adv.* **1.** in an instant; without delay; immediately **2.** [Archaic] urgently; pressingly —*conj.* as soon as; the instant that

**instant replay** the immediate reshowing of an action or play on videotape, as in sports, often in slow motion

**in·state** (in stāt′) *vt.* **-stat′ed, -stat′ing** to put in a particular status, position, or rank; install —**in·state′ment** *n.*

**in·stead** (in sted′) *adv.* [IN + STEAD] in place of the person or thing mentioned [to feel like crying and laugh *instead*] —**instead of** in place of

**in·step** (in′step′) *n.* **1.** the upper part of the arch of the foot, between the ankle and the toes **2.** the part of a shoe or stocking covering this

INSTEP

**in·sti·gate** (in′stə gāt′) *vt.* **-gat′ed, -gat′ing** [< L. pp. of *instigare*, to incite] **1.** to urge on or incite to some action **2.** to cause by inciting [to *instigate* a rebellion] —**in′sti·ga′tion** *n.* —**in′sti·ga′tive** *adj.* —**in′sti·ga′tor** *n.*

**in·still, in·stil** (in stil′) *vt.* **-stilled′, -still′ing** [< MFr. < L. *instillare*, ult. < *in-*, in + *stilla*, a drop] **1.** to put in drop by drop **2.** to put (an idea, feeling, etc.) in or into gradually —**in′stil·la′tion** *n.* —**in·still′er** *n.* —**in·still′ment, in·stil′ment** *n.*

**in·stinct** (in′stiŋkt; *for adj.* in stiŋkt′) *n.* [< L. pp. of *instinguere*, to impel] **1.** (an) inborn tendency to behave in a way characteristic of a species; natural, unacquired response to stimuli [suckling is an *instinct* in mammals] **2.** a natural or acquired tendency or talent; knack; gift [an *instinct* for doing the right thing] —*adj.* filled or charged (with) [a look *instinct* with pity] —**in·stinc·tu·al** (in stiŋk′chōō wəl) *adj.*

**in·stinc·tive** (in stiŋk′tiv) *adj.* **1.** of, or having the nature of, instinct **2.** prompted or done by instinct —**in·stinc′tive·ly** *adv.*

**in·sti·tute** (in′stə tōōt′, -tyōōt′) *vt.* **-tut′ed, -tut′ing** [< L. pp. of *instituere* < *in-*, in + *statuere*, to set up] **1.** to set up; establish; found **2.** to start; initiate [to *institute* a search] **3.** to install in office —*n.* something instituted; specif., *a)* an established principle, law, or custom *b)* an organization for the promotion or teaching of art, science, research, etc. *c)* a school specializing in art, music, technical subjects, etc. *d) same as* INSTITUTION (sense 3) —**in′sti·tut′er, in′sti·tu′tor** *n.*

**in·sti·tu·tion** (in′stə tōō′shən, -tyōō′-) *n.* **1.** an instituting or being instituted; establishment **2.** an established law, custom, practice, etc. **3.** *a)* an organization having a social, educational, or religious purpose, as a school, church, reformatory, etc. *b)* the building housing it **4.** [Colloq.] a well-established person or thing

**in·sti·tu·tion·al** (-'l) *adj.* **1.** of, or having the nature of, an institution **2.** of or to institutions, rather than individuals **3.** of advertising intended primarily to gain prestige rather than immediate sales —**in′sti·tu′tion·al·ly** *adv.*

**in·sti·tu·tion·al·ize** (-īz′) *vt.* **-ized′, -iz′ing 1.** to make into an institution **2.** to make institutional **3.** to place in an institution, as for treatment —**in′sti·tu′tion·al·i·za′tion** *n.*

**instr. 1.** instructor **2.** instrument

**in·struct** (in strukt′) *vt.* [< L. pp. of *instruere*, to erect < *in-*, in + *struere*, to pile up] **1.** to communicate knowledge to; teach **2.** to inform or guide [the judge *instructs* the jury] **3.** to order or direct

**in·struc·tion** (in struk′shən) *n.* **1.** an instructing; education **2.** *a)* knowledge, information, etc. given or taught *b)* a lesson or rule **3.** *a)* a command or order *b)* [*pl.*] directions —**in·struc′tion·al** *adj.*

**in·struc·tive** (-tiv) *adj.* serving to instruct; giving knowledge or information —**in·struc′tive·ly** *adv.* —**in·struc′tive·ness** *n.*

**in·struc·tor** (-tər) *n.* **1.** a teacher **2.** a college teacher ranking below an assistant professor —**in·struc′tor·ship′** *n.* —**in·struc′tress** *n.fem.*

**in·stru·ment** (in′strə mənt) *n.* [< OFr. < L. *instrumentum < instruere*: see INSTRUCT] **1.** *a)* a thing by means of which something is done; means *b)* a person used by another to bring something about **2.** a tool or implement **3.** a device for indicating or measuring conditions, performance, etc., or, sometimes, for controlling operations, esp. in aircraft **4.** any of various devices producing musical sound **5.** *Law* a document, as a deed, contract, etc. —*vt.* to provide with instruments

**in·stru·men·tal** (in′strə men′t'l) *adj.* **1.** serving as a means; helpful (*in* bringing something about) **2.** of or performed with an instrument or tool **3.** of, performed on, or written for a musical instrument or instruments —**in′stru·men′tal·ly** *adv.*

**in·stru·men·tal·ist** (-men′t'l ist) *n.* a person who performs on a musical instrument

**in·stru·men·tal·i·ty** (-men tal′ə tē) *n., pl.* **-ties 1.** a being instrumental **2.** a means or agency

**in·stru·men·ta·tion** (-tā′shən) *n.* **1.** the arrangement of music for instruments  2. a using or equipping with instruments, esp. scientific instruments  3. the instruments used  4. *same as* INSTRUMENTALITY

**in·stru·ment panel** (or **board**) a panel or board with instruments, gauges, etc. mounted on it, as in an automobile or airplane

**in·sub·or·di·nate** (in'sə bôr'd'n it) *adj.* not submitting to authority; disobedient —*n.* an insubordinate person —**in'-sub·or'di·nate·ly** *adv.* —**in'sub·or'di·na'tion** *n.*

**in·sub·stan·tial** (in'səb stan'shəl) *adj.* not substantial; specif., *a*) not real; imaginary  *b*) not solid or firm —**in'-sub·stan'ti·al'i·ty** (-shē al'ə tē) *n.*

**in·suf·fer·a·ble** (in suf'ər ə b'l) *adj.* not sufferable; intolerable; unbearable —**in·suf'fer·a·bly** *adv.*

**in·suf·fi·cien·cy** (in'sə fish'ən sē) *n., pl.* **-cies**  1. lack of sufficiency; deficiency; inadequacy  2. inability of an organ, etc. to function normally

**in·suf·fi·cient** (-ənt) *adj.* not sufficient; inadequate —**in'-suf·fi'cient·ly** *adv.*

**in·su·lar** (in'sə lər, -syoo-) *adj.* [< L. < *insula*, island]  1. of, or in the form of, an island  2. living or situated on an island  3. like an island  4. of or like islanders, esp. when regarded as narrow-minded, illiberal, etc. —**in'su·lar'i·ty** (-lar'ə tē), **in'su·lar·ism** *n.* —**in'su·lar·ly** *adv.*

**in·su·late** (-lāt') *vt.* **-lat'ed, -lat'ing** [< L. *insulatus*, made like an island < *insula*, island]  1. to set apart; detach from the rest; isolate  2. to separate or cover with a nonconducting material in order to prevent the passage or leakage of electricity, heat, sound, etc.

**in·su·la·tion** (in'sə lā'shən, -syoo-) *n.*  1. an insulating or being insulated  2. any material used to insulate

**in·su·la·tor** (in'sə lāt'ər, -syoo-) *n.* anything that insulates; esp., a device of glass or porcelain for insulating electric wires

**in·su·lin** (in'sə lin, -syoo-) *n.* [< L. *insula*, island + -IN[1]: referring to islands of special tissue in the pancreas]  1. a secretion of the pancreas, which helps the body use sugar and other carbohydrates  2. an extract from the pancreas of sheep, oxen, etc., used hypodermically in the treatment of diabetes mellitus

**in·sult** (in sult'; *for n.* in'sult) *vt.* [< MFr. < L. *insultare* < *in-*, in, on + *saltare*, freq. of *salire*, to leap] to treat or speak to with scorn, insolence, or disrespect —*n.*  1. an insulting act, remark, etc.  2. *Med.* injury to tissues or organs —**in·sult'er** *n.* —**in·sult'ing** *adj.* —**in·sult'ing·ly** *adv.*

**in·su·per·a·ble** (in soo'pər ə b'l, -syoo'-) *adj.* not superable; that cannot be overcome or passed over; insurmountable —**in·su'per·a·bil'i·ty** *n.* —**in·su'per·a·bly** *adv.*

**in·sup·port·a·ble** (in'sə pôrt'ə b'l) *adj.* not supportable; specif., *a*) intolerable  *b*) incapable of being upheld —**in'sup·port'a·bly** *adv.*

**in·sur·ance** (in shoor'əns) *n.*  1. an insuring or being insured against loss by fire, accident, death, etc.  2. *a*) a contract (**insurance policy**) whereby the insurer guarantees the insured that a certain sum will be paid for a specified loss  *b*) the premium specified for such a contract  3. the amount for which life, property, etc. is insured  4. the business of insuring against loss

**in·sure** (in shoor') *vt.* **-sured', -sur'ing** [SEE ENSURE]  1. to take out or issue insurance on (something or someone)  2. *same as* ENSURE —*vi.* to give or take out insurance —**in·sur'a·bil'i·ty** *n.* —**in·sur'a·ble** *adj.*

**in·sured** (in shoord') *n.* a person whose life, property, etc. is insured against loss

**in·sur·er** (in shoor'ər) *n.* a person or company that insures others against loss or damage

**in·sur·gence** (in sur'jəns) *n.* a rising in revolt; insurrection: also **in·sur'gen·cy**

**in·sur·gent** (-jənt) *adj.* [< L. prp. of *insurgere* < *in-*, upon + *surgere*, to rise: see SURGE] rising up against established authority —*n.* one engaged in insurgent activity —**in·sur'-gent·ly** *adv.*

**in·sur·mount·a·ble** (in'sər moun'tə b'l) *adj.* not surmountable; that cannot be overcome —**in'sur·mount'a·bil'i·ty** *n.* —**in'sur·mount'a·bly** *adv.*

**in·sur·rec·tion** (in'sə rek'shən) *n.* [< MFr. < LL. < pp. of L. *insurgere*: see INSURGENT] a rising up against established authority; rebellion; revolt —**in'sur·rec'tion·al** *adj.* —**in'sur·rec'tion·ar'y** *adj., n., pl.* **-ar'ies** —**in'sur·rec'tion·ist** *n.*

**in·sus·cep·ti·ble** (in'sə sep'tə b'l) *adj.* not susceptible (*to* or *of*); not easily affected or influenced —**in'sus·cep'ti·bil'i·ty** *n.* —**in'sus·cep'ti·bly** *adv.*

**int.**  1. interest  2. interior  3. internal  4. international  5. intransitive

**in·tact** (in takt') *adj.* [< L. < *in-*, not + *tactus*, pp. of *tan-*

*gere*, to touch] with nothing missing or injured; kept or left whole —**in·tact'ness** *n.*

**in·ta·gli·o** (in tal'yō, -tāl'-) *n., pl.* **-ios** [It. < *in-*, in + *tagliare*, to cut < LL. *taliare*: see TAILOR]  1. a design or figure carved or engraved below the surface  2. a gem or stone ornamented in this way  3. the art of making such designs or figures —*vt.* **-ioed, -io·ing** to carve, etc. in intaglio

**in·take** (in'tāk') *n.*  1. a taking in  2. the amount or thing taken in  3. the place at which a fluid is taken into a pipe, channel, etc.

**in·tan·gi·ble** (in tan'jə b'l) *adj.* not tangible; specif., *a*) that cannot be touched  *b*) representing value that is neither intrinsic nor material [good will is an *intangible* asset]  *c*) hard to define or grasp —*n.* something intangible —**in·tan'gi·bil'i·ty** *n., pl.* **-ties** —**in·tan'gi·bly** *adv.*

**in·te·ger** (in'tə jər) *n.* [L., untouched, whole]  1. anything complete in itself; whole  2. any whole number or zero: distinguished from FRACTION

**in·te·gral** (in'tə grəl; *also, exc. for adj. 4*, in teg'rəl) *adj.* [< prec.]  1. necessary for completeness; essential  2. whole or complete  3. made up of parts forming a whole  4. *Math.* of or having to do with integers; not fractional —*n.* a whole —**in'te·gral'i·ty** (-gral'ə tē) *n.* —**in'te·gral·ly** *adv.*

**integral calculus** the branch of higher mathematics dealing with the process (*integration*) of finding the quantity or function of which a given quantity or function is the differential

**in·te·grate** (-grāt') *vt.* **-grat'ed, -grat'ing** [< L. pp. of *integrare* < *integer*, whole]  1. to make whole or complete  2. to bring (parts) together into a whole; unify  3. to indicate the sum or total of  4. to remove legal and social barriers imposing segregation upon (racial groups) or in (schools, etc.) —*vi.* to become integrated —**in'te·gra'-tion** *n.* —**in'te·gra'tive** *adj.* —**in'te·gra'tor** *n.*

**integrated circuit** an electronic circuit containing interconnected amplifying devices formed on a single body, or chip, of semiconductor material

**in·te·gra·tion·ist** (-grā'shən ist) *n.* one who advocates integration, esp. of racial groups —*adj.* believing in or advocating integration

**in·teg·ri·ty** (in teg'rə tē) *n.* [see INTEGER]  1. a being complete; wholeness  2. unimpaired condition; soundness  3. uprightness, honesty, and sincerity

**in·teg·u·ment** (in teg'yoo mənt) *n.* [< L. < *in-*, upon + *tegere*, to cover] an outer covering, as of the body or of a plant; skin, shell, hide, etc. —**in·teg'u·men'ta·ry** *adj.*

**in·tel·lect** (in't'l ekt') *n.* [< L. < pp. of *intellegere*, to understand < *inter-*, between + *legere*, to choose]  1. the ability to reason or understand  2. great mental ability; high intelligence  3. *a*) a mind or intelligence  *b*) a person of high intelligence

**in·tel·lec·tu·al** (in't'l ek'choo wəl) *adj.*  1. of, pertaining to, or appealing to the intellect  2. *a*) requiring or involving the intellect  *b*) inclined toward intellectual activities  3. showing high intelligence —*n.* a person having intellectual tastes or work —**in'tel·lec'tu·al'i·ty** (-choo wal'ə tē) *n.* —**in'tel·lec'tu·al·ly** *adv.*

**in·tel·lec·tu·al·ism** (-iz'm) *n.* a being intellectual; devotion to intellectual pursuits —**in'tel·lec'tu·al·ist** *n.* —**in'-tel·lec'tu·al·is'tic** *adj.*

**in·tel·li·gence** (in tel'ə jəns) *n.* [< OFr. < L. *intelligentia* < prp. of *intelligere*: see INTELLECT]  1. *a*) the ability to learn or understand from experience; mental ability  *b*) the ability to respond successfully to a new situation  *c*) any degree of cleverness, shrewdness, etc.  2. news or information  3. *a*) the gathering of secret information, as for military purposes  *b*) the persons or agency employed at this  4. an intelligent being

**intelligence quotient** a number indicating a person's level of intelligence: it is the mental age (as shown by intelligence tests) multiplied by 100 and divided by the chronological age

**intelligence test** a series of problems intended to test the intelligence of an individual

**in·tel·li·gent** (-jənt) *adj.*  1. having or using intelligence  2. having or showing high intelligence; bright, clever, wise, etc.  3. [Archaic] aware (*of* something) —**in·tel'li·gent·ly** *adv.*

**in·tel·li·gent·si·a** (in tel'ə jent'sē ə, -gent'-) *n.pl.* [*also with sing. v.*] [< Russ. < L.: see INTELLIGENCE] the people regarded as, or regarding themselves as, the educated class; intellectuals collectively

**in·tel·li·gi·ble** (in tel'i jə b'l) *adj.* [< L. < *intelligere*: see INTELLECT] that can be understood; clear; comprehensible —**in·tel'li·gi·bil'i·ty** *n.* —**in·tel'li·gi·bly** *adv.*

**in·tem·per·ance** (in tem'pər əns) *n.*  1. a lack of temperance or restraint; immoderation  2. excessive drinking of alcoholic liquor

**in·tem·per·ate** (-it) *adj.*  1. not temperate; specif., *a*) not moderate; excessive  *b*) severe or violent [an *intemper-*

COMMON GLASS

PETTICOAT

PORCELAIN

HIGH TENSION

INSULATORS

ate wind/ **2.** drinking too much alcoholic liquor —**in·tem'·per·ate·ly** *adv.*

**in·tend** (in tend') *vt.* [< OFr. < L. *intendere,* to aim at < *in-,* at + *tendere,* to stretch] **1.** to have in mind as a purpose; plan; purpose **2.** to mean (something) to be or be used (*for*); design; destine **3.** to mean or signify —*vi.* to have a purpose or intention —**in·tend'er** *n.*

**in·tend·ant** (in ten'dənt) *n.* [Fr. < L. prp. of *intendere:* see INTEND] a director, manager of a public business, superintendent, etc.

**in·tend·ed** (-did) *adj.* **1.** meant; planned; purposed **2.** prospective; future —*n.* [Colloq.] the person whom one has agreed to marry

**intens. 1.** intensified **2.** intensifier **3.** intensive

**in·tense** (in tens') *adj.* [< MFr. < L. pp. of *intendere:* see INTEND] **1.** occurring or existing in a high degree; very strong /an *intense* light/ **2.** strained to the utmost; earnest [*intense* thought] **3.** having or showing strong emotion, great seriousness, etc. **4.** characterized by much action, emotion, etc. —**in·tense'ly** *adv.* —**in·tense'ness** *n.*

**in·ten·si·fy** (in ten'sə fī') *vt., vi.* -**fied'**, -**fy'ing** to make or become intense or more intense; increase; strengthen —**in·ten'si·fi·ca'tion** *n.* —**in·ten'si·fi'er** *n.*

**in·ten·si·ty** (in ten'sə tē) *n., pl.* -**ties 1.** a being intense; specif., *a)* extreme degree of anything *b)* great energy or vehemence, as of emotion **2.** relative strength, magnitude, etc. **3.** the degree of purity of color; saturation **4.** *Physics* the amount of force or energy of heat, light, sound, etc. per unit area, volume, etc.

**in·ten·sive** (-siv) *adj.* **1.** of or characterized by intensity; thorough; exhaustive **2.** designating very attentive hospital care given to patients, as after surgery **3.** *Agric.* designating a system of farming which aims at the increase of crop yield per unit area **4.** *Gram.* giving force or emphasis (Ex.: "very" in "the very same man") —*n.* **1.** anything that intensifies **2.** an intensive word, prefix, etc. —**in·ten'sive·ly** *adv.* —**in·ten'sive·ness** *n.*

**in·tent** (in tent') *adj.* [< L. pp. of *intendere:* see INTEND] **1.** firmly directed; earnest **2.** *a)* having the attention firmly fixed; engrossed *b)* strongly resolved [*intent* on going/ —*n.* **1.** an intending **2.** something intended; specif., *a)* a purpose; aim *b)* meaning or import **3.** *Law* one's mental attitude at the time of doing an act —**to all intents and purposes** in almost every respect —**in·tent'ly** *adv.* —**in·tent'ness** *n.*

**in·ten·tion** (in ten'shən) *n.* **1.** an intending; determination to do a specified thing or act in a specified way **2.** *a)* anything intended; aim or purpose *b)* [*pl.*] purpose in regard to marriage

**in·ten·tion·al** (-shən 'l) *adj.* **1.** having to do with intention **2.** done purposely; intended —**in·ten'tion·al·ly** *adv.*

**in·ter** (in tʉr') *vt.* -**terred'**, -**ter'ring** [< OFr. < L. *in,* in + *terra,* earth] to put (a dead body) into a grave or tomb

**in·ter-** [L. < *inter, prep.*] *a combining form meaning:* **1.** between or among [*interstate*] **2.** with or on each other (or one another), together, mutual, reciprocal, mutually, or reciprocally [*interact*]

**in·ter·act** (in'tər akt') *vi.* to act on one another —**in'ter·ac'tion** *n.* —**in'ter·ac'tive** *adj.*

‡**in·ter a·li·a** (in'tər ā'lē ə) [L.] among other things

**in·ter·breed** (in'tər brēd') *vt., vi.* -**bred'**, -**breed'ing** *same as* HYBRIDIZE

**in·ter·ca·lar·y** (in tʉr'kə ler'ē) *adj.* [< L.: see ff.] added to the calendar: said of an extra day, month, etc. inserted in a calendar year to make it correspond to the solar year

**in·ter·ca·late** (-lāt') *vt.* -**lat'ed**, -**lat'ing** [< L. pp. of *intercalare,* to insert < *inter-,* between + *calare,* to call] **1.** to insert (a day, month, etc.) in the calendar **2.** to interpolate or insert —**in·ter'ca·la'tion** *n.*

**in·ter·cede** (in'tər sēd') *vi.* -**ced'ed**, -**ced'ing** [< L. < *inter-,* between + *cedere,* to go] **1.** to plead in behalf of another or others **2.** to intervene for the purpose of producing agreement; mediate —**in'ter·ced'er** *n.*

**in·ter·cel·lu·lar** (-sel'yoo lər) *adj.* located between or among cells

**in·ter·cept** (in'tər sept'; *for n.* in'tər sept') *vt.* [< L. pp. of *intercipere* < *inter-,* between + *capere,* to take] **1.** to seize, stop, or interrupt on the way; cut off /to *intercept* a message/ **2.** *Math.* to mark off between two points, lines, or planes —*n.* **1.** *Math.* the part of a line, plane, etc. intercepted **2.** *Mil.* the intercepting of enemy aircraft, missiles, etc. —**in'ter·cep'tion** *n.* —**in'ter·cep'tive** *adj.* —**in'ter·cep'tor, in'ter·cep'ter** *n.*

**in·ter·ces·sion** (in'tər sesh'ən) *n.* an interceding; mediation, pleading, or prayer in behalf of another or others

**in·ter·ces·sor** (in'tər ses'ər, in'tər ses'ər) *n.* a person who intercedes —**in'ter·ces'so·ry** *adj.*

**in·ter·change** (in'tər chānj'; *for n.* in'tər chānj') *vt.* -**changed'**, -**chang'ing 1.** to give and take mutually; exchange /to *interchange* ideas/ **2.** to put (each of two things) in the other's place **3.** to alternate /to *interchange* work with play/ —*vi.* to change places with each other —*n.* **1.** an interchanging **2.** a place on a freeway where traffic can enter or depart, usually by means of a cloverleaf

**in·ter·change·a·ble** (in'tər chān'jə b'l) *adj.* that can be interchanged, esp. in position or use —**in'ter·change'a·bil'i·ty** *n.* —**in'ter·change'a·bly** *adv.*

**in·ter·col·le·gi·ate** (-kə lē'jət, -jē ət) *adj.* between or among colleges and universities

**in·ter·com** (in'tər käm') *n.* a radio or telephone intercommunication system, as between rooms of a building

**in·ter·com·mu·ni·cate** (in'tər kə myoo'nə kāt') *vt., vi.* -**cat'ed**, -**cat'ing** to communicate with or to each other or one another —**in'ter·com·mu·ni·ca'tion** *n.*

**in·ter·con·nect** (-kə nekt') *vt., vi.* to connect with one another —**in'ter·con·nec'tion** *n.*

**in·ter·cos·tal** (-käs't'l) *adj.* [see INTER- & COSTAL] between the ribs —**in'ter·cos'tal·ly** *adv.*

**in·ter·course** (in'tər kôrs') *n.* [< OFr. < L.: see INTER- & COURSE] **1.** communication or dealings between or among people, countries, etc.; interchange of products, services, ideas, etc. **2.** the sexual joining of two individuals; copulation: in full, **sexual intercourse**

**in·ter·de·nom·i·na·tion·al** (in'tər di näm'ə nā'shən 'l) *adj.* between, among, shared by, or involving different religious denominations

**in·ter·de·part·men·tal** (-di pärt'men't'l) *adj.* between or among departments

**in·ter·de·pend·ence** (-di pen'dəns) *n.* dependence on each other; mutual dependence: also **in'ter·de·pend'en·cy** —**in'ter·de·pend'ent** *adj.* —**in'ter·de·pend'ent·ly** *adv.*

**in·ter·dict** (in'tər dikt'; *for n.* in'tər dikt') *vt.* [< OFr. < L. pp. of *interdicere,* to forbid < *inter-,* between + *dicere,* to speak] **1.** to prohibit (an action); forbid with authority **2.** to restrain from doing or using something **3.** to hinder (the enemy) or isolate (an area, etc.) by bombing, etc. **4.** *R.C.Ch.* to exclude (a person, parish, etc.) from certain acts or privileges —*n.* an official prohibition or restraint; specif., *R.C.Ch.* an interdicting of a person, parish, etc. —**in'ter·dic'tion** *n.* —**in'ter·dic'to·ry, in'ter·dic'tive** *adj.*

**in·ter·dis·ci·pli·nar·y** (-dis'ə pli ner'ē) *adj.* involving two or more disciplines, or branches of learning

**in·ter·est** (in'trist, in'tər ist; *for v. also* -tə rest') *n.* [< ML. *interesse,* compensation < L. < *inter-,* between + *esse,* to be: altered after OFr. *interest* < L., it interests] **1.** a right or claim to something **2.** *a)* a share or participation in something *b)* anything in which one participates or has a share **3.** [*often pl.*] advantage; welfare; benefit **4.** [*usually pl.*] a group of people having a common concern or dominant power in some industry, occupation, cause, etc. /the steel *interests*/ **5.** *a)* a feeling of intentness, concern, or curiosity about something *b)* the power of causing this feeling *c)* something causing this feeling **6.** importance; consequence /a matter of little *interest*/ **7.** *a)* money paid for the use of money *b)* the rate of such payment, expressed as a percentage per unit of time **8.** an increase over what is owed /to repay kindness with *interest*/ —*vt.* **1.** to cause to have an interest (*in*) **2.** to excite the attention or curiosity of —**in the interest** (or **interests**) **of** for the sake of

**in·ter·est·ed** (-id) *adj.* **1.** having an interest or share **2.** influenced by personal interest; prejudiced **3.** feeling or showing interest, or curiosity —**in'ter·est·ed·ly** *adv.*

**in·ter·est·ing** (-in) *adj.* exciting interest, curiosity, or attention —**in'ter·est·ing·ly** *adv.*

**in·ter·face** (in'tər fās') *n.* **1.** a plane forming the common boundary between two parts of matter or space **2.** a point or means of interaction between two systems, disciplines, groups, etc. —*vt., vi.* -**faced'**, -**fac'ing** to interconnect with another system, discipline, group, etc.

**in·ter·faith** (in'tər fāth') *adj.* between or involving persons adhering to different religions

**in·ter·fere** (in'tər fir') *vi.* -**fered'**, -**fer'ing** [< OFr. < *entre-,* INTER- + *férir* < L. *ferire,* to strike] **1.** to come into collision or opposition; clash; conflict **2.** to come between for some purpose; intervene **3.** *Sports* to be guilty of interference **4.** *Physics* to affect each other by interference: said of vibrating waves —**interfere with** to hinder; prevent —**in'ter·fer'er** *n.* —**in'ter·fer'ing·ly** *adv.*

**in·ter·fer·ence** (-fir'əns) *n.* **1.** an interfering **2.** something that interferes **3.** *a) Football* the legal blocking of opposing players in order to clear the way for the ball carrier b) *Sports* the illegal hindering of an opposing player **4.** *Physics* the mutual action of two waves of vibration, as of sound, light, etc., in reinforcing or neutralizing each other **5.** *Radio & TV* static, unwanted signals, etc., producing a distortion of sounds or images

**in·ter·fer·on** (-fir'än) *n.* [INTERFER(E) + -on, arbitrary suffix] a cellular protein produced by the body to inhibit growth of an infecting virus

**in·ter·fold** (-fōld') *vt., vi.* to fold together or inside one another

**in·ter·fuse** (-fyoōz') *vt.* -fused', -fus'ing **1.** to combine by mixing, blending, or fusing together **2.** to spread itself through; pervade —*vi.* to fuse; blend —**in'ter·fu'sion** *n.*

**in·ter·group** (in'tər grōōp') *adj.* between or involving different social, ethnic, or racial groups

**in·ter·im** (in'tər im) *n.* [L., meanwhile < *inter*, between] the period of time between; meantime —*adj.* temporary; provisional [an *interim* council]

**in·te·ri·or** (in tir'ē ər) *adj.* [< MFr. < L., compar. of *inter*, between] **1.** situated within; inner **2.** away from the coast, border, etc.; inland **3.** of the domestic affairs of a country **4.** private —*n.* **1.** the interior part of anything; specif., *a)* the inside of a room or building *b)* the inland part of a country or region *c)* the inner nature of a person or thing **2.** the domestic affairs of a country [the U.S. Department of the *Interior*] —**in·te'ri·or'i·ty** (-ôr'ə tē) *n.* —**in·te'ri·or·ly** *adv.*

**interior angle** any of the four angles formed on the inside of two straight lines by a straight line cutting across them: cf. EXTERIOR ANGLE

**interior decoration** the decorating and furnishing of the interior of a room, house, etc.

**in·te·ri·or·ize** (-īz') *vt.* -ized', -iz'ing to make (a concept, value, etc.) part of one's inner nature

**interj.** interjection

**in·ter·ject** (in'tər jekt') *vt.* [< L. pp. of *interjicere* < *inter-*, between + *jacere*, to throw] to throw in between; insert; interpose —**in'ter·jec'tor** *n.*

**in·ter·jec·tion** (-jek'shən) *n.* **1.** an interjecting **2.** something interjected, as a word or phrase **3.** *Gram.* an exclamatory word or phrase (Ex.: ah! well!) —**in'ter·jec'-tion·al, in'ter·jec'to·ry** *adj.*

**in·ter·lace** (-lās') *vt., vi.* -laced', -lac'ing [< OFr.: see IN-TER- & LACE] **1.** to unite by passing over and under each other; weave together **2.** to connect intricately —**in'ter·lace'ment** *n.*

**in·ter·lard** (-lärd') *vt.* [< Fr.: see INTER- & LARD] **1.** to intersperse; diversify [to *interlard* a lecture with quotations] **2.** to be intermixed in

**in·ter·lay** (-lā') *vt.* -laid' (-lād'), -lay'ing to lay or put between or among —**in'ter·lay'er** *n.*

**in·ter·leaf** (in'tər lēf') *n., pl.* -leaves' (-lēvz') a leaf, usually blank, bound between the other leaves of a book, for notes, etc. —**in'ter·leave'** (-lēv') *vt.* -leaved', -leav'ing

**in·ter·line**[1] (in'tər līn') *vt.* -lined', -lin'ing to write or print (something) between the lines of (a text, document, etc.) —**in'ter·lin'e·a'tion** (-lin'ē ā'shən) *n.*

**in·ter·line**[2] (in'tər līn') *vt.* -lined', -lin'ing to put a lining between the outer material and the ordinary lining of (a garment)

**in·ter·lin·e·ar** (in'tər lin'ē ər) *adj.* **1.** written or printed between the lines **2.** having the same text in different languages printed in alternate lines Also **in'ter·lin'e·al**

**in·ter·lin·ing** (in'tər lī'niŋ) *n.* a lining between the outer cloth and the ordinary lining

**in·ter·link** (in'tər liŋk') *vt.* to link together

**in·ter·lock** (-läk') *vt., vi.* to lock together; join with one another —*n.* a being interlocked

**interlocking directorates** boards of directors having some members in common, so that their corporations are more or less under the same control

**in·ter·loc·u·tor** (-läk'yə tər; *for 2, often* -läk'ə tər) *n.* [< L. pp. < *inter*, between + *loqui*, to talk] **1.** a person taking part in a conversation **2.** the master of ceremonies in a minstrel show

**in·ter·loc·u·to·ry** (-läk'yə tôr'ē) *adj.* **1.** of, having the nature of, or occurring in dialogue; conversational **2.** *Law* pronounced during the course of a suit, pending final decision

**in·ter·lop·er** (in'tər lō'pər) *n.* [prob. < INTER- + LOPE] a person who meddles in others' affairs

**in·ter·lude** (in'tər lōōd') *n.* [< OFr. < ML. < L. *inter*, between + *ludus*, play] **1.** a short, humorous play formerly presented between the parts of a miracle play or morality play **2.** any performance between the acts of a play **3.** music played between the parts of a song, play, etc. **4.** anything that fills time between two events

**in·ter·mar·ry** (in'tər mar'ē) *vi.* -ried, -ry·ing to become connected by marriage: said of persons of different races, religions, etc. —**in'ter·mar'riage** *n.*

**in·ter·med·dle** (-med'l) *vi.* -dled, -dling to meddle in the affairs of others —**in'ter·med'dler** *n.*

**in·ter·me·di·ar·y** (-mē'dē er'ē) *adj.* **1.** acting between two persons; acting as a mediator **2.** intermediate —*n., pl.* -ar'ies a go-between; mediator

**in·ter·me·di·ate** (-mē'dē it; *for v.* -āt') *adj.* [< ML. < L. < *inter-*, between + *medius*, middle] being or happening between; in the middle —*n.* **1.** anything intermediate **2.** *same as* INTERMEDIARY —*vi.* -at'ed, -at'ing to act as an intermediary; mediate —**in'ter·me'di·ate·ly** *adv.* —**in'ter·me'di·ate·ness, in'ter·me'di·a·cy** (-ə sē) *n.* —**in'ter·me'di·a'tion** *n.* —**in'ter·me'di·a'tor** *n.*

**in·ter·ment** (in tur'mənt) *n.* an interring; burial

**in·ter·mez·zo** (in'tər met'sō, -med'zō) *n., pl.* -zos, -zi (-sē, -zē) [It.] **1.** a short, light musical entertainment between the acts of a play or opera **2.** *Music a)* a short movement connecting the main parts of a composition *b)* any of certain short works similar to this

**in·ter·mi·na·ble** (in tur'mi nə b'l) *adj.* not terminable; lasting, or seeming to last, forever; endless —**in·ter'mi·na·bly** *adv.*

**in·ter·min·gle** (in'tər miŋ'g'l) *vt., vi.* -gled, -gling to mix together; mingle; blend

**in·ter·mis·sion** (-mish'ən) *n.* **1.** an intermitting or being intermitted; interruption **2.** an interval of time between periods of activity; pause, as between acts of a play

**in·ter·mit** (-mit') *vt., vi.* -mit'ted, -mit'ting [< L. < *inter-*, between + *mittere*, to send] to stop for a time; cease at intervals

**in·ter·mit·tent** (-mit''nt) *adj.* stopping and starting again at intervals; periodic —**in'ter·mit'tence** *n.* —**in'ter·mit'-tent·ly** *adv.*

**in·ter·mix** (-miks') *vt., vi.* to mix together; blend —**in'ter·mix'ture** *n.*

**in·tern** (in'tərn; *for vt. usually in* turn') *n.* [< Fr. < L. *internus*, internal] **1.** a doctor serving as an assistant resident in a hospital, generally just after graduation from medical school **2.** an apprentice teacher, journalist, etc. —*vi.* to serve as an intern —*vt.* to detain and confine within a country or a definite area [to *intern* aliens in time of war] —**in·tern'ment** *n.*

**in·ter·nal** (in tur'n'l) *adj.* [< ML. < L. *internus*] **1.** of or on the inside; inner **2.** to be taken inside the body [*internal* remedies] **3.** of or belonging to the inner nature of a thing; intrinsic [*internal* evidence] **4.** of or belonging to a person's inner nature or mind; subjective **5.** domestic; nonforeign [*internal* revenue] —**in'ter·nal'i·ty** (-nal'ə tē) *n.* —**in·ter'nal·ly** *adv.*

**in·ter·nal-com·bus·tion engine** (-kəm bus'chən) an engine, as in an automobile, in which the power is produced by the combustion of a fuel-and-air mixture within the cylinders

**in·ter·nal·ize** (in tur'n'l īz') *vt.* -ized', -iz'ing to make internal; specif., to make (others' ideas, values, etc.) a part of one's own patterns of thinking —**in·ter'nal·i·za'tion** *n.*

**internal medicine** the branch of medicine dealing with the diagnosis and nonsurgical treatment of diseases

**internal revenue** governmental income from taxes on income, profits, luxuries, etc.

**in·ter·na·tion·al** (in'tər nash'ən 'l) *adj.* **1.** between or among nations [an *international* treaty] **2.** concerned with the relations between nations [an *international* court] **3.** for the use of all nations [*international* waters] **4.** of, for, or by people in various nations —*n.* an international organization; esp., [I-] any of several international socialist organizations in existence variously from 1864 on —**in'ter·na'tion·al'i·ty** *n.* —**in'ter·na'tion·al·ly** *adv.*

**international date line** *same as* DATE LINE

**in·ter·na·tion·al·ism** (in'tər nash'ən 'l iz'm) *n.* the principle of international cooperation for the common good —**in'ter·na'tion·al·ist** *n.*

**in·ter·na·tion·al·ize** (-īz') *vt.* -ized', -iz'ing to make international; bring under international control —**in'ter·na'tion·al·i·za'tion** *n.*

**International Phonetic Alphabet** a set of phonetic symbols for international use: each symbol represents a single sound, whether the sound occurs in only one language or in more than one

**in·terne** (in'tərn) *n. same as* INTERN

**in·ter·ne·cine** (in'tər nē'sin, -sin; -nes'/'n) *adj.* [< L. < *inter-*, between + *necare*, to kill] mutually destructive or harmful [*internecine* warfare]

**in·ter·nee** (in'tər nē') *n.* a person interned as a prisoner of war or enemy alien

**in·ter·nist** (in'tər nist, in tur'nist) *n.* a doctor who specializes in internal medicine

**in·tern·ship** (in'tərn ship') *n.* **1.** the position of an intern **2.** the period of service as an intern

**in·ter·of·fice** (in'tər ôf'is, -äf'-) *adj.* between or among the offices within an organization

**in·ter·pel·late** (in'tər pel'āt, in tur'pə lāt') *vt.* -lat·ed, -lat·ing [< L. pp. of *interpellare*, to interrupt < *inter-*, between + *pellere*, to drive] to ask (a cabinet minister, etc.) formally for an explanation of his action or policy: a form of political challenge in some national legislatures —**in′ter·pel′lant** *adj., n.* —**in′ter·pel·la′tion** *n.*

**in·ter·pen·e·trate** (-pen′ə trāt′) *vt.* -trat′ed, -trat′ing to penetrate thoroughly; permeate —*vi.* to penetrate mutually —**in′ter·pen′e·tra′tion** *n.*

**in·ter·per·son·al** (-pur′sə n′l) *adj.* **1.** between persons **2.** of or involving relations between persons —**in′ter·per′son·al·ly** *adv.*

**in·ter·phone** (in′tər fōn′) *n.* an intercom telephone system, as between office departments

**in·ter·plan·e·tar·y** (in′tər plan′ə ter′ē) *adj.* **1.** between planets **2.** within the solar system but outside the atmosphere of any planet or the sun

**in·ter·play** (in′tər plā′) *n.* action, effect, or influence on each other or one another; interaction

**in·ter·po·late** (in tur′pə lāt′) *vt.* -lat′ed, -lat′ing [< L. < *inter-*, between + *polire*, to polish] **1.** to change (a book, text, etc.) by putting in new words, subject matter, etc. **2.** to insert between or among others [to *interpolate* a remark] **3.** *Math.* to estimate a missing value by taking an average of known values at neighboring points —*vi.* to make interpolations —**in·ter′po·lat′er, in·ter′po·la′tor** *n.* —**in·ter′po·la′tion** *n.* —**in·ter′po·la′tive** *adj.*

**in·ter·pose** (in′tər pōz′) *vt.* -posed′, -pos′ing **1.** to place between; insert **2.** to introduce by way of intervention **3.** to put in as an interruption —*vi.* **1.** to be or come between **2.** to intervene **3.** to interrupt —**in′ter·pos′al** *n.* —**in′ter·pos′er** *n.* —**in′ter·po·si′tion** (-pə zish′ən) *n.*

**in·ter·pret** (in tur′prit) *vt.* [< MFr. < L. *interpretari* < *interpres*, negotiator] **1.** to explain the meaning of; clarify **2.** to translate (oral remarks) **3.** to have one's own understanding of; construe [to *interpret* a laugh as derisive] **4.** to bring out the meaning of; esp., to give one's own conception of, as in performing a play —*vi.* to act as an interpreter; translate —**in·ter′pret·a·ble** *adj.* —**in·ter′pre·tive, in·ter′pre·ta′tive** *adj.*

**in·ter·pre·ta·tion** (in tur′prə tā′shən) *n.* **1.** the act or result of interpreting; explanation, translation, etc. **2.** the expression of a person's conception of a work of art, subject, etc. through acting, writing, etc. —**in·ter′pre·ta′tion·al** *adj.*

**in·ter·pret·er** (in tur′prə tər) *n.* a person who interprets; specif., a person whose work is translating a foreign language orally

**in·ter·ra·cial** (in′tər rā′shəl) *adj.* between, among, or for persons of different races

**in·ter·reg·num** (-reg′nəm) *n., pl.* -reg′nums, -reg′na (-nə) [L. < *inter-*, between + *regnum*, a REIGN] **1.** an interval between two successive reigns, when the country has no sovereign **2.** any period without the usual ruler, governor, etc. **3.** any break in a series or in a continuity

**in·ter·re·late** (-ri lāt′) *vt., vi.* -lat′ed, -lat′ing to make, be, or become mutually related —**in′ter·re·la′tion** *n.* —**in′ter·re·la′tion·ship** *n.*

**in·ter·ro·gate** (in ter′ə gāt′) *vt.* -gat′ed, -gat′ing [< L. pp. of *interrogare* < *inter-*, between + *rogare*, to ask] to ask questions of formally in examining [to *interrogate* a witness] —*vi.* to ask questions —**in·ter′ro·ga′tor** *n.*

**in·ter·ro·ga·tion** (in ter′ə gā′shən) *n.* **1.** an interrogating or being interrogated; examination **2.** a question —**in·ter′ro·ga′tion·al** *adj.*

**interrogation mark** (or **point**) *same as* QUESTION MARK

**in·ter·rog·a·tive** (in′tə räg′ə tiv) *adj.* asking, or having the form of, a question —*n.* an interrogative word, element, etc. (Ex.: what? where?) —**in′ter·rog′a·tive·ly** *adv.*

**in·ter·rog·a·to·ry** (-ə tôr′ē) *adj.* expressing a question —*n., pl.* -ries a formal set of questions —**in′ter·rog′a·to′ri·ly** *adv.*

**in·ter·rupt** (in′tə rupt′) *vt.* [< L. pp. of *interrumpere* < *inter-*, between + *rumpere*, to break] **1.** *a)* to break into (a discussion, etc.) *b)* to break in upon (a person) while he is speaking, working, etc. **2.** to make a break in the continuity of; obstruct —*vi.* to make an interruption —**in′ter·rupt′er** *n.* —**in′ter·rup′tive** *adj.*

**in·ter·rup·tion** (in′tə rup′shən) *n.* **1.** an interrupting or being interrupted **2.** anything that interrupts **3.** an intermission

**in·ter·scho·las·tic** (in′tər skə las′tik) *adj.* between or among schools [an *interscholastic* debate]

**in·ter·sect** (in′tər sekt′) *vt.* [< L. pp. of *intersecare* < *inter-*, between + *secare*, to cut] to divide into two parts by passing through or across —*vi.* to cross each other

**in·ter·sec·tion** (-sek′shən) *n.* **1.** an intersecting **2.** a place of intersecting; specif., *a)* the point or line where two lines or surfaces meet or cross *b)* the place where two streets cross

**in·ter·sec·tion·al** (-′l) *adj.* **1.** of or forming an intersection **2.** between sections or regions

**in·ter·sperse** (in′tər spurs′) *vt.* -spersed′, -spers′ing [< L. pp. of *interspergere* < *inter-*, among + *spargere*, to scatter] **1.** to scatter among other things; put here and there **2.** to decorate or diversify with things scattered here and there —**in′ter·sper′sion** (-spur′zhən, -shən) *n.*

**in·ter·state** (in′tər stāt′) *adj.* between states of a federal government [*interstate* commerce]

**in·ter·stel·lar** (in′tər stel′ər) *adj.* [INTER- + STELLAR] between or among the stars

**in·ter·stice** (in tur′stis) *n., pl.* -stic·es (-stis iz, -stə sēz′) [Fr. < LL. < *inter-*, between + *sistere*, to set < *stare*, to stand] a small space between things or parts; crevice; crack —**in·ter·sti·tial** (in′tər stish′əl) *adj.* —**in′ter·sti′tial·ly** *adv.*

**in·ter·twine** (in′tər twīn′) *vt., vi.* -twined′, -twin′ing to twine together; intertwist

**in·ter·twist** (-twist′) *vt., vi.* to twist together

**in·ter·ur·ban** (-ur′bən) *adj.* [INTER- + URBAN] between cities or towns —*n.* an interurban railway

**in·ter·val** (in′tər v′l) *n.* [< OFr. < L. < *inter-*, between + *vallum*, a WALL] **1.** a space between two things **2.** a period of time between two events **3.** the extent of difference between two qualities, conditions, etc. **4.** *Music* the difference in pitch between two tones —**at intervals 1.** now and then **2.** here and there —**in·ter·val′lic** (-val′ik) *adj.*

**in·ter·vene** (in′tər vēn′) *vi.* -vened′, -ven′ing [< L. < *inter-*, between + *venire*, to come] **1.** to come or be between **2.** to occur between two events, etc. **3.** to come or be in between something irrelevant **4.** to come between as an influencing force —**in′ter·ven′er, Law in′ter·ve′nor** *n.* —**in′ter·ven′ient** (-yənt) *adj.*

**in·ter·ven·tion** (in′tər ven′shən) *n.* **1.** an intervening **2.** any interference in the affairs of others, esp. of one state in the affairs of another —**in′ter·ven′tion·ist** *n., adj.*

**in·ter·view** (in′tər vyoo′) *n.* [< Fr.: see INTER- & VIEW] **1.** a meeting of people face to face, as for evaluating a job applicant **2.** *a)* a meeting in which a person is asked about his views, activities, etc., as by a reporter *b)* a published account of this —*vt.* to have an interview with —**in′ter·view·ee′** *n.* —**in′ter·view′er** *n.*

**in·ter·weave** (in′tər wēv′) *vt., vi.* -wove′, -wo′ven, -weav′ing **1.** to weave together; interlace **2.** to connect closely; intermingle

**in·tes·tate** (in tes′tāt, -tit) *adj.* [< L. < *in-*, not + pp. of *testari*, to make a will] **1.** having made no will **2.** not disposed of by a will —*n.* a person who has died intestate —**in·tes′ta·cy** (-tə sē) *n.*

**in·tes·tin·al** (in tes′ti n′l) *adj.* of or in the intestines —**in·tes′tin·al·ly** *adv.*

**in·tes·tine** (in tes′tin) *adj.* [< L. *intestinus* < *intus*, within] internal, with regard to a country or community; domestic —*n. [usually pl.]* the lower part of the alimentary canal, extending from the stomach to the anus and consisting of a convoluted upper part (**small intestine**) and a lower part of greater diameter (**large intestine**); bowel(s)

**in·thrall, in·thral** (in thrôl′) *vt.* -thralled′, -thrall′ing *same as* EN-THRALL

**in·ti·ma·cy** (in′tə mə sē) *n., pl.* -cies **1.** a being intimate; familiarity **2.** an intimate act; esp., *[usually pl.]* illicit sexual intercourse

**in·ti·mate** (in′tə mit; *for v.* -māt′) *adj.* [< Fr. < L. *intimus*, superl. of *intus*, within] **1.** fundamental; essential [the *intimate* structure of the atom] **2.** most private or personal [one's *intimate* feelings] **3.** closely associated; very familiar [an *intimate* friend] **4.** suggesting privacy, romance, etc. [an *intimate* nightclub] **5.** *a)* resulting from careful study *b)* very close [*intimate* kinship] **6.** having illicit sexual relations —*n.* an intimate friend or companion —*vt.* -mat′ed, -mat′ing [< L. pp. of *intimare*, to announce < *intimus*] to hint or imply —**in′ti·mate·ly** *adv.* —**in′ti·mate·ness** *n.* —**in′ti·ma′tion** (-mā′shən) *n.*

**in·tim·i·date** (in tim′ə dāt′) *vt.* -dat′ed, -dat′ing [< ML. pp. of *intimidare* < L. *in-*, in + *timidus*, afraid] **1.** to make timid; make afraid **2.** to force or deter with threats; cow —**in·tim′i·da′tion** *n.* —**in·tim′i·da′tor** *n.*

**in·ti·tle** (in tīt′′l) *vt.* -tled, -tling *same as* ENTITLE

**intl.** international

**in·to** (in′too, -too, -tə) *prep.* [OE.] **1.** to the inside of; toward and within [*into* a house] **2.** advancing to the

INTESTINES
(A, stomach; B, pancreas; C, descending colon; D, rectum; E, appendix; F, ileum; G, jejunum; H, ascending colon; I, transverse colon; J, duodenum; K, liver)

midst of (a period of time) *[dancing far into the night]* **3.** to the form, substance, etc. of *[divided into parts]* **4.** so as to strike *[to bump into a door]* **5.** to the work, activity, etc. of *[to go into teaching]*

**in·tol·er·a·ble** (in täl′ər ə b'l) *adj.* not tolerable; unbearable; too severe, painful, etc. to be endured —**in·tol′er·a·bil′i·ty, in·tol′er·a·ble·ness** *n.* —**in·tol′er·a·bly** *adv.*

**in·tol·er·ance** (in täl′ər əns) *n.* **1.** lack of tolerance, esp. of others' opinions, beliefs, etc.; bigotry **2.** a sensitivity to some food, medicine, etc.

**in·tol·er·ant** (-ənt) *adj.* not tolerant; unwilling to tolerate others' opinions, beliefs, etc. or persons of other races, background, etc.; bigoted —**intolerant of** not able or willing to tolerate —**in·tol′er·ant·ly** *adv.* —**in·tol′er·ant·ness** *n.*

**in·to·na·tion** (in′tə nā′shən) *n.* **1.** an intoning **2.** the manner of singing or playing tones with regard to accuracy of pitch **3.** variations in pitch in speaking that affect the meaning **4.** the manner of applying final pitch to a spoken sentence or phrase *[a question ending with a rising intonation]* —**in′to·na′tion·al** *adj.*

**in·tone** (in tōn′) *vt.* **-toned′, -ton′ing** *[< OFr. < ML.: see* IN-¹ *&* TONE*]* **1.** to utter or recite in a singing tone or in prolonged monotones; chant **2.** to give a particular intonation to —*vi.* to speak or recite in a singing tone or in prolonged monotones; chant —**in·ton′er** *n.*

**in to·to** (in tō′tō) [L.] as a whole; entirely

**in·tox·i·cant** (in täk′sə kənt) *n.* something that intoxicates; esp., alcoholic liquor —*adj.* intoxicating

**in·tox·i·cate** (-kāt′) *vt.* **-cat′ed, -cat′ing** *[< ML. pp. of intoxicare,* to poison, ult. *< L. in-,* in + *toxicum,* a poison: see TOXIC] **1.** to make drunk **2.** to excite to a point beyond self-control **3.** *Med.* to poison

**in·tox·i·ca·tion** (in täk′sə kā′shən) *n.* **1.** a making or becoming drunk **2.** a feeling of wild excitement; frenzy **3.** *Med.* a poisoning or becoming poisoned

**intr.** intransitive

**in·tra-** [L. *< intra,* within] *a combining form meaning* within, inside of *[intramural]*

**in·trac·ta·ble** (in trak′tə b'l) *adj.* not tractable; specif., *a)* hard to manage; unruly or stubborn *b)* hard to work, cure, etc. —**in·trac′ta·bil′i·ty, in·trac′ta·ble·ness** *n.* —**in·trac′ta·bly** *adv.*

**in·tra·dos** (in′trə däs′, -dōs′; in trā′dōs) *n.* [Fr. *< L. intra,* within + Fr. *dos < L. dorsum,* the back] the inside curve or surface of an arch or vault

**in·tra·mu·ral** (in′trə myoor′əl) *adj.* [INTRA- + MURAL] within the walls or limits of a city, college, etc. *[intramural athletics]* —**in′tra·mu′ral·ly** *adv.*

**in·tra·mus·cu·lar** (-mus′kyə lər) *adj.* located or injected within the muscle —**in′tra·mus′cu·lar·ly** *adv.*

**intrans.** intransitive

**in·tran·si·gent** (in tran′sə jənt) *adj.* [< Fr. < Sp. < L. *in-,* IN-² + prp. of *transigere,* to settle] refusing to compromise, be reconciled, etc. —*n.* one who is intransigent, esp. in politics —**in·tran′si·gence, in·tran′si·gen·cy** *n.* —**in·tran′si·gent·ly** *adv.*

**in·tran·si·tive** (in tran′sə tiv) *adj.* not transitive; designating a verb that does not require a direct object to complete its meaning —*n.* an intransitive verb —**in·tran′si·tive·ly** *adv.*

**in·tra·state** (in′trə stāt′) *adj.* within a state; esp., within a State of the U.S.

**in·tra·u·ter·ine** (-yōōt′ər in, -yōō′tə rīn′) *adj.* within the uterus

**intrauterine (contraceptive) device** any of various devices, as a coil or loop of plastic, inserted in the uterus as a contraceptive

**in·tra·ve·nous** (-vē′nəs) *adj.* [INTRA- + VENOUS] in, or directly into, a vein or veins *[an intravenous injection]* —**in′tra·ve′nous·ly** *adv.*

**in·trench** (in trench′) *vt., vi. same as* ENTRENCH

**in·trep·id** (in trep′id) *adj.* [< L. < *in-,* not + *trepidus,* alarmed] unafraid; bold; fearless; very brave —**in·tre·pid′i·ty** (-trə pid′ə tē), **in·trep′id·ness** *n.* —**in·trep′id·ly** *adv.*

**Int. Rev.** internal revenue

**in·tri·ca·cy** (in′tri kə sē) *n.* **1.** an intricate quality or state; complexity **2.** *pl.* **-cies** something intricate; involved matter, etc.

**in·tri·cate** (in′tri kit) *adj.* [< L. pp. of *intricare,* to entangle < *in-,* in + *tricae,* perplexities] **1.** hard to follow or understand because full of puzzling parts, details, or relationships *[an intricate problem]* **2.** full of elaborate detail —**in′tri·cate·ly** *adv.* —**in′tri·cate·ness** *n.*

**in·trigue** (in trēg′; *for n., also* in′trēg) *vi.* **-trigued′, -trigu′ing** [< Fr. < It. < L. *intricare:* see prec.] **1.** to carry on a secret love affair **2.** to plot or scheme secretly or underhandedly —*vt.* **1.** to get by secret or underhanded plotting **2.** to excite the interest or curiosity of *[movies intrigue her]* —*n.* **1.** secret or underhanded plotting **2.** a secret or underhanded plot or scheme **3.** a secret love affair —**in·trigu′er** *n.* —**in·trigu′ing·ly** *adv.*

**in·trin·sic** (in trin′sik, -zik) *adj.* [< MFr. < LL. *intrinsecus,* inward < L. < *intra-,* within + *secus,* close] belonging to the real nature of a thing; essential; inherent: also **in·trin′si·cal** —**in·trin′si·cal·ly** *adv.* —**in·trin′si·cal·ness** *n.*

**in·tro-** [L. *< intro,* on the inside] *a combining form meaning* into, within, inward *[introvert]*

**introd., intro.** **1.** introduction **2.** introductory

**in·tro·duce** (in′trə dōōs′, -dyōōs′) *vt.* **-duced′, -duc′ing** [< L. < *intro-,* within + *ducere,* to lead] **1.** to lead or bring in **2.** to put in; insert *[to introduce a drain into a wound]* **3.** to add as a new feature *[introduce some humor into the play]* **4.** to bring into use, knowledge, or fashion *[space science has introduced many new words]* **5.** *a)* to make acquainted; present *(to) [introduce me to her]* *b)* to present *(a person) to society* *c)* to give knowledge or experience of *[they introduced him to music]* **6.** to bring forward *[introduce a bill into Congress]* **7.** to start; begin *[to introduce a talk with a joke]* —**in′tro·duc′er** *n.* —**in′tro·duc′i·ble** *adj.*

**in·tro·duc·tion** (-duk′shən) *n.* **1.** an introducing or being introduced **2.** anything brought into use, knowledge, or fashion **3.** anything that introduces; specif., *a)* the preliminary section of a book, speech, etc. *b)* a preliminary guide or text *c)* an opening section of music **4.** the formal presentation of one person to another, to society, etc.

**in·tro·duc·to·ry** (-duk′tər ē) *adj.* used as an introduction; preliminary: also **in′tro·duc′tive** —**in′tro·duc′to·ri·ly** *adv.*

**in·tro·it** (in trō′it; in′trō it, -troit) *n.* [< MFr. < L. *introitus,* an entrance, ult. < *intro-,* within + *ire,* to go] **1.** a psalm or hymn at the opening of a Christian worship service **2.** [I-] *R.C.Ch.* the first variable part of the Mass, consisting of a few psalm verses followed by the *Gloria Patri* and then repeated

**in·tro·spec·tion** (in′trə spek′shən) *n.* [< L. < pp. of *introspicere,* ult. < *intro-,* within + *specere,* to look] a looking into one's own mind, feelings, etc. —**in′tro·spec′tive** *adj.* —**in′tro·spec′tive·ly** *adv.*

**in·tro·ver·sion** (-vur′zhən, -shən) *n.* [see ff.] *Psychol.* an attitude in which a person directs his interest to his own experiences and feelings rather than upon external objects or other persons: opposed to EXTROVERSION —**in′tro·ver′sive** *adj.*

**in·tro·vert** (in′trə vurt′; *for v., also* in′trə vurt′) *vt.* [< L. *intro,* within + *vertere,* to turn] **1.** to direct (one's interest, mind, etc.) upon oneself **2.** to bend (something) inward —*vi.* to become introverted —*n. Psychol.* a person characterized by introversion: opposed to EXTROVERT —*adj.* characterized by introversion: usually **in′tro·vert′ed**

**in·trude** (in trōōd′) *vt.* **-trud′ed, -trud′ing** [< L. < *in-,* in + *trudere,* to thrust] **1.** to push or force (something *in* or *upon*) **2.** to force (oneself) upon others without being asked or welcomed **3.** *Geol.* to force (liquid magma, etc.) into or between solid rocks —*vi.* to intrude oneself —**in·trud′er** *n.*

**in·tru·sion** (in trōō′zhən) *n.* **1.** an intruding **2.** *Geol. a)* the invasion of liquid magma, etc. into or between solid rock *b)* intrusive rock

**in·tru·sive** (-siv) *adj.* **1.** intruding **2.** *Geol.* formed by intruding —**in·tru′sive·ly** *adv.* —**in·tru′sive·ness** *n.*

**in·trust** (in trust′) *vt. same as* ENTRUST

**in·tu·it** (in tōō′it, -tyōō′-) *vt., vi.* to know or learn by intuition —**in·tu′it·a·ble** *adj.*

**in·tu·i·tion** (in′tōō wish′ən, -tyoo-) *n.* [LL. < L. pp. of *intueri < in-,* in + *tueri,* to look at] **1.** *a)* the direct knowing or learning of something without conscious reasoning *b)* the ability to do this **2.** something known or learned in this way —**in′tu·i′tion·al** *adj.* —**in′tu·i′tion·al·ly** *adv.*

**in·tu·i·tive** (in tōō′i tiv, -tyōō′-) *adj.* **1.** having to do with, having, or perceiving by intuition **2.** perceived by intuition *[an intuitive truth]* —**in·tu′i·tive·ly** *adv.* —**in·tu′i·tive·ness** *n.*

**in·un·date** (in′ən dāt′) *vt.* **-dat′ed, -dat′ing** [< L. pp. of *inundare < in-,* in + *undare,* to flood < *unda,* a wave] to cover as with a flood; deluge; flood —**in·un·dant** (in·un′dənt) *adj.* —**in′un·da′tion** *n.* —**in·un·da·to·ry** (-də tôr′ē) *adj.*

**in·ure** (in yoor′) *vt.* **-ured′, -ur′ing** [< ME. in + *ure,* practice, work < OFr. *ovre < L. opera,* a work] to make accustomed to something difficult, painful, etc. —*vi.* to come into use or take effect —**in·ure′ment** *n.*

**inv.** **1.** invented **2.** inventor **3.** invoice

**†in va·cu·o** (in vak′yōō ō′) [L.] in a vacuum

**in·vade** (in vād′) *vt.* **-vad′ed, -vad′ing** [< L. < *in-,* in + *vadere,* to go] **1.** to enter forcibly, as to conquer **2.** to crowd into; throng *[tourists invading the beaches]* **3.** to intrude upon; violate *[he invaded my privacy]* **4.** to spread through with harmful effects *[disease invades tissue]* —*vi.* to make an invasion —**in·vad′er** *n.*

**in·va·lid¹** (in′və lid) *adj.* [< Fr. < L.: see IN-² + VALID] **1.** not well; weak and sickly **2.** of or for invalids *[an in-*

valid home] —*n*. a weak, sickly person; esp., one who is chronically ill or disabled —*vt*. **1.** to disable or weaken **2.** [Chiefly Brit.] to remove (a soldier, sailor, etc.) from active duty because of injury or illness —**in′va·lid·ism** *n*.

**in·val·id²** (in val′id) *adj*. not valid; having no force; null or void —**in·va·lid·i·ty** (in′və lid′ə tē) *n*. —**in·val′id·ly** *adv*.

**in·val·i·date** (in val′ə dāt′) *vt*. **-dat′ed, -dat′ing** to make invalid; deprive of legal force —**in·val′i·da′tion** *n*. —**in·val′i·da′tor** *n*.

**in·val·u·a·ble** (in val′yoo wə b′l, -yə b′l) *adj*. too valuable to be measured; priceless —**in·val′u·a·ble·ness** *n*. —**in·val′u·a·bly** *adv*.

**in·var·i·a·ble** (in ver′ē ə b′l) *adj*. not variable; unchanging; constant; uniform —**in·var′i·a·bil′i·ty, in·var′i·a·ble·ness** *n*. —**in·var′i·a·bly** *adv*.

**in·va·sion** (in vā′zhən) *n*. an invading; specif., *a*) an entering or being entered by an attacking military force *b*) an intruding upon others *c*) the onset, as of a disease —**in·va′sive** *adj*.

**in·vec·tive** (in vek′tiv) *adj*. [< MFr. < LL. < L. pp. of *invehere*: see ff.] inveighing; vituperative —*n*. **1.** a violent verbal attack; insults, curses, etc. **2.** an abusive term; insult, curse, etc.—**in·vec′tive·ly** *adv*. —**in·vec′tive·ness** *n*.

**in·veigh** (in vā′) *vi*. [< L. *invehi*, to attack < *invehere* < *in-* + *vehere*, to carry] to make a violent verbal attack; talk or write bitterly (*against*); rail —**in·veigh′er** *n*.

**in·vei·gle** (in vē′g′l, -vā′-) *vt*. **-gled, -gling** [< MFr. *aveugler*, to blind < L. *ab*, from + *oculus*, an eye] to lead on with deception; entice or trick into doing something, etc. —**in·vei′gle·ment** *n*. —**in·vei′gler** *n*.

**in·vent** (in vent′) *vt*. [< L. pp. of *invenire* < *in-*, on + *venire*, to come] **1.** to think up; devise in the mind [to *invent* excuses] **2.** to think out or produce (a new device, etc.); devise for the first time

**in·ven·tion** (in ven′shən) *n*. **1.** an inventing or being invented **2.** the power of inventing; ingenuity **3.** something invented; specif., *a*) something thought up; esp., a falsehood *b*) a new device or contrivance **4.** *Music* a short composition developing a motif in counterpoint

**in·ven·tive** (-tiv) *adj*. **1.** of or characterized by invention **2.** skilled in inventing; creative —**in·ven′tive·ly** *adv*. —**in·ven′tive·ness** *n*.

**in·ven·tor** (-tər) *n*. a person who invents; esp., one who devises a new contrivance, method, etc.

**in·ven·to·ry** (in′vən tôr′ē) *n*., *pl*. **-ries** [< ML. < LL. < L. pp. of *invenire*: see INVENT] **1.** an itemized list of goods, property, etc., as of a business, often prepared annually **2.** the store of goods, etc. for such listing; stock **3.** any detailed list **4.** the act of making such a list —*vt*. **-ried, -ry·ing 1.** to make an inventory of **2.** to place on an inventory —**take inventory 1.** to make an inventory of stock on hand **2.** to make an appraisal, as of one's situation —**in′ven·to′ri·al** *adj*. —**in′ven·to′ri·al·ly** *adv*.

**In·ver·ness** (in′vər nes′) *n*. [after county in Scotland] [*often* **i-**] **1.** an overcoat with a long, removable cape **2.** the cape: also **Inverness cape**

**in·verse** (in vurs′, in′vurs′) *adj*. inverted; reversed in order or relation; directly opposite [an *inverse* ratio] —*n*. any inverse thing; direct opposite —**in·verse′ly** *adv*.

**in·ver·sion** (in vur′zhən, -shən) *n*. **1.** an inverting or being inverted **2.** something inverted; reversal **3.** *Gram. & Rhetoric* a reversal of the normal order of words in a sentence (Ex.: "said he" for "he said") **4.** *Math*. an interchange of the terms of a ratio **5.** *Meteorol*. an atmospheric condition in which a layer of warm air traps cooler air near the surface of the earth, preventing the normal rising of surface air **6.** *Music* the reversal of the position of the tones in an interval or chord, as by raising the lower tone by an octave —**in·ver′sive** *adj*.

**in·vert** (in vurt′; *for n.* in′vurt′) *vt*. [< L. < *in-*, to + *vertere*, to turn] **1.** to turn upside down **2.** to change to the direct opposite; reverse the order, position, direction, etc. of **3.** to subject to inversion —*n*. anything inverted —**in·vert′i·ble** *adj*.

**in·ver·te·brate** (in vur′tə brit, -brāt′) *adj*. **1.** not vertebrate; having no backbone, or spinal column **2.** of invertebrates —*n*. any animal without a backbone; any animal other than a fish, amphibian, reptile, bird, or mammal

**in·vert·er** (in vur′tər) *n*. *Elec*. a device for changing direct current into alternating current

**in·vest** (in vest′) *vt*. [< L. < *in-*, in + *vestire*, to clothe < *vestis*, clothing] **1.** to clothe; array **2.** *a*) to cover or surround as with a garment [fog *invests* the city] *b*) to endow with qualities, attributes, etc. **3.** to install in office with ceremony **4.** to furnish with power, privilege, or authority **5.** to put (money) into business, stocks, bonds, etc. for the

purpose of obtaining a profit **6.** to spend (time, effort, etc.) with the expectation of some satisfaction **7.** *Mil*. to besiege (a town, port, etc.) —*vi*. to invest money —**in·ves′tor** *n*.

**in·ves·ti·gate** (in ves′tə gāt′) *vt*. **-gat′ed, -gat′ing** [< L. pp. of *investigare*, to trace out, ult. < *vestigium*, a track] to search into; inquire into systematically —*vi*. to make an investigation —**in·ves′ti·ga·ble** (-gə b′l) *adj*. —**in·ves′ti·ga′tive, in·ves′ti·ga·to′ry** (-gə tôr′ē) *adj*. —**in·ves′ti·ga′tor** *n*.

**in·ves·ti·ga·tion** (in ves′tə gā′shən) *n*. **1.** an investigating or being investigated **2.** a careful examination or inquiry —**in·ves′ti·ga′tion·al** *adj*.

**in·ves·ti·ture** (in ves′tə chər) *n*. **1.** a formal investing with an office, power, authority, etc. **2.** anything that clothes or covers

**in·vest·ment** (in vest′mənt) *n*. **1.** an investing or being invested **2.** an outer covering **3.** *same as* INVESTITURE (sense 1) **4.** *a*) the investing of money *b*) the amount of money invested *c*) anything in which money is or may be invested

**in·vet·er·ate** (in vet′ər it) *adj*. [< L. pp. of *inveterare*, to age < *in-*, in + *vetus*, old] **1.** firmly established over a long period; deep-rooted **2.** settled in a habit, practice, prejudice, etc.; habitual —**in·vet′er·a·cy** *n*. —**in·vet′er·ate·ly** *adv*.

**in·vid·i·ous** (in vid′ē əs) *adj*. [< L. < *invidia*, ENVY] **1.** such as to excite ill will or envy; giving offense **2.** giving offense by discriminating unfairly [*invidious* comparisons] —**in·vid′i·ous·ly** *adv*. —**in·vid′i·ous·ness** *n*.

**in·vig·or·ate** (in vig′ə rāt′) *vt*. **-at′ed, -at′ing** [IN-¹ + VIG-OR + -ATE¹] to give vigor to; fill with energy; enliven —**in·vig′or·a′tion** *n*. —**in·vig′or·a′tive** *adj*. —**in·vig′or·a′tor** *n*.

**in·vin·ci·ble** (in vin′sə b′l) *adj*. [< MFr. < L.: see IN-² & VINCIBLE] that cannot be overcome; unconquerable —**in·vin′ci·bil′i·ty, in·vin′ci·ble·ness** *n*. —**in·vin′ci·bly** *adv*.

**in·vi·o·la·ble** (in vī′ə lə b′l) *adj*. **1.** not to be violated; not to be profaned or injured; sacred [an *inviolable* promise] **2.** that cannot be violated; indestructible —**in·vi′o·la·bil′i·ty** *n*. —**in·vi′o·la·bly** *adv*.

**in·vi·o·late** (in vī′ə lit, -lāt′) *adj*. not violated; kept sacred or unbroken —**in·vi′o·la·cy** (-lə sē), **in·vi′o·late·ness** *n*. —**in·vi′o·late·ly** *adv*.

**in·vis·i·ble** (in viz′ə b′l) *adj*. **1.** not visible; that cannot be seen **2.** out of sight **3.** imperceptible **4.** kept hidden [*invisible* assets] —*n*. an invisible thing or being —**the In·visible 1.** God **2.** the unseen world —**in·vis′i·bil′i·ty, in·vis′i·ble·ness** *n*. —**in·vis′i·bly** *adv*.

**in·vi·ta·tion** (in′və tā′shən) *n*. **1.** an inviting to come somewhere or do something **2.** the message or note used in inviting

**in·vi·ta·tion·al** (-′l) *adj*. participated in only by those invited [an *invitational* art exhibit]

**in·vite** (in vīt′; *for n.* in′vīt) *vt*. **-vit′ed, -vit′ing** [< Fr. < L. *invitare*] **1.** to ask courteously to come somewhere or do something **2.** to make a request for [to *invite* questions] **3.** to give occasion for [action that *invites* scandal] **4.** to tempt; entice —*n*. [Colloq.] an invitation

**in·vit·ing** (-vīt′iŋ) *adj*. tempting; enticing

**in·vo·ca·tion** (in′və kā′shən) *n*. **1.** an invoking of God, the Muses, etc. for blessing, help, etc. **2.** a formal prayer used in invoking, as at the beginning of a church service **3.** *a*) a conjuring of evil spirits *b*) an incantation —**in′vo·ca′tion·al** *adj*. —**in·voc′a·to′ry** (-väk′ə tôr′ē) *adj*.

**in·voice** (in′vois′) *n*. [prob. orig. pl. of ME. *envoie*, a message: see ENVOY¹] **1.** an itemized list of goods shipped to a buyer, stating quantities, prices, shipping charges, etc. **2.** a shipment of invoiced goods —*vt*. **-voiced, -voic·ing** to present an invoice for or to

**in·voke** (in vōk′) *vt*. **-voked′, -vok′ing** [< MFr. < L. < *in-*, on + *vocare*, to call] **1.** to call on (God, the Muses, etc.) for blessing, help, etc. **2.** to put into use (a law, penalty, etc.) as pertinent **3.** to call forth; cause **4.** to summon (evil spirits) by incantation; conjure **5.** to ask solemnly for; implore —**in·vok′er** *n*.

**in·vo·lu·cre** (in′və loo′kər) *n*. [< L. *involucrum*, wrapper < *involvere*, INVOLVE] *Bot*. a ring of bracts at the base of a flower, flower cluster, or fruit —**in′vo·lu′cral** (-krəl) *adj*.

**in·vol·un·tar·y** (in väl′ən ter′ē) *adj*. not voluntary; specif., *a*) not done of one's own free will *b*) unintentional; accidental *c*) not consciously controlled [sneezing is *involuntary*] —**in·vol′un·tar′i·ly** *adv*. —**in·vol′un·tar′i·ness** *n*.

**in·vo·lute** (in′və loot′) *adj*. [L. *involutus*, pp. of *involvere*, INVOLVE] **1.** intricate; involved **2.** rolled up or curled in a spiral; having the whorls wound closely [*involute* shells]

fat, āpe, cär; ten, ēven; is, bīte; gō, hôrn, tool, look; oil, out; up, fur; get; joy; yet; chin; she; thin, *th*en; zh, leisure; ŋ, ring; ə for *a* in *ago*, *e* in *agent*, *i* in *sanity*, *o* in *comply*, *u* in *focus*; ′ as in *able* (ā′b′l); Fr. bal; ë, Fr. coeur; ö, Fr. feu; Fr. mon; ô, Fr. coq; ü, Fr. duc; r, Fr. cri; H, G. ich; kh, G. doch; ‡foreign; *hypothetical; < derived from. See inside front cover.

**3.** *Bot.* rolled inward at the edges [*involute* leaves] —*vi.* -lut'ed, -lut'ing to become involute or undergo involution

in·vo·lu·tion (in'və lōō'shən) *n.* **1.** an involving or being involved; entanglement **2.** something involved; complication; intricacy —in'vo·lu'tion·al *adj.* —in'vo·lu'tion·ar'y *adj.*

in·volve (in välv') *vt.* -volved', -volv'ing [< L. < *in-,* in + *volvere,* to roll] **1.** orig., to enfold or envelop **2.** to make intricate or complicated **3.** to entangle in difficulty, danger, etc.; implicate **4.** to draw or hold within itself; include [a riot *involving* thousands] **5.** to include by necessity; entail; require [saving money *involves* thrift] **6.** to relate to or affect [his honor is *involved*] **7.** to make busy; occupy [*involved* in research] —in·volve'ment *n.*

in·vul·ner·a·ble (in vul'nər ə b'l) *adj.* **1.** that cannot be wounded or injured **2.** proof against attack —in·vul'ner·a·bil'i·ty *n.* —in·vul'ner·a·bly *adv.*

in·ward (in'wərd) *adj.* **1.** situated within; internal **2.** mental or spiritual **3.** directed toward the inside [the inward pull of a centrifuge] —*n.* **1.** the inside **2.** [*pl.*] the entrails —*adv.* **1.** toward the inside or center **2.** into the mind or spirit Also in'wards *adv.*

in·ward·ly (-lē) *adv.* **1.** in or on the inside; internally **2.** in the mind or spirit **3.** toward the inside or center

in·ward·ness (-nis) *n.* **1.** the inner nature or meaning **2.** spirituality **3.** introspection

in·weave (in wēv') *vt.* -wove', -wo'ven or -wove', -weav'ing to weave in

in·wrap (in rap') *vt.* -wrapped', -wrap'ping same as ENWRAP

in·wrought (in rôt') *adj.* **1.** worked or woven into a fabric: said of a pattern, etc. **2.** closely blended with other things

I·o (ī'ō) *Gr. Myth.* a maiden loved by Zeus and changed into a heifer by Hera

Io *Chem.* ionium

i·o·dide (ī'ə dīd') *n.* a compound of iodine with another element or with a radical

i·o·dine (ī'ə dīn', -din; *Brit. & among chemists,* -dēn') *n.* [Fr. *iode* (< Gr. *iōdēs,* violetlike < *ion,* a violet + *eidos,* a form) + -INE⁴] **1.** a nonmetallic chemical element of the halogen family, consisting of grayish-black crystals that volatilize into a violet-colored vapor: used as an antiseptic, in photography, etc.: symbol, I; at. wt., 126.9044; at. no., 53: a radioactive isotope (**iodine 131**) is used in medical diagnosis and therapy **2.** tincture of iodine, used as an antiseptic

i·o·dize (ī'ə dīz') *vt.* -dized', -diz'ing to treat with iodine or an iodide

**iodized salt** common table salt to which a small amount of sodium iodide or potassium iodide has been added

i·o·do·form (ī ō'də fôrm') *n.* [*iodo-* (< Fr. *iode,* IODINE) + FORM(IC)] a yellowish, crystalline compound of iodine, CHI₃, used as an antiseptic in surgical dressings

i·on (ī'ən, -än) *n.* [< Gr. *iōn,* prp. of *ienai,* to go] an electrically charged atom or group of atoms, the electrical charge of which results when a neutral atom or group of atoms loses or gains one or more electrons: such loss (resulting in a CATION), or gain (resulting in an ANION), occurs during electrolysis, by the action of certain forms of radiant energy, etc. —i·on·ic (ī än'ik) *adj.*

-ion [< Fr. < L. -*io* (gen. -*ionis*)] *a suffix meaning* the act, condition, or result of [*translation, correction*]

I·o·ni·a (ī ō'nē ə) ancient region along the W coast of Asia Minor, colonized by the Greeks in the 11th cent. B.C. —I·o'ni·an *adj., n.*

**Ionian Sea** section of the Mediterranean, between Greece, Sicily, & the S Italian peninsula

I·on·ic (ī än'ik) *adj.* **1.** of Ionia or its people **2.** designating or of that one of the three orders of Greek architecture distinguished by ornamental scrolls on the capitals: cf. CORINTHIAN, DORIC

i·o·ni·um (ī ō'nē əm) *n.* [ION + ModL. ending -*ium*] a radioactive isotope of thorium

i·on·ize (ī'ə nīz') *vt., vi.* -ized', -iz'ing to change or be changed into ions; dissociate into ions, as a salt dissolved in water, or become

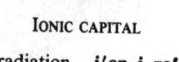
IONIC CAPITAL

electrically charged, as a gas under radiation —i'on·i·za'-tion *n.* —i'on·iz'er *n.*

i·on·o·sphere (ī än'ə sfir') *n.* the outer part of the earth's atmosphere, with changing layers characterized by an appreciable electron and ion content —i·on'o·spher'ic *adj.*

i·o·ta (ī ōt'ə) *n.* **1.** the ninth letter of the Greek alphabet (I, ι) **2.** a very small quantity; jot

IOU, I.O.U. (ī'ō'yōō') **1.** I owe you **2.** a signed note bearing these letters, acknowledging a debt

-ious (ē əs, yəs, əs) [see -OUS] *a suffix used to form adjectives corresponding to nouns that end in* -ION [*rebellious*] *or meaning* having, characterized by [*furious*]

I·o·wa (ī'ə wə; *occas.* -wā') [after an Indian tribe in the

area, prob. < AmInd. *Ayuba,* lit., sleepy ones] Middle Western State of the U.S.: 56,290 sq. mi.; pop. 2,913,000; cap. Des Moines: abbrev. Ia., IA —I'o·wan *adj., n.*

**IPA** International Phonetic Alphabet

ip·e·cac (ip'ə kak') *n.* [< Port. < Tupi] **1.** a tropical S. American plant of the madder family **2.** the dried roots of this plant **3.** an emetic made from the dried roots Also ip·e·cac·u·an·ha (ip'ə kak'yōō wan'ə)

Iph·i·ge·ni·a (if'ə jə nī'ə) *Gr. Myth.* a daughter of Agamemnon, offered by him as a sacrifice to Artemis

‡ip·se dix·it (ip'sē dik'sit) [L., he himself has said (it)] a dogmatic statement

ip·so fac·to (ip'sō fak'tō) [L.] by that very fact

**IQ, I.Q.** intelligence quotient

ir- *see* IN-¹ & IN-²

Ir *Chem.* iridium

**IR, ir, i-r** infrared

Ir. **1.** Ireland **2.** Irish

I·ra (ī'rə) [Heb. *'īrā,* lit., watchful] a masculine name

**IRA, I.R.A.** a retirement plan in which a worker may invest a limited amount of earnings, as in mutual funds, that is tax-free until retirement

**I.R.A., IRA** Irish Republican Army

I·ran (i ran', ī-; ē rän') country in SW Asia, between the Caspian Sea & the Persian Gulf: 636,000 sq. mi.; pop. 28,237,000; cap. Tehran

**Iran.** Iranian

I·ra·ni·an (i rā'nē ən, ī-) *adj.* of Iran, its people, their language, or culture —*n.* **1.** one of the people of Iran; Persian **2.** a subbranch of the Indo-European family of languages, including Persian

I·raq (i räk', -rak'; ē-) country in SW Asia, at the head of the Persian Gulf: 171,599 sq. mi.; pop. 9,431,000; cap. Baghdad: also sp. **Irak**

I·ra·qi (i rä'kē, -rak'ē) *n., pl.* -qis a native or inhabitant of Iraq **2.** the Arabic dialect spoken in Iraq —*adj.* of Iraq, its people, their language, or culture

i·ras·ci·ble (i ras'ə b'l, ī-) *adj.* [< MFr. < LL. < L. *irasci:* see ff.] easily angered; quick-tempered —i·ras'ci·bil'i·ty, i·ras'ci·ble·ness *n.* —i·ras'ci·bly *adv.*

i·rate (ī rāt', ī'rāt) *adj.* [L. *iratus* < *irasci,* to be angry < *ira,* ire] angry; wrathful; incensed —i·rate'ly *adv.* —i·rate'ness *n.*

**IRBM** intermediate range ballistic missile

ire (īr) *n.* [< OFr. < L. *ira*] anger; wrath —ire'ful *adj.* —ire'ful·ly *adv.* —ire'ful·ness *n.*

**Ire.** Ireland

Ire·land (īr'lənd) **1.** island of the British Isles, west of Great Britain **2.** republic comprising the S provinces of this island & three counties of Ulster province: 27,136 sq. mi.; pop. 2,921,000; cap. Dublin Cf. NORTHERN IRELAND

I·rene (ī rēn') [< Fr. < L. < Gr. *Eirēnē,* lit., peace] a feminine name

ir·i·des·cent (ir'ə des'nt) *adj.* [< L. *iris* (< Gr. *iris*), rainbow + -ESCENT] having or showing shifting changes in color or an interplay of rainbowlike colors —ir'i·des'cence *n.* —ir'i·des'cent·ly *adv.*

i·rid·i·um (i rid'ē əm, ī-) *n.* [ModL. < L. *iris* (< Gr. *iris*), rainbow: from the changing color of some of its salts] a white, heavy, brittle, metallic chemical element found in platinum ores: alloys of iridium are used for pen points and bearings of watches: symbol, Ir; at. wt., 192.2; at. no., 77

I·ris (ī'ris) [L. < Gr. *Iris:* see ff.] **1.** a feminine name **2.** *Gr. Myth.* the goddess of the rainbow and a messenger of the gods

i·ris (ī'ris) *n., pl.* i'ris·es, ir·i·des (ir'ə dēz', ī'rə-) [L. < Gr. *iris,* rainbow] **1.** a rainbow **2.** the round, pigmented membrane surrounding the pupil of the eye **3.** a plant with sword-shaped leaves and showy flowers composed of three petals and three drooping sepals **4.** the flower of this plant

I·rish (ī'rish) *adj.* of Ireland, its people, their language, or culture —*n.* **1.** same as IRISH GAELIC **2.** the English dialect of Ireland —the Irish the people of Ireland —I'rish·man *n., pl.* -men —I'rish·wom'an *n.fem., pl.* -wom'en

IRIS

**Irish bull** same as BULL³

**Irish Gaelic** the Celtic language of Ireland

**Irish potato** the common white potato

**Irish Sea** arm of the Atlantic between Ireland & Great Britain

**Irish setter** any of a breed of setter with a coat of long, silky, reddish-brown hair

**Irish stew** a stew of meat, potatoes, onions, etc.

**Irish terrier** any of a breed of small, lean dog with a wiry, reddish coat

**Irish wolfhound** any of a breed of very large, heavy, powerful dog with a rough coat

irk (ʉrk) *vt.* [ME. *irken,* to be weary of] to annoy, disgust, irritate, tire out, etc.

**irk·some** (-səm) *adj.* that tends to irk; tiresome or annoying —**irk′some·ly** *adv.* —**irk′some·ness** *n.*

**Ir·kutsk** (ir kōōtsk′) city in S Asiatic R.S.F.S.R., near Lake Baikal: pop. 428,000

**Ir·ma** (ur′mə) [G., orig. contr. of names beginning with *Irm-* < OHG. *Irmin,* name of a Gmc. god of war] a feminine name

**i·ron** (ī′ərn) *n.* see PLURAL, II, D, 3 [< OE. *iren, isern, isen* < Gmc.] **1.** a white, malleable, ductile, metallic chemical element: it is the most common and important of all metals: symbol, Fe; at. wt., 55.847; at. no., 26 **2.** any tool, device, etc. made of iron, as *a)* a device with a handle and flat undersurface, used, when heated, for pressing clothes or cloth *b)* a rodlike device with a brand at one end, heated for branding cattle: in full, **branding iron 3.** [*pl.*] iron shackles or chains **4.** firm strength; power **5.** *Golf* any of a set of numbered clubs with metal heads **6.** a medicine containing iron —*adj.* **1.** of or consisting of iron **2.** like iron, as *a)* firm [*an iron* will] *b)* strong **3.** cruel; merciless —*vt.* **1.** to furnish or cover with iron **2.** to press (clothes or cloth) with a hot iron —*vi.* to iron clothes or cloth —**have many** (or **several,** etc.) **irons in the fire** to be engaged in many (or several, etc.) activities —**iron out** to smooth out; eliminate —**strike while the iron is hot** to act at the opportune time

**Iron Age** a phase of human culture (in Europe, c. 1000 B.C.-100 A.D.) characterized by the introduction and development of iron tools and weapons

**i·ron·bound** (-bound′) *adj.* **1.** bound with iron **2.** hard; rigid; unyielding; inflexible **3.** edged with rocks or cliffs, as a coast

**i·ron·clad** (-klad′) *adj.* **1.** covered or protected with iron **2.** difficult to change or break [*an ironclad* lease] —*n.* formerly, a warship armored with thick iron plates

**iron curtain 1.** a barrier of secrecy and censorship regarded as isolating the Soviet Union and other countries in its sphere **2.** any similar barrier

**iron hand** firm, rigorous, severe control —**i′ron·hand′ed** *adj.*

**i·ron·i·cal** (ī rän′i k'l) *adj.* [< L. < Gr. < *eirōneia* (see IRONY) + -AL] **1.** meaning the contrary of what is expressed **2.** using or tending to use irony **3.** directly opposite to what might be expected Also **i·ron′ic** —**i·ron′i·cal·ly** *adv.*

**ironing board** (or **table**) a cloth-covered board or stand on which clothes are ironed

**iron lung** a large metal respirator enclosing all of the body but the head, used for maintaining artificial respiration

**i·ron·mon·ger** (ī′ərn muŋ′gər, -mäŋ′-) *n.* [Brit.] a dealer in hardware —**i′ron·mon′ger·y** *n.*

**iron pyrites** *same as* PYRITE

**I·ron·sides** (-sīdz′) **1.** nickname of Oliver CROMWELL **2.** *a)* his regiment *b)* his whole army —*n.pl.* [i-] [*with sing. v.*] *same as* IRONCLAD

**i·ron·stone** (-stōn′) *n.* a hard variety of white ceramic ware

**i·ron·ware** (-wer′) *n.* things made of iron

**i·ron·weed** (-wēd′) *n.* a plant of the composite family, with clusters of tubular, purple flowers

**i·ron·wood** (-wood′) *n.* **1.** any of various trees with extremely hard wood **2.** the wood

**i·ron·work** (-wurk′) *n.* articles or parts made of iron —**i′ron·work′er** *n.*

**i·ron·works** (-wurks′) *n.pl.* [*often with sing. v.*] a place where iron is smelted or heavy iron goods are made

**i·ro·ny** (ī′rən ē, ī′ər nē) *n., pl.* -**nies** [< Fr. < L. < Gr. *eirōneia* < *eirōn,* dissembler in speech < *eirein,* to speak] **1.** expression in which the intended meaning of the words is the direct opposite of their usual sense [the *irony* of calling a stupid plan "clever"] **2.** a set of circumstances or a result that is the opposite of what might be expected [an *irony* that the firehouse burned]

**Ir·o·quoi·an** (ir ə kwoi′ən) *adj.* of an important linguistic family of N. American Indians, including speakers of Huron, Cherokee, Mohawk, etc. —*n.* **1.** a member of an Iroquoian tribe **2.** the Iroquoian languages collectively

**Ir·o·quois** (ir′ə kwoi′) *n.* [Fr. < Algonquian *Irinakoiw,* lit., real adders] **1.** *pl.* -**quois** (-kwoi′, -kwoiz′) a member of a confederation of Iroquoian Indian tribes that lived in W and N New York and in adjacent Canada: see FIVE NATIONS **2.** the Iroquoian language family —*adj.* of the Iroquois

**ir·ra·di·ate** (i rā′dē āt′; *for adj. usually* -it) *vt.* -**at′ed**, -**at′ing** [< L. pp. of *irradiare:* see IN-¹ & RADIATE] **1.** to shine upon; light up; make bright **2.** to enlighten **3.** to radiate; diffuse **4.** to expose to or treat by exposing to X-rays, ultraviolet rays, etc. —*vi.* to emit rays; shine —*adj.* irradiated —**ir·ra′di·ance, ir·ra′di·an·cy** *n.* —**ir·ra′di·ant** *adj.* —**ir·ra′di·a·tion** *n.* —**ir·ra′di·a′tive** *adj.* —**ir·ra′di·a′tor** *n.*

**ir·ra·tion·al** (i rash′ən 'l) *adj.* **1.** lacking the power to reason **2.** senseless; unreasonable; absurd **3.** *Math.* designating a real number not expressible as an integer or a quotient of two integers —**ir·ra′tion·al′i·ty** (-ə nal′ə tē) *n., pl.* -**ties** —**ir·ra′tion·al·ly** *adv.*

**Ir·ra·wad·dy** (ir′ə wä′dē, -wô′-) river flowing from N Burma south into the Indian Ocean

**ir·re·claim·a·ble** (ir′i klā′mə b'l) *adj.* that cannot be reclaimed —**ir′re·claim′a·bil′i·ty** *n.* —**ir′re·claim′a·bly** *adv.*

**ir·rec·on·cil·a·ble** (i rek′ən sīl′ə b'l, i rek′ən sīl′-) *adj.* that cannot be reconciled; that cannot be brought into agreement; incompatible —*n.* one who is irreconcilable or refuses to compromise —**ir·rec′on·cil′a·bil′i·ty** *n.* —**ir·rec′on·cil′a·bly** *adv.*

**ir·re·cov·er·a·ble** (ir′i kuv′ər ə b'l) *adj.* that cannot be recovered, rectified, or remedied; irretrievable —**ir′re·cov′er·a·bly** *adv.*

**ir·re·deem·a·ble** (ir′i dēm′ə b'l) *adj.* **1.** that cannot be bought back **2.** that cannot be converted into coin, as certain kinds of paper money **3.** that cannot be changed or reformed —**ir′re·deem′a·bly** *adv.*

**ir·re·den·tist** (ir′i den′tist) *n.* [< It. < (*Italia*) *irredenta,* unredeemed (Italy)] a person who advocates a policy of recovering territory formerly a part of his country; specif., [*usually* I-] a member of an Italian political party, after 1878, with such a policy —**ir′re·den′tism** *n.*

**ir·re·duc·i·ble** (ir′i dōōs′ə b'l, -dyōōs′-) *adj.* that cannot be reduced —**ir′re·duc′i·bil′i·ty** *n.* —**ir′re·duc′i·bly** *adv.*

**ir·ref·ra·ga·ble** (i ref′rə gə b'l) *adj.* [< LL. < L. *in-,* IN-² + *refragari,* to oppose] that cannot be refuted; indisputable —**ir·ref′ra·ga·bil′i·ty** *n.* —**ir·ref′ra·ga·bly** *adv.*

**ir·ref·u·ta·ble** (i ref′yoo tə b'l, ir′i fyoot′ə b'l) *adj.* that cannot be refuted or disproved —**ir·ref′u·ta·bil′i·ty** *n.* —**ir·ref′u·ta·bly** *adv.*

**irreg. 1.** irregular **2.** irregularly

**ir·re·gard·less** (ir′i gärd′lis) *adj., adv. a substandard or humorous redundancy for* REGARDLESS

**ir·reg·u·lar** (i reg′yə lər) *adj.* **1.** not conforming to established rule, method, usage, standard, etc.; out of the ordinary **2.** immoral; lawless; disorderly **3.** not straight or even; not symmetrical; not uniform in shape, design, etc. **4.** uneven in occurrence; variable **5.** having minor flaws: said of merchandise **6.** *Gram.* not inflected in the usual way [go is an *irregular* verb] **7.** *Mil.* not belonging to the regularly established army —*n.* a person or thing that is irregular —**ir·reg′u·lar′i·ty** *n., pl.* -**ties** —**ir·reg′u·lar·ly** *adv.*

**ir·rel·e·vant** (i rel′ə vənt) *adj.* not relevant; not pertinent; not to the point —**ir·rel′e·vance, ir·rel′e·van·cy** *n., pl.* -**cies** —**ir·rel′e·vant·ly** *adv.*

**ir·re·li·gious** (ir′i lij′əs) *adj.* **1.** not religious **2.** indifferent or hostile to religion **3.** profane; impious —**ir′re·li′gion** *n.* —**ir′re·li′gion·ist** *n.* —**ir′re·li′gious·ly** *adv.*

**ir·re·me·di·a·ble** (ir′i mē′dē ə b'l) *adj.* that cannot be remedied; incurable —**ir′re·me′di·a·ble·ness** *n.* —**ir′re·me′di·a·bly** *adv.*

**ir·re·mis·si·ble** (-mis′ə b'l) *adj.* not remissible; specif., *a)* that cannot be excused or pardoned *b)* that cannot be shirked —**ir′re·mis′si·bly** *adv.*

**ir·re·mov·a·ble** (-mōō′və b'l) *adj.* not removable —**ir′re·mov′a·bil′i·ty** *n.* —**ir′re·mov′a·bly** *adv.*

**ir·rep·a·ra·ble** (i rep′ər ə b'l) *adj.* not reparable; that cannot be repaired, mended, remedied, etc. —**ir·rep′a·ra·bil′i·ty** *n.* —**ir·rep′a·ra·bly** *adv.*

**ir·re·place·a·ble** (ir′i plās′ə b'l) *adj.* not replaceable

**ir·re·press·i·ble** (-pres′ə b'l) *adj.* that cannot be repressed or restrained —**ir′re·press′i·bil′i·ty** *n.* —**ir′re·press′i·bly** *adv.*

**ir·re·proach·a·ble** (-prō′chə b'l) *adj.* blameless; faultless —**ir′re·proach′a·bil′i·ty, ir′re·proach′a·ble·ness** *n.* —**ir′re·proach′a·bly** *adv.*

**ir·re·sist·i·ble** (-zis′tə b'l) *adj.* that cannot be resisted; too strong, fascinating, etc. to be withstood —**ir′re·sist′i·bil′i·ty, ir′re·sist′i·ble·ness** *n.* —**ir′re·sist′i·bly** *adv.*

**ir·res·o·lute** (i rez′ə lōōt′) *adj.* not resolute; wavering in decision or purpose —**ir·res′o·lute′ly** *adv.* —**ir·res′o·lute′ness** *n.* —**ir·res′o·lu′tion** *n.*

**ir·re·spec·tive** (ir′i spek′tiv) *adj.* [Rare] showing disregard for persons or consequences —**irrespective of** regardless of —**ir′re·spec′tive·ly** *adv.*

**ir·re·spon·si·ble** (ir′i spän′sə b'l) *adj.* not responsible; specif., *a)* not accountable for actions *b)* showing the lack of a sense of responsibility —*n.* an irresponsible person —**ir′re·spon′si·bil′i·ty, ir′re·spon′si·ble·ness** *n.* —**ir′re·spon′si·bly** *adv.*

**ir·re·spon·sive** (-siv) *adj.* not responsive —**ir′re·spon′sive·ness** *n.*

**ir·re·triev·a·ble** (-trēv'ə b'l) *adj.* that cannot be retrieved, recovered, restored, or recalled —**ir're·triev'a·bil'i·ty** *n.* —**ir're·triev'a·bly** *adv.*

**ir·rev·er·ence** (i rev'ər əns) *n.* 1. lack of reverence 2. an act or statement showing this —**ir·rev'er·ent** *adj.* —**ir·rev'er·ent·ly** *adv.*

**ir·re·vers·i·ble** (ir'i vur'sə b'l) *adj.* not reversible; specif., *a)* that cannot be repealed or annulled *b)* that cannot be run backward, etc. —**ir're·vers'i·bil'i·ty** *n.* —**ir're·vers'i·bly** *adv.*

**ir·rev·o·ca·ble** (i rev'ə kə b'l) *adj.* that cannot be revoked or undone —**ir·rev'o·ca·bil'i·ty**, **ir·rev'o·ca·ble·ness** *n.* —**ir·rev'o·ca·bly** *adv.*

**ir·ri·ga·ble** (ir'i gə b'l) *adj.* that can be irrigated

**ir·ri·gate** (ir'ə gāt') *vt.* **-gat'ed**, **-gat'ing** [ < L. pp. of *irrigare* < *in-*, in + *rigare*, to water] 1. to supply (land) with water by means of artificial ditches, etc. 2. *Med.* to wash out (a cavity, wound, etc.) with water or other fluid —**ir'ri·ga'tion** *n.* —**ir'ri·ga'tive** *adj.* —**ir'ri·ga'tor** *n.*

**ir·ri·ta·ble** (ir'i tə b'l) *adj.* 1. easily annoyed or provoked; impatient 2. *Med.* excessively or pathologically sensitive to a stimulus 3. *Physiol.* able to respond to a stimulus —**ir'ri·ta·bil'i·ty**, **ir'ri·ta·ble·ness** *n.* —**ir'ri·ta·bly** *adv.*

**ir·ri·tant** (-tənt) *adj.* causing irritation —*n.* something causing irritation —**ir'ri·tan·cy** *n.*

**ir·ri·tate** (-tāt') *vt.* **-tat'ed**, **-tat'ing** [ < L. pp. of *irritare*, to excite] 1. to provoke to impatience or anger; annoy 2. to make (a part of the body) inflamed or sore 3. *Physiol.* to excite (an organ, muscle, etc.) to a characteristic action by a stimulus —**ir'ri·ta'tive** *adj.*

**ir·ri·ta·tion** (ir'ə tā'shən) *n.* 1. an irritating or being irritated 2. something that irritates 3. *Med.* an excessive response to stimulation in an organ or part; specif., a sore or inflamed condition

**ir·rupt** (i rupt') *vi.* [ < L. pp. of *irrumpere* < *in-*, in + *rumpere*, to break] 1. to burst violently (*into*) 2. *Ecol.* to increase abruptly in size of population —**ir·rup'tion** *n.* —**ir·rup'tive** *adj.*

**IRS, I.R.S.** Internal Revenue Service

**Ir·tysh** (ir tish') river in C Asia, flowing from NW China northwestward into the Ob River

**Ir·ving**[1] (ur'vin) [north Brit. surname, prob. orig. a place name] 1. a masculine name 2. **Washington**, 1783–1859; U.S. writer

**Ir·ving**[2] (ur'vin) [prob. an arbitrary selection] city in NE Tex.: suburb of Dallas: pop. 110,000

**Ir·win** (ur'win) [var. of ERWIN] a masculine name

**is** (iz) [OE.] *3d pers. sing., pres. indic., of* BE

**is.** 1. island(s) 2. isle(s)

**Isa., Is.** Isaiah

**I·saac** (ī'zək) [ < LL. < Gr. < Heb. *yitshāq*, lit., laughter] 1. a masculine name 2. *Bible* one of the patriarchs, son of Abraham and Sarah, and father of Jacob and Esau: Gen. 21:3

**Is·a·bel** (iz'ə bel') [Sp., prob. altered < *Elizabeth*] a feminine name: var. *Isabelle, Isabella*

**Is·a·bel·la** (iz'ə bel'ə) [It.] 1. a feminine name 2. **Isabella I** 1451–1504; wife of Ferdinand V & queen of Castile (1474–1504): gave help to Columbus in his expedition

**Is·a·dor·a** (iz'ə dôr'ə) [fem. of ISIDORE] a feminine name

**i·sa·go·ge** (ī'sə gō'jē) *n.* [L. < Gr., ult. < *eis-*, into + *agein*, to lead] an introduction, as to a branch of study —**i'sa·gog'ic** (-gäj'ik) *adj.*

**I·sa·iah** (ī zā'ə; *chiefly Brit.* -zī'-) [ < LL. < Gr. < Heb. *yĕsha'yah*, lit., God is salvation] 1. a masculine name 2. *Bible a)* a Hebrew prophet of the 8th cent. B.C. *b)* the book containing his teachings Also, in the Douay Bible, **I·sa'ias** (-əs)

**Is·car·i·ot** (is kar'ē ət) *see* JUDAS

**is·che·mi·a** (is kē'mē ə) *n.* [ModL. < Gr. < *ischein*, to hold + *haima*, blood] a lack of blood supply in an organ or tissue —**is·che'mic** *adj.*

**is·chi·um** (is'kē əm) *n., pl.* **-chi·a** (-ə) [L. < Gr. *ischion*, hip] the lowermost of the three sections of the hipbone

**-ise** (īz) *chiefly Brit. var. of* -IZE

**I·seult** (i sōolt') [Fr.] *same as* ISOLDE

**-ish** (ish) 1. [OE. *-isc*] *a suffix meaning: a)* of or belonging to (a specified people) [*Spanish*] *b)* like or characteristic of [*devilish*] *c)* tending to, verging on [*bookish, knavish*] *d)* somewhat, rather [*tallish*] *e)* [Colloq.] approximately, about [*thirtyish*] 2. [ < OFr.] *a suffix found in verbs of French origin* [*finish*]

**Ish·ma·el** (ish'mē əl, -mā-) [ < LL. < Heb. *yishmā'ē'l*, lit., God hears] *Bible* the son of Abraham and Hagar: he and his mother were made outcasts: Gen. 21:9–21 —*n.* an outcast

**Ish·ma·el·ite** (-ə līt') *n.* 1. a descendant of Ishmael, the traditional progenitor of Arab peoples 2. an outcast —**Ish'·ma·el·it'ish** *adj.*

**Ish·tar** (ish'tär) the Babylonian and Assyrian goddess of love and fertility

**Is·i·dore, Is·i·dor** (iz'ə dôr') [ult. < Gr. *Isidōros*, lit., gift of Isis] a masculine name: var. *Isadore, Isador*

**i·sin·glass** (ī'z'n glas', -zin-) *n.* [prob. < MDu. < *huizen*, sturgeon + *blas*, bladder] 1. a form of gelatin prepared from fish bladders, used as a clarifying agent and adhesive 2. mica, esp. in thin sheets

**I·sis** (ī'sis) the Egyptian goddess of fertility, sister and wife of Osiris

**isl.** *pl.* **isls.** 1. island 2. isle

**Is·lam** (is'läm, iz'-; -ləm, -lam; is läm') *n.* [Ar. *islām*, lit., submission (to God's will)] 1. the Moslem religion, a monotheistic religion in which the supreme deity is Allah and the founder and chief prophet is Mohammed 2. Moslems collectively 3. all the lands in which the Moslem religion predominates —**Is·lam'ic** (-lam'-, -läm'-), **Is'lam·it'ic** (-lə mit'ik) *adj.* —**Is'lam·ism** *n.* —**Is'lam·ite'** (-lə mīt') *n.*

**Is·lam·a·bad** (is läm'ə bäd') capital of Pakistan, in the NE part, near Rawalpindi: pop. 50,000

**Is·lam·ize** (is'lə mīz', iz'-) *vt., vi.* **-ized'**, **-iz'ing** to subject or adapt to Islam —**Is'lam·i·za'tion** *n.*

**is·land** (ī'lənd) *n.* [ < ME. *iland* (respelled after unrelated ISLE) < OE. *igland*, lit., island land & *ealand*, lit., water land] 1. a land mass not as large as a continent, surrounded by water 2. anything like an island in position or isolation 3. *Anat.* a cluster of cells differing from surrounding tissue in formation, etc. —*vt.* 1. to make into or like an island 2. to intersperse as with islands

**is·land·er** (-ər) *n.* a native or inhabitant of an island

**isle** (īl) *n.* [ < OFr. < ML. < L. *insula*] an island, esp. a small one —*vt.* **isled**, **isl'ing** *same as* ISLAND —*vi.* to live on an isle

**is·let** (ī'lit) *n.* a very small island

**islets** (or **islands**) **of Lang·er·hans** (läŋ'ər häns') [after P. Langerhans (1847–88), G. histologist] irregular groups of endocrine cells in the pancreas: they produce insulin

**ism** (iz'm) *n.* a doctrine, theory, system, etc., esp. one whose name ends in *-ism*

**-ism** (iz'm; iz əm) [ < OFr. & < L. *-isma* (< Gr. *-isma*) & *-ismus* (< Gr. *-ismos*)] *a suffix meaning:* 1. the act, practice, or result of [*terrorism*] 2. the condition of being [*pauperism*] 3. conduct or qualities characteristic of [*patriotism*] 4. the doctrine, school, or theory of [*socialism*] 5. devotion to [*nationalism*] 6. an instance, example, or peculiarity of [*witticism*] 7. an abnormal condition caused by [*alcoholism*]

**is·n't** (iz''nt) is not

**i·so-** [ < Gr. *isos*, equal] *a combining form meaning* equal, similar, alike, identical: also **is-**

**i·so·bar** (ī'sə bär') *n.* [ < prec. + Gr. *baros*, weight] 1. a line on a map connecting points on the earth's surface having equal barometric pressure 2. any of two or more forms of an atom having the same atomic weight but different atomic numbers —**i'so·bar'·ic** (-bar'ik) *adj.*

ISOBARS

**i·soch·ro·nal** (ī säk'rə n'l) *adj.* [ < ModL. < Gr. < *isos*, equal + *chronos*, time + -AL] 1. equal in length of time 2. occurring at equal intervals of time Also **i·soch'ro·nous** —**i·soch'ro·nism** *n.*

**i·so·cline** (ī'sə klīn') *n.* [ < ISO- + Gr. *klinein*, to slope] an anticline or syncline so compressed that the strata on both sides of the axis dip with equal inclination in the same direction —**i'so·cli'nal**, **i'so·clin'ic** (-klin'ik) *adj.* —**i'so·cli'nal·ly** *adv.*

**i·so·gon·ic** (ī'sə gän'ik) *adj.* [ISO- + -GON + -IC] 1. of or having equal angles 2. connecting or showing points on the earth's surface having the same magnetic declination —*n.* an isogonic line

**i·so·late** (ī'sə lāt', is'ə-; *for n., usually* -lit) *vt.* **-lat'ed**, **-lat'ing** [back-formation < *isolated* < It. < *isola* (< L. *insula*), island] 1. to set apart from others; place alone 2. *Chem.* to separate (an element or compound) in pure form from another compound or mixture 3. *Med.* to place (a patient with a contagious disease) apart from others to prevent the spread of infection —*n.* a person or group that is set apart —**i'so·la·ble** (-lə b'l) *adj.* —**i'so·la'tion** *n.* —**i'so·la'tor** *n.*

**i·so·la·tion·ist** (ī'sə lā'shən ist, is'ə-) *n.* a person who advocates isolation; specif., one who opposes the involvement of his country in international agreements, etc. —*adj.* of isolationists or their policy —**i'so·la'tion·ism** *n.*

**I·sol·de** (i sōl'də, i sōld') *see* TRISTRAM

**i·so·mer** (ī'sə mər) *n.* [ < Gr. < *isos*, equal + *meros*, a part] 1. any of two or more chemical compounds with the same elements in the same proportion by weight but differing in properties because of differences in the structure of their molecules  2. *Physics* any of two or more nuclei possessing the same number of neutrons and protons, but having different radioactive properties —i'so·mer'ic (-mer'ik) *adj.* —i·som·er·ism (ī säm'ər iz'm) *n.*

**i·som·er·ous** (ī säm'ər əs) *adj.* [see ISOMER] *Bot.* having the same number of parts in each whorl

**i·so·met·ric** (ī'sə met'rik) *adj.* [< Gr. < *isos*, equal + *metron*, a measure + -IC] **1.** of or having equality of measure: also **i'so·met'ri·cal**  **2.** of isometrics —*n.* [*pl.*] a method of physical exercise in which one set of muscles is briefly tensed in opposition to another set of muscles or to an immovable object —i'so·met'ri·cal·ly *adv.*

**i·so·mor·phic** (-môr'fik) *adj.* [ISO- + -MORPHIC] having similar or identical structure or form: also **i'so·mor'phous** (-fəs) —i'so·mor'phism *n.*

**i·so·prene** (ī'sə prēn') *n.* [< ISO- + PR(OPYL) + -ENE] a colorless, volatile liquid, $C_5H_8$, used in making synthetic rubber, resins, etc.

**i·sos·ce·les** (ī säs'ə lēz') *adj.* [LL. < Gr. *isoskeles* < *isos*, equal + *skelos*, a leg] designating a triangle with two equal sides

**i·so·therm** (ī'sə thurm') *n.* [< Fr. < *iso-*, ISO- + Gr. *thermē*, heat] a line on a map connecting points on the earth's surface having the same mean temperature or the same temperature at a given time

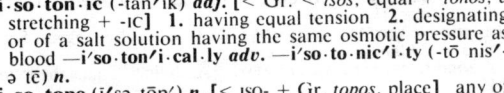

ISOSCELES TRIANGLES

**i·so·ther·mal** (ī'sə thur'm'l) *adj.* **1.** of or indicating equality or constancy of temperature  **2.** of isotherms —*n. same as* ISOTHERM —i'so·ther'mal·ly *adv.*

**i·so·ton·ic** (-tän'ik) *adj.* [< Gr. < *isos*, equal + *tonos*, a stretching + -IC] **1.** having equal tension  **2.** designating or of a salt solution having the same osmotic pressure as blood —i'so·ton'i·cal·ly *adv.* —i'so·to·nic'i·ty (-tō nis'-ə tē) *n.*

**i·so·tope** (ī'sə tōp') *n.* [< ISO- + Gr. *topos*, place] any of two or more forms of an element having the same or very closely related chemical properties and the same atomic number but different atomic weights [uranium *isotopes* U 235, U 238, U 239] —i'so·top'ic (-täp'ik, -tō'pik) *adj.*

**i·so·trop·ic** (ī'sə träp'ik, -trō'pik) *adj.* [ISO- + -TROPIC] having physical properties, as conductivity, elasticity, etc., that are the same regardless of the direction of measurement: also **i·sot·ro·pous** (ī sät'rə pəs) —i·sot'ro·py (-pē) *n.*

**Is·ra·el** (iz'rē əl, -rā-) [< OFr. < LL. < Gr. < Heb. *yisrā'ēl*, lit., contender with God] **1.** a masculine name  **2.** *Bible* Jacob: so named after wrestling with the angel: Gen. 32:28  **3.** the Jewish people, as descendants of Jacob  **4.** ancient land of the Hebrews, at the SE end of the Mediterranean  **5.** kingdom in the N part of this region  **6.** country between the Mediterranean Sea & the country of Jordan: a Jewish state: 7,992 sq. mi.; pop. 2,899,000; cap. Jerusalem

**Is·rae·li** (iz rā'lē) *adj.* of modern Israel or its people —*n.*, *pl.* **-lis, -li** a native or inhabitant of modern Israel

**Is·ra·el·ite** (iz'rē ə lit', -rā-) *n.* any of the people of ancient Israel or their descendants; Jew; Hebrew —*adj.* of ancient Israel or the Israelites; Jewish: also **Is'ra·el·it'ish** (-lit'ish), **Is'ra·el·it'ic** (-lit'ik)

**is·sei** (ē'sā) *n.*, *pl.* **-sei, -seis** [Jap., lit., 1st generation] [*also* I-] a Japanese who emigrated to the U.S. between 1907 and 1952

**is·su·ance** (ish'oo wəns) *n.* an issuing; issue

**is·sue** (ish'oo) *n.* [< OFr. pp. of *isser*. to go out < L. *exire* < *ex-*, out + *ire*, to go] **1.** an outgoing; outflow  **2.** a place or means of going out; exit; outlet  **3.** a result; consequence  **4.** offspring; a child or children  **5.** profits, as from property; proceeds  **6.** a point or matter under dispute  **7.** a sending or giving out  **8.** all that is put forth and circulated at one time [the May *issue* of a magazine, an *issue* of bonds]  **9.** *Med.* a discharge of blood, pus, etc. —*vi.* **-sued, -su·ing  1.** to go, pass, or flow out; emerge  **2.** to be descended; be born  **3.** to be derived or result (*from* a cause)  **4.** to end or result (*in* an effect)  **5.** to come as revenue  **6.** to be published; be put forth and circulated —*vt.* **1.** to let out; discharge  **2.** to give or deal out [to *issue* supplies]  **3.** to publish; put forth publicly or officially [to *issue* bonds, periodicals, an edict, etc.] —**at** (or **in**) **issue** in dispute; still to be decided —**join issue** to meet in conflict, argument, etc. —**take issue** to disagree —**is'su·a·ble** *adj.* —**is'su·er** *n.*

**-ist** (ist, əst) [< OFr. < L. < Gr. *-istēs*] *a suffix meaning:* **1.** a person who does, makes, or practices [*moralist, sati-*

rist]  **2.** a person skilled in or occupied with [*druggist, violinist*]  **3.** an adherent of [*anarchist*]

**Is·tan·bul** (is'tan bool', -tän-; -bool'; *Turk.* is täm'bool) seaport in NW Turkey, on the Bosporus: pop. 1,751,000 (met. area 2,150,000)

**isth·mi·an** (is'mē ən) *adj.* **1.** of an isthmus  **2.** [I-] *a*) of the Isthmus of Panama  *b*) of the Isthmus of Corinth —*n.* a native or inhabitant of an isthmus

**isth·mus** (is'məs) *n.*, *pl.* **-mus·es, -mi** (-mī) [L. < Gr. *isthmos*, a neck] a narrow strip of land having water at each side and connecting two larger bodies of land

**-is·tic** (is'tik) [< MFr. < L. < Gr. *-istikos*, or in Eng. < -IST + -IC] *a suffix used to form adjectives from nouns ending in* -ISM *and* -IST [*realistic, artistic*]: also **-is'ti·cal**

**is·tle** (ist'lē) *n.* [< AmSp. < Nahuatl *ichtli*] a fiber obtained from certain tropical American plants, used for baskets, etc.

**it** (it) *pron. for pl. see* THEY [OE. *hit*] the animal or thing under discussion  *It* is used as:  *a*) the subject of an impersonal verb [*it* is snowing]  *b*) the grammatical subject of a clause of which the actual subject is a following clause, etc. [*it* is settled that he will go]  *c*) an object of indefinite sense [to lord *it* over someone]  *d*) the antecedent to a relative pronoun from which it is separated by a predicate [*it* is your car that I want]  *e*) a reference to something indefinite but understood [*it*'s all right, no harm was done]  *f*) [Colloq.] an emphatic predicate pronoun referring to the person, thing, situation, etc. which is considered ultimate, final, or perfect [zero hour is here; this is *it*] —*n.* the player, as in the game of tag, who must do some specific thing —**with it** [Slang] alert, informed, or hip

**It., Ital. 1.** Italian  **2.** Italic  **3.** Italy

**ital.** italic (type)

**‡I·tal·ia** (ē täl'yä) *It. name of* ITALY

**I·tal·ian** (i tal'yən) *adj.* of Italy, its people, their language, etc. —*n.* **1.** a native or inhabitant of Italy  **2.** the Romance language of the Italians

**I·tal·ic** (i tal'ik) *adj.* **1.** of ancient Italy, its people, etc.  **2.** designating or of the subfamily of the Indo-European languages that includes Latin and the Romance languages —*n.* the Italic languages collectively

**i·tal·ic** (i tal'ik, ī-) *adj.* [< its first use in an *Italian* edition of Virgil] designating or of a type in which the characters slant upward to the right, used variously, as to emphasize words [this is *italic type*] —*n.* [usually *pl.*, sometimes with sing. v.] italic type or print

**i·tal·i·cize** (i tal'ə sīz') *vt.* **-cized', -ciz'ing  1.** to print in italics  **2.** to underscore (copy) to indicate it is to be printed in italics —i·tal'i·ci·za'tion *n.*

**It·a·ly** (it'l ē) country in S Europe, mostly on a peninsula & including Sicily & Sardinia: 116,304 sq. mi.; pop. 54,388,000; cap. Rome

**itch** (ich) *vi.* [OE. *giccan*] **1.** to feel an irritating sensation on the skin, with the desire to scratch  **2.** to have a restless desire —*vt.* **1.** to make itch  **2.** to irritate or annoy —*n.* **1.** an itching on the skin  **2.** a restless desire; hankering [an *itch* to travel] —**the itch** any of various skin disorders accompanied by severe irritation of the skin; specif., SCABIES

**itch·y** (-ē) *adj.* **itch'i·er, itch'i·est** like, feeling, or causing an itch —**itch'i·ly** *adv.* —**itch'i·ness** *n.*

**-ite** (īt) [< OFr. or L. < Gr. *-itēs*] *a suffix meaning:* **1.** a native or inhabitant of [*Brooklynite*]  **2.** a descendant from [*Israelite*]  **3.** an adherent or member of [*laborite*]  **4.** a commercially manufactured product [*dynamite*]  **5.** a fossil [*trilobite*]  **6.** a salt or ester of an acid whose name ends in -ous [*nitrite*]  **7.** a (specified) mineral or rock [*anthracite*]

**i·tem** (īt'əm) *adv.* [< L. < *ita*. so, thus]  also: used before each article in a series being enumerated —*n.* **1.** an article; unit; separate thing  **2.** a bit of news or information

**i·tem·ize** (-īz') *vt.* **-ized', -iz'ing** to specify the items of; set down by items [*itemize* the bill] —i'tem·i·za'tion *n.*

**it·er·ate** (it'ə rāt') *vt.* **-at'ed, -at'ing** [< L. pp. of *iterare* < *iterum*, again] to utter or do again or repeatedly —it'er·ant (-ər ənt) *adj.* —it'er·a'tion *n.* —it'er·a'tive *adj.*

**Ith·a·ca** (ith'ə kə) Gr. island off the W coast of Greece: legendary home of Odysseus

**i·tin·er·an·cy** (ī tin'ər ən sē, i-) *n.* **1.** an itinerating or being itinerant  **2.** official work requiring constant travel from place to place or frequent change of residence  Also **i·tin'er·a·cy** (-ə sē)

**i·tin·er·ant** (-ənt) *adj.* [< LL. prp. of *itinerari*. to travel < L. *iter*, a walk] traveling from place to place or on a circuit —*n.* a person who travels from place to place —i·tin'er·ant·ly *adv.*

**i·tin·er·ar·y** (ī tin'ə rer'ē, i-) *adj.* [see prec.] of traveling, journeys, routes, or roads —*n.*, *pl.* **-ar'ies  1.** a route

**2.** a record of a journey **3.** a guidebook for travelers **4.** a detailed plan or outline for a proposed journey

**i·tin·er·ate** (-rāt′) *vi.* **-at′ed, -at′ing** [< LL. pp. of *itinerari:* see ITINERANT] to travel from place to place or on a circuit —**i·tin′er·a′tion** *n.*

**-i·tion** (ish′ən) [< Fr. *-ition* or L. *-itio* (gen. *-itionis*)] *var. of* -ATION [*nutrition*]

**-i·tious** (ish′əs) [L. *-icius, -itius*] *a suffix that is used to form adjectives from nouns ending in* -ITION *and that means* of, having the nature of, characterized by [*nutritious*]

**-i·tis** (īt′əs, -is) [ModL. < L. < Gr. *-itis*] *a suffix meaning* inflammatory disease or inflammation of (a specified part or organ) [*sinusitis*]

**it′ll** (it′′l) **1.** it will **2.** it shall

**its** (its) *pron.* that or those belonging to it —*possessive pronominal adj.* of, belonging to, or done by it

**it's** (its) **1.** it is **2.** it has

**it·self** (it self′) *pron.* a form of the 3d pers. sing., neuter pronoun, used: *a)* as an intensive [the work *itself* is easy] *b)* as a reflexive [the dog bit *itself*] *c)* as a quasi-noun meaning "its real, true, or actual self" [the bird is not *itself* today]

**it·ty-bit·ty** (it′ē bit′ē) *adj.* [alteration < *little bit*] [Colloq.] very small; tiny **Also it·sy-bit·sy** (it′sē bit′sē)

**-i·ty** (ə tē, i-) [< OFr. *-ité* < L. *-itas*] *a suffix meaning* state, condition [*chastity, possibility*]

**IU, I.U.** international unit(s)

**IUD** intrauterine (contraceptive) device: also **IUCD**

**i.v.** **1.** initial velocity **2.** intravenous(ly)

**I·van** (ī′vən; Russ. i vän′) [Russ. < Gr.: see JOHN] **1.** a masculine name **2. Ivan III** 1440–1505; grand duke of Muscovy (1462–1505): called *the Great* **3. Ivan IV** 1530–84; grand duke of Muscovy (1533–84) & 1st czar of Russia (1547–84): called *the Terrible*

**I·va·no·vo** (ē vä′nô vô) city in C European R.S.F.S.R.: pop. 415,000

**I've** (īv) I have

**-ive** (iv) [< Fr. *-if*, fem. *-ive* < L. *-ivus*] *a suffix meaning:* **1.** of, relating to, having the nature of [*substantive*] **2.** tending to [*creative*]

**Ives** (īvz), **Charles Edward** 1874–1954; U.S. composer

**i·vied** (ī′vēd) *adj.* covered or overgrown with ivy

**i·vo·ry** (ī′vər ē, īv′rē) *n., pl.* **-ries** [< OFr. < L. < *ebur* < Egypt. *āb, ābu,* elephant] **1.** the hard, white substance forming the tusks of elephants, walruses, etc. **2.** any substance like ivory **3.** the color of ivory; creamy white **4.** a tusk of an elephant, etc. **5.** [*pl.*] things made of or suggesting ivory; specif., [Slang] *a)* piano keys *b)* teeth *c)* dice —*adj.* **1.** of or like ivory **2.** creamy-white

**Ivory Coast** country on the WC coast of Africa: 124,500 sq. mi.; pop. 3,750,000; cap. Abidjan

**ivory nut** *same as* VEGETABLE IVORY

**ivory tower** figuratively, a place of mental withdrawal from reality and action

**I·vy** (ī′vē) [< ff.] a feminine name

**i·vy** (ī′vē) *n., pl.* **i′vies** [OE. *ifig*] **1.** a climbing vine with a woody stem and evergreen leaves; English ivy **2.** any of various similar plants, as ground ivy, poison ivy, etc.

**Ivy League** [< the ivy-covered buildings] a group of colleges in the NE U.S. forming a league for intercollegiate sports: often used to describe the traditional fashions, attitudes, etc. associated with their students

**I.W.W., IWW** Industrial Workers of the World

**Ix·i·on** (ik sī′ən) *Gr. Myth.* a Thessalian king who was bound to a revolving wheel in Tartarus because he sought the love of Hera

**ix·tle** (iks′tlē, is′-) *n. same as* ISTLE

**I·yar** (ē yär′, ē′yär) *n.* [Heb.] the eighth month of the Jewish year: see JEWISH CALENDAR

**-i·za·tion** (ə zā′shən, ī-) *a suffix used to form nouns from verbs ending in* -IZE [*realization*]

**-ize** (īz) [< OFr. < LL. < Gr. *-izein*] *a suffix meaning:* **1.** to cause to be or become; make [*democratize*] **2.** to become or become like [*crystallize*] **3.** to treat or combine with [*oxidize*] **4.** to engage in; act in a specified way [*soliloquize, theorize*]

**Iz·mir** (iz mir′) seaport in W Turkey, on the Aegean Sea: pop. 412,000

**iz·zard** (iz′ərd) *n.* [var. of ZED] [Archaic or Dial.] the letter Z

# J

**J, j** (jā) *n., pl.* **J's, j's** **1.** the tenth letter of the English alphabet **2.** the sound of *J* or *j*

**j** *Physics a symbol for* joule

**J.** **1.** Journal **2.** Judge **3.** Justice

**Ja.** January

**J.A.** Judge Advocate

**jab** (jab) *vt., vi.* **jabbed, jab′bing** [< ME. *jobben*, to peck] **1.** to poke or thrust, as with a sharp instrument **2.** to punch with short, straight blows —*n.* a quick thrust, blow, or punch

**jab·ber** (jab′ər) *vi., vt.* [prob. echoic] to speak or say quickly, incoherently, or nonsensically; chatter —*n.* fast, incoherent, nonsensical talk —**jab′ber·er** *n.*

**ja·bot** (zha bō′, ja-) *n.* [Fr., bird's crop] a trimming or frill, as of lace, attached to the neck or front of a blouse, bodice, or shirt

**jac·a·ran·da** (jak′ə ran′də) *n.* [ModL. < Port. < Tupi] a tropical American tree with finely divided foliage and large clusters of lavender flowers

**ja·cinth** (jā′sinth, jas′inth) *n.* [< OFr. < L. *hyacinthus:* see HYACINTH] **1.** *same as* HYACINTH (sense 1 *b*) **2.** a reddish-orange color

**jack** (jak) [< OFr. < LL. *Jacobus*, JACOB] [J-] *a nickname for* JOHN —*n., pl.* for **5, 6, 7 jacks, jack:** see PLURAL, II, D, 1 [< nickname] **1.** [*often* J-] *a)* a man or boy; fellow *b)* a sailor **2.** *same as* BOOTJACK **3.** a fruit-flavored alcoholic drink, as applejack **4.** *a)* any of various devices used to lift or hoist something heavy a short distance [*hydraulic jack*, *automobile jack*] *b)* a device for turning a spit in roasting **5.** a male donkey **6.** *short for* JACK RABBIT **7.** any of various fishes, as the pickerel, pike, etc. **8.** [Old Slang] money **9.** *Elec.* a plug-in receptacle used to make electric contact **10.** *Games*

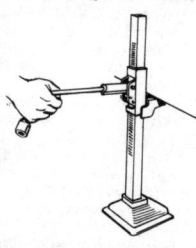

JACK (sense 4 *a*)

*a)* a playing card with a page boy's picture on it; knave *b)* any of the small pebbles or six-pronged metal pieces used in playing jacks: see JACKS *c)* in the game of bowls, the target ball **11.** *Naut.* a small flag flown on a ship's bow as a signal or to show nationality —*vt.* to raise by means of a jack —*adj.* male: of some animals —**every man jack** everyone —**jack up 1.** to raise by means of a jack **2.** [Colloq.] to raise (prices, salaries, etc.) **3.** [Colloq.] to encourage to perform one's duty

**jack-** [see prec.] *a combining form meaning:* **1.** male [*jackass*] **2.** large or strong [*jackboot*]; boy; fellow: used in hyphenated compounds [*jack-in-the-box*]

**jack·al** (jak′əl, -ôl) *n., pl.* **-als, -al:** see PLURAL, II, D, 1 [< Turk. < Per. *shagal* < Sans.] **1.** a yellowish-gray, meat-eating wild dog of Asia and N Africa, smaller than the wolf **2.** one who does dishonest or humiliating tasks for another

**jack·a·napes** (jak′ə nāps′) *n.* [< nickname of a 15th-c. Duke of Suffolk] **1.** formerly, a monkey **2.** a conceited, insolent fellow; saucy rascal

**jack·ass** (jak′as′) *n.* [JACK- + ASS] **1.** a male donkey **2.** a stupid or foolish person; nitwit

**jack·boot** (-bōōt′) *n.* [JACK- + BOOT¹] a heavy, sturdy military boot that reaches above the knee

**jack·daw** (-dô′) *n.* [JACK- + DAW] **1.** a European black bird related to the crow, but smaller **2.** *same as* GRACKLE

**jack·et** (jak′it) *n.* [< OFr. dim. of *jaque* < Sp. *jaco*, coat < Ar. *shakk*] **1.** a short coat **2.** an outer covering; specif., *a)* *same as* DUST JACKET *b)* a cardboard holder for a phonograph record *c)* the insulating casing on a boiler, etc. *d)* the skin of a potato, etc. —*vt.* **1.** to put a jacket, or coat, on **2.** to cover with a casing, wrapper, etc.

**Jack Frost** frost or cold weather personified

**jack·ham·mer** (-ham′ər) *n.* [JACK- + HAMMER] a portable type of pneumatic hammer, used for drilling rock, brick, etc.

**jack-in-the-box** (jak′in thə bäks′) *n., pl.* **-box′es** a toy consisting of a box from which a little figure on a spring jumps up when the lid is lifted: also **jack′-in-a-box′**

**jack-in-the-pul·pit** (-pool′pit) n., pl. **-pits** an American plant of the arum family, with a flower spike partly arched over by a hoodlike covering

**Jack Ketch** (kech) [Brit.] an official hangman

**jack·knife** (jak′nīf′) n., pl. **-knives′** (-nīvz′) [JACK- + KNIFE] 1. a large pocketknife 2. a dive in which the diver keeps his knees unbent, touches his feet with his hands, and then straightens out just before plunging into the water —vi. **-knifed′, -knif′ing** 1. to bend at the middle as in a jackknife dive 2. to turn on the hitch so as to form a sharp angle with each other: said of a vehicle and its trailer

JACK-IN-THE-PULPIT

**jack·leg** (-leg′) adj. not properly trained or qualified —n. a jackleg person or thing

**jack-of-all-trades** (jak′əv ôl′trādz′) n., pl. **jacks′-** [see JACK-, 3] [often J-] a person who can do many kinds of work acceptably; handyman

**jack-o′-lan·tern** (jak′ə lan′tərn) n., pl. **-terns** 1. a shifting, elusive light seen over marshes at night; will-o′-the-wisp 2. a hollow pumpkin, real or artificial, cut to look like a face and used as a lantern

**jack pine** a pine of Canada and the N U.S., having short needles and many woody cones

**jack·pot** (jak′pät′) n. [JACK, n. 10 a + POT] 1. cumulative stakes in a poker game, played for only when some player has a pair of jacks or better to open 2. any cumulative stakes, as in a slot machine **—hit the jackpot** [Slang] 1. to win the jackpot 2. to attain the highest success

**jack rabbit** [JACK(ASS) + RABBIT: from its long ears] a large hare of W N. America, with long ears and strong hind legs

**jacks** (jaks) n.pl. [< JACKSTONE] [with sing. v.] a children's game in which pebbles or small, six-pronged metal pieces are tossed and picked up in various ways, esp. while bouncing a small ball

**jack·screw** (jak′skroo′) n. [JACK- + SCREW] a machine for raising heavy things a short distance, operated by turning a screw

**Jack·son** (jak′s′n) [after A. JACKSON] capital of Miss., in the SW part: pop. 203,000

**Jack·son** (jak′s′n) 1. **Andrew,** 1767–1845; 7th president of the U.S. (1829–37) 2. **Thomas Jonathan,** (nickname **Stonewall Jackson**) 1824–63; Confederate general in the Civil War

**Jack·son·ville** (jak′s′n vil′) [after A. JACKSON] port in NE Fla.: pop. 541,000 (met. area 736,000)

**jack·stone** (jak′stōn′) n. [for dial. checkstone < check, pebble] 1. same as JACK (n. 10 b) 2. [pl., with sing. v.] same as JACKS

**jack·straw** (-strô′) n. [JACK- + STRAW] a narrow strip of wood, plastic, etc. used in a game (**jackstraws**) played by tossing a number of such strips into a jumbled heap and trying to remove them one at a time without moving any of the others

**Ja·cob** (jā′kəb) [< LL. < Gr. < Heb. ja′aqob, lit., seizing by the heel] 1. a masculine name: dim. **Jake** 2. Bible a son of Isaac and father of the founders of the twelve tribes of Israel: Gen. 25–50

**Jac·o·be·an** (jak′ə bē′ən) adj. [< Jacobus, Latinized form of James] 1. of James I of England 2. of the period in England when he was king (1603–25) —n. a poet, diplomat, etc. of this period

**Jac·o·bin** (jak′ə bin) n. [< the Church of St. Jacques in Paris, the society's meeting place] 1. any member of a society of radical democrats in France during the Revolution of 1789 2. a political radical —adj. of the Jacobins: also **Jac′o·bin′ic, Jac′o·bin′i·cal —Jac′o·bin·ism** n.

**Jac·o·bite** (jak′ə bīt′) n. [cf. JACOBEAN] a supporter of James II of England after his abdication, or of his descendants′ claims to the throne —**Jac′o·bit′ic** (-bit′ik), **Jac′o·bit′i·cal** adj.

**Jacob's ladder** 1. Bible the ladder to heaven that Jacob saw in a dream: Gen. 28:12 2. a ladder made of rope, wire, etc., used on ships

**Jac·quard** (jə kärd′) n. [after the Fr. inventor, J. M. Jacquard (1752–1834)] a loom (**Jacquard loom**) having an endless belt of cards punched with holes arranged to produce a figured weave (**Jacquard weave**)

**Jac·que·line** (jak′wə lin, jak′ə-) [Fr., fem. of Jacques, JACK] a feminine name: dim. **Jacky**

**Jacques-Car·tier** (zhàk kàr tyā′; E. zhak′kär tyā′) city in S Quebec, near Montreal: pop. 53,000

**jade**¹ (jād) n. [Fr. < Sp. < piedra de ijada, stone of the side: from the notion that it cured pains in the side] 1. a

hard stone, usually green, used in jewelry, carvings, etc. 2. a green color of medium hue —adj. 1. made of jade 2. green like jade

**jade**² (jād) n. [< ON. jalda, a mare < Finn.] 1. a horse, esp. a worn-out, worthless one 2. a loose or disreputable woman 3. [Now Rare] a saucy young woman —vt., vi. **jad′ed, jad′ing** to make or become tired, weary, or worn-out —**jad′ish** adj.

**jad·ed** (jā′did) adj. 1. tired; worn-out; wearied 2. satiated —**jad′ed·ly** adv. —**jad′ed·ness** n.

**jae·ger** (yā′gər) n. [< G. jäger, huntsman] any of several sea birds which force other, weaker birds to leave or give up their prey

**Jaf·fa** (yä′fə, jaf′ə) see TEL-AVIV-JAFFA

**jag**¹ (jag) n. [ME. jagge] 1. a sharp, toothlike projection 2. [Archaic] a notch or pointed tear, as in cloth —vt. **jagged, jag′ging** 1. to notch or pink (cloth, etc.) 2. to tear raggedly

**jag**² (jag) n. [< ?] [Slang] 1. an intoxicated condition due to liquor or drugs 2. a drunken spree 3. a period of uncontrolled activity [a crying jag]

**jag·ged** (jag′id) adj. having sharp projecting points; ragged or notched —**jag′ged·ly** adv. —**jag′ged·ness** n.

**jag·uar** (jag′wär, -yoo wär′) n., pl. **-uars, -uar:** see PLURAL, II, D, 1 [Port. < Tupi] a large cat, yellowish with black spots, found from SW U.S. to Argentina: it is similar to the leopard, but larger

**Jah·veh, Jah·ve, Jah·weh, Jah·we** (yä′ve) same as JEHO-VAH

**jai a·lai** (hī′lī′, hī′ə lī′) [Sp. < Basque jai, celebration + alai, merry] a Latin American game like handball, played with a curved basket fastened to the arm, for catching and hurling the ball

**jail** (jāl) n. [< OFr. gaole < LL. caveola, dim. of L. cavea, a cage] 1. a building for confining those awaiting trial or convicted of minor offenses 2. imprisonment —vt. to put or keep in jail

**jail·bird** (-burd′) n. [Colloq.] 1. a prisoner in a jail 2. a person often put in jail

**jail·break** (-brāk′) n. a breaking out of jail

**jail·er, jail·or** (-ər) n. a person in charge of a jail or of prisoners

**Jain** (jīn) n. [< Hindi Jaina < Sans. jina, saint] a believer in Jainism —adj. of the Jains or their religion Also **Jai·na** (jī′nə), **Jain′ist**

**Jain·ism** (jīn′iz′m) n. a Hindu religion founded in the 6th cent. B.C.: it emphasizes asceticism and reverence for all living things

**Jai·pur** (jī′poor) city in NW India: pop. 403,000

**Ja·kar·ta** (jə kär′tə) capital of Indonesia, on the NW coast of Java: pop. c.4,500,000

**jal·ap** (jal′əp) n. [Fr. < Sp. < Jalapa, city in Mexico] 1. the dried root of a Mexican plant, formerly used as a purgative 2. the plant

**ja·lop·y** (jə läp′ē) n., pl. **-lop′ies** [< ?] [Slang] an old, ramshackle automobile

**jal·ou·sie** (jal′ə sē′) n. [Fr. < OFr. gelosie, jealousy (see JEALOUS)] a window, shade, or door formed of adjustable, horizontal slats of wood, metal, or glass, for regulating the air or light entering

**jam**¹ (jam) vt. **jammed, jam′ming** [< ?] 1. to squeeze into or through a confined space 2. to bruise or crush 3. to push or crowd 4. to pack full or tight 5. to fill or block (a passageway, etc.) by crowding in 6. to wedge or make stick so that it cannot move or work 7. to make (radio or radar signals) unintelligible, as by sending out others on the same wavelength —vi. 1. to become wedged or stuck fast, esp. so as to become unworkable 2. to push against one another in a confined space 3. [Slang] Jazz to improvise —n. 1. a jamming or being jammed 2. a group of persons or things blocking a passageway, etc. [a traffic jam] 3. [Colloq.] a difficult situation

JALOUSIES

**jam**² (jam) n. [< ? prec.] a food made by boiling fruit with sugar to a thick mixture

**Ja·mai·ca** (jə mā′kə) country on an island of the West Indies, south of Cuba: a member of the Commonwealth: 4,411 sq. mi.; pop. 1,972,000; cap. Kingston —**Ja·mai′can** adj., n.

**jamb** (jam) n. [< OFr. jambe < LL. gamba, a leg] a side post of an opening for a door, window, etc.

**jam·ba·lay·a** (jum′bə lī′ə) n. [AmFr. < ModPr. jambalaia] a Creole stew made of rice and shrimp, oysters, crabs, ham, chicken, etc.

**jam·bo·ree** (jam′bə rē′) *n.* [< ?] **1.** [Colloq.] *a)* a boisterous party or revel *b)* a gathering with planned entertainment **2.** a national or international assembly of boy scouts

**James**[1] (jāmz) [< OFr. < LL. *Jacomus*, later form of *Jacobus*, JACOB] **1.** a masculine name **2.** *Bible a)* either of two Christian apostles *b)* a brother of Jesus; also, a book of the New Testament sometimes attributed to him **3. James I** 1566–1625; king of England (1603–25) **4. James II** 1633–1701; king of England (1685–88): deposed: son of CHARLES I **5. Henry,** 1843–1916; U.S. novelist, in England **6. Jesse (Woodson),** 1847–82; U.S. outlaw **7. William,** 1842–1910; U.S. psychologist & philosopher: brother of *Henry*

**James**[2] (jāmz) river in Va., flowing from the W part southeast into Chesapeake Bay

**James·town** (jāmz′toun′) [after JAMES I] colonial settlement (1607) at the mouth of the James River

**Jam·mu and Kashmir** (jum′ōō) state of N India, control of which is disputed by Pakistan

**jam-packed** (jam′pakt′) *adj.* tightly packed

**jam session** an informal gathering of jazz musicians to play improvisations

**Jan.** January

**Jane** (jān) [var. of JOANNA] a feminine name —*n.* [j-] [Slang] a girl or woman

**Jan·et** (jan′it) [dim. of prec.] a feminine name

**jan·gle** (jaŋ′g'l) *vi.* **-gled, -gling** [< OFr. *jangler*] **1.** to make a harsh, inharmonious sound, as of a bell out of tune **2.** to quarrel noisily —*vt.* **1.** to utter in a harsh, inharmonious manner **2.** to cause to make a harsh sound **3.** to irritate very much [to *jangle* one's nerves] —*n.* **1.** noisy talk or arguing **2.** a harsh sound —**jan′gler** *n.*

**Jan·ice** (jan′is) [< JANE, JANET] a feminine name

**jan·i·tor** (jan′i tər) *n.* [L., doorkeeper < *janua*, door] the custodian of a building, who does routine maintenance —**jan′i·to′ri·al** (-ə tôr′ē əl) *adj.*

**jan·i·zar·y** (jan′ə zer′ē) *n., pl.* **-zar′ies** [< Fr. < It. < Turk. < *yeni*, new + *cheri*, soldiery] [*often* **J-**] **1.** a Turkish soldier, orig. one in the former sultan's guard **2.** any very loyal supporter Also **jan′is·sar′y** (-ser′ē)

**Jan·u·ar·y** (jan′yōō wer′ē) *n., pl.* **-ar′ies** [< L. *Januarius* (*mensis*), (the month) of Janus] the first month of the year, having 31 days: abbrev. **Jan., Ja.**

**Ja·nus** (jā′nəs) *Rom. Myth.* the god who was guardian of portals and patron of beginnings and endings: his head is shown with two faces, one in front, the other at the back

**Jap.** **1.** Japan **2.** Japanese

**Ja·pan** (jə pan′) island country off the E coast of Asia, including Hokkaido, Honshu, Kyushu, Shikoku, & many smaller islands: 142,726 sq. mi.; pop. 102,833,000; cap. Tokyo

**ja·pan** (jə pan′) *n.* [orig. from Japan] **1.** a varnish giving a hard, glossy finish **2.** a liquid used as a paint drier **3.** objects decorated and varnished in the Japanese style —*vt.* **-panned′, -pan′ning** to varnish with japan

**Jap·a·nese** (jap′ə nēz′) *adj.* of Japan, its people, language, culture, etc. —*n.* **1.** *pl.* **-nese′** a native of Japan **2.** the language of Japan

**Japanese beetle** a shiny, green-and-brown beetle, orig. from Japan, which eats leaves, fruits, and grasses, and is damaging to crops

**Japanese lantern** *same as* CHINESE LANTERN

**Japanese quince** a spiny plant of the rose family, with pink or red flowers and green fruit

**jape** (jāp) *vi.* **japed, jap′ing** [ME. *japen*] **1.** to joke; jest **2.** to play tricks —*vt.* [Now Rare] to make fun of —*n.* **1.** a joke or jest **2.** a trick —**jap′er·y** *n., pl.* **-er·ies**

**Ja·pheth** (jā′fith) *Bible* the youngest of Noah's three sons: Gen. 5:32

**ja·pon·i·ca** (jə pän′i kə) *n.* [ModL., fem. of *Japonicus*, of Japan < *Japonia*, Japan < Fr. *Japon*] *a popular name for* JAPANESE QUINCE, CAMELLIA, etc.

**jar**[1] (jär) *vi.* **jarred, jar′ring** [ult. echoic] **1.** to make a harsh sound; grate **2.** to have a harsh, irritating effect (*on* one) **3.** to vibrate from a sudden impact **4.** to clash, disagree, or quarrel —*vt.* **1.** to make vibrate by sudden impact **2.** to cause to give a harsh or discordant sound **3.** to jolt or shock —*n.* **1.** a harsh, grating sound **2.** a vibration due to a sudden impact **3.** a jolt or shock **4.** a sharp clash or quarrel

**jar**[2] (jär) *n.* [Fr. *jarre* < OPr. or Sp. < Ar. *jarrah,* earthen water container] **1.** a container made of glass, stone, or earthenware, with a large opening and no spout **2.** as much as a jar will hold: also **jar′ful′**

**jar·di·niere** (jär′d'n ir′; *Fr.* zhàr dē nyer′) *n.* [< Fr. < *jardin,* a garden] **1.** an ornamental bowl, pot, or stand for flowers or plants **2.** a garnish for meats, of several vegetables cooked separately

**jar·gon** (jär′gən) *n.* [MFr., a chattering] **1.** incoherent speech; gibberish **2.** a language or dialect that seems incomprehensible or outlandish to one **3.** a hybrid language

or dialect; esp., pidgin **4.** the specialized vocabulary and idioms of those in the same work, profession, etc., as of sports writers: see SLANG —**jar′gon·is′tic** *adj.*

**Jas.** James

**jas·mine, jas·min** (jaz′min; *chiefly Brit.* jas′-) *n.* [< Fr. < Ar. < Per. *yāsamīn*] **1.** a tropical and subtropical plant of the olive family, with fragrant flowers of yellow, red, or white **2.** any of several other similar plants with fragrant flowers

**Ja·son** (jās′'n) [< L. *Iāson* < Gr., lit., healer] **1.** a masculine name **2.** *Gr. Myth.* a prince who led the Argonauts and got the Golden Fleece

**jas·per** (jas′pər) *n.* [< MFr. < L. < Gr. *iaspis*] **1.** an opaque variety of colored quartz, usually reddish, yellow, or brown **2.** *Bible* a precious stone, probably an opaque green quartz

**ja·to, JA·TO** (jā′tō) *n.* [ *j(et)-a(ssisted) t(ake)o(ff)*] an airplane takeoff assisted by small, solid-propellant rockets

**jaun·dice** (jôn′dis, jän′-) *n.* [< OFr. *jaunisse,* ult. < L. *galbinus,* greenish yellow < *galbus,* yellow] **1.** *a)* a condition in which the eyeballs, skin, and urine become abnormally yellow as a result of bile pigments in the blood *b)* popularly, a disease causing this, as hepatitis **2.** bitterness or prejudice caused by jealousy, envy, etc. —*vt.* **-diced, -dicing 1.** to cause to have jaundice **2.** to make bitter or prejudiced through jealousy, envy, etc.

**jaunt** (jônt, jänt) *vi.* [< ?] to take a short trip for pleasure —*n.* such a trip; excursion

**jaun·ty** (-ē) *adj.* **-ti·er, -ti·est** [< Fr. *gentil,* genteel] **1.** in fashion; chic **2.** gay and carefree; sprightly —**jaun′ti·ly** *adv.* —**jaun′ti·ness** *n.*

**Jav.** Javanese

**Ja·va** (jä′və, jav′ə) large island of Indonesia, southeast of Sumatra: 48,842 sq. mi. —*n.* **1.** a coffee grown on Java and nearby islands **2.** [*often* j-] [Slang] any coffee

**Java man** a type of primitive man (*Homo erectus erectus*) known from fossil remains found in Java

**Jav·a·nese** (jav′ə nēz′) *adj.* of Java, its people, etc. —*n.* **1.** *pl.* **-nese′** a native or inhabitant of Java **2.** the Indonesian language of Java

**jav·e·lin** (jav′lin, jav′ə lin) *n.* [MFr. *javeline,* fem. dim. < *javelot,* a spear] **1.** a light spear for throwing **2.** a pointed wooden or metal shaft, about 8½ ft. long, thrown for distance as a field event (**javelin throw**) in track and field meets

**jaw** (jô) *n.* [< ? OFr. *joue,* cheek] **1.** either of the two bony parts that hold the teeth and frame the mouth **2.** either of two parts that open and close to grip or crush something, as in a monkey wrench or vise **3.** [*pl.*] *a)* the mouth *b)* the entrance of a canyon, valley, etc. **4.** [Slang] talk; esp., abusive or boring talk —*vi.* [Slang] to talk, esp. in a boring or abusive way —*vt.* [Slang] to scold or reprove

**jaw·bone** (-bōn′) *n.* a bone of a jaw, esp. of the lower jaw —*vt., vi.* **-boned′, -bon′ing** to attempt to persuade by using the influence of one's high office or position

**jaw·break·er** (-brā′kər) *n.* **1.** a machine with jaws for crushing rocks, ore, etc. **2.** a hard, usually round candy **3.** [Slang] a word that is hard to pronounce

**jay** (jā) *n.* [< OFr. *gai* < LL. *gaius,* a jay] **1.** any of several birds of the crow family **2.** *same as* BLUE JAY **3.** [Colloq.] a stupid or foolish person

**Jay** (jā), **John** 1745–1829; Am. statesman & jurist: 1st chief justice of the U.S. (1789–95)

**Jay·hawk·er** (jā′hô′kər) *n.* [Colloq.] *a nickname for* a Kansan: also **Jay′hawk′**

**jay·walk** (jā′wôk′) *vi.* [JAY, 3 + WALK] [Colloq.] to walk in or across a street carelessly without obeying traffic rules and signals —**jay′walk′er** *n.* —**jay′walk′ing** *n.*

**jazz** (jaz) *n.* [< ? Creole patois *jass,* sexual term] **1.** a kind of music characterized by syncopation, rubato, melodic variations, and unusual tonal effects on the saxophone, clarinet, trumpet, trombone, etc. **2.** loosely, any popular dance music **3.** [Slang] remarks, acts, etc. regarded as hypocritical, tiresome, etc. —*adj.* of, in, or like jazz —*vt.* **1.** to play or arrange as jazz **2.** [Slang] to enliven or embellish (usually with *up*) —**jazz′i·ly** *adv.* —**jazz′i·ness** *n.* —**jazz′y** *adj.* **-i·er, -i·est**

**jazz·man** (jaz′man′) *n., pl.* **-men′** (-men′) a jazz musician

**jct.** junction

**JD** juvenile delinquency (or delinquent)

**Je.** June

**jeal·ous** (jel′əs) *adj.* [< OFr. *gelos* < ML. *zelosus:* see ZEAL] **1.** very watchful or careful in guarding or keeping [*jealous* of one's rights] **2.** *a)* resentfully suspicious, as of a rival [a husband *jealous* of other men] *b)* resentfully envious *c)* resulting from such feelings [a *jealous* rage] **3.** [Now Rare] requiring exclusive loyalty [a *jealous* God] —**jeal′ous·ly** *adv.* —**jeal′ous·ness** *n.*

**jeal·ous·y** (-ē) *n., pl.* **-ous·ies** **1.** the quality or condition of being jealous **2.** an instance of this; jealous feeling

**Jean** (jēn) **1.** [Fr., equiv. of JOHN] a masculine name **2.** [var. of JOANNA] a feminine name

**jean** (jēn) *n.* [< OFr. *Janne* < ML. < L. *Genua*, Genoa] **1.** a durable, twilled cotton cloth, used for work clothes and casual wear **2.** [*pl.*] trousers of this material, often blue, or of denim

**Jeanne** (jēn) [var. of JOANNA] a feminine name

**Jeanne d'Arc** (zhän därk) *see* JOAN OF ARC

**Jean·nette** (jə net′) [dim. of JEANNE] a feminine name

**Jeans** (jēnz), Sir **James** (**Hopwood**) 1877–1946; Eng. physicist, astronomer, & writer

**jee** (jē) *interj., n., vt., vi. same as* GEE¹

**jeep** (jēp) *n.* [after a creature in a comic strip by E. C. Segar (1894–1938)] a small, rugged, military automotive vehicle with a 1/4-ton capacity and a four-wheel drive —**[J-** ] *a trademark for* a similar vehicle for civilian use

**jee·pers** (jē′pərz) *interj.* [altered < JESUS] a mild exclamation of surprise, etc.

**jeer** (jir) *vt., vi.* [< ? CHEER] to make fun of (a person or thing) in a rude, sarcastic manner; mock; scoff (at) —*n.* a jeering remark; sarcastic or derisive comment —**jeer′er** *n.* —**jeer′ing·ly** *adv.*

**Jef·fer·son** (jef′ər s'n), **Thomas** 1743–1826; Am. statesman; 3d president of the U.S. (1801–09): drew up the Declaration of Independence —**Jef′fer·so′ni·an** (-sō′nē ən) *adj., n.*

**Jefferson City** [after T. JEFFERSON] capital of Mo., on the Missouri: pop. 34,000

**Jeff·rey** (jef′rē) [var. of GEOFFREY] a masculine name: dim. *Jeff*

**Je·hosh·a·phat** (ji häs′ə fat′, -häsh′-) *Bible* a king of Judah in the 9th cent. B.C.: II Chr. 17 ff.

**Je·ho·vah** (ji hō′və) [transliteration of Heb. sacred name for God] God; (the) Lord

**Jehovah's Witnesses** a proselytizing Christian sect founded by Charles T. Russell (1852–1916)

**je·hu** (jē′hōō, -hyōō) *n.* [< *Jehu* in the Bible: II Kings 9] [Colloq.] a fast, reckless driver

**je·june** (ji jōōn′) *adj.* [L. *jejunus*, empty] **1.** not nourishing **2.** not interesting or satisfying; dull **3.** not mature; childish —**je·june′ly** *adv.* —**je·june′ness** *n.*

**je·ju·num** (ji jōō′nəm) *n., pl.* **-na** (-nə) [< L.: see JEJUNE] the middle part of the small intestine, between the duodenum and the ileum —**je·ju′nal** *adj.*

**jell** (jel) *vi., vt.* [back-formation < JELLY] **1.** to become or make into jelly **2.** [Colloq.] to take or give definite form; crystallize /the plans didn't *jell*/ —*n.* [Dial.] *same as* JELLY

**jel·li·fy** (jel′ə fī′) *vt., vi.* **-fied′**, **-fy′ing** to change into jelly —**jel′li·fi·ca′tion** *n.*

**jel·ly** (jel′ē) *n., pl.* **-lies** [< OFr. pp. of *geler* < L. *gelare*, to freeze] **1.** a soft, partially transparent, gelatinous food resulting from the cooling of fruit juice boiled with sugar, or of meat juice cooked down **2.** any substance like this —*vt.* **-lied**, **-ly·ing 1.** to make into jelly **2.** to coat, fill, or serve with jelly —*vi.* to become jelly —**jel′ly·like′** *adj.*

**jel·ly·bean** (-bēn′) *n.* a small, bean-shaped, gelatinous candy with a colored sugar coating

**jel·ly·fish** (-fish′) *n., pl.* **-fish′**, **-fish′es**: see FISH **1.** an invertebrate sea animal with a body made up largely of jellylike substance and shaped like an umbrella: it has long, hanging tentacles with stinging cells on them **2.** [Colloq.] a weak-willed person

**jel·ly·roll** (-rōl′) *n.* a thin sheet of spongecake spread with jelly and rolled so as to form layers

**Jen·ghiz Khan** (jeŋ′gis) *same as* GENGHIS KHAN

**Jen·ner** (jen′ər), **Edward** 1749–1823; Eng. physician: introduced vaccination

**jen·net** (jen′it) *n.* [< MFr. < Sp. *jinete*, horseman < Ar. *Zenāta*, a tribe of Barbary] any of a breed of small Spanish horses

JELLYFISH
(to 16 in. long)

**Jen·ni·fer** (jen′i fər) [altered < GUINEVERE] a feminine name

**Jen·ny** (jen′ē) [dim. of JANE] a feminine name

**jen·ny** (jen′ē) *n., pl.* **-nies** [< prec.] **1.** *short for* SPINNING JENNY **2.** *a)* the female of some birds /a jenny wren/ *b)* a female donkey

**jeop·ard·ize** (jep′ər dīz′) *vt.* **-ized′**, **-iz′ing** to put in jeopardy; risk loss, failure, etc. of; endanger

**jeop·ard·y** (-dē) *n., pl.* **-ard·ies** [< OFr. *jeu parti*, lit., a game with even chances, ult. < L. *jocus*, a game + pp. of *partire*, to divide] **1.** great danger; peril **2.** *Law* the situation of an accused person on trial for a crime

**Jer.** Jeremiah

**jer·bo·a** (jər bō′ə) *n.* [Ar. *yarbū*] any of various small, nocturnal, leaping rodents of N Africa and Asia, with very long hind legs

**jer·e·mi·ad** (jer′ə mī′əd) *n.* a lamentation or tale of woe: in allusion to the *Lamentations of Jeremiah*

**Jer·e·mi·ah** (-ə) [< LL. < Gr. < Heb. *yirmeyāh*, lit., the Lord loosens (i.e., from the womb)] **1.** a masculine name: var. *Jeremy* **2.** *Bible a)* a Hebrew prophet of the 7th and 6th cent. B.C. *b)* the book containing his warnings and prophecies Also, in the Douay Bible, **Jer′e·mi′as** (-əs)

**Jer·i·cho** (jer′i kō′) city in W Jordan: site of an ancient city whose walls (*Bible*, Josh. 6) were miraculously destroyed when trumpets were sounded

**jerk¹** (jurk) *vt.* [< ?] **1.** to pull, twist, push, or throw with a sudden, sharp movement **2.** [Colloq.] to make and serve (ice cream sodas) —*vi.* **1.** to move with a jerk or in jerks **2.** to twitch —*n.* **1.** a sharp, abrupt pull, twist, push, etc. **2.** a sudden muscular contraction caused by a reflex action **3.** [Slang] a person regarded as stupid, foolish, etc.

**jerk²** (jurk) *vt.* [altered (after prec.) < JERKY²] to preserve (meat) by slicing into strips and drying in the sun —*n. same as* JERKY²

**jer·kin** (jur′kin) *n.* [< ?] a closefitting, sleeveless jacket of a kind worn in the 16th and 17th cent.

**jerk·wa·ter** (jurk′wôt′ər, -wät′-) *n.* [JERK¹ + WATER] a train on an early branch railroad —*adj.* [Colloq.] small, unimportant, etc. /a jerkwater town/

**jerk·y¹** (-ē) *adj.* **jerk′i·er**, **jerk′i·est 1.** characterized by jerks; making sudden starts and stops; spasmodic **2.** [Slang] stupid, dull, foolish, etc. —**jerk′i·ly** *adv.*

**jer·ky²** (jur′kē) *n.* [< Sp. *charqui* < Quechua] meat, esp. beef, that has been preserved by being sliced into strips and dried in the sun

**Je·rome** (jə rōm′) [Fr. < L. < Gr. < *hieros*, holy + *onyma*, name] **1.** a masculine name: dim. *Jerry* **2.** Saint, (born *Eusebius Hieronymus Sophronius*) 340?–420 A.D.; monk & church scholar: author of the Vulgate

**jer·ry·built** (jer′ē bilt′) *adj.* [prob. < name *Jerry*, infl. by JURY²] built poorly, of cheap materials

**Jer·sey** (jur′zē) largest of the Channel Islands —*n., pl.* **-seys 1.** any of a breed of small, reddish-brown dairy cattle, originally from Jersey **2.** **[j-]** *a)* a soft, elastic, knitted cloth *b)* any closefitting, knitted upper garment

**Jersey City** city in NE N.J., across the Hudson from New York: pop. 224,000 (met. area 555,000)

**Je·ru·sa·lem** (jə rōō′sə ləm) capital of Israel (sense 6), in the C part: pop. 266,000

**Jerusalem artichoke** [altered (after prec.) < It. *girasole*, sunflower] **1.** a tall N. American sunflower with edible potatolike tubers **2.** such a tuber

**jess** (jes) *n.* [< OFr. *gets*, pl. < L. *jactus*, a casting] a strap for a falcon's leg, with a ring for attaching a leash —*vt.* to fasten jesses on

**jes·sa·mine** (jes′ə min) *n. same as* JASMINE

**Jes·se** (jes′ē) [Heb. *yīshai*] **1.** a masculine name: dim. *Jess* **2.** *Bible* the father of David: I Sam. 16

**Jes·si·ca** (jes′i kə) a feminine name: var. *Jessie*

**jest** (jest) *n.* [OFr. *geste*, an exploit < L. pp. of *gerere*, to perform] **1.** a mocking remark; gibe; taunt **2.** a joke or humorous remark **3.** mere fun; joking /said in *jest*/ **4.** something to be laughed at or joked about —*vi.* **1.** to jeer; mock **2.** to be playful in speech and actions; joke

**jest·er** (-ər) *n.* one who jests; esp., a professional fool employed by a medieval ruler to amuse him

**Je·su** (jē′zōō, -sōō; jā′-) *archaic var. of* JESUS

**Jes·u·it** (jezh′ōo wit, jez′-; -yoo-) *n.* a member of the Society of Jesus, a Roman Catholic religious order for men founded by Ignatius Loyola in 1534

**Je·sus** (jē′zəs) [LL. *Iesus* < Gr. *Iēsous* < Heb. *yēshū'a*, contr. of *yĕhōshu'a*, help of Jehovah] c. 8–4 B.C.–29? A.D. (see CHRISTIAN ERA): founder of the Christian religion: also called **Jesus Christ, Jesus of Nazareth**: see also CHRIST

**jet¹** (jet) *vt., vi.* **jet′ted**, **jet′ting** [< MFr. *jeter*, ult. < L. *jactare*, freq. of *jacere*, to throw] **1.** to spout, gush, or shoot out in a stream **2.** to travel or convey by jet airplane —*n.* **1.** a stream of liquid or gas emitted or forced out, as from a spout **2.** a spout or nozzle for emitting a jet **3.** a jet-propelled airplane: in full, **jet** (**air**) **plane** —*adj.* **1.** jet-propelled **2.** of jet propulsion or jet-propelled aircraft /the jet age/

**jet²** (jet) *n.* [< OFr. < L. < Gr. *gagatēs*, jet < *Gagas*, town in Asia Minor] **1.** a hard, black variety of lignite: sometimes used in jewelry **2.** a deep, lustrous black —*adj.* **1.** made of jet **2.** black like jet

**jet-black** (-blak′) *adj.* glossy black, like jet

**jet·lin·er** (-lī′nər) *n.* a commercial jet aircraft for carrying passengers

**jet·port** (-pôrt′) *n.* an airport with long runways, for use by jet airplanes

**jet·pro·pelled** (-prə peld′) *adj.* driven by jet propulsion
**jet propulsion** a method of propelling airplanes, boats, etc. by the reaction caused when gases are emitted under pressure through a rear vent or vents
**jet·sam** (jet′səm) *n.* [var. of JETTISON] **1.** that part of the cargo thrown overboard to lighten a ship in danger: cf. FLOTSAM **2.** such discarded cargo washed ashore **3.** discarded things
**jet stream 1.** any of several bands of high-velocity winds moving from west to east around the earth at altitudes of from 8 to 10 mi. **2.** the stream of exhaust from a rocket engine
**jet·ti·son** (jet′ə s'n, -z'n) *n.* [< Anglo-Fr. < OFr. *getaison* < L. < *jactare,* to throw] **1.** a throwing overboard of goods to lighten a ship, airplane, etc. in an emergency **2.** *same as* JETSAM —*vt.* **1.** to throw (goods) overboard **2.** to discard (something)
**jet·ty** (jet′ē) *n., pl.* **-ties** [< OFr. *jetée,* orig. pp. of *jeter:* see JET¹] **1.** a kind of wall built out into the water to restrain currents, protect a harbor, etc. **2.** a landing pier **3.** a projecting part of a building —*vi.* **-tied, -ty·ing** to project, or jut out
**Jew** (jōō) *n.* [< OFr. < L. *Judaeus* < Gr. < Heb. *yehūdī,* member of the tribe of Judah] **1.** a person descended, or regarded as descended, from the ancient Hebrews **2.** a person whose religion is Judaism
**jew·el** (jōō′əl) *n.* [< OFr. *joel* < *jeu,* a trifle < L. *jocus,* a joke] **1.** a valuable ring, necklace, etc., esp. one set with gems **2.** a precious stone; gem **3.** any person or thing that is very precious or valuable **4.** a small gem or gemlike bit used as one of the bearings in a watch —*vt.* **-eled** or **-elled, -el·ing** or **-el·ling** to decorate or set with jewels
**jew·el·er, jew·el·ler** (-ər) *n.* a person who makes, deals in, or repairs jewelry, watches, etc.
**jew·el·ry** (jōō′əl rē) *n.* jewels collectively: Brit. sp. **jew′el·ler·y**
**jew·el·weed** (-wēd′) *n.* any of a group of plants bearing yellow or orange-yellow flowers and seedpods that split at the touch when ripe
**Jew·ess** (jōō′is) *n.* a Jewish woman or girl: term avoided by those who regard the *-ess* suffix as patronizing or discriminatory
**jew·fish** (-fish′) *n., pl.* **-fish′, -fish′es:** see FISH any of several large fish found in warm seas, as a grouper found off Florida
**Jew·ish** (-ish) *adj.* of or having to do with Jews or Judaism —*n.* [Colloq.] *same as* YIDDISH —**Jew′ish·ness** *n.*
**Jewish calendar** a calendar used by the Jews in calculating holidays, etc., based on the lunar month and reckoned from 3761 B.C., the traditional date of the Creation

**Months of the Jewish Calendar**

1. Tishri (30 days)
2. Heshvan (29 or 30 days)
3. Kislev (29 or 30 days)
4. Tebet (29 days)
5. Shebat (30 days)
6. Adar (29 or 30 days)
7. Nisan (30 days)
8. Iyar (29 days)
9. Sivan (30 days)
10. Tammuz (29 days)
11. Ab (30 days)
12. Elul (29 days)

N.B. About once every three years an extra month, **Veadar** or **Adar Sheni** (29 days), falls between *Adar* and *Nisan.* *Tishri* begins in late September or early October

**Jew·ry** (jōō′rē) *n., pl.* **-ries 1.** formerly, a district inhabited by Jews; ghetto **2.** Jewish people collectively [American *Jewry*]
**jew's-harp, jews'-harp** (jōōz′härp′) *n.* a small musical instrument consisting of a lyre-shaped metal frame held between the teeth and played by plucking a projecting bent piece with the finger
**Jez·e·bel** (jez′ə bel′, -b'l) [Heb.] *Bible* the wicked woman who married Ahab, king of Israel —*n.* [*also* j-] any shameless, wicked woman

JEW'S-HARP

**jg, j.g.** junior grade: designation of the lower rank of lieutenant in the U.S. Navy
**jib¹** (jib) *n.* [prob. < GIBBET] **1.** the projecting arm of a crane **2.** the boom of a derrick
**jib²** (jib) *vi., vt.* **jibbed, jib′bing** [< Dan. *gibbe,* to jibe] *Naut.* to jibe; shift —*n.* a triangular sail projecting ahead of the foremast —**cut of one's jib** [Colloq.] one's appearance
**jib³** (jib) *vi.* **jibbed, jib′bing** [prob. < *prec.*] **1.** to stop and refuse to go forward; balk **2.** to start or shy (*at* something) —*n.* an animal that jibs, as a horse —**jib′ber** *n.*
**jib boom** a spar fixed to and extending beyond the bowsprit of a ship: the jib is attached to it
**jibe¹** (jib) *vi.* **jibed, jib′ing** [< Du. *gijpen*] **1.** to shift from one side of a ship to the other, as a fore-and-aft sail when the course is changed in a following wind **2.** to change the course of a ship so that the sails shift thus **3.** [Colloq.] to be in harmony, agreement, or accord —*vt. Naut.* to cause to jibe —*n.* a shift of sail or boom from one side of a ship to another
**jibe²** (jīb) *vi., vt., n. same as* GIBE —**jib′er** *n.*

**Jid·da, Jid·dah** (jid′ə) seaport in Saudi Arabia, on the Red Sea: pop. c.300,000
**jif·fy** (jif′ē) *n., pl.* **-fies** [< ?] [Colloq.] a very short time; instant [done in a *jiffy*]: also **jiff**
**jig** (jig) *n.* [prob. < MFr. *giguer,* to dance < *gigue,* a fiddle] **1.** *a)* a fast, gay, springy dance, usually in triple time *b)* the music for such a dance **2.** any of various fishing lures that are jiggled up and down in the water **3.** any of several mechanical devices operated in a jerky manner, as a sieve for separating ores, a drill, etc. **4.** a device used as a guide for a tool or as a template —*vi., vt.* **jigged, jig′ging 1.** to dance (a jig) **2.** to move jerkily up and down or to and fro —**the jig is up** [Slang] all chances for success are gone: said of a risky or improper activity
**jig·ger¹** (jig′ər) *n.* [prob. of Afr. origin] *same as* CHIGGER
**jig·ger²** (jig′ər) *n.* **1.** one who jigs **2.** *a)* a small glass used to measure liquor, containing usually 1½ fluid ounces *b)* the quantity of liquor in a jigger **3.** any device or contraption whose name does not occur to one; gadget **4.** *same as* JIG (*n.* 2) **5.** *Mech.* any of several devices that operate with a jerky, up-and-down motion **6.** *Naut. a)* a small tackle *b)* a small sail *c) same as* JIGGER MAST
**jigger mast** a mast in the stern of a ship
**jig·gle** (jig′'l) *vt., vi.* **-gled, -gling** [freq. of *jig,* v.] to move in a succession of quick, slight jerks; rock lightly —*n.* a jiggling movement
**jig·gly** (jig′lē) *adj.* moving or tending to move with a jiggle; unsteady
**jig·saw** (jig′sô′) *n.* a saw with a narrow blade set in a frame, that moves with an up-and-down motion for cutting along curved or irregular lines, as in scrollwork: also **jig saw** —*vt.* to cut or form with a jigsaw

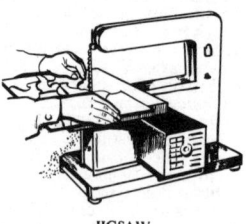

**jigsaw puzzle** a puzzle made by cutting up a picture into pieces of irregular shape, which must be put together again to re-form the picture
**Jill** (jil) [< proper name *Gillian* < L. *Juliana*] a feminine name —*n.* [*often* j-] [Now Rare] a girl or woman; esp., a sweetheart

JIGSAW

**jilt** (jilt) *n.* [< *jillet,* dim. of *prec.*] a woman who rejects a lover or suitor after accepting or encouraging him —*vt.* to reject or cast off (a previously accepted lover or sweetheart)
**Jim** (jim) a nickname for JAMES
**Jim Crow** [name of an early Negro minstrel song] [*also* j-c-] [Colloq.] discrimination against or segregation of Negroes —**Jim′-Crow′** *vt., adj.* —**Jim Crow′ism**
**jim·my** (jim′ē) *n., pl.* **-mies** [< dim. of JAMES] a short crowbar, used by burglars to pry open windows, etc. —*vt.* **-mied, -my·ing** to pry open with a jimmy or similar tool
**jim·son weed** (jim′s'n) [< JAMESTOWN, Va.] a poisonous annual weed of the nightshade family, with foul-smelling leaves, prickly fruit, and trumpet-shaped flowers
**jin·gle** (jiŋ′g'l) *vi.* **-gled, -gling** [ME. *gingelen,* prob. echoic] **1.** to make light, ringing sounds, as small bells or bits of metal striking together; tinkle **2.** to have obvious, easy rhythm, simple repetitions of sound, etc., as some poetry and music —*vt.* to cause to jingle —*n.* **1.** a jingling sound **2.** a verse that jingles [advertising *jingles*] —**jin′gly** (-glē) *adj.*
**jin·go** (jiŋ′gō) *n., pl.* **-goes** [< phr. *by jingo* in a patriotic Brit. music-hall song (1878)] one who boasts of his patriotism and favors an aggressive, warlike foreign policy; chauvinist —*adj.* of jingoes —**jin′go·ism** *n.* —**jin′go·ist** *n.* —**jin′go·is′tic** *adj.* —**jin′go·is′ti·cal·ly** *adv.*
**jinn** (jin) *n. pl. of* JINNI: popularly regarded as a singular, with the pl. **jinns**
**jin·ni** (ji nē′, jin′ē) *n., pl.* **jinn** [< Ar.] *Moslem Legend* a supernatural being that can take human or animal form and influence human affairs
**jin·rik·i·sha** (jin rik′shô, -shä) *n.* [< Jap. < *jin,* a man + *riki,* power + *sha,* carriage] a small, two-wheeled carriage with a hood, pulled by one or two men, esp. formerly in the Orient: also sp. **jin·rick′sha, jin·rik′sha**
**jinx** (jiŋks) *n.* [< L. *iynx* < Gr. *iynx,* the wryneck (bird used in black magic)] [Colloq.] **1.** a person or thing supposed to bring bad luck **2.** a spell of bad luck —*vt.* [Colloq.] to bring bad luck to
**jit·ney** (jit′nē) *n., pl.* **-neys** [c. 1903 < ? Fr. *jeton,* a token] **1.** [Old Slang] a five-cent coin; nickel **2.** a small bus or car that carries passengers for a low fare, originally five cents
**jit·ter** (jit′ər) *vi.* [? echoic] [Colloq.] to be nervous; have the jitters; fidget —**the jitters** [Colloq.] a very uneasy, nervous feeling; the fidgets —**jit′ter·y** *adj.*
**jit·ter·bug** (-bug′) *n.* [prec. + BUG] **1.** a dance for couples, esp. in the early 1940's, involving fast, acrobatic movements to swing music **2.** a dancer of the jitterbug —*vi.* **-bugged′, -bug′ging** to dance the jitterbug

**jiu·jit·su, jiu·jut·su** (jōō jit'sōō) *n. var. of* JUJITSU
**jive** (jīv) *vt.* **jived, jiv'ing** [altered < JIBE²] [Slang] to use jive, or nonsense talk, in speaking to, esp. in an effort to mislead —*n.* **1.** [Slang] foolish, exaggerated, or insincere talk **2.** *former term* (c. 1930–45) *for* JAZZ *or* SWING
**Jl.** July
**jo** (jō) *n., pl.* **joes** [var. of JOY] [Scot.] a sweetheart
**Joan** (jōn) [var. of ff.] a feminine name
**Jo·an·na** (jō an'ə) [ML., fem. of *Johannes:* see JOHN] a feminine name: var. *Joanne, Johanna*
**Joan of Arc** (ärk), Saint (Fr. name *Jeanne d'Arc*) 1412–31; Fr. heroine: defeated the English at Orléans (1429): burned at the stake for witchcraft: called the *Maid of Orléans*
**Job** (jōb) *Bible* **1.** a man who endured much suffering but did not lose his faith in God **2.** the book telling of him
**job** (jäb) *n.* [< ?] **1.** a specific piece of work, as in one's trade, or done by agreement for pay **2.** a task; chore; duty **3.** the thing or material being worked on or the resulting product **4.** a position of employment; work **5.** [Colloq.] a criminal act or deed, as a theft, etc. **6.** [Colloq.] any happening, affair, matter, object, etc. —*adj.* hired or done by the job —*vi.* **jobbed, job'bing 1.** to do odd jobs **2.** to act as a jobber or broker **3.** [Chiefly Brit.] to engage in jobbery —*vt.* **1.** to buy and sell (goods) as a wholesaler **2.** to let or sublet (work, contracts, etc.) —**odd jobs** miscellaneous pieces of work —**on the job 1.** while working at one's job **2.** [Slang] attentive to one's task or duty —**job'less** *adj.*
**job·ber** (jäb'ər) *n.* **1.** a wholesaler; middleman **2.** a person who works by the job or who does piecework
**job·ber·y** (-ər ē, -rē) *n.* [Chiefly Brit.] the carrying on of public business dishonestly for private gain
**Job Corps** a U.S. government program for training underprivileged youth for employment
**job·hold·er** (-hōl'dər) *n.* a person who has a steady job; specif., a government employee
**job lot 1.** an assortment of goods for sale as one quantity **2.** any random assortment
**Jo·cas·ta** (jō kas'tə) *Gr. Myth.* the queen who unwittingly married her own son, Oedipus
**jock** (jäk) *n. clip for:* **1.** JOCKEY **2.** JOCKSTRAP
**jock·ey** (jäk'ē) *n., pl.* **-eys** [< Scot. dim. of JACK¹] **1.** a person whose work is riding horses in races **2.** [Slang] the operator of a specified vehicle, machine, etc. —*vt., vi.* **-eyed, -ey·ing 1.** to ride (a horse) in a race **2.** to cheat; swindle **3.** to maneuver for position or advantage **4.** [Slang] to be the operator, pilot, etc. (of)
**jock·strap** (jäk'strap') *n.* [*jock,* penis + STRAP] **1.** an elastic belt with a pouch to support the genitals, worn by men **2.** [Slang] an athlete
**jo·cose** (jō kōs', jə-) *adj.* [< L. < *jocus,* a joke] joking or playful; humorous —**jo·cose'ly** *adv.* —**jo·cos'i·ty** (-käs'ə tē) *pl.* **-ties, jo·cose'ness** *n.*
**joc·u·lar** (jäk'yə lər) *adj.* [< L. dim. of *jocus,* a joke] **1.** joking; full of fun **2.** said as a joke —**joc'u·lar'i·ty** (-lar'ə tē) *n., pl.* **-ties** —**joc'u·lar·ly** *adv.*
**joc·und** (jäk'ənd, jō'kənd) *adj.* [< OFr. < LL. < L. *jucundus,* pleasant < *juvare,* to help] cheerful; genial; gay —**jo·cun·di·ty** (jō kun'də tē) *n., pl.* **-ties** —**joc'und·ly** *adv.*
**jodh·pur** (jäd'pər) *n.* [after *Jodhpur,* former state in India] **1.** [*pl.*] riding breeches made loose and full above the knees and tight from knees to ankles **2.** an ankle-high boot, often with an adjustable buckle and strap
**Joe** (jō) *a nickname for* JOSEPH —*n.* [Slang] **1.** [*often* j-] fellow; guy **2.** [j-] coffee
**Jo·el** (jō'əl) [< LL. < Gr. < Heb. *yō'ēl,* lit., the Lord is God] **1.** a masculine name **2.** *Bible a)* a Hebrew prophet of about 400 B.C. *b)* the book of his preachings
**jog¹** (jäg) *vt.* **jogged, jog'ging** [ME. *joggen,* to spur] **1.** *a)* to give a little shake or jerk to *b)* to nudge **2.** to shake up or revive (a person's memory) **3.** to cause to jog —*vi.* to move along at a slow, steady, jolting pace or trot —*n.* **1.** a little shake or nudge **2.** a slow, steady, jolting motion or trot —**jog'ger** *n.*
**jog²** (jäg) *n.* [var. of JAG¹] **1.** a projecting or notched part, esp. one at right angles, in a surface or line **2.** a sharp, temporary change of direction —*vi.* **jogged, jog'ging** to form or make a jog
**jog·ging** (jäg'iŋ) *n.* the practice of trotting at a slow, steady pace for some distance as a form of exercise
**jog·gle¹** (jäg''l) *vt., vi.* **-gled, -gling** [freq. of JOG¹] to shake or jolt slightly —*n.* a slight jolt
**jog·gle²** (jäg''l) *n.* [< JOG²] **1.** a joint made by putting a notch in one surface and a projection in the other to fit into it **2.** the notch or projection —*vt.* **-gled, -gling** to join by joggles
**Jo·han·nes·burg** (jō han'is burg', yō hän'-) city in the Transvaal, South Africa: pop. 1,295,000

**John** (jän) [< OFr. < ML. *Johannes* < LL. < Gr. < Heb. contr. of *yehōḫānān,* lit., Yahweh is gracious] **1.** a masculine name: dim. *Johnnie, Johnny* **2.** 1167?–1216; king of England (1199–1216): forced to sign the Magna Charta (1215) **3.** *Bible a)* a Christian apostle, credited with having written the fourth Gospel, the three Epistles of John, and Revelation: called *the Evangelist* and *the Divine b)* the fourth book of the New Testament *c)* same as JOHN THE BAPTIST **4. John XXIII** 1881–1963; Pope (1958–63)
**john** (jän) *n.* [Slang] a toilet
**John Barleycorn** corn liquor, etc., personified
**John Bull** England, or an Englishman, personified
**John Doe** *see* DOE
**John Hancock** [Colloq.] one's signature
**john·ny·cake** (jän'ē kāk') *n.* [< Eng. dial. *jannock,* bread of oatmeal] corn bread baked on a griddle
**John·ny-jump-up** (-jump'up') *n.* **1.** same as *a)* WILD PANSY *b)* DAFFODIL **2.** any of various American violets
**John Paul I** 1912–1978; Pope (1978)
**John Paul II** 1920– ; Pope (1978– )
**John·son** (jän's'n) **1. Andrew,** 1808–75; 17th president of the U.S. (1865–69) **2. Lyn·don Baines** (lin'dən bānz), 1908–73; 36th president of the U.S. (1963–69) **3. Samuel,** 1709–84; Eng. lexicographer, writer, & critic: known as *Dr. Johnson*
**Johns·town** (jänz'toun') [after J. *Johns,* local landowner] city in SW Pa.: site of a disastrous flood (1889): pop. 35,000
**John the Baptist** *Bible* the forerunner and baptizer of Jesus: Matt. 3
**Jo·hore** (jə hôr') state of Malaya, at the tip of the Malay Peninsula
**‡joie de vi·vre** (zhwåd vē'vr') [Fr.] joy of living
**join** (join) *vt.* [< OFr. < L. *jungere*] **1.** to bring together; connect; combine **2.** to make into one; unite [*join* forces, *joined* in wedlock] **3.** to become a part or member of (a club, etc.) **4.** to go to and combine with [the path *joins* the highway] **5.** to enter into the company of; accompany [*join* us soon] **6.** [Colloq.] to adjoin —*vi.* **1.** to come together; meet **2.** to enter into association or become a member: often with *up* **3.** to participate (*in* a conversation, singing, etc.) —*n.* a place of joining, as a seam in a coat —**join battle** to start fighting
**join·er** (-ər) *n.* **1.** a person or thing that joins **2.** a workman who finishes interior woodwork, as doors or molding **3.** [Colloq.] a person given to joining various organizations
**join·er·y** (-ər ē) *n.* the work or skill of a joiner
**joint** (joint) *n.* [< OFr. < L. pp. of *jungere,* to join] **1.** a place where, or way in which, two things or parts are joined **2.** one of the parts of a jointed whole **3.** a large cut of meat with the bones still in it, as for a roast **4.** [Slang] *a)* a cheap bar, restaurant, etc. *b)* any building, etc. **5.** [Slang] a marijuana cigarette **6.** *Anat.* a place or part where two bones, etc. are joined, usually so that they can move **7.** *Bot.* a point where a branch or leaf grows out of the stem —*adj.* **1.** common to two or more as to ownership or action [*joint* property] **2.** sharing with someone else [a *joint* owner] —*vt.* **1.** to fasten together by a joint or joints **2.** to give a joint or joints to **3.** to cut (meat) into joints —**out of joint 1.** not in place at the joint; dislocated **2.** disordered —**joint'ed** *adj.* —**joint'er** *n.*
**joint·ly** (-lē) *adv.* in common; together
**joint resolution** a resolution passed by a legislature with two houses: it becomes a law if signed by the chief executive or passed over his veto
**joint return** a single income tax return filed by a married couple, combining their incomes
**joint-stock company** (-stäk') a business firm owned by the stockholders in shares which each may sell or transfer independently
**join·ture** (join'chər) *n.* [< OFr. < L. < *jungere,* to join] *Law* **1.** an arrangement by which a husband grants real property to his wife for her use after his death **2.** the property thus settled
**joist** (joist) *n.* [< OFr. *giste,* a bed; ult. < L. *jacere,* to lie] any of the parallel beams that hold up the planks of a floor or the laths of a ceiling —*vt.* to provide with joists

JOISTS

**joke** (jōk) *n.* [L. *jocus*] **1.** anything said or done to arouse laughter; a funny anecdote or amusing trick **2.** a thing done or said merely in fun **3.** a person or thing to be laughed at —*vi.* **joked, jok'ing 1.** to tell or play jokes **2.** to say or do something as a joke; jest —*vt.* to bring to a specified condition by joking —**jok'ing·ly** *adv.*
**jok·er** (jō'kər) *n.* **1.** a person who jokes **2.** a hidden provision put into a law, legal document, etc. to

make it different from what it seems to be **3.** any hidden, unsuspected difficulty **4.** an extra playing card used in some games

**Jo·li·et** (jō′lē et′, jō′lē et′) [after L. *Joliet*, 17th-c. Fr.-Canad. explorer] city in NE Ill.: pop. 78,000

**jol·li·fy** (jäl′ə fī′) *vt., vi.* **-fied′, -fy′ing** [Colloq.] to make or be jolly or merry —**jol′li·fi·ca′tion** *n.*

**jol·li·ty** (-ə tē) *n.* a being jolly; fun; gaiety

**jol·ly** (jäl′ē) *adj.* **-li·er, -li·est** [< OFr. *joli*, joyful; prob. < ON. *jol*, YULE] **1.** full of high spirits and good humor **2.** [Colloq.] enjoyable; pleasant —*adv.* [Brit. Colloq.] very; altogether —*vt., vi.* **-lied, -ly·ing** [Colloq.] **1.** to try to make (a person) feel good or agreeable by coaxing, flattering, etc. (often with *along*) **2.** to make fun of (someone) —**jol′li·ly** *adv.* —**jol′li·ness** *n.*

**jolly (boat)** [< MDu.] *jolle*, yawl] a ship's small boat

**Jolly Roger** a black flag of pirates, with white skull and crossbones

**jolt** (jōlt) *vt.* [earlier *jot*, to jog, orig. echoic: prob. infl. by *jowl*, to strike] **1.** to shake up or jar, as with a bumpy ride or sharp blow **2.** to shock or surprise —*vi.* to move along in a bumpy, jerky manner —*n.* **1.** a sudden jerk, bump, etc., as from a blow **2.** a shock or surprise —**jolt′er** *n.* —**jolt′ing·ly** *adv.* —**jolt′y** *adj.*

**Jo·nah** (jō′nə) [< LL. < Gr. < Heb. *yōnāh*, lit., a dove] **1.** a masculine name: var. *Jonas* **2.** *Bible a)* a Hebrew prophet: thrown overboard in a storm, he was swallowed by a big fish, but later was cast up unharmed *b)* the book telling Jonah's story Also, esp. in the Douay Bible, **Jo′nas** (-nəs) —*n.* any person said to bring bad luck by his presence

**Jon·a·than** (jän′ə thən) [< Heb. < *yehōnāthān*, lit., Yahweh has given] **1.** a masculine name **2.** *Bible* Saul's oldest son, a close friend of David: I Sam. 18–20 —*n.* a late fall variety of apple

**Jones** (jōnz) **1.** In·i·go (in′i gō′), 1573–1652; Eng. architect & stage designer **2.** **John Paul**, (born *John Paul*) 1747–92; Am. naval officer in the Revolutionary War, born in Scotland

**jon·gleur** (jäŋ′glər; *Fr.* zhōn glër′) *n.* [Fr. < OFr. *jogleor*, juggler: see JUGGLE] a wandering minstrel in medieval France and England

**jon·quil** (jäŋ′kwəl, jän′-) *n.* [< Fr. < Sp. dim. *junquillo* < L. *juncus*, a rush] **1.** a species of narcissus having relatively small yellow flowers and long, slender leaves **2.** its bulb or flower

**Jon·son** (jän′s'n), **Ben** 1572?–1637; Eng. dramatist & poet —**Jon·so′ni·an** (-sō′nē ən) *adj.*

**Jor·dan** (jôr′d'n) **1.** river in the Near East, flowing into the Dead Sea **2.** country in the Near East, east of Israel: 37,300 sq. mi.; pop. 2,133,000; cap. Amman —**Jor·da′ni·an** (-dā′nē ən) *adj., n.*

**Jordan almond** [prob. < OFr. *jardin*, garden] a variety of large Spanish almond used in candies

**Jo·seph** (jō′zəf, -səf) [LL. < Gr. < Heb. *yōsēph*, lit., may he add] **1.** a masculine name **2.** *Bible a)* Jacob's eleventh son, who was sold into slavery in Egypt by his jealous brothers but became a high official there: Gen. 37, 39–41 *b)* the husband of Mary, mother of Jesus: Matt. 1:18–25

**Jo·se·phine** (jō′zə fēn, -sə-) [< Fr. fem. of prec.] **1.** a feminine name: dim. **Jo, Josie 2.** 1763–1814; wife of Napoleon (1796–1809) & empress of France (1804–09)

**Jo·se·phus** (jō sē′fəs), **(Flavius)** 37–95? A.D.; Jewish historian

**josh** (jäsh) *vt., vi.* [< ?] [Colloq.] to ridicule in a good-humored way; tease jokingly; banter —**josh′er** *n.* —**josh′ing·ly** *adv.*

**Josh·u·a** (jäsh′oo wə) [Heb. *yehōshū′a*, lit., help of Jehovah] **1.** a masculine name **2.** *Bible a)* Moses' successor, and leader of the Israelites into the Promised Land *b)* the book telling about him: also, in the Douay Bible, **Jos·u·e** (jäs′yoo wē′)

**joss** (jäs) *n.* [PidE. < Port. *deos* < L. *deus*, a god] a figure of a Chinese god

**joss house** a Chinese temple

**joss stick** a thin stick of dried, fragrant wood dust, burned by the Chinese as incense

**jos·tle** (jäs′'l) *vt., vi.* **-tled, -tling** [earlier *justle*, freq.: see JOUST] **1.** to bump or push, as in a crowd; shove roughly **2.** to contend (*with* someone *for* something) —*n.* a jostling —**jos′tler** *n.*

**jot** (jät) *n.* [< L. < Gr. *iōta*, the letter *i*, the smallest letter] a trifling amount; the smallest bit —*vt.* **jot′ted, jot′ting** to make a brief note of (usually with *down*) —**jot′ter** *n.*

**jo·ta** (hō′tä) *n.* [Sp. < OSp. < *sotar*, to dance] a Spanish dance in 3/4 time performed by a man and woman to the rhythm of castanets

**jot·ting** (jät′iŋ) *n.* a short note jotted down

**joule** (jōōl, joul) *n.* [after J. P. *Joule*, 19th.-c. Eng. physicist] *Physics* a unit of work or energy equal to 10,000,000 ergs

**jounce** (jouns) *n., vt., vi.* jounced, jounc′ing [< ?] jolt or bounce —**jounc′y** *adj.*

**jour·nal** (jur′n'l) *n.* [< OFr., lit., daily < L. *diurnalis* < *dies*, day] **1.** a daily record of happenings, as a diary **2.** a record of the transactions of a legislature, club, etc. **3.** a ship's logbook **4.** a newspaper, magazine, etc. **5.** *Bookkeeping* a book of original entry for recording every transaction with an indication of its proper account **6.** *Mech.* the part of a rotatory axle or shaft that turns in a bearing

**journal box** *Mech.* a housing for a journal

**jour·nal·ese** (jur′n'l ēz′) *n.* a style of writing characteristic of many newspapers, magazines, etc.; facile style, with many clichés

**jour·nal·ism** (jur′n'l iz′m) *n.* **1.** the work of gathering, writing, and publishing or disseminating news, as through newspapers, etc. or by radio and TV **2.** newspapers and magazines collectively

**jour·nal·ist** (-ist) *n.* a person whose occupation is journalism; reporter, news editor, etc. —**jour′nal·is′tic** *adj.* —**jour′nal·is′ti·cal·ly** *adv.*

**jour·ney** (jur′nē) *n., pl.* **-neys** [< OFr. *journee* < LL. < L. *diurnus*, daily: see JOURNAL] a traveling from one place to another; trip —*vi.* **-neyed, -ney·ing** to go on a trip; travel

**jour·ney·man** (-mən) *n., pl.* **-men** [ME. < *journee*, day's work + *man*] **1.** formerly, a worker qualified to work at his trade, after serving his apprenticeship **2.** now, a worker who has learned his trade **3.** an experienced craftsman of average ability

**joust** (joust, just, jōōst) *n.* [< OFr. < *juster* < L. *juxta*, beside] **1.** a combat with lances between two knights on horseback **2.** [*pl.*] a tournament —*vi.* to engage in a joust —**joust′er** *n.*

**Jove** (jōv) *same as* JUPITER —**by Jove!** an exclamation of astonishment, emphasis, etc. —**Jo·vi·an** (jō′vē ən) *adj.*

**jo·vi·al** (jō′vē əl, -vyəl) *adj.* [Fr. < LL. *Jovialis*, of Jupiter < L. *Jovis*: see prec.] full of hearty, playful good humor; genial and gay —**jo′vi·al′i·ty** (-al′ə tē) *n.* —**jo′vi·al·ly** *adv.*

**jowl¹** (joul, jōl) *n.* [< OE. *ceafl*, jaw] **1.** a jaw; esp., the lower jaw with the chin and cheeks **2.** the cheek **3.** the meat of a hog's cheek

**jowl²** (joul, jōl) *n.* [< OE. *ceole*, throat] [*often pl.*] the fleshy, hanging part under the lower jaw —**jowl′y** *adj.*

**joy** (joi) *n.* [< OFr. *joie* < LL. < L. *gaudium*, joy] **1.** a very glad feeling; happiness; delight **2.** anything causing this **3.** the expression of such feeling —*vi.* to be full of joy

**Joyce** (jois) [< L. fem. of *jocosus*, merry] **1.** a feminine name **2.** **James (Augustine Aloysius)**, 1882–1941; Ir. novelist & poet —**Joyc·e·an** (jois′ē ən) *adj.*

**joy·ful** (joi′fəl) *adj.* feeling, expressing, or causing joy; glad; happy —**joy′ful·ly** *adv.* —**joy′ful·ness** *n.*

**joy·less** (-lis) *adj.* without joy; unhappy; sad —**joy′less·ly** *adv.* —**joy′less·ness** *n.*

**joy·ous** (-əs) *adj.* full of joy; happy; gay; glad —**joy′ous·ly** *adv.* —**joy′ous·ness** *n.*

**joy ride** [Colloq.] an automobile ride merely for pleasure, often with reckless speed and, sometimes, in a stolen car —**joy rider** —**joy riding**

**J.P.** justice of the peace

**Jpn.** **1.** Japan **2.** Japanese

**Jr., jr.** junior

**Ju.** June

**ju·bi·lant** (jōō′b'l ənt) *adj.* [L. *jubilans*, prp. of *jubilare*: see ff.] joyful and triumphant; elated —**ju′bi·lance** *n.* —**ju′bi·lant·ly** *adv.*

**ju·bi·late** (jōō′bə lāt′) *vi.* **-lat′ed, -lat′ing** [< L. pp. of *jubilare*, to shout for joy < *jubilum*, wild shout] to rejoice, as in triumph; exult

**ju·bi·la·tion** (jōō′bə lā′shən) *n.* **1.** a jubilating **2.** a happy celebration, as of victory

**ju·bi·lee** (jōō′bə lē′, jōō′bə lē′) *n.* [< OFr. < LL. < Gr. < Heb. *yōbēl*, a ram's horn (trumpet): infl. by L. *jubilum*, wild shout] **1.** *Jewish History* a celebration held every fifty years in which all bondmen were freed, mortgaged lands restored to the owners, etc.: Lev. 25:8–17 **2.** a 50th or 25th anniversary **3.** a time or occasion of rejoicing **4.** jubilation; rejoicing **5.** *R.C.Ch.* a year proclaimed as a solemn time for gaining a plenary indulgence

**Ju·dah** (jōō′də) [Heb. *yehūdhāh* < ?] **1.** a masculine name **2.** *Bible a)* the fourth son of Jacob *b)* the tribe descended from him **3.** the kingdom in the S part of ancient Palestine formed by the tribes of Judah and Benjamin

**Ju·da·ic** (jōō dā′ik) *adj.* of the Jews or Judaism; Jewish —**Ju·da′i·cal·ly** *adv.*

**Ju·da·ism** (jōō′də iz′m, -dē-) *n.* **1.** the Jewish religion, a monotheistic religion based on the laws and teachings of the Holy Scripture and the Talmud **2.** observance of Jewish morality, traditions, etc. —**Ju′da·ist** *n.* —**Ju′da·is′tic** *adj.*

**Ju·da·ize** (-īz′) *vi., vt.* **-ized′, -iz′ing** to conform to, or make conform to, Judaism —**Ju′da·i·za′tion** *n.*

**Ju·das** (jōō′dəs) [var. of JUDAH] **1.** Judas Iscariot, the disciple who betrayed Jesus **2.** *same as* JUDE (sense 1) —*n.* a traitor or betrayer

**Judas tree** a tree of the legume family, with clusters of rose-pink flowers

**Jude** (jōōd) *Bible* **1.** a Christian apostle: also called *Judas* (not Iscariot) **2.** *a)* a book of the New Testament, the Epistle of Jude *b)* its author

**Ju·de·a** (jōō dē′ə) ancient region of S Palestine: it corresponded roughly to the Biblical Judah: also sp. **Judaea** —Ju·de′an *adj., n.*

**Ju·de·o-** (jōō dē′ō, -dā′-) *a combining form meaning:* **1.** Judaic; Jewish **2.** Jewish and [*Judeo*-Christian]

**Judg.** Judges

**judge** (juj) *n.* [< OFr. < L. *judex* < *jus*, law + *dicere*, to say] **1.** a public official with authority to hear and decide cases in a court of law **2.** a person designated to determine the winner, settle a controversy, etc. **3.** a person qualified to decide on the relative worth of anything [a good *judge* of music] **4.** any of the governing leaders of the ancient Israelites before the time of the kings —*vt., vi.* **judged, judg′ing** **1.** to hear and pass judgment (*on*) in a court of law **2.** to determine the winner of (a contest) or settle (a controversy) **3.** to form an opinion about **4.** to criticize or censure **5.** to think or suppose **6.** *Jewish History* to govern —**judg′er** *n.* —**judge′ship′** *n.*

**judge advocate** *pl.* **judge advocates** a military legal officer; esp., an officer designated to act as prosecutor at a court-martial

**Judg·es** (juj′iz) a book of the Bible telling the history of the Jews from the death of Joshua to the birth of Samuel

**judg·ment** (juj′mənt) *n.* **1.** a judging; deciding **2.** a legal decision; order or sentence given by a judge or law court **3.** a debt resulting from a court order **4.** an opinion or estimate **5.** criticism or censure **6.** power of comparing and deciding; understanding **7.** [J-] *short for* LAST JUDGMENT Also sp. **judge′ment** —**judg·men′tal** (-men′t'l) *adj.*

**Judgment Day** *Theol.* the time of God's final judgment of all people; end of the world

**ju·di·ca·to·ry** (jōō′di kə tôr′ē) *adj.* [< LL. < L. pp. of *judicare*, to judge < *judex*, a JUDGE] having to do with administering justice; judging —*n., pl.* **-ries** **1.** a court of law; tribunal **2.** law courts collectively

**ju·di·ca·ture** (-chər) *n.* **1.** the administering of justice **2.** the position, functions, or legal power of a judge **3.** the extent of legal power of a judge or court of law **4.** a court of law **5.** judges or courts of law collectively

**ju·di·cial** (jōō dish′əl) *adj.* [< OFr. < L. *judicialis* < *judex*, a JUDGE] **1.** of judges, law courts, or their functions **2.** allowed, enforced, or set by order of a judge or law court **3.** like or befitting a judge **4.** fair; unbiased —**ju·di′cial·ly** *adv.*

**ju·di·ci·ar·y** (jōō dish′ē er′ē, -dish′ər ē) *adj.* of judges, law courts, or their functions —*n., pl.* **-ar′ies** **1.** the part of government that administers justice **2.** a system of law courts **3.** judges collectively

**ju·di·cious** (-dish′əs) *adj.* [< Fr. < L. *judicium*, judgment < *judex*, a JUDGE] having, applying, or showing sound judgment; wise and careful —**ju·di′cious·ly** *adv.* —**ju·di′cious·ness** *n.*

**Ju·dith** (jōō′dith) [LL. < Gr. < Heb. *yehūdhīth*, woman of Judah] **1.** a feminine name: dim. *Judy* **2.** *a)* a book of the Apocrypha and the Douay Bible *b)* the Jewish heroine told about in this book

**ju·do** (jōō′dō) *n.* [Jap. < *jū*, soft + *dō*, art] a form of jujitsu, esp. as a means of self-defense

**jug** (jug) *n.* [a pet form of JUDITH or JOAN] **1.** *a)* a container for liquids, with a small opening and a handle *b)* the contents of a jug **2.** [Slang] a jail —*vt.* **jugged, jug′ging** **1.** to put into a jug **2.** to stew in a covered earthenware container **3.** [Slang] to jail —**jug′ful** (-fool) *n.*

**ju·gate** (jōō′gāt, -git) *adj.* [< L. pp. of *jugare*, to yoke < *jugum*, a yoke] *Biol.* paired or connected

**Jug·ger·naut** (jug′ər nôt′) *n.* [< Hindi < Sans. < *jagat*, world + *nātha*, lord] **1.** an incarnation of the Hindu god Vishnu: his worshipers reputedly threw themselves to be crushed under the wheels of a large car carrying his idol **2.** [*usually* j-] *a)* anything that exacts blind devotion *b)* any terrible, irresistible force

**jug·gle** (jug′'l) *vt.* **-gled, -gling** [< OFr. *jogler* < L. *joculari*, to joke < *jocus*, a joke] **1.** to perform skillful tricks of sleight of hand with (balls, knives, etc.) **2.** to make awkward attempts to catch or hold (a ball, etc.) **3.** to use trickery on to deceive or cheat [to *juggle* figures to show a profit] —*vi.* to toss up a number of balls, knives, etc. and keep them continuously in the air —*n.* **1.** a juggling **2.** a clever trick or deception —**jug′gler** (jug′lər) *n.* —**jug′gler·y** *n., pl.* **-gler·ies**

**Ju·go·sla·vi·a** (yōō′gō slä′vē ə) *same as* YUGOSLAVIA —**Ju′go·slav′** *adj., n.* —**Ju′go·sla′vi·an** *adj., n.* —**Ju′go·slav′ic** *adj.*

**jug·u·lar** (jug′yoo lər, jōōg′-) *adj.* [< LL. < L. *jugulum*, collarbone < *jugum*, a yoke] **1.** of the neck or throat **2.** of a jugular vein —*n.* either of two large veins in the neck carrying blood back from the head to the heart: in full, **jugular vein**

**juice** (jōōs) *n.* [< OFr. < L. *jus*] **1.** the liquid part of a plant, fruit, or vegetable **2.** a liquid in or from animal tissue [gastric *juice*] **3.** [Colloq.] energy; vitality **4.** [Slang] *a)* electricity *b)* gasoline, oil, or any liquid fuel **5.** [Slang] alcoholic liquor —*vt.* **juiced, juic′ing** to extract juice from —**juice up** to add power, vigor, excitement, etc. to —**juice′less** *adj.* —**juic′er** *n.*

**juic·y** (jōō′sē) *adj.* **juic′i·er, juic′i·est** **1.** full of juice; succulent **2.** [Colloq.] full of interest; piquant; spicy **3.** [Colloq.] highly profitable —**juic′i·ly** *adv.* —**juic′i·ness** *n.*

**ju·jit·su** (jōō jit′sōō) *n.* [< Jap. < *jū*, soft + *jutsu*, art] a Japanese system of wrestling in which the strength and weight of an opponent are used against him: also **ju·jut·su** (-jit′sōō, -jut′-)

**ju·jube** (jōō′jōōb; *for 3, often* jōō′jōō bē′) *n.* [Fr. < ML. < L. *zizyphum* < Gr. *zizyphon*] **1.** the edible, datelike fruit of a tree or shrub growing in warm climates **2.** this tree or shrub **3.** a lozenge of gelatinous, fruit-flavored candy

**juke·box** (jōōk′bäks′) *n.* [Gullah *juke*, wicked (as in *jukehouse*, house of prostitution), WAfr. orig.] a coin-operated electric phonograph: a record is chosen by pushing a button: also **juke box**

**ju·lep** (jōō′ləp) *n.* [< MFr. < Ar. < Per. < *gul*, rose + *āb*, water] *same as* MINT JULEP

**Jul·ia** (jōōl′yə) [L., fem. of JULIUS] a feminine name: var. *Julie*

**Jul·ian** (jōōl′yən) [< L. < *Julius*: see JULIUS] a masculine name —*adj.* of Julius Caesar

**Julian calendar** the calendar introduced by Julius Caesar in 46 B.C., in which the ordinary year had 365 days and every fourth year (leap year) had 366 days: replaced by the Gregorian calendar

**ju·li·enne** (jōō′lē en′; *Fr.* zhü lyen′) *n.* [Fr., origin obscure] a clear soup containing vegetables cut into strips or bits —*adj. Cooking* cut into strips: said of vegetables

**Ju·li·et** (jōōl′yət, -ē ət, jōō′lē et′) [< Fr. < L. *Julia*] **1.** a feminine name **2.** the heroine of Shakespeare's tragedy *Romeo and Juliet*

**Jul·ius** (jōōl′yəs) [L., name of a Roman gens] a masculine name

**Julius Caesar** *see* Julius CAESAR

**Ju·ly** (jōō lī′, jōō-, jə-) *n., pl.* **-lies′** [< Anglo-Fr. < L. < *mensis Julius*, the month of Julius (Caesar)] the seventh month of the year, having 31 days: abbrev. **Jul., Jl., Jy.**

**jum·ble** (jum′b'l) *vt.* **-bled, -bling** [? blend of JUMP + TUMBLE] **1.** to mix in a confused, disorderly heap **2.** to confuse mentally —*vi.* to be jumbled —*n.* **1.** a confused mixture or heap **2.** a muddle

**jum·bo** (jum′bō) *n., pl.* **-bos** [< Gullah *jamba*, elephant; infl. by P. T. BARNUM's use of it for his elephant, *Jumbo*] a very large person, animal, or thing —*adj.* very large

**Jum·na** (jum′nə) river in N India, flowing from the Himalayas southwest into the Ganges

**jump** (jump) *vi.* [< ?] **1.** to move oneself suddenly from the ground, etc. by using the leg muscles; leap; spring **2.** to jerk; bob; bounce **3.** to leap from an aircraft, using a parachute **4.** to act or react eagerly (often with *at*) **5.** to pass suddenly as from one topic to another **6.** to rise suddenly, as prices **7.** [Slang] to be lively and animated **8.** *Bridge* to make an unnecessarily high bid (**jump bid**) to increase the previous bid **9.** *Checkers* to move a piece over an opponent's piece, thus capturing it —*vt.* **1.** *a)* to leap over *b)* to skip over **2.** to cause to leap [to *jump* a horse over a fence] **3.** to advance (a person) by bypassing others **4.** to leap upon; spring aboard **5.** to cause (prices, etc.) to rise suddenly **6.** [Colloq.] to attack suddenly **7.** [Colloq.] to react to prematurely, in anticipation **8.** [Slang] to leave suddenly [to *jump* town] **9.** *Checkers* to capture (an opponent's piece) —*n.* **1.** a jumping; leap **2.** a distance jumped **3.** a descent from an aircraft by parachute **4.** a thing to be jumped over **5.** a sudden transition **6.** a sudden rise, as in prices **7.** a sudden, nervous start or jerk; twitch **8.** *Athletics* a contest in jumping **9.** *Checkers* a move by which an opponent's piece is captured —**get (or have) the jump on** [Slang] to get (or have) an advantage over —**jump a claim** to seize land claimed by someone else —**jump bail** to forfeit one's bail by running away —**jump on (or all over)** [Slang] to scold; censure —**jump the track** to go suddenly off the rails —**on the jump** [Colloq.] very busy

**jump·er¹** (jum′pər) *n.* **1.** a person, animal, or thing that jumps **2.** a short wire used to make a temporary electrical connection

---

fat, āpe, cär; ten, ēven; is, bīte; gō, hôrn, tōol, look; oil, out; up, fʉr; get; joy; yet; chin; she; thin, then; zh, leisure; ŋ, ring; ə for *a* in *ago*, *e* in *agent*, *i* in *sanity*, *o* in *comply*, *u* in *focus*; ′ as in *able* (ā′b'l); Fr. bål; ë, Fr. coeur; ö, Fr. feu; Fr. mo*n*; ô, Fr. coq; ü, Fr. duc; *r*, Fr. cri; H, G. ich; kh, G. doch; ‡foreign; *hypothetical; < derived from. See inside front cover.

**jump·er²** (jum′pər) *n.* [< dial. *jump*, short coat, prob. < Fr. *jupe* < Sp. < Ar. *jubbah*, undergarment]
**1.** a loose jacket or blouse, worn as to protect clothing or as part of a sailor's outfit **2.** a sleeveless dress worn over a blouse or sweater **3.** [*pl.*] rompers: see ROMPER (sense 2)

**jumping bean** the seed of a Mexican plant, which is made to jump or roll about by the movements of a moth larva inside it

**jumping jack** a child's toy consisting of a little jointed figure made to jump about by pulling a string

**jump suit 1.** a coverall worn by paratroops, etc. **2.** any one-piece garment like this

**jump·y** (jum′pē) *adj.* jump′i·er, jump′i·est **1.** moving in jumps, jerks, etc. **2.** easily startled; apprehensive —**jump′i·ly** *adv.* —**jump′i·ness** *n.*

**Jun., jun.** junior

**jun·co** (juŋ′kō) *n., pl.* **-cos** [< ModL. < Sp. < L. *juncus*, a rush] a sparrowlike bird of North and Central America, with a gray or black head

**junc·tion** (juŋk′shən) *n.* [< L. < *jungere*, to join] **1.** a joining or being joined **2.** a place or point of joining or crossing, as of highways or railroads **3.** the region separating two kinds of semiconductor material —**junc′tion·al** *adj.*

**junc·ture** (-chər) *n.* [< L.: see prec.] **1.** a joining or being joined **2.** a point or line of joining or connection; joint **3.** a point of time **4.** a crisis **5.** a state of affairs **6.** *Linguis.* the transition marking the boundary between one speech sound and the next

**June** (jōōn) [< L. *Junius*, name of a Roman gens] a feminine name —*n.* [< OFr. < L. < *mensis Junius*, the month of JUNO] the sixth month of the year, having 30 days

**Ju·neau** (jōō′nō) [after J. *Juneau*, a prospector] capital of Alas., on the SE coast: pop. 20,000

**June·ber·ry** (jōōn′ber′ē, -bər ē) *n., pl.* **-ries 1.** any of various N. American shrubs and trees of the rose family, with white flowers and purple-black fruits **2.** the fruit

**June bug 1.** a large, scarabaeid beetle appearing in May or June in the N U.S.: also **June beetle 2.** *same as* FIGEATER

**Jung** (yŏŏŋ), **Carl G(ustav)** 1875–1961; Swiss psychologist & psychiatrist —**Jung′i·an** *adj., n.*

**Jung·frau** (yŏŏŋ′frou′) mountain in the Alps of S Switzerland

**jun·gle** (juŋ′g'l) *n.* [< Hindi < Sans. *jangala*, desert] **1.** land with a dense growth of trees, vines, etc., as in the tropics, usually inhabited by predatory animals **2.** any tangled growth **3.** [Slang] a hobos' camp **4.** [Slang] a place where people compete ruthlessly —**jun′gly** *adj.*

**jun·ior** (jōōn′yər) *adj.* [L. compar. of *juvenis*, young] **1.** the younger: written *Jr.* after the name of a son who bears the same name as his father **2.** of more recent position or lower status [a *junior* partner] **3.** of later date **4.** made up of younger members **5.** relating to juniors in a high school or college —*n.* **1.** a younger person **2.** a person of lower standing or rank **3.** a student in the next-to-last year of a high school or college —**one's junior** a person younger than oneself

**junior college** a school offering courses two years beyond the high school level

**junior high school** a school intermediate between elementary school and senior high school: it usually includes the 7th, 8th, and 9th grades

**Junior League** an organization of young society women with leisure to do volunteer welfare work —**Junior Leaguer**

**junior varsity** a team that represents a school, college, etc. in a secondary level of competition

**ju·ni·per** (jōō′nə pər) *n.* [L. *juniperus*] a small evergreen shrub or tree with scalelike foliage and berrylike cones

**junk¹** (juŋk) *n.* [< ? Port. *junco*, a reed < L. *juncus*] **1.** orig., old rope used for making oakum, mats, etc. **2.** old metal, paper, rags, etc. **3.** [Colloq.] useless stuff; rubbish **4.** [Slang] a narcotic drug; esp., heroin —*vt.* [Colloq.] to throw away or sell as junk; discard —**junk′y** *adj.*

**junk²** (juŋk) *n.* [Sp. & Port. *junco* < Jav. *joñ*] a Chinese flat-bottomed ship

**Jun·ker** (yŏŏŋ′kər) *n.* [G. < MHG. < OHG. *jung*, young + *herro*, lord] a German of the militaristic, land-owning class; Prussian aristocrat

**jun·ket** (juŋ′kit) *n.* [ult. < L. *juncus*, a rush: orig. sold in reed baskets] **1.** formerly, curds with cream **2.** milk sweetened, flavored, and thickened into curd with rennet **3.** a feast or picnic **4.** an excursion for pleasure **5.** an excursion by an official, paid for with public funds —*vi.* to go on a junket —*vt.* to entertain at a feast —**jun′ket·eer′** (-kə tir′), **jun′ket·er** *n.*

JUMPER

JUNK

**junk food** any of various snack foods processed as with chemical additives and of low nutritional value

**junk·ie, junk·y** (juŋ′kē) *n., pl.* **junk′ies** [Slang] **1.** a narcotics addict, esp. one addicted to heroin **2.** a person who is addicted to a specified interest, activity, food, etc. [a TV *junkie*]

**junk mail** advertisements, requests for aid, etc. mailed impersonally to a large number of people

**junk·man** (juŋk′man′) *n., pl.* **-men′** (-men′) a dealer in old metal, paper, rags, etc.

**junk·yard** (-yärd′) *n.* a place where old cars are junked or where old metal, etc. is kept, sorted, and sold

**Ju·no** (jōō′nō) [L.] *Rom. Myth.* wife of Jupiter; queen of the gods and goddess of marriage: identified with the Greek goddess Hera

**jun·ta** (hoon′tə, jun′-) *n.* [Sp. < L. pp. of *jungere*, to join] **1.** a Spanish or Latin American legislature or council **2.** a group of political intriguers; also, a group of military men in power after a coup d'état: also **jun·to** (jun′tō), *pl.* **-tos**

**Ju·pi·ter** (jōō′pə tər) [L.] **1.** the chief Roman god: identified with the Greek god Zeus **2.** the largest planet of the solar system and the fifth in distance from the sun: diameter, c.88,000 mi.

**Ju·ra Mountains** (joor′ə) mountain range along the border of France & Switzerland

**Ju·ras·sic** (joo ras′ik) *adj.* [Fr. *jurassique* < *Jura* (Mountains)] designating or of the second period of the Mesozoic Era, following the Triassic —**the Jurassic** the Jurassic Period or its rocks: see GEOLOGY, chart

**ju·rid·i·cal** (joo rid′i k'l) *adj.* [< L. < *jus*, law + *dicere*, to declare] of judicial proceedings, or of law

**ju·ris·dic·tion** (joor′is dik′shən) *n.* [< OFr. < L. < *jus*, law + *dictio* < *dicere*, to declare] **1.** the administering of justice; authority to hear and decide cases **2.** authority or power in general **3.** the range of authority —**ju′ris·dic′tion·al** *adj.* —**ju′ris·dic′tion·al·ly** *adv.*

**ju·ris·pru·dence** (-prōō′d'ns) *n.* [< L. < *jus*, law + *prudentia*, a foreseeing] **1.** the science or philosophy of law **2.** a part or division of law —**ju′ris·pru·den′tial** (-den′shəl) *adj.* —**ju′ris·pru·den′tial·ly** *adv.*

**ju·rist** (joor′ist) *n.* [< MFr. < ML. < L. *jus*, law] **1.** an expert in law; writer on law **2.** a judge

**ju·ris·tic** (joo ris′tik) *adj.* of jurists or jurisprudence; relating to law —**ju·ris′ti·cal·ly** *adv.*

**ju·ror** (joor′ər) *n.* **1.** a member of a jury **2.** a person taking an oath, as of allegiance

**ju·ry¹** (joor′ē) *n., pl.* **-ries** [< OFr. < ML. < L. *jurare*, to swear < *jus*, law] **1.** a group of people sworn to hear evidence in a law case and to give a decision **2.** a group selected to decide the winners in a contest

**ju·ry²** (joor′ē) *adj.* [< ?] *Naut.* for temporary use; makeshift [a *jury* mast]

**just¹** (just) *adj.* [< OFr. < L. *justus*, lawful < *jus*, law] **1.** right or fair [a *just* decision] **2.** righteous; upright [a *just* man] **3.** deserved; merited [*just* praise] **4.** lawful **5.** proper, fitting, etc. **6.** well-founded [a *just* suspicion] **7.** correct or true **8.** accurate; exact —*adv.* **1.** precisely; exactly [*just* one o'clock] **2.** almost at the point of [*just* leaving] **3.** only [*just* a taste] **4.** barely [*just* missed the train] **5.** a very short time ago [*just* left the room] **6.** immediately [*just* to my right] **7.** [Colloq.] quite; really [feeling *just* fine] —**just now** a moment ago —**just the same** [Colloq.] nevertheless —**just′ness** *n.*

**just²** (just) *n., vi. same as* JOUST

**jus·tice** (jus′tis) *n.* **1.** a being righteous **2.** fairness **3.** a being correct **4.** sound reason; rightfulness **5.** reward or penalty as deserved **6.** the use of authority to uphold what is right, just, or lawful **7.** the administration of law **8.** *same as:* a) JUDGE b) JUSTICE OF THE PEACE —**bring to justice** to cause (a wrongdoer) to be tried in court and duly punished —**do justice to 1.** to treat fitly or fairly **2.** to enjoy properly —**do oneself justice** to do something in a manner worthy of one's abilities —**jus′tice·ship′** *n.*

**justice of the peace** a local magistrate, authorized to decide minor cases, perform marriages, etc.

**jus·ti·fi·a·ble** (jus′tə fī′ə b'l, jus′tə fī′ə b'l) *adj.* that can be justified or defended as correct —**jus′ti·fi′a·bly** *adv.*

**jus·ti·fi·ca·tion** (jus′tə fi kā′shən) *n.* **1.** a justifying or being justified **2.** a fact that justifies

**justification by faith** *Theol.* the act by which a sinner is freed through faith from the penalty of his sin and is accepted by God as righteous

**jus·ti·fy** (jus′tə fī′) *vt.* **-fied′, -fy′ing** [< OFr. < LL., ult. < L. *justus*, just + *facere*, to make] **1.** to show to be just, right, or reasonable **2.** *Theol.* to free from blame **3.** to supply good grounds for **4.** to space (type) to make the lines correct in length —*vi.* *Law* to show an adequate reason for something done —**jus′ti·fi′er** *n.*

**Jus·tin·i·an I** (jəs tin′ē ən) (L. name *Flavius Ancius Justinianus*) 483–565 A.D.; Byzantine emperor (527–565): known for the codification of Roman law (**Justinian code**): called *the Great*

**just·ly** (just′lē) *adv.* **1.** in a just manner **2.** rightly **3.** deservedly

**jut** (jut) *vi., vt.* **jut′ted, jut′ting** [prob. var. of JET¹] to stick out; project —*n.* a part that juts

**Jute** (jōōt) *n.* a member of any of several early Germanic tribes in Jutland: Jutes settled in SE England in the 5th cent. A.D. —**Jut′ish** *adj.*

**jute** (jōōt) *n.* [Hindi *jhuto* < Sans. *jūṭa*, matted hair] **1.** a strong fiber used for making burlap, sacks, rope, etc. **2.** either of two East Indian plants yielding this fiber

**Jut·land** (jut′lənd) peninsula of N Europe, forming the mainland of Denmark

**Ju·ve·nal** (jōō′və n'l) (L. name *Decimus Junius Juvenalis*) 60?–140? A.D.; Rom. satirical poet

**ju·ven·ile** (jōō′və n'l, -nīl′) *adj.* [< L. < *juvenis*, young] **1.** *a)* young; youthful *b)* immature; childish **2.** of, characteristic of, or suitable for children or young persons —*n.* **1.** a young person; child or youth **2.** an actor who plays youthful roles **3.** a book for children **4.** *Biol.* an immature animal or plant —**ju′ve·nil′i·ty** (-nil′ə tē) *n.*

**juvenile court** a law court for cases involving children under a specified age, usually 18

**juvenile delinquency** behavior by minors of not more than a specified age, usually 18, that is antisocial or unlawful —**juvenile delinquent**

**jux·ta·pose** (juk′stə pōz′) *vt.* **-posed′, -pos′ing** [< Fr. < *juxta-* (< L. *juxta*, near) + *poser*, POSE¹] to put side by side or close together —**jux′ta·po·si′tion** *n.*

**Jy.** July

**Jyl·land** (yül′län) *Dan. name of* JUTLAND

# K

**K, k** (kā) *n., pl.* **K's, k's** **1.** the eleventh letter of the English alphabet **2.** the sound of K or k

**K** **1.** karat (carat) **2.** *Physics* Kelvin **3.** *Chess* king **4.** knit **5.** [ModL. *kalium*] *Chem.* potassium

**K., k.** **1.** *Elec.* capacity **2.** karat (carat) **3.** *Physics* Kelvin **4.** kilo **5.** knight

**K2** (kā′tōō′) *same as* GODWIN AUSTEN

**Kaa·ba** (kä′bə, kä′ə bə) [Ar. *ka'bah*, lit., square building < *ka'b*, a cube] the sacred Moslem shrine at Mecca, toward which believers turn when praying: it contains a black stone supposedly given to Abraham by the angel Gabriel

**kab·a·la, kab·ba·la** (kab′ə lə, kə bä′lə) *n. same as* CABALA

**ka·bob** (kə bäb′) *n. same as* KEBAB

**Ka·bu·ki** (kä bōō′kē, kə-) [Jap. < *kabu*, music and dancing + *ki*, spirit] [*also* k-] a form of Japanese drama with formalized pantomime, dance, and song, and with male actors in all roles

**Ka·bul** (kä′bool) capital of Afghanistan, in the NE part: pop. 456,000

**ka·di** (kä′dē, kä′-) *n. same as* CADI

**kaf·fee·klatsch** (kä′fā kläch′, kô′fē klach′) *n.* [G.] [*also* K-] an informal gathering, as of housewives during the day, to drink coffee and chat: also **kaffee klatsch**

**Kaf·fir** (kaf′ər) *n.* [Ar. *kāfir*, infidel < prp. of *kafara*, to be skeptical] **1.** a member of any of several Bantu-speaking tribes in South Africa **2.** [k-] *same as* KAFIR

**kaf·fi·yeh** (kä fē′yə) *n.* [< Ar.] a headdress of draped cotton cloth worn by Arabs

**kaf·ir** (kaf′ər) *n.* [Ar. *kāfir:* see KAFFIR] **1.** a grain sorghum grown in dry regions for grain and fodder **2.** [K-] *same as* KAFFIR

**Kaf·ka** (käf′kə), **Franz** (fränts) 1883–1924; Austrian writer, born in Prague

**kaf·tan** (kaf′tən, käf tän′) *n. same as* CAFTAN

**kai·ak** (kī′ak) *n. same as* KAYAK

**kai·ser** (kī′zər) *n.* [Gmc. borrowing < L. *Caesar*] emperor: the title [K-] of the rulers of the Holy Roman Empire (962–1806), of Austria (1804–1918), and of Germany (1871–1918)

**Kal·a·ma·zoo** (kal′ə mə zōō′) [< Fr. < Ojibwa < ?] city in SW Mich.: pop. 80,000

**kale** (kāl) *n.* [Scot. var. of COLE] a hardy, nonheading cabbage with loose, spreading, curled leaves

**ka·lei·do·scope** (kə lī′də skōp′) *n.* [< Gr. *kalos*, beautiful + *eidos*, form + -SCOPE] **1.** a small tube containing loose bits of colored glass, plastic, etc. reflected by mirrors so that various symmetrical patterns appear when the tube is rotated **2.** anything that constantly changes —**ka·lei′do·scop′ic** (-skäp′ik) *adj.* —**ka·lei′do·scop′i·cal·ly** *adv.*

**kal·ends** (kal′əndz) *n.pl. same as* CALENDS

**Ka·le·va·la** (kä′lə vä′lä) [Finn., lit., land of heroes] a Finnish epic poem

**Ka·li** (kä′lē) a Hindu goddess viewed both as destroying life and giving it

**Ka·li·man·tan** (kä′lē män′tän) S part of the island of Borneo, belonging to Indonesia

**Kal·muck, Kal·muk** (kal′muk) *n.* **1.** a member of a group of Mongol peoples living chiefly in the NE Caucasus and N Sinkiang **2.** their western Mongolic language

**kal·so·mine** (kal′sə mīn′, -min) *n., vt.* **-mined′, -min′ing** *same as* CALCIMINE

**Ka·ma·su·tra** (kä′mə sōō′trə) [Sans. < *kāma*, love + *sūtra*, manual] a Hindu love manual written in the 8th cent.: also **Kama Sutra**

**Kam·chat·ka** (käm chät′kä; E. kam chat′kə) peninsula in NE Siberia, between the Sea of Okhotsk & the Bering Sea

**kam·pong** (käm′pôṇ′) *n.* [Malay] a small Malay village or cluster of native huts

**Kam·pu·che·a** (kam′poo chē′ə), **Democratic** *official name of* CAMBODIA

**Ka·nak·a** (kə nak′ə, kan′ə kə) *n.* [Haw., man] **1.** a Hawaiian **2.** a native of the South Sea Islands

**Kan·din·sky** (kan din′skē), **Was·si·ly** (vas′ə lē) 1866–1944; Russ. painter in Germany & France

**kan·ga·roo** (kaṇ′gə rōō′) *n., pl.* **-roos′, -roo′:** see PLURAL, II, D, 1 [said (by James COOK) to be native name] a leaping, plant-eating mammal native to Australia and neighboring islands, with short forelegs, strong, large hind legs, and a long, thick tail: the female has a pouch in front, in which she carries her young

**kangaroo court** [Colloq.] an unauthorized, irregular court illegally passing and executing judgment, as among frontiersmen or prison inmates

**kangaroo rat** a small, jumping, mouselike rodent of desert regions in the SW U.S. and Mexico

**Kan·pur** (kän′poor) city in N India, on the Ganges: pop. 895,000

**Kan·sas** (kan′zəs) [Fr. < Siouan tribal name] **1.** Middle Western State of the U.S.: 82,264 sq. mi.; pop. 2,363,000; cap. Topeka: abbrev. **Kans., KS 2.** river in NE Kans., flowing east into the Missouri —**Kan′san** *adj., n.*

**Kansas City 1.** city in W Mo., on the Missouri River: pop. 448,000 **2.** adjoining city in Kans., on the Missouri & Kansas rivers: pop. 161,000 (Both are in a single met. area, pop. 1,322,000)

**Kant** (kant; *G.* känt), **Immanuel** 1724–1804; Ger. philosopher —**Kant′i·an** *adj., n.*

**ka·o·lin** (kā′ə lin) *n.* [Fr. < Chin. *kao-ling,* name of hill where found] a fine white clay used in making porcelain

**ka·on** (kā′än) *n.* [*ka* (the letter K) + (MES)ON] any of four mesons having a mass approximately 970 times that of an electron

**ka·pok** (kā′päk) *n.* [Malay *kapoq*] the silky fibers around the seeds of a tropical tree: used for stuffing mattresses, sleeping bags, etc.

**kap·pa** (kap′ə) *n.* [Gr.] the tenth letter of the Greek alphabet (Κ, κ)

**Ka·ra·chi** (kə rä′chē) seaport in Pakistan, on the Arabian Sea: pop. 3,060,000

**Ka·ra·gan·da** (kä′rə gän′də) city in EC Kazakh S.S.R.: pop. 505,000

**Ka·ra·ko·ram** (kä′rä kôr′əm, kar′ə-) NW range of the Himalayas, in India, near the Chinese border

**kar·a·kul** (kar′ə kəl) *n.* [< *Kara Kul,* lake in SC U.S.S.R.] **1.** a broad-tailed sheep of C Asia **2.** *same as* BROADTAIL (sense 2)

**kar·at** (kar′ət) *n.* [var. of CARAT] one 24th part (of pure gold) *[14-karat* gold is 14 parts pure gold and 10 parts alloy]

---

fat, āpe, cär, ten, ēven, is, bīte; gō, hôrn, tōōl, look; oil, out; up, fur; get; joy; yet; chin; she; thin, then; zh, leisure; ŋ, ring; ə for *a* in *ago, e* in *agent, i* in *sanity, o* in *comply, u* in *focus;* as in *able* (ā′b'l); Fr. bāl; ë, Fr. coeur; ö, Fr. feu; Fr. mon; ō, Fr. coq; ü, Fr. duc; r, Fr. cri; H, G. ich; kh, G. doch; ‡foreign; *hypothetical; < derived from. See inside front cover.

**ka·ra·te** (kə rät′ē) *n.* [Jap. < *kara*, empty + *te*, hand] a Japanese system of self-defense in which blows are struck with the side of the open hand

**Ka·re·li·a** (kə rēl′yə; *Russ.* kä rē′lē ä) division of the R.S.F.S.R., east of Finland —**Ka·re′li·an** *adj., n.*

**Kar·en** (kar′ən) [Scand. var. of CATHERINE] a feminine name

**Karl** (kärl) [var. of CARL] a masculine name

**Karl-Marx-Stadt** (kärl′märks′shtät′) city in S East Germany: pop. 295,000

**Karls·ruh·e** (kärls′rōō ə; *E.* kärlz′rōō ə) city in SW West Germany, on the Rhine: pop. 253,000

**kar·ma** (kär′mə, kur′-) *n.* [Sans., a deed, fate] *Buddhism & Hinduism* a person's actions in one reincarnation thought of as determining his fate in the next

**Kar·nak** (kär′nak) village in S Egypt, on the Nile: site of ancient Thebes

**kart** (kärt) *n.* [altered < CART] **1.** any of various small vehicles **2.** a small, flat, 4-wheeled, motorized vehicle for one person, used in racing (**karting**)

**kar·y·o-** (ModL. < Gr. *karyon*, a nut, kernel] *a combining form meaning:* **1.** nut, kernel **2.** *Biol.* the nucleus of a cell

**kas·bah** (käz′bä) *n. same as* CASBAH

**Kash·mir** (kash′mir) region in SE Asia, between Afghanistan & Tibet: part of Jammu & Kashmir: see JAMMU AND KASHMIR —**Kash·mir′i·an** *adj., n.*

**kash·rut, kash·ruth** (käsh rōōt′, käsh′rōōt) *n.* the dietary regulations of Judaism: see KOSHER

**Kas·sel** (käs′əl) city in C West Germany: pop. 212,000

**kat·a-** *same as* CATA-: also, before a vowel, **kat-**

**Kath·ar·ine, Kath·er·ine** (kath′ər in, kath′rin) [see CATHERINE] a feminine name: dim. *Kate, Kay*

**Kath·leen** (kath′lēn, kath lēn′) [Ir. var. of CATHERINE] a feminine name

**Kat·man·du** (kät′män dōō′) capital of Nepal, in the C part: pop. 195,000: also sp. **Kath′man·du′**

**Ka·to·wi·ce** (kä′tô vē′tse) city in S Poland: pop. 290,000

**Kat·te·gat** (kat′i gat′) strait between SW Sweden & E Jutland, Denmark

**ka·ty·did** (kät′ē did′) *n.* [echoic of shrill sound made by the males] a large, green tree insect resembling the grasshopper

**Kau·nas** (kou′näs) city in SC Lithuanian S.S.R.: pop. 292,000

**kau·ri** (kou′rē) *n.* [Maori] **1.** a tall pine tree of New Zealand **2.** its wood **3.** a resin (**kauri resin, kauri gum**) from this tree, used in varnishes, etc.

**Ka·wa·sa·ki** (kä′wä sä′kē) city in C Honshu, Japan, between Tokyo & Yokohama: pop. 855,000

**kay·ak** (kī′ak) *n.* [Esk.] an Eskimo canoe made of skins completely covering a wooden frame except for an opening for the paddler

**kay·o** (kā′ō′) *vt.* **-oed′, -o′ing** [< KO] [Slang] *Boxing* to knock out —*n.* [Slang] *Boxing* a knockout

**Ka·zakh Soviet Socialist Republic** (kä zäk′) republic of the U.S.S.R., in W Asia: 1,048,000 sq. mi.; pop. 12,700,000; cap. Alma-Ata: also **Ka·zakh·stan** (kä′zäk stän′)

**Ka·zan** (kä zän′; *Russ.* kå zän′y′) city in W R.S.F.S.R., on the Volga: pop. 837,000

KAYAK

**ka·zoo** (kə zōō′) *n.* [echoic] a toy musical instrument consisting of a small, open tube with a top hole covered by a membrane that vibrates to give a buzzing quality to tones hummed through the tube

**kc, kc.** kilocycle; kilocycles

**K.C. 1.** King's Counsel **2.** Knight(s) of Columbus

**kcal.** kilocalorie; kilocalories

**Kčs** koruna; korunas

**ke·a** (kā′ə, kē′ə) *n.* [Maori] a large, green parrot of New Zealand that sometimes kills sheep by tearing at their backs to eat the kidney fat

**Keats** (kēts), **John** 1795–1821; Eng. poet

**ke·bab** (kə bäb′) *n.* [Ar. *kabāb*] **1.** [*often pl.*] a dish consisting of small pieces of marinated meat broiled or roasted on a skewer, often with alternating pieces of onion, tomato, etc. **2.** a piece of such meat

**Kech·ua** (kech′wä) *n. same as* QUECHUA —**Kech′uan** *adj., n.*

**kedge** (kej) *vt., vi.* **kedged, kedg′ing** [ME. *caggen*, to fasten < ?] to move (a ship) by hauling on a rope fastened to an anchor dropped at some distance —*n.* a light anchor, esp. for such use: also **kedge anchor**

**keel** (kēl) *n.* [< ON. *kjǫlr*] **1.** the chief timber or steel piece along the entire length of the bottom of a ship or boat **2.** anything like a ship's keel in position, appearance, etc. —*vt., vi.* to turn over on its side so as to turn up the keel

—**keel over 1.** to turn over; upset **2.** to fall in a faint, etc. —**on an even keel** upright and level, steady, stable, etc.

**keel·haul** (-hôl′) *vt.* to haul (a person) under the keel of a ship as a punishment

**keel·son** (kel′s'n, kēl′-) *n.* [prob. via Du. *kolsem* < Dan. < *kjøl*, KEEL + *sville*, sill] a beam or set of timbers or metal plates fastened inside a ship's hull along the keel for added strength

**keen¹** (kēn) *adj.* [OE. *cene*, wise] **1.** having a sharp edge or point **2.** sharp in force; piercing [a *keen* wind] **3.** sharp and quick in seeing, hearing, thinking, etc.; acute **4.** eager; enthusiastic **5.** strong or intense, as a desire **6.** [Slang] good, fine, excellent, etc. —**keen′ly** *adv.* —**keen′ness** *n.*

**keen²** (kēn) *n.* [< Ir. < *caoinim*, I wail] [Irish] a wailing for the dead; dirge —*vt., vi.* [Irish] to lament or wail for (the dead)

**keep** (kēp) *vt.* **kept, keep′ing** [< OE. *cepan*, to behold, lay hold of] **1.** to observe with due ceremony; celebrate [keep the Sabbath] **2.** to fulfill (a promise, etc.) **3.** to follow (a routine, diet, etc.) **4.** to go on maintaining [keep pace] **5.** to protect; guard; defend **6.** to watch over; take care of; tend **7.** to raise (livestock) **8.** to maintain in good order or condition; preserve **9.** to provide for; support **10.** to supply with food or lodging for pay [to keep boarders] **11.** to have in one's service or for one's use [to keep servants] **12.** to make regular entries in, detailing transactions, happenings, etc. [to keep books, a diary, etc.] **13.** to carry on; conduct; manage **14.** to make stay in a specified condition, position, etc. [to keep an engine running] **15.** to hold for future use or a long time **16.** to have regularly in stock for sale **17.** to hold in custody **18.** to detain **19.** to restrain from action **20.** to withhold **21.** to conceal (a secret) **22.** to continue to have or hold; not lose or give up **23.** to stay in or at (a path, course, or place) —*vi.* **1.** to stay in a specified condition, position, etc. **2.** to continue; go on; persevere (often with *on*) **3.** to hold oneself back; refrain [to keep from telling someone] **4.** to stay fresh; not spoil; last **5.** to require no immediate attention [a task that will keep] —*n.* **1.** orig., care, charge, or custody **2.** *a)* a donjon *b)* a fort; castle **3.** food and shelter; support; livelihood —**for keeps** [Colloq.] **1.** with the winner keeping what he wins **2.** forever — **keep at** to continue doing; persist in —**keep to 1.** to persevere in **2.** to adhere to **3.** to remain in —**keep to oneself 1.** to avoid others **2.** to refrain from telling —**keep up 1.** to maintain in good condition **2.** to continue **3.** to maintain the pace **4.** to remain informed about (with *on* or *with*)

**keep·er** (-ər) *n.* a person or thing that keeps; specif., *a)* a guard, as of prisoners, animals, etc. *b)* a guardian or protector *c)* a caretaker

**keep·ing** (-iŋ) *n.* **1.** observance (of a rule, holiday, etc.) **2.** care; charge **3.** maintenance or means of this; keep **4.** reservation for future use; preservation —**in keeping with** in conformity or accord with

**keep·sake** (-sāk′) *n.* something kept, or to be kept, in memory of the giver; memento

**keg** (keg) *n.* [< or akin to ON. *kaggi*, keg] **1.** a small barrel, usually of less than ten gallons **2.** a unit of weight for nails, equal to 100 lbs.

**keg·ler** (keg′lər) *n.* [G. < *kegel*, (nine)pin] [Colloq.] a person who bowls; bowler

**keis·ter, kees·ter** (kēs′tər) *n.* [prob. via Yid. < MHG. *kiste*, a chest, ult. < L.] [Slang] **1.** a satchel, suitcase, etc. **2.** the buttocks; rump

**Kel·ler** (kel′ər), **Helen Adams** 1880–1968; U.S. writer & lecturer: blind & deaf from infancy, she was taught to speak & read

**Kel·ly (green)** (kel′ē) [*also* k-] a bright, yellowish green

**ke·loid** (kē′loid) *n.* [< Fr. < Gr. *chēlē*, claw + *-oeidēs*, -OID] an excessive growth of scar tissue on the skin —**ke·loi′dal** *adj.*

**kelp** (kelp) *n.* [ME. *culp*] **1.** any of various large, coarse, brown seaweeds **2.** ashes of seaweed, from which iodine is obtained

**kel·pie, kel·py** (kel′pē) *n., pl.* **-pies** [Scot. < ? Gael. *calpa*, colt] *Gaelic Folklore* a water spirit, supposed to take the form of a horse and drown people

**kel·son** (kel′s'n) *n. same as* KEELSON

**Kelt** (kelt) *n. same as* CELT —**Kelt′ic** *adj., n.*

**kel·ter** (kel′tər) *n.* [Colloq.] *same as* KILTER

**Kel·vin** (kel′vin) *adj.* designating, of, or according to the Kelvin scale

**Kelvin scale** [after 1st Baron *Kelvin*, 19th-c. Brit. physicist] *Physics* a scale of temperature measured in degrees Celsius from absolute zero (−273.15°C)

**Ke·mal A·ta·turk** (ke mäl′ ät ä turk′) 1881–1938; 1st president of Turkey: also called **Mus·ta·fa Kemal** (mōōs′-tä fä) & **Kemal Pasha**

**Kem·pis** (kem′pis), **Thomas à** (born *Thomas Hamerken* or *Hammerlein*) 1380?–1471; Ger. monk & scholar

**ken** (ken) *vt., vi.* **kenned, ken'ning** [OE. *cennan,* lit., to cause to know] [Scot.] to know (*of* or *about*) —*n.* range of knowledge; understanding

**Ken·ne·dy** (ken'ə dē), **Cape** [after ff.] *former name (1963–73) of* Cape CANAVERAL

**Ken·ne·dy** (ken'ə dē), **John Fitzgerald** 1917–63; 35th president of the U.S. (1961–63): assassinated

**ken·nel** (ken''l) *n.* [< OFr. *chenil* < L. *canis,* a dog] **1.** a doghouse **2.** [*often pl.*] a place where dogs are bred or kept **3.** a pack of dogs —*vt.* **-neled** or **-nelled, -nel·ing** or **-nel·ling** to place or keep in a kennel —*vi.* to live or take shelter in a kennel

**Ken·neth** (ken'ith) [Scot. < Gael. *Caioneach,* lit., handsome] a masculine name: dim. *Ken*

**ke·no** (kē'nō) *n.* [< Fr. *quine,* five winning numbers < L.] a gambling game resembling lotto

**Ke·no·sha** (ki nō'shə) [< Fr. < Algonquian *kinōzhan,* lit., pickerel] city in SW Wis., on Lake Michigan: pop. 78,000

**Kent** (kent) county of SE England, on the English Channel: formerly an Anglo-Saxon kingdom

**Ken·tuck·y** (kən tuk'ē, ken-) [< Iroquoian, level land] EC State of the U.S.: 40,395 sq. mi.: pop. 3,661,000; cap. Frankfort: abbrev. **Ky., KY** —**Ken·tuck'i·an** *adj., n.*

**Ken·ya** (ken'yə, kēn'-) country in EC Africa, on the Indian Ocean: a member of the Commonwealth: 224,960 sq. mi.; pop. 10,890,000; cap. Nairobi —**Ken'yan** *adj., n.*

**Ke·ogh plan** (kē'ō) [after E. J. *Keogh* (1907– ), U.S. congressman] a retirement plan like an IRA but for self-employed persons and certain groups of employees

**kep·i** (kep'ē, kā'pē) *n., pl.* **kep'is** [Fr. *képi* < G. dial. *käppi,* dim. of *kappe,* a CAP] a visored cap with a flat, round top, worn by French soldiers

**Kep·ler** (kep'lər), **Jo·hann** (yō'hän) 1571–1630; Ger. astronomer & mathematician

**kept** (kept) *pt. & pp. of* KEEP —*adj.* maintained as a mistress [a *kept* woman]

**ker·a·tin** (ker'ət 'n) *n.* [< Gr. *keras* (gen. *keratos*), horn + -IN¹] a tough, fibrous, insoluble protein, the principal matter of hair, nails, horn, etc.

**kerb** (kurb) *n. Brit. sp. of* CURB (*n.* 4)

**ker·chief** (kur'chif) *n.* [< OFr. *covrechef* < *covrir,* to cover + *chef,* the head] **1.** a piece of cloth worn over the head or around the neck **2.** a handkerchief

**kerf** (kurf) *n.* [OE. *cyrf* < *ceorfan,* to CARVE] the cut made by a saw —*vt.* to make a kerf in

**ker·mes** (kur'mēz) *n.* [< Fr. < Ar. & Per. *qirmiz,* crimson] **1.** the dried bodies of certain Mediterranean insects, used to make a purple-red dye **2.** the dye

**ker·mis, ker·mess** (kur'mis) *n.* [< Du. < *kerk,* a church + *mis,* MASS] **1.** in the Netherlands, Belgium, etc., an outdoor fair or carnival **2.** any similar fair or entertainment, usually for charity

**kern** (kurn) *n.* [Fr. *carne,* a hinge < OFr. < L. *cardo*] that part of the face of a letter of type which projects beyond the body

**ker·nel** (kur'n'l) *n.* [OE. *cyrnel,* dim. of *corn,* seed] **1.** a grain or seed, as of corn, wheat, etc. **2.** the inner, softer part of a nut, fruit pit, etc. **3.** the central, most important part of something; essence —*vt.* **-neled** or **-nelled, -nel·ing** or **-nel·ling** to enclose as a kernel

**ker·o·sene** (ker'ə sēn', ker'ə sēn') *n.* [Gr. *kēros,* wax + -ENE] a thin oil distilled from petroleum or shale oil, used as a fuel, solvent, etc.: also, esp. in science and industry, sp. **kerosine**

**ker·sey** (kur'zē) *n., pl.* **-seys** [< *Kersey,* village in England] a coarse, lightweight woolen cloth, usually ribbed and with a cotton warp

**kes·trel** (kes'trəl) *n.* [OFr. *cresserelle:* origin echoic] a small, brown-and-gray European falcon that can hover in the air against the wind

**ketch** (kech) *n.* [< ME. *cacchen,* to catch: orig. used of fishing vessels] a fore-and-aft rigged sailing vessel with a mainmast toward the bow and a relatively tall mizzenmast, forward of the rudderpost, toward the stern: distinguished from YAWL

**ketch·up** (kech'əp) *n.* [Malay *kēchap,* a fish sauce < Chin. *ke-tsiap*] a sauce for meat, fish, etc.; esp., a thick sauce (**tomato ketchup**) made of tomatoes flavored with onion, salt, sugar, and spice

**ke·tone** (kē'tōn) *n.* [G. *keton,* var. of Fr. *acétone:* see ACETONE] an organic chemical compound containing the bivalent radical CO in combination with two hydrocarbon radicals

**Ket·ter·ing** (ket'ər iŋ) [after C. *Kettering,* 1876–1958, U.S. inventor] city in SW Ohio: suburb of Dayton: pop. 61,000

**ket·tle** (ket''l) *n.* [ON. *ketill* < L. dim. of *catinus,* bowl] **1.** a metal container for boiling or cooking things; pot **2.** a teakettle **3.** a kettledrum

**ket·tle·drum** (-drum') *n.* a percussion instrument consisting of a hollow hemisphere and a parchment top that can be tightened or loosened to change the pitch; timpano

KETTLEDRUMS

**kettle of fish** a difficult situation

**kev, Kev** (kev) *n., pl.* **kev, Kev** [K(ILO-)E(LECTRON-)V(OLTS)] a unit of energy equal to one thousand (10³) electronvolts

**key**¹ (kē) *n., pl.* **keys** [OE. *cæge*] **1.** an instrument, usually of metal, for moving the bolt of a lock and thus locking or unlocking something **2.** anything like this; specif., *a*) a device to turn a bolt, etc. [a skate *key*] *b*) a pin, bolt, etc. put into a hole or space to hold parts together *c*) any of the levers, or the disks, etc. connected to them, pressed down to operate a piano, clarinet, typewriter, etc. *d*) a device for opening or closing an electric circuit **3.** a place so located as to give control of a region **4.** a thing that explains or solves, as a book of answers **5.** a controlling or essential person or thing **6.** tone of voice; pitch **7.** tone of thought or expression [in a cheerful *key*] **8.** *Music* a system of notes forming a given scale; tonality —*adj.* controlling; essential; important —*vt.* **keyed, key'ing 1.** to fasten or lock with a key **2.** to furnish with a key **3.** to set the tone or pitch of **4.** to bring into harmony —**key up** to make tense or excited

**key**² (kē) *n., pl.* **keys** [Sp. *cayo*] a reef or low island

**key**³ (kē) *n.* [< Sp. pron. of 1st syllable of *kilogramo, kilogram*] [Slang] a kilogram as of marijuana

**Key** (kē), **Francis Scott** 1779–1843; U.S. lawyer: wrote "The Star-Spangled Banner"

**key·board** (kē'bôrd') *n.* **1.** the row(s) of keys of a piano, typewriter, etc. **2.** an electronic piano as in a rock or jazz group —*vt., vi.* to set (type) using a keyboard typesetting machine

**key·board·ist** (-ist) *n.* a performer on a keyboard

**keyed** (kēd) *adj.* **1.** having keys, as some musical instruments **2.** pitched in a specified key **3.** made appropriate

**key·hole** (kē'hōl') *n.* an opening (in a lock) into which a key is inserted

**Keynes** (kānz), **John May·nard** (mā'nərd), 1st Baron Keynes, 1883–1946; Eng. economist —**Keynes'i·an** *adj., n.*

**key·note** (kē'nōt') *n.* **1.** the lowest, basic note or tone of a musical scale **2.** the basic idea or ruling principle, as of a speech, policy, etc. —*vt.* **-not'ed, -not'ing 1.** to give the keynote of **2.** to give the keynote speech at —**key'not'er** *n.*

**keynote speech** (or **address**) a speech, as at a convention, setting forth the main line of policy

**key punch** a keyboard machine that records data by punching holes in cards, later fed into machines for sorting, etc.

**key ring** a metal ring for holding keys

**key signature** *Music* one or more sharps or flats after the clef on the staff, showing the key

**key·stone** (-stōn') *n.* **1.** the central, topmost stone of an arch **2.** a main or supporting part or principle

**Key West** westernmost island of a chain of islands (**Florida Keys**) off the S tip of Fla.

KEYSTONE

**kg, kg.** **1.** keg(s) **2.** kilogram(s)

**KGB, K.G.B.** [Russ. *K(omitet) G(osudarstvennoye) B(ezopastnosti),* Committee of State Security] the security police, or intelligence agency, of the Soviet Union

**Kha·cha·tu·ri·an** (kach'ə toor'ē ən; Russ. khä'chä too ryän'), **A·ram** (ar'əm) 1903?–1978; Russ. composer

**kha·ki** (kak'ē, kä'kē) *adj.* [< Hindi < Per. *khāk,* dust] **1.** dull yellowish-brown **2.** made of khaki (cloth) —*n., pl.* **-kis** **1.** a dull yellowish brown **2.** strong, twilled cloth of this color **3.** [*often pl.*] a khaki uniform or pants

**khan**¹ (kän, kan) *n.* [< Turki *khān,* lord, prince] **1.** a title of Turkish, Tatar, and Mongol rulers in the Middle Ages **2.** a title of honor in Iran, Afghanistan, etc. —**khan'ate** (-āt) *n.*

**khan**² (kän, kan) *n.* [Ar. *khān*] in Turkey and other Eastern countries, an inn or caravansary

**Khar·kov** (kär'kôf; *Russ.* khär'kôf) city in NE Ukrainian S.S.R.: pop. 1,148,000

**Khar·toum** (kär tōōm') capital of Sudan, on the Nile: pop. 185,000 (met. area 490,000)

**Khayyám, Omar** *see* OMAR KHAYYÁM

**khe·dive** (kə dēv') *n.* [< Fr. < Per. *khidīw,* prince] the title of the Turkish viceroys of Egypt (1867–1914)

**Khrush·chev** (krōōs'chev, -chôf; *Russ.* khrōōsh'chyôf), **Ni·ki·ta (Sergeyevich)** (ni kē'tä) 1894–1971; premier of the U.S.S.R. (1958–64)

**Khu·fu** (kōō′fōō) fl. c. 2650 B.C.; king of Egypt: builder of the Great Pyramid near Gîza

**Khy·ber Pass** (kī′bər) mountain pass in the Hindu Kush, between Afghanistan & Pakistan

**kHz** kilohertz

**Ki.** Kings

**kib·ble** (kib′'l) *vt.* **-bled, -bling** [< ?] to grind into coarse bits —*n.* kibbled food for dogs, etc.

**kib·butz** (ki bōōts′, -bŏŏts′) *n., pl.* **kib·but·zim** (kē′bŏŏ-tsēm′) [ModHeb.] an Israeli collective settlement, esp. a collective farm

**kib·itz** (kib′its) *vi.* [Colloq.] to act as a kibitzer

**kib·itz·er** (-ər) *n.* [Yid. < colloq. G. *kiebitzen < kiebitz*, meddlesome onlooker] [Colloq.] **1.** an onlooker at a card game, etc., esp. one who volunteers advice **2.** a giver of unwanted advice

**ki·bosh** (kī′bäsh) *n.* [< ? Yid.] [Slang] orig., nonsense —**put the kibosh on** to squelch; veto

**kick** (kik) *vi.* [ME. *kiken* < ?] **1.** to strike out with the foot or feet **2.** to spring back suddenly, as a gun when fired; recoil **3.** [Colloq.] to object; complain **4.** *Football* to kick the ball —*vt.* **1.** to strike suddenly with the foot or feet **2.** to drive (a ball, etc.) in this way **3.** to make (one's way) by kicking **4.** to score (a goal or point in football) by kicking **5.** [Slang] *a)* to stop taking (a narcotic drug) *b)* to get rid of (a habit) —*n.* **1.** a blow with the foot **2.** a kicking **3.** [Colloq.] an objection; complaint **4.** [Colloq.] a stimulating effect, as of alcoholic liquor **5.** [Colloq.] [*often pl.*] pleasure; thrill **6.** *Football a)* a kicking of the ball *b)* the kicked ball —**kick around** (or **about**) [Colloq.] **1.** to treat roughly **2.** to move from place to place **3.** to lie about unnoticed **4.** to think about or discuss —**kick back** **1.** [Colloq.] to recoil suddenly and unexpectedly **2.** [Slang] to give back (part of one's pay, etc.) —**kick in** [Slang] to pay (one's share) —**kick off** **1.** to put a football into play with a place kick **2.** to start (a campaign, etc.) **3.** [Slang] to die —**kick on** [Colloq.] **1.** to turn on (a switch, etc.) **2.** to begin operating —**kick out** [Colloq.] to get rid of; expel —**kick up** [Colloq.] to cause (trouble, etc.) —**on** (or **off**) **a kick** [Slang] currently (or no longer) enthusiastic about an activity

**kick·back** (-bak′) *n.* **1.** [Colloq.] a sharp reaction **2.** [Slang] *a)* a giving back of part of one's pay, etc. *b)* the money returned

**kick·er** (-ər) *n.* **1.** one that kicks **2.** [Slang] *a)* a surprise ending *b)* a hidden difficulty

**kick·off** (-ôf′) *n.* **1.** the act of kicking off in football **2.** the start of a campaign, etc.

**kick·shaw** (kik′shô′) *n.* [< Fr. *quelque chose*, something] **1.** a fancy food or dish; delicacy **2.** a trinket; trifle; gewgaw Also **kick′shaws′** (-shôz′)

**kick·stand** (kik′stand′) *n.* a short metal bar fastened to a bicycle or motorcycle: when kicked down it holds the stationary cycle upright

**kid** (kid) *n.* [prob. < Anglo-N.] **1.** a young goat **2.** its flesh, used as food **3.** leather from the skin of young goats, used for gloves, shoes, etc. **4.** [Colloq.] a child or young person —*adj.* **1.** made of kidskin **2.** [Colloq.] younger [*my kid* sister] —*vt., vi.* **kid′ded, kid′ding** [Colloq.] to deceive, fool, or tease playfully —**kid′der** *n.* —**kid′like′, kid′dish** *adj.*

**Kidd** (kid), Captain (**William**) 1645?–1701; Brit. privateer & pirate, born in Scotland: hanged

**kid·dy, kid·die** (kid′ē) *n., pl.* **-dies** [dim. of KID] [Colloq.] a child

**kid gloves** soft, smooth gloves made of kidskin —**handle with kid gloves** [Colloq.] to treat with care, tact, etc.

**kid·nap** (-nap′) *vt.* **-napped′** or **-naped′, -nap′ping** or **-nap′ing** [KID + dial. *nap*, NAB] **1.** to steal (a child) **2.** to seize and hold (a person) against his will, by force or fraud, often for ransom —**kid′nap′per, kid′nap′er** *n.*

**kid·ney** (kid′nē) *n., pl.* **-neys** [ME. *kidenei* < ?] **1.** either of a pair of glandular organs in vertebrates, which separate waste products from the blood and excrete them as urine **2.** an animal kidney, used as food **3.** *a)* temperament *b)* kind; sort

**kidney bean** the kidney-shaped seed of the common garden bean of the legume family

**kidney stone** a hard mineral deposit formed in the kidney from phosphates, urates, etc.

**kid·skin** (kid′skin′) *n.* leather from the skin of young goats, used for gloves, shoes, etc.

**Kiel** (kēl) seaport in N West Germany, on a canal (**Kiel Canal**) connecting the North Sea & the Baltic Sea: pop. 270,000

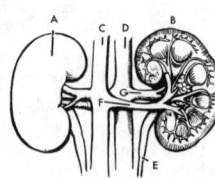

KIDNEYS
(A, right kidney; B, left kidney; C, vena cava; D, aorta; E, ureter; F, renal vein; G, renal artery; left kidney shown in cross section)

**kiel·ba·sa** (kēl bä′sə) *n., pl.* **-si** (-sē), **-sas** [Pol.] a smoked Polish sausage spiced with garlic

**Kier·ke·gaard** (kir′kə gärd′; *Dan.* kir′kə gôr′), **Sø·ren** (**Aabye**) (sö′rən) 1813–55; Dan. philosopher & theologian

**Ki·ev** (kē′ef; *E.* kē ev′, kē′ev) capital of the Ukrainian S.S.R., on the Dnepr: pop. 1,476,000

**kil.** kilometer; kilometers

**Kil·i·man·ja·ro** (kil′ə män jä′rō) mountain in NE Tanzania, near the Kenya border: highest mountain in Africa: 19,340 ft.

**kill**[1] (kil) *vt.* [ME. *killen* < ? OE. *cwellan*] **1.** to cause the death of; make die **2.** *a)* to destroy the vital or active qualities of *b)* to destroy; put an end to **3.** to defeat or veto (legislation) **4.** to spend (time) on trivial matters **5.** to stop (an engine, etc.), turn off (a light, etc.), or muffle (sound) **6.** to prevent publication of (a newspaper story) **7.** to spoil the effect of: said of colors, etc. **8.** [Colloq.] to overcome with laughter, chagrin, etc. **9.** [Colloq.] to make feel great pain or exhaustion **10.** [Slang] to drink the last, or all, of (a bottle of liquor, etc.) —*vi.* **1.** to destroy life **2.** to be killed [plants that *kill* easily] —*n.* **1.** an act of killing **2.** an animal or animals killed **3.** an enemy plane, ship, etc. destroyed

**kill**[2] (kil) *n.* [< Du. < MDu. *kille*] a stream; channel; creek: used esp. in place names

**kill·deer** (kil′dir′) *n., pl.* **-deers′, -deer′**: see PLURAL, II, D, 1 [echoic of its cry] a small, N. American bird of the plover family, with a high, piercing cry: also **kill′dee′** (-dē′)

**kill·er** (kil′ər) *n.* **1.** a person, animal, or thing that kills, esp. habitually **2.** *same as* KILLER WHALE

**killer whale** any of several fierce, grayish to black, small whales that hunt in large packs and prey on large fish, seals, and other whales

**kil·li·fish** (kil′ē fish′) *n., pl.* **-fish′, -fish′es**: see FISH [< KILL[2] + -IE + FISH] any of several minnowlike freshwater fishes used in mosquito control and as bait: also **kil′lie** (-ē), *pl.* **-lies**

**kill·ing** (kil′iŋ) *adj.* **1.** causing death; deadly **2.** exhausting **3.** [Colloq.] very comical —*n.* **1.** slaughter; murder **2.** [Colloq.] a sudden, great profit or success —**kill′ing·ly** *adv.*

**kill·joy** (-joi′) *n.* a person who destroys or lessens other people's enjoyment: also **kill′joy′**

**kiln** (kil, kiln) *n.* [< OE. *cylne* < L. *culina*, cookstove] a furnace or oven for drying, burning, or baking something, as bricks, pottery, or grain —*vt.* to dry, burn, or bake in a kiln

**kiln-dry** (-drī′) *vt.* **-dried′, -dry′ing** to dry in a kiln

**ki·lo** (kē′lō, kil′ō) *n., pl.* **-los** [Fr.] *short for:* **1.** KILOGRAM **2.** KILOMETER

**kil·o-** [Fr. < Gr. *chilioi*, thousand] *a combining form meaning* a thousand *[kilogram]*

**kilo.** **1.** kilogram **2.** kilometer

**kil·o·bar** (kil′ə bär′) *n.* [see KILO- & BAR[2]] a metric unit of pressure equal to 1,000 bars

**kil·o·cal·o·rie** (kil′ə kal′ər ē) *n.* 1,000 calories; great calorie

**kil·o·cy·cle** (-sī′k'l) *n. former name for* KILOHERTZ

**kil·o·gram** (-gram′) *n.* a unit of weight and mass, equal to 1,000 grams (2.2046 lb.): also, chiefly Brit., **kil′o·gramme′**

**kil·o·hertz** (-hurts′) *n., pl.* **-hertz′** 1,000 hertz

**kil·o·li·ter** (-lēt′ər) *n.* a unit of capacity, equal to 1,000 liters, or one cubic meter (264.18 gal., or 1.308 cu. yd.): also, chiefly Brit., **kil′o·li′tre**

**ki·lo·me·ter** (ki läm′ə tər, kil′ə mēt′ər) *n.* a unit of length or distance, equal to 1,000 meters (3,280.8 ft., or about 5/8 mi.): also, chiefly Brit., **ki·lo′me·tre —kil·o-met·ric** (kil′ə met′rik) *adj.*

**kil·o·ton** (kil′ə tun′) *n.* the explosive force of 1,000 tons of TNT

**kil·o·volt** (-vōlt′) *n.* 1,000 volts

**kil·o·watt** (-wät′) *n.* a unit of electrical power, equal to 1,000 watts

**kil·o·watt-hour** (-our′) *n.* a unit of electrical energy or work, equal to that done by one kilowatt acting for one hour

**kilt** (kilt) *vt.* [ME. *kilten*, prob. < Scand.] **1.** [Scot.] to tuck up (a skirt, etc.) **2.** to pleat **3.** to provide a kilt for —*n.* a pleated skirt reaching to the knees; esp., the tartan skirt worn sometimes by men of the Scottish Highlands

**kil·ter** (kil′tər) *n.* [< ?] [Colloq.] good condition; proper order: now chiefly in **out of kilter**

**Kim·ber·ley** (kim′bər lē) city in N Cape of Good Hope province, South Africa: diamond-mining center: pop. 95,000

**ki·mo·no** (kə mō′nə, -nō) *n., pl.* **-nos** [Jap.] **1.** a loose outer garment with short, wide sleeves and a sash, a traditional costume of Japanese men and women **2.** a woman's dressing gown like this

KILT

**kin** (kin) *n.* [< OE. *cynn*] relatives; family; kindred —*adj.* related, as by blood —**(near) of kin** (closely) related

**-kin** (kin) [< MDu. *-ken, -kijn,* dim. suffix] *a suffix meaning little [lambkin]*

**kind** (kīnd) *n.* [< OE. *cynd*] **1.** [Archaic] *a)* origin *b)* nature *c)* manner **2.** a natural group or division [the rodent *kind*] **3.** essential character **4.** sort; class —*adj.* **1.** sympathetic, friendly, gentle, generous, etc. **2.** cordial [*kind* regards] —**in kind 1.** in goods or produce instead of money **2.** with something like that received —**kind of** [Colloq.] somewhat; rather —**of a kind 1.** of the same kind; alike **2.** mediocre or inferior

**kin·der·gar·ten** (kin'dər gär't'n) *n.* [G., lit., garden of children] a school or class for children, usually four to six years old, preparing them for first grade by games, music, simple handicraft, etc. —**kin'der·gart'ner, kin'der·gar'ten·er** *n.*

**kind·heart·ed** (kīnd'här'tid) *adj.* having or resulting from a kind heart; sympathetic; kindly —**kind'heart'ed·ly** *adv.* —**kind'heart'ed·ness** *n.*

**kin·dle** (kin'd'l) *vt.* **-dled, -dling** [ME. *kindlen,* freq. < ON. *kynda*] **1.** to set on fire; ignite **2.** to start (a fire) **3.** to excite (interest, feelings, etc.) **4.** to make bright —*vi.* **1.** to catch fire **2.** to become excited —**kin'dler** *n.*

**kin·dling** (kin'dliŋ) *n.* bits of dry wood or other easily lighted material for starting a fire

**kind·ly** (kīnd'lē) *adj.* **-li·er, -li·est 1.** kind; gracious; benign **2.** agreeable; pleasant [a *kindly* climate] —*adv.* **1.** in a kind, gracious way **2.** agreeably **3.** please [*kindly* reply] —**take kindly to 1.** to be naturally attracted to **2.** to accept willingly —**kind'li·ness** *n.*

**kind·ness** (-nis) *n.* **1.** the state, quality, or habit of being kind **2.** kind act or treatment

**kin·dred** (kin'drid) *n.* [< OE. *cynn,* kin + *rǣden,* condition] **1.** formerly, family relationship **2.** relatives or family; kin —*adj.* of like nature

**kine** (kīn) [ME. *kin < cou* (< OE. *cy,* pl. of *cu,* COW¹) + *-(e)n*] [Archaic] cows; cattle

**kin·e·mat·ics** (kin'ə mat'iks) *n.pl.* [with sing. *v.*] [< Fr. < Gr. *kinēma,* motion < *kinein,* to move + -ICS] the branch of mechanics dealing with abstract motion, without reference to force or mass —**kin'e·mat'ic, kin'e·mat'i·cal** *adj.*

**kin·e·scope** (kin'ə skōp') *n.* [< Gr. < *kinein,* to move + -SCOPE] **1.** a cathode-ray tube used in television receivers, etc. for picture display **2.** a motion-picture record of such display

**ki·ne·sics** (ki nē'siks, kī-) *n.pl.* [with sing. *v.*] [< Gr. *kinēsis,* motion + -ICS] the study of bodily movements, facial expressions, etc. as ways of communication —**ki·ne'sic** *adj.*

**kin·es·the·si·a** (kin'is thē'zhə, -zhē ə) *n.* [ModL. < Gr. *kinein,* to move + *aisthēsis,* perception] the sensation of position, movement, etc. of bodily parts, perceived through nerve end organs in muscles, tendons, and joints: also **kin'es·the'sis** (-sis) —**kin'es·thet'ic** (-thet'ik) *adj.*

**ki·net·ic** (ki net'ik) *adj.* [Gr. *kinētikos < kinein,* to move] **1.** of or resulting from motion **2.** energetic or dynamic

**kinetic art** sculpture or assemblage involving the use of moving parts, sounds, shifting lights, etc.

**ki·net·ics** (ki net'iks) *n.pl.* [with sing. *v.*] same as DYNAMICS (sense 1)

**kin·folk** (kin'fōk') *n.pl.* family; relatives; kin; kindred: also **kin'folks'**

**king** (kiŋ) *n.* [OE. *cyning*] **1.** the male ruler of a monarchy; male monarch, limited or absolute **2.** *a)* a man who is supreme in some field [an oil *king*] *b)* something supreme in its class **3.** a playing card with a picture of a king on it **4.** *Checkers* a piece crowned upon reaching the opponent's base and hence movable backward and forward **5.** *Chess* the chief piece, movable one square in any direction: see CHECKMATE —*adj.* chief (in size, importance, etc.)

**King** (kiŋ), **Martin Luther, Jr.** 1929–68; U.S. clergyman & civil rights leader

**king·bird** (-bʉrd') *n.* any of several American flycatchers

**king·bolt** (-bōlt') *n.* a vertical bolt connecting the front axle of a wagon, etc., or the truck of a railroad car, with the body, to allow pivoting

**king crab 1.** same as HORSESHOE CRAB **2.** any of various very large crabs

**king·dom** (-dəm) *n.* [OE. *cyningdom:* see KING & -DOM] **1.** a government or country headed by a king or queen; monarchy **2.** a realm; domain [the *kingdom* of poetry] **3.** any of the three great divisions of things in nature (the animal, vegetable, and mineral kingdoms)

**king·fish** (-fish') *n.* **1.** *pl.* **-fish', -fish'es:** see FISH any of various large food fishes of the Atlantic or Pacific coast **2.** [Colloq.] a person holding absolute power in some group or place

**king·fish·er** (-fish'ər) *n.* a bright-colored bird with a large, crested head, a large, strong beak, and a short tail

**King James Version** *same as* AUTHORIZED VERSION

**King Lear** (lir) **1.** a tragedy by Shakespeare **2.** its main character, a legendary British king

**king·ly** (kiŋ'lē) *adj.* **-li·er, -li·est** of, like, or fit for a king; royal; regal; noble —*adv.* [Archaic] in the manner of a king —**king'li·ness** *n.*

**king·mak·er** (-mā'kər) *n.* a politically powerful person who manages to get candidates into high office

**king·pin** (-pin') *n.* **1.** same as KINGBOLT **2.** the headpin or center pin in bowling, etc. **3.** [Colloq.] the main or essential person or thing

**king post** *Carpentry* a vertical supporting post between the apex of a triangular truss and the base, or tie beam

**Kings** (kiŋz) **1.** either of two books of the Bible (I Kings, II Kings) about the reigns of the Jewish kings after David **2.** any of four books of the Douay Bible including I & II Samuel and I & II Kings

KING POST

**king salmon** *same as* CHINOOK SALMON

**king's** (or **queen's**) **English, the** standard (esp. British) English

**king·ship** (kiŋ'ship') *n.* **1.** the position, rank, or dignity of a king **2.** the rule of a king

**king-size** (-sīz') *adj.* [Colloq.] bigger than normal [a *king-size* bed] : also **king'-sized'**

**king snake** any of several large, harmless snakes of C and S North America: they eat mice, etc.

**Kings·ton** (kiŋz'tən, kiŋ'stən) **1.** seaport & capital of Jamaica: pop. 123,000 (met. area 422,000) **2.** port in SE Ontario, Canada: pop. 59,000

**kink** (kiŋk) *n.* [< Scand.] **1.** a short twist, curl, or bend in a rope, hair, etc. **2.** a painful cramp, as in the neck **3.** an eccentricity; quirk **4.** a difficulty or defect, as in a plan —*vi., vt.* to form or cause to form a kink

**kin·ka·jou** (kiŋ'kə jōō') *n.* [Fr., *quincajou,* a misapplication of AmInd. name, whence CARCAJOU] a nocturnal, tree-dwelling, raccoonlike mammal of Central and South America, with large eyes and a long, prehensile tail

**kink·y** (kiŋ'kē) *adj.* **kink'i·er, kink'i·est 1.** full of kinks; tightly curled [kinky hair] **2.** [Slang] weird, bizarre, etc.; specif., sexually abnormal —**kink'i·ness** *n.*

**kins·folk** (kinz'fōk') *n.pl. var. of* KINFOLK

**Kin·sha·sa** (kēn shä'sä) capital of Zaire, in the W part: pop. 902,000

**kin·ship** (kin'ship') *n.* **1.** family relationship **2.** relationship; close connection

**kins·man** (kinz'mən) *n., pl.* **-men** a relative; esp., a male relative —**kins'wom'an** (-woom'ən) *n.fem., pl.* **-wom'en**

**ki·osk** (kē'äsk, kē äsk') *n.* [< Fr. < Turk. < Per. *kūshk,* palace] **1.** in Turkey and Persia, an open summerhouse or pavilion **2.** a somewhat similar small structure open at one or more sides, used as a newsstand, bandstand, etc.

**kip¹** (kip) *n.* [prob. < Du.] the untanned hide of a calf, lamb, or other young or small animal

**kip²** (kip) *n., pl.* **kips, kip** [Thai] *see* MONETARY UNITS, table (Laos)

**kip³** (kip) *n.* [KI(LO) + P(OUND)¹] a unit of weight equal to 1,000 pounds

**Kip·ling** (kip'liŋ), (**Joseph**) **Rud·yard** (rud'yərd) 1865–1936; Eng. writer, born in India

**kip·per** (kip'ər) *vt.* [< ? the *n.*] to cure (herring, salmon, etc.) by salting and drying or smoking —*n.* [OE. *cypera*] **1.** a male salmon or sea trout during or shortly after the spawning season **2.** a kippered herring, salmon, etc.

**Kir·ghiz** (kir gēz') *n.* **1.** *pl.* **-ghiz', -ghiz'es** a member of a Mongolian people of SC Asia **2.** their Turkic language Also sp. **Kir·giz'**

**Kirghiz** (or **Kirgiz**) **Soviet Socialist Republic** republic of the U.S.S.R., in SC Asia: 76,460 sq. mi.; pop. 2,800,000; cap. Frunze: also **Kir·ghi'zia** (-gē'zhə, -zhē ə) —**Kir·ghi'zian** *adj., n.*

**Kir·i·bati** (kir'ə bas') country consisting principally of three groups of atolls in the WC Pacific: a member of the Commonwealth: 264 sq. mi.; pop. 58,000

**kirk** (kʉrk; *Scot.* kirk) *n.* [ME. *kirke* < OE. *cirice,* CHURCH] [Scot. & North Eng.] a church

**kir·mess** (kʉr'mis) *n. var. of* KERMIS

**kir·tle** (kʉr't'l) *n.* [OE. *cyrtel,* ult. < L. *curtus,* short + *-el,* dim. suffix] [Archaic] **1.** a man's tunic or coat **2.** a woman's dress or skirt

**Ki·shi·nev** (ki shi nyôf'; *E.* kish'i nef') capital of the Moldavian S.S.R.: pop. 317,000

**Kis·lev** (kis'lef) *n.* [Heb.] the third month of the Jewish year: see JEWISH CALENDAR

---

fat, āpe, cär, ten, ēven, is, bīte; gō, hôrn, tōol, look; oil, out; up, fʉr; get; joy; yet; chin; she; thin, *then*; zh, leisure; ŋ, ring; ə for *a* in *ago, e* in *agent, i* in *sanity, o* in *comply, u* in *focus;* as in *able* (ā'b'l); Fr. bál; ë, Fr. coeur; ö, Fr. feu; Fr. mon; ô, Fr. coq; ü, Fr. duc; r, Fr. cri; H, G. ich; kh, G. doch; ‡foreign; *hypothetical; < derived from. See inside front cover.

**kis·met** (kiz′met, kis′-) *n.* [< Turk. < Ar. *qismah*, a portion, fate] fate; destiny

**kiss** (kis) *vt.* [OE. *cyssan*] **1.** to touch or caress with the lips in affection, greeting, etc. **2.** to touch lightly —*vi.* to kiss each other —*n.* **1.** a kissing **2.** any of various candies —**kiss goodbye 1.** to kiss in leaving **2.** [Colloq.] to give up all hope of gaining or regaining —**kiss′a·ble** *adj.*

**kiss·er** (-ər) *n.* **1.** a person who kisses **2.** [Slang] *a)* the mouth or lips *b)* the face

**kit** (kit) *n.* [prob. < MDu. *kitte*, a wooden tub] **1.** personal equipment, esp. as packed for travel **2.** a set of tools, articles for special use, parts to be assembled, etc. **3.** a container for such equipment, tools, etc. **4.** [Colloq.] lot; collection: now chiefly in **the whole kit and caboodle**, everybody or everything

**Ki·ta·kyu·shu** (kē′tä kyōō′shōō) seaport on the N coast of Kyushu, Japan: pop. 1,042,000

**kitch·en** (kich′ən) *n.* [< OE. *cycene* < VL. < LL. *coquina* < L. *coquere*, to cook] **1.** a room or place for preparing and cooking food; also, the equipment used **2.** a staff that cooks and serves food

**Kitch·e·ner** (kich′ə nər) city in SE Ontario, Canada: pop. 132,000

**Kitch·e·ner** (kich′ə nər), **Horatio Herbert**, 1st Earl, Kitchener of Khartoum, 1850–1916; Brit. military officer & statesman, born in Ireland

**kitch·en·ette** (kich′ə net′) *n.* a small, compact kitchen

**kitchen midden** [transl. of Dan. *kökkenmödding*] a mound of shells, animal bones, etc. marking the site of a prehistoric settlement

**kitchen police 1.** soldiers detailed to assist the cooks in an army kitchen **2.** this duty

**kitch·en·ware** (kich′ən wer′) *n.* kitchen utensils

**kite** (kīt) *n.* [OE. *cyta*] **1.** a bird of the hawk family, with long, pointed wings and, usually, a forked tail **2.** a light wooden frame covered with paper or cloth, to be flown in the wind at the end of a string **3.** [*pl.*] the highest sails of a ship **4.** a bad check or the like used to raise money or maintain credit temporarily —*vi.* **kit′ed**, **kit′ing 1.** [Colloq.] *a)* to fly like a kite *b)* to move lightly and rapidly **2.** to get money or credit by using bad checks, etc. —*vt.* to issue (a bad check, etc.) as a kite

**kith** (kith) *n.* [OE. *cyth* < base of *cuth*, known: see UNCOUTH] friends, acquaintances, or neighbors: now only in **kith and kin**, friends, acquaintances, and relatives; also, often, relatives, or kin

**kitsch** (kich) *n.* [G., gaudy trash < dial. *kitschen*, to smear] pretentious but shallow art, writing, etc., designed for popular appeal —**kitsch′y** *adj.*

**kit·ten** (kit′'n) *n.* [< OFr. var. of *chaton*, dim. of *chat*, cat] a young cat

**kit·ten·ish** (-ish) *adj.* like a kitten; playful; frisky; often, playfully coy —**kit′ten·ish·ly** *adv.* —**kit′ten·ish·ness** *n.*

**kit·ti·wake** (kit′i wāk′) *n., pl.* **-wakes′**, **-wake′**: see PLURAL, II, D, 1 [echoic of its cry] any of several sea gulls of the Arctic and North Atlantic

**Kit·ty** (kit′ē) [dim. of CATHERINE] a feminine name

**kit·ty**[1] (kit′ē) *n., pl.* **-ties 1.** a kitten **2.** *a pet name for* a cat of any age

**kit·ty**[2] (kit′ē) *n., pl.* **-ties** [prob. < KIT] **1.** in poker, etc., *a)* the stakes or pot *b)* a pool from the winnings, to pay for refreshments, etc. **2.** any money pooled for some special use

**kit·ty-cor·nered** (kit′ē kôr′nərd) *adj., adv. same as* CATER-CORNERED: also **kit′ty-cor′ner**

**Kitty Hawk** [< AmInd.] village on an offshore island of N.C., near where the first controlled & sustained airplane flight was made by Orville & Wilbur Wright in 1903

**Ki·wa·nis** (kə wä′nis) *n.* [said to be < AmInd. *keewanis*, to make (oneself) known] an international club of business and professional men —**Ki·wa′ni·an** (-nē ən) *adj., n.*

**ki·wi** (kē′wē) *n., pl.* **-wis** [Maori: echoic of its cry] a tailless New Zealand bird with undeveloped wings, hairlike feathers, and a long, slender bill

**KJV, K.J.V.** King James Version (of the Bible)

**K.K.K., KKK** Ku Klux Klan

**kl, kl.** kiloliter; kiloliters

**Klan** (klan) *n. short for* KU KLUX KLAN —**Klans′man** *n., pl.* **-men**

**klatch, klatsch** (kläch, klach) *n.* [G. *klatsch*, gossip] [Colloq.] an informal gathering, as to chat

**Klax·on** (klak′s'n) *a trademark for* a kind of electric horn with a loud, shrill sound —*n.* [**k-**] such a horn

**Klee** (klā), **Paul** 1879–1940; Swiss abstract painter

**Klee·nex** (klē′neks) *a trademark for* soft tissue paper used as a handkerchief, etc. —*n.* [*occas.* **k-**] a piece of such paper

**klep·to·ma·ni·a** (klep′tə mā′nē ə) *n.* [ModL. < Gr. *kleptēs*, thief + -MANIA] an abnormal, persistent impulse to steal —**klep′to·ma′ni·ac′** (-ak′) *n.*

**klieg light** (klēg) [after A. & J. *Kliegl*, 20th-c. U.S.

inventors] a very bright, hot arc light used to light motion-picture sets: also sp. **kleig**

**Klon·dike** (klän′dīk) gold-mining region along a tributary (**Klondike River**) of the Yukon River, in W Yukon Territory, Canada

**klys·tron** (klīs′trən, klis′-; -trän) *n.* [< Gr. < *klyzein*, to wash + (ELEC)TRON] an electron tube used as an oscillator, amplifier, etc. in ultrahigh frequency circuits to modify the velocity of an electron stream

**km, km.** kilometer; kilometers

**knack** (nak) *n.* [ME. *knak*, sharp blow] **1.** a clever way of doing something **2.** ability to do something easily

**knack·wurst** (näk′wurst′; G. knäk′vŏorsht′) *n.* [G.] a thick, highly seasoned sausage

**knap·sack** (nap′sak′) *n.* [Du. *knapzak* < *knappen*, to eat + *zak*, a sack] a leather or canvas bag or case worn on the back, as by hikers, for carrying equipment or supplies

**knave** (nāv) *n.* [OE. *cnafa*, boy] **1.** [Archaic] *a)* a male servant *b)* a man of humble status **2.** a tricky rascal; rogue **3.** a jack (the playing card)

**knav·er·y** (nāv′ər ē) *n., pl.* **-er·ies** behavior or an act characteristic of a knave; rascality

**knav·ish** (-ish) *adj.* like a knave; esp., dishonest; tricky —**knav′ish·ly** *adv.* —**knav′ish·ness** *n.*

**knead** (nēd) *vt.* [OE. *cnedan*] **1.** to work (dough, clay, etc.) into a pliable mass by pressing and squeezing, usually with the hands **2.** to massage with similar movements **3.** to make or form as by kneading —**knead′er** *n.*

**knee** (nē) *n.* [OE. *cneow*] **1.** the joint between the thigh and the lower part of the human leg **2.** any similar or corresponding joint, as in an animal's forelimb **3.** anything like a knee, esp. like a bent knee **4.** the part of a stocking, trouser leg, etc. covering the knee —*vt.* **kneed**, **knee′ing** to hit or touch with the knee

**knee·cap** (-kap′) *n.* a movable bone at the front of the human knee; patella: also **knee′pan′** (-pan′)

**knee-deep** (-dēp′) *adj.* **1.** sunk to the knees, as in water **2.** so deep as to reach the knees

**knee-jerk** (-jurk′) *adj.* [< the reflex when the kneecap is tapped] [Colloq.] designating or characterized by an automatic, predictable response *[a knee-jerk bigot]*

**kneel** (nēl) *vi.* **knelt** or **kneeled**, **kneel′ing** [OE. *cneowlian* < *cneow*, knee] to bend or rest on a knee or the knees —**kneel′er** *n.*

**knee·pad** (nē′pad′) *n.* a pad worn to protect the knee, as by a basketball player

**knell** (nel) *vi.* [OE. *cnyllan*] **1.** to ring in a slow, solemn way; toll **2.** to sound ominously or mournfully —*vt.* to call or announce as by a knell —*n.* **1.** the sound of a tolling bell **2.** an omen of death, failure, etc.

**knelt** (nelt) *alt. pt. and pp. of* KNEEL

**knew** (nōō, nyōō) *pt. of* KNOW

**Knick·er·bock·er** (nik′ər bäk′ər) *n.* [< Diedrich *Knickerbocker*, fictitious Du. author of Washington Irving's *History of New York*] **1.** a descendant of the early Dutch settlers of New York **2.** any New Yorker **3.** [k-] [*pl.*] short, loose trousers gathered just below the knees; knickers

**knick·ers** (nik′ərz) *n.pl.* [contr. < prec.] **1.** knickerbockers **2.** [Chiefly Brit.] a woman's underpants

**knick·knack** (nik′nak′) *n.* [redupl. of KNACK] a small ornamental article or contrivance

**knife** (nīf) *n., pl.* **knives** [OE. *cnif*] **1.** a cutting or stabbing instrument with a sharp blade, single-edged or double-edged, set in a handle **2.** a cutting blade, as in a machine —*vt.* **knifed**, **knif′ing 1.** to cut or stab with a knife **2.** [Colloq.] to hurt, defeat, etc. by treachery —*vi.* to pass into or through something quickly, like a sharp knife —**under the knife** [Colloq.] under surgery —**knife′like′** *adj.*

**knight** (nīt) *n.* [OE. *cniht*, boy] **1.** in the Middle Ages, *a)* a military attendant of the king or other feudal superior, typically holding land in fief *b)* later, a man of high birth who after serving as page and squire was formally raised to honorable military rank and pledged to chivalrous conduct **2.** in Great Britain, a man who for some achievement is given honorary nonhereditary rank next below a baronet, entitling him to use *Sir* before his given name **3.** [*usually* K-] a member of any society that officially calls its members *knights* **4.** [Poet.] a lady's devoted champion or attendant **5.** *Chess* a piece typically shaped like a horse's head —*vt.* to make (a man) a knight

**knight-er·rant** (-er′ənt) *n., pl.* **knights′-er′rant 1.** a medieval knight wandering in search of adventure **2.** a chivalrous or quixotic person —**knight′-er′rant·ry** (-er′ən trē) *n., pl.* **-ries**

**knight·hood** (-hood′) *n.* **1.** the rank or vocation of a knight **2.** knightly conduct **3.** knights

**knight·ly** (-lē) *adj.* **1.** of or like a knight; chivalrous, brave, etc. **2.** consisting of knights —**knight′li·ness** *n.*

**Knights of Columbus** an international fraternal society of Roman Catholic men

**Knight Templar** *pl.* **Knights Templars** for 1, **Knights Templar** for 2 **1.** a member of a military and religious order established among the Crusaders c. 1118 **2.** a member of a certain order of Masons

**knit** (nit) *vt., vi.* **knit'ted** *or* **knit, knit'ting** [OE. *cnyttan* < base of *cnotta*, a knot] **1.** to make (cloth or clothing) by looping yarn or thread together with special needles **2.** to form into cloth in this way **3.** to join closely and firmly **4.** to draw (the brows) together —*n.* cloth or a garment made by knitting —**knit'ter** *n.*

**knit·ting** (-iŋ) *n.* **1.** the action of a person or thing that knits **2.** knitted work

**knitting needle** an eyeless, long needle used in pairs, etc. in knitting by hand

**knit·wear** (-wer') *n.* knitted clothing

**knives** (nīvz) *n. pl. of* KNIFE

**knob** (näb) *n.* [< or akin to MLowG. *knobbe*, a knot, bud, etc.] **1.** a rounded lump or protuberance **2.** a handle, usually round, of a door, drawer, etc. **3.** a rounded hill or mountain —**knobbed** *adj.*

**knob·by** (näb'ē) *adj.* **-bi·er, -bi·est** **1.** covered with knobs **2.** like a knob —**knob'bi·ness** *n.*

**knock** (näk) *vi.* [OE. *cnocian*] **1.** to strike a blow, as with the fist; esp., to rap on a door **2.** to bump; collide **3.** to make a thumping or rattling noise, as an engine **4.** [Colloq.] to find fault —*vt.* **1.** to hit; strike **2.** to make by hitting or striking [to *knock* a hole in the wall] **3.** [Colloq.] to find fault with —*n.* **1.** a knocking **2.** a sharp blow; rap, as on a door **3.** a thumping or rattling noise, as in an engine **4.** [Colloq.] an adverse criticism **5.** [Colloq.] a misfortune or trouble —**knock about** (or **around**) [Colloq.] **1.** to wander about; roam **2.** to treat roughly —**knock back** [Colloq.] to gulp down (an alcoholic drink) —**knock down 1.** to strike down **2.** to take apart **3.** to indicate the sale of at an auction **4.** [Slang] to earn as pay —**knock it off!** [Slang] quit it! specif., stop talking! —**knock off 1.** [Colloq.] to stop working **2.** [Colloq.] to deduct **3.** [Colloq.] to do **4.** [Slang] to kill, overcome, etc. —**knock (oneself) out** to exert oneself as to point of exhaustion —**knock out 1.** *Boxing* to score a knockout over **2.** to make unconscious or exhausted **3.** to defeat, destroy, etc. **4.** [Colloq.] to do; make; specif., to compose, write, etc., esp. casually or hastily —**knock together** to make or compose hastily or crudely —**knock up 1.** [Brit. Colloq.] *a)* to exhaust *b)* to wake (someone) by knocking at the door **2.** [Slang] to make pregnant

**knock·a·bout** (-ə bout') *n.* **1.** a small, one-masted yacht with a mainsail, jib, and centerboard or keel, but no bowsprit **2.** something for knockabout use —*adj.* **1.** rough; noisy; boisterous **2.** made or suitable for rough use

**knock·down** (-doun') *adj.* **1.** that knocks down; overwhelming **2.** made so as to be easily taken apart [a *knockdown* table] —*n.* **1.** a knocking down; felling **2.** a blow that knocks down

**knock·er** (-ər) *n.* one that knocks; specif., a small metal ring, knob, etc. on a door, for knocking

**knock-knee** (-nē') *n.* a condition in which the legs curve inward at the knees —**knock'-kneed'** *adj.*

**knock·out** (-out') *adj.* that knocks out, as a blow —*n.* **1.** *a)* a knocking out or being knocked out **2.** *a)* a blow that knocks out *b) Boxing* a victory won when the opponent is knocked down and cannot rise before an official count of ten **3.** [Slang] a very attractive or striking person or thing

**knockout drops** [Slang] a drug put into a drink to cause the drinker to become unconscious

**knock·wurst** (näk'wurst') *n. same as* KNACKWURST

**knoll** (nōl) *n.* [OE. *cnoll*] a hillock; mound

**Knos·sos** (näs'əs) *same as* CNOSSUS

**knot** (nät) *n.* [OE. *cnotta*] **1.** a lump or knob in a thread, cord, etc., as formed by a tangle drawn tight **2.** a fastening made by intertwining or tying together pieces of string, rope, etc. **3.** an ornamental bow of ribbon or twist of braid **4.** a small group or cluster **5.** something that ties closely or intricately; esp., the bond of marriage **6.** a problem; difficulty **7.** a knotlike part, as in a tense muscle; specif., *a)* a hard lump on a tree where a branch grows out *b)* a cross section of such a lump, appearing cross-grained in a board *c)* a joint on a plant stem where leaves grow out **8.** *Naut.* a unit of speed of one nautical mile (6,076.12 feet) an hour [a speed of 10 *knots*] —*vt.* **knot'ted, knot'ting 1.** to tie or intertwine in or with a knot **2.** to tie closely or intricately; entangle —*vi.* **1.** to form a knot or knots **2.** to make knots for fringe —**tie the knot** [Colloq.] to get married —**knot'ted** *adj.* —**knot'ter** *n.*

**knot·grass** (nät'gras') *n.* a common weed with slender stems and narrow leaves: also **knot'weed'** (-wēd')

**knot·hole** (-hōl') *n.* a hole in a board, etc. where a knot has fallen out

**knot·ty** (-ē) *adj.* **-ti·er, -ti·est** **1.** full of knots [a *knotty* board] **2.** hard to solve; puzzling [a *knotty* problem] —**knot'ti·ness** *n.*

**knout** (nout) *n.* [Russ. *knut* < Sw., a knot] a leather whip formerly used in Russia to flog criminals

**know** (nō) *vt.* **knew, known, know'ing** [OE. *cnawan*] **1.** to be well informed about [to *know* the facts] **2.** to be aware of; have perceived or learned [to *know* that one is loved] **3.** to have securely in the memory [the actor *knows* his lines] **4.** to be acquainted or familiar with **5.** to have understanding of or skill in as a result of study or experience [to *know* music] **6.** to recognize [I'd *know* that face anywhere] **7.** to recognize as distinct; distinguish [to *know* right from wrong] **8.** [Archaic] to have sexual intercourse with —*vi.* **1.** to have knowledge **2.** to be sure, informed, or aware —**in the know** [Colloq.] having confidential information —**know'a·ble** *adj.* —**know'er** *n.*

**know-how** (-hou') *n.* [Colloq.] knowledge of how to do something well; technical skill

**know·ing** (-iŋ) *adj.* **1.** having knowledge or information **2.** shrewd; clever **3.** implying shrewd understanding or secret knowledge [a *knowing* look] **4.** deliberate —**know'ing·ly** *adv.* —**know'ing·ness** *n.*

**knowl·edge** (näl'ij) *n.* **1.** the act, fact, or state of knowing **2.** acquaintance with facts; range of information, awareness, or understanding **3.** what is known; learning; enlightenment **4.** the body of facts, principles, etc. accumulated by mankind —**to (the best of) one's knowledge** as far as one knows; within the range of one's information

**knowl·edge·a·ble** (-ə b'l) *adj.* having or showing knowledge or intelligence —**knowl'edge·a·bil'i·ty, knowl'edge·a·ble·ness** *n.* —**knowl'edge·a·bly** *adv.*

**known** (nōn) *pp. of* KNOW

**know-noth·ing** (nō'nuth'iŋ) *n.* **1.** an ignoramus **2.** [K- N-] a member of a U.S. secret political party in the 1850's with a program of excluding from public office anyone not a native-born American

**Knox** (näks), **John** 1505?-72; Scot. Protestant clergyman & religious reformer

**Knox·ville** (näks'vil) [after Gen. H. *Knox* (1750-1806), 1st secretary of war] city in E Tenn., on the Tennessee River: pop. 183,000

**knuck·le** (nuk''l) *n.* [< or akin to MDu. & MLowG. *knokel*, little bone] **1.** a joint of the finger; esp., the joint connecting a finger to the rest of the hand **2.** the knee or hock joint of a pig or other animal, used as food **3.** [*pl.*] *same as* BRASS KNUCKLES —*vt.* **-led, -ling** to strike, press, or touch with the knuckles —**knuckle down 1.** to rest the knuckles on the ground in shooting a marble **2.** to work energetically or seriously —**knuckle under** to yield; give in

**knuck·le·head** (-hed') *n.* [Colloq.] a stupid person

**knurl** (nurl) *n.* [prob. blend of ME. *knur*, a knot + GNARL] **1.** a knot, knob, nodule, etc. **2.** any of a series of small beads or ridges, as along the edge of a coin —*vt.* to make knurls on —**knurled** *adj.*

**knurl·y** (-ē) *adj.* **knurl'i·er, knurl'i·est** full of knurls, as wood; gnarled

**Knut** (k'nōōt) *same as* CANUTE

**KO** (kā'ō') *vt.* **KO'd, KO'ing** [Slang] *Boxing* to knock out —*n., pl.* **KO's** [Slang] *Boxing* a knockout Also **K.O., k.o.**

**ko·a·la** (kō ä'lə) *n.* [< the native name] an Australian, tree-dwelling marsupial animal with thick, gray fur: it feeds on eucalyptus leaves and buds

**Ko·be** (kō'bā'; *E.* kō'bē) seaport on the S coast of Honshu, Japan: pop. 1,217,000

**Ko·ben·havn** (kö'b'n houn') *Dan. name of* COPENHAGEN

**kob·o** (käb'ō) *n., pl.* **kob'o** [native name of a former coin] see MONETARY UNITS, table (Nigeria)

**Koch** (kōk; *G.* kôkh), **Robert** 1843-1910; Ger. bacteriologist & physician

**ko·di·ak bear** (kō'dē ak') a very large, brown bear found on Kodiak Island and in adjacent areas

**Ko·di·ak Island** (kō'dē ak') [< Russ. < ? native name meaning "island"] island off the SW coast of Alas., in the State of Alas.

**Koh·i·noor, Koh-i-noor** (kō'ə noor') [< Per.] a famous large Indian diamond, now one of the British crown jewels

**kohl** (kōl) *n.* [Ar. *kuhl*] a cosmetic preparation used, esp. in Eastern countries, for eye makeup

**kohl·ra·bi** (kōl'rä'bē, kōl'rä'bē) *n., pl.* **-bies** [G. < It., pl. of *cavolo rapa*, cole rape: cf. COLE & RAPE²] a garden vegetable related to the cabbage, with an edible bulbous stem

KOALA (27-35 in. long)

fat, āpe, cär, ten, ēven, is, bīte; gō, hôrn, tōōl, look; oil, out; up, fʉr; get; joy; yet; chin; she; thin, *then*; zh, leisure; ŋ, ring; ə for *a* in *ago, e* in *agent, i* in *sanity, o* in *comply, u* in *focus;* as in *able* (ā'b'l); Fr. bal; ë, Fr. coeur; ö, Fr. feu; Fr. mon; ō, Fr. coq; ü, Fr. duc; r, Fr. cri; H, G. ich; kh, G. doch; ‡foreign; *hypothetical; < derived from. See inside front cover.

**ko·la** (kō′lə) *n. same as* COLA
**kola nut** the seed of the cola
**ko·lin·sky** (kə lin′skē, kō-) *n., pl.* **-skies** [< Russ. < *Kola*, Russian district] 1. any of several weasels of Asia 2. the golden-brown fur of such a weasel
**Köln** (köln) *Ger. name of* COLOGNE
**Kol Nid·re** (kōl nē′drä, nid′rə) [Aram. *kōl nidhrē*, lit., all our vows] 1. the prayer of atonement recited in synagogues at the opening of Yom Kippur eve services 2. the music for this
**koo·doo** (kōō′dōō) *n., pl.* **-doos, -doo:** see PLURAL, II, D, 1 *same as* KUDU
**kook** (kōōk) *n.* [< ? *cuckoo*] [Slang] a person regarded as silly, eccentric, crazy, etc. —**kook′y, kook′ie** *adj.* **kook′i·er, kook′i·est**
**ko·peck, ko·pek** (kō′pek) *n.* [< Russ. < *kopye*, a lance] a monetary unit, and a coin, equal to 1/100 of a ruble: see MONETARY UNITS, table (U.S.S.R.)
**Ko·ran** (kō ran′, -rän′; kō-, kə-) *n.* [Ar. *qur'ān*, lit., book, reading < *gara'a*, to read] the sacred book of the Moslems: its contents are reported revelations made to Mohammed by Allah —**Ko·ran′ic** *adj.*
**Ko·re·a** (kō rē′ə, kō-) peninsula in E Asia, extending south from NE China: divided (1948) into two countries: *a*) **North Korea**, occupying the N half of the peninsula, 47,255 sq. mi., pop. 11,568,000, cap. Pyongyang, and *b*) **South Korea**, occupying the S half, 38,030 sq. mi., pop. 31,738,000, cap. Seoul
**Ko·re·an** (-ən) *adj.* of Korea, its people, etc. —*n.* 1. a native of Korea 2. the language of the Koreans
**ko·ru·na** (kō rōō′nä) *n., pl.* **ko·ru′nas, ko·run′** [Czech < L. *corona*, a crown] *see* MONETARY UNITS, table (Czechoslovakia)
**Kos·ci·us·ko** (käs′ē us′kō; *Pol.* kồsh chōōsh′kồ), **Thad·de·us** (thad′ē əs) (born *Tadeusz Kościuszko*) 1746–1817; Pol. patriot & general: served in the Am. army in the American Revolution
**ko·sher** (kō′shər; *for v., usually* käsh′ər) *adj.* [Heb. *kāshēr*, fit, proper] 1. *Judaism a*) clean or fit to eat according to the dietary laws: Lev. 11 *b*) dealing in such food 2. [Slang] all right, proper, etc. —*n.* kosher food —*vt.* to make kosher
**Kos·suth** (käs′ōōth; *Hung.* kồ′shoot), **Louis** (Hung. name *Lajos Kossuth*) 1802–94; Hung. patriot & statesman
**kow·tow** (kou′tou′, kō′-) *n.* [Chin. *k'o-t'ou*, lit., knock head] the act of kneeling and touching the ground with the forehead to show great deference, submissive respect, homage, etc. —*vi.* 1. to make a kowtow 2. to show submissive respect (*to*)
**KP, K.P.** kitchen police
**Kr** *Chem.* krypton
**kraal** (kräl, krôl) *n.* [Afrik. < Port. *curral*, pen for cattle] 1. a village of South African natives, usually surrounded by a stockade 2. a fenced enclosure for cattle or sheep in South Africa
**krait** (krīt) *n.* [Hindi *karait*] a very poisonous, yellow-banded snake, found in SC and SE Asia
**Kra·ków** (kra′kou′; *Pol.* krä′koof) city in S Poland, on the Vistula: pop. 535,000
**Kras·no·dar** (kräs′nô där′) city in SW R.S.F.S.R., in the N Caucasus: pop. 420,000
**Kras·no·yarsk** (kräs′nồ yärsk′) city in C R.S.F.S.R., in NC Asia: pop. 592,000
**Kre·feld** (krā′felt) city in W West Germany, on the Rhine: pop. 224,000
**Kreis·ler** (krīs′lər), **Fritz** (frits) 1875–1962; U.S. violinist & composer, born in Austria
**krem·lin** (krem′lin) *n.* [Fr. < Russ. *kreml'*] in Russia, the citadel of a city —**the Kremlin** 1. the citadel of Moscow, formerly housing government offices of the Soviet Union 2. the government of the Soviet Union
**krim·mer** (krim′ər) *n.* [G. < *Krim*, Crimea] a grayish, tightly curled fur made from the pelts of Crimean lambs
**kris** (krēs) *n.* [Malay *kerīs*] a Malay dagger with a wavy blade: creese
**Krish·na** (krish′nə) an important Hindu god, an incarnation of Vishnu —**Krish′na·ism** *n.*
**Kriss Krin·gle** (kris′ krin′g'l) [< G. < *Christ*, Christ + *kindl*, dim. of *kind*, child] *same as* SANTA CLAUS
**Kri·voi Rog** (kri voi′ rồk′) city in SC Ukrainian S.S.R.: pop. 523,000
**kro·na** (krō′nə; *Sw.* krōō′nə) *n., pl.* **-nor** (-nôr) [Sw. < L. *corona*, crown] *see* MONETARY UNITS, table (Sweden)
**kró·na** (krō′nə) *n., pl.* **-nur** (-nər) [Ice. < ML. *corona*, a crown] *see* MONETARY UNITS, table (Iceland)
**kro·ne** (krō′nə) *n., pl.* **-ner** (-nər) [Dan. < L. *corona*, crown] *see* MONETARY UNITS, table (Denmark, Norway)

**Kru·ger** (krōō′gər), **Paul** (born *Stephanus Johannes Paulus Kruger*) 1825–1904; South African statesman
**krul·ler** (krul′ər) *n. same as* CRULLER
**Krupp** (krup; *G.* kroop) family of Ger. steel & munitions manufacturers in the 19th & 20th cent.
**kryp·ton** (krip′tän) *n.* [< Gr. neut. of *kryptos*, hidden < *kryptein*, to hide] a rare, inert, gaseous chemical element present in very small quantities in air: symbol, Kr; at. wt., 83.80; at. no., 36
**KS** Kansas
**Kt** *Chess* knight
**kt.** 1. karat 2. kiloton(s)
**Kua·la Lum·pur** (kwä′lə loom poor′) city in the SW Malay Peninsula: capital of Malaysia: pop. c.400,000
**Ku·blai Khan** (kōō′blī kän′, -blə) 1216?–94; Mongol emperor of China (1260?–94): founder of the Mongol dynasty: grandson of GENGHIS KHAN
**ku·chen** (kōō′kən, -khən) *n.* [G., cake] a coffeecake made of yeast dough and often frosted or filled with raisins, nuts, etc.
**ku·dos** (kōō′däs, -dôs; kyōō′-) *n.* [Gr. *kydos*, glory] praise for an achievement; glory; fame
**ku·du** (kōō′dōō) *n., pl.* **-dus, -du:** see PLURAL, II, D, 1 [Hottentot] a large, grayish-brown African antelope with long, twisted horns
**Kui·by·shev** (kwē′bi shef′) city in SW R.S.F.S.R., on the Volga: pop. 1,014,000
**Ku Klux** (kōō′kluks′, kyōō′) [< Gr. *kyklos*, a circle] 1. *short for* KU KLUX KLAN 2. a member of the Ku Klux Klan: also **Ku Klux′er**
**Ku Klux Klan** (klan) [prec. + *klan*, arbitrary sp. for CLAN] 1. a secret society of white men founded in the S States after the Civil War to reestablish and maintain white supremacy 2. a U.S. secret, terrorist society organized in 1915: it is anti-Negro, anti-Semitic, anti-Catholic, etc.
**ku·lak** (kōō läk′) *n.* [Russ., lit., fist < Estonian] a well-to-do farmer in Russia who profited from the labor of poorer peasants and who opposed the Soviet collectivization of the land
**ku·miss** (kōō′mis) *n.* [G. < Russ. < Tatar *kumiz*] mare's or camel's milk fermented and used as a drink by Tatar nomads of Asia
**küm·mel** (kim′'l; *G.* küm′əl) *n.* [G., caraway < OHG. *kumil* < L. *cuminum:* see CUMIN] a colorless liqueur flavored with caraway seeds, anise, cumin, etc.
**kum·quat** (kum′kwät, -kwôt) *n.* [< Chin. *chin-chü*, golden orange] 1. a small, orange-colored, oval fruit, with a sour pulp and a sweet rind, used in preserves 2. a tree that bears this fruit
**kung fu** (koon′ fōō′, goon′) [< Chin.] a Chinese system of self-defense, like karate but emphasizing circular rather than linear movements
**Kuo·min·tang** (kwō′min taη′; *Chin.* gwō′min′däη′) [Chin.] nationalist political party of China, organized chiefly by Sun Yat-sen in 1911 and afterward controlled and led by Chiang Kai-shek
**Kurd** (kurd, koord) *n.* [Turk. & Ar.] any of a nomadic Moslem people living chiefly in Kurdistan —**Kurd′ish** *adj., n.*
**Kur·dis·tan** (kur′di stan′, koor′-; -stän′) region occupying SE Turkey, N Iraq, & NW Iran
**Ku·ril** (or **Ku·rile**) **Islands** (kōō′ril, koo rēl′) chain of islands of the U.S.S.R., between N Hokkaido, Japan, and Kamchatka Peninsula
**Kush·it·ic** (kush it′ik) *adj., n. same as* CUSHITIC
**Ku·wait** (kōō wät′, -wīt′) independent Arab state in E Arabia, on the NW coast of the Persian Gulf: 6,000 sq. mi.; pop. 555,000
**kw.** kilowatt; kilowatts
**kwa·cha** (kwä′chä) *n., pl.* **-cha** [native term, lit., dawn] *see* MONETARY UNITS, table (Malawi, Zambia)
**Kwang·chow** (kwän′chō′; *Chin.* gwän′jō′) port in SE China: pop. 2,200,000: also sp. **Kwangchou**
**kwa·shi·or·kor** (kwä′shē ôr′kôr) *n.* [< name in Ghana] a severe disease of young children, caused by chronic deficiency of protein and calories and characterized by stunted growth, edema, etc.
**kwh, K.W.H., kw.-hr., kw-hr** kilowatt-hour
**Ky., KY** Kentucky
**ky·ak** (kī′ak) *n. same as* KAYAK
**kyat** (kyät) *n.* [Burmese] *see* MONETARY UNITS, table (Burma)
**Kym·ric** (kim′rik) *adj., n. same as* CYMRIC
**Kym·ry, Kym·ri** (-rē) *n.pl. same as* CYMRY
**Kyo·to** (kyō′tồ′; *E.* kē ōt′ō) city in S Honshu, Japan: pop. 1,365,000
**Kyu·shu** (kyōō′shōō′) one of the four main islands of Japan, south of Honshu: 16,223 sq. mi.

# L

**L, l** (el) *n., pl.* **L's, l's**   **1.** the twelfth letter of the English alphabet   **2.** the sound of *L* or *l*

**L** (el) *n., pl.* **L's**   **1.** an object shaped like L; esp., an extension of a building that gives the whole a shape resembling L   **2.** a Roman numeral for 50 —*adj.* shaped like L

**L.**   **1.** Latin   **2.** Licentiate

**L., l.**   **1.** lake   **2.** latitude   **3.** law   **4.** leaf   **5.** league   **6.** left   **7.** length   **8.** *pl.* **LL., ll.** line   **9.** link   **10.** lira; lire   **11.** liter   **12.** low   **13.** [L. *libra,* pl. *librae*] pound(s)

**la¹** (lä, lô) *interj.* [Dial. or Archaic] an exclamation of surprise or emphasis

**la²** (lä) *n.* [see GAMUT] *Music* a syllable representing the sixth tone of the diatonic scale

**La** *Chem.* lanthanum

**La., LA** Louisiana

**L.A.** [Colloq.] Los Angeles

**lab** (lab) *n.* [Colloq.] a laboratory

**la·bel** (lā'b'l) *n.* [OFr., a rag, strip < Gmc.]   **1.** a card, strip of paper, etc. marked and attached to an object to indicate its nature, contents, ownership, destination, etc.   **2.** a descriptive word or phrase applied to a person, group, etc. as a convenient generalized classification   **3.** an identifying brand of a company —*vt.* **-beled** or **-belled, -bel·ing** or **-bel·ling**   **1.** to attach a label to   **2.** to classify as; call; describe —**la'bel·er, la'bel·ler** *n.*

**la·bi·a** (lā'bē ə) *n., pl. of* LABIUM

**la·bi·al** (-əl) *adj.* [< ML. < L. *labium,* a lip]   **1.** of the labia, or lips   **2.** *Phonet.* formed mainly with the lips: said esp. of *b, m,* and *p* —*n.* a labial sound —**la'bi·al·ly** *adv.*

**la·bi·ate** (lā'bē āt', -it) *adj.* [< L. *labium,* a lip]   **1.** formed or functioning like a lip   **2.** having a lip or lips   **3.** *Bot.* having the calyx or corolla so divided that one part overlaps the other like a lip

**la·bile** (lā'b'l, -bīl) *adj.* [< L. < *labi,* to slip] liable to change; unstable —**la·bil'i·ty** *n.*

**la·bi·o·den·tal** (lā'bē ō den't'l) *adj.* [< L. *labium,* a lip + DENTAL] *Phonet.* formed with the lower lip against the upper teeth, as the sounds of *f* and *v* —*n.* a labiodental sound

**la·bi·um** (lā'bē əm) *n., pl.* **-bi·a** (-ə) [L., a lip] *Anat., Bot.,* etc. a lip or liplike organ; specif., [*pl.*] the outer folds of skin (**labia majora**) or the inner folds of mucous membrane (**labia minora**) of the vulva

**la·bor** (lā'bər) *n.* [< OFr. < L. *labor*]   **1.** physical or mental exertion; work; toil   **2.** a specific task   **3.** *a)* all wage-earning workers as a group: distinguished from CAPITAL¹ or MANAGEMENT   *b)* all manual workers whose work is characterized largely by physical exertion   **4.** labor unions collectively   **5.** [L-] *same as* LABOR PARTY   **6.** the work accomplished by workers collectively   **7.** *Med.* the process of giving birth to a child —*vi.* [< OFr. < L. *laborare* < the *n.*]   **1.** to work; toil   **2.** to work hard   **3.** to move slowly and with difficulty [the car *labored* up the hill]   **4.** to be burdened (with *under*) [to *labor* under a delusion]   **5.** to undergo, and suffer the pains of, childbirth —*vt.* to develop in too great detail [to *labor* a point]

**lab·o·ra·to·ry** (lab'rə tôr'ē, -ər ə tôr'ē; Brit. lə bär'ə-tər ē, -ə trē) *n., pl.* **-ries** [< ML. < L.: see LABOR, *vi.*]   **1.** a room or building for scientific experimentation or research   **2.** a place for preparing chemicals, drugs, etc.   **3.** a place where theories, methods, etc., as in education, are tested, demonstrated, etc. —*adj.* of or performed in, or as in, a laboratory

**Labor Day** in the U.S. & Canada, the first Monday in September, a legal holiday in honor of labor

**la·bored** (lā'bərd) *adj.* made or done with great effort; not easy and natural; strained

**la·bor·er** (lā'bər ər) *n.* one who labors; esp., a wage-earning worker whose work is characterized largely by physical exertion

**la·bo·ri·ous** (lə bôr'ē əs) *adj.*   **1.** involving or calling for much hard work; difficult   **2.** industrious; hard-working —**la·bo'ri·ous·ly** *adv.* —**la·bo'ri·ous·ness** *n.*

**la·bor·ite** (lā'bə rīt') *n.*   **1.** a member or supporter of a labor party   **2.** [L-] a member or supporter of the British Labor Party: Brit. sp. **La'bour·ite'**

**labor party**   **1.** a political party organized to protect and further the rights of workers, or one dominated by organized labor   **2.** [L- P-] such a party in Great Britain: Brit. sp. **Labour Party**

**la·bor·sav·ing** (lā'bər sā'viŋ) *adj.* eliminating or lessening physical labor [*labor-saving* appliances]

**labor union** an association of workers to promote and protect the welfare, interests, and rights of its members, mainly by collective bargaining

**la·bour** (lā'bər) *n., vi., vt. Brit. sp. of* LABOR

**Lab·ra·dor** (lab'rə dôr')   **1.** region along the E coast of Canada, constituting the mainland part of the province of Newfoundland   **2.** large peninsula occupied by this region & most of Quebec

**Labrador retriever** any of a breed of medium-sized hunting dog used in retrieving game, having a black, brown, or yellow coat of short, thick hair

**la·bur·num** (lə bur'nəm) *n.* [L.] a small, poisonous tree or shrub of the legume family, with drooping racemes of yellow flowers

**lab·y·rinth** (lab'ə rinth') *n.* [< L. < Gr. *labyrinthos*]   **1.** a structure containing an intricate network of winding passages hard to follow without losing one's way; maze; specif., [L-] *Gr. Myth.* such a structure built for King Minos, to house the Minotaur   **2.** a complicated, perplexing arrangement, condition, etc.   **3.** *Anat.* the inner ear

**lab·y·rin·thine** (lab'ə rin'thin, -thēn) *adj.* of, constituting, or like a labyrinth; intricate: also **lab'y·rin'thi·an** (-thē ən), **lab'y·rin'thic**

LABYRINTH

**lac** (lak) *n.* [< Hindi < Sans. *lākṣā*]   **1.** a resinous substance secreted on various trees in S Asia by certain scale insects: when melted, strained, and rehardened, it forms shellac   **2.** *same as* LAKH

**lace** (lās) *n.* [OFr. *laz* < L. *laqueus,* a noose]   **1.** a string, ribbon, etc. used to draw together and fasten the parts of a shoe, corset, etc.   **2.** braid of gold or silver, as for trimming uniforms   **3.** a fine netting or openwork fabric of linen, silk, etc., woven in ornamental designs —*vt.* **laced, lac'ing**   **1.** to draw the ends of (a garment, shoe, etc.) together and fasten with a lace   **2.** to compress the waist of by lacing a corset, etc.   **3.** to pass (a cord, etc.) in and out *through* eyelets, fabric, etc.   **4.** to weave together; intertwine   **5.** to ornament with lace   **6.** to streak, as with color; interspersed   **7.** to thrash; beat   **8.** to add a dash of alcoholic liquor to (a beverage) —*vi.*   **1.** to be fastened with a lace [these shoes *lace*]   **2.** [Colloq.] to attack physically or verbally (with *into*)

**lac·er·ate** (las'ə rāt'; *also for adj.* -ər it) *vt.* **-at'ed, -at'ing** [< L. pp. of *lacerare* < *lacer,* mangled]   **1.** to tear jaggedly; mangle   **2.** to hurt (one's feelings, etc.) deeply —*adj.*   **1.** torn; mangled   **2.** *Bot.* having jagged edges

**lac·er·a·tion** (las'ə rā'shən) *n.*   **1.** a lacerating   **2.** the result of lacerating; jagged tear or wound

**lace·wing** (lās'wiŋ') *n.* any of a large group of insects with four delicate, gauzy wings

**lace·work** (-wurk') *n.* lace, or any openwork decoration like lace

**lach·es** (lach'iz) *n.* [OFr. *laschesse,* ult. < L. *laxus,* lax] *Law* failure to do the required thing at the proper time; inexcusable delay

**Lach·e·sis** (lak'ə sis) *Gr. & Rom. Myth.* that one of the three Fates who determines the span of life

**lach·ry·mal** (lak'rə məl) *adj.* [< ML. < L. *lacrima,* TEAR²]   **1.** of, characterized by, or producing tears   **2.** *same as* LACRIMAL (sense 1)

**lach·ry·ma·to·ry** (-mə tôr'ē) *adj.* of, causing, or producing tears

**lach·ry·mose** (-mōs') *adj.* [< L. < *lacrima,* TEAR²]   **1.** inclined to shed many tears; tearful   **2.** causing tears; sad —**lach'ry·mose'ly** *adv.*

---

**lac·ing** (lās′iŋ) *n.* **1.** the act of a person who laces **2.** a thrashing; beating **3.** a cord or lace, as a shoelace **4.** gold or silver braid used to trim a uniform, etc.

**lack** (lak) *n.* [< or akin to MLowG., MDu. *lak*] **1.** the fact or condition of not having enough; shortage; deficiency **2.** the fact or condition of not having any; complete absence **3.** the thing that is lacking or needed —*vi.* **1.** to be wanting or missing **2.** *a)* to be short (with *in* or *for*) *b)* to be in need —*vt.* **1.** to be deficient in or entirely without **2.** to fall short by *[lacking* one ounce of being a pound*]*

**lack·a·dai·si·cal** (lak′ə dā′zi k'l) *adj.* [ult. < *alack the day*] showing lack of interest or spirit; listless; languid —**lack′a·dai′si·cal·ly** *adv.*

**lack·ey** (lak′ē) *n., pl.* **-eys** [< Fr. < Sp. *lacayo*] **1.** a male servant of low rank, usually in uniform; footman **2.** a servile follower; toady

**lack·lus·ter** (lak′lus′tər) *adj.* lacking brightness; dull *[lackluster* eyes*]* Also, chiefly Brit. sp., **lack′lus′tre**

**La·co·ni·a** (lə kō′nē ə) ancient region on the S coast of the Peloponnesus, dominated by the city of Sparta

**la·con·ic** (lə kän′ik) *adj.* [< L. < Gr. < *Lakōn*, a Laconian, Spartan] brief or terse in speech or expression; using few words —**la·con′i·cal·ly** *adv.*

**lac·quer** (lak′ər) *n.* [< Fr. < Port. < *laca*, gum lac] **1.** a coating substance of natural or synthetic resins, nitrocellulose, etc. dissolved in a solvent that evaporates rapidly leaving a tough, adherent film: pigments are often added to form **lacquer enamels 2.** a natural resin varnish obtained from certain trees in China and Japan, or woodenware (in full, **lac′quer·ware′, lac′quer·work′**) coated with it —*vt.* to coat with or as with lacquer —**lac′quer·er** *n.*

**lac·ri·mal** (lak′rə məl) *adj.* **1.** *Anat.* designating, of, or near the glands that secrete tears **2.** *same as* LACHRYMAL (sense 1)

**lac·ri·ma·tion** (lak′rə mā′shən) *n.* [< L. < pp. of *lacrimare*, to weep < *lacrima*, TEAR²] normal or excessive secretion or shedding of tears

**la·crosse** (lə krôs′, -kräs′) *n.* [CanadFr. < Fr. *la*, the + *crosse*, a crutch] a ball game in which two teams of ten men each, using long-handled, pouched rackets, try to advance a small rubber ball across the field into the opponents' goal

**La Crosse** (lə krôs′, kräs′) [< prec.] city in W Wis., on the Mississippi: pop. 51,000

**lac·tate** (lak′tāt) *vi.* **-tat·ed, -tat·ing** [< L. pp. of *lactare* < *lac* (see LACTO-)] to secrete milk —*n.* any salt or ester of lactic acid

**lac·ta·tion** (lak tā′shən) *n.* **1.** the secretion of milk by a mammary gland **2.** the period during which milk is secreted **3.** the suckling of young

LACROSSE

**lac·te·al** (lak′tē əl) *adj.* [< L. *lacteus* < *lac* (see LACTO-) + -AL] **1.** of or like milk; milky **2.** containing or carrying chyle, the milky fluid that is a product of digestion —*n.* any of the lymphatic vessels that carry chyle from the small intestine to the blood

**lac·tic** (lak′tik) *adj.* [< Fr.: see LACTO- & -IC] of or obtained from milk

**lactic acid** a yellowish or clear, syrupy organic acid, $C_3H_6O_3$, produced by the fermentation of lactose when milk sours

**lac·to-** [< L. *lac* (gen. *lactis*), milk] *a combining form meaning:* **1.** milk **2.** *Chem.* lactic acid or lactate Also, before a vowel, **lact-**

**lac·tose** (lak′tōs) *n.* [LACT(O)- + -OSE¹] a white, crystalline sugar, $C_{12}H_{22}O_{11}$, found in milk and used in infant foods, medicine, etc.

**la·cu·na** (lə kyōō′nə) *n., pl.* **-nas, -nae** (-nē) [L., a ditch < *lacus*, lake] **1.** a space where something has been omitted or has come out; missing part; gap; hiatus **2.** *Anat., Biol.* any of the very small cavities in bone that are filled with bone cells —**la·cu′nar** (-nər), **la·cu′nal** *adj.*

**lac·y** (lā′sē) *adj.* **lac′i·er, lac′i·est** of lace; like lace; having a delicate open pattern —**lac′i·ly** *adv.* —**lac′i·ness** *n.*

**lad** (lad) *n.* [ME. *ladde*] **1.** a boy or youth **2.** [Colloq.] any man; fellow: familiar term

**lad·der** (lad′ər) *n.* [OE. *hlæder*] **1.** a framework of two parallel sidepieces connected by rungs or crosspieces on which a person steps in climbing up or down **2.** anything by means of which a person climbs or rises *[the ladder* of success*]* **3.** [Chiefly Brit.] a run as in a stocking

**lad·die** (lad′ē) *n.* [Chiefly Scot.] a young lad

**lade** (lād) *vt., vi.* **lad′ed, lad′ed** or **lad′en, lad′ing** [OE. *hladan*] **1.** to load **2.** to bail; ladle

**lad·en** (lād′'n) *alt. pp. of* LADE —*adj.* **1.** loaded **2.** burdened; afflicted *[laden* with sorrow*]*

**la-di-da, la-de-da** (lä′dē dä′) *adj.* [Colloq.] affected in speech, manners, etc.; pretentiously refined

**Ladies' Day** a special day on which women may attend a particular event, as a baseball game, free or at reduced cost

**lad·ing** (lā′diŋ) *n.* **1.** the act of one that lades **2.** a load; cargo; freight

**la·dle** (lā′d'l) *n.* [OE. *hlædel* < *hladan*, to draw water] a long-handled, cuplike spoon for dipping out liquids —*vt.* **-dled, -dling 1.** to dip out with or as with a ladle **2.** to carry in a ladle —**la′dle·ful′** *n., pl.* **-fuls′** —**la′dler** *n.*

**La·do·ga** (lä′dô gä), **Lake** lake in NW R.S.F.S.R., near the border of Finland: c.7,000 sq. mi.

**la·dy** (lā′dē) *n., pl.* **-dies** [OE. *hlæfdige* < *hlaf*, loaf + base of *dæge*, kneader] **1.** a woman with the rights, rule, or authority of a lord **2.** *a)* a woman of high social position *b)* a woman who is polite, refined, and well-mannered **3.** any woman **4.** [L-] the Virgin Mary (usually with *Our*) **5.** [L-] in Great Britain, the title given to women of certain ranks —*adj.* female *[a lady* barber*]*

**la·dy·bug** (-bug′) *n.* a small, roundish beetle with a spotted back, that feeds chiefly on insect pests and their eggs: also **la′dy·bird′** (beetle) , **lady beetle**

**Lady Day** *Brit. name for* ANNUNCIATION (sense 2 *b*)

**la·dy·fin·ger** (-fiŋ′gər) *n.* a small spongecake shaped somewhat like a finger

**la·dy-in-wait·ing** (-in wāt′iŋ) *n., pl.* **la′dies-in-wait′ing** a woman attending, or waiting upon, a queen or princess

**la·dy·like** (-līk′) *adj.* like or suitable for a lady; refined

**la·dy·love** (-luv′) *n.* a sweetheart

**la·dy·ship** (-ship′) *n.* the rank or position of a lady: used in speaking to or of a woman having the title of *Lady*, always preceded by *your* or *her*

**la·dy-slip·per** (-slip′ər) *n.* any of certain orchids whose flowers somewhat resemble a slipper: also **la′dy's-slip′per**

**la·e·trile** (lā′ə tril′) *n.* [*lae(vo-rotatory glycosidic ni)trile*] any of several organic compounds obtained from various related plant substances, as apricot kernels and almond seeds, and claimed to be effective in treating cancers

LADY-SLIPPER

**La·fa·yette** (laf′ī yet′, lä′fi-, lə fā′it) [after ff.] city in SC La.: pop. 82,000

**La·fa·yette** (lä′fi yet′, laf′i-; *Fr.* là fà yet′), **marquis de** 1757–1834; Fr. general & statesman: served in Am. army in the American Revolution

**La Fol·lette** (lə fäl′it), **Robert Marion** 1855–1925; U.S. legislator & Progressive Party leader

**La Fon·taine** (là fōn ten′; *E.* lə fän tān′), **Jean de** (zhän də) 1621–95; Fr. poet & writer of fables

**lag** (lag) *vi.* **lagged, lag′ging** [? akin to MDan. *lakke*, to go slowly] **1.** *a)* to fall, move, or stay behind; loiter *b)* to be retarded in motion, development, etc. **2.** to wane; flag —*n.* **1.** a falling behind or being retarded in motion, development, etc. **2.** the amount of such falling behind —**lag′ger** *n.*

**lag bolt** *same as* LAG SCREW

**la·ger** (beer) (lä′gər) [G. *lagerbier*, lit., storehouse beer] a beer which is stored for several months for aging after it has been brewed

**lag·gard** (lag′ərd) *n.* [< LAG + -ARD] a slow person, esp. one who is always falling behind —*adj.* slow or late in doing things; falling behind —**lag′gard·ly** *adv., adj.* —**lag′gard·ness** *n.*

**la·gniappe, la·gnappe** (lan yap′, lan′yap) *n.* [Creole < Fr. *la*, the + Sp. *ñapa*, lagniappe < Quechua *yapa*] **1.** [Chiefly South] a small gift given to a customer with a purchase **2.** a gratuity

**la·goon** (lə gōōn′) *n.* [< Fr. *lagune* & It. *laguna* < L. *lacuna*, lake] **1.** a shallow lake or pond, esp. one connected with a larger body of water **2.** the water enclosed by a circular coral reef **3.** shallow salt water separated from the sea by dunes

**La·gos** (lā′gäs, -gos) capital of Nigeria; seaport on the Atlantic: pop. 665,000

**lag screw** a wood screw with a boltlike head

**lah-di-dah, lah-de-dah** (lä′dē dä′) *adj. same as* LA-DI-DA

**La·hore** (lə hôr′, lä-) city in NE Pakistan: pop. 1,296,000

**la·ic** (lā′ik) *adj.* [< LL. *laicus* < Gr. < *laos*, the people] of the laity; secular; lay: also **la′i·cal** —*n.* a layman

**la·i·cize** (lā′ə sīz′) *vt.* **-cized′, -ciz′ing** [LAIC + -IZE] to turn over to laymen; secularize

**laid** (lād) *pt. & pp. of* LAY¹

**laid-back** (-bak′) *adj.* [Slang] relaxed, restrained, easygoing, etc.; not frenetic or hurried

**lain** (lān) *pp. of* LIE¹

**lair** (ler) *n.* [OE. *leger*] the den or cave of a wild animal

**laird** (lerd; *Scot.* lärd) *n.* [Scot. form of LORD] in Scotland, a landowner, esp. a wealthy one

**lais·sez faire** (les′ā fer′, lez′-) [Fr., let (people) do (as they please)] noninterference; specif., the policy of letting the owners of industry and business operate without governmental regulation or control: also sp. **lais'ser faire'** —**lais'-sez-faire'** *adj.*

**la·i·ty** (lā'ət ē) *n., pl.* **-ties** [< LAY³] **1.** all the people not included among the clergy; laymen collectively **2.** all the people not belonging to any given profession

**lake¹** (lāk) *n.* [OE. *lacu* & OFr. *lac,* both < L. *lacus,* lake] **1.** a large, inland body of water, usually fresh water **2.** a pool of oil or other liquid

**lake²** (lāk) *n.* [see LAC] **1.** *a)* a dark-red pigment prepared from cochineal *b)* its color **2.** an insoluble coloring compound precipitated from a solution of a dye by adding a metallic salt

**Lake Charles** [after *Charles* Sallier, an early settler] city in SW La.: pop. 75,000

**Lake District** (or **Country**) lake & mountain region in NW England: home of Wordsworth, Coleridge, & Southey (the **Lake poets** )

**lake dwelling** a dwelling built on wooden piles rising above the surface of a lake, esp. in prehistoric times —**lake dweller**

**lak·er** (lā'kər) *n.* **1.** a fish, esp. a trout, found in lakes **2.** a lake ship, esp. one on the Great Lakes

**lake trout** a large, gray game fish of deep, cold lakes of the N U.S. and Canada

**Lake·wood** (lāk'wood) **1.** city in NC Colo.: suburb of Denver: pop. 113,000 **2.** city in SW Calif.: suburb of Los Angeles: pop. 75,000 **3.** city in NE Ohio: suburb of Cleveland: pop. 62,000

**lakh** (lak) *n.* [< Hindi (see LAC): prob. in reference to the abundance of the insects] in India and Pakistan, **1.** the sum of 100,000: said of rupees **2.** any indefinitely large number

**lal·ly·gag** (läl'ē gag') *vi.* **-gagged'**, **-gag'ging** [Colloq.] *same as* LOLLYGAG

**lam¹** (lam) *vt., vi.* **lammed, lam'ming** [< Scand., as in ON. *lemja*] [Slang] to beat; thrash; flog

**lam²** (lam) *n.* [< ? prec.] [Slang] headlong flight, usually to escape arrest or punishment: used in phrase **on the lam** —*vi.* **lammed, lam'ming** [Slang] to flee; escape —**take it on the lam** [Slang] to flee; escape

**Lam.** Lamentations

**la·ma** (lä'mə) *n.* [Tibetan *blama*] a priest or monk in Lamaism: cf. DALAI LAMA

**La·ma·ism** (lä'mə iz'm) *n.* a form of Buddhism practiced in Tibet and Mongolia, characterized by elaborate ritual and a strong hierarchal organization —**La'ma·ist** *adj., n.* —**La'ma·is'tic** *adj.*

**La·marck** (là màrk'; *E.* lə märk'), chevalier de 1744-1829; Fr. naturalist who advanced the evolutionary theory that acquired characters can be inherited (see ACQUIRED CHARACTER) —**La·marck'i·an** *adj., n.* —**La·marck'ism** *n.*

**la·ma·ser·y** (lä'mə ser'ē) *n., pl.* **-ser'ies** [< Fr.] a monastery of lamas

**lamb** (lam) *n.* [OE.] **1.** a young sheep **2.** its flesh used as food **3.** lambskin **4.** a gentle or innocent person, esp. a child **5.** a dear **6.** a person easily tricked or outwitted —*vi.* to give birth: said of a ewe —**the Lamb** Jesus —**lamb'like'** *adj.*

**Lamb** (lam), **Charles** 1775-1834; Eng. essayist & critic

**lam·baste** (lam bāst', -bast') *vt.* **-bast'ed, -bast'ing** [LAM¹ + BASTE³] [Colloq.] **1.** to beat soundly; thrash **2.** to scold or criticize severely Also sp. **lam·bast'**

**lamb·da** (lam'də) *n.* the eleventh letter of the Greek alphabet (Λ, λ)

**lam·bent** (lam'bənt) *adj.* [< L. prp. of *lambere,* to lick] **1.** playing lightly over a surface; flickering **2.** softly glowing **3.** light and graceful *[lambent wit]* —**lam'ben·cy** *n.*

**lamb·kin** (lam'kin) *n.* **1.** a little lamb **2.** a child or young person: a term of affection

**Lamb of God** John 1:29, 36

**lamb·skin** (lam'skin') *n.* **1.** the skin of a lamb, esp. with the fleece left on it **2.** leather or parchment made from the skin of a lamb

**lamb's-quar·ters** (lamz'kwôr'tərz) *n.* an annual weed of the goosefoot family, with mealy leaves sometimes used for greens

**lame** (lām) *adj.* [OE. *lama*] **1.** crippled; esp., having an injured leg or foot that makes one limp **2.** stiff and very painful *[a lame back]* **3.** poor, weak, ineffectual, etc. *[a lame excuse]* —*vt.* **lamed, lam'ing** to make lame —**lame'ly** *adv.* —**lame'ness** *n.*

**la·mé** (la mā') *n.* [Fr., laminated < *lame,* metal plate] a cloth interwoven with metallic threads

**lame·brain** (lām'brān') *n.* [Colloq.] a slow-witted or stupid person —**lame'brained'** *adj.*

**lame duck** **1.** a disabled, ineffectual, or helpless person or thing **2.** an elected official whose term extends beyond the time of the election at which he was not reelected

**la·mel·la** (lə mel'ə) *n., pl.* **-lae** (-ē), **-las** [L., dim. of LAMINA] *Biol.* a thin, platelike part, layer, organ, or structure —**la·mel'lar, lam·el·late** (lam'ə lāt', lə mel'āt) *adj.* —**la·mel'lar·ly** *adv.*

**la·mel·li·branch** (lə mel'i braŋk') *n.* [see prec. & BRANCHIAE] any of a class of mollusks, including the clams, oysters, etc., having platelike gills and bivalve shells

**la·ment** (lə ment') *vi.* [< Fr. < L. < *lamentum,* a wailing] to feel or express deep sorrow; mourn; grieve —*vt.* **1.** to mourn or grieve for **2.** to regret deeply —*n.* **1.** a lamentation; wail **2.** a song, poem, etc. mourning a loss, death, etc.; elegy or dirge —**la·ment'er** *n.* —**la·ment'ing·ly** *adv.*

**lam·en·ta·ble** (lam'ən tə b'l, lə men'tə b'l) *adj.* to be lamented; regrettable; distressing —**lam'en·ta·bly** *adv.*

**lam·en·ta·tion** (lam'ən tā'shən) *n.* a lamenting

**Lam·en·ta·tions** (-shənz) a book of the Bible attributed to Jeremiah

**la·ment·ed** (lə men'tid) *adj.* mourned for: usually said of someone dead —**la·ment'ed·ly** *adv.*

**lam·i·na** (lam'ə nə) *n., pl.* **-nae'** (-nē'), **-nas** [L.] **1.** a thin flake, scale, or layer **2.** the flat, expanded part of a leaf —**lam'i·nar** (-nər), **lam'i·nal** *adj.*

**lam·i·nate** (lam'ə nāt'; *for adj. & n. usually* -nit) *vt.* **-nat'ed, -nat'ing** **1.** to form or press into a thin sheet or layer **2.** to separate into thin layers **3.** to cover with or bond to thin layers, as of clear plastic **4.** to make by building up in layers —*vi.* to split into thin layers —*adj. same as* LAMINATED —*n.* something made by laminating —**lam'i·na·ble** (-nə b'l) *adj.* —**lam'i·na'tion** *n.* —**lam'i·na'tor** *n.*

**lam·i·nat·ed** (-nāt'id) *adj.* composed of or built in thin sheets or layers, as of fabric, wood, plastic, etc., that have been bonded or pressed together

**lamp** (lamp) *n.* [< OFr. < VL. *lampade,* ult. < Gr. *lampein,* to shine] **1.** a container with a wick for burning oil, alcohol, etc. to produce light or heat **2.** any device for producing light or therapeutic rays, as a gas jet with a mantle, an electric light bulb, or an ultraviolet bulb **3.** a holder, stand, or base for such a device

**lamp·black** (-blak') *n.* fine soot produced by the incomplete combustion of oils and other forms of carbon: used as a pigment in paint, ink, etc.

**lam·per eel** (lam'pər) *same as* LAMPREY

**lam·poon** (lam poon') *n.* [< Fr. < *lampons,* let us drink (refrain in a drinking song)] a piece of strongly satirical writing, usually attacking or ridiculing someone —*vt.* to attack or ridicule in a lampoon —**lam·poon'er, lam·poon'ist** *n.* —**lam·poon'er·y** *n.*

**lamp·post** (lam'pōst', lamp'-) *n.* a post supporting a street lamp

**lam·prey** (lam'prē) *n., pl.* **-preys** [< OFr. < ML. *lampreda*] an eellike parasitic fish with a funnel-shaped, jawless, sucking mouth: it preys on other fish

**la·nai** (lä nī', la-) *n.* [Haw.] a veranda or open-sided living room of a kind found in Hawaii

**Lan·cas·ter¹** (laŋ'kəs tər) ruling family of England (1399-1461) —**Lan·cas·tri·an** (-kas'trē ən) *adj., n.*

**Lan·cas·ter²** (laŋ'kas'tər) [ult. < prec.] city in SE Pa.: pop. 55,000

**lance** (lans) *n.* [OFr. < L. *lancea*] **1.** a thrusting weapon consisting of a long wooden shaft with a sharp metal head **2.** a lancer **3.** any sharp instrument like a lance, as a fish spear **4.** a surgical lancet —*vt.* **lanced, lanc'ing 1.** to attack or pierce with a lance **2.** to cut open as with a lancet

**lance corporal** **1.** *Brit. Army* a private acting temporarily as a corporal **2.** *U.S. Marine Corps* an enlisted man ranking below a corporal and above a private first class

**lance·let** (lans'lit) *n.* [LANCE + -LET] a small, invertebrate, fishlike sea animal closely related to the vertebrates; amphioxus

**Lan·ce·lot** (lan'sə lät', -lət) *Arthurian Legend* the bravest and most celebrated of the Knights of the Round Table: he was Guinevere's lover

**lan·ce·o·late** (lan'sē ə lāt', -lit) *adj.* [< LL. < *lanceola,* little lance] narrow and tapering like the head of a lance, as certain leaves

**lanc·er** (lan'sər) *n.* a cavalry soldier armed with a lance or a member of a cavalry regiment originally armed with lances

**lanc·ers** (-sərz) *n.pl.* [*with sing. v.*] [< prec.] **1.** a 19th-cent. quadrille **2.** music for this

**lance sergeant** *Brit. Army* a corporal acting temporarily as a sergeant

**lan·cet** (lan'sit) *n.* [< OFr. dim. of *lance,* LANCE] **1.** a small, pointed surgical knife, usually two-edged, used for making small incisions, skin punctures, etc. **2.** *same as: a)* LANCET ARCH *b)* LANCET WINDOW

**lancet arch** a narrow, sharply pointed arch

**lancet window** a narrow, sharply pointed window without tracery, set in a lancet arch

**lance·wood** (lans'wŏŏd') *n.* **1.** a tough, elastic wood used for fishing rods, billiard cues, etc. **2.** a tropical tree yielding such wood

**land** (land) *n.* [OE.] **1.** the solid part of the earth's surface not covered by water **2.** *a)* a country, region, etc. *b)* a country's people **3.** ground or soil *[rich land, high land]* **4.** ground considered as property *[to invest in land]* **5.** rural regions *[to return to the land]* **6.** *Econ.* natural resources —*vt.* **1.** to put or set on shore from a ship **2.** to bring into or end up in a particular place or condition *[a fight landed him in jail]* **3.** to set (an aircraft) down on land or water **4.** to catch *[to land a fish]* **5.** [Colloq.] to get or win *[to land a job]* **6.** [Colloq.] to deliver (a blow) —*vi.* **1.** to leave a ship and go on shore **2.** to come to a port or to shore: said of a ship **3.** to arrive at a specified place **4.** to alight or come to rest, as after a flight, jump, or fall —**land on** [Colloq.] to scold or criticize severely

**lan·dau** (lan'dou, -dô) *n.* [ < *Landau,* German town where orig. made] **1.** a four-wheeled carriage with the top in two sections, either of which can be lowered independently **2.** a former style of automobile with a top whose back could be folded down

**land contract** a contract in which a purchaser of real estate, upon making an initial payment, agrees to pay set amounts at specified intervals until the total purchase price is paid, at which time the seller transfers his interest in the property

**land·ed** (lan'did) *adj.* **1.** owning land *[landed gentry]* **2.** consisting of land or real estate *[a landed estate]*

**land·fall** (land'fôl') *n.* **1.** a sighting of land from a ship at sea **2.** the land sighted **3.** a landing by ship or airplane

**land·fill** (-fil') *n.* **1.** the disposal of garbage, rubbish, etc. by burying it in the ground **2.** the site or fill used

**land grant** a grant of public land by the government for a railroad, State college, etc.

**land·grave** (-grāv') *n.* [ < G. < *land,* land + *graf,* a count] **1.** in medieval Germany, a count having jurisdiction over a specified territory **2.** later, the title of certain German princes

**land·hold·er** (-hōl'dər) *n.* an owner or occupant of land —**land'hold'ing** *adj., n.*

**land·ing** (lan'diŋ) *n.* **1.** the act of coming to shore or putting ashore **2.** the place where a ship is unloaded or loaded **3.** a platform at the end of a flight of stairs **4.** the act of alighting, as after a flight, jump, or fall

**landing craft** naval craft designed to bring troops and equipment close to shore

**landing field** a field with a smooth surface to enable airplanes to land and take off easily

**landing gear** the undercarriage of an aircraft, including wheels, pontoons, etc.

**landing net** a baglike net attached to a long handle, for taking a hooked fish from the water

**landing strip** *same as* AIRSTRIP

**land·la·dy** (land'lā'dē) *n., pl.* **-dies** a woman landlord

**land·less** (-lis) *adj.* not owning land

**land·locked** (-läkt') *adj.* **1.** entirely or almost entirely surrounded by land, as a bay or a country **2.** cut off from the sea and confined to fresh water *[landlocked salmon]*

**land·lord** (-lôrd') *n.* **1.** a person, esp. a man, who rents or leases land, houses, etc. to others **2.** a man who keeps a rooming house, inn, etc.

**land·lub·ber** (-lub'ər) *n.* a person who has had little experience at sea, and is therefore awkward aboard a ship: a sailor's term of contempt

**land·mark** (-märk') *n.* **1.** any fixed object used to mark the boundary of a piece of land **2.** any prominent feature of the landscape, as a tree, identifying a particular locality **3.** an event, discovery, etc. considered as a high point or turning point in the development of something

**land·mass** (-mas') *n.* a very large area of land; esp., a continent

**land mine** an explosive charge hidden under the surface of the ground and detonated by pressure upon it

**land office** a government office that handles and records the sales and transfers of public lands —**land'-of'fice business** [Colloq.] a booming business

**Land of Promise** *same as* PROMISED LAND

**land·own·er** (land'ō'nər) *n.* one who owns land —**land'own'er·ship'** *n.* —**land'own'ing** *adj., n.*

**land reform** the redistribution of agricultural land by breaking up large landholdings and apportioning shares to small farmers, peasants, etc.

**land·scape** (-skāp') *n.* [ < Du. < *land,* land + *-schap,* -SHIP] **1.** a picture representing natural, inland scenery **2.** an expanse of natural scenery seen in one view —*vt.* **-scaped', -scap'ing** to change the natural features of (a plot of ground) so as to make it more attractive, as by adding lawns, bushes, trees, etc. —**land'scap'er** *n.*

**landscape architecture** the art or profession of planning or changing the natural scenery of a place for a desired effect —**landscape architect**

**landscape gardening** the art or work of arranging lawns, trees, etc. on a plot of ground to make it more attractive —**landscape gardener**

**land·scap·ist** (-skāp'ist) *n.* a painter of landscapes

**land·slide** (-slīd') *n.* **1.** the sliding of a mass of rocks or earth down a hillside or slope **2.** the mass sliding down **3.** an overwhelming majority of votes for a candidate, party, etc. in an election

**land·slip** (-slip') *n.* [Chiefly Brit.] *same as* LANDSLIDE (senses 1 & 2)

**lands·man** (landz'mən) *n., pl.* **-men** **1.** a person who lives on land: distinguished from SEAMAN **2.** [partly via Yid. < MHG.] a fellow countryman

**land·ward** (land'wərd) *adv.* toward the land: also **land'wards** —*adj.* situated or facing toward the land

**lane** (lān) *n.* [OE. *lanu*] **1.** a narrow way between hedges, walls, etc.; narrow country road or city street **2.** any narrow way, as an opening in a crowd **3.** *same as: a)* AIR LANE *b)* SEA LANE **4.** a marked strip of road wide enough for a single line of cars, etc. **5.** any of the parallel courses marked off for contestants in a race **6.** *Bowling* a long, narrow strip of highly polished wood, along which the balls are rolled; alley

**lang.** language

**Lang·er** (laŋ'ər), **Susanne K(atherina)** (born *Susanne Katherina Knauth*) 1895– ; U.S. philosopher

**Lang·ley** (laŋ'lē), **Samuel Pier·pont** (pir'pänt) 1834–1906; U.S. astronomer & pioneer in airplane construction

**lang·syne** (laŋ'sīn', -zīn') *adv.* [Scot. < *lang,* LONG¹ + *syne,* since] [Scot.] long ago —*n.* [Scot.] the long ago; bygone days Also **lang syne**

**lan·guage** (laŋ'gwij) *n.* [ < OFr. < *langue,* tongue < L. *lingua*] **1.** *a)* human speech *b)* the ability to communicate by human speech *c)* the vocal sounds used in speech, or the written symbols for them **2.** *a)* any means of communicating, as gestures, animal sounds, etc. *b)* a special set of symbols, rules, etc. used for transmitting information, as in a computer **3.** all the vocal sounds, words, and ways of combining them common to a particular nation, tribe, etc. **4.** the special words, phrases, and style of expression of a particular group, writer, etc. *[the language of teen-agers]* **5.** the study of language or languages; linguistics

**lan·guid** (laŋ'gwid) *adj.* [ < Fr. < L. < *languere,* to be faint] **1.** without vigor or vitality; drooping; weak **2.** without interest or spirit; listless **3.** sluggish; slow —**lan'guid·ly** *adv.* —**lan'guid·ness** *n.*

**lan·guish** (-gwish) *vi.* [ < OFr. < L. < *languere:* see prec.] **1.** to lose vigor or vitality; become weak; droop **2.** to live under distressing conditions *[to languish in poverty]* **3.** to become slack or dull *[his interest languished]* **4.** to suffer with longing; pine **5.** to put on a sentimental or wistful air —**lan'guish·er** *n.* —**lan'guish·ing** *adj.* —**lan'guish·ing·ly** *adv.* —**lan'guish·ment** *n.*

**lan·guor** (laŋ'gər) *n.* [ < OFr. < L. < *languere:* see LANGUID] **1.** a lack of vigor or vitality; weakness **2.** a lack of interest or spirit; listlessness **3.** tenderness of mood or feeling **4.** the condition of being still, sluggish, or dull —**lan'guor·ous** *adj.* —**lan'guor·ous·ly** *adv.* —**lan'guor·ous·ness** *n.*

**lan·gur** (luŋ'gŏŏr') *n.* [ < Hindi < Sans. *lāṅgūlin,* lit., having a tail] any of certain monkeys of SE Asia, with a long tail and a chin tuft

**lan·iard** (lan'yərd) *n. same as* LANYARD

**La·nier** (lə nir'), **Sidney** 1842–81; U.S. poet

**lank** (laŋk) *adj.* [OE. *hlanc*] **1.** long and slender; lean **2.** straight and limp; not curly: said of hair —**lank'ly** *adv.* —**lank'ness** *n.*

**lank·y** (laŋ'kē) *adj.* **lank'i·er, lank'i·est** awkwardly tall and lean or long and slender —**lank'i·ly** *adv.* —**lank'i·ness** *n.*

**lan·o·lin** (lan''l in) *n.* [ < L. *lana,* wool + *oleum,* oil + -IN¹] a fatty substance obtained from sheep wool and used in ointments, cosmetics, etc.: also **lan'o·line** (-in, -ēn)

**Lan·sing** (lan'siŋ) [after J. *Lansing* (1751–1829), U.S. jurist] capital of Mich.: pop. 130,000

**lan·tern** (lan'tərn) *n.* [ < OFr. < L. *lanterna* < Gr. *lamptēr* < *lampein,* to shine] **1.** a transparent case for holding a light and protecting it from wind and weather **2.** the room containing the lamp at the top of a lighthouse **3.** an open or windowed structure on the roof of a building, in a tower, etc. to admit light and air

**lantern jaw** **1.** a projecting lower jaw **2.** *[pl.]* long, thin jaws, with sunken cheeks, that give the face a gaunt look —**lan'tern-jawed'** *adj.*

**lantern slide** a photographic slide for projection, as, originally, by a magic lantern

**lan·tha·nide series** (lan'thə nīd') [ < ff.] the rare-earth group of chemical elements from element 57 (lanthanum) through element 71 (lutetium)

**lan·tha·num** (-nəm) *n.* [ModL. < Gr. *lanthanein,* to be concealed] a silvery, metallic chemical element of the rare-earth group: symbol, La; at. wt., 138.91; at. no., 57

**lan·yard** (lan'yərd) *n.* [< MFr. *laniere* < OFr. < *lasne*, noose: altered after YARD¹] **1.** a short rope used on board ship for holding or fastening something **2.** a cord used by sailors, etc. to hang a knife, whistle, etc. around the neck **3.** a cord for firing certain types of cannon

**La·oc·o·ön** (lā äk'ə wän') *Gr. Legend* a Trojan priest who, with his two sons, was destroyed by two huge sea serpents after he had warned against the wooden horse

**La·os** (lä'ōs, lous) country in the NW part of the Indochinese peninsula: 91,429 sq. mi.; pop. 2,893,000; cap. Vientiane —**La·o·tian** (lā ō'shən) *adj., n.*

**Lao-tse** (lou'dzu') 604? B.C.–?; Chin. philosopher: reputed founder of Taoism: also sp. **Lao-tzu, Lao-tsze**

**lap¹** (lap) *n.* [OE. *læppa*] **1.** [Now Rare] the loose lower part of a garment, which may be folded over **2.** *a)* the front part from the waist to the knees of a person in a sitting position *b)* the part of the clothing covering this **3.** that in which one is cared for, sheltered, etc. **4.** *a)* an overlapping part *b)* such overlapping *c)* amount or place of this **5.** one complete circuit around a race track **6.** a lapping —*vt.* **lapped, lap'ping 1.** to fold (*over* or *on*) **2.** to wrap; enfold **3.** to hold as in the lap; envelop **4.** to place partly upon something else *[to lap one board over another]* **5.** to lie partly upon; overlap *[one board laps the other]* **6.** to get a lap ahead of (an opponent) in a race —*vi.* **1.** to lie partly on something or on one another; overlap **2.** to extend beyond something in space or time (with *over*) —**drop** (or **dump, etc.) into someone's lap** to cause to be someone's responsibility

**lap²** (lap) *vi., vt.* **lapped, lap'ping** [OE. *lapian*] **1.** to drink (a liquid) by dipping it up with the tongue as a dog does **2.** to move or strike gently with a light splash: said of waves, etc. —*n.* **1.** a lapping **2.** the sound of lapping —**lap up 1.** to take up (liquid) by lapping **2.** [Colloq.] to take in eagerly —**lap'per** *n.*

**La Paz** (lä päs'; *E.* lə päz') city in W Bolivia: seat of government (cf. SUCRE): pop. 482,000

**lap dissolve** *Motion Pictures & TV* a dissolving view in which a new scene is blended in with a scene being faded out, as by lapping two exposures on one film

**lap dog** a pet dog small enough to hold in the lap

**la·pel** (lə pel') *n.* [dim. of LAP¹] either of the front parts of a coat folded back and forming a continuation of the collar

**lap·ful** (lap'fool) *n., pl.* **-fuls** as much as a lap can hold

**lap·i·dar·y** (lap'ə der'ē) *n., pl.* **-dar'ies** [< LL. *lapidarius* < L. < *lapis*, a stone] a workman who cuts, polishes, and engraves precious stones —*adj.* **1.** of or connected with the art of cutting and engraving precious stones **2.** like an inscription on a monument; short, precise, and elegant

**lap·in** (lap'in) *n.* [Fr., rabbit] rabbit fur, generally dyed in imitation of more valuable skins

**lap·is laz·u·li** (lap'is laz'yoo lī', lazh'-; -lē') [ModL. < L. *lapis*, a stone + ML. gen. of *lazulus*, azure < Ar.: see AZURE] an azure-blue, opaque, semiprecious stone

**lap joint** a joint made by overlapping parts: also **lapped joint** —**lap'-joint'** *vt.*

**La·place** (lä pläs'), marquis **Pierre Si·mon de** (pyer sē mōn' də) 1749–1827; Fr. mathematician & astronomer

**Lap·land** (lap'land') region of N Europe, including the N parts of Scandinavia & Finland & a NW section of the U.S.S.R., inhabited by the Lapps

LAP JOINT

**La Pla·ta** (lä plä'tä) seaport in E Argentina, on the Río de la Plata: pop. 337,000

**Lapp** (lap) *n.* **1.** a member of a Mongoloid people living in Lapland: also **Lap'land'er 2.** their Finno-Ugric language: also **Lap'pish**

**lap·pet** (lap'it) *n.* [dim. of LAP¹] a small fold or flap, as of a garment or as of flesh

**lap robe** a heavy blanket, fur wrap, etc. laid over the lap and legs for warmth, as when watching outdoor sports

**lapse** (laps) *n.* [L. *lapsus*, a fall < pp. of *labi*, to slip] **1.** a slip or small error *[a lapse of memory]* **2.** *a)* a falling away from a moral standard; moral slip *b)* a falling or slipping into a lower or worse condition, esp. for a short time **3.** a passing away, as of time **4.** *Law* the termination of a right or privilege through disuse, failure of some contingency, or failure to meet stated obligations —*vi.* **lapsed, laps'ing 1.** to slip into a specified state *[to lapse into a coma]* **2.** to slip or deviate from a higher standard or fall into former erroneous ways; backslide **3.** to pass away: said of time **4.** to come to an end; stop *[his subscription lapsed]* **5.** to become forfeit or void because of failure to pay the premium at the stipulated time: said of an insurance policy —**laps'a·ble, laps'i·ble** *adj.*

**lap·wing** (lap'wiŋ') *n.* [altered by folk etym. < OE. *hleapewince < hleapan*, to leap + *wince < wincian*, WINK] an old-world crested plover noted for its irregular, wavering flight

**lar·board** (lär'bərd, -bôrd') *n.* [< OE. *hladan*, to lade + *bord*, side] the left-hand side of a ship as one faces forward; port —*adj.* on or of this side Now largely replaced by PORT⁴

**lar·ce·ny** (lär'sə nē) *n., pl.* **-nies** [< Anglo-Fr. < OFr. < L. < *latrocinari*, to rob < *latro*, robber] *Law* the unlawful taking away of another's property with the intention of depriving him of it; theft: sometimes differentiated as **grand larceny** (more than a stated amount varying in States from $25 to $60) and **petit**, or **petty, larceny** (less than this amount) —**lar'ce·nist** *n.* —**lar'ce·nous** *adj.*

**larch** (lärch) *n.* [< G. < L. *larix*] **1.** a tree of the pine family, found throughout the N Hemisphere, bearing cones and needlelike leaves that are shed annually **2.** the tough wood of this tree

**lard** (lärd) *n.* [< OFr. < L. *lardum*] the fat of hogs, melted down and clarified —*vt.* **1.** to smear with lard or other fat; grease **2.** to put strips of fat pork, bacon, etc. on (meat or poultry) before cooking **3.** to add to; embellish *[a talk larded with jokes]* —**lard'y** *adj.* **-i·er, -i·est**

**lard·er** (lär'dər) *n.* [< OFr. *lardier* < ML. < L. *lardum*, lard] **1.** a place where the food supplies of a household are kept; pantry **2.** a supply of food

**La·re·do** (lə rā'dō) [after *Laredo*, town in Spain] city in S Tex., on the Rio Grande: pop. 91,000

**lar·es** (ler'ēz, lā'rēz) *n.pl., sing.* **lar** (lär) [L.] in ancient Rome, guardian ancestral spirits

**lares and penates 1.** the household gods of the ancient Romans **2.** the treasured belongings of a family or household

**large** (lärj) *adj.* **larg'er, larg'est** [OFr. < L. *largus*] **1.** big; great; specif., *a)* taking up much space; bulky *b)* enclosing much space; spacious *[a large office] c)* of great extent or amount *[a large sum]* **2.** big as compared with others of its kind **3.** operating on a big scale *[a large manufacturer]* —*adv.* in a large way *[to write large]* —**at large 1.** free; not confined **2.** fully; in complete detail **3.** in general; taken altogether **4.** representing an entire State or area rather than only a subdivision *[a congressman at large]* —**large'ness** *n.*

**large·heart·ed** (-här'tid) *adj.* generous; kindly

**large·ly** (-lē) *adv.* **1.** much; in great amounts **2.** for the most part; mainly

**large-scale** (-skāl') *adj.* **1.** drawn to a large scale: said of a map, etc. **2.** of wide scope; extensive *[large-scale business operations]*

**lar·gess, lar·gesse** (lär jes', lär'jis) *n.* [OFr. < *large*, LARGE] **1.** generous giving **2.** a gift or gifts generously given

**lar·ghet·to** (lär get'ō) *adj., adv.* [It. < *largo*: see LARGO] *Music* relatively slow, but faster than largo —*n., pl.* **-tos** a larghetto movement or passage

**larg·ish** (lär'jish) *adj.* rather large

**lar·go** (lär'gō) *adj., adv.* [It., large, slow < L. *largus*, large] *Music* slow and stately —*n., pl.* **-gos** a largo movement or passage

**lar·i·at** (lar'ē it) *n.* [Sp. *la reata*, the rope] **1.** a rope used for tethering grazing horses, etc. **2.** *same as* LASSO —*vt.* to tie or catch with a lariat

**lark¹** (lärk) *n.* [OE. *læwerce*] **1.** any of a large family of chiefly old-world songbirds; esp., the skylark **2.** any of various similar birds, as the meadowlark

**lark²** (lärk) *vi.* [? altered after prec. < dial. *lake* < ME. *laike*, to play] to play or frolic —*n.* a frolic or spree —**lark'ish, lark'y** *adj.*

**lark·spur** (lärk'spur') *n. a common name for* DELPHINIUM

**La Roche·fou·cauld** (lä rôsh foo kō'), duc **Fran·çois de** (frän swä' də) 1613–80; Fr. moralist & writer of maxims

**La·rousse** (lä rōōs'), **Pierre A·tha·nase** (pyer à tá näz') 1817–75; Fr. lexicographer

**lar·rup** (lar'əp) *vt.* [akin to or < Du. *larpen*] [Colloq.] to whip; flog; beat

**lar·va** (lär'və) *n., pl.* **-vae** (-vē), **-vas** [L., ghost] the early, free-living, immature form of any animal that changes structurally when it becomes an adult *[the caterpillar is the larva of the butterfly]* —**lar'val** *adj.*

**la·ryn·ge·al** (lə rin'jē əl) *adj.* **1.** of, in, or near the larynx **2.** used for treating the larynx

**lar·yn·gi·tis** (lar'ən jīt'əs) *n.* [ff. + -ITIS] inflammation of the larynx, often with a temporary loss of voice —**lar'yn·git'ic** (-jit'ik) *adj.*

**la·ryn·go-** [< Gr.] *a combining form meaning:* **1.** the larynx **2.** laryngeal and Also **laryng-**

**la·ryn·go·scope** (lə rin'gə skōp') *n.* [prec. + -SCOPE] an instrument for examining the larynx —**lar·yn·gos·co·py** (lar'in gäs'kə pē) *n.*

**lar·ynx** (lar'iŋks) *n., pl.* **lar'ynx·es, la·ryn·ges** (lə rin'jēz) [< Gr. *larynx*] **1.** the structure of muscle and cartilage at the upper end of the human trachea, containing the vocal cords and serving as the organ of voice: see EPIGLOTTIS, illus. **2.** a similar structure in other animals

**la·sa·gna** (lə zän'yə) *n.* [It., the noodle < L. *lasanum* (< Gr. *lasanon*), a pot] a dish of wide, flat noodles baked in layers with cheese, tomato sauce, and ground meat

**La Salle** (lȧ sȧl'; *E.* lə sal'), sieur **Ro·bert Cave·lier de** (rŏ ber' kȧv lyā' də) 1643–87; Fr. explorer in N. America

**las·car** (las'kər) *n.* [< Hindi < Per. *lashkar* < Ar. *al-'askar*, army] an Oriental sailor, esp. one who is a native of India

**las·civ·i·ous** (lə siv'ē əs) *adj.* [< ML. < L. < *lascivus*, wanton] **1.** characterized by or expressing lust or lewdness; wanton **2.** tending to excite lust —**las·civ'i·ous·ly** *adv.* —**las·civ'i·ous·ness** *n.*

**lase** (lāz) *vi.* **lased, las'ing** to emit laser light

**la·ser** (lā'zər) *n.* [*l(ight) a(mplification by) s(timulated) e(mission of) r(adiation)*] a device that amplifies focused light waves and concentrates them in a narrow, very intense beam

**lash¹** (lash) *n.* [ME. *lassche* < ?] **1.** a whip, esp. the flexible striking part **2.** a stroke as with a whip **3.** an eyelash —*vt.* **1.** to strike or drive as with a lash; flog **2.** to swing quickly or angrily; switch *[the cat lashed her tail]* **3.** to strike with great force *[waves lashed the cliffs]* **4.** to attack violently in words; censure or rebuke **5.** to incite by appealing to the emotions —*vi.* **1.** to move quickly or violently; switch **2.** to make strokes as with a whip —**lash out 1.** to strike out violently **2.** to speak angrily —**lash'er** *n.*

**lash²** (lash) *vt.* [< OFr. *lachier:* see LACE] to fasten or tie with a rope, etc.

**lash·ing¹** (-iŋ) *n.* **1.** a whipping **2.** a strong rebuke

**lash·ing²** (-iŋ) *n.* **1.** the act of fastening or tying with a rope, etc. **2.** a rope, etc. so used

**lash-up** (lash'up') *n.* [Colloq.] an improvised contrivance

**Las Pal·mas** (läs päl'məs) seaport, & largest city, in the Canary Islands: pop. 244,000

**lass** (las) *n.* [ME. *lasse*, prob. < ON.] **1.** a young woman; girl **2.** a sweetheart

**las·sie** (las'ē) *n.* [dim. of prec.] [Scot.] **1.** a young girl **2.** a sweetheart

**las·si·tude** (las'ə tōōd', -tyōōd') *n.* [Fr. < L. < *lassus*, faint] a state or feeling of being tired and listless; weariness; languor

**las·so** (las'ō, -ōō) *n., pl.* **-sos, -soes** [Sp. *lazo* < L. *laqueus*, noose] a long rope with a sliding noose at one end, used to catch cattle or horses —*vt.* **-soed, -so·ing** to catch with a lasso —**las'so·er** *n.*

**last¹** (last) *adj. alt. superl.* of LATE [< OE. *latost*, superl. of *læt:* see LATE] **1.** being or coming after all others in place or time; furthest from the first; final **2.** only remaining **3.** most recent *[last month]* **4.** least likely *[the last person to suspect]* **5.** utmost; greatest **6.** lowest in rank, as a prize **7.** newest *[the last thing in hats]* **8.** conclusive *[the last word in scientific research]* **9.** individual: a redundant intensive *[eat every last bite]* —*adv.* **1.** after all others; at the end **2.** most recently **3.** finally —*n.* **1.** someone or something which comes last *[the last of the kings]* **2.** end *[friends to the last]* —**at (long) last** finally —**see the last of** to see for the last time

**last²** (last) *vi.* [< OE. *læstan*] **1.** to remain in existence or operation; continue; endure **2.** to remain in good condition **3.** to continue unconsumed, unspent, etc.; be enough (for) *[food to last (for) a month]* —*vt.* to continue or endure throughout: often with *out [doubtful whether he can last (out) the year]* —**last'er** *n.*

**last³** (last) *n.* [OE. *læste < last*, footstep] a form shaped like a foot, on which shoes are made or repaired —*vt.* to form with a last —**stick to one's last 1.** to keep to one's own work **2.** to mind one's own business —**last'er** *n.*

**last-ditch** (-dich') *adj.* made, done, etc. in a final, often desperate effort to resist or oppose

**Las·tex** (las'teks) [< (E)LAS(TIC) + TEX(TILE)] *a trademark for* a fine, round rubber thread wound with cotton, silk, etc. and woven, etc. into cloth

**last·ing** (las'tiŋ) *adj.* that lasts a long time; enduring; durable *[a lasting peace]* —**last'ing·ly** *adv.* —**last'ing·ness** *n.*

**Last Judgment** *Theol.* the final judgment of mankind at the end of the world

**last·ly** (last'lē) *adv.* in conclusion; finally

**last rites 1.** final rites for a dead person **2.** sacraments administered to a dying person

**last straw** [from the last straw that broke the camel's back in the fable] the last of a sequence of troubles or annoyances that results in a breakdown, loss of patience, etc.

**Last Supper** the last supper eaten by Jesus with his disciples before the Crucifixion

**last word 1.** *a)* the final word or speech, regarded as settling the argument *b)* final authority **2.** something regarded as perfect **3.** [Colloq.] the very latest style

**Las Ve·gas** (läs vā'gəs) [Sp., the plains or meadows] city in SE Nev.: pop. 165,000

**Lat.** Latin

**lat.** latitude

**La·ta·ki·a** (lat'ə kē'ə) *n.* [< *Latakia*, a seaport in Syria] a fine grade of Turkish smoking tobacco

**latch** (lach) *n.* [OE. *læccan*, to catch] **1.** a fastening for a door or gate consisting of a bar that falls into a notch on the doorjamb or gatepost: now often used of a spring lock on a door **2.** a fastening for a window, etc. —*vt., vi.* to fasten with a latch —**latch onto** [Colloq.] to get or obtain —**on the latch** fastened by the latch but not bolted

**latch·key** (-kē') *n.* a key for drawing back or unfastening the latch of a door

**latch·string** (-striŋ') *n.* a cord fastened to a latch so that it can be raised from the outside

**late** (lāt) *adj.* **lat'er** or **lat'ter, lat'est** or **last** [OE. *læt*] **1.** happening, coming, etc. after the usual or expected time; tardy **2.** *a)* happening, continuing, etc. far on in the day, night, year, etc. *[a late party] b)* far advanced in a period, development, etc. *[the late Middle Ages]* **3.** recent *[a late news bulletin]* **4.** having been so recently but not now **5.** having recently died —*adv.* **lat'er, lat'est** or **last 1.** after the usual or expected time **2.** at or until an advanced time of the day, night, year, etc. **3.** toward the end of a period, development, etc. **4.** recently *[as late as yesterday]* —**of late** lately —**late'ness** *n.*

**la·teen** (la tēn', lə-) *adj.* [< Fr. < (*voile*) *latine*, Latin (sail)] **1.** designating or of a triangular sail attached to a long yard suspended from a short mast: used chiefly on Mediterranean vessels **2.** having such a sail —*n.* a vessel with such a sail

**Late Greek** the Greek language of the period after classical Greek, seen chiefly in writings from c.200 to c.600 A.D.

**Late Latin** the Latin language of the period after classical Latin, seen chiefly in writings from c.200 to c.600 A.D.

LATEEN SAIL

**late·ly** (lāt'lē) *adv.* recently; a short while ago

**la·tent** (lāt'nt) *adj.* [< L. prp. of *latere*, to lurk] lying hidden and undeveloped within a person or thing; concealed, dormant, etc. *[a latent talent]* —**la'ten·cy** *n.* —**la'tent·ly** *adv.*

**lat·er** (lāt'ər) *adj. alt. compar.* of LATE —*adv. compar.* of LATE at a later time; subsequently —**later on** subsequently

**lat·er·al** (lat'ər əl) *adj.* [< L. < *latus* (gen. *lateris*), a side] of, at, from, or toward the side; sideways *[lateral movement]* —*n.* **1.** any lateral part, growth, etc. **2.** *Football short for* LATERAL PASS —**lat'er·al·ly** *adv.*

**lateral pass** *Football* a short pass parallel to the goal line or in a slightly backward direction

**lat·est** (lāt'ist) *alt. superl.* of LATE —**at the latest** no later than (the time specified) —**the latest** the most recent thing, development, etc.

**la·tex** (lā'teks) *n., pl.* **lat·i·ces** (lat'ə sēz'), **la'tex·es** [L., a fluid] **1.** a milky liquid in certain plants and trees, as the rubber tree, milkweed, etc.: used esp. as the basis of rubber **2.** an emulsion in water of particles of synthetic rubber or plastic: used in rubber goods, adhesives, paints, etc.

**lath** (lath) *n., pl.* **laths** (lathz, laths) [OE. *læt*] **1.** any of the thin, narrow strips of wood used in building lattices or nailed to two-by-fours, rafters, etc. as a groundwork for plastering, tiling, etc. **2.** any framework for plaster, as wire screening or expanded metal **3.** laths collectively —*vt.* to cover with laths

**lathe** (lāth) *n.* [prob. < MDu. *lade*] a machine for shaping an article of wood, metal, etc. by holding and turning it rapidly against the edge of a cutting tool —*vt.* **lathed, lath'ing** to shape on a lathe

**lath·er** (lath'ər) *n.* [OE. *leathor*, washing soda or soap] **1.** the foam formed by soap or other detergent in water **2.** foamy sweat, as on a race horse **3.** [Slang] an agitated state —*vt.* to cover with lather —*vi.* to form, or become covered with, lather —**lath'er·y** *adj.*

**lath·ing** (lath'iŋ) *n.* **1.** laths collectively, esp. when used as a base for plaster **2.** the putting up of laths on walls, etc. Also **lath'work'** (-wurk')

**Lat·in** (lat'n) *adj.* **1.** of ancient Latium or its people **2.** of ancient Rome or its people **3.** of or in the language of ancient Latium and ancient Rome **4.** designating or of the languages derived from Latin, the peoples who speak them, their countries, etc. —*n.* **1.** a native or inhabitant of ancient Latium or ancient Rome **2.** the Italic language of ancient Latium and ancient Rome **3.** a person, as a Spaniard or Italian, whose language is derived from Latin

**Latin America** that part of the Western Hemisphere, south of the U.S., where Spanish, Portuguese, & French are official languages —**Latin American**

**Lat·in·ate** (-āt′) *adj.* of, derived from, or similar to Latin: also **La·tin·ic** (la tin′ik)

**Latin Church** *same as* ROMAN CATHOLIC CHURCH

**Lat·in·ism** (-iz′m) *n.* a Latin idiom or expression, used in another language

**Lat·in·ist** (-ist) *n.* a scholar in Latin

**Lat·in·ize** (-īz′) *vt.* **-ized′, -iz′ing** **1.** to translate into Latin **2.** to give Latin form or characteristics to —*vi.* to use Latin expressions, forms, etc. —**Lat′in·i·za′tion** *n.* —**Lat′in·iz′er** *n.*

**Latin Quarter** [transl. of Fr. *Quartier Latin*] a section of Paris, south of the Seine, where many artists and students live

**Latin Rite** the Latin liturgy used in the Roman Catholic Church

**lat·ish** (lāt′ish) *adj., adv.* somewhat late

**lat·i·tude** (lat′ə tōōd′, -tyōōd′) *n.* [OFr. < L. *latitudo* < *latus*, wide] **1.** extent; scope; range of applicability **2.** freedom from narrow restrictions **3.** *Geog. a)* angular distance, measured in degrees, north or south from the equator *b)* a place or region in relation to its latitude —**lat′i·tu′di·nal** *adj.* —**lat′i·tu′di·nal·ly** *adv.*

**lat·i·tu·di·nar·i·an** (lat′ə tōōd′′n er′ē ən, -tyōōd′-) *adj.* [see prec. & -ARIAN] liberal in one's views; permitting free thought, esp. in religious matters —*n.* one who is very liberal in his views and, in religion, cares little about particular creeds and forms —**lat′i·tu′di·nar′i·an·ism** *n.*

**La·ti·um** (lā′shē əm) ancient country on the central coast of Italy, southeast of Rome

**la·trine** (la trēn′) *n.* [Fr. < L. *latrina* < *lavare*, to wash] a toilet, privy, etc. for the use of a large number of people, as in an army camp

**-la·try** (lə trē) [< Gr. < *latreia*, service] *a combining form meaning* worship of or excessive devotion to [*idolatry*]

**lat·ter** (lat′ər) *adj. alt. compar. of* LATE [OE. *lættra*, compar. of *læt*, late] **1.** *a)* later; more recent *b)* nearer the end or close [the *latter* part of May] **2.** last mentioned of two: opposed to FORMER¹: often a noun (with *the*)

**lat·ter-day** (-dā′) *adj.* of recent or present time

**Lat·ter-day Saint** *see* MORMON

**lat·ter·ly** (lat′ər lē) *adv.* lately; recently

**lat·tice** (lat′is) *n.* [OFr. *lattis* < MHG. *latte*, a lath] **1.** an openwork structure of crossed strips of wood, metal, etc. used as a screen, support, etc. **2.** a door, shutter, trellis, etc. formed of such a structure **3.** *Physics* a three-dimensional pattern of points in space, as of atoms in a solid or crystal —*vt.* **-ticed, -tic·ing** **1.** to arrange like a lattice **2.** to furnish with a lattice

**lat·tice·work** (-wʉrk′) *n.* **1.** a lattice **2.** lattices collectively Also **lat′tic·ing**

LATTICE

**Lat·vi·a** (lat′vē ə) republic of the U.S.S.R., in NE Europe, on the Baltic Sea: 24,594 sq. mi.; pop. 2,300,000; cap. Riga: in full, **Latvian Soviet Socialist Republic** — **Lat′vi·an** *adj., n.*

**laud** (lôd) *n.* [< OFr. < ML. *laudes*, pl. < L. *laus*, praise] **1.** praise **2.** any song of praise **3.** [*pl.*] *Eccles.* [*often* L-] the service of dawn which constitutes the second (or, together with matins, the first) of the canonical hours and includes psalms of praise to God —*vt.* to praise; extol

**laud·a·ble** (-ə b'l) *adj.* worthy of being lauded; praiseworthy —**laud′a·bil′i·ty, laud′a·ble·ness** *n.* —**laud′a·bly** *adv.*

**laud·a·num** (lôd′′n əm) *n.* [ModL., altered use of ML. var. of L. *ladanum*, mastic] **1.** formerly, any of various opium preparations **2.** a solution of opium in alcohol

**lau·da·tion** (lô dā′shən) *n.* a lauding or being lauded; praise; commendation

**laud·a·to·ry** (lôd′ə tôr′ē) *adj.* expressing praise; eulogistic: also **laud′a·tive**

**laugh** (laf) *vi.* [OE. *hleahhan*] **1.** to make the vocal sounds and facial movements that express mirth, amusement, ridicule, etc. **2.** to feel or suggest joyousness —*vt.* **1.** to express with laughter **2.** to cause to be by means of laughter [to *laugh* oneself hoarse] —*n.* **1.** the act or sound of laughing **2.** anything that provokes or is fit to provoke laughter **3.** [*pl.*] [Colloq.] mere diversion or pleasure —**have the last laugh** to win after apparent defeat —**laugh at** **1.** to be amused by **2.** to make fun of **3.** to be indifferent to or contemptuous of —**laugh off** to scorn, avoid, or reject by laughter or ridicule —**laugh out of** (or **on**) **the other** (or **wrong**) **side of the mouth** to change from joy to sorrow, from amusement to annoyance, etc. —**no laughing matter** a serious matter —**laugh′er** *n.*

**laugh·a·ble** (-ə b'l) *adj.* of such a nature as to cause laughter; amusing or ridiculous —**laugh′a·ble·ness** *n.* —**laugh′a·bly** *adv.*

**laugh·ing** (-iŋ) *adj.* **1.** that laughs or seems to laugh [a *laughing* brook] **2.** uttered with laughter —*n.* laughter —**laugh′ing·ly** *adv.*

**laughing gas** nitrous oxide used as an anesthetic: it may cause laughter and exhilaration

**laugh·ing·stock** (laf′iŋ stäk′) *n.* a person or thing made the object of ridicule

**laugh·ter** (laf′tər) *n.* **1.** the action or sound of laughing **2.** an indication of amusement [with *laughter* in her eyes]

**launch¹** (lônch, länch) *vt.* [< OFr. *lanchier* < LL. < L. *lancea*, LANCE] **1.** to hurl, discharge, or send off (a weapon, blow, rocket, etc.) **2.** to cause (a newly built vessel) to slide into the water; set afloat **3.** to set in operation; start [to *launch* an attack] **4.** to start (a person) on some course —*vi.* **1.** to put to sea (often with *out* or *forth*) **2.** to start on some new course or enterprise (often with *out* or *forth*) **3.** to throw oneself (*into*) with vigor; plunge [to *launch* into a tirade] —*n.* the act or process of launching a ship, spacecraft, etc. —*adj.* designating or of facilities, sites, etc. used in launching spacecraft or missiles —**launch′er** *n.*

**launch²** (lônch, länch) *n.* [Sp. or Port. *lancha* < ?] **1.** formerly, the largest boat carried by a warship **2.** an open, or partly enclosed, motorboat

**launch pad** the platform from which a rocket, guided missile, etc. is launched: also **launching pad**

**laun·der** (lôn′dər, län′-) *vt.* [< OFr. < ML. < LL. *lavandaria*, things to be washed < L. < *lavare*, to wash] to wash, or wash and iron, (clothes, etc.) —*vi.* **1.** to withstand washing [this fabric *launders* well] **2.** to do laundry —**laun′der·er** *n.*

**Laun·der·ette** (lôn′də ret′, län′-) *a service mark for* a self-service laundry —*n.* [l-] such a laundry

**laun·dress** (lôn′dris, län′-) *n.* a woman whose work is washing clothes, ironing, etc.

**Laun·dro·mat** (lôn′drə mat′, län′-) [< a trademark for an automatic washing machine] *a service mark for* a self-service laundry —*n.* [l-] such a laundry

**laun·dry** (lôn′drē, län′-) *n., pl.* **-dries** **1.** a laundering **2.** a place where laundering is done **3.** clothes, etc. laundered or to be laundered

**laun·dry·man** (-mən) *n., pl.* **-men** a man who works for a laundry, esp. one who collects and delivers laundry

**laun·dry·wom·an** (-wōōm′ən) *n., pl.* **-wom′en** *same as* LAUNDRESS

**Lau·ra** (lôr′ə) [fem. of LAURENCE] a feminine name

**lau·re·ate** (lôr′ē it) *adj.* [< L. < *laurea* (*corona*), laurel (wreath) < *laurus*, laurel] **1.** crowned with a laurel wreath as a mark of honor **2.** honored —*n.* **1.** one on whom honor is conferred **2.** *same as* POET LAUREATE —**lau′re·ate·ship′** *n.*

**lau·rel** (lôr′əl, lär′-) *n.* [< OFr. < L. *laurus*] **1.** an evergreen tree or shrub, native to S Europe, with large, glossy, aromatic leaves **2.** the foliage of this tree, esp. as woven into wreaths such as those used by the ancient Greeks to crown victors in contests **3.** [*pl.*] *a)* fame; honor *b)* victory **4.** a tree or shrub resembling the true laurel, as the mountain laurel —*vt.* **-reled** or **-relled, -rel·ing** or **-rel·ling** **1.** to crown with laurel **2.** to honor —**look to one's laurels** to beware of having one's achievements surpassed —**rest on one's laurels** to be satisfied with what one has already achieved

**Lau·rence** (lôr′əns, lär′-) [L. *Laurentius*, prob. < *laurus*, laurel] a masculine name

**Lau·ren·tian Mountains** (lô ren′shən) mountain range in S Quebec, Canada, extending along the St. Lawrence River valley

**Lau·sanne** (lō zan′) city in W Switzerland, on Lake Geneva: pop. 137,000

**la·va** (lä′və, lav′ə) *n.* [It. < dial. *lave* < L. *labes*, a fall < *labi*, to slide] **1.** melted rock issuing from a volcano **2.** such rock when cool and solid

**La·val** (lə val′) city in SW Quebec, near Montreal: pop. 196,000: also **Ville de La·val** (vēl də là vàl′)

**lav·a·liere, lav·a·lier** (lav′ə lir′, lä′və-) *n.* [Fr. *lavallière*, kind of tie] an ornament hanging from a chain, worn around the neck

**lav·a·to·ry** (lav′ə tôr′ē) *n., pl.* **-ries** [LL. *lavatorium* < L. *lavare*, to wash] **1.** a washbowl **2.** a room equipped with a washbowl, flush toilet, etc.

**lave** (lāv) *vt., vi.* **laved, lav′ing** [< OE. *lafian* & OFr. *laver*, both < L. *lavare*, to wash] [Poet.] to wash or bathe

**lav·en·der** (lav′ən dər) *n.* [< Anglo-Fr. < ML. *lavandria* < L. *lavare*, to wash] **1.** a fragrant European plant of the mint family, having spikes of pale-purplish flowers and yielding an aromatic oil (**oil of lavender**) **2.** the dried flow-

---

fat, āpe, cär; ten, ēven; is, bīte; gō, hôrn, tōol, look; oil, out; up, fʉr; get; joy; yet; chin; she; thin, then; zh, leisure; ŋ, ring; ə for a in ago, e in agent, i in sanity, o in comply, u in focus; ′ as in able (ā′b'l); Fr. bàl; ë, Fr. coeur; ö, Fr. feu; Fr. mon; ô, Fr. coq; ü, Fr. duc; r, Fr. cri; H, G. ich; kh, G. doch; ‡foreign; *hypothetical; < derived from. See inside front cover.

ers, leaves, and stalks of this plant, used to perfume clothes, linens, etc. **3.** a pale purple —*adj.* pale-purple

**la·ver** (lā'vər) *n.* [< OFr. < L. < *lavare,* to wash] [Archaic] a large basin to wash in

**lav·ish** (lav'ish) *adj.* [< MFr. < OFr. *lavasse,* torrent of rain, prob. < *laver* < L. *lavare,* to wash] **1.** very generous or liberal in giving or spending, often extravagantly so **2.** more than enough; very abundant *[lavish* entertainment*]* —*vt.* to give or spend liberally —**lav'ish·ly** *adv.* —**lav'ish·ness** *n.*

**La·voi·sier** (lá vwá zyā'; *E.* lə vwä'zē ā'), **An·toine Lau·rent** (än twän' lô rän') 1743–94; Fr. pioneer in chemistry

**law** (lô) *n.* [OE. *lagu* < Anglo-N.] **1.** *a)* all the rules of conduct established and enforced by the authority, legislation, or custom of a given community or other group *b)* any one of such rules **2.** the condition existing when obedience to such rules is general *[to* establish *law* and order*]* **3.** the branch of knowledge dealing with such rules; jurisprudence **4.** the system of courts in which such rules are referred to in securing justice *[to* resort to *law]* **5.** all such rules dealing with a particular activity *[business law]* **6.** common law, as distinguished from equity **7.** the profession of lawyers, judges, etc. (often with *the*) **8.** *a)* a sequence of events in nature or in human activities occurring with unvarying uniformity under the same conditions: often **law of nature** *b)* the formulation in words of such a sequence **9.** any rule or principle expected to be observed *[the* laws of health*]* **10.** *Eccles.* a divine commandment **11.** *Math., Logic,* etc. a general principle to which all applicable cases must conform *[the* laws of exponents*]* —**go to law** to take a dispute to a law court for settlement —**lay down the law 1.** to give orders in an authoritative manner **2.** to give a scolding (*to*) —**read law** to study to become a lawyer —**the Law 1.** the Mosaic law, or the part of the Hebrew Scriptures containing it; specif., the Pentateuch **2.** [l-] [Colloq.] a policeman or the police

**law·a·bid·ing** (lô'ə bīd'iŋ) *adj.* obeying the law

**law·break·er** (-brā'kər) *n.* a person who violates the law —**law'break'ing** *adj., n.*

**law court** a court for administering justice under the law

**law·ful** (-fəl) *adj.* **1.** in conformity with the law; permitted by law *[a lawful* act*]* **2.** recognized by law; just *[lawful* debts*]* —**law'ful·ly** *adv.* —**law'ful·ness** *n.*

**law·giv·er** (-giv'ər) *n.* one who draws up or enacts a code of laws for a nation or people; lawmaker; legislator —**law'giv'ing** *n., adj.*

**law·less** (-lis) *adj.* **1.** without law; not regulated by the authority of law *[a lawless* city*]* **2.** not in conformity with law; illegal *[lawless* practices*]* **3.** not obeying the law; unruly —**law'less·ly** *adv.* —**law'less·ness** *n.*

**law·mak·er** (-mā'kər) *n.* one who makes or helps to make laws; esp., a legislator —**law'mak'ing** *adj., n.*

**law·man** (-man') *n., pl.* **-men'** (-men') a law officer; esp., a marshal, sheriff, etc.

**lawn¹** (lôn) *n.* [< OFr. < Bret. *lann,* country] land covered with grass kept closely mowed, esp. around a house —**lawn'y** *adj.*

**lawn²** (lôn) *n.* [< *Laon,* city in France, where made] a fine, sheer cloth of linen or cotton, used for blouses, curtains, etc. —**lawn'y** *adj.*

**lawn mower** a hand-propelled or power-driven machine for cutting the grass of a lawn

**lawn tennis** *see* TENNIS

**Law·rence¹** (lôr'əns, lär'-) **1.** a masculine name: see LAURENCE **2.** D(avid) H(erbert), 1885–1930; Eng. novelist & poet **3.** T(homas) E(dward), (changed name, 1927, to *Thomas Edward Shaw*) 1888–1935; Brit. adventurer & writer: called **Lawrence of Arabia**

**Law·rence²** (lôr'əns, lär'-) [after A. *Lawrence* (1814–86) of Boston] city in NE Mass.: pop. 63,000

**law·ren·ci·um** (lô ren'sē əm, lä-) *n.* [after E. O. *Lawrence,* 20th-c. U.S. physicist] a radioactive chemical element produced by nuclear bombardment of californium: symbol, Lr; at. wt., 256 (?); at. no., 103

**law·suit** (lô'sōōt') *n.* a suit at law between private parties; case before a civil court

**Law·ton** (lôt'n) [after Gen. H. W. *Lawton* (1843–99)] city in SW Okla.: pop. 80,000

**law·yer** (lô'yər) *n.* a person whose profession is advising others in matters of law or representing them in lawsuits

**lax** (laks) *adj.* [L. *laxus*] **1.** loose; slack; not rigid or tight **2.** not strict or exact; careless *[lax* morals*]* —**lax'ly** *adv.* —**lax'ness** *n.*

**lax·a·tive** (lak'sə tiv) *adj.* [< OFr. < ML. *laxativus* < LL. < pp. of L. *laxare* < *laxus,* loose] tending to make lax; specif., making the bowels loose and relieving constipation —*n.* any laxative medicine

**lax·i·ty** (lak'sə tē) *n.* lax quality or condition

**lay¹** (lā) *vt.* **laid, lay'ing** [OE. *lecgan* < pt. base of OE. *licgan,* to LIE¹] **1.** to cause to fall with force; knock down *[one punch laid* him low*]* **2.** to place or put so as to rest, lie, etc.; deposit (with *on, in,* etc.) *[lay* the pen on the desk*]*

**3.** *a)* to put down (bricks, carpeting, etc.) in the correct way for a specific purpose *b)* to situate in a particular place *[the* scene is *laid* in France*]* **4.** to place; put; set *[to lay* emphasis on accuracy*]* **5.** to produce and deposit (an egg or eggs) **6.** *a)* to cause to settle *[to lay* the dust*]* *b)* to allay, overcome, or appease *[to lay* one's fears*]* **7.** to smooth down *[to lay* the nap of cloth*]* **8.** to stake as a bet; wager **9.** to impose (a tax, penalty, etc. *on* or *upon*) **10.** to work out; devise *[to lay* plans*]* **11.** to set (a table) with silverware, plates, etc. **12.** to present or assert *[to lay* claim to property*]* **13.** to attribute; charge; impute *[to lay* the blame on Tom*]* —*vi.* **1.** to lay an egg or eggs **2.** to lie; recline: a dialectal or substantial usage **3.** *Naut.* to go; proceed *[all* hands *lay* aft to the fantail*]* —*n.* the way in which something is situated or arranged *[the* lay of the land*]* —**lay aside** to set aside for the future; save: also **lay away, lay by** —**lay down 1.** to sacrifice (one's life) **2.** to declare emphatically **3.** to store away, as wine in a cellar —**lay for** [Colloq.] to be waiting to attack —**lay in** to get and store away —**lay into** [Slang] to attack with blows or words —**lay it on (thick)** [Colloq.] **1.** to exaggerate **2.** to flatter effusively —**lay off 1.** to discharge (an employee), esp. temporarily **2.** to mark off the boundaries of **3.** [Slang] to cease —**lay on 1.** to spread on **2.** to attack with force —**lay oneself open** to expose oneself to attack, blame, etc. —**lay open 1.** to cut open **2.** to expose —**lay out 1.** to spend **2.** to arrange according to a plan **3.** to spread out (clothes, equipment, etc.) **4.** to make (a dead body) ready for burial **5.** [Slang] to scold (someone) —**lay over** to stop a while in a place before going on —**lay to 1.** to attribute to **2.** to apply oneself with vigor —**lay up 1.** to store for future use **2.** to disable; confine to bed or the sickroom

**lay²** (lā) *pt. of* LIE¹

**lay³** (lā) *adj.* [< OFr. < LL. *laicus* < Gr. < *lāos,* the people] **1.** of the laity, or ordinary people, as distinguished from the clergy **2.** not belonging to or connected with a given profession *[a* legal handbook for *lay* readers*]*

**lay⁴** (lā) *n.* [OFr. *lai*] **1.** a short poem, esp. a narrative poem, for singing **2.** [Archaic or Poet.] a song or melody

**lay·a·bout** (lā'ə bout') *n.* [Chiefly Brit. Colloq.] a lazy idler or loafer; bum

**lay analyst** a psychoanalyst who is not a medical doctor

**lay·a·way (plan)** (lā'ə wā') a method of buying by making a deposit on something which is delivered only after it is paid for in full

**lay·er** (lā'ər) *n.* **1.** a person or thing that lays **2.** a single thickness, coat, fold, or stratum **3.** a shoot (of a living plant) bent down and partly covered with earth so that it may take root —*vt., vi.* to grow (a plant) by means of a layer

**layer cake** a cake of two or more layers, with icing, preserves, etc. between them

**lay·ette** (lā et') *n.* [Fr., dim. of *laie,* drawer < Fl. < MDu. *lade,* a chest] a complete outfit for a newborn baby, including clothes, bedding, etc.

**lay figure** [earlier *layman* < Du. < MDu. *led,* limb + *man,* man] **1.** an artist's jointed model of the human form, on which drapery is arranged **2.** a person who is a mere puppet or a nonentity

**lay·man** (lā'mən) *n., pl.* **-men** [LAY³ + MAN] **1.** a member of the laity; person not a clergyman **2.** a person not belonging to or skilled in a given profession

**lay·off** (lā'ôf') *n.* the act of laying off; esp., temporary unemployment, or the period of this

**lay of the land 1.** the arrangement of the natural features of an area **2.** the existing state of affairs Also **lie of the land**

**lay·out** (lā'out') *n.* **1.** the act of laying something out **2.** the manner in which anything is laid out; arrangement; specif., the plan or makeup of a newspaper, page, advertisement, etc. **3.** the thing laid out **4.** an outfit or set **5.** [Colloq.] a residence, factory, etc., esp. when large

**lay·o·ver** (-ō'vər) *n.* a stopping for a while in some place during a journey

**la·zar** (laz'ər, lā'zər) *n.* [< ML. *lazarus,* leper < LL. < Gr. *Lazaros,* LAZARUS] [Rare] a poor, diseased, esp. leprous person

**laz·a·ret·to** (laz'ə ret'ō) *n., pl.* **-tos** [It. < Santa Madonna di *Nazaret,* Venetian church used as a plague hospital; initial *l-* after *lazzaro,* leper] formerly, a public hospital for poor people having contagious diseases, esp. for lepers: also **laz'a·ret'**, **laz'a·rette'** (-ret')

**Laz·a·rus** (laz'ə rəs) *Bible* **1.** the brother of Mary and Martha, raised from the dead by Jesus: John 11 **2.** the diseased beggar in Jesus' parable: Luke 16:19–31

**laze** (lāz) *vi.* **lazed, laz'ing** to be lazy or idle —*vt.* to spend (time, etc.) in idleness

**la·zy** (lā'zē) *adj.* **-zi·er, -zi·est** [prob. < MLowG. or MDu.] **1.** not eager or willing to work or exert oneself; indolent; slothful **2.** slow and heavy; sluggish *[a lazy* river*]* —*vi., vt.* **-zied, -zy·ing** same as LAZE —**la'zi·ly** *adv.* —**la'zi·ness** *n.*

**la·zy·bones** (-bōnz') *n.* [Colloq.] a lazy person
**Lazy Susan** a revolving tray with sections for relishes, condiments, etc.
**lb.** [L. *libra*, pl. *librae*] pound; pounds
**lbs.** pounds
**L/C, l/c** letter of credit
**l.c. 1.** [L. *loco citato*] in the place cited **2.** *Printing* lower case
**LCD** [*l(iquid)-c(rystal) d(isplay)*] a device for alphanumeric displays, as on digital watches, with a sealed-in liquid crystal activated by an external light source
**L.C.D., l.c.d.** least (or lowest) common denominator
**L.C.M., l.c.m.** least (or lowest) common multiple
**LDC** less developed country
**lea** (lē) *n.* [OE. *leah*] [Chiefly Poet.] a meadow, grassy field, or pasture; grassland
**leach** (lēch) *vt.* [prob. < OE. *leccan*, to water] **1.** to cause (a liquid) to filter down through some material **2.** to wash (wood ashes, etc.) with a filtering liquid **3.** to extract (a soluble substance) from some material [lye is *leached* from wood ashes] —*vi.* **1.** to lose soluble matter through a filtering liquid **2.** to dissolve and be washed away —*n.* **1.** a leaching **2.** a sievelike container used in leaching —**leach'·a·ble** *adj.* —**leach'er** *n.*
**lead**¹ (lēd) *vt.* **led, lead'ing** [OE. *lædan*] **1.** *a)* to direct the course of by going before or along with; conduct; guide *b)* to mark the way for [lights to *lead* you there] **2.** to guide by physical contact, pulling a rope, etc. [to *lead* a horse] **3.** to conduct (water, steam, rope, etc.) in a certain direction, channel, etc. **4.** to direct by influence, etc. to a course of action or thought; cause; prompt **5.** to be the head or leader of (an expedition, orchestra, etc.) **6.** *a)* to be at the head of [to *lead* one's class] *b)* to be ahead of by a specified margin **7.** to live; spend [to *lead* a hard life] **8.** *Card Games* to begin the play with (a card or suit) —*vi.* **1.** to show the way by going before or along; act as guide **2.** to submit to being led: said esp. of a horse **3.** to be or form a way (*to, from, under,* etc.); go **4.** to come, or bring one, as a result (with *to*) [one thing *led* to another] **5.** to be or go first **6.** *Boxing* to aim a first blow **7.** *Card Games* to play the first card —*n.* **1.** leadership **2.** example [follow his *lead*] **3.** *a)* first or front place; precedence *b)* the amount or distance ahead [to hold a safe *lead*] **4.** *same as* LEASH **5.** anything that leads, as a clue **6.** *Baseball* a position taken by a base runner away from his base in the direction of the next **7.** *Boxing* a blow used in leading **8.** *Card Games* the right of playing first, or the card or suit played **9.** *Elec.* a wire carrying current from one point to another in a circuit **10.** *Journalism* the opening paragraph of a news story **11.** *Mining* a stratum of ore **12.** *Music* the main melody in a harmonic composition **13.** *Theater a)* a main role *b)* an actor or actress playing such a role —*adj.* acting as leader [the *lead* horse] —**lead off** to begin —**lead on 1.** to conduct further **2.** to lure —**lead up to 1.** to prepare the way for **2.** to approach (a subject, etc.) in an indirect way
**lead**² (led) *n.* [OE.] **1.** a heavy, soft, malleable, bluish-gray metallic chemical element used for piping and in numerous alloys: symbol, Pb; at. wt., 207.19; at. no., 82 **2.** anything made of this metal; specif., *a)* a weight for sounding depths at sea, etc. *b)* *Printing* a thin strip of type metal inserted to increase the space between lines of type **3.** bullets **4.** a thin stick of graphite, used in pencils —*adj.* made of or containing lead —*vt.* **1.** to cover, line, or weight with lead **2.** *Printing* to increase the space between (lines of type) by inserting leads
**lead·en** (led''n) *adj.* **1.** made of lead **2.** having the heaviness of lead; hard to move **3.** sluggish; dull **4.** depressed; gloomy **5.** of a dull gray —**lead'en·ly** *adv.*
**lead·er** (lē'dər) *n.* **1.** a person or thing that leads; guiding head **2.** a horse harnessed before all others or in the foremost span **3.** a pipe for carrying fluid **4.** a tendon **5.** a section of blank film or recording tape at the beginning of a reel **6.** a featured, low-priced article of trade **7.** *Bot.* the central stem of a plant **8.** *Fishing* a short piece of catgut, etc. attaching the hook, lure, etc. to the fish line **9.** *Music a)* a conductor, esp. of a band *b)* the main performer, as in a vocal section **10.** [pl.] *Printing* dots, dashes, etc. in a line, used to direct the eye across the page —**lead'er·less** *adj.* —**lead'er·ship'** *n.*
**lead glass** (led) glass that contains lead oxide
**lead-in** (lēd'in') *n.* **1.** the wire leading from an aerial or antenna to a receiver or transmitter **2.** an introduction —*adj.* that is a lead-in
**lead·ing**¹ (led'iŋ) *n.* **1.** a covering or being covered with lead **2.** strips or sheets of lead
**lead·ing**² (lē'diŋ) *n.* guidance; direction —*adj.* **1.** that leads; guiding **2.** principal; chief **3.** playing the lead in a play, motion picture, etc.

**lead·ing edge** (lē'diŋ) *Aeron.* the front edge of a propeller blade or airfoil
**lead·ing light** (lē'diŋ) an important or influential member of a club, community, etc.
**lead·ing question** (lē'diŋ) a question put in such a way as to suggest the answer sought
**lead-off** (lēd'ôf') *n.* the first in a series of actions, moves, etc. or in a baseball lineup
**lead pencil** (led) a pencil consisting of a slender stick of graphite encased in wood, etc.
**lead poisoning** (led) an acute or chronic poisoning caused by the absorption of lead into the body
**lead tetraethyl** *same as* TETRAETHYL LEAD
**lead time** (lēd) the period of time from the decision to make a product to its actual production
**leaf** (lēf) *n., pl.* **leaves** [OE. *leaf*] **1.** any of the flat, thin, expanded organs, usually green, growing from the stem of a plant **2.** popularly, *a)* the blade of a leaf *b)* a petal **3.** leaves collectively [choice tobacco *leaf*] **4.** a sheet of paper with a page on each side **5.** *a)* a thin sheet of metal *b)* such sheets collectively [gold *leaf*] **6.** *a)* a hinged section of a table top *b)* a board inserted into a table top to increase its surface **7.** a flat, hinged or movable part of a folding door, shutter, etc. —*vi.* **1.** to bear leaves (often with *out*) **2.** to turn the pages of a book, etc. (with *through*) —*vt.* to turn the pages of —**in leaf** with foliage —**take a leaf from someone's book** to follow someone's example —**turn over a new leaf** to start anew —**leaf'less** *adj.* —**leaf'like'** *adj.*
**leaf·age** (-ij) *n.* leaves collectively; foliage
**leaf bud** a bud from which only stems and leaves develop
**leaf hopper** an insect that leaps from one plant to another, sucking the juices and often transmitting plant diseases
**leaf lard** a high-grade lard, made from the heavily layered fat (**leaf fat**) around the kidneys of a hog
**leaf·let** (-lit) *n.* **1.** one of the divisions of a compound leaf **2.** a small or young leaf **3.** a separate sheet of printed matter, often folded but not stitched
**leaf·stalk** (-stôk') *n.* the slender portion of a leaf, which supports the blade and is attached to the stem
**leaf·y** (lē'fē) *adj.* **leaf'i·er, leaf'i·est 1.** of, consisting of, or like a leaf or leaves **2.** having many leaves **3.** having broad leaves, as spinach —**leaf'i·ness** *n.*
**league**¹ (lēg) *n.* [< OFr. < It. *liga* < *legare* < L. *ligare,* to bind] **1.** a covenant made by nations, groups, or individuals for promoting common interests, etc. **2.** an association or alliance formed by such a covenant **3.** *Sports* a group of teams organized to compete against one another **4.** [Colloq.] a division according to grade or quality —*vt., vi.* **leagued, leagu'ing** to form into a league —**in league** allied —**leagu'er** *n.*
**league**² (lēg) *n.* [< OFr. < LL. *leuga,* Gallic mile < Celt.] a measure of distance varying in different times and countries, usually about 3 miles in English-speaking countries
**League of Nations** an association of nations (1920–46) to promote international cooperation and peace: it was succeeded by the United Nations
**Le·ah** (lē'ə) [? Heb. *lē'āh,* gazelle, or ? *lā'āh,* to tire, weary] **1.** a feminine name **2.** *Bible* the elder of the sisters who were wives of Jacob: Gen. 29:13–30
**leak** (lēk) *vi.* [< ON. *leka,* to drip] **1.** to let a fluid substance out or in accidentally [the boat *leaks*] **2.** to enter or escape in this way, as a fluid (often with *in* or *out*) **3.** to become known little by little [the truth *leaked* out] —*vt.* **1.** to allow to leak **2.** to allow to become known —*n.* **1.** an accidental hole or crack that lets something out or in **2.** any means of escape for something that ought not to be let out, lost, etc. **3.** leakage **4.** a disclosure, supposedly accidental but actually intentional: in full, **news leak 5.** *a)* a loss of electrical charge through faulty insulation *b)* the point where this occurs
**leak·age** (-ij) *n.* **1.** an act or instance of leaking; leak **2.** something that leaks in or out **3.** the amount that leaks in or out
**leak·y** (lē'kē) *adj.* **leak'i·er, leak'i·est** having a leak or leaks —**leak'i·ness** *n.*
**leal** (lēl) *adj.* [< OFr. < L. *legalis:* see LEGAL] [Archaic or Scot.] loyal; true —**leal'ly** *adv.*
**lean**¹ (lēn) *vi.* **leaned** or **leant, lean'ing** [OE. *hlinian*] **1.** to bend or deviate from an upright position; stand at a slant; incline **2.** to bend the body so as to rest part of one's weight upon something [he *leaned* on the desk] **3.** to depend for aid, etc.; rely (*on* or *upon*) **4.** to have a particular mental inclination; tend (*toward* or *to*) —*vt.* to cause to lean —*n.* an inclination; slant —**lean'er** *n.*
**lean**² (lēn) *adj.* [OE. *hlæne*] **1.** with little flesh or fat; thin; spare **2.** containing little or no fat: said of meat **3.** lacking in richness, profit, etc.; meager —*n.* meat containing little or no fat —**lean'ly** *adv.* —**lean'ness** *n.*

**Le·an·der** (lē an′dər) *Gr. Legend* the lover of Hero: see HERO

**lean·ing** (lē′niŋ) *n.* **1.** the act of a person or thing that leans **2.** tendency; inclination

**leant** (lent) *alt. pt. & pp. of* LEAN[1]

**lean-to** (lēn′tōō′) *n., pl.* **lean′-tos′** **1.** a shed with a sloping roof resting against trees, etc. **2.** a structure whose sloping roof abuts a wall or building

**leap** (lēp) *vi.* **leaped** or **leapt** (lept, lēpt), **leap′ing** [OE. *hleapan*] **1.** to jump; spring **2.** to move suddenly or swiftly, as if by jumping; bound **3.** to accept eagerly something offered (with *at*) —*vt.* **1.** to pass over by a jump **2.** to cause to leap [to *leap* a horse over a wall] —*n.* **1.** a jump; spring **2.** the distance covered in a jump **3.** a place that is, or is to be, leaped over or from —**by leaps and bounds** very rapidly —**leap in the dark** a risky act whose consequences cannot be foreseen —**leap′er** *n.*

**leap·frog** (-frôg′, -fräg′) *n.* a game in which each player in turn jumps over the bent back of each of the other players —*vi.* **-frogged′, -frog′ging** **1.** to skip (*over*) **2.** to progress in jumps or stages —*vt.* to jump or skip over

**leap year** a year of 366 days, occurring every fourth year: the additional day is February 29: a leap year is a year whose number is exactly divisible by four, or, in the case of century years, by 400

**Lear** (lir) **1.** *see* KING LEAR **2.** Edward, 1812–88; Eng. humorist

**learn** (lurn) *vt.* **learned** or **learnt** (lurnt), **learn′ing** [OE. *leornian*] **1.** to get knowledge of (a subject) or skill in (an art, trade, etc.) by study, experience, etc. **2.** to come to know [to *learn* what happened] **3.** to come to know how [to *learn* to swim] **4.** to memorize **5.** to acquire as a habit or attitude **6.** [Dial.] to teach —*vi.* **1.** to gain knowledge or skill **2.** to be informed; hear (*of* or *about*) —**learn′a·ble** *adj.* —**learn′er** *n.*

**learn·ed** (lur′nid; *for 3* lurnd) *adj.* **1.** having or showing much learning; erudite **2.** of or characterized by study and learning **3.** acquired by study, experience, etc. [a *learned* response] —**learn′ed·ly** *adv.* —**learn′ed·ness** *n.*

**learn·ing** (lur′niŋ) *n.* **1.** the acquiring of knowledge or skill **2.** acquired knowledge or skill

**lease** (lēs) *n.* [< Anglo-Fr. *les* < OFr. < L. *laxare*, to loosen (< *laxus*, loose] a contract by which a landlord gives to a tenant the use of lands, buildings, etc. for a specified time and for fixed payments; also, the period of time specified —*vt.* **leased, leas′ing** **1.** to give by a lease; let **2.** to get by a lease —**new lease on life** another chance to lead a happy life, be successful, etc. because of a new turn of events —**leas′a·ble** *adj.* —**leas′er** *n.*

**leash** (lēsh) *n.* [< OFr. < L. *laxa*, fem. of *laxus*, loose] a cord, strap, etc. by which a dog or other animal is held in check —*vt.* **1.** to put a leash on **2.** to control as by a leash —**hold in leash** to control —**strain at the leash** to be impatient to be free

**least** (lēst) *adj. alt. superl. of* LITTLE [< OE. *læsest, læst*, superl. of *læssa*, LESS] smallest in size, degree, importance, etc. —*adv.* in the smallest degree —*n.* the smallest in size, amount, importance, etc. —**at (the) least** **1.** with no less **2.** at any rate —**not in the least** not at all

**least common denominator** the least common multiple of the denominators of two or more fractions

**least common multiple** the smallest positive whole number that is exactly divisible by two or more given whole numbers [the *least common multiple* of 4, 5, and 10 is 20]

**least·wise** (-wīz′) *adv.* [Colloq.] at least; anyway Also [Chiefly Dial.] **least′ways** (-wāz′)

**leath·er** (leth′ər) *n.* [OE. *lether-*] **1.** animal skin prepared for use by removing the hair and tanning **2.** any article made of this —*adj.* of or made of leather —*vt.* [Colloq.] to whip with a leather strap

**Leath·er·ette** (leth′ə ret′) a trademark for imitation leather made of paper or cloth —*n.* [l-] such imitation leather

**leath·ern** (leth′ərn) *adj.* made of or like leather

**leath·er·neck** (leth′ər nek′) *n.* [from the leather-lined collar, formerly part of the Marine uniform] [Slang] a U.S. Marine

**leath·er·y** (-ē) *adj.* like leather; tough and flexible —**leath′er·i·ness** *n.*

**leave**[1] (lēv) *vt.* **left, leav′ing** [OE. *læfan*, lit., to let remain] **1.** to allow to remain [leave some cake for me] **2.** to make, place, etc., and cause to remain behind one [to *leave* footprints] **3.** to have remaining after one [the deceased *leaves* a widow] **4.** to bequeath **5.** to entrust (with *to* or *up to*) [to *leave* a decision to another] **6.** to give as a remainder [ten minus two *leaves* eight] **7.** to go away from **8.** to cause to be in a certain condition [the flood *left* them homeless] **9.** to abandon; forsake **10.** to stop living in, working for, or belonging to **11.** [Dial.] to let or allow [*leave* us go now] —*vi.* to go away or set out —**leave off** **1.** to stop; cease **2.** to stop doing or using —**leave out** **1.** to omit **2.** to fail to consider —**leave (someone) alone** to refrain from bothering (someone) —**leav′er** *n.*

**leave**[2] (lēv) *n.* [OE. *leaf*] **1.** permission **2.** *a*) permission to be absent from duty or work *b*) the period for which this is granted —**by your leave** with your permission —**on leave** absent from duty with permission —**take leave of** to say goodbye to —**take one's leave** to depart

**leave**[3] (lēv) *vi.* **leaved, leav′ing** [see LEAF] to put forth, or bear, leaves; leaf

**leaved** (lēvd) *adj.* having leaves [narrow-*leaved*]

**leav·en** (lev′'n) *n.* [< OFr. < L. *levamen*, alleviation < *levare*, to raise] **1.** a small piece of fermenting dough used for producing fermentation in a fresh batch of dough **2.** *same as* LEAVENING —*vt.* **1.** to make (batter or dough) rise with a leavening agent **2.** to spread through, causing a gradual change

**leav·en·ing** (-iŋ) *n.* **1.** a substance, such as yeast, used to make batter or dough rise by the formation of gas: also **leavening agent** **2.** any influence working on something to bring about a gradual change

**Leav·en·worth** (lev′'n wurth′) [after U.S. Army Col. H. *Leavenworth* (1783–1834)] city in NE Kans.: site of a Federal prison: pop. 34,000

**leave of absence** a leave from work or duty, esp. for a long time; also, the period of time

**leaves** (lēvz) *n. pl. of* LEAF

**leave-tak·ing** (lēv′tāk′iŋ) *n.* the act of taking leave, or saying goodbye

**leav·ings** (-iŋz) *n.pl.* leftovers, remnants, refuse, etc.

**Leb·a·non** (leb′ə nən) country in SW Asia, on the Mediterranean: c.4,000 sq. mi.; pop. 2,367,000; cap. Beirut —**Leb·a·nese′** (-nēz′) *adj., n., pl.* **-nese′**

**lech·er** (lech′ər) *n.* [< OFr. < *lechier*, to be a debauchee, lit., lick] a lewd, grossly sensual man

**lech·er·ous** (-əs) *adj.* lustful; lewd —**lech′er·ous·ly** *adv.* —**lech′er·ous·ness** *n.*

**lech·er·y** (-ē) *n., pl.* **-er·ies** gross sensuality

**lec·i·thin** (les′ə thin) *n.* [< Gr. *lekithos*, yolk of an egg + -IN[1]] a fatty compound found in nerve tissue, blood, egg yolk, and some vegetables: used in medicines, foods, cosmetics, etc.

**Le Cor·bu·sier** (lə kôr bü zyā′) (pseud. of *Charles-Édouard Jeanneret-Gris*) 1887–1965; Swiss architect in France

**lec·tern** (lek′tərn) *n.* [< OFr. < ML. *lectrum* < L. pp. of *legere*, to read] **1.** a reading desk in a church; esp., such a desk from which a part of the Scriptures is read during the service **2.** a stand for holding the notes, speech, etc., as of a lecturer

**lec·ture** (lek′chər) *n.* [< ML. *lectura* < pp. of *legere*, to read] **1.** an informative talk given before an audience, class, etc., and usually prepared beforehand **2.** a lengthy scolding —*vi.* **-tured, -tur·ing** to give a lecture —*vt.* to give a lecture to —**lec′tur·er** *n.* —**lec′ture·ship′** *n.*

LECTERN

**led** (led) *pt. & pp. of* LEAD[1]

**LED** [*l(ight-)e(mitting) d(iode)*] a semiconductor diode that emits light when voltage is applied: used in lamps, digital watches, etc.

**Le·da** (lē′də) *Gr. Myth.* the mother of Clytemnestra and Castor and Pollux and (by Zeus, who visited her in the form of a swan) of Helen of Troy

**ledge** (lej) *n.* [prob. < ME. *leggen*: see ff.] **1.** a shelf **2.** a projecting ridge of rocks **3.** *Mining* a vein

**ledg·er** (lej′ər) *n.* [prob. < ME. *leggen*, to lay, or *liggen*, to lie] *Bookkeeping* the book of final entry, in which a record of debits, credits, and all money transactions is kept

**ledger line** *same as* LEGER LINE

**Lee** (lē) **1.** [var. of LEIGH] a masculine or feminine name **2.** **Henry,** 1756–1818; Am. general in the Revolutionary War: called *Light-Horse Harry Lee* **3.** **Robert E(dward),** 1807–70; Confederate commander in chief: son of *Henry*

**lee** (lē) *n.* [OE. *hleo*, shelter] **1.** shelter; protection **2.** a sheltered place, esp. one on the side away from the wind **3.** *Naut.* the side or part away from the wind —*adj.* of or on the side away from the wind

**leech**[1] (lēch) *n.* [OE. *læce*] **1.** formerly, a physician **2.** any of a number of annelid worms with suckers, living in water or wet earth: one bloodsucking species was formerly used to bleed patients **3.** a person who is a parasite —*vt.* **1.** to bleed with leeches **2.** to drain dry —*vi.* to act as a parasite

**leech**[2] (lēch) *n.* [LME. *lyche*] the free or outside edge of a sail

**Leeds** (lēdz) city in Yorkshire, N England: pop. 506,000

**leek** (lēk) *n.* [OE. *leac*] an onionlike vegetable having a bulb with a cylindrical stem, and broad leaves

**leer** (lir) *n.* [OE. *hleor*] a sly, sidelong look showing salaciousness, malicious triumph, etc. —*vi.* to look with a leer —**leer′ing·ly** *adv.*

LEECH
(to 3 in. long)

**leer·y** (lir′ē) *adj.* **leer′i·er, leer′i·est** wary; suspicious
**lees** (lēz) *n.pl.* [< OFr. < ML. *lia*] dregs or sediment, as of wine
**lee·ward** (lē′wərd; *naut.* lōō′ərd) *adj.* in the direction toward which the wind blows; of the lee side: opposed to WINDWARD —*n.* the lee part or side —*adv.* toward the lee
**Lee·ward Islands** (lē′wərd) N group of islands in the Lesser Antilles of the West Indies
**lee·way** (lē′wā′) *n.* **1.** the leeward drift of a ship or aircraft from the true course **2.** [Colloq.] *a)* margin of time, money, etc. *b)* room for freedom of action
**left**[1] (left) *adj.* [OE. *lyft*, weak] **1.** *a)* designating or of that side of one's body which is toward the west when one faces north, the side of the less-used hand in most people *b)* designating or of the corresponding side of anything *c)* closer to the left side of a person directly facing the thing mentioned **2.** of the bank of a river on the left of a person facing downstream **3.** of the political left; radical or liberal —*n.* **1.** *a)* all or part of the left side *b)* a direction or location on the left side *c)* a turn toward the left side **2.** *Boxing a)* the left hand *b)* a blow delivered with the left hand **3.** [*often* L-] *Politics* a radical or liberal position, party, etc. (often with *the*): from the location of their seats in some European legislatures —*adv.* on or toward the left hand or left side
**left**[2] (left) *pt. & pp. of* LEAVE[1]
**left-hand** (left′hand′) *adj.* **1.** on or directed toward the left **2.** of, for, or with the left hand
**left-hand·ed** (-han′did) *adj.* **1.** using the left hand more skillfully than the right **2.** done with the left hand **3.** clumsy; awkward **4.** designating an insincere or ambiguous compliment **5.** made for use with the left hand **6.** turning from right to left —*adv.* with the left hand [to write *left-handed*] —**left′-hand′ed·ly** *adv.* —**left′-hand′ed·ness** *n.* —**left′-hand′er** *n.*
**left·ist** (-ist) *n.* a person whose political position is radical or liberal; member of the left —*adj.* radical or liberal —**left′ism** *n.*
**left·o·ver** (-ō′vər) *n.* something left over, as from a meal —*adj.* remaining unused, etc.
**left·ward** (-wərd) *adv., adj.* on or toward the left: also **left′wards** *adv.*
**left wing** the more radical or liberal section of a political party, group, etc. —**left′-wing′** *adj.* —**left′-wing′er** *n.*
**left·y** (lef′tē) *n., pl.* **left′ies** [Slang] a left-handed person: often used as a nickname
**leg** (leg) *n.* [< ON. *leggr*] **1.** one of the parts of the body by means of which animals stand and walk: in human beings, either of the two lower limbs **2.** a cut of meat consisting of the leg **3.** the part of a garment covering the leg **4.** anything resembling a leg in shape or use, as one of the supports of a piece of furniture **5.** any of the stages of a course or journey **6.** *Math.* either of the sides of a triangle other than its base or, in a right-angled triangle, its hypotenuse —*vi.* **legged, leg′ging** [Colloq.] to walk or run: used chiefly in the phr. **leg it** —**get up on one's hind legs** [Colloq.] to become assertive, aggressive, etc. —**not have a leg to stand on** [Colloq.] to have absolutely no defense, excuse, etc. —**on one's** (or **its**) **last legs** [Colloq.] not far from death, breakdown, etc. —**pull someone's leg** [Colloq.] to make fun of or fool someone —**shake a leg** [Slang] to hurry —**stretch one's legs** to walk, esp. after sitting a long time —**leg′less** *adj.*
**leg.** **1.** legal **2.** legislative **3.** legislature
**leg·a·cy** (leg′ə sē) *n., pl.* **-cies** [< OFr. *legacie* < ML. < L. *legatus:* see LEGATE] **1.** money or property left to someone by a will **2.** anything handed down from, or as from, an ancestor
**le·gal** (lē′gəl) *adj.* [< MFr. < L. *legalis* < *lex* (gen. *legis*), *law*] **1.** of, based on, or authorized by law **2.** permitted by law [a *legal* act] **3.** that can be enforced in a court of law **4.** of or applicable to lawyers [*legal* ethics] **5.** in terms of the law [a *legal* offense] —**le′gal·ly** *adv.*
**le·gal·ese** (lē′gə lēz′) *n.* the special vocabulary of legal forms, documents, etc., often thought of by the layman as incomprehensible
**legal holiday** a holiday set by statute
**le·gal·ism** (lē′gəl iz'm) *n.* strict, often too strict and literal, adherence to law —**le′gal·ist** *n.* —**le′gal·is′tic** *adj.*
**le·gal·i·ty** (li gal′ə tē) *n., pl.* **-ties** quality, condition, or instance of being legal or lawful
**le·gal·ize** (lē′gəl līz′) *vt.* **-ized′, -iz′ing** to make legal or lawful —**le′gal·i·za′tion** *n.*
**legal tender** money that may be legally offered in payment of an obligation and that a creditor must accept
**leg·ate** (leg′it) *n.* [< OFr. < L. pp. of *legare*, to send as ambassador < *lex*, law] an envoy or ambassador, esp. one officially representing the Pope —**leg′ate·ship′** *n.*

**leg·a·tee** (leg′ə tē′) *n.* one to whom a legacy is bequeathed
**le·ga·tion** (li gā′shən) *n.* **1.** a diplomatic minister and his staff, representing their government in a foreign country and ranking just below an embassy **2.** their headquarters
**le·ga·to** (li gät′ō) *adj., adv.* [It., pp. of *legare* < L. *ligare*, to tie] *Music* in a smooth, even style, with no noticeable interruption between the notes
**leg·end** (lej′ənd) *n.* [< OFr. < ML. *legenda*, things to be read < L. neut. pl. gerundive of *legere*, to read] **1.** *a)* a story handed down for generations and popularly believed to have a historical basis: cf. MYTH *b)* all such stories belonging to a particular group of people **2.** *a)* a notable person much talked about in his own time *b)* the stories of his exploits **3.** an inscription on a coin, medal, etc. **4.** a descriptive title, key, etc., as under an illustration
**leg·end·ar·y** (lej′ən der′ē) *adj.* of, based on, or presented in legends; traditional
**leg·end·ry** (-drē) *n.* legends collectively
**leg·er·de·main** (lej′ər di mān′) *n.* [< MFr. *leger de main*, lit., light of hand] **1.** sleight of hand; tricks of a stage magician **2.** trickery; deceit
**leg·er line** (lej′ər) [altered < *ledger line*] *Music* a short line written above or below the staff, for notes beyond the range of the staff
**leg·ged** (leg′id, legd) *adj.* having (a specified number or kind of) legs [long-*legged*]
**leg·ging** (leg′in, -ən) *n.* a covering of canvas, leather, etc. for protecting the leg below the knee
**leg·gy** (leg′ē) *adj.* **-gi·er, -gi·est** **1.** having long and awkward legs [a *leggy* colt] **2.** [Colloq.] having long, well-shaped legs —**leg′gi·ness** *n.*
**Leg·horn** (leg′hôrn, leg′ərn) city in Tuscany, W Italy: pop. 172,000 —*n.* [after prec.] **1.** [*sometimes* l-] any of a breed of small chicken, orig. developed in the Mediterranean region **2.** [l-] *a)* a plaiting made of an Italian wheat straw *b)* a broad-brimmed hat of this straw
**leg·i·ble** (lej′ə b'l) *adj.* [< LL. *legibilis* < *legere*, to read] **1.** that can be read or deciphered **2.** that can be read easily —**leg′i·bil′i·ty** *n.* —**leg′i·bly** *adv.*
**le·gion** (lē′jən) *n.* [< OFr. < L. *legio* < *legere*, to select] **1.** *Rom. History* a military division varying at times from 3,000 to 6,000 foot soldiers, with additional cavalrymen **2.** a large group of soldiers; army **3.** a large number; multitude
**le·gion·ar·y** (-er′ē) *adj.* of or constituting a legion —*n., pl.* **-ar′ies** a member of a legion
**le·gion·naire** (lē′jə ner′) *n.* [< Fr. < L.] a member of a legion
**leg·is·late** (lej′is lāt′) *vi.* **-lat′ed, -lat′ing** [< LEGISLATOR] to make or pass a law or laws —*vt.* to cause to be, become, go, etc. by making laws
**leg·is·la·tion** (lej′is lā′shən) *n.* [< LL. < L. *lex* (gen. *legis*), law + *latio*, a proposing < pp. of *ferre*, to BEAR[1]] **1.** the making of a law or laws **2.** the law or laws made
**leg·is·la·tive** (lej′is lāt′iv) *adj.* **1.** of legislation **2.** of a legislature or its members **3.** having the power to make laws [a *legislative* assembly] **4.** enforced by legislation —*n.* a legislature —**leg′is·la′tive·ly** *adv.*
**leg·is·la·tor** (-lāt′ər) *n.* [< L.: see LEGISLATION] a member of a legislative assembly; lawmaker
**leg·is·la·ture** (-lā′chər) *n.* a body of persons given the responsibility and power to make laws for a country, State, etc.
**le·git** (lə jit′) *n.* [Slang] the legitimate theater, drama, etc. —*adj.* [Slang] legitimate
**le·git·i·ma·cy** (lə jit′ə mə sē) *n.* a being legitimate
**le·git·i·mate** (-mit; *for v.* -māt′) *adj.* [< ML. pp. of *legitimare*, to make lawful, ult. < L. *lex*, law] **1.** born of parents legally married to each other **2.** *a)* lawful *b)* conforming to the law **3.** ruling by the rights of heredity [a *legitimate* king] **4.** *a)* logically correct [a *legitimate* inference] *b)* justifiable or justified **5.** conforming to established rules, standards, etc. **6.** *Theater* designating or of stage plays, as distinguished from motion pictures, vaudeville, etc. —*vt.* -**mat′ed, -mat′ing** *same as* LEGITIMIZE —**le·git′i·mate·ly** *adv.* —**le·git′i·ma′tion** *n.*
**le·git·i·mize** (lə jit′ə mə tīz′) *vt.* **-tized′, -tiz′ing** *same as* LEGITIMIZE
**le·git·i·mist** (-mist) *n.* a supporter of legitimate authority or, esp., of claims to monarchy based on the rights of heredity —**le·git′i·mism** *n.*
**le·git·i·mize** (-mīz′) *vt.* **-mized′, -miz′ing** **1.** to make or declare legitimate **2.** to make seem just, right, or reasonable —**le·git′i·mi·za′tion** *n.*
**leg·man** (leg′man′) *n., pl.* **-men′** a newspaperman who gathers information at the scene of events or at various sources
**leg-of-mut·ton** (leg′ə mut′'n, -əv-) *adj.* shaped like a leg

of mutton: said of a sleeve that puffs out toward the shoulder, etc.

**leg·room** (leg'rōōm') *n.* adequate space for the legs while seated, as in a car

**leg·ume** (leg'yōōm, li gyōōm') *n.* [< Fr. < L. *legumen* < *legere*, to gather] 1. any of a large family of plants, including the peas, beans, clovers, etc., with fruit that is a pod splitting along two sutures: many legumes are nitrogen-fixing 2. the pod or seed of some members of this family, used for food

**le·gu·mi·nous** (li gyōō'min əs) *adj.* 1. of, having the nature of, or bearing legumes 2. of the family of plants to which peas and beans belong

**leg·work** (leg'wurk') *n.* [Colloq.] travel away from the center of work as a routine part of a job, as of a legman

**Le Ha·vre** (lə häv'rə; *Fr.* lə à'vr') seaport in NW France, on the English Channel: pop. 200,000

**lei** (lā, lā'ē) *n., pl.* **leis** [Haw.] in Hawaii, a wreath of flowers and leaves

**Leib·niz** (līp'nits), Baron **Gott·fried Wil·helm von** (gôt'frēt vil'helm fôn) 1646–1716; Ger. philosopher & mathematician: also sp. **Leibnitz**

**Leices·ter** (les'tər) city in C England: pop. 280,000

**Leicester**, Earl of (*Robert Dudley*) 1532–88; Eng. courtier & general: favorite of Elizabeth I

**Lei·den** (līd'n) city in W Netherlands: pop. 103,000

**Leigh** (lē) [< surname *Leigh* < OE. *leah*, LEA] a masculine or feminine name

**Leip·zig** (līp'sig, -sik; *G.* līp'tsiH) city in SC East Germany: pop. 592,000

**lei·sure** (lē'zhər, lezh'ər) *n.* [< OFr. < L. *licere*, to be permitted] free, unoccupied time that can be used for rest, recreation, etc. —*adj.* 1. free and unoccupied; spare *[leisure time]* 2. having much leisure *[the leisure class]* —**at leisure** 1. having free time 2. with no hurry 3. not occupied or engaged —**at one's leisure** when one has the time or opportunity —**lei'sured** *adj.*

**lei·sure·ly** (-lē) *adj.* without haste; slow —*adv.* in an unhurried manner —**lei'sure·li·ness** *n.*

**leit·mo·tif, leit·mo·tiv** (līt'mō tēf') *n.* [< G. < *leiten*, to lead + *motiv*, MOTIVE] 1. a short musical phrase representing and recurring with a given character, situation, etc. as in Wagner's operas 2. a dominant theme or underlying pattern

**lek** (lek) *n. see* MONETARY UNITS, table (Albania)

**lem·an** (lem'ən, lē'mən) *n.* [ME. *lemman* < *lef*, dear (see LIEF) + *man*] [Archaic] a sweetheart or lover (man or woman); esp., a mistress

**Le·man** (lē'mən), **Lake** *same as* Lake GENEVA: Fr. name **Lac Lé·man** (làk lā män')

**lem·ming** (lem'iŋ) *n., pl.* **-mings, -ming**: see PLURAL, II, D, 1 [Dan. < ON.] a small arctic rodent resembling the mouse but having a short tail and fur-covered feet

**lem·on** (lem'ən) *n.* [< MFr. < Ar. *laimūn* < Per. *līmūn*] 1. a small, edible citrus fruit with a pale-yellow rind and a juicy, sour pulp 2. the small, spiny, semitropical tree bearing this fruit 3. pale yellow 4. [Slang] *a)* something that is defective *b)* an inadequate person —*adj.* 1. pale-yellow 2. made with or flavored like lemon —**lem'on·y** *adj.*

**lem·on·ade** (lem'ə nād') *n.* a drink made of lemon juice and water, usually sweetened

**lem·pi·ra** (lem pir'ə) *n., pl.* **-ras** [AmSp., after *Lempira*, native chief] *see* MONETARY UNITS, table (Honduras)

**le·mur** (lē'mər) *n.* [< L. *lemures*, ghosts] a small primate related to the monkey, with large eyes and soft, woolly fur: found mainly in the old-world tropics and active mostly at night

**Le·na** (lē'nə; *also, for 2, Russ.* lye'nä) 1. [dim. of HELEN] a feminine name 2. river in EC R.S.F.S.R., flowing northeast into the Arctic Ocean

**lend** (lend) *vt.* **lent, lend'ing** [OE. *lænan* < *læn*, a loan] 1. to let another use or have (a thing) temporarily 2. to let out (money) at interest 3. to give; impart *[to lend an air of mystery]* —*vi.* to make a loan or loans —**lend itself (or oneself) to** to be useful for or open to —**lend'er** *n.*

**lending library** a library from which books may be borrowed, usually for a daily fee

**lend-lease** (-lēs') *n.* in World War II, material aid in the form of munitions, tools, food, etc. granted to foreign countries whose defense was deemed vital to the defense of the U.S. —**lend'-lease'** *vt.* **-leased', -leas'ing**

**length** (leŋkth, lenth) *n.* [OE. *lengthu* < base of *lang*, long + -TH¹] 1. the measure of how long a thing is from end to end; the greatest dimension of anything 2. extent in space or time 3. a long stretch or extent 4. the state or fact of being long 5. a piece of a certain length *[a length of pipe]* 6. a unit of measure consisting of the length of an object or animal in a race *[the boat won by two lengths]* —**at full length** completely extended —**at length** 1. finally 2. in full —**go to any length** (or **great lengths**) to do whatever is necessary

**length·en** (-'n) *vt., vi.* to make or become longer —**length'-en·er** *n.*

**length·wise** (-wīz') *adv., adj.* in the direction of the length: also **length'ways'** (-wāz')

**length·y** (-ē) *adj.* **length'i·er, length'i·est** long; esp., too long —**length'i·ly** *adv.* —**length'i·ness** *n.*

**le·ni·ent** (lē'ni ənt, lēn'yənt) *adj.* [< L. prp. of *lenire*, to soften < *lenis*, soft] not harsh or severe in disciplining, judging, etc.; mild; merciful —**le'ni·en·cy,** *pl.* **-cies, le'ni·ence** *n.* —**le'ni·ent·ly** *adv.*

**Len·in** (len'in; *Russ.* lye'nyin), **V(ladimir) I(lyich)** (orig. surname *Ulyanov*: also called *Nikolai Lenin*) 1870–1924; Russ. Communist revolutionary leader; premier of the U.S.S.R. (1917–24)

**Len·in·grad** (len'in grad'; *Russ.* lye'nin grät') seaport in NW R.S.F.S.R., on the Gulf of Finland: pop. 3,752,000

**Len·in·ism** (len'in iz'm) *n.* the communist theories and policies of Lenin, including his theory of the dictatorship of the proletariat —**Len'in·ist** *n., adj.*

**len·i·tive** (len'ə tiv) *adj.* [< ML. < L. pp. of *lenire*, to soften] soothing or assuaging; lessening pain —*n.* a lenitive medicine, etc.

**len·i·ty** (-tē) *n.* [< OFr. < L. < *lenis*, mild: see LENIENT] 1. a being lenient; mildness; gentleness 2. *pl.* **-ties** a lenient act

**Le·nore** (lə nôr') [var. of ELEANOR] a feminine name

**lens** (lenz) *n.* [L., lentil: a double-convex lens is shaped like the seed] 1. *a)* a piece of glass, or other transparent substance, with two curved surfaces, or one plane and one curved, bringing together or spreading rays of light passing through it: lenses are used in optical instruments *b)* a combination of two or more lenses 2. a transparent biconvex body of the eye: it focuses upon the retina light rays entering the pupil

LENS
(A, plano-convex; B, double-convex; C, divergent meniscus; D, double-concave; E, plano-concave)

**Lent** (lent) *n.* [OE. *lengten*, the spring < *lang*, long: because the spring days lengthen] the period of forty weekdays from Ash Wednesday to Easter, observed variously in Christian churches by fasting and penitence

**lent** (lent) *pt. & pp. of* LEND

**-lent** (lənt) [L. *-lentus, -ful*] *a suffix meaning* full of, characterized by *[virulent, fraudulent]*

**Lent·en** (lent''n) *adj.* [*also* l-] of, connected with, or suitable for Lent

**len·til** (lent''l) *n.* [< OFr. < L. *lenticula*, dim. of *lens*, lentil] 1. an old-world leguminous plant with small, edible seeds shaped like double-convex lenses 2. the seed of this plant

**len·to** (len'tō) *adv., adj.* [It. < L. *lentus*, slow] *Music* slow —*n., pl.* **-tos** a lento passage or movement

**Le·o** (lē'ō) [L.: see LION] 1. a masculine name: var. *Leon* 2. a N constellation between Cancer and Virgo 3. the fifth sign of the zodiac: see ZODIAC, illus. 4. **Leo I,** Saint 400?–461 A.D.; Pope (440–461): called *the Great* 5. **Leo XIII** 1810–1903; Pope (1878–1903)

**Le·ón** (le ôn') region in NW Spain: formerly a kingdom

**Le·o·na** (lē ō'nə) [< LEO] a feminine name

**Leon·ard** (len'ərd) [< Fr. < OFr. < OHG. < *lewo*, lion + *hart*, strong] a masculine name

**le·one** (lē ōn') *n. see* MONETARY UNITS, table (Sierra Leone)

**Le·o·nids** (lē'ə nidz) *n.pl.* a shower of meteors visible yearly about November 15, appearing to radiate from the constellation Leo: also **Le·on·i·des** (lē än'ə dēz')

**le·o·nine** (lē'ə nīn') *adj.* [< OFr. < L. < *leo*, LION] of, characteristic of, or like a lion

**leop·ard** (lep'ərd) *n., pl.* **-ards, -ard**: see PLURAL, II, D, 1 [< OFr. < LL. < Gr. *leopardos* < *leōn*, lion + *pardos*, panther] 1. a large, ferocious animal of the cat family, with a black-spotted tawny coat, found in Africa and Asia 2. *same as* JAGUAR —**leop'ard·ess** *n.fem.*

**Le·o·pold** (lē'ə pōld') [G. < OHG. < *liut*, people + *balt*, strong] a masculine name

**Lé·o·pold·ville** (lē'ə pōld vil', lā'-) *former name of* KINSHASA

**le·o·tard** (lē'ə tärd') *n.* [after J. *Léotard*, 19th-c. Fr. aerialist] a one-piece, tightfitting garment for the torso, worn by acrobats, dancers, etc.

**lep·er** (lep'ər) *n.* [< OFr. < L. < Gr. *lepros*, rough, scaly < *lepein*, to peel] 1. a person having leprosy 2. a person to be shunned

**lep·i·dop·ter·an** (lep'ə däp'tər ən) *n.* [< ModL. < Gr. *lepis*, a scale + -PTER(OUS) + -AN] any of a large order of insects, including the butterflies and moths, characterized by two pairs of broad, membranous wings covered with very fine scales —**lep'i·dop'ter·ous** *adj.*

**lep·re·chaun** (lep'rə kôn', -kän') *n.* [Ir. *lupracān* < OIr. < *lu*, little + dim. of *corp* (< L. *corpus*), body] *Irish Folklore* a fairy in the form of a little old man who can reveal a buried crock of gold to anyone who catches him

**lep·ro·sy** (lep′rə sē) *n.* [see LEPER] a chronic, infectious disease caused by a bacterium that attacks the skin, flesh, nerves, etc.: it is characterized by ulcers, white scaly scabs, deformities, and wasting of body parts

**lep·rous** (-rəs) *adj.* 1. of or like leprosy 2. having leprosy

**-lep·sy** (lep′sē) [< Gr. *-lepsia* < *lēpsis*, an attack] *a combining form meaning* a fit, attack, seizure *[catalepsy]*: also **-lep′si·a**

**lep·ton** (lep′tän) *n., pl.* **-ta** (-tə) [Gr. < *leptos*, thin, small < *lepein*, to peel] *see* MONETARY UNITS, table (Greece)

**Le·roy** (lə roi′, lē′roi) [< Fr. *le roi*, the king] a masculine name

**les·bi·an** (lez′bē ən) *adj.* [in allusion to Sappho and her followers, in Lesbos] [*sometimes* L-] of homosexuality between women —*n.* [*sometimes* L-] a homosexual woman —**les′bi·an·ism** *n.*

**Les·bos** (lez′bäs, -bəs) Gr. island in the Aegean, off the coast of Asia Minor

**lese maj·es·ty** (lēz′ maj′əs tē) [< Fr. < L. fem. of *laesus*, pp. of *laedere*, to hurt + *majestas*, majesty] 1. a crime against the sovereign; treason 2. any insolence toward one to whom deference is due

**le·sion** (lē′zhən) *n.* [< MFr. < L. *laesio* < pp. of *laedere*, to harm] 1. an injury; hurt 2. an injury, sore, etc. in an organ or tissue of the body resulting in impairment or loss of function

**Les·lie** (les′lē, lez′-) [ult. < *less lee* (lea), i.e., smaller meadow] a masculine or feminine name

**Le·sot·ho** (le sut′hō, -sō′thō) country in SE Africa, surrounded by South Africa: a member of the Commonwealth: 11,716 sq. mi.; pop. 997,000

**less** (les) *adj. alt. compar. of* LITTLE [OE. *læs, læssa*] not so much, so many, so great, etc.; smaller; fewer —*adv. compar. of* LITTLE not so much; to a smaller extent —*n.* a smaller amount —*prep.* minus *[$5,000 less taxes]* —**less and less** decreasingly —**no less a person than** a person of no lower importance, rank, etc. than

**-less** (lis, ləs) [OE. *-leas* < *leas*, free] *a suffix meaning:* 1. without, lacking *[valueless]* 2. that does not *[tireless]* 3. that cannot be *[dauntless]*

**les·see** (les ē′) *n.* [see LEASE] a person to whom property is leased; tenant

**less·en** (les′'n) *vt.* 1. to make less; decrease 2. [Archaic] to disparage —*vi.* to become less

**less·er** (les′ər) *adj. alt. compar. of* LITTLE [LESS + -ER] smaller, less, or less important —*adv.* less

**Lesser Antilles** group of islands in the West Indies, southeast of Puerto Rico, including the Leeward Islands & the Windward Islands

**lesser panda** a reddish, raccoonlike mammal of the Himalayan region

**les·son** (les′'n) *n.* [< OFr. *leçon* < L. < pp. of *legere*, to read] 1. something to be learned; specif., *a)* an exercise that a student is to prepare or learn *b)* something that needs to be learned for one's safety, etc. *c)* [*pl.*] course of instruction *[music lessons]* 2. a selection from the Bible, read as part of a church service 3. a rebuke; reproof

**les·sor** (les′ôr, les ôr′) *n.* [Anglo-Fr. < *lesser*: see LEASE] one who gives a lease; landlord

**lest** (lest) *conj.* [< OE. < *thy læs the*, lit., by the less that] 1. for fear that; in case *[speak low lest you be overheard]* 2. that: used after expressions denoting fear *[afraid lest he should fall]*

**Les·ter** (les′tər) [< LEICESTER] a masculine name

**let¹** (let) *vt.* **let** or obs. **let′ted, let′ting** [OE. *lætan*, to leave behind] 1. to leave; abandon: now only in **let alone** (or **let be**), to refrain from bothering, etc. 2. *a)* to rent; hire out *b)* to assign (a contract) 3. to allow or cause to escape *[to let blood]* 4. to allow to pass, come, or go *[let me in]* 5. to allow; permit *[let me help]* 6. to cause to: usually with *know* or *hear [let me hear from you]* 7. to suppose; assume When used in commands, suggestions, or dares, *let* serves as an auxiliary *[let us go]* —*vi.* to be rented or leased *[house to let]* —**let down** 1. to lower 2. to slow up 3. to disappoint —**let off** 1. to give forth (steam, etc.) 2. to deal leniently with —**let on** [Colloq.] 1. to indicate one's awareness of a fact 2. to pretend —**let out** 1. to release 2. to rent out 3. to reveal (a secret, etc.) 4. to make a garment larger by reducing (the hem, etc.) 5. to dismiss or be dismissed, as school —**let up** 1. to relax 2. to cease

**let²** (let) *vt.* **let′ted** or **let, let′ting** [OE. *lettan*, lit., to make late] [Archaic] to hinder; obstruct —*n.* 1. an obstacle or impediment: used in **without let or hindrance** 2. in tennis, etc., an interference with the course of the ball in some specific way, making it necessary to play the point over again

**-let** (lit, lət) [< MFr. *-el* (< L. *-ellus*) + *-et*, both dim. suffixes] *a suffix meaning:* 1. small *[ringlet]* 2. a small object worn as a band or *[anklet]*

**let·down** (let′doun′) *n.* 1. a slowing up or feeling of dejection, as after great excitement, effort, etc. 2. a disappointment or disillusionment

**le·thal** (lē′thəl) *adj.* [L. *let(h)alis* < *letum*, death] 1. causing or capable of causing death; fatal or deadly 2. of or suggestive of death —**le·thal′i·ty** (-thal′ə tē) *n.* —**le′thal·ly** *adv.*

**le·thar·gic** (li thär′jik) *adj.* 1. of or producing lethargy 2. abnormally drowsy or dull, sluggish, etc. —**le·thar′gi·cal·ly** *adv.*

**leth·ar·gize** (leth′ər jīz′) *vt.* **-gized′, -giz′ing** to make lethargic

**leth·ar·gy** (leth′ər jē) *n., pl.* **-gies** [< OFr. < LL. < Gr. < *lēthargos*, forgetful < *lēthē* (see ff.) + *argos*, idle < *a-*, not + *ergon*, work] 1. a condition of abnormal drowsiness or torpor 2. a great lack of energy; sluggishness, apathy, etc.

**Le·the** (lē′thē) [L. < Gr. *lēthē*, oblivion] *Gr. & Rom. Myth.* the river of forgetfulness, in Hades, whose water produced loss of memory in those who drank of it —*n.* oblivion; forgetfulness —**Le·the·an** (lē thē′ən) *adj.*

**let's** (lets) let us

**Lett** (let) *n.* 1. a member of a people living in Latvia and adjacent Baltic regions 2. *same as* LETTISH

**let·ter** (let′ər) *n.* [< OFr. < L. *littera*] 1. any of the characters of the alphabet, theoretically representing a speech sound 2. a written or printed message, usually sent by mail 3. [*usually pl.*] an official document authorizing someone or something 4. [*pl.*] *a)* literature generally *b)* learning; knowledge 5. literal meaning; exact wording 6. the first letter of the name of a school or college, awarded and worn for superior performance in sports, etc. —*vt.* 1. to mark with letters *[to letter a poster]* 2. to set down in hand-printed letters —*vi.* 1. to make hand-printed letters 2. [Colloq.] to earn a school letter —**to the letter** just as written or directed —**let′ter·er** *n.*

**letter carrier** *same as* MAIL CARRIER

**let·tered** (let′ərd) *adj.* 1. able to read and write 2. very well educated 3. inscribed with letters

**let·ter·head** (let′ər hed′) *n.* 1. the name, address, etc. of a person or firm printed as a heading on sheets of letter paper 2. such a sheet

**let·ter·ing** (-iŋ) *n.* 1. the process of putting letters on something by inscribing, printing, etc. 2. the letters so made

**let·ter·man** (-man′) *n., pl.* **-men′** (-men′) a student who has won a school letter

**letter of credit** a letter from a bank asking that the holder of the letter be allowed to draw specified sums of money from other banks or agencies

**let·ter-per·fect** (-pur′fikt) *adj.* 1. correct in every respect 2. knowing one's lesson, theatrical role, etc. perfectly

**let·ter·press** (-pres′) *n.* 1. *a)* the method of printing from raised surfaces, as set type *b)* matter printed by this method 2. [Chiefly Brit.] reading matter, as distinguished from illustrations

**letters** (or **letter**) **of marque** formerly, a government document authorizing an individual to arm a ship and capture enemy merchant ships: also **letters** (or **letter**) **of marque and reprisal**

**letters patent** a document granting a patent

**Let·tish** (let′ish) *adj.* of the Letts or their language —*n.* the Baltic language of the Letts; Latvian

**let·tuce** (let′is) *n.* [< OFr. < L. *lactuca* < *lac*, milk: from its milky juice] 1. a hardy, annual composite plant, grown for its crisp, succulent, green leaves 2. the leaves, much used for salads 3. [Slang] paper money

**let·up** (let′up′) *n.* [< phr. *let up*] [Colloq.] 1. a slackening or lessening 2. a stop or pause

**le·u** (le′oo) *n., pl.* **lei** (lā) [Romanian < L. *leo*, lion] *see* MONETARY UNITS, table (Romania)

**leu·ke·mi·a** (loo kē′mē ə) *n.* [ModL.: see ff. + -EMIA] any of a group of diseases of the blood-forming organs, resulting in an abnormal increase in the production of leukocytes: also sp. **leu·kae′mi·a** —**leu·ke′mic** (-mik) *adj.* —**leu·ke′moid** (-moid) *adj.*

**leu·ko-** [< Gr. *leukos*, white] *a combining form meaning* white or colorless: also, before a vowel, **leuk-**

**leu·ko·cyte** (loo′kə sīt′) *n.* [see prec. & -CYTE] any of the small, colorless cells in the blood, lymph, and tissues, which are important in the body's defenses against infection; white blood corpuscle —**leu′ko·cyt′ic** (-sit′ik) *adj.*

**lev** (lef) *n., pl.* **le·va** (le′və) [Bulg., ult. < Gr. *leōn*, lion] *see* MONETARY UNITS, table (Bulgaria)

**Lev.** Leviticus

---

fat, āpe, cär; ten, ēven; is, bīte; gō, hôrn, tōōl, look; oil, out; up, fur; get; joy; yet; chin; she; thin, then; zh, leisure; ŋ, ring; ə for *a* in *ago, e* in *agent, i* in *sanity, o* in *comply, u* in *focus*; ' as in *able* (ā′b'l); Fr. bal; ë, Fr. coeur; ö, Fr. feu; Fr. mon; ō, Fr. coq; ü, Fr. duc; r, Fr. cri; H, G. ich; kh, G. doch; ‡foreign; *hypothetical; < derived from. See inside front cover.

**Le·vant** (lə vant′) [< Fr. < It. *levante* (< L. prp. of *levare*, to raise), applied to the East, where the sun "rises"] region on the E Mediterranean, including all countries bordering the sea between Greece & Egypt —*n.* [l-] *same as* LEVANT MOROCCO —**Lev·an·tine** (lev′ən tīn′, -tēn′; lə van′tin) *adj., n.*

**Levant morocco** a fine morocco leather with a large, irregular grain, used esp. in bookbinding

**le·va·tor** (lə vāt′ər) *n., pl.* **lev·a·to·res** (lev′ə tôr′ēz), **le·va′tors** [ModL. < pp. of L. *levare*, to raise] a muscle that raises a limb or other part of the body

**lev·ee¹** (lev′ē) *n.* [< Fr. pp. of *lever*, to raise < L. *levare*] 1. an embankment built alongside a river to prevent high water from flooding bordering land 2. a quay 3. a low ridge of earth around a field to be irrigated —*vt.* **lev′eed**, **lev′ee·ing** to build a levee along

**lev·ee²** (lev′ē; lə vē′, -vā′) *n.* [< Fr. < *se lever*, to rise: see prec.] formerly, a morning reception held by a sovereign or person of high rank upon arising

**lev·el** (lev′'l) *n.* [< OFr. < L. *libella*, dim. of *libra*, a balance] 1. an instrument for determining whether a surface is evenly horizontal 2. *a*) a horizontal plane or line; esp., such a plane as a basis for measuring elevation *[sea level] b*) the height of such a plane 3. a horizontal area 4. the same horizontal plane *[the seats are on a level]* 5. normal position

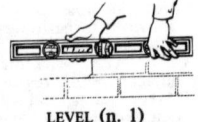

LEVEL (n. 1)

or proper place *[water seeks its level]* 6. position, rank, degree of concentration, etc. in a scale of values *[levels of income] —adj.* 1. perfectly flat and even 2. not sloping 3. even in height (*with*) 4. even with the top of the container *[a level teaspoonful]* 5. *a*) equal in importance, rank, degree, etc. *b*) conforming to a specified level *[high-level talks] c*) equally advanced in development *d*) uniform in tone, color, pitch, volume, rate, etc. 6. *a*) well-balanced; equable *b*) calm or steady 7. *[Slang]* honest —*vt.* **-eled** or **-elled**, **-el·ing** or **-el·ling** 1. to make level, even, flat, equal (as in rank), etc. 2. to knock to the ground; demolish 3. to raise (a gun, etc.) for firing 4. to aim or direct —*vi.* 1. to aim a gun, etc. (*at*) 2. to bring people or things to an equal rank, condition, etc. (usually with *down* or *up*) 3. *[Slang]* to be frank (*with* someone) —**level off** 1. to give a flat, horizontal surface to 2. *Aeron.* to come or bring to a horizontal line of flight: also **level out** 3. to become stable or constant —**one's level best** *[Colloq.]* the best one can do —**on the level** *[Slang]* honest(ly) and fair(ly) —**lev′el·er**, **lev′el·ler** *n.* —**lev′el·ly** *adv.* —**lev′el·ness** *n.*

**lev·el·head·ed** (-hed′id) *adj.* having or showing an even temper and sound judgment —**lev′el·head′ed·ly** *adv.* —**lev′el·head′ed·ness** *n.*

**lev·er** (lev′ər, lē′vər) *n.* [< OFr. < *lever*, to raise < L. *levare* < *levis*, LIGHT²] 1. a bar used as a pry 2. a means to an end 3. *Mech.* a device consisting of a bar turning about a fixed point, the fulcrum, using power or force applied at a second point to lift or sustain a weight at a third point; hence, any handle, etc. used to operate something —*vt.* to move, lift, etc. with a lever —*vi.* to use a lever

**lev·er·age** (-ij) *n.* 1. the action of a lever 2. the mechanical power resulting from this 3. increased means of accomplishing some purpose

LEVERS

**lev·er·et** (lev′ər it) *n.* [< MFr. dim. of *levre* < L. *lepus*, hare] a hare during its first year

**Le·vi** (lē′vī) *Bible* the third son of Jacob and Leah: see also LEVITE

**le·vi·a·than** (lə vī′ə thən) *n.* [LL. < Heb. *liwyāthān*] 1. *Bible* a sea monster, thought of as a reptile or a whale 2. anything huge or very powerful

**lev·i·er** (lev′ē ər) *n.* one who levies taxes, etc.

**Le·vi's** (lē′vīz) [after *Levi* Strauss, the U.S. maker] *a trademark for* closefitting trousers of heavy denim, reinforced at the seams, etc. with small copper rivets —*n.pl.* such trousers: usually written **le′vis**

**lev·i·tate** (lev′ə tāt′) *vt.* **-tat′ed**, **-tat′ing** [< L. *levis*, LIGHT² by analogy with GRAVITATE] to cause to rise and float in the air —*vi.* to rise and float in the air

**lev·i·ta·tion** (lev′ə tā′shən) *n.* 1. a levitating or being levitated 2. the illusion of raising and keeping a heavy body in the air with little or no support

**Le·vite** (lē′vīt) *n. Bible* any member of the tribe of Levi, chosen to assist the priests in the Temple

**Le·vit·i·cal** (lə vit′i k'l) *adj.* 1. of the Levites 2. of Leviticus or its laws

**Le·vit·i·cus** (-kəs) the third book of the Bible, containing the laws relating to priests and Levites

**lev·i·ty** (lev′ə tē) *n., pl.* **-ties** [< OFr. < L. *levitas < levis*,

LIGHT²] 1. *[Rare]* buoyancy 2. lightness of disposition, conduct, etc.; esp., improper gaiety; frivolity 3. fickleness

**lev·u·lose** (lev′yoo lōs′) *n. same as* FRUCTOSE

**lev·y** (lev′ē) *n., pl.* **lev′ies** [< MFr. fem. pp. of *lever*: see LEVER] 1. an imposing and collecting of a tax, fine, etc. 2. the amount levied 3. *a*) the enlistment, usually compulsory, of personnel, as for military service *b*) a group so enlisted —*vt.* **lev′ied**, **lev′y·ing** 1. to impose or collect (a tax, fine, etc.) 2. to enlist (troops) for military service, usually by force 3. to wage (war) —*vi.* 1. to make a levy 2. *Law* to seize property to satisfy a judgment

**lewd** (lood) *adj.* [OE. *læwede*, lay, unlearned] showing, or intended to excite, lust or sexual desire, esp. in an offensive way —**lewd′ly** *adv.* —**lewd′ness** *n.*

**Lew·is** (loo′is) 1. [see LOUIS] a masculine name: dim. *Lew* 2. **John L**(lewellyn), 1880-1969; U.S. labor leader 3. **Mer·i·weth·er** (mer′ē weth′ər), 1774-1809; Am. explorer, with William Clark, of the Northwest 4. **Sinclair**, 1885-1951; U.S. novelist

**lew·is·ite** (loo′ə sīt′) *n.* [after W.L. *Lewis* (1878-1943), U.S. chemist] a pale-yellow, odorless, arsenical compound, $ClCH\text{-}CHAsCl_2$, used as a blistering poison gas

**‡lex** (leks) *n., pl.* **le·ges** (lē′jēz, lā′gās) [L.] law

**lex·i·cog·ra·pher** (lek′sə käg′rə fər) *n.* [< LGr. < Gr. *lexikon*, LEXICON + *graphein*, to write] a person who writes or compiles a dictionary

**lex·i·cog·ra·phy** (-fē) *n.* [see prec.] the act, art, or work of writing or compiling a dictionary —**lex·i·co·graph·ic** (lek′si kə graf′ik), **lex′i·co·graph′i·cal** *adj.*

**lex·i·con** (lek′si kən, -kän′) *n.* [Gr. *lexikon < lexis*, a word < *legein*, to say] 1. a dictionary, esp. of an ancient language 2. the special vocabulary of a particular author, field of study, etc.

**Lex·ing·ton** (lek′siŋ tən) 1. [after ff.] city in NC Ky.: coextensive with Fayette county with which it constitutes a metropolitan government (**Lexington-Fayette**): pop. 204,000 2. [after the 2d Baron of *Lexington* (1661-1723)] suburb of Boston, in E Mass.: with Concord, site of one of the 1st battles of the Revolutionary War: pop. 29,000

**Ley·den jar** (or **vial**) (līd′'n) [< LEIDEN, where invented] a condenser for static electricity, consisting of a glass jar with a coat of tinfoil outside and inside and a metallic rod connecting with the inner lining and passing through the lid

**Ley·te** (lāt′ē) island of the EC Philippines, between Luzon & Mindanao

**LF, L.F., lf, l.f.** low frequency

**lf., lf** 1. *Baseball* left field (or fielder) 2. lightface

**LG., L.G.** Low German

**LGr., L.Gr.** Late Greek

**l.h., L.H., LH** left hand

**Lha·sa** (lä′sə) capital of Tibet: pop. 70,000

**Li** *Chem.* lithium

**L.I.** Long Island

**li·a·bil·i·ty** (lī′ə bil′ə tē) *n., pl.* **-ties** 1. the state of being liable 2. anything for which a person is liable 3. *[pl.] Accounting* all the entries on a balance sheet showing the debts of a person or business, as accounts and notes payable 4. something that works to one's disadvantage

**li·a·ble** (lī′ə b'l; *also, esp. for 3,* lī′b'l) *adj.* [prob. via Anglo-Fr. < OFr. *lier* < L. *ligare*, to bind] 1. legally bound, as to make good a loss; responsible 2. likely to have, suffer from, etc.; subject to *[liable to heart attacks]* 3. likely (*to* do, have, get, etc. something unpleasant or unwanted) *[liable to cause hard feelings]*

**li·ai·son** (lē′ə zän′, -zōn′; lē ā′zän; *occas.* lā′ə zän′; *for 3,* lē′ə zōn′; *Fr.* lye zōn′) *n.* [Fr. < OFr. < L. *ligare*, to bind] 1. a connecting of the parts of a whole, as of military units, in order to bring about proper coordination of activities 2. an illicit love affair 3. in spoken French, the linking of words by pronouncing the final consonant of one word as though it were the initial consonant of the following word, as in the phrase *chez elle* (pronounced shā zel′)

**li·a·na** (lē än′ə, -an′ə) *n.* [NormFr. *liane*, ult. < L. *viburnum*, wayfaring tree] any luxuriantly growing, woody, tropical vine that roots in the ground and climbs, as around tree trunks: also **li·ane′** (-än′, -an′)

**li·ar** (lī′ər) *n.* a person who tells lies

**lib** (lib) *n. clipped form of* LIBERATION

**lib.** 1. [L. *liber*] book 2. librarian 3. library

**li·ba·tion** (lī bā′shən) *n.* [< L. *libatio < libare*, to pour out] 1. the ritual of pouring out wine or oil upon the ground as a sacrifice to a god 2. the liquid so poured out 3. an alcoholic drink: used humorously —**li·ba′tion·al** *adj.*

**li·bel** (lī′b'l) *n.* [OFr. < L. *libellus*, dim. of *liber*, a book] 1. any false and malicious written or printed statement, or any sign, picture, etc., tending to injure a person's reputation unjustly 2. the act of publishing such a thing 3. anything that gives an unflattering or damaging picture of the subject it is dealing with —*vt.* **-beled** or **-belled**, **-bel·ing** or **-bel·ling** 1. to publish or make a libel against 2. to give an unflattering or damaging picture of —**li′bel·er**, **li′bel·ler** *n.*

**li·bel·ous, li·bel·lous** (-əs) *adj.* **1.** of or involving a libel **2.** given to writing and publishing libels; defamatory —**li'bel·ous·ly, li'bel·lous·ly** *adv.*

**lib·er·al** (lib'ər əl, lib'rəl) *adj.* [OFr. < L. *liberalis* < *liber*, free] **1.** orig., suitable for a freeman; not restricted: now only in LIBERAL ARTS, LIBERAL EDUCATION, etc. **2.** giving freely; generous **3.** ample; abundant *[a liberal reward]* **4.** not restricted to the literal meaning *[a liberal interpretation of the Bible]* **5.** broad-minded **6.** favoring reform or progress, as in religion, education, etc.; specif., favoring political reforms tending toward democracy **7.** [L-] designating or of a political party upholding liberal principles, as in England or Canada —*n.* **1.** a person favoring liberalism **2.** [L-] a member of a liberal political party —**lib'er·al·ly** *adv.* —**lib'er·al·ness** *n.*

**liberal arts** the subjects of an academic college course, including literature, philosophy, languages, history, etc., as distinguished from professional or technical subjects

**liberal education** an education mainly in the liberal arts, providing a broad cultural background

**lib·er·al·ism** (-iz'm) *n.* the quality or state of being liberal, esp. in politics or religion

**lib·er·al·i·ty** (lib'ə ral'ə tē) *n., pl.* -ties the quality or state of being liberal; specif., *a)* generosity *b)* tolerance; broadmindedness

**lib·er·al·ize** (lib'ər ə līz', lib'rə-) *vt., vi.* -ized', -iz'ing to make or become liberal —**lib'er·al·i·za'tion** *n.* —**lib'er·al·iz'er** *n.*

**lib·er·ate** (lib'ə rāt') *vt.* -at'ed, -at'ing [< L. pp. of *liberare*, to free < *liber*, free] **1.** to release from slavery, enemy occupation, etc. **2.** [Slang] to steal or loot, esp. from a defeated enemy in wartime **3.** *Chem.* to free from combination in a compound —**lib'er·a'tion** *n.* —**lib'er·a'tor** *n.*

**Li·ber·i·a** (lī bir'ē ə) country on the W coast of Africa: founded by freed slaves from the U.S.: 43,000 sq. mi.; pop. 1,200,000; cap. Monrovia —**Li·ber'i·an** *adj., n.*

**lib·er·tar·i·an** (lib'ər ter'ē ən) *n.* a person who advocates full civil liberties —*adj.* of or upholding such liberties —**lib'er·tar'i·an·ism** *n.*

**lib·er·tine** (lib'ər tēn', -tin) *n.* [< L. < *libertus*, freedman < *liber*, free] a man who leads an unrestrained, sexually immoral life; rake —*adj.* licentious —**lib'er·tin·ism, lib'er·tin·age** *n.*

**lib·er·ty** (lib'ər tē) *n., pl.* -ties [< OFr. < L. *libertas* < *liber*, free] **1.** freedom from slavery, captivity, or any other form of arbitrary control **2.** the sum of rights possessed in common by the people of a community, state, etc.: see also CIVIL LIBERTIES **3.** a particular right, franchise, freedom, etc. **4.** a too free, too familiar, or impertinent action or attitude **5.** the limits within which a certain amount of freedom may be exercised *[to have the liberty of the third floor]* **6.** *U.S. Navy* permission given to an enlisted person to be absent from duty for a period of 72 hours or less **7.** *Philos.* freedom to choose —**at liberty 1.** not confined; free **2.** allowed (to do or say something) **3.** not busy or in use —**take liberties 1.** to be too familiar or impertinent in action or speech **2.** to deal (*with* facts, etc.) in a distorting way

**Liberty Bell** the bell of Independence Hall in Philadelphia, rung on July 8, 1776, to proclaim the independence of the U.S.

**li·bid·i·nous** (li bid''n əs) *adj.* [see ff.] full of or characterized by lust; lewd; lascivious —**li·bid'i·nous·ly** *adv.* —**li·bid'i·nous·ness** *n.*

**li·bi·do** (li bē'dō, -bī'-) *n.* [L., desire, wantonness < *libet*, it pleases] **1.** the sexual urge or instinct **2.** *Psychoanalysis* energy of the psyche associated with the positive, loving instincts —**li·bid'i·nal** (-bid''n əl) *adj.* —**li·bid'i·nal·ly** *adv.*

**Li·bra** (lī'brə, lē'-) [L., a balance] **1.** a S constellation between Virgo and Scorpio **2.** the seventh sign of the zodiac: see ZODIAC, illus.

**li·bra** (lī'brə) *n., pl.* -brae (-brē) [L.] pound

**li·brar·i·an** (lī brer'ē ən) *n.* **1.** a person in charge of a library **2.** a library worker trained in library science —**li·brar'i·an·ship'** *n.*

**li·brar·y** (lī'brer'ē, -brə rē) *n., pl.* -brar'ies [< OFr. < *libraire*, copyist < L. < *liber*, a book] **1.** a room or building where a collection of books, periodicals, etc. is kept for reading or reference **2.** a public or private institution in charge of the care and circulation of such a collection **3.** a collection of books, periodicals, etc.

**library science** the study of library organization and management

**li·bret·tist** (li bret'ist) *n.* a writer of librettos

**li·bret·to** (li bret'ō) *n., pl.* -tos, -ti (-ē) [It., dim. of *libro*, a book < L. *liber*] **1.** the words, or text, of an opera, oratorio, etc. **2.** a book containing these words

**Lib·ri·um** (lib'rē əm) *a trademark for* a tranquilizing drug

**Lib·y·a** (lib'ē ə) **1.** ancient Greek & Roman name of N Africa, west of Egypt **2.** country in N Africa, on the Mediterranean: 679,359 sq. mi.; pop. 1,869,000; caps. Benghazi & Tripoli —**Lib'y·an** *adj., n.*

**lice** (līs) *n. pl. of* LOUSE

**li·cense** (līs''ns) *n.* [< OFr. < L. *licentia* < prp. of *licere*, to be permitted] **1.** formal or legal permission to do something specified *[license to marry, hunt, etc.]* **2.** a document, tag, etc. indicating that such permission has been granted **3.** *a)* freedom to deviate from strict conduct, rule, or practice *[poetic license] b)* an instance of this **4.** excessive, undisciplined freedom, constituting an abuse of liberty Also, Brit. sp., **licence** —*vt.* **-censed, -cens'ing** to give license or a license to or for; permit formally —**li'cens·a·ble** *adj.*

**li·cen·see** (līs''n sē') *n.* a person to whom a license is granted

**li·cens·er** (līs''n sər) *n.* a person with authority to grant licenses: also sp., *Law*, **li'cen·sor**

**li·cen·ti·ate** (lī sen'shē it, -āt') *n.* **1.** a person licensed to practice a specified profession **2.** in certain European and Canadian universities, an academic degree between that of bachelor and that of doctor —**li·cen'ti·ate·ship'** *n.*

**li·cen·tious** (lī sen'shəs) *adj.* [< L. < *licentia*: see LICENSE] **1.** [Rare] disregarding accepted rules and standards **2.** morally unrestrained, esp. in sexual activity; lascivious —**li·cen'tious·ly** *adv.* —**li·cen'tious·ness** *n.*

**li·chee** (lē'chē') *n. same as* LITCHI

**li·chen** (lī'kən) *n.* [L. < Gr., prob. < *leichein*, to lick] any of a large group of small plants composed of a fungus and an alga growing in close association to form a dual plant, commonly adhering in colored patches to rock, wood, soil, etc. —**li'chen·ous, li'chen·ose'** (-ōs') *adj.*

**licht** (likht) *adj., adv., n., vi., vt. Scot. var. of* LIGHT

**lic·it** (lis'it) *adj.* [< L. pp. of *licere*, to be permitted] permitted; lawful —**lic'it·ly** *adv.* —**lic'it·ness** *n.*

**lick** (lik) *vt.* [OE. *liccian*] **1.** to pass the tongue over *[to lick one's lips]* **2.** to bring into a certain condition by passing the tongue over *[to lick one's fingers clean]* **3.** to pass lightly over like a tongue *[flames licking the logs]* **4.** [Colloq.] *a)* to whip; thrash *b)* to vanquish —*vi.* to move lightly and quickly, as a flame —*n.* **1.** the act of licking with the tongue **2.** a small quantity; bit **3.** *short for* SALT LICK **4.** [Colloq.] *a)* a sharp blow *b)* a short, rapid burst of activity *c)* a fast pace; clip **5.** [Slang] a phrase of jazz music, esp. an interpolated improvisation **6.** [*often pl.*] [Slang] chance; turn *[to get one's licks in]* —**lick and a promise** a hasty, superficial effort —**lick into shape** [Colloq.] to bring into proper condition —**lick one's chops** to anticipate eagerly —**lick up** to consume as by licking

**lick·er·ish** (lik'ər ish) *adj.* [< Anglo-Fr. form of OFr. *lecheros*] [Archaic] **1.** lecherous; lustful; lewd **2.** greedy or eager, esp. to eat or taste

**lick·e·ty-split** (lik'ə tē split') *adv.* [fanciful formation based on LICK, *n.* 4 *c*] [Colloq.] at great speed

**lick·spit·tle** (lik'spit''l) *n.* a servile flatterer; toady

**lic·o·rice** (lik'ər ish, -is; lik'rish) *n.* [< OFr. < LL. *liquiritia*, ult. < Gr. *glykys*, sweet + *rhiza*, root] **1.** a European plant of the legume family **2.** its dried root or the black flavoring extract made from this **3.** candy flavored with or as with this extract

**lic·tor** (lik'tər) *n.* [L.] a minor Roman official who carried the fasces and cleared the way for the chief magistrates

**lid** (lid) *n.* [OE. *hlid*] **1.** a movable cover, as for a box, pot, etc. **2.** *short for* EYELID **3.** [Colloq.] a curb or restraint **4.** [Slang] a cap, hat, etc. —**lid'ded** *adj.* —**lid'less** *adj.*

**lie'** (lī) *vi.* **lay, lain, ly'ing** [OE. *licgan*] **1.** to be or put oneself in a reclining position along a relatively horizontal surface (often with *down*) **2.** to rest on a support in a more or less horizontal position: said of inanimate things **3.** to be or remain in a specified condition *[motives that lie hidden]* **4.** to be situated *[Canada lies to the north]* **5.** to extend *[the road that lies before us]* **6.** to be; exist *[the love that lies in her eyes]* **7.** to be buried or entombed **8.** [Archaic] to stay overnight or for a short while **9.** [Archaic] to have sexual intercourse (*with*) —*n.* **1.** the way in which something is situated or arranged; lay **2.** an animal's lair —**lie down on the job** [Colloq.] to put forth less than one's best efforts —**lie in** to be in confinement for childbirth —**lie off** *Naut.* to stay at a distance from shore or another ship —**lie over** to stay and wait until some future time —**lie to** *Naut.* to lie stationary with the head to the wind: said of a ship —**li'er** *n.*

**lie²** (lī) *vi.* **lied, ly'ing** [OE. *leogan*] **1.** to make a statement or statements that one knows to be false, esp. with intent to deceive **2.** to give a false impression —*vt.* to bring, put, accomplish, etc. by lying [to *lie* oneself into office] —*n.* **1.** a thing said or done in lying; falsehood **2.** anything that gives or is meant to give a false impression —**give the lie to 1.** to charge with telling a lie **2.** to prove to be false

**Liech·ten·stein** (lēH'tən shtīn') country in WC Europe, on the Rhine: 61 sq. mi.; pop. 21,000

**lied** (lēd; *G.* lēt) *n., pl.* **lied'er** (lē'dər; *G.* -dər) [G.] a German song, esp. one of a lyrical, often popular, character

**Lie·der·kranz** (lē'dər krants') [G., lit., garland of songs] *a trademark for* a soft cheese having a strong odor and flavor

**lie detector** a polygraph used on persons suspected of lying to record the physiological changes assumed to occur when the subject lies in answering questions

**lief** (lēf) *adj.* [OE. *leof*] [Archaic or Obs.] **1.** dear; beloved **2.** willing —*adv.* willingly; gladly: only in **would** (or **had**) **as lief**, etc.

**Liège** (lē āzh'; *Fr.* lyezh) city in E Belgium, on the Meuse: pop. 152,000

**liege** (lēj) *adj.* [< OFr., prob. < Frank. base but infl. by L. *ligare*, to bind] **1.** *Feudal Law a*) entitled to the service and allegiance of his vassals [a *liege* lord] *b*) bound to give service and allegiance to the lord [*liege* subjects] **2.** loyal; faithful —*n. Feudal Law* **1.** a lord or sovereign **2.** a subject or vassal

**liege·man** (-mən) *n., pl.* **-men 1.** a vassal **2.** a loyal follower Also **liege man**

**li·en** (lēn, lē'ən) *n.* [Fr. < L. *ligamen*, a band < *ligare*, to bind] *Law* a claim on the property of another as security for the payment of a debt

**lieu** (lōō) *n.* [OFr. < L. *locus*, place] place: now chiefly in **in lieu of**, instead of

**lieu·ten·ant** (lōō ten'ənt; *Brit. & Canad. army* lef ten'-) *n.* [< MFr. < *lieu*, place + *tenant*, holding < L. *tenere*, to hold] **1.** one who acts for a superior, as during the latter's absence **2.** an officer ranking below a captain, as in a police department **3.** *U.S. Mil.* an officer ranking below a captain: see also FIRST LIEUTENANT, SECOND LIEUTENANT **4.** *U.S. Navy* an officer ranking just above a lieutenant junior grade Abbrev. **Lieut., Lt.** —**lieu·ten'an·cy** (-ən sē) *n., pl.* **-cies**

**lieutenant colonel** *U.S. Mil.* an officer ranking above a major

**lieutenant commander** *U.S. Navy* an officer ranking above a lieutenant

**lieutenant general** *U.S. Mil.* an officer ranking above a major general

**lieutenant governor 1.** an elected official of a State who ranks below and substitutes for the governor in case of the latter's absence or death **2.** the official head of government of a Canadian province, appointed by the governor general: also **lieu·ten'ant-gov'er·nor** *n.*

**lieutenant junior grade** *U.S. Navy* an officer ranking above an ensign

**life** (līf) *n., pl.* **lives** [OE. *lif*] **1.** that property of plants and animals (ending at death and distinguishing them from inorganic matter) which makes it possible for them to take in food, get energy from it, grow, etc. **2.** the state of possessing this property [brought back to *life*] **3.** a living being, esp. a human being [the *lives* lost in wars] **4.** living things collectively [plant *life*] **5.** the time a person or thing is alive, or a specific portion of such time [his early *life*] **6.** a sentence of imprisonment for the rest of one's life **7.** one's manner of living [a *life* of ease] **8.** the people and activities of a given time, or in a given setting or class [military *life*, low *life*] **9.** human existence and activity [to learn from *life*] **10.** *a*) an individual's lifetime experiences *b*) an account of this **11.** the existence of the soul [eternal *life*] **12.** something essential to the continued existence of something else [freedom of speech is the *life* of democracy] **13.** the source of vigor or liveliness [the *life* of the party] **14.** vigor; liveliness **15.** the period of flourishing, usefulness, functioning, etc. [fads have a short *life*] **16.** representation in art from living models [a class in *life*] **17.** [Colloq.] another chance [to get a *life*] —*adj.* of, in, or for life —**as large (or big) as life 1.** life-size **2.** in actual fact —**for dear life** with a desperate intensity —**for life 1.** for the duration of one's life **2.** in order to save one's life —**from life** from a living model —**see life** to have a wide variety of experiences —**take life** to kill —**take one's (own) life** to commit suicide —**to the life** like the living original; exactly —**true to life** true to reality

**life belt** a life preserver in the form of a belt

**life·blood** (-blud') *n.* **1.** the blood necessary to life **2.** a vital element or animating influence

**life·boat** (-bōt') *n.* any of the small boats carried by a ship for use if the ship must be abandoned

**life buoy** *same as* LIFE PRESERVER

**life expectancy** the number of years that an individual of a given age may expect on the average to live, as projected in statistical tables

**life-giv·ing** (-giv'iŋ) *adj.* **1.** that gives or can give life **2.** refreshing —**life'-giv'er** *n.*

**life·guard** (-gärd') *n.* an expert swimmer employed at a beach, a pool, etc. to prevent drownings

**life insurance** insurance in which a stipulated sum is paid to the beneficiary or beneficiaries at the death of the insured, or to the insured when he reaches a specified age

**life jacket** (or **vest**) a life preserver in the form of a sleeveless jacket or vest

**life·less** (-lis) *adj.* **1.** without life; specif., *a*) inanimate *b*) dead **2.** dull; listless —**life'less·ly** *adv.* —**life'less·ness** *n.*

**life·like** (-līk') *adj.* **1.** resembling actual life **2.** closely resembling a real person or thing

**life·line** (-līn') *n.* **1.** a rope for saving life, as one thrown to a person in the water **2.** the rope used to raise or lower a diver **3.** a commercial route or transport line of vital importance

**life·long** (-lôŋ') *adj.* lasting or not changing during one's whole life [a *lifelong* love]

**life net** a strong net used by firemen, etc. as to catch people jumping from a burning building

**life preserver** a buoyant device for saving a person from drowning by keeping his body afloat, as a ring or sleeveless jacket of canvas-covered cork

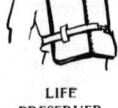

LIFE PRESERVER

**lif·er** (līf'ər) *n.* [Slang] a person sentenced to imprisonment for life

**life raft** a small, inflatable raft or boat

**life·sav·er** (-sā'vər) *n.* **1.** a person or thing that saves people from drowning, as a lifeguard **2.** [Colloq.] a person or thing that is of great timely help —**life'sav'ing** *adj., n.*

**life-size** (-sīz') *adj.* of the same size as the person or thing represented: said of a picture, sculpture, etc.: also **life'-sized'**

**life span 1.** *same as* LIFETIME **2.** the longest period of time that a typical individual can be expected to live

**life style** one's way of life as typified by one's activities, attitudes, possessions, etc.

**life·time** (-tīm') *n.* the length of time that someone lives, or that something lasts, functions, etc. —*adj.* lasting for such a period [a *lifetime* job]

**life·work** (-wurk') *n.* the work or task to which a person devotes his life; chief work in life

**lift** (lift) *vt.* [< ON. *lypta* < *lopt*, air] **1.** to bring up to a higher position; raise **2.** to pick up and move or set [*lift* the box down from the shelf] **3.** to hold up **4.** to raise in rank, condition, spirits, etc.; elevate; exalt **5.** to pay off (a mortgage, debt, etc.) **6.** to end (a blockade, siege, etc.) by withdrawing forces **7.** to revoke or rescind (a ban or order) **8.** to subject to FACE LIFTING **9.** [Colloq.] to plagiarize [to *lift* a passage from another writer] —*vi.* **1.** to exert strength in raising or trying to raise something **2.** to rise and vanish; be dispelled [the fog *lifted*] **3.** to become raised; go up —*n.* **1.** a lifting, raising, or rising **2.** the amount lifted **3.** the distance through which something is lifted **4.** lifting force, power, or influence **5.** elevation of spirits or mood **6.** elevated position or carriage, as of the neck, head, etc. **7.** a ride in the direction one is going **8.** help of any kind **9.** a rise in the ground **10.** the means by which something is lifted; specif., *a*) any layer of leather in the heel of a shoe *b*) [Brit.] an elevator *c*) a device used to transport people up or down a slope —**lift'er** *n.*

**lift-off** (-ôf') *n.* the vertical thrust and rise of a spacecraft, missile, etc. as it is launched

**lig·a·ment** (lig'ə mənt) *n.* [< L. < *ligare*, to bind] **1.** a bond or tie **2.** *Anat.* a band of tough tissue connecting bones or holding organs in place

**li·gate** (lī'gāt) *vt.* **-gat·ed, -gat·ing** to tie with a ligature, as a bleeding artery —**li·ga'tion** *n.*

**lig·a·ture** (lig'ə chər) *n.* [< MFr. < LL. < pp. of L. *ligare*, to bind] **1.** a tying or binding together **2.** a thing used for this; tie, bond, etc. **3.** a written or printed character containing two or more letters united, as æ, fl, th **4.** *Music a*) a curved line indicating a slur *b*) the notes slurred **5.** *Surgery* a thread or wire used to tie up an artery, etc. —*vt.* **-tured, -tur·ing** to tie or bind together with a ligature

**li·ger** (lī'gər) *n.* [LI(ON) + (TI)GER] the offspring of a male lion and a female tiger

**light¹** (līt) *n.* [OE. *leoht*] **1.** *a*) the form of electromagnetic radiation that acts upon the retina of the eye, optic nerve, etc., making sight possible: the speed of light is 186,000 miles per second *b*) a similar form of radiant energy not acting on the normal retina, as ultraviolet and infrared radiation **2.** the sensation that light stimulates in the organs of sight **3.** brightness; illumination, often of a specified kind **4.** a source of light, as the sun, a lamp, etc. **5.** *same as* TRAFFIC LIGHT **6.** the light from the sun; daylight or dawn **7.** a thing by means of which something can be started burning [a *light* for a cigar] **8.** the means by which light is let in; window **9.** knowledge or information; enlightenment /to shed *light* on the past/ **10.** spiritual inspiration **11.** public knowledge or view **12.** the way in which something is seen; aspect /presented in a favorable *light*/ **13.** facial expression /a *light* of recognition in his eyes/ **14.** an outstanding figure /one of the shining *lights* of the school/ —*adj.* **1.** having light; bright **2.** pale in color; whitish; fair —*adv.* palely /a *light* blue color/ —*vt.* **light′ed** or **lit, light′ing 1.** to set on fire; ignite /to *light* a bonfire/ **2.** to cause to give off light /to *light* a lamp/ **3.** to furnish with light /lamps *light* the streets/ **4.** to brighten; animate **5.** to show the way to by giving light —*vi.* **1.** to catch fire **2.** to be lighted; brighten (usually with *up*) — **according to one's lights** as one's opinions, information, or standards may direct —**in the light of** considering —**see the light (of day) 1.** to come into existence **2.** to come into public view **3.** to understand

**light²** (līt) *adj.* [OE. *leoht*]. **1.** having little weight; not heavy **2.** having little weight for its size **3.** below the usual or defined weight /a *light* coin/ **4.** less than usual or normal in amount, extent, force, intensity, etc.; specif., *a*) striking with little force /a *light* blow/ *b*) of less than the usual quantity or density /a *light* rain/ *c*) not coarse, massive, etc.; graceful /light tracery/ *d*) soft, muted, or muffled /a *light* sound/ *e*) not prolonged or intense /light applause/ **5.** of little importance; not serious /light conversation/ **6.** easy to bear; not burdensome /a *light* tax/ **7.** easy to do; not difficult /light work/ **8.** gay; happy; buoyant /light spirits/ **9.** flighty; frivolous; capricious **10.** loose in morals; wanton **11.** dizzy; giddy **12.** of an amusing or nonserious nature /light reading/ **13.** containing little alcohol /light wine/ **14.** *a*) not as full as usual /a *light* meal/ *b*) easy to digest **15.** well leavened; soft and spongy /a *light* cake/ **16.** loose in consistency; porous /light sand/ **17.** moving with ease and nimbleness /light on one's feet/ **18.** carrying little weight **19.** unstressed or slightly stressed: said of syllables **20.** designating or of industry equipped with relatively light machinery and producing small products **21.** designating, of, or equipped with light weapons, armor, etc. —*adv.* lightly —*vi.* **light′ed** or **lit, light′ing 1.** [Now Dial.] to dismount; alight **2.** to come to rest after traveling through the air /ducks *lighting* on the pond/ **3.** to come or happen (*on* or *upon*) by chance **4.** to strike suddenly, as a blow —**light in the head 1.** dizzy **2.** simple; foolish —**light into** [Colloq.] **1.** to attack **2.** to scold —**light out** [Colloq.] to depart suddenly —**make light of** to treat as unimportant —**light′ish** *adj.*

**light air** a wind speed of 1 to 3 miles per hour
**light breeze** a wind speed of 4 to 7 miles per hour
**light·en¹** (-'n) *vt.* **1.** to make light; illuminate **2.** to make light or pale —*vi.* **1.** to become light; grow brighter **2.** to shine brightly; flash **3.** to give off flashes of lightning — **light′en·er** *n.*
**light·en²** (-'n) *vt.* **1.** *a*) to make lighter in weight *b*) to reduce the load of **2.** to make less severe, harsh, etc. **3.** to make more cheerful —*vi.* **1.** to become lighter in weight **2.** to become more cheerful —**light′en·er** *n.*
**light·er¹** (-ər) *n.* a person or thing that lights something or starts it burning
**light·er²** (-ər) *n.* [< MDu. < *lichten*, to make light < *licht*, LIGHT²] an open barge used to load or unload larger ships lying offshore —*vt., vi.* to transport in a lighter
**light·er·age** (-ər ij) *n.* **1.** the loading or unloading of a ship by means of a lighter **2.** the charge for this
**light·face** (līt′fās′) *n. Printing* type having thin, light lines — *adj.* having thin, light lines: also **light′faced′**
**light-fin·gered** (-fiŋ′gərd) *adj.* skillful at stealing, esp. by picking pockets
**light-foot·ed** (-foot′id) *adj.* stepping lightly and gracefully: also [Poet.] **light′-foot′ —light′-foot′ed·ly** *adv.*
**light-hand·ed** (-han′did) *adj.* **1.** having a light, delicate touch **2.** having little to carry
**light-head·ed** (-hed′id) *adj.* **1.** mentally confused or feeling giddy; dizzy **2.** flighty; frivolous —**light′head′ed·ly** *adv.* —**light′head′ed·ness** *n.*
**light-heart·ed** (-här′tid) *adj.* free from care; gay —**light′-heart′ed·ly** *adv.* —**light′heart′ed·ness** *n.*
**light heavyweight** a boxer or wrestler between a middleweight and a heavyweight (in boxing, 161–175 pounds)
**light·house** (-hous′) *n.* a tower located at some place important or dangerous to navigation: it has a very bright light at the top, and often foghorns, sirens, etc., by which ships are guided and warned
**light·ing** (-iŋ) *n.* **1.** a giving light or being lighted; illumination; ignition **2.** the distribution of light and shade, as in a painting **3.** the art or manner of arranging stage lights

**light·ly** (-lē) *adv.* **1.** with little weight or pressure; gently **2.** to a small degree or amount /to spend *lightly*/ **3.** nimbly; deftly **4.** cheerfully; merrily **5.** with indifference or neglect **6.** with little or no reason **7.** with little or no punishment /to let someone off *lightly*/
**light-mind·ed** (-mīn′did) *adj.* not serious; frivolous — **light′-mind′ed·ly** *adv.* —**light′-mind′ed·ness** *n.*
**light·ness¹** (-nis) *n.* **1.** the quality or intensity of lighting; brightness **2.** *a*) paleness *b*) the relative amount of light reflected by an object
**light·ness²** (-nis) *n.* **1.** the state of being light, not heavy **2.** mildness, nimbleness, delicacy, cheerfulness, lack of seriousness, etc.
**light·ning** (-niŋ) *n.* [< ME. *lightnen*, to LIGHTEN¹] **1.** a flash of light in the sky caused by the discharge of atmospheric electricity from one cloud to another or between a cloud and the earth **2.** such a discharge of electricity —*vi.* to give off such a discharge —*adj.* like lightning
**lightning bug** (or **beetle**) *same as* FIREFLY
**lightning rod** a pointed metal rod placed high on a building, etc. and grounded to divert lightning from the structure
**light opera** a short, amusing musical play
**lights** (līts) *n.pl.* [from their light weight] [Dial.] the lungs of animals, used as food
**light·ship** (līt′ship′) *n.* a ship moored in a place dangerous to navigation and bearing lights, foghorns, sirens, etc. to warn or guide pilots
**light·some** (-səm) *adj.* **1.** nimble, graceful, or lively **2.** lighthearted; gay **3.** frivolous
**light·weight** (-wāt′) *n.* **1.** one below normal weight **2.** a boxer or wrestler between a featherweight and a welterweight (in boxing, 127–135 pounds) **3.** [Colloq.] a person of limited influence, intelligence, etc. —*adj.* **1.** light in weight **2.** not serious
**light-year** (-yir′) *n. Astron.* a unit of distance equal to the distance that light travels in a vacuum in one year, approximately 6 trillion miles
**lig·ne·ous** (lig′nē əs) *adj.* [< L. *ligneus* < *lignum*, wood] of, or having the nature of wood; woody
**lig·nite** (lig′nīt) *n.* [< Fr.: see LIGNEOUS & -ITE] a soft, brownish-black coal in which the texture of the original wood can still be seen —**lig·nit′ic** (-nit′ik) *adj.*
**lig·num vi·tae** (lig′nəm vīt′ē) [ModL. < L., wood of life] **1.** *same as* GUAIACUM (sense 1) **2.** *commercial name for* the very hard wood of the guaiacum
**Li·gu·ri·a** (li gyoor′ē ə) region of NW Italy, on an arm (**Ligurian Sea**) of the Mediterranean: chief city, Genoa — **Li·gu′ri·an** *adj., n.*
**lik·a·ble** (līk′ə b'l) *adj.* having qualities that inspire liking; attractive, genial, etc. —**lik′a·ble·ness, lik′a·bil′i·ty** *n.*
**like¹** (līk) *adj.* [OE. *gelic*] **1.** having almost or exactly the same characteristics; similar; equal /a cup of sugar and a *like* amount of flour/ **2.** [Dial.] likely —*adv.* [Colloq.] likely /like as not, he is already there/ —*prep.* **1.** similar to; resembling /she is *like* a bird/ **2.** similarly to /she sings *like* a bird/ **3.** characteristic of /not *like* her to cry/ **4.** in the mood for; desirous of /to feel *like* sleeping/ **5.** indicative of /it looks *like* a clear day tomorrow/ **6.** as for example /fruit, *like* pears, for dessert/ *Like* was originally an adjective in senses 1, 3, 4, 5, and an adverb in sense 2, and is still considered so by some grammarians —*conj.* [Colloq.] **1.** as /it was just *like* you said/ **2.** as if /it looks *like* he is late/ — *n.* a person or thing regarded as the equal or counterpart of another or of the person or thing being discussed /did you ever see the *like* of it?/ —*vt.* **liked, lik′ing** [Obs.] to liken —*vi.* [Dial.] to be about (*to* have done something) *Like* is also used without meaning or syntactical function, as in hip talk /it's *like* hot/ —**and the like** and others of the same kind —**like anything** [Colloq.] very much —**like blazes** (or **crazy, the devil, mad,** etc.) [Colloq.] with furious energy, speed, etc. —**nothing like** not at all like —**something like** almost like; about —**the like** (or **likes**) **of** [Colloq.] any person or thing like
**like²** (līk) *vi.* **liked, lik′ing** [OE. *lician*] to be so inclined; choose /leave whenever you *like*/ —*vt.* **1.** to be pleased with; have a preference for; enjoy **2.** to want or wish /I would *like* to go/ —*n.* [*pl.*] preferences or tastes —**lik′er** *n.*
**-like** (līk) [see LIKE¹] *a suffix meaning* like, characteristic of, suitable for /doglike, homelike/
**like·a·ble** (līk′ə b'l) *adj. same as* LIKABLE
**like·li·hood** (līk′lē hood′) *n.* (a) probability
**like·ly** (līk′lē) *adj.* **-li·er, -li·est** [prob. < OE. *geliclic* or < ? cognate ON. *likligr*] **1.** credible; probable /a *likely* cause/ **2.** reasonably to be expected /it is *likely* to rain/ **3.** suitable /a *likely* man for the job/ **4.** promising /a *likely* lad/ —*adv.* probably /he will very *likely* go/

**like-mind·ed** (līk'mīn'did) *adj.* having the same ideas, tastes, etc.; agreeing mentally —**like'-mind'ed·ly** *adv.* —**like'-mind'ed·ness** *n.*

**lik·en** (-'n) *vt.* to represent or describe as being like, or similar; compare

**like·ness** (-nis) *n.* **1.** the state or quality of being like; similarity **2.** (the same) form or shape *[Zeus took on the likeness of a bull]* **3.** something that is like; copy, facsimile, portrait, etc.

**like·wise** (-wīz') *adv.* [short for *in like wise*] **1.** in the same manner **2.** also; too; moreover

**lik·ing** (lī'kiŋ) *n.* **1.** fondness; affection **2.** preference; taste; pleasure *[not to my liking]*

**li·ku·ta** (lē kōō'tä) *n., pl.* **ma·ku·ta** (mä-) *see* MONETARY UNITS, table (Zaire)

**li·lac** (lī'lək, -läk, -lak) *n.* [Fr. < Ar. < Per. *nīlak,* bluish < *nīl,* indigo] **1.** a shrub or tree of the olive family, with large clusters of tiny, fragrant flowers ranging in color from white to lavender or crimson **2.** the flower cluster of this plant **3.** a pale-purple color —*adj.* pale-purple

**li·lan·gen·i** (li'län gen'i) *n., pl.* **em'a·lan·gen·i** (em'ə-) [native name, royal] *see* MONETARY UNITS, table (Swaziland)

**Lil·i·an, Lil·li·an** (lil'ē ən) [prob. < L. *lilium,* lily] a feminine name: dim. *Lil, Lily, Lilly*

**Lille** (lēl) city in N France: pop. 191,000

**Lil·li·put** (lil'ə put', -pət) in Swift's *Gulliver's Travels,* a. land inhabited by tiny people

**Lil·li·pu·tian** (lil'ə pyōō'shən) *adj.* **1.** of Lilliput or its people **2.** very small; tiny **3.** narrow-minded —*n.* **1.** an inhabitant of Lilliput **2.** a very small person **3.** a narrow-minded person

**lilt** (lilt) *vt., vi.* [ME. *lilten*] to sing, speak, or play with a light, graceful rhythm —*n.* **1.** a gay song or tune with a swingy rhythm **2.** a light, swingy, and graceful rhythm or movement —**lilt'ing** *adj.* —**lilt'ing·ly** *adv.*

**lil·y** (lil'ē) *n., pl.* **lil'ies** [< OE. < L. *lilium*] **1.** any of a large genus of plants of the lily family, grown from a bulb and having typically trumpet-shaped flowers, white or colored **2.** the flower or the bulb of any of these **3.** any of several similar plants, as the waterlily **4.** the fleur-de-lis, as in the royal arms of France —*adj.* **1.** designating a family of plants including the lilies, tulips, onions, etc. **2.** like a lily, as in whiteness, delicacy, purity, etc. —**gild the lily** to attempt vain improvements on something that is already excellent or perfect

**lil·y-liv·ered** (lil'ē liv'ərd) *adj.* cowardly; timid

**lily of the valley** *pl.* **lilies of the valley** a plant of the lily family which has a single pair of oblong leaves and a single raceme of very fragrant, small, white, bell-shaped flowers

**lil·y-white** (-hwīt', -wīt') *adj.* **1.** white as a lily **2.** innocent and pure: often used sarcastically **3.** practicing discrimination against, or segregation of, nonwhites, esp. Negroes

**Li·ma** (lē'mə; *for 2,* lī'-) **1.** capital of Peru, in the WC part: pop. 1,795,000 **2.** [after prec.] city in W Ohio: pop. 47,000

**li·ma bean** (lī'mə) [after LIMA, Peru] [*also* L-b-] **1.** a bean plant with creamy flowers and broad pods **2.** its broad, flat, nutritious seed

LILY OF THE VALLEY

**limb¹** (lim) *n.* [OE. *lim*] **1.** an arm, leg, or wing **2.** a large branch of a tree **3.** a part that projects like an arm or leg **4.** a person or thing regarded as a part or agent —**out on a limb** [Colloq.] in a precarious position or situation —**limb'less** *adj.*

**limb²** (lim) *n.* [< Fr. < ML. < L. *limbus,* edge] a border or edge; specif., *Astron.* the apparent outer edge of a heavenly body

**limbed** (limd) *adj.* having (a specified number or kind of) limbs *[four-limbed]*

**lim·ber¹** (lim'bər) *adj.* [< ? LIMB¹] **1.** easily bent; flexible **2.** able to bend the body easily; lithe —*vt.* to make limber —*vi.* to make oneself limber, as by exercises (usually with *up*) —**lim'ber·ness** *n.*

**lim·ber²** (lim'bər) *n.* [< ?] the two-wheeled, detachable front part of a gun carriage —*vt., vi.* to attach the limber to (a gun carriage)

**lim·bo** (lim'bō) *n., pl.* **-bos** [< L. *(in) limbo,* (in or on) the border] **1.** [*often* L-] in some Christian theologies, a region bordering on hell, the abode after death of unbaptized children and righteous people who lived before Jesus **2.** a place or condition of oblivion or neglect **3.** an indeterminate state midway between two others

**Lim·bur·ger (cheese)** (lim'bər gər) [< *Limburg,* a Belgian province] a semisoft cheese of whole milk, with a strong odor: also **Lim'burg (cheese)**

**lime¹** (līm) *n.* [OE. *lim*] **1.** *short for* BIRDLIME **2.** a white substance, calcium oxide, CaO, obtained by the action of heat on limestone, shells, etc. and used in making mortar and cement and in neutralizing acid soil —*vt.* **limed, lim'ing** **1.** to cement **2.** to smear with birdlime **3.** to catch with birdlime **4.** to treat with lime

**lime²** (līm) *n.* [Fr. < Pr. < Ar. *līma:* cf. LEMON] **1.** a small, lemon-shaped, greenish-yellow citrus fruit with a juicy, sour pulp **2.** the small, semitropical tree that it grows on —*adj.* **1.** made with or of limes **2.** having a flavor like that of limes

**lime³** (līm) *n.* [< earlier *line* < ME. *lind:* see LINDEN] *same as* LINDEN

**lime·ade** (līm'ād') *n.* a drink of lime juice and water, usually sweetened

**lime·kiln** (līm'kil', -kiln') *n.* a furnace in which limestone, shells, etc. are burned to make lime

**lime·light** (-līt') *n.* **1.** a brilliant light created by the incandescence of lime, formerly used in theaters to throw an intense beam of light upon a particular part of the stage, an actor, etc. **2.** a prominent or conspicuous position before the public

**lim·er·ick** (lim'ər ik, lim'rik) *n.* [prob. < Ir. refrain containing the name *Limerick,* a county of Ireland] a rhymed, nonsense poem of five anapestic lines

**lime·stone** (līm'stōn') *n.* rock consisting mainly of calcium carbonate, from which building stones, lime, etc. are made: cf. MARBLE

**lime·wa·ter** (-wôt'ər, -wät'ər) *n.* a solution of calcium hydroxide in water, used to neutralize acids

**lim·ey** (lī'mē) *n.* [from the LIME² juice formerly served to British sailors to prevent scurvy] [Slang] **1.** an English sailor or, sometimes, soldier **2.** any Englishman —*adj.* [Slang] British

**lim·it** (lim'it) *n.* [< OFr. < L. *limes* (gen. *limitis*)] **1.** the point, line, or edge where something ends or must end; boundary **2.** [*pl.*] bounds **3.** the greatest amount allowed *[a catch of ten trout is the limit,* a ten-cent *limit* on raising a bet in poker] —*vt.* to set a limit to; restrict; curb —**the limit** [Colloq.] any person or thing regarded as unbearable, remarkable, etc. to an extreme degree —**lim'it·a·ble** *adj.* —**lim'it·er** *n.*

**lim·i·ta·tion** (lim'ə tā'shən) *n.* **1.** a limiting or being limited **2.** qualification; restriction **3.** *Law* a period of time, fixed by statute, during which legal action can be brought, as for settling a claim —**lim'i·ta'tive** *adj.*

**lim·it·ed** (lim'it id) *adj.* **1.** *a)* confined within bounds; restricted *b)* narrow in scope **2.** making a restricted number of stops, and often charging extra fare: said of a train, bus, etc. **3.** exercising governmental powers under constitutional restrictions *[a limited monarch]* **4.** [Chiefly Brit.] restricting the liability of each partner or shareholder to the amount of his actual investment *[a limited company]* —*n.* a limited train, bus, etc. —**lim'it·ed·ly** *adv.* —**lim'it·ed·ness** *n.*

**lim·it·ing** (-iŋ) *adj. Gram.* designating or of any of a class of adjectives that limit or restrict the words modified (Ex.: *several, four,* etc.)

**lim·it·less** (-lis) *adj.* without limits; unbounded; vast —**lim'it·less·ly** *adv.* —**lim'it·less·ness** *n.*

**limn** (lim) *vt.* **limned, limn·ing** (lim'iŋ, -niŋ) [< OFr. *enluminer* < L. *illuminare,* to make light] **1.** to paint or draw **2.** to portray in words; describe —**limn·er** (lim'ər, -nər) *n.*

**Li·moges** (lē mōzh'; *Fr.* lē mōzh') city in WC France: pop. 133,000 —*n.* fine porcelain made there: also **Limoges ware**

**lim·ou·sine** (lim'ə zēn', lim'ə zēn') *n.* [Fr., lit., a hood] **1.** any large, luxurious sedan, esp. one driven by a chauffeur **2.** a buslike sedan used to carry passengers to or from an airport, etc.

**limp¹** (limp) *vi.* [< a sense of OE. *limpan,* to befall] **1.** to walk with or as with a lame leg **2.** to move jerkily, laboriously, etc. —*n.* a halt or lameness in walking —**limp'er** *n.* —**limp'ing·ly** *adv.*

**limp²** (limp) *adj.* [< base of prec.] **1.** lacking stiffness; drooping, wilted, etc. **2.** lacking firmness or vigor —**limp'ly** *adv.* —**limp'ness** *n.*

**limp·et** (lim'pit) *n.* [< OE. < ML. *lempreda*] a mollusk which clings to rocks, timbers, etc. by means of a thick, fleshy foot

**lim·pid** (lim'pid) *adj.* [< Fr. < L. *limpidus* < OL. *limpa,* water] **1.** perfectly clear; transparent *[limpid waters]* **2.** clear and simple *[limpid prose]* —**lim·pid'i·ty, lim'pid·ness** *n.* —**lim'pid·ly** *adv.*

**lim·y** (lī'mē) *adj.* **lim'i·er, lim'i·est** **1.** covered with, consisting of, or like birdlime; sticky **2.** of, like, or containing lime —**lim'i·ness** *n.*

**lin·age** (lī'nij) *n.* **1.** the number of written or printed lines on a page **2.** payment based on the number of lines produced by a writer

**linch·pin** (linch'pin') *n.* [< OE. *lynis,* linchpin] **1.** a pin that goes through the end of an axle outside the wheel to keep the wheel from coming off **2.** anything serving to hold together the parts of a whole

**Lin·coln** (liŋ'kən) [after Pres. LINCOLN] capital of Nebr., in the SE part: pop. 172,000

**Lin·coln** (liŋ'kən), **Abraham** 1809–65; 16th president of the U.S. (1861–65): assassinated —**Lin·coln·i·an** (liŋ kō'nē ən) *adj.*

**Lind** (lind), **Jenny** (born *Johanna Maria Lind*) 1820–87; Swed. soprano

**Lin·da** (lin′də) [dim. of BELINDA] a feminine name

**Lind·bergh** (lind′bərg, lin′-), **Charles Augustus** 1902–74; U.S. aviator

**lin·den** (lin′dən) *n.* [ME., *adj.* < OE. *lind*, linden] a tree with dense, heart-shaped leaves

**line**[1] (līn) *n.* [merging of OE. *line*, a cord, with OFr. *ligne* (both < L. *linea*, lit., linen thread < *linum*, flax)] **1.** *a*) a cord, rope, wire, or string *b*) a fine, strong cord with a hook, used in fishing *c*) a cord, steel tape, etc. used in measuring or leveling **2.** a wire or system of wires connecting stations in a telephone or telegraph system **3.** any wire, pipe, etc., or system of these, for conducting gas, water, electricity, etc. **4.** a very thin, threadlike mark; specif., *a*) a long, thin mark made by a pencil, pen, chalk, knife, etc. *b*) a thin crease in the palm or on the face **5.** a border or boundary [the State *line*] **6.** a limit; demarcation **7.** outline; contour **8.** [*usually pl.*] a plan of making or doing **9.** a row or series of persons or things; specif., a row of written or printed characters across a page or column **10.** *same as* LINEAGE[1] **11.** the descendants of a common ancestor or of a particular breed **12.** *a*) a transportation system consisting of regular trips by buses, ships, etc. between points *b*) a company operating such a system *c*) one branch of such a system *d*) a single track of a railroad **13.** the course or direction anything moving takes [the *line* of fire] **14.** course of conduct, action, explanation, etc. **15.** a person's trade or occupation, or the things he deals in [what's his *line?*] **16.** a stock of goods of a particular quality, quantity, variety, etc. **17.** *a*) the field of one's special knowledge or interest *b*) a source or piece of information [a *line* on a bargain] **18.** a short letter, note, or card [drop me a *line*] **19.** a verse of poetry **20.** [*pl.*] all the speeches of any one character in a play **21.** [Colloq.] flattering talk that is insincere **22.** *Football* the players arranged in a row even with the ball at the start of each play, or those directly opposite them **23.** *Geog.* an imaginary circle of the earth or of the celestial sphere, as the equator **24.** *Math. a*) the path of a moving point *b*) such a path when considered perfectly straight **25.** *Mil. a*) a formation of ships, troops, etc. abreast of each other *b*) the area or position in closest contact with the enemy during combat *c*) the troops in this area *d*) the combatant branches of the army as distinguished from the supporting branches and the staff **26.** *Music* any of the long parallel marks forming the staff —*vt.* **lined, lin′ing 1.** to mark with lines **2.** to trace with or as with lines **3.** to bring into alignment (often with *up*) **4.** to form a line along **5.** to place objects along the edge of **6.** *Baseball* to hit as a line drive —*vi.* **1.** to form a line (usually with *up*) **2.** *Baseball* to hit a line drive —**all along the line 1.** everywhere **2.** at every turn of events —**bring** (or **come, get**) **into line** to bring (or come) into alignment —**down the line** completely; entirely —**draw the** (or **a**) **line** to set a limit —**get a line on** [Colloq.] to find out about —**hold the line** to stand firm —**in** (or **out of**) **line** in (or not in) alignment, agreement, or conformity —**in line for** being considered for —**lay** (or **put**) **it on the line 1.** to pay up **2.** to speak frankly and in detail —**line out** *Baseball* to be put out by hitting a line drive that is caught by a fielder —**line up** to bring into or take a specified position —**on a line** in the same plane; level —**read between the lines** to discover a hidden meaning or purpose in something written, said, or done —**lin′a·ble, line′a·ble** *adj.*

**line**[2] (līn) *vt.* **lined, lin′ing** [< OE. *lin*, ult. < or akin to L. *linum*, flax] **1.** to put a layer or lining of a different material on the inside of **2.** to be used as a lining in **3.** to fill; stuff: now chiefly in **line one's pockets,** to make money, esp. greedily or unethically

**lin·e·age**[1] (lin′ē ij) *n.* [< OFr. *lignage* < *ligne*: see LINE[1]] **1.** direct descent from an ancestor **2.** ancestry; family; stock **3.** *same as* LINE[1] (*n.* 11)

**line·age**[2] (lī′nij) *n. same as* LINEAGE

**lin·e·al** (lin′ē əl) *adj.* **1.** in the direct line of descent from an ancestor **2.** hereditary **3.** of or composed of lines; linear —**lin′e·al·ly** *adv.*

**lin·e·a·ment** (lin′ē ə mənt) *n.* [< L. *lineamentum* < *linea*, LINE[1]] **1.** any of the features of the body, usually of the face, esp. with regard to its outline **2.** a distinctive feature Usually used in pl.

**lin·e·ar** (lin′ē ər) *adj.* **1.** of or relating to a line or lines **2.** made of or using lines **3.** extended in a line **4.** designating or of a style of art in which line is emphasized **5.** having an effect directly proportional to its cause **6.** *Algebra* of the first degree —**lin′e·ar′i·ty** (-ē ar′ə tē) *n.* —**lin′e·ar·ly** *adv.*

**linear measure 1.** measurement of length **2.** a system of measuring length, esp. the system in which 12 inches = 1

foot or that in which 100 centimeters = 1 meter: see TABLE OF WEIGHTS AND MEASURES in Supplements

**line·back·er** (līn′bak′ər) *n. Football* any player on defense stationed directly behind the line

**line drawing** a drawing done entirely in lines, from which a cut (**line cut**) can be photoengraved for printing

**line drive** *Baseball* a hard-hit ball that travels close to, and nearly parallel with, the ground

**line·man** (līn′mən) *n., pl.* **-men 1.** a man who carries a surveying line, tape, etc. **2.** a man whose work is setting up and repairing telephone, telegraph, or electric power lines **3.** *Football* one of the players in the line

**linemen's climber** a device with sharp spikes, fastened to the shoe or strapped to the leg to aid in climbing telephone poles, etc.

**lin·en** (lin′ən) *n.* see PLURAL, II, D, 3 [OE. < *lin*, flax] **1.** thread or cloth made of flax **2.** [*often pl.*] things made of linen, or of cotton, etc., as tablecloths, sheets, etc. —*adj.* **1.** spun from flax [*linen* thread] **2.** made of linen

**line of fire 1.** the course of a bullet, shell, etc. **2.** a position open to attack of any kind

**line of force** a line in a field of electrical or magnetic force that indicates the direction taken by the force at any point

**line of scrimmage** *Football* an imaginary line, parallel to the goal lines, on which the ball rests at the start of each play

**lin·er**[1] (lī′nər) *n.* **1.** a person or thing that traces lines **2.** a steamship, passenger airplane, etc. in regular service for a specific line **3.** *same as* LINE DRIVE **4.** a cosmetic applied in a fine line, as along the eyelid

**lin·er**[2] (lī′nər) *n.* **1.** a person who makes or attaches linings **2.** a lining **3.** the jacket of a long-playing record

**lines·man** (līnz′mən) *n., pl.* **-men 1.** *same as* LINEMAN **2.** *Football* an official who measures and marks the gains or losses in ground **3.** *Tennis* an official who reports whether the ball is inside or outside the lines he is assigned to watch

**line·up** (līn′up′) *n.* an arrangement of persons or things in or as in a line; specif., *a*) a group of suspected criminals lined up by the police for identification *b*) *Football, Baseball*, etc. the list of a team's players arranged according to playing position, order at bat, etc.

**ling**[1] (liŋ) *n., pl.* **ling, lings:** see PLURAL, II, D, 2 [akin to MDu. *lange*, ON. *langa*] an edible fish related to the cod, found in the North Atlantic

**ling**[2] (liŋ) *n.* [ON. *lyng*] *same as* HEATHER

**-ling**[1] (liŋ) [OE.] *a suffix added to nouns, meaning:* **1.** small [*duckling*] **2.** having a connection, esp. of an unimportant or contemptible kind, with the specified thing [*hireling*]

**-ling**[2] (liŋ) [OE.] [Archaic or Dial.] *a suffix meaning* extent or condition [*darkling*]

**ling.** linguistics

**lin·ger** (liŋ′gər) *vi.* [< North ME. freq. of *lengen*, to delay < OE. < base of *lang*, LONG[1]] **1.** to continue to stay, esp. through reluctance to leave **2.** to continue to live although very close to death **3.** to be unnecessarily slow in doing something; loiter —**lin′ger·er** *n.* —**lin′ger·ing** *adj.* —**lin′ger·ing·ly** *adv.*

**lin·ge·rie** (län′zhə rā′, -rē′; lan′-; -jə-) *n.* [Fr.] women's underwear and night clothes of silk, nylon, lace, etc.

**lin·go** (liŋ′gō) *n., pl.* **-goes** [Pr. < L. *lingua*, tongue] language; esp., a dialect, jargon, or special vocabulary that one is not familiar with: a humorous or disparaging term

**lin·gua fran·ca** (liŋ′gwə fraŋ′kə) *pl.* **lin′gua fran′cas, linguae fran·cae** (liŋ′gwē fran′sē) [It., lit., Frankish language] **1.** a hybrid language of Italian, Spanish, French, Greek, Arabic, and Turkish elements, spoken in certain Mediterranean ports **2.** any hybrid language used for communication between different peoples, as pidgin English

**lin·gual** (liŋ′gwəl) *adj.* [< ML. < L. *lingua*, the tongue] **1.** of the tongue **2.** of language or languages **3.** articulated with the tongue —*n. Phonet.* a lingual sound, as *l* or *t* —**lin′gual·ly** *adv.*

**lin·gui·ne** (liŋ gwē′nē) *n.* [< It. pl. of *linguina*, dim. of *lingua*, tongue] a kind of pasta like spaghetti but flat, often served with seafood

**lin·guist** (liŋ′gwist) *n.* [< L. *lingua*, the tongue + -IST] **1.** a specialist in linguistics **2.** *same as* POLYGLOT (sense 1)

**lin·guis·tic** (liŋ gwis′tik) *adj.* **1.** of language **2.** of linguistics —**lin·guis′ti·cal·ly** *adv.*

**linguistic atlas** an atlas charting the geographical distribution of linguistic forms and usages

**lin·guis·tics** (liŋ gwis′tiks) *n.pl.* [with *sing. v.*] **1.** the science of language, including phonology, morphology, syntax, and semantics: often **general linguistics 2.** the study of the structure, development, etc. of a particular language

**lin·i·ment** (lin′ə mənt) *n.* [< LL. < L. *linere*, to smear] a medicated liquid to be rubbed on the skin to soothe sore, sprained, or inflamed areas

**lin·ing** (lī′niŋ) *n.* [see LINE²] the material covering an inner surface

**link¹** (liŋk) *n.* [< Scand.] **1.** any of the series of rings or loops making up a chain **2.** *a)* a section of something resembling a chain [a *link* of sausage] *b)* an element in a series of circumstances [a weak *link* in the evidence] **3.** anything serving to connect or tie [a *link* with the past] **4.** one division (1/100) of a surveyor's chain, equal to 7.92 in. **5.** *Chem. same as* BOND¹ —*vt., vi.* to join together with a link or links —**link′er** *n.*

**link²** (liŋk) *n.* [prob. < ML. < L. *lychnus*, a light] a torch made of tow and pitch

**link·age** (liŋ′kij) *n.* **1.** a linking or being linked **2.** a series or system of links

**linking verb** a verb that functions chiefly as a connection between a subject and a predicate complement (Ex.: *be, seem, become,* etc.); copula

**links** (liŋks) *n.pl.* [OE. *hlinc*, a slope] *same as* GOLF COURSE

**link·up** (liŋk′up′) *n.* a joining together of two objects, factions, interests, etc.

**Lin·nae·an, Lin·ne·an** (li nē′ən) *adj.* [after C. *Linnaeus,* 18th-c. Swed. botanist] designating or of a system of classifying plants and animals by using a double name, the first word naming the genus, and the second the species

**lin·net** (lin′it) *n.* [OFr. *linette* < *lin* (< L. *linum*), flax: the bird feeds on flaxseed] a small finch found in Europe, Asia, and Africa

**li·no·cut** (lī′nə kut′) *n.* [< ff. + CUT] **1.** a design cut into the surface of a linoleum block **2.** a print made from this

**li·no·le·um** (li nō′lē əm) *n.* [coined < L. *linum,* flax + *oleum,* oil] a hard, washable floor covering made of a mixture of ground cork, ground wood, and oxidized linseed oil with a canvas backing

**Lin·o·type** (lin′ə tīp′) [< *line of type*] a trademark for a typesetting machine that casts an entire line of type in one bar, or slug —*n.* [often **l-**] **1.** a machine of this kind **2.** matter set in this way —*vt., vi.* [**l-**] **-typed′, -typ′ing** to set (matter) with this machine —**lin′o·typ′ist, lin′o·typ′er** *n.*

**lin·seed** (lin′sēd′) *n.* [OE. *linsæd*] the seed of flax

**linseed oil** a yellowish oil extracted from flaxseed, used in oil paints, etc.

**lin·sey-wool·sey** (lin′zē wool′zē) *n., pl.* **-wool′seys** [ME. < *lin,* flax + *wolle,* wool] a coarse cloth made of linen (or cotton) and wool: also **lin′sey**

**lint** (lint) *n.* [prob. < *lin,* linen] **1.** scraped and softened linen formerly used as a dressing for wounds **2.** bits of thread, ravelings, or fluff from cloth or yarn —*vi.* to give off lint —**lint′less** *adj.* —**lint′y** *adj.* **lint′i·er, lint′i·est**

**lin·tel** (lin′t'l) *n.* [OFr., ult. < L. *limen,* threshold] the horizontal crosspiece over a door, window, etc., carrying the weight of the structure above it

**lin·ters** (lin′tərz) *n.pl.* the short, fuzzy fibers clinging to cotton seeds after ginning, used in making cotton batting, etc.

**lin·y** (lī′nē) *adj.* **lin′i·er, lin′i·est** **1.** like a line; thin **2.** marked with lines

**Linz** (lints) city in N Austria: pop. 196,000

**li·on** (lī′ən) *n., pl.* **-ons, lī′on:** see PLURAL, II, D, 1 [OFr. < L. *leo* (gen. *leonis*) < Gr. *leōn*] **1.** a large, powerful member of the cat family, found in Africa and SW Asia, with a tawny coat, a tufted tail, and, in the adult male, a shaggy mane **2.** a person of great courage or strength **3.** a celebrity —**li′on·ess** *n.fem.*

**li·on-heart·ed** (lī′ən här′tid) *adj.* very brave

**li·on·ize** (lī′ə nīz′) *vt.* **-ized′, -iz′ing** to treat as a celebrity —**li′on·i·za′tion** *n.* —**li′on·iz′er** *n.*

**lion's share** the biggest and best portion

**lip** (lip) *n.* [OE. *lippa*] **1.** either of the two fleshy folds forming the edges of the mouth **2.** anything like a lip, as in structure or in being an edge or rim; specif., *a)* the projecting rim of a pitcher, cup, etc. *b)* the mouthpiece of a wind instrument *c) same as* LABIUM **3.** [Slang] insolent talk —*vt.* **lipped, lip′ping** **1.** to touch with the lips; specif., to place the lips in the proper position for playing (a wind instrument) **2.** to utter softly —*adj.* **1.** formed with a lip or the lips; labial **2.** from the lips only; spoken, but insincere —**bite one's lips** to keep back one's anger, annoyance, etc. —**hang on the lips of** to listen to with close attention —**keep a stiff upper lip** [Colloq.] to avoid becoming frightened or discouraged —**lip′less** *adj.*

**li·pase** (lī′pās, lip′ās) *n.* [< ff. + -ASE] an enzyme that aids in digestion by hydrolizing fats into fatty acids and glycerol

**lip·o-** [< Gr. *lipos,* fat] *a combining form meaning* of or like fat, fatty: also, before a vowel, **lip-**

**li·poid** (lip′oid, lī′poid) *adj.* [LIP(O)- + -OID] *Biochem., Chem.* resembling fat: also **li·poi′dal**

**lipped** (lipt) *adj.* having a lip or lips: often in compounds [*tight-lipped*]

**lip·py** (lip′ē) *adj.* **-pi·er, -pi·est** [Slang] impudent, brash, or insolent —**lip′pi·ness** *n.*

**lip-read** (lip′rēd′) *vt., vi.* **-read′** (-red′), **-read′ing** to recognize (a speaker's words) by lip reading —**lip reader**

**lip reading** the act or skill of recognizing a speaker's words by watching the movement of his lips: it is taught esp. to the deaf

**lip·stick** (-stik′) *n.* a small stick of cosmetic paste, set in a case, for coloring the lips

**liq. 1.** liquid **2.** liquor

**liq·ue·fa·cient** (lik′wə fā′shənt) *n.* [< L.: see LIQUEFY] something that causes liquefaction

**liq·ue·fac·tion** (-fak′shən) *n.* a liquefying or being liquefied

**liq·ue·fy** (lik′wə fī′) *vt., vi.* **-fied′, -fy′ing** [< Fr. < L. < *liquere,* to be liquid + *facere,* to make] to change into a liquid —**liq′ue·fi′a·ble** *adj.* —**liq′ue·fi′er** *n.*

**li·ques·cent** (li kwes′'nt) *adj.* [< L. prp. of *liquescere* < *liquere,* to be liquid] becoming liquid; melting —**li·ques′cence** *n.*

**li·queur** (li kur′) *n.* [Fr.] any of certain sweet, syrupy alcoholic liquors, variously flavored

**liq·uid** (lik′wid) *adj.* [< OFr. < L. *liquidus* < *liquere,* to be liquid] **1.** readily flowing; fluid; specif., that can move freely, unlike a solid, but does not expand indefinitely like a gas **2.** clear; limpid [*liquid* eyes] **3.** flowing smoothly and gracefully [*liquid* verse] **4.** readily convertible into cash [*liquid* assets] **5.** without friction and like a vowel, as the consonants *l* and *r* —*n.* a liquid substance —**liq·uid′i·ty, liq′uid·ness** *n.* —**liq′uid·ly** *adv.*

**liquid air** air brought to a liquid state by being subjected to great pressure and then cooled by its own expansion

**liq·ui·date** (lik′wə dāt′) *vt.* **-dat′ed, -dat′ing** [< ML. pp. of *liquidare,* to make clear < L. *liquidus,* liquid] **1.** to settle the amount of (indebtedness, damages, etc.) **2.** to settle the accounts of (a bankrupt business, etc.) by apportioning assets and debts **3.** to pay or settle (a debt) **4.** to convert (holdings or assets) into cash **5.** to dispose of or get rid of, as by killing —*vi.* to liquidate debts, accounts, etc. —**liq′ui·da′tion** *n.* —**liq′ui·da′tor** *n.*

**liq·uid·ize** (lik′wə dīz′) *vt.* **-ized′, -iz′ing** to cause to have a liquid quality

**liquid measure 1.** the measurement of liquids **2.** a system of measuring liquids; esp., the system in which 2 pints = 1 quart, 4 quarts = 1 gallon, etc.: see TABLE OF WEIGHTS AND MEASURES in Supplements

**liquid oxygen** a light-bluish liquid boiling at −183°C, produced by fractionation of liquid air

**liq·uor** (lik′ər) *n.* [< OFr. *licor* < L. *liquor*] **1.** any liquid or juice **2.** an alcoholic drink, esp. one made by distillation, as whiskey or rum —*vt., vi.* [Colloq.] to drink or cause to drink alcoholic liquor, esp. to the point of intoxication

**li·ra** (lir′ə) *n., pl.* **-re** (-ā), for 2 **-ras** [It. < L. *libra,* a balance] the monetary unit of **1.** Italy **2.** Turkey See MONETARY UNITS, table

**Lis·bon** (liz′bən) capital, & a seaport, of Portugal: pop. 826,000 (met. area 1,450,000): Port. name **Lis·bo·a** (lēzh-bô′ə)

**lisle** (līl) *n.* [< *Lisle,* earlier sp. of LILLE, France] **1.** a fine, hard, extra-strong cotton thread: in full, **lisle thread** **2.** a fabric, or stockings, gloves, etc., knit or woven of lisle —*adj.* made of lisle

**lisp** (lisp) *vi.* [< OE. < *wlisp,* a lisping] **1.** to substitute the sounds (th) and (*th*) for the sounds of *s* and *z* **2.** to speak imperfectly or like a child —*vt.* to utter with a lisp —*n.* **1.** the act or speech defect of lisping **2.** the sound of lisping —**lisp′er** *n.* —**lisp′ing·ly** *adv.*

**lis·some, lis·som** (lis′əm) *adj.* [altered < lithesome] moving gracefully or with ease and lightness; lithe, limber, agile, etc. —**lis′some·ly, lis′som·ly** *adv.* —**lis′some·ness, lis′som·ness** *n.*

**list¹** (list) *n.* [merging of OE. *liste* & Anglo-Fr. *liste* < OFr. < Gmc.] **1.** formerly, a narrow strip or border; specif., *a)* a strip of cloth *b)* a stripe of color *c)* a boundary **2.** the selvage of cloth **3.** a series of names, words, numbers, etc. set forth in order; catalog, roll, etc. **4.** *same as* LIST PRICE See also LISTS —*vt.* **1.** formerly, to edge with, or arrange in, stripes or bands **2.** *a)* to set forth (a series of names, items, etc.) in order *b)* to enter in a list, directory, catalog, etc. —*vi.* to be listed for sale, as in a catalog (at the price specified) —**list′er** *n.* —**list′ing** *n.*

**list²** (list) *vt.* [OE. *lystan* < base of *lust,* desire] [Archaic] to be pleasing to; suit —*vi.* [Archaic] to wish; like; choose

**list³** (list) *vt., vi.* [prob. specialized use of prec.] to tilt to one side, as a ship —*n.* a tilting or inclining to one side

**list⁴** (list) *vt., vi.* [OE. *hlystan* < base of *hlyst,* hearing] [Archaic] to listen (to)

**lis·ten** (lis′'n) *vi.* [OE. *hlysnan:* for base see prec.] **1.** to make a conscious effort to hear; attend closely, so as to hear **2.** to give heed; take advice —*n.* the act of listening —**listen in 1.** to listen to others' conversation; esp., to eavesdrop **2.** to listen to a broadcast —**lis′ten·er** *n.*

**list·er** (lis'tər) *n.* [< LIST[1] + -ER] a plow with a double moldboard, which heaps earth on both sides of the furrow

**Lis·ter** (lis'tər), **Joseph** 1827–1912; Eng. surgeon: introduced antiseptic surgery

**list·less** (list'lis) *adj.* [LIST[2] + -LESS] having or showing no interest in what is going on, as because of illness, weariness, dejection, etc.; spiritless; languid —**list'less·ly** *adv.* —**list'less·ness** *n.*

**list price** retail price as given in a list or catalog, discounted in sales to dealers, etc.

**lists** (lists) *n.pl.* [ME. *listes,* specialized use of *liste,* strip, border] **1.** *a)* the high fence enclosing an area where knights held tournaments *b)* this area itself or the tournament held there **2.** any place or realm of combat, conflict, etc. —**enter the lists** to enter a contest or struggle

**Liszt** (list), **Franz** (fränts) 1811–86; Hung. composer & pianist

**lit** (lit) *alt. pt. & pp. of* LIGHT

**lit. 1.** liter(s) **2.** literal **3.** literally **4.** literary **5.** literature

**lit·a·ny** (lit''n ē) *n., pl.* **-nies** [< OFr. < LL. < Gr. *litaneia* < *litē,* a request] **1.** a form of prayer in which the clergy and the congregation take part alternately, with recitation of supplications and fixed responses **2.** any dreary recital

**li·tchi** (lē'chē') *n.* [Chin. *li-chih*] **1.** a Chinese evergreen tree **2.** the dried or preserved fruit of this tree (**litchi nut**), with a single seed, a sweet, edible pulp, and a rough, brown, papery shell

**-lite** (līt) [Fr., for *-lithe:* see -LITH] *a combining form meaning* stone: used in the names of minerals, rocks, and fossils [*chrysolite*]

**li·ter** (lēt'ər) *n.* [Fr. *litre* < ML. < Gr. *litra,* a pound] the basic unit of capacity in the metric system, equal to 1 cubic decimeter (1.0567 liquid quarts or .908 dry quart)

**lit·er·a·cy** (lit'ər ə sē) *n.* the state or quality of being literate; ability to read and write

**lit·er·al** (lit'ər əl) *adj.* [< MFr. < LL. *litteralis* < L. *littera,* a letter] **1.** following the exact words of the original [*a literal translation*] **2.** based on the actual words in their ordinary meaning; in a basic or strict sense [*the literal* meaning of a passage] **3.** habitually interpreting statements or words according to their actual denotation; matter-of-fact [*a literal* mind] **4.** real; not going beyond the actual facts [*the literal* truth] : often used intensively to mean "virtual" —**lit'er·al'i·ty** (-ə ral'ə tē) *n., pl.* **-ties** —**lit'er·al·ly** *adv.* —**lit'er·al·ness** *n.*

**lit·er·al·ism** (-iz'm) *n.* **1.** the tendency to take words, statements, etc. in their literal sense **2.** thoroughgoing realism in art —**lit'er·al·ist** *n.* —**lit'er·al·is'tic** *adj.*

**lit·er·al·ize** (-ə līz') *vt.* **-ized', -iz'ing** to interpret literally

**lit·er·ar·y** (lit'ə rer'ē) *adj.* **1.** *a)* of or dealing with literature *b)* of or having to do with books [*literary* agents] **2.** of the relatively formal language of literature **3.** *a)* versed in literature *b)* making literature a profession

**lit·er·ate** (lit'ər it) *adj.* [< L. < *littera,* a letter] **1.** able to read and write **2.** having or showing extensive learning or culture —*n.* a literate person —**lit'er·ate·ly** *adv.*

**lit·e·ra·ti** (lit'ə rät'ē, -rä'tī) *n.pl.* [It. < L.] men of letters; scholarly or learned people

‡**lit·e·ra·tim** (-rät'im, -rät'-) *adv.* [ML. < L. *littera,* a letter] letter for letter; literally

**lit·er·a·ture** (lit'ər ə chər, lit'rə choor') *n.* [< OFr. < L. *litteratura* < *littera,* a letter] **1.** the profession of an author **2.** *a)* all the writings of a particular time, country, etc., esp. those of an imaginative or critical character valued for excellence of form and expression [*American literature*] *b)* all the writings on a particular subject **3.** [Colloq.] printed matter of any kind

**-lith** (lith) [Fr. *-lithe* < Gr. *lithos,* stone] *a combining form meaning* stone [*monolith*]

**Lith. 1.** Lithuania **2.** Lithuanian

**lith., litho., lithog. 1.** lithograph **2.** lithography

**lith·arge** (lith'ärj, li thärj') *n.* [< OFr. < L. < Gr. *lithargyros* < *lithos,* a stone + *argyros,* silver] an oxide of lead, PbO, used in storage batteries, paints, etc.

**lithe** (līth) *adj.* **lith'er, lith'est** [OE. *lithe,* soft, mild] bending easily; supple; limber: also **lithe'some** (-səm) —**lithe'ly** *adv.* —**lithe'ness** *n.*

**lith·i·a** (lith'ē ə) *n.* [ModL. < Gr. *lithos,* stone] lithium oxide, Li₂O, a white, crystalline compound

**-lith·ic** (lith'ik) *a combining form meaning* of a (specified) stage in the use of stone [*neolithic*]

**lith·i·um** (lith'ē əm) *n.* [ModL. < LITHIA] a soft, silver-white, metallic chemical element, the lightest known metal: symbol, Li; at. wt., 6.939; at. no., 3

**lithium carbonate** a white, powdery salt, Li₂CO₃, used in the manufacture of glass, dyes, etc. and in psychiatry to treat manic-depressive disorders

**lith·o** (lith'ō) *n., pl.* **-os**; *vt., vi.* **-oed, -o·ing** *clipped form of* LITHOGRAPH

**lith·o-** [< Gr. *lithos,* a stone] *a combining form meaning* stone, rock: also, before a vowel, **lith-**

**lith·o·graph** (lith'ə graf') *n.* a print made by lithography —*vi., vt.* to make (prints or copies) by lithography —**li·thog·ra·pher** (li thäg'rə fər) *n.*

**li·thog·ra·phy** (li thäg'rə fē) *n.* [LITHO- + -GRAPHY] the art or process of printing from a flat stone or metal plate: the design is put on the surface with a greasy material, and then water and printing ink are successively applied; the greasy parts, which repel water, absorb the ink, but the wet parts do not —**lith·o·graph·ic** (lith'ə graf'ik) *adj.* —**lith'o·graph'i·cal·ly** *adv.*

**lith·o·sphere** (lith'ə sfir') *n.* [LITHO- + SPHERE] the solid, rocky part of the earth; earth's crust

**li·thot·o·my** (li thät'ə mē) *n., pl.* **-mies** [< LL. < Gr.: see LITHO- & -TOMY] the surgical removal of a stone from the bladder

**Lith·u·a·ni·a** (lith'oo wā'nē ə) republic of the U.S.S.R., in NE Europe, on the Baltic Sea: 25,170 sq. mi.; pop. 3,100,000; cap. Vilnius: in full, **Lithuanian Soviet Socialist Republic** —**Lith'u·a'ni·an** *adj., n.*

**lit·i·ga·ble** (lit'i gə b'l) *adj.* that gives cause for litigation, or a lawsuit; actionable

**lit·i·gant** (lit'ə gənt) *n.* a party to a lawsuit

**lit·i·gate** (-gāt') *vt.* **-gat'ed, -gat'ing** [< L. pp. of *litigare* < *lis* (gen. *litis*), dispute + *agere,* to do] to contest in a lawsuit —*vi.* to carry on a lawsuit —**lit'i·ga'tor** *n.*

**lit·i·ga·tion** (lit'ə gā'shən) *n.* **1.** the carrying on of a lawsuit **2.** a lawsuit

**li·ti·gious** (li tij'əs) *adj.* **1.** *a)* given to carrying on litigations *b)* quarrelsome **2.** disputable at law **3.** of lawsuits —**li·ti'gious·ly** *adv.* —**li·ti'gious·ness** *n.*

**lit·mus** (lit'məs) *n.* [ON. *litmose,* lichen used in dyeing < *litr,* color + *mosi,* moss] a purple coloring matter obtained from various lichens: it turns blue in bases and red in acids

**litmus paper** absorbent paper treated with litmus and used as an acid-base indicator

**li·tre** (lēt'ər) *n. chiefly Brit. sp. of* LITER

**Litt.D.** [L. *Lit(t)erarum Doctor*] Doctor of Letters; Doctor of Literature

**lit·ter** (lit'ər) *n.* [< OFr. *litiere* < ML. < L. *lectus,* a couch] **1.** a framework having long horizontal shafts near the bottom and enclosing a couch on which a person can be carried **2.** a stretcher for carrying the sick or wounded **3.** straw, hay, etc. used as bedding for animals, as a covering for plants, etc. **4.** the young borne at one time by a dog, cat, etc. **5.** things lying about in disorder; esp., bits of scattered rubbish **6.** untidiness; disorder —*vt.* **1.** to bring forth (a number of young) at one time: said of certain animals **2.** to make messy with things scattered about **3.** to scatter about carelessly —*vi.* to bear a litter of young

**lit·té·ra·teur** (lit'ər ə tur') *n.* [Fr.] a literary man; man of letters: also written **litterateur**

**lit·ter·bug** (lit'ər bug') *n.* a person who litters a public place with trash, garbage, etc.

**lit·tle** (lit''l) *adj.* **lit'tler** or **less** or **less'er, lit'tlest** or **least** [OE. *lytel*] **1.** small in size; not big, large, or great **2.** small in amount, number, or degree **3.** short in duration or distance; brief **4.** small in importance or power [*the rights of the little* man] **5.** small in force, intensity, etc.; weak **6.** trivial; trifling **7.** lacking in breadth of vision; narrow-minded [*a little* mind] **8.** young: said of children or animals *Little* is sometimes used to express endearment [*bless your little* heart] —*adv.* **less, least 1.** in a small degree; only slightly; not much **2.** not in the least [*he little* suspects the plot] —*n.* **1.** *a)* a small amount, degree, etc. *b)* not much [*little* was done] **2.** a short time or distance —**little by little** gradually —**make little of** to treat as unimportant —**not a little** very much; very —**lit'tle·ness** *n.*

**Little America** five operational bases established by U.S. expeditions on the Ross Ice Shelf, Antarctica

**Little Bear** the constellation URSA MINOR

**Little Dipper** a dipper-shaped group of stars in the constellation Ursa Minor

**Little League** a league of baseball teams for youngsters

**Little Rock** [after a rocky cape in the river] capital of Ark., on the Arkansas River: pop. 158,000

**little slam** *Bridge* the winning of all but one trick

**little theater 1.** a small theater, as of a college, art group, etc., usually noncommercial and amateur **2.** drama produced by such theaters

**lit·to·ral** (lit'ər əl) *adj.* [L. *litoralis* < *litus* (gen. *litoris*), seashore] of, on, or along the shore —*n.* the region along the shore

**li·tur·gi·cal** (li tur'jə k'l) *adj.* **1.** of or constituting a liturgy **2.** used in or using a liturgy —**li·tur'gi·cal·ly** *adv.*

**lit·ur·gy** (lit′ər jē) *n., pl.* **-gies** [< Fr. < ML. < Gr. *leitourgia,* public service, ult. < *leōs,* people + *ergon,* work] **1.** prescribed forms or ritual for public worship in any of various religions **2.** the Eucharistic service

**liv·a·ble** (liv′ə b'l) *adj.* **1.** fit or pleasant to live in, as a house **2.** that can be lived through; endurable  Also sp. **liveable** —**liv′a·bil′i·ty, liv′a·ble·ness** *n.*

**live¹** (liv) *vi.* **lived, liv′ing** [OE. *libban*] **1.** to be alive; have life **2.** *a)* to remain alive *b)* to endure **3.** *a)* to pass one's life in a specified manner [to *live* happily] *b)* to conduct one's life [to *live* by a strict moral code] **4.** to enjoy a full and varied life **5.** *a)* to maintain life [to *live* on a pension] *b)* to be dependent for a living (with *off*) **6.** to feed; subsist [to *live* on fruits and nuts] **7.** to make one's dwelling; reside —*vt.* **1.** to carry out in one's life [to *live* one's faith] **2.** to spend; pass [to *live* a useful life] —**live down** to live in such a way as to wipe out the shame of (some fault, misdeed, etc.) —**live high** (or **well**) to live in luxury —**live in** to sleep at the place where one is in domestic service —**live it up** [Slang] to indulge in pleasures, extravagances, etc. that one usually forgoes —**live up to** to act according to (ideals, promises, etc.) —**live with** to bear; endure

**live²** (līv) *adj.* [< ALIVE] **1.** having life; not dead **2.** of the living state or living beings **3.** having positive qualities, as of warmth, vigor, vitality, brilliance, etc. [a *live* organization] **4.** of immediate or present interest [a *live* issue] **5.** *a)* still burning or glowing [a *live* spark] *b)* not extinct [a *live* volcano] **6.** unexploded [a *live* shell] **7.** unused; unexpended [live steam] **8.** carrying electrical current [a *live* wire] **9.** *a)* involving a performance in person, not one on film, tape, etc.; transmitted during the actual performance *b)* recorded at a public performance **10.** *Mech.* imparting motion or power

**-lived** (līvd; *occas.* livd) [see LIFE & -ED] *a combining form* meaning having (a specified kind or duration of) life [short-lived]

**live·li·hood** (līv′lē hood′) *n.* [OE. *liflad* < *lif,* life + *-lad,* course] means of supporting life; subsistence

**live·long** (liv′lôŋ′) *adj.* [ME. *lefe longe,* lit., lief long (cf. LIEF), phr. in which *lief* is merely intens.] long or tediously long in passing; whole; entire [the *livelong* day]

**live·ly** (līv′lē) *adj.* **-li·er, -li·est** [OE. *liflic*] **1.** full of life; active; vigorous **2.** full of spirit; exciting; animated [a *lively* debate] **3.** gay; cheerful **4.** moving quickly and lightly, as a dance **5.** vivid; keen [*lively* colors] **6.** bounding back with great resilience [a *lively* ball] —*adv.* in a lively manner —**live′li·ness** *n.*

**liv·en** (lī′vən) *vt., vi.* to make or become lively; cheer (*up*)

**live oak** **1.** *a)* an evergreen oak of the SE U.S. *b)* an oak of California **2.** the hard wood of these trees

**liv·er¹** (liv′ər) *n.* [OE. *lifer*] **1.** the largest glandular organ in vertebrate animals: it secretes bile and has an important function in metabolism **2.** the liver of cattle, fowl, etc. used as food

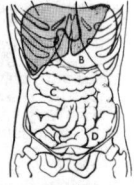

LIVER (A, liver; B, stomach; C, small intestine; D, large intestine)

**liv·er²** (liv′ər) *n.* a person who lives (in a specified way or place) [a clean *liver*]

**liv·er·ied** (liv′ər ēd, liv′rēd) *adj.* wearing a livery

**liv·er·ish** (liv′ər ish) *adj.* [Colloq.] **1.** bilious **2.** peevish; cross —**liv′er·ish·ness** *n.*

**Liv·er·pool** (liv′ər pool′) seaport in NW England: pop. 688,000 —**Liv′er·pud′li·an** (-pud′lē ən) *adj., n.*

**liver spot** a brownish spot on the skin, formerly attributed to faulty functioning of the liver

**liv·er·wort** (liv′ər wurt′) *n.* any of a class of plants, often forming dense, green mosslike mats on rocks, soil, etc. in moist places

**liv·er·wurst** (-wurst′) *n.* [LIVER¹ + G. *wurst,* sausage] a sausage containing ground liver: also **liver sausage**

**liv·er·y** (liv′ər ē, liv′rē) *n., pl.* **-er·ies** [< OFr. *livree,* gift of clothes to a servant < *livrer,* to deliver < L. *liberare,* to free] **1.** an identifying uniform such as is worn by servants or those in some particular group, trade, etc. **2.** the people wearing such uniforms **3.** characteristic dress or appearance **4.** *a)* the keeping and feeding of horses for a fixed charge *b)* the keeping of horses, vehicles, or both, for hire *c)* a stable providing these services: also **livery stable**

**liv·er·y·man** (-mən) *n., pl.* **-men** a person who owns or works in a livery stable

**lives** (līvz) *n. pl. of* LIFE

**live·stock** (līv′stäk′) *n.* domestic animals kept for use on a farm or raised for sale and profit

**live wire** **1.** a wire carrying an electric current **2.** [Colloq.] an energetic and enterprising person

**liv·id** (liv′id) *adj.* [< Fr. < L. *lividus*] **1.** discolored by a bruise; black-and-blue **2.** grayish-blue; lead-colored [*livid* with rage] : sometimes taken to mean pale, white, or red —**li·vid·i·ty** (li vid′ə tē), **liv′id·ness** *n.*

**liv·ing** (liv′iŋ) *adj.* **1.** alive; having life **2.** in active operation or use [a *living* institution] **3.** of persons alive [within *living* memory] **4.** in its natural state or place, or having its natural force, etc. [hewn from the *living* rock] **5.** still spoken and undergoing changes [a *living* language] **6.** true to reality; lifelike [the *living* image] **7.** of life or the sustaining of life [living conditions] **8.** suited for social and recreational activities in a house [the *living* area] **9.** presented in person before a live audience [living theater] **10.** very [the *living* daylights] —*n.* **1.** the state of being alive **2.** the means of sustaining life; livelihood **3.** manner of existence [the standard of *living*] **4.** in England, a church benefice —**the living** those that are still alive

**living death** a life of unrelieved misery

**living room** a room in a home, with sofas, chairs, etc., used for socializing, entertaining, etc.

**Liv·ing·stone** (liv′iŋ stən), **David** 1813–73; Scot. missionary & explorer in Africa

**living wage** a wage sufficient to maintain a person and that person's family in reasonable comfort

**living will** a document, legal in some States, directing that all measures to support life be ended if the signer should be dying of an incurable condition

**Li·vo·ni·a** (li vō′nē ə) [after *Livonia,* former Russian province] city in SE Mich.: suburb of Detroit: pop. 105,000

**Li·vor·no** (lē vôr′nô) *It. name of* LEGHORN

**Liv·y** (liv′ē) (L. name *Titus Livius*) 59 B.C.–17 A.D.; Rom. historian

**liz·ard** (liz′ərd) *n.* [< OFr. *lesard* < L. *lacerta*] **1.** any of a group of reptiles with a long slender body and tail, a scaly skin, and four legs (sometimes vestigial), as the gecko, chameleon, and iguana **2.** loosely, any of various similar animals, as alligators or salamanders

**Lju·blja·na** (lyōō′blyä nä) city in Slovenia, NW Yugoslavia: pop. 157,000

**'ll** *contraction of* will or shall [I'll go]

**LL., L.L.** Late Latin

**ll., ll** lines

**lla·ma** (lä′mə) *n., pl.* **-mas, -ma:** see PLURAL, II, D, 1 [Sp. < Quechua] a S. American animal related to the camel but smaller and without humps: it is used as a beast of burden and for its wool, flesh, and milk

**lla·no** (lä′nō; *Sp.* lyä′nô) *n., pl.* **-nos** (-nōz; *Sp.* -nôs) [Sp. < L. *planus,* plain] a grassy plain in the Southwest and in Spanish America

**LL.B.** [L. *Legum Baccalaureus*] Bachelor of Laws

**LL.D.** [L. *Legum Doctor*] Doctor of Laws

**Llew·el·lyn** (loo wel′ən) [W. *Llewelyn,* lit., prob., lionlike] a masculine name

**Lloyd** (loid) [W. *Llwyd,* lit., gray] a masculine name

**Lloyd George, David** 1863–1945; Brit. statesman; prime minister (1916–22)

**lo** (lō) *interj.* [OE. *la*] look! see!

**loach** (lōch) *n.* [< OFr. *loche*] a small, old-world, freshwater fish with barbels around the mouth

**load** (lōd) *n.* [OE. *lad,* a course, way] **1.** something carried or to be carried at one time; burden **2.** the amount that can be carried: a measure of weight or quantity varying with the type of conveyance [a *carload* of coal] **3.** something carried with difficulty; specif., *a)* a heavy burden or weight *b)* a great mental burden [a *load* off one's mind] **4.** the weight that a structure bears or the stresses that are put upon it **5.** a single charge, as of powder and bullets, for a firearm **6.** the amount of work carried by a person or a group [the class *load* of a teacher] **7.** [*often pl.*] [Colloq.] a great amount or number [loads of friends] **8.** *Elec.* the amount of power delivered by a generator, motor, etc. or carried by a circuit **9.** *Mech.* the external resistance offered to an engine by the machine that it is operating —*vt.* **1.** to put something to be carried into or upon; fill with a load [to *load* a truck] **2.** to put into or upon a carrier [to *load* coal] **3.** to burden; oppress **4.** to supply in abundance [to *load* one with honors, *loaded* with money] **5.** to put ammunition into (a gun or firearm), film into (a camera), etc. **6.** to weight (dice) unevenly for fraudulent use **7.** to add extra costs, a filler, etc. to **8.** to phrase (a question, etc.) so as to elicit a desired response **9.** *Baseball* to have or cause to have runners on (all bases) —*vi.* **1.** to put in or receive a charge, cartridge, etc. **2.** to put on or take on passengers, goods, etc. —**get a load of** [Slang] **1.** to listen to or hear **2.** to look at or see —**have a load on** [Slang] to be intoxicated —**load′ed** *adj.* —**load′er** *n.* —**load′ing** *n.*

**load·star** (lōd′stär′) *n. same as* LODESTAR

**load·stone** (lōd′stōn′) *n. same as* LODESTONE

**loaf¹** (lōf) *n., pl.* **loaves** (lōvz) [OE. *hlaf*] **1.** a portion of bread baked in one piece, commonly of oblong shape **2.** any mass of food shaped somewhat like a loaf of bread and baked [a salmon *loaf*]

**loaf²** (lōf) *vi.* [prob. < ff.] to spend time idly; loiter or lounge about; idle, dawdle, etc. —*vt.* to spend (time) idly (often with *away*)

**loaf·er** (-ər) *n.* [prob. < G. *landlaüfer,* a vagabond] a person who loafs —[L-] *a trademark for* a moccasinlike sport shoe; also, [l-] a shoe like this

**loam** (lōm) *n.* [OE. *lam*] **1.** a rich soil of clay, sand, and organic matter **2.** popularly, any rich, dark soil —*vt.* to fill or top with loam —**loam′y** *adj.*

**loan** (lōn) *n.* [< ON. *lān*] **1.** the act of lending **2.** something lent; esp., a sum of money lent, often at interest —*vt., vi.* to lend —**on loan** lent for temporary use or service

**loan·er** (-ər) *n.* **1.** one who loans **2.** a car, radio, etc. lent in place of one left for repair

**loan shark** [Colloq.] a person who lends money at exorbitant or illegal rates of interest

**loan·word** (-wurd′) *n.* [after G. *lehnwort*] a word of one language taken into another and naturalized (Ex.: KINDERGARTEN < G.)

**loath** (lōth) *adj.* [OE. *lath*, hostile] unwilling; reluctant *[to be loath to depart]* —**nothing loath** willing(ly)

**loathe** (lōth) *vt.* **loathed, loath′ing** [OE. *lathian*, to be hateful] to feel intense dislike or disgust for; abhor; detest —**loath′er** *n.*

**loath·ing** (lōth′iŋ) *n.* intense dislike, disgust, or hatred; abhorrence

**loath·ly¹** (lōth′lē) *adv.* [Rare] unwillingly

**loath·ly²** (lōth′lē) *adj. rare var. of* LOATHSOME

**loath·some** (lōth′səm, lōth′-) *adj.* causing loathing; disgusting —**loath′some·ly** *adv.* —**loath′some·ness** *n.*

**loaves** (lōvz) *n. pl. of* LOAF¹

**lob** (läb) *n.* [ME. *lobbe-*, lit., "heavy, thick"] *Tennis* a stroke in which the ball is sent high into the air, dropping into the back of the opponent's court —*vt.* **lobbed, lob′bing** to send (a ball) in a lob —*vi.* **1.** to move heavily and clumsily **2.** to lob a ball —**lob′ber** *n.*

**lo·bar** (lō′bər, -bär) *adj.* of a lobe or lobes

**lo·bate** (-bāt) *adj.* having or formed into a lobe or lobes —**lo′bate·ly** *adv.*

**lo·ba·tion** (lō bā′shən) *n.* **1.** the condition of having lobes **2.** the process of forming lobes **3.** a lobe

**lob·by** (läb′ē) *n., pl.* **-bies** [LL. *lobia:* see LODGE] **1.** a hall or large anteroom, as a waiting room of a hotel, theater, etc. **2.** a group of lobbyists —*vi.* **-bied, -by·ing** to act as a lobbyist —*vt.* to get or try to get legislators to vote for or against (a measure) by lobbying

**lob·by·ist** (-ist) *n.* a person, acting for a special interest group, who tries to influence the voting on legislation or the decisions of government administrators —**lob′by·ism** *n.*

**lobe** (lōb) *n.* [Fr. < LL. < Gr. *lobos*] a rounded projecting part; specif., *a)* the fleshy lower end of the human ear *b)* any of the main divisions of an organ *[a lobe of the brain, lung, or liver]* *c)* any of the rounded divisions of the leaves of certain trees —**lobed** *adj.*

**lo·be·li·a** (lō bēl′yə, -bē′lē ə) *n.* [ModL., after Matthias de *L'Obel* (1538–1616), Fl. botanist] any of a genus of plants with white, blue, or red flowers of very irregular shape

**lob·lol·ly** (läb′läl′ē) *n., pl.* **-lies** [prob. < dial. *lob*, to boil + dial. *lolly*, broth] **1.** a common pine of the SE U.S., having long needles **2.** the wood of this tree: also **loblolly pine**

**lo·bo** (lō′bō) *n.* [Sp. < L. *lupus*] *same as* GRAY WOLF

**lo·bot·o·my** (lō bät′ə mē) *n., pl.* **-mies** [< LOBE + -TOMY] a surgical operation in which a lobe of the brain is cut into or across

**lob·ster** (läb′stər) *n., pl.* **-sters, -ster:** see PLURAL, II, D, 1 [OE. *lopustre* < *loppe*, spider (from external resemblance) + -*estre:* see -STER] **1.** a large, edible sea crustacean with compound eyes, long antennae, and five pairs of legs, the first pair of which are modified into large pincers **2.** any similar crustacean, as the spiny lobster **3.** the flesh of these animals used as food

LOBSTER
(to 24 in. long)

**lobster tail** a tail of a lobster (sense 2), or its flesh used as food, often broiled in the shell

**lob·ule** (läb′yool) *n.* **1.** a small lobe **2.** a subdivision of a lobe —**lob′u·lar** (-yoo lər) *adj.* —**lob′u·late′** (-lāt′) *adj.*

**lo·cal** (lō′k'l) *adj.* [OFr. < LL. *localis* < L. *locus,* a place] **1.** relating to place **2.** of, characteristic of, or confined to a particular place or district *[items of local interest]* **3.** not broad; narrow *[local outlook]* **4.** of or for a particular part of the body **5.** making all stops along its run *[a local bus]* —*n.* **1.** a local train, bus, etc. **2.** a newspaper item of local interest only **3.** a chapter or branch, as of a labor union —**lo′cal·ly** *adv.*

**local color** behavior, speech, etc. characteristic of a certain region or time, introduced into a novel, play, etc. to supply

**lo·cale** (lō kal′) *n.* [Fr. *local*] a place or locality, esp. with reference to events, etc. connected with it, often as a setting for a story, etc.

**lo·cal·ism** (lō′k'l iz'm) *n.* **1.** a local custom **2.** a word, meaning, expression, pronunciation, etc. peculiar to one locality **3.** provincialism

**lo·cal·i·ty** (lō kal′ə tē) *n., pl.* **-ties 1.** position with regard to surrounding objects, landmarks, etc. **2.** a place; district

**lo·cal·ize** (lō′kə līz′) *vt.* **-ized′, -iz′ing** to make local; limit, confine, or trace to a particular place, area, or locality —**lo′cal·iz′a·ble** *adj.* —**lo′cal·i·za′tion** *n.*

**local option** the right to decide by a vote of the residents whether something, esp. the sale of liquor, shall be permitted in their locality

**lo·cate** (lō′kāt, lō kāt′) *vt.* **-cat·ed, -cat·ing** [< L. pp. of *locare* < *locus,* a place] **1.** to designate the site of (a mining claim, etc.) **2.** to establish in a certain place *[offices located downtown]* **3.** to discover the position of after a search *[to locate a lost object]* **4.** to show the position of *[to locate Guam on a map]* **5.** to assign to a particular place, etc. —*vi.* [Colloq.] to settle *[to locate in Boston]* —**lo′cat·er, lo′ca·tor** *n.*

**lo·ca·tion** (lō kā′shən) *n.* **1.** a locating or being located **2.** position; place; situation **3.** an area marked off for a specific purpose **4.** *Motion Pictures* an outdoor set or setting, away from the studio, where scenes are photographed: chiefly in **on location** —**lo·ca′tion·al** *adj.*

**loc·a·tive** (läk′ə tiv) *adj.* [< L. pp. of *locare:* see LOCATE] *Linguis.* expressing place at which or in which —*n.* **1.** the locative case (in Latin, Greek, etc.) **2.** a word in this case

**loc. cit.** [L. *loco citato*] in the place cited

**loch** (läk, läkh) *n.* [< Gael. & OIr.] [Scot.] **1.** a lake **2.** an arm of the sea, esp. when narrow and nearly surrounded by land

**lo·ci** (lō′sī) *n. pl. of* LOCUS

**lock¹** (läk) *n.* [OE. *loc,* a bolt, enclosure] **1.** a mechanical device for fastening a door, strongbox, etc. by means of a key or combination **2.** anything that fastens something else and prevents it from operating **3.** a locking together; jam **4.** an enclosed part of a canal, waterway, etc. equipped with gates so that the level of the water can be changed to raise or lower boats from one level to another **5.** the mechanism of a firearm used to explode the ammunition charge **6.** *same as* AIR LOCK **7.** *Wrestling* a hold in which a part of the opponent's body is firmly gripped —*vt.* **1.** to fasten (a door, trunk, etc.) by means of a lock **2.** to shut (*up, in,* or *out*); confine *[locked in jail]* **3.** to fit closely; link *[we locked arms]* **4.** to embrace tightly **5.** to jam together so as to make immovable *[locked gears]* **6.** to put in a fixed position **7.** to move (a ship) through a lock —*vi.* **1.** to become locked **2.** to intertwine or interlock —**lock out** to keep (workers) from a place of employment in seeking to force terms upon them —**lock, stock, and barrel** [Colloq.] completely

**lock²** (läk) *n.* [OE. *loc*] **1.** a curl, tress, or ringlet of hair **2.** [*pl.*] [Poet.] the hair of the head **3.** a tuft of wool, cotton, etc.

**Locke** (läk), **John** 1632–1704; Eng. philosopher

**lock·er** (läk′ər) *n.* **1.** a person or thing that locks **2.** a chest, closet, drawer, etc. which can be locked, esp. one for individual use **3.** a large freezer compartment, as one rented in a cold-storage plant

**locker room** a room equipped with lockers

**lock·et** (läk′it) *n.* [< OFr. *locquet,* dim. of *loc,* a latch < Frank.] a small, hinged ornamental case of gold, silver, etc., for holding a picture, lock of hair, etc.: it is usually worn on a necklace

**lock·jaw** (läk′jô′) *n.* [short for earlier *locked jaw*] *same as* TETANUS

**lock·out** (-out′) *n.* the locking out of workers by an employer

**lock·smith** (-smith′) *n.* a person whose work is making or repairing locks and keys

**lock step** a way of marching in very close file

**lock·up** (-up′) *n.* a jail

**lo·co** (lō′kō) *n.* [MexSp. < Sp., mad < L. *ulucus,* owl] [Western] *same as:* **1.** LOCOWEED **2.** LOCO DISEASE —*vt.* **-coed, -co·ing** to poison with locoweed —*adj.* [Slang] crazy; demented

**lo·co-** [< L. *locus,* a place] *a combining form meaning* from place to place *[locomotion]*

**‡lo·co ci·ta·to** (lō′kō sī tät′ō) [L.] in the place cited or quoted

**loco disease** a nervous disease of horses, sheep, and cattle, caused by locoweed poisoning: also **lo′co·ism** *n.*

**lo·co·mo·tion** (lō′kə mō′shən) *n.* [LOCO- + MOTION] motion, or the power of moving, from one place to another

**lo·co·mo·tive** (-mōt′iv) *adj.* **1.** of locomotion **2.** moving or capable of moving from one place to another **3.** designating or of engines that move under their own power *[locomotive design]* —*n.* an engine that can move about by its own power; esp., an electric, steam, or diesel engine on wheels, designed to push or pull a railroad train

**lo·co·mo·tor** (lō′kə mōt′ər) *n.* a person or thing with power of locomotion —*adj.* of locomotion

**locomotor ataxia** *same as* TABES DORSALIS

**lo·co·weed** (lō′kō wēd′) *n.* any of several plants of the legume family, which are common in western N. America and cause loco disease

**lo·cus** (lō′kəs) *n., pl.* **lo·ci** (-sī) [L.] **1.** a place **2.** *Math.* a line, plane, etc. every point of which satisfies a given condition

**lo·cust** (lō′kəst) *n.* [< L. *locusta*] **1.** any of various large grasshoppers; specif., a migratory grasshopper often traveling in great swarms destroying vegetation **2.** *same as* SEVENTEEN-YEAR LOCUST **3.** *a)* a spiny tree of the legume family, native to eastern and central U.S. and having racemes of fragrant white flowers *b)* the yellowish, hard wood of this tree **4.** *same as* HONEY LOCUST

LOCUST
(to 2 in. long)

**lo·cu·tion** (lō kyōō′shən) *n.* [< L. *locutio* < pp. of *loqui*, to speak] **1.** a word, phrase, or expression **2.** a particular style of speech

**lode** (lōd) *n.* [var. of LOAD (< OE. *lad*, course)] *Mining* **1.** a vein containing metallic ore and filling a fissure in rock **2.** any deposit of ore separated from the adjoining rock **3.** any rich source

**lo·den** (lō′d'n) *adj.* [G. < MHG. < OHG. *lodo*, coarse cloth] **1.** designating or of a fulled, waterproof wool cloth, used for coats **2.** of a dark, olive green often used for this cloth

**lode·star** (lōd′stär′) *n.* [see LODE & STAR] **1.** a star by which one directs his course; esp., the North Star **2.** a guiding principle or ideal

**lode·stone** (-stōn′) *n.* **1.** a strongly magnetic variety of the mineral magnetite **2.** something that attracts as with magnetic force

**lodge** (läj) *n.* [< OFr. *loge*, arbor < LL. *lobia* < Gmc.] **1.** *a)* a small house for special or seasonal use *[a hunting lodge]* *b)* a resort hotel or motel **2.** *a)* the meeting place of a local chapter, as of a fraternal organization *b)* such a local chapter **3.** the den of certain animals, esp. beavers **4.** *a)* the hut or tent of an American Indian *b)* those who live in it —*vt.* **lodged, lodg′ing 1.** to house, esp. temporarily **2.** to rent rooms to **3.** to deposit for safekeeping **4.** to place or land by shooting, thrusting, etc. (with *in*) **5.** to bring (a complaint, etc.) before legal authorities **6.** to confer (powers) upon (with *in*) —*vi.* **1.** to live in a certain place for a time **2.** to live (*with* another or *in* his home) as a paying guest **3.** to come to rest and remain firmly fixed (*in*)

**lodg·er** (läj′ər) *n.* a person or thing that lodges; esp., one who rents a room in another's home

**lodg·ing** (-iŋ) *n.* **1.** a place to live in, esp. temporarily **2.** *[pl.]* a room or rooms rented in a private home

**lodging house** *same as* ROOMING HOUSE

**lodg·ment** (-mənt) *n.* **1.** a lodging or being lodged **2.** a lodging place **3.** an accumulation of deposited material Also sp. **lodge′ment**

**Łódź** (looj) city in C Poland: pop. 749,000

**lo·ess** (les, lō′es) *n.* [G. *löss* < *lösch*, loose] a fine-grained, yellowish-brown, extremely fertile loam deposited by the wind —**lo·ess′i·al** *adj.*

**loft** (lôft, läft) *n.* [OE. < ON. *lopt*, upper room, sky] **1.** *a)* an attic or atticlike space just below the roof of a house, barn, etc. *b)* an upper story of a warehouse or factory **2.** a gallery *[the choir loft in a church]* **3.** *a)* the slope given to the face of a golf club to aid in hitting the ball in a high curve *b)* the height of a ball hit in a high curve —*vt.* **1.** to store in a loft **2.** *a)* to hit or throw (a golf ball, baseball, etc.) into the air in a high curve *b)* to throw (a bowling ball) so that it strikes the alley sharply some distance past the foul line —*vi.* to loft a ball —**loft′er** *n.*

**loft·y** (lôf′tē) *adj.* **loft′i·er, loft′i·est 1.** very high *[a lofty mountain]* **2.** elevated; noble; grand **3.** haughty; too proud; arrogant —**loft′i·ly** *adv.* —**loft′i·ness** *n.*

**log¹** (lôg, läg) *n.* [ME. *logge*, prob. < or akin to ON. *lāg*, felled tree] **1.** a section of the trunk or of a large branch of a felled tree **2.** a device (orig. a quadrant of wood) for measuring the speed of a ship: see also LOG CHIP **3.** a daily record of a ship's speed, progress, etc. and of the events in its voyage; logbook **4.** *a)* a similar record of an aircraft's flight *b)* a record of a pilot's flying time, experience, etc. **5.** any record of progress or occurrences —*adj.* made of a log or logs —*vt.* **logged, log′ging 1.** to saw (trees) into logs **2.** to cut down the trees of (a region) **3.** to enter or

record in a log **4.** to sail or fly (a specified distance) —*vi.* to cut down trees and transport the logs to a sawmill

**log²** (lôg, läg) *n. clipped form of* LOGARITHM

**-log** *same as* -LOGUE

**Lo·gan** (lō′gən), **Mount** mountain in SW Yukon, Canada: highest mountain in Canada: 19,850 ft.

**lo·gan·ber·ry** (lō′gən ber′ē) *n., pl.* **-ries** [after J. H. *Logan* (1841-1928), U.S. horticulturist] **1.** a hybrid bramble developed from the blackberry and the red raspberry **2.** its purplish-red fruit

**log·a·rithm** (lôg′ə rith′m, läg′-) *n.* [ModL. < Gr. *logos*, a ratio + *arithmos*, number] *Math.* the exponent of the power to which a fixed number (the *base*) must be raised in order to produce a given number (the *antilogarithm*): logarithms are normally computed to the base of 10 and are used for shortening mathematical calculations —**log′a·rith′mic** *adj.* —**log′a·rith′mi·cal·ly** *adv.*

**log·book** (lôg′book′, läg′-) *n. same as* LOG¹ (senses 3, 4, & 5)

**log chip** a flat piece of wood attached to a line (**log line**) and reel (**log reel**) and thrown into the water to measure a ship's rate of speed

**loge** (lōzh) *n.* [Fr.: see LODGE] **1.** a box in a theater **2.** the forward section of a balcony in a theater

**log·ger** (lôg′ər, läg′-) *n.* a person whose work is logging; lumberjack

**log·ger·head** (lôg′ər hed′, läg′-) *n.* [dial. *logger*, block of wood (< LOG¹) + HEAD] **1.** a sea turtle of the Atlantic with a large head: also **loggerhead turtle 2.** [Dial.] a stupid fellow —**at loggerheads** in disagreement; quarreling

**log·gi·a** (lä′jē ə, lä′jə; lō′-; *It.* lôd′jä) *n., pl.* **-gi·as;** *It.* **log′gie** (-je) [It.: see LODGE] an arcaded or roofed gallery built into or projecting from the side of a building, often one overlooking an open court

**log·ging** (lôg′iŋ, läg′-) *n.* the occupation of cutting down trees, cutting them into logs, and transporting them to the sawmill

LOGGIA

**log·ic** (läj′ik) *n.* [< OFr. < L. < Gr. *logikē (technē)*, logical (art) < *logos*, word, speech,, thought] **1.** the science of correct reasoning, dealing with relationships among propositions **2.** a book on this science **3.** correct reasoning; valid induction or deduction **4.** way of reasoning *[poor logic]* **5.** necessary connection or outcome, as of events **6.** the systematized interconnections in an electronic digital computer

**log·i·cal** (läj′i k'l) *adj.* **1.** of or used in the science of logic **2.** according to the principles of logic, or correct reasoning **3.** necessary or expected because of what has gone before **4.** using correct reasoning —**log′i·cal′i·ty** (-kal′ə-tē), **log′i·cal·ness** *n.* —**log′i·cal·ly** *adv.*

**-log·i·cal** (läj′i k'l) *a suffix used to form adjectives from nouns ending in* -LOGY *[biological]*: also **-log·ic**

**lo·gi·cian** (lō jish′ən) *n.* an expert in logic

**lo·gis·tics** (lō jis′tiks) *n.pl.* [with sing. v.] [< Fr. < *logis*, lodgings < *loger*, to quarter] the branch of military science having to do with procuring, maintaining, and transporting materiel, personnel, and facilities —**lo·gis′tic, lo·gis′ti·cal** *adj.* —**lo·gis′ti·cal·ly** *adv.*

**log·jam** (lôg′jam′, läg′-) *n.* **1.** logs jammed together in a stream **2.** an accumulation of many items to deal with

**log·roll** (lôg′rōl′, läg′-) *vi.* to take part in logrolling —*vt.* to get passage of (a bill) by logrolling —**log′roll′er** *n.*

**log·roll·ing** (-rōl′iŋ) *n.* **1.** the act of rolling logs away, as by a group clearing land **2.** mutual aid, esp. among politicians, as by voting for each other's bills **3.** *same as* BIRLING

**-logue** (lôg, läg) [Fr. < L. < Gr. < *logos*: see LOGIC] *a combining form meaning:* **1.** a (specified kind of) speaking or writing *[monologue]* **2.** a student or scholar

**log·wood** (lôg′wood′, läg′-) *n.* [so named from being imported in logs] **1.** the hard, brownish-red wood of a Central American and West Indian tree: it yields a dye used as a stain **2.** this tree or dye

**lo·gy** (lō′gē) *adj.* **-gi·er, -gi·est** [< ? Du. *log*, heavy, dull] [Colloq.] dull or sluggish, as from overeating —**lo′gi·ness** *n.*

**-lo·gy** (lə jē) [ult. < Gr. < *logos*: see LOGIC] *a combining form meaning:* **1.** a (specified kind of) speaking *[eulogy]* **2.** science, doctrine, or theory of *[biology, theology]*

**Lo·hen·grin** (lō′ən grin′) *Ger. Legend* a knight of the Holy Grail, son of Parsifal

**loin** (loin) *n.* [< OFr. *loigne*, ult. < L. *lumbus*] **1.** [*usually pl.*] the lower part of the back on either side of the backbone between the hipbones and the ribs **2.** the front part of the hindquarters of beef, lamb, veal, etc. with the flank removed **3.** [*pl.*] the hips and the lower abdomen regarded as a part of the body to be clothed or as the region of strength and procreative power —**gird (up) one's loins** to prepare to do something difficult

**loin·cloth** (-klôth′, -kläth′) *n.* a cloth worn about the loins, as by some tribes in warm climates

**Loire** (lwär) river flowing from S France north & west into the Bay of Biscay

**Lo·is** (lō′is) [LL. < Gr. *Lōis*] a feminine name

**loi·ter** (loit′ər) *vi.* [< MDu. *loteren*] **1.** to spend time idly (often with *about*); linger **2.** to move slowly and lazily, with frequent pauses —*vt.* to spend (time) idly —**loi′ter·er** *n.*

**Lo·ki** (lō′kē) *Norse Myth.* the god who constantly created discord and mischief

**loll** (läl) *vi.* [< MDu. *lollen*] **1.** to lean or lounge about in a lazy manner **2.** to hang in a relaxed manner; droop —*vt.* to let droop —**loll′er** *n.*

**lol·la·pa·loo·za, lol·la·pa·loo·sa** (läl′ə pə lŏo′zə) *n.* [< ?] [Slang] something very striking or exceptional: also **lol·lypalooza,** etc.

**Lol·lard** (läl′ərd) *n.* [< MDu. *lollaerd,* lit., a mutterer (of prayers)] any of the followers of John Wycliffe in 14th- and 15th-cent. England

**lol·li·pop, lol·ly·pop** (läl′ē päp′) *n.* [prob. < dial. *lolly,* the tongue + *pop*] a piece of hard candy fixed to the end of a small stick; sucker

**lol·lop** (läl′əp) *vi.* [extended < LOLL, prob. after GALLOP] [Chiefly Brit.] **1.** to lounge about; loll **2.** to move in a clumsy or relaxed, bobbing way

**lol·ly** (läl′ē) *n., pl.* -**lies** [contr. < *lollypop:* see LOLLIPOP] [Brit. Slang] **1.** money **2.** a piece of hard candy

**lol·ly·gag** (läl′ē gag′) *vi.* -**gagged′**, -**gag′ging** [< ?] [Colloq.] to waste time in trifling activity

**Lom·bard** (läm′bərd, lum′-) *n.* **1.** a native or inhabitant of Lombardy **2.** one of a Germanic tribe that settled in the Po Valley —*adj.* of Lombardy or the Lombards: also **Lom·bar′dic**

**Lom·bar·dy** (läm′bər dē, lum′-) region of N Italy, on the border of Switzerland: chief city, Milan

**Lombardy poplar** a tall, slender poplar with upward curving branches

**Lo·mond** (lō′mənd), **Loch** lake in WC Scotland

**Lon·don** (lun′dən) **1.** administrative county in SE England, consisting of the City of London & 28 metropolitan boroughs; capital of England, the United Kingdom, & the Brit. Commonwealth **2.** this county with its suburbs: pop. 11,025,000: called **Greater London 3.** city in SE Ontario, Canada: pop. 240,000 **4. City of,** historic center of the county of London: pop. 4,800 —**Lon′don·er** *n.*

**Lon·don** (lun′dən), **Jack** 1876–1916; U.S. writer

**London broil** a boneless cut of beef, as of the flank, that is marinated, then broiled, and served in thin slices

**Lon·don·der·ry** (lun′dən der′ē) seaport in NW Northern Ireland: pop. 56,000

**lone** (lōn) *adj.* [< ALONE] **1.** by oneself; solitary **2.** lonesome **3.** unmarried or widowed **4.** *a)* isolated *b)* unfrequented —**lone′ness** *n.*

**lone·ly** (-lē) *adj.* -**li·er**, -**li·est 1.** alone; solitary **2.** *a)* isolated *b)* unfrequented **3.** unhappy at being alone; longing for friends, etc. **4.** causing such a feeling —**lone′li·ly** *adv.* —**lone′li·ness** *n.*

**lon·er** (lō′nər) *n.* [Colloq.] one who avoids the company of others

**lone·some** (lōn′səm) *adj.* **1.** having or causing a lonely feeling **2.** unfrequented; desolate —*n.* [Colloq.] self [all by my *lonesome*] —**lone′some·ly** *adv.* —**lone′some·ness** *n.*

**long¹** (lôŋ) *adj.* [OE. *long, lang*] **1.** measuring much from one end or point to the other in space or time **2.** of a specified extent in length [a foot *long*] **3.** of greater than usual or standard length, quantity, etc. [a long toe, a long list] **4.** overextended in length **5.** tedious; slow **6.** extending to what is distant in space or time; far-reaching [a long view of the matter] **7.** large; big [long odds, a long chance] **8.** well supplied [long on excuses] **9.** holding a supply of a commodity or security in anticipation of a rise in price **10.** requiring a relatively long time to pronounce: said of a speech sound —*adv.* **1.** for a long time **2.** for the duration of [all day long] **3.** at a much earlier or a much later time [to stay *long* after midnight] —*n.* **1.** a variation of a clothing size longer than average for that size **2.** a signal, syllable, etc. of long duration **3.** a long time [it won't take *long*] —**as** (or so) **long as 1.** during the time that **2.** seeing that; since **3.** provided that —**before long** soon —**the long and (the) short of** the whole story of in a few words

**long²** (lôŋ) *vi.* [OE. *langian*] to feel a strong yearning; wish earnestly [to *long* to go home]

**long.** longitude

**Long Beach** seaport in SW Calif., on the Pacific: pop. 361,000

**long·boat** (lôŋ′bōt′) *n.* the largest boat carried on a merchant sailing ship

**long·bow** (-bō′) *n.* a large bow drawn by hand and shooting a long, feathered arrow: cf. CROSSBOW

**long·cloth** (-klôth′, -kläth′) *n.* a soft cotton fabric of fine quality

**long distance** a telephone service or system for calls to distant places —**long′-dis′tance** *adj., adv.*

**long division** the process of dividing one number by another and putting the steps down in full

**long-drawn** (-drôn′) *adj.* continuing for a long time; prolonged: also **long′-drawn′-out′**

**lon·gev·i·ty** (län jev′ə tē, lôn-) *n.* [< L. < *longus,* long + *aevum,* age] **1.** *a)* great span of life *b)* length of life **2.** length of service

**long face** a glum, disconsolate look —**long′-faced′** *adj.*

**Long·fel·low** (lôŋ′fel′ō), **Henry Wads·worth** (wädz′wurth′) 1807–82; U.S. poet

**long green** *slang term for* PAPER MONEY

**long·hair** (lôŋ′her′) *adj.* [Colloq.] designating or of intellectuals or their tastes; specif., preferring classical music to jazz or popular tunes: also **long′haired′** —*n.* [Colloq.] **1.** an intellectual; specif., a longhair musician **2.** *same as* HIPPIE

**long·hand** (-hand′) *n.* ordinary handwriting, with the words written out in full

**long-head·ed, long·head·ed** (-hed′id) *adj.* **1.** having a long head **2.** having much foresight; shrewd —**long′-head′ed·ly** *adv.* —**long′-head′ed·ness** *n.*

**long·horn** (-hôrn′) *n.* any of a breed of long-horned cattle formerly raised in great numbers in the Southwest

**long house** a communal home or council hall among the Iroquois and other Indian tribes

**long·ing** (-iŋ) *n.* strong desire; yearning —*adj.* feeling or showing a yearning —**long′ing·ly** *adv.*

**long·ish** (-ish) *adj.* somewhat long

**Long Island** island in SE N.Y., between Long Island Sound & the Atlantic: pop. 6,728,000

**Long Island Sound** arm of the Atlantic, between N Long Island & S Conn.

**lon·gi·tude** (län′jə tōod′, -tyōod′) *n.* [< L. *longitudo* < *longus,* LONG¹] **1.** length **2.** distance east or west on the earth's surface, measured as an arc of the equator (in degrees up to 180° or by the difference in time) between the meridian passing through a particular place and a standard or prime meridian, usually the one passing through Greenwich, England

**lon·gi·tu·di·nal** (län′jə tōod′'n əl, -tyōod′-) *adj.* **1.** of or in length **2.** running or placed lengthwise **3.** of longitude —**lon′gi·tu′di·nal·ly** *adv.*

**long johns** [Colloq.] long underwear: also **long′ies**

**long jump** a track and field event that is a jump for distance rather than height

**long-lived** (lôŋ′līvd′, -livd′) *adj.* having or tending to have a long life span or existence

**long-play·ing** (lôŋ′plā′iŋ) *adj.* designating or of a phonograph record with microgrooves, for playing at 33 1/3 revolutions per minute

**long-range** (-rānj′) *adj.* **1.** having a range of great distance **2.** taking the future into consideration [long-range plans]

**long·shore·man** (-shôr′mən) *n., pl.* -**men** [(*a*)longshore + *man*] a person who works on the waterfront loading and unloading ships

**long shot** [Colloq.] a betting choice that has little chance of winning and, hence, carries great odds —**not by a long shot** [Colloq.] not at all

**long·sight·ed** (-sīt′id) *adj. same as* FARSIGHTED

**long·stand·ing** (-stan′diŋ) *adj.* having continued for a long time

**long-suf·fer·ing** (-suf′ər iŋ) *adj.* bearing injuries, insults, trouble, etc. patiently for a long time —*n.* long and patient endurance of trials —**long′-suf′fer·ing·ly** *adv.*

**long suit 1.** the suit in which a card player holds the most cards **2.** something at which one excels

**long-term** (-turm′) *adj.* **1.** for or extending over a long time **2.** designating or of a capital gain, loan, etc. that involves a relatively long period

**long-time** (-tīm′) *adj.* over a long period of time

**long ton** the British ton, equal to 2,240 pounds

**‡lon·gueur** (lôn gër′; E. lôŋ gur′) *n.* [Fr.] a long, boring section, as in a novel, musical work, etc.

**long-waist·ed** (lôŋ′wās′tid) *adj.* with a low waistline

**long·ways** (-wāz′) *adv. same as* LENGTHWISE: also **long′wise′** (-wīz′)

**long-wind·ed** (-win′did) *adj.* **1.** not easily winded by exertion **2.** *a)* speaking or writing at great length *b)* tiresomely long —**long′-wind′ed·ly** *adv.* —**long′-wind′ed·ness** *n.*

**loo¹** (lōo) *n.* [< Fr. *lanturelu*] a card game played for a pool made up of stakes and forfeits

**loo²** (lōo) *n.* [< Fr. *lieux,* short for *les lieux d'aisances;* lit., places of conveniences] [Brit. Slang] a toilet

look (look) *vi.* [OE. *locian*] **1.** to see **2.** *a)* to direct one's eyes in order to see *b)* to direct one's attention mentally upon something **3.** to search **4.** to appear; seem **5.** to be facing in a specified direction **6.** to expect (followed by an infinitive) —*vt.* **1.** to direct one's eyes on *[look* him in the face*]* **2.** to express by one's looks *[to look* one's disgust*]* **3.** to appear as having attained (some age) *[he looks* his years*]* —*n.* **1.** the act of looking; glance **2.** outward aspect *[the look* of a beggar*]* **3.** [Colloq.] *a)* [*usually pl.*] appearance *[from the looks* of things*]* *b)* [*pl.*] personal appearance, esp. of a pleasing nature *[to have looks* and youth*]* —*interj.* **1.** see! **2.** pay attention! —**look after** to take care of —**look alive** (or **sharp**)! be alert! —**look down on** (or **upon**) to regard with contempt —**look for 1.** to search for **2.** to expect —**look forward to** to anticipate, esp. eagerly —**look in** (**on**) to pay a brief visit (to) —**look on 1.** to be an observer or spectator **2.** to consider; regard —**look** (**like**) **oneself** to seem in normal health, spirits, etc. —**look out** to be on the watch; be careful —**look out for 1.** to be wary about **2.** to take care of —**look over** to examine; inspect —**look to 1.** to take care of **2.** to rely upon; resort to **3.** to expect —**look up 1.** to search for in a reference book, etc. **2.** [Colloq.] to pay a visit to **3.** [Colloq.] to improve —**look up to** to admire —**look′er** *n.*

look·er-on (look′ər än′) *n., pl.* look′ers-on′ an observer or spectator; onlooker

looking glass a (glass) mirror

look·out (look′out′) *n.* **1.** a careful watching for someone or something **2.** a place for keeping watch, esp. a high place **3.** a person detailed to watch **4.** [Chiefly Brit.] outlook **5.** [Colloq.] concern; worry

loom¹ (loom) *n.* [OE. (*ge*)*loma*, tool, utensil] a machine for weaving thread or yarn into cloth —*vt.* to weave on a loom

loom² (loom) *vi.* [< ?] to appear, take shape, or come in sight indistinctly, esp. in a large or threatening form *[the* peak *loomed* up before us, disaster *loomed* ahead*]*

loon¹ (loon) *n.* [earlier *loom* < ON. *lomr*] a fish-eating, diving bird with a sharp bill and webbed feet: noted for its weird cry

loon² (loon) *n.* [Scot. *loun* < ?] **1.** a clumsy, stupid person **2.** a crazy person

loon·y (loo′nē) *adj.* loon′i·er, loon′i·est [< LUNATIC] [Slang] crazy; demented —*n., pl.* loon′ies [Slang] a loony person Also loon′ey

loop (loop) *n.* [< Anglo-N. forms corresponding to ON. *hlaup*, a leap, *hlaupa*, to run] **1.** the figure formed by a line, thread, wire, etc. that curves back to cross itself **2.** anything having or forming this figure, as a written *l* **3.** a sharp bend, as in a mountain road **4.** a ring-shaped fastening or ornament **5.** a plastic intrauterine contraceptive device (usually with *the*) **6.** *Aeron.* a maneuver in which an airplane describes a closed curve or circle in the vertical plane —*vt.* **1.** to make a loop or loops in or of **2.** to wrap around one or more times *[loop* the wire around the post*]* **3.** to fasten with a loop or loops —*vi.* **1.** to form a loop or loops **2.** *Aeron.* to perform a loop or loops —**knock** (or **throw**) **for a loop** [Slang] to throw into a state of confusion or shock —**loop the loop** to make a vertical loop in the air, as in an airplane —**loop′er** *n.*

loop·hole (-hōl′) *n.* [prob. < MDu. *lupen*, to peer + HOLE] **1.** a hole or narrow slit in the wall of a fort, etc. for looking or shooting through **2.** a means of evading an obligation, a law, etc.

loose (loos) *adj.* [< ON. *lauss*] **1.** not confined or restrained; free **2.** not put up in a package *[loose* salt*]* **3.** readily available *[loose* cash*]* **4.** not firmly fastened down or in *[a loose* wheel*]* **5.** not taut; slack **6.** not tight *[loose* clothing*]* **7.** not compact or compactly constructed *[loose* soil, a *loose* frame*]* **8.** not restrained *[loose* talk*]* **9.** not precise; inexact *[a loose* translation*]* **10.** sexually immoral; lewd **11.** *a)* not strained *[a loose* cough*]* *b)* moving freely or excessively *[loose* bowels*]* **12.** [Colloq.] relaxed; easy —*adv.* loosely; in a loose manner —*vt.* loosed, loos′ing **1.** to make loose; specif., *a)* to set free; unbind *b)* to make less tight *c)* to make less compact *d)* to free from restraint; relax **2.** to let fly; release *[he loosed* the arrow*]* —*vi.* to loose something or become loose —**break loose** to free oneself; escape —**cast loose** to untie or unfasten —**let loose** (**with**) to release; let go —**on the loose 1.** not confined or bound; free **2.** [Colloq.] having fun in a free, unrestrained manner —**set** (or **turn**) **loose** to make free; release —**loose′ly** *adv.* —**loose′ness** *n.*

loose ends minor bits of unfinished work, etc. —**at loose ends** unsettled, unoccupied, unemployed, etc.

loose-joint·ed (-join′tid) *adj.* **1.** having loose joints **2.** moving freely; limber —**loose′-joint′ed·ly** *adv.* —**loose′-joint′ed·ness** *n.*

loose-leaf (-lēf′) *adj.* having leaves, or sheets, that can easily be removed or changed

loos·en (loos′'n) *vt., vi.* to make or become loose or looser —**loosen up** [Colloq.] **1.** to talk freely **2.** to give money generously **3.** to relax —**loos′en·er** *n.*

loose·strife (-strīf′) *n.* [transl. of L. *lysimachia* < Gr. < *lyein*, to slacken + *machē*, battle] **1.** a plant with leafy stems and loose spikes of white, rose, or yellow flowers **2.** a plant (**purple loosestrife**) with spikes of purple flowers

loot (loot) *n.* [Hindi *lūt* < Sans. *lunt*, to rob] **1.** goods stolen or taken by force; plunder; spoils **2.** [Slang] money, gifts, etc. —*vt., vi.* to plunder —**loot′er** *n.*

lop¹ (läp) *vt.* lopped, lop′ping [OE. *loppian*, prob. < Scand.] **1.** to trim (a tree, etc.) by cutting off branches or twigs **2.** to remove by or as by cutting off —*n.* something lopped off —**lop′per** *n.*

lop² (läp) *vi.* lopped, lop′ping [prob. akin to LOB] **1.** to hang down loosely **2.** to move in a halting way —*adj.* hanging down loosely

lope (lōp) *vi.* loped, lop′ing [< ON. *hlaupa*, to leap] to move with a long, swinging stride or in an easy canter —*vt.* to cause to lope —*n.* a long, easy, swinging stride

lop-eared (läp′ird′) *adj.* having ears that droop or hang down

lop·sid·ed (-sīd′id) *adj.* **1.** noticeably heavier, bigger, or lower on one side **2.** not balanced; uneven —**lop′sid′ed·ly** *adv.* —**lop′sid′ed·ness** *n.*

lo·qua·cious (lō kwā′shəs) *adj.* [< L. *loquax* < *loqui*, to speak] very talkative; fond of talking —**lo·qua′cious·ly** *adv.* —**lo·qua′cious·ness** *n.*

lo·quac·i·ty (-kwas′ə tē) *n.* talkativeness, esp. when excessive

Lo·rain (lō rān′) [ult. after LORRAINE (France)] city in N Ohio, on Lake Erie: pop. 75,000

Lor·an (lôr′an) *n.* [< *Lo*(*ng*) *Ra*(*nge*) *N*(*avigation*)] [*also* l-] a system by which a ship or aircraft can determine its position by the difference in time between radio signals sent from two or more known stations

lord (lôrd) *n.* [OE. *hlaford* < *hlaf*, loaf + *weard*, keeper] **1.** a person having great power and authority; ruler; master **2.** the head of a feudal estate **3.** [L-] *a)* God *b)* Jesus Christ **4.** in Great Britain, *a)* a nobleman holding the rank of baron, viscount, earl, or marquess; member of the House of Lords *b)* a man who by courtesy or because of his office is given the title of Lord **5.** [L-] [*pl.*] the House of Lords in the British Parliament (usually with *the*) **6.** [L-] in Great Britain, the title of a lord, variously used —*interj.* [*often* L-] an exclamation of surprise or irritation —**lord it** (**over**) to domineer (over)

lord·ly (-lē) *adj.* -li·er, -li·est of, like, characteristic of, or suitable to a lord; specif., *a)* noble; grand *b)* haughty; overbearing —*adv.* in the manner of a lord —**lord′li·ness** *n.*

Lord of hosts Jehovah; God

Lord's day Sunday

lord·ship (lôrd′ship′) *n.* **1.** the rank or authority of a lord **2.** rule; dominion **3.** [*also* L-] a title used in speaking of or to a lord: with *his* or *your*

Lord's Prayer the prayer beginning *Our Father*, which Jesus taught his disciples: Matt. 6:9–13

lords spiritual the archbishops and bishops who are members of the British House of Lords

Lord's Supper **1.** *same as* LAST SUPPER **2.** Holy Communion; Eucharist

lords temporal those members of the British House of Lords who are not clergymen

lore (lôr) *n.* [OE. *lar*] knowledge or learning; specif., all the knowledge concerning a particular subject, esp. that of a traditional nature

Lor·e·lei (lôr′ə lī′) [G.] *German Legend* a siren whose singing on a rock in the Rhine lured sailors to shipwreck on the reefs

Lo·ret·ta (lō ret′ə, lə-) [dim. of LAURA] a feminine name

lor·gnette (lôr nyet′) *n.* [Fr. < *lorgner*, to spy, peep < OFr. *lorgne*, squinting] a pair of eyeglasses, or an opera glass, attached to a handle

lorn (lôrn) *adj.* [ME., pp. of *losen*, to lose] **1.** [Obs.] lost; ruined **2.** [Archaic] forsaken, forlorn, bereft, or desolate

Lor·raine (lō rān′; *Fr.* lô ren′) [Fr.] **1.** a feminine name **2.** former province of NE France: see ALSACE-LORRAINE

LORGNETTE

lor·ry (lôr′ē, lär′-) *n., pl.* -ries [prob. < dial. *lurry, lorry*, to tug] **1.** a low, flat wagon without sides **2.** [Brit.] a motor truck

lo·ry (lôr′ē) *n., pl.* -ries [Malay *lūrī*] a small, brightly colored parrot native to Australia and nearby islands

Los An·gel·es (lôs an′jə ləs, läs; an′gə ləs; -lēz′) [Sp., lit., the angels] city & seaport on the SW coast of Calif.: pop. 2,967,000 (met. area 7,446,000)

lose (looz) *vt.* lost, los′ing [< OE. *losian*, to be lost + *leosan*, to lose] **1.** to bring to ruin or destruction **2.** to become unable to find; mislay *[I lost* my key*]* **3.** to have taken from one by accident, death, removal, etc.; suffer the loss of **4.** to get rid of *[dieting to lose* weight*]* **5.** to fail to keep or maintain *[to lose* one's temper, to *lose* one's job*]* **6.** *a)* to fail to see, hear, or understand *b)* to fail to keep in sight, mind, etc. **7.** to fail to have, get, take, etc.; miss **8.** to fail to win *[to lose* a game*]* **9.** to cause the loss of *[it lost* him his job*]* **10.** to wander from and not be able to find (one's way, etc.). **11.** to confuse, bewilder, or alienate **12.** to waste; squander *[to lose* time*]* **13.** to outdistance **14.** to engross or preoccupy *[to be lost* in reverie*]* **15.** to go slower by *[my watch lost* a minute*]* —*vi.* **1.** to suffer loss **2.** to be defeated in a contest, etc. **3.** to be slow: said of a timepiece —**lose oneself 1.** to go astray; become bewildered **2.** to become engrossed —**lose out** [Colloq.] to fail —**lose out on** [Colloq.] to fail to take advantage of or gain —**los'·a·ble** *adj.*

**los·er** (lōō'zər) *n.* **1.** one that loses; esp., [Colloq.] one that seems doomed to lose **2.** a person who reacts to loss as specified *[a poor loser]*

**los·ing** (-ziŋ) *n.* *[pl.]* losses by gambling —*adj.* **1.** that loses *[a losing team]* **2.** resulting in loss *[a losing game]*

**loss** (lôs, läs) *n.* *[< ? OE. los,* ruin*]* **1.** a losing or being lost **2.** the damage, disadvantage, etc. caused by losing something **3.** the person, thing, or amount lost **4.** *Insurance a)* death, damage, etc. that is the basis for a valid claim *b)* the amount paid by the insurer **5.** *Mil. a)* the losing of military personnel in combat by death, injury, or capture *b)* *[pl.]* those lost in this way *c)* *[pl.]* ships, aircraft, etc. lost in battle —**at a loss (to)** puzzled or uncertain (how to)

**loss leader** any article that a store sells cheaply or below cost to attract customers

**lost** (lôst, läst) *pt. & pp. of* LOSE —*adj.* **1.** destroyed; ruined **2.** not to be found; missing **3.** no longer held, possessed, seen, heard, or known **4.** not gained or won **5.** having wandered from the way **6.** bewildered; ill at ease **7.** wasted; squandered —**lost in** engrossed in —**lost on** without effect on —**lost to 1.** no longer in the possession of **2.** no longer available to **3.** insensible to

**lost tribes** the ten tribes making up the kingdom of Israel that were carried off into Assyrian captivity about 722 B.C.: II Kings 17:6

**lot** (lät) *n.* *[OE. hlot]* **1.** any of a number of counters, etc. drawn from at random to decide a matter by chance **2.** the use of such a method *[to choose men by lot]* **3.** the decision arrived at by this means **4.** what one receives as the result of such a decision; share **5.** one's portion in life; fortune *[her unhappy lot]* **6.** a plot of ground **7.** *a)* a number of persons or things regarded as a group *b)* a quantity of material processed at the same time **8.** *[often pl.]* [Colloq.] a great number or amount **9.** [Colloq.] sort (of person) *[he's a bad lot]* **10.** a motion-picture studio —*adv.* very much *[a lot richer]* : also **lots** —*vt.* **lot'ted, lot'ting** to divide into lots —*vi.* to draw or cast lots —**cast** (or **throw**) **in one's lot with** to share the fortunes of —**draw** (or **cast**) **lots** to decide an issue by using lots —**the lot** [Colloq.] the entire amount or number

**Lot** (lät) *Bible* Abraham's nephew, who, warned by angels, fled from Sodom: his wife looked back to see it destroyed and was turned into a pillar of salt: Gen. 19:1–26

**loth** (lōth) *adj. alt. sp. of* LOATH

**Lo·thar·i·o** (lō ther'ē ō') *n., pl.* **-i·os'** [after the young rake in a play by Nicholas Rowe (1674–1718)] *[often* l-] a light-hearted seducer of women

**lo·tion** (lō'shən) *n.* *[< L. < pp. of lavare,* to wash*]* a liquid preparation used, as on the skin, for washing, soothing, healing, etc.

**lot·ter·y** (lät'ər ē) *n., pl.* **-ter·ies** *[< MFr. < MDu. < lot,* lot*]* **1.** a game of chance in which people buy numbered chances on prizes, the winning numbers being drawn by lot **2.** any undertaking involving chance selection, as by the drawing of lots *[military draft lottery]*

**lot·to** (lät'ō) *n.* *[It. < Fr. < MDu. lot,* lot*]* a game of chance played with cards having squares numbered in rows: counters are placed on those numbers corresponding to numbered disks drawn by lot

**lo·tus, lo·tos** (lōt'əs) *n.* *[L. < Gr. lōtos < Heb. lōṭ]* **1.** *Gr. Legend* a plant whose fruit induced a dreamy languor and forgetfulness **2.** any of several tropical African and Asiatic waterlilies, as the **white lotus** of Egypt **3.** a plant of the legume family, with irregular leaves and yellow, purple, or white flowers

**lo·tus-eat·er** (-ēt'ər) *n.* in the *Odyssey,* one of a people who ate the fruit of the lotus and became indolent, dreamy, and forgetful of duty

**lotus position** in yoga, an erect sitting posture with the legs crossed, each foot resting on the opposite thigh

**loud** (loud) *adj.* *[OE. hlud]* **1.** strongly audible: said of sound **2.** sounding with great intensity *[a loud bell]* **3.** noisy **4.** clamorous; emphatic *[loud denials]* **5.** [Colloq.] too vivid; flashy *[a loud pattern]* **6.** [Colloq.] unrefined;

vulgar —*adv.* in a loud manner —**loud'ish** *adj.* —**loud'ly** *adv.* —**loud'ness** *n.*

**loud-mouthed** (-moutht', -mouthd') *adj.* talking in a loud, irritating voice —**loud'mouth'** *n.*

**loud·speak·er** (-spē'kər) *n.* a device for converting electric current into sound waves and for amplifying this sound

**Lou·is** (lōō'ē; *for 1, usually* lōō'is; *Fr.* lwē) [Fr., ult. < OHG. *Hluodowig* < Gmc. bases meaning "famous in war"] **1.** a masculine name: dim. *Lou, Louie* **2. Louis XIV** 1638–1715; king of France (1643–1715) **3. Louis XV** 1710–74; king of France (1715–74): great-grandson of *prec.* **4. Louis XVI** 1754–93; king of France (1774–92): guillotined: grandson of *prec.*

**lou·is d'or** (lōō'ē dôr') [Fr., gold louis] **1.** an old French gold coin of varying value **2.** a later French gold coin worth 20 francs

**Lou·ise** (lōō wēz') [Fr., fem. of LOUIS] **1.** a feminine name: dim. *Lou;* var. *Louisa* **2.** Lake, small lake in SW Alberta, Canada

**Lou·i·si·an·a** (lōō wē'zē an'ə, lōō'ə zē-) [< Fr., ult. after LOUIS XIV] Southern State of the U.S., on the Gulf of Mexico: 48,523 sq. mi.; pop. 4,204,000; cap. Baton Rouge: abbrev. **La., LA** —**Lou·i'si·an'·i·an, Lou·i'si·an'an** *adj., n.*

**Louis Napoleon** (surname *Bonaparte*) 1808–73; president of France (1848–52) &, as Napoleon III, emperor (1852–70): deposed: nephew of NAPOLEON I

**Lou·is·ville** (lōō'ē vil; *locally* lōō'ə vəl) [after LOUIS XVI] city in N Ky.: pop. 298,000 (met. area 902,000)

**lounge** (lounj) *vi.* **lounged, loung'ing** [Scot. dial. < ? *lungis,* laggard] **1.** to stand, move, sit, etc. in a relaxed or lazy way **2.** to spend time in idleness —*vt.* to spend (time) by lounging —*n.* **1.** an act or time of lounging **2.** a room, as in a hotel or theater, with comfortable furniture and, often, an adjoining toilet or toilets **3.** a couch or sofa —**loung'er** *n.*

**loupe** (lōōp) *n.* [Fr., ult. prob. < OHG. *luppa,* shapeless mass] a small, high-powered magnifying lens held close to the eye, used by jewelers, etc.

**lour** (lour) *vi., n. same as* LOWER²

**Lourdes** (lōōrd, lōōrdz; *Fr.* lōōrd) town in SW France: site of a famous Catholic shrine

**louse** (lous; *also, for v.,* louz) *n., pl.* **lice** [OE. *lus* (pl. *lys*)] **1.** *a)* a small, wingless, parasitic insect that infests the hair or skin of man and some other mammals *b)* any of various arthropods that suck blood or juice from other animals or plants **2.** any similar insect, arachnid, etc., as the wood louse **3.** *pl.* **lous'es** [Slang] a person regarded as mean, contemptible, etc. —*vt.* **loused, lous'ing** [Rare] to delouse —**louse up** [Slang] to botch; spoil; ruin

**lous·y** (lou'zē) *adj.* **lous'i·er, lous'i·est 1.** infested with lice **2.** [Slang] dirty, disgusting, or contemptible **3.** [Slang] poor; inferior: a generalized epithet of disapproval **4.** [Slang] oversupplied (*with*) —**lous'i·ly** *adv.* —**lous'i·ness** *n.*

**lout** (lout) *n.* [prob. < ME. *lutien,* to lurk < OE. *lutian*] a clumsy, stupid fellow; boor —**lout'ish** *adj.* —**lout'ish·ly** *adv.* —**lout'ish·ness** *n.*

**lou·ver** (lōō'vər) *n.* [MFr. *lover* < MDu. *love,* theater gallery] **1.** an opening fitted with sloping slats so as to admit light and air but shed rain **2.** any of these slats: also **louver board 3.** any set of slats or fins used to control ventilation, etc. Also **lou'vre** —**lou'vered** *adj.*

**Lou·vre** (lōō'vrə, lōōv; *Fr.* lōō'vr') ancient royal palace in Paris, now an art museum

**lov·a·ble** (luv'ə b'l) *adj.* inspiring love; easily loved; endearing: also sp. **love'a·ble** —**lov'a·bil'i·ty, lov'a·ble·ness** *n.* —**lov'a·bly** *adv.*

**love** (luv) *n.* [OE. *lufu*] **1.** a deep affection for or attachment or devotion to someone, or the expression of this **2.** good will toward others **3.** *a)* a strong liking for or interest in something *[a love* of music*]* *b)* the object of such liking **4.** *a)* a strong, usually passionate, affection of one person for another *b)* the object of this; sweetheart **5.** sexual passion or intercourse **6.** [L-] *a)* Cupid *b)* [Rare] Venus **7.** *Tennis* a score of zero —*vt.* **loved, lov'ing 1.** to feel love for **2.** to show love for by fondling, kissing, etc. **3.** to take great pleasure in *[to love* books*]* **4.** to benefit from *[plants love* light*]* —*vi.* to feel the emotion of love —**fall in love (with)** to begin to feel love (for) —**for the love of** for the sake of —**in love** feeling love —**make love 1.** to embrace, kiss, etc. **2.** to have sexual intercourse

**love affair** an amorous relationship between two people not married to each other

**love apple** [Archaic] the tomato

**love·bird** (-burd') *n.* any of various small parrots, often kept as cage birds: the mates appear to be greatly attached to each other

**love-hate** (-hāt') *adj.* characterized simultaneously by feelings of love and hate *[a love-hate* relationship*]*

**Love·lace** (luv′lās′), Richard 1618–58; Eng. poet

**love·less** (-lis) *adj.* without love; specif., *a)* feeling no love *b)* unloved —**love′less·ly** *adv.,* —**love′less·ness** *n.*

**love-lies-bleed·ing** (-līz′blēd′iŋ) *n.* a cultivated amaranth with spikes of small, red flowers

**love·lorn** (-lôrn′) *adj.* deserted by one's sweetheart; pining from love

**love·ly** (-lē) *adj.* **-li·er, -li·est** having qualities that inspire love, admiration, etc.; specif., *a)* beautiful *b)* morally or spiritually attractive *c)* [Colloq.] highly enjoyable *[a lovely party]* —*n.,* *pl.* **-lies** [Colloq.] a beautiful young woman —**love′li·ly** *adv.,* —**love′li·ness** *n.*

**love·mak·ing** (-mā′kiŋ) *n.* the act of making love

**love potion** a magic drink supposed to arouse in the drinker love for a certain person

**lov·er** (-ər) *n.* a person who loves; specif., *a)* a sweetheart *b)* *[pl.]* a couple in love with each other *c)* a partner, esp. the male partner, in a love affair *d)* a person who greatly enjoys some (specified) thing *[a lover of good music]* —**lov′er·ly** *adj., adv.*

**love seat** a small sofa seating two persons

**love·sick** (-sik′) *adj.* **1.** so much in love as to be unable to act normally **2.** expressive of such a condition —**love′sick′ness** *n.*

**lov·ing** (-iŋ) *adj.* feeling or expressing love —**lov′ing·ly** *adv.*

**loving cup** a large drinking cup with two handles, formerly passed among guests at banquets: now often given as a trophy in sports, etc.

**lov·ing·kind·ness** (-kīnd′nis) *n.* kindness resulting from or expressing love

**low¹** (lō) *adj.* [ME. *lah* < ON. *lagr*] **1.** *a)* not high or tall *b)* not far above the ground **2.** depressed below the surrounding surface *[low land]* **3.** of little depth; shallow **4.** of little quantity, degree, value, etc. **5.** of less than normal height, depth, degree, etc. **6.** below others in order, position, etc. **7.** near the horizon *[the sun is low]* **8.** near the equator *[low latitudes]* **9.** exposing the neck and shoulders *[a dress with a low neckline]* **10.** in hiding *[stay low]* **11.** deep *[a low bow]* **12.** lacking energy; weak **13.** depressed; melancholy **14.** not of high rank; humble **15.** vulgar; coarse **16.** mean; contemptible *[a low trick]* **17.** unfavorable *[to have a low opinion of someone]* **18.** having less than a normal amount of some usual element *[low in calories]* **19.** not advanced in evolution, development, etc. *[a low form of plant life]* **20.** relatively recent *[a manuscript of low date]* **21.** designating or of the gear ratio of a motor vehicle transmission which produces the lowest speed and greatest power **22.** *a)* not well supplied with *[low on fuel]* *b)* [Colloq.] short of ready cash **23.** *a)* not loud *b)* deep in pitch **24.** very informal in matters of ceremony, doctrine, etc. **25.** *Phonet.* produced with the tongue held low in the mouth: said of some vowels, as (ä) —*adv.* **1.** in, to, or toward a low position, level, etc. **2.** in a low manner **3.** quietly; softly **4.** with a deep pitch —*n.* something low; specif., *a)* low gear (see *adj.* 21), or a similar arrangement in an automatic transmission *b)* a low level, point, degree, etc. *c)* *Meteorol.* an area of low barometric pressure —**lay low 1.** to cause to fall by hitting **2.** to overcome or kill —**lie low 1.** to keep oneself hidden **2.** to wait patiently —**low′ness** *n.*

**low²** (lō) *vi.* [OE. *hlowan*] to make the characteristic sound of a cow; moo —*n.* the characteristic sound of a cow

**low·born** (-bôrn′) *adj.* of humble birth

**low·boy** (-boi′) *n.* a chest of drawers mounted on short legs to about the height of a table

**low·bred** (-bred′) *adj.* ill-mannered; vulgar

**low·brow** (-brou′) *n.* [Colloq.] a person lacking intellectual tastes —*adj.* [Colloq.] of or for a lowbrow

**low-cal** (-kal′) *adj.* having a low caloric value

**Low Church** that party of the Anglican Church which attaches little importance to the priesthood or to traditional rituals, doctrines, etc. —**Low′-Church′** *adj.*

**low comedy** comedy that gets its effect mainly from action and situation, as burlesque, farce, etc.

**Low Countries** the Netherlands, Belgium, & Luxembourg

**low·down** (lō′doun′; *for adj.* -doun′) *n.* [Slang] the pertinent facts (with *the*) —*adj.* [Colloq.] mean; contemptible; despicable

**Low·ell** (lō′əl) [after F.C. *Lowell* (1775–1817), industrialist] city in NE Mass.: pop. 92,000

**Low·ell** (lō′əl) **1. Amy,** 1874–1925; U.S. poet **2. James Russell,** 1819–91; U.S. poet, essayist, & editor **3. Robert,** 1917–77; U.S. poet

**low·er¹** (lō′ər) *adj. compar. of* LOW¹ **1.** below or farther down in place, rank, dignity, etc. **2.** less in quantity, value, intensity, etc. **3.** farther south, closer to the mouth of a river, etc. **4.** [L-] *Geol.* earlier: used of a division of a period —*vt.* **1.** to let or put down *[lower the window]* **2.** to reduce in height, amount, value, etc. *[to lower prices]* **3.** to weaken or lessen *[to lower one's resistance]* **4.** to demean; degrade **5.** to reduce (a sound) in volume or in pitch —*vi.* to become lower; sink; fall

**low·er²** (lou′ər) *vi.* [ME. *louren*] **1.** to scowl or frown **2.** to appear dark and threatening —*n.* a lowering look

**Lower California** *same as* BAJA CALIFORNIA

**lower case** small-letter type used in printing, as distinguished from capital letters (*upper case*) —**low′er-case′** *adj.* —**low′er-case′** *vt.* - **cased′,** -**cas′ing**

**lower class** the social class below the middle class; working class, or proletariat

**low·er·class·man** (lō′ər klas′mən) *n., pl.* **-men** a student who is a freshman or sophomore

**Lower House** [*often* l- h-] the larger and more representative branch of a legislature having two branches, as the U.S. House of Representatives

**low·er·ing** (lou′ər iŋ) *adj.* **1.** scowling; frowning darkly **2.** dark, as if about to rain or snow —**low′er·ing·ly** *adv.*

**lower world 1.** *same as* NETHER WORLD **2.** the earth

**low frequency** any radio frequency between 30 and 300 kilohertz

**Low German 1.** *same as* PLATTDEUTSCH **2.** the West Germanic languages, other than High German, including Plattdeutsch, English, Dutch, Frisian, etc.

**low-grade** (lō′grād′) *adj.* **1.** of inferior quality **2.** of low degree *[a low-grade infection]*

**low-key** (-kē′) *adj.* of low intensity, tone, etc.; subdued or restrained: also **low′-keyed′**

**low·land** (lō′lənd; *also, for n.,* -land′) *n.* land that is below the level of the surrounding land —*adj.* of, in, or from such a region —**the Lowlands** lowland region in SC Scotland —**low′land·er, Low′land·er** *n.*

**Low Latin** nonclassical, esp. medieval, Latin

**low·life** (-līf′) *n.* [Slang] a disgusting person

**low·ly** (-lē) *adj.* **-li·er, -li·est 1.** of or suited to a low position or rank **2.** humble; meek **3.** ordinary —*adv.* **1.** humbly; meekly **2.** in a low manner, position, etc. **3.** softly; gently —**low′li·ness** *n.*

**Low Mass** a Mass said, not sung, less ceremonial than High Mass, and offered by one priest

**low-mind·ed** (-mīn′did) *adj.* having or showing a coarse, vulgar mind —**low′-mind′ed·ly** *adv.* —**low′-mind′ed·ness** *n.*

**low-pitched** (-picht′) *adj.* **1.** low in pitch **2.** having little slope, as a roof **3.** of low intensity; restrained

**low-pres·sure** (-presh′ər) *adj.* **1.** *a)* having or using a relatively low pressure *b)* having a low barometric pressure **2.** not energetic or forceful

**low profile** an unobtrusive presence, or concealed activity

**low-proof** (-prōōf′) *adj.* low in alcohol content

**low-rise** (-rīz′) *adj.* designating or of a building, esp. an apartment house, having only a few stories

**low-spir·it·ed** (-spir′i tid) *adj.* in low spirits; sad; depressed —**low′-spir′it·ed·ly** *adv.*

**low-test** (-test′) *adj.* vaporizing at a relatively high temperature: said of gasoline

**low tide 1.** the lowest level reached by the ebbing tide **2.** the time when the tide is at this level **3.** the lowest point reached by anything

**low water 1.** *same as* LOW TIDE **2.** water at its lowest level, as in a stream

**low-wa·ter mark** (-wôt′ər, -wät′-) **1.** a mark showing low water **2.** the lowest point reached

**lox¹** (läks) *n.* [via Yid. < G. *lachs,* salmon] a variety of salty smoked salmon

**lox²** (läks) *n.* [*l(iquid) ox(ygen)*] oxygen in a liquid state, used in a fuel mixture for rockets

**loy·al** (loi′əl) *adj.* [Fr. < OFr. < L. *legalis:* see LEGAL] **1.** faithful to one's country **2.** faithful to those persons, ideals, etc. that one is under obligation to defend or support **3.** relating to or indicating loyalty —**loy′al·ly** *adv.*

**loy·al·ist** (-ist) *n.* **1.** a person who supports the established government of his country during times of revolt **2.** [*often* L-] in the American Revolution, a colonist who was loyal to the British government **3.** [L-] in the Spanish Civil War, one who remained loyal to the Republic, opposing Franco —**loy′al·ism** *n.*

**loy·al·ty** (-tē) *n., pl.* **-ties** quality, state, or instance of being loyal; faithful adherence, etc.

**Loyola** *see* IGNATIUS (OF) LOYOLA

**loz·enge** (läz′′nj) *n.* [OFr. *losenge,* prob. < Gaul.] **1.** a plane figure with four equal sides and two obtuse angles; diamond **2.** a cough drop, candy, etc., orig. in this shape

**LP** [*L(ong) P(laying)*] *a trademark for* a long-playing record —*n.* a long-playing record

**LPG** liquefied petroleum gas: also **LP-gas**

**LPN, L.P.N.** Licensed Practical Nurse

**Lr** *Chem.* lawrencium

**LSD** [*l(y)s(ergic acid) d(iethylamide)*] a psychedelic drug that produces behavior and symptoms, as hallucinations, delusions, etc., like those of certain psychoses

**L.S.D., £.s.d., l.s.d.** [L. *librae, solidi, denarii*] pounds, shillings, pence

**Lt.** Lieutenant

**Ltd., ltd.** limited

**Lu** *Chem.* lutetium

**Lu·an·da** (loo än′də, -an′-) capital of Angola, on the Atlantic: pop. 347,000

**lu·au** (loo ou′, loo′ou′) n. [Haw.] a Hawaiian feast, usually with entertainment

**lub·ber** (lub′ər) n. [< ME. < lobbe- (see LOB)] 1. a big, slow, clumsy person 2. a landlubber —lub′ber·li·ness n. —lub′ber·ly adj., adv.

**Lub·bock** (lub′ək) [after T.S. Lubbock, Confederate officer] city in NW Tex.: pop. 174,000

**lube** (loob) n. 1. a lubricating oil: also **lube oil** 2. [Colloq.] a lubrication

**Lü·beck** (lü′bek; E. loo′-) city & port in N West Germany: pop. 243,000

**lu·bri·cant** (loo′brə kənt) adj. reducing friction by providing a smooth film as a covering over parts that move against each other —n. a substance for reducing friction in this way, as oil or grease

**lu·bri·cate** (-kāt′) vt. -cat′ed, -cat′ing [< L. pp. of lubricare < lubricus, smooth] 1. to make slippery or smooth 2. to apply a lubricant to —vi. to serve as a lubricant —lu′bri·ca′tion n. —lu′bri·ca′tive adj. —lu′bri·ca′tor n.

**lu·bric·i·ty** (loo bris′ə tē) n., pl. -ties [< Fr. < LL. lubricitas] 1. slipperiness; smoothness 2. trickiness 3. lewdness —lu·bri′cious (-brish′əs), lu′bri·cous (-bri kəs) adj.

**lu·cent** (loo′s'nt) adj. [< L. prp. of lucere, to shine] 1. giving off light; shining 2. translucent or clear —lu′cen·cy n. —lu′cent·ly adv.

**Lu·cerne** (loo surn′; Fr. lü sern′), **Lake (of)** lake in C Switzerland

**lu·cerne, lu·cern** (loo surn′) n. [< Fr. < ModPr., ult. < L. lucerna, a lamp < lucere, to shine] [Chiefly Brit.] same as ALFALFA

**Lu·cia** (loo′shə) [It. < L., fem. of LUCIUS] a feminine name

**Lu·cian** (loo′shən) [< L.: see LUCIUS] a masculine name

**lu·cid** (loo′sid) adj. [< L. < lucere, to shine] 1. [Poet.] bright; shining 2. transparent 3. designating an interval of sanity in a mental disorder 4. clear to the mind; readily understood 5. clearheaded; rational —lu·cid′i·ty, lu′cid·ness n. —lu′cid·ly adv.

**Lu·ci·fer** (loo′sə fər) [OE. < L. < lux (gen. lucis), LIGHT[1] + ferre, to BEAR[1]] 1. [Poet.] the planet Venus when it is the morning star 2. Theol. Satan, esp. as leader of the revolt of the angels before his fall —n. [l-] an early type of friction match

**Lu·cille, Lu·cile** (loo sēl′) [var. of LUCY] a feminine name

**Lu·cite** (loo′sīt) [< L. lux, light + -ITE] a trademark for a transparent or translucent acrylic resin or plastic

**Lu·cius** (loo′shəs) [L. < lux, LIGHT[1]] a masculine name

**luck** (luk) n. [prob. < MDu. luk, contr. < gelucke] 1. the seemingly chance happening of events which affect one; fortune; fate 2. good fortune, success, etc. —vi. [Colloq.] to be lucky enough to come (into, on, through, etc.) —**crowd (or push) one's luck** [Slang] to take superfluous risks —**down on one's luck** in misfortune; unlucky —**in luck** lucky —**luck out** [Colloq.] to have things turn out favorably for one —**out of luck** unlucky —**try one's luck** to try to do something without being sure of the outcome —**worse luck** unfortunately

**luck·less** (-lis) adj. having no good luck; unlucky —**luck′-less·ly** adv. —**luck′less·ness** n.

**Luck·now** (luk′nou) city in NC India: pop. 595,000

**luck·y** (luk′ē) adj. **luck′i·er, luck′i·est** 1. having good luck; fortunate 2. resulting fortunately 3. believed to bring good luck —**luck′i·ly** adv. —**luck′i·ness** n.

**lu·cra·tive** (loo′krə tiv) adj. [< L. pp. of lucrari, to gain < lucrum: see ff.] producing wealth or profit; profitable remunerative [a lucrative investment] —**lu′cra·tive·ly** adv. —**lu′cra·tive·ness** n.

**lu·cre** (loo′kər) n. [< L. lucrum, gain, riches] riches; money: chiefly derogatory, as in **filthy lucre**

**Lu·cre·tius** (loo krē′shəs) (born Titus Lucretius Carus) 96?–55? B.C.; Rom. poet & philosopher

**lu·cu·brate** (loo′kyoo brāt′) vi. **-brat′ed, -brat′ing** [< L. pp. of lucubrare, to work by candlelight < lux, light] 1. to work, study, or write laboriously, esp. late at night 2. to write in a scholarly manner —**lu′cu·bra′tor** n.

**lu·cu·bra·tion** (loo′kyoo brā′shən) n. 1. a lucubrating 2. a learned or carefully elaborated work [often pl.] any literary composition: humorous usage suggesting pedantry

**Lu·cul·lus** (loo kul′əs), **(Lucius Licinius)** 110?–57? B.C.; Rom. general: proverbial for his wealth —**Lu·cul′lan** (-ən), **Lu·cul′li·an** (-ē ən) adj.

**Lu·cy** (loo′sē) [prob. via Fr. < L. Lucia, fem. of LUCIUS] a feminine name

**lu·di·crous** (loo′di krəs) adj. [L. ludicrus < ludus, a game] causing laughter because absurd or ridiculous —**lu′di·crous·ly** adv. —**lu′di·crous·ness** n.

**luff** (luf) n. [< ODu. loef, weather side (of a ship)] 1. a sailing close to the wind 2. the forward edge of a fore-and-aft sail —vi. to turn the bow of a ship toward the wind

**lug**[1] (lug) vt. **lugged, lug′ging** [ME. luggen, prob. < Scand.] to carry or drag with effort —n. 1. an earlike projection by which a thing is held or supported 2. a heavy nut used with a bolt to secure a wheel to an axle 3. a shallow box in which fruit is shipped 4. [Slang] a loutish fellow

**lug**[2] (lug) n. clipped form of LUGSAIL

**lug**[3] (lug) n. clipped form of LUGWORM

**luge** (loozh) n. [Fr.] a racing sled for one or two persons —vi. luged, luge′ing to race with luges

**Lu·ger** (loo′gər) [G.] a trademark for a German semiautomatic pistol —n. [often l-] this pistol

**lug·gage** (lug′ij) n. [LUG[1] + -AGE] suitcases, valises, trunks, etc.; baggage

**lug·ger** (lug′ər) n. a small vessel equipped with a lugsail or lugsails

**lug·sail** (lug′s'l, -sāl′) n. [< ? LUG[1]] a four-sided sail attached to an upper yard that hangs obliquely on the mast

**lu·gu·bri·ous** (loo goo′brē əs, -gyoo′-) adj. [L. lugubris < lugere, to mourn + -OUS] very sad or mournful, esp. in a way that seems exaggerated or ridiculous —**lu·gu′bri·ous·ly** adv. —**lu·gu′bri·ous·ness** n.

**lug·worm** (lug′wurm′) n. [< ? + WORM] a bristly, segmented worm that burrows in muddy sand along the shore and is used for bait

LUGSAIL

**Luke** (look) [< LL. < Gr.] 1. a masculine name 2. Bible a) one of the four Evangelists, a physician and the reputed author of the third Gospel b) this book, the third in the New Testament

**luke·warm** (look′wôrm′) adj. [ME. luke, tepid + warm, warm] 1. barely or moderately warm: said of liquids 2. not very eager or enthusiastic —**luke′warm′ly** adv. —**luke′warm′ness** n.

**lull** (lul) vt. [ME. lullen, origin echoic] 1. to calm by gentle sound or motion: chiefly in **lull to sleep** 2. to bring into a specified condition by soothing and reassuring 3. to quiet; allay [to lull one's fears] —vi. to become calm —n. a short period of quiet or of comparative calm

**lull·a·by** (lul′ə bī′) n., pl. **-bies′** a song for lulling a baby to sleep —vt. **-bied′, -by′ing** to lull as with a lullaby

**lum·ba·go** (lum bā′gō) n. [< L. lumbus, loin] backache, esp. in the lower back

**lum·bar** (lum′bər, -bär) adj. [< L. lumbus, loin] of or near the loins; specif., designating or of the vertebrae, nerves, arteries, etc. in the part of the body just below the thoracic part

**lum·ber**[1] (lum′bər) n. [< ? LOMBARD: orig., pawnshop, hence pawned or stored articles] 1. discarded household articles, furniture, etc. stored away or taking up room 2. timber sawed into beams, boards, etc. of convenient sizes —vt. 1. to clutter with useless articles or rubbish 2. to remove (timber) from (an area) —vi. to cut down timber and saw it into lumber —**lum′ber·er** n. —**lum′ber·ing** n.

**lum·ber**[2] (lum′bər) vi. [ME. lomeren < ? Scand.] 1. to move heavily, clumsily, and, often, noisily 2. to rumble —**lum′ber·ing** adj. —**lum′ber·ing·ly** adv.

**lum·ber·jack** (lum′bər jak′) n. same as LOGGER

**lum·ber·man** (-mən) n., pl. **-men** 1. same as LOGGER 2. one who deals in lumber

**lum·ber·yard** (-yärd′) n. a place where lumber is kept for sale

**lu·men** (loo′mən) n., pl. **-mi·na** (-mi nə), **-mens** [ModL. < L., light] 1. a unit of measure for the flow of light, equal to the amount of flow from a uniform point source of one candle 2. the bore of a hollow needle, catheter, etc. 3. Anat. the passage within a tubular organ

**lu·mi·nance** (loo′mə nəns) n. [< L. lumen (see LUMEN) + -ANCE] 1. a being luminous 2. luminous intensity, expressed in candles per unit projected area

**lu·mi·nar·y** (-mə ner′ē) n., pl. **-nar′ies** [< OFr. < LL. < L. luminare < lumen, light] 1. a body that gives off light, such as the sun or moon 2. a) a famous intellectual b) any notable person

**lu·mi·nesce** (loo′mə nes′) vi. **-nesced′, -nesc′ing** [backformation < ff.] to be or become luminescent

**lu·mi·nes·cence** (-'ns) n. [< L. lumen, a light + -ESCENCE] any giving off of light caused by the absorption of radiant energy, etc. and not by incandescence; any cold light —**lu′mi·nes′cent** adj.

**lu·mi·nif·er·ous** (-nif′ər əs) adj. [< L. lumen, a light + -FEROUS] giving off or transmitting light

**lu·mi·nous** (lōō′mə nəs) *adj.* [L. *luminosus* < *lumen*, a light] **1.** giving off light; bright **2.** illuminated **3.** glowing in the dark, as paint with a phosphor in it **4.** enlightened or enlightening —**lu′mi·nos′i·ty** (-näs′ə tē), *pl.* **-ties**, **lu′mi·nous·ness** *n.* —**lu′mi·nous·ly** *adv.*

**lum·mox** (lum′əks) *n.* [< ?] [Colloq.] a clumsy, stupid person

**lump**[1] (lump) *n.* [ME. *lumpe*] **1.** a solid mass of no special shape; hunk **2.** a small cube, or oblong piece, etc., specif. of sugar **3.** a swelling; bulge **4.** a large amount; mass **5.** a clodlike person **6.** [*pl.*] [Colloq.] hard blows, criticism, or the like: in **get** (or **take**) **one's lumps** or **give someone his lumps** —*adj.* in lumps [*lump* sugar] —*vt.* **1.** to put together in a lump or lumps **2.** to treat or deal with in a mass, or collectively **3.** to make lumps in —*vi.* to become lumpy —**in the lump** all together —**lump in one's throat** a tight feeling in the throat, as from restrained emotion

**lump**[2] (lump) *vt.* [Early ModE., to look sour] [Colloq.] to put up with (something disagreeable) [if you don't like it, you can *lump* it]

**lump·ish** (lump′ish) *adj.* **1.** like a lump **2.** clumsy, dull, etc. —**lump′ish·ly** *adv.* —**lump′ish·ness** *n.*

**lump sum** a gross, or total, sum paid at one time

**lump·y** (lum′pē) *adj.* **lump′i·er**, **lump′i·est** **1.** full of lumps [*lumpy* pudding] **2.** covered with lumps **3.** rough: said of water **4.** like a lump; heavy; clumsy —**lump′i·ly** *adv.* —**lump′i·ness** *n.*

**Lu·na** (lōō′nə) [L., moon] **1.** *Rom. Myth.* the goddess of the moon **2.** the moon personified

**lu·na·cy** (lōō′nə sē) *n.*, *pl.* **-cies** [LUNA(TIC) + -CY] **1.** [Now Rare] insanity **2.** utter foolishness

**luna moth** a large N. American moth with crescent-marked wings, the hind pair of which end in elongated tails

**lu·nar** (lōō′nər) *adj.* [< L. < *luna*, the moon] of, on, or like the moon

**lunar eclipse** *see* ECLIPSE (sense 1)

**lunar month** *see* MONTH (sense 3)

**lunar year** a period of twelve lunar months

**lu·nate** (lōō′nāt) *adj.* [< L. < *luna*, the moon] crescent-shaped: also **lu′nat·ed** —**lu′nate·ly** *adv.*

**lu·na·tic** (lōō′nə tik) *adj.* [< OFr. < LL. *lunaticus*, moon-struck, crazy < L. *luna*, the moon] **1.** [Now Rare] *a)* insane *b)* of lunacy *c)* of or for insane persons **2.** utterly foolish —*n.* an insane person

**lunatic fringe** the minority considered fanatical in any political, social, or other movement

**lunch** (lunch) *n.* [earlier, a piece: ? < Sp. *lonja*, slice of ham] any light meal; esp., the midday meal between breakfast and dinner —*vi.* to eat lunch —*vt.* to provide lunch for —**lunch′er** *n.*

**lunch·eon** (lun′chən) *n.* [< prec., prob. after dial. *nunch-eon*, a snack] a lunch; esp., a formal lunch with others

**lunch·eon·ette** (lun′chə net′) *n.* [see -ETTE] a small restaurant where light lunches can be had

**lunch·room** (lunch′rōōm′) *n.* a restaurant where light, quick meals, as lunches, are served

**lung** (lun) *n.* [OE. *lungen*] either of the two spongelike respiratory organs in the thorax of vertebrates, that oxygenate the blood and remove carbon dioxide from it —**at the top of one's lungs** in one's loudest voice

**lunge** (lunj) *n.* [< Fr. < *allonger*, to lengthen < *a*- (< L. *ad*), to + *long* (< L. *longus*), long] **1.** a sudden thrust, as with a sword **2.** a sudden plunge forward —*vi.*, *vt.* **lunged**, **lung′ing** to move, or cause to move, with a lunge —**lung′er** *n.*

**lung·fish** (lun′fish′) *n.*, *pl.* **-fish′**, **-fish′es:** see FISH any of various fishes having lungs as well as gills

**lung·wort** (-wurt′) *n.* [OE. *lungenwyrt*] a plant with large, spotted leaves and clusters of blue or purple flowers

**Lu·per·ca·li·a** (lōō′pər kā′lē ə, -kāl′yə) *n.pl.* an ancient Roman fertility festival, held in February: also **Lu′per·cal′** (-kal′) *n.sing.* —**Lu′per·ca′li·an** *adj.*

**lu·pine**[1] (lōō′pin) *n.* [< L. < *lupus*, a wolf] **1.** a plant of the legume family, with racemes of white, rose, yellow, or blue flowers and pods containing beanlike seeds **2.** the seed of this plant, used in some parts of Europe as food

**lu·pine**[2] (lōō′pīn) *adj.* [< L. < *lupus*, a wolf] **1.** of a wolf or wolves **2.** wolflike; fierce

**lu·pus** (lōō′pəs) *n.* [ModL. < L., a wolf] any of various diseases with skin lesions, esp. tuberculosis of the skin

**lurch**[1] (lurch) *vi.* [< ?] **1.** to roll, pitch, or sway suddenly forward or to one side **2.** to stagger —*n.* a lurching movement

**lurch**[2] (lurch) *vi.* [var. of LURK] [Obs.] to lurk —*vt.* [Archaic] to cheat; steal; rob

**lurch**[3] (lurch) *n.* [Fr. *lourche*, name of a 16th-c. game, prob. < OFr. *lourche*, duped] a situation in certain card games, in which the loser has less than half the score of the winner —**leave in the lurch** to leave in a difficult situation

**lure** (loor) *n.* [< MFr. < OFr. *loirre*, prob. < Gmc.] **1.** a feathered device on the end of a long cord, used in falconry to recall the hawk **2.** *a)* the power of attracting or enticing *b)* anything having this power **3.** a bait used in fishing —*vt.* **lured**, **lur′ing** to attract; entice —**lur′er** *n.*

**lu·rid** (loor′id) *adj.* [L. *luridus*, pale yellow, ghastly] **1.** [Rare] deathly pale **2.** glowing through a haze, as flames enveloped by smoke **3.** *a)* startling; sensational *b)* characterized by violent passion or crime —**lu′rid·ly** *adv.* —**lu′rid·ness** *n.*

**lurk** (lurk) *vi.* [ME. *lurken*, akin to *louren*, LOWER[2]] **1.** to stay hidden, ready to attack, etc. **2.** to exist unobserved, be present as a latent threat, etc. **3.** to move furtively —**lurk′er** *n.*

**lus·cious** (lush′əs) *adj.* [ME. *lucius*, prob. var. of *licious*, DELICIOUS, infl. by ff.] **1.** very pleasing to taste or smell; delicious **2.** *a)* delighting any of the senses *b)* voluptuous —**lus′cious·ly** *adv.* —**lus′cious·ness** *n.*

**lush**[1] (lush) *adj.* [< OFr. *lasche*, lax, loose, ult. < L. *laxus*] **1.** tender and full of juice **2.** of or characterized by rich growth [*lush* vegetation, *lush* fields] **3.** characterized by richness, abundance, or extravagance —**lush′ly** *adv.* —**lush′ness** *n.*

**lush**[2] (lush) *n.* [< ? *Lushington*, former actors' club in London] [Slang] **1.** alcoholic liquor **2.** an alcoholic —*vi.*, *vt.* [Slang] to drink (liquor)

**lust** (lust) *n.* [OE., pleasure, appetite] **1.** a desire to satisfy one's sexual needs; esp., strong sexual desire **2.** *a)* excessive desire [a *lust* for power] *b)* great zest —*vi.* to feel an intense desire, esp. sexual desire —**lust′ful** *adj.* —**lust′ful·ly** *adv.* —**lust′ful·ness** *n.*

**lus·ter** (lus′tər) *n.* [< Fr. < It. < L. *lustrare*, to illumine] **1.** gloss; sheen **2.** brightness; radiance **3.** *a)* radiant beauty *b)* fame; glory **4.** a glossy fabric of cotton and wool **5.** the reflecting quality and brilliance of the surface of a mineral **6.** the metallic, sometimes iridescent appearance of glazed pottery —*vt.* **1.** to give a lustrous finish to **2.** to add glory to —*vi.* to be or become lustrous

**lus·ter·ware** (-wer′) *n.* highly glazed earthenware decorated by the application of metallic oxides to the glaze: also, chiefly Brit. sp., **lustreware**

**lus·trate** (lus′trāt) *vt.* **-trat·ed**, **-trat·ing** [< L. pp. of *lustrare:* see LUSTRUM] to purify by means of certain ceremonies —**lus·tra′tion** *n.*

**lus·tre** (lus′tər) *n.*, *vt.*, *vi.* **-tred**, **-tring** chiefly Brit. sp. of LUSTER

**lus·trous** (-trəs) *adj.* having luster; shining; bright —**lus′trous·ly** *adv.* —**lus′trous·ness** *n.*

**lus·trum** (lus′trəm) *n.*, *pl.* **-trums**, **-tra** (-trə) [L., orig., prob. illumination] **1.** in ancient Rome, a purification of all the people by means of ceremonies held every five years **2.** a five-year period

**lust·y** (lus′tē) *adj.* **lust′i·er**, **lust′i·est** full of vigor; strong, robust, hearty, etc. —**lust′i·ly** *adv.* —**lust′i·ness** *n.*

**Lü·ta** (lōō′dä′) urban complex in NE China, including two seaports on the Yellow Sea: pop. 3,600,000

**lu·ta·nist, lu·te·nist** (lōōt′'n ist) *n.* a lute player

**lute**[1] (lōōt) *n.* [< MFr. < OFr. < Ar. *al'ūd*, lit., the wood] an early stringed instrument with a rounded back and a long, fretted neck often bent in a sharp angle

**lute**[2] (lōōt) *n.* [< OFr. < L. *lutum*, mud, clay] a clayey cement used as a sealing agent for the joints of pipes, etc. —*vt.* **lut′ed**, **lut′ing** to seal with lute

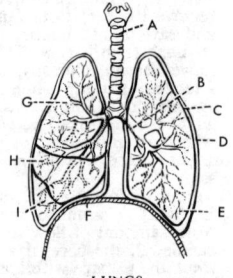

LUTE

**lu·te·in·iz·ing hormone** (lōōt′ē in′īz′in) [ult. < (CORPUS) LUTEUM] a hormone of the pituitary that esp. stimulates ovulation and the development of the corpus luteum

**lu·te·ti·um** (lōō tē′shē əm) *n.* [ModL. < L. *Lutetia*, ancient Rom. name of Paris] a metallic chemical element of the rare-earth group: symbol, Lu; at. wt., 174.97; at. no., 71

**Lu·ther** (lōō′thər) [G. < OHG. *Chlothar* < Gmc. bases meaning "famous fighter"] **1.** a masculine name **2.** Martin, 1483–1546; Ger. theologian: leader of the Protestant Reformation in Germany

**Lu·ther·an** (-ən) *adj.* **1.** of Martin Luther **2.** of the Protestant denomination founded by Luther, or of its doctrines, etc. —*n.* a member of a Lutheran church —**Lu′ther·an·ism** *n.*

**lut·ist** (lōōt′ist) *n.* a lute player

---

LUNGS
(A, trachea; B, bronchus; C, visceral pleura; D, parietal pleura; E, bronchiole; F, diaphragm; G, upper lobe; H, middle lobe; I, lower lobe)

**Lux·em·bourg** (luk′səm bʉrg′; *Fr.* lük sän bōōr′) **1.** grand duchy in W Europe, bounded by Belgium, West Germany, & France: 998 sq. mi.; pop. 337,000 **2.** its capital: pop. 79,000 Also sp. **Luxemburg**

**Lux·or** (luk′sôr, look′-) city in S Egypt, on the Nile, near the ruins of ancient Thebes

**lux·u·ri·ant** (lug zhoor′ē ənt, luk shoor′-) *adj.* [< L. prp. of *luxuriare:* see ff.] **1.** growing with vigor and in abundance; lush; teeming **2.** richly or extravagantly full, varied, elaborate, etc. **3.** *same as* LUXURIOUS —**lux·u′ri·ance, lux·u′ri·an·cy** *n.* —**lux·u′ri·ant·ly** *adv.*

**lux·u·ri·ate** (-āt′) *vi.* -**at′ed, -at′ing** [< L. pp. of *luxuriare,* to be too fruitful < *luxuria,* LUXURY] **1.** to grow with vigor and in great abundance **2.** to live in great luxury **3.** to revel (*in*) —**lux·u′ri·a′tion** *n.*

**lux·u·ri·ous** (-əs) *adj.* **1.** fond of or indulging in luxury **2.** filled with or providing luxury; splendid, rich, comfortable, etc. —**lux·u′ri·ous·ly** *adv.* —**lux·u′ri·ous·ness** *n.*

**lux·u·ry** (luk′shə rē, lug′zhə-) *n., pl.* -**ries** [< OFr. < L. *luxuria* < *luxus,* luxury] **1.** the enjoyment of the best and most costly things that offer the greatest comfort and satisfaction **2.** anything giving such enjoyment, usually something considered unnecessary to life and health **3.** any unusual pleasure or comfort —*adj.* characterized by luxury

**Lu·zon** (lōō zän′) main island of the Philippines: 40,420 sq. mi.; chief city, Manila

**Lvov** (lvôf) city in W Ukrainian S.S.R.: pop. 524,000

**LXX** Septuagint

**-ly**[1] (lē) [OE. *-lic*] *a suffix used to form adjectives and meaning:* **1.** like, characteristic of, suitable to [*manly*] **2.** happening (once) every (specified period of time) [*monthly*]

**-ly**[2] (lē) [OE. *-lice* < *-lic*] *a suffix used to form adverbs and meaning:* **1.** in a (specified) manner, to a (specified) extent or direction, in or at a (specified) time or place [*harshly, outwardly, hourly*] **2.** in the (specified) order of sequence [*secondly*]

**‡ly·cée** (lē sā′) *n.* [Fr. < L.: see ff.] in France, a public, college-preparatory secondary school

**Ly·ce·um** (lī sē′əm, lī′sē-) [L. < Gr. *Lykeion,* the Lyceum: from the temple of *Apollōn Lykeios* near it] the grove at Athens where Aristotle taught —*n.* [l-] **1.** a lecture hall **2.** an organization presenting public lectures or discussions, concerts, etc.

**Ly·cur·gus** (lī kʉr′gəs) real or legendary Spartan lawgiver of about the 9th cent. B.C.

**Lyd·i·a** (lid′ē ə) [LL. < Gr. fem. of *Lydios,* Lydian] **1.** a feminine name **2.** ancient kingdom in W Asia Minor —**Lyd′i·an** *adj., n.*

**lye** (lī) *n.* [OE. *leag*] **1.** orig., a strong alkaline solution obtained by leaching wood ashes **2.** any strongly alkaline substance Lye is used in cleaning and in making soap

**ly·ing**[1] (lī′iŋ) *prp. of* LIE[1]

**ly·ing**[2] (lī′iŋ) *prp. of* LIE[2] —*adj.* false; not truthful —*n.* the telling of a lie or lies

**ly·ing-in** (-in′) *n.* confinement in childbirth —*adj.* of or for childbirth [*a lying-in hospital*]

**Lyl·y** (lil′ē), **John** 1554?-1606; Eng. writer

**lymph** (limf) *n.* [L. *lympha,* spring water (infl. by Gr. *nymphē,* NYMPH)] a clear, yellowish fluid resembling blood plasma, found in the lymphatic vessels of vertebrates

**lym·phat·ic** (lim fat′ik) *adj.* **1.** of, containing, or conveying lymph **2.** sluggish; without energy —*n.* a lymphatic vessel

**lymph node** any of many small, compact structures lying in groups along the course of the lymphatic vessels and producing lymphocytes: also, esp. formerly, **lymph gland**

**lym·pho-** *a combining form meaning* of lymph or the lymphatics: also, before a vowel, **lymph-**

**lym·pho·cyte** (lim′fə sīt′) *n.* [prec. + -CYTE] a variety of leukocyte formed in lymphatic tissue —**lym′pho·cyt′ic** (-sit′ik) *adj.*

**lymph·oid** (lim′foid) *adj.* of or like lymph or the tissue of the lymph nodes

**lynch** (linch) *vt.* [< LYNCH LAW] to murder (an accused person) by mob action and without lawful trial, as by hanging —**lynch′er** *n.* —**lynch′ing** *n.*

**Lynch·burg** (linch′bʉrg) [after J. *Lynch,* reputed founder] city in C Va.: pop. 67,000

**lynch law** [after Capt. William *Lynch* (1742-1820), member of a vigilance committee in Pittsylvania, Virginia, in 1780] the practice of killing by lynching

**Lynn** (lin) [prob. < Brit. place name *Lynn* < Celt.] **1.** a masculine or feminine name **2.** city in NE Mass.: suburb of Boston: pop. 78,000

**lynx** (liŋks) *n., pl.* **lynx′es, lynx:** see PLURAL, II, D, 1 [L. < Gr. *lynx*] any of a group of wildcats found throughout the Northern Hemisphere and characterized by a short tail, long, tufted ears, and keen vision

**lynx-eyed** (-īd′) *adj.* having very keen sight

**Lyon** (lyōn) city in EC France, on the Rhone: pop. 528,000: Eng. name **Ly·ons** (lī′ənz)

**ly·on·naise** (lī′ə nāz′; *Fr.* lyô nez′) *adj.* [Fr., fem. of *Lyon-nais,* of Lyon] prepared with finely sliced onions, as potatoes with fried onions

**Ly·ra** (lī′rə) a N constellation: it contains Vega

**ly·rate** (lī′rāt) *adj.* shaped like a lyre

**lyre** (līr) *n.* [< L. < Gr. *lyra*] a small stringed instrument of the harp family, played by the ancient Greeks

**lyre·bird** (-bʉrd′) *n.* an Australian songbird: the long tail feathers of the male resemble a lyre when spread

**lyr·ic** (lir′ik) *adj.* [< Fr. or L.: both < Gr. *lyrikos*] **1.** suitable for singing, as to the accompaniment of a lyre; songlike; specif., designating poetry expressing the poet's emotions and thoughts: sonnets, odes, etc. are lyric poems **2.** writing lyric poetry **3.** *same as* LYRICAL **4.** having a relatively high voice with a light, flexible quality [*a lyric tenor*] —*n.* **1.** a lyric poem **2.** [*usually pl.*] the words of a song, as distinguished from the music

LYRE

**lyr·i·cal** (-i k'l) *adj.* **1.** *same as* LYRIC **2.** expressing rapture or great enthusiasm —**lyr′i·cal·ly** *adv.*

**lyr·i·cism** (lir′ə siz′m) *n.* lyric quality, style, expression, etc.

**lyr·i·cist** (-sist) *n.* a writer of lyrics, esp. lyrics for popular songs

**Ly·san·der** (lī san′dər) ?-395 B.C.; Spartan naval & military commander

**ly·sin** (lī′s'n) *n.* [< Gr. *lysis* (see ff.) + -IN[1]] any antibody capable of dissolving bacteria, blood corpuscles, etc.

**ly·sis** (lī′sis) *n.* [ModL. < Gr. *lysis,* a loosening < *lyein,* to loose] **1.** cell destruction by lysins **2.** the gradual ending of disease symptoms

**-ly·sis** (lə sis) [see prec.] *a combining form meaning* a loosing, dissolution, dissolving, destruction [*catalysis, paralysis*]

**-lyte** (līt) [< Gr. *lytos* < *lyein:* see LYSIS] *a combining form meaning* a substance subjected to a process of decomposition [*hydrolyte*]

**-lyt·ic** (lit′ik) **1.** *a combining form used to form adjectives corresponding to nouns ending in* -LYSIS [*catalytic*] **2.** *Biochem. a combining form meaning* hydrolysis by enzymes

**-lyze** (līz) *a combining form used to form verbs corresponding to nouns ending in* -LYSIS [*electrolyze*]

# M

**M, m** (em) *n., pl.* **M's, m's 1.** the thirteenth letter of the English alphabet **2.** the sound of M or m

**M** (em) *n.* a Roman numeral for 1,000

**M. 1.** Manitoba **2.** Medieval **3.** *Music* mezzo **4.** Monday **5.** *pl.* **MM.** Monsieur

**M., m. 1.** majesty **2.** male **3.** married **4.** masculine **5.** *Physics* mass **6.** meridian **7.** mile(s) **8.** mill(s) **9.** minim

**10.** minute(s) **11.** month **12.** [L. *meridies*] noon [*A.M., P.M.*]

**m, m.** meter; meters

**ma** (mä; *dial.* mô) *n.* [Colloq.] mamma; mother

**MA** Massachusetts

**MA, M.A.** *Psychol.* mental age

**M.A.** [L. *Magister Artium*] Master of Arts

---

fat, āpe, cär, ten, ēven, is, bīte; gō, hôrn, tōōl, look; oil, out; up, fʉr; get; joy; yet; chin; she; thin, *then*; zh, leisure; ŋ, ring; ə for *a* in *ago, e* in *agent, i* in *sanity, o* in *comply, u* in *focus;* as in *able* (ā′b'l); Fr. bäl; ë, Fr. coeur; ö, Fr. feu; ô, Fr. mon; б, Fr. coq; ü, Fr. duc; r, Fr. cri; H, G. ich; kh, G. doch; ‡foreign; *hypothetical; < derived from. See inside front cover.

**ma'am** (mam, mäm; *unstressed* məm, 'm) *n.* [Colloq.] madam: used in direct address

**Ma·bel** (mā'b'l) [< *Amabel* < L. *amabilis*, lovable] a feminine name

**ma·ca·bre** (mə käb'rə, mə käb', -kä'bər) *adj.* [Fr. < OFr. (*danse*) *Macabré*, (dance) of death] gruesome; grim and horrible: also **ma·ca'ber** (-kä'bər)

**mac·ad·am** (mə kad'əm) *n.* [after J. L. McAdam (1756–1836), Scot. engineer] **1.** small broken stones used in making roads, usually combined with tar or asphalt **2.** a macadamized road

**mac·a·dam·i·a nut** (mak'ə dā'mē ə) [after John Macadam (d. 1865), Scot. chemist in Australia] a spherical, hard-shelled, edible nut from an Australian tree cultivated in Hawaii, etc.

**mac·ad·am·ize** (mə kad'əm mīz') *vt.* **-ized', -iz'ing** to make, repair, or cover (a road) by rolling successive layers of macadam on it

**Ma·cao** (mə kou') Port. territory consisting of a peninsula on the SE coast of China & two small nearby islands: also, Port. sp., **Macau**

**ma·caque** (mə käk') *n.* [Fr. < Port. *macaco*] any of a group of monkeys of Asia, Africa, and the East Indies, with a nonprehensile tail

**mac·a·ro·ni** (mak'ə rō'nē) *n.* [It. *maccaroni*, pl. < LowGr. *makaria*, broth of barley, ult. < Gr. *makar*, blessed] **1.** pasta in the form of tubes, etc., often baked with cheese, ground meat, etc. **2.** *pl.* **-nies** an 18th-cent. English dandy

**mac·a·roon** (mak'ə rōōn') *n.* [< Fr. < It. *maccaroni*, MACARONI] a small cookie made chiefly of egg white, crushed almonds or coconut, and sugar

**Ma·cau·lay** (mə kô'lē), **Thomas Bab·ing·ton** (bab'iŋ tən), 1st Baron Macaulay, 1800–59; Eng. historian, essayist, & statesman

**ma·caw** (mə kô') *n.* [Port. *macao*, prob. < Braz. (Tupi) native name] a large, bright-colored, harsh-voiced parrot of Central and South America

**Mac·beth** (mək beth', mak-) **1.** a tragedy (c. 1606) by Shakespeare **2.** its title character

**Mac·ca·bae·us** (mak'ə bē'əs), **Judas** see MACCABEES

**Mac·ca·bees** (mak'ə bēz') **1.** family of Jewish patriots who, under Judas Maccabaeus, headed a successful revolt against Syria (175–164 B.C.) **2.** *Bible* two books of the Old Testament Apocrypha that tell of this revolt —**Mac'ca·be'an** *adj.*

**Mac·Dow·ell** (mək dou'əl), **Edward Alexander** 1861–1908; U.S. composer & pianist

**Mace** (mās) [< ff.] *a trademark* (in full, **Chemical Mace**) *for* a chemical compound used as a tear gas and a nerve gas

**mace**[1] (mās) *n.* [< OFr. *masse*] **1.** a heavy, spiked, armor-breaking club, used in the Middle Ages **2.** *a)* a staff used as a symbol of authority by certain officials *b)* a person who carries a mace: also **mace'bear'er**

**mace**[2] (mās) *n.* [< OFr. *macis* < ML. < L. < Gr. *makir*, a fragrant resin] a spice, usually ground, made from the dried outer covering of the nutmeg

**Mac·e·do·ni·a** (mas'ə dō'nē ə, -dōn'yə) **1.** ancient kingdom in SE Europe, now divided among Greece, Yugoslavia, & Bulgaria **2.** republic of Yugoslavia, in the SE part: 9,928 sq. mi.; cap. Skopje —**Mac'e·do'ni·an** *adj., n.*

**mac·er·ate** (mas'ə rāt') *vt.* **-at'ed, -at'ing** [< L. pp. of *macerare*, to soften] **1.** to soften and break down the parts of by soaking in liquid for some time **2.** to steep (fruit or vegetables) as in wine or liquor **3.** loosely, to break, tear, chop, etc. into bits **4.** to cause to waste away or grow thin —*vi.* to waste away; grow thin —**mac'er·a'tion** *n.*

**Mach** (mäk) *n. clipped form of* MACH NUMBER

**mach.** **1.** machine **2.** machinery **3.** machinist

**ma·che·te** (mə shet'ē, -chet'ē) *n.* [Sp., dim. of *macho*, ult. < L. *marcus*, a hammer] a large, heavy-bladed knife used for cutting down sugar cane or underbrush in Central and South America

**Mach·i·a·vel·li** (mä'kyä vel'lē; *E.* mak'ē ə vel'ē), **Nic·co·lò (di Bernardo)** (nē'kō lō') 1469–1527; Florentine statesman & writer on government

**Mach·i·a·vel·li·an** (mak'ē ə vel'ē ən, -vel'yən) *adj.* of or like Machiavelli or the political principles and methods of him

MACHETE

craftiness and duplicity advocated by him —*n.* a follower of such principles and methods —**Mach'i·a·vel'li·an·ism** *n.*

**ma·chic·o·late** (mə chik'ə lāt') *vt.* **-lat'ed, -lat'ing** [< ML. pp. of *machicolare* < MFr., prob. < L. *masticare*, MASTICATE + *col*, the neck: from use of machicolations to drop stones, etc.] to put machicolations in (a parapet, etc.)

**ma·chic·o·la·tion** (mə chik'ə lā'shən) *n.* an opening, as in the floor of a parapet, through which hot liquids, rocks, etc. could be dropped by the defenders of a fortress

**mach·i·nate** (mak'ə nāt'; *sometimes* mash'-) *vi., vt.* **-nat'ed, -nat'ing** [< L. pp. of *machinari*, to plot < *machina*, a

MACHINE] to devise, plan, or plot artfully, esp. to do evil —**mach'i·na'tor** *n.*

**mach·i·na·tion** (mak'ə nā'shən; *sometimes* mash'-) *n.* an artful plot or scheme, esp. an evil one: *usually used in pl.*

**ma·chine** (mə shēn') *n.* [Fr. < L. *machina* < Gr. < *mēchos*, contrivance] **1.** a vehicle, as an automobile: old-fashioned term **2.** a structure consisting of a framework and various fixed and moving parts, for doing some kind of work; mechanism *[a sewing machine]* **3.** a person or organization regarded as acting like a machine; esp., a smoothly functioning complex organization **4.** the members of a political party who control policy and confer patronage **5.** *Mech.* a device, as a lever or pulley, that transmits, or changes the application of, energy —*adj.* **1.** of a machine or machines **2.** made or done by machinery **3.** standardized; stereotyped —*vt.* **-chined', -chin'ing** to make, shape, etc. by machinery —**ma·chin'a·ble** *adj.*

**machine gun** an automatic gun, usually with a cooling apparatus, firing a rapid stream of bullets fed into it by a belt —**ma·chine'-gun'** (-gun') *vt.* **-gunned', -gun'ning**

**ma·chin·er·y** (mə shēn'ər ē, -shēn'rē) *n., pl.* **-er·ies** **1.** machines collectively **2.** the working parts of a machine **3.** any means by which something is kept in action or a desired result is obtained *[the machinery of government]*

**machine shop** a factory for making or repairing machines or machine parts

**machine tool** a power-driven tool, as an electric lathe or drill —**ma·chine'-tool'** *adj., vt.*

**ma·chin·ist** (-ist) *n.* **1.** a person who makes or repairs machinery **2.** a worker skilled in using machine tools or one who operates a machine

‡**ma·chis·mo** (mä chēz'mō) *n.* [< Sp. *macho* (see MACHO)] strong or aggressive masculinity; virility

**Mach number** (mäk) [after Ernst *Mach* (1838–1916), Austrian physicist] *[also* m-*]* a number representing the ratio of the speed of an object to the speed of sound through the same medium, as air

‡**ma·cho** (mä'chō) *adj.* [Sp. < Port., ult. < L. *masculus*, MASCULINE] masculine, virile, courageous, etc.

**Mac·ken·zie** (mə ken'zē) river in NW Canada, flowing from the Great Slave Lake into the Arctic Ocean

**mack·er·el** (mak'ər əl, mak'rəl) *n., pl.* **-el, -els:** see PLURAL, II, D, 2 [< OFr. *makerel* < ?] an edible fish of the North Atlantic, with a striped back and a silvery belly

**mackerel sky** a sky with rows of small, fleecy clouds, like the streaks on a mackerel's back

**Mack·i·nac** (mak'ə nô'), **Straits of** [see MACKINAW (COAT)] strait connecting Lake Huron & Lake Michigan

**Mackinac Island** small island in the Straits of Mackinac

**Mack·i·naw (coat)** (mak'ə nô') [CanadFr. *Mackinac* < AmInd. *mitchimakinak*, large turtle] a short, double-breasted coat made of heavy woolen cloth, usually plaid

**mack·in·tosh, mac·in·tosh** (mak'in täsh') *n.* [after C. *Macintosh* (1766–1843), the Scot. inventor] a waterproof raincoat, or the fabric for it

**Ma·con** (mā'kən) [after N. *Macon* (1758–1837), N.C. patriot] city in C Ga.: pop. 117,000

**mac·ra·mé** (mak'rə mā') *n.* [Fr. < It. < Turk. *makrama*, napkin < Ar. *miqramah*, a veil] a coarse fringe or lace of thread or cord knotted in designs

**mac·ro-** [< Gr. *makros*, long] *a combining form meaning* long (in extent or duration), large, enlarged, or elongated: also, before a vowel, **macr-**

**mac·ro·bi·ot·ics** (mak'rō bī ät'iks) *n.pl.* [*with sing. v.*] [< prec. + Gr. *biōtikos* < *bios*, life] the art of prolonging life, as by a special diet —**mac'ro·bi·ot'ic** *adj.*

**mac·ro·ceph·a·ly** (mak'rə sef'ə lē) *n.* [MACRO- + CEPHAL(O)- + -Y[3]] a condition in which the head or cranial capacity is abnormally large —**mac'ro·ceph'a·lous, mac'·ro·ce·phal'ic** (-si fal'ik) *adj.*

**mac·ro·cosm** (mak'rə käz'm) *n.* [< Fr. < ML.: see MACRO- & COSMOS] **1.** the universe **2.** any large, complex entity —**mac'ro·cos'mic** *adj.*

**mac·ro·e·co·nom·ics** (mak'rō ē'kə näm'iks, -ek'ə-) *n.pl.* [*with sing. v.*] a branch of economics dealing with all the forces at work in an economy or with the interrelationship of large sectors, as in employment or income

**mac·ro·mol·e·cule** (mak'rə mäl'ə kyōōl') *n.* a very large molecule, as a polymer molecule, composed of hundreds or thousands of atoms: also **mac'ro·mole'** (-mōl')

**ma·cron** (mā'krən, -krän) *n.* [< Gr. neut. of *makros*, long] a short, straight mark (‾) placed horizontally over a vowel to indicate that it is long or is to be pronounced in a certain way

**mac·u·la** (mak'yoo lə) *n., pl.* **-lae** (-lē') **-las** [L.] a spot, blotch, etc.; esp., *a)* a discolored spot on the skin *b)* a sunspot —**mac'u·lar** *adj.*

**macula lu·te·a** (lōōt'ē ə) [ModL., lit., yellowish spot] a small yellowish area of especially keen vision on the retina

**mad** (mad) *adj.* **mad'der, mad'dest** [< OE. pp. of (ge)*mædan*, to drive mad] **1.** mentally ill; insane **2.** frenzied; frantic *[mad with fear]* **3.** foolish and rash; unwise

**4.** foolishly enthusiastic or fond *[mad* about clothes*]* **5.** wildly amusing; hilarious **6.** having rabies *[a mad* dog*]* **7.** *a)* angry (often with *at) b)* showing anger —**have a mad on** [Colloq.] to be angry —**mad as a hatter** (or **March hare**) completely crazy

**Mad·a·gas·car** (mad'ə gas'kər) country that is an island off the SE coast of Africa: 228,000 sq. mi.; pop. 6,750,000

**mad·am** (mad'əm) *n., pl.* **mad'ams;** for 1, usually **mes·dames** (mā däm') [< Fr., orig. *ma dame* < L. *mea domina,* my lady] **1.** a woman; lady: a polite term of address **2.** the mistress of a household **3.** a woman in charge of a brothel

**mad·ame** (mad'əm; *Fr.* mȧ dȧm') *n., pl.* **mes·dames** (mā däm'; *Fr.* mā däm') [Fr.: see prec.] a married woman: French title equivalent to *Mrs.:* abbrev. **Mme., Mdme.**

**mad·cap** (mad'kap') *n.* [MAD + CAP, fig. for head] a reckless, impulsive person, esp. a girl —*adj.* reckless and impulsive

**mad·den** (mad'n) *vt., vi.* to make or become mad; make or become insane, angry, or wildly excited —**mad'den·ing** *adj.* —**mad'den·ing·ly** *adv.*

**mad·der** (mad'ər) *n.* [OE. mædere] **1.** any of various plants of the madder family; esp., a perennial vine with small, yellow flowers **2.** *a)* the red root of this vine *b)* a red dye made from this **3.** crimson —*adj.* designating a family of chiefly tropical herbs, shrubs, and trees, including bedstraw, bluet, coffee, etc.

**mad·ding** (-iŋ) *adj.* [Rare] **1.** raving; frenzied *["the madding* crowd"] **2.** making mad

**made** (mād) *pt. & pp. of* MAKE —*adj.* **1.** constructed; formed **2.** produced artificially *[made* flowers] **3.** invented; contrived *[a made* word] **4.** prepared from various ingredients *[a made* dish] **5.** sure of success *[a made* man] —**have (got) it made** [Slang] to be assured of success

**Ma·deir·a** (mə dir'ə) **1.** group of Port. islands in the Atlantic, off the W coast of Morocco **2.** largest island of this group —*n. [also* m-] a strong white wine made on this island

**mad·e·leine** (mad'l in) *n.* [Fr., after *Madeleine* Paulnier, 19th-c. Fr. cook] a small, rich cupcake

**Mad·e·line** (mad'l in, -īn') [< MAGDALENE] a feminine name

**ma·de·moi·selle** (mad'ə mə zel', mam zel'; *Fr.* mȧd mwȧ zel') *n.,* Fr. *pl.* **mesde·moi·selles** (mād mwȧ zel') [Fr. < *ma,* my + *demoiselle,* young lady] an unmarried woman or girl: French title equivalent to *Miss:* abbrev. **Mlle., Mdlle.**

**made-to-or·der** (mad'tə ôr'dər) *adj.* made to conform to the customer's specifications; custom-made

**made-up** (-up') *adj.* **1.** put together; arranged *[a made-up* page of type] **2.** invented; false *[a made-up* story] **3.** with cosmetics applied

**Madge** (maj) [dim. of MARGARET] a feminine name

**mad·house** (mad'hous') *n.* **1.** [Archaic] a place of confinement for the mentally ill **2.** any place of turmoil, noise, and confusion

**Mad·i·son** (mad'i s'n) [after ff.] capital of Wis., in the SC part: pop. 171,000

**Mad·i·son** (mad'i s'n), **James** 1751–1836; 4th president of the U.S. (1809–1817)

**mad·ly** (mad'lē) *adv.* **1.** insanely **2.** wildly; furiously **3.** foolishly **4.** extremely

**mad·man** (mad'man', -mən) *n., pl.* **-men'** (-men', -mən) an insane person; lunatic; maniac —**mad'wom'an** *n.fem., pl.* **-wom'en**

**mad money** [Colloq.] **1.** a small amount of money carried by a woman for emergencies, as on a date to enable her to get home alone if she wishes **2.** money saved for minor purchases, often for spending frivolously

**mad·ness** (-nis) *n.* **1.** insanity **2.** great anger **3.** great folly **4.** wild excitement **5.** rabies

**Ma·don·na** (mə dän'ə) *n.* [It. < *ma,* my (< L. *mea*) + *donna,* lady < L. *domina*] **1.** Mary, mother of Jesus **2.** a picture or statue of Mary

**Ma·dras** (mə dras', -dräs') seaport on the SE coast of India: pop. 1,729,000

**ma·dras** (mad'rəs, mäd'-; mə dras', -dräs') *n.* [< prec.] a fine, firm cotton cloth, usually striped or plaid

‡**ma·dre** (mä'dre) *n.* [Sp.] mother

**mad·re·pore** (mad'rə pôr') *n.* [< Fr. < It. < *madre,* mother + *poro,* a pore] any of various branching corals that form reefs and islands in tropical seas

**Ma·drid** (mə drid'; *Sp.* mä thrēth') capital of Spain, in the C part: pop. 2,867,000

**mad·ri·gal** (mad'ri gəl) *n.* [< It. *madrigale* < ?] **1.** a short poem, usually of love, that can be set to music **2.** a contrapuntal part song, without accompaniment, popular in the 15th to 17th cent. **3.** loosely, any song —**mad'ri·gal·ist** *n.*

**Ma·du·ra** (mä door'ä) island of Indonesia, northeast of Java: 1,770 sq. mi.

**Ma·du·rai** (mä də rī') city in S India: pop. 425,000

**Mae** (mā) [dim. of MARY] a feminine name

**Mae·ce·nas** (mi sē'nəs), (**Gaius Cilnius**) 70?–8 B.C.; Rom. statesman & patron of Horace & Virgil —*n.* any wealthy, generous patron

**Mael·strom** (māl'strəm) [Early ModDu. < *malen,* to grind + *stroom,* a stream] a dangerous whirlpool off the W coast of Norway —*n.* [m-] **1.** any large or violent whirlpool **2.** a violently agitated state of mind, emotions, affairs, etc.

**mae·nad** (mē'nad) *n.* [< L. < Gr. < *mainesthai,* to rave] **1.** [*often* M-] a female worshiper of Dionysus; bacchante **2.** a frenzied woman —**mae·nad·ic** (mi nad'ik) *adj.*

**ma·es·to·so** (mīs tō'sō; *It.* mä'e stō'sō) *adj., adv.* [It.] *Music* with majesty or dignity

**ma·es·tro** (mīs'trō; mä es'-) *n., pl.* **-tros, -tri** (-trē) [It. < L. *magister,* a MASTER] a master in any art; esp., a great composer, conductor, or teacher of music

**Mae·ter·linck** (māt'ər liŋk', met'-), **Count Maurice** 1862–1949; Belgian playwright & poet

**Ma·fi·a, Maf·fi·a** (mä'fē ə) *n.* [It. *maffia,* hostility to law] an alleged secret society of criminals in the U.S. and other countries

**Ma·fi·o·si** (mä'fē ō'sē) *n.pl., sing.* **-so'** (-sō') [It.] members of the Mafia

**mag. 1.** magazine **2.** magnetism **3.** magnitude

**mag·a·zine** (mag'ə zēn', mag'ə zēn') *n.* [< Fr. < OFr. < It. < Ar. < *makhzan,* a granary < *khazana,* to store up] **1.** a warehouse or military supply depot **2.** a space in which explosives are stored, as in a fort or warship **3.** a supply chamber, as the space in a rifle from which the cartridges are fed, the space in a camera from which the film is fed, etc. **4.** things kept in a magazine, as munitions or supplies **5.** a publication that appears at regular intervals and contains stories, articles, etc. and, usually, advertisements **6.** a television program, appearing regularly, with brief documentary segments

**Mag·da·lene** (mag'də lēn, -lin) [LL. < Gr. < *Magdala,* town in Galilee] *same as* MARY MAGDALENE —*n.* [m-] a reformed and repentant prostitute

**Mag·de·burg** (mäg'də boork; *E.* mag'də burg') city & port in W East Germany, on the Elbe: pop. 268,000

**Ma·gel·lan** (mə jel'ən), **Ferdinand** 1480?–1521; Port. navigator in the service of Spain

**Magellan, Strait of** channel between the S. American mainland & Tierra del Fuego

**ma·gen·ta** (mə jen'tə) *n.* [< *Magenta,* town in Italy] purplish red —*adj.* purplish-red

**mag·got** (mag'ət) *n.* [ME. *magotte*] **1.** a wormlike insect larva, as the legless larva of the housefly **2.** an odd notion; whim —**mag'got·y** *adj.*

**Ma·gi** (mā'jī) *n.pl., sing.* **Ma'gus** (-gəs) [L., pl. of *magus* < Gr. < OPer. *magus*] **1.** the priestly caste in ancient Media and Persia **2.** *Douay Bible* the wise men from the East who brought gifts to the infant Jesus: Matt. 2:1–13

**mag·ic** (maj'ik) *n.* [< OFr. < L. < Gr. < *magikos,* of the MAGI] **1.** the use of charms, spells, etc. in seeking or pretending to control events or forces **2.** any power or influence that seems mysterious or hard to explain *[the magic* of love] **3.** the art of producing illusions by sleight of hand, etc. —*adj.* **1.** of, produced by, or using magic **2.** producing extraordinary results, as if by magic —**mag'i·cal** *adj.* —**mag'i·cal·ly** *adv.*

**ma·gi·cian** (mə jish'ən) *n.* [< OFr. *magicien*] an expert in magic; specif., *a)* a sorcerer; wizard *b)* a performer skilled in magic (sense 3)

**magic lantern** *old-fashioned term for* a slide projector

**mag·is·te·ri·al** (maj'is tir'ē əl) *adj.* [< ML. < LL. < L. *magister,* a MASTER] **1.** of or suitable for a magistrate or master **2.** authoritative **3.** domineering; pompous —**mag'is·te'ri·al·ly** *adv.*

**mag·is·tra·cy** (maj'is trə sē) *n., pl.* **-cies 1.** the position, office, or jurisdiction of a magistrate **2.** magistrates collectively

**mag·is·trate** (-trāt', -trit) *n.* [< L. < *magister,* MASTER] **1.** a civil officer empowered to administer the law: the President of the U.S. may be called the *chief magistrate* **2.** a minor judicial official, as a justice of the peace

**mag·ma** (mag'mə) *n.* [L. < Gr. < *massein,* to knead] molten rock deep in the earth, from which igneous rock is formed

**Mag·na Char·ta** (or **Car·ta**) (mag'nə kär'tə) [ML., lit., great charter] **1.** the charter that King John was forced by the English barons to grant at Runnymede, June 15, 1215, interpreted as guaranteeing certain civil and political liberties **2.** any constitution guaranteeing certain liberties

‡**mag·na cum lau·de** (mäg'nä koom lou'de, mag'nə kum

lô′dē [L.] with great praise: phrase used to signify graduation with high honors from a university or college

**mag·na·nim·i·ty** (mag′nə nim′ə tē) *n.* **1.** a magnanimous quality or state **2.** *pl.* **-ties** a magnanimous act

**mag·nan·i·mous** (mag nan′ə məs) *adj.* [< L. < *magnus*, great + *animus*, soul] generous in overlooking injury or insult; rising above pettiness —**mag·nan′i·mous·ly** *adv.*

**mag·nate** (mag′nāt) *n.* [< LL. < L. *magnus*, great] a very influential person, esp. in business

**mag·ne·sia** (mag nē′zhə, -shə) *n.* [ModL., ult. < Gr. *Magnēsia*, area in Thessaly] magnesium oxide, MgO, a white, tasteless powder used as a mild laxative and antacid, and as an insulating substance —**mag·ne′sian** *adj.*

**mag·ne·si·um** (mag nē′zē əm, -zhē əm, -zhəm) *n.* [ModL. < prec.] a light, silver-white, malleable metallic chemical element: it burns with a hot, white light, and is used in photographic flashbulbs, etc.: symbol, Mg; at. wt., 24.312; at. no., 12

**mag·net** (mag′nit) *n.* [< OFr. < L. *magnes* < Gr. *Magnētis* (*lithos*), (stone) of Magnesia: see MAGNESIA] **1.** any piece of iron, steel, or lodestone that has the property of attracting iron, steel, etc. **2.** a person or thing that attracts

**mag·net·ic** (mag net′ik) *adj.* **1.** having the properties of a magnet **2.** of, producing, or caused by magnetism **3.** of the earth's magnetism **4.** that can be magnetized **5.** powerfully attractive *[a magnetic personality]* —**mag·net′i·cal·ly** *adv.*

**magnetic bottle** *Physics* a geometrical configuration whose extent is outlined by magnetic lines of force that will confine a hot plasma

**magnetic field** a region of space in which there is an appreciable magnetic force

**magnetic force** the attracting or repelling force between a magnet and a ferromagnetic material, between a magnet and a current-carrying conductor, etc.

**magnetic mine** a naval mine exploded when the metal hull of a ship passing near it deflects a magnetic needle, thus detonating the charge

**magnetic needle** a slender bar of magnetized steel which, when swinging freely on a pivot, as in a compass, points toward the magnetic poles

**magnetic north** the direction toward which a magnetic needle points, usually not true north

**magnetic pickup** a phonograph pickup in which a part of the stylus assembly vibrates in a magnetic field between two coils so as to induce a current

**magnetic pole** **1.** either pole of a magnet **2.** either point on the earth's surface toward which a magnetic needle points: the north and south magnetic poles do not precisely coincide with the geographical poles

**magnetic recording** the recording of electrical signals by means of changes in areas of magnetization on a tape (**magnetic tape**) or disc

**mag·net·ism** (mag′nə tiz′m) *n.* **1.** the property or quality of being magnetic **2.** the force to which this is due **3.** the branch of physics dealing with magnetic phenomena **4.** personal charm

**mag·net·ite** (-tīt′) *n.* a black iron oxide, Fe₃O₄, an important iron ore: called *lodestone* when magnetic

**mag·net·ize** (mag′nə tīz′) *vt.* **-ized′, -iz′ing** **1.** to give magnetic properties to (steel, iron, etc.) **2.** to attract or charm (a person) —*vi.* to become magnetic —**mag′net·iz′a·ble** *adj* —**mag′net·i·za′tion** *n.* —**mag′net·iz′er** *n.*

**mag·ne·to** (mag nēt′ō) *n., pl.* **-tos** a dynamo in which one or more permanent magnets produce the magnetic field; esp., a small machine of this sort connected with an internal-combustion engine to generate the current providing a spark for the ignition

**mag·ne·to-** [see MAGNET] *a combining form meaning:* **1.** magnetism, magnetic force **2.** magnetoelectric

**mag·ne·to·e·lec·tric** (-i lek′trik) *adj.* designating or of electricity produced by changing magnetic fields in the vicinity of electric conductors —**mag·ne′to·e·lec′tric′i·ty** (-tris′ə tē) *n.*

**mag·ne·tom·e·ter** (mag′nə täm′ə tər) *n.* an instrument for measuring magnetic forces

**mag·ne·to·mo·tive** (mag nēt′ō mōt′iv) *adj.* designating or of a force that causes magnetic flux

**mag·ne·to·sphere** (mag nēt′ə sfir′) *n.* [MAGNETO- + -SPHERE] that region surrounding a planet in which the planetary magnetic field is stronger than the interplanetary field

**mag·ne·tron** (mag′nə trän′) *n.* [MAGNE(T) + (ELEC)TRON] an electron tube in which the flow of electrons is acted upon by an externally applied magnetic field to produce microwave frequencies

**magnet school** a public school which offers innovative courses, specialized training, etc. in order to attract students from a broad urban area and thereby help to bring about desegregation

**mag·ni-** [< L. *magnus*, great] *a combining form meaning* great, big, large *[magnificent]*

**Mag·nif·i·cat** (mag nif′i kat′, män yif′i kät′) *n.* [L.] **1.** the hymn of the Virgin Mary in Luke 1:46–55 **2.** any musical setting for this

**mag·ni·fi·ca·tion** (mag′nə fi kā′shən) *n.* **1.** a magnifying or being magnified **2.** the power of magnifying **3.** a magnified image or model

**mag·nif·i·cence** (mag nif′ə s′ns) *n.* [OFr. < L. < *magnificus*, noble < *magnus*, great + *facere*, to do] richness and splendor, as of furnishings, color, dress, etc.; stately or imposing beauty; grandeur

**mag·nif·i·cent** (-s′nt) *adj.* [OFr. < LL. *magnificens*: see prec.] **1.** beautiful and grand or stately; rich or sumptuous, as in construction, decoration, etc. **2.** exalted: said of ideas, etc. **3.** [Colloq.] very good; excellent —**mag·nif′i·cent·ly** *adv.*

**mag·nif·i·co** (-kō′) *n., pl.* **-coes′, -cos′** [It. < L. *magnificus*: see MAGNIFICENCE] a person of high rank

**mag·ni·fy** (mag′nə fī′) *vt.* **-fied′, -fy′ing** [< OFr. < L. *magnificare*: see MAGNIFICENCE] **1.** [Rare] to make greater **2.** to exaggerate *[to magnify* one's sufferings] **3.** to increase the apparent size of, esp. by means of a lens **4.** [Archaic] to praise; extol —*vi.* to have the power of increasing the apparent size of an object —**mag′ni·fi′er** *n.*

**magnifying glass** a lens that increases the apparent size of an object seen through it

**mag·nil·o·quent** (mag nil′ə kwənt) *adj.* [< L. < *magnus*, great + prp. of *loqui*, to speak] **1.** pompous or grandiose in speech or style of expression **2.** boastful or bombastic — **mag·nil′o·quence** *n.* —**mag·nil′o·quent·ly** *adv.*

**mag·ni·tude** (mag′nə tōōd′, -tyōōd′) *n.* [< L. < *magnus*, great] **1.** greatness; specif., *a)* size *b)* of extent *c)* of influence **2.** *a)* size *b)* loudness (of sound) *c)* importance **3.** *Astron.* the degree of brightness of a fixed star: the brightest stars are of the first magnitude **4.** *Math.* a number given to a quantity for purposes of comparison with other quantities of the same class —**of the first magnitude** of the greatest importance

**mag·no·li·a** (mag nō′lē ə, -nōl′yə) *n.* [ModL., after P. *Magnol* (1638–1715), Fr. botanist] **1.** any of a group of trees or shrubs with large, fragrant flowers of white, pink, or purple **2.** the flower

**mag·num** (mag′nəm) *n.* [L., neut. sing. of *magnus*, great] a wine bottle holding twice as much as the usual bottle, or about 2/5 of a gallon

‡**mag·num o·pus** (mag′nəm ō′pəs) [L.] **1.** a great work, esp. of art or literature; masterpiece **2.** a person's greatest work or undertaking

**mag·pie** (mag′pī′) *n.* [< *Mag*, dim. of MARGARET + PIE³] **1.** a noisy bird related to the crows and jays, with black-and-white coloring and a long, tapering tail **2.** a person who chatters **3.** a person who collects odds and ends

**mag·uey** (mag′wā: *Sp.* mä ge′ē) *n.* [Sp.] **1.** a fleshy-leaved, fiber-yielding agave of the SW U.S., Mexico, and Central America; esp., the century plant **2.** its fiber

**Mag·yar** (mag′yär; *Hung.* môd′yär) *n.* [Hung.] **1.** a member of the people constituting the main ethnic group in Hungary **2.** their language; Hungarian —*adj.* of the Magyars, their language, etc.

**Ma·ha·bha·ra·ta** (mə hä′bä′rə tə) [Sans.] one of the two great epics of India, written in Sanskrit about 200 B.C.

**ma·ha·ra·jah, ma·ha·ra·ja** (mä′hə rä′jə) *n.* [< Sans. < *mahā*, great + *rājā*, king] formerly in India, a prince; specif., the sovereign prince of a native state

**ma·ha·ra·ni, ma·ha·ra·nee** (-nē) *n.* [< Hindi < *mahā*, great + *rānī*, queen] in India, the wife of a maharajah

**ma·hat·ma** (mə hat′mə, -hät′-) *n.* [< Sans. < *mahā*, great + *ātman*, soul] *Theosophy & Buddhism* any of a class of wise and holy persons held in special regard or reverence

**Ma·hi·can** (mə hē′kən) *n.* [< Algonquian, lit., a wolf] **1.** a confederacy or tribe of Algonquian Indians who lived chiefly in the upper Hudson Valley **2.** an Indian of this confederacy **3.** *same as* MOHEGAN —*adj.* of the Mahicans

**mah-jongg, mah·jong** (mä′jôn′, -jän′, -zhôn′, -zhän′) *n.* [< Chin. *ma-ch'iao*, lit., house sparrow (a figure on one of the tiles)] a game of Chinese origin, played with 136 or 144 small tiles

**Mah·ler** (mä′lər), **Gus·tav** (gōōs′täf) 1860–1911; Austrian composer & conductor, born in Bohemia

**ma·hog·a·ny** (mə häg′ə nē, -hôg′-) *n., pl.* **-nies** [< ?] **1.** any of various tropical trees, esp. one of tropical America, with hard, reddish-brown wood valued for furniture **2.** the wood of any of these trees **3.** reddish brown —*adj.* **1.** made of mahogany **2.** reddish-brown

**Ma·hom·et** (mə häm′it) *same as* MOHAMMED

**ma·hout** (mə hout′) *n.* [< Hindi < Sans. *mahāmātra*, lit., great in measure] in India and the East Indies, an elephant driver or elephant keeper

**maid** (mād) *n.* [< ME. contr. < *maiden*] **1.** *a)* a girl or young unmarried woman *b)* a virgin **2.** a girl or woman servant

**maid·en** (mād′'n) *n.* [OE. *mægden*] **1.** *a)* a girl or young unmarried woman *b)* a virgin **2.** a race horse that has never won a race —*adj.* **1.** of, characteristic of, for, or suitable for a maiden or maidens **2.** *a)* unmarried *b)* virgin **3.** untried; unused; new; fresh **4.** first or earliest [a *maiden voyage]*

**maid·en·hair** (-her′) *n.* any of various ferns with delicate brown to black fronds: also **maidenhair fern**

**maid·en·head** (-hed′) *n.* **1.** [Archaic] maidenhood; virginity **2.** the hymen

**maid·en·hood** (-hood′) *n.* the state or time of being a maiden: also **maid′hood′**

**maid·en·ly** (-lē) *adj.* **1.** of a maiden **2.** like or suitable for a maiden; modest, gentle, etc. —*adv.* [Archaic] in a maidenly manner —**maid′en·li·ness** *n.*

**maiden name** the surname of a woman before her marriage

**maid of honor** **1.** an unmarried woman acting as chief attendant to the bride at a wedding **2.** an unmarried woman, usually of noble birth, attending a queen or princess

**maid·ser·vant** (-sur′vənt) *n.* a girl or woman servant

**mail**[1] (māl) *n.* [OFr. *male*, ult. < OHG. *malaha*, wallet] **1.** *a)* letters, papers, packages, etc. transported and delivered by the post office *b)* their collection or delivery at a certain time **2.** [*also pl.*] the postal system —*adj.* of mail —*vt.* to send by mail, as by putting into a mailbox —**mail′a·bil′i·ty** *n.* —**mail′a·ble** *adj.* —**mail′er** *n.*

**mail**[2] (māl) *n.* [OFr. *maille* < L. *macula*, a mesh of a net] **1.** a flexible body armor made of small metal rings, loops of chain, or scales **2.** the hard protective covering of some animals, as turtles —*vt.* to cover or protect as with mail —**mailed** *adj.*

**mail·bag** (māl′bag′) *n.* **1.** a bag, as of leather, in which a mailman carries the mail he delivers: also **mail pouch 2.** a heavy canvas bag in which mail is transported: also **mail sack**

**mail·box** (-bäks′) *n.* **1.** a box into which mail is put when delivered **2.** a box, as on a street, into which mail is put for collection Also **mail box**

**mail carrier** one whose work is carrying and delivering mail; mailman; postman

**Mail·gram** (māl′gram′) *a trademark for* a telegram delivered with the regular mail —*n.* [*also* m-] such a telegram

**mail·ing list** (māl′iŋ) a special list of names and addresses used by an organization, business, etc. in mailing out its literature, advertising matter, etc.

**mail·man** (māl′man′, -mən) *n., pl.* **-men′** (-men′, -mən) *same as* MAIL CARRIER

**mail order** an order for goods to be sent through the mail —**mail′-or′der** *adj.*

**mail-order house** a business that takes mail orders

**maim** (mām) *vt.* [OFr. *mahaigner*] to deprive of the use of some necessary part of the body; cripple; mutilate; disable

**Mai·mon·i·des** (mī män′ə dēz′) (born *Moses ben Maimon*) 1135–1204; Sp. rabbi, physician, & philosopher, in Egypt

**Main** (mīn; *E.* mān) river in S West Germany, flowing west into the Rhine

**main**[1] (mān) *n.* [OE. *mægen*] **1.** physical strength; force: now only in **with might and main**, with all one's strength **2.** the principal part or point: usually in **in the main**, mostly, chiefly **3.** a principal pipe or line in a distributing system for water, gas, etc. **4.** [Poet.] the ocean **5.** [Archaic] the mainland **6.** [Obs.] any broad expanse —*adj.* **1.** orig., strong; powerful **2.** chief in size, importance, etc.; principal —**by main force** (or **strength**) by sheer force (or strength)

**main**[2] (mān) *n.* [prob. < prec.] a series of matches in cockfighting

**main clause** in a complex sentence, a clause that can function syntactically as a complete sentence by itself

**main drag** [Slang] the main street of a city or town

**Maine** (mān) [prob. from its being the *main* part of New England] New England State of the U.S.: 33,215 sq. mi.; pop. 1,125,000; cap. Augusta: abbrev. **Me., ME**

**main·frame** (mān′frām′) *n.* the central processing unit of a computer

**main·land** (mān′land′, -lənd) *n.* the main land mass of a continent, as distinguished from nearby islands, etc. —**main′land′er** *n.*

**main·line** (-līn′) *n.* the principal road, course, etc. —*vt.* **-lined′**, **-lin′ing** [Slang] to inject (a narcotic drug) directly into a large vein —**main′lin′er** *n.*

**main·ly** (-lē) *adv.* chiefly; principally; in the main

**main·mast** (-məst, -mast′) *n.* the principal mast of a vessel

**main·sail** (-s'l, -sāl′) *n.* **1.** in a square-rigged vessel, the sail set from the main yard: also **main course 2.** in a fore-and-aft-rigged vessel, the large sail set from the mainmast

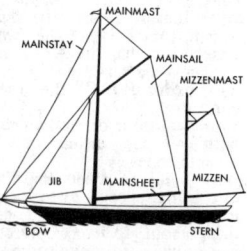

**main·sheet** (-shēt′) *n.* the line controlling the angle at which a mainsail is set

**main·spring** (-spriŋ′) *n.* **1.** the principal, or driving, spring in a clock, watch, etc. **2.** the chief motive, incentive, or impelling cause

**main·stay** (-stā′) *n.* **1.** the supporting line run forward from the mainmast **2.** a chief support

**main stem** [Slang] *same as* MAIN DRAG

**main·stream** (-strēm′) *n.* the main current or prevailing trend of thought, action, etc.

**Main Street 1.** the principal street of any small town **2.** the typical inhabitants of a small town, regarded as provincial and conservative

**main·tain** (mān tān′) *vt.* [< OFr. *maintenir*, ult. < L. *manu tenere*, to hold in the hand] **1.** to keep or keep up; carry on **2.** *a)* to keep in continuance [food *maintains* life] *b)* to keep in a certain condition, as of repair [to *maintain* roads] **3.** to hold (a place, etc.) against attack **4.** *a)* to uphold or defend, as by argument *b)* to declare positively; assert **5.** to support by aid, influence, etc. **6.** to provide the means of existence for [to *maintain* a family] —**main·tain′a·ble** *adj.* —**main·tain′er** *n.*

**main·te·nance** (mān′t'n əns) *n.* **1.** a maintaining or being maintained; upkeep, continuance, support, defense, etc. **2.** means of support or sustenance; livelihood

**main·top** (mān′täp′) *n.* a platform at the head of the lower section of the mainmast

**main·top·mast** (mān′täp′məst) *n.* the section of the mainmast above the maintop

**main·top·sail** (-s'l, -sāl) *n.* the sail above the mainsail on the mainmast

**main yard** the lower yard on the mainmast

**mai·tre d'** (māt′ər dē′) [< ff.] [Colloq.] a headwaiter

‡**maî·tre d'hô·tel** (me′tr′ dô tel′) [Fr., lit., master of the house] **1.** a butler or steward **2.** a headwaiter

**maize** (māz) *n.* [Sp. *maíz* < WInd. *mahiz*] **1.** *chiefly Brit.* name for CORN[1] (sense 2) **2.** the color of ripe corn; yellow —*adj.* yellow

**Maj.** Major

**ma·jes·tic** (mə jes′tik) *adj.* having majesty; grand, stately, dignified, lofty, etc.: also **ma·jes′ti·cal** —**ma·jes′ti·cal·ly** *adv.*

**maj·es·ty** (maj′is tē) *n., pl.* **-ties** [< OFr. < L. *majestas* < base of *major*, compar. of *magnus*, great] **1.** sovereign power or dignity **2.** [M-] a title used in speaking to or of a sovereign, preceded by *His, Her,* or *Your* **3.** grandeur or stateliness

**ma·jol·i·ca** (mə jäl′i kə, -yäl′-) *n.* [It. *maiolica* < *Maiolica*, MAJORCA] a variety of Italian pottery, enameled, glazed, and richly decorated

**ma·jor** (mā′jər) *adj.* [L., compar. of *magnus*, great] **1.** *a)* greater in size, amount, or extent *b)* greater in importance or rank **2.** of full legal age **3.** constituting the majority **4.** *Educ.* designating a field of study in which a student specializes **5.** *Music a)* designating an interval greater than the corresponding minor by a semitone *b)* characterized by major intervals, scales, etc. [the *major* key] *c)* based on the scale pattern of the major mode: see MAJOR SCALE —*vi. Educ.* to pursue a major subject [to *major* in physics] —*n.* **1.** a superior in some class or group **2.** *U.S. Mil.* an officer ranking above a captain **3.** *Educ. a)* a major field of study *b)* a student specializing in a (specified) subject **4.** *Law* a person of full legal age **5.** *Music* a major interval, key, etc. —**the Majors** *Baseball* the Major Leagues

**Ma·jor·ca** (mə jôr′kə) largest of the Balearic Islands

**ma·jor-do·mo** (mā′jər dō′mō) *n., pl.* **-mos** [< Sp. or It. < LL. < L. *major*, greater, an elder + gen. of *domus*, house] **1.** a man in charge of a great or royal household; chief steward **2.** any steward or butler: humorous usage

**ma·jor·ette** (mā′jər et′) *n. short for* DRUM MAJORETTE

**major general** *pl.* **major generals** *U.S. Mil.* an officer ranking above a brigadier general

**ma·jor·i·ty** (mə jôr′ə tē, -jär′-) *n., pl.* **-ties** [< Fr. < ML. < L. *major:* see MAJOR] **1.** the greater part or larger number; more than half **2.** the excess of the larger number of votes cast for one candidate, bill, etc. over all the rest of the votes **3.** the group or party with the majority of votes **4.** the state or time of being legally an adult **5.** *Mil.* the rank or position of a major

**major league** a principal league in a professional sport; specif., **[M- L-]** *[pl.]* the two main leagues of professional baseball clubs, the National League and the American League —**ma′jor-league′** *adj.* —**ma′jor-leagu′er** *n.*

**major order** *R.C.Ch.* the order of priest, deacon, or subdeacon

**major scale** one of the two standard diatonic musical scales, with half steps instead of whole steps after the third and seventh tones

**make** (māk) *vt.* **made, mak′ing** [OE. *macian*] **1.** to bring into being; specif., *a)* to form by shaping or putting parts, ideas, etc. together; build, create, devise, etc. *b)* to cause; bring about *[to make* corrections*] c)* to cause to be available; provide *[to make* room*]* **2.** to cause to be, become, or seem *[make* him chairman*]* : sometimes used reflexively *[make* yourself comfortable*]* **3.** to prepare for use *[make* the beds*]* **4.** to amount to *[two* pints *make* a quart*]* **5.** to have, or prove to have, the qualities of or for *[to make* a fine leader*]* **6.** to set up; establish *[to make* rules*]* **7.** *a)* to acquire, as by one's behavior *[to make* friends*] b)* to get by earning, investing, etc. *[to make* a fortune*]* **8.** to cause the success of *[that venture made* him*]* **9.** to understand *[what do you make* of that?*]* **10.** to estimate to be *[I make* the distance about 500 miles*]* **11.** *a)* to do, execute, accomplish, etc. *[to make* a quick turn*] b)* to engage in *[to make* war*]* **12.** to deliver (a speech) or utter (remarks, etc.) **13.** to cause or force *[make* him behave*]* **14.** to arrive at; reach *[the* ship *made* port*]* **15.** to go or travel; traverse *[to make* 500 miles the first day*]* **16.** [Colloq.] to succeed in getting a position on, etc. *[to make* the team*]* **17.** [Slang] to seduce sexually **18.** *Elec.* to close (a circuit); effect (a contact) —*vi.* **1.** to start (to do something) *[she made* to go*]* **2.** to tend, extend, or point (*to, toward,* etc.) **3.** to behave in a specified manner *[make* bold, *make* merry*]* **4.** to cause something to be in a specified condition *[make* ready*]* —*n.* **1.** the act or process of making **2.** the amount made; output **3.** the way in which something is made; style; build **4.** type, sort, or brand **5.** character; nature *[a* man of this *make]* **6.** *Elec.* the closing of a circuit —**make after** to chase or follow —**make away with 1.** to steal **2.** to get rid of **3.** to kill —**make believe** to pretend —**make for 1.** to head for **2.** to attack **3.** to help effect —**make it** [Colloq.] to do or achieve a certain thing —**make like** [Slang] to imitate —**make off with** to steal —**make or break** to cause the success or failure of —**make out 1.** to see with some difficulty **2.** to understand **3.** to write out **4.** to fill out (a blank form, etc.) **5.** to (try to) show or prove to be **6.** to succeed; get along **7.** [Slang] *a)* to kiss and caress as lovers *b)* to have sexual intercourse —**make over 1.** to change; renovate **2.** to transfer the ownership of **3.** [Colloq.] to be demonstrative toward or about —**make up 1.** to put together; compose **2.** to form; constitute **3.** to invent **4.** to complete by providing what is lacking **5.** to compensate *(for)* **6.** to become friendly again after a quarrel **7.** to put cosmetics on **8.** to decide (one's mind) **9.** to select and arrange type, illustrations, etc. for (a book, page, etc.) —**make up to** to try to ingratiate oneself with —**on the make 1.** [Colloq.] trying to succeed, esp. in an aggressive way **2.** [Slang] seeking a lover

**make-be·lieve** (māk′bə lēv′) *n.* **1.** pretense; feigning **2.** a pretender —*adj.* pretended; feigned

**mak·er** (-ər) *n.* **1.** a person or thing that makes **2.** **[M-]** God —**meet one's Maker** to die

**make·shift** (-shift′) *n.* a thing that will do for a while as a substitute; temporary expedient —*adj.* that will do for a while as a substitute

**make·up, make-up** (-up′) *n.* **1.** the way in which something is put together; composition **2.** nature; disposition **3.** the cosmetics, wigs, costumes, etc. put on for theatrical roles **4.** cosmetics generally **5.** the arrangement of type, illustrations, etc. in a book, newspaper, etc.

**make-work** (-wurk′) *adj.* designating a job, project, assignment, etc. that serves no useful purpose other than to give an otherwise idle or unemployed person something to do

**Ma·key·ev·ka** (mä kā′yif kä′) city in SE Ukrainian S.S.R., in the Donets river valley: pop. 415,000

**mak·ing** (māk′iŋ) *n.* **1.** the act of one that makes or the process of being made **2.** the cause of success or advancement *[an* experience that will be the *making* of him*]* **3.** *a)* something made *b)* the quantity made at a single time **4.** *[often pl.]* the material or potential qualities needed *[to* have the *making(s)* of a good doctor*]*

**mal-** [Fr. < L. < *male,* badly < *malus,* bad*] a prefix meaning* bad or badly, wrong, ill *[maladjustment]*

**Mal. 1.** Malachi **2.** Malay **3.** Malayan

**Ma·la·bo** (mä lä′bō) capital of Equatorial Guinea; seaport on the island portion of the country: pop. 20,000

**Ma·lac·ca** (mə lak′ə) **Strait of,** strait between Sumatra & the Malay Peninsula

**Mal·a·chi** (mal′ə kī′) *Bible* **1.** a Hebrew prophet of the 5th cent. B.C. **2.** the book containing prophecies attributed to him

**mal·a·chite** (mal′ə kīt′) *n.* [< L. < Gr. *malachē,* mallow: from its color] native basic copper carbonate, $CuCO_3$-$Cu(OH)_2$, a green mineral used as a source of copper and for table tops, vases, etc.

**mal·ad·just·ed** (mal′ə jus′tid) *adj.* poorly adjusted, esp. to the circumstances of one's life —**mal′ad·just′ment** *n.*

**mal·ad·min·is·ter** (mal′ad min′ə stər) *vt.* to administer badly or corruptly —**mal′ad·min′is·tra′tion** *n.*

**mal·a·droit** (mal′ə droit′) *adj.* [Fr.: see MAL- & ADROIT] awkward; clumsy; bungling —**mal′a·droit′ly** *adv.* —**mal′a·droit′ness** *n.*

**mal·a·dy** (mal′ə dē) *n., pl.* **-dies** [< OFr. *malade,* sick < VL. *male habitus,* out of condition: see MAL- & HABIT] a disease; illness; sickness

**Má·la·ga** (mä′lä gä′; *E.* mal′ə gə) seaport in S Spain, on the Mediterranean: pop. 330,000

**Mal·a·ga** (mal′ə gə) *n.* **1.** a large, white, oval grape **2.** a white, sweet wine, orig. from Málaga

**Mal·a·gas·y** (mal′ə gas′ē) *n.* **1.** *pl.* **-gas′y, -gas′ies** a native or inhabitant of Madagascar **2.** the Indonesian language of the Malagasy

**Malagasy Republic** *former name of* MADAGASCAR

**ma·laise** (ma lāz′) *n.* [Fr. < *mal,* bad (see MAL-) + *aise,* EASE] a vague feeling of physical discomfort or uneasiness, as early in an illness

**mal·a·mute** (mal′ə myoot′) *n.* [< *Malemute,* name of an Eskimo tribe] a strong dog with a thick coat of gray or black-and-white and a bushy tail: it was developed as a sled dog by the Alaskan Eskimo: in full, **Alaskan malamute:** also sp. **malemute, malemiut**

**mal·a·prop** (mal′ə prāp′) *adj.* [< ff.] using or characterized by malapropisms: also **mal′a·prop′i·an** (-ē ən) —*n.* *same as* MALAPROPISM

**mal·a·prop·ism** (mal′ə prāp iz'm) *n.* [after Mrs. *Malaprop,* a character in Sheridan's *The Rivals*] **1.** ludicrous misuse of words, esp. of words that sound somewhat alike **2.** an instance of this

**mal·ap·ro·pos** (mal′ap rə pō′, mal ap′-) *adj., adv.* [Fr.: see MAL- & APROPOS] inappropriate(ly); inopportune(ly)

**ma·lar·i·a** (mə ler′ē ə) *n.* [It., contr. of *mala aria,* bad air] an infectious disease, generally recurrent, caused by protozoans transmitted to man by the bite of an infected mosquito, esp. the anopheles: it is characterized by severe chills and fever —**ma·lar′i·al, ma·lar′i·an, ma·lar′i·ous** *adj.*

**ma·lar·key, ma·lar·ky** (mə lär′kē) *n.* [< ? Irish surname] [Slang] insincere talk; nonsense

**mal·a·thi·on** (mal′ə thī′än) *n.* an organic phosphate, $C_{10}H_{19}O_6S_2P$, used as an insecticide

**Ma·la·wi** (mä′lä wē) country in SE Africa: a member of the Commonwealth: 46,066 sq. mi.; pop. 4,530,000

**Ma·lay** (mā′lā, mə lā′) *n.* **1.** a member of a large group of brown-skinned peoples living in the Malay Peninsula, the Malay Archipelago, and nearby islands **2.** their Indonesian language —*adj.* of the Malays, their country, language, culture, etc.

**Ma·lay·a** (mə lā′ə) **1.** *same as* MALAY PENINSULA **2.** group of eleven states at the S end of the Malay Peninsula: it is a part of Malaysia and is called *West Malaysia*

**Ma·lay·an** (mə lā′ən) *adj. same as* INDONESIAN (sense 2) —*n.* **1.** *same as* MALAY (sense 1) **2.** *same as* INDONESIAN (sense 3)

**Malay Archipelago** large group of islands between the mainland of SE Asia & Australia

**Ma·lay·o-Pol·y·ne·sian** (mə lā′ō päl′ə nē′zhən, -shən) *adj.* designating or of a family of languages spoken over a large area in the C & W Pacific, including Polynesian, Indonesian, etc. —*n.* these languages

**Malay Peninsula** peninsula in SE Asia, including the S part of Thailand & the states of Malaya

**Ma·lay·sia** (mə lā′zhə, -shə) country in SE Asia, consisting of the states of Malaya and two states on N Borneo: a member of the Commonwealth: 128,654 sq. mi.; pop. 10,190,000; cap. Kuala Lumpur —**Ma·lay′sian** *adj., n.*

**Mal·colm** (mal′kəm) [Celt. *Maolcolm,* lit., servant of (St.) Columba] a masculine name

**mal·con·tent** (mal′kən tent′) *adj.* [OFr.: see MAL- & CONTENT[1]] dissatisfied or rebellious —*n.* a dissatisfied or rebellious person

**‡mal de mer** (mál də mer′) [Fr.] seasickness

**Mal·den** (môl′dən) [after *Maldon,* town in England] city in E Mass.: suburb of Boston: pop. 53,000

**Mal·dive Islands** (mal′dīv) country on a group of islands in the Indian Ocean, southwest of Ceylon: 115 sq. mi.; pop. 104,000: also **Mal′dives**

**male** (māl) *adj.* [< OFr. < L. *masculus,* dim. of *mas,* a male] **1.** designating or of the sex that fertilizes the ovum of the female and begets offspring **2.** of, like, or suitable for members of this sex; masculine **3.** consisting of men or boys **4.** designating or having a part shaped to fit into a corresponding hollow part **5.** *Bot.* designating or of fertilizing bodies, organs, etc. —*n.* **1.** a male person; man or boy **2.** a male animal or plant —**male′ness** *n.*

**mal·e·dic·tion** (mal′ə dik′shən) *n.* [OFr. < LL. *maledictio* < L., abuse: see MAL- & DICTION] a calling down of evil on someone; curse

**mal·e·fac·tion** (-fak′shən) *n.* wrongdoing; crime

**mal·e·fac·tor** (mal′ə fak′tər) *n.* [L. < pp. of *malefacere* < *male*, evil + *facere*, to do] an evildoer or criminal

**ma·lef·i·cent** (mə lef′ə s'nt) *adj.* [see prec.] harmful; hurtful; evil —**ma·lef′i·cence** *n.*

**ma·lev·o·lent** (mə lev′ə lənt) *adj.* [< OFr. < L. < *male*, evil + prp. of *velle*, to wish] wishing evil or harm to others; spiteful; malicious —**ma·lev′o·lence** *n.* —**ma·lev′o·lent·ly** *adv.*

**mal·fea·sance** (mal fē′z'ns) *n.* [obs. Fr. *malfaisance* < *mal*, evil + prp. of *faire*, to do] wrongdoing or misconduct, esp. by a public official: distinguished from MISFEASANCE, NONFEASANCE —**mal·fea′sant** *adj.*

**mal·for·ma·tion** (mal′fôr mā′shən) *n.* faulty, irregular, or abnormal formation of a body or part —**mal·formed′** (-fôrmd′) *adj.*

**mal·func·tion** (mal fuŋk′shən) *vi.* to fail to function as it should —*n.* the act or an instance of malfunctioning

**Ma·li** (mä′lē) country in W Africa, south & east of Mauritania: 464,873 sq. mi.; pop. 4,929,000

**mal·ic acid** (mal′ik, mā′lik) [< Fr. < L. < Gr. *mēlon*, apple] a colorless acid, $C_4H_6O_5$, occurring in apples and other fruits

**mal·ice** (mal′is) *n.* [OFr. < L. < *malus*, bad] **1.** active ill will; desire to harm another; spite **2.** *Law* evil intent —**malice aforethought** a deliberate intention and plan to do something unlawful

**ma·li·cious** (mə lish′əs) *adj.* having, showing, or caused by malice; spiteful —**ma·li′cious·ly** *adv.* —**ma·li′ciousness** *n.*

**ma·lign** (mə līn′) *vt.* [< OFr. < LL. < L. *malignus*, wicked < *male*, ill + base of *genus*, born] to speak evil of; slander —*adj.* **1.** showing ill will; malicious **2.** evil; sinister **3.** very harmful; malignant —**ma·lign′er** *n.*

**ma·lig·nan·cy** (mə lig′nən sē) *n.* **1.** a being malignant: also **ma·lig′nance 2.** *pl.* **-cies** a malignant tumor

**ma·lig·nant** (-nənt) *adj.* [< LL. < L. *malignus:* see MALIGN] **1.** having an evil influence; malign **2.** wishing evil; malevolent **3.** very harmful **4.** very virulent; causing or likely to cause death [a cancer is a *malignant* growth] —**ma·lig′nant·ly** *adv.*

**ma·lig·ni·ty** (-nə tē) *n.* **1.** intense ill will or desire to harm others; great malice **2.** the quality of being very harmful or dangerous **3.** *pl.* **-ties** a malignant act, event, or feeling

**ma·lines** (mə lēn′; *Fr.* mà lēn′) *n.* [< *Malines*, Belgian city] a thin, somewhat stiff, silk net: also **ma·line′**

**ma·lin·ger** (mə liŋ′gər) *vi.* [< Fr. *malingre*, sickly] to pretend to be ill in order to escape duty or work; shirk —**ma·lin′ger·er** *n.*

**mall** (môl, mal) *n.* [var. of MAUL] **1.** a shaded walk or public promenade **2.** *a)* a street for pedestrians only, with shops on each of the sides *b)* a completely enclosed, air-conditioned shopping center like this

**mal·lard** (mal′ərd) *n., pl.* **-lards, -lard:** see PLURAL, II, D, 1 [OFr. *malart*] the common wild duck, from which the domestic duck is descended: the male has a green head and a band of white around the neck

**Mal·lar·mé** (mà làr mā′), **Sté·phane** (stā fàn′) 1842–98; Fr. poet

**mal·le·a·ble** (mal′ē ə b'l) *adj.* [< ML. < L. *malleare*, to hammer < *malleus*, a hammer] **1.** that can be hammered, pounded, or pressed into various shapes without breaking **2.** pliable; adaptable —**mal′le·a·bil′i·ty, mal′le·a·ble·ness** *n.*

**mal·let** (mal′it) *n.* [< MFr. dim. of *mail* < OFr. *maile:* see MAUL] **1.** a kind of hammer, usually with a wooden head and a short handle, for driving a chisel, etc. **2.** *a)* a long-handled hammer used in playing croquet *b)* a similar instrument used in playing polo **3.** a small, light hammer used for playing a vibraphone, xylophone, etc.

**mal·le·us** (mal′ē əs) *n., pl.* **mal′le·i′** (-ī′) [L., a hammer] the outermost of the three small bones in the middle ear of mammals, shaped somewhat like a hammer

**Mal·lor·ca** (mäl yôr′kä, mä-) *Sp. name of* MAJORCA

**mal·low** (mal′ō) *n.* [OE. *mealuwe* < L. *malva*] **1.** any of a group of plants, with dissected or lobed leaves and large, showy flowers **2.** any of various other related plants, as the marsh mallow

**Malm·ö** (mälm′ö; *E.* mal′mō) seaport in S Sweden: pop. 254,000

**malm·sey** (mäm′zē) *n.* [< ML. < Gr. *Monembasia*, Greek town] **1.** a strong, full-flavored, sweet white wine **2.** the grape from which this is made

**mal·nour·ished** (mal nur′isht) *adj.* improperly nourished

**mal·nu·tri·tion** (mal′nōō trish′ən) *n.* faulty or inadequate nutrition; poor nourishment

**mal·o·dor·ous** (mal ō′dər əs) *adj.* having a bad odor; stinking —**mal·o′dor·ation** —**mal·o′dor·ous·ly** *adv.*

**Mal·o·ry** (mal′ər ē), **Sir Thomas** ?-1471?; Eng. compiler & translator of Arthurian tales taken mostly from Fr. sources

**mal·prac·tice** (mal prak′tis) *n.* **1.** injurious or unprofessional treatment of a patient by a physician or surgeon **2.** misconduct or improper practice in any professional or official position —**mal′prac·ti′tion·er** (-tish′ən ər) *n.*

**malt** (môlt) *n.* [OE. *mealt*] **1.** barley or other grain softened by soaking and then kiln-dried: used for brewing and distilling certain alcoholic liquors **2.** such liquor, esp. beer, ale, etc. **3.** [Colloq.] *same as* MALTED MILK —*adj.* made with malt —*vt.* **1.** to change (barley, etc.) into malt **2.** to prepare (milk, etc.) with malt or malt extract —*vi.* **1.** to be changed into malt **2.** to change barley, etc. into malt —**malt′y** *adj.* **malt′i·er, malt′i·est**

**Mal·ta** (môl′tə) **1.** country on a group of islands in the Mediterranean, south of Sicily: a member of the Commonwealth: 122 sq. mi.; pop. 328,000 **2.** main island of this group

**malted milk** a drink made by mixing a powdered preparation of dried milk and malted cereals with milk and, usually, ice cream and a flavoring

**Mal·tese** (môl tēz′) *adj.* of Malta, its inhabitants, etc. —*n.* **1.** *pl.* **-tese′** a native or inhabitant of Malta **2.** the Arabic language of Malta **3.** a variety of domestic cat with bluish-gray fur: in full, **Maltese cat**

**Maltese cross** a cross whose arms look like arrowheads pointing inward

**malt extract** a sticky, sugary substance obtained from malt soaked in water

**Mal·thu·sian** (mal thōō′zhən, -zē ən) *adj.* [after R. *Malthus* (1766–1834), Eng. economist] designating or of a theory that the increasing population of the world is naturally restricted by war, famine, and disease —*n.* a supporter of this theory

**malt liquor** beer, ale, etc. made from malt by fermentation

**malt·ose** (môl′tōs) *n.* a white, crystalline sugar, $C_{12}H_{22}O_{11} \cdot H_2O$, obtained by the action of the diastase of malt on starch: also called **malt sugar**

**mal·treat** (mal trēt′) *vt.* [< Fr.: see MAL- & TREAT] to treat roughly, unkindly, or brutally; abuse —**mal·treat′ment** *n.*

**malt·ster** (môlt′stər) *n.* one who makes malt

**mam·bo** (mäm′bō) *n.* [AmSp.] a rhythmic ballroom dance to music of Cuban Negro origin in 4/4 time with a heavy accent on the second and fourth beats —*vi.* to dance the mambo

**mam·ma¹** (mä′mə; *occas.* mə mä′) *n.* [like L. *mamma*, mother, Sans. *mā*, Gr. *mammē* < baby talk] mother: a child's word: also **ma′ma**

**mam·ma²** (mam′ə) *n., pl.* **-mae** (-ē) [L., breast] a gland for secreting milk, present in the female of all mammals; mammary gland

**mam·mal** (-əl) *n.* [< ModL. < LL. < L. *mamma:* see prec.] any of a large class of warmblooded vertebrates whose offspring are fed with milk secreted by the female mammary glands —**mam·ma·li·an** (mə mā′lē ən, ma-) *adj., n.*

**mam·ma·ry** (mam′ər ē) *adj.* designating or of the milk-secreting glands; of the mammae

**mam·mon** (mam′ən) *n.* [< LL. < Gr. < Aram. *māmōnā*, riches] [often M-] riches regarded as an object of worship and greedy pursuit —**mam′mon·ism** *n.*

**mam·moth** (mam′əth) *n.* [Russ. *mamont*] an extinct elephant with a hairy skin and long tusks curving upward —*adj.* very big; huge; enormous

**mam·my** (mam′ē) *n., pl.* **-mies** [dial. var. of MAMMA¹] **1.** mamma; mother: a child's word **2.** a Negro woman who takes care of white children, esp. in the southern States

**man** (man) *n., pl.* **men** (men) [OE. *mann*] **1.** a human being; person; specif., one of that species (see HOMO SAPIENS) of primates having the most highly developed brain and articulate speech **2.** the human race; mankind: used without the *or* a **3.** an adult male human being **4.** *a)* an adult male servant, follower, subordinate, etc. *b)* a male employee *c)* [Archaic] a vassal **5.** a husband or a lover **6.** a person

HAIRY MAMMOTH
(to 13 ft. high
at shoulder)

with qualities conventionally regarded as manly **7.** any of the pieces used in chess, checkers, etc. **8.** [Slang] fellow; chap —*vt.* **manned, man'ning 1.** to furnish with men for work, defense, etc. /to *man* a ship/ **2.** to take assigned places in, on, or at /*man* the guns!/ **3.** to strengthen; brace /to *man* oneself for an ordeal/ —*interj.* [Slang] an exclamation of emphasis: often used neutrally to preface or resume one's remarks —*adj.* male —**as a** (or one) **man** in unison; unanimously —**be one's own man 1.** to be free and independent **2.** to be in full control of oneself —**man and boy** first as a boy and then as a man —**the Man** [Slang] the person having authority over one, as a policeman —**to a man** with no one as an exception

**-man** (mən, man) *a combining form meaning* man or person of a specified kind, in a specified activity, etc. [*Frenchman, sportsman*]

**Man. 1.** Manila (paper) **2.** Manitoba

**Man** (man), **Isle of** one of the Brit. Isles, between Northern Ireland & England: 227 sq. mi.; pop. 48,000

**ma·na** (mä'nä) *n.* [ < Polynesian] the supernatural force to which certain primitive peoples attribute good fortune, magical powers, etc.

**man about town** a worldly man who spends much time in fashionable restaurants, clubs, etc.

**man·a·cle** (man'ə k'l) *n.* [ < OFr. < L. *manicula,* dim. of *manus,* hand] **1.** a handcuff; fetter or shackle for the hand **2.** any restraint *Usually used in pl.* —*vt.* **-cled, -cling 1.** to put handcuffs on; fetter **2.** to restrain; hamper

**man·age** (man'ij) *vt.* **-aged, -ag·ing** [It. *maneggiare* < *mano,* hand < L. *manus*] **1.** orig., to train (a horse) in his paces **2.** to control the movement or behavior of **3.** to have charge of; direct /to *manage* a household/ **4.** [Rare] to handle or use carefully **5.** to get (a person) to do what one wishes, esp. by tact, flattery, etc. **6.** to succeed in accomplishing; contrive —*vi.* **1.** to conduct or direct affairs; carry on business **2.** to contrive to get along; succeed in handling matters

**man·age·a·ble** (man'ij ə b'l) *adj.* that can be managed; controllable —**man'age·a·bil'i·ty, man'age·a·ble·ness** *n.* —**man'age·a·bly** *adv.*

**managed currency** a currency regulated through procedures that alter the amount of money in circulation so as to control credit, prices, etc.

**man·age·ment** (man'ij mənt) *n.* **1.** the act, art, or manner of managing, controlling, etc. **2.** skillful managing **3.** executive ability **4.** the persons managing a business, institution, etc.

**man·ag·er** (-ij ər) *n.* a person who manages the affairs of a business, institution, client, team, etc. —**man'ag·er·ship'** *n.*

**man·a·ge·ri·al** (man'ə jir'ē əl) *adj.* of a manager or management —**man'a·ge'ri·al·ism** *n.* —**man'a·ge'ri·al·ly** *adv.*

**Ma·na·gua** (mä nä'gwä) **1.** lake in W Nicaragua **2.** capital of Nicaragua, on this lake: pop. 300,000 (1967): devastated by an earthquake, 1972

‡**ma·ña·na** (mä nyä'nä) *n.* [Sp.] tomorrow —*adv.* **1.** tomorrow **2.** at some indefinite future time

**Ma·nas·seh** (mə nas'ə) *Bible* **1.** the elder son of Joseph **2.** the tribe of Israel descended from him

**man-at-arms** (man'ət ärmz') *n., pl.* **men'-at-arms'** (men'-) formerly, a soldier; esp., a heavily armed medieval soldier on horseback

**man·a·tee** (man'ə tē', man'ə tē') *n.* [Sp. *manatí* < native (Carib) name] a large, plant-eating aquatic mammal living in shallow tropical waters, having flippers and a broad, flat, rounded tail; sea cow

**Man·ches·ter** (man'ches'tər, -chi stər) **1.** city & port in NW England: pop. 603,000 **2.** [after prec.] city in S N.H.: pop. 91,000

**Man·chu** (man chōo', man'chōo) *n.* **1.** *pl.* **-chus', -chu'** a member of a Mongolian people of Manchuria: the Manchus conquered China in 1643–44 and ruled until 1912 **2.** the language of the Manchus —*adj.* of Manchuria, the Manchus, their language, etc.

**Man·chu·ri·a** (man choor'ē ə) region of NE China, north of Korea —**Man·chu'ri·an** *adj., n.*

**-man·cy** (man'sē) [ < OFr. < LL. < Gr. *manteia,* divination] *a combining form meaning* divination [*chiromancy*]

**man·da·la** (mun'də lə) *n.* [Sans. *maṇḍala*] a circular design of concentric geometric forms symbolizing the universe or wholeness in Hinduism and Buddhism

**Man·da·lay** (man'də lā', man'də lā') city in C Burma, on the Irrawaddy River: pop. 322,000

**man·da·mus** (man dā'məs) *n.* [L., we command] *Law* a writ commanding that a specified thing be done, issued by a higher court to a lower one, or to a corporation, agency, official, etc.

**man·da·rin** (man'də rin) *n.* [ < Port. < Hindi *mantrī,* minister of state < Sans. < *mantra,* counsel] **1.** a high official of China under the Empire **2.** a member of any elite group **3.** [M-] the official or main dialect of Chinese **4.** a small, sweet orange with a loose rind: in full, **mandarin orange**

—*adj.* elegant or overrefined, as in literary style —**man'da·rin·ism** *n.*

**man·date** (man'dāt) *n.* [ < L. neut. pp. of *mandare,* to command < *manus,* a hand + pp. of *dare,* to give] **1.** an authoritative order or command **2.** *a)* formerly, a commission from the League of Nations to a country to administer some region, colony, etc. *b)* the area that is so administered **3.** the wishes of constituents expressed to a representative, etc. and regarded as an order **4.** *Law* an order from a higher court or official to a lower one —*vt.* **-dat·ed, -dat·ing** to assign (a region, etc.) as a mandate —**man·da'tor** *n.*

**man·da·to·ry** (man'də tôr'ē) *adj.* **1.** of, like, or containing a mandate **2.** authoritatively commanded or required; obligatory **3.** holding a mandate (sense 2) —**man'da·to'ri·ly** *adv.*

**man·di·ble** (man'də b'l) *n.* [OFr. < LL. < *mandibulum* < L. *mandere,* to chew] the jaw; specif., *a)* the lower jaw of a vertebrate *b)* either of the most forward pair of biting jaws of an insect or other arthropod *c)* either jaw of a beaked animal —**man·dib'u·lar** (-dib'yōō lər) *adj.*

**man·do·lin** (man'd'l in', man'də lin') *n.* [ < Fr. < It. dim. of *mandola* < LL. < LGr. *pan·doura,* kind of lute] a musical instrument with four or five pairs of strings and a deep, rounded sound box: it is played with a plectrum —**man'do·lin'ist** *n.*

MANDOLIN

**man·drake** (man'drāk) *n.* [by folk etym. < OE. *mandragora* < LL. < L. < Gr. *mandragoras*] **1.** *a)* a poisonous plant of the nightshade family, with a short stem and a thick root *b)* the root, formerly used in medicine as a narcotic Also **man·drag·o·ra** (man drag'ər ə) **2.** *same as* MAY APPLE

**man·drel, man·dril** (man'drəl) *n.* [prob. < Fr. *mandrin*] **1.** a spindle or bar inserted into something to hold it while it is being machined **2.** a metal bar used as a core around which metal, glass, etc. is cast, molded, or shaped

**man·drill** (man'dril) *n.* [MAN + DRILL[4]] a large, fierce, strong baboon of W Africa

**mane** (mān) *n.* [OE. *manu*] the long hair growing from the top or sides of the neck of certain animals, as the horse, lion, etc. —**maned** *adj.* —**mane'less** *adj.*

**ma·nège, ma·nege** (ma nezh', -näzh') *n.* [Fr. < It. *maneggio:* see MANAGE] **1.** the art of riding and training horses **2.** a school teaching this art **3.** the paces of a trained horse

**ma·nes** (mā'nēz) *n.pl.* [L.] [*often* M-] *Ancient Rom. Religion* the deified souls of the dead, esp. of dead ancestors

**Ma·net** (má nā') **, É·douard** (ā dwär') 1832–83; Fr. impressionist painter

**ma·neu·ver** (mə nōō'vər, -nyōō'-) *n.* [Fr. *manoeuvre* < VL. < L. *manu operare,* to work by hand] **1.** a planned and controlled movement of troops, warships, aircraft, etc. **2.** [*pl.*] large-scale practice movements of troops, warships, aircraft, etc. **3.** any skillful change of movement or direction in driving a vehicle, controlling an aircraft, etc. **4.** a stratagem; scheme —*vi., vt.* **1.** to perform or cause to perform maneuvers **2.** to manage or plan skillfully; scheme **3.** to move, get, put, make, etc. by some stratagem —**ma·neu'ver·a·bil'i·ty** *n.* —**ma·neu'ver·a·ble** *adj.*

**man Friday** *see* FRIDAY

**man·ful** (man'fəl) *adj.* manly; brave, resolute, strong, etc. —**man'ful·ly** *adv.* —**man'ful·ness** *n.*

**man·ga·nese** (maŋ'gə nēs', -nēz') *n.* [ < Fr. < It., by metathesis < ML. *magnesia:* see MAGNESIA] a grayish-white, metallic chemical element, usually hard and brittle, which rusts like iron but is not magnetic: used in various alloys: symbol, Mn; at. wt., 54.9380; at. no., 25

**mange** (mānj) *n.* [ < OFr. *mangeue,* an itch, ult. < L. *manducare:* see MANGER] a skin disease of mammals caused by parasitic mites and characterized by itching, loss of hair, etc.

**man·gel-wur·zel** (maŋ'g'l wur'z'l, -wərt'-) *n.* [G., ult. < *mangold,* beet + *wurzel,* a root] a variety of large beet, used as food for cattle, esp. in Europe: also **mangel**

**man·ger** (mān'jər) *n.* [OFr. *mangeure,* ult. < L. *manducare,* to eat < *mandere,* to chew] a box or trough to hold hay, etc. for horses or cattle to eat

**man·gle**[1] (maŋ'g'l) *vt.* **-gled, -gling** [Anglo-Fr. *mangler* < OFr. *mehaigner,* to maim] **1.** to mutilate by repeatedly and roughly cutting, hacking, etc. **2.** to spoil; botch; mar —**man'gler** *n.*

**man·gle**[2] (maŋ'g'l) *n.* [Du. *mangel* < G. < MHG. < L. < Gr. *manganon,* war machine] a machine for pressing and smoothing cloth, esp. sheets and other flat pieces, between heated rollers —*vt.* **-gled, -gling** to press in a mangle —**man'gler** *n.*

**man·go** (maŋ'gō) *n., pl.* **-goes, -gos** [Port. *manga* < Malay < Tamil *mān-kāy*] **1.** a yellow-red, somewhat acid tropical fruit with a thick rind and juicy pulp **2.** the tree on which it grows

**man·grove** (maŋ'grōv) *n.* [altered (after GROVE) < Port. *mangue* < Sp. *mangle* < the WInd. name] a tropical tree with branches that spread and send down roots, thus forming more trunks

**man·gy** (mān'jē) *adj.* **-gi·er, -gi·est** 1. having or caused by the mange 2. shabby and filthy; squalid 3. mean and low; despicable —**man'gi·ly** *adv.* —**man'gi·ness** *n.*

**man·han·dle** (man'han'd'l) *vt.* **-dled, -dling** 1. [Rare] to move or do by human strength only, without mechanical aids 2. to handle roughly

**Man·hat·tan** (man hat''n, mən-) [< Du.] 1. island in SE N.Y., between the Hudson & East rivers: also **Manhattan Island** 2. borough of New York City, of which this island forms the major part: pop. 1,428,000 —*n.* [*often* m-] a cocktail made of whiskey and vermouth, usually with a dash of bitters

**man·hole** (man'hōl') *n.* a hole through which a man can get into a sewer, conduit, ship's tank, etc. for repair work or inspection

**man·hood** (man'hood') *n.* 1. the state or time of being a man 2. manly qualities; virility, courage, resolution, etc. 3. men collectively

**man-hour** (-our') *n.* an industrial time unit equal to one hour of work done by one person

**man·hunt** (-hunt') *n.* a hunt for a man, esp. for a fugitive: also **man hunt**

**ma·ni·a** (mā'nē ə, mān'yə) *n.* [LL. < Gr. *mania* < *mainesthai*, to rage] 1. wild or violent mental disorder; specif., the manic phase of manic-depressive psychosis, characterized generally by abnormal excitability, excessive activity, etc. 2. an excessive, steady enthusiasm; obsession; craze

**-ma·ni·a** (mā'nē ə, mān'yə) [see prec.] *a combining form meaning:* 1. a (specified) type of mental disorder [*kleptomania*] 2. a continuing, intense enthusiasm or craving for [*bibliomania*]

**ma·ni·ac** (mā'nē ak') *adj.* wildly insane; raving —*n.* a violently insane person; lunatic —**ma·ni·a·cal** (mə nī'ə k'l) *adj.* —**ma·ni'a·cal·ly** *adv.*

**man·ic** (man'ik; *chiefly Brit.* mā'nik) *adj.* having, characterized by, or like mania

**man·ic-de·pres·sive** (-di pres'iv) *adj.* designating, of, or having a psychosis characterized by alternating periods of mania and mental depression —*n.* a person who has this psychosis

**Man·i·chae·ism, Man·i·che·ism** (man'ə kē'iz'm) *n.* [after *Manichaeus*, 3d-cent. Persian prophet] a religious philosophy of the 3d to 7th cent. A.D. emphasizing a universal conflict between good and evil: also **Man'i·chae'an·ism** —**Man'i·chae'an** *n., adj.*

**man·i·cot·ti** (man'i kät'ē; *It.* mä'nē kôt'tē) *n.* [It., pl., lit., muffs] broad tubes of pasta, stuffed with cheese and baked with a tomato sauce

**man·i·cure** (man'ə kyoor') *n.* [Fr. < L. *manus*, a hand + *cura*, care] the care of the hands; esp., a trimming, polishing, etc. of the fingernails —*vt.* **-cured', -cur'ing** 1. *a)* to trim, polish, etc. (the fingernails) *b)* to give a manicure to 2. [Colloq.] to trim, clip, etc. meticulously [to *manicure* a lawn] —**man'i·cur'ist** *n.*

**man·i·fest** (man'ə fest') *adj.* [Fr. < L. *manifestus*, lit., struck by the hand, palpable] apparent to the senses, esp. to sight, or to the mind; evident; obvious —*vt.* 1. to make clear or evident; reveal 2. to prove; be evidence of —*vi.* to appear to the senses —*n.* 1. an itemized list of a ship's cargo, to be shown to customs officials 2. a list of passengers and cargo on an aircraft —**man'i·fest'ly** *adv.*

**man·i·fes·ta·tion** (man'ə fes tā'shən, -fəs-) *n.* 1. a manifesting or being manifested 2. something that manifests [his smile was a *manifestation* of joy] 3. any of the forms in which a being is thought to manifest itself 4. a public demonstration

**man·i·fes·to** (man'ə fes'tō) *n., pl.* **-toes** [It. < *manifestare*, to MANIFEST] a public declaration of motives and intentions by a government or by an important person or group

**man·i·fold** (man'ə fōld') *adj.* [OE. *manigfeald*: see MANY & -FOLD] 1. having many and various forms, parts, etc. 2. of many sorts [*manifold* duties] 3. being such in many ways [a *manifold* villain] 4. made up of or operating several units or parts of one kind —*n.* 1. something that is manifold 2. a pipe with one inlet and several outlets or with one outlet and several inlets, for connecting with other pipes, as the cylinder exhaust system in an automobile —*vt.* 1. to make manifold 2. to make a number of copies of [to *manifold* a letter with carbon paper] —**man'i·fold'er** *n.* —**man'i·fold'ly** *adv.*

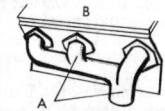
MANIFOLD
(A, manifold;
B, cylinder)

**man·i·kin** (man'ə k'n) *n.* [Du. *manneken* < *man*, man + dim. suffix *-ken*] 1. a little man; dwarf 2. *same as* MANNEQUIN

**Ma·nil·a** (mə nil'ə) capital & seaport of the Philippines, in SW Luzon: pop. 1,499,000 (met. area 3,100,000) —*n.* [*often* m-] *same as:* 1. MANILA HEMP 2. MANILA PAPER Also, for *n.,* **Ma·nil'la**

**Manila hemp** [*often* m-] a strong, tough fiber from the leafstalks of the abacá, used in making rope, paper, etc.

**Manila paper** [*often* m-] strong, buff or brownish paper orig. made of Manila hemp, now of various fibers

**man in the street** the average person

**man·i·oc** (man'ē äk') *n.* [Fr. < Tupi *manioca*] *same as* CASSAVA

**man·i·ple** (man'ə p'l) *n.* [ult. < L. *manus*, a hand] a silk band worn over the left forearm by priests at Mass

**ma·nip·u·late** (mə nip'yə lāt') *vt.* **-lat'ed, -lat'ing** [ult. < Fr. < L. *manipulus*, handful < *manus*, a hand + base of *plere*, to fill] 1. to work, operate, or treat with or as with the hands, esp. with skill 2. to manage or control artfully, often in an unfair or fraudulent way 3. to change or falsify (figures, accounts, etc.) for one's own purposes —**ma·nip'u·la·ble, ma·nip'u·lat'a·ble** *adj.* —**ma·nip'u·la'tion** *n.* —**ma·nip'u·la'tive** *adj.*

**ma·nip·u·la·tor** (-lāt'ər) *n.* 1. a person or thing that manipulates 2. a mechanical device operated by remote control, as for handling radioactive materials

**Man·i·to·ba** (man'ə tō'bə) 1. province of SC Canada: 251,000 sq. mi.; pop. 1,022,000; cap. Winnipeg: abbrev. **Man.** 2. **Lake**, lake in S Manitoba

**man·i·tou** (man'ə tōō') *n.* [< Algonquian name] any of various nature spirits believed in by Algonquian Indians: also **man'i·tu', man'i·to'** (-tō')

**man·kind** (man'kīnd'; *also, & for 2 always,* man'kīnd') *n.* 1. all human beings; the human race 2. all human males

**man·like** (man'līk') *adj.* 1. like or characteristic of a man or men 2. fit for a man; masculine

**man·ly** (-lē) *adj.* **-li·er, -li·est** 1. having qualities regarded as befitting a man; strong, brave, resolute, etc. 2. fit for a man; masculine [*manly* sports] —*adv.* in a manly way —**man'li·ness** *n.*

**man-made** (-mād') *adj.* made by man; synthetic

**Mann** (man; *for 2* män) 1. **Horace**, 1796–1859; U.S. educator 2. **Thom·as** (G. tō'mäs), 1875–1955; Ger. novelist in the U.S. & Switzerland

**man·na** (man'ə) *n.* [OE. < LL. < Gr. < Aram. *mannā* < Heb. *mān*] 1. *Bible* food miraculously provided for the Israelites in the wilderness: Ex. 16:14–36 2. anything badly needed that comes unexpectedly

**man·ne·quin** (man'ə kin) *n.* [Fr. < Du.: see MANIKIN] 1. a model of the human body, used by window dressers, artists, etc. 2. a woman whose work is modeling clothes in stores, etc.

**man·ner** (man'ər) *n.* [< OFr., ult. < L. *manuarius*, of the hand < *manus*, a hand] 1. a way or method in which something is done or happens 2. a way of acting; personal, esp. customary, behavior or bearing 3. [*pl.*] *a)* ways of social life [a comedy of *manners*] *b)* ways of social behavior; deportment [good *manners*] *c)* polite ways of social behavior [the child lacks *manners*] 4. characteristic style or method in art, etc. 5. *a)* kind; sort [what *manner* of man is he?] *b)* [*with pl. v.*] kinds; sorts [all *manner* of things] —**by all manner of means** of course; surely —**by any manner of means** in any way; at all —**by no manner of means** in no way; definitely not —**in a manner of speaking** in a certain sense or way —**to the manner born** accustomed from birth to the way or usage spoken of —**man'ner·less** *n.*

**man·nered** (-ərd) *adj.* 1. having manners or a manner of a specified sort [ill-*mannered*, soberly *mannered*] 2. artificial, stylized, or affected

**man·ner·ism** (man'ər iz'm) *n.* 1. excessive use of some distinctive manner in art, literature, speech, or behavior 2. a peculiarity of manner in behavior, speech, etc. that has become a habit —**man'ner·ist** *n.* —**man'ner·is'tic** *adj.*

**man·ner·ly** (-lē) *adj.* showing good manners; polite —*adv.* politely —**man'ner·li·ness** *n.*

**Mann·heim** (man'hīm; G. män'-) city in SW West Germany, on the Rhine: pop. 324,000

**man·ni·kin** (man'ə kin) *n. alt. sp. of* MANIKIN

**man·nish** (man'ish) *adj.* of, like, or fit for a man [she walks with a *mannish* stride] —**man'nish·ly** *adv.* —**man'nish·ness** *n.*

**ma·noeu·vre** (mə nōō'vər, -nyōō'-) *n., vi., vt.* **-vred, -vring** *chiefly Brit. var. of* MANEUVER

**man of God** 1. a holy man; saint, hermit, etc. 2. a clergyman; minister, priest, rabbi, etc.

**man of letters** a writer, scholar, etc., esp. one whose work is in the field of literature

fat, āpe, cär, ten, ēven, is, bīte; gō, hôrn, tōōl, look; oil, out; up, fur; get; joy; yet; chin; she; thin, then; zh, leisure; ŋ, ring; ə for a in ago, e in agent, i in sanity, o in comply, u in focus; ' as in able (ā'b'l); Fr. bāl; ë, Fr. coeur; ö, Fr. feu; Fr. mon; ö, Fr. coq; ü, Fr. duc; r, Fr. cri; H, G. ich; kh, G. doch; ‡foreign; *hypothetical; < derived from. See inside front cover.

man of the world a man familiar with and tolerant of various sorts of people and their ways

man-of-war (man'əv wôr', -ə wôr') n., pl. men'-of-war' an armed naval vessel; warship

man-of-war bird same as FRIGATE BIRD

ma·nom·e·ter (mə näm'ə tər) n. [< Fr. < Gr. manos, rare (in sense "thin, sparse") + Fr. -mètre, -METER] an instrument for measuring the pressure of gases or liquids —man·o·met·ric (man'ə met'rik), man'o·met'ri·cal adj.

man·or (man'ər) n. [< OFr. < manoir, to dwell < L. manere, to remain] 1. in England, a landed estate, orig. of a feudal lord and subject to the jurisdiction of his court 2. in colonial America, a district granted as a manor and leased to tenants 3. a mansion, as on an estate —ma·no·ri·al (mə nôr'ē əl) adj.

manor house the house of the lord of a manor

man·pow·er (man'pou'ər) n. 1. power furnished by human physical strength 2. the collective strength or availability for work of the people in a given area, nation, etc. Also man power

‡man·qué (mäŋ kā') adj. [Fr. < It. < L. mancus, defective] 1. that falls short of the goal; unsuccessful 2. potential but unrealized; would-be Placed after the noun it modifies /a scholar manqué/

man·sard (roof) (man'särd) [after F. Mansard, 17th-c. Fr. architect] a roof with two slopes on each of the four sides, the lower steeper than the upper

manse (mans) n. [< ML. < pp. of L. manere, to dwell] 1. a parsonage 2. [Archaic] a mansion

man·ser·vant (man'sur'vənt) n., pl. men·ser·vants (men'sur'vənts) a male servant: also man servant

MANSARD ROOF

Mans·field (manz'fēld', mans'-) [after J. Mansfield (1759-1830), surveyor] city in NC Ohio: pop. 54,000

man·sion (man'shən) n. [OFr. < L. mansio, a dwelling < pp. of manere, to dwell] a large, imposing house

man-sized (man'sīzd') adj. [Colloq.] of a size fit for a man; large; big: also man'-size'

man·slaugh·ter (-slôt'ər) n. the killing of a human being by another, esp. when unlawful but without malice

man·ta (ray) (man'tə) [Sp. < LL. mantum, a cloak] same as DEVILFISH (sense 1)

man·tel (man't'l) n. [see MANTLE] 1. the facing of stone, marble, etc. about a fireplace, including a shelf or slab above it 2. the shelf or slab

man·tel·et (man't'l it, mant'lit) n. [OFr., dim. of prec.] 1. a short mantle or cape 2. a protective shelter or screen: also mant'let

man·tel·piece (man't'l pēs') n. a mantel shelf, or this shelf and the side elements framing the fireplace in front

man·til·la (man til'ə, -tē'ə) n. [Sp. < LL. < L. mantellum, a mantle] a woman's scarf, as of lace, worn over the hair and shoulders, as in Spain or Mexico

man·tis (man'tis) n., pl. -tis·es, -tes (-tēz) [ModL. < Gr. mantis, prophet, seer] a long, slender insect that feeds on other insects and grasps its prey with stout, spiny forelegs often held up together as if praying

man·tis·sa (man tis'ə) n. [L., (useless) addition] the decimal part of a logarithm

man·tle (man't'l) n. [< OE. & OFr. < L. mantellum] 1. a loose, sleeveless cloak or cape 2. anything that cloaks or envelops 3. a small, mesh hood which becomes white-hot over a flame and gives off light 4. same as MANTEL 5. Geol. a) the layer of the earth's interior between the crust and the core b) same as MANTLEROCK 6. Zool. the glandular flap or folds of the body wall of a mollusk, etc., typically secreting a shell-forming fluid —vt. -tled, -tling to cover with or as with a mantle; cloak —vi. 1. to be or become covered, as a surface with froth 2. to blush or flush

man·tle·rock (-räk') n. the loose, unconsolidated material on the solid rock of the earth's crust

man·tra (mun'trə, man'-) n. [Sans., akin to mantar, thinker] Hinduism a hymn or text, esp. from the Veda, chanted as an incantation or prayer

man·u·al (man'yoo wəl) adj. [< OFr. < L. < manus, a hand] 1. of a hand or the hands 2. made, done, worked, or used by the hands 3. involving or doing hard physical work requiring use of the hands —n. 1. a handy book of instructions, etc. for use as a guide 2. a keyboard of an organ console or harpsichord 3. prescribed drill in the handling of a rifle: also manual of arms —man'u·al·ly adv.

manual training training in practical arts and crafts, as metalworking, etc.

man·u·fac·ture (man'yə fak'chər) n. [Fr. < ML. < L. < manus, a hand + factura, a making < facere, to make] 1. the making of goods by hand or, esp., by machinery, often on a large scale and with division of labor 2. anything so made 3. the making of something in a way regarded as mechanical —vt. -tured, -tur·ing 1. to make by hand or,

esp., by machinery, often on a large scale, etc. 2. to work (wool, steel, etc.) into usable form 3. to produce (something) in a way regarded as mechanical 4. to make up (excuses, evidence, etc.)

man·u·fac·tur·er (-chər ər) n. a person or company in the business of manufacturing; esp., a factory owner

man·u·mis·sion (man'yə mish'ən) n. [see ff.] a freeing or being freed from slavery; emancipation

man·u·mit (-mit') vt. -mit'ted, -mit'ting [< OFr. < L. < manus, a hand + mittere, to send] to free from slavery —man'u·mit'ter n.

ma·nure (mə noor', -nyoor') vt. -nured', -nur'ing [< Anglo-Fr. < OFr. manouvrer, to work with the hands, cultivate] to put manure on or into (soil) —n. animal excrement or other substance used to fertilize soil

man·u·script (man'yə skript') adj. [< L. < manus, a hand + pp. of scribere, to write] 1. written by hand or with a typewriter 2. designating writing that consists of unconnected letters resembling print; not cursive —n. 1. a written or typewritten book, article, etc.; esp., an author's copy of his work, as submitted to a publisher or printer 2. writing as distinguished from print

Manx (maŋks) adj. of the Isle of Man, its people, etc. —n. their Goidelic language, now nearly extinct —the Manx the people of the Isle of Man

Manx cat [also m-] any of a breed of domestic cat that has no tail

Manx·man (-mən) n., pl. -men a native or inhabitant of the Isle of Man —Manx'wom'an n.fem., pl. -wom'en

man·y (men'ē) adj. more, most [OE. manig] 1. consisting of some large, indefinite number; numerous 2. relatively numerous (preceded by as, too, etc.) —n. a large number (of persons or things) —pron. many persons or things Many a (or an, another) with a singular noun or pronoun is equivalent to many with the plural (e.g., many a man) —a good many [with pl. v.] a relatively large number —a great many [with pl. v.] an extremely large number —the many 1. the majority of people 2. the people; the masses

man·y-sid·ed (-sīd'id) adj. 1. having many sides or aspects 2. having many possibilities, qualities, interests, or accomplishments —man'y-sid'ed·ness n.

man·za·ni·ta (man'zə nēt'ə) n. [AmSp. < Sp., dim. of manzana, apple] any of several shrubs or small trees of the heath family, found in the W U.S.

Mao·ism (mou'iz'm) n. the communist theories and policies of Mao Tse-tung —Mao'ist adj., n.

Ma·o·ri (mou'rē, mä'ô rē; mä ôr'ē) n. 1. pl. -ris, -ri any of a brown-skinned people native to New Zealand, of Polynesian origin 2. their Polynesian language —adj. of the Maoris, their language, etc.

mao-tai (mou'tī') n. [after Mao-t'ai, town in SW China] a strong, colorless, Chinese distilled liquor made from grain: also written mao tai

Mao Tse-tung (mou' dzu'doŏŋ') 1893-1976; Chin. statesman; chairman of the People's Republic of China (1949-59) & of the Chin. Communist Party (1949-76)

map (map) n. [< ML. mappa (mundi), map (of the world) < L. mappa, napkin] 1. a representation, usually flat, of all or part of the earth's surface, ordinarily showing countries, bodies of water, cities, etc. 2. a similar representation of the sky, showing stars, planets, etc. 3. any maplike representation 4. [Slang] the face —vt. mapped, map'ping 1. to make a map of; represent on a map 2. to plan in detail /to map out a project/ 3. to survey for making a map —put on the map to make well known —wipe off the map to put out of existence —map'per n.

ma·ple (mā'p'l) n. [OE. mapel(treo)] 1. any of a large group of trees with opposite leaves and two-winged fruits, grown for wood, sap, or shade 2. the hard, fine-grained, light-colored wood 3. the flavor of maple syrup or of maple sugar —adj. 1. of maple 2. flavored with maple

maple sugar sugar from boiled-down maple syrup

maple syrup syrup made by boiling down the sap of the sugar maple

Ma·pu·to (mə pōōt'ō) capital of Mozambique; seaport on the Indian Ocean: pop. 799,000

ma·quis (mä kē'; Fr. mȧ kē') n. [Fr. < It. macchia, a thicket] 1. a zone of shrubby, evergreen plants in the Mediterranean area, used as a hiding place by guerrilla fighters, etc. 2. [often M-] pl. -quis' (-kēz'; Fr. -kē') a member of the French underground in World War II

mar (mär) vt. marred, mar'ring [OE. mierran, to hinder] to hurt or spoil the looks, value, perfection, etc. of; impair

Mar. March

mar·a·bou (mar'ə bōō') n. [Fr. < Port. < Ar. murābit, hermit] 1. any of certain large storks; esp., a) a dark-green African species b) the Indian adjutant 2. soft feathers from the wings and tail of the marabou

ma·ra·ca (mə rä'kə) n. [Port. maracá < the Braz. native name] a percussion instrument consisting of a dried gourd or a gourd-shaped rattle with loose pebbles in it, shaken to beat out a rhythm

**Mar·a·cai·bo** (mar′ə kī′bō; *Sp.* mä′rä kī′bô) seaport in NW Venezuela: pop. 625,000
**mar·a·schi·no** (mar′ə skē′nō, -shē′-) *n.* [It. < *marasca*, kind of cherry < *amaro*, bitter] a strong, sweet liqueur made from the fermented juice of a black wild cherry
**maraschino cherries** cherries in a syrup flavored with maraschino
**Ma·rat** (má rä′), **Jean Paul** (zhän pôl) 1743–93; Fr. Revolutionary leader, born in Switzerland
**Mar·a·thon** (mar′ə thän′) ancient Greek village in E Attica, or a plain nearby, where the Athenians defeated the Persians (490 B.C.)
**mar·a·thon** (mar′ə thän′) *n.* **1.** a footrace of 26 miles, 385 yards: so called in allusion to the Greek runner who carried word of the victory at Marathon to Athens **2.** any long-distance or endurance contest
**mar·a·thon·er** (mar′ə thän′ər) *n.* a person who competes in a marathon
**ma·raud** (mə rôd′) *vi.* [< Fr. < *maraud*, vagabond, prob. < dial. *maraud*, tomcat, echoic of cry] to rove in search of plunder; make raids —*vt.* to raid; plunder —**ma·raud′er** *n.*
**mar·ble** (mär′b'l) *n.* [< OFr. < L. < Gr. *marmaros*, white glistening stone] **1.** a hard, metamorphic limestone, white or colored and sometimes streaked or mottled, which can take a high polish **2.** *a)* a piece or slab of this stone, used as a monument, etc. *b)* a sculpture in marble **3.** anything like marble in hardness, coldness, etc. **4.** *a)* a little ball of stone, glass, or clay, used in games *b)* [*pl.,* with sing. *v.*] a children's game in which a marble is propelled with the thumb at other marbles in a marked circle **5.** [*pl.*] [Slang] brains; good sense /to lose one's *marbles*] —*adj.* of or like marble —*vt.* **-bled, -bling 1.** to stain (book edges) to look mottled or streaked like marble **2.** to cause fat to be evenly distributed in narrow streaks through (meat) —**mar′bled, mar′bly** *adj.*
**mar·ble·ize** (-īz′) *vt.* **-ized′, -iz′ing** to make, color, grain, or streak in imitation of marble
**Marc Antony** *see* ANTONY
**mar·ca·site** (mär′kə sīt′) *n.* [< Fr. < ML. < Ar. *marqashīṭā*] **1.** a pale, crystallized pyrite (**white iron pyrite**) **2.** this mineral or polished steel cut and used like brilliants
**mar·cel** (mär sel′) *n.* [after *Marcel* Grateau, early 20th-c. Fr. hairdresser] a series of even waves put in the hair with a curling iron: also **marcel wave** —*vt.* **-celled′, -cel′ling** to put such waves in (hair)
**March** (märch) *n.* [< OFr. < L. *Martius (mensis)*, (month) of Mars] the third month of the year, having 31 days: abbrev. **Mar.**
**march**[1] (märch) *vi.* [Fr. *marcher* < OFr., prob. < Frank.] **1.** to walk with regular, steady steps, as in a military formation **2.** to walk in a grave, stately way **3.** to advance or progress steadily —*vt.* to make march or go —*n.* **1.** a marching **2.** a steady advance; progress **3.** a regular, steady step or pace **4.** the distance covered in marching /a day's *march*] **5.** a long, tiring walk **6.** a piece of music for marching **7.** an organized walk by people demonstrating on a public issue /a peace *march*] —**on the march** marching —**steal a march on** to get an advantage over secretly —**march′er** *n.*
**march**[2] (märch) *n.* [OFr. *marche* < Frank. hyp. *marka*, boundary] a boundary, border, or frontier
**March hare** a hare in breeding time, proverbially regarded as an example of madness
**marching orders** orders to march, go, or leave
**mar·chion·ess** (mär′shə nis, mär′shə nes′) *n.* [< ML. fem. of *marchio*, prefect of the marches, or borderlands] **1.** the wife or widow of a marquess **2.** a lady whose own rank equals that of a marquess
**march·pane** (märch′pān′) *n. same as* MARZIPAN
**Mar·cia** (mär′shə) [< L., ult. < *Mars*, MARS] a feminine name
**Mar·co·ni** (mär kō′nē; *It.* mär kô′nē), **Marchese Gugliel·mo** (gōō lyel′mô) 1874–1937; It. physicist: developed wireless telegraphy
**Marco Polo** *see* POLO
**Mar·cus Aurelius** (mär′kəs) *see* AURELIUS
**Mar·di gras** (mär′di grä′) [Fr., lit., fat Tuesday] Shrove Tuesday, the last day before Lent: a day of carnival, as in New Orleans
**mare**[1] (mer) *n.* [OE. *mere,* fem. of *mearh,* horse] a fully mature female horse, mule, donkey, etc.
**ma·re**[2] (merē, märē) *n., pl.* **-ri·a** (-ē ə) [L., sea] **1.** a sea **2.** a large, dark area on the surface of the moon or of Mars
**mare's-nest** (merz′nest′) *n.* **1.** a hoax; delusion **2.** a disorderly or confused condition; mess
**mare's-tail** (-tāl′) *n.* long, narrow formations of cirrus cloud, shaped somewhat like a horse's tail
**Mar·ga·ret** (mär′grit, -gər it) [< OFr. < L. *margarita,* a

pearl] a feminine name: dim. *Marge;* var. *Margery, Margot, Marguerite*
**mar·ga·rine** (mär′jə rin) *n.* [Fr.] a spread or cooking fat made of refined vegetable oils processed to the consistency of butter, often churned with pasteurized skim milk, and generally fortified with vitamins A and D: also **mar′ga·rin**
**marge** (märj) *n.* [Fr. < L. *margo,* margin] [Archaic or Poet.] a border; edge; margin
**mar·gin** (mär′jən) *n.* [L. *margo* (gen. *marginis*)] **1.** a border, edge, or brink **2.** the blank border of a printed or written page **3.** a limit to what is desirable or possible **4.** *a)* an amount of money, supplies, etc. beyond what is needed *b)* provision for increase, addition, or advance **5.** the amount by which something is higher or lower **6.** *Business, Finance a)* the difference between the cost and selling price of goods *b)* money or collateral deposited with a broker, etc. either to meet legal requirements or to insure him against loss on contracts which he undertakes for a buyer or seller of stocks, etc. **7.** *Econ.* the minimum return of profit needed to continue activities —*vt.* **1.** to provide with a margin **2.** *Business* to deposit a margin upon
**mar·gin·al** (-'l) *adj.* **1.** written or printed in the margin **2.** of a margin **3.** at, on, or close to the margin —**mar′gin·al′i·ty** (-al′ə tē) *n.* —**mar′gin·al·ly** *adv.*
**mar·gin·ate** (mär′jə nāt′; *also for adj.* -nit) *vt.* **-at′ed, -at′ing** to provide with a margin —*adj.* having a distinct margin: also **mar′gin·at′ed** —**mar′gin·a′tion** *n.*
**mar·grave** (mär′grāv) *n.* [< MDu. < MHG. < OHG. < *marc,* a border + *graf,* a count] **1.** orig., a military governor of a border province in Germany **2.** the title of certain princes of Germany
**mar·gra·vine** (mär′grə vēn′) *n.* a margrave's wife
**mar·gue·rite** (mär′gə rēt′) *n.* [Fr., a pearl] **1.** *same as* DAISY (sense 1) **2.** a cultivated chrysanthemum with a single flower **3.** any of various daisylike plants of the composite family
**Ma·ri·a** (mə rī′ə, -rē′-) [see MARY] a feminine name
**ma·ri·a** (mer′ē ə, mär′-) *n. pl. of* MARE[2]
**ma·ri·a·chi** (mär′ē ä′chē) *n., pl.* **-chis** [MexSp. < ?] **1.** one of a strolling band of musicians in Mexico **2.** such a band **3.** their music
**Mar·i·an** (mer′ē ən, mar′-) [var. of MARION] a feminine name: var. *Marianne* —*adj.* of the Virgin Mary
**Ma·ri·an·a Islands** (mer′ē an′ə, mar′-) group of islands in the W Pacific: (except Guam); a commonwealth of the U.S. called **Northern Marianas**: pop. 15,000
**Maria Theresa** 1717–80; queen of Bohemia & Hungary & archduchess of Austria (1740–80): mother of MARIE ANTOINETTE
**mar·i·cul·ture** (mar′ə kul′chər) *n.* [< L. *mare,* sea + CULTURE] saltwater aquaculture
**Ma·rie** (mə rē′) [var. of MARY] a feminine name
**Marie An·toi·nette** (an′twə net′, -tə-), (**Joséphe Jeanne**) 1755–93; wife of Louis XVI; queen of France (1774–92): guillotined
**Marie Louise** 1791–1847; 2d wife of Napoleon I & empress of France (1810–15)
**mar·i·gold** (mar′ə gōld′) *n.* [< *Marie* (prob. the Virgin Mary) + *gold,* GOLD] **1.** a plant of the composite family, with red, yellow, or orange flowers **2.** its flower **3.** any of several unrelated plants
**ma·ri·jua·na, ma·ri·hua·na** (mar′ə wä′nə, mär′-; -hwä′-) *n.* [AmSp. < ? native word] **1.** *same as* HEMP (sense 1 *a*) **2.** its dried leaves and flowers, smoked for the psychological effects
**Mar·i·lyn** (mar′ə lin) [var. of MARY] a feminine name
**ma·rim·ba** (mə rim′bə) *n.* [< Afr. (Bantu), a kind of percussive instrument] a kind of xylophone, usually with resonators under the wooden bars
**ma·ri·na** (mə rē′nə) *n.* [It. & Sp., seacoast < L. *marinus*: see MARINE] a small harbor with dockage, supplies, and services for small pleasure craft
**mar·i·nade** (mar′ə nād′) *n.* [Fr. < Sp. < *marinar,* to pickle, ult. < L. *marinus*: see MARINE] **1.** a spiced pickling solution, esp. with oil and wine or vinegar, in which meat, fish, or salad is steeped **2.** meat, etc. so steeped —*vt.* **-nad′ed, -nad′ing** *same as* MARINATE
**mar·i·nate** (mar′ə nāt′) *vt.* **-nat′ed, -nat′ing** [< It. < *marinare,* to pickle: see prec.] to steep (meat, etc.) in a marinade —**mar′i·na′tion** *n.*
**ma·rine** (mə rēn′) *adj.* [< L. *marinus* < *mare,* the sea] **1.** of, found in, or formed by the sea or ocean **2.** *a)* of navigation on, or shipping by, the sea; nautical; maritime *b)* naval **3.** used, or to be used, at sea **4.** *a)* trained for service at sea, etc., as certain troops *b)* of such troops —*n.* **1.** one of a marine military force; specif. [*often* M-], a member of the MARINE CORPS **2.** naval or merchant ships collectively; fleet /the merchant *marine*] **3.** in some countries, the

governmental department of naval affairs  **4.** a picture of a ship or sea scene

**Marine Corps** a branch of the U.S. armed forces trained for land, sea, and aerial combat

**mar·i·ner** (mar′ə nər) *n.* [< Anglo-Fr. < ML. < L. *marinus*, MARINE] a sailor; seaman

**Mar·i·on** (mar′ē ən, mer′-) [Fr., orig. dim. of *Marie*, MARY] a masculine or feminine name

**mar·i·o·nette** (mar′ē ə net′) *n.* [Fr., dim. of MARION] a puppet or little jointed doll moved by strings or wires from above, often on a little stage

**Mar·i·po·sa lily** (or **tulip**) (mar′ə pō′zə, -sə) [AmSp. < Sp. *mariposa*, butterfly] **1.** a plant of the lily family, of W N. America, with tuliplike flowers **2.** its flower

**Ma·ri·tain** (má rē taṇ′), **Jacques** (zhàk) 1882–1973; Fr. philosopher

**mar·i·tal** (mar′ə t′l) *adj.* [< L. < *maritus*, a husband] of marriage —**mar′i·tal·ly** *adv.*

**mar·i·time** (mar′ə tīm′) *adj.* [L. *maritimus* < *mare*, the sea] **1.** on, near, or living near the sea **2.** of sea navigation, shipping, etc. **3.** nautical

**Maritime Provinces** Canad. provinces of Nova Scotia, New Brunswick, & Prince Edward Island

**mar·jo·ram** (mär′jər əm) *n.* [< OFr. < ML., prob. < L. *amaracus* < Gr. *amarakos*] any of various perennial plants of the mint family; esp., **sweet marjoram,** having aromatic leaves used in cooking

**Mar·jo·rie, Mar·jo·ry** (mär′jər ē) [var. of MARGARET] a feminine name

**Mark** (märk) **1.** [< L. *Marcus* < *Mars*, MARS] a masculine name **2.** *Bible a)* one of the four Evangelists, the reputed author of the second Gospel *b)* this book, the second in the New Testament

**mark¹** (märk) *n.* [OE. *mearc*, orig., boundary] **1.** a line, spot, stain, scratch, mar, etc. on a surface **2.** a sign, symbol, or indication; specif., *a)* a printed or written sign or stroke *[punctuation marks] b)* a brand, label, etc. put on an article to show the owner, maker, etc. *c)* a sign of some quality, character, etc. *[courtesy is the mark of a gentleman] d)* a grade; rating *[a mark of B in history] e)* a cross, etc. made by a person unable to write his signature **3.** a standard of quality, etc. *[up to the mark]* **4.** importance; distinction *[a man of mark]* **5.** impression; influence *[left his mark in history]* **6.** a visible object of known position, serving as a guide **7.** a line, dot, etc. used to indicate position, as on a graduated scale **8.** an object aimed at; target; end; goal **9.** the butt of an attack, criticism, etc. **10.** a taking notice; heed **11.** *Sports a)* the starting line of a race *b)* a spare or strike in bowling —*vt.* **1.** to put or make a mark or marks on **2.** to identify as by a mark **3.** to draw, write, record, etc. **4.** to show by a mark **5.** to show plainly; manifest *[a smile marking joy]* **6.** to distinguish; characterize **7.** to take notice of; heed **8.** to grade; rate **9.** to put price tags on **10.** to keep (score, etc.); record —*vi.* **1.** to make a mark or marks **2.** to observe; take note **3.** *Games* to keep score —**hit the mark 1.** to achieve one's aim **2.** to be right —**make one's mark** to achieve fame —**mark down 1.** to write down; record **2.** to mark for sale at a reduced price —**mark off** (or **out**) to mark the limits of —**mark time 1.** to keep time while at a halt by lifting the feet as if marching **2.** to suspend progress for a time —**mark up 1.** to cover with marks **2.** to mark for sale at an increased price —**miss the mark 1.** to fail in achieving one's aim **2.** to be inaccurate —**wide of** (or **beside**) **the mark 1.** not striking the point aimed at **2.** irrelevant —**mark′er** *n.*

**mark²** (märk) *n.* [< OE. < ON. *mǫrk*, a half pound of silver] a monetary unit of the old German Empire, superseded by the reichsmark, and of East Germany: see MONETARY UNITS, table

**Mark Antony** *see* ANTONY

**mark·down** (märk′doun′) *n.* **1.** a marking for sale at a reduced price **2.** the amount of reduction

**marked** (märkt) *adj.* **1.** having a mark or marks **2.** singled out as an object of hostility, etc. *[a marked man]* **3.** noticeable; distinct *[a marked change]* —**mark′ed·ly** (märk′kid lē) *adv.* —**mark′ed·ness** *n.*

**mar·ket** (mär′kit) *n.* [< ONormFr. < L. *mercatus*, trade < pp. of *mercari*, to trade < *merx*, merchandise] **1.** *a)* a gathering of people for buying and selling things *b)* the people gathered **2.** an open space or a building with goods for sale from stalls, etc.: also **mar′ket·place′ 3.** a store selling provisions *[a meat market]* **4.** a region where goods can be bought and sold *[the European market]* **5.** *a)* trade in goods, stocks, etc. *[an active market] b)* trade in a specified commodity *[the wheat market] c)* the people associated in such trade **6.** *short for* STOCK MARKET **7.** demand (for goods or services) *[a good market for new products]* **8.** supply (of goods or services) *[reduced labor market]* —*vt.* **1.** to send or take to market **2.** to offer for sale **3.** to sell —*vi.* **1.** to buy or sell **2.** to buy provisions —**be in the market for** to be seeking to buy —**be on the**

**market** to be offered for sale —**buyer's market** a state of trade favorable to the buyer (relatively heavy supply and low prices) —**put on the market** to offer for sale —**seller's market** a state of trade favorable to the seller (relatively heavy demand and high prices) —**mar′ket·a·bil′i·ty** *n.* —**mar′ket·a·ble** *adj.* —**mar′ket·er, mar′ket·eer′** (-kə tir′) *n.* —**mar′ket·ing** *n.*

**market price** the prevailing price of a commodity

**market value** the price that a commodity can be expected to bring in a given market

**mark·ing** (märk′iŋ) *n.* **1.** the act of making a mark or marks **2.** a mark or marks **3.** the characteristic arrangement of marks, as on fur or feathers

**mark·ka** (märk′kä) *n., pl.* **-kaa** (-kä) [Finn. < Sw. *mark*: see MARK²] *see* MONETARY UNITS, table (Finland)

**marks·man** (märks′mən) *n., pl.* **-men** a person who shoots, esp. with skill —**marks′man·ship′** *n.*

**mark·up** (märk′up′) *n.* **1.** a marking for sale at an increased price **2.** the amount of increase

**marl** (märl) *n.* [< OFr. < ML. dim. of L. *marga*, marl < Gaul.] a crumbly mixture of clay, sand, and limestone, usually with shell fragments —*vt.* to cover or fertilize with marl —**marl′y** *adj.*

**Marl·bor·ough** (märl′bur′ō, -ə; *Brit.* môl′bər ə), **1st Duke of,** (*John Churchill*) 1650–1722; Eng. general & statesman

**mar·lin** (mär′lin) *n., pl.* **-lin, -lins:** see PLURAL, II, D, 2 [< MARLINSPIKE] any of several large, slender deep-sea fishes related to the sailfish, esp. the **blue marlin** of the Atlantic

**mar·line** (mär′lin) *n.* [Du. *marlijn*, altered (after *lijn*, LINE¹)] a small cord of two loose strands for winding around the ends of ropes to prevent fraying: also **mar′lin, mar′ling** (-liŋ)

**mar·line·spike, mar·lin·spike** (-spīk′) *n.* a pointed iron instrument for separating rope strands, as in splicing: also **mar′ling·spike′** (-liŋ-)

**Mar·lowe** (mär′lō), **Christopher** 1564–93; Eng. dramatist & poet

**mar·ma·lade** (mär′mə lād′) *n.* [< OFr. < Port. < *marmelo*, quince < L. *melimelum* < Gr. < *meli*, honey + *mēlon*, apple] a jamlike preserve made of oranges or some other fruits and sugar

**Mar·ma·ra** (mär′mə rə), **Sea of** sea between European & Asiatic Turkey, connected with the Black Sea by the Bosporus & with the Aegean Sea by the Dardanelles: also sp. **Marmora**

**mar·mo·re·al** (mär môr′ē əl) *adj.* [< L. < *marmor*, marble + -AL] of or like marble: also **mar·mo′re·an** —**mar·mo′re·al·ly** *adv.*

**mar·mo·set** (mär′mə zet′, -set′) *n.* [< OFr. *marmouset*, grotesque figure] a very small monkey of South and Central America, with thick, soft fur

**mar·mot** (mär′mət) *n.* [< Fr. < earlier *marmottaine*, prob. < L. *mus montanus*, mountain mouse] any of a group of thick-bodied, gnawing and burrowing rodents with coarse fur and a short, bushy tail, as the woodchuck

**Marne** (märn) river in NE France, flowing northwest into the Seine at Paris

**ma·roon¹** (mə rōōn′) *n., adj.* [Fr. *marron*, chestnut < It. *marrone*] dark brownish red

**ma·roon²** (mə rōōn′) *n.* [< Fr. < AmSp. *cimarrón*, wild < OSp. *cimarra*, thicket] in the West Indies and Surinam, **1.** orig., a fugitive Negro slave **2.** a descendant of such slaves —*vt.* **1.** to put (a person) ashore in some desolate place and abandon him there **2.** to leave abandoned, helpless, etc.

MARMOSET
(body to 15 in. long; tail to 17 in. long)

**mar·plot** (mär′plät′) *n.* a person or, sometimes, a thing spoiling a plan by officious interference

**Marq. 1.** Marquess **2.** Marquis

**marque¹** (märk) *n.* [MFr. < Pr. *marca*] reprisal: obsolete except in LETTERS OF MARQUE

**marque²** (märk) *n.* [Fr., ult. < OIt. *marca*, a mark] an identifying nameplate or emblem on an automobile

**mar·quee** (mär kē′) *n.* [< Fr. *marquise* (misunderstood as pl.), orig. a canopy over an officer's tent] **1.** [Chiefly Brit.] a large tent, as for an outdoor entertainment **2.** a rooflike projection or awning over an entrance, as to a theater

**mar·quess** (mär′kwis) *n.* **1.** a British nobleman ranking above an earl and below a duke **2.** *same as* MARQUIS —**mar′quess·ate** (-kwə zit) *n.*

**mar·que·try, mar·que·terie** (mär′kə trē) *n.* [< Fr. < *marque*, a mark] decorative inlaid work of wood, ivory, etc., as in furniture or flooring

**Mar·quette** (mär ket′), **Jacques** (zhàk) 1637–75; Fr. Jesuit missionary & explorer, in N. America: called *Père Marquette*

**mar·quis** (mär′kwis; *Fr.* màr kē′) *n., pl.* **-quis·es;** *Fr.* **-quis′** (-kē′) [< OFr. < ML. *marchisus*, prefect of a frontier town < *marca*, borderland] in some European countries, a nobleman ranking above an earl or count and below a duke: cf. MARQUESS —**mar′quis·ate** (-kwə zit) *n.*

**mar·quise** (mär kēz′; *Fr.* màr kēz′) *n.* **1.** the wife or widow of a marquis **2.** a lady whose rank in her own right equals that of a marquis **3.** a gem cut as a pointed oval

**mar·qui·sette** (mär′ki zet′, -kwi-) *n.* [dim. of Fr. *marquise*, awning: see MARQUEE] a thin, meshlike fabric used for curtains, dresses, etc.

**Mar·ra·kech, Mar·ra·kesh** (mə rä′kesh, mar′ə kesh′) city in C Morocco; traditional S capital: pop. 295,000

**mar·riage** (mar′ij) *n.* [OFr. < *marier*: see MARRY] **1.** the state of being married; relation between husband and wife; wedlock **2.** the act or rite of marrying; wedding **3.** any close union

**mar·riage·a·ble** (mar′i jə b′l) *adj.* old enough to get married —**mar′riage·a·bil′i·ty** *n.*

**marriage portion** *same as* DOWRY

**mar·ried** (mar′ēd) *adj.* **1.** living together as husband and wife **2.** having a husband or wife **3.** of marriage or married people **4.** closely joined —*n.* a married person: chiefly in **young marrieds**

**mar·row** (mar′ō) *n.* [OE. *mearg*] **1.** the soft, vascular, fatty tissue that fills the cavities of most bones **2.** the innermost, essential, or choicest part; pith —**mar′row·y** *adj.*

**mar·row·bone** (-bōn′) *n.* a bone having marrow

**mar·row·fat** (-fat′) *n.* a variety of large, rich pea: also **marrowfat pea, marrow pea**

**mar·ry**[1] (mar′ē) *vt.* **-ried, -ry·ing** [< OFr. *marier* < L. *maritus*, a husband] **1.** *a)* to join as husband and wife *b)* to join (a man) to a woman as her husband, or (a woman) to a man as his wife **2.** to take as husband or wife **3.** to join closely —*vi.* **1.** to get married **2.** to enter into a close relationship —**marry off** to give in marriage: said of a parent or guardian —**mar′ri·er** *n.*

**mar·ry**[2] (mar′ē) *interj.* [euphemistic respelling of (the Virgin) *Mary*] [Archaic or Dial.] an exclamation of surprise, anger, etc.

**Mars** (märz) **1.** *Rom. Myth.* the god of war: identified with the Greek god Ares **2.** *a personification of* war **3.** a planet of the solar system, fourth in distance from the sun: diameter, c.4,200 miles

**Mar·sa·la** (mär sä′lä) *n.* [< *Marsala*, seaport in W Sicily] a light, sweet white wine

**Mar·seil·laise** (mär′sə lāz′; *Fr.* màr se yez′) [Fr., lit., of Marseille] the French national anthem, composed (1792) during the French Revolution

**Mar·seille** (màr se′y′; *E.* mär sā′) seaport in SE France, on the Mediterranean: pop. 889,000

**Mar·seilles** (mär sā′; *chiefly Brit.* -sālz′; *for n.* -sālz′) *Eng. sp. of* MARSEILLE —*n.* a thick, strong cotton cloth with a raised weave

**marsh** (märsh) *n.* [OE. *merisc*] a tract of low, wet, soft land; swamp; bog; morass

**Mar·shal** (mär′shəl) [< ff.] a masculine name

**mar·shal** (mär′shəl) *n.* [< OFr. *mareschal* < OHG. < *marah*, horse + *scalh*, servant] **1.** a high official of a medieval royal household **2.** a military commander; specif., *a) same as* FIELD MARSHAL *b)* in various foreign armies, a general officer of the highest rank **3.** an official in charge of ceremonies, processions, etc. **4.** a U.S. officer of various kinds; specif., *a)* a Federal officer appointed to a judicial district to perform functions like those of a sheriff *b)* the head of a police or fire department in some cities —*vt.* **-shaled** or **-shalled, -shal·ing** or **-shal·ling 1.** to arrange (troops, things, ideas, etc.) in order; dispose **2.** *a)* to direct as a marshal; manage *b)* to lead or guide ceremoniously —**mar′shal·cy, mar′shal·ship′** *n.*

**Mar·shall** (mär′shəl) **1.** George C(atlett), 1880–1959; U.S. general & statesman **2.** John, 1755–1835; U.S. jurist; chief justice of the U.S. (1801–35)

**Mar·shall Islands** (mär′shəl) group of islands in the W Pacific: see Trust Territory of the PACIFIC ISLANDS

**marsh gas** a gaseous product, chiefly methane, formed from decomposing vegetable matter

**marsh·mal·low** (marsh′mel′ō, -mal′ō) *n.* **1.** orig., a confection made from the root of the marsh mallow **2.** a soft, spongy confection of sugar, starch, corn syrup, and gelatin

**marsh mallow** a pink-flowered, perennial, European plant with a root sometimes used in medicine

**marsh marigold** a marsh plant of the buttercup family, with bright-yellow flowers

**marsh·y** (mär′shē) *adj.* **marsh′i·er, marsh′i·est 1.** of, like, or containing a marsh or marshes; swampy **2.** growing in marshes —**marsh′i·ness** *n.*

**mar·su·pi·al** (mär sōō′pē əl) *adj.* **1.** of or like a mar-

supium **2.** of an order of mammals whose young are carried by the female for several months after birth in an external pouch of the abdomen —*n.* an animal of this kind, as a kangaroo, opossum, etc.

**mar·su·pi·um** (-əm) *n., pl.* **-pi·a** (-ə) [ModL. < L. < Gr. dim. of *marsypos*, a pouch] the pouch on the abdomen of a female marsupial

**mart** (märt) *n.* [MDu., var. of *markt*] a market

**Mar·tel** (mär tel′), **Charles** 688?–741 A.D.; ruler of the Franks (714–741): grandfather of CHARLEMAGNE

**mar·ten** (mär′t′n) *n., pl.* **-tens, -ten:** see PLURAL, II, D, 1 [< OFr. < *martre*] **1.** a small, flesh-eating mammal like a weasel but larger, with soft, thick, valuable fur **2.** the fur

**Mar·tha** (mär′thə) [LL. < Gr. < Aram. *Mārthā*, lit., lady] **1.** a feminine name **2.** *Bible* a woman rebuked by Jesus for fussing over chores while he talked with her sister Mary: Luke 10:40

**Mar·tial** (mär′shəl) (*Marcus Valerius Martialis*) 40?–104? A.D.; Rom. epigrammatist & poet

**mar·tial** (mär′shəl) *adj.* [< L. *martialis*, of Mars] **1.** of or connected with war, soldiers, etc.; military [*martial* music] **2.** warlike; militaristic [*martial* spirit] —**mar′tial·ism** *n.* —**mar′tial·ist** *n.* —**mar′tial·ly** *adv.*

**martial law** temporary rule by the military authorities over the civilians, as in time of war

**Mar·tian** (mär′shən) *adj.* of Mars (god or planet) —*n.* an imagined inhabitant of the planet Mars

**Mar·tin** (mär′t′n) [Fr. < L. < *Mars* (gen. *Martis*), Mars: hence, lit., warlike] **1.** a masculine name **2.** Saint, 315?–397? A.D.; bishop of Tours: see MARTINMAS

**mar·tin** (mär′t′n) *n.* [Fr.] **1.** a stout-billed bird of the swallow family, as the purple martin **2.** any of various swallowlike birds

**mar·ti·net** (mär′t′n et′) *n.* [after Gen. J. *Martinet*, 17th-c. Fr. drillmaster] a very strict disciplinarian or stickler for rigid regulations

**mar·tin·gale** (mär′t′n gāl′) *n.* [Fr., prob. < Sp. *almártaga*, check, rein < Ar.] **1.** the strap of a horse's harness passing from the noseband to the girth between the forelegs, to keep the horse from rearing or throwing back its head **2.** a lower stay for the jib boom of a sailing vessel Also **mar′tin·gal′** (-gal′)

**mar·ti·ni** (mär tē′nē) *n., pl.* **-nis** [altered < earlier *Martinez:* reason for name unc.] [*also* M-] a cocktail of gin (or vodka) and dry vermouth

**Mar·ti·nique** (mär′tə nēk′) French island possession in the Windward group of the West Indies

**Mar·tin·mas** (mär′t′n məs) *n.* [see -MAS] Saint Martin's Day, a church festival held on November 11

**mar·tyr** (mär′tər) *n.* [OE. < LL. < Gr. *martyr*, a witness] **1.** a person tortured or killed because of his faith or beliefs **2.** a person suffering great pain or misery a long time —*vt.* to make a martyr of —**mar′tyr·dom** *n.*

**mar·tyr·ize** (mär′tə rīz′) *vt.* **-ized′, -iz′ing** to make a martyr of —*vi.* to be or become a martyr —**mar′tyr·i·za′tion** *n.*

**mar·tyr·ol·o·gy** (mär′tə räl′ə jē) *n., pl.* **-gies 1.** a list of martyrs **2.** a historical account of religious martyrs **3.** such accounts collectively —**mar′tyr·ol′o·gist** *n.*

**mar·vel** (mär′v′l) *n.* [< OFr. *merveille* < VL. < L. neut. pl. of *mirabilis*, wonderful < *mirari*, to admire] a wonderful or astonishing thing; prodigy or miracle —*vi.* **-veled** or **-velled, -vel·ing** or **-vel·ling** to be amazed; wonder —*vt.* to wonder at or about (followed by a clause)

**Mar·vell** (mär′v′l), **Andrew** 1621–78; Eng. poet

**mar·vel·ous** (mär′v′l əs) *adj.* **1.** causing wonder; astonishing, extraordinary, incredible, etc. **2.** [Colloq.] fine; splendid Also, chiefly Brit. sp., **mar′vel·lous** —**mar′vel·ous·ly** *adv.* —**mar′vel·ous·ness** *n.*

**Mar·vin** (mär′vin) [prob. ult. < Gmc. bases meaning "sea" & "friend"] a masculine name

**Marx** (märks), **Karl** (**Heinrich**) 1818–83; Ger. social philosopher & political economist whose doctrines are the basis of modern socialism

**Marx·ism** (märk′siz′m) *n.* the system of thought developed by Karl Marx, his co-worker Friedrich Engels, and their followers: also **Marx′i·an·ism** —**Marx′ist, Marx′i·an** *adj., n.*

**Mar·y** (mer′ē, mar′ē, mā′rē) [< OE. < LL. *Maria* < Gr. < Heb. *Miryām* or Aram. *Maryam*, lit., rebellion] **1.** a feminine name **2. Mary I** (*Mary Tudor*) 1516–58; queen of England (1553–58): daughter of HENRY VIII & wife of PHILIP II of Spain **3. Mary II** 1662–94; queen of England, Scotland, & Ireland, ruling jointly with her husband, WILLIAM III **4.** *Bible a)* mother of Jesus: Matt. 1:18–25 *b)* sister of Martha: Luke 10:38–42 *c) same as* MARY MAGDALENE

**Mary Janes** *a trademark for* low-heeled, patent-leather slippers with a strap, for little girls

**Mar·y·land** (mer′ə lənd) [after Queen Henrietta *Maria,* wife of CHARLES I of England] E State of the U.S., on the Atlantic: 10,577 sq. mi.; pop. 4,216,000; cap. Annapolis: abbrev. **Md., MD**

**Mary Magdalene** *Bible* woman out of whom Jesus cast seven devils: Luke 8:2: identified with the repentant woman in Luke 7:37 ff.

**Mary, Queen of Scots** (*Mary Stuart*) 1542–87; queen of Scotland (1542–67): beheaded

**mar·zi·pan** (mär′zi pan′) *n.* [G. < It. *marzapane,* confection < ML. < Ar.] a confection of various shapes and colors made of a paste of ground almonds, sugar, and egg white

**-mas** (mas) *a combining form for* MASS *meaning* a (specified) church festival *[Martinmas]*

**Ma·sai** (mä sī′) *n.* **1.** *pl.* **-sai′, -sais′** any member of a pastoral people of Kenya and Tanzania **2.** their language

**masc., mas.** masculine

**Mas·ca·gni** (mäs kä′nyē), **Pie·tro** (pye′trô) 1863–1945; It. composer of operas

**mas·ca·ra** (mas kar′ə) *n.* [< Sp. < It. *maschera:* see MASK] a cosmetic for coloring the eyelashes —*vt.* **-ca′raed, -ca′ra·ing** to put mascara on

**mas·con** (mäs′kän′) *n.* [*mas(s) con(centration)*] a concentration of very dense material beneath the surface of the moon

**mas·cot** (mas′kät, -kət) *n.* [< Fr. < Pr. dim. of *masco,* sorcerer] any person, animal, or thing supposed to bring good luck by being present

**mas·cu·line** (mas′kyə lin) *adj.* [< OFr. < L. < *masculus,* male < *mas,* male] **1.** male; of men or boys **2.** having qualities regarded as characteristic of men and boys, as strength, vigor, etc. **3.** suitable for or typical of a man **4.** mannish **5.** *Gram.* designating or of the gender of words referring to males or things orig. regarded as male **6.** *Prosody* designating or of a rhyme of stressed final syllables (Ex.: enjoy, destroy) —*n. Gram.* **1.** the masculine gender **2.** a word or form in this gender —**mas′cu·line·ly** *adv.* —**mas′cu·lin′i·ty** *n.*

**mas·cu·lin·ize** (-li nīz′) *vt.* **-ized′, -iz′ing** to make masculine; esp., to produce male characteristics in (a female) —**mas′cu·lin′i·za′tion** *n.*

**Mase·field** (mās′fēld, māz′-), **John** 1878–1967; Eng. writer, esp. of poetry

**ma·ser** (mā′zər) *n.* [*m(icrowave) a(mplification) by) s(timulated) e(mission of) r(adiation)*] a device, operating at microwave, infrared, etc. frequencies, in which atoms in a crystal or gas are concentrated, raised to a higher energy level, then emitted in a very narrow beam

**mash** (mash) *n.* [< OE. *masc-,* in *mascwyrt,* infused malt] **1.** crushed or ground malt or meal soaked in hot water for making wort, used in brewing beer **2.** a mixture of bran, meal, etc. in warm water for feeding horses, etc. **3.** any soft mixture or mass —*vt.* **1.** to mix (crushed malt, etc.) in hot water for making wort **2.** to change into a soft mass by beating, crushing, etc. **3.** to crush and injure or damage

**mash·er** (-ər) *n.* **1.** one that mashes; specif., a device for mashing vegetables, etc. **2.** [Slang] a man who makes unwanted advances to women not acquainted with him, esp. in public places

**mask** (mask) *n.* [Fr. *masque* < It. *maschera,* prob. < Ar. *maskhara,* buffoon] **1.** a covering to conceal or disguise all or part of the face **2.** anything that conceals or disguises **3.** a masque or masquerade **4.** a person wearing a mask **5.** *a)* a sculptured or molded likeness of the face *b)* a grotesque or comic representation of a face, worn to amuse or frighten **6.** a protective covering for the face or head [a gas *mask*] **7.** a covering for the mouth and nose, as for administering an anesthetic, preventing infection, etc. **8.** the face or head of a dog, fox, etc. —*vt.* to conceal, cover, disguise, etc. with or as with a mask —*vi.* **1.** to put on a mask **2.** to hide or disguise one's true motives, character, etc. —**masked** *adj.* —**mask′er** *n.*

MASKS

**masked ball** a ball at which masks and fancy costumes are worn

**mask·ing tape** (mas′kiŋ) an adhesive tape for covering borders, etc., as during painting

**mas·och·ism** (mas′ə kiz′m, maz′-) *n.* [after L. von Sacher-*Masoch* (1835–1895), Austrian writer] the getting of pleasure, specif. sexual pleasure, from being dominated or hurt physically or psychologically —**mas′och·ist** *n.* —**mas′och·is′tic** *adj.* —**mas′och·is′ti·cal·ly** *adv.*

**ma·son** (mās′n) *n.* [< OFr. < ML. *matio*] **1.** a person whose work is building with stone, brick, etc. **2.** [M-] *same as* FREEMASON

**Ma·son-Dix·on line** (mā′s′n dik′s′n) [after C. *Mason* & J. *Dixon,* who surveyed it, 1763–67] boundary line between Pa. & Md., regarded as separating the North from the South: also **Mason and Dixon's line**

**Ma·son·ic** (mə sän′ik) *adj.* [*also* m-] of Masons (Freemasons) or Masonry (Freemasonry)

**Ma·son·ite** (mā′s′n īt′) [after W. H. *Mason* (1877–1947?), U.S. engineer] *a trademark for* a kind of hardboard made from pressed wood fibers, used as building material, etc. —*n.* such hardboard

**Mason jar** [patented in 1858 by J. *Mason* of New York] [*also* m-] a wide-mouthed glass jar with a screw top, for preserving foods, esp. in home canning

**ma·son·ry** (mā′s′n rē) *n., pl.* **-ries** **1.** the trade or art of a mason **2.** something built by a mason or masons; brickwork or stonework **3.** [*usually* M-] *same as* FREEMASONRY

**masque** (mask) *n.* [see MASK] **1.** a masquerade; masked ball **2.** a former kind of dramatic entertainment with a mythical or allegorical theme and lavish costumes, music, etc. —**masqu′er** *n.*

**mas·quer·ade** (mas′kə rād′) *n.* [< Fr. < It. dial. var. of *mascherata* (< *maschera*): see MASK] **1.** a ball or party at which masks and fancy costumes are worn **2.** a costume for such a ball, etc. **3.** *a)* a disguise; pretense *b)* a living or acting under false pretenses —*vi.* **-ad′ed, -ad′ing** **1.** to take part in a masquerade **2.** to live or act under false pretenses —**mas′quer·ad′er** *n.*

**Mass** (mas) *n.* [OE. *mæsse* < LL. < *missa* in L. *ite, missa est* (*contio*), go, (the meeting) is dismissed] [*also* m-] **1.** the service of the Eucharist in the Roman Catholic Church and some other churches, consisting of a series of prayers and ceremonies **2.** a musical setting for certain parts of this service

**mass** (mas) *n.* [OFr. *masse* < L. < Gr. *maza,* barley cake] **1.** a piece or amount of indefinite shape or size [a *mass* of clay, a *mass* of cold air] **2.** a large quantity or number [a *mass* of bruises] **3.** bulk; size **4.** the main part; majority **5.** *Physics* the quantity of matter in a body as measured in its relation to inertia —*adj.* **1.** *a)* of a large number of things [*mass* production] *b)* of a large number of persons [a *mass* demonstration] **2.** of, like, or for the masses [*mass* education] —*vt., vi.* to gather or form into a mass —**in the mass** collectively —**the masses** the great mass of common people; specif., the working people

**Mas·sa·chu·setts** (mas′ə choo′sits) [< Algonquian *Massaadchu-es-et,* lit., at the big hill] New England State of the U.S.: 8,257 sq. mi.; pop. 5,737,000; cap. Boston: abbrev. **Mass., MA**

**mas·sa·cre** (mas′ə kər) *n.* [Fr. < OFr. *maçacre,* shambles] **1.** the indiscriminate, merciless killing of human beings **2.** a large-scale slaughter of animals —*vt.* **-cred, -cring** to kill indiscriminately and mercilessly and in large numbers —**mas′sa·crer** (-krər) *n.*

**mas·sage** (mə säzh′) *n.* [Fr. < *masser,* to massage < Ar. *massa,* to touch] a rubbing, kneading, etc. of part of the body, as to stimulate circulation and make muscles or joints supple —*vt.* **-saged′, -sag′ing** to give a massage to —**mas·sag′er** *n.*

**mass·cult** (mas′kult′) *n.* [MASS + CULT(URE)] [Colloq.] an artificial, commercialized culture popularized for the masses through the mass media

**Mas·se·net** (mas′ə nā′; *Fr.* màs ne′), **Jules** (Émile Frédéric) (zhül) 1842–1912; Fr. composer

**mas·sé** (shot) (ma sā′) [Fr. < *masse,* billiard cue] a stroke in billiards made by hitting the cue ball off center with the cue held vertically so as to make the ball move in a curve

**mas·seur** (ma sur′, mə-; *Fr.* mà sër′) *n.* [Fr.] a man whose work is giving massages —**mas·seuse′** (-sooz′, -sōōz′; *Fr.* -söz′) *n.fem.*

**mas·sive** (mas′iv) *adj.* **1.** *a)* forming or consisting of a large mass; big and solid; bulky *b)* larger or greater than normal [a *massive* dose of drugs] **2.** large and imposing or impressive **3.** large-scale; extensive —**mas′sive·ly** *adv.* —**mas′sive·ness** *n.*

**mass media** those means of communication that reach and influence large numbers of people, esp. newspapers, magazines, radio, and television

**mass meeting** a large public meeting to discuss public affairs, demonstrate public approval or disapproval, etc.

**mass noun** a noun used to denote an abstraction or something that is uncountable (Ex.: *love, girlhood, butter, news*)

**mass number** *Physics, Chem.* the number of neutrons and protons in the nucleus of an atom

**mass production** quantity production of goods, esp. by machinery and division of labor —**mass′-pro·duce′** *vt.* **-duced′, -duc′ing**

**mast**[1] (mast) *n.* [OE. *mæst*] **1.** a tall spar or hollow metal structure rising vertically from the keel or deck of a vessel and used to support the sails, yards, radar and radio equipment, etc. **2.** any vertical pole, as in a crane —*vt.* to put masts on —**before the mast** [Now Rare] as a common sailor

**mast**[2] (mast) *n.* [OE. *mæst*] beechnuts, acorns, chestnuts, etc., esp. as food for hogs

**mas·ta·ba, mas·ta·bah** (mas′tə bə) *n.* [< Ar.] an oblong structure with a flat roof and sloping sides, built over the opening of a mummy chamber or burial pit in ancient Egypt and used as a tomb

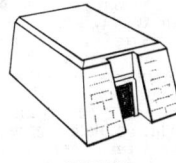

MASTABA

**mas·ter** (mas′tər) *n.* [< OE. mægester & OFr. maistre; both < L. magister < base of L. magnus, great] **1.** a man who rules others or has control, authority, or power over something; specif., *a)* a man who is head of a household or institution *b)* an employer *c)* an owner of an animal or slave *d)* the captain of a merchant ship *e)* a victor *f)* [Chiefly Brit.] a male schoolteacher *g)* a person whose teachings in religion, philosophy, etc. one follows *h)* [M-] Jesus Christ (with *our, the,* etc.) **2.** a person very skilled in some work, profession, etc.; expert; specif., *a)* a highly skilled workman qualified to follow his trade independently *b)* an artist regarded as great **3.** [M-] a title variously applied to *a)* any man or youth: now superseded by the variant *Mister,* usually written *Mr. b)* a boy regarded as too young to be addressed as *Mr. c)* a man who heads some institution, group, etc. *d)* in Scotland, the heir apparent of a viscount or baron *e)* a person who is a MASTER OF ARTS (or SCIENCE, etc.) **4.** *Law* any of several court officers appointed to assist the judge —*adj.* **1.** being a master **2.** of a master **3.** chief; main; controlling; specif., designating a mechanism or contrivance that controls others, sets a standard or norm, etc. [a *master* switch] —*vt.* **1.** to become master of; control, conquer, etc. **2.** to become an expert in (an art, science, etc.)
**master builder 1.** a person skilled in building; esp., formerly, an architect **2.** a building contractor
**mas·ter·ful** (-fəl) *adj.* **1.** fond of acting the part of a master; imperious **2.** having or showing the ability of a master; expert; skillful —**mas′ter·ful·ly** *adv.* —**mas′ter·ful·ness** *n.*
**master key** a key that will open every one of a set of locks
**mas·ter·ly** (-lē) *adj.* showing the ability or skill of a master; expert —*adv.* in a masterly manner —**mas′ter·li·ness** *n.*
**master mechanic** a skilled mechanic, esp. one serving as foreman
**mas·ter·mind** (-mīnd′) *n.* a very intelligent person, esp. one with the ability to plan or direct a group project —*vt.* to be the mastermind of (a project)
**Master of Arts** (or **Science,** etc.) **1.** a degree given by a college or university to a person who has completed a prescribed course of graduate study in the humanities (or in science, etc.) **2.** a person who has this degree
**master of ceremonies 1.** a person who supervises a ceremony. **2.** a person who presides over an entertainment, introducing the participants, filling in the intervals with jokes, etc.
**mas·ter·piece** (-pēs′) *n.* **1.** a thing made or done with masterly skill **2.** the greatest work made or done by a person or group: also **mas′ter·work′**
**Mas·ters** (mas′tərz), **Edgar Lee** 1869-1950; U.S. poet
**master sergeant** *U.S. Mil.* a noncommissioned officer of high rank
**mas·ter·ship** (mas′tər ship′) *n.* **1.** the state of being a master; rule; control **2.** the position, duties, or term of office of a master **3.** masterly ability
**mas·ter·stroke** (-strōk′) *n.* a masterly action, move, or achievement
**mas·ter·y** (mas′tər ē, -trē) *n., pl.* **-ter·ies 1.** mastership **2.** ascendancy or victory; the upper hand **3.** expert skill or knowledge [his *mastery* of chess]
**mast·head** (mast′hed′) *n.* **1.** the top part of a ship's mast **2.** that part of a newspaper or magazine stating its address, publishers, editors, etc. —*vt.* to display at the masthead
**mas·tic** (mas′tik) *n.* [OFr. < LL. < L. < Gr. *mastichē*] **1.** a yellowish resin obtained from a Mediterranean evergreen tree, used as an astringent and in making varnish, adhesives, etc. **2.** the tree: in full, **mastic tree**
**mas·ti·cate** (mas′ti kāt′) *vt.* **-cat′ed, -cat′ing** [< LL. pp. of *masticare* < Gr. *mastichan,* to gnash < *mastax,* a mouth] **1.** to chew up (food, etc.) **2.** to grind, cut, or knead (rubber, etc.) to a pulp —**mas′ti·ca′tion** *n.* —**mas′ti·ca′tor** *n.*
**mas·ti·ca·to·ry** (-kə tôr′ē) *adj.* of or for mastication; specif., adapted for chewing —*n., pl.* **-ries** any substance chewed but not swallowed, to increase saliva flow
**mas·tiff** (mas′tif) *n.* [< OFr. *mastin,* ult. < L. *mansuetus,* tame] a large, powerful, smooth-coated dog with hanging lips and drooping ears
**mas·to-** [< Gr. *mastos,* the breast] a combining form meaning of or like a breast: also **mast-**

**mas·to·don** (mas′tə dän′) *n.* [ModL. < Fr. < Gr. *mastos,* a breast + *odous,* a tooth: from the nipplelike processes on its molars] a large, extinct animal resembling the elephant but larger
**mas·toid** (mas′toid) *adj.* [< Gr. < *mastos,* a breast + *eidos,* form] **1.** shaped like a breast or nipple **2.** designating, of, or near a projection of the temporal bone behind the ear —*n.* **1.** the mastoid projection **2.** [Colloq.] same as MAS-TOIDITIS
**mas·toid·i·tis** (mas′toi dīt′is) *n.* inflammation of the mastoid
**mas·tur·bate** (mas′tər bāt′) *vi., vt.* **-bat′ed, -bat′ing** [< L. pp. of *masturbari,* ult. < *manus,* hand + *stuprum,* defilement] to manipulate one's own genitals, or the genitals of (another), for sexual gratification —**mas′tur·ba′tion** *n.* —**mas′tur·ba′tor** *n.* —**mas′tur·ba·to′ry** (-bə tôr′ē) *adj.*
**mat¹** (mat) *n.* [< OE. *meatt* < LL. *matta* < Phoen.] **1.** a flat, coarse fabric of woven or plaited hemp, straw, etc. **2.** a piece of this or of corrugated rubber, etc., used as a doormat, etc. **3.** a flat piece of cloth, woven straw, etc. put under a vase, dish, etc. **4.** a thickly padded floor covering, as in a gymnasium for wrestling, etc. **5.** anything growing or interwoven in a thick tangle [a *mat* of hair] —*vt.* **mat′ted, mat′ting 1.** to cover as with a mat **2.** to form into a thick tangle —*vi.* to become felted or thickly tangled
**mat²** (mat) *adj.* [Fr. < OFr. *mat,* defeated, prob. < L. *mattus,* drunk < *madere,* to be drunk] same as MATTE —*n.* **1.** same as MATTE **2.** a border, as of cardboard or cloth, put around a picture, usually between the picture and the frame —*vt.* **mat′ted, mat′ting 1.** to produce a dull surface or finish on **2.** to frame (a picture) with a mat
**mat³** (mat) *n.* [Colloq.] a matrix; printing mold
**mat·a·dor** (mat′ə dôr′) *n.* [Sp. < *matar,* to kill < *mate,* checkmate] the bullfighter who kills the bull with a sword after performing a series of actions with a cape to anger and tire the animal
**Ma·ta·mo·ros** (mä′tä mô′rôs; *E.* mat′ə môr′əs) city in NE Mexico, on the Rio Grande, opposite Brownsville, Tex.: pop. 175,000
**match¹** (mach) *n.* [< OFr. *mesche,* prob. < L. *myxa,* lamp wick < Gr.] **1.** orig., a wick or cord prepared to burn at a uniform rate, used for firing guns or explosives **2.** a slender piece of wood, cardboard, etc. tipped with a composition that catches fire by friction, sometimes only on a specially prepared surface
**match²** (mach) *n.* [OE. (ge)mæcca, a mate] **1.** any person or thing equal or similar to another in some way; specif., *a)* a person, group, or thing able to cope with another as an equal *b)* a counterpart or facsimile **2.** two or more persons or things that go together in appearance, size, etc. **3.** a contest or game; competition **4.** a marriage or mating **5.** a person regarded as a suitable mate —*vt.* **1.** to join in marriage; mate **2.** to compete with successfully **3.** to put in opposition (*with*); pit (*against*) **4.** to be equal, similar, or suitable to **5.** to make, show, or get a competitor, counterpart, or equivalent to [*match* this cloth] **6.** to suit or fit (one thing) to another **7.** to fit (things) together **8.** to compare **9.** *a)* to flip or reveal (coins) to decide something contested, the winner being determined by the combination of faces thus exposed *b)* to match coins with (another person) —*vi.* to be equal, similar, suitable, etc. in some way —**match′a·ble** *adj.* —**match′er** *n.*
**match·box** (-bäks′) *n.* a small box for holding matches
**match·less** (mach′lis) *adj.* having no equal; peerless —**match′less·ly** *adv.* —**match′less·ness** *n.*
**match·lock** (-läk′) *n.* **1.** an old type of gunlock in which the charge of powder was ignited by a slow-burning match (wick or cord) **2.** a musket with such a gunlock
**match·mak·ing¹** (-mā′kiŋ) *n.* the work or business of making matches (for burning) —**match′mak′er** *n.*
**match·mak·ing²** (-mā′kiŋ) *n.* **1.** the arranging of marriages for others **2.** the arranging of wrestling or boxing matches, etc. —**match′mak′er** *n.*
**match play** *Golf* a form of play in which the score is calculated by counting holes won rather than strokes taken: cf. MEDAL PLAY
**mate¹** (māt) *n.* [MDu. < *gemate* < Gmic.] **1.** a companion or fellow worker **2.** one of a matched pair **3.** *a)* a husband or wife *b)* the male or female of paired animals **4.** *Naut. a)* an officer of a merchant ship, ranking below the captain *b)* an assistant **5.** *U.S. Navy* any of various petty officers [a carpenter's *mate*] —*vt., vi.* **mat′ed, mat′ing 1.** to join as a pair **2.** to couple in marriage or sexual union
**mate²** (māt) *n., interj., vt.* **mat′ed, mat′ing** same as CHECK-MATE
**ma·té** (mä′tā, mat′ā) *n.* [AmSp. < Quechua *mati,* calabash (used to steep the brew)] **1.** a beverage made from the

dried leaves of a S. American tree **2.** this tree or its leaves Also sp. **mate**

**ma·ter** (māt'ər, mät'-) *n.* [L.] [Chiefly Brit. Colloq.] mother: often preceded by *the*

**ma·te·ri·al** (mə tir'ē əl) *adj.* [< LL. < L. *materia*, matter] **1.** of matter; relating to or consisting of what occupies space; physical *[a material object]* **2.** *a)* of the body or bodily needs, etc. *[material pleasures]* *b)* of or fond of comfort, wealth, etc.; worldly *[material success]* **3.** important, essential, etc. *(to the matter under discussion)* —*n.* **1.** what a thing is, or may be, made of; elements or parts **2.** ideas, notes, etc. that may be worked up; data **3.** cloth or other fabric **4.** *[pl.]* tools, articles, etc. for a specified use *[writing materials]* —**ma·te·ri·al'i·ty** (-al'ə tē) *n.*

**ma·te·ri·al·ism** (-iz'm) *n.* **1.** the philosophical doctrine that everything in the world, including thought, will, and feeling, can be explained only in terms of matter **2.** the tendency to be more concerned with material than with spiritual values —**ma·te'ri·al·ist** *adj., n.* —**ma·te·ri·al·is'tic** *adj.* —**ma·te'ri·al·is'ti·cal·ly** *adv.*

**ma·te·ri·al·ize** (mə tir'ē ə līz') *vt.* -**ized'**, -**iz'ing** **1.** to represent in material form **2.** to make (a spirit, etc.) appear in bodily form —*vi.* **1.** to become fact; be realized *[a plan that never materialized]* **2.** to take on, or appear in, bodily form: said of spirits, etc. **3.** to appear suddenly or unexpectedly —**ma·te'ri·al·i·za'tion** *n.*

**ma·te·ri·al·ly** (-lē) *adv.* **1.** with regard to the matter, content, etc. and not the form **2.** physically **3.** to a great extent; considerably

**ma·te·ri·a med·i·ca** (mə tir'ē ə med'i kə) [ML. < L. *materia*, matter + fem. of *medicus*, medical] **1.** the drugs and other remedial substances used in medicine **2.** the branch of medical science that deals with such substances, their uses, etc.

**ma·te·ri·el, ma·té·ri·el** (mə tir'ē el') *n.* [Fr.: see MATE-RIAL] the necessary materials and tools; specif., weapons, supplies, etc. of armed forces

**ma·ter·nal** (mə tur'n'l) *adj.* [< MFr. < L. < *mater*, a mother] **1.** of or like a mother; motherly **2.** derived or inherited from a mother **3.** related through the mother's side of the family *[maternal grandparents]* —**ma·ter'nal·ly** *adv.*

**ma·ter·ni·ty** (mə tur'nə tē) *n.* **1.** the state of being a mother; motherhood **2.** the qualities of a mother; motherliness —*adj.* **1.** for pregnant women *[a maternity dress]* **2.** for the care of women giving birth and of newborn babies *[a maternity ward]*

**math** (math) *n. clipped form of* MATHEMATICS

**math.** **1.** mathematical **2.** mathematician **3.** mathematics

**math·e·mat·i·cal** (math'ə mat'i k'l) *adj.* [< ML. < L. < Gr. < *mathēma*, what is learned < *manthanein*, to learn] **1.** of, like, or concerned with mathematics **2.** rigorously precise, accurate, etc. —**math'e·mat'i·cal·ly** *adv.*

**math·e·ma·ti·cian** (math'ə mə tish'ən, math'mə-) *n.* an expert or specialist in mathematics

**math·e·mat·ics** (math'ə mat'iks) *n.pl.* [*with sing. v.*] [see MATHEMATICAL & -ICS] the group of sciences (arithmetic, geometry, algebra, calculus, etc.) dealing with quantities, magnitudes, and forms, and their relationships, attributes, etc., by the use of numbers and symbols

**Math·er** (math'ər) **1.** Cot·ton (kät''n), 1663–1728; Am. clergyman & writer: son of *ff.* **2.** In·crease (in'krēs), 1639–1723; Am. clergyman & writer

**Ma·til·da, Ma·thil·da** (mə til'də) [< ML. < OHG. < *maht*, power + *hiltia*, battle] a feminine name

**mat·in** (mat''n) *n.* [OFr. < L. *matutinus*, of the morning < *Matuta*, goddess of dawn] **1.** *[pl.] [often* M-] *a)* R.C.Ch. the first of the seven canonical hours *b)* Anglican Ch. the service of public morning prayer **2.** [Poet.] a morning song —*adj.* **1.** of matins **2.** of morning —**mat'in·al** *adj.*

**mat·i·nee, mat·i·née** (mat''n ā', mat''n ā') *n.* [< Fr.: see prec.] a daytime reception, etc.; esp., a performance, as of a play, in the afternoon

**Ma·tisse** (mà tēs'), **Hen·ri** (än rē') 1869–1954; Fr. painter

**ma·tri-** [< L. *mater* (gen. *matris*), a mother] *a combining form meaning* mother *[matriarch]*

**ma·tri·arch** (mā'trē ärk') *n.* [prec. + -ARCH] a mother who rules her family or tribe; specif., a woman who is head of a matriarchy —**ma'tri·ar'chal** (-är'k'l) *adj.*

**ma·tri·ar·chy** (-trē är'kē) *n., pl.* -**chies** **1.** a form of social organization in which the mother is head of the family or tribe, descent being traced through the female line **2.** rule or domination by women —**ma'tri·ar'chic** *adj.*

**mat·ri·cide** (mat'rə sīd', mā'trə-) *n.* [< L. < *mater*, mother + *caedere*, to kill] **1.** the act of killing one's mother **2.** a person who kills his mother —**mat'ri·ci'dal** *adj.*

**ma·tric·u·late** (mə trik'yoo lāt'; also, for n., -lit) *vt., vi.* -**lat'ed**, -**lat'ing** [< ML. pp. of *matriculare*, to register < LL. dim. of *matrix*, MATRIX] to enroll, esp. as a student in a college or university —*n.* a person so enrolled —**ma·tric'u·lant** *n.* —**ma·tric'u·la'tion** *n.*

**mat·ri·mo·ny** (mat'rə mō'nē) *n., pl.* -**nies** [< OFr. < L.

*matrimonium* < *mater*, a mother] **1.** the act or rite of marriage **2.** the state of being husband and wife **3.** married life —**mat'ri·mo'ni·al** *adj.* —**mat'ri·mo'ni·al·ly** *adv.*

**ma·trix** (mā'triks) *n., pl.* -**tri·ces'** (mā'trə sēz', mat'rə-), -**trix·es** [LL., womb, ult. < L. *mater* (gen. *matris*), mother] **1.** orig., the womb; uterus **2.** that within which something originates, takes form, etc.; specif., a die or mold for casting or shaping **3.** *Printing a)* a metal mold for casting the face of type *b)* an impression, as of papier-mâché, from which a plate can be made

**ma·tron** (mā'trən) *n.* [< OFr. < L. *matrona* < *mater*, a mother] **1.** a wife or widow, esp. one with a mature manner **2.** a woman manager of the domestic arrangements of a hospital, prison, or other institution **3.** a woman guard, as in a jail —**ma'tron·al** *adj.* —**ma'tron·li·ness** *n.* —**ma'tron·ly** *adj.*

**matron of honor** a married woman acting as principal attendant to the bride at a wedding

**Matt.** Matthew

**matte** (mat) *n.* [var. of MAT²] a dull surface or finish, often roughened —*adj.* not shiny or glossy; dull Also sp. **matt** —**mat'ted** *adj.*

**mat·ted** (mat'id) *adj.* **1.** closely tangled together in a dense mass **2.** covered with matting or mats

**mat·ter** (mat'ər) *n.* [< OFr. < L. *materia*, material] **1.** what a thing is made of; constituent material **2.** whatever occupies space and is perceptible to the senses in some way: in modern physics, matter and energy are regarded as mutually convertible equivalents **3.** any specified sort of substance *[coloring matter]* **4.** material or content of thought or expression, as distinguished from style or form **5.** an amount or quantity *[a matter of a few days]* **6.** *a)* a thing or affair *[business matters]* *b)* cause or occasion *[no laughing matter]* **7.** importance; significance *[it's of no matter]* **8.** trouble; difficulty (with *the)* *[what's the matter?]* **9.** mail *[second-class matter]* **10.** pus **11.** *Printing a)* copy *b)* type set up —*vi.* **1.** to be of importance; have significance **2.** to form and discharge pus; suppurate —**as a matter of fact** in fact; really —**for that matter** as far as that is concerned: also **for the matter of that** —**no matter 1.** it is of no importance **2.** regardless of *[no matter what you say]*

**Mat·ter·horn** (mat'ər hôrn') mountain of the Pennine Alps, on the border between Switzerland & Italy

**mat·ter-of-course** (mat'ər əv kôrs') *adj.* **1.** coming naturally in the course of events; routine **2.** reacting to events in a calm and natural way

**matter of course** a thing to be expected as a natural or logical occurrence

**mat·ter-of-fact** (-əv fakt', -ə fakt') *adj.* sticking strictly to facts; literal, unimaginative, etc. —**mat'ter-of-fact'ly** *adv.* —**mat'ter-of-fact'ness** *n.*

**Mat·thew** (math'yoo) [< OFr. < LL. < Gr. < Heb. *mattithyāh*, lit., gift of God] **1.** a masculine name: dim. *Mat(t)*; var. *Matthias* **2.** *Bible a)* one of the four Evangelists and the reputed author of the first Gospel *b)* this book, the first of the New Testament

**mat·ting¹** (mat'iŋ) *n.* **1.** a fabric of fiber, as straw or hemp, for mats, floor covering, wrapping, etc. **2.** mats collectively **3.** the making of mats

**mat·ting²** (mat'iŋ) *n.* [see MATTE] **1.** the production of a dull surface or finish **2.** such a surface or finish **3.** a mat, or border

**mat·tins** (mat'nz) *n.pl.* Brit. var. of MATINS (see MATIN, *n.* 1)

**mat·tock** (mat'ək) *n.* [OE. *mattuc*] a tool like a pickax but with at least one flat blade, for loosening the soil, digging up roots, etc.

**mat·tress** (mat'ris) *n.* [< OFr. < It. *materasso* < Ar. *matrah*, cushion] **1.** a casing of strong cloth filled with cotton, hair, foam rubber, etc., and usually coiled springs, and used on or as a bed **2.** an inflatable pad used in the same way: in full, **air mattress**

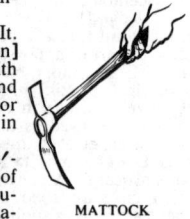

MATTOCK

**mat·u·rate** (mach'oo rāt', mat'-yoo-) *vi.* -**rat'ed**, -**rat'ing** [< L. pp. of *maturare*, to MATURE] **1.** to suppurate; discharge pus **2.** to ripen; mature —**ma·tur·a·tive** (mə tyoor'ə tiv, mach'oo rāt'iv, mat'yoos-) *adj.* —**mat'u·ra'tion** *n.*

**ma·ture** (mə toor', -choor', -tyoor') *adj.* [< L. *maturus*, ripe] **1.** *a)* full-grown, as plants or animals *b)* ripe, as fruits *c)* fully developed, as a person **2.** fully developed, perfected, etc. *[a mature scheme]* **3.** of a state of full development *[of mature age]* **4.** due: said of a note, bond, etc. —*vt.* -**tured'**, -**tur'ing** **1.** to bring to full growth, or to ripeness **2.** to develop fully —*vi.* **1.** to become fully grown or ripe **2.** to become due: said of a note, etc. —**ma·ture'ly** *adv.* —**ma·ture'ness** *n.*

**ma·tu·ri·ty** (-ə tē) *n.* **1.** *a)* a being full-grown, ripe, or fully developed *b)* a being perfect, complete, or ready

**2.** *a*) a becoming due *b*) the time at which a note, etc. becomes due

**ma·tu·ti·nal** (mə tōōt'n əl, -tyōōt'-; *chiefly Brit.* mach'ōō tī'n'l) *adj.* [< L. < *matutinus:* see MATIN] of or in the morning; early —**ma·tu'ti·nal·ly** *adv.*

**mat·zo** (mät'sə, -sō) *n., pl.* **mat'zot, mat'zoth** (-sōt), **mat'zos** [< Heb. *matstsāh,* unleavened] flat, thin unleavened bread eaten by Jews during the Passover, or a piece of this

**Maud, Maude** (môd) [< MATILDA] a feminine name

**maud·lin** (môd'lin) *adj.* [< ME. *Maudeleyne,* (Mary) Magdalene (often represented as weeping)] **1.** foolishly and tearfully or weakly sentimental **2.** tearfully sentimental from too much liquor

**Maugham** (môm), **(William) Som·er·set** (sum'ər set') 1874–1965; Eng. novelist & playwright

**mau·gre, mau·ger** (mô'gər) *prep.* [< OFr. *maugré,* lit., with displeasure] [Archaic] in spite of

**Mau·i** (mou'ē) [Haw.] island of Hawaii, southeast of Oahu

**maul** (môl) *n.* [< OFr. < L. *malleus,* a hammer] a very heavy hammer or mallet for driving stakes, etc. —*vt.* **1.** to bruise or lacerate **2.** to handle roughly —**maul'er** *n.*

**Mau·na Lo·a** (mou'nə lō'ə) [Haw., lit., long mountain] active volcano on the island of Hawaii

**maun·der** (môn'dər) *vi.* [prob. freq. of obs. *maund,* to beg] **1.** to move or act in a vague, aimless way **2.** to talk in an incoherent, rambling way —**maun'der·er** *n.*

**Maun·dy Thursday** (môn'dē) [OFr. *mandé* < LL. *mandatum,* commandment of God < L.: from use in a prayer on that day] the Thursday before Easter

**Mau·pas·sant** (mō'pə sänt'; *Fr.* mō pä sän') **(Henri René Albert) Guy de** (gē də) 1850–93; Fr. writer

**Mau·re·ta·ni·a** (môr'ə tā'nē ə, -tän'yə) ancient country & Roman province in NW Africa

**Mau·rice** (môr'is, mär'-; mô rēs') [Fr. < LL. *Maurus,* a Moor] a masculine name

**Mau·ri·ta·ni·a** (môr'ə tā'nē ə, -tän'yə) country in W Africa, on the Atlantic: 419,230 sq. mi.; pop. 1,120,000 — **Mau'ri·ta'ni·an** *adj., n.*

**Mau·ri·ti·us** (mô rish'ē əs, -rish'əs) island country in the Indian Ocean, east of Madagascar: a member of the Commonwealth: 809 sq. mi.; pop. 810,000

**Mau·so·le·um** (mô'sə lē'əm, -zə-) the tomb of Mausolus, king of an ancient land in Asia Minor —*n.* [m-] *pl.* -**le'ums, -le'a** (-lē'ə) a large, imposing tomb

**mauve** (mōv, môv) *n.* [Fr., mallow < L. *malva,* mallow] any of several shades of delicate purple

**ma·ven** (mā'vən) *n.* [Yid. < LHeb. *mēvin*] an expert or connoisseur, often, specif., a self-proclaimed one

**mav·er·ick** (mav'ər ik, mav'rik) *n.* [after S. *Maverick,* 19th-c. Texas rancher who did not brand his cattle] **1.** an unbranded animal, esp. a strayed calf, formerly the property of the first one who branded it **2.** [Colloq.] a person who acts independently of his political party or group

**ma·vis** (mā'vis) *n.* [< OFr.] *same as* SONG THRUSH

**maw** (mô) *n.* [OE. *maga*] **1.** *orig.,* the stomach **2.** the throat, gullet, jaws, etc. of a voracious animal **3.** anything thought of as devouring without end

**mawk·ish** (mô'kish) *adj.* [lit., maggoty < ON. *mathkr,* maggot] **1.** insipid or nauseating **2.** sentimental in a weak, insipid way, so as to be sickening —**mawk'ish·ly** *adv.* — **mawk'ish·ness** *n.*

**max.** maximum

**max·i-** [< MAXI(MUM)] *a combining form meaning* maximum, very large, very long *[maxicoat]*

**max·il·la** (mak sil'ə) *n., pl.* -**lae** (-ē) [L.] **1.** in vertebrates, the upper jaw, or a major bone or cartilage of it **2.** in insects, crabs, etc., one of the first or second pair of jaws or head appendages situated just behind the mandibles

**max·il·lar·y** (mak'sə ler'ē; *chiefly Brit.* mak sil'ə rē) *adj.* designating, of, or near the jaw or jawbone —*n., pl.* -**lar'ies** *same as* MAXILLA

**max·im** (mak'sim) *n.* [< MFr. < ML. < LL. *maxima* (*propositio*), the greatest (premise): see MAXIMUM] a concisely expressed rule of conduct; precept

**max·i·ma** (mak'sə mə) *n. alt. pl. of* MAXIMUM

**max·i·mal** (-m'l) *adj.* highest or greatest possible; of or constituting a maximum —**max'i·mal·ly** *adv.*

**Max·i·mil·ian** (mak'sə mil'yən) [? a blend of the L. names *Maximus & Aemilianus*] **1.** a masculine name: dim. *Max* **2.** (*Ferdinand Maximilian Joseph*) 1832–67; archduke of Austria; emperor of Mexico (1864–67): executed

**max·i·mize** (mak'sə mīz') *vt.* -**mized', -miz'ing** to increase to the maximum —**max'i·mi·za'tion** *n.* —**max'i·miz'er** *n.*

**max·i·mum** (-məm) *n., pl.* -**mums, -ma** (-mə) [L., neut. of *maximus,* superl. of *magnus,* great] **1.** the greatest quantity, number, etc. possible or permissible **2.** the highest degree

or point reached or recorded —*adj.* **1.** greatest possible, permissible, or reached **2.** marking a maximum

**Max·ine** (mak sēn') [fem. of *Max:* see MAXIMILIAN] a feminine name

**May¹** (mā) *n.* [OFr. < L. < *Maia,* goddess of increase] **1.** the fifth month of the year, having 31 days **2.** the springtime of life; youth

**May²** (mā) [contr. of MARY, MARGARET] a feminine name

**may** (mā) *v.aux. pt.* **might** [OE. *mæg*] an auxiliary preceding an infinitive (without *to*) and expressing: **1.** *orig.,* ability or power: now generally replaced by *can* **2.** possibility or likelihood *[it may rain]* **3.** permission *[you may go]* **4.** contingency, as in clauses of purpose, result, concession, or condition *[they died that we may be free]* **5.** wish, hope, or prayer *[may he rest in peace]*

**Ma·ya** (mä'yə) *n.* **1.** *pl.* **Ma'yas, Ma'ya** a member of a tribe of Indians in SE Mexico and Central America, who had a highly developed civilization **2.** their language —*adj.* of the Mayas —**Ma'yan** *adj., n.*

**Ma·ya·güez** (mä'yä gwes') seaport in W Puerto Rico: pop. 69,000

**May apple 1.** a woodland plant with shield-shaped leaves and a single large, white flower, found in the E U.S. **2.** its edible, yellow, oval fruit

**may·be** (mā'bē) *adv.* [ME. (for *it may be*)] perhaps

**May·day** (mā'dā') *n.* [< Fr. (*venez*) *m'aider,* (come) help me] the international radiotelephone signal for help, used by ships and aircraft in distress

**May Day** May 1: as a traditional spring festival, often celebrated by dancing, crowning a May queen, etc.; as an international labor holiday, observed in many countries by parades, demonstrations, etc.

**may·est** (mā'ist) *archaic 2d pers. sing., pres. indic., of* MAY: *used with* thou

**May·fair** (mā'fer') a fashionable residential district of the West End of London

**may·flow·er** (-flou'ər) *n.* a plant that flowers in early spring; esp., *a*) in the U.S., the trailing arbutus, etc. *b*) in England, the cowslip, marsh marigold, etc. —[M-] the ship on which the Pilgrims came to America (1620)

**may·fly** (-flī') *n., pl.* -**flies'** a slender insect with gauzy wings held vertically when at rest: the adult lives only a few hours or a few days

**may·hap** (mā'hap', mā'hap') *adv.* [< *it may hap(pen)*] [Archaic] perhaps; maybe: also **may'hap'pen**

**may·hem** (mā'hem, mā'əm) *n.* [see MAIM] **1.** *Law* the offense of maiming a person; specif., *a*) orig., injury inflicted on another so as to cause loss of a part or function necessary for self-defense *b*) any intentional mutilation of another's body **2.** loosely, any deliberate destruction or violence

MAYFLY (body to 1 in.)

**May·ing** (mā'iŋ) *n.* [*also* m-] the celebration of May Day, as by gathering flowers, dancing, etc.

**May·nard** (mā'nərd, -närd) [< Anglo-Fr. < OHG. < *magan,* power + *hart,* strong] a masculine name

**may·n't** (mā'nt, mānt) may not

**may·o** (mā'ō) *n.* [Colloq.] *clipped form of* MAYONNAISE

**may·on·naise** (mā'ə nāz') *n.* [Fr., prob. ult. < *Mahón,* Minorca] a creamy salad dressing made by beating together egg yolks, oil, lemon juice or vinegar, and seasoning

**may·or** (mā'ər, mer) *n.* [< OFr. *maire* < L. *major,* greater] the chief administrative official (or, under a city-manager plan, the formal head) of a city, town, or other municipality —**may'or·al** *adj.*

**may·or·al·ty** (-əl tē) *n., pl.* -**ties** the office or term of office of a mayor

**May·pole** (mā'pōl') *n.* a high pole wreathed with streamers, around which merrymakers dance on May Day

**May queen** a girl chosen to be queen of the merrymakers on May Day

**mayst** (māst) *archaic 2d pers. sing., pres. indic., of* MAY: *used with* thou

**May·time** (mā'tīm') *n.* the month of May: also **May'tide'**

**Ma·za·rin** (mà zà ran'; *E.* maz'ər in), **Jules** (zhül), Cardinal, (born *Giulio Mazarini*) 1602–61; Fr. statesman & prelate, born in Italy

**maze** (māz) *n.* [< OE. *amasian,* to amaze & pp. *amasod,* puzzled] **1.** a confusing, intricate network of winding pathways; labyrinth, specif. one used in psychological experiments and tests **2.** a state of confusion or bewilderment —**ma′zy** adj. -zi·er, -zi·est —**ma′zi·ly** adv. —**ma′-zi·ness** n.

‡**maz·el tov** (mä′z'l tōv′, tôf′) [Heb. (often via Yid.)] good luck: an expression of congratulation: also **maz′el·tov′**, **maz′zel tov**

**ma·zur·ka, ma·zour·ka** (mə zur′kə, -zoor′-) n. [Pol. mazurka, woman from Mazovia, region of C Poland] 1. a lively Polish dance like the polka 2. music for this, generally in 3/4 or 3/8 time

**Maz·zi·ni** (mät tsē′nē, mäd dzē′nē), **Giu·sep·pe** (jōō zep′pe) 1805–72; It. patriot & revolutionist

**M.B.A.** Master of Business Administration

**MBS** Mutual Broadcasting System

**M.C.** 1. Master of Ceremonies 2. Member of Congress

**Mc·Car·thy·ism** (mə kär′thē iz'm) n. [after J. McCarthy, U.S. senator (1946–57)] the use of indiscriminate, often unfounded, accusations, inquisitorial investigative methods, etc., ostensibly in the suppression of communism

**Mc·Clel·lan** (mə klel′ən), **George Brin·ton** (brin′t'n) 1826–85; Union general in the Civil War

**Mc·Cor·mick** (mə kôr′mik), **Cyrus Hall** (hôl) 1809–84, U.S. inventor of the reaping machine

**Mc·Coy** (mə koi′), **the** (**real**) [Slang] the real person or thing, not a substitute

**Mc·In·tosh** (mak′in täsh′) n. [after J. McIntosh, of Ontario, Can., who first cultivated it (1796)] a late-maturing variety of red apple: also **McIntosh Red**

**Mc·Kin·ley** (mə kin′lē), **Mount** [after ff.] mountain in SC Alas.: highest peak in N. America: 20,320 ft.

**Mc·Kin·ley** (mə kin′lē), **William** 1843–1901; 25th president of the U.S. (1897–1901): assassinated

**Md** Chem. mendelevium

**Md., MD** Maryland

**M.D.** [L. Medicinae Doctor] Doctor of Medicine

**Mdlle.** pl. **Mdlles.** Mademoiselle

**Mdm.** pl. **Mdms.** Madam

**Mdme.** pl. **Mdmes.** Madame

**mdse.** merchandise

**MDu.** Middle Dutch

**me** (mē) pron. [OE.] objective case of I: also used colloquially as a predicate complement with a linking verb (Ex.: that's me)

**ME.** Middle English

**Me., ME** Maine

**M.E.** 1. Master of Education 2. Mechanical Engineer 3. Methodist Episcopal 4. Mining Engineer

‡**me·a cul·pa** (mē′ə kul′pə, mä′ä kool′pä) [L.] (by) my fault; I am to blame

**mead**[1] (mēd) n. [OE. meodu] an alcoholic drink made from fermented honey, often with spices, fruit, malt, etc. added

**mead**[2] (mēd) n. [OE. mæd] [Poet.] a meadow

**Mead** (mēd), **Lake** [after E. Mead (1858–1936), U.S. engineer] lake in SE Nev. & NW Ariz., formed by the Hoover Dam on the Colorado River

**Mead** (mēd), **Margaret** 1901–78; U.S. anthropologist

**Meade** (mēd), **George Gordon** 1815–72; Union general in the Civil War

**mead·ow** (med′ō) n. [< OE. mædwe, oblique case of mæd] 1. a piece of grassland, esp. one whose grass is grown for use as hay 2. low, level grassland near a stream, etc. —**mead′ow·y** adj.

**mead·ow·lark** (-lärk′) n., pl. **-larks′, -lark′**: see PLURAL, II, D, 1 either of two N. American songbirds having brown-and-black upper parts and a yellow breast

**mea·ger** (mē′gər) adj. [< OFr. < L. macer, lean] 1. thin; lean; emaciated 2. of poor quality or small amount; inadequate Also, Brit., **mea′gre** —**mea′ger·ly** adv. —**mea′ger·ness** n.

**meal**[1] (mēl) n. [OE. mæl] 1. any of the times for eating; breakfast, lunch, dinner, etc. 2. the food served or eaten at such a time

**meal**[2] (mēl) n. [OE. melu] 1. any edible grain, coarsely ground and unbolted [cornmeal] 2. any substance similarly ground or powdered

**meal·ie** (mēl′ē) n. [Afrik. milje < Port. milho, millet] in South Africa, 1. [pl.] same as CORN[1] (sense 2) 2. an ear of corn

**meal ticket** 1. a ticket entitling one to a specified value in meals at a particular restaurant 2. [Slang] a person, job, skill, etc. depended on as one's means of support

**meal·time** (mēl′tīm′) n. the usual time for serving or eating a meal

**meal·y** (mēl′ē) adj. **meal′i·er, meal′i·est** 1. like meal; powdery, dry, soft, etc. 2. of or containing meal 3. covered with meal 4. floury in color; pale 5. mealy-mouthed —**meal′i·ness** n.

**meal·y-mouthed** (-mouthd′, -moutht′) adj. evasive, euphemistic, insincere, etc. in what one says

**mean**[1] (mēn) vt. **meant** (ment), **mean′ing** [OE. mænan] 1. to have in mind; intend; purpose [he means to go] 2. a) to

intend for a certain person or purpose [a gift meant for you] b) to destine [he was meant to be a doctor] 3. to intend to express or imply [to say what one means] 4. to signify; denote [the German word "ja" means "yes"] —vi. 1. to have a purpose in mind: chiefly in **mean well**, to have good intentions 2. to have a (specified) degree of importance, effect, etc. [she means little to him] —**mean well by** to have good intentions toward

**mean**[2] (mēn) adj. [OE. (ge)mæne] 1. low in quality, value, or importance; poor [paid no mean sum] 2. poor in appearance; shabby [a mean dwelling] 3. ignoble; base; petty 4. stingy; miserly 5. bad-tempered; unmanageable: said of a horse, etc. 6. contemptibly bad-tempered, selfish, etc. 7. humiliated 8. [Colloq.] in poor health 9. [Slang] hard to cope with; difficult —**mean′ly** adv. —**mean′ness** n.

**mean**[3] (mēn) adj. [< OFr. < L. medianus < medius, middle] 1. halfway between extremes; intermediate as to quantity, quality, etc. 2. average; middling —n. 1. what is between extremes; intermediate state, quality, course, etc. 2. moderation 3. Math. a) a number between the smallest and largest values of a set of quantities, obtained by some prescribed method: unless otherwise qualified, same as ARITHMETIC MEAN b) the second or third term of a four-term proportion See also MEANS

**me·an·der** (mē an′dər) n. [< L. < Gr. maiandros < the name of a winding river in Asia Minor] 1. [pl.] windings or convolutions, as of a stream 2. an aimless wandering —vi. 1. to take a winding course: said of a stream 2. to wander aimlessly or idly —**me·an′drous** (-drəs) adj.

**mean·ie, mean·y** (mē′nē) n., pl. **mean′ies** [Colloq.] a person who is mean, selfish, cruel, etc.

**mean·ing** (mē′niŋ) n. 1. what is meant; what is intended to be, or in fact is, signified, indicated, etc.; import, sense, or significance [the meaning of a word] 2. [Archaic] intention —adj. 1. that has meaning; significant 2. intending

**mean·ing·ful** (-fəl) adj. full of meaning; having significance or purpose —**mean′ing·ful·ly** adv. —**mean′ing·ful·ness** n.

**mean·ing·less** (-lis) adj. having no meaning; without significance or purpose —**mean′ing·less·ly** adv. —**mean′ing·less·ness** n.

**means** (mēnz) n.pl. [< MEAN[3], n.] 1. [with sing. or pl. v.] that by which something is done or obtained; agency [a fast means of travel] 2. resources or wealth [a person of means] —**by all means** 1. without fail 2. certainly —**by any means** in any way possible; somehow —**by means of** by using; with the aid of —**by no (manner of) means** not at all; certainly not —**means to an end** a method of getting what one wants

**mean (solar) time** time having exactly equal divisions

**means test** a financial investigation of a person's eligibility for welfare aid, public housing, etc.

**meant** (ment) pt. & pp. of MEAN[1]

**mean·time** (mēn′tīm′) adv. 1. in or during the intervening time 2. at the same time —n. the intervening time Also, and for adv. now usually, **mean′while′** (-hwīl′)

**mea·sles** (mē′z'lz) n.pl. [with sing. v.] [ME. maseles, ? infl. by ME. mesel, leper < OFr. < L. misellus, wretch] 1. an acute, infectious, communicable virus disease, characterized by small red spots on the skin, high fever, nasal discharge, etc., and occurring most frequently in childhood 2. any of various similar but milder diseases; esp., rubella (called German measles)

**mea·sly** (mēz′lē) adj. **-sli·er, -sli·est** 1. infected with measles 2. [Colloq.] contemptibly slight, worthless, or skimpy

**meas·ur·a·ble** (mezh′ər ə b'l) adj. that can be measured —**meas′ur·a·bil′i·ty** n. —**meas′ur·a·bly** adv.

**meas·ure** (mezh′ər, mā′zhər) n. [< OFr. mesure < L. mensura < pp. of metiri, to measure] 1. the extent, dimensions, capacity, etc. of anything, esp. as determined by a standard 2. a determining of extent, dimensions, etc.; measurement 3. a) unit of measurement, as an inch, yard, or bushel b) any standard of valuation; criterion 4. a system of measurement [dry measure] 5. an instrument or container for measuring [a quart measure] 6. a definite quantity measured out 7. an extent or degree not to be exceeded [remain within measure] 8. proportion, quantity, or degree [in large measure] 9. course of action; step [reform measures] 10. a statute; law 11. a) rhythm in verse; meter b) a metrical unit; foot of verse 12. a dance or dance movement 13. [pl.] Geol. strata: now chiefly in **coal measures** 14. Music a) the notes or rests, or both, contained between two bars on the staff b) musical time —vt. **-ured, -ur·ing** 1. to find out or estimate the extent, dimensions, etc. of, esp. by a standard 2. to set apart or mark off by measuring (often with off or out) 3. to make a judgment of

MEASURES

by comparing [to *measure* one's foe] **4.** to bring into comparison or rivalry (*against*) **5.** to be a device for measuring [a clock *measures* time] —*vi.* **1.** to get or take measurements **2.** to be of specified measurements **3.** to allow of measurement **—beyond** (or **above**) **measure** exceedingly; extremely **—for good measure** as a bonus or something extra **—in a measure** to some extent; somewhat **—made to measure** custom-made: said of clothes **—measure up** to prove to be qualified **—measure up to** to meet (expectations, a standard, etc.) **—take measures** to do things to accomplish a purpose **—take someone's measure** to estimate someone's ability, character, etc. **—meas′ur·er** *n.*

**meas·ured** (-ərd, -zhərd) *adj.* **1.** determined by a standard **2.** regular or uniform **3.** *a*) rhythmical *b*) metrical **4.** calculated, deliberate, etc., as speech **—meas′ured·ly** *adv.*

**meas·ure·less** (mezh′ər lis, mā′zhər-) *adj.* too large to be measurable; vast; immense **—meas′ure·less·ly** *adv.* **—meas′ure·less·ness** *n.*

**meas·ure·ment** (-mənt) *n.* **1.** a measuring or being measured **2.** extent or quantity determined by measuring **3.** a system of measuring

**measuring worm** the caterpillar larva of any geometrid moth

**meat** (mēt) *n.* [OE. *mete*] **1.** food: now dialectal except in **meat and drink 2.** the flesh of animals used as food; esp., the flesh of mammals and, sometimes, of fowl **3.** the edible, inner part [the *meat* of a nut] **4.** the substance or essence [the *meat* of a story] **5.** [Archaic] a meal **—one's meat** [Slang] something that one especially enjoys or is skillful at [golf's my *meat*] **—meat′less** *adj.*

**meat·ball** (-bôl′) *n.* a small ball of ground meat, seasoned and cooked, often with sauce, etc.

**meat·pack·ing** (-pak′iŋ) *n.* the process or industry of slaughtering animals and preparing their meat for market **—meat′pack′er** *n.*

**me·a·tus** (mē āt′əs) *n., pl.* **-tus·es, -tus** [LL. < L., a passage, pp. of *meare*, to pass] a natural passage or duct in the body, or its opening

**meat·y** (mēt′ē) *adj.* **meat′i·er, meat′i·est 1.** of, like, or having the flavor of, meat **2.** full of meat **3.** full of substance; thought-provoking; pithy **—meat′i·ness** *n.*

**Mec·ca** (mek′ə) religious capital of Saudi Arabia: birthplace of Mohammed, to which Muslims make pilgrimages: pop. c.250,000 **—***n.* [*often* **m-**] any place that many people feel drawn to **—Mec′can** *adj., n.*

**mech. 1.** mechanical **2.** mechanics

**me·chan·ic** (mə kan′ik) *adj.* [< L. < Gr. *mēchanē*, a machine] *rare or archaic var.* of MECHANICAL **—***n.* a worker skilled in using tools or in making, operating, and repairing machines

**me·chan·i·cal** (-i k′l) *adj.* **1.** having to do with, or having skill in the use of, machinery or tools **2.** produced or operated by machinery **3.** of, or in accordance with, the science of mechanics **4.** automatic, as if from force of habit; machinelike **—me·chan′i·cal·ly** *adv.*

**mechanical advantage** the rates of the output force of a mechanism to the input force

**mechanical drawing** drawing done, as by a draftsman, with T squares, scales, compasses, etc.

**mech·a·ni·cian** (mek′ə nish′ən) *n.* a person skilled in the design, operation, care, etc. of machinery

**me·chan·ics** (mə kan′iks) *n.pl.* [*with sing. v.*] **1.** the branch of physics that deals with the motion of material bodies and the action of forces on bodies: cf. STATICS, DYNAMICS, KINEMATICS **2.** knowledge of machinery **3.** the mechanical aspect; technical part [the *mechanics* of writing]

**mech·a·nism** (mek′ə niz′m) *n.* [< ModL. < Gr. *mēchanē*, a machine] **1.** the working parts of a machine; works [the *mechanism* of a clock] **2.** *a*) a system whose parts work together as in a machine [the *mechanism* of the universe] *b*) any physical or mental process by which some result is produced **3.** the mechanical aspect; technical part **4.** the theory that all phenomena can ultimately be explained in terms of physics and chemistry **—mech′a·nist** *n.* **—mech′a·nis′tic** *adj.* **—mech′a·nis′ti·cal·ly** *adv.*

**mech·a·nize** (mek′ə nīz′) *vt.* **-nized′, -niz′ing 1.** to make mechanical **2.** to do or operate by machinery, not by hand **3.** to bring about the use of machinery in (an industry, etc.) **4.** to equip (an army, etc.) with motor vehicles, tanks, etc. **—mech′a·ni·za′tion** *n.* **—mech′a·niz′er** *n.*

**mech·an·o·ther·a·py** (mek′ə nō ther′ə pē) *n.* [< Gr. *mēchanē*, a machine + THERAPY] the treatment of disease by mechanical means, such as massage

**med. 1.** medical **2.** medicine **3.** medieval **4.** medium

**M.Ed.** Master of Education

**med·al** (med′'l) *n.* [< Fr. < It. *medaglia*, ult. < LL. *medialis*, MEDIAL] **1.** a small, flat piece of metal with a design or inscription on it, made to commemorate some event, or awarded for some distinguished action, merit, etc. **2.** a disk bearing a religious symbol, blessed as by a priest and worn as a religious token

**med·al·ist** (-′l ist, -list) *n.* **1.** a person who designs or makes medals **2.** a person who has been awarded a medal **3.** *Golf* the low scorer in a qualifying round of medal play preliminary to a tournament Also, Brit. sp., **med′al·list**

**me·dal·lion** (mə dal′yən) *n.* [< Fr. < It.: see MEDAL] **1.** a large medal **2.** any of various designs, carvings, etc. like a medal in shape, used decoratively, as in architecture **3.** a small, thin, round or oval portion of meat, as beef or veal

**medal play** *Golf* a form of play in which the score is calculated by counting the total number of strokes taken to play the designated number of holes: cf. MATCH PLAY

**med·dle** (med′'l) *vi.* **-dled, -dling** [< OFr. *medler* < VL. < L. *miscere*, to mix] **1.** to concern oneself with other people's affairs without being asked or needed; interfere (*in* or *with*) **2.** to tamper (*with*) **—med′dler** *n.*

**med·dle·some** (-səm) *adj.* meddling or inclined to meddle **—med′dle·some·ness** *n.*

**Mede** (mēd) *n.* a native or inhabitant of Media

**Me·de·a** (mi dē′ə) *Gr. Myth.* a sorceress who helped Jason get the Golden Fleece

**Me·del·lín** (me′de yēn′) city in northwestern Colombia: pop. 968,000

**Med·ford** (med′fərd) [? for the meadlike marshes once there] city in E Mass.: suburb of Boston: pop. 58,000

**Me·di·a** (mē′dē ə) ancient kingdom in the part of SW Asia that is now NW Iran **—Me′di·an** *adj., n.*

**me·di·a** (mē′dē ə) *n. alt. pl. of* MEDIUM: see MEDIUM (*n.* 3)

**me·di·ae·val** (mē′dē ē′v′l, med′ē-, mid′ē-) *adj. same as* MEDIEVAL **—me′di·ae′val·ism** *n.*

**me·di·al** (mē′dē əl) *adj.* [< LL. < L. *medius*, middle] **1.** of or in the middle; median **2.** average; mean **—me′di·al·ly** *adv.*

**me·di·an** (-ən) *adj.* [< L. < *medius*, middle] **1.** middle; intermediate **2.** *a*) designating a line from a vertex of a triangle to the middle of the opposite side *b*) designating a line joining the midpoints of the nonparallel sides of a trapezoid **3.** *Statistics* designating the middle number in a series arranged in order of size, or, if there is no middle value, the average of the two middle numbers **—***n.* **1.** a median number, point, or line **2.** a strip of land separating opposing traffic on a divided highway: in full, **median strip** **—me′di·an·ly** *adv.*

**me·di·ate** (mē′dē āt′; *for adj.* -it) *vi.* **-at′ed, -at′ing** [< LL. pp. of *mediare* < L. *medius*, middle] **1.** to be in an intermediate position **2.** to be an intermediary between persons or sides **—***vt.* **1.** to settle by mediation **2.** to be the medium for bringing about (a result) **—***adj.* dependent on, acting by, or connected through some intervening agency **—me′di·ate·ly** *adv.* **—me′di·a′tor** *n.*

**me·di·a·tion** (mē′dē ā′shən) *n.* a mediating; intervention for settling differences between persons, nations, etc. **—me′di·a′tive** *adj.* **—me′di·a·to′ry** (-ə tôr′ē) *adj.*

**med·ic¹** (med′ik) *n.* [Colloq.] **1.** a physician or surgeon **2.** a medical student or intern **3.** a member of a military medical corps

**med·ic²** (med′ik) *n.* [< L. < Gr. *mēdikē* (*poa*), (grass) of Media] any of various leguminous plants, as alfalfa: also sp. **med′ick**

**med·i·ca·ble** (med′i kə b′l) *adj.* that can be cured, healed, or relieved by medical treatment

**Med·i·caid** (med′i kād′) *n.* [MEDIC(AL) + AID] [*also* **m-**] a State and Federal public health plan for persons with low income or no income

**med·i·cal** (med′i k′l) *adj.* [< Fr. < LL. < L. *medicus*, physician] of or connected with the practice or study of medicine **—med′i·cal·ly** *adv.*

**medical jurisprudence** the application of medical knowledge to questions of law, as in determining cause of death, proper medical practice, etc.

**med·i·ca·ment** (med′i kə mənt, mə dik′ə-) *n. same as* MEDICATION (sense 2)

**Med·i·care** (med′i ker′) *n.* [MEDI(CAL) + CARE] [*also* **m-**] a national health program for providing medical and hospital care for the aged from Federal, mostly social security, funds

**med·i·cate** (med′ə kāt′) *vt.* **-cat′ed, -cat′ing** [< L. pp. of *medicari*, to heal] **1.** to treat with medicine **2.** to add a medicinal substance to **—med′i·ca′tive** *adj.*

**med·i·ca·tion** (med′ə kā′shən) *n.* **1.** a medicating or being medicated **2.** a medicine; substance for curing or healing, or for relieving pain

**Med·i·ci** (med′ə chē′; *It.* me′dē chē′) family of rich, powerful bankers, merchants, & rulers of Florence & Tuscany in the 14th to 16th cent.; specif., *a)* **Catherine de'**, 1519–89; queen of Henry II of France (1547–59) *b)* **Lorenzo de'** (lô ren'tsô de), 1449–92; ruler of Florence (1469–92) *c)* **Maria de'**, 1573–1642; queen of Henry IV of France (1600–10); queen regent (1610–17) —**Med'i·ce'an** (-sē'ən, -chē'ən) *adj.*

**me·dic·i·nal** (mə dis''n 'l) *adj.* of, or having the properties of, medicine; curing, healing, or relieving —**me·dic'i·nal·ly** *adv.*

**med·i·cine** (med'ə s'n; *Brit.* med'sin) *n.* [< OFr. < L. < *medicus,* physician] **1.** the science and art of diagnosing, treating, and preventing disease **2.** the branch of this science that makes use of drugs, diet, etc., as distinguished esp. from surgery **3.** any substance, as a drug, used in treating disease, healing, relieving pain, etc. **4.** among North American Indians, *a)* any object, rite, etc. supposed,tf to have supernatural powers as a remedy, preventive, etc. *b)* magical power —*vt.* **-cined, -cin·ing** to give medicine to —**take one's medicine** to endure just punishment, etc.

**medicine ball** a large, heavy, leather-covered ball, tossed from one person to another for exercise

**medicine man** among North American Indians, etc., a man supposed to have supernatural powers of curing disease and controlling spirits; shaman

**med·i·co** (med'i kō') *n., pl.* **-cos'** [It.] [Colloq.] **1.** a doctor **2.** a medical student

**me·di·e·val** (mē'dē ē'v'l, med'ē-, mid'ē-) *adj.* [< L. *medius,* middle + *aevum,* age] of, like, characteristic of, or suggestive of the Middle Ages —**me'di·e'val·ly** *adv.*

**Medieval Greek** the Greek language as it was used in the Middle Ages, from c.600–c.1500 A.D.

**me·di·e·val·ism** (-iz'm) *n.* **1.** medieval spirit, beliefs, customs, etc. **2.** devotion to these **3.** a belief, custom, etc. of the Middle Ages

**me·di·e·val·ist** (-ist) *n.* **1.** a specialist in medieval history, literature, art, etc. **2.** a person devoted to medieval customs, beliefs, etc.

**Medieval Latin** the Latin language used in Europe in the Middle Ages, from c.600–c.1500 A.D.

**Me·di·na** (mə dē'nə) city in NW Saudi Arabia: site of Mohammed's tomb: pop. c.60,000

**me·di·o·cre** (mē'dē ō'kər, mē'dē ō'kər) *adj.* [< Fr. < L. *mediocris < medius,* middle + *ocris,* a peak] **1.** neither very good nor very bad; ordinary; average **2.** not good enough; inferior

**me·di·oc·ri·ty** (mē'dē äk'rə tē) *n., pl.* **-ties 1.** a being mediocre **2.** mediocre ability or attainment **3.** a person of mediocre abilities, etc.

**med·i·tate** (med'ə tāt') *vt.* **-tat'ed, -tat'ing** [< L. pp. of *meditari*] **1.** [Rare] to study; ponder **2.** to plan or intend — *vi.* to think deeply and continuously; reflect —**med'i·ta'tive** *adj.* —**med'i·ta'tive·ly** *adv.* —**med'i·ta'tor** *n.*

**med·i·ta·tion** (med'ə tā'shən) *n.* **1.** act of meditating; deep reflection, esp. on sacred matters **2.** [*often pl.*] oral or written material, as a sermon, based on meditation

**Med·i·ter·ra·ne·an** (med'i tə rā'nē ən) *adj.* [< L. < *medius,* middle + *terra,* land] **1.** of the Mediterranean Sea or nearby regions **2.** designating of a style of furniture made to simulate the massive lines and ornate carving of a kind of Renaissance furniture —*n.* a person who lives near the Mediterranean Sea

**Mediterranean Sea** large sea surrounded by Europe, Africa, & Asia: c.2,300 mi. long

**me·di·um** (mē'dē əm) *n., pl.* **-di·ums;** also (except sense 7), and for sense 3 usually, **-di·a** (-ə) [L., neut. of *medius,* middle] **1.** *a)* something intermediate *b)* a middle state or degree; mean **2.** an intervening thing through which a force acts **3.** any means, agency, etc.; specif., a means of communication that reaches the general public and carries advertising: in this sense, a singular form **media** (*pl.* **medias**) is now sometimes heard **4.** any surrounding substance in which bodies exist **5.** environment **6.** a nutritive substance, as agar, for cultivating bacteria, etc. **7.** a person through whom communications are supposedly sent from the spirits of the dead **8.** any material or technique as used in art **9.** a liquid mixed with pigments to give fluency — *adj.* **1.** intermediate in quality, amount, degree, size, etc. **2.** neither rare nor well-done: said of meat

**medium frequency** any radio frequency between 300 kilohertz and 3 megahertz

**med·lar** (med'lər) *n.* [< OFr. < L. < Gr. *mespilon*] **1.** a small tree of the rose family, growing in Europe and Asia **2.** its applelike fruit, eaten when partly decayed

**med·ley** (med'lē) *n., pl.* **-leys** [< OFr. < pp. of *medler:* see MEDDLE] **1.** a mixture of things not usually placed together **2.** a musical piece made up of passages from other works

**me·dul·la** (mi dul'ə) *n., pl.* **-dul'las, -dul'lae** (-ē) [L., the marrow] **1.** *Anat. a)* same as MEDULLA OBLONGATA *b)* the

inner substance of an organ *c)* bone marrow **2.** *Bot.* same as PITH (n. 1) —**med·ul·lar·y** (med'ə ler'ē, mej'-) *adj.*

**me·dul·la ob·lon·ga·ta** (äb'lôn gät'ə, -gät'-) [ModL., oblong medulla] the widening continuation of the spinal cord forming the lowest part of the brain: it controls breathing, circulation, etc.

**Me·du·sa** (mə do̅o̅'sə, -dyo̅o̅'-; -zə) *Gr. Myth.* one of the three Gorgons, slain by Perseus —*n.* [m-] *pl.* **-sas, -sae** (-sē, -zē) *Zool.* same as JELLYFISH —**me·du'san** *adj., n.*

**meed** (mēd) *n.* [OE. *med*] [Archaic] a merited reward

**meek** (mēk) *adj.* [< ON. *miukr,* gentle] **1.** patient and mild; not inclined to anger or resentment **2.** too submissive; spineless; spiritless —**meek'ly** *adv.* —**meek'ness** *n.*

**meer·schaum** (mir'shəm, -shôm) *n.* [G. < *meer,* sea + *schaum,* foam] **1.** a soft, white, claylike mineral used for tobacco pipes, etc. because heat-resistant **2.** a pipe made of this

**meet**[1] (mēt) *vt.* **met, meet'ing** [OE. *metan*] **1.** to come upon; esp., to come face to face with **2.** to be present at the arrival of [to *meet* a bus] **3.** to come into contact, connection, etc. with [the ball *met* the bat] **4.** *a)* to come into the presence of *b)* to be introduced to; get acquainted with *c)* to keep an appointment with **5.** *a)* to contend with *b)* to face [to *meet* angry words with a laugh] *c)* to deal with effectively [to *meet* an objection] **6.** to experience [to *meet* disaster] **7.** to come within the perception of (the eye, ear, etc.) **8.** *a)* to comply with; satisfy (a demand, etc.) *b)* to pay (a bill, etc.) —*vi.* **1.** to come together, as from different directions **2.** to come into contact, connection, etc. **3.** to become acquainted; be introduced **4.** to be opposed in or as in battle; fight **5.** to be united **6.** to assemble **7.** to come together for discussion, etc. (*with*) —*n.* **1.** a meeting, gathering, etc. [a track *meet*] **2.** the people who meet or the place of meeting —**meet with 1.** to experience **2.** to receive **3.** to encounter

**meet**[2] (mēt) *adj.* [< OE. (ge)*mæte,* fitting] [Now Rare] suitable; proper; fit —**meet'ly** *adv.*

**meet·ing** (mēt'iŋ) *n.* **1.** a coming together of persons or things **2.** an assembly; gathering of people **3.** an assembly or place of assembly for worship **4.** a series of horse or dog races **5.** a point of contact; junction

**meet·ing·house** (-hous') *n.* a building used for public meetings, esp. for public worship

**meg·a-** [Gr. < *megas,* great] *a combining form meaning:* **1.** large, great, powerful [*megaphone*] **2.** a million (of) [*megaton*] Also, before a vowel, **meg-**

**meg·a·death** (meg'ə deth') *n.* [see MEGA-] one million dead persons, as from a hypothetical nuclear explosion

**meg·a·hertz** (-hurts') *n., pl.* **-hertz'** [see MEGA-] one million hertz: formerly **meg'a·cy'cle** (-sī'k'l)

**meg·a·lo-** [ModL. < Gr. < *megas,* large] *a combining form meaning:* **1.** large, great, powerful [*megalomania*] **2.** abnormal enlargement

**meg·a·lo·ma·ni·a** (meg'ə lō mā'nē ə, -mān'yə) *n.* [ModL.: see prec. & MANIA] a mental disorder characterized by delusions of grandeur, wealth, power, etc. —**meg'a·lo·ma'ni·ac'** (-ak') *adj., n.* —**meg'a·lo·ma·ni'a·cal** (-mə nī'ə k'l) *adj.* —**meg'a·lo·man'ic** (-man'ik) *adj.*

**meg·a·lop·o·lis** (meg'ə läp'ə ləs) *n.* [Gr., great city] a vast, heavily populated urban area, including many cities — **meg'a·lo·pol'i·tan** (-lə päl'ə t'n) *adj., n.*

**meg·a·phone** (meg'ə fōn') *n.* [see MEGA-] a large, funnel-shaped device for increasing the volume of the voice and directing it —*vt., vi.* **-phoned', -phon'ing** to magnify or direct (the voice) with a megaphone —**meg'a·phon'ic** (-fän'ik) *adj.*

**meg·a·ton** (-tun') *n.* [see MEGA-] the explosive force of a million tons of TNT —**meg'a·ton'nage** *n.*

**me·grim** (mē'grəm) *n.* [< OFr.: see MIGRAINE] **1.** [Archaic] a whim; fancy **2.** [*pl.*] [Rare] low spirits

**mei·o·sis** (mī ō'sis) *n.* [ModL. < Gr. < *meioun,* to make smaller] the process of nuclear division in the formation of germ cells that halves the number of chromosomes present in the somatic cells of an animal or plant —**mei·ot'ic** (-ät'ik) *adj.*

**Meis·ter·sing·er** (mīs'tər siŋ'ər, -ziŋ'ər) *n., pl.* **-sing'er** [G., lit., master singer] a member of one of the German guilds organized in the 14th-16th cent. for cultivating music and poetry

**Mé·ji·co** (me'hē kô') *Sp.* name of MEXICO

**Me·kong** (mā'käŋ', -kôŋ') river flowing from SW China through Indochina into the South China Sea

**mel·a·mine** (mel'ə mēn') *n.* [G. *melamin*] a white, crystalline compound, $C_3H_6N_6$, used in making synthetic resins

**mel·an·cho·li·a** (mel'ən kō'lē ə, -kōl'yə) *n.* [ModL. < LL.: see ff.] a mental disorder characterized by extreme depression, brooding, etc. —**mel'an·cho'li·ac'** (-kō'lē ak') *adj., n.*

**mel·an·chol·y** (mel'ən käl'ē) *n., pl.* **-chol'ies** [< OFr. < LL. < Gr. *melancholia < melas,* black + *cholē,* bile: orig., referring to black bile as the humor causing this] **1.** *a)* sadness and depression of spirits *b)* a tendency to be sad or depressed **2.** pensiveness —*adj.* **1.** sad and depressed; gloomy **2.** causing sadness or depression **3.** pensive —**mel′an·chol′ic** *adj.* —**mel′an·chol′i·cal·ly** *adv.*

**Mel·a·ne·sia** (mel′ə nē′zhə, -shə) a major division of the Pacific islands, south of the equator, west of the international date line, & east of Australia & New Guinea

**Mel·a·ne·sian** (-zhən, -shən) *adj.* of Melanesia, its people, or their languages —*n.* **1.** a member of the dark-skinned native people of Melanesia **2.** the branch of Malayo-Polynesian languages of Melanesia

**mé·lange** (mā länzh′, -länj′) *n.* [Fr. < *mêler*, to mix] a mixture or medley; hodgepodge

**mel·a·nin** (mel′ə nin) *n.* [< Gr. *melas*, black + -IN¹] a brownish-black pigment found in skin, hair, etc.

**Mel·ba toast** (mel′bə) [after Nellie *Melba* (1861–1931), Australian soprano] [*also* **m-**] slightly stale bread sliced thin and toasted until brown and crisp

**Mel·bourne** (mel′bərn) seaport in SE Australia: pop. 2,110,000

**meld** (meld) *vt., vi.* [G. *melden*, to announce] *Card Games* to declare (a combination of cards in one's hand), esp. by putting them face up on the table —*n.* **1.** a melding **2.** the cards melded

**me·lee, mê·lée** (mā′lā, mā lā′) *n.* [Fr. *mêlée* < OFr.: see MEDLEY] a noisy, confused, hand-to-hand fight among a number of people

**mel·io·rate** (mēl′yə rāt′) *vt., vi.* **-rat′ed, -rat′ing** [< LL. pp. of *meliorare* < L. *melior*, better] to make or become better; improve —**mel′io·ra·ble** (-yər ə b'l) *adj.* —**mel′io·ra′tion** *n.* —**mel′io·ra′tive** *adj.* —**mel′io·ra′tor** *n.*

**mel·lif·lu·ous** (mə lif′loo wəs) *adj.* [< L. < *mel*, honey + *fluere*, to flow] sounding sweet and smooth; honeyed *[mellifluous tones]* : also **mel·lif′lu·ent** (-wənt) —**mel·lif′lu·ous·ly** *adv.* —**mel·lif′lu·ous·ness** *n.*

**mel·low** (mel′ō) *adj.* [prob. < OE. *melu*, MEAL²] **1.** soft, sweet, and juicy because ripe: said of fruit **2.** full-flavored; matured: said of wine, etc. **3.** full, rich, soft, and pure: said of sound, light, etc. **4.** moist and rich: said of soil **5.** grown gentle and understanding —*vt., vi.* to make or become mellow —**mel′low·ly** *adv.* —**mel′low·ness** *n.*

**me·lo·de·on** (mə lō′dē ən) *n.* [G. *melodion* < *melodie*, melody] a small keyboard organ in which air is drawn through metal reeds by means of a bellows

**me·lod·ic** (mə läd′ik) *adj.* **1.** of or like melody **2.** *same as* MELODIOUS —**me·lod′i·cal·ly** *adv.*

**me·lo·di·ous** (mə lō′dē əs) *adj.* **1.** containing or producing melody **2.** pleasing to hear; tuneful —**me·lo′di·ous·ly** *adv.* —**me·lo′di·ous·ness** *n.*

**mel·o·dist** (mel′ə dist) *n.* a singer or composer of melodies

**mel·o·dra·ma** (mel′ə drä′mə, -dram′ə) *n.* [< Fr., ult. < Gr. *melos*, a song + *drama*, drama] **1.** orig., a sensational or romantic stage play with interspersed songs **2.** now, a drama with exaggerated conflicts and emotions, stereotyped characters, etc. **3.** any sensational, highly emotional action, utterance, etc. —**mel′o·dram′a·tist** (-dram′ə tist) *n.*

**mel·o·dra·mat·ic** (mel′ə drə mat′ik) *adj.* of or like melodrama; sensational and extravagantly emotional —**mel′o·dra·mat′i·cal·ly** *adv.* —**mel′o·dra·mat′ics** *n.pl.*

**mel·o·dy** (mel′ə dē) *n., pl.* **-dies** [< OFr. < LL. < Gr. *melōidia* < *melos*, song + *aeidein*, to sing] **1.** any pleasing series of sounds **2.** *Music a)* a sequence of single tones to produce a rhythmic whole; often, a tune, song, etc. *b)* the leading part in a harmonic composition

**mel·on** (mel′ən) *n.* [< OFr. < LL. *melo* for L. *melopepo* < Gr. < *mēlon*, apple + *pepōn*, melon] the large, juicy, many-seeded fruit of certain trailing plants of the gourd family, as the watermelon, cantaloupe, etc. —**cut a melon** [Slang] to distribute profits, etc., as among stockholders

**Mel·pom·e·ne** (mel päm′ə nē′) *Gr. Myth.* the Muse of tragedy

**melt** (melt) *vt., vi.* **melt′ed, melt′ing,** archaic pp. **molt′en** [OE. *meltan, vi., mieltan, vt.*] **1.** to change from a solid to a liquid state, generally by heat **2.** to dissolve; disintegrate **3.** to disappear or cause to disappear gradually (often with *away*) **4.** to merge gradually; blend *[the sea melts into the sky]* **5.** to soften *[a tale to melt hearts]* —*n.* a melting or being melted —**melt down** to melt (previously formed metal) so that it can be cast or molded again —**melt in one's mouth 1.** to require little chewing **2.** to taste especially delicious —**melt′a·ble** *adj.* —**melt′er** *n.* —**melt′ing·ly** *adv.*

**melt·down** (-doun′) *n.* a situation in which dangerous radiation is released by a nuclear reactor if the fuel rods melt because of a defect in the cooling system

**melting point** the temperature at which a specified solid becomes liquid: abbrev. **melt. pt.**

**melting pot** a country, etc. in which people of various nationalities and races are assimilated

**mel·ton** (mel′t'n) *n.* [< *Melton* Mowbray, England] a heavy woolen cloth with a short nap

**Mel·ville** (mel′vil), **Herman** 1819–91; U.S. novelist

**Mel·vin** (mel′vin) [< ? OE. *mæl*, council + *wine*, friend] a masculine name

**mem. 1.** member **2.** memorandum

**mem·ber** (mem′bər) *n.* [< OE. < L. *membrum*] **1.** a limb or other part or organ of a person, animal, or plant **2.** a distinct part of a whole, as of a series, an equation, a structure, etc. **3.** a person belonging to an organization or group

**mem·ber·ship** (-ship′) *n.* **1.** the state of being a member **2.** all the members of a group **3.** the number of members

**mem·brane** (mem′brān) *n.* [L. *membrana* < *membrum*, member] a thin, soft, pliable layer of animal or plant tissue that covers or lines an organ or part —**mem′braned** *adj.* —**mem′bra·nous** (-brə nəs) *adj.* —**mem′bra·nous·ly** *adv.*

**me·men·to** (mi men′tō, mə-) *n., pl.* **-tos, -toes** [L., imperative of *meminisse*, to remember] anything serving as a reminder; esp., a souvenir

‡**me·men·to mo·ri** (mi men′tō mō′rī, -rē) [L., remember you must die] any reminder of death

**mem·o** (mem′ō) *n., pl.* **-os** *clipped form of* MEMORANDUM

**mem·oir** (mem′wär) *n.* [< Fr. *mémoire* < L. *memoria*, MEMORY] **1.** a biography **2.** [*pl.*] an autobiography **3.** [*pl.*] a record of events based on the writer's personal observation or knowledge **4.** a report of a scientific study, etc.

**mem·o·ra·bil·i·a** (mem′ər ə bil′ē ə, -bil′yə; -bēl′-) *n.pl., sing.* **mem′o·rab′i·le** (-ə rab′ə lē) [L.] things worth remembering or recording and collecting

**mem·o·ra·ble** (mem′ər ə b'l, mem′rə-) *adj.* worth remembering; notable —**mem′o·ra·bil′i·ty** *n.* —**mem′o·ra·bly** *adv.*

**mem·o·ran·dum** (mem′ə ran′dəm) *n., pl.* **-dums, -da** (-də) [L.] **1.** *a)* a short note written to help one remember something *b)* a record, as of events, for future use **2.** an informal written communication, as in a business office **3.** a short written statement of the terms of an agreement, contract, or transaction

**me·mo·ri·al** (mə môr′ē əl) *adj.* [see MEMORY] serving to help people remember some person or event —*n.* **1.** anything meant to help people remember some person or event, as a statue, holiday, etc. **2.** a statement of facts, often with a petition for action, sent to a government, official, etc.

**Memorial Day** a U.S. holiday (the last Monday in May in most States) in memory of dead servicemen of all wars

**me·mo·ri·al·ize** (-īz′) *vt.* **-ized′, -iz′ing 1.** to commemorate **2.** to present a petition to

**mem·o·rize** (mem′ə rīz′) *vt.* **-rized′, -riz′ing** to commit to memory —**mem′o·ri·za′tion** *n.*

**mem·o·ry** (mem′ər ē, mem′rē) *n., pl.* **-ries** [< OFr. < L. *memoria* < *memor*, mindful] **1.** the power, act, or process of recalling to mind facts or experiences **2.** the total of what one remembers **3.** a person, thing, etc. remembered **4.** the period over which remembering extends *[within the memory of living men]* **5.** commemoration or remembrance *[in memory of his son]* **6.** reputation after death **7.** the components of a computer, etc. that retain information

**Mem·phis** (mem′fis) **1.** capital of ancient Egypt, on the Nile just south of Cairo **2.** [after prec.] city in SW Tenn., on the Mississippi: pop. 646,000 (met. area 910,000)

**mem·sa·hib** (mem sä′ib, -säb′) *n.* [Anglo-Ind.: *mem* for MA'AM + Hindi *sāhib*, SAHIB] in India formerly, a term of address for a European married woman as used by servants, etc.

**men** (men) *n. pl. of* MAN

**men·ace** (men′is) *n.* [< OFr. < L. *minacia* < *minax*, threatening < *minari*, to threaten] **1.** a threat or threatening **2.** anything threatening harm or evil **3.** [Colloq.] an annoying person —*vt., vi.* **-aced, -ac·ing** to threaten —**men′ac·ing·ly** *adv.*

**me·nad** (mē′nad) *n. alt. sp. of* MAENAD

**mé·nage, me·nage** (mā näzh′, mə-) *n.* [< Fr. < OFr. *manage* < *manoir* (see MANOR)] **1.** a household **2.** the management of a household

**me·nag·er·ie** (mə naj′ər ē, -nazh′-) *n.* [< Fr. < *ménage*: see prec.] **1.** a collection of wild animals kept in cages for exhibition **2.** a place where such animals are kept

**Men·cken** (men′k'n), **H(enry) L(ouis)** 1880–1956; U.S. writer, editor, & critic

**mend** (mend) *vt.* [ME. *menden*, shortened from *amenden*, AMEND] **1.** to repair; restore to good condition **2.** to make better; improve; reform *[mend your manners]* **3.** to atone for: now only in **least said, soonest mended** —*vi.* **1.** to improve, esp. in health **2.** to grow together again or heal,

---

fat, āpe, cär, ten, ēven, is, bīte; gō, hôrn, tōol, look; oil, out; up, fur; get; joy; yet; chin; she; thin, *then*; zh, leisure; ŋ, ring; ə for *a* in *ago*, *e* in *agent*, *i* in *sanity*, *o* in *comply*, *u* in *focus*; ´ as in *able* (ā′b'l); Fr. bal; ë, Fr. coeur; ö, Fr. feu; Fr. mon; ö, Fr. coq; ü, Fr. duc; r, Fr. cri; H, G. ich; kh, G. doch; ‡foreign; *hypothetical; < derived from. See inside front cover.

as a fracture —*n.* **1.** a mending; improvement **2.** a mended place —**on the mend** improving, esp. in health —**mend′a·ble** *adj.* —**mend′er** *n.*

**men·da·cious** (men dā′shəs) *adj.* [< L. *mendax* (gen. *mendacis*)] not truthful; lying; false —**men·da′cious·ly** *adv.* —**men·da′cious·ness** *n.* —**men·dac·i·ty** (-das′ə tē) *n., pl.* **-ties**

**Men·del** (men′d'l), **Gre·gor Jo·hann** (grā′gôr yō′hän) 1822–84; Austrian monk & botanist: see MENDEL'S LAWS —**Men·de′li·an** (-dē′lē ən, -dēl′yən) *adj.* —**Men′del·ism** *n.* —**Men′del·ist** *adj., n.*

**men·de·le·vi·um** (men′də lē′vē əm) *n.* [ModL., after D.I. *Mendeleev* (1834–1907), Russ. chemist] a radioactive chemical element of the actinide series: symbol, Md; at. wt., 258(?); at. no., 101

**Mendel's laws** the principles of hereditary phenomena discovered and formulated by Mendel, holding that characters, as height, color, etc., are inherited in definite, predictable combinations

**Men·dels·sohn** (men′d'l sən; *G.* -dəls zōn′), **Fe·lix** (fā′liks) 1809–47; Ger. composer

**men·di·cant** (men′di kənt) *adj.* [< L. prp. of *mendicare*, to beg] asking for alms; begging [*mendicant* friars] —*n.* **1.** a beggar **2.** a mendicant friar —**men′di·can·cy, men·dic·i·ty** (mən dis′ə tē) *n.*

**Men·e·la·us** (men′ə lā′əs) *Gr. Myth.* a king of Sparta, brother of Agamemnon, and husband of Helen

**men·folk** (men′fōk′) *n.pl.* [Dial. or Colloq.] men: also **men′folks′**

**men·ha·den** (men hād′'n) *n., pl.* **-den, -dens:** see PLURAL, II, D, 2 [< Algonquian name] a sea fish related to the herring, common along the Atlantic coast: used for making oil and fertilizer

**me·ni·al** (mē′nē əl, mēn′yəl) *adj.* [< Anglo-Fr. < OFr. *meisniee*, household < L. *mansio:* see MANSION] **1.** of or fit for servants **2.** servile; low; mean —*n.* **1.** a domestic servant **2.** a servile, low person —**me′ni·al·ly** *adv.*

**me·nin·ges** (mə nin′jēz) *n.pl., sing.* **me·ninx** (mē′niŋks) [ModL., pl. of *meninx* < Gr. *mēninx*, a membrane] the three membranes that envelop the brain and spinal cord —**me·nin′ge·al** (-jē əl) *adj.*

**men·in·gi·tis** (men′in jīt′is) *n.* inflammation of the meninges, esp. as the result of infection —**men′in·git′ic** (-jit′ik) *adj.*

**me·nis·cus** (mi nis′kəs) *n., pl.* **-nis′cus·es, -nis′ci** (-nis′ī, -kī) [ModL. < Gr. *mēniskos*, dim. of *mēnē*, the moon] **1.** a crescent-shaped thing **2.** a lens convex on one side and concave on the other **3.** the curved upper surface of a column of liquid

**Men·non·ite** (men′ə nīt′) *n.* [after *Menno* Simons (1496?–1561?), a leader] a member of an evangelical Christian sect: Mennonites oppose the taking of oaths and military service, and favor plain dress

MENISCUS
(left, mercury;
right, water)

**‡me·no** (me′nō) *adv.* [It.] *Music* less

**men·o·pause** (men′ə pôz′) *n.* [< Gr. *mēn*, month + *pauein*, to make cease] the permanent cessation of menstruation; change of life —**men′o·paus′al** *adj.*

**men·o·rah** (mə nō′rə, -nôr′ə) *n.* [Heb., lamp stand] a candelabrum with seven branches, a symbol of Judaism, or with nine branches, used during Hanuka

**Me·nor·ca** (me nôr′kä) *Sp. name of* MINORCA

**Me·not·ti** (me nät′ē), **Gian Car·lo** (jän kär′lō) 1911– ; It. operatic composer, in U.S. since 1928

**men·ses** (men′sēz) *n.pl.* [L., pl. of *mensis*, month] the periodic flow of blood from the uterus: normally every four weeks, from puberty to menopause

**Men·she·vik** (men′shə vik′) *n., pl.* **-viks′, -vik′i** (-vē′kē) [Russ. < *menshe*, the smaller] [*also* m-] a member of the minority faction of the Social Democratic Party of Russia, which opposed the Bolsheviks from 1903 on —**Men′she·vism** *n.* —**Men′she·vist** *n., adj.*

**men·stru·ate** (men′strōō wāt′, -strāt) *vi.* **-at′ed, -at′ing** [< L. pp. of *menstruare* < *mensis*, month] to have a discharge of the menses —**men′stru·al** *adj.* —**men′stru·a′tion** *n.*

**men·sur·a·ble** (men′shər ə b'l, -sər-) *adj.* that can be measured; measurable —**men′sur·a·bil′i·ty** *n.*

**men·su·ra·tion** (men′shə rā′shən, -sə-) *n.* [< LL. < pp. of *mensurare* < L. *mensura*, MEASURE] **1.** a measuring **2.** the branch of mathematics dealing with the determination of length, area, or volume —**men′su·ra′tive** (-rāt′iv) *adj.*

**-ment** (mənt, mint) [< OFr. < L. *-mentum*] a suffix meaning: **1.** a result or product [*improvement*] **2.** a means or instrument [*adornment*] **3.** the act, process, or art [*movement*] **4.** the state, fact, or degree [*disappointment*]

**men·tal** (men′t'l) *adj.* [< MFr. < LL. < L. *mens* (gen. *mentis*), the mind] **1.** of or for the mind [*mental* aids] **2.** done by or in the mind [*mental* arithmetic] **3.** mentally ill [a *mental* patient] **4.** for the mentally ill [a *mental* hospital] **5.** having to do with telepathy, etc. —**men′tal·ly** *adv.*

**mental healing** the treatment of diseases by mental concentration or hypnotic suggestion

**men·tal·i·ty** (men tal′ə tē) *n., pl.* **-ties** mental capacity, power, or activity; mind

**mental reservation** a qualification (of a statement) that one thinks but does not express

**mental retardation** congenital subnormality of intelligence: it ranges from *mild* (IQ of 70–85) to *moderate* (IQ of 50–70) and *severe* (IQ below 50): these terms have replaced *moron, imbecile,* and *idiot:* formerly called **mental deficiency**

**men·thol** (men′thôl, -thôl, -thäl) *n.* [G. < L. *mentha*, MINT² + *-ol*, -OL¹] a white, waxy, crystalline alcohol, $C_{10}H_{19}OH$, obtained from oil of peppermint and used in medicine, cosmetics, etc.

**men·tho·lat·ed** (men′thə lāt′id) *adj.* containing or impregnated with menthol

**men·tion** (men′shən) *n.* [OFr. < L. *mentio* < stem of *mens,* the mind] **1.** a brief reference or statement **2.** a citing for honor —*vt.* **1.** to refer to or speak about briefly or incidentally **2.** to cite for honor —**make mention of** to mention —**not to mention** without even mentioning —**men′tion·a·ble** *adj.*

**Men·tor** (men′tər, -tôr) *Gr. Myth.* the loyal friend and adviser of Odysseus —*n.* [m-] **1.** a wise, loyal adviser **2.** a teacher or coach

**men·u** (men′yōō, mān′-) *n., pl.* **men′us** [Fr., small, detailed < L. *minutus:* see MINUTE²] **1.** a detailed list of the foods served at a meal or available at a restaurant **2.** the foods served

**me·ow, me·ou** (mē ou′, myou) *n.* [echoic] the characteristic vocal sound made by a cat —*vi.* to make such a sound

**me·per·i·dine** (mə per′ə dēn′) *n.* a synthetic narcotic, $C_{15}H_{21}O_2N$, used as a sedative and analgesic

**Meph·i·stoph·e·les** (mef′ə stäf′ə lēz′) a devil in medieval legend to whom Faust sells his soul for knowledge and power —*n.* a crafty, powerful, sardonic person Also **Me·phis·to** (mə fis′tō) —**Me·phis·to·phe·le·an, Me·phis·to·phe·li·an** (mef′is tə fē′lē ən, mə fis′-) *adj.*

**me·phit·ic** (mə fit′ik) *adj.* [< L. *mephitis,* a stench] **1.** bad-smelling **2.** poisonous; noxious

**me·pro·ba·mate** (mə prō′bə mat′) *n.* a bitter, white powder, $C_9H_{18}N_2O_4$, used as a tranquilizer

**mer·can·tile** (mur′kən til, -tīl′, -tēl′) *adj.* [Fr. < It. < *mercante,* a merchant < L. prp. of *mercari:* see MERCHANT] **1.** of or characteristic of merchants or trade; commercial **2.** of mercantilism

**mer·can·til·ism** (-iz'm) *n.* the earlier doctrine that the economic interests of a nation could be strengthened by the government through protective tariffs, by a balance of exports over imports, etc. —**mer′can·til·ist** *n., adj.*

**Mer·ca·tor projection** (mər kāt′ər) [after G. *Mercator* (1512–94), Fl. cartographer] a method of making maps on which the meridians are equally spaced parallel straight lines and the parallels of latitude are parallel straight lines spaced farther apart as they get farther from the equator: areas are increasingly distorted toward the poles

**mer·ce·nar·y** (mur′sə ner′ē) *adj.* [< L. < *merces,* wages] **1.** working or done for payment only; venal; greedy **2.** designating a soldier serving for pay in a foreign army —*n., pl.* **-nar′ies 1.** a mercenary soldier **2.** a hireling —**mer′ce·nar′i·ly** *adv.* —**mer′ce·nar′i·ness** *n.*

**mer·cer** (mur′sər) *n.* [< OFr. < *merz,* goods < L. *merx*] [Brit.] a dealer in textiles

**mer·cer·ize** (mur′sə rīz′) *vt.* **-ized′, -iz′ing** [after J. *Mercer* (1791–1866), Eng. calico dealer] to treat (cotton thread or fabric) with a caustic soda solution in order to strengthen it, give it a silky luster, and make it more receptive to dyes

**mer·chan·dise** (mur′chən dīz′; *for n., also* -dis′) *n.* [< OFr. < *marchant:* see ff.] things bought and sold; goods; wares —*vt., vi.* **-dised′, -dis′ing 1.** to buy and sell; carry on trade in (some kind of goods) **2.** to promote and organize the sale of (a product) Also sp. **merchandize** —**mer′chan·dis′er** *n.*

**mer·chant** (mur′chənt) *n.* [OFr. *marchant,* ult. < L. *mercari,* to trade < *merx,* wares] **1.** a person whose business is buying and selling goods for profit **2.** a person who sells goods at retail; storekeeper —*adj.* **1.** of or used in trade **2.** of the merchant marine —*vt.* to deal in; trade

**mer·chant·a·ble** (-ə b'l) *adj.* that can be sold; marketable

**mer·chant·man** (-mən) *n., pl.* **-men** a ship used in commerce

**merchant marine 1.** all the ships of a nation that are used in commerce **2.** their personnel

**‡mer·ci** (mer sē′) *interj.* [Fr.] thank you

**Mer·cia** (mur′shə) former Anglo-Saxon kingdom in central and southern England

**Mer·cian** (-shən) *adj.* of Mercia, its people, etc. —*n.* **1.** a native or inhabitant of Mercia **2.** the Old English dialect of the Mercians

**mer·ci·ful** (mur'si fəl) *adj.* full of mercy; having, feeling, or showing mercy; lenient; clement —**mer'ci·ful·ly** *adv.* —**mer'ci·ful·ness** *n.*

**mer·ci·less** (-lis) *adj.* without mercy; having, feeling, or showing no mercy; pitiless; cruel —**mer'ci·less·ly** *adv.* —**mer'ci·less·ness** *n.*

**mer·cu·ri·al** (mər kyoor'ē əl) *adj.* 1. [M-] of Mercury (the god or planet) 2. of or containing mercury 3. caused by the use of mercury 4. having qualities suggestive of mercury; quick, quick-witted, changeable, fickle, etc. —*n.* a drug or preparation containing mercury —**mer·cu'ri·al·ly** *adv.* —**mer·cu'ri·al·ness** *n.*

**mer·cu·ric** (mər kyoor'ik) *adj.* of or containing mercury, esp. with a valence of two

**mercuric chloride** a very poisonous, white, crystalline compound, $HgCl_2$, used as an antiseptic, etc.

**Mer·cu·ro·chrome** (mər kyoor'ə krōm') [see MERCURY, *n.* & -CHROME] *a trademark for* a compound used as an antiseptic in the form of a red solution —*n.* [m-] this solution

**mer·cu·rous** (mər kyoor'əs, mur'kyoo rəs) *adj.* of or containing mercury, esp. with a valence of one

**Mer·cu·ry** (mur'kyoo rē) [L. *Mercurius*] 1. *Rom. Myth.* the messenger of the gods, god of commerce, manual skill, eloquence, and cleverness: identified with the Greek god Hermes 2. the smallest planet in the solar system and the one nearest to the sun: diameter, c.3,000 mi. —*n.* [< ML. < L., Mercury] [m-] 1. a heavy, silver-white metallic chemical element, liquid at ordinary temperatures; quicksilver: it is used in thermometers, dentistry, etc.: symbol, Hg; at. wt., 200.59; at. no., 80 2. the mercury column in a thermometer or barometer

**mer·cu·ry-va·por lamp** (-vā'pər) a discharge tube containing mercury vapor

**mer·cy** (mur'sē) *n., pl.* **-cies** [< OFr. < L. *merces*, payment, reward] 1. a refraining from harming or punishing offenders, enemies, etc.; kindness in excess of what may be expected 2. imprisonment rather than death for those found guilty of capital crimes 3. a disposition to forgive or be kind 4. the power to forgive or be kind; clemency 5. kind or compassionate treatment 6. a fortunate thing; blessing —*interj.* a mild exclamation of surprise, annoyance, etc. —**at the mercy of** completely in the power of

**mere**[1] (mir) *adj. superl.* **mer'est** [< L. *merus*, unmixed, pure] nothing more or other than; only (as said to be) *[a mere boy]*

**mere**[2] (mir) *n.* [OE.] 1. [Poet.] a lake or pond 2. [Obs.] the sea or an arm of the sea

**-mere** (mir) [< Gr. *meros*, a part] *a combining form meaning* part

**Mer·e·dith** (mer'ə dith), **George** 1828–1909; Eng. novelist & poet

**mere·ly** (mir'lē) *adv.* 1. no more than; and nothing else; only 2. [Obs.] absolutely

**mer·e·tri·cious** (mer'ə trish'əs) *adj.* [< L. < *meretrix*, a prostitute < *mereri*, to serve for hire] 1. alluring by false, showy charms; flashy; tawdry 2. superficially plausible; specious —**mer'e·tri'cious·ly** *adv.* —**mer'e·tri'cious·ness** *n.*

**mer·gan·ser** (mər gan'sər) *n., pl.* **-sers, -ser:** see PLURAL, II, D, 1 [ModL. < L. *mergus*, diver + *anser*, goose] a large, fish-eating, diving duck with a long, slender beak and, usually, a crested head

**merge** (murj) *vi., vt.* **merged, merg'ing** [L. *mergere*, to dip] 1. to lose or cause to lose identity by being absorbed, swallowed up, or combined 2. to unite; combine

**merg·er** (mur'jər) *n.* a merging; specif., the combination of several companies, corporations, etc. in one

**Mer·i·den** (mer'i dən) [MERRY + DEN (in obs. sense of "valley")] city in C Conn.: pop. 57,000

**me·rid·i·an** (mə rid'ē ən) *adj.* [< OFr. < L. < *meridies*, noon, ult. < *medius*, middle + *dies*, day] 1. of or at noon 2. of or passing through the highest point in the daily course of any heavenly body 3. of or at the highest point, as of power 4. of or along a meridian —*n.* 1. orig., the highest point reached by a heavenly body in its course 2. the highest point of power, prosperity, etc.; zenith 3. a great circle of the celestial sphere passing through the poles of the heavens and the zenith and nadir of any given point 4. *a)* a great circle of the earth passing through the

geographical poles and any given point on the earth's surface *b)* the half of such a circle between the poles *c)* any of the lines of longitude on a globe or map, representing such a half circle

**me·ringue** (mə raŋ') *n.* [Fr. < ?] 1. egg whites beaten stiff and mixed with sugar, often browned in the oven and used as a covering for pies, cakes, etc. 2. a baked shell made of this

**me·ri·no** (mə rē'nō) *n., pl.* **-nos** [Sp., prob. < (Beni) *Merin,* name of a nomadic Berber tribe] 1. one of a hardy breed of sheep with long, fine wool 2. the wool 3. a fine, soft yarn made from this wool 4. a soft, thin cloth made of this yarn —*adj.* designating or of this sheep, wool, etc.

**mer·it** (mer'it) *n.* [< OFr. < L. *meritum* < pp. of *mereri*, to earn] 1. [*sometimes pl.*] the state, fact, or quality of deserving well or ill; desert 2. worth; value; excellence 3. something deserving reward, praise, etc. 4. a mark, badge, etc. awarded for excellence 5. [*pl.*] essential rightness or wrongness *[to decide a case on its merits]* —*vt.* to deserve —**mer'it·less** *adj.*

**mer·i·toc·ra·cy** (mer'ə täk'rə sē) *n.* an intellectual elite, based on academic achievement —**mer'it·o·crat'** *n.* —**mer'it·o·crat'ic** *adj.*

**mer·i·to·ri·ous** (mer'ə tôr'ē əs) *adj.* having merit; deserving reward, praise, etc. —**mer'i·to'ri·ous·ly** *adv.* —**mer'i·to'ri·ous·ness** *n.*

**merit system** a system of hiring and promoting people to civil service positions on the basis of merit as determined by competitive examinations

**merl, merle** (murl) *n.* [< OFr. < L. *merula*] [Archaic or Poet.] the European blackbird

**Merle** (murl) [Fr., prob. < *merle*, blackbird: see prec.] a masculine or feminine name

**Mer·lin** (mur'lin) *Arthurian Legend* a magician and seer, helper of King Arthur

**mer·maid** (mur'mād') *n.* [see MERE[2] & MAID] 1. an imaginary sea creature with the body of a beautiful woman and the tail of a fish 2. a woman who swims well —**mer'man'** *n.masc., pl.* **-men'**

**-mer·ous** (mər əs) [< Gr. *meros*, a part] *a suffix meaning* having (a specified number of) parts

**Mer·o·vin·gi·an** (mer'ə vin'jē ən, -jən) *adj.* designating or of the Frankish line of kings who reigned in Gaul (ancient France) from c. 500 to 751 A.D. —*n.* a king of this line

**mer·ri·ment** (mer'i mənt) *n.* merrymaking; gaiety and fun; mirth; hilarity

**mer·ry** (mer'ē) *adj.* **-ri·er, -ri·est** [OE. *myrge*] 1. full of fun and laughter; gay; mirthful 2. festive *[the merry month of May]* —**make merry** to have fun —**mer'ri·ly** *adv.* —**mer'ri·ness** *n.*

**mer·ry-an·drew** (mer'ē an'drōō) *n.* [MERRY + ANDREW: orig. unc.] a buffoon; clown

**mer·ry-go-round** (-gō round') *n.* 1. a circular, revolving platform with wooden animals and seats on it, used as an amusement ride; carrousel 2. a whirl or busy round, as of pleasure

**mer·ry·mak·ing** (-mā'kiŋ) *n.* 1. a making merry and having fun; conviviality; festivity 2. a merry festival or entertainment —*adj.* taking part in merrymaking; gay and festive —**mer'ry·mak'er** *n.*

**Mer·sey** (mur'zē) river in NW England, flowing into the Irish Sea at Liverpool

**Mer·thi·o·late** (mər thī'ə lāt') [*sodium ethyl-*) *mer-(curi-)thio(salicy)late*] *a trademark for* a compound used chiefly in solutions as an antiseptic for surface wounds

**Mer·vin** (mur'vin) [prob. var. of MARVIN] a masculine name: var. **Mervyn, Merwin, Merwyn**

**Me·sa** (mā'sə) [see ff.] city in SC Ariz., near Phoenix: pop. 152,000

**me·sa** (mā'sə) *n.* [Sp. < L. *mensa*, a table] a small, high plateau or flat tableland with steep sides, esp. in the SW U.S.

**mes·cal** (mes kal') *n.* [Sp. *mezcal* < Nahuatl *mexcalli*] 1. a colorless, alcoholic, Mexican liquor made from the fermented juice of various agaves 2. any plant from which this liquor is made 3. a small cactus whose buttonlike tops (**mescal buttons**) when chewed cause hallucinations

**mes·ca·line** (mes'kə lēn', -lin) *n.* [prec. + -INE[4]] a white, crystalline alkaloid, $C_{11}H_{17}O_3N$, a psychedelic drug obtained from mescal buttons

**mes·dames** (mā däm'; Fr. mā dàm') *n. pl. of* MADAME, MADAM (sense 1), or MRS.: abbrev. **Mmes.**

**mes·de·moi·selles** (mā'də mə zel'; Fr. mād mwà zel') *n. pl. of* MADEMOISELLE: abbrev. **Mlles.**

**me·seems** (mē sēmz') *v.impersonal pt.* **me·seemed'** [Archaic] (it) seems to me: also **me·seem'eth**

**mes·en·ter·y** (mez'n ter'ē, mes'-) *n., pl.* **-ter'ies** [< ML. < Gr. < *mesos*, middle + *enteron*, intestine] a supporting

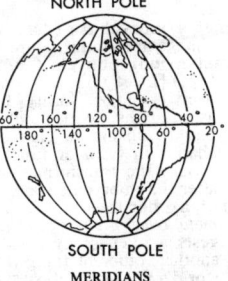

NORTH POLE

SOUTH POLE

MERIDIANS

membrane or membranes enfolding some internal organ and attaching it to the body wall or to another organ —**mes′en·ter′ic** *adj.*

**mesh** (mesh) *n.* [prob. < MDu. *maesche*] **1.** any of the open spaces of a net, screen, sieve, etc. **2.** [*pl.*] the threads, cords, etc. forming these openings **3.** a net or network **4.** a netlike, woven material, as that used for stockings **5.** a structure of interlocking metal links **6.** anything that entangles or snares —*vt., vi.* **1.** to entangle or become entangled **2.** to engage or become engaged: said of gears or gear teeth **3.** to interlock —**in mesh** in gear; interlocked —**mesh′y** *adj.*

‡**me·shu·ga** (mə shoog′ə) *adj.* [< Yid. < Heb.] crazy; insane: also **meshugga, meshugah,** etc.

**mesh·work** (mesh′wurk′) *n.* meshes; network

**mes·mer·ism** (mez′mər iz′m, mes′-) *n.* [after F. A. *Mesmer* (1734–1815), G. physician] **1.** hypnotism **2.** irresistible attraction —**mes·mer′ic** (-mer′ik) *adj.* —**mes·mer′i·cal·ly** *adv.* —**mes′mer·ist** *n.*

**mes·mer·ize** (-īz′) *vt.* **-ized′, -iz′ing** to hypnotize; esp., to spellbind, or fascinate —**mes′mer·i·za′tion** *n.* —**mes′mer·iz′er** *n.*

**mes·o-** [< Gr. *mesos*, middle] *a combining form meaning* in the middle, intermediate: also **mes-**

**mes·o·blast** (mes′ə blast′, mez′-) *n.* [MESO- + -BLAST] *same as* MESODERM —**mes′o·blas′tic** *adj.*

**mes·o·carp** (-kärp′) *n.* [MESO- + -CARP] the middle layer of the wall of a ripened ovary or fruit, as the flesh of a plum —**mes′o·car′pic** *adj.*

**mes·o·derm** (-durm′) *n.* [MESO- + -DERM] the middle layer of cells of an embryo, from which the skeleton, muscles, etc. develop —**mes′o·der′mal, mes′o·der′mic** *adj.*

**mes·o·lith·ic** (mes′ə lith′ik, mez′-) *adj.* [MESO- + -LITHIC] designating or of an old-world cultural period between the paleolithic and neolithic, during which certain animals and plants were domesticated

**mes·o·mor·phic** (-môr′fik) *adj.* [MESO- + -MORPHIC] designating or of the muscular type of human body, in which the structures developed from the mesoderm predominate —**mes′o·morph′** *n.*

**mes·on** (mes′än, mez′-; mē′sän, -zän) *n.* [MES(O)- + (ELECTR)ON] an unstable particle between the electron and proton in mass, first observed in cosmic rays —**me·son·ic** (me sän′ik, -zän′-; mē-) *adj.*

**Mes·o·po·ta·mi·a** (mes′ə pə tā′mē ə) ancient country in SW Asia, between the Tigris & Euphrates rivers: part of modern Iraq —**Mes′o·po·ta′mi·an** *adj., n.*

**Mes·o·zo·ic** (mes′ə zō′ik, mez′-) *adj.* [MESO- + ZO- + -IC] designating or of a geologic era after the Paleozoic and before the Cenozoic —**the Mesozoic** the Mesozoic Era or its rocks: see GEOLOGY, chart

**Mes·quite** (mes kēt′) [after the *mesquite* trees found there] city in NE Tex.: suburb of Dallas: pop. 67,000

**mes·quite, mes·quit** (mes kēt′, mes′kēt) *n.* [Sp. *mezquite* < Nahuatl *mizquitl*] a thorny tree or shrub common in the SW U.S. and in Mexico: its sugary, beanlike pods are used as fodder

**mess** (mes) *n.* [< OFr. < L. *missus*, a course (at a meal)] **1.** a quantity of food for a meal or dish **2.** a portion of soft food, as porridge **3.** unappetizing food **4.** *a)* a group of people who regularly have their meals together, as in the army *b)* the meal eaten by such a group **5.** a jumble; hodgepodge **6.** *a)* a state of trouble or difficulty *b)* a state of being untidy or dirty *c)* [Colloq.] a person in either of these states —*vt.* **1.** to supply meals to **2.** to make dirty or untidy; also, to bungle; botch: often with *up* —*vi.* **1.** to eat as one of a mess (sense 4 *a*) **2.** to make a mess **3.** to putter or meddle —**mess around (or about) 1.** to putter around **2.** [Colloq.] to get involved (*with*)

**mes·sage** (mes′ij) *n.* [OFr. < ML. < pp. of L. *mittere*, to send] **1.** a report, request, etc. sent between persons **2.** a formal, official report /the President's *message* to Congress] **3.** the chief idea that an artist, writer, etc. seeks to communicate in a work —*vt., vi.* **-saged, -sag·ing** to send (as) a message —**get the message** [Colloq.] to get the implications of a hint, etc.

**mes·sen·ger** (mes′'n jər) *n.* [< OFr. *messagier:* see MESSAGE] **1.** a person who carries a message or is sent on an errand **2.** [Archaic] a harbinger

**mess hall** a room or building where a group, as of soldiers, regularly have their meals

**Mes·si·ah** (mə sī′ə) [< LL. < Gr. *Messias* < Aram. < Heb. *māshīah*, lit., anointed] **1.** *Judaism* the promised and expected deliverer of the Jews **2.** *Christianity* Jesus Also **Mes·si′as** (-əs) —*n.* [m-] any expected savior —**Mes·si·an·ic** (mes′ē an′ik) *adj.*

**mes·sieurs** (mes′ərz; *Fr.* mā syö′) *n. pl. of* MONSIEUR: abbrev. MM.: see also MESSRS.

**Mes·si·na** (mə sē′nə, me-) seaport in NE Sicily, on a strait ( **Strait of Messina** ) between Sicily & Italy: pop. 269,000

**mess jacket** a man's short, closefitting jacket, as that worn by waiters or busboys

**mess kit** the compactly arranged metal or plastic plates and eating utensils carried by a soldier or camper for use in the field: also **mess gear**

**mess·mate** (mes′māt′) *n.* a person with whom one regularly has meals, as in the army

**Messrs.** (mes′ərz) Messieurs: now used chiefly as the pl. of MR.

**mess·y** (mes′ē) *adj.* **mess′i·er, mess′i·est** in or like a mess; untidy, disordered, dirty, etc. —**mess′i·ly** *adv.* —**mess′i·ness** *n.*

**mes·ti·zo** (mes tē′zō) *n., pl.* **-zos, -zoes** [Sp. < LL. *misticius,* of mixed race < L. pp. of *miscere,* to mix] a person of mixed parentage; esp., the offspring of a Spaniard and an American Indian —**mes·ti′za** (-zə) *n.fem.*

**met** (met) *pt. & pp. of* MEET¹

**met.** metropolitan

**met·a-** [< Gr. *meta,* along with, after, between] *a prefix meaning:* **1.** changed, transposed *[metamorphosis, metathesis]* **2.** after, beyond, higher *[metaphysics]* Also, before a vowel, **met-**

**me·tab·o·lism** (mə tab′ə liz′m) *n.* [< Gr. *metabolē,* change < *meta,* beyond + *ballein,* to throw] the continuous processes in living organisms and cells, comprising those by which food is built up into protoplasm and those by which protoplasm is broken down into simpler substances or waste matter, with the release of energy for all vital functions —**met·a·bol·ic** (met′ə bäl′ik) *adj.*

**me·tab·o·lize** (-līz′) *vt., vi.* **-lized′, -liz′ing** to change by or subject to metabolism —**me·tab′o·liz′a·ble** *adj.*

**me·tab·o·lous** (-ləs) *adj.* [< Gr. *metabolos,* changeable + -OUS] of or undergoing metamorphosis

**met·a·car·pus** (met′ə kär′pəs) *n., pl.* **-pi** (-pī) [ModL. < Gr. < *meta,* beyond + *karpos,* the wrist] **1.** the part of the hand consisting of the five bones between the wrist and the fingers **2.** the part of a land vertebrate's forelimb between the carpus and the phalanges —**met′a·car′pal** *adj., n.*

**met·al** (met′'l) *n.* [OFr. < L. *metallum* < Gr. *metallon,* mine] **1.** *a)* any of a class of chemical elements, as iron, gold, aluminum, etc., generally characterized by ductility, luster, conductivity of heat and electricity, and the ability to replace the hydrogen of an acid to form a salt *b)* an alloy of such elements, as brass, bronze, etc. **2.** any substance consisting of metal **3.** material; substance **4.** molten material for making glassware **5.** [Brit.] broken stones, cinders, etc. used as in making roads —*adj.* made of metal —*vt.* **-aled** or **-alled, -al·ing** or **-al·ling** to cover or supply with metal

**metal., metall. 1.** metallurgical **2.** metallurgy

**metal lath** lath of expanded metal or metal mesh

**me·tal·lic** (mə tal′ik) *adj.* **1.** of, or having the nature of, metal **2.** containing, yielding, or producing metal **3.** like or suggestive of metal /a *metallic* sound] —**me·tal′li·cal·ly** *adv.*

**met·al·lif·er·ous** (met′'l if′ər əs) *adj.* [< L. < *metallum,* metal + *ferre,* to BEAR¹ + -OUS] containing, yielding, or producing metal or ore

**met·al·lur·gy** (met′'l ur′jē) *n.* [ModL. < Gr. < *metallon,* metal, mine + *ergon,* work] the science of separating metals from their ores and preparing them for use, by smelting, refining, etc. —**met′al·lur′gi·cal, met′al·lur′gic** *adj.* —**met′al·lur′gi·cal·ly** *adv.* —**met′al·lur′gist** *n.*

**met·al·ware** (-wer′) *n.* kitchenware, etc. of metal

**met·al·work** (-wurk′) *n.* **1.** things made of metal **2.** the making of such things: also **met′al·work′ing** —**met′al·work′er** *n.*

**met·a·mor·phic** (met′ə môr′fik) *adj.* of, characterized by, causing, or formed by metamorphism or metamorphosis

**met·a·mor·phism** (-môr′fiz′m) *n.* **1.** *same as* METAMORPHOSIS **2.** change in the structure of rocks under pressure, heat, etc. which turns limestone into marble, granite into gneiss, etc.

**met·a·mor·phose** (-fōz, -fōs) *vt., vi.* **-phosed, -phos·ing** to change in form or nature; transform

**met·a·mor·pho·sis** (-môr′fə sis, -môr fō′sis) *n., pl.* **-ses** (-sēz) [L. < Gr. < *metamorphoun,* to transform < *meta,* over + *morphē,* form] **1.** *a)* change of form or structure, as, in myths, by magic *b)* the form resulting from this **2.** a marked change of character, appearance, etc. **3.** *Biol.* a change in form or function as a result of development; specif., the transformation undergone by various animals after the embryonic state, as of the tadpole to the frog

**met·a·phor** (met′ə fôr′, -fər) *n.* [< Fr. < L. < Gr., ult. < *meta,* over + *pherein,* to carry) a figure of speech that suggests a likeness by speaking of one thing as if it were another, different thing (Ex.: the curtain of night, "all the world's a stage"); cf. SIMILE —**mix metaphors** to use two or more inconsistent metaphors in a single expression (Ex.: the storm of protest was nipped in the bud) —**met′a·phor′i·cal, met′a·phor′ic** *adj.* —**met′a·phor′i·cal·ly** *adv.*

**met·a·phys·i·cal** (met′ə fiz′i k'l) *adj.* **1.** of, or having the nature of, metaphysics **2.** so subtle as to be hard to understand **3.** supernatural **4.** designating or of the school of early 17th-cent. English poets, whose verse is characterized by subtle and fanciful images —**met′a·phys′i·cal·ly** adv.

**met·a·phys·ics** (met′ə fiz′iks) n.pl. [with sing. v.] [< ML. < Gr. (ta) meta (ta) physika, lit., (that) after (the) Physics (in Aristotle's works)] **1.** the branch of philosophy that deals with first principles and seeks to explain the nature of being and of the origin and structure of the world **2.** speculative philosophy in general —**met′a·phy·si′cian** (-fə zish′ən) n.

**me·tas·ta·sis** (mə tas′tə sis) n., pl. **-ses′** (-sēz′) [ModL. < LL. < Gr. < meta, after + histanai, to place] the spread of disease from one part of the body to another unrelated to it, as of cancer cells by way of the bloodstream —**met·a·stat·ic** (met′ə stat′ik) adj. —**met′a·stat′i·cal·ly** adv.

**me·tas·ta·size** (-sīz′) vi. **-sized′, -siz′ing** to spread to other parts of the body by metastasis

**met·a·tar·sus** (met′ə tär′səs) n., pl. **-tar′si** (-sī) [ModL. < Gr. meta-, after + tarsus, sole of the foot] **1.** the part of the human foot consisting of the five bones between the ankle and toes **2.** the part of a land vertebrate's hind limb, between the tarsus and phalanges —**met′a·tar′sal** adj., n.

**me·tath·e·sis** (mə tath′ə sis) n., pl. **-ses′** (-sēz′) [LL. < Gr. < meta, over + tithenai, to place] transposition or interchange; specif., the transposition of letters or sounds in a word, as in clasp (from Middle English clapse) —**met·a·thet·ic** (met′ə thet′ik), **met′a·thet′i·cal** adj.

**met·a·zo·an** (met′ə zō′ən) n. [ModL. metazoa (see META- & -ZOA) + -AN] any of the very large zoological division made up of all animals whose bodies are composed of many cells arranged into definite organs —adj. of the metazoans

**mete¹** (mēt) vt. **met′ed, met′ing** [OE. metan] **1.** to allot; apportion (usually with out) **2.** [Archaic] to measure

**mete²** (mēt) n. [OFr. < L. meta] a boundary

**me·tem·psy·cho·sis** (mi temp′si kō′sis, -tem′-; met′əm-sī-) n., pl. **-ses** (-sēz) [LL. < Gr. < meta, over + empsychoun, to put a soul into < en, in + psychē, soul] the supposed passing of the soul at death into another body; transmigration

**me·te·or** (mēt′ē ər) n. [< ML. < Gr. < meteōra, things in the air < meta, beyond + eōra, a hovering in the air] **1.** the flash and streak of light, the ionized trail, etc. occurring when a meteoroid is heated by its entry into the earth's atmosphere: popularly called shooting (or falling) star **2.** loosely, a meteoroid or meteorite

**me·te·or·ic** (mēt′ē ôr′ik, -är′-) adj. **1.** atmospheric or meteorological **2.** of a meteor or meteors **3.** like a meteor; momentarily brilliant, flashing, or swift —**me′te·or′i·cal·ly** adv.

**me·te·or·ite** (mēt′ē ə rīt′) n. that part of a relatively large meteoroid that falls to earth as a mass of metal or stone —**me′te·or·it′ic** (-rit′ik) adj.

**me·te·or·oid** (mēt′ē ə roid′) n. any of the many small, solid bodies traveling through outer space, which are seen as meteors when they enter the earth's atmosphere

**me·te·or·o·log·i·cal** (mēt′ē ər ə läj′i k'l) adj. **1.** of weather or climate **2.** of meteorology: also **me′te·or·o·log′ic** —**me′te·or·o·log′i·cal·ly** adv.

**me·te·or·ol·o·gy** (mēt′ē ə räl′ə jē) n. [< Gr.: see METE-OR & -LOGY] the science of the atmosphere and its phenomena; study of weather and climate —**me′te·or·ol′o·gist** n.

**me·ter¹** (mēt′ər) n. [< OFr. < L. < Gr. metron, measure] **1.** a) rhythm in verse; measured, patterned arrangement of syllables, primarily according to stress and length b) the specific rhythmic pattern of a stanza **2.** rhythm in music; esp., the division into measures, or bars, having a uniform number of beats **3.** the basic unit of length in the metric system, equal to 39.37 inches

**me·ter²** (mēt′ər) n. **1.** [< METE¹ + -ER] a person who measures **2.** [< ff.] a) an instrument or apparatus for measuring and recording the quantity or rate of flow of gas, electricity, water, etc. passing through it b) same as PARK-ING METER —vt. to measure or record with a meter

**-me·ter** (mēt′ər, mi tər) [Fr. -mètre or ModL. -metrum, both < Gr. metron, a measure] a suffix meaning: **1.** a device for measuring [barometer] **2.** a) (a specified number of) meters [kilometer] b) (a specified fraction of) a meter [centimeter] **3.** having (a specified number of) metrical feet [pentameter]

**me·ter·age** (mēt′ər ij) n. measurement as by a meter, or the charge for this

**me·ter-kil·o·gram-sec·ond** (-kil′ə gram sek′ənd) adj. designating or of a system of measurement in which the meter, kilogram, and second are used as the units of length, mass, and time, respectively

**Meth.** Methodist

**meth·a·done** (meth′ə dōn′) n. [an acronym of the chemical name] a synthetic narcotic drug, $C_{21}H_{27}ON$, sometimes used in the treatment of hard-drug addicts

**meth·ane** (meth′ān) n. [METH(YL) + -ANE] a colorless, odorless, flammable gas, $CH_4$, present in marsh gas, firedamp, and natural gas: it is used as a fuel, etc.

**methane series** a series of saturated hydrocarbons having the general formula $C_nH_{2n+2}$: methane is the first member

**meth·a·nol** (meth′ə nôl′, -nōl′) n. [METHAN(E) + -OL¹] a colorless, flammable, poisonous liquid, $CH_3OH$, obtained by the destructive distillation of wood and used as a fuel, solvent, and antifreeze, and in the making of paints, etc.

**me·thinks** (mi thiŋks′) v.impersonal pt. **me·thought′** [< OE. < me, to me + thyncth, it seems < thyncan, to seem] [Archaic] it seems to me

**meth·od** (meth′əd) n. [< Fr. < L. < Gr. methodos, pursuit < meta, after + hodos, a way] **1.** a way of doing anything; mode; process; esp., a regular, orderly procedure or way of teaching, investigating, etc. **2.** a system in doing things or handling ideas **3.** regular, orderly arrangement

**me·thod·i·cal** (mə thäd′i k'l) adj. characterized by method; orderly; systematic: also **me·thod′ic** —**me·thod′i·cal·ly** adv. —**me·thod′i·cal·ness** n.

**Meth·od·ism** (meth′ə diz′m) n. **1.** the doctrines, organization, etc. of the Methodists **2.** [m-] excessive adherence to systematic procedure

**Meth·od·ist** (-dist) n. a member of a Protestant Christian denomination that developed from the evangelistic teachings of John and Charles Wesley —adj. of or characteristic of the Methodists or Methodism: also **Meth′od·is′tic**

**meth·od·ize** (-dīz′) vt. **-ized′, -iz′ing** to make methodical; systematize —**meth′od·iz′er** n.

**meth·od·ol·o·gy** (meth′ə däl′ə jē) n., pl. **-gies** [ModL.: see METHOD & -LOGY] **1.** the science of method, or orderly arrangement **2.** a system of methods, as in any particular science —**meth′od·o·log′i·cal** (-də läj′i k'l) adj. —**meth′od·o·log′i·cal·ly** adv. —**meth′od·ol′o·gist** n.

**me·thought** (mi thôt′) pt. of METHINKS

**Me·thu·se·lah** (mə thōō′zə lə, -thyōō′-) Bible one of the patriarchs, who lived 969 years: Gen. 5:27

**meth·yl** (meth′əl) n. [< Fr., ult. < Gr. methy, wine + hylē, wood] the monovalent hydrocarbon radical $CH_3$, normally existing only in combination

**methyl alcohol** same as METHANOL

**methyl chloride** a gas, $CH_3Cl$, which when compressed becomes a sweet, transparent liquid: it is used as a refrigerant and local anesthetic

**me·tic·u·lous** (mə tik′yoo ləs) adj. [L. meticulosus, fearful < metus, fear] extremely or excessively careful about details; scrupulous or finicky —**me·tic′u·lous·ly** adv. —**me·tic′u·lous·ness, me·tic′u·los′i·ty** (-läs′ə tē) n.

**mé·tier** (mā tyā′) n. [Fr. < OFr. mestier < L.: see MINIS-TRY] a trade, profession, or occupation

**me·ton·y·my** (mə tän′ə mē) n., pl. **-mies** [< LL. < Gr. < meta, change + onyma, name] use of the name of one thing for that of another associated with it (Ex.: "the press" for "journalists") —**met·o·nym·ic** (met′ə nim′ik) adj.

**me·tre** (mē′tər) n. chiefly Brit. sp. of METER¹

**met·ric** (met′rik) adj. **1.** same as METRICAL **2.** a) of the meter (unit of length) b) designating or of the system of measurement based on the meter: see METRIC SYSTEM

**met·ri·cal** (-ri k'l) adj. **1.** of or composed in meter or verse **2.** of, involving, or used in measurement; metric —**met′ri·cal·ly** adv.

**met·ri·ca·tion** (met′rə kā′shən) n. the process of changing over to the metric system of weights and measures

**met·ri·cize** (met′rə sīz′) vt. **-cized′, -ciz′ing** to change into the metric system of weights and measures

**metric system** a decimal system of weights and measures in which the gram, the meter, and the liter are the basic units of weight, length, and capacity, respectively: see TABLES OF WEIGHTS AND MEASURES in Supplements

**metric ton** a measure of weight equal to 1,000 kilograms or 2,204.62 pounds

**met·ro·nome** (met′rə nōm′) n. [< Gr. metron, measure + nomos, law] a clockwork device with an inverted pendulum that beats time, as in setting a musical tempo, at a rate determined by the position of a sliding weight on the pendulum —**met′ro·nom′ic** (-näm′ik) adj.

**me·trop·o·lis** (mə träp′'l is) n., pl. **-lis·es** [L. < Gr. < mētēr, a mother + polis, a city] **1.** the main city, often the capital, of a country, state, etc. **2.** any large city or center of population, culture, etc. **3.** the main diocese of an ecclesiastical province

METRONOME

**met·ro·pol·i·tan** (met′rə päl′ə t'n) adj. **1.** of or constituting a metropolis (senses 1

---

fat, āpe, cär; ten, ēven; is, bīte; gō, hôrn, tōōl, look; oil, out; up, fur; get; joy; yet; chin; she; thin, then; zh, leisure; ŋ, ring; ə for a in ago, e in agent, i in sanity, o in comply, u in focus; ′ as in able (ā′b'l); Fr. bal; ë, Fr. coeur; ö, Fr. feu; Fr. mon; ô, Fr. coq; ü, Fr. duc; r, Fr. cri; H, G. ich; kh, G. doch; ‡foreign; *hypothetical; < derived from. See inside front cover.

& 2) **2.** designating or of a metropolitan (sense 2) **3.** designating or of a population area consisting of a central city and smaller surrounding communities —*n.* **1.** a person who lives in and is wise in the ways of a metropolis (senses 1 & 2) **2.** *a)* an archbishop having authority over the bishops of a church province *b)* a bishop just below a Patriarch in the Orthodox Eastern Church

**-me·try** (mə trē) [< Gr. < *metron*, measure] *a terminal combining form meaning* the process, art, or science of measuring *[geometry]*

**Met·ter·nich** (met′ər nik; *G.* met′ər niH′), Prince (**Klemens Wenzel Nepomuk Lothar**) **von** 1773–1859; Austrian statesman & diplomat

**met·tle** (met′'l) *n.* [var. of METAL, used figuratively] quality of character; spirit; courage; ardor —**on one's mettle** prepared to do one's best

**met·tle·some** (met′'l səm) *adj.* full of mettle; spirited

**Meuse** (myo͞oz; *Fr.* möz) river flowing from NE France, through Belgium & the Netherlands into the North Sea

**mev, Mev** (mev) *n., pl.* **mev, Mev** [M(ILLION) E(LECTRON)-V(OLTS)] a unit of energy equal to one million electron-volts

**mew**[1] (myo͞o) *n.* [< OFr. < *muer* < L. *mutare*, to change] **1.** a cage, as for hawks while molting **2.** a secret place or den See also MEWS —*vt.* to confine in or as in a cage

**mew**[2] (myo͞o) *n.* [echoic] the characteristic vocal sound made by a cat —*vi.* to make this sound

**mew**[3] (myo͞o) *n.* [OE. *mæw*] a sea gull

**mewl** (myo͞ol) *vi.* [freq. of MEW[1]] to cry weakly, like a baby; whimper or whine —**mewl′er** *n.*

**mews** (myo͞oz) *n.pl.* [*usually with sing. v.*] [< MEW[1]] [Chiefly Brit.] **1.** stables or carriage houses, now often converted into dwellings, as along an alley **2.** such an alley

**Mex. 1.** Mexican **2.** Mexico

**Mex·i·cal·i** (mek′sə kal′ē) city in Baja California, NW Mexico, on the U.S. border: pop. 427,000

**Mex·i·can** (mek′si kən) *adj.* of Mexico, its people, their dialect of Spanish, or their culture —*n.* **1.** a native or inhabitant of Mexico **2.** Nahuatl

**Mexican War** a war between the U.S. and Mexico (1846–48)

**Mex·i·co** (mek′si kō′) **1.** country in N. America, south of the U.S.: 760,373 sq. mi.; pop. 48,313,000; cap. Mexico City **2.** Gulf of, arm of the Atlantic, east of Mexico & south of the U.S. Mexican name **Méx·i·co** (me′hē kô′), Spanish name, MÉJICO

**Mexico City** capital of Mexico, in a federal district, **México, D(istrito) F(ederal)**, in the SC part of Mexico: pop. 3,484,000 (of district, 5,584,000)

**me·zu·za** (mə zo͞o′zə) *n., pl.* **-zot** (-zōt), **-zas** [Heb. *mĕzūzāh*, doorpost] *Judaism* a small scroll inscribed with Biblical verses (Deuteronomy 6:4–9 & 11:13–21) and attached in a case to the doorpost of the home: also sp. **me·zu′zah**

**mez·za·nine** (mez′ə nēn′, mez′ə nēn′) *n.* [Fr. < It. < *mezzano*, middle, ult. < L. *medius*] **1.** a low-ceilinged story between two main stories in a building, usually in the form of a balcony projecting partly over the main floor: also **mezzanine floor 2.** the first few rows of a theater balcony

**mez·zo** (met′sō, med′zō, mez′ō) *adj.* [It. < L. *medius*, middle] *Music* medium; moderate; half —*adv. Music* moderately; somewhat —*n., pl.* **-zos** clipped form of: **1.** MEZZO-SOPRANO **2.** MEZZOTINT

**mez·zo-so·pra·no** (-sə pran′ō, -prä′nō) *n., pl.* **-nos, -ni** (-ē, -nē) [It.] **1.** a woman's voice or part between soprano and contralto **2.** a singer with such a voice

**mez·zo·tint** (-tint′) *n.* [< It.: see MEZZO & TINT] **1.** a method of engraving on a copper or steel plate by scraping or polishing parts of a roughened surface to produce impressions of light and shade **2.** an engraving so produced —*vt.* to engrave by this method

**MF, M.F., mf, m.f.** medium frequency

**mf** *Music* mezzo forte

**mfg.** manufacturing

**MFr.** Middle French

**mfr.** *pl.* **mfrs.** manufacturer

**Mg** *Chem.* magnesium

**mg, mg.** milligram; milligrams

**MGr.** Medieval (or Middle) Greek

**Mgr. 1.** Manager **2.** Monseigneur **3.** Monsignor

**MHG.** Middle High German

**MHz, Mhz** megahertz

**MI** Michigan

**mi** (mē) *n.* [ML.: see GAMUT] *Music* a syllable representing the third tone of the diatonic scale

**mi. 1.** mile(s) **2.** mill(s)

**Mi·am·i** (mī am′ē, -ə) [< Fr.] city on the SE coast of Fla.: pop. 347,000 (met. area 1,574,000)

**Miami Beach** resort city in SE Fla., on an island opposite Miami: pop. 96,000

**mi·aou, mi·aow, mi·au** (mē ou′, myou) *n., vi. same as* MEOW

**mi·as·ma** (mī az′mə, mē-) *n., pl.* **-mas, -ma·ta** (-mə tə) [ModL. < Gr. < *miainein*, to pollute] **1.** a vapor rising as

from marshes or decomposing organic matter, formerly supposed to poison the air **2.** an unwholesome atmosphere, influence, etc. —**mi·as′mal, mi′as·mat′ic** (-mat′ik), **mi·as′-mic** *adj.*

**Mic.** Micah

**mi·ca** (mī′kə) *n.* [ModL. < L., a crumb, infl. by *micare*, to shine] any of a group of minerals that crystallize in thin, somewhat flexible, easily separated layers, resistant to heat and electricity: a transparent form is often called ISINGLASS

**Mi·cah** (mī′kə) *Bible* **1.** a Hebrew prophet of the 8th cent. B.C. **2.** the book containing his prophecy

**mice** (mīs) *n. pl. of* MOUSE

**Mich. 1.** Michaelmas **2.** Michigan

**Mi·chael** (mī′k'l) [LL. < Gr. < Heb. *mīkhā′ĕl*, lit., who is like God?] **1.** a masculine name: dim. *Mike, Mickey* **2.** *Bible* one of the archangels

**Mich·ael·mas** (-məs) *n.* [see -MAS] the feast of the archangel Michael, celebrated on September 29 (**Michaelmas Day**)

**Mi·chel·an·ge·lo** (Buonarroti) (mī′k'l an′jə lō′, mik′'l-) 1475–1564; It. sculptor, painter, architect, & poet

**Mi·chel·son** (mī′k'l s'n), **Albert Abraham** 1852–1931; U.S. physicist, born in Germany

**Mich·i·gan** (mish′i gən) [< Fr. < Algonquian, lit., great water] **1.** Middle Western State of the U.S.: 58,216 sq. mi.; pop. 9,258,000; cap. Lansing: abbrev. **Mich., MI 2. Lake,** one of the Great Lakes, between Mich. & Wis.: 22,178 sq. mi. —**Mich′i·gan′der** (-gan′dər) *n.* —**Mich′i·ga′ni·an** (-gā′nē ən), **Mich′i·gan·ite′** (-īt′) *adj., n.*

**Mick·ey Finn** (mik′ē fin′) [*also* m- f-] [Slang] a drink of liquor to which a drug or purgative has been secretly added: often shortened to **Mick′ey, mick′ey** *n., pl.* **-eys**

**Mickey Mouse** [< a trademark for a cartoon character created by Walt Disney (1901–66), U.S. motion-picture producer] [Slang] [m- m-] childish, oversimplified, unrelated to reality, etc.

**mick·le** (mik′'l) *adj., adv., n.* [OE. *micel*] [Scot.] much

**Mic·mac** (mik′mak) *n., pl.* **-macs, -mac** [Algonquian, lit., allies] a member of a tribe of Indians in Newfoundland and the Maritime Provinces of Canada

**mi·cra** (mī′krə) *n. alt. pl. of* MICRON

**mi·cro-** [< Gr. < *mikros*, small] *a combining form meaning:* **1.** little; small; minute *[microfilm]* **2.** enlarging or amplifying *[microscope, microphone]* **3.** microscopic *[microchemistry]* **4.** one millionth part of (a specified unit) *[microgram]*

**mi·crobe** (mī′krōb) *n.* [Fr. < Gr. *mikros*, small + *bios*, life] a microscopic organism; esp., a disease germ —**mi·cro′bic, mi·cro′bi·al, mi·cro′bi·an** *adj.*

**mi·cro·bi·ol·o·gy** (mī′krō bī äl′ə jē) *n.* the branch of biology that deals with microorganisms —**mi′cro·bi′o·log′i·cal** (-ə läj′ə k'l) *adj.* —**mi′cro·bi·ol′o·gist** *n.*

**mi·cro·ceph·a·ly** (mī′krə sef′'l ē) *n.* [MICRO- + CEPHAL(O)- + -Y[3]] a condition in which the head or cranial capacity is abnormally small —**mi′cro·ceph′a·lous, mi′cro·ce·phal′ic** (-sə fal′ik) *adj.*

**mi·cro·chem·is·try** (-kem′is trē) *n.* the chemistry of microscopic or submicroscopic quantities or objects

**mi·cro·com·put·er** (mī′krō kəm pyo͞ot′ər) *n.* a very small computer controlled by a tiny silicon chip containing all the logical elements for handling data, performing calculations, etc.

**mi·cro·cop·y** (mī′krə käp′ē) *n., pl.* **-cop′ies** a copy of printed matter, etc. produced in very greatly reduced size, as by microfilming

**mi·cro·cosm** (mī′krə käz'm) *n.* a little world; miniature universe; specif., man, a community, etc. regarded as a miniature of the world —**mi′cro·cos′mic** *adj.*

**mi·cro·fiche** (mī′krə fēsh′) *n.* [Fr. < *micro-*, MICRO- + *fiche*, a small card] a small sheet of microfilm, containing a number of pages of microcopy

**mi·cro·film** (-film′) *n.* film on which documents, printed pages, etc. are photographed in a reduced size as for easier storage —*vt., vi.* to photograph on microfilm

**mi·cro·form** (-fôrm′) *n.* any form of photographically reduced document, print, etc., as microfilm

**mi·cro·gram** (-gram′) *n.* one millionth of a gram: also, chiefly Brit. sp., **mi′cro·gramme′**

**mi·cro·groove** (-gro͞ov′) *n.* a very narrow needle groove, as for a long-playing phonograph record

**mi·crom·e·ter** (mī kräm′ə tər) *n.* [< Fr.: see MICRO- & -METER] **1.** an instrument for measuring very small distances, angles, etc., used on a telescope or microscope **2.** *same as* MICROMETER CALIPER

**micrometer caliper** (or **calipers**) calipers with a micrometer screw, for extremely accurate measurement

MICROMETER

**micrometer screw** a finely threaded screw of definite pitch, with a head graduated to show how much the screw has been moved in or out

**mi·crom·e·try** (-trē) *n.* measurement with micrometers

**mi·cron** (mī′krän) *n., pl.* **-crons, -cra** (-krə) [ModL. < Gr. *mikros,* small] one millionth of a meter, or one thousandth of a millimeter

**Mi·cro·ne·sia** (mī′krə nē′zhə, -shə) a major division of the Pacific islands, north of the equator, west of the international date line, & east of the Philippines

**Mi·cro·ne·sian** (-zhən, -shən) *adj.* of Micronesia, its people, their language, etc. —*n.* **1.** a native of Micronesia **2.** any of the Malayo-Polynesian languages of Micronesia

**mi·cro·or·gan·ism** (mī′krō ôr′gə niz′m) *n.* any microscopic or ultramicroscopic animal or vegetable organism; esp., any of the bacteria, viruses, etc.

**mi·cro·phone** (mī′krə fōn′) *n.* [MICRO- + -PHONE] an instrument containing a device that converts the mechanical energy of sound waves into an electric signal, as for radio —**mi′cro·phon′ic** (-fän′ik) *adj.*

**mi·cro·print** (-print′) *n.* a photographic copy so greatly reduced that it can be read only through a magnifying device

**mi·cro·scope** (mī′krə skōp′) *n.* [< ModL.: see MICRO- & -SCOPE] an instrument consisting essentially of a lens or combination of lenses, for making very small objects, as microorganisms, look larger

**mi·cro·scop·ic** (mī′krə skäp′ik) *adj.* **1.** so small as to be invisible or obscure except through a microscope; minute **2.** of or with a microscope **3.** like or suggestive of a microscope Also **mi′cro·scop′i·cal** —**mi′cro·scop′i·cal·ly** *adv.*

**mi·cros·co·py** (mī kräs′kə pē; *occas.* mī′krə skō′pē) *n.* the use of a microscope; investigation by means of a microscope —**mi·cros′co·pist** *n.*

**mi·cro·wave** (mī′krə wāv′) *adj.* **1.** designating or of the electromagnetic spectrum lying between the far infrared and some lower frequency limit, usually between 300,000 and 300 megahertz **2.** designating an oven that cooks quickly by causing microwaves to penetrate the food, generating internal heat —*n.* any electromagnetic wave of microwave frequency —*vt.* **-waved′, -wav′ing** to cook in a microwave oven

**mic·tu·rate** (mik′chōō rāt′) *vi.* **-rat′ed, -rat′ing** [< L. pp. of *micturire* < *mingere,* to urinate] to urinate —**mic′tu·ri′tion** (-rish′ən) *n.*

**mid**[1] (mid) *adj.* [OE. *midd*] **1.** *same as* MIDDLE **2.** *Phonet.* produced with the tongue in a position midway between high and low: said of some vowels, as (e)

**mid**[2] (mid) *prep.* [Poet.] amid: also **′mid**

**mid-** *a combining form meaning* middle or middle part of [*midbrain, midday*]

**mid·air** (-er′) *n.* any point in space, not in contact with the ground or other surface

**Mi·das** (mī′dəs) *Gr. Myth.* a king of Phrygia able to turn everything that he touched into gold

**mid·brain** (mid′brān′) *n.* the middle part of the brain

**mid·day** (mid′dā′) *n.* [OE. *middæg*] the middle part of the day; noon —*adj.* of midday

**mid·den** (mid′′n) *n.* [prob. < Scand.] **1.** [Brit.] a dunghill or refuse heap **2.** *short for* KITCHEN MIDDEN

**mid·dle** (mid′′l) *adj.* [OE. *middel*] **1.** halfway between two given points, times, limits, etc.; also, equally distant from the ends, etc.; in the center **2.** in between; intermediate **3.** [M-] *Geol.* designating a division, as of a period, between *Upper* and *Lower* **4.** [M-] *Linguis.* designating a stage in language development intermediate between *Old* and *Modern* [*Middle* English] —*n.* **1.** a point or part halfway between extremes; middle point, time, etc. **2.** something intermediate **3.** the middle part of the body; waist —*vt., vi.* **-dled, -dling** to put in the middle

**middle age** the time of life between youth and old age: now usually the years from about 40 to about 65 —**mid′dle-aged′** *adj.*

**Middle Ages** the period of European history between ancient and modern times, 476 A.D.-c.1450 A.D.

**Middle America 1.** Mexico, Central America, and, sometimes, the West Indies **2.** the American middle class, esp. of the Middle West

**Middle Atlantic States** New Jersey, New York, & Pennsylvania

**mid·dle·brow** (mid′′l brou′) *n.* [Colloq.] a person regarded as having the conventional, anti-intellectual tastes or opinions of the middle class —*adj.* [Colloq.] of or for a middlebrow

**middle C** the musical note of the first leger line below the treble staff and the first above the bass staff

**middle class** the social class between the aristocracy or very wealthy and the lower working class —**mid′dle-class′** *adj.*

**middle ear** the eardrum and the adjacent cavity containing the hammer, the anvil, and the stirrup

**Middle East 1.** area from Afghanistan to Egypt, including Arabia, Cyprus, & Asiatic Turkey **2.** sometimes, the Near East, excluding the Balkans —**Middle Eastern**

**Middle English** the English language as written and spoken between c.1100 and c.1500

**Middle French** the French language as written and spoken between the 14th and 16th centuries

**Middle Greek** *same as* MEDIEVAL GREEK

**Middle High German** the High German language as written and spoken between c.1100 and c.1500

**Middle Irish** the Irish language as written and spoken from the 11th to the 15th century

**Middle Latin** *same as* MEDIEVAL LATIN

**Middle Low German** the Low German language as written and spoken between c.1100 and c.1500

**mid·dle·man** (mid′′l man′) *n., pl.* **-men** (-men′) **1.** a trader who buys commodities from the producer and sells them to the retailer or, sometimes, directly to the consumer **2.** a go-between

**mid·dle·most** (-mōst′) *adj. same as* MIDMOST

**mid·dle-of-the-road** (-əv thə rōd′) *adj.* avoiding extremes, esp. of the political left or right

**middle school** a school between elementary school and high school, variously between grades 5 and 9

**mid·dle·weight** (-wāt′) *n.* a boxer or wrestler between a welterweight and a light heavyweight (in boxing, 148–160 pounds)

**Middle West** region of the NC U.S. between the Rocky Mountains & the E border of Ohio, north of the Ohio River & the S borders of Kans. & Mo. —**Middle Western**

**mid·dling** (mid′liŋ) *adj.* of middle size, quality, grade, state, etc.; medium —*adv.* [Colloq.] moderately; somewhat —*n.* **1.** [*pl.*] products of medium quality, size, or price **2.** [*pl.*] particles of coarsely ground grain, often mixed with bran —**fair to middling** [Colloq.] moderately good or well

**mid·dy** (mid′ē) *n., pl.* **-dies 1.** [Colloq.] a midshipman **2.** a loose blouse with a sailor collar, worn by women and children: in full, **middy blouse**

**Mid·gard** (mid′gärd′) *Norse Myth.* the earth: also **Mid′garth′** (-gärth′)

**midge** (mij) *n.* [OE. *mycg*] **1.** a small, two-winged, gnatlike insect **2.** a very small person

**midg·et** (mij′it) *n.* **1.** a very small person **2.** anything very small of its kind —*adj.* very small of its kind; miniature

**Mi·di** (mē dē′) [Fr.] southern France

**mid·i·ron** (mid′ī′ərn) *n.* a golf club with a metal head, used for fairway shots of medium distance: now usually called *number 2 iron*

**Mid·land** (mid′lənd) [from being about midway between Fort Worth & El Paso] city in WC Tex.: pop. 71,000

**mid·land** (mid′lənd) *n.* **1.** the middle region of a country; interior **2.** [M-] *a)* an English dialect of the Midlands *b)* a dialect of American English spoken chiefly in the area that extends westward to the Coast across the middle of the U.S. from the Middle Atlantic States —*adj.* **1.** of or in the midland; inland **2.** [M-] of the Midlands —**the Midlands** region in WC England, around Birmingham

**mid·most** (mid′mōst′) *adj.* exactly in the middle, or nearest the middle —*adv.* in the middle or midst —*prep.* in the middle or midst of —*n.* the middle part

**mid·night** (-nīt′) *n.* the middle of the night; twelve o'clock at night —*adj.* **1.** of or at midnight **2.** like midnight; very dark —**burn the midnight oil** to study very late at night

**midnight sun** the sun visible at midnight in the arctic or antarctic regions during the summer

**mid·point** (-point′) *n.* a point at or close to the middle or center, or equally distant from the ends

**mid·rib** (-rib′) *n.* the central vein of a leaf

**mid·riff** (-rif) *n.* [< OE. < *midd,* MID[1] + *hrif,* belly] **1.** *same as* DIAPHRAGM (sense 1) **2.** the middle part of the torso, between the abdomen and the chest —*adj.* designating or of a garment that bares this part

**mid·ship** (-ship′) *adj.* of the middle of a ship

**mid·ship·man** (-ship′mən) *n., pl.* **-men 1.** a student in training for the rank of ensign; specif., such a student at the U.S. Naval Academy at Annapolis **2.** formerly, a junior British naval officer ranking just above a naval cadet

**mid·ships** (-ships′) *adv. same as* AMIDSHIPS

**midst**[1] (midst, mitst) *n.* the middle; central part: now mainly in phrases as below —**in our** (or **your, their**) **midst** among us (or you, them) —**in the midst of 1.** in the middle of **2.** during

**midst**[2] (midst, mitst) *prep.* [Poet.] in the midst of; amidst

**mid·stream** (mid′strēm′) *n.* the middle of a stream

**mid·sum·mer** (-sum′ər) *n.* **1.** the middle of summer **2.** popularly, the time of the summer solstice, about June 21 —*adj.* of, in, or like midsummer

**mid·term** (-turm′) *adj.* occurring in the middle of the term —*n.* [Colloq.] a midterm examination, as in a college course

**mid-Vic·to·ri·an** (mid′vik tôr′ē ən) *adj.* **1.** of or characteristic of the middle part of Queen Victoria's reign in

Great Britain (c.1850–1890) **2.** old-fashioned, prudish, morally strict, etc. —*n.* **1.** a person who lived during this period **2.** a person of mid-Victorian ideas, manners, etc.

**mid·way** (mid′wā′; *also, for adj. & adv.,* -wā′) *n.* **1.** orig., a middle way or course **2.** that part of a fair or exposition where sideshows and other amusements are located —*adj., adv.* in the middle

**Midway Islands** U.S. territory in the North Pacific, northwest of Hawaii, consisting of an atoll & two islets

**mid·week** (-wēk′) *n., adj.* (in) the middle of the week

**Mid·west** (mid′west′) *n. same as* MIDDLE WEST —*adj. same as* MIDWESTERN

**Mid·west·ern** (-ərn) *adj.* of, in, or characteristic of the Middle West —**Mid′west′ern·er** *n.*

**mid·wife** (mid′wīf′) *n., pl.* **-wives′** (-wīvz′) [OE. *mid,* with + *wif,* woman] a person whose work is helping women in childbirth —**mid′wife′ry** (-wīf′ə rē, -wīf′rē) *n.*

**mid·win·ter** (-win′tər) *n.* **1.** the middle of the winter **2.** popularly, the time of the winter solstice, about December 22 —*adj.* of, in, or like midwinter

**mid·year** (-yir′) *adj.* occurring in the middle of the (calendar or academic) year —*n.* [Colloq.] a midyear examination, as in a college course

**mien** (mēn) *n.* [< DEMEAN[2], but altered after Fr. *mine,* look, air] **1.** a way of carrying and conducting oneself; manner **2.** a way of looking; appearance

**miff** (mif) *n.* [prob. echoic of a sound of disgust] [Colloq.] a trivial quarrel or fit of the sulks; tiff or huff —*vt., vi.* [Colloq.] to offend or take offense

**MIG, MiG** (mig) *n.* [after A. *Mi*koyan & M. *Gu*revich, its Soviet designers] a small, fast jet military aircraft

**might**[1] (mīt) *v.* [OE. *mihte*] **1.** *pt. of* MAY **2.** an auxiliary with present or future sense, generally equivalent to *may [*it *might* rain*]*

**might**[2] (mīt) *n.* [OE. *miht*] **1.** great or superior strength, power, force, or vigor **2.** strength or power of any degree

**might·y** (-ē) *adj.* [OE. *mihtig*] **might′i·er, might′i·est 1.** having might; powerful; strong **2.** remarkably large, extensive, etc.; great —*adv.* [Colloq.] very; extremely —**might′i·ly** *adv.* —**might′i·ness** *n.*

**mi·gnon** (min′yän; *Fr.* mē nyōn′) *adj.* [Fr.] small and delicate —**mi·gnonne** (min′yän; *Fr.* mē nyôn′) *adj.fem.*

**mi·gnon·ette** (min′yə net′) *n.* [< Fr. dim. of *mignon:* see prec.] a plant bearing spikes of small greenish, whitish, or reddish flowers

**mi·graine** (mī′grān) *n.* [Fr. < OFr. < LL. *hemicrania* < Gr. < *hēmi-,* half + *kranion,* skull] a type of intense, periodically returning headache, usually limited to one side of the head —**mi·grain′ous** *adj.*

**mi·grant** (mī′grənt) *adj.* migrating; migratory —*n.* a person, bird, or animal that migrates; specif., a farm laborer who moves from place to place to harvest seasonal crops

**mi·grate** (mī′grāt) *vi.* **-grat·ed, -grat·ing** [< L. pp. of *migrare,* to migrate] **1.** to move from one place to another, esp. to another country **2.** to move from one region to another with the change in seasons, as many birds **3.** to move from place to place to harvest seasonal crops —**mi′gra·tor** *n.*

**mi·gra·tion** (mī grā′shən) *n.* **1.** a migrating **2.** a group of people or birds, fishes, etc. migrating together **3.** *Chem. a)* the shifting of position of one or more atoms within a molecule *b)* the movement of ions toward an electrode —**mi·gra′tion·al** *adj.*

**mi·gra·to·ry** (mī′grə tôr′ē) *adj.* **1.** migrating; characterized by migration **2.** of migration **3.** roving; wandering

**mi·ka·do** (mi kä′dō) *n., pl.* **-dos** [Jap. < *mi,* exalted + *kado,* gate] [*often* M-] the emperor of Japan: title no longer used

**mike** (mīk) *n.* [Colloq.] a microphone —*vt.* **miked, mik′ing** [Colloq.] to record, amplify, etc. by means of a microphone

**mil** (mil) *n.* [< L. *mille,* thousand] **1.** a unit of length, equal to 1/1000 inch, used in measuring the diameter of wire **2.** a unit of angle measurement for artillery fire, missile launching, etc., equal to 1/6400 of the circumference of a circle **3.** *see* MONETARY UNITS, table (Cyprus)

**mil. 1.** military **2.** militia

**mi·la·dy, mi·la·di** (mi lā′dē) *n.* [Fr. < E. *my lady*] **1.** an English noblewoman or gentlewoman **2.** a woman of fashion: advertisers' term

**mil·age** (mīl′ij) *n. alt. sp. of* MILEAGE

**Mi·lan** (mi lan′) city in NW Italy: pop. 1,684,000: It. name **Mi·la·no** (mē lä′nō) —**Mil·a·nese** (mil′ə nēz′) *adj., n., pl.* **-nese′**

**milch** (milch) *adj.* [OE. *-milce*] giving milk; kept for milking *[milch* cows*]*

**mild** (mīld) *adj.* [OE. *milde*] **1.** *a)* gentle or kind in disposition, action, or effect; not severe, harsh, etc. *b)* not extreme; moderate *[a mild* winter*]* **2.** having a soft, pleasant flavor; not strong, bitter, etc.: said of tobacco, cheese, etc. —**mild′ly** *adv.* —**mild′ness** *n.*

**mil·dew** (mil′dōō′, -dyōō′) *n.* [OE. *meledeaw,* lit., honeydew] **1.** a fungus that attacks various plants or appears on damp cloth, paper, etc. as a furry, whitish coating **2.** any such coating or discoloration —*vt., vi.* to affect or become affected with mildew —**mil′dew′y** *adj.*

**Mil·dred** (mil′drid) [< OE. < *milde,* mild + *thryth,* power] a feminine name: dim. *Millie, Milly*

**mile** (mīl) *n., pl.* **miles,** dial. **mile** [< OE. < L. *milia* (*passuum*), thousand (paces)] a unit of linear measure, equal to 1,760 yards (5,280 feet or 1,609.35 meters): in full, **statute mile:** see NAUTICAL MILE

**mile·age** (-ij) *n.* **1.** an allowance per mile for traveling expenses **2.** total number of miles traveled, etc. **3.** rate per mile **4.** the amount of use one can get from something

**mile·post** (-pōst′) *n.* a signpost showing the distance in miles from a specified place

**mil·er** (mīl′ər) *n.* one who competes in mile races

**Miles** (mīlz) [OFr. < OHG. *Milo,* lit., mild, peaceful] a masculine name

**mile·stone** (mīl′stōn′) *n.* **1.** a stone or pillar set up to show the distance in miles from a specified place **2.** a significant event in history, in one's career, etc.

**Mil·ford** (mil′fərd) [? after *Milford,* town in England] city in SW Conn., near Bridgeport: pop. 49,000

**Mil·haud** (mē yō′), **Da·rius** (dä ryüs′) 1892–1974; Fr. composer

**mi·lieu** (mēl yoo′; *Fr.* mē lyö′) *n., pl.* **-lieus′;** Fr. **-lieux′** (-lyö′) [Fr. < OFr. *mi,* middle + *lieu,* a place] environment; esp., social setting

**mil·i·tant** (mil′i tənt) *adj.* [< L. prp. of *militare,* to serve as a soldier < *miles* (gen. *militis*), a soldier] **1.** fighting **2.** ready and willing to fight; esp., vigorous in support of a cause —*n.* a militant person —**mil′i·tan·cy** *n.* —**mil′i·tant·ly** *adv.*

**mil·i·ta·rism** (mil′ə tər iz′m) *n.* **1.** military spirit or its dominance in a nation **2.** the policy of maintaining a strong military organization in aggressive preparedness for war —**mil′i·ta·rist** *n.* —**mil′i·ta·ris′tic** *adj.* —**mil′i·ta·ris′ti·cal·ly** *adv.*

**mil·i·ta·rize** (mil′i tə rīz′) *vt.* **-rized′, -riz′ing 1.** to equip and prepare for war **2.** to fill with warlike spirit —**mil′i·ta·ri·za′tion** *n.*

**mil·i·tar·y** (mil′ə ter′ē) *adj.* [< Fr. < L. *militaris* < *miles:* see MILITANT] **1.** of, characteristic of, for, fit for, or done by soldiers or the armed forces **2.** of, for, or fit for war **3.** of the army —**the military** the army or the armed forces; esp., army officers as an influential force —**mil′i·tar′i·ly** (*also* mil′ə ter′ə lē) *adv.*

**military attaché** an army officer attached to his nation's embassy or legation in a foreign country

**military police** soldiers assigned to carry on police duties for the army

**mil·i·tate** (mil′ə tāt′) *vi.* **-tat′ed, -tat′ing** [< L. pp. of *militare:* see MILITANT] to be directed (*against*); operate or work (*against* or, rarely, *for*): said of facts, actions, etc.

**mi·li·tia** (mə lish′ə) *n.* [L., soldiery < *miles:* see MILITANT] any army composed of citizens rather than professional soldiers, called up in time of emergency —**mi·li′tia·man** (-mən) *n., pl.* **-men**

**milk** (milk) *n.* [OE. *meolc*] **1.** a white liquid secreted by the mammary glands of female mammals for suckling their young **2.** cow's milk, etc. drunk by humans as a food or used to make butter, cheese, etc. **3.** any liquid or juice like this *[coconut milk, milk* of magnesia*]* —*vt.* **1.** to draw milk from the mammary glands of (a cow, etc.) **2.** to extract (something) as if by milking *[to milk* venom from a snake*]* **3.** to extract something from as if by milking *[to milk* a rich uncle for his money*]* —*vi.* **1.** to give milk **2.** to draw milk —**cry over spilt milk** to mourn or regret something that cannot be undone —**milk′ing** *n.*

**milk-and-wa·ter** (-ən wôt′ər, -wät′-) *adj.* insipid; weak; wishy-washy; namby-pamby

**milk·er** (mil′kər) *n.* **1.** a person who milks **2.** a machine for milking **3.** a cow or other animal that gives milk

**milk glass** a nearly opaque whitish glass

**milk leg** *a former term for* a painful swelling of the leg, caused by clotting in the femoral veins, as in childbirth

**milk·maid** (milk′mād′) *n.* a girl or woman who milks cows or works in a dairy; dairymaid

**milk·man** (-man′) *n., pl.* **-men′** (-men′) a man who sells or delivers milk for a dairy

**milk of magnesia** a milky-white fluid, a suspension of magnesium hydroxide, $Mg(OH)_2$, in water, used as a laxative and antacid

**milk·shake** (-shāk′) *n.* a drink made of milk, flavoring, and, usually, ice cream, mixed until frothy

**milk·shed** (-shed′) *n.* [MILK + (WATER)SHED] all the dairy farms supplying milk for a given city

**milk snake** a harmless snake, gray or reddish with black-rimmed markings: it feeds on rodents, etc.

**milk·sop** (-säp′) *n.* an unmanly man or boy; sissy

**milk sugar** *same as* LACTOSE

**milk tooth** any of the temporary, first set of teeth in a child or the young of other mammals

**milk·weed** (-wēd') *n.* any of a group of plants with a milky juice and pods which when ripe burst to release plumed seeds

**milk·y** (mil'kē) *adj.* **milk'i·er, milk'-i·est** **1.** like milk; esp., white as milk **2.** of or containing milk **3.** timid, meek, etc. —**milk'i·ness** *n.*

**Milky Way** a broad, faint band of light seen as an arch across the sky at night, created by billions of distant stars and masses of gas

**mill¹** (mil) *n.* [OE. *mylen,* ult. < LL. *molina* < L. *mola,* millstone] **1.** *a)* a building with machinery for grinding grain into flour or meal *b)* a machine for grinding grain **2.** a machine for grinding or crushing any solid material *[a coffee mill]* **3.** *a)* any of various machines for cutting, stamping, shaping, etc. *b)* [Colloq.] a place where things are done, produced, issued, etc. in a rapid, mechanical way *[a diploma mill]* **4.** a factory *[a textile mill]* **5.** a raised edge, ridged surface, etc. made by milling —*vt.* **1.** to grind, work, form, etc. by, in, or as in a mill **2.** to raise and ridge the edge of (a coin) —*vi.* to move slowly in a circle, as cattle, or aimlessly, as a confused crowd (often with *around* or *about*) —**in the mill** in preparation —**through the mill** [Colloq.] through a hard, painful, instructive experience —**milled** *adj.*

**mill²** (mil) *n.* [for L. *millesimus,* thousandth < *mille,* thousand] one tenth of a cent; $.001: a unit used in calculating but not as a coin

**Mill** (mil), **John Stuart** 1806–73; Eng. philosopher & political economist

**mill·age** (mil'ij) *n.* [MILL² + -AGE] taxation in mills per dollar of valuation

**Mil·lais** (mi lā'), **Sir John Everett** 1829–96; Eng. painter

**Mil·lay** (mi lā'), **Edna St. Vincent** 1892–1950; U.S. poet

**mill·dam** (mil'dam') *n.* a dam built across a stream to raise its level enough to provide water power for turning a mill wheel

**mil·len·ni·um** (mi len'ē əm) *n., pl.* **-ni·ums, -ni·a** (-ə) [ModL. < L. *mille,* thousand + *annus,* year] **1.** a period of 1,000 years **2.** *Theol.* the period of a thousand years during which some believe Christ will reign on earth (with *the*): Rev. 20:1–5 **3.** a period of peace and happiness for everyone —**mil·len'ni·al** *adj.* —**mil·len'ni·al·ism** *n.*

**mil·le·pede** (mil'ə pēd') *n. same as* MILLIPEDE

**mil·le·pore** (mil'ə pôr') *n.* [< Fr. < *mille,* thousand + *pore* < L. *porus,* PORE²] any of a genus of hydrozoans that form leaflike, porous masses of coral

**mill·er** (mil'ər) *n.* **1.** a person who owns or operates a mill, esp. a flour mill **2.** a tool used for milling **3.** a moth with wings that look dusty, suggesting a miller's clothes

**Mil·ler** (mil'ər) **1.** **Arthur,** 1915– ; U.S. playwright **2.** **Joaquin** (wä kēn'), (pseud. of *Cincinnatus Heine Miller*) 1839?–1913; U.S. poet

**mill·er's-thumb** (mil'ərz thum') *n.* any of several small freshwater fishes with spiny fins and a broad, flat head

**mil·let** (mil'it) *n.* see PLURAL, II, D, 3 [< MFr., dim. of *mil* < L. *milium,* millet] **1.** a cereal grass whose small grain is used for food in Europe and Asia **2.** the grain

**Mil·let** (mē le'; *E.* mi lā'), **Jean Fran·çois** (zhän frän'swä') 1814–75; Fr. painter

**mil·li-** [< L. *mille,* thousand] *a combining form meaning* a 1000th part of *[millimeter]*

**mil·li·am·pere** (mil'ē am'pir) *n.* one thousandth of an ampere

**mil·liard** (mil'yərd, -yärd') *n.* [Fr. < *million* (see MILLION) + -*ard* (see -ARD), orig. "large million"] [Brit.] 1,000 millions; billion

**Mil·li·cent** (mil'ə s'nt) [< OFr. < OHG. < *amal,* work + hyp. *swind,* strong] a feminine name

**mil·lieme** (mēl yem', mē-) *n.* [< Fr. < MFr. < *mille,* a thousand < L.] *see* MONETARY UNITS, table (Libya)

**mil·li·gram** (mil'ə gram') *n.* one thousandth of a gram: also, chiefly Brit. sp., **mil'li·gramme'**

**mil·li·li·ter** (-lēt'ər) *n.* one thousandth of a liter: also, chiefly Brit. sp., **mil'li·li'tre**

**mil·lime** (mil'ēm, -im) *n.* [Fr.: see MILLIEME] *see* MONETARY UNITS, table (Tunisia)

**mil·li·me·ter** (mil'ə mēt'ər) *n.* one thousandth of a meter: also, chiefly Brit. sp., **mil'li·me'tre**

**mil·li·mi·cron** (mil'ə mī'krän) *n., pl.* **-crons, -cra** (-krə) one thousandth of a micron, or ten angstroms: a unit of length for measuring waves of light, etc.

**mil·li·ner** (mil'ə nər) *n.* [< *Milaner,* importer of dress wares from Milan] a person who designs, makes, trims, or sells women's hats

MILKWEED PODS

**mil·li·ner·y** (mil'ə ner'ē; *chiefly Brit.* -nər i) *n.* **1.** women's hats, headdresses, etc. **2.** the work or business of a milliner

**mill·ing** (mil'iŋ) *prp. of* MILL¹ —*n.* **1.** the process or business of grinding grain into flour or meal **2.** the grinding, cutting, or processing of metal, cloth, etc. in a mill

**milling machine** a machine with a table on which material rests as it is fed against a rotating cutter (**milling cutter**) for cutting, grinding, shaping, etc.

**mil·lion** (mil'yən) *n.* [OFr. < It. *milione* < *mille,* thousand < L.] a thousand thousands; 1,000,000 —*adj.* **1.** amounting to one million in number **2.** very many —**mil'lionth** *adj., n.*

**mil·lion·aire** (mil'yə ner') *n.* [< Fr.] a person worth at least a million dollars, pounds, etc.

**mil·li·pede** (mil'ə pēd') *n.* [< L. < *mille,* thousand + *pes* (gen. *pedis*), a foot] a many-legged arthropod with two pairs of legs on most of its segments

**mill·pond** (mil'pänd') *n.* a pond from which water flows for driving a mill wheel

**mill·race** (-rās') *n.* **1.** the current of water that drives a mill wheel **2.** the channel in which it runs

**mill-run** (-run') *adj.* just as it comes out of the mill; ordinary; average

**mill·stone** (-stōn') *n.* **1.** either of a pair of large, flat, round stones between which grain or other substances are ground **2.** a heavy burden **3.** something that grinds, pulverizes, or crushes

**mill·stream** (-strēm') *n.* water flowing in a millrace

**mill wheel** the wheel, usually a water wheel, that drives the machinery in a mill

**mill·work** (-wurk') *n.* **1.** doors, windows, etc. made in a planing mill **2.** work done in a mill —**mill'work'er** *n.*

**mill·wright** (-rīt') *n.* **1.** one who designs, builds, or installs mills or their machinery **2.** a worker who installs or repairs the machinery in a plant

**Milne** (miln), **A(lan) A(lexander)** 1882–1956; Eng. playwright & writer of children's books

**mi·lord** (mi lôrd') *n.* [Fr. < E. *my lord*] an English nobleman: used as a term of address

**milque·toast** (milk'tōst') *n.* [< Caspar *Milquetoast,* comic-strip character by H. T. Webster (1885–1952), U.S. cartoonist] a timid, apologetic person

**milt** (milt) *n.* [prob. < Scand.] **1.** the reproductive glands of male fishes, esp. when filled with germ cells and the milky fluid containing them **2.** fish sperm —*adj.* breeding: said of male fishes —*vt.* to fertilize (fish roe) with milt —**milt'er** *n.*

**Mil·ti·a·des** (mil tī'ə dēz') ?–489? B.C.; Athenian general: defeated the Persians at Marathon

**Mil·ton** (mil't'n) [< OE. *Middel-tun,* Middletown, or *Mylen-tun,* Mill town] **1.** a masculine name: dim. *Milt* **2.** **John,** 1608–74; Eng. poet —**Mil·ton'ic** (-tän'ik), **Mil·to'ni·an** (-tō'nē ən) *adj.*

**Mil·wau·kee** (mil wô'kē) [< Fr. < Algonquian, lit., good land] city in SE Wis., on Lake Michigan: pop. 636,000 (met. area 1,393,000)

**mime** (mīm) *n.* [< L. < Gr. *mimos*] **1.** an ancient Greek or Roman farce, in which people and events were mimicked and burlesqued **2.** the representation of an action, character, mood, etc. by means of gestures rather than words **3.** an actor who performs in mimes —*vt.* **mimed, mim'ing** to mimic or act out as a mime —*vi.* to act as a mime, usually without speaking —**mim'er** *n.*

**mim·e·o·graph** (mim'ē ə graf', mim'yə-) *n.* [a former trademark < Gr. *mimeomai,* I imitate + -GRAPH] a machine for making copies of written, drawn, or typewritten matter by means of a stencil —*vt.* **1.** to make copies of on such a machine **2.** to make (copies) on such a machine

**mi·met·ic** (mi met'ik, mī-) *adj.* [< Gr. < *mimeisthai,* to imitate] **1.** of or characterized by imitation; imitative **2.** of or characterized by mimicry —**mi·met'i·cal·ly** *adv.*

**mim·ic** (mim'ik) *adj.* [< L. < Gr. < *mimos,* a mime] **1.** imitative **2.** of, or having the nature of, mimicry or imitation **3.** make-believe; mock —*n.* a person or thing that imitates; esp., an actor skilled in mimicry —*vt.* **mim'icked, mim'ick·ing** **1.** to imitate in speech or action, as in ridicule **2.** to copy closely **3.** to take on the appearance of —**mim'ick·er** *n.*

**mim·ic·ry** (-rē) *n., pl.* **-ries** **1.** the practice, art, instance, or way of mimicking **2.** close resemblance, in color, form, or behavior, of one organism to another or to some object in its environment

**mi·mo·sa** (mi mō'sə) *n.* [ModL. < L. *mimus:* see MIME] a tree, shrub, or herb of the legume family, growing in warm regions, with heads or spikes of small white, yellow, or pink flowers

**min.** **1.** mineralogy **2.** minim(s) **3.** minimum **4.** mining **5.** minor **6.** minute(s)

**mi·na** (mī'nə) *n. same as* MYNA: also sp. **mi'nah**

**min·a·ret** (min′ə ret′, min′ə ret′) *n.* [Fr. < Turk. < Ar. *manārah,* lighthouse] a high, slender tower attached to a Moslem mosque, with balconies from which a muezzin calls the people to prayer

**min·a·to·ry** (min′ə tôr′ē) *adj.* [< OFr. < LL. < pp. of L. *minari,* to threaten] menacing; threatening

**mince** (mins) *vt.* **minced, minc′ing** [OFr. *mincier,* ult. < L. *minutus,* small] **1.** to cut up (meat, etc.) into very small pieces **2.** to express or do with affected elegance or daintiness **3.** to lessen the force of; weaken [to *mince* no words] —*vi.* **1.** to speak or act with affected elegance or daintiness **2.** to walk with short steps or in an affected, dainty manner —*n. same as* MINCEMEAT —**not mince matters** to speak frankly —**minc′er** *n.*

MINARET

**mince·meat** (-mēt′) *n.* a mixture of chopped apples, spices, suet, raisins, etc., and sometimes meat, used as a pie filling —**make mincemeat of** to defeat or refute completely

**mince pie** a pie with a filling of mincemeat

**minc·ing** (min′siŋ) *adj.* **1.** affectedly elegant or dainty **2.** with short steps or affected daintiness [a *mincing* walk] —**minc′ing·ly** *adv.*

**mind** (mīnd) *n.* [OE. (ge)*mynd*] **1.** memory or remembrance [to bring to *mind* a story] **2.** what one thinks; opinion [speak your *mind*] **3.** *a*) that which thinks, perceives, feels, etc.; the seat of consciousness *b*) the intellect *c*) attention *d*) the psyche (sense 2) **4.** reason; sanity [to lose one's *mind*] **5.** a person having intelligence [the great *minds* of today] **6.** way, state, or direction of thinking and feeling [the reactionary *mind*] —*vt.* **1.** to direct one's mind to; specif., *a*) [Now Dial.] to perceive; observe *b*) to pay attention to; heed *c*) to obey *d*) to take care of; look after [*mind* the baby] *e*) to be careful about [*mind* those rickety stairs] **2.** *a*) to care about; feel concern about *b*) to object to; dislike [to *mind* the cold] **3.** [Dial.] to remember **4.** [Dial. or Archaic] to remind —*vi.* **1.** to pay attention; give heed **2.** to be obedient **3.** to be careful **4.** *a*) to care; feel concern *b*) to object —**bear** (or **keep**) **in mind** to remember —**be in one's right mind** to be sane —**blow one's mind** [Slang] **1.** to be hallucinated as by drugs **2.** to be amazed, confused, etc. —**call to mind 1.** to remember **2.** to be a reminder of —**change one's mind** to change one's opinion or one's intention —**give (someone) a piece of one's mind** to criticize or rebuke sharply —**have a** (**good** or **great**) **mind to** to feel (strongly) inclined to —**have half a mind to** to be somewhat inclined to —**have in mind 1.** to remember **2.** to think of **3.** to intend; purpose —**know one's own mind** to know one's own real thoughts, desires, etc. —**make up one's mind** to form a definite opinion or decision —**meeting of (the) minds** an agreement —**never mind** don't be concerned; it doesn't matter —**on one's mind 1.** occupying one's thoughts **2.** worrying one —**out of one's mind 1.** insane **2.** frantic (*with* worry, grief, etc.) —**put in mind** to remind —**set one's mind on** to be determinedly desirous of —**take one's mind off** to turn one's thoughts or attention from —**to one's mind** in one's opinion —**mind′er** *n.*

**Min·da·na·o** (min′də nou′, -nä′ō) 2d largest island of the Philippines, at the S end of the group: 36,906 sq. mi.

**mind·ed** (mīn′did) *adj.* **1.** having a (specified kind of) mind [high-*minded*] **2.** inclined; disposed

**mind·ful** (mīnd′f'l) *adj.* having in mind; aware or careful (*of*) [to be *mindful* of the danger] —**mind′ful·ly** *adv.* —**mind′ful·ness** *n.*

**mind·less** (-lis) *adj.* **1.** showing little or no intelligence; thoughtless **2.** taking no thought; heedless (*of*) —**mind′-less·ly** *adv.* —**mind′less·ness** *n.*

**Min·do·ro** (min dôr′ō) island of the Philippines, south of Luzon: 3,759 sq. mi.

**mind reader** one who professes to be able to perceive another's thoughts —**mind reading**

**mind's eye** the imagination

**mine¹** (mīn) *pron.* [OE. *min*] that or those belonging to me: used without a following noun [this is mine, mine are better]: also used after *of* to indicate possession [a friend of *mine*] —**possessive pronominal adj.** [Mainly Archaic] my: formerly used before a vowel or *h* [mine eyes, mine honor], now used after a noun in direct address [daughter *mine*]

**mine²** (mīn) *n.* [< MFr. < ? Celt.] **1.** *a*) a large excavation made in the earth, from which to extract metallic ores, coal, etc. *b*) a deposit of ore, coal, etc. **2.** any great source of supply [a *mine* of information] **3.** a firework that explodes in the air and scatters a number of smaller fireworks **4.** *Mil. a*) a tunnel dug under an enemy's trench, fort, etc., in which an explosive is placed to destroy the enemy fortifications *b*) an explosive charge in a container, buried in the ground for destroying enemy troops on land, or placed in the sea for destroying enemy ships —*vi.* **mined, min′ing**

to dig a mine; specif., *a*) to dig ores, coal, etc. from the earth *b*) to dig or lay military mines —*vt.* **1.** *a*) to dig in (the earth) for ores, coal, etc. *b*) to dig (ores, coal, etc.) from the earth **2.** to take from (a source) **3.** to place explosive mines in or under **4.** to undermine slowly by secret methods

**mine detector** an electromagnetic device for locating the position of hidden explosive mines

**mine field** an area on land or in water where explosive mines have been set

**mine·lay·er** (mīn′lā′ər) *n.* a ship especially equipped to lay explosive mines in the water

**min·er** (-ər) *n.* a person whose work is digging coal, ore, etc. in a mine

**min·er·al** (min′ər əl, min′rəl) *n.* [OFr. < ML. neut. of *mineralis* < *minera,* a mine] **1.** an inorganic substance occurring naturally in the earth and having distinctive physical properties and a composition expressible by a chemical formula: sometimes applied to organic substances in the earth, such as coal **2.** an ore **3.** any substance that is neither vegetable nor animal **4.** any of certain elements, as iron, vital to animals and plants —*adj.* of, like, or containing a mineral or minerals

**mineral. 1.** mineralogical **2.** mineralogy

**min·er·al·ize** (min′ər ə līz′, min′rə-) *vt.* **-ized′, -iz′ing 1.** to convert (organic matter) into a mineral **2.** to impregnate (water, etc.) with minerals **3.** to convert (a metal) into an ore —**min′er·al·i·za′tion** *n.* —**min′er·al·iz′-er** *n.*

**min·er·al·o·gy** (min′ə räl′ə jē, -ral′-) *n.* **1.** the scientific study of minerals **2.** *pl.* **-gies** a book about minerals —**min′er·a·log′i·cal** (-ər ə läj′i k'l) *adj.* —**min′er·a·log′i·cal·ly** *adv.* —**min′er·al′o·gist** *n.*

**mineral oil 1.** any oil found in the rock strata of the earth; specif., petroleum **2.** a colorless, tasteless oil derived from petroleum and used as a laxative

**mineral water** water naturally or artificially impregnated with mineral salts or gases

**mineral wool** a fibrous material made from rock and melted slag and used to insulate buildings

**Mi·ner·va** (mi nur′və) [L.] **1.** a feminine name **2.** the ancient Roman goddess of wisdom, technical skill, and invention: identified with the Greek goddess Athena

**mi·ne·stro·ne** (min′ə strō′nē; *occas.* -strōn′) *n.* [It., ult. < L. *ministrare,* to serve] a thick vegetable soup containing vermicelli, barley, etc. in a meat broth

**mine sweeper** a ship for destroying enemy mines

**Ming** (miŋ) Chin. dynasty (1368–1644): period noted for scholarly achievements & artistic works

**min·gle** (miŋ′g'l) *vt.* **-gled, -gling** [< OE. *mengan,* to mix] to mix together; combine; blend —*vi.* **1.** to be or become mixed, blended, etc. **2.** to join or unite with others —**min′gler** *n.*

**min·i-** [< MINI(ATURE)] *a combining form meaning:* **1.** miniature, very small, very short [*miniskirt*] **2.** of less scope, extent, etc. than usual [*mini-crisis*]

**min·i·a·ture** (min′ē ə chər, min′i chər) *n.* [< It. *miniatura* < ML. < L. *miniare,* to paint red < *minium,* red lead] **1.** *a*) a very small painting, esp. a portrait *b*) the art of making these **2.** a copy or model on a very small scale —*adj.* on or done on a very small scale; minute —**in miniature** on a small scale; greatly reduced —**min′i·a·tur·ist** *n.*

**min·i·a·tur·ize** (-īz′) *vt.* **-ized′, -iz′ing** to make in a small and compact form —**min′i·a·tur′i·za′tion** *n.*

**min·im** (min′im) *n.* [< L. *minimus:* see MINIMUM] **1.** the smallest liquid measure, 1/60 fluid dram, or about a drop **2.** a tiny portion **3.** [Brit.] *same as* HALF NOTE —*adj.* smallest; tiniest

**min·i·mize** (min′ə mīz′) *vt.* **-mized′, -miz′ing** to reduce to or estimate at a minimum, or the least possible amount, degree, etc. —**min′i·mi·za′tion** *n.* —**min′i·miz′er** *n.*

**min·i·mum** (-məm) *n., pl.* **-mums, -ma** (-mə) [L., neut. of *minimus,* least < *minor,* minor] **1.** the smallest quantity, number, or degree possible or permissible **2.** the lowest degree or point reached or recorded —*adj.* **1.** smallest possible, permissible, or reached **2.** of, marking, or setting a minimum or minimums —**min′i·mal** *adj.* —**min′i·mal·ly** *adv.*

**minimum wage** a wage established by contract or by law as the lowest that may be paid to employees doing a specified type of work

**min·ing** (mī′niŋ) *n.* the act, process, or work of removing ores, coal, etc. from a mine

**min·ion** (min′yən) *n.* [Fr. *mignon,* darling] **1.** a favorite, esp. one who is a servile follower: term of contempt **2.** a subordinate official **3.** *Printing* a size of type, 7 point —*adj.* [Rare] dainty

**minion of the law** *same as* POLICEMAN

**min·is·cule** (min′ə skyōōl′) *adj. mistaken sp. of* MINUSCULE

**min·i·skirt** (min′ē skurt′) *n.* [MINI- + SKIRT] a very short skirt ending well above the knee

**min·is·ter** (min′is tər) *n.* [< OFr. < L. *minister,* a servant

< *minor,* lesser] **1.** a person appointed to take charge of some governmental department **2.** a diplomatic officer sent to a foreign nation to represent his government **3.** anyone authorized to carry out the spiritual functions of a church, conduct worship, preach, etc.; pastor **4.** any person or thing thought of as serving as the agent of some power, force, etc. —*vt.* [Archaic] to administer —*vi.* **1.** to serve as a minister in a church **2.** to give help (*to*)

**min·is·te·ri·al** (min'is tir'ē əl) *adj.* **1.** of a minister or (the) ministry **2.** subordinate or instrumental **3.** administrative; executive —**min'is·te'ri·al·ly** *adv.*

**minister plenipotentiary** *pl.* **ministers plenipotentiary** a diplomatic representative with full authority to negotiate

**min·is·trant** (min'is trənt) *adj.* serving as a minister; ministering —*n.* a person who ministers, or serves

**min·is·tra·tion** (min'is trā'shən) *n.* **1.** the act of serving as a minister or clergyman **2.** the act of giving help

**min·is·try** (min'is trē) *n., pl.* **-tries 1.** the act of ministering, or serving **2.** *a)* the office or function of a minister of religion *b)* such ministers collectively; clergy **3.** *a)* the department under a minister of government *b)* his term of office *c)* his headquarters *d)* such ministers collectively

**min·i·ver** (min'ə vər) *n.* [ < OFr. < *menu,* small + *vair,* kind of fur < L. *varius,* variegated] a white fur used for trimming garments, esp. ceremonial robes, as of royalty

**mink** (miŋk) *n., pl.* **minks, mink:** see PLURAL, II, D, 1 [ < Scand.] **1.** a slim, carnivorous mammal with partly webbed feet; esp., a dark-brown weasel living in water part of the time **2.** its valuable fur, soft, thick, and white to brown in color

**Minn.** Minnesota

MINK
(17–28 in. long, including tail)

**Min·ne·ap·o·lis** (min'ē ap''l is) [after a nearby waterfall ( < Sioux *minne,* water, and *haha,* waterfall) + Gr. *polis,* city] city in E Minn., on the Mississippi: pop. 371,000 (met. area, with adjacent St. Paul, 2,109,000)

**min·ne·sing·er** (min'i siŋ'ər) *n.* [G. < MHG. *minne,* love + *senger,* singer] any of a number of German lyric poets and singers of the 12th to 14th cent.

**Min·ne·so·ta** (min'ə sōt'ə) [ < Sioux, lit., milky blue water] Middle Western State of the U.S.: 84,068 sq. mi.; pop. 4,077,000; cap. St. Paul: abbrev. **Minn., MN** —**Min'ne·so'tan** *adj., n.*

**min·now** (min'ō) *n., pl.* **-nows, -now:** see PLURAL, II, D, 1 [ < or akin to OE. *myne*] **1.** any of a large number of usually small freshwater fishes, used commonly as bait **2.** any very small fish Also [Dial. or Colloq.] **min'ny** (-ē), *pl.* **-nies**

**Mi·no·an** (mi nō'ən) *adj.* [ < MINOS + -AN] designating or of an advanced prehistoric culture that flourished in Crete from c.2800–c.1100 B.C.

**mi·nor** (mī'nər) *adj.* [L.] **1.** *a)* lesser in size, amount, or extent *b)* lesser in importance or rank **2.** under full legal age **3.** constituting the minority **4.** sad; melancholy **5.** *Educ.* designating a field of study in which a student specializes, but to a lesser degree than in his major **6.** *Music a)* designating an interval smaller than the corresponding major by a semitone *b)* characterized by minor intervals, scales, etc. *c)* based on the scale pattern of the minor mode: see MINOR SCALE —*vi. Educ.* to pursue a minor subject [*to minor* in French] —*n.* **1.** a person under full legal age **2.** *Educ.* a minor field of study **3.** *Music* a minor interval, key, etc. —**the minors** the minor leagues, esp. in baseball

**Mi·nor·ca** (mi nôr'kə) 2d largest of the Balearic Islands

**mi·nor·i·ty** (mə nôr'ə tē, mī-; -när'-) *n., pl.* **-ties 1.** the lesser part or smaller number; less than half **2.** a racial, religious, or political group smaller than and differing from the larger, controlling group **3.** the period or condition of being under full legal age

**minor league** any league in a professional sport, as baseball, other than the major leagues —**mi'nor-league'** *adj.* —**mi'-nor-leagu'er** *n.*

**minor order** *R.C.Ch.* any of the four lower orders below that of subdeacon, requisite for aspirants to major orders

**minor scale** one of the two standard diatonic scales, with half steps instead of whole steps, in ascending, after the second and seventh tones ( **melodic minor scale** ) or after the second, fifth, and seventh tones ( **harmonic minor scale** )

**minor suit** *Bridge* diamonds or clubs

**Mi·nos** (mī'nəs, -näs) *Gr. Myth.* a king of Crete who after he died became a judge of the dead in the lower world

**Min·o·taur** (min'ə tôr') *Gr. Myth.* a monster with the body of a man and the head of a bull, confined by Minos in a labyrinth and annually fed young Athenians, until killed by Theseus

**Minsk** (minsk; *Russ.* mēnsk) capital of the Byelorussian S.S.R.: pop. 818,000

**min·ster** (min'stər) *n.* [OE. *mynster* < LL. *monasterium,* MONASTERY] **1.** the church of a monastery **2.** any of various large churches or cathedrals

**min·strel** (min'strəl) *n.* [ < OFr., servant, orig., official < LL. < L. *ministerium,* ministry] **1.** any of a class of lyric poets and singers of the Middle Ages, who traveled from place to place singing and reciting **2.** [Poet.] a poet, singer, or musician **3.** a performer in a minstrel show

**minstrel show** a comic variety show presented by a company of performers in blackface, who sing, tell jokes, etc.

**min·strel·sy** (-sē) *n., pl.* **-sies 1.** the art or occupation of a minstrel **2.** a group of minstrels **3.** a collection of minstrels' ballads or songs

**mint¹** (mint) *n.* [OE. *mynet,* coin < L. < *Moneta,* epithet of Juno, in whose temple money was coined] **1.** a place where money is coined by the government **2.** a large amount [a *mint* of ideas] **3.** a source of manufacture or invention —*adj.* new, as if freshly minted [a postage stamp in *mint* condition] —*vt.* **1.** to coin (money) **2.** to invent or create; fabricate —**mint'er** *n.*

**mint²** (mint) *n.* [OE. *minte*] **1.** a plant of the mint family with leaves used for flavoring and in medicine **2.** a candy flavored with mint —*adj.* designating a family of plants, as the spearmint, peppermint, and basil, with aromatic leaves, volatile oil, and square stems

**mint·age** (min'tij) *n.* **1.** the act or process of minting money **2.** money so produced **3.** the cost of minting money **4.** the impression made on a coin

**mint jelly (or sauce)** a jelly (or sauce) flavored with mint leaves, served esp. with lamb

**mint julep** a frosted drink consisting of whiskey or brandy, sugar, and mint leaves

**min·u·end** (min'yoo wend') *n.* [ < L. gerundive of *minuere:* see MINUTE²] *Arith.* the number or quantity from which another is to be subtracted

**min·u·et** (min'yoo wet') *n.* [Fr. *menuet* (see MENU), orig., very small: from the small steps taken] **1.** a slow, stately dance of the 17th and 18th cent., for groups of couples **2.** the music for this, in 3/4 time

**mi·nus** (mī'nəs) *prep.* [L., neut. sing. of *minor,* less] **1.** reduced by the subtraction of, less [four *minus* two] **2.** [Colloq.] without [*minus* a toe] —*adj.* **1.** indicating subtraction [a *minus* sign] **2.** negative [a *minus* quantity] **3.** somewhat less than [a grade of A *minus*] **4.** *Elec.* same as NEGATIVE [the *minus* terminal] —*n.* **1.** a minus sign **2.** a negative quantity

**mi·nus·cule** (mi nus'kyōōl, min'ə skyōōl') *adj.* [Fr. < L. *minusculus,* rather small] very small

**minus sign** *Math.* a sign (–), indicating subtraction or negative quantity

**min·ute¹** (min'it) *n.* [ < OFr. < ML. *minuta* < L. (*pars*) *minuta* (*prima*), (first) small (part): see ff.] **1.** the sixtieth part of any of certain units; specif., *a)* 1/60 of an hour; sixty seconds *b)* 1/60 of a degree of an arc **2.** a moment; instant **3.** a specific point in time **4.** a measure of the distance usually covered in a minute [ten *minutes* from downtown] **5.** a note or memorandum; specif., [*pl.*] an official record of what was said and done at a meeting, etc. —*vt.* **-ut·ed, -ut·ing** to make minutes of; record —**the minute (that)** just as soon as —**up to the minute** in the latest style, fashion, etc.

**mi·nute²** (mī nōot', mi-; -nyōot') *adj.* [ < L. pp. of *minuere,* to lessen < *minor,* less] **1.** very small; tiny **2.** of little importance; trifling **3.** of or attentive to tiny details; exact; precise —**mi·nute'ness** *n.*

**minute hand** the longer hand of a clock or watch, which indicates the minutes and moves around the dial once every hour

**mi·nute·ly** (mī nōot'lē, mi-; -nyōot'-) *adv.* **1.** in a minute manner or in minute detail **2.** into tiny pieces

**min·ute·man** (min'it man') *n., pl.* **-men'** (-men') [*also* M-] a member of the American citizen army during the American Revolution who volunteered to be ready for military service at a minute's notice

**min·ute steak** (min'it) a small, thin steak that can be cooked quickly

**mi·nu·ti·ae** (mi nōō'shi ē', -nyōō'-) *n.pl., sing.* **-ti·a** (-shē ə, -shə) [L. < *minutus,* MINUTE²] small or relatively unimportant details

**minx** (miŋks) *n.* [ < ?] a pert, saucy young woman

**Mi·o·cene** (mī'ə sēn') *adj.* [ < Gr. *meiōn,* less + *kainos,* recent] designating or of the fourth epoch of the Tertiary Period in the Cenozoic Era —**the Miocene** the Miocene Epoch or its rocks: see GEOLOGY, chart

**Mi·ra·beau** (mir'ə bō', Fr. mē rà bō'), comte (**Honoré Gabriel Riqueti**) **de** 1749–91; Fr. revolutionist & statesman

fat, āpe, cär, ten, ēven, is, bīte; gō, hôrn, tōōl, look; oil, out; up, fʉr; get; joy; yet; chin; she; thin, *then;* zh, leisure; ŋ, ring; ə for *a* in *ago, e* in *agent, i* in *sanity, o* in *comply, u* in *focus;* as in *able* (ā'b'l); Fr. bàl; ë, Fr. coeur; ö, Fr. feu; Fr. mon; ỏ, Fr. coq; ü, Fr. duc; r, Fr. cri; H, G. ich; kh, G. doch; ‡foreign; *hypothetical; < derived from. See inside front cover.

**mir·a·cle** (mir'ə k'l) *n.* [OFr. < L. *miraculum* < *mirari*, to wonder at < *mirus*, wonderful] **1.** an event or action that apparently contradicts known scientific laws [the *miracles* in the Bible] **2.** a remarkable thing; marvel **3.** a wonderful example [a *miracle* of tact] **4.** *same as* MIRACLE PLAY

**miracle play** any of a class of medieval religious dramas dealing with events in the lives of the saints: cf. MYSTERY PLAY

**mi·rac·u·lous** (mi rak'yoo ləs) *adj.* **1.** having the nature of a miracle; supernatural **2.** like a miracle; marvelous **3.** able to work miracles —**mi·rac'u·lous·ly** *adv.* —**mi·rac'u·lous·ness** *n.*

**mi·rage** (mi räzh') *n.* [Fr. < *(se) mirer*, to be reflected < VL. *mirare*, to look at, for L. *mirari*: see MIRACLE] **1.** an optical illusion in which the image of a distant object, as an oasis, is made to appear nearby: it is caused by the refraction of light rays from the object through layers of air of different temperatures and densities **2.** something that falsely appears to be real

**mire** (mir) *n.* [< ON. *myrr*] **1.** an area of wet, soggy ground; bog **2.** deep mud or slush —*vt.* **mired, mir'ing 1.** to cause to get stuck in or as in mire **2.** to soil with mud or dirt —*vi.* to sink or stick in mud

**Mir·i·am** (mir'ē əm) [< Heb.: see MARY] **1.** a feminine name **2.** *Bible* the sister of Moses and Aaron: Ex. 15:20

**mirk** (mʉrk) *n. alt. sp. of* MURK —**mirk'y** *adj.* **mirk'i·er, mirk'i·est**

**Mi·ró** (mē rō'), Joan (hwän) 1893– ; Sp. painter

**mir·ror** (mir'ər) *n.* [< OFr. < VL. *mirare*: see MIRAGE] **1.** a smooth surface that reflects images; esp., a looking glass **2.** anything that truly pictures or describes [a play that is a *mirror* of life] —*vt.* to reflect as in a mirror

**mirth** (mʉrth) *n.* [OE. *myrgth* < base of *myrig*, pleasant] joyfulness, gaiety, or merriment, esp. when characterized by laughter

**mirth·ful** (-fəl) *adj.* full of, expressing, or causing mirth; merry —**mirth'ful·ly** *adv.* —**mirth'ful·ness** *n.*

**mirth·less** (-lis) *adj.* without mirth or joy —**mirth'less·ly** *adv.* —**mirth'less·ness** *n.*

**mir·y** (mir'ē) *adj.* **mir'i·er, mir'i·est 1.** boggy; swampy **2.** muddy; dirty —**mir'i·ness** *n.*

**mis-** [OE. *mis-* or OFr. *mes-*] *a prefix meaning:* **1.** wrong or wrongly, bad or badly [*misplace, misrule*] **2.** no, not [*mistrust, misfire*]

**mis·ad·ven·ture** (mis'əd ven'chər) *n.* an unlucky accident; bad luck; mishap

**mis·ad·vise** (-əd viz') *vt.* **-vised', -vis'ing** to advise badly —**mis'ad·vice'** (-vis') *n.*

**mis·al·li·ance** (-ə li'əns) *n.* an improper alliance; esp., an unsuitable marriage

**mis·al·ly** (-ə li') *vt.* **-lied', -ly'ing** to ally unsuitably or inappropriately

**mis·an·thrope** (mis'ən thrōp', miz'-) *n.* [< Gr. < *misein*, to hate + *anthrōpos*, a man] one who hates or distrusts all people: also **mis·an·thro·pist** (mis an'thrə pist) —**mis'an·throp'ic** (-thrăp'ik), **mis'an·throp'i·cal** *adj.* —**mis'an·throp'i·cal·ly** *adv.*

**mis·an·thro·py** (mis an'thrə pē) *n.* hatred or distrust of all people

**mis·ap·ply** (mis'ə pli') *vt.* **-plied', -ply'ing** to apply or use badly or improperly [to *misapply* one's energies, a trust fund, etc.] —**mis'ap·pli·ca'tion** *n.*

**mis·ap·pre·hend** (-ap rə hend') *vt.* to misunderstand —**mis'ap·pre·hen'sion** (-hen'shən) *n.*

**mis·ap·pro·pri·ate** (mis'ə prō'prē āt') *vt.* **-at'ed, -at'ing** to appropriate to a bad, incorrect, or dishonest use —**mis'ap·pro'pri·a'tion** *n.*

**mis·be·come** (-bi kum') *vt.* **-came', -come', -com'ing** to be unbecoming to; be unsuitable for

**mis·be·got·ten** (-bi gät''n) *adj.* wrongly or unlawfully begotten; specif., born out of wedlock: also **mis'be·got'**

**mis·be·have** (-bi hāv') *vi.* **-haved', -hav'ing** to behave wrongly —*vt.* to conduct (oneself) improperly —**mis'be·hav'er** *n.* —**mis'be·hav'ior** (-yər) *n.*

**mis·be·lief** (-bə lēf') *n.* wrong, false, or unorthodox belief

**misc.** **1.** miscellaneous **2.** miscellany

**mis·cal·cu·late** (mis kal'kyə lāt') *vt., vi.* **-lat'ed, -lat'ing** to calculate incorrectly; miscount or misjudge —**mis'cal·cu·la'tion** *n.*

**mis·call** (-kôl') *vt.* to call by a wrong name

**mis·car·riage** (-kar'ij) *n.* **1.** failure to carry out what was intended [a *miscarriage* of justice] **2.** failure of mail, freight, etc. to reach its destination **3.** the expulsion of a fetus from the womb before it is sufficiently developed to survive: see ABORTION

**mis·car·ry** (-kar'ē) *vi.* **-ried, -ry·ing 1.** *a)* to go wrong; fail: said of a plan, project, etc. *b)* to go astray; fail to arrive: said of mail, freight, etc. **2.** to suffer a miscarriage of a fetus

**mis·cast** (-kast') *vt.* **-cast', -cast'ing** to cast (an actor or a play) unsuitably

**mis·ce·ge·na·tion** (mis'i jə nā'shən, mi sej'ə-) *n.*

[coined (c.1863) < L. *miscere*, to mix + *genus*, race + -ATION] marriage or sexual relations between a man and woman of different races, esp., in the U.S., between a white and a black

**mis·cel·la·ne·ous** (mis'ə lā'nē əs, -yəs) *adj.* [< L. < *miscellus*, mixed < *miscere*, to mix] **1.** consisting of various kinds; varied; mixed **2.** having various qualities, etc.; many-sided —**mis'cel·la'ne·ous·ly** *adv.* —**mis'cel·la'ne·ous·ness** *n.*

**mis·cel·la·ny** (mis'ə lā'nē; *Brit.* mi sel'ə nē) *n., pl.* **-nies** [see prec.] **1.** a miscellaneous collection, esp. of literary works **2.** [*often pl.*] such a collection of writings, as in a book

**mis·chance** (mis chans') *n.* bad luck; misadventure

**mis·chief** (mis'chif) *n.* [< OFr. < *meschever*, to come to grief < *mes-*, mis- + *chief*, end] **1.** harm or damage, esp. that done by a person **2.** *a)* action that causes harm or trouble *b)* a person causing damage or annoyance **3.** a tendency to annoy with playful tricks **4.** *a)* a prank; playful, annoying trick *b)* playful, harmless teasing

**mis·chief-mak·er** (-mā'kər) *n.* a person who causes mischief; esp., one who creates trouble by gossiping —**mis'chief-mak'ing** *n., adj.*

**mis·chie·vous** (mis'chi vəs) *adj.* **1.** causing mischief; specif., *a)* injurious; harmful *b)* prankish; teasing **2.** inclined to annoy with playful tricks; naughty —**mis'chie·vous·ly** *adv.* —**mis'chie·vous·ness** *n.*

**mis·ci·ble** (mis'ə b'l) *adj.* [< ML. < L. *miscere*, to mix] that can be mixed —**mis'ci·bil'i·ty** *n.*

**mis·con·ceive** (mis'kən sēv') *vt., vi.* **-ceived', -ceiv'ing** to conceive or interpret wrongly; misunderstand —**mis'con·cep'tion** (-sep'shən) *n.*

**mis·con·duct** (-kən dukt'; *for n.* mis kän'dukt) *vt.* **1.** to manage badly or dishonestly **2.** to conduct (oneself) improperly —*n.* **1.** bad or dishonest management **2.** willfully improper behavior

**mis·con·strue** (-kən strōō') *vt.* **-strued', -stru'ing** to construe wrongly; misinterpret —**mis'con·struc'tion** (-struk'-shən) *n.*

**mis·count** (mis kount'; *for n. usually* mis'kount) *vt., vi.* to count incorrectly —*n.* an incorrect count

**mis·cre·ant** (mis'krē ənt) *adj.* [OFr. *mescreant,* unbelieving < *mes-*, mis- + prp. of *croire*, to believe] **1.** villainous; evil **2.** [Archaic] unbelieving —*n.* **1.** a criminal; villain **2.** [Archaic] an unbeliever —**mis'cre·an·cy** *n.*

**mis·cue** (mis kyōō') *n.* **1.** *Billiards* a shot spoiled by the cue's slipping off the ball **2.** [Colloq.] a mistake; error —*vi.* **-cued', -cu'ing 1.** to make a miscue **2.** *Theater* to miss one's cue

**mis·date** (-dāt') *vt.* **-dat'ed, -dat'ing** to date (a letter, etc.) incorrectly —*n.* a wrong date

**mis·deal** (-dēl') *vt., vi.* **-dealt', -deal'ing** to deal (playing cards) wrongly —*n.* a wrong deal —**mis'deal'er** *n.*

**mis·deed** (mis dēd') *n.* a wrong or wicked act; crime, sin, etc.

**mis·de·mean** (mis'di mēn') *vt., vi.* [Rare] to conduct (oneself) badly; misbehave

**mis·de·mean·or** (-ər) *n.* **1.** [Rare] a misbehaving **2.** *Law* any minor offense, as the breaking of a municipal ordinance, for which statute provides a lesser punishment than for a felony, usually a fine or a short term in a local jail, workhouse, etc. *Brit. sp.* **mis'de·mean'our**

**mis·di·rect** (mis'də rekt', -dī-) *vt.* to direct wrongly or badly —**mis'di·rec'tion** *n.*

**mis·do** (mis'dōō') *vt.* **-did', -done', -do'ing** to do wrongly —**mis·do'er** *n.* —**mis·do'ing** *n.*

**mis·doubt** (-dout') *vt.* [Archaic] **1.** to distrust **2.** to fear —*vi.* [Archaic] to have doubts —*n.* [Archaic] suspicion; doubt

‡**mise en scène** (mē zän sen') [Fr.] **1.** the staging of a play, motion picture, etc. including the setting, arrangement of the actors, etc. **2.** surroundings; environment

**mis·em·ploy** (mis'em ploi') *vt.* to employ wrongly or badly; misuse —**mis'em·ploy'ment** *n.*

**mi·ser** (mi'zər) *n.* [L., wretched] a greedy, stingy person who hoards money for its own sake, even at the expense of his own comfort

**mis·er·a·ble** (miz'ər ə b'l, miz'rə-) *adj.* [< Fr. < L. *miserabilis* < *miser*, wretched] **1.** in a condition of misery; wretched **2.** causing misery, discomfort, etc. [*miserable* weather] **3.** bad; inferior; inadequate [a *miserable* performance] **4.** pitiable **5.** shameful —**mis'er·a·ble·ness** *n.* —**mis'er·a·bly** *adv.*

**Mis·e·re·re** (miz'ə rer'ē, -rir'-) *n.* [LL., have mercy: first word of the psalm in the Vulgate] **1.** the 51st Psalm (50th in the Douay Version) **2.** a musical setting for this

**mi·ser·ly** (mi'zər lē) *adj.* like or characteristic of a miser; greedy and stingy —**mi'ser·li·ness** *n.*

**mis·er·y** (miz'ər ē) *n., pl.* **-er·ies** [< OFr. < L. < *miser*, wretched] **1.** a condition of great wretchedness or suffering, because of pain, sorrow, poverty, etc.; distress **2.** a cause of such suffering; pain, sorrow, poverty, squalor, etc.

**mis·fea·sance** (mis fē'z'ns) *n.* [< OFr. < *mes-*, mis- + *faire* (< L. *facere*), to do] *Law* wrongdoing; specif., the doing of a lawful act in an unlawful or improper manner infringing on the rights of others: distinguished from MAL- FEASANCE, NONFEASANCE —**mis·fea'sor** (-zər) *n.*

**mis·file** (-fīl') *vt.* -**filed'**, -**fil'ing** to file (papers, etc.) in the wrong place or order

**mis·fire** (-fīr') *vi.* -**fired'**, -**fir'ing** 1. to fail to ignite properly: said of an internal-combustion engine 2. to fail to be discharged: said of a firearm, missile, etc. 3. to fail to achieve the desired effect —*n.* an act or instance of misfiring

**mis·fit** (mis fit'; *for n. also, & for 3 always,* mis'fit') *vt., vi.* -**fit'ted**, -**fit'ting** to fit badly —*n.* 1. a misfitting 2. a garment, etc. that misfits 3. a person not suited to his position, associates, etc.

**mis·for·tune** (mis fôr'chən) *n.* 1. bad luck; ill fortune; trouble; adversity 2. an instance of this; unlucky accident; mishap

**mis·give** (-giv') *vt.* -**gave'**, -**giv'en**, -**giv'ing** to cause fear, doubt, or suspicion in [his heart *misgave* him] —*vi.* to feel fear, doubt, etc.

**mis·giv·ing** (-giv'iŋ) *n.* [*often pl.*] a disturbed feeling of fear, doubt, apprehension, etc.

**mis·gov·ern** (-guv'ərn) *vt.* to govern or administer badly —**mis·gov'ern·ment** *n.*

**mis·guide** (-gīd') *vt.* -**guid'ed**, -**guid'ing** to guide wrongly; lead into error or misconduct; mislead —**mis·guid'ance** *n.* —**mis·guid'ed·ly** *adv.* —**mis·guid'ed·ness** *n.*

**mis·han·dle** (mis han'd'l) *vt.* -**dled**, -**dling** to handle badly or roughly; abuse, mismanage, etc.

**mis·hap** (mis'hap') *n.* an unlucky accident

**mish·mash** (mish'mash') *n.* a hodgepodge; jumble: also **mish'mosh'** (-mäsh)

**Mish·na, Mish·nah** (mish nä', mish'nə) *n., pl.* **Mish·na·yot** (mish'nä yōt') [< ModHeb. < Heb. *shānāh*, to repeat, learn] the first part of the Talmud, containing interpretations of scriptural ordinances, compiled by the rabbis about 200 A.D.

**mis·in·form** (mis'in fôrm') *vt.* to supply with false or misleading information —**mis'in·form'ant**, **mis'in·form'er** *n.* —**mis'in·for·ma'tion** *n.*

**mis·in·ter·pret** (-in tur'prit) *vt.* to interpret wrongly; understand or explain incorrectly —**mis'in·ter·pre·ta'tion** *n.* —**mis'in·ter'pret·er** *n.*

**mis·judge** (mis juj') *vt., vi.* -**judged'**, -**judg'ing** to judge wrongly or unfairly —**mis·judg'ment**, **mis·judge'ment** *n.*

**mis·la·bel** (-lā'b'l) *vt., vi.* -**beled** or -**belled**, -**bel·ing** or -**bel·ling** to label incorrectly

**mis·lay** (-lā') *vt.* -**laid'**, -**lay'ing** 1. to put in a place afterward forgotten 2. to put down or install improperly [to *mislay* floor tiles]

**mis·lead** (-lēd') *vt.* -**led'**, -**lead'ing** 1. to lead in a wrong direction; lead astray 2. to deceive or delude 3. to lead into wrongdoing —**mis·lead'ing** *adj.* —**mis·lead'ing·ly** *adv.*

**mis·man·age** (-man'ij) *vt., vi.* -**aged**, -**ag·ing** to manage or administer badly —**mis·man'age·ment** *n.*

**mis·match** (-mach') *vt.* to match badly or unsuitably —*n.* a bad or unsuitable match

**mis·mate** (mis māt') *vt., vi.* -**mat'ed**, -**mat'ing** to mate badly or unsuitably

**mis·name** (-nām') *vt.* -**named'**, -**nam'ing** to give or apply a wrong name to

**mis·no·mer** (mis nō'mər) *n.* [< OFr. < *mes-*, mis- + *nomer*, to name < L. *nominare*: see NOMINATE] 1. the use of a wrong name or epithet for some person or thing 2. a name or epithet wrongly used

**mis·o-** [< Gr. < *misein*, to hate] *a combining form meaning* hatred or hating [*misogyny*]: also **mis-**

**mi·sog·a·my** (mi säg'ə mē) *n.* [prec. + -GAMY] hatred of marriage —**mi·sog'a·mist** *n.*

**mi·sog·y·ny** (mi säj'ə nē) *n.* [< Gr.: see MISO- & -GYNY] hatred of women —**mi·sog'y·nist** *n.* —**mi·sog'y·nous**, **mi·sog'y·nic** *adj.*

**mis·place** (mis plās') *vt.* -**placed'**, -**plac'ing** 1. to put in a wrong place 2. to bestow (one's trust, affection, etc.) unwisely 3. *same as* MISLAY (sense 1) —**mis·place'ment** *n.*

**mis·play** (-plā') *vt., vi.* to play wrongly or badly, as in a game —*n.* a wrong or bad play

**mis·print** (mis print'; *for n. usually* mis'print') —*vt.* to print incorrectly —*n.* an error in printing

**mis·pri·sion** (mis prizh'ən) *n.* [< OFr. < pp. of *mesprendre*, to take wrongly < *mes-*, mis- + *prendre* < L. *prehendere*, to take] *Law* 1. misconduct or neglect of duty, esp. by a public official 2. act of contempt against a government or court

**misprision of felony** (or **treason**) *Law* the offense of concealing knowledge of another's felony (or treason)

**mis·prize** (mis prīz') *vt.* -**prized'**, -**priz'ing** [< OFr. < *mes-*, mis- + LL. *pretiare*, to value < L. *pretium*, a price] to despise or undervalue

**mis·pro·nounce** (mis'prə nouns') *vt., vi.* -**nounced'**, -**nounc'ing** to give (a word) a pronunciation different from any of the accepted standard pronunciations —**mis'pro·nun'ci·a'tion** (-nun'sē ā'shən) *n.*

**mis·quote** (mis kwōt') *vt., vi.* -**quot'ed**, -**quot'ing** to quote incorrectly —**mis'quo·ta'tion** *n.*

**mis·read** (-rēd') *vt., vi.* -**read'** (-red'), -**read'ing** (-rēd'iŋ) to read wrongly, esp. so as to misinterpret or misunderstand

**mis·rep·re·sent** (mis'rep ri zent') *vt.* 1. to represent falsely; give an untrue idea of 2. to be a bad representative of —**mis'rep·re·sen·ta'tion** *n.*

**mis·rule** (mis rool') *vt.* -**ruled'**, -**rul'ing** to rule badly or unjustly; misgovern —*n.* 1. misgovernment 2. disorder or riot —**mis·rul'er** *n.*

**miss**[1] (mis) *vt.* [OE. *missan*] 1. to fail to hit, meet, catch, do, see, hear, etc. 2. to let (an opportunity, etc.) go by 3. to escape; avoid [he *missed* being hit] 4. to fail or forget to do, keep, attend, etc. [he *missed* a class] 5. to notice, feel, or regret the absence or loss of —*vi.* 1. to fail to hit something aimed at 2. to fail to be successful 3. to misfire, as an engine —*n.* a failure to hit, obtain, etc.

**miss**[2] (mis) *n., pl.* **miss'es** [contr. of MISTRESS] 1. [M-] a title used in speaking to or of an unmarried woman or girl, placed before the name [*Miss* Smith, the *Misses* Smith] 2. a young unmarried woman or girl 3. [*pl.*] a series of sizes in clothing for women and girls of average proportions

**Miss.** Mississippi

**miss.** 1. mission 2. missionary

**mis·sal** (mis''l) *n.* [< ML. < LL. *missa*, MASS] *R.C.Ch.* a book containing all the prayers, rites, etc. for the Mass throughout the year

**mis·shape** (mis shāp') *vt.* -**shaped'**, -**shaped'** or archaic -**shap'en**, -**shap'ing** to shape badly; deform

**mis·shap·en** (-'n) *adj.* badly shaped; deformed —**mis·shap'en·ly** *adv.* —**mis·shap'en·ness** *n.*

**mis·sile** (mis''l) *adj.* [L. *missilis* < pp. of *mittere*, to send] that can be, or is, thrown or shot —*n.* a weapon or other object, as a spear, bullet, rocket, etc., designed to be thrown or launched toward a target; often, specif., a guided missile

**mis·sile·ry, mis·sil·ry** (-rē) *n.* 1. the science of building and launching guided missiles 2. guided missiles collectively

**miss·ing** (mis'iŋ) *adj.* absent; lost; lacking; specif., absent after combat, but not definitely known to be dead or taken prisoner

**mis·sion** (mish'ən) *n.* [L. *missio* < pp. of *mittere*, to send] 1. a sending out or being sent out with authority to perform a special duty, as by a church, government, etc. 2. *a)* a group of persons sent by a church to spread its religion, esp. in a foreign land *b)* its headquarters *c)* [*pl.*] organized missionary work 3. a diplomatic delegation; embassy 4. a group of technicians, etc. sent to a foreign country 5. the special duty or function for which someone is sent 6. the special task for which a person is apparently destined in life; calling 7. any charitable or religious organization for doing welfare work for the needy 8. *Mil.* an assigned combat operation; esp., a single combat flight by an airplane or group of airplanes —*adj.* of a mission or missions —*vt.* to send on a mission

**mis·sion·ar·y** (-er'ē) *adj.* of or characteristic of religious missions or missionaries —*n., pl.* -**ar'ies** a person sent on a mission; specif., a person sent out by his church to preach, teach, and proselytize, as in a foreign country considered heathen: also **mis'sion·er**

**mis·sis** (mis'əz) *n.* [altered < MRS.] [Dial.] one's wife: also used with *the:* also **mis'sus**

**Mis·sis·sip·pi** (mis'ə sip'ē) [< Fr. < Algonquian, lit., big river] 1. river in C U.S., flowing from N Minn. to the Gulf of Mexico: 2,348 mi. 2. Southern State of the U.S.: 47,716 sq. mi.; pop. 2,521,000; cap. Jackson: abbrev. **Miss., MS**

**Mis·sis·sip·pi·an** (-ən) *adj.* 1. of the Mississippi River 2. of the State of Mississippi 3. designating or of the first coal-forming period of the Paleozoic Era in N. America —*n.* a native or inhabitant of Mississippi —**the Mississippian** the Mississippian Period or its rocks: see GEOLOGY, chart

**mis·sive** (mis'iv) *n.* [Fr. < ML. < L. pp. of *mittere*, to send] a letter or written message

**Mis·sour·i** (mi zoor'ē) [< Algonquian, lit., people of the big canoes] 1. river in WC U.S., flowing from NW Mont. to the Mississippi: 2,466 mi. 2. Middle Western State of the C U.S.: 69,686 sq. mi.; pop. 4,917,000; cap. Jefferson City: abbrev. **Mo., MO** —from Missouri [Colloq.] not easily convinced —**Mis·sour'i·an** *adj., n.*

**mis·speak** (mis spēk′) *vt., vi.* **-spoke′, -spok′en, -speak′-ing** to speak or say incorrectly

**mis·spell** (-spel′) *vt., vi.* **-spelled′** or **-spelt′, -spell′ing** to spell incorrectly

**mis·spell·ing** (-spel′iŋ) *n.* (an) incorrect spelling

**mis·spend** (-spend′) *vt.* **-spent′, -spend′ing** to spend improperly or wastefully

**mis·state** (-stāt′) *vt.* **-stat′ed, -stat′ing** to state incorrectly or falsely —**mis·state′ment** *n.*

**mis·step** (mis step′) *n.* **1.** a wrong or awkward step **2.** a mistake in conduct; faux pas

**mist** (mist) *n.* [OE.] **1.** a large mass of water vapor like a light fog **2.** a cloud of dust, gas, etc. **3.** a fine spray, as of perfume **4.** a film before the eyes, blurring the vision [through a *mist* of tears] **5.** anything that obscures the understanding, memory, etc. —*vt., vi.* to obscure with or as with a mist

**mis·take** (mi stāk′) *vt.* **-took′, -tak′en** or obs. **-took′, -tak′ing** [ON. *mistaka,* to take wrongly] **1.** to understand or perceive wrongly **2.** to take to be another [he *mistook* me for another] —*vi.* to make a mistake —*n.* **1.** a fault in understanding, interpretation, etc. **2.** a blunder; error —**and no mistake** [Colloq.] certainly —**mis·tak′a·ble** *adj.*

**mis·tak·en** (-stāk′'n) *adj.* **1.** wrong; having an incorrect understanding, perception, etc.: said of persons **2.** incorrect; misunderstood: said of ideas, etc. —**mis·tak′en·ly** *adv.*

**mis·ter** (mis′tər) *n.* [weakened form of MASTER] **1.** [M-] *a)* a title used in speaking to or of a man, placed before his name or office and usually written *Mr. b)* a title before the name of a place, occupation, etc. to designate an outstanding man in it **2.** [Colloq.] sir: in direct address, not followed by a name **3.** [Dial.] one's husband: also used with *the*

**mis·time** (mis tīm′) *vt.* **-timed′, -tim′ing** **1.** to do at an inappropriate time **2.** to judge incorrectly the time of

**mis·tle·toe** (mis′'l tō′) *n.* [< OE. < *mistel,* mistletoe + *tan,* a twig] **1.** an evergreen plant with yellowish-green leaves and waxy white, poisonous berries, parasitic on trees **2.** a sprig of this, hung as a Christmas decoration

**mis·took** (mi stook′) *pt. & obs. pp. of* MISTAKE

**mis·tral** (mis′trəl, mi strȧl′) *n.* [Fr. < Pr., lit., master-wind < L. < *magister,* MASTER] a cold, dry, north wind that blows over the Mediterranean coast of France and nearby regions

**mis·treat** (mis trēt′) *vt.* to treat wrongly or badly —**mis·treat′ment** *n.*

**mis·tress** (mis′tris) *n.* [< OFr. fem. of *maistre,* MASTER] **1.** a woman who rules others or controls something; specif., *a)* a woman head of a household or institution *b)* [Chiefly Brit.] a woman schoolteacher **2.** [sometimes M-] something regarded as feminine that has control, power, etc. [England was *Mistress* of the seas] **3.** a woman who has sexual relations with, and may be supported by, a man to whom she is not married **4.** [Archaic] a sweetheart **5.** [M-] formerly, a title prefixed to the name of a woman: now replaced by *Mrs.* or *Miss*

**mis·tri·al** (mis trī′əl) *n. Law* a trial made void because of an error in the proceedings, or because the jury cannot reach a verdict

**mis·trust** (-trust′) *n.* lack of trust or confidence; suspicion —*vt., vi.* to have no trust or confidence in; doubt —**mis·trust′ful** *adj.* —**mis·trust′ful·ly** *adv.* —**mis·trust′ful·ness** *n.*

**mist·y** (mis′tē) *adj.* **mist′i·er, mist′i·est** **1.** of or like mist **2.** characterized by or covered with mist **3.** *a)* blurred or dimmed, as by mist *b)* obscure or vague —**mist′i·ly** *adv.* —**mist′i·ness** *n.*

**mis·un·der·stand** (mis′un dər stand′, mis un′-) *vt.* **-stood′, -stand′ing** to fail to understand correctly; miscomprehend or misinterpret

**mis·un·der·stand·ing** (-stan′diŋ) *n.* **1.** a failure to understand correctly **2.** a quarrel; disagreement

**mis·un·der·stood** (-stood′) *adj.* **1.** not properly understood **2.** not properly appreciated

**mis·us·age** (mis yōō′sij, -zij) *n.* **1.** incorrect usage, as of words **2.** bad or harsh treatment

**mis·use** (mis yōōz′; *for n.* -yōōs′) *vt.* **-used′, -us′ing** **1.** to use improperly; misapply **2.** to treat badly or harshly; abuse —*n.* incorrect or improper use —**mis·us′er** *n.*

**mis·val·ue** (-val′yōō) *vt.* **-ued, -u·ing** to fail to value properly or adequately

**mis·word** (-wurd′) *vt.* to word incorrectly

**mis·write** (-rīt′) *vt.* **-wrote′, -writ′ten, -writ′ing** to write incorrectly

**Mitch·ell** (mich′əl), **Maria** 1818–89; U.S. astronomer

**mite**[1] (mīt) *n.* [OE.] any of a large number of tiny arachnids, often parasitic upon animals, insects, or plants, or infesting prepared foods

**mite**[2] (mīt) *n.* [< MDu., ult. same as prec.] **1.** *a)* a very small sum of money *b)* formerly, a coin of very small value **2.** a bit; a little [a *mite* slow] **3.** a very small creature

**mi·ter**[1] (mīt′ər) *n.* [< OFr. < L. < Gr. *mitra,* a headband] **1.** a tall, ornamented cap with peaks in front and back, worn by bishops and abbots as a mark of office **2.** the office or rank of a bishop —*vt.* to invest with the office of bishop

**mi·ter**[2] (mīt′ər) *n.* [prob. < prec.] *Carpentry* **1.** a kind of joint formed by fitting together two pieces, beveled to form a corner (usually a right angle): also **miter joint** **2.** either of the facing surfaces of such a joint —*vt.* **1.** to fit together in a miter **2.** to bevel the edges of to form a miter

MITER

MITER JOINT

**mit·i·gate** (mit′ə gāt′) *vt., vi.* **-gat′ed, -gat′ing** [< L. pp. of *mitigare,* to make mild < *mitis,* mild + *agere,* to drive] to make or become milder, less severe, or less painful —**mit′i·ga·ble** (-i gə b'l) *adj.* —**mit′i·ga′tion** *n.* —**mit′i·ga′tive** *adj.* —**mit′i·ga·tor** *n.* —**mit′i·ga·to′ry** (-gə tôr′ē) *adj.*

**Mit·i·lí·ni** (mit′'l ē′nē) *same as* LESBOS

**mi·to·sis** (mī tō′sis, mi-) *n., pl.* **-ses** (-sēz) [ModL. < Gr. *mitos,* thread + -OSIS] *Biol.* the indirect method of nuclear division of cells: the nuclear chromatin first appears as long threads which in turn break into chromosomes that are split lengthwise —**mi·tot′ic** (-tät′ik) *adj.* —**mi·tot′i·cal·ly** *adv.*

**mi·tral** (mī′trəl) *adj.* of or like a miter

**mitral valve** the valve between the left atrium and left ventricle of the heart

**mi·tre** (mīt′ər) *n., vt.* **-tred, -tring** *Brit. sp. of* MITER

**mitt** (mit) *n.* [contr. < MITTEN] **1.** a woman's glove covering part of the arm, the hand, and sometimes part of the fingers **2.** *same as* MITTEN **3.** [Slang] a hand **4.** *a)* *Baseball* a padded glove worn for protection [catcher's *mitt*] *b)* a boxing glove

**mit·ten** (mit′'n) *n.* [< OFr. *mitaine*] **1.** a glove with a thumb but no separately divided fingers **2.** *earlier var. of* MITT (sense 1)

**mix** (miks) *vt.* **mixed** or **mixt, mix′ing** [prob. < *mixt,* mixed < Fr. < L. pp. of *miscere,* to mix] **1.** to blend together in a single mass or compound **2.** to make by blending ingredients [to *mix* a cake] **3.** to join; combine [to *mix* work and play] **4.** to cause to associate [to *mix* boys with girls in a school] —*vi.* **1.** to be mixed; be blended; mingle **2.** to associate or get along —*n.* **1.** a mixing or being mixed **2.** a state of confusion **3.** a mixture, as of ingredients for making something **4.** soda, ginger ale, etc. for mixing with alcoholic liquor —**mix up 1.** to mix thoroughly **2.** to confuse **3.** to involve (*in* some matter) —**mix′a·ble** *adj.*

**mixed** (mikst) *adj.* **1.** joined or blended in a single mass or compound **2.** made up of different parts, elements, races, etc. **3.** consisting of or involving both sexes [mixed company] **4.** confused; muddled

**mixed bag** a random assortment or mixture, esp. of diverse elements, types of people, etc.

**mixed marriage** marriage between persons of different religions or races

**mixed media** **1.** the use of more than two media for an effect, as by combining acting, flashing lights, tape recordings, etc. **2.** *Painting* the use of different media, as oil and crayon, in the same composition

**mixed number** a number consisting of a whole number and a fraction, as 3 2/3

**mix·er** (mik′sər) *n.* **1.** one that mixes; specif., *a)* a person with reference to his sociability *b)* a machine or an electric appliance for mixing **2.** [Slang] a social gathering for getting people acquainted

**mix·ture** (miks′chər) *n.* **1.** a mixing or being mixed **2.** something mixed **3.** *Chem.* a substance containing two or more ingredients: distinguished from COMPOUND[1] in that the constituents are not in fixed proportions, retain their individual characteristics, and are physically separable

**mix-up** (miks′up′) *n.* **1.** a condition or instance of confusion **2.** [Colloq.] a fight

**miz·zen, miz·en** (miz′'n) *adj.* [< or akin to MFr. *misaine* < It. < L. *medianus:* see MEDIAN] of the mizzenmast —*n.* **1.** a fore-and-aft sail set on the mizzenmast **2.** clipped form of MIZZENMAST

**miz·zen·mast** (-məst, -mast′) *n.* the mast nearest the stern in a ship with two or three masts

**mk.** *pl.* **mks.** **1.** mark (monetary unit) **2.** markka

**mks., m.k.s., M.K.S.** meter-kilogram-second

**mkt.** market

**ML.** Medieval (or Middle) Latin

**ml.** **1.** mail **2.** milliliter(s): also **ml**

**Mlle.** *pl.* **Mlles.** Mademoiselle

**MLowG.** Middle Low German

**mm, mm.** 1. millimeter(s) 2. [L. *millia*] thousands

**MM.** Messieurs

**Mme.** Madame

**Mmes.** Mesdames

**MN** Minnesota

**Mn** *Chem.* manganese

**mne·mon·ic** (nē män′ik) *adj.* [< Gr. < *mnēmōn,* mindful < *mnasthai,* to remember] 1. helping, or meant to help, the memory 2. of mnemonics or memory —**mne·mon′i·cal·ly** *adv.*

**mne·mon·ics** (-iks) *n.pl.* 1. [*with sing. v.*] a technique for improving memory by the use of certain formulas 2. such formulas

**-mo** (mō) [< L. abl. ending] *a suffix meaning* having (a specified number of) leaves as a result of folding a sheet of paper [*twelvemo*]

**Mo** *Chem.* molybdenum

**Mo.** 1. Missouri: also **MO** 2. Monday

**mo.** 1. money order 2. *pl.* **mos.** month

**M.O., MO** 1. Medical Officer 2. money order

**m.o.** money order

**mo·a** (mō′ə) *n.* [< native (Maori) name] any of an extinct group of very large, flightless birds of New Zealand, resembling the ostrich

**Mo·ab** (mō′ab) ancient kingdom east & south of the Dead Sea —**Mo′ab·ite′** (-ə bīt′) *adj., n.*

**moan** (mōn) *n.* [< base of OE. *mænan,* to complain] 1. formerly, a lamentation 2. a low, mournful sound of sorrow or pain 3. any similar sound, as of the wind —*vi.* 1. to make a moan 2. to complain, lament, etc. —*vt.* 1. to say with a moan 2. to bewail [to *moan* one's fate]

**moat** (mōt) *n.* [OFr. *mote*] a deep, broad ditch dug around a fortress or castle, and often filled with water, for protection against invasion —*vt.* to surround with or as with a moat

**mob** (mäb) *n.* [< L. *mobile* (*vulgus*), movable (crowd)] 1. a disorderly and lawless crowd; rabble 2. any crowd 3. the common people: contemptuous term 4. [Slang] a gang of criminals —*vt.* **mobbed, mob′bing** 1. to crowd around and attack, jostle, annoy, etc. 2. to throng

**mob·cap** (mäb′kap′) *n.* [< MDu. *mop,* woman's cap + CAP] formerly, a woman's cap, worn indoors, with a high, puffy crown, often tied under the chin

**Mo·bile** (mō′bēl, mō′bēl) [< Fr. < AmInd.] seaport in SW Ala., on an arm (**Mobile Bay**) of the Gulf of Mexico: pop. 200,000

**mo·bile** (mō′b'l, -bīl; *also, & for n. usually,* -bēl) *adj.* [OFr. < L. *mobilis < movere,* to move] 1. *a)* moving, or able to move, from place to place *b)* movable by means of a motor vehicle [a *mobile* home] 2. that can change rapidly or easily, as to suit moods or needs; flexible, adaptable, fluid, etc. 3. designating or of a society in which one may move freely or advance from one class to another —*n.* an abstract sculpture with parts that can move, as a suspended arrangement of thin forms, rings, etc. —**mo·bil·i·ty** (mō bil′ə tē) *n.*

**mobile home** a movable dwelling with no permanent foundation, but connected to utility lines and set more or less permanently at a location

**mo·bi·lize** (mō′bə līz′) *vt.* **-lized′, -liz′ing** 1. *a)* to make movable *b)* to put into motion, circulation, or use 2. to make ready for immediate active service in war 3. to organize (people, resources, etc.) for any active service or use —*vi.* to become mobilized, as for war —**mo′bi·liz′a·ble** *adj.* —**mo′bi·li·za′tion** *n.* —**mo′bi·liz′er** *n.*

**Mö·bi·us strip** (mā′bē əs, mō′-) [after A. *Möbius* (1790–1868), G. mathematician] a surface with only one side, formed from a narrow strip of paper given a half twist and then pasted together

**mob·oc·ra·cy** (mäb äk′rə sē) *n., pl.* **-cies** [MOB + (DEM)OCRACY] 1. rule by a mob 2. the mob as ruler

**mob·ster** (mäb′stər) *n.* [Slang] a gangster

**Mo·çam·bi·que** (moo′səm bē′kə) Port. name of MOZAMBIQUE

**moc·ca·sin** (mäk′ə s'n) *n.* [< Algonquian] 1. a heelless slipper of soft, flexible leather, worn orig. by N. American Indians 2. a similar slipper, but with a hard sole and heel 3. *same as* WATER MOCCASIN

**moccasin flower** *same as* LADY-SLIPPER

**mo·cha** (mō′kə) *n.* [after Mocha, seaport in Yemen] 1. a choice grade of coffee grown orig. in Arabia 2. [Colloq.] any coffee 3. a flavoring made from coffee or coffee and chocolate 4. a type of soft, velvety leather —*adj.* 1. flavored with coffee or coffee and chocolate 2. reddish-brown

MOCCASINS

**mock** (mäk) *vt.* [OFr. *mocquer,* to mock] 1. to hold up to scorn or contempt; ridicule 2. to mimic, as in fun or derision 3. to lead on and disappoint; deceive 4. to defy and make futile —*vi.* to express scorn, ridicule, etc. —*n.* 1. a mocking 2. an object of ridicule 3. an imitation —*adj.* sham; imitation —**mock′er** *n.* —**mock′ing·ly** *adv.*

**mock·er·y** (-ər ē) *n., pl.* **-er·ies** 1. a mocking 2. an object of ridicule 3. a false, derisive, or impertinent imitation 4. vain effort; futility

**mock-he·ro·ic** (-hi rō′ik) *adj.* mocking, or burlesquing, heroic manner, action, or character —**mock′-he·ro′i·cal·ly** *adv.*

**mock·ing·bird** (mäk′iŋ bʉrd′) *n.* an American songbird able to imitate many birdcalls

**mock orange** any of a genus of shrubs with fragrant white flowers like those of the orange

**mock turtle soup** a soup made from calf's head, veal, etc., spiced to taste like green turtle soup

**mock-up** (mäk′up′) *n.* a scale model or replica of a structure or apparatus, used for instructional or experimental purposes

**mod** (mäd) *adj.* [< MOD(ERN)] [*also* M-] designating a flamboyant style of clothing popular among young people, originating in England in the 1960's

**mod.** 1. moderate 2. modern

**mod·al** (mōd′'l) *adj.* of or indicating a mode or mood; specif., *Gram.* of or expressing mood —**mo·dal·i·ty** (mō dal′ə tē) *n., pl.* **-ties** —**mod′al·ly** *adv.*

**modal auxiliary** an auxiliary verb used with another to indicate its mood: *can, may, might, must, should,* and *would* are *modal auxiliaries*

**mode** (mōd) *n.* [L. *modus,* measure, manner] 1. a manner or way of acting, doing, or being 2. [Fr. < L. *modus*] customary usage, or current fashion or style 3. *Gram. same as* MOOD² 4. *Music* the arrangement, or any specific arrangement, of tones and semitones in a scale 5. *Statistics* the value, number, etc. that appears most frequently in a given series

**mod·el** (mäd′'l) *n.* [< Fr. < It. *modello,* dim. of *modo* < L. *modus,* MODE] 1. *a)* a small copy or representation of an existing or planned object, as a ship, building, etc. *b) same as* ARCHETYPE (sense 1) *c)* a representation of the supposed structure of something *d)* a piece of sculpture in wax or clay from which a finished work in bronze, marble, etc. is to be made 2. a person or thing considered as a standard of excellence to be imitated 3. a style or design [a 1972 *model*] 4. *a)* a person who poses for an artist or photographer *b)* any person or thing serving as a subject for an artist *c)* a person employed to display clothes by wearing them —*adj.* 1. serving as a model, or standard of excellence 2. representative; typical —*vt.* **-eled** *or* **-elled, -el·ing** *or* **-el·ling** 1. *a)* to make a model of *b)* to plan or form after a model *c)* to make conform to a standard of excellence 2. to shape or form in or as in clay, wax, etc. 3. to display (a dress, etc.) by wearing —*vi.* 1. to make a model or models 2. to serve as a model (sense 4) —**mod′el·er, mod′el·ler** *n.*

**mod·er·ate** (mäd′ər it; *for v.* -ə rāt′) *adj.* [< L. pp. of *moderare,* to restrain] 1. within reasonable limits; avoiding extremes; temperate 2. mild; not violent [*moderate* weather] 3. of average or medium quality, range, etc. [*moderate* skills] —*n.* a person holding moderate views, as in politics or religion —*vt., vi.* **-at′ed, -at′ing** 1. to make or become moderate 2. to preside over (a meeting, etc.) —**mod′er·ate·ly** *adv.* —**mod′er·ate·ness** *n.*

**mod·er·a·tion** (mäd′ə rā′shən) *n.* 1. a moderating, or bringing within bounds 2. avoidance of extremes 3. absence of violence; calmness —**in moderation** to a moderate degree; without excess

**mod·e·ra·to** (-rät′ō) *adj., adv.* [It.] *Music* with moderation in tempo

**mod·er·a·tor** (mäd′ə rāt′ər) *n.* a person or thing that moderates; specif., a person who presides at a meeting, debate, etc. —**mod′er·a′tor·ship′** *n.*

**mod·ern** (mäd′ərn) *adj.* [< Fr. < LL. *modernus* < L. *modo,* just now, orig. abl. of *modus,* measure] 1. of the present or recent times; specif., *a)* of the latest styles, methods, ideas, etc.; up-to-date *b)* designating or of certain contemporary trends in art, music, literature, dance, etc. 2. of the period of history from c.1450 A.D. to now 3. [*often* M-] designating the most recent stage of a language [*Modern English*] —*n.* 1. a person living in modern times 2. a person with modern ideas, standards, etc. —**mo·der′ni·ty** (mä dʉr′nə tē, mə-) *n., pl.* **-ties** —**mod′ern·ly** *adv.* —**mod′ern·ness** *n.*

**Modern English** the English language since about the mid-15th cent.: cf. EARLY MODERN ENGLISH

**Modern Hebrew** Hebrew in post-Biblical times, esp. as the language of modern Israel

**mod·ern·ism** (-iz'm) *n.* **1.** *a)* modern practices, ideas, etc., or sympathy with these *b)* a modern idiom, practice, or usage **2.** [M-] *Christianity* any movement redefining doctrine in the light of modern science, etc. —**mod'ern·ist** *n., adj.* —**mod'ern·is'tic** *adj.* —**mod'ern·is'ti·cal·ly** *adv.*

**mod·ern·ize** (mäd'ər nīz') *vt., vi.* **-ized', -iz'ing** to make or become modern in style, design, methods, etc. —**mod'ern·i·za'tion** *n.* —**mod'ern·iz'er** *n.*

**Modern Latin** the Latin used since c.1500, chiefly in scientific literature

**mod·est** (mäd'ist) *adj.* [< Fr. < L. *modestus* < *modus,* measure] **1.** having or showing a moderate opinion of one's own value, abilities, etc.; not vain **2.** not forward; shy or reserved *[modest behavior]* **3.** behaving, dressing, etc. decorously or decently **4.** moderate or reasonable; not extreme *[a modest request]* **5.** quiet and humble in appearance, style, etc. *[a modest home]* —**mod'est·ly** *adv.*

**Mo·des·to** (mə des'tō) [Sp., lit., modest] city in C Calif.: pop. 106,000

**mod·es·ty** (mäd'is tē) *n.* the quality or state of being modest; specif., *a)* unassuming or humble behavior *b)* moderation *c)* decency; decorum

**ModGr.** Modern Greek

**ModHeb.** Modern Hebrew

**mod·i·cum** (mäd'i kəm) *n.* [L., neut. of *modicus,* moderate] a small amount; bit

**mod·i·fi·ca·tion** (mäd'ə fi kā'shən) *n.* a modifying or being modified; specif., *a)* a partial or slight change in form *b)* a product of this *c)* a slight reduction *d)* a qualification or limitation of meaning

**mod·i·fi·er** (mäd'ə fī'ər) *n.* a person or thing that modifies; esp., a word, phrase, or clause that limits the meaning of another word or phrase *[adjectives and adverbs are modifiers]*

**mod·i·fy** (mäd'ə fī') *vt.* **-fied', -fy'ing** [< MFr. < L. *modificare,* to limit < *modus,* measure + *facere,* to make] **1.** to change or alter, esp. slightly or partially **2.** to limit or lessen slightly; moderate *[to modify a penalty]* **3.** *Gram.* to limit the meaning of; qualify *["old" modifies "man" in old man]* **4.** *Linguis.* to change (a vowel) by umlaut —*vi.* to be modified —**mod'i·fi'a·ble** *adj.*

**Mo·di·glia·ni** (mō'dē lyä'nē), **A·me·de·o** (ä'me de'ō) 1884–1920; It. painter, in France

**mod·ish** (mōd'ish) *adj.* in the latest style; fashionable —**mod'ish·ly** *adv.* —**mod'ish·ness** *n.*

**mo·diste** (mō dēst') *n.* [Fr. < *mode:* see MODE] a woman who makes or deals in fashionable clothes, hats, etc. for women: somewhat old-fashioned term

**ModL.** Modern Latin

**mod·u·lar** (mäj'ə lər) *adj.* **1.** of a module or modulus **2.** designating or of units of standardized size, design, etc. that can be arranged or fitted together in various ways

**mod·u·late** (-lāt') *vt.* **-lat'ed, -lat'ing** [< L. pp. of *modulari* < dim. of *modus,* measure] **1.** to regulate, adjust, or adapt **2.** to vary the pitch, intensity, etc. of (the voice) **3.** *Radio* to vary the amplitude, frequency, or phase of (an oscillation, as a carrier wave) in accordance with some signal —*vi.* to shift from one key to another within a musical composition —**mod'u·la'tion** *n.* —**mod'u·la'tor** *n.* —**mod'u·la·to'ry** *adj.*

**mod·ule** (mäj'ōol) *n.* [Fr. < L. dim. of *modus,* measure] **1.** a standard or unit of measurement, as in architecture **2.** *a)* any of a set of units, as cabinets, designed to be arranged or joined in various ways *b)* a detachable section, compartment, or unit with a specific function, as in a spacecraft *c) Electronics* a compact assembly functioning as a component of a larger unit

**mod·u·lus** (mäj'ə ləs) *n., pl.* **-u·li'** (-lī') [ModL. < L.: see prec.] *Physics* a constant expressing the measure of some property, as elasticity

‡**mo·dus o·pe·ran·di** (mō'dəs äp'ə ran'dī, -dē) [L.] mode of operation; procedure

‡**modus vi·ven·di** (vi ven'dī, -dē) [L.] **1.** mode of living **2.** a temporary compromise in a dispute

**Mo·gul** (mō'gul, -g'l; mō gul') *n.* [Per. *Mughul*] **1.** a Mongol, or Mongolian; esp., any of the Mongolian conquerors of India or their descendants **2.** [m-] a powerful or important person

**mo·hair** (mō'her) *n.* [< OIt. < Ar. *mukhayyar*] **1.** the hair of the Angora goat **2.** yarn or a fabric made from this hair —*adj.* of mohair

**Mo·ham·med** (mō ham'id) 570?–632 A.D.; Arabian prophet: founder of the Moslem religion

**Mo·ham·med·an** (mō ham'i d'n) *adj.* of Mohammed or the Moslem religion —*n. same as* MOSLEM: term used mainly by non-Moslems

**Mo·ham·med·an·ism** (-iz'm) *n. same as* ISLAM: term used mainly by non-Moslems

**Mo·ha·ve** (mō hä'vē) *n.* [< Mohave words for "three" & "mountain"] **1.** *pl.* **-ves, -ve** a member of an Indian tribe living along the Colorado River in Arizona **2.** their language —*adj.* of the Mohaves

**Mo·hawk¹** (mō'hôk) *n.* [< Algonquian word meaning "man-eaters"] **1.** *pl.* **-hawks, -hawk** a member of an Iroquoian Indian tribe orig. of the Mohawk Valley, New York, now in Canada and New York **2.** their language —*adj.* of the Mohawks

**Mo·hawk²** (mō'hôk') [< prec.] river in C & E N.Y., flowing into the Hudson

**Mo·he·gan** (mō hē'gən) *n.* [< Algonquian, lit., a wolf] **1.** *pl.* **-gans, -gan** a member of a Mahican tribe of Algonquian Indians who lived in Connecticut **2.** *same as* MAHICAN —*adj.* of the Mohegans

**Mo·hi·can** (mō hē'kən) *n., adj. same as* MAHICAN

**moi·e·ty** (moi'ə tē) *n., pl.* **-ties** [< OFr. < L. < *medius,* middle] **1.** a half **2.** an indefinite part

**moil** (moil) *vi.* [< OFr. *moillier,* to moisten < L. *mollis,* soft] to toil —*vt.* [Archaic] to moisten or soil —*n.* **1.** toil **2.** turmoil —**moil'er** *n.*

**moire** (mwär, môr) *n.* [Fr., watered silk < E. MOHAIR] a fabric, as silk, rayon, or acetate, having a watered, or wavy, pattern

**moi·ré** (mwä rā', mô-; môr'ā) *adj.* [Fr.] having a watered, or wavy, pattern —*n.* **1.** a watered pattern pressed into cloth, etc. with engraved rollers **2.** *same as* MOIRE

**moist** (moist) *adj.* [OFr. *moiste* < L. *mucidus,* moldy < *mucus,* mucus] **1.** slightly wet; damp **2.** tearful —**moist'ly** *adv.* —**moist'ness** *n.*

**mois·ten** (mois''n) *vt., vi.* to make or become moist —**mois'ten·er** *n.*

**mois·ture** (-chər) *n.* water, etc. causing a slight wetness or dampness —**mois'ture·less** *adj.*

**mois·tur·ize** (-īz') *vt., vi.* **-ized', -iz'ing** to add or restore moisture to (the skin, air, etc.) —**mois'tur·iz'er** *n.*

**Mo·ja·ve** (mō hä'vē) *n., adj. same as* MOHAVE

**Mojave Desert** desert in SE Calif.

**mol** (mōl) *n. same as* MOLE⁴

**MOL** manned orbiting laboratory

**mol.** **1.** molecular **2.** molecule

**mo·lar** (mō'lər) *adj.* [< L. < *mola,* millstone] **1.** used for or capable of grinding **2.** designating or of a tooth or teeth adapted for grinding —*n.* a molar tooth: in man there are twelve molars

**mo·las·ses** (mə las'iz) *n.* [< Port. *melaco* < LL. *mellaceum,* must < L. *mel,* honey] a thick, usually dark brown syrup produced during the refining of sugar, or from sorghum, etc.

**mold¹** (mōld) *n.* [OFr. *molle* < L. *modulus:* see MODULE] **1.** a hollow form for shaping something plastic or molten **2.** a frame, shaped core, etc, on or around which something is modeled **3.** a pattern or model for something **4.** something formed in or on, or as if in or on, a mold; often, specif., a gelatin dessert, aspic, etc. so formed **5.** form or shape, esp. that given by a mold **6.** distinctive character or nature —*vt.* **1.** to make or shape in or on, or as if in or on, a mold **2.** to influence (opinion, etc.) strongly **3.** to fit closely to the contours of **4.** to ornament by or with molding **5.** to make a mold of for a casting —**mold'a·ble** *adj.* —**mold'er** *n.*

**mold²** (mōld) *n.* [ME. *moul:* sp. prob. infl. by ff.] **1.** a downy or furry fungous growth on organic matter, esp. in the presence of dampness or decay **2.** any fungus producing such a growth —*vt., vi.* to make or become moldy

**mold³** (mōld) *n.* [OE. *molde,* earth] loose, soft soil, esp. when rich with decayed organic matter

**Mol·da·vi·a** (mäl dā'vē ə, -dāv'yə) **1.** region in E Romania **2.** republic of the U.S.S.R., adjacent to this region: 13,000 sq. mi.; pop. 3,500,000; cap. Kishinev: in full, **Moldavian Soviet Socialist Republic** —**Mol·da'vi·an** *adj., n.*

**mold·board** (mōld'bôrd') *n.* **1.** a curved iron plate on a plowshare, for turning over the soil **2.** a large plate like this at the front of a bulldozer or snowplow, angled to push material aside **3.** one of the boards used to form a mold for concrete

**mold·er** (mōl'dər) *vi., vt.* [see MOLD³ & -ER] to crumble into dust; decay

**mold·ing** (mōl'diŋ) *n.* **1.** the act of one that molds **2.** something molded **3.** *a)* the ornamental contour of a cornice, jamb, etc. *b)* a cornice or similar projecting or sunk ornamentation *c)* a shaped strip of wood, etc., for finishing or decorating walls or near the ceiling), furniture, etc.

**mold·y** (mōl'dē) *adj.* **mold'i·er, mold'i·est** **1.** covered with a growth of mold **2.** musty or stale, as from age or decay —**mold'i·ness** *n.*

**mole¹** (mōl) *n.* [OE. *mal*] a small, congenital spot on the human skin, usually dark-colored and slightly raised, often hairy

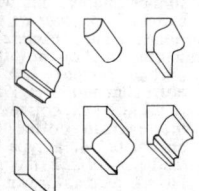

MOLDINGS

**mole²** (mōl) *n.* [< or akin to MDu. *mol*] a small, burrowing, insect-eating mammal with small eyes and ears, shovel-like forefeet, and soft fur: moles live mainly underground

**mole³** (mōl) *n.* [< Fr. < LGr. < L. *moles*, a mass] 1. a breakwater 2. a harbor formed by a breakwater

**mole⁴** (mōl) *n.* [< G. *mol*] *Chem.* the quantity of a substance having a weight in grams numerically equal to its molecular weight

**Mo·lech** (mō′lek) *Bible* an ancient god of the Phoenicians, etc., to whom children were sacrificed by burning —*n.* anything demanding terrible sacrifice

**mo·lec·u·lar** (mə lek′yə lər) *adj.* of, produced by, or existing between molecules —**mo·lec′u·lar′i·ty** (-lar′ə tē) *n.* —**mo·lec′u·lar·ly** *adv.*

**molecular biology** the branch of biology dealing with the chemical and physical structure and activities of the molecules in living matter

**molecular weight** the sum of the atomic weights of all atoms in a given molecule

**mol·e·cule** (mäl′ə kyool′) *n.* [< Fr. < ModL. *molecula*, dim. of L. *moles*, a mass] 1. the smallest particle of an element or compound that can exist in the free state and still retain the characteristics of the element or compound 2. a small particle

**mole·hill** (mōl′hil′) *n.* a small ridge or mound of earth, formed by a burrowing mole

**mole·skin** (-skin′) *n.* 1. the soft, dark-gray skin of the mole, used as fur 2. *a)* a strong cotton fabric with a soft nap, used for work clothes, etc. *b)* [*pl.*] trousers of this 3. a soft fabric, often with an adhesive backing, used for foot pads

**mo·lest** (mə lest′, mō-) *vt.* [< OFr. < L. < *molestus*, troublesome < *moles*, a burden] 1. to annoy or meddle with so as to trouble or harm 2. to make improper sexual advances to (esp. a child) —**mo·les·ta·tion** (mō′les tā′shən, mäl′əs-) *n.* —**mo·lest′er** *n.*

**Mo·lière** (mōl yer′; *Fr.* mô lyer′) (pseud. of *Jean Baptiste Poquelin*) 1622–73; Fr. dramatist

**moll** (mäl) *n.* [< var. of name MOLLY] [Slang] 1. a gangster's mistress 2. a prostitute

**mol·lah** (mäl′ə) *n. same as* MULLAH

**mol·li·fy** (mäl′ə fī′) *vt.* -fied′, -fy′ing [< MFr. < LL. < L. *mollis*, soft + *facere*, to make] 1. to soothe, pacify, or appease 2. to make less severe or violent —**mol′li·fi·ca′tion** *n.* —**mol′li·fi′er** *n.*

**mol·lusk, mol·lusc** (mäl′əsk) *n.* [< Fr. < ModL. < L. *molluscus*, soft < *mollis*, soft] any of a large group of invertebrate animals, including clams, oysters, snails, squids, etc., having a soft, usually unsegmented body often enclosed in a hard shell and usually having gills and a foot —**mol·lus·kan, mol·lus·can** (mə lus′kən) *adj., n.*

**Mol·ly** (mäl′ē) [dim. of MARY] a feminine name: also **Mol′lie**

**mol·ly** (mäl′ē) *n., pl.* -lies [< ModL. < F. N. *Mollien* (1758–1850), Fr. statesman] any of certain brightly colored tropical and subtropical American fishes often kept in aquariums: also **mol′lie**

**mol·ly·cod·dle** (mäl′ē käd′'l) *n.* [MOLLY + CODDLE] a man or boy used to being coddled, or protected, pampered, etc. —*vt.* -dled, -dling to pamper; coddle —**mol′ly·cod′dler** *n.*

**Mo·loch** (mō′läk, mäl′ək) *same as* MOLECH

**Mo·lo·kai** (mō′lō kī′) [Haw.] island of Hawaii: site of a leper colony

**Mo·lo·tov cocktail** (mô′lə täf) [after V. M. *Molotov* (1890– ), Russ. statesman] [Slang] a bottle of gasoline, etc., plugged with a rag, ignited, and hurled as a grenade against vehicles, etc.

**molt** (mōlt) *vi.* [OE. (*be*)*mutian*, to exchange < L. *mutare*, to change] to shed skin, feathers, etc., prior to replacement by a new growth: said of reptiles, birds, etc. —*vt.* to shed thus —*n.* 1. a molting 2. the parts shed —**molt′er** *n.*

**mol·ten** (mōl′t'n) *archaic pp. of* MELT —*adj.* 1. melted or liquefied by heat 2. made by being melted and cast in a mold

**mol·to** (mōl′tō) *adv.* [It.] *Music* very; much

**Mo·luc·cas** (mō luk′əz) group of islands in Indonesia, between Celebes & New Guinea: also **Molucca Islands**

**mol. wt.** molecular weight

**mo·lyb·de·nite** (mə lib′də nīt′) *n.* a scaly or foliated, lead-gray ore of molybdenum, MoS₂

**mo·lyb·de·num** (-nəm) *n.* [ModL. < L. *molybdaena* < Gr. < *molybdos*, lead] a soft, lustrous, silver-white metallic chemical element, used in alloys, etc.: symbol, Mo; at. wt., 95.94; at. no., 42

**mom** (mäm) *n.* [Colloq.] mother

**Mom·ba·sa** (mäm bä′sə, -bas′ə) seaport on the SE coast of Kenya: pop. 180,000

**mo·ment** (mō′mənt) *n.* [< L. *momentum*, movement < *movere*, to move] 1. an indefinitely brief period of time; instant 2. a definite point in time 3. a brief time of being important or outstanding 4. importance; consequence [news of great *moment*] 5. *Mech. a)* the tendency to cause rotation about a point or axis *b)* a measure of this —**the moment** the present time

**mo·men·tar·i·ly** (mō′mən ter′ə lē) *adv.* 1. for a moment or short time 2. in an instant 3. from moment to moment; at any moment

**mo·men·tar·y** (mō′mən ter′ē) *adj.* 1. lasting for only a moment; passing 2. [Now Rare] recurring every moment 3. likely to occur at any moment —**mo′men·tar′i·ness** *n.*

**mo·ment·ly** (mō′mənt lē) *adv.* 1. every moment 2. at any moment 3. for a single moment

**mo·men·tous** (mō men′təs) *adj.* of great moment; very important [a *momentous* decision] —**mo·men′tous·ly** *adv.* —**mo·men′tous·ness** *n.*

**mo·men·tum** (mō men′təm) *n., pl.* -tums, -ta (-tə) [ModL. < L.: see MOMENT] 1. the impetus of or as of a moving object 2. *Physics & Mech.* the quantity of motion of a moving body, equal to the product of its mass and its velocity

**mom·my** (mäm′ē) *n., pl.* -mies *child's term for* MOTHER¹

**mon-** *same as* MONO-: used before a vowel

**Mon.** 1. Monastery 2. Monday 3. Monsignor

**mon.** 1. monastery 2. monetary

**Mon·a·co** (män′ə kō, mə nä′kō) principality on the Mediterranean; enclave in SE France: 1/2 sq. mi.; pop. 23,000

**mo·nad** (mō′nad, män′ad) *n.* [LL. *monas* (gen. *monadis*) < Gr. < *monos*, alone] 1. a unit; something simple and indivisible 2. *Biol.* any simple, single-celled organism 3. *Chem.* an atom, element, or radical with a valence of one —*adj.* of a monad or monads —**mo·nad′ic, mo·nad′i·cal** *adj.*

**mon·arch** (män′ərk, -ärk) *n.* [< LL. < Gr. < *monos*, alone + *archein*, to rule] 1. the hereditary head of a state; king, queen, etc. 2. a person or thing surpassing others of the same kind 3. a large, migrating butterfly of N. America

**mo·nar·chal** (mə när′k'l) *adj.* of a monarch: also **mo·nar′chi·al** (-kē əl) —**mo·nar′chal·ly** *adv.*

**mo·nar·chi·cal** (-ki k'l) *adj.* 1. of or like a monarch or monarchy 2. favoring a monarchy Also **mo·nar′chic** —**mo·nar′chi·cal·ly** *adv.*

**mon·ar·chism** (män′ər kiz'm, -är-) *n.* monarchical principles or the advocacy of these —**mon′ar·chist** *n., adj.* —**mon′ar·chis′tic** *adj.*

**mon·ar·chy** (-kē) *n., pl.* -ar·chies a government or state headed by a monarch

**mon·as·ter·y** (män′ə ster′ē) *n., pl.* -ter′ies [< LL. < LGr. *monastērion* < *monazein*, to be alone < *monos*, alone] the residence of a group of people, esp. monks, retired from the world under religious vows —**mon′as·te′ri·al** (-stir′ē əl) *adj.*

**mo·nas·tic** (mə nas′tik) *adj.* 1. of or characteristic of monasteries 2. of or characteristic of monks or nuns; ascetic; self-denying Also **mo·nas′ti·cal** —*n.* a monastic person —**mo·nas′ti·cal·ly** *adv.*

**mo·nas·ti·cism** (-tə siz'm) *n.* the monastic system, state, or way of life

**mon·au·ral** (män ôr′'l) *adj.* [MON(O)- + AURAL] designating or of sound reproduction that uses only one source of sound, giving a monophonic effect —**mon·au′ral·ly** *adv.*

**mon·a·zite** (män′ə zīt′) *n.* [G. *monazit* < Gr. *monazein*, to be alone] a native phosphate of the rare-earth metals, a major source of cerium, lanthanum, etc. and thorium

**Mon·day** (mun′dē, -dā) *n.* [OE. *monandæg*, moon's day] the second day of the week

**Mon·days** (-dēz, -dāz) *adv.* on or during every Monday

**‡monde** (mōnd) *n.* [Fr.] the world; society

**‡mon Dieu** (môn dyö′) [Fr.] my God

**Mon·dri·an** (môn′drē än′), **Piet** (pēt) (born *Pieter Cornelis Mondriaan*) 1872–1944; Du. painter

**mo·ne·cious** (mə nē′shəs, mō-) *adj. same as* MONOECIOUS

**Mo·nel metal** (mō nel′) [after A. *Monell* (d. 1921), U.S. manufacturer] *a trademark for* an alloy mainly of nickel and copper, very resistant to corrosion

**Mo·net** (mō nā′, mə-; *Fr.* mô ne′), **Claude** 1840–1926; Fr. painter

**mon·e·tar·y** (män′ə ter′ē, mun′-) *adj.* [< LL. < L. *moneta*, a MINT¹] 1. of the coinage or currency of a country: see table of MONETARY UNITS on next page 2. of money; pecuniary —**mon′e·tar′i·ly** *adv.*

**mon·e·tize** (-tīz′) *vt.* -tized′, -tiz′ing [< L. *moneta*, a MINT¹ + -IZE] 1. to coin into money 2. to legalize as money —**mon′e·ti·za′tion** *n.*

**mon·ey** (mun′ē) *n., pl.* -eys, -ies [< OFr. < L. *moneta*, a

# Monetary Units of All Nations
### (The exchange rates in this list are unofficial.)

| Country | Basic Unit | Equiv. in U.S. Currency | Chief Fractional Unit |
|---|---|---|---|
| Afghanistan | afghani | .028 | pul |
| Albania | lek | .215 | qintar |
| Algeria | dinar | .268 | centime |
| Andorra | franc | .22 | centime |
|  | peseta | .013 | centimo |
| Angola | kwanza | .041 | lwei |
| Argentina | peso | .0005 | centavo |
| Australia | dollar | 1.18 | cent |
| Austria | schilling | .07 | groschen |
| Bahamas | dollar | 1.01 | cent |
| Bahrain | dinar | 2.66 | fils |
| Bangladesh | taka | .07 | paisa |
| Barbados | dollar | .52 | cent |
| Belgium | franc | .032 | centime |
| Benin | franc | .004 | centime |
| Bhutan | ngultrum | .11 | chhetrum |
| Bolivia | peso boliviano | .05 | centavo |
| Botswana | pula | 1.32 | thebe |
| Brazil | cruzeiro | .017 | centavo |
| Bulgaria | lev | 1.17 | stotinka |
| Burma | kyat | .158 | pya |
| Burundi | franc | .012 | centime |
| Cameroun | franc | .005 | centime |
| Canada | dollar | .84 | cent |
| Cape Verde | escudo | .03 | centavo |
| Central African Republic | franc | .004 | centime |
| Chad | franc | .004 | centime |
| Chile | peso | .0275 | centavo |
| China | yuan | .66 | fen |
| China (Taiwan) | dollar | .029 | cent |
| Colombia | peso | .023 | centavo |
| Comoros | franc | .004 | centime |
| Congo | franc | .004 | centime |
| Costa Rica | colon | .12 | centimo |
| Cuba | peso | 1.49 | centavo |
| Cyprus | pound | 2.90 | mil |
| Czechoslovakia | koruna | .19 | haler |
| Denmark | krone | .167 | ore |
| Djibouti | franc | .006 | centime |
| Dominica | dollar | .40 | cent |
| Dominican Republic | peso | 1.00 | centavo |
| Ecuador | sucre | .04 | centavo |
| Egypt | pound | 1.45 | piaster |
| El Salvador | colon | .40 | centavo |
| Equatorial Guinea | ekuele | .017 | centimo |
| Ethiopia | birr | .49 | santim |
| Fiji | dollar | 1.26 | cent |
| Finland | markka | .27 | penni |
| France | franc | .22 | centime |
| Gabon | franc | .004 | centime |
| Gambia | dalasi | .60 | butut |
| Germany, East | mark | .29 | pfennig |
| Germany, West | deutsche mark | .51 | pfennig |
| Ghana | cedi | .37 | pesewa |
| Greece | drachma | .024 | lepton |
| Grenada | dollar | .40 | cent |
| Guatemala | quetzal | 1.00 | centavo |
| Guinea | syli | .06 | kori |
| Guinea-Bissau | peso | .025 | centavo |
| Guyana | dollar | .42 | cent |
| Haiti | gourde | .20 | centime |
| Honduras | lempira | .50 | centavo |
| Hungary | forint | .05 | fillér |
| Iceland | króna | .002 | eyrir |
| India | rupee | .13 | paisa |
| Indonesia | rupiah | .002 | sen |
| Iran | rial | .014 | dinar |
| Iraq | dinar | 3.41 | fils |
| Ireland | pound | 1.90 | penny |
| Israel | shekel | .195 | agora |
| Italy | lira | .001 | centesimo |
| Ivory Coast | franc | .004 | centime |
| Jamaica | dollar | .57 | cent |
| Japan | yen | .0049 | sen |
| Jordan | dinar | 3.39 | fils |
| Kampuchea | (no currency) |  |  |
| Kenya | shilling | .14 | cent |
| Kiribati | dollar | 1.18 | cent |
| Korea, North | won | .52 | chon |
| Korea, South | won | .002 |  |
| Kuwait | dinar | 3.68 | fils |
| Laos | kip | .003 | at |
| Lebanon | pound | .28 | piaster |
| Lesotho | loti | 1.34 | lisente |
| Liberia | dollar | 1.00 | cent |
| Libya | dinar | 3.42 | millieme |
| Liechtenstein | franc | .56 | rappen |
| Luxembourg | franc | .032 | centime |
| Madagascar | franc | .004 | centime |
| Malawi | kwacha | 1.25 | tambala |
| Malaysia | ringgit | .45 | cent |
| Maldive Is. | rupee | .12 | cent |
| Mali | franc | .002 | centime |
| Malta | pound | 2.93 | penny |
| Mauritania | ouguya | .023 | khoms |
| Mauritius | rupee | .128 | cent |
| Mexico | peso | .045 | centavo |
| Monaco | franc | .235 | centime |
| Mongolia | tugrik | .30 | mongo |
| Morocco | dirham | .243 | franc |
| Mozambique | metical | .035 | centavo |
| Nauru | dollar | 1.18 | cent |
| Nepal | rupee | .087 | pice |
| Netherlands | guilder | .47 | cent |
| New Zealand | dollar | .96 | cent |
| Nicaragua | cordoba | .143 | centavo |
| Niger | franc | .004 | centime |
| Nigeria | naira | 1.91 | kobo |
| Norway | krone | .194 | ore |
| Oman | rial | 2.90 | paisa |
| Pakistan | rupee | .102 | paisa |
| Panama | balboa | 1.00 | centesimo |
| Papua New Guinea | kina | 1.54 | toea |
| Paraguay | guarani | .008 | centimo |
| Peru | sol | .004 | centavo |
| Philippines | peso | .135 | centavo |
| Poland | zloty | .035 | grosz |
| Portugal | escudo | .02 | centavo |
| Qatar | riyal | .28 | dirham |
| Romania | leu | .23 | ban |
| Rwanda | franc | .011 | centime |
| San Marino | lira | .001 | centesimo |
| São Tomé and Príncipe | dobra | .029 | centavo |
| Saudi Arabia | riyal | .30 | qursh |
| Senegal | franc | .004 | centime |
| Seychelles | rupee | .19 | cent |
| Sierra Leone | leone | .99 | cent |
| Singapore | dollar | .478 | cent |
| Solomon Is. | dollar | 1.18 | cent |
| Somalia | shilling | .16 | cent |
| South Africa | rand | 1.34 | cent |
| Spain | peseta | .013 | centimo |
| Sri Lanka | rupee | .057 | cent |
| St. Lucia | dollar | .40 | cent |
| St. Vincent | dollar | .40 | cent |
| Sudan | pound | 2.02 | piaster |
| Surinam | guilder | .57 | cent |
| Swaziland | lilangeni | 1.34 | cent |
| Sweden | krona | .23 | ore |
| Switzerland | franc | .56 | rappen |
| Syria | pound | .26 | piaster |
| Tanzania | shilling | .12 | cent |
| Thailand | baht | .051 | satang |
| Togo | franc | .004 | centime |
| Tonga | pa'anga | 1.40 | seniti |
| Trinidad & Tobago | dollar | .43 | cent |
| Tunisia | dinar | 2.50 | millime |
| Turkey | lira | .012 | piaster |
| Tuvalu | dollar | 1.18 | cent |
| Uganda | shilling | .13 | cent |
| United Arab Emirates | dirham | .27 | fils |
| United Kingdom | pound | 2.40 | penny |
| United States | dollar | 1.00 | cent |
| Upper Volta | franc | .004 | centime |
| Uruguay | peso | .11 | centesimo |
| U.S.S.R. | ruble | 1.56 | kopeck |
| Vanuatu | pound | 2.40 | penny |
|  | franc | .004 | centime |
| Vatican City | lira | .001 | centesimo |
| Venezuela | bolívar | .233 | centimo |
| Vietnam | dong | .456 | sau |
| Western Samoa | tala | 1.35 | sene |
| Yemen, People's Democratic Republic of | dinar | 2.95 | fils |
| Yemen Arab Rep. | riyal | .22 | bugshah |
| Yugoslavia | dinar | .04 | para |
| Zaire | zaire | .34 | likuta |
| Zambia | kwacha | 1.32 | ngwee |
| Zimbabwe | dollar | 1.53 | cent |

**MINT¹** 1. *a)* pieces of gold, silver, copper, etc., stamped by government authority and used as a medium of exchange; coin or coins: also called **hard money** *b)* any paper note authorized to be so used; bank notes; bills: see PAPER MONEY 2. anything used as a medium of exchange 3. any sum of money 4. wealth 5. *same as* MONEY OF ACCOUNT —**for one's money** [Colloq.] in one's opinion —**in the money** [Slang] wealthy —**make money** to gain profits —**one's money's worth** full value or benefit —**place** (or **put**) **money on** to bet on —**put money into** to invest money in —**mon′ey·less** *adj.*

**mon·ey·bag** (-bag′) *n.* 1. a bag for money 2. [*pl.*, *with sing. v.*] [Colloq.] a rich person

**mon·ey-chang·er** (-chān′jər) *n.* 1. a person whose business is money-changing 2. a device holding stacked coins for making change quickly

**mon·ey-chang·ing** (-chān′jiŋ) *n.* the exchanging of currency, usually of different countries, esp. at an established or official rate

**mon·eyed** (mun′ēd) *adj.* 1. wealthy; rich 2. of, from, or representing money [*moneyed* interests]

**mon·ey·lend·er** (-len′dər) *n.* a person whose business is lending money at interest

**mon·ey·mak·er** (-mā′kər) *n.* a person or thing that makes money or a profit —**mon′ey·mak′ing** *adj.*, *n.*

**money of account** a monetary denomination used in keeping accounts, etc., esp. one not issued in coin or in paper money (e.g., the U.S. mill)

**money order** an order for the payment of a specified sum of money, as one issued for a fee at one post office or bank and payable at another

**Mong.** 1. Mongolia 2. Mongolian

**mon·ger** (muŋ′gər, mäŋ′-) *n.* [OE. *mangere* < L. *mango*, dealer] a dealer or trader: usually in compounds [*fishmonger*]: sometimes used figuratively [*scandalmonger*]: chiefly Brit. in literal uses

**mon·go** (mäŋ′gō) *n.*, *pl.* **-gos** *see* MONETARY UNITS, table (Mongolia)

**Mon·gol** (mäŋ′g'l, -gōl) *adj. same as* MONGOLIAN —*n.* 1. a native of Mongolia (sense 1) or of an adjacent region in E Siberia 2. *same as* MONGOLOID 3. any Mongolic language, esp. that of the Mongolian People's Republic

**Mongol.** Mongolian

**Mon·go·li·a** (mäŋ gō′lē ə, män-; -gōl′yə) 1. region in EC Asia, consisting of Inner Mongolia & Mongolia (sense 2) 2. country in EC Asia, north of China: 592,600 sq. mi.; pop. 1,174,000: in full, **Mongolian People's Republic**

**Mon·go·li·an** (-ən, -yən) *adj.* 1. of Mongolia, its people, or their culture 2. *same as* MONGOLOID 3. same as MONGOLIC (*adj.* 1) —*n.* 1. a native of Mongolia 2. *same as* MONGOLOID 3. any Mongolic language

**Mon·gol·ic** (mäŋ gäl′ik, män-) *adj.* 1. designating or of a subfamily of Altaic languages spoken by the Mongols and including Kalmuck 2. *a)* MONGOLIAN (*adj.* 1) *b)* MONGOLOID (*adj.* 1 & 2) —*n.* any Mongolic language

**Mon·gol·ism** (mäŋ′gə liz'm) *n.* [*often* m-] earlier term for DOWN'S SYNDROME

**Mon·gol·oid** (-loid′) *adj.* 1. of or characteristic of the natives of Mongolia 2. designating or of one of the major groups of mankind: it includes most of the peoples of Asia, the Eskimos, the N. American Indians, etc. 3. [*often* m-] of or having Down's syndrome —*n.* 1. a member of the Mongoloid group 2. a person having Down's syndrome

**mon·goose** (mäŋ′gōōs) *n.*, *pl.* **-goos·es** [< native name] an old-world, ferretlike, flesh-eating mammal, noted for its ability to kill rodents, snakes, etc.

**mon·grel** (muŋ′grəl, mäŋ′-) *n.* [< base of OE. *mengan*, to mix] 1. an animal or plant produced by crossing breeds or varieties; esp., a dog of this kind 2. anything produced by indiscriminate mixture —*adj.* of mixed breed, race, origin, or character Often a derogatory usage —**mon′grel·i·za′tion** *n.* —**mon′grel·ize′** *vt.* -ized′, -iz′ing

MONGOOSE
(body 9–25 in. long; tail 9–20 in. long)

**'mongst, mongst** (muŋst) *prep. archaic var. of* AMONGST

**mon·ied** (mun′ēd) *adj. same as* MONEYED

**mon·ies** (mun′ēz) *n. alt. pl. of* MONEY

**mon·i·ker, mon·ick·er** (män′i kər) *n.* [< ?] [Slang] a person's name or nickname

**mo·nism** (mō′niz'm, män′iz'm) *n.* [ModL. *monismus* < Gr. *monos*, single] *Philos.* the doctrine that there is only one ultimate substance or principle, whether mind (*idealism*), matter (*materialism*), or something that is the basis of both —**mo′nist** *n.* —**mo·nis′tic, mo·nis′ti·cal** *adj.* —**mo·nis′ti·cal·ly** *adv.*

**mo·ni·tion** (mō nish′ən) *n.* [OFr. < L. < pp. of *monere*, to warn] 1. admonition; warning; caution 2. an official or legal notice

**mon·i·tor** (män′ə tər) *n.* [L. < pp. of *monere*, to warn] 1. [Rare] one who advises or warns 2. in some schools, a student chosen to help keep order, record attendance, etc. 3. a reminder 4. a large, flesh-eating lizard of Africa, S Asia, and Australia 5. formerly, an armored warship with a low, flat deck and heavy guns in revolving turrets 6. a person who monitors 7. a device or instrument used for monitoring 8. *Radio & TV* a receiver or speaker, as in a control room, for checking the quality of transmission —*vt.*, *vi.* 1. to watch or check on (a person or thing) for some reason 2. to check on or regulate the performance of (a machine, airplane, etc.) 3. to test for radioactive contamination with a monitor 4. to listen in on (a broadcast, another's telephone conversation, etc.) to gather some specified type of information 5. *Radio & TV* to check with a monitor —**mon′i·to′ri·al** (-tôr′ē əl) *adj.* —**mon′i·tor·ship′** *n.*

**mon·i·to·ry** (män′ə tôr′ē) *adj.* giving monition; admonishing —*n.*, *pl.* **-ries** a monitory letter

**monk** (muŋk) *n.* [OE. *munuc* < LL. < LGr. < Gr. *monos*, alone] 1. orig., a man living in solitary self-denial for religious reasons 2. a member of certain male religious orders, generally under vows, as of poverty, obedience, and chastity —**monk′ish** *adj.* —**monk′ish·ly** *adv.*

**mon·key** (muŋ′kē) *n.*, *pl.* **-keys** [prob. < or akin to MLowG. *Moneke*, the son of Martin the Ape in the medieval beast epic *Reynard the Fox*] 1. any of the primates except man and the lemurs; specif., any of the smaller, long-tailed primates 2. a person regarded as like a monkey, as a mischievous child —*vi.* [Colloq.] to play, trifle, or meddle

**monkey business** [Colloq.] foolish, mischievous, or deceitful tricks or behavior

**mon·key·shine** (-shīn′) *n.* [Colloq.] a mischievous trick or prank: *usually used in pl.*

**monkey wrench** a wrench with one movable jaw, adjusted by a screw to fit various sizes of nut, etc.

**monk's cloth** a heavy cloth, as of cotton, with a basket weave, used for drapes, etc.

**monks·hood** (muŋks′hood′) *n. same as* ACONITE (sense 1)

**mon·o** (män′ō) *adj. clipped form of* MONOPHONIC —*n. clipped form of* MONONUCLEOSIS

**mon·o-** [Gr. < *monos*, single] *a prefix meaning* one, alone, single [*monograph*]

**mon·o·bas·ic** (män′ə bā′sik) *adj. Chem.* designating an acid whose molecule contains one hydrogen atom replaceable by a metal or positive radical

**mon·o·chro·mat·ic** (-krō mat′ik) *adj.* [< L. < Gr.: see ff. & -IC] of or having one color: also **mon′o·chro′ic** (-krō′ik) —**mon′o·chro·mat′i·cal·ly** *adv.*

**mon·o·chrome** (män′ə krōm′) *n.* [< ML. < Gr. < *monos*, single + *chrōma*, color] a painting, drawing, or photograph in one color or shades of one color —**mon′o·chro′mic** *adj.* —**mon′o·chro′mist** *n.*

**mon·o·cle** (män′ə k'l) *n.* [Fr. < LL. *monoculus*, one-eyed < Gr. *monos*, single + L. *oculus*, eye] an eyeglass for one eye only —**mon′o·cled** *adj.*

**mon·o·cli·nal** (män′ə klī′n'l) *adj. Geol.* designating or of strata dipping in one direction —*n. same as* MONOCLINE

**mon·o·cline** (män′ə klīn′) *n.* [< MONO- + Gr. *klinein*, to incline] a monoclinal rock fold or structure

**mon·o·clin·ic** (män′ə klin′ik) *adj.* [see prec. & -IC] designating a crystalline form that has three unequal axes, two of which intersect at right angles while the third is oblique to one of the others

**mon·o·cli·nous** (män′ə klī′nəs) *adj.* [< ModL. < MONO- + Gr. *klinē*, a bed] *Bot.* having stamens and pistils in the same flower

**mon·o·cot·y·le·don** (män′ə kät′'l ē′d'n) *n.* a flowering plant with one seed leaf (cotyledon) —**mon′o·cot′y·le·don·ous** *adj.*

**mon·o·dy** (män′ə dē) *n.*, *pl.* **-dies** [< LL. < Gr. *monōidia* < *monos*, alone + *aeidein*, to sing] 1. a solo lament or dirge, as in ancient Greek tragedy 2. a poem mourning someone's death 3. *Music a)* a style of composition in which the melody is carried by one part, or voice *b)* a composition in this style —**mo·nod·ic** (mə näd′ik), **mo·nod′i·cal** *adj.* —**mo·nod′i·cal·ly** *adv.*

**mo·noe·cious** (mə nē′shəs, mō-) *adj.* [< MON(O)- + Gr. *oikos*, a house] *Bot.* having separate male flowers and female flowers on the same plant, as in maize —**mo·noe′cism** (-siz′m) *n.*

**mo·nog·a·my** (mə näg′ə mē) *n.* [< Fr. < LL. < Gr.: see MONO- & -GAMY] 1. the practice or state of being married to only one person at a time 2. *Zool.* the practice of having only one mate —mo·nog′a·mist *n.* —mo·nog′a·mous, mon·o·gam·ic (män′ə gam′ik) *adj.*

**mon·o·gram** (män′ə gram′) *n.* [< LL. < Gr. *mono-*, MONO- + *gramma*, letter] the initials of a name, combined in a single design —*vt.* **-grammed′, -gram′ming** to put a monogram on —mon′o·gram·mat′ic (-grə mat′ik) *adj.*

**mon·o·graph** (män′ə graf′) *n.* [MONO- + -GRAPH] a writing, esp. a scholarly one, on a single subject or aspect of a subject —mon′o·graph′ic *adj.*

**mon·o·lith** (män′ə lith′) *n.* [< Fr. < L. < Gr. < *monos*, single + *lithos*, stone] **1.** a single large block or piece of stone **2.** something made of this, as an obelisk **3.** something like a monolith in size, unity of structure or purpose, etc. —mon′o·lith′ic *adj.* —mon′o·lith′ism *n.*

**mon·o·logue, mon·o·log** (män′ə lôg′, -läg′) *n.* [Fr. < Gr. < *monos*, alone + *legein*, to speak] **1.** a long speech, esp. one monopolizing a conversation **2.** a poem, etc. in the form of a soliloquy **3.** a part of a play in which one character speaks alone; soliloquy **4.** a play, skit, or recitation for one actor only —mon′o·logu′ist, mo·nol·o·gist (mə näl′ə jist) *n.*

**mon·o·ma·ni·a** (män′ə mā′nē ə) *n.* **1.** an excessive interest in or enthusiasm for some one thing; craze **2.** a mental disorder characterized by irrational preoccupation with one subject —mon·o·ma′ni·ac′ (-mā′nē ak′) *n.* —mon′o·ma·ni′a·cal (-mə nī′ə k′l) *adj.*

**mon·o·mer** (män′ə mər) *n.* [MONO- + Gr. *meros*, a part] a simple molecule that can form polymers by combining with identical or similar molecules —mon′o·mer′ic (-mer′ik) *adj.*

**mon·o·met·al·lism** (män′ə met′′l iz′m) *n.* the use of only one metal, usually gold or silver, as the monetary standard —mon′o·me·tal′lic (-mə tal′ik) *adj.* —mon′o·met′al·list *n.*

**mo·no·mi·al** (mō nō′mē əl, mä-) *adj.* [MO(NO)- + (BI)NOMIAL] consisting of only one term, esp. in algebra —*n.* a monomial expression, quantity, etc.

**Mo·non·ga·he·la** (mə näŋ′gə hē′lə) [< Algonquian] river in N W.Va. & SW Pa., joining the Allegheny to form the Ohio: 128 mi.

**mon·o·nu·cle·o·sis** (män′ə nōō′klē ō′sis, -nyōō-) *n.* [MONO- + NUCLE(US) + -OSIS] **1.** *same as* INFECTIOUS MONONUCLEOSIS **2.** presence in the blood of too many cells with a single nucleus

**mon·o·phon·ic** (-fän′ik) *adj.* designating or of sound reproduction using a single channel

**mon·o·plane** (män′ə plān′) *n.* an airplane with only one pair of wings

**mo·nop·o·list** (mə näp′ə list) *n.* **1.** a person who has a monopoly **2.** a person who favors monopoly —mo·nop′o·lis′tic *adj.* —mo·nop′o·lis′ti·cal·ly *adv.*

**mo·nop·o·lize** (-līz′) *vt.* **-lized′, -liz′ing 1.** to get, have, or exploit a monopoly of **2.** to get full possession or control of; dominate or occupy completely —mo·nop′o·li·za′tion *n.* —mo·nop′o·liz′er *n.*

**mo·nop·o·ly** (-lē) *n., pl.* **-lies** [< L. < Gr. < *monopōlia*, exclusive sale < *monos*, single + *pōlein*, to sell] **1.** exclusive control of a commodity or service in a given market, or control that makes possible the fixing of prices **2.** such control granted by a government **3.** any exclusive possession or control **4.** something held or controlled as a monopoly **5.** a company, etc. that has a monopoly

**mon·o·rail** (män′ə rāl′) *n.* **1.** a single rail serving as a track for cars suspended from it or balanced on it **2.** a railway with such a track

**mon·o·so·di·um glu·ta·mate** (män′ə sō′dē əm glōō′tə māt′) a white, crystalline powder, C₅H₈O₄NaN, used in foods as a flavor enhancer

**mon·o·syl·lab·ic** (män′ə si lab′ik) *adj.* **1.** having only one syllable **2.** consisting of, using, or speaking in monosyllables —mon′o·syl·lab′i·cal·ly *adv.*

**mon·o·syl·la·ble** (män′ə sil′ə b′l) *n.* a word of one syllable

**mon·o·the·ism** (män′ə thē iz′m) *n.* [MONO- + THEISM] the doctrine or belief that there is only one God —mon′o·the·ist *n.* —mon′o·the·is′tic, mon′o·the·is′ti·cal *adj.* —mon′o·the·is′ti·cal·ly *adv.*

**mon·o·tint** (män′ə tint′) *n. same as* MONOCHROME

**mon·o·tone** (-tōn′) *n.* **1.** utterance of successive words without change of pitch or key **2.** monotony of tone, style, color, etc. **3.** a single, unchanging musical tone **4.** recitation, singing, etc. in such a tone **5.** a person who sings in such a tone —*adj. same as* MONOTONOUS —mon′o·ton′ic (-tän′ik) *adj.*

**mo·not·o·nous** (mə nät′′n əs) *adj.* [< LL. < Gr.: see MONO- & TONE] **1.** going on in the same tone without variation **2.** having little or no variation or variety **3.** tiresome because unvarying —mo·not′o·nous·ly *adv.* —mo·not′o·nous·ness *n.*

**mo·not·o·ny** (-ē) *n.* **1.** sameness of tone or pitch **2.** lack of variety **3.** tiresome sameness

**mon·o·treme** (män′ə trēm′) *n.* [< ModL. < Gr. *monos*, single + *trēma*, hole] any of the lowest order of mammals (platypuses and echidnas), which lay eggs and have a single

opening for the excretory and genital organs —mon′o·trem′a·tous (-trem′ə təs, -trē′mə-) *adj.*

**mon·o·type** (-tīp′) *n.* [MONO- + -TYPE] **1.** *Biol.* the only type of its group **2.** *Printing* type produced by Monotype —[M- ] *a trademark for* either of a pair of machines for casting and setting up type in separate characters: one, a casting machine, is controlled by a paper tape perforated on the other, a keyboard machine

**mon·o·va·lent** (män′ə vā′lənt) *adj. Chem. same as* UNIVALENT —mon′o·va′lence, mon′o·va′len·cy *n.*

**mon·ox·ide** (mə näk′sīd, män äk′-) *n.* an oxide with one atom of oxygen in each molecule

**Mon·roe** (mən rō′) [after ff.] city in N La.: pop. 58,000

**Mon·roe** (mən rō′), **James** 1758–1831; 5th president of the U.S. (1817–25)

**Monroe Doctrine** the doctrine, stated by President Monroe, that the U.S. would regard as an unfriendly act any attempt by a European nation to interfere in the affairs of, or increase its possessions in, the Americas

**Mon·ro·vi·a** (mən rō′vē ə) capital of Liberia; seaport on the Atlantic: pop. c.100,000

**Mon·sei·gneur** (män′sen yʉr′; *Fr.* mōn se nyēr′) *n., pl.* **Mes·sei·gneurs** (mes′en yʉrz′; *Fr.* mā se nyēr′) [Fr., lit., my lord] **1.** a French title of honor given to persons of high birth or rank, as princes, bishops, etc. **2.** [*often* m-] a person with this title

**mon·sieur** (mə syʉr′; *Fr.* mə syö′) *n., pl.* **mes·sieurs** (mes′ərz; *Fr.* mā syö′) [Fr., lit., my lord] a man; gentleman: French title [M-], equivalent to *Mr.* or *Sir:* abbrev. **M., Mons.**

**Monsig. 1.** Monseigneur **2.** Monsignor

**Mon·si·gnor** (män sēn′yər; *It.* mōn′sē nyōr′) *n., pl.* **-gnors** (-yərz); *It.* **-gno′ri** (-nyō′rē) [It., lit., my lord] **1.** a title of certain Roman Catholic prelates **2.** [*often* m-] a person with this title

**mon·soon** (män sōōn′) *n.* [< MDu. < Port. < Ar. *mausim*, a season] **1.** a seasonal wind of the Indian Ocean and S Asia, blowing from the southwest from April to October, and from the northeast the rest of the year **2.** the rainy season, when this wind blows from the southwest —mon·soon′al *adj.*

**mon·ster** (män′stər) *n.* [< OFr. < L. *monstrum*, divine portent < *monere*, to warn] **1.** any plant or animal greatly malformed, lacking parts, etc. **2.** any imaginary creature with striking incongruities in form, as a centaur or unicorn **3.** something monstrous **4.** any very cruel or wicked person **5.** any huge animal or thing —*adj.* huge; enormous; monstrous

**mon·strance** (män′strəns) *n.* [OFr. < ML. < L. *monstrare*, to show] *R.C.Ch.* a receptacle in which the consecrated Host is exposed for adoration

**mon·stros·i·ty** (män sträs′ə tē) *n.* **1.** the state or quality of being monstrous **2.** *pl.* **-ties** a monstrous thing or creature

**mon·strous** (män′strəs) *adj.* **1.** abnormally large; enormous **2.** very unnatural in shape, type, or character **3.** having the character or appearance of a monster **4.** horrible; hideous; shocking **5.** hideously wrong or evil; atrocious —*adv.* [Chiefly Dial.] very; extremely —mon′strous·ly *adv.* —mon′strous·ness *n.*

**mon·tage** (män täzh′, mōn-) *n.* [Fr. < *monter*, MOUNT²] **1.** *a)* the art or process of making a composite picture from a number of different pictures *b)* a picture so made **2.** *Motion Pictures a)* the art or process of producing a sequence of abruptly alternating or superimposed scenes or images *b)* such a sequence **3.** any technique, as in literature, with a similar sequence of elements —*vt.* **-taged′, -tag′ing** to incorporate in a montage

**Mon·ta·gnard** (män′tən yärd′) *n.* [Fr., lit., mountaineer] a member of a people living in the hills of central Vietnam

**Mon·taigne** (män tān′; *Fr.* mōn ten′y′), **Mi·chel Ey·quem de** (mē shel′ e kem′ də) 1533–92; Fr. essayist

**Mon·tan·a** (män tan′ə) [L. *montana*, mountainous region] Mountain State of the NW U.S.: 147,138 sq. mi.; pop. 787,000; cap. Helena: abbrev. **Mont., MT** —Mon·tan′an *adj., n.*

**Mont·calm** (mōn kälm′; *E.* mänt käm′), marquis **Louis Jo·seph de** (zhō zef′ də) 1712–59; Fr. general defeated & killed by Brit. forces at Quebec

**mon·te** (män′tē) *n.* [Sp., lit., mountain, hence heap of cards] a game in which players bet on the color of cards to be turned up

**Mon·te Car·lo** (män′ti kär′lō) town in Monaco: gambling resort: pop. 9,500

**Mon·te·ne·gro** (män′tə nē′grō) republic of S Yugoslavia: 5,333 sq. mi. —Mon′te·ne′grin (-grin) *adj., n.*

**Mon·te·rey Park** (män′tə rā′) city in SW Calif: suburb of Los Angeles: pop. 54,000

**Mon·ter·rey** (män′tə rā′; *Sp.* mōn′ter rā′) city in NE Mexico: pop. 1,012,000

**Mon·tes·quieu** (mōn tes kyö′; *E.* män′təs kyōō′), (Baron de la Brède et de) 1689–1755; Fr. philosophical writer on history

**Mon·tes·so·ri method** (or **system**) (män'tə sôr'ē) [after Maria *Montessori* (1870–1952), It. educator who devised it] a system of teaching young children which emphasizes training of the senses and guidance intended to encourage self-education

**Mon·te·ver·di** (môn'te ver'dē), **Clau·dio (Giovanni Antonio)** (klou'dyô) 1567–1643; It. composer

**Mon·te·vid·e·o** (män'tə vi dā'ō; *Sp.* môn'te vē *the*'ð) capital of Uruguay, on the Rīo de la Plata: pop. 1,204,000

**Mon·te·zu·ma II** (män'tə zōō'mə) 1479?–1520; Aztec emperor of Mexico (1502–20)

**Mont·gom·er·y** (mənt gum'ər ē, mänt-, mən-; -gum'rē) [after Gen. R. *Montgomery* (1736?–75)] capital of Ala., in the SC part: pop. 178,000

**month** (munth) *n.* [OE. *monath*] **1.** any of the twelve parts into which the calendar year is divided: also **calendar month 2.** *a)* the time from any day of one month to the corresponding day of the next *b)* a period of four weeks or 30 days **3.** the period of a complete revolution of the moon (in full, **lunar month**) **4.** one twelfth of the solar year (in full, **solar month**) —**month after month** every month —**month by month** each month —**month in, month out** every month

**month·ly** (munth'lē) *adj.* **1.** continuing or lasting for a month **2.** done, happening, payable, etc. every month —*n.*, *pl.* **-lies 1.** a periodical published once a month **2.** [Colloq.] [*also pl.*] the menses —*adv.* once a month; every month

**Mon·ti·cel·lo** (män'tə sel'ō, -chel'ō) [It., little mountain] home of Thomas Jefferson, in C Va.

**Mont·mar·tre** (môn mär'tr') district in Paris, in N part: noted for its cafés and as an artists' quarter

**Mont·pel·ier** (mänt pēl'yər) [after ff.] capital of Vt., in the NC part: pop. 8,000

**Mont·pel·lier** (môn pel yā') city in S France: pop. 162,000

**Mont·re·al** (män'trē ôl', mun'-) seaport in SW Quebec, Canada, on an island in the St. Lawrence River: pop. 1,081,000 (met. area 2,802,000): Fr. name **Mont·ré·al** (môn rā äl')

**Montreal North** suburb of Montreal: pop. 97,000: Fr. name **Montréal Nord** (nôr)

**Mont-St-Mi·chel** (môn san mē shel') islet off the NW coast of France: noted for its fortified abbey: also **Mont Saint Michel**

**mon·u·ment** (män'yə mənt) *n.* [OFr. < L. *monumentum* < *monere*, to remind] **1.** something set up to keep alive the memory of a person or event, as a tablet, statue, building, etc. **2.** a writing, etc. serving as a memorial **3.** *a)* a work of enduring significance [*monuments* of learning] *b)* an outstanding example [*a monument* of bigotry] **4.** a stone boundary marker **5.** [Obs.] a tomb

**mon·u·men·tal** (män'yə men't'l) *adj.* **1.** of, suitable for, or serving as a monument **2.** like a monument; massive, enduring, etc. **3.** of lasting importance; historically notable **4.** very great; colossal [*monumental* pride] —**mon'u·men'tal·ly** *adv.*

**mon·u·men·tal·ize** (-īz') *vt.* **-ized', -iz'ing** to memorialize as by a monument; make monumental

**-mo·ny** (mō'nē) [L. *-monia, -monium*] *a suffix meaning* a resulting thing or state [*patrimony*]

**moo** (mōō) *n., pl.* **moos** [echoic] the vocal sound made by a cow; lowing sound —*vi.* **mooed, moo'ing** to make this sound; low

**mooch** (mōōch) *vi., vt.* [ult. < OFr. *muchier*, to hide] [Slang] to get (food, money, etc.) by begging or sponging —**mooch'er** *n.*

**mood¹** (mōōd) *n.* [OE. *mod*, mind] **1.** a particular state of mind or feeling; humor, or temper **2.** a prevailing feeling, spirit, or tone **3.** [*pl.*] fits of morose, sullen, or uncertain temper

**mood²** (mōōd) *n.* [< MODE, altered after prec.] *Gram.* that aspect of verbs which indicates whether the action or state expressed is regarded as a fact (*indicative mood*), as a matter of supposition, desire, etc. (*subjunctive mood*), or as a command (*imperative mood*)

**mood·y** (mōō'dē) *adj.* **mood'i·er, mood'i·est 1.** subject to or characterized by gloomy, sullen, or changing moods **2.** resulting from or indicating such a mood —**mood'i·ly** *adv.* —**mood'i·ness** *n.*

**moon** (mōōn) *n.* [OE. *mona*] **1.** the satellite of the earth, that revolves around it once in 29½ days and shines at night by reflecting the sun's light **2.** this body as it appears at a particular time of the month: see NEW MOON, HALF-MOON, FULL MOON, OLD MOON **3.** a month; esp., a lunar month **4.** *same as* MOONLIGHT **5.** anything shaped like the

PHASES OF THE MOON

moon (i.e., an orb or crescent) **6.** any satellite of a planet —*vi.* to behave in an idle, dreamy, or abstracted way —*vt.* to pass (time) in mooning

**moon·beam** (-bēm') *n.* a ray of moonlight

**moon·calf** (-kaf') *n.* **1.** an idiot or fool **2.** a youth who spends time mooning about

**moon-faced** (-fāst') *adj.* round-faced

**moon·fish** (-fish') *n., pl.* **-fish', -fish'es:** see FISH an oval-shaped sea fish found in the warmer coastal waters of North and South America

**moon·let** (-lit) *n.* a small moon or artificial satellite

**moon·light** (-līt') *n.* the light of the moon —*adj.* **1.** of moonlight **2.** lighted by the moon **3.** done or occurring by moonlight, or at night

**moon·light·ing** (-līt'iŋ) *n.* [from the usual night hours of such jobs] the practice of holding a second regular job in addition to one's main job

**moon·lit** (-lit') *adj.* lighted by the moon

**moon·quake** (-kwāk') *n.* a trembling of the surface of the moon, thought to be caused by internal rock slippage or, possibly, meteorite impact

**moon·scape** (-skāp') *n.* [MOON + (LAND)SCAPE] the surface of the moon or a representation of it

**moon·shine** (-shīn') *n.* **1.** the light of the moon **2.** foolish or empty talk, notions, etc. **3.** [Colloq.] whiskey unlawfully made or smuggled

**moon·shin·er** (-shī'nər) *n.* [Colloq.] a person who makes and sells alcoholic liquor unlawfully

**moon·shot** (-shät') *n.* the launching of a rocket to the moon

**moon·stone** (-stōn') *n.* a translucent feldspar with a pearly luster, used as a gem

**moon·struck** (-struk') *adj.* **1.** crazed; lunatic **2.** romantically dreamy **3.** dazed or distracted Also **moon'strick'en** (-strik''n)

**moon·walk** (-wôk') *n.* a walking about by an astronaut on the surface of the moon

**moon·y** (-ē) *adj.* **moon'i·er, moon'i·est** mooning; listless; dreamy

**Moor** (moor) *n.* [< OFr. < L. < Gr. *Mauros*] **1.** a member of a Moslem people of mixed Arab and Berber descent living in NW Africa **2.** a member of a group of this people that invaded and occupied Spain in the 8th cent. A.D. —**Moor'ish** *adj.*

**moor¹** (moor) *n.* [OE. *mor*] [Brit.] a tract of open wasteland, usually covered with heather and often marshy; heath

**moor²** (moor) *vt.* [< or akin to MDu. *maren*, LowG. *moren*, to tie] **1.** to hold (a ship, etc.) in place by cables or chains as to a pier or buoy **2.** to cause to be held in place; secure —*vi.* **1.** to moor a ship, etc. **2.** to be secured as by cables —**moor'age** (-ij) *n.*

**Moore** (moor, môr) **1. George (Augustus)**, 1852–1933; Ir. novelist & playwright **2. Henry**, 1898– ; Eng. sculptor **3. Thomas**, 1779–1852; Ir. poet

**moor·hen** (moor'hen') *n.* a common gallinule of Europe and the E U.S.

**moor·ing** (-iŋ) *n.* **1.** [*often pl.*] the lines, cables, etc. by which a ship, etc. is moored **2.** [*pl.*] a place where a ship, etc. is moored **3.** [*often pl.*] beliefs, habits, ties, etc. that make one feel secure

**moor·land** (-land') *n.* [Brit.] *same as* MOOR¹

**moose** (mōōs) *n., pl.* **moose** [< Algonquian] **1.** the largest animal of the deer family, native to the N U.S. and Canada: the male has huge antlers **2.** *same as* ELK (sense 1)

**moot** (mōōt) *n.* [OE. *mot, gemot*, a meeting] **1.** an early English assembly of freemen to administer justice, etc. **2.** a discussion or argument, esp. of a case in a moot court: see ff. —*adj.* **1.** debatable **2.** so hypothetical as to be meaningless —*vt.* **1.** to debate or discuss **2.** to propose for discussion or debate

MOOSE
(4½–6 ft. high at shoulder)

**moot court** a mock court in which hypothetical cases are tried as an exercise for law students

**mop** (mäp) *n.* [ult. < ? L. *mappa*, napkin] **1.** a bundle of rags or yarn, or a sponge, etc., fastened to the end of a stick, as for washing floors **2.** anything suggestive of this, as a thick head of hair —*vt.* **mopped, mop'ping** to wash, wipe, or remove with or as with a mop —**mop up** [Colloq.] to finish —**mop'per** *n.*

**mope** (mōp) *vi.* **moped, mop'ing** [akin to MDu. *mopen*] to be gloomy and apathetic —*n.* **1.** a person who mopes **2.** [*pl.*] low spirits —**mop'er** *n.* —**mop'ey, mop'y, mop'ish** *adj.* —**mop'ish·ly** *adv.*

**mo·per·y** (mō′pər ē) *n.* [MOP(E) + -ERY] [Slang] a trivial or imaginary violation of law

**mop·pet** (mäp′it) *n.* [< ?] [Colloq.] a little child: a term of affection

**Mor.** Morocco

**mo·raine** (mə rān′, mô-) *n.* [Fr. < *morre,* a muzzle] a mass of rocks, gravel, sand, etc. deposited by a glacier, along its side (**lateral moraine**), at its lower end (**terminal moraine**), or beneath the ice (**ground moraine**) —**mo·rain′al, mo·rain′ic** *adj.*

**mor·al** (môr′əl, mär′-) *adj.* [< L. < *mos,* pl. *mores,* manners, morals] **1.** relating to, dealing with, or capable of distinguishing between, right and wrong in conduct **2.** of, teaching, or in accordance with, the principles of right and wrong **3.** good or right in conduct or character; sometimes, specif., sexually virtuous **4.** designating support, etc. that involves sympathy without action **5.** being virtually such because of its effect on thoughts, attitudes, etc. [a *moral* victory] **6.** based on strong probability [a *moral* certainty] —*n.* **1.** a moral lesson taught by a fable, event, etc. **2.** [*pl.*] principles, standards, or habits with respect to right or wrong in conduct; ethics; sometimes, specif., standards of sexual behavior —**mor′al·ly** *adv.*

**mo·rale** (mə ral′, mô-) *n.* [Fr., fem. of *moral:* see prec.] moral or mental condition with respect to courage, discipline, confidence, enthusiasm, etc. [the *morale* of the troops was low]

**mor·al·ist** (môr′əl ist, mär′-) *n.* **1.** a person who moralizes **2.** a person who adheres to a system of moral teaching **3.** a person who seeks to impose his morals on others —**mor′al·is′tic** *adj.* —**mor′al·is′ti·cal·ly** *adv.*

**mo·ral·i·ty** (mə ral′ə tē, mô-) *n., pl.* **-ties 1.** moral quality or character; rightness or wrongness, as of an action **2.** a being in accord with the principles or standards of right conduct; virtue **3.** principles of right and wrong in conduct; ethics **4.** moral instruction or lesson **5.** a narrative with a moral lesson **6.** *same as* MORALITY PLAY

**morality play** any of a class of allegorical dramas of the 15th and 16th cent., whose characters were personifications, as Everyman, Vice, etc.

**mor·al·ize** (môr′ə līz′, mär′-) *vi.* **-ized′, -iz′ing** to consider or discuss matters of right and wrong, often in a self-righteous way —*vt.* **1.** *a)* to explain in terms of right and wrong *b)* to draw a moral from **2.** to improve the morals of —**mor′al·i·za′tion** *n.* —**mor′al·iz′er** *n.*

**moral philosophy** *same as* ETHICS

**mo·rass** (mə ras′, mô-) *n.* [< Du. < OFr. < Frank. *marisk,* a swamp] a tract of low, soft, watery ground; bog; swamp: often used figuratively of a difficult or troublesome state of affairs

**mor·a·to·ri·um** (môr′ə tôr′ē əm, mär′-) *n., pl.* **-ri·ums, -ri·a** (-ə) [ModL. < LL. < L. < *mora,* a delay] **1.** a legal authorization, usually by an emergency law, to delay payment of money due **2.** the effective period of such an authorization **3.** any authorized delay or stopping of some specified activity

**Mo·ra·vi·a** (mô rā′vē ə, mə-) region in C Czechoslovakia: chief city, Brno

**Mo·ra·vi·an** (mô rā′vē ən, mə-) *adj.* **1.** of Moravia, its people, etc. **2.** of the religious sect of Moravians —*n.* **1.** a native or inhabitant of Moravia **2.** the Czech dialect of Moravia **3.** a member of a Protestant sect founded by people from Moravia (c.1722)

**mo·ray** (môr′ā; mô rā′, mə-) *n.* [< Port. < L. *muraena,* kind of fish < Gr. *myraina*] a voracious, brilliantly colored eel, found esp. among coral reefs: in full, **moray eel**

**mor·bid** (môr′bid) *adj.* [L. *morbidus,* sickly < *morbus,* disease] **1.** of, having, or caused by disease; diseased **2.** having or showing an interest in gruesome or gloomy matters **3.** gruesome; horrible [*morbid* details of a crime] —**mor·bid′i·ty, mor′bid·ness** *n.* —**mor′bid·ly** *adv.*

**mor·dant** (môr′d'nt) *adj.* [< OFr. prp. of *mordre* < L. *mordere,* to bite] **1.** biting, caustic, or sarcastic [*mordant* wit] **2.** corrosive **3.** acting as a mordant —*n.* **1.** a substance used in dyeing to fix the colors **2.** an acid, etc. used in etching to bite lines, areas, etc. into the surface —**mor′dancy** *n.* —**mor′dant·ly** *adv.*

**more** (môr) *adj. superl.* MOST [OE. *mara*] **1.** greater in amount, quantity, or degree: used as the comparative of MUCH **2.** greater in number: used as the comparative of MANY **3.** additional; further [take *more* tea] —*n.* **1.** a greater amount, quantity, or degree **2.** [with *pl. v.*] a greater number (*of*) [*more* of us are going] **3.** something additional or further [*more* can be said] —*adv. superl.* MOST **1.** in or to a greater degree or extent: used with many adjectives and adverbs (regularly with those of three or more syllables) to form comparatives **2.** in addition; further —**more and more 1.** increasingly **2.** a constantly increasing amount, quantity, etc. —**more or less 1.** somewhat **2.** approximately

**More** (môr), Sir **Thomas** 1478-1535; Eng. statesman & writer: executed: canonized in 1935

**mo·rel** (mə rel′, mô-) *n.* [< Fr. < MDu. < OHG. *morhila,* dim. of *morha,* carrot] an edible mushroom that looks like a sponge on a stalk

**more·o·ver** (môr ō′vər) *adv.* in addition to what has been said; besides; further; also

**mo·res** (môr′ēz, -āz) *n.pl.* [L., pl. of *mos,* custom] folkways that, through general observance, develop the force of law

**Mor·gan** (môr′gən), **J(ohn) P(ierpont)** 1837-1913; U.S. financier

MOREL

**mor·ga·nat·ic** (môr′gə nat′ik) *adj.* [< ML. < *morganaticum,* altered < OHG. *morgengeba,* morning gift given to one's bride (in lieu of a dower)] designating or of a form of marriage in which a man of royalty or nobility marries a woman of inferior social status with the provision that neither she nor their offspring may lay claim to his rank or property —**mor′ga·nat′i·cal·ly** *adv.*

**morgue** (môrg) *n.* [Fr.] **1.** a place where the bodies of unknown dead persons or those dead of unknown causes are kept to be examined, identified, etc. **2.** a newspaper office's reference library of back numbers, clippings, etc.

**mor·i·bund** (môr′ə bund′) *adj.* [< L. *moribundus* < *mori,* to die] **1.** dying **2.** coming to an end **3.** having little or no vitality left —**mor′i·bund′i·ty** *n.*

**mo·ri·on** (môr′ē än′) *n.* [Fr. < Sp. < *morra,* crown of the head] a crested, visorless helmet of the 16th and 17th cent., with a curved brim coming to a peak in front and in back

**Mo·ris·co** (mə ris′kō, mô-) *adj.* [Sp. < *Moro,* Moor] Moorish —*n., pl.* **-cos, -coes** a Moor; esp., one of the Moors of Spain

**Mor·mon** (môr′mən) *n.* a member of the Church of Jesus Christ of Latter-day Saints (commonly called the *Mormon Church*), founded in the U.S. in 1830 by Joseph Smith —*adj.* of the Mormons or their religion —**Mor′mon·ism** *n.*

**morn** (môrn) *n.* [OE. *morne*] [Poet.] morning

**morn·ing** (môr′niŋ) *n.* [ME. *morweninge* (by analogy with EVENING) < OE. *morgen*] **1.** the first or early part of the day, from midnight, or esp. dawn, to noon **2.** the first or early part [the *morning* of life] **3.** dawn; daybreak —*adj.* of, suited to, or occurring, appearing, etc. in the morning

**morning dress** formal daytime dress for men, including a cutaway (**morning coat**)

**morning glory** a twining annual vine with heart-shaped leaves and trumpet-shaped flowers of lavender, blue, pink, or white

**morn·ings** (-niŋz) *adv.* during every morning or most mornings

**morning star** a planet, esp. Venus, visible in the eastern sky before sunrise

**Mo·ro** (môr′ō) *n.* [Sp., a Moor] **1.** *pl.* **-ros, -ro** a member of a group of Moslem Malay tribes living in the S Philippines **2.** their language

**Mo·roc·co** (mə rä′kō) kingdom on the NW coast of Africa: c.171,300 sq. mi.; pop. 15,102,000; cap. Rabat —*n.* [m-] a fine, soft leather made, orig. in Morocco, from goatskins: also **morocco leather** —**Mo·roc′can** *adj., n.*

**mo·ron** (môr′än) *n.* [arbitrary use of Gr. neut. of *mōros,* foolish] **1.** a person having mild mental retardation: an obsolescent term: see MENTAL RETARDATION **2.** a very stupid person —**mo·ron′ic** *adj.* —**mo·ron′i·cal·ly** *adv.* —**mo·ron′i·ty, mo′ron·ism** *n.*

**mo·rose** (mə rōs′, mô-) *adj.* [L. *morosus,* fretful < *mos* (gen. *moris*), manner] **1.** ill-tempered; gloomy, sullen, etc. **2.** characterized by gloom —**mo·rose′ly** *adv.* —**mo·rose′ness** *n.*

**-morph** (môrf) [< Gr. *morphē,* form] *a combining form meaning* one having a (specified) form

**mor·pheme** (môr′fēm) *n.* [< Fr. < Gr. *morphē,* form] the smallest meaningful unit or form in a language: it may be an affix (*re-* in *refill*), a base (*do* in *undo*), or an inflectional form (*-s* in *girls*) —**mor·phe′mic** *adj.* —**mor·phe′mi·cal·ly** *adv.*

**Mor·pheus** (môr′fē əs, -fyōōs) *Gr. Myth.* the god of dreams

**-mor·phic** (môr′fik) [< Gr. *morphē,* form + -IC] *a combining form meaning* having a (specified) form or shape [*anthropomorphic*]

**mor·phine** (môr′fēn) *n.* [< G. or Fr. < ModL. *morphium* < L. *Morpheus,* MORPHEUS] a bitter, white or colorless, crystalline alkaloid derived from opium and used in medicine to relieve pain

**mor·phol·o·gy** (môr fäl′ə jē) *n.* [< G. < Gr. *morphē,* form + -LOGY] **1.** the branch of biology dealing with the form and structure of animals and plants **2.** the branch of linguistics dealing with the internal structure and forms of words —**mor′pho·log′i·cal** (-fə läj′i k'l), **mor′pho·log′ic** *adj.* —**mor′pho·log′i·cal·ly** *adv.* —**mor·phol′o·gist** *n.*

**-mor·phous** (môr′fəs) [< Gr. *morphē,* form] *same as* -MORPHIC

**Mor·ris** (môr′is, mär′-) **1.** [var. of MAURICE] a masculine name **2. William,** 1834–96; Eng. poet, artist, craftsman, & socialist

**Morris chair** [after Wm. MORRIS] an armchair with an adjustable back

**mor·ro** (mär′ō) *n., pl.* **-ros** [Sp.] a rounded hill or point of land

**mor·row** (mär′ō, môr′ō) *n.* [< OE. *morgen,* morning] [Poet.] **1.** morning **2.** the next day **3.** the time just after some particular event

**Morse** (môrs) *adj.* [after ff.] [*often* m-] designating or of a code, or alphabet, consisting of a system of dots and dashes, or short and long sounds, used in telegraphy, etc. —*n.* the Morse code

**Morse** (môrs), **Samuel F(inley) B(reese)** 1791–1872; U.S. inventor of the telegraph

**mor·sel** (môr′s'l) *n.* [< OFr. dim. of *mors* < L. *morsum,* a bite < pp. of *mordere,* to bite] **1.** a small bite or portion of food **2.** a small amount; bit

**mor·tal** (môr′t'l) *adj.* [< OFr. < L. *mortalis* < *mors* (gen. *mortis*), death] **1.** that must eventually die **2.** of man as a being who must eventually die **3.** of this world **4.** of death **5.** causing death; fatal **6.** to the death [*mortal combat*] **7.** not to be pacified [a *mortal* enemy] **8.** very intense; grievous [*mortal* terror] **9.** [Colloq.] *a*) extreme; very great *b*) very long and tedious *c*) possible [of no *mortal* good to anyone] **10.** R.C.Ch. causing spiritual death: said of sins regarded as serious —*n.* a being who must eventually die; esp., a human being —*adv.* [Dial.] extremely —**mor′tal·ly** *adv.*

**mor·tal·i·ty** (môr tal′ə tē) *n.* **1.** the mortal nature of man **2.** death on a large scale, as from disease or war **3.** the proportion of deaths to the population of a region, nation, etc.; death rate **4.** the proportion that fail **5.** human beings collectively

**mor·tar** (môr′tər) *n.* [< OE. & OFr. < L. *mortarium*] **1.** a very hard bowl in which substances are ground or pounded to a powder with a pestle **2.** a short-barreled cannon with a low muzzle velocity, which hurls shells in a high trajectory **3.** a mixture of cement or lime with sand and water, used between bricks, etc., or as plaster —*vt.* **1.** to plaster together with mortar **2.** to attack with mortar shells

**mor·tar·board** (-bôrd′) *n.* **1.** a square board with a handle beneath, on which mortar is carried **2.** an academic cap with a square, flat top, worn at commencements, etc.

**mort·gage** (môr′gij) *n.* [< OFr. < *mort,* dead + *gage,* GAGE¹] *Law* **1.** the pledging of property to a creditor as security for the payment of a debt **2.** the deed by which this pledge is made —*vt.* **-gaged, -gag·ing 1.** *Law* to pledge (property) by a mortgage **2.** to put an advance claim or liability on [he *mortgaged* his future]

**mort·ga·gee** (môr′gə jē′) *n.* a person to whom property is mortgaged

**mort·ga·gor, mort·gag·er** (môr′gi jər) *n.* a person who mortgages property

**mor·tice** (môr′tis) *n., vt. alt. sp. of* MORTISE

**mor·ti·cian** (môr tish′ən) *n.* [< L. *mors,* death + -ICIAN] *same as* FUNERAL DIRECTOR

**mor·ti·fi·ca·tion** (môr′tə fi kā′shən) *n.* **1.** a mortifying or being mortified; specif., *a*) the control of physical desires by self-denial, fasting, etc. *b*) shame, humiliation, etc. **2.** something causing shame, humiliation, etc. **3.** *old term for* GANGRENE

**mor·ti·fy** (môr′tə fī′) *vt.* **-fied′, -fy′ing** [< OFr. < LL. *mortificare,* to kill < L. *mors,* death + *facere,* to make] **1.** to punish (one's body) or control (one's physical desires) by self-denial, fasting, etc. **2.** to shame, humiliate, etc. **3.** [Now Rare] to make gangrenous —*vi.* [Now Rare] to become gangrenous —**mor′ti·fi′er** *n.*

**mor·tise** (môr′tis) *n.* [MFr. *mortaise* < Ar. *murtazza,* joined] a notch or hole cut, as in a piece of wood, to receive a projecting part (*tenon*) shaped to fit —*vt.* **-tised, -tis·ing 1.** to join or fasten securely, esp. with a mortise and tenon **2.** to cut a mortise in

**mort·main** (môrt′mān′) *n.* [< OFr. < ML. < L. pp. of *mori,* to die + *manus,* hand] *Law* a transfer of lands or houses to a corporate body, as a church, for perpetual ownership

**Mor·ton** (môr′t'n) [< OE. < *mor,* moor + *tun,* town] a masculine name

**mor·tu·ar·y** (môr′chŏo wer′ē) *n., pl.* **-ar′ies** [< LL. < L. *mortuus,* dead] a place where dead bodies are kept before burial or cremation, as a morgue or funeral home —*adj.*

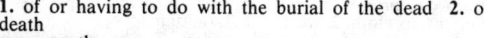

*TENON*

*MORTISE*

**1.** of or having to do with the burial of the dead **2.** of death

**mos.** months

**Mo·sa·ic** (mō zā′ik) *adj.* of Moses or the writings, principles, etc. attributed to him

**mo·sa·ic** (mō zā′ik) *n.* [< OFr. < ML. *musaicum* < LL. < L. *musa,* MUSE] **1.** the process of making pictures or designs by inlaying small bits of colored stone, glass, etc. in mortar **2.** a picture or design so made **3.** anything resembling this **4.** the photosensitive plate in a television camera tube —*adj.* of or resembling mosaic or a mosaic —*vt.* **-icked, -ick·ing** to make by or as by mosaic —**mo·sa′i·cal·ly** *adv.* —**mo·sa′i·cist** (-ə sist) *n.*

**Mosaic law** the ancient Hebrew law, ascribed to Moses and contained mainly in the Pentateuch

**Mos·cow** (mäs′kou, -kō) capital of the U.S.S.R. & the R.S.F.S.R., in W R.S.F.S.R.: pop. 6,942,000 (met. area 7,061,000): Russ. name, **Mos·kva** (môs kvä′)

**Mo·selle** (mō zel′) river in NE France & N West Germany, flowing into the Rhine

**Mo·ses** (mō′ziz) [LL. < Gr. < Heb. *mōsheh,* prob. < Egypt. *mes,* child] **1.** a masculine name **2.** *Bible* the leader who brought the Israelites out of slavery in Egypt and led them to the Promised Land, and who received the Ten Commandments

**mo·sey** (mō′zē) *vi.* [< *vamose,* var. of VAMOOSE] [Slang] **1.** to amble along **2.** to go away

**Mos·lem** (mäz′ləm, muz′-, mäs′-) *n.* [Ar. *muslim,* true believer < *aslama,* to resign oneself (to God)] an adherent of Islam —*adj.* of Islam or the Moslems: also **Mos·lem′ic** (-lem′ik) —**Mos′lem·ism** *n.*

**mosque** (mäsk) *n.* [< MFr. < It. < Ar. *masjid* < *sajada,* to pray] a Moslem temple or place of worship

**mos·qui·to** (mə skēt′ō, -ə) *n., pl.* **-toes, -tos** [Sp. & Port., dim. of *mosca* < L. *musca,* a fly] a two-winged insect, the female of which has skin-piercing, bloodsucking mouthparts: some varieties transmit diseases, as malaria and yellow fever —**mos·qui′to·ey** (-ē) *adj.*

**mosquito net** (or **netting**) a fine mesh curtain for keeping out mosquitoes

**moss** (môs, mäs) *n.* [OE. *mos,* a swamp] **1.** a very small, green plant growing in velvety clusters on rocks, trees, moist ground, etc. **2.** any of various similar plants, as some lichens, algae, etc. —*vt.* to cover with a growth of moss —**moss′like′** *adj.*

**moss agate** agate with mosslike markings

**moss·back** (-bak′) *n.* [Colloq.] an old-fashioned or very conservative person

**moss rose 1.** *same as* PORTULACA **2.** a variety of the cabbage rose with a roughened, mossy flower stalk and calyx

**moss·y** (-ē) *adj.* **moss′i·er, moss′i·est 1.** full of or covered with moss or a mosslike growth **2.** like moss —**moss′i·ness** *n.*

**most** (mōst) *adj. compar.* MORE [OE *mast*] **1.** greatest in amount, quantity, or degree: used as the superlative of MUCH **2.** greatest in number: used as the superlative of MANY **3.** in the greatest number of instances [*most* fame is fleeting] —*n.* **1.** the greatest amount, quantity, or degree **2.** [with pl. v.] the greatest number (of) —*adv.* **1.** *compar.* MORE in or to the greatest degree or extent: used with many adjectives and adverbs (regularly with those of three or more syllables) to form superlatives **2.** very [a *most* beautiful morning] **3.** [Colloq.] almost; nearly —**at (the) most** at the very limit; not more than —**make the most of** to take the fullest advantage of

**-most** (mōst) [OE. *-mest*] *a suffix used in forming superlatives* [foremost, hindmost]

**most·ly** (mōst′lē) *adv.* **1.** for the most part **2.** chiefly; principally **3.** generally

**Mo·sul** (mō sŏol′) city in N Iraq, on the Tigris River: pop. 243,000

**mot** (mō) *n.* [Fr., a word < L. *muttum,* a grunt] a witticism or pithy remark

**mote** (mōt) *n.* [OE. *mot*] a speck, as of dust

**mo·tel** (mō tel′) *n.* [MO(TORIST) + (HO)TEL] a hotel for those traveling by car, with accessible parking

**mo·tet** (mō tet′) *n.* [< OFr. dim. of *mot,* a word] a contrapuntal, polyphonic song of a sacred nature

**moth** (môth) *n., pl.* **moths** (môthz, môths) [OE. *moththe*] a four-winged, chiefly night-flying insect related to the butterfly but generally smaller and less brightly colored; specif., a small moth (**clothes moth**) whose larvae eat holes in woolens, furs, etc.

**moth·ball** (-bôl′) *n.* a small ball of naphthalene, the fumes of which repel moths, as from woolens, furs, etc. —*vt.* to store with protective covering —*adj.* in storage or reserve [a *mothball* fleet] —**in** (or **out of**) **mothballs** put into (or taken from) storage

**moth-eat·en** (-ēt'n) *adj.* **1.** gnawed away in patches by moths, as cloth **2.** worn-out **3.** outdated

**moth·er**¹ (muth'ər) *n.* [OE. *modor*] **1.** a woman who has borne a child; esp., a woman as she is related to her child **2.** *a)* a stepmother *b)* a mother-in-law **3.** the female parent of a plant or animal **4.** that which is the origin, source, or nurturer of something **5.** *a)* a woman having the responsibility and authority of a mother *b)* a woman who is the head (**mother superior**) of a religious establishment **6.** an elderly woman: used as a title of affectionate respect —*adj.* **1.** of, like, or like that of a mother **2.** native [*mother tongue*] —*vt.* **1.** to be the mother of **2.** to care for as a mother does —**moth'er·less** *adj.*

**moth·er**² (muth'ər) *n.* [altered (after prec.) < MDu. *moeder*] *same as* MOTHER OF VINEGAR

**Mother Car·ey's chicken** (ker'ēz) [< ?] any of various oceanic petrels; esp., *same as* STORMY PETREL (sense 1)

**mother country** *same as* MOTHERLAND

**Mother Goose** the imaginary creator of a collection of English nursery rhymes

**moth·er·hood** (muth'ər hood') *n.* **1.** the state of being a mother **2.** the qualities or character of a mother

**Mother Hub·bard** (hub'ərd) a full, loose gown for women

**mother image** (or **figure**) a person substituted in one's mind for one's mother

**moth·er-in-law** (-ən lô') *n., pl.* **moth'ers-in-law'** the mother of one's husband or wife

**moth·er·land** (-land') *n.* a person's native land or, sometimes, the land of his ancestors

**mother lode** the main vein of ore in a region

**moth·er·ly** (-lē) *adj.* of, like, or befitting a mother; maternal —**moth'er·li·ness** *n.*

**moth·er-of-pearl** (-əv purl') *n.* the hard, pearly internal layer of certain marine shells, as of the pearl oyster, used for making pearl buttons, etc.; nacre

**mother of vinegar** [see MOTHER²] a stringy, gummy, slimy substance formed by bacteria in vinegar or on the surface of fermenting liquids

**Mother's Day** the second Sunday in May, a day set aside (in the U.S.) in honor of mothers

**mother tongue 1.** one's native language **2.** a language from which another derives

**mother wit** native intelligence; common sense

**moth·proof** (môth'prōōf') *adj.* treated chemically so as to repel moths —*vt.* to make mothproof

**moth·y** (môth'ē) *adj.* **moth'i·er, moth'i·est 1.** infested with moths **2.** moth-eaten

**mo·tif** (mō tēf') *n.* [Fr.: see MOTIVE] **1.** a main element, idea, etc.; specif., a theme or subject that is repeated with various changes, as in a piece of music, a book, etc. **2.** a repeated figure in a design

**mo·tile** (mōt''l) *adj.* [< L. pp. of *movere*, to move + -ILE] *Biol.* capable of or exhibiting spontaneous motion —**mo·til·i·ty** (mō til'ə tē) *n.*

**mo·tion** (mō'shən) *n.* [< L. *motio* < pp. of *movere*, to move] **1.** a moving from one place to another; movement **2.** a moving of the body or any of its parts **3.** a meaningful movement of the hand, eyes, etc.; gesture **4.** a suggestion; esp., a proposal formally made in an assembly or meeting —*vi.* to make a meaningful movement of the hand, head, etc. —*vt.* to direct or command by a meaningful gesture —**go through the motions** to do something in a mechanical or merely formal way —**in motion** moving or in operation —**mo'tion·less** *adj.* —**mo'tion·less·ly** *adv.*

**motion picture 1.** a sequence of photographs or drawings projected on a screen in such rapid succession as to create the optical illusion of moving persons and objects **2.** a play, story, etc. photographed as a motion picture

**motion sickness** sickness characterized by nausea, dizziness, etc., and caused by the motion of an aircraft, boat, etc.

**mo·ti·vate** (mōt'ə vāt') *vt.* **-vat'ed, -vat'ing** to provide with, or affect as, a motive or motives; incite —**mo'ti·va'tion** *n.* —**mo'ti·va'tion·al** *adj.* —**mo'ti·va'tive** *adj.* —**mo'ti·va'tor** *n.*

**mo·tive** (mōt'iv) *n.* [< OFr. *motif* < ML. < L. pp. of *movere*, to move] **1.** some inner drive, impulse, etc. that causes one to act in a certain way; incentive; goal **2.** *same as* MOTIF —*adj.* of, causing, or tending to cause motion —*vt.* **-tived, -tiv·ing** *same as* MOTIVATE —**mo'tive·less** *adj.*

**-mo·tive** (mōt'iv) [< prec. (adj.)] *a suffix meaning* moving, of motion [*automotive, locomotive*]

**mot·ley** (mät'lē) *adj.* [< ?] **1.** of many colors **2.** wearing many-colored garments [*a motley fool*] **3.** of many different elements [*a motley group*] —*n.* **1.** cloth of mixed colors **2.** a garment of various colors, worn by a jester **3.** a combination of diverse elements

**mo·to·cross** (mō'tō krôs') *n.* [Fr. < *motocyclette*, motorcycle + Eng. *cross-country*] a cross-country race for lightweight motorcycles

**mo·tor** (mōt'ər) *n.* [L., a mover < pp. of *movere*, to move] **1.** anything that produces or imparts motion **2.** an engine; esp., an internal-combustion engine for propelling a vehicle **3.** *Elec.* a machine for converting electrical energy into mechanical energy —*adj.* **1.** producing motion **2.** of or powered by a motor [*a motor bicycle*] **3.** of, by, or for motor vehicles [*a motor trip*] **4.** for motorists [*a motor inn*] **5.** designating or of a nerve carrying impulses from the central nervous system to a muscle producing motion **6.** of, manifested by, or involving muscular movements [*motor skills*] —*vi.* to travel by automobile

**mo·tor·bike** (-bīk') *n.* [Colloq.] **1.** a bicycle propelled by a motor **2.** a light motorcycle

**mo·tor·boat** (-bōt') *n.* a boat propelled by a motor

**mo·tor·bus** (-bus') *n.* a passenger bus propelled by a motor: also **motor coach**

**mo·tor·cade** (-kād') *n.* [MOTOR + (CAVAL)CADE] a procession of automobiles

**mo·tor·car** (-kär') *n.* **1.** *same as* AUTOMOBILE **2.** a small, open car propelled by a motor and used on a railroad by workmen: also **motor car**

**mo·tor·cy·cle** (-sī'k'l) *n.* a two-wheeled vehicle, like a bicycle, propelled by an internal-combustion engine —*vi.* **-cled, -cling** to ride a motorcycle —**mo'tor·cy'clist** *n.*

**motor hotel** *same as* MOTEL: also **motor court, motor inn, motor lodge**

**mo·tor·ist** (mōt'ər ist) *n.* a person who drives an automobile or travels by automobile

**mo·tor·ize** (mōt'ə rīz') *vt.* **-ized', -iz'ing 1.** to equip with motor-driven vehicles **2.** to make mobile by mounting on a motor vehicle **3.** to equip (a vehicle, etc.) with a motor —**mo'tor·i·za'tion** *n.*

**mo·tor·man** (mōt'ər mən) *n., pl.* **-men** a person who drives an electric streetcar or motor locomotive

**motor pool** a group of motor vehicles kept for use as needed, as by military personnel

**motor truck** a motor-driven truck for hauling loads

**motor vehicle** a vehicle on wheels having its own motor and not running on rails, for use on streets or highways, as an automobile or bus

**mot·tle** (mät''l) *vt.* **-tled, -tling** [back-formation < *mottled* < MOTLEY + -ED] to mark with blotches or streaks of different colors —**mot'tled** *adj.*

**mot·to** (mät'ō) *n., pl.* **-toes, -tos** [It., a word: see MOT] **1.** a word, phrase, or sentence chosen as expressive of the goals or ideals of a nation, group, etc. and inscribed on something **2.** a maxim adopted as a principle of behavior

**‡moue** (mōō) *n., pl.* **moues** (mōō) [Fr. < OFr. *moue*, a grimace] a pouting grimace

**mould** (mōld) *n., vt., vi.* chiefly Brit. sp. of MOLD (all terms and senses) —**mould'y** *adj.* **mould'i·er, mould'i·est**

**mould·board** (-bôrd') *n.* chiefly Brit. sp. of MOLDBOARD

**mould·ing** (mōl'diŋ) *n.* chiefly Brit. sp. of MOLDING

**moult** (mōlt) *n., vt., vi.* chiefly Brit. sp. of MOLT

**mound** (mound) *n.* [< ? MDu. *mond*, protection, infl. by MOUNT¹] **1.** a heap or bank of earth, sand, etc., whether built or natural; small hill **2.** *Baseball* the slightly raised area on which the pitcher must stand when pitching —*vt.* to heap up in a mound

**Mound Builders** the early Indian peoples who built the burial mounds and other earthworks found in the Middle West and the Southeast

**mount**¹ (mount) *n.* [< OE. *munt* & OFr. *mont*, both < L. *mons*] a mountain or hill: now poetic or [M-] before a proper name [*Mount* McKinley]

**mount**² (mount) *vi.* [< OFr. *munter*, ult. < L. *mons*: see prec.] **1.** to climb; ascend (often with *up*) **2.** to climb up on something; esp., to get on a horse or bicycle, etc. for riding **3.** to increase in amount [profits are *mounting*] —*vt.* **1.** to go up; ascend; climb [to *mount* stairs] **2.** *a)* to get up on (a horse, bicycle, etc.) for riding *b)* to set on or provide with a horse *c)* to get up on (a platform, stool, etc.) **3.** to place on something raised (with *on*) [*mount* the statue on a pedestal] **4.** to place or fix on or in the proper support, backing, etc., as a gem in a setting, a specimen on a microscope slide, a picture on a mat, etc. **5.** to arrange (a skeleton, dead animal, etc.) for exhibition **6.** to furnish the costumes, settings, etc. for producing (a play) **7.** to prepare for and undertake (an expedition, campaign, etc.) **8.** *Mil. a)* to place (a gun) into position for use *b)* to be armed with (cannon) [this ship *mounts* six cannon] *c)* to post (a guard) on sentry duty *d)* to go on (guard) as a sentry —*n.* **1.** the act or manner of mounting (a horse, etc.) **2.** a horse, bicycle, etc. for riding **3.** the support, setting, etc. on or in which something is mounted

**moun·tain** (moun't'n) *n.* [< OFr. *montaigne*, ult. < L. *mons*, MOUNT¹] **1.** a natural raised part of the earth's surface, larger than a hill **2.** [pl.] a chain or group of such elevations: also **mountain chain, mountain range 3.** a large pile, heap, or mound **4.** a very large amount —*adj.*

**1.** of mountains **2.** situated, living, or used in the mountains **3.** like a mountain

**mountain ash** a small tree with clusters of white flowers and red berries

**mountain dew** [Colloq.] whiskey, esp. when illegally distilled, as by mountaineers

**moun·tain·eer** (moun't'n ir') *n.* **1.** a person who lives in a mountainous region **2.** a mountain climber —*vi.* to climb mountains, as for sport

**mountain goat** *same as* ROCKY MOUNTAIN GOAT

**mountain laurel** an evergreen shrub of E N. America, with pink and white flowers and shiny leaves

**mountain lion** *same as* COUGAR

**moun·tain·ous** (moun't'n əs) *adj.* **1.** full of mountains **2.** like a mountain; esp., very large

**mountain sheep** any of various wild sheep found in mountain regions; esp., *same as* BIGHORN

**moun·tain·side** (-sīd') *n.* the side of a mountain

**Mountain Standard Time** *see* STANDARD TIME

**Mountain State** any of the eight States of the W U.S. through which the Rocky Mountains pass

**moun·tain·top** (-täp') *n.* the top of a mountain

**Mountain View** city in W Calif., near San Jose: pop. 59,000

**moun·te·bank** (moun'tə baŋk') *n.* [< It. < *montare,* to mount + *in,* on + *banco,* a bench] **1.** orig., a person who sold quack medicines in a public place, attracting an audience by tricks, stories, etc. **2.** any charlatan, or quack —*vi.* to act as a mountebank —**moun'te·bank'er·y** *n.*

**mount·ed** (moun'tid) *adj.* provided with a mount, or horse, vehicle, support, etc. *[mounted police]*

**Mount·ie, Mount·y** (moun'tē) *n., pl.* **-ies** [Colloq.] a member of the Royal Canadian Mounted Police

**mount·ing** (moun'tiŋ) *n.* something serving as a backing, support, setting, etc.

**Mount Vernon 1.** [after E. *Vernon* (see GROG)] home of George Washington, in N Va., on the Potomac **2.** [after prec.] city in SE N.Y.: suburb of New York City: pop. 67,000

**mourn** (môrn) *vi., vt.* [OE. *murnan*] **1.** to feel or express sorrow for (something regrettable) **2.** to grieve for (someone who has died) —**mourn'er** *n.*

**mourn·ful** (-fəl) *adj.* **1.** of mourning; feeling or expressing grief or sorrow **2.** causing sorrow; melancholy —**mourn'ful·ly** *adv.* —**mourn'ful·ness** *n.*

**mourn·ing** (môr'niŋ) *n.* **1.** a sorrowing; specif., the expression of grief at someone's death, or the period of this **2.** black clothes, drapery, etc., worn or displayed as a sign of grief —*adj.* of or expressing mourning —**mourn'ing·ly** *adv.*

**mourning dove** a gray, wild dove of the U.S.: so called because of its cooing, regarded as mournful

**mouse** (mous; *for v., usually* mouz) *n., pl.* **mice** [OE. *mus*] **1.** any of numerous small rodents found throughout the world; esp., the **house mouse,** which infests human dwellings **2.** a timid or spiritless person **3.** [Slang] a dark, swollen bruise under the eye —*vi.* **moused, mous'ing 1.** to hunt for mice **2.** to search for something busily and stealthily —*vt.* to hunt for

**mous·er** (mou'zər, -sər) *n.* a cat, dog, etc. with reference to its ability to catch mice

**mous·ey** (mou'sē, -zē) *adj. same as* MOUSY

**mousse** (mōōs) *n.* [Fr., foam, prob. < L. *mulsa,* kind of mead] a light chilled or frozen food made with egg white, gelatin, whipped cream, etc., often served with fruit or flavoring for dessert

**mous·tache** (mə stash', mus'tash) *n. var. of* MUSTACHE

**mous·y** (mou'sē, -zē) *adj.* **mous'i·er, mous'i·est 1.** of, characteristic of, or like a mouse; quiet, timid, etc. **2.** infested with mice —**mous'i·ness** *n.*

**mouth** (mouth; *for v.* mouth) *n., pl.* **mouths** (mouthz) [OE. *muth*] **1.** the opening through which an animal takes in food; specif., the cavity in the head which contains the teeth and tongue and through which sounds are uttered **2.** the mouth regarded as the organ of eating and speaking **3.** a grimace **4.** any opening regarded as like the mouth *[the mouth of a river, of a jar, of a cavern, etc.]* —*vt.* **1.** to say, esp. in an affected or pompous manner **2.** to form (a word) with the mouth soundlessly **3.** to rub with the mouth or lips —*vi.* to speak in a pompous manner; declaim —**down in** (or **at**) **the mouth** [Colloq.] depressed; unhappy —**mouth'er** (mouth'-) *n.* —**mouth'like'** *adj.*

**-mouthed** (mouthd) *a combining form meaning* having a (specified kind of) mouth, voice, etc. *[loudmouthed]*

**mouth·ful** (mouth'fool') *n., pl.* **-fuls' 1.** as much as the mouth can hold **2.** the usual amount taken into the mouth **3.** a small amount **4.** [Slang] a pertinent remark: chiefly in **say a mouthful**

**mouth organ** *same as* HARMONICA

**mouth·part** (-pärt') *n.* any of various structures or organs around the mouth in arthropods, used for biting, grasping, etc.: *usually used in pl.*

**mouth·piece** (-pēs') *n.* **1.** a part placed at, or forming, a mouth **2.** the part of a musical instrument held in or to the mouth **3.** a person, periodical, etc. used by others to express their views, ideas, etc. **4.** [Slang] a criminal's lawyer

**mouth·wash** (-wôsh', -wäsh') *n.* a flavored liquid used for rinsing the mouth or gargling

**mouth·wa·ter·ing** (-wôt'ər iŋ, -wät'ər-) *adj.* appetizing enough to make the mouth water; tasty

**mouth·y** (mou'*th*ē, -thē) *adj.* **mouth'i·er, mouth'i·est** overly talkative, esp. in a bombastic or rude way —**mouth'i·ly** *adv.* —**mouth'i·ness** *n.*

**mou·ton** (mōō'tän) *n.* [Fr., sheep: see MUTTON] lambskin, processed to resemble beaver, seal, etc.

**mov·a·ble** (mōō'və b'l) *adj.* **1.** that can be moved from one place to another **2.** changing in date from one year to the next *[movable holidays]* —*n.* **1.** something movable **2.** *Law* personal property, as furniture: *usually used in pl.* Also **move'a·ble** —**mov'a·bil'i·ty** *n.* —**mov'a·bly** *adv.*

**move** (mōōv) *vt.* **moved, mov'ing** [< Anglo-Fr. < OFr. < L. *movere*] **1.** to change the place or position of **2.** to set or keep in motion; impel, stir, etc. **3.** to cause (*to act, do, say,* etc.); prompt **4.** to arouse the emotions, passions, etc. of **5.** to propose; esp., to propose formally, as in a meeting **6.** to cause (the bowels) to evacuate **7.** *Commerce* to dispose of (goods) by selling —*vi.* **1.** to change place or position **2.** to change one's residence **3.** to be active *[to move in artistic circles]* **4.** to make progress; advance **5.** to take action **6.** to be, or be set, in motion; turn, revolve, etc. **7.** to make a formal application (*for*) *[move for a new trial]* **8.** to evacuate: said of the bowels **9.** [Colloq.] to depart *[time to be moving on]* **10.** *Chess, Checkers,* etc. to change the position of a piece **11.** *Commerce* to be disposed of by sale: said of goods —*n.* **1.** act of moving; movement **2.** one of a series of actions toward some goal **3.** a change of residence **4.** *Chess, Checkers,* etc. the act of moving or one's turn to move —**get a move on** [Slang] **1.** to start moving **2.** to hurry —**move in on** [Slang] to draw near to and try to gain control of —**move up** to promote or be promoted —**on the move** [Colloq.] moving about from place to place

**move·ment** (-mənt) *n.* **1.** the act, process, or manner of moving; specif., *a)* an action of a person or group *b)* a shift in position *c)* an evacuation (of the bowels) *d) Mil.* a change in the location of troops, ships, etc., as part of a maneuver **2.** *a)* organized action by people working together toward some goal *b)* those active in this way **3.** a tendency; trend **4.** the progress of events in a literary work; action **5.** the effect of motion in painting, sculpture, etc. **6.** *Mech.* the moving parts of a mechanism *[the movement* of a clock*]* **7.** *Music a)* any of the principal divisions of a symphony or other long composition *b) same as* TEMPO or RHYTHM **8.** *Prosody* rhythmic flow

**mov·er** (-ər) *n.* a person or thing that moves; specif., a person whose work or business is moving furniture, etc. for those changing residence

**mov·ie** (mōō'vē) *n.* [contr. < MOVING PICTURE] **1.** a motion picture **2.** a motion-picture theater —**the movies 1.** the motion-picture industry **2.** a showing of a motion picture

**mov·ie·go·er** (-gō'ər) *n.* a person who goes to see motion pictures, esp. often or regularly

**mov·ing** (mōō'viŋ) *adj.* **1.** that moves; specif., *a)* changing, or causing to change, place or position *b)* causing motion or action *c)* stirring the emotions **2.** involving a moving motor vehicle *[a moving violation (of a traffic law)]* —**mov'ing·ly** *adv.*

**moving picture** *same as* MOTION PICTURE

**moving staircase** (or **stairway**) *same as* ESCALATOR

**mow**[1] (mō) *vt., vi.* **mowed, mowed** or **mown, mow'ing** [OE. *mawan*] **1.** to cut down (standing grass or grain) with a sickle, lawn mower, etc. **2.** to cut grass or grain from (a lawn, field, etc.) —**mow down 1.** to cause to fall like grass or grain being cut **2.** to kill or destroy **3.** to overwhelm (an opponent) —**mow'er** *n.*

**mow**[2] (mou) *n.* [OE. *muga*] **1.** a stack or heap of hay, grain, etc., esp. in a barn **2.** the part of a barn where hay or grain is stored

**mown** (mōn) *alt. pp. of* MOW[1]

**Mo·zam·bique** (mō'zəm bēk') country on the SE coast of Africa: formerly a Port. territory: c. 302,300 sq. mi.; pop. 8,519,000; cap. Maputo

**Mo·zart** (mō'tsärt), **Wolf·gang A·ma·de·us** (vôlf'gäŋk' ä'mä dā'oos) 1756–91; Austrian composer

**moz·za·rel·la** (mät'sə rel'ə) *n.* [It.] a soft, white, mild-flavored Italian cheese

**MP, M.P.** Military Police

**mp** [It. *mezzo piano*] *Music* moderately soft

**M.P. 1.** Member of Parliament **2.** Mounted Police
**M.P., m.p.** melting point
**mpg, m.p.g.** miles per gallon
**mph, m.p.h.** miles per hour
**Mr.** (mis′tər) *pl.* **Messrs.** (mes′ərz) mister: used before the name or title of a man
**Mrs.** (mis′iz) *pl.* **Mmes.** (mā däm′) mistress: now used as a title before the name of a married woman
**MS 1.** Mississippi **2.** multiple sclerosis
**MS., ms., ms** *pl.* **MSS., mss., mss** manuscript
**Ms.** (miz, mis) a title, free of reference to marital status, used before the name of a woman in place of either *Miss* or *Mrs.*
**M.S., M.Sc.** Master of Science
**MScand.** Middle Scandinavian
**MSG** monosodium glutamate
**Msgr.** Monsignor
**MSgt, M/Sgt** Master Sergeant
**m′sieur** (mə syur′; *Fr.* mə syö′) *n.* monsieur
**MST, M.S.T.** Mountain Standard Time
**MT** Montana
**Mt., mt.** *pl.* **mts. 1.** mount **2.** mountain
**M.T.** metric ton
**mtg. 1.** meeting **2.** mortgage: also **mtge.**
**mtn.** mountain
**mu** (myōō, mōō) *n.* [< Gr.] the twelfth letter of the Greek alphabet (M, μ)
**much** (much) *adj.* **more, most** [OE. *mycel*] great in quantity, amount, degree, etc. —*adv.* **1.** to a great degree or extent [*much* happier] **2.** just about; nearly [*much* the same] **3.** at frequent intervals; often [do you dine out *much?*] —*n.* **1.** a great amount or quantity [*much* to be done] **2.** something great, outstanding, etc. [not *much* to look at] —**as much as 1.** to the degree that **2.** practically; virtually —**make much of** to treat or consider as of great importance —**much as 1.** almost as **2.** however —**much′ness** *n.*
**mu·ci·lage** (myōō′s'l ij) *n.* [< MFr. < LL. *mucilago*, musty juice < L. *mucere*, to be moldy] **1.** any of various thick, sticky substances produced in certain plants **2.** any watery solution of gum, glue, etc. used as an adhesive
**mu·ci·lag·i·nous** (myōō′sə laj′ə nəs) *adj.* **1.** of or like mucilage; sticky **2.** producing mucilage
**muck** (muk) *n.* [< or akin to ON. *myki*, dung] **1.** moist manure **2.** black earth containing decaying matter, used as a fertilizer **3.** anything unclean or degrading; dirt; filth —*vt.* **1.** to fertilize with muck **2.** [Colloq.] to dirty as with muck —**muck′y** *adj.* **muck′i·er, muck′i·est**
**muck·er** (-ər) *n.* [prob. < G. < *mucken*, to grumble] [Slang] a coarse or vulgar person; cad
**muck·rake** (-rāk′) *vi.* **-raked′, -rak′ing** [coined c.1906: see MUCK & RAKE[1]] to search for and publicize corruption by public officials, businessmen, etc. —**muck′rak′er** *n.*
**mu·cous** (myōō′kəs) *adj.* **1.** of, containing, or secreting mucus **2.** like mucus or covered with or as with mucus; slimy
**mucous membrane** a mucus-secreting membrane lining body cavities and canals, as the mouth, etc., connecting with the external air
**mu·cus** (myōō′kəs) *n.* [L.] the slimy secretion that moistens and protects the mucous membranes
**mud** (mud) *n.* [prob. < a LowG. source] wet, soft, sticky earth —*vt.* **mud′ded, mud′ding** to cover or soil with or as with mud
**mud·der** (mud′ər) *n.* a race horse that performs especially well on a wet, muddy track
**mud·dle** (mud′'l) *vt.* **-dled, -dling** [< MUD] **1.** to mix up; jumble; bungle **2.** to confuse; befuddle, as with liquor —*vi.* to act or think in a confused way —*n.* mess, confusion, etc. —**muddle through** [Chiefly Brit.] to succeed in spite of confusion
**mud·dler** (-lər) *n.* a stick to stir mixed drinks
**mud·dy** (-ē) *adj.* **-di·er, -di·est 1.** full of or spattered with mud **2.** not clear; cloudy [*muddy* coffee] **3.** confused, obscure, etc. [*muddy* thinking] —*vt., vi.* **-died, -dy·ing** to make or become muddy —**mud′di·ly** *adv.* —**mud′di·ness** *n.*
**mud·fish** (-fish′) *n., pl.* **-fish′, -fish′es:** see FISH any of various fishes that live in mud or muddy water
**mud·guard** (-gärd′) *n.* older name for FENDER (sense *a*)
**mud hen** any of various birds that live in marshes, as the coot, gallinule, etc.
**mud·pack** (-pak′) *n.* a paste made up of fuller's earth, astringents, etc., used as a facial
**mud puppy** a N. American salamander that lives in mud under water
**mud·sling·ing** (-sliŋ′iŋ) *n.* unscrupulous attacks against an opponent, as in a political campaign —**mud′sling′er** *n.*
**mud snake** a long, bluish-black snake with a spine at the tip of the tail, found in the SE U.S.
**mud turtle** a small turtle of North and Central America that lives in muddy ponds, streams, etc.

**Muen·ster** (mun′stər, moon′-) *n.* [after *Munster*, in E France] a semisoft, mild cheese
**mu·ez·zin** (myōō ez′in) *n.* [< Ar. *mu'adhdhin* < *adhana*, to proclaim] a Moslem crier who calls the people to prayer at the proper hours
**muff** (muf) *n.* [Du. *mof* < Walloon < Fr. *moufle*, a mitten] **1.** a cylindrical covering of fur, etc. into which the hands are placed from either end for warmth **2.** *a*) *Baseball*, etc. a failure to hold the ball when catching it *b*) any bungling action —*vt., vi.* to do (something) badly or awkwardly; specif., to bungle (a play), as in baseball
**muf·fin** (muf′'n) *n.* [? akin to OFr. *moufflet*, soft] a quick bread made with eggs, baked in a small, cup-shaped mold and usually eaten hot
**muf·fle** (muf′'l) *vt.* **-fled, -fling** [prob. akin to OFr. *en-mouflé*, muffled < *moufle*, a mitten] **1.** to wrap in a shawl, blanket, etc. so as to hide, keep warm, etc. **2.** to wrap or cover in order to deaden or prevent sound **3.** to deaden (a sound) **4.** to stifle —*n.* a covering, mask, etc. used for muffling
**muf·fler** (-lər) *n.* **1.** a scarf worn around the throat, as for warmth **2.** a device for silencing noises, as a section in the exhaust pipe of an internal-combustion engine
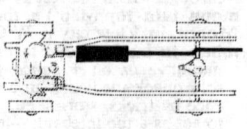
**muf·ti** (muf′tē) *n., pl.* **-tis** [Ar. < *āftā*, to judge] **1.** in Moslem countries, an interpreter of religious law **2.** ordinary clothes, esp. when worn by one who usually wears a uniform
**mug** (mug) *n.* [prob. < Scand.] **1.** a heavy drinking cup of earthenware or metal with a handle **2.** as much as a mug will hold

MUFFLER
**3.** [Slang] *a*) the face *b*) the mouth —*vt.* **mugged, mug′ging 1.** to assault, esp. from behind and usually with intent to rob **2.** [Slang] to photograph, as for police records —*vi.* **1.** to mug, or assault, someone **2.** [Slang] to grimace, esp. in overacting —**mug′ger** *n.*
**mug·gy** (mug′ē) *adj.* **-gi·er, -gi·est** [prob. < or akin to ON. *mugga*, a drizzle] hot, damp, and close [*muggy* weather] —**mug′gi·ness** *n.*
**mug·wump** (mug′wump′) *n.* [< Algonquian *mugquomp*, chief] an independent, esp. in politics
**Mu·ham·mad** (moo ham′əd) *same as* MOHAMMED —**Mu·ham′mad·an** *adj., n.* —**Mu·ham′mad·an·ism** *n.*
**‡mu·jik** (mōō zhēk′, mōō′zhik) *n. same as* MUZHIK
**Muk·den** (mook′dən, mook den′) *former name of* SHENYANG
**muk·luk** (muk′luk′) *n.* [Esk. *muklok*, a large seal] **1.** an Eskimo boot made of sealskin or reindeer skin **2.** a canvas or rubber boot like this
**mu·lat·to** (mə lat′ō, myoo-) *n., pl.* **-toes** [Sp. & Port. *mulato*, of mixed breed < *mulo*, mule < L. *mulus*] **1.** a person who has one Negro parent and one white parent **2.** popularly, any person with mixed Negro and Caucasoid ancestry
**mul·ber·ry** (mul′ber′ē, -bər ē) *n., pl.* **-ries** [OE. *morberie* < L. *morum*, mulberry + OE. *berie*, a berry] **1.** any of several trees that bear edible fruits resembling the raspberry **2.** this fruit **3.** purplish red —*adj.* designating a family of plants including the mulberry, fig, and breadfruit
**mulch** (mulch) *n.* [ME. *molsh*, soft] leaves, straw, peat moss, etc., spread on the ground around plants to prevent evaporation of water from the soil, freezing of roots, etc. —*vt.* to apply mulch to
**mulct** (mulkt) *vt.* [L. *mulctare* < *multa*, a fine] **1.** to punish by a fine or by depriving of something **2.** to extract (money) from (someone), as by fraud —*n.* a fine or similar penalty
**mule**[1] (myōol) *n.* [< OFr. < L. *mulus*] **1.** the (usually sterile) offspring of a donkey and a horse, esp. of a jackass and a mare **2.** a machine that draws and spins cotton fibers into yarn and winds the yarn **3.** [Colloq.] a stubborn person
**mule**[2] (myōol) *n.* [Fr., ult. < L. *mulleus*, red shoe] a lounging slipper that does not cover the heel
**mule deer** a long-eared deer of the western U.S.
**mule skinner** [Colloq.] a driver of mules
**mu·le·ta** (mōō lāt′ə, -let′ə) *n.* [Sp.] a red flannel cloth draped over a stick and manipulated by the matador in a bullfight
**mu·le·teer** (myōō′lə tir′) *n.* [< OFr.] a driver of mules
**Mül·heim** (mül′hīm′) city in W West Germany, on the Ruhr: pop. 189,000
**mul·ish** (myōol′ish) *adj.* like a mule; stubborn; obstinate —**mul′ish·ly** *adv.* —**mul′ish·ness** *n.*
**mull**[1] (mul) *vt., vi.* [OE. *myl*, dust] [Colloq.] to cogitate or ponder (usually with *over*)

**mull²** (mul) *vt.* [< ?] to heat, sweeten, and flavor with spices (ale, cider, wine, etc.)

**mul·lah, mul·la** (mul′ə, mool′-) *n.* [Turk., Per., & Hindi *mulla* < Ar. *mawlā*] a Moslem teacher or interpreter of the religious law: used as a title of respect for a learned man

**mul·lein** (mul′in) *n.* [OFr. *moleine*, ult. < L. *mollis*, soft] a tall plant of the figwort family, with spikes of yellow, lavender, or white flowers

**mul·let** (mul′it) *n., pl.* -**lets,** -**let:** see PLURAL, II, D, 1 [OFr. *mulet*, dim. < L. *mullus*, red mullet] any of a group of edible, spiny-rayed fishes found in fresh and salt waters; specif., the **striped** (or **gray) mullet**

**mul·li·gan** (mul′i g′n) *n.* [prob. < personal name] 1. [Slang] a stew made of odd bits of meat and vegetables, esp. as made by hobos: also **mulligan stew** 2. *Golf* a free drive, esp. off the first tee after a poor shot

**mul·li·ga·taw·ny** (mul′i gə tô′nē) *n.* [Tamil *milagutaṇṇir*, pepper water] an East Indian soup of meat, etc., flavored with curry

**mul·lion** (mul′yən) *n.* [prob. < OFr. *moienel* < L. *medianus*, middle] a slender, vertical dividing bar between the lights of windows, panels, etc. —*vt.* to furnish with mullions —**mul′lioned** *adj.*

**mul·tan·gu·lar** (mul taŋ′gyoo lər) *adj.* having many angles: also **mul′ti·an′gu·lar** (mul′tē aŋ′-)

**mul·ti-** [L. < *multus*, much, many] *a combining form meaning:* 1. having many [*multicolored*] 2. more than two [*multilateral*] 3. many times more than [*multimillionaire*] Also, before a vowel, **mult-** The meanings of the following words can be determined by combining the meanings of their component elements:

MULLIONS

| | | |
|---|---|---|
| multicellular | multilingual | multiracial |
| multicolored | multilobate | multispeed |
| multidimensional | multinational | multispiral |
| multidirectional | multinucleate | multistoried |
| multifold | multiphase | multivalve |
| multifoliate | multipinnate | multivitamin |
| multilevel | multipolar | multivoiced |
| multilinear | multipurpose | multivolume |

**mul·ti·far·i·ous** (mul′tə far′ē əs, -fer′-) *adj.* [L. *multifarius* < *multus*, many] having many kinds of parts or elements; of great variety —**mul′ti·far′i·ous·ly** *adv.* —**mul′ti·far′i·ous·ness** *n.*

**mul·ti·flo·ra rose** (-flôr′ə) a rose with thick clusters of small flowers, grown esp. for hedges

**mul·ti·lat·er·al** (mul′ti lat′ər əl) *adj.* 1. many-sided 2. involving more than two nations, etc. [a *multilateral* treaty] —**mul′ti·lat′er·al·ly** *adv.*

**mul·ti·me·di·a** (-mē′dē ə) *n. same as* MIXED MEDIA

**mul·ti·mil·lion·aire** (-mil′yə ner′) *n.* a person whose wealth amounts to many millions of dollars, francs, pounds, etc.

**mul·ti·na·tion·al** (-nash′ə n′l) *adj.* 1. of or involving a number of nations 2. designating or of a corporation with branches in a number of countries 3. comprising persons of many nationalities —*n.* a multinational corporation

**mul·tip·a·rous** (mul tip′ər əs) *adj.* [< ModL.: see MULTI- & -PAROUS] *Zool.* normally bearing more than one offspring at a delivery

**mul·ti·par·tite** (mul′ti pär′tīt) *adj.* 1. divided into many parts 2. *same as* MULTILATERAL (sense 2)

**mul·ti·ple** (mul′tə p′l) *adj.* [Fr. < L. *multiplex* < *multus*, many + -*plex*, -fold: see DUPLEX] 1. having or consisting of many parts, elements, etc.; manifold 2. *Elec.* designating or of a circuit with two or more conductors in parallel —*n.* a number that is a product of some specified number and another number [10 is a *multiple* of 5]

**multiple sclerosis** a disease of the central nervous system, marked by speech defects, lack of coordination, etc.

**mul·ti·plex** (-pleks′) *adj.* [L. *multiplex*, MULTIPLE] 1. multiple 2. designating or of a system for transmitting or receiving simultaneously two or more messages or signals over a common circuit, carrier wave, etc. —*vt.* to send (messages or signals) by a multiplex system

**mul·ti·pli·cand** (mul′tə pli kand′) *n.* [< L. *multiplicandus*, to be multiplied] *Math.* the number that is, or is to be, multiplied by another (the *multiplier*)

**mul·ti·pli·ca·tion** (-pli kā′shən) *n.* a multiplying or being multiplied; specif., *Math.* a method used to find the result of adding a specified quantity repeated a specified number of times

**mul·ti·plic·i·ty** (-plis′ə tē) *n.* [< LL. < L. *multiplex,*

MULTIPLE] 1. a being manifold or various 2. a great number

**mul·ti·pli·er** (mul′tə plī′ər) *n.* 1. a person or thing that multiplies or increases 2. *Math.* the number by which another number (the *multiplicand*) is, or is to be, multiplied

**mul·ti·ply¹** (mul′tə plī′) *vt.* -**plied′,** -**ply′ing** [< OFr. < L. *multiplicare* < *multiplex*, MULTIPLE] 1. to cause to increase in number, amount, degree, etc. 2. *Math.* to find the product of by multiplication —*vi.* 1. to increase in number, amount, etc., esp. by procreation 2. *Math.* to do multiplication

**mul·ti·ply²** (mul′tə plē) *adv.* in multiple ways

**mul·ti·stage** (mul′ti stāj′) *adj.* having several propulsion systems, used and discarded in sequence: said of a rocket or missile

**mul·ti·tude** (mul′tə tood′, -tyood′) *n.* [OFr. < L. *multitudo* < *multus*, many] 1. a large number of persons or things; host, myriad, etc. 2. the masses (preceded by *the*)

**mul·ti·tu·di·nous** (mul′tə tood′'n əs, -tyood′-) *adj.* 1. many 2. consisting of many parts, elements, etc.

**mul·ti·va·lent** (mul′ti vā′lənt, mul tiv′ə lənt) *adj. Chem.* *same as* POLYVALENT (sense 2) —**mul′ti·va′lence** *n.*

**mul·ti·ver·si·ty** (mul′tə vur′sə tē) *n., pl.* -**ties** the modern large and complex university with its many colleges, extensions, etc., regarded as being impersonal, bureaucratic, etc.

**mum¹** (mum) *vi.* **mummed, mum′ming** [< OFr. *momer* < *momo*, echoic for grimace] to wear a mask or costume in fun; specif., to act as a mummer at Christmas time

**mum²** (mum) *n.* [Colloq.] a chrysanthemum

**mum³** (mum) *adj.* [ME. *momme*, echoic of sound made with closed lips] silent; not speaking —*interj.* do not speak! —**mum's the word** say nothing

**mum·ble** (mum′b′l) *vt., vi.* -**bled, -bling** [ME. *momelen*] 1. to speak or say indistinctly, as with the mouth partly closed 2. [Rare] to chew gently and ineffectively —*n.* a mumbled utterance —**mum′bler** *n.* —**mum′bling·ly** *adv.*

**mum·ble·ty·peg** (mum′b′l tē peg′) *n.* a game in which a jackknife is tossed in various ways to make it land with the blade in the ground

**mum·bo jum·bo** (mum′bō jum′bō) [of Afr. orig.: < ?] 1. [M- J-] among certain West African tribes, an idol or god supposed to protect the people from evil 2. any idol or fetish 3. meaningless ritual, gibberish, etc.

**mum·mer** (mum′ər) *n.* [see MUM¹] 1. one who wears a mask or disguise for fun; specif., in England, any of the masked and costumed persons who act out pantomimes at Christmas time 2. any actor

**mum·mer·y** (-ē) *n., pl.* -**mer·ies** 1. performance by mummers 2. any show or ceremony regarded as hypocritical

**mum·mi·fy** (mum′ə fī′) *vt.* -**fied′,** -**fy′ing** to make into or like a mummy —*vi.* to shrivel or dry up —**mum′mi·fi·ca′tion** *n.*

**mum·my** (mum′ē) *n., pl.* -**mies** [< Fr. < ML. < Ar. *mūmiyā* < Per. *mum*, wax] 1. a dead body preserved by embalming, as by the ancient Egyptians 2. any well-preserved dead body

**mumps** (mumps) *n.pl.* [*with sing. v.*] [pl. of obs. *mump*, a grimace] an acute communicable disease, caused by a virus and characterized by swelling of the salivary glands

**mun.** municipal

**munch** (munch) *vt., vi.* [ME. *monchen*, echoic] to chew steadily, often with a crunching sound

**Mun·chau·sen** (mun′chou′zən, moon′-; -chô′-), Baron 1720–97; Ger. soldier & adventurer known for his exaggerated tales of his exploits

**Mun·cie** (mun′sē) [after the *Munsee* (Delaware) Indians] city in EC Ind.: pop. 77,000

**mun·dane** (mun dān′, mun′dān) *adj.* [< OFr. < L. < *mundus*, world] 1. of the world; esp., worldly, as distinguished from heavenly, spiritual, etc. 2. commonplace; everyday; ordinary

**Mu·nich** (myoo′nik) city in SE West Germany; capital of Bavaria: pop. 1,244,000: Ger. name **Mün·chen** (mün′Hən)

**mu·nic·i·pal** (myoo nis′ə p′l) *adj.* [< L. < *municeps*, citizen of a free town < *munia*, official duties + *capere*, to take] 1. of or having to do with a city, town, etc. or its local government 2. having local self-government —**mu·nic′i·pal·ly** *adv.*

**mu·nic·i·pal·i·ty** (myoo nis′ə pal′ə tē) *n., pl.* -**ties** a city, town, etc. having its own incorporated government

**mu·nic·i·pal·ize** (myoo nis′ə pə līz′) *vt.* -**ized′,** -**iz′ing** 1. to bring under the control or ownership of a municipality 2. to make a municipality of —**mu·nic′i·pal·i·za′tion** *n.*

**mu·nif·i·cent** (myoo nif′ə s'nt) *adj.* [< L. < *munificus*, bountiful < *munus,*] a gift + *facere*, to make] 1. very generous in giving 2. given with great generosity —**mu·nif′i·cence** *n.* —**mu·nif′i·cent·ly** *adv.*

**mu·ni·tion** (myōō nish′ən) *vt.* to provide with munitions
**mu·ni·tions** (-ənz) *n.pl.* [< MFr. < L. < *munire*, to fortify] war supplies; esp., weapons and ammunition
**Mün·ster** (mün′stər) city in NW West Germany: pop. 203,000
**mu·on** (myōō′än) *n.* [MU + (MES)ON] a positively or negatively charged subatomic particle with a mass 207 times that of an electron
**mu·ral** (myoor′əl) *adj.* [Fr. < L. *muralis* < *murus*, a wall] 1. of, on, in, or for a wall 2. like a wall —*n.* a picture or photograph, esp. a large one, painted or applied directly on a wall —**mu′ral·ist** *n.*
**Mur·ci·a** (mur′shə, -shē ə; *Sp.* mōōr′thyä) city in SE Spain: pop. 262,000
**mur·der** (mur′dər) *n.* [OE. *morthor* & OFr. *mordre*] the unlawful and malicious or premeditated killing of one human being by another —*vt.* 1. to kill unlawfully and with malice 2. to spoil or botch, as in performance [she *murdered* that song] —*vi.* to commit murder —**get away with murder** [Slang] to escape detection or punishment for a blameworthy act —**mur′der·er** *n.* —**mur′der·ess** *n.fem.*
**mur·der·ous** (-əs) *adj.* 1. of, having the nature of, or characteristic of murder; brutal 2. capable or guilty of, or intending, murder 3. [Colloq.] very dangerous, trying, etc.—**mur′der·ous·ly** *adv.* —**mur′der·ous·ness** *n.*
**mu·ri·at·ic acid** (myoor′ē at′ik) [< Fr. < L. < *muria*, brine] hydrochloric acid: a commercial term
**Mu·ri·el** (myoor′ē əl) [prob. < Celt. < *muir*, sea + *geal*, bright] a feminine name
**Mu·ril·lo** (mōō rē′lyô; *E.* myoo ril′ō), **Bar·to·lo·mé Es·te·ban** (bär′tô lô me′ es te′bän) 1617–82; Sp. painter
**murk** (murk) *n.* [< ON. *myrkr*, dark] darkness; gloom —*adj.* [Archaic] dark or dim
**murk·y** (mur′kē) *adj.* **murk′i·er, murk′i·est** 1. dark or gloomy 2. heavy and obscure with smoke, mist, etc. —**murk′i·ly** *adv.* —**murk′i·ness** *n.*
**Mur·mansk** (mōōr mänsk′) seaport on the NW coast of the U.S.S.R., on the Arctic Ocean: pop. 296,000
**mur·mur** (mur′mər) *n.* [< OFr. < L.: echoic word] 1. a low, indistinct, continuous sound, as of a stream, far-off voices, etc. 2. a mumbled complaint 3. *Med.* any abnormal sound heard by auscultation, esp. such a sound in the region of the heart —*vi.* 1. to make a murmur 2. to mumble a complaint —*vt.* to say in a murmur —**mur′mur·er** *n.* —**mur′mur·ing** *adj.* —**mur′mur·ous** *adj.*
**Mur·phy bed** (mur′fē) [after W. L. *Murphy*, its U.S. inventor (c.1900)] a bed that swings up or folds into a closet or cabinet when not in use
**mur·rain** (mur′in) *n.* [< OFr. *morine* < L. *mori*, to die] 1. any of various infectious diseases of cattle 2. [Archaic] a pestilence; plague
**Mur·ray¹** (mur′ē) [< the surname *Murray*] a masculine name
**Mur·ray²** (mur′ē) river in SE Australia, flowing into the Indian Ocean
**mur·ther** (mur′thər) *n., vt., vi.* dial. var. *of* MURDER
**mus.** 1. museum 2. music 3. musical
**mus·ca·dine** (mus′kə din, -dīn) *n.* [altered < MUSCATEL] a variety of grape grown in the SE U.S.
**mus·cat** (mus′kət, -kat) *n.* [Fr. < Pr. < It. *moscato*, musk, wine < LL. *muscus*, musk] 1. a variety of sweet European grape from which muscatel and raisins are made 2. *same as* MUSCATEL (sense 1)
**mus·ca·tel** (mus′kə tel′) *n.* [OFr. *muscadel*, ult. < It. *moscato*, MUSCAT] 1. a rich, sweet wine made from the muscat 2. *same as* MUSCAT (sense 1) Also **mus′ca·del′** (-del′)
**mus·cle** (mus′'l) *n.* [Fr. < L. *musculus*, dim. of *mus*, a mouse] 1. any of the body organs consisting of bundles of fibers that can be contracted and expanded to produce bodily movements 2. the tissue making up such an organ 3. muscular strength; brawn 4. [Colloq.] power based on force —*vi.* **-cled, -cling** [Colloq.] to make one's way by sheer force (usually with *in*)
**mus·cle-bound** (-bound′) *adj.* having some of the muscles enlarged and less elastic, as from too much exercise
**Mus·co·vite** (mus′kə vīt′) *n.* a Russian, esp. of Moscow —*adj.* of Russia or of Moscow
**Mus·co·vy** (mus′kə vē) 1. former grand duchy surrounding & including Moscow 2. *former name of* RUSSIA
**Muscovy duck** [altered < *musk duck*] a common domesticated duck with a large crest and red wattles
**mus·cu·lar** (mus′kyə lər) *adj.* 1. of, consisting of, or accomplished by a muscle or muscles 2. having well-developed muscles; strong; brawny —**mus′cu·lar′i·ty** (-lar′ə tē) *n.* —**mus′cu·lar·ly** *adv.*
**muscular dystrophy** a chronic disease·characterized by a progressive wasting of the muscles
**mus·cu·la·ture** (mus′kyə lə chər) *n.* [Fr.] the arrangement of the muscles of a body or of some part of the body; muscular system
**Muse** (myōōz) *n.* [< OFr. < L. < Gr. *mousa*] 1. *Gr. Myth.* any of the nine goddesses who presided over literature and

the arts and sciences 2. [m-] the spirit regarded as inspiring a poet or artist
**muse** (myōōz) *vi.* **mused, mus′ing** [< OFr. *muser*, to loiter] to think deeply; meditate —*vt.* to think or say meditatively —*n.* deep meditation
**mu·se·um** (myōō zē′əm) *n.* [L. < Gr. *mouseion*, place for the Muses < *mousa*, a Muse] a building, room, etc. for preserving and exhibiting artistic, historical, or scientific objects
**mush¹** (mush) *n.* [prob. var. of MASH] 1. a thick porridge of boiled cornmeal 2. any thick, soft mass 3. [Colloq.] maudlin sentimentality
**mush²** (mush) *interj.* [prob. < *mush on*, altered < Fr. *marchons*, let's go] in Canada and Alaska, a shout commanding sled dogs to start or to go faster —*vi.* to travel on foot over snow, usually with a dog sled —*n.* a journey by mushing
**mush·room** (mush′rōōm′, -room′) *n.* [OFr. *moisseron* < LL. *mussirio*] 1. any of various rapid-growing, fleshy fungi having a stalk with an umbrellalike top; popularly, any edible variety, as distinguished from the poisonous ones (*toadstools*) 2. anything like a mushroom in shape or rapid growth —*adj.* 1. of or made with mushrooms 2. like a mushroom in shape or rapid growth —*vi.* 1. to grow or spread rapidly 2. to flatten out at the end so as to resemble a mushroom
**mush·y** (mush′ē) *adj.* **mush′i·er, mush′i·est** 1. like mush; thick and soft 2. [Colloq.] maudlin and sentimental —**mush′i·ly** *adv.* —**mush′i·ness** *n.*
**mu·sic** (myōō′zik) *n.* [< OFr. < L. < Gr. *mousikē* (*technē*), musical (art) < *mousa*, a Muse] 1. the art and science of combining tones in varying melody, harmony, etc., esp. so as to form complete and expressive compositions 2. the tones so arranged, or their arrangement 3. any rhythmic sequence of pleasing sounds, as of birds, etc. 4. a musical composition or compositions; esp., the written or printed score 5. ability to respond to or take pleasure in music —**face the music** [Colloq.] to accept the consequences, however unpleasant —**set to music** to compose music for (a poem, etc.)
**mu·si·cal** (-zi k'l) *adj.* 1. of or for the creation or performance of music 2. melodious or harmonious 3. fond of or skilled in music 4. set to music —*n.* a theatrical or film production with dialogue and a musical score with popular songs and dances: in full, **musical comedy** (or **play**, or **drama**) —**mu′si·cal′i·ty** (-kal′ə tē) *n.* —**mu′si·cal·ly** *adv.*
**musical chairs** a game in which the players march to music around empty chairs (one fewer than the number of players) and rush to sit down each time the music stops: the player with no seat drops out
**mu·si·cale** (myōō′zə kal′) *n.* [Fr.] a party or social affair featuring a musical program
**music box** a mechanical musical instrument containing a bar with tuned steel teeth that are struck by pins so arranged on a revolving cylinder as to produce a certain tune or tunes
**music hall** 1. an auditorium for musical productions 2. [Brit.] a vaudeville theater
**mu·si·cian** (myōō zish′ən) *n.* a person skilled in music; esp., a professional performer of music —**mu·si′cian·ly** *adv.* —**mu·si′cian·ship′** *n.*
**mu·si·col·o·gy** (myōō′zi käl′ə jē) *n.* [< It.: see MUSIC & -LOGY] the systematized study of the science, history, and methods of music —**mu′si·co·log′i·cal** (-kə läj′i k'l) *adj.* —**mu′si·col′o·gist.n.**
**mus·ing** (myōō′ziŋ) *adj.* that muses; meditative —*n.* meditation; reflection —**mus′ing·ly** *adv.*
**musk** (musk) *n.* [< OFr. < LL. < Gr. < Per. *mušk*, musk < Sans. *muṣka*, testicle] 1. a substance with a strong, penetrating odor, obtained from a small sac (**musk bag**) under the skin of the abdomen in the male musk deer: used as the basis of numerous perfumes 2. the odor of this substance, now often created synthetically —**musk′like′** *adj.*
**musk deer** a small, hornless deer of the uplands of C Asia: the male secretes musk
**mus·kel·lunge** (mus′kə lunj′) *n., pl.* **-lunge′** [< Ojibway *maskinoje*] a large pike of the Great Lakes and upper Mississippi: also called **mus′kie** (-kē)
**mus·ket** (mus′kit) *n.* [< MFr. < It. *moschetto*, orig. fledged arrow < L. *musca*, a fly] a smooth-bore, long-barreled firearm, used, as by infantry soldiers, before the invention of the rifle
**mus·ket·eer** (mus′kə tir′) *n.* a soldier armed with a musket
**mus·ket·ry** (mus′kə trē) *n.* 1. the skill of firing muskets or other small arms 2. muskets or musketeers, collectively
**musk·mel·on** (musk′mel′ən) *n.* [MUSK + MELON] any of several roundish fruits growing on a vine of the gourd family, as the cantaloupe: they have a thick rind and sweet, juicy flesh
**Mus·ko·ge·an** (mus kō′gē ən, -jē-) *adj.* designating or of a N. American Indian language family of the SE U.S.: also **Mus·kho′ge·an**

**musk ox** a hardy ox of arctic America and Greenland, with a long, coarse, hairy coat, large, curved horns, and a musk-like odor

**musk·rat** (musk′rat′) *n., pl.* **-rats′, -rat′**: see PLURAL, II, D, 1  **1.** a N. American rodent living in water and having glossy brown fur and a musklike odor  **2.** its fur

**musk·y** (mus′kē) *adj.* **musk′i·er, musk′i·est** of, like, or smelling of musk —**musk′i·ness** *n.*

**Mus·lim** (muz′ləm, mooz′-) *n., adj. same as* MOSLEM

**mus·lin** (muz′lin) *n.* [< Fr. < It. *mus-solino* < *Mussolo*, Mosul, city in Iraq] a strong, often sheer cotton cloth of plain weave; esp., a heavy variety used for sheets, pillowcases, etc.

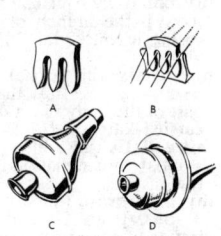
MUSKRAT
(body 9–13 in. long; tail 7–11 in. long)

**muss** (mus) *n.* [prob. var. of MESS] **1.** [Now Rare] a mess  **2.** [Old Slang or Dial.] a squabble —*vt.* to make messy (often with *up*)

**mus·sel** (mus′'l) *n.* [< OE., ult. < L. *musculus*, mussel, MUSCLE] any of various bivalve mollusks; specif., *a*) an edible saltwater variety *b*) a large freshwater variety with a pearly shell formerly made into buttons

**Mus·so·li·ni** (moo͞os′ṣö lē′nē; *E.* mooz′ə lē′nē, mus′-), **Be·ni·to** (be nē′tö) 1883–1945; It. dictator; Fascist prime minister of Italy (1922–43): executed

**Mus·sorg·sky** (moo sôrg′skē), **Mo·dest Pe·tro·vich** (mô′dyest′ pyi trô′vich) 1839–81; Russ. composer

**Mus·sul·man** (mus′'l mən) *n., pl.* **-mans** [< Per. < Ar. *muslim*] [Now Rare] a Moslem

**muss·y** (mus′ē) *adj.* **muss′i·er, muss′i·est** [Colloq.] messy; disordered, rumpled, etc. —**muss′i·ness** *n.*

**must¹** (must; *unstressed* məst) *v.aux. pt.* **must** [< OE. *moste*, pt. of *motan*, may] an auxiliary used with the infinitive of various verbs (without *to*) to express: **1.** compulsion, obligation, or necessity *[I must pay her]*  **2.** probability *[you must be my cousin]*  **3.** certainty *[all men must die]*  *Must* is sometimes used with the verb understood *[shoot if you must]* —*n.* [Colloq.] something that must be done, had, read, seen, etc. *[this book is a must]* —*adj.* [Colloq.] that must be done, etc.

**must²** (must) *n.* [OE. < L. *mustum*, new wine < *mustus*, fresh] the juice pressed from grapes or other fruit before it has fermented

**must³** (must) *n.* a musty quality or state

**mus·tache** (mə stash′, mus′tash) *n.* [< Fr. < It. *mostacchio* < MGr. < Gr. *mystax*, upper lip] **1.** the hair on the upper lip of men  **2.** the hair or bristles growing about an animal's mouth

**mus·ta·chio** (məs tä′shō, -shē ō′) *n., pl.* **-chios** [< Sp. or It.] a mustache, esp. a large, bushy one —**mus·ta′chioed** *adj.*

**Mustafa Kemal** *same as* KEMAL ATATURK

**mus·tang** (mus′taŋ) *n.* [< AmSp. < Sp. *mesteño*, belonging to the graziers, wild] a small wild or half-wild horse of the SW plains of the U.S.

**mus·tard** (mus′tərd) *n.* [< OFr. *moustarde* < L. *mustum*, MUST² (orig. added to the condiment)] **1.** any of several plants with yellow flowers and slender pods  **2.** the ground or powdered seeds from these pods, often prepared as a paste, used as a pungent seasoning  **3.** a dark yellow —*adj.* designating or of a family of plants with cross-shaped flowers, including cabbage, turnip, radish, alyssum, etc. —**cut the mustard** [Colloq.] to do the work required of one

**mustard gas** [from its mustardlike odor] a volatile liquid, ($CH_2ClCH_2)_2S$, used as a poison gas in war

**mustard plaster** a plaster made with powdered mustard, applied to the skin as a counterirritant

**mus·ter** (mus′tər) *vt.* [< OFr. < ML. < L. *monstrare*, to show < *monere*, to warn] **1.** to assemble (troops, etc.)  **2.** to gather up; collect; summon (often with *up*) *[to muster up strength]*  **3.** to total in number —*vi.* to assemble as for inspection or roll call —*n.* **1.** an assembling, as of troops for inspection  **2.** *a*) the persons or things assembled *b*) the total of these  **3.** the list of persons in a military or naval unit: also **muster roll** —**muster in** (or **out**) to enlist in (or discharge from) military service —**pass muster** to measure up to required standards

**must·n't** (mus′'nt) must not

**mus·ty** (mus′tē) *adj.* **-ti·er, -ti·est** [ult. < ? MOIST] **1.** having a stale, moldy smell or taste  **2.** stale, trite, or antiquated *[musty ideas]* —**mus′ti·ly** *adv.* —**mus′ti·ness** *n.*

**mu·ta·ble** (myoo͞o′tə b'l) *adj.* [< L. < *mutare*, to change] **1.** that can be changed  **2.** given to changing; inconstant  **3.** subject to mutation —**mu′ta·bil′i·ty, mu′ta·ble·ness** *n.* —**mu′ta·bly** *adv.*

**mu·tant** (myoo͞ot′'nt) *adj.* [< L. prp. of *mutare*, to change]

undergoing mutation —*n.* an animal or plant with inheritable characters that differ from those of the parents

**mu·tate** (myoo͞o′tāt) *vi., vt.* **-tat·ed, -tat·ing** [< L. pp. of *mutare*, to change] to change; specif., to undergo or cause to undergo mutation

**mu·ta·tion** (myoo͞o tā′shən) *n.* **1.** a changing or being changed  **2.** a change, as in form, nature, etc.  **3.** *Biol. a*) a sudden variation in some inheritable character of an animal or plant  *b*) an individual resulting from such variation; mutant —**mu·ta′tion·al** *adj.* —**mu·ta′tion·al·ly** *adv.*

**mute** (myoo͞ot) *adj.* [< OFr. < L. *mutus*] **1.** not speaking; voluntarily silent  **2.** unable to speak  **3.** not spoken *[a mute appeal]*  **4.** not pronounced; silent, as the *e* in *mouse*  **5.** *Law* refusing to plead when arraigned —*n.* **1.** a person who does not speak; specif., one who cannot speak because deaf; deaf-mute  **2.** a letter that is not pronounced  **3.** *Law* a defendant who refuses to plead when arraigned  **4.** *Music* a device used to soften the tone of an instrument —*vt.* **mut′ed, mut′ing** **1.** to soften the sound of, as with a mute  **2.** to tone down (a color) —**mute′ly** *adv.* —**mute′ness** *n.*

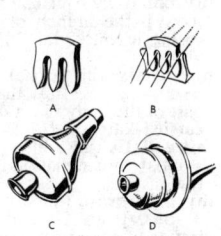
MUTES
(A, violin mute; B, on violin bridge; C, trumpet mute; D, in bell of trumpet)

**mu·ti·late** (myoo͞ot′'l āt′) *vt.* **-lat′ed, -lat′ing** [< L. pp. of *mutilare* < *mutilus*, maimed] **1.** to cut off or damage a limb, etc. of (a person or animal)  **2.** to damage or otherwise make imperfect, esp. by removing an essential part or parts —**mu′ti·la′tion** *n.* —**mu′ti·la′tive** *adj.* —**mu′ti·la′tor** *n.*

**mu·ti·neer** (myoo͞ot′'n ir′) *n.* one guilty of mutiny

**mu·ti·nous** (myoo͞ot′'n əs) *adj.* **1.** taking part or likely to take part in a mutiny  **2.** of or having to do with mutiny —**mu′ti·nous·ly** *adv.* —**mu′ti·nous·ness** *n.*

**mu·ti·ny** (myoo͞ot′'n ē) *n., pl.* **-nies** [< Fr. < OFr. *mutin*, riotous < *meute*, a revolt, ult. < L. *movere*, to move] forcible revolt against constituted authority; esp., rebellion of soldiers or sailors against their officers —*vi.* **-nied, -ny·ing** to take part in a mutiny; revolt

**mutt** (mut) *n.* [prob. < *muttonhead*, a dolt] [Slang] **1.** a stupid person; blockhead  **2.** a mongrel dog; cur

**mut·ter** (mut′ər) *vi., vt.* [ME. *moteren*] to speak or say in low tones with the lips almost closed, often in a complaining way; grumble —*n.* **1.** a muttering  **2.** something muttered —**mut′ter·er** *n.*

**mut·ton** (mut′'n) *n.* [OFr. *moton*, a ram < ML. *multo*, sheep] the flesh of sheep, esp. a grown sheep, used as food —**mut′ton·y** *adj.*

**mutton chop** **1.** a piece cut from the rib of a sheep for broiling or frying  **2.** *[pl.]* side whiskers shaped like mutton chops

**mu·tu·al** (myoo͞o′choo wəl) *adj.* [< MFr. < L. *mutuus*, reciprocal < *mutare*, to change] **1.** *a*) done, felt, etc. by each of two or more for or toward the other or others; reciprocal *[mutual admiration]*  *b*) of each other *[mutual enemies]*  **2.** shared in common; joint *[our mutual friend]* —**mu′tu·al′i·ty** (-wal′ə tē) *n., pl.* **-ties** —**mu′tu·al·ly** *adv.*

**mutual fund** a trust or corporation that invests funds from its shareholders in various securities

**mu·tu·el** (myoo͞o′choo wəl) *n. same as* PARIMUTUEL

**muu-muu** (moo͞o′moo͞o) *n.* [< Haw., lit., cut off] a full, long, loose garment for women, usually in a bright print as orig. worn in Hawaii

**Mu·zak** (myoo͞o′zak) *a trademark for* a system of transmitting recorded music to restaurants, factories, etc. —*n.* the music transmitted

**‡mu·zhik, mu·zjik** (moo͞o zhēk′, moo͞o′zhik) *n.* [Russ.] in czarist Russia, a peasant

**muz·zle** (muz′'l) *n.* [< OFr. *musel*, snout < ML. *musum* < ?] **1.** the part of the head of a dog, horse, etc. including the mouth, nose, and jaws  **2.** a device, as of straps, fastened over the mouth of an animal to prevent its biting or eating  **3.** anything that prevents free speech  **4.** the front end of the barrel of a firearm —*vt.* **-zled, -zling** **1.** to put a muzzle on (an animal)  **2.** to prevent from talking or expressing an opinion —**muz′zler** *n.*

**muz·zle·load·er** (-lōd′ər) *n.* any firearm loaded through the muzzle —**muz′zle·load′ing** *n.*

**my** (mi; *unstressed, often* mə) *possessive pronominal adj.* [OE. *min*] of, belonging to, made, or done by me —*interj.* an exclamation of surprise, dismay, etc.

**my·ce·li·um** (mi sē′lē əm) *n., pl.* **-li·a** (-ə) [ModL. < Gr. *mykēs*, a mushroom] the thallus, or vegetative part, of a fungus, made of a mass of threadlike tubes —my·ce′li·al adj.

My·ce·nae (mī sē′nē) ancient city in the NE Peloponnesus

My·ce·nae·an (mī′sə nē′ən) adj. 1. of Mycenae 2. designating or of a civilization that existed in Greece, Asia Minor, etc. from 1500 to 1100 B.C.

-my·cete (mī′sēt, mī sēt′) [< ModL. < Gr. < mykēs, a mushroom] a combining form meaning one of a specified class of fungi

my·co- [< Gr. mykēs, fungus] a combining form meaning fungus: also, before a vowel, myc-

my·col·o·gy (mī käl′ə jē) n. [< ModL.: see prec. & -LOGY] the branch of botany dealing with fungi —my·co·log·ic (mī′kə läj′ik), my′co·log′i·cal adj. —my·col′o·gist n.

my·co·sis (mī kō′sis) n., pl. -ses (-sēz) [ModL.: see MYC(O)- & -OSIS] 1. the growth of parasitic fungi in any part of the body 2. a disease caused by such fungi —my·cot′ic (-kät′ik) adj.

my·e·li·tis (mī′ə līt′is) n. [ModL. < Gr. myelos, marrow + -ITIS] inflammation of the spinal cord or the bone marrow

my·e·lo·gram (mī′ə lō gram′) n. [< Gr. myelos, marrow + -GRAM] an X-ray of the spinal cord, taken after the injection of a contrast substance —my′e·log′ra·phy (-läg′rə-fē) n.

My·lar (mī′lär) a trademark for a polyester used for recording tapes, fabrics, etc. —n. [m-] this substance

my·na, my·nah (mī′nə) n. [Hindi mainā] any of a group of tropical birds of SE Asia related to the starling: some species can mimic speech

my·o- [< Gr. mys (gen. myos), a muscle] a combining form meaning muscle: also, before a vowel, my-

my·o·car·di·um (mī′ə kär′dē əm) n. [ModL.: see prec. + CARDIO-] the muscular substance of the heart —my′o·car′di·al adj.

my·o·pi·a (mī ō′pē ə) n. [ModL. < Gr. < myein, to close + ōps, an eye] abnormal vision in which light rays from distant objects focus in front of the retina instead of on it, so that the objects are not seen distinctly; nearsightedness —my·op′ic (-äp′ik) adj. —my·op′i·cal·ly adv.

My·ra (mī′rə) [< ? Ir. Moira] a feminine name

myr·i·ad (mir′ē əd) n. [< Gr. myrias (gen. myriados), ten thousand < myrios, countless] 1. orig., ten thousand 2. any indefinitely large number 3. a great number of persons or things —adj. 1. countless; innumerable 2. of a highly varied nature

myr·i·a·pod (mir′ē ə päd′) adj. [see prec. & -POD] having many legs; specif., of a large group of arthropods having a long body of many segments, each with one or more pairs of jointed legs, as the centipedes —n. any animal of this group

Myr·mi·don (mur′mə dän′, -dən) n., pl. -dons, Myr·mid·o·nes (mər mid′ə nēz′) 1. Gr. Legend any of a tribe of Thessalian warriors who fought under Achilles, their king, in the Trojan War 2. [m-] an unquestioning follower or subordinate

myrrh (mur) n. [< OE. & OFr. < L. < Gr. myrrha < Ar. murr] a fragrant, bitter-tasting gum resin exuded from any of several plants of Arabia and E Africa, used in making incense, perfume, etc. 2. any of these plants

Myr·tle (mur′t'l) [< ff.] a feminine name

myr·tle (mur′t'l) n. [< OFr. < ML. dim. of L. myrtus < Gr. myrtos] 1. a shrub with evergreen leaves, white or pink flowers, and dark berries 2. any of various other evergreen plants, as the periwinkle —adj. designating a family of evergreen trees and shrubs, including myrtle, eucalyptus, guava, clove, and blue gum

my·self (mī self′, mə-) pron. a form of the 1st pers. sing. pronoun, used: a) as an intensive [I went myself] b) as a reflexive [I hurt myself] c) as a quasi-noun meaning "my real or true self" [I am not myself today]

My·sore (mī sôr′) city in S India: pop. 254,000

mys·te·ri·ous (mis tir′ē əs) adj. of, containing, implying, or characterized by mystery —mys·te′ri·ous·ly adv. —mys·te′ri·ous·ness n.

mys·ter·y¹ (mis′tə rē, -trē) n., pl. -ter·ies [< L. < Gr. mystērion, ult. < myein, to initiate into the mysteries, orig., to close (eyes or mouth)] 1. something unexplained, unknown, or kept secret 2. a) anything that remains so secret or obscure as to excite curiosity b) a novel, play, etc. involving an event of this kind, esp. one about a crime and its solution 3. obscurity or secrecy 4. [pl.] secret rites or doctrines known only to the initiated [the Eleusinian mysteries] 5. same as MYSTERY PLAY 6. Theol. any religious truth divinely revealed and to be accepted on faith

mys·ter·y² (mis′tə rē) n., pl. -ter·ies [< ML. misterium, altered < L. ministerium, office, by confusion with mysterium, a secret rite] [Archaic] a craft or craft guild

mystery play any of a class of medieval dramatic representations of Biblical events

mys·tic (mis′tik) adj. [< L. < Gr. mystikos < mystēs, one initiated] 1. same as MYSTICAL 2. mysterious, secret, occult, awe-inspiring, etc. [mystic rites, mystic powers] —n. one who professes to undergo mystical experiences by which he learns truths beyond human understanding

mys·ti·cal (-ti k'l) adj. 1. of mystics or mysticism; esp., based on intuition, meditation, etc. of a spiritual nature 2. spiritually symbolic 3. same as MYSTIC (sense 2) —mys′ti·cal·ly adv.

mys·ti·cism (-tə siz′m) n. 1. the beliefs or practices of mystics 2. the doctrine that knowledge of spiritual truths can be acquired by intuition and meditation 3. vague or obscure thinking or belief

mys·ti·fy (mis′tə fī′) vt. -fied′, -fy′ing [< Fr. < mystère, mystery + -fier, -FY] 1. a) to puzzle or perplex b) to bewilder deliberately 2. to involve in mystery; make obscure —mys′ti·fi·ca′tion n.

mys·tique (mis tēk′) n. [Fr., mystic] the quasi-mystical attitudes and feelings surrounding some person, institution, activity, etc.

myth (mith) n. [< LL. < Gr. mythos, a word, legend] 1. a traditional story of unknown authorship, serving usually to explain some phenomenon of nature, the origin of man, or the customs, religious rites, etc. of a people: cf. LEGEND 2. such stories collectively; mythology 3. any fictitious story 4. any imaginary person or thing

myth. mythology

myth·i·cal (-i k'l) adj. 1. of, or having the nature of, a myth or myths 2. existing only in myth 3. imaginary or fictitious; not based on fact Also myth′ic —myth′i·cal·ly adv.

my·thol·o·gize (mi thäl′ə jīz′) vi. -gized′, -giz′ing to relate, compile, or explain myths —vt. to make into a myth: also myth·i·cize (mith′ə sīz′) -cized′, -ciz′ing —my·thol′o·giz′er n.

my·thol·o·gy (mi thäl′ə jē) n., pl. -gies [< LL. < Gr. < mythos, myth + -logia, -LOGY] 1. the study of myths 2. myths collectively; esp., all the myths of a specific people or about a specific being —myth·o·log·i·cal (mith′ə läj′i k'l), myth′o·log′ic adj. —myth′o·log′i·cal·ly adv. —my·thol′o·gist n.

myth·os (mith′äs, mī′thäs) n. 1. a myth or body of myths 2. the attitudes, beliefs, etc. most characteristic of a particular group or society

Myt·i·le·ne (mit′'l ē′nē) same as LESBOS

# N

N, n (en) n., pl. N's, n's 1. the fourteenth letter of the English alphabet 2. the sound of N or n

n (en) n. 1. Math. the symbol for an indefinite number 2. Physics the symbol for neutron

N Chem. nitrogen

N, N., n, n. 1. north 2. northern

n. 1. net 2. neuter 3. noon 4. noun 5. number

Na [L. natrium] Chem. sodium

N.A. North America

NAACP, N.A.A.C.P. National Association for the Advancement of Colored People

nab (nab) vt. nabbed, nab′bing [prob. var. of dial. nap, to snatch < Scand.] [Colloq.] 1. to seize suddenly; snatch 2. to arrest or catch (a felon or wrongdoer) —nab′ber n.

na·bob (nā′bäb) n. [< Hindi < Ar. nuwwāb, pl. of nā′ib, deputy] 1. a native provincial deputy or governor of the old Mogul Empire in India 2. a very rich man

na·celle (nə sel′) n. [Fr. < LL. navicella, dim. of L. navis, a ship] a streamlined enclosure on an aircraft, esp. that which houses an engine

na·cre (nā′kər) n. [Fr. < It. < Ar. naqqārah, drum] same as MOTHER-OF-PEARL

**na·cre·ous** (-krē əs) *adj.* **1.** of or like nacre **2.** yielding nacre **3.** iridescent; lustrous

**Na·dine** (nə dēn′, nā-) [Fr. < Russ. *nadezhda*, hope] a feminine name

**na·dir** (nā′dər, -dir) *n.* [< MFr. < ML. < Ar. *naẓīr* (*assamt*), opposite (the zenith)] **1.** that point of the celestial sphere directly opposite to the zenith and directly below the observer **2.** the lowest point

**nae** (nā) *adv.* [Scot.] no; not —*adj.* no

**nag**[1] (nag) *vt.* **nagged, nag′ging** [< Scand.] **1.** to annoy by continual scolding, faultfinding, urging, etc. **2.** to keep troubling, worrying, etc. —*vi.* **1.** to urge, scold, etc. constantly **2.** to cause continual discomfort, pain, etc. —*n.* a person, esp. a woman, who nags: also **nag′ger** —**nag′ging·ly** *adv.* —**nag′gy** *adj.* **-gi·er, -gi·est**

**nag**[2] (nag) *n.* [ME. *nagge* < ?] **1.** a horse that is worn-out, old, etc. **2.** [Slang] a racehorse, esp. an inferior one

**Na·ga·sa·ki** (nä′gə sä′kē) seaport on the W coast of Kyushu, Japan: partly destroyed (Aug. 9, 1945) by a U.S. atomic bomb: pop. 405,000

**Na·go·ya** (nä′gô yä′) seaport in S Honshu, Japan: pop. 1,935,000

**Nag·pur** (näg′poor) city in C India: pop. 690,000

**Na·hua·tl** (nä′wät 'l) *n.* [Nahuatl] **1.** *pl.* **Na′hua·tls, Na′hua·tl** a member of any of a number of Indian tribes of Mexico **2.** their Uto-Aztecan language **3.** a branch of the Uto-Aztecan language family, spoken in Mexico and C America

**Na·hum** (nā′əm, -həm) *Bible* **1.** a Hebrew prophet of the 7th cent. B.C. **2.** the book containing his prophecies: abbrev. **Nah.**

**nai·ad** (nā′ad, nī′-; -əd) *n., pl.* **-ads, -a·des′** (-ə dēz′) [< Fr. < L. < Gr. *Naïas* < *naein*, to flow] **1.** [*also* N-] *Gr. & Rom. Myth.* any of the nymphs living in and giving life to springs, fountains, rivers, etc. **2.** a girl or woman swimmer **3.** *Zool.* the aquatic nymph of certain insects

**na·if, na·ïf** (nä ēf′) *adj.* [Fr.] *same as* NAIVE

**nail** (nāl) *n.* [OE. *nægl*] **1.** *a*) the thin, horny substance growing out at the ends of the fingers and toes *b*) a claw **2.** a tapered piece of metal, commonly pointed and with a head, driven with a hammer to hold pieces of wood together, serve as a peg, etc. —*vt.* **1.** to attach, fasten together, or fasten shut with nails **2.** to fix (the eyes, attention, etc.) steadily on an object **3.** to discover or expose (a lie, etc.) **4.** [Colloq.] to catch, capture, etc. **5.** [Colloq.] to hit squarely —**hit the nail on the head** to do or say whatever is exactly right —**nail down** to settle definitely; make sure —**nail′er** *n.*

**nail file** a small, flat file for trimming the fingernails

NAILS
(A, common wire; B, flooring; C, finishing; D, boat; E, screw; F, masonry)

**nail polish** a kind of lacquer, usually colored, applied to the fingernails or toenails as a cosmetic

**nail set** a tool for sinking a nail so that it is below the surface of the wood

**nain·sook** (nān′sook) *n.* [< Hindi < *nain*, the eye + *sukh*, pleasure] a thin, lightweight cotton fabric

**nai·ra** (nī′rə) *n., pl.* **nai′ra** [dim. of NIGERIA] the monetary unit of Nigeria: see MONETARY UNITS, table

**Nai·ro·bi** (nī rō′bē) capital of Kenya: pop. 479,000

**na·ive, na·ïve** (nä ēv′) *adj.* [Fr., fem. of *naïf* < L. *nativus*, natural] **1.** unaffectedly or foolishly simple; artless; unsophisticated **2.** not suspicious; credulous —**na·ive′ly, na·ive′ly** *adv.*

**na·ive·té, na·ïve·té** (nä ēv tā′, -ēv′tā) *n.* [Fr.] **1.** a being naive **2.** a naive action or remark Also **na·ive′ness, na·ïve′ness, na·ive′ty** (-tē), **na·ïve′ty**

**na·ked** (nā′kid) *adj.* [OE. *nacod*] **1.** *a*) completely unclothed; nude *b*) uncovered; exposed: said of parts of the body **2.** destitute **3.** without protection or defense **4.** without its usual covering; specif., *a*) out of its sheath [a *naked* sword] *b*) without decoration, etc. [a *naked* wall] **5.** without additions, etc.; plain [the *naked* truth] **6.** not aided by a microscope, telescope, etc. [the *naked* eye] —**na′ked·ly** *adv.* —**na′ked·ness** *n.*

**NAM, N.A.M.** National Association of Manufacturers

**nam·by-pam·by** (nam′bē pam′bē) *adj.* [orig. satirical nickname of *Ambrose Philips*, 18th-c. Eng. poet] weakly sentimental; insipidly pretty or nice —*n., pl.* **-bies 1.** namby-pamby talk or writing **2.** a namby-pamby person

**name** (nām) *n.* [OE. *nama*] **1.** a word or phrase by which a person, thing, or class of things is known; title **2.** a word or phrase expressing some quality considered descriptive; epithet **3.** *a*) reputation *b*) good reputation **4.** a family or clan **5.** appearance only, not reality [chief in *name* only] **6.** a famous person —*adj.* **1.** well-known [a *name* brand] **2.** carrying a name [a *name* tag] —*vt.* **named, nam′ing 1.** to give a name or title to **2.** to designate or refer to by name **3.** to identify by the right name [*name* the oceans] **4.** to nominate or appoint to a post or office **5.** to set or specify (a day, price, etc.) **6.** to speak about; mention —**call names** to swear at —**in the name of 1.** in appeal to **2.** by the authority of **3.** as belonging to —**to one's name** belonging to one —**name′a·ble, nam′a·ble** *adj.* —**nam′er** *n.*

**name-call·ing** (-kôl′iŋ) *n.* the use of abusive names in attacking another —**name′-call′er** *n.*

**name-drop·per** (-dräp′ər) *n.* a person who tries to impress others by often mentioning famous persons in a familiar way —**name′-drop′ping** *n.*

**name·less** (-lis) *adj.* **1.** without a name **2.** left unnamed **3.** not well known **4.** illegitimate **5.** indescribable **6.** too horrid to specify [*nameless* crimes] —**name′less·ly** *adv.* —**name′less·ness** *n.*

**name·ly** (-lē) *adv.* that is to say; to wit

**name·plate** (-plāt′) *n.* a piece of metal, etc. on which a name is inscribed

**name·sake** (-sāk′) *n.* a person with the same name as another, esp. if named after the other

**Na·mib·i·a** (nä mib′ē ə) *official* (*UN*) *name for* SOUTH WEST AFRICA

**Nan·cy** (nan′sē) [prob. by faulty division of MINE[1] + *Ancy*, dim. of ME. *Annis*, Agnes] a feminine name

**nan·keen** (nan kēn′) *n.* [< ff.] **1.** a buff-colored, durable cotton cloth, orig. from China **2.** [*pl.*] trousers made of this

**Nan·king** (nan′kiŋ′, nän′-) city in E China, on the Yangtze River: pop. 2,700,000

**Nan·nette, Na·nette** (na net′) [dim. of ANNA] a feminine name

**nan·ny** (nan′ē) *n., pl.* **-nies** [< *Nan*, dim. of ANN(A)] [Brit.] a child's nurse

**nanny goat** [see prec.] [Colloq.] a female goat

**na·no-** [< Gr. *nanos*, dwarf] *a combining form meaning* one billionth part of

**na·no·sec·ond** (nan′ō sek′ənd) *n.* one billionth of a second

**Nan·sen** (nän′sən), **Fridt·jof** (frit′yäf) 1861–1930; Norw. arctic explorer, naturalist, & statesman

**Nantes** (nänt; *E.* nants) **1.** city in W France, on the Loire: pop. 259,000 **2. Edict of,** a decree issued (1598) in France, giving political equality to the Huguenots: it was revoked in 1685

**Nan·tuck·et** (nan tuk′it) [AmInd., lit., faraway land] island of Mass., south of Cape Cod

**Na·o·mi** (nā ō′mē, na-; nā′ə mī′) [Heb. *nā'omi*, lit., my delight] **1.** a feminine name **2.** *Bible* the mother-in-law of Ruth: Ruth 1

**nap**[1] (nap) *vi.* **napped, nap′ping** [OE. *hnappian*] **1.** to sleep lightly for a short time **2.** to be careless or unprepared —*n.* a brief, light sleep

**nap**[2] (nap) *n.* [< or akin to MDu. & MLowG. *noppe*] **1.** the downy or hairy surface of cloth formed by short hairs or fibers, raised by brushing, etc. **2.** any similar surface, as of the flesh side of leather —*vt.* **napped, nap′ping** to raise a nap on by brushing, etc. —**nap′less** *adj.* —**napped** *adj.*

**na·palm** (nā′päm) *n.* [*na*(*phthene*) + *palm*(*itate*), salt of palmitic acid] a jellylike substance with gasoline or oil in it, used in flame throwers and bombs —*vt.* to attack or burn with napalm

**nape** (nāp, nap) *n.* [ME.] the back of the neck

**na·per·y** (nā′pər ē) *n.* [< MFr. < OFr. *nappe*: see NAPKIN] household linen; esp., table linen

**naph·tha** (naf′thə, nap′-) *n.* [L. < Gr. < Per. *neft*, pitch] **1.** a flammable, volatile liquid made by distilling petroleum, coal tar, wood, etc. and used as a fuel, solvent, etc. **2.** *same as* PETROLEUM

**naph·tha·lene** (-lēn′) *n.* [prec. + -*l*- + -ENE] a white, crystalline, aromatic hydrocarbon, $C_{10}H_8$, made by distilling coal tar and used in moth repellents and in certain dyes, etc.: also **naph′tha·lin′** —**naph′tha·len′ic** (-lē′nik, -len′ik) *adj.*

**naph·thol** (naf′thôl, -thôl; nap′-) *n.* [NAPHTH(ALENE) + -OL[1]] either of two white, crystalline compounds, $C_{10}H_7OH$, derived from naphthalene and used as antiseptics and in dyes, etc.

**nap·kin** (nap′kin) *n.* [< OFr. *nappe* < L. *mappa*, cloth] **1.** a small cloth or paper used while eating for protecting the clothes and wiping the fingers or lips **2.** any small cloth, towel, etc.

**Na·ples** (nā′p'lz) **1.** seaport in S Italy, on the Bay of Naples: pop. 1,263,000 **2. Bay of,** inlet of the Tyrrhenian Sea, on the S coast of Italy

**na·po·le·on** (nə pō'lē ən, -pōl'yən) *n.* [after ff.] **1.** a former gold coin of France, equivalent to 20 francs **2.** a card game similar to euchre **3.** a layered puff pastry with a custardlike filling

**Na·po·le·on I** (nə pō'lē ən, -pōl'yən) (full Fr. name *Napoléon Bonaparte*) 1769–1821; Fr. military leader & emperor of France (1804–15) —**Na·po'le·on'ic** (-pō'lē än'ik) *adj.*

**Napoleon III** *see* LOUIS NAPOLEON

**Na·po·li** (nä'pō lē') *It. name of* NAPLES

**nap·py**[1] (nap'ē) *n., pl.* -**pies** [< obs. *nap*, a bowl < OE. *hnæp*] a shallow bowl for serving food

**nap·py**[2] (nap'ē) *adj.* -**pi·er, -pi·est** covered with nap; downy, shaggy, etc. —**nap'pi·ness** *n.*

**Nar·ba·da** (nur'bud'ə) river in C India, flowing west into the Arabian Sea: c.800 mi.

**nar·cis·sism** (när'sə siz'm; *chiefly Brit.* när sis'iz'm) *n.* [< G.: see NARCISSUS & -ISM] **1.** self-love **2.** *Psychoanalysis* the first stage of libidinal development, in which the self is an erotic object Also **nar'cism** —**nar'cis·sist** *n., adj.* —**nar'cissis'tic** *adj.*

**Nar·cis·sus** (när sis'əs) *Gr. Myth.* a beautiful youth who pined away for love of his own reflection in a spring and was changed into the narcissus —*n.* [n-] *pl.* -**cis'sus, -cis'sus·es, -cis'si** (-ī) [ModL. < L. < Gr. *narkissos,* ? akin to *narkē* (see NARCOTIC): in reference to the narcotic properties] any of a genus of bulb plants with smooth leaves and white, yellow, or orange flowers, including the daffodils and jonquils

**nar·co-** [< Gr. *narkē,* stupor] *a combining form meaning* narcosis, sleep, stupor: also, before a vowel, **narc-**

**nar·co·sis** (när kō'sis) *n.* a condition of deep stupor which passes into unconsciousness, caused by a narcotic or certain chemicals

**nar·co·syn·the·sis** (när'kō sin'thə sis) *n.* [NARCO- + SYNTHESIS] a method of treating an acute traumatic neurosis by working with a patient while he is under the influence of a hypnotic drug

**nar·cot·ic** (när kät'ik) *n.* [< OFr. < ML. < Gr. *narkoun,* to benumb < *narkē,* numbness] **1.** a drug, as opium, used to relieve pain and induce sleep: narcotics are often addictive and in excessive doses can cause stupor, coma, or death **2.** anything with a soothing, lulling, or dulling effect —*adj.* **1.** of, like, or producing narcosis **2.** of, by, or for narcotic addicts

**nar·co·tism** (när'kə tiz'm) *n.* **1.** *same as* NARCOSIS **2.** addiction to narcotics

**nar·co·tize** (när'kə tīz') *vt.* -**tized', -tiz'ing 1.** to subject to a narcotic; stupefy **2.** to lull or dull the senses of —**nar'co·ti·za'tion** *n.*

**nard** (närd) *n.* [< OFr. < L. < Gr. *nardos,* ult. < Sans.] *same as* SPIKENARD (sense 2)

**nar·es** (ner'ēz) *n.pl., sing.* **nar'is** (-is) [L.] the nasal passages; esp., the nostrils —**nar'i·al** (-ē əl), **nar'ine** (-in, -īn) *adj.*

**nar·ghi·le** (när'gə lē', -lā') *n.* [< Turk. & Per. < Per. *nargīl,* coconut tree: orig. made of coconut shell] *same as* HOOKAH: also sp. **nar'gi·le', nar'gi·leh'**

**Nar·ra·gan·sett Bay** (nar'ə gan'sit) [after an extinct tribe of Algonquian Indians who lived around the bay] inlet of the Atlantic, extending into R.I.

**nar·rate** (nar'āt, na rāt') *vt., vi.* -**rat·ed, -rat·ing** [< L. pp. of *narrare,* to relate] **1.** to tell (a story) **2.** to give an account of (events)

**nar·ra·tion** (na rā'shən) *n.* **1.** a narrating **2.** *same as* NARRATIVE **3.** writing or speaking that narrates, as fiction —**nar·ra'tion·al** *adj.*

**nar·ra·tive** (nar'ə tiv) *adj.* **1.** in story form **2.** concerned with narration —*n.* **1.** a story; account; tale **2.** the art or practice of relating stories or accounts —**nar'ra·tive·ly** *adv.*

**nar·ra·tor** (nar'āt ər, na rāt'ər) *n.* **1.** a person who relates a story, etc. **2.** a person who reads narrative passages, as between scenes of a play

**nar·row** (nar'ō, ner'ō) *adj.* [OE. *nearu*] **1.** small in width; not wide **2.** limited in meaning, size, amount, or extent [a *narrow* majority] **3.** limited in outlook; not liberal; prejudiced **4.** close; careful [a *narrow* inspection] **5.** with barely enough space, time, etc. [a *narrow* escape] **6.** limited in means [*narrow* circumstances] **7.** *Phonetics* tense: said of the tongue —*vi., vt.* to decrease or limit in width, extent, or scope —*n.* **1.** a narrow part or place, esp. in a valley, road, etc. **2.** [*usually pl.*] a narrow passage; strait —**nar'row·ly** *adv.* —**nar'row·ness** *n.*

**narrow gauge 1.** a width (between railroad rails) less than standard (56½ in.) **2.** a narrow-gauge railroad or car —**nar'row-gauge', nar'row-gauged'** *adj.*

**nar·row-mind·ed** (-mīn'did) *adj.* limited in outlook; not liberal; prejudiced —**nar'row-mind'ed·ly** *adv.* —**nar'row-mind'ed·ness** *n.*

**nar·thex** (när'theks) *n.* [LGr., exterior portico] **1.** in early Christian churches, a porch or portico **2.** a church vestibule leading to the nave

**nar·whal** (när'wəl, -hwəl) *n.* [< Scand., as in Norw. & Dan. *narhval*] an arctic cetacean valued for its oil and ivory: the male has a long, spiral tusk extending from the upper jaw: also **nar'wal** (-wəl), **nar'whale'** (-hwāl)

**nar·y** (ner'ē) *adj.* [< *ne'er a,* never a] [Dial.] not any; no (with *a* or *an*) [*nary* a doubt]

**NASA** (nas'ə) National Aeronautics and Space Administration

**na·sal** (nā'z'l) *adj.* [< ModL. < L. *nasus,* a nose] **1.** of the nose **2.** produced by making breath go through the nose, as the sounds of *m, n, ng* (ŋ) **3.** characterized by such sounds [a *nasal* voice] —*n.* a nasal sound —**na·sal·i·ty** (nā zal'ə tē) *n.* —**na'sal·ly** *adv.*

NARWHAL
(body 11–16 ft.
long; tusk to
9 ft. long)

**na·sal·ize** (nā'zə līz') *vt., vi.* -**ized', -iz'ing** to pronounce or speak with a nasal sound or sounds —**na'sal·i·za'tion** *n.*

**Nas·by** (naz'bē), **Pe·tro·le·um V.** (pə trō'lē əm) (pseud. of *David Ross Locke*) 1833–88; U.S. humorist

**nas·cent** (nas'ʼnt, nā's'nt) *adj.* [< L. prp. of *nasci,* to be born] **1.** coming into being; being born **2.** beginning to form, grow, or develop: said of ideas, cultures, etc. —**nas'cence, nas'cen·cy** *n.*

**Nash·u·a** (nash'oo wə) [< Algonquian, lit., ? the land between] city in S N.H.: pop. 68,000

**Nash·ville** (nash'vil) [after Gen. F. *Nash* (1720–77)] capital of Tenn., on the Cumberland River: coextensive with Davidson county with which it constitutes a metropolitan government (**Nashville-Davidson**): pop. 456,000 (met. area 829,000)

**na·so-** [< L. *nasus,* nose] *a combining form meaning:* **1.** nose, nasal **2.** nasal and

**Nas·sau** (nas'ô) capital of the Bahamas: pop., with the island on which it is located, 81,000

**Nas·ser** (nas'ər), **Ga·mal Ab·del** (gä mäl' äb'dəl) 1918–70; Egypt. president of the United Arab Republic (1958–70)

**na·stur·tium** (nə stur'shəm, na-) *n.* [L. < *nasus,* nose + pp. of *torquere,* to twist: from its pungent odor] **1.** a plant with shield-shaped leaves and red, yellow, or orange flowers **2.** the flower

**nas·ty** (nas'tē) *adj.* -**ti·er, -ti·est** [< ? or akin to Du. *nestig,* dirty] **1.** very dirty; filthy **2.** nauseating **3.** morally offensive; indecent **4.** very unpleasant, mean, or harmful —**nas'ti·ly** *adv.* —**nas'ti·ness** *n.*

**nat. 1.** national **2.** native **3.** natural

**Na·tal** (nə tal', -täl') province of E South Africa, on the Indian Ocean

**na·tal** (nāt'ʼl) *adj.* [< L. *natalis* < pp. of *nasci,* to be born] **1.** of or connected with one's birth **2.** dating from birth **3.** native: said of a place

**Nat·a·lie** (nat'ʼl ē) [Fr. < LL. < L. *natalis (dies),* natal (day), name given to children born on Christmas Day] a feminine name

**na·tant** (nāt'ʼnt) *adj.* [< L. prp. of *natare,* to swim] swimming or floating

**na·ta·to·ri·al** (nāt'ə tôr'ē əl) *adj.* [< LL. < L. *natator,* swimmer (see prec.) + -AL] of, characterized by, or adapted for swimming: also **na'ta·to'ry**

**na·ta·to·ri·um** (-əm) *n., pl.* -**ri·ums, -ri·a** (-ə) [LL.] a swimming pool

**natch** (nach) *adv.* [Slang] naturally; of course

**na·tes** (nā'tēz) *n.pl.* [L.] the buttocks

**Na·than** (nā'thən) [Heb. *nāthān,* lit., gift] a masculine name: dim. *Nat, Nate*

**Na·than·a·el** (nə than'yəl, -ē əl) [LL. < Gr. < Heb. *nĕthan'ēl,* lit., gift of God] a masculine name: dim. *Nat:* also sp. **Nathaniel**

**nathe·less** (nāth'lis, nath'-) *adv.* [< OE. < *na,* never + *the,* the + *læs,* less] [Archaic] nevertheless —*pre* [Archaic] notwithstanding Also **nath'less** (nath'-)

**na·tion** (nā'shən) *n.* [< OFr. < L. *natio* < pp. of *nasci,* be born] **1.** a community of people with a territory, history, economic life, culture, and language in common **2.** the people of a territory united under a single government; country **3.** a people or tribe —**na'tion·hood'** (-hood') *n.*

**na·tion·al** (nash'ə n'l) *adj.* **1.** of a nation or the nation **2.** affecting a (or the) nation as a whole **3.** maintained by the Federal government —*n.* a citizen of a nation —**na'tion·al·ly** *adv.*

**national bank 1.** a bank or system of banks owned and operated by a government **2.** in the U.S., a member bank of the Federal Reserve System

**National Guard** in the U.S., the organized militia forces of individual States, part of the U.S. Army when called into active Federal service

**na·tion·al·ism** (-iz'm) *n.* **1.** a) patriotism b) narrow, jingoist patriotism **2.** the putting of national interests and security above international considerations **3.** the desire for or advocacy of national independence —**na′tion·al·ist** (-ist) *n., adj.* —**na′tion·al·is′tic** *adj.* —**na′tion·al·is′ti·cal·ly** *adv.*

**na·tion·al·i·ty** (nash′ə nal′ə tē) *n., pl.* **-ties** **1.** national quality or character **2.** the status of belonging to a particular nation by birth or naturalization **3.** the condition or fact of being a nation **4.** a national group, esp. of immigrants from some other country: in full, **nationality group**

**na·tion·al·ize** (nash′ə nə līz′) *vt.* **-ized′, -iz′ing** **1.** to make national **2.** to transfer ownership or control of (land, industries, etc.) to the nation —**na′tion·al·i·za′tion** *n.* —**na′tion·al·iz′er** *n.*

**National Weather Service** the division of the Department of Commerce that gathers data on weather conditions, on which weather forecasts are based

**na·tion·wide** (nā′shən wīd′) *adj.* by or throughout the whole nation; national

**na·tive** (nāt′iv) *adj.* [< MFr. < L. *nativus* < pp. of *nasci*, to be born] **1.** inborn; innate; natural **2.** belonging to a locality or country by birth, production, or growth; indigenous [a *native* Bostonian, *native* plants] **3.** *a)* being the place of one's birth [one's *native* land] *b)* belonging to one because of the place of one's birth [one's *native* language] **4.** as found in nature; unaltered by man **5.** occurring in a pure state in nature [*native* gold] **6.** of or characteristic of the people born in a certain place —*n.* **1.** a person born in the region indicated, esp. one whose ancestors were also born there or as distinguished from an invader, colonist, etc. **2.** a plant or animal indigenous to a place and growing or living there naturally **3.** a permanent resident, not a mere visitor —**go native** to adopt a simple way of life —**na′tive·ly** *adv.* —**na′tive·ness** *n.*

**na·tive-born** (-bôrn′) *adj.* born in a specified place or country

**na·tiv·i·ty** (nə tiv′ə tē, nā-) *n., pl.* **-ties** [see NATIVE] **1.** birth **2.** *Astrol.* the horoscope for one's birth —**the Nativity** **1.** the birth of Jesus **2.** Christmas Day

**natl.** national

**NATO** (nā′tō) North Atlantic Treaty Organization

**nat·ty** (nat′ē) *adj.* **-ti·er, -ti·est** [< ? NEAT[1]] trim and smart in appearance or dress [a *natty* suit] —**nat′ti·ly** *adv.* —**nat′ti·ness** *n.*

**nat·u·ral** (nach′ər əl, nach′rəl) *adj.* [< OFr. < L. *naturalis*, by birth] **1.** of or arising from nature; produced or existing in nature; not artificial **3.** dealing with nature [a *natural* science] **4.** as found in nature; unaltered by man **5.** real or physical, rather than spiritual, intellectual, or imaginary **6.** *a)* innate; inborn [*natural* abilities] *b)* having certain qualities innately [a *natural* comedian] **7.** based on instinctive moral feeling [*natural* rights] **8.** true to nature; lifelike [a *natural* likeness] **9.** normal or usual [a *natural* outcome] **10.** customarily expected [a *natural* courtesy] **11.** free from affectation **12.** *a)* illegitimate [a *natural* child] *b)* not adoptive [*natural* parents] **13.** *Music a)* without flats or sharps *b)* neither sharped nor flatted —*n.* **1.** an idiot **2.** [Colloq.] a person who is naturally expert **3.** [Colloq.] a sure success **4.** *Music a)* the sign (♮) canceling a preceding sharp or flat: in full, **natural sign** *b)* the note affected *c)* a white key on the piano —**nat′u·ral·ness** *n.*

**natural gas** a mixture of gaseous hydrocarbons, chiefly methane, occurring naturally in the earth and conveyed through pipes to be used as a fuel

**natural history** the study of the animal, vegetable, and mineral world, esp. in a popular way

**nat·u·ral·ism** (-iz′m) *n.* **1.** action or thought based on natural desires or instincts **2.** *Literature, Art*, etc. faithful adherence to nature; realism: specif. applied to the realism of a group of 19th-cent. French writers **3.** *Philos.* the belief that the natural world is all that exists

**nat·u·ral·ist** (-ist) *n.* **1.** a person who studies animals and plants **2.** a person who believes in or practices naturalism —*adj. same as* NATURALISTIC

**nat·u·ral·is·tic** (nach′ər ə lis′tik) *adj.* **1.** of natural history or naturalists **2.** of or characterized by naturalism **3.** in accordance with, or in imitation of, nature —**nat′u·ral·is′ti·cal·ly** *adv.*

**nat·u·ral·ize** (nach′ər ə līz′, nach′rə-) *vt.* **-ized′, -iz′ing** **1.** to confer citizenship upon (an alien) **2.** to adopt and make common (a custom, word, etc.) from another place **3.** to adapt (a plant or animal) to a new environment —*vi.* to become naturalized —**nat′u·ral·i·za′tion** *n.*

**nat·u·ral·ly** (nach′ər əl ē, nach′rə lē) *adv.* **1.** in a natural manner **2.** by nature; innately **3.** as one might expect; of course

**natural number** any positive integer, as 1, 2, etc.

**natural philosophy** *earlier name for* NATURAL SCIENCE (specif., physics)

**natural resources** the forms of wealth supplied by nature, as coal, oil, water power, etc.

**natural science** the systematized knowledge of nature, including biology, chemistry, physics, etc.

**natural selection** the process in evolution by which those individuals (of a species) with characters that help them to become adapted to their specific environment tend to transmit their characters, while those less able to become adapted tend to die out

**na·ture** (nā′chər) *n.* [< OFr. < L. *natura* < pp. of *nasci*, to be born] **1.** the quality or qualities that make something what it is; essence **2.** inborn character, disposition, or tendencies **3.** kind; sort **4.** the basic biological functions, instincts, drives, etc. **5.** normal or acceptable behavior **6.** the sum total of all things in the physical universe **7.** [*sometimes* N-] the power, force, etc. that seems to regulate this **8.** the primitive state of man **9.** a simple way of life close to or in the outdoors **10.** natural scenery, and the plants and animals in it —**by nature** naturally; inherently —**of** (or in) **the nature of** having the essential character of; like

**-na·tured** (nā′chərd) *a combining form meaning* having or showing a (specified kind of) nature, disposition, or temperament [good-*natured*]

**Naug·a·hyde** (nôg′ə hīd′) [arbitrary coinage] *a trademark for* a kind of imitation leather, used for upholstery —*n.* [n-] this material

**naught** (nôt) *n.* [< OE. < *na*, no + *wiht*, a person] **1.** nothing **2.** *Arith.* the figure zero (0) —*adj.* [Archaic or Obs.] **1.** worthless **2.** evil —**set at naught** to defy; scorn

**naugh·ty** (nôt′ē) *adj.* **-ti·er, -ti·est** [< obs. *naught*, wicked] **1.** not behaving properly; disobedient: used esp. of children **2.** improper or obscene —**naugh′ti·ly** *adv.* —**naugh′ti·ness** *n.*

**Na·u·ru** (nä ō̄o′rō̄o) country on an island in the W Pacific, near the equator: 8 sq. mi.; pop. 7,000

**nau·se·a** (nô′shə, -sē ə, -zē ə, -zhə) *n.* [L. < Gr. *nausia*, seasickness < *naus*, a ship] **1.** a feeling of sickness at the stomach, with an urge to vomit **2.** disgust —**nau′se·ant** *adj., n.*

**nau·se·ate** (-shē āt′, -sē-, -zē-, -zhē-) *vt., vi.* **-at′ed, -at′ing** to feel or cause to feel nausea —**nau′se·at′ing·ly** *adv.* —**nau′se·a′tion** *n.*

**nau·seous** (nô′shəs, -zē əs, -sē-) *adj.* **1.** causing nausea; sickening **2.** [Colloq.] feeling nausea —**nau′seous·ly** *adv.* —**nau′seous·ness** *n.*

**naut.** nautical

**nautch** (nôch) *n.* [< Hindi < Prakrit < Sans. *nṛtya*, dancing < *nṛt*, to dance] in India, a performance by professional dancing girls (**nautch girls**)

**nau·ti·cal** (nôt′i k'l) *adj.* [< Fr. < L. < Gr. < *nautēs*, sailor < *naus*, a ship] of or relating to sailors, ships, or navigation —**nau′ti·cal·ly** *adv.*

**nautical mile** an international unit of distance for sea and air navigation, equal to 6,076.11549 ft. (1,852 meters)

**nau·ti·lus** (nôt′'l əs) *n., pl.* **-lus·es, -li′** (-ī′) [ModL. < L. < Gr. *nautilos*, sailor < *naus*, a ship] **1.** any of a genus of tropical, cephalopod mollusks with a many-chambered, spiral shell having a pearly interior **2.** *same as* PAPER NAUTILUS

**nav.** **1.** naval **2.** navigation **3.** navigator

**Nav·a·ho** (nav′ə hō′) *n.* [< Sp. < AmInd. *Navahú*, lit., great fields] **1.** *pl.* **-hos′, -ho′, -hoes′** a member of an Indian tribe, the largest in the U.S., of Arizona, New Mexico, and Utah **2.** their Athapascan language Also sp. **Nav′a·jo′**

NAUTILUS
(shown in
cross section)

**na·val** (nā′v'l) *adj.* [< Fr. < L. *navalis* < *navis*, a ship] of, having, characteristic of, or for a navy, its ships, personnel, etc.

**Na·varre** (nə vär′) region in NE Spain & SW France: formerly a kingdom

**nave**[1] (nāv) *n.* [ML. *navis* < L., a ship] the main part of a church, extending between side aisles from the chancel to the principal entrance

**nave**[2] (nāv) *n.* [OE. *nafu*] the hub of a wheel

**na·vel** (nā′v'l) *n.* [OE. *nafela*] the small scar or depression in the middle of the abdomen, where the umbilical cord was attached to the fetus

**navel orange** a seedless orange having a navellike depression containing a small, secondary fruit

**navig.** **1.** navigation **2.** navigator

**nav·i·ga·ble** (nav′i gə b'l) *adj.* [see ff.] **1.** wide or deep enough, or free enough from obstructions, for ships, etc. to go through **2.** that can be steered or directed *[a navigable balloon]* —**nav′i·ga·bil′i·ty** *n.* —**nav′i·ga·bly** *adv.*

**nav·i·gate** (nav′ə gāt′) *vi.* -**gat′ed, -gat′ing** [< L. pp. of *navigare* < *navis*, a ship + *agere*, to lead] **1.** to steer, or direct, a ship or aircraft **2.** [Colloq.] to make one's way; walk —*vt.* **1.** to travel through or over (water, air, or land) in a ship or aircraft **2.** to steer, or direct the course of (a ship or aircraft) **3.** [Colloq.] to make one's way on or through

**nav·i·ga·tion** (nav′ə gā′shən) *n.* **1.** the act or practice of navigating; esp., the science of locating the position and plotting the course of ships and aircraft **2.** traffic by ship —**nav′i·ga′tion·al** *adj.* —**nav′i·ga′tion·al·ly** *adv.*

**nav·i·ga·tor** (nav′ə gāt′ər) *n.* **1.** a person who navigates; esp., one skilled in the navigation of a ship or aircraft **2.** an explorer by ship

**nav·vy** (nav′ē) *n.*, *pl.* **-vies** [abbrev. of prec.] [Brit.] an unskilled laborer, as on canals, roads, etc.

**na·vy** (nā′vē) *n.*, *pl.* **-vies** [< OFr. *navie*, ult. < L. *navis*, a ship] **1.** [Archaic] a fleet of ships **2.** all warships of a nation **3.** [*often* N-] *a)* the entire sea force of a nation, including vessels, personnel, stores, yards, etc. *b)* the governmental department in charge of this **4.** *same as* NAVY BLUE

**navy bean** [from common use in the U.S. Navy] a small, white variety of kidney bean

**navy blue** [from the color of the Brit. naval uniform] very dark, purplish blue

**navy yard** a dockyard for building and repairing naval ships, storing naval supplies, etc.

**na·wab** (nə wäb′, -wôb′) *n.* [Hindi *navāb*] *same as* NABOB

**nay** (nā) *adv.* [< ON. < *ne*, not + *ei*, ever] **1.** no: now seldom used except in a voice vote **2.** not that only, but also *[he is well-off, nay, rich]* —*n.* **1.** a refusal or denial **2.** a negative vote or a person voting in the negative **3.** a negative answer

**Naz·a·rene** (naz′ə rēn′, naz′ə rēn′) *adj.* of Nazareth or the Nazarenes —*n.* **1.** a native or inhabitant of Nazareth **2.** a member of an early sect of Jewish Christians —**the Nazarene** Jesus

**Naz·a·reth** (naz′ər əth) town in Galilee, N Israel, where Jesus lived as a child

**Naz·a·rite, Naz·i·rite** (naz′ə rīt′) *n.* [< LL. < Gr. < Heb. *nāzar*, to consecrate] among the ancient Hebrews, a person adhering to certain strict religious vows

**Na·zi** (nät′sē, nat′-) *adj.* [G., contr. of *Nationalsozialistische* in party name] designating or of the German fascist political party (*National Socialist German Workers' Party*), that ruled Germany under Hitler (1933–45) —*n.* **1.** a member of this party **2.** [*often* n-] a supporter of this party or its ideology; fascist —**Na′zi·fi·ca′tion** *n.* —**Na′zi·fy′, na′zi·fy′** *vt.* **-fied′, -fy′ing** —**Na′zism** (-siz′m), **Na′zi·ism** (-sē iz′m) *n.*

**Nb** *Chem.* niobium

**N.B.** New Brunswick

**N.B., n.b.** [L. *nota bene*] note well

**NBA, N.B.A.** **1.** National Basketball Association **2.** National Boxing Association

**NBC** National Broadcasting Company

**NBS, N.B.S.** National Bureau of Standards

**N.C., NC** **1.** no charge **2.** North Carolina **3.** nurse corps

**NCAA, N.C.A.A.** National Collegiate Athletic Association

**NCO, N.C.O.** noncommissioned officer

**Nd** *Chem.* neodymium

**N.D., n.d.** no date

**N.Dak., ND** North Dakota

**ne-** *same as* NEO-: used before a vowel

**Ne** *Chem.* neon

**NE** Nebraska

**NE, N.E., n.e.** **1.** northeast **2.** northeastern

**N.E.** **1.** Naval Engineer **2.** New England

**NEA, N.E.A.** National Education Association

**Neal** (nēl) [prob. < Ir. *Niul* < *niadh*, a champion] a masculine name

**Ne·an·der·thal** (nē an′dər thôl′, -täl′) *adj.* [name of German valley where remains were found] **1.** designating or of a form of primitive man of the paleolithic period **2.** *a)* crude or primitive *b)* reactionary; regressive

**neap** (nēp) *adj.* [OE. *nep-* in *nepflod*, neap tide] designating either of the two lowest monthly tides, occurring just after the first and third quarters of the lunar month —*n.* neap tide

**Ne·a·pol·i·tan** (nē′ə päl′ə t′n) *adj.* of Naples —*n.* a native or inhabitant of Naples

**near** (nir) *adv.* [OE. *near*, nearer, compar. of *neah*, nigh] **1.** at a short distance in space or time **2.** relatively close in degree; almost *[near night]*: now usually *nearly* **3.** closely; intimately —*adj.* **1.** close in distance or time; not far **2.** close in relationship; akin **3.** close in friendship; intimate **4.** *a)* close in degree; narrow *[a near escape]* *b)* almost happening *[a near accident]* **5.** on the left side, facing forward: said of an animal in double harness, a wagon wheel, etc.: opposed to OFF **6.** short or direct *[the near way]* **7.** stingy

**8.** somewhat resembling; approximating —*prep.* close to in space, time, degree, etc. —*vt., vi.* to draw near (to); approach —**near at hand** very close in time or space —**near′ness** *n.*

**near·by** (nir′bī′) *adj., adv.* near; close at hand

**Near East** **1.** countries near the E end of the Mediterranean, including those of SW Asia, NE Africa, &, sometimes, the Balkans **2.** [Brit.] the Balkans

**near·ly** (-lē) *adv.* almost; not quite *[nearly finished]* —**not nearly** not at all; far from

**near·sight·ed** (-sīt′id) *adj.* having better vision for near things than for far ones; myopic —**near′sight′ed·ly** *adv.* —**near′sight′ed·ness** *n.*

**neat¹** (nēt) *adj.* [< Fr. < L. *nitidus*, shining, trim < *nitere*, to shine] **1.** *a)* clean and orderly; trim; tidy *b)* tidy, skillful, and precise *[a neat worker]* *c)* free of superfluities; simple **2.** unmixed; straight *[to drink whiskey neat]* **3.** well-proportioned; shapely **4.** cleverly or smartly phrased or done; adroit **5.** [Slang] nice, pleasing, etc. —**neat′ly** *adv.* —**neat′ness** *n.*

**neat²** (nēt) *n.*, *pl.* **neat** [OE. *neat*] [Now Rare] a bovine animal; ox, cow, calf

**neat·en** (nēt′n) *vt.* to make neat

**'neath, neath** (nēth) *prep.* [Poet.] beneath

**neat·herd** (nēt′hurd′) *n.* [Now Rare] a cowherd

**neat's-foot oil** (nēts′foot′) a light-yellow oil obtained by boiling the feet and shinbones of cattle, used mainly as a dressing for leather

**neb** (neb) *n.* [OE. *nebb*] [Now Chiefly Brit. Dial.] **1.** a beak, nose, or snout **2.** a nib

**Ne·bras·ka** (nə bras′kə) [< Siouan name of Platte River, lit., flat water] Middle Western State of the U.S.: 77,227 sq. mi.; pop. 1,570,000; cap. Lincoln: abbrev. **Nebr., NE** —**Ne·bras′kan** *adj., n.*

**Neb·u·chad·nez·zar** (neb′yə kəd nez′ər, neb′ə-) ?–562 B.C.; king of Babylonia (605?–562), who conquered Jerusalem & deported many Jews into Babylonia: II Kings 24; Dan. 1–4 Also **Neb′u·chad·rez′zar** (-rez′ər)

**neb·u·la** (neb′yə lə) *n.*, *pl.* **-lae′** (-lē′), **-las** [ModL. < L., fog] any of several vast cloudlike patches seen in the night sky, consisting of very distant groups of stars or of gaseous masses or of galaxies —**neb′u·lar** *adj.*

**nebular hypothesis** the theory that the solar system was formed by the condensation of a nebula

**neb·u·los·i·ty** (neb′yə läs′ə tē) *n.* **1.** a nebulous quality or condition **2.** *pl.* **-ties** a nebula

**neb·u·lous** (neb′yə ləs) *adj.* **1.** of or like a nebula **2.** unclear; vague; indefinite Also **neb′u·lose′** (-lōs′) —**neb′u·lous·ly** *adv.* —**neb′u·lous·ness** *n.*

**nec·es·sar·i·ly** (nes′ə ser′ə lē, nes′ə ser′-) *adv.* **1.** because of necessity **2.** as a necessary result

**nec·es·sar·y** (nes′ə ser′ē) *adj.* [< L. < *necesse*, unavoidable < *ne-*, not + *cedere*, to give way] **1.** that cannot be done without; essential; indispensable **2.** that must happen; inevitable **3.** that must be done; required **4.** that follows logically; undeniable —*n.*, *pl.* **-sar′ies** a thing necessary to life, to some purpose, etc.: *often used in pl.*

**ne·ces·si·tate** (nə ses′ə tāt′) *vt.* **-tat′ed, -tat′ing** **1.** to make (something) necessary or unavoidable **2.** [Now Rare] to compel —**ne·ces′si·ta′tion** *n.*

**ne·ces·si·tous** (-təs) *adj.* **1.** needy **2.** necessary **3.** urgent —**ne·ces′si·tous·ly** *adv.*

**ne·ces·si·ty** (-tē) *n.*, *pl.* **-ties** [< OFr. < L. < *necesse*: see NECESSARY] **1.** natural causation; fate **2.** anything inevitable, unavoidable, etc. **3.** *a)* the compulsion of circumstances, custom, law, etc. *b)* what is required by this **4.** great need **5.** something that cannot be done without; necessary thing: *often used in pl.* **6.** the state or quality of being necessary —**of necessity** necessarily

**neck** (nek) *n.* [OE. *hnecca*] **1.** that part of man or animal joining the head to the body **2.** a narrow part between the head, or end, and the body, or base, of any object, as of a violin **3.** that part of a garment which covers or is nearest the neck **4.** a narrow, necklike part; specif., *a)* a narrow strip of land *b)* the narrowest part of a bottle, vase, etc. or of an organ of the body *c)* a strait —*vt., vi.* [Slang] to hug, kiss, and caress in making love —**get it in the neck** [Slang] to be severely reprimanded or punished —**neck and neck** very close or even, as in a race —**neck of the woods** a region or locality —**risk one's neck** to put one's life, career, etc. in danger —**stick one's neck out** to expose oneself to possible failure, ridicule, etc. —**neck′er** *n.* —**neck′ing** *n.*

**neck·band** (-band′) *n.* **1.** a band worn around the neck **2.** the part of a garment that encircles the neck; esp., the part fastened to the collar

**neck·er·chief** (nek′ər chif, -chēf′) *n.* a kerchief worn around the neck

**neck·lace** (nek′lis) *n.* [NECK + LACE] a string of beads, jewels, etc. or a fine chain of gold, silver, etc. worn as an ornament around the neck

**neck·line** (-līn′) *n.* the line formed by the edge of a garment around or nearest the neck

**neck·piece** (-pēs′) *n.* **1.** a decorative scarf, esp. of fur **2.** a piece of armor for the neck

**neck·tie** (-tī′) *n.* a decorative band for the neck, tied in front in a slipknot or bow

**neck·wear** (-wer′) *n.* articles worn about the neck, as neckties, scarfs, etc.

**nec·ro-** [< Gr. *nekros*, dead body] *a combining form meaning* death, corpse: also **necr-**

**ne·crol·o·gy** (ne kräl′ə jē) *n., pl.* **-gies** [see prec. & -LOGY] **1.** a list of people who have died **2.** an obituary —**nec·ro·log·i·cal** (nek′rə läj′i k'l) *adj.* —**nec′ro·log′i·cal·ly** *adv.* —**ne·crol′o·gist** *n.*

**nec·ro·man·cy** (nek′rə man′sē) *n.* [< OFr. < ML. *nigromantia* < L. < Gr. *nekros*, corpse + *manteia*, divination] **1.** divination by alleged communication with the dead **2.** sorcery —**nec′ro·man′cer** *n.* —**nec′ro·man′tic** *adj.*

**ne·crop·o·lis** (nə kräp′ə lis) *n., pl.* **-lis·es** [< Gr. < *nekros*, dead body + *polis*, city] a cemetery, esp. one belonging to an ancient city

**ne·cro·sis** (ne krō′sis) *n., pl.* **-ses** (-sēz) [ModL. < LL. < Gr. < *nekroun*, to make dead < *nekros*, dead body] the death or decay of tissue in a part of a living body or plant, as from disease —**ne·crose** (ne krōs′, nek′rōs) *vt., vi.* **-crosed′, -cros′ing** —**ne·crot′ic** (-krät′ik) *adj.*

**nec·tar** (nek′tər) *n.* [L. < Gr. *nektar*, lit., that overcomes death] **1.** *Gr. Myth.* the drink of the gods **2.** any very delicious beverage **3.** *Bot.* the sweetish liquid in many flowers, made into honey by bees —**nec′tar·ous** *adj.*

**nec·tar·ine** (nek′tə rēn′, nek′tə rēn′) *n.* [orig. adj. of *nectar*] a variety of peach having a smooth skin without down

**nec·ta·ry** (nek′tər ē) *n., pl.* **-ries** a nectar-secreting flower part —**nec·tar′i·al** (-ter′ē əl) *adj.*

**Ne·der·land** (nā′dər länt′) *Du. name of* NETHERLANDS

**nee, née** (nā; *now often* nē) *adj.* [Fr., fem. pp. of *naitre* < L. *nasci*, to be born] born: used to indicate the maiden name of a married woman *[Mrs. Helen Jones, nee Smith]*

**need** (nēd) *n.* [OE. *nied*] **1.** necessity or obligation **2.** lack of something required or desired **3.** something required or desired *[one's daily needs]* **4.** *a)* a condition of deficiency, or one requiring relief or supply *[a friend in need]* *b)* poverty; extreme want —*vt.* to have need of; lack; require *Need* is often used as an auxiliary followed by an infinitive with or without *to*, meaning "to be obliged, must" *[he need not come, he needs to be careful]* —*vi.* **1.** [Archaic] to be necessary *[it needs not]* **2.** to be in need See also NEEDS —**have need to** to be compelled to; must —**if need be** if it is required —**need′er** *n.*

**need·ful** (-fəl) *adj.* **1.** necessary **2.** [Archaic] needy —**need′ful·ly** *adv.* —**need′ful·ness** *n.*

**nee·dle** (nēd′'l) *n.* [OE. *nædl*] **1.** a small, slender, sharp-pointed piece of steel with a hole for thread, used for sewing **2.** *a)* a slender, hooked rod of steel, bone, etc., for crocheting *b)* a similar but hookless rod, for knitting **3.** a short, pointed piece of metal, etc. that moves in phonograph-record grooves to transmit vibrations **4.** a pointed instrument for etching or engraving **5.** the pointer of a compass, gauge, meter, etc. **6.** the thin, short, pointed leaf of the pine, spruce, etc. **7.** a thin rod that opens or closes a passage in a valve (**needle valve**) **8.** the sharp, very slender metal tube at the end of a hypodermic syringe **9.** *same as* ELECTRIC NEEDLE **10.** a needlelike structure or part —*vt.* **-dled, -dling** **1.** to sew, puncture, etc. with a needle **2.** [Colloq.] *a)* to goad *b)* to tease or heckle —**nee′dle·like′** *adj.* —**nee′dler** *n.*

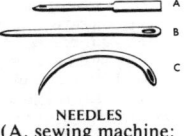

NEEDLES
(A, sewing machine; B, straight; C, surgical)

**nee·dle·point** (-point′) *n.* **1.** an embroidery of woolen threads on canvas, as in tapestry **2.** lace made on a paper pattern, with a needle instead of a bobbin: in full, **needlepoint lace**

**need·less** (nēd′lis) *adj.* not needed; unnecessary —**need′less·ly** *adv.* —**need′less·ness** *n.*

**nee·dle·wom·an** (nēd′'l woom′ən) *n., pl.* **-wom′en** a woman who does needlework; esp., a seamstress

**nee·dle·work** (-wurk′) *n.* work done with a needle; sewing or fancywork —**nee′dle·work′er** *n.*

**need·n't** (nēd′'nt) need not

**needs** (nēdz) *adv.* [OE. *nedes*] of necessity; necessarily (with *must*) *[he must needs obey]*

**need·y** (nēd′ē) *adj.* **need′i·er, need′i·est** in need; very poor; destitute —**need′i·ness** *n.*

**ne'er** (ner) *adv.* [Poet.] never

**ne'er-do-well** (-dōō wel′) *n.* a shiftless, irresponsible person —*adj.* lazy, worthless, etc.

**ne·far·i·ous** (ni fer′ē əs) *adj.* [< L. < *nefas*, crime < *ne-*,

not + *fas*, lawful] very wicked; iniquitous —**ne·far′i·ous·ly** *adv.* —**ne·far′i·ous·ness** *n.*

**neg. 1.** negative **2.** negatively

**ne·gate** (ni gāt′) *vt.* **-gat′ed, -gat′ing** [see ff.] **1.** to deny the existence or truth of **2.** to make ineffective —**ne·ga′tor, ne·gat′er** *n.*

**ne·ga·tion** (ni gā′shən) *n.* [< Fr. < L. < pp. of *negare*, to deny] **1.** a denying; denial **2.** the lack or opposite of something positive

**neg·a·tive** (neg′ə tiv) *adj.* [see prec.] **1.** expressing denial or refusal; saying "no" **2.** opposite to or lacking what is positive *[a negative personality]*; specif., *a) Biol.* directed away from the source of a stimulus *[negative tropism]* *b) Math.* less than zero; minus *c) Med.* not indicating the presence of symptoms, bacteria, etc. *d) Photog.* reversing the relation of light and shade of the original subject **3.** *Elec. a)* of, generating, or charged with NEGATIVE ELECTRICITY *b)* having an excess of electrons —*n.* **1.** a word, phrase, statement, etc. expressing denial, rejection, or refusal **2.** the point of view opposing the positive or affirmative **3.** an impression of a sculpture, etc. that shows it in reverse **4.** the plate in a voltaic battery where the lower potential is **5.** *Math.* a negative quantity **6.** *Photog.* an exposed and developed negative film or plate, from which positive prints are made —*vt.* **-tived, -tiv·ing** **1.** *a)* to refuse; reject *b)* to veto **2.** to deny; contradict **3.** to disprove **4.** to neutralize —**in the negative** **1.** in refusal or denial of a plan, etc. **2.** with a negative answer —**neg′a·tive·ly** *adv.* —**neg′a·tive·ness, neg′a·tiv′i·ty** *n.*

**negative electricity** the kind of electricity in a body of resin rubbed with wool: it has an excess of electrons

**neg·a·tiv·ism** (neg′ə tiv iz′m) *n. Psychol.* an attitude characterized by ignoring or resisting suggestions or orders from others —**neg′a·tiv·ist** *n., adj.* —**neg′a·tiv·is′tic** *adj.*

**Ne·gev** (neg′ev) region in S Israel of partially reclaimed desert: also **Ne′geb** (-eb)

**neg·lect** (ni glekt′) *vt.* [< L. pp. of *neglegere* < *neg-*, not + *legere*, to gather] **1.** to ignore or disregard **2.** to fail to attend to properly **3.** to leave undone —*n.* **1.** a neglecting or being neglected **2.** lack of proper care —**neg·lect′er, neg·lec′tor** *n.*

**neg·lect·ful** (-fəl) *adj.* negligent (often with *of*) —**neg·lect′ful·ly** *adv.* —**neg·lect′ful·ness** *n.*

**neg·li·gee** (neg′lə zhā′, neg′lə zhā′) *n.* [< Fr., fem. pp. of *négliger*, to neglect] **1.** a woman's loosely fitting dressing gown **2.** any informal or careless attire —*adj.* carelessly or incompletely dressed

**neg·li·gence** (neg′li jəns) *n.* **1.** the quality or condition of being negligent **2.** an instance of this

**neg·li·gent** (-jənt) *adj.* [< OFr. < L. prp. of *negligere:* see NEGLECT] **1.** habitually failing to do the required thing **2.** careless, lax, inattentive, etc. —**neg′li·gent·ly** *adv.*

**neg·li·gi·ble** (neg′li jə b'l) *adj.* that can be neglected or disregarded because small, unimportant, etc. —**neg′li·gi·bil′i·ty** *n.* —**neg′li·gi·bly** *adv.*

**ne·go·ti·a·ble** (ni gō′shē ə b'l, -shə b'l) *adj.* that can be negotiated; specif., *a)* legally transferable, as a promissory note *b)* that can be passed, crossed, etc. —**ne·go′ti·a·bil′i·ty** *n.*

**ne·go·ti·ate** (-shē āt′) *vi.* **-at′ed, -at′ing** [< L. pp. of *negotiari* < *negotium*, business < *nec-*, not + *otium*, ease] to confer or discuss with a view to reaching agreement —*vt.* **1.** to settle or conclude (a transaction, treaty, etc.) **2.** to transfer or sell (negotiable paper) **3.** to succeed in crossing, moving through, etc. —**ne·go′ti·a′tor** *n.*

**ne·go·ti·a·tion** (ni gō′shē ā′shən) *n.* a negotiating; specif., *[often pl.]* a conferring or bargaining to reach agreement —**ne·go′ti·a·to′ry** (-ə tôr′ē) *adj.*

**Ne·gress** (nē′gris) *n.* a Negro woman or girl: term regarded by some as patronizing or discriminatory

**Ne·gri·to** (nə grēt′ō) *n., pl.* **-tos, -toes** [Sp., dim. of *negro*, NEGRO] a member of any of various groups of dwarfish Negroid peoples of the East Indies, the Philippines, and Africa —**Ne·grit′ic** (-grit′ik) *adj.*

**ne·gri·tude** (neg′rə tōōd′, nē′grə-; -tyōōd′) *n.* [Fr. *négritude*, coined < *nègre*, black + *-i-* + *-tude*, -TUDE] *[also* N-] the affirmation by Negroes of their distinctive cultural heritage, esp. in Africa

**Ne·gro¹** (nē′grō) *n., pl.* **-groes** [Sp. & Port. *negro* < L. *niger*, black] **1.** a member of the Negroid peoples of Africa, living chiefly south of the Sahara **2.** *same as* NEGROID **3.** any person with Negro ancestors See BLACK (*n.* 3) —*adj.* of Negroes

**Ne·gro²** (nā′grō; *Port.* -grōō; *Sp.* -grô) river in N Brazil, flowing southeast into the Amazon: c.1,400 mi.

**Ne·groid** (nē′groid) *adj.* designating or of a major group of mankind that includes the dark-skinned peoples of Africa and of Melanesia, New Guinea, etc. —*n.* a Negroid person

**Ne·gros** (nā′grōs) island of the C Philippines, between Cebu & Panay: 4,905 sq. mi.

**ne·gus** (nē′gəs) *n.* [after Col. Francis *Negus* (d. 1732), who first made it] a beverage of hot water, wine, and lemon juice, sweetened and spiced

**Ne·he·mi·ah** (nē′ə mī′ə) *Bible* **1.** a Hebrew leader of about the 5th cent. B.C. **2.** the book that tells about his work: abbrev. **Neh.** In the Douay Bible, **Ne′he·mi′as** (-əs)

**Neh·ru** (nā′rōō), **Ja·wa·har·lal** (jə wä′hər läl′) 1889–1964; prime minister of India (1947–64)

**neigh** (nā) *vi.* [OE. *hnǽgan*] to utter the characteristic cry of a horse; whinny —*n.* this cry

**neigh·bor** (nā′bər) *n.* [< OE. < *neah* (see NIGH) + *gebur*, farmer] **1.** a person who lives near another **2.** a person or thing situated near another **3.** a fellow man —*adj.* nearby; adjacent —*vt.*, *vi.* to live or be situated near or nearby Also, Brit. sp., **neighbour**

**neigh·bor·hood** (-hood′) *n.* **1.** a being neighbors **2.** a district or area, esp. with regard to some characteristic **3.** people living near one another; community —**in the neighborhood of** [Colloq.] **1.** near (a place) **2.** approximately

**neigh·bor·ly** (nā′bər lē) *adj.* like or appropriate to neighbors; friendly —**neigh′bor·li·ness** *n.*

**Neil** (nēl) [var. of NEAL] a masculine name

**nei·ther** (nē′thər, nī′-) *adj., pron.* [OE. *na-hwæther*, lit., not whether] not either [*neither* boy went, *neither* of them sings] —*conj.* **1.** not either: in the pair of correlatives *neither . . . nor* [can *neither* laugh *nor* cry] **2.** nor [he doesn't smoke, *neither* does he drink] —*adv.* [Dial. or Colloq.] also (after negative expressions) [if she won't go, I won't *neither*]

**Nejd** (nezhd) district in C & E Saudi Arabia

**Nell** (nel) [dim. of HELEN] a feminine name

**Nel·lie, Nel·ly** (nel′ē) [dim. of HELEN] a feminine name

**Nel·son** (nel′s'n) [< the surname *Nelson*, Neal's son] **1.** a masculine name **2. Horatio**, Viscount Nelson, 1758–1805; Eng. admiral

**nel·son** (nel′s'n) *n.* [< personal name *Nelson*] a wrestling hold; specif., a hold (**half nelson**) in which one arm is placed under the opponent's arm from behind with the hand pressing the back of his neck, or a hold (**full nelson**) in which both arms are so placed under the opponent's arms

**nem·a·tode** (nem′ə tōd′) *n.* [< ModL. < Gr. *nēma* (gen. *nēmatos*), thread + -ODE] any of a phylum of long, cylindrical worms, as the hookworm

**Nem·e·sis** (nem′ə sis) [L. < Gr. < *nemein*, to deal out] *Gr. Myth.* the goddess of retribution or vengeance —*n.* [*usually* n-] *pl.* **-ses′** (-sēz′) **1.** *a)* just punishment *b)* one who imposes it **2.** anyone or anything that it seems will surely defeat or thwart one

**N.Eng. 1.** New England **2.** North England

**ne·o-** [< Gr. *neos*, new] *a combining form meaning:* **1.** [*often* N-] new, recent [*neolithic*] **2.** in a new or different way [*neocolonialism*]

**ne·o·clas·sic** (nē′ō klas′ik) *adj.* designating or of a revival of classic style in art, literature, etc.: also **ne′o·clas′si·cal** —**ne′o·clas′si·cism** *n.* —**ne′o·clas′si·cist** *n.*

**ne·o·co·lo·ni·al·ism** (-kə lō′nē əl iz′m) *n.* the survival or revival of colonialism, as by the exploitation of a supposedly independent region by a foreign power —**ne′o·co·lo′ni·al** *adj.* —**ne′o·co·lo′ni·al·ist** *n., adj.*

**ne·o·dym·i·um** (nē′ə dim′ē əm) *n.* [< NEO- + (DI)DYMIUM] a metallic chemical element of the rare-earth group: symbol, Nd; at. wt., 144.24; at. no., 60

**ne·o·lith·ic** (nē′ə lith′ik) *adj.* [NEO- + -LITHIC] designating or of the later part of the Stone Age, during which polished stone tools and metal tools were first used

**ne·ol·o·gism** (nē äl′ə jiz′m) *n.* [< Fr.: see NEO-, -LOGY, & -ISM] **1.** a new word or a new meaning for an established word **2.** the use of these Also **ne·ol′o·gy**, *pl.* **-gies** —**ne·ol′o·gis′tic, ne·ol′o·gis′ti·cal** *adj.*

**ne·ol·o·gize** (-jīz′) *vi.* **-gized′, -giz′ing** to invent or use neologisms —**ne·ol′o·gist** *n.*

**ne·o·my·cin** (nē′ə mī′sin) *n.* [< NEO- + Gr. *mykēs*, fungus + -INⁱ] a broad-spectrum antibiotic used esp. in treating infections of the skin and eye

**ne·on** (nē′än) *n.* [ModL. < Gr. *neon*, neut. of *neos*, new] a rare, colorless, and inert gaseous chemical element: symbol, Ne; at. wt., 20.183; at. no., 10

**neon lamp** a tube containing neon, which glows red when an electric current is sent through it

**ne·o·phyte** (nē′ə fīt′) *n.* [< LL. < Gr. < *neos*, new + *phytos* < *phyein*, to produce] **1.** a new convert **2.** any beginner; novice

**ne·o·plasm** (-plaz′m) *n.* [NEO- + -PLASM] an abnormal growth of tissue, as a tumor —**ne′o·plas′tic** *adj.*

**ne·o·prene** (nē′ə prēn′) *n.* [NEO- + (chloro)prene] an acetylene derivative] a synthetic rubber highly resistant to oil, heat, light, and oxidation

**Ne·pal** (ni pôl′, ne-; -päl′) country in the Himalayas, between India & Tibet: 54,362 sq. mi.; pop. 10,845,000; cap. Katmandu —**Nep·a·lese** (nep′ə lēz′) *adj., n., pl.* **-lese′**

**ne·pen·the** (ni pen′thē) *n.* [L. < Gr. < *nē-*, not + *penthos*, sorrow] **1.** a drug supposed by the ancient Greeks to cause forgetfulness of sorrow **2.** anything causing this Also **ne·pen′thes** (-thēz) —**ne·pen′the·an** (-thē ən) *adj.*

**neph·ew** (nef′yōō; *chiefly Brit.* nev′-) *n.* [< OFr. < L. *nepos*] **1.** the son of one's brother or sister **2.** the son of one's brother-in-law or sister-in-law

**ne·phrid·i·um** (ne frid′ē əm) *n., pl.* **-i·a** (-ə) [ModL. < Gr. dim. of *nephros*, kidney] **1.** an excretory tubule of many invertebrates, as worms, mollusks, etc. **2.** any of the excretory tubules of a vertebrate embryo

**ne·phrit·ic** (ne frit′ik) *adj.* [< LL. < Gr. < *nephros*, kidney] **1.** of a kidney or the kidneys; renal **2.** of or having nephritis

**ne·phri·tis** (ne frīt′əs) *n.* [see ff. & -ITIS] disease of the kidneys, characterized by inflammation, fibrosis, etc.

**neph·ro-** [< Gr. *nephros*, kidney] *a combining form meaning* kidney: also, before a vowel, **nephr-**

**ne plus ul·tra** (nē plus ul′trə) [L., no more beyond] the highest point of perfection

**nep·o·tism** (nep′ə tiz′m) *n.* [< Fr. < It. < L. *nepos* (gen. *nepotis*), nephew] favoritism shown to relatives, esp. in appointment to desirable positions —**nep′o·tist** *n.* —**nep′o·tis′tic** *adj.*

**Nep·tune** (nep′tōōn, -tyōōn) **1.** *Rom. Myth.* the god of the sea: identified with the Greek god Poseidon **2.** a planet of the solar system, eighth in distance from the sun: diameter, c.29,500 mi.

**nep·tu·ni·um** (nep tōō′nē əm, -tyōō′-) *n.* [ModL.: named after the planet Neptune] a radioactive chemical element produced by irradiating uranium atoms with neutrons: symbol, Np; at. wt., 237.00; at. no., 93

**nerd** (nurd) *n.* [< ?] [Slang] a person regarded as contemptibly ineffective, dull, unsophisticated, etc.

**Ne·re·id** (nir′ē id) *n. Gr. Myth.* any of the sea nymphs, the fifty daughters of Nereus

**Ne·re·us** (nir′ōōs, -ē əs) *Gr. Myth.* a benevolent sea god, father of the fifty Nereids

**Ne·ro** (nir′ō) (*Nero Claudius Caesar Drusus Germanicus*) 37–68 A.D.; emperor of Rome (54–68)

**ner·va·tion** (nər vā′shən) *n. same as* VENATION

**nerve** (nurv) *n.* [< OFr. < L. *nervus*] **1.** a tendon: now chiefly in **strain every nerve**, to try as hard as possible **2.** any of the cordlike fibers carrying impulses between the body organs and the central nervous system **3.** emotional control; courage [a man of *nerve*] **4.** strength; vigor **5.** [*pl.*] the nervous system regarded as indicating health, emotional stability, etc. **6.** [*pl.*] nervousness **7.** [Colloq.] impudent boldness; audacity **8.** *Biol.* a vein in a leaf or insect's wing —*vt.* **nerved, nerv′ing** to give strength or courage to —**get on one's nerves** [Colloq.] to make one irritable

**nerve block** a method of local anesthesia by stopping the impulses through a particular nerve

**nerve cell 1.** *same as* NEURON **2.** occasionally, a nerve cell body without its processes

**nerve center 1.** any group of nerve cells that function together in controlling some specific sense or bodily activity, as breathing **2.** a control center; headquarters

**nerve gas** any of several liquids whose vapors can paralyze the respiratory and central nervous systems when absorbed through the eyes, lungs, or skin

**nerve impulse** an electrical wave transmitted along a nerve that has been stimulated

**nerve·less** (nurv′lis) *adj.* **1.** without strength, force, courage, etc.; weak; unnerved **2.** not nervous; calm **3.** *Biol.* without nerves —**nerve′less·ly** *adv.* —**nerve′less·ness** *n.*

**nerve-rack·ing, nerve-wrack·ing** (-rak′iŋ) *adj.* very trying to one's patience or equanimity

**nerv·ous** (nur′vəs) *adj.* **1.** orig., strong; sinewy **2.** vigorous in expression; animated **3.** of the nerves **4.** made up of or containing nerves **5.** characterized by or having a disordered state of the nerves **6.** emotionally tense, restless, agitated, etc. **7.** fearful; apprehensive —**nerv′ous·ly** *adv.* —**nerv′ous·ness, ner·vos′i·ty** (-väs′ə tē) *n.*

**nervous breakdown** a psychotic or neurotic disorder that impairs the ability to function normally: a popular, nontechnical term

**nervous system** all the nerve cells and nervous tissues in an organism, including, in the vertebrates, the brain, spinal cord, nerves, etc.

**ner·vure** (nur′vyoor) *n.* [Fr.: see NERVE & -URE] *Zool.* same as VEIN (*n.* 2)

**nerv·y** (nur′vē) *adj.* **nerv′i·er, nerv′i·est** **1.** [Brit.] nervous; excitable **2.** full of courage; bold **3.** [Colloq.] brazen; impudent —**nerv′i·ly** *adv.* —**nerv′i·ness** *n.*

**nes·ci·ent** (nesh′ənt, -ē ənt) *adj.* [< L. prp. of *nescire* < *ne-*, not + *scire*, to know] ignorant —**nes′ci·ence** *n.*

**-ness** (nis, nəs) [OE. *-nes(s)*] *a suffix meaning* state, quality, or instance of being [*greatness, sadness, weakness*]

**nest** (nest) *n.* [OE.] **1.** the structure made or the place chosen by birds for laying their eggs and sheltering their young **2.** the place used by hornets, fish, etc. for spawning or breeding **3.** a cozy place to live; retreat **4.** a resort, haunt, or den or its frequenters [*a nest of thieves*] **5.** a swarm or colony of birds, insects, etc. **6.** a set of similar things, each fitting within the one next larger *—vt.* **1.** to build or live in a nest **2.** to fit one into another *—vt.* **1.** to make a nest for **2.** to place in or as in a nest **3.** to fit (an object) closely within another **—nest'a·ble** *adj.*

‡**n'est-ce pas?** (nes pä') [Fr.] isn't that so?

**nest egg 1.** an artificial or real egg left in a nest to induce a hen to lay more eggs there **2.** money, etc. put aside as a reserve or to set up a fund

**nes·tle** (nes'l) *vi.* **-tled, -tling** [OE. *nestlian*] **1.** to settle down comfortably and snugly **2.** to press close for comfort or in affection **3.** to lie sheltered or partly hidden, as a house among trees *—vt.* **1.** to rest or press in a snug, affectionate manner **2.** to shelter as in a nest **—nes'tler** *n.*

**nest·ling** (nest'liŋ, nes'-) *n.* **1.** a young bird not yet ready to leave the nest **2.** a young child

**Nes·tor** (nes'tər) *Gr. Myth.* a wise old counselor who fought with the Greeks at Troy

**net¹** (net) *n.* [OE. *nett*] **1.** a fabric of string, cord, etc., loosely knotted in an openwork pattern and used to snare birds, fish, etc. **2.** a trap; snare **3.** a meshed fabric used to hold, protect, or mark off something [*a hairnet, tennis net*] **4.** a fine, meshed, lacelike cloth **5.** *same as* NETWORK (sense 2) *—vt.* **net'ted, net'ting 1.** to make into a net **2.** to snare as with a net **3.** to shelter or enclose as with a net *—vi.* to make nets or network **—net'like'** *adj.*

**net²** (net) *adj.* [Fr.: see NEAT!] **1.** remaining after certain deductions or allowances have been made, as for expenses, weight of containers, etc. **2.** final [*net result*] *—n.* a net amount, profit, weight, price, etc. *—vt.* **net'ted, net'ting** to gain as profit, etc.

**neth·er** (neth'ər) *adj.* [OE. *neothera*] lower or under [*the nether* world, *nether garments*]

**Neth·er·lands** (neth'ər ləndz) **1.** country in W Europe, on the North Sea: 12,978 sq. mi.; pop. 13,033,000; cap. Amsterdam; seat of govt. The Hague **2.** kingdom consisting of the independent states of the Netherlands & Netherlands Antilles (used with *the* Abbrev. Neth. **—Neth'er·land'er** (-lan'dər, -lən dər) *n.*

**Netherlands Antilles** three islands off the coast of Venezuela & two islands & part of another in the Leeward Islands, together constituting a state of the Netherlands

**neth·er·most** (neth'ər mōst') *adj.* lowest

**nether world** *Theol. & Myth.* the world of the dead or of punishment after death; hell

**Net·tie, Net·ty** (net'ē) [dim. of ANTOINETTE, etc.] a feminine name

**net·ting** (net'iŋ) *n.* **1.** the act or process of making nets or fishing with them **2.** netted material

**net·tle** (net'l) *n.* [OE. *netele*] any of a number of related weeds with stinging hairs *—vt.* **-tled, -tling 1.** to sting with or as with nettles **2.** to irritate; annoy; vex

**net ton** *same as* SHORT TON

**net·work** (net'wurk') *n.* **1.** any arrangement or fabric of parallel wires, threads, etc. crossed at regular intervals by others so as to leave open spaces **2.** a thing resembling this; specif., *a)* a system of connecting roads, canals, etc. *b)* Radio & TV a chain of transmitting stations controlled and operated as a unit *c)* a system, etc. of cooperating individuals *—adj.* broadcast over the stations of a network

**Neuf·châ·tel (cheese)** (nōō'shə tel', nyōō-) [after a town in N France] a soft, white cheese prepared from whole or skim milk

**neu·ral** (noor'əl, nyoor'-) *adj.* [NEUR(O)- + -AL] of a nerve, nerves, or the nervous system

**neu·ral·gia** (noo ral'jə, nyoo-) *n.* [ModL.: see NEURO- & -ALGIA] severe pain along the course of a nerve **—neu·ral'gic** (-jik) *adj.*

**neu·ras·the·ni·a** (noor'əs thē'nē ə, nyoor'-) *n.* [ModL. < NEUR(O)- + Gr. *astheneia*, weakness] a type of neurosis, usually the result of emotional conflicts, characterized by irritability, fatigue, anxiety, etc. **—neu'ras·then'ic** (-then'ik) *adj., n.*

**neu·ri·tis** (noo rīt'əs, nyoo-) *n.* [ModL.: see ff. & -ITIS] inflammation of a nerve or nerves, accompanied by pain **—neu·rit'ic** (-rit'ik) *adj.*

**neu·ro-** [< Gr. *neuron*, nerve] *a combining form meaning of* a nerve, nerves, or the nervous system [*neuropathy*] : also, before a vowel, **neur-**

**neu·rol·o·gy** (noo räl'ə jē, nyoo-) *n.* [ModL.: see prec. & -LOGY] the branch of medicine dealing with the nervous system and its diseases **—neu·ro·log·i·cal** (noor'ə läj'i k'l, nyoor'-) *adj.* **—neu·rol'o·gist** *n.*

**neu·ron** (noor'än, nyoor'-) *n.* [ModL. < Gr. *neuron*, nerve] the structural and functional unit of the nervous system, consisting of the nerve cell body and all its processes: also **neu'rone** (-ōn) **—neu'ro·nal** (-ə nəl), **neu·ron·ic** (noo rän'ik, nyoo-) *adj.*

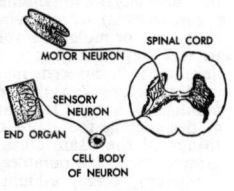

SPINAL CORD / MOTOR NEURON / SENSORY NEURON / END ORGAN / CELL BODY OF NEURON

NEURON

**neu·rop·a·thy** (noo räp'ə thē, nyoo-) *n.* [NEURO- + -PATHY] any disease of the nerves or the nervous system **—neu·ro·path·ic** (noor'ə path'ik, nyoor'-) *adj.*

**neu·ro·psy·chi·a·try** (noor'ō sə kī'ə trē, nyoor'-) *n.* a branch of medicine combining neurology and psychiatry

**neu·rop·ter·an** (noo räp'tər ən, nyoo-) *n.* [< ModL. < NEURO- + Gr. *pteron*, wing + -AN] any of an order of insects with four membranous wings and biting mouthparts **—neu·rop'ter·ous** *adj.*

**neu·ro·sis** (noo rō'sis, nyoo-) *n., pl.* **-ses** (-sēz) [ModL.: see NEURO- & -OSIS] a functional mental disorder characterized by combinations of anxiety, compulsions and obsessions, phobias, depression, etc.

**neu·ro·sur·ger·y** (noor'ō sur'jər ē, nyoor'-) *n.* the branch of surgery involving some part of the nervous system, including the brain and spinal cord **—neu'ro·sur'geon** *n.*

**neu·rot·ic** (noo rät'ik, nyoo-) *adj.* of or having a neurosis *—n.* a neurotic person **—neu·rot'i·cal·ly** *adv.* **—neu·rot'i·cism** (-ə siz'm) *n.*

**neut.** neuter

**neu·ter** (nōot'ər, nyōot'-) *adj.* [< MFr. < L. < *ne*-, not + *uter*, either] **1.** [Archaic] neutral **2.** *Biol. a)* having no sexual organs; asexual *b)* having undeveloped or imperfect sexual organs in the adult, as the worker bee **3.** *Gram.* designating or of the gender that refers to things regarded as neither male nor female *—n.* **1.** a castrated or spayed animal **2.** *Biol.* a neuter plant or animal **3.** *Gram. a)* the neuter gender *b)* a neuter word *—vt.* to castrate or spay

**neu·tral** (nōo'trəl, nyōo'-) *adj.* [Fr. < ML. < L. *neuter*: see prec.] **1.** not taking part in either side of a quarrel or war **2.** of or characteristic of a nation not taking part in a war or not taking sides in a power struggle **3.** not one thing or the other; indifferent **4.** having little or no decided color **5.** *Biol. same as* NEUTER **6.** *Chem.* neither acid nor alkaline **7.** *Elec.* neither negative nor positive **8.** *Phonet.* pronounced as the vowel is in most unstressed syllables, which tends to become (ə) *—n.* **1.** a nation not taking part in a war **2.** a neutral person **3.** a neutral color **4.** *Mech.* a disengaged position of gears, when they do not transmit power from the engine **—neu'tral·ly** *adv.*

**neu·tral·ism** (-iz'm) *n.* a policy, or the advocacy of a policy, of remaining neutral, esp. in international power conflicts **—neu'tral·ist** *adj., n.* **—neu'tral·is'tic** *adj.*

**neu·tral·i·ty** (nōo tral'ə tē, nyōo-) *n.* **1.** the quality, state, or character of being neutral **2.** the status or policy of a nation not participating directly or indirectly in a war between other nations

**neu·tral·ize** (nōo'trə līz', nyōo'-) *vt.* **-ized', -iz'ing 1.** to declare (a nation, etc.) neutral in war **2.** to destroy or counteract the effectiveness, force, etc. of **3.** *Chem.* to destroy the active properties of [*an alkali neutralizes an acid*] **4.** *Elec.* to make electrically neutral **—neu'tral·i·za'tion** *n.* **—neu'tral·iz'er** *n.*

**neutral spirits** ethyl alcohol of 190 proof or over, used in blended whiskeys, liqueurs, cordials, etc.

**neu·tri·no** (nōo trē'nō, nyōo-) *n., pl.* **-nos** [It., coined by E. FERMI < *neutrone* (< NEUTRON) + dim. suffix *-ino*] *Physics* a neutral particle having a mass approaching zero

**neu·tron** (nōo'trän, nyōo'-) *n.* [NEUTR(AL) + (ELECTR)ON] a fundamental particle in the nucleus of an atom: neutrons are uncharged and have about the same mass as protons

**neutron bomb** a small thermonuclear warhead for battlefield use, intended to disable or kill enemy soldiers without destroying buildings, vehicles, etc.

**neutron star** a heavenly object hypothesized to be a collapsed star consisting of immense numbers of densely packed neutrons

**Ne·vad·a** (nə vad'ə, -vä'də) [< (SIERRA) NEVADA] Mountain State of the U.S.: 110,540 sq. mi.; pop. 799,000; cap. Carson City: abbrev. Nev., NV **—Ne·vad'an** *adj., n.*

**nev·er** (nev'ər) *adv.* [OE. *næfre* < *ne*, not + *æfre*, ever] **1.** not ever; at no time **2.** not at all; in no case

**nev·er·more** (nev'ər môr') *adv.* never again

**never-never land** [after the fairyland in J. M. Barrie's *Peter Pan*] an unreal or unrealistic place or situation nev·er·the·less (nev'ər thə les') adv. in spite of that; nonetheless; however

Nev·il, Nev·ille (nev''l) [< Neuville, town in Normandy (lit., new city)] a masculine name

ne·vus (nē'vəs) n., pl. ne'vi (-vī) [ModL. < L. naevus] a birthmark or mole —ne'void (-void) adj.

new (nōō, nyōō) adj. [OE. niwe] 1. appearing, thought of, developed, discovered, made, etc. for the first time; never existing before 2. a) different [a new hairdo] b) strange; unfamiliar 3. not yet familiar or accustomed [new to the job] 4. designating the more or most recent of two or more things of the same class [the new library] 5. recently grown; fresh [new potatoes] 6. not previously used or worn 7. modern; recent; fashionable 8. more; additional 9. starting as a repetition of a cycle, series, etc. [the new year] 10. having just reached a position, rank, place, etc. [a new arrival] 11. refreshed in spirits, health, etc. [a new man] 12. [N-] same as MODERN (sense 3) —n. something new (with the) —adv. 1. again 2. newly; recently —new'ish adj. —new'ness n.

New Amsterdam Du. colonial town on Manhattan Island: renamed (1664) New York by the British

New·ark (nōō'ərk, nyōō'-) [after Newark, England] city in NE N.J.: pop. 329,000 (met. area 1,964,000)

new ball game [Colloq.] a situation so drastically changed as to require new approaches, solutions, etc.

New Bed·ford (bed'fərd) [after W. Russell, Duke of Bedford (1639–83)] seaport in SE Mass.: pop. 98,000

new blood new people, regarded as a potential source of fresh ideas, renewed vigor, etc.

new·born (nōō'bôrn', nyōō'-) adj. 1. recently born; just born 2. reborn

New Britain city in C Conn.: pop. 74,000

New Brunswick province of SE Canada, on the Gulf of St. Lawrence: 28,354 sq. mi.; pop. 677,000; cap. Fredericton: abbrev. N.B.

New·burg (-bərg) adj. served in a rich, creamy sauce made with butter, egg yolks, and wine

New Caledonia Fr. island in the SW Pacific, west of Australia

new candle see CANDLE (n. 3)

New·cas·tle (nōō'kas''l, nyōō'-; -käs'-) seaport in N England: pop. 254,000: in full, New'cas'tle-up·on-Tyne' (-tīn') —carry coals to Newcastle 1. to take things to a place where they are plentiful 2. to do an unnecessary thing

new·com·er (nōō'kum'ər, nyōō'-) n. a recent arrival

New Deal the economic and political principles and policies adopted by President Franklin D. Roosevelt in the 1930's to advance economic and social welfare —New Dealer

New Delhi capital of India, adjacent to the old city of Delhi: pop. 261,000

new·el (nōō'əl, nyōō'-) n. [< OFr. < LL. nucalis, like a nut < L. nux, nut] 1. the upright pillar around which the steps of a winding staircase turn 2. the post at the top or bottom of a flight of stairs, supporting the handrail: also newel post

New England [so named (1616) by Capt. John SMITH] the six NE States of the U.S.: Me., Vt., N.H., Mass., R.I., and Conn. —New Englander

New English Bible a British translation of the Bible, published in 1970

new·fan·gled (nōō'faŋ'g'ld, nyōō'-) adj. [< ME. < newe, new + -fangel < base of OE. fon, to take] new; novel: a humorously derogatory term

New·found·land (nōō'fənd land', -lənd; nyōō'-; nyōō found'land') 1. an island of Canada, off the E coast 2. province of E Canada, including this island & Labrador: 156,185 sq. mi.; pop. 558,000; cap. St. John's: abbrev. Nfld. —New'found·land'er n.

Newfoundland dog any of a North American breed of large, powerful, shaggy-haired dogs

New·gate (nōō'gāt, nyōō'-) former prison in London: torn down in 1902

New Guinea large island in the East Indies, north of Australia: divided between West Irian (in Indonesia) & the country of Papua New Guinea

New Hamp·shire (hamp'shir, ham'-) [after Hampshire, county in England] New England State of the U.S.: 9,304 sq. mi.; pop. 921,000; cap. Concord: abbrev. N.H., NH

New Ha·ven (hā'vən) city in S Conn., on Long Island Sound: pop. 126,000

New Hebrides group of islands in the SW Pacific, which in 1980 became the independent nation of VANUATU

New High German see GERMAN, HIGH GERMAN

New Jersey [after the island of JERSEY] Eastern State of the U.S.: 7,836 sq. mi.; pop. 7,364,000; cap. Trenton: abbrev. N.J., NJ —New Jer'sey·ite' (-īt')

New Jerusalem Bible heaven: Rev. 21:2

new·ly (nōō'lē, nyōō'-) adv. 1. recently; lately 2. anew; afresh 3. in a new way or style

new·ly·wed (-wed') n. a recently married person

New·man (nōō'mən, nyōō'-), John Henry, Cardinal Newman, 1801–90; Eng. theologian & writer

new math a system for teaching basic mathematics based on the use of sets

New Mexico [transl. of Sp. Nuevo Méjico] Mountain State of the U.S.: 121,666 sq. mi.; pop. 1,300,000; cap. Santa Fe: abbrev. N.Mex., NM —New Mexican

new moon the moon when it is between the earth and the sun, with its dark side toward the earth: it emerges as a crescent curving to the right

New Neth·er·land (neth'ər lənd) Du. colony (1613–64) in E N. America: taken by England & divided into the colonies of New York & New Jersey

New Or·le·ans (ôr'lē ənz, ôr lēnz'; chiefly Southern ôr'lənz) [after ORLÉANS, France] city in SE La., on the Mississippi: pop. 557,000 (met. area 1,184,000)

New·port (nōō'pôrt', nyōō'-) seaport in SE Wales: pop. 112,000

Newport News [< ?] seaport in SE Va.: pop. 145,000

New Ro·chelle (rə shel') [after La Rochelle, France] city in SE N.Y., on Long Island Sound: pop. 71,000

news (nōōz, nyōōz) n.pl. [with sing. v.] [after OFr. noveles or ML. nova, pl. of novum, what is new] 1. new information about anything; information previously unknown 2. reports of recent happenings, esp. those broadcast, printed in a newspaper, etc. 3. any person or thing featured in such reports —make news to do something reported as news

news·boy (-boi') n. a boy who sells or delivers newspapers

news·cast (-kast') n. [NEWS + (BROAD)CAST] a program of news broadcast over radio or TV —news'cast'er n.

news·deal·er (-dēl'ər) n. a person who sells newspapers, magazines, etc., esp. as a retailer

news·let·ter (-let'ər) n. a news bulletin issued at regular intervals to a special group

news·man (-man', -mən) n., pl. -men (-men', -mən) a newsperson, esp. a male —news'wom'an n.fem., pl. -wom'en

New South Wales state of SE Australia, on the Pacific

news·pa·per (-pā'pər) n. a regular publication, usually a daily or weekly, containing news, opinions, advertisements, etc. —news'pa'per·man' n., pl. -men' —news'pa'per·wom'an n.fem., pl. -wom'en

new·speak (nōō'spēk', nyōō'-) n. [sometimes N-] the use of ambiguous and deceptive talk, as by government officials, in seeking to mold public opinion

news·per·son (nōōz'pʉr's'n, nyōōz'-) n. a person involved in the gathering, writing, editing, or reporting of news, often specif. for TV or radio

news·print (nōōz'print', nyōōz'-) n. a cheap paper, made mainly from wood pulp, for newspapers, etc.

news·reel (-rēl') n. a short motion picture of news events

news·stand (-stand') n. a stand at which newspapers, magazines, etc. are sold

New Style the method of reckoning time in accordance with the Gregorian calendar

news·wor·thy (nōōz'wʉr'thē, nyōōz'-) adj. timely and important or interesting

news·y (-ē) adj. news'i·er, news'i·est [Colloq.] containing much news

newt (nōōt, nyōōt) n. [by syllabic merging of ME. an eute < OE. efeta, eft] any of various small salamanders that can live on land or in water

New Testament the part of the Bible containing the life and teachings of Jesus and his followers

New·ton[1] (nōōt'n, nyōōt'n) [< New Towne, orig. name of Cambridge, Mass.] city in E Mass.: suburb of Boston: pop. 84,000

NEWT (3–4 in. long)

New·ton[2] (nōōt'n, nyōōt'n) [< surname Newton < Eng. place name < OE. neowa tun, new town] 1. a masculine name 2. Sir Isaac, 1642–1727; Eng. mathematician & natural philosopher —New·to'ni·an (-tō'nē ən) adj., n.

new·ton (nōōt'n, nyōōt'n) n. [after Sir Isaac NEWTON] the unit of force in the mks system: the force which imparts to a mass of 1 kilogram an acceleration of 1 meter per second per second

New Town 1. any of a number of planned communities built in Great Britain since World War II 2. [often n- t-] any housing development like this

New World the Western Hemisphere —new'-world' adj.

new year [also N- Y-] 1. the year just about to begin or just begun (usually with the) 2. the first day or days of the new year

New Year's (Day) January 1, the first day of a calendar year, usually a legal holiday

New Year's Eve the evening before New Year's Day

New York [after the Duke of York] 1. State of the NE U.S.: 49,576 sq. mi.; pop. 17,557,000; cap. Albany: abbrev. N.Y., NY 2. city in SE N.Y., at the mouth of the Hudson:

often called **New York City:** pop. 7,071,000 (met. area 10,803,000) —**New York′er**

**New York State Barge Canal** system of waterways, including the Erie Canal, connecting Lake Erie & the Hudson River

**New Zea·land** (zē′lənd) country made up of two large islands & several small islands in the S Pacific, southeast of Australia: a member of the Commonwealth: 103,736 sq. mi.; pop. 2,809,000; cap. Wellington —**New Zea′land·er**

**next** (nekst) *adj. older superl. of* NIGH [OE. *neahst,* superl. of *neah,* nigh] nearest; immediately preceding or following —*adv.* **1.** in the time, place, degree, or rank immediately preceding or following **2.** on the first subsequent occasion *[when next we meet]* —*prep.* beside; nearest to *[sit next the tree]* —*n.* the one immediately following —**get next to** [Slang] to become friendly or intimate with —**next door (to) 1.** in or at the house adjacent (to) **2.** almost

**next-door** (neks′dôr′) *adj.* in or at the next house, building, etc.

**next of kin** one's relative(s) most nearly related

**nex·us** (nek′səs) *n., pl.* **-us·es, nex′us** [L. < pp. of *nectere,* to bind] **1.** a connection, tie, or link between individuals of a group, members of a series, etc. **2.** the group or series connected

**Nez Per·cé** (nez′ pər sā′, pʉrs′) *pl.* **Nez Per·cés′, Nez Per·cé′** [Fr., lit., pierced nose: from the false notion that they pierced the nose] a member of a N. American Indian tribe of the Northwest

**Nfld., Nfd.** Newfoundland

**N.G. 1.** National Guard: also **NG 2.** New Guinea

**N.G., n.g.** [Slang] no good

**ngul·trum** (′n o͞ol′tro͞om) *n.* [Bhutanese] *see* MONETARY UNITS, table (Bhutan)

**ngwee** (′n gwē′) *n., pl.* **ngwee** [native term, lit., bright] *see* MONETARY UNITS, table (Zambia)

**N.H., NH** New Hampshire

**Ni** *Chem.* nickel

**N.I.** Northern Ireland

**ni·a·cin** (nī′ə sin) *n.* [NI(COTINIC) AC(ID) + -IN[1]] a white, odorless substance, $C_6H_5O_2N$, found in protein foods: it is a member of the vitamin B complex, used in treating pellagra

**Ni·ag·a·ra** (nī ag′rə, -ər ə) [ < Iroquoian town name] river between W N.Y. & SE Ontario, Canada, flowing from Lake Erie into Lake Ontario

**Niagara Falls 1.** waterfall on the Niagara River: divided by an island into two falls, Horseshoe, or Canadian, Falls & American Falls **2.** city in W N.Y., at Niagara Falls: pop. 71,000 **3.** city in SE Ontario, opposite Niagara Falls, N.Y.: pop. 69,000

**nib** (nib) *n.* [var. of NEB] **1.** the bill or beak of a bird **2.** the point of a pen **3.** the projecting end of anything; point

**nib·ble** (nib′'l) *vt., vi.* **-bled, -bling** [prob. akin to MLowG. *nibbelen*] **1.** to eat (food) with quick, small bites, as a mouse does **2.** to bite at with small, gentle bites —*n.* **1.** a small bite or morsel **2.** a nibbling —**nib′bler** *n.*

**Ni·be·lung** (nē′bə lo͞oŋ′) *n.* [G.] *Germanic Legend* any of a race of dwarfs who owned a magic ring and a hoard of gold, taken from them by Siegfried

**Ni·be·lung·en·lied** (nē′bə lo͞oŋ′ən lēt′) a Middle High German epic poem by an unknown author of the 13th cent.: see SIEGFRIED

**nibs** (nibz) *n.* [ < ?] [Colloq.] an important, or esp. self-important, person (with *his*)

**Nic·a·ra·gua** (nik′ə rä′gwə) **1.** country in Central America, on the Caribbean & the Pacific: 54,342 sq. mi.; pop. 1,984,000; cap. Managua **2. Lake,** lake in S Nicaragua —**Nic′a·ra′guan** *adj., n.*

**Nice** (nēs) seaport & resort in SE France: pop. 322,000

**nice** (nīs) *adj.* **nic′er, nic′est** [OFr., stupid < L. *nescius,* ignorant < *ne-,* not + *scire,* to know] **1.** difficult to please; fastidious **2.** delicate; precise; discriminative; subtle *[a nice distinction]* **3.** calling for accuracy, care, tact, etc. *[a nice problem]* **4.** *a)* finely discriminating *b)* minutely accurate **5.** morally scrupulous **6.** *a)* agreeable; pleasant *b)* attractive; pretty *c)* kind; considerate *d)* respectable *e)* good; excellent —*adv.* pleasingly, attractively, etc.: regarded as substandard, dialectal, or colloquial —**nice and** [Colloq.] altogether; very *[my tea is nice and hot]* —**nice′ly** *adv.* —**nice′ness** *n.*

**Ni·cene Creed** (nī′sēn, nī sēn′) [ < *Nicaea,* ancient city in Asia Minor where it was formulated] a confession of faith for Christians adopted in 325 A.D.: now used in various forms by most denominations

**ni·ce·ty** (nī′sə tē) *n., pl.* **-ties 1.** a being nice; specif., *a)* scrupulosity *b)* precision; accuracy, as of discrimination or perception *c)* fastidiousness; refinement **2.** the quality of calling for delicacy or precision in handling **3.** a subtle or

minute detail, distinction, etc. **4.** something choice or dainty —**to a nicety** exactly

**niche** (nich) *n.* [Fr. < OFr., ult. < L. *nidus,* a nest] **1.** a recess in a wall for a statue, bust, or vase **2.** a place or position particularly suitable to the person or thing in it **3.** *Ecol.* the particular role of an organism in its total environment —*vt.* **niched, nich′ing** to place in a niche

STATUE IN NICHE

**Nich·o·las** (nik′'l əs) [ < OFr. < L. < Gr. < *nikē,* victory + *laos,* the people] **1.** a masculine name: dim. **Nick 2. Nicholas I** 1796–1855; czar of Russia (1825–55) **3. Nicholas II** 1868–1918; last czar of Russia (1894–1917): forced to abdicate; executed **4. Saint,** 4th cent. A.D.: patron saint of Russia, of Greece, & of young people, sailors, etc.: cf. SANTA CLAUS

**nick** (nik) *n.* [prob. akin to *nocke,* notch] a small cut, chip, etc. made on the edge or surface of wood, metal, china, etc.; notch —*vt.* **1.** to make a nick or nicks in **2.** *a)* to wound slightly *b)* to strike glancingly **3.** to hit or catch at the right time **4.** [Slang] *a)* to fine *b)* to overcharge or cheat —**in the nick of time** just before it is too late; exactly when needed

**nick·el** (nik′'l) *n.* [Sw. < G. *kupfernickel,* copper demon: so called because the copperlike ore contains no copper] **1.** a hard, silver-white, malleable metallic chemical element, used in alloys and for plating: symbol, Ni; at. wt., 58.71; at. no., 28 **2.** a U.S. or Canadian coin made of an alloy of nickel and copper and equal to five cents —*vt.* **-eled** or **-elled, -el·ing** or **-el·ling** to plate with nickel

**nick·el·o·de·on** (nik′ə lō′dē ən) *n.* [ < NICKEL + Fr. *odéon,* concert hall] **1.** formerly, a motion-picture theater, etc. where admission was five cents **2.** a player piano or early type of jukebox operated by the insertion of a nickel in a slot

**nickel plate** a thin layer of nickel deposited by electrolysis on metallic objects to prevent rust —**nick′el-plate′** *vt.* -**plat′ed, -plat′ing**

**nickel silver** a hard, tough, ductile, malleable alloy composed essentially of nickel, copper, and zinc

**nick·er** (nik′ər) *vi.* [prob. < freq. of NEIGH] to utter a low, whinnying sound: said of a horse —*n.* this sound

**nick·nack** (nik′nak′) *n. same as* KNICKKNACK

**nick·name** (nik′nām′) *n.* [by syllabic merging of ME. *an ekename,* a surname] **1.** a substitute, often descriptive name given to a person or thing, as in fun, affection, etc., as "Doc," "Shorty," etc. **2.** a familiar form of a name, as "Dick" for "Richard" —*vt.* **-named′, -nam′ing** to give a nickname to

**Nic·o·si·a** (nik′ə sē′ə) capital of Cyprus: pop. 109,000

**nic·o·tine** (nik′ə tēn′, -tin) *n.* [Fr. < ModL., after J. *Nicot,* 16th-c. Fr. diplomat who introduced tobacco into France] a poisonous alkaloid, $C_{10}H_{14}N_2$, found in tobacco leaves and used as an insecticide —**nic′o·tin′ic** (-tin′ik, -tē′nik) *adj.*

**nicotinic acid** *same as* NIACIN

**nic·tate** (nik′tāt) *vi.* **-tat·ed, -tat·ing** *same as* NICTITATE

**nic·ti·tate** (nik′tə tāt′) *vi.* **-tat′ed, -tat′ing** [ < ML. pp. of *nictitare,* freq. < L. *nictare,* to wink] to wink or blink rapidly, as birds and animals with a nictitating membrane —**nic′ti·ta′tion** *n.*

**nictitating membrane** a transparent third eyelid hinged at the inner side or lower lid of the eye of various animals

**niece** (nēs) *n.* [ < OFr. < LL. < L. *neptis*] **1.** the daughter of one's brother or sister **2.** the daughter of one's brother-in-law or sister-in-law

**Nie·tzsche** (nē′chə), **Frie·drich Wil·helm** (frē′driH vil′helm) 1844–1900; Ger. philosopher —**Nie′tzsche·an** (-chē ən) *adj., n.*

**nif·ty** (nif′tē) *adj.* **-ti·er, -ti·est** [prob. < MAGNIFICENT] [Slang] attractive, smart, stylish, enjoyable, etc. —*n., pl.* **-ties** a nifty thing; esp., a clever remark

**Ni·ger** (nī′jər) **1.** river in W Africa, flowing from Guinea through Mali, Niger, & Nigeria into the Atlantic **2.** country in WC Africa, north of Nigeria: c.458,500 sq. mi.; pop. 4,016,000

**Ni·ge·ri·a** (nī jir′ē ə) country in WC Africa, on the Atlantic: a member of the Commonwealth: 327,186 sq. mi.; pop. 61,450,000; cap. Lagos —**Ni·ger′i·an** *adj., n.*

**nig·gard** (nig′ərd) *n.* [prob. < Scand.] a stingy person; miser —*adj.* stingy; miserly

**nig·gard·ly** (-lē) *adj.* **1.** stingy; miserly **2.** small, few, or scanty —*adv.* stingily —**nig′gard·li·ness** *n.*

**nig·gle** (nig′'l) *vi.* **-gled, -gling** [prob. akin to Norw. dial.

*nigla*] to work fussily; be finicky —**nig′gler** *n.* —**nig′gling** *adj., n.*

**nigh** (nī) *adv.* [OE. *neah*] [Chiefly Archaic or Dial.] 1. near in time, place, etc. 2. almost —*adj.* **nigh′er, nigh′est** or, older, **next** [Chiefly Archaic or Dial.] 1. near; close 2. direct or short 3. on the left: said of animals, vehicles, etc. —*prep.* [Chiefly Archaic or Dial.] near —*vi., vt.* [Archaic] to approach

**night** (nīt) *n.* [OE. *niht*] 1. the period of darkness between sunset and sunrise 2. the evening at the end of a specified day [Christmas *night*] 3. the darkness of night 4. any period or condition of darkness or gloom; specif., *a*) a period of intellectual or moral degeneration *b*) a time of grief *c*) death —*adj.* 1. of, for, or at night 2. active or working at night —**make a night of it** to celebrate all night —**night and day** continuously or continually

**night blindness** imperfect vision in the dark or in dim light: a symptom of vitamin A deficiency

**night-bloom·ing cereus** (-blōō′miŋ) any of various cactuses that bloom at night

**night·cap** (-kap′) *n.* 1. a cap worn in bed, esp. formerly, to protect the head from cold 2. [Colloq.] an alcoholic drink taken at bedtime

**night clothes** clothes to be worn in bed, as pajamas

**night·club** (-klub′) *n.* a place of entertainment open at night for eating, drinking, dancing, etc.

**night crawler** any large earthworm that comes to the surface at night, commonly used as fish bait

**night·fall** (-fôl′) *n.* the close of day; dusk

**night·gown** (-goun′) *n.* a loose gown worn in bed by women or girls

**night·hawk** (-hôk′) *n.* 1. any of a group of new-world night birds related to the goatsuckers and the whippoorwill 2. *same as:* *a*) NIGHTJAR *b*) NIGHT OWL

**night·ie** (nīt′ē) *n. colloq. dim. of* NIGHTGOWN

**night·in·gale** (nīt′'n gāl′, -iŋ-) *n.* [< OE. < *niht*, night + base of *galan*, to sing] a small European thrush with a russet back and buff underparts, known for the melodious singing of the male, esp. at night

**Night·in·gale** (nīt′'n gāl′, -iŋ-), **Florence** 1820–1910; Eng. nurse: pioneer in modern nursing

**night·jar** (nīt′jär′) *n.* [NIGHT + JAR¹] the European goatsucker

**night latch** a door latch with a bolt opened from the outside by a key and from the inside by a knob

**night letter** a long telegram sent at night at a cheaper rate than a regular telegram

**night light** a small, dim light kept on all night, as in a hallway, bathroom, sickroom, etc.

**night·long** (-lôŋ′) *adj.* lasting the entire night —*adv.* during the entire night

**night·ly** (-lē) *adj.* 1. of or like the night 2. done or occurring every night —*adv.* 1. at night 2. every night

**night·mare** (-mer′) *n.* [< ME. < *niht*, night + *mare*, demon] 1. a frightening dream, often accompanied by a feeling of oppression and helplessness 2. any frightening experience —**night′mar′ish** *adj.*

**night owl** a person who works at night or otherwise stays up late

**nights** (nīts) *adv.* on every night or most nights

**night school** a school held in the evening, as for adults unable to attend by day

**night·shade** (nīt′shād′) *n.* [OE. *nihtscada*] 1. any of a large genus of flowering plants of the nightshade family, including BLACK NIGHTSHADE 2. *same as* BELLADONNA (sense 1) —*adj.* designating a large family of poisonous and nonpoisonous plants, including the tobacco, tomato, potato, petunia, and eggplant

**night·shirt** (-shurt′) *n.* a long, loose, shirtlike garment, worn in bed, esp. formerly, by men or boys

**night·spot** (-spät′) *n. colloq. var. of* NIGHTCLUB

**night stand** a small table at the bedside

**night stick** a club carried by a policeman

**night·time** (-tīm′) *n.* the period of darkness from sunset to sunrise

**night·wear** (-wer′) *n. same as* NIGHT CLOTHES

**night·y** (-ē) *n., pl.* **night′ies** *alt. sp. of* NIGHTIE

**NIH, N.I.H.** National Institutes of Health

**ni·hil·ism** (nī′ə liz′m, nē′-, ni′hi-) *n.* [< L. *nihil*, nothing + -ISM] 1. *Philos.* *a*) the denial of the existence of any basis for knowledge *b*) the general rejection of customary beliefs in morality, religion, etc. 2. the belief that there is no meaning or purpose in existence 3. *a*) [N-] a revolutionary movement in Russia (c.1860–1917) which advocated the destruction of existing social, political, and economic institutions *b*) loosely, any terroristic revolutionary movement —**ni′hil·ist** *n.* —**ni′hil·is′tic** *adj.*

**Ni·ke** (nī′kē) *Gr. Myth.* the winged goddess of victory

**nil** (nil) *n.* [L., contr. of *nihil*] nothing

**Nile** (nīl) river in NE Africa, flowing through Egypt into the Mediterranean: with one of its principal headstreams, over 4,000 mi.

**nil·gai** (nil′gī) *n., pl.* **-gais, -gai:** see PLURAL, II, D, 1 [Per. *nīlgāw*, blue cow] a large, gray Indian antelope: also **nil′gau** (-gô)

**nim·ble** (nim′b'l) *adj.* **-bler, -blest** [< OE. *numol* < *niman*, to take] 1. quick-witted; alert [a *nimble* mind] 2. showing mental quickness [a *nimble* reply] 3. moving quickly and lightly —**nim′ble·ness** *n.* —**nim′bly** *adv.*

**nim·bo·stra·tus** (nim′bō strāt′əs, -strat′əs) *n.* [ModL.: see ff. & STRATUS] an extensive, dark, low-level cloud, commonly bringing rain or snow

**nim·bus** (nim′bəs) *n., pl.* **-bi** (-bī), **-bus·es** [L., rain cloud] 1. orig., any rain-producing cloud 2. a bright cloud supposedly surrounding gods or goddesses appearing on earth 3. an aura of splendor about any person or thing 4. a halo surrounding the heads of saints, etc., as in pictures

**Nim·rod** (nim′räd) *Bible* a mighty hunter: Gen. 10:8–9 —*n.* [*often* n-] a hunter

**nin·com·poop** (nin′kəm pōōp′, niŋ′-) *n.* [< ?] a stupid, silly person; fool; simpleton

**nine** (nīn) *adj.* [OE. *nigon*] totaling one more than eight —*n.* 1. the cardinal number between eight and ten; 9; IX 2. anything having nine units or members, or numbered nine; specif., a baseball team —**the Nine** the nine Muses —**to the nines** 1. to perfection 2. in the most elaborate manner [dressed *to the nines*]

**nine·fold** (-fōld′) *adj.* [see -FOLD] 1. having nine parts 2. having nine times as much or as many —*adv.* nine times as much or as many

**nine·pins** (-pinz′) *n.pl.* [*with sing. v.*] a British version of tenpins, in which nine pins are used

**nine·teen** (-tēn′) *adj.* [OE. *nigontyne*] nine more than ten —*n.* the cardinal number between eighteen and twenty; 19; XIX

**nine·teenth** (-tēnth′) *adj.* 1. preceded by eighteen others in a series; 19th 2. designating any of the nineteen equal parts of something —*n.* 1. the one following the eighteenth 2. any of the nineteen equal parts of something; 1/19

**nine·ti·eth** (nīn′tē ith) *adj.* 1. preceded by eighty-nine others in a series; 90th 2. designating any of the ninety equal parts of something —*n.* 1. the one following the eighty-ninth 2. any of the ninety equal parts of something; 1/90

**nine·ty** (nīn′tē) *adj.* [OE. *nigontig*] nine times ten —*n., pl.* **-ties** the cardinal number between eighty-nine and ninety-one; 90; XC (or LXXXX) —**the nineties** the numbers or years, as of a century, from ninety through ninety-nine

**Nin·e·veh** (nin′ə və) capital of ancient Assyria

**nin·ny** (nin′ē) *n., pl.* **-nies** [prob. by syllabic merging and contr. of *an innocent*] a fool; dolt

**ninth** (nīnth) *adj.* [OE. *nigonthe*] 1. preceded by eight others in a series; 9th 2. designating any of the nine equal parts of something —*n.* 1. the one following the eighth 2. any of the nine equal parts of something; 1/9 —**ninth′ly** *adv.*

**Ni·o·be** (nī′ə bē′) *Gr. Myth.* a queen of Thebes, daughter of Tantalus, who, weeping for her slain children, was turned into a stone from which tears continued to flow

**ni·o·bi·um** (nī ō′bē əm) *n.* [ModL. < L. *Niobe*, NIOBE: from association with tantalum: see TANTALUM] a gray or white metallic chemical element used in chromium steels, in jet engines and rockets, etc.: symbol, Nb; at. wt., 92.906; at. no., 41

**nip¹** (nip) *vt.* **nipped, nip′ping** [prob. < MLowG. *nippen* or ON. *hnippa*] 1. to pinch or squeeze, as between two surfaces; bite 2. to sever (shoots, etc.) as by pinching or clipping 3. to check the growth of 4. to have a painful or injurious effect on because of cold [frost *nipped* the plants] —*vi.* to give a nip or nips —*n.* 1. a nipping; pinch; bite 2. a piece nipped off 3. a stinging quality, as in cold air 4. stinging cold; frost —**nip and tuck** so close or critical as to leave the outcome in doubt

**nip²** (nip) *n.* [prob. < Du. < base of *nippen*, to sip] a small drink of liquor; dram; sip —*vt., vi.* to drink (liquor) in nips

**nip·per** (nip′ər) *n.* 1. anything that nips, or pinches 2. [*pl.*] any of various tools for grasping or severing, as pliers, pincers, or forceps 3. the pincerlike claw of a crab, lobster, etc. 4. [Brit. Colloq.] a small boy

**nip·ple** (nip′'l) *n.* [prob. < dim. of NEB] 1. the part of a breast or udder through which a baby or young animal sucks milk from its mother; teat 2. a teatlike part, as of rubber, for a baby's bottle 3. any projection or thing resembling a nipple in shape or function

**Nip·pon** (nip′än, ni pän′) *a Jap. name for* JAPAN —**Nip′pon·ese′** (-ə nēz′) *adj., n., pl.* **-ese′**

**nip·py** (nip′ē) *adj.* **-pi·er, -pi·est** 1. tending to nip 2. cold in a stinging way —**nip′pi·ness** *n.*

**nir·va·na** (nir vä′nə, nər-; -van′ə) *n.* [< Sans.] [*also* N-] *Buddhism* the state of perfect blessedness achieved by the extinction of the self and by the absorption of the soul into the supreme spirit, or by the extinction of all desires or passions

**Ni·san** (nē sän′, nis′ən) *n.* [Heb.] the seventh month of the Jewish year: see JEWISH CALENDAR

**ni·sei** (nē′sā) *n., pl.* **ni′sei, ni′seis** [Jap., lit., second generation] [*also* N-] a native U.S. or Canadian citizen born of immigrant Japanese parents

**nit** (nit) *n.* [OE. *hnitu*] **1.** the egg of a louse or similar insect **2.** a young louse, etc.

**ni·ter** (nīt′ər) *n.* [ < MFr. < L. < Gr. *nitron*] same as: **1.** POTASSIUM NITRATE **2.** SODIUM NITRATE Also, chiefly Brit., **ni′tre**

**nit-pick·ing** (nit′pik′iŋ) *adj., n.* paying too much attention to petty details —**nit′-pick′er** *n.*

**ni·trate** (nī′trāt) *n.* [Fr. < *nitre*, NITER] **1.** a salt or ester of nitric acid **2.** potassium nitrate or sodium nitrate, used as a fertilizer —*vt.* **-trat·ed, -trat·ing** to treat or combine with nitric acid or a nitrate —**ni·tra′tion** *n.*

**ni·tric** (nī′trik) *adj.* **1.** of or containing nitrogen **2.** designating or of compounds in which nitrogen has a higher valence than in the corresponding nitrous compounds

**nitric acid** a colorless, corrosive acid, $HNO_3$

**ni·tride** (nī′trīd) *n.* [NITR(O)- + -IDE] a compound of nitrogen with a more electropositive element

**ni·tri·fy** (nī′trə fī′) *vt.* **-fied′, -fy′ing** [ < Fr.: see NITER & -FY] **1.** to impregnate (soil, etc.) with nitrates **2.** to cause the oxidation of (ammonium salts, atmospheric nitrogen, etc.) to nitrites and nitrates, as by the action of soil bacteria, etc. —**ni′tri·fi·ca′tion** *n.* —**ni′tri·fi′er** *n.*

**ni·trite** (nī′trīt) *n.* a salt or ester of nitrous acid

**ni·tro-** [see NITER] *a combining form used to indicate:* **1.** the presence of nitrogen compounds made as by the action of nitric or nitrous acid [*nitrocellulose*] **2.** the presence of the $NO_2$ radical [*nitrobenzene*] Also, before a vowel, **nitr-**

**ni·tro·ben·zene** (nī′trō ben′zēn) *n.* a poisonous yellow liquid, $C_6H_5NO_2$, prepared by treating benzene with nitric acid, used in dyes, etc.

**ni·tro·cel·lu·lose** (-sel′yoo lōs′) *n.* a substance produced by the action of nitric acid upon wood, cotton, etc.: used in making explosives, plastics, etc. —**ni′tro·cel′lu·los′ic** *adj.*

**ni·tro·gen** (nī′trə jən) *n.* [ < Fr.: see NITRO- & -GEN] a colorless, tasteless, odorless gaseous chemical element forming nearly four fifths of the atmosphere: it is a component of all living things: symbol N; at. wt., 14.0067; at. no., 7 —**ni·trog·e·nous** (nī trä′jə nəs) *adj.*

**nitrogen dioxide** a poisonous, reddish-brown gas, $NO_2$, used in making nitric acid, as a rocket-fuel oxidizer, etc.

**nitrogen fixation** **1.** the conversion of atmospheric nitrogen into nitrates by soil bacteria (**nitrogen fixers**) in the nodules of legumes **2.** the conversion of free nitrogen into useful nitrogenous compounds by various industrial processes —**ni′tro·gen-fix′ing** *adj.*

**ni·trog·e·nize** (nī träj′ə nīz′, nī′trə jə-) *vt.* **-nized′, -niz′ing** to combine with nitrogen or its compounds

**nitrogen mustard** any of a class of compounds similar to mustard gas, used in cancer research and treatment

**ni·tro·glyc·er·in, ni·tro·glyc·er·ine** (nī′trə glis′ər in, -trō-) *n.* a thick, explosive oil, $C_3H_5(ONO_2)_3$, prepared by treating glycerin with a mixture of nitric and sulfuric acids: used in medicine and in making dynamites and propellants

**ni·trous** (nī′trəs) *adj.* **1.** of, like, or containing niter **2.** designating or of compounds in which nitrogen has a lower valence than in the corresponding nitric compounds

**nitrous acid** an acid, $HNO_2$, known only in solution or in the form of its salts (*nitrites*)

**nitrous oxide** a colorless, nonflammable gas, $N_2O$, used as an anesthetic and in aerosols

**nit·ty** (nit′ē) *adj.* **-ti·er, -ti·est** full of nits

**nit·ty-grit·ty** (-grit′ē) *n.* [rhyming extension of GRITTY] [Slang] the actual, basic facts, elements, issues, etc.

**nit·wit** (nit′wit′) *n.* [*nit* ( < G. dial. for G. *nicht*, not) or ? NIT + WIT[1]] a stupid person

**nix[1]** (niks) *n., pl.* **nix′es**, G. **nix′e** (nik′sə) [G.] *Germanic Myth.* a water sprite —**nix·ie** (nik′sē) *n.fem.*

**nix[2]** (niks) *adv.* [G. *nichts*] [Slang] **1.** no; not so **2.** not at all —*interj.* [Slang] an exclamation meaning: **1.** stop! **2.** I forbid, refuse, disagree, etc. —*n.* [Slang] **1.** nothing **2.** rejection —*vt.* [Slang] to disapprove of or put a stop to

**Nix·on** (nik′s′n), **Richard M**(ilhous) 1913– ; 37th president of the U.S. (1969-74)

**N.J., NJ** New Jersey

**NLRB, N.L.R.B.** National Labor Relations Board

**N.Mex.** New Mexico: also NM, N.M.

**NNE, N.N.E., n.n.e.** north-northeast

**NNW, N.N.W., n.n.w.** north-northwest

**no[1]** (nō) *adv.* [OE. *na* < *ne a*, lit., not ever] **1.** [Scot. or Rare] not [*whether or no*] **2.** not in any degree [*no worse*] **3.** nay; not so: the opposite of YES, used to deny, refuse, or disagree —*adj.* not any; not a [*no errors*] —*n., pl.* **noes, nos** **1.** refusal or denial **2.** a negative vote or voter

**no[2]** (nō) *n., pl.* **no** [Jap. *nō*] [*often* N-] a classic form of Japanese drama with music and dancing

**No** *Chem.* nobelium

**No.** **1.** north **2.** northern **3.** number: also **no.**

**NOAA** National Oceanic and Atmospheric Administration

**no-ac·count** (nō′ə kount′) *adj.* [Colloq.] worthless; good-for-nothing —*n.* a shiftless person

**No·ah** (nō′ə) [Heb. *nōaḥ*, lit., rest, comfort] **1.** a masculine name **2.** *Bible* the patriarch commanded by God to build the ark on which he, his family, and two of every kind of creature survived the Flood: Gen. 5:28–10:32

**nob·by** (näb′ē) *adj.* **-bi·er, -bi·est** [ < ? slang *nob*, the head] [Chiefly Brit. Slang] stylish

**No·bel** (nō bel′), **Al·fred Bern·hard** (àl′fred ber′nàrd) 1833–96; Swed. industrialist & inventor of dynamite: established the Nobel prizes

**No·bel·ist** (nō bel′ist) *n.* a person who has been awarded a Nobel prize

**no·bel·i·um** (nō bel′ē əm) *n.* [after *Nobel* Institute in Stockholm, where discovered] a radioactive chemical element produced by the nuclear bombardment of curium: symbol, No; at. wt., 255(?); at. no., 102

**Nobel prizes** annual international prizes given by the Nobel Foundation for distinction in physics, chemistry, medicine, economics, and literature, and for promoting peace

**no·bil·i·ty** (nō bil′ə tē) *n., pl.* **-ties** **1.** a being noble **2.** high station or rank in society **3.** the class of people of noble rank: in Great Britain, the peerage (with *the*)

**no·ble** (nō′b′l) *adj.* **-bler, -blest** [OFr. < L. *nobilis*, lit., well-known] **1.** famous or renowned **2.** having or showing high moral qualities **3.** having excellent qualities **4.** grand; stately [*a noble view*] **5.** of high rank or title; aristocratic —*n.* a person having hereditary rank or title; nobleman; peer —**no′ble·ness** *n.* —**no′bly** *adv.*

**no·ble·man** (-mən) *n., pl.* **-men** a member of the nobility; peer —**no′ble·wom′an** *n.fem., pl.* **-wom′en**

**no·blesse o·blige** (nō bles′ ō blēzh′) [Fr., lit., nobility obliges] the obligation of people of high rank or social position to be kind and generous

**no·bod·y** (nō′bud′ē, -bäd′ē, -bəd ē) *pron.* not anybody; no one —*n., pl.* **-bod′ies** a person of no importance

**nock** (näk) *n.* [ < Scand.] **1.** a notch for holding the string at either end of a bow **2.** the notch in the end of an arrow, for the bowstring

**noc·tu·id** (näk′chōō wid) *n.* [ < ModL. < L. *noctua*, night owl < *nox*, night] any of a large family of moths which fly at night, including many of those flying into lighted houses

**noc·tur·nal** (näk tur′n'l) *adj.* [LL. *nocturnalis* < L. < *nox*, night] **1.** of, done, or happening in the night **2.** active during the night —**noc·tur′nal·ly** *adv.*

**noc·turne** (näk′tərn) *n.* [Fr.] **1.** a painting of a night scene **2.** a romantic, dreamy musical composition, appropriate to night

**nod** (näd) *vi.* **nod′ded, nod′ding** [ME. *nodden*] **1.** to bend the head forward quickly, as in agreement, greeting, command, etc. **2.** to let the head fall forward involuntarily because of drowsiness **3.** to be careless; make a slip **4.** to sway to and fro, as plumes —*vt.* **1.** to bend (the head) forward quickly **2.** to signify (assent, approval, etc.) by doing this —*n.* **1.** a nodding **2.** [N-] the imaginary realm of sleep and dreams: usually **land of Nod**

**nodding acquaintance** a slight, not intimate, acquaintance with a person or thing

**nod·dy** (näd′ē) *n., pl.* **-dies** [ < ? NOD] **1.** a fool; simpleton **2.** a tropical sea bird with dark feathers and a short tail

**node** (nōd) *n.* [L. *nodus*, knot] **1.** a knot; knob; swelling **2.** a central point **3.** *Astron.* either of the two diametrically opposite points at which the orbit of a heavenly body intersects a fundamental plane **4.** *Bot.* that part of a stem from which a leaf starts to grow **5.** *Physics* the point, line, or surface of a vibrating object where there is comparatively no vibration —**nod′al** *adj.*

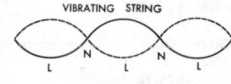

VIBRATING STRING

NODES
(N, nodes formed when vibrating string is stopped at intervals along its length; L, loops between nodes)

**nod·ule** (näj′ōōl) *n.* [L. *nodulus*, dim of *nodus*, a knot] **1.** a small knot or rounded lump **2.** *Bot.* a knot on a root, containing nitrogen-fixing bacteria —**nod′u·lar, nod′u·lose, nod′u·lous** *adj.*

**no·el, no·ël** (nō el′) *n.* [Fr. *noël* < OFr. < L. *natalis*, NATAL] **1.** a Christmas carol **2.** [N-] same as CHRISTMAS

**no-fault** (nō′fôlt′) *adj.* **1.** designating of insurance in which the victim of an accident collects damages although blame for the accident is not established **2.** designating a divorce granted without blame being indicated

**nog, nogg** (näg) *n.* [< East Anglian dial.] 1. [Brit.] a strong ale 2. *same as* EGGNOG

**nog·gin** (näg′in) *n.* [prob. < prec.] 1. a small cup or mug 2. one fourth of a pint: a measure for ale or liquor 3. [Colloq.] the head

**no-good** (nō′good′) *adj.* [Slang] contemptible

**No·gu·chi** (nō goo′chē), **Hi·de·yo** (hē′de yō′) 1876–1928; Jap. bacteriologist in the U.S.

**no-hit·ter** (nō′hit′ər) *n.* a baseball game in which the pitcher allows the opposing team no base hits

**no·how** (nō′hou′) *adv.* [Dial.] in no manner

**noise** (noiz) *n.* [OFr. < L. *nausea:* see NAUSEA] 1. *a)* loud shouting; clamor *b)* any loud, disagreeable sound 2. sound *[the noise of rain]* 3. any unwanted electrical signal within a communication system —*vt.* noised, nois′ing to spread (a report, rumor, etc.)

**noise·less** (-lis) *adj.* with little or no noise; silent —**noise′less·ly** *adv.* —**noise′less·ness** *n.*

**noi·some** (noi′səm) *adj.* [see ANNOY & -SOME¹] 1. injurious to health; harmful 2. foul-smelling; offensive —**noi′some·ly** *adv.* —**noi′some·ness** *n.*

**nois·y** (noi′zē) *adj.* **nois′i·er, nois′i·est** 1. making noise 2. making more sound than is expected or customary 3. full of noise; clamorous —**nois′i·ly** *adv.* —**nois′i·ness** *n.*

‡**no·lens vo·lens** (nō′lenz vō′lenz) [L.] unwilling (or) willing; whether or not one wishes it

**nol·le pros·e·qui** (näl′ē präs′ə kwī′) [L., to be unwilling to prosecute] *Law* formal notice that prosecution in a criminal case or civil suit will be partly or entirely ended

**no·lo con·ten·de·re** (nō′lō kən ten′də rē) [L., I do not wish to contest (it)] *Law* a plea by the defendant in a criminal case declaring that he will not make a defense, but not admitting guilt

**nol-pros** (näl′präs′) *vt.* **-prossed′, -pros′sing** [< abbrev. of NOLLE PROSEQUI] to abandon (all or part of a suit) by entering a nolle prosequi on the court records

**nom.** nominative

**no·mad** (nō′mad) *n.* [< L. < Gr. < *nemein*, to pasture] 1. a member of a tribe or people having no permanent home, but moving about constantly in search of food, pasture, etc. 2. a wanderer —*adj.* wandering: also **no·mad′ic** —**no·mad′i·cal·ly** *adv.* —**no′mad·ism** *n.*

**no man's land** 1. a piece of land to which no one has a recognized title 2. the area on a battlefield separating the combatants 3. an indefinite area of operation, involvement, etc.

**nom de guerre** (näm′ də ger′) *pl.* **noms′ de guerre′** [Fr., lit., a war name] a pseudonym

**nom de plume** (näm′ də ploom′) *pl.* **noms′ de plume′** [Fr.] a pen name; pseudonym

**Nome** (nōm) [< nearby Cape *Nome*, prob. < *? name*, query on an early map, misread as *C. Nome*] city in W Alas., on the Bering Sea: pop. 2,500

**no·men·cla·ture** (nō′mən klā′chər) *n.* [< L. < *nomen*, name + pp. of *calare*, to call] 1. the system of names used in a branch of learning, or for the parts of a mechanism 2. a system of naming

**nom·i·nal** (näm′i n′l) *adj.* [< L. < *nomen*, a name] 1. of, or having the nature of, a name 2. of or having to do with a noun 3. in name only, not in fact *[the nominal leader]* 4. relatively very small *[a nominal fee]* —*n.* a noun; also, any word or phrase, as an adjective, used like a noun —**nom′i·nal·ly** *adv.*

**nom·i·nate** (näm′ə nāt′) *vt.* **-nat′ed, -nat′ing** [< L. < pp. of *nominare* < *nomen*, a name] 1. to name or appoint to an office or position 2. *a)* to name as a candidate for election or appointment *b)* to propose as a candidate for an award or honor —**nom′i·na′tion** *n.* —**nom′i·na′tor** *n.*

**nom·i·na·tive** (näm′ə nə tiv; *for adj. 1, also* -nāt′iv) *adj.* 1. named or appointed to a position or office 2. *Gram.* designating or of the case of the subject of a finite verb and the words (appositives, predicate adjectives, etc.) that agree with it; active case —*n.* 1. the nominative case 2. a word in this case

**nom·i·nee** (näm′ə nē′) *n.* [NOMIN(ATE) + -EE] a person who is nominated, esp. a candidate for election

**-no·my** [< Gr. < *nomos*, law] *a combining form meaning* the systematized knowledge of *[astronomy]*

**non-** [< L. *non*, not] *a prefix meaning* not: used to give a negative force, esp. to nouns, adjectives, and adverbs: *non-* is less emphatic than *in-* and *un-*, which often give a word an opposite meaning (Ex.: *nonhuman, inhuman*) The list below includes the more common compounds formed with *non-* that do not have special meanings; they will be understood if *not* is used before the meaning of the base word

**non·age** (nän′ij, nō′nij) *n.* [< Anglo-Fr. < OFr.: see NON- & AGE] 1. *Law* the state of being under full legal age, usually twenty-one 2. the period of immaturity

**non·a·ge·nar·i·an** (nän′ə ji ner′ē ən, nō′nə-) *adj.* [< L. < *nonaginta*, ninety] ninety years old, or between the ages of ninety and one hundred —*n.* a person of this age

**non·ag·gres·sion pact** (nän′ə gresh′ən) an agreement between two nations not to attack each other, usually for a specified period of years

**non·a·gon** (nän′ə gän′) *n.* [< L. *nonus*, ninth + -GON] a polygon with nine angles and nine sides

**non·a·ligned** (nän′ə līnd′) *adj.* not aligned with either side in a conflict —**non′a·lign′ment** *n.*

**nonce** (näns) *n.* [ME. *(for the) nonce*, formed by syllabic merging < *(for then) ones*, lit., for the once] the present use, occasion, or time; time being: chiefly in **for the nonce**

**nonce word** a word coined and used for a single or particular occasion

**non·cha·lant** (nän′shə länt′, nän′shə lənt) *adj.* [Fr. < *non*, not + *chaloir*, to care for < L. *calere*, to be warm] 1. without warmth or enthusiasm 2. showing cool lack of concern; casually indifferent —**non′cha·lance′** *n.* —**non′cha·lant′ly** *adv.*

**non·com** (nän′käm′) *n. colloq. clipped form of* NONCOMMISSIONED OFFICER

**non·com·bat·ant** (nän käm′bə tənt, nän′kəm bat′ənt) *n.* 1. a member of the armed forces whose activities do not include actual combat, as a chaplain 2. any civilian in wartime —*adj.* of noncombatants

**non·com·mis·sioned officer** (nän′kə mish′ənd) an enlisted person of any of various grades in the armed forces, as, in the U.S. Army, from corporal to sergeant major: see also PETTY OFFICER

**non·com·mit·tal** (-kə mit′′l) *adj.* not committing one to any point of view or course of action —**non′com·mit′tal·ly** *adv.*

**non·com·pli·ance** (-kəm plī′əns) *n.* failure or refusal to comply —**non′com·pli′ant** *adj.*

**non com·pos men·tis** (nän′ käm′pəs men′tis) [L.] *Law* not of sound mind; mentally incapable of handling one's own affairs: often **non compos**

| | | | |
|---|---|---|---|
| nonabrasive | non-Anglican | nonbelieving | nonclassical |
| nonabsorbent | nonantagonistic | nonbelligerent | nonclassifiable |
| nonacademic | nonapologetic | non-Biblical | nonclerical |
| nonacceptance | nonapostolic | nonblooming | nonclinical |
| nonacid | nonappearance | nonbreakable | noncoagulating |
| nonactinic | nonappearing | non-British | noncoalescing |
| nonactive | nonapplicable | non-Buddhist | noncoercive |
| nonaddictive | nonaquatic | nonbudding | noncohesive |
| nonadjacent | non-Arab | nonbureaucratic | noncollapsible |
| nonadjectival | non-Arabic | nonburnable | noncollectable |
| nonadjustable | nonaristocratic | nonbusiness | noncollectible |
| nonadministrative | nonarithmetical | noncaloric | noncollegiate |
| nonadvantageous | nonartistic | noncancerous | noncombat |
| nonadverbial | non-Aryan | noncanonical | noncombining |
| nonaesthetic | non-Asiatic | noncapitalistic | noncombustible |
| nonaffiliated | nonassertive | noncarbonated | noncommercial |
| non-African | nonassessable | noncarnivorous | noncommunicable |
| nonaggressive | nonassignable | noncategorical | noncommunicant |
| nonagreement | nonassimilable | non-Catholic | noncommunicating |
| nonagricultural | nonassimilation | non-Caucasoid | non-Communist |
| nonalcoholic | nonathletic | noncellular | noncompensating |
| nonalgebraic | nonatmospheric | noncereal | noncompetency |
| nonallergenic | nonattendance | noncertified | noncompetent |
| nonallergic | nonattributive | nonchargeable | noncompeting |
| nonalphabetic | nonautomatic | nonchemical | noncompetitive |
| nonamendable | nonbacterial | non-Christian | noncomplacent |
| non-American | nonbasic | noncitizen | noncompletion |
| nonanalytic | nonbeliever | noncivilized | noncomplying |

**non·con·duc·tor** (nän'kən duk'tər) *n.* a substance that does not readily transmit certain forms of energy, as electricity, sound, heat, etc.

**non·con·form·ist** (-kən fôr'mist) *adj.* not following established customs, beliefs, etc. —*n.* a person who is nonconformist; esp. [N-], a Protestant in England who is not a member of the Anglican Church —**non'con·form'ism,** **non'con·form'i·ty** *n.*

**non·co·op·er·a·tion** (-kō äp'ə rā'shən) *n.* **1.** failure to work together or act jointly **2.** refusal to cooperate with a government, as by nonpayment of taxes: used as a form of protest —**non'co·op'er·a'tion·ist** *n.* —**non'co·op'er·a·tive** *adj.* —**non'co·op'er·a'tor** *n.*

**non·de·script** (nän'di skript', nän'di skript') *adj.* [< L. *non,* not + pp. of *describere,* DESCRIBE] belonging to no definite class or type; hard to classify or describe —*n.* a nondescript person or thing

**non·du·ra·ble goods** (-door'ə b'l, -dyoor'-) goods usable for a relatively short time, as food, apparel, or fabrics: also **nondurables** *n.pl.*

**none¹** (nun) *pron.* [OE. *nan* < *ne,* not + *an,* one] **1.** no one; not anyone [*none* but Jack can do it] **2.** [*usually with pl. v.*] no persons or things; not any [there are *none* on the table] —*n.* no part; nothing [I want *none* of it] —*adv.* in no way; not at all [*none* the worse for wear]

**none²** (nōn) *n.* [OE. *non:* see NOON] *Eccles.* [often N-] the fifth of the canonical hours

**non·en·ti·ty** (nän en'tə tē) *n., pl.* -ties **1.** the state of not

existing **2.** something that exists only in the mind **3.** a person of no importance

**nones** (nōnz) *n.pl.* [< L. < *nonus,* ninth < *novem,* nine] **1.** in the ancient Roman calendar, the ninth day before the ides of a month **2.** *same as* NONE²

**non·es·sen·tial** (nän'i sen'shəl) *adj.* not essential; of relatively no importance; unnecessary —*n.* a nonessential person or thing

**none·such** (nun'such') *n.* a person or thing unrivaled or unequaled; nonpareil

**none·the·less** (nun'*th*ə les') *adv.* in spite of that; nevertheless: also **none the less**

**non-Eu·clid·e·an** (nän'yōō klid'ē ən) *adj.* designating or of a geometry that rejects any of Euclid's postulates

**non·fea·sance** (nän fē'z'ns) *n. Law* failure to do what duty requires to be done

**non·fer·rous** (-fer'əs) *adj.* **1.** not made of or containing iron **2.** designating or of metals other than iron

**non·he·ro** (nän'hir'ō) *n. same as* ANTIHERO

**no·nil·lion** (nō nil'yən) *n.* [Fr. < L. *nonus,* ninth + Fr. *million*] **1.** in the U.S. and France, the number represented by 1 followed by 30 zeros **2.** in Great Britain and Germany, the number represented by 1 followed by 54 zeros —*adj.* amounting to one nonillion in number

**non·in·ter·ven·tion** (nän'in tər ven'shən) *n.* the state or fact of not intervening; esp., a refraining by one nation from interference in the affairs of another —**non'in·ter·ven'tion·ist** *adj., n.*

---

| | | | |
|---|---|---|---|
| noncompressible | nondeductible | nonelastic | nonforfeiture |
| noncompression | nondefamatory | nonelective | nonformal |
| noncompulsory | nondefensive | nonelectric | nonfreezing |
| nonconciliating | nondefilement | nonelectrolyte | non-French |
| nonconclusive | nondefining | nonemotional | nonfulfillment |
| nonconcurrence | nondehiscent | nonendemic | nonfunctional |
| noncondensing | nondelivery | nonenforceable | nonfundamental |
| nonconducive | nondemand | non-English | nongaseous |
| nonconducting | nondemocratic | nonentailed | nongenetic |
| nonconferrable | nondenominational | nonepiscopal | non-Germanic |
| nonconfidential | nondepartmental | nonequal | nongovernmental |
| nonconflicting | nondeparture | nonequivalent | nongranular |
| nonconformance | nondependence | nonerotic | non-Greek |
| nonconforming | nondepositor | noneternal | nongregarious |
| noncongealing | nondepreciating | nonethical | nonhabitable |
| noncongenital | nonderivative | noneugenic | nonhabitual |
| non-Congressional | nonderogatory | non-European | nonhabituating |
| nonconnective | nondestructive | nonevangelical | nonhazardous |
| nonconscious | nondetachable | nonevolutionary | non-Hellenic |
| nonconsecutive | nondetonating | nonexchangeable | nonhereditary |
| nonconsent | nondevelopment | nonexclusive | nonheritable |
| nonconservative | nondevotional | nonexcusable | nonhistoric |
| nonconstitutional | nondialectal | nonexecutive | nonhuman |
| nonconstructive | nondictatorial | nonexempt | nonhumorous |
| nonconsultative | nondidactic | nonexistence | nonidentical |
| noncontagious | nondifferentiation | nonexistent | nonidiomatic |
| noncontemporary | nondiffractive | nonexpansive | nonimaginary |
| noncontentious | nondiffusible | nonexpendable | nonimitative |
| noncontiguous | nondiffusing | nonexperienced | nonimmune |
| noncontinental | nondiplomatic | nonexperimental | nonimmunized |
| noncontinuance | nondirectional | nonexpert | nonimportation |
| noncontinuous | nondisappearing | nonexplosive | nonimpregnated |
| noncontraband | nondischarging | nonexportable | noninclusive |
| noncontradictory | nondisciplinary | nonextension | nonindependent |
| noncontributory | nondiscrimination | nonextraditable | non-Indian |
| noncontrolled | nondiscriminatory | nonfactual | nonindictable |
| noncontroversial | nondisparaging | nonfading | nonindividualistic |
| nonconventional | nondisposal | nonfat | nonindustrial |
| nonconvergent | nondistinctive | nonfatal | noninfected |
| nonconvertible | nondivergent | nonfatalistic | noninfectious |
| nonconviction | nondivisible | nonfattening | noninflammable |
| noncoordinating | nondoctrinal | nonfederal | noninflammatory |
| noncorrective | nondocumentary | nonfederated | noninflationary |
| noncorresponding | nondogmatic | nonfertile | noninflectional |
| noncorrodible | nondramatic | nonfestive | noninformative |
| noncorroding | nondrinker | nonfiction | noninheritable |
| noncorrosive | nondriver | nonfictional | noninjurious |
| noncreative | nondrying | nonfigurative | noninstructional |
| noncriminal | nondutiable | nonfilterable | noninstrumental |
| noncritical | nondynastic | nonfinancial | nonintegrated |
| noncrucial | nonearning | nonfireproof | nonintellectual |
| noncrystalline | nonecclesiastical | nonfiscal | nonintelligent |
| nonculpable | noneconomic | nonfissionable | nonintercourse |
| noncumulative | nonedible | nonflammable | noninterference |
| noncurrent | noneditorial | nonflowering | noninternational |
| nondamageable | noneducable | nonflowing | nonintersecting |
| nondecaying | noneducational | nonfluctuating | nonintoxicant |
| nondeceptive | noneffective | nonflying | nonintoxicating |
| nondeciduous | nonefficient | nonfocal | nonintuitive |

---

fat, āpe, cär; ten, ēven; is, bīte; gō, hôrn, tōōl, look; oil, out; up, fur; get; joy; yet; chin; she; thin, then; zh, leisure; ŋ, ring; ə for *a* in *ago,* *e* in *agent,* *i* in *sanity,* *o* in *comply,* *u* in *focus;* ' as in *able* (ā'b'l); Fr. bȧl; ë, Fr. coeur; ö, Fr. feu; Fr. mon; ɔ̃, Fr. coq; ü, Fr. duc; r, Fr. cri; H, G. ich; kh, G. doch; ‡foreign; *hypothetical; < derived from. See inside front cover.

**non·ju·ror** (nän joor'ər) *n.* a person who refuses to take an oath of allegiance, as to his ruler or government —**non·ju'ring** *adj.*

**non·met·al** (-met''l) *n.* an element lacking the characteristics of a metal; specif., any of the elements (e.g., oxygen, carbon, nitrogen, fluorine) whose oxides form acids —**non'me·tal'lic** *adj.*

**non·mor·al** (-môr'əl, -mär'-) *adj.* not connected in any way with morality; not moral and not immoral

**non·nu·cle·ar** (-nōō'klē ər) *adj.* not nuclear; specif., not operated by or using nuclear energy

**non·ob·jec·tive** (nän'əb jek'tiv) *adj. same as* NONREPRESENTATIONAL —**non'ob·jec'tiv·ism** *n.*

**non·pa·reil** (nän'pə rel') *adj.* [Fr. < *non*, not + *pareil*, equal, ult. < L. *par*, equal] unequaled; peerless —*n.* **1.** someone or something unequaled or unrivaled **2.** a small wafer of chocolate covered with tiny sugar pellets **3.** *Printing* a size of type between agate and minion; 6 point

**non·par·ti·san** (nän pär'tə z'n) *adj.* not partisan; esp., not controlled by, or supporting, any single political party: also **non·par'ti·zan** —**non·par'ti·san·ship'** *n.*

**non·per·son** (nän'pur's'n) *n.* a person who is officially ignored by the government of his country

**non·plus** (nän plus', nän'plus') *n.* [L. *non*, not + *plus*, more] a condition of perplexity in which one is unable to go, speak, or act further —*vt.* **-plused'** or **-plussed', -plus'ing** or **-plus'sing** to put in a nonplus; bewilder

**non·pro·duc·tive** (nän'prə duk'tiv) *adj.* **1.** not productive **2.** not directly related to the production of goods, as clerks, salesmen, etc. —**non'pro·duc'tive·ly** *adv.*

**non·prof·it** (nän präf'it) *adj.* not intending or intended to earn a profit

**non·pro·lif·er·a·tion** (nän'prō lif'ə rā'shən) *n.* a not proliferating; specif., the limitation of production of nuclear weapons

**non-pros** (-präs') *vt.* **-prossed', -pros'sing** to enter a judgment of non prosequitur against (a plaintiff or his suit)

**non pro·se·qui·tur** (nän' prō sek'wi tər) [L., he does not prosecute] *Law* a judgment entered against a plaintiff who fails to appear at the court proceedings of his suit

**non·rat·ed** (nän rāt'id) *adj. U.S. Navy* designating an enlisted man who is not a petty officer

**non·rep·re·sen·ta·tion·al** (nän'rep ri zən tā'shən 'l) *adj.* designating or of art that does not attempt to represent in recognizable form any object in nature; abstract —**non'rep·re·sen·ta'tion·al·ism** *n.*

**non·res·i·dent** (nän rez'ə dənt) *adj.* not residing in a specified place; esp., not residing in the locality where one works, attends school, etc. —*n.* a nonresident person —**non·res'i·dence, non·res'i·den·cy** *n.* —**non'res·i·den'tial** *adj.*

**non·re·sist·ant** (nän'ri zis'tənt) *adj.* not resistant; submitting to force or arbitrary authority —*n.* a person who believes that force should not be used to oppose arbitrary authority, however unjust —**non're·sist'ance** *n.*

**non·re·stric·tive** (-ri strik'tiv) *adj. Gram.* designating a clause, phrase, or word felt as not essential to the sense, or purely descriptive, and hence usually set off by commas (Ex.: John, *who is six feet tall*, is younger than Bill)

**non·sched·uled** (nän skej'ōōld) *adj.* designating or of an airline, plane, etc. making commercial flights on demand, not on a regular schedule

**non·sec·tar·i·an** (nän'sek ter'ē ən) *adj.* not sectarian; not confined to any specific religion

**non·sense** (nän'sens, -səns) *n.* [NON- + SENSE] **1.** words or actions that convey an absurd meaning or no meaning at all **2.** things of relatively no importance or value **3.** impudent or foolish behavior —*adj.* designating or of syllables or words constructed so as to have no meaning —*interj.* how foolish! how absurd!

**non·sen·si·cal** (nän sen'si k'l) *adj.* unintelligible, foolish, absurd, etc. —**non·sen'si·cal·ly** *adv.*

**non se·qui·tur** (nän' sek'wi tər) [L., lit., it does not follow] **1.** a conclusion or inference that does not follow

| | | | |
|---|---|---|---|
| noninvolvement | nonnational | nonpoisonous | nonreligious |
| noniodized | nonnative | nonpolitical | nonremovable |
| nonionized | nonnatural | nonporous | nonrenewable |
| nonirradiated | nonnavigable | nonpossession | nonrepayable |
| nonirritant | nonnegotiable | nonpredatory | nonrepentance |
| nonirritating | non-Negro | nonpredictable | nonrepresentative |
| non-Islamic | nonneutral | nonpreferential | nonreproductive |
| non-Jewish | nonnucleated | nonprejudicial | nonresidual |
| nonjudicial | nonnutritious | nonprescriptive | nonresonant |
| non-Latin | nonnutritive | nonproducer | nonrestricted |
| nonlegal | nonobedience | nonprofessional | nonretentive |
| nonlethal | nonobligatory | nonprofessorial | nonretiring |
| nonlicensed | nonobservance | nonprofitable | nonretractile |
| nonlinear | nonobservant | nonprogressive | nonreturnable |
| nonliquefying | nonobstructive | nonprohibitive | nonreversible |
| nonliquid | nonoccupational | nonprolific | nonrevertible |
| nonliquidating | nonoccurrence | nonprophetic | nonrevolving |
| nonliterary | nonodorous | nonproportional | nonrhetorical |
| nonliterate | nonofficial | nonproprietary | nonrhyming |
| nonliving | nonoperating | nonproscriptive | nonrhythmic |
| nonlocal | nonoperational | nonprotective | nonrigid |
| nonmagnetic | nonoperative | nonprotein | nonritualistic |
| nonmailable | non-Oriental | non-Protestant | nonrival |
| nonmaintenance | nonorthodox | nonpsychic | non-Roman |
| nonmalignant | nonoxidizing | nonpublic | nonromantic |
| nonmalleable | nonoxygenated | nonpuncturable | nonrotating |
| nonmarital | nonpalatal | nonpunishable | nonroyal |
| nonmaritime | nonpapal | nonpurulent | nonrural |
| nonmarrying | nonparallel | nonracial | nonsacred |
| nonmartial | nonparasitic | nonradiating | nonsacrificial |
| nonmaterial | nonparental | nonradical | nonsalable |
| nonmaterialistic | nonparishioner | nonradioactive | nonsalaried |
| nonmaternal | nonparliamentary | nonratable | nonsalutary |
| nonmathematical | nonparochial | nonrational | nonsaturated |
| nonmechanical | nonparticipant | nonreactive | non-Scandinavian |
| nonmedicinal | nonpaying | nonreader | nonscholastic |
| nonmelodious | nonpayment | nonrealistic | nonscientific |
| nonmember | nonperceptual | nonreality | nonscoring |
| nonmercantile | nonperforated | nonreciprocal | nonseasonal |
| nonmetaphysical | nonperformance | nonreciprocating | nonsecret |
| nonmetropolitan | nonperiodical | nonrecognition | nonsecretory |
| nonmigratory | nonperishable | nonrecoverable | nonsectional |
| nonmilitant | nonpermanent | nonrecurrent | nonsecular |
| nonmilitary | nonpermeable | nonrecurring | nonsedentary |
| nonmineral | nonpermissible | nonredeemable | nonseditious |
| nonmortal | nonperpendicular | nonrefillable | nonsegregated |
| non-Moslem | nonpersecution | nonregenerating | nonsegregation |
| nonmotile | nonpersistent | nonregimented | nonselective |
| nonmunicipal | nonphilosophical | nonregistered | non-Semitic |
| nonmuscular | nonphysical | nonregistrable | nonsensitive |
| nonmystical | nonphysiological | nonregulation | nonsensitized |
| nonmythical | nonplastic | nonreigning | nonsensory |
| nonnarcotic | nonpoetic | nonrelative | nonsensuous |

from the premises **2.** a remark having no bearing on what has just been said

**non·skid** (nän′skid′) *adj.* so constructed as to reduce skidding: said of a tire tread, etc.

**non·stand·ard** (nän stan′dərd) *adj.* not standard; specif., designating or of locutions, pronunciations, etc. not considered to be standard speech, as slang usages, obscenities, etc.

**non·stop** (-stäp′) *adj., adv.* without a stop

**non·such** (nun′such′) *n. same as* NONESUCH

**non·suit** (nän′sōōt′) *n.* [ < Anglo-Fr.: see NON- & SUIT] *Law* a judgment against a plaintiff due to his failure to proceed to trial or to establish a valid case or adequate evidence —*vt.* to bring a nonsuit against (a plaintiff or his case)

**non·sup·port** (nän′sə pôrt′) *n.* failure to provide for a legal dependent

**non trop·po** (nän trō′pō) [It.] *Music* not too much; moderately

**non·un·ion** (nän yōōn′yən) *n.* failure to mend or unite: said of a broken bone —*adj.* **1.** not belonging to a labor union **2.** not made or serviced under conditions required by a labor union **3.** refusing to recognize a labor union —**non·un′ion·ism** *n.* —**non·un′ion·ist** *n.*

**non·vi·o·lence** (-vī′ə ləns) *n.* an abstaining from violence or physical force, as in opposing government policy —**non·vi′o·lent** *adj.*

**non·vot·er** (nän vōt′ər) *n.* a person who does not vote or is not permitted to vote —**non·vot′ing** *adj.*

**noo·dle**[1] (nōō′d′l) *n.* [prob. < earlier *noddle,* the head] **1.** a simpleton; fool **2.** [Slang] the head

**noo·dle**[2] (nōō′d′l) *n.* [G. *nudel*] a flat, narrow strip of dry dough, usually made with egg and served in soup, etc.

**noo·dle**[3] (nōō′d′l) *vi.* **-dled, -dling** [prob. var. of DOODLE] [Colloq.] **1.** to play idly or improvise on a musical instrument **2.** to explore an idea

**nook** (nook) *n.* [ME. *nok*] **1.** a corner, esp. of a room **2.** a small recess or secluded spot

**noon** (nōōn) *n.* [OE. *non* < L. *nona* (*hora*), ninth (hour): cf. NONES, now recited at midday] **1.** twelve o'clock in the daytime; midday **2.** the highest point or culmination —*adj.* of or occurring at noon (midday)

**noon·day** (-dā′) *n., adj.* noon (midday)

**no one** no person; not anybody; nobody

**noon·time** (-tīm′) *n., adj.* noon (midday): also **noon′tide′**

**noose** (nōōs) *n.* [prob. via Pr. < L. *nodus*] **1.** a loop formed in a rope, cord, etc. by means of a slipknot so that the loop tightens as the rope is pulled **2.** anything that restricts one's freedom; tie, bond, etc. —*vt.* **noosed, noos′ing 1.** to catch or hold as in a noose **2.** to form a noose in (a rope, etc.) —**the noose** death by hanging

**no-par** (nō′pär′) *adj.* having no stated par value [a *no-par* certificate of stock]

**nope** (nōp) *adv.* [Slang] no: a negative reply

**nor** (nôr; *unstressed* nər) *conj.* [ME., contr. of *nother,* neither] and not; and not either: used as the second of the correlatives *neither. . . nor* or after some other negative [I can *neither* go *nor* stay; not for sale, *nor* for rent]

**nor′, nor** (nôr) north: used especially in compounds [*nor′western*]

**Nor. 1.** North **2.** Norway **3.** Norwegian

**No·ra** (nôr′ə) [Ir., dim. of ELEANOR] a feminine name

**Nor·dic** (nôr′dik) *adj.* [ < ModL. < Fr. < *nord,* north < OE. *north*] designating or of a physical type of the Caucasoid peoples exemplified by the long-headed, tall, blond people of Scandinavia

**nor·ep·i·neph·rine** (nôr′ep′ə nef′rin, -rēn) *n.* [ < NOR(MAL) + EPINEPHRINE] a hormone, $C_8H_{11}NO_3$, of the adrenal medulla, that constricts blood vessels, helps transmit nerve impulses, etc.

**Nor·folk** (nôr′fək) [after *Norfolk,* county in England] seaport in SE Va., on Hampton Roads & Chesapeake Bay: pop. 267,000

**Norfolk jacket** (or **coat**) a loose-fitting, single-breasted, belted jacket with box pleats

**Nor·ge** (nôr′gə) *Norw. name of* NORWAY

**no·ri·a** (nôr′ē ə) *n.* [Sp. < Ar. *nā′ūrah*] in Spain and the Orient, a water wheel with buckets at its circumference to raise and discharge water

**norm** (nôrm) *n.* [ < L. *norma,* carpenter's square] a standard, model, or pattern; esp., *a*) a standard of achievement as represented by the average achievement of a large group *b*) an ideal standard of conduct or one typical of a certain group

**Norm.** Norman

**Nor·ma** (nôr′mə) [ < ? L. *norma:* see NORM] a feminine name

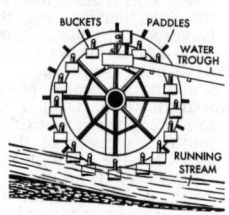

BUCKETS    PADDLES

WATER TROUGH

RUNNING STREAM

NORIA

**nor·mal** (nôr′m′l) *adj.* [ < L. < *norma,* a rule] **1.** conforming with or constituting an accepted standard or norm; esp., corresponding to the average of a large group; natural; usual; regular **2.** naturally occurring [*normal* immunity] **3.** *Chem. a*) designating or of a salt formed by replacing all the replaceable hydrogen of an acid *b*) designating a solution of an acid or base containing 1.00797 grams of hydrogen ions per liter **4.** *Math.* perpendicular; at right angles **5.** *Med., Psychol. a*) free from disease, disorder, etc.; esp., average in intelligence or development *b*) mentally sound —*n.* **1.** anything normal **2.** the usual state, amount, degree, etc. **3.** *Math.* a perpendicular —**nor′mal·cy, nor·mal′i·ty** (-mal′ə tē) *n.*

**nor·mal·ize** (nôr′mə līz′) *vt., vi.* **-ized′, -iz′ing 1.** to bring or come to the normal, or usual, state **2.** to bring or come into conformity with a standard —**nor′mal·i·za′tion** *n.* —**nor′mal·iz′er** *n.*

**nor·mal·ly** (-lē) *adv.* **1.** in a normal manner **2.** under normal circumstances; ordinarily

**normal school** esp. formerly, a school for training high-school graduates to become teachers

**Nor·man**[1] (nôr′mən) **1.** [ < OE. < OHG. *Nordemann,* lit., Northman] a masculine name: dim. *Norm* **2.** [ult. after A. *Norman,* railroad surveyor] city in C Okla., near Oklahoma City: pop. 68,000

**Nor·man**[2] (nôr′mən) *n.* [ < OFr. *Normant* or ML. *Normannus,* both < Frank.] **1.** any of the Scandinavians who oc-

fat, āpe, cär, ten, ēven, is, bīte; gō, hôrn, tōōl, look; oil, out; up, fur; get; joy; yet; chin; she; thin, *then*; zh, leisure; ŋ, ring; ə for *a* in *ago, e* in *agent, i* in *sanity, o* in *comply, u* in *focus;* ′ as in *able* (ā′b′l); Fr. bâl; ë, Fr. coeur; ö, Fr. feu; ô, Fr. mon; ô, Fr. coq; ü, Fr. duc; r, Fr. cri; H, G. ich; kh, G. doch; ‡foreign; *hypothetical; < derived from. See inside front cover.

cupied Normandy in the 10th cent. A.D. **2.** a descendant of the Normans and French who conquered England in 1066 **3.** *same as* NORMAN FRENCH **4.** a native or inhabitant of Normandy —*adj.* of Normandy, the Normans, their language, or culture —**Nor′man·esque′** (-esk′) *adj.*
**Norman Conquest** the conquest of England by the Normans under William the Conqueror in 1066
**Nor·man·dy** (nôr′mən dē) region & former province in NW France, on the English Channel
**Norman French** the French spoken in England by the Norman conquerors; Anglo-French —**Nor′man-French′** *adj.*
**norm·a·tive** (nôr′mə tiv) *adj.* of or establishing a norm, or standard —**norm′a·tive·ly** *adv.*
**Nor·ris** (nôr′is, när′-) **Frank,** (born *Benjamin Franklin Norris, Jr.*) 1870–1902; U.S. novelist
**Norse** (nôrs) *adj.* [prob. < Du. *Noorsch,* a Norwegian < *noord,* north] Scandinavian, esp. West Scandinavian —*n.* **1.** the Scandinavian, esp. the West Scandinavian, group of languages **2.** *same as* NORWEGIAN —**the Norse 1.** the Scandinavians **2.** the West Scandinavians
**Norse·man** (-mən) *n., pl.* **-men** a member of the ancient Scandinavian people; Northman
**north** (nôrth) *n.* [OE.] **1.** the direction to the right of a person facing the sunset (0° or 360° on the compass, opposite south) **2.** a region or district in or toward this direction **3.** [*often* N-] the northern part of the earth, esp. the arctic regions —*adj.* **1.** in, of, to, or toward the north **2.** from the north **3.** [N-] designating the northern part of a country, etc. —*adv.* in or toward the north —**the North** that part of the U.S. bounded on the south by Maryland, the Ohio River, and S Missouri
**North, Frederick,** 2d Earl of Guilford; 1732–92; Eng. statesman; prime minister of Great Britain (1770–82): called *Lord North*
**North America** N continent in the Western Hemisphere: including adjacent islands, c.9,330,000 sq. mi.; pop. 376,000,000 —**North American**
**north·bound** (-bound′) *adj.* going northward
**North Carolina** [see CAROLINA[1]] Southern State of the U.S.: 52,712 sq. mi.; pop. 5,874,000; cap. Raleigh: abbrev. **N.C., NC** —**North Carolinian**
**North Charleston** city in SE S.C., near Charleston: pop. 66,000
**North Dakota** [see DAKOTA[1]] Middle Western State of the U.S.: 70,665 sq. mi.; pop. 653,000; cap. Bismarck: abbrev. **N.Dak., ND** —**North Dakotan**
**north·east** (nôrth′ēst′; *nautical,* nôr-) *n.* **1.** the direction halfway between north and east; 45° east of due north **2.** a region or district in or toward this direction —*adj.* **1.** in, of, to, or toward the northeast **2.** from the northeast, as a wind —*adv.* in, toward, or from the northeast —**the Northeast** the northeastern part of the U.S., esp. New England
**north·east·er** (nôrth′ēs′tər; *nautical,* nôr-) *n.* a storm or strong wind from the northeast
**north·east·er·ly** (-tər lē) *adj., adv.* **1.** in or toward the northeast **2.** from the northeast
**north·east·ern** (-tərn) *adj.* **1.** in, of, or toward the northeast **2.** from the northeast **3.** [N-] of or characteristic of the Northeast or New England —**North′east′ern·er** *n.*
**north·east·ward** (nôrth′ēst′wərd; *nautical,* nôr-) *adv., adj.* toward the northeast: also **north′east′wards** *adv.* —*n.* a northeastward direction, point, or region
**north·east·ward·ly** (-lē) *adj., adv.* **1.** toward the northeast **2.** from the northeast, as a wind
**north·er** (nôr′thər) *n.* a storm or strong wind from the north
**north·er·ly** (-lē) *adj., adv.* **1.** toward the north **2.** from the north
**north·ern** (nôr′thərn) *adj.* **1.** in, of, or toward the north **2.** from the north **3.** [N-] of or characteristic of the North —**north′ern·most′** *adj.*
**north·ern·er** (nôr′thər nər, -thə nər) *n.* a native or inhabitant of the north, specif. [N-] of the northern part of the U.S.
**Northern Hemisphere** that half of the earth north of the equator
**Northern Ireland** division of the United Kingdom, in the NE part of the island of Ireland: 5,462 sq. mi.; pop. 1,512,000; cap. Belfast
**northern lights** *same as* AURORA BOREALIS
**Northern Rhodesia** *former name of* ZAMBIA
**Northern Spy** a yellowish-red winter apple
**Northern Territory** territory of N Australia, on the Pacific
**North Island** N island of the two main islands of New Zealand
**north·land** (nôrth′land′, -lənd) *n.* [*also* N-] the northern region of a country —**north′land′er** *n.*
**North Little Rock** city in C Ark., on the Arkansas River opposite Little Rock: pop. 64,000
**North·man** (-mən) *n., pl.* **-men** *same as* NORSEMAN
**north-north·east** (nôrth′nôrth′ēst′; *nautical,* nôr′nôr-) *n.*

the direction halfway between due north and northeast; 22°30′ east of due north —*adj., adv.* **1.** in or toward this direction **2.** from this direction
**north-north·west** (-west′) *n.* the direction halfway between due north and northwest; 22°30′ west of due north —*adj., adv.* **1.** in or toward this direction **2.** from this direction
**North Pole** the northern end of the earth's axis
**North Sea** arm of the Atlantic, between Great Britain & the European mainland, esp. Norway & Denmark
**North Star** Polaris, the bright star almost directly above the North Pole; polestar
**North·um·bri·a** (nôr thum′brē ə) former Anglo-Saxon kingdom in Great Britain, south of the Firth of Forth
**North·um·bri·an** (-ən) *adj.* of Northumbria, its people, or their dialect —*n.* **1.** a native or inhabitant of Northumbria **2.** the Old English dialect of Northumbria
**north·ward** (nôrth′wərd; *nautical,* nôr′thərd) *adv., adj.* toward the north: also **north′wards** *adv.* —*n.* a northward direction, point, etc.
**north·ward·ly** (-lē) *adj., adv.* **1.** toward the north **2.** from the north
**north·west** (nôrth′west′; *nautical,* nôr-) *n.* **1.** the direction halfway between north and west; 45° west of due north **2.** a district or region in or toward this direction —*adj.* **1.** in, of, or toward the northwest **2.** from the northwest —*adv.* in, toward, or from the northwest —**the Northwest** the northwestern part of the U.S., esp. Wash., Oreg., and Ida.
**north·west·er** (nôrth′wes′tər; *nautical,* nôr-) *n.* a storm or strong wind from the northwest
**north·west·er·ly** (-tər lē) *adj., adv.* **1.** in or toward the northwest **2.** from the northwest
**north·west·ern** (-tərn) *adj.* **1.** in, of, or toward the northwest **2.** from the northwest **3.** [N-] of or characteristic of the Northwest —**North′west′ern·er** *n.*
**Northwest Territories** division of Canada, on the Arctic Ocean: 1,304,903 sq. mi.; pop. 43,000; cap. Yellowknife: abbrev. **N.W.T.**
**Northwest Territory** region north of the Ohio River, between Pa. & the Mississippi (established 1787): it now forms Ohio, Ind., Ill., Mich., Wis., & part of Minn.
**north·west·ward** (nôrth′west′wərd; *nautical,* nôr-) *adv., adj.* toward the northwest: also **north′west′wards** *adv.* —*n.* a northwestward direction, point, or region
**north·west·ward·ly** (-lē) *adj., adv.* **1.** toward the northwest **2.** from the northwest, as a wind
**Norw. 1.** Norway **2.** Norwegian
**Nor·walk** (nôr′wôk′) [< AmInd.] **1.** city in SW Calif.; suburb of Los Angeles: pop. 85,000 **2.** city in SW Conn., on Long Island Sound: pop. 78,000
**Nor·way** (nôr′wā′) country in N Europe, occupying the W & N parts of the Scandinavian Peninsula: 125,064 sq. mi.; pop. 3,851,000; cap. Oslo
**Nor·we·gian** (nôr wē′jən) *adj.* of Norway, its people, their language, etc. —*n.* **1.** a native or inhabitant of Norway **2.** the North Germanic language of the Norwegians
**Nor·wich** (nôr′ij, -ich; när′-) city in E England: pop. 119,000
**Nos., nos.** numbers
**nose** (nōz) *n.* [OE. *nosu*] **1.** the part of the human face between the mouth and the eyes, having two openings for breathing and smelling **2.** the corresponding part in animals; snout, muzzle, etc. **3.** the sense of smell **4.** power to track or perceive as by scent [a *nose* for news] **5.** anything noselike in shape or position; projecting part, as a prow, front of an airplane, etc. —*vt.* **nosed, nos′ing 1.** to discover or perceive as by smell **2.** to rub with the nose **3.** to push with the nose` (with *aside,* etc.) **4.** to push (a way, etc.) with the front forward —*vi.* **1.** to smell; sniff **2.** to pry inquisitively **3.** to advance; move forward —**by a nose 1.** by the length of the animal's nose in horse racing, etc. **2.** by a very small margin —**lead by the nose** to dominate completely —**look down one's nose at** [Colloq.] to be disdainful of —**nose out 1.** to defeat by a very small margin **2.** to discover, as by smelling —**nose over** to turn over on its nose: said of an airplane moving on the ground —**on the nose** [Slang] **1.** that (a specified horse, etc.) will finish first in a race **2.** precisely; exactly —**pay through the nose** to pay an unreasonable price —**turn up one's nose at** to sneer at; scorn —**under one's (very) nose** in plain view
**nose bag** *same as* FEED BAG
**nose·band** (nōz′band′) *n.* that part of a bridle or halter which passes over the animal's nose
**nose·bleed** (-blēd′) *n.* a bleeding from the nose
**nose cone** the cone-shaped foremost part of a rocket or missile, resistant to intense heat
**nose dive 1.** a swift, downward plunge of an airplane, nose first **2.** any sudden, sharp drop —**nose′-dive′** *vi.* **-dived′, -div′ing**
**nose drops** medication administered through the nose with a dropper
**no-see-um** (nō sē′əm) *n.* [alt. after *no see* (th)*em*: in reference to its very small size] *same as* BITING MIDGE

**nose·gay** (nōz′gā′) *n.* [NOSE + GAY (in obs. sense of "gay object")] a small bouquet

**nose·piece** (-pēs′) *n.* **1.** that part of a helmet which protects the nose **2.** *same as* NOSEBAND **3.** anything nose-like in form or position **4.** the bridge of a pair of eyeglasses

**nos·ey** (nō′zē) *adj. nos′i·er, nos′i·est same as* NOSY

**nosh** (näsh) *vt., vi.* [< Yid. < G. *naschen*, to nibble] [Slang] to eat (a snack) —*n.* [Slang] a snack —**nosh′er** *n.*

**no-show** (nō′shō′) *n.* [Colloq.] a person who fails to claim or cancel a reservation, as for a flight

**nos·tal·gia** (näs tal′jə, nəs-, -nôs-; -jē ə) *n.* [ModL. < Gr. *nostos*, a return + -ALGIA] **1.** a longing for home; homesickness **2.** a longing for something far away or of former times —**nos·tal′gic** (-jik) *adj.* —**nos·tal′gi·cal·ly** *adv.*

**nos·tril** (näs′tral) *n.* [OE. *nosthyrl* < *nosu*, nose + *thyrel*, hole] either of the openings into the nose

**nos·trum** (näs′trəm) *n.* [L., ours] **1.** *a)* a medicine made by the person selling it *b)* a quack medicine **2.** a pet scheme for solving some problem

**nos·y** (nō′zē) *adj. nos′i·er, nos′i·est* [Colloq.] prying; inquisitive —**nos′i·ly** *adv.* —**nos′i·ness** *n.*

**Nosy Par·ker** (pär′kər) [NOSY + proper name *Parker*] [*also* n- p-, n- P-] [Colloq.] a nosy person

**not** (nät) *adv.* [ME., unstressed form of *nought*] in no manner; to no degree: a term of negation

‡**no·ta be·ne** (nō′tə bē′nē, nō′tä be′nä) [L.] note well; take particular notice

**no·ta·bil·i·ty** (nōt′ə bil′ə tē) *n.* **1.** *pl.* **-ties** a notable person **2.** the quality of being notable

**no·ta·ble** (nōt′ə b'l) *adj.* [OFr. < L. *notabilis* < *notare*, to note] worthy of notice; remarkable —*n.* a famous or well-known person —**no′ta·bly** *adv.*

**no·tar·i·al** (nō ter′ē əl) *adj.* of or done by a notary public —**no·tar′i·al·ly** *adv.*

**no·ta·rize** (nōt′ə rīz′) *vt.* **-rized′, -riz′ing** to certify or attest (a document) as a notary public —**no′ta·ri·za′tion** *n.*

**no·ta·ry** (nōt′ər ē) *n., pl.* **-ries** [< OFr. < L. < *notare*, to note] *clipped form of* NOTARY PUBLIC

**notary public** *pl.* **notaries public, notary publics** an official authorized to certify or attest documents, take depositions and affidavits, etc.

**no·ta·tion** (nō tā′shən) *n.* [< L. < *notare*, to NOTE] **1.** the use of a system of signs or symbols for words, quantities, etc. **2.** any such system used in algebra, music, etc. **3.** a brief note jotted down **4.** the noting of something in writing —**no·ta′tion·al** *adj.*

**notch** (näch) *n.* [by syllabic merging of ME. *an oche* < OFr. *oche*, a notch] **1.** a V-shaped cut in an edge or surface **2.** a narrow, deep pass; gap **3.** [Colloq.] a step; degree [*a notch below average*] —*vt.* **1.** to cut a notch or notches in **2.** to record or tally, as by notches —**notched** *adj.* —**notch′er** *n.*

**note** (nōt) *n.* [OFr. < L. *nota*, a mark, sign < pp. of *noscere*, to know] **1.** a distinguishing feature [*a note of joy*] **2.** importance or distinction [*a man of note*] **3.** *a)* a brief, written statement of a fact, etc., as to aid memory *b)* [*pl.*] a record of experiences, etc. **4.** a comment or explanation, as at the foot of a page **5.** notice; heed [*worthy of note*]

NOTES
(A, whole; B, half; C, quarter; D, eighth; E, sixteenth; F, thirty-second; G, sixty-fourth)

**6.** *a)* a short, informal letter *b)* a formal diplomatic or other official communication **7.** *a)* any of certain commercial papers relating to debts or payment of money [*a promissory note*] *b)* a piece of paper currency **8.** a cry or call, as of a bird; a signal or intimation [*a note of warning*] **10.** [Archaic] a tune or song **11.** *Music a)* a tone of definite pitch *b)* a symbol for a tone, indicating pitch and duration *c)* a key of a piano, etc. —*vt.* **not′ed, not′ing 1.** to heed; observe **2.** to put in writing; make a note of **3.** to mention specially **4.** to signify or indicate —**compare notes** to exchange views —**take notes** to write down notes, as during a lecture —**note′less** *adj.*

**note·book** (-book′) *n.* a book for memorandums

**not·ed** (nōt′id) *adj.* distinguished; renowned; eminent —**not′ed·ly** *adv.* —**not′ed·ness** *n.*

**note paper** paper for writing notes, or letters

**note·wor·thy** (-wur′thē) *adj.* worthy of note; outstanding; remarkable —**note′wor′thi·ly** *adv.* —**note′wor′thi·ness** *n.*

**noth·ing** (nuth′iŋ) *n.* [OE. *na thing*] **1.** *a)* no thing; not anything *b)* no part, trace, etc. **2.** nothingness **3.** a thing that does not exist **4.** *a)* something of little or no value, importance, etc. *b)* a person considered of no value or importance **5.** a nought; zero —*adv.* not at all —**for nothing 1.** at no cost; free **2.** in vain **3.** without reason —**in nothing flat** [Colloq.] in almost no time at all —**make nothing of 1.** to treat as of little importance **2.** to fail to understand —**nothing but** nothing other than —**nothing doing** [Colloq.] **1.** no: used in refusal **2.** no result, accomplishment, etc. —**nothing less than** no less than: also **nothing short of** —**think nothing of 1.** to attach no importance to **2.** to regard as easy to do

**noth·ing·ness** (-nis) *n.* **1.** nonexistence **2.** lack of value, meaning, etc. **3.** unconsciousness or death **4.** anything nonexistent, useless, etc.

**no·tice** (nōt′is) *n.* [MFr. < L. *notitia* < *notus*: see NOTE] **1.** announcement or warning **2.** a brief mention or review of a book, play, etc. **3.** a written or printed sign giving some public information, warning, or rule **4.** *a)* attention; regard; heed *b)* courteous attention **5.** a formal warning of intention to end an agreement or contract at a certain time [*to give a tenant notice*] —*vt.* **-ticed, -tic·ing 1.** *a)* to refer to or comment on *b)* to review briefly **2.** *a)* to observe; pay attention to *b)* to be courteous or responsive to —**serve notice** to give formal warning, as of intentions; announce —**take notice** to pay attention; observe

**no·tice·a·ble** (-ə b'l) *adj.* **1.** readily noticed; conspicuous **2.** significant —**no′tice·a·bly** *adv.*

**no·ti·fi·ca·tion** (nōt′ə fi kā′shən) *n.* **1.** a notifying or being notified **2.** the notice given or received **3.** the letter, form, etc. notifying

**no·ti·fy** (nōt′ə fī′) *vt.* **-fied′, -fy′ing** [< MFr. < L. < *notus* (see NOTE) + *facere*, to make] **1.** to give notice to; inform **2.** [Chiefly Brit.] to give notice of; announce —**no′ti·fi′er** *n.*

**no·tion** (nō′shən) *n.* [Fr. < L. < *notus*: see NOTE] **1.** *a)* a mental image *b)* a vague thought **2.** a belief; opinion; view **3.** an inclination; whim **4.** an intention **5.** [*pl.*] small, useful articles, as needles, thread, etc., sold in a store

**no·tion·al** (-'l) *adj.* **1.** of or expressing notions, or concepts **2.** imaginary; not actual **3.** having visionary ideas; fanciful

**no·to·ri·e·ty** (nōt′ə rī′ə tē) *n.* the quality or state of being notorious

**no·to·ri·ous** (nō tôr′ē əs) *adj.* [ML. *notorius* < LL. < L. *notus*: see NOTE] **1.** well-known **2.** widely but unfavorably known or talked about —**no·to′ri·ous·ly** *adv.* —**no·to′ri·ous·ness** *n.*

**no-trump** (nō′trump′) *adj. Bridge* with no suit being trumps —*n. Bridge* a no-trump bid or hand

**Not·ting·ham** (nät′iŋ əm) city in C England: pop. 305,000

**not·with·stand·ing** (nät′with stan′diŋ, -with-) *prep.* in spite of [*he flew on, notwithstanding the storm*] —*adv.* all the same; nevertheless [*he will go, notwithstanding*] —*conj.* although

**nou·gat** (nōō′gət) *n.* [Fr. < Pr. < *noga* < L. *nux*, nut] a confection of sugar paste with nuts

**nought** (nôt) *n.* [OE. *nowiht* < *ne*, not + *awiht*, aught] **1.** nothing **2.** *Arith.* the figure zero (0) —*adj.* [Archaic or Obs.] **1.** worthless **2.** evil —*adv.* [Archaic] in no way; not at all —**set at nought** to defy; scorn

**noun** (noun) *n.* [< OFr. < L. *nomen*, a name] *Gram.* **1.** any of a class of words naming or denoting a person, thing, action, quality, etc. [Ex.: *boy, water,* and *truth* are *nouns*] **2.** any word, phrase, or clause so used —**noun′al** *adj.*

**nour·ish** (nur′ish) *vt.* [< OFr. *norrir* < L. *nutrire*] **1.** to feed or sustain with substances necessary to life and growth **2.** to foster; develop; promote (a feeling, attitude, habit, etc.) —**nour′ish·er** *n.* —**nour′ish·ing** *adj.* —**nour′ish·ing·ly** *adv.*

**nour·ish·ment** (-mənt) *n.* **1.** a nourishing or being nourished **2.** something that nourishes

**nou·veau riche** (nōō′vō rēsh′) *pl.* **nou·veaux riches** (nōō′vō rēsh′) [Fr., newly rich] a newly rich person: often connoting lack of culture

**Nov.** November

**no·va** (nō′və) *n., pl.* **-vae** (-vē), **-vas** [ModL. < L. *nova* (*stella*), new (star)] *Astron.* a star that suddenly becomes vastly brighter and then loses brightness through months or years

**No·va Sco·tia** (nō′və skō′shə) province of SE Canada, consisting of a peninsula & an island at the mouth of the Gulf of St. Lawrence: 21,425 sq. mi.; pop. 829,000; cap. Halifax: abbrev. N.S. —**No′va Sco′tian**

**nov·el** (näv′'l) *adj.* [< OFr. < L. *novellus*, dim. of *novus*, new] new and unusual —*n.* [< It. < L. *novella*, new things < *novellus*] **1.** a relatively long fictional prose narrative with a more or less complex plot **2.** the literary form including all such narratives (with *the*) —**nov′el·is′tic** *adj.*

**nov·el·ette** (näv′ə let′) *n.* a short novel

**nov·el·ist** (näv′'l ist) *n.* a person who writes novels

**nov·el·ize** (näv′ə līz′) *vt.* **-ized′, -iz′ing** to make into or like a novel —**nov′el·i·za′tion** *n.*

**no·vel·la** (nō vel'ə; *It.* nô vel'lä) *n., pl.* **-las, -le** (-ē; *It.* -le) [It.] **1.** a short prose narrative, often satiric, as a tale by Boccaccio **2.** a short novel; novelette

**nov·el·ty** (näv''l tē) *n., pl.* **-ties 1.** the quality of being novel **2.** something novel; innovation **3.** a small, often cheap, cleverly made article, as for play: *usually used in pl.*

**No·vem·ber** (nō vem'bər) *n.* [< OFr. < L. < *novem,* nine: the ancient Roman year began with March] the eleventh month of the year, having 30 days: abbrev. **Nov., N.**

**no·ve·na** (nō vē'nə) *n.* [ML. < L. < *novem,* nine] *R.C.Ch.* a nine-day period of devotions

**nov·ice** (näv'is) *n.* [OFr. < L. *novicius* < *novus,* new] **1.** a person on probation in a religious group before taking vows **2.** a person new to an activity, etc.; beginner

**no·vi·ti·ate** (nō vish'ē it, -āt'; -vish'it) *n.* **1.** the period or state of being a novice **2.** a novice **3.** the quarters of religious novices

**No·vo·cain** (nō'və kān') [L. *nov*(*us*), new + (C)OCAIN(E)] *a trademark for* PROCAINE: also sp. **Novocaine**

**No·vo·kuz·netsk** (nô'vô kōōz nyetsk') city in SC R.S.F.S.R.: pop. 495,000

**No·vo·si·birsk** (-si birsk') city in the SC R.S.F.S.R., on the Ob River: pop. 1,079,000

**now** (nou) *adv.* [OE. *nu*] **1.** *a*) at the present time *b*) at once **2.** at the time referred to; then; next *[now* the war began*]* **3.** *a*) very recently *[he* left just *now] b*) very soon *[he's* leaving just *now]* **4.** with things as they are *[now* I'll never know*] Now* is often used for emphasis or in making transitions *[now* look here*] —conj.* since; seeing that *[now* that you know*] —n.* the present time *[that's* all for *now] —adj.* of the present time *[the now* generation*] —interj.* an exclamation of warning, reproach, etc. —**now and then** sometimes: also **now and again**

**now·a·days** (nou'ə dāz') *adv.* in these days; at the present time —*n.* the present time

**no·way** (nō'wā') *adv.* in no manner; by no means; not at all; nowise: also **no'ways'** (-wāz')

**no·where** (nō'hwer', -wer') *adv.* not in, at, or to any place; not anywhere: also [Dial. or Colloq.] **no'wheres' —n. 1.** a place that is nonexistent, remote, etc. **2.** a place or state of obscurity —**nowhere near** not nearly

**no-win** (-win') *adj.* designating or of a situation, policy, etc. that will be unsuccessful no matter what is done

**no·wise** (-wīz') *adv.* in no manner; noway

**nox·ious** (näk'shəs) *adj.* [< L. < *noxa,* injury < *nocere, to hurt*] harmful to health or morals; injurious; unwholesome —**nox'ious·ly** *adv.* —**nox'ious·ness** *n.*

**noz·zle** (näz'l) *n.* [dim. of NOSE] **1.** a spout at the end of a hose, etc., for controlling a stream of liquid or gas **2.** [Slang] the nose

**Np** *Chem.* neptunium

**N.P., n.p.** Notary Public

**NRC, N.R.C.** Nuclear Regulatory Commission

**N/S, n/s** *Banking* not sufficient funds: also **N.S.F.**

**N.S. 1.** New Style **2.** Nova Scotia

**N.S.W.** New South Wales

**-n't** a contracted form of *not [aren't]*

**NT, N.T., N.T.** New Testament

**nth** (enth) *adj.* **1.** expressing the ordinal equivalent to *n* **2.** of the indefinitely large or small quantity represented by *n* —**to the nth degree (or power) 1.** to an indefinite degree or power **2.** to an extreme

**nt. wt.** net weight

**nu** (nōō, nyōō) *n.* [Gr.] the thirteenth letter of the Greek alphabet (N, ν)

**nu·ance** (nōō'äns, nyōō'-; nōō äns') *n.* [Fr. < *nuer,* to shade, ult. < L. *nubes,* a cloud] a slight or delicate variation in tone, color, meaning, etc. —**nu'anced** *adj.*

**nub** (nub) *n.* [var. of *knub,* for KNOB] **1.** *a*) a knob or lump *b*) small piece **2.** [Colloq.] the point of a story or gist of a matter

**nub·bin** (nub'in) *n.* [dim. of NUB] **1.** a small or imperfect ear of Indian corn **2.** anything small or undeveloped *[nubbins* of coal]

**nub·ble** (nub''l) *n.* [dim. of NUB] a small knob or lump —**nub'bly** *adj.* **-bli·er, -bli·est**

**nub·by** (-ē) *adj.* **-bi·er, -bi·est** covered with small nubs, or lumps; having a rough, knotted surface *[a nubby* fabric] —**nub'bi·ness** *n.*

**Nu·bi·a** (nōō'bē ə, nyōō'-) region & former kingdom in NE Africa, between the Red Sea & the Sahara, in Egypt & Sudan —**Nu'bi·an** *adj., n.*

**nu·bile** (nōō'b'l, nyōō'-; -bīl) *adj.* [Fr. < L. < *nubere,* to marry] marriageable: said of a young woman with reference to her age or physical development —**nu·bil'i·ty** *n.*

**nu·cle·ar** (nōō'klē ər, nyōō'-) *adj.* **1.** of, like, or forming a nucleus **2.** of or relating to atomic nuclei *[nuclear* energy] **3.** of or operated by atomic energy *[nuclear weapons]* **4.** of, having, or involving nuclear weapons *[nuclear* war]

**nuclear fission** the splitting of the nuclei of atoms, with conversion of some mass into energy, as in an atomic bomb

**nuclear fusion** the fusion of atomic nuclei into a nucleus of

heavier mass, with a resultant loss in the combined mass, which is converted into energy, as in a hydrogen bomb

**nuclear reactor** a device for initiating and maintaining a controlled nuclear chain reaction in a fissionable fuel for the production of energy or additional fissionable material

**nu·cle·ase** (nōō'klē ās', nyōō'-) *n.* [NUCLE(O)- + -ASE] any of various enzymes that speed up the hydrolysis of nucleic acids

**nu·cle·ate** (-it; *also, & for v. always,* -āt') *adj.* having a nucleus —*vt.* **-at'ed, -at'ing** to form into or around a nucleus —*vi.* to form a nucleus —**nu'cle·a'tion** *n.* —**nu'cle·a'tor** *n.*

**nu·cle·i** (nōō'klē ī', nyōō'-) *n. pl. of* NUCLEUS

**nu·cle·ic acid** (nōō klē'ik, nyōō-) any of a group of complex organic acids found esp. in the nucleus of all living cells and essential to life

**nu·cle·o-** *a combining form meaning:* **1.** nucleus **2.** nuclear **3.** nucleic acid Also **nu·cle-**

**nu·cle·o·lus** (nōō klē'ə ləs, nyōō-) *n., pl.* **-li'** (-lī') [ModL. < LL., dim. of L. *nucleus*] a conspicuous, usually spherical body in the nucleus of most cells: also **nu'cle·ole'** —**nu·cle'o·lar** *adj.*

**nu·cle·on** (nōō'klē än', nyōō'-) *n.* [NUCLE(US) + (PROT)ON] a neutron or proton, either of the fundamental particles of the atomic nucleus —**nu'cle·on'ic** *adj.*

**nu·cle·on·ics** (nōō'klē än'iks, nyōō'-) *n.pl.* [*with sing. v.*] the branch of physics dealing with nucleons or with nuclear phenomena

**nu·cle·us** (nōō'klē əs, nyōō'-) *n., pl.* **-cle·i'** (-ī'), **-cle·us·es** [ModL. < L., a kernel] **1.** a central thing or part around which other things or parts are grouped **2.** any center of growth or development **3.** *Astron.* the bright central part of a comet head **4.** *Biol.* the central, usually rounded mass of protoplasm in most plant and animal cells, necessary to growth, reproduction, etc. **5.** *Chem., Physics* the central part of an atom, the fundamental particles of which are the proton and neutron: it carries a positive charge **6.** *Organic Chem.* a stable arrangement of atoms that may occur in many compounds

**nu·clide** (-klīd) *n.* [NUCL(EUS) + -*ide* < Gr. *eidos,* form] a specific type of atom that exists for a measurable time and is characterized by a distinct nuclear structure —**nu·clid'ic** (-klid'ik) *adj.*

**nude** (nōōd, nyōōd) *adj.* [L. *nudus*] completely unclothed or uncovered; naked; bare —*n.* **1.** a nude person **2.** a nude figure in painting, sculpture, etc. **3.** the condition of being nude *[in the nude]* —**nude'ly** *adv.* —**nude'ness** *n.*

**nudge** (nuj) *vt.* **nudged, nudg'ing** [prob. akin to Norw. dial. *nyggja,* to push] to push gently, esp. with the elbow, so as to get attention, etc. —*n.* a gentle push with the elbow, etc. —**nudg'er** *n.*

**nud·ism** (nōō'diz'm) *n.* the practice or cult of going nude for hygienic reasons —**nud'ist** *n., adj.*

**nu·di·ty** (-də tē) *n.* **1.** a being nude; nakedness **2.** *pl.* **-ties** a nude figure, as in art

**nud·nik** (nood'nik) *n.* [< Yid. < Russ.] [Slang] a dull, tiresome person

**nu·ga·to·ry** (nōō'gə tôr'ē, nyōō'-) *adj.* [< L. < pp. of *nugari,* to trifle] **1.** trifling; worthless **2.** not operative; invalid

**nug·get** (nug'it) *n.* [prob. dim. of E. dial. *nug,* lump] a lump, esp. of native gold

**nui·sance** (nōō's'ns, nyōō'-) *n.* [< OFr. < *nuisir* < L. *nocere,* to annoy] an act, thing, person, etc. causing trouble, annoyance, or inconvenience

**nuisance tax** a tax considered a nuisance because paid in very small amounts by the consumer

**null** (nul) *adj.* [< MFr. < L. *nullus,* none < *ne-,* not + *ullus,* any] **1.** without legal force; invalid: usually in **null and void 2.** amounting to nought; nil **3.** of no value, effect, etc.; insignificant **4.** *Math.* designating, of, or being zero

**nul·li·fy** (nul'ə fī') *vt.* **-fied', -fy'ing** [< LL. < L. *nullus,* none + *facere,* to make] **1.** to make legally null; make void **2.** to make valueless or useless **3.** to cancel out —**nul'li·fi·ca'tion** *n.* —**nul'li·fi'er** *n.*

**nul·li·ty** (nul'ə tē) *n.* **1.** a being null **2.** *pl.* **-ties** anything that is null

**Num.** (the book of) Numbers

**num. 1.** number **2.** numeral(s)

**numb** (num) *adj.* [< ME. *nomen,* pp. of *nimen,* to take] weakened in or deprived of the power of feeling or moving; deadened; insensible —*vt.* to make numb —**numb'ly** *adv.* —**numb'ness** *n.*

**num·ber** (num'bər) *n.* [< OE. < L. *numerus*] **1.** a symbol or word, or a group of either of these, showing how many or which one in a series: see CARDINAL NUMBER, ORDINAL NUMBER **2.** [*pl.*] *same as* ARITHMETIC **3.** the sum or total of persons or units **4.** a collection of persons or things; assemblage **5.** *a*) *[often pl.]* a large group *b*) *[pl.]* numerical superiority **6.** quantity, as consisting of units **7.** *a*) a single issue of a periodical *[the May number] b*) a single song, skit, etc. in a program **8.** [Colloq.] a person or thing singled out [this hat is a smart *number*] 9. *Gram. a)* the differentiation in form to show whether one or more than one is meant *b)* the form itself See SINGULAR, PLURAL 10. [*pl.*] *a)* metrical form; meter *b)* metrical lines; verses —*vt.* 1. to count; enumerate 2. to give a number to; designate by number 3. to include as one of a group (*among*) 4. to limit the number of [his days are *numbered*] 5. to comprise; total —*vi.* 1. to total; count 2. to be numbered —a **number of** several or many —**beyond** (or **without**) **number** too many to be counted —**do a number on** [Slang] to abuse in some way, as by injuring, cheating, etc. —**get** (or **have**) **one's number** [Slang] to discover (or know) one's true character or motives —**one's number is up** [Slang] one's time to die, suffer punishment, etc. has arrived —**the numbers** an illegal lottery involving small bets on the order of numbers in a tabulation, as of published financial reports: also called **numbers pool** (or **racket,** etc.) —**without number** too numerous to be counted —**num′ber·er** *n.*

**num·ber·less** (-lis) *adj.* 1. innumerable; countless 2. without a number or numbers

**number one** [Colloq.] 1. oneself 2. the first, usually the very best, quality or grade

**Num·bers** (num′bərz) [so named from containing the census of the Hebrews after the Exodus] the fourth book of the Pentateuch in the Bible

**numb·skull** (num′skul′) *n. same as* NUMSKULL

**nu·mer·a·ble** (n$\overline{oo}$′mər ə b′l, ny$\overline{oo}$′-) *adj.* that can be numbered or counted

**nu·mer·al** (-mər əl) *adj.* [< LL. < L. *numerus,* number] of, expressing, or denoting a number or numbers —*n.* a figure, letter, or word, or a group of any of these, expressing a number: see ARABIC NUMERALS, ROMAN NUMERALS

**nu·mer·ate** (-mə rāt′) *vt.* -**at′ed, -at′ing** 1. *same as* ENUMERATE 2. to read as words (numbers expressed in figures)

**nu·mer·a·tion** (n$\overline{oo}$′mə rā′shən, ny$\overline{oo}$′-) *n.* 1. a numbering or counting 2. a system of numbering 3. a numerating (sense 2)

**nu·mer·a·tor** (n$\overline{oo}$′mə rāt′ər, ny$\overline{oo}$′-) *n.* 1. a person or thing that numbers 2. *Math.* the term above the line in a fraction, indicating how many of the specified parts of a unit are taken

**nu·mer·i·cal** (noo mer′i k′l, nyoo-) *adj.* 1. of, or having the nature of, number 2. in or by numbers 3. denoting a number 4. expressed by numbers, not letters —**nu·mer′i·cal·ly** *adv.*

**nu·mer·ol·o·gy** (n$\overline{oo}$′mə räl′ə jē, ny$\overline{oo}$′-) *n.* [< L. *numerus,* a number + -LOGY] divination based on assigning meanings to numbers, as those of birth dates

**nu·mer·ous** (n$\overline{oo}$′mər əs, ny$\overline{oo}$′-) *adj.* [< L. < *numerus,* a number] 1. consisting of many 2. very many —**nu′mer·ous·ly** *adv.* —**nu′mer·ous·ness** *n.*

**Nu·mid·i·a** (n$\overline{oo}$ mid′ē ə, ny$\overline{oo}$-) ancient country in N Africa, mainly in what is now E Algeria —**Nu·mid′i·an** *adj., n.*

**nu·mis·mat·ic** (n$\overline{oo}$′miz mat′ik, ny$\overline{oo}$′-; -mis-) *adj.* [< Fr. < L. *numisma,* a coin < Gr. < *nomizein,* to sanction < *nomos,* law] 1. of coins or medals 2. of or having to do with currency 3. of numismatics

**nu·mis·mat·ics** (-iks) *n.pl.* [*with sing. v.*] the study or collection of coins, medals, etc. —**nu·mis·ma·tist** (n$\overline{oo}$ miz′mə tist, ny$\overline{oo}$-; -mis′-) *n.*

**num·skull** (num′skul′) *n.* [NUM(B) + SKULL] a stupid person; dolt; dunce

**nun** (nun) *n.* [< OE. < LL. *nonna*] a woman devoted to a religious life, esp. in a convent under vows of poverty, chastity, and obedience

**Nunc Di·mit·tis** (nuŋk′ di mit′is, nooŋk′) [L., now thou lettest depart] 1. a hymn based on the words in Luke 2: 29–32 2. [n- d-] *a)* departure or farewell *b)* dismissal

**nun·ci·o** (nun′shē ō′, -sē-) *n., pl.* -**ci·os′** [It. < L. *nuntius,* messenger] an ambassador of the Pope to a foreign state

**nun·ner·y** (nun′ər ē) *n., pl.* -**ner·ies** *a former name for* CONVENT

**nup·tial** (nup′shəl) *adj.* [< L. < *nuptiae,* marriage < pp. of *nubere,* to marry] 1. of marriage 2. of mating —*n.* [*pl.*] a wedding

**Nu·rem·berg** (noor′əm burg′, nyoor′-) city in NC Bavaria, West Germany: pop. 472,000: Ger. name **Nürn·berg** (nürn′berkh′)

**nurse** (nurs) *n.* [< OFr. < LL. < L. *nutrix < nutrire,* to nourish] 1. a woman hired to take full care of another's young child or children 2. a person trained to take care of the sick or aged, assist surgeons, etc. 3. a person or thing that fosters, protects, etc. —*vt.* **nursed, nurs·ing** 1. to give milk from the breast to (an infant) 2. to suck milk from the breast of 3. to take care of (a child or children) 4. to bring up; rear 5. to tend (the sick or aged) 6. to nourish or foster [to *nurse* a grudge] 7. to treat, or try to cure [to

nurse a cold] 8. *a)* to use, handle, etc. carefully, so as to avoid pain, etc. [to *nurse* an injured leg] *b)* to consume, spend, etc. slowly or carefully so as to conserve [to *nurse* a drink] 9. to hold carefully —*vi.* 1. to feed at the breast 2. to suckle a child 3. to tend the sick, etc. as a nurse

**nurse·maid** (-mād′) *n.* a woman hired to take care of a child or children: also **nurs′er·y·maid′**

**nurs·er·y** (nur′sə rē, nurs′rē) *n., pl.* -**er·ies** 1. a room in a home, set aside for the children 2. *same as: a)* NURSERY SCHOOL *b)* DAY NURSERY 3. a place where young trees or plants are raised for sale, etc.

**nurs·er·y·man** (-mən) *n., pl.* -**men** (-mən) one who owns, operates, or works for a nursery (sense 3)

**nursery rhyme** a short poem for children

**nursery school** a prekindergarten school for young children aged usually 3 to 5

**nursing home** a residence providing care for the infirm, chronically ill, disabled, etc.

**nurs·ling** (nurs′liŋ) *n.* 1. a young baby still being nursed 2. anything that is being carefully tended Also **nurse′ling**

**nur·ture** (nur′chər) *n.* [< OFr. < LL. pp. of L. *nutrire,* to nourish] 1. anything that nourishes; food 2. training, upbringing, fostering, etc.: also **nur′tur·ance** 3. the environmental influences as distinguished from genetic nature —*vt.* -**tured, -tur·ing** 1. to nourish 2. to train, rear, foster, etc. —**nur′tur·ant, nur′tur·al** *adj.* —**nur′tur·er** *n.*

**nut** (nut) *n.* [OE. *hnutu*] 1. a dry, one-seeded fruit, consisting of a kernel, often edible, in a woody or leathery shell, as the walnut, chestnut, pecan, acorn, etc. 2. the kernel itself 3. loosely, any hard-shelled fruit keeping more or less indefinitely, as a peanut 4. a small, usually metal block with a center threaded hole for screwing onto a bolt, etc. 5. [Colloq.] the cost of an undertaking that must be recovered before a profit can be made 6. [Slang] *a)* a foolish, crazy, or eccentric person *b)* a devotee; fan See also NUTS —*vi.* **nut′ted, nut′ting** to hunt for or gather nuts —**hard** (or **tough**) **nut to crack** a person or thing hard to understand or deal with —**off one's nut** [Slang] foolish, silly, or crazy

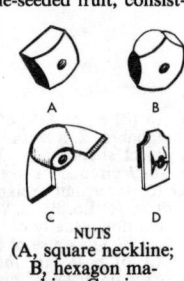

NUTS
(A, square neckline; B, hexagon machine; C, wing; D, snap-on)

**nut·crack·er** (-krak′ər) *n.* a device, usually hinged, for cracking the shells of nuts

**nut·gall** (-gôl′) *n.* a small, nut-shaped gall on the oak and other trees

**nut·hatch** (-hach′) *n.* a small, nut-eating bird with a sharp beak and short tail

**nut·meat** (-mēt′) *n.* the kernel of a nut

**nut·meg** (nut′meg′) *n.* [ME. *notemygge,* partial transl. of OFr. *noiz muscade,* lit., musky nut] 1. the hard, aromatic seed of an East Indian tree: it is grated and used as a spice 2. the tree

**nut·pick** (nut′pik′) *n.* a small, sharp instrument for digging out the kernels of cracked nuts

**nu·tri·a** (n$\overline{oo}$′trē ə, ny$\overline{oo}$′-) *n.* [Sp. < L. *lutra,* otter] 1. a S. American water-dwelling rodent with webbed feet and a long, almost hairless tail 2. its short-haired, soft, brown fur

**nu·tri·ent** (n$\overline{oo}$′trē ənt, ny$\overline{oo}$′-) *adj.* [< L. prp. of *nutrire,* to nourish] nutritious; nourishing —*n.* anything nutritious

**nu·tri·ment** (-trə mənt) *n.* [< L. < *nutrire,* to nourish] anything that nourishes; food

**nu·tri·tion** (n$\overline{oo}$ trish′ən, ny$\overline{oo}$-) *n.* [< L. *nutrire,* to nourish] 1. a nourishing or being nourished; esp., the series of processes by which an organism takes in and assimilates food for promoting growth and repairing tissues 2. nourishment 3. the science or study of proper diet —**nu·tri′tion·al** *adj.* —**nu·tri′tion·al·ly** *adv.* —**nu·tri′tion·ist** *n.*

**nu·tri·tious** (-əs) *adj.* nourishing; of value as food —**nu·tri′tious·ly** *adv.* —**nu·tri′tious·ness** *n.*

**nu·tri·tive** (n$\overline{oo}$′trə tiv, ny$\overline{oo}$′-) *adj.* 1. having to do with nutrition 2. nutritious —**nu′tri·tive·ly** *adv.*

**nuts** (nuts) *adj.* [see NUT, 6] [Slang] crazy; foolish —*interj.* [Slang] an exclamation of disgust, scorn, refusal, etc.: often in the phrase **nuts to** (someone or something) —**be nuts about** [Slang] to love or like very much

**nuts and bolts** [Colloq.] the basic elements or practical aspects of something —**nuts′-and-bolts′** *adj.*

**nut·shell** (nut′shel′) *n.* the shell enclosing the kernel of a nut —**in a nutshell** concisely

**nut·ty** (nut′ē) *adj.* -**ti·er, -ti·est** 1. containing or producing nuts 2. nutlike in flavor 3. [Slang] *a)* very enthusiastic *b)* crazy —**nut′ti·ly** *adv.* —**nut′ti·ness** *n.*

**nux vom·i·ca** (nuks'väm'i kə) [ML. < L. *nux*, nut + *vomere*, to vomit] **1.** the poisonous seed of an Asiatic tree, containing strychnine **2.** the tree
**nuz·zle** (nuz''l) *vt.* **-zled, -zling** [< NOSE] to push against or rub with the nose, snout, etc. —*vi.* **1.** to push or rub with the nose, etc. against or into something **2.** to nestle; snuggle —**nuz'zler** *n.*
**NV** Nevada
**NW, N.W., n.w. 1.** northwest **2.** northwestern
**N.W.T.** Northwest Territories
**N.Y., NY** New York
**Nya·sa** (nyä'sä, nī as'ə), **Lake** lake in SE Africa, between Malawi & Mozambique
**Nya·sa·land** (-land') *former name of* MALAWI
**N.Y.C.** New York City
**nyc·ta·lo·pi·a** (nik'tə lō'pē ə) *n.* [LL. < Gr. < *nyx* (gen. *nyktos*), night + *alaos*, blind + *ōps*, eye] *same as* NIGHT BLINDNESS —**nyc'ta·lop'ic** (-läp'ik) *adj.*
**nyl·ghai** (nil'gī) *n. same as* NILGAI

**ny·lon** (nī'län) *n.* [arbitrary coinage] **1.** a synthetic polymeric amide made into fiber, bristles, etc. of great strength and elasticity **2.** any of the materials made from nylon; specif., [*pl.*] stockings of nylon yarn
**nymph** (nimf) *n.* [< OFr. < L. < Gr. *nymphē*] **1.** *Gr. & Rom. Myth.* any of a group of minor nature goddesses, represented as beautiful maidens living in rivers, trees, etc. **2.** a lovely young woman **3.** *Entomology* the young of an insect with incomplete metamorphosis —**nymph'al, nymph'e·an** *adj.*
**nymph·et** (nim'fət, nim fet') *n.* [< Fr. dim. of *nymphe:* see prec.] a pubescent girl, esp. one who is sexually precocious —**nym·phet'ic** *adj.*
**nym·pho·ma·ni·a** (nim'fə mā'nē ə, -mān'yə) *n.* [ModL. < Gr. *nymphē*, bride, nymph + -MANIA] abnormal and uncontrollable desire by a woman for sexual intercourse —**nym'pho·ma'ni·ac'** (-ak') *adj., n.*
**Nyx** (niks) [Gr.] *Gr. Myth.* the goddess of night
**N.Z., N.Zeal.** New Zealand

# O

**O, o** (ō) *n., pl.* **O's, o's 1.** the fifteenth letter of the English alphabet **2.** a sound of *O* or *o* **3.** the numeral zero **4.** an object shaped like O or o **5.** *Physics the symbol for* ohm —*adj.* circular or oval in shape
**O** (ō) *interj.* an exclamation variously used: **1.** in direct address *[O Lord!]* **2.** to express surprise, fear, wonder, pain, etc.: now usually *oh* **3.** at the end of a line in some ballads —*n., pl.* **O's** a use of this exclamation
**o'** (ə, ō) *prep. an abbreviated form of:* **1.** of *[o'clock]* **2.** [Archaic or Dial.] on
**O 1.** *Linguis.* Old *[OFr.]* **2.** *Chem.* oxygen
**O. 1.** Ocean **2.** October **3.** Ohio **4.** Ontario
**O., o. 1.** octavo **2.** old **3.** [L. *octarius*] *Pharmacy* pint
**oaf** (ōf) *n.* [< ON. *alfr*, elf] a stupid, clumsy fellow; lout —**oaf'ish** *adj.* —**oaf'ish·ly** *adv.* —**oaf'ish·ness** *n.*
**O·a·hu** (ō ä'hōō) [Haw. < ?] chief island of Hawaii, on which Honolulu is located
**oak** (ōk) *n.* see PLURAL, II, D, 3 [OE. *ac*] **1.** a large hardwood tree or bush bearing nuts called *acorns* **2.** its wood **3.** any of various plants resembling an oak —*adj.* of oak: also **oak'en**
**oak apple** an applelike gall on oak trees
**Oak·land** (ōk'lənd) [after *oak* groves orig. there] seaport in W Calif., on San Francisco Bay, opposite San Francisco: pop. 339,000: see SAN FRANCISCO
**Oak Ridge** [after the many *oak* trees there] city in E Tenn.: center for atomic research: pop. 28,000
**oak tag** a kind of sturdy cardboard originally made from oak fibers, used for posters, folders, etc.
**oa·kum** (ō'kəm) *n.* [OE. *acumba* < *a-*, out + *camb*, a comb] loose, stringy, hemp fiber got by taking apart old ropes: used in caulking
**oar** (ôr) *n.* [OE. *ar*] **1.** a long pole with a broad blade at one end, used in rowing **2.** a person who uses an oar; rower —*vt., vi.* to row —**put one's oar in** to meddle —**rest on one's oars** to stop to rest or relax —**oared** *adj.*
**oar·fish** (ôr'fish') *n., pl.* **-fish', -fish'es:** see FISH a narrow, serpentlike, deep-sea fish, up to 30 ft. long, with a fin the length of the back
**oar·lock** (-läk') *n.* a device, often U-shaped, for holding the oar in place in rowing
**oars·man** (ôrz'mən) *n., pl.* **-men** a man who rows; esp., an expert at rowing —**oars'man·ship'** *n.*
**OAS, O.A.S.** Organization of American States
**o·a·sis** (ō ā'sis; *occas.* ō'ə sis) *n., pl.* **-ses** (-sēz) [L. < Gr. *ōasis:* orig. Coptic] **1.** a fertile place in a desert, due to the presence of water **2.** any place or thing offering welcome relief in the midst of difficulty, dullness, etc.
**oat** (ōt) *n.* [OE. *ate*] **1.** [*usually pl.*] *a)* a hardy cereal grass *b)* its edible grain **2.** any related grass; esp., the wild oat **3.** [Obs. or Poet.] a musical pipe made of an oat stalk —**feel one's oats** [Slang] **1.** to be frisky **2.** to feel and act important —**oat'en** *adj.*
**oat·cake** (-kāk') *n.* a thin, flat cake of oatmeal
**oath** (ōth) *n., pl.* **oaths** (ō*th*z, ōths) [OE. *ath*] **1.** *a)* a ritualistic declaration, as by appeal to God, that one will speak the truth, keep a promise, etc. *b)* the thing declared **2.** the profane use of the name of God or of a sacred thing in anger or emphasis **3.** a swearword —**take oath** to promise or declare with an oath

**oat·meal** (ōt'mēl') *n.* **1.** oats ground or rolled into meal or flakes **2.** a porridge made from this
**Ob** (ōb; *Russ.* ôb'y') river in W Siberia, flowing northwest & north into the Arctic Ocean: 2,495 mi.
**ob-** [< L. *ob*] *a prefix meaning:* **1.** to, toward, before *[object]* **2.** opposed to, against *[obnoxious]* **3.** upon, over *[obfuscate]* **4.** completely, totally *[obsolete]* **5.** inversely, oppositely *[objurgate]* In words of Latin origin, *ob-* assimilates to *o-* before *m, oc-* before *c, of-* before *f,* and *op-* before *p*
**OB, O.B. 1.** obstetrician **2.** obstetrics
**ob.** [L. *obiit*] he (or she) died
**O·ba·di·ah** (ō'bə dī'ə) *Bible* **1.** a minor Hebrew prophet **2.** the book containing his prophecies: abbrev. **Ob., Obad.**
**ob·bli·ga·to** (äb'lə gät'ō) *adj.* [It., lit., obliged < L.] *Music* indispensable: said earlier of a required accompaniment but now usually of an optional one —*n., pl.* **-tos, -ti** (-ē) such an accompaniment
**ob·du·rate** (äb'door ət, -dyoor-) *adj.* [< L. pp. of *obdurare* < *ob-*, intens. + *durare*, to harden] **1.** hardhearted **2.** hardened and unrepenting **3.** stubborn —**ob'du·ra·cy** (-ə sē) *n.* —**ob'du·rate·ly** *adv.*
**o·be·di·ence** (ō bē'dē əns, ə-) *n.* the state, fact, or an instance of obeying; a being obedient
**o·be·di·ent** (-ənt) *adj.* [< OFr. < L. prp. of *obedire*, OBEY] obeying or willing to obey; submissive —**o·be'di·ent·ly** *adv.*
**o·bei·sance** (ō bā's'ns, -bē'-) *n.* [< OFr. < prp. of *obeir*, OBEY] **1.** a gesture of respect or reverence, as a bow **2.** homage; deference —**o·bei'sant** *adj.*
**ob·e·lisk** (äb'ə lisk, ōb'ə-) *n.* [< L. < Gr. *obeliskos*, dim. of *obelos*, a spit] a tall, four-sided stone pillar tapering toward its pyramidal top
**O·ber·am·mer·gau** (ō'bər äm'ər gou') village in Bavaria, S West Germany: site of a Passion play performed usually every ten years
**O·ber·hau·sen** (ō'bər hou'z'n) city in W West Germany: pop. 260,000
**O·ber·on** (ō'bə rän', -bər ən) in early folklore, the king of fairyland and husband of Titania
**o·bese** (ō bēs') *adj.* [< L. pp. of *obedere* < *ob-* (see OB-) + *edere*, to eat] very fat —**o·be'si·ty** *n.*
**o·bey** (ō bā', ə-) *vt.* [< OFr. < L. *obedire* < *ob-* (see OB-) + *audire*, to hear] **1.** to carry out the orders of **2.** to carry out (an order) **3.** to be guided by *[to obey one's conscience]* —*vi.* to be obedient —**o·bey'er** *n.* —**o·bey'ing·ly** *adv.*
**ob·fus·cate** (äb'fəs kāt', äb fus'kāt) *vt.* **-cat'ed, -cat'ing** [< L. pp. of *obfuscare* < *ob-* (see OB-) + *fuscare*, to obscure < *fuscus*, dark] **1.** to darken; obscure **2.** to muddle; confuse —**ob'fus·ca'tion** *n.*
**o·bi** (ō'bē) *n.* [Jap.] a broad sash with a bow in back, worn with a Japanese kimono
**o·bit** (ō'bit, äb'it) *n. same as* OBITUARY
**ob·i·ter dic·tum** (äb'i tər dik'təm) *pl.* **ob'i·ter dic'ta** (-tə) [L.] **1.** an incidental opinion expressed by a judge **2.** any incidental remark
**o·bit·u·ar·y** (ō bich'ōō wer'ē, ə-) *n., pl.* **-ar'ies** [ult. < L. *obitus*, death < pp. of *obire*, to die < *ob-* (see OB-) + *ire*,

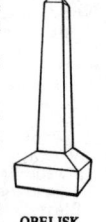

OBELISK

to go] a notice of someone's death, usually with a brief biography —*adj.* of or recording a death or deaths

**obj.** 1. object 2. objection 3. objective

**ob·ject** (äb′jikt; *for v.* əb jekt′, äb-) *n.* [< ML. *objectum,* something thrown in the way < L. pp. of *objicere* < *ob-* (see OB-) + *jacere,* to throw] 1. a thing that can be seen or touched; material thing 2. a person or thing to which action, thought, or feeling is directed 3. aim; purpose; goal 4. *Gram.* a noun or substantive receiving the action of a verb (see DIRECT OBJECT, INDIRECT OBJECT), or one governed by a preposition 5. *Philos.* anything that can be perceived by the mind —*vt.* to state in opposition or disapproval —*vi.* 1. to put forward an objection; be opposed 2. to feel or express disapproval —**ob′ject·less** *adj.* —**ob·jec′tor** *n.*

**object glass** *same as* OBJECTIVE (*n.* 4)

**ob·jec·ti·fy** (əb jek′tə fī′, äb-) *vt.* **-fied′, -fy′ing** to make objective —**ob·jec′ti·fi·ca′tion** *n.*

**ob·jec·tion** (əb jek′shən, äb-) *n.* 1. an objecting 2. a feeling or expression of opposition, disapproval, or dislike 3. a reason for opposing, disapproving, or disliking

**ob·jec·tion·a·ble** (-ə b'l) *adj.* causing objection; disagreeable; offensive —**ob·jec′tion·a·bly** *adv.*

**ob·jec·tive** (əb jek′tiv, äb-) *adj.* 1. of or having to do with a known or perceived object that is not merely in the mind 2. having existence independent of the mind; real 3. concerned with the actual features of the thing dealt with rather than the thoughts, feelings, etc. of the artist, writer, or speaker [an *objective* description] 4. without bias or prejudice 5. being the aim or goal 6. minimizing subjective factors in answering and grading, as a multiple-choice or true-false test 7. *Gram.* designating or of the case of an object (sense 4) —*n.* 1. anything external to or independent of the mind; reality 2. aim; goal 3. *Gram. a)* the objective case *b)* a word in this case 4. *Optics* the lens or lenses nearest the object observed, as in a microscope or telescope —**ob·jec′tive·ly** *adv.* —**ob·jec′tive·ness** *n.*

**ob·jec·tiv·i·ty** (äb′jek tiv′ə tē) *n.* 1. the state or quality of being objective 2. objective reality

**ob·jec·tiv·ize** (əb jek′tə vīz′, äb-) *vt.* **-ized′, -iz′ing** to make objective —**ob·jec′ti·vi·za′tion** *n.*

**object lesson** an actual or practical demonstration or exemplification of some principle

**ob·jet d'art** (äb′zhä där′, ub′-) *pl.* **ob·jets d'art** (äb′zhä-, ub′-) [Fr.] a relatively small object of artistic value, as a figurine, vase, etc.

**ob·jur·gate** (äb′jər gāt′, əb jur′gāt) *vt.* **-gat′ed, -gat′ing** [< L. pp. of *objurgare* < *ob-* (see OB-) + *jurgare,* to chide] to chide vehemently; upbraid sharply; berate —**ob′jur·ga′tion** *n.* —**ob·jur′ga·to′ry** (-gə tôr′ē) *adj.*

**obl.** 1. oblique 2. oblong

**ob·late¹** (äb′lāt, äb lāt′) *adj.* [ModL. *oblatus* < OB- + *-latus* as in *prolatus:* see PROLATE] *Geom.* flattened at the poles [an *oblate* spheroid]

**ob·late²** (äb′lāt) *n.* [< ML. *oblatus* < L. pp. of *offerre,* to OFFER] *R.C.Ch.* a person living in or associated with a religious community but not bound by vows

**ob·la·tion** (ä blā′shən) *n.* [OFr. < L. < *oblatus,* pp. of *offerre:* see OFFER] an offering made to God or a god —**ob·la′tion·al** *adj.*

**ob·li·gate** (äb′lə gāt′) *vt.* **-gat′ed, -gat′ing** [< L. pp. of *obligare:* see OBLIGE] to bind by a contract, promise, sense of duty, etc.

**ob·li·ga·tion** (äb′lə gā′shən) *n.* 1. an obligating or being obligated 2. *a)* a legal or moral responsibility *b)* the thing that such a responsibility binds one to do 3. binding power of a contract, promise, etc. 4. indebtedness for a favor, service, etc. —**ob′li·ga′tion·al** *adj.*

**ob·li·ga·to** (äb′lə gät′ō) *adj., n., pl.* **-tos, -ti** (-ē) *same as* OBBLIGATO

**ob·lig·a·to·ry** (ə blig′ə tôr′ē, äb′lig ə-) *adj.* legally or morally binding; required —**ob·lig′a·to′ri·ly** *adv.* —**ob·lig′a·to′ri·ness** *n.*

**o·blige** (ə blīj′, ō-) *vt.* **o·bliged′, o·blig′ing** [< OFr. < L. *obligare* < *ob-* (see OB-) + *ligare,* to bind] 1. to compel by moral, legal, or physical force; constrain 2. to make indebted for a kindness; do a favor for —*vi.* to do a favor —**o·blig′er** *n.*

**o·blig·ing** (ə blī′jiŋ) *adj.* ready to do favors; helpful; accommodating —**o·blig′ing·ly** *adv.*

**ob·lique** (ə blēk′, ō-; *also, esp. in mil. use,* -blīk′) *adj.* [< L. *obliquus* < *ob-* (see OB-) + *liquis,* awry] 1. neither perpendicular nor horizontal; slanting 2. not straight to the point; indirect 3. evasive, underhanded, etc. 4. indirectly aimed at or attained 5. *Gram.* designating or of any case but the nominative and vocative —*n.* an oblique angle, muscle, etc. —*vi.* **-liqued′, -liqu′ing** to veer from the perpendicular; slant —**ob·lique′ly** *adv.* —**ob·liq·ui·ty** (ə blik′wə tē, ō-), **ob·lique′ness** *n.*

**oblique angle** any angle other than a right angle; acute or obtuse angle

**ob·lit·er·ate** (ə blit′ə rāt′, ō-) *vt.* **-at′ed, -at′ing** [< L. pp. of *obliterare,* to blot out < *ob-* (see OB-) + *litera,* a letter] 1. to blot out or wear away, leaving no traces; efface 2. to do away with; destroy —**ob·lit′er·a′tion** *n.* —**ob·lit′er·a′tive** *adj.* —**ob·lit′er·a′tor** *n.*

**ob·liv·i·on** (ə bliv′ē ən, ō-) *n.* [< OFr. < L. < *oblivisci,* to forget] 1. a forgetting or having forgotten; forgetfulness 2. a being forgotten

**ob·liv·i·ous** (-əs) *adj.* 1. forgetful or unmindful (usually with *of* or *to*) 2. causing forgetfulness —**ob·liv′i·ous·ly** *adv.* —**ob·liv′i·ous·ness** *n.*

**ob·long** (äb′lôŋ) *adj.* [< L. < *ob-* (see OB-) + *longus,* long] longer than broad; elongated; specif., rectangular and longer in one direction than in the other —*n.* an oblong figure

**ob·lo·quy** (äb′lə kwē) *n., pl.* **-quies** [< LL. < *obloqui,* to speak against < *ob-* (see OB-) + *loqui,* to speak] 1. verbal abuse of a person or thing; esp., widespread censure 2. disgrace or infamy resulting from this

**ob·nox·ious** (əb näk′shəs, äb-) *adj.* [< L. < *obnoxius,* in danger < *ob-* (see OB-) + *noxa,* a harm] very unpleasant; objectionable; offensive —**ob·nox′ious·ly** *adv.* —**ob·nox′ious·ness** *n.*

**o·boe** (ō′bō) *n.* [It. < Fr. *hautbois:* see HAUTBOY] a double-reed woodwind instrument having a high, penetrating, melancholy tone —**o′bo·ist** *n.*

**Obs., obs.** obsolete

**ob·scene** (äb sēn′, əb-) *adj.* [< Fr. < L. *obscenus,* filthy, repulsive] 1. offensive to one's feelings, or to prevailing notions, of modesty or decency; lewd 2. disgusting; repulsive —**ob·scene′ly** *adv.* —**ob·scen′i·ty** (-sen′ə tē) *n., pl.* **-ties**

OBOE

**ob·scu·rant·ism** (äb skyoor′ənt·iz′m, əb-) *n.* [< L. *obscurans,* obscuring] 1. opposition to human progress or enlightenment 2. the practice of being deliberately obscure or vague —**ob·scu′rant·ist** *n., adj.*

**ob·scure** (əb skyoor′, äb-) *adj.* [< OFr. < L. *obscurus,* lit., covered over] 1. lacking light; dim; dark [the *obscure* night] 2. not easily perceived; not clear or distinct [an *obscure* figure] 3. not easily understood; vague; ambiguous [an *obscure* answer] 4. in an inconspicuous position; hidden 5. not well-known [an *obscure* scientist] —*vt.* **-scured′, -scur′ing** 1. to make obscure; specif., *a)* to darken; make dim *b)* to conceal from view *c)* to overshadow [success *obscured* his failures] *d)* to confuse [his testimony *obscured* the issue] 2. *Phonet.* to pronounce (a vowel) as (ə) or (i) —**ob·scure′ly** *adv.* —**ob·scure′ness** *n.*

**ob·scu·ri·ty** (-skyoor′ə tē) *n.* 1. the quality or condition of being obscure 2. *pl.* **-ties** an obscure person or thing

**ob·se·quies** (äb′sə kwēz) *n.pl.* [< OFr. < ML. *obsequiae* (pl.) (< L. *obsequium:* see ff.), substituted for L. *exsequiae,* funeral] funeral rites

**ob·se·qui·ous** (əb sē′kwē əs, äb-) *adj.* [< L. < *obsequium,* compliance < *obsequi,* to comply with] showing too great a willingness to serve or obey; fawning —**ob·se′qui·ous·ly** *adv.* —**ob·se′qui·ous·ness** *n.*

**ob·serv·a·ble** (əb zur′və b'l, äb-) *adj.* 1. that can be observed; visible; noticeable 2. deserving of attention 3. that can or must be kept or celebrated [an *observable* holiday] —**ob·serv′a·bly** *adv.*

**ob·serv·ance** (-vəns) *n.* 1. the act or practice of observing a law, duty, custom, etc. 2. a customary act, rite, etc. 3. observation 4. *R.C.Ch.* the rule to be observed by a religious order

**ob·serv·ant** (-vənt) *adj.* 1. strict in observing a rule, custom, etc. (often with *of*) 2. paying careful attention 3. perceptive or alert —**ob·serv′ant·ly** *adv.*

**ob·ser·va·tion** (äb′zər vā′shən) *n.* 1. *a)* the act, practice, or power of noticing *b)* something noticed 2. a being seen or noticed 3. *a)* a noting and recording of facts and events, as for some scientific study *b)* the data so noted and recorded 4. a comment based on something observed 5. the act of determining the altitude of the sun, a star, etc., in order to find a ship's position at sea —*adj.* for observing —**ob′ser·va′tion·al** *adj.*

**ob·serv·a·to·ry** (əb zur′və tôr′ē, äb-) *n., pl.* **-ries** 1. a building or institution equipped for scientific observation, esp. one with a large telescope for astronomical research 2. any building or place providing an extensive view of the surrounding land

**ob·serve** (əb zʉrv′, äb-) *vt.* **-served′, -serv′ing** [< OFr. < L. *observare*, to watch < *ob-* (see OB-) + *servare*, to keep] **1.** to adhere to or keep (a law, custom, duty, etc.) **2.** to celebrate (a holiday, etc.) according to custom **3.** *a)* to notice or perceive (something) *b)* to pay special attention to **4.** to conclude after study **5.** to say casually; remark **6.** to examine scientifically —*vi.* **1.** to take notice or make observations **2.** to comment (*on* or *upon*) —**ob·serv′er** *n.* —**ob·serv′ing·ly** *adv.*

**ob·sess** (əb ses′, äb-) *vt.* [< L. *obsessus*, pp. of *obsidere*, to besiege < *ob-* (see OB-) + *sedere*, to sit] to haunt or trouble in mind, esp. to an abnormal degree; preoccupy greatly —**ob·ses′sive** *adj.* —**ob·ses′sive·ly** *adv.* —**ob·ses′sive·ness** *n.*

**ob·ses·sion** (-sesh′ən) *n.* **1.** the fact or state of being obsessed with an idea, desire, emotion, etc. **2.** such a persistent idea, desire, etc. —**ob·ses′sion·al** *adj.*

**ob·sid·i·an** (əb sid′ē ən, äb-) *n.* [< ModL. < L. *Obsidianus*, a faulty reading for *Obsianus*, after Obsius, who, according to Pliny, discovered it] a hard, dark volcanic glass, used as a gemstone

**ob·so·lesce** (äb′sə les′) *vi.* **-lesced′, -lesc′ing** to be or become obsolescent

**ob·so·les·cent** (-les′′nt) *adj.* in the process of becoming obsolete —**ob′so·les′cence** *n.* —**ob′so·les′cent·ly** *adv.*

**ob·so·lete** (äb′sə lēt′, äb′sə lēt′) *adj.* [< L. pp. of *obsolescere* < *ob-* (see OB-) + *solere*, to become accustomed] **1.** no longer in use or practice; discarded **2.** out-of-date; passé —*vt.* **-let′ed, -let′ing** to make obsolete, as by replacing with something newer —**ob′so·lete′ly** *adv.* —**ob′so·lete′ness** *n.*

**ob·sta·cle** (äb′sti k'l) *n.* [OFr. < L. *obstaculum* < *ob-* (see OB-) + *stare*, to stand] anything that gets in the way or hinders; obstruction

**ob·stet·ric** (əb stet′rik, äb-) *adj.* [< ModL. < L. < *obstetrix*, midwife, lit., she who stands before] of childbirth or obstetrics: also **ob·stet′ri·cal** —**ob·stet′ri·cal·ly** *adv.*

**ob·ste·tri·cian** (äb′stə trish′ən) *n.* a medical doctor who specializes in obstetrics

**ob·stet·rics** (əb stet′riks, äb-) *n.pl.* [*with sing. v.*] the branch of medicine concerned with the care and treatment of women in pregnancy, childbirth, and the period immediately following

**ob·sti·na·cy** (äb′stə nə sē) *n.* **1.** the state or quality of being obstinate **2.** *pl.* **-cies** an obstinate act, attitude, etc.

**ob·sti·nate** (äb′stə nit) *adj.* [< L. pp. of *obstinare*, to resolve on, ult. < *ob-* (see OB-) + *stare*, to stand] **1.** unreasonably determined to have one's own way; stubborn; dogged **2.** resisting treatment [*an obstinate fever*] **3.** not easily subdued, ended, etc. —**ob′sti·nate·ly** *adv.* —**ob′sti·nate·ness** *n.*

**ob·strep·er·ous** (əb strep′ər əs, äb-) *adj.* [< L., ult. < *ob-* (see OB-) + *strepere*, to roar] noisy, boisterous, or unruly, esp. in resisting or opposing —**ob·strep′er·ous·ly** *adv.* —**ob·strep′er·ous·ness** *n.*

**ob·struct** (əb strukt′, äb-) *vt.* [< L. pp. of *obstruere* < *ob-* (see OB-) + *struere*, to pile up] **1.** to block (a passage) with obstacles; clog **2.** to hinder (progress, an activity, etc.); impede **3.** to block (the view) —**ob·struct′er, ob·struc′tor** *n.* —**ob·struc′tive** *adj.* —**ob·struc′tive·ly** *adv.* —**ob·struc′tive·ness** *n.*

**ob·struc·tion** (əb struk′shən, äb-) *n.* **1.** an obstructing or being obstructed **2.** anything that obstructs; hindrance

**ob·struc·tion·ist** (-ist) *n.* anyone who obstructs progress; esp., a member of a legislature who hinders legislation by technical maneuvers —*adj.* of obstructionists: also **ob·struc′tion·is′tic** —**ob·struc′tion·ism** *n.*

**ob·tain** (əb tān′, äb-) *vt.* [< OFr. < L. *obtinere* < *ob-* (see OB-) + *tenere*, to hold] to get possession of by effort; procure —*vi.* to be in force or in effect; prevail [*peace will obtain*] —**ob·tain′a·ble** *adj.* —**ob·tain′er** *n.* —**ob·tain′ment** *n.*

**ob·trude** (əb trōōd′, äb-) *vt.* **-trud′ed, -trud′ing** [< L. *obtrudere* < *ob-* (see OB-) + *trudere*, to thrust] **1.** to thrust forward; push out; eject **2.** to force (oneself, one's opinions, etc.) upon others unasked or unwanted —*vi.* to obtrude oneself (*on* or *upon*) —**ob·trud′er** *n.* —**ob·tru′sion** (-trōō′zhən) *n.*

**ob·tru·sive** (-trōō′siv) *adj.* **1.** inclined to obtrude **2.** obtruding itself —**ob·tru′sive·ly** *adv.* —**ob·tru′sive·ness** *n.*

**ob·tuse** (äb tōōs′, əb-; -tyōōs′) *adj.* [< L. pp. of *obtundere*, to blunt < *ob-* (see OB-) + *tundere*, to strike] **1.** not sharp or pointed; blunt **2.** greater than 90 degrees and less than 180 degrees [*an obtuse angle*] **3.** slow to understand or perceive; dull or insensitive **4.** not acute [*an obtuse pain*] —**ob·tuse′ly** *adv.* —**ob·tuse′ness, ob·tu′si·ty** *n.*

**ob·verse** (äb vʉrs′, əb-; *also, &* *for n. always,* äb′vʉrs) *adj.* [< L.

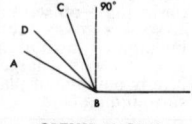

OBTUSE ANGLES
(ABE, DBE, CBE)

pp. of *obvertere* < *ob-* (see OB-) + *vertere*, to turn] **1.** turned toward the observer **2.** narrower at the base than at the top [*an obverse leaf*] **3.** forming a counterpart —*n.* **1.** the side, as of a coin or medal, bearing the main design **2.** the front or main surface of anything **3.** a counterpart —**ob·verse′ly** *adv.*

**ob·vi·ate** (äb′vē āt′) *vt.* **-at′ed, -at′ing** [< L. pp. of *obviare* < *obvius*: see OBVIOUS] to do away with or prevent by effective measures; make unnecessary —**ob′vi·a′tion** *n.*

**ob·vi·ous** (äb′vē əs) *adj.* [L. *obvius*, in the way: see OB- & VIA] easy to see or understand; evident —**ob′vi·ous·ly** *adv.* —**ob′vi·ous·ness** *n.*

**oc-** see OB-

**o/c** overcharge

**Oc., oc.** ocean

**oc·a·ri·na** (äk′ə rē′nə) *n.* [It., dim. of *oca* < LL. *auca*, a goose: from its shape] a small, simple wind instrument with finger holes and a mouthpiece: it produces soft, hollow tones

**O'Ca·sey** (ō kā′sē), **Sean** (shôn) 1880–1964; Ir. playwright

**occas.** **1.** occasion **2.** occasional **3.** occasionally

**oc·ca·sion** (ə kā′zhən) *n.* [< OFr. < L. < pp. of *occidere* < *ob-* (see OB-) + *cadere*, to fall] **1.** a favorable time; opportunity **2.** a fact or event that makes something else possible **3.** *a)* a happening; occurrence *b)* a particular time [*on the occasion of his birth*] **4.** a special time or event, suitable for celebration **5.** need arising from circumstances —*vt.* to give occasion to; cause —**on occasion** once in a while; sometimes —**rise to the occasion** to meet an emergency —**take (the) occasion** to use the opportunity (to do something)

**oc·ca·sion·al** (-'l) *adj.* **1.** occurring on a particular occasion **2.** of or for a special occasion **3.** acting only on special occasions **4.** happening now and then; infrequent —**oc·ca′sion·al·ly** *adv.*

**oc·ci·dent** (äk′sə dənt) *n.* [< OFr. < L. *occidens*, direction of the setting sun < *occidere*: see OCCASION] the west: now rare, except [O-] the part of the world west of Asia, esp. Europe and the Americas —**oc′ci·den′tal, Oc′ci·den′tal** *adj., n.*

**oc·cip·i·tal** (äk sip′ə t'l) *adj.* of the occiput or the occipital bone —*n. same as* OCCIPITAL BONE —**oc·cip′i·tal·ly** *adv.*

**occipital bone** the bone that forms the back part of the skull

**oc·ci·put** (äk′si put′) *n., pl.* **oc·cip′i·ta** (-sip′ə tə), **-puts′** [< MFr. < L. < *ob-* (see OB-) + *caput*, head] the back part of the skull or head

**oc·clude** (ə klōōd′, ä-) *vt.* **-clud′ed, -clud′ing** [< L. *occludere* < *ob-* (see OB-) + *claudere*, to shut] **1.** to close or block (a passage) **2.** to shut in or out **3.** *Chem.* to retain or absorb (a gas, liquid, or solid) —*vi. Dentistry* to meet with the cusps fitting closely —**oc·clud′ent** *adj.* —**oc·clu′sion** (-klōō′zhən) *n.* —**oc·clu′sive** *adj.*

**oc·cult** (ə kult′, ä′kult) *adj.* [< L. pp. of *occulere*, to conceal < *ob-* (see OB-) + *celare*, hide] **1.** hidden **2.** secret; esoteric **3.** beyond human understanding; mysterious **4.** designating or of such alleged mystic arts as alchemy, astrology, etc. —*vt., vi.* to hide or become hidden —**the occult** the occult arts —**oc·cult′ism** *n.* —**oc·cult′ist** *n.* —**oc·cult′ly** *adv.* —**oc·cult′ness** *n.*

**oc·cul·ta·tion** (äk′ul tā′shən) *n.* **1.** the state of becoming hidden or disappearing from view **2.** *Astron.* an eclipse in which the eclipsed body seems much smaller than the eclipsing body

**oc·cu·pan·cy** (äk′yə pən sē) *n., pl.* **-cies** **1.** an occupying; a taking or keeping in possession **2.** *Law* the taking possession of a previously unowned object

**oc·cu·pant** (-pənt) *n.* **1.** one who occupies a house, post, etc. **2.** one who acquires possession by occupancy

**oc·cu·pa·tion** (äk′yə pā′shən) *n.* **1.** an occupying or being occupied; specif., the seizure and control of a country or area by military forces **2.** (one's) trade, profession, or business —**oc′cu·pa′tion·al** *adj.* —**oc′cu·pa′tion·al·ly** *adv.*

**occupational disease** a disease commonly acquired by people in a particular occupation [*silicosis is an occupational disease of miners*]

**occupational therapy** therapy by means of work, as arts and crafts, designed to divert the mind or to correct a physical defect

**oc·cu·py** (äk′yə pī′) *vt.* **-pied′, -py′ing** [< OFr. < L. *occupare*, to possess < *ob-* (see OB-) + *capere*, to seize] **1.** to take possession of by settlement or seizure **2.** to hold possession of by tenure; specif., *a)* to dwell in *b)* to hold (a position or office) **3.** to take up or fill up (space, time, etc.) **4.** to employ or busy (oneself, one's mind, etc.) —**oc′cu·pi′er** *n.*

**oc·cur** (ə kʉr′) *vi.* **-curred′, -cur′ring** [< L. *occurrere* <

*ob-* (see OB-) + *currere*, to run] **1.** to be found; exist /fish *occur* in most waters/ **2.** to present itself; come to mind /an idea *occurred* to him/ **3.** to take place; happen

**oc·cur·rence** (-əns) *n.* **1.** the act or fact of occurring **2.** an event; incident —**oc·cur'rent** *adj.*

**o·cean** (ō'shən) *n.* [ < OFr. < L. *oceanus* < Gr. *Ōkeanos*] **1.** the great body of salt water that covers about 71% of the earth's surface **2.** any of its five principal divisions: the Atlantic, Pacific, Indian, Arctic, or Antarctic Ocean **3.** any great expanse or quantity —**o·ce·an·ic** (ō'shē an'ik) *adj.*

**o·cean·aut** (-ôt') *n.* [ < OCEAN + Gr. *nautēs*, sailor] *same as* AQUANAUT

**o·cean·go·ing** (-gō'iŋ) *adj.* of, having to do with, or made for, travel on the ocean

**O·ce·an·i·a** (ō'shē an'ē ə) islands in the Pacific, including Melanesia, Micronesia, & Polynesia &, sometimes, Australia, New Zealand, & the Malay Archipelago: also **O'ce·an'i·ca** (-i kə) —**O'ce·an'i·an** *adj., n.*

**o·ce·an·og·ra·phy** (ō'shə näg'rə fē, ō'shē ə-) *n.* the study of the environment in the oceans —**o'ce·an·og'ra·pher** *n.* —**o'ce·an·o·graph'ic** (-nə graf'ik), **o'ce·an·o·graph'i·cal** *adj.*

**o·ce·an·ol·o·gy** (-näl'ə jē) *n.* **1.** the study of the sea in all its aspects, including oceanography **2.** *same as* OCEANOGRA-PHY —**o'ce·an·ol'o·gist** *n.*

**ocean sunfish** a large, sluggish ocean fish, with a globelike body and stumpy tail

**o·cel·lus** (ō sel'əs) *n., pl.* **-li** (-ī) [L., dim. of *oculus*, an eye] **1.** the simple eyespot of certain invertebrates **2.** an eyelike spot —**o·cel'lar** *adj.*

**o·ce·lot** (äs'ə lät', ō'sə-) *n., pl.* **-lots**, **-lot**: see PLURAL, II, D, 1 [Fr. < Nahuatl *ocelotl*, jaguar] a large cat of N. and S. America, with a yellow or gray coat marked with black spots

**OCelt.** Old Celtic

**o·cher** (ō'kər) *n.* [ < L. < Gr. < *ōchros*, pale-yellow] **1.** a yellow or reddish-brown clay colored by iron oxide, used as a pigment **2.** the color of this; *esp.*, dark yellow —*vt.* to color with ocher —**o'cher·ous** *adj.*

**o·chre** (ō'kər) *n., vt.* **o'chred**, **o'chring** *alt. sp. of* OCHER —**o'chre·ous** (-kər əs, -krē əs) *adj.*

**-ock** (ək) [OE. *-oc, -uc,* dim.] *a suffix used orig. to form the diminutive [hillock]*

**o'clock** (ə kläk', ō-) *adv.* **1.** of or according to the clock **2.** as if on a clock dial

**oct-** *same as:* **1.** OCTA- **2.** OCTO- Used before a vowel

**Oct.** October

**oct.** octavo

**oc·ta-** [Gr. *okta-* < *oktō*, eight] *a combining form meaning* eight *[octagon]*

**oc·ta·gon** (äk'tə gän') *n.* [ < L. < Gr.: see OCTA- & -GON] a plane figure with eight angles and eight sides —**oc·tag'o·nal** (-tag'ə n'l) *adj.* —**oc·tag'o·nal·ly** *adv.*

**oc·ta·he·dron** (äk'tə hē'drən) *n., pl.* **-drons**, **-dra** (-drə) [ < Gr.: see OCTA- & -HEDRON] a solid figure with eight plane surfaces —**oc'ta·he'dral** *adj.*

**oc·tane** (äk'tān) *n.* [ < OCT(O)- + -ANE] an oily paraffin hydrocarbon, $C_8H_{18}$, found in petroleum

**octane number** (or **rating**) a number representing the antiknock quality of a gasoline, etc.: the higher the number, the greater this quality

**oc·tave** (äk'tiv, -tāv) *n.* [ < OFr. < L. *octavus*, eighth < *octo*, eight] **1.** *a)* the eighth day inclusive following a church festival *b)* the period between the festival and this day **2.** the first eight lines of a sonnet **3.** any group of eight **4.** *Music a)* the eighth full tone above or below a given tone *b)* the interval of eight diatonic degrees between a tone and either of its octaves *c)* the series of tones (a full scale) within this interval, or the keys of an instrument producing such a series *d)* a tone and either of its octaves sounded together —*adj.* consisting of eight, or an octave —**oc·ta·val** (äk tā'v'l, äk'tə v'l) *adj.*

**Oc·ta·vi·an** (äk tā'vē ən) *see* AUGUSTUS (sense 2)

**oc·ta·vo** (äk tā'vō, -tä'-) *n., pl.* **-vos** [ < L. (*in*) *octavo*, (in) eight] **1.** the page size (about 6 by 9 inches) of a book made up of printer's sheets folded into eight leaves **2.** a book with pages of this size Also written **8vo** or **8°** —*adj.* with pages of this size

**oc·tet**, **oc·tette** (äk tet') *n.* [ < OCT(O)- + (DU)ET] **1.** any group of eight; *esp.*, an octave (sense 2) **2.** *Music a)* a composition for eight voices or eight instruments *b)* the eight performers of this

**oc·to-** [Gr. *oktō-* < *oktō*, eight] *a combining form meaning* eight

**Oc·to·ber** (äk tō'bər) *n.* [OE. < L. < *octo*, eight: it was the eighth month of the ancient Roman year] the tenth month of the year, having 31 days: abbrev. **Oct., O.**

**oc·to·ge·nar·i·an** (äk'tə ji ner'ē ən) *adj.* [ < L. < *octoginta*, eighty] eighty years old, or between the ages of eighty and ninety —*n.* a person of this age

**oc·to·pus** (äk'tə pəs) *n., pl.* **-pus·es, -pi'** (-pī'), **oc·top·o·des** (äk täp'ə dēz') [ModL. < Gr. < *oktō*, eight + *pous*, a foot] **1.** a mollusk with a soft body and eight arms covered with suckers **2.** anything suggesting an octopus; *esp.*, a powerful organization with many branches

OCTOPUS
(diameter with outspread arms, from 1 in. to 25 ft.)

**oc·to·roon** (äk'tə rōōn') *n.* [OCTO- + (QUAD)ROON] a person with one eighth Negro ancestry

**oc·tu·ple** (äk'too p'l, -tyoo-; äk tōō'-, -tyōō'-) *adj.* [ < L. < *octo*, eight + *-plus*, -fold] eightfold —*n.* something that is eight times as great as something else —*vt.* **-pled, -pling** to multiply by eight

**oc·u·lar** (äk'yə lər) *adj.* [ < LL. < L. *oculus*, the eye] **1.** of, for, or like the eye **2.** by eyesight /an *ocular* demonstration/ —*n.* the eyepiece of an optical instrument

**oc·u·list** (-list) *n.* [ < Fr. < L. *oculus*, the eye] *earlier term for* OPHTHALMOLOGIST

**OD** (ō'dē') *n., pl.* **ODs, OD's** [Slang] an overdose, *esp.* of a narcotic —*vi.* **OD'd** or **ODed, OD'ing** or **ODing** [Slang] to take an overdose, *esp.* a fatal overdose of a narcotic

**OD, O.D.** **1.** Officer of the Day **2.** olive drab

**o·da·lisque, o·da·lisk** (ōd'''l isk) *n.* [Fr. < Turk. *ōdalik*, chambermaid] a female slave or concubine in a harem

**odd** (äd) *adj.* [ < ON. *oddi*, triangle, hence (from the third angle) odd number] **1.** *a)* remaining or separated from a pair, a set, etc. /an *odd* glove, a few *odd* volumes of Dickens/ *b)* remaining after the others are paired, grouped, taken, etc. **2.** having a remainder of one when divided by two; not even: said of numbers **3.** numbered with an odd number /the *odd* months/ **4.** *a)* in addition to that mentioned in a round number /ten dollars and some *odd* change/ *b)* with a relatively small number over that specified /thirty *odd* years ago/ **5.** occasional; incidental /odd jobs/ **6.** *a)* singular; peculiar *b)* queer; eccentric **7.** out-of-the-way /in *odd* corners/ —**odd'ly** *adv.* —**odd'ness** *n.*

**odd·ball** (-bôl) *n.* [ODD + BALL¹] [Slang] an eccentric or nonconforming person —*adj.* strange or unconventional

**odd·i·ty** (äd'ə tē) *n.* **1.** queerness; peculiarity **2.** *pl.* **-ties** an odd person or thing

**odd·ment** (-mənt) *n.* something odd or left over

**odds** (ädz) *n.pl.* **1.** [Now Rare] difference **2.** difference in favor of one side over the other; advantage **3.** an equalizing advantage given by a bettor or competitor in proportion to the assumed chances in his favor —**at odds** in disagreement; quarreling —**by (all) odds** by far —**the odds are** the likelihood is

**odds and ends** scraps; remnants; oddments

**odds-on** (-än', -ôn') *adj.* having better than an even chance of winning /an *odds-on* favorite/

**ode** (ōd) *n.* [Fr. < LL. < Gr. *ōidē*, song < *aeidein*, to sing] a lyric poem typically addressed to some person or thing and characterized by lofty feeling and dignified style —**od'ic** (ō'dik) *adj.*

**-ode** (ōd) [ < Gr. *hodos*] *a suffix meaning* way, path

**O·der** (ō'dər) river in C Europe, flowing northeast through Czechoslovakia & Poland into the Baltic

**O·des·sa** (ō des'ə; *Russ.* ô de'sä) **1.** seaport in S Ukrainian S.S.R., on the Black Sea: pop. 797,000 **2.** city in WC Tex.: pop. 90,000

**O·din** (ō'din) *Norse Myth.* the chief god: identified with the Teutonic god Woden

**o·di·ous** (ō'dē əs) *adj.* [ < OFr. < L. < *odium:* see ff.] arousing or deserving hatred or loathing; disgusting —**o'di·ous·ly** *adv.* —**o'di·ous·ness** *n.*

**o·di·um** (-əm) *n.* [L. *odium*, hatred < *odi*, I hate] **1.** *a)* hatred *b)* a being hated **2.** the disgrace brought on by hateful action; opprobrium

**O·do·a·cer** (ō'dō ā'sər) 435?-493 A.D.; 1st barbarian ruler of Italy (476-493)

**o·dom·e·ter** (ō däm'ə tər) *n.* [ < Fr. < Gr. < *hodos*, way + *metron*, a measure] an instrument for measuring the distance traveled by a vehicle

**-o·dont** (ə dänt') [ < Gr. *odōn* (gen. *odontos*)] *a combining form meaning* tooth

**o·dont·o-** [see prec.] *a combining form meaning* tooth or teeth: also, before a vowel, **odont-**

**o·don·tol·o·gy** (ō'dän täl'ə jē) *n.* [ < Fr.: see prec. & -LOGY] the science dealing with the structure, growth, and diseases of the teeth —**o·don′to·log′i·cal** (-tə läj′i k'l) *adj.* —**o·don′to·log′i·cal·ly** *adv.* —**o′don·tol′o·gist** *n.*

**o·dor** (ō′dər) *n.* [< OFr. < L.] **1.** *a*) that characteristic of a substance which makes it perceptible to the sense of smell *b*) a smell, whether pleasant or unpleasant; fragrance, stench, etc. **2.** [Archaic] a perfume —**be in bad** (or **ill**) **odor** to be in ill repute —**o′dor·less** *adj.*

**o·dor·if·er·ous** (ō′də rif′ər əs) *adj.* giving off an odor, often, a fragrant one —**o′dor·if′er·ous·ly** *adv.* —**o′dor·if′er·ous·ness** *n.*

**o·dor·ous** (ō′dər əs) *adj.* having an odor; esp., fragrant —**o′dor·ous·ly** *adv.* —**o′dor·ous·ness** *n.*

**o·dour** (ō′dər) *n. Brit. sp. of* ODOR

**-o·dus** (ə dəs) [ModL. < Gr. *-odous* < *odōn*, tooth] *a combining form meaning* having teeth, toothed

**-o·dyn·i·a** (ə din′ē ə, -dīn′-) [ModL. < Gr. < *odynē*, pain] *a combining form meaning* pain in (a specified organ or part)

**O·dys·se·us** (ō dis′yo͞os, -dis′ē əs) the hero of the *Odyssey*, a king of Ithaca and one of the Greek leaders in the Trojan War: Latin name, *Ulysses*

**Od·ys·sey** (äd′ə sē) an ancient Greek epic poem, ascribed to Homer, about the wanderings of Odysseus during the ten years after the fall of Troy —*n.* [*sometimes* o-] *pl.* **-seys** any extended wandering

**oe-** an earlier variant spelling for many words of Gr. and L. origin now usually written with *e*-

**OE., OE, O.E.** Old English

**OED, O.E.D.** Oxford English Dictionary

**Oed·i·pal** (ed′ə pəl, ē′də-) *adj.* [*also* o-] of or relating to the Oedipus complex

**Oed·i·pus** (-pəs) *Gr. Myth.* a king of Thebes who unwittingly killed his father and married his mother

**Oedipus complex** *Psychoanalysis* the unconscious tendency of a child, sometimes unresolved in adulthood, to be attached to the parent of the opposite sex and hostile toward the other parent

**o'er** (ôr) *prep., adv. chiefly poet. contr. of* OVER

**oe·soph·a·gus** (i säf′ə gəs) *n. chiefly Brit. sp. of* ESOPHAGUS

**oes·trus** (es′trəs, ēs′-) *adj. Brit. sp. of* ESTRUS

**of** (uv, äv; *unstressed* əv, ə) *prep.* [OE., unstressed var. of *af*, *æf*, away (from)] **1.** from; specif., *a*) derived or coming from [men *of* Ohio] *b*) as relates to [how wise *of* her] *c*) resulting from; through [to die *of* fever] *d*) at a distance from [east *of* the city] *e*) proceeding as a product from; by [the poems *of* Poe] *f*) separated from [robbed *of* his money] *g*) from the whole constituting [part *of* the time] *h*) made from [a sheet *of* paper] **2.** belonging to [pages *of* a book] **3.** *a*) possessing [a man *of* property] *b*) containing [a bag *of* nuts] **4.** specified as [a height *of* six feet] **5.** with (something specified) as object, goal, etc. [a reader *of* books] **6.** characterized by [a man *of* honor] **7.** concerning; about [think well *of* me] **8.** set aside for [a day *of* rest] **9.** during [*of* late years] **10.** before: used in telling time [ten *of* nine] **11.** [Archaic] by [rejected *of* men] *Of* is also used in various idiomatic expressions, many of which are entered in this dictionary under the key words

**of-** *see* OB-

**off** (ôf) *adv.* [LME. variant of *of*, OF] **1.** so as to be or keep away or at a distance [to move *off*, to ward *off*] **2.** so as to be measured, divided, etc. [to mark *off*] **3.** so as to be no longer on, attached, etc. [take *off* your hat] **4.** (a specified distance) away in space or time [200 yards *off*, two weeks *off*] **5.** so as to be no longer in operation, function, etc. [turn the motor *off*] **6.** so as to be less, smaller, etc. [5% *off* for cash] **7.** so as to lose consciousness [to doze *off*] **8.** away from one's work [take a day *off*] —*prep.* **1.** no longer (or not) on, attached, etc. [the car is *off* the road] **2.** away from [to live *off* the campus] **3.** *a*) from the substance of; on [to live *off* the land] *b*) at the expense of **4.** branching out from [an alley *off* Main Street] **5.** free or relieved from [*off* duty] **6.** not up to the usual level, standard, etc. of [*off* one's game] **7.** [Colloq.] no longer using, supporting, etc. [to be *off* liquor] **8.** [Colloq.] from [to buy it *off* him] —*adj.* **1.** not on, attached, etc. [his hat is *off*] **2.** not in operation, function, etc. [the motor is *off*] **3.** on the way [be *off* to bed] **4.** less, smaller, etc. [sales are *off*] **5.** away from work, etc. [the maid is *off* today] **6.** not up to what is usual, standard, etc. [an *off* day] **7.** more remote; further [on the *off* chance] **8.** designating the horse on the right in double harness, etc. **9.** in (specified) circumstances [to be well *off*] **10.** not correct; in error [his figures are *off*] **11.** *Cricket* designating the side of the field facing the batsman **12.** *Naut.* toward the sea —*n.* the fact or condition of being off —*interj.* go away! stay away! —**off and on** now and then —**off with!** take off! remove! —**off with you!** go away! depart!

**off.** **1.** office **2.** officer **3.** official

**of·fal** (ôf′'l, äf′-) *n.* [ME. *ofall*, lit., off-fall] **1.** [*with sing. or pl. v.*] the entrails, etc. of a butchered animal **2.** refuse; garbage

**off·beat** (ôf′bēt′) *adj.* [< a rhythm in jazz music] [Colloq.] not conforming to the usual pattern or trend; unconventional, unusual, etc.

**off-Broad·way** (-brôd′wā′) *adj., adv.* outside the main commercial theatrical district in New York City —*n.* off-Broadway theaters and their productions Also written **Off Broadway**

**off-col·or** (-kul′ər) *adj.* **1.** varying from the usual, standard, or required color **2.** not quite proper; risqué [an *off-color* joke]

**Of·fen·bach** (ôf′'n bäk′), **Jacques** (zhȧk) (born *Jakob Ebersch*) 1819?–80; Fr. composer, born in Germany

**of·fence** (ə fens′) *n. Brit. sp. of* OFFENSE

**of·fend** (ə fend′) *vi.* [< OFr. < L. *offendere* < *ob*- (see OB-) + *fendere*, to hit] **1.** to commit a sin or crime; do wrong **2.** to create resentment, anger, etc. —*vt.* **1.** to hurt the feelings of; make resentful, angry, etc. **2.** to be displeasing to (the taste, sense, etc.) —**of·fend′er** *n.*

**of·fense** (ə fens′; ō′fens, ä′-) *n.* **1.** an offending; specif., *a*) a breaking of the law; sin or crime *b*) a creating of resentment, anger, etc. **2.** a being offended; esp., a feeling hurt, resentful, or angry **3.** [Rare] something that causes wrongdoing **4.** something that causes resentment, anger, etc. **5.** *a*) the act of attacking *b*) the action of seeking to score in any contest **6.** *a*) the person, army, etc. that is attacking *b*) the side that is seeking to score in any contest —**give offense** to anger, insult, etc.; offend —**take offense** to become offended; feel hurt, angry, etc. —**of·fense′less** *adj.*

**of·fen·sive** (ə fen′siv) *adj.* **1.** attacking; aggressive **2.** of or for attack **3.** designating or of the side that is seeking to score in any contest **4.** unpleasant; disgusting; repugnant [an *offensive* odor] **5.** causing resentment, anger, etc.; insulting —*n.* **1.** attitude or position of attack **2.** an attack or hostile action, esp. by armed forces —**of·fen′sive·ly** *adv.* —**of·fen′sive·ness** *n.*

**of·fer** (ôf′ər, äf′-) *vt.* [OE. *offrian* < LL. *offerre*, to sacrifice < *ob*- (see OB-) + *ferre*, to bring] **1.** to present in an act of worship [to *offer* prayers] **2.** to present for acceptance or consideration [to *offer* one's services, a suggestion, etc.] **3.** to express willingness or intention (to do something) [to *offer* to go] **4.** to show or give signs of [to *offer* resistance] **5.** *a*) to present for sale *b*) to bid (a price, etc.) —*vi.* **1.** to make a presentation in worship **2.** to occur; present itself [when the opportunity *offers*] —*n.* the act of offering or thing offered —**of′fer·er, of′fer·or** *n.*

**of·fer·ing** (-iŋ) *n.* **1.** the act of making an offer **2.** something offered; specif., *a*) a contribution *b*) a presentation made in an act of worship *c*) something offered for sale *d*) a theatrical presentation

**of·fer·to·ry** (ôf′ər tôr′ē, äf′-) *n., pl.* **-ries** [< ML. < LL. *offertorium*, place for offerings < *offerre*, OFFER] [*often* O-] **1.** that part of Holy Communion during which the Eucharistic bread and wine are offered to God **2.** any collection of money at a church service, or the part of the service for this **3.** the prayers or music accompanying the offertory

**off·hand** (ôf′hand′) *adv.* without prior preparation; extemporaneously —*adj.* **1.** said or done offhand; extemporaneous **2.** casual, curt, etc. Also **off′hand′ed** —**off′·hand′ed·ly** *adv.* —**off′hand′ed·ness** *n.*

**of·fice** (ôf′is, äf′-) *n.* [< OFr. < L. *officium* < *opus*, a work + *facere*, to do] **1.** something done for another; (specified kind of) service [done through his good (or ill) *offices*] **2.** an assigned duty, esp. one that is an essential part of one's work; function; task **3.** a position of authority or trust, esp. in a government, business, etc. **4.** *a*) any of the branches of the U.S. Government ranking next below the departments [the Printing *Office*] *b*) [Chiefly Brit.] a governmental department [the Foreign *Office*] **5.** a place where work or business that is clerical, administrative, professional, etc. is carried on **6.** a religious ceremony or rite; specif., *a*) [O-] *shortened form of* DIVINE OFFICE *b*) [*often pl.*] any special rites

**office boy** a boy who works in an office, doing odd jobs and errands

**of·fice·hold·er** (-hōl′dər) *n.* a government official

**of·fi·cer** (ôf′ə sər, äf′-) *n.* **1.** anyone holding an office or position of authority in a government, business, society, etc. **2.** a policeman **3.** a person holding a position of authority in the armed forces; specif., *same as* COMMISSIONED OFFICER **4.** the captain or any of the mates of a nonnaval ship —*vt.* **1.** to provide with officers **2.** to command; direct

**officer of the day** the military officer in overall charge of the interior guard and security of his garrison for any given day

**of·fi·cial** (ə fish′əl) *adj.* **1.** of or holding an office, or position of authority **2.** by, from, or with the proper authority; authorized or authoritative [an *official* request] **3.** formal or ceremonious and often involving persons of authority **4.** formally set or prescribed [the *official* date of publication] —*n.* **1.** a person holding office **2.** *Sports* one who supervises an athletic contest —**of·fi′cial·ly** *adv.*

**of·fi·cial·dom** (-dəm) *n.* **1.** officials collectively **2.** the domain or position of officials

**of·fi·cial·ese** (ə fish'ə lēz') *n.* the pompous, wordy, and involved language typical of official communications and reports

**of·fi·cial·ism** (ə fish'əl iz'm) *n.* **1.** the characteristic practices of officials **2.** officials collectively

**of·fi·ci·ate** (ə fish'ē āt') *vi.* **-at'ed, -at'ing 1.** to perform the duties of an office **2.** to perform the functions of a priest, minister, rabbi, etc. at a religious ceremony **3.** *Sports* to act as referee, umpire, etc. —**of·fi'ci·a'tion** *n.*

**of·fi·cious** (ə fish'əs) *adj.* [< L. < *officium*, OFFICE] offering unwanted advice or services; meddlesome —**of·fi'cious·ly** *adv.* —**of·fi'cious·ness** *n.*

**off·ing** (ôf'iŋ) *n.* [< OFF] **1.** the distant part of the sea visible from the shore **2.** distance, or position at a distance, from the shore —**in the offing 1.** at some distance but in sight **2.** at some indefinite time in the future

**off·ish** (ôf'ish) *adj.* [Colloq.] aloof; standoffish —**off'ish·ly** *adv.* —**off'ish·ness** *n.*

**off-key** (ôf'kē') *adj.* **1.** not on the right note; flat or sharp **2.** not quite in accord with what is normal, fitting, etc.

**off-lim·its** (-lim'its) *adj.* ruled to be a place that cannot be entered, visited, patronized, etc. by a specific group

**off·scour·ing** (-skour'iŋ) *n.* [*usually pl.*] something scoured off; refuse, dregs, etc.

**off·set** (ôf'set'; *for v. usually* ôf set') *n.* **1.** an offshoot; extension; branch; spur **2.** anything that balances or compensates for something else **3.** a ledge formed in a wall by a reduction in its thickness above **4.** *Mech.* a bend in a pipe, etc. to permit it to pass an obstruction **5.** *a*) *same as* OFFSET PRINTING *b*) an impression made by this process —*adj.* **1.** of, relating to, or being an offset **2.** that is offset —*vt.* **-set', -set'ting 1.** to balance, compensate for, etc. **2.** to make an offset in **3.** to make (an impression) by offset printing —*vi.* to project or develop as an offset

**offset printing** a lithographic printing process in which the inked impression is first made on a rubber-covered roller, then transferred to paper

**off·shoot** (ôf'shoot') *n.* **1.** a shoot growing from the main stem of a plant **2.** anything that branches off, or derives from, a main source

**off·shore** (-shôr') *adj.* **1.** moving away from the shore **2.** at some distance from shore **3.** engaged in outside the U.S., as by U.S. banks or manufacturers [*offshore* investments, *offshore* production*]* —*adv.* **1.** away from the shore **2.** outside the U.S. [to borrow money *offshore*]

**off·side** (-sīd') *adj. Sports* not in the proper position for play, as, in football, ahead of the ball before the play has begun —*n.* an offside play

**off·spring** (-spriŋ') *n., pl.* **-spring', -springs' 1.** a child or animal as related to its parent **2.** progeny **3.** a result

**off·stage** (-stāj') *n.* that part of a stage, as the wings, not seen by the audience —*adj.* in or from the offstage —*adv.* **1.** to the offstage **2.** when not actually appearing before the public

**off-white** (-hwīt', -wīt') *adj.* of any of various shades of grayish-white or yellowish-white

**off year 1.** a year in which a major election does not take place **2.** a year of little production, poor crops, etc.

**OFr.** Old French

**oft** (ôft) *adv.* [OE.] *chiefly poet. var. of* OFTEN

**of·ten** (ôf'n, ôf't'n) *adv.* [ME. var. of prec.] many times; frequently —*adj.* [Archaic] frequent

**of·ten·times** (-tīmz') *adv. same as* OFTEN: also [Chiefly Poet.] **oft'times'**

**Og·den** (äg'dən, ôg'-) [after P. *Ogden*, local fur trader] city in N Utah: pop. 64,000

**o·gee** (ō'jē, ō jē') *n.* [< OFr. *ogive*] **1.** an S-shaped curve, line, molding, etc. **2.** a pointed arch formed with the curve of an ogee on each side: also **ogee arch**

**o·gle** (ō'g'l, ä'-) *vi., vt.* **o'gled, o'gling** [prob. < LowG. *oegeln* < *oog*, the eye] to keep looking (at) boldly and with obvious desire; make eyes (at) —*n.* an ogling look —**o'gler** *n.*

**o·gre** (ō'gər) *n.* [Fr. < ? L. *Orcus*, Pluto, Hades] **1.** in fairy tales and folklore, a man-eating monster or giant **2.** a hideous or cruel man —**o'gre·ish, o'grish** *adj.* —**o'gress** *n.fem.*

OGEE ARCH

**oh** (ō) *interj.* **1.** an exclamation of surprise, fear, wonder, pain, etc. **2.** a word used in direct address [*oh,* waiter!] —*n., pl.* **oh's, ohs** any instance of this exclamation

**OH** Ohio

**O. Henry** *see* HENRY

**OHG, OHG., O.H.G.** Old High German

**O·hi·o** (ō hī'ō) **1.** [after the river] Middle Western State of the U.S.: 41,222 sq. mi.; pop. 10,797,000; cap. Columbus: abbrev. **O., OH 2.** [ult. < Iroquoian, lit., large river] river flowing from SW Pa. southwestward into the Mississippi —**O·hi'o·an** *adj., n.*

**ohm** (ōm) *n.* [after G. S. *Ohm* (1789–1854), G. physicist] the mks unit of electrical resistance, equal to the resistance of a circuit in which an electromotive force of one volt maintains a current of one ampere —**ohm'ic** *adj.*

**ohm·me·ter** (-mēt'ər) *n.* an instrument for measuring directly electrical resistance in ohms

**-oid** (oid) [< Gr. < *eidos*, a form, shape] *a suffix meaning* like, resembling [*crystalloid*]

**oil** (oil) *n.* [< OFr. < L. *oleum* < Gr. *elaion*, (olive) oil] **1.** any of various greasy, combustible substances obtained from animal, vegetable, and mineral sources: oils are liquid at ordinary temperatures and soluble in certain organic solvents, as ether, but not in water **2.** *same as* PETROLEUM **3.** any of various substances with the consistency of oil **4.** *same as: a*) OIL COLOR *b*) OIL PAINTING —*vt.* to lubricate or supply with oil —*adj.* of, from, like, or yielding oil, or having to do with the production or use of oil —**oiled** *adj.* —**oil'er** *n.*

**oil cake** a mass of crushed linseed, cottonseed, etc. from which the oil has been extracted, used as livestock feed and as a fertilizer

**oil·cloth** (-klôth', -kläth') *n.* cloth made waterproof with oil or with heavy coats of paint

**oil color** paint made by grinding a pigment in oil

**oil of vitriol** *same as* SULFURIC ACID

**oil painting 1.** a picture painted in oil colors **2.** the art of painting in oil colors

**oil·pa·per** (-pā'pər) *n.* paper made transparent and waterproof by treatment with oil

**oil·skin** (-skin') *n.* **1.** cloth made waterproof by treatment with oil **2.** [*often pl.*] a garment or outfit made of this

**oil slick** a film of oil on water, forming a smooth area

**oil·stone** (-stōn') *n.* a whetstone treated with oil

**oil well** a well bored through layers of rock, etc. to a supply of petroleum

**oil·y** (-ē) *adj.* **oil'i·er, oil'i·est 1.** of, like, or containing oil **2.** covered with oil; greasy **3.** too smooth; unctuous —**oil'i·ly** *adv.* —**oil'i·ness** *n.*

**oink** (oiŋk) *n.* the grunt of a pig, or a sound imitating it —*vi.* to grunt as or like a pig

**oint·ment** (oint'mənt) *n.* [< OFr., ult. < L. *unguentum:* see UNGUENT] a fatty substance applied to the skin as a salve or cosmetic; unguent

**O·jib·wa** (ō jib'wā, -wä, -wə) *n.* [Algonquian *ojibway*, to pucker: from the puckered seam on their moccasins] **1.** *pl.* **-was, -wa** a member of a group of N. American tribes living from Michigan to North Dakota **2.** their Algonquian language —*adj.* of these tribes Also **O·jib'way** (-wā)

**OK, O.K.** (ō'kā'; *also, & for v. & n. usually,* ō'kā') *adj., adv., interj.* [abbrev. for "oll korrect," jocular misspelling of *all correct*] all right; correct —*n., pl.* **OK's, O.K.'s** approval —*vt.* **OK'd, O.K.'d, OK'ing, O.K.'ing** to put an OK on; approve

**OK** Oklahoma

**o·ka·pi** (ō kä'pē) *n., pl.* **-pis, -pi:** see PLURAL, II, D, 1 [native Afr. name] an African animal related to the giraffe, but having a much shorter neck

**o·kay** (ō'kā') *adj., adv., interj., n., vt. colloq. var. of* OK

**O·kee·cho·bee** (ō'kē chō'bē), **Lake** [< AmInd.] lake in SE Fla., at the N edge of the Everglades

**O·ke·fe·no·kee Swamp** (ō'kə fə nō'kē) [< AmInd., lit., trembling earth] swamp in SE Ga. & NE Fla.

**O·khotsk** (ō kätsk'; *Russ.* ô khôtsk'), **Sea** of arm of the Pacific, off the E coast of Siberia

**O·kie** (ō'kē) *n.* [OK(LAHOMA) + -IE] a migratory farm worker, esp. one forced from Oklahoma by drought, farm foreclosure, etc., in the late 1930's

OKAPI
(to 5 ft. high at shoulder)

**O·ki·na·wa** (ō'kə nä'wə) largest island of the Ryukyus, northeast of Taiwan

**O·kla·ho·ma** (ō'klə hō'mə) [< Choctaw *okla*, people + *homma*, red] State of the SC U.S.: 69,919 sq. mi.; pop. 3,025,000; cap. Oklahoma City: abbrev. **Okla., OK** —**O'kla·ho'man** *adj., n.*

**Oklahoma City** capital of Okla., in the central part: pop. 403,000 (met. area 830,000)

**o·kra** (ō'krə) *n.* [< WAfr. name] **1.** a tall plant with slender, ribbed, sticky green pods **2.** the pods, used as a cooked vegetable, in soups, etc.

**-ol¹** (ôl, ōl) [< (ALCOH)OL] *a suffix used in chemistry to mean an alcohol or phenol [menthol]*

**-ol²** (ôl, ōl) *var. of* -OLE

**OL., O.L.** Old Latin

**old** (ōld) *adj.* **old′er** or **eld′er, old′est** or **eld′est** [OE. *ald*] **1.** having lived or existed for a long time; aged **2.** of or characteristic of aged people **3.** of a certain age *[a boy ten years old]* **4.** made some time ago; not new **5.** known from the past *[up to his old tricks]* **6.** [*often* O-] designating the earliest stage of a language *[Old English]* **7.** worn out by age or use; shabby **8.** former **9.** having had long experience *[an old hand at this work]* **10.** having existed long ago; ancient *[an old civilization]* **11.** of long standing *[an old joke]* **12.** designating the earlier or earliest of two or more *[the Old World]* **13.** [Colloq.] dear: a term of affection *[old boy]* Also used as a colloquial intensive *[a fine old time]* —*n.* **1.** time long past; yore *[days of old]* **2.** a person of a specified age: used in hyphenated compounds *[a six-year-old]* **3.** something old (with *the*) —**old′ish** *adj.* —**old′ness** *n.*

**old age** the advanced years of life, when strength and vigor decline: cf. MIDDLE AGE

**old country** the country from which an immigrant came, esp. a country in Europe

**old·en** (ōl′d′n) *adj.* [Poet.] (of) old; ancient

**Old English** the West Germanic, Low German language of the Anglo-Saxons, spoken in England from c. 400 to c. 1100 A.D.

**old-fash·ioned** (ōld′fash′ənd) *adj.* suited to or favoring the styles, ideas, etc. of past times; out-of-date —*n.* [*also* O- F-] a cocktail made with whiskey, soda water, bitters, sugar, and fruit

**old fogy, old fogey** *see* FOGY

**Old French** the French language from c. 800 to c. 1550 A.D., esp. from the 9th to the 14th century

**Old Glory** the flag of the United States

**old gold** a soft, yellowish, metallic color

**Old Guard** [after Napoleon's imperial guard (1804)] **1.** any group that has long defended a cause **2.** the conservative element of a group, party, etc.

**old hand** a person with much skill or experience

**old hat** [Slang] **1.** old-fashioned **2.** well-known to the point of being trite or commonplace

**Old High German** the High German language from the 8th to the 12th century

**old·ie, old·y** (ōl′dē) *n., pl.* **old′ies** [Colloq.] an old joke, song, movie, etc.

**Old Irish** Irish Gaelic before the 11th century

**old lady** [Slang] **1.** one's mother **2.** one's wife

**Old Latin** the Latin language before c. 75 B.C.

**old-line** (ōld′līn′) *adj.* **1.** old and well-established **2.** following tradition; conservative

**Old Low German** the Low German language from its earliest period to the 12th century A.D.

**old maid 1.** a woman, esp. an older woman, who has never married; spinster **2.** a prim, prudish, fussy person —**old′-maid′ish** *adj.*

**old man** [Slang] **1.** one's father **2.** one's husband **3.** [*usually* O- M-] any man in authority, as the head of a company, captain of a vessel, etc.

**old master 1.** any great European painter before the 18th cent. **2.** a painting by any of these

**old moon** the moon in its last quarter, when it appears as a crescent curving to the left

**Old Nick** [prob. contr. < NICHOLAS] the Devil; Satan: also **Old Harry**

**Old Norman French** *same as* NORMAN FRENCH

**Old Norse** the North Germanic language of the Scandinavian peoples before the 14th century

**Old Prussian** a Baltic language which became extinct in the 17th century

**old rose** grayish or purplish red —**old′-rose′** *adj.*

**Old Saxon** a West Germanic language known chiefly from manuscripts of the 9th and 10th centuries A.D.

**old school** a group of people who cling to traditional or conservative ideas, methods, etc.

**Old South** the South before the Civil War

**old·ster** (ōld′stər) *n.* [Colloq.] a person who is no longer a youngster; old or elderly person

**old style 1.** an old style of type with narrow, light letters **2.** [O- S-] the old method of reckoning time according to the Julian calendar, which was off one day every 128 years —**old′-style′** *adj.*

**Old Testament** *Christian designation for* the Holy Scriptures of Judaism, the first of the two general divisions of the Christian Bible

**old-time** (ōld′tīm′) *adj.* **1.** of or like past times **2.** of long standing or experience

**old-tim·er** (-tī′mər) *n.* [Colloq.] **1.** a longtime resident, employee, etc. **2.** an old-fashioned person

**old wives' tale** a silly story or superstition such as gossipy old women might pass around

**old-wom·an·ish** (-woom′ən ish) *adj.* like, typical of, or suitable for an old woman; fussy

**Old World** the Eastern Hemisphere, often esp. Europe —**old′-world′** *adj.*

**-ole** (ōl) [< L. *oleum,* oil] *a suffix used in chemistry indicating:* **1.** a five-member, closed-chain compound **2.** a compound without hydroxyl

**o·le·ag·i·nous** (ō′lē aj′i nəs) *adj.* [< Fr. < L. < *olea,* olive tree] oily; unctuous —**o′le·ag′i·nous·ness** *n.*

**o·le·an·der** (ō′lē an′dər, ō′lē an′dər) *n.* [ML.] a poisonous evergreen shrub with fragrant white, pink, or red flowers

**o·le·ate** (ō′lē āt′) *n.* a salt or ester of oleic acid

**o·le·ic** (ō lē′ik, ō′lē-) *adj.* [< L. *oleum,* oil + -IC] **1.** of or from oil **2.** of oleic acid

**oleic acid** an oily acid, $C_{17}H_{33}COOH$, present in most fats and oils as an ester, used in soaps, etc.

**o·le·in** (ō′lē in) *n.* [< Fr. < L. *oleum,* an oil] **1.** a liquid glyceride, present in olive oil, etc. **2.** the liquid part of a fat

**o·le·o** (ō′lē ō′) *n.* clipped form of OLEOMARGARINE

**o·le·o-** [< L. *oleum,* an oil] *a combining form meaning* oil, olein, or oleic *[oleomargarine]*

**o·le·o·mar·ga·rine, o·le·o·mar·ga·rin** (ō′lē ō mär′jə rin) *n.* [< Fr.: see prec. & MARGARINE] *full name of* MARGARINE

**o·le·o·res·in** (ō′lē ō rez′'n) *n.* **1.** a mixture of a resin and an essential oil, as turpentine, occurring naturally in various plants **2.** a prepared solution of resin in an essential oil

**ol·fac·tion** (äl fak′shən, ōl-) *n.* [see ff.] **1.** the sense of smell **2.** the act of smelling

**ol·fac·to·ry** (-tər ē, -trē) *adj.* [< L. pp. of *olfacere,* to smell < *olere,* to have a smell + *facere,* to make] of the sense of smell: also **ol·fac′tive** —*n., pl.* **-ries** [*usually pl.*] an organ of smell

**OLG, OLG., O.L.G.** Old Low German

**ol·i·garch** (äl′ə gärk′) *n.* any of the rulers of an oligarchy

**ol·i·gar·chy** (-gär′kē) *n., pl.* **-chies** [Gr. *oligarchia:* see OLIGO- & -ARCHY] **1.** a form of government with the ruling power belonging to a few **2.** a state so governed **3.** those ruling such a state —**ol′i·gar′chic, ol′i·gar′chi·cal, ol′i·gar′chal** (-k′l) *adj.*

**ol·i·go-** [Gr. < *oligos,* small] *a combining form meaning* few, small, a deficiency of: also **olig-**

**Ol·i·go·cene** (äl′ə gō sēn′) *adj.* [< prec. + Gr. *kainos,* new] designating or of the third epoch of the Tertiary Period in the Cenozoic Era —**the Oligocene** the Oligocene Epoch or its rocks: see GEOLOGY, chart

**ol·i·gop·o·ly** (äl′ə gäp′ə lē) *n., pl.* **-lies** [OLIG(O)- + (MON)OPOLY] control of a commodity or service by a few companies or suppliers —**ol′i·gop′o·list** *n.* —**ol′i·gop′o·lis′tic** *adj.*

**o·li·o** (ō′lē ō′) *n., pl.* **o′li·os′** [< Sp. *olla:* see OLLA] **1.** a spicy stew **2.** a medley or miscellany

**ol·ive** (äl′iv) *n.* [OFr. < L. *oliva* < Gr. *elaia*] **1.** *a)* an evergreen tree of the olive family, native to S Europe and the Near East, with an edible fruit *b)* the small, oval fruit, eaten green or ripe, or pressed to extract its oil *c)* the wood of this tree **2.** an olive branch or wreath **3.** the dull, yellowish-green color of the unripe fruit —*adj.* **1.** of the olive **2.** olive-colored **3.** designating a family of trees and shrubs with loose clusters of four-parted flowers, including the olives, ashes, lilacs, etc.

**olive branch 1.** the branch of the olive tree, a symbol of peace **2.** any peace offering

**olive drab 1.** a shade of greenish brown **2.** woolen cloth dyed this color and used for U.S. Army uniforms **3.** [*pl.*] such a uniform —**ol′ive-drab′** *adj.*

**olive oil** a light-yellow oil pressed from ripe olives, used in cooking, soap, etc.

**Ol·i·ver** (äl′ə vər) [Fr. *Olivier,* prob. < MLowG. < *alf,* elf + *hari,* an army] a masculine name

**ol·i·vine** (äl′ə vēn′) *n.* [OLIV(E) + -INE⁴] a green silicate of magnesium and iron

**ol·la** (äl′ə; *Sp.* ōl′yä) *n.* [Sp. < L.] **1.** a large-mouthed pot or jar **2.** a spicy stew

**Ol·mec** (äl′mek) *n., pl.* **-mecs, -mec** a member of an ancient Indian people in Mexico —*adj.* of the Olmecs

**ol·o·gy** (äl′ə jē) *n., pl.* **-gies** [< -LOGY] a branch of learning; science: humorous usage

**O·lym·pi·a** (ō lim′pē ə, ə-) **1.** plain in the W Peloponnesus: site of the ancient Olympic games **2.** [ult. < Mount OLYMPUS] capital of Wash., on Puget Sound: pop. 27,000

**O·lym·pi·ad** (-ad′) *n.* [*often* o-] **1.** in ancient Greece, a four-year period between Olympic games **2.** a celebration of the modern Olympic games

**O·lym·pi·an** (-ən) *n.* **1.** *Gr. Myth.* any of the gods on Mount Olympus **2.** a native of Olympia **3.** a participant in the Olympic games —*adj.* **1.** of Olympia or Mount Olympus **2.** exalted; majestic; celestial **3.** of the ancient Olympic games

**O·lym·pic** (ō lim′pik, ə-) *adj. same as* OLYMPIAN —*n.* [*pl.*] the Olympic games (preceded by *the*)

**Olympic games 1.** an ancient Greek festival with contests in athletics, poetry, and music, held every four years at Olympia to honor Zeus **2.** a modern international athletic competition held every four years in a selected city

**O·lym·pus** (ō lim′pəs, ə-), **Mount** mountain in N Greece, between Thessaly & Macedonia: in Greek mythology, the home of the gods

**-o·ma** (ō′mə) [ModL. < Gr. *-ōma*] *a suffix meaning* tumor [*sarcoma*]

**O·ma·ha** (ō′mə hô, -hä) [ult. < Siouan tribal name, lit., ? upstream people] city in E Nebr., on the Missouri River: pop. 312,000 (met. area 566,000)

**O·man** (ō män′) country in SE Arabia, on the Arabian Sea: 82,000 sq. mi.; pop. c.750,000

**O·mar Khay·yám** (ō′mär kī yäm′, ō′mər kī yam′) ?–1123?; Persian poet & mathematician

**o·ma·sum** (ō mā′səm) *n., pl.* **-sa** (-sə) [ModL. < L., bullock's tripe < Gaul.] the third division in the stomach of a cud-chewing animal, as the cow

**O.M.B.** Office of Management and Budget

**om·buds·man** (äm′bədz mən) *n., pl.* **-men** [Sw.] a public official appointed to investigate citizens' complaints that government agencies may be violating their rights

**o·me·ga** (ō mā′gə, -meg′ə, -mē′gə) *n.* [Gr. *o mega,* lit., great (i.e., long) *o*] **1.** the twenty-fourth and final letter of the Greek alphabet (Ω, ω) **2.** the last (of any series); end

**om·e·let, om·e·lette** (äm′lit, äm′ə let) *n.* [< Fr., ult. < L. *lamella,* small plate] eggs beaten up, often with milk or water, cooked as a pancake in a frying pan and served usually folded over and often with a filling, as of jelly

**o·men** (ō′mən) *n.* [L.] a thing or happening supposed to foretell a future event; augury —*vt.* to be an omen of

**om·i·cron, om·i·kron** (äm′ə krän′, ō′mə-; *Brit.* ō mī′krən) *n.* [Gr. *o mikron,* lit., small *o*] the fifteenth letter of the Greek alphabet (O, o)

**om·i·nous** (äm′ə nəs) *adj.* [L. *ominosus*] of or serving as an evil omen; threatening; sinister —**om′i·nous·ly** *adv.* —**om′i·nous·ness** *n.*

**o·mis·si·ble** (ō mis′ə b'l) *adj.* that can be omitted

**o·mis·sion** (ō mish′ən) *n.* [< LL. *omissio*] **1.** an omitting or being omitted **2.** anything omitted

**o·mit** (ō mit′) *vt.* **o·mit′ted, o·mit′ting** [< L. *omittere* < *ob-* (see OB-) + *mittere,* to send] **1.** to fail to include; leave out **2.** to fail to do; neglect —**o·mit′ter** *n.*

**omni-** [L. < *omnis,* all] *a combining form meaning* all, everywhere [*omniscient*]

**om·ni·bus** (äm′nə bəs, -ni bus′) *n., pl.* **-bus·es** [Fr. < L., lit., for all] **1.** *same as* BUS (sense 1) **2.** a one-volume collection of previously published works —*adj.* providing for many things at once

**omnibus bill** a legislative bill containing many miscellaneous provisions, appropriations, etc.

**om·ni·far·i·ous** (äm′nə fer′ē əs) *adj.* [< L. *omnifarius* < *omnis,* all + *fari,* to speak] of all kinds, varieties, or forms

**om·nip·o·tence** (äm nip′ə təns) *n.* **1.** the state or quality of being omnipotent **2.** [O-] God

**om·nip·o·tent** (-tənt) *adj.* [OFr. < L. < *omnis,* all + *potens,* able] having unlimited power or authority; all-powerful —**the Omnipotent** God —**om·nip′o·tent·ly** *adv.*

**om·ni·pres·ent** (äm′ni prez′'nt) *adj.* [< ML. < L. *omnis,* all + *praesens,* present] present in all places at the same time —**om′ni·pres′ence** *n.*

**om·nis·cient** (äm nish′ənt) *adj.* [< ML. < L. *omnis,* all + prp. of *scire,* to know] knowing all things —**the Omniscient** God —**om·nis′cience** *n.* —**om·nis′cient·ly** *adv.*

**om·ni·um-gath·er·um** (äm′nē əm gath′ər əm) *n.* [L. *omnium,* all + Latinized form of GATHER] a miscellaneous collection of persons or things

**om·niv·o·rous** (äm niv′ər əs) *adj.* [< L.: see OMNI- & -VOROUS] **1.** eating any sort of food **2.** taking in everything indiscriminately [an *omnivorous* reader] —**om·niv′o·rous·ly** *adv.* —**om·niv′o·rous·ness** *n.*

**Omsk** (ômsk) city in W Siberia, on the Irtysh River: pop. 800,000

**on** (än, ôn) *prep.* [OE. *on, an*] **1.** above, but in contact with and supported by; upon **2.** in contact with; covering or attached to **3.** so as to be supported by [to lean *on* one's elbow] **4.** in the surface of **5.** near to [a cottage *on* the lake] **6.** at the time of [*on* entering] **7.** with (something specified) as the basis [*on* purpose] **8.** connected with, as a part [*on* the faculty] **9.** engaged in [*on* a trip] **10.** in a state of [*on* parole] **11.** as a result of [a profit *on* the sale] **12.** in the direction of [a light shone *on* us] **13.** so as to affect [to put a curse *on* someone] **14.** through the use or medium of [to live *on* bread] **15.** concerning [an essay *on* war] **16.** coming after [insult *on* insult] **17.** [Colloq.] chargeable to [a drink *on* the house] **18.** [Slang] using; addicted to [to be *on* drugs] —*adv.* **1.** in a situation of contacting, being supported by, or covering [put your shoes *on*] **2.** in a direction toward [looked *on*] **3.** forward; ahead [move *on*] **4.** continuously [she sang *on*] **5.** into operation or action [turn the light *on*] **6.** *Baseball* on base **7.** *Theater* on stage —*adj.* **1.** in action or operation [the TV is *on*] **2.** planned for [tomorrow's game is still *on*] —**and so on** and more like the preceding —**on and off** intermittently —**on and on** continuously —**on to** [Slang] aware of, esp. aware of the real nature of

**-on** (än) *a suffix designating:* **1.** [< *-on* in *argon*] an inert gas [*radon*] **2.** [< *-on* in *ion*] a subatomic particle [*electron*]

**ON., ON, O.N.** Old Norse

**o·nan·ism** (ō′nə niz′m) *n.* [< *Onan* (Gen. 38:9)] **1.** withdrawal in coition before ejaculation **2.** masturbation —**o′nan·ist** *n.* —**o′nan·is′tic** *adj.*

**once** (wuns) *adv.* [ME. *ones,* gen. of *on,* ONE] **1.** one time; one time only **2.** at any time; ever **3.** formerly **4.** by one degree [a cousin *once* removed] —*conj.* as soon as; if ever —*adj.* former —*n.* one time [go this *once*] —**all at once 1.** all at the same time **2.** suddenly —**at once 1.** immediately **2.** at the same time —**for once** for at least one time —**once (and) for all** conclusively —**once in a while** occasionally —**once or twice** a few times —**once upon a time** long ago

**once-o·ver** (wuns′ō′vər) *n.* [Colloq.] **1.** a swiftly appraising glance **2.** a quick cleaning or going-over

**on·com·ing** (än′kum′iŋ) *adj.* approaching [*oncoming* traffic] —*n.* approach

**one** (wun) *adj.* [OE. *an*] **1.** being a single thing **2.** forming a whole; united **3.** designating a person or thing as contrasted with another [from *one* day to another] **4.** being uniquely the person or thing specified [the *one* solution to the problem] **5.** single in kind; the same [all of *one* mind] **6.** a certain but unspecified [*one* day last week]: also used as an intensive substitute for the indefinite article [she's *one* beautiful girl] —*n.* **1.** the number expressing unity or designating a single unit; the first and lowest cardinal number; 1; I **2.** a single person or thing **3.** anything consisting of a single unit or numbered one; specif., [Colloq.] a one-dollar bill —*pron.* **1.** some, or a certain, person or thing **2.** any person or thing **3.** the person or thing previously mentioned —**all one** making no difference —**at one** in accord —**one and all** everybody —**one another** each one the other; each other: see EACH OTHER, under EACH —**one of those things** something inevitable

**-one** (ōn) [arbitrary use of Gr. *-ōnē*] *a suffix used in chemistry, meaning* a ketone [*acetone*]

**one-horse** (wun′hôrs′) *adj.* **1.** drawn by or using one horse **2.** [Colloq.] small, unimportant, etc.

**O·nei·da** (ō nī′də) *n.* [Iroquois *Oneiute,* lit., standing rock] **1.** *pl.* **-das, -da** a member of a tribe of Indians orig. of New York State but now also of Wisconsin and Ontario **2.** their Iroquoian language

**O'Neill** (ō nēl′), **Eugene** 1888–1953; U.S. playwright

**one·ness** (wun′nis) *n.* **1.** singleness; unity **2.** unity of mind, feeling, etc. **3.** sameness; identity

**one-night stand** (wun′nīt′) a single appearance in a town by a traveling show, lecturer, etc.

**one-on-one** (wun′än wun′, -ôn-) *adj., adv.* **1.** contending individually against a single opposing player, as in basketball **2.** in direct, personal confrontation

**on·er·ous** (än′ər əs, ō′nər-) *adj.* [< MFr. < L. *onerosus* < *onus,* a load] burdensome; oppressive —**on′er·ous·ly** *adv.*

**one·self** (wun′self′, wunz′-) *pron.* a person's own self: also **one's self** —**be oneself 1.** to function normally **2.** to be natural —**by oneself** alone; unaccompanied —**come to oneself** to recover one's senses or capacity for judgment

**one-sid·ed** (wun′sīd′id) *adj.* **1.** on, having, or involving only one side **2.** larger, heavier, etc. on one side; lopsided **3.** favoring one side; unfair **4.** uneven or unequal [a *one-sided* race] —**one′-sid′ed·ly** *adv.* —**one′-sid′ed·ness** *n.*

**one-step** (-step′) *n.* an old ballroom dance with quick walking steps in 2/4 time

**one-time** (-tīm′) *adj.* at a past time; former

**one-to-one** (wun′tə wun′) *adj.* **1.** permitting the pairing of an element of one group uniquely with a corresponding element of another group **2.** *Math.* with each member of one set having a partner in the other set

**one-track** (wun′trak′) *adj.* **1.** having a single track **2.** [Colloq.] able or willing to deal with only one thing at a time [a *one-track* mind]

**one-up** (-up′) *adj.* [Colloq.] having an advantage (over another): often **be one-up on** —*vt.* **-upped′, -up′ping** [Colloq.] to have or seize an advantage over (another) —**one′-up′man·ship** *n.*

**one-way** (-wā′) *adj.* **1.** moving, or allowing movement, in one direction only *[a one-way street]* **2.** without reciprocal action or obligation

**on·go·ing** (än′gō′iŋ) *adj.* going on; in process

**on·ion** (un′yən) *n.* [< OFr. < L. *unio,* a kind of single onion] **1.** a plant of the lily family, with an edible bulb having a strong, sharp smell and taste **2.** the bulb

**on·ion·skin** (-skin′) *n.* a tough, thin, translucent paper, often used for carbon copies

**on-line** (än′līn′, ôn′-) *adj.* designating or of instruments, equipment, or devices directly connected to and controlled by the unit of a computer that interprets and executes instructions

**on·look·er** (än′look′ər) *n.* one who watches without taking part; spectator —**on′look′ing** *adj.,* **n.**

**on·ly** (ōn′lē) *adj.* [OE. *anlic* < *an,* one + *-lic,* -LY¹] **1.** alone of its or their kind; sole **2.** alone in superiority; best —*adv.* **1.** and no other; and no (or nothing) more; solely *[drink water only]* **2.** (but) in what follows or in the end *[to meet one crisis, only to face another]* **3.** as recently as *[only last fall]* —*conj.* [Colloq.] except that; but *[I'd go, only it's late]* —*if* ... *only* would that; I wish that —**only too** very

**on·o·mat·o·poe·ia** (än′ə mat′ə pē′ə, -mät′-) *n.* [LL. < Gr. < *onoma,* a name + *poiein,* to make] **1.** formation of a word by imitating the sound associated with as in object or action (Ex.: *buzz*) **2.** the use of such words, as in poetry —**on′o·mat′o·poe′ic, on′o·mat′o·po·et′ic** (-pō et′ik) *adj.*

**On·on·da·ga** (än′ən dô′gə, ôn′-; -dä′-) *n.* [Iroquois *Ononta′ge′,* lit., on top of the hill] **1.** *pl.* **-gas, -ga** a member of a tribe of Indians orig. of New York State but now also of Ontario **2.** their Iroquoian language —**On′on·da′gan** *adj.*

**ONormFr.** Old Norman French

**on·rush** (än′rush′, ôn′-) *n.* a headlong dash forward; strong onward rush —**on′rush′ing** *adj.*

**on·set** (-set′) *n.* **1.** an attack **2.** a beginning

**on·shore** (-shôr′) *adj.* **1.** moving onto or toward the shore **2.** on land *[an onshore patrol]* —*adv.* toward the shore

**on·slaught** (-slôt′) *n.* [< Du. *annslag* < *slagen,* to strike] a violent, intense attack

**On·tar·i·o** (än ter′ē ō) **1.** [after the lake, below] province of SC Canada, between the Great Lakes & Hudson Bay: 412,582 sq. mi.; pop. 8,264,000; cap. Toronto: abbrev. **Ont. 2.** [after prec.] city in S Calif.: pop. 89,000 **3. Lake,** [ult. < Iroquoian, lit., fine lake] smallest & easternmost of the Great Lakes, between N.Y. & Ontario, Canada: 7,313 sq. mi. —**On·tar′i·an** *adj.,* **n.**

**on·to** (än′tōō, ôn′-; -tə) *prep.* **1.** to a position on **2.** [Slang] aware of the real nature, etc. of *[he's onto our schemes]* Also **on to**

**on·to-** [< Gr. prp. of *einai,* to be] *a combining form meaning:* **1.** being; existence **2.** organism

**on·tog·e·ny** (än täj′ə nē) *n.* [prec. + -GENY] the development of an individual organism: distinguished from PHYLOGENY: also **on·to·gen·e·sis** (än′tə jen′ə sis) —**on′to·ge·net′ic** (-jə net′ik), **on′to·gen′ic** *adj.*

**on·tol·o·gy** (än täl′ə jē) *n.* the study of the nature of being or reality —**on·to·log·i·cal** (än′tə läj′i k′l) *adj.*

**o·nus** (ō′nəs) *n.* [L.] **1.** a hard or unpleasant task, duty, etc.; burden **2.** responsibility for a wrong; blame **3.** same *as* BURDEN OF PROOF

**on·ward** (än′wərd) *adv.* toward or at a position ahead; forward: also **on′wards** —*adj.* moving or directed ahead; advancing

**on·yx** (än′iks; *occas.* ō′niks) *n.* [< OFr. < L. < Gr. *onyx,* nail, claw: its color resembles that of the fingernail] **1.** a variety of agate with alternate colored layers **2.** a translucent, often banded, stalagmitic calcite: also **onyx marble**

**o·o-** [< Gr. *ōion*] *a combining form meaning* egg or ovum: also written **oö-**

**oo·dles** (ōō′d′lz) *n.pl.* [< ? HUDDLE] [Colloq.] a great amount; very many

**o·o·lite** (ō′ə līt′) *n.* [< Fr.: see OO- & -LITE] **1.** a tiny calcium carbonate particle with concentric layers, formed in the sea: also **o′o·lith** (-lith) **2.** a rock of these —**o′o·lit′ic** (-lit′ik) *adj.*

**o·ol·o·gy** (ō äl′ə jē) *n.* [OO- + -LOGY] the study of birds' eggs —**o·o·log·i·cal** (ō′ə läj′i k′l) *adj.* —**o·ol′o·gist** *n.*

**oo·long** (ōō′lôŋ) *n.* [< Chin. *wulung,* lit., black dragon] a dark Chinese tea, partly fermented before being dried

**oo·mi·ac, oo·mi·ak** (ōō′mē ak′) *n.* same as UMIAK

**o·o·pho·ro-** (ō′ə fə rō′) [< Gr. *ōion,* an egg + *-phoros,* bearing] *a combining form meaning* ovary or ovaries: also, before a vowel, **oophor-**

**oops** (ōōps, oops) *interj.* same as WHOOPS

**ooze**¹ (ōōz) *n.* [OE. *wos,* sap] an oozing or something that oozes —*vi.* **oozed, ooz′ing 1.** to flow or pass slowly, as through tiny holes; seep **2.** to give forth moisture, as through pores —*vt.* to exude

**ooze**² (ōōz) *n.* [OE. *wase*] **1.** soft mud or slime; esp., the sediment at the bottom of a lake, ocean, etc. **2.** a bog

**oo·zy**¹ (ōō′zē) *adj.* **-zi·er, -zi·est** oozing moisture —**oo′zi·ly** *adv.* —**oo′zi·ness n.**

**oo·zy**² (ōō′zē) *adj.* **-zi·er, -zi·est** full of or like ooze; slimy —**oo′zi·ly** *adv.* —**oo′zi·ness n.**

**op-** *see* OB-

**op. 1.** opera **2.** operation **3.** opposite **4.** opus

**O.P.** Order of Preachers (Dominicans)

**O.P., OP, o.p.,** op out of print

**o·pac·i·ty** (ō pas′ə tē) *n.* **1.** opaque state, quality, or degree **2.** *pl.* **-ties** an opaque thing

**o·pal** (ō′p'l) *n.* [< L. < Gr. *opallios* < Sans. *upala,* precious stone] an amorphous silica, of various colors, typically iridescent: some varieties are semiprecious stones

**o·pal·es·cent** (ō′pə les′'nt) *adj.* iridescent like opal —**o′pal·esce′** *vi.* **-esced′, -esc′ing** —**o′pal·es′cence n.**

**o·pal·ine** (ō′p'l in, -ēn′, -īn′) *adj.* of or like opal —*n.* a translucent, milky glass

**o·paque** (ō pāk′) *adj.* [L. *opacus,* shady] **1.** not letting light through **2.** not reflecting light or not shining **3.** hard to understand; obscure **4.** slow in understanding; obtuse —*n.* anything opaque —*vt.* **o·paqued′, o·paqu′ing** to make opaque —**o·paque′ly** *adv.* —**o·paque′ness n.**

**op** (art) (äp) [< OP(TICAL)] abstract painting using geometrical patterns to create various optical effects, such as the illusion of movement

**op. cit.** [L. *opere citato*] in the work cited

**ope** (ōp) *adj., vt., vi.* **oped, op′ing** [Poet.] open

**OPEC** (ō′pek) Organization of Petroleum Exporting Countries

**o·pen** (ō′p'n) *adj.* [OE.] **1.** allowing access, entrance, or exit; not closed or shut **2.** allowing freedom of view or passage; unenclosed or unobstructed **3.** unsealed; unwrapped **4.** *a)* not covered *b)* unprotected or undefended **5.** spread out; unfolded **6.** having spaces, gaps, etc. *[open ranks]* **7.** free from ice **8.** *a)* not excluding anyone *[an open meeting] b)* ready to admit customers, clients, etc. **9.** free to be argued; not settled *[an open question]* **10.** *a)* not prejudiced or narrow-minded *b)* liberal; generous **11.** *a)* free from legal or discriminatory restrictions *[open housing] b)* free from effective regulation *[the city is wide open] c)* not regulated, organized, or conducted along traditional lines *[open marriage, open education]* **12.** socially mobile, politically free, etc. *[an open society]* **13.** in force or operation *[an open account]* **14.** *a)* not already taken or engaged *[the job is open] b)* free to be accepted or rejected **15.** accessible; available **16.** not secret; public **17.** frank; candid **18.** *Music a)* not stopped by the finger: said of a string *b)* not closed at the top: said of an organ pipe *c)* produced by an open string or pipe or without a slide or key: said of a tone *d)* not muted **19.** *Phonetics a)* low *b)* fricative *c)* ending in a vowel or diphthong: said of a syllable —*vt.* **1.** to make open, or no longer closed, shut, obstructed, etc. **2.** *a)* to make an opening in *b)* to produce (a hole, way, etc.) **3.** to spread out; expand **4.** to expose (to an influence or action) **5.** to make available without restriction, fee, etc. **6.** *a)* to free from prejudice *b)* to make liberal and generous **7.** to reveal; disclose **8.** to begin (bidding, a session, etc.) **9.** to start operating, going, etc. *[to open a new shop]* —*vi.* **1.** to become open **2.** to spread out; expand; unfold **3.** to become revealed, disclosed, etc. **4.** to give access (with *to, into, on,* etc.) **5.** to begin; start **6.** to start operating, going, etc.; specif., in the stock exchange, to show an indicated initial price level *[steel opened high]* **7.** to begin a series of performances, games, etc. —*n.* [*usually* O-] any of various golf tournaments for both professionals and amateurs —**open out 1.** to expand **2.** to develop **3.** to reveal —**open to 1.** willing to receive, discuss, etc. **2.** liable to **3.** available or accessible to or for —**open up 1.** to make or become open **2.** to unfold **3.** to start; begin **4.** [Colloq.] to begin firing a gun or guns **5.** [Colloq.] to speak freely **6.** [Colloq.] to go or make go faster —**the open 1.** any open, unobstructed area **2.** the outdoors **3.** public knowledge —**o′pened** *adj.* —**o′pen·er** *n.* —**o′pen·ly** *adv.* —**o′pen·ness n.**

**open air** the outdoors —**o′pen-air′** *adj.*

**o·pen-and-shut** (ō′p'n 'n shut′) *adj.* easily decided; obvious *[an open-and-shut case]*

**open chain** the structural form of certain molecules in which the chain of atoms does not form a ring

**open city** a city left open to enemy occupation to gain immunity from attack

**open door 1.** unrestricted admission **2.** equal, unrestricted opportunity for all nations to trade with a given nation —**o′pen-door′** *adj.*

**o·pen-end** (-end′) *adj.* **1.** of an investment company not limiting the shares issued **2.** allowing additional borrowing on the original security *[an open-end mortgage]* **3.** same as OPEN-ENDED

**o·pen-end·ed** (-en′did) *adj.* **1.** unrestricted in duration, scope, etc., as a discussion **2.** open to change **3.** allowing for a freely formulated answer rather than one chosen from among predetermined answers: said of a question

**o·pen-eyed** (-īd′) *adj.* with the eyes open or wide open, as in awareness or amazement

**o·pen-faced** (-fāst′) *adj.* **1.** having a frank, honest face **2.** designating a sandwich without a top slice of bread: also **o′pen-face′**

**o·pen-hand·ed** (-han′did) *adj.* generous —**o′pen-hand′ed·ly** *adv.* —**o′pen·hand′ed·ness** *n.*

**o·pen-heart·ed** (-här′tid) *adj.* **1.** not reserved; frank **2.** kindly; generous —**o′pen·heart′ed·ly** *adv.* —**o′pen-heart′ed·ness** *n.*

**o·pen-hearth** (-härth′) *adj.* designating or using a furnace with a wide, saucer-shaped hearth and a low roof, for making steel

**o·pen-heart surgery** (-härt′) heart surgery with the chest opened and the blood recirculated and oxygenated by mechanical means

**open house** informal reception of visitors freely coming and going, at one's home, a school, etc.

**o·pen·ing** (-iŋ) *n.* **1.** a becoming or making open **2.** an open place; hole; gap **3.** a clearing in a wooded area **4.** *a)* a beginning *b)* a first performance **5.** an opportunity **6.** a job available **7.** *Chess, Checkers,* etc. the series of first moves

OPEN-HEARTH FURNACE
(A, lining; B, metal; C, heater ports; D, gas; E, air: fired alternately from either end)

**open letter** a letter written as to a specific person but published in a newspaper, etc. for all to read

**open market** *same as* FREE MARKET

**o·pen-mind·ed** (-mīn′did) *adj.* open to new ideas; not biased —**o′pen-mind′ed·ly** *adv.* —**o′pen-mind′ed·ness** *n.*

**o·pen-mouthed** (-mouthd′, -moutht′) *adj.* **1.** having the mouth open **2.** gaping, as in astonishment

**open primary** a primary election in which the voter need not declare party affiliation

**open punctuation** punctuation characterized by relatively few commas or other marks

**open sea** **1.** the expanse of sea away from coastlines, bays, inlets, etc. **2.** *same as* HIGH SEAS

**open secret** something supposed to be secret but known to almost everyone

**open sesame** **1.** magic words spoken to open the door of the thieves' den in the story of Ali Baba **2.** any sure means of achieving an end

**open shop** a factory, business, etc. employing workers regardless of union membership

**open stock** merchandise, as dishes, available in sets, with individual pieces kept in stock

**o·pen·work** (-wurk′) *n.* ornamental work, as in cloth, with openings in the material

**op·er·a¹** (äp′ər ə, äp′rə) *n.* [It. < L., a work] **1.** a play with most or all the text sung to orchestral accompaniment and usually with elaborate costuming, sets, and choreography **2.** the art of such plays **3.** the score, libretto, or performance of an opera **4.** a theater for operas

**o·pe·ra²** (ō′pə rə, äp′ər ə) *n. pl. of* OPUS

**op·er·a·ble** (äp′ər ə b'l) *adj.* [< ML.: see OPERATE & -ABLE] **1.** practicable **2.** treatable surgically —**op′er·a·bil′i·ty** *n.* —**op′er·a·bly** *adv.*

**‡o·pé·ra bouffe** (ȯ pä rà bo͞of′; E. äp′ər ə bo͞of′) [Fr.] comic, esp. farcical, opera

**opera glasses** a small binocular telescope used at the opera, in theaters, etc.

**opera hat** a man's tall, collapsible silk hat

**opera house** a theater chiefly for operas

**op·er·ant** (äp′ər ənt) *adj.* operating, or producing an effect or effects —*n.* one that operates

**op·er·ate** (äp′ə rāt′) *vi.* **-at′ed, -at′ing** [< L. pp. of *operari,* to work < *opus* (gen. *operis*), a work] **1.** to be in action; work **2.** to produce a certain effect **3.** to carry on military movements **4.** to perform a surgical operation —*vt.* **1.** [Now Rare] to effect **2.** *a)* to put or keep in action; work (a machine, etc.) *b)* to conduct or manage (a business, etc.) **3.** [Colloq.] to do a surgical operation on

**op·er·at·ic** (äp′ə rat′ik) *adj.* of or like the opera —**op′er·at′i·cal·ly** *adv.*

**op·er·a·tion** (äp′ə rā′shən) *n.* **1.** the act, process, or method of operating **2.** the condition of being in action or at work **3.** a procedure that is part of a series in some work **4.** any strategic military movement; also, *[pl.]* a center where this is monitored or supervised **5.** any specific plan, project, etc. *[Operation Cleanup]* **6.** any surgical procedure to remedy a physical ailment or defect **7.** *Math.*

any process, as addition, involving a change in quantity —**in operation** **1.** in action; working **2.** in force

**op·er·a·tion·al** (-'l) *adj.* **1.** of the operation of a device, system, process, etc. **2.** *a)* that can be used or operated *b)* in use; operating **3.** of or ready for use in a military operation —**op′er·a′tion·al·ly** *adv.*

**op·er·a·tion·al·ize** (-'l īz′) *vt.* **-ized′, -iz′ing** to make operational; put into operation —**op′er·a′tion·al·i·za′tion** *n.*

**operations research** systematic, scientific analysis of problems, as in government, military, or business operations: also **operations analysis**

**op·er·a·tive** (äp′ə rā′tiv, äp′ər ə-) *adj.* **1.** capable of or in operation **2.** effective **3.** connected with physical work or mechanical action **4.** of or resulting from a surgical operation —*n.* **1.** a worker, esp. a skilled industrial worker **2.** a detective or spy —**op′er·a′tive·ly** *adv.*

**op·er·a·tor** (äp′ə rāt′ər) *n.* **1.** one who operates; specif., *a)* a person who effects something; agent *b)* a person who works a machine *c)* a person engaged in commercial or industrial operations or enterprises **2.** [Slang] a clever person who generally manages to achieve his ends

**o·per·cu·lum** (ō pur′kyo͞o ləm) *n., pl.* **-la** (-lə), **-lums** [ModL. < L., lid, dim. < *operire,* to close] any of various covering flaps or lidlike structures in plants and animals, as the bony covering protecting the gills of fishes —**o·per′cu·lar** *adj.* —**o·per′cu·late** (-lit, -lāt′), **o·per′cu·lat′ed** *adj.*

**op·er·et·ta** (äp′ə ret′ə) *n.* [It., dim. of *opera,* OPERA¹] a light, amusing opera with spoken dialogue

**oph·thal·mi·a** (äf thal′mē ə) *n.* [< LL. < Gr. < *ophthalmos,* the eye] severe inflammation of the eyeball or conjunctiva

**oph·thal·mic** (-mik) *adj.* of the eye; ocular

**oph·thal·mo-** [< Gr. *ophthalmos,* the eye] *a combining form meaning* the eye: also **oph·thalm-**

**oph·thal·mol·o·gy** (äf′thal mäl′ə jē, äp′-; -thə-) *n.* the branch of medicine dealing with the structure, functions, and diseases of the eye —**oph′thal·mo·log′i·cal** (-mə läj′i·k'l) *adj.* —**oph′thal·mol′o·gist** *n.*

**oph·thal·mo·scope** (äf thal′mə skōp′, äp-) *n.* [OPHTHALMO- & -SCOPE] an instrument for examining the interior of the eye —**oph·thal′mo·scop′ic** (-skäp′ik) *adj.* —**oph·thal·mos′co·py** (-thəl mäs′kə pē) *n.*

**-o·pi·a** (ō′pē ə) [< Gr. < *ōps,* an eye] *a combining form meaning* a (specified kind of) eye defect

**o·pi·ate** (ō′pē it, -āt′) *n.* **1.** any medicine containing opium or any of its derivatives, and acting as a sedative and narcotic **2.** anything quieting, soothing, etc. —*adj.* **1.** containing opium **2.** bringing sleep, quiet, etc.; narcotic

**o·pine** (ō pīn′) *vt., vi.* **o·pined′, o·pin′ing** [< MFr. < L. *opinari,* to think] to hold or express (some opinion): now usually humorous

**o·pin·ion** (ə pin′yən) *n.* [< OFr. < L. < *opinari,* to think] **1.** a belief not based on certainty or knowledge but on what seems true, valid, or probable **2.** an evaluation, estimation, etc. **3.** an expert's formal judgment **4.** *Law* the formal statement by a judge, court referee, etc. of the law bearing on a case

**o·pin·ion·at·ed** (-āt′id) *adj.* holding unreasonably or obstinately to one's own opinions —**o·pin′ion·at′ed·ly** *adv.* —**o·pin′ion·at′ed·ness** *n.*

**o·pin·ion·a·tive** (-āt′iv, -ə tiv) *adj.* **1.** of, or of the nature of, opinion **2.** opinionated —**o·pin′ion·a′tive·ly** *adv.* —**o·pin′ion·a′tive·ness** *n.*

**o·pi·um** (ō′pē əm) *n.* [L. < Gr. < *opos,* vegetable juice] a narcotic drug made from the juice of the seed capsules of the opium poppy, used as an intoxicant and medicinally to relieve pain and produce sleep

**opium poppy** an annual poppy with large, white or purple flowers, the source of opium

**O·por·to** (ō pôr′tō) seaport in N Portugal: pop. 305,000

**o·pos·sum** (ə päs′əm) *n., pl.* **-sums, -sum:** see PLURAL, II, D, 1 [< Algonquian, lit., white beast] any of several American marsupials; esp., the **American** (or **Virginian**) **opossum,** a small, tree-dwelling mammal: it is active at night and pretends to be dead when trapped

**opp.** **1.** opposed **2.** opposite

**op·po·nent** (ə pō′nənt) *n.* [< L. prp. of *opponere* < *ob-* (see OB-) + *ponere,* to set] one who opposes, as in a fight, game, etc.; adversary —*adj.* opposing; antagonistic

**op·por·tune** (äp′ər to͞on′, äp′ər tyo͞on′) *adj.* [< MFr. < L. *opportunus,* lit., before the port < *ob-* (see OB-) + *portus,* a port] **1.** right

OPOSSUM
(body 12–20 in. long; tail 10–21 in. long)

for the purpose: said of time **2.** happening or done at the right time; timely —**op′por·tune′ly** *adv.*

**op·por·tun·ism** (-iz′m) *n.* the adapting of one's actions, judgments, etc. to circumstances, as in politics, for one's own benefit without regard for principles —**op′por·tun′ist** *n.* —**op′por·tun·is′tic** *adj.* —**op′por·tun·is′ti·cal·ly** *adv.*

**op·por·tu·ni·ty** (äp′ər tōō′nə tē, -tyōō′-) *n., pl.* **-ties 1.** a combination of circumstances favorable for the purpose **2.** a good chance or occasion

**op·pos·a·ble** (ə pō′zə b′l) *adj.* **1.** that can be resisted **2.** that can be placed opposite something else —**op·pos′a·bil′i·ty** *n.*

**op·pose** (ə pōz′) *vt.* **-posed′, -pos′ing** [< OFr. < L. *op-ponere:* see OB- & POSITION] **1.** to set against; place opposite, in balance or contrast **2.** to contend with in speech or action; resist —*vi.* to act in opposition —**op·pos′er** *n.*

**op·po·site** (äp′ə zit) *adj.* [OFr. < L. pp. of *opponere:* see prec.] **1.** set against, facing, or back to back; at the other end or side (often with *to*) **2.** hostile; resistant **3.** entirely different; exactly contrary **4.** *Bot.* growing in pairs, but separated by a stem —*n.* anything opposed or opposite —*adv.* on opposing sides or in an opposite position —*prep.* across from —**op′po·site·ly** *adv.* —**op′po·site·ness** *n.*

**op·po·si·tion** (äp′ə zish′ən) *n.* **1.** an opposing **2.** an opposed condition; resistance, contrast, etc. **3.** anything that opposes; specif., [*often* O-] a political party opposing the party in power **4.** *Astrol., Astron.* the position of two heavenly bodies 180° apart in longitude —**op′po·si′tion·al** *adj.* —**op′po·si′tion·ist** *n., adj.*

**op·press** (ə pres′) *vt.* [< OFr. < ML. < L. pp. of *op-primere* < *ob-* (see OB-) + *premere*, PRESS[1]] **1.** to weigh heavily on the mind, spirits, or senses of **2.** to keep down by the cruel or unjust use of power; tyrannize over —**op·pres′sor** *n.*

**op·pres·sion** (ə presh′ən) *n.* **1.** an oppressing or being oppressed **2.** a thing that oppresses **3.** physical or mental distress

**op·pres·sive** (ə pres′iv) *adj.* **1.** hard to put up with **2.** cruelly overbearing; tyrannical **3.** weighing heavily on the mind, etc.; distressing —**op·pres′sive·ly** *adv.* —**op·pres′sive·ness** *n.*

**op·pro·bri·ous** (ə prō′brē əs) *adj.* **1.** expressing opprobrium; abusive **2.** [Now Rare] disgraceful —**op·pro′bri·ous·ly** *adv.* —**op·pro′bri·ous·ness** *n.*

**op·pro·bri·um** (-əm) *n.* [L. < *opprobrare*, to reproach < *ob-* (see OB-) + *probrum*, a disgrace] **1.** the disgrace or infamy attached to conduct viewed as grossly shameful **2.** anything bringing shame or disgrace **3.** reproachful contempt

**-op·sis** (äp′sis) [< Gr. < *opsis*, a sight] *a combining form meaning* sight or view

**opt** (äpt) *vi.* [< Fr. < L. *optare*] to make a choice (often with *for*) —**opt out (of)** to choose not to be or continue in (an activity, group, etc.)

**opt. 1.** optical **2.** optician **3.** optional

**op·ta·tive** (äp′tə tiv) *adj.* [< Fr. < LL. < L. *optare*, to desire] expressing wish or desire, as a mood in Greek grammar —*n.* the optative mood, or a verb in this mood

**op·tic** (äp′tik) *adj.* [< Fr. < ML. < Gr. *optikos*] of the eye or sense of sight

**op·ti·cal** (-′l) *adj.* **1.** of the sense of sight; visual **2.** of optics **3.** for aiding vision [*optical* instruments] —**op′ti·cal·ly** *adv.*

**op·ti·cian** (äp tish′ən) *n.* a person who makes or deals in optical instruments, esp. one who prepares and dispenses eyeglasses

**optic nerve** either of a pair of nerves which connect the retina of the eye with the brain

**op·tics** (äp′tiks) *n.pl.* [*with sing. v.]* [< OPTIC] the branch of physics dealing with the nature and properties of light and vision

**op·ti·mal** (äp′tə məl) *adj.* most favorable or desirable; best; optimum —**op′ti·mal·ly** *adv.*

**op·ti·mism** (-miz′m) *n.* [< Fr. < L. *optimus*, best] **1.** *Philos. a)* the doctrine that the existing world is the best possible *b)* the belief that good ultimately prevails over evil **2.** the tendency to take the most hopeful or cheerful view of matters —**op′ti·mist** (-mist) *n.* —**op′ti·mis′tic** (-mis′tik), **op′ti·mis′ti·cal** *adj.* —**op′ti·mis′ti·cal·ly** *adv.*

**op·ti·mum** (-məm) *n., pl.* **-mums, -ma** (-mə) [L., neut. of *op-timus*, best < *ops*, riches] the best or most favorable degree, condition, amount, etc. —*adj.* most favorable or desirable; best

**op·tion** (äp′shən) *n.* [Fr. < L. *optio* < *optare*, to wish] **1.** a choosing; choice **2.** the right or liberty of choosing **3.** something that is or can be chosen **4.** the right to buy, sell, or lease at a fixed price, sign a contract, etc. within a specified time

**op·tion·al** (-′l) *adj.* left to one's option, or choice; elective —**op′tion·al·ly** *adv.*

**op·tom·e·try** (äp täm′ə trē) *n.* [see OPTIC & -METRY] **1.** measurement of the range and power of vision **2.** the profession of examining the eyes for errors in refraction and of prescribing glasses to correct such defects —**op·to·met·ric** (äp′tə met′rik), **op′to·met′ri·cal** *adj.* —**op·tom′e·trist** *n.*

**op·u·lent** (äp′yə lənt) *adj.* [< L. < *ops*, wealth] **1.** wealthy; rich **2.** abundant; profuse —**op′u·lence, op′u·len·cy** *n.* —**op′u·lent·ly** *adv.*

**o·pus** (ō′pəs) *n., pl.* **o·pe·ra** (ō′pə rə, äp′ər ə), **o′pus·es** [L., a work] a work; composition; esp., any of the musical works of a composer numbered in order of composition or publication

**-o·py** (ō′pē) *same as* -OPIA

**or[1]** (ôr; *unstressed* ər) *conj.* [ME., in form a contr. of *other*, either, but actually < OE. *oththe*] a coordinating conjunction introducing: *a)* an alternative possibility [beer *or* wine, either go *or* stay] *b)* a synonymous term [ill, *or* sick]

**or[2]** (ôr) *n.* [Fr. < L. *aurum*, gold] *Heraldry* gold

**-or** (ər; *occas.* ôr) [< OFr. < L. *-or*] *a suffix meaning:* **1.** a person or thing that [*inventor*] **2.** quality or condition [*error*] : in Brit. usage, often **-our**

**OR** Oregon

**or·a·cle** (ôr′ə k′l, är′-) *n.* [OFr. < L. *oraculum* < *orare*, to pray < *os* (gen. *oris*), the mouth] **1.** in ancient Greece and Rome, *a)* the place where, or medium by which, deities were consulted *b)* the revelation of a medium or priest **2.** *a)* any person or agency believed to be in communication with a deity *b)* any person of great wisdom *c)* opinion or statements of any such oracle

**o·rac·u·lar** (ō rak′yoo lər) *adj.* of or like an oracle; wise, mysterious, etc. —**o·rac′u·lar·ly** *adv.*

**o·ral** (ôr′əl) *adj.* [< L. *os* (gen. *oris*), the mouth] **1.** uttered; spoken **2.** of or using speech **3.** of, at, or near the mouth **4.** *Psychoanalysis* of an early stage of psychosexual development focusing on mouth functions —*n.* a spoken examination, as in a college —**o′ral·ly** *adv.*

**oral history 1.** the gathering of historical data consisting of personal recollections, usually in the form of tape-recorded interviews **2.** such an interview or interviews

**O·ran** (ō ran′) seaport in N Algeria, on the Mediterranean: pop. 430,000

**Or·ange** (ôr′inj, är′-; *also, for 3,* Fr. ô ränzh′) **1.** [prob. after the *orange* groves there] city in SW Calif.: suburb of Los Angeles: pop. 92,000 **2.** river in South Africa, flowing from NE Lesotho into the Atlantic **3.** former principality in W Europe, in what is now SE France

**or·ange** (ôr′inj, är′-) *n.* [< OFr. < Pr. *auranja* < Sp. < Ar. < Per. < Sans. *naranga*] **1.** a reddish-yellow, round, edible citrus fruit with a sweet, juicy pulp **2.** the evergreen tree it grows on **3.** reddish yellow —*adj.* **1.** reddish-yellow **2.** of oranges —**or′ang·y** (-in jē) *adj.*

**or·ange·ade** (-ād′) *n.* a drink made of orange juice and water, usually sweetened

**Orange Free State** province of South Africa, west of Lesotho

**Or·ange·man** (ôr′inj mən, är′-) *n., pl.* **-men** [after the Prince of *Orange*, later WILLIAM III] a member of a secret society organized in northern Ireland in 1795 to support Protestantism

**orange pekoe** a black tea of Ceylon and India

**orange stick** an orangewood stick, for manicuring

**or·ange·wood** (ôr′inj wood′, är′-) *n.* the wood of the orange tree —*adj.* of orangewood

**o·rang·u·tan** (ô raŋ′oo tan′, ə-; -taŋ′) *n.* [< Malay < *oraŋ*, man + *utan*, forest] an ape of Borneo and Sumatra, with shaggy, reddish-brown hair, very long arms, small ears, and a hairless face: also sp. **o·rang′ou·tang′** (-taŋ′)

**o·rate** (ô rāt′, ôr′āt) *vi.* **o·rat′ed, o·rat′ing** [< ff.] to make an oration; speak pompously or bombastically: a humorously derogatory term

**o·ra·tion** (ô rā′shən) *n.* [< L. *oratio* < *orare*, to speak] a formal speech, as at a ceremony

**or·a·tor** (ôr′ət ər, är′-) *n.* **1.** a person who delivers an oration **2.** an eloquent public speaker

**or·a·tor·i·cal** (ôr′ə tôr′i k′l, är′-) *adj.* **1.** of or characteristic of orators or oratory **2.** given to oratory —**or′a·tor′i·cal·ly** *adv.*

ORANGUTAN
(standing height
to 60 in.)

**or·a·to·ri·o** (ôr′ə tôr′ē ō′, är′-) *n., pl.* **-os′** [It., small chapel: from performances at a chapel in Rome] a long, dramatic musical work, usually on a religious theme, consisting of arias, recitatives, choruses, etc. with orchestral accompaniment but without stage action, scenery, etc.

**or·a·to·ry** (ôr′ə tôr′ē, är′-) *n., pl.* **-ries** [L. *oratoria*] **1.** the art of an orator; skill in public speaking **2.** [< LL. < L. *oratorius* < *orator*] a small chapel, esp. for private prayer

**orb** (ôrb) *n.* [L. *orbis*, a circle] **1.** a globe; sphere **2.** any heavenly sphere, as the sun or moon **3.** a small globe with a cross, as a symbol of royal power **4.** [Poet.] the eye —*vt.*

**1.** to form into a sphere or circle **2.** [Poet.] to enclose or encircle —**orbed** *adj.* —**orb′y** *adj.*

**or·bic·u·lar** (ôr bik′yo͞o lər) *adj.* [< LL. < L. dim. of *orbis,* a circle] **1.** in the form of an orb; spherical or circular **2.** *Bot.* round and flat, as some leaves Also **or·bic′u·late** (-lit, -lāt′), **or·bic′u·lat′ed** (-lāt′id) —**or·bic′u·lar′i·ty** (-lar′ə tē) *n.* —**or·bic′u·lar·ly** *adv.*

**or·bit** (ôr′bit) *n.* [< MFr. < ML. < L. *orbita,* path < *orbis,* a circle] **1.** the bony cavity containing the eye; eye socket **2.** *a)* the path of a heavenly body in its revolution around another *b)* the path of an artificial satellite or spacecraft around a heavenly body **3.** the range of one's experience or activity —*vi.* to move in an orbit or circle —*vt.* **1.** to put into an orbit in space **2.** to move in an orbit around —**or′bit·al** *adj.*

**or·bit·er** (-ər) *n.* one that moves in an orbit; specif., an artificial satellite designed to orbit a planet, etc.

**or·chard** (ôr′chərd) *n.* [< OE. *ortgeard,* ult. < L. *hortus,* a garden + OE. *geard,* enclosure] **1.** an area of land where fruit trees or nut trees are grown **2.** such trees

**or·ches·tra** (ôr′kis trə, -kes′-) *n.* [L. < Gr. *orchēstra,* space for the chorus in front of the stage < *orcheisthai,* to dance] **1.** the space in front of and below the stage, where the musicians sit: in full, **orchestra pit 2.** *a)* the main-floor seats of a theater, esp. the front section *b)* the main floor itself **3.** *a)* a group of musicians playing together; esp., *same as* SYMPHONY ORCHESTRA *b)* their instruments —**or·ches′tral** (-kes′trəl) *adj.* —**or·ches′tral·ly** *adv.*

**or·ches·trate** (ôr′kis trāt′) *vt., vi.* -**trat′ed,** -**trat′ing 1.** to compose or arrange (music) for an orchestra **2.** to furnish (a ballet, etc.) with an orchestral score **3.** to combine harmoniously —**or′ches·tra′tion** *n.* —**or′ches·tra′tor, or′·ches·trat′er** *n.*

**or·chid** (ôr′kid) *n.* [< L.: see ff.] **1.** any of a family of plants having bulbous roots and flowers with three petals, one lip-shaped **2.** the flower **3.** a light bluish red —*adj.* of this color

**or·chis** (ôr′kis) *n.* [L. < Gr. *orchis,* lit., testicle: from the shape of the roots] an orchid; specif., one with small flowers growing in spikes

**ord.** **1.** order **2.** ordinal **3.** ordinance

**or·dain** (ôr dān′) *vt.* [< OFr. < L. *ordinare* < *ordo,* an order] **1.** to decree; order; establish; enact **2.** to invest with the functions or office of a minister, priest, or rabbi —*vi.* to command; decree —**or·dain′er** *n.* —**or·dain′ment** *n.*

**or·deal** (ôr dēl′, -dē′əl; ôr′dēl) *n.* [OE. *ordal*] **1.** an old method of trial exposing the accused to physical dangers from which he was supposedly protected if innocent **2.** a painful or severe test

**or·der** (ôr′dər) *n.* [< OFr. < L. *ordo,* straight row] **1.** social position **2.** a state of peace; orderly conduct **3.** arrangement of things or events; series **4.** a fixed or definite plan; system **5.** a group set off from others by some quality **6.** a group of persons organized for military, monastic, or social purposes *[the Masonic Order]* **7.** *a)* a group of persons distinguished by having received a certain award or citation *b)* the group's insignia **8.** a condition in which everything is in its right place and functioning properly **9.** condition in general *[in working order]* **10.** a command, direction, etc., usually backed by authority **11.** class; kind; sort *[sentiments of a high order]* **12.** an established method, as of conduct in meetings, court, etc. **13.** *a)* a request or commission to supply something *b)* the goods supplied *c)* a single portion of some food, as in a restaurant **14.** *Archit. a)* any of several classical styles of structure, as Doric, determined chiefly by the type of column and entablature *b)* a style of building **15.** *Biol.* a classification ranking above a family and below a class **16.** *Finance* written instructions to pay money or surrender property **17.** *Theol. a)* any of the nine grades of angels *b)* any rank in the Christian clergy *c)* [*pl.*] the position of ordained minister —*vt.* **1.** to put or keep in order; arrange **2.** *a)* to command *b)* to command to go (*to, out of,* etc.) **3.** to request or direct (something to be supplied) —*vi.* **1.** to give a command **2.** to request that something be supplied —**by order of** according to the command of —**call to order** to request to be quiet, as to start a (meeting) —**in** (or **out of**) **order 1.** in (or not in) proper sequence or position **2.** in (or not in) good condition **3.** in (or not in) accordance with the rules **4.** being (or not being) suitable to the occasion —**in order that** so that; to the end that —**in order to** as a means to —**in short order** without delay —**on order** ordered but not yet supplied —**on the order of 1.** similar to **2.** approximately —**to order** as specified by the buyer —**or′der·er** *n.*

**or·der·ly** (ôr′dər lē) *adj.* **1.** *a)* neatly arranged *b)* conforming to some regular order; systematic **2.** well-behaved; law-abiding —*adv.* in proper order; methodically —*n., pl.* -**lies 1.** *Mil.* an enlisted man assigned as a personal attendant or

given a specific task **2.** a male hospital attendant —**or′der·li·ness** *n.*

**or·di·nal** (ôr′d'n əl) *adj.* [< LL. *ordinalis* < L. *ordo,* an order] **1.** expressing order, specif. of a number in a series: see ORDINAL NUMBER **2.** of an order of animals or plants —*n.* **1.** *same as* ORDINAL NUMBER **2.** [*often* O-] a book of religious rituals

**ordinal number** a number used to indicate order (e.g., ninth, 25th, etc.) in a series: distinguished from CARDINAL NUMBER

**or·di·nance** (ôr′d'n əns) *n.* [< OFr. < *ordener:* see ORDAIN] **1.** an authoritative command **2.** an established practice, rite, etc. **3.** a governmental, now esp. municipal, statute or regulation

**or·di·nar·i·ly** (ôr′d'n er′ə lē) *adv.* **1.** usually; as a rule **2.** in an ordinary way

**or·di·nar·y** (ôr′d'n er′ē) *n., pl.* -**nar′ies** [< OFr. < ML. < L. *ordinarius,* an overseer < *ordo,* an order] **1.** an official of church or court whose power is original, not delegated **2.** [Brit.] *a)* a set meal at a fixed price *b)* an inn, etc. serving such meals **3.** *Eccles.* [*often* O-] the unvarying part of the Mass —*adj.* **1.** customary; usual **2.** *a)* unexceptional; common *b)* relatively inferior —**in ordinary** in regular service —**out of the ordinary** unusual —**or′di·nar′i·ness** *n.*

**or·di·nate** (ôr′d'n it, -āt′) *n.* [< ModL. (*linea*) *ordinate* (*applicata*), line applied in an ordered manner] *Math.* in a system of coordinates, the distance of a point from the horizontal axis as measured along a line parallel to the vertical axis: cf. ABSCISSA

**or·di·na·tion** (ôr′d'n ā′shən) *n.* an ordaining or being ordained

**ord·nance** (ôrd′nəns) *n.* [contr. < ORDINANCE] **1.** cannon or artillery **2.** all military weapons together with ammunition, vehicles, equipment, etc. **3.** a military unit supplying and storing ordnance

**Or·do·vi·cian** (ôr′də vish′ən) *adj.* [< L. *Ordovices,* a tribe in Wales] designating or of the second period of the Paleozoic Era —**the Ordovician** the Ordovician Period or its rocks: see GEOLOGY, chart

**or·dure** (ôr′jər, -dyoor) *n.* [OFr. < *ord,* filthy < L. *horridus,* horrid] dung; excrement

**ore** (ôr) *n.* [OE. *ar,* brass, copper] **1.** any natural combination of minerals, esp. one from which a metal or metals can be profitably extracted **2.** a natural substance from which a nonmetallic material, as sulfur, can be extracted

**ö·re** (ö′rə) *n., pl.* **ö′re** [Sw., ult. < L. *aurum,* gold] *see* MONETARY UNITS, table (Sweden)

**o·re** (ö′rə) *n., pl.* **o′re** [Dan. & Norw.: see prec.] *see* MONETARY UNITS, table (Denmark, Norway)

**o·reg·a·no** (ô reg′ə nō, ə-) *n.* [Sp. *orégano,* ult. < Gr. *origanon*] any of several plants of the mint family, with fragrant leaves used for seasoning

**Or·e·gon** (ôr′i gən, är′-; *also, but not locally,* -gän′) [prob. < AmInd. name of the Columbia River] NW State of the U.S.: 96,981 sq. mi.; pop. 2,633,000; cap. Salem: abbrev. **Oreg., OR** —**Or′e·go′ni·an** (-gō′nē ən) *adj., n.*

**O·res·tes** (ô res′tēz, ə-) *Gr. Myth.* brother of Electra: see ELECTRA

**Ö·re·sund** (Swed. ö′rə sund′) strait between Sweden & the Danish island of Zealand

**or·gan** (ôr′gən) *n.* [< OFr. & OE. < L. *organum* < Gr. *organon,* an instrument < *ergon,* work] **1.** *a)* a large wind instrument consisting of various sets of pipes which, opened by keys on one or more keyboards, allow passage to a column of compressed air causing sound by vibration: also called **pipe organ** *b)* any of several musical instruments producing similar sounds, as a reed organ **2.** in animals and plants, a part composed of specialized tissues and adapted to perform a specific function or functions **3.** a means for performing some action **4.** a means of communicating ideas, as a periodical

**or·gan·dy, or·gan·die** (ôr′gən dē) *n., pl.* -**dies** [Fr. *organdi* < ?] a very sheer, crisp cotton fabric, used for dresses, curtains, etc.

**or·gan·elle** (ôr′gə nel′) *n.* [ult. < L. *organum,* a tool + *-ella,* dim. suffix] a specialized structure within a cell, as a chloroplast or cilium

**organ grinder** a person who makes a living by playing a barrel organ in the streets

**or·gan·ic** (ôr gan′ik) *adj.* **1.** of or having to do with an organ **2.** inherent; constitutional **3.** made up of systematically interrelated parts; organized **4.** *a)* designating or of any chemical compound containing carbon *b)* designating or of the branch of chemistry dealing with carbon compounds **5.** of, like, or derived from living organisms **6.** grown with only animal or vegetable fertilizers **7.** *Law* designating or of fundamental, or constitutional, law **8.**

*Med.* producing or involving alteration in the structure of an organ: cf. FUNCTIONAL —**or·gan′i·cal·ly** *adv.*

**or·gan·ism** (ôr′gə niz′m) *n.* **1.** any animal or plant with organs and parts that function together to maintain life **2.** anything like a living thing in its complexity of structure or functions —**or′gan·is′mic** *adj.* —**or′gan·is′mi·cal·ly** *adv.*

**or·gan·ist** (ôr′gə nist) *n.* one who plays the organ

**or·gan·i·za·tion** (ôr′gə ni zā′shən, -nī-) *n.* **1.** an organizing or being organized **2.** the way in which the parts of a thing are organized **3.** any unified group or systematized whole; esp., *a)* a body of persons organized for some purpose, as a club, union, etc. *b)* the administrative or executive structure of a business or political party —**or′gan·i·za′tion·al** *adj.* —**or′gan·i·za′tion·al·ly** *adv.*

**or·gan·ize** (ôr′gə nīz′) *vt.* **-ized′, -iz′ing 1.** to provide with an organic structure; esp., *a)* to arrange in an orderly way *b)* to bring into a unified, coherent form *c)* to make plans and arrange for **2.** to bring into being; establish **3.** to enlist in, or cause to form, a labor union **4.** [Colloq.] to set (oneself) into an orderly state of mind —*vi.* **1.** to become organized **2.** to form an organization, esp. a labor union —**or′gan·iz′a·ble** *adj.* —**or′gan·iz′er** *n.*

**or·gan·za** (ôr gan′zə) *n.* [< ?] a stiff, sheer fabric of rayon, silk, etc.

**or·gasm** (ôr′gaz′m) *n.* [< Fr. < Gr. *orgasmos* < *organ*, to swell with moisture] a frenzy; esp., the climax of a sexual act —**or·gas′mic, or·gas′tic** *adj.*

**or·gy** (ôr′jē) *n., pl.* **-gies** [< Fr. < L. < Gr. *orgia*, pl., secret rites] **1.** [*usually pl.*] in ancient Greece and Rome, wild celebration in worship of certain gods **2.** any wild, licentious merrymaking **3.** unrestrained indulgence in any activity —**or′gi·as′tic** (-as′tik) *adj.* —**or′gi·as′ti·cal·ly** *adv.*

**o·ri·el** (ôr′ē əl) *n.* [< OFr. < ? ML. *oriolum*, porch] a large window built out from a wall and resting on a bracket or corbel

**o·ri·ent** (ôr′ē ənt; *also, and for v. usually,* -ent′) *n.* [OFr. < L. *oriens*, direction of the rising sun, prp. of *oriri*, to arise] the east: now rare, except [O-] the East, or Asia; esp., the Far East —*adj.* **1.** shining, as pearls **2.** [Poet.] *a)* eastern; oriental *b)* rising, as the sun —*vt.* **1.** to arrange with reference to the east **2.** to set (a map or chart) in agreement with the points of the compass **3.** to adjust or adapt to a particular situation (often used reflexively)

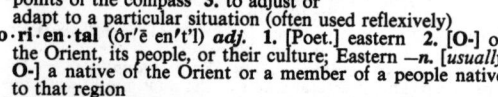

ORIEL

**o·ri·en·tal** (ôr′ē en′t'l) *adj.* **1.** [Poet.] eastern **2.** [O-] of the Orient, its people, or their culture; Eastern —*n.* [*usually* O-] a native of the Orient or a member of a people native to that region

**O·ri·en·tal·ism** (-iz′m) *n.* **1.** any trait, quality, etc. associated with people of the East **2.** study of Eastern culture —**O′ri·en′tal·ist** *n.*

**Oriental poppy** a perennial poppy often grown for its red, pink, or white flowers

**Oriental rug** (or **carpet**) a carpet hand-woven in the Orient, usually with intricate, colorful designs

**o·ri·en·tate** (ôr′ē ən tāt′, -en-) *vt.* **-tat′ed, -tat′ing** same as ORIENT —*vi.* **1.** to face east, or in any specified direction **2.** to adjust to a situation

**o·ri·en·ta·tion** (ôr′ē ən tā′shən, -en-) *n.* **1.** an orienting or being oriented **2.** *a)* awareness of one's environment as to time, space, objects, and persons *b)* a period of introduction and adjustment

**or·i·en·teer·ing** (ôr′ē en tir′iŋ) *n.* [< Swed. *orientering*, lit., orientation] a timed cross-country competition in which runners follow a course, using compass and map

**or·i·fice** (ôr′ə fis, är′-) *n.* [Fr. < LL. *orificium* < L. *os* (gen. *oris*), mouth + *facere*, to make] an opening or mouth, as of a tube or cavity

**or·i·flamme** (ôr′ə flam′, är′-) *n.* [Fr. < OFr. < L. < *aurum*, gold + *flamma*, flame] **1.** the ancient royal standard of France, a red silk banner with flame-shaped streamers **2.** any battle standard

**orig.** **1.** origin **2.** original **3.** originally

**o·ri·ga·mi** (ôr′ə gä′mē) *n.* [Jap.] **1.** a traditional Japanese art of folding paper to form flowers, animal figures, etc. **2.** an object so made

**or·i·gin** (ôr′ə jin, är′-) *n.* [< MFr. < L. *origo* (gen. *originis*) < *oriri*, to rise] **1.** a coming into existence or use; beginning **2.** parentage; birth; lineage **3.** source; root **4.** *Math.* the point at which coordinate axes intersect

**o·rig·i·nal** (ə rij′ə n'l) *adj.* **1.** having to do with an origin; first; earliest **2.** never having been before; new; novel **3.** capable of creating something new, or thinking or acting in an independent, fresh way; inventive **4.** coming from someone as the originator, maker, author, etc. **5.** being that from which copies, reproductions, translations, etc. have been made —*n.* **1.** a primary type that has given rise to varieties **2.** an original work of art, writing, etc., as dis-

tinguished from a copy, etc. **3.** the person or thing depicted in a painting, etc. **4.** a person of original mind and unusual creativity —**o·rig′i·nal·ly** *adv.*

**o·rig·i·nal·i·ty** (ə rij′ə nal′ə tē) *n.* **1.** a being original **2.** the ability to be original, inventive, or creative

**original sin** *Christian Theology* sinfulness and depravity regarded as innate in man as a direct result of Adam's sin

**o·rig·i·nate** (ə rij′ə nāt′) *vt.* **-nat′ed, -nat′ing** to bring into being; esp., to create (something original); invent —*vi.* to come into being; begin; start —**o·rig′i·na′tion** *n.* —**o·rig′i·na′tive** *adj.* —**o·rig′i·na′tor** *n.*

**O·ri·no·co** (ôr′ə nō′kō) river in Venezuela, flowing from N Brazil into the Atlantic: c. 1,700 mi.

**o·ri·ole** (ôr′ē ōl′) *n.* [< OFr. < ML. < L. *aureolus*, golden < *aurum*, gold] **1.** any of a family of yellow and black birds found from Europe to Australia **2.** any of a group of American birds, including the Baltimore oriole, that have orange and black plumage and build hanging nests

**O·ri·on** (ō rī′ən, ô-) an equatorial constellation near Taurus, containing the bright star Rigel

**or·i·son** (ôr′i z'n, är′-; -s'n) *n.* [< OFr. < LL. *oratio*, prayer < L.: see ORATION] a prayer

**Ork·ney Islands** (ôrk′nē) group of islands north of Scotland, constituting a region (**Orkney**) of Scotland

**Or·lan·do** (ôr lan′dō) [after *Orlando* Reeves, an Indian runner] city in C Fla.: pop. 128,000 (met. area 695,000)

**Or·lé·ans** (ôr′lē än′; *E.* ôr′lē ənz) city in NC France, on the Loire: pop. 96,000

**Or·lon** (ôr′län) [arbitrary coinage, after (NYL)ON] a *trademark for* a synthetic fiber somewhat like nylon, or a fabric made from this fiber —*n.* [o-] this fiber or fabric

**Or·mazd** (ôr′məzd) [Per.] *Zoroastrianism* the supreme deity and creator of the world: also sp. **Or′muzd**

**or·mo·lu** (ôr′mə lōō′) *n.* [< Fr. *or moulu*, ground gold] an imitation gold consisting of an alloy of copper and tin, used as decoration, etc.

**or·na·ment** (ôr′nə mənt; *for v.* -ment′) *n.* [< OFr. < L. *ornamentum* < *ornare*, to adorn] **1.** anything that adorns; decoration; embellishment **2.** a person whose character or talent adds luster to his surroundings, society, etc. **3.** an adorning or being adorned **4.** mere external display **5.** *Music* an embellishing trill, arpeggio, etc. —*vt.* to furnish with ornaments or be an ornament to; decorate

**or·na·men·tal** (ôr′nə men′t'l) *adj.* serving as an ornament; decorative —*n.* something ornamental; specif., a decorative plant —**or′na·men′tal·ly** *adv.*

**or·na·men·ta·tion** (-men tā′shən) *n.* **1.** an ornamenting or being ornamented **2.** ornaments collectively

**or·nate** (ôr nāt′) *adj.* [< L. pp. of *ornare*, to adorn] **1.** heavily ornamented; overadorned **2.** showy or flowery, as some literary styles —**or·nate′ly** *adv.* —**or·nate′ness** *n.*

**or·ner·y** (ôr′nər ē) *adj.* [altered < ORDINARY] [Chiefly Dial.] **1.** having an ugly or mean disposition **2.** obstinate **3.** base; low —**or′ner·i·ness** *n.*

**or·ni·thol·o·gy** (ôr′nə thäl′ə jē) *n.* [< ModL. < Gr. *ornis* (gen. *ornithos*), bird + -LOGY] the branch of zoology dealing with birds —**or·ni·tho·log·i·cal** (ôr′ni thə läj′i k'l) *adj.* —**or′ni·tho·log′i·cal·ly** *adv.* —**or′ni·thol′o·gist** *n.*

**o·ro·tund** (ôr′ə tund′) *adj.* [< L. *ore rotundo*, lit., with round mouth] **1.** clear, strong, and deep: said of the voice **2.** bombastic or pompous, as speech —**o′ro·tun′di·ty** *n.*

**O·roz·co** (ô rôs′kô), **Jo·sé Cle·men·te** (hô se′ kle men′te) 1883–1949; Mex. painter

**or·phan** (ôr′fən) *n.* [< LL. < Gr. *orphanos*] a child whose parents are dead —*adj.* **1.** being an orphan **2.** of or for orphans —*vt.* to cause to become an orphan

**or·phan·age** (-ij) *n.* **1.** the state of being an orphan **2.** an institution housing orphans

**Or·phe·us** (ôr′fē əs, -fyōōs) *Gr. Myth.* a poet-musician with magic musical powers who lost his chance to lead his wife, Eurydice, out from the world of the dead when he looked back at her

**Or·phic** (-fik) *adj.* **1.** of or characteristic of Orpheus **2.** [*also* o-] *a)* like the music attributed to Orpheus; entrancing *b)* mystic; occult

**or·pine** (ôr′pin) *n.* [< MFr. < OFr. < L. *auripigmentum*, pigment of gold] a plant with fleshy leaves and white, yellow, or purple flowers

**or·ris** (ôr′is, är′-) *n.* [prob. < MIt. < L. *iris*, iris] any of several European irises, esp. a species whose rootstocks yield orrisroot

**or·ris·root** (-rōōt′) *n.* the rootstock of the orris, ground and used in perfumery, tooth powders, etc.

**or·tho-** [< Gr. *orthos*, straight] *a combining form meaning:* **1.** straight [*orthodontics*] **2.** right angle [*orthoclase*] **3.** correct or standard [*orthography*] **4.** *Med.* correction of deformities [*orthopedics*] Also, before a vowel, **orth-**

**or·tho·clase** (ôr′thə klās′, -klāz′) *n.* [< G. < Gr. *orthos* (see ORTHO-) + *klasis*, fracture, because of 90° cleavage] potassium feldspar, common in granitic rocks

**or·tho·don·tics** (ôr′thə dän′tiks) *n.pl.* [*with sing. v.*] [<

ModL.: see ORTH(O)-, -ODONT, & -ICS] the branch of dentistry concerned with correcting irregularities of the teeth and poor occlusion: also or′tho·don′ti·a (-dän′shə, -shē ə) —or′tho·don′tic adj. —or′tho·don′tist n.

or·tho·dox (ôr′thə däks′) adj. [< Fr. < LL. < LGr. < Gr. orthos, correct + doxa, opinion < dokein, to think] 1. conforming to the usual beliefs or established doctrines, esp. in religion; conventional; specif., a) conforming to the Christian faith as formulated in the early creeds b) [O-] strictly observing the ceremonial rites and traditions of Judaism, such as kashrut, the Sabbath, etc. 2. [O-] designating or of any church in the Orthodox Eastern Church —or′tho·dox′y n., pl. -dox′ies

**Orthodox Eastern Church** the Christian church dominant in E Europe, W Asia, and N Africa, orig. made up of four patriarchates (Constantinople, Alexandria, Antioch, Jerusalem), now also including the autonomous churches of the Soviet Union, Greece, Romania, Bulgaria, etc.

or·tho·e·py (ôr thō′ə pē, ôr′thō-) n. [< ModL. < Gr. < orthos, right + epos, a word] 1. the study of pronunciation; phonology 2. the standard pronunciation of a language —or·tho·ep·ic (ôr′thō ep′ik), or′tho·ep′i·cal adj. —or′tho·ep′i·cal·ly adv. —or·tho′e·pist n.

or·thog·ra·phy (ôr thäg′rə fē) n., pl. -phies [< MFr. < L. < Gr.: see ORTHO- & -GRAPHY] 1. spelling in accord with accepted usage 2. any method of spelling 3. spelling as a subject for study —or·thog′ra·pher n. —or·tho·graph·ic (ôr′thə graf′ik), or′tho·graph′i·cal adj. —or′tho·graph′i·cal·ly adv.

or·tho·pe·dics, or·tho·pae·dics (ôr′thə pē′diks) n.pl. [with sing. v.] [< Fr. < Gr. orthos, straight + paideia, training of children < pais, child] the branch of surgery dealing with the treatment of deformities, diseases, and injuries of the bones, joints, etc. —or′tho·pe′dic, or′tho·pae′dic adj. —or′tho·pe′dist, or′tho·pae′dist n.

or·thop·ter·an (ôr thäp′tər ən) n. [< ORTHO- + Gr. pteron, wing] any of an order of insects, including crickets, grasshoppers, etc., having chewing mouthparts and hard forewings covering membranous hind wings —or·thop′ter·ous adj.

or·to·lan (ôr′t'l ən) n. [Fr. < Pr. < It. < L. hortulanus, dim. of hortus, a garden] an old-world bunting, prized as choice food

**Or·well** (ôr′wel, -wəl), **George** (pseud. of Eric Arthur Blair) 1903-50; Eng. writer —Or·well′i·an adj.

-o·ry (ôr′ē, ər ē) [< OFr. < L. -orius, -oria, -orium] a suffix meaning: 1. of, having the nature of [contradictory] 2. a place or thing for [laboratory]

o·ryx (ôr′iks, är′-) n., pl. o′ryx·es, o′ryx: see PLURAL, II, D, 1 [ModL. < L., wild goat < Gr., lit., pickax] any of a group of large African and Asian antelopes with long horns

‡os¹ (äs) n., pl. os′sa (-ə) [L.] a bone

‡os² (äs) n., pl. o·ra (ôr′ə) [L.] a mouth; opening

**Os** Chem. osmium

**OS, O.S.** Old Style

**OS., OS, O.S.** Old Saxon

**O·sage orange** (ō sāj′, ō′sāj) [< Osage, AmInd. tribe] 1. a thorny tree with hard, yellow wood, used for hedges, etc. 2. its orangelike, inedible fruit

**O·sa·ka** (ō′sä kä′; E. ō sä′kə) seaport in S Honshu, Japan: pop. 3,156,000

**Os·car** (äs′kər) [< OE. < os, a god + gar, a spear] a masculine name —n. [< ?] [Slang] any of the statuettes awarded annually in the U.S. for achievements in motion pictures

os·cil·late (äs′ə lāt′) vi. -lat′ed, -lat′ing [< L. pp. of oscillare, to swing] 1. to swing back and forth 2. to be indecisive; vacillate 3. Physics to vary between maximum and minimum values, as electric current —vt. to cause to oscillate —os′cil·la′tor n. —os′cil·la·to′ry adj.

os·cil·la·tion (äs′ə lā′shən) n. 1. an oscillating 2. fluctuation; instability 3. Physics a) variation between maximum and minimum values, as of current b) a single swing of an oscillating object

os·cil·lo·graph (ä sil′ə graf′, ə-) n. [< L. oscillare, to swing + -GRAPH] an instrument for displaying or recording electrical oscillations in a wavy line (oscillogram) —os·cil′lo·graph′ic adj.

os·cil·lo·scope (-skōp′) n. [< L. oscillare, to swing + -SCOPE] a type of oscillograph that visually displays an electrical wave on a fluorescent screen, as of a cathode-ray tube —os·cil′lo·scop′ic (-skäp′ik) adj.

os·cine (äs′in, -īn) adj. [< ModL. < L. oscen, bird whose notes were used in divining] designating or of a group of perching birds, as the finches, larks, etc., typically with highly developed vocal organs —n. an oscine bird

os·cu·late (äs′kyə lāt′) vt., vi. -lat′ed, -lat′ing [< L. pp. of osculari < osculum, kiss, dim. of os, a mouth] 1. to kiss: a jocular usage 2. to touch closely —os′cu·lant adj. —os′cu·la′tion n. —os′cu·la·to′ry adj.

-ose¹ (ōs) [Fr. < (gluc)ose: see GLUCOSE] a suffix designating: 1. a carbohydrate [sucrose] 2. the product of a protein hydrolysis [proteose]

-ose² (ōs) [L. -osus] a suffix meaning full of, having the qualities of, like [verbose]

**Osh·a·wa** (äsh′ə wə, -wô) city in SE Ontario, Canada, on Lake Ontario: pop. 107,000

**Osh·kosh** (äsh′käsh) [after Oshkosh (1795-1850), Am. Indian chief] city in E Wis.: pop. 50,000

o·sier (ō′zhər) n. [< OFr. < ML. ausaria, bed of willows] 1. any of several willows whose branches or stems are used for baskets and furniture 2. a willow branch used for wickerwork

**O·si·ris** (ō sī′ris) the ancient Egyptian god of the lower world, brother and husband of Isis

-o·sis (ō′sis) [L. < Gr. -ōsis] a suffix meaning: 1. state, condition, action [osmosis] 2. an abnormal or diseased condition [neurosis]

-os·i·ty (äs′ət ē) [< Fr. < L. -ositas] a suffix used to form nouns from adjectives ending in -OSE² or -OUS

**Os·lo** (äs′lō, äz′-; Norw. ōōs′lōō) capital of Norway; seaport in the SE part: pop. 487,000

**Os·man·li** (äz man′lē, äs-) n. [Turk. < Osman (1259-1326), leader & founder of the Ottoman Empire] 1. pl. -lis an Ottoman Turk 2. same as TURKISH (n. 1) —adj. same as TURKISH

os·mics (äz′miks) n.pl. [with sing. v.] [< Gr. osmē, odor + -ICS] the science of smell

os·mi·um (äz′mē əm) n. [ModL. < Gr. osmē, odor: after the odor of one of its oxides] a very hard, bluish-white, metallic chemical element that occurs in the form of an alloy with platinum and iridium: symbol, Os; at. wt., 190.2; at. no., 76

os·mose (äs′mōs, äz′-) vt., vi. -mosed, -mos·ing to undergo osmosis

os·mo·sis (äs mō′sis, äz-) n. [ModL., ult. < Gr. ōsmos, impulse < ōthein, to push] 1. the tendency of a solvent to pass through a semipermeable membrane, as the wall of a living cell, so as to equalize concentrations on both sides of the membrane 2. the diffusion of fluids through a porous partition —os·mot′ic (-mät′ik) adj. —os·mot′i·cal·ly adv.

os·prey (äs′prē) n., pl. -preys [< L. ossifraga, lit., the bonebreaker < os, a bone + frangere, to break] a large diving bird of prey of the hawk family with a blackish back and white breast, that feeds solely on fish

OSPREY
(20-24 in. long)

**Os·sa** (äs′ə) mountain in Thessaly, NE Greece: see PELION

‡os·sa (äs′ə) n. pl. of OS¹

os·se·ous (äs′ē əs) adj. [< L. < os, a bone] composed of, containing, or like bone; bony

**Os·sian** (äsh′ən, äs′ē ən) Gaelic Folklore a bard and hero of the 3d cent. —Os′si·an′ic adj.

os·si·fy (äs′ə fī′) vt., vi. -fied, -fy′ing [< L. os (gen. ossis), a bone + -FY] 1. to change or develop into bone 2. to settle or fix rigidly in a practice, custom, etc. —os′si·fi·ca′tion n.

**Os·si·ning** (äs′ə niŋ) [< Delaware ossingsing, lit., at the standing stone] village in SE N.Y., on the Hudson: site of Sing Sing, a State prison

os·te·al (äs′tē əl) adj. osseous; bony

os·te·i·tis (äs′tē īt′əs) n. [OSTE(O)- + -ITIS] inflammation of the bone or bony tissue

**Ost·end** (äs tend′, äs′tend) seaport & summer resort in NW Belgium, on the North Sea: pop. 58,000

os·ten·si·ble (äs ten′sə b'l, əs-) adj. [Fr. < ML. < L. ostendere, to show < ob(s)-, against + tendere, to stretch] apparent; seeming; professed —os·ten′si·bly adv.

os·ten·sive (äs ten′siv) adj. 1. directly pointing out; clearly demonstrative 2. same as OSTENSIBLE —os·ten′sive·ly adv.

os·ten·ta·tion (äs′tən tā′shən) n. [< L., ult. < ostendere: see OSTENSIBLE] showy display, as of wealth, knowledge, etc.; pretentiousness —os·ten·ta′tious adj. —os′ten·ta′tious·ly adv. —os′ten·ta′tious·ness n.

os·te·o- [< Gr. osteon] a combining form meaning a bone or bones [osteopath]: also, before a vowel, oste-

os·te·ol·o·gy (äs′tē äl′ə jē) n. [ModL.: see prec. & -LOGY] the study of the structure and function of bones —os′te·o·log′i·cal (-ə läj′i k'l) adj. —os′te·ol′o·gist n.

os·te·o·ma (äs′tē ō′mə) n., pl. -mas, -ma·ta (-mə tə) [ModL.: see OSTEO- & -OMA] a tumor composed of bony tissue

os·te·o·ma·la·cia (-ō mə lā′shə) n. [ModL. < OSTEO- + malacia, a softness of tissue] a bone disease characterized by a softening of the bones from a deficiency in calcium salts

**os·te·o·my·e·li·tis** (-ō mī'ə līt'is) *n.* [ModL.: see OSTEO- & MYELITIS] infection of bone marrow or structures

**os·te·op·a·thy** (äs'tē äp'ə thē) *n.* [ModL.: see OSTEO- & -PATHY] a school of medicine and surgery emphasizing the interrelationship of the musculoskeletal system to all other body parts —**os'te·o·path'** (-ə path') *n.* —**os'te·o·path'ic** *adj.* —**os'te·o·path'i·cal·ly** *adv.*

**os·te·o·po·ro·sis** (-ō pô rō'sis) *n.* [ModL. < OSTEO- + *porosis*, a porous condition] a bone disease in which the bones become brittle because of a loss of calcium

**Os·ter·reich** (ös'tər rīH') *Ger. name of* AUSTRIA

**ost·ler** (äs'lər) *n. same as* HOSTLER

**os·tra·cism** (äs'trə siz'm) *n.* [see ff.] **1.** in ancient Greece, the temporary banishment of a citizen by popular vote **2.** an exclusion by general consent, as from society

**os·tra·cize** (-sīz') *vt.* -**cized'**, -**ciz'ing** [Gr. *ostrakizein*, to exile by votes written on potsherds < *ostrakon*, a potsherd] to banish, exclude, etc. by ostracism

**os·trich** (ôs'trich, äs'-) *n., pl.* -**trich·es**, -**trich**: see PLURAL, II, D, 1 [< OFr. < VL. < L. *avis*, bird + *struthio*, ostrich] **1.** a swift-running, non-flying bird of Africa and the Near East, the largest living bird, with a long neck and legs and small wings **2.** *same as* RHEA (*see* RHEA 1)

**Os·tro·goth** (äs'trə gäth') *n.* an East Goth; esp., a member of the tribe which conquered Italy in the 5th cent. A.D. — **Os'tro·goth'ic** *adj.*

**Oś·wie·cim** (ôsh vyan'tsim) *Pol. name of* AUSCHWITZ

**OT., OT, O.T.** Old Testament

**O·thel·lo** (ə thel'ō, ô-) a tragedy by Shakespeare in which the title character, made madly jealous by the villainous Iago, kills his faithful wife, Desdemona

OSTRICH
(to 8 ft. high)

**oth·er** (uth'ər) *adj.* [OE.] **1.** being the remaining one or ones of two or more [Bill and the *other* boy(s)] **2.** different or distinct from that or those implied [some *other* girl] **3.** different [it is *other* than you think] **4.** additional [to have no *other* coat] **5.** former [in *other* times] —*pron.* **1.** the other one [each loved the *other*] **2.** some other person or thing [to do as others do] —*adv.* otherwise; differently [he can't do *other* than go] —**of all others** above all others —**the other day** (or **night, etc.**) not long ago —**oth'er·ness** *n.*

**oth·er·wise** (-wīz') *adv.* **1.** in another manner; differently [to believe *otherwise*] **2.** in all other respects [an *otherwise* intelligent man] **3.** in other circumstances —*adj.* different [his answer could not be *otherwise*]

**other world** a supposed world after death

**oth·er·world·ly** (-wurld'lē) *adj.* being apart from earthly interests —**oth'er·world'li·ness** *n.*

**-ot·ic** (ät'ik) [Gr. -*ōtikos*] *a suffix meaning:* **1.** of or affected with [sclerotic] **2.** producing [narcotic]

**o·ti·ose** (ō'shē ōs', ōt'ē-) *adj.* [< L. < *otium*, leisure] **1.** idle; indolent **2.** ineffective; futile **3.** useless; superfluous —**o'ti·ose'ly** *adv.* —**o'ti·os'i·ty** (-äs'ə tē) *n.*

**O·tis** (ōt'əs) **1.** [orig. family name] a masculine name **2.** **James**, 1725–83; Am. Revolutionary statesman

**o·ti·tis** (ō tīt'əs) *n.* [ModL.: see OTO- & -ITIS] inflammation of the ear

**o·to-** [< Gr. *ous* (gen. *ōtos*), the ear] *a combining form meaning* the ear [otology] : also, before a vowel, **ot-**

**o·tol·o·gy** (ō täl'ə jē) *n.* [OTO- + -LOGY] the branch of medicine dealing with the ear and its disorders —**o·to·log·i·cal** (ōt'ə läj'i k'l) *adj.* —**o·tol'o·gist** *n.*

**o·to·scle·ro·sis** (ōt'ō skli rō'sis) *n.* [OTO- + SCLEROSIS] a growth of spongy bone in the inner ear causing deafness

**O·tran·to** (ō trän'tō) **Strait of** strait between Italy & Albania, connecting the Adriatic & Ionian seas

**Ot·ta·wa¹** (ät'ə wə, -wä') *n.* **1.** *pl.* -**was**, -**wa** a member of a tribe of Indians who lived in SE Canada and in Michigan **2.** their Algonquian language —*adj.* of the Ottawas

**Ot·ta·wa²** (ät'ə wə, -wä') capital of Canada, in SE Ontario: pop. 304,000

**ot·ter** (ät'ər) *n., pl.* -**ters**, -**ter**: see PLURAL, II, D, 1 [OE. *oter*] **1.** a furry, flesh-eating mammal related to the weasel and mink, with webbed feet and a long tail **2.** its fur **3.** *same as* SEA OTTER

**Ot·to** (ät'ō) [< OHG. < *auda*, rich] **1.** a masculine name **2.** **Otto I** 912–973 A.D.; king of Germany (936–973) & emperor of the Holy Roman Empire (962–973): called *the Great*

**Ot·to·man** (ät'ə mən) *adj.* [ult. < Ar. *'Uthmāni*, of Osman: see OSMANLI] *same as* TURKISH —*n., pl.* -**mans** **1.** a Turk **2.** [o-] *a)* a low, cushioned seat or couch without a back or arms *b)* a cushioned footstool

**Ottoman Empire** empire (c.1300–1918) of the Turks, in-

cluding at its peak much of SE Europe, SW Asia, & NE Africa

**ouch** (ouch) *interj.* an exclamation of pain

**ought¹** (ôt) *v.aux.* [orig., pt. of *owe* < OE. pp. of *agan*, to owe] an auxiliary used with infinitives to express obligation or duty [he *ought* to pay his debts] or desirability [you *ought* to eat more] or probability [it *ought* to be over soon]

**ought²** (ôt) *n.* [var. of AUGHT] anything whatever; aught —*adv.* [Archaic] to any degree; aught

**ought³** (ôt) *n.* [by faulty division of *a nought*] a nought; the figure zero (0)

**ought·n't** (-'nt) ought not

**toui** (wē) *adv.* [Fr.] yes

**Oui·ja** (wē'jə, -jē) [Fr. *oui*, yes + G. *ja*, yes] *a trademark for* a device consisting of a planchette and a board bearing the alphabet and other symbols, used in spiritualistic séances, etc.

**ounce¹** (ouns) *n.* [< OFr. < L. *uncia*, a twelfth] **1.** a unit of weight equal to 1/16 pound avoirdupois, or 1/12 pound troy **2.** *same as* FLUID OUNCE **3.** any small amount Abbrev. **oz.** (*sing. & pl.*)

**ounce²** (ouns) *n.* [< OFr. *l'once* < VL. < L. *lynx*, lynx] *same as* SNOW LEOPARD

**our** (our, är) *possessive pronominal adj.* [OE. *ure*] of, belonging to, made, or done by us

**Our Father** *same as* LORD'S PRAYER

**ours** (ourz, ärz) *pron.* that or those belonging to us: used without a following noun [ours are better] : also used after *of* to indicate possession [a friend of *ours*]

**our·self** (our self', är-) *pron.* a form corresponding to OURSELVES, used, as in royal proclamations, by one person

**our·selves** (-selvz') *pron.* a form of the 1st pers. pl. pronoun, used: *a)* as an intensive [we went *ourselves*] *b)* as a reflexive [we hurt *ourselves*] *c)* as a quasi-noun meaning "our real or true selves" [we are not *ourselves* today]

**-ous** (əs) [< OFr. < L. -*osus*] *a suffix meaning:* **1.** having, full of, characterized by [dangerous] **2.** *Chem.* having a lower valence than is indicated by the suffix -*ic* [nitrous]

**ou·sel** (ōō'z'l) *n. same as* OUZEL

**oust** (oust) *vt.* [< Anglo-Fr. < OFr. *ouster* < L. *ostare* < *ob-*, against + *stare*, to stand] to force or drive out; expel, dispossess, eject, etc.

**oust·er** (ou'stər) *n.* **1.** a person or thing that ousts **2.** *Law* an ousting or being ousted, esp. from real property; legal eviction or unlawful dispossession

**out** (out) *adv.* [OE. *ut*] **1.** *a)* away or forth from a place, position, etc. [they live ten miles *out*] *b)* away from home *c)* away from shore *d)* on strike **2.** into the open air [come *out* and play] **3.** into existence or activity [disease broke *out*] **4.** *a)* to a conclusion [argue it *out*] *b)* completely [tired *out*] *c)* in full bloom, or in leaf **5.** into sight or notice [the moon came *out*] **6.** *a)* into or in circulation [to put *out* a new style] *b)* into or in society [debutantes who come *out*] **7.** from existence or activity [fade *out*] **8.** so as to remove from power or office [vote them *out*] **9.** aloud [sing *out*] **10.** beyond a regular surface, condition, etc. [stand *out*, eke *out*] **11.** away from the interior or midst [spread *out*] **12.** from one state, as of composure, to another, as of annoyance [friends may fall *out*] **13.** into disuse, discard, etc. [long skirts went *out*] **14.** from a number or stock [pick *out*] **15.** [Slang] into unconsciousness [pass *out*] **16.** *Baseball*, etc. in a manner that results in an out [to fly *out*] —*adj.* **1.** external: usually in combination [outpost] **2.** beyond regular limits **3.** outlying **4.** directed outward [an *out* flight] **5.** away from work, etc. **6.** deviating from what is accurate **7.** *a)* not in operation, use, etc. *b)* turned off; extinguished **8.** not to be considered; not possible **9.** not in power **10.** [Colloq.] having suffered a loss [out five dollars] **11.** [Colloq.] outmoded **12.** *Baseball* having failed to get on base —*prep.* **1.** out of; through to the outside **2.** along the way of [to drive *out* a driveway] **3.** [Poet.] forth from: usually after *from* —*n.* **1.** something that is out **2.** a person, group, etc. that is not in power, etc.: *usually used in pl.* **3.** [Slang] a way out; means of avoiding **4.** *Baseball* the failure of a batter or runner to reach base safely **5.** *Tennis, Squash*, etc. a service or return that lands out of bounds —*vi.* to come out; esp., to become known —*vt.* to put out —*interj.* get out! —**on the outs** [Colloq.] on unfriendly terms —**out and away** by far; without comparison —**out and out** completely; thoroughly —**out for** making a determined effort to get or do —**out of 1.** from inside of **2.** from the number of **3.** beyond **4.** from (material, etc.) [made *out* of stone] **5.** because of [out of spite] **6.** having no [out of gas] **7.** not in a condition of [out of order] **8.** so as to deprive [cheat *out* of money] —**out one's way** [Colloq.] to or near one's neighborhood —**out** to making a determined effort to

**out-** [< OUT] *a combining form meaning:* **1.** at or from a point away, outside [outbuilding] **2.** going away or forth, outward [outbound] **3.** better, greater, or more than *[outdo]* : a frequent usage as in the following self-explanatory terms:

| | | |
|---|---|---|
| **outact** | **outhit** | **outscore** |
| **outbox** | **outperform** | **outshout** |
| **outfight** | **outproduce** | **outspend** |

**out·age** (out′ij) *n.* [OUT- + -AGE] an accidental suspension of operation, as of electric power

**out-and-out** (out′'n out′) *adj.* complete; thorough

**out·back** (out′bak′) *n.* [*also* O-] the sparsely settled, flat, arid inland region of Australia

**out·bal·ance** (out′bal′əns) *vt.* **-anced, -anc·ing** to be greater than in weight, value, etc.

**out·bid** (-bid′) *vt.* **-bid′, -bid′ding** to bid or offer more than (someone else)

**out·board** (out′bôrd′) *adj., adv.* **1.** outside the hull or bulwarks of a ship or boat **2.** away from the fuselage or hull of an aircraft **3.** outside the main body of a spacecraft —*n.* **1.** *same as* OUTBOARD MOTOR **2.** a boat with an outboard motor

**outboard motor** a portable gasoline engine mounted outboard on a boat to propel it

**out·bound** (-bound′) *adj.* outward bound

**out·break** (-brāk′) *n.* a breaking out; sudden occurrence, as of disease, war, rioting, etc.

**out·build·ing** (-bil′diŋ) *n.* a structure, as a garage, separate from the main building

**out·burst** (-burst′) *n.* a sudden release, as of feeling

**out·cast** (-kast′) *adj.* driven out; rejected —*n.* a person or thing cast out or rejected

**out·class** (out′klas′) *vt.* to surpass; excel

**out·come** (out′kum′) *n.* result; consequence

**out·crop** (out′kräp′; *for v.* -kräp′) *n.* **1.** the emergence of a mineral from the earth so as to be exposed on the surface **2.** the mineral —*vi.* **-cropped′, -crop′ping 1.** to emerge in this way **2.** to break forth

**out·cry** (-krī′) *n., pl.* **-cries′ 1.** a crying out **2.** a strong protest or objection

**out·dat·ed** (out′dāt′id) *adj.* no longer popular

**out·dis·tance** (-dis′təns) *vt.* **-tanced, -tanc·ing** to leave behind, as in a race

**out·do** (-doo′) *vt.* **-did′, -done′, -do′ing** to exceed or surpass —**outdo oneself** to do better than one expected to

**out·door** (out′dôr′) *adj.* **1.** being or taking place outdoors **2.** of, or fond of, the outdoors

**out·doors** (-dôrz′) *adv.* in or into the open; outside —*n.* **1.** any area outside a building **2.** countryside, etc. where there are few houses

**out·er** (out′ər) *adj.* **1.** located farther out; exterior **2.** relatively far removed *[the outer regions]*

**out·er·coat** (-kōt′) *n.* a topcoat, overcoat, etc.

**Outer Mongolia** *former name of* MONGOLIAN PEOPLE'S REPUBLIC

**out·er·most** (-mōst′) *adj.* located farthest without

**outer space 1.** space beyond the atmosphere of the earth **2.** space beyond the solar system

**out·er·wear** (-wer′) *n.* outer garments, as topcoats

**out·face** (out′fās′) *vt.* **-faced′, -fac′ing 1.** to subdue with a look or stare **2.** to defy or resist

**out·field** (out′fēld′) *n. Baseball* **1.** the playing area beyond the infield **2.** the outfielders

**out·field·er** (-ər) *n. Baseball* a player whose position is in the outfield

**out·fit** (-fit′) *n.* **1.** *a)* a set of articles for equipping *b)* the equipment used in any craft or activity **2.** articles of clothing worn together **3.** a group of people associated in some activity, as a military unit —*vt.* **-fit′ted, -fit′ting** to equip —*vi.* to obtain an outfit —**out′fit′ter** *n.*

**out·flank** (out′flaŋk′) *vt.* **1.** to go around and beyond the flank of (enemy troops) **2.** to thwart; outwit

**out·flow** (out′flō′) *n.* **1.** the act of flowing out **2.** *a)* that which flows out *b)* amount flowing out

**out·fox** (out′fäks′) *vt.* to outwit; outsmart

**out·gen·er·al** (-jen′ər əl) *vt.* **-aled** or **-alled, -al·ing** or **-al·ling** to surpass, as in leadership

**out·go** (out′gō′; *for n.* out′gō′) *vt.* **-went′, -gone′, -go′ing** to surpass; go beyond —*n., pl.* **-goes′ 1.** a going out **2.** that which goes or is paid out; outflow or expenditure

**out·go·ing** (out′gō′iŋ) *adj.* **1.** going out; leaving **2.** sociable, friendly, etc. —*n.* the act of going out

**out·grow** (out′grō′) *vt.* **-grew′, -grown′, -grow′ing 1.** to grow faster or larger than **2.** to lose or get rid of by becoming mature **3.** to grow too large for

**out·growth** (out′grōth′) *n.* **1.** a growing out **2.** a result; consequence; development **3.** an offshoot

**out·guess** (out′ges′) *vt.* to outwit; anticipate

**out·house** (out′hous′) *n.* an outbuilding; specif., a small outbuilding with a toilet over a pit

**out·ing** (-iŋ) *n.* **1.** a pleasure trip or holiday away from home **2.** an outdoor walk, ride, etc.

**out·land·er** (-lan′dər) *n.* a foreigner; stranger

**out·land·ish** (out lan′dish) *adj.* **1.** very odd; fantastic **2.** remote; out-of-the-way —**out·land′ish·ly** *adv.*

**out·last** (-last′) *vt.* **1.** to endure longer than **2.** to outlive

**out·law** (out′lô′) *n.* [OE. *utlaga* < ON. *utlagr*] **1.** orig., a person deprived of legal rights and protection **2.** a notorious criminal who is a fugitive from the law —*vt.* **1.** orig., to declare to be an outlaw **2.** to remove the legal force of (contracts, etc.) **3.** to declare illegal **4.** to bar, or ban —**out′law′ry** *n., pl.* **-ries**

**out·lay** (out′lā′; *for v., usually* out′lā′) *n.* **1.** a spending (of money, energy, etc.) **2.** money, etc. spent —*vt.* **-laid′, -lay′ing** to spend (money)

**out·let** (out′let′) *n.* **1.** a passage for letting something out **2.** a means of expression *[an outlet for rage]* **3.** a stream, river, etc. that flows out from a lake **4.** *a)* a market for goods *b)* a store, etc. that sells the goods of a specific manufacturer or wholesaler **5.** a point in a wiring system at which electric current may be taken by inserting a plug

**out·line** (out′līn′) *n.* **1.** a line bounding the limits of an object **2.** a sketch showing the contours of an object **3.** *[also pl.]* an undetailed general plan **4.** a systematic listing of the important points of a subject —*vt.* **-lined′, -lin′ing 1.** to draw in outline **2.** to list the main points of

**out·live** (out′liv′) *vt.* **-lived′, -liv′ing 1.** to live or endure longer than **2.** to live through; outlast

**out·look** (out′look′) *n.* **1.** *a)* a place for looking out *b)* the view from such a place **2.** a looking out **3.** viewpoint **4.** prospect; probable result

**out·ly·ing** (-lī′iŋ) *adj.* relatively far out from a certain point or center; remote

**out·man** (out′man′) *vt.* **-manned′, -man′ning** to surpass in number of men

**out·ma·neu·ver, out·ma·noeu·vre** (-mə noo′vər) *vt.* **-vered** or **-vred, -ver·ing** or **-vring** to maneuver with better effect than; outwit

**out·match** (-mach′) *vt.* to surpass; outdo

**out·mi·grant** (out′mī′grənt) *adj.* leaving one region, etc. to go to another —*n.* an out-migrant person

**out·mod·ed** (out′mōd′id) *adj.* no longer in fashion or accepted; obsolete

**out·most** (out′mōst′) *adj.* most remote; outermost

**out·num·ber** (out′num′bər) *vt.* to exceed in number

**out-of-date** (out′əv dāt′) *adj.* no longer in style or use; outmoded; old-fashioned

**out-of-door** (-dôr′) *adj. same as* OUTDOOR

**out-of-doors** (-dôrz′) *adv., n. same as* OUTDOORS

**out-of-the-way** (-thə wā′) *adj.* **1.** secluded **2.** unusual **3.** not conventional

**out·pa·tient** (out′pā′shənt) *n.* a patient, not an inmate, receiving treatment at a hospital

**out·play** (out′plā′) *vt.* to play better than

**out·point** (-point′) *vt.* to score more points than

**out·post** (out′pōst′) *n.* **1.** *Mil. a)* a small group stationed at a distance from the main force, to prevent a surprise attack *b)* the station so occupied *c)* any military base in a foreign country **2.** a frontier settlement

**out·pour** (out′pôr′; *for v.* out′pôr′) *n.* **1.** a pouring out **2.** outflow Also **out′pour′ing** —*vt., vi.* to pour out

**out·put** (out′poot′) *n.* **1.** the work done or amount produced, esp. over a given period **2.** in computers, *a)* information transferred or delivered *b)* the act or process of transferring or delivering this information *c)* any of various devices involved in this process **3.** *Elec. a)* the useful current delivered by amplifiers, generators, etc. or by a circuit *b)* the terminal where such energy is delivered

**out·rage** (out′rāj′) *n.* [< OFr. < *outre,* beyond < L. *ultra*] **1.** an extremely vicious or violent act **2.** a deep insult or offense **3.** great anger, indignation, etc. aroused by such an act or offense —*vt.* **-raged′, -rag′ing 1.** to commit an outrage upon; specif., *a)* to offend, insult, or wrong *b)* to rape **2.** to cause great anger, etc. in

**out·ra·geous** (out rā′jəs) *adj.* **1.** involving or doing great injury or wrong **2.** very offensive or shocking —**out·ra′geous·ly** *adv.* —**out·ra′geous·ness** *n.*

**out·rank** (out′raŋk′) *vt.* to exceed in rank

‡**ou·tré** (ōō trā′; *E.* -trā′) *adj.* [Fr.] **1.** exaggerated **2.** eccentric; bizarre

**out·reach** (out′rēch′; *for n.* out′rēch′) *vt., vi.* **1.** to reach farther (than); surpass **2.** to reach out; extend —*n.* **1.** a reaching out **2.** the extent of reach

**out·ride** (out′rīd′) *vt.* **-rode′, -rid′den, -rid′ing 1.** to surpass in riding **2.** to endure successfully

**out·rid·er** (out′rīd′ər) *n.* **1.** an attendant on horseback who rides ahead of or beside a carriage **2.** a cowboy who rides over a range to prevent cattle from straying **3.** a trailblazer; forerunner

**out·rig·ger** (-rig′ər) *n.* **1.** any framework extended beyond the rail of a ship, as a projecting brace for an oarlock **2.** a timber rigged out from the side of a native canoe to prevent tipping; also, a canoe of this type

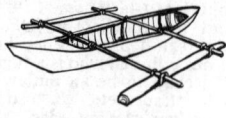

OUTRIGGER

**out·right** (out′rīt′; *for adv.* out′rīt′) *adj.* **1.** without reservation; downright **2.** straightforward **3.** complete; whole —*adv.* **1.** entirely **2.** openly **3.** at once —**out′right′- ness** *n.*

**out·run** (out′run′) *vt.* **-ran′, -run′, -run′ning 1.** to run faster or farther than **2.** to exceed **3.** to escape (a pursuer) as by running

**out·sell** (-sel′) *vt.* **-sold′, -sell′ing 1.** to sell in greater amounts than **2.** to excel in salesmanship

**out·set** (out′set′) *n.* a setting out; beginning

**out·shine** (out′shīn′) *vt.* **-shone′** *or* **-shined′, -shin′ing 1.** to shine brighter or longer than (another) **2.** to surpass; excel —*vi.* to shine forth

**out·shoot** (out′shoot′; *for n.* out′shoot′) *vt., vi.* **-shot′, -shoot′ing** to shoot better than (another) —*n.* that which shoots out or protrudes

**out·side** (out′sīd′, out′-; -sīd′) *n.* **1.** the outer side, part, or surface; exterior **2.** *a)* outward aspect or appearance *b)* that which is obvious or superficial **3.** any place or area not inside —*adj.* **1.** of or on the outside; outer **2.** coming from or situated beyond given limits; from some other place, person, group, etc. /to accept no *outside* help/ **3.** extreme [an *outside* estimate] **4.** mere; slight [an *outside* chance] —*adv.* **1.** on or to the outside **2.** beyond certain limits **3.** outdoors —*prep.* **1.** on or to the outer side of **2.** beyond the limits of —**at the outside** at the very most —**out·side of 1.** outside **2.** [Colloq.] other than

**out·sid·er** (out′sīd′ər) *n.* one who is outside or not included; esp., one not a member of a given group

**out·sit** (-sit′) *vt.* **-sat′, -sit′ting** to sit longer than or beyond the time of

**out·size** (out′sīz′) *n.* **1.** an odd size; esp., an unusually large size **2.** a garment, etc. of such a size —*adj.* of nonstandard size; esp., unusually large: also **out′sized′**

**out·skirts** (-skurts′) *n.pl.* the outer areas, as of a city

**out·smart** (out′smärt′) *vt.* [Colloq.] to overcome by cunning or cleverness; outwit

**out·spo·ken** (out′spō′kən) *adj.* **1.** unrestrained in speech; frank **2.** spoken boldly or candidly —**out′spo′ken·ly** *adv.* —**out′spo′ken·ness** *n.*

**out·spread** (out′spred′; *for adj. & n.* out′spred′) *vt., vi.* **-spread′, -spread′ing** to spread out; extend; expand —*n.* a spreading out —*adj.* spread out; extended; expanded

**out·stand·ing** (out′stand′iŋ) *adj.* **1.** projecting **2.** prominent; distinguished **3.** unsettled **4.** unpaid **5.** that have been issued and sold: said of stocks and bonds —**out′- stand′ing·ly** *adv.*

**out·stare** (-ster′) *vt.* **-stared′, -star′ing** to outdo in staring; stare down; outface

**out·stay** (-stā′) *vt.* **1.** to stay longer than **2.** to stay beyond the time of; overstay

**out·stretch** (-strech′) *vt.* **1.** to extend **2.** to stretch beyond —**out′stretched′** *adj.*

**out·strip** (-strip′) *vt.* **-stripped′, -strip′ping 1.** to go at a faster pace than; get ahead of **2.** to surpass; excel

**out·talk** (-tôk′) *vt.* to talk more skillfully, loudly, or forcibly than; surpass in talking

**out·think** (-thiŋk′) *vt.* **-thought′, -think′ing 1.** to think deeper, faster, or more cunningly than **2.** to outwit by such thinking

**out·vote** (-vōt′) *vt.* **-vot′ed, -vot′ing** to defeat or surpass in voting

**out·ward** (out′wərd) *adj.* **1.** having to do with the outside; outer **2.** readily seen; visible **3.** to or toward the outside **4.** having to do with the physical as opposed to the mind or spirit **5.** superficial or external —*adv.* **1.** toward the outside; away **2.** visibly; publicly Also **out′wards** *adv.* —*n.* that which is outward —**out′ward·ness** *n.*

**out·ward·ly** (-lē) *adv.* **1.** toward or on the outside **2.** in regard to outward appearance or action

**out·wear** (out′wer′) *vt.* **-wore′, -worn′, -wear′ing 1.** to wear out **2.** to be more lasting than

**out·weigh** (-wā′) *vt.* **1.** to weigh more than **2.** to be more important, valuable, etc. than

**out·wit** (-wit′) *vt.* **-wit′ted, -wit′ting** to get the better of by cunning or cleverness

**out·work** (out′wurk′; *for v.* out′wurk′) *n.* a lesser fortifica-

tion built out beyond the main defenses —*vt.* **-worked′** *or* **-wrought′, -work′ing** to work better or harder than

**ou·zel** (oo′z′l) *n.* [OE. *osle*] any of several perching birds including the dippers, of Europe, Asia, and the New World; esp., *same as* WATER OUZEL

**o·va** (ō′və) *n. pl. of* OVUM

**o·val** (ō′v′l) *adj.* [ < Fr. < L. *ovum,* an egg] **1.** shaped like the cross section of an egg lengthwise; elliptical **2.** having the form of an egg —*n.* anything oval —**o′val·ly** *adv.*

**Oval Office** the oval-shaped office of the President in the White House; also, his position, authority, or power

**o·var·i·ec·to·my** (ō ver′ē ek′tə mē) *n., pl.* **-mies** [see -ECTOMY] the surgical removal of one or both ovaries

**o·va·ry** (ō′vər ē) *n., pl.* **-ries** [ < ModL. < L. *ovum,* an egg] **1.** *Anat., Zool.* either of the pair of female reproductive glands producing eggs and, in vertebrates, sex hormones **2.** *Bot.* the enlarged hollow part of the pistil, containing ovules —**o·var·i·an** (ō ver′ē ən) *adj.*

**o·vate** (ō′vāt) *adj.* [ < L. < *ovum,* an egg] **1.** egg-shaped **2.** *Bot.* shaped like the longitudinal section of an egg, esp. with the broader end at the base, as some leaves —**o′vate·ly** *adv.*

**o·va·tion** (ō vā′shən) *n.* [L. *ovatio* < *ovare,* to celebrate a triumph] an enthusiastic outburst of applause or an enthusiastic public welcome

**ov·en** (uv′ən) *n.* [OE. *ofen*] a compartment or receptacle for baking or roasting food or for heating or drying things

**ov·en·bird** (-burd′) *n.* a N. American warbler that builds a domelike nest on the ground

**o·ver** (ō′vər) *prep.* [OE. *ofer*] **1.** *a)* in, at, or to a position up from; above *b)* across and down from /to fall *over* a cliff/ **2.** while engaged in /discuss it *over* dinner/ **3.** upon the surface of /spread icing *over* the cake/ **4.** so as to cover /shutters *over* the windows/ **5.** upon, as an effect or influence /he cast a spell *over* us/ **6.** with care, concern, etc. for /watch *over* the flock/ **7.** in authority, power, etc. **8.** along or across, or above and to the other side of /fly *over* the lake/ **9.** on the other side of /a city *over* the border/ **10.** through all or many parts of /over the whole State/ **11.** during /over a decade/ **12.** more than /over ten dollars/ **13.** up to and including /stay *over* Easter/ **14.** rather than **15.** concerning; about **16.** through the medium of /over the radio/ —*adv.* **1.** *a)* above, across, or to the other side *b)* across the brim or edge **2.** more; beyond /three hours or *over*/ **3.** longer or till a time later /please stay *over*/ **4.** covering the entire area /the wound healed *over*/ **5.** from start to finish /count the money *over*/ **6.** *a)* from an upright position /he fell *over*/ *b)* upside down /turn the cup *over*/ **7.** again /do it *over*/ **8.** at or on the other side, as of an intervening space /over in Spain/ **9.** from one side, viewpoint, person, etc. to another /they won him *over*/ —*adj.* **1.** upper, outer, superior, excessive, or extra: often in combination /overcoat, overseer, oversupply/ **2.** finished; past /his life is *over*/ **3.** having reached the other side **4.** [Colloq.] as a surplus; extra /an hour *over* for the week/ —*n.* something in addition; surplus —*interj.* turn the page, etc. over —**over again** another time; anew —**over all** from end to end —**over and above** more than —**over and over (again)** repeatedly

**o·ver-** *a combining form meaning:* **1.** above in position, outer, upper, superior /overhead, overlord/ **2.** passing across or beyond /overrun/ **3.** involving a movement downward from above /overflow/ **4.** excessive(ly), too much /overload, oversell/ : the list below includes some common compounds formed with *over-* that can be understood if *too* or *too much* is added to the meaning of the base word

| | | |
|---|---|---|
| overabundance | overeager | overpayment |
| overabundant | overeat | overpeopled |
| overactive | overemotional | overpopulate |
| overambitious | overemphasize | overpraise |
| overanxious | overenthusiastic | overprecise |
| overattentive | overexercise | overrefined |
| overbold | overexert | overreligious |
| overbuild | overexpand | overripe |
| overburden | overexpose | oversensitive |
| overbusy | overexpand | oversentimental |
| overbuy | overfed | oversolicitous |
| overcapitalize | overfond | overspecialize |
| overcareful | overgenerous | overstimulate |
| overcareless | overgreedy | overstretch |
| overcautious | overhasty | overstrict |
| overcompensate | overheat | overstudy |
| overconfident | overindulge | oversubtle |
| overconscientious | overindulgence | oversufficient |
| overconservative | overinflate | oversuspicious |
| overcook | overinvert | overtire |
| overcritical | overladen | overuse |
| overcrowd | overlong | overvalue |
| overdecorate | overnice | overwind |
| overdependent | overorganize | overvalue |
| overdye | overpay | overzealous |

o·ver·act (ō′vər akt′) *vt., vi.* to act with exaggeration

o·ver·age¹ (ō′vər āj′) *adj.* 1. over the age fixed as a standard 2. so old as to be of no use

o·ver·age² (ō′vər ij) *n.* [OVER- + -AGE] a surplus or excess, as of goods

o·ver·all (ō′vər ôl′; *for adv.* -ôl′) *adj.* 1. from end to end 2. including everything; total —*adv.* 1. from end to end 2. in general

o·ver·alls (-ôlz′) *n.pl.* loose-fitting trousers, often with an attached bib, worn over other clothing to protect against dirt and wear

o·ver·arm (-ärm′) *adj.* performed by raising the arm above the shoulder, as in swimming

o·ver·awe (ō′vər ô′) *vt.* -awed′, -aw′ing to overcome or subdue by inspiring awe

o·ver·bal·ance (ō′vər bal′əns; *for n.* ō′vər bal′əns) *vt.* -anced, -anc·ing 1. *same as* OUTWEIGH 2. to throw off balance —*n.* something that overbalances

o·ver·bear (ō′vər ber′) *vt.* -bore′, -borne′, -bear′ing 1. to press down by weight or physical power 2. to dominate or subdue —*vi.* to be too fruitful

o·ver·bear·ing (-iŋ) *adj.* 1. arrogant or domineering 2. dominant or overriding —o′ver·bear′ing·ly *adv.* —o′ver·bear′ing·ness *n.*

o·ver·bid (ō′vər bid′; *for n.* ō′vər bid′) *vt., vi.* -bid′, -bid′ding 1. to outbid (another person) 2. to bid more than the worth of (a thing, as one's hand in bridge) —*n.* a higher or excessive bid

o·ver·blown¹ (ō′vər blōn′) *adj.* past the stage of full bloom

o·ver·blown² (ō′vər blōn′) *adj.* 1. stout; obese 2. *a)* overdone; excessive *b)* pompous; bombastic

o·ver·board (ō′vər bôrd′) *adv.* 1. over a ship's side 2. from a ship into the water —go overboard [Colloq.] to go to extremes

o·ver·cast (ō′vər kast′; *for v. 1, usually* ō′vər kast′) *n.* a covering, esp. of clouds —*adj.* 1. cloudy: said of the sky or weather 2. *Sewing* made with overcasting —*vt., vi.* -cast′, -cast′ing 1. to overcloud 2. *Sewing* to sew over (an edge) with long, loose stitches to prevent raveling

o·ver·charge (ō′vər chärj′; *for n.* ō′vər chärj′) *vt., vi.* -charged′, -charg′ing 1. to charge too high a price 2. to overload 3. to exaggerate —*n.* 1. an excessive charge 2. too full or heavy a load

o·ver·cloud (-kloud′) *vt., vi.* 1. to darken or cover over with clouds; dim 2. to make or become gloomy, angry, etc. in appearance

o·ver·coat (ō′vər kōt′) *n.* a coat, esp. a heavy coat, worn over the usual clothing for warmth

o·ver·come (ō′vər kum′) *vt.* -came′, -come′, -com′ing 1. to get the better of; defeat; conquer 2. to master, prevail over, or surmount [to *overcome* obstacles] 3. to overpower or overwhelm [overcome by laughter] —*vi.* to win

o·ver·de·vel·op (-di vel′əp) *vt.* 1. to develop too much 2. *Photog.* to develop (a film, plate, etc.) too long or in too strong a developer —o′ver·de·vel′op·ment *n.*

o·ver·do (-dōō′) *vt.* -did′, -done′, -do′ing 1. to do too much, or to excess 2. to spoil the effect of by exaggeration 3. to cook too long 4. to exhaust; tire —*vi.* to do too much

o·ver·dose (ō′vər dōs′; *for v.* ō′vər dōs′) *n.* too large a dose —*vt.* -dosed′, -dos′ing to dose to excess

o·ver·draft (ō′vər draft′) *n.* 1. an overdrawing of money from a bank 2. the amount overdrawn

o·ver·draw (ō′vər drô′) *vt.* -drew′, -drawn′, -draw′ing 1. to spoil the effect of by exaggeration 2. to draw on in excess of the amount credited to the drawer

o·ver·dress (-dres′) *vt., vi.* to dress too warmly, too showily, or too formally for the occasion

o·ver·drive (ō′vər drīv′) *n.* a gear that automatically reduces an engine's power output without reducing its driving speed

o·ver·due (ō′vər dōō′, -dyōō′) *adj.* 1. past or delayed beyond the time set for payment, arrival, etc. 2. that should have come about sooner

o·ver·es·ti·mate (-es′tə māt′; *for n.* -mit) *vt.* -mat′ed, -mat′ing to set too high an estimate on or for —*n.* an estimate that is too high —o′ver·es′ti·ma′tion *n.*

o·ver·ex·tend (-ik stend′) *vt.* to extend beyond reasonable limits or beyond one's capacity to meet obligations —o′ver·ex·ten′sion (-ik sten′shən) *n.*

o·ver·flow (ō′vər flō′; *for n.* ō′vər flō′) *vt.* 1. to flow or spread across; flood 2. to flow over the brim or edge of 3. to cause to overflow by filling beyond capacity —*vi.* 1. to run over 2. to be superabundant —*n.* 1. an overflowing or being overflowed 2. the amount that overflows; surplus 3. an outlet for overflowing liquids

o·ver·fly (ō′vər flī′) *vt.* -flew′, -flown′, -fly′ing to fly an aircraft over (a specified area) or beyond (a specified place), as for reconnaissance —o′ver·flight′ *n.*

o·ver·grow (-grō′) *vt.* -grew′, -grown′, -grow′ing 1. to overspread with growth or foliage so as to cover up 2. to outgrow —*vi.* 1. to grow too large or too fast 2. to grow beyond normal size —o′ver·grown′ *adj.* —o′ver·growth′ *n.*

o·ver·hand (ō′vər hand′) *adj.* 1. with the hand over the object it grasps 2. done with the hand raised above the shoulder 3. designating or of sewing in which the stitches are passed over two edges to sew them together —*adv.* in an overhand manner —*vt.* to sew overhand —*n. Sports* an overhand stroke

o·ver·hang (ō′vər haŋ′; *for n.* ō′vər haŋ′) *vt.* -hung′, -hang′ing 1. to hang or project over or beyond 2. to impend; threaten —*vi.* to project or jut out over something —*n.* 1. the projection of one thing over or beyond another 2. an overhanging or projecting part

o·ver·haul (ō′vər hôl′; *for n.* ō′vər hôl′) *vt.* 1. to haul over, as for examination 2. *a)* to check thoroughly for needed repairs, adjustments, etc. *b)* to make such repairs, etc., as on a motor 3. to catch up with —*n.* an overhauling

o·ver·head (ō′vər hed′; *for adv.* ō′vər hed′) *adj.* 1. located or operating above the level of the head 2. in the sky 3. on a higher level, with reference to related objects —*n.* the regular costs of running a business, as of rent, maintenance, taxes, etc. —*adv.* above the head; aloft

o·ver·hear (ō′vər hir′) *vt.* -heard′, -hear′ing to hear (something spoken or a speaker) without the speaker's knowledge or intention

o·ver·joy (-joi′) *vt.* to give great joy to; delight

o·ver·kill (ō′vər kil′) *n.* 1. the capacity of a nation's nuclear weapon stockpile to kill many times the total population of any given nation 2. much more of something than is necessary, appropriate, etc.; esp., an excess of effort in trying to achieve some end

o·ver·land (-land′, -lənd) *adv., adj.* by, on, or across land

O·ver·land Park (ō′vər lənd) [after the *Overland*, or Santa Fe, Trail which passed through the area] city in NE Kans.: suburb of Kansas City: pop. 82,000

o·ver·lap (ō′vər lap′; *for n.* ō′vər lap′) *vt., vi.* -lapped′, -lap′ping to lap over; to extend over (something or each other) so as to coincide in part —*n.* 1. an overlapping 2. a part that overlaps 3. the extent or place of overlapping

o·ver·lay (ō′vər lā′; *for n.* ō′vər lā′) *vt.* -laid′, -lay′ing 1. to lay or spread over 2. to cover, as with a decorative layer —*n.* 1. a covering 2. a decorative layer or the like 3. a transparent flap showing additional details, areas of color, etc. placed over a map, art work, etc.

o·ver·leaf (ō′vər lēf′) *adj., adv.* on the other side of the page or sheet

o·ver·leap (ō′vər lēp′) *vt.* 1. to leap over or across 2. to omit; pass over 3. to overreach (oneself) by leaping too far

o·ver·lie (-lī′) *vt.* -lay′, -lain′, -ly′ing to lie on or over

o·ver·load (ō′vər lōd′; *for n.* ō′vər lōd′) *vt.* to put too great a load in or on —*n.* too great a load

o·ver·look (ō′vər look′; *for n.* ō′vər look′) *vt.* 1. to look at from above 2. to give a view of from above 3. to rise above 4. *a)* to look beyond and not see *b)* to ignore; neglect 5. to pass over indulgently; excuse 6. to oversee; supervise —*n.* a height or the view from it

o·ver·lord (ō′vər lôrd′) *n.* a lord ranking above other lords, esp. in the feudal system

o·ver·ly (-lē) *adv.* too or too much; excessively

o·ver·man (ō′vər man′) *vt.* -manned′, -man′ning to supply with more men than necessary

o·ver·mas·ter (-mas′tər) *vt.* to overcome; conquer

o·ver·match (-mach′) *vt.* 1. to be more than a match for 2. to match against a superior opponent

o·ver·much (ō′vər much′) *adj., adv.* too much —*n.* too great a quantity; excessive amount

o·ver·night (ō′vər nīt′; *for adj.* ō′vər nīt′) *adv.* 1. during the night 2. on or during the previous evening 3. very suddenly —*adj.* 1. done or going on during the night 2. of the previous evening 3. for one night [an *overnight* guest] 4. of or for a brief trip [an *overnight* bag]

o·ver·pass (ō′vər pas′) *n.* a bridge or other passageway over a road, railway, etc.

o·ver·play (ō′vər plā′) *vt.* 1. to overact, overdo, or over-emphasize 2. *Card Games* to overestimate the strength of (one's hand)

o·ver·pop·u·late (-päp′yə lāt′) *vt.* -lat′ed, -lat′ing to populate (an area) too heavily for the available resources —o′ver·pop′u·la′tion *n.*

o·ver·pow·er (-pou′ər) *vt.* 1. to get the better of; make helpless; subdue; overwhelm 2. to supply with more power than is needed —o′ver·pow′er·ing *adj.* —o′ver·pow′er·ing·ly *adv.*

o·ver·print (ō′vər print′; *for n.* ō′vər print′) *vt.* to print over (a previously printed surface) —*n.* anything over-printed, as (on) a stamp

**o·ver·pro·duce** (ō'vər prə dōōs', -dyōōs') *vt., vi.* **-duced',** **-duc'ing** to produce in a quantity that exceeds the need or demand —**o'ver·pro·duc'tion** *n.*

**o·ver·pro·tect** (-prə tekt') *vt.* to protect more than is necessary; specif., to seek to shield (one's child, etc.) from normal hurts or conflicts —**o'ver·pro·tec'tive** *adj.*

**o·ver·rate** (-rāt') *vt.* **-rat'ed, -rat'ing** to rate or estimate too highly

**o·ver·reach** (-rēch') *vt.* **1.** to reach beyond or above **2.** to reach too far for and miss **3.** to outwit or cheat —*vi.* to reach too far —**overreach oneself 1.** to fail because of trying more than one can do **2.** to fail because of being too crafty or eager —**o'ver·reach'er** *n.*

**o·ver·re·act** (-rē akt') *vi.* to react in an extreme, highly emotional way, as by undue use of force

**o·ver·ride** (-rīd') *vt.* **-rode', -rid'den, -rid'ing 1.** to ride over **2.** to trample down **3.** to suppress or prevail over **4.** to disregard, overrule, or nullify **5.** to fatigue (a horse, etc.) by riding too long

**o·ver·rule** (-rōōl') *vt.* **-ruled', -rul'ing 1.** to set aside or decide against, as by higher authority; rule against or rule out **2.** to prevail over

**o·ver·run** (-run'; *for n.* ō'vər run') *vt.* **-ran', -run', -run'ning 1.** to spread out over so as to cover **2.** to swarm over, as vermin, or ravage, as an army **3.** to invade or conquer by a rapid advance **4.** to spread swiftly throughout, as ideas **5.** to run beyond (certain limits) *[to overrun second base]* —*vi.* **1.** to overflow **2.** to run over or beyond certain limits —*n.* **1.** an act or instance of overrunning **2.** the amount that overruns

**o·ver·seas** (ō'vər sēz') *adv.* over or beyond the sea —*adj.* **1.** foreign **2.** over or across the sea Also, chiefly Brit., **o'ver·sea'**

**o·ver·see** (ō'vər sē') *vt.* **-saw', -seen', -see'ing 1.** to supervise; superintend **2.** to catch sight of secretly or accidentally **3.** to survey; watch

**o·ver·se·er** (ō'vər sē'ər) *n.* a person who directs the work of others; supervisor

**o·ver·sell** (ō'vər sel') *vt.* **-sold', -sell'ing 1.** to sell more than can be supplied **2.** to promote to an extreme degree that defeats one's purposes

**o·ver·set** (ō'vər set'; *for n.* ō'vər set') *vt.* **-set', -set'ting 1.** to upset **2.** to overturn or overthrow —*vi.* to tip over —*n.* an overturning

**o·ver·shad·ow** (ō'vər shad'ō) *vt.* **1.** *a)* to cast a shadow over *b)* to darken **2.** to be more significant or important than by comparison

**o·ver·shoe** (ō'vər shōō') *n.* a kind of boot of rubber or fabric worn over the regular shoe to protect against cold or dampness; galosh

**o·ver·shoot** (ō'vər shōōt') *vt.* **-shot', -shoot'ing 1.** to shoot or pass over or beyond (a target, mark, etc.) **2.** to go farther than (an intended or normal limit); exceed —*vi.* to shoot or go too far

**o·ver·shot** (ō'vər shät') *adj.* **1.** with the upper part or half extending past the lower *[an overshot jaw]* **2.** driven by water flowing onto the upper part *[an overshot water wheel]*

**o·ver·sight** (-sīt') *n.* a careless mistake or omission

**o·ver·sim·pli·fy** (ō'vər sim'plə fī') *vt., vi.* **-fied', -fy'ing** to simplify to an extent that distorts, as by ignoring essential details —**o'ver·sim'pli·fi·ca'tion** *n.*

**o·ver·size** (-sīz') *adj.* **1.** too large **2.** larger than the normal or usual Also **o'ver·sized'** —*n.* a size larger than regular sizes

**o·ver·skirt** (-skurt') *n.* an outer skirt

**o·ver·sleep** (ō'vər slēp') *vi.* **-slept', -sleep'ing** to sleep past the intended time for getting up

**o·ver·spread** (-spred') *vt.* **-spread', -spread'ing** to spread over; cover the surface of

**o·ver·state** (-stāt') *vt.* **-stat'ed, -stat'ing** to give a magnified account of (facts, truth, etc.); exaggerate —**o'ver·state'ment** *n.*

**o·ver·stay** (-stā') *vt.* to stay beyond the time, duration, or limits of

**o·ver·step** (-step') *vt.* **-stepped', -step'ping** to go beyond the limits of; exceed

**o·ver·stock** (ō'vər stäk'; *for n.* ō'vər stäk') *vt.* to stock more of than is needed —*n.* too large a stock

**o·ver·strung** (ō'vər strun') *adj.* too highly strung; tense

**o·ver·stuff** (-stuf') *vt.* **1.** to stuff with too much of something **2.** to upholster (furniture) with deep stuffing —**o'ver·stuffed'** *adj.*

**o·ver·sub·scribe** (-səb skrīb') *vt., vi.* **-scribed', -scrib'ing** to subscribe for more (of) than is available or asked —**o'ver·sub·scrip'tion** (-skrip'shən) *n.*

**o·ver·sup·ply** (-sə plī') *vt.* **-plied', -ply'ing** to supply in excess —*n., pl.* **-plies** too great a supply

**o·vert** (ō vurt', ō'vurt) *adj.* [< MFr. pp. of *ovrir* < L. *aperire,* to open] **1.** not hidden; open **2.** *Law* done publicly, without attempt at concealment —**o·vert'ly** *adv.* —**o·vert'ness** *n.*

**o·ver·take** (ō'vər tāk') *vt.* **-took', -tak'en, -tak'ing 1.** to catch up with and, often, go beyond **2.** to come upon unexpectedly or suddenly

**o·ver·tax** (-taks') *vt.* **1.** to tax too heavily **2.** to make excessive demands on

**o·ver·throw** (ō'vər thrō'; *for n.* ō'vər thrō') *vt.* **-threw', -thrown', -throw'ing 1.** to throw or turn over; upset **2.** to conquer; end **3.** to throw a ball, etc. beyond (the intended receiver or target) —*n.* **1.** an overthrowing or being overthrown **2.** destruction; end

**o·ver·time** (ō'vər tīm'; *for v.* -tīm') *n.* **1.** time beyond the established limit, as of working hours **2.** pay for work done in such time **3.** *Sports* an extra period added to the game to decide a tie —*adj., adv.* of, for, or during (an) overtime —*vt.* **-timed', -tim'ing** to allow too much time for (a photographic exposure, etc.)

**o·ver·tone** (ō'vər tōn') *n.* **1.** any of the attendant higher tones heard with a fundamental musical tone **2.** an implication; nuance: *usually used in pl.* *[a reply full of overtones]*

**o·ver·top** (ō'vər täp') *vt.* **-topped', -top'ping 1.** to rise above **2.** to excel; surpass

**o·ver·ture** (ō'vər chər, ō'və-) *n.* [< OFr. < L. *apertura,* APERTURE] **1.** an introductory proposal or offer **2.** a musical introduction to an opera, oratorio, etc.

**o·ver·turn** (ō'vər turn'; *for n.* ō'vər turn') *vt.* **1.** to turn over; upset **2.** to conquer —*vi.* to tip over; capsize —*n.* an overturning or being overturned

**o·ver·view** (ō'vər vyōō') *n.* a general survey

**o·ver·ween·ing** (ō'vər wē'niŋ) *adj.* [< OE. *oferwenan:* see OVER- & WEEN] **1.** arrogant; excessively proud **2.** exaggerated; excessive —**o'ver·ween'ing·ly** *adv.*

**o·ver·weigh** (-wā') *vt.* **1.** *same as* OUTWEIGH **2.** to burden; oppress

**o·ver·weight** (ō'vər wāt'; *for adj. & v.,* ō'vər wāt') *n.* extra or surplus weight —*adj.* above the normal, desirable, or allowed weight —*vt. same as* OVERWEIGH

**o·ver·whelm** (ō'vər hwelm', -welm') *vt.* [see OVER- & WHELM] **1.** to pour down on and bury beneath **2.** to crush; overpower —**o'ver·whelm'ing** *adj.* —**o'ver·whelm'ing·ly** *adv.*

**o·ver·work** (ō'vər wurk'; *for n.* ō'vər wurk') *vt.* to work or use to excess —*vi.* to work too hard or too long —*n.* work that is severe or burdensome

**o·ver·write** (ō'vər rīt') *vt., vi.* **-wrote', -writ'ten, -writ'ing 1.** to write over (other writing) **2.** to write too much, or in a labored style, about (some subject) **3.** to receive a commission on the sales of (a subagent)

**o·ver·wrought** (ō'vər rôt') *adj.* **1.** very nervous or excited **2.** with the surface adorned **3.** too elaborate

**o·vi-** [< L. *ovum,* an egg] *a combining form meaning* egg or ovum *[oviduct, oviform]*

**Ov·id** (äv'id) (L. name, *Publius Ovidius Naso*) 43 B.C.–17? A.D.; Rom. poet

**o·vi·duct** (ō'vi dukt') *n.* [< ModL.: see OVI- & DUCT] a duct or tube through which the ovum passes from an ovary to the uterus or to the outside

**o·vi·form** (-fôrm') *adj.* [OVI- & -FORM] egg-shaped

**o·vip·a·rous** (ō vip'ər əs) *adj.* [< L.: see OVI- & -PAROUS] producing eggs which hatch after leaving the body —**o·vip'a·rous·ly** *adv.*

**o·vi·pos·i·tor** (ō'vi päz'i tər) *n.* [ModL. < OVI- + L. *positor,* one who places < *ponere,* to place] a special organ of many female insects, usually at the end of the abdomen, for depositing eggs

**o·void** (ō'void) *adj.* [OV(I)- + -OID] egg-shaped: also **o·void'al** —*n.* anything of ovoid form

**o·vu·late** (ō'vyə lāt', äv'yə-) *vi.* **-lat'ed, -lat'ing** [OVUL(E) + -ATE¹] to produce and discharge ova from the ovary —**o'vu·la'tion** *n.* —**o'vu·la·to'ry** (-lə tôr'ē) *adj.*

**o·vule** (ō'vyōōl, äv'yōōl) *n.* [Fr. < ModL. dim. of L. *ovum,* egg] a small egg or seed, esp. one in an early stage of development; specif., *a) Bot.* the part of a plant which develops into a seed after fertilization *b) Zool.* the immature ovum —**o'vu·lar** *adj.*

**o·vum** (ō'vəm) *n., pl.* **o·va** (ō'və) [L., an egg] *Biol.* a mature female germ cell

**ow** (ou) *interj.* a cry of pain

**owe** (ō) *vt.* **owed, ow'ing** [OE. *agan,* to own] **1.** to be indebted to (someone) for (a specified amount or thing) **2.** to feel the need to do, give, etc. **3.** to cherish (a feeling) toward another: only in **owe a grudge** —*vi.* to be in debt

**O·wens·bor·o** (ō'ənz bur'ō) [after a Col. Owens (1769–1811)] city in NW Ky., on the Ohio: pop. 54,000

**ow·ing** (ō'iŋ) *adj.* **1.** that owes **2.** due; unpaid *[ten dollars owing on a bill]* —**owing to** because of; as a result of

**owl** (oul) *n.* [OE. *ule*] a night bird of prey found throughout the world, having a large face, large eyes, a short, hooked beak, and feathered legs with sharp talons: applied figuratively to a person who is active at night, looks solemn, etc. —**owl'ish** *adj.* —**owl'ish·ly** *adv.* —**owl'like'** *adj.*

**owl·et** (-it) *n.* a young or small owl

**own** (ōn) *adj.* [OE. *agen,* pp. of *agan,* to possess] belonging or relating to oneself or itself: used to strengthen a preceding possessive *[his* own *book]* —*n.* that which belongs to oneself *[the car is his* own*]* —*vt.* **1.** to possess; have **2.** to admit; acknowledge —*vi.* to confess *(to)* —**come into one's own** to receive what properly belongs to one, esp. recognition —**of own's own** belonging strictly to oneself —**on one's own** [Colloq.] by one's own efforts; independent —**own up (to)** to confess (to) —**own'er** *n.* —**own'er·less** *adj.* —**own'er·ship'** *n.*

**ox** (äks) *n.,* pl. **ox'en,** rarely **ox:** see PLURAL, II, D, 1 [OE. *oxa*] **1.** any of several bovine mammals, as the buffalo, bison, yak, etc. **2.** a castrated bull, used as a draft animal —*ox'-like' adj.*

**ox·al·ic acid** (äk sal'ik) [< Fr. < L. < Gr. *oxalis,* sorrel < *oxys,* acid] a colorless, poisonous, crystalline acid, $(COOH)_2$, found in many plants and used in dyeing, bleaching, etc.

**ox·blood** (äks'blud') *n.* a deep red color

**ox·bow** (-bō') *n.* **1.** the U-shaped part of an ox yoke which passes under and around the animal's neck **2.** something shaped like this, as a bend in a river

**ox·en** (äk's'n) *n.* pl. *of* OX

**ox·eye** (äks'ī') *n.* **1.** any of several composite plants, as a sunflowerlike perennial of E N. America **2.** any of various birds, as the dunlin

**ox-eyed** (-īd') *adj.* having large, full eyes

**oxeye daisy** *same as* DAISY (sense 1)

**Ox·ford** (äks'fərd) city in SC England: site of Oxford University: pop. 109,000

**ox·ford** (äks'fərd) *n.* [after prec.] [*sometimes* O-] **1.** a low shoe laced over the instep: also **oxford shoe 2.** a cotton or rayon fabric with a basketlike weave, used for shirts, etc.: also **oxford cloth**

**Oxford gray** a very dark gray, nearly black

**ox·heart** (äks'härt') *n.* a large, heart-shaped cherry

**ox·i·dant** (äk'sə dənt) *n.* an oxidizing agent

**ox·i·da·tion** (äk'sə dā'shən) *n.* an oxidizing or being oxidized —*ox'i·da'tive adj.*

**ox·ide** (äk'sīd) *n.* [Fr. < Gr. *oxys,* sour + Fr. *(ac)ide,* acid] a binary compound of oxygen with another element or a radical

**ox·i·dize** (äk'sə dīz') *vt.* **-dized', -diz'ing** [< prec. + -IZE] **1.** to unite with oxygen, as in burning or rusting **2.** to increase the positive valence or decrease the negative valence of (an element or ion) —*vi.* to become oxidized —*ox'i·diz'-a·ble adj.* —*ox'i·diz'er n.*

**ox·lip** (äks'lip') *n.* [< OE. < *oxa,* ox + *slyppe,* dropping] a perennial plant related to the primrose, having yellow flowers in early spring

**Ox·nard** (äks'närd) [after H. *Oxnard,* local businessman] city in SW Calif.: pop. 108,000

**Ox·o·ni·an** (äk sō'nē ən) *adj.* of Oxford (England) or Oxford University —*n.* **1.** a student or alumnus of Oxford University **2.** a native or inhabitant of Oxford, England

**ox·tail** (äks'tāl') *n.* the tail of an ox or steer, esp. when skinned and used in soup or stew

**ox·y-**[1] [< OXY(GEN)] *a combining form meaning* containing oxygen

**ox·y-**[2] [< Gr. *oxys,* sharp] *a combining form meaning* sharp, pointed, or acid *[oxymoron, oxygen]*

**ox·y·a·cet·y·lene** (äk'sē ə set''l ēn') *adj.* of or using a mixture of oxygen and acetylene, as for producing an extremely hot flame used in welding or cutting metals *[oxyacetylene* torch*]*

**ox·y·gen** (äk'si jən) *n.* [< Fr.: see OXY-[2] & -GEN] a colorless, odorless, tasteless, gaseous chemical element, the most abundant of all elements: it occurs free in the atmosphere, forming one fifth of its volume, and is able to combine with nearly all other elements; it is essential to life processes and to combustion: symbol, O; at. wt., 15.9994; at. no., 8 —*ox'-y·gen'ic* (-jen'ik) *adj.*

**ox·y·gen·ate** (äk'si jə nāt') *vt.* **-at'ed, -at'ing** to mix, treat, or combine with oxygen: also **ox'y·gen·ize', -ized', -iz'ing** —*ox'y·gen·a'tion n.* —*ox'y·gen·a'tor n.*

**oxygen tent** a transparent enclosure into which oxygen is released, fitted around a bed patient to help him breathe

**ox·y·hy·dro·gen** (äk'si hī'drə jən) *adj.* of or using a mixture of oxygen and hydrogen, as for producing a hot flame used in welding *[oxyhydrogen* torch*]*

**ox·y·mo·ron** (äk'si môr'än) *n.,* pl. **-mo'ra** (-ə) [LGr. < *oxys,* sharp + *moros,* dull] a figure of speech in which contradictory ideas or terms are combined (Ex.: sweet sorrow)

**o·yez, o·yes** (ō'yez', -yes', -yā') *interj.* [Anglo-Fr., hear ye, ult. < L. *audire,* to hear] hear ye! attention!: usually cried out three times by an official to command silence before a proclamation is made —*n.* a cry of "oyez"

**oys·ter** (oi'stər) *n.* [< OFr. < L. *ostrea* < Gr. *ostreon*] **1.** a marine mollusk with an irregular, bivalve shell, found esp. on the ocean floor and widely used as food **2.** any of several similar bivalve mollusks

**oyster bed** a natural or artificially prepared place on the ocean floor for breeding oysters

**oyster crab** any of various small crabs that live in the gill cavities of oysters, clams, etc.

**oyster cracker** a small, round, salted soda cracker

**oyster plant** *same as* SALSIFY

**oz.** pl. **oz., ozs.** ounce

**O·zark Mountains** (ō'zärk) [< Fr. *aux Arcs,* to the (region of the) Arc (Arkansa) Indians, a Siouan-speaking tribe] highland region in NW Ark., SW Mo., & NE Okla.: also **Ozarks**

**o·zone** (ō'zōn) *n.* [Fr. < Gr. *ozein,* to smell] **1.** a pale-blue gas, $O_3$, with a strong odor: it is an allotropic form of oxygen, formed by a silent electrical discharge in air and used as a bleaching agent, water purifier, etc. **2.** [Slang] pure, fresh air —*o·zon'ic* (-zän'ik, -zō'nik) *adj.*

**o·zon·ize** (ō'zō nīz') *vt.* **-ized', -iz'ing 1.** to change (oxygen) into ozone **2.** to treat with ozone —*o'zon·i·za'-tion n.* —*o'zon·iz'er n.*

# P

**P, p** (pē) *n.,* pl. **P's, p's 1.** the sixteenth letter of the English alphabet **2.** the sound of *P* or *p* —**mind one's p's and q's** to be careful what one does

**P 1.** *Chess* pawn **2.** *Chem.* phosphorus **3.** police **4.** *Physics* power or pressure

**p** [Brit.] penny; pennies

**P., p. 1.** pitcher **2.** power **3.** pressure

**p. 1.** pl. **pp.** page **2.** participle **3.** past **4.** penny **5.** per **6.** piano **7.** pint

**pa** (pä; *dial. often* pô) *n.* [Colloq.] father; papa

**Pa** *Chem.* protactinium

**Pa., PA** Pennsylvania

**P.A.** public address (system)

**pa·'an·ga** (pä äŋ'ä) *n.,* pl. **pa·'an'ga** [Polynesian (Tongan), a kind of seedpod] *see* MONETARY UNITS, table (Tonga)

**Pab·lum** (pab'ləm) [< ff.] *a trademark for* a soft, bland cereal food for infants —*n.* [p-] any oversimplified or tasteless writing, ideas, etc.

**pab·u·lum** (pab'yσσ ləm) *n.* [L.] **1.** food **2.** nourishment for the mind **3.** *same as* PABLUM

**pac** (pak) *n.* [< AmInd. *pacu,* moccasin] a high, insulated, waterproof, laced boot

**pace** (pās) *n.* [< OFr. *pas* < L. *passus,* a step] **1.** a step in walking, running, etc. **2.** the length of a step or stride (30 in. to 40 in.) **3.** the rate of speed in walking, etc. **4.** rate of movement, progress, development, etc. **5.** a particular way of walking, etc.; gait **6.** the gait of a horse in which both legs on the same side are raised together —*vt.* **paced, pac'ing 1.** to walk back and forth across **2.** to measure by paces (often with *off)* **3.** to train or guide the pace of (a horse) **4.** to set the pace for (a runner, etc.) **5.** to go before and lead **6.** to cover (a certain distance) —*vi.* **1.** to walk with regular steps **2.** to raise both legs on the same side at the same time in moving: said of a horse —**change of pace** variation in tempo or mood or in speed of delivery —**keep pace (with)** to maintain the same speed or rate of progress (as) —**put through one's paces** to test one's abilities, etc. —**set the pace 1.** to go at a speed that others try to equal, as in a race **2.** to do or be something for others to emulate —**pac'er n.**

---

fat, āpe, cär, ten, ēven, is, bīte; gō, hôrn, tōol, look; oil, out; up, fur; get; joy; yet; chin; she; thin, *then;* zh, leisure; ŋ, ring; ə for *a* in *ago, e* in *agent, i* in *sanity, o* in *comply, u* in *focus;* ' as in *able* (ā'b'l); Fr. bál; ĕ, Fr. coeur; ŏ, Fr. feu; Fr. mon; ö, Fr. coq; ü, Fr. duc; r, Fr. cri; H, G. ich; kh, G. doch; ‡foreign; *hypothetical; < derived from. See inside front cover.

**pace·mak·er** (-mā'kər) *n.* **1.** *a)* a runner, horse, etc. that sets the pace for others, as in a race *b)* a person, group, or thing that serves as a model Also **pace'set'ter 2.** *Med.* an electronic device surgically implanted in the body to stimulate or regulate the heartbeat —**pace'mak'ing** *n.*

**pa·chi·si** (pə chē'zē) *n.* [< Hindi < *pacīs,* twenty-five (the highest throw)] **1.** in India, a game in which the moves of pieces around a board are determined by the throwing of cowrie shells **2.** *same as* PARCHEESI

**pach·y·derm** (pak'ə durm') *n.* [< Fr. < Gr. *pachys,* thick + *derma,* a skin] **1.** a large, thick-skinned, hoofed animal, as the elephant, rhinoceros, or hippopotamus **2.** an insensitive, stolid person —**pach'y·der'mal, pach'y·der'mic** *adj.* —**pach'y·der'ma·tous, pach'y·der'mous** *adj.*

**pach·y·san·dra** (pak'ə san'drə) *n.* [ModL. < Gr. *pachys,* thick + ModL. *-andrus,* -ANDROUS] a low, dense-growing, hardy evergreen plant, often used for a ground cover

**Pa·cif·ic** (pə sif'ik) [< ff., after its tranquil appearance] largest of the earth's oceans, between Asia and the American continents —*adj.* of, in, on, or near this ocean

**pa·cif·ic** (pə sif'ik) *adj.* [< Fr. < L. < *pacificare,* PACIFY] **1.** making or tending to make peace **2.** peaceful; calm; tranquil —**pa·cif'i·cal·ly** *adv.*

**pa·cif·i·cate** (-ə kāt') *vt.* **-cat'ed, -cat'ing** *same as* PACIFY —**pac·i·fi·ca·tion** (pas'ə fi kā'shən) *n.* —**pa·cif'i·ca'tor** *n.* —**pa·cif'i·ca·to'ry** (-kə tôr'ē) *adj.*

**Pacific Islands, Trust Territory of the** U.S. trust territory in the W Pacific, consisting of the Caroline & Marshall islands: 420 sq. mi.; pop. 110,000

**Pacific Standard Time** *see* STANDARD TIME

**pac·i·fi·er** (pas'ə fī'ər) *n.* **1.** a person or thing that pacifies **2.** a nipple or teething ring for babies

**pac·i·fism** (-fiz'm) *n.* [< Fr.: see PACIFIC & -ISM] opposition to the use of force under any circumstances; specif., refusal for reasons of conscience to participate in war —**pac'i·fist** *n., adj.* —**pac'i·fis'tic** *adj.* —**pac'i·fis'ti·cal·ly** *adv.*

**pac·i·fy** (pas'ə fī') *vt.* **-fied', -fy'ing** [< Fr. < L. *pacificare* < *pax,* peace + *facere,* to make] **1.** to make peaceful or calm; appease; tranquilize **2.** *a)* to secure peace in (a nation, etc.) *b)* to seek to neutralize or win over (people in occupied areas) —**pac'i·fi'a·ble** *adj.*

**pack¹** (pak) *n.* [MDu. *pak* < MFl. *pac*] **1.** a bundle of things tied up for carrying, as on the back; load; burden **2.** a container in which something may be stored compactly *[parachute pack]* **3.** a group or set *[a pack* of lies or liars*];* specif., *a)* a package of a standard number *[a pack* of cigarettes*] b)* a set of playing cards; deck *c)* a set of hunting hounds *d)* a group of wild animals living and hunting together **4.** *same as* ICE PACK **5.** *a)* treatment by wrapping a patient in sheets, etc. that are wet or dry and hot or cold *b)* the sheets so used **6.** a cosmetic paste applied to the skin and left to dry *[mudpack]* **7.** *a)* the amount of food put in cans, etc. in a season or year *b)* a method of packing or canning —*vt.* **1.** to make a pack of **2.** *a)* to put together in a box, trunk, etc. *b)* to fill (a box, trunk, etc.) **3.** to put (food) in (cans, etc.) for preservation **4.** *a)* to crowd; cram *[the hall was packed] b)* to crowd (people) together **5.** to fill in tightly, as for prevention of leaks *[to pack* valves*]* **6.** to press together firmly *[packed* earth*]* **7.** to load (an animal) with a pack **8.** to carry (goods, etc.) in a pack: said of an animal **9.** to send (*off*) **10.** [Slang] to wear or carry (a gun, etc.) as part of one's equipment **11.** [Slang] *a)* to deliver (a blow, punch, etc.) with force *b)* to provide or contain *[a play that packs* a message*]* —*vi.* **1.** to make up packs **2.** to put one's clothes, etc. into luggage for a trip **3.** to crowd together in a small space **4.** to admit of being folded compactly, put in a container, etc. *[this suit packs* well*]* **5.** to settle into a compact mass —*adj.* **1.** used in or suitable for packing **2.** formed into packs **3.** used for carrying packs, loads, etc. *[a pack* animal*]* —**send packing** to dismiss (a person) abruptly —**pack'a·bil'i·ty** *n.* —**pack'a·ble** *adj.*

**pack²** (pak) *vt.* [orig. unc., but infl. by prec.] to choose (a jury, court, etc.) in such a way as to get desired results

**-pack** (pak) *a combining form meaning* a carton of (a specified number of) bottles or cans, as of beer

**pack·age** (pak'ij) *n.* **1.** orig., the act or process of packing **2.** a wrapped or boxed thing; parcel **3.** a container, wrapping, etc., esp. one in which a commodity is packed for sale **4.** a number of items, plans, etc. offered as an inseparable unit —*vt.* **-aged, -ag·ing** to put into a package

**package store** a store where alcoholic liquor is sold by the bottle to be drunk off the premises

**pack·er** (pak'ər) *n.* a person or thing that packs; specif., *a)* one who packs goods for shipping, sale, etc. *b)* one who owns or manages a packing house

**pack·et** (-it) *n.* **1.** a small package **2.** *same as* PACKET BOAT —*vt.* to make up into a packet

**packet boat** a boat that travels a regular route carrying passengers, freight, and mail

**pack·ing** (pak'iŋ) *n.* **1.** the act or process of a person or thing that packs; specif., the large-scale processing and packaging of meats, fruits, etc. **2.** material used to pack

**pack·ing·house** (-hous') *n.* a plant where meats are processed and packed for sale; also, a similar plant for packing fruits and vegetables

**pack rat** a N. American rat that often hides small articles in its nest

**pack·sad·dle** (-sad''l) *n.* a saddle with fastenings to secure the load carried by a pack animal

**pack·thread** (-thred') *n.* strong, thick thread or twine for tying bundles, packages, etc.

**pack train** a procession of pack animals

**pact** (pakt) *n.* [< OFr. < L. < pp. of *paciscere,* to agree < *pax,* peace] an agreement between persons or nations

**pad¹** (pad) *n.* [echoic, but infl. by PAD³] the dull sound made by a footstep or staff on the ground

**pad²** (pad) *n.* [? var. of POD] **1.** a soft, stuffed saddle **2.** anything made of or stuffed with soft material to fill out a shape, protect from friction, jarring, blows, etc. *[a shoulder pad]* **3.** a piece of folded gauze, etc. used as a dressing on a wound, etc. **4.** *a)* the foot of certain animals, as the wolf, fox, etc. *b)* any of the cushionlike parts on the underside of such a foot **5.** the floating leaf of a water plant, as the waterlily **6.** a tablet of paper for writing on **7.** a small cushion soaked with ink for inking a rubber stamp: in full, **stamp pad** or **ink pad 8.** *same as* LAUNCH PAD **9.** [Slang] *a)* a bed *b)* the room, apartment, etc. where one lives —*vt.* **pad'ded, pad'ding 1.** to stuff, cover, or line with a pad or padding **2.** to lengthen (a speech or writing) with unnecessary material **3.** to fill (an expense account, etc.) with invented or inflated entries

**pad³** (pad) *vi.* **pad'ded, pad'ding** [< Du. *pad,* path] **1.** to travel on foot; walk **2.** to walk or run with a soft step

**pad·ding** (pad'iŋ) *n.* **1.** the action of one who pads **2.** any soft material used to pad, as cotton, felt, etc. **3.** unnecessary material used to lengthen a speech or writing

**pad·dle¹** (pad''l) *n.* [< ?] **1.** a short oar with a wide blade, used without an oarlock **2.** any of various implements shaped like this and used as in washing clothes, working butter, flogging, hitting a ball in some games, etc. **3.** any of the propelling boards in a water wheel or paddle wheel —*vt., vi.* **-dled, -dling 1.** to propel (a canoe, etc.) with a paddle **2.** to punish by beating as with a paddle; spank **3.** to stir, work, etc. with a paddle —**paddle one's own canoe** to depend entirely on oneself —**pad'dler** *n.*

**pad·dle²** (pad''l) *vi.* **-dled, -dling** [prob. freq. of PAD³] **1.** to move the hands or feet about in the water; dabble **2.** to walk like a small child; toddle —**pad'dler** *n.*

**paddle ball** a game similar to handball, but played with a short-handled, perforated paddle

**pad·dle·fish** (-fish') *n., pl.* **-fish', -fish'es:** see FISH a large fish of the Mississippi and Yangtze river systems, with a paddle-shaped snout

**paddle wheel** a wheel with paddles around it for propelling a steamboat

**pad·dock** (pad'ək) *n.* [< OE. *pearruc,* enclosure] **1.** a small enclosure near a stable, in which horses are exercised **2.** an enclosure at a race track, where horses are saddled and walked before a race

**pad·dy** (pad'ē) *n., pl.* **-dies** [Malay *padi*] **1.** rice in the husk, growing or gathered **2.** rice in general **3.** a rice field: often **rice paddy**

**paddy wagon** *slang name for* PATROL WAGON

PADDLE WHEEL

**Pa·de·rew·ski** (pä'de ref'skē; *E.* pad'ə ref'skē), **I·gnace (Jan)** (ē'nyás') 1860-1941; Pol. pianist & composer

**pad·lock** (pad'läk') *n.* [< ME. < *pad* (< ?) + *lokke,* LOCK¹] a removable lock with a hinged link to be passed through a staple, chain, or eye —*vt.* to fasten or keep shut as with a padlock

**pa·dre** (pä'drā, -drē; *It.* -dre; *Sp.* -thre) *n., pl.* **-dres** (-drāz, -drēz; *Sp.* -thres); *It.* **pa'dri** (-drē) [Sp., It., Port. < L. *pater,* a father] **1.** father: the title of a priest in Italy, Spain, Portugal, and Latin America **2.** [Slang] a priest or chaplain

**Pad·u·a** (paj'ōō ə, pad'yōō ə) city in N Italy: pop. 226,000: It. name **Pa·do·va** (pä'dô vä)

**pae·an** (pē'ən) *n.* [L. < Gr. < *Paian,* epithet of Apollo] a song of joy, triumph, praise, etc.

**pae·do-** *same as* PEDO-: also **paed-**

**pa·el·la** (pä yel'ə; *Sp.* pä e'lyä) *n.* [Catalan, ult. < L. *patella,* a small pan] a dish of rice cooked with chicken, seafood, etc., seasoned with saffron

**pa·gan** (pā'gən) *n.* [LL. *paganus,* a heathen < L., a peasant < *pagus,* country] **1.** anyone not a Christian, Moslem, or Jew; heathen **2.** a person who has no religion —*adj.* **1.** of pagans **2.** not religious —**pa'gan·dom** *n.* —**pa'gan·ish** *adj.* —**pa'gan·ism** *n.*

**Pa·ga·ni·ni** (pä'gä nē'nē; *E.* pag'ə nē'nē), **Ni·co·lò** (nē'kô lô') 1782-1840; It. violinist & composer

**pa·gan·ize** (pā'gə nīz') *vt., vi.* **-ized', -iz'ing** to make or become pagan —**pa'gan·iz'er** *n.*
**page**[1] (pāj) *n.* [Fr. < L. *pagina* < base of *pangere,* to fasten] **1.** *a*) one side of a leaf of a book, newspaper, etc. *b*) the printing or writing on it *[the sports pages]* *c*) an entire leaf in a book, etc. **2.** *[often pl.]* a record of events *[the pages of history]* **3.** an event or series of events that might fill a page *[a colorful page in his life]* —*vt.* **paged, pag'ing** to number the pages of —*vi.* to turn pages in scanning (*through* a book, etc.)
**page**[2] (pāj) *n.* [OFr. < It. *paggio*] **1.** formerly, a boy training for knighthood **2.** a boy attendant, esp. one serving a person of high rank, as in court **3.** a boy, or sometimes a girl, who runs errands, carries messages, etc., as in a hotel, legislature, etc. —*vt.* **paged, pag'ing** to try to find (a person) by calling his name, as a hotel page does
**pag·eant** (paj'ənt) *n.* [Anglo-L. *pagina,* scene displayed on a stage, stage < L., PAGE[1]] **1.** a spectacular exhibition, elaborate parade, etc., as a procession with floats **2.** a drama, often staged outdoors, celebrating a historical event or events **3.** empty pomp or display
**pag·eant·ry** (-ən trē) *n., pl.* **-ries** **1.** grand spectacle; gorgeous display **2.** empty show or display
**pag·i·nate** (paj'ə nāt') *vt.* **-nat'ed, -nat'ing** to number the pages of (a book, etc.)
**pag·i·na·tion** (paj'ə nā'shən) *n.* **1.** the numbering of the pages of a book, etc. **2.** the figures with which pages are numbered in sequence
**pa·go·da** (pə gō'də) *n.* [< Port., prob. < Per. < *but,* idol + *kadah,* house, prob. infl. by Prakrit *bhagodi,* divine] in the Orient, a temple that is a tapering tower with rooflike, upward curving projections between its several stories
**Pa·go Pa·go** (päŋ'ō päŋ'ō, pä'gō pä'gō) seaport on the S coast of Tutuila Island, American Samoa: pop. 2,500
**paid** (pād) *pt. & pp. of* PAY[1]
**pail** (pāl) *n.* [OE. *pægel,* small measure < LL. *pagella,* in VL. a measure of area or volume] **1.** a cylindrical container, usually with a hoop-shaped handle, for carrying liquids, etc.; bucket **2.** the amount held by a pail: also **pail'ful',** *pl.* **-fuls'**
**pain** (pān) *n.* [< OFr. < L. *poena,* punishment < Gr. *poinē,* penalty] **1.** orig., penalty or punishment **2.** a sensation of hurting caused by injury, disease, etc., transmitted by the nervous system **3.** the distress or suffering caused by anxiety, grief, disappointment, etc. **4.** [*pl.*] the labor of childbirth **5.** [*pl.*] great care *[to take pains with one's work]* **6.** [Slang] an annoyance —*vt.* to cause pain to; hurt —*vi.* to have or cause pain —**on** (or **upon** or **under**) **pain of** at the risk of bringing upon oneself (punishment, death, etc.) — **pain'less** *adj.* —**pain'less·ly** *adv.* —**pain'less·ness** *n.*
**Paine** (pān), **Thomas** 1737–1809; Am. Revolutionary patriot, writer, & political theorist, born in England
**pained** (pānd) *adj.* **1.** hurt or distressed; offended **2.** showing hurt feelings or resentment
**pain·ful** (pān'fəl) *adj.* **1.** causing pain; hurting; distressing **2.** having pain; aching **3.** exacting and difficult **4.** annoying —**pain'ful·ly** *adv.* —**pain'ful·ness** *n.*
**pains·tak·ing** (pānz'tā'kiŋ) *n.* great care or diligence —*adj.* **1.** very careful; diligent **2.** characterized by great care — **pains'tak'ing·ly** *adv.*
**paint** (pānt) *vt.* [< OFr. pp. of *peindre* < L. *pingere*] **1.** *a*) to make (a picture, etc.) in colors applied to a surface *b*) to depict with paints *[to paint a landscape]* **2.** to describe colorfully; depict in words **3.** to cover or decorate with paint *[to paint a wall]* **4.** to apply such cosmetics as lipstick, rouge, etc. to **5.** to apply (a medicine, etc.) with a brush or swab —*vi.* **1.** to practice the art of painting pictures **2.** to use cosmetics —*n.* **1.** a mixture of pigment with oil, water, etc. used as a covering or coloring or for making pictures on canvas, etc. **2.** a dried coat of paint **3.** *a*) coloring matter, as lipstick, rouge, etc., used as a cosmetic *b*) *same as* GREASEPAINT **4.** [Dial.] a piebald horse; pinto —**paint out** to cover up as with a coat of paint —**paint the town (red)** [Slang] to go on a boisterous spree —**paint'a·ble** *adj.* — **paint'y** *adj.* —**paint'i·er, paint'i·est**
**paint·brush** (-brush') *n.* a brush used for applying paint
**paint·er**[1] (pānt'ər) *n.* **1.** an artist who paints pictures **2.** a person whose work is covering surfaces, as walls, with paint
**paint·er**[2] (pānt'ər) *n.* [< OFr., ult. < L. *pendere,* to hang] a rope attached to the bow of a boat for tying it to a dock, etc.
**paint·er**[3] (pānt'ər) *n.* [altered < PANTHER] *dial. var. of* COUGAR
**paint·ing** (pānt'iŋ) *n.* **1.** the work or art of one who paints **2.** a picture made with paints

**pair** (per) *n., pl.* **pairs;** sometimes, after a number, **pair** [< OFr. < L. neut. pl. of *par,* equal] **1.** two similar or corresponding things associated or used together *[a pair of shoes]* **2.** a single thing with two joined corresponding parts *[a pair of pants]* **3.** two persons or animals; specif., *a*) a married, engaged, or courting couple *b*) two mated animals *c*) two people with something in common *[a pair of thieves]* *d*) a brace; span *[a pair of oxen]* *e*) two legislators on opposing sides of a question who agree to withhold their vote so as to offset each other; also, such an agreement **4.** two playing cards of the same denomination —*vt.* **1.** to make a pair of (two persons or things) or of (one *with* another) by matching, joining, etc. **2.** to arrange in pairs — *vi.* **1.** to form a pair; match **2.** to mate —**pair off 1.** to join (two people or things) in a pair **2.** to separate into pairs
**pai·sa** (pī'sä) *n., pl.* **-se** (-se) [Hindi *paisā*] *see* MONETARY UNITS, table (Bangladesh, India, Pakistan)
**pais·ley** (pāz'lē) *adj.* [after *Paisley,* city in Scotland where orig. made] *[also P-]* **1.** of or having an elaborate, colorful pattern of intricate, curved figures **2.** made of cloth having such a pattern —*n.* *[also P-]* a paisley cloth, shawl, necktie, etc.

PAISLEY PATTERN

**Pai·ute** (pī'yōōt, pī yōōt') *n.* [< Shoshonean *pah-ute,* lit., water Ute] **1.** *pl.* **-utes, -ute** a member of any of various groups of N. American Indians living in Nevada, California, Utah, and Arizona **2.** any of their Shoshonean dialects
**pa·ja·mas** (pə jam'əz, -jä'məz) *n.pl.* [< Hindi < Per. *pāi,* a leg + *jāma,* garment] a loosely fitting sleeping or lounging suit consisting of jacket and trousers —**pa·ja'ma** *adj.*
**Pa·ki·stan** (pä'ki stän', pak'i stan') country in S Asia, on the Arabian Sea: 310,403 sq. mi.; pop. 42,900,000; cap. Islamabad
**Pa·ki·stan·i** (pä'ki stä'nē, pak'i stan'ē) *adj.* of Pakistan or its people —*n.* a native or inhabitant of Pakistan
**pal** (pal) *n.* [Eng. Romany < Sans. *bhrātr,* brother] [Colloq.] an intimate friend; comrade; chum —*vi.* **palled, pal'ling** [Colloq.] **1.** to associate as pals **2.** to be a pal (*with* another)
**pal·ace** (pal'is) *n.* [< OFr. < L. < *Palatium,* one of the seven hills of Rome, where Augustus lived] **1.** the official residence of a king, emperor, etc. **2.** any large, magnificent house or building
**pal·a·din** (pal'ə din) *n.* [< Fr. < It. < L. *palatinus,* a palace officer: see prec.] **1.** any of the twelve legendary peers of Charlemagne's court **2.** a knight or heroic champion
**pa·lae·o-** *same as* PALEO-: also **pa·lae-**
**pal·an·quin, pal·an·keen** (pal'ən kēn') *n.* [< Port. < Jav. < Sans. *palyaṅka*] formerly in eastern Asia, a covered litter for one person, carried by poles on men's shoulders
**pal·at·a·ble** (pal'it ə b'l) *adj.* [PALAT(E) + -ABLE] **1.** pleasant or acceptable to the taste **2.** acceptable to the mind — **pal'at·a·bil'i·ty, pal'at·a·ble·ness** *n.* —**pal'at·a·bly** *adv.*
**pal·a·tal** (pal'it 'l) *adj.* **1.** of the palate **2.** pronounced with the tongue raised against or near the hard palate, as *y* in *yes* —*n.* a palatal sound —**pal'a·tal·ly** *adv.*
**pal·a·tal·ize** (-īz') *vt.* **-ized', -iz'ing** to pronounce as a palatal (the *t* in *nature* is palatalized to ch] —**pal'a·tal·i·za'tion** *n.*
**pal·ate** (pal'it) *n.* [L. *palatum*] **1.** the roof of the mouth, consisting of a hard, bony forward part (the *hard palate*) and a soft, fleshy back part (the *soft palate*) **2.** taste

PALATE

**pa·la·tial** (pə lā'shəl) *adj.* [see PALACE] **1.** of, suitable for, or like a palace **2.** large and ornate; magnificent —**pa·la'tial·ly** *adv.*
**pa·lat·i·nate** (pə lat'n āt', -it) *n.* the territory ruled by a palatine
**pal·a·tine** (pal'ə tīn, -tin) *adj.* [< OFr. < L. *palatium,* palace] **1.** of a palace **2.** having royal privileges *[a count palatine]* **3.** of or belonging to a count palatine or earl palatine —*n.* a medieval vassal lord having the rights of royalty in his own territory, or palatinate —[P-] one of the SEVEN HILLS OF ROME
**pa·lav·er** (pə lav'ər) *n.* [Port. *palavra,* a word, speech < LL. *parabola,* PARABLE] **1.** a conference, as orig. between West African natives and European explorers **2.** talk; esp., idle

chatter **3.** flattery; cajolery —*vi.* **1.** to talk, esp. idly or flatteringly **2.** to confer —*vt.* to flatter or wheedle

**Pa·la·wan** (pä lä′wän) island in the W Philippines, southwest of Mindoro: 4,550 sq. mi.

**pale**[1] (pāl) *adj.* [OFr. < L. < *pallere,* to be pale] **1.** of a whitish or colorless complexion; pallid; wan **2.** lacking intensity; faint: said of color, light, etc. **3.** feeble; weak [a *pale* imitation] —*vi., vt.* **paled, pal′ing** to make or become pale —**pale′ly** *adv.* —**pale′ness** *n.* —**pal′ish** *adj.*

**pale**[2] (pāl) *n.* [< MFr. < L. *palus,* a stake] **1.** a narrow, pointed stake used in fences; picket **2.** a fence; enclosure; boundary: now chiefly figurative **3.** a district enclosed within bounds

**pale·face** (pāl′fās′) *n.* a white person: a term allegedly first used by N. American Indians

**pa·le·o-** [< Gr. *palaios,* ancient] *a combining form meaning* ancient, prehistoric, primitive, etc. [*Paleozoic, paleolithic*] : also **pa·le-**

**Pa·le·o·cene** (pā′lē ə sēn′, pal′ē-) *adj.* [< prec. + Gr. *kainos,* recent] designating or of the first epoch of the Tertiary Period in the Cenozoic Era —**the Paleocene** the Paleocene Epoch or its rocks: see GEOLOGY, chart

**pa·le·og·ra·phy** (pā′lē äg′rə fē, pal′ē-) *n.* **1.** ancient writing or forms of writing **2.** the study of describing or deciphering ancient writings —**pa′le·og′ra·pher** *n.* —**pa′le·o·graph′ic** (-ə graf′ik), **pa′le·o·graph′i·cal** *adj.*

**pa·le·o·lith·ic** (pā′lē ə lith′ik, pal′ē-) *adj.* [PALEO- + -LITHIC] designating or of the middle part of the early Stone Age, during which stone and bone tools were used

**pa·le·on·tol·o·gy** (pā′lē än täl′ə jē) *n.* [< Fr.: see PALE(O)- & ONTO- & -LOGY] the branch of geology that deals with prehistoric life through the study of fossils —**pa′le·on′to·log′i·cal** (-tə läj′i k′l), **pa′le·on′to·log′ic** *adj.* —**pa′le·on·tol′o·gist** *n.*

**Pa·le·o·zo·ic** (-ə zō′ik) *adj.* [PALEO- + ZO- + -IC] designating or of the era between the Precambrian and the Mesozoic —**the Paleozoic** the Paleozoic era or its rocks: see GEOLOGY, chart

**Pa·ler·mo** (pə lər′mō; *It.* pä ler′mô) seaport on the N coast of Sicily: pop. 659,000

**Pal·es·tine** (pal′əs tīn′) **1.** region on the E coast of the Mediterranean, the country of the Jews in Biblical times **2.** Brit. mandated territory (1923–48) in this region, west of the Jordan River, before the establishment of the state of Israel —**Pal′es·tin′i·an** (-tin′ē ən) *adj., n.*

**Pal·es·tri·na** (päl′is trē′nä), **Gio·van·ni** (jô vän′nē) **da** (jō vän′nē dä) 1525?–94; It. composer

**pal·ette** (pal′it) *n.* [Fr. < L. *pala,* a shovel] **1.** a thin board with a hole for the thumb at one end, on which an artist arranges and mixes his paints **2.** the colors used, as by a particular artist

**pal·frey** (pôl′frē) *n., pl.* **-freys** [< OFr. < ML., ult. < Gr. *para,* beside + L. *veredus,* post horse] [Archaic] a saddle horse, esp. one for a woman

**Pa·li** (pä′lē) *n.* the Old Indic dialect which has become the religious language of Buddhism

**pal·imp·sest** (pal′imp sest′) *n.* [< L. < Gr. < *palin,* again + *psēn,* to rub smooth] a parchment, tablet, etc. that has been written upon several times, with previous, erased texts still partly visible

PALETTE

**pal·in·drome** (pal′in drōm′) *n.* [< Gr. < *palin,* again + *dramein,* to run] a word, phrase, or sentence that reads the same backward or forward (Ex.: madam)

**pal·ing** (pāl′iŋ) *n.* **1.** a fence made of pales **2.** the action of making such a fence **3.** a pale, or pales collectively

**pal·i·sade** (pal′ə sād′, pal′ə sād′) *n.* [< Fr. < Pr. < L. *palus,* a stake] **1.** any of a row of large pointed stakes set in the ground to form a fence as for fortification **2.** such a fence **3.** [*pl.*] a line of steep cliffs —*vt.* **-sad′ed, -sad′ing** to fortify or defend with a palisade

**pall**[1] (pôl) *vi.* **palled, pall′ing** [ME. *pallen,* short for *appallen,* APPALL] **1.** to become cloying, insipid, etc. **2.** to become satiated or bored —*vt.* to satiate, bore, or disgust

**pall**[2] (pôl) *n.* [< OE. < L. *pallium,* a cover] **1.** a piece of velvet, etc. used to cover a coffin, hearse, or tomb **2.** a dark or gloomy covering [a *pall* of smoke] **3.** a cloth, or cardboard covered with cloth, used to cover the chalice in some Christian churches —*vt.* **palled, pall′ing** to cover as with a pall

**Pal·la·dio** (päl lä′dyô), **An·dre·a** (än dre′ä) (born *Andrea di Pietro*) 1518–80; It. architect —**Pal·la·di·an** (pə lā′dē ən, -lä′-) *adj.*

**Pal·la·di·um** (pə lā′dē əm) *n., pl.* **-di·a** (-ə) **1.** the legendary statue of Pallas Athena in Troy believed to guard the city **2.** [p-] any safeguard

**pal·la·di·um** (pə lā′dē əm) *n.* [ModL., ult. < Gr. *Pallas,* the goddess] a rare, silvery-white, metallic chemical element: it is used as a catalyst, or in alloys with gold, silver, etc.: symbol, Pd; at. wt., 106.4; at. no., 46

**Pal·las** (pal′əs) *Gr. Myth.* Athena, goddess of wisdom: also **Pallas Athena** —**Pal·la·di·an** (pə lā′dē ən) *adj.*

**pall·bear·er** (pôl′ber′ər) *n.* [PALL[2] + BEARER] one of the persons who bear the coffin at a funeral

**pal·let**[1] (pal′it) *n.* [< MFr.: see PALETTE] **1.** a wooden tool consisting of a flat blade with a handle; esp., such a tool for smoothing pottery **2.** *same as* PALETTE (sense 1) **3.** a low, portable platform for storing goods in warehouses, etc. **4.** any of the clicks or pawls in the escapement of a clock, etc. which engage the ratchet wheel to regulate the speed

**pal·let**[2] (pal′it) *n.* [< MFr. < OFr. *paille,* straw < L. *palea,* chaff] a small, inferior bed or a mattress filled as with straw and used on the floor

**pal·li·ate** (pal′ē āt′) *vt.* **-at′ed, -at′ing** [< LL. pp. of *palliare,* to conceal < *pallium,* a cloak] **1.** to lessen the pain or severity of without curing; alleviate **2.** to make appear less serious or offensive; excuse —**pal′li·a′tion** *n.* —**pal′li·a′tive** (-āt′iv, -ə tiv) *adj., n.* —**pal′li·a′tor** *n.*

**pal·lid** (pal′id) *adj.* [L. *pallidus,* PALE[1]] faint in color; pale —**pal′lid·ly** *adv.* —**pal′lid·ness** *n.*

**Pall Mall** (pel′mel′, pal′mal′, pôl′môl′) a London street, noted for its clubs for men

**pal·lor** (pal′ər) *n.* [L. < *pallere:* see PALE[1]] lack of color; unnatural paleness, as of the face

**palm**[1] (päm; *occas.* pälm) *n.* [OE. < L. *palma:* from its handlike fronds] **1.** any of a family of tropical or subtropical trees with a tall, branchless trunk and a bunch of large leaves at the top **2.** a leaf of this tree carried as a symbol of victory, triumph, etc. **3.** victory; triumph —*adj.* designating or of a family of plants including the coconut palm, date palm, etc. —**bear** (or **carry off) the palm** to be the winner —**pal·ma·ceous** (pal mā′shəs, pä-) *adj.*

**palm**[2] (päm; *occas.* pälm) *n.* [< OFr. < L. *palma*] **1.** the inner surface of the hand between the fingers and wrist **2.** the part of a glove, etc. that covers the palm **3.** the broad, flat part of an antler, as of a moose **4.** a unit of measure based either on the width of the hand (3 to 4 inches) or its length (7 to 9 inches) **5.** any broad, flat part at the end of an arm, handle, etc. —*vt.* to hide (something) in the palm or between the fingers, as in a sleight-of-hand trick —**have an itching palm** [Colloq.] to desire money greedily —**palm off** to pass off by fraud or deceit —**pal·mar** (pal′mər, pä′-) *adj.*

**Pal·ma** (päl′mä) seaport on Majorca: chief city of the Balearic Islands: pop. 208,000: in full, **Palma de Mallorca**

**pal·mate** (pal′māt, pä′-) *adj.* [< L. < *palma,* PALM[2]] shaped like a hand with the fingers spread; specif., *a) Bot.* having veins or lobes radiating from a common center, as some leaves *b) Zool.* web-footed Also **pal′mat·ed** —**pal′mate·ly** *adv.* —**pal·ma′tion** *n.*

**Palm Beach** resort town on the SE coast of Fla.

**palm·er** (päm′ər, päl′mər) *n.* **1.** a pilgrim who carried a palm leaf as a sign that he had been to the Holy Land **2.** any pilgrim

**Palm·er·ston** (päm′ər stən), **3d Viscount,** (*Henry John Temple*) 1784–1865; Brit. statesman; prime minister (1855–58; 1859–65)

**pal·met·to** (pal met′ō) *n., pl.* **-tos, -toes** [Sp. *palmito,* dim. < *palma* < L., PALM[1]] any of several new-world palms with fan-shaped leaves, as the cabbage palm

**palm·is·try** (päm′is trē, päl′mis-) *n.* [< ME., prob. contr. < *paume,* PALM[2] + *maistrie,* mastery] the pretended art of telling a person's fortune by the lines, etc. on the palm of his hand —**palm′ist** *n.*

**pal·mit·ic acid** (pal mit′ik, pä-) [< Fr.] a fatty acid found in many natural fats and oils

**palm leaf** the leaf of a palm tree, esp. of a palmetto, used to make fans, hats, etc.

**palm oil** an oil obtained from the fruit of certain palms, used in making soap, candles, etc.

**Palm Springs** resort city in S Calif.

**Palm Sunday** the Sunday before Easter, commemorating Jesus' triumphal entry into Jerusalem

**palm·y** (päm′ē, päl′mē) *adj.* **palm′i·er, palm′i·est 1.** abounding in or shaded by palm trees **2.** of or like a palm **3.** prosperous [*palmy* days]

**pal·my·ra** (pal mī′rə) *n.* [< Port. < *palma* < L., PALM[1]] a palm tree grown in India, Ceylon, and Africa for its durable wood, its leaves used for thatching, etc.

**Pal·o Al·to** (pal′ō al′tō) [Sp., lit., tall tree (the redwood)] city in W Calif., near San Francisco: pop. 55,000

**pal·o·mi·no** (pal′ə mē′nō) *n., pl.* **-nos** [AmSp. < Sp., dove-colored, ult. < L. *palumbes,* pigeon] a cream, golden, or light-chestnut horse with white mane and tail

**palp** (palp) *n. same as* PALPUS —**pal′pal** *adj.*

**pal·pa·ble** (pal′pə b′l) *adj.* [< LL. < L. *palpare,* to touch] **1.** that can be touched, felt, etc.; tangible **2.** easily perceived by the senses; recognizable, perceptible, etc. **3.** obvious; plain —**pal′pa·bil′i·ty** *n.* —**pal′pa·bly** *adv.*

**pal·pate** (pal′pāt) *vt.* **-pat·ed, -pat·ing** [< L. pp. of *pal-*

*pare,* to touch] to examine by touching, as for medical diagnosis —**pal·pa′tion** *n.*

**pal·pi·tate** (pal′pə tāt′) *vi.* **-tat′ed, -tat′ing** [< L. pp. of *palpitare,* freq. of *palpare,* to feel] **1.** to beat rapidly or flutter: said of the heart **2.** to throb; quiver —**pal′pi·tant** *adj.* —**pal′pi·ta′tion** *n.*

**pal·pus** (pal′pəs) *n., pl.* **pal′pi** (-pī) [ModL. < L. *palpus,* the soft palm of the hand] a jointed organ or feeler for touching or tasting, attached to one of the head appendages of insects, lobsters, etc.

**pal·sy** (pôl′zē) *n., pl.* **-sies** [< OFr. < L. *paralysis,* PARALYSIS] paralysis of any voluntary muscle, sometimes accompanied by uncontrollable tremors —*vt.* **-sied, -sy·ing** to afflict with or as with palsy; paralyze

**pal·ter** (pôl′tər) *vi.* [freq. < dial. *palt,* a rag] **1.** to talk or act insincerely; prevaricate **2.** to trifle **3.** to quibble

**pal·try** (pôl′trē) *adj.* **-tri·er, -tri·est** [prob. < LowG. *paltrig* < *palte,* a rag] worthless; trifling; petty —**pal′tri·ness** *n.*

**pam·pas** (pam′pəz; *for adj., usually* -pəs) *n.pl.* [AmSp., pl. of *pampa* < Quechua, plain] the extensive treeless plains of S. America, esp. of Argentina —*adj.* of the pampas — **pam·pe·an** (pam′pē ən, pam pē′-) *adj., n.*

**pam·per** (pam′pər) *vt.* [< LowG. source] **1.** orig., to feed too much; glut **2.** to be overindulgent with; coddle [to *pamper a child]* —**pam′per·er** *n.*

**pam·phlet** (pam′flit) *n.* [< OFr. *Pamphilet,* popular name of a ML. poem] **1.** a small, unbound booklet, usually with a paper cover **2.** a treatise in this form, as on some topic of current interest

**pam·phlet·eer** (pam′flə tir′) *n.* a writer of pamphlets, esp. those dealing with political or social issues —*vi.* to write or publish pamphlets

**Pan** (pan) *Gr. Myth.* a god of fields, forests, wild animals, flocks, and shepherds, represented with the legs of a goat

**pan¹** (pan) *n.* [OE. *panne*] **1.** any broad, shallow container, usually of metal and without a cover, used in cooking, etc.: often in combination *[saucepan]* **2.** a pan-shaped part or object; specif., *a)* a container for washing out gold, etc. from gravel *b)* either receptacle in a pair of scales **3.** *same as* HARDPAN (sense 1) **4.** the part holding the powder in a flintlock **5.** [Slang] a face —*vt.* **panned, pan′ning 1.** to cook in a pan **2.** [Colloq.] to criticize unfavorably, as in reviewing **3.** *Mining a)* to wash (gravel) in a pan *b)* to separate (gold, etc.) from gravel in this way —*vi. Mining* **1.** to wash gravel in a pan **2.** to yield gold in this process —**pan out 1.** *Mining* to yield gold, as gravel, a mine, etc. **2.** [Colloq.] to turn out; esp., to turn out well

**pan²** (pan) *vt., vi.* **panned, pan′ning** [< PAN(ORAMA)] to move (a motion-picture or television camera) so as to get a panoramic effect or follow a moving object —*n.* the act of panning

**pan-** [< Gr. *pan,* neut. of *pas,* all, every] *a combining form meaning:* **1.** all *[pantheism]* **2.** [P-] *a)* of, comprising, or common to every *[Pan-American] b)* (belief in the) union or cooperation of all members of (a specified group) *[Pan-Americanism]* In sense 2, usually with a hyphen, as in the following words:

| | |
|---|---|
| **Pan-African** | **Pan-European** |
| **Pan-Arabic** | **Pan-Islamic** |
| **Pan-Asiatic** | **Pan-Slavic** |

**pan·a·ce·a** (pan′ə sē′ə) *n.* [L. < Gr. < *pan,* all + *akeisthai,* to cure] a supposed remedy or cure for all diseases or ills; cure-all —**pan′a·ce′an** *adj.*

**pa·nache** (pə nash′) *n.* [Fr., ult. < LL. *pinnaculum,* plume] **1.** a plume on a helmet **2.** carefree self-confidence or style; flamboyance

**Pan·a·ma** (pan′ə mä′, -mô′) **1.** country in Central America, on the Isthmus of Panama: 29,201 sq. mi.; pop. 1,425,000 **2.** its capital, on the Pacific: pop. 412,000: also **Panama City 3. Isthmus of,** strip of land connecting South America & Central America —**Pan′a·ma′ni·an** (-mä′nē ən) *adj., n.*

**Panama Canal** ship canal across the Isthmus of Panama, connecting the Caribbean Sea & the Pacific Ocean: 50.7 mi. long

**Panama (hat)** [< *Panama* (city)] a fine, hand-plaited hat made from select leaves of a Central and South American plant

**Pan-A·mer·i·can** (pan′ə mer′ə kən) *adj.* of North, Central, and South America, collectively

**Pan-A·mer·i·can·ism** (-iz′m) *n.* a policy of political and economic cooperation, mutual cultural understanding, etc. among the Pan-American nations

**pan·a·tel·a, pan·a·tel·la** (pan′ə tel′ə) *n.* [AmSp., orig. a long biscuit < It., dim. of *pane,* bread] a long, slender cigar

**Pa·nay** (pä nī′; *E.* pə nī′) island of the C Philippines, between Mindoro & Negros: 4,446 sq. mi.

**pan·broil** (pan′broil′) *vt.* to fry in a pan with little or no fat

**pan·cake** (pan′kāk′) *n.* **1.** a thin, flat cake of batter fried on a griddle or in a pan; griddlecake; flapjack **2.** a landing in which the plane levels off, stalls, then drops almost vertically: in full, **pancake landing** —*vi., vt.* **-caked′, -cak′ing** to make, or cause to make, a pancake landing

**pancake makeup** a thin cake of compressed powder used as cosmetic or theatrical makeup

**pan·chro·mat·ic** (pan′krō mat′ik) *adj.* sensitive to light of all colors *[panchromatic* film] —**pan·chro·ma·tism** (pan krō′mə tiz′m) *n.*

**pan·cre·as** (pan′krē əs, paŋ′-) *n.* [ModL. < Gr. < *pan,* all + *kreas,* flesh] a large, elongated gland that secretes an alkaline digestive juice (**pancreatic juice**) into the small intestine: the pancreas of animals, used as food, is called *sweetbread* —**pan′cre·at′ic** (-at′ik) *adj.*

**pan·da** (pan′də) *n.* [Fr. < native name in Nepal] *clipped form of:* **1.** GIANT PANDA **2.** LESSER PANDA

**pan·dem·ic** (pan dem′ik) *adj.* [< LL. < Gr. < *pan,* all + *dēmos,* the people] epidemic over a large region —*n.* a pandemic disease

**Pan·de·mo·ni·um** (pan′də mō′nē əm) [ModL. < Gr. *pan-* + *daimōn,* demon] the capital of Hell in Milton's *Paradise Lost* —*n.* [p-] wild disorder, noise, or confusion, or a place where this exists

**pan·der** (pan′dər) *n.* [< L. *Pandarus,* who, in the story of Troilus and Cressida, acts as their go-between] **1.** a go-between in a sexual intrigue; pimp **2.** one who provides the means of helping to satisfy the ambitions, vices, etc. of another Also **pan′der·er** —*vi.* to act as a pander (*to*)

**pan·dit** (pun′dit, pan′-) *n.* [var. of PUNDIT] in India, a learned man: used [P-] as a title of respect

**P. and L., P. & L.** profit and loss

**Pan·do·ra** (pan dôr′ə) [L. < Gr. < *pan,* all + *dōron,* a gift] *Gr. Myth.* the first mortal woman, who in curiosity opened a box, letting out all human ills into the world

**pan·dow·dy** (pan dou′dē) *n., pl.* **-dies** [prob. < obs. E. dial. *pandoulde,* custard] deep-dish apple pie, having a top crust only

**pane** (pān) *n.* [< OFr. < L. *pannus,* piece of cloth] **1.** a flat piece, side, or face **2.** *a)* a single division of a window, etc., consisting of a sheet of glass in a frame *b)* such a sheet of glass **3.** a panel, as of a door

**pan·e·gyr·ic** (pan′ə jir′ik) *n.* [Fr. < L. < Gr. *panēgyris,* public meeting < *pan,* all + *ageirein,* to bring together] **1.** a formal speech or writing praising a person or event **2.** high or exaggerated praise —**pan′e·gyr′i·cal** *adj.* —**pan′e·gyr′i·cal·ly** *adv.* —**pan′e·gyr′ist** *n.* —**pan′e·gyr·ize′** (-jə rīz′) *vt., vi.* **-rized′, -riz′ing**

**pan·el** (pan′'l) *n.* [< OFr., ult. < L. *pannus,* piece of cloth] **1.** a section or division of a surface; specif., *a)* a flat piece, usually rectangular, forming a part of the surface of a wall, door, etc., usually raised, recessed, framed, etc. *b)* a similar piece used as a cover, a light diffuser, a built-in heating element, etc. *c)* a pane of a window *d)* a board, or flat surface, for instruments or controls **2.** *a)* a thin board for an oil painting *b)* a painting on such a board *c)* a picture much longer than it is wide **3.** *a)* a list of persons summoned for jury duty *b)* the jury itself **4.** a group of persons selected for a specific purpose, as for judging a contest, discussing an issue, etc. **5.** a lengthwise strip, as of contrasting material, in a skirt or dress —*vt.* **-eled** or **-elled, -el·ing** or **-el·ling** to provide, decorate, etc. with panels

**panel discussion** a discussion carried on by a selected group of speakers before an audience

**pan·el·ing, pan·el·ling** (-iŋ) *n.* **1.** panels collectively; series of panels in a wall, etc. **2.** sections of plastic, wood, etc. from which to cut panels

**pan·el·ist** (-ist) *n.* a member of a panel (*n.* 4)

**panel truck** a small, enclosed pickup truck

**pan·e·tel·a, pan·e·tel·la** (pan′ə tel′ə) *n. same as* PANATELA

**pan fish** a fish that can be fried whole in a pan

**pan-fry** (pan′frī′) *vt.* **-fried′, -fry′ing** to fry in a shallow skillet or frying pan

**pang** (paŋ) *n.* [< ?] a sudden, sharp, brief pain, physical or emotional; spasm of distress

**pan·go·lin** (paŋ gō′lin) *n.* [Malay *pĕngulin,* roller < *gulin,* to roll] any of various toothless, scaly mammals of Asia and Africa, able to roll into a ball when attacked

**pan·han·dle¹** (pan′han′d'l) *n.* **1.** the handle of a pan **2.** [often P-] a strip of land like the handle of a pan, as the northern extension of Texas

**pan·han·dle²** (pan′han′d'l) *vt., vi.* **-dled, -dling** [ult. < PAN¹ + HANDLE, *vt.*] [Colloq.] to beg (from), esp. on the streets —**pan′han′dler** *n.*

---

fat, āpe, cär; ten, ēven; is, bīte; gō, hôrn, tōōl, lŏŏk; oil, out; up, fur; get; joy; yet; chin; she; thin, then; zh, leisure; ŋ, ring; ə for *a* in *ago, e* in *agent, i* in *sanity, o* in *comply, u* in *focus;* ′ as in *able* (ā′b'l); Fr. bal; ë, Fr. coeur; ö, Fr. feu; Fr. mon; ô, Fr. coq; ü, Fr. duc; r, Fr. cri; H, G. ich; kh, G. doch; ‡foreign; *hypothetical; < derived from. See inside front cover.

**Pan·hel·len·ic** (pan'hə len'ik) *adj.* **1.** of all the Greek peoples **2.** of all Greek-letter fraternities and sororities

**pan·ic**[1] (pan'ik) *n.* [L. *panicum*, kind of millet < *panus*, a swelling] any of several related grasses, as millet, used as fodder: also **panic grass**

**pan·ic**[2] (pan'ik) *adj.* [< Fr. < Gr. *panikos*, of Pan] **1.** literally, of Pan or of sudden fear supposedly inspired by him **2.** like, showing, or resulting from, panic —*n.* **1.** a sudden, unreasoning, hysterical fear, often spreading quickly **2.** a widespread fear of financial collapse, resulting in stock-market decline, withdrawals of bank deposits, etc. **3.** [Slang] a very comical person or thing —*vt.* **-icked, -icking 1.** to affect with panic **2.** [Slang] to convulse (an audience, etc.) with laughter, etc. —*vi.* to give way to or show panic —**push** (or **press, hit,** etc.) **the panic button** [Slang] to react to a crisis by some frantic action —**pan'i·cal·ly** *adv.* —**pan'ick·y** *adj.*

**pan·i·cle** (pan'i k'l) *n.* [< L. dim. of *panus*, a swelling, ear of millet] a loose, irregularly branched flower cluster; compound raceme —**pan·i·cled, pa·nic·u·late** (pa nik'yə lit, -lāt') *adj.*

**pan·ic-strick·en** (pan'ik strik''n) *adj.* stricken with panic; badly frightened: also **panic-struck**

**pan·jan·drum** (pan jan'drəm) *n.* [arbitrary coinage] a self-important, pompous official

**pan·nier, pan·ier** (pan'yər, -ē ər) *n.* [< MFr. < L. *panarium*, breadbasket < *panis*, bread] **1.** *a*) a large basket for carrying loads on the back *b*) either of a pair of baskets hung across the back of a donkey, horse, etc. **2.** *a*) a framework, as of wire, used formerly to puff out a skirt at the hips *b*) a skirt so puffed

PANICLE OF OATS

**pan·ni·kin** (pan'ə kin) *n.* [Chiefly Brit.] a small pan or cup

**pa·no·cha** (pə nō'chə) *n.* [AmSp. < Sp. *pan*, bread < L. *panis*] **1.** a coarse Mexican sugar **2.** *var. of* PENUCHE: also **pa·no'che** (-chē)

**pan·o·ply** (pan'ə plē) *n., pl.* **-plies** [< Gr. < *pan*, all + *hopla*, arms] **1.** a complete suit of armor **2.** any complete or magnificent covering or array —**pan'o·plied** *adj.*

**pan·o·ra·ma** (pan'ə ram'ə) *n.* [< PAN- + Gr. *horama*, a view] **1.** *a*) a picture unrolled in such a way as to give the impression of a continuous view *b*) *same as* CYCLORAMA (sense 1) **2.** an open view in all directions **3.** a full review of a subject **4.** a constantly changing scene *[the panorama* of the waterfront*]* —**pan'o·ram'ic** *adj.* —**pan'o·ram'i·cal·ly** *adv.*

**pan·pipe** (pan'pīp') *n.* [*also* P-] a primitive musical instrument made of a row of reeds or tubes of graduated lengths, played by blowing across the open ends: also **panpipes, Pan's pipes**

**pan·sy** (pan'zē) *n., pl.* **-sies** [Fr. *pensée*, a thought < *penser*, to think] **1.** a small, flowering plant with flat, broad, velvety petals in many colors **2.** [Slang] a male homosexual

**pant**[1] (pant) *vi.* [prob. < OFr. *pantaisier*, ult. < L. *phantasia*, nightmare] **1.** to breathe rapidly and heavily, as from running fast **2.** to beat rapidly; throb **3.** to yearn eagerly (with *for* or *after*) —*vt.* to gasp out —*n.* **1.** any of a series of rapid, heavy breaths; gasp **2.** a throb, as of the heart **3.** a puff of an engine

**pant**[2] (pant) *n., adj. see* PANTS

**pan·ta·lets, pan·ta·lettes** (pan't'l ets') *n.pl.* [dim. of ff.] **1.** long, loose drawers showing below the skirt, worn by women in the 19th cent. **2.** detachable ruffles for the legs of drawers

**pan·ta·loon** (pan't'l ōōn') [< Fr. < It., ult. after the Venetian patron saint *Pantalone*] [P-] **1.** a foolish old man in early Italian comedy, typically slender and in tightfitting trousers **2.** a similar buffoon in modern pantomime —*n.* [*pl.*] trousers

**pant·dress** (pant'dres') *n.* a woman's garment with the lower part like pants instead of a skirt

**pan·the·ism** (pan'thē iz'm) *n.* **1.** the belief that God is not a personality but the sum of all beings, things, forces, etc. in the universe **2.** the worship of all gods —**pan'the·ist** *n.* —**pan'the·is'tic, pan'the·is'ti·cal** *adj.* —**pan'the·is'ti·cal·ly** *adv.*

**pan·the·on** (pan'thē än', -ən) *n.* [< L. < Gr. < *pan*, all + *theos*, a god] **1.** a temple for all the gods; esp., [P-] a temple built in Rome in 27 B.C.: used since 609 A.D. as a Christian church **2.** all the gods of a people **3.** [*often* P-] a building in which the famous dead of a nation are entombed or commemorated

**pan·ther** (pan'thər) *n., pl.* **-thers, -ther:** *see* PLURAL, II, D, 1 [< OFr. < L. < Gr. *panthēr*] **1.** a leopard; specif., *a*) a black leopard *b*) a leopard that is very large or fierce **2.** *same as: a*) COUGAR *b*) JAGUAR —**pan'ther·ess** *n.fem.*

**pant·ies** (pan'tēz) *n.pl.* women's or children's short underpants: also **pan'tie** (-tē)

**pan·to-** [< Gr. *pantos*, gen. of *pan*, all, every] *a combining form meaning* all or every: also **pant-**

**pan·to·graph** (pan'tə graf') *n.* [< Fr.: see prec. & -GRAPH] a mechanical device for reproducing a drawing on the same or a different scale

**pan·to·mime** (pan'tə mīm') *n.* [< L. < Gr. < *pantos* (see PANTO-) + *mimos*, a mimic] **1.** *a*) a play, skit, etc. performed without words, using actions and gestures only *b*) the art of acting in this way **2.** actions and gestures without words —*vt., vi.* **-mimed', -mim'ing** to express or act in pantomime —**pan'to·mim'ic** (-mim'ik) *adj.* —**pan'to·mim'ist** (-mī'mist, -mim'ist) *n.*

**pan·to·then·ic acid** (pan'tə then'ik) [< Gr. *pantothen*, from every side] a yellow, viscous oil, $C_9H_{17}O_5N$, a member of the vitamin B complex, found in all living tissues

**pan·try** (pan'trē) *n., pl.* **-tries** [< OFr. < ML. *panetaria* < L. *panis*, bread] **1.** a small room off the kitchen where cooking ingredients and utensils, china, etc. are kept **2.** *same as* BUTLER'S PANTRY

**pants** (pants) *n.pl.* [abbrev. of PANTALOON(s)] **1.** trousers **2.** drawers or panties As an adjective or in compounds, usually **pant** [*pant* legs, *pantdress*]

**pant·suit** (pant'sōōt') *n.* a woman's outfit of a matched jacket and pants: also **pants suit**

**pan·ty** (pan'tē) *n., pl.* **-ties** *same as* PANTIES

**panty girdle** a girdle with a crotch like panties

**panty hose** a woman's undergarment combining panties with hose: also **pan'ty·hose'** (-hōz') *n.*

**pan·ty·waist** (-wāst') *n.* **1.** orig., a child's two-piece undergarment **2.** [Slang] a sissy

**pan·zer** (pan'zər; *G.* pän'tsər) *adj.* [G., armor] armored [*a panzer* division]

**Pao·tou** (bou'dō') city in Inner Mongolia, NE China: pop. 1,500,000: also sp. **Paotow**

**pap**[1] (pap) *n.* [prob. orig. < baby talk] [Archaic] a nipple or teat

**pap**[2] (pap) *n.* [orig. < baby talk] **1.** any soft food for babies or invalids **2.** any oversimplified or tasteless writing, ideas, etc.

**pa·pa** (pä'pə; *now less freq.* pə pä') *n.* [< baby talk, as also in Fr. & L. *papa*] father: a child's word

**pa·pa·cy** (pā'pə sē) *n., pl.* **-cies** [< ML. < LL. *papa*, pope] **1.** the position or authority of the Pope **2.** the period during which a pope rules **3.** the succession of popes **4.** [*also* P-] the government of the Roman Catholic Church, headed by the Pope

**pa·pal** (pā'pəl) *adj.* [< MFr. < ML.: see POPE & -AL] **1.** of the Pope or the papacy **2.** of the Roman Catholic Church —**pa'pal·ly** *adv.*

**pa·paw** (pô'pô, pə pô') *n.* [prob. < ff.] **1.** *same as* PAPAYA **2.** *a*) a tree of central and southern U.S. having a yellowish, edible fruit with many seeds *b*) its fruit

**pa·pa·ya** (pə pä'yə) *n.* [Sp. < Carib name] **1.** a palmlike tropical American tree bearing a large, yellowish-orange fruit like a melon **2.** its fruit

**pa·per** (pā'pər) *n.* [< OFr. < L. *papyrus*, PAPYRUS] **1.** a thin, flexible material usually in sheets, made from wood pulp, rags, etc., and used for writing or printing on, for packaging, etc. **2.** a single piece or sheet of this **3.** a printed or written paper; specif., *a*) an official document *b*) an essay, dissertation, etc. *c*) a written examination, report, etc. **4.** *same as: a*) COMMERCIAL PAPER *b*) PAPER MONEY **5.** *clipped form of: a*) NEWSPAPER *b*) WALLPAPER **6.** a small wrapper of paper, usually including its contents [*a paper* of pins] **7.** any material like paper, as papyrus **8.** [*pl.*] *a*) documents identifying a person; credentials *b*) a collection of letters, writings, etc. —*adj.* **1.** of paper; made of paper **2.** like paper; thin **3.** existing only in written form; theoretical [*paper* profits] —*vt.* **1.** to cover with paper, esp. wallpaper **2.** to wrap in paper —*vi.* to hang wallpaper —**on paper 1.** in written or printed form **2.** in theory —**pa'per·er** *n.* —**pa'per·like', pa'per·y** *adj.*

**pa·per·back** (-bak') *n.* a book bound in paper —**pa'per·backed', pa'per·bound'** (-bound') *adj.*

**paper birch** the N. American birch having white or ash-colored paperlike bark

**pa·per·boy** (-boi') *n.* a boy or man who sells or delivers newspapers

**paper clip** a flexible clasp of metal wire for holding loose sheets of paper together

**paper cutter 1.** *same as* PAPER KNIFE **2.** a device for cutting and trimming several sheets of paper at a time

**pa·per·hang·er** (-haŋ'ər) *n.* a person whose work is covering walls with wallpaper —**pa'per·hang'ing** *n.*

**paper knife** a knifelike blade, as of metal, used to slit sealed envelopes and uncut book pages

**paper money** noninterest-bearing notes, as dollar bills, issued by a government or its banks, circulating as legal tender

**paper nautilus** an eight-armed mollusk related to the octopus: the female has a paperlike shell in which the young develop

**paper tiger** a person, nation, etc. that seems to pose a threat but is actually powerless

**pa·per·weight** (-wāt′) *n.* any small, heavy object set on papers to keep them from being scattered

**paper work** the keeping of records, filing of reports, etc. incidental to some work or task

**pa·pier-mâ·ché** (pā′pər mə shā′) *n.* [Fr. *papier,* paper + pp. of *mâcher,* to chew] a material made from paper pulp mixed with size, glue, etc., that is easily molded when moist and dries strong and hard —*adj.* made of papier-mâché

**pa·pil·la** (pə pil′ə) *n., pl.* **-lae** (-ē) [L., dim. of *papula,* pimple] 1. a small bulge of flesh, as at the root of a hair, a developing tooth, etc., or on the surface of the tongue 2. *Bot.* a tiny, protruding cell —**pap·il·lar·y** (pap′ə ler′ē, pə pil′ər ē) *adj.* —**pap·il·late** (pap′ə lāt′, pə pil′it) *adj.*

**pap·il·lo·ma** (pap′ə lō′mə) *n., pl.* **-ma·ta** (-mə tə), **-mas** [ModL.: see PAPILLA & -OMA] a benign tumor of the skin or mucous membrane, consisting of a thickened and enlarged papilla or group of papillae, as a corn or wart

**pa·pist** (pā′pist) *n.* [< ModL. < LL. *papa,* POPE] 1. one who believes in papal supremacy 2. a Roman Catholic —*adj.* Roman Catholic A hostile term

**pa·poose** (pa pōōs′, pə-) *n.* [< Algonquian *papoos*] a North American Indian baby

**pap·pus** (pap′əs) *n., pl.* **pap′pi** (-ī) [ModL. < L. < Gr. *pappos,* old man] *Bot.* a tuft of bristles, hairs, etc.

**pap·py** (pap′ē) *n., pl.* **-pies** [Dial. or Colloq.] father

**pa·pri·ka** (pa prē′kə, pə-; pap′ri kə) *n.* [Hung. < Serb. < Gr. *peperi,* pepper] a mild, red condiment ground from the fruit of certain peppers

**Pap test** (pap) [after G. *Papanicolaou* (1883–1962), U.S. anatomist] the microscopic examination of a smear (**Pap smear**) taken from the cervix of a woman: a test for cancer

**Pap·u·a New Guinea** (pap′yoo wə, pä′poo wə) country occupying the E half of the island of New Guinea, and nearby islands: c. 180,000 sq. mi.; pop. 2,756,000

**pap·ule** (pap′yōōl) *n.* [L. *papula*] a pimple —**pap′u·lar** (-lər) *adj.* —**pap′u·lose′** (-lōs′) *adj.*

**pa·py·rus** (pə pī′rəs) *n., pl.* **-ri** (-rī), **-rus·es** [L. < Gr. *papyros,* prob. < Egypt.] 1. a tall water plant abundant in the Nile region in Egypt 2. a writing material made from this plant by the ancient Egyptians, Greeks, and Romans 3. any ancient document or manuscript on papyrus

**par** (pär) *n.* [L., an equal] 1. the established value of the money of one country in terms of the money of another 2. an equal status, footing, level, etc.: usually in **on a par (with)** 3. the average state, condition, etc. /work that is above par/ 4. *Commerce* the face value of stocks, bonds, etc. 5. *Golf* the number of strokes established as a skillful score for a hole or course —*adj.* 1. of or at par 2. average; normal —*vt.* **parred, par′ring** *Golf* to score par on (a given hole or course)

**par.** 1. paragraph 2. parallel 3. parenthesis 4. parish

**Pa·rá** (pä rä′) river in NE Brazil, forming the S estuary of the Amazon

**pa·ra** (pä rä′, pär′ə) *n.* [Turk. < Per. *pārah,* a piece] *see* MONETARY UNITS, table (Yugoslavia)

**par·a-** [< Gr. < *para,* at the side of] *a prefix meaning:* 1. by or at the side of, beyond, aside from *[paramilitary]* 2. *Med.* a) in a secondary capacity b) functionally disordered, abnormal c) like or resembling *[paratyphoid]*

**par·a·mi·no·ben·zo·ic acid** (par′ə ə mē′nō ben zō′ik, -am′ə nō′-) a crystalline compound, $C_7H_7NO_2$, considered a member of the vitamin B complex

**par·a·ble** (par′ə b′l) *n.* [< MFr. < LL. < L. < Gr. *parabolē,* a comparing; ult. < *para,* beside + *ballein,* to throw] a short, simple story teaching a moral or religious lesson

**pa·rab·o·la** (pə rab′ə lə) *n.* [ModL. < Gr. *parabolē:* see prec.] *Geom.* a plane curve formed by the intersection of a cone with a plane parallel to its side

**par·a·bol·ic¹** (par′ə bäl′ik) *adj.* of, like, or expressed by a parable: also **par′a·bol′i·cal** —**par′a·bol′i·cal·ly** *adv.*

**par·a·bol·ic²** (par′ə bäl′ik) *adj.* 1. of or like a parabola 2. concave with the regular outline of a parabola, as a reflector —**par′a·bol′i·cal·ly** *adv.*

**Par·a·cel·sus** (par′ə sel′səs), **Phi·lip·pus Au·re·o·lus** (fi lip′əs ô rē′ə ləs) (born *Theophrastus Bombastus von Hohenheim*) 1493–1541; Swiss physician & alchemist

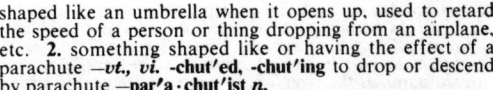

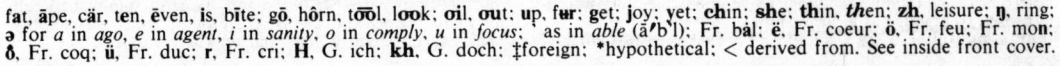

PARABOLA

**par·a·chute** (par′ə shōōt′) *n.* [Fr. < *para-* (< It. *parare,* to ward off) + *chute,* a fall] 1. a large cloth contrivance shaped like an umbrella when it opens up, used to retard the speed of a person or thing dropping from an airplane, etc. 2. something shaped like or having the effect of a parachute —*vt., vi.* **-chut′ed, -chut′ing** to drop or descend by parachute —**par′a·chut′ist** *n.*

**pa·rade** (pə rād′) *n.* [Fr. < Sp. *parada,* ult. < L. *parare,* to prepare] 1. ostentatious display 2. *a)* a military assembly; esp., a review of marching troops *b)* a place where troops assemble regularly for parade 3. any organized procession or march, as for display 4. *a)* a public walk or promenade *b)* persons promenading —*vt.* **-rad′ed, -rad′ing** 1. to bring together (troops, etc.) for inspection or display 2. to march or walk through (the streets, etc.), as for display 3. to show off /he *parades* his knowledge/ —*vi.* 1. to march in a parade 2. to walk about ostentatiously 3. to assemble in military formation for review or display —**on parade** on display —**pa·rad′er** *n.*

**par·a·digm** (par′ə dim, -dīm′) *n.* [< Fr. < LL. < Gr. < *para,* beside + *deigma,* example < *deiknynai,* to show] 1. a pattern, example, or model 2. *Gram.* an example of a declension or conjugation, giving all the inflectional forms of a word —**par′a·dig·mat′ic** (-dig mat′ik) *adj.*

**par·a·dise** (par′ə dīs′) *n.* [< OFr. < LL. < L. < Gr. *paradeisos,* a garden] 1. [P-] the garden of Eden 2. *same as* HEAVEN 3. any place or state of perfection, happiness, etc. —**par′a·di·si′a·cal** (-di sī′ə k′l), **par′a·dis′i·ac′** (-dis′ē ak′) *adj.*

**par·a·dox** (par′ə däks′) *n.* [< L. < Gr. < *para,* beyond + *doxa,* opinion < *dokein,* to think] 1. a statement that seems contradictory, absurd, etc. but may be true in fact 2. a statement that contradicts itself and is false 3. a person, situation, etc. that seems inconsistent or full of contradictions —**par′a·dox′i·cal** *adj.* —**par′a·dox′i·cal·ly** *adv.*

**par·af·fin** (par′ə fin) *n.* [G. < L. *parum,* too little + *affinis,* akin: from its chemical inertness] 1. a white, waxy substance consisting of a mixture of hydrocarbons, distilled from petroleum and used for making candles, sealing jars, etc. 2. *Chem.* any hydrocarbon of the methane series —*vt.* to coat or impregnate with paraffin

**paraffin series** *same as* METHANE SERIES

**par·a·gon** (par′ə gän′, -gən) *n.* [MFr. < It. *paragone,* touchstone < Gr. < *para,* against + *akonē,* whetstone] a model of perfection or excellence

**par·a·graph** (par′ə graf′) *n.* [< OFr. < ML. < Gr. *paragraphos* < *para,* beside + *graphein,* to write] 1. a distinct section of a chapter, letter, etc. dealing with a particular point: it is begun on a new line, often indented 2. a mark (¶) used as by proofreaders to indicate the beginning of a paragraph 3. a brief item in a newspaper or magazine —*vt.* 1. to write about in paragraphs 2. to arrange in paragraphs —**par′a·graph′ic** *adj.*

**Par·a·guay** (par′ə gwä′, -gwī′; Sp. pä rä gwī′) 1. inland country in SC S. America: 157,042 sq. mi.; pop. 2,303,000; cap. Asunción 2. river flowing from S Brazil through Paraguay into the Paraná —**Par′a·guay′an** *adj., n.*

**Paraguay tea** *same as* MATÉ

**par·a·keet** (par′ə kēt′) *n.* [MFr. *paroquet,* prob. < *perrot,* parrot] any of various small, slender parrots with a long, tapering tail

**par·a·le·gal** (par′ə lē′gəl) *adj.* [PARA- + LEGAL] designating or of persons trained to aid lawyers but not licensed to practice law —*n.* a person doing paralegal work

**par·al·lax** (par′ə laks′) *n.* [< Fr. < Gr. < *para,* beyond + *allassein,* to change] 1. the apparent change in the position of an object resulting from a change in the viewer's position 2. the amount of such change; specif., *Astron.* the apparent difference in the position of a heavenly body with reference to some point on the surface of the earth and some other point, as the center of the earth —**par′al·lac′tic** *adj.*

**par·al·lel** (par′ə lel′, -ləl) *adj.* [< Fr. < L. < Gr. < *para,* side by side + *allēlos,* one another] 1. extending in the same direction and at a constant distance apart, so as never to meet, as lines, planes, etc. 2. having parallel parts or movements, as some machines 3. *a)* similar or corresponding, as in purpose, time, or essential parts *b)* having a balanced arrangement, esp. of phrases or clauses *[parallel structure]* 4. *Elec.* designating a circuit in parallel —*adv.* in a parallel manner —*n.* 1. a parallel line, surface, etc. 2. any person or thing similar or corresponding to another; counterpart 3. a being parallel 4. any comparison showing likeness 5. *a)* any of the imaginary lines parallel to the equator and representing degrees of latitude *b)* such a line drawn on a map or globe: in full, **parallel of latitude** 6. [*pl.*] a sign (∥) used as a reference mark 7. *Elec.* a circuit connection in which the negative terminals are joined to

one conductor and the positive to another: usually in phrase, **in parallel** —*vt.* **-al·leled'** or **-al·lelled', -al·lel·ing** or **-al·lel·ling 1.** *a)* to make (one thing) parallel to another *b)* to make parallel to each other **2.** to be parallel with /the road *parallels* the river/ **3.** to compare (things) in order to show similarity **4.** to be or find a counterpart for; match
**parallel bars** two parallel, horizontal bars set on adjustable upright posts: used in gymnastics
**par·al·lel·e·pi·ped** (par'ə lel'ə pī'pid, -pip'id) *n.* [< Gr. *parallēlos*, parallel + *epipedos*, plane] a solid with six faces, each of which is a parallelogram: also **par'al·lel'·e·pip'e·don'** (-pip'ə dän')

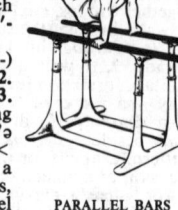

PARALLEL BARS

**par·al·lel·ism** (par'ə lel iz'm, -ləl-) *n.* **1.** the state of being parallel **2.** close resemblance; similarity **3.** use of parallel structure in writing
**par·al·lel·o·gram** (par'ə lel'ə gram') *n.* [< Fr. < L. < Gr. *parallēlos*, PARALLEL + *grammē*, a line] a plane figure with four sides, having the opposite sides parallel and equal
**pa·ral·y·sis** (pə ral'ə sis) *n., pl.* **-ses'** (-sēz') [L. < Gr. < *paralyein*, to loosen at the side < *para-*, beside + *lyein*, to loose] **1.** partial or complete loss of the power of motion or sensation, esp. voluntary motion, in some part or all of the body **2.** any condition of helpless inactivity or inability to act —**par·a·lyt·ic** (par'ə lit'ik) *adj., n.*
**par·a·lyze** (par'ə līz') *vt.* **-lyzed', -lyz'ing 1.** to cause paralysis in **2.** to make inactive, ineffective, or powerless —**par'a·ly·za'tion** *n.* —**par'a·lyz'er** *n.*
**Par·a·mar·i·bo** (par'ə mar'i bō') seaport & capital of Suriname: pop. c.150,000
**par·a·me·ci·um** (par'ə mē'shē əm, -sē əm) *n., pl.* **-ci·a** (-ə) [ModL. < Gr. *paramēkēs*, oval] a one-celled, elongated protozoan that moves by means of cilia
**par·a·med·ic¹** (par'ə med'ik) *n.* [< PARA(CHUTE) + MEDIC¹] a medic, esp. a medical corpsman, who parachutes to combat or rescue areas
**par·a·med·ic²** (par'ə med'ik) *n.* [back-formation < ff.] a person in paramedical work
**par·a·med·i·cal** (par'ə med'i k'l) *adj.* [PARA- + MEDICAL] designating or of auxiliary medical personnel, as midwives, corpsmen, nurses' aides, etc.
**pa·ram·e·ter** (pə ram'ə tər) *n.* [< ModL. < Gr. *para*, alongside + *metron*, measure] **1.** *Math.* a quantity whose value varies with the circumstances of its application **2.** any constant, with variable values, used as a reference for other variables —**par·a·met·ric** (par'ə met'rik) *adj.*
**par·a·mil·i·tar·y** (par'ə mil'ə ter'ē) *adj.* [PARA- + MILITARY] designating or of forces working along with, or in place of, a regular military organization, often as a semiofficial or secret auxiliary
**par·a·mount** (par'ə mount') *adj.* [< Anglo-Fr. < OFr. *par* (L. *per*), by + *amont* (< L. *ad montem*), uphill] ranking higher than any other; chief; supreme —*n.* a supreme ruler; overlord —**par'a·mount'cy** (-sē) *n.* —**par'a·mount'ly** *adv.*
**par·a·mour** (par'ə moor') *n.* [< OFr. *par amour*, with love] **1.** a lover; esp., the illicit sexual partner of a married person **2.** [Archaic] a sweetheart
**Pa·ra·ná** (pä'rä nä') river flowing from S Brazil through NE Argentina into the Río de la Plata
**par·a·noi·a** (par'ə noi'ə) *n.* [ModL. < Gr. < *para-*, beside + *nous*, the mind] a mental disorder characterized by systematized delusions, as of grandeur or, esp., persecution —**par'a·noid', par'a·noi'ac** (-ak) *adj., n.* —**par'a·noi'dal** *adj.*
**par·a·pet** (par'ə pit, -pet') *n.* [Fr. < It. < *parare*, to guard + *petto*, breast < L. *pectus*] **1.** a wall or bank for screening troops from enemy fire **2.** a low wall or railing, as on a balcony or bridge
**par·a·pher·na·li·a** (par'ə fər nāl'yə, -fə näl'-; -nā'lē ə) *n.pl.* [often with sing. v.] [ML. < LL. *parapherna* < Gr. < *para-*, beyond + *phernē*, a dowry] **1.** personal belongings **2.** equipment; apparatus; gear
**par·a·phrase** (par'ə frāz') *n.* [Fr. < L. < Gr. *paraphrasis*, ult. < *para-*, beyond + *phrazein*, to tell] a rewording of the meaning of something spoken or written —*vt., vi.* **-phrased', -phras'ing** to express in a paraphrase —**par'a·phras'er, par'a·phrast'** (-frast') *n.* —**par'a·phras'tic** *adj.*
**par·a·ple·gi·a** (par'ə plē'jē ə, -jə) *n.* [ModL. < Gr. *paraplēgia*, a stroke at one side: see PARA- & -PLEGIA] paralysis of the entire lower half of the body —**par'a·ple'gic** (-plē'jik, -plej'ik) *adj., n.*
**par·a·pro·fes·sion·al** (-prə fesh'ən 'l) *n.* a worker trained to perform certain functions, as in medicine, but not licensed to practice as a professional
**par·a·psy·chol·o·gy** (-sī käl'ə jē) *n.* [PARA- + PSYCHOLOGY] the study of such psychic phenomena as telepathy, ESP, etc.
**Pará rubber** crude rubber obtained from several tropical S. American trees
**par·a·site** (par'ə sīt') *n.* [< L. < Gr. *parasitos*, one who eats at the table of another < *para-*, beside + *sitos*, food] **1.** a person who lives at others' expense without making any useful return **2.** a plant or animal that lives on or within another from which it derives sustenance —**par'a·sit'ic** (-sit'ik), **par'a·sit'i·cal** *adj.* —**par'a·sit'i·cal·ly** *adv.* —**par'a·sit'ism** (-sīt'iz'm) *n.*
**par·a·sit·ize** (-si tīz', -sī-) *vt.* **-ized', -iz'ing 1.** to live on, in, or with as a parasite **2.** to infest with parasites
**par·a·si·tol·o·gy** (par'ə sī tä'lə jē, -sī-) *n.* the science dealing with parasites —**par'a·si·tol'o·gist** *n.*
**par·a·sol** (par'ə sôl', -säl') *n.* [Fr. < It. < *parare*, to ward off + *sole*, the sun] a light umbrella carried as a sunshade
**par·a·sym·pa·thet·ic** (par'ə sim'pə thet'ik) *adj.* [PARA- + SYMPATHETIC] designating or of that part of the autonomic nervous system whose functions include the slowing of the heartbeat and stimulation of certain digestive glands: cf. SYMPATHETIC
**par·a·thi·on** (par'ə thī'än) *n.* [< Gr. *para-*, alongside + *theion*, sulfur] a poisonous insecticide, $C_{10}H_{14}O_5NPS$
**par·a·thy·roid** (-thī'roid) *adj.* [PARA- + THYROID] designating or of any of four small glands on or near the thyroid gland: their hormonal secretions help control the body's calcium-phosphorus balance —*n.* a parathyroid gland
**par·a·troops** (par'ə trōops) *n.pl.* [< PARA(CHUTE) + TROOP] troops trained and equipped to parachute into a combat area —**par'a·troop'** *adj.* —**par'a·troop'er** *n.*
**par·a·ty·phoid** (par'ə tī'foid) *adj.* [PARA- + TYPHOID] designating, of, or causing a disease similar to typhoid fever but milder and caused by various bacteria
**‡par·a·vion** (pár á vyōn') [Fr.] by air mail
**par·boil** (pär'boil') *vt.* [< OFr. < *par* (< L. *per*), through + *boullir* (< L. *bullire*), to boil: meaning infl. by Eng. *part*] **1.** to boil until partly cooked, as before roasting **2.** to make uncomfortably hot
**par·buck·le** (pär'buk''l) *n.* [altered (after BUCKLE¹) < Early ModE. *parbunkel*] a sling for a log, barrel, etc. made by passing a doubled rope around the object and pulling the ends through the loop —*vt.* **-led, -ling** to raise or lower by using a parbuckle
**Par·cae** (pär'sē) *n.pl. Rom. Myth.* the three Fates
**par·cel** (pär's'l) *n.* [< MFr., ult. < L. *particula*: see PARTICLE] **1.** a small, wrapped bundle; package **2.** a quantity of items put up for sale **3.** a group; pack /a *parcel* of fools/ **4.** a piece, as of land —*vt.* **-celed** or **-celled, -cel·ing** or **-cel·ling 1.** to separate into parts and distribute (with *out*) **2.** to make up in or as a parcel
**parcel post** a postal service for carrying and delivering parcels (fourth-class mail)
**parch** (pärch) *vt.* [< ?] **1.** to expose (corn, etc.) to great heat, so as to dry or roast **2.** to make hot and dry **3.** to make very thirsty **4.** to dry up and shrivel with cold —*vi.* to become very hot, dry, thirsty, etc.
**Par·chee·si** (pär chē'zē) *a trademark for* a game like pachisi, in which dice are thrown —*n.* [**p-**] this game or the game of pachisi: also sp. **par·che'si, par·chi'si**
**parch·ment** (pärch'mənt) *n.* [< OFr., ult. < L. (*charta*) *Pergamena*, (paper) of Pergamum, city in Asia Minor] **1.** an animal skin, as of a sheep or goat, prepared as a surface for writing or painting **2.** paper treated to resemble this **3.** a manuscript, diploma, etc. on parchment
**pard** (pärd) *n.* [< OFr. < L. < Gr. *pardos*] [Archaic or Poet.] a leopard, or panther
**pard·ner** (pärd'nər) *n.* [altered < PARTNER] [Chiefly Dial.] a partner: often clipped to **pard**
**par·don** (pär'd'n) *vt.* [< OFr. < LL. < L. *per-*, through + *donare*, to give] **1.** to release (a person) from punishment **2.** to cancel penalty for (an offense); forgive **3.** to excuse (a person) for (a minor fault, discourtesy, etc.) —*n.* **1.** a pardoning or being pardoned; forgiveness **2.** an official document granting a pardon **3.** *R.C.Ch.* same as INDULGENCE —**par'don·a·ble** *adj.* —**par'don·a·bly** *adv.*
**par·don·er** (-ər) *n.* **1.** in the Middle Ages, a person authorized to sell ecclesiastical pardons, or indulgences **2.** a person who pardons
**pare** (per) *vt.* **pared, par'ing** [< MFr. < L. *parare*, to prepare] **1.** to cut or trim away (the rind, skin, covering, etc.) of (anything); peel **2.** to reduce gradually —**par'er** *n.*
**par·e·gor·ic** (par'ə gôr'ik, -gär'-) *n.* [< LL. < Gr. < *parēgoros*, speaking, consoling < *para-*, beside + *agora*, assembly] **1.** orig., a medicine that lessens pain **2.** a camphorated tincture of opium, used to relieve diarrhea
**pa·ren·chy·ma** (pə reŋ'ki mə) *n.* [ModL. < Gr., ult. < *para-*, beside + *en-*, in + *chein*, to pour] **1.** *Anat.* the functional tissue of an organ, as distinguished from its connective tissue, etc. **2.** *Bot.* a soft tissue of thin-walled cells in plant leaves and stems, fruit pulp, etc. —**pa·ren'chy·mal, par·en·chym·a·tous** (par'eŋ kim'ə təs) *adj.*

**par·ent** (per'ənt, par'-) *n.* [OFr. < L. *parens*, parent, orig. prp. of *parere*, to beget] **1.** a father or mother **2.** a progenitor or ancestor **3.** any organism in relation to its offspring **4.** a source; origin —**pa·ren·tal** (pə ren't'l) *adj.* —**pa·ren'tal·ly** *adv.* —**par'ent·hood'** *n.*

**par·ent·age** (-ij) *n.* **1.** descent from parents or ancestors; lineage **2.** the position or relation of a parent; parenthood

**pa·ren·the·sis** (pə ren'thə sis) *n., pl.* **-ses'** (-sēz') [LL. < Gr., ult. < *para-*, beside + *entithenai*, to insert] **1.** a word, clause, remark, etc. added as an explanation or comment within a complete sentence and usually marked off by curved lines, commas, etc. **2.** either or both of the curved lines ( ) so used **3.** an episode or interlude —**par·en·thet·i·cal** (par'ən thet'i k'l), **par'en·thet'ic** *adj.* —**par'en·thet'·i·cal·ly** *adv.*

**pa·ren·the·size** (-sīz') *vt.* **-sized'**, **-siz'ing 1.** to insert (a word, etc.) as a parenthesis **2.** to put into parentheses (sense 2)

**par·ent·ing** (per'ənt iŋ, par'-) *n.* the work or skill of a parent in raising a child or children

**pa·re·sis** (pə rē'sis, par'ə sis) *n., pl.* **-ses** (-sēz) [ModL. < Gr. < *parienai*, to relax] **1.** partial or slight paralysis **2.** a syphilitic brain disease marked by dementia, paralytic attacks, etc.: in full, **general paresis** —**pa·ret'ic** (-ret'ik, -rē'tik) *n., adj.*

**par ex·cel·lence** (pär ek'sə läns') [Fr.] in the greatest degree of excellence; beyond comparison

**par·fait** (pär fā') *n.* [Fr., lit., perfect] **1.** a frozen dessert of cream, eggs, syrup, etc. in a tall, slender, short-stemmed glass **2.** a dessert of layers of ice cream, crushed fruit, etc. in such a glass

**par·he·li·on** (pär hē'lē ən, -hēl'yən) *n., pl.* **-li·a** (-ə, -yə) [ < L. < Gr. < *para-*, beside + *hēlios*, the sun] a bright, colored spot of light on a solar halo —**par·he'lic** *adj.*

**pa·ri·ah** (pə rī'ə; *chiefly Brit.* par'ē ə) *n.* [ < Tamil *paṛaiyan*, a drummer: the pariah was a hereditary drumbeater] **1.** a member of a low caste in India **2.** any outcast

**pa·ri·e·tal** (pə rī'ə t'l) *adj.* [ < Fr. < LL. < L. *paries*, a wall] *Anat.* of the walls of a cavity, etc.; esp., designating either of two bones forming part of the top and sides of the skull

**par·i·mu·tu·el** (par'ə myōō'choo wəl) *n.* [Fr., lit., a mutual bet] **1.** a system of betting on races in which the winning bettors share the total amount bet, minus a percentage for the track operators, taxes, etc. **2.** a machine for recording such bets and computing payoffs

**par·ing** (per'iŋ) *n.* a thin piece or strip pared off

‡**pa·ri pas·su** (per'ē pas'ōō, par'ē) [L.] **1.** with equal speed **2.** in equal proportion

**Par·is¹** (par'is) *Gr. Legend* a son of Priam: he kidnapped Helen, thus causing the Trojan War

**Par·is²** (par'is; *Fr.* pà'rē') capital of France, on the Seine: pop. 2,591,000 (urbanized area, 8,197,000) —**Pa·ri·sian** (pə rizh'ən, -rē'zhən) *adj., n.*

**Paris green** a poisonous, bright-green chemical powder used chiefly as an insecticide

**par·ish** (par'ish) *n.* [ < OFr. < LL. < LGr. *paroikia*, diocese, ult. < Gr. *para-*, beside + *oikos*, dwelling] **1.** a district of British local government **2.** an administrative district of various churches, esp. a part of a diocese, under the charge of a priest or minister **3.** *a)* the members of a church congregation *b)* the territory they live in **4.** a civil division in Louisiana, corresponding to a county

**pa·rish·ion·er** (pə rish'ə nər) *n.* a member of a parish

**par·i·ty** (par'ə tē) *n., pl.* **-ties** [ < Fr. < L. < *par*, equal] **1.** a being the same in power, value, etc.; equality **2.** resemblance; similarity **3.** equivalence in value of a currency in terms of another country's currency **4.** equality of value at a given ratio between different kinds of money, commodities, etc. **5.** a controlled price for farm products, to keep the farmers' purchasing power at a specified level

**park** (pärk) *n.* [ < OFr. < ML. *parricus*] **1.** land with woods, lakes, etc., held as part of a private estate or as a hunting preserve **2.** an area of public land; specif., *a)* an area for parking motor vehicles **6.** *Mil.* an area for storing and servicing motor vehicles and other equipment —*vt.* **1.** to enclose as in a park **2.** to assemble (military equipment) in a park **3.** to leave (a vehicle) in a certain place temporarily **4.** to maneuver (a vehicle) into a space for parking **5.** [Colloq.] to put, leave, or deposit in a certain place —*vi.* to park a vehicle

**par·ka** (pär'kə) *n.* [Aleutian < Russ.] **1.** a hip-length pullover fur garment with a hood, worn in arctic regions **2.** a similar hooded jacket

**parking lot** an area for parking motor vehicles

**parking meter** a coin-operated timing device at a parking space to show the length of time that a parked vehicle may occupy that space

**Par·kin·son's disease** (pär'kin sənz) [after J. *Parkinson* (1755–1824), Eng. physician] a brain disease characterized by a tremor and muscular rigidity

**park·land** (pärk'land') *n.* wooded land set aside as, or suitable for, a public park

**Park·man** (pärk'mən), **Francis** 1823–93; U.S. historian

**park·way** (pärk'wā') *n.* **1.** a broad roadway edged or divided with plantings of trees, bushes, and grass **2.** the landscaped center strip or border

**Parl. 1.** Parliament **2.** Parliamentary

**parl·ance** (pär'ləns) *n.* [ < Anglo-Fr. < OFr. < *parler*, to speak] a style or manner of speaking or writing; language; idiom [military *parlance*]

**par·lan·do** (pär län'dō) *adj., adv.* [It.] *Music* to be sung in a style suggesting or approximating speech

**par·lay** (pär'lā, -lē; *for v., also* pär lā') *vt., vi.* [ < Fr. < It. < *paro*, an equal < L. *par*] **1.** to bet (an original wager plus its winnings) on another race, etc. **2.** to exploit (an asset) successfully [to *parlay* one's voice into fame] —*n.* a bet or series of bets made by parlaying

**par·ley** (pär'lē) *vi.* [ < Fr. *parler*, to speak < LL. < *parabola*, PARABLE] to confer, esp. with an enemy —*n., pl.* **-leys** a conference; specif., a military conference with an enemy to discuss terms

**par·lia·ment** (pär'lə mənt) *n.* [ < OFr. *parlement* < *parler:* see prec.] **1.** an official conference or council concerned with government **2.** [P-] the national legislative body of Great Britain, composed of the House of Commons and the House of Lords **3.** [P-] a similar body in other countries

**par·lia·men·tar·i·an** (pär'lə men ter'ē ən, -mən-) *n.* a person skilled in parliamentary rules or debate

**par·lia·men·ta·ry** (pär'lə men'tər ē, -trē) *adj.* **1.** of, like, or established by a parliament **2.** conforming to the rules of a parliament or other public assembly **3.** having or governed by a parliament; specif., of a government in which the prime minister holds office only so long as he commands a majority in the parliament

**par·lor** (pär'lər) *n.* [ < OFr. < *parler:* see PARLEY] **1.** *a)* orig., a room set aside for the entertainment of guests *b)* any living room: old-fashioned term **2.** a small, semiprivate room in a hotel, etc., used as for conferences **3.** a business establishment, esp. one with specialized services [a beauty *parlor*] *Brit. sp.* **parlour**

**par·lous** (pär'ləs) *adj.* [ME., contr. of *perilous*] [Chiefly Archaic] **1.** perilous **2.** cunning, shrewd, etc. —*adv.* [Chiefly Archaic] extremely

**Par·ma** (pär'mə; *for 1, also It.* pär'mä) **1.** city in N Italy: pop. 172,000 **2.** [ult. after prec.] city in NE Ohio: suburb of Cleveland: pop. 93,000

**Par·men·i·des** (pär men'ə dēz') 5th cent. B.C.; Gr. philosopher

**Par·me·san (cheese)** (pär'mə zän', -zən, -zan') [Fr. < It. < *Parma*, city in Italy] a very hard, dry Italian cheese made from skim milk and usually grated for sprinkling on spaghetti, soup, etc.

**Par·nas·sus** (pär nas'əs) mountain in C Greece: sacred to Apollo and the Muses in ancient times —*n.* **1.** poetry or poets collectively **2.** any center of poetic or artistic activity —**Par·nas'si·an** (-ē ən) *adj.*

**Par·nell** (pär'n'l, pär nel'), **Charles Stewart** 1846–91; Ir. nationalist leader

**pa·ro·chi·al** (pə rō'kē əl) *adj.* [OFr. < ML. < LL. *parochia:* see PARISH] **1.** of or in a parish or parishes **2.** narrow; provincial; limited —**pa·ro'chi·al·ism** *n.* —**pa·ro'chi·al·ist** *n.* —**pa·ro'chi·al·ly** *adv.*

**parochial school** a school supported and controlled by a church

**par·o·dy** (par'ə dē) *n., pl.* **-dies** [ < Fr. < L. < Gr. *parōidia* < *para-*, beside + *ōidē*, song] **1.** a literary or musical composition imitating the style of a writer or composer in a nonsensical way, as in ridicule **2.** a weak imitation —*vt.* **-died, -dy·ing** to make a parody of —**pa·rod·ic** (pə räd'ik), **pa·rod'i·cal** *adj.* —**par'o·dist** *n.* —**par'o·dis'tic** *adj.*

**pa·role** (pə rōl') *n.* [Fr. < LL. *parabola*, PARABLE] **1.** word of honor; esp., the promise of a prisoner of war not to fight further if released **2.** the condition of being on parole **3.** *a)* the release of a prisoner before his sentence has expired, on condition of future good behavior *b)* the freedom thus granted, or its duration —*vt.* **-roled', -rol'ing** to release on parole —**on parole** at liberty under conditions of parole

---

**pa·rol·ee** (pə rō′lē′) *n.* a person on parole from prison
**pa·rot·id** (pə rät′id) *adj.* [< ML. < L. < Gr. *parōtis* < *para-*, beside + *ous* (gen. *ōtos*, ear] designating or of either of the salivary glands below and in front of each ear —*n.* a parotid gland
**-par·ous** (pər əs) [< L. < *parere*, to bear] *a combining form meaning* bringing forth, producing, bearing *[viviparous]*
**par·ox·ysm** (par′ək siz′m) *n.* [< Fr. < ML. < Gr. < *para-*, beyond + *oxynein*, to sharpen < *oxys*, sharp] **1.** a sudden attack, or intensification of the symptoms, of a disease, usually recurring periodically **2.** a sudden outburst of laughter, rage, etc.; fit; spasm —**par′ox·ys′mal** (-siz′m′l) *adj.*
**par·quet** (pär kā′) *n.* [Fr. < MFr. dim. of *parc*, a park] **1.** the main floor of a theater, esp. from the orchestra pit to the parquet circle: usually called *orchestra* **2.** a flooring of parquetry —*vt.* **-queted′** (-kād′), **-quet′ing** (-kā′iŋ) **1.** to use parquetry to make (a floor, etc.) **2.** to decorate the floor of (a room) with parquetry
**parquet circle** the part of a theater beneath the balcony and behind the parquet
**par·quet·ry** (pär′kə trē) *n.* inlaid woodwork in geometric forms: used esp. in flooring
**parr** (pär) *n., pl.* **parrs, parr:** see PLURAL, II, D, 1 [< ?] a young salmon before it enters salt water
**par·ra·keet** (par′ə kēt′) *n. alt. sp.* of PARAKEET
**par·ri·cide** (par′ə sīd′) *n.* [Fr. < L. *parricida*, a relative + *-cida*, -CIDE] **1.** a person who murders his parent or another near relative **2.** the act of a parricide —**par′ri·ci′dal** *adj.*
**par·rot** (par′ət) *n.* [Fr. dial. *perrot*] **1.** any of several related tropical or subtropical birds with a hooked bill, brightly colored feathers, and feet having two toes pointing forward and two backward: some parrots can learn to imitate human speech **2.** a person who mechanically repeats the words or acts of others —*vt.* to repeat or imitate, esp. without understanding

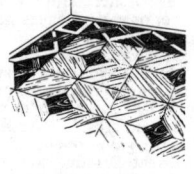

PARQUETRY

**parrot fever** *same as* PSITTACOSIS
**parrot fish** any of various related, brightly colored, tropical ocean fishes with parrotlike jaws
**par·ry** (par′ē) *vt.* **-ried, -ry·ing** [prob. < imper. of Fr. *parer* < It. *parare*, to ward off < L. *parare*, to prepare] **1.** to ward off or deflect (a blow, sword thrust, etc.) **2.** to turn aside (a question, etc.) as by a clever or evasive reply —*vi.* to make a parry —*n., pl.* **-ries 1.** a warding off of a blow, etc. **2.** an evasive reply
**parse** (pärs) *vt., vi.* **parsed, pars′ing** [< L. *pars* (*orationis*), part (of speech)] [Now Rare] **1.** to separate (a sentence) into its parts, explaining the grammatical form, function, etc. of each part **2.** to describe the form, part of speech, etc. of (a word in a sentence)
**Par·see, Par·si** (pär′sē, pär sē′) *n.* [Per. *Pārsī*, a Persian] a member of a Zoroastrian religious sect in India descended from Persian refugees from the Moslem persecutions of the 7th and 8th cent. —**Par′see·ism, Par′si·ism** *n.*
**Par·si·fal** (pär′si fäl′, -fəl) the title character in Wagner's opera (1882) about the knights of the Holy Grail
**par·si·mo·ny** (pär′sə mō′nē) *n.* [< L. *parcimonia* < *parcere*, to spare] a tendency to be very careful in spending; stinginess —**par′si·mo′ni·ous** *adj.* —**par′si·mo′ni·ous·ly** *adv.* —**par′si·mo′ni·ous·ness** *n.*
**pars·ley** (pärs′lē) *n.* [< OE. & OFr. < L. *petroselinum* < Gr. < *petros*, a rock + *selinon*, celery] a plant of the parsley family, with aromatic, often curled leaves used to flavor or garnish some foods —*adj.* designating a family of hollow-stemmed, herbaceous plants having umbels, including the parsnip, carrot, etc.
**pars·nip** (pärs′nip) *n.* [altered (after ME. *nepe*, turnip) < OFr. < L. *pastinaca* < *pastinare*, to dig up] **1.** a plant of the parsley family, with a long, thick, sweet, white root used as a vegetable **2.** its root
**par·son** (pär′s'n) *n.* [< OFr. < ML. *persona*, orig., person < L.: see PERSON] **1.** a clergyman in charge of a parish **2.** any clergyman
**par·son·age** (-ij) *n.* the dwelling provided by a church for the use of its parson
**part** (pärt) *n.* [OE. & OFr., both < L. *pars* (gen. *partis*)] **1.** a division or portion of a whole; specif., *a)* any of several equal quantities, numbers, pieces, etc. into which something can be divided *b)* an essential, separable element *[radio parts] c)* a certain amount but not all *d)* a segment or organ as of the body **2.** a share assigned or given; specif., *a)* duty *[to do one's part] b)* interest; concern *[to have some part in a matter] c)* [*usually pl.*] talent; ability *[a man of parts] d)* a role in a play *e)* Music any voice or instrument in an ensemble, or the score for

it **3.** a region; esp., [*usually pl.*] a portion of a country; district **4.** one of the sides in a transaction, dispute, etc. **5.** the dividing line made by combing the hair in different directions —*vt.* [< OFr. < L. *partire* < the *n.*] **1.** to break or divide into parts **2.** to comb (the hair) so as to leave a part **3.** to break up or separate; break or hold apart **4.** [Archaic] to apportion —*vi.* **1.** to break or divide into parts **2.** to separate and go different ways **3.** to cease associating **4.** *a)* to go away *b)* to die —*adj.* not total; partial —*adv.* not fully; partly —**for one's part** as far as one is concerned —**for the most part** mostly; generally —**in good part** good-naturedly —**in part** to some extent or degree; partly —**on the part of one 1.** as far as one is concerned **2.** by or coming from one Also **on one's part** —**part with** to give up; relinquish —**play a part 1.** to behave unnaturally in trying to deceive **2.** to participate: also **take part** —**take someone's part** to side with someone
**part. 1.** participial **2.** participle
**par·take** (pär tāk′) *vi.* **-took′, -tak′en, -tak′ing** [< *partaker*, contr. of *part taker*] **1.** to take part (*in* an activity); participate **2.** to take a portion; specif., to eat or drink, esp. with others (usually with *of*) **3.** to have or show a trace (*of*); have some of the qualities (*of*) —**par·tak′er** *n.*
**par·terre** (pär ter′) *n.* [Fr. < *par*, on + *terre*, earth] **1.** an ornamental garden area **2.** *same as* PARQUET CIRCLE
**par·the·no·gen·e·sis** (pär′thə nō jen′ə sis) *n.* [ModL. < Gr. *parthenos*, virgin + *genesis*, origin] reproduction by the development of an unfertilized ovum, seed, or spore, as in certain insects, algae, etc. —**par′the·no·ge·net′ic** (-jə net′ik) *adj.* —**par′the·no·ge·net′i·cal·ly** *adv.*
**Par·the·non** (pär′thə nän′, -nən) [L. < Gr. < *parthenos*, a virgin (i.e., Athena)] the Doric temple of Athena built (5th cent. B.C.) on the Acropolis
**Par·thi·a** (pär′thē ə) ancient country southeast of the Caspian Sea —**Par′thi·an** *adj., n.*
**Parthian shot** any hostile gesture or remark made in leaving: Parthian cavalrymen shot at the enemy while retreating or pretending to retreat
**par·tial** (pär′shəl) *adj.* [MFr. < ML. < L. *pars*, PART] **1.** favoring one person, faction, etc. more than another; biased **2.** not complete or total —**partial to** fond of —**par′tial·ly** *adv.*
**par·ti·al·i·ty** (pär′shē al′ə tē, pär shal′-) *n.* **1.** the state or quality of being partial; bias **2.** particular fondness or liking
**par·tic·i·pant** (pär tis′ə pənt, pər-) *adj.* participating —*n.* a person who participates
**par·tic·i·pate** (-pāt′) *vi.* **-pat′ed, -pat′ing** [< L. pp. of *participare* < *pars*, PART + *capere*, to take] to have or take a share with others (*in* an activity, etc.) —**par·tic′i·pa′tion, par·tic′i·pance** *n.* —**par·tic′i·pa′tive** *adj.* —**par·tic′i·pa′tor** *n.* —**par·tic′i·pa·to′ry** (-pə tōr′ē) *adj.*
**par·ti·cip·i·al** (pär′tə sip′ē əl) *adj.* of, based on, or having the nature and use of a participle —**par′ti·cip′i·al·ly** *adv.*
**par·ti·ci·ple** (pär′tə sip′'l) *n.* [OFr. < L. < *particeps*, partaking < *pars*, PART + *capere*, to take] a verbal form having the qualities of both verb and adjective Participles are used: *a)* in verb phrases (are *asking*) *b)* as verbs (*seeing* her, he stopped) *c)* as adjectives (the *beaten* path) *d)* as nouns (*seeing* is *believing*) *e)* as adverbs (*raving* mad) *f)* as connectives (*saving* those present)
**par·ti·cle** (pär′ti k'l) *n.* [< MFr. < L. *particula*, dim. of *pars*, PART] **1.** *a)* a tiny fragment *b)* the slightest trace; speck **2.** *Gram. a)* a short, usually uninflected part of speech used to show syntactical relationships, as an article, preposition, conjunction, or interjection *b)* an uninflected stem **3.** *Physics* a piece of matter so small as to be considered without magnitude
**par·ti-col·ored** (pär′tē kul′ərd) *adj.* [< Fr. pp. of *partir:* see PARTY] **1.** having different colors in different parts **2.** diversified
**par·tic·u·lar** (pər tik′yə lər, pär-) *adj.* [< MFr. < LL. < L. *particula*, PARTICLE] **1.** of or belonging to a single, definite person, group, or thing **2.** regarded separately; specific **3.** unusual; special **4.** itemized; detailed **5.** hard to please; exacting —*n.* **1.** a distinct fact, item, or instance **2.** a detail; item —**in particular** particularly; especially
**par·tic·u·lar·i·ty** (pər tik′yə lar′ə tē, pär-) *n., pl.* **-ties 1.** the state, quality, or fact of being particular; specif., *a)* individuality *b)* attention to detail **2.** something particular; specif., *a)* a peculiarity *b)* a minute detail
**par·tic·u·lar·ize** (-tik′yə lə rīz′) *vt.* **-ized′, -iz′ing** to specify; itemize —*vi.* to give particulars or details —**par·tic′u·lar·i·za′tion** *n.*
**par·tic·u·lar·ly** (-tik′yə lər lē) *adv.* **1.** in detail **2.** especially; unusually **3.** specifically
**par·tic·u·late** (pär tik′yə lit, -lāt′) *adj.* [< L. *particula*, particle + -ATE¹] of or pertaining to tiny, separate particles —*n.* a tiny particle
**part·ing** (pärt′iŋ) *adj.* **1.** dividing; separating **2.** departing **3.** given, spoken, done, etc. at parting —*n.* **1.** a

breaking or separating **2.** a dividing point or line **3.** something that separates or divides **4.** a leave-taking or departure **5.** death

**par·ti·san** (pärt′ə z'n, -s'n) *n.* [MFr. < It. *partigiano* < L. *pars,* PART] **1.** a strong supporter of a side, party, or person; often, specif., an unreasoning, emotional adherent **2.** any of a group of guerrilla fighters, esp. in a civilian force —*adj.* of or like a partisan Also sp. **par′ti·zan** —**par′ti·san·ship′** *n.*

**par·ti·ta** (pär tēt′ə) *n.* [It. < fem. pp. of *partire,* to divide < L. *pars,* part] *Music* **1.** a kind of suite, esp. of the 18th cent. **2.** an air with variations

**par·tite** (pär′tīt) *adj.* [ < L. pp. of *partire,* to part] in parts: often in compounds *[tripartite]*

**par·ti·tion** (pär tish′ən, pər-) *n.* [ < L. *partitio*] **1.** division into parts **2.** something that divides, as a wall separating rooms **3.** a part or section —*vt.* **1.** to divide into parts **2.** to divide by a partition —**par·ti′tion·er** *n.*

**par·ti·tive** (pärt′ə tiv) *adj.* [ < ML.: see PARTITE & -IVE] **1.** making a division **2.** *Gram.* restricting to or involving only a part of a whole —*n.* a partitive word or form —**par′ti·tive·ly** *adv.*

**part·ly** (pärt′lē) *adv.* in part; not fully

**part·ner** (pärt′nər) *n.* [altered (after *part*) < *parcener,* joint inheritor] one who takes part in an activity with another or others; specif., *a)* one of two or more persons heading the same business enterprise *b)* a husband or wife *c)* either of two persons dancing together *d)* either of two players on the same side or team playing against two others —*vt.* **1.** to join (others) together as partners **2.** to be or provide a partner for

**part·ner·ship** (-ship′) *n.* **1.** the state of being a partner **2.** the relationship of partners; joint interest **3.** *a)* an association of partners in a business enterprise *b)* the contract for this

**part of speech** any of the classes of words of a given language, variously based on form, function, meaning, etc.: in traditional English grammar, the parts of speech are noun, verb, adjective, adverb, pronoun, preposition, conjunction, and interjection

**par·took** (pär took′) *pt. of* PARTAKE

**par·tridge** (pär′trij) *n., pl.* **-tridg·es, -tridge:** see PLURAL, II, D, 1 [ < OFr. < L. < Gr. *perdix*] **1.** a quaillike game bird, orig. of Europe and now also of N. America, with an orange-brown head, grayish neck, and rust-colored tail **2.** any of various game birds like the partridge, as the pheasant

**part song** a song for several voices singing in harmony, usually unaccompanied: also **part′-song′** *n.*

**part-time** (pärt′tīm′) *adj.* designating, of, or engaged in work, study, etc. for periods regarded as taking less time than a full schedule

**part time** as a part-time employee, student, etc. *[to work part time]*

PARTRIDGE
(to 14 in. long;
wingspread to
13 in.)

**par·tu·ri·ent** (pär tyoor′ē ənt, -toor′-) *adj.* [ < L. prp. of *parturire,* to be in labor < *parere,* to produce] **1.** giving birth or about to give birth to young **2.** of childbirth —**par·tu′ri·en·cy** *n.*

**par·tu·ri·tion** (pär′choo rish′ən, -tyoo-, -too-) *n.* [ < L.: see prec.] a giving birth; childbirth

**part·way** (pärt′wā′) *adv.* to some point, degree, etc.

**par·ty** (pär′tē) *n., pl.* **-ties** [ < OFr. < *partir,* to divide < L. < *pars,* PART] **1.** a group working to establish or promote certain principles of government; esp., a political group which tries to elect its candidates to office **2.** any group acting together to accomplish or do something *[a surveying party]* **3.** a gathering for social entertainment, or the entertainment itself *[a cocktail party]* **4.** a participant in an action, plan, etc. (often with *to*) *[he is a party to the plan]* **5.** either of the persons or sides concerned in a legal matter **6.** [Colloq.] a person —*adj.* **1.** of a political party **2.** for a social gathering *[party clothes]* —*vi.* **-tied, -ty·ing** to attend or hold social parties —*vt.* to be host to at a party

**party line 1.** a single circuit connecting two or more telephone users with the exchange **2.** the line of policy followed by a political party —**par′ty-lin′er** *n.*

**par value** the value of a stock, bond, etc. fixed at the time of its issue; face value

**par·ve·nu** (pär′və nōō′, -nyōō′) *n.* [Fr., pp. of *parvenir* < L. *parvenire,* to arrive] a person who has suddenly acquired wealth or power and is considered an upstart —*adj.* like or characteristic of a parvenu

**pas** (pä) *n., pl.* **pas** (päz; Fr. pä) [Fr. < L. *passus,* a step] a step or series of steps in dancing; in ballet, a **pas de deux**

(pä′də dōō′) is a dance for two, a **pas de trois** (pät trwä′) is for three, a **pas de qua·tre** (pät kä′t'r′) is for four

**Pas·a·de·na** (pas′ə dē′nə) **1.** [ < Ojibwa, lit., valley town] city in SW Calif., near Los Angeles: pop. 119,000 **2.** [after prec.] city in SE Tex., near Houston: pop. 113,000

**Pas·cal** (pás kál′; *E.* pas kal′), **Blaise** (blez) 1623–62; Fr. mathematician, physicist, & philosopher

**Pas·cal celery** (pas′k'l) [ < ?] a large, dark-green variety of celery with firm stalks

**Pasch** (pask) *n.* [ < OFr. < LL. < Gr. *pascha* < Heb. *pesah,* the Passover] *same as:* **1.** PASSOVER **2.** EASTER —**pas′chal** (pas′k'l) *adj.*

**pasch flower** (pask) *same as* PASQUEFLOWER

**pa·sha** (pə shä′, pä′shə, pash′ə) *n.* [Turk. *pasha*] formerly, in Turkey, **1.** a title of honor placed after the name **2.** a high official

**Pash·to** (push′tō, päsh′-) *n.* an Iranian language of Afghanistan and West Pakistan

**pasque·flow·er** (pask′flou′ər) *n.* [ < MFr. < *passer,* PASS² + *fleur,* a flower, altered after Fr. *pasque,* PASCH] any of several plants of the buttercup family; esp., a N. American wildflower with hairy leaves and cup-shaped, bluish flowers

**pass¹** (pas) *n.* [see PACE] a narrow passage or opening, esp. between mountains; gap; defile

**pass²** (pas) *vi.* [ < OFr. *passer,* ult. < L. *passus,* a step] **1.** to go forward, through, or out **2.** to extend; lead *[a road passing around the hill]* **3.** to be handed on from person to person **4.** to go or be conveyed from one place, condition, possession, etc. to another **5.** to be exchanged between persons, as greetings **6.** *a)* to cease *[the fever passed]* *b)* to go away; depart **7.** to die (usually with *away, on*) **8.** to go by or past **9.** to slip by or elapse *[an hour passed]* **10.** to make a way (with *through* or *by*) **11.** to take place or be accepted without question **12.** to be sanctioned or approved, as by a legislative body **13.** *a)* to go through a test, course, etc. successfully; satisfy requirements *b)* to be barely acceptable as a substitute **14.** to take place; happen **15.** to give a judgment, sentence, etc.; decide (*on* or *upon*) **16.** to be rendered or pronounced *[the judgment passed against us]* **17.** *Card Games* to decline a chance to bid, play, etc. **18.** *Sports* to make a pass of the ball, etc. —*vt.* **1.** to go by, beyond, past, over, or through; specif., *a)* to leave behind *b)* to undergo (usually with *through*) *c)* to go by without noticing *d)* to omit paying (a regular dividend) *e)* to go through (a test, course, etc.) successfully *f)* to surpass; excel **2.** to cause or allow to go or move; specif., *a)* to send; dispatch *b)* to guide into position *[to pass a rope around a stake]* *c)* to cause to go through *d)* to make move past *e)* to cause or allow to get by an obstacle, etc. *f)* to ratify, enact, or approve *g)* to cause or allow to go through a test, course, etc. successfully *h)* to spend (time) *i)* to excrete; void *j)* *Baseball* to walk (a batter) **3.** to make move from place to place or person to person; specif., *a)* to hand to another *b)* to put into circulation *[to pass a bad check]* *c)* to throw or hit (a ball, etc.) from one player to another **4.** *a)* to give (an opinion or judgment) *b)* to utter (a remark) —*n.* **1.** an act of passing; passage **2.** *a)* the successful completion of a course or test in school, esp. without honors *b)* a mark indicating this **3.** condition or situation *[a strange pass]* **4.** *a)* a ticket, etc. giving one free entry or exit *b)* a ticket that permits unlimited rides on a bus, etc. for a specified period *c)* *Mil.* a written leave of absence for a brief period **5.** a motion of the hands meant to deceive, as in card tricks **6.** a motion of the hand, as in hypnotism **7.** *a)* a motion of the hand as if to strike *b)* a tentative attempt **8.** [Slang] an attempt to embrace or kiss, often an overly familiar one **9.** *Aeron.* a flight over a specified point or at a target **10.** *Card Games* a declining of a chance to bid, play, etc. **11.** *Sports a)* an intentional transfer of the ball, etc. to another player during play *b)* a lunge or thrust in fencing *c)* a walk in baseball —**bring to pass** to make happen —**come to pass** to happen —**pass for** to be accepted or looked upon as *[it is a sham but passes for the real thing]* —**pass off 1.** to cease **2.** to take place, as a transaction **3.** to be or cause to be accepted as genuine, etc., esp. through deceit —**pass out 1.** to distribute **2.** to faint —**pass over 1.** to disregard; ignore; omit **2.** to not consider (someone) for a promotion, etc. —**pass up** [Colloq.] to reject, refuse, or let go by, as an opportunity —**pass′er** *n.*

**pass. 1.** passenger **2.** passim **3.** passive

**pass·a·ble** (pas′ə b'l) *adj.* **1.** that can be passed, traveled over, or crossed **2.** that can be circulated, as coin **3.** barely satisfactory; fair **4.** that can be enacted, as a proposed law —**pass′a·ble·ness** *n.* —**pass′a·bly** *adv.*

**pas·sage** (pas′ij) *n.* [OFr. < *passer:* see PASS² & -AGE] **1.** the act of passing; specif., *a)* migration *b)* transition *c)* the enactment of a law by a legislature **2.** permission, right, or a chance to pass **3.** a journey, esp. by water; voyage **4.** *a)* passenger accommodations, esp. on a ship *b)* the charge for this **5.** a way or means of passing; specif., *a)* a road or path *b)* a channel, duct, etc. *c)* a passageway **6.** an interchange, as of blows or words **7.** a short section of something written or spoken or of a musical composition

**pas·sage·way** (-wā′) *n.* a narrow way for passage, as a hall, corridor, or alley

**Pas·sa·ic** (pə sā′ik) [after *Passaic* River (on which the city is located) < Delaware *passajeck*, valley] city in NE N.J.: pop. 52,000

**pass·book** (pas′book′) *n. same as* BANKBOOK

**pas·sé** (pa sā′, pas′ā) *adj.* [Fr., lit., past] **1.** out-of-date; old-fashioned **2.** rather old

**passed ball** *Baseball* a pitch that the catcher should have caught but that gets by him, allowing a base runner to advance

**pas·sen·ger** (pas′'n jər) *n.* [< MFr. < OFr. *passage*, PASSAGE] a person traveling in a vehicle, esp. when not operating it

**passenger pigeon** a N. American pigeon formerly abundant but now extinct

**pass·er·by** (pas′ər bī′) *n., pl.* **pass′ers·by′** a person who passes by

**pas·ser·ine** (pas′ər in, -ə rīn′) *adj.* [< L. < *passer*, a sparrow] of the order of perching songbirds to which most birds belong —*n.* a bird of this order

‡**pas·sim** (pas′im) *adv.* [L.] here and there; in various parts (of a book, etc.)

**pass·ing** (pas′iŋ) *adj.* **1.** going by, beyond, past, over, or through **2.** only brief; momentary **3.** casual; incidental *[a passing remark]* **4.** satisfying requirements *[a passing grade]* —*adv.* [Chiefly Archaic] very —*n.* **1.** the act of one that passes; specif., death **2.** a means or place of passing —**in passing 1.** casually **2.** incidentally

**passing shot** *Tennis* a sharp shot sent past an opposing player who is at the net or moving toward it

**pas·sion** (pash′ən) *n.* [OFr. < LL. < L. pp. of *pati*, to suffer] **1.** orig., suffering, as of a martyr **2.** [P-] the suffering of Jesus during the Crucifixion or after the Last Supper **3.** *a)* any emotion, as hate, grief, love, etc. *b)* [*pl.*] all of these emotions **4.** extreme emotion; specif., *a)* rage; fury *b)* enthusiasm *[a passion for music] c)* strong love or affection *d)* sexual desire; lust **5.** the object of strong desire or fondness —**pas′sion·al** *adj.* —**pas′sion·less** *adj.*

**pas·sion·ate** (-it) *adj.* **1.** having or showing strong emotions **2.** hot-tempered **3.** intense; ardent **4.** readily aroused sexually —**pas′sion·ate·ly** *adv.*

**pas·sion·flow·er** (-flou′ər) *n.* [from the supposed resemblance of parts of the flowers to Jesus' wounds, crown of thorns, etc.] any of a number of tropical plants with variously colored flowers and yellow or purple, egglike fruit **(passion fruit)**

**Passion play** a religious play representing the Passion of Jesus

**pas·sive** (pas′iv) *adj.* [< L. *passivus* < pp. of *pati*, to suffer] **1.** acted upon without acting in return **2.** not resisting; submissive **3.** taking no active part; inactive **4.** *Gram.* denoting the voice or form of a verb whose subject is the receiver (object) of the action of the verb —*n. Gram.* the passive voice —**pas′sive·ly** *adv.* —**pas′sive·ness, pas·siv·i·ty** (pa siv′ə tē) *n.*

**passive resistance** opposition, as to a government, by refusal to comply with orders, or by such nonviolent acts as fasting, public demonstrations, etc.

**pass·key** (pas′kē′) *n.* **1.** *same as: a)* MASTER KEY *b)* SKELETON KEY **2.** any private key

**Pass·o·ver** (pas′ō′vər) *n.* [PASS² & OVER] a Jewish holiday (*Pesach*) of eight (or seven) days beginning on the 14th of Nisan and commemorating the ancient Hebrews' deliverance from slavery in Egypt: Ex. 12

**pass·port** (-pôrt′) *n.* [< Fr. < *passer*, PASS² & *port*, PORT¹] **1.** a government document issued to a citizen for travel abroad, subject to visa requirements, certifying his identity and citizenship and entitling him to protection **2.** anything making a person accepted or admitted

**pass-through** (-throo′) *n.* an opening in a wall, as for passing food, etc. from a kitchen to another room

**pass·word** (-wurd′) *n.* **1.** a secret word or phrase that must be uttered by someone wishing to pass a guard **2.** any means of gaining entrance, etc.

**past** (past) *rare pp. of* PASS² —*adj.* **1.** gone by; ended **2.** of a former time **3.** just gone by *[the past week]* **4.** having served formerly *[a past chairman]* **5.** *Gram.* indicating a time or condition gone by or an action completed or in progress at a former time —*n.* **1.** time gone by **2.** the history or former life of a person, group, etc.: often used to indicate a hidden or questionable past *[a woman with a past]* **3.** *Gram. a)* the past tense *b)* a verb form in this tense —*prep.* **1.** later than **2.** farther on than **3.** beyond in amount or degree **4.** beyond the extent, power, etc. of *[past*

belief*]* —*adv.* to and beyond a point in time or space —**not put it past someone** to believe someone is not unlikely (to do a certain thing) *[I would not put it past him to lie]*

**pas·ta** (päs′tə) *n.* [It. < LL.: see ff.] **1.** dough made as of semolina and shaped and dried in the form of spaghetti, macaroni, etc. **2.** spaghetti, macaroni, etc. cooked in some way

**paste** (pāst) *n.* [OFr. < LL. *pasta* < Gr. *pastē*, barley porridge] **1.** *a)* dough for making rich pastry *b) same as* PASTA **2.** any soft, moist, smooth-textured substance *[toothpaste]* **3.** a foodstuff, pounded or ground until creamy *[almond paste]* **4.** a mixture of flour or starch, water, resin, etc., used as an adhesive for paper, etc. **5.** the moistened clay used to make pottery or porcelain **6.** *a)* a hard, brilliant glass for making artificial gems *b)* such a gem or gems **7.** [Slang] a blow or punch —*vt.* **past′ed, past′ing 1.** to make adhere, as with paste **2.** to cover with pasted material **3.** [Slang] to punch —**past′er** *n.*

**paste·board** (-bôrd′) *n.* a stiff material made of layers of paper pasted together or of pressed and dried paper pulp —*adj.* **1.** of pasteboard **2.** flimsy

**pas·tel** (pas tel′) *n.* [Fr. < It. *pastello* < LL. *pasta*, PASTE] **1.** *a)* ground coloring matter formed into a crayon *b)* the crayon **2.** a picture drawn with such crayons **3.** drawing with pastels as an art form **4.** a soft, pale shade of any color —*adj.* **1.** soft and pale: said of colors **2.** of pastel **3.** drawn with pastels —**pas·tel′ist, pas·tel′list** *n.*

**pas·tern** (pas′tərn) *n.* [< MFr. < *pasture*, a tether, ult. < L. *pastor*: see PASTOR] the part of a horse's foot between the fetlock and the hoof

**Pas·teur** (pas tur′; *Fr.* pås tër′), **Louis** 1822–95; Fr. chemist & bacteriologist

**pas·teur·i·za·tion** (pas′chər i zā′shən, pas′tər-) *n.* a method of destroying and checking bacteria in milk, beer, etc. by heating the liquid to a specified temperature for a specified period of time

**pas·teur·ize** (pas′chə rīz′, pas′tə-) *vt.* **-ized′, -iz′ing** [after L. PASTEUR] to subject (milk, beer, etc.) to pasteurization —**pas′teur·iz′er** *n.*

PASTERN

**pas·tiche** (pas tēsh′) *n.* [Fr. < It. *pasticcio*] **1.** *a)* a literary, artistic, or musical composition made up of bits from various sources; potpourri *b)* such a composition intended to imitate or ridicule another artist's style **2.** a jumbled mixture; hodgepodge

**pas·tie** (pas′tē) *n. same as* PASTY²

**pas·tille** (pas tēl′) *n.* [Fr. < L. *pastillus*, lozenge < *pascere*, to feed] **1.** a small tablet or lozenge containing medicine, flavoring, etc. **2.** a pellet of aromatic paste, burned for fumigating or deodorizing Also **pas·til** (pas′til) *n.*

**pas·time** (pas′tīm′) *n.* [transl. of Fr. *passe-temps*] a way of spending spare time pleasantly

**past master 1.** a former master, as in a lodge **2.** an expert —**past mistress** *fem.*

**pas·tor** (pas′tər) *n.* [< OFr. < L., a shepherd < *pascere*, to feed] a clergyman in charge of a church or congregation —**pas′tor·ship′** *n.*

**pas·to·ral** (-tər əl) *adj.* [< L. < *pastor*, a shepherd] **1.** of shepherds or their work, etc. **2.** of or characteristic of rural life idealized as peaceful, simple, and natural **3.** of a pastor or his duties —*n.* **1.** a poem, play, etc. having an idealized pastoral setting with shepherds, etc. **2.** a pastoral picture or scene **3.** a letter from a pastor or bishop to those in his charge **4.** *same as* PASTORALE —**pas′to·ral·ly** *adv.*

**pas·to·rale** (pas′tə ral′, -rä′lē) *n.* [It., lit., pastoral] *Music* a composition suggesting rural scenes or life

**pas·tor·ate** (pas′tər it) *n.* **1.** the position, rank, or term of office of a pastor **2.** a group of pastors

**past participle** a participle used: *a)* with auxiliaries and typically expressing completed action or a time or state gone by (as *started* in "he has started") *b)* as an adjective (as *grown* in "a grown man")

**past perfect 1.** a tense indicating an action or state as completed before a specified or implied time in the past **2.** a verb form in this tense (Ex.: had gone)

**pas·tra·mi** (pə strä′mē) *n.* [Yid. < Romanian < *pastra*, to preserve] highly spiced, smoked beef

**pas·try** (pās′trē) *n., pl.* **-tries** [see PASTE & -ERY] **1.** *a)* flour dough made with shortening, for pie crust, tarts, etc. *b)* foods made with this **2.** all fancy baked goods **3.** a single pie, cake, etc.

**pas·tur·age** (pas′chər ij) *n. same as* PASTURE

**pas·ture** (pas′chər) *n.* [OFr. < LL. *pastura* < L. *pascere*, to feed] **1.** grass or other growing plants used as food by grazing animals **2.** ground suitable, or a field set aside, for grazing —*vt.* **-tured, -tur·ing 1.** to put (cattle, etc.) out to graze in a pasture **2.** to graze on (grass, etc.) **3.** to provide with pasture: said of land —*vi.* to graze —**put out to pasture 1.** to pasture (cattle) **2.** to cause to retire from work —**pas′tur·a·ble** *adj.* —**pas′tur·er** *n.*

**past·y**¹ (pās′tē) *adj.* **past′i·er, past′i·est** of or like paste in color or texture —**past′i·ness** *n.*

**pas·ty**² (pas′tē, päs′-, päs′-) *n., pl.* **pas′ties** [< OFr. < *paste,* PASTE] [Chiefly Brit.] a meat pie

**pat**¹ (pat) *adj.* [prob. < ff.] **1.** apt; timely; opportune **2.** exactly suitable *[a pat* hand in poker] **3.** so glibly plausible as to seem contrived —*adv.* in a pat manner —**have (down) pat** [Colloq.] to know or have memorized thoroughly —**stand pat** to stick to an opinion, course of action, etc. —**pat′ly** *adv.* —**pat′ness** *n.*

**pat**² (pat) *n.* [prob. echoic] **1.** a gentle tap or stroke with the hand or other flat surface **2.** the sound made by this **3.** a small lump, as of butter —*vt.* **pat′ted, pat′ting 1.** *a)* to tap or stroke gently, esp. with the hand, as in affection, sympathy, etc. *b)* to tap lightly with a flat surface **2.** to shape, apply, etc. by patting —*vi.* **1.** to pat a surface **2.** to move with a patting sound

**pat. 1.** patent **2.** patented

**Pat·a·go·ni·a** (pat′ə gō′nē ə, -gōn′yə) dry, grassy region in the S parts of Argentina & Chile, east of the Andes —**Pat′a·go′ni·an** *adj., n.*

**patch** (pach) *n.* [prob. < OFr. *pieche,* PIECE] **1.** a piece of material to cover or mend a hole or tear or to strengthen a weak spot **2.** a dressing for a wound **3.** a shield worn over an injured eye **4.** a differing part of a surface area *[patches* of blue sky] **5.** a small plot of ground *[a* potato *patch]* **6.** *a)* a scrap of material; remnant *b) same as* BEAUTY SPOT (sense 1) **7.** *Mil.* a cloth insignia of unit identification worn high on the sleeve —*vt.* **1.** to put a patch on **2.** to be a patch for **3.** to make (a quilt, etc.) out of patches **4.** to make or put together crudely or hurriedly (often with *up* or *together*) —**patch up** to end or settle (differences, a quarrel, etc.) —**patch′er** *n.*

**patch·ou·li, patch·ou·ly** (pach′oo lē, pə choo′lē) *n.* [Fr., altered < E. *patch leaf* < Tamil < *paccu,* green + *ilai,* leaf] **1.** an East Indian plant that yields a heavy, darkbrown, fragrant oil **2.** a perfume made from this oil

**patch pocket** a pocket made by sewing a patch of shaped material to the outside of a garment

**patch test** a test for determining allergy to a specific substance, made by attaching a sample of it to the skin and observing the reaction

**patch·work** (pach′wurk′) *n.* **1.** anything made of odd, miscellaneous parts; jumble **2.** needlework, as a quilt, made of odd patches of cloth sewn together at the edges **3.** any design or surface like this

**patch·y** (pach′ē) *adj.* **patch′i·er, patch′i·est 1.** of or like patches **2.** not consistent or uniform; irregular —**patch′i·ly** *adv.* —**patch′i·ness** *n.*

**pate** (pāt) *n.* [< ?] **1.** the head, esp. the top of the head **2.** the brain or intellect A humorous term

**pâ·té** (pä tā′) *n.* [Fr.] **1.** a pie **2.** a meat paste

**pâ·té de foie gras** (pä tā′ də fwä′ grä′, pät′ā) [Fr.] a paste made of the livers of fattened geese

**pa·tel·la** (pə tel′ə) *n., pl.* **-las, -lae** (-ē) [L., dim. of *patina,* a pan < Gr. *patanē] same as* KNEECAP —**pa·tel′lar** *adj.*

**pat·en** (pat′'n) *n.* [< OFr. < L. *patina:* see prec.] a metal plate, esp. for the Eucharistic bread

**pa·ten·cy** (pāt′'n sē, pat′-) *n.* the state or quality of being patent, or obvious

**pat·ent** (pat′'nt; *Brit.,* & *for adj.* 2, 3, & 4, *usually* pāt′-) *adj.* [MFr. < L. prp. of *patere,* to be open] **1.** *a)* open to public inspection: said of a document granting a right, esp. to an invention *[letters patent] b)* granted or appointed by letters patent **2.** generally accessible or available **3.** obvious; evident *[a patent* lie] **4.** open or unobstructed **5.** *a)* protected by a patent *b)* of or having to do with patents *c)* made or sold under a patent —*n.* **1.** an official document granting a right or privilege; letters patent; esp., a document granting the exclusive right to produce, sell, or get a profit from an invention, process, etc. for a specific period **2.** *a)* the right so granted *b)* the thing so protected **3.** any exclusive right or license —*vt.* **1.** to grant a patent to or for **2.** to get a patent for —**pat′ent·a·ble** *adj.* —**pat·ent·ee** (pat′'n tē′) *n.* —**pat·en·tor** (pat′'n tər) *n.*

**patent leather** leather with a hard, glossy, usually black finish: formerly patented

**pa·tent·ly** (pāt′'nt lē, pat′-) *adv.* in a patent manner; clearly; obviously; openly

**patent medicine** a trademarked medical preparation obtainable without a prescription

**pa·ter** (pāt′ər) *n.* [L.] [Chiefly Brit. Colloq.] father

**Pa·ter** (pāt′ər), **Walter (Horatio)** 1839–94; Eng. essayist & critic

**pa·ter·fa·mil·i·as** (pāt′ər fə mil′ē əs, pät′-) *n.* [L.] the father of a family

**pa·ter·nal** (pə tur′n'l) *adj.* [< ML. < L. < *pater,* father] **1.** of or like a father; fatherly **2.** derived or inherited from

a father **3.** related through the father's side of the family *[paternal* grandparents] —**pa·ter′nal·ly** *adv.*

**pa·ter·nal·ism** (-iz′m) *n.* the system of controlling a country, employees, etc. as a father might his children —**pa·ter′nal·ist** *n., adj.* —**pa·ter′nal·is′tic** *adj.* —**pa·ter′nal·is′ti·cal·ly** *adv.*

**pa·ter·ni·ty** (pə tur′nə tē) *n.* **1.** the state of being a father **2.** male parentage **3.** origin in general

**pa·ter·nos·ter** (pät′ər nôs′tər; pat′ər näs′tər, pāt′-) *n.* [L., our father] **1.** the Lord's Prayer, esp. in Latin: often **Pater Noster 2.** each large bead on a rosary on which this is said

**Pat·er·son** (pat′ər s'n) [after W. *Paterson* (1745–1806), State governor] city in NE N.J.: pop. 138,000

**path** (path) *n.* [OE. *pæth]* **1.** a way worn by footsteps **2.** a walk for use by people on foot, as in a park **3.** a course along which something moves **4.** a course of conduct or procedure —**path′less** *adj.*

**pa·thet·ic** (pə thet′ik) *adj.* [< LL. < Gr. *pathētikos,* akin to *pathos,* suffering] **1.** expressing or arousing pity, sympathy, etc.; pitiful **2.** pitifully unsuccessful, ineffective, etc. **3.** of the emotions: now only in PATHETIC FALLACY Also **pa·thet′i·cal** —**pa·thet′i·cal·ly** *adv.*

**pathetic fallacy** the ascribing of human feelings, etc. to nonhuman things (Ex.: the angry sea)

**path·find·er** (path′fīn′dər) *n.* one who makes a way where none had existed, as in a wilderness

**-path·i·a** (path′ē ə) [ModL.] *same as* -PATHY

**-path·ic** (path′ik) *a combining form used to form adjectives from nouns ending in* -PATHY

**path·o-** [< Gr. *pathos,* suffering] *a combining form meaning* suffering, disease, feeling: also, before a vowel, **path-**

**path·o·gen** (path′ə jən) *n.* [prec. + -GEN] any microorganism or virus that can cause disease —**path′o·gen′ic** (-jen′ik) *adj.* —**path′o·gen′i·cal·ly** *adv.*

**path·o·gen·e·sis** (path′ə jen′ə sis) *n.* [ModL.: see PATHO- & GENESIS] the development of a disease: also **pa·thog·e·ny** (pə thäj′ə nē) —**path′o·ge·net′ic** (-jə net′ik) *adj.*

**pa·thol·o·gy** (pə thäl′ə jē, pa-) *n., pl.* **-gies** [< Fr. or ModL. < Gr.: see ff. & -LOGY] **1.** the branch of medicine dealing with the nature of disease, esp. with the structural and functional changes caused by disease **2.** all the conditions, processes, or results of a particular disease —**path·o·log·i·cal** (path′ə läj′i k'l), **path′o·log′ic** *adj.* —**path′o·log′i·cal·ly** *adv.* —**pa·thol′o·gist** *n.*

**pa·thos** (pā′thäs, -thôs) *n.* [Gr., suffering] **1.** the quality in something experienced or observed which arouses feelings of pity, sorrow, sympathy, or compassion **2.** the feeling aroused

**path·way** (path′wā′) *n. same as* PATH

**-pa·thy** (pə thē) [< ModL. < Gr. < *pathos,* suffering] *a combining form meaning:* **1.** feeling, suffering *[antipathy]* **2.** disease, treatment of disease *[osteopathy]*

**pa·tience** (pā′shəns) *n.* [< OFr. < L. *patientia* < *pati,* to suffer] **1.** the state, quality, or fact of being patient **2.** [Chiefly Brit.] any game of solitaire

**pa·tient** (pā′shənt) *adj.* [< OFr. < L. prp. of *pati,* to suffer] **1.** enduring pain, trouble, etc. with composure and without complaint **2.** calmly tolerating insult, delay, confusion, etc. **3.** showing calm endurance *[a patient* face] **4.** diligent; persevering *[a patient* worker] —*n.* a person receiving medical care —**pa′tient·ly** *adv.*

**pat·i·na** (pat′'n ə, pə tē′nə) *n.* [Fr. < It.] **1.** a fine greenish crust formed by oxidation on bronze or copper, often valued as ornamental **2.** any surface change due to age, as on old wood

**pa·ti·o** (pat′ē ō′, pät′-) *n., pl.* **-ti·os′** [Sp.] **1.** a courtyard or inner area open to the sky, as in Spanish and Spanish-American architecture **2.** a paved area, as one next to a house, with chairs, tables, etc. for outdoor lounging, dining, etc.

**pat·ois** (pat′wä; *Fr.* pȧ twä′) *n., pl.* **-ois** (-wäz; *Fr.* -twä′) [Fr.] **1.** a form of a language differing from the accepted standard, as a provincial or local dialect **2.** *same as* JARGON (sense 4)

**pat. pend.** patent pending

**pat·ri-** [L. < G. < *patēr,* father] *a combining form meaning* father

**pa·tri·arch** (pā′trē ärk′) *n.* [< OFr. < LL. < Gr., ult. < *patēr,* father + *archein,* to rule] **1.** the father and ruler of a family or tribe: in the Bible, Abraham, Isaac, Jacob, and Jacob's twelve sons were patriarchs **2.** a person regarded as the founder of a religion, business, etc. **3.** a man of great age and dignity **4.** *[often* P-] *a)* any of certain bishops in the early Christian Church *b)* R.C.Ch. the Pope **(Patriarch of the West),** or any of certain Eastern bishops *c) Orthodox Eastern Ch.* the highest-ranking bishop at Constantinople, Alexandria, Antioch, Jerusalem, Moscow, etc. —**pa′tri·ar′chal** *adj.*

**pa·tri·ar·chate** (-är′kit, -kāt) *n.* the position, rank, jurisdiction, etc. of a patriarch

**pa·tri·ar·chy** (-är′kē) *n., pl.* **-chies** 1. a form of social organization in which the father is the head of the family or tribe, descent being traced through the male line 2. rule or domination by men —**pa′tri·ar′chic** *adj.*

**Pa·tri·cia** (pə trish′ə, -trē′shə) [L., fem. of *patricius:* see PATRICK] a feminine name: dim. *Pat, Patty*

**pa·tri·cian** (pə trish′ən) *n.* [< MFr. < L. *patricius < patres,* pl. of *pater,* father] 1. in ancient Rome, *a)* orig., a member of any of the Roman citizen families *b)* later, a member of the nobility 2. an aristocrat —*adj.* 1. of or characteristic of patricians 2. noble; aristocratic

**pat·ri·cide** (pat′rə sīd′) *n.* [< ML.: see PATRI- & -CIDE] 1. the act of killing one's father 2. a person who kills his father —**pat′ri·ci′dal** *adj.*

**Pat·rick** (pat′rik) [< L. *patricius,* patrician] 1. a masculine name 2. Saint, 385?–461? A.D.; Brit. missionary in, and patron saint of, Ireland

**pat·ri·mo·ny** (pat′rə mō′nē) *n., pl.* **-nies** [< OFr. < L. *patrimonium < pater,* father] 1. property inherited from one's father or ancestors 2. property endowed to a church, etc. 3. anything inherited; heritage —**pat′ri·mo′ni·al** *adj.*

**pa·tri·ot** (pā′trē ət, -ät′; *chiefly Brit.* pat′rē-) *n.* [< Fr. < LL. < Gr. < *patris,* fatherland] a person who loves and loyally or zealously supports his own country —**pa′tri·ot′ic** *adj.* —**pa′tri·ot′i·cal·ly** *adv.*

**pa·tri·ot·ism** (-ə tiz′m) *n.* love and loyal or zealous support of one's own country

**pa·tris·tic** (pə tris′tik) *adj.* [< G. < L. *patres,* pl. of *pater,* father] of the early leaders, or fathers, of the Christian Church or their writings, etc.: also **pa·tris′ti·cal** —**pa·tris′ti·cal·ly** *adv.*

**pa·trol** (pə trōl′) *vt., vi.* **-trolled′, -trol′ling** [Fr. *patrouiller* < OFr. *patouiller,* to paddle] to make a regular, repeated circuit of (an area, camp, etc.), as in guarding —*n.* 1. a patrolling 2. a person or group patrolling 3. a group of ships, airplanes, etc. used in patrolling 4. a subdivision of a troop of Boy Scouts or Girl Scouts —**pa·trol′ler** *n.*

**pa·trol·man** (-mən) *n., pl.* **-men** a policeman assigned to patrol a specific beat

**patrol wagon** a small, enclosed truck used by the police in transporting prisoners

**pa·tron** (pā′trən) *n.* [< OFr. < ML., ult. < L. *pater,* father] 1. a person who is like a father in some respects; protector; benefactor 2. a wealthy or influential person who sponsors and supports some person, activity, etc. 3. a regular customer —**pa′tron·ess** *n.fem.*

**pa·tron·age** (pā′trən ij, pat′rən-) *n.* 1. *a)* the function or status of a patron *b)* support, sponsorship, etc. given by a patron 2. favor, courtesy, etc. shown to people considered inferior; condescension 3. *a)* clientele; customers *b)* business; trade 4. *a)* the power to appoint to office or grant other political favors *b)* the distribution of such offices or favors *c)* the offices, etc. thus distributed

**pa·tron·ize** (pā′trə nīz′, pat′rə-) *vt.* **-ized′, -iz′ing** 1. to act as a patron toward; sponsor; support 2. to treat kindly but as an inferior 3. to be a regular customer of (a store, etc.)

**patron saint** a saint looked upon as the special guardian of a person, place, institution, etc.

**pat·ro·nym·ic** (pat′rə nim′ik) *n.* [< LL. < Gr. < *patēr,* father + *onyma,* a name] a name showing descent from a given person as by the addition of a prefix or suffix (e.g., *Stevenson,* son of Steven, *O'Brien,* descendant of Brien)

**pa·troon** (pə trōōn′) *n.* [Du., protector < Fr. *patron,* PATRON] a person who held an estate with manorial rights under the old Dutch governments of New York and New Jersey

**pat·sy** (pat′sē) *n., pl.* **-sies** [prob. < It. *pazzo,* an insane person] [Slang] a person easily imposed upon or victimized

**pat·ten** (pat′'n) *n.* [MFr. *patin,* a clog < *pate,* a paw] a thick wooden sandal or clog

**pat·ter** (pat′ər) *vi.* [freq. of PAT²] to make, or move so as to make, a patter —*n.* a series of quick, light taps

**pat·ter²** (pat′ər) *vi., vi.* [< *pater,* in PATERNOSTER] to speak rapidly or glibly; recite mechanically —*n.* 1. language peculiar to a group, class, etc.; jargon 2. glib, rapid speech, as of salesmen, comedians, etc. 3. idle, meaningless chatter

**pat·ter³** (pat′ər) *n.* a person or thing that pats

**pat·tern** (pat′ərn) *n.* [< OFr. *patron,* patron, hence model, pattern] 1. a person or thing considered worthy of imitation or copying 2. a model, plan, or set of forms used as a guide in making things *[a dress pattern]* 3. something representing a class or type; sample 4. an arrangement of form; design *[wallpaper patterns]* 5. a regular, mainly unvarying way of acting *[behavior patterns]* 6. a predictable or prescribed route, movement, etc. *[traffic pattern]* —*vt.* to make, do, shape, or plan in imitation of a model or pattern (with *on, upon,* or *after*)

**pat·tern·mak·er** (-māk′ər) *n.* a person who makes patterns, as for molds or for various articles to be mass-produced: also **pattern maker**

**pat·ty** (pat′ē) *n., pl.* **-ties** [Fr. *pâté,* a pie] 1. a small pie 2. a small, flat cake of ground meat, fish, etc., usually fried 3. any disk-shaped piece, as of candy

**patty shell** a pastry case in which individual portions of creamed foods, etc. are served

**pau·ci·ty** (pô′sə tē) *n.* [< MFr. < L. < *paucus,* few] 1. fewness; small number 2. scarcity; insufficiency

**Paul** (pôl) [L. *Paulus,* Rom. surname, prob. < *paulus,* small] 1. a masculine name 2. *Bible* the apostle to the Christianity to the Gentiles, author of many Epistles: also *Saint Paul* 3. **Paul VI** 1897–1978; Pope (1963–78)

**Paul·a** (-ə) [L., fem. of prec.] a feminine name

**Paul Bun·yan** (bun′yən) *American Folklore* a giant lumberjack, who, with the help of his blue ox, Babe, performed various superhuman feats

**Paul·ine¹** (pô lēn′) [L. *Paulina,* fem. of *Paulinus:* see ff.] a feminine name

**Paul·ine²** (pôl′īn, -ēn) *adj.* [ModL. *Paulinus*] of the Apostle Paul, his writings, or doctrines

**Paul·ing** (pôl′iŋ), **Li·nus (Carl)** (lī′nəs) 1901– ; U.S. chemist

**paunch** (pônch) *n.* [< MFr. < L. *pantex,* belly] the abdomen, or belly; esp., a potbelly —**paunch′i·ness** *n.* —**paunch′y** *adj.*

**pau·per** (pô′pər) *n.* [L., poor person] 1. a person who lives on charity, esp. public charity 2. an extremely poor person

**pau·per·ism** (-iz′m) *n.* 1. the condition of being a pauper 2. paupers collectively Also **pau′per·dom** (-dəm)

**pau·per·ize** (pô′pə rīz′) *vt.* **-ized′, -iz′ing** to make a pauper of —**pau′per·i·za′tion** *n.*

**pause** (pôz) *n.* [MFr. < L. < Gr. *pausis,* a stopping < *pauein,* to stop] 1. a temporary stop or rest, as in working or speaking 2. hesitation; delay *[pursuit without pause]* 3. *Music* same as FERMATA 4. *Prosody* a rhythm break or caesura —*vi.* **paused, paus′ing** 1. to make a pause; stop; hesitate 2. to dwell or linger (*on* or *upon*) —**give one pause** to make one hesitant or uncertain —**paus′er** *n.*

**pave** (pāv) *vt.* **paved, pav′ing** [< OFr. *paver,* ult. < L. *pavire,* to beat] 1. to cover the surface of (a road, etc.), as with concrete, asphalt, etc. 2. to be the top surface of —**pave the way (for)** to prepare the way (for) —**pav′er** *n.*

**pave·ment** (pāv′mənt) *n.* 1. a paved surface, as of concrete, brick, etc.; specif., a paved street or road 2. the material used in paving

**pa·vil·ion** (pə vil′yən) *n.* [< OFr. < L. *papilio,* butterfly, also tent] 1. a large tent, usually with a peaked top 2. a building, often partly open, for exhibits, etc., as at a fair or park 3. part of a building jutting out 4. any of the separate or connected parts of a group of related buildings, as of a hospital —*vt.* to furnish with or shelter in a pavilion

**pav·ing** (pā′viŋ) *n.* 1. a pavement 2. material for a pavement

**Pav·lov** (päv′lôf; *E.* pav′lôv), **I·van Pe·tro·vich** (i vän′ trō′vich) 1849–1936; Russ. physiologist —**Pav·lov·i·an** (pav lô′vē ən) *adj.*

**Pav·lo·va** (päv′lô vä; *E.* päv lō′və), **An·na (Matveyevna)** (än′ä) 1885?–1931; Russ. ballet dancer

**paw** (pô) *n.* [< OFr. *poue* < Frank.] 1. the foot of a four-footed animal having claws 2. [Colloq.] a hand —*vt., vi.* 1. to touch, dig, strike, etc. with the paws or feet 2. to handle clumsily, roughly, or overintimately —**paw′er** *n.*

**pawl** (pôl) *n.* [akin ? to Du. *pal,* pole] a mechanical device allowing rotation in only one direction, as a hinged tongue which engages the notches of a ratchet wheel, preventing backward motion

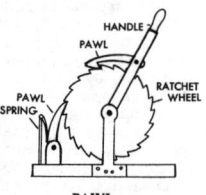

PAWL

**pawn¹** (pôn) *n.* [< MFr. *pan*] 1. anything given as security, as for a debt; pledge 2. the state of being pledged *[his ring was in pawn]* 3. the act of pawning —*vt.* 1. to put in pawn 2. to stake or risk —**pawn′age** *n.* —**pawn′er, pawn′nor** *n.*

**pawn²** (pôn) *n.* [< OFr. < ML. *pedo,* foot soldier, ult. < L. *pes,* foot] 1. a chessman of the lowest value 2. a person used to advance another's purposes

**pawn·bro·ker** (-brō′kər) *n.* a person licensed to lend money at interest on personal belongings left with him as security —**pawn′bro′king** *n.*

**Paw·nee** (pô nē′) *n.* [< ? Algonquian *pani,* slave] 1. *pl.* **-nees′, -nee′** a member of an Indian tribe formerly living in Nebraska and now in N Oklahoma 2. their language —*adj.* of this tribe or their language

**pawn·shop** (pôn′shäp′) *n.* a pawnbroker's shop

**pawn ticket** a receipt for goods in pawn

**paw·paw** (pô′pô′) *n. same as* PAPAW

**Paw·tuck·et** (pô tuk′it) [< Algonquian, little falls] city in NE R.I., adjacent to Providence: pop. 71,000

**‡pax vo·bis·cum** (paks vō bis′kəm, päks-) [L.] peace (be) with you

**pay**[1] (pā) *vt.* **paid** or obs. (except in phrase *pay out*, sense 2) **payed, pay′ing** [< OFr. < L. *pacare*, to pacify < *pax*, peace] **1.** to give to (a person) what is due, as for goods or services; remunerate **2.** to give (what is due) in return, as for goods or services **3.** to make a deposit or transfer of (money) *[to pay $10 into savings]* **4.** to settle (a debt, etc.) **5.** *a)* to give (a compliment, respects, etc.) *b)* to make (a visit, etc.) **6.** to yield as a recompense *[this job pays $90]* **7.** to be profitable to *[it will pay him to listen]* —*vi.* **1.** to give due compensation; make payment **2.** to be profitable **3.** to yield return as specified *[that stock pays poorly]* —*n.* **1.** a paying or being paid; payment **2.** money paid; esp., wages or salary —*adj.* **1.** operated or made available by depositing a coin *[a pay telephone]* **2.** designating a service, facility, etc. paid for by subscription, fees, etc. *[pay TV]* —**in the pay of** employed and paid by —**pay as you go** to pay expenses as they arise —**pay back 1.** to repay **2.** to get even with —**pay for 1.** to undergo punishment because of **2.** to atone for —**pay off 1.** to pay all that is owed **2.** to take revenge on (a wrongdoer) or for (a wrong done) —**pay out 1.** to give out (money, etc.) **2.** to let out a rope, cable, etc. gradually —**pay up** to pay in full or on time —**pay′er** *n.*

**pay**[2] (pā) *vt.* **payed, pay′ing** [ONormFr. *peier* < L. < *pix*, pitch] to coat (the seams of a vessel, etc.) as with tar, in order to make waterproof

**pay·a·ble** (pā′ə b'l) *adj.* **1.** that can be paid **2.** that is to be paid (*on* a specified date); due

**pay·check** (-chek′) *n.* a check in payment of wages, etc.

**pay·day** (-dā′) *n.* the day on which wages, etc. are paid

**pay dirt** soil, gravel, ore, etc. rich enough in minerals to make mining profitable —**hit** (or **strike**) **pay dirt** [Colloq.] to discover a source of wealth, success, etc.

**pay·ee** (pā ē′) *n.* the person to whom a check, note, money, etc. is payable

**pay·load** (pā′lōd′) *n.* **1.** a cargo, or the part of a cargo, producing income: also **pay load 2.** *a)* the warhead of a ballistic missile, the spacecraft launched by a rocket, etc. *b)* the weight of this

**pay·mas·ter** (-mas′tər) *n.* the official in charge of paying employees —**pay′mis′tress** *n.fem.*

**pay·ment** (-mənt) *n.* **1.** a paying or being paid **2.** something paid **3.** penalty or reward

**pay·nim** (pā′nim) *n.* [< OFr. < LL. *paganismus*, paganism] [Archaic] **1.** a pagan or the pagan world **2.** a non-Christian; esp., a Moslem

**pay·off** (pā′ôf′) *n.* **1.** the act or time of payment **2.** settlement or reckoning **3.** that which is paid off; recompense **4.** [Colloq.] a bribe **5.** [Colloq.] an unexpected or improbable climax or outcome

**pay·o·la** (pā ō′lə) *n.* [PAY[1] + -ola, as in *Pianola* (trademark for a player piano)] [Slang] **1.** the paying of bribes or graft for commercial advantage or special favors, as to a disc jockey for promoting a song unfairly **2.** such a bribe or graft

**pay·roll** (pā′rōl′) *n.* **1.** a list of employees to be paid, with the amount due to each **2.** the total amount needed for this for a given period

**payt., pay′t** payment

**pa·zazz** (pə zaz′) *n. same as* PIZAZZ

**Pb** [L. *plumbum*] *Chem.* lead

**PBS** Public Broadcasting Service

**PBX, P.B.X.** [< *p(rivate) b(ranch) ex(change)*] the telephone connections on the switchboard of an office, company, etc.

**pc. 1.** piece **2.** price(s)

**p.c. 1.** percent: also **pct. 2.** postal card **3.** post card

**Pd** *Chem.* palladium

**pd.** paid

**P.D. 1.** per diem: also **p.d. 2.** Police Department **3.** postal district

**pea** (pē) *n., pl.* **peas,** archaic or Brit. dial. **pease** [< ME. *pese*, a pea, taken as pl. < OE. *pise* < L. < Gr. *pison*] **1.** a climbing plant with white or pinkish flowers and green seedpods **2.** its small, round seed, eaten as a vegetable **3.** any similar plant —**as like as two peas (in a pod)** exactly alike

**peace** (pēs) *n.* [< OFr. *pais* < L. *pax*] **1.** freedom from or a stopping of war **2.** a treaty or agreement to end war **3.** freedom from public disturbance; law and order **4.** harmony in a group; concord **5.** an undisturbed state of mind; serenity: in full, **peace of mind 6.** calm; quiet —*vi.* [Obs. except in imperative] to be or become silent or quiet —**at peace** free from war, conflict, etc. —**hold** (or **keep**) **one's peace** to be silent —**keep the peace** to maintain law and order —**make peace** to end hostilities

**peace·a·ble** (-ə b'l) *adj.* **1.** fond of or promoting peace; not quarrelsome **2.** at peace; peaceful —**peace′a·bly** *adv.*

**peace conference** a conference for ending a war or for seeking ways to establish lasting peace

**Peace Corps** an agency of the U.S., established to provide volunteers skilled in teaching, construction, etc. to assist underdeveloped areas abroad

**peace·ful** (-fəl) *adj.* **1.** not quarrelsome; peaceable **2.** free from disturbance; calm **3.** of or characteristic of a time of peace —**peace′ful·ly** *adv.* —**peace′ful·ness** *n.*

**peace·mak·er** (-mā′kər) *n.* a person who makes peace, as by settling the quarrels of others —**peace′mak′ing** *n., adj.*

**peace pipe** *same as* CALUMET

**peace·time** (-tīm′) *n.* a time of peace —*adj.* of or characteristic of such a time

**peach**[1] (pēch) *n.* [< OFr. < VL., ult. < L. *Persicum (malum)*, Persian (apple)] **1.** a small tree with pink blossoms and round, juicy, orange-yellow fruit with a fuzzy skin and a rough pit **2.** its fruit **3.** the color of this fruit **4.** [Slang] any person or thing well liked —**peach′like′** *adj.*

**peach**[2] (pēch) *vi.* [ult. < OFr. *empechier*, IMPEACH] [Old Slang] to inform against another

**peach·y** (pē′chē) *adj.* **peach′i·er, peach′i·est 1.** peach-like, as in color or texture **2.** [Old Slang] fine; excellent —**peach′i·ness** *n.*

**pea·cock** (pē′käk′) *n., pl.* **-cocks′, -cock′:** see PLURAL, II, D, 1 [< OE. *pea* < L. *pavo*, peacock + *cok*, COCK[1]] **1.** the male of a species of peafowls, with a crest and long tail coverts having rainbow-colored, eyelike spots: these coverts can be erected and fanned out **2.** any male peafowl **3.** a vain, strutting person —*vi.* to display vanity in behavior, dress, etc. —**pea′cock′ish, pea′cock′y** *adj.*

**pea·fowl** (-foul′) *n., pl.* **-fowls, -fowl′:** see PLURAL, II, D, 1 any of a genus of pheasantlike birds of S Asia and the East Indies, including the peacock that is widely domesticated

**pea green** a light yellowish green

**pea·hen** (-hen′) *n.* a female peafowl

**pea jacket** [< Du. < *pij*, coarse cloth + *jekker*, jacket] a hip-length, heavy woolen coat worn as by seamen: also **pea′coat′** *n.*

**peak** (pēk) *n.* [var. of *pike* (summit)] **1.** a pointed end or top, as of a cap, roof, etc. **2.** *a)* the summit of a mountain ending in a point *b)* a mountain with such a summit **3.** the highest point or degree; maximum *[the peak of production]* **4.** *Naut. a)* the top rear corner of a fore-and-aft sail *b)* the upper end of the gaff *c)* the narrowed part of the hull, front or rear —*adj.* maximum *[peak production]* —*vt., vi.* **1.** to bring or come to a vertical position, as a sail yard **2.** to come or cause to come to a peak

**peaked**[1] (pēkt; *occas.* pē′kid) *adj.* having a peak

**peak·ed**[2] (pē′kid) *adj.* [< ?] thin and drawn, or weak and wan, as from illness —**peak′ed·ness** *n.*

**peal** (pēl) *n.* [ME. *pele* < *apele*, appeal] **1.** the loud ringing of a bell or bells **2.** a set of bells; chimes **3.** any loud, prolonged sound, as of gunfire, laughter, etc. —*vt., vi.* to sound in a peal; resound; ring

**pe·an** (pē′ən) *n. alt. sp. of* PAEAN

**pea·nut** (pē′nut′) *n.* **1.** an annual vine of the legume family, with brittle pods ripening underground and containing edible seeds **2.** the pod or its seed **3.** *[pl.]* [Slang] a trifling sum

**peanut butter** a food paste or spread made by grinding roasted peanuts

**pear** (per) *n.* [< OE. < VL. *pira* < L. pl. of *pirum*] **1.** a tree with soft, juicy fruit, round at the base and narrowing toward the stem **2.** this fruit

**Pearl** (purl) [< ff.] a feminine name

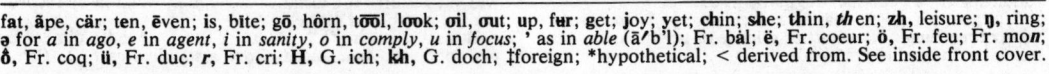

PEANUT PLANT

**pearl** (purl) *n.* [< MFr., ult. < L. *perna*, a sea mussel] **1.** a smooth, hard, usually white or bluish-gray, roundish growth formed around a foreign body within the shell of some oysters and other mollusks: it is used as a gem **2.** *same as* MOTHER-OF-PEARL **3.** anything pearllike in size, color, beauty, value, etc. **4.** the color of some pearls, a bluish gray —*vi.* to fish for pearl-bearing mollusks —*adj.* **1.** of or having pearls **2.** like a pearl in shape or color **3.** made of mother-of-pearl *[pearl buttons]* —**pearl′er** *n.* —**pearl′i·ness** *n.* —**pearl′y** *adj.* **-i·er, -i·est**

**pearl ash** a refined potash

**pearl diver** (or **fisher**) a person who dives for pearl-bearing mollusks

**pearl gray** a pale bluish gray

**Pearl Harbor** [after the *pearl* oysters once there] inlet on the S coast of Oahu, Hawaii, near Honolulu: site of a U.S. naval base bombed by Japan, Dec. 7, 1941

---

fat, āpe, cär; ten, ēven; is, bīte; gō, hôrn, tōol, look; oil, out; up, fur; get; joy; yet; chin; she; thin, then; zh, leisure; ŋ, ring; ə for *a* in *ago*, *e* in *agent*, *i* in *sanity*, *o* in *comply*, *u* in *focus*; ′ as in *able* (ā′b'l); Fr. bàl; ë, Fr. coeur; ö, Fr. feu; Fr. mon; ô, Fr. coq; ü, Fr. duc; r, Fr. cri; H, G. ich; kh, G. doch; ‡foreign; *hypothetical; < derived from. See inside front cover.

**Pearly Gates** [Colloq.] the gates of heaven: cf. Rev. 21:21
**pear-shaped** (per'shāpt') *adj.* 1. shaped like a pear 2. full, clear, and resonant: said of sung tones
**peart** (pirt) *adj.* [var. of PERT] [Dial.] lively, chipper, sprightly, smart, etc. —**peart'ly** *adv.* —**peart'ness** *n.*
**Pear·y** (pir'ē), Robert Edwin 1856-1920; U.S. arctic explorer, the first to reach the North Pole
**peas·ant** (pez''nt) *n.* [< Anglo-Fr. < MFr. < OFr. < *país*, country < LL. < *pagus*, district] 1. any person of the class of small farmers or of farm laborers, as in Europe or Asia 2. a person regarded as coarse, boorish, ignorant, etc.
**peas·ant·ry** (-'n trē) *n.* peasants collectively
**pease** (pēz) *n.* 1. *pl.* **peas'es, peas'en** (-'n) [Obs.] a pea 2. *archaic or Brit. dial. pl. of* PEA
**pease·cod, peas·cod** (pēz'käd') *n.* [Archaic] the pod of the pea plant
**peat** (pēt) *n.* [ML. *peta*, piece of turf < Celt.] 1. partly decayed plant matter found in ancient bogs and swamps 2. a dried block of this used as fuel —**peat'y** *adj.* **peat'i·er, peat'i·est**
**peat moss** 1. *same as* SPHAGNUM 2. peat composed of residues of mosses, used as a mulch
**pea·vey** (pē'vē) *n., pl.* **-veys** [prob. after J. *Peavey*, said to be its inventor, c. 1872] a heavy wooden lever with a pointed tip and hinged hook near the end: used by lumbermen in handling logs: also sp. **pea'vy,** *pl.* **-vies**
**peb·ble** (peb''l) *n.* [< OE. *papol*(*stan*), pebble (stone)] 1. a small stone worn smooth and round, as by the action of water 2. clear, transparent quartz or a lens made from it 3. a surface treated to make it irregular or indented, as on leather (**pebble leather**), paper, etc. —*vt.* **-bled, -bling** 1. to cover as with pebbles 2. to stamp (leather) so as to give it a pebble surface
**peb·bly** (-lē) *adj.* **-bli·er, -bli·est** 1. having many pebbles 2. having a pebble surface
**pe·can** (pi kan', -kän'; pē'kan, -kän) *n.* [< Algonquian *pakan*] 1. an olive-shaped, edible nut with a thin shell 2. the N. American tree on which it grows
**pec·ca·dil·lo** (pek'ə dil'ō) *n., pl.* **-loes, -los** [< Sp. dim. of *pecado* < L. < *peccare*, to sin] a minor or petty sin; slight fault
**pec·cant** (pek'ənt) *adj.* [< L. prp. of *peccare*, to sin] sinful; sinning —**pec'can·cy** *n.,* **-cies** —**pec'cant·ly** *adv.*
**pec·ca·ry** (pek'ər ē) *n., pl.* **-ries, -ry:** see PLURAL, II, D, 1 [AmSp. *pecari* < native Carib name] a grayish, piglike animal of N. and S. America, with sharp tusks and porklike flesh
**peck**[1] (pek) *vt.* [< ME. var. of *picken,* PICK[2]] 1. to strike with a pointed object, as a beak 2. to make by doing this [to *peck* a hole] 3. to pick up or get by pecking —*vi.* to make strokes as with a pointed object —*n.* 1. a stroke so made, as with the beak 2. a mark made as by pecking 3. [Colloq.] a quick, casual kiss —**peck at** 1. to make a pecking motion at 2. [Colloq.] to eat very little of 3. [Colloq.] to criticize constantly —**peck'er** *n.*
**peck**[2] (pek) *n.* [< OFr. *pek*] 1. a unit of dry measure equal to 1/4 bushel or eight quarts 2. any container that will hold a peck 3. [Colloq.] a large amount, as of trouble
**pec·tin** (pek'tin) *n.* [< Gr. *pēktos,* congealed + -IN[1]] a water-soluble carbohydrate obtained from certain ripe fruits, which yields a gel that is the basis of jellies and jams —**pec'tic, pec'tin·ous** *adj.*
**pec·to·ral** (pek'tər əl) *adj.* [< L. *pectus* (gen. *pectoris*), breast] 1. of or located in or on the breast or chest 2. worn on the chest or breast [a *pectoral* cross] —*n.* a pectoral fin or muscle
**pectoral fin** either of a pair of fins just behind the head of a fish
**pec·u·late** (pek'yə lāt') *vt., vi.* **-lat'ed, -lat'ing** [< L. pp. of *peculari,* to embezzle] to steal or misuse (money or property in one's care); embezzle —**pec'u·la'tion** *n.* —**pec'u·la'tor** *n.*
**pe·cu·liar** (pi kyōōl'yər) *adj.* [< L. < *peculium,* private property] 1. of only one person, thing, group, etc.; exclusive 2. particular; special [a matter of *peculiar* interest] 3. queer; odd; strange —**pe·cul'iar·ly** *adv.*
**pe·cu·li·ar·i·ty** (pi kyōō'lē ar'ə tē, -kyōōl'yar'-) *n.* 1. a being peculiar 2. *pl.* **-ties** something that is peculiar, as a trait
**pe·cu·ni·ar·y** (pi kyōō'nē er'ē) *adj.* [< L. < *pecunia,* money] 1. of or involving money 2. involving a money penalty, or fine —**pe·cu'ni·ar'i·ly** *adv.*
**ped-** *same as:* 1. PEDO- 2. PEDI- Used before a vowel
**ped·a·gog·ic** (ped'ə gäj'ik, -gō'jik) *adj.* [see ff.] of or characteristic of teachers or of teaching: also **ped'a·gog'i·cal** —**ped'a·gog'i·cal·ly** *adv.*
**ped·a·gogue, ped·a·gog** (ped'ə gäg', -gôg') *n.* [< OFr. < L. < Gr. < *pais,* a child + *agein,* to lead] a teacher; often specif., a pedantic, dogmatic teacher
**ped·a·go·gy** (-gō'jē, -gäj'ē) *n.* [see prec.] 1. the profession of teaching 2. the art or science of teaching; esp., instruction in teaching methods

**ped·al** (ped''l; *also, for adj. 1,* pēd'-) *adj.* [< L. < *pes* (gen. *pedis*), a foot] 1. of the foot or feet 2. of or operated by a pedal —*n.* a lever operated by the foot to transmit motion, as in a bicycle, or to change the tone or volume of an organ, harp, etc. —*vt., vi.* **-aled** or **-alled, -al·ing** or **-al·ling** to operate by a pedal or pedals; use the pedals (of)
**pedal pushers** calf-length pants for women or girls, used originally for bicycle riding
**ped·ant** (ped''nt) *n.* [< Fr. < It. *pedante,* ult. < Gr. *paidagōgos:* see PEDAGOGUE] 1. a person who emphasizes trivial points of learning, showing a scholarship lacking in judgment 2. a narrow-minded teacher who insists on exact adherence to rules —**pe·dan'tic** (pi dan'tik) *adj.* —**pe·dan'ti·cal·ly** *adv.*
**ped·ant·ry** (ped''n trē) *n., pl.* **-ries** 1. the qualities, practices, etc. of a pedant; showy display of knowledge, or an instance of this 2. adherence to rules
**ped·ate** (ped'āt) *adj.* [< L. < *pes,* foot] 1. *Bot.* palmately divided into three main divisions 2. *Zool. a)* having a foot or feet *b)* footlike
**ped·dle** (ped''l) *vi.* **-dled, -dling** [back-formation < *peddler* < ? ME. *ped,* a basket] to go from place to place selling small articles —*vt.* 1. to carry from place to place and offer for sale 2. to deal out or circulate (gossip, etc.) —**ped'dler** *n.*
**-pede** (pēd) [< L. *pes,* a foot] *a combining form meaning* foot or feet [*centipede*]: also **-ped**
**ped·er·as·ty** (ped'ə ras'tē, pē'də-) *n.* [< ModL. < Gr. < *pais* (gen. *paidos*), boy + *eran,* to love] sodomy between males, esp. by a man with a boy —**ped'er·ast'** *n.* —**ped'er·as'tic** *adj.* —**ped'er·as'ti·cal·ly** *adv.*
**ped·es·tal** (ped'is t'l) *n.* [< Fr. < It. < *piè* (< L. *pes*), a foot + *di,* of + *stal* (< Gmc. hyp. *stal*), a rest] 1. the bottom support of a column, statue, etc. 2. any foundation, base, etc. —*vt.* **-taled** or **-talled, -tal·ing** or **-tal·ling** to furnish with a pedestal —**put** (or **set**) **on a pedestal** to idolize
**pe·des·tri·an** (pə des'trē ən) *adj.* [< L. *pedester* < *pes* (gen. *pedis*), a foot + -IAN] 1. going or done on foot 2. of or for pedestrians [a *pedestrian* crossing] 3. lacking interest or imagination; prosaic; dull —*n.* one who goes on foot; a walker —**pe·des'tri·an·ism** *n.*
**ped·i-** [< L. *pes* (gen. *pedis*), a foot] *a combining form meaning foot or feet [pedicure]*
**pe·di·a·tri·cian** (pē'dē ə trish'ən) *n.* a specialist in pediatrics: also **pe'di·at'rist** (-at'rist)
**pe·di·at·rics** (-at'riks) *n.pl.* [*with sing. v.*] [< PED(O)- + -IATRICS] the branch of medicine dealing with the care of infants and children and the treatment of their diseases —**pe'di·at'ric** *adj.*
**ped·i·cab** (ped'i kab') *n.* [PEDI- + CAB] a three-wheeled passenger vehicle, esp. in SE Asia, which the driver propels by pedaling like a bicycle
**ped·i·cel** (ped'i s'l) *n.* [< ModL. dim. of L. *pediculus,* dim. of *pes,* a foot] 1. *Bot.* the stalk of a single flower, fruit, grass spikelet, etc. 2. *Zool. a)* a small, stalklike structure *b)* a small, footlike part Also **ped'i·cle** (-k'l) —**ped'i·cel·late** (-sel'it, -āt) *adj.*
**pe·dic·u·lo·sis** (pi dik'yə lō'sis) *n.* [< L. dim. of *pedis,* a louse + -OSIS] infestation with lice —**pe·dic'u·lous** (-ləs) *adj.*
**ped·i·cure** (ped'i kyoor') *n.* [< Fr. < L. *pes,* a foot + *cura,* care] 1. *early term for* PODIATRIST 2. care of the feet; esp., a trimming, polishing, etc. of the toenails —**ped'i·cur'ist** *n.*
**ped·i·gree** (ped'ə grē') *n.* [< MFr. *piè de grue,* lit., crane's foot: from the lines in the genealogical tree] 1. a list of ancestors; family tree 2. descent; lineage 3. a recorded line of descent, esp. of a purebred animal —**ped'i·greed'** *adj.*
**ped·i·ment** (ped'ə mənt) *n.* [altered (after L. *pes,* gen. *pedis,* a foot) < earlier *periment,* prob. < PYRAMID] 1. a low-pitched gable on the front of some buildings of Grecian architecture 2. any similar triangular piece, as over a doorway, etc. —**ped'i·men'tal** *adj.* —**ped'i·men'ted** *adj.*
**ped·i·palp** (ped'i palp') *n.* [< ModL.: see PEDI- & PALPUS] either of the second pair of appendages of arachnids, developed for grasping, sensing, etc.

PEDIMENT

**ped·lar, ped·ler** (ped'lər) *n.* one who peddles; peddler
**pe·do-** [< Gr. *pais* (gen. *paidos*), a child] *a combining form meaning* child, children
**pe·dom·e·ter** (pi däm'ə tər) *n.* [< Fr. < L. *pes* (gen. *pedis*), a foot + Gr. *metron,* a measure] an instrument which measures the distance covered in walking by recording the number of steps
**pe·dun·cle** (pi duŋ'k'l, pē'duŋ k'l) *n.* [< ModL. dim. of L. *pes,* foot] 1. *Anat., Med., Zool.* a stalklike part 2. *Bot.* a

stalk of a flower cluster or solitary flower —**pe·dun'cu·lar** (-kyə lər) *adj.* —**pe·dun'cu·late** (-kyə lit, -lāt') *adj.*

**peek** (pēk) *vi.* [< ?] to glance or look quickly and furtively, as through an opening —*n.* such a glance

**peek·a·boo** (pēk'ə bōō') *n.* a child's game in which someone hides his face, as behind his hands, and then suddenly reveals it, calling "peekaboo!" —*adj.* made of openwork or sheer fabric, as a blouse

**peel**[1] (pēl) *vt.* [< OFr. < L. *pilare*, to make bald < *pilus*, a hair] to cut away or strip off (the rind, skin, surface, etc.) of (anything); pare —*vi.* 1. to shed skin, bark, etc. 2. to come off in layers or flakes, as old paint 3. [Slang] to undress —*n.* the rind or skin of fruit —**peel off** *Aeron.* to veer away from a flight formation abruptly —**peel rubber** (or **tires**) [Slang] to accelerate an automobile quickly —**peel'er** *n.*

**peel**[2] (pēl) *n.* [< OFr. < L. *pala*, a spade] a long shovellike tool used by bakers for moving bread into and out of ovens

**Peel** (pēl), Sir **Robert** 1788–1850; Brit. statesman; prime minister (1834–35; 1841–46)

**peel·ing** (pēl'iŋ) *n.* a peeled-off strip, as of apple skin

**peen** (pēn) *n.* [prob. < Scand.] the part of certain hammer heads opposite to the flat striking surface: often ball-shaped (**ball peen**) or wedge-shaped —*vt.* to hammer, bend, etc. with a peen

**peep**[1] (pēp) *vi.* [orig. echoic] 1. to make the short, high-pitched cry of a young bird 2. to speak in a weak voice, as from fear —*n.* 1. a short, high-pitched sound 2. a slight vocal sound —**peep'er** *n.*

**peep**[2] (pēp) *vi.* [? akin to ME. *piken*, peek] 1. to look through a small opening or from a place of hiding 2. to peer slyly or secretly 3. to show or appear gradually or partially *[stars peeped* through the clouds] —*vt.* to cause to appear or protrude —*n.* 1. a brief look; secret or furtive glimpse 2. the first appearance, as of dawn

**peep·er** (-ər) *n.* 1. a person who peeps or pries 2. [Slang] *a*) [*pl.*] the eyes *b*) a private detective

**peep·hole** (-hōl') *n.* a hole to peep through

**Peeping Tom** 1. *Eng. Legend* the tailor who was struck blind after peeping at Lady Godiva 2. [**p- T-**] a person who gets pleasure, esp. sexual pleasure, from furtively watching others

**peer**[1] (pir) *n.* [< OFr. *per* < L. *par*, an equal] 1. one that has the same rank, value, etc. as another; specif., an equal before the law 2. a noble; esp., a British duke, marquess, earl, viscount, or baron

**peer**[2] (pir) *vi.* [? short for APPEAR] 1. to look closely, as in trying to see more clearly 2. to come partly into sight 3. [Poet.] to appear

**peer·age** (pir'ij) *n.* 1. all the peers of a particular country 2. the rank or dignity of a peer 3. a book or list of peers with their lineage

**peer·ess** (-is) *n.* 1. the wife of a peer 2. a woman having the rank of peer in her own right

**peer group** a group of people of about the same age and status and having the same set of values

**peer·less** (-lis) *adj.* without equal; unrivaled —**peer'less·ly** *adv.* —**peer'less·ness** *n.*

**peeve** (pēv) *vt.* **peeved, peev'ing** [< ff.] [Colloq.] to make peevish —*n.* [Colloq.] 1. an object of dislike; annoyance 2. a peevish state

**pee·vish** (pē'vish) *adj.* [< ?] 1. irritable; fretful 2. showing ill humor or impatience, as a remark —**pee'vish·ly** *adv.* —**pee'vish·ness** *n.*

**pee·wee** (pē'wē') *n.* [prob. echoic redupl. of WEE] [Colloq.] an unusually small person or thing

**peg** (peg) *n.* [prob. < LowG. source] 1. a short pin or bolt used to hold parts together, close an opening, hang things on, fasten ropes to, mark the score in a game, etc. 2. *a*) the distance between pegs *b*) a step or degree *c*) a fixed level, as for a price 3. any of the pins that regulate the tension of the strings of a violin, etc. 4. a point or prong for tearing, hooking, etc. 5. a point of reference, esp. an excuse or reason 6. [Colloq.] the foot or leg 7. [Colloq.] an act of throwing —*vt.* **pegged, peg'ging** 1. to put a peg or pegs into so as to fasten, mark, etc. 2. to maintain (prices, etc.) at a fixed level 3. to score (points) in cribbage 4. [Colloq.] to identify or categorize *[pegged* him as a scholar] 5. [Colloq.] to throw (a ball) —*vi.* 1. to keep score with pegs, as in cribbage 2. to move energetically (with *along*, etc.) —**peg away** (**at**) to work steadily and persistently (at) —**round peg in a square hole** one in a position, etc. for which he is unfitted: also **square peg in a round hole** —**take down a peg** to lower the pride or conceit of

**Peg·a·sus** (peg'ə səs) 1. *Gr. Myth.* a winged horse, symbol of poetic inspiration 2. a large northern constellation

**peg·board** (peg'bôrd') *n.* 1. a small board with holes in it for inserting scoring pegs for cribbage 2. a piece of board-like material with rows of holes for hooks to hold displays, tools, etc.: a trademark, **Peg-Board**

**Peg·gy** (peg'ē) [dim. of MARGARET] a feminine name

**peg leg** [Colloq.] 1. a wooden leg 2. a person with a wooden leg

**peg-top** (peg'täp') *adj.* designating trousers that are full at the hips and narrow at the cuffs

**peg top** 1. a child's spinning top, pear-shaped with a metal tip 2. [*pl.*] peg-top trousers

**P.E.I.** Prince Edward Island

**peign·oir** (pān wär', pen-; pän'wär, pen'-) *n.* [Fr. < *peigner*, to comb, ult. < L. *pecten*, a comb] a negligee

**Pei·ping** (bā'piŋ') *former name of* PEKING

**Peirce** (pɜrs), **Charles San·ders** (san'dərz) 1839–1914; U.S. philosopher & mathematician

**pe·jo·ra·tion** (pē'jə rā'shən, pej'ə-) *n.* [see ff.] 1. a worsening 2. a change for the worse in the meaning of a word

**pe·jo·ra·tive** (pi jôr'ə tiv, pej'ə rāt'iv) *adj.* [< L. pp. of *pejorare*, to make worse < *pejor*, worse] 1. declining; making or becoming worse: said of a word whose basic meaning has changed for the worse (Ex.: *cretin*) 2. disparaging or derogatory —*n.* a pejorative word or form

**Pe·king** (pē'kiŋ'; *Chin.* bā'jiŋ') capital of China, in the NE part: pop. c. 7,000,000

**Pe·king·ese** (pē'kiŋ ēz'; *for n. 3, usually* -kə nēz') *adj.* of Peking, China, or its people —*n., pl.* **Pekingese** 1. a native or inhabitant of Peking 2. the Chinese dialect of Peking 3. a small dog with long, silky hair, short legs, and a pug nose Also **Pe'kin·ese'** (-kə nēz')

**Peking man** a type of early man of the Pleistocene age, known from fossil remains found near Peking

**pe·koe** (pē'kō; *Brit. often* pek'ō) *n.* [< Chin. *pek-ho*, lit., white down (on the young leaves used)] a black, small-leaved tea of Ceylon and India

**pe·lag·ic** (pi laj'ik) *adj.* [< L. < Gr. < *pelagos*, the sea] of the open sea or ocean

**pel·ar·go·ni·um** (pel'är gō'nē əm) *n.* [ModL. < Gr. *pelargos*, stork] any of a group of plants with lobed leaves and showy flowers; geranium

**pelf** (pelf) *n.* [akin to MFr. *pelfre*, booty] 1. orig., booty 2. wealth regarded with contempt

**pel·i·can** (pel'i kən) *n.* [< OE. < LL. < Gr. *pelekan*] a large water bird with webbed feet and an expandable pouch in the lower bill for scooping up fish

**Pe·li·on** (pē'lē ən) mountain in NE Greece: in Greek mythology, the Titans piled Pelion on Ossa and both on Olympus in a futile attempt to attack the gods

**pe·lisse** (pə lēs') *n.* [Fr., ult. < L. *pellicius*, made of skins < *pellis*, a skin] a long cloak or outer coat, esp. one of fur

**pel·la·gra** (pə lag'rə, -lā'grə) *n.* [It. < *pelle* (< L. *pellis*), the skin + *-agra* < Gr. *agra*, seizure] a chronic disease caused by a deficiency of niacin in the diet and causing skin eruptions and mental disorders —**pel·la'grous** *adj.*

**pel·let** (pel'ət) *n.* [< OFr. *pelote* < VL. dim. of L. *pila*, a ball] 1. a little ball, as of clay, paper, medicine, compressed food, etc. 2. *a*) a crude projectile, as used in a catapult *b*) a bullet, or imitation bullet *c*) a small lead shot —*vt.* 1. to make pellets of 2. to shoot or hit with pellets

**pel·let·ize** (-īz') *vt.* **-ized', -iz'ing** to make pellets of the iron-containing particles recovered from low-grade iron (ore) —**pel'let·i·za'tion** *n.*

**pell-mell, pell·mell** (pel'mel') *adv., adj.* [< Fr. < OFr. *pesle mesle*, redupl. < *mesler*, to mix] 1. in a jumbled, confused mass or manner 2. in reckless haste; headlong —*n.* confusion; disorder

**pel·lu·cid** (pə lōō'sid) *adj.* [< L. < *pellucere* < *per*, through + *lucere*, to shine] 1. transparent or translucent; clear 2. clear and simple in style —**pel'lu·cid'i·ty, pel·lu'cid·ness** *n.* —**pel·lu'cid·ly** *adv.*

**Pel·o·pon·ne·sus, Pel·o·pon·ne·sos** (pel'ə pə nē'səs) peninsula forming the S part of the mainland of Greece —**Pel'o·pon·ne'sian** (-shən, -zhən) *adj., n.*

**pelt**[1] (pelt) *vt.* [? ult. < L. *pillare*, to drive] 1. to throw things at 2. to beat heavily and repeatedly 3. to throw (missiles) —*vi.* 1. to strike heavily or steadily, as hard rain 2. to hurry —*n.* a blow —(**at**) **full pelt** at full speed

**pelt**[2] (pelt) *n.* [prob. < PELTRY] 1. the skin of a fur-bearing animal, esp. after it is stripped from the carcass 2. the humorous usage

**pel·tate** (pel'tāt) *adj.* [< L. *pelta*, light shield + -ATE[1]] *Bot.* shield-shaped: having the stalk attached to the lower surface within the margin: said of a leaf —**pel'tate·ly** *adv.*

---

**pelt·ry** (pel'trē) *n., pl.* **-ries** [< OFr. < *peletier,* furrier < *pel,* a skin] pelts, or fur-bearing skins, collectively

**pel·vis** (pel'vis) *n., pl.* **-vis·es, -ves** (-vēz) [ModL. < L., a basin] *Anat., Zool.* any basinlike structure; specif., *a)* the basinlike cavity in the posterior part of the trunk of man and many other vertebrates *b)* the ring of bones forming this cavity: also **pelvic girdle** —**pel'vic** *adj.*

**pem·mi·can** (pem'i kən) *n.* [< Cree *pemikkân,* fat meat < *pimiy,* fat] **1.** dried lean meat, pounded into a paste with fat and preserved as pressed cakes **2.** a concentrated food of dried beef, suet, dried fruit, etc., used for emergency rations, as by explorers

**pen¹** (pen) *n.* [OE. *penn*] **1.** a small yard or enclosure for domestic animals **2.** the animals inside it **3.** any small enclosure —*vt.* **penned** or **pent, pen'ning** to confine or enclose as in a pen

**pen²** (pen) *n.* [< OFr. < L. *penna,* a feather] **1.** orig., a heavy quill trimmed to a split point, for writing with ink **2.** any of various devices used in writing or drawing with ink, often with a metal point split into two nibs: see also BALL POINT PEN, FOUNTAIN PEN **3.** the metal point for this device **4.** *a)* writing as a profession *b)* literary style —*vt.* **penned, pen'ning** to write as with a pen

**pen³** (pen) *n.* [Slang] a penitentiary

**pen⁴** (pen) *n.* [< ?] a female swan

**Pen., pen.** peninsula

**pe·nal** (pē'n'l) *adj.* [< L. < *poena,* punishment] **1.** of, for, or involving punishment, esp. legal punishment **2.** making one liable to punishment, as an offense —**pe'nal·ly** *adv.*

**penal code** a body of law dealing with various crimes or offenses and their legal penalties

**pe·nal·ize** (pē'n'l īz', pen'l-) *vt.* **-ized', -iz'ing** **1.** to set a penalty for **2.** to impose a penalty on, as for breaking some rule **3.** to put at a disadvantage —**pe'nal·i·za'tion** *n.*

**pen·al·ty** (pen'l tē) *n., pl.* **-ties** **1.** a punishment fixed by law, as for a crime **2.** the handicap, fine, forfeit, etc. imposed upon an offender or one who does not fulfill a contract or obligation **3.** any unfortunate consequence **4.** *Sports* a loss of yardage, the removal of a player, etc. imposed for breaking a rule

**pen·ance** (pen'əns) *n.* [< OFr. < L. < *paenitens:* see PENITENT] **1.** *R.C.Ch. & Orthodox Eastern Ch.* a sacrament involving the confession of sin, repentance, and submission to penalties imposed, followed by absolution **2.** any voluntary suffering to show repentance for wrongdoing —*vt.* **-anced, -anc·ing** to impose a penance on —**do penance** to perform an act of penance

**Pe·nang** (pi naŋ') seaport in Malaysia, on an island **(Penang)** off the NW coast of the Malay Peninsula: pop. 325,000

**pe·na·tes** (pi nāt'ēz) *n.pl.* [L.] the household gods of the ancient Romans: see LARES AND PENATES

**pence** (pens; *in compounds,* pəns) *n.* [Brit.] *pl. of* PENNY: used also in compounds *[twopence]*

**pen·chant** (pen'chənt; *Fr.* pän shän') *n.* [Fr. < *pencher,* to incline, ult. < L. *pendere,* to hang] a strong liking or fondness; inclination

**pen·cil** (pen's'l) *n.* [< MFr. < L. *penicillus* < dim. of *penis,* a tail] **1.** orig., an artist's brush **2.** the style of a given artist **3.** a pointed, rod-shaped instrument with a core of graphite or crayon, used for writing, drawing, etc. **4.** something shaped or used as a pencil *[a styptic pencil]* **5.** a series of lines coming to or spreading out from a point —*vt.* **-ciled** or **-cilled, -cil·ing** or **-cil·ling** **1.** to write, draw, etc. as with a pencil **2.** to use a pencil on —**pen'cil·er, pen'cil·ler** *n.*

**pend** (pend) *vi.* [< OFr. < L. *pendere,* to hang] to await judgment or decision

**pend·ant** (pen'dənt) *n.* [< OFr. prp. of *pendre* < L. *pendere,* to hang] **1.** an ornamental hanging object, as from an earring **2.** anything hanging, as the pull chain on a lamp **3.** a decorative piece suspended from a ceiling or roof —*adj. same as* PENDENT —**pend'ant·ly** *adv.*

**pend·ent** (pen'dənt) *adj.* [see prec.] **1.** suspended **2.** overhanging **3.** undecided; pending —*n. same as* PENDANT —**pend'en·cy** *n.* —**pend'ent·ly** *adv.*

**pend·ing** (pen'diŋ) *adj.* **1.** not decided or established *[patent pending]* **2.** impending —*prep.* **1.** throughout the course of; during **2.** while awaiting; until *[pending his arrival]*

**pen·drag·on** (pen drag'ən) *n.* [W. *pen,* head + *dragon,* leader < L. *draco,* cohort's standard] supreme chief or leader: a title used in ancient Britain

**pen·du·lous** (pen'joo ləs, -dyoo-) *adj.* [L. *pendulus* < *pendere,* to hang] **1.** hanging freely or loosely; suspended so as to swing **2.** drooping —**pen'du·lous·ly** *adv.* —**pen'du·lous·ness** *n.*

**pen·du·lum** (pen'joo ləm, -dyoo-, -d'l əm) *n.* [ModL. < L.: see prec.] a body hung from a fixed point so as to swing freely to and fro under the combined forces of gravity and momentum: often used to regulate clock movements —**pen'du·lar** *adj.*

**Pe·nel·o·pe** (pə nel'ə pē) [L. < Gr. *Pēnelopē*] **1.** a feminine name: dim. *Penny* **2.** Ulysses' wife, who waited faithfully for his return

**pen·e·tra·ble** (pen'i trə b'l) *adj.* that can be penetrated —**pen'e·tra·bil'i·ty, pen'e·tra·ble·ness** *n.* —**pen'e·tra·bly** *adv.*

**pen·e·trate** (pen'ə trāt') *vt.* **-trat'ed, -trat'ing** [< L. pp. of *penetrare* < base of *penitus,* inward] **1.** to find or force a way into or through; enter as by piercing **2.** to see into the interior of **3.** to have an effect throughout; permeate **4.** to affect or move deeply **5.** to understand —*vi.* **1.** to make a way into or through something **2.** to have a marked effect on the mind or emotions

**pen·e·trat·ing** (-trāt'iŋ) *adj.* **1.** that can penetrate *[a penetrating oil]* **2.** sharp; piercing *[a penetrating smell]* **3.** that has entered deeply *[a penetrating wound]* **4.** discerning *[a penetrating mind]* Also **pen'e·tra'tive** —**pen'e·trat'ing·ly, pen'e·tra'tive·ly** *adv.*

**pen·e·tra·tion** (pen'ə trā'shən) *n.* **1.** a penetrating **2.** the depth to which something penetrates **3.** sharp discernment; insight

**pen·guin** (peŋ'gwin, pen'-) *n.* [prob. < W. *pen gwyn,* lit., white head] any of a group of flightless birds of the Southern Hemisphere, having webbed feet and paddlelike flippers for swimming

**pen·hold·er** (pen'hōl'dər) *n.* **1.** the holder into which a pen point fits **2.** a container for a pen

**pen·i·cil·lin** (pen'ə sil'in) *n.* [< ff. + -IN¹] any of several antibiotic compounds obtained from certain molds or produced synthetically

**pen·i·cil·li·um** (-ē əm) *n., pl.* **-li·ums, -li·a** (-ə) [ModL. < L. *penicillus,* a brush: from the tuftlike ends] any of a group of fungi growing as green mold on stale bread, decaying fruit, etc.

PENGUIN
(to 4 ft. high)

**pen·in·su·la** (pə nin'sə lə, -syoo-) *n.* [< L. < *paene,* almost + *insula,* an isle] **1.** a land area almost entirely surrounded by water, connected with the mainland by an isthmus **2.** any land area projecting into the water —**pen·in'su·lar** *adj.*

**pe·nis** (pē'nis) *n., pl.* **-nis·es, -nes** (-nēz) [L., a tail, penis] the male organ of sexual intercourse: in mammals it is also the organ through which urine is ejected —**pe'nile** (-nīl, -nil) *adj.*

**pen·i·tent** (pen'ə tənt) *adj.* [< OFr. < L. prp. of *paenitere,* to repent] sorry for having done wrong and willing to atone; repentant —*n.* **1.** a penitent person **2.** *R.C.Ch.* a person undergoing penance —**pen'i·tence** *n.* —**pen'i·tent·ly** *adv.*

**pen·i·ten·tial** (pen'ə ten'shəl) *adj.* of, constituting, or expressing penitence or penance —*n.* **1.** a penitent **2.** a list or book of rules governing religious penance —**pen'i·ten'tial·ly** *adv.*

**pen·i·ten·tia·ry** (pen'ə ten'shə rē) *adj.* [< ML. < L.: see PENITENT] **1.** of or for penance **2.** used in punishing and reforming **3.** making one liable to imprisonment in a penitentiary —*n., pl.* **-ries** a prison; specif., a State or Federal prison for persons convicted of serious crimes

**pen·knife** (pen'nīf') *n., pl.* **-knives'** (-nīvz') a small pocketknife; orig., one used in making quill pens

**pen·light, pen·lite** (pen'līt') *n.* a flashlight that is as small and slender as a fountain pen

**pen·man** (pen'mən) *n., pl.* **-men** **1.** a person employed to write or copy; scribe **2.** a person skilled in penmanship **3.** an author

**pen·man·ship** (-ship') *n.* **1.** handwriting as an art or skill **2.** a style of handwriting

**Penn** (pen), **William** 1644–1718; Eng. Quaker leader: founder of Pennsylvania

**Penn., Penna.** Pennsylvania

**pen name** a name used by an author in place of his true name; nom de plume

**pen·nant** (pen'ənt) *n.* [< PENNON, altered after PENDANT] **1.** any long, narrow flag **2.** any such flag symbolizing a championship, esp. in baseball

**pen·ni** (pen'ē) *n., pl.* **-ni·a** (-ə), **-nis, -ni** [Finn., akin to PENNY] *see* MONETARY UNITS, table (Finland)

**pen·ni·less** (pen'i lis) *adj.* without even a penny; extremely poor —**pen'ni·less·ness** *n.*

**Pen·nine Alps** (pen'īn, -in) division of the W Alps, along the Swiss-Italian border

**pen·non** (pen'ən) *n.* [< OFr. < *penne:* see PEN²] **1.** a long, narrow, triangular or swallow-tailed flag used as an ensign by knights or lancers **2.** any flag or pennant **3.** a pinion; wing

**Penn·syl·va·ni·a** (pen's'l vān'yə, -vā'nē ə) [after Wm. PENN + L. *sylvania,* wooded (land), ult. < *sylva,* forest] State of the NE U.S.: 45,333 sq. mi.; pop. 11,867,000; cap. Harrisburg: abbrev. **Pa., PA**

**Pennsylvania Dutch** 1. the descendants of early German immigrants, who settled mainly in E Pennsylvania 2. their High German dialect: also called **Pennsylvania German** 3. their folk art, featuring stylized decorations of flowers, birds, etc. —**Penn′syl·va′ni·a-Dutch′** adj.

**Penn·syl·va·ni·an** (pen′s'l vān′yən, -vā′nē ən) adj. 1. of Pennsylvania 2. designating or of the sixth period of the Paleozoic Era in N. America —n. a native or inhabitant of Pennsylvania —**the Pennsylvanian** the Pennsylvanian Period or its rocks: see GEOLOGY, chart

**pen·ny** (pen′ē) n., pl. **-nies**; for 1 (esp. collectively), **pence** [OE. pening, ult. < L. pannus, cloth (a medium of exchange)] 1. in the United Kingdom and certain Commonwealth countries, a) formerly, a unit of currency equal to one twelfth of a shilling b) a unit of currency equal to one 100th part of a pound: in full, **new penny** 2. a U.S. or Canadian cent 3. a sum of money —**a pretty penny** [Colloq.] a large sum of money

**-pen·ny** (pen′ē) a combining form meaning costing (a specified number of) pennies [sixpenny] : as applied to nails, now a measure of their length

**penny arcade** a public amusement hall with various coin-operated game and vending machines

**penny pincher** a person who is extremely frugal or stingy —**pen′ny-pinch′ing** n., adj.

**pen·ny·roy·al** (pen′ē roi′əl) n. [< Anglo-Fr. < OFr. poliol (< L. pulegium, fleabane) + real, royal] 1. a European mint with lavender flowers 2. a similar N. American mint that yields an aromatic oil

**pen·ny·weight** (pen′ē wāt′) n. a unit of weight, equal to 24 grains or 1/20 ounce troy weight

**pen·ny-wise** (pen′ē wīz′) adj. careful or thrifty in small matters —**penny-wise and pound-foolish** thrifty in small matters but wasteful in major ones

**pen·ny·worth** (-wurth′) n. 1. the amount that can be bought for one penny 2. the value in money of something paid for 3. a small amount

**pe·nol·o·gy** (pē näl′ə jē) n. [Gr. poinē, penalty + -LOGY] the study of the reformation and rehabilitation of criminals and of prison management —**pe·no·log·i·cal** (pē′nə läj′i k'l) adj. —**pe·nol′o·gist** n.

**pen pal** a person, esp. a stranger in another country, with whom one arranges to exchange letters

**Pen·sa·co·la** (pen′sə kō′lə) [< Choctaw, hair people < pansha, hair + okla, people] seaport in NW Fla., on the Gulf of Mexico: pop. 58,000

**pen·sion** (pen′shən; for n. 3, pän′sē än′, Fr. pän syōn′) n. [< MFr. < L. pensio < pp. of pendere, to pay] 1. a regular payment, not wages, to one who has fulfilled certain requirements, as of service, age, disability, etc. 2. a regular payment, not a fee, given to an artist, etc. by his patron; subsidy 3. in France, etc., a) a boardinghouse b) room and board —vt. to grant a pension to —**pension off** to dismiss from service with a pension —**pen′sion·a·ble** adj. —**pen′sion·ar′y** adj., n. —**pen′sion·er** n.

**pen·sive** (pen′siv) adj. [< OFr. < penser < L. pensare, to consider, freq. of pendere, to weigh] 1. thinking deeply, often of sad or melancholy things 2. expressing deep thoughtfulness, often with some sadness —**pen′sive·ly** adv. —**pen′sive·ness** n.

**pen·stock** (pen′stäk′) n. [PEN + STOCK] 1. a sluice for controlling the flow of water 2. a tube or trough for carrying water to a water wheel

**pent** (pent) alt. pt. & pp. of PEN[1] —adj. held or kept in; penned (often with up)

**penta-** [Gr. penta- < pente, five] a combining form meaning five: also, before a vowel, **pent-**

**pen·ta·gon** (pen′tə gän′) n. [< L. < Gr.: see prec. & -GON] a plane figure with five angles and five sides —**the Pentagon** a five-sided building in Arlington, Va., housing the Department of Defense; hence, the U.S. military establishment —**pen·tag′o·nal** (-tag′ə n'l) adj.

**pen·ta·he·dron** (pen′tə hē′drən) n., pl. **-drons, -dra** (-drə) [ModL.: see PENTA- & -HEDRON] a solid figure with five plane surfaces —**pen′ta·he′dral** adj.

**pen·tam·er·ous** (pen tam′ər əs) adj. [PENTA- + -MEROUS] Biol. made up of five parts: also written **5-merous**

**pen·tam·e·ter** (-ə tər) n. [L. < Gr.: see PENTA- & METER[1]] 1. a line of verse containing five metrical feet 2. verse consisting of pentameters —adj. having five metrical feet

**Pen·ta·teuch** (pen′tə tōōk′, -tyōōk′) n. [< LL. < Gr. < penta-, five + teuchos, a book] the first five books of the Bible

**pen·tath·lon** (pen tath′län, -lən) n. [< Gr. < penta-, five + athlon, a contest] an athletic contest in which each contestant takes part in five track and field events

**pen·ta·va·lent** (pen′tə vā′lənt) adj. 1. having a valence of five 2. same as QUINQUEVALENT (sense 1)

**Pen·te·cost** (pen′tə kôst′, -käst′) n. [< LL. < Gr. pentēkostē (hēmera), the fiftieth (day) after Passover] 1. same as SHAVUOT 2. a Christian festival on the seventh Sunday after Easter, celebrating the descent of the Holy Spirit upon the Apostles; Whitsunday —**Pen′te·cos′tal** adj.

**pent·house** (pent′hous′) n. [< MFr. apentis, ult. < L. appendere, APPEND] 1. a small structure with a sloping roof, or such a roof, attached to the side of a building 2. an apartment or houselike structure built on the roof of a building

**pen·tode** (pen′tōd) n. [PENT(A)- + -ODE] an electron tube containing five electrodes, usually a cathode, anode, and three grids

**Pen·to·thal Sodium** (pen′tə thôl′) a trademark for THIOPENTAL SODIUM: often clipped to **Pentothal**

**pent-up** (pent′up′) adj. held in check; curbed; confined [pent-up emotion]

**pe·nu·che, pe·nu·chi** (pə nōō′chē) n. [var. of PANOCHA] a fudgelike candy made of brown sugar, milk, butter, and, sometimes, nuts

**pe·nult** (pē′nult, pi nult′) n. [< L. < paene, almost + ultimus, last] the one next to the last; specif., the second last syllable in a word

**pe·nul·ti·mate** (pi nul′tə mit) adj. 1. next to the last 2. of the penult —n. same as PENULT —**pe·nul′ti·mate·ly** adv.

**pe·num·bra** (pi num′brə) n., pl. **-brae** (-brē), **-bras** [ModL. < L. paene, almost + umbra, shade] 1. the partly lighted area surrounding the complete shadow of a body, as the moon, in full eclipse 2. the less dark region around the central area of a sunspot 3. a vague, indefinite, or borderline area —**pe·num′bral** adj.

**pe·nu·ri·ous** (pə nyoor′ē əs, -noor′-) adj. 1. unwilling to part with money or possessions; miserly; stingy 2. characterized by penury; destitute —**pe·nu′ri·ous·ly** adv. —**pe·nu′ri·ous·ness** n.

**pen·u·ry** (pen′yə rē) n. [< L. penuria, want] lack of money, property, or necessities; destitution

**pe·on** (pē′än, -ən) n. [< Sp. < ML. pedo, foot soldier] 1. in Latin America, a person of the laboring class 2. in the SW U.S., formerly, a person forced into servitude to work off a debt 3. an exploited laborer

**pe·on·age** (pē′ə nij) n. 1. the condition of a peon 2. the system by which debtors or legal prisoners are forced to labor for their creditors or for persons who lease their services from the state

**pe·o·ny** (pē′ə nē) n., pl. **-nies** [< OE. & OFr. < L. < Gr. Paiōn, epithet for Apollo, god of medicine: from its former medicinal use] 1. any of a group of plants with large pink, white, red, or yellow, showy flowers 2. the flower

**peo·ple** (pē′p'l) n., pl. **-ple**; for 1 & 10, **-ples** [< Anglo-Fr. < OFr. < L. populus, nation] 1. all the persons of a racial, national, religious, linguistic, or cultural group; nation, race, ethnic group, etc. 2. the persons belonging to a certain place, community, or class [the people of Ohio, ple of wealth] 3. the persons under the leadership or control of a particular person or body 4. the members of (someone's) class, occupation, set, race, etc. [the miner spoke for his people] 5. one's relatives or ancestors; family 6. persons without wealth, privilege, etc.; populace 7. the electorate of a state 8. persons considered indefinitely [what will people say?] 9. human beings 10. a group of creatures [the ant people] —vt. **-pled, -pling** to fill with or as with people; populate

**people's front** same as POPULAR FRONT

**Pe·o·ri·a** (pē ôr′ē ə) [< Fr. < Algonquian piwarea, ? he carries a pack] city in C Ill.: pop. 124,000

**pep** (pep) n. [< PEPPER] [Colloq.] energy; vigor; liveliness —vt. **pepped, pep′ping** [Colloq.] to fill with pep; invigorate; stimulate (with up)

**pep·lum** (pep′ləm) n., pl. **-lums, -la** (-lə) [L. < Gr. peplos, a shawl] 1. a large scarf worn draped about the body by women in ancient Greece 2. a flounce attached to the waist of a dress, coat, etc. and extending around the hips

**pep·per** (pep′ər) n. see PLURAL, II, D, 3 [< OE. < L. piper < Gr. peperi] 1. a) a pungent condiment obtained from the small, dried fruits of an East Indian plant: see BLACK PEPPER, WHITE PEPPER b) the plant itself 2. any of various plants possessing aromatic and pungent properties, used as flavoring 3. a) same as CAPSICUM b) the fruit of the capsicum: see RED PEPPER, GREEN PEPPER, SWEET PEPPER 4. any of various pungent spices, as cayenne pepper —vt. 1. to season with ground pepper 2. to sprinkle thickly 3. to shower with many small objects [a roof peppered with hailstones] 4. to beat or hit with quick jabs

**pep·per-and-salt** (-'n sôlt′) adj. speckled with contrasting colors, esp. black and white

**pep·per·corn** (-kôrn′) n. [OE. piporcorn] the dried berry of the black PEPPER (n. 1)

**pep·per·grass** (-gras′) *n.* a plant of the mustard family, with small, whitish flowers and flattened pods

**pepper mill** a hand mill used to grind peppercorns

**pep·per·mint** (-mint′, -mənt) *n.* **1.** a plant of the mint family, with lance-shaped leaves and whitish or purplish flowers **2.** the pungent oil it yields, used for flavoring **3.** a candy flavored with this oil

**pep·per·o·ni** (pep′ə rō′nē) *n., pl.* **-nis, -ni** [< It. *peperoni*] a highly spiced Italian sausage

**pepper pot** any of various stews or soups of vegetables, meat, etc. flavored with hot spices

**pepper shaker** a container with a perforated top, for sprinkling ground pepper: also **pep′per·box′** (-bäks′) *n.*

**pepper tree** a S. American ornamental tree with loose clusters of yellowish flowers and pinkish-red berries

**pep·per·y** (-ē) *adj.* **1.** of, like, or highly seasoned with pepper **2.** sharp or fiery, as speech or writing **3.** hot-tempered; irritable —**pep′per·i·ness** *n.*

**pep pill** [Slang] any of various pills containing a stimulant, esp. amphetamine

**pep·py** (pep′ē) *adj.* **-pi·er, -pi·est** [Colloq.] full of pep, or energy; brisk; vigorous; spirited —**pep′pi·ly** *adv.* —**pep′pi·ness** *n.*

**pep·sin** (pep′s'n) *n.* [G. < Gr. < *peptein*, to digest] **1.** an enzyme secreted in the stomach, aiding in the digestion of proteins **2.** an extract of pepsin from the stomachs of calves, etc., formerly used to help in digesting food

**pep talk** a talk, as to an athletic team by its coach, to instill enthusiasm, etc.

**pep·tic** (pep′tik) *adj.* [< L. < Gr. < *peptein*, to digest] **1.** of or aiding digestion **2.** of or relating to pepsin **3.** related to, or caused to some extent by, digestive secretions [a *peptic* ulcer]

**pep·tone** (-tōn) *n.* [< G. < Gr. *peptos*, digested] any of a group of soluble and diffusible derived proteins formed by the action of enzymes on proteins, as in digestion —**pep·ton′ic** (-tän′ik) *adj.*

**Pepys** (pēps; *occas.* peps, pep′is, pē′pis), **Samuel** 1633-1703; Eng. government official, known for his diary

**Pe·quot** (pē′kwät) *n.* [< Algonquian *paquatanog*, destroyers] **1.** *pl.* **-quots, -quot** any member of a tribe of Indians in Connecticut until dispersed in 1637 **2.** their Algonquian language —*adj.* of this tribe

**per** (pur; *unstressed* pər) *prep.* [L.] **1.** through; by; by means of **2.** for each [fifty cents *per* yard] **3.** [Colloq.] according to [*per* his instructions]

**per-** [< L. *per*, through] *a prefix meaning:* **1.** through; throughout [*perceive, percolate*] **2.** thoroughly; very [*persuade*] **3.** *Chem.* containing a specified element or radical in its maximum, or a relatively high, valence [*peroxide*]

**Per.** **1.** Persia **2.** Persian

**per.** **1.** period **2.** person

**per·ad·ven·ture** (pur′əd ven′chər) *adv.* [< OFr. < *par*, by + *aventure*, chance] [Archaic] **1.** possibly **2.** by chance —*n.* chance; doubt

**per·am·bu·late** (pər am′byoo lāt′) *vt.* **-lat′ed, -lat′ing** [< L. pp. of *perambulare* < *per*, through + *ambulare*, to walk] to walk through, over, around, etc., as in inspecting —*vi.* to stroll —**per·am′bu·la′tion** *n.* —**per·am′bu·la·to′ry** (-lə tôr′ē) *adj.*

**per·am·bu·la·tor** (-lāt′ər) *n.* **1.** a person who perambulates **2.** [Chiefly Brit.] a baby carriage

**per an·num** (pər an′əm) [L.] by the year; yearly

**per·cale** (pər kāl′, -kal′) *n.* [Fr. < Per. *pargāla*] closely woven cotton cloth, used for sheets, etc.

**per cap·i·ta** (pər kap′ə tə) [ML., lit., by heads] for each person

**per·ceive** (pər sēv′) *vt., vi.* **-ceived′, -ceiv′ing** [< OFr. < L. *percipere* < *per*, through + *capere*, to take] **1.** to grasp or take in mentally **2.** to become aware (of) through the senses —**per·ceiv′a·ble** *adj.* —**per·ceiv′a·bly** *adv.* —**per·ceiv′er** *n.*

**per·cent** (pər sent′) *adv., adj.* [< It. *per centum*] in or for every hundred [a 20 *percent* rate means 20 in every hundred]: symbol, %: also **per cent** or, now rare, **per cent.**, **per cen·tum** (sen′təm) —*n.* **1.** a hundredth part **2.** [Colloq.] percentage **3.** [*pl.*] bonds, etc. bearing regular interest of a (stated) percentage [the four *percents*]

**per·cent·age** (-ij) *n.* **1.** a given part or amount in every hundred **2.** any amount, as of interest, stated in percent **3.** part; portion [a *percentage* of the audience] **4.** [Colloq.] *a)* use; advantage *b)* [*usually pl.*] a risk based on favorable odds

**per·cen·tile** (pər sen′til, -sent′'l) *n.* *Statistics* **1.** any value in a series dividing the distribution of its members into 100 groups of equal frequency **2.** any of these groups —*adj.* of a percentile

**per·cept** (pur′sept) *n.* [< PERCEPTION] a recognizable sensation or impression received by the mind through the senses

**per·cep·ti·ble** (pər sep′tə b'l) *adj.* that can be perceived —**per·cep′ti·bil′i·ty** *n.* —**per·cep′ti·bly** *adv.*

**per·cep·tion** (-shən) *n.* [< L. < pp. of *percipere*: see PERCEIVE] **1.** *a)* the act of perceiving or the ability to perceive; awareness *b)* insight or intuition **2.** the understanding, knowledge, etc. or a specific idea, concept, etc. got by perceiving —**per·cep′tion·al** *adj.* —**per·cep′tu·al** (-chōō əl) *adj.*

**per·cep·tive** (-tiv) *adj.* **1.** of or capable of perception **2.** able to perceive quickly and easily —**per·cep′tive·ly** *adv.* —**per·cep′tive·ness**, **per′cep·tiv′i·ty** *n.*

**perch**[1] (purch) *n., pl.* **perch, perch′es:** see PLURAL, II, D, 2 [< OFr. < L. < Gr. *perkē*] **1.** a small, spiny-finned, freshwater food fish **2.** any of various bony, spiny-rayed, usually saltwater fishes

**perch**[2] (purch) *n.* [< OFr. < L. *pertica*, a pole] **1.** a horizontal pole, branch, etc. serving as a roost for birds **2.** any resting place, esp. a high or insecure one **3.** *a)* a measure of length, equal to 5½ yards *b)* a measure of area, equal to 30¼ square yards —*vi., vt.* to alight and rest, or place, on or as on a perch —**perch′er** *n.*

**per·chance** (pər chans′) *adv.* [< OFr. *par*, by + *chance*, chance] [Archaic] **1.** by chance **2.** perhaps; possibly

**Per·che·ron** (pur′chə rän′, -shə-) *n.* [Fr. < *Perche*, region in France] a breed of large, fast-trotting draft horses: also **Percheron Norman**

**per·cip·i·ent** (pər sip′ē ənt) *adj.* perceiving, esp. keenly or readily —*n.* a person who perceives —**per·cip′i·ence, per·cip′i·en·cy** *n.* —**per·cip′i·ent·ly** *adv.*

**Per·ci·val** (pur′sə v'l) [< OFr., prob. < *perce val*, pierce valley] **1.** a masculine name **2.** a knight in Arthurian legend, who saw the Holy Grail: usually **Per′ci·vale** (-v'l)

**per·co·late** (pur′kə lāt′) *vt.* **-lat′ed, -lat′ing** [< L. pp. of *percolare* < *per*, through + *colare*, to strain] **1.** to pass (a liquid) gradually through a porous substance; filter **2.** to drain or ooze through (a porous substance); permeate **3.** to brew (coffee) in a percolator —*vi.* **1.** to ooze through a porous substance **2.** to permeate **3.** to start bubbling up, as percolated coffee —**per′co·la′tion** *n.*

**per·co·la·tor** (-lāt′ər) *n.* a coffeepot in which boiling water bubbles up through a tube and filters back down through the ground coffee

**per·cus·sion** (pər kush′ən) *n.* [< L. < pp. of *percutere*, to strike] **1.** the hitting of one body against another, as the hammer of a firearm against a powder cap **2.** the impact of sound waves on the ear **3.** percussion instruments collectively **4.** *Med.* the tapping of the chest, back, etc. with the fingers to determine from the sound produced the condition of internal organs —**per·cus′sive** *adj.* —**per·cus′sive·ly** *adv.* —**per·cus′sive·ness** *n.*

**percussion cap** a small paper or metal container holding a charge that explodes when struck

**percussion instrument** a musical instrument in which the tone is produced when some part is struck, as the drums, cymbals, xylophone, etc.

**per·cus·sion·ist** (-ist) *n.* a musician who plays percussion instruments

**Per·cy** (pur′sē) **1.** a masculine name: see PERCIVAL **2.** **Sir Henry,** 1364-1403; Eng. soldier & rebel against Henry IV

**per di·em** (dē′əm, dī′əm) [L.] **1.** by the day; daily **2.** a daily allowance, as for expenses

**per·di·tion** (pər dish′ən) *n.* [< OFr. < LL. < L. pp. of *perdere*, to lose] **1.** [Archaic] complete and irreparable loss; ruin **2.** *Theol. a)* the loss of the soul; damnation *b)* same as HELL

**†père** (per) *n.* [Fr.] father: often used after the surname, like English *Senior* [Dumas *père*]

**per·e·gri·nate** (per′ə gri nāt′) *vt., vi.* **-nat′ed, -nat′ing** [< L. pp. of *peregrinari* < *peregrinus*: see PILGRIM] to travel, esp. walk (along or through) —**per′e·gri·na′tion** *n.* —**per′e·gri·na′tor** *n.*

**per·e·grine (falcon)** (per′ə grin, -grēn′) [see prec.] a very swift European falcon with a spotted breast: used in falconry

**per·emp·to·ry** (pə remp′tər ē) *adj.* [< LL. < L. < pp. of *perimere*, to destroy < *per-*, intens. + *emere*, to take] **1.** *Law a)* barring further action, debate, etc.; final; decisive *b)* not requiring that any cause be shown [a *peremptory* challenge of a juror] **2.** that cannot be denied, delayed, etc., as a command **3.** intolerantly positive; dogmatic [a *peremptory* manner] —**per·emp′to·ri·ly** *adv.* —**per·emp′to·ri·ness** *n.*

**per·en·ni·al** (pə ren′ē əl) *adj.* [< L. < *per*, through + *annus*, a year] **1.** lasting or active throughout the whole year **2.** continuing for a long time [a *perennial* youth] **3.** becoming active again and again; perpetual **4.** having a life cycle of more than two years: said of plants —*n.* a perennial plant —**per·en′ni·al·ly** *adv.*

**perf.** **1.** perfect **2.** perforated

**per·fect** (pur′fikt; *for v., usually* pər fekt′) *adj.* [< OFr. < L. pp. of *perficere* < *per*, through + *facere*, to do] **1.** complete in all respects; flawless **2.** in a condition of excellence, as in skill or quality **3.** completely accurate; exact *[a perfect* copy*]* **4.** utter; absolute *[a perfect* fool*]* **5.** *Gram.* expressing a state or action completed at the time of speaking or at the time indicated: verbs have three perfect tenses: present perfect, past perfect, and future perfect **6.** *Music* designating an interval, as an octave, whose character is not altered by inversion and which has no alternative major and minor forms —*vt.* **1.** to bring to completion **2.** to make perfect or more nearly perfect according to a given standard, as by training, etc. —*n.* **1.** the perfect tense **2.** a verb form in this tense —**per·fect′er** *n.* —**per′·fect·ness** *n.*

**per·fect·i·ble** (pər fek′tə b'l) *adj.* that can become, or be made, perfect or more nearly perfect —**per·fect′i·bil′i·ty** *n.*

**per·fec·tion** (pər fek′shən) *n.* **1.** the act or process of perfecting **2.** a being perfect **3.** a person or thing that is the perfect embodiment of some quality —**to perfection** completely; perfectly

**per·fec·tion·ism** (-iz'm) *n.* extreme or obsessive striving for perfection, as in one's work —**per·fec′tion·ist** *n., adj.* —**per·fec′tion·is′tic** *adj.*

**per·fect·ly** (pur′fikt lē) *adv.* **1.** to a perfect degree **2.** completely; fully

**per·fec·to** (pər fek′tō) *n., pl.* **-tos** [Sp., perfect] a cigar of a standard shape, thick in the center and tapering to a point at each end

**perfect participle** *same as* PAST PARTICIPLE

**perfect pitch** *a popular term for* ABSOLUTE PITCH

**per·fer·vid** (pər fur′vid) *adj.* extremely fervid

**per·fi·dy** (pur′fə dē) *n., pl.* **-dies** [< Fr. < L. *perfidia* < *per fidem (decipi)*, (to deceive) through faith] betrayal of trust; treachery —**per·fid·i·ous** (pər fid′ē əs) *adj.* —**per·fid′i·ous·ly** *adv.*

**per·fo·li·ate** (pər fō′lē it, -āt′) *adj.* [< ModL. < L. *per*, through + *folium*, a leaf] having a stem that seems to pass through it: said of a leaf —**per·fo′li·a′tion** *n.*

**per·fo·rate** (pur′fə rāt′; *for adj., usually* -rit) *vt., vi.* **-rat′ed, -rat′ing** [< L. pp. of *perforare* < *per*, through + *forare*, to bore] **1.** to make a hole or holes through, as by punching or boring **2.** to pierce with holes in a row, as a pattern, computer tape, etc. —*adj.* pierced with holes, esp. in a row, for easy tearing: also **per′fo·rat′ed** —**per′fo·ra·ble** *adj.* —**per′fo·ra′tor** *n.*

PERFOLIATE LEAVES

**per·fo·ra·tion** (pur′fə rā′shən) *n.* **1.** a perforating or being perforated **2.** a hole made by piercing, ulceration, etc. **3.** any of a series of punched holes, as those between postage stamps on a sheet

**per·force** (pər fôrs′) *adv.* [< OFr.: see PER & FORCE] by or through necessity; necessarily

**per·form** (pər fôrm′) *vt.* [< Anglo-Fr. < OFr. *parfournir*, to consummate < *par* (< L. *per-*, intens.) + *fornir*, to accomplish] **1.** to act on so as to complete; do (a task, process, etc.) **2.** to fulfill (a promise, etc.) **3.** to render or enact (a piece of music, a dramatic role, etc.) —*vi.* to execute an action or process; esp., to act in a play, dance, etc. before an audience —**per·form′a·ble** *adj.* —**per·form′er** *n.*

**per·form·ance** (-fôr′məns) *n.* **1.** the act of performing; execution, accomplishment, etc. **2.** functioning, usually with regard to effectiveness, as of a machine **3.** a deed or feat **4.** *a)* a formal exhibition or presentation before an audience, as a play; show *b)* one's part in this

**per·fume** (pər fyoom′; *for n., usually* pur′fyoom) *vt.* **-fumed′, -fum′ing** [< MFr. < It. < L. *per-*, intens. + *fumare*, to smoke] **1.** to fill with a pleasing odor **2.** to put perfume on —*n.* **1.** a sweet scent; fragrance **2.** a substance producing a pleasing odor; esp., a volatile oil, as that extracted from flowers

**per·fum·er** (pər fyoo′mər) *n.* **1.** one who makes or sells perfumes **2.** one who or that which perfumes

**per·fum·er·y** (-ē) *n., pl.* **-er·ies** **1.** the trade or art of a perfumer **2.** perfumes collectively **3.** a place where perfume is made or sold

**per·func·to·ry** (pər funk′tər ē) *adj.* [< LL. < L. pp. of *perfungi* < *per-*, intens. + *fungi*, to perform] **1.** done merely as a routine; superficial *[a perfunctory* examination*]* **2.** without concern; indifferent *[a perfunctory* teacher*]* —**per·func′to·ri·ly** *adv.* —**per·func′to·ri·ness** *n.*

**per·go·la** (pur′gə lə) *n.* [It., arbor < L. *pergula*, projecting cover] an arbor, esp. one with an open roof of cross rafters supported on columns, usually with climbing vines

**per·haps** (pər haps′, -aps′) *adv.* [PER + *haps*, pl. of HAP] possibly; maybe

**pe·ri** (pir′ē) *n.* [Per. *part*] *Persian Myth.* **1.** a fairy or elf **2.** any fairylike being

**per·i-** [< Gr. < *peri*] *a prefix meaning:* **1.** around, about *[periscope]* **2.** near *[perigee]*

**per·i·anth** (per′ē anth′) *n.* [< ModL. < Gr. *peri-*, around + *anthos*, a flower] the outer envelope of a flower, including the calyx and corolla

**per·i·car·di·tis** (per′ə kär dīt′is) *n.* inflammation of the pericardium

**per·i·car·di·um** (-kär′dē əm) *n., pl.* **-di·a** (-ə) [ModL. < Gr. < *peri-*, around + *kardia*, heart] in vertebrates, the thin, membranous sac around the heart —**per′i·car′di·al, per′i·car′di·ac′** *adj.*

**per·i·carp** (per′ə kärp′) *n.* [< ModL. < Gr.: see PERI- & -CARP] *Bot.* the wall of a ripened ovary —**per′i·car′pi·al** *adj.*

**Per·i·cles** (per′ə klēz′) 495?–429 B.C.; Athenian statesman & general —**Per′i·cle′an** (-klē′ən) *adj.*

**per·i·cra·ni·um** (per′ə krā′nē əm) *n., pl.* **-ni·a** (-ə) [ModL. < Gr. < *peri-*, around + *kranion*, skull] the tough membrane covering the skull

**per·i·gee** (per′ə jē′) *n.* [< Fr. < ModL. < Gr. < *peri-*, near + *ge*, earth] **1.** the point nearest to the earth, the moon, or another planet, in the orbit of a satellite or spacecraft around it **2.** the lowest or nearest point —**per′i·ge′an, per′i·ge′al** *adj.*

**per·i·he·li·on** (per′ə hē′lē ən, -hēl′yən) *n., pl.* **-li·ons, -li·a** (-ə) [ModL. < Gr. *peri-*, around + *helios*, the sun] the point nearest the sun in the orbit around it of a planet, comet, or man-made satellite: cf. APHELION

**per·il** (per′əl) *n.* [OFr. < L. *periculum*, danger] **1.** exposure to harm or injury; danger **2.** something that may cause harm or injury —*vt.* **-iled** or **-illed, -il·ing** or **-il·ling** to expose to danger

**per·il·ous** (-əs) *adj.* involving peril or risk; dangerous —**per′il·ous·ly** *adv.* —**per′il·ous·ness** *n.*

**pe·rim·e·ter** (pə rim′ə tər) *n.* [< L. < Gr. < *peri-*, around + *metron*, a measure] **1.** the outer boundary of a figure or area **2.** the total length of this —**per′i·met′ric** (per′ə-met′rik), **per′i·met′ri·cal** *adj.* —**per′i·met′ri·cal·ly** *adv.*

**per·i·ne·um** (per′ə nē′əm) *n., pl.* **-ne′a** (-ə) [ModL. < Gr. < *peri-*, around + *inein*, to discharge] the region between the thighs; specif., the small area between the anus and the vulva or the scrotum —**per′i·ne′al** *adj.*

**pe·ri·od** (pir′ē əd) *n.* [< MFr. < L. < Gr. *periodos*, a cycle < *peri-*, around < *hodos*, way] **1.** the interval between the successive occurrences of an astronomical event, as between two full moons **2.** a portion of time distinguished by certain processes, conditions, etc.; stage *[a period of change]* **3.** any of the portions of time into which a game, school day, etc. is divided **4.** the full course, or one of the stages, of a disease **5.** the menses **6.** an end or conclusion *[death put a period to his plans]* **7.** a subdivision of a geologic era **8.** *Gram.* a) a sentence, esp. a well-balanced sentence b) the pause in speaking or a mark of punctuation (.) used at the end of a declarative sentence c) the dot (.) following many abbreviations **9.** *Physics* the interval of time necessary for a complete cycle of a regularly recurring motion —*adj.* of or like that of an earlier period or age *[period furniture]*

**pe·ri·od·ic** (pir′ē äd′ik) *adj.* **1.** appearing or recurring at regular intervals *[a periodic fever]* **2.** occurring from time to time; intermittent **3.** of or characterized by periods **4.** of a sentence (**periodic sentence**) in which the essential elements are withheld until the end

**pe·ri·od·i·cal** (-i k'l) *adj.* **1.** *same as* PERIODIC **2.** published at regular intervals, as weekly, monthly, etc. **3.** of a periodical —*n.* a periodical publication —**pe′ri·od′i·cal·ly** *adv.*

**pe·ri·o·dic·i·ty** (pir′ē ə dis′ə tē) *n., pl.* **-ties** the tendency or fact of recurring at regular intervals

**periodic law** the law that properties of chemical elements recur periodically when the elements are arranged in order of their atomic numbers

**periodic table** an arrangement of the chemical elements according to their atomic numbers, to exhibit the periodic law

**per·i·o·don·tal** (per′ē ə dän′t'l) *adj.* [PERI- + -ODONT + -AL] occurring around a tooth or affecting the gums

**per·i·os·te·um** (per′ē äs′tē əm) *n., pl.* **-te·a** (-ə) [ModL. < L. < Gr. < *peri-*, around + *osteon*, a bone] the membrane of connective tissue covering all bones except at the joints —**per′i·os′te·al** *adj.*

**per·i·pa·tet·ic** (per′i pə tet′ik) *adj.* [< Fr. < L. < Gr., ult. < *peri-*, around + *patein*, to walk] **1.** [P-] of the philosophy or followers of Aristotle, who walked about while he was teaching **2.** walking or moving about; itinerant —*n.* **1.** [P-] a follower of Aristotle **2.** a person who walks from place to place —**per′i·pa·tet′i·cal·ly** *adv.*

**pe·riph·er·al** (pə rif′ər əl) *adj.* **1.** of, belonging to, or forming a periphery **2.** *Anat.* of, at, or near the surface of the body **3.** merely incidental; tangential *[of peripheral interest]* —*n.* a piece of equipment that can be used with a computer to increase its functional range or efficiency, as a printer or disc —**pe·riph′er·al·ly** *adv.*

**pe·riph·er·y** (-ē) *n., pl.* **-er·ies** [< MFr. < LL. < Gr. < *peri-*, around + *pherein*, to bear] **1.** a boundary line or outside surface, esp. of a rounded figure **2.** surrounding space or area

**pe·riph·ra·sis** (pə rif′rə sis) *n., pl.* **-ses′** (-sēz′) [L. < Gr. < *peri-*, around + *phrazein*, to speak] the use of many words where a few would do; roundabout way of speaking: also **per·i·phrase** (per′ə frāz′)

**per·i·phras·tic** (per′ə fras′tik) *adj.* **1.** of, like, or expressed in periphrasis **2.** *Gram.* formed with a particle or auxiliary verb instead of by inflection, as the phrase *did sing* used for *sang* —**per′i·phras′ti·cal·ly** *adv.*

**pe·rique** (pə rēk′) *n.* [AmFr.] a strong, rich black tobacco grown in Louisiana, used in blending

**per·i·sarc** (per′ə särk′) *n.* [< PERI- + Gr. *sarx*, flesh] the tough, nonliving, outer skeleton layer of many hydroid colonies

**per·i·scope** (per′ə skōp′) *n.* [PERI- + -SCOPE] an optical instrument consisting of a tube equipped with lenses and mirrors or prisms, so arranged that a person looking through one end can see objects reflected at the other end; used on submerged submarines, etc. —**per′i·scop′ic** (-skäp′ik) *adj.*

**per·ish** (per′ish) *vi.* [< OFr. < L. *perire*, to perish < *per-*, intens. + *ire*, to go] **1.** to be destroyed, ruined, or wiped out **2.** to die; esp., to die a violent or untimely death —**perish the thought!** do not even consider such a possibility!

**per·ish·a·ble** (-ə b'l) *adj.* that may perish; esp., liable to spoil, as some foods —*n.* something, esp. a food, liable to spoil or deteriorate —**per′ish·a·bil′i·ty, per′ish·a·ble·ness n.**

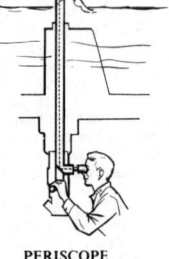

PERISCOPE

**per·i·stal·sis** (per′ə stôl′sis, -stal′-) *n., pl.* **-ses** (-sēz) [ModL. < Gr. < *peri-*, around + *stellein*, to place] the wavelike muscular contractions and dilations of the walls of the alimentary canal and certain other hollow organs, that move the contents onward —**per′i·stal′tic** *adj.*

**per·i·style** (per′ə stil′) *n.* [< Fr. < L. < Gr. < *peri-*, around + *stylos*, a column] **1.** a row of columns forming an enclosure or supporting a roof **2.** any area so formed, as a court —**per′i·sty′lar** (-sti′lər) *adj.*

**per·i·to·ne·um** (per′it ′n ē′əm) *n., pl.* **-ne′a** (-ə), **-ne′ums** [LL. < Gr. < *peri-*, around + *teinein*, to stretch] the serous membrane lining the abdominal cavity and covering the visceral organs —**per′i·to·ne′al** *adj.*

**per·i·to·ni·tis** (-it′əs) *n.* inflammation of the peritoneum

**per·i·wig** (per′ə wig′) *n.* [earlier *perwyke* < Fr. *perruque*, PERUKE] a wig, formerly worn by men

**per·i·win·kle¹** (per′ə win′k'l) *n.* [< OE. < L. *pervinca*] a European creeper with blue, white, or pink flowers, grown as a ground cover

**per·i·win·kle²** (per′ə win′k'l) *n.* [OE. *pinewincle*] **1.** any of various small saltwater snails having a thick, cone-shaped shell **2.** such a shell

**per·jure** (pur′jər) *vt.* **-jured, -jur·ing** [< OFr. < L. < *per*, through + *jurare*, to swear] to make (oneself) guilty of perjury —**per′jur·er n.**

**per·jured** (-jərd) *adj.* guilty of, or characterized by, perjury: also **per·ju·ri·ous** (pər jur′ē əs)

**per·ju·ry** (-jər ē) *n., pl.* **-ries** [< OFr. < L. < *perjurus*, false] **1.** the willful telling of a lie while under oath **2.** the breaking of any oath

**perk¹** (purk) *vt.* [< ? ONormFr. *perquer*, to perch] **1.** to raise (the head, ears, etc.) briskly (often with *up*) **2.** to make smart in appearance (often with *up* or *out*) **3.** to give or restore freshness, vivacity, etc. to (usually with *up*) —*vi.* **1.** to straighten one's posture jauntily **2.** to become lively or recover one's spirits (with *up*)

**perk²** (purk) *vt., vi. colloq.* clip of PERCOLATE

**perk³** (purk) *n.* [Chiefly Brit. Colloq.] clipped form of PERQUISITE

**perk·y** (pur′kē) *adj.* **perk′i·er, perk′i·est 1.** self-confident **2.** sprightly; jaunty —**perk′i·ly** *adv.* —**perk′i·ness n.**

**Perm** (perm) city in E European R.S.F.S.R.: pop. 850,000

**per·ma·frost** (pur′mə frôst′, -fräst′) *n.* [PERMA(NENT) + FROST] permanently frozen subsoil

**per·ma·nence** (pur′mə nəns) *n.* the state or quality of being permanent

**per·ma·nen·cy** (-nən sē) *n.* **1.** *same as* PERMANENCE **2.** *pl.* **-cies** something permanent

**per·ma·nent** (-nənt) *adj.* [MFr. < L. prp. of *permanere* <

*per*, through + *manere*, to remain] lasting or intended to last indefinitely or for a relatively long time —*n. colloq.* clip of PERMANENT WAVE —**per′ma·nent·ly** *adv.*

**permanent wave** a hair wave, produced by applying heat or chemicals, that is relatively long lasting

**per·man·ga·nate** (pər maŋ′gə nāt′) *n.* a salt of permanganic acid, generally dark purple

**per·man·gan·ic acid** (pur′man gan′ik) an unstable acid, $HMnO_4$, that is an oxidizing agent

**per·me·a·bil·i·ty** (pur′mē ə bil′ə tē) *n.* **1.** a being permeable **2.** *Physics a)* the measure of ease with which magnetic lines of force are carried *b)* the rate of diffusion of a fluid through a porous body

**per·me·a·ble** (pur′mē ə b'l) *adj.* that can be permeated, as by liquids —**per′me·a·bly** *adv.*

**per·me·ate** (-āt′) *vt.* **-at′ed, -at′ing** [< L. pp. of *permeare* < *per*, through + *meare*, to glide] to pass into or through and affect every part of; spread through *[ink permeates blotting paper]* —*vi.* to spread or diffuse (with *through* or *among*) —**per′me·a′tion, per′me·ance n.** —**per′me·a′tive** (-āt′iv) *adj.*

**Per·mi·an** (pur′mē ən) *adj.* [after *Perm*, former province of Russia] designating or of the seventh and last period of the Paleozoic Era —**the Permian** the Permian Period or its rocks: see GEOLOGY, chart

**per·mis·si·ble** (pər mis′ə b'l) *adj.* that can be permitted; allowable —**per·mis′si·bil′i·ty n.** —**per·mis′si·bly** *adv.*

**per·mis·sion** (pər mish′ən) *n.* the act of permitting; esp., formal consent; leave

**per·mis·sive** (-mis′iv) *adj.* **1.** giving permission **2.** allowing freedom; indulgent —**per·mis′sive·ly** *adv.* —**per·mis′sive·ness n.**

**per·mit** (pər mit′; *for n., usually* pur′mit) *vt.* **-mit′ted, -mit′ting** [< L. < *per*, through + *mittere*, to send] **1.** to allow; consent to *[smoking is not permitted]* **2.** to give permission to; authorize *[to permit women to vote]* **3.** to give opportunity for *[to permit light to enter]* —*vi.* to give opportunity *[if time permits]* —*n.* **1.** *same as* PERMISSION **2.** a document granting permission; license —**per·mit′ter n.**

**per·mu·ta·tion** (pur′myoo tā′shən) *n.* **1.** any radical alteration **2.** *Math.* any one of the total number of groupings, or subsets, into which a group, or set, of elements can be arranged: the permutations of 1, 2, and 3 taken two at a time are 12, 21, 13, 31, 23, 32 —**per′mu·ta′tion·al** *adj.*

**per·mute** (pər myoot′) *vt.* **-mut′ed, -mut′ing** [< L. < *permutare* < *per-*, intens. + *mutare*, to change] to rearrange the order or sequence of —**per·mut′a·ble** *adj.*

**Per·nam·bu·co** (pur′nəm boo′kō; *Port.* per′näm boo′koo) *same as* RECIFE

**per·ni·cious** (pər nish′əs) *adj.* [< Fr. < L. < *pernecare* < *per*, thoroughly + *necare*, to kill < *nex* (gen. *necis*), death] **1.** causing great injury, destruction, or ruin **2.** [Rare] wicked; evil —**per·ni′cious·ly** *adv.* —**per·ni′cious·ness n.**

**pernicious anemia** a form of anemia characterized by a reduction of the red blood cells and by gastrointestinal and nervous disturbances, etc.

**per·nick·et·y** (pər nik′ə tē) *adj. same as* PERSNICKETY

**per·o·rate** (per′ə rāt′) *vi.* **-rat′ed, -rat′ing 1.** to make a lengthy oration **2.** to sum up or conclude a speech

**per·o·ra·tion** (per′ə rā′shən) *n.* [< L. < pp. of *perorare* < *per*, through + *orare*, to speak] **1.** the concluding part of a speech, including a summing up **2.** a bombastic speech

**per·ox·ide** (pə räk′sīd) *n.* [PER- + OXIDE] any oxide containing the oxygen ($O_2$) group linked by a single bond; specif., hydrogen peroxide —*vt.* **-id·ed, -id·ing** to bleach (hair, etc.) with hydrogen peroxide —*adj.* bleached with hydrogen peroxide

**per·pen·dic·u·lar** (pur′pən dik′yə lər) *adj.* [< OFr. < L. < *perpendiculum*, plumb line < *per-*, intens. + *pendere*, to hang] **1.** at right angles to a given plane or line **2.** exactly upright; vertical **3.** very steep —*n.* **1.** a line at right angles to another line or plane **2.** a perpendicular position —**per′pen·dic′u·lar′i·ty** (-lar′ə tē) *n.* —**per′pen·dic′u·lar·ly** *adv.*

PERPENDICULAR

**per·pe·trate** (pur′pə trāt′) *vt.* **-trat′ed, -trat′ing** [< L. pp. of *perpetrare* < *per*, thoroughly + *patrare*, to effect] **1.** to do (something evil, criminal, or offensive) **2.** to commit (a blunder), impose (a hoax), etc. —**per′pe·tra′tion n.** —**per′pe·tra′tor n.**

**per·pet·u·al** (pər pech′oo wəl) *adj.* [< OFr. < L. < *perpetuus*, constant] **1.** lasting forever or for an indefinitely long time **2.** continuing indefinitely without interruption; constant *[a perpetual nuisance]* —**per·pet′u·al·ly** *adv.*

**perpetual motion** the motion of a hypothetical device which, once set in motion, would operate indefinitely by creating its own energy

**per·pet·u·ate** (pər pech′oo wāt′) *vt.* **-at′ed, -at′ing** to make perpetual; cause to continue or be remembered —**per·pet′u·a′tion n.** —**per·pet′u·a′tor n.**

**per·pe·tu·i·ty** (pur'pə tōō'ə tē, -tyōō'-) *n., pl.* -ties 1. a being perpetual 2. something perpetual, as a pension to be paid indefinitely 3. unlimited time; eternity —**in perpetuity** forever

**per·plex** (pər pleks') *vt.* [< MFr. < L. *perplexus*, confused < *per*, through + pp. of *plectere*, to twist] 1. to make (a person) uncertain, hesitant, etc.; confuse 2. to make intricate or complicated —**per·plexed'** *adj.* —**per·plex'ing** *adj.* —**per·plex'ing·ly** *adv.*

**per·plex·i·ty** (-plek'sə tē) *n.* 1. the state of being perplexed; bewilderment 2. *pl.* -ties something that perplexes

**per·qui·site** (pur'kwə zit) *n.* [< ML. < pp. of *perquirere*, to obtain < L. < *per-*, intens. + *quaerere*, to seek] 1. something additional to regular profit or pay, resulting from one's employment 2. a tip or gratuity 3. a prerogative or right, by virtue of one's status, position, etc.

**Per·ry** (per'ē) 1. [? < Fr. < L. *Petrus*, Peter] a masculine name 2. **Matthew Cal·braith** (kal'brāth), 1794–1858; U.S. naval officer 3. **Oliver Haz·ard** (haz'ərd), 1785–1819; U.S. naval officer: brother of *prec.*

**Pers.** 1. Persia 2. Persian

**pers.** 1. person 2. personal

**per se** (pur' sē', sā') [L.] by (or in) itself; intrinsically

**per second per second** for each second every second: used of a rate of acceleration

**per·se·cute** (pur'sə kyōōt') *vt.* -cut'ed, -cut'ing [< MFr. < L. < *persequi*, to pursue < *per*, through + *sequi*, to follow] 1. to afflict constantly so as to injure or distress, esp. for reasons of religion, politics, or race 2. to annoy constantly [*persecuted* by mosquitoes] —**per'se·cu'tion** *n.* —**per'se·cu'tive** *adj.* —**per'se·cu'tor** *n.*

**Per·seph·o·ne** (pər sef'ə nē) *Gr. Myth.* the daughter of Zeus and Demeter, abducted by Hades (Pluto) to be his wife: identified with the Roman goddess Proserpina

**Per·seus** (pur'syōōs, -sē əs) 1. *Gr. Myth.* a son of Zeus and slayer of Medusa: he married Andromeda after rescuing her from a sea monster 2. a N constellation

**per·se·ver·ance** (pur'sə vir'əns) *n.* 1. the act of persevering 2. persistence; steadfastness

**per·sev·er·ate** (pər sev'ə rāt') *vi.* -at'ed, -at'ing to experience or display perseveration

**per·sev·er·a·tion** (pər sev'ə rā'shən) *n.* the tendency of an idea, experience, or response to persist in an individual

**per·se·vere** (pur'sə vir') *vi.* -vered', -ver'ing [< OFr. < L. < *perseverus* < *per-*, intens. + *severus*, severe] to continue in some effort, course of action, etc. in spite of difficulty, opposition, etc.; persist —**per'se·ver'ing·ly** *adv.*

**Per·shing** (pur'shing), **John Joseph** 1860–1948; U.S. general: commander of U.S. forces in World War I

**Per·sia** (pur'zhə, -shə) 1. *former official name of* IRAN 2. *same as* PERSIAN EMPIRE

**Per·sian** (-zhən, -shən) *adj.* of Persia, its people, their language, etc.; Iranian —*n.* 1. a native or inhabitant of Persia 2. the Iranian language of Iran

**Persian Empire** ancient empire in SW Asia, including at its peak the area from the Indus River to the W borders of Asia Minor & Egypt: founded by Cyrus the Great & conquered by Alexander the Great

**Persian Gulf** arm of the Arabian Sea, between SW Iran & Arabia

**Persian lamb** 1. the lamb of the karakul sheep 2. the black or gray pelt of newborn karakul lambs, having small, tight curls

**Persian rug** (or **carpet**) an Oriental rug made in Persia, with a richly colored, intricate pattern

**per·si·flage** (pur'sə fläzh') *n.* [Fr. < *persifler*, to banter < *per-* (see PER-) + *siffler*, to whistle] 1. a light, frivolous style of writing or speaking 2. talk or writing of this kind

**per·sim·mon** (pər sim'ən) *n.* [< AmInd.] 1. any of various trees with white flowers, hard wood, and plumlike fruit 2. the fruit, sour and astringent when green, but sweet and edible when ripe

**per·sist** (pər sist', -zist') *vi.* [< MFr. < L. < *per*, through + *sistere*, to cause to stand] 1. to refuse to give up, esp. when faced with opposition 2. to continue insistently, as in repeating a question 3. to endure; remain; last

**per·sist·ence** (-sis'təns, -zis'-) *n.* 1. a persisting; stubborn continuance 2. a persistent or lasting quality; tenacity: also **per·sist'en·cy**

**per·sist·ent** (-tənt) *adj.* 1. continuing, esp. in the face of opposition, etc.; stubborn 2. continuing to exist or endure 3. constantly repeated; continued —**per·sist'ent·ly** *adv.*

**per·snick·e·ty** (pər snik'ə tē) *adj.* [< Scot. dial.] [Colloq.] 1. too particular or precise; fussy 2. showing or requiring careful treatment

**per·son** (pur's'n) *n.* [< OFr. < L. *persona*, lit., actor's mask, hence a person] 1. a human being; individual man, woman, or child 2. *a*) a living human body *b*) bodily

appearance [to be neat about one's *person*] 3. personality; self 4. *Gram. a*) division into three sets of pronouns (**personal pronouns**), and, usually, corresponding verb forms, to identify the subject: see FIRST PERSON, SECOND PERSON, THIRD PERSON *b*) any of these sets 5. *Law* any individual or incorporated group having certain legal rights and responsibilities —**in person** actually present

**-per·son** (pur's'n) *a combining form meaning* person (of either sex) in a specified activity: used in coinages to avoid the masculine implication of *-man* ["chairperson"]

**per·so·na** (pər sō'nə) *n., pl.* -nae (-nē); for sense 2, -nas [L.: see prec.] 1. [*pl.*] the characters of a drama, novel, etc. 2. *Psychol.* the outer personality presented to others by an individual

**per·son·a·ble** (pur's'n ə b'l) *adj.* having a pleasing appearance and personality; attractive —**per'son·a·ble·ness** *n.* —**per'son·a·bly** *adv.*

**per·son·age** (-ij) *n.* 1. an important person 2. any person 3. a character in history, a play, novel, etc.

‡**per·so·na gra·ta** (pər sō'nə grät'ə, grāt'ə) [L.] a person who is acceptable or welcome

**per·son·al** (pur's'n əl) *adj.* 1. private; individual 2. done in person or by oneself [a *personal* interview] 3. involving human beings [*personal* relationships] 4. of the body or physical appearance 5. *a*) having to do with the character, conduct, etc. of a certain person [a *personal* remark] *b*) tending to make personal remarks [to get *personal* in an argument] 6. of or like a person or rational being 7. *Gram.* indicating grammatical person, as the inflectional endings of verbs in Latin and Greek 8. *Law* of property (**personal property**) that is movable or not attached to the land —*n.* 1. a local news item about a person or persons 2. a classified advertisement about a personal matter

**per·son·al·i·ty** (pur'sə nal'ə tē) *n., pl.* -ties 1. the quality or fact of being a person 2. the quality or fact of being a particular person; individuality 3. *a*) distinctive individual qualities of a person, considered collectively *b*) such qualities applied to a group, nation, etc. 4. *a*) the sum of such qualities as impressing others *b*) personal attractiveness 5. a person; esp., a notable person 6. [*pl.*] any offensive remarks aimed at a person

**per·son·al·ize** (pur's'n ə līz') *vt.* -ized', -iz'ing 1. to apply to a particular person, esp. to oneself 2. *same as* PERSONIFY 3. to have marked with one's name or initials [*personalized* checks]

**per·son·al·ly** (-ə lē) *adv.* 1. without the help of others; in person 2. as a person [I dislike him *personally*, but admire his art] 3. in one's own opinion 4. as though directed at oneself [to take a remark *personally*]

**per·son·al·ty** (-əl tē) *n., pl.* -ties *same as* PERSONAL PROPERTY: see PERSONAL (sense 8)

‡**per·so·na non gra·ta** (pər sō'nə nän grät'ə, grāt'ə) [L.] a person who is not acceptable

**per·son·ate** (pur'sə nāt') *vt.* -at'ed, -at'ing 1. to act the part of, as in a drama 2. *Law* to assume the identity of with intent to defraud —**per'son·a'tion** *n.* —**per'son·a'tive** *adj.* —**per'son·a'tor** *n.*

**per·son·i·fi·ca·tion** (pər sän'ə fi kā'shən) *n.* 1. a personifying or being personified 2. a person or thing thought of as representing some quality, idea, etc.; perfect example [Cupid is the *personification* of love] 3. a figure of speech in which a thing or idea is represented as a person

**per·son·i·fy** (pər sän'ə fī') *vt.* -fied', -fy'ing 1. to think or speak of (a thing or idea) as a person [to *personify* a ship by referring to it as "she"] 2. to symbolize (an abstract idea) by a human figure, as in art 3. to be a symbol or perfect example of (something); typify —**per·son'i·fi'er** *n.*

**per·son·nel** (pur'sə nel') *n.* [Fr.] 1. persons employed in any work, enterprise, service, etc. 2. a personnel department or office for hiring employees, etc. —*adj.* of or in charge of personnel

**per·spec·tive** (pər spek'tiv) *adj.* [< LL. < L. *perspicere* < *per*, through + *specere*, to look] 1. of perspective 2. drawn in perspective —*n.* 1. the art of picturing objects or a scene, e.g., by converging lines, so as to show them as they appear to the eye with reference to relative distance or depth 2. *a*) the appearance of objects as determined by their relative distance and positions *b*) the effect of relative distance and position 3. the relationship of the parts of a whole, regarded from a particular standpoint or point in time 4. *a*) a specific point of view in judging things or events *b*) the ability to see things in a true relationship —**per·spec'tive·ly** *adv.*

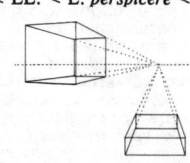

PERSPECTIVE

**per·spi·ca·cious** (pur'spə kā'shəs) *adj.* [L. *perspicax* < *perspicere:* see prec.] having keen judgment or understanding; discerning —**per'spi·ca'cious·ly** *adv.* —**per'spi·cac'·i·ty** (-kas'ə tē), **per'spi·ca'cious·ness** *n.*

**per·spic·u·ous** (pər spik'yoo wəs) *adj.* [L. *perspicuus,* transparent < *perspicere:* see PERSPECTIVE] clear in statement or expression; easily understood —**per·spi·cu·i·ty** (pur'spə kyoo'ə tē), **per·spic'u·ous·ness** *n.* —**per·spic'u·ous·ly** *adv.*

**per·spi·ra·tion** (pur'spə rā'shən) *n.* [Fr.] **1.** a perspiring; sweating **2.** sweat —**per·spi·ra·to·ry** (pər spīr'ə tôr'ē) *adj.*

**per·spire** (pər spīr') *vt., vi.* -**spired'**, -**spir'ing** [< Fr. < L. *perspirare* < *per,* through + *spirare,* to breathe] to give forth a (characteristic salty moisture) through the pores of the skin; sweat

**per·suade** (pər swād') *vt.* -**suad'ed**, -**suad'ing** [< MFr. < L. *persuadere* < *per-,* intens. + *suadere,* to urge] to cause to do something, esp. by reasoning, urging, etc.; induce; convince —**per·suad'a·ble, per·sua·si·ble** (-swā'sə b'l) *adj.* —**per·suad'er** *n.* —**per·sua'si·bil'i·ty** *n.*

**per·sua·sion** (pər swā'zhən) *n.* **1.** a persuading or being persuaded **2.** power of persuading **3.** a strong belief; conviction **4.** *a)* a particular religious belief *b)* a particular sect, party, group, etc. **5.** [Colloq.] kind, sort, sex, etc.: used jocularly

**per·sua·sive** (-siv) *adj.* having the power, or tending, to persuade —**per·sua'sive·ly** *adv.* —**per·sua'sive·ness** *n.*

**pert** (purt) *adj.* [aphetic for *apert* < OFr. < L. *apertus,* open] **1.** bold or impudent in speech or behavior; saucy **2.** chic and jaunty **3.** [Dial.] lively; brisk —**pert'ly** *adv.* —**pert'ness** *n.*

**per·tain** (pər tān') *vi.* [< OFr. < L. *pertinere,* to reach < *per-,* intens. + *tenere,* to hold] **1.** to belong; be connected or associated; be a part, etc. **2.** to be appropriate *[conduct that pertains to a lady]* **3.** to have reference; be related *[laws pertaining to the case]*

**Perth** (purth) capital of Western Australia: pop. 626,000

**per·ti·na·cious** (pur'tə nā'shəs) *adj.* [< L. *pertinax* (gen. *pertinacis*), firm < *per-,* intens. + *tenax* < *tenere,* to hold] **1.** holding firmly or stubbornly to some purpose, belief, or action **2.** hard to get rid of; persistent —**per'ti·na'cious·ly** *adv.* —**per'ti·nac'i·ty** (-nas'ə tē) *n.*

**per·ti·nent** (pur't'n ənt) *adj.* [< MFr. < L. prp. of *pertinere:* see PERTAIN] of or connected with the matter at hand; relevant —**per'ti·nence, per'ti·nen·cy** *n.* —**per'ti·nent·ly** *adv.*

**per·turb** (pər turb') *vt.* [< MFr. < L. < *per-,* intens. + *turbare,* to disturb] **1.** to cause to be alarmed, agitated, or upset; disturb or trouble greatly **2.** to cause confusion in —**per·turb'a·ble** *adj.* —**per·turb'ed·ly** *adv.* —**per·turb'er** *n.*

**per·tur·ba·tion** (pur'tər bā'shən) *n.* **1.** a perturbing or being perturbed **2.** a disturbance **3.** *Astron.* an irregularity in the orbit of a heavenly body, caused by the attraction of a body other than the one around which it orbits —**per'·tur·ba'tion·al** *adj.*

**per·tus·sis** (pər tus'is) *n.* [ModL. < L. *per-,* intens. + *tussis,* a cough] *same as* WHOOPING COUGH

**Pe·ru** (pə roo') country in W S.America, on the Pacific: 496,222 sq. mi.; pop. 13,586,000; cap. Lima —**Pe·ru·vi·an** (pə roo'vē ən) *adj., n.*

**pe·ruke** (pə rook') *n.* [< Fr. *perruque*] *same as* PERIWIG

**pe·rus·al** (pə roo'z'l) *n.* a perusing

**pe·ruse** (pə rooz') *vt.* -**rused'**, -**rus'ing** [prob. < L. *per-,* intens. + ME. *usen,* to use] **1.** to read carefully; study **2.** to read —**pe·rus'er** *n.*

**per·vade** (pər vād') *vt.* -**vad'ed**, -**vad'ing** [< L. *pervadere* < *per,* through + *vadere,* to go] **1.** to pass through; spread throughout **2.** to be prevalent throughout —**per·va'sion** (-vā'zhən) *n.* —**per·va'sive** *adj.* —**per·va'sive·ly** *adv.* —**per·va'sive·ness** *n.*

**per·verse** (pər vurs') *adj.* [< OFr. < L. pp. of *pervertere:* see PERVERT] **1.** deviating from what is considered right or good; improper; wicked, etc. **2.** persisting in error; stubbornly contrary **3.** obstinately disobedient **4.** obstinate; stubborn —**per·verse'ly** *adv.* —**per·verse'ness, per·ver'·si·ty** *n., pl.* -**ties**

**per·ver·sion** (-vur'zhən, -shən) *n.* **1.** a perverting or being perverted **2.** something perverted **3.** any sexual act or practice considered abnormal

**per·vert** (pər vurt'; *for n.* pur'vərt) *vt.* [< OFr. < L. < *per-,* intens. + *vertere,* to turn] **1.** to lead astray from what is right or good; misdirect; corrupt **2.** to misuse **3.** to misinterpret; distort **4.** to debase —*n.* a perverted person; esp., one who practices sexual perversion —**per·ver'sive** (-vur'siv) *adj.* —**per·vert'ed** *adj.* —**per·vert'er** *n.*

**per·vi·ous** (pur'vē əs) *adj.* [< L. < *per,* through + *via,* way] **1.** allowing passage through; permeable **2.** having a mind open to influence, argument etc. —**per'vi·ous·ly** *adv.* —**per'vi·ous·ness** *n.*

**Pe·sach** (pā'säkh) *n.* [Heb. *pesaḥ,* a passing over] *same as* PASSOVER

**pe·se·ta** (pə sāt'ə; *Sp.* pe se'tä) *n.* [Sp., dim. of *peso,* PESO] the monetary unit and a coin of Spain: see MONETARY UNITS, table

**pes·e·wa** (pes'ə wä) *n., pl.* -**e·was**, -**e·wa** [< native word *kpesaba,* a seed] the monetary unit of Ghana: see MONETARY UNITS, table (Ghana)

**pes·ky** (pes'kē) *adj.* -**ki·er**, -**ki·est** [prob. var. of *pesty* < PEST + -Y²] [Colloq.] annoying; troublesome —**pes'ki·ly** *adv.* —**pes'ki·ness** *n.*

**pe·so** (pā'sō; *Sp.* pe'sô) *n., pl.* -**sos** [Sp. < L. pp. of *pendere,* to weigh] the monetary unit of Argentina, Colombia, Cuba, Mexico, etc.: see MONETARY UNITS, table

**peso bo·liv·i·a·no** (bô lē'vyä'nô) *pl.* **pesos bolivianos** *see* MONETARY UNITS, table (Bolivia)

**pes·sa·ry** (pes'ər ē) *n., pl.* -**ries** [< LL. < L. < Gr. *pessos,* pebble] a device worn in the vagina to support the uterus or prevent conception

**pes·si·mism** (pes'ə miz'm) *n.* [< Fr. < L. *pessimus,* worst, superl. of *pejor,* worse] **1.** *a)* the belief that the existing world is the worst possible *b)* the belief that the evil in life outweighs the good **2.** the tendency to expect the worst outcome in any circumstance; a looking on the dark side of things —**pes'si·mist** *n.* —**pes'si·mis'tic** *adj.* —**pes'si·mis'·ti·cal·ly** *adv.*

**pest** (pest) *n.* [< Fr. < L. *pestis,* a plague] **1.** a person or thing that causes trouble, annoyance, etc.; nuisance; specif., any destructive insect, small animal, weed, etc. **2.** [Rare] bubonic plague

**pes·ter** (pes'tər) *vt.* [< OFr. *empestrer,* orig., to hobble a horse: infl. by prec.] to annoy repeatedly with petty irritations; bother —**pes'ter·er** *n.*

**pest·hole** (pest'hōl') *n.* a place infested or likely to be infested with an epidemic disease

**pes·ti·cide** (pes'tə sīd') *n.* any chemical used for killing insects, weeds, etc. —**pes'ti·ci'dal** *adj.*

**pes·tif·er·ous** (pes tif'ər əs) *adj.* [< L. < *pestis,* a plague + *ferre,* to bear] **1.** orig., *a)* bringing or carrying disease *b)* infected with an epidemic disease **2.** dangerous to the welfare of society; evil **3.** [Colloq.] annoying; bothersome —**pes·tif'er·ous·ly** *adv.* —**pes·tif'er·ous·ness** *n.*

**pes·ti·lence** (pes't'l əns) *n.* [see ff.] **1.** any contagious or infectious disease that is fatal or very harmful, esp. an epidemic of such disease, as bubonic plague **2.** anything, as a doctrine, regarded as harmful —**pes'ti·len'tial** (-tə len'shəl) *adj.* —**pes'ti·len'tial·ly** *adv.*

**pes·ti·lent** (-ənt) *adj.* [< L. < *pestis,* plague] **1.** likely to cause death; deadly **2.** dangerous to the security and welfare of society; pernicious **3.** annoying; troublesome —**pes'·ti·lent·ly** *adv.*

**pes·tle** (pes''l) *n.* [< OFr. < L. *pistillum* < *pinsere,* to pound] **1.** a tool used to pound or grind substances, as in a mortar **2.** a heavy bar used in pounding or stamping —*vt., vi.* -**tled**, -**tling** to pound, grind, crush, etc. with or as with a pestle

**pes·to** (pes'tō) *n.* [It., ult. < L. *pinsere:* see PESTLE] a sauce of ground fresh basil and garlic mixed with olive oil, used esp. over pasta

**pet¹** (pet) *n.* [orig. Scot. dial.] **1.** an animal that is domesticated and kept as a companion or treated with fondness **2.** a person who is liked or treated better than others; favorite —*adj.* **1.** kept or treated as a pet **2.** especially liked; favorite **3.** greatest; particular *[one's pet peeve]* **4.** showing fondness *[a pet name]* —*vt.* **pet'ted**, **pet'ting** **1.** to stroke or pat gently; fondle; caress **2.** to pamper —*vi.* [Colloq.] to kiss, fondle intimately, etc. in making love —**pet'ter** *n.*

**pet²** (pet) *n.* [< obs. phr. *to take the pet* < ?] a state of sulky peevishness or ill humor

**Pet. Peter**

**pet·al** (pet''l) *n.* [< ModL. < Gr. < *petalos,* outspread] any of the component parts, or leaves, of a corolla —**pet'·aled, pet'alled** *adj.* —**pet'al·like'** *adj.* —**pet'al·ous** *adj.*

**pe·tard** (pi tärd') *n.* [< Fr. < *péter,* ult. < L. *pedere,* to break wind] a metal cone filled with explosives: formerly used to break an opening in a wall or gate

**pet·cock** (pet'käk') *n.* [< obs. *pet,* breaking wind + COCK¹] a small valve for draining excess water or air from pipes, radiators, boilers, etc.

**Pe·ter** (pē'tər) [< LL. < Gr. < *petros,* a rock] **1.** a masculine name: dim. *Pete* **2.** *Bible a)* ?-64? A.D.; one of the Twelve Apostles, a fisherman and the reputed author of the Epistles of Peter: also called *Simon Peter b)* either of these books **3.** **Peter I** 1672-1725; czar of Russia (1682-1725): called *Peter the Great*

**pe·ter** (pē'tər) *vi.* [< ?] [Colloq.] to become gradually smaller, weaker, etc. and cease (with *out*)

**Pe·ter·bor·ough** (pē'tər bur'ō) city in SE Ontario, Canada, near Toronto: pop. 56,000

**pet·i·ole** (pet'ē ōl') *n.* [< ModL. < L. *petiolus,* dim. of *pes,* a foot] **1.** *Bot. same as* LEAFSTALK **2.** *Zool.* a stalklike part; peduncle —**pet'i·o·lar** (-ə lər) *adj.* —**pet'i·o·late'** (-ə lāt', -lit) *adj.*

**pet·it** (pet'ē; *Fr.* pə tē') *adj.* [< OFr.: see PETTY] small; petty: now used chiefly in law

**Philippine mahogany** the reddish wood of various trees of the Philippines and SE Asia

**Phil·ip·pines** (fil′ə pēnz′) country occupying a group of c. 7,100 islands (**Philippine Islands**) in the SW Pacific off the SE coast of Asia: 114,830 sq. mi.; pop. 43,751,000; cap. Manila

**Phi·lis·ti·a** (fə lis′tē ə) country of the Philistines, in ancient SW Palestine

**Phil·is·tine** (fil′is tēn′; fi lis′tin, -tēn) *n.* **1.** a member of a non-Semitic people who lived in Philistia and repeatedly warred with the Israelites **2.** [*often* p-] a person regarded as smugly conventional, indifferent to cultural values, etc. —*adj.* **1.** of the ancient Philistines **2.** [*often* p-] smugly conventional, lacking in culture, etc. —**Phil′is·tin·ism** *n.*

**Phil·lips** (fil′əps) [after H. *Phillips* (?–1958), its U.S. developer] *a trademark for* a screwdriver (**Phillips screwdriver**) with a tip that can be used on a screw (**Phillips screw**) that has two slots crossing at the center of the head

**phil·o-** [< Gr. *philos,* loving] *a combining form meaning* loving, liking, having a predilection for [*philology*] : also, before a vowel, **phil-**

**phil·o·den·dron** (fil′ə den′drən) *n.* [ModL. < Gr. *philos,* loving + *dendron,* a tree] a tropical American vine of the arum family, often with heart-shaped leaves

**phi·log·y·ny** (fi läj′ə nē) *n.* [< Gr. < *philein,* to love + *gynē,* woman] love of or fondness for women —**phi·log′y·nist** *n.* —**phi·log′y·nous** *adj.*

**phi·lol·o·gy** (fi läl′ə jē) *n.* [< Fr. < L. < Gr. *philologia,* love of literature < *philein,* to love + *logos,* a word] **1.** the study of literary texts, meaning, etc. **2.** *earlier term for* LINGUISTICS —**phil·o·log·i·cal** (fil′ə läj′i k′l), **phil′o·log′ic** *adj.* —**phil′o·log′i·cal·ly** *adv.* —**phi·lol′o·gist** *n.*

**philos.** philosophy

**phi·los·o·pher** (fi läs′ə fər) *n.* [< OFr. < L. < Gr. *philos,* loving + *sophos,* wise] **1.** a person who studies or is learned in philosophy **2.** a person who lives by a system of philosophy **3.** *a)* a person who meets difficulties with calmness and composure *b)* a person who philosophizes

**philosophers′** (or **philosopher′s**) **stone** an imaginary substance that alchemists believed would change base metals into gold or silver

**phil·o·soph·ic** (fil′ə säf′ik) *adj.* **1.** of a philosophy or philosopher **2.** devoted to or learned in philosophy **3.** calm, as in a difficult situation; rational Also **phil′o·soph′i·cal** —**phil′o·soph′i·cal·ly** *adv.*

**phi·los·o·phize** (fi läs′ə fīz′) *vi.* -**phized′, -phiz′ing** **1.** to deal philosophically with abstract matter; reason like a philosopher **2.** to express superficial philosophic ideas, truisms, etc.; esp., to moralize —**phi·los′o·phiz′er** *n.*

**phi·los·o·phy** (-fē) *n., pl.* -**phies** [< OFr. < L. < Gr.: see PHILOSOPHER] **1.** theory or logical analysis of the principles underlying conduct, thought, knowledge, and the nature of the universe **2.** the general principles of a field of knowledge [*the philosophy* of economics] **3.** a particular system of principles for the conduct of life **4.** *a)* a study of human morals, character, and behavior *b)* mental composure; calmness

**-phi·lous** (fi ləs) [< Gr. *philos,* loving] *a combining form meaning* loving, liking

**phil·ter** (fil′tər) *n.* [< MFr. < L. < Gr. *philtron* < *philein,* to love] **1.** a potion or charm thought to arouse sexual love, esp. toward a specific person **2.** any magic potion —*vt.* to charm or arouse with a philter

**phle·bi·tis** (fli bīt′is) *n.* [see ff. & -ITIS] inflammation of a vein —**phle·bit′ic** (-bit′ik) *adj.*

**phleb·o-** [< Gr. *phleps* (gen. *phlebos*), a vein] *a combining form meaning* vein: also, before a vowel, **phleb-**

**phle·bot·o·my** (fli bät′ə mē) *n., pl.* -**mies** [< OFr. < LL. < Gr.: see prec. & -TOMY] the act of bloodletting as a therapeutic measure —**phle·bot′o·mist** *n.*

**phlegm** (flem) *n.* [< MFr. < LL. < Gr. *phlegma,* inflammation < *phlegein,* to burn] **1.** the thick secretion of the mucous glands of the respiratory tract, discharged from the throat, as during a cold **2.** [Obs.] that one of the four humors believed to cause sluggishness **3.** *a)* sluggishness *b)* calmness; composure —**phlegm′y** *adj.*

**phleg·mat·ic** (fleg mat′ik) *adj.* [ult. < Gr. *phlegma:* see prec.] hard to rouse to action; specif., *a)* sluggish; dull; apathetic *b)* calm; cool; stolid Also **phleg·mat′i·cal** —**phleg·mat′i·cal·ly** *adv.*

**phlo·em** (flō′em) *n.* [G. < Gr. *phloos,* bark] the cell tissue serving as a path for the distribution of food material in a plant

**phlo·gis·ton** (flō jis′tän, -tən) *n.* [ModL., ult. < Gr. *phlegein,* to burn] an imaginary element formerly believed to cause combustion; principle of fire —**phlo·gis′tic** *adj.*

**phlox** (fläks) *n.* [ModL. < L. < Gr. *phlox,* a flame < *phlegein,* to burn] any of a group of chiefly N. American plants, with opposite leaves and white, pink, red, or bluish flowers

**Phnom Penh** (p′nôm′ pen′) capital of Kampuchea (see CAMBODIA): pop. c. 300,000 (in 1979): also **Pnom-Penh**

**-phobe** (fōb) [Fr. < L. < Gr. *phobos,* a fear] a suffix meaning one who fears or hates [*Francophobe*]

**pho·bi·a** (fō′bē ə) *n.* [< Gr. *phobos,* a fear] an irrational, persistent fear of some particular thing or situation —**pho′bic** *adj.*

**-pho·bi·a** (fō′bē ə) [see prec.] *a combining form meaning* fear, dread, hatred [*claustrophobia*]

PHLOX

**Phoe·be** (fē′bē) [L. < Gr. < *phoibos,* bright] **1.** a feminine name **2.** *Gr. Myth.* same as ARTEMIS

**phoe·be** (fē′bē) *n.* [echoic, with sp. after prec.] any of several American flycatchers with a gray or brown back and a short crest

**Phoe·bus** (fē′bəs) *Gr. Myth.* same as APOLLO

**Phoe·ni·cia** (fə nish′ə, -nē′shə) ancient region of city-states at the E end of the Mediterranean, in the region of present-day Syria & Lebanon

**Phoe·ni·cian** (-nish′ən, -nē′shən) *adj.* of Phoenicia, its people, their language, etc. —*n.* **1.** a native of Phoenicia **2.** the extinct Semitic language of the Phoenicians

**Phoe·nix** (fē′niks) capital of Ariz., in the SC part: pop. 765,000 (met. area 1,512,000)

**phoe·nix** (fē′niks) *n.* [< OE. & OFr. *fenix* < L. *phoenix* < Gr. *phoinix*] *Egyptian Myth.* a beautiful bird which lived for 500 or 600 years and then consumed itself in fire, rising renewed from the ashes: a symbol of immortality

**phon** (fän) *n.* [< Gr. *phōnē,* a sound] a measure of the apparent loudness of a sound

**pho·nate** (fō′nāt) *vi.* -**nat·ed, -nat·ing** [< Gr. *phōnē,* a voice + -ATE¹] to utter a voiced sound —**pho·na′tion** *n.*

**phone¹** (fōn) *n.* [Gr. *phōnē,* a sound] any single speech sound: a phoneme is composed of phones

**phone²** (fōn) *n., vt., vi.* **phoned, phon′ing** *colloq. shortened form of* TELEPHONE

**-phone** (fōn) [< Gr. *phōnē,* a sound] *a combining form meaning:* **1.** a device producing or transmitting sound [*saxophone*] **2.** a telephone [*radiophone*]

**pho·neme** (fō′nēm) *n.* [< Fr. < Gr. *phōnēma,* a sound < *phōnē,* a voice] *Linguis.* a set of similar sounds in a language that are heard as the same sound and represented in phonemic transcription by the same symbol, as the sounds of *p* in *pin, spin,* and *tip*

**pho·ne·mic** (fə nē′mik, fō-) *adj.* **1.** of, characterized by, or based on, phonemes **2.** of phonemics

**pho·ne·mics** (fə nē′miks, fō-) *n.pl.* [with *sing. v.*] **1.** the branch of language study dealing with the phonemic systems of languages **2.** the description and classification of the phonemes of a language —**pho·ne′mi·cist** (-mə sist) *n.*

**pho·net·ic** (fə net′ik, fō-) *adj.* [< ModL. < Gr. < *phōnētos,* to be spoken, ult. < *phōnē,* a sound] **1.** of speech sounds **2.** of phonetics **3.** conforming to pronunciation [*phonetic* spelling] —**pho·net′i·cal·ly** *adv.*

**pho·net·ics** (-iks) *n.pl.* [with *sing. v.*] **1.** the branch of language study dealing with speech sounds, their production and combination, and their representation by written symbols **2.** the phonetic system of a particular language —**pho·ne·ti·cian** (fō′nə tish′ən), **pho·net·ist** (fō′nə tist) *n.*

**pho·ney** (fō′nē) *adj., n.* [Colloq.] *same as* PHONY

**phon·ic** (fän′ik, fō′nik) *adj.* [< Gr. *phōnē,* a sound] **1.** of, or having the nature of, sound; esp., of speech sounds **2.** of phonics —**phon′i·cal·ly** *adv.*

**phon·ics** (fän′iks, fō′niks) *n.pl.* [with *sing. v.*] [< prec.] a method of teaching beginners to read by learning the usual sounds of certain letters or groups of letters

**pho·no-** [< Gr. *phōnē,* a sound] *a combining form meaning* sound, speech: also, before a vowel, **phon-**

**pho·no·gram** (fō′nə gram′) *n.* [prec. + -GRAM] a symbol representing a word, syllable, or sound, as in shorthand —**pho′no·gram′ic, pho′no·gram′mic** *adj.*

**pho·no·graph** (fō′nə graf′) *n.* [PHONO- + -GRAPH] an instrument for reproducing sound that has been transcribed in a spiral groove on a disk or cylinder: a needle or stylus follows this groove —**pho′no·graph′ic** *adj.* —**pho′no·graph′i·cal·ly** *adv.*

**pho·nog·ra·phy** (fō näg′rə fē) *n.* [PHONO- + -GRAPHY] **1.** a written representation of the sounds of speech **2.** any system of shorthand based on a phonetic transcription of speech

**pho·nol·o·gy** (fō näl'ə jē, fə-) *n.* [PHONO- + -LOGY] **1.** phonetics or phonemics or, esp., both considered as a system of speech sounds **2.** the study of the changes in speech sounds in a language or dialect —**pho·no·log·i·cal** (fō'nə läj'i k'l), **pho'no·log'ic** *adj.* —**pho'no·log'i·cal·ly** *adv.* —**pho·nol'o·gist** *n.*

**pho·non** (fō'nän) *n.* [PHON(O)- + -on, as in PHOTON] a quantum of sound energy that is a carrier of heat

**pho·ny** (fō'nē) *adj.* -ni·er, -ni·est [< Brit. thieves' argot *fawney*, a gilt ring (passed off as gold) < Ir. *fáinne*] [Colloq.] not genuine; false, counterfeit, pretentious, etc. —*n.*, *pl.* -nies [Colloq.] **1.** something not genuine; fake **2.** a person who deceives, dissembles, is insincere, etc.; fraud —**pho'ni·ness** *n.*

**-pho·ny** (fə nē, fō'nē) [< Gr. *phōnē*, a sound] *a combining form meaning* a (specified kind of) sound: also **-pho·ni·a** (fō'nē ə)

**-phore** (fôr) [< ModL. < Gr. *-phoros* < *pherein*, to bear] *a combining form meaning* bearer, producer

**-phor·ous** (fər əs) [see prec.] *a combining form meaning* bearing, producing

**phos·gene** (fäs'jēn) *n.* [< Gr. *phōs*, light + -*gene* (for -GEN)] a colorless, volatile liquid, $COCl_2$, used as a poison gas, in making dyes, etc.

**phos·phate** (fäs'fāt) *n.* [Fr.] **1.** a salt or ester of phosphoric acid **2.** a fertilizer containing phosphates **3.** a soft drink made with soda water, syrup, and, orig., a few drops of phosphoric acid —**phos·phat'ic** (-fat'ik) *adj.*

**phos·pha·tide** (fäs'fə tīd') *n.* [PHOSPHAT(E) + -IDE] any of a group of fatty compounds, as lecithin, found in animal and plant cells

**phos·phide** (-fīd) *n.* a compound consisting of trivalent phosphorus with another element or a radical

**phos·phite** (-fīt) *n.* [Fr.] a salt or ester of phosphorous acid

**phos·pho-** [< PHOSPHORUS] *a combining form meaning* phosphorous or phosphoric acid: also **phospho-**

**Phos·phor** (fäs'fər) [see PHOSPHORUS] [Poet.] the morning star, esp. Venus —*n.* [p-] **1.** *same as* PHOSPHORUS: now esp. in **phosphor bronze**, a bronze with a little phosphorus in it **2.** a phosphorescent or fluorescent substance

**phos·pho·rate** (-fə rāt') *vt.* -rat'ed, -rat'ing to combine or impregnate with phosphorus

**phos·pho·resce** (fäs'fə res') *vi.* -resced', -resc'ing to show or undergo phosphorescence

**phos·pho·res·cence** (-res''ns) *n.* [Fr.: see PHOSPHORUS & -ESCENCE] **1.** *a)* the condition or property of giving off light after exposure to radiant energy, as light, X-rays, etc. *b)* such light **2.** a giving off of light without noticeable heat, as from phosphorus —**phos'pho·res'cent** *adj.*

**phos·pho·ret·ed, phos·pho·ret·ted** (fäs'fə ret'id) *adj.* combined or impregnated with phosphorus: also **phos'phu·ret'ed** (-fyoo-), **phos'phu·ret'ted**

**phos·phor·ic** (fäs fôr'ik, -fär'-) *adj.* of, like, or containing phosphorus, esp. with a valence of five

**phosphoric acid** any of several oxygen acids of phosphorus

**phos·pho·ro-** *a combining form meaning* phosphorus or phosphorescence: also **phosphor-**

**phos·pho·rous** (fäs'fər əs, fäs fôr'əs) *adj.* of, like, or containing phosphorus, esp. with a valence of three

**phosphorous acid** a white or yellowish, crystalline acid, $H_3PO_3$, that absorbs oxygen readily

**phos·pho·rus** (fäs'fər əs) *n.* [ModL. < L. *Phosphorus*, morning star < Gr. < *phōs*, a light + *pherein*, to bear] **1.** orig., any phosphorescent substance or object **2.** a nonmetallic chemical element, normally a white, phosphorescent, waxy solid, becoming yellow when exposed to light: it is poisonous and ignites spontaneously at room temperature: when heated in sealed tubes it becomes red, nonpoisonous, and less flammable: symbol, P; at. wt., 30.9738; at. no., 15: a radioactive isotope (**phosphorus 32**) is used in medical treatment, as a tracer in research, etc.

**pho·tic** (fōt'ik) *adj.* [< Gr. *phōs* (gen. *phōtos*), a light + -IC] **1.** of light, esp. in its effect on organisms **2.** designating or of the upper layer (**photic zone**) in a body of water into which daylight penetrates and influences living organisms

**pho·to** (fōt'ō) *n., pl.* -tos clipped form of PHOTOGRAPH

**pho·to-** [< Gr. *phos* (gen. *phōtos*), a light] *a combining form meaning:* **1.** of or produced by light [*photograph*] **2.** of a photograph or photography

**pho·to·chem·is·try** (fōt'ō kem'is trē) *n.* the branch of chemistry having to do with the effect of light, etc. in producing chemical action, as in photography —**pho'to·chem'i·cal** (-i k'l) *adj.*

**pho·to·com·po·si·tion** (-käm'pə zish'ən) *n.* any of various methods of preparing matter for printing by projecting light images of the letters on a photosensitive surface to produce a negative from which plates can be made —**pho'to·com·pose'** (-kəm pōz') *vt.* -posed', -pos'ing

**pho·to·con·duc·tive** (-kən duk'tiv) *adj.* designating or of a substance, as selenium, whose conductivity varies with the illumination striking it —**pho'to·con·duc'tor** *n.*

**pho·to·cop·y** (fōt'ə käp'ē) *n., pl.* -cop'ies a photographic copy of printed or other graphic material —*vt.* -cop'ied, -cop'y·ing to make a photocopy of

**pho·to·de·tec·tor** (fōt'ō di tek'tər) *n.* a demodulator that is sensitive to light

**pho·to·e·lec·tric** (-i lek'trik) *adj.* of or having to do with the electric effects produced by light or other radiation, esp. as in the emission of electrons by certain substances when subjected to radiation of suitable wavelength

**photoelectric cell** any device in which light controls the electron emission from a cathode, the electrical resistance of an element, etc.: usually used in an electric circuit for mechanical devices, as for opening doors, etc.; electric eye

**pho·to·e·lec·tron** (-i lek'trän) *n.* an electron emitted by a photoelectric effect

**pho·to·en·grav·ing** (-in grā'viŋ) *n.* **1.** a photomechanical process by which photographs are reproduced in relief on printing plates **2.** a plate so made **3.** a print from such a plate —**pho'to·en·grave'** *vt.* -graved', -grav'ing —**pho'to·en·grav'er** *n.*

**photo finish 1.** a race so close that the winner can be determined only from a photograph at the finish line **2.** any close finish of a game, contest, etc.

**pho·to·fin·ish·ing** (-fin'ish iŋ) *n.* the developing and printing of photographs —**pho'to·fin'ish·er** *n.*

**pho·to·flash** (fōt'ə flash') *adj. Photog.* designating or of a light, esp. a flashbulb, electrically synchronized with the shutter —*n.* a photoflash bulb, lamp, photograph, etc.

**pho·to·flood** (-flud') *adj. Photog.* designating or of a high-intensity electric lamp used for sustained illumination —*n.* a photoflood bulb, lamp, photograph, etc.

**photog. 1.** photographic **2.** photography

**pho·to·gen·ic** (fōt'ə jen'ik) *adj.* [PHOTO- + -GENIC] **1.** giving off light **2.** that looks or is likely to look attractive in photographs: said esp. of a person —**pho'to·gen'i·cal·ly** *adv.*

**pho·to·graph** (fōt'ə graf') *n.* a picture made by photography —*vt.* to take a photograph of —*vi.* **1.** to take photographs **2.** to appear (as specified) in photographs [to *photograph* well] —**pho·tog·ra·pher** (fə täg'rə fər) *n.*

**pho·to·graph·ic** (fōt'ə graf'ik) *adj.* **1.** of or like a photograph or photography **2.** used in or made by photography **3.** retaining or recalling in precise detail [a *photographic* memory] —**pho'to·graph'i·cal·ly** *adv.*

**pho·tog·ra·phy** (fə täg'rə fē) *n.* [PHOTO- + -GRAPHY] the art or process of producing images of objects upon a photosensitive surface by the chemical action of light or other radiant energy

**pho·to·gra·vure** (fōt'ə grə vyoor') *n.* [Fr.] **1.** a photomechanical process by which photographs are reproduced on intaglio printing plates **2.** a plate so made **3.** a print from such a plate, usually with a satinlike finish

**pho·to·li·thog·ra·phy** (-li thäg'rə fē) *n.* a printing process combining photography and lithography

**pho·tol·y·sis** (fō täl'ə sis) *n.* [see PHOTO- & -LYSIS] chemical decomposition due to the action of light —**pho·to·lyt·ic** (fōt'ə lit'ik) *adj.*

**pho·to·me·chan·i·cal** (fōt'ō mə kan'i k'l) *adj.* designating or of any process by which printing plates are made by a photographic method —**pho'to·me·chan'i·cal·ly** *adv.*

**pho·tom·e·ter** (fō täm'ə tər) *n.* [PHOTO- + -METER] a device used to measure the intensity of light

**pho·tom·e·try** (-trē) *n.* the measurement of the intensity of light, esp. as a branch of optics —**pho·to·met·ric** (fōt'ə met'rik) *adj.* —**pho'to·met'ri·cal·ly** *adv.*

**pho·to·mon·tage** (fōt'ə män täzh', -mōn-) *n.* montage done in or with photographs

**pho·to·mu·ral** (-myoor'əl) *n.* a very large photograph used as a mural

**pho·ton** (fō'tän) *n.* [PHOT(O)- + (ELECTR)ON] a quantum of electromagnetic energy, as of light, X-rays, etc., having both particle and wave behavior

**pho·to-off·set** (fōt'ō ôf'set') *n.* a method of offset printing in which the pictures or text are photographically transferred to a metal plate from which inked impressions are made on the rubber roller

**pho·to·re·cep·tor** (-ri sep'tər) *n. Biol.* a sense organ, as an eye, specialized to detect light —**pho'to·re·cep'tive** *adj.*

**pho·to·sen·si·tive** (-sen'sə tiv) *adj.* reacting or sensitive to radiant energy, esp. to light —**pho'to·sen'si·tiv'i·ty** *n.* —**pho'to·sen'si·tize'** (-tīz') *vt.* -tized', -tiz'ing

**pho·to·sphere** (fōt'ə sfir') *n.* [PHOTO- + SPHERE] the visible surface of the sun —**pho'to·spher'ic** (-sfer'ik) *adj.*

**Pho·to·stat** (-stat') [PHOTO- + -STAT] *a trademark for* a device for making photographic copies of printed matter, drawings, etc. directly as positives upon special paper —*n.* [p-] a copy so made —*vt.* [p-] -stat'ed or -stat'ted, -stat'ing or -stat'ting to make a photostat of —**pho'to·stat'ic** *adj.*

**pho·to·syn·the·sis** (fōt'ə sin'thə sis) *n.* the formation in green plants of organic substances, chiefly sugars, from carbon dioxide and water in the presence of light and chlorophyll —**pho'to·syn'the·size'** (-sīz') *vt., vi.* -sized', -siz'ing

—**pho′to·syn·thet′ic** (-sin thet′ik) *adj.* —**pho′to·syn·thet′·i·cal·ly** *adv.*

**pho·tot·ro·pism** (fō tät′rə piz′m) *n. Bot.* movement of a part of a plant toward or away from light sources: see HE-LIOTROPISM —**pho·to·trop·ic** (fōt′ə träp′ik) *adj.*

**phrase** (frāz) *n.* [< L. *phrasis,* diction < Gr. < *phrazein,* to speak] **1.** a manner or style of speech or expression **2.** a short, colorful or forceful expression **3.** *Gram.* a sequence of two or more words conveying a single thought or form-ing a distinct part of a sentence but not containing a sub-ject and predicate: cf. CLAUSE **4.** *Music* a short, distinct passage, usually of two, four, or eight measures —*vt.* **phrased, phras′ing 1.** to express in words or in a phrase **2.** *Music* to mark off (notes) into phrases —**phras′al** *adj.*

**phra·se·ol·o·gy** (frā′zē äl′ə jē) *n., pl.* **-gies** [< ModL.: see PHRASE & -LOGY] choice and pattern of words; way of speaking or writing —**phra′se·ol′o·gist** *n.*

**phre·net·ic** (fri net′ik) *adj.* [< OFr. < L. < Gr. *phrenētikos,* mad] *earlier sp. of* FRENETIC

**phre·nol·o·gy** (fri näl′ə jē) *n.* [< Gr. *phrēn,* mind + -LOGY] a system, now rejected, by which character and mental faculties are analyzed by studying the shape and protuberances of the skull —**phren·o·log·i·cal** (fren′ə läj′i k′l) *adj.* —**phre·nol′o·gist** *n.*

**Phryg·i·a** (frij′ē ə) ancient country in WC Asia Minor —**Phryg′i·an** *adj., n.*

**PHS, P.H.S.** Public Health Service

**phthi·sis** (thī′sis, tī′-, fthī′-) *n.* [L. < Gr. < *phthiein,* to waste away] *old term for* any wasting disease, esp. tuber-culosis of the lungs —**phthis·ic** (tiz′ik) *adj., n.* —**phthis′ic·al, phthis′ick·y** *adj.*

**phy·co·my·cete** (fī′kō mī′sēt, -mī sēt′) *n.* [< Gr. *phykos,* seaweed + -MYCETE] any of a class of fungi resembling the algae —**phy′co·my·ce′tous** (-mī sēt′əs) *adj.*

**Phyfe** (fīf), **Duncan** (born *Duncan Fife*) 1768-1854; U.S. cabinetmaker & furniture designer, born in Scotland

**phy·la** (fī′lə) *n. pl. of* PHYLUM

**phy·lac·ter·y** (fi lak′tər ē, -trē) *n., pl.* **-ter·ies** [< ML. < LL. < Gr. *phylaktērion,* a safeguard < *phylassein,* to guard] a small leather case holding slips inscribed with Scripture passages: one is worn on the forehead and one on the left arm by Orthodox or Conservative Jewish men during morning prayer

**-phyll** (fil) [ModL. < Gr. *phyllon,* a combining form meaning leaf *[chlorophyll]*

**Phyl·lis** (fil′is) [L. < Gr. *Phyllis,* lit., a leaf] a feminine name

**phyl·lo-** [< Gr. *phyllon,* a leaf] *a com-bining form meaning* leaf: also, before a vowel, **phyll-**

PHYLACTERIES

**phyl·lo·tax·is** (fil′ə tak′sis) *n.* [ModL. < prec. + Gr. *taxis,* arrangement] *Bot.* **1.** the arrangement of leaves on a stem **2.** the study or principles of such arrangement Also **phyl′lo·tax′y** (-sē) —**phyl′lo·tac′tic** (-tik) *adj.*

**-phyl·lous** (fil′əs) [see PHYLLO- & -OUS] *a combining form meaning* having a (specified number or kind of) leaves, leaflets, etc.

**phyl·lox·e·ra** (fil′ək sir′ə, fi läk′sər ə) *n., pl.* **-rae** (-ē), **-ras** [ModL. < Gr. *phyllon,* a leaf + *xēros,* dry] any of various plant lice that attack the leaves and roots of certain plants, as grapevines

**phy·lo-** [< Gr. *phylon,* tribe] *a combining form meaning* tribe, race, phylum, etc.: also **phyl-**

**phy·log·e·ny** (fī läj′ə nē) *n., pl.* **-nies** [< G.: see PHYLO- & -GENY] descent, development, or evolution, as of a species or race: distinguished from ONTOGENY Also **phy·lo·gen·e·sis** (fī′lə jen′ə sis) —**phy′lo·ge·net′ic** (-jə net′ik), **phy′lo·gen′ic** (-jen′ik) *adj.* —**phy′lo·ge·net′i·cal·ly** *adv.*

**phy·lum** (fī′ləm) *n., pl.* **-la** (-lə) [< Gr. *phylon,* tribe] **1.** any principal division of the animal kingdom: sometimes, unof-ficially, a main subdivision of the plant kingdom **2.** *a)* a language stock *b)* loosely, a language family

**phys. 1.** physical **2.** physician **3.** physics

**phys. ed.** physical education

**phys·ic** (fiz′ik) *n.* [< OFr. < L. *physica,* natural science < Gr. < *physis,* nature < *phyein,* to produce] **1.** [Archaic] medical science **2.** a medicine, esp. a cathartic —*vt.* **-icked, -ick·ing 1.** to dose with medicine, esp. with a cathartic **2.** to cure; heal

**phys·i·cal** (fiz′i k′l) *adj.* [< ML. < L.: see prec.] **1.** of na-ture and all matter; natural; material **2.** of natural science **3.** of or according to the laws of nature **4.** of, or produced by the forces of, physics **5.** of the body as opposed to the

mind —*n.* a general medical examination: in full, **physical examination** —**phys′i·cal·ly** *adv.*

**physical chemistry** chemistry dealing with physical proper-ties in relation to chemical properties

**physical education** instruction in the exercise, hygiene, etc. of the human body; esp., a course in gymnastics, athletics, etc., as in a school or college

**physical geography** the study of the features and nature of the earth's surface, atmosphere, climate, etc.

**physical science** any science dealing with inanimate matter or energy, as physics, chemistry, etc.

**physical therapy** therapy using exercise, massage, heat, etc. instead of drugs —**physical therapist**

**phy·si·cian** (fə zish′ən) *n.* [< OFr. < L.: see PHYSIC] **1.** a person licensed to practice medicine **2.** a medical doctor other than a surgeon **3.** any person or thing that heals or relieves

**phys·i·cist** (fiz′ə sist) *n.* a specialist in physics

**phys·ics** (fiz′iks) *n.pl. [with sing. v. in senses 1 & 2]* [transl. of L. *physica,* physics] **1.** orig., natural science **2.** *a)* the science dealing with the properties, changes, etc. of matter and energy, with energy considered either as continuous (**classical physics**) or as discrete (**quantum physics**) *b)* a specific system of physics **3.** physical properties or processes

**phys·i·o-** [< Gr. *physis,* nature] *a combining form meaning:* **1.** nature; natural *[physiography]* **2.** physical *[physiotherapy]* Also, before a vowel, **physi-**

**phys·i·og·no·my** (fiz′ē äg′nə mē; *chiefly Brit.* -än′ə-) *n.* [< MFr. < ML. < Gr. *physis,* nature + *gnōmon,* one who knows] **1.** the practice of trying to judge character and mental qualities by observation of bodily, esp. facial, fea-tures **2.** facial features, esp. as supposedly indicative of character **3.** outward features —**phys′i·og·nom′ic** (-äg näm′ik, -ə näm′-), **phys′i·og·nom′i·cal** *adj.* —**phys′i·og·nom′i·cal·ly** *adv.* —**phys′i·og′no·mist** *n.*

**phys·i·og·ra·phy** (fiz′ē äg′rə fē) *n.* [PHYSIO- + -GRAPHY] **1.** a description of the features and phenomena of nature **2.** *same as* PHYSICAL GEOGRAPHY —**phys′i·og′ra·pher** *n.* —**phys′i·o·graph′ic** (-ə graf′ik), **phys′i·o·graph′i·cal** *adj.*

**physiol. 1.** physiological **2.** physiology

**phys·i·ol·o·gy** (fiz′ē äl′ə jē) *n.* [< Fr. < L. < Gr.: see PHYSIO- & -LOGY] **1.** the study of the functions and vital processes of living organisms or their parts and organs **2.** the functions and vital processes (*of* an organism, etc.) —**phys′i·o·log′i·cal** (-ə läj′i k′l), **phys′i·o·log′ic** *adj.* —**phys′i·o·log′i·cal·ly** *adv.* —**phys′i·ol′o·gist** *n.*

**phys·i·o·ther·a·py** (fiz′ē ō ther′ə pē) *n. same as* PHYSICAL THERAPY —**phys′i·o·ther′a·pist** *n.*

**phy·sique** (fi zēk′) *n.* [Fr.] the structure, constitution, strength, or appearance of the body

**-phyte** (fīt) [< Gr. *phyton,* a plant] *a combining form mean-ing:* **1.** a plant growing in a (specified) way or place *[sporophyte]* **2.** plantlike *[zoophyte]*

**phy·to-** [< Gr. *phyton,* a plant] *a combining form meaning* a plant, vegetation: also, before a vowel, **phyt-**

**pi¹** (pī) *n., pl.* **pies** [see PIE²] **1.** a mixed, disordered collec-tion of printing type **2.** any jumble or mixture —*vt.* **pied, pie′ing** or **pi′ing** to make jumbled; mix up (type)

**pi²** (pī) *n.* [Gr.] **1.** the sixteenth letter of the Greek alphabet (Π, π) **2.** *a)* the symbol (π) designating the ratio of the cir-cumference of a circle to its diameter *b)* this ratio, equal to 3.14159265+

**pi·a ma·ter** (pī′ə māt′ər, pē′ə mät′ər) [ML., lit., gentle mother < L.] the vascular membrane that is the innermost of the three membranes around the brain and spinal cord

**pi·an·ism** (pē an′iz′m, pē′ən-) *n.* a pianist's technique

**pi·a·nis·si·mo** (pē′ə nis′ə mō′) *adj., adv.* [It., superl. of *piano,* soft] *Music* very soft: a direction to the performer —*n., pl.* **-mos′, -mi′** (-mē′) a pianissimo note or passage

**pi·an·ist** (pē an′ist, pyan′-, pē′ən-) *n.* a person who plays the piano, esp. skillfully

**pi·an·o¹** (pē an′ō, pyan′ō) *n., pl.* **-os** [It., contr. < *pianoforte*] a large, stringed percussion instrument played from a keyboard: each key operates a felt-covered hammer that strikes and vibrates a rigid steel wire or set of wires

**pi·a·no²** (pē an′ō, pyä′-) *adj., adv.* [It., soft, smooth < L. *planus,* smooth] *Music* soft: a direction to the performer —*n., pl.* **-nos** a note or passage played softly

**pi·an·o·for·te** (pē an′ə fôrt′, pē an′ə fôr′tē) *n.* [It. < *piano,* soft + *forte,* strong] *same as* PIANO¹

**pi·as·ter** (pē as′tər) *n.* [< Fr. < It., ult. < L. *emplastrum,* plaster] a unit of currency in Egypt, Lebanon, Sudan, Syria, and Turkey: see MONETARY UNITS, table Also, Brit. sp., **pi·as′tre**

**pi·az·za** (pē az′ə, -at′sə; *It.* pyät′tsä) *n.* [It. < L. *platea:* see

PLACE] **1.** in Italy, an open public square, esp. with buildings around it **2.** a covered gallery or arcade **3.** a large, covered porch

**pi·broch** (pē′bräk) *n.* [< Gael. *piobaireachd*, ult. < *piob*, bagpipe] a piece of music for the bagpipe, usually martial but sometimes dirgelike

**pi·ca** (pī′kə) *n.* [< ? ML., directory: perhaps in reference to the type used in printing it] **1.** a size of type, 12 point **2.** the height of this type, about 1/6 inch: used as a unit of measure

**pic·a·dor** (pik′ə dôr′) *n.* [Sp. < *picar*, to prick] in bullfighting, any of the horsemen who prick the bull's neck with a lance to weaken him

**Pic·ar·dy** (pik′ər dē) region & former province of N France: Fr. **Pi·car·die** (pē kár dē′)

**pic·a·resque** (pik′ə resk′) *adj.* [< Sp. < *pícaro*, a rascal] of or dealing with sharp-witted vagabonds and their adventures *[a picaresque novel]*

**Pi·cas·so** (pi kä′sō, -kas′ō), **Pa·blo** (pä′blō) 1881–1973 ; Sp. painter & sculptor in France

**pic·a·yune** (pik′ē ōōn′, -ə yōōn′) *n.* [Fr. *picaillon*, small coin < Pr.] **1.** a coin of small value **2.** anything trivial or worthless —*adj.* trivial; petty; small or small-minded: also **pic′a·yun′ish**

**Pic·ca·dil·ly** (pik′ə dil′ē) street in London, a traditional center of fashionable shops, clubs, & hotels

**pic·ca·lil·li** (pik′ə lil′ē) *n.* [prob. < PICKLE] a relish of chopped vegetables, mustard, spices, etc.

**pic·co·lo** (pik′ə lō′) *n., pl.* **-los′** [It., small] a small flute, pitched an octave above the ordinary flute

**pice** (pīs) *n., pl.* **pice** [Hindi *paisā*] *see* MONETARY UNITS, table (Nepal)

**pick**[1] (pik) *n.* [var. of PIKE[4]] **1.** a heavy tool with a long, pointed metal head set at a right angle to the handle, used for breaking up soil, rock, etc. **2.** a pointed instrument for picking *[toothpick]* **3.** *same as* PLECTRUM **4.** a pin used to hold hair rollers in place

**pick**[2] (pik) *vt.* [ME. *picken*, akin to ON. *pikka*, to pierce] **1.** to break up, pierce, or dig up (soil, rock, etc.) with something pointed **2.** to make (a hole) with something pointed **3.** *a)* to dig, probe, or scratch at in trying to remove *b)* to clear something from (the teeth, etc.) in this way **4.** to remove by pulling; specif., to gather (flowers, berries, etc.) **5.** to clear thus, as a fowl of its feathers or a tree of its fruit **6.** to eat sparingly or daintily **7.** to pull (fibers, rags, etc.) apart **8.** to choose **9.** to find occasion for (a quarrel or fight) **10.** to search out *[to pick flaws]* **11.** *a)* to pluck (the strings on a guitar, etc.) *b)* to play (a guitar, etc.) thus **12.** to open (a lock) with a wire, etc. instead of a key **13.** to steal from (another's pocket, etc.) —*vi.* **1.** to eat sparingly or fussily **2.** to thieve **3.** to use a pick **4.** to gather growing berries, flowers, etc. **5.** to select, esp. in a fussy way —*n.* **1.** a stroke or blow with something pointed **2.** the act of choosing or a thing chosen **3.** the best or most desirable one(s) **4.** the amount of a crop gathered at one time —**pick and choose** to choose or select carefully —**pick at 1.** to eat small portions of, esp. in a fussy way **2.** [Colloq.] to find fault with **3.** to toy with; finger —**pick off 1.** to pluck **2.** to hit with a carefully aimed shot —**pick on 1.** to choose **2.** [Colloq.] to single out for abuse, criticism, etc. —**pick one's way** to move slowly and cautiously —**pick out 1.** to choose **2.** to single out from among a group; distinguish **3.** to make out (meaning) **4.** to play (a tune) note by note —**pick over** to sort out, item by item —**pick up 1.** to grasp and lift **2.** to get or learn, esp. by chance or casually **3.** to stop for and take along **4.** to take into custody; arrest **5.** to gain (speed) **6.** to regain (health, power, etc.); improve **7.** to resume (an activity, etc.) after a pause **8.** to bring into range of sight, hearing, radio or TV reception, etc. **9.** to make (a room, etc.) tidy **10.** [Colloq.] to get to know casually, esp. for lovemaking —**pick′er** *n.*

**pick·a·back** (pik′ə bak′, pik′ē-) *adv., adj.* [var. of *pick-apack*, redupl. of PACK[1]] *same as* PIGGYBACK

**pick·ax, pick·axe** (pik′aks′) *n.* [altered (after *ax*) < OFr. *picquois*] a pick with a point at one end of the head and a chisellike edge at the other —*vt., vi.* **-axed′**, **-ax′ing** to use a pickax (on)

**picked** (pikt) *adj.* [< PICK[2]] **1.** selected with care **2.** gathered directly from plants, as berries

**pick·er·el** (pik′ər əl, pik′rəl) *n., pl.* **-el, -els:** see PLURAL, II, D, 2 [dim. of PIKE[3]] **1.** any of various small N. American freshwater fishes related to the pike **2.** *a local name for* WALLEYED PIKE

PICKAX

**pick·er·el·weed** (-wēd′) *n.* any of certain N. American aquatic plants, esp. a shallow-water plant with arrow-shaped leaves and bluish flowers

**pick·et** (pik′it) *n.* [< Fr. dim. of *pic*, PIKE[2]] **1.** a stake, usually pointed, used in a fence, as a hitching post, etc. **2.** a soldier or soldiers stationed to guard troops from surprise attack **3.** a ship or airplane patrol **4.** a person stationed, as by a labor union, outside a factory, store, public building, etc. to demonstrate protest, keep strikebreakers out, etc. —*vt.* **1.** to enclose with a picket fence **2.** to hitch (an animal) to a picket **3.** *a)* to post as a military picket *b)* to guard (troops) with a picket **4.** to place pickets, or serve as a picket, at (a factory, etc.) —*vi.* to serve as a picket (sense 4) —**pick′et·er** *n.* —**pick′et·ing** *n.*

**picket fence** a fence made of upright stakes

**picket line** a line of people serving as pickets

**pick·ing** (pik′iŋ) *n.* **1.** the act of one that picks **2.** [*usually pl.*] something picked, or the amount of this; specif., *a)* small scraps that may be gleaned *b)* something got by effort; returns or spoils

**pick·le** (pik′'l) *n.* [< MDu. *pekel*] **1.** any brine, vinegar, or spicy solution used to preserve or marinate food **2.** a vegetable, specif. a cucumber, so preserved **3.** a chemical bath to clear metal of scale, preserve wood, etc. **4.** [Colloq.] an awkward or difficult situation —*vt.* **-led, -ling** to treat or preserve in a pickle solution —**pick′ler** *n.*

**pick·led** (-'ld) *adj.* [Slang] intoxicated; drunk

**pick-me-up** (pik′mē up′) *n.* [Colloq.] an alcoholic drink taken to raise one's spirits

**pick·pock·et** (-päk′it) *n.* a thief who steals from the pockets of persons, as in crowds

**pick-up** (pik′up′) *n.* **1.** a picking up **2.** an increasing in speed; acceleration **3.** a small, open truck for light loads **4.** [Colloq.] a casual acquaintance, as for lovemaking **5.** [Colloq.] improvement, as in business **6.** [Colloq.] *a)* a stimulant *b)* stimulation **7.** *a)* in an electric phonograph, a device producing audio-frequency currents from the vibrations of a needle in a record groove *b)* the pivoted arm holding this **8.** *Radio & TV a)* reception of sound or light for conversion into electrical energy in the transmitter *b)* the apparatus used *c)* any place outside a studio where a broadcast originates *d)* the electrical system connecting this place to the broadcasting station —*adj.* [Colloq.] assembled, organized, etc. informally or hastily

**pick·y** (pik′ē) *adj.* **pick′i·er, pick′i·est** [Colloq.] overly fastidious or exacting; fussy

**pic·nic** (pik′nik) *n.* [< Fr., prob. < *piquer*, to pick + *nique*, a trifle] **1.** a pleasure outing, with an outdoor meal **2.** a shoulder cut of pork, cured like ham: also **picnic ham, picnic shoulder 3.** [Slang] *a)* a pleasant experience *b)* an easy task —*vi.* **-nicked, -nick·ing** to hold or attend a picnic —**pic′nick·er** *n.*

**pi·co-** [prob. < It. *piccolo*, small] *a combining form meaning* one trillionth

**Pi·co Ri·ver·a** (pē′kō rə ver′ə) [after P. *Pico*, gov. of Mexican Calif. + *Rivera*, from its being between two rivers] city in SW Calif.: suburb of Los Angeles: pop. 53,000

**pi·cot** (pē′kō) *n., pl.* **-cots** (-kōz) [Fr., dim. of *pic*, a point] any of the small loops in an ornamental edging on lace, ribbon, etc. —*vt., vi.* **-coted** (-kōd), **-cot·ing** (-kō iŋ) to edge with these

**pic·ric acid** (pik′rik) [< Fr. < Gr. *pikros*, bitter] a poisonous, yellow, crystalline, bitter acid, $C_6H_3O_7N_3$, used in dyes, explosives, etc.

**Pict** (pikt) *n.* any of an ancient people of Great Britain, driven into Scotland by the Britons and Romans —**Pict′ish** *adj., n.*

**pic·to·graph** (pik′tə graf′) *n.* [< L. *pictus* (see PICTURE) + -GRAPH] **1.** a picture or picturelike symbol representing an idea, as in ancient writing **2.** a diagram using pictured objects to convey ideas —**pic′to·graph′ic** *adj.* —**pic′to·graph′i·cal·ly** *adv.* —**pic·tog′ra·phy** (-täg′rə fē) *n.*

**pic·to·ri·al** (pik tôr′ē əl) *adj.* **1.** of, containing, or expressed in pictures **2.** suggesting a mental image; graphic —*n.* a periodical featuring many pictures —**pic·to′ri·al·i·za′tion** *n.* —**pic·to′ri·al·ize′** *vt.* **-ized′, -iz′ing** —**pic·to′ri·al·ly** *adv.*

**pic·ture** (pik′chər) *n.* [< L. *pictura* < *pictus*, pp. of *pingere*, to paint] **1.** *a)* a likeness of an object, person, or scene produced on a flat surface, as by painting or photography *b)* a printed reproduction of this **2.** anything resembling or typifying something else *[he's the picture of health]* **3.** anything regarded as like a painting, etc. **4.** a mental image; idea **5.** a vivid description **6.** all the facts of an event **7.** *same as: a)* TABLEAU *b)* MOTION PICTURE **8.** the image on a TV screen —*vt.* **-tured, -tur·ing 1.** to make a picture of by painting, drawing, etc. **2.** to make visible; show clearly **3.** to describe or explain **4.** to imagine —**in (or out of) the picture** considered as involved (or not involved) in a situation

**pic·tur·esque** (pik′chə resk′) *adj.* **1.** like a picture; specif., *a)* having a wild beauty, as mountain scenery *b)* pleasantly unfamiliar; quaint **2.** suggesting a mental picture; vivid —**pic′tur·esque′ly** *adv.* —**pic′tur·esque′ness** *n.*

**picture tube** *same as* KINESCOPE (sense 1)

**picture window** a large window, esp. in a living room, that seems to frame the outside view

**picture writing** writing that uses pictographs

**pid·dle** (pid′'l) *vi.*, *vt.* **-dled**, **-dling** [child's word for URINATE] to dawdle —**pid′dler** *n.*

**pid·dling** (pid′liŋ) *adj.* trifling; petty

**pidg·in** (pij′in) *n.* [a supposed Chin. pronun. of BUSINESS] a jargon, as pidgin English, incorporating the vocabulary of one or more languages

**pidgin English** **1.** a simplified form of English with a Chinese or Melanesian syntax, used by Orientals, etc. as a trade language **2.** any jargon similarly intermixed with English

**pie¹** (pī) *n.* [akin ? to PIE³] **1.** a baked dish consisting of fruit, meat, etc. with an under or upper crust, or both **2.** a layer cake with a filling of custard, jelly, etc. **3.** [Slang] something extremely good or easy —**(as) easy as pie** [Colloq.] extremely easy

**pie²** (pī) *n.*, *vt.* [< ? prec.] *chiefly Brit. sp. of* PI¹

**pie³** (pī) *n.* [OFr. < L. *pica*] *same as* MAGPIE

**pie·bald** (pī′bôld′) *adj.* [PIE³ + BALD] covered with patches or spots of two colors, esp. white and black —*n.* a piebald horse or other animal

**piece** (pēs) *n.* [OFr. *pece*, prob. < Gaul.] **1.** a part broken or separated from the whole **2.** a section or quantity of a whole, regarded as complete in itself **3.** a single thing, specimen, etc.; specif., *a*) an artistic work, as of music *b*) an action or its result *[a piece of business]* *c*) a firearm *d*) a coin or token *e*) one of a set, as of china *f*) a counter as used in games **4.** the quantity or size, as of cloth, manufactured as a unit **5.** an amount of work constituting a single job **6.** [Archaic or Dial.] an amount of time or space —*vt.* **pieced, piec′ing 1.** to add pieces to, as in repairing or enlarging **2.** to join (*together*) the pieces of, as in mending —**go to pieces 1.** to fall apart **2.** to lose all self-control —**of a (or one) piece** of the same sort; alike —**speak one's piece** to vent one's views or opinions —**piec′er** *n.*

**‡pièce de ré·sis·tance** (pyes′ də rā zēs täns′) [Fr., piece of resistance] **1.** the principal dish of a meal **2.** the main item or event in a series

**piece goods** *same as* YARD GOODS

**piece·meal** (pēs′mēl′) *adv.* [< ME. < *pece*, PIECE + *-mele*, a measure] piece by piece; in small amounts or degrees —*adj.* made or done in pieces or one piece at a time

**piece of eight** the obsolete Spanish dollar

**piece·work** (-wurk′) *n.* work paid for at a fixed rate (**piece rate**) per piece —**piece′work′er** *n.*

**pied** (pīd) *adj.* covered with spots or patches of two or more colors; piebald; variegated

**Pied·mont** (pēd′mänt) **1.** hilly, upland region of the E U.S., between the Atlantic coastal plain & the Appalachians **2.** region of NW Italy, on the border of Switzerland & France: chief city, Turin

**pied·mont** (pēd′mänt) *adj.* [< PIEDMONT, Italy] at the base of a mountain —*n.* a piedmont area, etc.

**pie·plant** (pī′plant′) *n.* [PIE¹ + PLANT] the rhubarb: so called from its use in pies

**pier** (pir) *n.* [ML. *pera*, ult. < ? or akin to L. *petra*, stone] **1.** a heavy structure supporting the spans of a bridge **2.** a structure built out over water and supported by pillars: used as a landing place, pavilion, etc. **3.** *Archit.* *a*) a heavy supporting column *b*) the part of a wall between windows or other openings *c*) a buttress

**pierce** (pirs) *vt.* **pierced, pierc′ing** [OFr. *percer*, ult. < L. *per*, through + *tundere*, to strike] **1.** to pass into or through as a pointed instrument does; stab **2.** to affect sharply the senses or feelings of **3.** to make a hole in; perforate; bore **4.** to make (a hole), as by boring **5.** to break into or through **6.** to sound sharply through **7.** to penetrate with the sight or mind —*vi.* to penetrate —**pierc′er** *n.* —**pierc′ing·ly** *adv.*

**Pierce** (pirs), **Franklin** 1804–69; 14th president of the U.S. (1853–57)

**pier glass** a tall mirror set in the pier, or wall section, between windows

**Pi·er·i·an** (pī ir′ē ən) *adj.* **1.** of a region (**Pieria**) in northern Greece, where the Muses were worshiped **2.** of the Muses or the arts

**Pi·erre¹** (pē er′; *Fr.* pyer) [Fr., var. of PETER] a masculine name

**Pierre²** (pir) [after *Pierre* Chonteau, early fur trader] capital of S.Dak., on the Missouri River: pop. 12,000

**Pi·er·rot** (pē′ə rō′; *Fr.* pye rō′) [Fr., dim. of *Pierre*, PETER] a stock comic character in old French pantomime, having a whitened face and loose white pantaloons and jacket

**pi·e·tism** (pī′ə tiz′m) *n.* religious piety, esp. when exaggerated —**pi′e·tis′tic, pi′e·tis′ti·cal** *adj.*

**pi·e·ty** (pī′ə tē) *n.*, *pl.* **-ties** [< OFr. < LL. *pietas* < L. <

*pius*, pious] **1.** devotion to religious duties and practices **2.** loyalty and devotion to parents, family, etc. **3.** a pious act, statement, etc.

**piezoelectric effect** the property exhibited by certain crystals of generating voltage when subjected to pressure, and, conversely, undergoing mechanical stress when subjected to voltage: a piezoelectric crystal when ground and cut to a particular size oscillates or resonates at a precise frequency

**pi·e·zo·e·lec·tric·i·ty** (pē ā′zō i lek′tris′ə tē) *n.* [< Gr. *piezein*, to press + ELECTRICITY] electricity resulting from the piezoelectric effect —**pi·e′zo·e·lec′tric, pi·e′zo·e·lec′-tri·cal** *adj.* —**pi·e′zo·e·lec′tri·cal·ly** *adv.*

**pif·fle** (pif′'l) *n.* [< Brit. dial.] [Colloq.] talk, action, etc. regarded as insignificant or nonsensical —*interj.* nonsense! —**pif′fling** *adj.*

**pig** (pig) *n.*, *pl.* **pigs, pig:** see PLURAL, II, D, 1 [ME. *pigge*, orig., young pig] **1.** a domesticated animal with a long, broad snout and a thick, fat body covered with coarse bristles; swine; hog **2.** a young hog of less than c. 100 lbs. **3.** pork **4.** a person regarded as piggish or like a pig **5.** [Slang] a slattern or slut **6.** *a*) an oblong casting of iron, etc. poured from the smelting furnace *b*) the mold used *c*) *clipped form of* PIG IRON —*vi.* **pigged, pig′ging 1.** to bear pigs **2.** to live like a pig, esp. in the phrase **pig it** —**buy a pig in a poke** to buy, get, or agree to something without sight or knowledge of it in advance

**pi·geon¹** (pij′ən) *n.*, *pl.* **-geons, -geon:** see PLURAL, II, D, 1 [< MFr. < LL. *pipio*, chirping bird < *pipire*, to peep] **1.** any of various related birds with a small head, plump body, and short legs, larger than doves **2.** *same as* CLAY PIGEON **3.** a young woman **4.** [Slang] a dupe

**pi·geon²** (pij′ən) *n. same as* PIDGIN

**pigeon breast** a deformity of the human chest, as from rickets, in which the sternum projects sharply like that of a pigeon —**pi′geon-breast′ed** *adj.*

**pigeon hawk** a small N. American falcon

**pi·geon·hole** (-hōl′) *n.* **1.** a small recess for pigeons to nest in **2.** a small, open compartment, as in a desk, for filing papers —*vt.* **-holed′, -hol′ing 1.** to put in the pigeonhole of a desk, etc. **2.** to put aside indefinitely **3.** to classify

**pi·geon-toed** (-tōd′) *adj.* having the toes or feet turned in

**pig·ger·y** (pig′ər ē) *n.*, *pl.* **-ies** *chiefly Brit. var. of* PIGPEN

**pig·gish** (pig′ish) *adj.* like a pig; gluttonous or filthy —**pig′-gish·ly** *adv.* —**pig′gish·ness** *n.*

**pig·gy** (pig′ē) *n.*, *pl.* **-gies** a little pig: also sp. **pig′gie** —*adj.* **-gi·er, -gi·est** *same as* PIGGISH

**pig·gy·back** (pig′ē bak′) *adv.*, *adj.* [alt. of PICKABACK] **1.** on the shoulders or back **2.** of or by a system in which loaded truck trailers are carried on railroad flatcars —*vt.* to carry piggyback

**piggy bank** any small savings bank, often in the form of a pig, with a slot for coins

**pig·head·ed** (-hed′id) *adj.* stubborn; obstinate —**pig′head′-ed·ly** *adv.* —**pig′head′ed·ness** *n.*

**pig iron** [see PIG, *n.* 6] crude iron, as it comes from the blast furnace

**pig·let** (pig′lit) *n.* a little pig, esp. a suckling

**pig·ment** (pig′mənt) *n.* [< L. *pigmentum* < base of *pingere*, to paint] **1.** coloring matter, usually as an insoluble powder mixed with oil, water, etc. to make paints **2.** coloring matter in the cells and tissues of plants or animals —*vi.*, *vt.* to take on or make take on pigment: also **pig′ment·ize′ -ized′, -iz′ing** —**pig′men·tar′y** (-mən ter′ē) *adj.*

**pig·men·ta·tion** (pig′mən tā′shən) *n.* coloration in plants or animals due to pigment in the tissue

**Pig·my** (pig′mē) *adj.*, *n.*, *pl.* **-mies** *same as* PYGMY

**pig·nut** (pig′nut′) *n.* **1.** any of several bitter-tasting hickory nuts **2.** any tree they grow on

**pig·pen** (-pen′) *n.* a pen where pigs are confined

**pig·skin** (-skin′) *n.* **1.** the skin of a pig **2.** leather made from this **3.** [Colloq.] a football

**pig·stick·ing** (-stik′iŋ) *n.* the hunting of wild boars, esp. on horseback with spears —**pig′stick′er** *n.*

**pig·sty** (-stī′) *n.*, *pl.* **-sties′** *same as* PIGPEN

**pig·tail** (-tāl′) *n.* **1.** tobacco in a twisted roll **2.** a braid of hair hanging at the back of the head

**pi·ka** (pī′kə) *n.* [< E. Siberian name] any of various small, rabbitlike mammals of rocky, usually high areas in western N. America and in Asia

**pike¹** (pīk) *n. clipped form of* TURNPIKE

**pike²** (pīk) *n.* [< Fr. < *piquer*, to pierce < ? L. *picus*, woodpecker] a weapon, formerly used by foot soldiers, with a metal spearhead on a long, wooden shaft —*vt.* **piked, pik′ing** to pierce with a pike —**pike′man** (-mən) *n.*, *pl.* **-men**

**pike³** (pīk) *n.*, *pl.* **pike, pikes:** see PLURAL, II, D, 2 [prob. < *pike* (see PIKE²), from the pointed head] **1.** a slender, voracious, freshwater game fish of northern waters, having a narrow, pointed head and sharp teeth: also **northern pike**

**2.** any of several related fishes, as the pickerel **3.** a fish resembling the true pike, as the walleyed pike

**pike⁴** (pīk) *n.* [OE. *pic,* a pickax] a spike or point, as the pointed tip of a spear

**pik·er** (pī′kər) *n.* [orig., prob. one from *Pike* County, Mo.] [Slang] a person who does things in a petty or very cautious way

**Pikes Peak** (pīks) [after Z. *Pike* (1779-1813), Am. explorer] mountain in C Colo.: 14,110 ft.

**pike·staff** (pīk′staf′) *n., pl.* **-staves** (-stāvz′) **1.** the shaft of a pike **2.** a traveler's staff with a sharp point

**pi·laf, pi·laff** (pi läf′, pē′läf) *n.* [Pers. & Turk. *pilâw*] a dish of rice boiled in a seasoned liquid, and usually containing meat or fish

**pi·las·ter** (pi las′tər) *n.* [< Fr. < It. *pilastro* < L. *pila,* a pile] a rectangular support projecting partially from a wall and treated architecturally as a column, with a base, shaft, and capital

**Pi·late** (pī′lət), **Pon·tius** (pän′shəs, -chəs, -tē əs) 1st cent. A.D.; Rom. governor of Judaea & Samaria (26?-36?) who condemned Jesus to be crucified

**pi·lau, pi·law** (pi lô′) *n. same as* PILAF

**pil·chard** (pil′chərd) *n.* [earlier *pilcher* < ?] **1.** a small saltwater fish of the herring family, the commercial sardine of western Europe **2.** any of several related fishes; esp., the **Pacific sardine,** found off the western coast of the U.S.

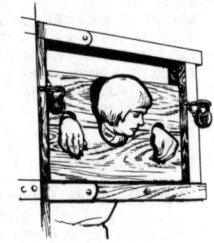

PILASTER

**Pil·co·ma·yo** (pēl′kô mä′yô) river flowing from Bolivia along the Argentine-Paraguay border into the Paraguay River

**pile¹** (pīl) *n.* [< MFr. < L. *pila,* a pillar] **1.** a mass of things heaped together **2.** a heap of wood, etc. on which a corpse or sacrifice is burned **3.** a large building or group of buildings **4.** [Colloq.] *a)* a large amount or number *b)* a lot of money **5.** *Elec. a)* orig., a series of alternate plates of unlike metals with acid-saturated cloth or paper between them, for making an electric current *b)* any similar arrangement that produces an electric current; battery **6.** *an earlier name for* NUCLEAR REACTOR —*vt.* **piled, pil′ing 1.** to put in a pile; heap up **2.** to cover with a pile; load **3.** to accumulate Often with *up* —*vi.* **1.** to form a pile or heap **2.** to move confusedly in a mass (with *in, out, on,* etc.)

**pile²** (pīl) *n.* [< L. *pilus,* a hair] **1.** a soft, velvety, raised surface on a rug, fabric, etc., consisting of yarn loops that are often sheared **2.** soft, fine hair, as on wool, fur, etc. —**piled** *adj.*

**pile³** (pīl) *n.* [OE. *pil*] **1.** a long, heavy beam driven into the ground, sometimes under water, to support a bridge, dock, etc. **2.** any similar support —*vt.* **piled, pil′ing 1.** to drive piles into **2.** to support with piles

**pi·le·ate** (pī′lē it, pil′ē-; -āt′) *adj.* [< L. *pileus,* cap] having a crest extending from the bill to the nape, as some birds Also **pi′le·at′ed** (-āt′id)

**pileated woodpecker** a N. American woodpecker with a black and white body and a red crest

**pile driver** (or **engine**) a machine with a drop hammer for driving piles

**pi·le·ous** (pī′lē əs, pil′ē-) *adj.* [< L. *pilus,* a hair + -EOUS] hairy or furry

**piles** (pīlz) *n.pl.* [< L. *piloe,* pl. of *pila,* a ball] *same as* HEMORRHOIDS (see HEMORRHOID)

**pi·le·um** (pī′lē əm, pil′ē-) *n., pl.* **-le·a** (-ə) [ModL. < L. *pilleum,* felt cap] the top of a bird's head from the bill to the nape

**pile-up** (pīl′up′) *n.* **1.** a piling up **2.** [Colloq.] a collision involving several vehicles

**pi·le·us** (pī′lē əs, pil′ē-) *n., pl.* **-le·i** (-ī′) [< L. *pilleus* (or *pilleum*), felt cap] *Bot.* the cap of a mushroom, or a similar part of other fungi

**pil·fer** (pil′fər) *vt., vi.* [MFr. *pelfrer* < *pelfre,* booty] to steal (esp. small sums, petty objects, etc.) —**pil′fer·age** *n.* —**pil′fer·er** *n.*

**pil·grim** (pil′grəm) *n.* [< OFr. < LL. < L. *peregrinus,* foreigner, ult. < *per,* through + *ager,* country] **1.** a wanderer **2.** a traveler to a shrine or holy place **3.** [P-] any member of the band of English Puritans who founded Plymouth Colony in 1620

**pil·grim·age** (-ij) *n.* **1.** a pilgrim's journey, esp. to a shrine, etc. **2.** any similar long journey

**Pilgrim Fathers** the Pilgrims

**Pilgrim's Progress** a religious allegory by John Bunyan (1678)

**pil·ing** (pī′liŋ) *n.* **1.** piles collectively **2.** a structure of piles

**Pil·i·pi·no** (pil′ə pē′nō) *n.* [Tag. < obs. Sp. *Philippino,* FILIPINO] *same as* TAGALOG (sense 2): official national language of the Philippines

**pill** (pil) *n.* [contr. < L. *pilula,* dim. of *pila,* a ball] **1.** a small ball, tablet, or capsule of medicine to be swallowed

whole **2.** a thing that is unpleasant but unavoidable **3.** [Slang] a baseball, golf ball, etc. **4.** [Slang] an unpleasant person —*vt.* to dose with pills —*vi.* to form into small balls of fuzz on a fabric —**the pill** [Colloq.] a contraceptive taken as a pill by women

**pil·lage** (pil′ij) *n.* [< MFr. < *piller,* to rob] **1.** a plundering **2.** booty; loot —*vt.* **-laged, -lag·ing 1.** to deprive of money or property by violence; loot **2.** to take as booty or loot —*vi.* to take loot —**pil′lag·er** *n.*

**pil·lar** (pil′ər) *n.* [< OFr., ult. < L. *pila,* a column] **1.** a slender, vertical structure used as a support; column **2.** a column standing alone as a monument **3.** a person who is a main support of an institution, movement, etc. —*vt.* to support as with pillars —**from pillar to post** from one predicament, place of appeal, etc. to another

**Pillars of Hercules** two headlands on either side of the Strait of Gibraltar

**pill·box** (pil′bäks′) *n.* **1.** a small, shallow box, often cylindrical, for pills **2.** a low, enclosed gun emplacement of concrete and steel

**pil·lion** (pil′yən) *n.* [< Gael. < *peall,* a hide, ult. < L. *pellis,* a skin] **1.** a cushion behind a saddle for an extra rider, esp. a woman **2.** an extra saddle behind the driver's on a motorcycle

**pil·lo·ry** (pil′ər ē) *n., pl.* **-ries** [OFr. *pilori*] **1.** a wooden board with holes for the head and hands, in which petty offenders were formerly locked and exposed to public scorn **2.** any exposure to public scorn —*vt.* **-ried, -ry·ing 1.** to punish by placing in a pillory **2.** to lay open to public ridicule, scorn, or abuse

**pil·low** (pil′ō) *n.* [OE. *pyle*] **1.** a cloth case filled with feathers, foam rubber, etc., used as a support, as for the head in sleeping **2.** anything like a pillow in form or function —*vt.* **1.** to rest as on a pillow **2.** to be a pillow for —*vi.* to rest the head as on a pillow —**pil′low·y** *adj.*

PILLORY

**pil·low·case** (-kās′) *n.* a removable cloth case to cover a pillow: also **pil′low·slip′** (-slip′)

**pillow sham** a decorative cover for a bed pillow

**pi·lose** (pī′lōs) *adj.* [< L. < *pilus,* a hair] covered with hair, esp. fine, soft hair: also **pi′lous** (-ləs) —**pi·los·i·ty** (pī läs′ə tē) *n.*

**pi·lot** (pī′lət) *n.* [< MFr. < It. *pilota,* ult. < Gr. *pēdon,* oar blade] **1.** a steersman; specif., a person licensed to direct or steer ships into or out of a harbor or through difficult waters **2.** a qualified operator of an aircraft **3.** a guide; leader **4.** a device guiding the action of a machine or machine part **5.** *same as: a)* COWCATCHER *b)* PILOT LIGHT *c)* PILOT FILM (OR TAPE) —*vt.* **1.** to act as a pilot of, on, in, or over **2.** to guide; lead —*adj.* **1.** that guides or activates **2.** that serves as a testing unit —**pi′lot·less** *adj.*

**pi·lot·age** (-ij) *n.* a piloting, or the fee for it

**pilot balloon** a small balloon sent up to determine the direction and velocity of the wind

**pilot biscuit** (or **bread**) *same as* HARDTACK

**pilot film** (or **tape**) a film (or videotape) of a single segment of a projected television series, for showing to prospective commercial sponsors

**pilot fish** any of various fishes seemingly acting as pilots, as the remora

**pi·lot·house** (-hous′) *n.* an enclosed place on the upper deck of a ship, for the helmsman

**pilot lamp** an electric lamp placed in an electric circuit to indicate when the current is on

**pilot light 1.** a small gas burner kept lighted to rekindle a principal burner when needed: also **pilot burner 2.** *same as* PILOT LAMP

**Pil·sener, Pil·sner** (pilz′nər, pils′-) *adj.* [after Pilsen (*Plzeň*), city in Bohemia, where first made] [*often* p-] designating a light, Bohemian lager beer often served in a tall, conical glass (**Pilsener glass**)

**Pilt·down man** (pilt′doun′) a supposed species of prehistoric man presumed on the basis of bone fragments found in Piltdown (Sussex, England) in 1911 and exposed as a hoax in 1953

**Pi·ma** (pē′mə) *n.* [< Sp. < Pima] **1.** *pl.* **-mas, -ma** any member of a N. American Indian tribe in Arizona **2.** their language —**Pi′man** *adj.*

**Pima cotton** [< *Pima* County, Ariz.] a strong, smooth cotton grown in the SW U.S.

**pi·men·to** (pi men′tō) *n., pl.* **-tos** [< Sp. < L. *pigmentum,* lit., PIGMENT (in VL. & ML., spice)] **1.** a sweet variety of the capsicum pepper, or its red fruit, used as a relish, etc. **2.** *same as* ALLSPICE

**pimento cheese** a cheese containing pimentos

**pi·mien·to** (pi myen′tō, -men′-) *n. same as* PIMENTO
**pimp** (pimp) *n.* [prob. < or akin to MFr. *pimper*, to allure] a man who is an agent for prostitutes —*vi.* to act as a pimp
**pim·per·nel** (pim′pər nel′, -nəl) *n.* [< OFr. < LL., ult. < L. *piper*, PEPPER: its fruit resembles peppercorns] any of certain related plants with clustered flowers and leafless stems; esp., the **scarlet pimpernel**, with red, white, or blue, starlike flowers which close in bad weather
**pim·ple** (pim′p'l) *n.* [prob. < or akin to OE. *piplian*, to break out in pimples] any small, rounded, usually inflamed swelling of the skin
**pim·ply** (pim′plē) *adj.* **-pli·er, -pli·est** having pimples: also **pim′pled** (-p'ld)
**pin** (pin) *n.* [OE. *pinn*] **1.** a peg of wood, metal, etc., used for fastening things together, as a support to hang things, etc. **2.** a little piece of stiff wire with a pointed end and flattened or rounded head, for fastening things together **3.** something worthless or insignificant; trifle **4.** *clipped form of* CLOTHESPIN, SAFETY PIN, COTTER PIN, etc. **5.** anything like a pin in form, use, etc. **6.** an ornament, badge, or emblem with a pin or clasp for fastening to clothes **7.** a peg for regulating the tension of a string in a piano, harp, etc. **8.** [Colloq.] the leg: *usually used in pl.* **9.** *Bowling* any of the wooden clubs at which the ball is rolled **10.** *Golf* a pole with a flag attached, in and marking the hole of a green **11.** *Naut.* a) *same as* THOLE b) a peg or bolt to fasten rigging —*vt.* **pinned, pin′ning 1.** to fasten as with a pin **2.** to pierce with a pin **3.** to hold firmly in one position **4.** [Slang] to give one's fraternity pin to, as an informal token of betrothal —**pin down 1.** to get (someone) to commit himself as to his opinion, plans, etc. **2.** to determine or confirm (a fact, details, etc.) —**pin someone's ears back** [Colloq.] to beat, defeat, or scold someone soundly —**pin (something) on someone** [Colloq.] to lay the blame for (something) on someone
**pin·a·fore** (pin′ə fôr′) *n.* [PIN + AFORE] **1.** a sleeveless, apronlike garment worn by little girls over the dress **2.** a sleeveless housedress
**pin·ball machine** (pin′bôl′) a game machine with an inclined board having pins, holes, etc. marked with scores for a spring-driven ball to contact
**pince-nez** (pans′nā′, pins′-; *Fr.* pans nā′) *n., pl.* **pince′-nez′** (-nāz′; *Fr.* -nā′) [Fr., nose-pincher] eyeglasses without sidepieces, kept in place by a spring gripping the bridge of the nose
**pin·cers** (pin′sərz) *n.pl.* [*occas. with sing. v.*] [< OFr. *pincier*, to pinch] **1.** a tool with two pivoted parts for gripping or nipping things **2.** a grasping claw, as of a crab —**pin′cer·like′** *adj.*
**pinch** (pinch) *vt.* [ult. < OFr. *pincier*] **1.** to squeeze as between finger and thumb or between two edges **2.** to nip off the end of (a plant shoot) **3.** to press painfully upon (a part of the body) **4.** to cause distress or discomfort to **5.** to make thin, cramped, etc., as by hunger or cold **6.** to restrict closely; straiten: usually in the passive **7.** [Slang] a) to steal b) to arrest —*vi.* **1.** to squeeze painfully **2.** to be stingy or frugal —*n.* **1.** a pinching; squeeze **2.** a quantity graspable between finger and thumb; small amount **3.** distress; hardship **4.** an emergency **5.** [Slang] a) a theft b) an arrest —**pinch pennies** to be very frugal —**pinch′er** *n.*
**pinch·beck** (pinch′bek′) *n.* [after C. *Pinchbeck*, 18th-cent. Eng. jeweler] **1.** an alloy of copper and zinc used to imitate gold in jewelry **2.** anything cheap or imitation —*adj.* of or like pinchbeck
**pinch·ers** (pinch′ərz) *n.pl. same as* PINCERS
**pinch-hit** (pinch′hit′) *vi.* **-hit′, -hit′ting 1.** *Baseball* to bat in place of the batter whose turn it is, esp. when a hit is needed **2.** to act as a substitute (*for*) in an emergency —**pinch hitter**
**pin·cush·ion** (pin′koosh′ən) *n.* a small cushion to stick pins and needles in, to keep them handy
**Pin·dar** (pin′dər) 522?-438? B.C.; Gr. lyric poet —**Pin·dar·ic** (pin dar′ik) *adj.*
**pine¹** (pīn) *n.* see PLURAL, II, D, 3 [OE. *pin* < L. *pinus*, pine tree] **1.** any of various evergreen trees of the pine family: many pines are valuable for wood and for resin, from which turpentine, tar, etc. are obtained **2.** the wood —*adj.* designating a family of trees with needlelike leaves and, usually, woody cones and valuable wood, including the pines, firs, hemlocks, etc.
**pine²** (pīn) *vi.* **pined, pin′ing** [OE. *pinian*, to torment < *pin* < L. *poena*, a pain] **1.** to waste (*away*) with grief, longing, etc. **2.** to have an intense desire; yearn (*for* or *after*)
**pin·e·al body** (pin′ē əl) [< Fr. < L. *pinea*, a pine cone] a

small, cone-shaped body on the dorsal portion of the brain of all vertebrates: its function is obscure
**pine·ap·ple** (pīn′ap′'l) *n.* [ME. *pinappel*, pine cone (see PINE¹ & APPLE) **1.** a juicy, edible tropical fruit somewhat resembling a pine cone **2.** the plant it grows on, with spiny-edged leaves
**Pine Bluff** city in central Ark., on the Arkansas River: pop. 57,000
**pine tar** a thick, dark liquid obtained from pine wood, used in disinfectants, tar paints, etc.
**pin·ey** (pī′nē) *adj.* **pin′i·er, pin′i·est 1.** abounding in pines **2.** of or like pines
**pin·feath·er** (pin′feth′ər) *n.* an undeveloped feather that is just emerging through the skin
**ping** (piŋ) *n.* [echoic] a sharp sound, as of a bullet striking, an engine knocking, etc. —*vi., vt.* to make or cause to make such a sound
**Ping-Pong** (piŋ′pôŋ′, -päŋ′) [echoic] *a trademark for* table tennis equipment —*n.* [p- p-] *same as* TABLE TENNIS
**pin·head** (pin′hed′) *n.* **1.** the head of a pin **2.** anything tiny or trifling **3.** a stupid or silly person —**pin′head′ed** *adj.* —**pin′head′ed·ness** *n.*
**pin·hole** (-hōl′) *n.* **1.** a tiny hole made as by a pin **2.** a hole into which a pin or peg goes
**pin·ion¹** (pin′yən) *n.* [< Fr., ult. < L. *pinna*, bucket of a paddle wheel, lit., feather] a small cogwheel with teeth that fit into a gearwheel or rack
**pin·ion²** (pin′yən) *n.* [< OFr. < L. *pinna*, a feather] **1.** the end joint of a bird's wing **2.** a wing **3.** any wing feather —*vt.* **1.** to cut off or bind the pinions of (a bird) to keep it from flying **2.** to bind (the wings) **3.** to disable or impede by binding the arms of **4.** to confine
**pink¹** (piŋk) *n.* [< ?] **1.** any of certain annual and perennial plants of the pink family **2.** the flower **3.** pale red **4.** the finest example, degree, etc. **5.** [Colloq.] a person of somewhat radical political views: a derogatory term —*adj.* **1.** designating a family of plants with bright-colored flowers, including the carnation, sweet william, etc. **2.** pale-red **3.** [Colloq.] somewhat radical —**in the pink** [Colloq.] in good physical condition; healthy —**pink′ish** *adj.* —**pink′ness** *n.*
**pink²** (piŋk) *vt.* [akin ? to OE. *pyngan*, to prick] **1.** to ornament (cloth, paper, etc.) by making perforations in a pattern **2.** to cut a saw-toothed edge on (cloth, etc.) to prevent unraveling or for decoration **3.** to prick or stab **4.** to adorn or embellish —**pink′er** *n.*
**pink·eye** (piŋk′ī′) *n.* an acute, contagious form of conjunctivitis, in which the eyeball also is inflamed
**pink·ie, pink·y** (piŋk′kē) *n., pl.* **pink′ies** [prob. < Du. dim. of *pink*, little finger] the fifth, or smallest, finger
**pink·ing shears** (piŋk′iŋ) shears with notched blades, for pinking the edges of cloth, etc.
**pink salmon** a widespread species of salmon, often canned
**pink tea** [Colloq.] a frivolous social gathering
**pin money 1.** orig., an allowance given to a wife for small personal expenses **2.** any small sum of money, as for incidental minor expenses
**pin·na** (pin′ə) *n., pl.* **-nae** (-ē), **-nas** [L., a feather] **1.** *Anat.* the external ear **2.** *Bot.* a leaflet of a pinnately compound leaf **3.** *Zool.* a feather, wing, fin, etc. —**pin′nal** *adj.*
**pin·nace** (pin′is) *n.* [< Fr. < Sp., ult. < L. *pinus*, PINE¹] **1.** a small sailing ship **2.** a ship's boat
**pin·na·cle** (pin′ə k'l) *n.* [< MFr. < LL. dim. of L. *pinna*, wing] **1.** a small turret or spire on a buttress, etc. **2.** a slender, pointed formation, as a mountain peak **3.** the highest point; acme —*vt.* **-cled, -cling 1.** to set on a pinnacle **2.** to furnish with pinnacles **3.** to form the pinnacle of
**pin·nate** (pin′āt, -it) *adj.* [ModL. < L. < *pinna*, a feather] **1.** resembling a feather **2.** *Bot.* with featherlike leaflets on each side of a common axis —**pin′nate·ly** *adv.* —**pin·na′tion** *n.*
**pi·noch·le, pi·noc·le** (pē′nuk′'l, -näk′'l) *n.* [earlier *binochle* < G. dial. < Fr. *binocle*, eyeglasses] a card game using a 48-card deck made up of two of every card above the eight
**pi·ñon** (pin′yən, -yōn; *Sp.* pē nyôn′) *n., pl.* **-ñons**; *Sp.* **-ño′nes** (-nyô′nes) [< AmSp. < Sp., ult. < L. *pinus*, PINE¹] **1.** any of several small pines with large, edible seeds, found in western N. America **2.** the seed
**pin·point** (pin′point′) *vt.* **1.** to show the location of (a place on a map, etc.) by sticking in a pin **2.** to locate, define, or focus on precisely —*n.* **1.** the point of a pin **2.** something trifling
**pin·prick** (-prik′) *n.* **1.** a tiny hole made as by a pin **2.** a minor irritation or annoyance
**pins and needles** a prickling feeling as in a numb limb —**on pins and needles** in anxious suspense

*fat, āpe, cär; ten, ēven; is, bīte; gō, hôrn, tool, look; oil, out; up, fur; get; joy; yet; chin; she; thin, then; zh, leisure; ŋ, ring; ə for a in ago, e in agent, i in sanity, o in comply, u in focus; ' as in able (ā′b'l); Fr. bal; ë, Fr. coeur; ö, Fr. feu; Fr. mon; ô, Fr. coq; ü, Fr. duc; r, Fr. cri; H, G. ich; kh, G. doch; ‡foreign; \*hypothetical; < derived from. See inside front cover.*

**pin·set·ter** (-set'ər) *n.* **1.** a person that sets up bowling pins on the alley **2.** a device that does this automatically Also **pin'spot'ter** (-spät'ər)

**pin stripe 1.** a very thin stripe, as in some suits **2.** a pattern of such stripes in parallel

**pint** (pīnt) *n.* [< MFr. < ML. *pinta:* orig. prob. a painted spot marking the level in a measure] **1.** a measure of capacity (liquid or dry) equal to 1/2 quart **2.** a pint container Abbrev. **pt., p.**

**pin·tail** (pin'tāl') *n., pl.* **-tails', -tail'**: see PLURAL, II, D, 1 **1.** any of several ducks, esp. one with long, pointed middle tail feathers **2.** a grouse with a long, pointed tail — **pin'tailed'** *adj.*

**pin·tle** (pin't'l) *n.* [OE. *pintel,* penis] a pin or bolt upon which some other part pivots or turns

**pin·to** (pin'tō) *adj.* [AmSp. < Sp., ult. < L. pp. of *pingere,* to paint] marked with patches of white and another color —*n., pl.* **-tos 1.** a pinto horse **2.** *same as* PINTO BEAN

PINTLE

**pinto bean** a mottled kidney bean grown in the southwestern U.S. for food and fodder

**pint-size** (pīnt'sīz') *adj.* tiny: also **pint'-sized'**

**pin·up** (pin'up') *adj.* **1.** that is or can be pinned up on or fastened to a wall *[a pinup lamp]* **2.** [Colloq.] designating or of a girl whose sexual attractiveness makes her a suitable subject for the kind of pictures often pinned up on walls, as of a barracks —*n.* [Colloq.] a pinup girl, picture, etc.

**pin·wheel** (-hwēl', -wēl') *n.* **1.** a small wheel with colored vanes of paper, etc., pinned to a stick so as to revolve in the wind **2.** a firework that revolves when set off

**pin·worm** (-wurm') *n.* a small, unsegmented worm sometimes parasitic in the human large intestine

**pin·y** (pī'nē) *adj.* **pin'i·er, pin'i·est** *same as* PINEY

**pi·on** (pī'än') *n.* [PI² + (MES)ON] any of three mesons, positive, negative, or neutral, with a mass approximately 270 times that of an electron

**pi·o·neer** (pī'ə nir') *n.* [< Fr. < OFr. *peonier,* foot soldier < *peon:* see PEON] one who goes before, preparing the way for others, as an early settler or a scientist in research —*adj.* of a pioneer —*vi.* to be a pioneer —*vt.* **1.** to prepare or open (a way, etc.) **2.** to be a pioneer in or of

**pi·ous** (pī'əs) *adj.* [L. *pius*] **1.** having or showing religious devotion **2.** springing from actual or pretended religious devotion **3.** virtuous in a hypocritical way **4.** sacred —**pi'ous·ly** *adv.* —**pi'ous·ness** *n.*

**pip¹** (pip) *n.* [contr. < PIPPIN] a small seed, as of an apple, pear, orange, etc.

**pip²** (pip) *n.* [earlier *peep* < ?] **1.** any of the spots on playing cards, dice, etc. **2.** *same as* BLIP (sense 1)

**pip³** (pip) *vi.* **pipped, pip'ping** [prob. var. of PEEP¹] to peep or chirp, as a young bird —*vt.* to break through (the shell): said of a hatching bird

**pip⁴** (pip) *n.* [< MDu., ult. < L. *pituita,* phlegm] **1.** a contagious disease of fowl, characterized by the secretion of mucus in the throat **2.** [Colloq.] any unspecified human ailment: a jocular usage

**pipe** (pīp) *n.* [OE., ult. < L. *pipare,* to chirp] **1.** a cylindrical tube, as of wood or metal, into which air is blown to make musical sounds; specif., *[pl.] same as:* **a)** PANPIPE **b)** BAGPIPE **2.** any of the tubes in an organ that produce the tones **3.** a boatswain's whistle **4.** a high, shrill sound, as of a birdcall **5.** *[often pl.]* the vocal organs, esp. as used in singing **6.** a long tube of concrete, metal, etc., for conveying water, oil, etc. **7.** a tubular organ of the body; esp., *[pl.]* the respiratory organs **8.** anything tubular in form **9.** **a)** a tube with a small bowl at one end, in which tobacco, etc. is smoked **b)** enough tobacco, etc. to fill such a bowl **10.** **a)** a cask holding about 126 gallons **b)** this volume as a unit of measure —*vi.* **piped, pip'ing 1.** to play on a pipe **2.** to utter shrill sounds —*vt.* **1.** to play (a tune, etc.) on a pipe **2.** to utter in a shrill voice **3.** to bring, call, etc. by piping **4.** to convey (water, oil, etc.) by pipes **5.** to provide with pipes **6.** to trim (a dress, etc.) with piping **7.** [Slang] to look at —**pipe down** [Slang] to become quiet, stop shouting, etc. —**pipe up 1.** to begin to play or sing (music) **2.** to speak up or say, esp. in a piping voice

**pipe clay** a white, plastic clay used for making tobacco pipes, whitening leather, etc.

**pipe cleaner** a short length of wires twisted to hold tiny tufts of yarn, for cleaning pipestems

**pipe cutter** a tool that is rotated around a metal pipe and cuts it by sharp disks in a curved jaw

**pipe dream** [Colloq.] a fantastic idea or vain hope, such as an opium smoker might have

**pipe fitter** a mechanic who installs and maintains plumbing pipes, etc. —**pipe fitting**

**pipe·ful** (pīp'fool') *n., pl.* **-fuls'** the amount (of tobacco, etc.) put in a pipe at one time

**pipe·line** (-līn') *n.* **1.** a line of pipes for conveying water, gas, oil, etc. **2.** any means whereby something is conveyed *[a pipeline of information]* —*vt.* **-lined', -lin'ing** to convey by, or supply with, a pipeline

**pipe of peace** *same as* CALUMET

**pipe organ** *same as* ORGAN (sense 1 *a*)

**pip·er** (-ər) *n.* a person who plays on a pipe; esp., a bagpiper —**pay the piper** to suffer the consequences of doing as one pleases

**pipe·stem** (-stem') *n.* **1.** the slender stem of a tobacco pipe **2.** anything like this in form

**pi·pette, pi·pet** (pī pet', pi-) *n.* [Fr., dim. of *pipe,* a pipe] a slender tube for measuring or transferring small amounts of liquids

**pip·ing** (pīp'iŋ) *n.* **1.** the act of one who pipes **2.** music made by pipes **3.** a shrill sound **4.** a system of pipes **5.** material used for pipes **6.** a narrow, rounded fold of material with which edges or seams are trimmed —*adj.* **1.** playing on a pipe **2.** shrill —**piping hot** so hot as to sizzle; very hot

**pip·it** (pip'it) *n.* [echoic of its cry] a small songbird with a slender bill and streaked breast

**pip·kin** (pip'kin) *n.* [? dim. of PIPE, *n.* 10] a small earthenware pot

**pip·pin** (pip'in) *n.* [OFr. *pepin,* seed, pip] any of a number of varieties of apple

**pip·sis·se·wa** (pip sis'ə wə) *n.* [< Algonquian] a N. American evergreen plant with jagged, leathery leaves formerly used in medicine

**pip·squeak** (pip'skwēk') *n.* [PIP³ + SQUEAK] [Colloq.] a person, etc. regarded as small or insignificant

**pi·quant** (pē'kənt, -känt; *now occas.* -kwänt) *adj.* [Fr. prp. of *piquer,* to prick] **1.** pleasantly sharp or spicy to the taste **2.** exciting interest; stimulating; provocative —**pi'quan·cy** (-kən sē), **pi'quant·ness** *n.* —**pi'quant·ly** *adv.*

**pique** (pēk) *n.* [Fr. < *piquer,* to prick] **1.** resentment at being slighted; ruffled pride **2.** a fit of displeasure —*vt.* **piqued, piqu'ing 1.** to arouse resentment in, as by slighting **2.** to arouse (one's curiosity, etc.)

**pi·qué** (pē kā') *n.* [Fr., pp. of *piquer,* to prick] a firmly woven cotton fabric with ribbed wales

**pi·quet** (pi ket', -kā') *n.* [Fr. < *pic,* orig., a sting] a game of cards for two, played with 32 cards

**pi·ra·cy** (pī'rə sē) *n., pl.* **-cies** [< ML: see PIRATE] **1.** robbery of ships on the high seas **2.** the unauthorized publication or use of a copyrighted or patented work

**Pi·rae·us** (pī rē'əs) seaport in SE Greece: part of Athens metropolitan area: pop. 184,000

**Pi·ran·del·lo** (pir'ən del'ō; *It.* pē'rän del'lô), **Lu·i·gi** (lōō ē'jē) 1867–1936; It. playwright & novelist

**pi·ra·nha** (pi rän'yə, -rän'-) *n.* [Braz. Port. < Tupi, toothed fish] a small, fiercely voracious freshwater fish of South America

**pi·rate** (pī'rət) *n.* [< L. < Gr. *peiratēs* < *peiran,* to attack] **1.** a person who practices piracy; esp., a robber of ships on the high seas **2.** a pirates' ship —*vt., vi.* **-rat·ed, -rat·ing 1.** to practice piracy (upon) **2.** to take (something) by piracy **3.** to publish or reproduce without authorization (a literary work, musical recording, etc.), esp. in violation of a copyright —**pi·rat·i·cal** (pī rat'i k'l), **pi·rat'ic** *adj.* —**pi·rat'i·cal·ly** *adv.*

**pi·rogue** (pi rōg') *n.* [< Fr. < Sp. *piragua* < Carib] a canoe made by hollowing out a log

**pir·ou·ette** (pir'ou wet') *n.* [Fr., spinning top; prob. < dial. *piroue,* a top] a whirling around on one foot or the point of the toe, esp. in ballet —*vi.* **-et'ted, -et'ting** to do a pirouette

**Pi·sa** (pē'zə; *It.* pē'sä) city in W Italy: famous for its Leaning Tower, a bell tower which leans more than 17 ft. from the perpendicular: pop. 103,000

**pis·ca·to·ri·al** (pis'kə tôr'ē əl) *adj.* [< L. < *piscator,* fisherman] of fishermen or fishing: also **pis'ca·to'ry** —**pis'ca·to'ri·al·ly** *adv.*

**Pis·ces** (pī'sēz, pis'ēz) [L., pl. of *piscis,* a fish] **1.** a constellation south of Andromeda **2.** the twelfth sign of the zodiac: see ZODIAC, illus.

**pis·ci-** [< L. *piscis,* a fish] a combining form meaning fish *[pisciculture]*

**pis·ci·cul·ture** (pis'i kul'chər) *n.* [prec. + CULTURE] the breeding of fish as a science or industry

**pis·cine** (pis'īn, -ēn; pī'sēn) *adj.* [< L. *piscis,* a fish] of or resembling fish

**Pi·sis·tra·tus** (pī sis'trə təs, pi-) 600?–527 B.C.; tyrant of Athens (560–527, with two interruptions)

**pis·mire** (pis'mīr', piz'-) *n.* [< ME. < *pisse,* urine + *mire,* ant: from the odor of ants' formic acid] an ant

**pis·mo clam** (piz'mō) [after *Pismo* Beach, Calif.] a heavy-shelled, edible clam found on sandy beaches of California and Mexico

**Pis·sar·ro** (pē sà rō'; *E.* pi sär'ō), **Ca·mille** (kà mē'y') 1830–1903; Fr. painter

**pis·ta·chi·o** (pi stä'shē ō', -stash'ē ō', -stash'ō) *n., pl.*

**-chi·os′** [< It. < L. < Gr. *pistakē* < OPer. *pistah*] **1.** a small tree related to the cashew **2.** its edible, greenish seed (**pistachio nut**) **3.** the flavor of this nut **4.** a light yellow-green color

**pis·til** (pis′t'l) *n.* [Fr. < L. *pistillum*, PESTLE] the seedbearing organ of a flowering plant, consisting of one carpel or of several united carpels

**pis·til·late** (pis′tə lit, -lāt′) *adj.* having a pistil or pistils; specif., having pistils but no stamens

**pis·tol** (pis′t'l) *n.* [< Fr. < G. < Czech *pišt'al*, prob. < *pisk,* a whistling sound] **1.** a small firearm held and fired with one hand **2.** such a firearm in which the chamber is part of the barrel: cf. REVOLVER —*vt.* -toled or -tolled, -tol·ing or -tol·ling to shoot with a pistol

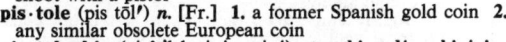

PISTIL

**pis·tole** (pis tōl′) *n.* [Fr.] **1.** a former Spanish gold coin **2.** any similar obsolete European coin

**pis·tol-whip** (pis′t'l hwip′, -wip′) *vt.* -whipped′, -whip′ping to beat with a pistol, esp. about the head

**pis·ton** (pis′t'n) *n.* [Fr. < It. < *pistare,* to beat, ult. < L. *pinsere,* to pound] **1.** a disk or short cylinder closely fitted in a hollow cylinder and moved back and forth by the pressure of a fluid so as to transmit reciprocating motion to a rod (**piston rod**), or moved by the rod so as to exert pressure on the fluid **2.** *Music* a sliding valve moved in the cylinder of a brass-wind instrument to change the pitch

**piston ring** a split metal ring placed around a piston to make it fit the cylinder closely

**pit¹** (pit) *n.* [Du. < MDu. *pitte*] the hard stone, as of the plum, peach, etc., which contains the seed —*vt.* pit′ted, pit′ting to remove the pit from

**pit²** (pit) *n.* [OE. *pytt,* ult. < L. *puteus,* a well] **1.** a hole in the ground **2.** an abyss **3.** hell: used with *the* **4.** a covered hole used to trap wild animals; pitfall **5.** any concealed danger; trap **6.** an enclosed area in which animals are kept or made to fight *[a bear pit]* **7.** *a)* the shaft of a coal mine *b)* the mine itself **8.** a hollow on a part of the human body *[an armpit]* **9.** a small hollow in a surface; specif., a smallpox scar on the skin **10.** [Brit.] *a)* the rear part of the ground floor of a theater *b)* the spectators in that section **11.** the sunken section in front of the stage, where the orchestra sits **12.** the part of the floor of an exchange where a special branch of business is transacted *[the corn pit]* **13.** an area off the side of a racing speedway for servicing cars —*vt.* pit′ted, pit′ting **1.** to put or store in a pit **2.** to make pits in **3.** to mark with small scars **4.** to set (cocks, etc.) in a pit to fight **5.** to set in competition (*against*) —*vi.* to become marked with pits —**the pits** [Slang] the worst possible place, condition, etc.

**pi·ta** (pē′tä, -tə) *n.* [Heb. < *pāt,* loaf] a round, flat bread of the Middle East that can be split open to form a pocket for a filling

**pit·a·pat** (pit′ə pat′) *adv.* [echoic] with rapid beating; palpitatingly —*n.* a rapid succession of beats —*vi.* -pat′ted, -pat′ting to go pitapat

**Pit·cairn Island** (pit′kern) Brit. island in Polynesia, South Pacific: settled by Brit. mutineers in 1790

**pitch¹** (pich) *n.* [OE. *pic* < L. *pix*] **1.** a black, sticky substance formed in the distillation of coal tar, petroleum, etc. and used for waterproofing, pavements, etc. **2.** natural asphalt **3.** a resin from certain evergreen trees —*vt.* to cover or smear as with pitch

**pitch²** (pich) *n.* [ME. *picchen*] **1.** to set up *[to pitch a tent]* **2.** to throw; fling; toss **3.** to fix or set at a particular point, level, degree, etc. **4.** *Baseball a)* to throw (the ball) to the batter *b)* to serve as pitcher for (a game) **5.** *Golf* to loft (a ball), esp. in making an approach **6.** *Music* to set the key of (a tune, an instrument, or the voice) —*vi.* **1.** to encamp **2.** to take up one's position; settle **3.** to hurl or toss anything, as hay, a baseball, etc. **4.** to fall or plunge forward or headlong **5.** to incline downward; dip **6.** to toss with the bow and stern rising and falling: said of a ship **7.** to move in a like manner in the air: said of an aircraft **8.** to act as pitcher in a ball game —*n.* **1.** act or manner of pitching **2.** a throw; toss **3.** the pitching of a ship or aircraft in rough sea or air **4.** anything pitched **5.** the amount pitched **6.** a point or degree *[emotion was at a high pitch]* **7.** the degree of slope or inclination **8.** a card game in which the suit of the first card led becomes trump **9.** [Slang] a line of talk, such as a salesman or hawker uses **10.** *Machinery* the distance between corresponding points,

as on two adjacent gear teeth or on two adjacent threads of a screw **11.** *Music,* etc. *a)* that quality of a tone or sound determined by the frequency of vibration of the sound waves: the greater the frequency, the higher the pitch *b)* a standard of pitch for tuning instruments —**make a pitch for** [Slang] to speak in favor of —**pitch in** [Colloq.] **1.** to set to work energetically **2.** to make a contribution —**pitch into** [Colloq.] to attack

**pitch-black** (pich′blak′) *adj.* very black

**pitch·blende** (-blend′) *n.* [< G. < *pech,* PITCH¹ + *blende,* BLENDE] a brown to black lustrous mineral, the chief ore of uranium

**pitch-dark** (-därk′) *adj.* very dark

**pitched battle** (picht) **1.** a battle in which placement of troops and the line of combat are fixed before the action **2.** a hard-fought battle

**pitch·er¹** (pich′ər) *n.* [< OFr. < VL. *bicarium,* a jug, cup: see BEAKER] a container, usually with a handle and lip, for holding and pouring liquids —**pitch′er·ful′** *n., pl.* -fuls′

**pitch·er²** (pich′ər) *n.* [PITCH² + -ER] *Baseball* the player who pitches the ball to opposing batters

**pitcher plant** a plant with pitcherlike leaves which attract and trap insects

**pitch·fork** (pich′fôrk′) *n.* a large, long-handled fork used for lifting and tossing hay, etc. —*vt.* to lift and toss as with a pitchfork

**pitch·man** (-mən) *n., pl.* -men **1.** a person who hawks novelties, etc. from a stand, as at a carnival **2.** [Slang] any high-pressure salesman or advertiser

**pitch·out** (-out′) *n. Baseball* a ball pitched deliberately away from the plate so that the catcher can try to throw out a runner who is off base

**pitch pine** a resinous pine from which pitch or turpentine is obtained

**pitch pipe** a small pipe which produces a fixed tone as a standard for tuning instruments, etc.

**pitch·y** (pich′ē) *adj.* pitch′i·er, pitch′i·est **1.** full of or smeared with pitch **2.** thick and sticky like pitch **3.** black

**pit·e·ous** (pit′ē əs) *adj.* arousing or deserving pity —**pit′e·ous·ly** *adv.* —**pit′e·ous·ness** *n.*

**pit·fall** (pit′fôl′) *n.* [< ME. < *pit,* PIT² + *falle,* a trap < OE. *fealle*] **1.** a lightly covered pit used as a trap for animals **2.** any hidden danger or difficulty

**pith** (pith) *n.* [OE. *pitha*] **1.** the soft, spongy tissue in the center of certain plant stems **2.** any soft core, as of a bone **3.** the essential part; gist **4.** importance: now usually in the phrase **of great pith and moment** —*vt.* **1.** to remove the pith from (a plant stem) **2.** to pierce or sever the spinal cord of (an animal)

**Pith·e·can·thro·pus e·rec·tus** (pith′ə kan′thrə pəs i rek′təs, -kan thrō′pəs) [ModL. < Gr. *pithēkos,* an ape + *anthrōpos,* man] *an earlier name for* JAVA MAN

**pith·y** (pith′ē) *adj.* pith′i·er, pith′i·est **1.** of, like, or full of pith **2.** terse and full of substance or meaning —**pith′i·ly** *adv.* —**pith′i·ness** *n.*

**pit·i·a·ble** (pit′ē ə b'l) *adj.* arousing or deserving pity, sometimes mixed with scorn or contempt —**pit′i·a·ble·ness** *n.* —**pit′i·a·bly** *adv.*

**pit·i·ful** (pit′i fəl) *adj.* **1.** exciting or deserving pity **2.** deserving contempt; despicable —**pit′i·ful·ly** *adv.* —**pit′i·ful·ness** *n.*

**pit·i·less** (-lis) *adj.* without pity; merciless —**pit′i·less·ly** *adv.* —**pit′i·less·ness** *n.*

**pit·man** (pit′mən) *n., pl.* -men a person who works in a pit; esp., a coal miner

**pi·ton** (pē′tän; *Fr.* pē tōn′) *n., pl.* -tons (-tänz; *Fr.* -tōn′) [Fr. < MFr., a spike] a metal spike that is driven into rock or ice for support in mountain climbing: it has an eye to which a rope can be secured

**Pitt** (pit), **William 1.** 1st Earl of Chatham, 1708–78; Eng. statesman; prime minister (1766–68) **2.** 1759–1806; Eng. statesman; prime minister (1783–1801; 1804–06): son of prec.

**pit·tance** (pit′'ns) *n.* [< OFr. *pitance,* food allowed a monk, ult. < L. *pietas,* PIETY] **1.** a meager allowance of money **2.** a small amount or share

**pit·ter-pat·ter** (pit′ər pat′ər) *n.* [echoic] a rapid succession of light beating or tapping sounds, as of raindrops —*adv.* with a pitter-patter —*vi.* to fall, etc. with a pitter-patter

**Pitts·burgh** (pits′bərg) [after Wm. PITT (the father)] city in SW Pa.: pop. 424,000 (met. area 2,261,000)

**Pitts·field** (pits′fēld′) [after Wm. PITT (the father)] city in W Mass.: pop. 52,000

**pi·tu·i·tar·y** (pi tōō′ə ter′ē, -tyōō′-) *adj.* [< L. < *pituita,* phlegm] of the pituitary gland —*n., pl.* -tar′ies same as PITUITARY GLAND

**pituitary gland** (or **body**) a small, oval endocrine gland attached to the base of the brain: it secretes hormones influencing body growth, the activity of other endocrine glands, etc.

**pit viper** any of a family of poisonous snakes, as the rattlesnake, copperhead, etc., with a pit on each side of the head

**pit·y** (pit′ē) *n., pl.* **pit′ies** [< OFr. < L. *pietas*, PIETY] 1. sorrow for another's suffering or misfortune; compassion 2. a cause for sorrow or regret —*vt., vi.* **pit′ied**, **pit′y·ing** to feel pity (for) —**have** (or **take**) **pity on** to show pity for —pit′i·er *n.* —pit′y·ing·ly *adv.*

**‡più** (pyoo) *adv.* [It.] more: a direction in music, as in *più allegro*, more quickly

**Pi·us** (pī′əs) name of twelve popes; esp., **Pius XII** 1876–1958; Pope (1939–58)

**piv·ot** (piv′ət) *n.* [Fr.] 1. a point, shaft, etc. on which something turns 2. a person or thing on which something turns or depends 3. a pivoting movement —*adj.* same as PIVOTAL —*vt.* to provide with or mount on a pivot —*vi.* to turn as on a pivot

**piv·ot·al** (-'l) *adj.* 1. of or acting as a pivot 2. on which something turns or depends; crucial

**pix·ie, pix·y** (pik′sē) *n., pl.* **pix′ies** [< Brit. dial.] a fairy or sprite, esp. one that is puckish —pix′ie·ish, pix′y·ish *adj.*

**pix·i·lat·ed** (pik′sə lāt′id) *adj.* [altered < *pixy-led*, lost] eccentric, daft, puckish, etc.

**Pi·zar·ro** (pē thär′rō; *E.* pi zä′rō), **Fran·cis·co** (frän-thēs′kō) 1470?–1541; Sp. conqueror of Peru

**pi·zazz, piz·zazz** (pə zaz′) *n.* [prob. echoic of exuberant cry] [Slang] 1. energy, vitality, spirit, etc. 2. smartness, style, flair, etc. —pi·zaz′zy, piz·zaz′zy *adj.*

**piz·za** (pēt′sə) *n.* [It.] an Italian dish made by baking a thin layer of dough covered with a spiced preparation of tomatoes, cheese, etc.

**piz·ze·ri·a** (pēt′sə rē′ə) *n.* [It.] a place where pizzas are prepared and sold

**piz·zi·ca·to** (pit′sə kät′ō; *It.* pēt′tsē kä′tò) *adj.* [It.] *Music* plucked: a direction to pluck the strings of a violin, viola, etc. —*adv.* in a pizzicato manner —*n., pl.* **-ca′ti** (-ē; *It.* -tē) a note or passage played in this way

**pk.** *pl.* **pks.** 1. pack 2. park 3. peak 4. peck

**pkg.** package; packages

**pkwy.** parkway

**pl.** 1. place 2. plate 3. plural

**plac·a·ble** (plak′ə b'l, plā′kə-) *adj.* [< OFr. < L. < *placare*, to soothe] capable of being placated; forgiving —plac′a·bil′i·ty *n.* —plac′a·bly *adv.*

**plac·ard** (plak′ärd, -ərd) *n.* [< MFr. < MDu. *placke*, a piece] 1. a notice for display in a public place; poster 2. a small card or plaque —*vt.* 1. to place placards on or in 2. to advertise by means of placards 3. to display as a placard —*vi.* to set up placards

**pla·cate** (plā′kāt, plak′āt) *vt.* -**cat·ed**, -**cat·ing** [< L. pp. of *placare*, to appease] to stop from being angry; appease; pacify —pla′cat·er *n.* —pla·ca′tion *n.* —pla′ca·tive *adj.* —pla′ca·to′ry *adj.*

**place** (plās) *n.* [OFr. < L. *platea* < Gr. *plateia*, a street < *platys*, broad] 1. a square or court in a city 2. a short street 3. space; room 4. a region or locality 5. *a)* the part of space occupied by a person or thing *b)* situation or state 6. a city, town, or village 7. a residence; dwelling 8. a building or space devoted to a special purpose [a *place* of amusement] 9. a particular spot on or part of something [a sore *place* on the leg] 10. a particular passage or page in a book, etc. 11. position or standing, esp. one of importance [one's *place* in history] 12. a step or point in a sequence [in the first *place*] 13. the customary or proper position, time, or character 14. a space reserved or occupied by a person, as a seat in a theater, etc. 15. a job or position; employment 16. official position 17. the duties of any position 18. one's duty or business 19. *Arith.* the position of an integer, as in noting decimals [the third decimal *place*] 20. *Racing* the first, second, or third position at the finish, specif. the second position —*vt.* **placed**, **plac′ing** 1. *a)* to put in a particular place, condition, or relation *b)* to identify by associating with the correct place or circumstances 2. to find employment or a position for 3. to assign (a value) 4. to offer for consideration, etc. 5. to repose (trust, etc.) *in* a person or thing 6. to finish in (a specified position) in a competition —*vi.* to finish among the first three in a contest; specif., to finish second in a horse or dog race —**give place** 1. to make room 2. to yield —**go places** [Slang] to achieve success —**in** (or **out of**) **place** 1. in (or out of) the customary or proper place 2. being (or not being) fitting or timely —**in place of** instead of —**put someone in his place** to humble someone who is overstepping bounds —**take place** to occur —**take the place of** to be a substitute for

**pla·ce·bo** (plə sē′bō) *n., pl.* -**bos**, -**boes** [L., I shall please] *Med.* a sugar pill or the like given merely to humor a patient

**place card** a small card with the name of a guest, set at the place that he is to occupy at a table

**place kick** *Football* a kick made while the ball is held in place on the ground, as in attempting a field goal —**place′-kick′** *vi.*

**place mat** a small mat serving as an individual table cover for a person at a meal

**place·ment** (plās′mənt) *n.* 1. a placing or being placed 2. the finding of employment for a person 3. location or arrangement

**pla·cen·ta** (plə sen′tə) *n., pl.* -**tas**, -**tae** (-tē) [ModL. < L., lit., a cake, ult. < Gr. *plax*, a flat object] a vascular organ developed within the uterus, connected by the umbilical cord to the fetus and supplying it with nourishment —pla·cen′tal, pla·cen′tate *adj.*

**plac·er¹** (plās′ər) *n.* a person who places

**plac·er²** (plas′ər) *n.* [AmSp. < Catal. < *plassa*, a place] a waterborne or glacial deposit of gravel or sand containing particles of gold, platinum, etc. that can be washed out

**placer mining** (plas′ər) mining in placer deposits by washing, dredging, etc.

**place setting** the china, silverware, etc. for setting one place at a table for a meal

**plac·id** (plas′id) *adj.* [L. *placidus*] undisturbed; tranquil; calm —pla·cid·i·ty (plə sid′ə tē), plac′id·ness *n.* —plac′id·ly *adv.*

**plack·et** (plak′it) *n.* [prob. < PLACARD, in related obs. sense] a slit at the waist of a skirt or dress to make it easy to put on and take off

**pla·gia·rism** (plā′jə riz'm, -jē ə riz'm) *n.* [ < L. *plagiarius*, kidnapper] 1. the act of plagiarizing 2. an idea, plot, etc. that has been plagiarized Also pla′gia·ry, *pl.* -ries —pla′gia·rist *n.* —pla′gia·ris′tic *adj.*

**pla·gia·rize** (-rīz′) *vt., vi.* -**rized**, -**riz′ing** to take (ideas, writings, etc.) from (another) and pass them off as one's own —pla′gia·riz′er *n.*

**pla·gi·o·clase** (plā′jē ə klās′) *n.* [< G. < Gr. *plagios*, oblique + *klasis*, a cleaving] any of a series of common rock-forming feldspars

**plague** (plāg) *n.* [< MFr. < L. *plaga* < Gr. *plēgē*, misfortune] 1. anything that afflicts or troubles; calamity 2. any deadly epidemic disease; specif., same as BUBONIC PLAGUE 3. [Colloq.] a nuisance —*vt.* **plagued**, **plagu′ing** 1. to afflict with a plague 2. to vex; torment —plagu′er *n.*

**plaice** (plās) *n., pl.* **plaice**, **plaic′es**: see PLURAL, II, D, 2 [< OFr. < LL. *platessa*, flatfish < Gr. *platys*, broad] a kind of American or European flatfish

**plaid** (plad) *n.* [Gael. *plaide*, a blanket] 1. a long woolen cloth with a crossbarred pattern, worn over the shoulder by Scottish Highlanders 2. a fabric with such a pattern 3. any pattern of this kind —*adj.* having such a pattern: also **plaid′ed**

**plain** (plān) *adj.* [OFr. < L. *planus*, flat] 1. orig., flat; level 2. not obstructed; open [in *plain* view] 3. clearly understood; obvious [his meaning was *plain*] 4. *a)* outspoken; frank [*plain* talk] *b)* downright [*plain* nonsense] 5. not luxurious [a *plain* coat] 6. not complicated; simple [*plain* sewing] 7. homely [a *plain* face] 8. unfigured, undyed, etc. [*plain* cloth] 9. unmixed [*plain* soda] 10. not of high rank; ordinary [a *plain* man] —*n.* an extent of level country —*adv.* clearly or simply —plain′ly *adv.* —plain′ness *n.*

**plain·clothes man** (plān′klōz′, -klōthz′) a police detective who wears civilian clothes on duty: also **plain′clothes′man** (-mən) *n., pl.* -**men**

**plains·man** (plānz′mən) *n., pl.* -**men** an inhabitant of the plains; esp., a frontiersman on the Great Plains

**plain·song** (plān′sôŋ′) *n.* early Christian church music, still used in some churches, in free rhythm and sung in unison: also **plain′chant′** (-chant′)

**plain-spo·ken** (plān′spō′k'n) *adj.* speaking or spoken plainly or frankly —plain′-spo′ken·ness *n.*

**plaint** (plānt) *n.* [< OFr. < L. < pp. of *plangere*, to lament] 1. [Poet.] lament. 2. a complaint

**plain·tiff** (plān′tif) *n.* [< OFr. < *plaindre*, to complain: see prec.] a person who brings a suit into a court of law; complainant

**plain·tive** (-tiv) *adj.* [< OFr.: see prec.] expressing sorrow or melancholy; sad —plain′tive·ly *adv.* —plain′tive·ness *n.*

**plait** (plāt; *chiefly Brit.* plat) *n.* [< OFr. < L. pp. of *plicare*, to fold] 1. same as PLEAT 2. a braid of hair, ribbon, etc. —*vt.* 1. same as PLEAT 2. to braid or make by braiding —plait′er *n.*

**plan** (plan) *n.* [Fr., plan: merging of *plan* (< L. *planus*, flat) with MFr. *plant* < It. *pianta* < L. *planta*, sole of the foot] 1. a diagram showing the arrangement in horizontal section of a structure, piece of ground, etc. 2. *a)* a scheme for making, doing, or arranging something; project, schedule, etc. *b)* a method of proceeding 3. any outline or sketch —*vt.* **planned**, **plan′ning** 1. to make a plan of (a structure, etc.) 2. to devise a scheme for doing, making, etc. 3. to have in mind as a project or purpose —*vi.* to make plans —plan′ner *n.*

**plan·chette** (plan chet′, -shet′) *n.* [Fr., dim. of *planche,* PLANK] a small, three-cornered device used on a Ouija board: it is believed to move without guidance to letters or words as the fingers rest on it

**Planck** (pläŋk), **Max** (mäks) 1858–1947; Ger. physicist

**plane**[1] (plān) *n.* [< MFr. < L. < Gr. < *platys,* broad: from its broad leaves] any of several trees with maplelike leaves and bark that comes off in large patches: also **plane tree**

**plane**[2] (plān) *adj.* [L. *planus*] 1. flat; level 2. *Math. a)* on a surface that is a plane *b)* of such surfaces —*n.* 1. a surface that wholly contains a straight line joining any two points lying in it 2. a flat or level surface 3. a level of achievement, existence, etc. 4. *clipped form of* AIRPLANE 5. any airfoil; esp., a wing of an airplane

**plane**[3] (plān) *n.* [< OFr. < LL. < *planare,* to make level < L. *planus,* level] a carpenter's tool for shaving a wood surface to make it smooth, level, etc. —*vt.* **planed, plan′ing** 1. to make smooth or level with a plane 2. to remove with a plane (with *off* or *away*) —*vi.* 1. to work with a plane 2. to do the work of a plane —**plan′er** *n.*

**plane**[4] (plān) *vi.* **planed, plan′ing** [Fr. *planer* < OFr. (term used in falconry)] 1. to soar or glide 2. to rise from the water, as a hydroplane does 3. to travel by airplane

PLANE

**plane geometry** the branch of geometry dealing with plane figures

**plan·et** (plan′it) *n.* [< OFr. < LL. < Gr. *planētēs,* wanderer < *planan,* to wander] 1. orig., any heavenly body with apparent motion, including the sun, moon, Venus, Mars, etc. 2. now, any heavenly body shining by reflected sunlight and revolving about the sun: the major planets, in their order from the sun, are Mercury, Venus, Earth, Mars, Jupiter, Saturn, Uranus, Neptune, and Pluto 3. *Astrol.* any heavenly body regarded as influencing human lives

**plan·e·tar·i·um** (plan′ə ter′ē əm) *n., pl.* **-i·ums, -i·a** (-ə) [ModL. < LL. *planeta,* PLANET + L. (*sol*)*arium,* SOLARIUM] 1. an arrangement for projecting the images of the sun, moon, planets, and stars inside a large dome by means of a complex optical instrument that is revolved to show the celestial motions 2. the room or building containing this

**plan·e·tar·y** (plan′ə ter′ē) *adj.* 1. of a planet or the planets 2. terrestrial; global 3. wandering; erratic 4. moving in an orbit, like a planet 5. designating or of an epicyclic train of gears, as in an automobile transmission 6. *Astrol.* under the influence of a planet

**plan·e·tes·i·mal** (plan′ə tes′i m'l) *adj.* [PLANET + (IN)FINIT)ESIMAL] of very small bodies in space that move in planetary orbits: according to the **planetesimal hypothesis** the planets were formed by the uniting of planetesimals —*n.* any of these bodies

**plan·et·oid** (plan′ə toid′) *n.* [PLANET + -OID] *same as* ASTEROID (*n.* 1)

**plank** (plaŋk) *n.* [< ONormFr. < OFr. < LL. *planca,* ult. < Gr. *phalanx,* PHALANX] 1. a long, broad, thick board 2. timber cut into planks 3. something that supports 4. any of the principles in a platform, as of a political party —*vt.* 1. to cover, lay, etc. with planks 2. to broil and serve (steak, etc.) on a board 3. [Colloq.] *a)* to lay or set (*down*) with force *b)* to pay (usually with *down* or *out*) —**walk the plank** to walk off a plank projecting out from a ship's side, as pirates' victims were forced to do

**plank·ing** (-iŋ) *n.* 1. the act of laying planks 2. planks collectively

**plank·ton** (plaŋk′tən) *n.* [G. < Gr. *planktos,* wandering < *plazesthai,* to wander] the microscopic animal and plant life floating in bodies of water, used as food by fish — **plank·ton′ic** (-tän′ik) *adj.*

**planned parenthood** the planning of the number and spacing of the births of one's children

**pla·no-** [< L. *planus,* flat] *a combining form meaning:* 1. plane, flat 2. having one side plane and (the other as specified)

**pla·no·con·cave** (plā′nō kän kāv′, -kän′kāv) *adj.* having one side plane and the other concave

**pla·no·con·vex** (-kän veks′, -kän′veks) *adj.* having one side plane and the other convex

**plan position indicator** a circular radarscope on which the center represents the location of the transmitter and echoes represent the location of objects

**plant** (plant) *n.* [OE. *plante* < L. *planta,* a sprout] 1. a living organism that, unlike an animal, cannot move voluntarily, synthesizes food from carbon dioxide, and has no sense organs 2. a young tree, shrub, or herb, ready to put into other soil to mature 3. a soft-stemmed organism of this kind, as distinguished from a tree or shrub 4. the machinery, buildings, etc. of a factory 5. the equipment, buildings, etc. of an institution, as a school 6. the apparatus for a certain mechanical operation [a ship's power *plant*] 7. [Slang] a person placed, or thing used, to trick or trap —*vt.* 1. *a)* to put into the ground to grow *b)* to set plants in (a piece of ground) 2. to set firmly in position 3. to fix in the mind; implant 4. to settle; found; establish 5. to stock with animals 6. to put a stock of (fish, etc.) in a body of water 7. [Slang] to deliver (a punch, etc.) with force 8. [Slang] *a)* to place (a person or thing) in such a way as to trick, trap, etc. *b)* to place (an ostensible news item) in a newspaper, etc. 9. [Slang] to hide or conceal —*plant′like′ adj.*

**Plan·tag·e·net** (plan taj′ə nit) the ruling family of England (1154–1399), or any member of it

**plan·tain**[1] (plan′tin) *n.* [OFr. < L. *plantago*] any of various related plants with leaves at the base of the stem and spikes of tiny, greenish flowers

**plan·tain**[2] (plan′tin) *n.* [< Sp. *plá(n)tano,* lit., plane tree < L. *platanus:* see PLANE[1]] 1. a tropical banana plant with a coarse fruit eaten as a cooked vegetable 2. this fruit

**plantain lily** a plant of the lily family, with broad leaves and white or bluish flowers

**plan·tar** (plan′tər) *adj.* [< L. < *planta,* sole of the foot] of or on the sole of the foot

**plan·ta·tion** (plan tā′shən) *n.* [< L. < *plantare,* to plant] 1. formerly, a colony 2. an area growing cultivated crops 3. an estate, as in the South, cultivated by workers living on it 4. a large, cultivated planting of trees

**plant·er** (plan′tər) *n.* 1. the owner of a plantation 2. a person or machine that plants 3. a decorative container for house plants

**plan·ti·grade** (plan′tə grād′) *adj.* [Fr. < L. *planta,* sole + Fr. *-grade,* -GRADE] walking on the whole sole of the foot, as a bear, man, etc. —*n.* a plantigrade animal

**plant louse** *same as* APHID

**plaque** (plak) *n.* [Fr. < MDu. *placke,* a disk] 1. *a)* any thin, flat piece of metal, wood, etc. with a design, etc. used as a wall ornamentation *b)* a wall tablet commemorating or identifying something 2. a platelike brooch 3. *a)* an abnormal patch on the skin, mucous membrane, etc. *b)* a thin, transparent film on a tooth surface

**plash**[1] (plash) *n.* [OE. *plæsc,* prob. echoic] a pool or puddle —**plash′y** *adj.* **plash′i·er, plash′i·est**

**plash**[2] (plash) *vt., vi., n.* [echoic] *same as* SPLASH

**-pla·si·a** (plā′zhə, -zhē ə) [ModL. < Gr. < *plassein,* to mold] *a combining form meaning* change, development

**-plasm** (plaz′'m) [see ff.] *a combining form meaning:* 1. the fluid substances of an animal or vegetable cell 2. protoplasm [*ectoplasm*]

**plas·ma** (plaz′mə) *n.* [G. < Gr., something molded < *plassein,* to form] 1. the fluid part of blood, without the corpuscles 2. the fluid part of lymph, milk, or intramuscular liquid 3. *same as* PROTOPLASM 4. a high-temperature, ionized gas composed of nearly equal numbers of electrons and positive ions —**plas·mat′ic** (-mat′ik) *adj.*

**plasma membrane** a very thin living membrane surrounding the cytoplasm of a plant or animal cell

**plas·ter** (plas′tər) *n.* [< OE. & OFr. < LL. *plastrum* < L. *emplastrum* < Gr. < *emplassein,* to daub over] 1. a pasty mixture of lime, sand, and water, hard when dry, for coating walls, ceilings, etc. 2. *same as* PLASTER OF PARIS 3. a pasty preparation spread on cloth and applied to the body as a medicine —*vt.* 1. to cover, smear, etc. as with plaster 2. to apply or affix like a plaster [to *plaster* posters on walls] 3. to make lie smooth and flat 4. [Colloq.] to affect or strike with force —**plas′ter·er** *n.* —**plas′ter·y** *adj.*

**plas·ter·board** (-bôrd′) *n.* a thin board formed of layers of plaster and paper, used in wide sheets

**plas·tered** (plas′tərd) *adj.* [Slang] intoxicated; drunk

**plaster of Paris** [from use of gypsum from Paris, France] a heavy white powder, calcined gypsum, which, when mixed with water, forms a thick paste that sets quickly: used for casts, statuary, etc.

**plas·tic** (plas′tik) *adj.* [< L. < Gr. *plastikos* < *plassein,* to form] 1. molding or shaping matter; formative 2. *a)* that can be molded or shaped *b)* made of a plastic 3. in a flexible state; impressionable 4. dealing with molding or modeling 5. *Physics* capable of change of shape without breaking apart —*n.* any of various nonmetallic compounds, synthetically produced, which can be molded and hardened, or formed into pliable sheets, etc. —**plas′ti·cal·ly** *adv.* — **plas·tic′i·ty** (-tis′ə tē) *n.*

**-plas·tic** (plas′tik) [< Gr.: see prec.] *a combining form meaning* forming, developing

**Plas·ti·cine** (plas′tə sēn′) [PLASTIC + -INE[4]] *a trademark*

*for* an oil-base modeling paste, used like clay or wax —*n.* [p-] this paste: also **plas'ti·cene'** (-sēn)
**plas·ti·cize** (-sīz') *vt., vi.* **-cized', -ciz'ing** to make or become plastic
**plas·ti·ciz·er** (-sī'zər) *n.* any substance added to a plastic material to keep it soft and viscous
**plastic surgery** surgery dealing with the repair of injured, deformed, or destroyed parts of the body, esp. by transferring skin, bone, etc. from other parts —**plastic surgeon**
**plas·tid** (plas'tid) *n.* [< G. < Gr. < *plastēs,* molder < *plassein,* to form] a specialized protoplasmic structure in the cytoplasm of some plant cells
**plas·tron** (plas'trən) *n.* [Fr. < It. < *piastra,* thin plate of metal] **1.** a metal breastplate **2.** a chest protector for a fencer **3.** the under shell of a turtle
**-plas·ty** (plas'tē) [< Gr. < *plastos,* formed < *plassein,* to mold] *a combining form meaning* plastic surgery
**plat¹** (plat) *vt.* **plat'ted, plat'ting** [see PLAIT] [Dial.] to plait or braid —*n.* [Dial.] a plait or braid
**plat²** (plat) *n.* [var. of PLOT] **1.** a small piece of ground **2.** a map or plan, esp. of a piece of land divided into building lots —*vt.* **plat'ted, plat'ting** to make a map or plan of
**Pla·ta** (plä'tä), **Rí·o de la** (rē'ō de lä) estuary of the Paraná & Uruguay rivers, between Argentina & Uruguay
**plate** (plāt) *n.* [OFr., flat object, ult. < Gr. *platys,* flat] **1.** a smooth, flat, thin piece of metal, etc. **2.** *same as* SHEET METAL. **3.** *a)* any of the thin sheets of metal used in one kind of armor (**plate armor**) *b)* such armor. **4.** *a)* a thin, flat piece of metal on which an engraving is cut *b)* an impression taken from this **5.** a print of a woodcut, lithograph, etc. **6.** a full-page book illustration printed on special paper **7.** dishes, utensils, etc. of, or plated with, gold or silver **8.** a shallow dish from which food is eaten **9.** *same as* PLATEFUL **10.** the food in a dish; course *[a fruit plate]* **11.** food and service for an individual at a meal *[a dollar a plate]* **12.** a container passed in churches, etc. for donations of money **13.** a thin cut of beef from the forequarter, just below the short ribs **14.** *Anat., Zool.* a thin layer or scale, as of horny tissue, etc. **15.** *Archit.* a horizontal wooden girder that supports the trusses of a roof **16.** *Baseball short for* HOME PLATE **17.** *Dentistry a)* that part of a denture which fits to the mouth and holds the teeth *b)* [*often pl.*] loosely, a full set of false teeth **18.** *Elec. same as* ANODE (sense 1) **19.** *Philately* the impression surface from which a sheet of stamps is printed **20.** *Photog.* a sheet of glass, metal, etc. coated with a film sensitive to light, upon which the image is formed **21.** *Printing* a cast, to be printed from, made from a molded set of type by the electrotype or stereotype process —*vt.* **plat'ed, plat'ing 1.** to coat with gold, tin, etc. **2.** to cover with metal plates for protection **3.** *Printing* to make a plate of
**pla·teau** (pla tō') *n., pl.* **-teaus', -teaux'** (-tōz') [Fr. < OFr. < *plat:* see PLATE] **1.** an elevated tract of more or less level land **2.** a period of little change or progress, as represented by a flat extent on a graph, etc.
**plat·ed** (plāt'id) *adj.* **1.** protected with plates, as of armor **2.** coated with a metal *[silver-plated]*
**plate·ful** (-fool') *n., pl.* **-fuls'** as much as a plate will hold
**plate glass** polished, clear glass in thick sheets, used for shop windows, mirrors, etc.
**plate·let** (plāt'lit) *n.* [PLATE + -LET] any of certain roundish disks, smaller than a red blood cell, found in the blood of mammals and associated with blood clotting
**plat·en** (plat'n) *n.* [< OFr. *platine,* flat plate < *plat:* see PLATE] **1.** a flat metal plate, as that in a printing press which presses the paper against the inked type **2.** in a typewriter, the roller against which the keys strike
**plat·er** (plāt'ər) *n.* a person or thing that plates
**plate tec·ton·ics** (tek tän'iks) [SEE TECTONIC] the theory that the earth's surface consists of plates, or large crustal slabs, whose constant motion accounts for continental drift, mountain building, etc.
**plat·form** (plat'fôrm') *n.* [Fr. *plate-forme,* lit., flat form: see PLATE & FORM] **1.** a raised horizontal surface; specif., *a)* a raised flooring beside railroad tracks, etc. *b)* a vestibule at the end of a railroad car *c)* a raised stage for performers, speakers, etc. **2.** a statement of principles, as of a political party —*adj.* **1.** *a)* designating a woman's shoe with a thick sole of cork, leather, etc. *b)* designating such a sole **2.** designating a rocking chair (**platform rocker**) that rocks atop an attached, stationary base
**plat·ing** (plāt'iŋ) *n.* **1.** the act or process of one that plates **2.** an external layer of metal plates **3.** a thin coating of gold, silver, tin, etc.
**plat·i·num** (plat'n əm) *n.* [ModL. < Sp. *platina* < *plata,* silver] a steel-gray, ductile metallic chemical element, resistant to corrosion and electrochemical attack: used as a chemical catalyst, for dental alloys, jewelry, etc.: symbol, Pt; at. wt., 195.09; at. no., 78

**platinum blonde 1.** a girl or woman with very light, silvery blonde hair **2.** such a color
**plat·i·tude** (plat'ə tōōd', -tyōōd') *n.* [Fr. < *plat,* flat (see PLATE), after *latitude,* etc.] **1.** dullness or triteness of ideas, etc. **2.** a trite remark, esp. one uttered as though it were fresh —**plat'i·tu'di·nous** *adj.* —**plat'i·tu'di·nous·ly** *adv.*
**plat·i·tu·di·nize** (plat'ə tōō'd'n īz', -tyōō'-) *vi.* **-nized', -niz'ing** to write or speak platitudes
**Pla·to** (plā'tō) 427?-347? B.C.; Gr. philosopher
**Pla·ton·ic** (plə tän'ik, plā-) *adj.* **1.** of or characteristic of Plato or his philosophy **2.** idealistic or impractical **3.** [*usually* p-] not amorous or sexual, but purely spiritual or intellectual *[platonic love]* —**pla·ton'i·cal·ly** *adv.*
**Pla·to·nism** (plāt'n iz'm) *n.* the idealistic philosophy of Plato or his school —**Pla'to·nist** *n.* —**Pla'to·nis'tic** *adj.*
**pla·toon** (plə tōōn') *n.* [Fr. *peloton,* a ball, group < *pelote,* a ball] **1.** a military unit composed of two or more squads **2.** a group like this *[a platoon of police]* **3.** any of the specialized squads on a team, as an offensive or defensive squad in football —*vt.* to divide into, or use as or on, a platoon
**Platt·deutsch** (plät'doich', plat'-) *n.* [G. < Du. *plat,* clear, lit., flat + *duitsch,* German, Dutch] any Low German vernacular dialect of N Germany
**Platte** (plat) [Fr. *Rivière Platte,* lit., flat river] river formed in C Nebr. & flowing east into the Missouri
**plat·ter** (plat'ər) *n.* [< Anglo-Fr. < OFr. *plat:* see PLATE] **1.** a large, shallow dish, usually oval, from which food, esp. meat or fish, is served **2.** [Slang] a phonograph record
**plat·y-** [< Gr. *platys,* flat] *a combining form meaning* broad or flat *[platypus]* : also, before a vowel, **plat-**
**plat·y·hel·minth** (plat'ē hel'minth) *n.* [prec. + HELMINTH] any of a large group of flattened worms, as the tapeworms, flukes, etc.: many are parasitic —**plat'y·hel·min'thic** *adj.*
**plat·y·pus** (plat'ə pəs) *n., pl.* **-pus·es, -pi'** (-pī') [ModL. < Gr. < *platys,* flat + *pous,* a foot] a small, aquatic, egg-laying mammal of Australia and Tasmania, with webbed feet, a tail like a beaver's, and a bill like a duck's: in full, **duckbill platypus**

PLATYPUS
(16–24 in. long, including tail)

**plau·dit** (plô'dit) *n.* [< L. pl. imper. of *plaudere,* to applaud] [*usually pl.*] **1.** a round of applause **2.** any strong expression of approval or praise
**plau·si·ble** (plô'zə b'l) *adj.* [< L. *plausibilis* < *plaudere,* to applaud] **1.** seemingly true, acceptable, etc.: often implying disbelief **2.** seemingly honest, trustworthy, etc.: often implying distrust —**plau'si·bil'i·ty** *n.* —**plau'si·bly** *adv.*
**Plau·tus** (plô'təs), (**Titus Maccius**) 254?-184 B.C.; Rom. writer of comic dramas
**play** (plā) *vi.* [OE. *plegan*] **1.** to move lightly, rapidly, etc. *[sunlight playing on the waves]* **2.** to have fun; amuse oneself **3.** to take part in a game or sport **4.** to gamble **5.** to handle or treat carelessly or lightly; trifle (*with* a thing or person) **6.** to perform on a musical instrument **7.** to give out musical sounds, etc.: said of an instrument, phonograph record, etc. **8.** *a)* to act in a specified way *[to play fair]* *b)* to pretend to be *[to play dumb]* **9.** to perform on the stage, etc. **10.** to be performed in a theater, on the radio, etc. **11.** to impose (*on* another's feelings or weaknesses) —*vt.* **1.** *a)* to take part in (a game or sport) *b)* to be stationed at (a specified position) in a sport **2.** to oppose (a person, team, etc.) in a game or contest **3.** to use (a player, etc.) in a game **4.** to do (something), as in fun or to deceive *[to play tricks]* **5.** *a)* to bet *b)* to bet on *[to play the horses]* *c)* to act on the basis of *[to play a hunch]* **6.** to speculate in (the stock market) **7.** to cause to move, act, etc.; wield **8.** to put (a specified card) into play **9.** to cause or effect *[to play havoc]* **10.** to perform (music, a drama, etc.) **11.** *a)* to perform on (an instrument) *b)* to put (a phonograph, a recording, etc.) into operation **12.** to act the part of *[to play Iago]* **13.** to imitate the activities of for amusement *[to play teacher, school, etc.]* **14.** to give performances in *[to play Boston]* **15.** to direct (a light, a stream of water, etc.) repeatedly or continuously (*on, over,* or *along*) **16.** to let (a hooked fish) tire itself by tugging at the line **17.** to use or exploit (a person) *[played him for a fool]* —*n.* **1.** motion or activity, esp. when free and rapid **2.** freedom or looseness of movement in a mechanical part *[too much play in a wheel]* **3.** activity for amusement or recreation; sport, games, etc. **4.** fun; joking *[to do a thing in play]* **5.** the playing of, or the way of playing, a game **6.** a move or act in a game **7.** gambling **8.** a dramatic composition or performance; drama —**in** (or **out of**) **play** *Sports* in (or not in) the condition for continuing play: said of a ball, etc. —**make a play for** [Colloq.] to

employ one's arts or skills to obtain, win, etc.; court —**play along (with)** to cooperate (with), often just for expediency —**play around 1.** to behave in a frivolous way **2.** to be sexually unfaithful or promiscuous —**play at 1.** to pretend to be engaged in **2.** to work at halfheartedly —**play down** to make seem not too important —**played out 1.** finished **2.** exhausted —**play into (someone's) hands** to act in a way that gives the advantage to (someone) —**play it** to act in a (specified) manner /to *play it* smart/ —**play off 1.** to pit (one) against another **2.** to break (a tie) by playing once more —**play out 1.** to play to the finish; end **2.** to pay out (a rope, etc.) —**play up** to give prominence to —**play up to** [Colloq.] to try to please by flattery —**play'a·ble** *adj.*

**play·act** (plā'akt') *vi.* **1.** to act in a play **2.** to pretend **3.** to behave in an affected or dramatic manner

**play·back** (-bak') *n.* the playing of a phonograph record or tape to listen to or check the sound recorded on it

**play·bill** (-bil') *n.* **1.** a poster or circular advertising a play **2.** a program of a play

**play·boy** (-boi') *n.* a man of means who is given to pleasure-seeking, sexual promiscuity, etc.

**play·er** (-ər) *n.* **1.** a person who plays a game **2.** an actor **3.** a person who plays a musical instrument **4.** a gambler **5.** a thing that plays; specif., a RECORD PLAYER

**player piano** a piano that can play mechanically.

**play·ful** (-fəl) *adj.* **1.** fond of play or fun; frisky; frolicsome **2.** said or done in fun; jocular —**play'ful·ly** *adv.* —**play'-ful·ness** *n.*

**play·go·er** (-gō'ər) *n.* a person who goes to the theater frequently —**play'go'ing** *n., adj.*

**play·ground** (-ground') *n.* a place, often part of a school-yard, for outdoor games and play

**play hook·y** (hook'ē) [*hooky* prob. < *hook it,* to run away] to stay away from school without permission

**play·house** (plā'hous') *n.* **1.** a theater **2.** a small house for children to play in **3.** a doll house

**playing cards** cards used in playing various games, arranged in four suits (spades, hearts, diamonds, and clubs): a standard deck has 52 cards

**play·let** (-lit) *n.* a short drama

**play·mate** (-māt') *n.* a companion in games and recreation: also **play'fel'low** (-fel'ō)

**play-off** (-ôf') *n.* a game or any of a series of games played to break a tie or to decide a championship

**play on words** a pun or punning

**play·pen** (-pen') *n.* a small, portable enclosure in which an infant can play, crawl, etc.

**play·thing** (-thiŋ') *n.* a thing to play with; toy

**play·time** (-tīm') *n.* time for play or recreation

**play·wright** (-rīt') *n.* a writer of plays; dramatist

**pla·za** (plä'zə, plaz'ə) *n.* [Sp. < L. *platea*] **1.** a public square in a city or town **2.** *same as* SHOPPING CENTER **3.** an area along a superhighway, with a restaurant, service station, etc.

**plea** (plē) *n.* [< OFr. < L. *placitum,* an opinion < pp. of *placere,* to please] **1.** a statement in defense **2.** an appeal; entreaty **3.** *Law* a defendant's statement, answering the charges against him or showing why he should not answer

**plea bargaining** pretrial negotiations in which the defendant agrees to plead guilty to a lesser charge in exchange for having more serious charges dropped

**plead** (plēd) *vi.* **plead'ed** or **pled** or **plead** (pled), **plead'ing** [< OFr.: see PLEA] **1.** to present a case or a plea in a law court **2.** to make an appeal; beg /to *plead* for mercy/ —*vt.* **1.** to argue (a law case) **2.** to declare oneself to be (guilty or not guilty) of a charge **3.** to offer as an excuse /to *plead* ignorance/ —**plead'a·ble** *adj.* —**plead'er** *n.*

**plead·ings** (-iŋz) *n.pl.* the statements setting forth to the court the claims of the plaintiff and the answer of the defendant

**pleas·ance** (plez''ns) *n.* [< MFr. < *plaisant:* see ff.] a pleasant area or garden, as on an estate

**pleas·ant** (-'nt) *adj.* [< MFr. prp. of *plaisir,* to please] **1.** agreeable to the mind or senses; pleasing **2.** having an agreeable manner, appearance, etc. —**pleas'ant·ly** *adv.* —**pleas'ant·ness** *n.*

**pleas·ant·ry** (plez''n trē) *n., pl.* **-ries 1.** pleasant jocularity in conversation **2.** *a)* a humorous remark or action *b)* a polite social remark

**please** (plēz) *vt.* **pleased, pleas'ing** [MFr. *plaisir* < L. *placere*] **1.** to be agreeable to; give pleasure to; satisfy **2.** to be the will or wish of /it *pleased* him to remain/ —*vi.* **1.** to satisfy; give pleasure; satisfy /to aim to *please*/ **2.** to have the will or wish; like /to do as one *pleases*/ *Please* is also used for politeness in requests to mean "be obliging enough (to)" /*please* sit down/ —**if you please** if you wish or like

**pleas·ing** (plē'ziŋ) *adj.* giving pleasure; agreeable —**pleas'-ing·ly** *adv.* —**pleas'ing·ness** *n.*

**pleas·ur·a·ble** (plezh'ər ə b'l) *adj.* pleasant; enjoyable —**pleas'ur·a·ble·ness** *n.* —**pleas'ur·a·bly** *adv.*

**pleas·ure** (plezh'ər, plā'zhər) *n.* **1.** a pleased feeling; delight **2.** one's wish, will, or choice /what is your *pleasure*?/ **3.** a thing that gives delight or satisfaction **4.** sensual satisfaction **5.** amusement; fun —**pleas'ure·ful** *adj.*

**pleat** (plēt) *n.* [ME. *pleten:* cf. PLAIT] a flat double fold in cloth or other material, pressed or stitched in place —*vt.* to lay and press (cloth) in a pleat or pleats —**pleat'er** *n.*

**plebe** (plēb) *n.* [short for PLEBIAN] a member of the freshman class at the U.S. Military Academy or Naval Academy

**ple·be·ian** (pli bē'ən) *n.* [< L. < *plebs,* common people] **1.** a member of the ancient Roman lower class **2.** one of the common people **3.** a vulgar, coarse person —*adj.* **1.** of or characteristic of the lower class in ancient Rome or of the common people anywhere **2.** vulgar or common

**pleb·i·scite** (pleb'ə sīt', -sit) *n.* [< Fr. < L. < *plebs,* common people + *scitum,* decree] a direct vote of the people on a political issue, as on a choice between independence for their region or union with another nation

**plec·trum** (plek'trəm) *n., pl.* **-trums, -tra** (-trə) [L. < Gr. *plēktron* < *plēssein,* to strike] a thin piece of metal, bone, plastic, etc., used for plucking the strings of a guitar, mandolin, etc.

**pled** (pled) *alt. pt. & pp. of* PLEAD

**pledge** (plej) *n.* [< OFr. or ML., prob. < OS. *plegan,* to guarantee] **1.** the condition of being given or held as security for a contract, payment, etc. **2.** a person or thing given or held as such security; something pawned; hostage **3.** a token **4.** the drinking of a toast to someone **5.** a promise or agreement **6.** something promised, esp. money to be donated **7.** a person undergoing a trial period before initiation into a fraternity —*vt.* **pledged, pledg'ing 1.** to present as security, esp. for the repayment of a loan; pawn **2.** to drink a toast to **3.** to bind by a promise **4.** to promise to give (loyalty, a donation, etc.) **5.** *a)* to accept tentative membership in (a fraternity) *b)* to accept as a pledge (*n.* 7) —**take the pledge** to vow not to drink alcoholic liquor —**pledg'er** *n.*

**pledg·ee** (plej ē') *n.* a person to whom a pledge is delivered: distinguished from PLEDGOR

**pledg·or** (plej'ər, plej'ôr') *n. Law* a person who delivers something as security

**-ple·gia** (plē'jē ə, -jə) [ModL. < Gr. < *plēgē,* a stroke] *a combining form meaning paralysis [paraplegia]*

**Ple·ia·des** (plē'ə dēz', plī'-) *n.pl., sing.* **Ple'iad** (-ad) **1.** *Gr. Myth.* the seven daughters of Atlas, placed by Zeus among the stars **2.** *Astron.* a cluster of stars in the constellation Taurus

**Plei·o·cene** (plī'ə sēn') *adj. same as* PLIOCENE

**Pleis·to·cene** (plīs'tə sēn') *adj.* [< Gr. *pleistos,* most + *kainos,* recent] designating or of the first epoch of the Quaternary Period in the Cenozoic Era —**the Pleistocene** the Pleistocene Epoch or its rocks: see GEOLOGY, chart

**ple·na·ry** (plē'nə rē, plen'ə-) *adj.* [< LL. < L. *plenus,* full] **1.** full; complete /*plenary* power/ **2.** for attendance by all members /a *plenary* session/ —**ple'na·ri·ly** (-rə lē) *adv.*

**plenary indulgence** *R.C.Ch.* an indulgence remitting in full the temporal punishment due a sinner

**plen·i·po·ten·ti·ar·y** (plen'i pə ten'shē er'ē, -shə rē) *adj.* [< ML. < LL. < L. *plenus,* full + *potens,* powerful] having or giving full authority —*n., pl.* **-ar'ies** a person given full authority to act as diplomatic representative of a government

**plen·i·tude** (plen'ə tood', -tyood') *n.* [OFr. < L. < *plenus,* full] **1.** fullness; completeness **2.** abundance; plenty —**plen'i·tu'di·nous** *adj.*

**plen·te·ous** (plen'tē əs) *adj.* plentiful; abundant —**plen'te·ous·ly** *adv.* —**plen'te·ous·ness** *n.*

**plen·ti·ful** (plen'ti fəl) *adj.* **1.** having or yielding plenty **2.** ample or abundant —**plen'ti·ful·ly** *adv.* —**plen'ti·ful·ness** *n.*

**plen·ty** (plen'tē) *n., pl.* **-ties** [< MFr. < L. *plenitas* < *plenus,* full] **1.** prosperity; opulence **2.** an ample supply; enough **3.** a large number /*plenty* of errors/ —*adj.* [Colloq.] ample; enough —*adv.* [Colloq.] quite /*plenty* good/

**ple·o·nasm** (plē'ə naz'm) *n.* [< LL. < Gr. < *pleonazein,* to be in excess < *pleōn,* more, compar. of *polys,* much] **1.** the use of more words than are necessary for the meaning **2.** a redundant word or expression —**ple'o·nas'tic** *adj.*

**pleth·o·ra** (pleth'ə rə) *n.* [ML. < Gr. < *plēthos,* fullness] the state of being too full; overabundance; excess —**pleth·or·ic** (plə thôr'ik, pleth'ə rik) *adj.*

**pleu·ra** (ploor′ə) *n.*, *pl.* **-rae** (-ē) [ML. < Gr. *pleura*, a rib] the thin serous membrane lining each half of the chest cavity and covering a lung —**pleu′ral** *adj.*

**pleu·ri·sy** (ploor′ə sē) *n.* [< MFr. < LL. < L. < Gr. < *pleura*, a rib] inflammation of the pleura, characterized by painful breathing —**pleu·rit·ic** (ploo rit′ik) *adj.*

**pleu·ro-** [< Gr. *pleura*, a rib] *a combining form meaning:* **1.** on or near the side **2.** of, involving, or near the pleura Also, before a vowel, **pleur-**

**Plex·i·glas** (plek′sə glas′) [< L. *plexus*, a twining + GLASS] *a trademark for* a lightweight, transparent, thermoplastic resin, used for aircraft canopies, lenses, etc. —*n.* this material: also **plex′i·glass′**

**plex·us** (plek′səs) *n.*, *pl.* **-us·es**, **-us** [ModL. < L. < pp. of *plectere*, to twine] a network; specif., *Anat.* a network of blood vessels, nerves, etc.

**pli·a·ble** (plī′ə b'l) *adj.* [< MFr. < *plier*, to bend < L. *plicare*, to fold] **1.** easily bent; flexible **2.** easily influenced or persuaded **3.** adjusting readily; adaptable —**pli′a·bil′i·ty**, **pli′a·ble·ness** *n.* —**pli′a·bly** *adv.*

**pli·ant** (plī′ənt) *adj.* [see prec.] **1.** easily bent; pliable **2.** adaptable or compliant —**pli′an·cy**, **pli′ant·ness** *n.*

**pli·cate** (plī′kāt) *adj.* [< L. pp. of *plicare*, to fold] having lengthwise folds —**pli·ca′tion** *n.*

**pli·er** (plī′ər) *n.* a person or thing that plies

**pli·ers** (plī′ərz) *n.pl.* [< PLY¹] small pincers for gripping small objects, bending wire, etc.

**plight¹** (plīt) *n.* [< Anglo-Fr. *plit*, for OFr. *pleit*, a fold] a condition or state of affairs; esp., an awkward, sad, or dangerous situation

**plight²** (plīt) *vt.* [OE. *plihtan*, to pledge < *pliht*, danger] to pledge or promise, or bind by a pledge —**plight one's troth** to make a promise of marriage

**Plim·soll mark** (or **line**) (plim′səl, -säl, -sôl) [after S. *Plimsoll* (1824-98), Eng. statesman] a line or set of lines on the outside of merchant ships, showing the water level to which they may legally be loaded

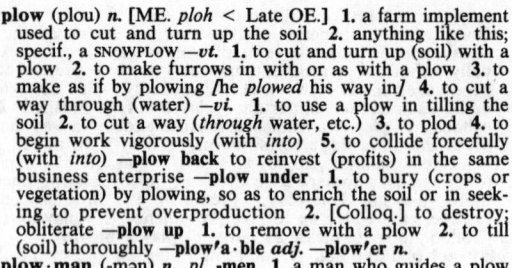

PLIERS
(A, slip joint; B, needle nose; C, arc joint)

**plink** (pliŋk) *n.* [echoic] a light, sharp, ringing or clinking sound —*vt.*, *vi.* **1.** to make such sounds on (a piano, banjo, etc.) **2.** to shoot at (tin cans, etc.) —**plink′er** *n.*

**plinth** (plinth) *n.* [< L. < Gr. *plinthos*, a brick, tile] **1.** the square block at the base of a column, pedestal, etc. **2.** the base on which a statue rests

**Plin·y** (plin′ē) **1.** (L. name *Gaius Plinius Secundus*) 23-79 A.D.; Rom. naturalist & writer: called *the Elder* **2.** (L. name *Gaius Plinius Caecilius Secundus*) 62?-113? A.D.; Rom. writer & statesman: called *the Younger*: nephew of *prec.*

**Pli·o·cene** (plī′ə sēn′) *adj.* [< Gr. *pleōn*, more + *kainos*, new] designating or of the last epoch of the Tertiary Period in the Cenozoic Era —**the Pliocene** the Pliocene Epoch or its rocks: see GEOLOGY, chart

**plis·sé**, **plis·se** (pli sā′) *n.* [< Fr. < pp. of *plisser*, to pleat] **1.** a crinkled finish given to cotton, nylon, etc. with a caustic soda solution **2.** a fabric with this finish

**PLO**, **P.L.O.** Palestine Liberation Organization

**plod** (pläd) *vi.* **plod′ded**, **plod′ding** [prob. echoic] **1.** to walk or move heavily and laboriously; trudge **2.** to work steadily and monotonously; drudge —*n.* **1.** the act of plodding **2.** the sound of a heavy step —**plod′der** *n.* —**plod′ding·ly** *adv.*

**plonk** (pläŋk, pluŋk) *vt.*, *vi.*, *n.* same as PLUNK

**plop** (pläp) *vt.*, *vi.* **plopped**, **plop′ping** [echoic] **1.** to drop with a sound like that of something flat falling into water **2.** to drop heavily —*n.* the act of plopping or the sound made by this —*adv.* with a plop

**plo·sive** (plō′siv) *adj.* [< (EX)PLOSIVE] *Phonet.* produced by the stoppage and sudden release of the breath, as the sounds of *k*, *p*, and *t* when used initially —*n.* a plosive sound

**plot** (plät) *n.* [OE., a piece of land] **1.** a small area of ground [a garden *plot*] **2.** a chart or diagram, as of a building or estate **3.** a secret, usually evil, scheme **4.** the plan of action of a play, novel, etc. —*vt.* **plot′ted**, **plot′ting 1.** *a)* to draw a plan of (a ship's course, etc.) *b)* to mark the position or course of on a map **2.** to make secret plans for **3.** to plan the action of (a story, etc.) **4.** *a)* to determine the location of (a point) on a graph by means of coordinates *b)* to represent (an equation) by joining points on a graph to form a curve —*vi.* to scheme or conspire —**plot′less** *adj.* —**plot′less·ness** *n.* —**plot′ter** *n.*

**plough** (plou) *n.*, *vt.*, *vi.* chiefly Brit. sp. of PLOW

**plov·er** (pluv′ər, plō′vər) *n.*, *pl.* **plov′ers**, **plov′er**: see PLURAL, II, D, 1 [< OFr., ult. < L. *pluvia*, rain] a shore bird with a short tail, long, pointed wings, and a short beak

**plow** (plou) *n.* [ME. *ploh* < Late OE.] **1.** a farm implement used to cut and turn up the soil **2.** anything like this; specif., a SNOWPLOW —*vt.* **1.** to cut and turn up (soil) with a plow **2.** to make furrows in with or as with a plow **3.** to make as if by plowing [he *plowed* his way in] **4.** to cut a way through (water) —*vi.* **1.** to use a plow in tilling the soil **2.** to cut a way (*through* water, etc.) **3.** to plod **4.** to begin work vigorously (with *into*) **5.** to collide forcefully (with *into*) —**plow back** to reinvest (profits) in the same business enterprise —**plow under 1.** to bury (crops or vegetation) by plowing, so as to enrich the soil or in seeking to prevent overproduction **2.** [Colloq.] to destroy; obliterate —**plow up 1.** to remove with a plow **2.** to till (soil) thoroughly —**plow′a·ble** *adj.* —**plow′er** *n.*

**plow·man** (-mən) *n.*, *pl.* **-men 1.** a man who guides a plow **2.** a farm worker

**plow·share** (-sher′) *n.* the share, or cutting blade, of a moldboard plow

**ploy** (ploi) *n.* [? < (EM)PLOY] an action or maneuver intended to outwit or disconcert another person

**pluck** (pluk) *vt.* [OE. *pluccian*] **1.** to pull off or out; pick **2.** to drag or snatch **3.** to pull feathers or hair from [to *pluck* a chicken, *pluck* eyebrows] **4.** to pull at (the strings of a musical instrument) and release quickly to sound tones **5.** [Slang] to rob or swindle —*vi.* **1.** to pull; tug; snatch (often with *at*) **2.** to pluck a musical instrument —*n.* **1.** a pulling; tug **2.** courage to meet danger or difficulty; fortitude —**pluck′er** *n.*

**pluck·y** (-ē) *adj.* **pluck′i·er**, **pluck′i·est** brave; spirited; resolute —**pluck′i·ly** *adv.* —**pluck′i·ness** *n.*

**plug** (plug) *n.* [MDu. *plugge*] **1.** an object used to stop up a hole, drain, etc. **2.** *a)* a cake of pressed tobacco *b)* a piece of chewing tobacco **3.** a device, as with projecting prongs, for fitting into an electric outlet, appliance, etc. to make electrical contact **4.** *same as: a)* SPARK PLUG *b)* FIREPLUG **5.** [Colloq.] a defective or shopworn article **6.** [Slang] an old, worn-out horse **7.** [Colloq.] a boost, advertisement, etc. esp. one slipped into the entertainment part of a radio or TV program, a magazine article, etc. —*vt.* **plugged, plug′ging 1.** to stop up (a hole, etc.) with a plug (often with *up*) **2.** to insert (something) as a plug **3.** [Colloq.] *a)* to promote (a song) by frequent performance *b)* to promote with a plug (*n.* 7) **4.** [Slang] to shoot a bullet into —*vi.* [Colloq.] to work or study hard and steadily; plod —**plug in** to connect (an electrical device) with an outlet, etc. by inserting a plug in a socket or jack —**pull the plug** [Colloq.] **1.** to disconnect a device being used to maintain a terminal patient's life **2.** to put an end to something

**plum** (plum) *n.* [OE. *plume*] **1.** *a)* any of various small trees bearing a smooth-skinned, edible fruit with a flattened stone *b)* the fruit **2.** a raisin, when used in pudding or cake **3.** the dark bluish-red or reddish-purple color of some plums **4.** something choice or desirable

**plum·age** (plōō′mij) *n.* [MFr. < L. *pluma*, a feather] a bird's feathers

**plumb** (plum) *n.* [< MFr. < L. *plumbum*, LEAD²] a lead weight (**plumb bob**) hung at the end of a line (**plumb line**), used to determine how deep water is or whether a wall, etc. is vertical —*adj.* perfectly vertical —*adv.* **1.** straight down; directly **2.** [Colloq.] entirely; absolutely [*plumb* crazy] —*vt.* **1.** to test or sound with a plumb **2.** to discover the facts of; solve **3.** to make vertical —**out of** (or **off**) **plumb** not vertical

**plumb·er** (plum′ər) *n.* [< MFr. < L. < *plumbarius*, lead-worker < *plumbum*, LEAD²] a skilled worker who installs and repairs pipes, fixtures, etc., as of water or gas systems

**plumb·ing** (plum′iŋ) *n.* **1.** the using of a plumb **2.** the work of a plumber **3.** the pipes and fixtures with which a plumber works

PLUMB

**plume** (plōōm) *n.* [OFr. < L. *pluma*] **1.** *a)* a feather, esp. a large, showy one *b)* a cluster of these **2.** an ornament made of such a feather or feathers, or a feathery tuft of hair, esp. when worn on a hat, helmet, etc. **3.** a token of worth or achievement; prize **4.** something like a plume in shape or lightness [a *plume* of smoke] —*vt.* **plumed, plum′ing 1.** to provide, cover, or adorn with plumes **2.** to preen (its feathers): said of a bird **3.** to pride (oneself)

**plum·met** (plum′it) *n.* [< MFr. dim. of *plombe*: see PLUMB] **1.** a plumb **2.** a thing that weighs heavily —*vi.* to fall or drop straight downward

**plu·mose** (plōō′mōs) *adj.* [< L. < *pluma*, a feather] **1.** feathered **2.** like a feather —**plu·mos·i·ty** (-mäs′ə tē) *n.*

**plump¹** (plump) *adj.* [< MDu. *plomp*, bulky] full and rounded in form; chubby —*vt.*, *vi.* to make plump; fill out (sometimes with *up* or *out*) —**plump′ish** *adj.* —**plump′ly** *adv.* —**plump′ness** *n.*

**plump²** (plump) *vi.* [< MDu. *plompen*: orig. echoic] **1.** to fall or bump (*against*) suddenly or heavily **2.** to offer strong support (*for* someone or something) —*vt.* to drop, throw, or put down heavily or all at once —*n.* a sudden or heavy fall or the sound of this —*adv.* **1.** suddenly or heavily **2.** straight down **3.** in plain words; bluntly — *adj.* blunt; direct

**plum pudding** [orig. made with plums] a rich pudding made of raisins, currants, flour, suet, etc., boiled or steamed, as in a linen bag

**plu·mule** (plōōm′yōōl) *n.* [< L. dim. of *pluma*, a feather] **1.** the growing stem tip of the embryo of a plant seed **2.** a down feather

**plum·y** (plōō′mē) *adj.* **plum′i·er, plum′i·est 1.** covered or adorned with plumes **2.** like a plume; feathery

**plun·der** (plun′dər) *vt.* [< G. *plunder*, baggage] **1.** to rob (a person or place) by force, esp. in warfare **2.** to take (property) by force or fraud —*vi.* to engage in plundering —*n.* **1.** the act of plundering; pillage **2.** goods taken by force or fraud; loot; booty —**plun′der·er** *n.* —**plun′der·ous** *adj.*

**plunge** (plunj) *vt.* **plunged, plung′ing** [< OFr. *plongier*, ult. < L. *plumbum*, LEAD²] to thrust or throw suddenly (*into* a liquid, hole, condition, etc.) —*vi.* **1.** to dive or rush, as into water, a fight, etc. **2.** to move violently and rapidly downward or forward **3.** to pitch, as a ship **4.** to extend far down in a revealing way [a *plunging* neckline] **5.** [Colloq.] to spend, gamble, or speculate heavily —*n.* **1.** *a)* a dive or downward leap *b)* a swim **2.** any sudden, violent plunging motion **3.** [Colloq.] a heavy, rash investment —**take the plunge** to start on some new and uncertain enterprise, esp. after some hesitation

**plung·er** (plun′jər) *n.* **1.** a person who plunges **2.** a large, rubber suction cup with a long handle, used to free clogged drains **3.** any cylindrical device that operates with a plunging motion, as a piston

**plunk** (pluŋk) *vt.* [echoic] **1.** to pluck or strum (a banjo, guitar, etc.) **2.** to throw or put down heavily; plump —*vi.* **1.** to give out a twanging sound, as a banjo **2.** to fall heavily **3.** [Colloq.] *same as* PLUMP² (*vi.* 2) —*n.* the act or sound of plunking —*adv.* with a twang or thud —**plunk down** [Colloq.] to pay —**plunk′er** *n.*

**plu·per·fect** (plōō pur′fikt) *adj.* [abbrev. of L. *plus quam perfectum*, more than perfect] designating a tense in any of certain languages corresponding to the past perfect in English —*n.* a pluperfect tense or a form in this tense

**plu·ral** (ploor′əl) *adj.* [L. *pluralis* < *plus* (gen. *pluris*), more] **1.** of or including more than one **2.** of or involving a plurality of persons or things [*plural* marriage] **3.** *Gram.* designating or of that category of number referring to more than one, or in languages having dual number, more than two —*n. Gram.* **1.** the plural number **2.** a plural form of a word **a word in plural form** The plurals of nouns are formed in English according to the principles listed below. Words with alternative plurals in the regular -(e)s form are marked (*).

**I. REGULAR ENGLISH PLURALS**
  A. Add -s in all cases except as noted below
  B. Add -es after final -ss, -sh, -ch, -s, -x, -z, and -zz: glass-es, ash-es, witch-es, gas-es, box-es, adz-es, buzz-es
  C. Add -es after -y preceded by a consonant or by -qu-, and change the -y to -i-: fly, fli-es; soliloquy, soliloqui-es; etc. (Add -s after -y preceded by a vowel: day, day-s; monkey, monkey-s; etc.)
  D. Add -s to most words ending in -o preceded by a consonant, and to all words ending in -o preceded by a vowel: piano-s, radio-s, studio-s, etc. (Add -es to some words ending in -o preceded by a consonant: *buffalo-es, *domino-es, echo-es, hero-es, potato-es, etc.)

**II. OTHER ENGLISH PLURALS**
  A. Change -f to -v in many words, and add -es: half, self, life, leaf, *scarf¹, *wharf, etc.
  B. Plural formed by:
    1. -en: ox-en
    2. -ren: child-ren
    3. Vowel change: man, men; foot, feet; mouse, mice; etc.
  C. Plural the same as the singular: alms, barracks, Chinese, deer (occas. deers), forceps, gross, means, moose, sheep, etc.
  D. Plural either different from or the same as the singular:
    1. Plural usually different, but sometimes the same, esp. in the usage of hunters and fishermen: antelope, badger, brant, buffalo, cougar, giraffe, mullet, shrimp, sturgeon, tarpon, etc.
    2. Plural usually the same, but different if referring to different kinds, species, varieties, etc. [the *fishes* of the South Pacific]: cod, elk, gar, mackerel, shad, springbok, trout, etc.

  3. Plural usually lacking, but given in -(e)s form when different kinds are referred to [the many *steels* produced]: brass, coffee, fruit, iron, linen, wool, etc.
  4. Plural and collective singular interchangeable: seeds, seed; etc.

**III. FORMS SINGULAR OR PLURAL ONLY**
  A. Singular only (or when a generalized abstraction): clearness, fishing, information, knowledge, luck, music, nonsense, truth, etc.
  B. Plural only (even when singular in meaning), including certain senses of nouns otherwise singular: Balkans, blues (depression), glasses, overalls, pliers, remains (corpse), scissors, tongs, trousers, etc.
  C. Plural in form but used with singular verbs: checkers (game), measles, mumps, news, etc.
  D. Nouns ending in -ics are singular when they denote scientific subjects, as mathematics, physics, etc., and plural when they denote activities or qualities, as acrobatics, acoustics, etc.

**IV. LATIN AND GREEK PLURALS**
  A. With Latin suffix -i replacing singular ending -us: alumnus, alumn-i; *focus, foc-i; *nucleus, nucle-i; *radius, radi-i; etc.
  B. With Latin suffix -ae replacing singular ending -a: alumna, alumn-ae; *formula, formul-ae; etc.
  C. With suffix -a replacing singular ending:
    1. Latin nouns in -um: *agendum, agend-a; datum, dat-a; *medium, medi-a; etc.
    2. Greek nouns in -on: *criterion, criteri-a; *phenomenon, phenomen-a; etc.
  D. With suffix -es:
    1. Latin suffix -ex or -ix replaced by -ices: *appendix, append-ices; *index, ind-ices; etc.
    2. Latin or Greek suffix -is replaced by -es: analysis, analys-es; axis, ax-es; etc.
  E. Miscellaneous Latin and Greek plurals: *phalanx, phalang-es; *stigma, stigma-ta; corpus, corp-ora; *genus, gen-era; etc.

**V. OTHER FOREIGN PLURALS**
  A. Hebrew: *cherub, cherub-im; kibbutz, kibbutz-im; *matzo, matzo-t(h)
  B. Italian: *bandit, bandit-ti; *dilettante, dilettant-i; *virtuoso, virtuos-i; etc.
  C. French: bijou, bijou-x; *château, château-x; *portmanteau, portmanteau-x; etc.

**VI. PLURALS OF NUMBERS, LETTERS, SIGNS, WORDS** (when thought of as things), etc. add -'s (or now often -s): 8's (or 8s), B's (or Bs), &'s (or &s), but's (or buts)

**plu·ral·ism** (ploor′əl iz'm) *n.* **1.** a being plural, or existing in more than one part or form **2.** the existence within a society of groups that differ ethnically, culturally, etc. **3.** *Philos.* the theory that reality is composed of a number of ultimate beings, principles, or substances —**plu′ral·ist** *n., adj.* —**plu′ral·is′tic** *adj.* —**plu′ral·is′ti·cal·ly** *adv.*

**plu·ral·i·ty** (ploo ral′ə tē) *n., pl.* **-ties 1.** a being plural or numerous **2.** a great number; multitude **3.** *a)* the total number of votes received by the leading candidate in an election *b)* the number of votes that the leading candidate of more than two obtains over the next highest candidate **4.** *same as* MAJORITY

**plu·ral·ize** (ploor′ə līz′) *vt., vi.* **-ized′, -iz′ing** to make or become plural —**plu′ral·i·za′tion** *n.* —**plu′ral·iz′er** *n.*

**plu·ral·ly** (-ə lē) *adv.* in the plural number

**plu·ri-** [L. < *plus* (gen. *pluris*), several] *a combining form meaning* several or many

**plus** (plus) *prep.* [L., more] **1.** added to [2 *plus* 2 equals 4] **2.** in addition to [salary *plus* bonus] —*adj.* **1.** designating a sign (**plus sign**) indicating addition [+ is a *plus* sign] **2.** positive [a *plus* quantity] **3.** somewhat higher than [a grade of B *plus*] **4.** involving extra gain or advantage [a *plus* factor] **5.** [Colloq.] and more [she has personality *plus*] **6.** *Elec. same as* POSITIVE [the *plus* terminal] —*adv.* [Colloq.] moreover [he has the time *plus* he has the money] —*n., pl.* **plus′es, plus′ses 1.** a plus sign **2.** an added or favorable quantity or thing **3.** a positive quantity

**plus fours** [orig. indicating added length of material for overlap below the knee] loose knickerbockers worn, esp. formerly, for active sports

**plush** (plush) *n.* [< Fr. < *peluche*, ult. < L. *pilus*, hair] a fabric with a soft, thick, deep pile —*adj.* **1.** of plush **2.** [Slang] luxurious, as in furnishings —**plush′i·ly** *adv.* —**plush′i·ness** *n.* —**plush′y** *adj.* **plush′i·er, plush′i·est**

**Plu·tarch** (plōō′tärk) 46?–120? A.D.; Gr. biographer & historian

**Plu·to** (plōōt′ō) **1.** *Gr. & Rom. Myth.* the god ruling the lower world **2.** the outermost planet of the solar system: diameter, c. 3,700 mi. —**Plu·to′ni·an** *adj.*

**plu·toc·ra·cy** (plōō tăk'rə sē) *n., pl.* **-cies** [< Gr. < *ploutos*, wealth + *kratein*, to rule] **1.** government by the wealthy **2.** a group of wealthy people who control a government

**plu·to·crat** (plōōt'ə krat') *n.* **1.** a member of a wealthy ruling class **2.** a person whose wealth gives him control or great influence —**plu'to·crat'ic** *adj.* —**plu'to·crat'i·cal·ly** *adv.*

**plu·ton·ic** (plōō tän'ik) *adj.* [after PLUTO] *Geol.* formed far below the surface of the earth by intense heat and slow cooling, as some rocks

**plu·to·ni·um** (plōō tō'nē əm) *n.* [ModL. after *Pluto* (planet)] a radioactive, metallic chemical element: symbol, Pu; at. wt., 239.05; at. no., 94

**plu·vi·al** (plōō'vē əl) *adj.* [< L. < *pluvia*, rain] **1.** *a)* of or having to do with rain *b)* having much rain **2.** *Geol.* formed by the action of rain

**ply¹** (plī) *vt.* **plied, ply'ing** [< OFr. < L. *plicare*, to fold] [Now Rare] to bend, twist, fold, or mold —*n., pl.* **plies 1.** a single thickness or layer, as of plywood, doubled cloth, etc. **2.** one of the twisted strands in rope, yarn, etc. **3.** bias or inclination —*adj.* having (a specified number of) layers, strands, etc. [three-*ply*]

**ply²** (plī) *vt.* **plied, ply'ing** [ME. *plien*, short for *applien*, APPLY] **1.** to work with; wield or use (a tool, faculty, etc.) **2.** to work at (a trade) **3.** to address (someone) urgently (*with* questions, etc.) **4.** to keep supplying (*with* gifts, food, etc.) **5.** to sail back and forth across [boats *ply* the channel] —*vi.* **1.** to keep busy or work (*at* something or *with* a tool, etc.) **2.** to travel regularly (*between* places): said of ships, buses, etc.

**Ply·mouth** (plim'əth) **1.** seaport in SW England, on the English Channel: pop. 257,000 **2.** village on the SE coast of Mass.: settled by the Pilgrims (1620) as **Plymouth Colony**

**Plymouth Rock 1.** boulder at Plymouth, Mass., where the Pilgrims are said to have landed **2.** any of a breed of American chickens

**ply·wood** (plī'wood') *n.* [PLY¹ + WOOD] a material made of thin layers of wood glued and pressed together, usually with the grains at right angles

**Pm** *Chem.* promethium

**pm. 1.** phase modulation **2.** premium

**P.M. 1.** Paymaster **2.** Postmaster **3.** Prime Minister

**P.M., p.m., PM** [L. *post meridiem*] after noon: used to designate the time from noon to midnight

**p.m.** post-mortem

**pmk.** postmark

**pneu·mat·ic** (nōō mat'ik, nyōō-) *adj.* [< L. < Gr. < *pneuma*, breath] **1.** of or containing wind, air, or gases **2.** *a)* filled with compressed air [*pneumatic* tire] *b)* worked by compressed air [*pneumatic* drill] —**pneu·mat'i·cal·ly** *adv.*

**pneu·mat·ics** (-iks) *n.pl.* [*with sing. v.*] the branch of physics dealing with such properties of air and other gases as pressure, density, etc.

**pneu·mo·coc·cus** (nōō'mə käk'əs, nyōō'-) *n., pl.* **-coc'ci** (-käk'sī) [ModL. < Gr. *pneumōn*, a lung + COCCUS] a bacterium that is a causative agent of pneumonia —**pneu'mo·coc'cal** (-käk''l), **pneu'mo·coc'cic** (-käk'sik) *adj.*

**pneu·mo·en·ceph·a·lo·gram** (-en sef'ə lō gram') *n.* [< Gr. *pneumōn*, a lung + en-, in + *kephalē*, the head + -GRAM] an X-ray photograph of the brain made after cerebrospinal fluid has been replaced with air or oxygen

**pneu·mo·ni·a** (nōō mōn'yə, nyōō-; -mō'nē ə) *n.* [ModL. < Gr. < *pneumōn*, a lung < *pnein*, to breathe] inflammation or infection of the alveoli of the lungs, caused by any of various agents, such as bacteria or viruses —**pneu·mon'ic** (-män'ik) *adj.*

**Pnom-Penh** (p'nôm'pen') *same as* PHNOM PENH

**Po** (pō) river in N Italy, flowing from the Alps east into the Adriatic

**Po** *Chem.* polonium

**P.O., p.o. 1.** petty officer: also **PO 2.** post office **3.** post office box

**poach¹** (pōch) *vt.* [< MFr. < *poche*, a pocket: the yolk is "pocketed" in the white] to cook (fish, an egg without its shell, etc.) in water or other liquid near the boiling point, or in a small receptacle put over boiling water —**poach'er** *n.*

**poach²** (pōch) *vt.* [< Fr. < OFr. *pochier*, to tread upon < MHG. *puchen*, to plunder] **1.** to trample **2.** *a)* to trespass on (private property), esp. for hunting or fishing *b)* to hunt or catch (game or fish) illegally, esp. by trespassing **3.** to steal —*vi.* to hunt or fish illegally, esp. as a trespasser —**poach'er** *n.*

**Po·ca·hon·tas** (pō'kə hän'təs) 1595?-1617; Am. Indian princess: reputed to have saved Captain John Smith from execution

**pock** (päk) *n.* [OE. *pocc*] **1.** a pustule, esp. one caused by smallpox **2.** *same as* POCKMARK —**pocked** *adj.* —**pock'y** *adj.* **pock'i·er, pock'i·est**

**pock·et** (päk'it) *n.* [< Anglo-Fr. < ONormFr. dim. of *poque*, a bag] **1.** *a)* a little bag or pouch, now usually sewn into or on clothing, for carrying money and small articles *b)* any usually small container, compartment, pouch, etc. **2.** a cavity for holding something **3.** a small area or group [a *pocket* of poverty] **4.** a confining or frustrating situation **5.** funds [a drain on one's *pocket*] **6.** *Aeron. same as* AIR POCKET **7.** any of the pouches at the sides and corners of a billiard or pool table **8.** *Geol. a)* a cavity filled with ore, oil, gas, or water *b)* a small deposit of ore, etc. —*adj.* **1.** *a)* that is or can be carried in a pocket *b)* smaller than standard **2.** not widespread; isolated [*pocket* resistance] —*vt.* **1.** to put into a pocket **2.** to provide with pockets **3.** to envelop; enclose **4.** to take dishonestly; appropriate (money, etc.) for one's own use **5.** to put up with (an insult, etc.) without answering or showing anger **6.** to hide, suppress, or set aside [*pocket* one's pride] —**out of pocket** from money at hand

**pocket battleship** a small battleship within certain treaty limits as to tonnage and guns

**pocket billiards** *same as* POOL² (*n.* 2)

**pock·et·book** (-book') *n.* **1.** a case, as of leather, for carrying money and papers in one's pocket; billfold **2.** a woman's purse **3.** monetary resources

**pocket book** a book small enough to be carried in one's pocket

**pock·et·ful** (-fool') *n., pl.* **-fuls'** as much as a pocket will hold

**pock·et·knife** (-nīf') *n., pl.* **-knives'** (-nīvz') a knife with blades that fold into the handle

**pocket money** cash for small expenses

**pock·et·size** (-sīz') *adj.* of a small size; esp., of a size to fit in a pocket: also **pock'et·sized'**

**pocket veto** the indirect veto by the President of the U.S. of a bill presented to him by Congress within ten days of its adjournment, by his failing to sign and return the bill before Congress adjourns

**pock·mark** (päk'märk') *n.* a scar or pit left by a pustule, as of smallpox, or any mark like this —*vt.* to cover with pockmarks —**pock'marked'** *adj.*

**po·co** (pō'kō) *adv.* [It.] *Music* somewhat

**pod** (päd) *n.* [< ?] **1.** a dry fruit or seed vessel enclosing one or more seeds, as a legume **2.** a contoured enclosure, as the housing of a jet engine —*vi.* **pod'ded, pod'ding 1.** to bear pods **2.** to swell out into a pod —**pod'like'** *adj.*

**-pod** (päd) [< Gr. *pous* (gen. *podos*), a foot] a combining form meaning: **1.** foot **2.** (one) having a (specified number or kind of) feet [tripod] Also **-pode** (pōd)

**podg·y** (päj'ē) *adj.* **podg'i·er, podg'i·est** *var. of* PUDGY

**po·di·a·try** (pō dī'ə trē, pə-) *n.* [< Gr. *pous* (see -POD) + -IATRY] the profession dealing with the care of the feet and with the treatment of foot disorders —**po·di'a·trist** *n.* —**po'di·at'ric** *adj.*

**po·di·um** (pō'dē əm) *n., pl.* **-di·a** (-ə); for 1 usually, **-di·ums** [L. < Gr. *podion*, dim. of *pous* (see -POD)] **1.** a low platform, esp. for the conductor of an orchestra **2.** *Zool.* a foot or footlike structure

**Po·dunk** (pō'dunk') [after a village in Mass. or Conn.] [Colloq.] any typically dull small town in the U.S.

**Poe** (pō), **Edgar Allan** 1809-49; U.S. poet, short-story writer, & critic

**po·em** (pō'əm) *n.* [< MFr. < L. < Gr. *poiēma* < *poiein*, to make] **1.** an arrangement of words written or spoken, traditionally a rhythmical or metrical composition, sometimes rhymed **2.** anything suggesting a poem in its effect

**po·e·sy** (pō'ə sē', -zē') *n., pl.* **-sies** [< OFr. < L. < Gr. *poiēsis* < *poiein*, to make] **1.** *old-fashioned var. of* POETRY **2.** [Obs.] a poem

**po·et** (pō'ət) *n.* [< OFr. < L. < Gr. *poiētēs* < *poiein*, to make] **1.** a person who writes poems **2.** a person who expresses himself with beauty of thought and language —**po'et·ess** [Now Rare] *n.fem.*

**poet. 1.** poetic **2.** poetry

**po·et·as·ter** (pō'ə tas'tər) *n.* [see POET & -ASTER] a writer of mediocre verse; rhymester

**po·et·ic** (pō et'ik) *adj.* **1.** of, like, or fit for a poet or poetry **2.** written in verse **3.** having the beauty, imagination, etc. of poetry **4.** imaginative or creative Also **po·et'i·cal** —**po·et'i·cal·ly** *adv.*

**po·et·i·cize** (-ə sīz') *vt.* **-cized', -ciz'ing 1.** to make poetic **2.** to express, or deal with, in poetry —*vi.* to write poetry

**poetic justice** justice, as in some plays, etc., in which good is rewarded and evil punished

**poetic license 1.** disregard of strict fact or of rigid form, as by a poet, for artistic effect **2.** freedom to do this

**po·et·ics** (pō et'iks) *n.pl.* [*with sing. v.*] **1.** *a)* the theory or structure of poetry *b)* a treatise on this **2.** the poetic theory or practice of a specific poet

**po·et·ize** (pō'ə tīz') *vt., vi.* **-ized', -iz'ing** *same as* POETICIZE

**poet laureate** *pl.* **poets laureate, poet laureates 1.** the court poet of England, appointed for life by the monarch to write poems celebrating official occasions, national events, etc. **2.** any official poet of any nation, region, etc.

**po·et·ry** (pō′ə trē) *n.* [< OFr. < ML. < L. *poeta*, a poet] **1.** the art, theory, or structure of poems **2.** poems **3.** *a)* poetic qualities *b)* the expression or embodiment of such qualities

**po·go stick** (pō′gō) [arbitrary coinage] a stilt with pedals and a spring at one end, used as a toy on which one can move along in a series of bounds

**po·grom** (pō gräm′, -grum′; pō′grəm) *n.* [Russ., devastation] an organized persecution and massacre of a minority group, esp. of Jews (as in Czarist Russia)

**poi** (poi, pō′ē) *n.* [Haw.] Hawaiian food made of mashed, fermented taro root

**poign·ant** (poin′yənt; *chiefly Brit.* -ənt) *adj.* [MFr. prp. of *poindre* < L. *pungere*, to prick] **1.** *a)* sharp or pungent to the smell or, formerly, the taste *b)* keenly affecting the other senses [*poignant* beauty] **2.** *a)* sharply painful to the feelings *b)* evoking pity, compassion, etc. **3.** sharp, biting, etc. [*poignant* wit] —**poign′an·cy** *n.* —**poign′ant·ly** *adv.*

**poi·kil·o·ther·mal** (poi kil′ō thʉr′m'l) *adj.* [< Gr. *poikilos*, variegated + THERMAL] *Zool.* same as COLD-BLOODED (sense 1)

**poin·ci·a·na** (poin′sē an′ə, -ā′nə) *n.* [ModL., after M. de *Poinci*, a governor of the Fr. West Indies] any of various small tropical trees with showy red, orange, or yellow flowers

**poin·set·ti·a** (poin set′ē ə, -set′ə) *n.* [ModL., after J. R. *Poinsett* (d. 1851), U.S. ambassador to Mexico] a Mexican and Central American plant with yellow flowers surrounded by petallike red leaves

**point** (point) *n.* [OFr., a dot, prick < L. < *punctus*, pp. of *pungere*, to prick] **1.** a minute mark or dot **2.** a dot in print or writing, as a period, decimal point, etc. **3.** *a)* an element in geometry having definite position, but no size, shape, or extension *b)* a particular position, location, spot, etc. [*points* on an itinerary] **4.** *a)* the position of a player, as in cricket *b)* the player **5.** the exact moment [at the *point* of death] **6.** a stage, condition, level, or degree reached [a boiling *point*] **7.** an item [explain it *point* by *point*] **8.** *a)* a distinguishing characteristic *b)* a physical characteristic of an animal, used as a standard in judging breeding **9.** a unit, as of measurement, value, game scores, etc. **10.** *a)* a sharp end; tip *b)* something with a sharp end **11.** needlepoint lace **12.** a projecting piece of land; cape **13.** a branch of a deer's antler [a ten-*point* buck] **14.** *a)* the essential fact or idea under consideration *b)* the main idea or feature of a story, etc. **15.** aim; purpose; object [there's no *point* in going] **16.** *a)* an impressive argument or fact [he has a *point* there!] *b)* a helpful hint **17.** the number that the thrower must make to win in craps **18.** *Ballet* the position of being on the tips of the toes **19.** *Elec.* either of the two tungsten or platinum contacts that make or break the circuit in a distributor **20.** *Finance a)* a standard unit of value, equal to $1, used in quoting prices, as of stocks *b)* a percentage of a mortgage required to be paid in advance by the borrower **21.** *Navigation a)* any of the 32 marks showing direction on a compass card *b)* the angle between two successive compass points **22.** *Printing* a measuring unit for type bodies and printed matter, equal to about 1/72 of an inch —*vt.* **1.** *a)* to put punctuation marks in *b)* to mark (*off* a sum, etc.) with (decimal) points **2.** to sharpen (a pencil, etc.) to a point **3.** to give (a story, remark, etc.) emphasis (usually with *up*) **4.** to show or call attention to (usually with *out*) [*point* the way] **5.** to aim or direct (a gun, finger, etc.) **6.** to extend the foot so as to bring (the toe) more nearly in line with the leg **7.** to show the location of (game) by standing still and facing toward it: said of hunting dogs **8.** *Masonry* to rake out mortar from the joints of (brickwork) and finish with fresh mortar —*vi.* **1.** to direct one's finger or the like (*at* or *to*) **2.** to call attention (*to*); hint (*at*) **3.** to aim or be directed (*to* or *toward*) **4.** to point game: said of a hunting dog —**at the point of** very close to —**beside the point** not pertinent —**in point of** in the matter of —**make a point of 1.** to make (something) one's strict rule, practice, etc. **2.** to call special attention to —**on** (or **upon**) **the point of** on the verge of —**stretch** (or **strain**) **a point** to make an exception or concession —**to the point** pertinent; apt: also in point —**point′a·ble** *adj.*

**point-blank** (-blaŋk′) *adj.* [POINT + BLANK (white center of the target)] **1.** aimed horizontally, straight at a mark **2.** straightforward; plain [a *point-blank* answer] —*adv.* **1.** in a direct line; straight **2.** without quibbling; bluntly [to refuse *point-blank*]

**point·ed** (poin′tid) *adj.* **1.** *a)* having a point, or sharp end *b)* tapering **2.** sharp; incisive, as an epigram **3.** aimed at someone [a *pointed* remark] **4.** very evident; emphasized —**point′ed·ly** *adv.* —**point′ed·ness** *n.*

**point·er** (-tər) *n.* **1.** a person or thing that points **2.** a long, tapered rod for pointing to things, as on a map **3.** an indicator on a clock, meter, etc. **4.** a large, lean hunting dog with a smooth coat: it smells out game and then points **5.** [Colloq.] a helpful hint —**the Pointers** *Astron.* the two stars in the Big Dipper that are almost in a line with the North Star

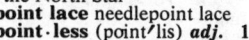
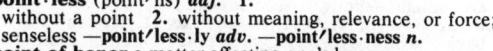

POINTER (26 in. high at shoulder)

**point lace** needlepoint lace

**point·less** (point′lis) *adj.* **1.** without a point **2.** without meaning, relevance, or force; senseless —**point′less·ly** *adv.* —**point′less·ness** *n.*

**point of honor** a matter affecting one's honor

**point of order** a question as to whether the rules of parliamentary procedure are being observed

**point of view 1.** the place from which, or way in which, something is viewed; standpoint **2.** a mental attitude

**point·y** (poin′tē) *adj.* **point′i·er**, **point′i·est 1.** that comes to a sharp point **2.** having many points

**poise** (poiz) *n.* [< OFr. < VL. < L. *pensum*, something weighed < *pendere*, to weigh] **1.** balance; stability **2.** ease and dignity of manner; composure **3.** the condition of being calm or serene **4.** carriage; bearing, as of the body —*vt.* **poised**, **pois′ing 1.** to balance; keep steady **2.** to suspend (usually passive or reflexive) —*vi.* **1.** to be suspended or balanced **2.** to hover

**poi·son** (poi′z'n) *n.* [< OFr. < L. *potio*, potion] **1.** a substance causing illness or death when eaten, drunk, or absorbed in small quantities **2.** anything harmful to happiness or welfare —*vt.* **1.** to harm or destroy by means of poison **2.** to put poison on or into **3.** to influence wrongfully [to *poison* one's mind] —*adj.* poisonous or poisoned —**poi′son·er** *n.*

**poison dogwood** same as POISON SUMAC

**poison ivy 1.** any of several plants having leaves of three leaflets and ivory-colored berries: it can cause a severe rash on contact **2.** such a rash

**poison oak** name variously used for: **1.** POISON IVY **2.** POISON SUMAC

**poi·son·ous** (poi′z'n əs) *adj.* capable of injuring or killing by or as by poison; full of poison; venomous —**poi′son·ous·ly** *adv.* —**poi′son·ous·ness** *n.*

POISON IVY

**poison sumac** a swamp plant with clusters of grayish fruit and leaves made up of 7 to 13 leaflets: it can cause a severe rash on contact

**poke¹** (pōk) *vt.* **poked**, **pok′ing** [MDu. or LowG. *poken*] **1.** *a)* to push or jab with a stick, finger, etc. *b)* [Slang] to hit with the fist **2.** to make (a hole, etc.) by poking **3.** to stir up (a fire) **4.** to thrust (something) forward; intrude [to *poke* one's head out a window] —*vi.* **1.** to jab with a stick, poker, etc. (*at*) **2.** to intrude; meddle **3.** to search (sometimes with *about* or *around*) **4.** to stick out; protrude **5.** to move slowly or lazily; loiter (often with *along*) —*n.* **1.** *a)* a poking; jab; thrust *b)* [Slang] a blow with the fist **2.** same as SLOWPOKE **3.** a poke bonnet —**poke fun (at)** to ridicule or deride

**poke²** (pōk) *n.* [OFr. *poke*, *poque* < Frank.] **1.** [Dial.] a sack or bag **2.** [Slang] *a)* a wallet or purse *b)* all of one's money

**poke³** (pōk) *n.* [< AmInd. *puccoon*] same as POKEWEED: also **poke′ber·ry** (-ber′ē), *pl.* **-ries**

**poke bonnet** a bonnet with a wide front brim

**pok·er¹** (pō′kər) *n.* [< ?] a card game in which the players bet on the value of their hands, forming a pool to be taken by the winner: see DRAW POKER, STUD POKER

**pok·er²** (pō′kər) *n.* **1.** a person or thing that pokes **2.** a bar, as of iron, for stirring a fire

**poker face** [Colloq.] an expressionless face, as of a poker player hiding the nature of his hand

**poke·weed** (pōk′wēd′) *n.* [see POKE³] a N. American plant with purplish-white flowers, reddish-purple berries, and poisonous roots

**pok·ey** (pō′kē) *n.*, *pl.* **pok′eys**, **pok′ies** [< ?] [Slang] a jail: also **pok′y**

**pok·y** (pō′kē) *adj.* **pok′i·er**, **pok′i·est** [POKE¹ + -Y²] **1.** slow; dull **2.** small; stuffy [a *poky* room] **3.** shabbily dressed Also **pok′ey** —**pok′i·ly** *adv.* —**pok′i·ness** *n.*

**pol** (päl) *n.* [Slang] an experienced politician

**Pol. 1.** Poland **2.** Polish

**Po·land** (pō′lənd) country in C Europe, on the Baltic Sea: 120,625 sq. mi.; pop. 32,807,000; cap. Warsaw

**Poland China** an American breed of large hog, usually black and white

**po·lar** (pō'lər) *adj.* [< ML. < L. *polus:* see POLE²] **1.** of or near the North or South Pole **2.** of a pole or poles **3.** having polarity **4.** opposite in character, direction, etc. **5.** guiding, like the polestar

**polar bear** a large, white bear of the Arctic regions

**polar circle** *same as:* **1.** ARCTIC CIRCLE **2.** ANTARCTIC CIRCLE

**Po·la·ris** (pō lar'is) [ModL. < ML. (*stella*) *polaris*, polar (star)] *same as* NORTH STAR

**po·lar·i·scope** (pō lar'ə skōp') *n.* [POLARI(ZE) + -SCOPE] an instrument for demonstrating or detecting the polarization of light —**po·lar'i·scop'ic** (-skäp'ik) *adj.*

**po·lar·i·ty** (pō lar'ə tē) *n., pl.* **-ties 1.** the tendency of bodies having opposite magnetic poles to become aligned so that their two extremities point to the two magnetic poles of the earth **2.** any tendency to turn, feel, etc. in a certain way, as if magnetized **3.** the having of two contrary qualities, powers, etc. **4.** the condition of being positive or negative with respect to some reference point or object

**po·lar·i·za·tion** (pō'lər i zā'shən) *n.* **1.** the producing or acquiring of polarity **2.** the accumulation of gases around the electrodes of an electric cell during electrolysis, causing a reduction in the flow of current **3.** *Optics* a condition, or the production of a condition, of light in which the transverse vibrations of the waves are in one plane or direction only

**po·lar·ize** (pō'lə rīz') *vt.* **-ized', -iz'ing** [< Fr. < *polaire*, POLAR] to give polarity to; produce polarization in —*vi.* to acquire polarity; specif., to separate into diametrically opposed groups, etc. —**po'lar·iz'a·ble** *adj.* —**po'lar·iz'er** *n.*

**Po·lar·oid** (pō'lə roid') [POLAR + -OID] *a trademark for:* **1.** a transparent material capable of polarizing light **2.** a camera that develops and prints snapshots: in full, **Polaroid (Land) camera**

**Pole** (pōl) *n.* a native or inhabitant of Poland

**pole¹** (pōl) *n.* [OE. *pal* < L. *palus*, a stake] **1.** a long, slender piece of wood, metal, etc. [a tent *pole*] **2.** a unit of measure, equal to one rod or one square rod **3.** the innermost position on a race track —*vt., vi.* **poled, pol'ing 1.** to propel (a boat or raft) with a pole **2.** to impel, support, etc. (something) as with a pole

**pole²** (pōl) *n.* [L. *polus* < Gr. *polos*] **1.** either end of any axis, as of the earth, of the celestial sphere, etc. **2.** the region around the North Pole or South Pole **3.** either of two opposed forces, parts, etc., such as the ends of a magnet, the terminals of a battery, etc. —**poles apart** widely separated

**pole·ax, pole·axe** (pōl'aks') *n., pl.* **-ax'es** (-ak'siz) [< *pol*, POLL + *ax*, AX] **1.** a long-handled battle-ax **2.** any ax with a spike, hook, etc. opposite the blade —*vt.* **-axed', -ax'ing** to attack with a poleax

**pole·cat** (pōl'kat') *n., pl.* **-cats', -cat':** see PLURAL, II, D, 1 [prob. < OFr. *poule:* see PULLET & CAT] **1.** a small, weasel-like carnivore of Europe **2.** *same as* SKUNK

**po·lem·ic** (pə lem'ik, pō-) *adj.* [< Fr. < Gr. *polemikos* < *polemos*, a war] **1.** of or involving dispute; controversial **2.** argumentative Also, esp. for 2, **po·lem'i·cal** —*n.* **1.** an argument or controversial discussion **2.** a person inclined to argument —**po·lem'i·cal·ly** *adv.*

**po·lem·ics** (-iks) *n.pl.* [*with sing. v.*] the art or practice of disputation —**po·lem'i·cist** (-ə sist) *n.*

**pole·star** (pōl'stär') *n.* **1.** Polaris, the North Star **2.** a guiding principle **3.** a center of attraction

**pole vault** *Track and Field* **1.** an event in which the contestants leap for height, vaulting over a bar with the aid of a long, flexible pole **2.** such a leap —**pole'-vault'** *vi.* —**pole'-vault'er** *n.*

**po·lice** (pə lēs') *n.* [Fr. < LL. < Gr. *politeia*, the state < *politēs*, citizen < *polis*, city] **1.** the regulation of morals, safety, etc.; law enforcement **2.** the governmental department (of a city, state, etc.) for keeping order, enforcing the law, and preventing and detecting crimes **3.** [*with pl. v.*] the members of such a department, or of a private organization like this [security *police*] **4.** *U.S. Army* a) the duty of keeping a camp, etc. clean and orderly b) [*with pl. v.*] the soldiers charged with this —*vt.* **-liced', -lic'ing 1.** to control, protect, etc. with police or the like [to *police* the streets] **2.** to keep (a camp, etc.) clean and orderly

**police dog** a dog specially trained to assist police; esp., in popular usage, a German shepherd dog

**po·lice·man** (-mən) *n., pl.* **-men** a member of a police force —**po·lice'wom'an** *n.fem., pl.* **-wom'en**

**police state** a government that uses a secret police force to suppress political opposition

**pol·i·clin·ic** (päl'i klin'ik) *n.* [< G. < Gr. *polis*, city + G. *klinik*, clinic] the department of a hospital where outpatients are treated

**pol·i·cy¹** (päl'ə sē) *n., pl.* **-cies** [< OFr. < L. < Gr. *politeia:* see POLICE] **1.** wise or prudent management **2.** any governing principle, plan, etc.

**pol·i·cy²** (päl'ə sē) *n., pl.* **-cies** [< MFr. < It. *polizza* < ML., ult. < Gr. *apodeixis*, proof < *apodeiknynai*, to display] a written contract (**insurance policy**) in which one party guarantees to insure another against a specified loss, injury, etc.

**policy (racket)** *same as* THE NUMBERS (see NUMBER)

**po·li·o** (pō'lē ō') *n. clipped form of* POLIOMYELITIS

**po·li·o·my·e·li·tis** (pō'lē ō mī'ə līt'əs) *n.* [ModL. < Gr. *polios*, gray + MYELITIS] an acute infectious disease, esp. of children, caused by a virus inflammation of the gray matter of the spinal cord, often resulting in muscular paralysis

**Pol·ish** (pō'lish) *adj.* of Poland, its people, their language, or culture —*n.* the West Slavic language of the Poles

**pol·ish** (päl'ish) *vt.* [< OFr. < L. *polire*] **1.** *a)* to smooth and brighten, as by rubbing *b)* to coat with wax, etc. and make glossy **2.** to improve or refine (manners, etc.) by removing crudeness **3.** to complete or embellish —*vi.* to take a polish; become glossy, refined, etc. —*n.* **1.** a surface gloss **2.** elegance; refinement **3.** a substance used for polishing **4.** a polishing or being polished —**polish off** [Colloq.] to finish or get rid of —**polish up** [Colloq.] to improve —**pol'ished** *adj.* —**pol'ish·er** *n.*

**Po·lit·bu·ro** (päl'it byoor'ō, pō'lit-) *n.* [< Russ. < *Politicheskoe*) *Byuro*, political bureau] the executive committee of the Communist Party of the Soviet Union and of certain other countries

**po·lite** (pə līt') *adj.* [< L. pp. of *polire*, to polish] **1.** polished; cultured; refined [*polite* society] **2.** having good manners; courteous —**po·lite'ly** *adv.* —**po·lite'ness** *n.*

**pol·i·tesse** (päl'ə tes') *n.* [Fr.] politeness

**pol·i·tic** (päl'ə tik) *adj.* [< MFr. < L. < Gr. < *politēs:* see POLICE] **1.** having practical wisdom; prudent **2.** crafty; unscrupulous **3.** artful; expedient [a *politic* plan] **4.** [Rare] political: see BODY POLITIC —*vi.* **-ticked, -tick·ing** to engage in political campaigning —**pol'i·tic·ly** *adv.*

**po·lit·i·cal** (pə lit'i k'l) *adj.* **1.** of or concerned with government, politics, etc. **2.** having a definite governmental organization **3.** engaged in politics [*political* parties] **4.** of or characteristic of political parties or politicians —**po·lit'i·cal·ly** *adv.*

**political economy** *earlier name for* ECONOMICS

**political science** the science of the principles, organization, and methods of government —**political scientist**

**pol·i·ti·cian** (päl'ə tish'ən) *n.* a person actively engaged in politics, often one holding or seeking political office: often used derogatorily of one who seeks only to advance himself or his party, as by scheming: cf. STATESMAN

**po·lit·i·co** (pə lit'i kō') *n., pl.* **-cos'** [Sp. or It.] *same as* POLITICIAN

**pol·i·tics** (päl'ə tiks) *n.pl.* [*with sing. or pl. v.*] **1.** the science of government; political science **2.** political affairs **3.** participation in political affairs **4.** political methods, tactics, etc. **5.** political opinions, principles, etc. **6.** fractional scheming for power within a group

**pol·i·ty** (päl'ə tē) *n., pl.* **-ties** [< MFr. < L. *politia:* see POLICY¹] **1.** the government organization of a state, church, etc. **2.** a society or institution with a government; state

**Polk** (pōk), **James Knox** 1795–1849; 11th president of the U.S. (1845–49)

**pol·ka** (pōl'kə) *n.* [Czech < Pol. fem. of *Polak*, a Pole] **1.** a fast dance for couples **2.** music for this dance, in duple time —*vi.* to dance the polka

**pol·ka dot** (pō'kə) **1.** one of the small round dots regularly spaced to form a pattern on cloth **2.** a pattern or cloth with such dots —**pol'ka-dot'** *adj.*

**poll** (pōl) *n.* [< or akin to MDu. *pol*, head] **1.** the head; esp., the crown, back, or hair of the head **2.** a counting, listing, etc. of persons, esp. of voters **3.** the number of votes recorded **4.** [*pl.*] a place where votes are cast and recorded **5.** *a)* a canvassing of a selected or random group to collect information, or to attempt to discover public opinion *b)* a report on this —*vt.* **1.** to cut off or cut short **2.** to trim the wool, branches, etc. of **3.** *a)* to register the votes of *b)* to require each member of (a jury, etc.) to declare his vote individually **4.** to receive (a certain number of votes) **5.** to cast (a vote) **6.** to canvass in a poll (sense 5 *a*) —*vi.* to vote in an election —**poll'er** *n.*

**pol·len** (päl'ən) *n.* [ModL. < L., dust] the yellow, powderlike male sex cells on the stamens of a flower

**pol·li·nate** (päl'ə nāt') *vt.* **-nat'ed, -nat'ing** to transfer pollen from a stamen to a pistil of (a flower) —**pol'li·na'tion** *n.* —**pol'li·na'tor** *n.*

**pol·li·wog** (päl'ē wäg', -wôg') *n.* [prob. < *pol*, POLL + *wigelen*, to WIGGLE] *same as* TADPOLE: also sp. **pol'ly·wog'**

**poll·ster** (pōl'stər) *n.* a person whose work is taking public opinion polls

**poll tax** a tax per head: in some States payment of a poll tax is a prerequisite for voting

**pol·lu·tant** (pə loot''nt) *n.* something that pollutes, as a harmful chemical discharged into the air

**pol·lute** (pə loot') *vt.* **-lut'ed, -lut'ing** [< L. pp. of *pol-*

*luere*] to make unclean, impure, or corrupt; defile —**pol-lut′er** *n.* —**pol·lu′tion** *n.*

**Pol·lux** (päl′əks) **1.** *Gr. & Rom. Myth.* the immortal twin of Castor **2.** the brightest star in the constellation Gemini

**Pol·ly·an·na** (päl′ē an′ə) *n.* [the heroine of novels by Eleanor H. Porter (1868–1920), U.S. writer] a persistently optimistic person

**po·lo** (pō′lō) *n.* [prob. < Tibet. *pulu*, the ball] **1.** a game played on horseback by two teams who try to drive a small wooden ball through the opponents' goal with long-handled mallets **2.** *same as* WATER POLO —**po′lo·ist** *n.*

**Po·lo** (pō′lō), **Mar·co** (mär′kō) 1254?–1324?; Venetian traveler in E Asia

**po·lo·naise** (päl′ə nāz′, pō′lə-) *n.* [Fr. < fem. of *polonais*, Polish] **1.** a stately Polish dance in triple time **2.** music for this dance

**po·lo·ni·um** (pə lō′nē əm) *n.* [ModL. < ML. *Polonia*, Poland: coinage of Marie Curie, its co-discoverer] a radioactive chemical element formed by the disintegration of radium: symbol, Po; at. wt., 210.05; at. no., 84

**polo shirt** a knitted pullover sport shirt

**Pol·ska** (pôl′skä) *Pol. name of* POLAND

**pol·troon** (päl trōōn′) *n.* [< Fr. < It. *poltrone*, coward < *poltro*, colt] a thorough coward —*adj.* cowardly —**pol-troon′er·y** *n.*

**pol·y-** [ModL. < Gr. *poly-* < *polys*, much, many] *a combining form meaning* much, many, more than one

**pol·y·an·dry** (päl′ē an′drē, päl′ē an′-) *n.* [< Gr. < *poly-*, many + *anēr*, a man] the state or practice of having two or more husbands at the same time —**pol′y·an′dric** *adj.* —**pol′y·an′drist** *n.* —**pol′y·an′drous** *adj.*

**pol·y·an·thus** (päl′ē an′thəs) *n.* [ModL. < Gr. < *poly-*, many + *anthos*, a flower] **1.** any of various primroses with many flowers **2.** a sweet-scented narcissus with clusters of star-shaped flowers

**pol·y·cen·tric** (päl′i sen′trik) *adj.* [POLY- + CENT(E)R + -IC] of or relating to independent centers of power within a political system —**pol′y·cen′trism** *n.* —**pol′y·cen′trist** *adj., n.*

**pol·y·clin·ic** (-klin′ik) *n.* [POLY- + CLINIC] a clinic or hospital treating various kinds of diseases

**pol·y·es·ter** (päl′ē es′tər) *n.* [POLY(MER) + ESTER] any of several polymeric synthetic resins used in making plastics, fibers, etc.

**pol·y·eth·yl·ene** (päl′ē eth′ə lēn′) *n.* [POLY(MER) + ETHYLENE] any of several thermoplastic resins, ($C_2H_4$)n, used in making plastics, films, etc.

**po·lyg·a·my** (pə lig′ə mē) *n.* [< Fr. < Gr.: see POLY- & -GAMY] the practice of having two or more wives or husbands at the same time —**po·lyg′a·mist** *n.* —**po·lyg′a·mous** *adj.* —**po·lyg′a·mous·ly** *adv.*

**pol·y·glot** (päl′i glät′) *adj.* [< Gr. < *poly-*, many + *glōtta*, the tongue] **1.** speaking or writing several languages **2.** containing or written in several languages —*n.* **1.** a polyglot person **2.** a polyglot book

**pol·y·gon** (päl′i gän′) *n.* [< LL. < Gr.: see POLY- & -GON] a closed plane figure, esp. one with more than four sides and angles —**po·lyg·o·nal** (pə lig′ə n'l) *adj.*

**pol·y·graph** (-graf′) *n.* **1.** an early device for reproducing writings or drawings **2.** an instrument for recording changes in blood pressure, pulse rate, etc.: see LIE DETECTOR —**pol′y·graph′ic** *adj.*

**po·lyg·y·ny** (pə lij′ə nē) *n.* [ModL. < POLY- + Gr. *gynē*, a woman] the practice of having two or more wives or concubines at the same time —**po·lyg′y·nous** (-nəs) *adj.*

**pol·y·he·dron** (päl′i hē′drən) *n., pl.* **-drons, -dra** (-drə) [ModL. < Gr.: see POLY- & -HEDRON] a solid figure, esp. one with more than six plane surfaces —**pol′y·he′dral** *adj.*

**Pol·y·hym·ni·a** (-him′nē ə) *Gr. Myth.* the Muse of sacred poetry: also **Po·lym′ni·a** (pə lim′-)

**pol·y·math** (päl′i math′) *n.* [< Gr. < *poly-* (see POLY-) + *manthanein*, to learn] a person of great and diversified learning —**pol′y·math′ic** *adj.*

**pol·y·mer** (päl′i mər) *n.* [G. < Gr.: see POLY- & -MEROUS] a naturally occurring or synthetic substance made up of giant molecules formed by polymerization

**pol·y·mer·ic** (päl′i mer′ik) *adj.* composed of the same chemical elements in the same proportions by weight, but differing in molecular weight —**pol′y·mer′i·cal·ly** *adv.*

**po·lym·er·i·za·tion** (pə lim′ər i zā′shən, päl′i mər-) *n.* the process of joining two or more like molecules to form a more complex molecule whose molecular weight is a multiple of the original and whose physical properties are different —**po·lym′er·ize′** (-īz′) *vt., vi.* **-ized′, -iz′ing**

**pol·y·mor·phous** (päl′i môr′fəs) *adj.* [< Gr.: see POLY- & -MORPH] having, occurring in, or passing through several or various forms: also **pol′y·mor′phic** —**pol′y·mor′phism** *n.* —**pol′y·mor′phous·ly** *adv.*

**Pol·y·ne·sia** (päl′ə nē′zhə, -shə) a major division of the Pacific islands east of the international date line, including Hawaii, Samoa, Tonga, Society Islands, etc.

**Pol·y·ne·sian** (-zhən, -shən) *adj.* of Polynesia, its people, their language, etc. —*n.* **1.** a member of the brown people of Polynesia, including the Hawaiians, Tahitians, Samoans, and Maoris **2.** the group of Malayo-Polynesian languages of Polynesia

**pol·y·no·mi·al** (päl′i nō′mē əl) *n.* [POLY- + (BI)NOMIAL] **1.** *Algebra* an expression consisting of two or more terms (Ex.: $x^3 + 3x + 2$) **2.** *Biol.* a species or subspecies name having two or more terms —*adj.* consisting of polynomials

**pol·yp** (päl′ip) *n.* [< Fr. < L. < Gr. < *poly-*, many + *pous*, a foot] **1.** any of various coelenterates having a mouth fringed with tentacles at the top of a tubelike body, as the sea anemone, hydra, etc. **2.** a projecting growth of mucous membrane inside the nose, bladder, etc. —**pol′yp·ous** *adj.*

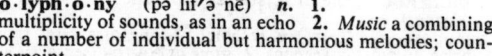

MOUTH

PERISARC

POLYP
(sense 1)

**pol·y·pet·al·ous** (-pet′'l əs) *adj.* [POLY- + PETAL + -OUS] *Bot.* having separate petals

**pol·y·phon·ic** (päl′i fän′ik) *adj.* [< Gr.: see POLY- & -PHONE] **1.** having or making many sounds **2.** *Music* of or characterized by polyphony; contrapuntal Also **po·lyph·o·nous** (pə-lif′ə nəs) —**pol′y·phon′i·cal·ly** *adv.*

**po·lyph·o·ny** (pə lif′ə nē) *n.* **1.** multiplicity of sounds, as in an echo **2.** *Music* a combining of a number of individual but harmonious melodies; counterpoint

**pol·y·pro·pyl·ene** (päl′i prō′pə lēn′) *n.* [POLY(MER) + PROPYLENE] polymerized propylene, a very light thermoplastic resin used in packaging, tubing, etc.

**pol·y·some** (päl′i sōm′) *n.* [POLY- + -SOME³] a group of ribosomes in which protein synthesis occurs

**pol·y·so·mic** (päl′i sō′mik) *adj.* [< prec. + -IC] *Genetics* having extra chromosomes, not in a set

**pol·y·sty·rene** (-stī′rēn) *n.* a tough plastic, a polymer of styrene, used to make containers, etc.

**pol·y·syl·lab·ic** (-si lab′ik) *adj.* **1.** having several, esp. four or more, syllables **2.** characterized by polysyllables Also **pol′y·syl·lab′i·cal** —**pol′y·syl·lab′i·cal·ly** *adv.*

**pol·y·syl·la·ble** (päl′i sil′ə b'l) *n.* a polysyllabic word

**pol·y·tech·nic** (päl′i tek′nik) *adj.* [< Fr. < Gr. < *poly-*, many + *technē*, an art] of or providing instruction in many scientific and technical subjects —*n.* a polytechnic school

**pol·y·the·ism** (päl′i the iz′m) *n.* [< Fr. < Gr. < *poly-*, many + *theos*, god] belief in more than one god —**pol′y·the·ist** *adj., n.* —**pol′y·the·is′tic, pol′y·the·is′ti·cal** *adj.* —**pol′y·the·is′ti·cal·ly** *adv.*

**pol·y·un·sat·u·rat·ed** (päl′i un sach′ə rāt′id) *adj.* [POLY- + UNSATURATED] containing more than one double or triple bond in the molecule, as certain vegetable and animal fats and oils

**pol·y·u·re·thane** (-yoor′ə thān′) *n.* [POLY- + *urethane*, a chemical compound with the basic structure of polyurethane] any of certain synthetic rubber polymers used in cushions, molded products, etc.

**pol·y·va·lent** (-vā′lənt) *adj.* **1.** designating a vaccine for two or more strains of the same microorganism **2.** *Chem.* a) having a valence of more than two b) having more than one valence —**pol′y·va′lence** *n.*

**pol·y·wa·ter** (-wôt′ər, -wät′-) *n.* [POLY(MERIC) + WATER] a viscous substance variously identified as a new form of water, highly contaminated water, etc.

**pom·ace** (pum′is) *n.* [ML. *pomacium*, cider < L. *pomum*, a fruit] **1.** the crushed pulp of apples or other fruit pressed for juice **2.** the crushed matter of anything pressed, as seeds for oil

**po·ma·ceous** (pō mā′shəs) *adj.* [< L. *pomum*, a fruit] of or like apples or other pomes

**po·made** (pä mād′, pō-, pə-; -mäd′) *n.* [< Fr. < It. *pomata*, ult. < L. *pomum*, fruit: orig. perfumed with apple pulp] a perfumed preparation, as for grooming the hair: also **po·ma′tum** (pō māt′əm) —*vt.* **-mad′ed, -mad′ing** to apply pomade to

**pome** (pōm) *n.* [OFr., ult. < L. *pomum*, fruit] any fleshy fruit with a core and seeds, as the apple, pear, etc.

**pome·gran·ate** (päm′gran′it, päm′ə-; pum′-) *n.* [< OFr. < *pome*, apple + *granade* < L. *granatum*, lit., having seeds] **1.** a round fruit with a thick, red rind and many seeds covered with red, juicy, edible flesh **2.** the bush or small tree that bears it

**Pom·er·a·ni·a** (päm′ə rā′nē ə) region in C Europe, on the Baltic, now divided between Poland & East Germany

**Pom·er·a·ni·an** (-ən) *adj.* of Pomerania or its people —*n.*

1. a native or inhabitant of Pomerania 2. any of a breed of small dog with long, silky hair, pointed ears, and a bushy tail

**pom·mel** (pum′'l; *also, for n.,* päm′'l) *n.* [< OFr. dim. of *pome:* see POME] 1. a round knob on the end of some sword hilts 2. the rounded, upward-projecting front part of a saddle —*vt.* -meled or -melled, -mel·ing or -mel·ling *same as* PUMMEL

**po·mol·o·gy** (pō mäl′ə jē) *n.* [< ModL.: see POME & -LOGY] the science of fruit cultivation —**po′mo·log′i·cal** (-mə läj′i k′l) *adj.* —**po·mol′o·gist** *n.*

**Po·mo·na** (pə mō′nə) [after *Pomona,* Rom. goddess of fruits & fruit trees] city in S Calif., east of Los Angeles: pop. 93,000

**pomp** (pämp) *n.* [< MFr. < L. < Gr. *pompē,* solemn procession] 1. stately display; splendor 2. ostentatious show or display

**pom·pa·dour** (päm′pə dôr′) *n.* [after ff.] a hairdo in which the hair is swept or brushed up high from the forehead

**Pom·pa·dour** (päm′pə dôr′, -door′; *Fr.* pōn pá dōōr′), marquise de (də) 1721–64; mistress of Louis XV

**pom·pa·no** (päm′pə nō′) *n., pl.* **-no′, -nos′:** see PLURAL, II, D, 2 [Sp. *pámpano*] a spiny-finned, saltwater food fish of N. America and the West Indies

**Pom·pei·i** (päm pā′ē, -pā′) ancient city on the S coast of Italy: destroyed by the eruption of Mount Vesuvius (79 A.D.) —**Pom·pei′an** (-pā′ən) *adj., n.*

**Pom·pey** (päm′pē) (L. name *Gnaeus Pompeius*) 106–48 B.C.; Rom. general & statesman: called *the Great* (L. *Magnus*)

**pom-pom** (päm′päm′) *n.* [echoic] 1. any of several rapid-firing automatic weapons 2. *same as* POMPON (sense 1): also **pom′pom′**

**pom·pon** (päm′pän′, -päm′) *n.* [Fr.] 1. an ornamental ball or tuft as of silk or wool, worn as on hats or waved by cheerleaders 2. *a*) a kind of chrysanthemum, dahlia, etc. with small, round flowers *b*) the flower

**pom·pous** (päm′pəs) *adj.* 1. full of pomp; magnificent 2. pretentious, as in speech or manner; self-important —**pom·pos′i·ty** (-päs′ə tē), *pl.* **-ties, pom′pous·ness** *n.* —**pom′pous·ly** *adv.*

**Pon·ce** (pôn′se) seaport on the S coast of Puerto Rico: pop. 126,000

**Pon·ce de Le·ón** (pôn′the *the* le ôn′; *E.* päns′ də lē′ən), **Juan** (hwän) 1460?–1521; Sp. explorer: discovered Florida

**pon·cho** (pän′chō) *n., pl.* **-chos** [< SAmInd.] 1. a cloak like a blanket with a hole in the middle for the head 2. a garment, esp. a raincoat, like this

**pond** (pänd) *n.* [< ME. var. of POUND[3]] a body of standing water smaller than a lake, often man-made

**pon·der** (pän′dər) *vt., vi.* [< MFr. < L. *ponderare,* to weigh < *pondus,* a weight] to think deeply (about); deliberate —**pon′der·a·bil′i·ty** *n.* —**pon′der·a·ble** *adj.* —**pon′der·er** *n.*

**pon·der·o·sa** (pine) (pän′də rō′sə) [< ModL. (*Pinus*) *ponderosa,* lit., heavy (pine)] 1. a yellow pine of western N. America 2. its wood

**pon·der·ous** (pän′dər əs) *adj.* [< L. < *pondus* (gen. *ponderis*), a weight] 1. very heavy 2. unwieldy because of weight 3. bulky; massive 4. labored; dull [*a ponderous style*] —**pon′der·ous·ly** *adv.* —**pon′der·ous·ness, pon′der·os′i·ty** (-äs′ə tē) *n.*

**pond lily** *same as* WATERLILY

**pond scum** a mass of filamentous algae forming a green scum on the surface of ponds, etc.

**pond·weed** (pänd′wēd′) *n.* any of various related water plants, with submerged or floating leaves

**pone** (pōn) *n.* [< Algonquian] [Chiefly Southern] 1. corn bread in small, oval loaves 2. such a loaf

**pon·gee** (pän jē′) *n.* [< Chin. dial. *pen-chi,* domestic loom] 1. a soft, thin silk cloth, usually left in its natural light-brown color 2. a cloth like this

**pon·iard** (pän′yərd) *n.* [< Fr., ult. < L. *pugnus,* fist] a dagger —*vt.* to stab with a poniard

**pons** (pänz) *n., pl.* **pon·tes** (pän′tēz) [L., a bridge] *Anat., Zool.* a piece of connecting tissue

**Pon·ti·ac[1]** (pän′tē ak′) 1720?–69; Ottawa Indian chief

**Pon·ti·ac[2]** (pän′tē ak′) [after prec.] city in SE Mich., just north of Detroit: pop. 77,000

**pon·ti·fex** (pän′tə feks′) *n., pl.* **pon·tif·i·ces** (pän tif′ə sēz′) [L.: see ff.] in ancient Rome, a member of the supreme college of priests

**pon·tiff** (pän′tif) *n.* [< Fr. < LL. *pontifex,* bishop < L., high priest] 1. a bishop; specif., [P-] the Pope (in full, **Supreme Pontiff**) 2. a high priest

**pon·tif·i·cal** (pän tif′i k′l) *adj.* 1. having to do with a high priest 2. celebrated by a bishop or other highranking prelate [*a pontifical* Mass] 3. papal 4. having the pomp, dogmatism, and dignity of a pontiff; sometimes, specif., arrogant or haughty —*n.* 1. [*pl.*] a pontiff's vestments and insignia 2. a book of rites as performed by a bishop —**pon·tif′i·cal·ly** *adv.*

**pon·tif·i·cate** (-kit; *also, and for v. always,* -kāt′) *n.* the office or tenure of a pontiff —*vi.* **-cat′ed, -cat′ing** 1. to officiate as a pontiff 2. to speak in a pompous or dogmatic way —**pon·tif′i·ca′tor** *n.*

**Pon·tine Marshes** (pän′tēn, -tīn) region in C Italy, southeast of Rome: formerly swampy, now reclaimed

**pon·toon** (pän tōōn′) *n.* [Fr. < L. *ponto* < *pons,* a bridge] 1. a flat-bottomed boat 2. any of a number of these, or of hollow, floating cylinders, etc., used to support a temporary bridge (**pontoon bridge**) 3. a float on an aircraft Also **pon′ton** (-t′n)

**po·ny** (pō′nē) *n., pl.* **-nies** [< Scot., prob. < OFr. dim. of *poulain,* a colt, ult. < L. *pullus,* foal] 1. a small horse of any of several breeds, usually not over 58 in. high at the withers 2. something small of its kind; specif., a small liqueur glass or its contents 3. [Colloq.] a literal translation of a foreign work, used in doing schoolwork, often dishonestly 4. [Slang] a racehorse —*vt., vi.* **-nied, -ny·ing** [Slang] to pay (money), as to settle an account (with *up*)

**po·ny·tail** (pō′nē tāl′) *n.* a hairdo in which long hair, tied tight high at the back of the head, hangs free

**pooch** (pōōch) *n.* [Slang] a dog

**poo·dle** (pōō′d′l) *n.* [G. *pudel* < LowG. < *pudeln,* to splash] any of a breed of dog with a solid-colored, curly coat

**pooh[1]** (pōō) *interj.* [prob. echoic] an exclamation of disdain, disbelief, or impatience

**pooh[2]** (pōō) *vt.* [Slang] *same as* POOP[2]

**pooh-pooh** (pōō′pōō′) *vt.* [redupl. of POOH[1]] to minimize; make light of; belittle

**pool[1]** (pōōl) *n.* [< OE. *pol*] 1. a small pond, as in a garden 2. a puddle 3. *same as* SWIMMING POOL 4. a deep, still spot in a river 5. a natural underground accumulation of oil or gas —*vi.* to form, or accumulate in, a pool

**pool[2]** (pōōl) *n.* [Fr. *poule* < LL. *pulla,* hen: associated in E. with prec.] 1. the total stakes played for, as in a single deal of a card game 2. a game of billiards played with object balls numbered 1 to 15 and a cue ball, on a table with six pockets 3. *a*) a combination of resources, funds, etc. for some common purpose *b*) the persons or parties forming it 4. a combination of business firms for creating a monopoly 5. a supply of equipment, personnel, etc. shared by a group —*vt., vi.* to contribute to a common fund; form a pool (of)

**Poo·na** (pōō′nə) city in W India: pop. 737,000

**poop[1]** (pōōp) *n.* [< MFr., ult. < L. *puppis*] 1. orig., the stern of a ship 2. on sailing ships, a raised deck at the stern, sometimes forming the roof of a cabin: also **poop deck** —*vt.* to break over the poop or stern of: said of waves

**poop[2]** (pōōp) *vt.* [echoic] [Slang] to tire: usually in the passive voice —**poop out** [Slang] 1. to become exhausted 2. to cease functioning

**poop[3]** (pōōp) *n.* [prob. < *poop,* feces] [Slang] 1. a contemptible person 2. the pertinent facts

**poor** (poor) *adj.* [< OFr. < L. *pauper,* poor] 1. *a*) having little or no means to support oneself; needy *b*) indicating or characterized by poverty 2. lacking in some quality or thing; specif., *a*) scanty; inadequate [*poor crops*] *b*) barren; sterile [*poor soil*] *c*) lacking nourishment; feeble *d*) lacking excellence; inferior *e*) mean-spirited; contemptible *f*) lacking pleasure or comfort [to have a *poor time*] *g*) lacking skill [*a poor cook*] 3. worthy of pity; unfortunate —**the poor** poor, or needy, people —**poor′ly** *adv.* —**poor′ness** *n.*

**poor-boy sandwich** (poor′boi′) *same as* HERO SANDWICH

**poor·house** (-hous′) *n.* formerly, an institution for paupers, supported from public funds

**poor-mouth** (-mouth′) *vi.* [Colloq.] to complain about one's lack of money: also **talk** (or **cry**) **poor-mouth**

**poor white** a white person, esp. in the South, who lives in great poverty: often an offensive term

**pop[1]** (päp) *n.* [echoic] 1. a sudden, short, light explosive sound 2. a shot with a revolver, rifle, etc. 3. any carbonated, nonalcoholic beverage 4. *Baseball* a ball popped into the infield: also **pop′-up′** —*vi.* **popped, pop′ping** 1. to make, or burst with, a pop 2. to move, go, come, etc. suddenly and quickly 3. to open wide suddenly, or protrude: said of the eyes 4. to shoot a pistol, etc. 5. *Baseball* to hit the ball high in the air into the infield —*vt.* 1. to cause (corn) to pop, as by roasting, etc. 2. *a*) to fire (a pistol, etc.) *b*) to shoot 3. to put suddenly or quickly [to *pop* one's head in the door] 4. [Slang] to swallow (a pill, capsule, etc.) 5. *Baseball* to hit (the ball) high in the air into the infield —*adv.* with or like a pop —**pop off** [Slang] 1. to die suddenly 2. to speak or write emotionally, etc. 3. [Chiefly Brit.] to leave hastily —**pop the question** [Colloq.] to propose marriage

**pop[2]** (päp) *n.* [< PAPA] [Slang] father: also a familiar term of address for any elderly man

**pop[3]** (päp) *adj. clipped form of* POPULAR [*pop music*]

**pop.** 1. popular 2. popularly 3. population

**pop (art)** (päp) a realistic style of painting and sculpture, using techniques and popular subjects from commercial art and mass media, such as comic strips

**pop concert** a popular concert, chiefly of semiclassical and light classical music

**pop·corn** (-kôrn′) *n.* **1.** a variety of Indian corn with small ears and hard grains which pop open in a white, puffy mass when heated **2.** the popped grains, often salted for eating

**pope** (pōp) *n.* [OE. *papa* < LL., ult. < Gr. *pappas*, father] [*usually* **P-**] *R.C.Ch.* the bishop of Rome and head of the Church —**pope′dom** (-dəm) *n.*

**Pope** (pōp), Alexander 1688–1744; Eng. poet

**pop·er·y** (pōp′ər ē) *n.* the doctrines and rituals of the Roman Catholic Church: a hostile term

**pop·eyed** (päp′īd′) *adj.* having protruding eyes

**pop·gun** (-gun′) *n.* a toy gun that shoots pellets by air compression, with a pop

**pop·in·jay** (päp′in jā′) *n.* [< MFr. *papagai* < Ar. *babaghā*, parrot] a talkative, conceited person

**pop·ish** (pōp′ish) *adj.* having to do with popery: a hostile term —**pop′ish·ly** *adv.* —**pop′ish·ness** *n.*

**pop·lar** (päp′lər) *n.* [< OFr. *poplier*, ult. < L. *populus*] **1.** any of various tall, fast-growing trees with alternate leaves and catkins **2.** the wood of any of these **3.** *same as:* a) TULIP TREE b) TULIPWOOD (sense 1)

**pop·lin** (päp′lən) *n.* [Fr. *papeline*, prob. < (*draps de*) *Poperinghes*, (cloths from) Poperinge, city in Flanders] a sturdy fabric of cotton, rayon, etc. with fine ribbing

**Po·po·ca·té·petl** (pô pō′kä te′pet'l; *E.* pō′pə kat′ə-pet′'l) volcano in SC Mexico

**pop·o·ver** (päp′ō′vər) *n.* a puffy, hollow muffin

**pop·per** (-ər) *n.* **1.** a person or thing that pops **2.** a covered wire basket or pan for popping corn

**pop·pet** (päp′it) *n.* [var. of PUPPET] a valve that moves into and from its seat, as in a gasoline engine: in full, **poppet valve**

**pop·py** (päp′ē) *n.*, *pl.* **-pies** [OE. *popæg* < L. *papaver*] **1.** any of various related plants with a milky juice and showy, variously colored flowers **2.** the flower of any of these **3.** an extract, as opium, made from poppy juice **4.** yellowish red, the color of some poppies: also **poppy red**

**pop·py·cock** (-käk′) *n.* [Du. *pappekak*, dung] [Colloq.] nonsense

**poppy seed** the small, dark seed of the poppy, used in baking, etc. as a flavoring or topping

**Pop·si·cle** (päp′si k'l) [blend < POP¹ + (I)CICLE] *a trademark for* a flavored ice frozen around a stick —*n.* [p-] such a confection

**pop·u·lace** (päp′yə lis) *n.* [ Fr. < It. < L. *populus*, PEOPLE] **1.** the common people; the masses **2.** *same as* POPULATION (sense 1 *a*)

**pop·u·lar** (päp′yə lər) *adj.* [< L. < *populus*, PEOPLE] **1.** of or carried on by people generally **2.** suitable or intended for the general public [*popular music*] **3.** within the means of the ordinary person [*popular* prices] **4.** common; prevalent [a *popular* notion] **5.** liked by very many people [a *popular* actor] **6.** having many friends —**pop′u·lar′i·ty** (-lar′ə tē) *n.* —**pop′u·lar·ly** *adv.*

**popular front** a political coalition of leftist and liberal groups, as in France (1936–39) to combat fascism

**pop·u·lar·ize** (päp′yə lə rīz′) *vt.* **-ized′**, **-iz′ing** **1.** to make popular **2.** to make understandable to the general public —**pop′u·lar·i·za′tion** *n.* —**pop′u·lar·iz′er** *n.*

**pop·u·late** (päp′yə lāt′) *vt.* **-lat′ed**, **-lat′ing** [< ML. pp. of *populare* < L. *populus*, PEOPLE] **1.** to inhabit **2.** to supply with inhabitants

**pop·u·la·tion** (päp′yə lā′shən) *n.* **1.** *a*) all the people in a country, region, etc. *b*) the number of these *c*) a (specified) part of the people in a given area [the Japanese *population* of Hawaii] **2.** a populating or being populated **3.** *Biol.* all the organisms living in a given area **4.** *Statistics* a group of persons or things

**population explosion** the very great and continuing increase in human population in modern times

**Pop·u·list** (päp′yə list) *n.* [< L. *populus*, PEOPLE] a member of a U.S. political party (**Populist party** or **People's party**, 1891–1904) advocating free coinage of gold and silver, public ownership of utilities, an income tax, etc. —*adj.* of this party: also **Pop′u·lis′tic** —**Pop′u·lism** *n.*

**pop·u·lous** (päp′yə ləs) *adj.* full of people; thickly populated —**pop′u·lous·ly** *adv.* —**pop′u·lous·ness** *n.*

**por·ce·lain** (pôr′s'l in, pôrs′lin) *n.* [< Fr. < It. *porcellana*, a kind of shell, shaped like a pig, ult. < L. *porcus*, pig] **1.** a hard, white, nonporous, translucent ceramic ware, made of kaolin, feldspar, and quartz or flint **2.** porcelain dishes or ornaments, collectively —*adj.* made of porcelain —**por′ce·la′ne·ous**, **por′cel·la′ne·ous** (-sə lā′nē əs) *adj.*

**por·ce·lain·ize** (-īz′) *vt.* **-ized′**, **-iz′ing** to coat with porcelain or a substance like it

**porch** (pôrch) *n.* [< OFr. < L. *porticus* < *porta*, a gate] **1.** a covered entrance to a building, usually with a roof that is held up by posts **2.** an open or enclosed room on the outside of a building **3.** [Obs.] a portico

**por·cine** (pôr′sīn, -sin) *adj.* [< Fr. < L. < *porcus*, a hog] of or like pigs or hogs

**por·cu·pine** (pôr′kyə pīn′) *n.*, *pl.* **-pines′**, **-pine′**: see PLURAL, II, D, 1 [< MFr. < OIt. < L. *porcus*, a pig + *spina*, a spine] any of various large, related rodents having coarse hair mixed with long, stiff, sharp spines

**pore¹** (pôr) *vi.* **pored**, **por′ing** [< ?] **1.** to read or study carefully [to *pore* over a book] **2.** to ponder (with *over*)

**pore²** (pôr) *n.* [< L. < Gr. *poros*, a passage] **1.** a tiny opening, as in plant leaves, skin, etc., through which fluids may be absorbed or discharged **2.** a similar tiny opening in rocks or other substances

**por·gy** (pôr′gē) *n.*, *pl.* **-gies**, **-gy**: see PLURAL, II, D, 1 [prob. < Sp. or Port. *pargo* < L. *pagrus* < Gr. *phagros*, sea bream] **1.** a saltwater food fish having spiny fins and a wide body, as the scup **2.** any of various other fishes, as the menhaden

**pork** (pôrk) *n.* [< OFr. < L. *porcus*, a pig] the flesh of a pig or hog used, fresh or cured, as food

**pork barrel** [Colloq.] government money spent for political patronage, as for local improvements to please the voters in a district —**pork′-bar′rel·ing** *n.*

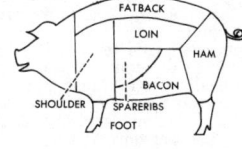

CUTS OF PORK

**pork·er** (pôr′kər) *n.* a hog, esp. a young one, fattened for use as food

**pork pie 1.** a meat pie made with chopped pork **2.** a man's soft hat with a round, flat crown: now often **pork′pie′** *n.*, **porkpie hat**

**pork·y** (pôr′kē) *adj.* **pork′i·er**, **pork′i·est** **1.** of or like pork **2.** fat, as though overfed **3.** [Slang] saucy, cocky, etc.

**por·nog·ra·phy** (pôr näg′rə fē) *n.* [< Gr. < *porne*, a prostitute + *graphein*, to write] writings, pictures, etc. intended primarily to arouse sexual desire —**por·nog′ra·pher** *n.* —**por′no·graph′ic** (-nə graf′ik) *adj.* —**por′no·graph′i·cal·ly** *adv.*

**po·rous** (pôr′əs) *adj.* full of pores, through which fluids, air, or light may pass —**po·ros·i·ty** (pō räs′ə tē, pə-), **po′rous·ness** *n.* —**po′rous·ly** *adv.*

**por·phy·ry** (pôr′fər ē) *n.*, *pl.* **-ries** [< OFr. < ML., ult. < Gr. *porphyros*, purple] **1.** orig., an Egyptian rock with large feldspar crystals in a purplish rock mass **2.** any igneous rock resembling this —**por′phy·rit′ic** (-fə rit′ik) *adj.*

**por·poise** (pôr′pəs) *n.*, *pl.* **-pois·es**, **-poise**: see PLURAL, II, D, 1 [< OFr. *porpeis* < L. *porcus*, a pig + *piscis*, a fish] **1.** any of a number of small, toothed whales with a blunt snout, found in most seas, esp. the **harbor porpoise 2.** a dolphin or any of several other small cetaceans

**por·ridge** (pôr′ij, pär′-) *n.* [altered < POTTAGE by confusion with ME. *porrey* < OFr. < VL. *porrata*, leek broth < L. *porrum*, leek] [Chiefly Brit.] a soft food made of cereal or meal boiled in water or milk

**por·rin·ger** (-in jər) *n.* [< Fr. *potager*, soup dish: altered after prec.] a bowl for porridge, cereal, etc., esp. one of metal used by children

**port¹** (pôrt) *n.* [OFr. & OE. < L. *portus*, a haven] **1.** a harbor **2.** a city with a harbor where ships can load and unload cargo **3.** *same as* PORT OF ENTRY

**port²** (pôrt) *n.* [< *Oporto*, city in Portugal] a sweet, fortified, usually dark-red wine

**port³** (pôrt) *vt.* [< MFr. < L. *portare*, to carry] to hold or place (a rifle or sword) diagonally in front of one, as for inspection —*n.* way of carrying the head and body

**port⁴** (pôrt) *n.* [prob. < PORT¹] the left-hand side of a ship or airplane as one faces forward, toward the bow —*adj.* of or on the port —*vt.*, *vi.* to move or turn (the helm) to the port side

**port⁵** (pôrt) *n.* [< OFr. < L. *porta*, a door] **1.** *a*) *same as* PORTHOLE *b*) a porthole covering **2.** an opening, as in a valve face, for the passage of steam, gas, etc.

**Port. 1.** Portugal **2.** Portuguese

**port·a·ble** (pôr′tə b'l) *adj.* [< MFr. < LL. < L. *portare*, to carry] **1.** that can be carried **2.** *a*) easily carried or moved, esp. by hand [a *portable* TV] *b*) that can be used anywhere because battery-operated [a *portable* radio] —*n.* something portable —**port′a·bil′i·ty** *n.*

**por·tage** (pôr′tij; *for n.* 2 & *v.*, *also Canad.* pôr tàzh′) *n.* [MFr. < ML. *portaticum* < L. *portare*, to carry] **1.** the act of carrying **2.** *a*) a carrying of boats and supplies overland between navigable rivers, lakes, etc. *b*) any route over which this is done —*vt.*, *vi.* **-taged**, **-tag·ing** to carry (boats, etc.) over a portage

**por·tal** (pôr′t'l) *n.* [MFr. < ML. < L. *porta*, a gate] a doorway, gate, or entrance, esp. a large or imposing one

**Port Arthur** [after *Arthur* Stilwell, local philanthropist] seaport in SE Tex.: pop. 61,000

**Port-au-Prince** (pôr′ō prins′; *Fr.* pôr tō prans′) capital of Haiti; seaport on the Caribbean: pop. 250,000

**port authority** a government commission in charge of the traffic, regulations, etc. of a port

**port·cul·lis** (pôrt kul′is) *n.* [< MFr. < *porte*, a gate + *coleïce*, sliding < L. *colare*, to filter] a heavy iron grating suspended by chains and lowered between grooves to bar the gateway of a castle or fortified town

**Port du Sa·lut** (pôr′ doo sa loo′) [Fr.] a semihard, whole-milk, yellowish cheese

**porte-co·chere, porte-co·chère** (pôrt′kō sher′) *n.* [Fr., coach gate] **1.** a large gateway into a courtyard **2.** a kind of porch roof projecting over a driveway at an entrance to a house, etc.

**Port Elizabeth** seaport in S Cape Province, South Africa: pop. 381,000

**por·tend** (pôr tend′) *vt.* [< L. *portendere* < *por-*, akin to *per-*, through + *tendere*, to stretch] **1.** to be an omen or warning of; foreshadow; presage **2.** to be an indication of; signify

**por·tent** (pôr′tent) *n.* **1.** something that portends an event about to occur, esp. an unfortunate event; omen **2.** a portending; significance **3.** a marvel

**por·ten·tous** (pôr ten′təs) *adj.* **1.** being a portent; ominous **2.** marvelous; amazing **3.** pompous —**por·ten′tous·ly** *adv.* —**por·ten′tous·ness** *n.*

**por·ter¹** (pôr′tər) *n.* [< OFr. < LL. *portarius* < L. *porta*, a gate] a doorman or gatekeeper

**por·ter²** (pôr′tər) *n.* [< OFr. < LL. < L. *portare*, to carry] **1.** a man whose work is to carry luggage, as at a railroad station **2.** a man who sweeps, cleans, does errands, etc. in a bank, store, etc. **3.** a railroad employee who waits on passengers in a sleeper or parlor car **4.** [abbrev. of *porter's ale*] a dark-brown beer resembling light stout, made from charred or browned malt

**Por·ter** (pôr′tər) **1.** *Katherine Anne,* 1890–1980; U.S. short-story writer & novelist **2.** *William Sydney, see* O. HENRY

**por·ter·house** (-hous′) *n.* **1.** formerly, a place serving beer, porter, etc. (and sometimes steaks and chops) **2.** a choice cut of beef from the loin just before the sirloin: in full, **porterhouse steak**

**port·fo·li·o** (pôrt fō′lē ō′) *n., pl.* **-li·os′** [< It. *portafoglio* < L. *portare*, to carry + *folium*, a leaf] **1.** a flat, portable case for carrying loose papers, drawings, etc. **2.** such a case for state documents **3.** the office of a minister of state **4.** a list of an investor's stocks, bonds, etc. **5.** a selection of representative works, as of an artist

**port·hole** (pôrt′hōl′) *n.* **1.** an opening in a ship's side, as for admitting light and air **2.** an opening to shoot through; embrasure **3.** any similar opening

**por·ti·co** (pôr′tə kō′) *n., pl.* **-coes′, -cos′** [It. < L. *porticus*: see PORCH] a porch or covered walk, consisting of a roof supported by columns

**por·tiere, por·tière** (pôr tyer′, -tē er′) *n.* [Fr. < *porte*, a door] a curtain hung in a doorway

**por·tion** (pôr′shən) *n.* [< OFr. < L. *portio* (gen. *portionis*)] **1.** a part, esp. as allotted to a person, set aside for some purpose, etc.; share **2.** the part of an estate received by an heir **3.** a dowry **4.** one's lot; destiny **5.** a helping of food —*vt.* **1.** to divide into portions **2.** to give as a portion to **3.** to give a portion to —**por′tion·less** *adj.*

PORTICO

**Port·land** (pôrt′lənd) **1.** [after ff.] city & port in NW Oreg., on the Columbia River: pop. 366,000 (met. area 1,236,000) **2.** [after *Portland*, town in England] seaport on the coast of SE Maine: pop. 62,000

**portland cement** [concrete made from it resembles stone from the Isle of *Portland*, England] [*sometimes* P-] a kind of cement that hardens under water, made by burning limestone and clay

**port·ly** (pôrt′lē) *adj.* **-li·er, -li·est** [PORT³ + -LY¹] **1.** large and heavy in a dignified or stately way **2.** stout; corpulent —**port′li·ness** *n.*

**port·man·teau** (pôrt man′tō, pôrt′man tō′) *n., pl.* **-teaus, -teaux** (-tōz) [< Fr. < *porter*, to carry + *manteau*, a cloak] a stiff leather suitcase that opens like a book into two compartments

**portmanteau word** a word that is a combination of two others (Ex.: *smog*, from *smoke* and *fog*)

**Pôr·to** (pôr′too) *Port. name of* OPORTO

**Pôr·to A·le·gre** (ä le′grə) seaport in S Brazil, on the Atlantic: pop. 641,000

**port of call** a regular stopover port for ships

**port of entry** any place where customs officials check people and foreign goods entering a country

**Port-of-Spain** (pôrt′əv spān′) seaport on NW Trinidad; capital of Trinidad and Tobago: pop. 98,000

**Por·to No·vo** (pôr′tō nō′vō) capital of Benin; seaport on the Atlantic: pop. 100,000

**Por·to Ri·co** (pôr′tə rē′kō) *former name of* PUERTO RICO

**por·trait** (pôr′trit, -trāt) *n.* [MFr., pp. of *portraire*: see PORTRAY] **1.** a painting, photograph, etc. of a person, esp. of his face **2.** a description, portrayal, etc. of a person —**por′trait·ist** *n.*

**por·trai·ture** (pôr′tri chər) *n.* **1.** the making of portraits **2.** a portrait

**por·tray** (pôr trā′) *vt.* [MFr. *portraire* < L. < *pro-*, forth + *trahere*, to draw] **1.** to make a picture or portrait of **2.** to make a word picture of; describe **3.** to play the part of in a play, movie, etc. —**por·tray′a·ble** *adj.* —**por·tray′al** *n.*

**Port Sa·id** (sä ēd′, sä′id) seaport in NE Egypt, at the Mediterranean end of the Suez Canal: pop. 244,000

**Ports·mouth** (pôrts′məth) **1.** seaport in S England, on the English Channel: pop. 212,000 **2.** [after prec.] seaport in SE Va., on Hampton Roads: pop. 105,000

**Por·tu·gal** (pôr′chə gəl; *Port.* pôr′too gäl′) country in SW Europe, on the Atlantic, including the Azores & Madeira: 35,509 sq. mi.; pop. 9,526,000; cap. Lisbon

**Por·tu·guese** (pôr′chə gēz′) *adj.* of Portugal, its people, their language, etc. —*n.* **1.** *pl.* **-guese′** a native or inhabitant of Portugal **2.** the Romance language spoken in Portugal and Brazil

**Portuguese man-of-war** a large, warm-sea animal having long, dangling tentacles that sting, and a large, bladderlike sac that enables it to float on water

**por·tu·lac·a** (pôr′chə lak′ə) *n.* [ModL. < L., purslane] a fleshy annual plant with yellow, pink, or purple flowers

**pose¹** (pōz) *vt.* **posed, pos′ing** [< OFr. *poser* < VL. < LL. *pausare*, to pause: infl. by L. *positus*, pp. of *ponere*, to place] **1.** to put forth; assert [to *pose* a claim] **2.** to propose (a question, problem, etc.) **3.** to put (a model, photographic subject, etc.) in a certain attitude —*vi.* **1.** to assume a certain attitude, as in modeling for an artist **2.** to strike attitudes for effect [look at her *posing*] **3.** to pretend to be what one is not [to *pose* as an officer] —*n.* **1.** a bodily attitude, esp. one held for an artist, photographer, etc. **2.** behavior or speech assumed for effect; pretense

**pose²** (pōz) *vt.* **posed, pos′ing** [< APPOSE, OPPOSE] to baffle, as by a difficult question

**Po·sei·don** (pō sī′d'n, pə-) *Gr. Myth.* god of the sea: identified with the Roman god Neptune

**pos·er¹** (pō′zər) *n.* **1.** a person who poses **2.** a person who behaves in an affected way

**pos·er²** (pō′zər) *n.* a baffling question or problem

**po·seur** (pō zur′) *n.* [Fr.] a person who assumes attitudes or manners merely for their effect upon others

**posh** (päsh) *adj.* [prob. < obs. Brit. slang *posh*, a dandy] [Colloq.] luxurious and fashionable; elegant —**posh′ly** *adv.* —**posh′ness** *n.*

**pos·it** (päz′it) *vt.* [< L. *positus*, pp. of *ponere*, to place] **1.** to set in place or position; situate **2.** to set down or assume as fact; postulate

**po·si·tion** (pə zish′ən) *n.* [MFr. < L. *positio* < pp. of *ponere*, to place] **1.** the manner in which a person or thing is placed or arranged; attitude **2.** one's attitude toward or opinion on a subject; stand **3.** the place where a person or thing is, esp. in relation to others; location or situation **4.** the usual or proper place; station [the players are in *position*] **5.** a location or condition of advantage [to jockey for *position*] **6.** a person's relative place, as in society; rank; status **7.** a place high in society, business, etc. [a man of *position*] **8.** a post of employment; job; office —*vt.* to put in a particular position; place —**po·si′tion·al** *adj.* —**po·si′tion·er** *n.*

**pos·i·tive** (päz′ə tiv) *adj.* [< OFr. < L. *positivus* < pp. of *ponere*, to place] **1.** *a)* definitely set; explicit; specific [*positive* instructions] *b)* allowing no doubt; certain; sure **2.** *a)* sure in mind; confident; assured [a *positive* person] *b)* overconfident or dogmatic **3.** showing resolution or agreement; affirmative [a *positive* answer] **4.** tending in the direction regarded as that of increase, progress, etc. **5.** making a definite contribution; constructive [*positive* criticism] **6.** unrelated to anything else; absolute; unqualified **7.** having real existence in itself [a *positive* good] **8.** based on reality or facts [*positive* proof] **9.** concerned only with real things and experience; empirical; practical **10.** [Colloq.] complete; downright [a *positive* fool] **11.** *Biol.* directed toward the source of a stimulus [*positive* tropism] **12.** *Elec. a)* of, generating, or charged with POSITIVE ELECTRICITY *b)* having a deficiency of electrons **13.** *Gram.* of an adjective or adverb in its uninflected or unmodified form or degree: neither comparative nor superlative **14.** *Math.* greater than zero; plus **15.** *Med.* indicating the presence or existence of a condition, symptoms, bacteria, etc. **16.** *Photog.* with the relation of light and shade the same as in the thing photographed —*n.* something positive, as a degree, quality, etc.; specif., *a)* the plate in a voltaic battery where the higher potential is *b) Gram.* the positive degree, or a word in it *c) Math.* a positive quantity *d) Photog.* a positive print —**pos′i·tive·ly** *adv.* —**pos′i·tive·ness** *n.*

**positive electricity** the kind of electricity in a glass body rubbed with silk; it is deficient in electrons

**pos·i·tiv·ism** (päz′ə tiv iz′m) *n.* **1.** a being positive; certainty; assurance **2.** overconfidence or dogmatism **3.** a system of philosophy based solely on observable scientific facts and rejecting speculation about ultimate origins —**pos′i·tiv·ist** *n., adj.* —**pos′i·tiv·is′tic** *adj.*

**pos·i·tron** (päz′ə trän′) *n.* [POSI(TIVE) + (ELEC)TRON] the positive antiparticle of an electron, with about the same mass and magnitude of charge

**poss. 1.** possession **2.** possessive **3.** possibly

**pos·se** (päs′ē) *n.* [ML., short for *posse comitatus*, power of the county] a body of men summoned by a sheriff, to assist him in keeping the peace

**pos·sess** (pə zes′) *vt.* [< MFr. < L. pp. of *possidere*] **1.** to have as something that belongs to one; own **2.** to have as an attribute, quality, etc. [to *possess* wisdom] **3.** to gain or keep influence or control over; dominate [*possessed* by an idea] **4.** to cause (someone) to have property, facts, etc. (usually with *of*) **5.** [Archaic] to seize; gain —**pos·ses′sor** *n.*

**pos·sessed** (pə zest′) *adj.* **1.** owned **2.** controlled as by an evil spirit; crazed —**possessed of** having

**pos·ses·sion** (pə zesh′ən) *n.* **1.** a possessing or being possessed; ownership, hold, etc. **2.** anything possessed **3.** [*pl.*] property; wealth **4.** territory ruled by an outside country **5.** *Sports* actual control of the ball or puck in play

**pos·ses·sive** (pə zes′iv) *adj.* **1.** of possession, or ownership **2.** showing or desiring possession [a *possessive* person] **3.** *Gram.* designating or of a case, form, or construction expressing possession (Ex.: *men′s, of men, her, whose)* —*n. Gram.* **1.** the possessive case **2.** a possessive form —**pos·ses′sive·ly** *adv.* —**pos·ses′sive·ness** *n.*

**pos·set** (päs′it) *n.* [< ?] a hot drink made of milk and ale, wine, etc., usually spiced

**pos·si·bil·i·ty** (päs′ə bil′ə tē) *n.* **1.** a being possible **2.** *pl.* **-ties** something that is possible

**pos·si·ble** (päs′ə b′l) *adj.* [OFr. < L. < *posse*, to be able] **1.** that can be **2.** that may or may not happen **3.** that can be done, known, chosen, etc., depending on circumstances **4.** permissible

**pos·si·bly** (-blē) *adv.* **1.** by any possible means [it can′t *possibly* work] **2.** perhaps; maybe

**pos·sum** (päs′əm) *n.* [Colloq.] *same as* OPOSSUM —**play possum** to feign death, unawareness, etc.

**post¹** (pōst) *n.* [OE. < L. *postis*] **1.** a piece of wood, metal, etc., usually long and square or cylindrical, set upright to support a building, sign, fence, etc. **2.** the starting point of a horse race —*vt.* **1.** to put up (a notice, etc.) on (a wall, post, etc.) **2.** to announce or publicize thus [*post* a reward] **3.** to warn persons against trespassing on (grounds, etc.) by posted notices **4.** to put (a name) on a posted or published list

**post²** (pōst) *n.* [< Fr. < It., ult. < L. *positum*, neut. pp. of *ponere*, to place] **1.** the place where a soldier, guard, etc. is stationed **2.** *a)* a place where troops are stationed *b)* the troops there; garrison **3.** a local unit of a veterans′ organization **4.** a place where a person or group is stationed, as at a machine **5.** an assigned or appointed position, job, or duty **6.** *clipped form of* TRADING POST —*vt.* **1.** to station at or assign to a post **2.** to put up or deposit (a bond, etc.)

**post³** (pōst) *n.* [< Fr. < It. < L. fem. pp. of *ponere:* see prec.] **1.** formerly, any of a number of riders or runners posted at intervals to carry mail, etc. in relays along a route *b)* a stage of a post route *c)* a post horse *d)* a packet boat **2.** [Chiefly Brit.] *a)* (the) mail *b)* a post office *c)* a mailbox —*vi.* **1.** formerly, to travel in posts or stages **2.** to travel fast **3.** to rise and sink back in the saddle in rhythm with the horse′s trot —*vt.* **1.** formerly, to send by post **2.** [Chiefly Brit.] to mail **3.** to inform, as of events: usually passive [keep me *posted*] **4.** *Bookkeeping a)* to transfer (an item) to the ledger *b)* to enter all necessary items in (a ledger, etc.) —*adv.* **1.** by post or postal courier **2.** speedily

**post-** [L. < *post*, after] *a prefix meaning:* **1.** after in time, following [*postglacial*] **2.** after in space, behind

**post·age** (pōs′tij) *n.* [< POST³ + -AGE] the amount charged for mailing a letter or package, esp. as represented by stamps or indicia

**postage meter** a machine that prints indicia on mail, indicating that postage has been paid

**postage stamp** a government stamp for a letter or package, showing postage paid

**post·al** (pōs′t′l) *adj.* having to do with mail or post offices —*n.* [Colloq.] a postal card

**postal card 1.** a card with a printed postage stamp, issued by a government at a rate lower than that for letters **2.** *same as* POST CARD

**post·bel·lum** (pōst bel′əm) *adj.* [L.] after the war; specif., after the American Civil War

**post·box** (pōst′bäks′) *n.* chiefly Brit. var. of MAILBOX

**post card 1.** an unofficial card, often a picture card, for mailing when a postage stamp is affixed **2.** *same as* POSTAL CARD

**post chaise** a closed, four-wheeled coach drawn by fast horses, formerly used to carry mail and passengers

**post·date** (pōst′dāt′) *vt.* **-dat′ed, -dat′ing 1.** to assign a later date to than the actual or current date **2.** to put such a date on **3.** to follow in time

**post·er** (pōs′tər) *n.* **1.** a person who posts notices, bills, etc. **2.** a large advertisement or notice, often illustrated, posted publicly

**pos·te·ri·or** (päs tir′ē ər, pōs-) *adj.* [L., compar. of *posterus*, following < *post*, after] **1.** later; following after **2.** coming after in order; succeeding **3.** at or toward the rear; hinder; back: opposed to ANTERIOR —*n.* [*formerly also pl.*] the buttocks —**pos·te′ri·or′i·ty** (-ôr′ə tē) *n.* —**pos·te′ri·or·ly** *adv.*

**pos·ter·i·ty** (päs ter′ə tē) *n.* [< MFr. < L. < *posterus:* see prec.] **1.** all of a person′s descendants **2.** all future generations

**pos·tern** (pōs′tərn, päs′-) *n.* [< OFr. < LL. *posterula* < *posterus:* see POSTERIOR] a back door or gate; private entrance at the side or rear —*adj.* of a postern; rear, etc.

**post exchange** a nonprofit general store at an army post, selling merchandise, as to servicemen

**post·gla·cial** (pōst′glā′shəl) *adj.* existing or happening after the disappearance of glaciers from a specific area

**post·grad·u·ate** (-graj′oo wit, -wāt′) *adj.* of or taking a course of study after graduation —*n.* a postgraduate student

**post·haste** (pōst′hāst′) *adv.* with great haste

**post horse** formerly, a horse kept at an inn (**post house**) for couriers or for hire to travelers

**post·hu·mous** (päs′choo məs, -tyoo-) *adj.* [< LL. < L. *postumus*, last, superl. of *posterus* (see POSTERIOR): altered after *humare*, to bury] **1.** born after the father′s death **2.** published after the author′s death **3.** arising or continuing after one′s death —**post′hu·mous·ly** *adv.*

**post·hyp·not·ic** (pōst′hip nät′ik) *adj.* of, or carried out in, the period following a hypnotic trance [*posthypnotic* suggestion]

**pos·til·ion, pos·til·lion** (pōs til′yən, päs-) *n.* [Fr. < It. < *posta*, POST³] a person riding the left-hand leading horse of a four-horse carriage or the left-hand horse of a two-horse carriage

**post·im·pres·sion·ism** (pōst′im presh′ən iz′m) *n.* the theory or practice of some late 19th-cent. painters reacting against impressionism and emphasizing what is subjective or formal —**post′im·pres′sion·ist** *adj., n.* —**post′im·pres′sion·is′tic** *adj.*

**post·lude** (pōst′lood′) *n.* [POST- + (PRE)LUDE] **1.** a solo on the organ at the end of a church service **2.** a concluding musical section

**post·man** (-mən) *n., pl.* **-men** *same as* MAIL CARRIER

**post·mark** (-märk′) *n.* a post-office mark stamped on a piece of mail, canceling the postage stamp and recording the date and place —*vt.* to stamp with a postmark

**post·mas·ter** (-mas′tər) *n.* a person in charge of a post office —**post′mas′ter·ship′** *n.* —**post′mis′tress** *n.fem.*

**postmaster general** *pl.* **postmasters general, postmaster generals** the head of a government′s postal system

**post·me·rid·i·an** (pōst′mə rid′ē ən) *adj.* [< L.: see POST- & MERIDIAN] of or in the afternoon

**post me·ri·di·em** (-ē əm) [L.] after noon: abbrev. **P.M., p.m., PM**

**post·mor·tem** (pōst′môr′təm) *adj.* [L., after death] **1.** happening or done after death **2.** designating or of an examination of a human body after death —*n.* **1.** a postmortem examination: see AUTOPSY **2.** a detailed evaluation of some event just ended

**post·na·sal drip** (pōst′nā′z′l) a dripping of mucus from behind the nose onto the pharynx

**post·na·tal** (pōst′nāt′′l) *adj.* after birth

**post office 1.** the governmental department in charge of the mails **2.** an office or building where mail is sorted, postage stamps are sold, etc.

**post·op·er·a·tive** (pōst′äp′ər ə tiv, -āp′rə-; -ə rāt′iv) *adj.* of or in the period after surgery —**post′op′er·a·tive·ly** *adv.*

**post·paid** (pōst′pād′) *adj.* with the postage prepaid

**post·pone** (pōst pōn′, pōs-) *vt.* **-poned′, -pon′ing** [< L.

*post*, after + *ponere*, to put] to put off until later; defer; delay —**post·pon′a·ble** *adj.* —**post·pone′ment** *n.* —**post·pon′er** *n.*

**post·pran·di·al** (pōst′pran′dē əl) *adj.* [< POST- + L. *prandium*, noonday meal] after a meal —**post′pran′di·al·ly** *adv.*

**post road** a road over which the post, or mail, is or formerly was carried

**post·script** (pōst′skript′, pōs′-) *n.* [< ModL. < L. pp. of *postscribere* < *post-*, after + *scribere*, to write] a note, paragraph, etc. added below the signature of a letter, or to a book, speech, etc. to give more facts, ideas, etc.

**post time** the scheduled starting time of a horse race

**pos·tu·lant** (päs′chə lant) *n.* [Fr. < L. prp. of *postulare*: see ff.] a petitioner, esp. for admission into a religious order

**pos·tu·late** (päs′chə lāt′; *for n., usually* -lit) *vt.* **-lat′ed, -lat′ing** [< L. pp. of *postulare*, to demand] **1.** to claim; demand; require **2.** to assume without proof to be true, real, or necessary, esp. as a basis for argument **3.** to take for granted; assume —*n.* **1.** something postulated; assumption or axiom **2.** a prerequisite **3.** a basic principle —**pos′tu·la′tion** *n.* —**pos′tu·la′tor** (-ər) *n.*

**pos·ture** (päs′chər) *n.* [MFr. < It. < L. *positura* < *ponere*, to place] **1.** the position or carriage of the body; bearing **2.** a position assumed as in posing for an artist **3.** the way things stand; condition [the *posture* of foreign affairs **4.** *a)* frame of mind *b)* an attitude assumed merely for effect **5.** an official stand on an issue —*vt.* **-tured, -tur·ing** to place in a posture; pose —*vi.* to assume a bodily or mental posture, esp. for effect; pose —**pos′tur·al** *adj.* —**pos′tur·er** *n.*

**pos·tur·ize** (-chə rīz′) *vt., vi.* **-ized′, -iz′ing** *same as* POSTURE

**post·war** (pōst′wôr′) *adj.* after the (or a) war

**po·sy** (pō′zē) *n., pl.* **-sies** [contr. < POESY] **1.** orig., a verse or motto inscribed inside a ring, etc. **2.** a flower or bouquet: an old-fashioned usage

**pot** (pät) *n.* [OE. *pott*] **1.** a round vessel of metal, etc., for holding liquids, cooking food, etc. **2.** a pot with its contents **3.** *same as* POTFUL **4.** a pot of liquor **5.** *shortened form for* FLOWERPOT, CHIMNEY POT, etc. **6.** a toilet: a vulgar usage **7.** [Colloq.] *a)* all the money bet at a single time *b)* a large amount of money **8.** [Colloq.] a potshot **9.** [Slang] *same as: a)* MARIJUANA *b)* POTBELLY —*vt.* **pot′ted, pot′ting 1.** to put into a pot **2.** to cook or preserve in a pot **3.** to shoot (game) for food, not for sport **4.** to hit or get as by a potshot —*vi.* to go to pot to go to ruin

**po·ta·ble** (pōt′ə b'l) *adj.* [Fr. < LL. < L. *potare*, to drink] fit to drink; drinkable —*n.* something drinkable; beverage —**po′ta·bil′i·ty, po′ta·ble·ness** *n.*

**‡po·tage** (pô tàzh′) *n.* [Fr.] soup or broth

**pot·ash** (pät′ash′) *n.* [< Du. < *pot*, pot + *asch*, ash] **1.** *same as: a)* POTASSIUM CARBONATE *b)* POTASSIUM HYDROXIDE **2.** any substance containing potassium; esp., any potassium compound used in fertilizers

**po·tas·si·um** (pə tas′ē əm) *n.* [ModL. < Du.: see prec.] a soft, silver-white, waxlike metallic chemical element: its native salts are used in fertilizers, glass, etc.: symbol, K; at. wt., 39.102; at. no., 19 —**po·tas′sic** *adj.*

**potassium bromide** a white, crystalline compound, KBr, used in photography, medicine, etc.

**potassium carbonate** an alkaline, crystalline compound, $K_2CO_3$, used in making soap, glass, etc.

**potassium chlorate** a crystalline salt, $KClO_3$, a strong oxidizing agent used in medicine and in making matches, etc.

**potassium chloride** a crystalline salt, KCl, used in fertilizers, as a source of potassium salts, etc.

**potassium cyanide** an extremely poisonous crystalline compound, KCN, used in metallurgy, in electroplating, etc.

**potassium hydroxide** a strongly alkaline, crystalline compound, KOH, used in making soap, glass, etc.

**potassium nitrate** a crystalline compound, $KNO_3$, used in fertilizers, gunpowder, etc. and as an oxidizing agent

**potassium permanganate** a dark-purple, crystalline compound, $KMnO_4$, used as an oxidizing agent, disinfectant, etc.

**po·ta·tion** (pō tā′shən) *n.* [< MFr. < L. *potare*, to drink] **1.** the act of drinking **2.** a drink or draft, esp. of liquor

**po·ta·to** (pə tāt′ō, -ə) *n., pl.* **-toes** [Sp. *patata* < WInd. name] **1.** orig., *same as* SWEET POTATO **2.** *a)* the starchy tuber of a widely cultivated plant of the nightshade family, cooked as a vegetable *b)* the plant

**potato beetle** (or **bug**) *same as* COLORADO BEETLE

**potato chip** a very thin slice of potato fried crisp and then salted: also, Brit., **potato crisp**

**pot·bel·ly** (pät′bel′ē) *n., pl.* **-lies** a protruding belly —**pot′bel′lied** *adj.*

**pot·boil·er** (-boil′ər) *n.* a piece of writing, etc., usually inferior, done quickly for money

**Po·tem·kin** (pä tyôm′kin; *E.* pō tem′kin), **Gri·go·ri**

**A·le·ksan·dro·vich** (grē gô′rē ä′lyek sän′drô vich) 1739–91; Russian field marshal & statesman; favorite of Catherine II

**po·tent** (pōt′'nt) *adj.* [L. *potens* (gen. *potentis*), prp. of *posse*, to be able] **1.** having authority or power; mighty **2.** convincing; cogent **3.** effective or powerful in action, as a drug **4.** able to have an erection and hence to engage in sexual intercourse —**po′ten·cy,** *pl.* **-cies, po′tence** *n.* —**po′tent·ly** *adv.*

**po·ten·tate** (pōt′'n tāt′) *n.* a ruler; monarch

**po·ten·tial** (pə ten′shəl) *adj.* [< ML. < L.: see POTENT] **1.** that can, but has not yet, come into being; possible; latent **2.** *Gram.* expressing possibility, capability, etc. ["I can go" is in the *potential* mood] —*n.* **1.** something potential **2.** *Elec.* the relative voltage at a point in an electric circuit or field with respect to some reference point in the same circuit or field —**po·ten′tial·ly** *adv.*

**potential energy** inactive energy resulting from position or structure instead of motion, as in a coiled spring

**po·ten·ti·al·i·ty** (pə ten′shē al′ə tē) *n.* **1.** possibility or capability of becoming, developing, etc.; latency **2.** *pl.* **-ties** something potential

**po·ten·ti·ate** (pə ten′shē āt′) *vt.* **-at′ed, -at′ing** [< L. *potentia*, potency + -ATE[1]] to increase (the effect of a drug or toxin) by previous or simultaneous use of another drug or toxin —**po·ten′ti·a′tion** *n.* —**po·ten′ti·a′tor** *n.*

**po·ten·ti·om·e·ter** (pə ten′shē äm′ə tər) *n.* [< POTENTIAL + -METER] an instrument for measuring, comparing, or controlling electric potentials

**pot·ful** (pät′fool) *n., pl.* **-fuls** as much as a pot will hold

**pot·head** (-hed′) *n.* [Slang] a habitual user of marijuana

**poth·er** (päth′ər) *n.* [< ?] **1.** a cloud of smoke, dust, etc. **2.** a commotion or fuss —*vt., vi.* to fuss or bother

**pot·herb** (pät′ʉrb′, -hʉrb′) *n.* any herb whose leaves and stems are boiled for food or used as a flavoring

**pot·hold·er** (-hōl′dər) *n.* a small pad, or piece of thick cloth, for handling hot pots, etc.

**pot·hole** (-hōl′) *n.* **1.** a deep hole or pit **2.** *chiefly Brit. var. of* CHUCKHOLE

**pot·hook** (-hook′) *n.* **1.** an S-shaped hook for hanging a pot or kettle over a fire **2.** a hooked rod for lifting hot pots, etc. **3.** a curved mark in writing

**pot·house** (-hous′) *n.* [Brit.] a small tavern

**po·tion** (pō′shən) *n.* [< OFr. < L. < *potare*, to drink] a drink or liquid dose, as of medicine or poison

**pot·luck** (pät′luk′) *n.* whatever the family meal happens to be [invited in to take *potluck*]

**Po·to·mac** (pə tō′mək) [< Algonquian town name, lit., ? where tribute is brought] river forming a boundary of W.Va., Md., & Va., and flowing into Chesapeake Bay

**pot·pie** (pät′pī′) *n.* **1.** a meat pie made in a pot or deep dish, usually with only a top crust **2.** a stew with dumplings

**pot·pour·ri** (pō′poo rē′, pät poor′ē) *n.* [Fr. < *pot*, a pot + pp. of *pourrir*, to rot] **1.** a mixture of dried flower petals with spices, kept in a jar for its fragrance **2.** a medley, miscellany, or anthology

**pot roast** meat, usually a large cut of beef, cooked in one piece by braising

**Pots·dam** (päts′dam′; *G.* pôts däm′) city in East Germany, near Berlin: pop. 111,000

**pot·sherd** (pät′shʉrd′) *n.* [see POT & SHARD] a piece of broken pottery

**pot·shot** (-shät′) *n.* **1.** an easy shot **2.** a random shot **3.** a haphazard try **4.** a random criticism

**pot·tage** (pät′ij) *n.* [< MFr. < *pot*, a pot < Du.] a thick soup or stew of vegetables, or meat and vegetables

**pot·ted** (pät′id) *adj.* **1.** put into a pot **2.** cooked or preserved in a pot or can **3.** [Slang] drunk

**pot·ter**[1] (-ər) *n.* a maker of earthenware pots, dishes, etc.

**pot·ter**[2] (pät′ər) *vi., vt.* [< OE. *potian*, to push] *chiefly Brit. var. of* PUTTER[3]

**potter's field** [cf. Matt. 27:7] a burial ground for paupers or unknown persons

**potter's wheel** a rotating horizontal disk upon which clay is molded into bowls, etc.

**pot·ter·y** (pät′ər ē) *n., pl.* **-ter·ies** [< MFr. < *potier*, a potter < *pot*, a pot] **1.** a potter's workshop or factory **2.** the art of a potter **3.** pots, bowls, etc. made of clay hardened by heat; earthenware

**pot·tle** (pät′'l) *n.* [< MFr. dim. of *pot*, a pot] **1.** formerly, a half-gallon liquid measure **2.** *a)* a pot holding a half gallon *b)* its contents; esp., alcoholic liquor

**pot·ty**[1] (pät′ē) *n., pl.* **-ties 1.** a child's small chamber pot **2.** a child's chair for toilet training, having an open seat with a pot beneath: in full, **potty chair 3.** a toilet: a child's word

POTTER'S
WHEEL

**pot·ty**[2] (pät′ē) *adj.* **-ti·er, -ti·est** [Brit. Colloq.] **1.** trivial **2.** slightly crazy —**pot′ti·ness** *n.*

**pouch** (pouch) *n.* [MFr. *poche,* var. of *poque,* a poke] **1.** a small bag or sack, as for pipe tobacco **2.** a mailbag **3.** any pouchlike cavity, part, etc. **4.** *a)* a saclike structure on the abdomen of some animals; marsupium *b)* a baglike part, as of a gopher's cheeks, for carrying food —*vt.* **1.** to put into a pouch **2.** to make into a pouch —*vi.* to form a pouch —**pouched** *adj.*

**poul·ter·er** (pōl'tər ər) *n.* [Brit.] a dealer in poultry and game: also [Archaic] **poul'ter**

**poul·tice** (pōl'tis) *n.* [ML. *pultes,* orig. pl. of L. *puls,* pap] a hot, soft, moist mass, as of flour, mustard, etc., applied, sometimes on a cloth, to a sore part of the body —*vt.* **-ticed, -tic·ing** to apply a poultice to

**poul·try** (pōl'trē) *n.* [< MFr. < OFr. *poulet:* see PULLET] domestic fowls, as chickens, raised for meat or eggs

**poul·try·man** (-mən) *n., pl.* **-men** a person who raises or deals in poultry

**pounce**[1] (pouns) *n.* [< ? MFr. *poinçon:* see PUNCHEON[1]] **1.** a claw or talon of a bird of prey **2.** the act of pouncing; swoop, leap, etc. —*vi.* **pounced, pounc'ing** to swoop down, spring, or leap (*on, upon,* or *at*) as in attacking —**pounc'er** *n.*

**pounce**[2] (pouns) *n.* [< Fr. < L. *pumex,* pumice] **1.** a fine powder, as of cuttlefish bone, formerly used to keep ink from blotting **2.** a fine powder sprinkled over a stencil to make a design, as on cloth —*vt.* **pounced, pounc'ing** to use pounce on

**pound**[1] (pound) *n., pl.* **pounds,** collectively **pound** [OE. *pund* < L. *pondo,* abl. of *pondus,* weight] **1.** a unit of weight, equal to 16 oz. (7,000 grains) avoirdupois or 12 oz. (5,760 grains) troy: abbrev. **lb. 2.** the monetary unit of the United Kingdom, equal to 20 shillings or 100 (new) pennies, symbol £, and of various other countries, as of Ireland, Israel, etc.: see MONETARY UNITS, table

**pound**[2] (pound) *vt.* [OE. *punian*] **1.** to beat to a pulp, powder, etc. **2.** to strike or drive with repeated heavy blows **3.** to make by pounding —*vi.* **1.** to deliver repeated, heavy blows (*at* or *on* a door, etc.) **2.** to move with heavy steps, thumps, etc. **3.** to beat heavily; throb —*n.* a pounding, or the sound of it —**pound one's ear** [Slang] to sleep —**pound out 1.** to flatten, smooth, etc. by pounding **2.** to produce (musical notes, typed copy, etc.) with a very heavy touch —**pound the pavement** [Slang] to walk the streets, as in looking for work —**pound'er** *n.*

**pound**[3] (pound) *n.* [< OE. *pund-*] **1.** a municipal enclosure for confining stray animals **2.** an enclosure for keeping animals **3.** an enclosure for trapping animals **4.** a place of confinement, as for arrested persons **5.** an enclosed area for catching or keeping fish

**pound·age** (poun'dij) *n.* **1.** a tax, etc. per pound (sterling or weight) **2.** weight in pounds

**pound·al** (poun'd'l) *n.* [< POUND[1]] a unit of force producing an acceleration of one foot per second every second on a one-pound mass

**pound·cake** (pound'kāk') *n.* a rich cake made with a pound each of flour, butter, sugar, etc.

**-pound·er** (poun'dər) *a combining form meaning* something weighing or worth (a specified number of pounds)

**pound-fool·ish** (pound'fōōl'ish) *adj.* not handling large sums of money wisely: see PENNY-WISE

**pour** (pôr) *vt.* [< ?] **1.** to make flow in a continuous stream **2.** to emit, utter, etc. profusely or steadily —*vi.* **1.** to flow freely, continuously, or copiously **2.** to rain heavily **3.** to swarm **4.** to act as a hostess by pouring tea, coffee, etc. for guests at a reception —*n.* **1.** a pouring **2.** a heavy rain —**pour it on** [Slang] **1.** to flatter **2.** to try or work very hard —**pour'er** *n.*

‡**pour·boire** (pōōr bwàr') *n.* [Fr. < *pour,* for + *boire,* to drink] a tip or gratuity

**pout**[1] (pout) *vi.* [ME. *pouten*] **1.** to thrust out the lips, as in sullenness **2.** to sulk **3.** to protrude: said of the lips —*vt.* **1.** to thrust out (the lips) **2.** to utter with a pout —*n.* **1.** a pouting **2.** a fit of sulking: also **the pouts**

**pout**[2] (pout) *n., pl.* **pout, pouts:** see PLURAL, II, D, 2 [OE. *-pute*] any of several stout-bodied fishes, as the horned pout, eelpout, etc.

**pout·er** (-ər) *n.* **1.** a person who pouts **2.** any of a breed of pigeon that can distend its crop: also **pouter pigeon**

**pov·er·ty** (päv'ər tē) *n.* [< OFr. < L. < *pauper,* poor] **1.** the condition or quality of being poor; need **2.** inferiority; inadequacy **3.** scarcity

**pov·er·ty-strick·en** (-strik''n) *adj.* very poor

**pow** (pou) *interj.* an exclamation suggesting the sound of a shot, explosion, etc.

**POW, P.O.W.** prisoner of war

**pow·der** (pou'dər) *n.* [< OFr. *poudre* < L. *pulvis*] **1.** any dry substance in the form of fine, dustlike particles, produced by crushing, grinding, etc. **2.** a specific kind of powder [face *powder*] **3.** *same as* GUNPOWDER —*vt.* **1.** to put powder on **2.** to make into powder —*vi.* **1.** to be made into powder **2.** to use powder as a cosmetic —**take a powder** [Slang] to run away; leave —**pow'der·er** *n.*

**powder blue** pale blue —**pow'der-blue'** *adj.*

**powder burn** a skin burn caused by gunpowder exploding at close range

**pow·dered sugar** (pou'dərd) granulated sugar ground to a powder

**powder horn** a container made of an animal's horn, for carrying gunpowder

**powder puff** a soft pad for applying cosmetic powder

**powder room** a lavatory for women

**pow·der·y** (pou'dər ē) *adj.* **1.** of, like, or in the form of, powder **2.** easily made into powder **3.** covered with or as if with powder

**pow·er** (pou'ər) *n.* [< OFr. *poeir,* earlier *poter,* ult. < L. *posse,* to be able] **1.** ability to do, act, or produce **2.** a specific ability or faculty [*the power* of sight] **3.** great ability to do, act, or affect; vigor; force **4.** *a)* the ability to control others; influence *b)* [*pl.*] special authority of a person or group in office *c)* legal authority **5.** *a)* physical force or energy [*water power*] *b)* the capacity to exert such force [*200 horsepower*] **6.** a person or thing of great influence, force, or authority **7.** a nation, esp. one dominating others **8.** a spirit or divinity **9.** military strength **10.** *Math. a)* the result of multiplying a quantity by itself [*4* is the second *power* of 2 ($2^2$)] *b)* *same as* EXPONENT (sense 3) **11.** *Optics* the degree of magnification of a lens, telescope, etc. —*vt.* to supply with power —*adj.* **1.** operated by electricity, etc. [*power tools*] **2.** using an auxiliary, engine-powered system [*power steering*] **3.** carrying electricity [*power lines*] —**in power 1.** in authority **2.** in office —**the powers that be** the persons in control —**pow'ered** *adj.*

POWDER HORN

**pow·er·boat** (-bōt') *n. same as* MOTORBOAT

**power dive** *Aeron.* a dive speeded by engine power —**pow'er-dive'** *vi., vt.* **-dived', -div'ing**

**pow·er·ful** (-fəl) *adj.* having much power; strong —*adv.* [Dial.] very —**pow'er·ful·ly** *adv.* —**pow'er·ful·ness** *n.*

**pow·er·house** (-hous') *n.* **1.** a building where electric power is generated **2.** [Colloq.] a powerful person, team, etc.

**pow·er·less** (-lis) *adj.* without power; weak, impotent, etc. —**pow'er·less·ly** *adv.* —**pow'er·less·ness** *n.*

**power of attorney** a written statement legally authorizing a person to act for one

**power pack** *Radio* a unit in an amplifier that converts power-line or battery voltage to required voltages

**power structure** those persons or groups who hold the ruling power in a nation, organization, etc. because of their social, economic, and institutional position

**pow·wow** (pou'wou') *n.* [< Algonquian *powwaw,* priest] **1.** a N. American Indian ceremony to effect a cure, success in war, etc. as by magic, attended by feasting, dancing, etc. **2.** a conference of or with N. American Indians **3.** [Colloq.] any conference or gathering —*vi.* **1.** to hold a powwow **2.** [Colloq.] to confer

**pox** (päks) *n.* [for *pocks:* see POCK] **1.** a disease characterized by skin eruptions, as smallpox **2.** syphilis

**Poz·nań** (pôz'nän'y') city in W Poland: pop. 462,000

**pp, pp.** *Music* pianissimo

**pp. 1.** pages **2.** past participle

**P.P., p.p. 1.** parcel post **2.** past participle **3.** postpaid **4.** prepaid

**ppd. 1.** postpaid **2.** prepaid

**PPI** print position indicator

**ppm, p.p.m., PPM** parts per million

**ppr., p.pr.** present participle

**P.P.S., p.p.s.** [L. *post postscriptum*] an additional postscript

**P.Q.** Province of Quebec

**Pr** *Chem.* praseodymium

**Pr. 1.** Prince **2.** Provençal

**pr. 1.** pair(s) **2.** present **3.** price **4.** pronoun

**P.R., PR 1.** Puerto Rico **2.** public relations

**prac·ti·ca·ble** (prak'ti kə b'l) *adj.* [< Fr. < *pratiquer:* see PRACTICE] **1.** that can be done or put into practice; feasible [a *practicable* plan] **2.** that can be used; usable [a *practicable* tool] —**prac'ti·ca·bil'i·ty, prac'ti·ca·ble·ness** *n.* —**prac'ti·ca·bly** *adv.*

**prac·ti·cal** (prak'ti k'l) *adj.* [obs. *practic* < LL. *practicus:* see PRACTICE] **1.** of or from practice or action [*practical* knowledge] **2.** *a)* usable; workable; useful and sensible [*practical* proposals] *b)* designed for use; utilitarian **3.**

concerned with application to useful ends, rather than theory, speculation, etc. *[practical science]* **4.** given to actual practice *[a practical farmer]* **5.** of, concerned with, or realistic and sensible about everyday activities, work, etc. **6.** that is so in practice; virtual **7.** matter-of-fact —**prac'ti·cal'i·ty** (-kal'ə tē), *pl.* -**ties, prac'ti·cal·ness** *n.*

**practical joke** a trick played on someone but meant in fun —**practical joker**

**prac·ti·cal·ly** (prak'tik lē, -tik 'l ē) *adv.* **1.** in a practical way **2.** from a practical viewpoint **3.** in effect; virtually **4.** [Colloq.] nearly

**practical nurse** a nurse, often licensed, with less training than a registered nurse

**prac·tice** (prak'tis) *vt.* -**ticed, -tic·ing** [< MFr. < *pratiquer* < ML. < LL. < Gr. *praktikos*, practical < *prassein*, to do] **1.** to do or engage in regularly; make a habit of *[to practice thrift]* **2.** to do repeatedly so as to gain skill **3.** *a)* to work at, esp. as a profession *[to practice law]* *b)* to observe, or adhere to (beliefs, ideals, etc.) *[to practice one's religion]* —*vi.* **1.** to do something repeatedly so as to gain skill **2.** to work at a profession —*n.* **1.** the act, result, etc. of practicing; specif., *a)* a usual action; habit *b)* a usual method or custom; convention **2.** *a)* repeated action for gaining skill *b)* the resulting condition of being skilled *[out of practice]* **3.** knowledge put into action **4.** *a)* exercise of a profession *b)* a business based on this *[to buy another's law practice]* —**prac'tic·er** *n.*

**prac·ticed** (-tist) *adj.* **1.** skilled through practice **2.** learned or perfected by practice

**practice teacher** *same as* STUDENT TEACHER —**practice teaching**

**prac·tise** (-tis) *vt., vi.* -**tised, -tis·ing** *chiefly Brit. sp. of* PRACTICE

**prac·ti·tion·er** (prak tish'ə nər) *n.* **1.** a person who practices a profession, art, etc. **2.** a Christian Science healer

**prae-** [L.: see PRE-] *same as* PRE-

**prae·no·men** (prē nō'mən) *n., pl.* -**no'mens, -nom'i·na** (-näm'i nə) [L. < *prae-*, before + *nomen*, a name] the first name of an ancient Roman

**prae·tor** (prēt'ər) *n.* [L., ult. < *prae-*, before + *ire*, to go] an ancient Roman magistrate, next below a consul in rank —**prae·to·ri·al** (pri tôr'ē əl) *adj.*

**prae·to·ri·an** (pri tôr'ē ən) *adj.* **1.** of a praetor **2.** *[often* P-*]* designating or of the bodyguard (**Praetorian Guard**) of a Roman emperor

**prag·mat·ic** (prag mat'ik) *adj.* [< L. < Gr. *pragmatikos* < *pragma*, business < *prassein*, to do] **1.** concerned with actual practice, not with theory; practical **2.** dealing with historical facts as causally related **3.** of pragmatism Also, for senses 1 & 3, **prag·mat'i·cal** —**prag·mat'i·cal·ly** *adv.*

**pragmatic sanction** any of various royal decrees that had the force of fundamental law

**prag·ma·tism** (prag'mə tiz'm) *n.* **1.** the quality or condition of being pragmatic **2.** a philosophy that tests all concepts by practical results —**prag'ma·tist** *n., adj.*

**Prague** (präg) capital of Czechoslovakia, in the W part: pop. 1,034,000: Czech name **Pra·ha** (prä'hä)

**prai·rie** (prer'ē) *n.* [Fr. < OFr. *praerie* < *pré* < L. *pratum*, meadow + *-erie, -ERY*] a large area of level or slightly rolling grassland

**prairie chicken** either of two brown-and-white henlike grouse, with a short, rounded tail, of N. American prairies and the coast of the Gulf of Mexico: also **prairie hen**

**prairie dog** a small, squirrellike, burrowing rodent of N. America, with a barking cry

**Prairie Provinces** Canad. provinces of Manitoba, Saskatchewan, & Alberta

**prairie schooner** a large covered wagon used by pioneers to cross the American prairies

**prairie wolf** *same as* COYOTE

**praise** (prāz) *vt.* **praised, prais'ing** [< OFr. < LL. < L. *pretium*, worth] **1.** to commend the worth of; express admiration of **2.** to laud the glory of (God, etc.), as in song; glorify —*n.* a praising or being praised; commendation; glorification —**sing someone's praise** (or **praises**) to praise someone highly —**prais'er** *n.*

PRAIRIE DOG
(to 15 in. long,
including tail)

**praise·wor·thy** (-wur'thē) *adj.* worthy of praise; laudable —**praise'wor'thi·ly** *adv.* —**praise'wor'thi·ness** *n.*

**Pra·krit** (prä'krit) *n.* [Sans. *prākṛta*, natural < *pra-*, before + *kṛ*, to do] any of several Old Indic languages not of Sanskrit origin, spoken in ancient India

**pra·line** (prā'lēn; *chiefly South* prä'-) *n.* [Fr., after Marshal Duplessis-*Praslin* (1598-1675), whose cook created it] **1.** a crisp candy made of a pecan, almond, etc. browned in boiling sugar **2.** a similar patty of pecans, brown sugar, etc.

**pram** (pram) *n.* [Brit. Colloq.] a perambulator

**prance** (prans) *vi.* **pranced, pranc'ing** [< ?] **1.** to rise up on the hind legs in a lively way, esp. while moving along: said of a horse **2.** to ride on a prancing horse **3.** to caper like a prancing horse **4.** to swagger; strut —*vt.* to make (a horse) prance —*n.* a prancing —**pranc'er** *n.* —**pranc'ing·ly** *adv.*

**prank**[1] (praŋk) *n.* [< ? or akin ? to ff.] a playful trick, often one causing some mischief —**prank'ish** *adj.* —**prank'ish·ly** *adv.* —**prank'ish·ness** *n.* —**prank'ster** *n.*

**prank**[2] (praŋk) *vt., vi.* [prob. < LowG. source] to dress up or adorn showily

**pra·se·o·dym·i·um** (prā'zē ō dim'ē əm, -sē-) *n.* [ModL. < Gr. *prasios*, green + (DI)DYMIUM] a metallic chemical element of the rare-earth group, whose salts are generally green: symbol, Pr; at. wt., 140.907; at. no., 59

**prat** (prat) *n.* [< ?] [Slang] the buttocks

**prate** (prāt) *vi.* **prat'ed, prat'ing** [< MDu. *praten*; prob. echoic] to talk on and on, foolishly; chatter —*vt.* to tell idly; blab —*n.* chatter —**prat'er** *n.* —**prat'ing·ly** *adv.*

**prat·fall** (prat'fôl') *n.* [Slang] a fall on the buttocks, esp. for comic effect, as in burlesque

**prat·tle** (prat''l) *vi., vt.* -**tled, -tling** [MLowG. *pratelen*] **1.** *same as* PRATE **2.** to speak childishly; babble —*n.* **1.** idle chatter **2.** childish babble —**prat'tler** *n.*

**prau** (prou, prä'ōō) *n. same as* PROA

**prawn** (prôn) *n.* [< ?] any of various related edible, shrimplike crustaceans or larger shrimp

**Prax·it·e·les** (prak sit'ə lēz') 4th cent. B.C.; Athenian sculptor

**pray** (prā) *vt.* [< OFr. < LL. < L. *precari* < *prex* (gen. *precis*), prayer] **1.** to implore: no longer used except in a shortened form of direct request *[(I) pray (you) tell me]* **2.** to ask for by prayer; beg for imploringly **3.** to recite (a prayer) **4.** to effect, get, etc. by praying —*vi.* to make supplication or offer prayers

PRAWN
(from 1 in. to
2 ft. long)

**prayer**[1] (prer) *n.* [< OFr. < ML. < L. *precarius*, got by begging < *precari*, to entreat] **1.** the act of praying **2.** an earnest request; entreaty **3.** *a)* an earnest request to God, etc. *b)* an utterance of praise, etc. to God *c)* a set of words used in praying *[evening prayer]* **4.** *[often pl.]* a religious prayer service **5.** something prayed for —**prayer'ful** *adj.* —**prayer'ful·ly** *adv.* —**prayer'ful·ness** *n.*

**pray·er**[2] (prā'ər) *n.* a person who prays

**prayer book** a book of formal religious prayers

**praying mantis** *same as* MANTIS

**pre-** [< Fr. *pré-* or L. *prae-* < L. *prae*, before] *a prefix meaning:* **1.** before in time, place, or rank *[prewar]* **2.** preliminary to *[preschool]*

**preach** (prēch) *vi.* [< OFr. < LL. < L. < *prae-*, before + *dicare*, to proclaim] **1.** to give a sermon **2.** to give moral or religious advice, esp. tediously —*vt.* **1.** to teach, advocate, or urge as by preaching **2.** to deliver (a sermon)

**preach·er** (prē'chər) *n.* a person who preaches; esp., a clergyman

**preach·i·fy** (-chə fī') *vi.* -**fied', -fy'ing** [Colloq.] to preach or moralize tiresomely

**preach·ment** (prēch'mənt) *n.* a preaching or sermon, esp. a long, tiresome one

**preach·y** (prē'chē) *adj.* **preach'i·er, preach'i·est** [Colloq.] given to or marked by preaching

**pre·am·ble** (prē'am'b'l, prē am'-) *n.* [< MFr., ult. < L. < *prae-*, before + *ambulare*, to go] **1.** an introduction, esp. to a constitution, statute, etc., stating its reason and purpose **2.** an introductory fact, event, etc.; preliminary

**pre·am·pli·fi·er** (prē am'plə fī'ər) *n.* in a radio, phonograph, etc., an amplifier to boost the voltage of a weak signal before it reaches the main amplifier

**pre·ar·range** (prē'ə rānj') *vt.* -**ranged', -rang'ing** to arrange beforehand —**pre'ar·range'ment** *n.*

**preb·end** (preb'ənd) *n.* [< MFr. < ML. *praebenda*, things to be supplied < L. *praebere*, to give] **1.** the amount paid a clergyman by his cathedral or collegiate church **2.** the church property yielding this amount **3.** *same as* PREBENDARY

**preb·en·dar·y** (preb'ən der'ē) *n., pl.* -**dar'ies** a person receiving a prebend

**prec.** preceding

**Pre·cam·bri·an** (prē kam'brē ən) *adj.* designating or of the geologic era covering all the time before the Cambrian Period —**the Precambrian** the Precambrian Era or its rocks: see GEOLOGY, chart

**pre·can·cel** (prē kan's'l) *vt.* -**celed** or -**celled, -cel·ing** or -**cel·ling** to cancel (a postage stamp) before use in mailing —*n.* a precanceled stamp

**pre·can·cer·ous** (-kan'sər əs) *adj.* that may or is likely to become cancerous

**pre·car·i·ous** (pri ker′ē əs) *adj.* [L. *precarius:* see PRAYER[1]] **1.** dependent upon circumstances; insecure [a *precarious* living] **2.** dependent upon chance; risky [a *precarious* foothold] —**pre·car′i·ous·ly** *adv.* —**pre·car′i·ous·ness** *n.*

**pre·cast concrete** (prē′kast) blocks, slabs, etc. of concrete cast into form before being put into position

**pre·cau·tion** (pri kô′shən) *n.* [< Fr. < LL. < L. pp. of *praecavere* < *prae-*, before + *cavere*, to take care] **1.** care taken beforehand **2.** a measure taken beforehand against possible danger, failure, etc. —**pre·cau′tion·ar′y** *adj.*

**pre·cede** (prē sēd′) *vt., vi.* **-ced′ed, -ced′ing** [< MFr. < L. < *prae-*, before + *cedere*, to go] to be, come, or go before in time, order, rank, importance, etc.

**prec·e·dence** (pres′ə dəns, pri sēd′′ns) *n.* **1.** the act, right, or fact of preceding; priority in time, order, rank, etc. **2.** a ranking of dignitaries in order of importance Also **prec′e·den·cy**

**prec·e·dent** (pri sēd′′nt; *for n.* pres′ə dənt) *adj.* that precedes —*n.* **1.** an act, decision, etc. that may serve as an example, reason, or justification for a later one **2.** a practice resulting from such precedents

**prec·e·den·tial** (pres′ə den′shəl) *adj.* **1.** of, like, or serving as a precedent **2.** having precedence

**pre·cen·tor** (pri sen′tər) *n.* [< LL. < L. < *prae*, before + *canere*, to sing] a person who directs church singing —**pre·cen·to·ri·al** (prē′sen tôr′ē əl) *adj.*

**pre·cept** (prē′sept) *n.* [< L. < *praecipere*, to teach < *prae-*, before + *capere*, to take] **1.** a direction meant as a rule of action or conduct (Ex.: Look before you leap) **2.** a rule of moral conduct **3.** a rule or direction, as in technical matters —**pre·cep′tive** *adj.*

**pre·cep·tor** (pri sep′tər) *n.* [see prec.] a teacher —**pre·cep·to·ri·al** (prē′sep tôr′ē əl) *adj.* —**pre·cep′tor·ship′** *n.* —**pre·cep′tress** *n.fem.*

**pre·ces·sion** (pri sesh′ən) *n.* **1.** a preceding; precedence **2.** *Mech.* a change in direction of the rotational axis of a spinning body, in which the axis describes a cone —**pre·ces′sion·al** *adj.*

**pre·cinct** (prē′siŋkt) *n.* [< ML. < L. pp. of *praecingere*, to encompass < *prae-*, before + *cingere*, to surround] **1.** [*usually pl.*] an enclosure between buildings, walls, etc. **2.** [*pl.*] environs; neighborhood **3.** *a)* a division of a city, as for police administration *b)* a subdivision of a ward, as for voting **4.** any limited area **5.** a boundary

**pre·ci·os·i·ty** (presh′ē äs′ə tē) *n., pl.* **-ties** [see PRECIOUS] great fastidiousness or affectation, esp. in language

**pre·cious** (presh′əs) *adj.* [< OFr. < L. *pretiosus* < *pretium*, a price] **1.** of great price or value; costly **2.** much loved or cherished; dear **3.** overrefined or affected **4.** very great [a *precious* liar] —*adv.* [Colloq.] very —**pre′cious·ly** *adv.* —**pre′cious·ness** *n.*

**precious stone** a rare and costly gem

**prec·i·pice** (pres′ə pis) *n.* [< Fr. < L. < *praeceps*, headlong < *prae-*, before + *caput*, a head] **1.** a vertical, almost vertical, or overhanging rock face; steep cliff **2.** the brink of disaster, defeat, etc.

**pre·cip·i·tant** (pri sip′ə tənt) *adj.* [< L. prp. of *praecipitare:* see ff.] *same as* PRECIPITATE —*n.* a substance causing formation of a precipitate —**pre·cip′i·tan·cy**, *pl.* **-cies, pre·cip′i·tance** *n.* —**pre·cip′i·tant·ly** *adv.*

**pre·cip·i·tate** (pri sip′ə tāt′; *also, for adj. & n.,* -tit) *vt.* **-tat′ed, -tat′ing** [< L. pp. of *praecipitare < praeceps:* see PRECIPICE] **1.** to throw headlong; hurl downward **2.** to make happen before expected, needed, etc.; hasten **3.** *Chem.* to cause (a dissolved substance) to become insoluble and separate out from a solution, as by a reagent **4.** *Meteorol.* to condense (vapor) and make fall as rain, snow, etc. —*vi.* **1.** *Chem.* to be precipitated **2.** *Meteorol.* to condense and fall as rain, snow, etc. —*adj.* **1.** falling steeply, rushing headlong, etc. **2.** acting, happening, or done very hastily or rashly; impetuous **3.** very sudden; abrupt —*n.* a substance precipitated out from a solution —**pre·cip′i·tate·ly** *adv.* —**pre·cip′i·tate·ness** *n.* —**pre·cip′i·ta′tive** *adj.* —**pre·cip′i·ta′tor** *n.*

**pre·cip·i·ta·tion** (pri sip′ə tā′shən) *n.* **1.** a precipitating or being precipitated **2.** sudden or rash haste **3.** *Chem.* a precipitating or precipitate **4.** *Meteorol. a)* rain, snow, etc. *b)* the amount of this

**pre·cip·i·tous** (pri sip′ə təs) *adj.* **1.** steep like a precipice **2.** having precipices **3.** *same as* PRECIPITATE —**pre·cip′i·tous·ly** *adv.* —**pre·cip′i·tous·ness** *n.*

**pré·cis** (prā sē′, prā′sē) *n., pl.* **pré·cis′** (-sēz′, -sēz) [Fr.: see ff.] a summary or abstract —*vt.* to make a précis of

**pre·cise** (pri sīs′) *adj.* [MFr. *precis* < L. pp. of *praecidere,* to cut off < *prae-*, before + *caedere,* to cut] **1.** strictly defined; accurately stated; definite **2.** speaking definitely or distinctly **3.** minutely exact **4.** *a)* very careful or strict

in following a procedure, rules, etc. *b)* finicky —**pre·cise′ly** *adv.* —**pre·cise′ness** *n.*

**pre·ci·sion** (pri sizh′ən) *n.* **1.** the quality of being precise; exactness, accuracy, etc. **2.** the degree of this —*adj.* characterized by precision, as in measurement, operation, etc. —**pre·ci′sion·ist** *n.*

**pre·clude** (pri klood′) *vt.* **-clud′ed, -clud′ing** [< L. *praecludere < prae-*, before + *claudere,* to shut] to make impossible, esp. in advance; shut out —**pre·clu′sion** (-kloo′zhən) *n.* —**pre·clu′sive** (-siv) *adj.* —**pre·clu′sive·ly** *adv.*

**pre·co·cious** (pri kō′shəs) *adj.* [L. *praecox,* ult. < *prae-*, before + *coquere,* to cook] **1.** matured beyond normal for one's age, esp. in mental capacity, talent, etc. **2.** of or showing premature development —**pre·co′cious·ly** *adv.* —**pre·co′cious·ness, pre·coc′i·ty** (-käs′ə tē) *n.*

**pre·cog·ni·tion** (prē′käg nish′ən) *n.* supposed perception, esp. extrasensory, of something before it occurs —**pre·cog′ni·tive** (-nə tiv) *adj.*

**pre·con·ceive** (prē′kən sēv′) *vt.* **-ceived′, -ceiv′ing** to form a conception or opinion of beforehand —**pre′con·cep′tion** *n.*

**pre·con·cert** (-kən surt′) *vt.* to arrange or settle beforehand —**pre′con·cert′ed** *adj.* —**pre′con·cert′ed·ly** *adv.*

**pre·con·di·tion** (-kən dish′ən) *vt.* to prepare (someone or something) to react, etc. in a certain way under certain conditions —*n.* a condition required in advance for something to occur, be done, etc.

**pre·cook** (prē kook′) *vt.* to cook partially or completely, for final preparation later

**pre·cur·sor** (pri kur′sər) *n.* [< L. < *praecurrere,* to run ahead] **1.** a person or thing that comes before and indicates, or prepares the way for, what will follow; forerunner **2.** a predecessor, as in office

**pre·cur·so·ry** (-sə rē) *adj.* **1.** serving as a precursor **2.** introductory; preliminary

**pred.** predicate

**pre·da·cious, pre·da·ceous** (pri dā′shəs) *adj.* [< L. *praedari,* to prey upon < *praeda,* a prey + -ACEOUS] preying on other animals —**pre·dac′i·ty** (-das′ə tē), **pre·da′cious·ness, pre·da′ceous·ness** *n.*

**pre·date** (prē dāt′) *vt.* **-dat′ed, -dat′ing 1.** to date before the actual date **2.** to come before in date

**pre·da·tion** (pri dā′shən) *n.* [< L. < pp. of *praedari:* see PREDACIOUS] **1.** a plundering or preying **2.** the method of existence of predatory animals

**pred·a·tor** (pred′ə tər) *n.* a predatory person or animal

**pred·a·to·ry** (-tôr′ē) *adj.* [< L. < *praeda,* a prey] **1.** plundering, robbing, or exploiting **2.** capturing and feeding upon other animals —**pred′a·to′ri·ly** *adv.* —**pred′a·to′ri·ness** *n.*

**pre·de·cease** (prē′di sēs′) *vt., vi.* **-ceased′, -ceas′ing** to die before (someone else)

**pred·e·ces·sor** (pred′ə ses′ər, pred′ə ses′ər; *chiefly Brit.* prē′di-) *n.* [< MFr. < LL. < L. *prae-*, before + *decessor,* retiring officer < *decessus:* see DECEASE] **1.** a person preceding another, as in office **2.** a thing replaced by another thing, as in use

**pre·des·ig·nate** (prē dez′ig nāt′) *vt.* **-nat′ed, -nat′ing** to designate beforehand —**pre·des′ig·na′tion** *n.*

**pre·des·ti·nate** (prē des′tə nit; *for v.* -nāt′) *adj.* predestined or foreordained —*vt.* **-nat′ed, -nat′ing** to foreordain, specif., *Theol.,* by divine decree —**pre·des′ti·na′tor** *n.*

**pre·des·ti·na·tion** (prē des′tə nā′shən) *n.* **1.** *Theol.* divine foreordaining of everything, specif. of certain souls to salvation and esp. in Calvinism, of others to damnation **2.** destiny; fate

**pre·des·tine** (prē des′tin) *vt.* **-tined, -tin·ing** to destine or decree beforehand; foreordain

**pre·de·ter·mine** (prē′di tur′mən) *vt.* **-mined, -min·ing 1.** to determine or decide beforehand **2.** to bias or prejudice beforehand —**pre′de·ter′mi·nate** (-mə nit) *adj.* —**pre′de·ter′mi·na′tion** *n.*

**pred·i·ca·ble** (pred′i kə b'l) *adj.* that can be predicated —*n.* something predicable —**pred′i·ca·bil′i·ty, pred′i·ca·ble·ness** *n.* —**pred′i·ca·bly** *adv.*

**pre·dic·a·ment** (pri dik′ə mənt) *n.* [< LL. *praedicamentum* < L. *praedicare:* see PREACH] a condition or situation, esp. one that is difficult, embarrassing, or comical

**pred·i·cate** (pred′ə kāt′; *for n. and adj.,* -kit) *vt.* **-cat′ed, -cat′ing** [< L. pp. of *praedicare:* see PREACH] **1.** orig., to proclaim; affirm **2.** to affirm as a quality, attribute, etc. [to *predicate* the honesty of one's motives] **3.** to base (something) *on* or *upon* facts, conditions, etc. **4.** to imply or connote —*vi.* to make an affirmation —*n.* **1.** *Gram.* the verb or verbal phrase, including any complements, objects, and modifiers, that is one of the two constituents of a sentence or clause, the other being the subject **2.** *Logic* something that is affirmed or denied about the subject of a proposition

(Ex.: *green* in "grass is green") —*adj. Gram.* of, or having the nature of, a predicate —**pred′i·ca′tion** *n.* —**pred′i·ca′tive** *adj.* —**pred′i·ca′tive·ly** *adv.*

**pre·dict** (pri dikt′) *vt., vi.* [< L. pp. of *praedicere* < *prae-*, before + *dicere*, to tell] to state (what one believes will happen); foretell —**pre·dict′a·bil′i·ty** *n.* —**pre·dict′a·ble** *adj.* —**pre·dict′a·bly** *adv.* —**pre·dic′tive** *adj.* —**pre·dic′tor** *n.*

**pre·dic·tion** (pri dik′shən) *n.* **1.** a predicting or being predicted **2.** something predicted

**pre·di·gest** (prē′di jest′, -dī-) *vt.* to digest beforehand; specif., to treat (food) as with enzymes for easier digestion —**pre′di·ges′tion** *n.*

**pre·di·lec·tion** (pred′'l ek′shən, prēd′-) *n.* [< Fr. < ML. < L. *prae-*, before + *diligere*, to prefer] a preconceived liking; partiality (*for*)

**pre·dis·pose** (prē′dis pōz′) *vt.* **-posed′, -pos′ing** to make receptive beforehand —**pre′dis·po·si′tion** (-pə zish′ən) *n.*

**pre·dom·i·nant** (pri däm′ə nənt) *adj.* **1.** having authority or influence over others; superior **2.** most frequent; prevailing —**pre·dom′i·nance, pre·dom′i·nan·cy** *n., pl.* **-cies, pre·dom′i·nant·ly** *adv.*

**pre·dom·i·nate** (-nāt′; *for adj.* -nit) *vi.* **-nat′ed, -nat′ing 1.** to have influence or authority (*over* others); hold sway **2.** to prevail; preponderate —*adj. same as* PREDOMINANT —**pre·dom′i·nate·ly** *adv.* —**pre·dom′i·na′tion** *n.*

**pre·em·i·nent, pre-em·i·nent** (prē em′ə nənt) *adj.* eminent above others; surpassing: also **pre·ëm′i·nent** —**pre·em′i·nence, pre-em′i·nence** *n.* —**pre·em′i·nent·ly, pre-em′i·nent·ly** *adv.*

**pre·empt, pre-empt** (-empt′) *vt.* [< ff.] **1.** to acquire (public land) by preemption **2.** to seize before anyone else can; appropriate **3.** *Radio & TV* to replace (a regularly scheduled program) —*vi. Bridge* to make a preemptive bid Also **pre·ëmpt′** —**pre·emp′tor, pre-emp′tor** *n.*

**pre·emp·tion, pre-emp·tion** (-emp′shən) *n.* [< ML. pp. of *preemere* < L. *prae-*, before + *emere*, to buy] **1.** the act or right of buying land, etc. before, or in preference to, others **2.** action taken to check other action beforehand Also **pre·ëmp′tion**

**pre·emp·tive, pre-emp·tive** (-emp′tiv) *adj.* **1.** having to do with preemption **2.** *Bridge* designating a high bid intended to shut out opposing bids Also **pre·ëmp′tive** —**pre·emp′tive·ly, pre-emp′tive·ly** *adv.*

**preen** (prēn) *vt.* [< OE. < *proinen*] **1.** to clean and trim (the feathers) with the beak: said of birds **2.** to dress up or adorn (oneself) **3.** to show satisfaction with or vanity in (oneself) —*vi.* to primp —**preen′er** *n.*

**pre·ex·ist, pre-ex·ist** (prē′ig zist′) *vt., vi.* to exist previously or before (another person or thing): also **pre′ëx·ist′** —**pre′ex·ist′ence, pre′-ex·ist′ence** *n.* —**pre′ex·ist′ent, pre′-ex·ist′ent** *adj.*

**pref. 1.** preface **2.** preferred **3.** prefix

**pre·fab** (prē′fab′) *n.* [Colloq.] a prefabricated building

**pre·fab·ri·cate** (prē fab′rə kāt′) *vt.* **-cat′ed, -cat′ing 1.** to fabricate beforehand **2.** to make (houses, etc.) in standardized sections for shipment and quick assembly —**pre′fab·ri·ca′tion** *n.*

**pref·ace** (pref′is) *n.* [< MFr. < ML. < L. *prae-*, before + pp. of *fari*, to speak] **1.** an introductory statement to an article, book, or speech, telling its subject, purpose, etc. **2.** something introductory —*vt.* **-aced, -ac·ing 1.** to furnish or introduce with a preface **2.** to be or serve as a preface to

**pref·a·to·ry** (pref′ə tôr′ē) *adj.* of, like, or serving as a preface: also **pref′a·to′ri·al** —**pref′a·to′ri·ly** *adv.*

**pre·fect** (prē′fekt) *n.* [< OFr. < L. pp. of *praeficere*, to set over < *prae-*, before + *facere*, to make] **1.** in ancient Rome, any of various officials in charge of governmental or military departments **2.** any of various administrators; specif., the head of a department of France

**pre·fec·ture** (prē′fek chər) *n.* the office, authority, territory, or residence of a prefect —**pre·fec′tur·al** *adj.*

**pre·fer** (pri fur′) *vt.* **-ferred′, -fer′ring** [< MFr. < L. *prae-*, before + *ferre,* BEAR¹] **1.** to promote; advance **2.** to put before a magistrate, court, etc. to be considered **3.** to choose before another; like better —**pre·fer′rer** *n.*

**pref·er·a·ble** (pref′ər ə b'l, pref′rə-) *adj.* to be preferred; more desirable —**pref′er·a·bil′i·ty, pref′er·a·ble·ness** *n.* —**pref′er·a·bly** *adv.*

**pref·er·ence** (pref′ər əns, pref′rəns) *n.* **1.** a preferring or being preferred **2.** the right, power, etc. of prior choice or claim **3.** something preferred **4.** a giving of advantage to one person, country, etc. over others, as in granting credit or setting tariff rates

**pref·er·en·tial** (pref′ə ren′shəl) *adj.* **1.** of, giving, or receiving preference **2.** offering a preference **3.** designating a union shop which gives preference to union members in hiring, layoffs, etc. —**pref′er·en′tial·ly** *adv.*

**pre·fer·ment** (pri fur′mənt) *n.* **1.** a preferring **2.** an advancement in rank or office; promotion **3.** an office, rank, or honor to which a person is advanced

**preferred stock** stock on which dividends must be paid before those of common stock

**pre·fig·ure** (prē fig′yər) *vt.* **-ured, -ur·ing** [< LL. < L. *prae-*, before + *figurare,* to fashion] **1.** to be a type of or foreshadow (something that will appear later) **2.** to imagine beforehand —**pre′fig·u·ra′tion** (-yə rā′shən) *n.* —**pre·fig′ur·a·tive** *adj.* —**pre·fig′ur·a·tive·ly** *adv.* —**pre·fig′ur·a·tive·ness** *n.* —**pre·fig′ure·ment** *n.*

**pre·fix** (prē′fiks; *also, for v.,* prē fiks′) *vt.* [< MFr. < L. pp. of *praefigere* < *prae-*, before + *figere*, to fix] to fix to the beginning of a word, etc.; esp., to add as a prefix —*n.* **1.** a syllable or group of syllables joined to the beginning of a word to alter its meaning or create a new word [*pre-* is a prefix added to *cool* to form *precool*] **2.** a title before a person's name, as *Dr.* —**pre′fix·al** *adj.* —**pre·fix′ion** *n.*

**pre·fron·tal** (prē frunt′'l) *adj.* in or situated near the front of the brain or of the head of a vertebrate

**preg·na·ble** (preg′nə b'l) *adj.* [< MFr. < *prendre,* to take] that can be captured or attacked —**preg′na·bil′i·ty** *n.*

**preg·nant** (preg′nənt) *adj.* [< L. *pregnans* (gen. *pregnantis*) < *prae-*, before + base of OL. *gnasci,* to be born] **1.** having (an) offspring developing in the uterus; with young or with child **2.** mentally fertile; inventive **3.** productive of results; fruitful **4.** full of meaning, significance, etc. **5.** filled (*with*) or rich (*in*); abounding —**preg′nan·cy** *n., pl.* **-cies** —**preg′nant·ly** *adv.*

**pre·hen·sile** (pri hen′s'l) *adj.* [< Fr. < L. pp. of *prehendere,* to take] adapted for seizing or grasping, esp. by wrapping itself around something as a monkey's tail does —**pre·hen·sil·i·ty** (prē′hen sil′ə tē) *n.*

**pre·his·tor·ic** (prē′his tôr′ik, -tär′-) *adj.* of the period before recorded history: also **pre′his·tor′i·cal** —**pre′his·tor′i·cal·ly** *adv.*

**pre·judge** (prē juj′) *vt.* **-judged′, -judg′ing** [< Fr. < L.: see PRE- & JUDGE] to judge beforehand, or without all the evidence —**pre·judg′ment, pre·judge′ment** *n.*

**prej·u·dice** (prej′ə dis) *n.* [< MFr. < L. < *prae-*, before + *judicium,* judgment] **1.** an opinion formed before the facts are known; preconceived idea, usually one that is unfavorable **2.** *a)* an opinion held in disregard of facts that contradict it; unreasonable bias *b)* the holding of such opinions **3.** intolerance or hatred of other races, creeds, etc. **4.** harm resulting as from some judgment or action of another —*vt.* **-diced, -dic·ing 1.** to harm or damage, as by some judgment or action **2.** to cause to have prejudice; bias

**prej·u·di·cial** (prej′ə dish′əl) *adj.* causing prejudice, or harm; injurious; detrimental —**prej′u·di′cial·ly** *adv.*

**prel·a·cy** (prel′ə sē) *n., pl.* **-cies 1.** *a)* the office or rank of a prelate *b)* prelates collectively Also **prel′a·ture** (-chər) **2.** church government by prelates: often a hostile term: also **prel′a·tism** (-it iz′m)

**prel·ate** (-it) *n.* [< OFr. < LL. < L. pp. of *praeferre,* to PRE-FER] a high-ranking ecclesiastic, as a bishop —**prel′ate·ship′** *n.* —**pre·lat·ic** (pri lat′ik) *adj.*

**pre·lim** (prē′lim) *n.* [Slang] *clipped form of* PRELIMINARY

**prelim.** preliminary

**pre·lim·i·nar·y** (pri lim′ə ner′ē) *adj.* [< Fr. or ModL. < L. *prae-*, before + *liminaris* < *limen,* threshold] leading up to the main action, business, etc.; introductory; preparatory —*n., pl.* **-nar′ies** [*often pl.*] **1.** a preliminary step, procedure, etc. **2.** a preliminary examination **3.** a contest before the main one —**pre·lim′i·nar′i·ly** *adv.*

**prel·ude** (prel′yōōd; prā′lōōd, prē-) *n.* [< Fr. < ML. < L. < *prae-*, before + *ludere,* to play] **1.** a preliminary part; preface; opening **2.** *Music a)* an introductory section of a suite, fugue, etc. *b)* since the 19th cent., any short, romantic composition —*vt., vi.* **-ud·ed, -ud·ing 1.** to serve as or be a prelude (*to*) **2.** to play (as) a prelude —**pre·lu·di·al** (prā lōō′dē əl, prē-) *adj.*

**pre·mar·i·tal** (prē mar′ə t'l) *adj.* before marriage

**pre·ma·ture** (prē′mə toor′, -choor′, -tyoor′) *adj.* [< L.: see PRE- & MATURE] happening, done, arriving, or existing before the proper or usual time; specif., born before the full period of gestation —**pre′ma·ture′ly** *adv.* —**pre′ma·tu′ri·ty, pre′ma·ture′ness** *n.*

**pre·med** (prē′med′) *adj. clipped form of* PREMEDICAL —*n.* a premedical student

**pre·med·i·cal** (prē med′i k'l) *adj.* designating or of the studies preparatory to the study of medicine

**pre·med·i·tate** (pri med′ə tāt′) *vt.* **-tat′ed, -tat′ing** to think out or plan beforehand —*vi.* to meditate beforehand —**pre·med′i·tat′ed** *adj.* —**pre·med′i·tat′ed·ly** *adv.* —**pre·med′i·ta′tive** *adj.* —**pre·med′i·ta′tor** *n.*

**pre·med·i·ta·tion** (pri med′ə tā′shən, prē′med-) *n.* **1.** a premeditating **2.** *Law* a degree of forethought sufficient to show intent to commit an act

**pre·mier** (pri mir′, -myir′; prē′mē ər) *adj.* [MFr. < L. *primarius* < *primus,* first] **1.** first in importance; chief **2.** first in time —*n.* a chief official; specif., *the title of a)* the prime minister in certain countries *b)* the governor of a Canadian province —**pre·mier′ship** *n.*

**pre·mière, pre·miere** (pri myer′, -mir′, -mē er′) *n.* [Fr., fem. of *premier:* see prec.] a first performance of a play, movie, etc. —*adj.* **1.** being the leading woman performer, as in ballet **2.** *same as* PREMIER —*vt., vi.* **-mièred′** or **-miered′, -mièr′ing** or **-mier′ing** to exhibit (a play, movie, etc.) for the first time

**prem·ise** (prem′is; *for v., also* pri mīz′) *n.* [< ML. < L. pp. of *praemittere* < *prae-*, before + *mittere*, to send] **1.** a previous statement serving as a basis for an argument; specif., either of the two propositions of a syllogism from which the conclusion is drawn: also sp. **prem′iss** **2.** [*pl.*] *a)* the part of a deed or lease that states the parties and property involved, etc. *b)* the property so mentioned **3.** [*pl.*] a piece of real estate [*keep off the premises*] —*vt.* **-ised, -is·ing** **1.** to state as a premise **2.** to preface (a discourse, etc.) —*vi.* to make a premise

**pre·mi·um** (prē′mē əm, prēm′yəm) *n., pl.* **-ums** [< L. < *prae-*, before + *emere*, to take] **1.** a reward or prize, esp. as an added inducement to buy or do something **2.** an amount paid in addition to the regular charge, interest, etc. **3.** a payment, as for an insurance policy **4.** very high value [*to put a premium on honesty*] **5.** the amount by which one form of money exceeds another (of the same nominal value), as in exchange value —*adj.* rated as superior and higher in price —**at a premium** **1.** at a value or price higher than normal **2.** very valuable, as because of scarcity

**pre·mo·lar** (prē mō′lər) *adj.* designating of any bicuspid tooth in front of the molars —*n.* a premolar tooth

**pre·mo·ni·tion** (prē′mə nish′ən, prem′ə-) *n.* [< MFr. < LL. < L. < *prae-*, before + *monere*, to warn] **1.** a forewarning **2.** a foreboding —**pre·mon·i·to·ry** (pri män′ə tôr′ē) *adj.*

**pre·na·tal** (prē nāt′′l) *adj.* [PRE- + NATAL] existing or taking place before birth —**pre·na′tal·ly** *adv.*

**pre·nup·tial** (prē nup′shəl, -chəl) *adj.* **1.** before a marriage or wedding **2.** before mating

**pre·oc·cu·pa·tion** (prē äk′yə pā′shən) *n.* a preoccupying or being preoccupied: also **pre·oc′cu·pan·cy,** *pl.* **-cies**

**pre·oc·cu·py** (-äk′yə pī′) *vt.* **-pied′, -py′ing** [< MFr. < L.: see PRE- & OCCUPY] **1.** to occupy completely the thoughts of; engross; absorb **2.** to occupy or take possession of before someone else or beforehand

**pre·or·dain** (prē′ôr dān′) *vt.* to ordain or decree beforehand —**pre′or·di·na′tion** (-d′n ā′shən) *n.*

**prep** (prep) *adj.* [Colloq.] *clipped form of* PREPARATORY —*vi.* **prepped, prep′ping** [Colloq.] to prepare oneself by study, etc. —*vt.* to prepare (one) for something; specif., to prepare (a patient) as for surgery

**prep.** **1.** preparation **2.** preparatory **3.** preposition

**pre·pack·age** (prē pak′ij) *vt.* **-aged, -ag·ing** to package (goods, esp. foods) in certain amounts or weights before selling

**pre·paid** (prē pād′) *pt. & pp. of* PREPAY

**prep·a·ra·tion** (prep′ə rā′shən) *n.* **1.** a preparing or being prepared **2.** a preparatory measure **3.** something prepared for a special purpose, as a medicine, cosmetic, etc.

**pre·par·a·tive** (pri par′ə tiv) *adj. same as* PREPARATORY —*n. same as* PREPARATION (sense 2, 3)

**pre·par·a·to·ry** (-tôr′ē) *adj.* **1.** that prepares or serves to prepare; introductory **2.** undergoing preparation, esp. for college entrance —**pre·par′a·to′ri·ly** *adv.*

**preparatory school** a private secondary school for preparing students to enter college

**pre·pare** (pri par′, -per′) *vt.* **-pared′, -par′ing** [< MFr. < L. < *prae-*, before + *parare*, to get ready] **1.** to make ready or suitable **2.** to make receptive; dispose **3.** to equip or furnish; fit out **4.** to put together; construct; compound [*to prepare a dinner or a medicine*] —*vi.* **1.** to make things ready **2.** to make oneself ready —**pre·par′ed·ly** (-id lē) *adv.*

**pre·par·ed·ness** (-id nis) *n.* the state of being prepared, esp. for waging war, as by stockpiling weapons

**pre·pay** (prē pā′) *vt.* **-paid′, -pay′ing** to pay or pay for in advance —**pre·pay′ment** *n.*

**pre·pense** (pri pens′) *adj.* [< OFr. < *pur-*, pro- + *penser*, to think] planned beforehand

**pre·pon·der·ant** (pri pän′dər ənt) *adj.* greater in amount, power, influence, etc.; predominant —**pre·pon′der·ance,** **pre·pon′der·an·cy** *n.* —**pre·pon′der·ant·ly** *adv.*

**pre·pon·der·ate** (-də rāt′) *vi.* **-at·ed, -at′ing** [< L. pp. of *praeponderare* < *prae-*, before + *ponderare*, to weigh < *pondus*, a weight] to be greater in amount, power, influence, etc.; predominate —**pre·pon′der·a′tion** *n.*

**prep·o·si·tion** (prep′ə zish′ən) *n.* [< L. < pp. of *praeponere* < *prae-*, before + *ponere*, to place] **1.** a relation word, as *in, by, for, with, to,* etc., that connects a noun or pronoun, or a noun phrase, to another element, as to another noun (Ex.: the sound *of* rain), to a verb (Ex.: he

went *to* the store), or to an adjective (Ex.: late *for* the tea party) **2.** any construction having a similar function (Ex.: *in back of*, equivalent to *behind*) —**prep′o·si′tion·al** *adj.* —**prep′o·si′tion·al·ly** *adv.*

**prepositional phrase** a preposition and its object

**pre·pos·sess** (prē′pə zes′) *vt.* **1.** orig., to occupy beforehand or before another **2.** to preoccupy to the exclusion of later thoughts, feelings, etc. **3.** to prejudice or bias **4.** to impress favorably at once —**pre′pos·ses′sion** *n.*

**pre·pos·sess·ing** (-iŋ) *adj.* that prepossesses, or impresses favorably; pleasing —**pre′pos·sess′ing·ly** *adv.* —**pre′pos·sess′ing·ness** *n.*

**pre·pos·ter·ous** (pri päs′tər əs) *adj.* [< L. < *prae-*, before + *posterus*, coming after < *post*, after] so contrary to nature, common sense, etc. as to be laughable; absurd —**pre·pos′ter·ous·ly** *adv.* —**pre·pos′ter·ous·ness** *n.*

**pre·puce** (prē′pyōōs) *n.* [< MFr. < L. *praeputium*] the fold of skin covering the end of the penis —**pre·pu′tial** (-pyōō′shəl) *adj.*

**Pre-Raph·a·el·ite** (prē raf′ē ə līt′, -rā′fē-) *n.* **1.** a member of a society of artists (**Pre-Raphaelite Brotherhood**) formed in England in 1848 to revive the qualities of Italian art before Raphael **2.** any artist with similar aims —*adj.* of or like Pre-Raphaelites —**Pre-Raph′a·el·it′ism** *n.*

**pre·re·cord** (prē′ri kôrd′) *vt. Radio & TV* to record (an announcement, program, etc.) in advance, for later broadcasting

**pre·req·ui·site** (pri rek′wə zit) *adj.* required beforehand, esp. as a necessary condition for something following —*n.* something prerequisite

**pre·rog·a·tive** (pri räg′ə tiv) *n.* [< MFr. < L. *prae-rogativa*, called upon to vote first, ult. < *prae-*, before + *rogare*, to ask] **1.** a prior or exclusive privilege, esp. one peculiar to a rank, class, etc. **2.** a superior advantage —*adj.* of or having a prerogative

**Pres.** **1.** Presbyterian: also **Presb.** **2.** President

**pres.** **1.** present **2.** presidency

**pres·age** (pres′ij; *for v., usually* pri sāj′) *n.* [< MFr. < L. < *prae-*, before + *sagire*, to perceive] **1.** a sign or warning of a future event; portent **2.** a foreboding **3.** foreshadowing quality [*of ominous presage*] —*vt.* **-aged′, -ag′ing** **1.** to give a warning of; portend **2.** to have a foreboding of **3.** to predict —*vi.* to make a prediction —**pres·ag′er** *n.*

**pres·by·ter** (prez′bi tər, pres′-) *n.* [LL.: see PRIEST] **1.** in the early Christian church and in the Presbyterian Church, an elder **2.** in the Episcopal Church, a priest or minister —**pres′by·te′ri·al** (-bə tir′ē əl), **pres·byt′er·al** (-bit′ər əl) *adj.*

**pres·by·ter·i·an** (prez′bə tir′ē ən, pres′-) *adj.* **1.** having to do with church government by presbyters **2.** [P-] designating or of a church of a Calvinistic Protestant denomination governed by presbyters, or elders —*n.* [P-] a member of a Presbyterian church —**Pres′by·te′ri·an·ism** *n.*

**pres·by·ter·y** (prez′bə ter′ē, pres′-) *n., pl.* **-ter′ies** **1.** *a)* in Presbyterian churches, a governing body made up of all the ministers and an equal number of elders from all the churches in a district *b)* such a district **2.** the part of a church reserved for the officiating clergy

**pre·school** (prē′skōōl′) *adj.* designating, of, or for a child between infancy and school age, usually between the ages of two and five (or six) —**pre·school′er** *n.*

**pre·sci·ence** (prē′shē əns, presh′əns) *n.* [< OFr. < LL., ult. < L. *prae-*, before + *scire*, to know] apparent knowledge of things before they happen; foreknowledge —**pre′sci·ent** *adj.* —**pre′sci·ent·ly** *adv.*

**pre·scribe** (pri skrīb′) *vt.* **-scribed′, -scrib′ing** [< L. < *prae-*, before + *scribere*, to write] **1.** to set down as a rule or direction; order **2.** to order or advise as a medicine or treatment: said of physicians, etc. —*vi.* **1.** to set down or impose rules **2.** to give medical advice or prescriptions —**pre·scrib′er** *n.*

**pre·script** (pri skript′; *also, and for n. always,* prē′skript) *adj.* prescribed —*n.* something prescribed; direction; rule

**pre·scrip·tion** (pri skrip′shən) *n.* **1.** a prescribing **2.** something prescribed; order **3.** *a)* a doctor's written direction for the preparation and use of a medicine, the grinding of eyeglass lenses, etc. *b)* a medicine so prescribed —*adj.* made according to, or purchasable only with, a doctor's prescription —**pre·scrip′tive** *adj.* —**pre·scrip′tive·ly** *adv.*

**pres·ence** (prez′′ns) *n.* **1.** the fact or condition of being present **2.** immediate surroundings [*admitted to his presence*] **3.** one that is present, esp. a person of high station or imposing appearance **4.** *a)* a person's bearing, appearance, etc. *b)* poised and confident bearing, as that of a performer before an audience (**stage presence**) **5.** a spirit or ghost felt to be present

**presence of mind** ability to think clearly and act quickly and intelligently in an emergency

**pres·ent** (prez′'nt; *for v.* pri zent′) *adj.* [OFr. < L. *praesens*, prp. of *praeesse* < *prae-*, before + *esse*, to be] **1.** *a)* being at the specified place; in attendance *b)* existing (*in a particular thing*) [nitrogen is *present* in the air] **2.** existing or happening now **3.** now being discussed, considered, etc. [the *present* writer] **4.** *Gram.* indicating action as now taking place (Ex.: he *goes*) or state as now existing (Ex.: the plums *are* ripe), action that is habitual (Ex.: he *speaks* softly), or action that is always true (Ex.: two and two *is* four) —*n.* **1.** the present time **2.** the present occasion **3.** *Gram.* the present tense or a verb in it **4.** [*pl.*] *Law* this very document [know by these *presents*] **5.** something presented, or given; gift —*vt.* [< OFr. < L. *praesentare*, to place in the presence of < *praesens*: see the *adj.*] **1.** to introduce (a person *to* someone) **2.** to offer for viewing or notice; exhibit; show **3.** to offer for consideration **4.** to give (a gift, award, etc.) to (someone) **5.** to hand over, send, etc. (a bill, credentials, etc.) to **6.** to point or aim (a weapon, etc.) —**present arms** *Mil.* **1.** to hold a rifle vertically in front of the body: a position of salute **2.** *a)* this position *b)* the command to assume it —**pre·sent′er** *n.*

**pre·sent·a·ble** (pri zen′tə b'l) *adj.* **1.** that can be presented; fit to be shown, given, etc. to others **2.** properly dressed for meeting people —**pre·sent′a·bil′i·ty, pre·sent′a·ble·ness** *n.* —**pre·sent′a·bly** *adv.*

**pre·sen·ta·tion** (prē′zen tā′shən, prez′'n-) *n.* **1.** a presenting or being presented **2.** something presented, as a theatrical performance, a gift, etc. —**pre′sen·ta′tion·al** *adj.*

**pres·ent-day** (prez′'nt dā′) *adj.* of the present time

**pre·sen·ti·ment** (pri zen′tə mənt) *n.* [MFr. < L.: see PRE- & SENTIMENT] a feeling that something, esp. of an unfortunate nature, is about to take place; foreboding

**pres·ent·ly** (prez′'nt lē) *adv.* **1.** in a little while; soon **2.** at present; now **3.** [Archaic] instantly

**pre·sent·ment** (pri zent′mənt) *n.* **1.** same as PRESENTATION **2.** a grand-jury report of an offense initiated by the jury without their having received a bill of indictment

**present participle** a participle used *a)* with auxiliaries to express present or continuing action or state of being [as *going* in "I am going"] *b)* as an adjective [as *going* in "a going concern"]

**present perfect 1.** a tense indicating an action or state as completed at the time of speaking but not at any definite time in the past **2.** a verb form in this tense (Ex.: has gone)

**pre·ser·va·tive** (pri zur′və tiv) *adj.* preserving —*n.* anything that preserves; esp., a substance added to food to keep it from spoiling

**pre·serve** (pri zurv′) *vt.* **-served′, -serv′ing** [< MFr., ult. < L. *prae-*, before + *servare*, to keep] **1.** to keep from harm, damage, etc.; protect; save **2.** to keep from spoiling or rotting **3.** to prepare (food), as by canning, salting, etc., for future use **4.** to keep up; maintain [to *preserve* liberty] —*vi.* to preserve fruit, etc. —*n.* **1.** [usually *pl.*] fruit preserved whole or in large pieces by cooking with sugar **2.** a place where game, fish, etc. are maintained and protected, esp. for regulated hunting and fishing **3.** the special domain or sphere of some person or group —**pre·serv′a·ble** *adj.* —**pres·er·va·tion** (prez′ər vā′shən) *n.* —**pre·serv′er** *n.*

**pre·set** (prē set′) *vt.* **-set′, -set′ting** to set (the controls of an automatic apparatus) beforehand

**pre-shrunk** (prē′shruŋk′) *adj.* shrunk by a special process in manufacture so as to minimize shrinkage in laundering or dry cleaning

**pre·side** (pri zīd′) *vi.* **-sid′ed, -sid′ing** [< Fr. < L. *praesidere* < *prae-*, before + *sedere*, to sit] **1.** to be in charge of an assembly; act as chairman **2.** to have authority, control, etc. (usually with *over*) —**pre·sid′er** *n.*

**pres·i·den·cy** (prez′i dən sē) *n., pl.* **-cies 1.** the office, function, or term of president **2.** [*often* P-] the office of President of the U.S.

**pres·i·dent** (prez′i dənt) *n.* [< MFr. < L. prp. of *praesidere*: see PRESIDE] **1.** the highest executive officer of a company, society, university, club, etc. **2.** [*often* P-] the chief executive, or sometimes the formal head, of a republic **3.** any presiding officer —**pres′i·den′tial** (-den′shəl) *adj.* —**pres′i·den′tial·ly** *adv.*

**pres·i·dent-e·lect** (-i lekt′) *n.* an elected president who has not yet taken office

**pre·sid·i·o** (pri sid′ē ō′) *n., pl.* **-i·os** [Sp. < L. *praesidium*] a military post, esp. in the SW U.S.

**pre·sid·i·um** (pri sid′ē əm) *n., pl.* **-i·a** (-ə), **-i·ums** [< Russ. < L. *praesidium*, a presiding over] **1.** in the Soviet Union, *a)* any of a number of permanent administrative committees *b)* [P-] the permanent administrative committee of the Supreme Soviet **2.** [P-] a chief administrative committee as in Albania, Romania, etc.

**pre·sig·ni·fy** (prē sig′nə fī′) *vt.* **-fied′, -fy′ing** to indicate beforehand; foreshadow

**press**[1] (pres) *vt.* [< MFr. < L. *pressare*, freq. of *premere* to press] **1.** to act on with steady force or weight; push steadily against; squeeze **2.** to squeeze (juice, etc.) from (grapes, etc.) **3.** *a)* to squeeze so as to make smooth, compact, etc.; compress *b)* to iron (clothes, etc.) with a heavy iron or a steam machine **4.** to embrace closely **5.** to force; compel; constrain **6.** to urge persistently; entreat **7.** to try to force acceptance of [she *pressed* the gift on us] **8.** to lay stress on; emphasize **9.** to distress or trouble [to be *pressed* for time] **10.** to urge on **11.** to shape (a phonograph record, plastic item, etc.), using a form **12.** [Archaic] to crowd; throng **13.** [Obs.] *same as* OPPRESS —*vi.* **1.** to exert pressure; specif., *a)* to weigh down; bear heavily *b)* to go forward with determined effort *c)* to force one's way *d)* to crowd; throng *e)* to be urgent or insistent *f)* to try too hard **2.** to iron clothes, etc. **3.** to undergo pressing in a specified way —*n.* **1.** a pressing or being pressed; pressure, urgency, etc. **2.** a crowd; throng **3.** an instrument or machine by which something is crushed, stamped, smoothed, etc. by pressure **4.** the condition of clothes as to smoothness, creases, etc. after pressing **5.** *a)* clipped form of PRINTING PRESS *b)* a printing or publishing establishment *c)* the art or business of printing *d)* newspapers, magazines, etc. or the persons who write for them *e)* publicity, criticism, etc., as in newspapers **6.** an upright closet for clothes, etc. —**go to press** to start to be printed —**press′er** *n.*

**press**[2] (pres) *vt.* [altered (after prec.) < obs. *prest*, to enlist for military service by advance pay < OFr., ult. < L. *praes*, surety + *stare*, to stand] **1.** to force into service, esp. military or naval service **2.** to use in a way different from the ordinary, esp. in an emergency

**press agent** a person whose work is to get publicity for an individual, organization, etc. —**press′-a′gent·ry** *n.*

**press box** a place reserved for reporters at sports events, etc.

**press conference** a collective interview granted to newsmen as by a celebrity or personage

**press gang** [for *prest gang*: see PRESS[2]] a group who round up others and force them into military or naval service

**press·ing** (pres′iŋ) *adj.* calling for immediate attention; urgent —*n.* something stamped, squeezed, etc. with a press [a *pressing* of phonograph records] —**press′ing·ly** *adv.*

**press·man** (-mən) *n., pl.* **-men 1.** an operator of a printing press **2.** [Brit.] a newspaperman

**press of sail** (or **canvas**) the maximum amount of sail that a ship can safely carry under given conditions

**pres·sure** (presh′ər) *n.* [OFr. < L. *pressura* < pp. of *premere*, to PRESS[1]] **1.** a pressing or being pressed; compression; squeezing **2.** a state of distress or strain **3.** a feeling as though a part of the body is being compressed **4.** a compelling influence [social *pressure*] **5.** pressing demands; urgency **6.** clipped form of: *a)* AIR PRESSURE *b)* BLOOD PRESSURE **7.** *Physics* the force pressing against a surface, expressed in units of force per unit of area —*vt.* **-sured, -sur·ing** to exert pressure on

**pressure cooker** an airtight container for quick cooking by steam under pressure —**pres′sure-cook′** *vt.*

**pressure group** any group exerting pressure on legislators and the public through lobbies, propaganda, etc. to affect legislation, etc.

**pressure suit** a type of G-suit designed to maintain normal respiration and circulation, esp. in spaceflights

**pres·sur·ize** (presh′ər īz′) *vt.* **-ized′, -iz′ing 1.** to keep nearly normal air pressure inside of (an airplane, spacesuit, etc.), as at high altitudes **2.** to subject to high pressure —**pres′sur·i·za′tion** *n.* —**pres′sur·iz′er** *n.*

**press·work** (pres′wurk′) *n.* **1.** the operation of a printing press **2.** work done by a printing press

**pres·ti·dig·i·ta·tion** (pres′tə dij′i tā′shən) *n.* [Fr. < *preste* < It. *presto*, quick + L. *digitus*, a finger] the doing of tricks by quick, skillful use of the hands; sleight of hand —**pres′ti·dig′i·ta′tor** *n.*

**pres·tige** (pres tēzh′, -tēj′) *n.* [Fr. < LL. *praestigium*, illusion, ult. < L. *praestringere*, to blind] **1.** the power to impress or influence, as because of success, wealth, etc. **2.** reputation based on high achievement, character, etc. —**pres·tige′ful, pres·ti′gious** (-tij′əs, -tē′jəs) *adj.*

**pres·tis·si·mo** (pres tis′ə mō′) *adv., adj.* [It., superl. of *presto*: see ff.] *Music* very fast —*n., pl.* **-mos** a prestissimo passage or movement

**pres·to** (pres′tō) *adv., adj.* [It., quick < L. *praestus*, ready] **1.** fast **2.** *Music* in fast tempo —*n., pl.* **-tos** *Music* a presto passage or movement

**pre-stressed concrete** (prē′strest′) concrete containing steel cables, wires, etc. under tension to produce compressive stress and lend greater strength

**pre·sume** (pri zōōm′, -zyōōm′) *vt.* **-sumed′, -sum′ing** [< OFr. < L. < *prae-*, before + *sumere*, to take] **1.** to take upon oneself without permission or authority; dare (to say or do something); venture **2.** to take for granted, lacking proof; suppose **3.** to constitute reasonable evidence for supposing [a signed invoice *presumes* receipt of goods]

—*vi.* **1.** to act presumptuously; take liberties **2.** to rely too much (*on* or *upon*), as in taking liberties —**pre·sum′a·ble** *adj.* —**pre·sum′a·bly** *adv.* —**pre·sum′ed·ly** *adv.*

**pre·sump·tion** (pri zump′shən) *n.* **1.** a presuming; specif., *a*) an overstepping of proper bounds; effrontery *b*) a taking of something for granted **2.** the thing presumed; supposition **3.** a ground or reason for presuming **4.** *Law* the inference that a fact exists, based on other known facts

**pre·sump·tive** (-tiv) *adj.* **1.** giving reasonable ground for belief [*presumptive* evidence] **2.** based on probability; presumed [an heir *presumptive*] —**pre·sump′tive·ly** *adv.*

**pre·sump·tu·ous** (-choo wəs) *adj.* too bold or forward; overstepping proper bounds; showing presumption —**pre·sump′tu·ous·ly** *adv.* —**pre·sump′tu·ous·ness** *n.*

**pre·sup·pose** (prē′sə pōz′) *vt.* -posed′, -pos′ing **1.** to suppose or assume beforehand; take for granted **2.** to require or imply as a preceding condition —**pre′sup·po·si′tion** (-sup ə zish′ən) *n.*

**pret.** preterit

**pre·tend** (pri tend′) *vt.* [< MFr. < L. < *prae-*, before + *tendere*, to stretch] **1.** to claim; profess [to *pretend* ignorance of the law] **2.** to claim or profess falsely; feign [to *pretend* illness] **3.** to make believe, as in play [to *pretend* to be astronauts] —*vi.* **1.** to lay claim (with *to*) **2.** to make believe in play or deception —**pre·tend′ed** *adj.*

**pre·tend·er** (-ten′dər) *n.* **1.** a person who pretends **2.** a person who lays claim to something, esp. to a throne

**pre·tense** (pri tens′, prē′tens) *n.* [< Anglo-Fr., ult. < L. pp. of *praetendere*: see PRETEND] **1.** a claim; pretension [making no *pretense* to being rich] **2.** a false claim or profession [a *pretense* of friendship] **3.** a false show of something **4.** a pretending, as at play; make-believe **5.** a pretext **6.** pretentiousness Also, Brit. sp., **pretence**

**pre·ten·sion** (pri ten′shən) *n.* [< ML. < L.: see prec.] **1.** a pretext or allegation **2.** a claim, as to a right, title, etc. **3.** assertion of a claim **4.** pretentiousness

**pre·ten·tious** (-shəs) *adj.* [< Fr.] claiming or pretending to be more important, elegant, etc. than is really so; affectedly grand; ostentatious —**pre·ten′tious·ly** *adv.* —**pre·ten′tious·ness** *n.*

**pret·er·it, pret·er·ite** (pret′ər it) *adj.* [< MFr. < L. pp. of *praeterire* < *praeter-*, beyond + *ire*, to go] *Gram.* expressing past action or state —*n.* **1.** the past tense **2.** a verb in this tense

**pre·ter·mit** (prēt′ər mit′) *vt.* -mit′ted, -mit′ting [< L. < *praeter-*, beyond + *mittere*, to send] to neglect, omit, or overlook —**pre′ter·mis′sion** *n.*

**pre·ter·nat·u·ral** (-nach′ər əl) *adj.* [< ML. < L. *praeter-*, beyond + *naturalis*, natural] **1.** differing from or beyond what is natural; abnormal **2.** *same as* SUPERNATURAL —**pre′ter·nat′u·ral·ism** *n.* —**pre′ter·nat′u·ral·ly** *adv.*

**pre·test** (prē′test′; *for v.* prē′test′) *n.* a preliminary test, as of a product —*vt., vi.* to test in advance

**pre·text** (prē′tekst) *n.* [< L. pp. of *praetexere*, to pretend: see PRE- & TEXTURE] **1.** a false reason or motive put forth to hide the real one; excuse **2.** a cover-up; front

**pre·tor** (prēt′ər) *n. same as* PRAETOR —**pre·to·ri·al** (pri-tôr′ē əl) *adj.* —**pre·to′ri·an** *adj., n.*

**Pre·to·ri·a** (pri tôr′ē ə) capital of the Transvaal & the seat of the government of South Africa: pop. 493,000

**pre·tri·al** (prē′trī′əl) *adj.* occurring, presented, etc. before a court trial begins [a *pretrial* motion]

**pret·ti·fy** (prit′ə fī′) *vt.* -fied′, -fy′ing to make pretty

**pret·ty** (prit′ē, pur′tē) *adj.* -ti·er, -ti·est [< OE. *prætig*, crafty < *prætt*, a trick] **1.** pleasing or attractive, esp. in a light, dainty, or graceful way **2.** *a*) fine; nice: often used ironically [a *pretty* fix] *b*) skillful [a *pretty* move] **3.** [Colloq.] considerable; quite large [a *pretty* price] —*adv.* **1.** fairly; somewhat; quite [*pretty* sure] **2.** [Colloq.] prettily [to talk *pretty*] —*n., pl.* -ties a pretty person or thing —*vt.* -tied, -ty·ing to make pretty (usually with *up*) —sitting pretty [Slang] in a favorable position —**pret′ti·ly** *adv.* —**pret′ti·ness** *n.* —**pret′ty·ish** *adj.*

**pret·zel** (pret′s'l) *n.* [G. *brezel* < OHG., ult. < L. *brachium*, an arm] a hard, brittle biscuit usually in the form of a loose knot or stick, sprinkled with salt

**pre·vail** (pri vāl′) *vi.* [< L. < *prae-*, before + *valere*, to be strong] **1.** to gain the advantage or mastery; be victorious (*over* or *against*) **2.** to be effective; succeed **3.** to be or become stronger or more widespread; predominate **4.** to exist widely; be prevalent —**prevail on** (or **upon, with**) to persuade; induce

PRETZEL

**pre·vail·ing** (-iŋ) *adj.* **1.** superior in strength, influence, or effect **2.** most frequent; predominant **3.** widely existing; prevalent —**pre·vail′ing·ly** *adv.*

**prev·a·lent** (prev′ə lənt) *adj.* [see PREVAIL] **1.** [Rare] dominant **2.** widely existing, practiced, or accepted; common —**prev′a·lence** *n.* —**prev′a·lent·ly** *adv.*

**pre·var·i·cate** (pri var′ə kāt′) *vi.* -cat′ed, -cat′ing [< L. pp. of *praevaricari*, lit., to walk crookedly < *prae-*, before + *varicare*, to straddle, ult. < *varus*, bent] **1.** to turn aside from, or evade, the truth; equivocate **2.** to tell an untruth; lie —**pre·var′i·ca′tion** *n.* —**pre·var′i·ca′tor** *n.*

**pre·vent** (pri vent′) *vt.* [< L. pp. of *praevenire* < *prae-*, before + *venire*, to come] **1.** to stop or keep (*from* doing something) **2.** to keep from happening; make impossible by prior action; hinder —**pre·vent′a·ble, pre·vent′i·ble** *adj.* —**pre·vent′er** *n.*

**pre·ven·tion** (pri ven′shən) *n.* **1.** a preventing **2.** [Now Rare] a means of preventing; preventive

**pre·ven·tive** (-tiv) *adj.* preventing or serving to prevent; esp., preventing disease —*n.* anything that prevents; esp., anything that prevents disease; prophylactic Also **pre·vent′a·tive** —**pre·ven′tive·ly** *adv.* —**pre·ven′tive·ness** *n.*

**pre·view** (prē′vyoō) *vt.* to view or show beforehand —*n.* **1.** a previous or preliminary view or survey **2.** *a*) a restricted showing, as of a movie, before exhibition to the public generally *b*) a showing of scenes from a movie, TV show, etc. to advertise it

**pre·vi·ous** (prē′vē əs) *adj.* [< L. < *prae-*, before + *via*, a way] **1.** occurring before in time or order; prior **2.** [Colloq.] too soon; premature —**previous to** before —**pre′vi·ous·ly** *adv.*

**previous question** the question, put as a motion, whether a matter under consideration by a parliamentary body should be voted on immediately

**pre·vi·sion** (prē vizh′ən) *n.* [< Fr. < ML. < L. pp. of *praevidere* < *prae-*, before + *videre*, to see] **1.** foresight or foreknowledge **2.** a prediction or prophecy —*vt.* to foresee —**pre·vi′sion·al, pre·vi′sion·ar′y** *adj.*

**pre·vue** (prē′vyoō) *n. same as* PREVIEW (esp. sense 2)

**pre·war** (prē′wôr′) *adj.* before a (or the) war

**prex·y** (prek′sē) *n., pl.* **prex′ies** [Slang] the president, esp. of a college, etc.

**prey** (prā) *n.* [OFr. *preie* < L. *praeda*] **1.** orig., plunder; booty **2.** an animal hunted for food by another animal **3.** a person or thing that falls victim to someone or something **4.** the mode of living by preying on other animals [a bird of *prey*] —*vi.* **1.** to plunder; rob **2.** to hunt other animals for food **3.** to profit by swindling **4.** to have a wearing or destructive influence Generally used with *on* or *upon* —**prey′er** *n.*

**Pri·am** (prī′əm) *Gr. Legend* the last king of Troy, who reigned during the Trojan War: father of Hector and Paris

**pri·ap·ic** (prī āp′ik) *adj.* [< PRIAPUS + -IC] **1.** *same as* PHALLIC **2.** overly concerned with one's virility

**Pri·a·pus** (prī ā′pəs) [L. < Gr.] *Gr. & Rom. Myth.* the god personifying the male procreative power

**price** (prīs) *n.* [< OFr. < L. *pretium*] **1.** the amount of money, etc. asked or paid for something; cost **2.** value or worth **3.** a reward for the capture or death of a person **4.** the cost, as in life, labor, etc., of obtaining some benefit —*vt.* priced, pric′ing **1.** to fix the price of **2.** [Colloq.] to ask or find out the price of —at any price no matter what the cost —beyond (or without) price priceless; invaluable —**pric′er** *n.*

**price control** the setting of ceiling prices on basic commodities by a government, as to fight inflation

**price index** *see* INDEX (sense 5 b)

**price·less** (prīs′lis) *adj.* **1.** too valuable to be measured by price **2.** [Colloq.] very amusing or absurd

**prick** (prik) *n.* [OE. *prica*, a dot] **1.** a very small puncture or dot made by a sharp point **2.** [Archaic] a pointed object, as a thorn **3.** a pricking **4.** a sharp pain caused as by being pricked —*vt.* **1.** to make (a tiny hole) in (something) with a sharp point **2.** to pain sharply [*pricked* by remorse] **3.** to mark by dots, points, or punctures **4.** to cause to point or stick up (with *up*) **5.** [Archaic] to goad —*vi.* **1.** to cause or feel a slight, sharp pain **2.** to point or stick up: said esp. of ears —prick up one's ears to listen closely —**prick′er** *n.*

**prick·le** (prik′'l) *n.* [OE. *pricel* < base of *prica*, prick] **1.** any sharp point; specif., a thornlike process on a plant **2.** a prickly sensation; tingling —*vt.* -led, -ling **1.** to prick as with a thorn **2.** to cause to feel a tingling sensation —*vi.* to tingle

**prick·ly** (-lē) *adj.* -li·er, -li·est **1.** full of prickles **2.** stinging; tingling —**prick′li·ness** *n.*

**prickly heat** an itching skin disease with small eruptions caused by inflammation of the sweat glands

**prickly pear 1.** any of various cactus plants, some of

which have barbed spines **2.** its pear-shaped, edible fruit
**pride** (prīd) *n.* [OE. *pryte* < *prut*, proud] **1.** *a)* an overhigh
opinion of oneself; exaggerated self-esteem *b)* haughtiness;
arrogance **2.** a sense of one's own dignity; self-respect **3.**
delight or satisfaction in one's achievements, one's children, etc. **4.** a person or thing that one is proud of **5.** the
best of a class, group, etc.; pick **6.** the best part; prime *[in
the pride of manhood]* **7.** *a)* a group or family (of lions) *b)*
[Colloq.] any impressive group —*vt.* prid′ed, prid′ing [Rare]
to make proud —**pride oneself on** to be proud of —**pride′ful**
*adj.* —**pride′ful·ly** *adv.* —**pride′ful·ness** *n.*
**prie-dieu** (prē′dyōō′) *n.* [Fr. < *prier*, to pray + *dieu*, God] a
narrow, upright frame with a ledge for kneeling on at
prayer and an upper ledge, as for a book
**pri·er** (prī′ər) *n.* a person who pries
**priest** (prēst) *n.* [OE. *preost* < LL. *presbyter*, an elder < Gr.
< *presbys*, old] **1.** a person whose function is to make sac-
rificial offerings and perform other religious rites **2.** in
some Christian churches, a clergyman authorized to administer the sacraments **3.** any clergyman —**priest′hood′** *n.*
—**priest′li·ness** *n.* —**priest′ly** *adj.* -li·er, -li·est
**priest·ess** (prēs′tis) *n.* a girl or woman priest, esp. of a
pagan religion
**Priest·ley** (prēst′lē), **Joseph** 1733–1804; Eng. scientist &
theologian: discoverer of oxygen
**prig** (prig) *n.* [< 16th-c. slang] an annoying person who is
excessively proper and smug in his moral behavior and attitudes —**prig′ger·y, prig′gism** *n.* —**prig′gish** *adj.* —**prig′-
gish·ly** *adv.* —**prig′gish·ness** *n.*
**prim** (prim) *adj.* **prim′mer, prim′mest** [< ? MFr. *prim*,
prime, sharp, neat < L. *primus*, first] stiffly formal, precise,
moral, etc.; proper; demure —*vt., vi.* primmed, prim′ming
to get a prim look on (one's face or mouth) —**prim′ly** *adv.*
—**prim′ness** *n.*
**prim.** 1. primary **2.** primitive
**pri·ma ballerina** (prē′mə) [It., lit., first ballerina] the principal woman dancer in a ballet company
**pri·ma·cy** (prī′mə sē) *n., pl.* -cies [< MFr. < ML. < LL.
*primas*: see PRIMATE] **1.** the state of being first in time,
order, rank, etc. **2.** the rank or authority of a primate
**pri·ma don·na** (prē′mə dän′ə, prim′ə) *pl.* **pri′ma don′nas**
[It., lit., first lady] **1.** the principal woman singer, as in an
opera **2.** [Colloq.] a temperamental or arrogant person
**pri·ma fa·ci·e** (prī′mə fā′shi ē′, fā′shē) [L.] at first sight:
used to designate legal evidence (**prima facie evidence**) that
is enough to establish a fact unless refuted
**pri·mal** (prī′m'l) *adj.* [< ML. < L. *primus*, first] **1.** first in
time; original **2.** first in importance; chief
**primal therapy** a treatment of mental disorder in which the
patient, often in group sessions, is induced to reenact his
infancy and to express his emotions violently in screams,
shouts, etc.: also **primal scream (therapy)**
**pri·ma·quine** (prī′mə kwēn′) *n.* a synthetic chemical compound, $C_{15}H_{21}N_3O$, used as a cure for malaria
**pri·ma·ri·ly** (prī mer′ə lē, prī′mer′-) *adv.* **1.** at first; originally **2.** mainly; principally
**pri·ma·ry** (prī′mer′ē, -mər ē) *adj.* [< L. *primarius* < *primus*,
first] **1.** first in time or order of development; primitive;
original **2.** *a)* from which others are derived; fundamental
*b)* designating colors regarded as basic, from which all
others may be derived: see COLOR (*n.* 2 & 3) **3.** first in importance; chief; principal *[a primary concern]* **4.**
firsthand; direct *[a primary source of information]* **5.** *Elec.*
designating or of an inducing current, input circuit, or
input coil in a transformer, etc. **6.** *Zool.* of the large feathers on the end joint of a bird's wing —*n., pl.* -ries **1.** something first in order, quality, etc. **2.** in the U.S., *a)* a local
meeting of voters of a given political party to nominate
candidates for public office, etc. *b)* same as DIRECT PRI-
MARY ELECTION **3.** any of the primary colors **4.** *Elec.* a primary coil **5.** *Zool.* a primary feather
**primary accent (or stress)** **1.** the heavier stress or force
given to one syllable in a spoken word or to one word in an
utterance **2.** the mark to show this (′)
**primary cell** a battery cell whose energy is derived from an
essentially irreversible electrochemical reaction
**primary school** same as ELEMENTARY SCHOOL
**pri·mate** (prī′māt; *also, for 1,* -mit) *n.* [< OFr. < LL. *primas*
(gen. *primatis*), chief < L. *primus*, first] **1.** an archbishop,
or the highest-ranking bishop in a province, etc. **2.** any of
an order of mammals, including man, the apes, monkeys,
etc. —**pri′mate·ship′** *n.* —**pri·ma′tial** (prī mā′shəl) *adj.*
**prime** (prīm) *adj.* [MFr. < L. *primus*, first < OL. *pri*, before]
**1.** first in time; original; primitive **2.** first in rank; chief
*[prime minister]* **3.** first in importance; principal *[a prime
advantage]* **4.** first in quality; first-rate *[prime beef]* **5.**
from which others are derived; fundamental **6.** *Finance*
designating the most favorable interest rate on bank loans
**7.** *Math. a)* of or being a prime number *b)* having no factor
in common except 1 *[9 and 16 are prime to each other]* —*n.*

[OE. *prim* < L. *prima* (*hora*), first (hour): see the *adj.*] **1.**
[*often* P-] the first daylight canonical hour **2.** the first or
earliest part; dawn, springtime, youth, etc. **3.** *a)* the best or
most vigorous period or stage of a person or thing *b)* the
best part; pick **4.** *a)* any of a number of equal parts, usually sixty, into which a unit, as a degree, is divided *b)* the
mark (′) indicating this: it is also used to distinguish a letter, etc. from another of the same kind, as A′ **5.** *Math.*
same as PRIME NUMBER **6.** *Music* same as UNISON —*vt.*
primed, prim′ing **1.** to make ready; prepare **2.** to prepare
(a gun) for firing or (a charge) for exploding by providing
with priming or a primer **3.** *a)* to get (a pump) into operation by pouring in water *b)* to get (an empty carburetor)
into operation by pouring in gasoline **4.** to undercoat, size,
etc. (a surface) for painting **5.** to provide (a person)
beforehand with information, answers, etc. —*vi.* to prime a
person or thing —**prime′ness** *n.*
**prime meridian** the meridian from which longitude is measured east and west; 0° longitude: see GREENWICH TIME
**prime minister** in parliamentary governments, the chief executive and, usually, head of the cabinet —**prime ministry**
**prime number** an integer that can be evenly divided by no
other whole number than itself and 1, as 2, 3, 5, or 7
**prim·er**[1] (prim′ər; *Brit.* prī′mər) *n.* [< ML. < L. *primus*,
first] **1.** a simple book for first teaching children to read **2.**
a textbook giving the first principles of any subject
**prim·er**[2] (prī′mər) *n.* a person or thing that primes; specif.,
*a)* a small cap, tube, etc. containing an explosive, used to
set off the main charge *b)* a preliminary coat of paint, etc.
**prime time** *Radio & TV* the hours, esp. the evening hours,
when the largest audience is readily available
**pri·me·val** (prī mē′v'l) *adj.* [< L. *primaevus* (< primus, first
+ *aevum*, an age) + -AL] of the earliest times or ages; pri-
mordial —**pri·me′val·ly** *adv.*
**prim·ing** (prī′miŋ) *n.* **1.** the explosive used to set off the
charge in a gun, etc. **2.** paint, sizing, etc. used as a primer
**prim·i·tive** (prim′ə tiv) *adj.* [< MFr. < L. *primitivus* <
*primus*, first] **1.** of or existing in the earliest times or ages;
original **2.** *a)* characteristic of the earliest ages *b)* crude,
simple, etc. **3.** not derivative; primary —*n.* **1.** a primitive
person or thing **2.** *a)* an artist or a work of art of an early
culture *b)* an artist or a work of art characterized by lack of
formal training —**prim′i·tive·ly** *adv.* —**prim′i·tive·ness** *n.*
**prim·i·tiv·ism** (-iz′m) *n.* **1.** belief in or practice of primitive ways, living, etc. **2.** the qualities, etc. of primitive art
or artists —**prim′i·tiv·ist** *n., adj.*
**pri·mo·gen·i·tor** (prī′mə jen′i tər) *n.* [LL. < L. *primus*,
first + *genitor*, a father] **1.** an ancestor; forefather **2.** the
earliest ancestor of a family, race, etc.
**pri·mo·gen·i·ture** (-chər) *n.* [< ML. < L. *primus*, first +
*genitura*, a begetting] **1.** the condition or fact of being the
firstborn of the same parents **2.** *Law* the exclusive right of
the eldest son to inherit his father's estate
**pri·mor·di·al** (prī môr′dē əl) *adj.* [< LL. < L. *primordium*,
the beginning < *primus*, first + *ordiri*, to begin] **1.** existing
at or from the beginning; primitive **2.** fundamental; original —**pri·mor′di·al·ly** *adv.*
**primp** (primp) *vt., vi.* [prob. extension of PRIM] to groom or
dress up in a fussy way
**prim·rose** (prim′rōz′) *n.* [< MFr. altered (after *rose*, ROSE[1])
< OFr. *primerole* < ML. *primula* < L. *primus*, first] **1.** any
of a number of related plants having variously colored,
tubelike flowers: also **prim′u·la** (-yoo lə) **2.** the flower of
any of these plants **3.** the light yellow of some primroses —
*adj.* **1.** of the primrose **2.** light-yellow
**primrose path** [cf. *Hamlet* I, iii] the path of pleasure, self-
indulgence, etc.
**prin.** 1. principal **2.** principle
**prince** (prins) *n.* [OFr. < L. *princeps*, chief < *primus*, first +
*capere*, to take] **1.** orig., any male monarch; esp., a king **2.**
a ruler whose rank is below that of a king; head of a principality **3.** a nonreigning male member of a royal family
**4.** in Great Britain, a son or grandson of the sovereign **5.**
*a)* a preeminent person in any class or group *[a merchant
prince]* *b)* [Colloq.] a fine, generous, helpful fellow —
**prince′dom** *n.*
**Prince Albert** a long, double-breasted frock coat
**prince consort** the husband of a queen or empress reigning
in her own right
**Prince Edward Island** island province of SE Canada, in
the Gulf of St. Lawrence: 2,184 sq. mi.; pop. 118,000; cap.
Charlottetown: abbrev. **P.E.I.**
**prince·ling** (prins′liŋ) *n.* a young, small, or subordinate
prince: also **prince′kin, prince′let**
**prince·ly** (-lē) *adj.* -li·er, -li·est **1.** of a prince; royal **2.**
characteristic or worthy of a prince; magnificent; generous
**Prince of Darkness** *a name sometimes given to* SATAN
**Prince of Peace** *a name sometimes given to* JESUS
**Prince of Wales** *title conferred on* the oldest son and heir
apparent of a British king or queen

**prin·cess¹** (prin′sis, -ses) *n.* **1.** orig., any female monarch **2.** a nonreigning female member of a royal family **3.** in Great Britain, a daughter of the sovereign or of a son of the sovereign **4.** the wife of a prince

**prin·cess²** (prin′sis, prin ses′) *adj.* [< Fr. *princesse*, a princess] of or designating a woman's one-piece, closefitting, gored dress, etc.: also **prin·cesse′** (-ses′)

**Prince·ton** (prins′tən) [after the *Prince* of Orange, later WILLIAM III] borough in C N.J., near Trenton: scene of a battle of the Revolutionary War: pop. 12,000

**prin·ci·pal** (prin′sə pəl) *adj.* [OFr. < L. *principalis* < *princeps:* see PRINCE] **1.** first in rank, authority, importance, etc. **2.** that is or has to do with principal (n. 3) —*n.* **1.** a principal person or thing; specif., *a)* a chief; head *b)* a governing officer, as of a school *c)* a main actor or other kind of performer **2.** any of the main end rafters of a roof **3.** *Finance a)* the amount of a debt, investment, etc. minus the interest *b)* the face value of a stock or bond *c)* the main portion of an estate, etc., as distinguished from income **4.** *Law a)* one who employs another to act as his agent *b)* the one primarily responsible for an obligation *c)* one who commits a crime: cf. ACCESSORY —**prin′ci·pal·ly** *adv.* —**prin′ci·pal·ship′** *n.*

**prin·ci·pal·i·ty** (prin′sə pal′ə tē) *n., pl.* -ties **1.** the rank, dignity, or jurisdiction of a prince **2.** the territory ruled by a prince

**principal parts** the principal inflected forms of a verb, from which the other forms may be derived: in English, they are the present infinitive, the past tense, the past participle, and, sometimes, the present participle (Ex.: *drink, drank, drunk, drinking; go, went, gone, going*)

**Prin·ci·pe** (prin′sə pē′; *Port.* prēn′sə pə) see SÃO TOMÉ

**prin·ci·ple** (prin′sə pəl) *n.* [< MFr. < L. *principium* < *princeps:* see PRINCE] **1.** the ultimate source or cause **2.** a natural or original tendency, faculty, etc. **3.** a fundamental truth, law, etc., upon which others are based *[moral principles]* **4.** *a)* a rule of conduct *b)* such rules collectively *c)* adherence to them; integrity *[a man of principle]* **5.** an essential element or quality *[the active principle of a medicine]* **6.** *a)* the scientific law that explains a natural action *[the principle of cell division]* *b)* the method of a thing's operation —**in principle** theoretically or in essence

**prin·ci·pled** (-pəld) *adj.* having or based on principles, as of conduct

**prink** (priŋk) *vt., vi.* [prob. < PRANK²] *same as* PRIMP

**print** (print) *n.* [< OFr. < pp. of *preindre* < L. *premere*, to PRESS¹] **1.** a mark made on a surface by pressing or hitting with an object; imprint *[the print of a heel]* **2.** an object for making such a mark, as a stamp, die, etc. **3.** a cloth printed with a design, or a dress, blouse, etc. made of this **4.** the condition of being printed **5.** printed lettering **6.** the impression made by inked type **7.** a picture or design printed from a plate, block, etc., as an etching or lithograph **8.** printed material *[newsprint]* **9.** a photograph, esp. one made from a negative —*vt.* **1.** to make a print on or in **2.** to stamp or draw, trace, etc. (a mark, letter, etc.) on or in a surface **3.** to produce on (paper, etc.) the impression of inked type, plates, etc. by means of a printing press **4.** to produce (a book, etc.) by typesetting, presswork, etc. **5.** to publish in print *[to print a story]* **6.** to write in letters resembling printed ones **7.** to produce (a photograph) from (a negative) **8.** in computers, to deliver (information) by means of a printer: often with *out* **9.** to impress upon the mind, memory, etc. —*vi.* **1.** to practice the trade of a printer **2.** to produce an impression, photograph, etc. **3.** to write in letters resembling printed ones **4.** to produce newspapers, books, etc. by means of a printing press —**in** (or **out of**) **print** still (or no longer) for sale by the publisher: said of books, etc. —**print′a·ble** *adj.*

**printed circuit** an electrical circuit formed by applying conductive material in fine lines or other shapes to an insulating surface

**print·er** (-ər) *n.* **1.** one whose work or business is printing **2.** a device that prints; esp., in computers, a device that produces information in printed form

**printer's devil** an apprentice in a printing shop

**print·ing** (-iŋ) *n.* **1.** the act of a person or thing that prints **2.** the production of printed matter **3.** the art of a printer **4.** something printed **5.** *same as* IMPRESSION (sense 5 *b*) **6.** written letters made like printed ones

**printing press** a machine for printing from inked type, plates, or rolls

**print·out** (-out′) *n.* the output of a computer presented in printed or typewritten form

**print shop 1.** a shop where printing is done: also **printing office 2.** a shop where prints, etchings, etc. are sold

**pri·or** (prī′ər) *adj.* [L., former, superior] **1.** preceding in time; earlier **2.** preceding in order or importance *[a prior choice]* —*n.* [OE. & OFr., both < ML. < L.] **1.** the head of a priory **2.** in an abbey, the person in charge next below the abbot —**prior to** before in time —**pri′or·ate** (-it), **pri′or·ship′** *n.* —**pri′or·ess** *n.fem.*

**pri·or·i·tize** (prī ôr′ə tīz′, -är′-) *vt.* -tized′, -tiz′ing **1.** to arrange (items) in order of priority **2.** to assign (an item) to a particular level of priority

**pri·or·i·ty** (prī ôr′ə tē, -är′-) *n., pl.* -ties **1.** a being prior; precedence **2.** *a)* a right to precedence over others in obtaining, buying, or doing something *b)* an order granting this **3.** something given or to be given prior attention

**pri·o·ry** (prī′ər ē) *n., pl.* -ries a monastery governed by a prior, or a convent governed by a prioress

**Pris·cil·la** (pri sil′ə) [L., ult. < *priscus*, ancient] a feminine name

**prise** (prīz) *vt.* prised, pris′ing [Chiefly Brit.] to prize, or pry, as with a lever

**prism** (priz′m) *n.* [< LL. < Gr. *prisma*, lit., something sawed < *prizein*, to saw] **1.** a solid figure whose ends are equal and parallel polygons and whose sides are parallelograms **2.** anything that refracts light, as a drop of water **3.** *Optics a)* a transparent body, as of glass, whose ends are equal and parallel triangles, and whose three sides are parallelograms: used for refracting or dispersing light, as into the spectrum *b)* any similar body of three or more sides

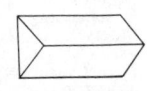
TRIANGULAR
PRISM

**pris·mat·ic** (priz mat′ik) *adj.* **1.** of or like a prism **2.** that refracts light as a prism **3.** that forms prismatic colors **4.** many-colored; brilliant —**pris·mat′i·cal·ly** *adv.*

**prismatic colors** the colors of the visible spectrum; red, orange, yellow, green, blue, indigo, and violet

**pris·on** (priz′'n) *n.* [OFr. < L. *prensio*, for *prehensio* < *prehendere*, to take] **1.** a place where persons are confined **2.** a building, usually with cells, where persons convicted by trial or awaiting trial are confined; specif., such a building maintained by a State or the Federal government **3.** imprisonment

**pris·on·er** (priz′nər, -'n ər) *n.* **1.** a person confined in prison, as for some crime **2.** a person held in custody **3.** a person captured or held captive *[a prisoner of love]*

**prisoner of war** a member of the regular or irregular armed forces of a nation at war held captive by the enemy

**pris·sy** (pris′ē) *adj.* -si·er, -si·est [prob. PR(IM) + (S)ISSY] [Colloq.] very prim or precise; fussy, prudish, etc. —**pris′si·ly** *adv.* —**pris′si·ness** *n.*

**pris·tine** (pris′tēn, -tin; pris tēn′) *adj.* [L. *pristinus*, former] **1.** characteristic of the earliest period or condition; original **2.** still pure; uncorrupted; unspoiled *[pristine beauty]* —**pris′tine·ly** *adv.*

**prith·ee** (prith′ē) *interj.* [< *pray thee*] [Archaic] I pray thee; please

**pri·va·cy** (prī′və sē; *Brit. also* priv′ə-) *n., pl.* -cies **1.** the quality or condition of being private; withdrawal from public view **2.** secrecy *[told in strict privacy]* **3.** one's private life or personal affairs *[an invasion of one's privacy]*

**pri·vate** (prī′vit) *adj.* [< L. *privatus*, belonging to oneself, ult. < *privus*, separate] **1.** of or concerning only one particular person or group; not general *[private property, his private affairs]* **2.** not open to or controlled by the public *[a private school]* **3.** for an individual person *[a private room]* **4.** not holding public office *[a private citizen]* **5.**, away from public view; secluded *[a private dining room]* **6.** secret; confidential *[a private matter]* **7.** not connected with an institution or organization; independent *[private medical practice; a private detective]* —*n.* an enlisted man of either of the two lowest ranks in the U.S. Army or of the lowest rank in the U.S. Marine Corps —**in private** not publicly —**pri′vate·ly** *adv.*

**private enterprise** *same as* FREE ENTERPRISE

**pri·va·teer** (prī′və tir′) *n.* [< PRIVAT(E) + -EER] **1.** a privately owned and manned armed ship commissioned in a war to attack and capture enemy ships, esp. merchant ships **2.** a commander or crew member of a privateer: also **pri′va·teers′man,** *pl.* -men —*vi.* to sail as a privateer

**private eye** [Slang] a private detective

**private first class** an enlisted man ranking just below a corporal in the U.S. Army and just below a lance corporal in the U.S. Marine Corps

**pri·va·tion** (prī vā′shən) *n.* [< L. *privatio:* see PRIVATE] **1.** deprivation; the loss or absence of some quality or condition **2.** lack of the ordinary necessities of life

**priv·a·tive** (priv′ə tiv) *adj.* **1.** depriving or tending to deprive **2.** *Gram.* indicating negation, absence, or loss —*n. Gram.* a privative term or affix, as *a-, un-, non-*, or *-less* —**priv′a·tive·ly** *adv.*

**priv·et** (priv′it) *n.* [< ?] any of various shrubs of the olive family, with bluish-black berries and white flowers

**priv·i·lege** (priv′'l ij, priv′lij) *n.* [< OFr. < L. *privilegium*, a law for or against an individual < *privus*, separate + *lex* (gen. *legis*), a law] **1.** a right, advantage, favor, etc. specially granted to a certain person, group, or class **2.** a basic civil right, guaranteed by a government [the *privilege* of trial by jury] —*vt.* **-leged, -leg·ing** to grant a privilege to

**priv·y** (priv′ē) *adj.* [< OFr. < L. *privatus*, PRIVATE] **1.** orig., private; personal **2.** [Archaic] hidden, secret, etc. —*n., pl.* **priv′ies** a toilet; esp., an outhouse —**privy to** privately informed about —**priv′i·ly** *adv.*

**privy council** a body of advisers or confidential counselors appointed by or serving a ruler —**privy councilor**

**privy seal** in Great Britain, the seal placed on documents which later receive the great seal or which are not important enough to receive it

**prize[1]** (prīz) *vt.* **prized, priz′ing** [see PRICE] **1.** formerly, to price or appraise **2.** to value highly; esteem —*n.* **1.** something offered or given to the winner of a contest, lottery, etc. **2.** a reward, premium, etc. **3.** anything worth striving for; any highly valued possession —*adj.* **1.** that has received a prize **2.** worthy of a prize **3.** given as a prize

**prize[2]** (prīz) *n.* [< OFr. *prise*, fem. pp. of *prendre* < L. *prehendere*, to take] something taken by force, as in war; esp., a captured enemy warship —*vt.* **prized, priz′ing 1.** to seize as a prize of war **2.** to pry, as with a lever

**prize court** a court that decides how captured property, esp. that taken at sea in wartime, is to be distributed

**prize·fight** (prīz′fīt′) *n.* a professional boxing match —**prize′fight′er** *n.* —**prize′fight′ing** *n.*

**prize ring 1.** a square platform, enclosed by ropes, for prizefights **2.** prizefighting

**pro[1]** (prō) *adv.* [L., for] on the affirmative side; favorably —*adj.* favorable —*prep.* in favor of; for —*n., pl.* **pros** a reason, vote, position, etc. in favor of something

**pro[2]** (prō) *adj., n., pl.* **pros** *short form of* PROFESSIONAL

**pro-[1]** [Gr. < *pro*, before] *a prefix meaning* before in place or time [*proboscis*]

**pro-[2]** [L. < *pro*, forward] *a prefix meaning:* **1.** forward or ahead [*progress*] **2.** forth [*produce*] **3.** substituting for, acting for [*pronoun*] **4.** supporting, favoring [*prolabor*]

**pro·a** (prō′ə) *n.* [Malay *prau*] a Malayan boat having a triangular sail and one outrigger

**prob. 1.** probable **2.** probably **3.** problem

**prob·a·bil·i·ty** (präb′ə-bil′ə tē) *n., pl.* **-ties 1.** the quality or state of being probable; likelihood **2.** a probable thing or event **3.** *Math.* the ratio of the number of times a particular event can occur to the total number of likely events involved —**in all probability** very likely

PROA

**prob·a·ble** (präb′ə b'l) *adj.* [MFr. < L. < *probare*, to prove] **1.** likely to occur or be; that can reasonably but not certainly be expected [the *probable* winner] **2.** reasonably so, as on the basis of evidence, but not proved [the *probable* cause of a disease] —**prob′a·bly** *adv.*

**pro·bate** (prō′bāt) *n.* [< L. pp. of *probare:* see PROBE] **1.** the act or process of proving or establishing that a document submitted for official certification and registration, as a will, is genuine **2.** all matters coming under the jurisdiction of probate courts —*adj.* having to do with probate or a probate court —*vt.* **-bat·ed, -bat·ing 1.** to establish officially the genuineness or validity of (a will) **2.** popularly, to certify in a probate court as mentally unsound —**pro′ba·tive** (-bə tiv, präb′ə-), **pro′ba·to′ry** (-tôr′ē) *adj.*

**probate court** a court having jurisdiction over the probating of wills, the administration of estates, and, usually, the guardianship of minors and incompetents

**pro·ba·tion** (prō bā′shən) *n.* [< OFr. < L. < *probare:* see PROBE] **1.** a testing or trial, as of a person's character, fitness for a position, etc. **2.** the suspension of sentence of a person convicted but not imprisoned, on condition of continued good behavior and regular reporting to a probation officer. **3.** *a*) the status of a person being tested or on trial *b*) the period of testing or trial —**pro·ba′tion·ar′y, pro·ba′tion·al** *adj.*

**pro·ba·tion·er** (-ər) *n.* a person on probation

**probation officer** an officer appointed by a court to supervise persons placed on probation

**probe** (prōb) *n.* [LL. *proba*, proof < L. *probare*, to test <

*probus*, proper] **1.** a slender, blunt surgical instrument for exploring a wound or the like **2.** the act of probing **3.** a searching examination; specif., *a*) an investigation, as by a legislative committee, into corruption, etc. *b*) an exploratory survey **4.** an instrumented spacecraft for exploring the upper atmosphere, outer space, another planet, etc. —*vt.* **probed, prob′ing 1.** to explore (a wound, etc.) with a probe **2.** to examine or investigate thoroughly —*vi.* to search; investigate —**prob′er** *n.*

**prob·i·ty** (prō′bə tē, präb′ə-) *n.* [< L. < *probus*, good] uprightness; honesty; integrity

**prob·lem** (präb′ləm) *n.* [< MFr. < L. < Gr. *problēma* < *pro-*, forward + *ballein*, to throw] **1.** a question or matter to be thought about or worked out [a math *problem*] **2.** a matter, person, etc. that is perplexing or difficult —*adj.* **1.** depicting a social problem [a *problem* play] **2.** very difficult to deal with, esp. to train or discipline [a *problem* child]

**prob·lem·at·ic** (präb′lə mat′ik) *adj.* **1.** having the nature of a problem; hard to solve or deal with **2.** uncertain Also **prob′lem·at′i·cal** —**prob′lem·at′i·cal·ly** *adv.*

‡**pro bo·no pu·bli·co** (prō bō′nō pub′li kō′) [ML.] for the public good or welfare

**pro·bos·cis** (prō bäs′is) *n., pl.* **-cis·es, -ci·des′** (-ə dēz′) [L. < Gr. < *pro-*, before + *boskein*, to feed] **1.** an elephant's trunk, or a long, flexible snout, as of a tapir **2.** any tubular organ for sucking, food-gathering, sensing, etc., as of some insects, worms, and mollusks **3.** a person's nose, esp. if large: a jocular usage

**pro·caine** (prō′kān) *n.* [PRO-[2] + (CO)CAINE] a synthetic crystalline compound used as a local anesthetic

**pro·ce·dure** (prə sē′jər, prō-) *n.* **1.** the act, method, or manner of proceeding in some action; esp., the order of steps to be followed **2.** a particular course or method of action **3.** the established way of carrying on the business of a legislature, law court, etc. —**pro·ce′dur·al** *adj.* —**pro·ce′dur·al·ly** *adv.*

**pro·ceed** (prō sēd′, prə-) *vi.* [< MFr. < L. < *procedere* < *pro-*, forward + *cedere*, to go] **1.** to advance or go on, esp. after stopping **2.** to go on speaking, esp. after an interruption **3.** to undertake and carry on some action [to proceed to build a fire] **4.** to move along or be carried on [things proceeded smoothly] **5.** to take legal action (often with *against*) **6.** to come forth, issue, or arise (*from*)

**pro·ceed·ing** (-iŋ) *n.* **1.** an advancing or going on with what one has been doing **2.** the carrying on of an action or course of action **3.** a particular action or course of action **4.** [*pl.*] a record of the business transacted by a learned society, etc. **5.** [*pl.*] legal action

**pro·ceeds** (prō′sēdz) *n.pl.* the sum or profit derived from a sale, venture, etc.

**proc·ess** (präs′es; *chiefly Brit. & Canad.,* prō′ses) *n.* [< OFr. < L. pp. of *procedere:* see PROCEED] **1.** a series of changes by which something develops or is brought about [the *process* of digestion, growth, etc.] **2.** a particular method of making or doing something, in which there are a number of steps **3.** *Biol.* a projecting part of a structure or organism **4.** *Law a*) an action or suit *b*) a written order, as a summons to appear in court —*vt.* to prepare by or subject to a special process —*adj.* prepared by a special process —**in process** in the course of being done —**in (the) process of** in or during the course of —**proc′es·sor, proc′ess·er** *n.*

**process cheese** a cheese made by heating and blending together several natural cheeses with an emulsifying agent: also **proc′essed cheese**

**pro·ces·sion** (prə sesh′ən, prō-) *n.* [OFr. < L. < *procedere:* see PROCEED] **1.** the act of proceeding, esp. in an orderly manner **2.** a number of persons or things moving forward, as in a parade, in an orderly, formal way

**pro·ces·sion·al** (-'l) *adj.* of or relating to a procession —*n.* **1.** a hymn sung at the beginning of a church service during the entrance of the clergy **2.** any musical composition to accompany a procession

**pro·claim** (prō klām′, prə-) *vt.* [< MFr. < L. < *pro-*, before + *clamare*, to cry out] **1.** to announce to the public officially; announce to be **2.** to show to be [acts that proclaimed him a friend] **3.** to praise or extol

**proc·la·ma·tion** (präk′lə mā′shən) *n.* **1.** a proclaiming or being proclaimed **2.** something that is proclaimed

**pro·cliv·i·ty** (prō kliv′ə tē) *n., pl.* **-ties** [L. *proclivitas* < *pro-*, before + *clivus*, a slope] a natural or habitual tendency or inclination

**pro·con·sul** (prō kän′s'l) *n.* [L. < *pro consule*, (acting) for the consul] a Roman official with consular authority who commanded an army in the provinces, often acting as provincial governor —**pro·con′sul·ar** (-ər) *adj.* —**pro·con′sul·ate** (-it), **pro·con′sul·ship′** *n.*

**pro·cras·ti·nate** (prō kras′tə nāt′, prə-) *vi., vt.* **-nat′ed, -nat′ing** [< L. pp. of *procrastinare*, ult. < *pro-*, forward + *cras*, tomorrow] to put off doing (something) until later; delay —**pro·cras′ti·na′tion** *n.* —**pro·cras′ti·na′tor** *n.*

**pro·cre·ate** (prō′krē āt′) *vt., vi.* -at′ed, -at′ing [< L. pp. of *procreare* < *pro-*, before + *creare*, to create] 1. to produce (young); beget 2. to produce or bring into existence —**pro′cre·ant** *adj.* —**pro′cre·a′tion** *n.* —**pro′cre·a′tive** *adj.* —**pro′cre·a′tor** *n.*

**Pro·crus·te·an** (prō krus′tē ən) *adj.* 1. of or like Procrustes or his actions 2. securing conformity at any cost

**Pro·crus·tes** (-tēz) *Gr. Myth.* a giant who seized travelers, tied them to a bedstead, and either stretched them or cut off their legs to make them fit it

**proc·tol·o·gy** (präk täl′ə jē) *n.* [< Gr. *prōktos*, anus + -LOGY] the branch of medicine dealing with the rectum and anus and their diseases —**proc′to·log′ic** (-tə läj′ik), **proc′to·log′i·cal** *adj.* —**proc·tol′o·gist** *n.*

**proc·tor** (präk′tər) *n.* [< ME., contr.: see PROCURATOR] 1. a person employed to manage another's affairs 2. a college or university official who maintains order, supervises examinations, etc. —*vt.* to supervise (an examination) —**proc·to·ri·al** (präk tôr′ē əl) *adj.* —**proc′tor·ship′** *n.*

**proc·u·ra·tor** (präk′yə rāt′ər) *n.* [< OFr. < L. < *procurare*: see ff.] 1. in the Roman Empire, an administrator of a province 2. a person employed to manage another's affairs; agent —**proc′u·ra·to′ri·al** (-yər ə tôr′ē əl) *adj.*

**pro·cure** (prō kyoor′, prə-) *vt.* -cured′, -cur′ing [< MFr. < L. < *pro*, for + *curare*, to attend to < *cura*, a care] 1. to get or bring about by some effort; obtain; secure 2. to obtain (women) for the purpose of prostitution —**pro·cur′a·ble** *adj.* —**pro·cure′ment, pro·cur′ance, pro·cur′al** *n.*

**pro·cur·er** (-ər) *n.* a person who procures; specif., a man who obtains women for the purpose of prostitution; pimp —**pro·cur′ess** *n.fem.*

**Pro·cy·on** (prō′sē än′) [L. < Gr. < *pro-*, before + *kyōn*, dog: it rises before the Dog Star] a star of the first magnitude in Canis Minor

**prod** (präd) *vt.* **prod′ded, prod′ding** [< ?] 1. to jab or poke as with a pointed stick 2. to urge or stir into action —*n.* 1. a prodding; jab, poke, thrust, etc. 2. something that prods; specif., a rod or pointed stick used in driving cattle —**prod′der** *n.*

**prod·i·gal** (präd′i gəl) *adj.* [MFr. < L. < *prodigere*, to waste < *pro-*, forth + *agere*, to drive] 1. wasteful in a reckless way 2. extremely generous; lavish 3. extremely abundant; profuse —*n.* a person who recklessly wastes his wealth, resources, etc. —**prod′i·gal′i·ty** (-gal′ə tē) *n., pl.* -ties —**prod′i·gal·ly** *adv.*

**prodigal son** *Bible* a wastrel son who repented and was welcomed home: Luke 15:11–32

**pro·di·gious** (prə dij′əs) *adj.* [< L.: see ff.] 1. wonderful; amazing 2. enormous; huge —**pro·di′gious·ly** *adv.* —**pro·di′gious·ness** *n.*

**prod·i·gy** (präd′ə jē) *n., pl.* -gies [L. *prodigium*, omen] a person or thing so extraordinary as to inspire wonder; specif., a child who is extremely talented or intelligent

**pro·duce** (prə dōōs′, -dyōōs′; *for n.* präd′ōōs, -yōōs; prō′dōōs, -dyōōs) *vt.* -duced′, -duc′ing [L. *producere* < *pro-*, forward + *ducere*, to lead] 1. to bring to view; offer for inspection [to *produce* identification] 2. to bring forth; bear; yield [a well that *produces* oil] 3. *a)* to make or manufacture *b)* to create 4. to cause; give rise to [war *produces* devastation] 5. to get ready and present (a play, movie, etc.); be the producer (sense 2) of 6. *Econ.* to create (anything having exchange value) 7. *Geom.* to extend (a line or plane) —*vi.* to bear, yield, create, manufacture, etc. something —*n.* something produced; yield; esp., fresh fruits and vegetables —**pro·duc′i·bil′i·ty** *n.* —**pro·duc′i·ble** *adj.*

**pro·duc·er** (prə dōōs′ər, -dyōōs′-) *n.* 1. a person or thing that produces; specif., one who produces goods and services: opposed to CONSUMER 2. a person in charge of the financing and coordination of all activities in connection with the production of a play, movie, etc.

**prod·uct** (präd′əkt) *n.* [< ML. < L. pp. of *producere*: see PRODUCE] 1. something produced by nature or by man 2. result; outgrowth 3. *Chem.* any substance resulting from a chemical change 4. *Math.* the quantity obtained by multiplying two or more quantities together

**pro·duc·tion** (prə duk′shən) *n.* 1. the act or process of producing 2. the rate of producing or the amount produced 3. *a)* something produced; product *b)* a work of art, literature, etc. *c)* a show, movie, etc. 4. the creation of economic value; producing of goods and services —**make a production (out) of** [Colloq.] to dwell on or fuss over needlessly

**pro·duc·tive** (-tiv) *adj.* 1. fertile 2. marked by abundant production or effective results 3. bringing as a result (with *of*) [war is *productive* of much misery] 4. of or engaged in the creating of economic value —**pro·duc′tive·ly** *adv.* —**pro·duc·tiv·i·ty** (prō′dək tiv′ə tē, präd′ək-, prə duk′-), **pro·duc′tive·ness** *n.*

**pro·em** (prō′em) *n.* [< MFr. < L. < Gr. < *pro-*, before + *oimē*, song] a brief introduction; preface

**prof** (präf) *n.* [Colloq.] *shortened form of* PROFESSOR

**Prof.** Professor

**prof·a·na·tion** (präf′ə nā′shən) *n.* a profaning or being profaned; desecration —**pro·fan·a·to·ry** (prə fan′ə tôr′ē, prō-) *adj.*

**pro·fane** (prə fān′, prō-) *adj.* [< MFr. < L. < *pro-*, before (i.e., outside of) + *fanum*, a temple] 1. not connected with religion; secular [*profane* art] 2. not hallowed 3. showing disrespect or contempt for sacred things; irreverent —*vt.* -faned′, -fan′ing 1. to treat (sacred things) with disrespect or contempt 2. to put to a base or improper use —**pro·fane′ly** *adv.* —**pro·fane′ness** *n.* —**pro·fan′er** *n.*

**pro·fan·i·ty** (-fan′ə tē) *n.* 1. the state or quality of being profane 2. *pl.* -ties something profane; esp., profane language or the use of profane language

**pro·fess** (prə fes′, prō-) *vt.* [< L. pp. of *profiteri* < *pro-*, before + *fateri*, to avow] 1. to make an open declaration of; affirm [to *profess* one's love] 2. to claim to have (some feeling, knowledge, etc.): often connoting insincerity or pretense 3. to practice as one's profession 4. to declare one's belief in [to *profess* Christianity]

**pro·fessed** (-fest′) *adj.* 1. openly declared; avowed 2. insincerely avowed; pretended 3. having made one's profession (sense 4) 4. professing to be duly qualified [a *professed* economist] —**pro·fess′ed·ly** (-fes′id lē) *adv.*

**pro·fes·sion** (prə fesh′ən) *n.* 1. a professing, or declaring; avowal, as of love, religious belief, etc. 2. a faith or religion professed 3. *a)* an occupation requiring advanced education and involving intellectual skills, as medicine, law, theology, engineering, teaching, etc. *b)* the body of persons in any such occupation *c)* loosely, any occupation 4. the act or ceremony of taking vows on entering a religious order —**the oldest profession** prostitution: a jocular usage

**pro·fes·sion·al** (-′l) *adj.* 1. of, engaged in, or worthy of the standards of, a profession 2. designating or of a school offering instruction in a profession 3. earning one's living from an activity, such as a sport, not normally thought of as an occupation 4. engaged in by professional players [*professional* hockey] 5. engaged in a specific occupation for pay [a *professional* writer] 6. being such in the manner of one practicing a profession [a *professional* hatemonger] —*n.* 1. a person who is professional (esp. in sense 3) 2. a person who does something with great skill —**pro·fes′sion·al·ism** *n.* —**pro·fes′sion·al·ly** *adv.*

**pro·fes·sion·al·ize** (-′l īz′) *vt.* -ized′, -iz′ing to cause to have professional qualities, status, etc. —**pro·fes′sion·al·i·za′tion** *n.*

**pro·fes·sor** (prə fes′ər) *n.* 1. a person who professes something 2. a teacher; specif., a college teacher of the highest rank —**pro·fes·so·ri·al** (prō′fə sôr′ē əl) *adj.* —**pro′fes·so′ri·al·ly** *adv.* —**pro·fes′sor·ship′, pro′fes·sor·ate** (-it) *n.*

**prof·fer** (präf′ər) *vt.* [< Anglo-Fr. & OFr. < *por-*, PRO-² + *offrir*, ult. < L. *offerre*, to offer] to offer (advice, friendship, etc.) —*n.* an offer or proposal

**pro·fi·cient** (prə fish′ənt) *adj.* [< L. prp. of *proficere*, to advance < *pro-*, forward + *facere*, to make] highly competent; skilled —*n.* an expert —**pro·fi′cien·cy** (-ən sē) *n., pl.* -cies —**pro·fi′cient·ly** *adv.*

**pro·file** (prō′fīl; *chiefly Brit.* -fēl) *n.* [< It. < *profilare*, to outline < *pro-* (< L. *pro-*), before + *filo* (< L. *filum*), a thread] 1. *a)* a side view of the face *b)* a drawing of this 2. outline [the *profile* of a hill] 3. a short, vivid biographical and character sketch 4. a graph, writing, etc. presenting data about a particular subject 5. *Archit.* a side or sectional elevation of a building, etc. —*vt.* -filed′, -fil·ing to sketch, write, or make a profile of

**prof·it** (präf′it) *n.* [OFr. < L. pp. of *proficere*, to profit: see PROFICIENT] 1. advantage; gain; benefit 2. [*often pl.*] income from money invested in stocks, bonds, etc. 3. [*often pl.*] the sum remaining after all costs are deducted from the income of a business —*vi.* 1. to make a profit 2. to benefit; gain —*vt.* to be of profit or advantage to —**prof′it·er** *n.* —**prof′it·less** *adj.*

**prof·it·a·ble** (-ə b'l) *adj.* yielding profit, gain, or benefit —**prof′it·a·bil′i·ty, prof′it·a·ble·ness** *n.* —**prof′it·a·bly** *adv.*

**prof·i·teer** (präf′ə tir′) *n.* [PROFIT + -EER] a person who makes an unfair profit by charging very high prices when there is a short supply of something that people need —*vi.* to be a profiteer

**profit sharing** the practice of dividing a share of the profits of a business among employees, in addition to paying them their wages —**prof′it-shar′ing** *adj.*

**prof·li·gate** (präf′lə git) *adj.* [< L. pp. of *profligare*, to rout, ruin < *pro-*, forward + *fligere*, to drive] 1. immoral and shameless; dissolute 2. recklessly extravagant —*n.* a profligate person —**prof′li·ga·cy** (-gə sē), **prof′li·gate·ness** *n.* —**prof′li·gate·ly** *adv.*

**pro·found** (prə found′) *adj.* [< OFr. < L. *profundus* < *pro-*, forward + *fundus*, bottom] 1. very deep or low *[a profound abyss, sigh, etc.]* 2. marked by intellectual depth *[profound talk]* 3. deeply or intensely felt *[profound grief]* 4. thoroughgoing *[profound changes]* 5. unbroken *[a profound silence]* —**pro·found′ly** *adv.* —**pro·found′ness** *n.*

**pro·fun·di·ty** (-fun′də tē) *n., pl.* -ties 1. depth 2. intellectual depth 3. a profound idea, matter, etc.

**pro·fuse** (prə fyōōs′) *adj.* [< L. pp. of *profundere* < *pro-*, forth + *fundere*, to pour] 1. giving freely; generous *[profuse in her apologies]* 2. given or poured forth freely and abundantly —**pro·fuse′ly** *adv.* —**pro·fuse′ness** *n.*

**pro·fu·sion** (-fyōō′zhən) *n.* 1. a pouring forth with great liberality or wastefulness 2. great liberality or wastefulness 3. rich or lavish supply; abundance

**pro·gen·i·tor** (prō jen′ə tər, prə-) *n.* [< MFr. < L., ult. < *pro-*, forth + *gignere*, to beget] 1. a forefather; ancestor in direct line 2. an originator or precursor

**prog·e·ny** (präj′ə nē) *n., pl.* -nies [< MFr. < L. < *progignere*: see prec.] children, descendants, or offspring

**pro·ges·ter·one** (prō jes′tə rōn′) *n.* [PRO-¹ + GE(STATION) + STER(OL) + -ONE] a steroid hormone, $C_{21}H_{30}O_2$, that prepares the uterus for the fertilized ovum and the mammary glands for milk secretion

**prog·na·thous** (präg′nə thəs, präg nā′-) *adj.* [PRO-¹ + Gr. *gnathos*, a jaw] having the jaws projecting beyond the upper face: also **prog·nath′ic** (-nath′ik) —**prog′na·thism** *n.*

**prog·no·sis** (präg nō′sis) *n., pl.* -no′ses (-sēz) [< LL. < Gr. < *pro-*, before + *gignōskein*, to know] a forecast or forecasting; esp., a prediction of the probable course of a disease in an individual and the chances of recovery

**prog·nos·tic** (-näs′tik) *n.* [see prec.] 1. a sign; omen 2. a forecast —*adj.* 1. foretelling 2. *Med.* of, or serving as a basis for, prognosis

**prog·nos·ti·cate** (-näs′tə kāt′) *vt.* -cat′ed, -cat′ing 1. to foretell or predict 2. to indicate beforehand —**prog·nos′ti·ca′tion** *n.* —**prog·nos′ti·ca′tive** (-kāt′iv) *adj.* —**prog·nos′ti·ca′tor** *n.*

**pro·gram** (prō′gram, -grəm) *n.* [< Fr. < LL. < Gr. *programma*, an edict < *pro-*, before + *graphein*, to write] 1. *a)* the acts, speeches, musical pieces, etc. that make up an entertainment, ceremony, etc. *b)* a printed list of these 2. a scheduled broadcast on radio or television 3. a plan or procedure 4. all the activities offered at a camp, resort, etc. 5. *a)* sequence of operations to be performed by a digital computer, as in solving a problem *b)* the coded instructions and data for this —*vt.* -grammed or -gramed, -gram·ming or -gram·ing 1. to schedule in a program 2. to prepare (a textbook) for use in programmed learning 3. *a)* to furnish (a computer) with a program *b)* to incorporate in a computer program —*vi.* to prepare a program Also, Brit. sp., **pro′gramme** —**pro·gram·mat·ic** (prō′grə mat′ik) *adj.* —**pro′gram·mer, pro′gram·er** *n.*

**programmed learning** learning that a pupil acquires on his own, step by step, from a textbook that has a series of questions with the answers given elsewhere in the book

**program music** instrumental music that is meant to suggest a particular scene, story, etc.

**prog·ress** (präg′res, -rəs; *chiefly Brit.* prō′gres; *for v.* prə-gres′) *n.* [< L. pp. of *progredi* < *pro-*, before + *gradi*, to step] 1. a moving forward or onward 2. forward course; development 3. advance toward perfection; improvement —*vi.* 1. to move forward or onward 2. to move forward toward completion, a goal, etc. 3. to advance toward perfection; improve —**in progress** going on

**pro·gres·sion** (prə gresh′ən) *n.* 1. a moving forward or onward 2. a succession, as of acts, happenings, etc. 3. *Math.* a series of numbers increasing or decreasing by a constant difference between terms: see ARITHMETIC PROGRESSION, GEOMETRIC PROGRESSION —**pro·gres′sion·al** *adj.*

**pro·gres·sive** (-gres′iv) *adj.* 1. moving forward or onward 2. continuing by successive steps 3. of, or concerned with, progression 4. designating a tax whose rate increases as the base increases 5. favoring or working for progress, as through political or social reform 6. of education that stresses self-expression, etc. 7. *Gram.* indicating continuing action: said of certain verb forms, as *am working* 8. *Med.* becoming more severe: said of a disease —*n.* 1. a person who is progressive, esp. one who favors political progress or reform 2. [P-] a member of a Progressive Party —**pro·gres′sive·ly** *adv.* —**pro·gres′sive·ness** *n.*

**Progressive Party** any of several U.S. political parties; specif., *a)* one formed in 1912 by followers of Theodore Roosevelt *b)* one formed in 1924 and led by Robert LaFollette *c)* one formed in 1948, orig. led by Henry Wallace (1888–1965)

**pro·hib·it** (prō hib′it, prə-) *vt.* [< L. pp. of *prohibere* < *pro-*, before + *habere*, to have] 1. to refuse to permit; forbid by law or by an order 2. to prevent; hinder —**pro·hib′it·er, pro·hib′i·tor** *n.*

**pro·hi·bi·tion** (prō′ə bish′ən) *n.* 1. a prohibiting or being prohibited 2. an order or law that forbids 3. the forbidding by law of the manufacture or sale of alcoholic liquors; specif., [P-] in the U.S., the period (1920–1933) of prohibition by Federal law —**pro′hi·bi′tion·ist** *n.*

**pro·hib·i·tive** (prō hib′ə tiv, prə-) *adj.* 1. prohibiting or tending to prohibit something 2. such as to prevent purchase, use, etc. *[prohibitive prices]* Also **pro·hib′i·to′ry** (-tôr′ē) —**pro·hib′i·tive·ly** *adv.*

**proj·ect** (präj′ekt, -ikt; *for v.* prə jekt′) *n.* [< L. pp. of *projicere* < *pro-*, before + *jacere*, to throw] 1. a proposal; plan 2. an organized undertaking, as a special unit of work, research, etc. in school 3. a complex of inexpensive apartments or houses, usually owned publicly —*vt.* 1. to propose (a plan of action) 2. to throw forward 3. *a)* to cause (one's voice) to be heard clearly and at a distance *b)* to get (ideas, feelings, etc.) across to others effectively 4. to send forth in one's imagination *[to project oneself into the future]* 5. to cause to jut out 6. to cause (a shadow, image, etc.) to fall upon a surface 7. *same as* EXTRAPOLATE 8. *Geom.* to transform the points of (a geometric figure) into the points of another figure, usually by lines of correspondence —*vi.* 1. to jut out 2. to project one's voice, ideas, etc.

**pro·jec·tile** (prə jek′t'l, -tīl) *n.* 1. an object designed to be shot forward, as a cannon shell, bullet, or rocket 2. anything thrown forward —*adj.* 1. designed to be hurled forward, as a javelin 2. hurling forward *[projectile energy]*

**pro·jec·tion** (-shən) *n.* 1. a projecting or being projected 2. something that projects, or juts out 3. something that is projected; specif., in map making, the representation on a plane of all or part of the earth's surface or of the celestial sphere 4. an extrapolation 5. *Psychiatry* the unconscious act of ascribing to others one's own ideas, impulses, or emotions 6. *Photog.* the process of projecting an image, as from a transparent slide, upon a screen, etc. —**pro·jec′tion·al** *adj.* —**pro·jec′tive** *adj.*

**pro·jec·tion·ist** (-ist) *n.* the operator of a motion-picture or slide projector

**pro·jec·tor** (prə jek′tər) *n.* a person or thing that projects; specif., a machine for throwing an image on a screen, as from a motion-picture film

**Pro·kof·iev** (prô kôf′yef; *E.* prə kō′fē ef′), **Ser·gei** (Sergeevich) (syer gyā′) 1891–1953; Russ. composer

**pro·lapse** (prō′laps; *also, and for v. usually,* prō laps′) *n.* [< ModL. < LL. < pp. of *prolabi* < *pro-*, forward + *labi*, to fall] *Med.* the slipping out of place of an internal organ, as the uterus: also **pro·lap′sus** (-lap′səs) —*vi.* -lapsed′, -laps′ing *Med.* to slip out of place

**pro·late** (prō′lāt) *adj.* [< L. pp. of *proferre*, to bring forward] extended or elongated at the poles *[a prolate spheroid]*

**pro·le·tar·i·at** (prō′lə ter′ē ət) *n.* [< Fr. < L. *proletarius*, a citizen of the poorest class, who served the state only by having children < *proles*, offspring] 1. [Rare] the class of lowest status in any society 2. the working class; esp., the industrial working class —**pro′le·tar′i·an** *adj., n.*

**pro·lif·er·ate** (prō lif′ə rāt′, prə-) *vt., vi.* -at′ed, -at′ing [ult. < ML. < L. *proles*, offspring + *ferre*, to bear] 1. to reproduce (new parts) in quick succession 2. to create in profusion; multiply rapidly —**pro·lif′er·a′tion** *n.* —**pro·lif′er·ous** (-rəs) *adj.*

**pro·lif·ic** (prə lif′ik, prō-) *adj.* [< Fr. < ML. < L. *proles*, offspring + *facere*, to make] 1. producing many young or much fruit 2. creating many products of the mind *[a prolific poet]* 3. fruitful; abounding (often with *in* or *of*) —**pro·lif′i·ca·cy** (-i kə sē) *n.* —**pro·lif′i·cal·ly** *adv.*

**pro·lix** (prō liks′, prō′liks) *adj.* [< L. *prolixus*, extended] 1. so wordy as to be tiresome; verbose 2. long-winded —**pro·lix′i·ty** *n.* —**pro·lix′ly** *adv.*

**pro·logue** (prō′lôg, -läg) *n.* [< MFr. < L. < Gr. < *pro-*, before + *logos*, a discourse] 1. an introduction to a poem, play, etc.; esp., introductory lines spoken before a dramatic performance 2. the actor speaking such lines 3. any preliminary act, event, etc.

**pro·long** (prə lôŋ′) *vt.* [< MFr. < LL. < L. *pro-*, forth + *longus*, long] to lengthen in time or space: also **pro·lon′gate** (-gāt) -gat·ed, -gat·ing —**pro·lon·ga·tion** (prō′lôŋ-gā′shən) *n.* —**pro·long′er** *n.*

**prom** (präm) *n.* [contr. < ff.] [Colloq.] a ball or dance, as of a particular class at a school or college

**prom·e·nade** (präm′ə näd′, -näd′) *n.* [Fr. < *promener*, to take for a walk < LL. < L. *pro-*, forth + *minare*, to herd] 1. a leisurely walk taken for pleasure, to display one's finery, etc. 2. a public place for such a walk, as an avenue

**3.** *a)* a ball, or formal dance *b)* a march of all the guests, beginning a formal ball —*vi., vt.* -nad′ed, -nad′ing to take a promenade (along or through); parade —prom′e-nad′er *n.*

**Pro·me·theus** (prə mē′thyo͞os, -thē əs) *Gr. Myth.* a Titan who stole fire from heaven to benefit mankind: in punishment, Zeus chained him to a rock where a vulture ate away at his liver —**Pro·me′the·an** (-thē ən) *adj., n.*

**pro·me·thi·um** (-thē əm) *n.* [ModL. < prec.] a metallic chemical element of the rare-earth group: symbol, Pm; at. wt., 145(?); at. no., 61

**prom·i·nence** (präm′ə nəns) *n.* **1.** a being prominent **2.** something prominent

**prom·i·nent** (-nənt) *adj.* [< L. prp. of *prominere*, to project] **1.** sticking out; projecting [a *prominent* chin] **2.** noticeable at once; conspicuous **3.** widely and favorably known [a *prominent* artist] —**prom′i·nent·ly** *adv.*

**pro·mis·cu·ous** (prə mis′kyo͞o wəs) *adj.* [< L. < *pro-*, forth + *miscere*, to mix] **1.** consisting of different elements mixed together without sorting **2.** showing little or no taste or care in choosing; specif., engaging in sexual intercourse with many persons casually **3.** without plan or purpose; casual —**prom·is·cu·i·ty** (präm′is kyo͞o′ə tē, prō′mis-), *pl.* -ties, **pro·mis′cu·ous·ness** *n.* —**pro·mis′cu·ous·ly** *adv.*

**prom·ise** (präm′is) *n.* [< L. *promissum*, ult. < *pro-*, forth + *mittere*, to send] **1.** an agreement to do or not to do something; vow **2.** a sign that gives reason for expecting success **3.** something promised —*vi.* -ised, -is·ing **1.** to make a promise **2.** to give a basis for expectation —*vt.* **1.** to make a promise of (something) *to* somebody **2.** to engage or pledge (with an infinitive or clause) [to *promise* to go] **3.** to give a basis for expecting **4.** [Colloq.] to assure —**prom′is·er,** *Law* **prom′i·sor′** (-i sôr′) *n.*

**Promised Land 1.** *Bible* Canaan, promised by God to Abraham and his descendants: Gen. 17:8 **2.** [p- l-] a place where one expects to have a better life

**prom·is·ing** (präm′i siŋ) *adj.* showing promise of success, excellence, etc. —**prom′is·ing·ly** *adv.*

**prom·is·so·ry** (präm′i sôr′ē) *adj.* **1.** containing a promise **2.** stipulating conditions that must be complied with to keep an insurance contract valid

**promissory note** a written promise to pay a certain sum of money to a certain person or bearer on demand or on a specified date

**prom·on·to·ry** (präm′ən tôr′ē) *n., pl.* -ries [< LL. < L. *promunturium*, prob. < *prominere*, to project] a peak of high land that juts out into a body of water; headland

**pro·mote** (prə mōt′) *vt.* -mot′ed, -mot′ing [< L. pp. of *promovere* < *pro-*, forward + *movere*, to move] **1.** to raise or advance to a higher position or rank [she was *promoted* to manager] **2.** to help bring about or further the growth or establishment of [to *promote* the general welfare] **3.** to further the popularity, sales, etc. of by publicizing and advertising [to *promote* a product] **4.** to move forward a grade in school —**pro·mot′a·ble** *adj.*

**pro·mot·er** (-mōt′ər) *n.* a person or thing that promotes; specif., a person who begins, secures financing for, and helps to organize an undertaking, as a business

**pro·mo·tion** (-mō′shən) *n.* a promoting; specif., *a)* advancement in rank, grade, or position *b)* furtherance of an enterprise, cause, etc. —**pro·mo′tion·al** *adj.*

**prompt** (prämpt) *adj.* [< MFr. < L. < pp. of *promere* < *pro-*, forth + *emere*, to take] **1.** quick to act or to do what is required; ready, punctual, etc. **2.** done, spoken, etc. at once or without delay —*n.* a notice of payment due —*vt.* **1.** to urge into action **2.** to remind (a person) of something he has forgotten; specif., to help (an actor, etc.) with a cue **3.** to move or inspire by suggestion —**prompt′ly** *adv.* —**prompt′ness** *n.*

**prompt·er** (prämp′tər) *n.* a person who prompts; specif., one who cues performers when they forget their lines

**promp·ti·tude** (-tə to͞od′, -tyo͞od′) *n.* the quality of being prompt; promptness

**prom·ul·gate** (präm′əl gāt′, prō mul′gāt) *vt.* -gat′ed, -gat·ing [< L. pp. of *promulgare*, to publish, altered < ? *pro-*, before + *vulgus*, the people] **1.** to publish or make known officially (a decree, law, dogma, etc.) **2.** to make widespread [to *promulgate* culture] —**prom′ul·ga′tion** *n.* —**prom′ul·ga′tor** *n.*

**pron. 1.** pronominal **2.** pronoun **3.** pronounced **4.** pronunciation

**prone** (prōn) *adj.* [< L. *pronus* < *pro*, before] **1.** lying or leaning face downward **2.** lying flat or prostrate **3.** having a natural bent; disposed or inclined (*to*) [*prone* to error] **4.** groveling —**prone′ly** *adv.* —**prone′ness** *n.*

**prong** (prôŋ) *n.* [akin to MLowG. *prangen*, to pinch] **1.** any of the pointed ends of a fork; tine **2.** any pointed projecting part, as the tip of an antler —*vt.* to pierce or break up with a prong —**pronged** *adj.*

**prong·horn** (prôŋ′hôrn′) *n., pl.* -horns′, -horn′: see PLURAL, II, D, 1 an antelopelike deer of Mexico and the western U.S., having curved horns

**pro·nom·i·nal** (prō näm′i n'l) *adj. Gram.* of, or having the function of, a pronoun —**pro·nom′i·nal·ly** *adv.*

**pro·noun** (prō′noun) *n.* [< MFr. < L. *pronomen* < *pro*, for + *nomen*, noun] *Gram.* a word that can assume the functions of a noun and be used in place of a noun: *I, you, them, it, ours, who, which, myself, anybody,* etc. are *pronouns*

**pro·nounce** (prə nouns′) *vt.* -nounced′, -nounc′ing [< OFr. < L. < *pro-*, before + *nuntiare*, to announce < *nuntius*, messenger] **1.** to say officially, solemnly, etc. [the judge *pronounced* sentence] **2.** to declare to be as specified [to *pronounce* a man guilty] **3.** *a)* to utter or articulate (a sound or word) *b)* to utter in the required or standard manner [he couldn't *pronounce* my name] —*vi.* **1.** to make a pronouncement (*on*) **2.** to pronounce words, syllables, etc. —**pro·nounce′a·ble** *adj.* —**pro·nounc′er** *n.*

**pro·nounced** (-nounst′) *adj.* **1.** spoken or uttered **2.** clearly marked; unmistakable; decided [a *pronounced* change] —**pro·nounc′ed·ly** (-noun′sid lē) *adv.*

**pro·nounce·ment** (-nouns′mənt) *n.* **1.** a pronouncing **2.** a formal statement of a fact, opinion, or judgment

**pron·to** (prän′tō) *adv.* [Sp. < L. *promptus:* see PROMPT] [Slang] at once; quickly; immediately

**pro·nun·ci·a·men·to** (prə nun′sē ə men′tō, prō-) *n., pl.* -tos [Sp. < L.: see PRONOUNCE] **1.** a public declaration; proclamation **2.** *same as* MANIFESTO

**pro·nun·ci·a·tion** (-ā′shən) *n.* **1.** the act or manner of pronouncing words **2.** *a)* any of the accepted or standard pronunciations of a word *b)* the representation in phonetic symbols of such a pronunciation —**pro·nun′ci·a′tion·al** *adj.*

**proof** (pro͞of) *n.* [< OFr. *prueve* < LL. *proba:* see PROBE] **1.** a proving, testing, or trying of something **2.** anything serving to establish the truth of something; conclusive evidence **3.** the establishment of the truth of something [to work on the *proof* of a theory] **4.** a test or trial of the truth, worth, quality, etc. of something **5.** the state of having been tested or proved **6.** tested or proved strength, as of armor **7.** the relative strength of an alcoholic liquor with reference to the standard for proof spirit: see PROOF SPIRIT **8.** *Law* all the facts, admissions, and conclusions which together operate to determine a verdict **9.** *Photog.* a trial print of a negative **10.** *Printing* an impression of composed type taken for checking errors and making changes —*adj.* **1.** of tested and proved strength **2.** able to resist, withstand, etc. (with *against*) [*proof* against criticism] **3.** used in proving or testing **4.** of standard strength: said of alcoholic liquors —*vt.* **1.** to make a proof of **2.** *clipped form of* PROOFREAD

**-proof** (pro͞of) *a combining form meaning:* **1.** impervious to [*waterproof*] **2.** protected from [*rustproof*] **3.** resistant to [*fireproof*]

**proof·read** (pro͞of′rēd′) *vt., vi.* to read and mark corrections on (printers' proofs, etc.) —**proof′read′er** *n.*

**proof spirit** an alcoholic liquor that is 100 proof and contains 50% of its volume of alcohol having a specific gravity of 0.7939 at 60° F

**prop**¹ (präp) *n.* [MDu. *proppe,* a prop] **1.** a support, as a stake or pole, placed under or against a structure or part **2.** a person or thing that gives support to a person, institution, etc. —*vt.* **propped, prop′ping 1.** to support or hold up, as with a prop (often with *up*) **2.** to place or lean (something) *against* a support **3.** to sustain or bolster

**prop**² (präp) *n. same as* PROPERTY (sense 5)

**prop**³ (präp) *n. clipped form of* PROPELLER

**prop. 1.** proper(ly) **2.** property **3.** proposition

**prop·a·gan·da** (präp′ə gan′də, prō′pə-) *n.* [ModL., short for *congregatio de propaganda fide*, congregation for propagating the faith] **1.** [P-] R.C.Ch. a committee of cardinals in charge of the foreign missions **2.** the systematic, widespread promotion of a certain set of ideas, doctrines, etc., esp. to further one's own cause: also **prop′a·gan′dism 3.** ideas, doctrines, or allegations so spread, esp. if regarded as spread by deception —**prop′a·gan′dist** *n., adj.* —**prop′a·gan·dis′tic** *adj.* —**prop′a·gan·dis′ti·cal·ly** *adv.*

**prop·a·gan·dize** (-dīz) *vt., vi.* -dized, -diz·ing **1.** to spread (certain ideas or propaganda) **2.** to subject (people) to propaganda

**prop·a·gate** (präp′ə gāt′) *vt.* -gat′ed, -gat′ing [< L. pp. of *propagare*, to peg down < *propago*, slip (of a plant)] **1.** to cause (a plant or animal) to reproduce itself; raise or breed **2.** to reproduce (itself): said of a plant or animal **3.** to spread (ideas, customs, etc.) **4.** to extend or transmit (sound waves, etc.) through air or water —*vi.* to reproduce, as plants or animals —**prop'a·ga'tion** *n.* —**prop'a·ga'tive** *adj.* —**prop'a·ga'tor** *n.*

**pro·pane** (prō'pān) *n.* [PROP(YL) + (METH)ANE] a heavy, gaseous hydrocarbon, C₃H₈, of the methane series, used as a fuel, in refrigerants, etc.

‡**pro pa·tri·a** (prō pā'trē ə) [L.] for (one's) country

**pro·pel** (prə pel') *vt.* **-pelled', -pel'ling** [< L. < *pro-*, forward + *pellere*, to drive] to push, drive, or impel onward, forward, or ahead —**pro·pel'lant** *n.* —**pro·pel'lent** *adj., n.*

**pro·pel·ler** (-ər) *n.* a person or thing that propels; specif., a device (**screw propeller**) consisting of blades twisted to move in a spiral as they rotate with the hub, and serving to propel a ship or aircraft forward

**pro·pen·si·ty** (prə pen'sə tē) *n., pl.* **-ties** [< L. pp. of *propendere*, to hang forward + -ITY] a natural inclination or tendency; bent

**prop·er** (präp'ər) *adj.* [< OFr. < L. *proprius*, one's own] **1.** specially adapted or suitable; appropriate [the *proper* tool for a job] **2.** naturally belonging or peculiar (*to*) [weather *proper* to May] **3.** conforming to an accepted standard or to good usage; correct **4.** fitting; seemly; right **5.** decent or decorous or exceedingly respectable **6.** in its most restricted sense; strictly so called [*Chicago proper* (i.e., apart from its suburbs)] **7.** [Chiefly Brit. Colloq.] complete; thorough [a *proper* scoundrel] **8.** [Archaic or Dial.] *a*) fine; excellent *b*) handsome **9.** *Gram.* designating a noun that names a specific individual, place, etc., is not used with an article, and is normally capitalized, as *Donald, Boston*, etc. —*adv.* [Dial.] completely; thoroughly —**prop'er·ly** *adv.* —**prop'er·ness** *n.*

**proper fraction** *Math.* a fraction in which the numerator is less than the denominator (Ex.: 2/5)

**prop·er·tied** (präp'ər tēd) *adj.* owning property

**prop·er·ty** (präp'ər tē) *n., pl.* **-ties** [< OFr. < L. *proprietas* < *proprius*, one's own] **1.** *a*) the right to possess, use, and dispose of something; ownership *b*) something, as a piece of writing, in which copyright or other rights are held **2.** a thing or things owned; possessions; esp., land or real estate owned **3.** a specific piece of land or real estate **4.** any trait or attribute proper to a thing; characteristic or essential quality [the *properties* of a chemical compound] **5.** any of the movable articles used as part of a stage setting, except the costumes, backdrops, etc.

**proph·e·cy** (präf'ə sē) *n., pl.* **-cies** [< OFr. < LL. < Gr. < *prophētēs*: see PROPHET] **1.** prediction of the future by a prophet, as supposedly influenced by the guidance of God or a god **2.** any prediction **3.** something prophesied

**proph·e·sy** (-sī') *vt., vi.* **-sied', -sy'ing 1.** to declare or predict (something) by or as by the influence of divine guidance; utter (prophecies) **2.** to predict (a future event) in any way —**proph'e·si'er** *n.*

**proph·et** (präf'it) *n.* [< OFr. < LL. < Gr. *prophētēs*, interpreter of a god's will < *pro-*, before + *phanai*, to speak] **1.** a person who claims to speak for God, or a religious leader who claims to be, or is thought to be, divinely inspired **2.** a spokesman for some cause, group, etc. **3.** a person who predicts the future —**the Prophet** *a name used for* MOHAMMED (by Moslems) *or for* Joseph SMITH (by Mormons) —**the Prophets 1.** the prophetic books of the Bible that include Isaiah, Jeremiah, etc. **2.** the authors or subjects of these books —**proph'et·ess** *n.fem.*

**pro·phet·ic** (prə fet'ik) *adj.* **1.** of, or having the powers of, a prophet **2.** of or containing a prophecy **3.** that predicts Also **pro·phet'i·cal** —**pro·phet'i·cal·ly** *adv.*

**pro·phy·lac·tic** (prō'fə lak'tik) *adj.* [< Gr., ult. < *pro-*, before + *phylassein*, to guard] preventive or protective; esp., preventing disease —*n.* a prophylactic medicine, device, etc.; esp., a condom

**pro·phy·lax·is** (-sis) *n., pl.* **-lax'es** (-sēz) the prevention of or protection from disease; specif., a cleaning of the teeth by a dentist, to remove plaque and tartar

**pro·pin·qui·ty** (prō piŋ'kwə tē) *n.* [< MFr. < L. < *propinquus*, near] **1.** nearness in time or place **2.** nearness of relationship; kinship

**pro·pi·ti·ate** (prə pish'ē āt', prō-) *vt.* **-at'ed, -at'ing** [< L. pp. of *propitiare* < *propitius*: see ff.] to win or regain the good will of; appease or conciliate —**pro·pi'ti·a·ble** *adj.* —**pro·pi'ti·a'tion** *n.* —**pro·pi'ti·a'tor** *n.* —**pro·pi'ti·a·to'ry** (-ə tôr'ē), **pro·pi'ti·a'tive** (-āt'iv) *adj.*

**pro·pi·tious** (prə pish'əs, prō-) *adj.* [< OFr. < L. *propitius* < *pro-*, before + *petere*, to seek] **1.** favorably inclined; gracious [the *propitious* gods] **2.** favorable; auspicious [a *propitious* omen] **3.** that favors [*propitious* winds] —**pro·pi'tious·ly** *adv.* —**pro·pi'tious·ness** *n.*

**prop·jet** (präp'jet') *n. same as* TURBOPROP

**pro·po·nent** (prə pō'nənt) *n.* [< L. prp. of *proponere* < *pro-*, forth + *ponere*, to place] **1.** a person who makes a proposal or proposition **2.** a person who espouses or supports a cause, etc.

**pro·por·tion** (prə pôr'shən) *n.* [< MFr. < L. < *pro-*, for + *portio*, a part] **1.** the comparative relation between things with respect to size, amount, etc.; ratio **2.** a part,

share, etc., esp. in its relation to the whole; quota **3.** balance or symmetry **4.** size, degree, etc. relative to a standard **5.** [*pl.*] dimensions **6.** *Math. a)* an equality between ratios (Ex.: 2 is to 6 as 3 is to 9): also called **geometrical proportion** *b) same as* RULE OF THREE —*vt.* **1.** to cause to be in proper relation, balance, etc. [*proportion* the penalty to the crime] **2.** to arrange the parts of (a whole) so as to be harmonious —**pro·por'tioned** *adj.* —**pro·por'tion·ment** *n.*

**pro·por·tion·al** (-'l) *adj.* **1.** of or determined by proportion; relative **2.** in proportion [pay *proportional* to work done] **3.** *Math.* having the same ratio —*n.* a quantity in a mathematical proportion —**pro·por'tion·al'i·ty** (-al'ə tē) *n.* —**pro·por'tion·al·ly** *adv.*

**proportional representation** a system of voting that allows each political party to be represented in a legislature in proportion to its share of the popular vote

**pro·por·tion·ate** (prə pôr'shə nit; *for v.* -nāt') *adj.* in proper proportion; proportional —*vt.* **-at'ed, -at'ing** to make proportionate —**pro·por'tion·ate·ly** *adv.*

**pro·pos·al** (prə pō'z'l) *n.* **1.** a proposing **2.** a plan or action proposed **3.** an offer of marriage

**pro·pose** (prə pōz') *vt.* **-posed', -pos'ing** [< OFr. < L. pp. of *proponere*: see PROPONENT] **1.** to put forth for consideration or acceptance **2.** to plan or intend **3.** to present as a toast in drinking **4.** to nominate for membership, office, etc. —*vi.* **1.** to make a proposal; form a purpose, etc. **2.** to offer marriage —**pro·pos'er** *n.*

**prop·o·si·tion** (präp'ə zish'ən) *n.* **1.** a proposing **2.** *a)* something proposed; plan *b)* [Colloq.] an immoral proposal, esp. in sexual relations **3.** [Colloq.] a proposed deal, as in business **4.** [Colloq.] a person, problem, etc. to be dealt with **5.** a subject to be discussed **6.** *Logic* an expression in which the predicate affirms or denies something about the subject **7.** *Math.* a theorem to be demonstrated or a problem to be solved —*vt.* to make a proposition, esp. an improper one, to —**prop'o·si'tion·al** *adj.*

**pro·pound** (prə pound') *vt.* [< L. *proponere*: see PROPONENT] to put forth for consideration; propose —**pro·pound'er** *n.*

**pro·pri·e·tar·y** (prə prī'ə ter'ē) *n., pl.* **-tar'ies** [< LL. < L. *proprietas*: see PROPERTY] **1.** a proprietor **2.** a group of proprietors **3.** proprietorship —*adj.* **1.** belonging to a proprietor **2.** holding property **3.** of property or proprietorship **4.** held under patent, trademark, or copyright [a *proprietary* medicine]

**pro·pri·e·tor** (prə prī'ə tər) *n.* [< PROPRIET(ARY) + -OR] **1.** a person who has exclusive right to some property; owner **2.** one who owns and operates a business establishment —**pro·pri'e·tor·ship'** *n.* —**pro·pri'e·tress** (-tris) *n.fem.*

**pro·pri·e·ty** (prə prī'ə tē) *n., pl.* **-ties** [< OFr.: see PROPERTY] **1.** the quality of being proper, fitting, etc.; fitness **2.** conformity with what is proper or fitting or with accepted standards of behavior —**the proprieties** accepted standards of behavior in polite society

**pro·pul·sion** (prə pul'shən) *n.* [< L. pp. of *propellere* (see PROPEL) + -ION] **1.** a propelling or being propelled **2.** something that propels; propelling or driving force —**pro·pul'sive, pro·pul'so·ry** *adj.*

**pro·pyl** (prō'pil) *n.* [< PRO(TO)- + Gr. *piōn*, fat + -YL] the monovalent radical C₃H₇, occurring in two isomeric forms —**pro·pyl'ic** *adj.*

**pro·pyl·ene** (prō'pə lēn') *n.* [prec. + -ENE] a flammable, colorless gas, used in making polypropylene, synthetic glycerol, etc.

**propylene glycol** a colorless, viscous liquid used as antifreeze, in making polyester resins, etc.

**pro ra·ta** (prō rāt'ə, rät'ə) [L. *pro rata (parte)*, according to the calculated (share)] in proportion; proportionate or proportionally

**pro·rate** (prō rāt', prō'rāt') *vt., vi.* **-rat'ed, -rat'ing** [< prec.] to divide, assess, or distribute proportionately —**pro·rat'a·ble** *adj.* —**pro·ra'tion** *n.*

**pro·rogue** (prō rōg') *vt., vi.* **-rogued', -rogu'ing** [< MFr. < L. *prorogare*, to defer < *pro-*, for + *rogare*, to ask] to discontinue or end a session of (a legislative assembly) —**pro'ro·ga'tion** (-rō gā'shən) *n.*

**pro·sa·ic** (prō zā'ik) *adj.* [< ML. < L. *prosa*, PROSE] **1.** of or like prose; unpoetic **2.** commonplace; dull —**pro·sa'i·cal·ly** *adv.* —**pro·sa'ic·ness** *n.*

**pro·sce·ni·um** (prō sē'nē əm) *n., pl.* **-ni·ums, -ni·a** (-ə) [L. < Gr. < *pro-*, before + *skēnē*, a tent] **1.** the apron of a stage **2.** the plane separating the stage proper from the audience and including the arch (**proscenium arch**) and its curtain

**pro·sciut·to** (prə shōōt'ō) *n.* [It. < *prosciugare*, to dry out] a spicy Italian ham, cured by drying and served in very thin slices

**pro·scribe** (prō skrīb') *vt.* **-scribed', -scrib'ing** [< L. < *pro-*, before + *scribere*, to write] **1.** in ancient Rome, to publish the name of (a person) condemned to death, banishment, etc. **2.** to deprive of the protection of the law; outlaw **3.** to banish; exile **4.** to denounce or forbid the

**practice of** —**pro·scrib′er** *n.* —**pro·scrip′tion** (-skrip′shən) *n.* —**pro·scrip′tive** *adj.* —**pro·scrip′tive·ly** *adv.*

**prose** (prōz) *n.* [MFr. < L. *prosa*, for *prorsa* (*oratio*), direct (speech), ult. < pp. of *provertere*, to turn forward] **1.** the ordinary form of language, without rhyme or meter: cf. VERSE, POETRY **2.** dull, commonplace talk —*adj.* **1.** of or in prose **2.** dull; prosaic —*vt.*, *vi.* **prosed, pros′ing** to speak or write in prose —**pros′er** *n.*

**pros·e·cute** (präs′ə kyo͞ot′) *vt.* -**cut′ed,** -**cut′ing** [< L. pp. of *prosequi* < *pro-*, before + *sequi*, to follow] **1.** to pursue (something) to a conclusion [to *prosecute* a war] **2.** to carry on; engage in **3.** *a)* to conduct legal proceedings against, esp. in court for a crime *b)* to try to get, enforce, etc. by legal process —*vi.* to institute and carry on a legal suit —**pros′e·cut′a·ble** *adj.* —**pros′e·cu′tor** *n.*

**prosecuting attorney** a public official who conducts criminal proceedings on behalf of the State; prosecutor

**pros·e·cu·tion** (präs′ə kyo͞o′shən) *n.* **1.** a prosecuting, or following up **2.** the conducting of a lawsuit **3.** the State as the party that institutes and carries on criminal proceedings in court

**pros·e·lyte** (präs′ə līt′) *n.* [< LL. < Gr. *prosēlytos*] a person who has been converted from one religion, belief, etc. to another —*vt.*, *vi.* -**lyt′ed,** -**lyt′ing 1.** to try to convert (a person), esp. to one's religion **2.** to persuade to do or join something —**pros′e·lyt′er** *n.* —**pros′e·lyt·ism** (-li tiz′m, -līt iz′m) *n.*

**pros·e·lyt·ize** (-li tīz′) *vi.*, *vt.* -**ized′,** -**iz′ing** same as PROSELYTE —**pros′e·lyt·iz′er** *n.*

**Pro·ser·pi·na** (prō sur′pi nə) *Rom. Myth.* the daughter of Ceres and wife of Pluto: identified with the Greek goddess Persephone: also **Pro·ser′pi·ne′** (-nē′, präs′ər pīn′)

**‡pro·sit** (prō′zit; *E.* prō′sit) *interj.* [G. < L. *prodesse*, to do good] to your health: a toast, esp. among Germans

**pros·o·dy** (präs′ə dē) *n.*, *pl.* -**dies** [< L. < Gr. *prosōidia*, tone, accent < *pros*, to + *ōidē*, song] the science or art of versification, including the study of metrical structure, rhyme, etc. **2.** a system of versification [Poe's *prosody*] —**pro·sod·ic** (prə säd′ik), **pro·sod′i·cal** *adj.* —**pro·sod′i·cal·ly** *adv.* —**pros′o·dist** *n.*

**pros·pect** (präs′pekt) *n.* [L. *prospectus*, lookout, ult. < *pro-*, forward + *specere*, to look] **1.** *a)* a broad view; scene *b)* a place from which one can see such a view **2.** a mental view; survey **3.** the view from any particular point; outlook **4.** a looking forward; anticipation **5.** *a)* something hoped for *b)* [*usually pl.*] apparent chance for success **6.** a likely customer, candidate, etc. —*vt.*, *vi.* to explore or search (*for*) [to *prospect* for gold] —**in prospect** expected

**pro·spec·tive** (prə spek′tiv, prä-) *adj.* **1.** looking toward the future **2.** expected; likely —**pro·spec′tive·ly** *adv.*

**pros·pec·tor** (präs′pek tər) *n.* a person who prospects for valuable ores, oil, etc.

**pro·spec·tus** (prə spek′təs, prä-) *n.* [L.: see PROSPECT] a statement outlining the main features of a new work, business enterprise, etc. or of an established institution

**pros·per** (präs′pər) *vi.* [< MFr. < L. < *prosperus*, favorable] to succeed, thrive, grow, etc. vigorously —*vt.* [Archaic] to cause to prosper

**pros·per·i·ty** (prä sper′ə tē) *n.* prosperous condition; good fortune, wealth, success, etc.

**pros·per·ous** (präs′pər əs) *adj.* **1.** prospering; flourishing **2.** well-to-do; well-off **3.** conducive to success; favorable —**pros′per·ous·ly** *adv.*

**pros·tate** (präs′tāt) *adj.* [< ML. < Gr. *prostatēs*, one standing before, ult. < *pro-*, before + *histanai*, to stand] of or relating to the prostate gland: also **pros·tat′ic** (-tat′ik) —*n.* same as PROSTATE GLAND

**prostate gland** a partly muscular gland surrounding the urethra at the base of the bladder in most male mammals

**pros·the·sis** (präs′thə sis; *for 2, often* präs thē′-) *n.*, *pl.* -**the·ses′** (-sēz′) [< LL. < Gr. < *pros*, to + *tithenai*, to place] *Med.* **1.** the replacement of a missing limb, eye, etc. by an artificial substitute **2.** such a substitute —**pros·thet′ic** (-thet′ik) *adj.*

**pros·ti·tute** (präs′tə to͞ot′, -tyo͞ot′) *vt.* -**tut′ed,** -**tut′ing** [< L. pp. of *prostituere* < *pro-*, before + *statuere*, to make stand] **1.** to sell the services of (oneself or another) for purposes of sexual intercourse **2.** to sell (oneself, one's integrity, etc.) for unworthy purposes —*n.* **1.** a woman who engages in promiscuous sexual intercourse for pay **2.** a writer, artist, etc. who sells his services for unworthy purposes —**pros′ti·tu′tion** *n.* —**pros′ti·tu′tor** *n.*

**pros·trate** (präs′trāt) *adj.* [< L. pp. of *prosternere* < *pro-*, before + *sternere*, to stretch out] **1.** lying with the face downward in humility or submission **2.** lying flat, prone, or supine **3.** thrown or fallen to the ground **4.** *a)* laid low; overcome *b)* physically weak or exhausted **5.** *Bot.* trailing on the ground —*vt.* -**trat·ed,** -**trat·ing 1.** to lay flat on the ground **2.** to lay low; overcome or exhaust —**pros·tra′tion** *n.*

**pro·style** (prō′stīl) *adj.* [< L. < Gr. < *pro*, before + *stylos*, pillar] having a portico with columns, usually four, across the front only —*n.* such a portico

**pros·y** (prō′zē) *adj.* **pros′i·er, pros′i·est 1.** like, or having the nature of, prose **2.** prosaic, dull, etc. —**pros′i·ly** *adv.* —**pros′i·ness** *n.*

**Prot.** Protestant

**pro·tac·tin·i·um** (prō′tak tin′ē əm) *n.* [ModL.: see PROTO- & ACTINIUM] a rare, radioactive, metallic chemical element: symbol, Pa; at. wt., 231.10; at. no., 91

**pro·tag·o·nist** (prō tag′ə nist) *n.* [< Gr. *prōtos*, first + *agōnistēs*, actor] **1.** the main character in a drama, novel, or story **2.** a person playing a leading or active part

**Pro·tag·o·ras** (prō tag′ər əs) 481?–411? B.C.; Gr. philosopher

**prot·a·sis** (prät′ə sis) *n.* [LL. < Gr. < *pro-*, before + *tei-nein*, to stretch] *Gram.* the clause that expresses the condition in a conditional sentence: cf. APODOSIS

**pro·te·an** (prōt′ē ən, prō tē′ən) *adj.* **1.** [P-] of or like Proteus **2.** readily taking on different shapes or forms

**pro·te·ase** (prōt′ē ās′) *n.* [PROTE(IN) + (DIAST)ASE] an enzyme that digests proteins

**pro·tect** (prə tekt′) *vt.* [< L. pp. of *protegere* < *pro-*, before + *tegere*, to cover] **1.** to shield from injury, danger, or loss; defend **2.** to set aside funds for paying (a note, draft, etc.) at maturity **3.** *Econ.* to guard (domestic goods) by tariffs on imports —**pro·tect′a·ble** *adj.*

**pro·tec·tion** (prə tek′shən) *n.* **1.** a protecting or being protected **2.** a person or thing that protects **3.** a passport **4.** [Colloq.] *a)* money extorted by racketeers threatening violence *b)* bribes paid by racketeers to avoid prosecution **5.** *Econ.* the system of protecting domestic goods by taxing imports

**pro·tec·tion·ism** (-iz′m) *n. Econ.* the system, theory, or policy of protection —**pro·tec′tion·ist** *n.*, *adj.*

**pro·tec·tive** (prə tek′tiv) *adj.* **1.** protecting or intended to protect **2.** *Econ.* intended to protect domestic products, industries, etc. in competition with foreign ones [a *protective* tariff] —**pro·tec′tive·ly** *adv.* —**pro·tec′tive·ness** *n.*

**pro·tec·tor** (prə tek′tər) *n.* **1.** one that protects; guardian **2.** *a)* a person ruling a kingdom during the minority, incapacity, etc. of the sovereign *b)* [P-] the title (in full **Lord Protector**) held by Oliver Cromwell (1653–1658) and his son Richard (1658–1659), during the Protectorate —**pro·tec′tor·ship′** *n.* —**pro·tec′tress** (-tris) *n.fem.*

**pro·tec·tor·ate** (-it) *n.* **1.** government by a protector **2.** the office or term of a protector **3.** [P-] the government of England under the Protectors (1653–1659) **4.** *a)* the relation of a strong state to a weaker state under its control and protection *b)* a state so controlled

**pro·té·gé** (prōt′ə zhā′, prōt′ə zhā′) *n.* [Fr., pp. of *protéger* < L.: see PROTECT] a person receiving guidance and help, esp. in furthering his career, from an influential person —**pro′té·gée′** (-zhā′, -zhā′) *n.fem.*

**pro·tein** (prō′tēn, prōt′ē in) *n.* [G. < Fr. < Gr. *prōteios*, prime < *prōtos*, first] any of a class of complex nitrogenous substances occurring in all animal and vegetable matter and essential to the diet of animals

**pro tem·po·re** (prō tem′pə rē′) [L.] for the time (being); temporary or temporarily: shortened to **pro tem**

**pro·te·ol·y·sis** (prōt′ē äl′ə sis) *n.* [ModL.: see PROTEIN & -LYSIS] *Biochem.* the breaking down of proteins, as by gastric juices, into simpler substances —**pro′te·o·lyt′ic** (-ə lit′ik) *adj.*

**pro·te·ose** (prōt′ē ōs′) *n.* [PROTE(IN) + -OSE¹] any of a class of water-soluble products, formed in the hydrolysis of proteins, that can be broken down into peptones

**pro·test** (prə test′; *for n.* präs′test) *vt.* [< MFr. < L. < *pro-*, forth + *testari*, to affirm < *testis*, a witness] **1.** to state positively; declare or affirm strongly **2.** to speak strongly against **3.** to make a written declaration of the nonpayment of (a promissory note, check, etc.) —*vi.* **1.** to make solemn affirmation **2.** to express disapproval; object —*n.* **1.** the act or an instance of protesting; objection **2.** a document formally objecting to something **3.** *Law* a formal declaration that a bill or note has not been honored by the drawer —**under protest** while expressing one's objections; unwillingly —**pro·test′er, pro·tes′tor** *n.*

**Prot·es·tant** (prät′is tənt; *for n. 2 & adj. 2, also* prə tes′tənt) *n.* [Fr. < G. < L. prp. of *protestari*: see prec.] **1.** a member of any of the Christian churches resulting or deriving from the Reformation under the leadership of Luther, Calvin, Wesley, etc. **2.** [p-] a person who protests —*adj.* **1.** of Protestants or Protestant beliefs, practices, etc. **2.** [p-] protesting —**Prot′es·tant·ism** *n.*

**Protestant Episcopal Church** the Protestant church in the

U.S. that conforms to the practices and principles of the Church of England

**prot·es·ta·tion** (prät′is tā′shən, prō′tes-) *n.* **1.** a strong declaration or affirmation **2.** the act of protesting **3.** a protest; objection

**Pro·teus** (prōt′ē əs, prō′tyōōs) *Gr. Myth.* a sea god who could change his own form at will

**pro·thal·li·um** (prō thal′ē əm) *n., pl.* **-li·a** (-ə) [ModL. < Gr. *pro-*, before + *thallos*, a shoot] the part of a fern that bears the sex organs, a small, flat, greenish disc usually attached to the ground by hairlike roots: also **pro·thal′lus** (-əs), *pl.* **-li** (-ī), **-lus·es**

**pro·throm·bin** (prō thräm′bin) *n.* [PRO-1 + THROMBIN] a factor in the blood plasma that is converted into thrombin during blood clotting

**pro·to-** [< Gr. < *prōtos*, first] *a combining form meaning:* **1.** first in time, original, primitive [*prototype*] **2.** first in importance, chief [*protagonist*] Also **prot-**

**pro·to·col** (prōt′ə kôl′, -käl′) *n.* [< MFr. < ML. < LGr. *prōtokollon*, first leaf glued to a manuscript (noting the contents) < Gr. *prōtos*, first + *kolla*, glue] **1.** an original draft or record of a document, negotiation, etc. **2.** the code of ceremonial forms and courtesies used in official dealings, as between heads of state or diplomats —*vt., vi.* **-colled′** or **-coled′**, **-col′ling** or **-col′ing** to draw up, or state in, a protocol

**pro·ton** (prō′tän) *n.* [ModL. < Gr. neut. of *prōtos*, first] a fundamental particle in the nucleus of all atoms: it carries a unit positive charge of electricity and has a mass approximately 1836 times that of an electron: cf. NEUTRON

**proton synchrotron** a synchrotron for accelerating protons and other heavy particles to very high energies

**pro·to·plasm** (prōt′ə plaz′m) *n.* [< G.: see PROTO- & PLASMA] a semifluid, colloidal substance that is the essential living matter of all animal and plant cells —**pro′to·plas′mic** *adj.*

**pro·to·type** (prōt′ə tīp′) *n.* [see PROTO- & TYPE] **1.** the first thing or being of its kind; original **2.** a model for another of its kind **3.** a perfect example of a particular type —**pro′-to·typ′al** (-tī′p′l), **pro′to·typ′ic** (-tip′ik), **pro′to·typ′i·cal** *adj.*

**pro·to·zo·an** (prōt′ə zō′ən) *n.* [ModL. *Protozoa* (see PROTO-& -ZOA) + -AN] any of a large group of mostly microscopic, one-celled animals living chiefly in water but sometimes parasitic: also **pro′to·zo′on** (-än), *pl.* **-zo′a** (-ə) —*adj.* of the protozoans: also **pro′to·zo′ic** (-ik)

**pro·tract** (prō trakt′) *vt.* [< L. pp. of *protrahere* < *pro-*, forward + *trahere*, to draw] **1.** to draw out in time; prolong **2.** to draw to scale, using a protractor and scale **3.** *Zool.* to thrust out; extend —**pro·tract′ed·ly** *adv.* —**pro·tract′ed·ness** *n.* —**pro·tract′i·ble** *adj.* —**pro·trac′tion** *n.* —**pro·trac′tive** *adj.*

**pro·trac·tile** (prō trak′t′l) *adj.* capable of being protracted or thrust out; extensible

**pro·trac·tor** (-tər) *n.* [ML.] **1.** a person or thing that protracts **2.** a graduated, semicircular instrument for plotting and measuring angles

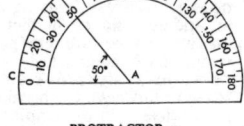

PROTRACTOR
(DAC, angle measured)

**pro·trude** (prō trōōd′) *vt., vi.* **-trud′ed**, **-trud′ing** [< L. < *pro-*, forth + *trudere*, to thrust] to thrust or jut out; project —**pro·tru′sion** (-trōō′zhən) *n.*

**pro·tru·sile** (-trōō′s′l) *adj.* that can be protruded, or thrust out, as a tentacle, etc.: also **pro·tru′si·ble**

**pro·tru·sive** (-trōō′siv) *adj.* **1.** protruding; jutting or bulging out **2.** *same as* OBTRUSIVE —**pro·tru′sive·ly** *adv.* —**pro·tru′sive·ness** *n.*

**pro·tu·ber·ance** (prō tōō′bər əns, -tyōō′-) *n.* **1.** a being protuberant **2.** a part or thing that protrudes; projection; bulge; swelling Also **pro·tu′ber·an·cy** (-ən sē), *pl.* **-cies**

**pro·tu·ber·ant** (-ənt) *adj.* [< LL. prp. of *protuberare*, to bulge out < L. *pro-*, forth + *tuber*, a bump] bulging or swelling out; protruding; prominent —**pro·tu′ber·ant·ly** *adv.*

**proud** (proud) *adj.* [OE. *prud* < OFr. < LL. *prode*, beneficial < L. *prodesse*, to be useful] **1.** having or showing a proper pride in oneself, one's position, etc. **2.** having or showing an overweening opinion of oneself; haughty; arrogant **3.** feeling or causing great pride or joy [his *proud* parents, a *proud* moment] **4.** caused by pride; presumptuous **5.** stately; splendid [a *proud* fleet] **6.** spirited [a *proud* stallion] —**do oneself proud** [Colloq.] to do extremely well —**proud of** highly pleased with —**proud′ly** *adv.*

**proud flesh** [< the notion of swelling up] an abnormal growth of flesh around a healing wound

**Proust** (prōōst), **Mar·cel** (mär sel′) 1871–1922; Fr. novelist —**Proust′i·an** *adj.*

**Prov. 1.** Provençal **2.** Proverbs **3.** Province

**prov. 1.** province **2.** provincial **3.** provisional **4.** provost

**prove** (prōōv) *vt.* **proved**, **proved** or **prov′en**, **prov′ing** [< OFr. *prover* < L.: see PROBE] **1.** to test by experiment, a standard, etc.; try out **2.** to establish as true; demonstrate to be a fact **3.** to establish the validity of (a will, etc.) **4.** to show (oneself) to be capable, dependable, etc. **5.** *Math.* to test the correctness of (a calculation, etc.) —*vi.* to be found by experience or trial; turn out to be —**prov′a·bil′-i·ty, prov′a·ble·ness** *n.* —**prov′a·ble** *adj.* —**prov′a·bly** *adv.* —**prov′er** *n.*

**prov·e·nance** (präv′ə nəns) *n.* [Fr. < L. < *pro-*, forth + *venire*, to come] origin; derivation; source

**Pro·ven·çal** (prō′vən säl′, präv′ən-) *adj.* of Provence, its people, their language, etc. —*n.* **1.** the vernacular of S France, a Romance language which, in its medieval form, was an important literary language **2.** a native or inhabitant of Provence

**Pro·vence** (prô väns′) region & former province of SE France, on the Mediterranean

**prov·en·der** (präv′ən dər) *n.* [< MFr. < ML. *praebenda:* see PREBEND] **1.** dry food for livestock, as hay, corn, etc. **2.** [Colloq.] provisions; food

**prov·erb** (präv′ərb) *n.* [< OFr. < L. < *pro-*, before + *verbum*, a word] **1.** a short, popular saying that expresses some obvious truth; adage; maxim **2.** a person or thing that has become commonly recognized as a type; byword

**pro·ver·bi·al** (prə vur′bē əl) *adj.* **1.** of, or having the nature of, a proverb **2.** expressed in a proverb **3.** well-known because commonly referred to —**pro·ver′bi·al·ly** *adv.*

**Prov·erbs** (präv′ərbz) a book of the Bible containing maxims ascribed to Solomon and others

**pro·vide** (prə vīd′) *vt.* **-vid′ed**, **-vid′ing** [< L. < *pro-*, before + *videre*, to see] **1.** to make available; supply **2.** to supply (someone *with* something) **3.** to state as a condition; stipulate —*vi.* **1.** to prepare (*for* or *against*) a possible situation, event, etc. **2.** to furnish the means of support (*for*) —**pro·vid′er** *n.*

**pro·vid·ed** (-vīd′id) *conj.* on the condition or understanding; if (often with *that*)

**Prov·i·dence** (präv′ə dəns) [named by Roger WILLIAMS] capital of Rhode Island, on Narragansett Bay: pop. 157,000 (met. area 918,000)

**prov·i·dence** (präv′ə dəns) *n.* [< MFr. < L. < prp. of *providere:* see PROVIDE] **1.** a looking to, or preparation for, the future; provision **2.** skill in management; prudence **3.** *a)* the benevolent guidance of God or nature *b)* an instance of this **4.** [P-] God

**prov·i·dent** (-dənt) *adj.* [< L. *providens*, prp. of *providere:* see PROVIDE] **1.** providing for future needs or events **2.** prudent or economical —**prov′i·dent·ly** *adv.*

**prov·i·den·tial** (präv′ə den′shəl) *adj.* of, by, or as if decreed by divine providence —**prov′i·den′tial·ly** *adv.*

**pro·vid·ing** (prə vīd′iŋ) *conj.* on the condition or understanding; provided (often with *that*)

**prov·ince** (präv′ins) *n.* [< OFr. < L. *provincia*] **1.** an outside territory governed by ancient Rome **2.** an administrative division of a country; specif., any of the ten main divisions of Canada **3.** *a)* a territorial district; territory *b)* [*pl.*] the parts of a country removed from the capital and major cities **4.** range of duties or functions **5.** a field of knowledge, activity, etc. **6.** a division of a country under the jurisdiction of an archbishop or metropolitan

**pro·vin·cial** (prə vin′shəl) *adj.* **1.** of or belonging to a province **2.** having the ways, speech, attitudes, etc. of a certain province **3.** rural; countrified; rustic **4.** narrow or limited in outlook; unsophisticated —*n.* **1.** a native of a province **2.** a provincial, esp. unsophisticated, person —**pro·vin′cial·ly** *adv.*

**pro·vin·cial·ism** (-iz′m) *n.* **1.** a being provincial **2.** narrowness of outlook **3.** a provincial custom, characteristic, etc. **4.** a word, phrase, etc. peculiar to a province Also **pro·vin′ci·al′i·ty** (-shē al′ə tē), *pl.* **-ties** —**pro·vin′cial·ist** *n.*

**proving ground** a place for testing new equipment, new theories, etc.

**pro·vi·sion** (prə vizh′ən) *n.* [MFr. < L. < pp. of *providere:* see PROVIDE] **1.** a providing or supplying **2.** something provided for the future; specif., [*pl.*] a stock of food **3.** a preparatory arrangement or measure taken in advance **4.** a clause, as in a legal document, stipulating some specific thing —*vt.* to supply with provisions, esp. with a stock of food —**pro·vi′sion·er** *n.*

**pro·vi·sion·al** (-′l) *adj.* conditional or temporary, pending a permanent arrangement —**pro·vi′sion·al·ly** *adv.*

**pro·vi·so** (prə vī′zō) *n., pl.* **-sos, -soes** [ML. *proviso* (*quod*), provided that] **1.** a clause, as in a document, making some condition **2.** a condition or stipulation

**pro·vi·so·ry** (-zər ē) *adj.* **1.** containing a proviso; conditional **2.** *same as* PROVISIONAL —**pro·vi′so·ri·ly** *adv.*

**Pro·vo** (prō′vō) [after Étienne *Provot*, early fur trader] city in NC Utah: pop. 74,000

**prov·o·ca·tion** (präv′ə kā′shən) *n.* **1.** a provoking **2.** something that provokes; esp., a cause of anger or irritation

**pro·voc·a·tive** (prə väk′ə tiv) *adj.* provoking or tending to provoke; stimulating, erotic, irritating, etc. —*n.* something that provokes —**pro·voc′a·tive·ly** *adv.* —**pro·voc′a·tive·ness** *n.*

**pro·voke** (prə vōk′) *vt.* **-voked′, -vok′ing** [< MFr. < L. < *pro-*, forth + *vocare*, to call] **1.** to excite to some action or feeling **2.** to anger or irritate **3.** to stir up (action or feeling) **4.** to evoke —**pro·vok′er** *n.* —**pro·vok′ing·ly** *adv.*

**pro·vo·lo·ne** (prō′və lō′nē, präv′ə-) *n.* [It.] a hard, light-colored Italian cheese, usually smoked

**pro·vost** (prō′vōst; *priv.′əst; esp. military* prō′vō) *n.* [< OE. & OFr., both < ML. *propositus*, for L. *praepositus*, chief, ult. < *prae-*, before + *ponere*, to place] **1.** a superintendent; official in charge **2.** the chief magistrate of a Scottish burgh **3.** the head of a cathedral chapter or principal church **4.** the head of, or an administrator in, some colleges and universities —**pro′vost·ship′** *n.*

**pro·vost guard** (prō′vō) a detail of military police under the command of an officer (**provost marshal**)

**prow** (prou) *n.* [< Fr., ult. < L. < Gr. *prōira*] **1.** the forward part of a ship **2.** anything like this

**prow·ess** (prou′is, prō′-) *n.* [< OFr. *prouesse* < *prou*, brave, var. of *prud*: see PROUD] **1.** bravery; valor **2.** superior ability, skill, etc.

**prowl** (proul) *vi., vt.* [ME. *prollen* < ?] to roam about furtively as in search of prey —*n.* a prowling —**on the prowl** prowling about —**prowl′er** *n.*

**prowl car** *same as* SQUAD CAR

**prox.** proximo

**prox·i·mal** (präk′sə m′l) *adj.* **1.** proximate; next or nearest **2.** situated near the point of attachment of a limb, etc. —**prox′i·mal·ly** *adv.*

**prox·i·mate** (präk′sə mit) *adj.* [< LL. pp. of *proximare*, to come near < L. *proximus*, nearest, superl. of *prope*, near] **1.** next or nearest in space, order, time, etc. **2.** approximate —**prox′i·mate·ly** *adv.*

**prox·im·i·ty** (präk sim′ə tē) *n.* [< MFr. < L. < *proximus*: see prec.] nearness in space, time, etc.

**prox·i·mo** (präk′sə mō′) *adv.* [L. *proximo* (*mense*), in the next (month)] in or of the next month [on the 9th *proximo*]

**prox·y** (präk′sē) *n., pl.* **prox′ies** [ME. *prokecie* < *procuracie*, office of a procurator] **1.** the function of a deputy **2.** *a)* the authority to act for another, or a person given this authority *b)* a document giving this authority, as in voting at a stockholders' meeting

**prs.** pairs

**prude** (prōōd) *n.* [Fr. < *prudefemme*, excellent woman] a person who is overly modest or proper in behavior, dress, speech, etc., esp. in a way that annoys others —**prud′ish** *adj.* —**prud′ish·ly** *adv.* —**prud′ish·ness** *n.*

**pru·dence** (prōōd′'ns) *n.* **1.** the quality or fact of being prudent **2.** careful management; economy

**pru·dent** (prōōd′'nt) *adj.* [OFr. < L. *prudens*, for *providens*, PROVIDENT] **1.** exercising sound judgment in practical matters, esp. as concerns one's own interests **2.** cautious in conduct; sensible; not rash **3.** managing carefully and with economy —**pru′dent·ly** *adv.*

**pru·den·tial** (prōō den′shəl) *adj.* **1.** characterized by or exercising prudence **2.** having an advisory function —**pru·den′tial·ly** *adv.*

**prud·er·y** (prōōd′ər ē) *n.* a being prudish

**prune**[1] (prōōn) *n.* [< MFr. < VL. < L. *prunum* < Gr. *proumnon*, plum] **1.** a plum dried for eating **2.** [Slang] a dull or otherwise unpleasant person

**prune**[2] (prōōn) *vt.* **pruned, prun′ing** [< MFr., prob. ult. < *provain* (< L. *propago*), a slip] **1.** to remove dead or living parts from (a plant), as to increase fruit or flower production **2.** to cut out as being unnecessary **3.** to shorten by removing unnecessary parts [to prune a novel] —*vi.* to remove unnecessary parts —**prun′er** *n.*

**pruning hook** a long tool or shears with a hooked blade, for pruning plants

**pru·ri·ent** (proor′ē ənt) *adj.* [L. *pruriens* < *prurire*, to itch, long for] **1.** having lustful ideas or desires **2.** full of or causing lust; lascivious; lewd —**pru′ri·ence, pru′ri·en·cy** *n.* —**pru′ri·ent·ly** *adv.*

**pru·ri·tus** (proo rīt′əs) *n.* [< L. pp. of *prurire*, to itch] intense itching without a rash —**pru·rit′ic** (-rit′ik) *adj.*

**Prus·sia** (prush′ə) former kingdom in N Europe (1701–1871) & the dominant state of the German Empire (1871–1919) —**Prus′sian** *adj., n.*

**Prussian blue** any of a group of dark-blue iron pigments used in paints, printing inks, etc.

**prus·sic acid** (prus′ik) *same as* HYDROCYANIC ACID

**pry**[1] (prī) *n., pl.* **pries** [back-formation < PRIZE[2]] **1.** a lever or crowbar **2.** leverage —*vt.* **pried, pry′ing 1.** to raise or move with a lever or crowbar **2.** to draw forth with difficulty

**pry**[2] (prī) *vi.* **pried, pry′ing** [ME. *prien* < ?] to look (*into*) closely or inquisitively; peer or snoop —*n., pl.* **pries 1.** a prying **2.** a person who is too inquisitive

**pry·er** (prī′ər) *n. same as* PRIER

**pry·ing** (-iŋ) *adj.* improperly curious or inquisitive —**pry′ing·ly** *adv.*

**Ps., Psa.** Psalm; Psalms

**ps.** pieces

**P.S. 1.** Privy Seal **2.** Public School

**P.S., p.s., PS** postscript

**psalm** (säm) *n.* [OE. *sealm* < LL. < Gr. *psalmos* < *psallein*, to pluck (a harp)] **1.** a sacred song or poem **2.** [*usually* P-] any of the sacred songs in praise of God that make up the Book of Psalms in the Bible

**psalm·book** (-book′) *n.* a collection of psalms for use in religious worship

**psalm·ist** (-ist) *n.* a composer of psalms —**the Psalmist** King David, to whom some or all of the Psalms are attributed

**psal·mo·dy** (säm′ə dē, sal′mə-) *n.* [< LL. < Gr. < *psalmos* (see PSALM) + *ōidē*, a song] **1.** the singing of psalms **2.** psalms collectively **3.** the arrangement of psalms for singing —**psal′mo·dist** *n.*

**Psalms** (sämz) a book of the Bible, consisting of 150 psalms: also **Book of Psalms**

**Psal·ter** (sôl′tər) *n.* [< OE. & OFr., both < L. < Gr. *psaltērion*, psaltery < *psallein*, to pluck] the Book of Psalms —*n.* [*also* p-] a version of the Psalms for use in religious services

**psal·ter·y** (sôl′tər ē, sôl′trē) *n., pl.* **-ter·ies** [< OFr. < L.: see PSALTER] an ancient stringed instrument with a shallow sound box, played by plucking the strings

PSALTERY

**pseud.** pseudonym

**pseu·do** (sōō′dō, syōō′-) *adj.* [see ff.] sham; false; spurious; pretended; counterfeit

**pseu·do-** [< LL. < Gr. < *pseudēs*, false < *pseudein*, to deceive] *a combining form meaning:* **1.** fictitious, sham [*pseudonym*] **2.** counterfeit, spurious **3.** closely or deceptively similar to (a specified thing): also **pseud-**

**pseu·do·nym** (sōō′də nim′, syōō′-) *n.* [< Fr. < Gr. < *pseudēs*, false + *onyma*, a name] a fictitious name, esp. one assumed by an author; pen name —**pseu′do·nym′i·ty** *n.* —**pseu·don′y·mous** (-dän′ə məs) *adj.* —**pseu·don′y·mous·ly** *adv.*

**pseu·do·po·di·um** (sōō′də pō′dē əm, syōō′də-) *n., pl.* **-di·a** (-ə) [ModL.: see PSEUDO- & PODIUM] a temporary jutting out of a part of a single cell, as in an amoeba, by means of which it can move about or take in food: also **pseu′do·pod′** (-päd′) —**pseu·dop′o·dal** (-däp′ə dəl) *adj.*

**pseu·do·sci·ence** (-dō sī′əns) *n.* any system of theories that claims to be a science but has no scientific basis —**pseu′do·sci′en·tif′ic** *adj.*

**psf, p.s.f.** pounds per square foot

**pshaw** (shô) *interj., n.* an exclamation of impatience, disgust, contempt, etc.

**psi** (sī, psē) *n.* [LGr. < Gr.] the twenty-third letter of the Greek alphabet (Ψ, ψ)

**psi, p.s.i.** pounds per square inch

**psi·lo·cy·bin** (sī′lə sī′bin, sil′ə-) *n.* [< ModL. *Psilocybe*, genus of mushrooms] a hallucinogenic drug obtained from certain mushrooms

**psit·ta·co·sis** (sit′ə kō′sis) *n.* [ModL. < L. < Gr. *psittakos*, a parrot + -OSIS] an acute, infectious virus disease of birds of the parrot family, often transmitted to man

**pso·ri·a·sis** (sə rī′ə sis) *n.* [ModL. < Gr. < *psōra*, an itch] a chronic skin disease in which scaly, reddish patches are formed —**pso·ri·at·ic** (sôr′ē at′ik) *adj.*

**psst** (pst) *interj.* a sound made to get someone's attention quickly and quietly

**PST, P.S.T.** Pacific Standard Time

**psych** (sīk) *vt.* **psyched, psych′ing** [clipped < PSYCHOANALYZE] [Slang] to figure out the motives of, esp. in order to outwit, control, etc. (often with *out*)

**Psy·che** (sī′kē) *n.* [L. < Gr. < *psychē*, the soul] *Rom. Myth.* a maiden who becomes the wife of Cupid and is made immortal

**psy·che** (sī′kē) *n.* [L. < Gr. < *psychē*, the soul] **1.** the human soul **2.** the human mind

**psy·che·del·ic** (sī′kə del′ik) *adj.* [< PSYCHE + Gr. *delein*, to make manifest] **1.** of or causing extreme changes in the conscious mind, with hallucinations, delusions, etc. **2.** of or like the intense, distorted sights, sounds, colors, etc. produced by such changes in the mind —*n.* a psychedelic drug —**psy′che·del′i·cal·ly** *adv.*

**psy·chi·a·trist** (sə kī′ə trist, sī-) *n.* a doctor of medicine specializing in psychiatry

**psy·chi·a·try** (-trē) *n.* [ModL.: see PSYCHO- & -IATRY] the branch of medicine dealing with disorders of the mind, including psychoses and neuroses —**psy·chi·at·ric** (sī′kē-at′rik), **psy′chi·at′ri·cal** *adj.* —**psy′chi·at′ri·cal·ly** *adv.*

**psy·chic** (sī′kik) *adj.* [< Gr. < *psychē*, the soul] **1.** of the psyche, or mind **2.** beyond natural or known physical processes **3.** apparently sensitive to supernatural forces Also **psy′chi·cal** —*n.* a person who is supposedly sensitive to supernatural forces —**psy′chi·cal·ly** *adv.*

**psy·cho** (sī′kō) *adj., n. colloq. clipped form of* PSYCHOTIC, PSYCHOPATHIC, PSYCHOPATH

**psy·cho-** [< Gr. *psychē*, soul] *a combining form meaning* the mind or mental processes [*psychology*]: also, before a vowel, **psych-**

**psy·cho·ac·tive** (sī′kō ak′tiv) *adj.* [PSYCHO- + ACTIVE] designating or of a drug, chemical, etc. that has a strong or specific effect on the mind

**psy·cho·a·nal·y·sis** (sī′kō ə nal′ə sis) *n.* [ModL.: see PSYCHO- & ANALYSIS] a method or practice, originated by Freud, of treating neuroses and some other mental disorders through analysis of emotional conflicts, repressions, etc. by getting the patient to talk freely, analyzing his dreams, etc. —**psy′cho·an′a·lyt′ic** (-an′ə lit′ik), **psy′cho·an′a·lyt′i·cal** *adj.* —**psy′cho·an′a·lyt′i·cal·ly** *adv.*

**psy·cho·an·a·lyst** (-an′əl ist) *n.* a specialist in psychoanalysis

**psy·cho·an·a·lyze** (-an′ə līz′) *vt.* **-lyzed′, -lyz′ing** to treat by means of psychoanalysis

**psy·cho·dra·ma** (sī′kə drä′mə) *n.* a form of psychotherapy in which each patient in a group acts out situations related to his problem —**psy′cho·dra·mat′ic** (-drə mat′ik) *adj.*

**psy·cho·dy·nam·ics** (sī′kō dī nam′iks) *n.pl.* [*with sing. v.*] the study of the mental and emotional motives underlying human behavior —**psy′cho·dy·nam′ic** *adj.* —**psy′cho·dy·nam′i·cal·ly** *adv.*

**psy·cho·gen·ic** (sī′kə jen′ik) *adj.* [PSYCHO- + -GENIC] caused by mental conflicts; psychic —**psy′cho·gen′i·cal·ly** *adv.*

**psy·cho·ki·ne·sis** (sī′kō ki nē′sis) *n.* [PSYCHO- + Gr. *kinēsis*, motion] the supposed ability to influence physical objects or events by thought processes —**psy′cho·ki·net′ic** (-net′ik) *adj.*

**psy·cho·log·i·cal** (sī′kə läj′i k′l) *adj.* **1.** of psychology **2.** of the mind; mental **3.** affecting or intended to affect the mind Also **psy′cho·log′ic** —**psy′cho·log′i·cal·ly** *adv.*

**psychological moment 1.** the moment when one is mentally ready for something **2.** the critical moment

**psychological warfare** the use of psychological means, as propaganda, to influence the thinking of or undermine the morale of an enemy

**psy·chol·o·gist** (sī käl′ə jist) *n.* a specialist in psychology

**psy·chol·o·gize** (-ə jīz′) *vi.* **-gized′, -giz′ing 1.** to study psychology **2.** to reason psychologically —*vt.* to analyze psychologically

**psy·chol·o·gy** (-jē) *n., pl.* **-gies** [< ModL.: see PSYCHO- & -LOGY] **1.** *a)* the science dealing with the mind and with mental and emotional processes *b)* the science of human and animal behavior **2.** the sum of a person's actions, traits, thoughts, etc. **3.** a system of psychology

**psy·cho·neu·ro·sis** (sī′kō noo rō′sis) *n., pl.* **-ro′ses** (-sēz) [ModL.: see PSYCHO- & NEUROSIS] *same as* NEUROSIS —**psy′cho·neu·rot′ic** (-rät′ik) *adj., n.*

**psy·cho·path** (sī′kə path′) *n. same as* PSYCHOPATHIC PERSONALITY (sense 1)

**psy·cho·path·ic** (sī′kə path′ik) *adj.* characterized by psychopathy; mentally ill —**psy′cho·path′i·cal·ly** *adv.*

**psychopathic personality 1.** a person with serious personality defects, whose behavior is amoral and asocial (often criminal), generally without psychotic symptoms **2.** the personality of such a person

**psy·cho·pa·thol·o·gy** (sī′kō pa thäl′ə jē) *n.* **1.** the science dealing with mental disorders **2.** the behavior of the mentally ill —**psy′cho·path′o·log′i·cal** (-path′ə läj′i k′l) *adj.* —**psy′cho·pa·thol′o·gist** *n.*

**psy·chop·a·thy** (sī käp′ə thē) *n.* [PSYCHO- + -PATHY] mental disorder

**psy·cho·phar·ma·col·o·gy** (sī′kō fär′mə käl′ə jē) *n.* the study of the effects of drugs on the mind —**psy′cho·phar′ma·co·log′i·cal** (-kə läj′i k′l), **psy′cho·phar′ma·co·log′ic** *adj.*

**psy·cho·sex·u·al** (-sek′shoo wəl) *adj.* having to do with the psychological aspects of sexuality in contrast to the physical aspects —**psy′cho·sex′u·al′i·ty** (-wal′ə tē) *n.*

**psy·cho·sis** (sī kō′sis) *n., pl.* **-cho′ses** (-sēz) [ModL.: see PSYCHO- & -OSIS] a major mental disorder in which the personality is very seriously disorganized and one's sense of reality is usually altered

**psy·cho·so·cial** (sī′kō sō′shəl) *adj.* of the psychological development of an individual in relation to his social environment

**psy·cho·so·mat·ic** (-sō mat′ik) *adj.* [PSYCHO- + SOMATIC] **1.** designating or of a physical disorder originating in or aggravated by one's psychic or emotional processes **2.** designating a system of medicine using a coordinated psychological and physiological approach toward such disorders —**psy′cho·so·mat′i·cal·ly** *adv.*

**psy·cho·ther·a·py** (-ther′ə pē) *n.* [PSYCHO- + THERAPY] treatment of mental disorder by counseling, psychoanalysis, etc. —**psy′cho·ther′a·peu′tic** *adj.* —**psy′cho·ther′a·pist** *n.*

**psy·chot·ic** (sī kät′ik) *adj.* of or having a psychosis —*n.* a person having a psychosis —**psy·chot′i·cal·ly** *adv.*

**psy·chot·o·mi·met·ic** (sī kät′ō mi met′ik) *adj.* [< PSYCHOT(IC) + -o- + MIMETIC] designating or of certain drugs, as LSD and mescaline, that produce hallucinations, psychotic symptoms, etc. —*n.* a psychotomimetic drug

**psy·cho·tox·ic** (sī′kō täk′sik) *adj.* [PSYCHO- + TOXIC] of or pertaining to substances capable of damaging the brain

**Pt** *Chem.* platinum

**pt.** *pl.* **pts. 1.** part **2.** pint **3.** point

**p.t. 1.** past tense **2.** pro tempore

**P.T.A.** Parent-Teacher Association

**ptar·mi·gan** (tär′mə gən) *n., pl.* **-gans, -gan:** see PLURAL, II, D, 1 [altered (after PTERO-) < Scot. *tarmachan*] any of several varieties of northern or alpine grouse, having feathered legs and undergoing seasonal color changes

**PT boat** [*p(atrol) t(orpedo) boat*] a high-speed motorboat equipped with torpedoes and machine guns

**pter·i·do·phyte** (ter′ə dō fīt′, tə rid′ə-) *n.* [< Gr. *pteris*, a fern + -PHYTE] a group of plants reproducing by means of spores and including the ferns —**pter′id·o·phyt′ic** (-fit′ik), **pter′i·doph′y·tous** (-däf′i təs) *adj.*

**pter·o-** [ModL. < Gr. *pteron*] *a combining form meaning* feather, wing [*pterodactyl*]

**pter·o·dac·tyl** (ter′ə dak′t′l) *n.* [< ModL.: see prec. & DACTYL] an extinct flying reptile, having wings of skin stretched between the hind limb and a long digit of the forelimb —**pter′o·dac′tyl·oid′, pter′o·dac′tyl·ous** *adj.*

PTERODACTYL
(wingspread to 20 ft.)

**-pter·ous** (tər əs) [see PTERO- & -OUS] *a combining form meaning* having (a specified number or kind of) wings [*homopterous*]

**Ptol·e·ma·ic** (täl′ə mā′ik) *adj.* **1.** of Ptolemy, the astronomer, or his theory that the earth is the center of the universe and that the heavenly bodies move around it **2.** of the Ptolemies who ruled Egypt

**Ptol·e·my** (täl′ə mē) **1.** (L. name *Claudius Ptolemaeus*) 2d cent. A.D.; Gr. astronomer, mathematician, & geographer of Alexandria **2.** *pl.* **-mies** Macedonian family whose members formed the ruling dynasty of Egypt (305?-30 B.C.); esp., *a)* **Ptolemy I** 367?-283; 1st king of this dynasty (305?-285) *b)* **Ptolemy II** 309?- 247?; king of Egypt (285-247?)

**pto·maine** (tō′mān) *n.* [< It. < Gr. *ptōma*, a corpse < *piptein*, to fall] any of a class of alkaloid substances, some of which are poisonous, formed in decaying animal or vegetable matter by bacteria

**ptomaine poisoning** *earlier term for* FOOD POISONING (erroneously thought to be from ptomaines)

**pty·a·lin** (tī′ə lin) *n.* [< Gr. < *ptyein*, to spit + -IN¹] an enzyme in the saliva of man (and some animals) that converts starch to dextrin and maltose

**Pu** *Chem.* plutonium

**pub** (pub) *n. chiefly Brit. colloq. clipped form of* PUBLIC HOUSE (sense 2)

**pub. 1.** public **2.** published **3.** publisher **4.** publishing

**pu·ber·ty** (pyoo′bər tē) *n.* [< L. < *puber*, adult] the state of physical development when sexual reproduction first becomes possible: the age is generally fixed in common law at 14 for boys and 12 for girls —**pu′ber·tal** *adj.*

**pu·bes¹** (pyoo′bēz) *n.* [L., pubic hair] **1.** the body hair appearing at puberty; esp., the hair surrounding the genitals **2.** the region of the abdomen covered by such hair

**pu·bes²** (pyoo′bēz) *n. pl. of* PUBIS

**pu·bes·cent** (pyoo bes′'nt) *adj.* [Fr. < L. prp. of *pubescere*, to reach puberty < *pubes*, adult] **1.** reaching or having reached puberty **2.** covered with a soft down, as many plants and insects —**pu·bes′cence** *n.*

**pu·bic** (pyoo′bik) *adj.* of or in the region of the pubes

**pu·bis** (-bis) *n., pl.* **pu′bes** (-bēz) [ModL. < L.: see PUBES¹] that part of either hipbone forming, with the other, the front arch of the pelvis

**pub·lic** (pub′lik) *adj.* [L. *publicus*, ult. < *populus*, the people] 1. of, belonging to, or concerning the people as a whole; of the community at large [the *public* welfare] 2. for the use or benefit of all; esp., government-supported [a *public* park] 3. acting in an official capacity on behalf of the people as a whole [the *public* prosecutor] 4. known by all or most people [a *public* figure] —*n.* 1. the people as a whole; community at large 2. a specific part of the people [the reading *public*] —**go public** *Finance* to offer corporation stock for sale to the public —**in public** openly; not in privacy or secret —**pub′lic·ly** *adv.*

**pub·li·can** (pub′li kən) *n.* 1. in ancient Rome, a tax collector 2. [Brit.] a saloonkeeper; innkeeper

**pub·li·ca·tion** (pub′lə kā′shən) *n.* [< L. < *publicare:* see PUBLISH] 1. a publishing or being published; public notification 2. the printing and distribution, usually for sale, of books, magazines, newspapers, etc. 3. something published, esp. a periodical

**public domain** 1. public lands, for the use of everyone 2. the condition of being free from copyright or patent, and available to anyone

**public enemy** a hardened criminal or other person who is a menace to society

**public house** 1. an inn 2. [Brit.] an establishment where alcoholic drinks are served; bar

**pub·li·cist** (pub′lə sist) *n.* 1. a specialist in international law 2. a journalist who writes about public affairs 3. a specialist in public relations

**pub·lic·i·ty** (pə blis′ə tē) *n.* 1. a being public, or commonly known 2. a) any information that makes a person, place, etc. known or well-known to the public b) the work of handling such information 3. a being noticed by the public 4. any procedure or act intended to gain public notice

**pub·li·cize** (pub′lə sīz′) *vt.* **-cized′, -ciz′ing** to give publicity to; draw public attention to

**public opinion** the opinion held by people generally

**public relations** relations of an organization with the public through publicity seeking to form public opinion

**public school** 1. in the U.S., an elementary or secondary school that is part of a system of free schools maintained by public taxes and supervised by local authorities 2. in England, any of several private, expensive, endowed boarding schools for boys, preparing them for the universities or the public service

**public servant** an elected or appointed government official or a civil-service employee

**pub·lic-spir·it·ed** (pub′lik spir′i tid) *adj.* having or showing zeal for the public welfare

**public utility** an organization that supplies water, electricity, transportation, etc. to the public: it may be operated either by a private corporation (**public-service corporation**) under governmental regulation or by the government itself

**public works** works constructed by the government for public use or service, as highways or dams

**pub·lish** (pub′lish) *vt.* [< OFr. < L. *publicare* < *publicus,* PUBLIC] 1. to make publicly known; announce; proclaim 2. *a)* to issue (a printed work, etc.) to the public, as for sale *b)* to issue the written work of (an author) —*vi.* 1. to issue books, newspapers, etc. to the public 2. to write books, etc. that are published —**pub′lish·a·ble** *adj.*

**pub·lish·er** (-ər) *n.* a person or firm that publishes books, newspapers, magazines, etc.

**Puc·ci·ni** (pōt chē′nē), **Gia·co·mo** (jä′kô mô′) 1858-1924; It. operatic composer

**puce** (pyōos) *n.* [Fr., lit., a flea] brownish purple

**puck¹** (puk) *n.* [akin to POKE¹] *Ice Hockey* a hard rubber disk which the players try to drive into the opponents' goal

**puck²** (puk) *n.* [OE. *puca*] a mischievous sprite or elf, as [P-] the one in Shakespeare's *A Midsummer Night's Dream* —**puck′ish** *adj.* —**puck′ish·ly** *adv.* —**puck′ish·ness** *n.*

**puck·a** (puk′ə) *adj.* same as PUKKA

**puck·er** (puk′ər) *vt., vi.* [freq. form of POKE²] to draw up into wrinkles or small folds —*n.* such a wrinkle or fold —**pucker up** to contract the lips as in preparing to kiss —**puck′er·y** *adj.*

**pud·ding** (pood′iŋ) *n.* [akin ? to OE. *puduc,* a swelling] 1. [Scot.] a kind of boiled sausage 2. a soft, mushy food, usually made with a base of flour, cereal, etc. and boiled or baked 3. a sweetened dessert of this kind, variously containing eggs, milk, fruit, etc.

**pud·dle** (pud′'l) *n.* [dim. < OE. *pudd,* a ditch] 1. a small pool of water, esp. stagnant or muddy water 2. a thick mixture of clay, and sometimes sand, with water —*vt.* **-dled, -dling** 1. to make muddy 2. to make a thick mixture of

(wet clay and sand) 3. to keep water from penetrating by using this mixture 4. to treat (iron) by the puddling process —*vi.* to dabble or wallow in muddy water —**pud′dler** *n.* —**pud′dly** *adj.* **-dli·er, -dli·est**

**pud·dling** (-liŋ) *n.* the process of making wrought iron from pig iron by heating and stirring it in the presence of oxidizing agents

**pu·den·dum** (pyōo den′dəm) *n., pl.* **-den′da** (-də) [ModL., ult. < L. *pudere,* to be ashamed] [*usually pl.*] the external human sex organs, esp. of the female —**pu·den′dal** (-d′l) *adj.*

**pudg·y** (puj′ē) *adj.* **pudg′i·er, pudg′i·est** [prob. < Scot. *pud,* belly] short and fat —**pudg′i·ness** *n.*

**Pueb·lo** (pweb′lō) [see ff.] city in SC Colo., on the Arkansas River: pop. 102,000

**pueb·lo** (pweb′lō) *n., pl.* **-los;** also, for 2, **-lo** [Sp. < L. *populus,* people] 1. an Indian village of the SW U.S.; specif., one in which the Indians live together in one or more terraced, flat-roofed structures of stone or adobe 2. [P-] an Indian, as a Hopi, living in a pueblo

**pu·er·ile** (pyōō′ər əl, pyoor′əl; -īl) *adj.* [< Fr. < L. < *puer,* boy] childish; silly; immature —**pu′er·ile·ly** *adv.* —**pu′er·il′i·ty** (-ə ril′ə tē) *n., pl.* **-ties**

**pu·er·per·al** (pyōō ur′pər əl) *adj.* [< L. < *puer,* boy + *parere,* to bear] of or connected with childbirth

**puerperal fever** septic poisoning occurring during childbirth: a term no longer used

**Puer·to Ri·co** (pwer′tə rē′kō, pôr′-) island in the West Indies, constituting a commonwealth associated with the U.S.: 3,421 sq. mi.; pop. 2,712,000; cap. San Juan: abbrev. **P.R., PR** —**Puer′to Ri′can**

**puff** (puf) *n.* [OE. *pyff* < the *v.*] 1. *a)* a short, sudden gust, as of wind, or an expulsion, as of breath *b)* a small quantity of vapor, smoke, etc. expelled at one time 2. a drawing into the mouth of smoke from a cigarette, etc. 3. a swelling or protuberance 4. a shell of light pastry filled with whipped cream, etc. 5. a soft, bulging mass of material, gathered in at the edges 6. a soft roll of hair on the head 7. a soft pad for dabbing powder on the skin or hair 8. a quilted bed covering with a filling of down, etc. 9. undue or exaggerated praise, as in a book review —*vi.* [OE. *pyffan*] 1. to blow in puffs, as the wind 2. *a)* to give forth puffs of smoke, steam, etc. *b)* to breathe rapidly and hard 3. to move (*away, out, in,* etc.), giving forth puffs 4. to fill, become inflated, or swell (*out* or *up*), as with air or pride 5. to take a puff or puffs on a cigarette, etc. —*vt.* 1. to blow, drive, etc. in or with a puff or puffs 2. to inflate; swell 3. to praise unduly, as in a book review 4. to smoke (a cigarette, etc.) 5. to set (the hair) in puffs —**puff′i·ly** *adv.* —**puff′i·ness** *n.* —**puff′y** *adj.* **puff′i·er, puff′i·est**

**puff adder** 1. a large, poisonous African snake which hisses or puffs loudly when irritated 2. *same as* HOGNOSE SNAKE

**puff·ball** (-bôl′) *n.* any of various round, white-fleshed fungi that burst at the touch when mature, and discharge a brown powder

**puff·er** (-ər) *n.* 1. one that puffs 2. any of various fishes that can expand the body by swallowing air or water

**puf·fin** (puf′in) *n.* [ME. *poffin* < ?] a northern sea bird with a short neck, ducklike body, and brightly colored triangular beak

**pug¹** (pug) *n.* [< ? PUCK²] 1. a small, short-haired dog with a wrinkled face, snub nose, and curled tail 2. *same as* PUG NOSE

**pug²** (pug) *vt.* **pugged, pug′ging** [< dial.: prob. echoic of pounding] 1. to mix (wet, plastic clay) for making bricks, earthenware, etc. 2. to fill in with clay, mortar, etc. for soundproofing —*n.* wet, plastic clay

PUFFIN
(to 13½ in. long)

**pug³** (pug) *n.* [Slang] a pugilist

**Pu·get Sound** (pyōo′jit) [after P. *Puget,* Eng. explorer] inlet of the Pacific, extending southward into NW Wash.

**pug·ging** (pug′iŋ) *n.* 1. the mixing of pug (wet clay) 2. clay, mortar, etc. used for soundproofing

**pu·gil·ism** (pyōo′jə liz'm) *n.* [< L. *pugil,* boxer, akin to *pugnare,* to fight + -ISM] *same as* BOXING —**pu′gil·ist** *n.* —**pu′gil·is′tic** *adj.*

**pug·na·cious** (pug nā′shəs) *adj.* [< L. < *pugnare,* to fight + -OUS] eager and ready to fight; quarrelsome —**pug·na′cious·ly** *adv.* —**pug·nac′i·ty** (-nas′ə tē), **pug·na′cious·ness** *n.*

**pug nose** a short, thick, turned-up nose —**pug′-nosed′** (-nōzd′) *adj.*

**pu·is·sant** (pyōo′i sənt, pyōo is′'nt, pwis′'nt) *adj.* [OFr.

< *poeir:* see POWER] [Archaic] powerful; strong —**pu′is-sance** *n.* —**pu′is·sant·ly** *adv.*

**puke** (pyōōk) *n., vi., vt.* **puked, puk′ing** [akin ? to G. *spucken,* to spit] *same as* VOMIT: avoided by some as vulgar

**puk·ka** (puk′ə) *adj.* [Hindi *pakka,* ripe] [Anglo-Indian] **1.** good or first-rate of its kind **2.** genuine; real

**pul** (pool) *n., pl.* **puls, pul** [< Per., ult. < L., orig., bellows, hence bag, moneybag] *see* MONETARY UNITS, table (Afghanistan)

**Pu·las·ki** (poo las′kē; *Pol.* pōō lä′skē), **Cas·i·mir** (kaz′i-mir) 1748–79; Pol. general in the Am. Revolutionary army

**pul·chri·tude** (pul′krə tōōd′, -tyōōd′) *n.* [< L. < *pulcher,* beautiful] physical beauty —**pul′chri·tu′di·nous** (-′n əs) *adj.*

**pule** (pyōōl) *vi.* **puled, pul′ing** [echoic] to whine or whimper, as a sick or fretful child

**Pul·it·zer** (pool′it sər; *now often* pyōō′lit-), **Joseph** 1847–1911; U.S. newspaper owner & philanthropist, born in Hungary

**Pulitzer Prize** any of various yearly prizes established by Joseph Pulitzer, for work in journalism, literature, and music

**pull** (pool) *vt.* [OE. *pullian,* to pluck] **1.** to exert force or influence on so as to make move toward or after the source of the force; drag, tug, draw, etc. **2.** *a)* to draw or pluck out; extract (a tooth, etc.) *b)* to pick or uproot (weeds, etc.) **3.** to draw apart; tear **4.** to stretch (taffy, etc.) back and forth repeatedly **5.** to strain and injure *[to pull a muscle]* **6.** [Colloq.] to carry out; perform *[to pull a raid]* **7.** [Colloq.] to restrain *[to pull one's punches]* **8.** [Colloq.] *a)* to take out (a gun, etc.) so as to threaten *b)* to force (a wheel, etc.) off or out **9.** *Baseball, Golf* to hit (the ball) so it goes to the left or, if left-handed, to the right **10.** *Printing* to take (a proof) on a hand press **11.** *Rowing a)* to work (an oar) by drawing it toward one *b)* to be rowed normally by *[this boat pulls four oars]* —*vi.* **1.** to exert force in or for dragging, tugging, or attracting something **2.** to take a deep draft of a drink, a puff on a cigarette, etc. **3.** to be capable of being pulled **4.** to move or drive a vehicle (*away, ahead, out,* etc.) —*n.* **1.** the act or force of pulling; specif., *a)* a dragging, tugging, attracting, etc. *b)* a drink, a puff on a cigarette, etc. *c)* a hard, steady effort *d)* the force to move something **2.** something to be pulled, as a drawer handle **3.** [Colloq.] *a)* influence or special advantage *b)* drawing power; appeal —**pull apart** to find fault with —**pull down 1.** to tear down **2.** to degrade; humble **3.** to reduce **4.** [Colloq.] to get (a specified wage, grade, etc.) —**pull for** [Colloq.] to cheer on, or hope for the success of —**pull in 1.** to arrive **2.** to draw in **3.** [Slang] to arrest and take to police headquarters —**pull off** [Colloq.] to accomplish or do —**pull oneself together** to regain one's poise, courage, etc. —**pull out 1.** to depart **2.** to withdraw or retreat **3.** to escape from a responsibility, etc. —**pull over** to drive (a vehicle) to or toward the curb —**pull through** to get over (an illness, difficulty, etc.) —**pull up 1.** to uproot **2.** to bring or come to a stop **3.** to drive (a vehicle) to a specified place **4.** to check or rebuke —**pull′er** *n.*

**pul·let** (pool′it) *n.* [< OFr. dim. of *poule,* hen < L. *pullus,* chicken] a young hen, usually not more than a year old

**pul·ley** (pool′ē) *n., pl.* **-leys** [< OFr. < ML. *poleia,* ult. < Gr. dim. of *polos,* axis] **1.** a small wheel with a grooved rim in which a rope or chain runs, as to raise a weight attached at one end by pulling on the other end **2.** a combination of such wheels, used to increase the applied power **3.** a wheel that turns or is turned by a belt, rope, chain, etc., so as to transmit power

**Pull·man** (pool′mən) *n.* **1.** [after G.M. *Pullman* (1831–1897), U.S. inventor] a railroad car with private compartments or seats that can be made up into berths for sleeping: also **Pullman car 2.** [*often* p-] a suitcase that opens flat and has a hinged divider inside: also **pullman case**

**Pullman kitchen** [*also* p-] a small, compact kitchen, typically built into an alcove, as in some apartments

**pull·out** (pool′out′) *n.* **1.** a pulling out; esp., a removal, withdrawal, etc. **2.** something to be pulled out, as a magazine insert

**pull·o·ver** (-ō′vər) *adj.* that is put on by being pulled over the head —*n.* a pullover sweater, shirt, etc.

**pull-up** (pool′up′) *n. Gym.* the act of chinning oneself

**pul·mo·nar·y** (pul′mə ner′ē, pool′-) *adj.* [< L. < *pulmo* (gen. *pulmonis*), a lung] **1.** of, like, or affecting the lungs **2.** having lungs **3.** designating the artery conveying blood from the heart to the lungs or any of the veins conveying blood from the lungs to the heart Also **pul·mon′ic** (-män′ik)

**Pul·mo·tor** (pool′mōt′ər, pul′-) [< L. *pulmo,* a lung + MOTOR] *a trademark for* an apparatus that gives artificial respiration by forcing oxygen into the lungs —*n.* [p-] such an apparatus

**pulp** (pulp) *n.* [< Fr. < L. *pulpa,* flesh] **1.** a soft, moist, formless mass **2.** the soft, juicy part of a fruit **3.** the soft pith of a plant stem **4.** the soft, sensitive substance under the dentin of a tooth **5.** ground-up, moistened fibers of wood, rags, etc., from which paper is made **6.** a magazine printed on rough, inferior paper, often featuring shocking stories about sex, crime, etc. —*vt.* **1.** to reduce to pulp **2.** to remove the pulp from —*vi.* to become pulp —**pulp′i·ly** *adv.* —**pulp′i·ness** *n.* —**pulp′y** *adj.* **pulp′i·er, pulp′i·est**

**pul·pit** (pool′pit, pul′-) *n.* [L. *pulpitum,* a stage] **1.** a raised platform from which a clergyman preaches in a church **2.** preachers as a group

**pulp·wood** (pulp′wood′) *n.* **1.** soft wood for making paper **2.** wood ground to pulp for paper

**pul·que** (pool′kē; *Sp.* pōōl′ke) *n.* [AmSp., prob. of Mex. Ind. origin] a fermented drink, popular in Mexico, made from the juice of an agave

**pul·sar** (pul′sär, -sər) *n.* [PULS(E)[1] + -AR] any of several small heavenly objects in the Milky Way that emit radio pulses at regular intervals

**pul·sate** (pul′sāt) *vi.* **-sat·ed, -sat·ing** [< L. pp. of *pulsare,* to beat] **1.** to beat or throb rhythmically, as the heart **2.** to vibrate; quiver —**pul·sa′tion** *n.* —**pul′sa·tive** (-sə tiv) *adj.* —**pul′sa·tor** *n.* —**pul′sa·to′ry** *adj.*

**pulse**[1] (puls) *n.* [< OFr., ult. < L. pp. of *pellere,* to beat] **1.** the regular beating in the arteries, caused by the contractions of the heart **2.** any regular or rhythmical beat, signal, etc. **3.** the underlying feelings of a group, the public, etc. **4.** a brief surge of electric current **5.** a very short burst of radio waves —*vi.* **pulsed, puls′ing** to pulsate —*vt.* to make pulsate —**puls′er** *n.*

**pulse**[2] (puls) *n.* [< OFr. < L. *puls,* a pottage] **1.** the edible seeds of peas, beans, lentils, and similar plants having pods **2.** any such plant

**pulse-jet (engine)** (-jet′) a jet engine in which the air-intake valves of the combustion chamber open and close in a pulselike manner

**pul·ver·ize** (pul′və rīz′) *vt.* **-ized′, -iz′ing** [< MFr. < LL. < L. *pulvis,* dust] **1.** to crush, grind, etc. into a powder or dust **2.** to demolish —*vi.* to be pulverized into a powder or dust —**pul′ver·iz′a·ble, pul′ver·a·ble** (-vər ə b′l) *adj.* —**pul′ver·i·za′tion** *n.* —**pul′ver·iz′er** *n.*

**pu·ma** (pyōō′mə, pōō′-) *n., pl.* **-mas, -ma:** see PLURAL, II, D, 1 [AmSp. < Quechua] *same as* COUGAR

**pum·ice** (pum′is) *n.* [< OFr. < L. *pumex*] a light, porous, volcanic rock used in solid or powdered form to scour, smooth, and polish: also **pumice stone** —*vt.* **-iced, -ic·ing** to scour, etc. with pumice —**pu·mi·ceous** (pyōō mish′əs) *adj.*

**pum·mel** (pum′'l) *vt.* **-meled** or **-melled, -mel·ing** or **-mel·ling** [< POMMEL] to beat or hit with repeated blows, esp. with the fist

**pump**[1] (pump) *n.* [< MDu. *pompe* < Sp. *bomba,* prob. of echoic origin] any of various machines that force a liquid or gas into or through, or draw it out of, something, as by suction or pressure —*vt.* **1.** to move (fluids) with a pump **2.** to remove water, etc. from, as with a pump **3.** to drive air into, as with a pump **4.** to force in, draw out, move up and down, etc. in the manner of a pump **5.** to apply force to with a pumping motion **6.** [Colloq.] *a)* to question closely and persistently *b)* to get (information) in this way —*vi.* **1.** to work a pump **2.** to move water, etc. with a pump **3.** to move or go up and down like a pump handle **4.** to flow in, out, or through by, or as if by, being pumped —**pump′er** *n.*

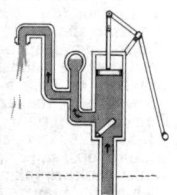

PUMP

**pump**[2] (pump) *n.* [< ? Fr. *pompe,* an ornament] a low-cut shoe without straps or ties

**pump·er·nick·el** (pum′pər nik′'l) *n.* [G.] a coarse, dark, sour bread made of unsifted rye

**pump·kin** (pum′kin, pump′-, pun′-) *n.* [< MFr. < L. < Gr. *pepon,* lit., ripe] **1.** a large, round, orange-yellow fruit with many seeds, cooked and eaten in pies, etc. **2.** the vine on which it grows **3.** [Brit.] any of several squashes

**pun** (pun) *n.* [< ? It. *puntiglio,* fine point] the humorous use of words that have the same sound or spelling, but have different meanings; a play on words —*vi.* **punned, pun′ning** to make a pun or puns —**pun′ner** *n.*

**Punch** (punch) [< PUNCHINELLO] the hero of the puppet show **Punch and Judy,** a humpbacked figure with a hooked nose, constantly fighting with his wife, Judy —**pleased as Punch** greatly pleased

**punch**[1] (punch) *n.* [see PUNCHEON[1]] **1.** *a)* a tool driven or

pressed against a surface that is to be shaped or stamped *b)* a tool driven against a nail, bolt, etc. that is to be worked in or out  **2.** a device or machine for making holes, cuts, etc.  **3.** the hole, cut, etc. so made —*vt.*  **1.** to pierce, stamp, etc. with a punch  **2.** to make (a hole, etc.) with a punch —**punch′er** *n.*
**punch²** (punch) *vt.* [ME. *punchen*]  **1.** to prod or poke with a stick  **2.** to herd (cattle) as by prodding  **3.** to strike with the fist —*n.*  **1.** a thrusting blow with the fist  **2.** [Colloq.] effective force; vigor —**pull one's punches** [Colloq.] to deliver blows, criticisms, etc. intended to have little or no effect —**punch a (time) clock** to insert a timecard into a time clock when arriving at or leaving work —**punch in (or out)** to record one's arrival (or departure) by punching a time clock —**punch′er** *n.*
**punch³** (punch) *n.* [Hindi *pāc*, five: it orig. had five ingredients]  a sweet drink of fruit juices, carbonated beverages, sherbet, etc., often mixed with wine or liquor, and served in cups from a large bowl (**punch bowl**)
**punch·board** (-bôrd′) *n.* a board or card with covered holes to be punched out, used as a game of chance: the holes contain slips or disks with hidden numbers, etc. usually designating prizes
**punch card** a card with holes or notches positioned in it, esp. by a key punch for data processing
**punch-drunk** (-druŋk′) *adj.* dazed, unsteady in gait, confused in speech, etc., as because of many blows to the head in boxing
**pun·cheon¹** (pun′chən) *n.* [< MFr., ult. < L. pp. of *pungere*, to prick]  **1.** a short, upright wooden post used in framework  **2.** a heavy piece of timber roughly dressed with one side flat  **3.** a device for punching, stamping, etc.
**pun·cheon²** (pun′chən) *n.* [OFr. *poinçon*]  a large cask of varying capacity (72–120 gal.), for beer, wine, etc.; also, as much as it will hold
**pun·chi·nel·lo** (pun′chə nel′ō) *n., pl.* **-los** [< a character's name in a Neapolitan puppet play]  a buffoon; clown
**punching bag** a stuffed or inflated leather bag hung up in order to be punched for exercise or practice
**punch line** the line carrying the point of a joke
**punch press** a press in which dies are fitted for cutting, shaping, or stamping metal
**punch·y** (pun′chē) *adj.* **punch′i·er, punch′i·est** [Colloq.]  **1.** forceful; vigorous  **2.** *same as* PUNCH-DRUNK
**punc·til·i·o** (puŋk til′ē ō′) *n., pl.* **-os′** [< Sp. or It., ult. < L. *punctum*, a point]  **1.** a nice point of conduct, ceremony, etc.  **2.** punctiliousness
**punc·til·i·ous** (-ē əs) *adj.*  **1.** very careful about every detail of behavior, ceremony, etc.  **2.** very exact; scrupulous —**punc·til′i·ous·ly** *adv.* —**punc·til′i·ous·ness** *n.*
**punc·tu·al** (puŋk′choo wəl) *adj.* [< ML. *punctualis* < L. *punctus*, a point]  on time; prompt —**punc′tu·al′i·ty** (-wal′ə tē) *n.* —**punc′tu·al·ly** *adv.* —**punc′tu·al·ness** *n.*
**punc·tu·ate** (puŋk′choo wāt′) *vt.* **-at′ed, -at′ing** [< ML. pp. of *punctuare* < L. *punctus*, a point]  **1.** *a)* to insert punctuation marks in  *b)* to function as a punctuation mark in  **2.** to break in on here and there [a speech *punctuated* with applause]  **3.** to emphasize; accentuate —*vi.* to use punctuation marks —**punc′tu·a′tor** *n.*
**punc·tu·a·tion** (puŋk′choo wā′shən) *n.*  **1.** a punctuating; specif., the use of standardized marks in writing and printing to separate sentences or sentence elements or to make meaning clearer  **2.** a punctuation mark or marks
**punctuation mark** any of the marks used in punctuation, as a period or comma
**punc·ture** (puŋk′chər) *n.* [< L. < *pungere*, to pierce]  **1.** a perforating or piercing  **2.** a hole made by a sharp point —*vt.* **-tured, -tur·ing**  **1.** to perforate or pierce with a sharp point  **2.** to reduce or put an end to [to *puncture* one's pride] —*vi.* to be punctured —**punc′tur·a·ble** *adj.*
**pun·dit** (pun′dit) *n.* [< Hindi < Sans. *paṇḍita*]  **1.** in India, a Brahman learned in Sanskrit, Hindu philosophy, etc.  **2.** a person who has great learning
**pun·gent** (pun′jənt) *adj.* [< L. prp. of *pungere*, to prick]  **1.** producing a sharp sensation of taste or smell; acrid  **2.** sharp to the mind; poignant  **3.** sharply penetrating; biting [*pungent* language]  **4.** keenly clever —**pun′gen·cy** *n.* —**pun′gent·ly** *adv.*
**Pu·nic** (pyoo′nik) *adj.* [L. *Punicus* < *Poeni*, the Carthaginians]  **1.** of ancient Carthage or its people  **2.** like the Carthaginians, regarded by the Romans as faithless and treacherous
**pun·ish** (pun′ish) *vt.* [< OFr. < L. *punire*, to punish < *poena*, punishment]  **1.** to cause to undergo pain, loss, or suffering for a crime or wrongdoing  **2.** to impose a penalty for (an offense)  **3.** to treat harshly  **4.** [Colloq.] to consume or use up —*vi.* to deal out punishment —**pun′ish·a·bil′i·ty** *n.* —**pun′ish·a·ble** *adj.* —**pun′ish·er** *n.*

**pun·ish·ment** (-mənt) *n.*  **1.** a punishing or being punished  **2.** a penalty imposed on an offender for wrongdoing  **3.** harsh treatment
**pu·ni·tive** (pyoo′nə tiv) *adj.* inflicting or concerned with punishment: also **pu′ni·to·ry** (-tôr′ē) —**pu′ni·tive·ly** *adv.* —**pu′ni·tive·ness** *n.*
**punitive damages** *same as* EXEMPLARY DAMAGES
**Pun·jab** (pun jäb′, pun′jäb, -jab)  **1.** region in NW India & NE Pakistan, between the Indus & Jumna rivers  **2.** state of India, in this region: 19,403 sq. mi.; pop. 11,147,000
**punk¹** (puŋk) *n.* [var. of SPUNK]  any substance, as decayed wood, that smolders when ignited, used as tinder; esp., a fungous substance shaped into slender, fragile sticks and used to light fireworks, etc.
**punk²** (puŋk) *n.* [< ?] [Slang]  **1.** a young hoodlum  **2.** anyone, esp. a youngster, regarded as inexperienced, insignificant, etc. —*adj.* [Slang] poor or bad in quality
**pun·kah, pun·ka** (puŋ′kə) *n.* [Hindi *pankhā*]  in India, a large fan made from the palmyra leaf, or a large, swinging fan hung from the ceiling
**pun·ster** (pun′stər) *n.* a person who is fond of making puns
**punt¹** (punt) *n.* [< slang of Rugby School, England]  *Football* a kick in which the ball is dropped from the hands and then kicked before it strikes the ground —*vt., vi.* to kick (a football) in this way —**punt′er** *n.*
**punt²** (punt) *n.* [OE. < L. *ponto:* see PONTOON]  a flat-bottomed boat with square ends, usually propelled by a long pole —*vt.*  **1.** to propel (a boat) by pushing with a pole against the bottom of a shallow river or lake  **2.** to carry in a punt —*vi.* to go in a punt —**punt′er** *n.*
**punt³** (punt) *vi.* [< Fr. < Sp. *punto* < L. *punctum*, a point]  **1.** in certain card games, to bet against the banker  **2.** [Brit.] to gamble; bet —**punt′er** *n.*
**pu·ny** (pyoo′nē) *adj.* **-ni·er, -ni·est** [< Fr. < OFr. *puis*, after + *né*, born]  of inferior size, strength, or importance; weak —**pu′ni·ness** *n.*
**pup** (pup) *n.*  **1.** *a)* a young dog; puppy  *b)* a young fox, wolf, etc.  **2.** a young seal, whale, etc. —*vi.* **pupped, pup′ping** to give birth to pups
**pu·pa** (pyoo′pə) *n., pl.* **-pae** (-pē), **-pas** [ModL. < L., a girl, doll]  an insect in the stage between the larval and adult forms: some pupae are enclosed in cocoons —**pu′pal** *adj.*
**pu·pate** (-pāt) *vi.* **-pat·ed, -pat·ing** to go through the pupal stage —**pu·pa′tion** *n.*

PUPA

**pu·pil¹** (pyoo′p'l) *n.* [< MFr. < L. *pupillus* (dim. of *pupus*, boy), *pupilla* (dim. of *pupa*, girl), ward]  a person being taught by a teacher or tutor, as in a school —**pu′pil·age, pu′pil·lage** *n.*
**pu·pil²** (pyoo′p'l) *n.* [< Fr. < L. *pupilla*, one's figure reflected in another's eye; special use of *pupilla:* see prec.]  the contractile circular opening in the center of the iris of the eye
**pup·pet** (pup′it) *n.* [< OFr., ult. < L. *pupa*, a girl, doll]  **1.** orig., a doll  **2.** a small, usually jointed figure, as of a human being, moved with the hands or by strings, wires, or rods, usually in a puppet show  **3.** a person whose actions, ideas, etc. are controlled by another
**pup·pet·eer** (pup′i tir′) *n.* a person who operates or designs puppets or produces puppet shows
**pup·pet·ry** (pup′i trē) *n.* the art or work of a puppeteer
**puppet show** a play or performance with puppets
**pup·py** (pup′ē) *n., pl.* **-pies** [< MFr. *popee*, doll < OFr.: see PUPPET]  **1.** a young dog  **2.** an insolent, conceited, or silly young man —**pup′py·ish** *adj.*
**puppy love** immature love between a boy and a girl
**pup tent** *same as* SHELTER TENT
**pur·blind** (pur′blind′) *adj.* [ME. *pur blind*, quite blind]  **1.** orig., completely blind  **2.** partly blind  **3.** slow in perceiving or understanding —**pur′blind′ness** *n.*
**Pur·cell** (pur′s'l), Henry 1659?–95; Eng. composer
**pur·chase** (pur′chəs) *vt.* **-chased, -chas·ing** [< OFr. < *pour*, for + *chacier*, to chase]  **1.** to get for money; buy  **2.** to get at a cost, as of suffering  **3.** *a)* to move or raise by applying mechanical power  *b)* to get a fast hold on so as to do this —*n.*  **1.** anything obtained by buying  **2.** a buying  **3.** *a)* a fast hold applied to move something mechanically or to keep from slipping  *b)* an apparatus for applying such a hold —**pur′chas·a·ble** *adj.* —**pur′chas·er** *n.*
**pur·dah** (pur′də) *n.* [Hindi & Per. *pardah*, a veil]  a curtain or veil used by some Hindus and Moslems to hide their women from strangers; also, this practice of hiding women
**pure** (pyoor) *adj.* [< OFr. < L. *purus*]  **1.** *a)* free from any adulterant [*pure* maple syrup]  *b)* free from anything harmful [*pure* water]  **2.** simple; mere [*pure* luck]  **3.** utter; absolute  **4.** free from defects  **5.** free from sin or

guilt **6.** virgin or chaste **7.** of unmixed stock; purebred **8.** abstract or theoretical [*pure* physics] —**pure′ly** *adv.* —**pure′ness** *n.*

**pure·bred** (-bred′) *adj.* belonging to a recognized breed through generations of unmixed descent —*n.* such a plant or animal

**pu·rée** (pyoo rā′; pyoor′ā, -ē) *n.* [Fr. < OFr. < L. < *purus,* pure] **1.** food prepared by putting cooked vegetables, fruits, etc. through a sieve or blender **2.** a thick, smooth soup made with this —*vt.* -réed′, -rée′ing to make a purée of  Also sp. **puree**

**pur·ga·tion** (pur gā′shən) *n.* the act of purging

**pur·ga·tive** (pur′gə tiv) *adj.* **1.** that purges **2.** causing bowel movement —*n.* a substance that purges; specif., a cathartic —**pur′ga·tive·ly** *adv.*

**pur·ga·to·ry** (pur′gə tôr′ē) *n., pl.* -ries [< OFr. < ML. < LL. < L. *purgare:* see ff.] **1.** [*often* P-] in R.C. and other Christian doctrine, a state or place in which those who have died in the grace of God expiate their sins **2.** any state or place of temporary punishment or remorse —**pur′ga·to′ri·al** *adj.*

**purge** (purj) *vt.* **purged, purg′ing** [< OFr. < L. *purgare* < *purus,* clean + *agere,* to do] **1.** to cleanse of impurities, foreign matter, etc. **2.** to cleanse of guilt, sin, etc. **3.** to remove by cleansing **4.** *a)* to rid (a nation, political party, etc.) of individuals regarded as disloyal or undesirable *b)* to kill or otherwise get rid of (such individuals) **5.** *Med.* *a)* to empty (the bowels) *b)* to make the bowels of (a person) become empty —*vi.* **1.** to become clean, clear, or pure **2.** to have or cause a thorough bowel movement —*n.* **1.** a purging **2.** that which purges; esp., a cathartic —**purg′er** *n.*

**pu·ri·fy** (pyoor′ə fī′) *vt.* -fied′, -fy′ing [< OFr. < L. *purificare* < *purus,* pure + *facere,* to make] **1.** to rid of impurities or pollution **2.** to free from guilt, sin, corruption, etc. —*vi.* to become purified —**pu′ri·fi·ca′tion** *n.* —**pu·rif·i·ca·to·ry** (pyoo rif′ə kə tôr′ē) *adj.* —**pu′ri·fi′er** *n.*

**Pu·rim** (poor′im, poo rēm′) *n.* [Heb. *pūrīm,* pl., lit., lots] a Jewish holiday celebrated on the 14th day of Adar, commemorating the deliverance of the Jews by Esther from a massacre: also called **Feast of Lots**

**pur·ism** (pyoor′iz′m) *n.* **1.** strict observance of or insistence on precise usage or style, as in applying formal rules of grammar, art, etc. **2.** an instance of this —**pur′ist** *n.* —**pu·ris′tic, pu·ris′ti·cal** *adj.* —**pu·ris′ti·cal·ly** *adv.*

**Pu·ri·tan** (pyoor′ə t′n) *n.* [see PURITY & -AN] **1.** a member of a Protestant group in England and America who, in the 16th and 17th centuries, wanted to make the Church of England simpler in its services and stricter about morals **2.** [p-] a person regarded as excessively strict in morals and religion —*adj.* **1.** of the Puritans **2.** [p-] puritanical —**Pu′ri·tan·ism, pu′ri·tan·ism** *n.*

**pu·ri·tan·i·cal** (pyoor′ə tan′i k′l) *adj.* **1.** [P-] of the Puritans **2.** excessively strict in morals and religion  Also **pu′ri·tan′ic** —**pu′ri·tan′i·cal·ly** *adv.*

**pu·ri·ty** (pyoor′ə tē) *n.* [< MFr. < LL. < L. *purus,* pure] the quality or condition of being pure; specif., *a)* freedom from adulterating matter *b)* cleanness; clearness *c)* innocence or chastity *d)* freedom from elements regarded as corrupting

**purl¹** (purl) *vi.* [< ? Scand.] **1.** to move in ripples or with a murmuring sound **2.** to eddy; swirl —*n.* a stream or rill that purls, or its murmuring sound

**purl²** (purl) *vt., vi.* [prob. < a Romance source] **1.** to edge (lace) with small loops **2.** to invert (stitches) in knitting —*n.* **1.** metal thread, for embroidery **2.** a small loop or chain of loops on the edge of lace **3.** an inversion of knitting stitches

**pur·lieu** (pur′loo, purl′yoo) *n.* [< Anglo-Fr. < OFr. < *pur-,* through + *aler,* to go] **1.** orig., an outlying part of a royal forest, returned to private owners **2.** a place one visits often **3.** [*pl.*] *a)* bounds; limits *b)* environs **4.** an outlying part

**pur·lin, pur·line** (pur′lin) *n.* [< ?] a horizontal timber supporting rafters of a roof

**pur·loin** (pər loin′, pur′loin) *vt., vi.* [< OFr. < *pur-,* for + *loin,* far] to steal; filch —**pur·loin′er** *n.*

**pur·ple** (pur′p′l) *n.* [OE. < L. *purpura* < Gr. *porphyra,* shellfish yielding purple dye] **1.** a dark color that is a blend of red and blue **2.** esp. formerly, *a)* deep crimson *b)* cloth or clothing of such color: an emblem of royalty or high rank —*adj.* **1.** of the color purple **2.** imperial; royal **3.** *a)* flowery [*purple* prose] *b)* strong and often offensive [*purple* language] —*vt., vi.* -pled, -pling to make or become purple —**born to** (*or* **in**) **the purple** of royal or high birth —**pur′plish, pur′ply** *adj.*

**Purple Heart** a decoration awarded to members of the U.S. armed forces wounded in action

**purple martin** a large N. American swallow with bluish-black plumage

**pur·port** (pər pôrt′; *also,* & *for n. always,* pur′pôrt) *vt.* [< Anglo-Fr. < OFr. < *por-,* forth + *porter,* to bear] **1.** to

profess or claim as its meaning or intent **2.** to give the appearance, often fa¹sely, of being, intending, etc. —*n.* meaning; main idea —**p .r·port′ed** *adj.* —**pur·port′ed·ly** *adv.*

**pur·pose** (pur′pəs) *vt., vi.* -posed, -pos·ing [< OFr. var. of *proposer,* to PROPOSE] to plan, intend, or resolve —*n.* **1.** what one plans to get or do; intention; aim **2.** resolution; determination **3.** the reason or use for something [a room with no *purpose*] —**on purpose** not by accident; intentionally —**to good purpose** advantageously —**to little** (*or* **no**) **purpose** with little or no effect —**to the purpose** apt; relevant —**pur′pose·less** *adj.* —**pur′pose·less·ly** *adv.* —**pur′pose·less·ness** *n.*

**pur·pose·ful** (-fəl) *adj.* **1.** resolutely aiming at a specific goal **2.** directed toward a specific end; not meaningless —**pur′pose·ful·ly** *adv.* —**pur′pose·ful·ness** *n.*

**pur·pose·ly** (-lē) *adv.* with a definite purpose; intentionally; deliberately

**pur·pos·ive** (pur′pə siv) *adj.* **1.** serving a purpose **2.** having purpose —**pur′pos·ive·ly** *adv.*

**purr** (pur) *n.* [echoic] **1.** a low, vibratory sound made by a cat when it seems to be pleased **2.** any sound like this —*vi., vt.* to make, or express by, such a sound

**purse** (purs) *n.* [OE. < ML. *bursa,* a bag < LL., a hide < Gr. *byrsa*] **1.** a small bag or pouch for carrying money **2.** finances; money **3.** a sum of money given as a present or prize **4.** a woman's handbag —*vt.* **pursed, purs′ing** to pucker (one's lips, brows, etc.)

**purs·er** (pur′sər) *n.* [ME., a purse bearer] a ship's officer in charge of accounts, freight, tickets, etc., esp. on a passenger vessel

**purse strings** a drawstring for certain purses —**hold the purse strings** to be in control of the money —**tighten** (*or* **loosen**) **the purse strings** to make funds less (or more) readily available

**purs·lane** (purs′lin, -lān) *n.* [< MFr. < LL. *porcilaca* < L. *portulaca*] any of a number of trailing weeds with pink, fleshy stems and small, yellow flowers; esp., an annual used as a potherb and in salads

**pur·su·ance** (pər soo′əns, -syoo′-) *n.* a pursuing, or carrying out, as of a project, plan, etc.

**pur·su·ant** (-ənt) *adj.* [Now Rare] pursuing —**pursuant to 1.** following upon **2.** in accordance with

**pur·sue** (pər soo′, -syoo′) *vt.* -sued′, -su′ing [< OFr. < VL. < L. < *pro-,* forth + *sequi,* to follow] **1.** to follow in order to overtake, capture, etc.; chase **2.** to follow or go on with (a specified course, action, etc.) **3.** to strive for; seek after [to *pursue* success] **4.** to have as one's occupation, profession, or study; devote oneself to **5.** to keep on harassing; hound —*vi.* **1.** to chase **2.** to go on; continue —**pur·su′a·ble** *adj.* —**pur·su′er** *n.*

**pur·suit** (-soot′, -syoot′) *n.* **1.** a pursuing **2.** a career, interest, etc. to which one devotes oneself

**pursuit plane** a fighter plane: see FIGHTER (sense 3)

**pur·sui·vant** (pur′si vənt, -swi-) *n.* [< OFr. < *poursuir:* see PURSUE] **1.** in England, an officer ranking below a herald **2.** a follower; attendant

**pur·sy¹** (pur′sē) *adj.* -si·er, -si·est [< Anglo-Fr. *pursif,* for OFr. *polsif* < *polser,* to push, pant < L. *pulsare,* to beat] **1.** short-winded, esp. from being fat **2.** fat —**pur′-si·ness** *n.*

**pur·sy²** (pur′sē) *adj.* -si·er, -si·est pursed; puckered

**pu·ru·lent** (pyoor′ə lənt, -yoo lənt) *adj.* [Fr. < L. < *pus* (gen. *puris*), pus] of, like, containing, or discharging pus —**pu′ru·lence, pu′ru·len·cy** *n.* —**pu′ru·lent·ly** *adv.*

**pur·vey** (pər vā′) *vt.* [< Anglo-Fr. < OFr. < L. *providere:* see PROVIDE] to supply (esp. food or provisions) —**pur·vey′ance** *n.* —**pur·vey′or** *n.*

**pur·view** (pur′vyoo) *n.* [< Anglo-Fr. *purvere* (*est*), (it is) provided, ult. < L. *providere:* see PROVIDE] **1.** the body and scope of an act or bill **2.** extent or range of control, activity, concern, etc.; province

**pus** (pus) *n.* [L.] the usually yellowish-white liquid matter produced in certain infections, consisting of bacteria, white corpuscles, serum, etc.

**Pu·san** (poo′sän′) seaport on the SE coast of South Korea: pop. 1,879,000

**push** (poosh) *vt.* [< MFr. < OFr. < L. *pulsare,* to beat < pp. of *pellere,* to drive] **1.** *a)* to exert pressure or force against, esp. so as to move *b)* to move in this way *c)* to thrust, shove, or drive (*up, down, in, out,* etc.) **2.** *a)* to urge on; impel *b)* to follow up vigorously; promote (a campaign, claim, etc.) *c)* to extend or expand (business activities, etc.) **3.** to bring into a critical state; press [be *pushed* for time] **4.** to urge or promote the use, sale, etc. of **5.** [Colloq.] to be near or close to [*pushing* sixty years] —*vi.* **1.** to press against a thing so as to move it **2.** to try hard to advance, succeed, etc. **3.** to move forward against opposition **4.** to move by being pushed —*n.* **1.** a pushing **2.** a vigorous effort, campaign, etc. **3.** pressure of circumstances **4.** [Colloq.] enterprise; drive —**push off** [Colloq.] to set out; depart —**push on** to go forward; proceed

**push button** a small knob or button that is pushed to cause something to operate, as by closing an electric circuit —**push'·but'ton** *adj.*

**push·cart** (poosh'kärt') *n.* a cart pushed by hand, esp. one used by street vendors

**push·er** (-ər) *n.* **1.** a person or thing that pushes **2.** [Slang] a person peddling drugs, esp. narcotics, illegally

**push·ing** (-iŋ) *adj.* **1.** aggressive; enterprising **2.** forward; officious —**push'ing·ly** *adv.*

**Push·kin** (poosh'kin; *E.* poosh'-), **A·lek·san·dr** (Ser·geyevich) (ä'lyik sän'dr') 1799–1837; Russ. poet

**push·o·ver** (poosh'ō'vər) *n.* [Slang] **1.** anything very easy to do **2.** a person, group, etc. easily persuaded, defeated, seduced, etc.

**Push·tu** (push'too) *n.* same as PASHTO

**push-up, push·up** (poosh'up') *n.* an exercise in which a person lying face down, with hands palm down under the shoulders, pushes the body up by straightening the arms and lowers it by bending the arms

**push·y** (poosh'ē) *adj.* **push'i·er, push'i·est** [Colloq.] annoyingly aggressive and persistent —**push'i·ness** *n.*

**pu·sil·lan·i·mous** (pyōō's'l an'ə məs) *adj.* [< LL. < L. *pusillus*, tiny + *animus*, the mind] **1.** timid or cowardly **2.** proceeding from or showing a lack of courage —**pu'sil·la·nim'i·ty** (-ə nim'ə tē) *n.* —**pu·sil·lan'i·mous·ly** *adv.*

**puss**[1] (poos) *n.* [orig. ? echoic of the spitting of a cat] **1.** a cat: pet name **2.** a girl: term of endearment

**puss**[2] (poos) *n.* [prob. < IrGael. *pus*, mouth] [Slang] **1.** the face **2.** the mouth

**pus·sy**[1] (pus'ē) *adj.* **-si·er, -si·est** containing or like pus

**puss·y**[2] (poos'ē) *n., pl.* **puss'ies** [dim. of PUSS[1]] a cat, esp. a kitten —*adj.* [dim.] of affection

**puss·y·foot** (-foot') *vi.* [Colloq.] **1.** to move with stealth, like a cat **2.** to shy away from giving a definite opinion, taking a firm stand, etc. —**puss'y·foot'er** *n.*

**pussy willow** any of several willows bearing silvery, velvet-like catkins before the leaves appear

**pus·tu·lant** (pus'chə lənt) *adj.* making pustules form

**pus·tu·lar** (-lər) *adj.* of, like, or covered with pustules: also **pus'tu·lous** (-ləs)

**pus·tu·late** (-lāt'; *for adj.* -lit) *vt., vi.* **-lat'ed, -lat'ing** [< LL. pp. of *pustulare* < *pustula*, a pustule] to form into pustules —*adj.* covered with pustules —**pus'tu·la'tion** *n.*

**pus·tule** (pus'chool) *n.* [L. *pustula*] **1.** a small swelling in the skin, containing pus **2.** any small swelling like a blister or pimple

**put** (poot) *vt.* **put, put'ting** [< or akin to OE. *potian*, to push] **1.** *a)* to drive or send by a blow, shot, or thrust *b)* to throw with an overhand thrust from the shoulder [*put the shot*] **2.** to make do something; impel; force **3.** to make be in a specified place, condition, relation, etc.; place; set [*put her at ease*] **4.** to make undergo; subject **5.** to impose (a burden, tax, etc.) **6.** *a)* to bring to bear (*on*); apply (*to*) *b)* to bring in; add; inject *c)* to bring about; effect **7.** to attribute; assign; ascribe [*put the blame on him*] **8.** to express; state [*put it plainly*] **9.** to translate **10.** to present for consideration, decision, etc. [*put the question*] **11.** *a)* to estimate as being (with *at*) [*to put the cost at $50*] *b)* to fix or set (a price, value, etc.) *on* **12.** to fit (words) to music **13.** *a)* to bet (money) *on* *b)* to invest (money) *in* or *into* —*vi.* to go (*in, out, back*, etc.) —*n.* a cast or thrust —*adj.* [Colloq.] fixed [*stay put*] —**put about** to turn from one tack or direction to another —**put across** [Colloq.] **1.** to make understood or accepted **2.** to carry out with success **3.** to carry out by trickery —**put aside** (or **by**) **1.** to keep for later **2.** to discard —**put away 1.** same as PUT ASIDE **2.** [Colloq.] *a)* to put in a jail, etc. *b)* to consume (food or drink) *c)* to kill (a pet) to prevent suffering —**put down 1.** to crush; repress *b)* to strip of power, rank, etc.; degrade **2.** to write down; record **3.** to attribute (*to*) **4.** to consider as; classify **5.** to land (an aircraft) **6.** [Slang] to belittle, reject, criticize, or humiliate —**put forth 1.** to grow (leaves, etc.) **2.** to exert (effort, etc.) **3.** to propose; offer **4.** to leave port —**put in 1.** to enter a port or haven **2.** to enter (a claim, etc.) **3.** [Colloq.] to spend (time) —**put in for** to apply for —**put it (or something) over on** [Colloq.] to deceive; trick —**put off 1.** to postpone; delay **2.** to evade or divert **3.** to perturb; upset —**put on 1.** to clothe, adorn, or cover oneself with **2.** to take on; add **3.** to assume or pretend **4.** to apply (a brake, etc.) **5.** to stage (a play) **6.** [Slang] to fool (someone) by taking advantage of his readiness to believe; hoax —**put on to** to inform (someone) about (something) —**put out 1.** to expel; dismiss **2.** to stop from burning; extinguish (a fire or light) **3.** to spend (money) **4.** to disconcert or vex **5.** to inconvenience **6.** to publish, produce, or supply **7.** *Baseball* to cause (a batter or runner) to be out by a fielding play —**put over** [Colloq.] same as PUT ACROSS —**put through 1.** to carry out successfully **2.** to

cause to do or undergo **3.** to connect (someone) by telephone with someone else —**put to it** to place in a difficult situation; press hard —**put up 1.** to offer, as for consideration, decision, sale, etc. **2.** to offer as a candidate **3.** to preserve or can (fruits, etc.) **4.** to erect; build **5.** to lodge, or provide lodgings for **6.** *a)* to advance or provide (money) *b)* [Slang] to do or produce what is needed or wanted **7.** to arrange (the hair) with curlers, bobby pins, etc. **8.** to carry on [*to put up a struggle*] **9.** [Colloq.] to incite (a person) *to* some action —**put upon** to impose on; victimize —**put up with** to tolerate; bear

**pu·ta·tive** (pyōōt'ə tiv) *adj.* [< L. < *putare*, to suppose] reputed; supposed —**pu'ta·tive·ly** *adv.*

**put-down** (poot'doun') *n.* [Slang] a belittling remark or crushing retort

**put-on** (poot'än') *adj.* feigned —*n.* [Slang] a fooling of someone by taking advantage of his readiness to believe

**put·out** (-out') *n. Baseball* a play in which the batter or runner is retired, or put out

**put-put** (put'put') *n., vi.* put'-put'ted, put'-put'ting same as PUTT-PUTT

**pu·tre·fac·tion** (pyōō'trə fak'shən) *n.* [see ff.] the rotting of organic matter by bacteria, fungi, and oxidation, with resulting foul-smelling products —**pu'tre·fac'tive** *adj.*

**pu·tre·fy** (pyōō'trə fī') *vt., vi.* **-fied', -fy'ing** [< L. *putrefacere* < *putris*, putrid + *facere*, to make] to make or become putrid or rotten —**pu'tre·fi'er** *n.*

**pu·tres·cent** (pyōō tres''nt) *adj.* [L. prp. of *putrescere*, to become rotten < *putris*, rotten] **1.** rotting **2.** of or relating to putrefaction —**pu·tres'cence** *n.*

**pu·trid** (pyōō'trid) *adj.* [< Fr. < L. *putridus* < *putrere*, to be rotten] **1.** rotten and smelling bad **2.** of or from decay **3.** corrupt or depraved **4.** [Colloq.] very unpleasant —**pu·trid'i·ty, pu'trid·ness** *n.* —**pu'trid·ly** *adv.*

‡**Putsch** (pooch) *n.* [G.] an uprising or rebellion, esp. an unsuccessful one

**putt** (put) *n.* [< PUT, *v.*] *Golf* a light stroke made on the putting green in trying to put the ball into the hole —*vt., vi.* to hit (the ball) thus

**put·tee** (pu tē', put'ē) *n.* [< Hindi *paṭṭī*, a bandage < Sans. *paṭṭa*, a strip of cloth] a cloth or leather legging or a cloth strip wound spirally to cover the leg from ankle to knee

**put·ter**[1] (poot'ər) *n.* a person or thing that puts

**putt·er**[2] (put'ər) *n. Golf* **1.** a short, straight-faced club used in putting **2.** a person who putts

**put·ter**[3] (put'ər) *vi.* [var. of POTTER[2]] to busy oneself in an ineffective or aimless way; dawdle (often with *around*, etc.) —*vt.* to fritter (*away*)

**putt·ing green** (put'iŋ) *Golf* the area of smooth, closely mowed turf in which the hole is sunk

PUTTEES

**putt-putt** (put'put') *n.* [echoic] **1.** the chugging or popping sounds of a motor-boat engine, etc. **2.** [Colloq.] a boat, etc. making such sounds —*vi.* **putt'-putt'ed, putt'-putt'ing** to make, move along, or operate with such sounds

**put·ty** (put'ē) *n.* [< Fr. *potée*, lit., potful < *pot*, a pot] **1.** a soft, plastic mixture of powdered chalk and linseed oil, used to hold glass panes in place, to fill small cracks, etc. **2.** any similar substance —*vt.* **-tied, -ty·ing** to cement, fill, etc. with putty —**put'ti·er** *n.*

**Pu·tu·ma·yo** (pōō'tōō mä'yō) river flowing from SW Colombia into the Amazon in NW Brazil

**put-up** (poot'up') *adj.* [Colloq.] planned secretly beforehand [*a put-up job*]

**puz·zle** (puz''l) *vt.* **-zled, -zling** [< ?] to perplex; bewilder —*vi.* **1.** to be perplexed, etc. **2.** to exercise one's mind, as on a problem —*n.* **1.** a puzzled state **2.** a puzzling problem, etc. **3.** a toy or problem to test skill or ingenuity —**puzzle out** to solve by deep thought —**puzzle over** to give deep thought to —**puz'zle·ment** *n.* —**puz'zler** *n.*

**Pvt.** *Mil.* Private

**PW** Prisoner of War

**PWA, P.W.A.** Public Works Administration

**pwt.** pennyweight(s)

**PX** post exchange

**pya** (pyä) *n., pl.* **pyas** [Burmese] *see* MONETARY UNITS, table (Burma)

**py·e·mi·a** (pī ē'mē ə) *n.* [ModL.: see PYO- & -EMIA] blood poisoning caused by pus-producing organisms —**py·e'mic** *adj.*

**Pyg·ma·li·on** (pig māl'yən, -mā'lē ən) *Gr. Legend* a sculptor who fell in love with his statue of a maiden, later brought to life as Galatea by Aphrodite

---

**Pyg·my** (pig′mē) *n., pl.* **-mies** [< L. < Gr. *pygmaios*, of the length of the *pygmē*, forearm and fist] **1.** a member of any of several African and Asian peoples of small stature **2.** [p-] any abnormally undersized or insignificant person or thing —*adj.* **1.** of Pygmies **2.** [p-] very small

**py·ja·mas** (pə jam′əz, -jä′məz) *n.pl. Brit. sp. of* PAJAMAS

**py·lon** (pī′län) *n.* [Gr. *pylōn*, gateway] **1.** a gateway, as of an Egyptian temple **2.** a towerlike structure, as for supporting electric lines, marking an aircraft course, etc.

**py·lo·rus** (pī lôr′əs, pə-) *n., pl.* **-ri** (-ī) [LL. < Gr. *pylōros*, gatekeeper < *pylē*, a gate + *ouros*, watchman] the opening from the stomach into the duodenum —**py·lor′ic** *adj.*

**py·o-** [< Gr. *pyon*, pus] *a combining form meaning:* **1.** pus **2.** pus-forming Also **py-**

**Pyong·yang** (pyuŋ′yäŋ′) capital of North Korea, in the W part: pop. 1,500,000

**py·or·rhe·a, py·or·rhoe·a** (pī′ə rē′ə) *n.* [ModL.: see PYO- & -RRHEA] a discharge of pus; specif., *short for* PYORRHEA ALVEOLARIS —**py′or·rhe′al, py′or·rhoe′al** *adj.*

**pyorrhea al·ve·o·la·ris** (al vē′ə ler′is) an infection of the gums and tooth sockets, in which pus forms and the teeth become loose

**pyr·a·mid** (pir′ə mid) *n.* [L. *pyramis* (gen. *pyramidis*) < Gr.] **1.** any huge structure with a square base and four sloping, triangular sides meeting at the top, as those built for royal tombs in ancient Egypt **2.** anything shaped like this **3.** *Geom.* a solid figure the base of which is a polygon whose sides are the bases of triangular surfaces meeting at a common vertex —*vi., vt.* to build up or grow as in the form of a pyramid —**py·ram·i·dal** (pi ram′ə d'l) *adj.* —**py·ram′i·dal·ly** *adv.* —**pyr′a·mid′ic, pyr′a·mid′i·cal** *adj.*

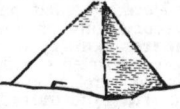
EGYPTIAN PYRAMID

**pyre** (pīr) *n.* [< L. < Gr. < *pyr*, a fire] a pile, esp. of wood, for burning a corpse in a funeral rite

**Pyr·e·nees** (pir′ə nēz′) mountain range along the border between France & Spain —**Pyr′e·ne′an** (-nē′ən) *adj.*

**py·re·thrum** (pī rē′thrəm) *n.* [ModL. < L. < Gr. *pyrethron*, feverfew] **1.** any of several chrysanthemums, with white, pink, red, or purple flower heads **2.** an insecticide made from the dried flower heads of certain chrysanthemums

**py·ret·ic** (pī ret′ik) *adj.* [< ModL. < Gr. *pyretos*, fever < *pyr*, a fire] of or causing fever

**Py·rex** (pī′reks) [arbitrary coinage < PIE[1] + *-r-* + *-ex*] a *trademark for* a heat-resistant glassware for cooking, etc.

**pyr·i·dine** (pir′ə dēn′, -din) *n.* [PYR(O)- + -ID + -INE[4]] a flammable, liquid base, $C_5H_5N$, with a sharp odor, produced by distilling coal tar, etc. and used in the synthesis of vitamins and drugs, etc.

**pyr·i·dox·ine** (pir′ə däk′sēn′, -sin) *n.* [PYRID(INE) + OX(Y)-[1] + -INE[4]] a pyridine derivative, $C_8H_{11}O_3N$, a vitamin of the B complex, found in cereal grains, liver, yeast, etc.

**py·rite** (pī′rīt) *n., pl.* **py·ri·tes** (pə rīt′ēz, pi-; pī′rīts) [< L. < Gr. *pyritēs*, flint < *pyr*, a fire] iron sulfide, $FeS_2$, a lus-

trous, yellow mineral that is an important ore of sulfur

**py·ri·tes** (pə rīt′ēz, pī-; pī′rīts) *n.* any of various native metallic sulfides, as pyrite —**py·rit′ic** (-rit′ik), **py·rit′i·cal** *adj.*

**py·ro-** [< Gr. *pyr*, a fire] *a combining form meaning* fire, heat [*pyromania*]: also **pyr-**

**Py·ro·ce·ram** (pī′rō sə ram′) [prec. + CERAM(IC)] a *trademark for* a heavy, glasslike, ceramic material highly resistant to heat and breakage

**py·rog·ra·phy** (pī räg′rə fē) *n.* [PYRO- + -GRAPHY] **1.** the art of burning designs on wood or leather with heated tools **2.** a design so made —**py·rog′ra·pher** *n.* —**py′ro·graph′ic** (-rə graf′ik) *adj.*

**py·ro·ma·ni·a** (pī′rə mā′nē ə, -mān′yə) *n.* [ModL.: see PYRO- & -MANIA] an uncontrollable desire to start destructive fires —**py′ro·ma′ni·ac′** (-nē ak′) *n., adj.* —**py′ro·ma·ni′a·cal** (-mə nī′ə k'l) *adj.*

**py·rom·e·ter** (pī räm′ə tər) *n.* [PYRO- + -METER] an instrument for measuring unusually high temperatures —**py′ro·met′ric** (-rə met′rik) *adj.* —**py′ro·met′ri·cal·ly** *adv.* —**py·rom′e·try** (-trē) *n.*

**py·ro·tech·nic** (pī′rə tek′nik) *adj.* [< Fr. < Gr. *pyr*, fire + *technē*, art] **1.** of fireworks **2.** designating or of spacecraft devices or materials that ignite or explode to activate propellants, etc. **3.** dazzling [*pyrotechnic wit*] Also **py′ro·tech′ni·cal** —**py′ro·tech′ni·cal·ly** *adv.*

**py·ro·tech·nics** (-niks) *n.pl.* **1.** [*with sing. v.*] the art of making and using fireworks: also **py′ro·tech′ny** (-nē) **2.** *a)* a display of fireworks *b)* fireworks; esp., rockets, flares, etc., as for signaling *c)* pyrotechnic devices in spacecraft **3.** a dazzling display, as of eloquence —**py′ro·tech′nist** *n.*

**py·rox·y·lin, py·rox·y·line** (pī räk′sə lin) *n.* [< Fr. < Gr. *pyr*, fire + *xylon*, wood] nitrocellulose, esp. in less explosive forms than guncotton, used in making paints, lacquers, etc.

**Pyr·rhic victory** (pir′ik) [after *Pyrrhus*, king of Epirus, who defeated the Romans in 280 and 279 B.C., suffering extremely heavy losses] a victory that is too costly

**Py·thag·o·ras** (pi thag′ər əs) 6th cent. B.C.; Gr. philosopher & mathematician —**Py·thag′o·re′an** (-ə rē′ən) *adj., n.*

**Pyth·i·an** (pith′ē ən) *adj.* [< L. < Gr. *Pythios*, of *Pythō*, older name for DELPHI] **1.** of Apollo as patron of Delphi and the Delphic oracle **2.** designating or of the games held at Delphi every four years in ancient Greece in honor of Apollo

**Pythias** *see* DAMON AND PYTHIAS

**py·thon** (pī′thän, -thən) *n.* [< L. < Gr. *Pythōn*, a serpent slain by Apollo] **1.** any of a group of large, nonpoisonous snakes of Asia, Africa, and Australia, that crush their prey to death **2.** popularly, any large snake that crushes its prey

**py·tho·ness** (pī′thə nis) *n.* [< MFr. < ML. < LL. < Gr. *Pythō*: see PYTHIAN] **1.** a priestess of Apollo at Delphi **2.** any woman soothsayer; prophetess

**pyx** (piks) *n.* [< L. < Gr. *pyxis*, a box < *pyxos*, the box tree] the container in which the consecrated wafer of the Eucharist is kept or carried

**pyx·is** (pik′sis) *n., pl.* **pyx′i·des′** (-sə dēz′) [L.: see prec.] *Bot.* a dry fruit whose upper portion splits off as a lid

# Q

**Q, q** (kyōō) *n., pl.* **Q's, q's** **1.** the seventeenth letter of the English alphabet **2.** the sound of *Q* or *q*

**Q** *Chess* queen

**Q.** **1.** Quebec **2.** Queen **3.** Question

**q.** **1.** quart **2.** quarter **3.** quarto **4.** queen **5.** question **6.** quetzal **7.** quintal: also **ql. 8.** quire

**Qa·tar** (kä′tär) independent Arab sheikdom occupying a peninsula in E Arabia on the Persian gulf: 8,500 sq. mi.; pop. 130,000

**Q.C.** Queen's Counsel

**Q.E.D.** [L. *quod erat demonstrandum*] which was to be proved

**qin·tar** (kin tär′) *n.* [Alb., ult. < L. *centum*, cent] *see* MONETARY UNITS, table (Albania)

**QM, Q.M.** Quartermaster

**qr.** *pl.* **qrs.** **1.** quarter **2.** quire

**qt.** **1.** quantity **2.** quart(s)

**Q.T., q.t.** [Slang] quiet: usually in **on the Q.T.** (or **q.t.**), in secret

**qto.** quarto

**qua** (kwā, kwä) *adv.* [L. < *qui*, who] in the function or capacity of [*the President* qua *Commander in Chief*]

**quack**[1] (kwak) *vi.* [echoic] to utter the sound or cry of a duck, or a sound like it —*n.* the sound made by a duck, or any sound like it

**quack**[2] (kwak) *n.* [short for QUACKSALVER] **1.** a person who practices medicine without having been trained, licensed, etc. **2.** any person who pretends to have knowledge or skill that he does not have; charlatan —*adj.* **1.** characterized by grand claims that have little or no foundation **2.** dishonestly claiming to bring about a cure —*vi.* to engage in quackery —**quack′ish** *adj.* —**quack′ish·ly** *adv.*

**quack·er·y** (-ər ē) *n.* the claims or methods of a quack

**quack·sal·ver** (-sal′vər) *n.* [< MDu. < *quacken*, to brag + *zalf*, salve] [Now Rare] a quack; charlatan

**quad**[1] (kwäd) *n.* same as: **1.** QUADRANGLE (of a college) **2.** QUADRUPLET

**quad**[2] (kwäd) *n.* [< QUAD(RAT)] *Printing* a piece of type metal lower than the face of the type, used for spacing, etc. —*vt.* **quad′ded, quad′ding** to fill out (a line) with quads

**Quad·ra·ges·i·ma** (kwäd′rə jes′i mə) *n.* [LL. < fem. of L. *quadragesimus*, fortieth] the first Sunday in Lent: also **Quadragesima Sunday**

**quad·ran·gle** (kwäd′raŋ′g'l) *n.* [< MFr. < LL. < L.: see QUADRI- & ANGLE[1]] **1.** a plane figure with four angles and four sides **2.** *a)* an area surrounded on four sides by buildings *b)* the buildings themselves —**quad·ran′gu·lar** (-gyə lər) *adj.*

**quad·rant** (kwäd′rənt) *n.* [< L. *quadrans*, fourth part] **1.** a fourth part of the circumference of a circle; an arc of 90° **2.** a quarter section of a circle **3.** an instrument for measuring altitudes or angular elevations in astronomy and navigation —**quad·ran′tal** (-ran′t'l) *adj.*

**quad·ra·phon·ic** (kwäd′rə fän′ik) *adj.* [< L. *quadra*, a square + PHONIC] designating or of sound reproduction, as on records or tapes or in broadcasting, using four channels to carry and reproduce through separate speakers a blend of sounds from separate sources

**quad·rat** (kwäd′rat) *n.* [var. of ff.] **1.** *same as* QUAD[2] **2.** *Ecol.* a plot of ground used to study plant and animal life

**quad·rate** (-rāt; *also, for adj. & n.,* -rit) *adj.* [< L. pp. of *quadrare*, to make square, ult. < *quattuor*, four] square or nearly square —*n.* **1.** a square or rectangle **2.** a square or rectangular space, thing, etc. —*vi.* **-rat·ed, -rat·ing** to square; agree (*with*) —*vt.* to make square

**quad·rat·ic** (kwäd rat′ik) *adj.* [< prec. + -IC] *Algebra* involving a quantity or quantities that are squared but none that are raised to a higher power —*n. Algebra* a quadratic term, expression, or equation —**quad·rat′i·cal·ly** *adv.*

**quadratic equation** *Algebra* an equation in which the second power, or square, is the highest to which the unknown quantity is raised

**quad·ra·ture** (kwäd′rə chər) *n.* [< LL. < L. pp. of *quadrare*: see QUADRATE] **1.** the act of squaring **2.** the determining of the dimensions of a square equal in area to a given surface **3.** *Astron.* the relative position of two heavenly bodies when 90° distant from each other

**quad·ren·ni·al** (kwäd ren′ē əl) *adj.* [< L. < *quadri-* (see ff.) + *annus*, a year] **1.** lasting four years **2.** occurring once every four years —*n.* a quadrennial event —**quad·ren′ni·al·ly** *adv.*

**quad·ri-** [L. < base of *quattuor*, four] *a combining form meaning* four times, fourfold: also, before a vowel, **quadr-**

**quad·ri·lat·er·al** (kwäd′rə lat′ər əl) *adj.* [< L.: see QUADRI- & LATERAL] four-sided —*n.* **1.** *Geom.* a plane figure having four sides and four angles **2.** a four-sided area —**quad′ri·lat′er·al·ly** *adv.*

**qua·drille** (kwə dril′, kwä-) *n.* [Fr. < Sp. *cuadrilla*, dim. < *cuadro*, a square] **1.** a square dance performed by four couples **2.** music for this dance

**quad·ril·lion** (kwäd ril′yən) *n.* [Fr. < *quadri-* (see QUADRI-) + (MI)LLION] **1.** in the U.S. and France, the number represented by 1 followed by 15 zeros **2.** in Great Britain and Germany, the number represented by 1 followed by 24 zeros —*adj.* amounting to one quadrillion in number —**quad·ril′lionth** *adj., n.*

QUADRILATERALS

**quad·ri·ple·gi·a** (kwäd′rə plē′jē ə, -jə) *n.* [ModL.: see QUADRI- & -PLEGIA] total paralysis of the body from the neck down —**quad′ri·ple′gic** (-plē′jik, -plej′ik) *adj., n.*

**quad·ri·va·lent** (kwäd′rə vā′lənt, kwä driv′ə-) *adj.* **1.** having four valences **2.** *same as* TETRAVALENT (sense 1) —**quad′ri·va′lence, quad′ri·va′len·cy** *n.*

**quad·roon** (kwä drōōn′) *n.* [< Sp. < *cuarto*, a fourth < L. *quartus:* see QUART] a person who has one Negro grandparent

**quad·ru·ped** (kwäd′rōō ped′) *n.* [< L. < *quadru-* (for *quadri-*), four + *pes*, a foot] an animal, esp. a mammal, with four feet —*adj.* having four feet —**quad·ru·pe·dal** (kwä drōō′pi d'l, kwäd′rə ped′'l) *adj.*

**quad·ru·ple** (kwä drōō′p'l, -drup′'l; kwäd′rōō-) *adj.* [MFr. < L. < *quadru-* (see prec.) + *-plus*, -fold] **1.** consisting of four **2.** four times as much or as many; fourfold **3.** *Music* having four beats to the measure —*n.* an amount four times as much or as many —*vt., vi.* **-pled, -pling** to make or become four times as much or as many

**quad·ru·plet** (kwä drup′lit, -drōō′plit; kwäd′rōō plit) *n.* [dim. of prec.] **1.** any of four offspring born at a single birth **2.** a group of four, usually of one kind

**quad·ru·pli·cate** (kwä drōō′plə kāt′; *for adj. & n., usually* -kit) *vt.* **-cat·ed, -cat·ing** [< L. pp. of *quadruplicare* < *quadru-* (see QUADRUPED) + *plicare*, to fold] to make four identical copies of —*adj.* **1.** fourfold **2.** designating the fourth of identical copies —*n.* any of four identical copies —**in quadruplicate** in four identical copies —**quad·ru′pli·ca′tion** *n.*

**quaes·tor** (kwes′tər, kwēs′-) *n.* [L. < pp. of *quaerere*, to inquire] in ancient Rome, **1.** orig., a judge in certain criminal cases **2.** later, any of certain state treasurers —**quaes·to′ri·al** (-tôr′ē əl) *adj.* —**quaes′tor·ship′** *n.*

**quaff** (kwäf, kwaf) *vt., vi.* [prob. by misreading of *-ss-* as *-ff-*) < LowG. *quassen*, to overindulge] to drink deeply in a hearty or thirsty way —*n.* **1.** a quaffing **2.** a drink that is quaffed —**quaff′er** *n.*

**quag·ga** (kwag′ə) *n., pl.* **-ga, -gas** see PLURAL, II, D, 2 [Afrik. < native name] a striped wild ass of Africa, now extinct

**quag·gy** (kwag′ē) *adj.* **-gi·er, -gi·est** **1.** like a quagmire; boggy; miry **2.** soft; flabby

**quag·mire** (kwag′mīr′) *n.* [< earlier *quag*, a bog + MIRE] **1.** wet, boggy ground, yielding under the feet **2.** a difficult or dangerous situation from which it is hard to escape [a *quagmire* of debts]

**qua·hog, qua·haug** (kwô′hôg, kō′-; -häg) *n.* [< AmInd. name] an edible clam of the eastern coast of N. America, having a very hard, solid shell

**quail**[1] (kwāl) *vi.* [prob. < OFr. *coaillier* < L. *coagulare*, to coagulate] to draw back in fear; lose courage; cower

**quail**[2] (kwāl) *n., pl.* **quails, quail:** see PLURAL, II, D, 1 [< OFr. < ML. *cuacula*, prob. < Gmc. echoic name] **1.** any of various small game birds, resembling partridges **2.** *same as* BOBWHITE

**quaint** (kwānt) *adj.* [< OFr. *cointe* < L. *cognitus*, known: see COGNITION] **1.** unusual or old-fashioned in a pleasing way **2.** unusual; curious **3.** fanciful; whimsical —**quaint′ly** *adv.* —**quaint′ness** *n.*

**quake** (kwāk) *vi.* **quaked, quak′ing** [OE. *cwacian*] **1.** to tremble or shake, as the ground does in an earthquake **2.** to shudder or shiver, as from fear or cold —*n.* **1.** a shaking or tremor **2.** an earthquake

**Quak·er** (kwāk′ər) *n.* [orig. mocking: said to be from founder's admonition to "quake" at the word of the Lord] *a popular name for* a member of the Society of Friends: see SOCIETY OF FRIENDS —**Quak′er·ess** [Now Rare] *n.fem.* —**Quak′er·ish** *n.* —**Quak′er·ism** *n.* —**Quak′er·ly** *adj., adv.*

**quaking aspen** a poplar with small, flat-stemmed leaves that tremble in the slightest breeze

**quak·y** (kwā′kē) *adj.* **quak′i·er, quak′i·est** inclined to quake; shaky —**quak′i·ly** *adv.* —**quak′i·ness** *n.*

**qual·i·fi·ca·tion** (kwäl′ə fi kā′shən) *n.* **1.** a qualifying or being qualified **2.** a thing or condition that qualifies or limits; modification or restriction **3.** any skill, knowledge, experience, etc. that fits a person for a position, office, etc. **4.** a condition that must be met, as to be eligible

**qual·i·fied** (kwäl′ə fīd′) *adj.* **1.** having met conditions or requirements set **2.** having the necessary or desirable qualities; competent **3.** modified [*qualified* approval] —**qual′i·fied′ly** *adv.* —**qual′i·fied′ness** *n.*

**qual·i·fy** (-fī′) *vt.* **-fied′, -fy′ing** [< Fr. < ML. < L. *qualis*, of what kind + *facere*, to make] **1.** to describe by giving the qualities or characteristics of **2.** to make fit for an office, position, etc. **3.** to make legally capable; license **4.** to modify; restrict; limit **5.** to moderate; soften **6.** to change the strength of (a liquor, etc.) **7.** *Gram.* to modify the meaning of (a word) —*vi.* to be or become qualified —**qual′i·fi′a·ble** *adj.* —**qual′i·fi′er** *n.* —**qual′i·fy′ing·ly** *adv.*

**qual·i·ta·tive** (-tāt′iv) *adj.* having to do with quality or qualities —**qual′i·ta′tive·ly** *adv.*

**qualitative analysis** the branch of chemistry dealing with the determination of the elements or ingredients of which a compound or mixture is composed

**qual·i·ty** (kwäl′ə tē) *n., pl.* **-ties** [< OFr. < L. *qualis*, of what kind] **1.** any of the features that make something what it is; characteristic; attribute **2.** basic nature; character; kind **3.** the degree of excellence which a thing possesses **4.** excellence; superiority **5.** [Archaic] *a)* high social position *b)* people of such position **6.** the property of a tone determined by its overtones; timbre

**quality control** a system for maintaining desired standards in a product, esp. by inspecting samples

**qualm** (kwäm) *n.* [OE. *cwealm*, disaster] **1.** a sudden feeling of sickness, faintness, or nausea **2.** a sudden feeling of uneasiness or doubt; misgiving **3.** a twinge of conscience; scruple —**qualm′ish** *adj.* —**qualm′ish·ly** *adv.* —**qualm′ish·ness** *n.*

**quan·da·ry** (kwän′drē, -dər ē) *n., pl.* **-ries** [< ? L. *quande*, how much] a state of perplexity; dilemma

**quan·ta** (kwän′tə) *n., pl. of* QUANTUM

**quan·ti·fy** (kwän′tə fī′) *vt.* **-fied′, -fy′ing** [ML. < L. *quantus*, how much + *facere*, to make] to determine or express the quantity of; measure —**quan′ti·fi′a·ble** *adj.* —**quan′ti·fi·ca′tion** *n.* —**quan′ti·fi′er** *n.*

**quan·ti·ta·tive** (kwän′tə tāt′iv) *adj.* **1.** having to do

with quantity **2.** capable of being measured —**quan′ti‧ta′tive‧ly** *adv.* —**quan′ti‧ta′tive‧ness** *n.*
**quantitative analysis** the branch of chemistry dealing with the measurement of the amounts or percentages of the various components of a compound or mixture
**quan‧ti‧ty** (kwän′tə tē) *n., pl.* **-ties** [< OFr. < L. < *quantus*, how much] **1.** an amount; portion **2.** any bulk, weight, or number not definitely specified **3.** the exact amount of something **4.** [*also pl.*] a great amount **5.** that property of anything which can be determined by measurement **6.** the relative length of a vowel, syllable, musical tone, etc. **7.** *Math. a)* a thing that has the property of being measurable in dimensions, amounts, etc. *b)* a number or symbol expressing a quantity
**quan‧tum** (-təm) *n., pl.* **-ta** (-tə) [L., neut. sing. of *quantus*, how much] *Physics* an (or the) elemental unit, as of energy: the **quantum theory** states that energy is not absorbed or radiated continuously, but discontinuously, in quanta
**quar‧an‧tine** (kwôr′ən tēn′, kwär′-) *n.* [It. *quarantina*, lit., forty days, ult. < L. *quadraginta*, forty] **1.** *a)* the period, orig. 40 days, during which a vessel suspected of carrying contagious disease is detained in a port in isolation *b)* the place where such a vessel is stationed **2.** any isolation or restriction on travel to keep contagious diseases, insect pests, etc. from spreading **3.** a place where persons, animals, or plants having such diseases, etc. are isolated **4.** the state of being quarantined —*vt.* **-tined′, -tin′ing 1.** to place under quarantine **2.** to isolate politically, commercially, socially, etc. —**quar′an‧tin′a‧ble** *adj.*
**quark** (kwôrk) *n.* [orig. a word coined by James Joyce in *Finnegan's Wake*] any of three proposed particles thought of as the building blocks of baryons and mesons
**quar‧rel¹** (kwôr′əl, kwär′-) *n.* [< OFr., ult. < dim. of L. *quadrus*, a square] **1.** a square-headed arrow shot from a crossbow **2.** a small, diamond-shaped or square pane of glass
**quar‧rel²** (kwôr′əl, kwär′-) *n.* [< OFr. < L. *querela*, complaint < *queri*, to complain] **1.** a cause for dispute **2.** a dispute, esp. one marked by anger and resentment **3.** a breaking up of friendly relations —*vi.* **-reled** or **-relled, -rel‧ing** or **-rel‧ling 1.** to find fault; complain **2.** to dispute heatedly **3.** to have a breach in friendship —**quar′rel‧er, quar′rel‧ler** *n.*
**quar‧rel‧some** (-səm) *adj.* inclined to quarrel —**quar′rel‧some‧ly** *adv.* —**quar′rel‧some‧ness** *n.*
**quar‧ry¹** (kwôr′ē, kwär′ē) *n., pl.* **-ries** [< OFr. *cuiree*, altered (after *cuir*, a hide) < pp. of *curer*, to eviscerate] **1.** an animal that is being hunted down **2.** anything pursued
**quar‧ry²** (kwôr′ē, kwär′ē) *n., pl.* **-ries** [< ML., ult. < L. *quadrare*, to square] a place where building stone, marble, or slate is excavated —*vt.* **-ried, -ry‧ing 1.** to excavate from a quarry **2.** to make a quarry (in land)
**quar‧ry‧man** (-mən) *n., pl.* **-men** a person who works in a stone quarry: also **quar‧ri‧er** (kwôr′ē ər, kwär′-)
**quart** (kwôrt) *n.* [< MFr. < OFr. < L. *quartus*, fourth < base of *quattuor*, four] **1.** a liquid measure, equal to 1/4 gallon (57.75 cu. in.) **2.** a dry measure, equal to 1/8 peck **3.** any container that can hold one quart
**quar‧ter** (kwôr′tər) *n.* [< OFr. < L. *quartarius*, a fourth < *quartus*, fourth] **1.** any of the four equal parts of something; fourth **2.** *a)* one fourth of a year; three months *b)* a school or college term, usually one fourth of a school year **3.** *a)* one fourth of an hour; 15 minutes *b)* the moment marking the end of each fourth of an hour **4.** *a)* one fourth of a dollar; 25 cents *b)* a coin of the U.S. and Canada equal to 25 cents: in the U.S., made of cupronickel **5.** any leg of a four-legged animal, with the adjoining parts **6.** *a)* any of the four main points of the compass *b)* any of the regions of the earth thought of as under these **7.** a particular district in a city [the Latin *quarter*] **8.** [*pl.*] lodgings; place of abode **9.** mercy granted to a surrendering foe **10.** a particular person, group, place, etc., esp. one serving as a source [news from the highest *quarters*] **11.** *a)* the period of time in which the moon makes one fourth of its revolution around the earth *b)* a phase of the moon when it is half lighted **12.** *Football, Basketball,* etc. any of the four periods into which a game is divided **13.** *Heraldry a)* any of the four equal divisions of a shield *b)* the charge occupying such a division **14.** *Naut.* the after part of a ship's side *b)* an assigned station or post —*vt.* **1.** to divide into four equal parts **2.** loosely, to separate into any number of parts **3.** to dismember (the body of a person put to death) into four parts **4.** to provide lodgings for; specif., to assign (soldiers) to lodgings **5.** to pass over (an area) in many directions, as hounds do in searching for game **6.** *Heraldry* to place (different coats of arms) on the quarters of a shield, or to add (a coat of arms) to a shield thus —*vi.* **1.** to be lodged or stationed (*at* or *with*) **2.** to range over a field, etc., as hounds in hunting **3.** *Naut.* to blow on the quarter of a ship: said of the wind —*adj.* constituting or equal to a quarter —**at close quarters** at close range —**cry quarter** to beg for mercy —**quar′ter‧ing** *adj., n.*

**quar‧ter‧back** (-bak′) *n. Football* the offensive back who calls the signals and directs the plays —*vt., vi.* **1.** to act as quarterback for (a team) **2.** to direct or lead; manage
**quarter day** any of the four days regarded as beginning a new quarter of the year, when quarterly payments on rents, etc. are due
**quar‧ter‧deck, quar‧ter‧deck** (-dek′) *n.* **1.** the after part of a ship's upper deck, usually reserved for officers **2.** *U.S. Navy* the part of a ship's upper deck reserved for official ceremonies
**quar‧tered** (kwôr′tərd) *adj.* **1.** divided into quarters **2.** provided with quarters or lodgings **3.** quartersawed
**quar‧ter‧fi‧nal** (kwôr′tər fī′n'l; *for n. usually* kwôr′tər‧fī′n'l) *adj.* coming just before the semifinals, as of a tournament —*n.* **1.** a quarterfinal match **2.** [*pl.*] a quarterfinal round —**quar′ter‧fi′nal‧ist** *n.*
**quarter horse** an American breed of horse with a low, compact, muscular body and great sprinting speed for distances up to a quarter of a mile
**quar‧ter‧ly** (kwôr′tər lē) *adj.* **1.** occurring or appearing at regular intervals four times a year **2.** consisting of a quarter —*adv.* once every quarter of the year —*n., pl.* **-lies** a publication issued every three months
**quar‧ter‧mas‧ter** (-mas′tər) *n.* **1.** *Mil.* an officer whose duty it is to provide troops with quarters, clothing, equipment, etc. **2.** a ship's petty officer who attends to navigation, signals, etc.
**quar‧tern** (kwôr′tərn) *n.* [< OFr.: see QUART] **1.** orig., a fourth part **2.** [Brit.] one fourth of a pint, a peck, etc.
**quarter note** *Music* a note having one fourth the duration of a whole note; crotchet: see NOTE, illus.
**quar‧ter‧saw** (kwôr′tər sô′) *vt.* **-sawed′, -sawed′** or **-sawn′, -saw′ing** to saw (a log) into quarters lengthwise and then into boards, in order to show off the grain of the wood
**quarter section** a division of public lands that is one fourth of a section (160 acres) and is half a mile square
**quarter sessions 1.** in England, a court that sits quarterly in civil proceedings, with limited criminal jurisdiction **2.** in the U.S., any of various courts that sit quarterly
**quar‧ter‧staff** (-staf′) *n., pl.* **-staves′** (-stāvz′) a stout, iron-tipped wooden staff, six to eight feet long, formerly used in England as a weapon
**quarter tone** *Music* an interval of one half of a semitone
**quar‧tet, quar‧tette** (kwôr tet′) *n.* [< Fr. < It. dim. of *quarto* < L. *quartus*, a fourth] **1.** any group of four **2.** *Music a)* a composition for four voices or four instruments *b)* the four performers of such a composition
**quar‧to** (kwôr′tō) *n., pl.* **-tos** [< L. (*in*) *quarto*, (in) a fourth] **1.** the page size (about 9 by 12 in.) of a book made up of printer's sheets folded into four leaves **2.** a book with pages of this size —*adj.* with pages of this size
**quartz** (kwôrts) *n.* [G. *quarz* < ?] a brilliant, crystalline mineral, silicon dioxide, $SiO_2$, occurring most often in a colorless, transparent form, but also as variously colored semiprecious stones —**quartz‧ose** (kwôrt′sōs) *adj.*
**quartz crystal** *Electronics* a thin plate or rod cut from quartz and ground so as to vibrate at a particular frequency
**quartz lamp** a mercury-vapor lamp with a quartz tube for transmitting ultraviolet rays
**qua‧sar** (kwā′sär, -zär, -sər) *n.* [< *quas(i-stell)ar* (*radio source*)] any of a number of extremely distant starlike objects that emit powerful radio waves
**quash¹** (kwäsh) *vt.* [< MFr. < LL. *cassare*, to destroy < L. *cassus*, empty] *Law* to annul or set aside (an indictment)
**quash²** (kwäsh) *vt.* [< MFr. < L. *quassare*, to shatter < pp. of *quatere*, to break] to put down or overcome as by force; suppress; quell [to *quash* an uprising]
**qua‧si** (kwā′sī, -zī; kwä′sē, -zē) *adv.* [L. < *quam*, as + *si*, as if; seemingly; in part —*adj.* seeming Often hyphenated as a prefix [*quasi*-judicial]
**qua‧si‧stel‧lar radio source** (-stel′ər) *same as* QUASAR
**quas‧si‧a** (kwäsh′ē ə, kwäsh′ə) *n.* [ModL. < Graman *Quassi*, Surinam Negro who prescribed it for fever, c. 1730] **1.** any of a group of tropical trees related to the ailanthus **2.** the wood of certain of these or a drug extracted from it
**qua‧ter‧na‧ry** (kwät′ər ner′ē, kwə tur′nər ē) *adj.* [< L. < *quaterni*, four each] **1.** consisting of four **2.** [Q-] designating or of the geologic period following the Tertiary in the Cenozoic Era —**the Quaternary** the Quaternary Period or its rocks: see GEOLOGY, chart
**quat‧rain** (kwä′trān) *n.* [Fr. < *quatre* < L. *quattuor*, four] a stanza or poem of four lines
**quat‧re‧foil** (kat′ər foil′, kat′rə-) *n.* [< MFr. < *quatre* (< L. *quattuor*), four + *feuille* (< L. *folium*), a leaf] **1.** a flower with four petals or a leaf with four leaflets **2.** *Archit.* a circular design of four converging arcs
**qua‧ver** (kwā′vər) *vi.* [ME. *cwafien*] **1.** to shake or tremble **2.** to be tremulous: said of the voice **3.** to make a trill in singing or playing —*vt.* **1.** to utter in a tremulous voice **2.** to sing or play with a trill —*n.* **1.** a tremulous quality in a voice or tone **2.** [Brit.] *same as* EIGHTH NOTE —**qua′ver‧er** *n.* —**qua′ver‧ing‧ly** *adv.* —**qua′ver‧y** *adj.*

**quay** (kē) *n.* [MFr. *cai* < Celt.] a wharf for loading and unloading ships, usually one of stone or concrete

**Que.** Quebec

**quean** (kwēn) *n.* [OE. *cwene*] 1. a hussy 2. a prostitute

**quea·sy** (kwē′zē) *adj.* -si·er, -si·est [ME. *qwesye* < Scand.] 1. causing or feeling nausea 2. squeamish; easily nauseated 3. uncomfortable; uneasy —**quea′si·ly** *adv.* —**quea′si·ness** *n.*

**Que·bec** (kwi bek′) 1. province of E Canada: 594,860 sq. mi.; pop. 6,234,000; abbrev. **Que.**, **P.Q.** 2. its capital, on the St. Lawrence River: pop. 177,000 (met. area 413,000) Fr. **Qué·bec** (kā bek′)

**Que·bec·ois** (ke′be kwä′) *n., pl.* -ois′ [CanadFr. *Québecois*] a French-speaking native or inhabitant of the province of Quebec

**Quech·ua** (kech′wä, -wə) *n.* [Sp. < Quechua name] 1. *pl.* -uas, -ua a member of any of a group of S. American Indian tribes dominant in the former Inca Empire 2. their language, still widely spoken —**Quech′uan** *adj., n.*

**queen** (kwēn) *n.* [OE. *cwen*] 1. the wife of a king 2. a woman who rules over a monarchy in her own right 3. a woman who is foremost among others, as in beauty or accomplishments 4. a place or thing regarded as the finest of its kind 5. the fully developed, reproductive female in a colony of bees, ants, etc. 6. a playing card with a picture of a queen on it 7. [Slang] a male homosexual, esp. one with feminine characteristics 8. *Chess* the most powerful piece: it can move in any straight or diagonal direction —**queen** it to act like a queen; domineer —**queen′dom** *n.* —**queen′hood′** *n.* —**queen′like′** *adj.*

**Queen Anne's lace** *same as* WILD CARROT

**queen consort** the wife of a reigning king

**queen dowager** the widow of a king

**queen·ly** (-lē) *adj.* -li·er, -li·est of, like, or fit for a queen; royal; regal —**queen′li·ness** *n.*

**queen mother** a queen dowager who is mother of a reigning sovereign

**queen post** *Carpentry* either of two vertical posts set between the rafters and the base of a truss, at equal distances from the apex

**Queens** (kwēnz) [after *Queen Catherine*, wife of CHARLES II of England] borough of New York City, on W Long Island: pop. 1,891,000

QUEEN POSTS

**queen's English** *see* KING'S ENGLISH

**queen-size** (kwēn′sīz′) *adj.* [Colloq.] larger than usual, but less than king-size

**Queens·land** (kwēnz′land′, -lənd) state of NE Australia

**queer** (kwir) *adj.* [< ? G. *quer*, crosswise] 1. differing from what is usual or ordinary: odd; strange 2. slightly ill; giddy, queasy, etc. 3. [Colloq.] doubtful; suspicious 4. [Colloq.] having mental quirks; eccentric 5. [Slang] counterfeit; not genuine 6. [Slang] homosexual —*vt.* [Slang] 1. to spoil the success of 2. to put (oneself) into an unfavorable position —*n.* [Slang] 1. counterfeit money 2. an eccentric person 3. a homosexual —**queer′ish** *adj.* —**queer′ly** *adv.* —**queer′ness** *n.*

**quell** (kwel) *vt.* [OE. *cwellan*, to kill] 1. to crush; subdue [to *quell* a mutiny] 2. to quiet; allay [to *quell* fears]

**quench** (kwench) *vt.* [OE. *cwencan*, caus. of *cwincan*, to go out] 1. to extinguish; put out [water *quenched* the fire] 2. to overcome; subdue 3. to satisfy; slake [he *quenched* his thirst] 4. to cool (hot steel, etc.) suddenly by plunging into water, oil, etc. —**quench′a·ble** *adj.* —**quench′er** *n.* —**quench′less** *adj.*

**quern** (kwurn) *n.* [OE. *cweorn*] a primitive hand mill, esp. for grinding grain

**quer·u·lous** (kwer′ə ləs, -yə-) *adj.* [< L. < *queri*, to complain] 1. inclined to find fault; complaining 2. full of complaint; peevish —**quer′u·lous·ly** *adv.* —**quer′u·lous·ness** *n.*

**que·ry** (kwir′ē) *n., pl.* -ries [< L. *quaere*, 2d pers. sing., imper., of *quaerere*, to ask] 1. a question; inquiry 2. a doubt 3. a question mark (?) —*vt.* -ried, -ry·ing 1. to call in question; ask about 2. to question (a person) 3. to question the accuracy of (written or printed matter) by marking with a question mark —*vi.* to ask questions or express doubt —**que′rist** *n.*

**ques.** question

**quest** (kwest) *n.* [< OFr. < ML., ult. < L. *quaesitus*, pp. of *quaerere*, to seek] 1. a seeking; hunt; search 2. a journey in search of adventure, etc., as those undertaken by knights-errant in medieval times 3. the persons participating in a quest —*vi.* to go in search or pursuit —*vt.* to seek —**quest′er** *n.*

**ques·tion** (kwes′chən) *n.* [< Anglo-Fr. < OFr. < L. *quaestio* < pp. of *quaerere*, to ask] 1. an asking; inquiry 2. something asked; interrogative sentence 3. doubt; uncertainty 4. something in controversy before a court 5. a problem; matter open to discussion or inquiry 6. a matter or case of difficulty [not a *question* of money] 7. *a)* a point being debated or a resolution brought up before an assembly *b)* the putting of such a matter to a vote —*vt.* 1. to ask questions of; interrogate 2. to express uncertainty about; doubt 3. to dispute; challenge —*vi.* to ask a question or questions —**beside the question** not relevant —**beyond (all) question** without any doubt —**in question** being considered, debated, etc. —**out of the question** impossible; not to be considered —**ques′tion·er** *n.* —**ques′tion·ing** *adj.*

**ques·tion·a·ble** (-ə b'l) *adj.* 1. that can or should be questioned; open to doubt 2. suspected with good reason of being immoral, dishonest, etc. 3. uncertain [of *questionable* excellence] —**ques′tion·a·bly** *adv.*

**question mark** 1. a mark of punctuation (?) put after a sentence, word, etc. to indicate a direct question, or to express doubt, uncertainty, etc. 2. an unknown factor

**ques·tion·naire** (kwes′chə ner′) *n.* [Fr.] a written or printed list of questions used in gathering information from one or more persons

**quet·zal** (ket säl′) *n.* [AmSp. < Nahuatl < *quetzalli*, tail feather] 1. a Central American bird, usually brilliant green above and red below, with long, streaming tail feathers in the male 2. *pl.* -zal′es (-sä′les) *see* MONETARY UNITS, table (Guatemala)

**queue** (kyōō) *n.* [Fr. < OFr. *coue* < L. *cauda*, tail] 1. a pigtail 2. [Chiefly Brit.] a line, as of persons waiting to be served —*vi.* queued, queu′ing [Chiefly Brit.] to form in a line (often with *up*)

**Que·zon** (ke′sôn; E. kā′zän), **Man·uel Lu·is** (mä nwel′ lōō ēs′) 1878–1944; Philippine statesman

**quib·ble** (kwib′'l) *n.* [< L. *quibus* (formerly common in legal documents), abl. pl. of *qui*, who, which] 1. a petty evasion; cavil 2. a petty objection or criticism —*vi.* -bled, -bling to evade the truth of a point under discussion by caviling —**quib′bler** *n.*

**‡quiche Lor·raine** (kēsh lô ren′) *pl.* **quiches Lor·raine** (kēsh) [Fr., lit., Lorraine pastry: *quiche* < G. dial. *küche*, dim. of *kuchen*, cake] a kind of custard pie made with cheese, bacon, etc. and served hot

QUETZAL (length, including plumes, to 42 in.)

**quick** (kwik) *adj.* [OE. *cwicu*, living] 1. [Archaic] living 2. *a)* rapid in action; swift [a *quick* walk, a *quick* worker] *b)* prompt [a *quick* reply] 3. lasting a short time [a *quick* look] 4. prompt to understand or learn 5. sensitive [a *quick* sense of smell] 6. easily stirred; fiery [a *quick* temper] —*adv.* quickly; rapidly —*n.* 1. the living, esp. in **the quick and the dead** 2. the sensitive flesh under a fingernail or toenail 3. the deepest feelings [cut to the *quick*] —**quick′ly** *adv.* —**quick′ness** *n.*

**quick bread** any bread, as muffins, corn bread, etc., leavened with baking powder, soda, etc., and baked as soon as the batter or dough is mixed

**quick·en** (kwik′ən) *vt.* 1. to animate; enliven 2. to stir; arouse; stimulate 3. to make move more rapidly; hasten —*vi.* 1. to become enlivened; revive 2. *a)* to begin to show signs of life *b)* to enter the stage of pregnancy in which the movement of the fetus can be felt 3. to become more rapid; speed up [the pulse *quickens* with fear] —**quick′en·er** *n.*

**quick-freeze** (-frēz′) *vt.* -froze′, -froz′en, -freez′ing to subject (food) to sudden freezing so that flavor and natural juices are retained and the food can be stored at low temperatures for a long time

**quick·ie** (-ē) *n.* [Slang] anything done or made quickly —*adj.* [Slang] done or made quickly

**quick·lime** (-līm′) *n.* lime, or calcium oxide, which gives off much heat in combining with water; unslaked lime

**quick·sand** (-sand′) *n.* [see QUICK & SAND] a deep deposit of loose, wet sand in which a person or heavy object may be easily engulfed

**quick·set** (-set′) *n.* [Chiefly Brit.] 1. a live slip or cutting, as of hawthorn, planted, as for a hedge 2. a hedge

**quick·sil·ver** (-sil′vər) *n.* the metal mercury —*vt.* to cover with mercury —*adj.* of or like mercury

**quick·step** (-step′) *n.* 1. the step used for marching in quick time 2. a march in the rhythm of quick time 3. a spirited dance step

**quick-tem·pered** (-tem′pərd) *adj.* easily angered

fat, āpe, cär, ten, ēven, is, bīte; gō, hôrn, tōōl, look; oil, out; up, fur; get; joy; yet; chin; she; thin, *then*; zh, leisure; ŋ, ring; ə for *a* in *ago*, *e* in *agent*, *i* in *sanity*, *o* in *comply*, *u* in *focus*; as in *able* (ā′b'l); Fr. bál; ë, Fr. coeur; ö, Fr. feu; Fr. mon; ô, Fr. coq; ü, Fr. duc; r, Fr. cri; H, G. ich; kh, G. doch; ‡foreign; *hypothetical; < derived from. See inside front cover.

**quick time** the normal rate of marching: in the U.S. Army, 120 (30-inch) paces a minute

**quick-wit·ted** (-wit′id) *adj.* nimble of mind; alert —**quick′-wit′ted·ly** *adv.* —**quick′-wit′ted·ness** *n.*

**quid¹** (kwid) *n.* [var. of *cud*] a piece, as of tobacco, to be chewed

**quid²** (kwid) *n., pl.* **quid** [Brit. Slang] a sovereign, or one pound sterling

**quid·di·ty** (kwid′ə tē) *n., pl.* **-ties** [< ML. < L. *quid,* what] 1. essential quality 2. a quibble

**quid·nunc** (kwid′nuŋk′) *n.* [L., lit., what now?] an inquisitive, gossipy person; busybody

**quid pro quo** (kwid′ prō kwō′) [L.] 1. one thing in return for another 2. something equivalent; substitute

**qui·es·cent** (kwī es′'nt) *adj.* [< L. prp. of *quiescere,* to become quiet] quiet; still; inactive —**qui·es′cence** *n.* —**qui·es′cent·ly** *adv.*

**qui·et** (kwī′ət) *adj.* [< OFr. < L. *quietus,* pp. of *quiescere,* to keep quiet < *quies* (gen. *quietis*), rest] 1. still; calm; motionless 2. *a)* not noisy; hushed *b)* not speaking; silent 3. not agitated; gentle [a *quiet* sea] 4. not easily excited [a *quiet* disposition] 5. not bright or showy [*quiet* furnishings] 6. not forward; unobtrusive [a *quiet* manner] 7. secluded [a *quiet* den] 8. peaceful; relaxing [a *quiet* evening] 9. *Commerce* not busy [a *quiet* market] —*n.* 1. a quiet state; calmness, stillness, etc. 2. a quiet or peaceful quality —*vt., vi.* to make or become quiet —*adv.* in a quiet manner —**qui′et·er** *n.* —**qui′et·ly** *adv.* —**qui′et·ness** *n.*

**qui·et·en** (-'n) *vt., vi.* [Brit. or Dial.] to make or become quiet

**qui·e·tude** (kwī′ə tōōd′, -tyōōd′) *n.* a state of being quiet; rest; calmness

**qui·e·tus** (kwī ēt′əs) *n.* [< ME. *quietus* (*est*) < ML., (he is) quit < L., QUIET] 1. discharge or release from debt, obligation, etc. 2. discharge or release from life; death 3. anything that kills

**quill** (kwil) *n.* [prob. < MLowG. or MDu.] 1. any of the large, stiff wing or tail feathers of a bird 2. *a)* the hollow, horny stem of a feather *b)* anything made from this, as a pen or plectrum 3. any of the spines of a porcupine or hedgehog

**quilt** (kwilt) *n.* [< OFr. < L. *culcita,* a bed] 1. a bedcover made of two layers of cloth filled with down, wool, etc. and stitched together in lines or patterns 2. anything like or used as a quilt —*vt.* 1. to stitch as or like a quilt [to *quilt* a potholder] 2. to fasten between two pieces of material 3. to line or pad with quilting —*vi.* to make a quilt or quilts —**quilt′er** *n.*

**quilt·ing** (-iŋ) *n.* 1. the act of making quilts 2. material for quilts 3. *same as* QUILTING BEE

**quilting bee** (or **party**) a social gathering of women at which they work together sewing quilts

**quince** (kwins) *n.* [orig. pl. of ME. *quyn* < OFr. < L. < Gr. *kydōnion*] 1. a golden or greenish-yellow, hard, apple-shaped fruit used in preserves 2. the tree that bears this fruit

**Quin·cy** (kwin′zē) [after J. *Quincy* (1689–1767), a local official] city in E Mass.: suburb of Boston: pop. 85,000

**qui·nine** (kwī′nīn; *chiefly Brit.* kwi nēn′) *n.* [< *quina,* cinchona bark (< Sp. < Quechua name) + -INE⁴] 1. a bitter, crystalline substance, $C_{20}H_{24}N_2O_2$, extracted from cinchona bark 2. any compound of this used in medicine, esp. for treating malaria

**quinine water** *same as* TONIC (*n.* 2)

**Quin·qua·ges·i·ma** (kwiŋ′kwə jes′i mə) *n.* [LL. *quinquagesima* (*dies*), fiftieth (day)] the Sunday before Lent: also **Quinquagesima Sunday**

**quin·quen·ni·al** (kwiŋ kwen′ē əl) *adj.* [< L. < *quinque,* five + *annus,* year] 1. lasting five years 2. taking place every five years —*n.* a quinquennial event —**quin·quen′ni·al·ly** *adv.*

**quin·que·va·lent** (kwiŋ′kwə vā′lənt) *adj.* [L. *quinque,* five + -VALENT] 1. having five valences 2. *same as* PENTAVALENT (sense 1) —**quin′que·va′lence, quin′que·va′len·cy** *n.*

**quin·sy** (kwin′zē) *n.* [< ML. *quinancia* < LL. *cynanche* < Gr. *kynanchē,* lit., dog-choking < *kyōn,* dog + *anchein,* to choke] *an earlier term for* TONSILLITIS

**quint** (kwint) *n. shortened form of* QUINTUPLET

**quin·tal** (kwin′t'l) *n.* [< MFr. < ML. < Ar. *qintār,* ult. < L. *centenarius:* see CENTENARY] 1. a hundredweight (100 lbs. in the U.S., 112 lbs. in Great Britain) 2. a metric unit of weight, equal to 100 kilograms (220.46 lbs.)

**quin·tes·sence** (kwin tes′'ns) *n.* [< MFr. < ML. *quinta essentia,* fifth essence, or ultimate substance] 1. the essence of something in its purest form 2. the perfect type or example of something —**quin′tes·sen′tial** (-tə sen′shəl) *adj.*

**quin·tet, quin·tette** (kwin tet′) *n.* [< Fr. < It. dim. of *quinto* < L. *quintus,* a fifth] 1. any group of five 2. *Music* *a)* a composition for five voices or five instruments *b)* the five performers of such a composition

**Quin·til·i·an** (kwin til′yən, -ē ən) (L. name *Marcus Fabius*

*Quintilianus*) 30?–96? A.D.; Rom. rhetorician, born in Spain

**quin·til·lion** (kwin til′yən) *n.* [< L. *quintus,* a fifth + (M)ILLION] 1. in the U.S. and France, the number represented by 1 followed by 18 zeros 2. in Great Britain and Germany, the number represented by 1 followed by 30 zeros —*adj.* amounting to one quintillion in number —**quin·til′lionth** *adj., n.*

**quin·tu·ple** (kwin tōō′p'l, -tyōō′-, -tup′'l; kwin′tōō p'l) *adj.* [MFr. < LL. < L. *quintus,* a fifth + *-plex,* -fold] 1. consisting of five 2. five times as much or as many; fivefold —*n.* an amount five times as much or as many —*vt., vi.* -**pled,** -**pling** to make or become five times as much or as many

**quin·tu·plet** (kwin tup′lit, -tōō′plit, -tyōō′-; kwin′tōō plit) *n.* [dim. of prec.] 1. any of five offspring born at a single birth 2. a group of five, usually of one kind

**quip** (kwip) *n.* [< L. *quippe,* indeed] 1. a witty, or, esp. formerly, sarcastic remark; jest 2. a quibble 3. something curious or odd —*vi.* **quipped, quip′ping** to utter quips —**quip′ster** *n.*

**quire¹** (kwīr) *n. archaic var. of* CHOIR

**quire²** (kwīr) *n.* [< OFr. < VL. *quaternum,* paper in sets of four < L. *quaterni,* four each] a set of 24 or 25 sheets of paper of the same size and stock

**quirk** (kwurk) *n.* [< ? ON. *kverk,* a bird's crop] 1. *a)* a sudden twist, turn, etc. [a *quirk* of fate] *b)* a flourish in writing 2. a quibble 3. a peculiar trait or mannerism —**quirk′i·ly** *adv.* —**quirk′i·ness** *n.* —**quirk′y** *adj.* **quirk′i·er, quirk′i·est**

**quirt** (kwurt) *n.* [AmSp. *cuarta*] a riding whip with a braided leather lash and a short handle —*vt.* to strike with a quirt

**quis·ling** (kwiz′liŋ) *n.* [after Vidkun *Quisling* (1887–1945), Norw. collaborationist with the Nazis] a traitor

**quit** (kwit) *vt.* **quit** or **quit′ted, quit′ting** [< OFr. < ML. *quietus,* free: see QUIET] 1. to free (oneself) *of* 2. to discharge (a debt); repay 3. to give up 4. to leave; depart from 5. to stop, discontinue, or resign from —*vi.* 1. *a)* to stop doing something *b)* to give up, as in discouragement 2. to give up one's job; resign —*adj.* clear, free, or rid, as of an obligation

**quitch** (kwich) *n.* [< OE. < *cwicu,* alive] *same as* COUCH GRASS

**quit·claim** (kwit′klām′) *n.* [< Anglo-Fr. & OFr.: see QUIT & CLAIM] 1. the relinquishment of a claim, right, title, etc. 2. a legal paper in which a person relinquishes to another a claim or title to some property or right: in full, **quitclaim deed** —*vt.* to give up a claim or title to

**quite** (kwīt) *adv.* [ME. form of QUIT, *adj.*] 1. completely; entirely 2. really; truly 3. to a considerable degree or extent —**quite a few** (or **bit,** etc.) [Colloq.] more than a few (or bit, etc.) —**quite (so)!** certainly!

**Qui·to** (kē′tō) capital of Ecuador: pop. 463,000

**quit·rent** (kwit′rent′) *n.* a rent paid in lieu of feudal services: also **quit rent**

**quits** (kwits) *adj.* [prob. contr. < ML. *quittus,* var. of *quietus:* see QUIETUS] on even terms, as by paying a debt, retaliating, etc. —**call it quits** [Colloq.] 1. to stop working, playing, etc. 2. to end an association or friendship; stop being intimate

**quit·tance** (kwit′'ns) *n.* [see QUIT] 1. *a)* payment of a debt or obligation *b)* a document certifying this; receipt 2. recompense; repayment

**quit·ter** (kwit′ər) *n.* [Colloq.] a person who quits or gives up easily, without trying hard

**quiv·er¹** (kwiv′ər) *vi.* to shake with a tremulous motion; tremble —*n.* the act or condition of quivering; tremor —**quiv′er·y** *adj.*

**quiv·er²** (kwiv′ər) *n.* [OFr. *coivre* < Gmc.] 1. a case for holding arrows 2. the arrows in it

**‡qui vive?** (kē vēv′) [Fr., (long) live who? (i.e., whose side are you on?)] who goes there?: a sentry's challenge —**on the qui vive** on the lookout; on the alert

**Quixote, Don** *see* DON QUIXOTE

**quix·ot·ic** (kwik sät′ik) *adj.* [*often* Q-] of or like Don Quixote 2. extravagantly chivalrous or romantically idealistic; visionary; impractical Also **quix·ot′i·cal** —**quix·ot′i·cal·ly** *adv.* —**quix′ot·ism** (-sə tiz′m) *n.*

**quiz** (kwiz) *n., pl.* **quiz′zes** [prob. arbitrary use of L. *quis,* what?] 1. formerly, a practical joke; hoax 2. a questioning; esp., a short examination to test one's knowledge —*vt.* **quizzed, quiz′zing** 1. [Obs.] to make fun of 2. to ask questions of, as in interrogating —**quiz′zer** *n.*

**quiz program** (or **show**) a radio or TV program in which a group of people compete in answering questions posed by a master of ceremonies ( **quizmaster** )

**quiz·zi·cal** (kwiz′i k'l) *adj.* 1. odd; comical 2. teasing; bantering 3. perplexed —**quiz′zi·cal′i·ty** (-kal′ə tē), **quiz′-zi·cal·ness** *n.* —**quiz′zi·cal·ly** *adv.*

**Qum·ran** (koom rän′) region in Palestine, near the Dead Sea: site of caves in which Dead Sea Scrolls have been found

**quoin** (koin, kwoin) *n*. [var. of COIN] **1.** the external corner of a building; esp., any of the stones forming the corner of a building **2.** a wedgelike piece of stone, etc., such as the keystone of an arch **3.** a wedge-shaped wooden or metal block used to lock something in place

**quoit** (kwoit; *chiefly Brit*. koit) *n*. [< Anglo-Fr., prob. < OFr. *coite*, a cushion] **1.** a ring of rope or metal thrown at an upright peg: the object of the game is to encircle the peg with the ring **2.** [*pl., with sing. v.*] this game

QUOINS

**quon·dam** (kwän′dəm) *adj*. [L.] that was at one time; former [*a quondam* pacifist]

**Quon·set hut** (kwän′sit) [< *Quonset* Point, R.I., where first manufactured] *a trademark for* a prefabricated metal shelter shaped like the longitudinal half of a cylinder resting on its flat surface

**quo·rum** (kwôr′əm) *n*. [L., gen. pl. of *qui*, who] the minimum number of members required to be present at an assembly or meeting before it can validly transact business

**quo·ta** (kwōt′ə) *n*. [ML., short for L. *quota pars*, how large a part] **1.** a share which each of a number is to contribute or receive; proportional share **2.** the number or proportion that is allowed or admitted [nationality *quotas* for immigrants to the U.S.]

**quot·a·ble** (kwōt′ə b'l) *adj*. worthwhile quoting or suitable for quotation —**quot′a·bil′i·ty** *n*. —**quot′a·bly** *adv*.

**quo·ta·tion** (kwō tā′shən) *n*. **1.** a quoting **2.** the words or passage quoted **3.** *Commerce* the current quoted price of a stock, bond, commodity, etc.

**quotation mark** either of a pair of punctuation marks (". . .") used to enclose a direct quotation, or of single marks ('. . .') for enclosing a quotation within a quotation

**quote** (kwōt) *vt*. **quot′ed, quot′ing** [< ML. *quotare*, to number (chapters, etc.) < L. *quotus*, of what number] **1.** to repeat a passage from or statement of **2.** to repeat (a passage, statement, etc.) **3.** to cite as an example or authority **4.** to state (the price of something) —*vi*. to make a quotation, as from a book —*n*. [Colloq.] *same as:* **1.** QUOTATION **2.** QUOTATION MARK —*interj*. I shall quote: used in speech before a quotation —**quot′er** *n*.

**quoth** (kwōth) *vt*. < OE. < *cwethan*, to speak] [Archaic] said: followed by a subject in the first or third person

**quoth·a** (-ə) *interj*. [< *quoth he*] [Archaic] indeed!

**quo·tid·i·an** (kwō tid′ē ən) *adj*. [< OFr. < L. < *quotidie*, daily < *quot*, as many as + *dies*, day] **1.** daily; recurring every day **2.** everyday; ordinary —*n*. anything, esp. a fever, that recurs daily

**quo·tient** (kwō′shənt) *n*. [< L. *quoties*, how often < *quot*, how many] *Arith*. the result obtained when one number is divided by another

**quo war·ran·to** (kwō wô ran′tō) *pl*. **quo war·ran′tos** [ML., by what warrant] a legal proceeding undertaken to recover an office, franchise, etc. from the one in possession

**qursh** (koorsh) *n*., *pl*. **qu·rush** (koo′rəsh) [< Ar. *taqrush*, to earn < *qrsh*, to collect] *see* MONETARY UNITS, table (Saudi Arabia)

**q.v.** [L. *quod vide*] which see

# R

**R, r** (är) *n*., *pl*. **R's, r's 1.** the eighteenth letter of the English alphabet **2.** a sound of *R* or *r*

**R 1.** *Math*. radical **2.** *Math*. ratio **3.** *Elec*. resistance **4.** *Chess* rook —**the three R's** reading, writing, and arithmetic, regarded as the basic studies

**R** restricted: a motion-picture rating meaning that no one under the age of seventeen will be admitted unless accompanied by a parent or guardian

**r 1.** *Math*. radius **2.** roentgen(s) **3.** ruble

**R. 1.** Radical **2.** Republic(an)

**R., r. 1.** [L. *Rex*] king **2.** [L. *Regina*] queen **3.** rabbi **4.** radius **5.** railroad **6.** right **7.** river **8.** road **9.** ruble **10.** *Baseball* runs **11.** *pl*. **Rs., Rs, rs.** rupee

**r. 1.** rare **2.** retired **3.** rod(s)

**Ra¹** (rä) the sun god and chief god of the ancient Egyptians, usually depicted as having the head of a hawk

**Ra²** *Chem*. radium

**Ra·bat** (rä bät′, rə-) capital of Morocco: pop. 435,000

**ra·bat** (rab′ē, rə bat′) *n*. [MFr.] a plain, black dickey worn with a clerical collar by some clergymen

**rab·bet** (rab′it) *n*. [< OFr. < *rabattre*: see REBATE] a groove or cut made in the edge of a board, etc. so that another piece may be fitted into it to form a joint (**rabbet joint**) —*vt*. **1.** to cut a rabbet in **2.** to join by means of a rabbet —*vi*. to be joined by a rabbet

**rab·bi** (rab′ī) *n*., *pl*. **-bis, -bies** [< LL. < Gr. < Heb. *rabbi*, my master] a teacher of the Jewish law, now usually one that is ordained and the spiritual head of a congregation

**rab·bin·ate** (rab′i nit, -nät′) *n*. **1.** the position or office of rabbi **2.** rabbis as a group

**Rab·bin·ic** (rə bin′ik) *adj*. **1.** designating the Hebrew language as used in the writings of rabbis of the Middle Ages **2.** [r-] *same as* RABBINICAL

**rab·bin·i·cal** (-i k'l) *adj*. of the rabbis, their doctrines, learning, language, etc., esp. in the early Middle Ages — **rab·bin′i·cal·ly** *adv*.

**rab·bit** (rab′it) *n*., *pl*. **-bits, -bit**: see PLURAL, II, D, 1 [ME. *rabette*] **1.** a burrowing mammal that is usually smaller than the hare, produces unfurred young, and has soft fur, long ears, and a stubby tail **2.** its fur —*vi*. to hunt rabbits

**rabbit ears** [Colloq.] an indoor TV antenna with two adjustable rods that swivel apart at a V-shaped angle

**rabbit fever** *same as* TULAREMIA

**rabbit punch** *Boxing* a sharp blow to the back of the neck

**rab·ble** (rab′l) *n*. [< ? or akin to ML. *rabulus*, noisy < L. *rabula*, a pettifogger] a noisy, disorderly crowd; mob —*vt*. **-bled, -bling** to attack by a rabble; mob —**the rabble** the common people; the masses: a term of contempt

**rab·ble-rous·er** (-rouz′ər) *n*. a person who tries to arouse people to violent action by appeals to emotions, prejudices, etc.; demagogue —**rab′ble-rous′ing** *adj*., *n*.

**Rab·e·lais** (ra ble′; E. rab′ə lā′), **Fran·çois** (frän swä′) 1495?–1553; Fr. satirist & humorist —**Rab·e·lai·si·an** (rab′ə lā′zhən, -zē ən) *adj*., *n*.

**rab·id** (rab′id; *for 3 occas*. rā′bid) *adj*. [< L. < *rabere*, to rage] **1.** violent; raging **2.** fanatical or unreasonably zealous **3.** of or having rabies —**ra·bid′i·ty** (rə bid′ə tē), **rab′id·ness** *n*. —**rab′id·ly** *adv*.

**ra·bies** (rā′bēz) *n*. [L., madness] an infectious virus disease of mammals, passed on to man by the bite of an infected animal: it causes choking, convulsions, etc.

**rac·coon** (ra koon′) *n*., *pl*. **-coons′, -coon′**: see PLURAL, II, D, 1 [< Algonquian *äräkun*, lit., scratcher] **1.** a small, tree-climbing, chiefly flesh-eating mammal of N. America, active largely at night and having long, yellowish-gray fur and a long, black-ringed tail **2.** its fur

**race¹** (rās) *n*. [< ON. *rās*, a running] **1.** a competition of speed in running, riding, etc. **2.** [*pl*.] a series of such competitions for horses, cars, etc., on a regular course **3.** any contest likened to a race [the *race* for mayor] **4.** a steady onward movement **5.** *a)* a swift current of water *b)* a channel for this, esp. one built to use the water in industry [a *millrace*] —*vi*. **raced, rac′ing 1.** to take part in a race **2.** to go or move very fast or too fast —*vt*. **1.** to compete with in a race **2.** to enter or run (a horse, etc.) in a race **3.** to make go very fast or too fast **4.** to run (an engine) at high speed while the transmission system not engaged

**race²** (rās) *n*. [Fr. < It. *razza*] **1.** any of the different varieties of mankind, mainly the Caucasoid, Mongoloid, or Negroid groups, distinguished by kind of hair, color of skin, stature, etc.: now often replaced in scientific use by *ethnic stock* or *group* **2.** any geographical, national, or tribal ethnic grouping **3.** any group of people having the same ancestry **4.** any group of people having the same habits, ideas, etc. **5.** *Biol. a)* a subspecies, or variety *b)* *same as* BREED (*n*. 1) —**the (human) race** mankind

**race·course** (-kôrs′) *n*. *same as* RACE TRACK

**race·horse** (-hôrs′) *n*. a horse bred and trained for racing

**ra·ceme** (rā sēm′, rə-) *n.* [L. *racemus,* cluster of grapes] a flower cluster with individual flowers growing on small stems at intervals along one central stem, as in the lupine —**rac·e·mose** (ras′ə mōs′) *adj.*

**rac·er** (rās′ər) *n.* 1. any person, animal, vehicle, etc. that takes part in races 2. any of several slim, swift, harmless snakes

**race riot** violence and fighting in a community, brought on by racial hostility

**race track** a course prepared for racing

**race·way** (rās′wā′) *n.* 1. a narrow channel for water 2. a race track for harness racing 3. a race track for drag races, racing stock cars, etc.

**Ra·chel** (rā′chəl) [LL. < Gr. < Heb. *rāḥēl,* lit., ewe] 1. a feminine name 2. *Bible* the younger of the two wives of Jacob: Gen. 29–35

**ra·chi·tis** (rə kīt′əs, ra-) *n.* [ModL. < Gr. *rhachitis,* inflammation of the spine < *rhachis,* spine] *same as* RICKETS —**ra·chit′ic** (-kit′ik) *adj.*

**Rach·ma·ni·noff** (räkh mä′nŭ nôf′; *E.* räk mä′ni nôf′), **Ser·gei V**(assilievich) (syer gā′) 1873–1943; Russ. composer, conductor, & pianist: also sp. **Rachmaninov**

**ra·cial** (rā′shəl) *adj.* 1. of a race, or ethnic group 2. of or between races —**ra′cial·ly** *adv.*

**ra·cial·ism** (-iz′m) *n.* 1. a doctrine or teaching, without scientific support, that claims to find racial differences in character, intelligence, etc. and that seeks to maintain the supposed superiority and purity of some one race 2. *same as* RACISM (sense 2) —**ra′cial·ist** *n., adj.*

**Ra·cine** (rə sēn′) [Fr., root, after the nearby Root River] city in SE Wis., on Lake Michigan: pop. 86,000

**Ra·cine** (rȧ sēn′; *E.* rə sēn′), **Jean Bap·tiste** (zhän bȧ tēst′) 1639–99; Fr. poet & dramatist

**rac·ism** (rā′siz′m) *n.* 1. *same as* RACIALISM (sense 1) 2. the practice of racial discrimination, segregation, etc., based on racialism —**rac′ist** *n., adj.*

**rack¹** (rak) *n.* [prob. < MDu. *rek* < *recken,* to stretch] 1. a framework, stand, etc. for holding things [clothes *rack*] 2. the triangular device in which the balls are set up at the start of a pool game 3. a device for lifting an automobile for repairs from below 4. a toothed bar that meshes with a cogwheel, etc. 5. a frame on which a victim is tortured by stretching his limbs out of place 6. any great torment 7. a wrenching or upheaval, as by a storm —*vt.* 1. to put in or on a rack 2. to torture on a rack 3. to torment or afflict 4. to oppress, as by demanding excessive rent —**off the rack** ready-made: said of clothing —**on the rack** in a very painful situation —**rack one's brains** (or **memory,** etc.) to try very hard to think of something —**rack up** [Slang] 1. to gain or score 2. to beat decisively

**rack²** (rak) *n., vi.* [< ?] *same as* SINGLE-FOOT

**rack³** (rak) *n.* [var. of WRACK] destruction: now only in **go to rack and ruin,** to become ruined

**rack⁴** (rak) *n.* [prob. < Scand.] a broken mass of clouds blown by the wind

**rack·et¹** (rak′it) *n.* [prob. echoic] 1. a noisy confusion; uproar 2. *a)* an obtaining of money illegally, as by fraud *b)* [Colloq.] any dishonest scheme 3. [Slang] *a)* an easy, profitable source of income *b)* any business, profession, etc. —*vi.* to make a racket, or uproar —**rack′et·y** *adj.*

**rack·et²** (rak′it) *n.* [MFr. *raquette* < ML. *rasceta* < Ar. *rāḥah,* palm of the hand] 1. a light bat for tennis, etc., with a network of catgut, nylon, etc. in an oval or round frame attached to a handle 2. loosely, a table-tennis paddle 3. [*pl., with sing. v.*] the game of racquets

**rack·et·eer** (rak′ə tir′) *n.* [see RACKET¹ & -EER] one who gets money illegally, as by fraud, blackmail, or, esp., extortion —*vi.* to get money thus —**rack′et·eer′ing** *n.*

**ra·clette** (rȧ klet′) *n.* [Fr. < *racler,* to scrape] a Swiss dish consisting of cheese that is melted, as over a fire, and scraped onto boiled potatoes or crusty bread

**rac·on·teur** (rak′än tur′) *n.* [Fr. < *raconter,* to recount] a person skilled at telling stories or anecdotes

**ra·coon** (ra kōōn′) *n., pl.* **-coons′, -coon′:** see PLURAL, II, D, 1 *same as* RACCOON

**rac·quet** (rak′it) *n.* 1. *same as* RACKET² 2. [*pl., with sing. v.*] a game similar to court tennis: see TENNIS

**rac·quet·ball** (-bôl′) *n.* a game similar to handball, but played with a short-handed racket

**rac·y** (rā′sē) *adj.* **rac′i·er, rac′i·est** [RACE² + -Y²] 1. having the taste or quality required to be genuine [*racy* fruit] 2.

RA-
CEME

RACKETS
(A, squash; B, tennis; C, badminton; D, racquetball)

lively; spirited 3. piquant; pungent 4. indecent; risqué —**rac′i·ly** *adv.* —**rac′i·ness** *n.*

**rad** (rad) *n.* [< *rad(iation)*] the unit of absorbed dose of ionizing radiation, equal to 100 ergs of energy per gram of matter

**rad.** 1. radical 2. radius

**ra·dar** (rā′där) *n.* [*ra(dio) d(etecting) a(nd) r(anging)*] a system or device for sending out radio waves in order to detect an object by the waves reflected back from the object and thus find out its direction, distance, height, or speed: used also in mapping, navigation, etc. —**ra′dar·man** (-mən) *n., pl.* **-men**

**ra·dar·scope** (rā′där skōp′) *n.* an instrument that displays on a screen the reflected radio waves picked up by radar

**ra·di·al** (rā′dē əl) *adj.* [< ML.: see RADIUS] 1. of or like a ray or rays; branching out in all directions from a common center 2. of or like a radius 3. *Anat.* of or near the radius —*n.* a radial part —**ra′di·al·ly** *adv.*

**radial (ply) tire** an automobile tire with the ply cords almost at right angles to the center line of the tread

**ra·di·ant** (rā′dē ənt) *adj.* [< L. prp. of *radiare:* see RADIATE] 1. shining brightly 2. filled with light 3. showing joy, love, well-being, etc. 4. issuing (from a source) in or as in rays —*n.* a source of heat or light rays —**ra′di·ance, ra′di·an·cy** *n.* —**ra′di·ant·ly** *adv.*

**radiant energy** energy traveling in waves; esp., electromagnetic radiation, as heat, light, X-rays, etc.

**radiant heating** a method of heating by radiation, as from electric coils or steam pipes in the floor or walls

**ra·di·ate** (rā′dē āt′) *vi.* **-at′ed, -at′ing** [< L. pp. of *radiare* < *radius:* see RADIUS] 1. to send out rays of heat, light, etc. 2. to spread out in rays 3. to branch out in lines from a center —*vt.* 1. to send out (heat, light, etc.) in rays 2. to give forth (happiness, love, etc.) —*adj.* having rays or raylike parts; radial —**ra′di·al·ly** *adv.*

**ra·di·a·tion** (rā′dē ā′shən) *n.* 1. a radiating; specif., the process in which radiant energy is sent out from atoms and molecules as they undergo internal change 2. such radiant energy 3. energetic nuclear particles, as alpha and beta particles, etc. —**ra′di·a′tion·al** *adj.* —**ra′di·a′tive** *adj.*

**radiation sickness** sickness produced by overexposure to radiation from X-rays, nuclear explosions, etc. and resulting in nausea, diarrhea, bleeding, etc.

**ra·di·a·tor** (rā′dē āt′ər) *n.* anything that radiates; specif., *a)* a series of pipes with hot water or steam circulating in them so as to radiate heat into a room, etc. *b)* a device of tubes and fins, as in a motor vehicle, through which circulating water passes so as to take away the extra heat and thus cool the engine

**rad·i·cal** (rad′i k'l) *adj.* [< LL. < L. *radix* (gen. *radicis*), a root] 1. *a)* of or from the root or source; fundamental; basic *b)* extreme; thorough 2. *a)* favoring basic or extreme change, as in the social or economic structure *b)* [R-] designating or of any of various modern political parties, as in Europe, ranging from moderate to conservative —*n.* 1. *a)* a basic part of something *b)* a fundamental 2. *a)* a person having radical views *b)* [R-] a member of a Radical party 3. *Chem.* a group of two or more atoms that acts as a single atom and goes through a reaction unchanged, or is replaced by a single atom 4. *Math. a)* an expression showing that a root is to be extracted *b)* *same as* RADICAL SIGN —**rad′i·cal·ly** *adv.* —**rad′i·cal·ness** *n.*

**rad·i·cal·ism** (-iz′m) *n.* 1. the quality or state of being radical 2. radical principles, methods, or practices

**rad·i·cal·ize** (-īz′) *vt., vi.* **-ized′, -iz′ing** to make or become politically radical —**rad′i·cal·i·za′tion** *n.*

**radical sign** *Math.* the sign used before a quantity to show that its root is to be extracted

**rad·i·cand** (rad′i kand′) *n. Math.* a quantity from which a root is to be extracted, shown with a radical sign

**rad·i·cle** (rad′i k'l) *n.* [< L. dim. of *radix,* a root] *Bot.* the lower part of the axis of an embryo seedling

**ra·di·i** (rā′dē ī′) *n. alt. pl. of* RADIUS

**ra·di·o** (rā′dē ō′) *n., pl.* **-os′** [contr. < RADIOTELEGRAPH] 1. a way of communicating over a distance by changing sounds or signals into electromagnetic waves that are sent through space, without wires, to a receiving set, which changes them back into sounds or signals 2. such a receiving set 3. broadcasting by radio as an industry, entertainment, etc. —*adj.* 1. of, using, used in, or sent by radio 2. of electromagnetic wave frequencies from c.10 kilohertz to c.300,000 megahertz —*vt., vi.* **-oed′, -o′ing** to send (a message, etc.) or communicate with (a person, etc.) by radio

**ra·di·o-** [Fr. < L. *radius,* ray: see RADIUS] *a combining form meaning:* 1. ray, raylike 2. by radio 3. using radiant energy [*radiotherapy*] 4. radioactive [*radioisotope*]

**ra·di·o·ac·tive** (rā′dē ō ak′tiv) *adj.* giving off radiant energy in particles or rays by the disintegration of the atomic nuclei: said of such elements as radium and uranium —**ra′di·o·ac′tive·ly** *adv.* —**ra′di·o·ac·tiv′i·ty** (-ak tiv′ə tē) *n.*

**radio astronomy** astronomy dealing with radio waves in space in order to get data about the universe

**radio beacon** a radio transmitter that gives off special signals to help ships or aircraft determine their positions or come in safely, as in a fog

**ra·di·o·broad·cast** (-brôd′kast′) *n.* a broadcast by radio — *vt., vi.* **-cast′** or **-cast′ed, -cast′ing** to broadcast by radio — **ra′di·o·broad′cast′er** *n.*

**ra·di·o·car·bon** (-kär′bən) *n. same as* CARBON 14: see CARBON

**radio frequency** any frequency between normally audible sound waves and infrared light, from c.10 kilohertz to c.300,000 megahertz

**ra·di·o·gram** (rā′dē ō gram′) *n.* **1.** a message sent by radio: also **ra′di·o·tel′e·gram′** **2.** *same as* RADIOGRAPH

**ra·di·o·graph** (-graf′) *n.* a picture made on a sensitized film or plate by X-rays **—ra′di·og′ra·pher** (-äg′rə fər) *n.* **—ra′di·o·graph′ic** *adj.* **—ra′di·og′ra·phy** *n.*

**ra·di·o·i·so·tope** (rā′dē ō ī′sə tōp′) *n.* a natural or artificial radioactive isotope of a chemical element

**ra·di·ol·o·gy** (rā′dē äl′ə jē) *n.* [RADIO- + -LOGY] the science dealing with X-rays and other radiant energy, esp. as used in medicine and radiotherapy **—ra′di·o·log′i·cal** (-ə läj′i k'l) *adj.* **—ra′di·o·log′i·cal·ly** *adv.* **—ra′di·ol′o·gist** *n.*

**ra·di·om·e·ter** (-äm′ə tər) *n.* an instrument for measuring radiant energy **—ra′di·om′e·try** *n.*

**ra·di·o·pho·to** (rā′dē ō fōt′ō) *n., pl.* **-tos** a photograph or picture transmitted by radio: also **ra′di·o·pho′to·graph′**

**ra·di·os·co·py** (-äs′kə pē) *n.* [RADIO- + -SCOPY] the direct examination of the inside structure of opaque objects by radiation, as by X-rays **—ra′di·o·scop′ic** (-ə skäp′ik) *adj.*

**ra·di·o·sonde** (rā′dē ō sänd′) *n.* [Fr. < *radio* (cf. RADIO) + *sonde*, a sounding line] a compact package made up of a radio transmitter and meteorological instruments sent into the upper atmosphere, as by balloon, to record and send back temperature, pressure, and humidity data

**radio spectrum** the complete range of frequencies of electromagnetic radiation useful in radio, from c.10 kilohertz to c.300,000 megahertz

**ra·di·o·tel·e·graph** (rā′dē ō tel′ə graf′) *n. same as* WIRELESS TELEGRAPHY: also **ra′di·o·te·leg′ra·phy** (-tə leg′rə fē) **—***vt., vi.* to send (a message, etc.) by radiotelegraph

**ra·di·o·tel·e·phone** (-tel′ə fōn′) *n.* the equipment needed at one station for two-way voice communication by radio: also **ra′di·o·phone′** **—ra′di·o·tel′e·phon′ic** (-fän′ik) *adj.* **—ra′di·o·te·leph′o·ny** (-ə lef′ə nē) *n.*

**radio telescope** a radio antenna or array of antennas for use in radio astronomy

**ra·di·o·ther·a·py** (-ther′ə pē) *n.* the treatment of disease by X-rays or by rays from a radioactive substance

**rad·ish** (rad′ish) *n.* [OE. *rædic* < L. *radix*, a root] **1.** an annual plant of the mustard family, with an edible root **2.** the pungent root, eaten raw as a relish or in a salad

**ra·di·um** (rā′dē əm) *n.* [ModL. < L. *radius*, a ray] a radioactive metallic chemical element, found in uranium minerals: symbol, Ra; at. wt., 226.00; at. no., 88

**radium therapy** the treatment of cancer or other diseases by the use of radium

**ra·di·us** (rā′dē əs) *n., pl.* **-di·i′** (-ī′), **-us·es** [L., a spoke (of a wheel), hence ray (of light)] **1.** a raylike part, as a spoke of a wheel **2.** *a)* a straight line from the center to the periphery of a circle or sphere *b)* its length **3.** *a)* the circular area or distance within the sweep of such a line [no house within a *radius* of five miles] *b)* the distance a ship or airplane can go and still get back without refueling **4.** any limited extent, scope, etc. [within the *radius* of one's experience] **5.** the shorter and thicker of the two bones of the forearm on the same side as the thumb

**RAdm** Rear Admiral

**ra·dome** (rā′dōm′) *n.* [RA(DAR) + DOME] a domed housing for a radar antenna, esp. on aircraft

**ra·don** (rā′dän) *n.* [RAD(IUM) + -ON] a radioactive gaseous chemical element formed in the atomic disintegration of radium: symbol, Rn; at. wt., 222.00; at. no., 86

**RAF, R.A.F.** Royal Air Force

**raf·fi·a** (raf′ē ə) *n.* [< Malagasy native name] **1.** a palm tree of Madagascar, with large, pinnate leaves **2.** fiber from its leaves, woven into baskets, hats, etc.

**raff·ish** (raf′ish) *adj.* [(RIFF)RAFF + -ISH] **1.** disreputable, rakish, etc. **2.** tawdry; vulgar; low **—raff′ish·ly** *adv.* **—raff′ish·ness** *n.*

**raf·fle** (raf′'l) *n.* [MFr. *rafle*, dice game < OHG. *raffel*, a rake] a lottery in which a chance or chances to win a prize are bought **—***vt.* **-fled, -fling** to offer as a prize in a raffle (often with *off*) **—raf′fler** *n.*

**raft¹** (raft) *n.* [< ON. *raptr*, a log] **1.** a flat structure of logs, boards, etc. fastened together and floated on water **2.** an inflatable boat or pad, as of rubber, for floating on water — *vt.* to carry on a raft —*vi.* to travel, work, etc. on a raft — **rafts′man** (-mən) *n., pl.* **-men**

**raft²** (raft) *n.* [< Brit. Dial. *raff*, rubbish] [Colloq.] a large number, collection, or quantity; lot

**raft·er** (raf′tər) *n.* [OE. *ræfter*] any of the beams that slope from the ridge of a roof to the eaves and serve to support the roof

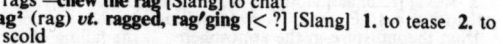

RAFTERS

**rag¹** (rag) *n.* [ult. < ON. *rögg*, tuft of hair] **1.** a waste piece of cloth, esp. an old or torn one **2.** a small cloth for dusting, washing, etc. **3.** anything regarded as having as little value as a rag **4.** [*pl.*] *a)* old, worn clothes *b)* any clothes: humorous term **5.** [Slang] any newspaper regarded with contempt **—***adj.* made of rags **—chew the rag** [Slang] to chat

**rag²** (rag) *vt.* **ragged, rag′ging** [< ?] [Slang] **1.** to tease **2.** to scold

**rag³** (rag) *n.* **1.** *clipped form of* RAGTIME **2.** a composition in ragtime **—***vt.* **ragged, rag′ging** to play in ragtime

**ra·ga** (rä′gə) *n.* [Sans. *raga*, lit., color] any of various traditional melodies used in improvising by Hindu musicians

**rag·a·muf·fin** (rag′ə muf′in) *n.* [ME. *Ragamoffyn*, name of a demon in *Piers Plowman*, a poem attributed to William Langland] a dirty, ragged person; esp., a poor, ragged child

**rag·bag** (rag′bag′) *n.* **1.** a bag for rags **2.** a collection of odds and ends

**rage** (rāj) *n.* [< OFr. < LL. < L. *rabies*, madness] **1.** furious, uncontrolled anger; esp., a brief spell of raving fury **2.** violence or intensity, as of the wind **3.** strong emotion, enthusiasm, or desire **—***vi.* **raged, rag′ing** **1.** to show violent anger in action or speech **2.** to be violent, uncontrolled, etc. [a *raging* sea] **3.** to spread unchecked, as a disease **—(all) the rage** anything thought of as a fad or craze

**rag·ged** (rag′id) *adj.* **1.** shabby or torn from wear **2.** wearing shabby or torn clothes **3.** uneven; rough **4.** shaggy; unkempt [*ragged* hair] **5.** not finished; imperfect **6.** harsh; strident **—run ragged** to make (someone) exhausted **—rag′ged·ly** *adv.* **—rag′ged·ness** *n.*

**rag·ged·y** (rag′i dē) *adj.* somewhat ragged, or tattered

**rag·lan** (rag′lən) *n.* [after Lord *Raglan* (1788–1855), Brit. general] a loose overcoat or topcoat without shoulder seams, each sleeve (**raglan sleeve**) continuing in one piece to the collar

**rag·man** (rag′man′) *n., pl.* **-men′** (-men′) a man who collects, buys, and sells rags, old paper, etc.

**ra·gout** (ra gōō′) *n.* [< Fr. < *ragoûter*, to revive the appetite of] a highly seasoned stew of meat and vegetables **—***vt.* **-gouted′** (-gōōd′), **-gout′ing** (-gōō′in) to make into a ragout

**rag·pick·er** (rag′pik′ər) *n.* a person who makes his living by picking up and selling rags and junk

**rag rug** a rug of rag strips woven or sewn together

**rag·tag (and bobtail)** (rag′tag′) [RAG¹ + TAG] the lowest classes; the rabble: term of contempt

**rag·time** (rag′tīm′) *n.* [prob. < *ragged time*] **1.** a type of strongly syncopated American music in fast, even time, popular 1890–1915 **2.** its rhythm

**rag·weed** (rag′wēd′) *n.* [from the tattered appearance of the leaves] any of a genus of chiefly N. American plants of the composite family, having tassellike, greenish flowers with a pollen that is a major cause of hay fever

**rag·wort** (-wurt′) *n.* [see prec.] *same as* GROUNDSEL

**rah** (rä) *interj.* hurrah; used as a cheer

**raid** (rād) *n.* [< ROAD, in obs. sense "a riding"] **1.** a sudden, hostile attack, as by troops, aircraft, bandits, etc. **2.** any sudden invasion of some place by police, to discover violations of the law **3.** an attempt to lure employees from a competitor **4.** an attempt by speculators to make stock market prices fall **—***vt., vi.* to make a raid (on) **—raid′er** *n.*

**rail¹** (rāl) *n.* [< OFr. < L. *regula*, a rule] **1.** a bar of wood, metal, etc. placed horizontally between posts as a barrier or support **2.** a fence or railing **3.** any of a series of parallel metal bars laid on crossties, etc. to make a track for trains, etc. **4.** a railroad as a means of transportation [travel by *rail*] **5.** the rim of a billiard table **6.** a narrow wooden piece at the top of a ship's bulwarks **—***vt.* to supply with rails or a railing; fence

**rail²** (rāl) *vi.* [< MFr. *railler* < Pr., ult. < LL. *ragere*, to bellow] to complain violently (with *against* or *at*)

**rail³** (rāl) *n., pl.* **rails, rail:** see PLURAL, II, D, 1 [< MFr. < *raaler*, to screech] any of a number of small, cranelike wading birds living in marshes and having short wings and tail, long toes, and a harsh cry

**rail·ing** (rāl'iŋ) *n.* **1.** material for rails **2.** rails collectively **3.** a fence or balustrade made of rails and posts

**rail·ler·y** (rāl'ər ē) *n., pl.* **-ler·ies** [Fr. *raillerie:* see RAIL² & -ERY] **1.** light ridicule; banter **2.** a teasing act or remark

**rail·road** (rāl'rōd') *n.* **1.** a road laid with parallel steel rails along which locomotives draw cars in a train **2.** a complete system of such roads, including land, rolling stock, etc. **3.** the corporation owning such a system —*vt.* **1.** to transport by railroad **2.** [Colloq.] to rush through quickly, so as to prevent careful consideration **3.** [Slang] to cause to go to prison on a trumped-up charge or after a hasty trial —*vi.* to work on a railroad —**rail'road'er** *n.*

**rail-split·ter** (-split'ər) *n.* a person who splits logs into rails —**the Rail-Splitter** *nickname of* Abraham LINCOLN

**rail·way** (-wā') *n.* **1.** *a)* a railroad for light vehicles *[a street railway] b)* [Brit.] any railroad **2.** any track with rails for guiding wheels

**rai·ment** (rā'mənt) *n.* [ME. *rayment* < *arayment:* see ARRAY & -MENT] [Archaic] clothing; wearing apparel

**rain** (rān) *n.* [OE. *regn*] **1.** water falling in drops condensed from the moisture in the atmosphere **2.** the falling of such drops; shower **3.** *a)* rainy weather *b)* [*pl.*] the rainy season (preceded by *the*) **4.** a rapid falling or propulsion of many small objects *[a rain of ashes]* —*vi.* **1.** to fall: said of rain *[it is raining]* **2.** to fall like rain **3.** to cause rain to fall —*vt.* **1.** to pour down (rain or something likened to rain) **2.** to give in large quantities —**rain cats and dogs** [Colloq.] to rain heavily —**rain out** to cause (an event) to be postponed or canceled because of rain —**rain'less** *adj.*

**rain·bow** (-bō') *n.* an arc containing the colors of the spectrum in bands, formed in the sky by the refraction, reflection, and dispersion of the sun's rays in falling rain or in mist —*adj.* of many colors

**rainbow trout** a game fish native to the mountain streams and rivers of the Pacific Coast of N. America

**rain check 1.** the stub of a ticket to a ball game, etc., entitling the holder to be admitted at a future date if the original event is rained out **2.** a bid for, or an offer of, a future invitation in place of one turned down

**rain·coat** (rān'kōt') *n.* a waterproof or water-repellent coat for giving protection from rain

**rain·drop** (-dräp') *n.* a single drop of rain

**rain·fall** (-fôl') *n.* **1.** a falling of rain; shower **2.** the amount of water falling as rain, snow, etc. over a given area in a given period of time: measured in inches of depth of water that has fallen into a rain gauge

**rain forest** a dense, evergreen forest in a tropical region having abundant rainfall throughout the year

**rain gauge** an instrument for measuring rainfall

**Rai·nier** (rā nir', rā'nir), Mount [after an 18th-cent. Brit. Adm. *Rainier*] mountain of the Cascade Range, in WC Wash.: 14,410 ft.

**rain·proof** (rān'prōof') *adj.* not letting rain through —*vt.* to make rainproof

**rain·storm** (-stôrm') *n.* a storm with a heavy rain

**rain·wa·ter** (-wôt'ər, -wät'ər) *n.* water that falls or has fallen as rain and is soft and fairly free of mineral matter

**rain·wear** (-wer') *n.* rainproof clothing

**rain·y** (rā'nē) *adj.* **rain'i·er, rain'i·est 1.** that has rain or much rain *[the rainy season]* **2.** wet with rain **3.** bringing rain —**rain'i·ness** *n.*

**rainy day** a possible future time of difficulty or need

**raise** (rāz) *vt.* **raised, rais'ing** [< ON. *reisa*] **1.** *a)* to make rise; lift *b)* to put upright **2.** to construct (a building, etc.) **3.** to stir up; arouse; incite *[to raise a revolt]* **4.** to increase in size, value, amount, etc. *[to raise prices]* **5.** to increase in degree, intensity, etc. *[to raise one's voice]* **6.** to improve the position or rank of *[to raise oneself from poverty]* **7.** to cause to arise, appear, or come; esp., to bring back as from death *[to raise the dead]* **8.** to produce; provoke *[the joke raised a laugh]* **9.** to bring forward for consideration *[to raise a question]* **10.** to collect or procure (an army, money, etc.) **11.** to utter (a cry, shout, etc.) **12.** to bring to an end *[to raise a siege]* **13.** to leaven (bread, etc.) **14.** *a)* to make (corn, etc.) grow *b)* to breed (cattle, etc.) *c)* to rear (children) **15.** to contact by radio **16.** to make (a blister) form **17.** to make (a nap on cloth) with teasels, etc. **18.** *Bridge* to increase (one's partner's bid in a suit) **19.** *Naut.* to come within sight of (land, etc.) **20.** *Poker* to bet more than (the highest preceding bet or bettor) —*vi.* **1.** [Dial.] to rise or arise **2.** *Poker* to increase the bet —*n.* **1.** a raising **2.** an increase in amount; specif., an increase in salary or wages —**raise Cain** (or **the devil, hell, a rumpus, the roof,** etc.) [Slang] to create a disturbance; cause trouble

**raised** (rāzd) *adj.* **1.** made in low relief; embossed **2.** having a napped surface **3.** leavened with yeast

**rai·sin** (rā'z'n) *n.* [< OFr. < L. *racemus,* cluster of grapes] a sweet, dried grape, usually seedless

**rai·son d'être** (rā'zōn det', det'rə; *Fr.* re zōn de'tr') [Fr.] reason for being; justification for existence

**raj** (räj) *n.* [see ff.] in India, rule; sovereignty; dominion

**ra·jah, ra·ja** (rä'jə) *n.* [< Hindi < Sans. *rājan* < *rāj,* to rule] **1.** formerly, a prince or chief in India **2.** esp. formerly, a Malay chief

**rake¹** (rāk) *n.* [OE. *raca*] a long-handled tool with teeth or prongs at one end, used for gathering loose grass, leaves, etc. —*vt.* **raked, rak'ing 1.** *a)* to gather with or as with a rake *b)* to make (a lawn, etc.) tidy with a rake **2.** to gather with great care **3.** to scratch or smooth as with a rake **4.** to search through carefully **5.** to direct gunfire along (a line of troops, etc.): often used figuratively —*vi.* **1.** to use a rake **2.** to search as if with a rake **3.** to scrape or sweep (with *over, across,* etc.) —**rake in** to gather an abundant amount of rapidly —**rake up** to uncover facts or gossip about (the past, a scandal, etc.)

**rake²** (rāk) *n.* [contr. of *rakehell,* prob. < ME. *rakel,* rash] a man who leads a wild, dissolute life: also **rake'hell'** (-hel')

**rake³** (rāk) *vi., vt.* **raked, rak'ing** [? akin to Sw. *raka,* to project] to be or make slightly inclined, as a ship's masts; slant —*n.* a slanting or inclining

**rake-off** (rāk'ôf') *n.* [Slang] a commission, rebate, or share, esp. one gained in a shady deal

**rak·ish¹** (rā'kish) *adj.* [< RAKE³ + -ISH] **1.** having a trim, neat appearance suggesting speed: said of a ship **2.** dashing and gay; jaunty —**rak'ish·ly** *adv.* —**rak'ish·ness** *n.*

**rak·ish²** (rā'kish) *adj.* like a rake; wild and carefree —**rak'ish·ly** *adv.* —**rak'ish·ness** *n.*

**Ra·leigh** (rô'lē, rä'-) [after ff.] capital of N.C., in the C part: pop. 150,000

**Ra·leigh** (rô'lē, rä'-), Sir Walter 1552?-1618; Eng. statesman, explorer, & poet: also sp. **Ralegh**

**ral·len·tan·do** (räl'ən tän'dō) *adj., adv.* [It., prp. of *rallentare,* to slow down] *Music* gradually slower: abbrev. **rall.**

**ral·ly¹** (ral'ē) *vt.* **-lied, -ly·ing** [< Fr. < OFr. < *re-,* again + *alier,* to join: see ALLY] **1.** to gather together (retreating troops) and restore to a state of order **2.** to bring (persons) together for a common purpose **3.** to revive (one's spirits, etc.) —*vi.* **1.** to return to a state of order: said esp. of retreating troops **2.** to come together for a common purpose **3.** to come in order to help *[to rally to a friend]* **4.** to revive; recover *[to rally from a fever]* **5.** *Commerce* to rise in price after having fallen: said of stocks, etc. **6.** *Sports* to come from behind in scoring **7.** *Tennis,* etc. to take part in a rally —*n., pl.* **-lies 1.** a rallying or being rallied; specif., a mass meeting **2.** an organized run, esp. of sports cars, over a course, designed to test driving skills: also sp. **ral'lye 3.** *Tennis,* etc. an exchange of several strokes before the point is won —**ral'li·er** *n.*

**ral·ly²** (ral'ē) *vt., vi.* **-lied, -ly·ing** [Fr. *rallier,* to RAIL²] to tease or mock playfully; banter

**Ralph** (ralf; *Brit. usually* rāf) [< ON. < *rath,* counsel + *ulfr,* a wolf] a masculine name

**ram** (ram) *n.* [OE. *ramm*] **1.** a male sheep **2.** same as BATTERING RAM **3.** *a)* formerly, a sharp projection at a prow, for piercing enemy vessels *b)* a ship with this **4.** same as HYDRAULIC RAM **5.** the striking part of a pile driver **6.** the plunger of a force pump —[R-] *Aries* —*vt.* **rammed, ram'ming 1.** to strike against with great force **2.** to force into place **3.** to force acceptance of (an idea, legislative bill, etc.) **4.** to stuff or cram (*with* something) —*vi.* **1.** to strike with force; crash **2.** to move rapidly —**ram'mer** *n.*

**Ram·a·dan** (ram'ə dän') *n.* [Ar. *ramaḍān,* lit., the hot month < *ramaḍa,* to be hot] the ninth month of the Moslem year, a period of daily fasting from sunrise to sunset

**Ra·ma·ya·na** (rä mä'yə nə) one of the two great epics of India, written in Sanskrit after the Mahabharata

**ram·ble** (ram'b'l) *vi.* **-bled, -bling** [< ME. *romblen,* freq. of *romen,* to roam] **1.** to roam about; esp., to stroll about idly **2.** to talk or write aimlessly, without sticking to any point **3.** to spread in all directions, as a vine —*vt.* to roam through —*n.* a rambling, esp. a stroll

**ram·bler** (ram'blər) *n.* **1.** a person or thing that rambles **2.** any of certain climbing roses

**ram·bunc·tious** (ram buŋk'shəs) *adj.* [altered < *robustious* < *robust*] wild, boisterous, unruly, etc. —**ram·bunc'tious·ly** *adv.* —**ram·bunc'tious·ness** *n.*

**ram·e·kin, ram·e·quin** (ram'ə kin) *n.* [Fr. *ramequin* < MDu. *rammeken,* cheese dish] **1.** a food mixture, specif. of bread crumbs, cheese, and eggs, baked in individual baking dishes **2.** a baking dish of this kind

**Ram·ses** (ram'ə sēz) *var. of* RAMSES

**ram·i·fi·ca·tion** (ram'ə fi kā'shən) *n.* **1.** a ramifying or being ramified **2.** *a)* a branch or offshoot *b)* a derived effect, consequence, or result

**ram·i·fy** (ram'ə fi') *vt., vi.* **-fied', -fy'ing** [< Fr. < ML. < L. *ramus,* a branch + *facere,* to make] to divide or spread out into branches or branchlike divisions

**ram·jet (engine)** (ram'jet') a jet engine in which the air for burning the fuel is compressed by being rammed into the inlet by the aircraft's velocity

**ra·mose** (rā'mōs, rə mōs') *adj.* [L. *ramosus* < *ramus,* a branch] **1.** bearing many branches or branchlike projections **2.** branching —**ra′mose·ly** *adv.*

**ra·mous** (rā′məs) *adj.* **1.** *same as* RAMOSE **2.** branchlike

**ramp¹** (ramp) *n.* [Fr. *rampe* < OFr.: see ff.] **1.** a sloping walk, road, plank, etc. joining different levels **2.** a wheeled staircase rolled up to an airplane for use in getting on or off **3.** a sloping runway for launching boats, as from trailers

**ramp²** (ramp) *vi.* [OFr. *ramper*, to climb] **1.** to rear up on the hind legs; specif., *Heraldry* to be shown rampant **2.** to rampage or rage —*n.* a ramping

**ram·page** (ram pāj′; *also, and for n.* always, ram′pāj) *vi.* **-paged′**, **-pag′ing** [prob. < RAMP²] to rush violently or wildly about; rage —*n.* a rampaging: chiefly in **on the** (or **a**) **rampage** —**ram·pa′geous** *adj.* —**ram·pag′er** *n.*

**ramp·ant** (ram′pənt) *adj.* [< OFr.: see RAMP²] **1.** growing or spreading unchecked; rife **2.** violent and uncontrollable **3.** standing up on the hind legs; specif., *Heraldry* shown so in profile, one forepaw above the other [a lion *rampant*] —**ramp′an·cy** *n.* —**ramp′ant·ly** *adv.*

**ram·part** (ram′pärt, -pərt) *n.* [Fr. < *re-*, again + *emparer* < Pr. *amparer*, to fortify < L. *ante*, before + *parare*, to prepare] **1.** a defensive embankment around a castle, fort, etc., with a parapet at the top **2.** any defense or bulwark

**ram·rod** (ram′räd′) *n.* a rod for ramming down the charge in a gun loaded through the muzzle

**Ram·ses** (ram′sēz) any of a number of Egyptian kings who ruled from c. 1315 to c. 1090 B.C.

**ram·shack·le** (ram′shak′′l) *adj.* [< freq. of RANSACK] loose and rickety; likely to fall to pieces

**ran** (ran) *pt. of* RUN

**ranch** (ranch) *n.* [< RANCHO] **1.** a large farm, esp. in western States, for raising many cattle, horses, or sheep **2.** any large farm for raising a particular crop or livestock [a fruit *ranch*] **3.** *same as* RANCH HOUSE —*vi.* to work on or manage a ranch —**ranch′er** *n.* —**ranch′man** (-mən) *n., pl.* **-men**

**ranch house 1.** the owner's residence on a ranch **2.** a house with all the rooms on one floor, usually with a garage attached

**ran·cho** (ran′chō, rän′-) *n., pl.* **-chos** [AmSp.] in Spanish America, *same as* RANCH

**ran·cid** (ran′sid) *adj.* [< L. < *rancere*, to be rank] having the bad smell or taste of spoiled fats or oils —**ran·cid′i·ty** (-sid′ə tē), **ran′cid·ness** *n.* —**ran′cid·ly** *adv.*

**ran·cor** (ran′kər) *n.* [OFr. < LL. < L. *rancere*, to be rank] a continuing and bitter hate or ill will; deep spite: also, Brit. sp., **ran′cour** —**ran′cor·ous** *adj.* —**ran′cor·ous·ly** *adv.*

**rand** (rand, ränd) *n., pl.* **rand** [Afrik., orig., shield] *see* MONETARY UNITS, table (South Africa)

**R & B, r & b** rhythm and blues

**R & D, R. and D.** research and development

**Ran·dolph** (ran′dälf, -dôlf) [< ML. < OE. *randwulf*, lit., shield wolf] a masculine name

**ran·dom** (ran′dəm) *n.* [< OFr. *randon*, violence, speed < *randir*, to run violently] haphazard movement: now only in **at random**, without careful choice, aim, plan, etc.; haphazardly —*adj.* **1.** made, done, etc. in an aimless or haphazard way **2.** not uniform **3.** *Statistics* with each in a set or group having an equal opportunity of occurring or of occurring with a particular frequency —**ran′dom·ly** *adv.* —**ran′dom·ness** *n.*

**ran·dom·ize** (-īz′) *vt.* **-ized′**, **-iz′ing** to pick at random so as to get an unbiased result, often using a table of random numbers —**ran′dom·i·za′tion** *n.*

**R & R, R and R** *Mil.* rest and recuperation (leave)

**ran·dy** (ran′dē) *adj.* **-di·er**, **-di·est** [prob. < *rand*, dial. var. of RANT + -Y²] sexually aroused; lustful

**ra·nee** (rä′nē) *n. alt. sp. of* RANI

**rang** (raŋ) *pt. of* RING¹

**range** (rānj) *vt.* **ranged**, **rang′ing** [< OFr. var. of *rengier* < *renc*, a row] **1.** to put in a certain order, esp. in a row or rows **2.** to classify **3.** to place with others in a cause, party, etc. [to *range* oneself with the rebels] **4.** to aim (a gun, telescope, etc.) properly **5.** to roam over or through **6.** to move along parallel to [*ranging* the coastline] **7.** to put out (cattle, etc.) to graze on a range —*vi.* **1.** to extend in a given direction [hills *ranging* south] **2.** to wander about; roam **3.** to vary between stated limits [ages *ranging* from 1 to 7] **4.** *Biol., Zool.* to be native to a specified region —*n.* **1.** a row, line, or series; rank **2.** a class, kind, or order **3.** a chain or single system of mountains **4.** *a)* the firing distance, either maximum or to a target, of a weapon *b)* the flight path of a missile or rocket **5.** the farthest distance a plane, etc. can go without refueling **6.** *a)* a place for shooting practice *b)* a place for testing rockets in flight **7.** the full extent over which something moves or is heard, seen, effective, etc.; scope **8.** the full extent of pitch, from

highest to lowest tones, of a voice, instrument, etc. **9.** a large, open area of land for grazing livestock **10.** the limits within which there are changes or differences in amount, degree, etc. [a wide *range* in price] **11.** a cooking unit typically with an oven and surface heating units **12.** *Biol., Zool.* the region to which a plant or animal is native —*adj.* of a range (sense 9)

**range finder** any of various instruments to determine the distance of a target or object from a gun, camera, etc.

**rang·er** (rān′jər) *n.* **1.** one who ranges; roamer **2.** *a)* a member of a special military or police force that patrols a region *b)* [*often* R-] a soldier of a group trained for raiding **3.** *a)* in England, the chief official of a royal park or forest *b)* in the U.S., a warden patrolling government forests

**Ran·goon** (raŋ gōōn′) capital of Burma, a seaport in the S part, on the Irrawaddy: pop. 1,759,000

**rang·y** (rān′jē) *adj.* **rang′i·er**, **rang′i·est 1.** ranging about **2.** long-limbed and slender **3.** having range —**rang′i·ness** *n.*

**ra·ni** (rä′nē) *n.* [< Hindi < Sans. fem. of *rājan:* see RAJAH] the wife of a rajah

**rank¹** (raŋk) *n.* [< MFr. < OFr. *renc*] **1.** a row, line, or series; specif., a set of organ pipes of the same kind **2.** an orderly arrangement **3.** a social class [people from all *ranks* of life] **4.** a high position in society [a man of *rank*] **5.** an official grade [the *rank* of captain] **6.** a relative position as measured by quality, etc. [a poet of the first *rank*] **7.** a row of soldiers, etc., side by side **8.** [*pl.*] all those in an organization, as the army, who are not officers or leaders [to rise from the *ranks*] : also **rank and file** —*vt.* **1.** to place in a rank or ranks **2.** to assign a relative position to **3.** to outrank —*vi.* **1.** to hold a certain position [to *rank* third] —**pull (one's) rank** [Slang] to use one's higher rank to get others to obey, etc.

**rank²** (raŋk) *adj.* [OE. *ranc*, strong] **1.** growing vigorously and coarsely; too luxuriant [*rank* grass] **2.** producing a luxuriant crop, often to excess **3.** very bad in smell or taste **4.** coarse; indecent **5.** utter; extreme [*rank* injustice] —**rank′ly** *adv.* —**rank′ness** *n.*

**rank·ing** (raŋ′kiŋ) *adj.* **1.** of the highest rank [the *ranking* officer] **2.** prominent or outstanding

**ran·kle** (raŋ′k′l) *vi., vt.* **-kled**, **-kling** [< OFr. < draoncle < ML. *dracunculus*, a fester < L. dim. of *draco*, dragon] **1.** orig., to fester **2.** to cause or fill with long-lasting rancor, resentment, etc.

**ran·sack** (ran′sak) *vt.* [< ON. < *rann*, a house + *sækja*, to search] **1.** to search through every part of **2.** to search through for plunder; pillage —**ran′sack·er** *n.*

**ran·som** (ran′səm) *n.* [< OFr. *raençon* < L. *redemptio*, REDEMPTION] **1.** the securing of the release of a captive or of seized property by paying money or meeting other demands **2.** the price so paid or demanded —*vt.* to get (a captive, etc.) released by paying the demanded price —**ran′som·er** *n.*

**rant** (rant) *vi., vt.* [< obs. Du. *ranten*, to rave] to talk or say in a loud, wild, extravagant way; declaim violently; rave —*n.* ranting talk —**rant′er** *n.* —**rant′ing·ly** *adv.*

**rap¹** (rap) *vt.* **rapped, rap′ping** [prob. echoic] **1.** to strike quickly and sharply; tap **2.** [Slang] to criticize sharply —*vi.* **1.** to knock quickly and sharply **2.** [Slang] to talk; chat —*n.* **1.** a quick, sharp knock; tap **2.** [Slang] a talking; chat **3.** [Slang] blame or punishment; specif., a judicial sentence, as to prison: usually in **beat** (escape) or **take** (receive) **the rap**, or **bum** (unfair) **rap** —**rap out** to utter sharply —**rap′per** *n.*

**rap²** (rap) *n.* [< ?] [Colloq.] the least bit: in **not care** (or **give**) **a rap**, not care anything at all

**ra·pa·cious** (rə pā′shəs) *adj.* [< L. *rapax* (gen. *rapacis*) < *rapere*, to seize] **1.** taking by force; plundering **2.** greedy; voracious **3.** living on captured prey; predatory —**ra·pa′cious·ly** *adv.* —**ra·pac·i·ty** (rə pas′ə tē), **ra·pa′cious·ness** *n.*

**rape¹** (rāp) *n.* [ME. < L. *rapere*, to seize] **1.** *a)* the crime of having sexual intercourse with a woman or girl forcibly and without her consent, or **(statutory rape)** with a girl below the age of consent *b)* any sexual assault upon a person **2.** [Now Rare] a seizing and carrying away by force **3.** any violent or outrageous assault —*vt., vi.* raped, rap′ing to commit rape (on) —**rap′ist** *n.*

**rape²** (rāp) *n.* [L. *rapa, rapum,* turnip] an annual old-world plant of the mustard family, with seed (**rape′seed′**) yielding an oil (**rape oil, rapeseed oil**) and with leaves used for fodder

**Raph·a·el** (rā′fē əl; *also, and for 2 usually,* raf′ē-) [LL. < Gr. < Heb. *repha′ēl*, lit., God hath healed] **1.** an archangel mentioned in the Apocrypha **2.** (born *Raffaello Santi* or *Sanzio*) 1483–1520; It. painter & architect

**rap·id** (rap′id) *adj.* [L. *rapidus* < *rapere*, to rush] moving, occurring, or acting with speed; swift; fast; quick —*n.* **1.** [*usually pl.*] a part of a river where the current is swift, as because of a narrowing of the river bed **2.** a rapid transit car, train, or system —**ra·pid·i·ty** (rə pid′ə tē), **rap′id·ness** *n.* —**rap′id·ly** *adv.*

**rap·id-fire** (-fīr′) *adj.* **1.** firing shots in rapid succession: said of guns **2.** done, carried on, etc. in a swift, sharp way

**rapid transit** a system of rapid public transportation in an urban area, using electric trains running along an unimpeded right of way

**ra·pi·er** (rā′pē ər, rāp′yər) *n.* [Fr. *rapière*] **1.** orig., a slender, two-edged sword with a large cup hilt **2.** later, a light, sharp-pointed sword used only for thrusting

**rap·ine** (rap′in) *n.* [OFr. < L. *rapina* < *rapere*, to seize] the act of seizing property by force; plunder; pillage

**rap·pel** (ra pel′, rə-) *n.* [Fr., lit., a recall] a descent down a steep cliff by a climber using a double rope secured above —*vi.* **-pelled′**, **-pel′ling** to make such a descent

**rap·pen** (räp′ən) *n., pl.* **-pen** [G. < *rappe*, raven: after the eagle on an earlier Alsatian coin] *see* MONETARY UNITS, table (Liechtenstein, Switzerland)

**rap·port** (ra pôr′, -pôrt′) *n.* [Fr. < OFr. < *re-*, again + *aporter* < L. < *ad-*, to + *portare*, to carry] relationship, esp. of a sympathetic kind; agreement; harmony

**rap·proche·ment** (ra prôsh′mäṅ; *Fr.* rȧ prôsh mäṅ′) *n.* [Fr.] an establishing or restoring of friendly relations

**rap·scal·lion** (rap skal′yən) *n.* [< earlier *rascallion*, extension of RASCAL] a rascal; rogue

**rapt** (rapt) *adj.* [< L. pp. of *rapere*, to seize] **1.** carried away with joy, love, etc.; full of or showing rapture **2.** absorbed (*in* meditation, study, etc.)

**rap·to·ri·al** (rap tôr′ē əl) *adj.* [< L. < pp. of *rapere*, to seize] **1.** predatory; specif., of or belonging to a group of birds of prey with a strong notched beak and sharp talons, as the eagle **2.** adapted for seizing prey [*raptorial* claws]

**rap·ture** (rap′chər) *n.* [RAPT + -URE] **1.** the state of being carried away with joy, love, etc.; ecstasy **2.** an expression of great joy, pleasure, etc. —**rap′tur·ous** *adj.*

**rare¹** (rer) *adj.* **rar′er**, **rar′est** [MFr. < L. *rarus*] **1.** not often seen, done, found, etc.; uncommon **2.** unusually good; excellent [a *rare* teacher] **3.** not dense; thin [*rare* atmosphere] —**rare′ness** *n.*

**rare²** (rer) *adj.* **rar′er**, **rar′est** [OE. *hrere*] not fully cooked; partly raw: said esp. of meat —**rare′ness** *n.*

**rare³** (rer) *vi.* **rared**, **rar′ing** **1.** dial. var. of REAR² *vi.* **2.** [Colloq.] to be eager: used in prp. [*raring* to go]

**rare·bit** (rer′bit) *n. same as* WELSH RABBIT

**rare earth 1.** any of certain similar basic oxides; specif., any of the oxides of the rare-earth metals **2.** any of the rare-earth metals

**rare-earth metals** (or **elements**) (rer′urth′) a group of rare metallic chemical elements with consecutive atomic numbers of 57 to 71 inclusive

**rar·e·fy** (rer′ə fī′) *vt., vi.* **-fied**, **-fy′ing** [< MFr. < L. < *rarus*, rare + *facere*, to make] **1.** to make or become thin, or less dense **2.** to make or become more refined, subtle, or lofty —**rar′e·fac′tion** (-fak′shən) *n.*

**rare·ly** (rer′lē) *adv.* **1.** not often; seldom **2.** beautifully, excellently, etc. **3.** uncommonly; unusually

**rar·i·ty** (rer′ə tē) *n.* **1.** a being rare; specif., *a)* uncommonness; scarcity *b)* excellence *c)* lack of density **2.** *pl.* **-ties** a rare or uncommon thing

**ras·cal** (ras′k'l) *n.* [OFr. *rascaille*, scrapings, ult. < L. pp. of *radere*, to scrape] a scoundrel; rogue; scamp; often used playfully, as of a mischievous child

**ras·cal·i·ty** (ras kal′ə tē) *n.* **1.** the character or behavior of a rascal **2.** *pl.* **-ties** a low, mean, or dishonest act

**ras·cal·ly** (ras′k'l ē) *adj.* of or like a rascal; base; dishonest; mean —*adv.* in a rascally way

**rase** (rāz) *vt.* **rased**, **ras′ing** *alt. Brit. sp. of* RAZE

**rash¹** (rash) *adj.* [ME. *rasch*] too hasty and careless; reckless —**rash′ly** *adv.* —**rash′ness** *n.*

**rash²** (rash) *n.* [MFr. *rasche*] **1.** a breaking out of red spots on the skin **2.** a sudden appearance of a large number [a *rash* of complaints]

**rash·er** (rash′ər) *n.* [< ? obs. *rash*, to cut] **1.** a thin slice of bacon or, rarely, ham, for frying or broiling **2.** a serving of several such slices

**rasp** (rasp) *vt.* [< OFr. < OHG. *raspon*, to scrape together] **1.** to scrape or rub as with a file **2.** to utter in a rough, grating tone **3.** to grate upon; irritate —*vi.* **1.** to scrape; grate **2.** to make a rough, grating sound —*n.* **1.** a type of rough file with sharp, projecting points **2.** a rough, grating sound —**rasp′er** *n.* —**rasp′ing·ly** *adv.*

**rasp·ber·ry** (raz′ber′ē, -bər ē) *n., pl.* **-ries** [earlier *raspis berry* < *raspis*, raspberry] **1.** the small, juicy, edible fruit of various brambles of the rose family: it is a cluster of red, purple, or black drupelets **2.** the bramble bearing this **3.** [Slang] a jeering sound made by blowing out so as to vibrate the tongue between the lips

**Ras·pu·tin** (räs po͞o′tin; *E.* ras pyo͞ot′'n), **Gri·go·ri E·fi·mo·vich** (gri gô′ri ye fē′mə vich) 1871?-1916; Russ. religious mystic & faith healer: assassinated

**rasp·y** (ras′pē) *adj.* **rasp′i·er**, **rasp′i·est 1.** rasping; grating **2.** easily irritated —**rasp′i·ness** *n.*

**ras·sle** (ras′'l) *n., vi., vt.* **-sled**, **-sling** *dial. or colloq. var. of* WRESTLE

**rat** (rat) *n.* [OE. *ræt*] **1.** *a)* any of numerous long-tailed rodents resembling, but larger than, the mouse, very destructive, and carriers of disease *b)* any of various ratlike rodents **2.** [Slang] a sneaky, contemptible person; informer, traitor, etc. —*vi.* **rat′ted**, **rat′ting 1.** to hunt rats **2.** [Slang] *a)* to desert or betray a cause, movement, etc. *b)* to act as an informer —*vt.* to tease (the hair) —**rats!** [Slang] an exclamation of disgust, disappointment, etc. —**smell a rat** to suspect a trick, plot, etc.

**rat·a·ble** (rāt′ə b'l) *adj.* **1.** that can be rated, or estimated, etc. **2.** figured at a certain rate; proportional **3.** [Brit.] taxable Also sp. **rate′a·ble** —**rat′a·bly**, **rate′a·bly** *adv.*

**rat-a-tat** (rat′ə tat′) *n.* [echoic] a series of sharp, quick rapping sounds: also **rat′-a-tat′-tat′**

**ra·ta·touille** (rä′tä twē′) *n.* [Fr. < *ra-*, intensifier + *ta-*, reduplicated syllable + *touiller*, to stir, mix < L. *tudiculare*, to stir about] a vegetable stew of eggplant, zucchini, tomatoes, etc. flavored with garlic and served hot or cold

**ratch·et** (rach′it) *n.* [< Fr. < It. *rocchetto*, dim. of *rocca*, distaff] **1.** a toothed wheel (in full, **ratchet wheel**) or bar whose teeth slope in one direction so as to catch and hold a pawl, which thus prevents backward movement **2.** such a pawl **3.** such a wheel (or bar) and pawl as a unit

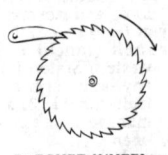

RATCHET WHEEL

**rate¹** (rāt) *n.* [OFr. < L. *rata* (*pars*), reckoned (part) < pp. of *reri*, to reckon] **1.** the amount, degree, etc. of anything in relation to units of something else [the *rate* of pay per month] **2.** a fixed ratio; proportion [the *rate* of exchange] **3.** a price or value; specif., the cost per unit of some commodity, service, etc. **4.** speed of movement or action **5.** a class or rank [of the first *rate*] **6.** [Brit.] a local property tax **7.** *U.S. Navy* any of the grades of an enlisted man with a rating —*vt.* **rat′ed**, **rat′ing 1.** to estimate the value, capacity, skill, etc. of; appraise **2.** *a)* to put into a particular class or rank *b) U.S. Navy* to assign a rate to **3.** to consider; esteem **4.** to fix or determine the rates for **5.** [Colloq.] to deserve —*vi.* **1.** to be classed or ranked **2.** to have value, status, or rating —**at any rate 1.** in any event **2.** anyway

**rate²** (rāt) *vt., vi.* **rat′ed**, **rat′ing** [ME. *raten*] to scold severely; chide

**rate·pay·er** (rāt′pā′ər) *n.* [Brit. & Canad.] one who pays rates, or local taxes

**-rat·er** (rāt′ər) *a combining form meaning* one of a (specified) rate, or class [*first-rater*]

**rath·er** (rath′ər; *for interj.* rä′thur′) *adv.* [OE. *hrathor*, compar. of *hrathe*, quickly] **1.** more willingly; preferably **2.** with more justice, reason, etc. **3.** more accurately; more precisely **4.** on the contrary **5.** to some degree; somewhat —*interj.* [Chiefly Brit.] certainly —**had** (or **would**) **rather 1.** would choose to **2.** would prefer that —**rather than** instead of

**raths·kel·ler** (rät′skel′ər, rath′-) *n.* [G. < *rat*, council + *keller*, cellar] a restaurant of the German type, usually below street level, where beer is served

**rat·i·fy** (rat′ə fī′) *vt.* **-fied**, **-fy′ing** [< MFr. < ML. < L. *ratus* (see RATE¹) + *facere*, to make] to approve or confirm; esp., to give official sanction to —**rat′i·fi·ca′tion** *n.*

**ra·ti·né** (rat′'n ā′) *n.* [Fr., frizzed: of the nap] a loosely woven fabric of cotton, wool, rayon, etc., with a nubby surface: also **ra·tine** (ra tēn′)

**rat·ing** (rāt′iŋ) *n.* **1.** a rank or grade; specif., a classification of armed-forces personnel according to specialties **2.** a placement in a certain rank or class **3.** an evaluation of the credit or financial standing of a businessman, firm, etc. **4.** an amount determined as a grade **5.** *Radio & TV* the relative popularity of a program, as shown by polls

**ra·tio** (rā′shō, -shē ō′) *n., pl.* **-tios** [L.: see REASON] **1.** a fixed relation in degree, number, etc. between two similar things; proportion [a *ratio* of two boys to three girls] **2.** *Math.* the quotient of one quantity divided by another of the same kind, usually expressed as a fraction

**ra·ti·o·ci·nate** (rash′ē ō′sə nāt′, rat′ē-; -äs′ə nāt′) *vi.* **-nat′ed**, **-nat′ing** [< L. pp. of *ratiocinari* < *ratio*: see REASON] to reason, esp. using formal logic —**ra′ti·o′ci·na′tion** *n.* —**ra′ti·o′ci·na′tive** *adj.* —**ra′ti·o′ci·na′tor** *n.*

**ra·tion** (rash′ən, rā′shən) *n.* [MFr. < ML. < L. *ratio*: see REASON] **1.** a fixed portion; share; allowance **2.** a fixed allowance of food or provisions, as a daily allowance for one soldier, etc. **3.** [*pl.*] food or food supply —*vt.* **1.** to give rations to **2.** to distribute (food, clothing, etc.) in rations, as in times of scarcity —**ra′tion·ing** *n.*

**ra·tion·al** (rash′ən 'l) *adj.* [L. *rationalis* < *ratio*: see REASON] **1.** of or based on reasoning **2.** able to reason; reasoning **3.** showing reason; sensible [a *rational* plan] **4.** *Math.* designating or of a number that can be expressed as the quotient of two integers or as an integer —**ra′tion·al′i·ty** (-ə nal′ə tē) *n., pl.* **-ties** —**ra′tion·al·ly** *adv.*

**ra·tion·a·le** (rash′ə nal′, -nä′lē) *n.* [L.: see prec.] **1.** the rational basis for something **2.** an explanation of reasons or principles

**ra·tion·al·ism** (rash′ən 'l iz'm) *n.* the principle or practice of accepting reason as the only source of knowledge and as the only basis for forming one's opinions, beliefs, or course of action —**ra′tion·al·ist** *n., adj.* —**ra′tion·al·is′tic** *adj.* —**ra′tion·al·is′ti·cal·ly** *adv.*

**ra·tion·al·ize** (rash′ən ə līz′) *vt.* **-ized′, -iz′ing 1.** to make rational; make conform to reason **2.** to explain on the basis of reason or logic **3.** *Psychol.* to think of explanations for (one's acts, beliefs, etc.) that seem to make sense but do not truly reveal one's motives —*vi.* **1.** to think in a rational or rationalistic manner **2.** to rationalize one's acts, beliefs, etc. —**ra′tion·al·i·za′tion** *n.* —**ra′tion·al·iz′er** *n.*

**rat·ite** (rat′īt) *adj.* [< L. < *ratis*, a raft] of a group of large, flightless birds having a flat breastbone without the keellike ridge of flying birds —*n.* any bird of this group, as the ostrich

**rat·line** (rat′lin) *n.* [altered by folk etym. < LME. *ratling* < ?] any of the small, thin pieces of tarred rope that join the shrouds of a ship and serve as a ladder: also sp. **rat′lin**

**rat race** [Slang] a mad scramble or intense competitive struggle, as in the business world

**rats·bane** (rats′bān′) *n.* [see BANE] rat poison

**rat-tail** (rat′tāl′) *adj.* shaped like a rat's tail; slim and tapering: also **rat′tailed′**

**rat·tan** (ra tan′) *n.* [Malay *rotan* < *raut*, to strip] **1.** a climbing palm with long, slender, tough stems **2.** these stems, used in making wickerwork, etc. **3.** a cane or switch made from such a stem

**rat·ter** (rat′ər) *n.* **1.** a dog or cat skilled at catching rats **2.** [Slang] a betrayer or informer

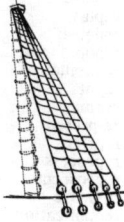

RATLINES

**rat·tle** (rat′'l) *vi.* **-tled, -tling** [ME. *ratelen*: prob. echoic] **1.** to make a rapid series of sharp, short sounds **2.** to move with such sounds [a cart *rattled* over the stones] **3.** to chatter (often with *on*) —*vt.* **1.** to cause to rattle [he *rattled* the handle] **2.** to utter or perform rapidly (usually with *off*) **3.** to confuse or upset [catcalls *rattled* the speaker] —*n.* **1.** a quick succession of short, sharp sounds **2.** a rattling noise in the throat, as of a dying person **3.** a noisy uproar **4.** the series of horny rings at the end of a rattlesnake's tail **5.** a device, as a baby's toy, intended to rattle when shaken —**rattle around in** to occupy (a place too big for one's needs) —**rat′tly** *adj.*

**rat·tle·brain** (-brān′) *n.* a frivolous, talkative person: also **rat′tle·pate′** (-pāt′) —**rat′tle·brained′** *adj.*

**rat·tler** (rat′lər) *n.* **1.** a person or thing that rattles **2.** a rattlesnake **3.** [Colloq.] a freight train

**rat·tle·snake** (rat′'l snāk′) *n.* any of various poisonous American pit vipers having a series of horny rings at the end of the tail that rattle when shaken

**rat·tle·trap** (-trap′) *n.* anything worn out, rickety, or rattling; esp., an old, worn-out automobile

**rat·tling** (rat′liŋ) *adj.* **1.** that rattles **2.** [Colloq.] very fast, good, etc. —*adv.* [Colloq.] very [a *rattling* good time]

**rat·ty** (rat′ē) *adj.* **-ti·er, -ti·est 1.** of, like, or full of rats **2.** [Slang] shabby or run-down

**rau·cous** (rô′kəs) *adj.* [L. *raucus*] **1.** hoarse; rough-sounding [a *raucous* shout] **2.** loud and rowdy [a *raucous* party] —**rau′cous·ly** *adv.* —**rau′cous·ness** *n.*

**raun·chy** (rôn′chē, rän′-) *adj.* **-chi·er, -chi·est** [< ?] [Slang] **1.** dirty, cheap, sloppy, etc. **2.** earthy, risqué, lustful, etc. —**raun′chi·ly** *adv.* —**raun′chi·ness** *n.*

**rau·wol·fi·a** (rô wool′fē ə, rou-) *n.* [ModL., after L. *Rauwolf*, 16th-c. G. botanist] **1.** any of a group of tropical trees and shrubs, some of which yield medicinal substances **2.** the root of one of these trees, a source of reserpine

**rav·age** (rav′ij) *n.* [Fr. < *ravir*: see RAVISH] **1.** the act or practice of violently destroying **2.** ruin; devastating damage —*vt.* **-aged, -ag·ing** to destroy violently; devastate; ruin —*vi.* to commit ravages —**rav′ag·er** *n.*

**rave** (rāv) *vi.* **raved, rav′ing** [prob. < OFr. *raver*] **1.** to talk incoherently or wildly, as when delirious or demented **2.** to talk with excessive enthusiasm (*about*) **3.** to rage, as a storm —*vt.* to utter incoherently —*n.* **1.** a raving **2.** [Colloq.] an excessively enthusiastic commendation: often used before a noun [a *rave* review] —**rav′er** *n.*

**rav·el** (rav′'l) *vt.* **-eled** or **-elled, -el·ing** or **-el·ling** [MDu. *ravelen*] **1.** orig., to make complicated or tangled **2.** to separate the parts, esp. threads, of; untwist **3.** to make clear; disentangle —*vi.* to become separated into its parts, esp. threads; fray (*out*) —*n.* a raveling, or a raveled thread —**rav′el·er, rav′el·ler** *n.*

**Ra·vel** (rȧ vel′; E. ra vel′), **Mau·rice (Joseph)** (mô rēs′) 1875-1937; Fr. composer

**rav·el·ing, rav·el·ling** (rav′'l iŋ, rav′liŋ) *n.* anything raveled, as a thread raveled from knitted or woven fabric

**ra·ven** (rā′vən) *n.* [OE. *hræfn*] a large bird of the crow family, with shiny black feathers and a sharp beak —*adj.* black and shiny

**rav·en·ing** (rav′'n iŋ) *adj.* [see RAVENOUS] greedily searching for prey

**rav·e·nous** (rav′ə nəs) *adj.* [< OFr. < *ravine* < L. *rapina*, RAPINE] **1.** greedily hungry **2.** greedy [*ravenous* for praise] **3.** rapacious —**rav′e·nous·ly** *adv.* —**rav′e·nous·ness** *n.*

**ra·vine** (rə vēn′) *n.* [Fr., flood < OFr.: see prec.] a long, deep hollow in the earth's surface, worn by a stream; gorge

**rav·ing** (rā′viŋ) *adj.* **1.** raging; delirious **2.** [Colloq.] exciting raving admiration [a *raving* beauty] —*adv.* so as to cause raving [*raving* mad] —*n.* delirious, incoherent speech

**ra·vi·o·li** (rav′ē ō′lē) *n.pl.* [*with sing. v.*] [It.] small casings of dough containing seasoned ground meat, cheese, etc., boiled and served usually in a savory tomato sauce

**rav·ish** (rav′ish) *vt.* [< stem of OFr. *ravir*, ult. < L. *rapere*, to seize] **1.** to seize and carry away forcibly **2.** to rape **3.** to enrapture —**rav′ish·er** *n.* —**rav′ish·ment** *n.*

**rav·ish·ing** (-iŋ) *adj.* causing great joy or delight; entrancing —**rav′ish·ing·ly** *adv.*

**raw** (rô) *adj.* [OE. *hreaw*] **1.** not cooked **2.** in its natural condition; not changed by art, manufacture, etc. [*raw* silk] **3.** not processed, edited, etc. [*raw* data] **4.** inexperienced [a *raw* recruit] **5.** with the skin rubbed off; sore and inflamed [a *raw* cut] **6.** uncomfortably cold and damp [a *raw* wind] **7.** *a)* brutal or coarse in frankness *b)* indecent; bawdy **8.** [Colloq.] harsh or unfair [a *raw* deal] —**in the raw 1.** in the natural state **2.** naked —**raw′ly** *adv.* —**raw′ness** *n.*

**Ra·wal·pin·di** (rä′wəl pin′dē) city in NE Pakistan: pop. 340,000

**raw·boned** (rô′bōnd′) *adj.* having little fat; lean; gaunt

**raw·hide** (-hīd′) *n.* **1.** an untanned or partially tanned cattle hide **2.** a whip made of this —*vt.* **-hid′ed, -hid′ing** to beat with such a whip

**Ray** (rā) [dim. of RAYMOND] a masculine name

**ray¹** (rā) *n.* [< OFr. < L. *radius*: see RADIUS] **1.** any of the thin lines, or beams, of light that appear to come from a bright source **2.** any of several lines coming out from a center **3.** a tiny amount [a *ray* of hope] **4.** *Bot., Zool.* any part of a structure with parts coming like rays from a center, as the petals of certain flowers, the limbs of a starfish, etc. **5.** *Physics a)* a stream of particles given off by a radioactive substance, or any of the particles *b)* a straight line along which any part of a wave of radiant energy is regarded as traveling —*vi.* **1.** to shine forth in rays **2.** to radiate —*vt.* **1.** to send out in rays **2.** to supply with rays or radiating lines —**ray′less** *adj.* —**ray′like′** *adj.*

**ray²** (rā) *n.* [< MFr. < L. *raia*] any of several fishes, as the stingray, electric ray, skate, etc., having a horizontally flat body with both eyes on top, wide fins at each side, and a slender or whiplike tail

**ray flower** any of the flowers around the margin of the head of certain composite plants, as the daisy: also **ray floret**

**Ray·mond** (rā′mənd) [< ONormFr. < Frank. *Raginmund*, lit., wise protection] a masculine name

**ray·on** (rā′än) *n.* [arbitrary coinage < RAY¹] **1.** any of various synthetic textile fibers produced by pressing a cellulose solution through very small holes and solidifying it in the form of filaments **2.** any fabric woven or knitted from such fibers

**raze** (rāz) *vt.* **razed, raz′ing** [< OFr. *raser*, ult. < L. pp. of *radere*, to scrape] to tear down completely; level to the ground; demolish

**ra·zor** (rā′zər) *n.* [< OFr. < *raser*: see prec.] **1.** a sharp-edged cutting instrument for shaving off or cutting hair **2.** same as SHAVER (sense 2)

**ra·zor·back** (-bak′) *n.* **1.** a wild or semiwild hog of the S U.S., with a ridged back and long legs **2.** a sharp ridge

**razz** (raz) *vt., vi.* [contr. < RASPBERRY] [Slang] to tease, ridicule, heckle, etc. —*n.* [Slang] *same as* RASPBERRY (sense 3)

**raz·zle-daz·zle** (raz′'l daz′'l) *n.* [Slang] a flashy display intended to confuse, bewilder, or deceive

**razz·ma·tazz** (raz′mə taz′) *n.* [Slang] **1.** lively spirit; excitement **2.** flashy display; showiness

**Rb** *Chem.* rubidium

**rbi, RBI, r.b.i.** *Baseball* run(s) batted in

**R.C. 1.** Red Cross **2.** Roman Catholic

**R.C.Ch.** Roman Catholic Church

**Rd., rd. 1.** road **2.** rod **3.** round

**R.D.** Rural Delivery

**re**[1] (rā) *n.* [It. < L. *re*(*sonare*): see GAMUT] *Music* a syllable representing the second tone of the diatonic scale

**re**[2] (rē, rā) *prep.* [L., abl. of *res*, thing] in the case or matter of; as regards: short for *in re*

**re-** [< Fr. *re-, ré-* < L. *re-, red-*, back] *a prefix meaning:* **1.** back [*repay*] **2.** again, anew [*reappear*] It is used with a hyphen: 1) to distinguish between a word in which the prefix means *again* or *anew* and a word having a special meaning (Ex.: *re-sound, resound*) 2) to avoid ambiguity in forming nonce words [*re-urge*] 3) esp. formerly, before words beginning with an *e* [*re-edit*]: now usually solid [*reedit*] The following list contains some of the more common words in which *re-* means *again* or *anew*

| | | |
|---|---|---|
| reabsorb | recommission | refashion |
| reabsorption | recompose | refasten |
| reaccuse | recompress | refigure |
| reaccustom | recompute | refile |
| reacquaint | reconduct | refilter |
| reacquire | recondense | refocus |
| readapt | reconfine | refold |
| readdress | reconfirm | reformulate |
| readjust | reconquer | refortify |
| readmission | reconquest | reframe |
| readmit | reconsecrate | refreeze |
| readmittance | reconsign | refuel |
| readopt | reconsolidate | refurnish |
| reaffiliate | reconstitute | regather |
| reaffirm | recontaminate | regild |
| reaffirmation | reconvene | reglaze |
| realliance | reconvey | reglorify |
| reallocation | recook | reglue |
| reallot | recopy | regrade |
| reappearance | recross | regrind |
| reapplication | recrystallize | regrow |
| reapply | recultivate | rehandle |
| reappoint | redecorate | rehang |
| reappointment | rededicate | rehire |
| rearrest | redefine | rehospitalize |
| reascend | redefinition | rehouse |
| reassemble | redeliver | reignite |
| reassembly | redemand | reimpose |
| reassert | redeposit | reimprisonment |
| reassertion | redescribe | reincorporate |
| reassess | redesign | reincur |
| reassign | redetermine | reinduce |
| reassociate | redevelop | reinfect |
| reassume | rediscover | reinflate |
| reassumption | rediscovery | reinform |
| reattach | redistribute | reinfuse |
| reattack | redistribution | reinoculate |
| reattain | redraft | reinsert |
| reattempt | redraw | reinspect |
| reawaken | redry | reinspire |
| rebaptism | redye | reinstall |
| rebaptize | reedit | reinstitute |
| rebeautify | reelect | reinstruct |
| rebid | reelection | reinsure |
| rebill | reembark | reinterment |
| rebind | reembody | reinterpret |
| reborn | reembrace | reinterrogate |
| rebuild | reemerge | reintroduce |
| rebury | reemergence | reintroduction |
| recalculate | reemphasize | reinvest |
| recapitalize | reenact | reinvestigate |
| recarry | reengage | reinvigorate |
| recertify | reenlist | reinvite |
| rechannel | reenlistment | reinvolve |
| recharge | reenter | reissue |
| recharter | reentrance | rekindle |
| recheck | reequip | reknit |
| rechew | reestablish | relabel |
| recirculate | reevaluate | relace |
| reclassification | reexamination | relaunder |
| reclassify | reexamine | relearn |
| reclothe | reexchange | relet |
| recode | reexperience | relight |
| recolor | reexplain | reload |
| recombine | reexport | reman |
| recommence | reface | remarriage |

| | | |
|---|---|---|
| remarry | reread | resummon |
| rematch | rerecord | resupply |
| remeasure | reroll | resurvey |
| remelt | resaddle | reswallow |
| remerge | reschedule | resynthesize |
| remilitarize | rescore | retabulate |
| remix | rescreen | retack |
| remodify | reseal | retape |
| remold | reseed | reteach |
| rename | reseize | retelevise |
| renegotiate | resell | retell |
| renominate | resend | retest |
| renotify | resentence | retestify |
| renumber | re-serve | rethread |
| reobtain | resettle | retie |
| reoccupy | resew | retitle |
| reoccur | reshape | retold |
| reoccurrence | resharpen | retrain |
| reopen | reshine | retransfer |
| reoppose | reshow | retranslate |
| reorient | reshuffle | re-treat |
| repack | re-sign | retrial |
| repaint | resilver | retrim |
| repanel | resituate | retry |
| repaper | resmooth | retune |
| repark | resolder | retwist |
| repartition | resolidify | retype |
| repave | re-solve | reupholster |
| rephotograph | re-sound | reusable |
| replan | respace | reuse |
| replant | respread | revaccinate |
| replaster | restabilize | revaluation |
| replate | restaff | revalue |
| replay | restage | revarnish |
| repolish | restamp | reverify |
| repopularize | restart | revibrate |
| repopulate | restimulate | revisit |
| repot | restitch | revisualize |
| repour | restock | revitalize |
| re-present | restraighten | revote |
| reprice | re-strain | rewaken |
| reprocess | restrengthen | rewarm |
| reprosecute | restretch | rewash |
| re-prove | restrike | reweave |
| republication | restring | reweigh |
| republish | restudy | reweld |
| repurchase | restyle | rewin |
| repurify | resubmit | rework |
| requalify | resubscribe | rezone |

**Re** *Chem.* rhenium

**reach** (rēch) *vt.* [OE. *ræcan*] **1.** to thrust out or extend (the hand, etc.) **2.** to extend to, or touch, by thrusting out **3.** to obtain and hand over [*reach* me the salt] **4.** to go as far as; attain **5.** to carry as far as [the news *reached* him late] **6.** to add up to [to *reach* hundreds of dollars] **7.** to influence; affect **8.** to get in touch with, as by telephone —*vi.* **1.** to thrust out the hand, foot, etc. **2.** to stretch, or be extended, in amount, influence, space, time, etc. **3.** to carry, as sight, sound, etc. **4.** to try to obtain something **5.** to try too hard to make a point, joke, etc. **6.** *Naut.* to sail on a reach —*n.* **1.** a stretching or thrusting out **2.** the power of stretching, obtaining, etc. **3.** the distance or extent covered in stretching, obtaining, etc. **4.** a continuous extent or stretch, esp. of water **5.** *Naut.* a tack sailed with the wind coming from abeam —**reach′a·ble** *adj.* —**reach′er** *n.*

**re·act** (rē akt′) *vi.* **1.** to act in return or reciprocally **2.** to act in opposition **3.** to go back to a former condition, stage, etc. **4.** to respond to a stimulus, influence, etc. **5.** *Chem.* to act with another substance in producing a chemical change —*vt.* to produce a chemical change in

**re-act** (rē′akt′) *vt.* to act or do again

**re·act·ance** (rē ak′təns) *n. Elec.* opposition to the flow of alternating current, caused by inductance or capacitance

**re·act·ant** (-tənt) *n.* any of the substances taking part in a chemical reaction

**re·ac·tion** (rē ak′shən) *n.* **1.** a returning or opposing action, influence, etc. **2.** a response, as to a stimulus **3.** a movement back to a former or less advanced condition, stage, etc.; esp., such a movement in politics **4.** *Chem. a)* the mutual action of substances undergoing chemical change *b)* a process that produces changes in an atomic nucleus **5.** *Med. a)* an action induced by resistance to another action *b)* the effect produced by an allergen *c)* depression or exhaustion following nervous tension, overstimulation, etc. *d)* increased activity following depression —**re·ac′tion·al** *adj.* —**re·ac′tive** *adj.* —**re·ac′tive·ly** *adv.* —**re′ac·tiv′i·ty** *n.*

**re·ac·tion·ar·y** (-shə ner′ē) *adj.* of, showing, or favoring reaction, esp. in politics —*n., pl.* **-ar′ies** a reactionary person

**reaction engine** an engine, as a rocket, that develops thrust by the reaction to the jet of gases ejected from it

**reaction time** *Psychol.* the time between stimulation and the beginning of the response

**re·ac·ti·vate** (rē ak′tə vāt′) *vt.* **-vat'ed, -vat'ing** to make active again; specif., to restore to active military status —*vi.* to be reactivated —**re·ac'ti·va'tion** *n.*

**re·ac·tor** (-tər) *n.* **1.** a person or thing that reacts **2.** *same as* NUCLEAR REACTOR

**read¹** (rēd) *vt.* **read** (red), **read'ing** (rēd′iŋ) [OE. *rædan,* to counsel] **1.** to get the meaning of (something written or printed) by interpreting its characters or signs /to *read* books, music, Braille, etc./ **2.** to utter aloud (something written or printed) **3.** to interpret movements of (the lips of a person speaking) **4.** to know (a language) well enough to interpret its written form **5.** to understand the nature, significance, or thinking of **6.** to interpret (dreams, omens, etc.) or foretell (the future) **7.** to interpret (a printed passage, a signal, etc.) as having a particular meaning **8.** to give as a reading in a certain passage /for "shew" *read* "show"/ **9.** to study /to *read* law/ **10.** to register /the thermometer *reads* 80°/ **11.** to put into a specified state by reading **12.** to obtain (information) from (punch cards, tape, etc.): said of a computer **13.** [Slang] to hear and understand /I *read* you loud and clear/ —*vi.* **1.** to read something written or printed **2.** to learn by reading (with *about* or *of*) **3.** to study **4.** to give a particular meaning when read **5.** to be drawn up in certain words /the sentence *reads* as follows/ **6.** to admit of being read /it *reads* well/ —**read into** (or **in**) to interpret in a certain way —**read out** to display or record with a readout device —**read out of** to expel from (a political party, society, etc.) —**read up (on)** to become well informed (about) by reading

**read²** (red) *pt. & pp. of* READ¹ —*adj.* having knowledge got from reading; informed /well-*read*/

**read·a·ble** (rēd′ə b'l) *adj.* **1.** interesting or easy to read **2.** capable of being read; legible —**read'a·bil'i·ty, read'a·ble·ness** *n.* —**read'a·bly** *adv.*

**Reade** (rēd), **Charles** 1814–84; Eng. novelist

**read·er** (rēd′ər) *n.* **1.** a person who reads **2.** a person who reads lessons, prayers, etc. aloud in church **3.** *a)* a schoolbook containing stories, poems, etc. for use in teaching how to read *b)* an anthology of stories, essays, etc.

**read·er·ship** (-ship′) *n.* all the people who read a particular publication, author, etc.

**Read·ing** (red′iŋ) **1.** city in SC England: pop. 127,000 **2.** [after prec.] city in SE Pa.: pop. 79,000

**read·ing** (rēd′iŋ) *adj.* **1.** that reads **2.** of or for reading —*n.* **1.** the act or practice of one who reads **2.** the reciting of a literary work in public **3.** material read or to be read **4.** the extent to which a person has read **5.** the amount measured by a barometer, thermometer, etc. **6.** the way something is written, read, performed, understood, etc. /a superb *reading* of Hamlet/

**read·out** (rēd′out′) *n.* **1.** a retrieving of information from storage in a digital computer **2.** this information, displayed visually or recorded, as by typewriter or on tape, for immediate use **3.** information immediately displayed or recorded from various electronic instruments

**read·y** (red′ē) *adj.* **read'i·er, read'i·est** [OE. *ræde*] **1.** prepared to act or be used immediately /*ready* to go, *ready* for occupancy/ **2.** unhesitant; willing /a *ready* worker/ **3.** *a)* likely or liable immediately /*ready* to cry/ *b)* apt; inclined /always *ready* to blame others/ **4.** done without delay; prompt /a *ready* reply/ **5.** available immediately /*ready* cash/ —*vt.* **read'ied, read'y·ing** to make ready (often used reflexively) —**at the ready** being prepared for immediate use /to hold a gun *at the ready*/ —**make ready** to prepare —**read'i·ly** *adv.* —**read'i·ness** *n.*

**read·y-made** (-mād′) *adj.* made so as to be ready for immediate use or sale; not made-to-order: also, as applied to clothing, **read'y-to-wear'** (-tə wer′)

**Rea·gan** (rā′gən), **Ronald (Wilson)** 1911– ; 40th president of the U.S. (1981– )

**re·a·gent** (rē ā′jənt) *n.* [RE- + AGENT] *Chem.* a substance used to detect or measure another substance or to convert one substance into another

**re·al¹** (rē′əl, rēl) *adj.* [OFr. < ML. *realis* < L. *res,* thing] **1.** existing or happening as or in fact; actual, true, etc. **2.** *a)* authentic; genuine *b)* not pretended; sincere **3.** designating wages or income as measured by purchasing power **4.** *Law* of or relating to permanent, immovable things /*real* property/ **5.** *Philos.* existing objectively —*adv.* [Colloq.] very —**for real** [Slang] real or really

**re·al²** (rē′əl; *Sp.* re äl′) *n., pl.* **re'als;** *Sp.* **re·al'es** (-ä′les) [Sp. & Port., lit., royal < L. *regalis:* see REGAL] a former silver coin of Spain

**re·al³** (re äl′) *n. sing. of* REIS

**real estate 1.** land, including the buildings or improvements on it and its natural assets, as minerals, water, timber, etc. **2.** ownership of or property in land, etc.

**re·a·lign** (rē′ə līn′) *vt., vi.* to align again; specif., to readjust alliances (between) —**re'a·lign'ment** *n.*

**re·al·ism** (rē′ə liz′m) *n.* **1.** a tendency to face facts and be practical **2.** the picturing in art and literature of people and things as they really appear to be, without idealizing **3.** *Philos. a)* the doctrine that universals are objectively actual *b)* the doctrine that material objects exist in themselves apart from the mind's consciousness of them —**re'al·ist** *n.*

**re·al·is·tic** (rē′ə lis′tik) *adj.* **1.** of, having to do with, or in the style of, realism or realists **2.** tending to face facts; practical rather than visionary —**re'al·is'ti·cal·ly** *adv.*

**re·al·i·ty** (rē al′ə tē) *n., pl.* **-ties 1.** the quality or fact of being real **2.** a person or thing that is real; fact **3.** the quality of being true to life **4.** *Philos.* that which is real —**in reality** in fact; actually

**re·al·ize** (rē′ə līz′) *vt.* **-ized', -iz'ing 1.** to make real; bring into being; achieve **2.** to make appear real **3.** to understand fully /to *realize* one's danger/ **4.** to convert (assets, rights, etc.) into money **5.** to gain; obtain /to *realize* a profit/ **6.** to be sold for, or bring as profit (a specified sum) —**re'al·iz'a·ble** *adj.* —**re'al·i·za'tion** *n.*

**re·al-life** (rē′əl līf′) *adj.* actual; not imaginary

**re·al·ly** (rē′ə lē, rēl′ē) *adv.* **1.** in reality; in fact; actually **2.** truly or genuinely /really hot/ —*interj.* indeed

**realm** (relm) *n.* [< OFr. *reaume* < L. *regimen,* rule, infl. by L. *regalis,* REGAL] **1.** a kingdom **2.** a region; sphere; area /the *realm* of imagination/

**real number** *Math.* any rational or irrational number

**real time 1.** time in which the occurrence and recording of an event are almost simultaneous **2.** the actual time used by a computer to solve a problem the answer to which is immediately available to control a process that is going on at the same time

**Re·al·tor** (rē′əl tər) *n.* [< ff. + -OR] a real estate broker who is a member of the National Association of Real Estate Boards

**re·al·ty** (rē′əl tē) *n.* [REAL¹ + -TY¹] *same as* REAL ESTATE

**ream¹** (rēm) *n.* [< MFr. < Ar. *rizma,* a bale] **1.** a quantity of paper varying from 480 sheets (20 quires) to 516 sheets **2.** [*pl.*] [Colloq.] a great amount

**ream²** (rēm) *vt.* [OE. *reman,* akin to *ryman,* lit., to make roomy < base of *rum,* room] **1.** *a)* to enlarge or taper (a hole) *b)* to enlarge the bore of (a gun) **2.** to remove (a defect) by reaming **3.** to squeeze the juice from a reamer **4.** [Slang] to cheat or deceive

**ream·er** (-ər) *n.* a person or thing that reams; specif., *a)* a sharp-edged tool for enlarging or tapering holes *b)* a utensil in which oranges, etc. are squeezed for juice

REAMER

**re·an·i·mate** (rē an′ə māt′) *vt.* **-mat'ed, -mat'ing** to give new life, power, vigor, courage, etc. to —**re·an'i·ma'tion** *n.*

**reap** (rēp) *vt.* [OE. *ripan*] **1.** to cut (grain) with a scythe, machine, etc. **2.** to gather (a crop, harvest, etc.) **3.** to harvest grain from (a field) **4.** to get as the result of action, work, etc. —*vi.* to reap a harvest, reward, etc.

**reap·er** (rē′pər) *n.* **1.** a person who reaps **2.** a machine for reaping grain —**the (Grim) Reaper** death

**re·ap·por·tion** (rē′ə pôr′shən) *vt.* to apportion again, as with the intent of having all legislative districts contain about the same number of people —**re'ap·por'tion·ment** *n.*

**re·ap·praise** (-prāz′) *vt.* **-praised', -prais'ing** to make a fresh appraisal of; reconsider —**re'ap·prais'al** *n.*

**rear¹** (rir) *n.* [< ARREAR(S)] **1.** the back part **2.** the position behind or at the back **3.** the part of an army, etc. farthest from the battle front **4.** [Slang] the buttocks: also **rear end** —*adj.* of, at, or in the rear —**bring up the rear** to come at the end, as of a procession

**rear²** (rir) *vt.* [OE. *ræran,* caus. of *risan,* to rise] **1.** to put upright; elevate **2.** to build; erect **3.** to grow or breed (animals or plants) **4.** to bring to maturity by educating, nourishing, etc. /to *rear* children/ —*vi.* **1.** to rise on the hind legs, as a horse **2.** to rise (*up*) in anger, etc.

**rear admiral** a naval officer next in rank above a captain and below a vice admiral

**rear guard** a military detachment to protect the rear of a main force or body

**re·arm** (rē ärm′) *vt., vi.* **1.** to arm again **2.** to arm with new or more effective weapons —**re·ar'ma·ment** *n.*

**rear·most** (rir′mōst′) *adj.* farthest in the rear

**re·ar·range** (rē′ə rānj′) *vt.* **-ranged', -rang'ing 1.** to arrange again  2. to arrange in a different manner —**re'ar·range'ment** *n.*

**rear·ward** (rir'wərd) *adj.* at, in, or toward the rear —*adv.* toward the rear: also **rear'wards**

**rea·son** (rē'z'n) *n.* [< OFr. < L. *ratio*, a reckoning < pp. of *reri*, to think]  1. an explanation or justification of an act, idea, etc.  2. a cause or motive  3. the ability to think, draw conclusions, etc.  4. sound thought or judgment; good sense  5. normal mental powers; sanity —*vi.* 1. to think logically; draw conclusions from facts known or assumed  2. to argue or talk in a logical way —*vt.* 1. to think logically about; analyze  2. to argue, conclude, or infer [he *reasoned* that the method was too costly]  3. to justify with reason  4. to persuade by reasoning (*into* or *out of* something) —**by reason of** because of —**in** (or **within**) **reason** in accord with what is reasonable —**out of all reason** unreasonable —**stand to reason** to be logical or reasonable —**with reason** justifiably; rightly —**rea'son·er** *n.*

**rea·son·a·ble** (-ə b'l) *adj.* 1. capable of reasoning or being reasoned with  2. using or showing reason, or sound judgment; sensible  3. *a)* not extreme or excessive  *b)* not expensive —**rea'son·a·ble·ness** *n.* —**rea'son·a·bly** *adv.*

**rea·son·ing** (-iŋ) *n.* 1. the drawing of inferences or conclusions from known or assumed facts  2. the reasons, proofs, etc. used in this process

**re·as·sure** (rē'ə shoor') *vt.* -sured', -sur'ing  1. to assure again or anew  2. to restore to confidence  3. [Brit.] to insure anew —**re·as·sur'ance** *n.* —**re·as·sur'ing·ly** *adv.*

**re·bate** (rē'bāt; *also for v.* ri bāt') *vt.* -bat·ed, -bat·ing [< OFr. < *re-*, re- + *abattre*: see ABATE]  1. to give back (part of an amount paid)  2. to make a deduction from (a bill) —*n.* a return of part of the amount paid, as for goods

**re·bec, re·beck** (rē'bek) *n.* [Fr. < OFr. *rebebe* < Ar. *rabāb*] a medieval pear-shaped instrument played with a bow like a violin

**Re·bec·ca** (ri bek'ə) [LL. < Gr. < Heb. *ribbqāh*, lit., noose]  1. a feminine name  2. *Bible* the wife of Isaac and mother of Jacob and Esau: usually sp. **Rebekah**

**reb·el** (reb'l; *for v.* ri bel') *n.* [< OFr. < L. < *re-*, again + *bellare*, to war < *bellum*, war]  1. a person who takes up arms against the government of his own country  2. a person who resists any authority or control  3. [*often* R-] *an epithet for* a Confederate soldier —*adj.* 1. rebellious  2. of rebels —*vi.* -elled', -el'ling  1. to be a rebel against the government of one's country  2. to resist any authority or control  3. to feel or show strong aversion

**re·bel·lion** (ri bel'yən) *n.* [< MFr. < L.: see prec.]  1. an act or state of armed, open resistance to one's government  2. defiance of any authority or control

**re·bel·lious** (-yəs) *adj.* 1. resisting authority; engaged in rebellion  2. of or like rebels or rebellion  3. opposing any control; defiant  4. difficult to treat or handle —**re·bel'lious·ly** *adv.* —**re·bel'lious·ness** *n.*

**re·birth** (rē burth', rē'burth') *n.* 1. a new or second birth  2. a reawakening; revival

**re·bound** (ri bound'; *also, & for n. usually*, rē'bound') *vi.* 1. to bound or spring back, as upon impact or in recovery  2. to reecho —*vt.* to make bound or spring back —*n.* 1. a rebounding; recoil  2. a basketball that bounds back after an attempted basket, or the play made in getting this ball —**on the rebound** 1. after bouncing off the ground, a wall, etc.  2. just after and while reacting to rejection, as in love

**re·bo·zo** (ri bō'zō; *Sp.* re bô'thô, -sô) *n., pl.* -zos (-zōz; *Sp.* -thôs, -sôs) [Sp., a shawl] a long scarf worn by women around the head and shoulders, as in Mexico

**re·broad·cast** (rē brôd'kast') *vt., vi.* -cast' or -cast'ed, -cast'ing  1. to broadcast again  2. to broadcast (a program, etc. received in a relay system from another station) —*n.* 1. a rebroadcasting  2. a program that is being or has been rebroadcast

**re·buff** (ri buf') *n.* [< MFr. < It. *rabbuffo*, ult. < Gmc.]  1. a blunt refusal of offered help, advice, etc.  2. any check or repulse —*vt.* 1. to refuse bluntly; snub  2. to check

**re·buke** (ri byook') *vt.* -buked', -buk'ing [< Anglo-Fr. < OFr. < *re-*, back + *buchier*, to beat] to blame or scold in a sharp way; reprimand —*n.* a sharp scolding or reprimand —**re·buk'er** *n.* —**re·buk'ing·ly** *adv.*

**re·bus** (rē'bəs) *n.* [L., lit., by things] a kind of puzzle consisting of pictures of things combined so as to suggest words or phrases [a picture of a bee plus the figure 4 is a *rebus* for "before"]

**re·but** (ri but') *vt.* -but'ted, -but'ting [< Anglo-Fr. < OFr. < *re-*, back + *buter*, to push] to contradict or oppose, esp. in a formal manner by argument, proof, etc. —*vi.* to provide opposing arguments —**re·but'ta·ble** *adj.* —**re·but'ter** *n.*

**re·but·tal** (-'l) *n.* a rebutting, as in law

**rec** (rek) *n. shortened form of* RECREATION in such compounds as **rec room, rec hall**

**rec.** 1. receipt  2. recipe  3. record(ed)

**re·cal·ci·trant** (ri kal'si trənt) *adj.* [< L. prp. of *recalcitrare* < *re-*, back + *calcitrare*, to kick < *calx*, a heel]  1. refusing to obey authority, regulation, etc.; stubbornly defiant  2. hard to handle or deal with —*n.* a recalcitrant person —**re·cal'ci·trance, re·cal'ci·tran·cy** *n.* —**re·cal'ci·trant·ly** *adv.*

**re·call** (ri kôl'; *for n. also* rē'kôl') *vt.* 1. to call back; order to return  2. to bring back to mind; remember  3. to take back; revoke  4. to bring back in awareness, attention, etc. —*n.* 1. a recalling  2. the ability to remember; memory  3. the process of removing, or the right to remove, a public official from office by popular vote —**re·call'a·ble** *adj.*

**re·cant** (ri kant') *vt., vi.* [< L. < *re-*, back + *cantare*, freq. of *canere*, to sing] to take back or confess being wrong about (former beliefs, statements, etc.), esp. formally or publicly —**re·can·ta·tion** (rē'kan tā'shən) *n.*

**re·cap**[1] (rē kap'; *also, & for n. always*, rē'kap') *vt.* -capped', -cap'ping [RE- + CAP] to cement, mold, and vulcanize a strip of rubber on the outer surface of (a worn pneumatic tire); retread —*n.* a recapped tire

**re·cap**[2] (rē'kap') *n.* a recapitulation, or summary —*vi., vt.* -capped', -cap'ping to recapitulate

**re·ca·pit·u·late** (rē'kə pich'ə lāt') *vi., vt.* -lat'ed, -lat'ing [see RE- & CAPITULATE] to tell again briefly; summarize

**re·ca·pit·u·la·tion** (-pich'ə lā'shən) *n.* 1. a recapitulating  2. a summary, or brief restatement —**re·ca·pit'u·la·tive, re·ca·pit'u·la·to·ry** (-lə tôr'ē) *adj.*

**re·cap·ture** (rē kap'chər) *vt.* -tured, -tur·ing  1. to capture again; retake; reacquire  2. to bring back by remembering —*n.* a recapturing or being recaptured

**re·cast** (rē kast'; *for n.* rē'kast') *vt.* -cast', -cast'ing  1. to cast again or anew  2. to improve the form of by redoing; reconstruct [to *recast* a sentence] —*n.* a recasting

**recd., rec'd.** received

**re·cede**[1] (ri sēd') *vi.* -ced'ed, -ced'ing [< L.: see RE- & CEDE]  1. to go or move back [the flood *receded*]  2. to withdraw [to *recede* from a promise]  3. to slope backward [her chin *recedes*]  4. to lessen, dim, etc.

**re·cede**[2] (rē'sēd') *vt.* -ced'ed, -ced'ing to cede back

**re·ceipt** (ri sēt') *n.* [< Anglo-Fr. < ML. < L. < pp. of *recipere*: see RECEIVE]  1. *old-fashioned var. of* RECIPE  2. a receiving or being received  3. a written acknowledgment that something, as goods, money, etc., has been received  4. [*pl.*] the thing or amount received, as of money taken in by a business —*vt.* 1. to mark (a bill) paid  2. to write a receipt for (goods, etc.)

**re·ceiv·a·ble** (ri sē'və b'l) *adj.* 1. that can be received  2. suitable for acceptance  3. due in payment from one's customers —*n.* [*pl.*] accounts or bills receivable

**re·ceive** (ri sēv') *vt.* -ceived', -ceiv'ing [< Anglo-Fr. < OFr. < L. *recipere* < *re-*, back + *capere*, to take]  1. to take or get (something given, offered, sent, etc.)  2. to meet with; experience [to *receive* acclaim]  3. to undergo; suffer [to *receive* a blow]  4. to take the force of; bear [each wheel *receives* equal weight]  5. to react to as specified [the song was well *received*]  6. to get knowledge of; learn [to *receive* news]  7. to accept as authentic, valid, etc.  8. *a)* to let enter; admit  *b)* to have room for; contain  9. to greet (visitors, etc.) —*vi.* 1. to be a recipient  2. to greet guests or visitors  3. *Radio & TV* to convert incoming electromagnetic waves into sound or light, thus reproducing the sounds or images being transmitted  4. *Sports* to catch a ball or be prepared to return a thrown, kicked, etc. ball

**re·ceiv·er** (ri sē'vər) *n.* 1. a person who receives (in various senses); specif., *Law* a person appointed by the court to administer or hold in trust property in bankruptcy or in a lawsuit  2. a thing that receives; specif., *a)* a receptacle  *b)* an apparatus that converts electrical signals, etc. into sound or light, as a radio or television receiving set, or that part of a telephone held to the ear

**re·ceiv·er·ship** (-ship') *n. Law* 1. the duties or office of a receiver  2. the state of being administered or held by a receiver

**receiving set** an apparatus for receiving radio or television signals; receiver

**re·cent** (rē's'nt) *adj.* [MFr. < L. *recens* < *re-*, again + base akin to Gr. *kainos*, new]  1. done, made, etc. just before the present time; modern; new  2. of a time just before the present  3. [R-] designating or of the present epoch, extending from the close of the Pleistocene —**the Recent** the Recent Epoch or its rocks: see GEOLOGY, chart —**re'cent·ly** *adv.* —**re'cent·ness** *n.*

**re·cep·ta·cle** (ri sep'tə k'l) *n.* [L. *receptaculum* < freq. of *recipere*: see RECEIVE]  1. anything used to contain or hold something else; container  2. *Bot. a)* the part of the stalk from which the flower grows  *b)* a cuplike or disklike part supporting spores, seeds, etc.

**re·cep·tion** (ri sep'shən) *n.* [OFr. < L. < pp. of *recipere*: see RECEIVE]  1. *a)* a receiving or being received  *b)* the manner of this [a friendly *reception*]  2. a social function, often formal, for the receiving of guests  3. *Radio & TV* the manner of receiving, with reference to quality [poor *reception*]

**re·cep·tion·ist** (-ist) *n.* an office employee who receives callers, gives information, etc.

**re·cep·tive** (ri sep′tiv) *adj.* **1.** receiving or tending to receive, admit, or contain **2.** able or ready to receive requests, suggestions, new ideas, etc. **3.** of reception or receptors —**re·cep′tive·ly** *adv.* —**re·cep′tiv′i·ty, re·cep′tive·ness** *n.*

**re·cep·tor** (-tər) *n. Physiol.* a nerve ending specialized for the reception of stimuli; sense organ

**re·cess** (rē′ses; *also, and for v. usually,* ri ses′) *n.* [< L. pp. of *recedere,* to recede] **1.** a receding or hollow place, as in a wall; niche **2.** a secluded or withdrawn place [the *recesses* of the subconscious] **3.** a temporary halting of work, study, etc. —*vt.* **1.** to place in a recess **2.** to form a recess in —*vi.* to take a recess

**re·ces·sion¹** (ri sesh′ən) *n.* [L. *recessio* < pp. of *recedere,* to recede] **1.** a going backward; withdrawal **2.** a departing procession, as of clergy and choir after a church service **3.** a receding part, as of a wall **4.** a temporary falling off of business activity during a prosperous period

**re·ces·sion²** (rē sesh′ən) *n.* [RE- + CESSION] a ceding back, as to a former owner

**re·ces·sion·al** (-′l) *adj.* of a recession —*n.* a hymn or other music sung or played during a church recession

**re·ces·sive** (ri ses′iv) *adj.* **1.** receding or tending to recede **2.** *Genetics* designating or of that one of any pair of allelic characters which, when both are present in the germ plasm, remains latent: opposed to DOMINANT —**re·ces′sive·ly** *adv.* —**re·ces′sive·ness** *n.*

**re·cher·ché** (rə sher′shā, -sher′shā′) *adj.* [Fr., pp. of *rechercher:* see RESEARCH] **1.** sought out with care; choice **2.** having refinement or contrived elegance **3.** too refined; too studied

**re·cid·i·vism** (ri sid′ə viz′m) *n.* [< L. < *recidere* < *re-,* back + *cadere,* to fall + -ISM] relapse, or tendency to relapse, esp. into crime or antisocial behavior —**re·cid′i·vist** *n., adj.* —**re·cid′i·vis′tic, re·cid′i·vous** *adj.*

**Re·ci·fe** (re sē′fə) seaport in NE Brazil, on the Atlantic: pop. 1,079,000

**rec·i·pe** (res′ə pē) *n.* [L., imperative of *recipere:* see RECEIVE] **1.** formerly, a medicinal prescription **2.** a list of ingredients and directions for preparing a dish or drink **3.** any procedure for bringing about a desired result

**re·cip·i·ent** (ri sip′ē ənt) *n.* [< L. prp. of *recipere:* see RECEIVE] a person or thing that receives —*adj.* receiving, or ready or able to receive —**re·cip′i·ence, re·cip′i·en·cy** *n.*

**re·cip·ro·cal** (ri sip′rə k′l) *adj.* [< L. *reciprocus,* returning] **1.** done, felt, given, etc. in return **2.** on both sides; mutual **3.** corresponding but reversed **4.** equivalent or interchangeable; complementary **5.** *Gram.* expressing mutual action or relation [each other is a *reciprocal* pronoun] **6.** *Math.* of reciprocals —*n.* **1.** anything that has a reciprocal relation to another; counterpart **2.** *Math.* the quantity resulting from the division of 1 by the given quantity [the *reciprocal* of 7 is 1/7] —**re·cip′ro·cal′i·ty** (-kal′ə tē) *n.* —**re·cip′ro·cal·ly** *adv.*

**re·cip·ro·cate** (-kāt′) *vt., vi.* -cat′ed, -cat′ing [< L. pp. of *reciprocare* < *reciprocus:* see prec.] **1.** *a)* to give and get reciprocally *b)* to give, do, feel, etc. (something similar) in return **2.** to move alternately back and forth —**re·cip′ro·ca′tion** *n.* —**re·cip′ro·ca′tive, re·cip′ro·ca·to′ry** (-kə tôr′ē) *adj.* —**re·cip′ro·ca′tor** *n.*

**rec·i·proc·i·ty** (res′ə präs′ə tē) *n., pl.* -ties [< Fr.] **1.** reciprocal state or relationship **2.** mutual exchange; esp., exchange of special privileges between two countries, as mutual reduction of tariffs

**re·cit·al** (ri sīt′'l) *n.* **1.** *a)* a reciting; specif., a telling in detail *b)* the account, story, etc. told **2.** a detailed statement **3.** a musical or dance program given by a soloist, soloists, or a small ensemble —**re·cit′al·ist** *n.*

**rec·i·ta·tion** (res′ə tā′shən) *n.* **1.** a recital (sense 1) **2.** *a)* the speaking aloud in public of something memorized *b)* the piece so presented **3.** a reciting by pupils of answers to questions on a prepared lesson, etc.

**rec·i·ta·tive** (res′ə tə tēv′) *n.* [It. *recitativo* < L. *recitare,* to RECITE] *Music* **1.** a type of declamatory singing, free in rhythm and tempo, as in the dialogue of operas **2.** a work or passage in this style **3.** music for such passages —*adj.* in the style of recitative

**re·cite** (ri sīt′) *vt., vi.* -cit′ed, -cit′ing [< OFr. < L. *recitare:* see RE- & CITE] **1.** to speak aloud, as from memory, (a lesson) in class or (a poem, etc.) before an audience **2.** to tell in detail or narrate (something) —**re·cit′er** *n.*

**reck** (rek) *vi., vt.* [OE. *reccan*] [Archaic] **1.** to have care or concern (*for*) or take heed (*of*) **2.** to concern or be of concern; matter (to)

**reck·less** (rek′lis) *adj.* [see prec. & -LESS] **1.** careless;

heedless **2.** not regarding consequences; rash —**reck′less·ly** *adv.* —**reck′less·ness** *n.*

**reck·on** (rek′ən) *vt.* [OE. *-recenian*] **1.** to count; figure up; compute **2.** *a)* to consider as; regard as being [*reckon* them friends] *b)* to judge; estimate **3.** [Colloq. or Dial.] to suppose —*vi.* **1.** to count up; figure **2.** [Colloq.] to rely (*with on*) **3.** [Colloq.] to suppose —**reckon with 1.** to settle accounts with **2.** to take into consideration

**reck·on·ing** (-iŋ) *n.* **1.** the act of one who reckons; count or computation **2.** a calculated guess **3.** *a)* a bill; account *b)* settlement of an account **4.** the giving of rewards or punishments [day of *reckoning*] **5.** *Naut.* the determination of the position of a ship; esp., *short for* DEAD RECKONING

**re·claim** (ri klām′) *vt.* [< OFr. < L. *reclamare:* see RE- & CLAIM] **1.** to rescue or bring back (someone) from error, vice, etc. **2.** to make (wasteland, etc.) capable of being cultivated or lived on, as by irrigating, etc. **3.** to recover (useful materials) from waste products —*n.* reclamation [beyond *reclaim*] —**re·claim′a·ble** *adj.* —**re·claim′ant, re·claim′er** *n.*

**re-claim** (rē′klām′) *vt.* to claim back; demand the return of; try to get back

**rec·la·ma·tion** (rek′lə mā′shən) *n.* a reclaiming or being reclaimed, as of wasteland or of useful materials from waste products

**re·cline** (ri klīn′) *vt., vi.* -clined′, -clin′ing [< L. < *re-,* back + *clinare,* to lean] to lie or cause to lie back or down; lean back —**rec·li·na·tion** (rek′lə nā′shən) *n.*

**re·clin·er** (-klī′nər) *n.* **1.** one that reclines **2.** an upholstered armchair that can be adjusted for reclining: also **reclining chair**

**rec·luse** (rek′lōōs, ri klōōs′) *adj.* [< OFr. < LL. < L. pp. of *recludere* < *re-,* back + *claudere,* to shut] secluded; solitary —*n.* a person who leads a secluded, solitary life —**re·clu·sion** (ri klōō′zhən) *n.* —**re·clu′sive** *adj.*

**rec·og·ni·tion** (rek′əg nish′ən) *n.* [< L. < pp. of *recognoscere:* see ff.] **1.** *a)* a recognizing or being recognized; acknowledgment *b)* approval, gratitude, etc. [in *recognition* of his services] **2.** formal acceptance by a government of the sovereignty of a newly established state or government **3.** identification of a person or thing as being known to one **4.** notice, as in passing; greeting —**re·cog·ni·to·ry** (ri käg′nə tôr′ē), **re·cog′ni·tive** *adj.*

**re·cog·ni·zance** (ri käg′ni zəns, -kän′i-) *n.* [< OFr. < L. < *re-,* again + *cognoscere,* to know: see COGNITION] *Law* **1.** a bond or obligation of record binding a person to some act, as to appear in court **2.** a sum of money that one must forfeit if this obligation is not fulfilled

**rec·og·nize** (rek′əg nīz′) *vt.* -nized′, -niz′ing [altered (after prec.) < OFr.: see prec.] **1.** to identify as known before **2.** to know by some detail, as of appearance **3.** to be aware of the significance of **4.** to acknowledge the existence, validity, etc. of [to *recognize* a claim] **5.** to accept as a fact; admit [to *recognize* defeat] **6.** to acknowledge as worthy of appreciation or approval **7.** to formally acknowledge the legal standing of (a government or state) **8.** to show acquaintance with (a person) by greeting **9.** to grant (a person) the right to speak, as in a meeting —**rec′og·niz′a·bil′i·ty** *n.* —**rec′og·niz′a·ble** *adj.* —**rec′og·niz′a·bly** *adv.* —**rec′og·niz′er** *n.*

**re·coil** (ri koil′; *also for n., esp. of weapons,* rē′koil′) *vi.* [< OFr. < *re-,* back + *cul* < L. *culus,* the buttocks] **1.** to draw, start, or shrink back, as in fear, surprise, disgust, etc. **2.** to fly back when released, as a spring, or kick back when fired, as a gun **3.** to return as to the starting point or source; react (*on* or *upon*) —*n.* **1.** a recoiling **2.** the state of having recoiled —**re·coil′er** *n.* —**re·coil′less** *adj.*

**re-coil** (rē′koil′) *vt., vi.* to coil anew or again

**rec·ol·lect** (rek′ə lekt′) *vt.* [< L.: see RE- & COLLECT¹] **1.** to call back to mind; remember, esp. with some effort **2.** to recall to (oneself) something temporarily forgotten —*vi.* to remember —**rec′ol·lec′tion** *n.* —**rec′ol·lec′tive** *adj.*

**re-col·lect** (rē′kə lekt′) *vt.* **1.** to collect again (what has been scattered) **2.** to rally (one's courage, etc.) **3.** to compose (oneself): in this sense sometimes written **recollect**

**rec·om·mend** (rek′ə mend′) *vt.* [< ML.: see RE- & COMMEND] **1.** to give in charge; entrust [*recommended* to his care] **2.** to suggest favorably as suited for some function, position, etc. **3.** to make acceptable or pleasing [his charm *recommends* him] **4.** to advise; counsel —**rec′om·mend′a·ble** *adj.* —**rec′om·mend′a·to·ry** *adj.* —**rec′om·mend′er** *n.*

**rec·om·men·da·tion** (-mən dā′shən) *n.* **1.** a recommending **2.** anything that recommends or makes a favorable or pleasing impression; specif., a letter recommending a person or thing **3.** advice; counsel

**re·com·mit** (rē′kə mit′) *vt.* **-mit′ted, -mit′ting** **1.** to commit again **2.** to refer (a question, bill, etc.) back to a committee —**re′com·mit′ment, re′com·mit′tal** *n.*

**rec·om·pense** (rek′əm pens′) *vt.* **-pensed′, -pens′ing** [< MFr. < LL.: see RE- & COMPENSATE] **1.** to repay (a person, etc.); reward **2.** to compensate (a loss, injury, etc.) —*n.* **1.** something given or done in return for something else; requital, reward, etc. **2.** something given or done to make up for a loss, injury, etc.; compensation

**rec·on·cile** (rek′ən sīl′) *vt.* **-ciled′, -cil′ing** [< OFr. < L.: see RE- & CONCILIATE] **1.** to make friendly again **2.** to settle (a quarrel, etc.) **3.** to make (facts, ideas, texts, etc.) consistent or compatible **4.** to make content or acquiescent (*to*) —**rec′on·cil′a·bil′i·ty** *n.* —**rec′on·cil′a·ble** *adj.* —**rec′on·cil′a·bly** *adv.* —**rec′on·cil′i·a′tion** (-sil′ē ā′shən), **rec′on·cile′ment** *n.* —**rec′on·cil′i·a·to·ry** (-sil′ē-ə tôr′ē) *adj.*

**rec·on·dite** (rek′ən dīt′, ri kän′dīt) *adj.* [< L. pp. of *recondere* < *re-*, back + *condere*, to store up, hide] **1.** beyond the grasp of ordinary understanding; profound **2.** dealing with abstruse or difficult subjects **3.** obscure or concealed —**rec′on·dite′ly** *adv.* —**rec′on·dite′ness** *n.*

**re·con·di·tion** (rē′kən dish′ən) *vt.* to put back in good condition by cleaning, repairing, etc.

**re·con·nais·sance** (ri kän′ə səns, -zəns) *n.* [Fr.: see RECOGNIZANCE] an exploratory survey or examination, as in seeking out information about enemy positions

**rec·on·noi·ter** (rē′kə noit′ər, rek′ə-) *vt., vi.* [< Fr. < OFr.: see RECOGNIZANCE] to make a reconnaissance (of): also, chiefly Brit. sp., **rec′on·noi′tre** **-tred, -tring** —**rec′on·noi′ter·er, rec′on·noi′trer** (-noi′trər) *n.*

**re·con·sid·er** (rē′kən sid′ər) *vt., vi.* to consider again; think over, as with a view to changing a decision —**re′con·sid′er·a′tion** *n.*

**re·con·sti·tute** (rē kän′stə toot′, -tyoot′) *vt.* **-tut′ed, -tut′ing** to constitute again or anew; specif., to restore (a dehydrated or condensed substance) to its full liquid form by adding water —**re′con·sti·tu′tion** *n.*

**re·con·struct** (rē′kən strukt′) *vt.* **1.** to construct again; make over **2.** to build up again (something in its original form), as from remaining parts —**re′con·struc′tive** *adj.*

**re·con·struc·tion** (-struk′shən) *n.* **1.** *a)* a reconstructing *b)* something reconstructed **2.** [R-] the period (1867-77) or the process, after the Civil War, of reestablishing the Southern States in the Union

**re·con·vert** (rē′kən vurt′) *vt., vi.* to change back, as to a former status, religion, etc. —**re′con·ver′sion** *n.*

**re·cord** (ri kôrd′; *for n. & adj.,* rek′ərd) *vt.* [< OFr. < L. *recordari,* to remember < *re-,* again + *cor* (gen. *cordis*), heart, mind] **1.** *a)* to put in writing, print, etc. for future use *b)* to make an official note of [to *record* a vote] **2.** *a)* to indicate automatically and permanently, as on a graph [a seismograph *records* earthquakes] *b)* to show, as on a dial **3.** to remain as evidence of **4.** *a)* to register (sound or visual images) in some permanent form, as on a phonograph disc, magnetic tape, etc. for reproduction on a playback device *b)* to register the performance of in this way —*vi.* **1.** to record something **2.** to admit of being recorded —*n.* **1.** the condition of being recorded **2.** *a)* an account of events *b)* anything that serves as evidence of an event, etc. *c)* an official report of public proceedings, as in a court **3.** anything that written evidence is put on or in, as a register, monument, etc. **4.** *a)* the known facts about anyone or anything, as about one's career *b)* the recorded offenses of a person who has been arrested one or more times **5.** a thin, flat, grooved disc for playing on a phonograph **6.** the best performance, highest speed, greatest amount, etc. achieved, esp. when officially recorded —*adj.* establishing a record as the best, largest, etc. [a *record* crop] —**go on record** to state one's opinions publicly or officially —**off the record** confidential(ly) —**on (the) record** publicly declared

**record changer** a phonograph device that automatically sets in place each record from a stack placed on a spindle

**re·cord·er** (ri kôr′dər) *n.* **1.** a public officer who keeps records of deeds or other official papers **2.** a machine or device that records; esp., *same as* TAPE RECORDER **3.** an early form of flute

**re·cord·ing** (ri kôr′diŋ) *adj.* that records —*n.* **1.** the act of one that records **2.** *a)* what is recorded, as on a disc or tape *b)* the record itself

**record player** a phonograph having the pickup, turntable, amplifier, speaker, etc. operate electrically or electronically

**re·count** (ri kount′) *vt.* [< Anglo-Fr.: see RE- & COUNT[1]] to tell in detail; narrate; enumerate —**re·count′-al** *n.*

**re-count** (rē′kount′; *for n.* rē′kount′) *vt.* to count again —*n.* a second or additional count, as of votes: also written **recount**

**re·coup** (ri kōōp′) *vt.* [< Fr. < *re-,* again + *couper,* to cut] **1.** *a)* to make up for [to *recoup* a loss] *b)* to regain [to *recoup* one's health] **2.** to pay back —*n.* a recouping —**re·coup′a·ble** *adj.* —**re·coup′ment** *n.*

**re·course** (rē′kôrs, ri kôrs′) *n.* [< OFr. < L. *recursus,* a running back: see RE- & COURSE] **1.** a turning for aid, safety, etc. [he had *recourse* to the law] **2.** that to which one turns seeking aid, safety, etc. [one's last *recourse*]

**re·cov·er** (ri kuv′ər) *vt.* [< OFr. < L. *recuperare:* see RECUPERATE] **1.** *a)* to get back (something lost, stolen, etc.) *b)* to regain (health, etc.) **2.** to compensate for [to *recover* losses] **3.** *a)* to get (oneself) back to a state of control, balance, etc. *b)* to save (oneself) from a slip, betrayal of feeling, etc. **4.** to reclaim (land from the sea, useful substances from waste, etc.) **5.** *Law* to get or get back by final judgment in a court —*vi.* **1.** to regain health, balance, control, etc. **2.** to save oneself from a slip, self-betrayal, etc. **3.** *Law* to receive judgment in one's favor —**re·cov′er·a·ble** *adj.*

**re-cov·er** (rē′kuv′ər) *vt.* to cover again or anew

**re·cov·er·y** (ri kuv′ər ē) *n., pl.* **-er·ies** the act or an instance of recovering; specif., *a)* a regaining of something lost or stolen *b)* a return to health, consciousness, etc. *c)* a regaining of balance, composure, etc. *d)* a retrieval of a capsule, nose cone, etc. after a spaceflight *e)* the removal of valuable substances from waste material, byproducts, etc.

**rec·re·ant** (rek′rē ənt) *adj.* [OFr. prp. of *recreire,* to surrender allegiance < ML. < L. *re-,* back + *credere,* believe] **1.** *a)* orig., crying for mercy *b)* cowardly **2.** disloyal; traitorous —*n.* **1.** a coward **2.** a disloyal person; traitor —**rec′re·an·cy** *n.* —**rec′re·ant·ly** *adv.*

**rec·re·ate** (rek′rē āt′) *vt.* **-at′ed, -at′ing** [< L. pp. of *recreare:* see RE- & CREATE] to refresh in body or mind —*vi.* to take recreation —**rec′re·a′tive** *adj.*

**re-cre·ate** (rē′krē āt′) *vt.* **-at′ed, -at′ing** to create anew —**re′-cre·a′tion** *n.* —**re′-cre·a′tive** *adj.*

**rec·re·a·tion** (rek′rē ā′shən) *n.* [see RECREATE] **1.** refreshment in body or mind, as after work, by some form of play, amusement, or relaxation **2.** any form of play, amusement, etc. used for this purpose, as games, sports, etc. —**rec′re·a′tion·al** *adj.*

**re·crim·i·nate** (ri krim′ə nāt′) *vi.* **-nat′ed, -nat′ing** [< ML.: see RE- & CRIMINATE] to answer an accuser by accusing him in return —**re·crim′i·na′tion** *n.* —**re·crim′i·na·to′ry** (-nə tôr′ē), **re·crim′i·na′tive** *adj.*

**re·cru·desce** (rē′krōō des′) *vi.* **-desced′, -desc′ing** [< L. < *re-,* again + *crudescere,* to become harsh < *crudus,* raw] to break out again after being relatively inactive —**re′cru·des′cence** *n.* —**re′cru·des′cent** *adj.*

**re·cruit** (ri krōōt′) *vt.* [< Fr. < pp. of *recroître,* to grow again < L. *re-,* again + *crescere,* to grow] **1.** to raise or strengthen (an army, navy, etc.) by enlisting personnel **2.** to enlist (personnel) into an army or navy **3.** *a)* to enlist (new members) for a party, organization, etc. *b)* to hire or engage the services of —*vi.* to enlist new personnel, esp. for a military force —*n.* **1.** a recently enlisted or drafted soldier, sailor, etc. **2.** a new member of any group, etc. —**re·cruit′er** *n.* —**re·cruit′ment** *n.*

**rec. sec.** recording secretary

**rec·tal** (rek′t′l) *adj.* of, for, or near the rectum —**rec′tal·ly** *adv.*

**rec·tan·gle** (rek′taŋ′g′l) *n.* [Fr. < ML.: see RECTI- & AN-GLE[1]] any four-sided plane figure with four right angles

**rec·tan·gu·lar** (rek taŋ′gyə lər) *adj.* **1.** shaped like a rectangle **2.** having right-angled corners, as a building **3.** right-angled —**rec·tan′gu·lar′i·ty** (-lar′ə tē) *n.* —**rec·tan′gu·lar·ly** *adv.*

RECTANGLES

**rec·ti-** [LL. < L. *rectus*] *a combining form meaning* straight, right [*rectilinear*]: also, before a vowel, **rect-**

**rec·ti·fi·er** (rek′tə fī′ər) *n.* **1.** a person or thing that rectifies **2.** *Elec.* a device that converts alternating current into direct current

**rec·ti·fy** (rek′tə fī′) *vt.* **-fied′, -fy′ing** [< MFr. < LL.: see RECTI- & -FY] **1.** to put right; correct **2.** *Chem.* to refine or purify (a liquid) by distillation **3.** *Elec.* to convert (alternating current) to direct current —**rec′ti·fi′a·ble** *adj.* —**rec′ti·fi·ca′tion** *n.*

**rec·ti·lin·e·ar** (rek′tə lin′ē ər) *adj.* [< LL. < *rectus,* straight + *linea,* LINE[1]] **1.** in or forming a straight line **2.** bounded, formed, or characterized by straight lines Also **rec′ti·lin′e·al** —**rec′ti·lin′e·ar·ly** *adv.*

**rec·ti·tude** (rek′tə tōōd′, -tyōōd′) *n.* [MFr. < L. *rectus,* straight] **1.** strict honesty; uprightness of character **2.** correctness of judgment or method

**rec·to** (rek′tō) *n., pl.* **-tos** [< ModL. (*folio*) *recto,* on (the page) to the right] *Printing* any right-hand page of a book; front side of a leaf: opposed to VERSO

RECORDER

**rec·tor** (rek'tər) *n.* [L. < pp. of *regere*, to rule] **1.** a clergyman or minister in charge of a parish, esp. in the Protestant Episcopal Church or an Anglican Church **2.** *R.C.Ch.* *a*) a priest in charge of a seminary, college, etc. *b*) [Brit.] the head priest of a parish **3.** in certain schools, colleges, etc., the head or headmaster —**rec'tor·ate** (-it) *n.* —**rec·to'·ri·al** (-tôr'ē əl) *adj.*

**rec·to·ry** (rek'tər ē) *n., pl.* **-ries** the residence of a clergyman who is a rector

**rec·tum** (rek'təm) *n., pl.* **-tums, -ta** (-tə) [ModL. < L. *rectum* (*intestinum*), straight (intestine)] the lowest, or last, segment of the large intestine, ending at the anus

**re·cum·bent** (ri kum'bənt) *adj.* [< L. < *re-*, back + *cumbere*, to lie down] **1.** lying down; reclining **2.** resting; idle —**re·cum'ben·cy** *n.* —**re·cum'bent·ly** *adv.*

**re·cu·per·ate** (ri kōō'pə rāt', -kyōō'-) *vt.* **-at'ed, -at'ing** [< L. pp. of *recuperare*, to recover] to get back, or recover (losses, health, etc.) —*vi.* **1.** to get well again **2.** to recover losses, etc. —**re·cu'per·a·tive** (-pə rāt'iv, -pər ə tiv) *adj.* —**re·cu'per·a'tor** *n.*

**re·cur** (ri kur') *vi.* **-curred', -cur'ring** [< L. *re-*, back + *currere*, to run] **1.** to have recourse (*to*) **2.** to return in thought, talk, etc. [to *recur* to a topic] **3.** to occur again, as in memory **4.** to happen or appear again or at intervals

**re·cur·rent** (ri kur'ənt) *adj.* **1.** appearing again or periodically **2.** turning back in the opposite direction, as some nerves —**re·cur'rence** *n.* —**re·cur'rent·ly** *adv.*

**re·curve** (ri kurv') *vt., vi.* **-curved', -curv'ing** to curve or bend back or backward —**re·cur·vate** (ri kur'vit, -vāt) *adj.*

**re·cy·cle** (rē sī'k'l) *vt., vi.* **-cled, -cling 1.** to pass through a cycle again, as for treating **2.** to use again and again, as a single supply of water

**red¹** (red) *n.* [OE. *read*] **1.** a primary color varying in hue from that of blood to pink **2.** a pigment producing this color **3.** [*often* R-] a political radical; esp., a communist **4.** anything colored red, as a red checker piece —*adj.* **red'der, red'dest 1.** of the color red **2.** having red hair **3.** *a*) having a reddish skin *b*) florid, flushed, or blushing *c*) bloodshot *d*) sore **4.** [R-] *a*) politically radical; esp., communist *b*) of the Soviet Union —**in the red** in debt or losing money —**see red** [Colloq.] to be or become angry —**red'dish** *adj.* —**red'ly** *adv.* —**red'ness** *n.*

**red²** (red) *vt., vi.* **red, red'ding** *var. of* REDD

**re·dact** (ri dakt') *vt.* [< L. pp. of *redigere*, to reduce to order] to arrange in proper form for publication; edit —**re·dac'tion** *n.* —**re·dac'tor** *n.*

**red algae** a group of red, brownish-red, pink, or purple algae that form shrublike masses in the depths of the oceans

**red·bait** (red'bāt') *vi., vt.* to denounce (a person or group) as being communist, esp. with little or no valid evidence —**red'bait'er** *n.*

**red blood cell** *same as* ERYTHROCYTE: also called **red blood corpuscle**

**red-blood·ed** (red'blud'id) *adj.* high-spirited and strong-willed; vigorous, lusty, etc.

**red·breast** (-brest') *n.* any of several birds with a reddish breast; esp., the American robin and the European robin

**red·bud** (-bud') *n. same as* JUDAS TREE

**red·cap** (-kap') *n.* a porter in a railway station, air terminal, etc.

**red carpet 1.** a long red carpet laid out for important guests to walk on, as at a reception **2.** a very grand welcome and entertainment (with *the*) —**roll out the red carpet (for)** to welcome and entertain in a very grand style —**red'-car'pet** *adj.*

**red·coat** (red'kōt') *n.* a British soldier in a uniform with a red coat, as during the American Revolution

**Red Cross 1.** a red cross on a white ground, emblem of neutrality in war, used since 1864 to mark hospitals, ambulances, etc. **2.** *a*) an international society (in full, **International Red Cross**) for the relief of suffering in time of war or disaster *b*) any national branch of this

**redd** (red) *vt., vi.* **redd** or **redd'ed, redd'ing** [< ? OE. *hreddan*, to free] [Colloq.] to make (a place) tidy (usually with *up*)

**red deer 1.** a deer native to Europe and Asia **2.** the white-tailed deer in its reddish summer coat

**red·den** (red''n) *vt.* to make red —*vi.* to become red; esp., to blush or flush

**re·deem** (ri dēm') *vt.* [< MFr. < L. *redimere* < *re(d)-*, back + *emere*, to get] **1.** to get or buy back; recover **2.** to pay off (a mortgage, etc.) **3.** *a*) to convert (paper money) into coin or bullion *b*) to convert (stocks, bonds, etc.) into cash *c*) to turn in (trading stamps or coupons) for a prize, premium, etc. **4.** *a*) to set free by paying a ransom *b*) to deliver from sin and its penalties **5.** to fulfill (a promise or pledge) **6.** *a*) to make amends or atone for *b*) to restore (oneself) to favor by making amends *c*) to make worthwhile —**re·deem'a·ble, re·demp'ti·ble** (-demp'tə b'l) *adj.* —**re·deem'er** *n.*

**re·demp·tion** (ri demp'shən) *n.* [OFr. < L. < pp. of *redimere:* see prec.] **1.** a redeeming or being redeemed **2.** something that redeems —**re·demp'tion·al** *adj.* —**re·demp'tive, re·demp'to·ry** *adj.*

**re·de·ploy** (rē'di ploi') *vt., vi.* to move (troops, etc.) from one front or area to another —**re'de·ploy'ment** *n.*

**red-eye** (red'ī') *adj.* [from the bloodshot eyes of one who has not slept] [Slang] designating a late-night or all-night commercial airline flight —*n.* [Slang] such a flight

**red fox 1.** the common European fox with reddish fur **2.** the similar related fox of N. America

**red-hand·ed** (red'han'did) *adv., adj.* **1.** with hands covered with a victim's blood **2.** in the very act of committing a crime **3.** in a situation that makes one seem guilty

**red·head** (red'hed') *n.* **1.** a person with red hair **2.** a N. American duck related to the canvasback: the male has a red head —**red'head'ed** *adj.*

**redheaded woodpecker** a N. American woodpecker with a bright-red head and neck

**red herring 1.** a smoked herring **2.** something used to turn attention away from the basic issue: from drawing a herring across the trace in hunting, to confuse the hounds

**red-hot** (red'hät') *adj.* **1.** hot enough to glow; very hot **2.** very excited, angry, etc. **3.** very new; up-to-the-minute [*red-hot* news] —*n.* [Colloq.] a frankfurter

**red·in·gote** (red'iŋ gōt') *n.* [Fr., altered < E. *riding coat*] **1.** formerly, a man's long, full-skirted overcoat **2.** a long, lightweight coat, open down the front, worn by women

**red·in·te·grate** (red in'tə grāt', ri din'-) *vt.* **-grat'ed, -grat'ing** [< L. pp. of *redintegrare:* see RE- & INTEGRATE] to make whole again; reunite —**red·in'te·gra'tion** *n.*

**re·di·rect** (rē'di rekt', -dī-) *vt.* to direct again or direct to a different place —*adj. Law* designating the examination of one's own witness again, after his cross-examination by the opposing lawyer —**re'di·rec'tion** *n.*

**re·dis·count** (rē dis'kount) *vt.* to discount (esp. commercial paper) for a second time —*n.* **1.** a rediscounting **2.** rediscounted commercial paper —**re'dis·count'a·ble** *adj.*

**re·dis·trict** (rē dis'trikt) *vt.* to divide anew into districts, esp. so as to reapportion representatives

**red lead** red oxide of lead, $Pb_3O_4$, used in making paint, in glassmaking, etc.

**red-let·ter** (red'let'ər) *adj.* designating a memorable or joyous day or event: from the custom of marking holidays on the calendar in red ink

**red light 1.** any warning signal **2.** a red stoplight

**red·lin·ing** (red'lī'niŋ) *n.* [from the practice of outlining such areas in red on a map] the systematic refusal by lending institutions or insurance companies to issue mortgage loans or insurance on property in certain neighborhoods regarded by them as deteriorating

**red man** a North American Indian

**red meat** meat that is red before cooking; esp., beef or mutton as distinguished from pork, veal, poultry, etc.

**re·do** (rē dōō') *vt.* **-did', -done', -do'ing 1.** to do again or do over **2.** to redecorate (a room, etc.)

**red·o·lent** (red''l ənt) *adj.* [OFr. < L. prp. of *redolere* < *re(d)-*, intens. + *olere*, to smell] **1.** sweet-smelling; fragrant **2.** smelling (*of*) [*redolent* of tar] **3.** suggestive (*of*) —**red'o·lence, red'o·len·cy** *n.* —**red'o·lent·ly** *adv.*

**Re·don·do Beach** (rə dän'dō) [< Sp. *redondo*, circular] city in SW Calif.: suburb of Los Angeles: pop. 57,000

**re·dou·ble** (rē dub''l) *vt.* **-bled, -bling** [MFr. *redoubler:* see RE- & DOUBLE] **1.** *a*) to increase fourfold *b*) to make twice as much or twice as great *c*) to make much greater **2.** to refold —*vi.* **1.** *a*) to become twice as great or twice as much *b*) to increase fourfold **2.** [Archaic] to reecho **3.** to turn sharply backward, as on one's tracks **4.** *Bridge* to double a bid that an opponent has already doubled —*n. Bridge* a redoubling

**re·doubt** (ri dout') *n.* [< Fr. < It. *ridotto* < ML. *reductus*, orig. pp. of L. *reducere:* see REDUCE] **1.** a breastwork outside or within a fortification **2.** any stronghold

**re·doubt·a·ble** (-ə b'l) *adj.* [< MFr. < *redouter*, to fear < L. *re-*, intens. + *dubitare*, to doubt] **1.** inspiring fear **2.** commanding respect —**re·doubt'a·bly** *adv.*

**re·dound** (ri dound') *vi.* [< MFr. < L. *redundare*, to overflow < *re(d)-*, intens. + *undare*, to surge] **1.** to have a result (*to* the credit or discredit of someone or something) **2.** to come back; recoil (*upon*): said of honor or disgrace

**red pepper 1.** a plant with a red, many-seeded fruit, as the cayenne **2.** the fruit **3.** the ground fruit or seeds, used for seasoning

**red·poll** (red'pōl') *n.* any of a number of finches the males of which usually have a red crown

**re·dress** (ri dres′; *for n., usually* rē′dres) *vt.* [< OFr.: see RE- & DRESS] **1.** to set right; rectify, as by making compensation for (a wrong, etc.) **2.** [Now Rare] to make amends to —*n.* **1.** compensation, as for a wrong **2.** a redressing —**re·dress′a·ble** *adj.* —**re·dress′er** *n.*

**re-dress** (rē′dres′) *vt.* to dress again

**Red River 1.** river flowing along the Tex.-Okla. border, through Ark. & La. into the Mississippi **2.** river flowing along the N.Dak.-Minn. border into Lake Winnipeg in Manitoba: in full, **Red River of the North**

**red salmon** *same as* SOCKEYE

**Red Sea** sea between NE Africa & W Arabia, connected with the Mediterranean Sea by the Suez Canal

**red·shirt** (red′shurt′) *vt.* [from red shirts worn by a scrimmage team] [Slang] to withdraw (a player) from the varsity team so that he will be eligible to play an extra year later —*n.* such a player

**red snapper** a reddish, deep-water food fish, found in the Gulf of Mexico and in adjacent Atlantic waters

**red spider** a small, red, vegetarian mite

**red squirrel** a N. American tree squirrel, with reddish fur

**red·start** (red′stärt′) *n.* [RED¹ + obs. *start*, tail] **1.** an American fly-catching warbler **2.** a small European warbler with a reddish tail

**red tape** [from the tape used to tie official papers] **1.** official forms and routines **2.** rigid adherence to routine and regulations, causing delay in getting business done

**red tide** a reddish discoloration of sea waters, caused by large numbers of certain red protozoans that release poisons that kill fishes and other organisms

**red·top** (-täp′) *n.* a grass grown in the cooler parts of N. America for hay, pasturage, and lawns

**re·duce** (ri dōōs′, -dyōōs′) *vt.* -**duced**′, -**duc**′**ing** [< L. < *re-*, back + *ducere*, to lead] **1.** *a)* to lessen in any way, as in size, amount, value, price, etc. *b)* to put into a simpler or more concentrated form **2.** to bring into a certain order; systematize **3.** to change to a different form, as by melting, grinding, etc. **4.** to lower, as in rank; demote **5.** *a)* to bring to order, obedience, etc., as by persuasion or force *b)* to subdue or conquer **6.** *a)* to bring into difficult circumstances *[reduced* to poverty] *b)* to compel by need *[reduced* to stealing] **7.** to make thin **8.** *Arith.* to change in denomination or form without changing in value *[to reduce* 4/8 to 1/2] **9.** *Chem. a)* to decrease the positive valence of (an atom or ion) *b)* to increase the number of electrons of (an atom or ion) *c)* to remove the oxygen from *d)* to combine with hydrogen *e)* to bring into the metallic state by removing nonmetallic elements **10.** *Photog.* to weaken the density of (a negative) **11.** *Surgery* to restore to normal position *[to reduce* a fracture] —*vi.* **1.** to become reduced **2.** to lose weight, as by being on a diet —**re·duc′er** *n.* —**re·duc′i·bil′i·ty** *n.* —**re·duc′i·ble** *adj.* —**re·duc′i·bly** *adv.*

**reducing agent** *Chem.* any substance that reduces another substance and is itself oxidized in the process

‡**re·duc·ti·o ad ab·sur·dum** (ri duk′tē ō′ ad ab sur′dəm, -shē ō′) [L., lit., reduction to absurdity] *Logic* the disproof of a proposition by showing the logical conclusions drawn from it to be absurd

**re·duc·tion** (ri duk′shən) *n.* **1.** *a)* a reducing or being reduced *b)* the amount of this **2.** anything made or brought about by reducing, as a smaller copy —**re·duc′tion·al** *adj.* —**re·duc′tive** *adj.* —**re·duc′tive·ly** *adv.*

**re·dun·dan·cy** (ri dun′dən sē) *n., pl.* -**cies** **1.** a being redundant **2.** an overabundance **3.** the use of redundant words **4.** the part of a statement that is redundant or unnecessary Also **re·dun′dance**

**re·dun·dant** (-dənt) *adj.* [< L. prp. of *redundare:* see REDOUND] **1.** more than enough; excess; superfluous **2.** wordy **3.** unnecessary to the meaning: said of words and affixes —**re·dun′dant·ly** *adv.*

**re·du·pli·cate** (ri dōō′plə kāt′, -dyōō′-; *for adj. & n., usually* -kit) *vt.* -**cat′ed**, -**cat′ing** [< ML.: see RE- & DUPLICATE] **1.** to redouble, double, or repeat **2.** to double (a syllable or word) to form a new word (as *tom-tom*), sometimes with changes (as *chitchat*) —*vi.* to become reduplicated —*adj.* reduplicated; doubled —*n.* something reduplicated —**re·du′pli·ca′tion** *n.* —**re·du′pli·ca′tive** *adj.*

**red·wing** (red′wiŋ′) *n.* **1.** a small European thrush with an orange-red patch on the underside of the wings **2.** *same as* RED-WINGED BLACKBIRD

**red-winged blackbird** a N. American blackbird with a bright-red patch on the top surface of the wings in the male: also **redwing blackbird**

**red·wood** (-wood′) *n.* **1.** a giant evergreen having enduring, soft wood, found on the coast of California and S Oregon **2.** *same as* BIG TREE **3.** the wood of these trees

**Redwood City** [after prec.] city in W Calif., on San Francisco Bay: suburb of San Francisco: pop. 55,000

**re·ech·o, re-ech·o** (rē ek′ō) *vt., vi.* -**ech′oed**, -**ech′o·ing** to echo back or again; resound —*n., pl.* -**ech′oes** the echo of an echo Also **re·ēch′o**

**reed** (rēd) *n.* [OE. *hreod*] **1.** *a)* any of various tall, slender grasses growing in wet or marshy land *b)* the stem of any of these *c)* such plants collectively **2.** a rustic musical pipe made from a hollow stem **3.** *Music a)* a thin strip of some flexible substance placed within the opening of the mouthpiece of certain wind instruments, as the clarinet: when vibrated by the breath, it produces a musical tone *b)* an instrument with a reed *c)* in some organs, a similar device that vibrates in a current of air

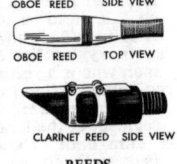
OBOE REED    SIDE VIEW

OBOE REED    TOP VIEW

CLARINET REED    SIDE VIEW

REEDS

**Reed** (rēd), **Walter** 1851-1902; U.S. army surgeon & bacteriologist

**reed organ** an organ with a set of free metal reeds instead of pipes to produce the tones

**re·ed·u·cate, re-ed·u·cate** (rē ej′ə kāt′) *vt.* -**cat′ed**, -**cat′-ing** to educate anew, esp. so as to rehabilitate or adapt to new situations: also **re·ĕd′u·cate′** —**re·ed′u·ca′tion, re-ed′u·ca′tion** *n.* —**re·ed′u·ca′tive, re-ed′u·ca′tive** *adj.*

**reed·y** (rēd′ē) *adj.* **reed′i·er, reed′i·est 1.** full of reeds **2.** made of reed or reeds **3.** like a reed; slender, fragile, etc. **4.** sounding like a reed instrument; thin; piping —**reed′i·ly** *adv.* —**reed′i·ness** *n.*

**reef¹** (rēf) *n.* [prob. < ON. *rif*, a rib] a ridge of rock, coral, or sand at or near the surface of the water

**reef²** (rēf) *n.* [< or akin to prec.] **1.** a part of a sail which can be folded and tied down to reduce the area exposed to the wind **2.** the act of reefing —*vt.* **1.** to reduce (a sail) by taking in part of it **2.** to lower (a spar or mast) or reduce the projection of (a bowsprit)

**reef·er** (rē′fər) *n.* **1.** a person who reefs **2.** a short, thick, double-breasted coat like a seaman's jacket **3.** [from the rolled appearance of a *reef* (of a sail)] [Slang] a marijuana cigarette

**reef knot** a square knot used for reefing

**reek** (rēk) *n.* [OE. *rec*] **1.** vapor; fume **2.** a strong, unpleasant smell; stench —*vi.* **1.** to fume **2.** to have a strong, offensive smell **3.** to be permeated with anything very unpleasant —*vt.* to emit or exude (vapor, fumes, etc.) —**reek′y** *adj.*

**reel¹** (rēl) *vi.* [< the *n.*] **1.** to give way or fall back; sway or stagger as from being struck **2.** to lurch or stagger about, as from drunkenness **3.** to go around and around; whirl **4.** to feel dizzy —*vt.* to cause to reel —*n.* [OE. *hreol*] a reeling motion; whirl, stagger, etc.

**reel²** (rēl) *n.* [prob. < REEL¹, *n.*] **1.** *a)* a lively Scottish dance *b)* *same as* VIRGINIA REEL **2.** music for either of these

**reel³** (rēl) *n.* [OE. *hreol*] **1.** a frame or spool on which thread, wire, film, etc. is wound **2.** such a frame on a fishing rod for winding line **3.** the quantity of wire, thread, film, etc. usually wound on one reel **4.** in a lawn mower, a set of spiral steel blades rotating on a horizontal bar —*vt., vi.* to wind on a reel —**reel in 1.** to wind on a reel **2.** to pull in (a fish) by winding a line on a reel —**reel off** to tell, write, etc. easily and quickly —**reel out** to unwind from a reel —**(right) off the reel** without hesitation

**re·en·force, re-en·force** (rē′in fôrs′) *vt.* -**forced′**, -**forc′ing** *same as* REINFORCE: also **re·ĕn′force′**

**re·en·try, re-en·try** (rē en′trē) *n., pl.* -**tries 1.** a reentering; specif., a coming back, as of a space vehicle, into the earth's atmosphere **2.** a second or repeated entry **3.** *Bridge, Whist* a card that will win a trick and regain the lead Also **re·ĕn′try**

**reeve¹** (rēv) *n.* [OE. *gerefa*] **1.** in English history, *a)* the chief officer of a town or district *b)* the overseer of a manor; steward **2.** the elected head of a town council in certain Canadian provinces

**reeve²** (rēv) *vt.* **reeved** or **rove, rove** or **rov′en, reev′ing** [prob. < Du. *reven*] *Naut.* **1.** to slip (a rope, etc.) through a block, ring, etc. **2.** *a)* to pass in, through, or around something *b)* to fasten by so doing **3.** to pass a rope through (a block or pulley)

**ref** (ref) *n., vt., vi. same as* REFEREE

**ref. 1.** referee **2.** reference **3.** reformed

**re·fec·tion** (ri fek′shən) *n.* [OFr. < L. < pp. of *reficere* < *re-*, again + *facere*, to make] **1.** food or drink taken to refresh oneself **2.** a light meal

**re·fec·to·ry** (-tər ē) *n., pl.* -**ries** a dining hall in a monastery, convent, college, etc.

**re·fer** (ri fur′) *vt.* -**ferred′**, -**fer′ring** [< MFr. < L. *referre* < *re-*, back + *ferre*, to bear] **1.** to assign or attribute (*to*) as cause or origin **2.** to assign or regard as belonging (*to* a kind, class, etc.) **3.** to submit (a quarrel, etc.) for settlement **4.** to direct (to someone or something) for aid, information, etc. —*vi.* **1.** to relate or apply (*to*) **2.** to direct attention, or make reference (*to*) [*to refer* to an earlier event] **3.** to turn for information, aid, etc. (*to*) [*to refer* to a map] —**ref·er·a·ble** (ref′ər ə b′l), **re·fer′ra·ble, re·fer′ri·ble** (ri fur′-) *adj.* —**re·fer′rer** *n.*

**ref·er·ee** (ref′ə rē′) *n.* **1.** a person to whom something is referred for decision **2.** an official who enforces the rules in certain sports contests **3.** *Law* a person appointed by a court to study, and report on, a matter —*vt., vi.* **-eed′, -ee′ing** to act as referee (in)

**ref·er·ence** (ref′ər əns, ref′rəns) *n.* **1.** a referring or being referred **2.** relation; regard [in *reference* to his letter] **3.** *a)* the direction of attention to a person or thing *b)* a mention or allusion **4.** *a)* an indication, as in a book, of some other work to be consulted *b)* the work so indicated *c)* a number or symbol (in full, **reference mark**) directing the reader to a footnote, etc. **5.** *a)* the giving of the name of a person who can offer information or recommendation *b)* the person so indicated *c)* a written statement giving the qualifications, abilities, etc. of someone seeking a position, etc. **6.** *a)* a source of information: often attributive [*reference* books] *b)* a book, etc. used for reference —*vt.* **-enced, -enc·ing** to provide with references —**make reference to** refer to; mention —**ref′er·en′tial** (-ə ren′shəl) *adj.* —**ref′er·en′tial·ly** *adv.*

**ref·er·en·dum** (ref′ə ren′dəm) *n., pl.* **-dums** or **-da** (-də) [ModL. < L., gerund of *referre:* see REFER] **1.** the submission of a law, proposed or already in effect, to a direct vote of the people **2.** the right of the people to vote on such laws, overruling the legislature **3.** the vote itself

**ref·er·ent** (ref′ər ənt) *n.* something referred to; specif., *Linguis.* the thing referred to by a term or expression

**re·fer·ral** (ri fur′əl) *n.* **1.** a referring or being referred, as for professional service **2.** a person who is referred or directed to another person, an agency, etc.

**re·fill** (rē fil′; *for n.* rē′fil) *vt., vi.* to fill again —*n.* a new filling; esp., *a)* a unit to replace the used-up contents of a container *b)* any additional filling of a prescription for medicine —**re·fill′a·ble** *adj.*

**re·fi·nance** (rē′fə nans′, rē fi′nans) *vt.* **-nanced′, -nanc′ing** to finance again; specif., to provide or obtain a new loan or more capital for

**re·fine** (ri fīn′) *vt., vi.* **-fined′, -fin′ing** [RE- + FINE¹, *v.*] **1.** to free or become free from impurities, dross, etc.; purify **2.** to free or become free from imperfection, coarseness, etc.; make or become more polished **3.** to make or become more subtle, as in thinking or speaking —**refine on** (or **upon**) to improve, as by adding refinements —**re·fin′er** *n.*

**re·fined** (ri fīnd′) *adj.* **1.** made free from impurities; purified **2.** free from coarseness; cultivated; elegant **3.** characterized by great subtlety, precision, etc.

**re·fine·ment** (ri fīn′mənt) *n.* **1.** *a)* a refining or being refined *b)* the result of this **2.** delicacy or elegance of language, speech, manners, etc.; polish **3.** a development; improvement; elaboration **4.** a fine distinction; subtlety

**re·fin·er·y** (ri fīn′ər ē) *n., pl.* **-er·ies** an establishment or plant for refining, or purifying, such raw materials as oil, metal, sugar, etc.

**re·fin·ish** (rē fin′ish) *vt.* to give a new surface to (wood, etc.) —**re·fin′ish·er** *n.*

**re·fit** (rē fit′; *also for n.* rē′fit) *vt., vi.* **-fit′ted, -fit′ting** to make or be made ready or fit for use again, as by repairing, reequipping, etc. —*n.* an act or instance of refitting

**refl. 1.** reflection **2.** reflex **3.** reflexive

**re·flect** (ri flekt′) *vt.* [< MFr. < L. < *re-*, back + *flectere*, to bend] **1.** to bend or throw back (light, heat, or sound) **2.** to give back an image of; mirror or reproduce **3.** to bring back as a consequence (with *on*) [deeds that *reflect* honor on him] **4.** to express or show [skills that *reflect* years of training] **5.** to recollect or realize after thought (*that*) **6.** to fold or turn back: *usually used in pp.* —*vi.* **1.** to be thrown back [light *reflecting* from the water] **2.** to throw back light, heat, etc. [a *reflecting* surface] **3.** *a)* to give back an image *b)* to be mirrored **4.** to think seriously; contemplate (*on* or *upon*) **5.** to cast blame or discredit (*on* or *upon*)

**re·flec·tance** (-flek′t'ns) *n. Physics* the ratio of the total electromagnetic radiation, usually light, reflected by a surface to the total striking the surface

**re·flec·tion** (ri flek′shən) *n.* **1.** a reflecting or being reflected **2.** the throwing back by a surface of sound, light, etc. **3.** anything reflected; specif., an image; likeness **4.** *a)* serious thought; contemplation *b)* an idea, remark, etc. that comes from such thought **5.** *a)* blame; discredit *b)* a statement casting, or an action bringing, blame or discredit **6.** *Anat.* a bending back on itself —**re·flec′tion·al** *adj.*

**re·flec·tive** (-tiv) *adj.* **1.** reflecting **2.** of or produced by reflection **3.** meditative; thoughtful —**re·flec′tive·ly** *adv.* —**re·flec′tive·ness**, **re′flec·tiv′i·ty** *n.*

**re·flec·tor** (-tər) *n.* **1.** a person or thing that reflects; esp., a surface, object, or device that reflects radiant energy, as light, sound, etc. **2.** a reflecting telescope: see TELESCOPE

**re·flex** (rē′fleks; *for v.* ri fleks′) *n.* [< L. pp. of *reflectere:* see REFLECT] **1.** reflection, as of light **2.** a reflected image or reproduction **3.** *a) Physiol.* a reflex action *b)* any quick, automatic or habitual response *c)* [*pl.*] ability to react quickly and effectively [a boxer with good *reflexes*] —*adj.* **1.** turned or bent back **2.** coming in reaction; esp., *Physiol.* designating or of an involuntary action, as a sneeze, resulting when a stimulus carried to a nerve center is directly transmitted to the muscle or gland that responds **3.** *Geom.* designating an angle greater than a straight angle (180°) —*vt.* to bend, turn, or fold back —**re′flex·ly** *adv.*

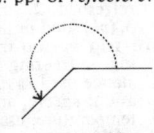

REFLEX ANGLE

**re·flex·ion** (ri flek′shən) *n. Brit. var. of* REFLECTION

**re·flex·ive** (-siv) *adj.* **1.** reflex **2.** *Gram. a)* designating a verb whose subject and direct object refer to the same person or thing (e.g., *wash* in "I wash myself") *b)* designating a pronoun used as the direct object of such a verb, as *myself* in the above example —*n.* a reflexive verb or pronoun —**re·flex′ive·ly** *adv.* —**re·flex′ive·ness**, **re·flex·iv′i·ty** (rē′flek siv′ə tē) *n.*

**re·for·est** (rē fôr′ist, -fär′-) *vt., vi.* to plant new trees on (land once forested) —**re′for·est·a′tion** *n.*

**re·form** (ri fôrm′) *vt.* [< OFr. < L. *reformare:* see RE- & FORM] **1.** to make better by removing faults; correct [to *reform* a calendar] **2.** *a)* to make better by stopping abuses, introducing better procedures, etc. *b)* to put a stop to (abuses, etc.) **3.** to cause (a person) to give up misconduct and behave better —*vi.* to become better; give up one's bad ways —*n.* **1.** a correction of faults or evils, as in government or society **2.** an improvement in character and conduct —*adj.* [R-] designating or of a movement in Judaism that emphasizes its ethical aspects rather than traditional ritual —**re·form′a·ble** *adj.* —**re·form′a·tive** *adj.* —**re·formed′** *adj.*

**re-form** (rē′fôrm′) *vt., vi.* to form again

**ref·or·ma·tion** (ref′ər mā′shən) *n.* **1.** a reforming or being reformed **2.** [R-] the 16th-cent. religious movement that aimed at reforming the Roman Catholic Church and resulted in establishing the Protestant churches —**ref′or·ma′tion·al** *adj.*

**re·form·a·to·ry** (ri fôr′mə tôr′ē) *adj.* reforming or aiming at reform —*n., pl.* **-ries 1.** an institution to which young law offenders are sent for training and discipline intended to reform them: also **reform school 2.** a penitentiary for women

**re·form·er** (ri fôr′mər) *n.* a person who seeks to bring about reform, esp. political or social reform

**re·form·ism** (-miz′m) *n.* the practice or advocacy of reform, esp. political or social reform —**re·form′ist** *n., adj.*

**re·fract** (ri frakt′) *vt.* [< L. *refractus*, pp. of *refringere* < *re-*, back + *frangere*, to break] **1.** to cause (a ray or wave of light, heat, or sound) to undergo refraction **2.** *Optics* to measure the degree of refraction of (an eye or lens) —**re·frac′tive** *adj.* —**re·frac′tive·ly** *adv.* —**re·frac·tiv·i·ty** (rē′frak tiv′ə tē), **re·frac′tive·ness** *n.*

**re·frac·tion** (ri frak′shən) *n.* **1.** the bending of a ray or wave of light, heat, or sound, as it passes obliquely from one medium to another of different density **2.** *Optics* the ability of the eye to refract light entering it, so as to form an image on the retina

**re·frac·tor** (ri frak′tər) *n.* **1.** something that refracts **2.** a refracting telescope: see TELESCOPE

**re·frac·to·ry** (ri frak′tər ē) *adj.* [< L. < *refractus:* see REFRACT] **1.** hard to manage; stubborn; obstinate **2.** resistant to heat; hard to melt or work: said of ores or metals **3.** not yielding to treatment, as a disease —**re·frac′to·ri·ly** *adv.* —**re·frac′to·ri·ness** *n.*

**re·frain¹** (ri frān′) *vi.* [< OFr. < L. < *re-*, back + *frenare*, to curb < *frenum*, a rein] to hold back; keep oneself (*from* doing something); forbear

**re·frain²** (ri frān′) *n.* [MFr., ult. < L. *refringere:* see REFRACT] **1.** a phrase or verse repeated at intervals in a song or poem, as after each stanza **2.** music for this

**re·fran·gi·ble** (ri fran′jə b'l) *adj.* [< RE- + L. *frangere*, to break + -IBLE] that can be refracted, as light rays —**re·fran·gi·bil′i·ty**, **re·fran′gi·ble·ness** *n.*

**re·fresh** (ri fresh′) *vt.* [< OFr.: see RE- & FRESH¹] **1.** to make fresh by cooling, wetting, etc. [rains *refreshing* parched plants] **2.** to make (another or oneself) feel cooler, stronger, etc., as by food, drink, or sleep **3.** to replenish, as by new supplies, etc. **4.** to revive (the memory, etc.) —*vi.* **1.** to become fresh again; revive **2.** to take refreshment, as food or drink —**re·fresh′er** *n.* —**re·fresh′ing** *adj.* —**re·fresh′ing·ly** *adv.*

**refresher course** a course of study reviewing material previously studied

**re·fresh·ment** (ri fresh'mənt) *n.* **1.** a refreshing or being refreshed **2.** something that refreshes, as food, drink, etc. **3.** [*pl.*] food or drink or both, esp. when not a full meal

**re·frig·er·ant** (ri frij'ər ənt) *adj.* **1.** that refrigerates; cooling or freezing **2.** reducing heat or fever —*n.* **1.** a substance used to reduce fever **2.** a substance used in refrigeration; specif., any of various liquids that vaporize at a low temperature, used in mechanical refrigeration

**re·frig·er·ate** (-ə rāt') *vt.* **-at'ed, -at'ing** [< L. pp. of *refrigerare* < re-, intens. + *frigerare*, to cool < *frigus*, cold] **1.** to make or keep cool or cold; chill **2.** to preserve (food, etc.) by keeping cold or freezing —**re·frig'er·a'tion** *n.* — **re·frig'er·a'tive, re·frig'er·a·to'ry** *adj.*

**re·frig·er·a·tor** (-rāt'ər) *n.* something that refrigerates; esp., a box, cabinet, or room in which food, etc. is kept cool, as by ice or mechanical refrigeration

**reft** (reft) *adj.* robbed or deprived (*of* something); bereft

**ref·uge** (ref'yōōj) *n.* [< OFr. < L., ult. < *re-*, back + *fugere*, to flee] **1.** shelter or protection from danger, difficulty, etc. **2.** a place of safety; shelter; safe retreat

**ref·u·gee** (ref'yoo jē', ref'yoo jē') *n.* a person who flees from his home or country to seek refuge elsewhere, as in a time of war, persecution, etc.

**re·ful·gent** (ri ful'jənt) *adj.* [< L. prp. of *refulgere*: see RE- & FULGENT] shining; radiant; resplendent —**re·ful'gence, re·ful'gen·cy** *n.* —**re·ful'gent·ly** *adv.*

**re·fund**[1] (ri fund') *for n.* rē'fund') *vt., vi.* [< MFr. < L. < *re-*, back + *fundere*, to pour] to give back (money, etc.); repay —*n.* the act of refunding or the amount refunded; repayment —**re·fund'a·ble** *adj.*

**re·fund**[2] (rē'fund') *vt.* to fund again or anew; specif., *Finance* to use borrowed money, as from the sale of a bond issue, to pay back (a loan)

**re·fur·bish** (ri fur'bish) *vt.* [RE- + FURBISH] to brighten, freshen, or polish up again; renovate —**re·fur'bish·ment** *n.*

**re·fus·al** (ri fyoo'z'l) *n.* **1.** the act of refusing **2.** the right or chance to accept or refuse something before it is offered to another; option

**re·fuse**[1] (ri fyooz') *vt.* **-fused', -fus'ing** [< OFr. *refuser*, ult. < L. pp. of *refundere*: see REFUND[1]] **1.** to decline to accept; reject **2.** to decline to do, give, grant, obey, etc.; deny [*to refuse* a request, to *refuse* to go] **3.** to stop short at (a fence, etc.) without jumping it: said of a horse —*vi.* to decline to accept, agree to, or do something —**re·fus'er** *n.*

**ref·use**[2] (ref'yoos, -yooz) *n.* [< OFr. pp. of *refuser*: see prec.] anything thrown away or rejected as worthless or useless; waste; rubbish —*adj.* thrown away or rejected as worthless or useless

**re·fute** (ri fyoot') *vt.* **-fut'ed, -fut'ing** [L. *refutare*, to repel: see RE- & CONFUTE] **1.** to prove (a person) to be wrong; confute **2.** to prove (an argument or statement) to be false or wrong, by argument or evidence —**re·fut'a·ble** (-fyoot'ə b'l, ref'yə tə-) *adj.* —**re·fut' a·bly** *adv.* —**ref·u·ta·tion** (ref'yə tā'shən), **re·fut'al** *n.* —**re·fut'er** *n.*

**reg. 1.** regiment **2.** region **3.** register **4.** registered **5.** registrar **6.** regular **7.** regulation

**re·gain** (ri gān') *vt.* **1.** to get back again; recover **2.** to succeed in reaching again; get back to

**re·gal** (rē'gəl) *adj.* [MFr. < L. *regalis* < *rex* (gen. *regis*), a king] **1.** of a king; royal **2.** characteristic of, like, or fit for a king; splendid, stately, etc. —**re·gal·i·ty** (rē gal'ə tē) *n.* — **re'gal·ly** *adv.*

**re·gale** (ri gāl') *vt.* **-galed', -gal'ing** [< Fr. < *ré-* (see RE-) + OFr. *gale*, joy] **1.** to entertain by providing a splendid feast **2.** to delight with something pleasing or amusing —*vi.* to feast —**re·gale'ment** *n.* —**re·gal'er** *n.*

**re·ga·li·a** (ri gāl'yə, -gā'lē ə) *n.pl.* [L., neut. pl. of *regalis*: see REGAL] **1.** the emblems and insignia of kingship, as a crown, scepter, etc. **2.** the insignia or decorations of any rank, society, etc. **3.** splendid clothes; finery

**re·gard** (ri gärd') *n.* [< OFr. < *regarder*: see RE- & GUARD] **1.** a firm, fixed look; gaze **2.** consideration; concern [have *regard* for your health] **3.** respect and affection; esteem [to have high *regard* for one's teachers] **4.** reference; relation [in *regard* to your plan] **5.** [*pl.*] good wishes; respects [give my *regards* to Bill] —*vt.* **1.** to look at with a firm, steady gaze **2.** to take into account; consider **3.** [Archaic] to give attentive heed to **4.** to hold in affection and respect **5.** to think of in a certain light [to *regard* taxes as a burden] **6.** to have relation to; concern [this *regards* your welfare] —*vi.* to look or pay heed —**as regards** concerning —**without regard to** without considering

**re·gard·ful** (-fəl) *adj.* **1.** mindful (*of*) **2.** respectful

**re·gard·ing** (-iŋ) *prep.* with regard to; concerning; about

**re·gard·less** (-lis) *adj.* heedless; careless —*adv.* [Colloq.] without regard for objections, difficulties, etc.; anyway — **regardless of** in spite of —**re·gard'less·ly** *adv.*

**re·gat·ta** (ri gät'ə, -gat'-) *n.* [It.] **1.** a boat race **2.** a series of such races

**re·gen·cy** (rē'jən sē) *n., pl.* **-cies 1.** the position, function,

or authority of a regent or group of regents **2.** a group of men serving as regents **3.** a country governed by a regent or a group of regents **4.** the time during which a regent or regency governs; specif., **[R-]** in England, the period between 1811 and 1820

**re·gen·er·ate** (ri jen'ər it; *for v.* -ə rāt') *adj.* [< L. pp. of *regenerare*: see RE- & GENERATE] **1.** spiritually reborn **2.** renewed or restored —*vt.* **-at'ed, -at'ing 1.** to cause to be spiritually reborn **2.** to cause to be completely reformed or improved **3.** to bring into existence again; reestablish **4.** *Biol.* to grow anew (a part to replace one hurt or lost) **5.** *Electronics* to increase the amplification of (a signal) by feeding energy back from an amplifier output to its input **6.** *Physics* to restore (a battery, etc.) to its original state or properties —*vi.* **1.** to form again, or be made anew **2.** to be regenerated, or spiritually reborn —**re·gen'er·a·cy** (-ə sē) *n.* —**re·gen'er·a'tion** *n.* —**re·gen'er·a'tive** *adj.*

**re·gent** (rē'jənt) *n.* [MFr. < ML. < L. prp. of *regere*, to rule] acting in place of a king or ruler [a prince *regent*] —*n.* **1.** a person appointed to rule a monarchy when the sovereign is absent, too young, or incapacitated **2.** a member of a governing board, as of a State university or a State system of schools —**re'gent·ship'** *n.*

**reg·i·cide** (rej'ə sīd') *n.* [< ML. < L. *rex* (see REGAL) + *-cida*: see -CIDE] **1.** a person who kills a king **2.** the killing of a king —**reg'i·ci'dal** *adj.*

**re·gime, ré·gime** (rə zhēm', rā-) *n.* [< Fr. < L. *regimen*: see ff.] **1.** *a*) a political system *b*) a form of government or rule **2.** a social system or order **3.** the period that a person or system is in power **4.** *same as* REGIMEN

**reg·i·men** (rej'ə mən) *n.* [L., rule < *regere*, to rule] a regulated system of diet, exercise, rest, etc. for promoting the health

**reg·i·ment** (rej'ə mənt; *for v.* -ment') *n.* [< MFr. < LL. *regimentum*, government < L. *regere*, to rule] **1.** a military unit consisting of two or more battalions **2.** a large number (of persons, etc.) —*vt.* **1.** to form into regiments **2.** to assign to a regiment **3.** to organize systematically, as into uniform groups **4.** to organize in a rigid system under strict discipline and control —**reg'i·men'tal** *adj.* —**reg'i·men'tal·ly** *adv.* —**reg'i·men·ta'tion** *n.*

**reg·i·men·tals** (rej'ə men't'lz) *n.pl.* **1.** a regiment's uniform and insignia **2.** military uniform

**Re·gi·na** (ri jī'nə) [L., a queen] capital of Saskatchewan, Canada, in the S part: pop. 150,000 —*n.* [*also* r-] queen

**Reg·i·nald** (rej'i nəld) [ult. < Gmc. bases meaning "wise ruler"] a masculine name: dim. *Reggie*

**re·gion** (rē'jən) *n.* [< Anglo-Fr. < OFr. < L. *regio* < *regere*, to rule] **1.** a part of the earth's surface, esp. a part having a specified position or feature [a coastal *region*, tropical *regions*] **2.** any area, place, space, etc. or sphere, realm, etc. [the upper *regions* of the air, a *region* of research] **3.** an administrative division of a country, as in Italy or the U.S.S.R. **4.** a division or part of the body

**re·gion·al** (-'l) *adj.* **1.** of a whole region, not just a locality **2.** of some particular region, district, etc. —**re'gion·al·ism** *n.* —**re'gion·al·ly** *adv.*

**reg·is·ter** (rej'is tər) *n.* [< MFr. < ML. *registrum* < LL. < L. pp. of *regerere*, to record] **1.** *a*) a record or list of names, events, items, etc. *b*) a book in which this is kept *c*) an entry in such a record **2.** registration; enrollment **3.** a device, as a meter or counter, for recording fares paid, money deposited, etc. [a cash *register*] **4.** an opening into a room by which the amount of air passing, as from a furnace, can be controlled **5.** *Music a*) a part of a range of tones of the human voice or of an instrument having a specified quality *b*) an organ stop, or the tone quality it produces **6.** *Printing* exact placing of lines, pages, colors, etc. —*vt.* **1.** to enter in or as in a record or list; enroll **2.** to indicate as on a scale [a thermometer *registers* temperature] **3.** to show, as by facial expression [to *register* surprise] **4.** to safeguard (mail) by having its committal to the postal system recorded, for a fee **5.** *Printing* to cause to be in register —*vi.* **1.** to enter one's name, as in a hotel register, a list of eligible voters, etc. **2.** to enroll in a school, college, etc. **3.** to make an impression —**reg'is·trant** (-trənt) *n.*

**reg·is·tered** (-tərd) *adj.* officially or legally recorded, enrolled, or certified

**registered nurse** a nurse who has completed extensive training and has passed a State examination so as to qualify for performing complete nursing services

**reg·is·trar** (rej'i strär', rej'i strär') *n.* **1.** an official who keeps records, as of the students in a college **2.** a trust company that keeps the records of stock transfers, etc.

**reg·is·tra·tion** (rej'i strā'shən) *n.* **1.** a registering or being registered **2.** an entry in a register **3.** the number of persons registered

**reg·is·try** (rej'is trē) *n., pl.* **-tries 1.** *same as* REGISTRATION **2.** an office where registers are kept **3.** an official record or list; register **4.** a certificate on which is shown the nationality of a merchant ship as recorded in an official register

**reg·nant** (reg′nənt) *adj.* [< L. prp. of *regnare*, to reign] **1.** reigning; ruling **2.** predominant **3.** prevalent; widespread —**reg′nan·cy** *n.*

**re·gorge** (ri gôrj′) *vt.* -gorged′, -gorg′ing [< Fr.: see RE- & GORGE] to throw up or back; disgorge

**re·gress** (rē′gres; *for v.* ri gres′) *n.* [< L. pp. of *regredi* < *re-*, back + *gradi*, to go] **1.** a going or coming back **2.** backward movement; retrogression —*vi.* **1.** to go back; move backward **2.** to revert to an earlier form or to earlier or more infantile behavior patterns —**re·gres′sion** *n.* —**re·gres′sive** *adj.* —**re·gres′sive·ly** *adv.* —**re·gres′sor** *n.*

**re·gret** (ri gret′) *vt.* -gret′ted, -gret′ting [< OFr. *regreter*, to mourn < a Gmc. base] **1.** to be sorry about or mourn for (a person or thing gone, lost, etc.) **2.** to feel troubled or remorseful over (an occurrence, one's acts, etc.) —*n.* **1.** a troubled feeling or remorse, esp. over one's acts or omissions **2.** sorrow over a person or thing gone, lost, etc. —(one's) **regrets** a polite expression of regret, as at declining an invitation —**re·gret′ful** *adj.* —**re·gret′ful·ly** *adv.* —**re·gret′ful·ness** *n.* —**re·gret′ta·ble** *adj.* —**re·gret′ta·bly** *adv.* —**re·gret′ter** *n.*

**re·group** (rē grōōp′) *vt., vi.* to group again; specif., *Mil.* to reorganize (one's forces), as after a battle

**reg·u·lar** (reg′yə lər) *adj.* [< MFr. < L. < *regula*: see RULE] **1.** conforming in form or arrangement to a rule, principle, type, etc.; orderly; symmetrical **2.** characterized by conforming to a fixed principle or procedure **3.** *a)* usual; customary *b)* not a substitute; established *[the regular quarterback]* **4.** consistent, habitual, steady, etc. *[a regular customer]* **5.** recurring at set times or functioning in a normal way **6.** conforming to a generally accepted rule of conduct; proper **7.** properly qualified *[a regular doctor]* **8.** [Colloq.] thorough; absolute *[a regular nuisance]* **9.** [Colloq.] pleasant, friendly, etc. *[a regular fellow]* **10.** *Bot.* having all similar parts of the same shape and size: said of flowers **11.** *Eccles.* belonging to a religious order, etc. and adhering to its rule **12.** *Gram.* conforming to the usual type as in inflection **13.** *Math.* having all angles and sides equal, as a polygon, or all faces equal, as a polyhedron **14.** *Mil. a)* designating or of the standing army of a country *b)* designating soldiers recognized in international law as legitimate combatants in warfare **15.** *Politics* designating, of, or loyal to the party leadership, candidates, etc. —*n.* **1.** a member of a religious order **2.** a member of a regular army **3.** a regular member of an athletic team **4.** a clothing size for men of average height **5.** *Politics* one who is loyal to the party leadership, candidates, etc. —**reg′u·lar′i·ty** (-lar′ə tē) *n., pl.* -ties —**reg′u·lar·ly** *adv.*

**reg·u·late** (reg′yə lāt′) *vt.* -lat′ed, -lat′ing [< LL. pp. of *regulare* < L. *regula*: see RULE] **1.** to control or direct according to a rule, principle, etc. **2.** to adjust to a standard, rate, degree, etc. *[regulate the heat]* **3.** to adjust (a clock, etc.) so as to make operate accurately **4.** to make uniform, methodical, etc. —**reg′u·la′tive, reg′u·la·to′ry** (-lə tôr′ē) *adj.*

**reg·u·la·tion** (reg′yə lā′shən) *n.* **1.** a regulating or being regulated **2.** a rule or law by which conduct, etc. is regulated —*adj.* **1.** required by regulation *[a regulation uniform]* **2.** usual; normal

**reg·u·la·tor** (reg′yə lāt′ər) *n.* a person or thing that regulates; specif., *a)* a mechanism for controlling the movement of machinery, fluids, etc.; governor *b)* the device in a watch or clock by which its speed is adjusted

**re·gur·gi·tate** (ri gur′jə tāt′) *vi., vt.* -tat′ed, -tat′ing [< ML. pp. of *regurgitare* < *re-*, back + LL. *gurgitare*, to surge] to surge or flow back, or cause to do this; specif., to bring (partly digested food) from the stomach back to the mouth —**re·gur′gi·tant** *adj.* —**re·gur′gi·ta′tion** *n.*

**re·ha·bil·i·tate** (rē′hə bil′ə tāt′, rē′ə-) *vt.* -tat′ed, -tat′ing [< ML.: see RE- & HABILITATE] **1.** to restore to rank, privileges, reputation, etc. which one has lost **2.** to put back in good condition **3.** *a)* to restore to a normal state of health, etc. as by medical treatment *b)* to make (the handicapped or disadvantaged) able to be employed by giving them special training —**re′ha·bil′i·ta′tion** *n.* —**re′ha·bil′i·ta′tive** *adj.*

**re·hash** (rē hash′; *for n.* rē′hash) *vt.* [RE- + HASH¹] to work up again or go over again *[to rehash the same old arguments]* —*n.* the act or result of rehashing

**re·hear** (rē hir′) *vt.* -heard′ (-hurd′), -hear′ing *Law* to hear (a case) a second time —**re·hear′ing** *n.*

**re·hears·al** (ri hur′s'l) *n.* a rehearsing; specif., a practice performance of a play, concert, etc.

**re·hearse** (ri hurs′) *vt.* -hearsed′, -hears′ing [< OFr. *re-*, again + *herser*, to harrow < *herse*, a harrow] **1.** to repeat aloud as heard or read; recite **2.** to tell in detail **3.** to perform (a play, concert, etc.) for practice in preparation

for a public performance **4.** to drill (a person) in what he is to do —*vi.* to rehearse a play, etc.

**re·heat** (rē hēt′) *vt.* to heat again; specif., to add heat to (a fluid), as in an afterburner —**re·heat′er** *n.*

**Reich** (rīk; *G.* rīH) *n.* [G.] Germany or the German government; specif., the German fascist state under the Nazis from 1933 to 1945 (**Third Reich**)

**reichs·mark** (rīks′märk′; *G.* rīHs′märk′) *n., pl.* -marks′, -mark′ [G.] the monetary unit of Germany from 1924 to 1948

**Reichs·tag** (rīks′täg′; *G.* rīHs′täkh′) *n.* [G.] formerly, the legislative assembly of Germany

**reign** (rān) *n.* [< OFr. < L. *regnum* < *regere*, to rule] **1.** royal power or rule **2.** dominance; prevalence *[the reign of fashion]* **3.** the period of rule, dominance, etc. —*vi.* **1.** to rule as a sovereign **2.** to be widespread; prevail *[peace reigns]*

**Reign of Terror** the period of the French Revolution from 1793 to 1794, during which many persons were executed

**re·im·burse** (rē′im burs′) *vt.* -bursed′, -burs′ing [RE- + archaic *imburse*, after Fr. *rembourser*] **1.** to pay back (money spent) **2.** to compensate (a person) for expenses, damages, losses, etc. —**re′im·burs′a·ble** *adj.* —**re′im·burse′ment** *n.*

**Reims** (rēmz; *Fr.* rans) city in NE France: pop. 153,000

**rein** (rān) *n.* [< OFr. *resne*, ult. < L. *retinere*: see RETAIN] **1.** a narrow strip of leather attached to each end of a horse's bit and held by the rider or driver to control the animal: *usually used in pl.* **2.** [*pl.*] a means of guiding, controlling, etc. *[the reins of government]* —*vt.* to guide, control, etc. as with reins —*vi.* to stop or slow down as with reins (with *in* or *up*) —**draw rein** to slow down or stop: also **draw in the reins** —**give (free) rein to** to allow to act without restraint

REINS

**re·in·car·nate** (rē′in kär′nāt) *vt.* -nat·ed, -nat·ing to cause to undergo reincarnation

**re·in·car·na·tion** (-kär nā′shən) *n.* **1.** a rebirth of the soul in another body, as in Hindu religious belief **2.** a new incarnation **3.** the doctrine that the soul reappears after death in another and different bodily form

**rein·deer** (rān′dir′) *n., pl.* -deer′, occas. -deers′ [< ON. < *hreinn*, reindeer + *dȳr*, deer] a large deer with branching antlers, found in northern regions: domesticated there as a beast of burden and for its milk, meat, and leather

**reindeer moss** an arctic lichen eaten by grazing animals

**re·in·force** (rē′in fôrs′) *vt.* -forced′, -forc′ing [RE- + var. of ENFORCE] **1.** to strengthen (a military or naval force) with more troops, ships, planes, etc. **2.** to strengthen, as by propping, adding new material, etc. **3.** to make more compelling *[to reinforce an argument]* —**re′in·forc′er** *n.*

**reinforced concrete** concrete masonry containing steel bars or mesh to increase its tensile strength

**re·in·force·ment** (-mənt) *n.* **1.** a reinforcing or being reinforced **2.** anything that reinforces; specif., [*pl.*] additional troops, ships, etc.

**reins** (rānz) *n.pl.* [< OFr. < L. pl. of *ren*, kidney] [Archaic] **1.** the kidneys **2.** the loins, thought of as the seat of the emotions and affections

**re·in·state** (rē′in stāt′) *vt.* -stat′ed, -stat′ing to instate again; restore to a former condition, position, etc. —**re′in·state′ment** *n.*

**reis** (rās) *n.pl., sing.* **re·al** (re äl′) [Port.] a former Portuguese and Brazilian money of account

**re·it·er·ate** (rē it′ə rāt′) *vt.* -at′ed, -at′ing [< L. pp. of *reiterare*: see RE- & ITERATE] to say or do again or repeatedly —**re·it′er·a′tion** *n.* —**re·it′er·a′tive** (-ə rāt′iv, -ər ə-tiv) *adj.* —**re·it′er·a′tive·ly** *adv.*

**re·ject** (ri jekt′; *for n.* rē′jekt) *vt.* [< L. pp. of *rejicere* < *re-*, back + *jacere*, to throw] **1.** to refuse to take, agree to, use, believe, etc. **2.** to discard or throw out as worthless **3.** to pass over (a phonograph record set by a record changer) **4.** to vomit **5.** to deny love or acceptance to (someone) **6.** *Physiol.* to be incompatible with (a part or organ transplanted into the body) —*n.* a rejected thing or person —**re·ject′ee′** *n.* —**re·ject′er, re·jec′tor** *n.* —**re·jec′tion** *n.* —**re·jec′tive** *adj.*

**re·joice** (ri jois′) *vi.* -joiced′, -joic′ing [< OFr. *rejoir* < *re-*, again + *joir* < L. *gaudere*, to rejoice] to be glad or happy (often with *at* or *in*) —*vt.* to make glad; delight —**re·joic′ing·ly** *adv.*

**re·join¹** (rē join′) *vt.* [< MFr.: see ff.] **1.** to come into the company of again **2.** to join together again; reunite **3.** to renew membership in (an organization) after a lapse —*vi.* to become joined together again

**re·join²** (ri join′) *vt.* [< Anglo-Fr. < MFr. *rejoindre:* see RE- & JOIN] to say in answer —*vi.* to answer

**re·join·der** (-dər) *n.* [< Anglo-Fr. substantive use of *rejoindre:* see prec.] **1.** *a)* an answer to a reply *b)* any answer **2.** *Law* the defendant's answer to the plaintiff's replication

**re·ju·ve·nate** (ri jōō′və nāt′) *vt.* -nat′ed, -nat′ing [<RE- + L. *juvenis*, young + -ATE¹] **1.** to make young again; bring back to youthful strength, appearance, etc. **2.** to make seem new or fresh again —**re·ju′ve·na′tion** *n.* —**re·ju′ve·na′tor** *n.*

**re·lapse** (ri laps′; *for n.*, *also* rē′laps) *vi.* -lapsed′, -laps′ing [< L. pp. of *relabi*, to slip back: see RE- & LAPSE] to slip back into a former condition, esp. after improvement or seeming improvement —*n.* **1.** a relapsing **2.** the recurrence of a disease after apparent improvement —**re·laps′er** *n.*

**re·late** (ri lāt′) *vt.* -lat′ed, -lat′ing [< L. pp. of *referre*, to bring back: see REFER] **1.** to tell the story of; narrate **2.** to connect, as in thought or meaning; show a relation between [to *relate* theory and practice] —*vi.* **1.** *a)* to have some connection (*to*) *b)* to show sympathy and understanding **2.** to have reference (*to*) —**re·lat′a·ble** *adj.* —**re·lat′er, re·la′tor** *n.*

**re·lat·ed** (-lāt′id) *adj.* **1.** narrated; told **2.** connected or associated, as by origin, kinship, marriage, etc.; of the same family —**re·lat′ed·ness** *n.*

**re·la·tion** (ri lā′shən) *n.* **1.** a narrating, telling, etc. **2.** what is narrated; recital **3.** connection, as in thought, meaning, etc. **4.** connection of persons by blood or marriage; kinship **5.** a person related to others by kinship; relative **6.** [*pl.*] *a)* the connections between or among persons, groups, nations, etc. *b)* sexual intercourse —**in** (or **with**) **relation to** concerning; regarding —**re·la′tion·al** *adj.*

**re·la·tion·ship** (-ship′) *n.* **1.** the state or an instance of being related **2.** connection by blood or marriage; kinship

**rel·a·tive** (rel′ə tiv) *adj.* **1.** related each to the other; referring to each other **2.** having to do with; relevant **3.** regarded in relation to something else; comparative **4.** meaningful only in relationship ["cold" is a *relative* term] **5.** *Gram. a)* designating a word that introduces a subordinate clause and refers to an antecedent ["which" is a *relative* pronoun in "the hat which you bought"] *b)* introduced by such a word [a *relative* clause] —*n.* **1.** a relative word or thing **2.** a person related to others by kinship; member of the same family —**relative to 1.** concerning; about **2.** corresponding to; in proportion to —**rel′a·tive·ness** *n.*

**relative humidity** *see* HUMIDITY

**rel·a·tive·ly** (-lē) *adv.* in a relative manner; in relation to or compared to something else; not absolutely [a *relatively* unimportant matter]

**rel·a·tiv·ism** (-iz′m) *n.* any theory of ethics or knowledge based on the idea that all values or judgments are relative, differing according to circumstances, persons, etc. —**rel′a·tiv·ist** *n.* —**rel′a·tiv·is′tic** *adj.*

**rel·a·tiv·i·ty** (rel′ə tiv′ə tē) *n.* **1.** a being relative **2.** *Physics* the fact, principle, or theory of the relative, rather than absolute, character of motion, velocity, mass, time, etc.: as developed esp. by Albert Einstein, the theory includes the statements that: 1) the velocity of light is constant; 2) the mass of a body in motion varies with its velocity; 3) matter and energy are equivalent; 4) space and time are interdependent and form a four-dimensional continuum

**re·lax** (ri laks′) *vt.*, *vi.* [< L. < *re-*, back + *laxare*, to loosen < *laxus*, loose] **1.** to make or become looser, or less firm, stiff, or tense **2.** to make or become less strict, severe, or intense, as discipline, effort, etc. **3.** to rest or give rest to, from work, worry, etc. —**re·laxed′** *adj.* —**re·lax′ed·ly** (-lak′sid lē) *adv.* —**re·lax′er** *n.*

**re·lax·ant** (-ənt) *adj.* of or causing relaxation, esp. of muscular tension —*n.* a relaxant drug or agent

**re·lax·a·tion** (rē′lak sā′shən) *n.* **1.** a relaxing or being relaxed; loosening, lessening of severity, etc. **2.** *a)* a lessening of or rest from work, worry, etc. *b)* recreation or other activity for bringing this about

**re·lay** (rē′lā; *for v.*, *also* ri lā′) *n.* [MFr. *relais* (pl.), orig. relays of hunting hounds < *re-*, back + *laier*, to leave] **1.** a fresh supply of horses, etc. ready to relieve others, as for a stage of a journey **2.** a crew of workers relieving others; shift **3.** *a) same as* RELAY RACE *b)* any of the laps of a relay race **4.** a conveying or transmitting as by relays **5.** *same as* SERVOMOTOR **6.** *Elec.* a device activated by variations in conditions in one electric circuit and controlling a larger current or activating other devices in the same or another circuit: used in telegraphy, etc. —*vt.* -layed, -lay·ing **1.** to convey by or as by relays [to *relay* news] **2.** *Elec.* to control, operate, or send on by a relay

**re·lay** (rē′lā′) *vt.* -laid′, -lay′ing to lay again or anew: also written **re′lay′**

**relay race** a race between teams, each runner going in turn only part of the total distance

**re·lease** (ri lēs′) *vt.* -leased′, -leas′ing [< OFr. < L. *relaxare:* see RELAX] **1.** to set free, as from confinement, duty, work, etc. **2.** to let (a missile, etc.) go **3.** to permit to be issued, published, broadcast, etc. **4.** *Law* to give up to someone else (a claim, right, etc.) —*n.* **1.** a freeing or being freed, as from prison, pain, an obligation, etc. **2.** relief from tension as by expressing emotion freely **3.** a document authorizing release, as from prison, etc. **4.** a letting loose of something caught, held, etc. **5.** a device for releasing a catch, etc., as on a machine **6.** *a)* a releasing to the public, as of a book, film, news, etc. *b)* the book, film, news, etc. released **7.** *Law a)* a giving up of a claim or right *b)* the document by which this is done

**re·lease** (rē′lēs′) *vt.* -leased′, -leas′ing to lease again

**released time** periods during school time when pupils in a public school may leave the school in order to receive religious instruction during this

**rel·e·gate** (rel′ə gāt′) *vt.* -gat′ed, -gat′ing [< L. pp. of *relegare* < *re-*, away + *legare*, to send] **1.** to exile or banish (*to*) **2.** to consign or assign to an inferior position **3.** to assign to a class, sphere, etc. **4.** to refer, commit, or hand over for decision or action —**rel′e·ga′tion** *n.*

**re·lent** (ri lent′) *vi.* [ult. < L. < *re-*, again + *lentus*, pliant] to soften in temper, resolution, etc.; become less severe, stern, or stubborn —**re·lent′ing·ly** *adv.*

**re·lent·less** (-lis) *adj.* **1.** not relenting; harsh; pitiless **2.** persistent; unremitting —**re·lent′less·ly** *adv.* —**re·lent′less·ness** *n.*

**rel·e·vant** (rel′ə vənt) *adj.* [< ML. prp. of *relevare:* see RELIEVE] bearing upon or relating to the matter in hand; pertinent; to the point —**rel′e·vance, rel′e·van·cy** *n.* —**rel′e·vant·ly** *adv.*

**re·li·a·ble** (ri lī′ə b'l) *adj.* that can be relied on; dependable —**re·li′a·bil′i·ty, re·li′a·ble·ness** *n.* —**re·li′a·bly** *adv.*

**re·li·ance** (-əns) *n.* **1.** the act of relying **2.** trust, dependence, or confidence **3.** a thing relied on

**re·li·ant** (-ənt) *adj.* having or showing trust, dependence, or confidence; dependent (*on*) —**re·li′ant·ly** *adv.*

**rel·ic** (rel′ik) *n.* [< OFr. < L. *reliquiae* (pl.), remains < *relinquere:* see RELINQUISH] **1.** *a)* an object, custom, etc. that has survived from the past *b)* a keepsake or souvenir **2.** [*pl.*] remaining fragments; ruins **3.** *R.C.Ch. & Orthodox Eastern Ch.* the bodily remains of a saint, martyr, etc., or an object associated with him, reverenced as a memorial

**rel·ict** (rel′ikt) *n.* [< L. pp. of *relinquere:* see RELINQUISH] [Archaic] a widow

**re·lief** (ri lēf′) *n.* [< OFr. *relever:* see ff.] **1.** an easing, as of pain, anxiety, a burden, etc. **2.** anything that lessens tension, or offers a pleasing change **3.** aid in the form of goods or money given, as by a government agency, to those unable to support themselves **4.** any aid given in times of need, danger, or disaster, as supplies sent into a flooded area **5.** *a)* release from work or duty *b)* the person or persons bringing such release by taking over a post **6.** *a)* the projection of sculptured figures and forms from a flat surface, so that they stand wholly or partly free *b)* a work of art so made **7.** *a)* the differences in height, collectively, of land forms in any particular area *b)* these differences as shown by lines, colors, or raised areas on a map (**relief map**) **8.** *Law* the assistance sought by a complainant as in a court of equity **9.** *a) Painting* the apparent solidity or projection of objects *b)* distinctness of outline; contrast —*adj. Baseball* designating a pitcher regularly used to replace another during a game —**in relief** carved or molded so as to project from a surface —**on relief** receiving relief from a government agency

**re·lieve** (ri lēv′) *vt.* -lieved′, -liev′ing [< OFr. < L. < *re-*, again + *levare*, to raise < *levis*, light] **1.** *a)* to ease, lighten, or reduce (pain, anxiety, etc.) *b)* to free from pain, distress, etc. **2.** to lighten (pressure, stress, etc.) on (something) **3.** to give or bring aid or assistance to [to *relieve* a besieged city] **4.** *a)* to set free from a burden, obligation, etc. *b)* to remove (a burden, etc.) **5.** to set free from duty or work by replacing with oneself or another [to *relieve* a nurse]; specif., *Baseball* to serve as a relief pitcher for **6.** to make less tedious, etc. by providing a pleasing change **7.** to set off by contrast; make distinct or prominent **8.** to ease (oneself) by urinating or defecating —**re·liev′a·ble** *adj.* —**re·liev′er** *n.*

**re·lie·vo** (ri lē′vō, ril yev′ō) *n.*, *pl.* -vos same as RELIEF (SENSE 6)

**re·li·gion** (ri lij′ən) *n.* [< OFr. < L. *religio* < ? < *re-*, back + *ligare*, to bind] **1.** *a)* belief in a superhuman power or powers to be obeyed and worshiped as the creator(s) and ruler(s) of the universe *b)* expression of this belief in conduct and ritual **2.** any specific system of belief, worship, etc., often involving a code of ethics [the Christian *religion*] **3.** the state or way of life of a person in a monastic order, etc. **4.** any object that is seriously or zealously pursued

**re·li·gi·os·i·ty** (ri lij′ē äs′ə tē) *n.* the quality of being excessively or mawkishly religious —**re·li′gi·ose′** (-ōs′) *adj.*

**re·li·gious** (ri lij′əs) *adj.* **1.** that believes in or supports a religion; devout; pious **2.** of or concerned with religion [*religious* books] **3.** belonging to a community of monks, nuns, etc. **4.** conscientiously exact; scrupulous —*n., pl.* **-gious** a member of a community of monks, nuns, etc. —**re·li′gious·ly** *adv.* —**re·li′gious·ness** *n.*

**re·line** (rē līn′) *vt.* **-lined′, -lin′ing** **1.** to mark with new lines **2.** to provide with a new lining

**re·lin·quish** (ri liŋ′kwish) *vt.* [< OFr. < L. < *re-*, from + *linquere*, to leave] **1.** to give up (a plan, policy, etc.) **2.** to surrender (something owned, a right, etc.) **3.** to let go (a grasp, etc.) —**re·lin′quish·ment** *n.*

**rel·i·quar·y** (rel′ə kwer′ē) *n., pl.* **-quar′ies** [< Fr. < L.: see RELIC] a small box, casket, or shrine in which relics are kept and shown

**rel·ique** (rel′ik, re lēk′) *n. archaic var. of* RELIC

**rel·ish** (rel′ish) *n.* [< OFr. *relais*, something remaining < *relaisser*: see RELEASE] **1.** the distinctive flavor something has **2.** a trace (of some quality) **3.** an appetizing flavor; pleasing taste **4.** *a)* pleasure; enjoyment *b)* liking or craving **5.** anything that gives pleasure, zest, etc. **6.** pickles, olives, etc. served with a meal to add flavor or as an appetizer —*vt.* to enjoy; like —*vi.* **1.** to have the flavor (*of* something) **2.** to have a pleasing taste

**re·live** (rē liv′) *vt.* **-lived′, -liv′ing** to experience again (a past event) as in the imagination

**re·lo·cate** (rē lō′kāt) *vt., vi.* **-cat·ed, -cat·ing** **1.** to locate again **2.** to move to a new location —**re′lo·ca′tion** *n.*

**re·luc·tance** (ri luk′təns) *n.* **1.** a being reluctant; unwillingness **2.** *Elec.* a measure of the opposition presented to the lines of force in a magnetic circuit

**re·luc·tant** (-tənt) *adj.* [< L. prp. of *reluctari* < *re-*, against + *luctari*, to struggle] **1.** unwilling or disinclined (*to* do something) **2.** marked by unwillingness [a *reluctant* answer] —**re·luc′tant·ly** *adv.*

**re·ly** (ri lī′) *vi.* **-lied′, -ly′ing** [< OFr. < L. *religare*: see RELIGION] to have confidence; depend (*with on* or *upon*)

**REM** (rem) *n., pl.* **REMs** [*r*(*apid*) *e*(*ye*) *m*(*ovement*)] the periodic, rapid, jerky movement of the eyeballs under closed lids while asleep and dreaming

**re·main** (ri mān′) *vi.* [< OFr. < L. < *re-*, back + *manere*, to stay] **1.** to be left over when the rest has been taken away, destroyed, etc. **2.** to stay on as while others go [to *remain* at home] **3.** to go on being [to *remain* a cynic] **4.** to continue to exist; persist [hope *remains*] **5.** to be left to be dealt with, done, etc.

**re·main·der** (-dər) *n.* **1.** those remaining **2.** what is left when a part is taken away **3.** a copy or copies of a book still held by the publisher when the sale has fallen off, usually disposed of at a very low price **4.** *Arith. a)* what is left when a smaller number is subtracted from a larger *b)* what is left undivided when one number is not evenly divisible by another —*vt.* to sell (books, etc.) as remainders

**re·mains** (ri mānz′) *n.pl.* **1.** what is left after part has been used, destroyed, etc. **2.** a dead body; corpse **3.** writings left unpublished by an author at his death

**re·make** (rē māk′; *for n.* rē′māk′) *vt.* **-made′, -mak′ing** to make again or anew —*n.* **1.** a remaking **2.** something remade, as a motion picture

**re·mand** (ri mand′) *vt.* [< OFr., ult. < L. *re-*, back + *mandare*, to order] **1.** to send back **2.** *Law a)* to send (a prisoner or accused person) back into custody, as to await trial, etc. *b)* to send (a case) back to a lower court for further proceedings —*n.* a remanding or being remanded

**re·mark** (ri märk′) *vt.* [Fr. *remarquer* < *re-*, again + *marquer*, to mark] **1.** to notice; observe; perceive **2.** to say or write as an observation or comment —*vi.* to make an observation or comment (*with on* or *upon*) —*n.* **1.** a noticing or observing **2.** something said briefly; comment

**re·mark·a·ble** (-ə b′l) *adj.* **1.** worthy of remark or notice **2.** unusual; extraordinary —**re·mark′a·ble·ness** *n.* —**re·mark′a·bly** *adv.*

**Rem·brandt (Harmensz) van Rijn** (rem′brant van rīn′; *Du.* rem′bränt vän rīn′) 1606–69; Du. painter & etcher

**re·me·di·a·ble** (ri mē′dē ə b′l) *adj.* that can be remedied —**re·me′di·a·ble·ness** *n.* —**re·me′di·a·bly** *adv.*

**re·me·di·al** (-əl) *adj.* **1.** providing, or intended to provide, a remedy **2.** *Educ.* of or being a course for helping students having difficulty in the subject [*remedial* reading] —**re·me′di·al·ly** *adv.*

**rem·e·dy** (rem′ə dē) *n., pl.* **-dies** [< Anglo-Fr. < OFr. < L. *remedium* < *re-*, again + *mederi*, to heal] **1.** any medicine or treatment that cures, heals, or relieves a disease or tends to restore health **2.** something that corrects or counteracts an evil or wrong; relief **3.** a legal means by which a violation of a right is prevented or compensated for —*vt.* **-died, -dy·ing** to act as a remedy for; cure, counteract, correct, etc. —**rem′e·di·less** *adj.*

**re·mem·ber** (ri mem′bər) *vt.* [< OFr. < LL. < L. *re-*, again + *memorare*, to bring to mind < *memor*, mindful] **1.** to have (an event, thing, person, etc.) come to mind again; think of again **2.** to bring back to mind by an effort; recall **3.** to bear in mind; be careful not to forget **4.** to keep (a person) in mind for a present, legacy, etc. **5.** to mention as sending greetings [*remember* me to your sister] —*vi.* **1.** to bear in mind or call back to mind **2.** to have memory

**re·mem·brance** (-brəns) *n.* **1.** a remembering or being remembered **2.** the power to remember **3.** a memory **4.** the extent of time over which one can remember **5.** a souvenir or keepsake **6.** commemoration **7.** [*pl.*] greetings

**Remembrance Day** a British and Canadian holiday in November, equivalent to VETERANS DAY

**re·mind** (ri mīnd′) *vt., vi.* [RE- + MIND, *v.*] to put (a person) in mind (*of* something); cause to remember —**re·mind′er** *n.*

**re·mind·ful** (-fəl) *adj.* reviving memory; reminding

**Rem·ing·ton** (rem′iŋ tən), **Frederic** 1861–1909; U.S. painter, sculptor, & illustrator

**rem·i·nisce** (rem′ə nis′) *vi.* **-nisced′, -nis′cing** [< ff.] to think, talk, or write about one's past experiences

**rem·i·nis·cence** (-′ns) *n.* [Fr. < LL. < L. prp. of *reminisci* < *re-*, again + *memini*, to remember] **1.** a remembering of past experiences **2.** a memory or recollection **3.** [*pl.*] an account, written or spoken, of remembered experiences

**rem·i·nis·cent** (-′nt) *adj.* **1.** characterized by or given to reminiscence **2.** bringing to mind something else; suggestive (*of*) —**rem′i·nis′cent·ly** *adv.*

**re·miss** (ri mis′) *adj.* [see REMIT] **1.** careless in, or negligent about, carrying out a task **2.** showing carelessness or negligence —**re·miss′ness** *n.*

**re·mis·si·ble** (-ə b′l) *adj.* that can be remitted

**re·mis·sion** (ri mish′ən) *n.* the act or an instance of remitting; forgiveness of sins or debts, lessening or leaving of pain or symptoms, etc. —**re·mis′sive** *adj.*

**re·mit** (ri mit′) *vt.* **-mit′ted, -mit′ting** [< L. *remittere* (pp. *remissus*) < *re-*, back + *mittere*, to send] **1.** to forgive or pardon (sins, etc.) **2.** to free someone from (a debt, tax, penalty, etc.) **3.** to let slacken; lessen [without *remitting* one's efforts] **4.** to refer (a matter) for consideration, judgment, etc.; specif., *Law* same as REMAND **5.** to send (money) in payment —*vi.* **1.** *a)* to moderate; slacken *b)* to have its symptoms lessen or disappear: said of an illness **2.** to send money in payment —**re·mit′ment** *n.* —**re·mit′ta·ble** *adj.* —**re·mit′ter** *n.*

**re·mit·tal** (-′l) *n. same as* REMISSION

**re·mit·tance** (-′ns) *n.* **1.** the sending of money, as by mail **2.** the money sent

**re·mit·tent** (-′nt) *adj.* remitting; abating for a while or at intervals, as a fever —**re·mit′tent·ly** *adv.*

**rem·nant** (rem′nənt) *n.* [< OFr. prp. of *remaindre*: see REMAIN] **1.** what is left over **2.** [*often pl.*] a small remaining part, amount, or number **3.** a trace; vestige **4.** a piece of cloth, ribbon, etc. left over, as at the end of the bolt —*adj.* remaining

**re·mod·el** (rē mäd′′l) *vt.* **-eled** or **-elled, -el·ing** or **-el·ling** **1.** to model again **2.** to make over; rebuild

**re·mon·strance** (ri män′strəns) *n.* a remonstrating; protest, complaint, etc., or a statement of this

**re·mon·strant** (-strənt) *adj.* remonstrating —*n.* a person who remonstrates —**re·mon′strant·ly** *adv.*

**re·mon·strate** (-strāt) *vt.* **-strat·ed, -strat·ing** [< ML. pp. of *remonstrare* < L. *re-*, again + *monstrare*, to show] to say or plead in protest, objection, etc. —*vi.* to present and urge reasons in opposition or complaint; protest —**re·mon·stra·tion** (rē′män strā′shən, rem′ən-) *n.* —**re·mon′stra·tive** (-strə tiv) *adj.* —**re·mon′stra·tive·ly** *adv.* —**re·mon′stra·tor** (-strät′ər) *n.*

**rem·o·ra** (rem′ər ə) *n.* [L., lit., hindrance] an ocean fish with a sucking disc on the head, by which it clings to sharks, ships, etc.

**re·morse** (ri môrs′) *n.* [< OFr. < LL. < L. pp. of *remordere* < *re-*, again + *mordere*, to bite] **1.** a deep, torturing sense of guilt over a wrong one has done; self-reproach **2.** pity: now only in *without remorse*, pitilessly —**re·morse′ful** *adj.* —**re·morse′ful·ly** *adv.* —**re·morse′ful·ness** *n.* —**re·morse′less** *adj.* —**re·morse′less·ly** *adv.* —**re·morse′less·ness** *n.*

REMORA
(7 in. to 3 ft. long)

**re·mote** (ri mōt′) *adj.* **-mot′er, -mot′est** [< L. pp. of *removere*, to remove] **1.** distant in space or time; far off **2.** far off and hidden; secluded **3.** distant in connection, relation, etc. [a question *remote* from the subject] **4.** distantly related [a *remote* cousin] **5.** distant in manner; aloof **6.** slight; faint [a *remote* chance] —re·mote′ly *adv.* —re·mote′ness *n.*

**remote control** control of aircraft, missiles, or other apparatus from a distance, as by radio waves

**re·mount** (rē mount′; *for n. usually* rē′mount′) *vt., vi.* to mount again —*n.* a fresh horse to replace another

**re·mov·a·ble** (ri mōō′və b′l) *adj.* that can be removed —re·mov′a·bil′i·ty *n.* —re·mov′a·bly *adv.*

**re·mov·al** (ri mōō′v′l) *n.* a removing or being removed; esp., *a)* a taking away *b)* dismissal, as from an office *c)* a moving to somewhere else, as of a store

**re·move** (ri mōōv′) *vt.* **-moved′, -mov′ing** [< OFr. < L. *removere:* see RE- & MOVE] **1.** to move (something) from where it is; take away **2.** to take off [*remove* your hat] **3.** *a)* to kill *b)* to dismiss, as from an office *c)* to get rid of [to *remove* the causes of war] **4.** to extract or separate (*from*) —*vi.* **1.** [Poet.] to go away **2.** to move away, as to another place of residence **3.** to be removable [paint that *removes* easily] —*n.* **1.** a removing **2.** the space or time in which a move is made **3.** any step, interval, or degree [but one *remove* from war] —re·mov′er *n.*

**re·moved** (ri mōōvd′) *adj.* **1.** distant by (a specified number of degrees of relationship) [one's first cousin once *removed* is the child of one's first cousin] **2.** remote; distant; unconnected (*from*)

**re·mu·ner·ate** (ri myōō′nə rāt′) *vt.* **-at′ed, -at′ing** [< L. pp. of *remunerari,* to reward < *re-,* again + *munus,* a gift] to pay (a person) for (a service, loss, etc.); reward; recompense —re·mu′ner·a·ble *adj.* —re·mu′ner·a′tion *n.* —re·mu′ner·a′tive *adj.* —re·mu′ner·a′tive·ly *adv.* —re·mu′ner·a′tive·ness *n.* —re·mu′ner·a′tor *n.*

**Re·mus** (rē′məs) [L.] *see* ROMULUS

**ren·ais·sance** (ren′ə säns′, -zäns′; *chiefly Brit.* ri nā′s′ns) *n.* [Fr. < *re-,* again + *naître* (ult. < L. *nasci*), to be born] **1.** a rebirth; revival **2.** [R-] *a)* the great revival of art, literature, and learning in Europe in the 14th, 15th, and 16th centuries *b)* the period of this *c)* the style of art, literature, architecture, etc. of this period *d)* any similar revival —*adj.* [R-] of, or in the style of, the Renaissance

**re·nal** (rē′n′l) *adj.* [< Fr. < L. *renalis* < *renes,* kidneys] of or near the kidneys

**re·nas·cence** (ri nas′ns, -nās′-) *n.* [*also* R-] *same as* RENAISSANCE

**re·nas·cent** (-'nt) *adj.* [< L.: see RE- & NASCENT] having or showing new life, strength, or vigor

**rend** (rend) *vt.* **rent, rend′ing** [OE. *rendan*] **1.** to tear or pull with violence (with *from, off,* etc.) **2.** to tear apart or split with violence: often figurative [a roar *rends* the air] —*vi.* to tear; split apart

**ren·der** (ren′dər) *vt.* [< OFr., ult. < L. < *re-,* back + *dare,* to give] **1.** to hand over, or submit, as for approval, consideration, payment, etc. [*render* an account of your actions] **2.** to give (*up*); surrender **3.** to give in return [*render* good for evil] **4.** to give or pay as due [to *render* thanks] **5.** to cause to be; make [to *render* one helpless] **6.** *a)* to give (aid, etc.) *b)* to do (a service, etc.) **7.** to represent; depict **8.** to recite (a poem, etc.), play (music), act (a role), etc. **9.** to translate **10.** to deliver (a judgment, verdict, etc.) **11.** to melt down (fat) —ren′der·a·ble *adj.* —ren′der·er *n.* —ren′der·ing *n.*

**ren·dez·vous** (rän′dā vōō′, -dē-, -də-) *n., pl.* **-vous′** (-vōōz′) [< Fr. *rendez vous,* betake yourself] **1.** a place set for a meeting, as of troops, ships, spacecraft, etc. **2.** a place where people gather; meeting place **3.** *a)* an agreement to meet at a certain time or place *b)* the meeting itself —*vi., vt.* **-voused′** (-vōōd′), **-vous′ing** (-vōō′iŋ) to bring or come together at a rendezvous

**ren·di·tion** (ren dish′ən) *n.* a rendering or result of rendering; specif., *a)* a performance (*of* a piece of music, a role, etc.) *b)* a translation

**ren·e·gade** (ren′ə gād′) *n.* [< Sp. pp. of *renegar,* to deny, ult. < L. *re-,* again + *negare,* to deny] a person who abandons his religion, party, principles, etc. to join the other side; apostate; traitor —*adj.* disloyal; traitorous

**re·nege** (ri nig′, -neg′, -nēg′) *vi.* **-neged′, -neg′ing** [ML. *renegare:* see prec.] **1.** to go back on a promise **2.** *Card Games* to play a card of another suit, against the rules, when holding any of the suit called for —*n. Card Games* an act of reneging —re·neg′er *n.*

**re·new** (ri nōō′, -nyōō′) *vt.* **1.** to make new or as if new again; make fresh or strong again **2.** to cause to exist again; reestablish **3.** to begin again; resume **4.** to go over again; repeat [*renew* a promise] **5.** to replace as by a fresh supply of **6.** to give or get an extension of [to *renew* a lease] —re·new′a·bil′i·ty *n.* —re·new′a·ble *adj.* —re·new′al *n.* —re·new′ed·ly *adv.* —re·new′er *n.*

**ren·i-** [< L. *renes,* kidneys] *a combining form meaning* kidney, kidneys

**Rennes** (ren) city in NW France: pop. 181,000

**ren·net** (ren′it) *n.* [< OE. *gerennan,* to coagulate] **1.** *a)* the membrane lining the stomach of an unweaned animal, esp. the fourth stomach of a calf *b)* the contents of such a stomach **2.** *a)* an extract of this membrane or of the stomach contents, used to curdle milk, as in making cheese or junket *b)* any substance used to curdle milk

**ren·nin** (ren′in) *n.* [RENN(ET) + -IN¹] a coagulating enzyme that can curdle milk, found in rennet

**Re·no** (rē′nō) [after U.S. Gen. J. L. *Reno* (1823–62)] city in W Nev.: pop. 101,000

**Re·noir** (rə nwär′; *E.* ren′wär), **Pierre Au·guste** (ô güst′) 1841–1919; Fr. painter

**re·nounce** (ri nouns′) *vt.* **-nounced′, -nounc′ing** [OFr. < L. < *re-,* back + *nuntiare,* to tell < *nuntius,* messenger] **1.** to give up formally (a claim, right, etc.) **2.** to give up (a pursuit, practice, belief, etc.) **3.** to cast off or disown [to *renounce* a son] —re·nounce′ment *n.*

**ren·o·vate** (ren′ə vāt′) *vt.* **-vat′ed, -vat′ing** [< L. pp. of *renovare* < *re-,* again + *novare,* to make new < *novus,* new] to make fresh or sound again, as though new; clean up, replace worn parts in, repair, rebuild, etc. —ren′o·va′tion *n.* —ren′o·va′tive *adj.* —ren′o·va′tor *n.*

**re·nown** (ri noun′) *n.* [< Anglo-Fr. < OFr. < *re-,* again + *nom(m)er,* to name < L. < *nomen,* a name] great fame or reputation —re·nowned′ *adj.*

**rent¹** (rent) *n.* [< OFr. < LL. hyp. form for L. *reddita* (*pecunia*), paid (money)] **1.** a stated payment at fixed intervals for the use of a house, land, etc. **2.** *Econ.* income from the use of land —*vt.* **1.** to get or give temporary possession of (a house, land, etc.) in return for rent **2.** to get or give temporary use of (a car, tool, etc.) in return for a fee —*vi.* to be leased or let for rent or a fee —**for rent** available to be rented —rent′a·ble *adj.* —rent′er *n.*

**rent²** (rent) *pt. & pp. of* REND

**rent³** (rent) *n.* [n. use of obs. var. of REND] **1.** a hole or gap made by tearing or splitting **2.** a split in an organization; schism

**rent·al** (ren′t′l) *n.* **1.** an amount paid or received as rent **2.** a house, apartment, car, etc. offered for rent —*adj.* of, in, or for rent

**re·nun·ci·a·tion** (ri nun′sē ā′shən) *n.* [< L.: see RENOUNCE] a renouncing, as of a right, claim, pursuit, etc. —re·nun′ci·a·tive, re·nun′ci·a·to′ry (-ə tôr′ē) *adj.*

**re·or·der** (rē ôr′dər) *n.* a repeated order for the same goods —*vt.* **1.** to order again **2.** to put in order again —*vi.* to order goods again

**re·or·gan·i·za·tion** (rē ôr′gə ni zā′shən, rē′ôr-) *n.* **1.** a reorganizing or being reorganized **2.** a thorough reconstruction of a business corporation as effected after, or in anticipation of, a failure

**re·or·gan·ize** (rē ôr′gə nīz′) *vt., vi.* **-ized′, -iz′ing** to organize again or anew; effect a reorganization (of) —re·or′gan·iz′er *n.*

**rep** (rep) *n.* [Fr. *reps* < Eng. *ribs*] a ribbed fabric of silk, wool, cotton, rayon, etc.

**Rep. 1.** Representative **2.** Republic **3.** Republican

**rep. 1.** repeat **2.** report(ed) **3.** reporter

**re·pack·age** (rē pak′ij) *vt.* **-aged, -ag·ing** to package again or anew, as in a more secure or attractive package

**re·paid** (rē pād′) *pt. & pp. of* REPAY

**re·pair¹** (ri per′) *vt.* [< OFr. < L. < *re-,* again + *parare,* to prepare] **1.** to put back in good condition after damage, decay, etc.; fix **2.** to renew; restore (one's health, etc.) **3.** to set right; remedy (a mistake, etc.) **4.** to make amends for (a wrong, etc.) —*n.* **1.** a repairing **2.** [*usually pl.*] an instance of, or work done in, repairing **3.** the state of being repaired [a car kept in *repair*] **4.** state with respect to being repaired [in bad *repair*] —re·pair′a·ble *adj.* —re·pair′er *n.*

**re·pair²** (ri per′) *vi.* [< OFr. < LL. *repatriare* < L. *re-,* back + *patria,* one's native country] to go (*to* a place)

**re·pair·man** (-mən, -man′) *n., pl.* **-men** (-mən, -men′) a man whose work is repairing things

**rep·a·ra·ble** (rep′ər ə b′l) *adj.* that can be repaired, remedied, etc. —rep′a·ra·bly *adv.*

**rep·a·ra·tion** (rep′ə rā′shən) *n.* [< MFr. < LL. < pp. of L. *reparare:* see REPAIR¹] **1.** a repairing or being repaired **2.** a making up for a wrong or injury **3.** compensation; specif., [*usually pl.*] compensation by a defeated nation for damage done by it in a war, payable in money, goods, etc.

**rep·ar·tee** (rep′ər tē′; -är-; -tä′) *n.* [< Fr. pp. of *repartir,* to reply < *re-,* back + *partir,* to part] **1.** a quick, witty reply; retort **2.** a series of such retorts; banter **3.** skill in making witty replies

**re·past** (ri past′) *n.* [< OFr. < *re-,* RE- + *past,* food < L. < pp. of *pascere,* to feed] food and drink; a meal

**re·pa·tri·ate** (rē pā′trē āt′; *for n. usually* -it) *vt., vi.* **-at′ed, -at′ing** [< LL. pp. of *repatriare:* see REPAIR²] to send back or return to the country of birth, citizenship, or allegiance [to *repatriate* prisoners of war] —*n.* a person who has been repatriated —re·pa′tri·a′tion *n.*

**re·pay** (ri pā′) *vt.* **-paid′, -pay′ing** [OFr. *repaier*] **1.** *a)* to pay back (money); refund *b)* to pay back (a person) **2.**

to make some return for [*repay* a kindness] **3.** to make some return to (a person), as for some service —*vi.* to make a repayment or return —**re·pay′a·ble** *adj.* —**re·pay′-ment** *n.*

**re·peal** (ri pēl′) *vt.* [< OFr. *rapeler:* see RE- & APPEAL] to revoke; cancel; annul [*to repeal* a law] —*n.* the act of repealing —**re·peal′a·ble** *adj.* —**re·peal′er** *n.*

**re·peat** (ri pēt′) *vt.* [< OFr. < L. < *re-*, again + *petere*, to seek] **1.** to say or utter again **2.** to say over; recite, as a poem **3.** to say (something) as said by someone else **4.** to tell to others [*to repeat* a secret] **5.** to do or make again [*repeat* an operation] **6.** to say again what has been said before by (oneself) —*vi.* **1.** to say or do again what has been said or done before **2.** to occur again; recur **3.** to vote (illegally) more than once in an election —*n.* **1.** a repeating **2.** *a*) anything said or done again *b*) a rebroadcast of a radio or TV program **3.** *Music a*) a passage repeated in playing *b*) a symbol for this —**re·peat′a·bil′i-ty** *n.* —**re·peat′a·ble** *adj.*

**re·peat·ed** (-id) *adj.* said, made, or done again, or again and again —**re·peat′ed·ly** *adv.*

**re·peat·er** (-ər) *n.* **1.** a person or thing that repeats **2.** *same as* REPEATING FIREARM **3.** a person who fraudulently votes more than once in the same election **4.** a student who repeats a course or grade in school

**repeating decimal** a decimal in which some digit or group of digits is repeated continuously (Ex.: .3333, .037037)

**repeating firearm** a firearm that can fire a number of shots (from a magazine or clip) without reloading

**re·pel** (ri pel′) *vt.* -pelled′, -pel′ling [< L. < *re-*, back + *pellere*, to drive] **1.** to drive back or force back [*to repel* an attack] **2.** to refuse, reject, or spurn [she *repelled* his attentions] **3.** to cause dislike in; disgust [the odor *repels* me] **4.** *a*) to be resistant to, or present an opposing force to [plastic *repels* water] *b*) to fail to mix with [water *repels* oil] —*vi.* to cause distaste, dislike, aversion, etc. —**re·pel′ler** *n.*

**re·pel·lent** (-ənt) *adj.* **1.** that repels; pushing away or driving back **2.** causing distaste, dislike, etc. **3.** able to resist the absorption of liquid, esp. water, to a limited extent —*n.* something that repels; specif., *a*) a solution applied to fabric to make it water-repellent *b*) any substance used to repel insects Also **re·pel′lant** —**re·pel′lence, re·pel′-len·cy** *n.* —**re·pel′lent·ly** *adv.*

**re·pent** (ri pent′) *vi., vt.* [< OFr. < VL. < L. *re-*, again + *paenitere*, to repent] **1.** to feel sorry for (a past error, sin, omission, etc.) **2.** to feel such regret over (some past act, intention, etc.) as to change one's mind —**re·pent′er** *n.*

**re·pent·ance** (-′ns) *n.* a repenting or being penitent; feeling of sorrow, etc., esp. for wrongdoing; remorse —**re·pent′ant** *adj.* —**re·pent′ant·ly** *adv.*

**re·peo·ple** (rē pē′p'l) *vt.* -pled, -pling to people anew; provide with new inhabitants

**re·per·cus·sion** (rē′pər kush′ən, rep′ər-) *n.* [< L. pp. of *repercutere:* see RE- & PERCUSSION] **1.** formerly, a recoil **2.** reflection, as of sound **3.** a reaction to some event or action: *usually used in pl.* —**re′per·cus′sive** *adj.*

**rep·er·toire** (rep′ər twär′, rep′ə-) *n.* [< Fr. < LL. *repertorium:* see ff.] **1.** the stock of plays, operas, roles, songs, etc. that a company, actor, singer, etc. knows and is ready to perform **2.** the stock of special skills of a certain person or group

**rep·er·to·ry** (rep′ər tôr′ē, rep′ə-) *n., pl.* -ries [LL. *repertorium* < L. pp. of *reperire*, to discover] **1.** a storehouse, or the things in it **2.** *same as* REPERTOIRE **3.** the system of play production used by a repertory theater

**repertory theater** a theater whose actors perform several plays a season, alternating them at regular intervals

**rep·e·ti·tion** (rep′ə tish′ən) *n.* [< MFr. < L. *repetitio*] **1.** a repeating; a doing or saying again **2.** something repeated **3.** a copy or imitation —**re·pet′i·tive** (ri pet′ə tiv) *adj.* —**re·pet′i·tive·ly** *adv.*

**rep·e·ti·tious** (-əs) *adj.* full of or using repetition, esp. tiresome or boring repetition —**rep′e·ti′tious·ly** *adv.* —**rep′e-ti′tious·ness** *n.*

**re·phrase** (rē frāz′) *vt.* -phrased′, -phras′ing to phrase again, esp. in a different way

**re·pine** (ri pīn′) *vi.* -pined′, -pin′ing [RE- + PINE²] to feel or express discontent; complain; fret —**re·pin′er** *n.* —**re·pin′ing·ly** *adv.*

**re·place** (ri plās′) *vt.* -placed′, -plac′ing **1.** to put back in a former or the proper place or position **2.** to take the place of **3.** to provide an equivalent for [*replace* a worn tire] **4.** to put back or pay back; restore [*replace* stolen goods] —**re·place′a·ble** *adj.* —**re·plac′er** *n.*

**re·place·ment** (-mənt) *n.* **1.** a replacing or being replaced **2.** a person or thing that takes the place of another that is lost, worn out, dismissed, etc.

**re·plen·ish** (ri plen′ish) *vt.* [< OFr. < L. *re-*, again + *plenus*, full] **1.** to make full or complete again, as with a new supply **2.** to supply again with fuel, etc. —**re·plen′ish·er** *n.* —**re·plen′ish·ment** *n.*

**re·plete** (ri plēt′) *adj.* [< OFr. < L. pp. of *replere* < *re-*, again + *plere*, to fill] **1.** well-filled; plentifully supplied **2.** stuffed with food and drink —**re·ple′tion** *n.*

**re·plev·in** (ri plev′in) *n.* [< OFr. *re-*, again + *plevir*, to pledge] *Law* **1.** the recovery by a person of goods claimed to be his, on his promise to test the matter in court and give up the goods if defeated **2.** the writ by which this is done —*vt.* to take back (goods) under such a writ: usually **re·plev′y** -plev′ied, -plev′y·ing

**rep·li·ca** (rep′li kə) *n.* [It. < ML. < L. *replicare:* see REPLY] a reproduction or close copy, esp. of a work of art

**rep·li·ca·tion** (rep′lə kā′shən) *n.* [< MFr. < L. < pp. of *replicare:* see ff.] *Law* the plaintiff's answer to the plea of the defendant

**re·ply** (ri plī′) *vi.* -plied′, -ply′ing [< OFr. < L. < *re-*, back + *plicare*, to fold] **1.** to answer in speech or writing **2.** to respond by some action [to *reply* to enemy fire] **3.** *Law* to answer a defendant's plea —*vt.* to say in answer [she *replied* that she agreed] —*n., pl.* -plies′ **1.** an answer in speech or writing **2.** a response by some action —**re·pli′er** *n.*

**re·port** (ri pôrt′) *vt.* [< OFr. < L. < *re-*, back + *portare*, to carry] **1.** to give an account of; give information about; recount **2.** to carry and repeat (a message, etc.) **3.** to write an account of for publication, as in a newspaper **4.** to make known the presence, approach, etc. of **5.** to give an official account of **6.** to present (something referred for study, etc.) with conclusions, recommendations, etc. [the committee *reported* the bill out] **7.** to make a charge about (an offense or offender) to a person in authority —*vi.* **1.** to make a report **2.** to work as a reporter —*n.* **1.** rumor; gossip [*report* has it that he will resign] **2.** reputation [a man of good *report*] **3.** a statement or account brought in and presented, often for publication **4.** a formal or official presentation of facts or of the record of an investigation, court case, etc. **5.** a loud noise, esp. one made by an explosion —**re·port′a·ble** *adj.* —**re·port′ed·ly** *adv.* —**re·port′ing** *n.*

**re·port·age** (-ij) *n.* the reporting of news events

**report card** a written report of a pupil's progress and behavior, sent to his parents or guardian at regular intervals

**re·port·er** (-ər) *n.* a person who reports; specif., *a*) a person who reports legal or legislative proceedings *b*) a person who gathers information and writes reports for a newspaper, magazine, etc. *c*) a person who reports news on radio or TV —**rep·or·to·ri·al** (rep′ər tôr′ē əl) *adj.* —**rep′or·to′ri·al·ly** *adv.*

**re·pose¹** (ri pōz′) *vt.* -posed′, -pos′ing [< OFr. < LL. < L. *re-*, again + LL. *pausare*, to rest] to lay or place for rest [to *repose* oneself on a bed] —*vi.* **1.** to lie at rest **2.** to rest from work, travel, etc. **3.** to rest in death or a grave **4.** to rest or be supported [the shale *reposes* on limestone] —*n.* **1.** a reposing, or resting **2.** *a*) rest *b*) sleep **3.** ease of manner; composure **4.** calm; peace —**re·pose′ful** *adj.* —**re·pose′ful·ly** *adv.*

**re·pose²** (ri pōz′) *vt.* -posed′, -pos′ing [< L. *repositus:* see ff.] **1.** to place (trust, etc.) in someone **2.** to place (power, etc.) in the control of someone

**re·pos·i·to·ry** (ri päz′ə tôr′ē) *n., pl.* -ries [< L. < pp. of *reponere* < *re-*, back + *ponere*, to place] **1.** a box, chest, closet, or room in which things may be placed for safekeeping **2.** a center for storing [a *repository* of information] **3.** a person to whom something is confided

**re·pos·sess** (rē′pə zes′) *vt.* to get possession of again; specif., to take back from a buyer who has failed to keep up payments —**re′pos·ses′sion** (-zesh′ən) *n.*

**rep·re·hend** (rep′ri hend′) *vt.* [< L. < *re-*, back + *prehendere*, to take] **1.** to reprimand or rebuke (a person) **2.** to find fault with (something done) —**rep·re·hen·sion** (-hen′shən) *n.* —**rep′re·hen′sive** *adj.* —**rep′re·hen′sive·ly** *adv.*

**rep·re·hen·si·ble** (-hen′sə b'l) *adj.* deserving to be reprehended —**rep′re·hen′si·bil′i·ty** *n.* —**rep′re·hen′si·bly** *adv.*

**rep·re·sent** (rep′ri zent′) *vt.* [< OFr. < L.: see RE- & PRESENT, *v.*] **1.** to present or picture to the mind **2.** to present or be a likeness of **3.** to describe or set forth, often in order to influence, persuade, etc. **4.** *a*) to be a sign or symbol for [x *represents* the unknown] *b*) to express by symbols, characters, etc. **5.** to be the equivalent of [a cave *represents* home to them] **6.** to act the part of (a character), as in a play **7.** to act in place of; be a substitute for

**8.** to speak and act for by conferred authority, as a legislator for his constituents **9.** to serve as a specimen, example, type, etc. of —**rep′re·sent′a·ble** *adj.*

**rep·re·sen·ta·tion** (rep′ri zen tā′shən) *n.* **1.** a representing or being represented **2.** legislative representatives, collectively **3.** a likeness, image, etc. **4.** [*often pl.*] an account of facts, arguments, etc. intended to influence action, etc. **5.** the production or performance of a play, etc.

**rep·re·sen·ta·tion·al** (-′l) *adj.* **1.** of representation **2.** designating or of art that represents in recognizable form objects in nature —**rep′re·sen·ta′tion·al·ism** *n.* —**rep′re·sen·ta′tion·al·ist** *n.* —**rep′re·sen·ta′tion·al·ly** *adv.*

**rep·re·sen·ta·tive** (rep′rə zen′tə tiv) *adj.* **1.** representing; specif., *a*) picturing; portraying *b*) acting in the place of or on behalf of another or others; esp., serving as an elected delegate **2.** of or based on representation of the people by elected delegates [*representative* government] **3.** typical —*n.* **1.** an example or type **2.** a person authorized to act or speak for others, as an elected legislator or a salesman, agent, etc. **3.** [R-] a member of the lower house of Congress or of a State legislature —**rep′re·sent′a·tive·ly** *adv.* —**rep′re·sent′a·tive·ness** *n.*

**re·press** (ri pres′) *vt.* [< L. pp. of *reprimere*: see RE- & PRESS¹] **1.** to hold back; restrain [*to repress* a sigh] **2.** to put down; subdue **3.** to control so strictly as to stifle free, natural behavior [*to repress* a child] **4.** *Psychiatry a*) to force (painful ideas, impulses, etc.) into the unconscious *b*) to prevent (unconscious ideas, etc.) from becoming conscious —**re·press′er, re·press′or** *n.* —**re·press′i·ble** *adj.* —**re·pres′sive** *adj.* —**re·pres′sive·ly** *adv.* —**re·pres′sive·ness** *n.*

**re-press** (rē′pres′) *vt.* to press again; esp., to make new copies of (a recording) from the original master

**re·pres·sion** (ri presh′ən) *n.* **1.** a repressing or being repressed **2.** *Psychiatry* what is repressed

**re·prieve** (ri prēv′) *vt.* **-prieved′, -priev′ing** [ult. < Fr. pp. of *reprendre*, to take back] **1.** to postpone the punishment of; esp., to postpone the execution of (a condemned person) **2.** to give temporary relief to, as from pain —*n.* a reprieving or being reprieved; specif., *a*) a postponement of a penalty, esp. of execution *b*) a temporary relief, as from trouble or pain

**rep·ri·mand** (rep′rə mand′; *also for v.*, rep′rə mand′) *n.* [< Fr. < L. *reprimendus*, that is to be repressed < *reprimere*, REPRESS] a severe or formal rebuke —*vt.* to rebuke severely or formally

**re·print** (rē print′; *for n. usually* rē′print′) *vt.* to print again; print an additional impression of —*n.* something reprinted; specif., an additional impression or edition, as of an earlier book, pamphlet, etc.

**re·pris·al** (ri prī′z′l) *n.* [< MFr. < It. < *riprendere*, to take back < L. *reprehendere*: see REPREHEND] **1.** the use of force, short of war, against another nation to obtain redress of grievances **2.** injury done in return for injury received, esp. in war, as the killing of prisoners

**re·prise** (ri prēz′) *n.* [< OFr. pp. of *reprendre*, to take back] in a musical play, the repetition of all or part of a song performed earlier —*vt.* **-prised′, -pris′ing** to present a reprise of (a song)

**re·pro** (rē′prō) *n., pl.* **-pros** *shortened form of* REPRODUCTION PROOF: also **repro proof**

**re·proach** (ri prōch′) *vt.* [OFr. *reprochier*: ult. < L. *re-*, back + *prope*, near] to accuse of and blame for a fault; rebuke; reprove —*n.* **1.** shame, disgrace, or blame, or a source or cause of this **2.** a blaming, or an expression of blame; rebuke —**re·proach′a·ble** *adj.* —**re·proach′er** *n.* —**re·proach′ing·ly** *adv.*

**re·proach·ful** (-fəl) *adj.* full of or expressing reproach —**re·proach′ful·ly** *adv.* —**re·proach′ful·ness** *n.*

**rep·ro·bate** (rep′rə bāt′) *vt.* **-bat′ed, -bat′ing** [< LL. pp. of *reprobare*: see REPROVE] **1.** to disapprove of strongly; condemn **2.** to reject or abandon —*adj.* **1.** depraved; corrupt **2.** *Theol.* lost in sin; rejected by God —*n.* a reprobate person —**rep′ro·ba′tion** *n.* —**rep′ro·ba′tive** *adj.*

**re·pro·duce** (rē′prə dōōs′, -dyōōs′) *vt.* **-duced′, -duc′ing** to produce again; specif., *a*) to bring forth others of (its kind), esp. by sexual intercourse *b*) to make (a lost part or organ) grow again *c*) to make a copy, imitation, etc. of (a picture, sound, etc.) *d*) to repeat —*vi.* **1.** to produce offspring, esp. by sexual intercourse **2.** to undergo copying, duplication, etc. —**re′pro·duc′er** *n.* —**re′pro·duc′i·ble** *adj.*

**re·pro·duc·tion** (rē′prə duk′shən) *n.* **1.** a reproducing or being reproduced **2.** something made by reproducing; copy **3.** the process by which animals and plants produce new individuals

**reproduction proof** an especially fine proof of type, etc. to be photographed for making a printing plate

**re·pro·duc·tive** (-tiv) *adj.* **1.** reproducing **2.** of or for reproduction —**re′pro·duc′tive·ly** *adv.* —**re′pro·duc′tive·ness** *n.*

**re·proof** (ri prōōf′) *n.* a reproving or something said in reproving; rebuke: also **re·prov′al** (-prōō′v′l)

**re·prove** (ri prōōv′) *vt.* **-proved′, -prov′ing** [< OFr. < LL. *reprobare*: see RE- & PROVE] **1.** to speak to in disapproval; rebuke **2.** to express disapproval of (something done or said) —**re·prov′a·ble** *adj.* —**re·prov′er** *n.* —**re·prov′ing·ly** *adv.*

**rep·tile** (rep′t′l, -tīl) *n.* [LL. < neut. of L. *reptilis*, crawling < pp. of *repere*, to creep] **1.** any of a group of coldblooded vertebrates having a body covered with scales or horny plates and including snakes, lizards, turtles, crocodiles, etc. and dinosaurs **2.** a mean, sneaky person —*adj.* of or like a reptile —**rep·til·i·an** (rep til′ē ən) *adj., n.*

**re·pub·lic** (ri pub′lik) *n.* [< MFr. < L. < *res*, thing + *publica*, public] **1.** a nation in which the supreme power rests in all the citizens entitled to vote and is exercised by representatives elected by them **2.** the government of such a state **3.** a nation with a president as its head **4.** any of certain divisions of the U.S.S.R. or Yugoslavia

**re·pub·li·can** (ri pub′li kən) *adj.* **1.** of or like a republic **2.** favoring a republic **3.** [R-] of the Republican Party —*n.* **1.** a person who favors a republican form of government **2.** [R-] a member of the Republican Party

**re·pub·li·can·ism** (-iz′m) *n.* **1.** republican government **2.** republican principles, or adherence to them **3.** [R-] the policies, etc. of the Republican Party

**Republican Party** one of the two major political parties in the U.S., organized in 1854

**re·pu·di·ate** (ri pyōō′dē āt′) *vt.* **-at′ed, -at′ing** [< L. pp. of *repudiare*, to divorce < *repudium*, separation] **1.** to disown or cast off publicly **2.** *a*) to refuse to accept or support (a belief, treaty, etc.) *b*) to deny the truth of (a charge, etc.) **3.** to refuse to acknowledge or pay (a debt, etc.) —**re·pu′di·a′tion** *n.* —**re·pu′di·a′tor** *n.*

**re·pug·nance** (ri pug′nəns) *n.* [< MFr. < L. < prp. of *repugnare* < *re-*, back + *pugnare*, to fight] **1.** inconsistency **2.** extreme dislike or distaste  Also **re·pug′nan·cy**

**re·pug·nant** (-nənt) *adj.* **1.** contradictory or opposed **2.** causing repugnance; offensive —**re·pug′nant·ly** *adv.*

**re·pulse** (ri puls′) *vt.* **-pulsed′, -puls′ing** [< L. pp. of *repellere*, REPEL] **1.** to drive back; repel (an attack, etc.) **2.** to repel with discourtesy, coldness, etc.; rebuff **3.** to be repulsive to —*n.* **1.** a repelling or being repelled **2.** a refusal, rejection, or rebuff

**re·pul·sion** (ri pul′shən) *n.* **1.** a repelling or being repelled **2.** strong dislike, distaste, or aversion **3.** *Physics* the mutual action by which bodies or particles of matter tend to repel each other: opposed to ATTRACTION

**re·pul·sive** (-siv) *adj.* **1.** tending to repel **2.** causing strong dislike or aversion **3.** of repulsion —**re·pul′sive·ly** *adv.* —**re·pul′sive·ness** *n.*

**rep·u·ta·ble** (rep′yoo tə b′l) *adj.* **1.** having a good reputation; respectable **2.** in proper or good usage [a *reputable* word] —**rep′u·ta·bil′i·ty** *n.* —**rep′u·ta·bly** *adv.*

**rep·u·ta·tion** (rep′yoo tā′shən) *n.* [< L. < pp. of *reputare*: see ff.] **1.** the regard, favorable or not, shown for a person or thing by the public, community, etc.; repute **2.** such regard when favorable [to lose one's *reputation*] **3.** fame; distinction

**re·pute** (ri pyōōt′) *vt.* **-put′ed, -put′ing** [< MFr. < L. < *re-*, again + *putare*, to think] to consider to be as specified [he is *reputed* to be rich] —*n. same as* REPUTATION (senses 1, 3)

**re·put·ed** (-id) *adj.* generally regarded as being such [the *reputed* owner] —**re·put′ed·ly** *adv.*

**re·quest** (ri kwest′) *n.* [< OFr. < ML., ult. < L. *requirere*: see REQUIRE] **1.** an asking for something; petition **2.** something asked for **3.** state of being asked for; demand [a song much in *request*] —*vt.* **1.** to ask for, esp. in a polite or formal way **2.** to ask (a person) to do something —**by request** in response to a request

**Re·qui·em** (rek′wē əm, rāk′-, rēk′-) *n.* [L., acc. of *requies*, rest: first word of the Mass] [*also* r-] **1.** *R.C.Ch. a*) a Mass for the repose of the dead *b*) a musical setting for this **2.** a dirge

‡**re·qui·es·cat in pa·ce** (rāk′wē es′kät in pä′chā, rek′-) [L.] may he (or she) rest in peace

**re·quire** (ri kwīr′) *vt.* **-quired′, -quir′ing** [< OFr. < L. *requirere* < *re-*, again + *quaerere*, to ask] **1.** to ask or insist upon, as by right or authority; demand **2.** to order; command [to *require* him to go] **3.** to need [to *require* help] **4.** to call for as needed [the work *requires* skill] —*vi.* to make a demand

**re·quire·ment** (-mənt) *n.* **1.** a requiring **2.** something required or demanded **3.** something needed; necessity

**req·ui·site** (rek′wə zit) *adj.* [< L. pp. of *requirere*: see REQUIRE] required; necessary; indispensable —*n.* something requisite

**req·ui·si·tion** (rek′wə zish′ən) *n.* **1.** a requiring, as by authority **2.** a formal written request, as for equipment **3.** the state of being demanded for use —*vt.* **1.** to demand or take, as by authority [to *requisition* food for troops] **2.** to demand from [to *requisition* a town for food] **3.** to submit a written request for (equipment, etc.)

**re·quite** (ri kwīt′) *vt.* -quit′ed, -quit′ing [RE- + *quite*, obs. var. of QUIT] to repay or make return to (a person, group, etc.) for (a benefit, service, etc. or an injury, wrong, etc.) —re·quit′al *n.* —re·quit′er *n.*

**rere·dos** (rir′däs, rer′ə-) *n.* [< Anglo-Fr. < OFr. *arere* (see ARREARS) + *dos*, back] an ornamental screen or partition wall behind an altar in a church

**re·route** (rē rōōt′, -rout′) *vt.* -rout′ed, -rout′ing to send by a new or different route

**re·run** (rē run′; *for n.* rē′run′) *vt.* -ran′, -run′ning to run again —*n.* 1. a rerunning; esp., a repeat showing of a movie, taped TV program, etc. 2. the movie, etc. so shown

**res** (räs, rēz) *n., pl.* **res** [L., a thing] *Law* 1. a thing; object 2. matter; case; point; action

**res.** 1. reserve 2. residence 3. resides 4. resolution

**re·sal·a·ble** (rē sāl′ə b′l) *adj.* that can be sold again

**re·sale** (rē′sāl′) *n.* the act of selling again

**re·scind** (ri sind′) *vt.* [L. *rescindere* < *re-*, back + *scindere*, to cut] to revoke, repeal, or cancel (a law, order, etc.) —re·scind′a·ble *adj.* —re·scind′er *n.*

**re·scis·sion** (ri sizh′ən) *n.* a rescinding

**re·script** (rē′skript) *n.* [< L. < pp. of *rescribere* < *re-*, back + *scribere*, to write] an official decree or order; specif., one issued by a court to its clerk

**res·cue** (res′kyōō) *vt.* -cued, -cu·ing [< OFr. < *re-*, again + *escorre*, to shake < L. < *ex-*, off + *quatere*, to shake] 1. to free or save from danger, evil, etc. 2. *Law* to take out of legal custody by force —*n.* a rescuing —res′cu·a·ble *adj.* —res′cu·er *n.*

**re·search** (ri surch′; *for n. equally* rē′surch) *n.* [< MFr.: see RE- & SEARCH] [*sometimes pl.*] systematic investigation in a field of knowledge, to discover or establish facts or principles —*vi., vt.* to do research (on or in) —re·search′a·ble *adj.* —re·search′er, re·search′ist *n.*

**re·seat** (rē sēt′) *vt.* 1. to seat again or in another seat 2. to supply with a new seat or seats

**re·sect** (ri sekt′) *vt.* [< L. pp. of *resecare* < *re-*, back + *secare*, to cut] *Surgery* to remove part of (an organ, bone, etc.) —re·sec′tion *n.*

**re·sem·blance** (ri zem′bləns) *n.* 1. a resembling; likeness 2. a point, degree, or sort of likeness

**re·sem·ble** (ri zem′b′l) *vt.* -bled, -bling [< OFr. < *re-*, again + *sembler* < L. *simulare*: see SIMULATE] to be like or similar to in appearance or nature

**re·sent** (ri zent′) *vt.* [< Fr. < OFr. < *re-*, again + *sentir* < L. *sentire*, to feel] to feel or show hurt or indignation at (some act, etc.) or toward (a person), from a sense of being offended —re·sent′ful *adj.* —re·sent′ful·ly *adv.* —re·sent′ful·ness *n.* —re·sent′ment *n.*

**re·ser·pine** (ri sur′pin, -pēn; res′ər pēn′) *n.* [G. *reserpin*] a crystalline alkaloid, $C_{33}H_{40}N_2O_9$, obtained from the root of a rauwolfia: used in the treatment of hypertension and as a sedative

**res·er·va·tion** (rez′ər vā′shən) *n.* 1. a reserving or the thing reserved; specif., *a)* public land set aside for some special use [an Indian *reservation*] *b)* an arrangement by which a hotel room, theater ticket, etc. is set aside for use at a certain time or until called for *c)* anything so reserved 2. a limiting condition or qualification, expressed or implied: see also MENTAL RESERVATION

**re·serve** (ri zurv′) *vt.* -served′, -serv′ing [< OFr. < L. < *re-*, back + *servare*, to hold] 1. to keep back, store up, or set apart for later use or a special purpose 2. to hold over to a later time 3. to set aside or have set aside (a theater seat, etc.) for someone 4. to retain for oneself [to *reserve* the right to refuse] —*n.* 1. something reserved 2. a limitation: now rare except in **without reserve** (see below) 3. the practice of keeping one's thoughts, feelings, etc. to oneself; aloofness; reticence; silence 5. restraint in artistic expression; freedom from exaggeration 6. [*pl.*] *a)* manpower kept out of action and ready for emergency use or for replacing others *b)* military forces not on active duty but subject to call; militia (with *the*) 7. cash, or any liquid assets, kept aside by a bank, business, etc. to meet expected or unexpected demands 8. land set apart for special use —*adj.* being, or having the nature of, a reserve —**in reserve** reserved for later use —**without reserve** subject to no limitation

**re·served** (ri zurvd′) *adj.* 1. set apart for some purpose, person, etc. 2. showing reserve; aloof or reticent —re·serv′ed·ly (-zur′vid lē) *adv.* —re·serv′ed·ness *n.*

**re·serv·ist** (ri zur′vist) *n.* a member of a country's military reserves

**res·er·voir** (rez′ər vwär′, rez′ə-; -vwôr′, -vôr′) *n.* [< Fr. < *réserver*: see RESERVE] 1. a place where anything is collected and stored; esp., a natural or artificial lake in which water is stored for use 2. a receptacle (in an apparatus) for a fluid, as oil or ink 3. a reserve supply

**re·set** (rē set′; *for n.* rē′set′) *vt.* -set′, -set′ting to set again —*n.* 1. a resetting 2. something reset 3. a device for resetting something

**re·ship** (rē ship′) *vt.* -shipped′, -ship′ping 1. to ship again 2. to transfer to another ship —re·ship′ment *n.*

**re·side** (ri zīd′) *vi.* -sid′ed, -sid′ing [< MFr. < L. *residere* < *re-*, back + *sedere*, to sit] 1. to dwell for a long time; live (*in* or *at*) 2. to be present or exist (*in*): said of qualities, etc. 3. to be vested (*in*): said of rights, powers, etc.

**res·i·dence** (rez′i dəns) *n.* 1. a residing 2. the fact or status of living or staying in a place while working or in training, school, etc. 3. the place where one resides; one's abode; esp., a house or mansion 4. the time during which a person resides in a place

**res·i·den·cy** (-dən sē) *n., pl.* -cies 1. *same as* RESIDENCE 2. a period of advanced, specialized medical or surgical training at a hospital

**res·i·dent** (-dənt) *adj.* 1. having a residence (*in* or *at*); residing 2. being in residence (sense 2) [a *resident* physician of a hospital] 3. present or existing (*in*) 4. not migratory: said of birds, etc. —*n.* 1. a person who lives in a place and is not a visitor or transient 2. a doctor who is serving a residency 3. a nonmigratory bird, etc.

**res·i·den·tial** (rez′ə dent′shəl) *adj.* 1. of or connected with residence 2. of or suitable for residences, or homes [a *residential* area] 3. chiefly for residents rather than transients [a *residential* hotel] —res′i·den′tial·ly *adv.*

**re·sid·u·al** (ri zij′oo wəl) *adj.* of or like a residue; leftover; remaining —*n.* 1. something remaining, as at the end of a process 2. [*pl.*] extra fees paid to performers for reruns, as on TV 3. *Math.* the difference between an actual and an estimated value —re·sid′u·al·ly *adv.*

**re·sid·u·ar·y** (-oo wer′ē) *adj.* 1. residual; leftover 2. *Law a)* relating to the residue of an estate *b)* receiving such a residue [a *residuary* legatee]

**res·i·due** (rez′ə dōō′, -dyōō′) *n.* [< MFr. < L. neut. of *residuus*, remaining < *residere*: see RESIDE] 1. what is left after part is removed; remainder 2. *Chem.* matter remaining after evaporation, combustion, etc. 3. *Law* that part of a testator's estate left after all claims and bequests have been satisfied

**res·id·u·um** (ri zij′oo wəm) *n., pl.* -u·a (-wə) [L.] *same as* RESIDUE

**re·sign** (ri zīn′) *vt., vi.* [< MFr. < L. < *re-*, back + *signare*, to sign] to give up or relinquish (a claim, office, position, etc.), esp. by formal notice (often with *from*) —**resign oneself (to)** to submit or become reconciled (to)

**res·ig·na·tion** (rez′ig nā′shən) *n.* 1. *a)* a resigning *b)* formal notice of this, esp. in writing 2. patient submission; acquiescence

**re·signed** (ri zīnd′) *adj.* feeling or showing resignation —re·sign′ed·ly (-zīn′id lē) *adv.* —re·sign′ed·ness *n.*

**re·sil·ience** (ri zil′yəns, -ē əns) *n.* the quality of being resilient: also **re·sil′ien·cy**

**re·sil·ient** (-yənt, -ē ənt) *adj.* [< L. prp. of *resilire* < *re-*, back + *salire*, to jump] 1. springing back into shape, position, etc. after being stretched, bent, or compressed 2. recovering strength, spirits, etc. quickly —re·sil′ient·ly *adv.*

**res·in** (rez′′n) *n.* [< MFr. < L. *resina*] 1. a solid or semisolid, viscous, organic substance exuded from various plants and trees: natural resins are used in varnishes and lacquers 2. *same as: a)* SYNTHETIC RESIN *b)* ROSIN —*vt.* to treat or rub with resin: also **res′in·ate′** (-ə nāt′) -at′ed, -at′ing —res′in·ous, res′in·y *adj.*

**re·sist** (ri zist′) *vt.* [< MFr. < L. < *re-*, back + *sistere*, to set] 1. to withstand; fend off; stand firm against 2. *a)* to oppose actively; fight or work against *b)* to refuse to cooperate with, submit to, etc. 3. to keep from yielding to or enjoying —*vi.* to oppose or withstand something; offer resistance —*n.* a resistant substance, as a protective coating —re·sist′er *n.* —re·sist′i·bil′i·ty *n.* —re·sist′i·ble *adj.* —re·sis′tive *adj.* —re·sis·tiv·i·ty (rē′zis tiv′ə tē, ri zis′-) *n.*

~~**re·sist·ance**~~ (ri zis′təns) *n.* 1. a resisting; opposition 2. power or capacity to resist; specif., the ability of an organism to ward off disease 3. opposition of some force, thing, etc. to another 4. a force that retards or opposes motion 5. [*often* R-] an underground movement in a country fighting against a foreign occupying power, etc. 6. *Elec. a)* the property by which a conductor opposes current flow and thus generates heat *b) same as* RESISTOR —re·sist′ant *adj.*

**re·sist·less** (ri zist′lis) *adj.* 1. that cannot be resisted; irresistible 2. without power to resist —re·sist′less·ly *adv.* —re·sist′less·ness *n.*

**re·sis·tor** (ri zis′tər) *n. Elec.* a device, as a wire coil, used to produce resistance in a circuit

**re·sole** (rē'sōl') *vt.* **-soled'**, **-sol'ing** to put a new sole on (a shoe, etc.) —*n.* a new sole for a shoe, etc.

**re·sol·u·ble** (ri zäl'yoo b'l, rez'əl-) *adj.* that can be resolved —**re·sol'u·bil'i·ty, re·sol'u·ble·ness** *n.*

**res·o·lute** (rez'ə lōōt') *adj.* [< L. pp. of *resolvere*: see RE- & SOLVE] having or showing a fixed, firm purpose; determined; resolved —**res'o·lute'ly** *adv.* —**res'o·lute'ness** *n.*

**res·o·lu·tion** (rez'ə lōō'shən) *n.* **1.** *a)* a resolving of something or breaking it up into its separate parts *b)* the result of this **2.** *a)* a determining or deciding *b)* a decision as to future action **3.** a resolute quality of mind **4.** a formal statement of opinion adopted by a group **5.** a solving or answering; solution **6.** the unraveling of the plot in a drama or narrative

**re·solve** (ri zälv', -zôlv') *vt.* **-solved'**, **-solv'ing** [< L.: see RE- & SOLVE] **1.** to break up into separate parts; analyze **2.** to change or transform [the talk *resolved* itself into a dispute] **3.** to cause to decide [this *resolved* him to go] **4.** to reach as a decision; determine [to *resolve* to go] **5.** *a)* to find an answer to; solve *b)* to make a decision about, esp. by vote or formally *c)* to explain or make clear (a problem, a fictional plot, etc.) *d)* to remove (doubt, etc.) **6.** *Music* to make (a dissonant chord or tone) become consonant —*vi.* **1.** to be resolved, as by analysis **2.** to come to a decision —*n.* **1.** a fixed purpose or intention **2.** a formal resolution, as by a group —**re·solv'a·bil'i·ty** *n.* —**re·solv'a·ble** *adj.* —**re·solv'er** *n.*

**re·solved** (-zälvd', -zôlvd') *adj.* firm and fixed in purpose; resolute —**re·solv'ed·ly** (-zäl'vid lē, -zôl'-) *adv.*

**res·o·nance** (rez'ə nəns) *n.* **1.** a being resonant **2.** the reinforcing and prolonging of a sound or musical tone by reflection and by sympathetic vibration of other bodies **3.** *Elec.* the condition arising in a circuit when an incoming current is at the same, or nearly the same, frequency as the circuit, thus producing much greater currents **4.** *Physics* the effect produced when the natural vibration frequency of a body is greatly amplified by vibrations at this same frequency from another body

**res·o·nant** (-nənt) *adj.* [< L. prp. of *resonare*, to resound] **1.** resounding or reechoing **2.** producing resonance [*resonant* walls] **3.** of, full of, or intensified by resonance [a *resonant* voice] —**res'o·nant·ly** *adv.*

**res·o·nate** (-nāt') *vi., vt.* **-nat'ed**, **-nat'ing** to be or make resonant

**res·o·na·tor** (-nāt'ər) *n.* **1.** a device for producing resonance or increasing sound by resonance **2.** *Electronics* an apparatus or system that can be put into oscillation by oscillations in another system

**re·sorb** (ri sôrb') *vt.* [< L. < *re-*, again + *sorbere*, to suck up] to absorb again —**re·sorp'tion** (-sôrp'shən) *n.*

**res·or·cin·ol** (ri zôr'si nōl', -nôl') *n.* [< RES(IN) + It. *or-cello*, a kind of lichen] a colorless crystalline compound, $C_6H_4(OH)_2$, used in making dyes, celluloid, pharmaceuticals, etc.: also **res·or'cin** (-sin)

**re·sort** (ri zôrt') *vi.* [< OFr. < *re-*, again + *sortir*, to go out] **1.** to go; esp., to go often **2.** to have recourse; turn (*to*) for help, support, etc. —*n.* **1.** a place people often go to for rest or recreation, as on a vacation **2.** a frequent getting together or visiting [a place of general *resort*] **3.** a person or thing one turns to for help, support, etc. **4.** a turning for help, support, etc.; recourse —**as a** (or **the**) **last resort** as the last available means

**re·sound** (ri zound') *vi.* [< OFr. < L. < *re-*, again + *sonare*, to sound] **1.** to echo or be filled with sound; reverberate **2.** to make a loud, echoing or prolonged sound **3.** to be echoed **4.** to be praised —*vt.* **1.** to give back (sound); echo **2.** to give forth or utter loudly

**re·sound·ing** (-iŋ) *adj.* **1.** reverberating **2.** thoroughgoing; complete [a *resounding* victory] **3.** high-sounding —**re·sound'ing·ly** *adv.*

**re·source** (rē'sôrs, -zôrs; ri sôrs', -zôrs') *n.* [< Fr. < OFr. < *re-*, again + *sourdre* (s to spring up < L. *surgere*, to rise] **1.** something ready for use or available as needed **2.** [*pl.*] wealth; assets **3.** [*pl.*] something useful, as coal or oil, that a country, state, etc. has **4.** a means to an end; expedient **5.** [*pl.*] a source of strength or ability within oneself: in full, **inner resources 6.** a being resourceful

**re·source·ful** (ri sôrs'fəl, -zôrs'-) *adj.* full of resource; able to deal promptly and effectively with difficulties, etc. —**re·source'ful·ly** *adv.* —**re·source'ful·ness** *n.*

**re·spect** (ri spekt') *vt.* [< L. pp. of *respicere* < *re-*, back + *specere*, to look at] **1.** to hold in high regard; show honor or courtesy to **2.** to show consideration for; avoid intruding upon, etc. [*respect* others' privacy] **3.** to concern; relate to —*n.* **1.** a feeling of high regard; esteem **2.** a being held in honor **3.** deference or dutiful regard [*respect* for law] **4.** courteous consideration **5.** [*pl.*] courteous expressions of regard: now chiefly in **pay one's respects**, to show polite regard as by visiting **6.** a particular point or detail [right in every *respect*] **7.** reference; relation [with *respect* to this] —**in respect of** with reference to —**re·spect'er** *n.*

**re·spect·a·ble** (ri spek'tə b'l) *adj.* **1.** worthy of respect or esteem **2.** socially acceptable; proper **3.** fairly good in quality **4.** fairly large **5.** good enough to be seen, worn, etc. —**re·spect'a·bil'i·ty** *n.* —**re·spect'a·bly** *adv.*

**re·spect·ful** (ri spekt'fəl) *adj.* full of or showing respect; polite —**re·spect'ful·ly** *adv.* —**re·spect'ful·ness** *n.*

**re·spect·ing** (ri spek'tiŋ) *prep.* concerning; about

**re·spec·tive** (-tiv) *adj.* as relates individually to each of two or more [their *respective* merits]

**re·spec·tive·ly** (-tiv lē) *adv.* in regard to each in the order named [the first and second prizes went to Mary and George, *respectively*]

**re·spell** (rē spel') *vt.* to spell again; specif., to spell differently in an attempt to show the pronunciation [to respell the word "calf" as (kaf)]

**res·pi·ra·tion** (res'pə rā'shən) *n.* **1.** act or process of respiring; breathing **2.** the processes by which a living organism or cell takes in oxygen, distributes and utilizes it in oxidation, and gives off products, esp. carbon dioxide **3.** a similar process in anaerobic organisms —**res'pi·ra'tion·al** *adj.*

**res·pi·ra·tor** (res'pə rāt'ər) *n.* **1.** a device, as of gauze, worn over the mouth and nose, as to prevent the inhaling of harmful substances **2.** an apparatus for giving artificial respiration

**res·pi·ra·to·ry** (res'pər ə tôr'ē, ri spir'ə-) *adj.* of, for, or involving respiration

**re·spire** (ri spīr') *vi., vt.* **-spired'**, **-spir'ing** [< OFr. < L. < *re-*, back + *spirare*, to breathe] to breathe; inhale and exhale (air)

**res·pite** (res'pit) *n.* [< OFr. < L. pp. of *respicere*: see RESPECT] **1.** a delay or postponement, esp. in carrying out a death sentence; reprieve **2.** a period of temporary relief, as from pain, work, etc. —*vt.* **-pit·ed**, **-pit·ing** to give a respite to

**re·splend·ent** (ri splen'dənt) *adj.* [< L. prp. of *resplendere* < *re-*, again + *splendere*, to shine] shining brightly; dazzling —**re·splend'ence, re·splend'en·cy** *n.* —**re·splend'ent·ly** *adv.*

**re·spond** (ri spänd') *vi.* [< OFr. < L. < *re-*, back + *spondere*, to pledge] **1.** to answer; reply **2.** to act in return, as if in answer **3.** to react favorably, as to medical treatment **4.** *Law* to be answerable or liable —*vt.* to say in answer

**re·spond·ent** (-spän'dənt) *adj.* responding; answering —*n.* **1.** a person who responds **2.** *Law* a defendant —**re·spond'ence, re·spond'en·cy** *n.*

**re·spond·er** (-dər) *n.* **1.** a person or thing that responds **2.** *Electronics* a device, as a transponder, that indicates reception of a signal

**re·sponse** (ri späns') *n.* [< ML. < L. pp. of *respondere*: see RESPOND] **1.** something said or done in answer; reply or reaction **2.** *Eccles.* a word, phrase, etc. sung or spoken in answer, as by a congregation or choir in answer to an officiating clergyman **3.** *Electronics* the ratio of output to input of a device or system **4.** *Physiol., Psychol.* a reaction to a stimulus

**re·spon·si·bil·i·ty** (ri spän'sə bil'ə tē) *n., pl.* **-ties 1.** a being responsible; obligation, accountability, etc. **2.** a person or thing that one is responsible for

**re·spon·si·ble** (ri spän'sə b'l) *adj.* [< MFr. < L.: see RESPONSE] **1.** expected or obliged to account (*for* something, *to* someone); answerable **2.** involving obligation or duties [a *responsible* job] **3.** that can be charged with being the cause, agent, etc. of something **4.** able to think and act rationally, and hence accountable for one's behavior **5.** dependable or reliable, as in meeting obligations —**re·spon'si·ble·ness** *n.* —**re·spon'si·bly** *adv.*

**re·spon·sive** (-siv) *adj.* **1.** answering **2.** reacting readily, as to suggestion [a *responsive* audience] **3.** containing responses [*responsive* reading in church] —**re·spon'sive·ly** *adv.* —**re·spon'sive·ness** *n.*

**rest¹** (rest) *n.* [OE.] **1.** *a)* peace, ease, and refreshment, as produced by sleep *b)* sleep or repose **2.** refreshing inactivity after work or exertion, or a period of this **3.** *a)* relief from anything distressing, tiring, etc. *b)* peace of mind **4.** the repose of death **5.** absence of motion **6.** a place for resting; lodging place, as for travelers **7.** a thing that supports [a foot *rest*] **8.** *Music a)* a measured interval of silence between tones *b)* a symbol for this —*vi.* **1.** *a)* to get refreshed by sleeping, lying down, ceasing work, etc. *b)* to sleep **2.** to be at ease or at peace **3.** to be dead **4.** to be quiet or still for a while **5.** to remain unchanged [let the matter rest] **6.** *a)* to lie, sit, or lean *b)* to be placed or based (*in, on,* etc.) **7.** to be or lie (where specified) [the fault *rests* with him] **8.** to be fixed [his eyes *rested* on her] **9.** to rely; depend **10.** *Law* to end voluntarily the introduction of evidence in a case —*vt.*

MUSICAL RESTS
(A, whole; B, half;
C, quarter; D,
eighth; E, sixteenth)

**1.** to give rest to; refresh by rest **2.** to put or lay for ease, support, etc. *[rest* your head on the pillow*]* **3.** to base; ground *[to rest* an argument on facts*]* **4.** to fix (the eyes, etc.) **5.** to bring to rest; stop **6.** *Law* to cause (a case) to rest —**at rest 1.** asleep **2.** immobile **3.** free from distress, care, etc. **4.** dead —**lay to rest** to bury —**rest′er** *n.*

**rest²** (rest) *n.* [< OFr. < L. *restare*, to remain < *re-*, back + *stare*, to stand] **1.** what is left; remainder **2.** [*with pl. v.*] the others Used with *the* —*vi.* to go on being *[rest* assured*]*

**re·state** (rē stāt′) *vt.* **-stat′ed, -stat′ing** to state again, esp. in a different way —**re·state′ment** *n.*

**res·tau·rant** (res′tə rənt, -ränt′) *n.* [Fr. < prp. of *restaurer:* see RESTORE] a place where meals can be bought and eaten

**res·tau·ra·teur** (res′tər ə tur′) *n.* [Fr.] a person who owns or operates a restaurant

**rest·ful** (rest′fəl) *adj.* **1.** full of or giving rest **2.** quiet; peaceful **3.** having a soothing effect —**rest′ful·ly** *adv.* —**rest′ful·ness** *n.*

**res·ti·tu·tion** (res′tə tōō′shən, -tyōō′-) *n.* [< MFr. < L. < pp. of *restituere*, to restore < *re-*, again + *statuere*, to set up] **1.** restoration to the rightful owner of something lost or taken away **2.** a making good for loss or damage **3.** a return to a former condition

**res·tive** (res′tiv) *adj.* [< OFr. < *rester:* see REST²] **1.** hard to control; unruly, balky, etc. **2.** nervous or impatient under restraint; restless —**res′tive·ly** *adv.* —**res′tive·ness** *n.*

**rest·less** (rest′lis) *adj.* **1.** unable to rest or relax **2.** giving no rest or relaxation; disturbed *[restless* sleep*]* **3.** never or seldom still; always moving **4.** seeking change; discontented —**rest′less·ly** *adv.* —**rest′less·ness** *n.*

**res·to·ra·tion** (res′tə rā′shən) *n.* **1.** a restoring or being restored, as of a person or thing to a former condition or position, or of something taken away or lost to its rightful owner **2.** a reconstruction of the original form of a building, fossil animal, etc. **3.** a restored thing —**the Restoration 1.** reestablishment of the monarchy in England in 1660 under Charles II **2.** the period of his reign (1660-85)

**re·stor·a·tive** (ri stôr′ə tiv) *adj.* of restoration **2.** restoring or able to restore health, consciousness, etc. —*n.* a thing that restores

**re·store** (ri stôr′) *vt.* **-stored′, -stor′ing** [< OFr. < L. < *re-*, again + *-staurare*, to place] **1.** to give back (something taken away, lost, etc.) **2.** to bring back to a former or normal condition, as by repairing, rebuilding, etc. **3.** to put (a person) back into a position, rank, etc. **4.** to bring back to health, strength, etc. **5.** to bring back into being, use, etc. —**re·stor′a·ble** *adj.* —**re·stor′er** *n.*

**restr.** restaurant

**re·strain** (ri strān′) *vt.* [< OFr. < L. < *re-*, back + *stringere*, to draw tight] **1.** to hold back from action; check; curb **2.** to keep under control **3.** to deprive of physical liberty, as by shackling **4.** to limit; restrict —**re·strain′a·ble** *adj.* —**re·strain′ed·ly** *adv.* —**re·strain′er** *n.*

**re·straint** (ri strānt′) *n.* **1.** a restraining or being restrained **2.** a restraining influence or action **3.** a means of restraining **4.** loss or limitation of liberty **5.** control of emotions, impulses, etc.; reserve

**restraint of trade** restriction or prevention of business competition, as by monopoly, price fixing, etc.

**re·strict** (ri strikt′) *vt.* [< L. pp. of *restringere:* see RESTRAIN] to keep within certain limits; limit; confine

**re·strict·ed** (ri strik′tid) *adj.* limited; confined; specif., *a)* that may be seen only by authorized personnel *[a restricted* document*] b)* excluding certain groups, esp. minorities

**re·stric·tion** (-shən) *n.* **1.** restricting or being restricted **2.** something that restricts; limitation

**re·stric·tion·ism** (-shən iz′m) *n.* the policy of favoring restriction, as of trade, immigration, etc. —**re·stric′tion·ist** *n., adj.*

**re·stric·tive** (ri strik′tiv) *adj.* **1.** restricting or tending to restrict **2.** *Gram.* designating a clause, phrase, or word felt as limiting what it modifies and so not set off with commas (Ex.: the man *who spoke to us* is my uncle) —**re·stric′tive·ly** *adj.* —**re·stric′tive·ness** *n.*

**rest·room** (rest′rōōm′) *n.* a room or rooms in a public building, with toilets, washbowls, and, sometimes, couches, etc.: also **rest room**

**re·struc·ture** (rē struk′chər) *vt.* **-tured, -tur·ing** to plan or provide a new structure or organization for

**re·sult** (ri zult′) *vi.* [< ML. < L. *resultare*, to rebound, freq. of *resilire:* see RESILIENT] **1.** to happen because of something else; follow as an effect (often with *from*) **2.** to end (*in* something) as an effect or development —*n.* **1.** *a)* what comes about from an action, process, etc.; consequence; outcome *b)* [*pl.*] desired effects **2.** the number, quantity, etc. obtained by mathematical calculation

**re·sult·ant** (-′nt) *adj.* that results —*n.* **1.** a result **2.** *Physics* a force, velocity, etc. with an effect equal to that of two or more such forces, etc. acting together

**re·sume** (ri zōōm′, -zyōōm′) *vt.* **-sumed′, -sum′ing** [< MFr. < L. < *re-*, again + *sumere*, to take] **1.** to take or occupy again **2.** to begin again or go on with again after interruption —*vi.* to begin again or go on again

**ré·su·mé** (rez′ŏŏ mā′, rā′zŏŏ-; rā′zŏŏ mā′) *n.* [Fr., pp. of *résumer:* see prec.] a summary; specif., a statement of a job applicant's previous employment experience, education, etc.: also written **resume, resumé**

**re·sump·tion** (ri zump′shən) *n.* [< L. < pp. of *resumere*] the act of resuming

**re·sur·face** (rē sur′fis) *vt.* **-faced, -fac·ing** to put a new surface on —*vi.* to come to the surface again

**re·surge** (ri surj′) *vi.* **-surged′, -surg′ing 1.** to rise again; revive **2.** to surge back again

**re·sur·gent** (-sur′jənt) *adj.* rising or tending to rise again; resurging —**re·sur′gence** *n.*

**res·ur·rect** (rez′ə rekt′) *vt.* [< ff.] **1.** *Theol.* to bring back to life **2.** to bring back into notice, use, etc. —*vi. Theol.* to rise from the dead

**res·ur·rec·tion** (rez′ə rek′shən) *n.* [< OFr. < LL. < L. *resurrectus*, pp. of *resurgere*, to rise again] **1.** *Theol. a)* a rising from the dead, or coming back to life *b)* the state of having so risen **2.** a return to notice, use, etc.; revival —**the Resurrection** *Theol.* **1.** the rising of Jesus from the dead **2.** the rising of all the dead at the Last Judgment —**res′ur·rec′tion·al** *adj.*

**resurrection plant** any of various small plants that curl up when dry and spread their branches or become green again when watered

**re·sus·ci·tate** (ri sus′ə tāt′) *vt., vi.* **-tat′ed, -tat′ing** [< L. pp. of *resuscitare* < *re-*, again + *suscitare*, to revive] to revive (someone who is unconscious, apparently dead, etc.) —**re·sus′ci·ta′tion** *n.* —**re·sus′ci·ta′tive** *adj.* —**re·sus′ci·ta′tor** *n.*

**ret** (ret) *vt.* **ret′ted, ret′ting** [MDu. *reten*] to dampen or soak (flax, hemp, etc.) in water to separate the fibers from woody tissue

**ret. 1.** retain **2.** retired **3.** return(ed)

**re·tail** (rē′tāl; *for v. 2, usually* ri tāl′) *n.* [< OFr. *retailler*, to cut up < *re-*, again + *tailler*, to cut] the sale of goods in small quantities directly to the consumer: cf. WHOLESALE —*adj.* having to do with the selling of goods in this way —*adv.* in small amounts or at a retail price —*vt.* **1.** to sell as retail goods **2.** to repeat or pass on (gossip, etc.) —*vi.* to be sold as retail goods —**re′tail·er** *n.*

**re·tain** (ri tān′) *vt.* [< OFr. < L. < *re-*, back + *tenere*, to hold] **1.** to keep in possession **2.** to keep in a fixed state **3.** to continue to hold (heat, etc.) **4.** to continue to use, etc. **5.** to keep in mind; remember **6.** to engage (a lawyer, etc.) by an advance fee called a retainer —**re·tain′ment** *n.*

**re·tain·er** (ri tā′nər) *n.* **1.** a person or thing that retains **2.** a servant, attendant, etc., as of a person or family of rank or wealth **3.** *Law a)* the retaining of the services of a lawyer, consultant, etc. *b)* a fee paid in advance to make such services available when needed

**retaining wall** a wall built to keep a bank of earth from sliding or water from flooding

**re·take** (rē tāk′; *for n.* rē′tāk′) *vt.* **-took′, -tak′en, -tak′ing 1.** to take again, take back, or recapture **2.** to photograph again —*n.* **1.** a retaking **2.** a movie scene, etc. rephotographed or to be rephotographed

**re·tal·i·ate** (ri tal′ē āt′) *vi.* **-at′ed, -at′ing** [< L. pp. of *retaliare* < *re-*, back + *talio*, punishment in kind] to return like for like; esp., to pay back injury for injury —*vt.* to return in kind (an injury, wrong, etc. suffered) —**re·tal′i·a′tion** *n.* —**re·tal′i·a′tive** *adj.* —**re·tal′i·a·to′ry** *adj.*

**re·tard** (ri tärd′) *vt.* [< OFr. < L. < *re-*, back + *tardare*, to make slow < *tardus*, slow] to hinder, delay, or slow the advance or progress of —*n.* a retarding; delay

**re·tard·ant** (-′nt) *n.* something that retards; esp., a substance that delays a chemical reaction: also **re·tard′er** —*adj.* tending to retard

**re·tard·ate** (ri tär′dāt) *n.* a mentally retarded person

**re·tar·da·tion** (rē′tär dā′shən) *n.* **1.** a retarding or being retarded **2.** something that retards **3.** *same as* MENTAL RETARDATION —**re·tard′a·tive** (ri tär′də tiv), **re·tard′a·to′ry** (-tôr′ē) *adj.*

**re·tard·ed** (ri tär′did) *adj.* delayed in development or progress, esp. because of mental retardation

**retch** (rech) *vi.* [OE. *hræcan*, to hawk, spit] to strain to vomit, esp. without bringing anything up

**retd. 1.** retained **2.** retired **3.** returned

**re·ten·tion** (ri ten′shən) *n.* [L.] **1.** a retaining or being retained **2.** power of or capacity for retaining **3.** *a)* memory *b)* ability to remember

**re·ten·tive** (-tiv) *adj.* **1.** retaining or able to retain **2.** having good recall or a good memory —**re·ten′tive·ly** *adv.* —**re·ten′tive·ness, re·ten·tiv·i·ty** (rē′ten tiv′ə tē) *n.*

**re·think** (rē thiŋk′) *vt.* **-thought′, -think′ing** to think over again, with a view to changing; reconsider

**ret·i·cence** (ret′ə s′ns) *n.* quality, state, or instance of being reticent; reserve: also **ret′i·cen·cy**

**ret·i·cent** (-s′nt) *adj.* [< L. prp. of *reticere* < *re-*, again + *tacere*, to be silent] **1.** not willing to say much; tending to keep one's thoughts, etc. to oneself; reserved **2.** having a restrained, quiet, or understated quality —**ret′i·cent·ly** *adv.*

**re·tic·u·lar** (ri tik′yə lər) *adj.* [see RETICULE] **1.** netlike **2.** intricate —**re·tic′u·lar·ly** *adv.*

**re·tic·u·late** (-lit; *also, and for v. always,* -lāt′) *adj.* [< L. < *reticulum:* see ff.] like a net or network, as the veins of some leaves: also **re·tic′u·lat′ed** —*vt., vi.* **-lat′ed, -lat′ing** to divide, mark, or be marked so as to look like network —**re·tic′u·late·ly** *adv.* —**re·tic′u·la′tion** *n.*

**ret·i·cule** (ret′ə kyōōl′) *n.* [< Fr. < L. *reticulum*, dim. of *rete*, a net] a woman's drawstring handbag, orig. of net

**re·tic·u·lum** (ri tik′yə ləm) *n., pl.* **-la** (-lə) [L.: see RETICULE] **1.** network **2.** the second division of the stomach of cud-chewing animals, as cows

**ret·i·na** (ret′′n ə) *n., pl.* **-nas, -nae′** (-ē′) [ML., prob. < L. *rete*, a net] the innermost coat of the back part of the eyeball, on which the image is formed by the lens —**ret′i·nal** *adj.*

**ret·i·nue** (ret′′n ōō′, -yōō′) *n.* [< OFr. < pp. of *retenir:* see RETAIN] a body of assistants, servants, etc. attending a person of rank or importance; train of attendants

**re·tire** (ri tīr′) *vi.* **-tired′, -tir′ing** [< Fr. < *re-*, back + *tirer*, to draw] **1.** to withdraw to a private or secluded place **2.** to go to bed **3.** to retreat, as in battle **4.** to give up one's work, career, etc., esp. because of advanced age **5.** to move back or away —*vt.* **1.** to withdraw or move (troops) in retreat **2.** to take (money, paid-off bonds, etc.) out of circulation **3.** to cause to retire from a job, etc. **4.** to withdraw (an outdated or worn-out thing) from use **5.** *Baseball*, etc. to end the batting turn of (a batter, side, etc.)

**re·tired** (ri tīrd′) *adj.* **1.** secluded or private **2.** *a)* that has given up one's work, etc., esp. because of advanced age *b)* of or for such retired persons

**re·tir·ee** (ri tīr′ē′) *n.* one who has retired from work, etc.: also **re·tir′ant** (-ənt)

**re·tire·ment** (ri tīr′mənt) *n.* **1.** a retiring or being retired, specif. from work, etc. **2.** *a)* privacy; seclusion *b)* a place of privacy or seclusion

**re·tir·ing** (-iŋ) *adj.* **1.** that retires **2.** reserved; modest; shy

**re·took** (rē tŏōk′) *pt. of* RETAKE

**re·tool** (rē tōōl′) *vt., vi.* to adapt the machinery of (a factory) for making a different product by changing the tools and dies

**re·tort**[1] (ri tôrt′) *vt., vi.* [< L. *retortus*, pp. of *retorquere* < *re-*, back + *torquere*, to twist] **1.** to return in kind (an insult, etc. received) **2.** to answer back, esp. in a sharp, quick, or clever way —*n.* a retorting or the response so made

**re·tort**[2] (ri tôrt′) *n.* [< Fr. < ML. *retorta* < L. fem. pp.: see prec.] **1.** a container for distilling, usually of glass and with a long tube **2.** a vessel for heating ore to extract metal, coal to produce gas, etc.

**re·touch** (rē tuch′; for n., also rē′tuch′) *vt.* to touch up or change details in (a painting, the negative or print of a photograph, etc.) —*n.* a retouching or thing retouched —**re·touch′er** *n.*

RETORT

**re·trace** (ri trās′) *vt.* **-traced′, -trac′ing** [Fr. *retracer:* see RE- & TRACE[1]] **1.** to go back over again, esp. in the reverse direction [to *retrace* one's steps] **2.** to trace again the story of, from the beginning

**re-trace** (rē′trās′) *vt.* **-traced′, -trac′ing** to trace the lines of (a drawing, engraving, etc.) over again

**re·tract** (ri trakt′) *vt., vi.* [< L.: ult. < *re-*, back + *trahere*, to draw] **1.** to draw back or in [to *retract* claws] **2.** to withdraw or take back (a statement, offer, charge, etc.); recant —**re·tract′a·bil′i·ty** *n.* —**re·tract′a·ble** *adj.* —**re·trac′tion** *n.* —**re·trac′tive** *adj.*

**re·trac·tile** (ri trak′t′l, -tīl) *adj.* [Fr.] that can be retracted, or drawn back or in, as the claws of a cat

**re·trac·tor** (-tər) *n.* one that retracts; esp., *a)* a muscle that retracts an organ, protruded part, etc. *b)* a surgical device for retracting a part or organ

**re·tread** (rē tred′; *for n.* rē′tred′) *vt., n. same as* RECAP[1]

**re·tread** (rē′tred′) *vt.* **-trod′, -trod′den** or **-trod′, -tread′-ing** to tread again

**re·treat** (ri trēt′) *n.* [< OFr., ult. < L. *re-*, back + *trahere*, to draw] **1.** a going back or backward; withdrawal in the face of opposition, etc. **2.** withdrawal to a safe or private place **3.** a safe, quiet, or secluded place **4.** a period of seclusion, esp. for religious contemplation, often as part of a group **5.** *Mil. a)* the forced withdrawal of troops under attack, or a signal for this *b)* a signal by bugle or drum at sunset for lowering the national flag, or this ceremony —*vi.* **1.** to withdraw; go back **2.** to slope backward —**beat a retreat** to retreat or withdraw in a hurry

**re·trench** (rē trench′) *vt., vi.* [< MFr.: see RE- & TRENCH] to cut down or reduce (esp. expenses); curtail, economize, etc. —**re·trench′ment** *n.*

**ret·ri·bu·tion** (ret′rə byōō′shən) *n.* [< OFr. < LL., ult. < L. < *re-*, back + *tribuere*, to pay] deserved punishment for evil done, or, sometimes, reward for good done —**re·trib·u·tive** (ri trib′yōō tiv), **re·trib′u·to·ry** (-tôr′ē) *adj.* —**re·trib′u·tive·ly** *adv.*

**re·triev·al** (ri trē′v′l) *n.* **1.** a retrieving **2.** possibility of recovery or restoration

**re·trieve** (ri trēv′) *vt.* **-trieved′, -triev′ing** [< OFr. < *re-*, again + *trouver*, to find] **1.** to get back; recover **2.** to restore; revive [to *retrieve* one's spirits] **3.** to rescue or save **4.** to set right or repair (a loss, error, etc.) **5.** to recall to mind **6.** to recover (information) from data stored in a computer **7.** *Hunting* to find and bring back (killed or wounded game): said of dogs **8.** *Tennis*, etc. to return (a ball hard to reach) —*vi. Hunting* to retrieve game —*n.* a retrieving —**re·triev′a·ble** *adj.*

**re·triev·er** (-ər) *n.* **1.** a person or thing that retrieves **2.** a dog trained to retrieve game; specif., any of several breeds of dog developed for this purpose

**ret·ro** (ret′rō) *n., pl.* **-ros** *clipped form of* RETROROCKET

**ret·ro-** [< L. *retro*, backward] *a combining form meaning* backward, back, behind [*retroactive*]

**ret·ro·ac·tive** (ret′rō ak′tiv) *adj.* applying to, or going into effect as of, the preceding period [a *retroactive* pay increase] —**ret′ro·ac′tive·ly** *adv.* —**ret′ro·ac·tiv′i·ty** *n.*

**ret·ro·cede** (ret′rə sēd′) *vi.* **-ced′ed, -ced′ing** [< L. < *retro-*, back + *cedere*, to yield, go] to go back; recede —*vt.* to cede (territory) back —**ret′ro·ces′sion** (-sesh′ən) *n.*

**ret·ro·fire** (ret′rə fīr′) *vi., vt.* **-fired′, -fir′ing** to ignite: said of a retrorocket —*n.* a retrofiring

**ret·ro·fit** (-fit′) *n.* [RETRO- + FIT[1]] a change in design, construction, etc., as of an aircraft, to incorporate later improvements —*vt., vi.* **-fit′ted, -fit′ting** to modify with a retrofit

**ret·ro·flex** (-fleks′) *adj.* [< L.: see RETRO- & FLEX] **1.** bent or turned backward **2.** *Phonet.* pronounced with the tip of the tongue raised and bent slightly backward Also **ret′ro·flexed′** —*n. Phonet.* a retroflex sound

**ret·ro·grade** (ret′rə grād′) *adj.* [< L. *retrogradi:* see RETRO- & GRADE] **1.** moving or directed backward **2.** going back to an earlier, esp. worse, condition —*vi.* **-grad′ed, -grad′ing** **1.** to go or move backward **2.** to deteriorate

**ret·ro·gress** (ret′rə gres′, ret′rə gres′) *vi.* [< L. pp. of *retrogradi:* see prec.] to move backward, esp. into an earlier or worse condition —**ret′ro·gres′sion** (-gresh′ən) *n.* —**ret′ro·gres′sive** *adj.* —**ret′ro·gres′sive·ly** *adv.*

**ret·ro·rock·et, ret·ro-rock·et** (ret′rō räk′it) *n.* a small rocket on a larger rocket or spacecraft, used to produce thrust against flight direction so as to reduce speed

**ret·ro·spect** (ret′rə spekt′) *n.* [< L. pp. of *retrospicere* < *retro-*, back + *specere*, to look] a looking back on or thinking about things past —**in retrospect** in reviewing the past —**ret′ro·spec′tion** *n.*

**ret·ro·spec·tive** (ret′rə spek′tiv) *adj.* **1.** looking or directed back, to the past, etc. **2.** retroactive —*n.* an art show of typical works of an artist over all or part of his lifetime —**ret′ro·spec′tive·ly** *adv.*

**ret·rous·sé** (ret′rōō sā′) *adj.* [Fr., turned up] turned up at the tip [a *retroussé* nose]

**ret·si·na** (ret′si nə) *n.* [ModGr.] a wine of Greece, flavored with pine resin

**re·turn** (ri turn′) *vi.* [< OFr. *retourner:* see RE- & TURN] **1.** to go or come back **2.** to answer; retort —*vt.* **1.** to bring, send, carry, or put back **2.** to pay back by doing or giving the same; reciprocate [to *return* a visit, a compliment, etc.] **3.** to produce (a profit, revenue, etc.); yield **4.** to report officially or formally **5.** to elect or reelect, as to a legislature **6.** to render (a verdict, etc.) **7.** *Sports* to hit back or throw back (a ball) —*n.* **1.** a coming or going back **2.** a bringing, sending, carrying, or putting back **3.** something returned **4.** repayment; requital; reciprocation **5.** *a)* profit made on an exchange of goods *b)* [*often pl.*] yield or profit, as from investments **6.** an answer; retort **7.** *a)* an official or formal report *b)* [*usually pl.*] a report on a vote count [election *returns*] *c)* a form for reporting income tax due: in full, **(income) tax return**—*adj.* **1.** of or for returning [a *return* ticket] **2.** given, sent, done, etc. again or in return [a *return* visit] **3.** returning or returned **—in return** as a return; as an equivalent, etc.

**re·turn·a·ble** (ri tur′nə b'l) *adj.* that can or may be returned **—n.** a container, as a glass beer bottle, that can be returned for reuse and for a refund of a deposit on it

**re·turn·ee** (ri tur′nē′) *n.* a person who returns, as home from military service

**Reu·ben** (rōō′bin) [via LL. < Gr. < Heb. *rĕ′ūbēn*, lit., behold, a son] **1.** a masculine name **2.** *Bible a)* the eldest son of Jacob *b)* the tribe of Israel descended from him

**Reuben (sandwich)** [? after *Reuben* Kay, Omaha grocer c. 1930] a sandwich made with rye bread, corned beef, sauerkraut, Swiss cheese, and a dressing and served hot

**re·u·ni·fy** (rē yōō′nə fī′) *vt., vi.* **-fied′, -fy′ing** to unify again after being divided **—re′u·ni·fi·ca′tion** *n.*

**Ré·un·ion** (rā ü nyōn′; *E.* rē yōōn′yən) French island possession in the Indian Ocean, east of Madagascar

**re·un·ion** (rē yōōn′yən) *n.* **1.** a reuniting **2.** a gathering of persons after separation *[a family reunion]*

**re·u·nite** (rē′yōō nīt′) *vt., vi.* **-nit′ed, -nit′ing** to unite again; bring or come together again

**rev** (rev) *n.* [Colloq.] a revolution, as of an engine **—vt., vi. revved, rev′ving** [Colloq.] to speed up (an engine, motor, etc.): usually with *up*

**Rev. 1.** *Bible* Revelation **2.** *pl.* **Revs.** Reverend

**rev. 1.** revenue **2.** reverse **3.** review(ed) **4.** revise(d) **5.** revision **6.** revolution **7.** revolving

**re·val·u·ate** (rē val′yoo wāt′) *vt.* **-at′ed, -at′ing** to make a new valuation or appraisal of **—re·val′u·a′tion** *n.*

**re·vamp** (rē vamp′) *vt.* **1.** to put a new vamp on (a shoe or boot) **2.** to make over; revise **—n.** a revamping

**re·vanch·ism** (rə vänsh′iz′m, -vänch′-) *n.* [ < Fr. *revanche*, revenge + -ISM] the revengeful spirit moving a defeated nation to aggressively seek restoration of territories, etc. **—re·vanch′ist** *adj., n.*

**re·veal** (ri vēl′) *vt.* [ < OFr. < L. *revelare*, lit., to draw back the veil < *re-*, back + *velum*, a veil] **1.** to make known (something hidden or secret); disclose **2.** to expose to view; show; display **—re·veal′a·ble** *adj.* **—re·veal′er** *n.*

**re·veil·le** (rev′ə lē; *Brit.* ri val′ē, -vel′-) *n.* [ < Fr. imper. of (*se*) *réveiller*, to wake up, ult. < L. *re-*, again + *vigilare*, to watch] *Mil.* **1.** a signal on a bugle, drum, etc. early in the morning to wake soldiers or sailors or call them to first assembly **2.** the first assembly of the day

**rev·el** (rev′'l) *vi.* **-eled** or **-elled, -el·ing** or **-el·ling** [ < MFr. < L. *rebellare*: see REBEL] **1.** to make merry; be noisily festive **2.** to take much pleasure (*in*) *[to revel in sports]* **—n. 1.** merrymaking; revelry **2.** [*often pl.*] an occasion of merrymaking **—rev′el·er, rev′el·ler** *n.*

**rev·e·la·tion** (rev′ə lā′shən) *n.* **1.** a revealing, or disclosing **2.** something disclosed, especially when it comes as a great surprise **3.** *Theol.* God's revealing of himself and his will to man **—[R- ]** the last book of the New Testament (in full, **The Revelation of Saint John the Divine**): also **Revelations** **—rev′e·la′tor** *n.* **—rev′e·la·to′ry** (-lə tôr′ē) *adj.*

**rev·el·ry** (rev′'l rē) *n., pl.* **-ries** reveling; noisy merrymaking; boisterous festivity

**re·venge** (ri venj′) *vt.* **-venged′, -veng′ing** [ < OFr. *re-*, again + *vengier*, to take vengeance < L. *vindicare*: see VINDICATE] **1.** to inflict injury or punishment in return for (an injury, insult, etc.) **2.** to avenge (a person, oneself, etc.) **—n. 1.** a revenging; vengeance **2.** what is done in revenging **3.** desire to take vengeance **4.** a chance to retaliate, as by a return match after a defeat **—be revenged** to get revenge **—re·veng′er** *n.* **—re·veng′ing·ly** *adv.*

**re·venge·ful** (-fəl) *adj.* full of or desiring revenge **—re·venge′ful·ly** *adv.* **—re·venge′ful·ness** *n.*

**rev·e·nue** (rev′ə nōō′, -nyōō′) *n.* [ < MFr. < *re-*, back + *venir* < L. *venire*, to come] **1.** the income or return from property or investment **2.** a source of income **3.** the income of a government from taxes, licenses, etc.

**rev·e·nu·er** (-ər) *n.* [Colloq.] a Treasury Department revenue agent, esp. one concerned with halting the illegal distilling of alcohol and bootlegging

**re·ver·ber·ant** (ri vur′bər ənt) *adj.* reverberating

**re·ver·ber·ate** (-bə rāt′) *vt.* **-at′ed, -at′ing** [ < L. *re-*, again + *verberare*, to beat < *verber*, a lash] **1.** to cause (a sound) to reecho **2.** to reflect (light, heat, etc.) **—vi. 1.** to reecho or resound **2.** to be reflected, as light or sound waves **3.** to recoil; rebound

**re·ver·ber·a·tion** (ri var′bə rā′shən) *n.* **1.** a reverberating or being reverberated; reflection of light or sound waves, etc. **2.** something reverberated, as reechoed sound **—re·ver′ber·a′tive** (-bə rāt′iv, -bər ə tiv) *adj.* **—re·ver′ber·a·tive·ly** *adv.* **—re·ver′ber·a·to′ry** (-bər ə tôr′ē) *adj.*

**Re·vere** (ri vir′), **Paul** 1735–1818; Am. patriot

**re·vere** (ri vir′) *vt.* **-vered′, -ver′ing** [ < Fr. < L. < *re-*, again + *vereri*, to fear] to regard with deep respect, love, and awe; venerate

**rev·er·ence** (rev′ər əns, rev′rəns) *n.* **1.** a feeling or attitude of deep respect, love, and awe; veneration **2.** a manifestation of this; specif., a bow or curtsy **3.** [R-] a title used in speaking to or of a clergyman: preceded by *your* or *his* **—vt. -enced, -enc·ing** to treat with reverence

**rev·er·end** (-ər ənd, -rənd) *adj.* [ < MFr. < L. *reverendus*, gerundive of *revereri*: see REVERE] worthy of reverence: used [*usually* **the R-**] as a title of respect for a clergyman, often before the name **—n.** *colloq. term for* CLERGYMAN

**rev·er·ent** (-ər ənt, -rənt) *adj.* feeling or showing reverence **—rev′er·ent·ly** *adv.*

**rev·er·en·tial** (rev′ə ren′shəl) *adj.* showing or caused by reverence **—rev′er·en′tial·ly** *adv.*

**rev·er·ie** (rev′ər ē) *n.* [ < Fr. < MFr. < *rever*, to wander] **1.** dreamy thinking, esp. of agreeable things; daydreaming **2.** a fanciful notion or daydream

**re·vers** (ri vir′, -ver′) *n., pl.* **-vers′** (-virz′, -verz′) [Fr. < L. *reversus*: see REVERSE] a part (of a garment) turned back to show the reverse side or facing, as a lapel: also **re·vere′**

**re·ver·sal** (ri vur′s'l) *n.* a reversing or being reversed

**re·verse** (ri vurs′) *adj.* [ < OFr. < L. pp. of *revertere*: see REVERT] **1.** *a)* turned backward; opposite or contrary, as in position, direction, etc. *b)* with the back showing **2.** reversing the usual effect, as to show white letters on a black background **3.** acting or moving in a way opposite or contrary to the usual **4.** causing movement backward or in the opposite direction **—n. 1.** the opposite or contrary **2.** the back, as the side of a coin or medal that does not show the main design **3.** a reversing; esp., a change from good fortune to bad; defeat; check **4.** a mechanism, etc. for reversing, as a gear or an arrangement in an automatic transmission that causes a machine or motor vehicle to run backward **—vt. -versed′, -vers′ing 1.** to turn in an opposite position or direction, upside down, or inside out **2.** to change to the opposite **3.** to cause to go in an opposite direction **4.** to transfer (the charges for a telephone call) to the party being called **5.** *Law* to revoke or annul (a decision, etc.) **—vi. 1.** to go or turn in the opposite direction **2.** to put a motor, engine, etc. in reverse **—re·verse′ly** *adv.* **—re·vers′er** *n.*

**re·vers·i·ble** (ri vur′sə b'l) *adj.* **1.** that can be reversed, as cloth, coats, etc. finished so that either side can be used as the outer side **2.** that can reverse, as a chemical reaction **—n.** a reversible coat, jacket, etc. **—re·vers′i·bil′i·ty** *n.*

**re·ver·sion** (ri vur′zhən, -shən) *n.* **1.** a return, as to a former state, custom, etc. **2.** *Biol.* a return to a former or primitive type; atavism **3.** *Law a)* the right of succession, future possession, etc. *b)* the return of an estate to the grantor and his heirs after a grant terminates **—re·ver′sion·ar′y, re·ver′sion·al** *adj.*

**re·vert** (ri vurt′) *vi.* [ < OFr. < L. < *re-*, back + *vertere*, to turn] **1.** to go back; return, as to a former practice, subject, etc. **2.** *Biol.* to return to an earlier type **3.** *Law* to go back to a former owner or his heirs **—re·vert′i·ble** *adj.*

**rev·er·y** (rev′ər ē) *n., pl.* **-er·ies** *same as* REVERIE

**re·vet·ment** (ri vet′mənt) *n.* [ < Fr. < OFr., ult. < L. *re-*, again + *vestire*, to clothe] **1.** a facing, as of stone, to protect an embankment, etc. **2.** *same as* RETAINING WALL

**re·view** (ri vyōō′) *n.* [ < MFr. < L. < *re-*, again + *videre*, to see] **1.** a looking at or looking over again **2.** a general survey or report **3.** a looking back, as on past events **4.** reexamination, as by a higher court of the decision of a lower court **5.** a critical report and evaluation, as in a newspaper, of a book, play, concert, etc. **6.** a magazine containing articles of criticism and evaluation *[a law review]* **7.** the act of going over a lesson again, as in recitation **8.** *same as* REVUE **9.** a formal inspection, as of troops on parade **—vt. 1.** to look back on (past events, etc.) **2.** to survey in thought, speech, or writing **3.** to inspect (troops, etc.) formally **4.** to give or write a critical report of (a book, play, etc.) **5.** to reexamine (a lower court's decision) **6.** to go over (lessons, etc.) again **—vi.** to review books, plays, etc.

**re·view·er** (-ər) *n.* a person who reviews; esp., one who reviews books, plays, etc. as for a newspaper

**re·vile** (ri vīl′) *vt.* **-viled′, -vil′ing** [ < OFr. *reviler*, to treat as vile: see RE- & VILE] to call bad names in talking to or about **—re·vile′ment** *n.* **—re·vil′er** *n.*

**re·vise** (ri vīz′) *vt.* **-vised′, -vis′ing** [ < Fr. < L. < *re-*, back + *visere*, to survey, freq. of *videre*, to see] **1.** to read (a manuscript, etc.) over carefully and correct and improve it **2.** to change or amend **—n.** a revising or a revision **—re·vis′al** *n.* **—re·vis′er, re·vi′sor** *n.*

**Revised Standard Version** a mid-20th-cent. revision of an earlier version of the Bible, made by certain U.S. scholars

**re·vi·sion** (ri vizh′ən) *n.* **1.** act, process, or work of revising **2.** a revised form, as of a book, etc. **—re·vi′sion·ar′y, re·vi′sion·al** *adj.*

**re·vi·sion·ist** (-ist) *n.* a person who favors the revision of some accepted theory, etc. —*adj.* of revisionists —**re·vi'·sion·ism** *n.*

**re·vi·so·ry** (ri vī'zər ē) *adj.* of, or having the nature or power of, revision

**re·viv·al** (ri vī'v'l) *n.* a reviving or being revived; specif., *a*) a bringing or coming back into use, being, etc. *b*) a new presentation of an earlier play, movie, etc. *c*) restoration to vigor and activity *d*) a bringing or coming back to life or consciousness *e*) a stirring up of religious feelings, usually by the excited preaching of evangelists at public meetings *f*) a series of such meetings

**re·viv·al·ist** (-ist) *n.* a person who promotes or conducts religious revivals —**re·viv'a·lism** *n.* —**re·viv'a·lis'tic** *adj.*

**re·vive** (ri vīv') *vi., vt.* -**vived'**, -**viv'ing** [< OFr. < L. < *re-*, again + *vivere*, to live] **1.** to come or bring back to life or consciousness **2.** to come or bring back to health and vigor **3.** to come or bring back into use, operation, or attention **4.** to come or bring to mind again **5.** to present (a play or movie) in a revival —**re·viv'a·bil'i·ty** *n.* —**re·viv'a·ble** *adj.* —**re·viv'er** *n.*

**re·viv·i·fy** (ri viv'ə fī') *vt., vi.* -**fied'**, -**fy'ing** to give or acquire new life or vigor; revive —**re·viv'i·fi·ca'tion** *n.* —**re·viv'i·fi'er** *n.*

**rev·o·ca·ble** (rev'ə kə b'l) *adj.* that can be revoked: also **re·vok·a·ble** (ri vōk'ə b'l) —**rev'o·ca·bil'i·ty** *n.* —**rev'o·ca·bly** *adv.*

**rev·o·ca·tion** (rev'ə kā'shən) *n.* a revoking or being revoked; repeal; annulment

**rev·o·ca·to·ry** (rev'ə kə tôr'ē) *adj.* revoking or tending to revoke

**re·voke** (ri vōk') *vt.* -**voked'**, -**vok'ing** [< MFr. < L. < *re-*, back + *vocare*, to call] to withdraw, repeal, or cancel (a law, permit, etc.) —*vi. same as* RENEGE (sense 2) —*n. same as* RENEGE —**re·vok'er** *n.*

**re·volt** (ri vōlt') *n.* [< Fr. < It., ult. < L. *revolvere:* see REVOLVE] **1.** a rising up against the government; rebellion **2.** any refusal to submit to authority **3.** the state of a person or persons revolting —*vi.* **1.** to rise up against the government **2.** to refuse to submit to authority; rebel **3.** to be disgusted or shocked (with *at* or *against*) —*vt.* to disgust —**re·volt'er** *n.*

**re·volt·ing** (-vōl'tiŋ) *adj.* **1.** rebellious **2.** causing revulsion; disgusting —**re·volt'ing·ly** *adv.*

**rev·o·lu·tion** (rev'ə loo'shən) *n.* [< OFr. < LL. < L. pp. of *revolvere:* see REVOLVE] **1.** *a*) movement of a body in an orbit or circle *b*) the time taken for a body to go around an orbit **2.** a turning motion of a body around its center or axis; rotation **3.** a complete cycle of events **4.** a complete or radical change of any kind **5.** overthrow of a government or social system, with another taking its place

**rev·o·lu·tion·ar·y** (-er'ē) *adj.* **1.** of, like, favoring, or causing a revolution in a government or social system **2.** bringing about a very great change **3.** [R-] having to do with the American Revolution **4.** revolving or rotating —*n., pl.* -**ar'ies** a revolutionist

**Revolutionary War** *see* AMERICAN REVOLUTION

**rev·o·lu·tion·ist** (-ist) *n.* a person who favors or takes part in a revolution

**rev·o·lu·tion·ize** (-īz') *vt.* -**ized'**, -**iz'ing** **1.** to make a complete and basic change in **2.** [Rare] to bring about a political revolution in

**re·volve** (ri välv') *vt.* -**volved'**, -**volv'ing** [< L. < *re-*, back + *volvere*, to roll] **1.** to turn over in the mind; reflect on **2.** to cause to travel in a circle or orbit **3.** to cause to rotate —*vi.* **1.** to move in a circle or orbit **2.** to rotate **3.** to seem to move (*around* or *about* something) **4.** to recur at intervals **5.** to be pondered on —**re·volv'a·ble** *adj.*

**re·volv·er** (ri väl'vər) *n.* a handgun with a revolving cylinder holding several bullets which can be fired without reloading

**re·volv·ing** (-viŋ) *adj.* **1.** that revolves **2.** designating a fund that is regularly replenished, for making loans, etc. **3.** designating credit, as for a charge account, renewed by regular payments to maintain a specified amount

**revolving door** a door consisting of four vanes hung on a central axle, and turned around by pushing on a vane

**re·vue** (ri vyoo') *n.* [Fr.: see REVIEW] a musical show consisting of skits, songs, and dances, often poking fun at personages, fashions, etc.

**re·vul·sion** (ri vul'shən) *n.* [< Fr. < L. < pp. of *revellere* < *re-*, back + *vellere*, to pull] **1.** a sudden, complete, and violent change of feeling **2.** extreme disgust —**re·vul'sive** *adj.*

**re·ward** (ri wôrd') *n.* [< ONormFr. (for OFr. *regarde*) < *regarder:* see REGARD] **1.** something given in return for good or, sometimes, evil, or for service or merit **2.** money offered, as for the capture of a criminal, etc. **3.** compensation; profit —*vt.* **1.** to give a reward to **2.** to give a reward for (service, etc.) —**re·ward'a·ble** *adj.* —**re·ward'er** *n.*

**re·ward·ing** (-iŋ) *adj.* giving a sense of reward, or return —**re·ward'ing·ly** *adv.*

**re·wind** (rē wīnd') *vt.* -**wound'**, -**wind'ing** to wind again; specif., to wind (film, tape, etc.) back on the reel —*n.* **1.** something rewound **2.** a rewinding

**re·wire** (-wīr') *vt., vi.* -**wired'**, -**wir'ing** to wire again; specif., *a*) to put new wires in or on (a house, motor, etc.) *b*) to telegraph again

**re·word** (rē wurd') *vt.* to state again in other words; change the wording of

**re·work** (-wurk') *vt.* to work again; specif., *a*) to rewrite or revise *b*) to process (something used) for use again

**re·write** (rē rīt'; *for n.* rē'rīt') *vt., vi.* -**wrote'**, -**writ'ten**, -**writ'ing** **1.** to write again **2.** to revise **3.** to write (news turned in by a reporter) in a different form for publication —*n.* an article so written —**re·writ'er** *n.*

**Rex** (reks) [L., a king] a masculine name —*n.* [*also* r-] king

**Rey·kja·vik** (rā'kyə vēk') capital of Iceland: seaport on the SW coast: pop. 81,000

**Reyn·ard** (ren'ərd, rā'nərd, rā'närd) [OFr. *Renard* < OHG.] the fox in the medieval beast epic *Reynard the Fox*; hence, a name for any fox

**Reyn·olds** (ren'əldz), Sir **Joshua** 1723–92; Eng. portrait painter

**RF, R.F., r.f.** **1.** radio frequency **2.** rapid-fire

**rf., rf** *Baseball* right field (or fielder)

**RFD, R.F.D.** Rural Free Delivery

**Rh** **1.** *see* RH FACTOR **2.** *Chem.* rhodium

**r.h.** relative humidity

**r.h., R.H., RH** right hand

**Rhad·a·man·thus** (rad'ə man'thəs) *Gr. Myth.* a son of Zeus who after he died became a judge of the dead in the lower world —**Rhad'a·man'thine** (-thin) *adj.*

**rhap·sod·ic** (rap säd'ik) *adj.* of, or having the nature of, rhapsody; extravagantly enthusiastic: also **rhap·sod'i·cal** —**rhap·sod'i·cal·ly** *adv.*

**rhap·so·dize** (rap'sə dīz') *vi., vt.* -**dized'**, -**diz'ing** to speak, write, or recite in a rhapsodic manner or form —**rhap'so·dist** *n.*

**rhap·so·dy** (-dē) *n., pl.* -**dies** [< Fr. < L. < Gr. *rhapsōidia*, ult. < *rhaptein*, to stitch together + *ōidē*, song] **1.** any ecstatic or extravagantly enthusiastic speech or writing **2.** great delight **3.** *Music* an instrumental composition of free, irregular form, suggesting improvisation

**Rhe·a** (rē'ə) *Gr. Myth.* the daughter of Uranus and Gaea, wife of Cronus, and mother of Zeus, Hera, etc. —*n.* [r-] a large S. American nonflying bird, resembling the African ostrich but smaller and having a feathered neck and head

**Rheims** (rēmz; *Fr.* rans) *former sp. of* REIMS

**Rhein** (rīn) *Ger. name of the* RHINE

**Rhein·gold** (rīn'gōld'; *G.* rīn'gôlt') [G., Rhine gold] *Germanic Legend* the hoard of gold guarded by the Rhine maidens and later owned by the Nibelungs and Siegfried

**Rhen·ish** (ren'ish) *adj.* of the Rhine or the regions around it —*n.* [Now Rare] *same as* RHINE WINE

**rhe·ni·um** (rē'nē əm) *n.* [ModL. < L. *Rhenus*, Rhine] a rare metallic chemical element resembling manganese: symbol, Re; at. wt., 186.2; at no., 75

**rhe·o-** [< Gr. *rheos*, current < *rhein*, to flow] *a combining form meaning* a flow, current [*rheostat*]

**rhe·o·stat** (rē'ə stat') *n.* [RHEO- + -STAT] a device for varying the resistance of an electric circuit without interrupting the circuit, used as to dim or brighten electric lights —**rhe'o·stat'ic** *adj.*

**rhe·sus** (rē'səs) *n.* [ModL. < L. < Gr. proper name] a brownish-yellow macaque of India, often kept in zoos and used in medical research: in full, **rhesus monkey**

**rhet·o·ric** (ret'ər ik) *n.* [< OFr. < L. < Gr. *rhētorikē* (*technē*), oratorical (art) < *rhētōr*, orator] **1.** the art of using words effectively in speaking or writing; esp., now, the art of prose composition **2.** a book on this **3.** artificial eloquence; showiness in literary style

**rhe·tor·i·cal** (ri tôr'i k'l, -tär'-) *adj.* **1.** of, having the nature of, or according to rhetoric **2.** artificially eloquent; showy and elaborate in literary style —**rhe·tor'i·cal·ly** *adv.*

**rhetorical question** a question asked only to produce an effect, no spoken answer being expected

**rhet·o·ri·cian** (ret'ə rish'ən) *n.* **1.** a person skilled in using or teaching the art of rhetoric **2.** a person who writes or speaks in a showy, elaborate way

**rheum** (room) *n.* [< OFr. < L. < Gr. *rheuma*, a flow] **1.** any watery discharge from the mucous membranes, as of the mouth, eyes, or nose **2.** a cold; rhinitis —**rheum'y** *adj.* **rheum'i·er, rheum'i·est**

**rheu·mat·ic** (roo mat'ik) *adj.* of, caused by, or having

RHESUS
MONKEY
(head & body
to 18 in.; tail
to 8 in.)

**rheumatism** —*n.* a person who has rheumatism —**rheu·mat'i·cal·ly** *adv.*

**rheumatic disease** any of a group of diseases of connective tissue, as rheumatoid arthritis, gout, etc.

**rheumatic fever** a disease in which there is fever, the joints ache and swell, and the heart becomes inflamed

**rheu·ma·tism** (rōō'mə tiz'm) *n.* [< L. < Gr. *rheumatismos:* see RHEUM] *a popular term for* any of various painful conditions in which the joints and muscles become inflamed and stiff, as rheumatoid arthritis, bursitis, etc.

**rheu·ma·toid** (-toid') *adj.* of or like rheumatism

**rheumatoid arthritis** a chronic disease in which the joints become inflamed, painful, and swollen often to the extent that fingers, toes, etc. become deformed

**Rh factor** (är'āch') [RH(ESUS): first discovered in rhesus monkeys] a group of antigens, usually present in human red blood cells, which may cause hemolytic reactions during pregnancy or after tranfusion of blood containing this factor into someone lacking it: people who have this factor are **Rh positive**; those who lack it are **Rh negative**

**Rhin** (ran) *Fr. name of the* RHINE

**rhi·nal** (rī'n'l) *adj.* [RHIN(O)- + -AL] of the nose; nasal

**Rhine** (rīn) river in W Europe, flowing from E Switzerland through Germany & the Netherlands into the North Sea

**Rhine·land** (rīn'land', -lənd) that part of Germany west of the Rhine

**rhine·stone** (rīn'stōn') *n.* [transl. of Fr. *caillou du Rhin:* so called because orig. made at Strasbourg (on the Rhine)] a bright, artificial gem made of hard, colorless glass, often cut to imitate a diamond

**Rhine wine** 1. any of various wines produced in the Rhine Valley, esp. any such light, dry white wine 2. a wine like this produced elsewhere

**rhi·ni·tis** (rī nīt'əs) *n.* [ModL.: see RHINO- & -ITIS] inflammation of the mucous membrane of the nose

**rhi·no** (rī'nō) *n., pl.* **-nos,** *-no shortened form of* RHINOCEROS

**rhi·no-** [< Gr. *rhis* (gen. *rhinos*), the nose] a combining form meaning nose: also, before a vowel, **rhin-**

**rhi·noc·er·os** (rī näs'ər əs) *n., pl.* **-os·es, -os:** see PLURAL, II, D, 1 [< L. < Gr. < *rhis* (see prec.) + *keras,* horn] any of various large, thick-skinned, plant-eating mammals of Africa and Asia, with one or two upright horns on the snout

**rhi·zo-** [< Gr. *rhiza,* a root] a combining form meaning root: also, before a vowel, **rhiz-**

**rhi·zoid** (rī'zoid) *adj.* [prec. + -OID] rootlike —*n.* any of the rootlike filaments in a moss, fern, etc. that attach the plant to the substratum —**rhi·zoi'dal** *adj.*

INDIAN
RHINOCEROS
(3–6½ ft. high
at shoulder)

**rhi·zome** (rī'zōm) *n.* [ModL. < Gr., ult. < *rhiza,* a root] a creeping stem lying, usually horizontally, at or under the surface of the soil: it has scale leaves, bears leaves or aerial shoots near its tips, and produces roots from its undersurface —**rhi·zom'a·tous** (-zäm'ə təs, -zō'mə-) *adj.*

**rhi·zo·pod** (rī'zə päd') *n.* [RHIZO- + -POD] any of a class of one-celled animals with pseudopodia, including the amoebas, foraminifers, etc. —**rhi·zop'o·dous** (-zäp'ə dəs) *adj.*

**rho** (rō) *n.* [Gr.] the seventeenth letter of the Greek alphabet (P, ρ)

RHIZOME
OF GRASS

**Rhode Island** (rōd) [< ? Du. *Roodt Eylandt,* red island or < ? RHODES] New England State of the U.S.: 1,214 sq. mi.; pop. 947,000; cap. Providence: abbrev. **R.I., RI** —**Rhode Islander**

**Rhode Island Red** any of a breed of American chickens with reddish-brown feathers and a black tail

**Rhode Island White** any of a breed of chickens similar to Rhode Island Reds, but with white feathers

**Rhodes** (rōdz) largest island of the Dodecanese, in the Aegean: 545 sq. mi. —**Rho·di·an** (rō'dē ən) *adj., n.*

**Rho·de·sia** (rō dē'zhə, -zhē ə) *former name of* ZIMBABWE —**Rho·de'sian** *adj., n.*

**Rhodesian man** [skeletal remains found in Northern *Rhodesia*] a form of primitive man of the later Pleistocene, with massive brow ridges

**rho·di·um** (rō'dē əm) *n.* [ModL. < Gr. *rhodon,* a rose: from the color of its salts in solution] a hard, gray-white metallic chemical element, used in alloys with platinum and gold: symbol, Rh; at. wt. 102.905; at. no., 45

**rho·do-** [< Gr. *rhodon,* a rose] a combining form meaning rose, rose-red: also, before a vowel, **rhod-**

**rho·do·den·dron** (rō'də den'drən) *n.* [L. < Gr. < *rhodon,* a rose + *dendron,* a tree] any of a genus of trees and shrubs, mainly evergreen, with showy flowers of pink, white, or purple

**rhom·boid** (räm'boid) *n.* [< Fr. < L. < Gr.: see RHOMBUS & -OID] a parallelogram with oblique angles and only the opposite sides equal —*adj.* shaped like a rhomboid or rhombus: also **rhom·boi'dal**

RHOMBOID

**rhom·bus** (räm'bəs) *n., pl.* **-bus·es, -bi** (-bī) [L. < Gr. *rhombos,* turnable object] an equilateral parallelogram, esp. one with oblique angles: also **rhomb** —**rhom'bic** *adj.*

**Rhone, Rhône** (rōn) river flowing from SW Switzerland south through France into the Mediterranean

**rhu·barb** (rōō'bärb) *n.* [< OFr. < ML. < LL. < Gr. *rhēon,* rhubarb + *barbaron,* foreign] 1. a perennial plant having large leaves whose long, thick, sour stalks are cooked into a sauce or baked in pies 2. the roots or rhizomes of certain Asiatic varieties, used as a cathartic 3. [Slang] a heated argument

RHOMBUS

**rhumb** (rum, rumb) *n.* [< Port. & Sp. *rumbo,* prob. < L. *rhombus,* RHOMBUS] any of the points of a mariner's compass

**rhum·ba** (rum'bə) *n. alt. sp. of* RUMBA

**rhumb line** a course keeping a constant compass direction, charted as a line cutting all meridians at the same angle

**rhyme** (rīm) *n.* [< OFr. < *rimer,* to rhyme, prob. < Frank. hyp. *rim,* a row: form infl. by L. *rhythmus,* rhythm] 1. likeness of sounds at the ends of words or lines of verse 2. a word that has the same end sound as another ["lazy" is a *rhyme* for "daisy"] 3. a poem, or verse in general, using such end sounds —*vi.* **rhymed, rhym'ing** 1. to make verse, esp. rhyming verse 2. to form a rhyme ["more" *rhymes* with "door"] 3. to be composed in metrical form with rhymes: said of verse —*vt.* 1. to put into rhyme 2. to compose in metrical form with rhymes 3. to use as a rhyme [to *rhyme* "new" with "true"] —**rhyme or reason** order or sense: preceded by *without, no,* etc. —**rhym'er** *n.*

**rhyme·ster** (rīm'stər) *n.* a maker of simple or inferior verse or rhymes; poetaster

**rhyming slang** 1. a word or phrase that rhymes with, and is a slang term for, a particular word (Ex.: *bees and honey* for *money*) 2. such words or phrases collectively

**rhythm** (rith'm, rith'əm) *n.* [< Fr. < L. < Gr. *rhythmos,* measure < *rhein,* to flow] 1. *a)* flow or movement having a regularly repeated pattern of accents, beats, etc. [the *rhythm* of the waves, of dancing, of the heartbeat, etc.] *b)* the pattern of this 2. *Biol.* a periodic occurrence in living organisms of specific physiological changes 3. *Music a)* regular, repeated grouping of strong and weak beats, or heavily and lightly accented tones *b)* the form or pattern of this [waltz *rhythm*] 4. *Prosody* the form or pattern of the regularly repeated stressed and unstressed or long and short syllables [iambic *rhythm*] —**rhyth'mic** (rith'mik), **rhyth'mi·cal** *adj.* —**rhyth'mi·cal·ly** *adv.*

**rhythm and blues** a form of popular U.S. Negro music, influenced by the blues and having a strong beat

**rhythm method** a method of seeking birth control by abstaining from sexual intercourse during the woman's probable monthly ovulation period

**R.I., RI** Rhode Island

**ri·al** (rī'əl) *n.* [Per. < Ar. < Sp. *real,* REAL²] *see* MONETARY UNITS, table (Iran and Oman)

**ri·al·to** (rē al'tō) *n., pl.* **-tos** [< *Rialto,* a bridge in Venice, Italy] a trading area or marketplace

**rib** (rib) *n.* [OE. *rib*] 1. any of the curved bones attached to the backbone and enclosing the chest cavity: in man there are twelve pairs of such bones: see TRUE RIBS, FALSE RIBS, FLOATING RIBS 2. a cut of meat having one or more ribs, as spareribs 3. a raised ridge in woven or knitted material 4. any riblike piece used to form a framework, or to shape or strengthen something [an umbrella *rib*] 5. any of the main veins of a leaf 6. [Slang] a playfully teasing remark or action —*vt.* **ribbed, rib'bing** 1. to provide, form, or strengthen with a rib or ribs 2. [Slang] to tease playfully —**ribbed** *adj.* —**rib'ber** *n.* —**rib'less** *adj.*

**rib·ald** (rib'əld) *adj.* [OFr. *ribaud,* debauchee, ult. < OHG. *riban,* to copulate] characterized by coarse joking; esp., dealing with sex in a humorously earthy or direct way —*n.* a ribald person

**rib·ald·ry** (-əl drē) *n.* ribald language or humor

**rib·and** (rib'ənd, -ən) *n. archaic var. of* RIBBON

**rib·bing** (rib'iŋ) *n.* an arrangement or series of ribs, as in knitted fabric, a ship's framework, etc.

**rib·bon** (rib'ən) *n.* [MFr. *riban*] 1. a narrow strip as of silk or rayon, used for decorating or tying, for badges, etc. **2.** anything suggesting such a strip [a *ribbon* of blue sky] **3.** [*pl.*] torn strips or shreds; tatters [a sleeve torn to *ribbons*] **4.** a narrow strip of cloth inked for use in a typewriter, etc. —*vt.* **1.** to decorate, trim, or mark with ribbons **2.** to tear into ribbonlike shreds —*vi.* to extend in a ribbonlike strip —**rib'bon·like'** *adj.*

**ri·bo·fla·vin** (rī'bə flā'vin) *n.* [ < *ribose*, a sugar + FLAVIN] a factor of the vitamin B complex, found in milk, eggs, liver, fruits, leafy vegetables, etc.: lack of riboflavin in the diet causes stunted growth, loss of hair, etc.

**ri·bo·nu·cle·ase** (rī'bō noo'klē ās', -nyoo'-) *n.* [RIBO(SE) + NUCLEASE] any of various enzymes that split ribonucleic acid

**ri·bo·nu·cle·ic acid** (-noo klē'ik, -nyoo-) [RIBO(SE) + NUCLEIC ACID] an essential component in the cytoplasm of all living cells, composed of long chains of phosphate and ribose along with several bases bonded to the ribose: one form carries the genetic information needed for protein synthesis in the cell

**ri·bose** (rī'bōs) *n.* [ < G. *rib(onsäure)*, an acid containing four OH radicals + -OSE¹] a sugar, $C_5H_{10}O_5$, derived from nucleic acids

**ri·bo·some** (rī'bə sōm') *n.* [RIBO(SE) + -SOME³] any of the minute particles composed of RNA and proteins, found in cell cytoplasm and functioning in the production of proteins —**ri'bo·so'mal** *adj.*

**-ric** (rik) [OE. *rice*, reign] *a combining form meaning* jurisdiction, realm [*bishopric*]

**rice** (rīs) *n.* [OFr. *ris* < It. < L. < Gr. *oryza*: of Oriental origin] **1.** a cereal grass of warm climates, planted in ground under water **2.** its starchy seeds or grain, used as food —*vt.* **riced, ric'ing** to form (cooked potatoes, etc.) into ricelike granules

**rice paper 1.** a thin paper made from the straw of rice **2.** a fine, delicate paper made by cutting and pressing the pith of an Asian plant (the **rice-paper plant**)

**ric·er** (rī'sər) *n.* a utensil for ricing cooked potatoes, etc. by forcing them through small holes

**rich** (rich) *adj.* [OE. *rice*, noble, powerful < OFr. < Gmc.] **1.** having much money or property; wealthy **2.** having abundant natural resources [a *rich* region] **3.** well supplied (*with*); abounding (*in*) **4.** valuable [a *rich* prize] **5.** costly and elegant; sumptuous [*rich* gifts] **6.** *a*) containing much butter (or other fat), cream, sugar, flavoring, etc. [*rich* foods] *b*) strong and flavorful [*rich* wine] **7.** *a*) full and mellow: said of sounds, the voice, etc. *b*) vivid: said of colors *c*) very fragrant: said of odors **8.** abundant; ample [a *rich* fund of stories] **9.** yielding in abundance, as soil, etc. **10.** [Colloq.] *a*) very amusing *b*) absurd; preposterous —**the rich** wealthy people collectively —**rich'ly** *adv.* —**rich'ness** *n.*

**Rich·ard** (rich'ərd) [ < OFr. < OHG. *Richart* < Gmc. bases meaning "strong king"] **1.** a masculine name **2. Richard I,** 1157–99; king of England (1189–99): called **Richard the Lion-Hearted** (Fr. *Richard Coeur de Lion*) **3. Richard II,** 1367–1400; king of England (1377–99) **4. Richard III,** 1452–85; king of England (1483–85)

**Rich·ard·son** (rich'ərd sən), **Samuel** 1689–1761; Eng. novelist

**Ri·che·lieu** (rish'ə loo'; *Fr.* rēsh lyö'), duc de (*Armand Jean du Plessis*) 1585–1642; Fr. cardinal & statesman

**rich·en** (rich''n) *vt.* to make rich or richer

**rich·es** (-iz) *n.pl.* [ME. *richess*, n. sing. < OFr. *richesse*] valuable possessions; much money, property, etc.; wealth

**Rich·mond** (rich'mənd) **1.** [after Duke of *Richmond*, son of CHARLES II] borough of New York City, including Staten Island: pop. 352,000 **2.** [after *Richmond*, city in SE England] *a*) capital of Va.: port on the James River: pop. 219,000 (met. area 631,000) *b*) seaport in W Calif., on San Francisco Bay: pop. 75,000

**Rich·ter scale** (rik'tər) [devised by C. *Richter* (1900– ), U.S. seismologist] a scale for measuring the magnitude of earthquakes, with each of its 10 steps about 60 times greater than the preceding step

**rick** (rik) *n.* [OE. *hreac*] a stack of hay, straw, etc. in a field, esp. one covered for protection from rain —*vt.* to pile (hay, etc.) into ricks

**rick·ets** (rik'its) *n.* [altered < ? RACHITIS] a disease, chiefly of children, characterized by a softening and, often, bending of the bones: it is caused by lack of vitamin D

**rick·ett·si·a** (ri ket'sē ə) *n., pl.* **-si·ae'** (-ē'), **-si·as** [ModL., after H. T. *Ricketts* (1871–1910), U.S. pathologist] any of a genus of microorganisms that cause certain diseases, as typhus, and are transmitted by the bite of certain lice and ticks —**rick·ett'si·al** *adj.*

**rick·et·y** (rik'it ē) *adj.* **1.** of or having rickets **2.** weak in the joints; tottering **3.** liable to fall apart or break down; shaky —**rick'et·i·ness** *n.*

**rick·rack** (rik'rak') *n.* [redupl. of RACK¹] flat, zigzag braid for trimming dresses, etc.

**rick·shaw, rick·sha** (rik'shô) *n. same as* JINRIKISHA

**ric·o·chet** (rik'ə shā', rik'ə shā'; *also, chiefly Brit.,* -shet') *n.* [Fr.] **1.** the rebound or skipping of a bullet, stone, etc. after striking a surface at an angle **2.** a bullet, etc. that ricochets —*vi.* **-cheted'** (-shād') or **-chet'ted** (-shet'id), **-chet'ing** (-shā'iŋ) or **-chet'ting** (-shet'iŋ) to move with such a motion

**ri·cot·ta** (ri kät'ə; *It.* rē kôt'tä) *n.* [It. < L. pp. of *recoquere*, to boil again] a soft, dry or moist Italian cheese made from whey left from making other cheeses

**rid** (rid) *vt.* **rid** or **rid'ded, rid'ding** [ON. *rythja*, to clear (land)] to free, clear, or relieve, as of something undesirable [to *rid* a garden of weeds] —**be rid of** to be freed from —**get rid of 1.** to get free from **2.** to do away with; dispose of

**rid·dance** (rid''ns) *n.* a ridding or being rid; clearance or removal, as of something undesirable —**good riddance!** welcome relief or deliverance!

**rid·den** (rid''n) *pp. of* RIDE —*adj.* controlled or obsessed (by the thing specified) [fear-*ridden*]

**rid·dle¹** (rid''l) *n.* [OE. *rædels*, akin to *rædan*, to guess] **1.** a puzzle in the form of a question or statement with a tricky meaning or answer that is hard to guess; conundrum **2.** any puzzling or perplexing person or thing; enigma —*vt.* **-dled, -dling** to solve or explain (a riddle) —*vi.* to utter riddles —**rid'dler** *n.*

**rid·dle²** (rid''l) *n.* [OE. *hriddel*] a coarse sieve —*vt.* **-dled, -dling 1.** to sift through a riddle **2.** *a*) to make many holes in, as with buckshot *b*) to affect every part of [*riddled* with errors]

**ride** (rīd) *vi.* **rode** or archaic **rid** (rid), **rid'den** or archaic **rid** or **rode, rid'ing** [OE. *ridan*] **1.** *a*) to sit on and control a horse or other animal in motion *b*) to be carried along (in a vehicle, on a bicycle, etc.) *c*) to move along as if so carried *d*) to be carried or supported in motion (on or upon) [tanks *ride* on treads] **2.** to admit of being ridden [the car *rides* smoothly] **3.** to move, lie, or float on the water **4.** to be dependent (on) [the change *rides* on his approval] **5.** to be placed as a bet (on) **6.** [Colloq.] to continue undisturbed, with no action taken —*vt.* **1.** to sit on or in and control so as to move along [to *ride* a horse] **2.** to move along on or be carried or supported on [to *ride* the waves] **3.** to move over, along, or through (a road, area, etc.) by horse, car, etc. **4.** to cover (a specified distance) by riding **5.** to engage in by riding [to *ride* a race] **6.** to cause to ride **7.** to control, dominate, or oppress [*ridden* by fear] **8.** [Colloq.] to torment or tease, as with ridicule, criticism, etc. —*n.* **1.** *a*) a riding; esp., a journey by horse, car, bicycle, etc. *b*) a way or chance to ride *c*) the way a car, etc. rides **2.** a road, etc. for riding **3.** a roller coaster, Ferris wheel, or other thing to ride, as at a carnival —**ride down 1.** to knock down by riding against **2.** to overtake by riding **3.** to overcome **4.** to exhaust (a horse, etc.) by riding —**ride herd (on)** to keep under close control —**ride out** to withstand or endure (a storm, crisis, etc.) successfully —**ride up** to move upward out of place, as an article of clothing —**take for a ride** [Slang] **1.** to take somewhere, as in a car, and kill **2.** to cheat or swindle —**rid'a·ble, ride'a·ble** *adj.*

**rid·er** (-ər) *n.* **1.** a person who rides **2.** *a*) an addition or amendment to a contract, etc. *b*) a clause, usually dealing with an unrelated matter, added to a legislative bill when it is up for passage **3.** any of various pieces moving or resting on something else —**rid'er·less** *adj.*

**rid·er·ship** (-ship') *n.* the passengers using a particular system of public transportation over a given period of time, or the estimated number of these

**ridge** (rij) *n.* [OE. *hrycg*] **1.** the long, narrow top or crest of something, as of an animal's back, a wave, etc. **2.** a long, narrow elevation of land or similar range of hills or mountains **3.** any narrow, raised strip, as on fabric **4.** the horizontal line formed by the meeting of two sloping surfaces [the *ridge* of a roof] —*vt., vi.* **ridged, ridg'ing** to form into or mark with a ridge or ridges —**ridge'like'** *adj.*

**ridge·pole** (-pōl') *n.* the horizontal timber or beam at the ridge of a roof: also **ridge'piece'**

**rid·i·cule** (rid'i kyool') *n.* [Fr. < L. *ridiculum*, a jest, wit. < *ridere*, to laugh] **1.** the act of making someone or something the object of scornful laughter by joking, mocking, etc.; derision **2.** words or actions used in doing this —*vt.* **-culed', -cul'ing** to make fun of or make others laugh at; deride; mock

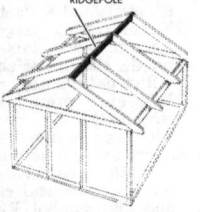

RIDGEPOLE

**ri·dic·u·lous** (ri dik'yə ləs) *adj.* deserving ridicule; absurd —**ri·dic'u·lous·ly** *adv.* —**ri·dic'u·lous·ness** *n.*

**rid·ing¹** (rīd'iŋ) *adj.* **1.** that rides or is ridden **2.** of or for riders on horseback —*n.* the act of one that rides

**rid·ing²** (rīd'iŋ) *n.* [OE. *-thrithing*, a third part] formerly, any of the three administrative divisions of Yorkshire, England

**Rif** (rif) mountain range along the Mediterranean coast of Morocco: also **Er Rif** (er)

**rife** (rīf) *adj.* [OE. *ryfe*] **1.** frequently or commonly occurring; widespread [gossip was *rife*] **2.** *a)* abundant *b)* abounding; filled [*rife* with error] —**rife′ness** *n.*

**Riff** (rif) *same as* RIF —*n.*, *pl.* **Riffs, Riff′i** (-ē) a member of a Berber people living in or near the Rif

**rif·fle** (rif′'l) *n.* [< ? or akin to G. *riffel*, a groove] **1.** *a)* a shoal, reef, etc. in a stream, producing a stretch of ruffled or choppy water *b)* a stretch of such water, or a ripple on it **2.** the act or a method of riffling cards —*vt.*, *vi.* **-fled, -fling 1.** to ruffle or ripple **2.** to leaf rapidly (through) by releasing pages, etc. along their edge with the thumb **3.** to shuffle (playing cards) by holding part of the deck in each hand and mixing the cards together with riffling motions

**riff·raff** (rif′raf′) *n.* [< OFr. *rif et raf* < *rifler*, to scrape + *rafle*, a raking in] **1.** those people regarded as worthless, insignificant, etc.; rabble **2.** [Dial.] trash

**ri·fle**[1] (rī′f'l) *vt.* **-fled, -fling** [Fr. *rifler*, to scrape < OFr. < MHG. *riffeln*, to scratch] **1.** to cut spiral grooves on the inside of (a gun barrel, etc.) **2.** to hurl or throw with great speed —*n.* **1.** a shoulder gun with spiral grooves cut into the inner surface of the barrel: see RIFLING **2.** [*pl.*] troops armed with rifles

**ri·fle**[2] (rī′f'l) *vt.* **-fled, -fling** [< OFr. *rifler*, to plunder, orig. to scratch: see prec.] **1.** to ransack and rob; pillage; plunder **2.** to take as plunder; steal —**ri′fler** *n.*

**ri·fle·man** (-mən) *n.*, *pl.* **-men 1.** a soldier armed with a rifle **2.** a man who uses a rifle

**rifle range** a place for target practice with a rifle

**ri·fle·ry** (-rē) *n.* the skill or practice of shooting at targets with rifles

**ri·fling** (rī′fliŋ) *n.* **1.** the cutting of spiral grooves within a gun barrel, to make the projectile spin when fired **2.** a system of such grooves

**rift** (rift) *n.* [Dan., a fissure < *rive*, to tear] **1.** an opening caused by splitting; fissure; cleft **2.** an open break in friendly relations —*vt.*, *vi.* to burst open; split

**rig** (rig) *vt.* **rigged, rig′ging** [< Scand.] **1.** *a)* to fit (a ship, mast, etc.) with sails, shrouds, etc. *b)* to fit (a ship's sails, shrouds, etc.) to the masts, yards, etc. **2.** to fit (*out*); equip **3.** to prepare for use, esp. in a hurry (often with *up*) **4.** to arrange in a dishonest way [to *rig* a contest] **5.** [Colloq.] to dress; clothe (usually with *out*) —*n.* **1.** the arrangement of sails, masts, etc. on a vessel **2.** equipment; gear **3.** *a)* a carriage, etc. with its horse or horses *b)* a tractor-trailer **4.** [Colloq.] dress; costume —**rig′ger** *n.*

**Ri·ga** (rē′gə) capital of the Latvian S.S.R.; seaport on the Baltic Sea: pop. 733,000

**rig·a·ma·role** (rig′ə mə rōl′) *n.* *var. of* RIGMAROLE

**rig·a·to·ni** (rig′ə tō′nē) *n.* [It., *pl.* < pp. of *rigare*, to mark with lines] short, ridged casings of pasta, often stuffed with ground meat, cheese, etc.

**Ri·gel** (rī′j'l, -g'l) [Ar. *rijl*, foot: in the left foot of Orion] a bright, bluish star, brightest in the constellation Orion

**rig·ging** (rig′iŋ) *n.* **1.** the chains, ropes, etc. used for supporting and working the masts, sails, etc. of a vessel **2.** equipment; gear

**right** (rīt) *adj.* [OE. *riht*] **1.** orig., straight [a *right* line] **2.** *a)* formed by a straight line perpendicular to a base [a *right* angle] *b)* having the axis perpendicular to the base [a *right* cylinder] **3.** in accordance with justice, law, morality, etc.; virtuous [*right* conduct] **4.** in accordance with fact, reason, etc.; correct; true [the *right* answer] **5.** *a)* fitting; suitable *b)* most convenient or favorable **6.** designating the side meant to be seen [the *right* side of cloth] **7.** having sound physical or mental health **8.** *a)* designating or of that side of one's body which is toward the east when one faces north *b)* designating or of the corresponding side of anything *c)* closer to the right side of a person facing the thing mentioned [the top *right* drawer] **9.** of the bank of a river on the right of a person facing downstream **10.** of the political right; conservative or reactionary —*n.* **1.** what is right, or just, lawful, proper, etc. **2.** *a)* a power, privilege, etc. that a person has or gets by law, nature, tradition, etc. [the *right* of free speech] *b)* [*often pl.*] an interest in property, real or intangible **3.** the true report, as of a happening (with *the*) **4.** *a)* the right side *b)* a turn toward the right side **5.** *Boxing a)* the right hand *b)* a blow delivered with the right hand **6.** [*often* R-] *Politics* a conservative or reactionary position, party, etc. (often with *the*): from the location of their seats in some European legislatures —*adv.* **1.** in a straight line; directly [go *right* home] **2.** in a way that is correct, proper, etc.; just, favorable, etc.; well **3.** completely [soaked *right* through his coat] **4.** exactly [*right* here] **5.** immediately [come *right* down] **6.** on or toward the right hand **7.** very [he knows *right* well]: colloquial except in certain

titles [the *right* reverend] —*interj.* agreed! I understand! —*vt.* **1.** to put in or restore to an upright position [we *righted* the boat] **2.** to correct **3.** to put in order [she *righted* the room] **4.** to make amends for —*vi.* to regain an upright position —**by right** (or **rights**) in justice; properly —**in one's own right** through one's own status, ability, etc. —**in the right** on the side supported by truth, justice, etc. —**right away** (or **off**) without delay; at once —**right on!** [Slang] precisely! exactly! that's right!: an exclamation of approval or encouragement —**to rights** [Colloq.] in or into proper condition or order —**right′a·ble** *adj.* —**right′er** *n.* —**right′ness** *n.*

**right·a·bout** (rīt′ə bout′) *n.* **1.** *same as* RIGHTABOUT-FACE **2.** the direction faced after turning completely about —*adv.*, *adj.* with, in, or by a rightabout-face

**right·a·bout-face** (-fās′) *n.* **1.** a turning directly about so as to face the opposite direction **2.** a complete reversal of belief, conduct, etc. —*interj.* a military command to perform a rightabout-face

**right angle** an angle of 90 degrees, made by the meeting of two straight lines perpendicular to each other

**right-an·gled** (rīt′aŋ′g'ld) *adj.* having or forming one or more right angles; rectangular: also **right′-an′gle**

**right·eous** (rī′chəs) *adj.* [altered < OE. *riht-wis*: see RIGHT & -WISE] **1.** acting justly; doing what is right; upright; virtuous [a *righteous* man] **2.** morally right or having a sound moral basis [*righteous* anger] —**right′eous·ly** *adv.* —**right′eous·ness** *n.*

RIGHT ANGLE

**right·ful** (rīt′fəl) *adj.* **1.** fair; just; right **2.** having a just, lawful claim [the *rightful* owner] **3.** belonging or owned by just or lawful claim [a *rightful* rank] **4.** proper; fitting —**right′ful·ly** *adv.* —**right′ful·ness** *n.*

**right-hand** (rīt′hand′) *adj.* **1.** on or directed toward the right **2.** of, for, or with the right hand **3.** most helpful or reliable [the president's *right-hand* man]

**right-hand·ed** (-han′did) *adj.* **1.** using the right hand more skillfully than the left **2.** done with the right hand **3.** made for use with the right hand **4.** turning from left to right; clockwise —*adv.* with the right hand [to throw *right-handed*] —**right′-hand′ed·ly** *adv.* —**right′-hand′ed·ness** *n.* —**right′-hand′er** *n.*

**right·ist** (rīt′ist) *n.* a person whose political position is conservative or reactionary; member of the right —*adj.* conservative or reactionary —**right′ism** *n.*

**right·ly** (rīt′lē) *adv.* **1.** with justice; fairly **2.** properly; suitably **3.** correctly

**right-mind·ed** (rīt′mīn′did) *adj.* thinking or believing what is right; having correct views or sound principles —**right′-mind′ed·ly** *adv.* —**right′-mind′ed·ness** *n.*

**right·o** (rīt′ō, rī′tō′) *interj.* [Chiefly Brit.] yes; certainly

**right of asylum** the right of a nation to extend protection to refugees, esp. political refugees, from another nation

**right of way 1.** the legal right to move in front of others, as at a traffic intersection **2.** the right to use a certain route, as over another's property **3.** *a)* a strip of land used by a railroad for its tracks *b)* land over which a public road, a power line, etc. passes Also **right′-of-way′**

**right-on** (rīt′än′, -ôn′) *adj.* [Slang] sophisticated, informed, current, etc.

**right-to-work** (rīt′tə wurk′) *adj.* designating or of laws prohibiting the union shop

**right triangle** a triangle with one right angle

**right·ward** (-wərd) *adv.*, *adj.* on or toward the right: also **right′wards** *adv.*

**right whale** a large-headed whalebone whale without teeth or dorsal fin

**right wing** [see RIGHT, *n.* 6] the more conservative or reactionary section of a political party, group, etc. —**right′-wing′** *adj.* —**right′-wing′er** *n.*

**rig·id** (rij′id) *adj.* [< L. < *rigere*, to be stiff] **1.** not bending or flexible; stiff [a *rigid* metal girder] **2.** not moving; set **3.** severe, strict, or rigorous [a *rigid* taskmaster, a *rigid* rule] **4.** *Aeron.* having a rigid framework that encloses containers for the gas, as a dirigible —**ri·gid·i·ty** (ri jid′ə-tē), **rig′id·ness** *n.* —**rig′id·ly** *adv.*

**ri·gid·i·fy** (ri jid′ə fī′) *vt.*, *vi.* **-fied′, -fy′ing** to make or become rigid —**ri·gid′i·fi·ca′tion** *n.*

**rig·ma·role** (rig′mə rōl′) *n.* [< *ragman roll* < ME. *rageman rolle*, a document] **1.** rambling talk; nonsense **2.** a fussy or time-wasting procedure

**rig·or** (rig′ər; *for 4, also* rī′gôr) *n.* [< MFr. < L. < *rigere*, to be rigid] **1.** harshness or severity; specif., *a)* strictness [the *rigor* of martial law] *b)* extreme hardship [the *rigors* of life] **2.** exact precision or accuracy **3.** a severe, harsh, or oppressive act, etc. **4.** stiffness or rigidity, esp. in body tissues Also, Brit. sp., **rig′our**

---

fat, āpe, cär; ten, ēven; is, bīte; gō, hôrn, tōōl, lŏŏk; oil, out; up, fur; get; joy; yet; chin; she; thin, *th*en; zh, leisure; ŋ, ring; ə for *a* in *ago*, *e* in *agent*, *i* in *sanity*, *o* in *comply*, *u* in *focus*; ' as in *able* (ā′b'l); Fr. bal; ë, Fr. coeur; ö, Fr. feu; Fr. mon; ö, Fr. coq; ü, Fr. duc; r, Fr. cri; H, G. ich; kh, G. doch; ‡foreign; *hypothetical; < derived from. See inside front cover.

**rig·or mor·tis** (rig'ər môr'tis, rī'gôr) [ModL., stiffness of death] the stiffening of the muscles after death

**rig·or·ous** (rig'ər əs) *adj.* **1.** very strict or harsh *[rigorous rules]* **2.** very severe or sharp *[a rigorous climate]* **3.** exactly precise or accurate *[rigorous scholarship]* —**rig'or·ous·ly** *adv.* —**rig'or·ous·ness** *n.*

**Ri·je·ka** (rē ye'kä) seaport in NW Yugoslavia, on the Adriatic: pop. 101,000

**Rijn** (rīn) *Du. name of the* RHINE

**rile** (rīl) *vt.* **riled, ril'ing** [var. of ROIL] [Colloq. or Dial.] **1.** *same as* ROIL **2.** to anger; irritate

**Ri·ley** (rī'lē), **James Whit·comb** (hwit'kəm, wit'-) 1849–1916; U.S. poet

**rill** (ril) *n.* [< Du. *ril* or LowG. *rille*] a little brook

**rim** (rim) *n.* [OE. *rima,* an edge] **1.** an edge, border, or margin, esp. of something circular **2.** *a)* the outer part of a wheel *b)* the metal flange of an automobile wheel, on which the tire is mounted **3.** *Basketball* the metal hoop to which the net is attached —*vt.* **rimmed, rim'ming 1.** to put a rim on or around **2.** to roll around the rim of *[the golf ball rimmed the hole]* —**rim'less** *adj.*

**Rim·baud** (ran bō'), **(Jean Nicolas) Ar·thur** (är tür') 1854–91; Fr. poet

**rime¹** (rīm) *n., vt., vi.* **rimed, rim'ing** *same as* RHYME —**rim'er** *n.*

**rime²** (rīm) *n.* [OE. *hrim*] a white frost on grass, leaves, etc.; hoarfrost —*vt.* **rimed, rim'ing** to coat with rime

**Rim·sky-Kor·sa·kov** (rēm'skē kôr'sä kôf'; *E.* rim'skē kôr'sə kôf'), **Ni·ko·lai (Andreyevich)** (nē kô lī') 1844–1908; Russ. composer: also sp. **Rimski-Korsakoff**

**rind** (rīnd) *n.* [OE.] a thick, hard, or tough outer layer or coating, as on fruit, cheese, bacon, etc.

**rin·der·pest** (rin'dər pest') *n.* [G. *rinder,* cattle + *pest,* plague] an acute infectious disease of cattle and, often, sheep and goats

**ring¹** (riŋ) *vi.* **rang** or now chiefly dial. **rung, rung, ring'ing** [OE. *hringan*] **1.** to give forth the clear, resonant sound of a bell **2.** to produce, as by sounding, a specified impression *[promises that ring false]* **3.** to cause a bell to sound, esp. as a summons *[to ring for a maid]* **4.** to sound loudly; resound *[the room rang with laughter]* **5.** to have a sensation as of ringing, etc.: said of the ears or head —*vt.* **1.** to cause (a bell, etc.) to ring **2.** to sound (a peal, knell, etc.) as by ringing a bell **3.** to signal, announce, etc. as by ringing **4.** to call by telephone (often with *up*) **5.** [Slang] to substitute fraudulently (often with *in*) —*n.* **1.** the sound of a bell **2.** any similar sound, esp. when loud and continued **3.** a characteristic sound or impression *[the ring of sincerity]* **4.** the act of ringing a bell, etc. **5.** a telephone call: chiefly in **give (someone) a ring,** to telephone (someone) —**ring a bell** to stir up a memory —**ring down (or up) the curtain 1.** to signal for a theater curtain to be lowered (or raised) **2.** to end (or begin) something —**ring up** to record (a specified amount) on a cash register

**ring²** (riŋ) *n.* [OE. *hring*] **1.** a small, circular band, esp. of precious metal, to be worn on the finger **2.** any similar band used for some special purpose *[a key ring]* **3.** a circular line, mark, or figure **4.** the outer edge, or rim, as of a wheel **5.** any of the circular marks seen in the cross section of a tree trunk: each ring represents a year's growth: in full, **annual ring 6.** a number of people or things grouped in a circle **7.** a group of people working together to advance their own selfish interests, as in politics, etc. **8.** an enclosed area, often circular, for contests, exhibitions, etc. *[a circus ring]* **9.** *a)* an enclosure, now a square, in which boxing and wrestling matches are held *b)* prizefighting (with *the*) **10.** a contest: often used in **throw one's hat into the ring,** to enter a contest, esp. one for political office **11.** *Chem.* a number of atoms united in such a way that they can be represented as a ring —*vt.* **ringed, ring'ing 1.** to encircle as with a ring **2.** to form into, or furnish with, a ring or rings **3.** in some games, to toss a ring, horseshoe, etc. so that it encircles (a peg) **4.** to cut a circle of bark from (a tree) —*vi.* to form in a ring or rings —**run rings around** [Colloq.] **1.** to run much faster than **2.** to excel greatly —**ringed** *adj.*

**ring·bolt** (-bōlt') *n.* a bolt with a ring at the head

**ring·dove** (-duv') *n.* **1.** the European wood pigeon **2.** a small dove of Europe and Asia, with a dark ring around the neck

**ring·er¹** (riŋ'ər) *n.* **1.** a horseshoe, quoit, etc. thrown so that it encircles the peg **2.** such a throw

**ring·er²** (riŋ'ər) *n.* **1.** a person or thing that rings a bell, chime, etc. **2.** [Slang] *a)* a horse, player, etc. fraudulently entered, or substituted for another, in a competition *b)* a person or thing very closely resembling another

**ring·git** (riŋ'git) *n., pl.* **ring'git** [native term] *see* MONETARY UNITS, table (Malaysia)

**ring·lead·er** (riŋ'lēd'ər) *n.* a person who leads others, esp. in unlawful acts, etc.

**ring·let** (-lit) *n.* **1.** a little ring **2.** a curl of hair, esp. a long one —**ring'let·ed** *adj.*

**ring·mas·ter** (riŋ'mas'tər) *n.* a man who directs the performances in a circus ring

**ring-necked pheasant** (-nekt') an Asian game fowl with a whitish collar around the neck in the male, now widespread in N. America

**ring·side** (-sīd') *n.* **1.** the place just outside the ring, as at a boxing match or circus **2.** any place that provides a close view of something

**ring·worm** (-wurm') *n.* any contagious skin disease caused by a fungus that produces ring-shaped patches

**rink** (riŋk) *n.* [< Scot. < OFr. *renc,* RANK¹] **1.** a smooth expanse of ice, often enclosed, for ice-skating or for playing hockey **2.** a smooth floor, usually of wood and enclosed, for roller-skating **3.** the building enclosing a rink

**rinse** (rins) *vt.* **rinsed, rins'ing** [< OFr. *rincer,* ult. < L. *recens,* fresh] **1.** to wash lightly, as by dipping into clear water **2.** *a)* to remove soap, dirt, etc. from by such washing *b)* to remove (soap, dirt, etc.) by such washing **3.** to flush (the mouth or teeth), as with clear water **4.** *a)* to dip (fabrics, etc.) into a dye solution *b)* to use a rinse on (the hair) —*vi.* to undergo rinsing —*n.* **1.** a rinsing **2.** the water or solution used in rinsing **3.** a substance mixed with water and used to tint hair —**rins'er** *n.*

**Ri·o de Ja·nei·ro** (rē'ō dā' zhə ner'ō, dē', də; jə nir'ō) seaport in SE Brazil, on the Atlantic: pop. 4,297,000

**Ri·o Grande** (rē'ō grand', gran'dē, grän'dā) river flowing from S Colo. through N.Mex., then southeast as the boundary of Texas & Mexico into the Gulf of Mexico: 1,885 mi.

**ri·ot** (rī'ət) *n.* [OFr. *riote* < *rihoter,* to make a disturbance] **1.** wild or violent disorder, confusion, etc.; tumult **2.** a violent, public disturbance of the peace by a number of persons (in law, usually three or more) assembled together **3.** a brilliant display *[a riot of color]* **4.** [Now Rare] *a)* debauchery *b)* unrestrained revelry or a wild revel **5.** [Colloq.] an extremely amusing person, thing, or event —*vi.* **1.** to take part in a riot or public disturbance **2.** [Now Rare] to revel —**read the riot act to** to command to stop doing something, under threat of punishment —**run riot 1.** to act in a wild, unrestrained manner **2.** to grow in profusion —**ri'ot·er** *n.*

**ri·ot·ous** (rī'ət əs) *adj.* **1.** *a)* having the nature of a disturbance of the peace *b)* engaging in rioting **2.** disorderly or boisterous **3.** debauched; immoral *[riotous living]* **4.** luxuriant or profuse —**ri'ot·ous·ly** *adv.* —**ri'ot·ous·ness** *n.*

**rip¹** (rip) *vt.* **ripped, rip'ping** [prob. < or akin to Fl. *rippen,* to tear] **1.** *a)* to cut or tear apart roughly *b)* to remove as by cutting or tearing (with *off, out,* etc.) *c)* to make (a hole) in this way *d)* to slash with a sharp instrument *e)* to cut or tear (stitches) so as to open (a seam, hem, etc.) **2.** to saw or split (wood) along the grain —*vi.* **1.** to become torn or split apart **2.** [Colloq.] to move with speed or violence —*n.* a torn place or burst seam; split —**rip into** [Colloq.] to attack violently, often with words —**rip off** [Slang]1. to steal or rob **2.** to cheat, exploit, etc. —**rip out** [Colloq.] to utter sharply, as in anger —**rip'per** *n.*

**rip²** (rip) *n.* [< ? prec.] an extent of rough water caused by cross currents or tides meeting

**rip³** (rip) *n.* [var. of *rep,* prob. abbrev. of REPROBATE] [Colloq.] a debauched, dissipated person

**R.I.P.** *abbrev. of* REQUIESCAT IN PACE

**ri·par·i·an** (ri per'ē ən, rī-) *adj.* [< L. < *ripa,* a bank] of, adjacent to, or living on the bank of a river or, sometimes, of a lake, pond, etc.

**rip cord** a cord, etc. pulled to open a parachute during descent

**ripe** (rīp) *adj.* [OE.] **1.** fully grown or developed; specif., ready to be harvested for food, as grain or fruit **2.** like ripe fruit, as in being ruddy and full *[ripe lips]* **3.** sufficiently processed to be ready for use *[ripe cheese]* **4.** fully or highly developed; mature *[ripe wisdom]* **5.** advanced in years *[the ripe age of ninety]* **6.** fully prepared *[ripe for marriage]* **7.** ready for some treatment or process *[a boil ripe for lancing]* **8.** far enough along *(for some purpose):* said of time —**ripe'ly** *adv.* —**ripe'ness** *n.*

**rip·en** (rī'pən) *vi., vt.* to become or make ripe; mature, age, cure, etc. —**rip'en·er** *n.*

**rip-off** (rip'ôf') *n.* [Slang] a stealing, robbing, cheating, exploiting, etc.

**ri·poste, ri·post** (ri pōst') *n.* [< Fr. < It. *risposta* < L. *respondere:* see RESPOND] **1.** *Fencing* a sharp, swift thrust made after parrying an opponent's lunge **2.** a sharp, swift retort —*vi.* **-post'ed, -post'ing** to make a riposte

**rip·ping** (rip'iŋ) *adj.* **1.** that rips or tears **2.** [Chiefly Brit. Slang] excellent; fine —**rip'ping·ly** *adv.*

**rip·ple** (rip''l) *vi.* **-pled, -pling** [prob. < RIP¹ + *-le,* freq. suffix] **1.** *a)* to form or have little waves on the surface, as water stirred by a breeze *b)* to flow with such waves on the surface **2.** to give the effect of rippling water, as by alternately rising and falling *[laughter rippling through the hall]* —*vt.* to cause to ripple —*n.* **1.** a small wave or undulation, as on the surface of water **2.** a movement, appear-

ance, etc. like this **3.** a sound like that of rippling water —**rip′pler** *n.* —**rip′ply** (-lē) *adj.* -**pli·er**, -**pli·est**
**ripple effect** the spreading effects experienced as the result of a single event
**rip-roar·ing** (-rôr′iŋ) *adj.* [Slang] boisterous; uproarious
**rip·saw** (-sô′) *n.* [RIP¹ + SAW¹] a saw with coarse teeth, for cutting wood along the grain
**rip·tide** (-tīd′) *n.* [RIP² + TIDE] a tide opposing another tide, producing rough waters
**rise** (rīz) *vi.* **rose, ris·en** (riz′'n), **ris′ing** [OE. *risan*] **1.** to stand or assume an erect or nearly erect position after sitting, lying etc. **2.** to get up after sleeping or resting **3.** to rebel; revolt **4.** to end an official assembly or meeting **5.** to return to life after dying **6.** to go to a higher place or position; ascend **7.** to appear above the horizon /the moon *rose*/ **8.** to attain a higher level /the river is *rising*/ **9.** to advance in status, rank, etc.; become rich, famous, etc. **10.** to become erect or rigid **11.** to extend or incline upward /hills *rising* steeply/ **12.** to increase in amount, degree, etc. **13.** to become louder, shriller, etc. **14.** to become stronger, more vivid, etc. **15.** to become larger and puffier, as dough with yeast **16.** to originate; begin **17.** to have its source: said of a stream **18.** to happen; occur **19.** to become apparent to the senses or the mind /land *rising* ahead of the ship/ **20.** to become aroused /to make one's temper *rise*/ **21.** to be built /the house *rose* quickly/ —*vt.* to cause to rise, as birds from cover —*n.* **1.** the appearance of the sun, moon, etc. above the horizon **2.** upward motion; ascent **3.** an advance in status, rank, etc. **4.** the appearance of a fish at the water's surface **5.** a piece of rising ground; hill **6.** a slope upward **7.** the vertical height of something, as a staircase **8.** *a)* an increase in height, as of water level *b)* an increase in pitch of a sound *c)* an increase in degree, amount, etc. **9.** a beginning, origin, etc. **10.** [Brit.] a raise (in wages) —**get a rise out of** [Slang] to draw a desired response from, as by teasing —**give rise to** to bring about; begin —**rise to** to prove oneself capable of coping with /to *rise to* the occasion/
**ris·er** (rīz′ər) *n.* **1.** a person or thing that rises **2.** a vertical piece between the steps in a stairway
**ris·i·bil·i·ty** (riz′ə bil′ə tē) *n., pl.* -**ties 1.** the quality or state of being risible **2.** [*usually pl.*] a sense of the ridiculous or amusing
**ris·i·ble** (riz′ə b'l) *adj.* [Fr. < LL. < L. pp. of *ridere*, to laugh] **1.** able or inclined to laugh **2.** of or connected with laughter **3.** causing laughter; laughable; funny
**ris·ing** (rī′ziŋ) *adj.* **1.** that rises; ascending, advancing, etc. **2.** growing; maturing /the *rising* generation/ **3.** [Colloq. or Dial.] somewhat more than; also, approaching /a man *rising* fifty/ : in these senses sometimes regarded as a preposition —*n.* **1.** the act of one that rises; esp., an uprising; revolt **2.** something that rises; projection
**risk** (risk) *n.* [Fr. *risque* < It. *risco*] **1.** the chance of injury, damage, or loss; dangerous chance; hazard **2.** *a)* the chance or likelihood that a person or thing·insured may suffer injury, damage, or loss *b)* the person or thing insured, in relation to such chance or likelihood —*vt.* **1.** to expose to risk; hazard /to *risk* one's life/ **2.** to take the chance of /to *risk* a fight/ —**run** (or **take**) **a risk** to expose oneself to a risk; take a chance —**risk′er** *n.*
**risk·y** (ris′kē) *adj.* **risk′i·er, risk′i·est** involving risk; hazardous; dangerous —**risk′i·ly** *adv.* —**risk′i·ness** *n.*
**ris·qué** (ris kā′) *adj.* [Fr., pp. of *risquer*, to risk] very close to being improper or indecent; daring; suggestive
**Ri·ta** (rēt′ə) [It.] a feminine name
**ri·tar·dan·do** (rē′tär dän′dō) *adj., adv.* [It., gerund of *ritardare*: see RETARD] *Music* becoming gradually slower
**rite** (rīt) *n.* [L. *ritus*] **1.** a solemn or ceremonial act or observance in accordance with prescribed rule, as in religious use /marriage *rites*/ **2.** any formal, customary observance, practice, or procedure /the *rites* of courtship/ **3.** *a)* a particular system or form of ceremonial procedure; ritual *b)* [*often* R-] liturgy; esp., any of the forms of the Eucharistic service **4.** [*often* R-] either of the two major divisions (**Eastern Rite** and **Western Rite**) of the Christian (Catholic) Church, according to the liturgy used
**rit·u·al** (rich′oo wəl) *adj.* [L. *ritualis*] of, having the nature of, or done as a rite —*n.* **1.** a system of rites, religious or otherwise **2.** the observance of set forms or rites, as in worship **3.** a book containing rites **4.** a practice, service, or procedure done as a rite —**rit′u·al·ly** *adv.*
**rit·u·al·ism** (-iz'm) *n.* **1.** the observance of ritual **2.** an excessive devotion to ritual **3.** the study of religious ritual —**rit′u·al·ist** *n., adj.* —**rit′u·al·is′tic** *adj.* —**rit′u·al·is′ti·cal·ly** *adv.*
**ritz·y** (rit′sē) *adj.* **ritz′i·er, ritz′i·est** [< the *Ritz* hotels] [Old Slang] luxurious, fashionable, elegant, etc. —**ritz′i·ness** *n.*

**ri·val** (rī′v'l) *n.* [Fr. < L. *rivalis*, orig., one using the same stream as another < *rivus*, a brook] **1.** a person who tries to get the same thing as another, or to equal or surpass another; competitor **2.** an equal or a satisfactory substitute /plastics are *rivals* of many metals/ —*adj.* acting as a rival; competing —*vt.* -**valed** or -**valled**, -**val·ing** or -**val·ling 1.** to try to equal or surpass **2.** to equal —*vi.* [Archaic] to be a rival
**ri·val·ry** (-rē) *n., pl.* -**ries** the act of rivaling or the fact or state of being a rival or rivals; competition
**rive** (rīv) *vt., vi.* **rived, rived** or **riv·en** (riv′'n), **riv′ing** [ON. *rifa*] **1.** to tear apart; rend **2.** to split; cleave
**riv·er** (riv′ər) *n.* [< OFr. < VL. < L. *riparius*: see RIPARIAN] **1.** a natural stream of water larger than a creek and emptying into an ocean, a lake, or another river **2.** any plentiful stream or flow —**sell down the river** to betray, deceive, etc. —**up the river** [Slang] to or confined in a penitentiary
**Ri·ve·ra** (rē ve′rä; *E.* ri ver′ə), **Die·go** (dye′gō) 1886–1957; Mex. painter, esp. of murals
**river basin** the area drained by a river and its tributaries
**riv·er·bed** (riv′ər bed′) *n.* the channel in which a river flows or has flowed
**Riv·er·side** (riv′ər sīd′) [< Santa Ana *River*, near which it is located] city in S Calif.: pop. 171,000
**riv·er·side** (riv′ər sīd′) *n.* the bank of a river —*adj.* on or near the bank of a river
**riv·et** (riv′it) *n.* [< MFr. < *river*, to clinch] **1.** a metal bolt with a head on one end, used to fasten beams together by being inserted through holes: the plain end is then hammered into a head **2.** a similar device used to strengthen seams, as on work clothes —*vt.* **1.** to fasten with rivets **2.** to hammer the end of (a bolt, etc.) into a head **3.** to fasten firmly **4.** to hold (the eyes, attention, etc.) firmly —**riv′et·er** *n.*
**Riv·i·er·a** (riv′ē er′ə; *It.* rē vye′rä) coastal strip of the Mediterranean in SE France & NW Italy: a famous resort area
**riv·u·let** (riv′yoo lit) *n.* [< It. *rivoletto*, ult. < L. *rivus*, a brook] a little stream
**Ri·yadh** (rē yäd′) political capital of Saudi Arabia: pop. c. 300,000: cf. MECCA
**ri·yal** (rē yäl′, -yôl′) *n., pl.* -**yals′** [Ar. *riyāl* < Sp. *real*: see REAL²] *see* MONETARY UNITS, table (Qatar, Saudi Arabia, Yemen)
**rm.** *pl.* **rms. 1.** ream **2.** room
**Rn** *Chem.* radon
**R.N. 1.** Registered Nurse: also **RN 2.** Royal Navy
**RNA** ribonucleic acid
**roach¹** (rōch) *n.* **1.** *same as* COCKROACH **2.** [Slang] the butt of a marijuana cigarette
**roach²** (rōch) *n., pl.* **roach, roach′es**: see PLURAL, II, D, 2 [OFr. *roche*, prob. < Gmc.] **1.** a freshwater fish of the carp family, found in N Europe **2.** any of various similar American fishes
**roach³** (rōch) *vt.* [< ?] **1.** to brush (a person's hair) so that it arches in a roll **2.** to cut (a horse's mane) so that it stands up
**road** (rōd) *n.* [OE. *rad*, a ride < *ridan*, to ride] **1.** *a)* a way made for traveling between places by automobile, horseback, etc.; highway *b) same as* ROADBED (sense 2) **2.** a way; path; course /the *road* to fortune/ **3.** *same as* RAILROAD **4.** [*often pl.*] a protected place near shore where ships can ride at anchor —**one for the road** [Slang] a last alcoholic drink before leaving —**on the road 1.** traveling, as a salesman **2.** on tour, as actors —**take to the road** to start traveling —**the road** the cities visited by touring theatrical companies
**road·a·bil·i·ty** (rōd′ə bil′ə tē) *n.* the degree of operating ease and riding comfort of a vehicle on the road
**road·bed** (rōd′bed′) *n.* **1.** a layer of crushed rock, cinders, etc. on which the ties and rails of a railroad are laid **2.** the foundation and surface of a road, or highway
**road·block** (-bläk′) *n.* **1.** a blockade set up in a road to prevent movement of vehicles **2.** any hindrance
**road·house** (-hous′) *n.* a tavern, inn, or, esp., nightclub along a country road, as in the 1920's
**road runner** a long-tailed, crested desert bird of the southwestern U.S. and northern Mexico, that can run swiftly
**road·side** (-sīd′) *n.* the side of a road —*adj.* on or at the side of a road /a *roadside* park/
**road·stead** (-sted′) *n. same as* ROAD (sense 4)
**road·ster** (-stər) *n.* an earlier type of open automobile with a single seat for two or three persons and, sometimes, a rumble seat
**road test** a test of a vehicle, tires, etc. under actual operating conditions —**road′-test′** *vt.*

RIVETS (A, rivet holding steel beams together; B, C, D, rivets)

fat, āpe, cär, ten, ēven, is, bīte; gō, hôrn, tōōl, look; oil, out; up, fur; get; joy; yet; chin; she; thin, *then*; zh, leisure; ŋ, ring; ə for a in ago, e in agent, i in sanity, o in comply, u in focus; ' as in able (ā′b'l); Fr. bal; ë, Fr. coeur; ö, Fr. feu; Fr. mon; ô, Fr. coq; ü, Fr. duc; r, Fr. cri; H, G. ich; kh, G. doch; ‡foreign; *hypothetical; < derived from. See inside front cover.

**road·way** (-wā′) *n.* **1.** a road **2.** that part of a road intended for cars, trucks, and other vehicles to travel on
**roam** (rōm) *vi.* [ME. *romen*] to travel from place to place, esp. with no special plan or purpose; wander —*vt.* to wander over or through [to *roam* the streets] —*n.* the act of roaming; ramble —**roam′er** *n.*
**roan** (rōn) *adj.* [OFr. < OSp. *roano*, ult. < *ravus*] of a solid color, as reddish-brown, black, etc., with a thick sprinkling of white hairs: said chiefly of horses —*n.* **1.** a roan color **2.** a roan horse or other animal
**Ro·a·noke** (rō′ə nōk′) [< Algonquian *Roanok*, northern people] **1.** city in SW Va.: pop. 100,000 **2.** island off the NE coast of N.C.: site of an abortive Eng. colony (1585–87)
**roar** (rôr) *vi.* [OE. *rarian*] **1.** to utter a loud, deep, rumbling sound, as a lion **2.** to talk or laugh loudly and boisterously **3.** to operate with a loud noise, as a motor or gun **4.** to resound with a noisy din —*vt.* **1.** to utter with a roar **2.** to make, put, etc. by roaring [to *roar* oneself hoarse] —*n.* **1.** a loud, deep, rumbling sound, as of a lion, bull, crowd shouting, etc. **2.** a loud noise, as of waves, a motor, etc.; din —**roar′er** *n.*
**roast** (rōst) *vt.* [OFr. *rostir* < Frank.] **1.** to cook (something) with little or no moisture, as in an oven or over an open fire **2.** to dry, parch, or brown (coffee, etc.) by exposure to heat **3.** to expose to great heat **4.** to heat (ore, etc.) in a furnace in order to remove impurities or cause oxidation **5.** [Colloq.] to criticize or ridicule severely —*vi.* **1.** to be cooked by being roasted **2.** to be or become very hot —*n.* **1.** roasted meat **2.** a cut of meat for roasting **3.** a roasting or being roasted **4.** a picnic at which food is roasted [a steer *roast*] —*adj.* roasted [roast pork] —**roast′ing** *adj.*
**roast·er** (rōs′tər) *n.* **1.** a person or thing that roasts **2.** a pan, oven, etc. for roasting meat **3.** a young pig, chicken, etc. suitable for roasting
**rob** (räb) *vt.* **robbed, rob′bing** [OFr. *rober* < Gmc.] **1.** *a)* Law to take personal property, money, etc. from unlawfully by using or threatening force *b)* popularly, to steal something from in any way **2.** to deprive (someone) of something belonging to or due him [the accident *robbed* him of health] —*vi.* to commit robbery —**rob′ber** *n.*
**rob·ber·y** (räb′ər ē) *n., pl.* **-ber·ies** a robbing; specif., the committing of a felony by taking another's property while he is present, by violence or threat of violence
**robe** (rōb) *n.* [OFr., a robe, orig., booty < Gmc.] **1.** a long, loose outer garment; specif., *a)* such a garment worn on formal occasions, to show rank or office, as by a judge *b)* a bathrobe or dressing gown **2.** [*pl.*] [Archaic] clothes; costume **3.** short for LAP ROBE —*vt., vi.* **robed, rob′ing** to dress in or cover with a robe
**Rob·ert** (räb′ərt) [< OFr. < OHG. < *hruod-*, fame + *perht*, bright] **1.** a masculine name: dim. *Bob, Rob, Robin* **2.** Robert I *see* BRUCE (sense 2)
**Ro·ber·ta** (rə bur′tə, rō-) [fem. of ROBERT] a feminine name
**Ro·bes·pierre** (rō′bes pyer′; *E.* rōbs′pyer, -pir), **Max·i·mi·lien** (François Marie Isidore de) (mȧk sē mē lyan′) 1758–94; Fr. revolutionist & Jacobin leader: guillotined
**rob·in** (räb′in) *n.* [< OFr. dim. of *Robert*] **1.** a large N. American thrush with a dull-red breast and belly **2.** a small European warbler with a yellowish-red breast Also **robin redbreast**
**Robin Good·fel·low** (good′fel′ō) *Eng. Folklore* a mischievous elf or fairy: identified with Puck
**Robin Hood** *Eng. Legend* an outlaw of the 12th cent. who lived with his followers in Sherwood Forest and robbed the rich to help the poor
**rob·in's-egg blue** (räb′inz eg′) a light greenish blue
**Rob·in·son** (räb′in s'n), **Edwin Ar·ling·ton** (är′liŋ tən) 1869–1935; U.S. poet
**Robinson Cru·soe** (krōō′sō) the hero of Defoe's novel (1719) of the same name, a sailor who is shipwrecked on a tropical island
**ro·bot** (rō′bət, -bät) *n.* [< Czech *robota*, forced labor < OBulg. < *rabu*, servant] **1.** *a)* any manlike mechanical being, as those in Karel Čapek's play *R.U.R. b)* any mechanical device operated automatically, esp. by remote control, to perform in a seemingly human way **2.** an automaton; esp., a person who acts or works mechanically —**ro′bot·ism** *n.*
**robot bomb** a small, jet-propelled bomb with wings, steered by an automatic pilot and carrying high explosives
**ro·bust** (rō büst′, rō′bust) *adj.* [L. *robustus* < *robur*, hard variety of oak] **1.** *a)* strong and healthy; hardy *b)* strongly built; muscular or sturdy **2.** suited to or requiring physical strength [*robust* work] **3.** rough; coarse; boisterous **4.** full and rich, as in flavor [a *robust* port wine] —**ro·bust′ly** *adv.* —**ro·bust′ness** *n.*
**roc** (räk) *n.* [< Ar. < Per. *rukh*] *Arabian & Persian Legend* a fabulous bird, so huge and strong that it could carry off large animals
**Rochelle salt** [after La *Rochelle*, France] a colorless, crys-

talline compound, $KNaC_4H_4O_6.4H_2O$, used as a piezoelectric material, etc.
**Roch·es·ter** (rä′ches′tər, räch′is-) **1.** [after N. *Rochester*, Revolutionary officer] city in W N.Y., on Lake Ontario: pop. 242,000 (met. area 970,000) **2.** [after prec.] city in SE Minn.: pop. 58,000
**roch·et** (räch′it) *n.* [< OFr. < *roc*, a cloak < MHG. < OHG. *roch*] a vestment of lawn or linen, like a surplice, worn by bishops
**rock¹** (räk) *n.* [< OFr. *roche*] **1.** a large mass of stone **2.** *a)* a large stone detached from the mass; boulder *b)* broken pieces of any size of such stone **3.** *a)* mineral matter formed in masses in the earth's crust *b)* a particular kind or mass of this **4.** anything like a rock, as in strength; esp., a firm support, basis, etc. **5.** [Colloq. or Dial.] any stone **6.** [Slang] a diamond or other gem —**on the rocks** [Colloq.] **1.** in a condition of ruin or catastrophe **2.** without money; bankrupt **3.** served undiluted over ice cubes: said of liquor, wine, etc.
**rock²** (räk) *vt.* [OE. *roccian*] **1.** to move back and forth or from side to side (a cradle, a child in the arms, etc.) **2.** to make or put by moving this way [to *rock* a baby to sleep] **3.** *a)* to sway strongly; shake [the explosion *rocked* the house] *b)* to upset emotionally —*vi.* **1.** to move back and forth or from side to side **2.** to sway strongly; shake —*n.* **1.** a rocking **2.** a rocking motion **3.** *a)* same as ROCK-AND-ROLL *b)* popular music evolved from rock-and-roll, variously containing elements of folk music, country music, etc.
**rock-and-roll** (räk′'n rōl′) *n.* a form of popular music, having a strong and regular rhythm, which evolved from jazz and the blues: also sp. **rock 'n' roll**
**rock bottom** the lowest level, point, or position; very bottom —**rock′-bot′tom** *adj.*
**rock-bound** (-bound′) *adj.* surrounded or covered by rocks [a *rock-bound* coast]
**rock candy** large, hard, clear crystals of sugar formed on a string dipped in a solution of boiled sugar
**Rock Cornish** (hen) *same as* CORNISH (sense 2 *b*)
**rock crystal** a transparent, esp. colorless, quartz
**Rock·e·fel·ler** (räk′ə fel′ər) **1.** **John D(avison)**, 1839–1937; U.S. industrialist & philanthropist **2.** **John D(avison), Jr.**, 1874–1960; U.S. industrialist & philanthropist: son of *prec.*
**rock·er** (räk′ər) *n.* **1.** either of the curved pieces on the bottom of a cradle, rocking chair, etc. **2.** same as ROCKING CHAIR **3.** any of various devices that work with a rocking motion —**off one's rocker** [Slang] crazy; insane
**rock·et** (räk′it) *n.* [It. *rocchetta*, a spool, orig. dim. of *rocca*, a distaff < OHG.] **1.** any of various devices, typically cylindrical, containing a combustible substance which when ignited produces gases that escape through a rear vent and drive the container forward by the principle of reaction: rockets are used as fireworks and projectile weapons and to propel spacecraft **2.** a spacecraft, missile, etc. propelled by a rocket —*vi.* **1.** to dart ahead swiftly like a rocket **2.** to travel in a rocket **3.** to soar [prices *rocketed*] —*vt.* to convey in a rocket —**rock·e·teer** (räk′ə tir′) *n.*
**rock·et·ry** (räk′ə trē) *n.* **1.** the science of designing, building, and launching rockets **2.** rockets collectively
**Rock·ford** (räk′fərd) [after the *rocky*-bottomed *ford* there] city in N Ill.: pop. 140,000
**rock garden** a garden with flowers and plants growing among rocks variously arranged
**Rock·ies** (räk′ēz) *same as* ROCKY MOUNTAINS
**rocking chair** a chair mounted on rockers or springs, so as to allow a rocking movement
**rocking horse** a toy horse mounted on rockers or springs and big enough for a child to ride
**Rock Island** [< the name of the *rocky island* in the river] city in NW Ill., on the Mississippi: pop. 47,000
**rock-ribbed** (räk′ribd′) *adj.* **1.** having rocky ridges [*rock-ribbed* coasts] **2.** firm; unyielding
**rock salt** common salt in solid masses
**rock wool** a fibrous material that looks like spun glass, made from molten rock or slag through which steam is forced: it is used for insulation, esp. in buildings
**rock·y¹** (räk′ē) *adj.* **rock′i·er, rock′i·est** **1.** full of rocks **2.** consisting of rock **3.** like a rock; firm, hard, unfeeling, etc. **4.** full of obstacles [the *rocky* road to success] —**rock′i·ness** *n.*
**rock·y²** (räk′ē) *adj.* **rock′i·er, rock′i·est** **1.** *a)* inclined to rock, or sway *b)* uncertain; shaky **2.** [Slang] weak or dizzy, as from illness; unwell —**rock′i·ness** *n.*
**Rocky Mountain goat** a white, goatlike antelope of the mountains of northwest N. America
**Rocky Mountains** mountain system in W N.America, extending from C N.Mex. to N Alas.
**Rocky Mountain sheep** *same as* BIGHORN
**Rocky Mountain spotted fever** an acute infectious disease caused by a rickettsia
**ro·co·co** (rə kō′kō; *occas.* rō′kə kō′) *n.* [Fr. < *rocaille*,

shell work] a style of architecture and decoration using elaborate ornamentation imitating foliage, shell work, scrolls, etc.: popular in the 18th cent. —*adj.* 1. of or in rococo 2. too elaborate; florid and tasteless

**rod** (räd) *n.* [OE. *rodd*] 1. *Bible* a branch of a family or tribe 2. any straight stick, bar, etc., as of wood, metal, etc. *[curtain rods]* 3. *a)* a stick for beating as punishment *b)* punishment 4. *a)* a staff, scepter, etc., carried as a symbol of office or rank *b)* power; authority 5. same as FISHING ROD 6. a stick used to measure something 7. *a)* a measure of length equal to 5½ yards *b)* a square rod, equal to 30¼ square yards 8. [Slang] a pistol or revolver 9. [Slang] same as HOT ROD 10. *Biol.* a rod-shaped cell, microorganism, etc. —**rod′like′** *adj.*

**rode** (rōd) *pt. & archaic pp. of* RIDE

**ro·dent** (rōd′'nt) *adj.* [< L. prp. of *rodere*, to gnaw] 1. gnawing 2. of or like rodents —*n.* any of various gnawing mammals, including rats, mice, beavers, etc., that have constantly growing incisors; esp., a rat or mouse

**ro·de·o** (rō′dē ō′; *also, esp. for 1*, rō dā′ō) *n., pl.* **-de·os′** [Sp. < *rodear*, surround < L. *rotare:* see ROTATE] 1. [Now Rare] a roundup of cattle 2. a public exhibition of the skills of cowboys, as broncobusting, lassoing, etc.

**Ro·din** (rō dan′; *E.* rō dan′), **(François) Au·guste (René)** (ō güst′) 1840–1917; Fr. sculptor

**rod·o·mon·tade** (räd′ə män täd′, rō′də-; -täd′) *n.* [Fr. < It. *Rodomonte*, boastful Saracen leader in *Orlando Furioso*, 16th-c. epic] arrogant boasting or blustering talk —*adj.* arrogantly boastful —*vi.* boasting —*vt.*, **-tad′ing** to boast

**roe**[1] (rō) *n.* [akin to or < ? ON. *hrogn*] fish eggs, esp. when still massed in the ovarian membrane

**roe**[2] (rō) *n., pl.* **roe, roes:** see PLURAL, II, D, 2 [OE. *ra*] a small, agile, graceful European and Asian deer

**roe·buck** (rō′buk′) *n., pl.* **-bucks′, -buck′:** see PLURAL, II, D, 1 the male of the roe deer

**roent·gen** (rent′gən, ren′chən) *n.* [after W. K. *Roentgen* (1845–1923), Ger. physicist] the international unit used in measuring ionizing radiation, as X-rays or gamma rays

**Roentgen ray** [*also* r-] same as X-RAY

**ro·ga·tion** (rō gā′shən) *n.* [< L. < *rogare*, to ask] a supplication or prayer, esp. as chanted during the three days **(Rogation Days)** before Ascension Day

**Rog·er** (räj′ər) [OFr. < OHG. < *hruod-*, fame + base meaning "spear"] a masculine name —*interj.* [< conventional name of international signal flag for *R*] [*also* r-] 1. received: term used in radiotelephony to indicate reception of a message 2. [Colloq.] right! OK!

**Ro·get** (rō zhā′), **Peter Mark** 1779–1869; Eng. writer: compiler of a thesaurus

**rogue** (rōg) *n.* [< ? L. *rogare*, to ask] 1. formerly, a vagabond 2. a scoundrel 3. a fun-loving, mischievous person 4. an animal that wanders alone and is fierce and wild —*vt.* **rogued, rogu′ing** to cheat —*vi.* to live or act like a rogue

**ro·guer·y** (rō′gər ē) *n., pl.* **-guer·ies** the behavior of a rogue; specif., *a)* trickery; cheating *b)* playful mischief

**rogues′ gallery** a collection of photographs of criminals, as used by police in identification

**ro·guish** (rō′gish) *adj.* of or like a rogue; specif., *a)* dishonest; unscrupulous *b)* playfully mischievous —**ro′guish·ly** *adv.* —**ro′guish·ness** *n.*

**roil** (roil) *vt.* [< Fr. < OFr. *rouil*, rust, ult. < L. *robigo*, rust] 1. to make (a liquid) cloudy, muddy, etc. by stirring up the sediment 2. to stir up; agitate 3. to make angry or irritable —*vi.* to be agitated —**roil′y** *adj.* **roil′i·er, roil′i·est**

**roist·er** (rois′tər) *vi.* [< OFr. < L. *rusticus:* see RUSTIC] 1. to boast or swagger 2. to be lively and noisy; revel boisterously —**roist′er·er** *n.* —**roist′er·ous** *adj.*

**Ro·land** (rō′lənd) [Fr. < OHG. < *hruod-*, fame + *land*, land] 1. a masculine name 2. a hero famous for his courage who appears in legends about Charlemagne

**role, rôle** (rōl) *n.* [Fr. *rôle*, a roll: from roll containing actor's part] 1. a part, or character, that an actor plays 2. a function assumed by someone [an advisory role]

**roll** (rōl) *vi.* [OFr. *roller*, ult. < L. *rotula* (or *rotulus*), dim. of *rota*, wheel] 1. to move by turning over and over 2. *a)* to move on wheels *b)* to travel in a wheeled vehicle 3. to pass [the years rolled by] 4. to move in a periodical revolution: said of stars, planets, etc. 5. *a)* to flow, as water, in a full, sweeping motion *b)* to be carried in a flow 6. to extend in gentle swells or undulations 7. to make a loud, rising and falling sound [thunder rolls] 8. to rise and fall in a full, mellow cadence, as speech 9. to trill 10. to be wound into a ball or cylinder, as yarn 11. to turn in a circular motion [with eyes rolling] 12. to rock from side to side, as a ship 13. to walk by swaying 14. to become spread under a roller 15. to make progress; advance 16. to start operating [the presses rolled] 17. [Colloq.] to abound (in) [rolling in wealth] 18. *Football* to move laterally: said of the

passer: in full, **roll out** —*vt.* 1. to move by turning over and over 2. to move on wheels or rollers 3. to cause to start operating 4. to beat (a drum) with light, rapid blows 5. to utter with a full, flowing sound 6. to say with a trill [to roll one's r's] 7. to give a swaying motion to 8. to move around or from side to side [to roll one's eyes] 9. to wind into a ball or cylinder [to roll a cigarette] 10. to wrap or enfold 11. to make flat or spread out, by using a roller, etc. 12. to iron (sleeves, etc.) without forming a crease 13. [Slang] to rob (a drunken or sleeping person) 14. *Printing* to spread ink on (type, a form, etc.) with a roller —*n.* 1. the act or an instance of rolling 2. *a)* a scroll *b)* something that is, or looks as if, rolled up 3. a register; catalog 4. a list of names for checking attendance 5. a measure of something rolled into a cylinder [a roll of wallpaper] 6. a cylindrical mass of something 7. any of various small cakes of bread, etc. 8. a roller (in various senses) 9. a swaying motion 10. a rapid succession of light blows on a drum 11. a loud, reverberating sound, as of thunder 12. a trill 13. a slight swell on the surface, as of land 14. [Slang] money; esp., a wad of paper money —**roll back** 1. to move back 2. to reduce (prices) to a previous level by government action —**roll in** to arrive or appear, usually in large numbers or amounts —**roll out** to spread out by unrolling —**roll over** 1. to refinance (a maturing note, etc.) 2. to reinvest (funds) so as to defer paying taxes —**roll up** 1. to increase by accumulation 2. [Colloq.] to arrive in a vehicle —**strike off** (or **from**) **the rolls** to expel from membership

**roll·a·way** (rōl′ə wā′) *adj.* having rollers for easy moving and storing when not in use [a rollaway bed]

**roll bar** a heavy metal bar reinforcing the roof of an automobile to reduce injury if the car should roll over

**roll call** the reading aloud of a roll, as in military formations, to find out who is absent

**roll·er** (rō′lər) *n.* 1. a person or thing that rolls 2. *a)* a cylinder on which something is rolled up *b)* a heavy rolling cylinder used to crush, smooth, or spread something 3. a long bandage in a roll 4. a long, heavy wave that breaks on the shoreline 5. a canary that trills its notes

**roller bearing** a bearing in which the shaft turns on rollers in a ringlike track

**roller coaster** an amusement ride in which small, open cars move on tracks that dip and curve sharply

**roller skate** a skate with wheels: see SKATE[1] (sense 2) —**roll′er-skate′** *vi.* **-skat′ed, -skat′ing** —**roller skater**

**rol·lick** (räl′ik) *vi.* [< ? FROLIC] to play or behave in a gay, carefree way —**rol′lick·ing, rol′lick·some** (-səm) *adj.*

**roll·ing** (rō′liŋ) *adj.* that rolls; specif., rotating or revolving, recurring, swaying, surging, resounding, trilling, etc. —*n.* the action, motion, or sound of something that rolls

**rolling mill** 1. a factory in which metal bars, sheets, etc. are rolled out 2. a machine used for such rolling

**rolling pin** a heavy, smooth cylinder of wood, glass, etc., usually with a handle at each end, used to roll out dough

**rolling stock** all the locomotives, cars, etc. of a railroad, or the trucks, trailers, etc. of a trucking company

**roll·o·ver** (-ō′vər) *n.* the act or an instance of rolling over a maturing note, etc. or invested funds

**roll-top** (rōl′täp′) *adj.* made with a flexible top of parallel slats that slides back [a roll-top desk]

**ro·ly-po·ly** (rō′lē pō′lē) *adj.* [redupl. of ROLL] short and plump; pudgy —*n., pl.* **-lies** 1. a roly-poly person or thing 2. [Chiefly Brit.] a pudding made of rich dough and jam

**rom, rom** (type)

**Rom.** 1. Roman 2. Romance 3. Romania 4. Romanian 5. Romanic 6. Romans (Epistle to the Romans)

**Ro·ma** (rō′mä) *It.* name of ROME

**Ro·ma·ic** (rō mā′ik) *n.* the everyday language of modern Greece —*adj.* of this language

**ro·maine** (rō mān′, rō′mān) *n.* [Fr. < fem. of *romain*, Roman] a kind of lettuce with long leaves that form a cylindrical or conical head: also **romaine lettuce**

**Ro·man** (rō′mən) *adj.* 1. of or characteristic of ancient or modern Rome, its people, etc. 2. of the Roman Catholic Church 3. [*usually* r-] designating or of the usual upright style of printing types; not italic —*n.* 1. a native, citizen, or inhabitant of ancient or modern Rome 2. [*usually* r-] roman type or characters

**Roman alphabet** the alphabet of the ancient Romans, used with little change in most modern European languages

**Roman arch** a semicircular arch

**Roman candle** a firework consisting of a long tube that sends out balls of fire, sparks, etc.

**Roman Catholic** 1. of the Roman Catholic Church 2. a member of this church —**Roman Catholicism**

**Roman Catholic Church** the Christian church headed by the Pope

**Ro·mance** (rō mans′, rō′mans) *adj.* [see ff.] designating or of any of the languages derived from Vulgar Latin, as Italian, Spanish, French, etc. —*n.* these languages

**ro·mance** (rō mans′; *also, for n.,* rō′mans) *n.* [OFr. *romanz,* Roman (i.e., the vernacular, not Latin), ult. < L. *Romanicus,* Roman] **1.** a long verse or prose narrative, orig. written in one of the Romance languages, about knights and chivalric deeds, adventure, and love **2.** a novel of love, adventure, etc. **3.** excitement, love, and adventure of the kind found in such literature **4.** the tendency to enjoy romantic adventures **5.** an exaggeration or fabrication **6.** a love affair —*vi.* **-manced′, -manc′ing 1.** to write or tell romances **2.** to think or talk about romantic things —*vt.* [Colloq.] to woo; court —**ro·manc′er** *n.*

**Roman Curia** *R.C.Ch. see* CURIA (sense 2)

**Roman Empire** empire established by Augustus, including, at its peak, W & S Europe, Britain, Asia Minor, N Africa, & the lands at the E end of the Mediterranean: it existed from 27 B.C. until 395 A.D.

**Ro·man·esque** (rō′mə nesk′) *adj.* designating or of a style of European architecture of the 11th and 12th cent., based on the Roman and using round arches and vaults, massive walls, etc. —*n.* this style of architecture

**Roman holiday** [after the ancient Roman gladiatorial contests] entertainment at the expense of others′ suffering, or a spectacle yielding such entertainment

**Ro·ma·nia, Ro·mâ·nia** (rō mān′yə, -mā′nē ə; *Romanian* rô mu′nyä) country in SE Europe, on the Black Sea: 91,700 sq. mi.; pop. 20,470,000; cap. Bucharest

**Ro·ma·nian** (-mān′yən, -mā′nē ən) *adj.* of Romania, its people, language, etc. —*n.* **1.** a native or inhabitant of Romania **2.** the Romance language of the Romanians

**Ro·man·ic** (-man′ik) *adj., n. same as* ROMANCE

**Ro·man·ism** (rō′mən iz′m) *n.* Roman Catholicism: hostile usage

**Ro·man·ize** (-īz′) *vt.* **-ized′, -iz′ing 1.** to make or become Roman in character, spirit, etc. **2.** to make or become Roman Catholic —**Ro′man·i·za′tion** *n.*

**Roman nose** a nose with a prominent bridge

**Roman numerals** the Roman letters used as numerals until the 10th cent. A.D.: in Roman numerals I = 1, V = 5, X = 10, L = 50, C = 100, D = 500, and M = 1,000 The value of a symbol following another of the same or greater value is added (e.g., III = 3, XV = 15); the value of a symbol preceding one of greater value is subtracted (e.g., IX = 9)

**Ro·ma·no** (rō mä′nō) *n.* [It., ROMAN] a dry, sharp, very hard Italian cheese, usually grated

**Ro·ma·nov** (rô mä′nôf; *E.* rō′mə nôf′) ruling family of Russia from 1613 to 1917: also sp. **Romanoff**

**Ro·mans** (rō′mənz) a book of the New Testament, an epistle from the Apostle Paul to the Christians of Rome

**ro·man·tic** (rō man′tik) *adj.* **1.** of, like, or characterized by romance **2.** without a basis in fact; fanciful or fictitious **3.** not practical; visionary *[a romantic scheme]* **4.** full of thoughts, feelings, etc. of romance **5.** *a)* of or concerned with idealized lovemaking *b)* suited for romance, or lovemaking *[a romantic night]* **6.** *[often* R-*]* of or associated with the ROMANTIC MOVEMENT —*n.* a romantic person —**ro·man′ti·cal·ly** *adv.*

**ro·man·ti·cism** (rō man′tə siz′m) *n.* **1.** romantic spirit, outlook, etc. **2.** *a) same as* ROMANTIC MOVEMENT *b)* the spirit, style, etc. of, or adherence to, the Romantic Movement: contrasted with CLASSICISM, etc. —**ro·man′ti·cist** *n.*

**ro·man·ti·cize** (-sīz′) *vt.* **-cized′, -ciz′ing** to treat or regard romantically —*vi.* to have romantic ideas, attitudes, etc. —**ro·man′ti·ci·za′tion** *n.*

**Romantic Movement** the revolt in the 18th and 19th cent. against neoclassicism in literature, music, art, etc.: it emphasized freedom of form, full expression of feeling, etc.

**Rom·a·ny** (räm′ə nē, rō′mə-) *n.* [Romany *romani,* Gypsy < *rom,* a man < Sans.] **1.** *pl.* **-ny, -nies** a Gypsy **2.** the Indic language of the Gypsies —*adj.* of the Gypsies, their language, etc. Also sp. **Rom′ma·ny**

**Rom. Cath.** Roman Catholic

**Rome** (rōm) **1.** capital of Italy, on the Tiber River: formerly, the capital of the Roman Empire: pop. 2,731,000 **2.** [after prec.] city in C N.Y., near Utica: pop. 44,000 **3.** *same as* ROMAN CATHOLIC CHURCH

**Ro·me·o** (rō′mē ō′) the hero of Shakespeare′s tragedy *Romeo and Juliet* (c. 1595), lover of Juliet —*n., pl.* **-os′** a man who is an ardent lover

**Rom·ney** (räm′nē, rum′-), **George** 1734–1802; Eng. painter

**romp** (rämp) *n.* [< earlier *ramp,* hussy, prob. < OFr. *ramper:* see RAMP[2]] **1.** a person who romps, esp. a girl **2.** boisterous, lively play **3.** *a)* an easy, winning gait in a race *[to win in a romp]* *b)* an easy victory —*vi.* **1.** to play in a boisterous, lively way **2.** to win with ease

**romp·er** (räm′pər) *n.* **1.** one who romps **2.** *[pl.]* a young child′s loose-fitting, one-piece outer garment with bloomer-like pants

**Rom·u·lus** (räm′yōō ləs) *Rom. Myth.* the founder and first king of Rome: he and his twin brother Remus, left as infants to die, were suckled by a she-wolf

**Ron·ald** (rän′ld) [Scot. < ON. *Rögnvaldr:* see REGINALD] a masculine name

**ron·deau** (rän′dō) *n., pl.* **-deaux** (-dōz) [Fr. < *rondel* < *rond,* round] a short lyrical poem of thirteen (or ten) lines and an unrhymed refrain that consists of the opening words and is used in two places

**ron·del** (-d′l, -del) *n.* [OFr.: see prec.] a kind of rondeau, usually with fourteen lines, two rhymes, and the first two lines used as a refrain in the middle and at the end

**ron·do** (rän′dō) *n., pl.* **-dos** [It. < Fr.: see RONDEAU] *Music* a composition or movement having its principal theme stated three or more times in the same key, separated by subordinate themes

**rood** (rōōd) *n.* [OE. *rod*] **1.** a crucifix **2.** in England, a measure of area usually equal to 1/4 acre (40 square rods)

**roof** (rōōf, roof) *n., pl.* **roofs** [OE. *hrof*] **1.** the outside top covering of a building **2.** figuratively, a house or home **3.** anything like a roof *[the roof of the mouth]* —*vt.* to cover as with a roof —**raise the roof** [Slang] to be very noisy, as in anger or joy —**roof′less** *adj.*

**roof·er** (-ər) *n.* a person who builds or repairs roofs

**roof garden 1.** a garden on the flat roof of a building **2.** the roof or top floor of a building, decorated as a garden and used as a restaurant, etc.

**roof·ing** (-iŋ) *n.* **1.** the act of covering with a roof **2.** material for roofs **3.** a roof

**roof·top** (-täp′) *n.* the roof of a building

**roof·tree** (-trē′) *n.* **1.** the ridgepole of a roof **2.** a roof

**rook**[1] (rook) *n.* [OE. *hroc*] **1.** a crowlike European bird **2.** a swindler; cheat —*vt., vi.* to swindle; cheat

**rook**[2] (rook) *n.* [< OFr. *roc* < Ar. < Per. *rukh*] *Chess* either of the two corner pieces shaped like a castle tower, movable only in a vertical or horizontal line; castle

**rook·er·y** (rook′ər ē) *n., pl.* **-er·ies** a breeding place or colony of rooks, or of seals, penguins, etc.

**rook·ie** (rook′ē) *n.* [altered < ? RECRUIT] [Slang] **1.** an inexperienced recruit in the army **2.** any novice, as on a police force or in a professional sport

**room** (rōōm, room) *n.* [OE. *rum*] **1.** space to contain something or in which to do something *[room for one more]* **2.** opportunity *[room for doubt]* **3.** a space within a building enclosed or set apart by walls **4.** *[pl.]* living quarters; lodgings **5.** the people in a room *[the whole room was silent]* —*vi., vt.* to have, or provide with, lodgings

**room and board** lodging and meals

**room clerk** a clerk at a hotel or motel who registers guests, assigns them rooms, etc.

**room·er** (rōō′mər, room′-) *n.* a person who rents lodgings

**room·ette** (rōō met′, roo-) *n.* a small compartment for one person in a railroad sleeping car

**room·ful** (rōōm′fool′, room′-) *n., pl.* **-fuls′ 1.** as much or as many as will fill a room **2.** the people or objects in a room, collectively

**rooming house** a house with furnished rooms for rent

**room·mate** (-māt′) *n.* a person with whom one shares a room or rooms

**room·y** (-ē) *adj.* **room′i·er, room′i·est** having plenty of room; spacious —**room′i·ly** *adv.* —**room′i·ness** *n.*

**roor·back, roor·bach** (roor′bak) *n.* [after a nonexistent book, *Roorback′s Tour,* containing spurious charges against presidential candidate James K. POLK] a slanderous story spread to damage the reputation of a political candidate

**Roo·se·velt** (rō′zə velt′, -vəlt; rōz′velt) **1. Franklin Del·a·no** (del′ə nō′), 1882–1945; 32d president of the U.S. (1933–45) **2. Theodore,** 1858–1919; 26th president of the U.S. (1901–09)

**roost** (rōōst) *n.* [OE. *hrost*] **1.** a perch on which birds, esp. domestic fowls, can rest or sleep **2.** a place with perches for birds **3.** a place for resting, sleeping, etc. —*vi.* **1.** to sit, sleep, etc. on a roost **2.** to settle down, as for the night —**come home to roost** to come back in an unfavorable way to the doer; boomerang —**rule the roost** to be master

**roost·er** (rōō′stər) *n.* the male of the chicken

**root**[1] (rōōt, root) *n.* [Late OE. *rote* < ON. *rot*] **1.** the part of a plant, usually below the ground, that lacks nodes, shoots, and leaves, holds the plant in place, and draws water and food from the soil **2.** loosely, any underground part of a plant **3.** the embedded part of a bodily structure, as of the teeth, hair, etc. **4.** the source or cause of an action, quality, condition, etc. **5.** an ancestor **6.** *[pl.]* the close ties one has with some place or people as through birth, upbringing, long association, etc. **7.** a supporting part; base **8.** an essential or basic part *[the root of the matter]* **9.** *Math. a)*

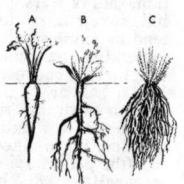

ROOTS
(A, B, taproot;
C, fibrous)

a quantity that, multiplied by itself a specified number of times, produces a given quantity [4 is the square *root* (4 x 4) of 16 and the cube *root* (4 x 4 x 4) of 64] *b*) a number that, when substituted for the unknown quantity in an equation, will satisfy the equation **10.** *Music* the basic tone of a chord **11.** *Linguis. same as* BASE[1] (*n.* 10) —*vi.* **1.** to begin to grow by putting out roots **2.** to become fixed, settled, etc. —*vt.* **1.** to fix the roots of in the ground **2.** to establish; settle —**root up** (or **out, away**) to pull out by the roots; remove completely —**take root 1.** to begin growing by putting out roots **2.** to become settled —**root′i·ness** *n.* —**root′y** *adj.*

**root²** (rōot, root) *vt.* [OE. *wrotan* < *wrot,* snout] to dig (*up* or *out*) with or as with the snout —*vi.* **1.** to dig in the ground, as with the snout **2.** to search about; rummage **3.** [Colloq.] *a*) to encourage a contestant or team by applauding and cheering *b*) to lend moral support to one seeking success, recovery, etc. Usually with *for* —**root′er** *n.*

**Root** (rōot, root), E·li·hu (el′ə hyōō′) 1845–1937; U.S. statesman; secretary of state (1905–09)

**root beer** a carbonated drink made of extracts from the roots and bark of certain plants, etc.

**root canal** a small, tubular channel, normally filled with pulp, in the root of a tooth

**root crop** a crop, as turnips, beets, etc., grown for the edible roots

**root hair** *Bot.* any of the hairlike tubular outgrowths from a growing root, which absorb water and minerals from the soil

**root·less** (-lis) *adj.* having no roots or ties —**root′less·ly** *adv.* —**root′less·ness** *n.*

**root·let** (-lit) *n.* a little root

**root·stock** (-stäk′) *n. Bot.* **1.** *same as* RHIZOME **2.** a plant onto which another is grafted as a new top

**rope** (rōp) *n.* [OE. *rap*] **1.** a thick, strong cord made of intertwisted strands of fiber, wires, etc. **2.** *a*) a noose for hanging a person *b*) death by hanging: with *the* **3.** *same as* LASSO **4.** a ropelike string of things [a *rope* of pearls] **5.** a ropelike, sticky formation, as in a liquid —*vt.* **roped, rop′ing 1.** to fasten or tie with a rope **2.** to connect by a rope **3.** to mark off or enclose with a rope (usually with *in, off,* or *out*) **4.** to catch with a lasso —*vi.* to become ropelike and sticky, as candy —**know the ropes** [Colloq.] to know the details or procedures, as of a job —**rope in** [Slang] to trick into doing something —**the end of one's rope** the end of one's endurance, resources, etc. —**rop′er** *n.*

**rope·walk** (-wôk′) *n.* a long, low, narrow shed, etc. in which ropes are made

**rope·walk·er** (-ər) *n.* a performer who walks or does tricks on a tightrope: also **rope′danc′er** (-dan′sər) —**rope′walk′ing** *n.*

**rop·y** (rō′pē) *adj.* **rop′i·er, rop′i·est 1.** forming sticky threads, as some liquids **2.** like rope —**rop′i·ness** *n.*

**Roque·fort (cheese)** (rōk′fərt) [ < *Roquefort,* France, where orig. made] a strong cheese with a bluish mold, made from goats' and ewes' milk

**ror·qual** (rôr′kwəl) *n.* [Fr. < Norw. *röyrkval* < ON. *reytharhvalr,* lit., red whale] any of the whalebone whales with a well-developed dorsal fin, esp. a finback whale with lengthwise furrows on its belly and throat

**Ror·schach test** (rôr′shäk) [after H. *Rorschach* (1884–1922), Swiss psychiatrist] *Psychol.* a test for personality analysis, in which the person being tested tells what is suggested to him by a standard series of inkblot designs: his responses are then interpreted

**ro·sa·ceous** (rō zā′shəs) *adj.* **1.** of the rose family of plants, as the strawberry, plum, etc. **2.** like a rose **3.** rose-colored

**Ros·a·lie** (rō′zə lē′, räz′ə-) [Fr., prob. ult. < L. *rosa,* rose] a feminine name

**Ros·a·lind** (räz′ə lind) [Sp. *Rosalinda,* as if from *rosa linda,* pretty rose] a feminine name

**Ro·sa·rio** (rō sä′ryō) city & port in EC Argentina, on the Paraná River: pop. 672,000

**ro·sa·ry** (rō′zər ē) *n., pl.* **-ries** [L. *rosarium,* ult. < *rosa,* a rose] *R.C.Ch.* **1.** a string of beads used to keep count in saying certain prayers **2.** [*also* R-] the prayers said with these beads

**Rose** (rōz) [see ff.] a feminine name

**rose¹** (rōz) *n.* [OE. < L. *rosa*] **1.** any of a genus of shrubs with prickly stems and five-parted, usually fragrant flowers of red, pink, white, yellow, etc. **2.** the flower of any of these **3.** any of several related plants **4.** pinkish red or purplish red **5.** anything like a rose in form, as a rosette, the perforated nozzle of a sprinkling can, a round cut of gem with many facets and a flat base, etc. —*adj.* **1.** of or having to do with roses **2.** rose-colored **3.** rose-scented **4.** designating a large family of wild and cultivated flowers,

shrubs, and trees, including the hawthorns, roses, strawberries, apples, peaches, almonds, etc. —*vt.* **rosed, ros′ing** to make rose-colored —**under the rose** *same as* SUB ROSA

**rose²** (rōz) *pt. of* RISE

**ro·sé** (rō zā′) *n.* [Fr., lit., pink] a light, pink wine made by removing the grape husks after partial fermentation

**ro·se·ate** (rō′zē it, -āt′) *adj.* **1.** rose-colored; rosy **2.** cheerful or optimistic —**ro′se·ate·ly** *adv.*

**rose·bud** (rōz′bud′) *n.* the bud of a rose

**rose·bush** (-boosh′) *n.* a shrub that bears roses

**rose chafer** a small N. American beetle that feeds on the leaves and flowers of roses and other plants: also called **rose bug**

**rose-col·ored** (-kul′ərd) *adj.* **1.** pinkish-red or purplish-red **2.** cheerful or optimistic —**through rose-colored glasses** with optimism

**rose fever** a kind of hay fever believed to be caused by the pollen of roses: also **rose cold**

**Rose·mar·y** (rōz′mer′ē; *chiefly Brit.* -mə ri) [see ff.] a feminine name

**rose·mar·y** (-mer′ē; *chiefly Brit.* -mə ri) *n.* [altered (after ROSE¹ & MARY), ult. < L. *ros marinus,* lit., dew of the sea] an evergreen plant of the mint family, with small, light-blue flowers and fragrant leaves used in perfumery, cooking, etc.

**rose of Sharon 1.** a plant with white, red, pink, or purplish, bell-shaped flowers **2.** [Chiefly Brit.] a Saint Johnswort shrub with large, yellow flowers

**ro·se·o·la** (rō zē′ə lə, rō′zē ō′lə) *n.* [ModL., dim. < L. *roseus,* rosy] *same as* RUBELLA: also called **rose rash**

**Ro·set·ta stone** (rō zet′ə) a stone tablet, found in 1799 at Rosetta, Egypt, bearing inscriptions that provided a key for deciphering Egyptian hieroglyphics

**ro·sette** (rō zet′) *n.* [Fr. < OFr., dim. of *rose,* ROSE¹] an ornament, arrangement, etc. resembling or suggesting a rose [a *rosette* of ribbon]

**Rose·ville** (rōz′vil) [after W. *Rose,* 1st local postmaster (1836)] city in SE Mich.: suburb of Detroit: pop. 54,000

**rose water** a preparation consisting of water and attar of roses, used as a perfume

**rose window** a circular window with roselike tracery or mullions arranged like the spokes of a wheel

**rose·wood** (rōz′wood′) *n.* [from its odor] **1.** any of a number of valuable hard, reddish, black-streaked woods, used in making furniture, etc. **2.** a tropical tree yielding such wood

ROSE WINDOW

**Rosh Ha·sha·na** (rōsh′ hə shô′nə, -shä′-; *Heb.* rōsh′ hä shä nä′) the Jewish New Year, celebrated on the 1st and 2d days of Tishri: also sp. **Rosh Hashona, Rosh Hashanah,** etc.

**ros·in** (räz′'n) *n.* [altered < MFr. *resine,* RESIN] the hard, brittle resin, light-yellow to almost black, left after the distillation of crude turpentine: it is rubbed on violin bows, used in making varnish, etc. —*vt.* to rub with rosin; put rosin on —**ros′in·ous, ros′in·y** *adj.*

**Ross** (rôs) **1. Bet·sy** (bet′sē), (*Mrs. Elizabeth Griscom Ross*) 1752–1836; Am. woman reputed to have made the first Am. flag **2. Sir James Clark,** 1800–62; Brit. polar explorer **3. Sir John,** 1777–1856; Brit. arctic explorer, born in Scotland: uncle of *prec.*

**Ros·set·ti** (rō zet′ē, -set′ē) **1. Chris·ti·na (Georgina)** (kris tē′nə), 1830–94; Eng. poet **2. Dante Gabriel,** 1828–82; Eng. painter & poet: brother of *prec.*

**Ross Ice Shelf** frozen S section of the Ross Sea: also called **Ross Shelf Ice**

**Ros·si·ni** (rôs sē′nē; *E.* rô sē′nē), Gio·ac·chi·no (Antonio) (jô′ä kē′nō) 1792–1868; It. composer

**Ross Sea** arm of the Pacific, along the coast of Antarctica

**Ros·tand** (rôs tän′; *E.* räs′tand), Ed·mond (ed môn′) 1868–1918; Fr. dramatist & poet

**ros·ter** (räs′tər) *n.* [Du. *rooster,* orig., gridiron, hence a list (from ruled paper used for lists)] **1.** a list of military or naval personnel, with their assignments, duties, etc. **2.** any list; roll

**Ros·tock** (rôs′tôk; *E.* räs′täk) seaport in N East Germany, on the Baltic: pop. 195,000

**Ros·tov** (rô stôf′; *E.* räs′täv) seaport in SW R.S.F.S.R., at the mouth of the Don: pop. 789,000: also called **Ros′tov-on-Don′**

**ros·trum** (räs′trəm) *n., pl.* **-trums, -tra** (-trə) [L., (ship's) beak, hence the speakers' platform in the Forum, decorated with ramming beaks taken from captured ships] **1.** any platform for public speaking **2.** public speaking, or public speakers collectively —**ros′tral** *adj.*

**ros·y** (rō′zē) *adj.* **ros′i·er, ros′i·est** **1.** like a rose, esp. in color; rose-red or pink *[rosy* cheeks*]* **2.** [Archaic] made with roses **3.** bright, promising, cheerful, etc. *[a rosy* future*]* —**ros′i·ly** *adv.* —**ros′i·ness** *n.*

**rot** (rät) *vi.* **rot′ted, rot′ting** [OE. *rotian*] **1.** to decompose gradually by the action of bacteria, etc.; decay **2.** to become unhealthy, etc. *[to rot* in prison*]* **3.** to become morally corrupt —*vt.* **1.** to cause to rot, or decompose **2.** *same as* RET —*n.* **1.** a rotting or being rotten; decay **2.** something rotting or rotten **3.** any of various plant and animal diseases, esp. of sheep, causing decay **4.** [Slang] nonsense —*interj.* an exclamation of disgust, anger, etc.

**ro·ta·ry** (rōt′ər ē) *adj.* [< ML. < L. *rota*, a wheel] **1.** turning around a central point or axis, as a wheel; rotating **2.** *a)* having a rotating part or parts *b)* having blades that rotate on a hub *[a rotary* lawn mower*]* —*n.*, *pl.* **-ries** a rotary machine or engine

**Rotary Club** any local organization of an international club (**Rotary International**) of business and professional men, founded in 1905 to promote community welfare —**Ro·tar·i·an** (rō ter′ē ən) *n.*, *adj.* —**Ro·tar′i·an·ism** *n.*

**rotary press** a printing press with curved plates mounted on rotating cylinders, for printing on paper fed from a roll

**ro·ta·ry-wing aircraft** (-wiŋ′) an aircraft, as the helicopter, sustained in the air by rotors

**ro·tate** (rō′tāt) *vi.*, *vt.* **-tat·ed, -tat·ing** [< L. pp. of *rotare* < *rota*, a wheel] **1.** to move or turn around, as a wheel **2.** to go or cause to go in a regular and recurring succession of changes *[to rotate* crops*]* —**ro′tat·a·ble** *adj.* —**ro·ta·tive** (rō′tāt iv, rōt′ə tiv) *adj.* —**ro′ta·tor** *n.*

**ro·ta·tion** (rō tā′shən) *n.* **1.** a rotating or being rotated **2.** regular and recurring succession of changes —**ro·ta′·tion·al** *adj.*

**rotation of crops** a system of rotating in a fixed order the kinds of crops grown in the same field, to maintain soil fertility

**ro·ta·to·ry** (rō′tə tôr′ē) *adj.* **1.** of, or having the nature of, rotation **2.** rotating; rotary **3.** going or following in rotation **4.** causing rotation

**ROTC, R.O.T.C.** Reserve Officers' Training Corps

**rote** (rōt) *n.* [< ?] a fixed, mechanical way of doing something; routine —**by rote** by memory alone, without thought

**ro·te·none** (rōt′'n ōn′) *n.* [Jap. *roten*, an East Indian plant + -ONE] a white, odorless, crystalline substance, $C_{23}H_{22}O_6$, used in insecticides

**rot·gut** (rät′gut′) *n.* [ROT + GUT] [Slang] raw, low-grade whiskey or other liquor

**Roth·schild** (rôth′chīld′, räths′-; *G.* rōt′shilt) family of European bankers of the 18th & 19th cent., originally of Germany

**ro·ti·fer** (rōt′ə fər) *n.* [ModL. < L. *rota*, wheel + -FER] any of various microscopic, invertebrate freshwater animals, having a ring or rings of cilia at the front end of the body —**ro·tif·er·al** (rō tif′ər əl), **ro·tif′er·ous**, **ro·tif′er·an** *adj.*

**ro·tis·ser·ie** (rō tis′ər ē) *n.* [Fr. < MFr., ult. < *rostir*, to ROAST] **1.** a shop where roasted meats are sold **2.** a grill with an electrically turned spit

**ro·to** (rōt′ō) *n.*, *pl.* **-tos** shortened form of ROTOGRAVURE

**ro·to·gra·vure** (rōt′ə grə vyoor′) *n.* [< L. *rota*, a wheel + GRAVURE] **1.** a printing process using photogravure cylinders on a rotary press **2.** a print or newspaper pictorial section printed by this process

**ro·tor** (rōt′ər) *n.* [< ROTATE] **1.** the rotating part of a motor, dynamo, etc. **2.** a device, as on a helicopter, consisting of generally horizontal airfoils with their hub

**Ro·to·till·er** (rōt′ə til′ər) *a trademark for* a motorized cultivator with rotary blades —*n.* [*also* r-] such a cultivator —**ro′to·till′** *vt.*

**rot·ten** (rät′'n) *adj.* [ON. *rotinn*] **1.** decayed; decomposed; spoiled **2.** smelling of decay; putrid **3.** morally corrupt or offensive; dishonest, etc. **4.** unsound or weak, as if decayed within **5.** [Slang] very bad, disagreeable, etc. *[a rotten* show*]* —**rot′ten·ly** *adv.* —**rot′ten·ness** *n.*

**rot·ter** (rät′ər) *n.* [< ROT] [Chiefly Brit. Slang] a despicable fellow; cad; bounder

**Rot·ter·dam** (rät′ər dam′; *Du.* rôt′ər däm′) seaport in SW Netherlands, in the Rhine delta: pop. 687,000

**ro·tund** (rō tund′) *adj.* [L. *rotundus*, akin to *rota*, a wheel] **1.** round or rounded out; plump or stout **2.** full-toned; sonorous *[a rotund* voice*]* —**ro·tun′di·ty, ro·tund′ness** *n.* —**ro·tund′ly** *adv.*

**ro·tun·da** (rō tun′də) *n.* [< It. < L. fem. of *rotundus*, rotund] a round building, hall, or room, esp. one with a dome

**Rou·ault** (roo ō′), **Georges** (zhôrzh) 1871-1958; Fr. painter

**rou·ble** (roo′b'l) *n. same as* RUBLE

**rou·é** (roo ā′) *n.* [Fr., pp. of *rouer*, to break on the wheel < L. *rota*, a wheel] a dissipated man; debauchee; rake

**Rou·en** (roo än′; *Fr.* rwän) city & port in NW France, on the Seine: pop. 120,000

**rouge** (roozh) *n.* [Fr., red < L. *rubeus*] **1.** any of various reddish cosmetic powders, pastes, etc. for coloring the cheeks and lips **2.** a reddish powder, mainly ferric oxide, for polishing jewelry, metal, etc. —*vi.*, *vt.* **rouged, roug′ing** to use cosmetic rouge (on)

**rough** (ruf) *adj.* [OE. *ruh*] **1.** *a)* not smooth or level; uneven *[a rough* surface*]* *b)* not easily traveled; overgrown, wild, etc. *[rough* country*]* **2.** shaggy *[a rough* coat*]* **3.** moving violently; agitated; specif., *a)* stormy; tempestuous *[rough* weather*]* *b)* boisterous or disorderly *[rough* play*]* **4.** harsh, rude, brutal, etc. *[a rough* temper*]* **5.** sounding, feeling, or tasting harsh **6.** lacking comforts and conveniences *[the rough* life of pioneers*]* **7.** not refined or polished *[a rough* diamond*]* **8.** not finished, perfected, etc. *[a rough* sketch, a *rough* estimate*]* **9.** needing strength rather than skill or intelligence *[rough* labor*]* **10.** [Colloq.] difficult, severe, etc. *[a rough* time*]* **11.** *Phonet.* pronounced with an aspirate; having the sound of *h* —*n.* **1.** rough ground **2.** rough material or condition **3.** a rough sketch or draft **4.** [Chiefly Brit.] a rough person; rowdy **5.** *Golf* any part of the course where grass, weeds, etc. grow uncut —*adv.* in a rough manner —*vt.* **1.** to make rough; roughen **2.** to treat roughly (often with *up*) **3.** to make or shape roughly (usually with *in* or *out*) *[rough* out a scheme*]* —*vi.* to behave roughly —**in the rough** in a rough or crude state —**rough it** to live without comforts and conveniences —**rough′ish** *adj.* —**rough′ly** *adv.* —**rough′ness** *n.*

**rough·age** (ruf′ij) *n.* rough or coarse substance; specif., coarse food or fodder, as bran, straw, etc., serving as a stimulus to peristalsis

**rough-and-read·y** (ruf′'n red′ē) *adj.* **1.** rough, or crude, rude, etc., but effective *[rough-and-ready* methods*]* **2.** characterized by rough vigor rather than refinement, formality, etc.

**rough-and-tum·ble** (-tum′b'l) *adj.* violent and disorderly, with no concern for rules —*n.* a fight or struggle of this kind

**rough·cast** (ruf′kast′) *n.* **1.** a coarse plaster for covering outside surfaces, as walls **2.** a rough pattern or crude model —*vt.* **-cast′, -cast′ing** **1.** to cover (walls, etc.) with roughcast **2.** to make or shape in a rough form

**rough-dry** (-drī′) *vt.* **-dried′, -dry′ing** to dry (washed laundry) without ironing: also **rough′dry′** *adj.* washed and dried but not ironed

**rough·en** (ruf′'n) *vt.*, *vi.* to make or become rough

**rough-hew** (ruf′hyoo′) *vt.* **-hewed′, -hewed′** or **-hewn′, -hew′ing** **1.** to hew (timber, stone, etc.) roughly, or without finishing or smoothing **2.** to form roughly Also **rough′hew′**

**rough·house** (ruf′hous′) *n.* [Slang] rough or boisterous play, fighting, etc. —*vt.* **-housed′, -hous′ing** [Slang] to treat roughly or boisterously —*vi.* [Slang] to take part in rough-house

**rough·neck** (-nek′) *n.* [Slang] a rough person; rowdy

**rough·rid·er** (-rīd′ər) *n.* **1.** a person who breaks horses for riding **2.** a person who does much hard, rough riding **3.** [R-] a member of Theodore Roosevelt's volunteer cavalry regiment in the Spanish-American War: also **Rough Rider**

**rough·shod** (-shäd′) *adj.* shod with horseshoes that have metal points to prevent slipping —**ride roughshod over** to treat in a harsh, arrogant, inconsiderate manner

**rou·lade** (roo läd′) *n.* [Fr. < *rouler*, to ROLL] **1.** a rapid series of tones sung to one syllable **2.** a slice of meat rolled and cooked

**rou·lette** (roo let′) *n.* [Fr. < OFr. dim. of *roele*, a small wheel, ult. < L. *rota*, a wheel] **1.** a gambling game played by rolling a small ball around a shallow bowl with a revolving inner disk (**roulette wheel**) with red and black numbered compartments **2.** a small toothed wheel for making rows of marks or dots, as between postage stamps —*vt.* **-let′ted, -let′ting** to make marks, dots, etc. in with a roulette

**Rou·ma·nia** (roo mān′yə, -mä′nē ə) *same as* ROMANIA — **Rou·ma′nian** *adj.*, *n.*

**round** (round) *adj.* [< OFr. < L. *rotundus*, rotund] **1.** shaped like a ball; spherical **2.** *a)* shaped like a circle, ring, etc.; circular or curved *b)* shaped like a cylinder; cylindrical **3.** plump or stout **4.** with or involving a circular motion *[a round* dance*]* **5.** full; complete *[a round* dozen*]* **6.** expressed by a whole number, or in tens, hundreds, etc. **7.** large in amount, size, etc. *[a round* sum*]* **8.** mellow and full in tone; sonorous **9.** brisk; vigorous *[a round* pace*]* **10.** outspoken; plain and blunt **11.** *Phonet.* pronounced with the lips forming an oval *[a round* vowel*]* —*n.* **1.** something round; thing that is spherical, circular, curved, etc. **2.** a rung of a ladder or a chair **3.** the part of a beef animal between the rump and the leg: in full, **round of beef** **4.** movement in a circular course **5.** *same as* ROUND DANCE **6.** a series or succession of actions, events, etc. *[a round* of parties*]* **7.** the complete extent *[the round* of human beliefs*]* **8.** [*often pl.*] a regular, customary circuit, as by a watchman of his station **9.** a single serving, as of drinks, for each in a group **10.** *a*) a single shot from a rifle, etc. or from a number of rifles fired together *b*) ammunition for such a shot **11.** a single outburst, as of applause **12.** *Games & Sports* a single period or division of action; specif., *a*) *Boxing* any of the timed periods of a fight *b*) *Golf* a number of holes as a unit of competition **13.** *Music* a short song for two or more persons or groups, in which the second starts when the first reaches the second phrase, etc. —*vt.* **1.** to make round **2.** to pronounce with rounded lips **3.** to make plump **4.** to express as a round number (usually with *off*) **5.** to complete; finish **6.** to make a circuit of [*we rounded* the island] **7.** to make a turn about [*to round* a corner] —*vi.* **1.** to make a complete or partial circuit **2.** to turn; reverse direction **3.** to become round or plump —*adv.* **1.** in a circle; along a circular course **2.** through a recurring period of time [*to work the year *round*] **3.** from one person or place to another [*the peddler came *round*] **4.** for each of several [not enough to go *round*] **5.** in circumference **6.** on all sides; in every direction **7.** about; near **8.** in a roundabout way **9.** here and there **10.** with a rotating movement **11.** in or to the opposite direction **12.** in or to an opposite viewpoint —*prep.* **1.** so as to encircle or surround **2.** on the circumference or border of **3.** on all sides of **4.** in the vicinity of **5.** in a circuit or course through **6.** here and there in **7.** so as to make a curve or circuit about In the U.S., *round* (*adv. & prep.*) is generally superseded by *around;* in Great Britain, *round* is preferred for most senses —**go the round** (or **rounds**) **1.** to be circulated widely, as a story, rumor, etc. **2.** to walk one's regular circuit: also **make one's rounds —in the round 1.** with the audience, etc. seated all around a central stage, etc. **2.** in full and completely rounded form, not in relief: said of sculpture **3.** in full detail —**out of round** not having perfect roundness —**round about 1.** in or to the opposite direction **2.** in every direction around —**round up 1.** to drive together in a herd, group, etc. **2.** [Colloq.] to gather or assemble — **round′ish** *adj.* —**round′ness** *n.*

**round·a·bout** (round′ə bout′) *adj.* **1.** not straight or straightforward; indirect [*roundabout* methods] **2.** encircling; enclosing —*n.* **1.** something that is indirect or circuitous **2.** a short, tight jacket formerly worn by men or boys **3.** *Brit. var. of* MERRY-GO-ROUND

**round dance 1.** a dance with the dancers moving in a circle **2.** any of several dances, as the waltz, polka, etc., in which the couples make circular movements

**round·ed** (roun′did) *adj.* **1.** made round **2.** having variety in tastes, abilities, etc. [a well-*rounded* person]

**roun·de·lay** (roun′də lā′) *n.* [< MFr. dim. of *rondel*, a rondel] a simple song in which some phrase, line, etc. is continually repeated

**round·er** (roun′dər) *n.* **1.** a person or thing that rounds, as a tool for rounding edges **2.** [Colloq.] a dissolute person or drunkard

**Round·head** (round′hed′) *n.* a member of the Parliamentary, or Puritan, party in England during the English civil war (1642-52)

**round·house** (-hous′) *n.* **1.** a building, generally circular, with a turntable in the center, for storing and repairing locomotives **2.** a cabin on the after part of a ship's quarter-deck **3.** *a*) *Baseball* a pitch with a wide curve *b*) *Boxing* a wide swing or hook, as to the head

**round·ly** (-lē) *adv.* **1.** in a round form **2.** in a round manner; specif., *a*) vigorously, severely, etc. *b*) fully

**round robin 1.** a petition, protest, etc. with the signatures written in a circle to conceal the order of signing **2.** a tournament in which every entrant is matched with every other one **3.** a letter circulated among the members of a group, forwarded by each in turn, often with added comments

**round-shoul·dered** (-shōl′dərd) *adj.* stooped because the shoulders are bent forward

**round steak** a cut from a round of beef: see ROUND (*n.* 3)

**Round Table 1.** the table around which King Arthur and his knights sat **2.** King Arthur and his knights, collectively **3.** [r- t-] *a*) an informal discussion group *b*) the informal discussion —**round′-ta′ble** *adj.*

**round-the-clock** (-thə kläk′) *adj., adv.* continuously

**round trip** a trip to a place and back again —**round′-trip′** *adj.*

**round·up** (-up′) *n.* **1.** *a*) the act of driving cattle, etc. together on the range and collecting them in a herd, as for branding *b*) the cowboys, horses, etc. that do this work **2.** any similar driving together or collecting **3.** a summary, as of news

**round·worm** (-wurm′) *n.* **1.** *same as* NEMATODE **2.** a species of nematode worms, living as parasites, esp. in the intestines of man and other mammals

**rouse** (rouz) *vt.* roused, rous′ing [prob. < Anglo-Fr. or

OFr.] **1.** to stir up (game) from cover to flight or attack **2.** to stir up, as to anger or action; excite **3.** to wake —*vi.* **1.** to leave cover: said of game **2.** to wake **3.** to become active —*n.* a rousing —**rous′er** *n.* —**rous′ing·ly** *adv.*

**Rous·seau** (roo sō′) **1.** Hen·ri (än rē′), 1844-1910; Fr. painter **2.** Jean Jacques (zhän zhäk), 1712-78; Fr. political philosopher & writer, born in Switzerland

**roust·a·bout** (roust′ə bout′) *n.* [*roust*, dial. var. of ROUSE + ABOUT] **1.** a deckhand or waterfront laborer **2.** an unskilled or transient laborer, as in a circus or on a ranch

**rout**[1] (rout) *n.* [< OFr. < L. *rupta*: see ROUTE] **1.** a disorderly crowd; rabble **2.** a disorderly flight, as of defeated troops **3.** an overwhelming defeat **4.** [Archaic] a group of people; company —*vt.* **1.** to put to disorderly flight **2.** to defeat overwhelmingly

**rout**[2] (rout) *vi.* [var. of ROOT[2]] **1.** to dig for food with the snout, as a pig **2.** to poke or rummage about —*vt.* **1.** to dig up with the snout **2.** to force out —**rout out 1.** to expose to view **2.** to scoop, gouge, or hollow out **3.** to make (a person) get out —**rout up 1.** to get by poking about **2.** to make (a person) get up —**rout′er** *n.*

**route** (root; *also, and for n.* 2 *usually,* rout) *n.* [OFr. < L. *rupta* (*via*), broken (path) < pp. of *rumpere*, to break] **1.** a road, etc. for traveling; esp., a highway **2.** *a*) a regular course traveled as in delivering mail, milk, etc. *b*) a set of customers to whom one regularly makes deliveries —*vt.* **rout′ed, rout′ing 1.** to send by a specified route [*to route* goods through Omaha] **2.** to fix the order of procedure of

**rou·tine** (roo tēn′) *n.* [Fr. < *route:* see prec.] **1.** a regular, unvarying procedure, customary, prescribed, or habitual, as of work **2.** a theatrical skit **3.** a series of dance steps **4.** a set of coded instructions for a computer —*adj.* having the nature of or using routine —**rou·tine′ly** *adv.* —**rou·tin′ism** *n.* —**rou·tin′ize** *vt.* -ized, -iz·ing

**roux** (roo) *n.* [Fr. *roux* (*beurre*), reddish-brown (butter)] a cooked mixture of butter (or other fat) and flour, used for thickening sauces, soups, gravies, etc.

**rove**[1] (rōv) *vi.* roved, rov′ing [< ?] **1.** to wander about; roam **2.** to look around: said of the eyes —*vt.* to wander over; roam through [he *roved* the woods] —*n.* a roving; ramble —**rov′er** *n.*

**rove**[2] (rōv) *vt.* [< ?] to twist (fibers) together and draw out into a strand (*roving*) before spinning

**rove**[3] (rōv) *alt. pt. & pp. of* REEVE[2]

**rov·en** (rōv′'n) *alt. pp. of* REEVE[2]

**row**[1] (rō) *n.* [OE. *ræw*] **1.** a number of people or things arranged in a line **2.** any of the lines of seats side by side in a theater, etc. **3.** a street with a line of buildings, as of a specified nature, on either side [fraternity *row*] —*vt.* to arrange or put in rows —**hard** (or **long**) **row to hoe** anything hard or tiring to do —**in a row** one after the other

**row**[2] (rō) *vt.* [OE. *rowan*] **1.** to move (a boat, etc.) on water by using oars **2.** to carry in a rowboat [*row* us across the lake] **3.** to use (oarsmen, a stroke, etc. as specified) in rowing **4.** to take part in (a race) by rowing —*vi.* **1.** to use oars in moving a boat **2.** to be moved by oars: said of a boat —*n.* **1.** a rowing **2.** a trip made by rowboat —**row′er** *n.*

**row**[3] (rou) *n.* [< ? ROUSE] a noisy quarrel, dispute, or disturbance; squabble or brawl —*vi.* to take part in a row

**row·an** (rō′ən, rou′-) *n.* [< Scand.] **1.** the mountain ash, a tree with white flowers and reddish berries **2.** its fruit: also **row′an·ber′ry**, *pl.* -ries

**row·boat** (rō′bōt′) *n.* a boat made to be rowed

**row·dy** (rou′dē) *n., pl.* -dies [< ? ROW[3]] a person whose behavior is rough, quarrelsome, and disorderly; hoodlum —*adj.* -di·er, -di·est of or like a rowdy —**row′di·ly** *adv.* —**row′di·ness** *n.* —**row′dy·ish** *adj.* —**row′dy·ism** *n.*

**row·el** (rou′əl) *n.* [< OFr. *roele:* see ROULETTE] a small wheel with sharp projecting points, forming the end of a spur —*vt.* -eled or -elled, -el·ing or -el·ling to spur or prick (a horse) with a rowel

**row·lock** (rul′ək, räl′-; rō′läk′) *n.* [altered (after ROW[2]) < OARLOCK] *chiefly Brit. term for* OARLOCK

**Roy** (roi) [as if < OFr. *roy* (Fr. *roi*), a king, but prob. < Gael. *rhu*, red] a masculine name

**roy·al** (roi′əl) *adj.* [< OFr. < L. *regalis:* see REGAL] **1.** of a king, queen, or other sovereign [a *royal* edict, the *royal* family] **2.** having the rank of a king or queen **3.** of a kingdom, its government, etc. [the *royal* fleet] **4.** *a*) founded or supported by a king or queen *b*) in the service of the Crown **5.** suitable for a king or queen; magnificent, stately, regal, etc. **6.** unusually large, fine, etc. —*n.* a small sail set on the royal mast —**roy′al·ly** *adv.*

**royal blue** a deep, vivid reddish or purplish blue

ROWEL

**royal flush** the highest poker hand, consisting of the ace, king, queen, jack, and ten of the same suit

**roy·al·ist** (-ist) *n.* a person who supports a king or a monarchy, esp. in times of revolution —**roy′al·ism** *n.*

**royal jelly** a highly nutritious food fed by worker bees to all very young larvae and continued to be fed to larvae chosen to be queens

**royal mast** a small mast above the topgallant mast

**Royal Oak** [after an oak in which CHARLES II is said to have hidden] city in SE Mich.: suburb of Detroit: pop. 71,000

**royal palm** any of a genus of tall, ornamental palm trees

**roy·al·ty** (roi′əl tē) *n., pl.* **-ties** 1. the rank, status, or power of a king or queen 2. a royal person or, collectively, royal persons 3. a kingdom 4. royal quality or character; regalness, nobility, etc. 5. [*usually pl.*] a right, privilege, etc. of a monarch 6. *a)* a share of the proceeds paid to the owner of a right, as a patent, for its use *b)* such a share paid to one who leases out lands rich in oil or minerals *c)* a share of the proceeds from his work paid to an author, composer, etc.

**rpm, r.p.m.** revolutions per minute

**R.R.** 1. railroad: also **RR** 2. Right Reverend

ROYAL PALM

**-rrha·gi·a** (rā′jē ə) [ModL. < Gr. < *rhēgnynai,* to burst] *a combining form meaning* abnormal discharge or flow: also **-rrhage** (rij), **-rrhag′y** (rā′jē)

**-rrhe·a, -rrhoe·a** (rē′ə) [ModL. < Gr. < *rhein,* to flow] *a combining form meaning* a flow, discharge

**Rs, rs.** rupees

**R.S.F.S.R., RSFSR** Russian Soviet Federated Socialist Republic

**RSV, R.S.V.** Revised Standard Version (of the Bible)

**R.S.V.P., r.s.v.p.** [Fr. *répondez s'il vous plâit*] please reply

**rt.** right

**rte.** route

**Ru** *Chem.* ruthenium

**rub** (rub) *vt.* **rubbed, rub′bing** [ME. *rubben,* akin to Dan. *rubbe*] 1. to move (one's hand, a cloth, etc.) back and forth over (something) firmly 2. to spread or apply (polish, salve, etc.) on a surface 3. to move (a thing) against something else, or move (things) over each other with pressure and friction 4. to put into a specified condition by applying pressure and friction [*rub* it *dry*] 5. to make sore by rubbing 6. to remove by rubbing (*out, off,* etc.) —*vi.* 1. to move with pressure and friction (*on, against,* etc.) 2. to rub something 3. to admit of being rubbed or removed by rubbing (often with *off, out,* etc.) —*n.* 1. a rubbing; specif., a massage 2. an obstacle or difficulty 3. something that irritates, annoys, etc. —**rub down** 1. to massage 2. to smooth, polish, etc. by rubbing —**rub it in** [Slang] to keep reminding someone of his failure or mistake —**rub off on** to be left on as a mark, as by rubbing on, figuratively, by close contact —**rub the wrong way** to annoy or irritate

**ru·ba·to** (rōō bät′ō) *adj., adv.* [It. < (*tempo*) *rubato,* stolen (time)] *Music* with some notes lengthened and others shortened in dropping strict tempo in a passage for effect —*n., pl.* **-toes** 1. the use of rubato 2. a rubato passage, phrase, etc.

**rub·ber**[1] (rub′ər) *n.* 1. a person or thing that rubs 2. [from use as an eraser] an elastic substance produced from the milky sap of various tropical plants, or synthetically 3. something made of this substance; specif., *a)* an eraser *b)* a low-cut overshoe *c)* [Slang] a condom 4. *Baseball* an oblong piece of rubber, etc. set into the pitcher's mound —*adj.* made of rubber —**rub′ber·like′** *adj.*

**rub·ber**[2] (rub′ər) *n.* [< ?] 1. *Bridge* a series limited to three games, two of which must be won to win the series 2. any game played to break a tie in games won: usually **rubber game**

**rubber band** a narrow, continuous band of rubber as for holding small objects together

**rubber cement** an adhesive made of unvulcanized rubber in a quickly evaporating solvent

**rub·ber·ize** (-īz′) *vt.* **-ized′, -iz′ing** to coat or impregnate with rubber

**rub·ber·neck** (-nek′) *n.* [Old Slang] a person who gazes about in curiosity, as a sightseer —*vi.* [Old Slang] to gaze about in this way

**rubber plant** 1. any plant yielding latex from which crude rubber is formed 2. a house plant with large, glossy, leathery leaves

**rubber stamp** 1. a stamp made of rubber, inked on a pad and used for printing signatures, dates, etc. 2. [Colloq.] *a)* a person, bureau, etc. that approves something in a routine way, without thought *b)* any routine approval —**rub′ber-stamp′** *vt., adj.*

**rub·ber·y** (rub′ər ē) *adj.* like rubber in appearance, elasticity, toughness, etc. —**rub′ber·i·ness** *n.*

**rub·bing** (rub′iŋ) *n.* an impression of a raised or incised design, etc. taken by placing a paper over it and rubbing with graphite, wax, etc.

**rub·bish** (rub′ish) *n.* [ult. < base of RUB] 1. any material thrown away as worthless; trash 2. worthless, foolish ideas, statements, etc.; nonsense —**rub′bish·y** *adj.*

**rub·ble** (rub′'l) *n.* [akin to RUBBISH, RUB] 1. rough, broken pieces of stone, brick, etc. 2. masonry made of such pieces: also **rub′ble·work′** 3. debris from buildings, etc., resulting from earthquake, bombing, etc. —**rub′bly** *adj.*

**rub·down** (rub′doun′) *n.* a massage

**rube** (rōōb) *n.* [< REUBEN] [Slang] a country person regarded as simple, unsophisticated, etc.

**Rube Gold·berg** (rōōb gōld′bərg) [< *Rube Goldberg* (1883–1970), U.S. cartoonist] designating a complicated device used to perform a simple operation

**ru·bel·la** (rōō bel′ə) *n.* [ModL. < L. *rubellus* < *ruber,* red] a contagious virus disease, characterized by swollen glands of the neck and small red spots on the skin; German measles

**Ru·bens** (rōō′bənz; *Fl.* rü′bəns), **Peter Paul** 1577–1640; Fl. painter

**ru·be·o·la** (rōō bē′ə lə, rōō′bē ō′lə) *n.* [ModL., neut. pl. dim. of L. *rubeus,* red] *same as* MEASLES (sense 1)

**Ru·bi·con** (rōō′bi kän′) small river in N Italy crossed by Caesar to march on Rome with his army (49 B.C.), starting a civil war —**cross the Rubicon** to make a decisive move that cannot be undone

**ru·bi·cund** (rōō′bi kund′) *adj.* [< Fr. < L. *ruber,* red] reddish; ruddy —**ru′bi·cun′di·ty** *n.*

**ru·bid·i·um** (rōō bid′ē əm) *n.* [ModL. < L. *rubidus,* red (from red lines in its spectrum)] a soft, silvery-white metallic chemical element, resembling potassium: symbol, Rb; at. wt., 85.47; at. no., 37

**ru·ble** (rōō′b'l) *n.* [Russ. *rubl′*] the monetary unit of the U.S.S.R.: see MONETARY UNITS, table

**ru·bric** (rōō′brik) *n.* [< MFr. < L. *rubrica,* rubric < *ruber,* red] 1. in early books and manuscripts, a chapter heading, initial letter, etc. printed or written in red, decorative lettering, etc. 2. a heading, title, etc., as of a chapter, a law, etc. 3. a direction in a prayer book 4. a note of comment; gloss 5. an established rule of procedure —**ru′bri·cal** *adj.* —**ru′bri·cal·ly** *adv.*

**ru·by** (rōō′bē) *n., pl.* **-bies** [< OFr. *rubi,* ult. < L. *rubeus,* red] 1. a clear, deep-red variety of corundum, valued as a precious stone 2. deep red —*adj.* deep-red

**ruche** (rōōsh) *n.* [Fr., lit., beehive < OFr. < Celt.] a fluting or pleating of lace, ribbon, net, etc. for trimming garments, esp. at the neck or wrist

**ruch·ing** (rōō′shiŋ) *n.* 1. ruches collectively 2. material used to make ruches

**ruck·sack** (ruk′sak′, rŏŏk′-) *n.* [G. < *rücken,* the back + *sack,* a sack] a kind of knapsack

**ruck·us** (ruk′əs) *n.* [prob. a merging of earlier *ruction,* an uproar & RUMPUS] [Colloq.] noisy confusion; uproar; row; disturbance

**rud·der** (rud′ər) *n.* [OE. *rother,* steering oar] 1. a broad, flat, movable piece of wood or metal hinged vertically at the stern of a boat or ship, used for steering 2. a piece like this on an aircraft, etc. —**rud′der·less** *adj.*

**rud·der·post** (-pōst′) *n.* the sternpost or the vertical shaft to which the rudder is fastened

**rud·dy** (rud′ē) *adj.* **-di·er, -di·est** [OE. *rudig*] 1. having a healthy red color 2. red or reddish —**rud′di·ness** *n.*

RUDDER

**ruddy duck** a small, N. American duck, the adult male of which has a brownish-red upper body

**rude** (rōōd) *adj.* **rud′er, rud′est** [OFr. < L. *rudis*] 1. crude or rough in form [*a rude* hut] 2. barbarous or ignorant [*rude* savages] 3. lacking refinement; coarse, uncouth, etc. 4. discourteous; impolite [*a rude* reply] 5. rough; harsh [*a rude* awakening] 6. harsh in sound; discordant 7. simple or primitive 8. not carefully worked out —**rude′ly** *adv.* —**rude′ness** *n.*

**ru·di·ment** (rōō′də mənt) *n.* [L. *rudimentum* < *rudis,* rude] 1. a first principle or element, as of a subject to be learned [the *rudiments* of physics] 2. a first slight beginning of something 3. *Biol.* an incompletely developed or vestigial organ or part

**ru·di·men·ta·ry** (rōō′də men′tər ē, -men′trē) *adj.* 1. of rudiments or first principles; elementary 2. incompletely developed 3. vestigial Also **ru′di·men′tal** —**ru′di·men·ta·ri·ly** *adv.* —**ru′di·men′ta·ri·ness** *n.*

**Ru·dolf I** (rōō′dälf, -dôlf) 1218–91; Ger. king & emperor of the Holy Roman Empire (1273–91)

**Ru·dolph** (rōō′dälf, -dôlf) [< G. < OHG. < *hruod-,* fame + *wolf,* a wolf] a masculine name: dim. *Rudy*

**rue**[1] (rōō) *vt., vi.* **rued, ru′ing** [OE. *hreowan*] to feel sorrow or remorse (for); regret; repent —*n.* [Archaic] sorrow or regret

**rue**[2] (rōō) *n.* [< OFr. < L. *ruta* < Gr. *rhytē*] a strong-scented herb with yellow flowers and bitter-tasting leaves formerly used in medicine

**rue·ful** (rōō′fəl) *adj.* **1.** causing sorrow or pity **2.** feeling or showing sorrow or regret, esp. in a wry way —**rue′ful·ly** *adv.* —**rue′ful·ness** *n.*

**ruff**[1] (ruf) *n.* [contr. of RUFFLE[1], *n.*] **1.** a high, frilled, stiff collar worn by men and women in the 16th and 17th cents. **2.** a ring of feathers or fur standing out about the neck of a bird or animal **3.** a Eurasian sandpiper the male of which grows a ruff in the breeding season —**ruffed** *adj.*

**ruff**[2] (ruf) *n.* [< OFr. *roffle*] *Card Games* the act of trumping —*vt., vi. Card Games* to trump

**ruffed grouse** a N. American game bird with neck feathers that can be spread into a ruff: also called *partridge* in the northern U.S. and *pheasant* in the southern U.S.

RUFF

**ruf·fi·an** (ruf′ē ən, ruf′yən) *n.* [< Fr. < It. *ruffiano*, a pander] a brutal, lawless person; hoodlum —*adj.* brutal and lawless: also **ruf′fi·an·ly** —**ruf′fi·an·ism** *n.*

**ruf·fle**[1] (ruf′'l) *vt.* **-fled, -fling** [< ON. or MLowG.] **1.** to disturb the smoothness of; ripple *[wind ruffling the water]* **2.** to gather into ruffles **3.** to put ruffles on **4.** to make (feathers, etc.) stand up as in a ruff **5.** to disturb or annoy **6.** *a)* to turn (pages) rapidly *b)* to shuffle (cards) —*vi.* **1.** to become uneven **2.** to become disturbed, annoyed, etc. —*n.* **1.** a strip of cloth, lace, etc. gathered in pleats or puckers and used for trimming **2.** a bird's ruff **3.** a disturbance; annoyance **4.** a ripple —**ruf′fly** *adj.*

**ruf·fle**[2] (ruf′'l) *n.* [prob. echoic] a low, continuous beating of a drum —*vi., vt.* **-fled, -fling** to beat (a drum, etc.) with a ruffle

**ru·fous** (rōō′fəs) *adj.* [L. *rufus*, red] brownish-red

**rug** (rug) *n.* [< Scand.] **1.** a piece of thick, often napped fabric, woven strips of rag, an animal skin, etc. used as a floor covering **2.** *chiefly Brit. term for* LAP ROBE

**Rug·by** (rug′bē) *n.* [first played at *Rugby*, a boys' school in C England] a kind of football in which there are 15 players on each side, action is continuous, and the oval ball may be kicked, thrown laterally, or run with

**rug·ged** (rug′id) *adj.* [< Scand.] **1.** having a surface that is uneven, rough, craggy, etc. *[rugged ground]* **2.** strong, irregular, and lined *[a rugged face]* **3.** stormy *[rugged weather]* **4.** sounding harsh **5.** severe *[a rugged life]* **6.** not polished or refined; rude **7.** strong; robust; vigorous; hardy **8.** [Colloq.] requiring skill, endurance, etc. —**rug′ged·ly** *adv.* —**rug′ged·ness** *n.*

**Ruhr** (rōor; G. rōōr) **1.** river in C West Germany, flowing west into the Rhine **2.** major coal-mining & industrial region in the valley of this river: also called **Ruhr Basin**

**ru·in** (rōō′in) *n.* [< OFr. < L. *ruina* < *ruere*, to fall] **1.** [*pl.*] the remains of a fallen building, city, etc., or of something destroyed, devastated, decayed, etc. **2.** anything that has been destroyed, etc. **3.** the state of being destroyed, dilapidated, etc. **4.** downfall, destruction, decay, etc., as of a thing or person, or the cause of this *[gambling was his ruin]* —*vt.* to bring to ruin; specif., *a)* to destroy, or damage greatly *b)* to make bankrupt *c)* to seduce (a chaste woman) —*vi.* to go or come to ruin

**ru·in·a·tion** (rōō′ə nā′shən) *n.* **1.** a ruining or being ruined **2.** anything that ruins

**ru·in·ous** (rōō′ə nəs) *adj.* **1.** falling or fallen into ruin **2.** bringing ruin; disastrous —**ru′in·ous·ly** *adv.*

**rule** (rōōl) *n.* [< OFr. < L. *regula*, straightedge < *regere*, to lead straight] **1.** *a)* an authoritative regulation for conduct, method, procedure, etc. *b)* an established practice that serves as a guide *[rules of grammar]* **2.** a set of regulations in a religious order **3.** a habit; custom **4.** customary course of events *[famine is the rule following war]* **5.** *a)* government; reign *b)* the period of a particular reign **6.** a ruler or straightedge **7.** *Law a)* a court regulation *b)* a decision, order, etc. made by a judge or court in regard to a specific question or point *c)* a legal principle **8.** *Printing* a thin strip of metal as high as type, used to print lines —*vt.* **ruled, rul′ing 1.** to have an influence over; guide **2.** to keep under control **3.** to have authority over; govern **4.** to settle by decree; determine **5.** to mark (lines) on (paper, etc.) as with a ruler —*vi.* **1.** to govern **2.** to prevail **3.** to issue a

formal decision —**as a rule** usually —**rule out** to decide to exclude from consideration

**rule of three** *Math.* the method of finding the fourth term of a proportion when three terms are given: the product of the first and last is equal to the product of the second and third

**rule of thumb 1.** a rule based on experience or practice rather than on scientific knowledge **2.** any practical, though crude, method of estimating

**rul·er** (rōō′lər) *n.* **1.** a person or thing that rules or governs **2.** a thin strip of wood, metal, etc. with a straight edge, used in drawing lines, measuring, etc.

**rul·ing** (-liŋ) *adj.* that rules; governing, predominating, etc. —*n.* **1.** a governing **2.** a decision made by a court **3.** *a)* the making of ruled lines *b)* the lines so made

**rum**[1] (rum) *n.* [short for *rumbullion*, orig. a dial. term, tumult < ?] **1.** an alcoholic liquor distilled from fermented sugar cane, molasses, etc. **2.** alcoholic liquor in general

**rum**[2] (rum) *adj.* [< obs. *rum*, good] [Chiefly Brit. Colloq.] **1.** odd; strange **2.** bad; poor, etc. *[a rum joke]*

**rum**[3] (rum) *n. same as* RUMMY[1]

**Ru·ma·nia** (rōō mān′yə, -mā′nē ə) *same as* ROMANIA —**Ru·ma′nian** *adj., n.*

**rum·ba** (rum′bə, room′-; Sp. rōōm′bä) *n.* [AmSp., prob. of Afr. origin] **1.** a dance of Cuban Negro origin **2.** a ballroom adaptation of this, characterized by rhythmic movements of the lower part of the body **3.** music for this dance —*vi.* to dance the rumba

**rum·ble** (rum′b'l) *vi.* **-bled, -bling** [prob. < MDu. *rommelen*] **1.** to make a deep, heavy rolling sound, as thunder **2.** to move with such a sound —*vt.* **1.** to cause to make, or move with, such a sound **2.** to utter with such a sound —*n.* **1.** a deep, heavy rolling sound **2.** a widespread expression of discontent **3.** [Slang] a gang fight —**rum′bler** *n.*

**rumble seat** in some earlier automobiles, an open rear seat that could be folded shut when not in use

**ru·men** (rōō′min) *n., pl.* **-mi·na** (-mi nə) [ModL. < L., gullet] the first stomach of a ruminant

**Rum·ford** (rum′fərd), Count *see* Benjamin THOMPSON

**ru·mi·nant** (rōō′mə nənt) *adj.* [< L. prp. of *ruminare*, to ruminate < *rumen*, RUMEN] **1.** chewing the cud **2.** of the cud-chewing animals **3.** meditative —*n.* any of a large group of four-footed, hoofed, even-toed, cud-chewing mammals, as the cattle, sheep, goat, deer, camel, etc. —**ru′mi·nant·ly** *adv.*

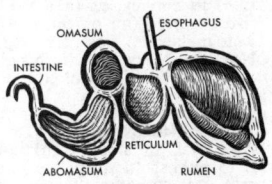

STOMACH OF A RUMINANT

**ru·mi·nate** (rōō′mə nāt′) *vt., vi.* **-nat′ed, -nat′ing** [< L. pp. of *ruminare*: see prec.] **1.** to chew (the cud), as a cow does **2.** to meditate (on); muse —**ru′mi·na′tion** *n.* —**ru′mi·na′tive** *adj.*

**rum·mage** (rum′ij) *n.* [< MFr. < *arrumer*, to stow cargo < *run*, ship's hold < Frank.] **1.** odds and ends **2.** a rummaging search —*vt.* **-maged, -mag·ing 1.** to search through (a place, etc.) thoroughly by moving the contents about **2.** to get or turn up by searching thoroughly (with *up* or *out*) —*vi.* to make a thorough search —**rum′mag·er** *n.*

**rummage sale** a sale of miscellaneous articles, used or new, to raise money for a charity

**rum·my**[1] (rum′ē) *adj.* **-mi·er, -mi·est** [RUM[2] + -Y[2]] [Chiefly Brit. Colloq.] odd; strange; queer —*n.* any of certain card games in which the object is to match cards into sets of the same denomination or sequences of the same suit

**rum·my**[2] (rum′ē) *n., pl.* **-mies** [RUM[1] + -Y[2]] [Slang] a drunkard —*adj.* **-mi·er, -mi·est** of or like rum

**ru·mor** (rōō′mər) *n.* [< OFr. < L., noise] **1.** general talk not based on definite knowledge; hearsay **2.** an unconfirmed report, story, etc. in general circulation —*vt.* to tell or spread by rumor Also, Brit. sp., **ru′mour**

**ru·mor·mon·ger** (-muŋ′gər, -mäŋ′-) *n.* a person who spreads rumors

**rump** (rump) *n.* [ON. *rumpr*] **1.** the hind part of an animal, where the legs and back join **2.** a cut of beef from this part, behind the loin and above the round **3.** the buttocks **4.** the last and unimportant part; remnant

**rum·ple** (rum′p'l) *n.* [< MDu. < *rompe*, a wrinkle] an uneven fold or crease; wrinkle —*vt., vi.* **-pled, -pling 1.** to make rumples (in); crumple **2.** to make or become disheveled —**rum′ply** *adj.*

**rum·pus** (rum′pəs) *n.* [< ?] [Colloq.] noisy disturbance

---

**rum·run·ner** (rum′run′ər) *n.* a person, ship, etc. engaged in smuggling alcoholic liquor —**rum′run′ning** *n.*

**run** (run) *vi.* **ran** or dial. **run, run, run′ning** [ON. *rinna* & OE. *rinnan*] **1.** to go by moving the legs faster than in walking **2.** *a)* to move swiftly [we *ran* to her aid] *b)* to go (*to*) for help [*run* to the doctor] **3.** to associate (*with*) **4.** to go, move, etc. easily and freely, without hindrance **5.** to flee **6.** to make a quick trip (*up to, down to,* etc.) for a brief stay **7.** *a)* to take part in a contest or race *b)* to be a candidate in an election **8.** to swim in migration: said of fish **9.** to go, as on a schedule [a bus *runs* between Chicago and Detroit] **10.** to pass lightly and rapidly [his eyes *ran* over the page] **11.** to be told repeatedly [a rumor *ran* through the town] **12.** to climb or creep, as a vine **13.** to ravel [her stocking *ran*] **14.** to operate with parts that revolve or slide [the machine is *running*] **15.** to flow [rivers *run* to the sea] **16.** to melt and flow, as wax **17.** *a)* to spread over cloth, etc. when moistened, as colors *b)* to be subject to this spreading, as fabric **18.** to be wet with a flow [her eyes *ran* with tears] **19.** *a)* to discharge pus, mucus, etc. *b)* to leak, as a faucet **20.** *a)* to appear in print, as in a newspaper *b)* to appear continuously [the play *ran* for a year] **21.** *a)* to continue in effect [the law *runs* for ten years] *b)* to continue to occur [talent *runs* in the family] **22.** to show a preference for (with *to*) [his taste *runs* to sweets] **23.** *a)* to extend in a continuous line [a fence *runs* through the woods] *b)* to extend in scope (*from* one thing *to* another) **24.** to pass into a specified condition, etc. [to *run* into trouble] **25.** to be written, expressed, etc. in a specified way [the adage *runs* like this] **26.** to be or continue at a specified size, price, etc. [apples *running* four to the pound] —*vt.* **1.** to follow (a specified course) **2.** to travel over [horses *ran* the range] **3.** to perform as by running [to *run* a race] **4.** to incur (a risk) **5.** *a)* to get past [to *run* a blockade] *b)* to go through without making a required stop [to *run* a red light] **6.** to hunt (game, etc.) **7.** to compete with as in a race **8.** *a)* to enter (a horse, etc.) in a race *b)* to put up as a candidate for election **9.** *a)* to make run, move, etc. *b)* to cause to go between points, as on a schedule *c)* to cause (an engine, etc.) to idle for a while **10.** to bring or force into a specified condition by running [to *run* oneself into debt] **11.** *a)* to convey, as in a vehicle *b)* to smuggle **12.** to drive or force (an object) into, against, etc. (something) **13.** to make pass, flow, etc., esp. rapidly, in a specified way, place, etc. [to *run* water into a glass] **14.** *a)* to manage [to *run* a household] *b)* to conduct (a test, etc.) *c)* to cause to undergo a test, etc. **15.** to cost (an amount) **16.** to mark or draw (lines, as on a map) **17.** to trace [to *run* a story back to its source] **18.** to undergo (a fever, etc.) **19.** to melt or smelt (ore) **20.** to cast or mold; found **21.** to publish (a story, etc.) as in a newspaper **22.** *Billiards,* etc. to complete successfully (a sequence of shots, etc.) **23.** *Bridge* to lead (a suit) taking a series of tricks —*n.* **1.** *a)* an act or period of running *b)* a running pace **2.** the distance covered or time spent in running **3.** a trip; journey; esp., *a)* a regular trip, as of a plane *b)* a route for making deliveries **4.** *a)* movement onward; progression *b)* a continuous course or period [a *run* of good luck] **5.** a continuous course of performances, etc., as of a play **6.** a continued series of demands, as for specified goods **7.** a continuous series or extent **8.** a flow or rush of water, etc., as of the tide **9.** a small, swift stream **10.** *a)* a period during which some fluid flows readily *b)* the amount of flow **11.** *a)* a period of operation of a machine *b)* the output during this period **12.** *a)* a kind or class, as of goods *b)* the usual or average kind **13.** *a)* an inclined pathway or course [a ski *run*] *b)* an enclosed area for domestic animals [a dog *run*] **14.** freedom to move about at will [to have the *run* of the house] **15.** *a)* a large number of fish migrating together *b)* such migration **16.** a ravel, as in a stocking **17.** *Baseball* a scoring point, made by a successful circuit of the bases **18.** *Billiards,* etc. a sequence of successful shots, etc. **19.** *Mil.* the approach to the target made by an airplane in bombing, etc. **20.** *Music* a rapid succession of tones —*adj.* **1.** melted **2.** poured while in a melted state [*run* metal] —**a run for one's money 1.** powerful competition **2.** satisfaction for what one has expended —**in the long run** in the final outcome; ultimately —**on the run 1.** running **2.** running away —**run across** to encounter by chance —**run along** to depart —**run away 1.** to flee **2.** to desert one's home or family **3.** to escape and run loose —**run away with 1.** to steal **2.** to carry out of control [his anger *ran away with* him] **3.** to outdo all others in (a contest, etc.) *b)* to get (a prize, etc.) in this way —**run down 1.** to stop operating **2.** to run or drive against so as to knock down **3.** to pursue and capture or kill **4.** to search out the source of **5.** to speak of with disapproval **6.** to make or become run-down **7.** to read through rapidly —**run for it** to run to escape something —**run in 1.** to include (something additional) **2.** [Colloq.] to make a quick visit **3.** [Slang] to arrest —**run**

**into 1.** to encounter by chance **2.** to collide with **3.** to add up to (a large sum of money): also **run to** —**run off 1.** to print, make copies of, etc. **2.** to cause to be run, played, etc. **3.** to drive (trespassers) away **4.** to drain **5.** *same as* RUN AWAY —**run on 1.** to continue or be continued **2.** to add (something) at the end **3.** to talk continuously —**run out 1.** to come to an end; expire **2.** to drive out —**run out of** to use up —**run out on** [Colloq.] to abandon or desert —**run over 1.** to ride or drive over **2.** to overflow **3.** to go beyond a limit **4.** to examine, rehearse, etc. rapidly —**run scared** [Slang] to behave as if expecting to fail —**run through 1.** to use up or spend quickly or recklessly **2.** to pierce **3.** to examine, rehearse, etc. rapidly —**run up 1.** to raise, rise, or make rapidly **2.** to let (bills, etc.) go without paying them **3.** to sew with a rapid succession of stitches

**run·a·bout** (run′ə bout′) *n.* **1.** a person who runs about from place to place **2.** a light, one-seated, open carriage or automobile **3.** a light motorboat

**run·a·round** (-ə round′) *n.* [Colloq.] a series of evasive excuses, delays, etc.: usually in **get** (or **give**) **the runaround**

**run·a·way** (-ə wā′) *n.* **1.** a fugitive **2.** a horse, etc. that runs away **3.** a running away —*adj.* **1.** running away or having run away **2.** of or done by runaways **3.** easily won, as a race **4.** *a)* rising rapidly, as prices *b)* having an uncontrolled rise of prices [*runaway* inflation]

**run-down** (-doun′) *adj.* **1.** not wound and therefore not running, as a clock **2.** in poor physical condition, as from overwork **3.** fallen into disrepair

**run·down** (-doun′) *n.* a concise summary

**rune** (rōōn) *n.* [OE. *run*] **1.** any of the characters of an ancient Germanic alphabet **2.** something inscribed in such characters **3.** *a)* a Finnish or Old Norse poem or canto *b)* [Poet.] any poem, song, etc. that is mystical or obscure

**rung[1]** (ruŋ) *n.* [OE. *hrung,* a staff] **1.** any sturdy stick, bar, or rod used as a crossbar, support, etc.; specif., *a)* any of the steps of a ladder *b)* a crosspiece between the legs of a chair, or across the back, etc. **2.** a degree, as of social status, success, etc.

**rung[2]** (ruŋ) *pp. & chiefly dial. pt. of* RING[1]

**ru·nic** (rōō′nik) *adj.* **1.** consisting of or set down in runes **2.** like runes in decorative effect **3.** mystical; obscure

**run-in** (run′in′) *adj. Printing* made continuous without a break or paragraph —*n.* **1.** *Printing* run-in matter **2.** [Colloq.] a quarrel, dispute, etc.

**run·nel** (run′'l) *n.* [OE. *rynel* < *rinnan,* to run] a small stream; little brook: also **run′let** (-lit)

**run·ner** (run′ər) *n.* **1.** one that runs; specif., *a)* a racer *b)* *same as* BASE RUNNER **2.** a messenger, as for a bank or broker **3.** a smuggler **4.** a person who operates a machine, etc. **5.** a long, narrow cloth or rug **6.** a long ravel, as in hose; run **7.** a long, trailing stem, as of a strawberry, that puts out roots along the ground, thus producing new plants **8.** something on or in which something else moves **9.** either of the long, narrow pieces on which a sled or sleigh slides **10.** the blade of a skate

**run·ner-up** (-up′) *n., pl.* **-ners-up′** a person or team that finishes second in a race, contest, etc.

**run·ning** (run′iŋ) *n.* **1.** the act of one that runs; racing, managing, etc. **2.** that which runs, or flows —*adj.* **1.** moving or advancing rapidly **2.** flowing [*running* water] **3.** cursive: said of handwriting **4.** melting; becoming liquid **5.** discharging pus [a *running* sore] **6.** creeping or climbing: said of plants **7.** in operation, as machinery **8.** in a straight line [a *running* foot] **9.** without interruption; continuous [a *running* commentary] **10.** prevalent **11.** current [a *running* account] **12.** simultaneous [a *running* translation] **13.** moving easily or smoothly **14.** slipping or sliding easily, as a knot **15.** moving when pulled, as a rope **16.** done in or by a run [a *running* jump] **17.** of the normal run (of a train, bus, etc.) [*running* time] —*adv.* in succession [for ten days *running*] —**in** (or **out of**) **the running** in (or out of) the competition

**running board** esp. formerly, a footboard along the lower part of the side of some automobiles

**running fire** a rapid succession of shots fired, remarks made, questions asked, etc.

**running head** (or **title**) a heading or title printed at the top of every, or every other, page

**running knot** *same as* SLIPKNOT

**running lights** the lights that a ship or aircraft traveling at night is required to display

**running mate** a candidate for a lesser office, as for the vice-presidency, in his relationship to the candidate for the greater office

**run·ny** (run′ē) *adj.* **-ni·er, -ni·est 1.** that flows, esp. too freely **2.** that keeps on discharging mucus [a *runny* nose]

**Run·ny·mede** (run′ē mēd′) meadow on the south bank of the Thames, southwest of London: see MAGNA CHARTA

**run-off** (run′ôf′) *n.* **1.** something that runs off, as rain in excess of the amount absorbed by the ground **2.** a deciding, final race, election, etc., as in case of a tie

**run-of-the-mill** (run′əv th̵ə mil′) *adj.* [see RUN, *n.*, 12 *b*] not selected or special; ordinary

**run-on** (run′än′) *adj. Printing* continuous without a break or new paragraph —*n.* run-on matter

**runt** (runt) *n.* [< ?] **1.** a stunted or undersized animal, plant, thing, or (usually in a contemptuous sense) person **2.** the smallest animal of a litter —**runt′i·ness** *n.* —**runt′y** *adj.* **runt′i·er, runt′i·est**

**run-through** (run′thr̵o̅o̅′) *n.* a full rehearsal without stopping

**run·way** (-wā′) *n.* a channel, track, chute, etc. in, on, or along which something moves; specif., *a*) a strip of leveled, usually paved ground for use by airplanes in taking off and landing *b*) a narrow extension of a stage out into the audience

**ru·pee** (r̵o̅o̅ pē′, r̵o̅o̅′pē) *n.* [< Hindi < Sans. *rūpya*, wrought silver] the monetary unit of India, Pakistan, Ceylon, etc.: see MONETARY UNITS, table

**ru·pi·ah** (r̵o̅o̅ pē′ə) *n.* [< Hindi] *see* MONETARY UNITS, table (Indonesia)

**rup·ture** (rup′chər) *n.* [< MFr. < L. < pp. of *rumpere*, to break] **1.** a breaking apart or being broken apart **2.** a breaking off of friendly or peaceful relations **3.** a hernia —*vt., vi.* **-tured, -tur·ing 1.** to break apart or burst **2.** to affect with or undergo a rupture

**ru·ral** (roor′əl) *adj.* [< MFr. < LL. *ruralis* < L. *rus* (gen. *ruris*), the country] **1.** of or like the country, country folk, etc.; rustic **2.** living in the country **3.** having to do with farming —**ru′ral·ly** *adv.*

**rural delivery** delivery of mail by carriers on routes in rural areas: formerly **rural free delivery**

**ru·ral·ism** (-iz′m) *n.* **1.** rural quality **2.** rural life **3.** a rural idiom, feature, etc. Also **ru·ral·i·ty** (r̵o̅o̅ ral′ə tē), *pl.* **-ties** —**ru′ral·ist** (-ist) *n.*

**ru·ral·ize** (roor′ə līz′) *vt.* **-ized′, -iz′ing** to make rural —*vi.* to live for a time in the country —**ru′ral·i·za′tion** *n.*

**Ru·ri·ta·ni·an** (roor′ə tā′nē ən) *adj.* [after *Ruritania*, imaginary kingdom in novels by A. Hope (1863–1933)] of or characteristic of some quaint, romantic, unreal place

**ruse** (r̵o̅o̅z) *n.* [< MFr. < OFr. *reuser*, to deceive < L. *recusare*, to refuse] a stratagem or trick

**rush**[1] (rush) *vi.* [< Anglo-Fr. < MFr. < OFr. *reuser:* see prec.] **1.** *a*) to move swiftly or impetuously *b*) to dash recklessly **2.** to make a sudden attack (*on* or *upon*) **3.** to pass, come, go, etc. swiftly or suddenly **4.** *Football* to advance the ball by a running play —*vt.* **1.** to move, send, push, etc. swiftly or violently **2.** to do, make, move, etc. with unusual speed or haste **3.** *a*) to attack suddenly *b*) to overcome or capture thus **4.** [Colloq.] *a*) to lavish attentions on, as in courting *b*) to entertain with parties, etc. prior to inviting to join a fraternity or sorority —*n.* **1.** a rushing **2.** an eager movement of many people to get to a place **3.** intense activity; haste; hurry **4.** a sudden attack **5.** a scrimmage contest between groups of college students **6.** great pressure, as of much business requiring quick or hasty attention **7.** [*usually pl.*] *Motion Pictures* a first print of a scene or scenes, shown for the director, etc. to inspect —*adj.* necessitating haste [*rush* orders] —**with a rush** suddenly and forcefully —**rush′er** *n.*

**rush**[2] (rush) *n.* [OE. *risc*] **1.** any of a genus of grasslike plants usually growing in wet places and having, in some species, round stems and pliant leaves used in making baskets, mats, etc. **2.** any of various similar plants, as bulrushes —**rush′y** *adj.* **rush′i·er, rush′i·est**

**rush candle** a candle made with the pith of a rush as the wick: also **rush′light**′ *n.*, **rush light**

**rush·ee** (rush ē′) *n.* a college student who is being rushed by a fraternity or sorority

**rush hour** a time of the day when business, traffic, etc. are especially heavy —**rush′-hour**′ *adj.*

**rusk** (rusk) *n.* [Sp. *rosca*, twisted bread roll] **1.** sweet, raised bread or cake toasted in an oven until crisp, usually after being sliced **2.** a piece of this

**Rus·kin** (rus′kin), **John** 1819–1900; Eng. writer, art critic, & social reformer

**Russ. 1.** Russia **2.** Russian

**Rus·sell** (rus′'l) **1.** [< surname *Russell*, orig. dim. of Fr. *roux*, red] a masculine name: dim. *Russ* **2. Bertrand (Arthur William)**, 3d Earl Russell, 1872–1970; Brit. philosopher, mathematician, & writer, born in Wales

**rus·set** (rus′it) *n.* [< OFr. < L. *russus*, reddish] **1.** yellowish (or reddish) brown **2.** a coarse, brownish cloth, formerly used for clothing by country folk **3.** a winter apple with a rough, mottled skin —*adj.* yellowish-brown or reddish-brown

**Rus·sia** (rush′ə) **1.** former empire (**Russian Empire**) in E. Europe & N Asia, 1547–1917, ruled by the czars **2.** *popular name for the* UNION OF SOVIET SOCIALIST REPUBLICS

**Russia leather** a fine, smooth leather, usually dyed dark red, orig. made in Russia: used in bookbinding, etc.

**Rus·sian** (rush′ən) *adj.* of Russia, its people, their language, etc. —*n.* **1.** *a*) a native or inhabitant of Russia, specif. of the R.S.F.S.R. *b*) popularly, any citizen of the U.S.S.R. **2.** a member of the chief Slavic people of Russia **3.** the East Slavic language of the Russians; esp., its principal dialect (**Great Russian**), the official language of the U.S.S.R.

**Russian dressing** mayonnaise mixed with chili sauce, chopped pickles, pimentos, etc.: used on salads, etc.

**Rus·sian·ize** (-īz′) *vt.* **-ized′, -iz′ing** to make Russian in character —**Rus′sian·i·za′tion** *n.*

**Russian Revolution** the revolution of 1917 in Russia in which the Czar's government was overthrown

**Russian roulette** a deadly game of chance in which a person spins the cylinder of a revolver holding only one bullet, aims at his head, and pulls the trigger

**Russian Soviet Federated Socialist Republic** largest republic of the U.S.S.R., from the Baltic Sea to the Pacific: 6,592,000 sq. mi.; pop. 130,100,000; cap. Moscow

**Russian wolfhound** *same as* BORZOI

**Rus·si·fy** (rus′ə fī′) *vt.* **-fied′, -fy′ing** *same as* RUSSIANIZE

**Rus·so-** *a combining form meaning:* **1.** Russia or Russian **2.** Russian and [*Russo-*Japanese]

**rust** (rust) *n.* [OE.] **1.** the reddish-brown coating (mainly ferric oxide) formed on iron or steel by oxidation, as during exposure to air and moisture **2.** any similar coating on other metals **3.** any stain or formation resembling iron rust **4.** any habit, influence, etc. injurious to usefulness, to the mind, etc. **5.** inactivity; idleness **6.** a reddish brown **7.** *a*) any of various plant diseases caused by parasitic fungi that produce reddish spots on stems and leaves *b*) such a fungus: in full, **rust fungus** —*vi., vt.* **1.** to affect or be affected by a rust fungus **2.** to become or cause to be coated with rust **3.** to spoil, as from lack of use **4.** to become or make rust-colored —**rust′-col′ored** *adj.* —**rust′less** *adj.*

**rus·tic** (rus′tik) *adj.* [< MFr. < L. *rusticus* < *rus:* see RURAL] **1.** of or living in the country, as distinguished from cities or towns; rural **2.** not refined or sophisticated; specif., *a*) simple, plain, or artless *b*) awkward, uncouth, or boorish **3.** made of bark-covered branches or roots [*rustic* furniture] —*n.* a country person, esp. one regarded as simple, awkward, uncouth, etc. —**rus′ti·cal·ly** *adv.* —**rus·tic′i·ty** (-tis′ə tē) *n.*

**rus·ti·cate** (rus′ti kāt′) *vi.* **-cat′ed, -cat′ing 1.** to go to the country **2.** to live in the country —*vt.* **1.** to send to live in the country **2.** [Brit.] to suspend (a student) temporarily from a university **3.** to make rustic —**rus′ti·ca′tion** *n.* —**rus′ti·ca′tor** *n.*

**rus·tle**[1] (rus′'l) *vi., vt.* **-tled, -tling** [ult. < WGmc. echoic base] to make or cause to make soft sounds, as of leaves moved by a breeze —*n.* a series of such sounds

**rus·tle**[2] (rus′'l) *vi., vt.* **-tled, -tling** [< ? RUSH[1] + HUSTLE] [Colloq.] **1.** to work with, or move or get by, energetic action **2.** to steal (cattle, etc.) —**rustle up** [Colloq.] to collect or get together, as by foraging around —**rus′tler** *n.*

**rust·proof** (rust′pr̵o̅o̅f′) *adj.* resistant to rust —*vt.* to make rustproof

**rust·y** (rus′tē) *adj.* **rust′i·er, rust′i·est 1.** coated with rust, as a metal, or affected by rust, as a plant **2.** of or caused by rust **3.** not working freely because of or as if because of rust **4.** *a*) impaired by disuse, neglect, etc. *b*) having lost one's skill through lack of practice **5.** rust-colored **6.** faded, old-looking, or shabby —**rust′i·ly** *adv.* —**rust′i·ness** *n.*

**rut**[1] (rut) *n.* [< ? MFr. *route*, ROUTE] **1.** a track or furrow, esp. one made by wheeled vehicles **2.** a fixed, routine procedure, way of acting, thinking, etc. —*vt.* **rut′ted, rut′-ting** to make a rut or ruts in

**rut**[2] (rut) *n.* [< OFr. < L. < *rugire*, to roar] **1.** the periodic sexual excitement of certain mammals, esp. males **2.** the period of this —*vi.* **rut′ted, rut′ting** to be in rut

**ru·ta·ba·ga** (r̵o̅o̅t′ə bā′gə, r̵o̅o̅t′ə bä′gə) *n.* [Sw. dial. *rotabagge*] a turnip with a large, yellow root

**Ruth** (r̵o̅o̅th) [LL. < Heb. *rūth*, prob. contr. < *rē'uth*, companion] **1.** a feminine name **2.** *Bible a*) a Moabite widow deeply devoted to her mother-in-law, Naomi *b*) the book of the Bible that tells her story **3. George Herman,** (nicknamed "**Babe**") 1895–1948; U.S. baseball player

**ruth** (r̵o̅o̅th) *n.* [ult. < OE. *hreowian*, to rue] [Now Rare] **1.** pity; compassion **2.** sorrow; grief; remorse

**Ru·the·ni·a** (r̵o̅o̅ thē′nē ə) region in W Ukrainian S.S.R. —**Ru·the′ni·an** *adj., n.*

**ru·the·ni·um** (r̵o̅o̅ thē′nē əm) *n.* [ModL. < ML. *Ruthenia*, Russia, where first found] a rare, very hard, silvery-gray metallic chemical element, used in alloys and as a catalyst: symbol, Ru; at. wt., 101.07; at. no., 44

**Ruth·er·ford** (ru*th*ər fərd), **Ernest,** 1st Baron Rutherford of Nelson, 1871–1937; Brit. physicist, born in New Zealand
**ruth·ful** (rōōth′fəl) *adj.* [Now Rare] full of ruth, or pity, sorrow, etc. —**ruth′ful·ly** *adv.* —**ruth′ful·ness** *n.*
**ruth·less** (-lis) *adj.* without ruth; pitiless and relentless, as in seeking some goal —**ruth′less·ly** *adv.* —**ruth′less-ness** *n.*
**rut·ty** (rut′ē) *adj.* **-ti·er, -ti·est** having or full of ruts *[a rutty road]* —**rut′ti·ness** *n.*
**Rwan·da** (ur wän′dä, rōō wän′də) country in EC Africa, east of Zaire: 10,169 sq. mi.; pop. 3,724,000 —**Rwan′dan** *adj., n.*
**Rwy., Ry.** Railway

**Rx** [< ℞, symbol for L. *recipe:* see RECIPE] *symbol for* PRESCRIPTION (sense 3) —*n.* a prescription for any disorder
**-ry** (rē) *shortened form of* -ERY *[dentistry, jewelry]*
**rye** (rī) *n.* see PLURAL, II, D, 3 [OE. *ryge*] **1.** a hardy cereal grass widely grown for its grain and straw **2.** the grain or seeds of this plant, used for making flour and whiskey, and as feed for livestock **3.** *a)* whiskey distilled from this grain *b)* in the eastern U.S., a blended whiskey
**rye bread** bread made altogether or partly of rye flour
**rye·grass** (-gras′) *n.* any of various grasses that are annuals or that live for only a few years
**Ryu·kyu Islands** (ryōō′kyōō′) chain of Jap. islands in the W Pacific, between Kyushu & Taiwan

# S

**S, s** (es) *n., pl.* **S's, s's** **1.** the nineteenth letter of the English alphabet **2.** a sound of *S* or *s*
**S** (es) *n.* **1.** something shaped like an *S* **2.** *Chem.* sulfur —*adj.* shaped like *S*
**-s** [alt. form of -ES] **1.** the plural ending of most nouns *[hips, shoes]* **2.** the ending of the third person singular, present indicative, of verbs *[gives, runs]* **3.** a suffix used to form some adverbs *[betimes, days]*
**-'s¹** [OE. *-es*] the ending of the possessive singular of nouns (and some pronouns) and of the possessive plural of nouns not ending in *s* *[boy's, one's, women's]*
**-'s²** *the unstressed and assimilated form of:* **1.** is *[he's here]* **2.** has *[she's eaten]* **3.** does *[what's it matter?]* **4.** us *[let's go]*
**S, S., s, s.** **1.** south **2.** southern
**S.** **1.** Saturday **2.** September **3.** Sunday
**S., s.** **1.** *pl.* **SS., ss.** saint **2.** school
**s.** **1.** second(s) **2.** shilling(s) **3.** singular
**SA** Seaman Apprentice
**S.A.** **1.** Salvation Army **2.** South America
**Saar** (sär, zär) **1.** river flowing from NE France north into the Moselle River, SW West Germany **2.** rich coal-mining region in the valley of this river: also called **Saar Basin**
**Saar·land** (sär′land, zär′-; *G.* zär′länt′) state of SW West Germany, in the Saar River Basin
**Sa·ba** (sä′bə) ancient kingdom in S Arabia in the region of modern Yemen: Biblical name, *Sheba*
**Sab·ba·tar·i·an** (sab′ə ter′ē ən) *adj.* of the Sabbath and its observance —*n.* **1.** a person, esp. a Christian, who observes the Sabbath (sense 1) **2.** a Christian favoring rigid observance of Sunday as the Sabbath —**Sab′ba·tar′i·an·ism** *n.*
**Sab·bath** (sab′əth) *n.* [< OFr. & OE. *sabat,* both < L. < Gr. < Heb. < *shābath,* to rest] **1.** the seventh day of the week (Saturday), observed as a day of rest and worship by Jews and some Christian sects **2.** Sunday as the usual Christian day of rest and worship —*adj.* of the Sabbath
**Sab·bat·i·cal** (sə bat′i k'l) *adj.* [< Fr. < LL. < Gr. *sabbatikos:* see prec.] **1.** of or suited to the Sabbath **2.** [s-] designating a year or shorter period of absence for study, rest, or travel, given at intervals, orig. every seven years, as to some college teachers —*n.* [s-] a sabbatical year or leave Also **Sab·bat′ic**
**sa·ber** (sä′bər) *n.* [< Fr. < G. *sabel* < MHG. < Pol. & Hung.] a heavy cavalry sword with a slightly curved blade —*vt.* to cut, wound, or kill with a saber
**Sa·bin** (sä′bin), **Albert B(ruce)** 1906– ; U.S. bacteriologist: developed an oral vaccine to prevent poliomyelitis
**Sa·bine** (sä′bīn) *n.* a member of an ancient tribe living in central Italy, conquered by the Romans, 3d century B.C.
**sa·ble** (sä′b'l) *n., pl.* **-bles, -ble:** see PLURAL, II, D, 1 [OFr. < ML. *sabelum,* ult. < Russian *sobol'*] **1.** *same as* MARTEN; esp., *a)* the **European marten,** with light-colored underfur *b)* the **American marten,** with a darker pelt **2.** *a)* the costly fur of the sable *b)* [*pl.*] a coat, etc. of this **3.** *Heraldry* the color black —*adj.* **1.** made of or with the fur of the sable **2.** black or dark brown; dark
**sa·bot** (sab′ō, sa bō′) *n.* [Fr., ult. < Ar. *sabbât,* sandal] **1.** a shoe shaped from a single piece of wood **2.** a heavy leather shoe with a wooden sole
**sab·o·tage** (sab′ə täzh′) *n.* [Fr. < *saboter,* to damage < *sabot:* see prec. & -AGE: from damage done to machinery by wooden shoes] **1.** intentional destruction of machines, waste of materials, etc.,

as during labor disputes **2.** destruction of railroads, bridges, etc. as by enemy agents or an underground resistance **3.** deliberate obstruction of or damage to any cause, effort, etc. —*vt.* **-taged′, -tag′ing** to injure or destroy by sabotage —*vi.* to engage in sabotage
**sab·o·teur** (sab′ə tur′) *n.* [Fr.] a person who sabotages
**sa·bra** (sä′brə) *n.* [ModHeb. *sābrāh,* lit., prickly fruit of a native cactus] a native-born Israeli
**sa·bre** (sä′bər) *n., vt.* **-bred, -bring** *same as* SABER
**sac** (sak) *n.* [Fr. < L. *saccus:* see SACK¹] a pouchlike part in a plant or animal, esp. one filled with fluid —**sac′like′** *adj.*
**SAC, S.A.C.** Strategic Air Command
**sac·cha·ride** (sak′ə rīd′) *n.* [see ff.] any of the carbohydrates; esp., any of the sugars, as glucose
**sac·cha·rin** (sak′ə rin) *n.* [< L. *saccharum,* sugar < Gr. *sakcharon,* ult. < Sans.] a white, crystalline coal-tar compound, $C_7H_5O_3NS$, about 500 times sweeter than cane sugar, used as a sugar substitute in diabetic diets, etc.
**sac·cha·rine** (-rin, -rīn′) *adj.* [see prec.] **1.** of, like, or producing sugar **2.** too sweet or syrupy *[a saccharine voice]* —*n. same as* SACCHARIN —**sac′cha·rine·ly** *adv.* —**sac′cha·rin′i·ty** (-rin′ə tē) *n.*
**sac·er·do·tal** (sas′ər dōt′'l, sak′-) *adj.* [< MFr. < L. < *sacerdos,* priest] of priests or the office of priest; priestly —**sac′er·do′tal·ly** *adv.*
**sa·chem** (sä′chəm) *n.* [< Algonquian *sâchimau*] among some N. American Indian tribes, the chief
**sa·chet** (sa shā′; *chiefly Brit.* sash′ā) *n.* [Fr. < OFr., dim. of *sac:* see SAC] **1.** a small bag, pad, etc. filled with perfumed powder and put in dresser drawers, etc. to scent clothing **2.** such powder: also **sachet powder**
**sack¹** (sak) *n.* [OE. *sacc* < L. *saccus* < Gr. < Heb. *śaq* **1.** *a)* a bag, esp. a large bag of coarse cloth, for holding grain, foodstuffs, etc. *b)* the contents or capacity of a sack **2.** a loose-fitting jacket or dress **3.** [Slang] dismissal from a job (with *the*) **4.** [Slang] a bed, bunk, etc. **5.** *Baseball* a base —*vt.* **1.** to put into sacks **2.** [Slang] to dismiss from a job; fire —**hit the sack** [Slang] to go to bed
**sack²** (sak) *n.* [< MFr. < It. *sacco,* plunder, lit., bag < L. *saccus:* see prec.] the plundering of a captured city, etc. —*vt.* to plunder (a city, etc.)
**sack³** (sak) *n.* [< Fr. (*vin) sec,* dry (wine) < L. *siccus,* dry] any of various dry white wines from Spain or the Canary Islands
**sack·but** (sak′but′) *n.* [Fr. *saquebute* < OFr. *saquer,* to pull + *bouter,* to push] a medieval wind instrument, forerunner of the trombone: the word is also incorrectly used in the King James Version of the Bible to translate an Aramaic word for a kind of lyre
**sack·cloth** (-klôth′, -kläth′) *n.* **1.** *same as* SACKING **2.** a rough cloth worn as a symbol of mourning or penitence —**in sackcloth and ashes** in a state of great mourning or penitence
**sack coat** a man's loose-fitting, straight-backed coat, usually part of a business suit
**sack·ful** (sak′fool′) *n., pl.* **-fuls′** **1.** the amount a sack holds **2.** a large quantity
**sack·ing** (-iŋ) *n.* a cheap, coarse cloth of flax, hemp, jute, etc., used esp. for sacks
**sa·cral¹** (sā′krəl) *adj.* [< L. neut. of *sacer,* sacred] of or for religious rites or observances
**sa·cral²** (sā′krəl) *adj.* [< ModL.: see SACRUM & -AL] of, or in the region of, the sacrum
**sac·ra·ment** (sak′rə mənt) *n.* [< OFr. < LL. *sacramentum,* ult. < L. *sacer,* sacred] **1.** any of certain rites variously observed by Christians as ordained by Jesus, as baptism,

SABOT

Holy Communion, etc. **2.** [*sometimes* **S-**] the Eucharist, or Holy Communion; also, the consecrated bread and wine, or sometimes the bread alone **3.** something regarded as sacred

**sac·ra·men·tal** (sak'rə men't'l) *adj.* of, like, or used in a sacrament —*n. R.C.Ch.* something like a sacrament but instituted by the Church, as holy water —**sac'ra·men'tal·ly** *adv.*

**Sac·ra·men·to** (sak'rə men'tō) [Sp., sacrament] **1.** river in C Calif., flowing south into San Francisco Bay **2.** capital of Calif., on this river: pop. 276,000 (met. area 1,011,000)

**sa·cred** (sā'krid) *adj.* [ < OFr. < L. < *sacer,* holy] **1.** consecrated to a god or deity; holy **2.** having to do with religion or religious rites **3.** given the respect accorded holy things; venerated **4.** dedicated to a person, place, purpose, etc. [*sacred* to his memory] **5.** that must not be broken, ignored, etc.; inviolate [a *sacred* promise] —**sa'cred·ly** *adv.* —**sa'cred·ness** *n.*

**sacred cow** any person or thing regarded as above criticism

**sac·ri·fice** (sak'rə fīs') *n.* [ < OFr. < L. *sacrificium* < *sacer,* sacred + *facere,* to make] **1.** *a)* an offering of the life of a person or animal, or of an object, in homage to a deity *b)* the thing offered **2.** *a)* a giving up, destroying, etc. of one thing for the sake of another *b)* the thing given up, etc. **3.** *a)* a selling or giving up of a thing at less than its value *b)* the loss incurred **4.** *Baseball same as* SACRIFICE BUNT —*vt.* **-ficed', -fic'ing** **1.** to offer as a sacrifice to a deity **2.** to give up, destroy, etc. for the sake of another thing **3.** to sell at less than value **4.** *Baseball* to advance (a base runner) by a sacrifice —*vi.* to make a sacrifice

**sacrifice bunt** *Baseball* a bunt by the batter hit so that while he is being put out a base runner advances to another base: also **sacrifice hit**

**sacrifice fly** *Baseball* a play in which the batter flies out and a runner scores from third base after the catch

**sac·ri·fi·cial** (sak'rə fish'əl) *adj.* of, like, used in, or offering a sacrifice —**sac'ri·fi'cial·ly** *adv.*

**sac·ri·lege** (sak'rə lij) *n.* [ < MFr. < L. < *sacrilegus,* temple robber < *sacer,* sacred + *legere,* to take away] **1.** misuse or violation of what is consecrated to God or religion **2.** a desecrating of anything held sacred

**sac·ri·le·gious** (sak'rə lij'əs, -lē'jəs) *adj.* **1.** that is or involves sacrilege **2.** guilty of sacrilege —**sac'ri·le'gious·ly** *adv.* —**sac'ri·le'gious·ness** *n.*

**sac·ris·tan** (sak'ris tən) *n.* a person in charge of a sacristy

**sac·ris·ty** (-tē) *n., pl.* **-ties** [ < Fr. < ML. < L. < *sacrista,* sacristan] a room in a church where the sacred vessels, vestments, etc. are kept

**sa·cro·il·i·ac** (sak'krō il'ē ak', sak'rō-) *adj.* [ < SACRUM + ILIAC] of the sacrum and the ilium; esp., designating the joint between them —*n.* the sacroiliac joint

**sac·ro·sanct** (sak'rō saŋkt') *adj.* [ < L. < *sacer,* sacred + *sanctus,* holy] very sacred, holy, or inviolable

**sa·crum** (sā'krəm, sak'rəm) *n., pl.* **-cra** (-krə, -rə) or **-crums** [ModL. < LL. (*os*) *sacrum,* sacred (bone): ? anciently used in sacrifices] a thick, triangular bone joining the ilia (see ILIUM) at the lower end of the spinal column

**sad** (sad) *adj.* **sad'der, sad'dest** [OE. *sæd,* sated] **1.** having or expressing low spirits or sorrow; unhappy; sorrowful **2.** causing or characterized by sorrow, dejection, etc. **3.** dark or dull in color; drab **4.** [Colloq.] very bad; deplorable **5.** [Dial.] heavy or soggy [a *sad* cake] —**sad'ly** *adv.* —**sad'ness** *n.*

**sad·den** (sad''n) *vt., vi.* to make or become sad

**sad·dle** (sad''l) *n.* [OE. *sadol*] **1.** a seat, usually of padded leather, for a rider on a horse, bicycle, etc. **2.** a padded part of a harness worn over a horse's back **3.** the part of an animal's back where a saddle is put **4.** anything like a saddle in form, position, etc. **5.** a ridge between two peaks **6.** a cut of lamb, etc. including part of the backbone and the two loins —*vt.* **-dled, -dling** **1.** to put a saddle upon **2.** to burden (a person) with (a debt, responsibility, obligation, etc.) —*vi.* to put a saddle on a horse and mount it (often with *up*) —**in the saddle** **1.** seated on a saddle **2.** having control

**sad·dle·bag** (-bag') *n.* **1.** a large bag, usually one of a pair, carried on either side of the back of a horse, etc., just behind the saddle **2.** a similar bag carried over the back wheel of a motorcycle, etc.

**sad·dle·bow** (-bō') *n.* the arched front part of a saddle, the top of which is the pommel

**sad·dle·cloth** (-klôth', -kläth') *n.* a thick cloth placed under a saddle on an animal's back

**saddle horse** a horse trained for riding

**sad·dler** (sad'lər) *n.* a person whose work is making, repairing, or selling saddles, harnesses, etc.

**saddle roof** a roof with two gables and a ridge

**sad·dler·y** (sad'lə rē) *n., pl.* **-dler·ies** **1.** the work of a sad-

dler **2.** articles made by a saddler **3.** a shop where these are sold

**saddle shoes** white oxford shoes with a band of contrasting leather across the instep

**saddle soap** a mild soap with neat's-foot oil in it, for cleaning and softening leather

**Sad·du·cee** (saj'oo sē', sad'yoo-) *n.* a member of an ancient Jewish party accepting only the written law and rejecting the oral, or traditional, law —**Sad'du·ce'an** *adj.*

**Sade** (säd), marquis de (full name, comte *Donatien Alphonse François de Sade*) 1740–1814; Fr. soldier & novelist

**sa·dhu** (sä'dōō) *n.* [Sans. < *sādhu,* straight] a Hindu holy man

**sad·i·ron** (sad'ī'ərn) *n.* [SAD (sense 5) + IRON] a heavy flatiron, pointed at both ends

**sad·ism** (sad'iz'm, sā'diz'm) *n.* [Fr., after marquis de SADE] the getting of pleasure, specif. sexual pleasure, from hurting or mistreating another or others —**sad'ist** *n.* —**sa·dis·tic** (sə dis'tik, sā-) *adj.* —**sa·dis'ti·cal·ly** *adv.*

**sad·o·mas·o·chism** (sā'dō mas'ə kiz'm, sad'ō-; -maz'-) *n.* sadism and masochism in the same individual —**sad'o·mas'o·chist** *n.* —**sad'o·mas'o·chis'tic** *adj.*

**sad sack** [Slang] a person who means well but is always blundering and in trouble

**sa·fa·ri** (sə fär'ē) *n., pl.* **-ris** [Swahili < Ar. < *safara,* to travel] a journey or hunting expedition, esp. in E Africa

**safe** (sāf) *adj.* **saf'er, saf'est** [OFr. *sauf* < L. *salvus*] **1.** *a)* free from danger, damage, etc.; secure *b)* having escaped injury; unharmed **2.** *a)* giving protection *b)* trustworthy **3.** unable to cause trouble or damage [*safe* in jail] **4.** taking or involving no risks **5.** *Baseball* having reached base without being put out —*n.* **1.** a strong, locking metal container for valuables **2.** any compartment, box, etc. to store food, etc. —**safe'ly** *adv.* —**safe'ness** *n.*

**safe-con·duct** (-kän'dukt) *n.* **1.** permission to travel through a dangerous area, as in time of war, with protection against arrest or harm **2.** a written pass giving this

**safe-de·pos·it** (-di päz'it) *adj.* designating or of a box or vault, esp. in a bank, for storing valuables: also **safe'ty-de·pos'it**

**safe·guard** (-gärd') *n.* any person or thing that protects or guards against loss or injury; a precaution or protection —*vt.* to protect or guard

**safe·keep·ing** (-kēp'iŋ) *n.* a keeping or being kept in safety; protection or custody

**safe·ty** (sāf'tē) *n., pl.* **-ties** **1.** a being safe; security **2.** a device to prevent accident, as a locking device (also **safety catch, safety lock**) on a firearm **3.** *Football* a) a play in which a player grounds the ball behind his own goal line when the ball was caused to pass the goal line by his own team: it scores two points for the opponents *b)* a player of a defensive backfield whose position is deep, behind the cornerbacks: in full, **safety man** —*adj.* giving safety

**safety belt** **1.** *same as* LIFE BELT **2.** a belt attaching a person working at heights to something to prevent falling **3.** *same as* SEAT BELT

**safety glass** glass made to be shatterproof by fastening together two sheets of glass with a transparent, plastic substance between them

**safety lamp** a miner's lamp designed to avoid fire, etc.

**safety match** a match that will light only when it is struck on a prepared surface

**safety pin** a pin bent back on itself so as to form a spring, the point being held with a guard

**safety razor** a razor with guards for the blade to protect the skin from cuts

**safety valve** **1.** an automatic valve for a steam boiler, etc., to release steam if the pressure is too great **2.** any outlet for emotion, energy, etc.

**saf·fi·an leather** (saf'ē ən) [G. *saffian,* ult. < Per. *säht,* hard] leather of sheepskin or goatskin tanned with sumac

**saf·flow·er** (saf'lou'ər) *n.* [ < Du. or MFr., ult. < Ar. *aṣ far,* a yellow plant] a thistlelike annual plant of the composite family, with orange flower heads yielding a dyestuff and with seeds yielding oil used in paints, foods, etc.

**saf·fron** (saf'rən) *n.* [ < OFr. *safran,* ult. < Ar. *za'farān*] **1.** a perennial old-world plant with funnel-shaped, purplish flowers having orange stigmas **2.** the dried, aromatic stigmas, used in flavoring and coloring foods **3.** orange yellow: also **saffron yellow** —*adj.* orange-yellow

**S. Afr.** **1.** South Africa **2.** South African

**sag** (sag) *vi.* **sagged, sag'ging** [prob. < Scand.] **1.** to sink or bend; esp. in the middle, from weight or pressure **2.** to hang down unevenly **3.** to lose firmness, strength, etc.; weaken **4.** to decline in price, sales, etc. —*vt.* to cause to sag —*n.* **1.** a sagging **2.** a sunken place

**sa·ga** (sä'gə) *n.* [ON., a tale] **1.** a medieval Scandinavian story of battles, etc., generally telling the legendary history

of a Norse family  **2.** any long story relating heroic deeds
**sa·ga·cious** (sə gā'shəs) *adj.* [< L. *sagax* (gen. *sagacis*),
wise] keenly perceptive or discerning, farsighted, etc. —**sa-
ga'cious·ly** *adv.* —**sa·ga'cious·ness** *n.*
**sa·gac·i·ty** (sə gas'ə tē) *n., pl.* -**ties** the quality or an instance of being sagacious
**sag·a·more** (sag'ə môr') *n.* [< AmInd. *sāgimau*] a chief of
second rank among certain tribes of N. American Indians
**sage**[1] (sāj) *adj.* **sag'er, sag'est** [< OFr., ult. < L. *sapiens,*
orig. prp. of *sapere,* to know] having or showing wisdom or
good judgment —*n.* a very wise man, esp. an old man respected for his wisdom, experience, etc. —**sage'ly** *adv.*
**sage**[2] (sāj) *n.* [< OFr. < L. < *salvus,* safe: it reputedly had
healing powers]  **1.** any of various plants of the mint
family, as the **scarlet sage,** with bright red flowers, or the
**garden sage,** with leaves dried for seasoning meats, etc.  **2.**
*same as* SAGEBRUSH
**sage·brush** (-brush') *n.* any of certain plants of the composite family, common in dry, alkaline areas of the western
U.S.; esp., the **big sagebrush,** with small, aromatic leaves
and minute flower heads
**sage grouse** a large grouse of sagebrush plains of western
N. America: also, esp. for the female, **sage hen**
**Sag·i·naw** (sag'ə nô') [< Ojibway village name, lit., at the
mouth of a river] city in EC Mich.: pop. 78,000
**Sag·it·ta·ri·us** (saj'i ter'ē əs) [L., archer]  **1.** a large S constellation in the Milky Way  **2.** the ninth sign of the zodiac:
see ZODIAC, illus.
**sag·it·tate** (saj'ə tāt') *adj.* [< ModL. < L. *sagitta,* arrow]
in the shape of an arrowhead, as some leaves
**sa·go** (sā'gō) *n., pl.* -**gos** [Malay *sāgū*]  **1.** an edible starch
prepared from certain palm trees and other plants  **2.** a
palm tree yielding sago: also **sago palm**
**sa·gua·ro** (sə gwä'rō, -wä'-) *n., pl.* -**ros** [MexSp. < native
name] a giant cactus with a thick, spiny stem and white
flowers, native to the southwestern U.S. and northern Mexico: also **sa·hua'ro** (-wä'-)
**Sa·ha·ra** (sə har'ə, -her'ə, -hä'rə) [Ar. *ṣahrā,* a desert] vast
desert region in N Africa —**Sa·ha'ran** *adj.*
**Sa·hel** (sä hel') region in NC Africa, south of the Sahara,
characterized by periodic drought
**sa·hib** (sä'ib, -hib, -ēb, -hēb) *n.* [< Hindi < Ar. *ṣāhib,*
master] sir; master: title formerly used by natives in
colonial India when speaking to or of a European
**said** (sed) *pt. & pp. of* SAY —*adj.* aforesaid; named before
**Sai·gon** (sī gän') seaport in S Vietnam; capital of the former
South Vietnam: now called **Ho Chi Minh City**
**sail** (sāl) *n.* [OE. *segl*]  **1.** any of the shaped sheets of canvas,
etc. spread to catch the wind and so drive certain vessels
forward  **2.** sails collectively  **3.** a sailing vessel or vessels
**4.** a trip in a ship or boat  **5.** anything like a sail, as an arm
of a windmill —*vi.*  **1.** to be moved forward by means of
sails or a propeller, etc.  **2.** to travel on water  **3.** to begin a
trip by water  **4.** to manage a sailboat, as in racing  **5.** to
glide through the air  **6.** to move smoothly, like a ship sailing  **7.** [Colloq.] to move quickly  **8.** [Colloq.] to throw oneself (*into*) with energy  **9.** [Colloq.] to attack or criticize
someone severely (with *into*) —*vt.*  **1.** to move through or
upon (a body of water) in a boat or ship  **2.** to manage or
navigate (a boat or ship) —**in sail** with sails set —**make sail
1.** to spread out a ship's sail  **2.** to begin a trip by water
—**set sail  1.** to hoist the sails for departure  **2.** to begin a
trip by water —**take in sail** to lower sails —**under sail** sailing; with sails set —**sail'ing** *n., adj.*
**sail·boat** (-bōt') *n.* a boat having a sail or sails
**sail·cloth** (-klôth', -kläth') *n.* canvas or other cloth used in
making sails, tents, etc.
**sail·er** (-ər) *n.* a ship or boat, esp. one with sails
**sail·fish** (-fish') *n., pl.* -**fish', -fish'es:** see FISH A large, tropical marine fish with a large, sail-
like dorsal fin and a sword-shaped
upper jaw
**sail·or** (-ər) *n.*  **1.** a person who
makes his living by sailing; seaman
**2.** *a)* an enlisted man in the navy
*b)* anyone in the navy  **3.** a voyager
on water, as affected by seasickness
[a bad *sailor*]  **4.** a straw hat with a
low, flat crown and flat brim
—**sail'or·ing** *n.* —**sail'or·ly** *adj.*
**sail·plane** (sāl'plān') *n.* a light
glider designed for soaring —*vi.*
-**planed', -plan'ing** to fly a sailplane

SAILFISH
(to 11 ft. long)

**saint** (sānt) *n.* [< OFr. < LL. <
L. *sanctus,* holy]  **1.** a holy person
**2.** a person who is unusually charitable, patient, etc.  **3.**
[*pl.*] those, esp. holy persons, who have died and are believed to be with God  **4.** *a)* in the New Testament, any
Christian *b)* [S-] a member of any religious group calling
themselves *Saints*  **5.** in certain Christian churches, a
deceased person officially recognized as having lived an exceptionally holy life —*vt.* to make a saint of  For names of

saints see the given name (as JOHN, PAUL, etc.); for other
terms, see ST. & ff. —**saint'hood'** *n.*
**Saint Agnes's Eve** the night of January 20, when a girl's
future husband was supposed to be revealed to her if she
performed certain rites
**Saint Ber·nard** (bər närd') a large, reddish-brown and
white dog of a breed formerly trained by monks at the St.
Bernard hospice, in the Swiss Alps, to rescue travelers
**saint·ed** (sān'tid) *adj.*  **1.** of or fit for a saint; saintly  **2.** regarded as a saint  **3.** holy; sacred
**Saint El·mo's fire** (or **light**) (el'mōz) [after *St. Elmo,* patron saint of sailors] a visible electric discharge from tips of
masts, spires, trees, etc. as during electrical storms
**Saint-Ex·u·pé·ry** (san teg zü pā rē'), **An·toine de** (än
twän' də) 1900–44; Fr. aviator & writer
**Saint-Gau·dens** (sānt gô'd'nz), **Augustus** 1848–1907; U.S.
sculptor, born in Ireland
**Saint Johns·wort** (jänz'wurt') [< ?] any of various plants
with usually yellow flowers and spotted leaves
**saint·ly** (sānt'lē) *adj.* -**li·er, -li·est** like or suitable for a
saint —**saint'li·ness** *n.*
**Saint Patrick's Day** March 17, observed by the Irish in
honor of Saint Patrick, the patron saint of Ireland
**Saint-Saëns** (san säns'), **Charles Ca·mille** (shárl ká mē'y')
1835–1921; Fr. composer
**Saint Valentine's Day** February 14, observed in honor of a
martyr of the 3d cent. and, coincidentally, as a day for
sending valentines to sweethearts, etc.
**Saint Vi·tus' dance** (vī'təs) [after *St. Vitus,* patron saint of
persons having chorea] *same as* CHOREA
**saith** (seth; *now also* sā'ith) *archaic* 3d pers. sing., pres.
*indic., of* SAY
**sake**[1] (sāk) *n.* [OE. *sacu,* suit at law]  **1.** purpose or reason;
motive [for the *sake* of peace]  **2.** advantage; behalf; benefit
[for my *sake*] —**for heaven's** (or **gosh** or **Pete's**) **sake!** a
mild exclamation of surprise, annoyance, etc.
**sa·ke**[2] (sä'kē) *n.* [Jap.] a Japanese alcoholic beverage made
from fermented rice: also sp. **sa'ki**
**Sa·kha·lin** (sä khä lēn'; *E.* sak'ə lēn') island of the
U.S.S.R., off the E coast of Siberia
**sal** (sal) *n.* [L.] *Pharmacy* salt
**sa·laam** (sə läm') *n.* [Ar. *salām,* peace]  **1.** a Moslem greeting ("peace")  **2.** an Oriental greeting made by bowing low
with the palm of the right hand placed on the forehead  **3.**
a greeting showing respect —*vt., vi.* to make a salaam
**sal·a·ble** (sāl'ə b'l) *adj.* that can be sold; marketable
**sa·la·cious** (sə lā'shəs) *adj.* [< L. < *salire,* to leap]  **1.**
lecherous; lustful  **2.** erotically stimulating; pornographic
—**sa·la'cious·ly** *adv.* —**sa·la'cious·ness, sa·lac'i·ty** (-las'ə
tē) *n.*
**sal·ad** (sal'əd) *n.* [< MFr. < Pr. < L. pp. of *salare,* to salt
< *sal,* salt]  **1.** a dish, usually cold, of vegetables, usually
raw, or fruits, served with a dressing, or molded in gelatin
**2.** any green plant or herb used for such a dish
**salad bar** a bar or counter in a restaurant at which one may
pick out vegetables to make a salad
**salad days** time of youth and inexperience
**salad dressing** a preparation of olive oil or other vegetable
oil, vinegar, spices, etc. served with a salad
**sal·a·man·der** (sal'ə man'dər) *n.* [< OFr. < L. *salaman-
dra* < Gr.]  **1.** a mythological reptile .that was said to live
in fire  **2.** any of a group of tailed amphibians related to
frogs and toads, with a soft, moist skin
**sa·la·mi** (sə lä'mē) *n.* [It., pl., preserved meat, ult. < L.
*sal,* salt] a highly spiced, salted sausage, orig. Italian, of
pork and beef, or of beef alone
**sal ammoniac** *same as* AMMONIUM CHLORIDE
**sal·a·ried** (sal'ə rēd) *adj.*  **1.** receiving a salary  **2.** yielding
a salary [a *salaried* position]
**sal·a·ry** (sal'ə rē) *n., pl.* -**ries** [< L. *salarium,* orig., part of
a Roman soldier's pay for buying salt < *sal,* salt] a fixed
payment at regular intervals for services, esp. when clerical
or professional
**sale** (sāl) *n.* [< OE. < ON. *sala*]  **1.** a selling; the exchange
of property or a service for an agreed sum of money or its
equivalent  **2.** opportunity to sell; market  **3.** an auction  **4.**
a selling at prices lower than usual  **5.** [*pl.*] receipts in business  **6.** [*pl.*] the work, department, etc. of selling [a job in
*sales*] —**for** (or **on**) **sale** to be sold
**sale·a·ble** (sāl'ə b'l) *adj. same as* SALABLE
**Sa·lem** (sā'ləm) [< Biblical place name]  **1.** capital of
Oreg., in the NW part: pop. 89,000  **2.** city on the NE
coast of Mass.: suburb of Boston: pop. 38,000
**sal·e·ra·tus** (sal'ə rāt'əs) *n.* [ModL. *sal aeratus,* aerated
salt] sodium bicarbonate; baking soda
**Sa·ler·no** (sä ler'nô; *E.* sə lur'nō) seaport in S Italy, on the
Tyrrhenian Sea: pop. 151,000
**sales·clerk** (sālz'klurk') *n.* a person employed to sell goods
in a store
**sales·man** (sālz'mən) *n., pl.* -**men  1.** a man who is a salesclerk  **2.** a traveling agent who sells goods or services
**sales·man·ship** (-ship') *n.* the skill or technique of selling

**sales·per·son** (sālz'pur's'n) *n.* a person employed to sell goods; esp., a salesclerk —**sales'peo'ple** (-pē'p'l) *n.pl.*

**sales resistance** resistance of potential customers to efforts aimed at getting them to buy

**sales·room** (-rōōm') *n.* a room in which goods are shown and offered for sale

**sales talk** any persuasion or argument used in trying to sell something or to persuade one to do something

**sales tax** a tax on sales and, sometimes, services

**sales·wom·an** (-wōōm'ən) *n., pl.* **-wom'en** (-wim'in) a woman salesclerk: also **sales'la'dy** (-lā'dē), *pl.* **-dies**

**Sal·ic law** (sal'ik, sā'lik) [< ML. < LL. *Salii,* a tribe of Franks] **1.** a code of laws of Germanic tribes, or any of these laws **2.** a law excluding women from succession to the throne in the French and Spanish monarchies

**sa·li·cy·late** (sə lis'ə lāt'; sal'ə sil'āt, -it) *n.* any salt or ester of salicylic acid

**sal·i·cyl·ic acid** (sal'ə sil'ik) [< Fr. *salicyle* (radical of the acid) < L. *salix,* willow + -IC] a white, crystalline compound, $C_7H_6O_3$, used in making aspirin, as a food preservative, etc.

**sa·lient** (sāl'yənt, sā'lē ənt) *adj.* [< L. prp. of *salire,* to leap] **1.** leaping **2.** pointing outward; projecting **3.** standing out; noticeable; prominent —*n.* **1.** the part of a battle line, fort, etc. projecting farthest toward the enemy **2.** a projecting angle, part, etc. —**sa'lience** *n.* —**sa'lien·cy** *n., pl.* **-cies** —**sa'lient·ly** *adv.*

**Sa·li·nas** (sə lē'nəs) [ult. < L. *salina,* salty < *sal,* salt] city in WC Calif., near San Jose: pop. 80,000

**sa·line** (sā'līn; *for n. 1 also* sə lēn') *adj.* [< L. < *sal,* salt] of, like, or containing salt; salty —*n.* **1.** a salt lick, salt marsh, etc. **2.** a salt of an alkali metal or of magnesium, used as a cathartic **3.** a saline solution —**sa·lin·i·ty** (sə lin'ə tē) *n.*

**Salis·bur·y** (sôlz'ber'ē, -bə rē) **1.** city in SC England: noted for its 13th-cent. cathedral: pop. 36,000 **2.** capital of Zimbabwe, in the NE part: pop. 385,000

**Salisbury,** 3d Marquess of, (*Robert Arthur Talbot Gascoyne-Cecil*) 1830–1903; Eng. statesman

**Salisbury steak** *same as* HAMBURGER (sense 2)

**sa·li·va** (sə lī'və) *n.* [L.] the thin, watery, slightly viscid fluid secreted by the salivary glands: it aids digestion by moistening and softening food, and contains an enzyme that converts starch to dextrin and maltose

**sal·i·var·y** (sal'ə ver'ē) *adj.* of or secreting saliva

**sal·i·vate** (-vāt') *vt.* **-vat'ed, -vat'ing** [< L. pp. of *salivare*] to produce an excessive flow of saliva in —*vi.* to secrete saliva —**sal'i·va'tion** *n.*

**Salk** (sôlk), **Jonas E(dward)** 1914– ; U.S. bacteriologist: developed a vaccine for injection to prevent poliomyelitis

**sal·low** (sal'ō) *adj.* [OE. *salu*] of a sickly, pale-yellowish complexion —*vt.* to make sallow —**sal'low·ness** *n.*

**Sal·ly** (sal'ē) [dim. of SARAH] a feminine name

**sal·ly** (sal'ē) *n., pl.* **-lies** [MFr. *saillie,* ult. < L. *salire,* to leap] **1.** a sudden rushing forth, as of troops to attack besiegers **2.** any sudden start into activity **3.** a quick witticism; quip **4.** an excursion; jaunt —*vi.* **-lied, -ly·ing 1.** to make a sally **2.** *a)* to go outdoors *b)* to set out on a trip Used with *forth* or *out*

**sal·ma·gun·di** (sal'mə gun'dē) *n.* [Fr. *salmigondis* < ? It. *salame conditi,* pickled meat] **1.** a dish of chopped meat, eggs, onions, etc. **2.** any mixture

**salm·on** (sam'ən) *n., pl.* **-on, -ons:** see PLURAL, II, D, 2 [< MFr. < OFr. *saumon* < L. *salmo*] **1.** any of various bony fishes; specif., any of several varieties of game and food fishes of the N Hemisphere, with silver scales and flesh that is pink when cooked: salmon spawn in fresh water but usually live in salt water **2.** yellowish pink: also **salmon pink**

**sal·mo·nel·la** (sal'mə nel'ə) *n., pl.* **-nel'lae** (-ē), **-nel'la, -nel'las** [ModL.: after D. *Salmon* (d. 1914), U.S. veterinarian] any of certain rod-shaped bacteria that cause various diseases, as typhoid fever, food poisoning, etc.

**Sa·lo·me** (sə lō'mē; *occas.* sal'ə mā') traditional name of the stepdaughter of Herod Antipas: her dancing pleased Herod so much that he granted her request for the head of John the Baptist: Matt. 14:8

**sa·lon** (sə län', sal'än; *Fr.* sá lōn') *n.* [Fr.: see SALOON] **1.** a large reception hall **2.** a drawing room of a French private home **3.** a regular gathering of distinguished persons, writers, artists, etc. in a celebrity's home **4.** *a)* an art gallery *b)* an art exhibition **5.** a shop or business place for performing some personal service /beauty *salon*/

**Sa·lo·ni·ka** (sal'ə nē'kə, -nī'-; sə län'i kə) **1.** seaport in N Greece, on the Gulf of Salonika: pop. 251,000 **2. Gulf of,** N arm of the Aegean Sea Also **sp. Salonica**

**sa·loon** (sə lōōn') *n.* [Fr. *salon* < It. *sala,* a hall] **1.** any large room or hall for receptions, exhibitions, etc.; specif., the main social cabin of a passenger ship **2.** a place where alcoholic drinks are sold to be drunk on the premises: an old-fashioned term

**sa·loon·keep·er** (-kēp'ər) *n.* a person who operates a saloon (sense 2)

**sal·sa** (säl'sə) *n.* [AmSp. < Sp., sauce] a kind of Latin American dance music of Afro-Cuban and Puerto Rican origin, influenced by jazz and rock

**sal·si·fy** (sal'sə fē', -fī') *n.* [< Fr. < It. *sassefrica*] a plant of the composite family, with white, edible, fleshy roots

**sal soda** crystallized sodium carbonate

**salt** (sôlt, sält) *n.* [OE. *sealt*] **1.** sodium chloride, NaCl, a white, crystalline substance found in natural beds, in sea water, etc., and used for seasoning and preserving food, etc. **2.** a chemical compound derived from an acid by replacing hydrogen, wholly or partly, with a metal or an electropositive radical **3.** that which lends tang or piquancy, as pungent wit **4.** *same as* SALTCELLAR **5.** [*pl.*] mineral salts used as a cathartic (as **Epsom salts**), to soften bath water (**bath salts**), as a restorative (**smelling salts**), etc. **6.** [Colloq.] a sailor —*adj.* **1.** containing salt **2.** preserved with salt **3.** tasting or smelling of salt **4.** *a)* flooded with salt water *b)* growing in salt water —*vt.* **1.** to sprinkle, season, or preserve with salt **2.** to treat or provide with salt **3.** to give tang to **4.** to put minerals in (a mine), oil in (a well), etc. so as to deceive prospective buyers —**salt away** (or **down**) **1.** to pack and preserve with salt **2.** [Colloq.] to store or save (money, etc.) —**with a grain** (or **pinch**) **of salt** with allowance or reserve; skeptically —**worth one's salt** worth one's wages, etc. —**salt'er** *n.* —**salt'ish** *adj.* —**salt'like'** *adj.* —**salt'ness** *n.*

**SALT** (sôlt, sält) Strategic Arms Limitation Talks

**salt-and-pep·per** (-'n pep'ər) *adj. same as* PEPPER-AND-SALT

**salt·box** (sôlt'bäks') *n.* **1.** a box for salt, with a sloping lid **2.** a house shaped like this, with two stories in front and one at the rear and a gable roof Also **salt box**

**salt·cel·lar** (-sel'ər) *n.* [< ME. < *salt,* salt + MFr. *salière,* saltcellar] a small dish or shaker for salt at the table

**salt·ine** (sôl tēn') *n.* [SALT + -INE⁴] a flat, crisp cracker sprinkled with salt

**Salt Lake City** capital of Utah, near the SE end of the Great Salt Lake: pop. 163,000 (met. area 935,000)

**salt lick 1.** an exposed natural deposit of rock salt which animals come to lick **2.** a block of rock salt placed in a pasture for cattle, etc. to lick

**salt marsh** grassland over which salt water flows at intervals

**salt pork** pork cured in salt

**salt·shak·er** (sôlt'shā'kər) *n.* a container for salt, with a perforated top for shaking out the salt

**salt·wa·ter** (-wôt'ər, -wät'ər) *adj.* of, having to do with, or living in salt water or the sea

**salt·works** (-wurks') *n., pl.* **-works'** a place where salt is made, as by evaporation of natural brines

**salt·wort** (-wurt') *n.* any of a genus of plants of the goosefoot family, growing on seashores or saline soils

**salt·y** (sôl'tē) *adj.* **salt'i·er, salt'i·est 1.** of, tasting of, or containing salt **2.** smelling of or suggesting the sea **3.** *a)* sharp; piquant *b)* coarse or earthy *c)* cross or caustic —**salt'i·ly** *adv.* —**salt'i·ness** *n.*

**sa·lu·bri·ous** (sə lōō'brē əs) *adj.* [L. *salubris* < *salus,* health] promoting health or welfare; healthful, wholesome, salutary, etc. —**sa·lu'bri·ous·ly** *adv.* —**sa·lu'bri·ty** (-brə tē), **sa·lu'bri·ous·ness** *n.*

**sal·u·tar·y** (sal'yoo ter'ē) *adj.* [< Fr. < L. < *salus* (gen. *salutis*), health] **1.** promoting health; healthful **2.** promoting some good purpose; beneficial —**sal'u·tar'i·ly** *adv.*

**sal·u·ta·tion** (sal'yoo tā'shən) *n.* [< MFr. < L. < pp. of *salutare:* see SALUTE] **1.** the act of greeting, addressing, etc. by gestures or words **2.** certain words serving as a greeting or as the opening of a letter, as "Dear Sir"

**sa·lu·ta·to·ri·an** (sə lōōt'ə tôr'ē ən) *n.* in some schools and colleges, the student, usually second highest in scholastic rank, who gives the salutatory

**sa·lu·ta·to·ry** (sə lōōt'ə tôr'ē) *adj.* of or expressing a salutation —*n., pl.* **-ries** an opening address, esp. at a school or college commencement exercise

**sa·lute** (sə lōōt') *vt.* **-lut'ed, -lut'ing** [< L. *salutare* < *salus:* see SALUTARY] **1.** to greet in a friendly way, as by bowing, tipping the hat, etc. **2.** to honor ceremonially and officially by firing cannon, raising the right hand to the forehead, etc. **3.** to present itself to, as if in greeting **4.** to acknowledge with praise; commend —*vi.* to make a salute —*n.* **1.** an act, remark, or gesture made in saluting **2.** *Mil.* the position of the hand, etc. assumed in saluting

**sal·va·ble** (sal'və b'l) *adj.* that can be saved or salvaged

**Sal·va·dor** (sal'və dôr'; *Port.* säl'və dôr') seaport in E Brazil, on the Atlantic: pop. 1,001,000

**Sal·va·do·ran** (sal'və dôr'ən) *adj.* of El Salvador, its people, or culture —*n.* a native or inhabitant of El Salvador Also **Sal'va·do'ri·an** (-dôr'ē ən)

**sal·vage** (sal'vij) *n.* [Fr. < MFr. < *salver,* to SAVE¹] **1.** *a)* the rescue of a ship and cargo at sea from fire, shipwreck, etc. *b)* compensation paid for such rescue *c)* the ship or cargo so rescued *d)* the bringing up of a sunken ship or its cargo by divers, caissons, etc. **2.** *a)* the saving of any goods, etc. from destruction or waste *b)* goods, etc. so saved *c)* the proceeds from sale of such goods, etc. as in settling insurance claims —*vt.* **-vaged, -vag·ing** to save or rescue from shipwreck, fire, flood, etc.; engage or succeed in the salvage of (ships, goods, etc.) —**sal'vage·a·bil'i·ty** *n.* —**sal'vage·a·ble** *adj.* —**sal'vag·er** *n.*

**sal·va·tion** (sal vā'shən) *n.* [< OFr. < LL. < L. pp. of *salvare,* to SAVE¹] **1.** a saving or being saved **2.** a person or thing that saves or rescues **3.** *Theol.* spiritual rescue from the consequences of sin —**sal·va'tion·al** *adj.*

**Salvation Army** a Christian organization that works to bring religion and help to the very poor

**salve¹** (sav) *n.* [OE. *sealf*] **1.** any soothing or healing ointment applied to wounds, burns, sores, etc. **2.** anything that soothes or heals; balm —*vt.* **salved, salv'ing** to soothe

**salve²** (salv) *vt.* **salved, salv'ing** *same as* SALVAGE

**sal·ver** (sal'vər) *n.* [< Fr. < Sp. *salva* < *salvar,* to taste (so as to prove food wholesome) < L. *salvare,* to SAVE¹] a tray on which something is served or presented

**sal·vi·a** (sal'vē ə) *n.* [ModL., genus name < L.] *same as* SAGE² (sense 1)

**sal·vo** (sal'vō) *n., pl.* **-vos, -voes** [< It. < L. *salve,* hail!] **1.** a discharge of a number of guns in succession or at the same time, either in salute or at a target **2.** the release of a load of bombs or the launching of several rockets at the same time **3.** a burst of cheers or applause

**sal vo·la·ti·le** (vō lat''l ē') [ModL., volatile salt] ammonium carbonate, used in smelling salts

**Sal·ween** (sal wēn') river in SE Asia, flowing from Tibet through Burma into the Indian Ocean

**Salz·burg** (zälts'boorkh; *E.* sôlz'bərg) city in C Austria: pop. 108,000

**SAM** (sam) surface-to-air missile

**Sam.** Samuel

**Sa·mar** (sä'mär) island of the E Philippines, southeast of Luzon: 5,181 sq. mi.

**sam·a·ra** (sam'ər ə, sə mer'ə) *n.* [ModL. < L., elm seed] a dry, winged, seeded fruit, as of the maple

**Sa·mar·i·a** (sə mer'ē ə, -mar'-) in ancient times, **1.** N kingdom of the Hebrews; Israel **2.** its capital **3.** district of Palestine between Galilee & Judea

**Sa·mar·i·tan** (-ə t'n) *n.* **1.** a native or inhabitant of Samaria **2.** *see* GOOD SAMARITAN —*adj.* of Samaria or its people

**sa·mar·i·um** (sə mer'ē əm, -mar'-) *n.* [ModL. < *samarskite,* a mineral, ult. < Col. *Samarski,* Russ. mining official] a metallic chemical element of the rare-earth group: symbol, Sm; at. wt., 150.35; at. no., 62

**SAMARAS** (A, maple; B, elm; C, ash; D, basswood)

**Sam·ar·kand** (sam'ər kand'; *Russ.* sä mär känt') city in E Uzbek S.S.R.: pop. 267,000

**sam·ba** (sam'bə, säm'-) *n.* [Port., prob. of Afr. origin] **1.** a Brazilian dance of African origin **2.** music for this dance —*vi.* to dance the samba

**Sam Browne belt** (sam' broun') [after 19th-c. Brit. Gen. *Samuel J. Browne*] a military officer's belt with a diagonal strap across the right shoulder

**same** (sām) *adj.* [ON. *samr*] **1.** being the very one; identical **2.** alike in kind, quality, amount, etc.; corresponding **3.** unchanged; not different [he looks the *same*] **4.** before-mentioned; just spoken of —*pron.* the same person or thing —*adv.* **1.** in the same way **2.** nevertheless The *adj.* & *pron.* are usually used with *the, this,* or *that;* the *adv.,* with *the* —**same'ness** *n.*

**sam·i·sen** (sam'ə sen') *n.* [Jap. < Chin. *san hsien,* three strings] a three-stringed Japanese musical instrument, somewhat like a banjo

**sam·ite** (sam'īt, sā'mīt) *n.* [< MFr. < ML. < MGr. < *hexamitos,* woven with six threads] a heavy silk fabric interwoven with gold or silver threads, worn in the Middle Ages

**Sa·mo·a** (sə mō'ə) group of islands in the South Pacific, north of Tonga: seven of these islands constitute a possession (**American Samoa**) of the U.S., 76 sq. mi., pop. 28,000: see also WESTERN SAMOA —**Sa·mo'an** *adj., n.*

**Sa·mos** (sā'mäs; *Gr.* sä'mồs) Gr. island in the Aegean, off the W coast of Turkey —**Sa·mi·an** (sā'mē ən) *adj., n.*

**Sam·o·thrace** (sam'ə thrās') Gr. island in the NE Aegean

**sam·o·var** (sam'ə vär', säm'ə vär') *n.* [Russ., lit., self-boiler] a Russian metal urn with an internal tube for heating water for tea

**Sam·o·yed, Sam·o·yede** (sam'ə yed') *n.* [Russ.] **1.** any of a Uralic people of Siberia **2.** their language **3.** any of a strong breed of Siberian dog, with a thick, white coat —*adj.* of the Samoyeds or their language: also **Sam'o·yed'ic**

**samp** (samp) *n.* [< Algonquian *nasaump,* softened by water] coarse cornmeal or a porridge of this

**SAMOVAR**

**sam·pan** (sam'pan) *n.* [Chin. *san-pan* < ? *san,* three + *pan,* a plank] any of various small boats used in China and Japan, rowed with a scull from the stern, and often having a sail and a small cabin formed of mats

**sam·ple** (sam'p'l) *n.* [< OFr.: see EXAMPLE] **1.** a part, piece, or item that shows what the whole thing or group is like; specimen or example [samples of wallpaper, a *sample* of his humor] **2.** *Statistics* a selected part of the population studied to gain knowledge of the whole —*vt.* **-pled, -pling** to take or test a sample of

**sam·pler** (-plər) *n.* **1.** a person who prepares or tests samples **2.** a cloth embroidered with designs, mottoes, etc. in different stitches

**Sam·son** (sam's'n) [LL. < Gr. < Heb. *shimshōn* < ? *shemesh,* sun] *Bible* an Israelite noted for his great strength: betrayed by Delilah: Judges 13–16

**Sam·u·el** (sam'yoo wəl, sam'yool) [LL. < Gr. < Heb. *shĕmū'ēl,* lit., name of God] **1.** a masculine name: dim. *Sam, Sammy* **2.** *Bible a)* a Hebrew judge and prophet *b)* either of two books (I Samuel, II Samuel) telling of Samuel, Saul, and David

**sam·u·rai** (sam'ə rī') *n., pl.* **-rai'** [Jap.] **1.** a member of a military class in feudal Japan **2.** a Japanese army officer or member of the military caste

**‡-san** (sän) [Jap.] a Japanese honorific suffix added to names, titles, etc.

**San An·ge·lo** (san an'jə lō') [after *Santa Angela,* a Mex. nun] city in WC Tex.: pop. 73,000

**San An·to·ni·o** (san' ən tō'nē ō', an-) [Sp., St. Anthony, 13th-c. Franciscan friar of Padua] city in SC Tex.: site of the Alamo: pop. 785,000 (met. area 1,070,000)

**san·a·to·ri·um** (san'ə tôr'ē əm) *n., pl.* **-ri·ums, -ri·a** (-ə) [ModL. < LL. *sanatorius,* giving health < L. *sanare,* to heal] *chiefly Brit. var. of* SANITARIUM

**San Ber·nar·di·no** (san' bur'nər dē'nō, -nə-) [Sp., St. Bernardine (of Siena)] city in S Calif., near Los Angeles: pop. 118,000

**sanc·ti·fied** (saŋk'tə fīd') *adj.* **1.** made holy; consecrated **2.** sanctimonious

**sanc·ti·fy** (saŋk'tə fī') *vt.* **-fied', -fy'ing** [< OFr. < LL. *sanctificare:* see SAINT & -FY] **1.** to make holy; specif., *a)* to set apart as holy; consecrate *b)* to make free from sin; purify **2.** to make binding or inviolable by sanction —**sanc'ti·fi·ca'tion** *n.* —**sanc'ti·fi'er** *n.*

**sanc·ti·mo·ni·ous** (saŋk'tə mō'nē əs) *adj.* pretending to be very pious; affecting sanctity or righteousness —**sanc'ti·mo'ni·ous·ly** *adv.* —**sanc'ti·mo'ni·ous·ness** *n.*

**sanc·ti·mo·ny** (saŋk'tə mō'nē) *n.* [< OFr. < L. *sanctimonia* < *sanctus,* holy] affected piety or righteousness

**sanc·tion** (saŋk'shən) *n.* [< Fr. < L. < *sanctus,* holy] **1.** the confirming or ratifying of an action by authority; authorization **2.** support; approval **3.** something that gives binding force to a law, as the penalty for breaking it or a reward for carrying it out **4.** something, as a moral principle or influence, that makes a rule of conduct, etc. binding **5.** [*usually pl.*] a boycott, blockade, or similar coercive measure, as against one nation by others to enforce international law —*vt.* to give sanction to; specif., *a)* to ratify or confirm *b)* to authorize or permit —**sanc'tion·a·ble** *adj.*

**sanc·ti·ty** (saŋk'tə tē) *n., pl.* **-ties** [< L. < *sanctus,* holy] **1.** saintliness or holiness **2.** a being sacred or inviolable **3.** anything held sacred

**sanc·tu·ar·y** (saŋk'choo wer'ē) *n., pl.* **-ies** [< MFr. < LL. < L. *sanctus,* sacred] **1.** a holy place, as a building set aside for worship; specif., *a)* the ancient Temple at Jerusalem *b)* any church, temple, etc. *c)* a holy place within a church, temple, etc., as the part around the altar, the holy of holies, etc. **2.** a place of refuge or protection **3.** refuge; immunity from punishment **4.** a reservation where animals or birds may not be hunted or trapped

**sanc·tum** (saŋk'təm) *n., pl.* **-tums, -ta** (-tə) [L., neut. of *sanctus,* holy] **1.** a sacred place **2.** a study or private room where one is not to be disturbed

**sanctum sanc·to·rum** (saŋk tôr'əm) [LL.] **1.** *same as* HOLY OF HOLIES **2.** a place of utmost privacy

**sand** (sand) *n.* [OE.] **1.** loose, gritty grains of disintegrated rock, as on beaches, in deserts, etc. **2.** [*usually pl.*] an area of sand; beach **3.** the sand in an hourglass **4.** [*pl.*] moments of time **5.** [Slang] grit; courage —*vt.* **1.** to sprinkle, fill, or mix with sand 2. to smooth or polish with sand or sandpaper —**sand'ed** adj. —**sand'er** n.

**Sand** (sand; Fr. sänd), **George** (pseud. of Amandine Aurore Lucie Dupin, Baronne Dudevant) 1804–76; Fr. novelist

**san·dal**[1] (san'd'l) n. [< L. < Gr. dim. of sandalon] 1. a kind of footwear consisting of a sole fastened in various ways to the foot by straps over the instep or toes, or around the ankles 2. any of various low slippers —**san'daled, san'dalled** adj.

**san·dal**[2] (san'd'l) n. same as SANDALWOOD

**san·dal·wood** (-wood') n. [< MFr. < ML., ult. < Sans. candana] 1. the hard, sweet-smelling heartwood of any of certain Asiatic trees, used for carving and cabinetmaking or burned as incense 2. any tree yielding such wood

**sand·bag** (sand'bag') n. 1. a bag filled with sand and used for ballast, in fortifications, for levees against floods, etc. 2. a small, sand-filled bag used as a bludgeon —vt. -**bagged'**, -**bag'ging** 1. to place sandbags in or around 2. to hit with a sandbag 3. [Colloq.] to force into doing something —**sand'bag'ger** n.

**sand bar** a ridge or narrow shoal of sand formed in a river or along a shore by the action of currents or tides

**sand·blast** (-blast') n. 1. a current of air or steam carrying sand at a high velocity, used in etching glass and in cleaning surfaces as of metals, stone, etc. 2. the machine used to apply this blast —vt. to engrave, clean, etc. with a sandblast —**sand'blast'er** n.

**sand·box** (-bäks') n. a box containing sand for children to play in

**Sand·burg** (sand'bərg, san'-), **Carl** 1878–1967; U.S. poet, writer, & ballad collector

**sand flea** 1. any of various crustaceans found on sandy sea beaches, that jump like fleas 2. same as CHIGGER

**sand·hog** (sand'hôg', -häg') n. a laborer in underground or underwater construction projects, working under compressed air, as in a caisson or tunnel

**San Di·e·go** (san' dē ā'gō) [after San Diego (St. Didacus), 15th-cent. Sp. friar] seaport in S Calif., on the Pacific: pop. 876,000 (met. area 1,860,000)

**sand·lot** (sand'lät') adj. having to do with games, esp. baseball, played by amateurs, orig. on a sandy lot or field —**sand'lot'ter** n.

**S & M, s & m** sexual sadism and masochism

**sand·man** (-man') n. in fairy tales, etc. a person supposed to make children sleepy by dusting sand in their eyes

**sand·pa·per** (-pā'pər) n. a strong paper with sand glued on one side, used for smoothing and polishing —vt. to smooth or polish with sandpaper

**sand·pip·er** (-pī'pər) n., pl. -**pip'ers**, -**pip'er**: see PLURAL, II, D, 1 a small shore bird with a long, soft-tipped bill

**San·dra** (san'drə, sän'-) [< Alexandra, fem. of ALEXANDER] a feminine name

**sand·stone** (sand'stōn') n. a common sedimentary rock much used for building, composed largely of sand grains, mainly quartz, cemented together by silica, etc.

**sand·storm** (-stôrm') n. a windstorm in which large quantities of sand are blown about

**sand trap** a hollow filled with sand, serving as a hazard on a golf course

**sand·wich** (sand'wich, san'-) n. [< 4th Earl of Sandwich (1718–1792)] two or more slices of bread with a filling of meat, cheese, etc. between them: now sometimes used of a single slice of bread covered with meat, gravy, etc. —vt. to place between other persons, things, materials, etc.

**sandwich man** a man who walks the streets with two signboards hung from his shoulders, front and back

**sand·y** (san'dē) adj. **sand'i·er, sand'i·est** 1. composed of, full of, or covered with sand 2. like sand; gritty, shifting, etc. 3. pale brown or dark yellow [sandy hair] —**sand'i·ness** n.

**sane** (sān) adj. **san'er, san'est** [L. sanus, healthy] 1. having a normal, healthy mind; able to make sound, rational judgments 2. showing good sense; sensible [a sane policy] —**sane'ly** adv. —**sane'ness** n.

**San·for·ize** (san'fə rīz') vt. -**ized'**, -**iz'ing** [from the trademark Sanforized: after Sanford L. Cluett (1874–1968), the inventor] to preshrink (cloth) permanently by a patented process before making garments

**San Fran·cis·co** (san' frən sis'kō) [prob. after St. FRANCIS OF ASSISI] seaport on the coast of C Calif., on an inlet (**San Francisco Bay**) of the Pacific: pop. 679,000 (met. area, incl. Oakland, 3,227,000)

**sang** (saŋ) pt. of SING

**Sang·er** (saŋ'ər), **Margaret** (born Margaret Higgins) 1883–1966; U.S. nurse: leader in birth-control education

**sang-froid** (saŋ'frwä'; Fr. sän frwȧ') n. [Fr., lit., cold blood] cool self-possession or composure

**san·gui·nar·y** (saŋ'gwi ner'ē) adj. [< L. < sanguis: see

ff.] 1. with much bloodshed or killing 2. of or stained with blood 3. bloodthirsty —**san'gui·nar'i·ly** adv. —**san'gui·nar'i·ness** n.

**san·guine** (saŋ'gwin) adj. [< OFr. < L. < sanguis (gen. sanguinis), blood] 1. of the color of blood; ruddy 2. [from medieval notion about those in whom blood is the main humor] cheerful; confident; optimistic —**san'guine·ly** adv. —**san'guine·ness** n.

**san·guin·e·ous** (saŋ gwin'ē əs) adj. [see prec.] same as: 1. SANGUINARY 2. SANGUINE

**San·he·drin** (san hed'rin, -hē'drin) n. [< Heb. < Gr. < syn-, together + hedra, seat] the highest court and council of the ancient Jewish nation, having religious and civic functions

**san·i·tar·i·um** (san'ə ter'ē əm) n., pl. -**i·ums**, -**i·a** (-ə) [ModL. < L. sanitas, health] a nursing home, hospital, etc. for the care of invalids or convalescents, esp. one for treating a specific disease or disorder

**san·i·tar·y** (san'ə ter'ē) adj. [< Fr. < L. sanitas, health] 1. of health or the rules and conditions of health; esp., promoting health by getting rid of dirt and of things that bring disease 2. free from dirt, etc. that could bring disease; clean; hygienic —**san'i·tar'i·ly** adv. —**san'i·tar'i·ness** n.

**sanitary napkin** an absorbent pad of cotton, etc. worn by women during menstruation

**san·i·ta·tion** (san'ə tā'shən) n. 1. the science and work of bringing about healthful and hygienic conditions 2. drainage and disposal of sewage

**san·i·tize** (san'ə tīz') vt. -**tized'**, -**tiz'ing** to make sanitary, as by sterilizing —**san'i·tiz'er** n.

**san·i·ty** (san'ə tē) n. [< OFr. < L. sanitas, health] 1. the condition of being sane; soundness of mind; mental health 2. soundness of judgment

**San Joa·quin** (san' wô kēn', wä-) [Sp., St. Joachim, reputed father of the Virgin Mary] river in C Calif., flowing south into the Sacramento River

**San Jo·se** (san' hō zā', ə zā') [Sp. San José, St. Joseph] city in WC Calif.: pop. 637,000 (met. area 1,290,000)

**San Jo·sé** (sän' hō se') capital of Costa Rica, in the C part: pop. 203,000

**San Juan** (san' hwän', wôn'; Sp. sän' hwän') [Sp., St. John] capital of Puerto Rico; seaport on the Atlantic: pop. 445,000 (met. area 851,000)

**sank** (saŋk) alt. pt. of SINK

**San Le·an·dro** (san' lē an'drō) [Sp., St. Leander, archbishop of Seville] city in W Calif., on San Francisco Bay: suburb of Oakland: pop. 64,000

**San Ma·ri·no** (sän' mä rē'nô; E. san' mə rē'nō) independent country within E Italy: 23 sq. mi.; pop. 19,000

**San Mar·tín** (sän' mär tēn'), **Jo·sé de** (hô se' de) 1778–1850; S. American revolutionary leader, born in Argentina

**San Ma·te·o** (san' mə tā'ō) [Sp., St. Matthew] city in W Calif.: suburb of San Francisco: pop. 78,000

**sans** (sanz; Fr. sän) prep. [< OFr. sanz (Fr. sans) < L. sine, without] without; lacking

**Sans.** Sanskrit

**San Sal·va·dor** (san sal'və dôr'; Sp. sän säl'vä thôr') 1. capital of El Salvador: pop. 256,000 2. island of the E Bahamas: prob. the place of Columbus' first landing (1492)

**sans-cu·lotte** (sanz'koo lät', -kyoo-) n. [Fr., without breeches] a revolutionary: term of contempt applied by the aristocrats to the republicans in the French Revolution, who wore pantaloons instead of knee breeches

**san·se·vi·e·ri·a** (san'sə vir'ē ə, -vi ē'rē ə) n. [ModL., after the Prince of Sanseviero (1710–71)] any of a genus of succulent plants with thick, lance-shaped leaves

**San·skrit** (san'skrit) n. [< Sans. samskrta, lit., made together, well arranged] the classical Old Indic literary language: important in the study of comparative Indo-European linguistics —adj. of or written in Sanskrit Also sp. **San'scrit** —**San·skrit'ic** adj. —**San·skrit·ist** n.

**sans-ser·if** (san ser'if) n. [see SANS & SERIF] a style of printing type with no serifs

**San·ta** (san'tə, -tä; for adj., also sän'tä) short for SANTA CLAUS —adj. [Sp. & It., saint, fem.] holy or saint: used in combinations [Santa Maria]

**San·ta An·a** (san'tə an'ə) [Sp., St. Anne] city in SW Calif.: suburb of Los Angeles: pop. 204,000

**San·ta An·na** (sän'tä ä'nä), **An·to·nio Ló·pez de** (än tô'nyô lô'pes de) 1795?–1876; Mex. revolutionist & general

**San·ta Bar·ba·ra** (san'tə bär'bə rə) [Sp., St. Barbara] city on the coast of SW Calif.: pop. 75,000

**Santa Cat·a·li·na** (kat''l ē'nə) island off the SW coast of Calif.: a tourist resort

**San·ta Cla·ra** (kler'ə) [Sp., St. Clare (of Assisi)] city in W Calif., near San Jose: pop. 88,000

**San·ta Claus, San·ta Klaus** (san'tə klôz', -ti) [< Du.

dial. < *Sant Nikolass,* St. NICHOLAS] *Folklore* a fat, white-bearded, jolly old man in a red suit, who distributes gifts at Christmas time: also called **Saint Nicholas, Saint Nick**

**San·ta Fe** (san′tə fā′) [Sp., holy faith] capital of N.Mex., in the NC part: pop. 49,000

**Santa Fe Trail** trade route between Santa Fe, N.Mex., & Independence, Mo.: important from 1821 to 1880

**San·ta Mon·i·ca** (san′tə män′i kə) [Sp., St. Monica, mother of St. AUGUSTINE (of North Africa)] city in SW Calif., on the Pacific: suburb of Los Angeles: pop. 88,000

**San·ta Ro·sa** (san′tə rō′zə) [Sp., holy rose] city in W Calif., north of San Francisco: pop. 83,000

**San·ta·ya·na** (san′tē an′ə, -ä′nə; *Sp.* sän′tä yä′nä), **George** (born *Jorge Augustín Nicolás de Santayana*) 1863–1952; Sp. philosopher & writer in English

**San·ti·a·go** (sän′tē ä′gō; *E.* sän′tē ä′gō) capital of Chile, in the C part: pop. 2,566,000 (met. area 3,120,000)

**san·tim** (sun tēm′) *n., pl.* **san′ti·motch** (-tē mäch′) [Amharic] *see* MONETARY UNITS, table (Ethiopia)

**San·to Do·min·go** (sän′tō dō min′gō; *E.* san′tō dō min′gō) capital of the Dominican Republic; seaport on the S coast: pop., of the district, 823,000

**Saône** (sōn) river in E France, flowing south into the Rhone

**São Pau·lo** (soun pou′loo) city in SE Brazil: pop. 5,902,000

**São To·mé and Prín·ci·pe** (tō mä′ ənd prin′sə pē′) country off the W coast of Africa, comprising two islands (*São Tomé* and *Príncipe*): 372 sq. mi.; pop. 75,000

**sap**[1] (sap) *n.* [OE. sæp] **1.** the juice that circulates through a plant, esp. a woody plant, bearing water, food, etc. **2.** any fluid considered vital to life or health **3.** vigor; energy **4.** [Slang] a stupid person: in full, **sap′head′** (-hed′) —*vt.* **sapped, sap′ping** to drain of sap

**sap**[2] (sap) *n.* [MFr. *sappe,* a hoe < It. *zappe*] a trench for approaching or undermining an enemy position —*vt.* **sapped, sap′ping 1.** to undermine by digging away foundations **2.** to undermine in any way; weaken; exhaust —*vi.* **1.** to dig saps **2.** to approach a position by saps

**sap**[3] (sap) *n.* [prob. orig. contr. < SAPLING] [Slang] a blackjack, short club, etc. —*vt.* **sapped, sap′ping** [Slang] to hit on the head, or knock out, with a sap

**sa·pi·ent** (sā′pē ənt) *adj.* [< L. prp. of *sapere,* to taste, know] full of knowledge; wise; discerning —**sa′pi·ence** *n.*

**sa·pi·en·tial** (sā′pē en′shəl) *adj.* [see prec.] having, providing, or expounding wisdom

**sap·ling** (sap′liŋ) *n.* **1.** a young tree **2.** a youth

**sap·o·dil·la** (sap′ə dil′ə) *n.* [< Sp. < Nahuatl *tzapotl*] **1.** a tropical American evergreen tree, yielding chicle and having a brown fruit with a yellowish pulp **2.** the fruit

**sap·o·na·ceous** (sap′ə nā′shəs) *adj.* [< ModL. < L. *sapo,* soap] soapy or soaplike

**sa·pon·i·fy** (sə pän′ə fī′) *vt.* **-fied′, -fy′ing** [< Fr. < L. *sapo* (gen. *saponis*), soap + *facere,* to make] to convert (a fat) into soap by reaction with an alkali —*vi.* to be made into soap —**sa·pon′i·fi′a·ble** *adj.* —**sa·pon′i·fi·ca′tion** *n.*

**sap·per** (sap′ər) *n.* **1.** a soldier employed in digging saps, laying mines, etc. **2.** a person or thing that saps

**sap·phire** (saf′īr) *n.* [< OFr. < L. < Gr. *sappheiros*] **1.** a hard, transparent precious stone of a clear, deep-blue corundum **2.** its color **3.** a hard variety of corundum, varying in color **4.** a gem made of this —*adj.* deep-blue

**Sap·pho** (saf′ō) 7th cent. B.C.; Gr. lyric poetess of Lesbos —**Sap′phic** (-ik) *adj.*

**Sap·po·ro** (sä′pō rō′) chief city on the island of Hokkaido, Japan: pop. 821,000

**sap·py** (sap′ē) *adj.* **-pi·er, -pi·est 1.** full of sap; juicy **2.** [Slang] foolish; silly; fatuous —**sap′pi·ness** *n.*

**sap·ro·phyte** (sap′rə fīt′) *n.* [< Gr. *sapros,* rotten + -PHYTE] any organism that lives on dead or decaying organic matter, as some fungi —**sap′ro·phyt′ic** (-fit′ik) *adj.*

**sap·suck·er** (sap′suk′ər) *n.* any of several small American woodpeckers that often drill holes in trees for the sap

**sap·wood** (sap′wood′) *n.* the soft wood between the inner bark of a tree and the heartwood, serving to conduct water

**sar·a·band** (sar′ə band′) *n.* [< Fr. < Sp., ult. < Per. *sarband,* kind of dance] **1.** a graceful, stately, slow Spanish dance in triple time **2.** music for this dance

**Sar·a·cen** (sar′ə s'n) *n.* any Arab or any Moslem, esp. at the time of the Crusades —*adj.* of the Saracens

**Sar·ah** (ser′ə, sar′ə) [Heb. *sārāh,* lit., princess] **1.** a feminine name: dim. *Sadie, Sally;* var. *Sara* **2.** *Bible* the wife of Abraham and mother of Isaac: also **Sa·rai** (ser′ī)

**Sa·ra·je·vo** (sä′rä′ye vō̇; *E.* sar′ə yā′vō̇) capital of Bosnia and Hercegovina, in C Yugoslavia: scene of the assassination of an Austrian archduke (June 28, 1914), which precipitated World War I: pop. 175,000

**sa·ran** (sə ran′) *n.* [arbitrary coinage] any of various thermoplastic resins obtained, as by polymerization, from certain vinyl compounds: used in making fabrics, a transparent wrapping material, etc.

**Sa·ra·tov** (sä rä′tôf) city & port in SC European R.S.F.S.R., on the Volga: pop. 758,000

**sar·casm** (sär′kaz'm) *n.* [< LL. < Gr. *sarkazein,* to tear

flesh like dogs < *sarx,* flesh] **1.** a taunting or sneering remark; gibe or jeer, generally ironical **2.** the making of such remarks **3.** sarcastic quality

**sar·cas·tic** (sär kas′tik) *adj.* **1.** of, like, or full of sarcasm; sneering, caustic, etc. **2.** using, or fond of using, sarcasm —**sar·cas′ti·cal·ly** *adv.*

**sar·co·carp** (sär′kə kärp′) *n.* [< Gr. *sarx,* flesh + -CARP] the fleshy part of a stone fruit, as in the plum

**sar·co·ma** (sär kō′mə) *n., pl.* **-mas, -ma·ta** (-mə tə) [ModL. < Gr. < *sarx,* flesh] any of various malignant tumors that begin in connective tissue —**sar·co′ma·to′sis** (-tō′sis) *n.*

**sar·coph·a·gus** (sär käf′ə gəs) *n., pl.* **-gi′** (-jī′), **-gus·es** [L. < Gr. < *sarx,* flesh + *phagein,* to eat: because the limestone orig. used hastened disintegration] a stone coffin, esp. one on display, as in a monumental tomb

**sard** (särd) *n.* [L. *sarda*] a very hard, deep orange-red variety of chalcedony, used in jewelry, etc.

**sar·dine** (sär dēn′) *n., pl.* **-dines′, -dine′:** see PLURAL, II, D, 1 [< MFr. < L. < *sarda,* kind of fish] any of various small ocean fishes preserved in tightly packed cans for eating; specif., *same as* PILCHARD

**Sar·din·i·a** (sär din′ē ə, -din′yə) It. island in the Mediterranean, south of Corsica: c.9,196 sq. mi.: It. name **Sar·de·gna** (sär dā′nyä) —**Sar·din′i·an** *adj., n.*

**sar·don·ic** (sär dän′ik) *adj.* [< Fr. < L. < Gr. < *sardanios,* bitter, scornful] disdainfully or bitterly sneering or sarcastic *[a sardonic smile]* —**sar·don′i·cal·ly** *adv.*

**sar·do·nyx** (sär′də niks) *n.* [L. < Gr. < *sardios,* sard + *onyx,* onyx] a variety of onyx made up of layers of white chalcedony and sard, used as a gem

**sar·gas·sum** (sär gas′əm) *n.* [ModL. < Port. < *sarga,* kind of grape] any of various floating, brown seaweeds having special branches with berrylike air sacs: also **sar·gas′so** (-ō), *pl.* **-sos, sargasso weed**

**Sar·gent** (sär′jənt), **John Sing·er** (siŋ′ər) 1856–1925; U.S. painter in Europe

**sa·ri** (sä′rē) *n.* [< Hindi < Sans.] an outer garment of Hindu women, a long cloth wrapped around the body with one end over the shoulder: also sp. **sa′ree**

**Sar·ni·a** (sär′nē ə) city & port in SE Ontario, Canada, at the S end of Lake Huron: pop. 55,000

**sa·rod, sa·rode** (sə rōd′) *n.* [Hindi *sarod* < Per.] a lutelike musical instrument of India, with many strings

**sa·rong** (sə rôŋ′) *n.* [Malay *sārung*] a garment of men and women in the Malay Archipelago, the East Indies, etc., consisting of a long cloth, often brightly colored and printed, worn like a skirt

**sar·sa·pa·ril·la** (sas′pə ril′ə, särs′-, sär′sə-) *n.* [< Sp. < *zarza,* bramble + dim. of *parra,* vine] **1.** a tropical American plant with fragrant roots **2.** its dried root, or an extract **3.** a carbonated drink flavored with sarsaparilla

SARI

**Sar·to** (sär′tō), **An·dre·a del** (än dre′ä del) 1486–1531; Florentine painter

**sar·to·ri·al** (sär tôr′ē əl) *adj.* [< LL. *sartor,* a tailor] **1.** of tailors or their work **2.** of men's clothing or dress

**Sar·tre** (sàr′tr′), **Jean-Paul** (zhän pôl) 1905–80; Fr. philosopher, playwright, & novelist

SASE self-addressed stamped envelope

**sash**[1] (sash) *n.* [Ar. *shāsh,* muslin] an ornamental ribbon or scarf worn over the shoulder or around the waist

**sash**[2] (sash) *n.* [taken as sing. of earlier *shashes* < Fr. *châssis,* a frame] **1.** a frame for holding the glass pane of a window or door, esp. a sliding frame **2.** such frames collectively

**sa·shay** (sa shā′) *vi.* [altered < *chassé* (dance)] [Colloq.] to move, walk, or go, esp. casually

**sash cord** a cord attached to either side of a sliding sash, having balancing weights (**sash weights**) for raising or lowering the window easily

**Sas·katch·e·wan** (sas kach′ə wän′, -wən) province of SC Canada: 251,700 sq. mi.; pop. 921,000; cap. Regina: abbrev. **Sask.**

**Sas·ka·toon** (sas′kə tōōn′) city in C Saskatchewan, Canada: pop. 134,000

**sas·quatch** (sas′kwach′) *n.* [< AmInd.] [*also* S-] a huge, hairy, manlike creature reputed to live in the mountains of NW North America

**sass** (sas) *n.* [var. of SAUCE] [Colloq.] impudent talk —*vt.* [Colloq.] to talk impudently to

**sas·sa·fras** (sas′ə fras′) *n.* [Sp. *sasafras*] **1.** a small eastern N. American tree bearing small, bluish fruits **2.** the dried root bark of this tree, used as a flavoring

**sass·y** (sas′ē) *adj.* **sass′i·er, sass′i·est** [dial. var. of SAUCY] [Colloq.] impudent; saucy —**sass′i·ly** *adv.* —**sass′i·ness** *n.*

**sat** (sat) *pt.* & *pp. of* SIT

**SAT, S.A.T.** Scholastic Aptitude Test

**Sat. 1.** Saturday **2.** Saturn

**Sa·tan** (sāt′'n) [OE., ult. < Heb. *sāṭan*, to plot against] *Christian Theol.* the chief evil spirit; the Devil

**sa·tang** (sä taŋ′) *n., pl.* **-tang′** [Siamese *satäŋ*] *see* MONETARY UNITS, table (Thailand)

**sa·tan·ic** (sā tan′ik, sə-) *adj.* of or like Satan; devilish; wicked: also **sa·tan′i·cal** —**sa·tan′i·cal·ly** *adv.*

**satch·el** (sach′əl) *n.* [ < OFr. < L. dim. of *saccus*, a sack] a small bag for carrying clothes, books, etc.

**sate¹** (sāt) *vt.* **sat′ed, sat′ing** [prob. < L. *satiare*, to fill full] **1.** to satisfy (an appetite, desire, etc.) to the full **2.** to satiate; surfeit; glut

**sate²** (sat, sāt) *archaic pt. & pp. of* SIT

**sa·teen** (sa tēn′, sə-) *n.* [ < SATIN] a smooth, glossy cotton cloth, made to imitate satin

**sat·el·lite** (sat′'l īt′) *n.* [Fr. < L. *satelles*, an attendant] **1.** *a)* an attendant of some important person *b)* an obsequious follower **2.** *a)* a small planet revolving around a larger one *b)* a man-made object put into orbit around the earth, the moon, or some other heavenly body **3.** a small state that is economically dependent on a larger state

**sa·tia·ble** (sā′shə b'l, sā′shē ə-) *adj.* that can be sated or satiated —**sa′tia·bil′i·ty** *n.* —**sa′tia·bly** *adv.*

**sa·ti·ate** (sā′shē āt′; *for adj., usually* -it) *adj.* [ < L. pp. of *satiare*, to satisfy < *satis*, enough] having had enough or more than enough —*vt.* **-at′ed, -at′ing 1.** [Rare] to sate; satisfy fully **2.** to provide with more than enough, so as to weary or disgust; glut; surfeit —**sa′ti·a′tion** *n.*

**sa·ti·e·ty** (sə tī′ə tē) *n.* a being satiated; surfeit

**sat·in** (sat′'n) *n.* [ < MFr. < Sp. < Ar. *zaitūnī*, of *Zaitūn*, former name of a Chinese seaport] a fabric of silk, nylon, rayon, etc. with a smooth, glossy finish on one side —*adj.* of or like satin; smooth and glossy —**sat′in·y** *adj.*

**sat·in·wood** (sat′'n wood′) *n.* **1.** any of several smooth, hard woods used in fine furniture, etc. **2.** a tree yielding such wood, esp. one in the East or one in the West Indies

**sat·ire** (sa′tīr) *n.* [Fr. < L. *satira*, orig. a dish of fruits, prob. < Etruscan] **1.** a literary work in which vices, follies, etc. are held up to ridicule and contempt **2.** such works collectively **3.** the use of ridicule, sarcasm, irony, etc. to attack or deride vices, follies, etc.

**sa·tir·i·cal** (sə tir′i k'l) *adj.* **1.** of, like, or containing satire **2.** using satire Also **sa·tir′ic** —**sa·tir′i·cal·ly** *adv.*

**sat·i·rist** (sat′ə rist) *n.* a writer of satires

**sat·i·rize** (-rīz′) *vt.* **-rized′, -riz′ing** to attack, ridicule, or criticize with satire —**sat′i·riz′er** *n.*

**sat·is·fac·tion** (sat′is fak′shən) *n.* **1.** a satisfying or being satisfied **2.** something that satisfies; specif., *a)* anything that brings pleasure or contentment *b)* settlement of debt *c)* reparation for injury or insult —**give satisfaction 1.** to satisfy **2.** to accept a challenge to duel or fight

**sat·is·fac·to·ry** (-fak′tə rē, -trē) *adj.* satisfying; fulfilling a need, wish, requirement, etc. adequately —**sat′is·fac′to·ri·ly** *adv.* —**sat′is·fac′to·ri·ness** *n.*

**sat·is·fy** (sat′is fī′) *vt.* **-fied′, -fy′ing** [ < OFr. < L. < *satis*, enough + *facere*, to make] **1.** to fulfill the needs or desires of; gratify **2.** to fulfill the requirements of **3.** to comply with (rules or obligations) **4.** *a)* to free from doubt; convince *b)* to answer (a doubt, etc.) adequately **5.** *a)* to give what is due to *b)* to discharge (a debt, etc.) **6.** to make reparation to or for —*vi.* to be adequate, sufficient, etc. —**sat′is·fi′a·ble** *adj.* —**sat′is·fi′er** *n.*

**sa·to·ri** (sä tôr′ē) *n.* [Jap.] *Zen Buddhism* spiritual enlightenment or illumination

**sa·trap** (sā′trap, sat′rap) *n.* [ < L. < Gr. *satrapēs* < OPer.] **1.** the governor of a province in ancient Persia **2.** a ruler of a dependency, esp. a petty tyrant

**sa·trap·y** (sā′trə pē, sat′rə-) *n., pl.* **-trap·ies** the government, authority, or province of a satrap

**sat·u·ra·ble** (sach′ər ə b'l) *adj.* that can be saturated

**sat·u·rate** (sach′ə rāt′) *vt.* **-rat′ed, -rat′ing** [ < L. pp. of *saturare*, to fill up < *satur*, full] **1.** to cause to be thoroughly soaked **2.** to cause to be so completely filled or supplied that no more can be taken up **3.** *Chem. a)* to cause (a substance) to combine to its full capacity with another *b)* to dissolve the maximum amount of (a gas, liquid, or solid) in a solution —**sat′u·ra′tor** *n.*

**sat·u·ra·tion** (sach′ə rā′shən) *n.* **1.** a saturating or being saturated **2.** the degree to which a color is free from mixture with white; intensity of hue

**saturation point 1.** the point at which the maximum amount has been absorbed **2.** the limit beyond which something cannot be continued, endured, etc.

**Sat·ur·day** (sat′ər dē, -dā′) *n.* [OE. *Sæterdæg*, Saturn's day] the seventh and last day of the week

**Saturday night special** [from their use in weekend crimes] [Slang] any small, cheap, short-barreled handgun

**Sat·ur·days** (-dēz, -dāz′) *adv.* on or during every Saturday

**Sat·urn** (sat′ərn) **1.** *Rom. Myth.* the god of agriculture:

identified with the Greek god Cronus **2.** a planet in the solar system, sixth in distance from the sun: diameter, c.72,000 mi. —**Sa·tur·ni·an** (sə tur′nē ən) *adj.*

**Sat·ur·na·li·a** (sat′ər nā′lē ə, -nāl′yə) *n.pl.* **1.** the ancient Roman festival of Saturn, held about December 17, with general feasting and revelry **2.** [s-] *[often with sing. v. & with a pl. -li·as]* a period of unrestrained revelry

**sat·ur·nine** (sat′ər nīn′) *adj.* **1.** *Astrol.* born under the supposed influence of the planet Saturn **2.** sluggish, grave, taciturn, etc. —**sat′ur·nine′ly** *adv.*

**sat·yr** (sāt′ər, sat′-) *n.* [ < L. < Gr. *satyros*] **1.** *Gr. Myth.* a lecherous woodland deity, attendant on Bacchus, represented as having pointed ears, short horns, the head and body of a man, and the legs of a goat **2.** a lecherous man

**sat·y·ri·a·sis** (sat′ə rī′ə sis) *n.* [see prec.] abnormal and uncontrollable desire by a man for sexual intercourse: cf. NYMPHOMANIA

**sau** (sou) *n.* [Vietnamese] *see* MONETARY UNITS, table (Vietnam)

**sauce** (sôs) *n.* [ < OFr. < L. *salsa*, salted food, ult. < *sal*, salt] **1.** *a)* a liquid or soft dressing served with food as a relish *b)* a flavored syrup put on ice cream **2.** stewed or preserved fruit **3.** something that adds interest or zest **4.** [Dial.] garden vegetables eaten as a side dish **5.** [Colloq.] impudence **6.** [Slang] alcoholic liquor: usually with *the* —*vt.* **sauced, sauc′ing 1.** to flavor with a sauce **2.** to give flavor to **3.** [Colloq.] to be impudent or saucy to

**sauce·pan** (-pan′) *n.* a small pot with a projecting handle, used for cooking

**sau·cer** (sô′sər) *n.* [MFr. *saussier* < *sause*, SAUCE] **1.** a small, round, shallow dish, esp. one with an indentation to hold a cup **2.** anything round and shallow like a saucer

**sau·cy** (sô′sē) *adj.* **-ci·er, -ci·est** [SAUC(E) - Y²] **1.** rude; impudent **2.** pert; sprightly *[a saucy smile]* **3.** stylish or smart —**sau′ci·ly** *adv.* —**sau′ci·ness** *n.*

**Sa·u·di** (sä ōō′dē, sou′dē) *adj.* of Saudi Arabia, its people, etc. —*n., pl.* **-dis** a native or inhabitant of Saudi Arabia

**Saudi Arabia** kingdom occupying most of Arabia: c. 617,000 sq. mi.; pop. 6,036,000; cap. Riyadh (Mecca is the religious capital)

**sau·er·bra·ten** (sour′brät′'n, zou′ər-) *n.* [G. < *sauer*, sour + *braten*, a roast] a dish made of beef marinated in vinegar with onion, spices, etc. before cooking

**sau·er·kraut** (sour′krout′) *n.* [G. *sauer*, sour + *kraut*, cabbage] chopped cabbage fermented in a brine of its own juice with salt

**sau·ger** (sô′gər) *n.* [ < ?] a small American pikeperch

**Saul** (sôl) [ < LL. < Gr. < Heb. *shā′ul*, lit., asked (i.e., of God)] **1.** a masculine name **2.** *Bible a)* the first king of Israel *b)* orig. name of the Apostle PAUL

**Sault Ste. Ma·rie** (sōō′ sänt′ mə rē′) [ < Fr. *Sault de Sainte Marie*, lit., falls of St. Mary] **1.** city in N Mich., on a river (*St. Marys River*) flowing from Lake Superior into Lake Huron: pop. 14,000 **2.** city opposite it, in Ontario, Canada: pop. 75,000 Also **Sault Sainte Marie** See also Soo

**sau·na** (sou′nə, sô′-) *n.* [Finn.] **1.** a Finnish bath, consisting of exposure to very hot, relatively dry air, with light beating of the skin with birch or cedar boughs **2.** the enclosure for such a bath

**saun·ter** (sôn′tər) *vi.* [ < ?] to walk about idly; stroll —*n.* **1.** a leisurely and aimless walk **2.** a slow, leisurely gait

**sau·ri·an** (sôr′ē ən) *n.* [ < Gr. *sauros*, a lizard] any of those reptiles that are lizards —*adj.* of or like lizards

**-sau·rus** (sôr′əs) [see prec.] *a combining form meaning* lizard

**sau·sage** (sô′sij) *n.* [ < ONormFr. < VL. < L. *salsus:* see SAUCE] pork or other meat, chopped fine, highly seasoned, and either stuffed into membranous casings or made into patties for cooking

**sau·té** (sō tā′, sô-) *adj.* [Fr., pp. of *sauter*, to leap] fried quickly in a little fat —*vt.* **-téed′, -té′ing** to fry quickly in a pan with a little fat —*n.* a sautéed dish

**sau·terne** (sō turn′, sô-) *n.* [ < *Sauternes*, town in France] a white, usually sweet table wine

**sav·age** (sav′ij) *adj.* [ < OFr. < VL. < L. *silvaticus*, wild < *silva*, a wood] **1.** wild; uncultivated *[a savage jungle]* **2.** fierce; untamed *[a savage tiger]* **3.** without civilization; barbarous *[a savage tribe]* **4.** crude; rude **5.** cruel; pitiless —*n.* **1.** a member of a primitive society or savage tribe **2.** a fierce, brutal person —*vt.* **-aged, -ag·ing** to attack violently, either physically or verbally —**sav′age·ly** *adv.*

**sav·age·ry** (-rē) *n., pl.* **-ries 1.** the condition of being savage, wild, primitive, etc. **2.** savage act or behavior

**sa·van·na, sa·van·nah** (sə van′ə) *n.* [ < Sp. < *zavana* < native name] a treeless plain or a grassland with scattered trees, esp. in or near the tropics

**Sa·van·nah** (sə van′ə) [ < the native name of the Shawnees] seaport in SE Ga.: pop. 142,000

**sa·vant** (sə vänt′, sav′ənt) *n.* [Fr., orig. prp. of *savoir* < L. *sapere*, to know] a learned person

**save¹** (sāv) *vt.* **saved, sav′ing** [< OFr. *salver* < L. < *salvus*, safe] **1.** to rescue or preserve from harm or danger **2.** to preserve for future use (often with *up*) **3.** to prevent loss or waste of [to *save* time] **4.** to avoid or lessen [to *save* wear and tear] **5.** to treat carefully in order to preserve, lessen wear, etc. **6.** *Theol.* to deliver from sin and punishment —*vi.* **1.** to avoid expense, loss, waste, etc. **2.** to keep something or someone from danger, harm, etc. **3.** to hoard money or goods **4.** to keep; last **5.** *Theol.* to exercise power to redeem from sin —*n. Sports* an action that keeps an opponent from scoring or winning —**sav′a·ble, save′a·ble** *adj.* —**sav′er** *n.*

**save²** (sāv) *prep.* [< OFr. *sauf*, lit., SAFE] except; but — *conj.* **1.** except; but **2.** [Archaic] unless

**sav·ing¹** (sā′viŋ) *adj.* that saves; specif., *a)* rescuing *b)* economical *c)* containing an exception [a *saving* clause] *d)* compensating; redeeming [a *saving* grace] —*n.* **1.** the act of one that saves **2.** [often *pl. with sing. v.*] any reduction in expense, time, etc. [a *saving(s)* of 10%] **3.** *a)* anything saved *b)* [*pl.*] sums of money saved

**sav·ing²** (sā′viŋ) *prep.* [Now Rare] **1.** with due respect for **2.** except; save —*conj.* [Now Rare] save

**savings account** an account in a bank or savings association which receives and invests depositors' savings, on which it pays interest

**savings and loan association** a depositor-owned establishment in which depositors' savings draw interest and are used for making real-estate loans

**sav·ior, sav·iour** (sāv′yər) *n.* [< OFr. < LL. *salvator* < *salvare*, to SAVE¹] a person who saves —**the Saviour** (or **Savior**) Jesus Christ

**sa·voir-faire** (sav′wär fer′) *n.* [Fr., to know (how) to do] ready knowledge of what to do or say, and of when and how to do or say it; social poise and tact

**sa·vor** (sā′vər) *n.* [< OFr. < L. *sapor*] **1.** the taste or smell of something; flavor **2.** characteristic quality **3.** noticeable trace **4.** power to excite interest, zest, etc. —*vi.* **1.** to have the particular taste, smell, or quality; smack (*of*) **2.** to show traces or signs (*of*) —*vt.* **1.** to season or flavor **2.** to taste or smell, esp. with relish **3.** to dwell on with delight; relish Also, Brit. sp., **savour** —**sa′vor·er** *n.* —**sa′vor·less** *adj.* —**sa′vor·ous** *adj.*

**sa·vor·y¹** (sā′vər ē) *adj.* [< OFr. pp. of *savourer*, to taste < *savour*, SAVOR] **1.** pleasing to the taste or smell **2.** pleasant, agreeable, etc. **3.** morally acceptable; respectable **4.** salty or piquant [a *savory* relish] —*n., pl.* **-vor·ies** in England, a small, highly seasoned portion of food served at the end of a meal or as an appetizer Also, Brit. sp., **savoury** —**sa′vor·i·ness** *n.*

**sa·vor·y²** (sā′vər ē) *n.* [< OFr. *savoreie*, altered (prob. after *savour*, SAVOR) < L. *satureia*, savory] a fragrant herb of the mint family, used in cooking

**Sa·voy¹** (sə voi′) ruling family of Piedmont, the duchy of Savoy, the kingdom of Sardinia, & (1861-1946) Italy

**Sa·voy²** (sə voi′) region in SE France, on the borders of Italy & Switzerland: formerly, a duchy

**Sa·voy·ard** (sə voi′ərd) *n.* [< the *Savoy*, London theater] an actor, producer, or admirer of Gilbert and Sullivan operas

**sav·vy** (sav′ē) *vi.* **-vied, -vy·ing** [altered < Sp. *sabe* (*usted*), do (you) know? < *saber*, to know] [Slang] to understand; get the idea —*n.* [Slang] **1.** shrewd understanding **2.** skill or know-how —*adj.* [Slang] shrewd or discerning

**saw¹** (sô) *n.* [OE. *sagu*] **1.** a cutting tool having a thin, metal blade or disk with sharp teeth along the edge **2.** a machine that operates a saw —*vt.* **sawed, sawed** or chiefly Brit. **sawn, saw′ing 1.** to cut or shape with a saw **2.** to make sawlike cutting motions through or with (something) or produce with such motions —*vi.* **1.** to cut with a saw or as a saw does **2.** to be cut with a saw [wood that *saws* easily] **3.** to make sawlike cutting motions —**saw′er** *n.*

**saw²** (sô) *n.* [OE. *sagu*] an old saying; maxim

**saw³** (sô) *pt. of* SEE¹

**saw·bones** (sô′bōnz′) *n.* [Slang] a surgeon

**saw·buck** (-buk′) *n.* **1.** [Du. *zaagbok*] a sawhorse with the legs projecting above the crossbar **2.** [from resemblance of the crossed legs of a sawbuck to an X (Roman numeral for 10)] [Slang] a ten-dollar bill

**saw·dust** (-dust′) *n.* tiny bits of wood formed in sawing

**sawed-off** (sôd′ôf′) *adj.* **1.** designating a shotgun with the barrel cut off short **2.** [Colloq.] short in stature

**saw·fish** (sô′fish′) *n., pl.* **-fish′, -fish′es:** see FISH any of a

genus of tropical giant rays having a long, flat, sawlike snout edged with teeth on both sides

**saw·fly** (-flī′) *n., pl.* **-flies′** any of a group of four-winged insects the female of which has a pair of sawlike organs that cut into plants, the eggs being then deposited in the cuts

**saw·horse** (-hôrs′) *n.* a rack on which wood is placed while being sawed

**saw·mill** (-mil′) *n.* **1.** a place where logs are sawed into boards **2.** a large sawing machine

**sawn** (sôn) *chiefly Brit. pp. of* SAW¹

**saw-toothed** (sô′tōŏtht′) *adj.* having notches like the teeth of a saw; serrate: also **saw′tooth′**

**saw·yer** (sô′yər) *n.* a person whose work is sawing wood, as into planks and boards

**sax** (saks) *n.* [Colloq.] a saxophone

**sax·horn** (saks′hôrn′) *n.* [after A. J. *Sax* (1814-1894), Belgian inventor] any of a group of valved brass-wind instruments with a full, even tone

**sax·i·frage** (sak′sə frij) *n.* [MFr. < L. < *saxum*, a rock + base of *frangere*, to break: the plant grows in rock crevices] any of a group of plants with white, yellow, purple, or pinkish small flowers, and leaves often at the base of the plant

**Sax·on** (sak′s'n) *n.* **1.** a member of an ancient Germanic people of northern Germany: some Saxons conquered parts of England in the 5th and 6th cent. A.D. **2.** *same as* ANGLO-SAXON (*n.* 1 & 4) **3.** a native or inhabitant of modern Saxony **4.** any of the Low German dialects of the Saxon peoples —*adj.* **1.** of the Saxons, their language, etc. **2.** of Saxony

**Sax·on·y** (sak′sə nē) **1.** region in S East Germany: formerly, a kingdom **2.** medieval duchy at the base of Jutland: now part of a West German state called *Lower Saxony*

**sax·o·phone** (sak′sə fōn′) *n.* [Fr., after A. J. *Sax* (see SAXHORN) & -PHONE] a single-reed, keyed wind instrument having a curved metal body —**sax′o·phon′ist** *n.*

SAXOPHONE

**say** (sā) *vt.* **said, say′ing; 3d pers. sing., pres. indic., says** (sez), archaic **saith** [OE. *secgan*] **1.** to utter; speak **2.** to express in words; state; declare **3.** to state positively or as an opinion [who can *say* what will be?] **4.** to indicate or show [the clock *says* ten] **5.** to recite; repeat [to *say* one's prayers] **6.** to estimate [he is, I'd *say*, forty] **7.** to allege; report [they *say* he's guilty] **8.** to communicate (an idea, feeling, etc.) [the painting *says* nothing] —*vi.* to make a statement; speak; express an opinion —*n.* **1.** a chance to speak [to have one's *say*] **2.** authority, as to make a final decision: often with *the* —*adv.* **1.** for example [any fish, *say* perch] **2.** about; nearly [costing, *say*, $5] —*interj.* an exclamation expressing surprise, admiration, etc. —**go without saying** to be too obvious to need explanation —**that is to say** in other words; that means —**to say the least** to understate —**say′er** *n.*

**say·ing** (sā′iŋ) *n.* something said; esp., an adage, proverb, or maxim

‡**sa·yo·na·ra** (sä′yô nä′rä) *n., interj.* [< Jap.] farewell

**say-so** (sā′sō′) *n.* [Colloq.] **1.** (one's) word, opinion, assurance, etc. **2.** right of decision; authority

**Sb** [L. *stibium*] *Chem.* antimony

**Sc** *Chem.* scandium

**SC, S.C.** South Carolina

**Sc. 1.** Scotch **2.** Scots **3.** Scottish

**sc. 1.** scene **2.** science **3.** scilicet

**s.c.** *Printing* small capitals

**scab** (skab) *n.* [ON. *skabb*] **1.** a crust that forms over a sore or wound as it is healing **2.** a mangy skin disease, esp. of sheep **3.** a plant disease characterized by roughened, scablike spots **4.** *a)* [Old Slang] a scoundrel *b)* a worker who refuses to join a union *c)* a worker who refuses to strike, or who takes the place of a striking worker —*vi.* **scabbed, scab′bing 1.** to become covered with a scab **2.** to work or act as a scab

**scab·bard** (skab′ərd) *n.* [< Anglo-Fr. *escaubers* (pl.) < ? OHG. *scar*, sword + *bergan*, to hide] a sheath or case to hold the blade of a sword, dagger, etc. —*vt.* to sheathe

**scab·by** (skab′ē) *adj.* **-bi·er, -bi·est 1.** covered with or consisting of scabs **2.** low; base; mean —**scab′bi·ly** *adv.* —**scab′bi·ness** *n.*

**sca·bies** (skā′bēz, -bē ēz) *n.* [L., itch < *scabere*, to scratch] a contagious skin disease caused by mites that burrow under the skin to deposit eggs, causing intense itching

**sca·bi·o·sa** (skā′bē ō′sə) *n.* [ModL., genus name < ML. < L.: see prec.: once considered a remedy for scabies] any of various related plants having showy flowers in flattened or dome-shaped heads: also **sca′bi·ous** (-əs)

**scab·rous** (skab′rəs, skā′brəs) *adj.* [< LL. < L. *scabere*, to scratch] **1.** rough, like a file; scaly, scabby, etc. **2.** full

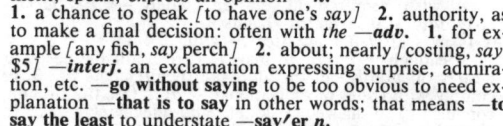
SAWS
(A, keyhole; B, hacksaw; C, hand-saw; D, crosscut)

of difficulties 3. indecent, scandalous, etc. —**scab′rous·ly** *adv.* —**scab′rous·ness** *n.*

**scad** (skad) *n.* [< ?] [*usually pl.*][Colloq.] a very large number or amount [*scads* of money]

**scaf·fold** (skaf′ld, -ōld) *n.* [OFr. *escafalt:* prob. akin to CATAFALQUE] **1.** a temporary framework for supporting workmen during the erecting, repairing, or painting of a building, etc. **2.** a raised platform on which criminals are executed, as by hanging **3.** any raised framework —*vt.* to furnish or support with a scaffold

**scaf·fold·ing** (-′l diŋ) *n.* **1.** the materials that form a scaffold **2.** a scaffold or scaffolds

**sca·lar** (skā′lər) *adj.* **1.** in, on, or of a scale **2.** *Math.* designating or of a quantity that has magnitude but no direction in space, as volume or temperature —*n.* a scalar quantity: distinguished from VECTOR (sense 2 *a*)

**scal·a·wag** (skal′ə wag′) *n.* [< ?] **1.** a scamp; rascal **2.** a white Southern Republican during the Reconstruction: an opprobrious term Also sp. **scallawag**

**scald¹** (skôld) *vt.* [< ONormFr. < OFr. < LL. *excaldare* < L. *ex-*, intens. + *calidus*, hot] **1.** to burn with hot liquid or steam **2.** to heat almost to the boiling point **3.** to use boiling liquid on, as in sterilizing, etc. —*vi.* to be or become scalded —*n.* **1.** a burn caused by scalding **2.** the act or an instance of scalding **3.** any of various plant diseases characterized by a whitening or browning of tissues

**scald²** (skôld, skäld) *n.* var. of SKALD —**scald′ic** *adj.*

**scale¹** (skāl) *n.* [< LL. *scala* < L., a ladder] **1.** orig., a ladder or flight of stairs **2.** *a)* a series of marks along a line, as at regular intervals, used in measuring or registering something [the *scale* of a thermometer] *b)* any instrument or ruler so marked **3.** *a)* the proportion that a map, model, etc. bears to the thing that it represents [a *scale* of one inch to a mile] *b)* a line marked off on a map to show this ratio **4.** *a)* a system of classifying in a series of degrees according to relative size, amount, rank, etc. [a wage *scale*] *b)* any point, level, or degree in such a series **5.** *Math.* a number system having a specified base [the binary *scale*] **6.** *Music* a sequence of tones, rising or falling in pitch, in accordance with any of various systems of intervals —*vt.* **scaled, scal′ing** **1.** to climb up or over **2.** to make according to a scale —*vi.* **1.** to climb; go up **2.** to go up in a graduated series —**on a large** (or **small** ) **scale** to a relatively large (or small) degree or extent —**scale down** (or **up**) to reduce (or increase) according to a ratio —**scal′er** *n.*

**scale²** (skāl) *n.* [< OFr. *escale*, husk & *escaille*, shell: both < Gmc.] **1.** any of the thin, flat, overlapping, horny plates forming the outer covering of many fishes and reptiles **2.** any thin, flaky or platelike layer or piece that forms part of, or peels off from, a surface **3.** a coating that forms on metals when heated or rusted [*scale* on the inside of a boiler] **4.** any small scalelike leaf or bract; esp., such a modified leaf covering the bud of a seed plant —*vt.* **scaled, scal′ing** **1.** to strip or scrape scales from **2.** to remove in thin layers; pare down **3.** to cause scales to form on —*vi.* **1.** to flake or peel off in scales **2.** to become covered with scale or scales —**scale′less** *adj.*

**scale³** (skāl) *n.* [ ON. *skál*, bowl] **1.** either of the shallow dishes or pans of a balance **2.** [*often pl.*] a balance or other weighing device —*vt.* **scaled, scal′ing** **1.** to weigh in scales **2.** to have a weight of —*vi.* to be weighed —**the Scales** same as LIBRA —**turn the scales** to determine; decide

**scale insect** any of a large group of small, homopterous insects destructive to plants: the females secrete a round, wax scale under which they live and lay their eggs

**sca·lene** (skā lēn′, skā′lēn) *adj.* [< LL. < Gr. *skalēnos*, uneven] *Geom.* **1.** having unequal sides and angles: said of a triangle **2.** having the axis not perpendicular to the base: said of a cone, etc.

**scaling ladder** a ladder used for climbing high walls

**scal·lion** (skal′yən) *n.* [< ONormFr. *escalogne*, ult. < L. (*caepa*) *Ascalonia*, (onion of) Ascalon (in Philistia)] any of three varieties of onion; specif., *a)* the shallot *b)* the leek *c)* a green onion with an almost bulbless root

**scal·lop** (skäl′əp, skal′-) *n.* [OFr. *escalope* < *escale:* see SCALE²] **1.** a kind of mollusk with two deeply grooved, curved shells, that swims by means of a large muscle that rapidly snaps its shells together **2.** this muscle, used as food **3.** a single shell of such a mollusk; specif., one used as a baking dish **4.** any of a series of curves, projections, etc. forming an ornamental edge on cloth, lace, etc. —*vt.* **1.** to cut the edge or border of in scallops **2.** to bake with a milk sauce and bread crumbs; escallop —*vi.* to gather scallops —**scal′lop·er** *n.*

SCALLOP
(sense 1)

**scal·ly·wag** (skal′ē wag′) *n.* same as SCALAWAG

**scalp** (skalp) *n.* [< Scand.] **1.** the skin on the top and back of the head, usually covered with hair **2.** a part of this, cut or torn from the head of an enemy for a trophy, as by certain N. American Indians, frontiersmen, etc. **3.** a symbol of victory, prowess, etc. —*vt.* **1.** to cut or tear the scalp from **2.** *a)* to cheat or rob *b)* to defeat decisively **3.** [Colloq.] to buy and sell in order to make small, quick profits **4.** [Colloq.] to buy (theater tickets, etc.) and sell later at higher than regular prices —*vi.* [Colloq.] to scalp tickets, etc. —**scalp′er** *n.*

**scal·pel** (skal′pəl) *n.* [< L. dim. of *scalprum*, a knife < *scalpere*, to cut] a small, light, straight knife with a very sharp blade, used by surgeons and in anatomical dissections

**scal·y** (skā′lē) *adj.* **scal′i·er, scal′i·est** having, covered with, or resembling scales —**scal′i·ness** *n.*

**scamp¹** (skamp) *n.* [< obs. *scamp*, to roam < MFr. *escamper*, to flee, ult. < L. *ex-*, out + *campus*, battlefield] a mischievous or roguish fellow; rascal —**scamp′ish** *adj.*

**scamp²** (skamp) *vt.* [akin to or < ON. *skammr*, short] to do in a careless, inadequate way —**scamp′er** *n.*

**scam·per** (skam′pər) *vi.* [prob. freq. of obs. *scamp:* see SCAMP¹] to run or go hurriedly or quickly —*n.* the act of scampering —**scam′per·er** *n.*

**scam·pi** (skam′pē) *n., pl.* **-pi, -pies** [It., pl. of *scampo*] a kind of large prawn, valued as food

**scan** (skan) *vt.* **scanned, scan′ning** [< L. *scandere*, to climb] **1.** to analyze (verse), as by marking off the metrical feet and showing the rhythmic structure **2.** to look at closely or in a broad, searching way; scrutinize **3.** to glance at quickly **4.** in computers, to examine in sequence (data), esp. with an electronic device **5.** *Radar* to traverse (a region) with a succession of transmitted radar beams **6.** *TV* to traverse (a surface) rapidly and point by point with a beam of light or electrons in transmitting or reproducing an image —*vi.* **1.** to scan verse **2.** to be in a certain poetic meter —*n.* a scanning —**scan′na·ble** *adj.* —**scan′ner** *n.*

**Scan., Scand.** **1.** Scandinavia **2.** Scandinavian

**scan·dal** (skan′d'l) *n.* [< OFr. < LL. *scandalum*, cause for stumbling < Gr. *skandalon*, a snare] **1.** any act, person, or thing that offends or shocks the moral feelings of people and leads to disgrace **2.** a reaction of shame, outrage, etc. caused by such an act, person, etc. **3.** disgrace or ignominy **4.** talk that harms a reputation; wicked gossip

**scan·dal·ize** (skan′də līz′) *vt.* **-ized′, -iz′ing** to outrage the moral feelings of by improper conduct —**scan′dal·iz′er** *n.*

**scan·dal·mon·ger** (skan′d'l muŋ′gər, -mäŋ′-) *n.* a person who gossips maliciously and spreads scandal

**scan·dal·ous** (-əs) *adj.* **1.** causing scandal; shocking to people's moral feelings; shameful **2.** consisting of or spreading slander; libelous —**scan′dal·ous·ly** *adv.* —**scan′dal·ous·ness** *n.*

**Scan·di·na·vi·a** (skan′də nā′vē ə) **1.** region in N Europe, including Norway, Sweden, & Denmark and, sometimes, Iceland **2.** peninsula in N Europe, consisting of Norway & Sweden: in full, **Scandinavian Peninsula**

**Scan·di·na·vi·an** (-ən) *adj.* of Scandinavia, its people, their languages, etc. —*n.* **1.** any of the people of Scandinavia **2.** the subbranch of the Germanic languages spoken by them; North Germanic

**scan·di·um** (skan′dē əm) *n.* [ModL. < ML. < L. *Scandia*, N European lands] a rare metallic chemical element: symbol, Sc; at. wt., 44.956; at. no., 21

**scan·sion** (skan′shən) *n.* the act of scanning verse

**scant** (skant) *adj.* [< ON. < *skammr*, short] **1.** inadequate in size or amount; not enough; meager **2.** not quite up to full measure —*vt.* **1.** to limit in size or amount; stint **2.** to fail to give full measure of **3.** to treat in an inadequate manner —*adv.* [Dial.] scarcely; barely —**scant′ly** *adv.* —**scant′ness** *n.*

**scant·ling** (skant′liŋ) *n.* [< ONormFr. < OFr. *eschandillon*, a measure] a small beam or timber; esp., a small upright timber, as in the frame of a structure

**scant·y** (skan′tē) *adj.* **scant′i·er, scant′i·est** [SCANT + -Y²] **1.** barely sufficient; not ample; meager **2.** insufficient; not enough —**scant′i·ly** *adv.* —**scant′i·ness** *n.*

**scape** (skāp) *n., vt., vi.* **scaped, scap′ing** [Archaic] same as ESCAPE: also **′scape**

**-scape** (skāp) [< (LAND)SCAPE] *a combining form meaning* (a drawing, etc. of) a specified view or scene [*cityscape*]

**scape·goat** (skāp′gōt′) *n.* [SCAPE + GOAT] **1.** a goat over which the high priest of the ancient Jews confessed the sins of the people, after which it was allowed to escape: Lev. 16:7-26 **2.** a person, group, or thing upon whom the blame for the mistakes or crimes of others is thrust

**scape·grace** (-grās′) *n.* [SCAPE + GRACE] a graceless, unprincipled fellow; scamp; rogue

**scap·u·la** (skap′yoo lə) *n., pl.* **-lae′** (-lē′), **-las** [ModL. < L.] same as SHOULDER BLADE

**scap·u·lar** (-lər) *adj.* of the shoulder or scapula —*n.* **1.** a sleeveless outer garment falling from the shoulders, worn by monks **2.** two small pieces of cloth joined by strings, worn on the chest and back, under the clothes, by some Roman Catholics as a token of religious devotion

**scar** (skär) *n.* [< MFr. < LL. < Gr. *eschara*, orig., fireplace] **1.** a mark left after a wound, burn, ulcer, etc. has healed **2.** any mark like this, as on a plant where a leaf was attached **3.** the lasting mental or emotional effects of suffering —*vt., vi.* **scarred, scar′ring** to mark with or form a scar

**scar·ab** (skar′əb) *n.* [< Fr. < L. *scarabaeus*] **1.** any of various beetles, mostly stout-bodied and often brilliantly colored **2.** *a)* the black, winged dung beetle, held sacred by the ancient Egyptians *b)* an image of this beetle, cut from a stone or gem and formerly worn as a charm

**scar·a·bae·id** (skar′ə bē′id) *n.* [< ModL. family name] *same as* SCARAB (sense 1) —*adj.* of the scarab beetles

**Scar·a·mouch** (skar′ə mōōsh′, -mōōch′, -mouch′) [< Fr. < It. *Scaramuccia*, lit., a skirmish] a stock character in old Italian comedy, depicted as a braggart and a coward

**scarce** (skers) *adj.* [ONormFr. *escars*, ult. < L. *excerpere*, to select] **1.** not common; rarely seen **2.** not plentiful; hard to get —*adv. literary var. of* SCARCELY —**make oneself scarce** [Colloq.] to go or stay away —**scarce′ness** *n.*

**scarce·ly** (-lē) *adv.* **1.** hardly; not quite **2.** probably not or certainly not [*scarcely* true]

**scar·ci·ty** (sker′sə tē) *n., pl.* **-ties 1.** the condition of being scarce; inadequate supply **2.** rarity; uncommonness

**scare** (sker) *vt.* **scared, scar′ing** [ON. *skirra*, to scare < *skjarr*, timid] to fill with fear or terror; esp., to frighten suddenly —*vi.* to become frightened, esp. suddenly —*n.* **1.** a sudden fear **2.** a state of widespread fear [a war *scare*] —**scare up** [Colloq.] to produce or gather quickly

**scare·crow** (-krō′) *n.* **1.** a figure of a man, etc. made with sticks, old clothes, etc., put in a field to scare birds away from crops **2.** anything that frightens one but is harmless **3.** a person who is dressed like a scarecrow

**scarf**[1] (skärf) *n., pl.* **scarfs, scarves** [ONormFr. *escarpe*, a purse hung from the neck < ML. < L. < *scirpus*, a bulrush] **1.** a long or broad piece of cloth worn about the neck, head, etc. for warmth or decoration **2.** a long, narrow covering for a table, etc. **3.** a sash worn by soldiers or officials —*vt.* to cover as with a scarf

**scarf**[2] (skärf) *n., pl.* **scarfs** [prob. < Scand.] **1.** a joint made by notching, grooving, or cutting the ends of two pieces and fastening them so that they join into one continuous piece: also **scarf joint 2.** the ends so cut —*vt.* **1.** to join by a scarf **2.** to make a scarf in the end of

**scar·i·fy** (skar′ə fī′) *vt.* **-fied′, -fy′ing** [< MFr., ult. < Gr. *skariphasthai*, to scratch < *skariphos*, a stylus] **1.** to make a series of small cuts or punctures in (the skin), as in surgery **2.** to criticize sharply **3.** *Agric.* to loosen or stir (the topsoil) —**scar′i·fi·ca′tion** *n.*

**scar·la·ti·na** (skär′lə tē′nə) *n.* [ModL. < ML. (*febris*) *scarlatina*] popular term for a mild form of SCARLET FEVER

**Scar·lat·ti** (skär lät′tē) **1.** A·les·san·dro (ä′les sän′drō), 1660?–1725; It. composer **2.** (Giuseppe) Do·me·ni·co (dō me′nē kō′), 1685–1757; It. composer: son of *prec.*

**scar·let** (skär′lit) *n.* [< OFr. < ML. *scarlatum*, scarlet cloth < Per. < Ar., ult. < Gr. *kyklas*, encircling] **1.** very bright red with a slightly orange tinge **2.** cloth or clothing of this color —*adj.* **1.** of this color **2.** sinful

**scarlet fever** an acute contagious disease in which one has a sore throat, fever, and a scarlet rash

**scarlet letter** a scarlet letter A worn in earlier times by a person convicted of adultery

**scarlet runner (bean)** a climbing bean plant of tropical America, having scarlet flowers, and pods with red-and-black seeds

**scarlet tanager** a songbird native to the U.S., the male of which has a scarlet body and black wings and tail

**scarp** (skärp) *n.* [< It. *scarpa*] **1.** a steep slope; specif., an escarpment or cliff along the edge of a plateau **2.** the outer slope of a rampart, or a rear slope of a ditch below the rampart —*vt.* to make into a steep slope

**scar tissue** the fibrous, contracted tissue of a scar

**scarves** (skärvz) *n. alt. pl. of* SCARF[1]

**scar·y** (sker′ē) *adj.* **scar′i·er, scar′i·est** [Colloq.] **1.** causing fear **2.** easily frightened —**scar′i·ness** *n.*

**scat**[1] (skat) *vi.* **scat′ted, scat′ting** [? a hiss + CAT] [Colloq.] to go away: usually in the imperative

**scat**[2] (skat) *adj.* [< ?] *Jazz* designating or of singing in which meaningless syllables are used, often to imitate the sounds of a musical instrument —*n.* such singing —*vi.* **scat′ted, scat′ting** to engage in scat singing

**scat**[3] (skat) *n.* [< Gr. *skōr*, excrement] excrement left by an animal, esp. a wild animal

**scathe** (skā*th*) *vt.* **scathed, scath′ing** [< ON. < *skathi*, harm] **1.** [Archaic or Dial.] *a)* to injure *b)* to wither or sear **2.** to denounce fiercely —*n.* [Archaic or Dial.] injury or harm —**scathe′less** *adj.*

**scath·ing** (skā′*thi*ŋ) *adj.* searing; harsh or caustic [*scathing* remarks] —**scath′ing·ly** *adv.*

**sca·tol·o·gy** (skə täl′ə jē) *n.* [< Gr. *skōr* (gen. *skatos*), excrement + -LOGY] obsession with the obscene, esp. with excrement or excretion, in literature —**scat·o·log·i·cal** (skat′ə läj′i k'l), **scat′o·log′ic** *adj.*

**scat·ter** (skat′ər) *vt.* [ME. *skateren*] **1.** to throw here and there or strew loosely; sprinkle **2.** to separate and drive in many directions; disperse —*vi.* to separate and go off in several directions [the crowd *scattered*] —*n.* **1.** a scattering **2.** what is scattered about —**scat′ter·er** *n.*

**scat·ter·brain** (-brān′) *n.* a person who is flighty and not able to think in a serious way —**scat′ter·brained′** *adj.*

**scatter rug** a small rug for covering only a limited area

**scaup** (skôp) *n., pl.* **scaups, scaup:** see PLURAL, II, D, 1 [obs. var. of *scalp*, mussel bed] any of several wild ducks related to the canvasback and redhead: also **scaup duck**

**scav·enge** (skav′inj) *vt.* **-enged, -eng·ing** [< ff.] **1.** to clean up (streets, etc.) **2.** to salvage (usable goods) by rummaging through refuse —*vi.* **1.** to act as a scavenger **2.** to look for food

**scav·eng·er** (-in jər) *n.* [< Anglo-Fr., ult. < Fl. *scawen* or OFrank. *scouwon*, to peer at] **1.** a person who gathers things that have been discarded by others **2.** any animal that eats refuse or decaying organic matter

**sce·nar·i·o** (si ner′ē ō′, -när′-) *n., pl.* **-i·os′** [It. < L. < *scaena*, stage, SCENE] **1.** a synopsis of a play, opera, or the like **2.** the working script of a movie, television play, etc. **3.** an outline for a planned series of events, real or imagined —**sce·nar′ist** *n.*

**scene** (sēn) *n.* [< MFr. < L. < Gr. *skēnē*, tent, stage] **1.** the place in which any event occurs [the *scene* of the crime] **2.** the setting of the action of a play, story, etc. [the *scene* of *Hamlet* is Denmark] **3.** a division of a play, usually part of an act **4.** a part of a play, story, etc. that constitutes a unit of action [a deathbed *scene*] **5.** *same as* SCENERY (sense 1) **6.** a view of people or places **7.** a display of strong feeling before others [she made a *scene* in court] **8.** an episode or event, real or imaginary, esp. as described **9.** [Colloq.] the locale or environment for a specified activity [the poetry *scene*] —**behind the scenes 1.** backstage **2.** in private or in secrecy; not for public knowledge —**make the scene** [Slang] **1.** to be present **2.** to participate actively or successfully

**sce·ner·y** (sē′nər ē) *n., pl.* **-ner·ies 1.** painted screens, backdrops, hangings, etc., used on the stage to represent places **2.** the features of a landscape

**sce·nic** (sē′nik, sen′ik) *adj.* **1.** *a)* of the stage; theatrical *b)* relating to stage effects or stage scenery **2.** *a)* having to do with natural scenery *b)* having beautiful scenery **3.** representing an action, event, etc. —**sce′ni·cal·ly** *adv.*

**scent** (sent) *vt.* [< OFr. < L. *sentire*, to feel] **1.** to smell **2.** to get a hint of; suspect **3.** to fill with an odor; perfume —*vi.* to hunt by the sense of smell —*n.* **1.** a smell; odor **2.** the sense of smell **3.** a perfume **4.** an odor left by an animal, by which it is tracked **5.** a track followed in hunting **6.** any clue by which something is followed —**scent′ed** *adj.* —**scent′less** *adj.*

**scep·ter** (sep′tər) *n.* [< OFr. < L. < Gr. *skēptron*, staff] **1.** a staff held by rulers on ceremonial occasions as a symbol of sovereignty **2.** royal authority; sovereignty —*vt.* to furnish with a scepter; invest with royal authority

**scep·tic** (skep′tik) *n., adj. chiefly Brit. sp. of* SKEPTIC —**scep′ti·cal** *adj. chiefly Brit. sp. of* SKEPTICAL —**scep′ti·cism** *n.*

**scep·tre** (sep′tər) *n., vt.* **-tred, -tring** *chiefly Brit. sp. of* SCEPTER

**sched·ule** (skej′ōōl, -əl; *Brit. & often Canad.* shed′yōōl, shej′ōōl) *n.* [< OFr. < LL. dim. of L. *scheda*, a leaf of paper < Gr. *schidē*, splinter of wood] **1.** a list or catalog of details, as of a bill of sale **2.** a list of times of recurring events, arriving and departing trains, etc.; timetable **3.** a timed plan for a project —*vt.* **-uled, -ul·ing 1.** to place in a schedule **2.** to make a schedule of **3.** to plan for a certain time

**Scheduled Castes** the groups of people in India formerly belonging to the class of untouchables

**Scheldt** (skelt) river flowing from N France through Belgium & the Netherlands into the North Sea: Du. name **Schel·de** (skhel′də)

**sche·ma** (skē′mə) *n., pl.* **-ma·ta** (-mə tə) [Gr.: see SCHEME] an outline, diagram, scheme, plan, etc.

**sche·mat·ic** (skē mat′ik, skə-) *adj.* of, or having the nature of, a scheme, schema, plan, diagram, etc. —*n.* a diagram, as of the wiring of an electric circuit —**sche·mat′i·cal·ly** *adv.*

**scheme** (skēm) *n.* [< L. < Gr. *schēma*, a form] **1.** *a)* a systematic program for attaining some object *b)* a secret or underhanded plan; plot *c)* a visionary plan **2.** an orderly combination of things on a definite plan [a color *scheme*] **3.** an outline showing different parts of an object or system —*vt.* **schemed, schem′ing** to plan as a scheme; devise; contrive; plot —*vi.* **1.** to make schemes **2.** to plot; intrigue —**schem′er** *n.*

**schem·ing** (skē'miŋ) *adj.* given to forming schemes or plots; crafty, tricky, etc. —**schem'ing·ly** *adv.*

**Sche·nec·ta·dy** (skə nek'tə dē) [< Du. < Iroquoian name (? lit., place of the pines) + Du. *stede*, place] city in E N.Y., on the Mohawk River: pop. 68,000

**scher·zan·do** (sker tsän'dō, -tsan'-) *adj.* [It. < *scherzo*: see ff.] *Music* playful —*adv. Music* playfully

**scher·zo** (sker'tsō) *n., pl.* **-zos, -zi** (-tsē) [It., a jest] a lively, playful movement, as of a sonata, in 3/4 time

**Schick test** (shik) [after B. *Schick* (1877–1967), U.S. pediatrician] a test for immunity to diphtheria, made by injecting dilute diphtheria toxin into the skin

**Schil·ler** (shil'ər), (**Johann Christoph**) **Fried·rich von** (frē'driH fôn) 1759–1805; Ger. dramatist & poet

**schil·ling** (shil'iŋ) *n.* [G.] *see* MONETARY UNITS, table (Austria)

**schism** (siz'm; *now occas.* skiz''m) *n.* [< OFr. < LL. < Gr. *schisma* < *schizein*, to cleave] **1.** a split in an organized group, esp. a church, caused by a difference of opinion **2.** the offense of trying to cause a split in a church

**schis·mat·ic** (siz mat'ik; *now occas.* skiz-) *adj.* **1.** of or having the nature of schism **2.** tending to or causing schism Also **schis·mat'i·cal** —*n.* a person who causes or participates in schism —**schis·mat'i·cal·ly** *adv.*

**schist** (shist) *n.* [< Fr. < L. < Gr. *schistos*, easily cleft < *schizein*, to cleave] any metamorphic rock of a type that splits easily into thin leaves —**schist'ose** (-ōs) *adj.*

**schis·to·so·mi·a·sis** (shis'tə sō mī'ə sis) *n.* [ModL. < Gr. *schistos*, cleft + *sōma*, body + -IASIS] a chronic disease, caused by parasitic flukes in the bloodstream, that produces disorders of the liver, bladder, lungs, etc.

**schiz·o** (skit'sō, skiz'ō) *adj., n., pl.* **schiz'os** *clipped form of* SCHIZOPHRENIC

**schiz·o-** [ModL. < Gr. *schizein*, to cleave] *a combining form meaning* split, division: also, before a vowel, **schiz-**

**schiz·o·carp** (skiz'ə kärp', skit'sə-) *n.* [prec. + -CARP] *Bot.* a dry fruit, as of the maple, that splits into one-seeded carpels —**schiz'o·car'pous, schiz'o·car'pic** *adj.*

**schiz·oid** (skit'soid, skiz'oid) *adj.* **1.** of, like, or having schizophrenia **2.** designating or of a type of person who is withdrawn, introverted, etc. —*n.* a schizoid person

**schiz·o·phre·ni·a** (skit'sə frē'nē ə, skiz'ə-) *n.* [ModL. < SCHIZO- + Gr. *phrēn*, the mind] a major mental disorder of unknown cause in which, typically, a person's emotions are displayed in bizarre behavior, his sense of reality is distorted by delusions and hallucinations, etc. —**schiz'o·phren'ic** (-fren'ik, -frē'nik) *adj., n.*

**schle·miel** (shlə mēl') *n.* [Yid. < Heb. proper name *Shelumiēl*] [Slang] a bungling person who habitually fails or is easily victimized: also sp. **schle·mihl'**

**Schles·wig-Hol·stein** (shles'wig hōl'stīn; *G.* shläs'viH hōl'shtīn) state of N West Germany, at the base of Jutland

**schmaltz** (shmälts, shmôlts) *n.* [via Yid. < G. *schmalz*, lit., melted fat] [Slang] **1.** highly sentimental and banal music, literature, etc. **2.** banal sentimentalism Also **schmalz** —**schmaltz'y** *adj.* **schmaltz'i·er, schmaltz'i·est**

**schnapps** (shnäps, shnaps) *n., pl.* **schnapps** [G., a dram] any strong alcoholic liquor: also sp. **schnaps**

**schnau·zer** (shnou'zər) *n.* [G. < *schnauzen*, to snarl] any of three breeds of sturdy, active dog with a close, wiry coat

**Schnitz·ler** (shnits'lər), **Ar·thur** (är'toor) 1862–1931; Austrian playwright & novelist

**schnoz·zle** (shnäz''l) *n.* [via Yid. < G. *schnauze*] [Slang] the nose: also **schnoz**

**schol·ar** (skäl'ər) *n.* [< OE. or OFr., both ult. < L. *schola*, a SCHOOL[1]] **1.** *a)* a learned person *b)* a specialist in a particular branch of learning, esp. in the humanities **2.** a student given scholarship aid **3.** any student or pupil

SCHNAUZER
(17–20 in. high
at shoulder)

**schol·ar·ly** (-lē) *adj.* **1.** of or relating to scholars **2.** showing much knowledge and critical ability **3.** devoted to learning; studious —*adv.* [Rare] like a scholar

**schol·ar·ship** (-ship') *n.* **1.** the quality of knowledge and learning shown by a student **2.** the systematized knowledge of a learned man, or of scholars collectively **3.** a gift of money or other aid to help a student

**scho·las·tic** (skə las'tik) *adj.* [< L. < Gr. < *scholazein*, to be at leisure < *scholē*, a SCHOOL[1]] **1.** of schools, colleges, students, teachers, etc.; academic **2.** [*also* S-] of or relating to scholasticism Also **scho·las'ti·cal** —*n.* [*also* S-] **1.** *same as* SCHOOLMAN **2.** a person who favors Scholasticism —**scho·las'ti·cal·ly** *adv.*

**scho·las·ti·cism** (-tə siz'm) *n.* **1.** [*often* S-] a medieval system of Christian thought based on Aristotelian logic **2.** an insistence upon traditional doctrines and methods

**scho·li·ast** (skō'lē əst) *n.* [< ModL. < MGr. < Gr. *scholion*, a comment < *scholē*, a SCHOOL[1]] an ancient interpreter and annotator of the classics —**scho'li·as'tic** *adj.*

**Schön·berg** (shän'bərg, shōn'-; *G.* shōn'berkh), **Arnold** 1874–1951; U.S. composer, born in Austria

**school[1]** (skōōl) *n.* [OE. *scol* < L. *schola* < Gr. *scholē*, leisure, school] **1.** a place or institution for teaching and learning, as a public school, dancing school, college or university, etc. **2.** *a)* the building or buildings, classrooms, etc. of a school *b)* all of its students and teachers *c)* a regular session of teaching at a school **3.** *a)* attendance at a school [to miss *school* for a week] *b)* the process of being educated at a school [he finished *school*] **4.** any situation or experience through which one gains knowledge, training, etc. [the *school* of hard knocks] **5.** a particular division of an institution of learning, esp. of a university [the *school* of law] **6.** a group following the same teachings, beliefs, methods, etc. [the Impressionist *school*] **7.** a way of life [a gentleman of the old *school*] —*vt.* **1.** to teach; instruct; educate **2.** to discipline or control —*adj.* of a school or schools

**school[2]** (skōōl) *n.* [Du., a crowd] a large number of fish or water animals of the same kind swimming or feeding together —*vi.* to move together in such a school

**school board** a group of people, elected or appointed, who are in charge of local public schools

**school·book** (skōōl'book') *n.* a book used for study in schools; textbook

**school·boy** (-boi') *n.* a boy attending school

**school bus** a vehicle for transporting students to and from school and on school-related trips

**school·child** (-chīld') *n., pl.* **-chil'dren** (-chil'drən) a child attending school

**school·fel·low** (-fel'ō) *n. same as* SCHOOLMATE

**school·girl** (-gurl') *n.* a girl attending school

**school guard** a person whose duty it is to escort children across streets near schools

**school·house** (-hous') *n.* a building used as a school

**school·ing** (-iŋ) *n.* **1.** training or education; esp., formal instruction at school **2.** cost of attending school

**school·man** (-mən; *for 2, often* -man') *n., pl.* **-men** (-mən; *for 2, often* -men') **1.** [*often* S-] any of the medieval teachers of scholasticism **2.** a teacher or educator

**school·marm** (-märm', -mäm') *n.* [Colloq.] a woman schoolteacher, hence any person, who tends to be oldfashioned and prudish: also **school'ma'am'** (-mam', -mam')

**school·mas·ter** (-mas'tər) *n.* **1.** a man who teaches in a school: an old-fashioned term **2.** [Brit.] a headmaster or master in a school —**school'mis'tress** (-mis'tris) *n.fem.*

**school·mate** (-māt') *n.* a person going to the same school at the same time as another

**school·room** (-rōōm') *n.* a classroom

**school·teach·er** (-tē'chər) *n.* a person whose work is teaching in a school

**school·work** (-wurk') *n.* lessons worked on in classes at school or done as homework

**school year** the part of a year when school is in session, usually from September to June

**schoon·er** (skōō'nər) *n.* [< ? Scot. dial. *scun*, to skip a flat stone across water] **1.** a ship with two or more masts, rigged fore and aft **2.** *short for* PRAIRIE SCHOONER **3.** a large beer glass

**Scho·pen·hau·er** (shō'pən hou'ər), **Arthur** 1788–1860; Ger. pessimist philosopher —**Scho'pen·hau'er·ism** *n.*

**schot·tische** (shät'ish) *n.* [< G. (*der*) *schottische* (*tanz*), (the) Scottish (dance)] **1.** a form of round dance in 2/4 time, similar to the polka **2.** music for this —*vi.* -**tisched**, -**tisch·ing** to dance a schottische

**Schu·bert** (shōō'bərt; *G.* shōō'bert), **Franz** (**Peter**) (fränts) 1797–1828; Austrian composer

**Schu·mann** (shōō'män), **Robert** (**Alexander**) 1810–56; Ger. composer

**schuss** (shoos) *n.* [G., lit., shot, rush] a straight run down a hill in skiing —*vi.* to make such a run

**schwa** (shwä) *n.* [G. < Heb. *sh'wā*] **1.** the neutral vowel sound of most unstressed syllables in English; sound of *a* in *ago, e* in *agent, i* in *sanity, o* in *comply, u* in *focus;* as in *able* (ā'b'l) **2.** the symbol (ə) for this sound

**Schweit·zer** (shvīt'sər; *E.* shwīt'sər), **Al·bert** (äl'bert) 1875–1965; Alsatian medical missionary, theologian, & musician in Africa

**sci. 1.** science **2.** scientific

**sci·at·ic** (sī at'ik) *adj.* [< MFr. < ML. < L. < Gr. *ischiadikos* < *ischion*, the hip] of, near, or affecting the hip or its nerves

**sci·at·i·ca** (sī at'i kə) *n.* any painful condition in the region of the hip and thighs; esp., neuritis of the long nerve (**sciatic nerve**) passing down the back of the thigh

**sci·ence** (sī'əns) *n.* [< OFr. < L. < prp. of *scire*, to know] **1.** orig., knowledge **2.** systematized knowledge derived from observation, study, and experimentation **3.** a branch of knowledge, esp. one concerned with establishing and systematizing facts, principles, and methods [the *science* of mathematics] **4.** *a*) the systematized knowledge of nature *b*) any branch of this See NATURAL SCIENCE **5.** skill based upon systematized training [the *science* of cooking] **6.** [S-] *shortened form of* CHRISTIAN SCIENCE

**science fiction** highly imaginative or fantastic fiction typically involving real or imagined scientific phenomena

**sci·en·tif·ic** (sī'ən tif'ik) *adj.* **1.** of, dealing with, or used in science [*scientific* study, *scientific* apparatus] **2.** *a*) based on, or using, the principles and methods of science; systematic and exact *b*) designating a method in which theories are based on data collected systematically and tested objectively **3.** *a*) done according to methods gained by systematic training [*scientific* boxing] *b*) having or showing such training —**sci'en·tif'i·cal·ly** *adv.*

**sci·en·tist** (sī'ən tist) *n.* **1.** a specialist in science, as in biology, chemistry, etc. **2.** [S-] a Christian Scientist

**sci-fi** (sī'fī') *adj., n. same as* SCIENCE FICTION

**scil·i·cet** (sil'i set') *adv.* [L., contr. of *scire licet*, it is permitted to know] namely; that is to say

**scim·i·tar, scim·i·ter** (sim'ə tər) *n.* [It. *scimitarra* < ?] a short, curved sword with an edge on the convex side, used chiefly by Turks, Arabs, etc.

**scin·til·la** (sin til'ə) *n.* [L.] **1.** a spark **2.** the least trace

**scin·til·late** (sin't'l āt') *vi.* -lat'ed, -lat'ing [< L. pp. of *scintillare* < *scintilla*, a spark] **1.** to give off sparks; flash; sparkle **2.** to sparkle with wit **3.** to twinkle, as a star — **scin'til·lant** *adj.* —**scin'til·la'tor** *n.*

**scin·til·la·tion** (sin't'l ā'shən) *n.* **1.** a scintillating, or flashing, twinkling, sparkling, etc. **2.** a spark or flash **3.** the flash of light made by ionizing radiation upon striking a crystal detector or a phosphor

**sci·o·lism** (sī'ə liz'm) *n.* [< L. dim. of *scius*, knowing < *scire*, to know] superficial knowledge or learning —**sci'o·list** *n.* —**sci'o·lis'tic** *adj.*

**sci·on** (sī'ən) *n.* [OFr. *cion* < ?] **1.** a shoot or bud of a plant, esp. one for grafting **2.** a descendant; offspring

**Scip·i·o** (sip'ē ō) **1.** (*Publius Cornelius Scipio Africanus* 237?–183? B.C.); Rom. general: defeated Hannibal (202): called *Major* or *the Elder* **2.** (*Publius Cornelius Scipio Aemilianus Africanus Numantinus*) 184?–129? B.C.; Rom. general & statesman: destroyed Carthage (146): grandson of *prec.*: called *Minor* or *the Younger*

**scis·sion** (sizh'ən, sish'-) *n.* [Fr. < LL. < L. pp. of *scindere*, to cut] a cutting or splitting, or the state of being cut

**scis·sor** (siz'ər) *vt.* to cut with scissors —*n. same as* SCISSORS

**scis·sors** (siz'ərz) *n.pl.* [< OFr. < LL. pl. of *cisorium*, cutting tool < L. *caedere*, to cut] **1.** a cutting instrument, smaller than shears, with two opposing blades which are pivoted together so that they work against each other: also **pair of scissors 2.** [*with sing. v.*] *a*) a gymnastic feat in which the legs are moved in a way suggestive of scissors *b*) *same as* SCISSORS HOLD

**scissors hold** a wrestling hold in which one contestant clasps the other with his legs

**scissors kick** a swimming kick in which one leg is bent at the knee and the other thrust backward, then both brought together with a snap

**scis·sor·tail** (siz'ər tāl') *n.* a pale gray and pink variety of flycatcher of the S U.S. and Mexico, having a forked tail

**SCLC, S.C.L.C.** Southern Christian Leadership Conference

**scle·ra** (sklir'ə) *n.* [< Gr. *sklēros*, hard] the tough, white, fibrous membrane covering all of the eyeball except the area covered by the cornea

**scle·ren·chy·ma** (skli ren'kə mə) *n.* [ModL. < Gr. *sklēros*, hard + *enchyma*, infusion] *Bot.* plant tissue of uniformly thick-walled, dead cells, as in nut shells

**scle·ro-** [< Gr. *sklēros*, hard] *a combining form meaning:* **1.** hard **2.** of the sclera Also, before a vowel, **scler-**

**scle·ro·sis** (skli rō'sis) *n., pl.* -ses (-sēz) [< ML. < Gr. < *sklēros*, hard] **1.** an abnormal hardening of body tissues, esp. of the nervous system or the walls of arteries **2.** a disease characterized by such hardening

**scle·rot·ic** (-rät'ik) *adj.* **1.** hard **2.** of, characterized by, or having sclerosis **3.** of the sclera

**scoff** (skôf, skäf) *n.* [prob. < Scand.] **1.** an expression of scorn or derision; jeer **2.** an object of mocking contempt, scorn, etc. —*vt.* to mock at or deride —*vi.* to show scorn or derision; jeer (*at*) —**scoff'er** *n.* —**scoff'ing·ly** *adv.*

**scoff·law** (-lô) *n.* [prec. + LAW] [Colloq.] a habitual or flagrant violator of laws, esp. traffic or liquor laws

**scold** (skōld) *n.* [< ON. *skald*, poet (prob. because of satirical verses)] a person, esp. a woman, who habitually uses abusive language —*vt.* to find fault with angrily; rebuke —*vi.* **1.** to find fault angrily **2.** to use abusive language habitually —**scold'er** *n.* —**scold'ing** *adj., n.*

**scol·lop** (skäl'əp) *n., vt. var. of* SCALLOP

**sconce[1]** (skäns) *n.* [< OFr., ult. < L. *abscondere*, to hide] a bracket attached to a wall for holding a candle, etc.

**sconce[2]** (skäns) *n.* [Du. *schans*, a fortress, orig. wickerwork] a small fort, bulwark, etc. —*vt.* **sconced, sconc'ing** [Archaic] **1.** to provide with a sconce **2.** to shelter or protect

**scone** (skōn) *n.* [Scot., contr. < ? MDu. *schoonbrot*, fine bread] a tea cake resembling a baking powder biscuit, usually baked on a griddle

**scoop** (skoōp) *n.* [< MDu. *schope*, bailing vessel & *schoppe*, a shovel] **1.** any of various small, shovellike utensils; specif., *a*) a kitchen utensil used to take up sugar, flour, etc. *b*) a small utensil with a round bowl, for dishing up ice cream, mashed potatoes, etc. **2.** the deep shovel of a dredge or steam shovel, which takes up sand, etc. **3.** the act or motion of taking up with or as with a scoop **4.** the amount taken up at one time by a scoop **5.** a hollowed-out place **6.** [Colloq.] a large profit made by speculation **7.** [Colloq.] *a*) advantage gained over a competitor by being first, specif. as in the publication of a news item *b*) such a news item —*adj.* designating a rounded, somewhat low neckline in a dress, etc. —*vt.* **1.** to take up or out as with a scoop **2.** to dig (*out*); hollow (*out*) **3.** to make by digging out **4.** to gather (*in* or *up*) as if with a scoop **5.** [Colloq.] to effect a scoop (*n.* 7) in competition with —**scoop'er** *n.*

**scoop·ful** (-fool') *n., pl.* -fuls' as much as a scoop will hold

**scoot** (skoōt) *vi., vt.* [prob. < ON. *skjóta*, to shoot] [Colloq.] to go or move quickly; hurry (off); dart —*n.* [Colloq.] the act of scooting

**scoot·er** (-ər) *n.* [< prec.] **1.** a child's toy for riding on, consisting of a low footboard with a wheel or wheels at each end, and a raised handlebar for steering: it is moved by pushing one foot against the ground **2.** a similar vehicle with a seat, propelled by a motor: in full, **motor scooter 3.** a sailboat with runners, for use on water or ice

**scope** (skōp) *n.* [< It. < L. < Gr. *skopos*, distant object viewed, watcher] **1.** the extent of the mind's grasp; range of understanding **2.** the range or extent of action, content, etc., or of an activity, concept, etc. [the *scope* of a book] **3.** room or opportunity for action or thought **4.** *short for* TELESCOPE, MICROSCOPE, RADARSCOPE, etc.

**-scope** (skōp) [< Gr. < *skopein*, to see] *a combining form meaning* an instrument, etc. for seeing or observing [*telescope*]

**sco·pol·a·mine** (skō päl'ə mēn', -min) *n.* [< G. < ModL. *Scopolia*, a genus of plants, after G. A. *Scopoli* (1723–1788), It. naturalist + G. *amin*, amine] an alkaloid, $C_{17}H_{21}O_4N$, used in medicine as a sedative, hypnotic, etc.

**-sco·py** (skə pē) [< Gr. < *skopein*, to see] *a combining form meaning* a seeing, observing [*bioscopy*]

**scor·bu·tic** (skôr byoōt'ik) *adj.* [< ModL. < ML. *scorbutus*, scurvy < Russ. *skórbnut*, to wither] of, like, or having scurvy: also **scor·bu'ti·cal**

**scorch** (skôrch) *vt.* [< ? Scand.] **1.** *a*) to char or discolor the surface of by superficial burning *b*) to parch or shrivel by heat **2.** to criticize very sharply **3.** to burn and destroy everything in (an area) before yielding it to the enemy [a *scorched*-earth policy] —*vi.* to become scorched —*n.* a superficial burning or burn

**scorch·er** (-ər) *n.* anything that scorches; esp., [Colloq.] *a*) a very hot day *b*) a withering remark

**score** (skôr) *n.* [OE. *scoru* < ON. *skor*] **1.** *a*) a scratch, mark, incision, etc. *b*) a drawn line, as one to mark a starting point *c*) notches, marks, etc. made to keep tally or account **2.** an amount due; debt **3.** a grievance one seeks to settle or get even for **4.** a reason or ground **5.** the number of points made in a game or contest **6.** a grade or rating, as on a test **7.** *a*) twenty people or things *b*) [*pl.*] very many **8.** [Colloq.] a successful action, remark, etc. **9.** [Colloq.] the way things really are: chiefly in **know the score 10.** [Slang] the victim of a swindle; mark **11.** *Music a*) a written or printed copy of a composition, showing all parts for the instruments or voices *b*) the music for a stage production, motion picture, etc. —*vt.* **scored, scor'ing 1.** to mark or mark out with notches, lines, gashes, etc. **2.** to crease or partly cut (paper, etc.) for accurate folding or tearing **3.** to keep account of by lines or notches **4.** *a*) to make (runs, hits, goals, etc.) in a game *b*) to record the score of *c*) to add (points) to one's score *d*) *Baseball* to bring (a runner) home on one's hit, etc. **5.** to gain [to *score* a success] **6.** to grade, as in testing **7.** *a*) to raise welts on by lashing *b*) to upbraid **8.** *Music* to arrange in a score —*vi.* **1.** to make points, as in a game **2.** to run up a score **3.** to keep score in a game **4.** to succeed in getting what one wants —**scor'er** *n.*

**score·board** (-bôrd') *n.* a large board for posting the score and other details of a game, as in a baseball stadium

**score card** **1.** a card for recording the score of a game, match, etc. **2.** a card printed with the names, positions, etc. of the players of competing teams Also **score'card'** *n.*

**score·keep·er** (-kēp'ər) *n.* a person keeping score, esp. officially, at a game, competition, etc.

**score·less** (-lis) *adj.* with no points scored

**sco·ri·a** (skôr′ē ə) *n.*, *pl.* **-ri·ae′** (-ē′) [L. < Gr. < *skōr*, dung] **1.** the refuse left after metal has been smelted from ore **2.** cinderlike lava —**sco′ri·a′ceous** (-ā′shəs) *adj.*

**scorn** (skôrn) *n.* [< OFr. < *escharnir*, to scorn] **1.** great contempt for someone or something, often with some indignation **2.** expression of this feeling **3.** the object of such contempt —*vt.* **1.** to regard with scorn; treat with contempt **2.** to refuse or reject as wrong or disgraceful —*vi.* [Obs.] to scoff; mock —**laugh to scorn** to ridicule

**scorn·ful** (-fəl) *adj.* filled with or showing scorn or contempt —**scorn′ful·ly** *adv.* —**scorn′ful·ness** *n.*

**Scor·pi·o** (skôr′pē ō′) [L.] **1.** a S constellation: also **Scor′pi·us** (-əs) **2.** *Astrol.* the eighth sign of the zodiac: see ZO-DIAC, illus.

**scor·pi·on** (-ən) *n.* [OFr. < L. < Gr. *skorpios*] **1.** any of various arachnids found in warm regions, with a long tail ending in a curved, poisonous sting **2.** *Bible* a whip or scourge —[S- ] *same as* SCORPIO

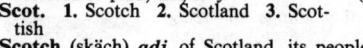

**Scot** (skät) *n.* **1.** any member of a Gaelic tribe of northern Ireland that migrated to Scotland in the 5th cent. A.D. **2.** a native or inhabitant of Scotland

SCORPION
(to 10 in. long)

**scot** (skät) *n.* [ON. *skot*, tribute] money assessed or paid; tax; levy

**Scot.** **1.** Scotch **2.** Scotland **3.** Scottish

**Scotch** (skäch) *adj.* of Scotland, its people, their language, etc.: cf. SCOTTISH —*n. same as:* **1.** SCOTTISH **2.** SCOTCH WHISKY

**scotch** (skäch) *vt.* [prob. < Anglo-Fr. < OFr. *coche*, a notch] **1.** to cut; scratch; notch **2.** to wound without killing; maim **3.** to put an end to; stifle [to *scotch* a rumor] —*n.* a cut or scratch

**Scotch-Irish** (-ī′rish) *adj.* designating or of those people of northern Ireland descended from Scottish settlers, esp. those who emigrated to America

**Scotch·man** (-mən) *n.*, *pl.* **-men** *var. of* SCOTSMAN

**Scotch pine** a hardy Eurasian pine, with yellow wood

**Scotch tape** [< *Scotch*, a trademark] a thin, transparent, cellulose adhesive tape

**Scotch terrier** *same as* SCOTTISH TERRIER

**Scotch whisky** whiskey, often having a smoky flavor, distilled in Scotland from malted barley

**sco·ter** (skōt′ər) *n.*, *pl.* **-ters, -ter:** see PLURAL, II, D, 1 [< ?] any of several large, dark-colored sea ducks found chiefly along the N coasts of Europe and N. America

**scot-free** (skät′frē′) *adj.* **1.** free from payment of scot, or tax **2.** unharmed or unpunished; free from penalty

**Sco·tia** (skō′shə) *n. poet. term for* SCOTLAND

**Scot·land** (skät′lənd) division of the United Kingdom, occupying the N half of Great Britain & nearby islands: 30,405 sq. mi.; pop. 5,217,000; cap. Edinburgh

**Scotland Yard** **1.** headquarters of the metropolitan London police: officially, **New Scotland Yard** **2.** the London police, esp. the detective bureau

**Scots** (skäts) *adj.*, *n. same as* SCOTTISH

**Scots·man** (skäts′mən) *n.*, *pl.* **-men** a native or inhabitant of Scotland, esp. a man: *Scotsman* or *Scot* is preferred to *Scotchman* in Scotland —**Scots′wom′an** *n.fem.*, *pl.* **-wom′en**

**Scott** (skät) **1.** **Robert Fal·con** (fôl′kən), 1868–1912; Eng. antarctic explorer **2.** **Sir Walter,** 1771–1832; Scot. poet & novelist

**Scot·ti·cism** (skät′ə siz′m) *n.* a Scottish idiom, expression, word, pronunciation, etc.

**Scot·tie, Scot·ty** (skät′ē) *n.*, *pl.* **-ties** *colloq.* name for SCOT-TISH TERRIER

**Scot·tish** (skät′ish) *adj.* of Scotland, its people, their English dialect, etc. *Scottish* is preferred in formal usage, but with some words, *Scotch* is almost invariably used (e.g., tweed, whisky), with others, *Scots* (e.g., law) —*n.* the dialect of English spoken in Scotland —**the Scottish** the Scottish people

**Scottish Gaelic** the Celtic language of the Scottish Highlands: see GAELIC

**Scottish terrier** any of a breed of terriers with short legs, a squarish muzzle, rough, wiry hair, and pointed, erect ears

**Scotts·dale** (skäts′dāl′) [after Rev. W. *Scott*, chaplain in the Civil War] city in SC Ariz.: suburb of Phoenix: pop. 88,000

**Scotus** *see* DUNS SCOTUS

**scoun·drel** (skoun′drəl) *n.* [prob. < Anglo-Fr. *escoundre*, ult. < L. *abscondere*, ABSCOND] a mean, immoral, or wicked person; villain; rascal —*adj.* characteristic of a scoundrel; mean: also **scoun′drel·ly**

**scour¹** (skour) *vt.* [MDu. *scuren* < ? OFr. *escurer* < VL. < L. *ex-*, intens. + *curare*, to take care of] **1.** to clean or polish by vigorous rubbing, as with abrasives **2.** to remove dirt and grease from (wool, etc.) **3.** *a*) to wash or clear as by a swift current of water; flush *b*) to wash away **4.** to clear of (something undesirable) —*vi.* **1.** to clean things by rubbing and polishing **2.** to become clean and bright by being scoured —*n.* **1.** the act of scouring **2.** a cleansing agent used in scouring **3.** [*usually pl., with sing. v.*] dysentery in cattle, etc. —**scour′er** *n.*

**scour²** (skour) *vt.* [< ? OFr. *escourre*, to run forth < VL. < L. *ex-*, out + *currere*, to run] to pass over quickly, or range over or through, as in search or pursuit [to *scour* a town for an escaped convict] —*vi.* to run or range about, as in search or pursuit —**scour′er** *n.*

**scourge** (skurj) *n.* [< OFr. < L. *ex*, off + *corrigia*, a whip] **1.** a whip or other instrument for flogging **2.** any means of severe punishment or any cause of great suffering [the *scourge* of war] —*vt.* **scourged, scourg′ing** **1.** to whip or flog **2.** to punish or make suffer severely —**scourg′er** *n.*

**scour·ings** (skour′iŋz) *n.pl.* dirt, refuse, or remains removed by or as if by scouring

**scout¹** (skout) *n.* [< OFr. < *escouter*, to hear < L. *auscultare*, to listen] **1.** a soldier, plane, etc. sent to spy out the strength, movements, etc. of the enemy **2.** a person sent out to learn the tactics of an opponent, to search out new talent, etc. [a baseball *scout*] **3.** a member of the Boy Scouts or Girl Scouts **4.** the act of reconnoitering **5.** [Slang] fellow; guy —*vt.* **1.** to follow closely so as to spy upon **2.** to look for; watch **3.** to find by looking around (often with *out, up*) —*vi.* **1.** to go out in search of information about the enemy; reconnoiter **2.** to go in search of something [*scout* around for some firewood] **3.** to work as a scout (*n.* 2) **4.** to be active in the Boy Scouts or Girl Scouts —**scout′er** *n.* —**scout′ing** *n.*

**scout²** (skout) *vt.* [prob. < ON. *skuti*, a taunt] to reject as absurd; scoff at —*vi.* to scoff (*at*)

**scout·mas·ter** (-mas′tər) *n.* the adult leader of a troop of Boy Scouts

**scow** (skou) *n.* [Du. *schouw*] a large, flat-bottomed boat with square ends, used for carrying coal, sand, etc. and often towed by a tug

**scowl** (skoul) *vi.* [prob. < Scand.] **1.** to contract the eyebrows and lower the corners of the mouth in showing displeasure; look angry, sullen, etc. **2.** to have a threatening look; lower —*vt.* to affect or express with a scowl —*n.* the act or expression of scowling; angry frown —**scowl′er** *n.*

**scrab·ble** (skrab′'l) *vi.* **-bled, -bling** [Du. *schrabbelen* < *schrabben*, to scrape] **1.** to scratch, scrape, or paw as though looking for something **2.** to struggle **3.** to scribble —*vt.* **1.** to scrape together quickly **2.** *a*) to scribble *b*) to scribble on —*n.* **1.** a scrabbling; a scramble, scribble, scrawl, etc. —[S-] *a trademark for* a word game played with lettered tiles placed as in a crossword puzzle —**scrab′bler** *n.*

**scrag** (skrag) *n.* [prob. < ON.] **1.** a thin, scrawny person, animal, or plant **2.** [Slang] the neck —*vt.* **scragged, scrag′-ging** [Slang] to choke or wring the neck of

**scrag·gly** (skrag′lē) *adj.* **-gli·er, -gli·est** [see ff. & -LY¹] sparse, scrubby, irregular, uneven, ragged, or the like [a *scraggly* beard] —**scrag′gli·ness** *n.*

**scrag·gy** (skrag′ē) *adj.* **-gi·er, -gi·est** [< SCRAG] **1.** rough or jagged **2.** lean; bony; skinny —**scrag′gi·ly** *adv.*

**scram** (skram) *vi.* **scrammed, scram′ming** [contr. of ff.] [Slang] to leave or get out, esp. in a hurry

**scram·ble** (skram′b'l) *vi.* **-bled, -bling** [< ? SCAMPER + SCRABBLE] **1.** to climb, crawl, or clamber hurriedly **2.** to scuffle or struggle for something **3.** to rush pell-mell, as to get something highly prized [to *scramble* for political office] —*vt.* **1.** *a*) to throw together haphazardly; jumble *b*) *Electronics* to modify (transmitted auditory or visual signals) so as to make unintelligible without special receiving equipment **2.** to cook (eggs) while stirring the mixed whites and yolks —*n.* **1.** a hard, hurried climb or advance as over rough, difficult ground **2.** a disorderly struggle or rush, as for something prized **3.** a jumble —**scram′bler** *n.*

**Scran·ton** (skrant′'n) [family name of the founders of a local ironworks] city in NE Pa.: pop. 88,000

**scrap¹** (skrap) *n.* [< ON. *skrap*] **1.** a small piece; fragment; bit **2.** a bit of something written **3.** *a*) discarded metal suitable only for reprocessing *b*) discarded articles of rubber, leather, paper, etc. **4.** [*pl.*] bits of leftover food —*adj.* **1.** in the form of pieces, leftovers, etc. **2.** used and discarded —*vt.* **scrapped, scrap′ping 1.** to make into scrap **2.** to discard; junk —**scrap′per** *n.*

**scrap²** (skrap) *n.* [prob. < *scrape*, orig., nefarious scheme] [Colloq.] a fight or quarrel —*vi.* **scrapped, scrap′ping** [Colloq.] to fight or quarrel —**scrap′per** *n.*

**scrap·book** (-book′) *n.* a book of blank pages for mounting clippings, pictures, etc.

---

fat, āpe, cär, ten, ēven, is, bīte; gō, hôrn, tōōl, look; oil, out; up, fur; get; joy; yet; chin; she; thin, *then*; zh, leisure; ŋ, ring; ə for *a* in *ago*, *e* in *agent*, *i* in *sanity*, *o* in *comply*, *u* in *focus*; as in *able* (ā′b'l); Fr. bal; ë, Fr. coeur; ö, Fr. feu; Fr. mon; δ, Fr. coq; ü, Fr. duc; r, Fr. cri; H, G. ich; kh, G. doch; ‡foreign; *hypothetical; < derived from. See inside front cover.

**scrape** (skrāp) *vt.* **scraped, scrap′ing** [< ON. *skrapa*] **1.** to rub over the surface of with something rough or sharp **2.** to make smooth or clean by rubbing with a tool or abrasive **3.** to remove by rubbing with something sharp or rough (with *off*, *out*, etc.) **4.** to scratch or abrade by a rough, rubbing contact **5.** to rub with a harsh, grating sound *[chalk scraping a blackboard]* **6.** to gather slowly and with difficulty *[to scrape up some money]* —*vi.* **1.** to rub against something harshly; grate **2.** to give out a harsh, grating noise **3.** to gather goods or money slowly and with difficulty **4.** to manage to get by (with *through*, *along*, *by*) **5.** to draw the foot back along the ground in bowing —*n.* **1.** a scraping **2.** a scraped place; abrasion **3.** a harsh, grating sound **4.** a disagreeable situation; predicament **5.** a fight or conflict —**scrap′er** *n.*
**scrap·ing** (skrā′piŋ) *n.* **1.** the act of a person or thing that scrapes **2.** the sound of this **3.** *[usually pl.]* something scraped off, together, or up
**scrap iron** discarded or waste pieces of iron, to be recast
**scrap·ple** (skrap′'l) *n.* [dim. of SCRAP[1]] cornmeal boiled with scraps of pork, allowed to set, sliced, and fried
**scrap·py[1]** (skrap′ē) *adj.* **-pi·er, -pi·est** [SCRAP[1] + -Y[2]] **1.** made of scraps **2.** disconnected *[scrappy memories]* —**scrap′pi·ly** *adv.* —**scrap′pi·ness** *n.*
**scrap·py[2]** (skrap′ē) *adj.* **-pi·er, -pi·est** [SCRAP[2] + -Y[2]] [Colloq.] fond of fighting —**scrap′pi·ly** *adv.* —**scrap′pi·ness** *n.*
**Scratch** (skrach) [altered (after ff.) < ON. *skratti*, devil] *[sometimes s-]* the Devil: usually **Old Scratch**
**scratch** (skrach) *vt.* [prob. altered < ME. *scratten*, to scratch, after *cracchen*] **1.** to mark or cut the surface of slightly with something pointed or sharp **2.** to tear or dig with the nails or claws **3.** *a)* to scrape lightly to relieve itching, etc. *b)* to chafe **4.** to rub or scrape with a grating noise **5.** to write or draw hurriedly or carelessly **6.** to strike out (writing, etc.) **7.** to gather with difficulty; scrape (*together* or *up*) **8.** *Politics* to strike out the name of (a candidate) on (a party ticket or ballot) **9.** *Sports* to withdraw (an entry) from a contest, specif. from a horse race —*vi.* **1.** to use nails or claws in digging or wounding **2.** to scrape the skin lightly to relieve itching, etc. **3.** to manage to get by **4.** to make a harsh, scraping noise **5.** to withdraw from a race or contest **6.** *Billiards, Pool* to commit a scratch —*n.* **1.** the act of scratching **2.** a mark, tear, or slight wound made by scratching **3.** a grating or scraping sound **4.** a scribble **5.** the starting line of a race **6.** [Slang] money **7.** *Billiards, Pool a)* a shot that results in a penalty *b)* a miss **8.** *Sports a)* the starting point or time of a contestant who receives no handicap *b)* such a contestant *c)* an entry withdrawn from a contest —*adj.* **1.** used for hasty notes, preliminary figuring, etc. *[scratch paper]* **2.** having no handicap in a contest **3.** put together hastily, without selection **4.** *Baseball* designating a chance hit credited to the batter for a ball not hit sharply —**from scratch 1.** from the starting line, as in a race **2.** from nothing; without advantage —**scratch the surface** to do, consider, or affect something superficially —**up to scratch** [Colloq.] up to a standard —**scratch′er** *n.*
**scratch·y** (-ē) *adj.* **scratch′i·er, scratch′i·est 1.** made with scratches **2.** making a scratching noise **3.** scratched together; haphazard **4.** that chafes, itches, etc. *[scratchy cloth]* —**scratch′i·ly** *adv.* —**scratch′i·ness** *n.*
**scrawl** (skrôl) *vt., vi.* [< ?] to write, draw, or mark hastily, carelessly, or awkwardly —*n.* **1.** sprawling handwriting, often hard to read **2.** something scrawled —**scrawl′er** *n.* —**scrawl′y** *adj.* **scrawl′i·er, scrawl′i·est**
**scraw·ny** (skrô′nē) *adj.* **-ni·er, -ni·est** [prob. < Scand.] **1.** very thin; skinny and bony **2.** stunted or scrubby —**scraw′ni·ness** *n.*
**scream** (skrēm) *vi.* [akin to WFl. *schreemen*, to scream, G. *schrei*, a cry] **1.** to utter or make a shrill, piercing cry or sound **2.** to laugh loudly or hysterically **3.** to have a startling effect **4.** to shout or yell in anger, hysteria, etc. —*vt.* **1.** to utter with or as with a scream **2.** to bring into a specified state by screaming *[to scream oneself hoarse]* —*n.* **1.** a sharp, piercing cry or sound **2.** [Colloq.] a hilariously funny person or thing
**scream·er** (-ər) *n.* **1.** a person who screams **2.** [Slang] a sensational headline **3.** any of various long-toed S. American wading birds
**scream·ing** (-iŋ) *adj.* **1.** that screams **2.** startling in effect **3.** causing screams of laughter —**scream′ing·ly** *adv.*
**screech** (skrēch) *vi.* [ON. *skraekja*] to utter or make a shrill, high-pitched, harsh shriek or sound —*vt.* to utter with a screech —*n.* a shrill, high-pitched, harsh shriek or sound —**screech′er** *n.* —**screech′y** *adj.* **screech′i·er, screech′i·est**
**screech owl 1.** a small owl with feathered ear tufts and an eerie, wailing cry **2.** [Brit.] *same as* BARN OWL
**screed** (skrēd) *n.* [ME. *screde*, var. of *schrede*, shred] a long, tiresome speech or piece of writing

**screen** (skrēn) *n.* [< OFr. *escren* < Gmc.] **1.** a curtain or movable partition, as a covered frame, used to separate, conceal, protect, etc. **2.** anything that functions to shield, conceal, etc. *[a smoke screen]* **3.** a coarse mesh of wire, etc. used as a sieve, as for grading coal **4.** a system for screening or testing persons **5.** a frame covered with a mesh, as of wire, used, as on a window, to keep insects out **6.** *a)* a white surface upon which movies, slides, etc. are projected *b)* the movie industry or art **7.** the surface area of a television or radar receiver on which the light pattern is traced —*vt.* **1.** to separate, conceal, or protect, as with a screen **2.** to enclose or provide with a screen **3.** to sift through a screen **4.** *a)* to interview or test in order to separate according to skills, personality, etc. *b)* to separate in this way (usually with *out*) **5.** *a)* to project (movies, etc.) upon a screen *b)* to photograph with a movie camera *c)* to adapt (a story, play, etc.) as for a movie —*vi.* to be screened or suitable for screening, as in movies —**screen′a·ble** *adj.* —**screen′er** *n.* —**screen′less** *adj.*
**screen·ing** (-iŋ) *n.* **1.** the act of one that screens **2.** *a)* a screen or set of screens *b)* mesh used in a screen **3.** *[pl.]* material separated out by a sifting screen
**screen·play** (-plā′) *n.* a story written, or adapted from a novel, etc., for production as a movie
**screw** (skrōō) *n.* [MFr. *escroue*, hole in which a screw turns < L. *scrofa*, sow, infl. by *scrobis*, vulva] **1.** *a)* a cylindrical or conical piece of metal for fastening things by being turned: it is threaded evenly with an advancing spiral ridge and usually has a slotted head: also called **male** (or **external**) **screw** *b)* the internal thread, as of a nut, into which a male screw can be turned: also called **female** (or **internal**) **screw** *c)* a turning of such a screw **2.** any of various devices operating or threaded like a screw, as a screw propeller **3.** [Slang] a prison guard **4.** [Chiefly Brit. Colloq.] a stingy person **5.** [Brit. Colloq.] a salary —*vt.* **1.** to twist; turn; tighten **2.** to fasten, tighten, insert, etc. as with a screw or screws **3.** to twist out of shape; contort **4.** to make stronger (often with *up*) **5.** to force or compel, as if by using screws **6.** [Slang] to cheat; swindle —*vi.* **1.** to go together or come apart by being turned like a screw *[a lid screws on]* **2.** to be fitted for screws **3.** to twist; turn; wind **4.** to cheat; swindle —**have a screw loose** [Slang] to be eccentric, odd, etc. —**put the screws on** (or **to**) to subject to force or great pressure —**screw up** [Slang] to make a mess of; bungle

MACHINE SCREW
MACHINE SCREW
WOOD SCREW
LAG SCREW
SETSCREW

**screw·ball** (-bôl′) *n.* **1.** *Baseball* a ball thrown by a right-handed pitcher that curves to the right, or by a left-handed pitcher that curves to the left **2.** [Slang] a person who seems irrational, unconventional, unbalanced, etc. —*adj.* [Slang] peculiar; irrational
**screw·driv·er** (-drī′vər) *n.* **1.** a tool used for turning screws, having an end that fits into the slot in the head of a screw **2.** a cocktail of orange juice and vodka
**screw eye** a screw with a loop for a head
**screw hook** a screw with a hook for a head
**screw propeller** *see* PROPELLER
**screw thread** the spiral ridge of a screw
**screw·y** (skrōō′ē) *adj.* **screw′i·er, screw′i·est** [Slang] **1.** mentally unbalanced; crazy **2.** peculiar, odd, etc. in a confusing way —**screw′i·ness** *n.*
**scrib·ble** (skrib′'l) *vt., vi.* **-bled, -bling** [< ML. < L. *scribere*, to write] **1.** to write carelessly, hastily, or illegibly **2.** to cover with or make marks that are meaningless or hard to read —*n.* scribbled writing, marks, etc.; scrawl —**scrib′bler** *n.*
**scribe** (skrīb) *n.* [L. *scriba*, public writer < *scribere*, to write] **1.** a penman who copied manuscripts before the invention of printing **2.** a writer; author **3.** a person learned in the Jewish law who makes handwritten copies of the Torah **4.** a person employed by the public to write letters, etc. —*vi.* **scribed, scrib′ing** to work as a scribe —**scrib′al** *adj.*
**scrim** (skrim) *n.* [< ?] a light, sheer, loosely woven cotton or linen cloth, often used in the theater as a backdrop or as a semitransparent curtain
**scrim·mage** (skrim′ij) *n.* [altered < SKIRMISH] **1.** a tussle; confused struggle **2.** *Football a)* the play that follows the pass from center *b)* football practice in the form of actual play —*vi.* **-maged, -mag·ing** to take part in a scrimmage
**scrimp** (skrimp) *vt.* [prob. < Scand.] **1.** to make too small, short, etc.; skimp **2.** to treat stingily; stint —*vi.* to be sparing and frugal —**scrimp′er** *n.* —**scrimp′ing·ly** *adv.*
**scrimp·y** (skrim′pē) *adj.* **scrimp′i·er, scrimp′i·est 1.** skimpy; scanty **2.** meager **3.** frugal or economical —**scrimp′i·ly** *adv.* —**scrimp′i·ness** *n.*
**scrim·shaw** (skrim′shô′) *n.* [< ?] **1.** carving done on shells, bone, ivory, etc., esp. by sailors **2.** an article or articles so made

**scrip** (skrip) *n.* [contr. < SCRIPT] **1.** a note, list, receipt, etc. **2.** a certificate of a right to receive something; specif., a certificate of indebtedness, issued as currency, as by a local government without funds

**script** (skript) *n.* [< MFr. < L. *scriptum*, neut. pp. of *scribere*, to write] **1.** handwriting, or a style of this **2.** *Printing* a typeface that looks like handwriting **3.** an original manuscript **4.** a copy of the text of a play or movie, or of a radio or television show —*vt.* [Colloq.] to write the script for (a movie, etc.)

**scrip·ture** (skrip′chər) *n.* [< L. < *scriptus*: see SCRIPT] **1.** [S-] [*often pl.*] *a*) the sacred writings of the Jews, identical with the Old Testament of the Christians *b*) the Christian Bible; Old and New Testaments **2.** any sacred writing —**scrip′tur·al** *adj.* —**scrip′tur·al·ly** *adv.*

**script·writ·er** (skript′rīt′ər) *n.* a person who writes scripts for movies, television shows, etc.

**scrive·ner** (skriv′nər, -'n ər) *n.* [< OFr., ult. < L. *scriba*, a SCRIBE] [Archaic] **1.** a scribe or clerk **2.** a notary

**scrod** (skräd) *n.* [prob. < MDu. *schrode*, strip] a young codfish or haddock, split and prepared for cooking

**scrof·u·la** (skräf′yə lə) *n.* [ML. < L. < dim. of *scrofa*, a sow] tuberculosis of the lymphatic glands, esp. of the neck, in which the glands become enlarged —**scrof′u·lous** *adj.* —**scrof′u·lous·ly** *adv.* —**scrof′u·lous·ness** *n.*

**scroll** (skrōl) *n.* [altered (? after *roll*) < ME. *scrowe* < OFr. *escroue*, roll of writings] **1.** a roll of parchment, paper, etc., usually with writing on it **2.** anything having the form of a loosely rolled sheet of paper, as an ornamental design in coiled or spiral form — **scrolled** *adj.*

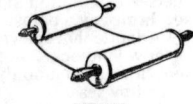

SCROLL

**scroll saw** a thin, ribbonlike saw for cutting thin wood into spiral or ornamental designs (scroll′work′)

**Scrooge** (skrooj) *n.* [after *Scrooge*, a character in Dickens' *A Christmas Carol*] [*also* s-] a hard, miserly old man

**scro·tum** (skrōt′əm) *n., pl.* -**ta** (-ə), -**tums** [L.] in most male mammals, the pouch of skin containing the testicles —**scro′tal** *adj.*

**scrounge** (skrounj) *vt.* **scrounged, scroung′ing** [< ?] [Colloq.] **1.** to get or find by hunting around **2.** to get by begging or sponging **3.** to pilfer —*vi.* [Colloq.] to search (*around*) for something —**scroung′er** *n.*

**scrub**[1] (skrub) *n.* [dial. var. of *shrub*, infl. ? by ON. *skroppa*, a lean creature] **1.** *a*) short, stunted trees or bushes growing thickly together *b*) land covered with such growth **2.** any person, animal, or thing smaller than the usual, or considered inferior **3.** *Sports a*) a player not on the regular team *b*) [*pl.*] a secondary team made up of such players —*adj.* **1.** mean; poor; inferior **2.** undersized; stunted **3.** *Sports* of or for the scrubs

**scrub**[2] (skrub) *vt.* **scrubbed, scrub′bing** [prob. < Scand.] **1.** to clean or wash by rubbing hard **2.** to rub hard **3.** to cleanse (a gas) of impurities **4.** [Colloq.] *a*) to cancel or call off *b*) to get rid of —*vi.* to clean something by rubbing, as with a brush —*n.* **1.** the act of scrubbing **2.** a person who scrubs —**scrub′ber** *n.*

**scrub·by** (skrub′ē) *adj.* -**bi·er, -bi·est** **1.** undersized or inferior; stunted **2.** covered with brushwood **3.** paltry; shabby, etc. —**scrub′bi·ly** *adv.* —**scrub′bi·ness** *n.*

**scruff** (skruf) *n.* [< ON. *skrufr*, tuft of hair] the back of the neck; nape

**scruff·y** (skruf′ē) *adj.* **scruff′i·er, scruff′i·est** [< dial. *scruff*, var. of SCURF + -Y[2]] shabby, unkempt, or untidy; grubby —**scruff′i·ly** *adv.* —**scruff′i·ness** *n.*

**scrum·mage** (skrum′ij) *n.* [dial. var. of SCRIMMAGE] *Rugby* a play in which the two sets of forwards, lined up facing each other, try to kick the ball back to their teammates —*vi.* -**maged, -mag·ing** to take part in a scrummage

**scrump·tious** (skrump′shəs) *adj.* [< SUMPTUOUS] [Colloq.] very pleasing, attractive, etc. —**scrump′tious·ly** *adv.*

**scru·ple** (skroo′p'l) *n.* [< MFr. < L. *scrupulus*, small sharp stone] **1.** a very small quantity **2.** an apothecaries' weight equal to 1/3 dram (20 grains) **3.** a doubt arising from difficulty in deciding what is right, proper, etc.; qualm —*vt., vi.* -**pled, -pling** to hesitate (at) from doubt; have scruples (about)

**scru·pu·lous** (skroo′pyə ləs) *adj.* **1.** having or showing scruples; conscientiously honest **2.** demanding or using precision, care, and exactness —**scru′pu·los′i·ty** (-läs′ə-tē), *pl.* -**ties, scru′pu·lous·ness** *n.* —**scru′pu·lous·ly** *adv.*

**scru·ti·nize** (skroot′'n īz′) *vt.* -**nized′, -niz′ing** to look at carefully or examine closely —**scru′ti·niz′er** *n.*

**scru·ti·ny** (-'n ē) *n., pl.* -**nies** [< LL. < L. *scrutari*, to search into carefully] **1.** a close examination **2.** a careful, continuous watch **3.** a lengthy, searching look

**scu·ba** (skoo′bə) *n.* [*s*(elf-)*c*(ontained) *u*(nderwater) *b*(reathing) *a*(pparatus)] a diver's apparatus with compressed-air tanks connected to a mouthpiece for breathing under water

**scud** (skud) *vi.* **scud′ded, scud′ding** [prob. < ON.] **1.** to move swiftly **2.** to be driven before the wind —*n.* **1.** a scudding **2.** spray, rain, or snow driven by the wind **3.** very low, dark, swiftly moving clouds

**scuff** (skuf) *vt.* [prob. < or akin to ON. *skufa*, to shove] **1.** to scrape (the ground, etc.) with the feet **2.** to wear a rough place on the surface of **3.** to scrape (one's feet) on the ground, etc. —*vi.* **1.** to walk without lifting the feet; shuffle **2.** to become scraped or worn in patches —*n.* **1.** a noise or act of scuffing **2.** a worn or rough spot **3.** a loose-fitting house slipper, esp. one without a counter

**scuf·fle** (skuf′'l) *vi.* -**fled, -fling** [freq. of prec.] **1.** to struggle or fight in rough confusion **2.** to move in a confused hurry **3.** to drag one's feet —*n.* **1.** a rough, confused fight **2.** the act or sound of feet shuffling

**scull** (skul) *n.* [prob. < Scand.] **1.** an oar mounted at the stern and worked from side to side to move a boat forward **2.** either of a pair of light oars used by a single rower **3.** a light racing boat for one, two, or four rowers —*vt., vi.* to propel with a scull or sculls —**scull′er** *n.*

**scul·ler·y** (skul′ər ē) *n., pl.* -**ler·ies** [< OFr., ult. < *escuelle*, a dish < L. *scutella*, a tray] a room adjoining the kitchen, where pots and pans are cleaned, etc.

**scul·lion** (skul′yən) *n.* [< OFr. < L. *scopa*, a broom] [Archaic] a servant doing the rough, dirty work in a kitchen

**scul·pin** (skul′pin) *n., pl.* -**pin, -pins:** see PLURAL, II, D, 2 [prob. < Fr. *scorpene* < L. *scorpaena*: see SCORPION] any of certain spiny sea fishes with a big head and wide mouth

**sculpt** (skulpt) *vt., vi.* [Fr. *sculpter*, ult. < L. *sculpere*: see SCULPTURE] **1.** to carve or model as a sculptor **2.** to give sculpturelike form to (hair, fabric, etc.) Also **sculp**

**sculp·tor** (skulp′tər) *n.* [L. < *sculpere*, to carve] an artist who models, carves, or fashions figures or forms of clay, stone, metal, wood, etc. —**sculp′tress** [Now Rare] *n.fem.*

**sculp·ture** (-chər) *n.* [< L. < pp. of *sculpere*, to carve] **1.** the art of carving wood, chiseling stone, casting or welding metal, modeling clay, etc. into statues, figures, or the like **2.** any work or works of sculpture —*vt.* -**tured, -turing** **1.** to carve, chisel, etc. into statues, figures, etc. **2.** to portray in sculpture **3.** to form like sculpture **4.** to decorate with sculpture —*vi.* to work as a sculptor —**sculp′tu·ral** *adj.* —**sculp′tu·ral·ly** *adv.*

**sculp·tur·esque** (skulp′chə resk′) *adj.* like sculpture

**scum** (skum) *n.* [< MDu. *schum*] **1.** a thin layer of impurities which forms on the top of liquids **2.** worthless parts or things; refuse **3.** a mean, despicable person, or such people collectively —*vi.* **scummed, scum′ming** to form scum

**scum·my** (skum′ē) *adj.* -**mi·er, -mi·est** **1.** of, like, or covered with scum **2.** [Colloq.] despicable; low; mean

**scup** (skup) *n., pl.* **scup, scups:** see PLURAL, II, D, 2 [< AmInd.] a brown-and-white porgy of the N Atlantic

**scup·per** (skup′ər) *n.* [< ?] **1.** an opening in a ship's side to allow water to run off the deck **2.** an opening in a wall to allow water to run off a floor or roof

**scup·per·nong** (skup′ər nôη′, -näη′) *n.* [< the *Scuppernong* River, N. Carolina] **1.** a golden-green grape of the southern U.S. **2.** sweet wine made from this grape

**scurf** (skurf) *n.* [< ON. hyp. *skurfr*] **1.** little, dry scales shed by the skin, as dandruff **2.** any scaly coating —**scurf′y** *adj.* **scurf′i·er, scurf′i·est**

**scur·ril·ous** (skur′ə ləs) *adj.* [< L. < *scurra*, buffoon] using or containing coarse, vulgar, or abusive language —**scur·ril′i·ty** (skə ril′ə tē) *n., pl.* -**ties** —**scur′ril·ous·ly** *adv.* —**scur′ril·ous·ness** *n.*

**scur·ry** (skur′ē) *vi.* -**ried, -ry·ing** [< HURRY-SCURRY] to run hastily —*vt.* to cause to scurry —*n.* a scurrying

**scur·vy** (skur′vē) *adj.* -**vi·er, -vi·est** [< SCURF] low; mean; contemptible —*n.* a disease resulting from a deficiency of vitamin C in the body and causing weakness, anemia, spongy gums, bleeding from the mucous membranes, etc. —**scur′vi·ly** *adv.* —**scur′vi·ness** *n.*

**scut** (skut) *n.* [< ?] **1.** a short, stumpy tail, esp. of a rabbit or deer **2.** a contemptible person

**scu·tate** (skyoo′tāt) *adj.* [ModL. < L. < *scutum*, a shield] **1.** *Bot.* same as PELTATE **2.** *Zool.* covered by bony or horny plates or scales

**scutch·eon** (skuch′ən) *n.* same as ESCUTCHEON

**scu·tel·lum** (skyoo tel′əm) *n., pl.* -**tel′la** (-ə) **1.** [ModL., mistaken for L. dim. of *scutum*, a shield] *Bot.* any shield-shaped part **2.** [ModL. < L. *scutella*: see ff.] *Zool.* a small, horny scale or plate

**scut·tle**[1] (skut′'l) *n.* [OE. *scutel*, a dish < L. *scutella*] a kind of bucket used for pouring coal on a fire: in full, **coal scuttle**

**scut·tle²** (skut′'l) *vi.* **-tled, -tling** [prob. akin to SCUD] to scurry, esp. away from trouble, etc. —*n.* a scurry

**scut·tle³** (skut′'l) *n.* [< MFr. < Sp. *escotilla*, dim. of *escote*, a notch] **1.** an opening in a wall or roof, fitted with a cover **2.** a small, covered opening in the hull or deck of a ship —*vt.* **-tled, -tling 1.** to make or open holes in the hull of (a ship) below the waterline; esp., to sink in this way **2.** to abandon (a plan, undertaking, etc.)

**scut·tle·butt** (-but′) *n.* [orig. < *scuttled butt*, lidded cask] **1.** *Naut.* a drinking fountain on shipboard **2.** [Colloq.] rumor or gossip

**scu·tum** (skyōōt′əm) *n., pl.* **scu′ta** (-ə) [L.] **1.** the long, leather-covered, wooden shield of Roman infantrymen **2.** *Zool.* a heavy, horny scale, as on certain reptiles or insects: also **scute** (skyōōt)

**Scyl·la** (sil′ə) a dangerous rock on the southern Italian coast, opposite the whirlpool Charybdis —**between Scylla and Charybdis** facing danger or evil on either hand

**scythe** (sīth) *n.* [altered (after L. *scindere*, to cut) < OE. *sithe*] a tool with a long, single-edged blade on a bent wooden shaft, used in cutting tall grass, grain, etc. by hand —*vt.* **scythed, scyth′ing** to cut with a scythe

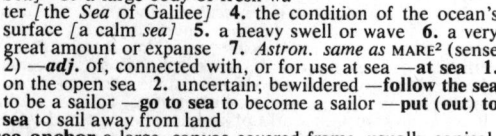
SCYTHE

**Scyth·i·a** (sith′ē ə) ancient region in SE Europe, on the N coast of the Black Sea —**Scyth′i·an** *adj., n.*

**S.Dak., SD** South Dakota

**Se** *Chem.* selenium

**SE, S.E., s.e. 1.** southeast **2.** southeastern

**sea** (sē) *n.* [OE. *sæ*] **1.** the ocean **2.** a large body of salt water wholly or partly enclosed by land [the Red *Sea*] **3.** a large body of fresh water [the *Sea* of Galilee] **4.** the condition of the ocean's surface [a calm *sea*] **5.** a heavy swell or wave **6.** a very great amount or expanse **7.** *Astron. same as* MARE² (sense 2) —*adj.* of, connected with, or for use at sea —**at sea 1.** on the open sea **2.** uncertain; bewildered —**follow the sea** to be a sailor —**go to sea** to become a sailor —**put (out) to sea** to sail away from land

**sea anchor** a large, canvas-covered frame, usually conical, let out from a ship as a drag to reduce drifting or to keep the ship heading into the wind

**sea anemone** a sea polyp having a firm, gelatinous body topped with colored, petallike tentacles

**sea bag** a large, cylindrical bag in which a sailor carries his clothes and personal belongings

**sea bass 1.** any of numerous sea fishes; esp., *a)* the **black sea bass,** a food fish with large scales and a wide mouth, found along the Atlantic coast of the U.S. *b)* the **giant sea bass,** found along the California coast **2.** any of various similar fishes, as the **white sea bass,** a drum found along the California coast

**Sea·bee** (sē′bē′) *n.* [< *CB*, short for *Construction Battalion*] a member of any of the construction and engineering battalions of the U.S. Navy

**sea bird** a bird living on or near the sea: also **sea fowl**

**sea·board** (-bôrd′) *n.* land or coastal region bordering on the sea —*adj.* bordering on the sea

**sea·borne** (-bôrn′) *adj.* **1.** carried on or by the sea **2.** afloat: said of ships

**sea breeze** a breeze blowing inland from the sea

**sea·coast** (-kōst′) *n.* land bordering on the sea

**sea cow 1.** any of several sea mammals, as the dugong or manatee **2.** *earlier name for* WALRUS

**sea cucumber** an echinoderm with a cucumber-shaped, flexible body and long tentacles around the mouth

**sea dog 1.** an experienced sailor **2.** any of various seals

**sea elephant** a large seal that is hunted for oil: the male has a long proboscis

**sea·far·er** (-fer′ər) *n.* a traveler by sea; esp., a sailor

**sea·far·ing** (-fer′iŋ) *adj.* of or engaged in life at sea —*n.* **1.** the occupation of a sailor **2.** travel by sea

**sea·food** (-fōōd′) *n.* food prepared from or consisting of saltwater fish or shellfish

**sea·girt** (-gurt′) *adj.* surrounded by the sea

**sea·go·ing** (-gō′iŋ) *adj.* **1.** made for use on the open sea [a *seagoing* schooner] **2.** *same as* SEAFARING

**sea green** a pale bluish green —**sea′-green′** *adj.*

**sea gull** *same as* GULL¹; esp., any gull living along a seacoast

**sea horse 1.** a small, semitropical marine fish with a slender tail, plated body, and a head somewhat like that of a horse **2.** a mythical sea creature, half fish and half horse

**Sea Islands** chain of islands off the coasts of S.C., Ga., & N Fla.

**seal¹** (sēl) *n.* [< OFr. < L. *sigillum*, a seal, dim. of *signum*, a sign] **1.** a design, initials, etc. placed on a letter, document, etc. to prove it is authentic: letters were once commonly sealed with a molten wax wafer impressed with such a design **2.** a stamp or signet ring for making such an im-

pression **3.** a wax wafer, piece of paper, etc. bearing an impressed design recognized as official **4.** *a)* something that closes or fastens tightly or securely *b)* a tight closure, as against the passage of air or water **5.** anything that guarantees; pledge **6.** a sign; token [a handshake as a *seal* of friendship] **7.** an ornamental paper stamp [a Christmas *seal*] —*vt.* **1.** to mark with a seal **2.** to secure the contents of (a letter, etc.) by closing with a wax seal, a gummed flap, etc. **3.** to confirm the truth of (a promise, etc.) by some action **4.** to certify as being official, accurate, exact, etc. by or as by fixing a seal to **5.** to settle or determine finally [to *seal* one's fate] **6.** *a)* to close, etc. as with a seal [to *seal* one's lips] *b)* to close completely as to make airtight or watertight *c)* to apply a nonpermeable coating to (a porous surface, as a wood) —**seal off** **1.** to close completely **2.** to surround with barriers, a cordon, etc. —**set one's seal to 1.** to mark with one's seal **2.** to endorse — **seal′a·ble** *adj.* —**seal′er** *n.*

**seal²** (sēl) *n., pl.* **seals, seal:** see PLURAL, II, D, 1 [OE. *seolh*] **1.** a sea mammal with a sleek coat and four flippers: it lives in cold waters and eats fish **2.** the fur of a fur seal **3.** leather made from sealskin —*vi.* to hunt seals

**Sea·lab** (sē′lab′) *n.* [SEA + LAB(ORATORY)] any of a series of underwater laboratories of the U.S. Navy for undersea exploration and research

**sea lamprey** a parasitic lamprey of the N Atlantic that spawns in streams and is now landlocked in the Great Lakes

**sea lane** a commonly used route for travel by sea

FUR SEAL
(5–7 ft. long)

**seal·ant** (sēl′ənt) *n.* [SEAL¹ + -ANT] a substance, as a wax, plastic, silicone, etc., used for sealing

**sea legs** the ability to walk without loss of balance on board ship, esp. in a rough sea

**seal·er·y** (sēl′ər ē) *n., pl.* **-er·ies 1.** a place where seals are hunted **2.** the work of hunting seals Also **seal fishery**

**sea level** the level of the surface of the sea, esp. the mean level between high and low tide: used as a standard in measuring heights and depths

**sea lily** a stalked and attached crinoid

**sealing wax** a hard mixture of resin and turpentine used for sealing letters, dry cells, etc.: it softens when heated

**sea lion** a large, eared seal of the N Pacific

**seal ring** *same as* SIGNET RING

**seal·skin** (sēl′skin′) *n.* **1.** the skin of the seal; esp., the soft undercoat dyed dark-brown or black **2.** a garment made of this —*adj.* made of sealskin

**Sea·ly·ham terrier** (sē′lē ham′, -əm) [< *Sealyham*, an estate in Wales] any of a breed of small, white terrier with short legs and square jaws

**seam** (sēm) *n.* [OE. *seam*] **1.** the line formed by sewing together two pieces of material **2.** any line marking joining edges, as of boards **3.** a mark, line, etc. like this, as a scar, wrinkle, etc. **4.** a layer or stratum of ore, coal, etc. —*vt.* **1.** to join together so as to form a seam **2.** to mark with a seamlike line, crack, etc. —**seam′less** *adj.*

**sea·man** (sē′mən) *n., pl.* **-men 1.** a sailor **2.** *U.S. Navy* a nonrated enlisted man whose duties are concerned with deck maintenance, equipment, etc. —**sea′man·like′** *adj.*

**sea·man·ship** (-ship′) *n.* skill in sailing, navigating, or working a ship

**seam·stress** (sēm′stris) *n.* a woman who sews expertly or who makes her living by sewing

**seam·y** (sē′mē) *adj.* **seam′i·er, seam′i·est 1.** having or showing seams **2.** unpleasant, squalid, or sordid [the *seamy* side of life] —**seam′i·ness** *n.*

**sé·ance** (sā′äns) *n.* [Fr. < OFr. *seoir* < L. *sedere*, to sit] a meeting at which spiritualists seek or profess to communicate with the dead

**sea otter** a web-footed sea mammal, found along the N Pacific coast: its dark-brown fur is valuable

**sea·plane** (sē′plān′) *n.* any airplane designed to land on and take off from water

**sea·port** (-pôrt′) *n.* **1.** a port or harbor used by ocean ships **2.** a town or city having such a port

**sear** (sir) *adj.* [OE.] withered; sere —*vt.* **1.** to dry up; wither **2.** to scorch or burn the surface of **3.** to brand with a hot iron **4.** to make callous or unfeeling —*n.* a mark produced by searing —**sear′ing·ly** *adv.*

**search** (surch) *vt.* [< OFr. *cercher* < LL. *circare*, to go about < *circus*, ring] **1.** to go over and look through in order to find something [*search* the records] **2.** to examine (a person) for something concealed **3.** to examine carefully; probe [to *search* one's soul] —*vi.* to make a search —*n.* the act of searching; examination —**in search of** trying to find —**search me** [Slang] I do not know —**search out** to seek and find by searching —**search′a·ble** *adj.* —**search′er** *n.*

**search·ing** (-iŋ) *adj.* **1.** examining thoroughly **2.** keen; piercing —**search′ing·ly** *adv.*

**search·light** (-līt′) *n.* **1.** an apparatus on a swivel, that projects a strong, far-reaching beam of light **2.** such a beam

**search warrant** a legal document authorizing a poiice search, as for stolen articles, etc.

**sea·scape** (sē′skāp′) *n.* [SEA + (LAND)SCAPE] **1.** a view of the sea **2.** a drawing, painting, etc. of this

**sea·shell** (-shel′) *n.* the shell of any saltwater mollusk

**sea·shore** (-shôr′) *n.* land along the sea; seacoast

**sea·sick·ness** (-sik′nis) *n.* nausea, dizziness, etc. caused by the rolling or pitching of a ship at sea —**sea′sick′** *adj.*

**sea·side** (-sīd′) *n.* land along the sea; seashore —*adj.* at or of the seaside

**sea·son** (sē′z′n) *n.* [< OFr. < VL. *satio*, sowing time < L. < base of *serere*, to sow] **1.** any of the four divisions into which the year is divided; spring, summer, fall (or autumn), or winter **2.** the time of the year when something specified takes place, is popular, permitted, at its best, etc. *[the harvest season,* the hunting *season]* **3.** a period of time *[the busy season* in a factory*]* **4.** the fitting or convenient time **5.** the time of a specified festival or holiday *[the Easter season] —vt.* **1.** to make (food) more tasty by adding salt, spices, etc. **2.** to add zest or interest to **3.** to make more fit for use, as by aging, curing, etc. **4.** to make used to; accustom *[a seasoned* traveler*]* **5.** to temper; soften —*vi.* to become seasoned, as wood by drying —**for a season** for a while —**in season 1.** available fresh for use as food **2.** at the legally established time for being hunted or caught: said of game, etc. **3.** in or at the proper time **4.** early enough: also **in good season 5.** in heat: said of animals —**out of season** not in season —**sea′son·er** *n.*

**sea·son·a·ble** (-ə b′l) *adj.* **1.** suitable to or usual for the time of year **2.** timely; opportune —**sea′son·a·bly** *adv.*

**sea·son·al** (-əl) *adj.* of or depending on a season or the seasons *[seasonal* rains, *seasonal* work*]* —**sea′son·al·ly** *adv.*

**sea·son·ing** (-iŋ) *n.* anything that adds zest: esp., salt, spices, etc. added to food to make it more tasty

**season ticket** a ticket or set of tickets as for a series of concerts, sports events, etc. or for transportation, etc. for a given period of time

**seat** (sēt) *n.* [ON. *sæti*] **1.** the manner of sitting, as on horseback **2.** *a)* a place to sit, or the right to such a place, esp. as shown by a ticket *b)* a thing to sit on; chair, bench, etc. **3.** *a)* the buttocks *b)* the part of a garment covering the buttocks *c)* the part of a chair, etc. that supports the buttocks **4.** the right to sit as a member; membership *[a seat* on the stock exchange*]* **5.** a part or surface on which another part rests or fits **6.** the chief location, or center *[the seat* of government*] —vt.* **1.** to put or set in or on a seat **2.** to lead to a seat **3.** to have seats for *[the car seats* six*]* **4.** to put a seat in or on; reseat **5.** to put in a certain place, position, etc. —**be seated 1.** to get in a seat; sit down: also **take a seat 2.** to be sitting **3.** to be located, settled, etc. —**seat′less** *adj.*

**seat belt** anchored straps buckled across the hips, to protect a seated passenger, as in an automobile or airplane

**-seat·er** (sēt′ər) *a combining form meaning* a vehicle, etc. having (a specified number of) seats *[a two-seater]*

**seat·ing** (-iŋ) *n.* **1.** a providing with a seat or seats **2.** material for covering chair seats, etc. **3.** the arrangement of seats

**SEATO** (sē′tō) Southeast Asia Treaty Organization

**Se·at·tle** (sē at′′l) [after *Seathl*, an Indian chief] seaport in WC Wash., on Puget Sound: pop. 494,000 (met. area 1,601,000)

**sea urchin** a small sea animal with a round body in a shell covered with long, movable spines

**sea wall** a wall made to break the force of the waves and to protect the shore from erosion

**sea·ward** (sē′wərd) *adj., adv.* toward the sea: also, for *adv.,* **sea′wards** —*n.* a seaward direction or position

**sea·way** (-wā′) *n.* **1.** a way or route by sea **2.** a ship's headway **3.** a rough sea **4.** an inland waterway to the sea for ocean ships

**sea·weed** (-wēd′) *n.* **1.** any sea plant or plants; esp., any marine alga: in full, **marine seaweed 2.** any similar freshwater plant: in full, **freshwater seaweed**

**sea·wor·thy** (-wʉr′thē) *adj.* fit to travel in on the open sea; sturdy: said of a ship —**sea′wor′thi·ness** *n.*

**se·ba·ceous** (si bā′shəs) *adj.* [< L. < *sebum*, tallow] of or like fat, tallow, or sebum; esp., designating certain skin glands that secrete sebum

**Se·bas·tian** (si bas′chən) [L. < Gr. < *Sebastia*, ancient city in Asia Minor] **1.** a masculine name **2.** Saint, ?–288? A.D.; Christian martyr of Rome

**se·bum** (sē′bəm) *n.* [L., tallow] the semiliquid, greasy secretion of the sebaceous glands

**SEC, S.E.C.** Securities and Exchange Commission

**sec** secant

**sec. 1.** second(s) **2.** secondary **3.** secretary **4.** section(s) **5.** sector **6.** security

**se·cant** (sē′kənt, -kant) *adj.* [< L. prp. of *secare*, to cut] cutting; intersecting —*n.* **1.** *Geom.* any straight line intersecting a curve at two or more points **2.** *Trigonometry* the ratio of the hypotenuse of a right triangle to either of the other two sides with reference to the enclosed angle

**se·cede** (si sēd′) *vi.* **-ced′ed, -ced′ing** [< L. < *se-,* apart + *cedere,* to go] to withdraw formally from a larger body, as from a political union —**se·ced′er** *n.*

**se·ces·sion** (si sesh′ən) *n.* **1.** a seceding **2.** [often S-] the withdrawal of the Southern States from the Federal Union at the start of the Civil War —**se·ces′sion·al** *adj.* —**se·ces′sion·ism** *n.* —**se·ces′sion·ist** *n.*

**Seck·el (pear)** (sek′′l) [after the Pa. fruitgrower who originated it] a small, sweet, juicy, reddish-brown pear

**se·clude** (si klood′) *vt.* **-clud′ed, -clud′ing** [< L. *secludere* < *se-,* apart + *claudere,* to shut] **1.** to keep away or shut off from others; isolate **2.** to make private or hidden

**se·clud·ed** (-klood′id) *adj.* shut off or kept apart from others; isolated; withdrawn —**se·clud′ed·ly** *adv.*

**se·clu·sion** (si kloo′zhən) *n.* **1.** a secluding or being secluded; retirement; isolation **2.** a secluded spot —**se·clu′sive** *adj.* —**se·clu′sive·ly** *adv.* —**se·clu′sive·ness** *n.*

**sec·ond¹** (sek′ənd) *adj.* [OFr. < L. *secundus* < *sequi,* to follow] **1.** coming next after the first in order; 2d or 2nd **2.** another; other; additional *[a second* helping*]* **3.** being of the same kind as another *[a second* Caesar*]* **4.** alternate *[every second* day*]* **5.** next below the first in rank, value, merit, etc. **6.** *Music a)* lower in pitch *b)* performing a part lower in pitch —*n.* **1.** the second person, thing, class, place, etc. **2.** the next after the first **3.** an article of merchandise that is not of the first quality **4.** an aid or assistant, as to a duelist or boxer **5.** the second forward gear ratio of a motor vehicle **6.** [Slang] *[pl.]* a second helping of food —*vt.* **1.** to act as an aid to; assist **2.** to give support or encouragement to; reinforce **3.** to indicate formal support of (a motion, etc.) so that it may be discussed or voted on —*adv.* in the second place, group, etc. —**sec′ond·er** *n.*

**sec·ond²** (sek′ənd) *n.* [ML. *(pars minuta) secunda,* second (small part): from being a further division (i.e., beyond the minute)] **1.** 1/60 of a minute of time **2.** 1/60 of a minute of angular measurement **3.** a very short time; instant **4.** a specific point in time

**Second Advent** *same as* SECOND COMING

**sec·ond·ar·y** (sek′ən der′ē) *adj.* **1.** second, or below the first, in rank, importance, place, etc.; subordinate; minor **2.** *a)* coming from something considered primary or original; derivative *b)* second-hand; not original *[a secondary* source of information*] c)* designating colors derived by mixing two primary colors: see COLOR (*n.* 3) **3.** coming after the first in a series of processes, events, stages, etc. **4.** *Elec.* designating or of an induced current or its circuit **5.** *Zool.* designating or of the long flight feathers on the second joint of a bird's wing —*n., pl.* **-ar′ies 1.** a person or thing that is secondary, subordinate, etc. **2.** any of the secondary colors **3.** *Elec.* an output winding of a transformer from which the power is taken **4.** *Football* the defensive backfield —**sec′ond·ar′i·ly** *adv.*

**secondary accent** (or **stress**) **1.** any accent or stress, that is weaker than the full, or primary, accent **2.** a mark (in this dictionary, ′) to show this

**secondary school** a school, as a high school, coming after elementary school

**second banana** [Slang] **1.** a subordinate performer in a show, esp. burlesque, as one who plays straight man to the top banana, or star comedian **2.** any person in a subordinate position

**second base** *Baseball* the base between first base and third base, located behind the pitcher

**second childhood** feeble and childish state due to old age

**sec·ond-class** (sek′ənd klas′) *adj.* **1.** of the class, rank, quality, etc. next below the highest **2.** designating or of travel accommodations next below the best **3.** designating or of a class of mail consisting of newspapers, periodicals, etc. **4.** inferior, inadequate, etc. —*adv.* **1.** with second-class accommodations **2.** as or by second-class mail

**Second Coming** in the theology of some Christian sects, the expected return of Christ, at the Last Judgment

**second cousin** the child of one's parent's first cousin

**second growth** tree growth on land stripped of virgin forest

**sec·ond-guess** (sek′ənd ges′) *vt., vi.* [Colloq.] to use hindsight in criticizing (someone or something), remaking (a decision), etc. —**sec′ond-guess′er** *n.*

**sec·ond·hand** (-hand′) *adj.* **1.** not direct from the original source; not original **2.** used or worn previously by another; not new   **3.** of or dealing in merchandise that is not new —*adv.* not firsthand; not directly

**second hand** the hand (of a clock or watch) that indicates the seconds and moves around the dial once every minute

**second lieutenant** a commissioned officer of the lowest rank in the U.S. Army, Air Force, or Marine Corps

**sec·ond·ly** (sek′ənd lē) *adv.* in the second place; second

**second nature** acquired habits, etc. fixed so deeply as to seem part of a person's nature

**second person** that form of a pronoun (as *you*) or verb (as *are*) which refers to the person(s) spoken to

**sec·ond-rate** (-rāt′) *adj.* **1.** second in quality, rank, etc,; second-class   **2.** inferior; mediocre —**sec′ond-rat′er** *n.*

**second sight** the supposed ability to see things not physically present, to foresee the future, etc.

**sec·ond-string** (-striŋ′) *adj.* [Colloq.]   **1.** *Sports* that is the second or a substitute choice for play at a specified position   **2.** second-rate; inferior —**sec′ond-string′er** *n.*

**second wind**   **1.** the return of normal ease in breathing after the feeling one has at first of being exhausted from hard exercise   **2.** recovered capacity for continuing any effort

**se·cre·cy** (sē′krə sē) *n., pl.* **-cies**   **1.** a being secret   **2.** the practice or habit of being secretive

**se·cret** (sē′krit) *adj.* [< OFr. < L. pp. of *secernere* < *se-*, apart + *cernere*, to sift, discern]   **1.** kept from the knowledge of others   **2.** remote; secluded   **3.** keeping one's affairs to oneself; secretive   **4.** beyond general understanding; mysterious   **5.** concealed from sight or notice; hidden [a *secret* drawer]   **6.** acting in secret [a *secret* society] —*n.*   **1.** something known only to some and kept from the knowledge of others   **2.** something not understood or explained; mystery   **3.** the true explanation, regarded as not obvious [the *secret* of success] —**in secret** without the knowledge of others; secretly —**se′cret·ly** *adv.*

**secret agent** a person who carries on espionage or similar work of a secret nature, as for a government

**sec·re·tar·i·at** (sek′rə ter′ē ət) *n.*   **1.** the office, position, or quarters of a secretary of high position in a government, etc.   **2.** a staff headed by a secretary-general

**sec·re·tar·y** (sek′rə ter′ē) *n., pl.* **-tar′ies** [ML. *secretarius*, one entrusted with secrets < L. *secretum:* see SECRET]   **1.** *a)* a person whose work is keeping records, handling correspondence, etc. as for an executive in a business office   *b)* an officer of a company, club, etc. having somewhat similar duties   **2.** an official in charge of a department of government   **3.** a writing desk, esp. one topped with a small bookcase —**sec′re·tar′i·al** *adj.* —**sec′re·tar′y·ship′** *n.*

**secretary bird** [from the penlike feathers of its crest] a large, grayish-blue and black African bird of prey with a long neck and long legs

**sec·re·tar·y-gen·er·al** (-jen′ər əl) *n., pl.* **-tar′ies-gen′er·al** the chief administrative officer of an organization, in charge of a secretariat

**se·crete** (si krēt′) *vt.* **-cret′ed, -cret′ing** [< L. pp. of *secernere:* see SECRET]   **1.** to hide; conceal   **2.** to form and release (a specified secretion) as a gland, etc. does

**se·cre·tion** (si krē′shən) *n.*   **1.** a hiding or concealing of something   **2.** *a)* the process by which a substance is formed from the blood or sap and then released into the organism or as a waste product   *b)* such a substance

**se·cre·tive** (sē′krə tiv; *also, & for 2 always,* si krēt′iv) *adj.* [SECRET + -IVE]   **1.** keeping one's affairs to oneself; not frank; reticent   **2.** *same as* SECRETORY —**se′cre·tive·ly** *adv.* —**se′cre·tive·ness** *n.*

**se·cre·to·ry** (si krēt′ər ē) *adj.* of, or having the function of, secretion —*n.* a secretory gland, etc.

**secret police** a police force that operates secretly, esp. in order to suppress opposition to the government

**secret service** a government service that carries on secret investigation; specif., [S- S-] a division of the U.S. Treasury Department for uncovering counterfeiters, protecting the President, etc.

**sect** (sekt) *n.* [< MFr. < L. < *sequi*, to follow]   **1.** a religious denomination, esp. one that has broken away from an established church   **2.** a group of people or a faction having a common leadership, philosophy, etc.

**sec·tar·i·an** (sek ter′ē ən) *adj.*   **1.** of or relating to a sect   **2.** devoted to some sect   **3.** narrow-minded —*n.*   **1.** a member of any religious sect   **2.** a person who is blindly devoted to a sect —**sec·tar′i·an·ism** *n.*

**sec·ta·ry** (sek′tər ē) *n., pl.* **-ries** a member of a sect

**sec·tion** (sek′shən) *n.* [< L. < pp. of *secare,* to cut]   **1.** a cutting or separating by cutting; specif., an incision in surgery   **2.** a part separated by cutting; slice; division   **3.** *a)* a division of a book, newspaper, etc.   *b)* a numbered paragraph of a law, etc.   **4.** any distinct or separate part [a bookcase in *sections*]   **5.** a segment of an orange, etc.   **6.** a division of public lands that is a mile square (640 acres)   **7.** a drawing, etc. of a thing as it would appear if cut straight through in a given plane   **8.** any one of two or more buses, trains, or airplanes for a particular run or flight   **9.** *Railroading a)* a part of a sleeping car containing an

upper and lower berth   *b)* a division of the right of way maintained by a single crew —*vt.*   **1.** to divide into sections   **2.** to represent in sections

**sec·tion·al** (sek′shən 'l) *adj.*   **1.** of or devoted to a given section or district   **2.** made up of or divided into sections —*n.* a sectional sofa, bookcase, etc. —**sec′tion·al·ly** *adv.*

**sec·tion·al·ism** (-iz'm) *n.* narrow-minded concern shown for one section of a country —**sec′tion·al·ist** *adj., n.*

**sec·tor** (sek′tər) *n.* [LL. < L., cutter < *secare,* to cut]   **1.** part of a circle bounded by any two radii and the included arc   **2.** a mathematical instrument, as for measuring angles, consisting of two scaled rulers jointed together at one end   **3.** any of the districts into which an area is divided for military operations   **4.** a distinct part of a society or of an economy, group, etc. —*vt.* to divide into sectors —**sec′tor·al,** **sec·to′ri·al** (-tôr′ē əl) *adj.*

**sec·u·lar** (sek′yə lər) *adj.* [< OFr. < LL. < L. < *saeculum,* an age, generation]   **1.** *a)* not related to church or religion; not sacred or religious; temporal; worldly [*secular* schools]   *b)* of secularism   **2.** living in the outside world and not bound by a monastic vow [the *secular* clergy] —*n.* a member of the secular clergy —**sec′u·lar·ly** *adv.*

**sec·u·lar·ism** (-iz'm) *n.*   **1.** worldly spirit, views, etc.; esp., a system of beliefs and practices that rejects any form of religious faith   **2.** the belief that religion should be strictly separated from the state or government, esp. from public education —**sec′u·lar·ist** *n., adj.* —**sec′u·lar·is′tic** *adj.*

**sec·u·lar·ize** (sek′yə lə rīz′) *vt.* **-ized′, -iz′ing**   **1.** to change from religious to civil ownership or use   **2.** to deprive of religious character, influence, etc.   **3.** to convert to secularism —**sec′u·lar·i·za′tion** *n.*

**se·cure** (si kyoor′) *adj.* [< L. < *se-,* free from + *cura,* care]   **1.** free from fear, care, doubt, etc.; not worried, troubled, etc.   **2.** free from danger; safe   **3.** in safekeeping   **4.** firm; stable [make the knot *secure*]   **5.** reliable; dependable —*vt.* **-cured′, -cur′ing**   **1.** to make secure, or safe; protect   **2.** to make sure or certain; guarantee, as with a pledge [to *secure* a loan with collateral]   **3.** to make firm, fast, etc. [*secure* the bolt]   **4.** to obtain; acquire; get [to *secure* aid]   **5.** to capture —*vi.* to give security —**se·cur′a·ble** *adj.* —**se·cure′ly** *adv.* —**se·cur′er** *n.*

**se·cu·ri·ty** (si kyoor′ə tē) *n., pl.* **-ties**   **1.** the state of being or feeling free from fear, anxiety, danger, doubt, etc.   **2.** protection or defense, as against attack, espionage, etc. [funds for national *security*]   **3.** *a)* something given as a pledge of repayment, etc.   *b)* a person who promises to pay another's debt if he fails to pay it   **4.** a stock certificate or bond: *usually used in pl.*

**Security Council** the United Nations council responsible for maintaining international peace and security

**secy., sec′y.** secretary

**se·dan** (si dan′) *n.* [< ? L. *sedere,* to sit]   **1.** *same as* SEDAN CHAIR   **2.** an enclosed automobile with two or four doors, and two wide seats, front and rear

**sedan chair** an enclosed chair for one person, carried on poles by two men

**se·date¹** (si dāt′) *adj.* [< L. pp. of *sedare,* to settle] calm or composed; esp., serious and unemotional; decorous —**se·date′ly** *adv.* —**se·date′ness** *n.*

**se·date²** (si dāt′) *vt.* **-dat′ed, -dat′-ing** [< SEDATIVE] to dose with a sedative

**se·da·tion** (si dā′shən) *n. Med.*   **1.** the reducing of excitement, nervousness, or irritation by means of sedatives   **2.** the calm state produced by sedatives

SEDAN CHAIR

**sed·a·tive** (sed′ə tiv) *adj.* [see SEDATE¹] tending to soothe or quiet; specif., *Med.* producing sedation —*n.* a sedative medicine

**sed·en·tar·y** (sed′'n ter′ē) *adj.* [< Fr. < L. < prp. of *sedere,* to sit]   **1.** *a)* tending to sit much of the time   *b)* keeping one seated much of the time [a *sedentary* job]   **2.** *a)* not migratory, as some birds   *b)* fixed to one spot, as a barnacle —**sed′en·tar′i·ly** *adv.* —**sed′en·tar′i·ness** *n.*

**Se·der** (sā′dər) *n., pl.* **Se·dar·im** (sə där′im), **Se′ders** [Heb. *sēdher,* arrangement] *Judaism* the Passover feast commemorating the exodus of the Jews from Egypt

**sedge** (sej) *n.* [OE. *secg*] any of several coarse, grasslike plants often found on wet ground or in water —**sedg′y** *adj.*

**sed·i·ment** (sed′ə mənt) *n.* [< Fr. < L. < *sedere,* to sit]   **1.** matter that settles to the bottom of a liquid   **2.** *Geol.* matter deposited by water or wind —**sed′i·men′tal** (-men′t'l) *adj.* —**sed′i·men·ta′tion** (-men tā′shən) *n.*

**sed·i·men·ta·ry** (sed′ə men′tər ē) *adj.*   **1.** of, like, or containing sediment   **2.** formed by the deposit of sediment, as certain rocks —**sed′i·men′ta·ri·ly** *adv.*

**se·di·tion** (si dish′ən) *n.* [OFr. < L. < *sed-,* apart + *itio,* a going < *ire,* to go] a stirring up of rebellion against the government —**se·di′tion·ist** *n.*

**se·di·tious** (si dish′əs) *adj.* **1.** of, like, or constituting sedition **2.** stirring up rebellion —**se·di′tious·ly** *adv.* —**se·di′tious·ness** *n.*

**se·duce** (si dōōs′, -dyōōs′) *vt.* **-duced′, -duc′ing** [< LL. < L. < *se-*, apart + *ducere*, to lead] **1.** *a*) to persuade to do something disloyal, disobedient, etc. *b*) to tempt to evil or wrongdoing; lead astray *c*) to persuade to engage in unlawful sexual intercourse, esp. for the first time **2.** to entice —**se·duce′ment** *n.* —**se·duc′er** *n.* —**se·duc′i·ble** *adj.*

**se·duc·tion** (si duk′shən) *n.* **1.** a seducing or being seduced **2.** something that seduces

**se·duc·tive** (-tiv) *adj.* tending to seduce, or lead astray; enticing —**se·duc′tive·ly** *adv.* —**se·duc′tive·ness** *n.*

**se·duc·tress** (-tris) *n.* a woman who seduces

**sed·u·lous** (sej′oo ləs) *adj.* [L. *sedulus*, ult. < *se-*, apart + *dolus*, trickery] working hard and steadily; diligent and persistent —**se·du·li·ty** (si dyōol′ə tē, -dōōl′-), **sed′u·lous·ness** *n.* —**sed′u·lous·ly** *adv.*

**se·dum** (sē′dəm) *n.* [ModL., genus name < L.] any of a genus of plants found on rocks and walls, with fleshy stalks and leaves and white, yellow, or pink flowers

**see¹** (sē) *vt.* **saw, seen, see′ing** [OE. *seon*] **1.** *a*) to get knowledge of through the eyes; look at *b*) to picture mentally **2.** *a*) to grasp mentally; understand *b*) to accept as proper [I can′t *see* him as president] *c*) to consider; judge [*saw* it as his duty] **3.** to find out; learn [*see* who′s there] **4.** to know by experience [has *seen* better days] **5.** to look over; inspect **6.** to make sure [*see* that he goes] **7.** *a*) to escort [to *see* someone home] *b*) to keep company with **8.** to encounter; meet **9.** to call on; visit or consult [*see* a lawyer] **10.** to admit to one′s presence; receive [too ill to *see* anyone] **11.** to be a spectator at; view or attend [*see* a show] **12.** *Card Games* to meet (a bet) of (another) by staking an equal sum —*vi.* **1.** to have the power of sight **2.** to discern objects, colors, etc. by using the eyes [able to *see* far] **3.** *a*) to take a look *b*) to investigate or inquire **4.** to understand **5.** to think something over; reflect [let′s *see,* where is it?] —*interj.* behold! look! —**see about 1.** to inquire into **2.** to attend to —**see after** to take care of —**see fit (to)** to think it is proper (to do something) —**see into 1.** to look into **2.** to perceive the true meaning or nature of —**see off** to go with and watch (another) leave by plane, boat, bus, etc. —**see out 1.** to go through with; finish **2.** to wait till the end of —**see through 1.** to perceive the true meaning or character of **2.** to carry out to the end; finish **3.** to help through a time of difficulty —**see to** to attend to —**see′a·ble** *adj.*

**see²** (sē) *n.* [< OFr. *sie* < L. *sedes,* a seat] **1.** the official seat, or center of authority, of a bishop **2.** the position, authority, or jurisdiction of a bishop

**seed** (sēd) *n., pl.* **seeds, seed:** see PLURAL, II, D, 4 [OE. *sæd*] **1.** the part of a flowering plant that contains the embryo and will develop into a new plant if sown **2.** loosely, *a*) any part, as a bulb, from which a new plant will grow *b*) a small, seedlike fruit **3.** seeds used for sowing **4.** source; origin [the *seeds* of revolt] **5.** family stock; ancestry **6.** descendants; posterity **7.** *same as* SPAT⁴ **8.** seed-bearing condition [in *seed*] **9.** *same as* SPORE (*n.* 2) **10.** sperm or semen **11.** something tiny, like a seed; esp., *a*) a tiny crystal or particle *b*) a tiny bubble, as in glassware **12.** *Sports* a seeded player —*vt.* **1.** to plant with seeds **2.** to sow (seeds) **3.** to remove the seeds from **4.** to sprinkle particles of dry ice, silver iodide, etc. into (clouds), as in trying to produce rainfall **5.** to provide with the means or stimulus for growing or developing **6.** *Sports a*) to distribute the names of contestants in (the draw for position in a tournament) so as to avoid matching the most skilled too early *b*) to treat (any of the most skilled players) thus —*vi.* **1.** to become ripe and produce seeds **2.** to shed seeds **3.** to sow seeds —**go** (or **run**) **to seed 1.** to shed seeds after flowering **2.** to become weak, useless, etc. —**seed′ed** *adj.* —**seed′er** *n.* —**seed′less** *adj.*

**seed·bed** (-bed′) *n.* a bed of soil, usually covered with glass, in which seedlings are grown for transplanting

**seed·case** (-kās′) *n. same as* SEED VESSEL

**seed coral** fragments of coral used in ornaments

**seed leaf** *same as* COTYLEDON

**seed·ling** (-liŋ) *n.* **1.** a plant grown from a seed, rather than from a cutting, etc. **2.** any young plant; esp., a young tree less than three feet high

**seed money** money made available to begin the financing of, or to attract additional funds for, a long-term project

**seed oysters** oyster spat; very young oysters, esp. at the stage suitable for relocation

**seed pearl** a very small pearl, often imperfect

**seed plant** *same as* SPERMATOPHYTE

**seed·pod** (-päd′) *n.* a carpel or pistil, enclosing ovules or seeds in angiosperms

**seeds·man** (sēdz′mən) *n., pl.* **-men 1.** a sower of seeds **2.** a dealer in seeds Also **seed′man**

**seed·time** (sēd′tīm′) *n.* the season for sowing seeds

**seed vessel** any dry, hollow fruit, as a pod, containing seed

**seed·y** (sēd′ē) *adj.* **seed′i·er, seed′i·est 1.** containing many seeds **2.** gone to seed **3.** shabby, run-down, or looking bad, ill, etc. —**seed′i·ly** *adv.* —**seed′i·ness** *n.*

**see·ing** (sē′iŋ) *n.* **1.** the sense or power of sight **2.** the use of the eyes to see —*adj.* having the sense of sight —*conj.* considering; inasmuch as

**Seeing Eye dog** [*also* s- e-] a guide dog, specif. one trained by Seeing Eye, Inc., near Morristown, N.J.

**seek** (sēk) *vt.* **sought, seek′ing** [OE. *secan*] **1.** to try to find; look for **2.** to go to; resort to [to *seek* the woods for peace] **3.** *a*) to try to get or find out by asking or searching [to *seek* an answer] *b*) to request; ask for **4.** to try for; aim at [*seeking* perfection] **5.** to try: used with an infinitive [to *seek* to please] —*vi.* to look for someone or something —**seek′er** *n.*

**seem** (sēm) *vi.* [prob. < ON. *sæma,* to conform to] **1.** *a*) to appear to be [to *seem* glad] *b*) to appear: usually used with an infinitive [he *seems* to know] *c*) to have the impression; think: used with an infinitive [I *seem* to recall] **2.** to appear to exist [there *seems* no end] **3.** to be apparently true [it *seems* he was here]

**seem·ing** (-iŋ) *adj.* that seems real, true, etc. without necessarily being so; apparent [her *seeming* anger] —*n.* outward appearance; semblance —**seem′ing·ly** *adv.*

**seem·ly** (sēm′lē) *adj.* **-li·er, -li·est** [< ON. < *sæmr,* fitting] **1.** pleasing in appearance **2.** suitable, proper, decorous, etc. —*adv.* in a seemly way —**seem′li·ness** *n.*

**seen** (sēn) *pp. of* SEE¹

**seep** (sēp) *vi.* [OE. *sipian,* to soak] to leak, drip, or flow out slowly through small openings; ooze —*n.* **1.** a seeping **2.** liquid that seeps —**seep′age** (-ij) *n.* —**seep′y** *adj.*

**seer** (sē′ər *for 1;* sir *for 2*) *n.* **1.** a person who sees **2.** a person with the supposed power to foretell the future

**seer·suck·er** (sir′suk′ər) *n.* [< Hindi < Per. *shir u shakar,* lit., milk and sugar] a light fabric of cotton, etc. woven with alternating crinkled stripes in various patterns

**see·saw** (sē′sô′) *n.* [redupl. of SAW¹] **1.** a plank balanced at the middle, used by children at play, who ride the ends so that when one goes up, the other comes down **2.** such a riding **3.** any up-and-down or back-and-forth movement or change —*adj.* moving up and down or back and forth —*vt., vi.* to move on a seesaw or like a seesaw

**seethe** (sēth) *vt.* **seethed, seeth′ing** [OE. *sēothan*] **1.** to cook by boiling **2.** to soak or saturate in liquid —*vi.* **1.** to boil or to surge, foam, etc. as if boiling **2.** to be violently agitated —*n.* a seething

**seg·ment** (seg′mənt; *for v.* -ment) *n.* [L. *segmentum* < *secare,* to cut] **1.** any of the parts into which something is separated or separable; section **2.** *Geom.* any part, esp. of a circle or sphere, cut off by a line or plane —*vt., vi.* to divide into segments —**seg·men′tal** (-men′t′l), **seg′men·tar′y** *adj.* —**seg·men′tal·ly** *adv.*

**seg·men·ta·tion** (seg′mən tā′shən, -men-) *n.* **1.** a dividing or being divided into segments **2.** *Biol.* the progressive growth and cleavage of a single cell into others to form a new organism

**se·go** (sē′gō) *n., pl.* **-gos** [< AmInd.] **1.** a perennial bulb plant with trumpet-shaped flowers, found in western N. America: in full, **sego lily 2.** its edible bulb

**seg·re·gate** (seg′rə gāt′; *for adj. usually* -git) *adj.* [< L. pp. of *segregare* < *se-,* apart + *grex* (gen. *gregis*), a flock] separate; set apart —*vt.* **1.** to set apart from others; isolate; specif., to impose a system of segregation on (racial groups, social facilities, etc.) —*vi.* to become segregated —**seg′re·ga′tive** *adj.*

**seg·re·gat·ed** (seg′rə gāt′id) *adj.* conforming to a system that segregates racial groups

**seg·re·ga·tion** (seg′rə gā′shən) *n.* a segregating or being segregated; specif., the policy or practice of compelling racial groups to live apart from each other, go to separate schools, etc. —**seg′re·ga′tion·ist** *n., adj.*

**se·gue** (seg′wā, sā′gwā) *vi.* **-gued, -gue·ing** [< It., ult. < L. *sequi,* to follow] to continue without break (*to* or *into*) the next part or what follows —*n.* a segueing

**sei·del** (zī′d′l, sī′-) *n., pl.* **-dels, -del** [G. < MHG. < L. *situla,* a bucket] a large beer mug, often with a hinged lid

**sei·gneur** (sen yur′, sān-, sēn-) *n.* [Fr. < MFr.: see SEIGNIOR] **1.** *same as* SEIGNIOR **2.** the owner of a seigneury (sense 2) —**sei·gneur′i·al** (-ē əl) *adj.*

**sei·gneur·y** (sen′yər ē, sān′-, sēn′-) *n., pl.* **-gneur·ies 1.** *same as* SEIGNIORY (sense 1) **2.** in French Canada, an estate granted by royal decree to 17th-cent. French settlers

**sei·gnior** (sēn′yər) *n.* [< Anglo-Fr. < OFr. < L. *senior:* see SENIOR] a lord or noble; specif., the lord of a fief

**sei·gnio·ri·al, sei·gno·ri·al** (sēn yôr′ē əl) *adj.* of or relating to a seignior: also **sei·gnior·al, sei·gnor·al** (sēn′-yər əl)

**sei·gnior·y** (sēn′yər ē) *n., pl.* **-gnior·ies 1.** the estate of a seignior **2.** the rights or authority of a feudal lord

**Seine** (sān; *Fr.* sen) river in N France, flowing through Paris into the English Channel

**seine** (sān) *n.* [OE. *segne*, ult. < L. < Gr. *sagēnē*] a large fishing net with floats along the top edge and weights along the bottom —*vt., vi.* **seined, sein′ing** to fish with a seine

**seis·mic** (sīz′mik, sīs′-) *adj.* [< Gr. *seismos*, an earthquake < *seiein*, to shake] of, relating to, or caused by an earthquake or earthquakes or similar, but man-made, tremors —**seis′mi·cal·ly** *adv.*

**seis·mo-** [< Gr. *seismos*: see prec.] *a combining form meaning* earthquake [*seismogram*]

**seis·mo·gram** (sīz′mə gram′, sīs′-) *n.* the chart of an earthquake as recorded by a seismograph

**seis·mo·graph** (-graf′) *n.* an instrument that records the intensity and duration of earthquakes and similar tremors —**seis·mog·ra·pher** (sīz mäg′rə fər, sīs-) *n.* —**seis′mo·graph′ic** *adj.* —**seis·mog′ra·phy** *n.*

**seis·mol·o·gy** (sīz mäl′ə jē, sīs-) *n.* [SEISMO- + -LOGY] a geophysical science dealing with earthquakes and related phenomena —**seis′mo·log′ic** (-mə läj′ik), **seis′mo·log′i·cal** *adj.* —**seis′mo·log′i·cal·ly** *adv.* —**seis·mol′o·gist** *n.*

**seize** (sēz) *vt.* **seized, seiz′ing** [< OFr. *saisir* < ML. *sacire*, prob. < Frank.] **1.** *a)* orig., to give a feudal holding to *b)* to give ownership to: in the passive voice [*seized* of the lands] **2.** *a)* to take possession of by legal power; confiscate [to *seize* contraband] *b)* to capture and put into custody; arrest; apprehend **3.** to take forcibly or quickly; grasp [to *seize* a weapon, to *seize* power] **4.** *a)* to suddenly fill the mind of [an idea *seized* him] *b)* to grasp with the mind, esp. suddenly **5.** to afflict suddenly [*seized* with tremors] **6.** *Naut.* to bind with cord, etc. —**seize on** (or **upon**) to grasp or take eagerly —**seiz′a·ble** *adj.* —**seiz′er** *n.*

**sei·zin** (sē′zin) *n.* [< OFr.: see prec.] legal possession, esp. of a freehold estate —**sei′zor** *n.*

**sei·zure** (sē′zhər) *n.* **1.** a seizing or being seized **2.** a sudden attack, as of disease

**sel. 1.** selected **2.** selection(s)

**sel·dom** (sel′dəm) *adv.* [OE. *seldan*] not often; rarely — *adj.* rare; infrequent —**sel′dom·ness** *n.*

**se·lect** (sə lekt′) *adj.* [L. *selectus*, pp. of *seligere* < *se-*, apart + *legere*, to choose] **1.** chosen in preference to others; specially picked **2.** choice; excellent **3.** careful in choosing; discriminating **4.** limited to certain people or groups; exclusive —*vt., vi.* to choose, as for excellence —**se·lect′ness** *n.* —**se·lec′tor** *n.*

**se·lect·ee** (sə lek′tē′) *n.* a person inducted into the armed forces under selective service

**se·lec·tion** (sə lek′shən) *n.* **1.** a selecting or being selected **2.** *a)* a thing, person, or group chosen *b)* a variety to choose from **3.** *Biol.* any process by which certain organisms or genetic characters naturally survive over others or are bred to do so: see NATURAL SELECTION

**se·lec·tive** (-tiv) *adj.* **1.** of or characterized by selection **2.** having the power of selecting, or tending to select **3.** *Radio* excluding undesired frequencies when tuned to a specific station —**se·lec′tive·ly** *adv.* —**se·lec′tive·ness** *n.*

**selective service** compulsory military training and service according to age, physical fitness, etc.

**se·lec·tiv·i·ty** (sə lek′tiv′ə tē) *n.* **1.** the state or quality of being selective **2.** the degree to which a radio receiver is selective

**se·lect·man** (sə lekt′mən; *locally, also* sē′lekt man′) *n., pl.* **-men** (-mən, -men′) any of a board of officers elected in New England towns to manage municipal affairs

**Se·le·ne** (si lē′nē) the Greek goddess of the moon

**sel·e·nite** (sel′ə nīt′) *n.* [< L. < Gr. *selēnitēs* (*lithos*), lit., moon (stone)] a kind of gypsum in crystalline form

**se·le·ni·um** (sə lē′nē əm) *n.* [ModL. < Gr. *selēnē*, the moon] a nonmetallic chemical element whose electrical conductivity varies with the intensity of light: used in photoelectric devices, etc.: symbol, Se; at. wt., 78.96; at. no., 34

**self** (self) *n., pl.* **selves** [OE.] **1.** the identity, character, or essential qualities of a person or thing **2.** one's own person or being as apart from all others **3.** one's own well-being or advantage —*pron.* [Colloq.] myself, himself, herself, or yourself [tickets for *self* and wife] —*adj.* **1.** uniform throughout **2.** of the same kind, color, material, etc. as the rest [a *self* lining]

**self-** *a prefix used in hyphenated compounds, meaning:* **1.** of oneself or itself [*self*-restraint] **2.** by oneself or itself [*self*-starting] **3.** in oneself or itself [*self*-centered] **4.** to, with, or for oneself or itself [*self*-addressed, *self*-pity]

**self-a·base·ment** (self′ə bās′mənt) *n.* abasement or humiliation of oneself

**self-ab·ne·ga·tion** (-ab′nə gā′shən) *n.* lack of consideration for oneself; self-denial

**self-ab·sorp·tion** (-əb zôrp′shən, -sôrp′-) *n.* absorption in one's own interests, affairs, etc. —**self′-ab·sorbed′** *adj.*

**self-a·buse** (-ə byōōs′) *n. a euphemism for* MASTURBATION

**self-act·ing** (-ak′tiŋ) *adj.* working by itself; automatic

**self-ad·dressed** (-ə drest′) *adj.* addressed to oneself [a *self-addressed* envelope]

**self-ad·vance·ment** (-əd vans′mənt) *n.* the advancing or promoting of one's own interests

**self-ap·point·ed** (-ə poin′tid) *adj.* acting as such on one's own, but not recognized as such by others [a *self-appointed* censor]

**self-as·ser·tion** (-ə sur′shən) *n.* the act of demanding recognition for oneself or of insisting upon one's rights, claims, etc. —**self′-as·ser′tive, self′-as·sert′ing** *adj.*

**self-as·sur·ance** (-ə shoor′əns) *n.* confidence in oneself, one's own ability, talent, etc. —**self′-as·sured′** *adj.*

**self-cen·tered** (-sen′tərd) *adj.* occupied or concerned only with one's own affairs; egocentric; selfish

**self-col·ored** (-kul′ərd) *adj.* **1.** of only one color **2.** of the natural or original color, as a fabric

**self-com·mand** (-kə mand′) *n. same as* SELF-CONTROL

**self-com·pla·cent** (-kəm plā′s'nt) *adj.* self-satisfied, esp. in a smug way —**self′-com·pla′cen·cy** *n.*

**self-con·ceit** (-kən sēt′) *n.* too high an opinion of oneself; conceit —**self′-con·ceit′ed** *adj.*

**self-con·fessed** (-kən fest′) *adj.* being such by one's own admission [a *self-confessed* thief]

**self-con·fi·dence** (-kän′fə dəns) *n.* confidence in oneself, one's own abilities, etc. —**self′-con′fi·dent** *adj.* —**self′-con′fi·dent·ly** *adv.*

**self-con·scious** (-kän′shəs) *adj.* **1.** unduly conscious of oneself as an object of notice; embarrassed or ill at ease **2.** showing embarrassment [a *self-conscious* cough] — **self′-con′scious·ly** *adv.* —**self′-con′scious·ness** *n.*

**self-con·tained** (-kən tānd′) *adj.* **1.** keeping one's affairs to oneself; reserved **2.** showing self-control **3.** having all working parts, complete with motive power, in an enclosed unit: said of machinery **4.** having within oneself or itself all that is necessary; self-sufficient, as a community —**self′-con·tain′ment** *n.*

**self-con·tent·ed** (-kən ten′tid) *adj.* contented with what one is or has —**self′-con·tent′, self′-con·tent′ment** *n.*

**self-con·tra·dic·tion** (-kän′trə dik′shən) *n.* **1.** contradiction of oneself or itself **2.** any statement or idea containing elements that contradict each other —**self′-con′tra·dic′to·ry** *adj.*

**self-con·trol** (-kən trōl′) *n.* control of oneself, or of one's own emotions, desires, actions, etc.

**self-de·cep·tion** (-di sep′shən) *n.* the deceiving of oneself as to one's true feelings, motives, circumstances, etc.: also **self′-de·ceit′, self′-de·lu′sion** (-di lōō′zhən) —**self′-de·ceiv′ing** *adj.*

**self-de·feat·ing** (-di fēt′iŋ) *adj.* that unwittingly defeats its own purpose or interests

**self-de·fense** (-di fens′) *n.* **1.** defense of oneself, one's rights, etc. **2.** boxing: usually in **manly art of self-defense** —**self′-de·fen′sive** *adj.*

**self-de·ni·al** (-di nī′əl) *n.* denial or sacrifice of one's own desires or pleasures —**self′-de·ny′ing** *adj.*

**self-de·struct** (-di strukt′) *vi. same as* DESTRUCT

**self-de·struc·tion** (-di struk′shən) *n.* destruction of oneself or itself; specif., suicide —**self′-de·struc′tive** *adj.*

**self-de·ter·mi·na·tion** (-di tur′mə nā′shən) *n.* **1.** determination or decision according to one's own mind or will, without outside influence **2.** the right of a people to decide upon its own political status or form of government —**self′-de·ter′mined** *adj.* —**self′-de·ter′min·ing** *adj.*

**self-dis·ci·pline** (-dis′ə plin) *n.* the disciplining or controlling of oneself, one's actions, etc. —**self′-dis′ci·plined** *adj.*

**self-doubt** (-dout′) *n.* lack of self-confidence

**self-ed·u·cat·ed** (-ej′ə kāt′id) *adj.* educated by oneself, with little or no formal schooling

**self-ef·face·ment** (-i fās′mənt) *n.* modest, retiring behavior —**self′-ef·fac′ing** *adj.*

**self-em·ployed** (-im ploid′) *adj.* working for oneself, with direct control over work, services, fees, etc. —**self′-em·ploy′ment** *n.*

**self-es·teem** (-ə stēm′) *n.* **1.** belief in oneself; self-respect **2.** undue pride in oneself; conceit

**self-ev·i·dent** (-ev′ə dənt) *adj.* evident without need of proof or explanation —**self′-ev′i·dent·ly** *adv.*

**self-ex·am·i·na·tion** (-ig zam′ə nā′shən) *n.* examination or analysis of oneself and one's conduct, motives, etc.

**self-ex·ist·ent** (-ig zis′tənt) *adj.* existing of or by itself without external cause —**self′-ex·ist′ence** *n.*

**self-ex·plan·a·to·ry** (-ik splan′ə tôr′ē) *adj.* explaining itself: also **self′-ex·plain′ing**

**self-ex·pres·sion** (-ik spresh′ən) *n.* expression of one's own personality or emotions, as in the arts

**self-ful·fill·ment** (-fəl fil′mənt) *n.* fulfillment of one's aspirations, hopes, etc. through one's own efforts

**self-gov·ern·ment** (-guv′ər mənt, -ərn-) *n.* government of a group by its own members, as in electing representatives —**self′-gov′ern·ing** *adj.*

**self-hate** (-hāt′) *n.* hate directed against oneself or one's own people, often in despair: also **self′-ha′tred**

**self·heal** (-hēl′) *n.* any of various plants supposed to have healing properties; esp., a common old-world weed of the mint family

**self-help** (-help′) *n.* care or betterment of oneself by one's own efforts, as through study

**self-hyp·no·sis** (-hip nō′sis) *n. same as* AUTOHYPNOSIS

**self-im·age** (-im′ij) *n.* one's concept of oneself and one's identity, abilities, worth, etc.

**self-im·por·tant** (-im pôr′t'nt) *adj.* having or showing an exaggerated opinion of one's own importance; pompous or officious —**self′-im·por′tance** *n.*

**self-im·posed** (-im pōzd′) *adj.* imposed on oneself by oneself, as a duty

**self-im·prove·ment** (-im prōōv′mənt) *n.* improvement of one's status, mind, etc. by one's own efforts

**self-in·crim·i·na·tion** (-in krim′ə nā′shən) *n.* incrimination of oneself by one's own statements or answers —**self′-in·crim′i·nat′ing** *adj.*

**self-in·duced** (-in dōost′) *adj.* 1. induced by oneself or itself 2. produced by self-induction

**self-in·duc·tion** (-in duk′shən) *n.* induction of a voltage in a circuit by the variation of current in that circuit

**self-in·dul·gence** (-in dul′jəns) *n.* indulgence of one's own desires, impulses, etc. —**self′-in·dul′gent** *adj.*

**self-in·flict·ed** (-in flik′tid) *adj.* inflicted on oneself by oneself, as an injury

**self-in·ter·est** (-in′trist, -in′tər ist) *n.* 1. one's own interest or advantage 2. an exaggerated regard for this, esp. at the expense of others

**self·ish** (sel′fish) *adj.* 1. too much concerned with one's own welfare or interests, with little or no thought or care for others 2. showing or prompted by self-interest —**self′ish·ly** *adv.* —**self′ish·ness** *n.*

**self-jus·ti·fi·ca·tion** (self′jus′tə fi kā′shən) *n.* the justifying or explaining away of one's actions or motives

**self·less** (self′lis) *adj.* devoted to others' welfare or interests and not one's own; unselfish —**self′less·ly** *adv.* —**self′less·ness** *n.*

**self-load·ing** (self′lōd′iŋ) *adj.* loading again by its own action [a *self-loading* gun]

**self-love** (-luv′) *n.* love of self or regard for oneself and one's own interests

**self-made** (-mād′) *adj.* 1. made by oneself or itself 2. successful, rich, etc. through one's own efforts

**self-o·pin·ion·at·ed** (-ə pin′yə nāt′id) *adj.* stubborn or conceited with regard to one's own opinions

**self-pit·y** (-pit′ē) *n.* pity for oneself

**self-pol·li·na·tion** (-päl′ə nā′shən) *n.* pollination of a flower by itself or by another flower on the same plant —**self′-pol′li·nat′ed** *adj.*

**self-por·trait** (-pôr′trit, -trāt) *n.* a painting, drawing, etc. of oneself, done by oneself

**self-pos·ses·sion** (-pə zesh′ən) *n.* full control of one's feelings, actions, etc.; self-control; composure —**self′-pos·sessed′** *adj.*

**self-pres·er·va·tion** (-prez′ər vā′shən) *n.* 1. preservation of oneself from danger, injury, or death 2. the urge to preserve oneself, regarded as instinctive

**self-pro·nounc·ing** (-prə noun′siŋ) *adj.* showing pronunciation by marks added to the original spelling, not by phonetic respelling

**self-pro·pelled** (-prə peld′) *adj.* propelled by its own motor or power: also **self′-pro·pel′ling**

**self-re·al·i·za·tion** (-rē′ə li zā′shən) *n.* fulfillment of oneself, one's capabilities, etc.

**self-re·cord·ing** (-ri kôr′diŋ) *adj.* recording its own operations automatically, as a seismograph

**self-re·gard** (-ri gärd′) *n.* 1. concern for oneself and one's own interests 2. *same as* SELF-RESPECT

**self-reg·u·lat·ing** (-reg′yə lāt′iŋ) *adj.* regulating oneself or itself automatically or without outside control —**self′-reg′u·la′tion** *n.*

**self-re·li·ance** (-ri lī′əns) *n.* reliance on oneself, one's abilities, etc. —**self′-re·li′ant** *adj.*

**self-re·proach** (-ri prōch′) *n.* blame of oneself; guilt feeling —**self′-re·proach′ful** *adj.*

**self-re·spect** (-ri spekt′) *n.* proper respect for oneself and one's worth as a person —**self′-re·spect′ing** *adj.*

**self-re·straint** (-ri strānt′) *n.* restraint of oneself; self-control —**self′-re·strained′** *adj.*

**self-re·veal·ing** (-ri vēl′iŋ) *adj.* revealing one's innermost thoughts, feelings, etc.: also **self′-rev′e·la·to′ry** (-rev′ə lə-tôr′ē) —**self′-rev′e·la′tion** *n.*

**self-right·eous** (-rī′chəs) *adj.* thinking oneself more righteous or moral than others —**self′-right′eous·ly** *adv.* —**self′-right′eous·ness** *n.*

**self-ris·ing** (-rīz′iŋ) *adj.* rising by itself: said specif. of flour sold with a leavening agent blended in for quick breads or cakes

**self-rule** (-rōōl′) *n. same as* SELF-GOVERNMENT

**self-sac·ri·fice** (-sak′rə fīs′) *n.* sacrifice of oneself or one's interests to benefit others —**self′-sac′ri·fic′ing** *adj.*

**self·same** (-sām′) *adj.* exactly the same; identical; (the) very same —**self′same′ness** *n.*

**self-sat·is·fied** (-sat′is fīd′) *adj.* pleased with oneself or with what one has done —**self′-sat′is·fac′tion** *n.*

**self-sat·is·fy·ing** (-sat′is fī′iŋ) *adj.* satisfying to oneself

**self-seal·ing** (-sēl′iŋ) *adj.* 1. automatically sealing punctures, etc., as some tires 2. sealable by pressure alone, as some envelopes

**self-seek·er** (-sē′kər) *n.* a person seeking only or mainly to further his own interests —**self′-seek′ing** *n., adj.*

**self-serv·ice** (-sur′vis) *n.* the practice of serving oneself in a store, cafeteria, etc. and then paying a cashier —*adj.* operating thus

**self-serv·ing** (-sur′viŋ) *adj.* serving one's own selfish interests, esp. at the expense of others

**self-sown** (-sōn′) *adj.* sown by wind, water, or other natural means, as some weeds

**self-styled** (-stīld′) *adj.* so named by oneself [he is a *self-styled* expert]

**self-suf·fi·cient** (-sə fish′ənt) *adj.* able to get along without help; independent —**self′-suf·fi′cien·cy** *n.*

**self-sup·port** (-sə pôrt′) *n.* support of oneself or itself without aid or reinforcement —**self′-sup·port′ing** *adj.*

**self-sus·tain·ing** (-sə stān′iŋ) *adj.* 1. supporting or able to support oneself or itself 2. able to continue once begun

**self-taught** (-tôt′) *adj.* 1. having taught oneself 2. learned by oneself without instruction

**self·ward** (-wərd) *adv.* toward oneself: also **self′wards** —*adj.* directed toward oneself

**self-willed** (-wild′) *adj.* stubborn about getting one's own way; willful —**self′-will′** *n.*

**self-wind·ing** (-wīn′diŋ) *adj.* winding automatically, as certain wristwatches

**sell** (sel) *vt.* **sold, sell′ing** [OE. *sellan*, to give] 1. to exchange (property, goods, services, etc.) for money or its equivalent 2. *a)* to offer for sale; deal in *b)* to make or try to make sales in or to [to *sell* chain stores] 3. *a)* to deliver (a person) to his enemies, into slavery, etc. *b)* to betray (a country, cause, etc.) 4. to give up (one's honor, etc.) for profit, etc. 5. to promote the sale of [television *sells* many products] 6. [Colloq.] *a)* to establish confidence or belief in [to *sell* oneself to the public] *b)* to persuade (someone) of the value of something (with *on*) [sell him on the idea] 7. [Slang] to cheat or dupe —*vi.* 1. to sell something 2. to work or act as a salesman or salesperson 3. to be a popular item on the market 4. to be sold (*for* or *at*) [belts *selling* for two dollars] 5. [Colloq.] to be accepted, approved, etc. [a scheme that won't *sell*] —*n.* [Slang] 1. a trick or hoax 2. selling or salesmanship — **sell out** 1. to dispose of completely by selling 2. [Colloq.] to betray (someone, a cause, etc.) —**sell short** 1. to sell securities, etc. not yet owned, expecting to cover later at a lower price 2. to undervalue —**sell′er** *n.*

**sell-off** (-ôf′) *n.* a price decline for all or certain stocks and bonds, due to pressure to sell

**sell·out** (-out′) *n.* [Colloq.] 1. a selling out, or betrayal 2. a show, etc. for which all seats have been sold

**Sel·ma** (sel′mə) [< ? Gr. *selma*, a ship] a feminine name

**Selt·zer** (selt′sər) *n.* [< *Niederselters*, village near Wiesbaden, Germany] 1. natural mineral water that is effervescent 2. [*often* s-] any carbonated water Also **Seltzer water**

**sel·vage, sel·vedge** (sel′vij) *n.* [< SELF + EDGE, after MDu. *selfegge*] 1. a specially woven edge to keep cloth from raveling 2. an edge of fabric or paper that is to be trimmed off or covered

**selves** (selvz) *n. pl. of* SELF

**Sem.** 1. Seminary 2. Semitic

**sem.** 1. semester 2. semicolon

**se·man·tic** (sə man′tik) *adj.* [Gr. *sēmantikos*, significant < *sēmainein*, to show < *sēma*, a sign] 1. of meaning, esp. in language 2. of semantics —**se·man′ti·cal·ly** *adv.*

**se·man·tics** (-tiks) *n.pl.* [*with sing. v.*] [see prec.] 1. the branch of linguistics dealing with the meanings given to words and the changes that occur to these meanings as time goes on 2. the relationships between symbols and the ideas given to them by their users 3. loosely, the twisting of meaning to mislead or confuse, as in some advertising and propaganda —**se·man′ti·cist** (-tə sist) *n.*

---

fat, āpe, cär; ten, ēven; is, bīte; gō, hôrn, tōōl, look; oil, out; up, fur; get; joy; yet; chin; she; thin, then; zh, leisure; ŋ, ring; ə for *a* in *ago*, *e* in *agent*, *i* in *sanity*, *o* in *comply*, *u* in *focus*; ′ as in *able* (ā′b'l); Fr. bäl; ë, Fr. coeur; ö, Fr. feu; Fr. mon; ô, Fr. coq; ü, Fr. duc; r, Fr. cri; H, G. ich; kh, G. doch; ‡foreign; *hypothetical; < derived from. See inside front cover.

**sem·a·phore** (sem′ə fôr′) *n.* [< Fr. < Gr. *sēma,* a sign + *-phoros:* see -PHOROUS] any device or system for signaling, as by lights, flags, mechanical arms, etc. —*vt., vi.* **-phored′, -phor′ing** to signal by semaphore —**sem′a·phor′ic** *adj.* —**sem′a·phor′ist** *n.*

**Se·ma·rang** (sə mä′räŋ) seaport in N Java, Indonesia: pop. 503,000

**sem·blance** (sem′bləns) *n.* [< OFr. < *sembler,* to seem, ult. < L. *similis,* like] **1.** outward look or show; seeming likeness **2.** a likeness, image, or representation **3.** a false, assumed, or deceiving form or appearance

**se·men** (sē′mən) *n.* [ModL. < L., a seed] the fluid secreted by the male reproductive organs, containing the spermatozoa

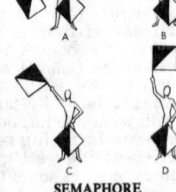

SEMAPHORE
(signals for letters A, B, C, D)

**se·mes·ter** (sə mes′tər) *n.* [G. < L. *semestris,* half-yearly < *sex,* six + *mensis,* month] either of the two terms which usually make up a school or college year —**se·mes′tral** *adj.*

**sem·i** (sem′ī, -ē) *n., pl.* **sem′is** *clipped form of* SEMITRAILER (sense 2)

**sem·i-** (sem′i; *also variously* -ē, -ī, -ə) [L.] *a prefix meaning:* **1.** half [*semicircle*] **2.** partly [*semiskilled*] **3.** twice in a (specified period) [*semiannually*]

**sem·i·an·nu·al** (sem′ē an′yōō wəl) *adj.* **1.** happening, presented, etc. every half year **2.** lasting only half a year, as some plants —**sem′i·an′nu·al·ly** *adv.*

**sem·i·a·quat·ic** (-ə kwät′ik, -kwat′-) *adj. Biol.* **1.** growing in or near water **2.** spending some time in water, as muskrats

**sem·i·au·to·mat·ic** (-ôt′ə mat′ik) *adj.* **1.** partly automatic and partly hand-controlled: said of machinery **2.** operating like an automatic firearm but requiring a trigger pull for each shot fired —*n.* a semiautomatic firearm

**sem·i·breve** (sem′i brēv′) *n.* [Brit.] *same as* WHOLE NOTE

**sem·i·cir·cle** (sem′i sur′k'l) *n.* a half circle —**sem′i·cir′cu·lar** (-kyə lər) *adj.*

**semicircular canal** any of the three loop-shaped, tubular structures of the inner ear that serve to maintain balance in the organism

**sem·i·co·lon** (sem′i kō′lən) *n.* a mark of punctuation (;) showing more separation than that marked by the comma and less than that marked by the period, etc.: used chiefly between units containing elements separated by commas and between some coordinate clauses

**sem·i·con·duc·tor** (sem′i kən duk′tər) *n.* a substance, as silicon, whose conductivity is improved by minute additions of certain substances or by application of heat, light, or voltage: used in transistors, etc.

**sem·i·con·scious** (-kän′shəs) *adj.* not fully conscious or awake —**sem′i·con′scious·ness** *n.*

**sem·i·de·tached** (-di tacht′) *adj.* partly separate, as two houses joined by a common wall

**sem·i·fi·nal** (sem′i fī′n'l; *for n., usually* sem′i fī′n'l) *adj.* coming just before the final match, as of a tournament —*n.* **1.** a semifinal match **2.** [*pl.*] a semifinal round —**sem′i·fi′nal·ist** *n.*

**sem·i·flu·id** (sem′i flōō′id) *adj.* heavy or thick but able to flow —*n.* a semifluid substance

**sem·i·for·mal** (-fôr′m'l) *adj.* designating or requiring attire that is less than strictly formal but not informal

**sem·i·hard** (-härd′) *adj.* somewhat hard, but easily cut

**sem·i·lit·er·ate** (-lit′ər it) *adj.* knowing how to read and write a little, or knowing only how to read

**sem·i·month·ly** (-munth′lē) *adj.* coming, happening, done, etc. twice a month —*n., pl.* **-lies** something coming, appearing, issued, etc. twice a month —*adv.* twice a month

**sem·i·nal** (sem′ə n'l) *adj.* [< MFr. < L. < *semen,* a seed] **1.** of or containing seed or semen **2.** of reproduction **3.** like seed in being a source or a first stage in development; germinal [*a seminal book*] **4.** being an early and influential example [*a seminal jazz band*]

**sem·i·nar** (sem′ə när′) *n.* [G. < L.: see ff.] **1.** a group of supervised students doing advanced study **2.** a course for such a group **3.** any similar group discussion

**sem·i·nar·y** (sem′ə ner′ē) *n., pl.* **-nar′ies** [< L. neut. of *seminarius,* of seed < *semen,* a seed] **1.** a school, esp. a private school for young women: an old-fashioned term **2.** a school or college where priests, ministers, or rabbis are trained —**sem′i·nar′i·an** (-ē ən) *n.*

**sem·i·nif·er·ous** (sem′ə nif′ər əs) *adj.* [< L. *semen,* a seed + -FEROUS] **1.** seed-bearing **2.** containing semen

**Sem·i·nole** (sem′ə nōl′) *n.* [Creek *Simanóle,* lit., runaway] **1.** *pl.* **-noles′, -nole′** any of an American Indian people of S Florida and Oklahoma **2.** their Muskogean language

**sem·i·of·fi·cial** (sem′ē ə fish′'l) *adj.* having some, but not full, official authority —**sem′i·of·fi′cial·ly** *adv.*

**se·mi·ot·ics** (sē′mē ät′iks) *n.pl.* [< Gr. *sēmeion,* a sign]

[*with sing. v.*] *Philos.* a general theory of signs and symbols; esp., the analysis of signs used in language

**sem·i·per·me·a·ble** (sem′i pur′mē ə b'l) *adj.* allowing some substances to pass; permeable to smaller molecules but not to larger ones

**sem·i·pre·cious** (-presh′əs) *adj.* designating gems, as garnets and opals, of lower value than precious gems

**sem·i·pri·vate** (-prī′vit) *adj.* partly but not completely private; specif., designating or of a hospital room with two, three, or, sometimes, four beds

**sem·i·pro** (sem′i prō′) *adj., n. shortened form of* SEMIPROFESSIONAL

**sem·i·pro·fes·sion·al** (sem′i prə fesh′ən 'l) *adj.* not fully professional; specif., *a*) engaging in a sport, etc. for pay but not as a regular occupation *b*) engaged in by semiprofessional players, etc. —*n.* a semiprofessional player, etc. —**sem′i·pro·fes′sion·al·ly** *adv.*

**sem·i·qua·ver** (sem′i kwā′vər) *n.* [Chiefly Brit.] a musical sixteenth note

**sem·i·rig·id** (sem′i rij′id) *adj.* somewhat or partly rigid; specif., designating an airship with a rigid internal keel

**sem·i·skilled** (-skild′) *adj.* **1.** partly skilled **2.** of or doing manual work that requires only limited training

**sem·i·soft** (-sôft′) *adj.* soft but firm and easily cut

**sem·i·sol·id** (-säl′id) *adj.* viscous and slowly flowing, as asphalt —*n.* a semisolid substance

**Sem·ite** (sem′īt; *chiefly Brit.* sē′mīt) *n.* [prob. < Fr. < ModL. < *Semiticus:* see ff.] a member of any people speaking a Semitic language, as a Hebrew, Arab, etc.

**Se·mit·ic** (sə mit′ik) *adj.* [< G. < ModL. *Semiticus,* ult. < Gr. *Sem* < Heb. *Shēm,* SHEM] **1.** of or like the Semites **2.** designating or of a major division of a family of languages of SW Asia and N Africa, including Hebrew, Arabic, etc. —*n.* this division, or any member of it

**Sem·i·tism** (sem′ə tiz'm) *n.* **1.** a Semitic word or idiom **2.** traits, customs, etc. of the Semites

**sem·i·tone** (sem′i tōn′) *n. Music* the difference in pitch between any two immediately adjacent keys on the piano

**sem·i·trail·er** (-trā′lər) *n.* **1.** a detachable trailer designed to be attached by a coupling to the rear part of a tractor (sense 2), on which it is partly supported **2.** a truck made up of such a trailer and tractor

**sem·i·trop·i·cal** (sem′i träp′i k'l) *adj.* somewhat like the tropics; nearly tropical: also **sem′i·trop′ic**

**sem·i·vow·el** (sem′i vou′əl) *n. Phonet.* a glide at the beginning of a syllable, as the sound of *w* in *wall*

**sem·i·week·ly** (sem′i wēk′lē) *adj.* appearing, happening, done, etc. twice a week —*n., pl.* **-lies** a semiweekly publication —*adv.* twice a week

**sem·i·year·ly** (-yir′lē) *adj.* coming, happening, done, etc. twice a year —*adv.* twice a year

**sem·o·li·na** (sem′ə lē′nə) *n.* [< It. dim. of *semola,* bran] coarsely ground durum, a byproduct in the milling of flour, used in making macaroni, puddings, etc.

‡**sem·per fi·de·lis** (sem′pər fi dā′lis) [L.] always faithful: motto of the U.S. Marine Corps

‡**semper pa·ra·tus** (pə rät′əs, -rāt′əs) [L.] always prepared: motto of the U.S. Coast Guard

**sem·pi·ter·nal** (sem′pi tur′n'l) *adj.* [< ML. < L. < *semper,* always + *aeternus,* ETERNAL] everlasting; eternal

**sen** (sen) *n., pl.* **sen** [Jap.] the 100th part of a yen: a former monetary unit of Japan, now used only as a money of account See also MONETARY UNITS, table (Indonesia)

**Sen., sen. 1.** senate **2.** senator **3.** senior

**sen·ate** (sen′it) *n.* [< OFr. < L. *senatus < senex,* old] **1.** the supreme council of the ancient Roman state **2.** a lawmaking assembly **3.** [S-] *a*) the upper branch of the legislature of the U.S., or of most of the States of the U.S. *b*) a similar body in other countries **4.** a governing body, as in some schools

**sen·a·tor** (sen′ə tər) *n.* a member of a senate —**sen′a·to′ri·al** (-tôr′ē əl) *adj.*

**send** (send) *vt.* **sent, send′ing** [OE. *sendan*] **1.** *a*) to cause to go or be carried; convey *b*) to dispatch or transmit (a message) by mail, radio, etc. **2.** to direct or command to go [*send him home*] **3.** to enable to go or attend [*to send one's son to college*] **4.** to cause to move by hitting, throwing, etc. [*he sent the ball over the fence*] **5.** to drive into some condition [*sent him to his ruin*] **6.** to cause to happen, come, etc. [*joy sent by the gods*] **7.** [Slang] to excite; thrill —*vi.* **1.** to send a message, messenger, etc. [*to send for help*] **2.** to transmit, as by radio —**send away** to dispatch or banish —**send down** [Brit.] to suspend or expel from a university —**send flying 1.** to dismiss hurriedly **2.** to stagger, as with a blow **3.** to put to flight **4.** to scatter abruptly in all directions —**send for 1.** to order to come; summon **2.** to request or order delivery of —**send forth** to give out or forth; produce, emit, etc. —**send in 1.** to dispatch or send to one receiving **2.** to put (a player) in a game —**send off 1.** to dispatch (a letter, gift, etc.) **2.** to dismiss **3.** to give a send-off to —**send up 1.** to cause to rise **2.** [Colloq.] to sentence to prison —**send′er** *n.*

**send-off** (send′ôf′) *n.* [Colloq.] **1.** a demonstration of friendly feeling toward someone starting out on a trip, career, etc. **2.** a start given to someone or something

**Sen·e·ca**[1] (sen′i kə) *n.* [< Oneida Indian name meaning "people of the standing rock"] **1.** *pl.* **-cas, -ca** any of a N. American Indian people of New York and Ontario **2.** their Iroquoian language —**Sen′e·can** *adj.*

**Sen·e·ca**[2] (sen′i kə) (*Lucius Annaeus Seneca*) 4? B.C.–65 A.D.; Rom. philosopher, dramatist, & statesman

**Sen·e·gal** (sen′i gôl′) **1.** country in W Africa, on the Atlantic: 76,124 sq. mi.; pop. 3,780,000; cap. Dakar **2.** river flowing from W Mali, along the Senegal border into the Atlantic —**Sen′e·ga·lese′** (-gə lēz′) *adj., n., pl.* **-lese′**

**se·nes·cent** (sə nes′′nt) *adj.* [< L. prp. of *senescere*, to grow old] growing old; aging —**se·nes′cence** (-′ns) *n.*

**sen·es·chal** (sen′ə shəl) *n.* [< OFr. < Frank. *siniskalk*, oldest servant] a steward in charge of a medieval household

**se·nile** (sē′nīl, sen′īl) *adj.* [L. *senilis* < *senex*, old] **1.** of or typical of old age **2.** showing the deterioration, esp. the mental confusion, memory loss, etc., often accompanying old age —**se′nile·ly** *adv.* —**se·nil·i·ty** (si nil′ə tē) *n.*

**sen·ior** (sēn′yər) *adj.* [L., compar. of *senex*, old] **1.** the older: written *Sr.* after the name of a father whose son bears the same name **2.** of higher rank or longer service **3.** of or for seniors in a high school or college —*n.* **1.** an older person **2.** a person of greater rank or longer service **3.** a student in the last year of a high school or college —**one's senior** a person older than oneself

**senior citizen** an elderly person, esp. one who is retired

**senior high school** high school, following junior high school: it usually includes the 10th, 11th, and 12th grades

**sen·ior·i·ty** (sēn yôr′ə tē, -yär′-) *n., pl.* **-ties 1.** a being senior, as in age or rank **2.** certain rights, esp. the right to continue to hold a certain job, based on length of service

**sen·i·ti** (sen′ə tē) *n., pl.* **sen′i·ti** [Polynesian (Tongan), cent] *see* MONETARY UNITS, table (Tonga)

**sen·na** (sen′ə) *n.* [< Ar. *sanā*] **1.** any of a genus of plants of the legume family, with yellow flowers **2.** the dried leaflets of various sennas, used, esp. formerly, as a laxative

‡**se·ñor** (se nyôr′) *n., pl.* **se·ño′res** (-nyô′res) [Sp. < L. *senior:* see SENIOR] a man; gentleman: Spanish title equivalent to *Mr.* or *Sir*

‡**se·ño·ra** (se nyô′rä) *n., pl.* **se·ño′ras** (-räs) [Sp.] a married woman: Spanish title equivalent to *Mrs.* or *Madam*

‡**se·ño·ri·ta** (se′nyô rē′tä) *n., pl.* **-ri′tas** (-täs) [Sp.] an unmarried woman or girl: Spanish title equivalent to *Miss*

**sen·sa·tion** (sen sā′shən) *n.* [< LL. < *sensatus*, intelligent < L. *sensus*, sense] **1.** the power or process of receiving conscious sense impressions through direct stimulation of the body organism *[the sensations of hearing, seeing, etc.]* **2.** a conscious feeling or sense impression *[a sensation of cold]* **3.** a generalized feeling *[a sensation of joy]* **4.** *a)* a state or feeling of general excitement *[the play caused a sensation]* *b)* the action, event, person, etc. causing this

**sen·sa·tion·al** (-′l) *adj.* **1.** of the senses or sensation **2.** *a)* intensely interesting or exciting *b)* intended to startle, shock, thrill, etc. **3.** [Colloq.] unusually good, fine, etc. —**sen·sa′tion·al·ize′** (-′l īz′) *vt.* **-ized′, -iz′ing** —**sen·sa′tion·al·ly** *adv.*

**sen·sa·tion·al·ism** (-′l iz′m) *n.* **1.** the use of subject matter, style, etc. intended to shock, thrill, etc. **2.** *Philos.* the belief that all knowledge is acquired through the senses —**sen·sa′tion·al·ist** *n.* —**sen·sa′tion·al·is′tic** *adj.*

**sense** (sens) *n.* [< Fr. < L. *sensus* < *sentire*, to feel] **1.** ability to receive and react to stimuli, as light, sound, etc.; specif., any of five faculties of receiving impressions through certain body organs (sight, touch, taste, smell, and hearing) **2.** these faculties collectively **3.** *a)* feeling, impression, or perception through the senses *[a sense of warmth]* *b)* a generalized feeling *[a sense of longing]* **4.** an ability to judge external conditions, sounds, etc. *[a sense of direction, pitch, etc.]* **5.** an ability to feel, appreciate, or understand some quality *[a sense of humor, honor, etc.]* **6.** *a)* sound thinking; normal intelligence and judgment *b)* something wise or reasonable *[to talk sense]* **7.** *[pl.]* normal ability to think or reason soundly *[to come to one's senses]* **8.** *a)* meaning; esp., any of several meanings of the same word or phrase *b)* essential meaning; gist **9.** the general opinion or attitude of a group —*vt.* **sensed, sens′ing 1.** to be aware of; perceive **2.** to understand **3.** to detect automatically, as by sensors —**in a sense** from one aspect; to a limited degree —**make sense** to be intelligible or logical

**sense·less** (-lis) *adj.* **1.** unconscious **2.** not showing good sense; stupid **3.** having no real point; meaningless —**sense′less·ly** *adv.* —**sense′less·ness** *n.*

**sense organ** any organ or structure, as an eye or a taste bud, that receives specific stimuli and transmits them as sensations to the brain

**sen·si·bil·i·ty** (sen′sə bil′ə tē) *n., pl.* **-ties** [< MFr. < LL. < L.: see ff.] **1.** the capacity for physical sensation; ability to feel **2.** *[often pl.] a)* the capacity for being affected emotionally or intellectually *b)* sensitive responsiveness to intellectual, moral, or aesthetic values

**sen·si·ble** (sen′sə b′l) *adj.* [< MFr. < L. *sensibilis* < pp. of *sentire*, to feel] **1.** that can cause physical sensation **2.** perceptible to the intellect **3.** easily perceived or noticed; striking **4.** capable of receiving sensation **5.** having appreciation or understanding; aware **6.** showing good sense or sound judgment; wise —**sen′si·bly** *adv.*

**sen·si·tive** (sen′sə tiv) *adj.* [< MFr. < ML. *sensitivus* < L. *sensus:* see SENSE] **1.** of the senses or sensation; sensory **2.** receiving and responding to stimuli **3.** keenly susceptible to stimuli *[a sensitive ear]* **4.** easily hurt; tender **5.** highly responsive to whatever is stimulating intellectually, artistically, etc. **6.** easily offended, shocked, irritated, etc. **7.** highly responsive as to light, radio signals, etc. *[sensitive equipment]* **8.** indicating or measuring small changes or differences **9.** of or dealing with secret or delicate government matters —**sen′si·tive·ly** *adv.* —**sen′si·tiv′i·ty** (-ə tē), **sen′si·tive·ness** *n.*

**sensitive plant** a tropical American plant with purplish flowers, whose leaflets fold and leafstalks droop when touched

**sensitivity training** a kind of psychotherapy in which a group of patients, under the guidance of a leader, seek a better understanding of themselves and others, as by the exchange of intimate feelings and experiences

**sen·si·tize** (sen′sə tiz′) *vt.* **-tized′, -tiz′ing** to make sensitive —**sen′si·ti·za′tion** *n.* —**sen′si·tiz′er** *n.*

**sen·sor** (sen′sər, -sôr) *n.* [< L. pp. of *sentire*, to feel + -OR] a device designed to detect, measure, or record physical phenomena, as radiation, and to respond, as by transmitting information or operating controls

**sen·so·ri·mo·tor** (sen′sə rē mōt′ər) *adj.* [< SENSORY + MOTOR] *Physiol., Psychol.* of or involving both sensory and motor functions

**sen·so·ry** (sen′sər ē) *adj.* **1.** of the senses or sensation **2.** connected with the reception and transmission of sense impressions Also **sen·so′ri·al** (-sôr′ē əl)

**sen·su·al** (sen′shoo wəl) *adj.* [L. *sensualis* < *sensus*, SENSE] **1.** of the body and the senses as distinguished from the intellect or spirit **2.** *a)* connected or preoccupied with bodily or sexual pleasures *b)* lustful; lewd —**sen′su·al·ly** *adv.*

**sen·su·al·ism** (-iz′m) *n.* **1.** frequent or excessive indulgence in sensual pleasures **2.** *a)* the belief that sensual pleasures are the greatest good for mankind *b)* expression of this belief, esp. in art —**sen′su·al·ist** *n.*

**sen·su·al·i·ty** (sen′shoo wal′ə tē) *n.* **1.** a being sensual; fondness for or indulgence in sensual pleasures **2.** lasciviousness; lewdness

**sen·su·al·ize** (sen′shoo wə līz′) *vt.* **-ized′, -iz′ing** to make sensual —**sen′su·al·i·za′tion** *n.*

**sen·su·ous** (sen′shoo wəs) *adj.* **1.** of, based on, or appealing to the senses **2.** enjoying or readily affected by sense impressions —**sen′su·ous·ly** *adv.* —**sen′su·ous·ness** *n.*

**sent** (sent) *pt. & pp. of* SEND

**sen·tence** (sen′t′ns) *n.* [< OFr. < L. *sententia*, opinion, ult. < prp. of *sentire*, to feel] **1.** *a)* a decision or judgment, as of a court; esp., the determination by a court of a convicted person's punishment *b)* the punishment **2.** *Gram.* a word or group of words stating, asking, commanding, or exclaiming something, usually having a subject and predicate: in writing, it begins with a capital letter and ends with a period, question mark, etc. —*vt.* **-tenced, -tenc′ing** to pronounce judgment upon (a convicted person); condemn (*to a specified punishment*) —**sen·ten′tial** (-ten′shəl) *adj.*

**sen·ten·tious** (sen ten′shəs) *adj.* [< L. < *sententia:* see prec.] **1.** expressing much in few words; short and pithy **2.** full of, or fond of using, maxims, proverbs, etc., esp. in a pompously trite or moralizing way —**sen·ten′tious·ly** *adv.*

**sen·tient** (sen′shənt, -shē ənt) *adj.* [< L. prp. of *sentire*, to feel] of, having, or capable of feeling or perception; conscious —**sen′tience, sen′tien·cy** *n.* —**sen′tient·ly** *adv.*

**sen·ti·ment** (sen′tə mənt) *n.* [< OFr. < ML. < L. *sentire*, to feel] **1.** a complex combination of feelings and opinions **2.** an opinion, attitude, etc.: *often used in the pl.* **3.** susceptibility to emotional appeal; sensibility **4.** appeal to the emotions in literature or art **5.** sentimentality; maudlin emotion **6.** a short sentence expressing some thought or wish **7.** the real thought or meaning behind something

**sen·ti·men·tal** (sen′tə men′t′l) *adj.* **1.** having or showing tender or delicate feelings, as in literature or art, often in an excessive or maudlin way **2.** influenced more by emotion than reason **3.** of or resulting from sentiment —**sen′ti·men′tal·ism** *n.* —**sen′ti·men′tal·ist** *n.* —**sen′ti·men′tal·ly** *adv.*

**sen·ti·men·tal·i·ty** (sen′tə men tal′ə tē) *n.* **1.** the quality or condition of being sentimental, esp. in a maudlin way **2.** *pl.* **-ties** any expression of this

**sen·ti·men·tal·ize** (-men′tə līz′) *vi.* **-ized′**, **-iz′ing** to be sentimental —*vt.* to regard or treat sentimentally —**sen′ti·men′tal·i·za′tion** *n.*

**sen·ti·nel** (sen′ti n'l) *n.* [< Fr. < It. *sentinella*, ult. < L *sentire*, to feel] a person or animal set to guard a group; specif., a sentry —*vt.* **-neled** or **-nelled**, **-nel·ing** or **-nel·ling** **1.** to guard as a sentinel **2.** to furnish with a sentinel **3.** to post as a sentinel

**sen·try** (sen′trē) *n., pl.* **-tries** [< ? obs. *centery*, guardhouse] a sentinel; esp., any member of a military guard posted to guard against, and warn of, danger

**Se·oul** (sōl; *Korean* syŏ′ool′) capital of South Korea, in the NW part: pop. 5,510,000

**se·pal** (sē′p'l; *chiefly Brit.* sep′'l) *n.* [< Fr. < ModL. *sepalum*, arbitrary blend < Gr. *skepē*, a covering + L. *petalum*, petal] *Bot.* any of the usually green, leaflike parts of the calyx —**se′paled, se′palled** *adj.*

SEPALS

**-sep·al·ous** (sep′'l əs) *a combining form meaning* having (a specified number or kind of) sepals

**sep·a·ra·ble** (sep′ər ə b'l, sep′rə-) *adj.* that can be separated —**sep′a·ra·bil′i·ty** *n.* —**sep′a·ra·bly** *adv.*

**sep·a·rate** (sep′ə rāt′; *for adj. & n.* sep′ər it, sep′rit) *vt.* **-rat′ed**, **-rat′ing** [< L. pp. of *separare* < *se-*, apart + *parare*, to arrange] **1.** to set apart into groups, sets, units, etc.; divide **2.** to tell apart; distinguish between **3.** to keep apart by being between [a wall *separates* the yards] **4.** to bring about a separation between (a man and wife) **5.** to set apart from others; segregate **6.** to take away (a part or ingredient) from a combination or mixture **7.** to discharge from military service or from a job —*vi.* **1.** to withdraw or secede **2.** to part, become disconnected, etc. **3.** to part company; go in different directions **4.** to stop living together as man and wife but without getting a divorce **5.** to become distinct or disengaged, as from a mixture —*adj.* **1.** set apart or divided from the rest or others **2.** not associated with others; distinct; individual **3.** having individual form or function **4.** not shared or held in common —*n.* [*pl.*] articles of dress designed to be worn as a set or separately —**sep′a·rate·ly** *adv.* —**sep′a·rate·ness** *n.* —**sep·a·ra·tive** (sep′ə rā′tiv, -ər ə tiv), **sep′a·ra·to′ry** (-ər ə tôr′ē) *adj.* —**sep′a·ra′tor** *n.*

**sep·a·ra·tion** (sep′ə rā′shən) *n.* **1.** a separating or being separated **2.** the place where this occurs; break; division **3.** something that separates **4.** an arrangement by which a man and wife live apart by agreement or court decree

**sep·a·ra·tism** (sep′ər ə tiz′m) *n.* a policy of or movement for political, religious, or racial separation —**sep·a·ra·tist** (sep′ər ə tist, -ə rāt′ist) *n., adj.*

**Se·phar·dim** (sə fär′dim, -fär dēm′) *n.pl., sing.* **Se·phard** (sə färd′), **Se·phar·di** (-fär′dē, -fär dē′) [< Heb.: cf. Obad. 20] the Jews of Spain and Portugal before the Inquisition, or their descendants —**Se·phar′dic** *adj.*

**se·pi·a** (sē′pē ə) *n.* [L., cuttlefish < Gr. *sēpia* < *sēpein*, to cause to rot (from the inky fluid)] **1.** a dark-brown pigment prepared from the inky secretion of cuttlefish **2.** a dark reddish-brown color **3.** a photographic print in this color —*adj.* **1.** of sepia **2.** dark reddish-brown

**se·poy** (sē′poi) *n.* [Port. *sipae* < Hindi & Per. *sipāhī* < *sipāh*, army] formerly, a native of India serving in the British army

**sep·pu·ku** (se pōo′kōo) *n.* [Jap.] *same as* HARA-KIRI

**sep·sis** (sep′sis) *n.* [ModL. < Gr. < *sēpein*, to make putrid] poisoning caused by the absorption into the blood of certain microorganisms and their products

**Sept.** **1.** September **2.** Septuagint

**sep·ta** (sep′tə) *n. alt. pl. of* SEPTUM

**Sep·tem·ber** (sep tem′bər, səp-) *n.* [< L. < *septem*, seven: the early Romans reckoned from March] the ninth month of the year, having 30 days

**sep·ten·ni·al** (sep ten′ē əl) *adj.* [< L. < *septum*, seven + *annus*, year] **1.** lasting seven years **2.** coming, happening, etc. every seven years —**sep·ten′ni·al·ly** *adv.*

**sep·tet, sep·tette** (sep tet′) *n.* [G. < L. *septem*, seven + G. (*du*)*ett*] **1.** a group of seven persons or things **2.** *Music a*) a composition for seven voices or instruments *b*) the performers of this

**sep·tic** (sep′tik) *adj.* [< L. < Gr. *sēptikos* < *sēpein*, to make putrid] caused by or involving microorganisms that are infecting or putrefying —**sep′ti·cal·ly** *adv.*

**sep·ti·ce·mi·a** (sep′tə sē′mē ə) *n.* [< Gr. *sēptikos*, putrefactive + *haima*, blood] a systemic disease caused by certain microorganisms and their toxic products in the blood —**sep′ti·ce′mic** *adj.*

**septic tank** an underground tank in which waste matter is putrefied and decomposed through bacterial action

**sep·til·lion** (sep til′yən) *n.* [Fr. < L. *septem*, seven + Fr. (*m*)*illion*] **1.** in the U.S. and France, the number represented by 1 followed by 24 zeros **2.** in Great Britain and Germany, the number represented by 1 followed by 42 zeros —*adj.* amounting to one septillion in number

**sep·tu·a·ge·nar·i·an** (sep′too wə ji ner′ē ən) *adj.* [< LL. < L. *septuageni*, seventy each < *septuaginta*, seventy] seventy years old, or between the ages of seventy and eighty —*n.* a person of this age

**Sep·tu·a·gint** (sep′too wə jint, -tyoo-, -choo-) [< L. *septuaginta*, seventy: in tradition, done by 70 or 72 translators] a Greek translation of the Hebrew Scriptures made in the 3d cent. B.C.

**sep·tum** (sep′təm) *n., pl.* **-tums**, **-ta** (-tə) [ModL. < L. *sepire*, to enclose < *saepes*, a hedge] *Biol.* a part that separates two cavities or masses of tissue, as in the nose, a fruit, etc.; partition —**sep′tal** *adj.*

**sep·tu·ple** (sep too′p'l, -tyoo′-, -tup′'l; sep′too p'l) *adj.* [LL. *septuplus* < L. *septem*, seven] **1.** consisting of seven **2.** seven times as much or as many —*vt., vi.* **-pled**, **-pling** to multiply by seven

**sep·ul·cher** (sep′'l kər) *n.* [< OFr. < L. *sepulcrum* < *sepelire*, to bury] a vault for burial; grave; tomb —*vt.* to bury in a sepulcher

**se·pul·chral** (sə pul′krəl) *adj.* **1.** of sepulchers, burial, etc. **2.** suggestive of the grave, etc.; dismal; gloomy **3.** deep and melancholy: said of sound —**se·pul′chral·ly** *adv.*

**sep·ul·chre** (sep′'l kər) *n., vt.* **-chred**, **-chring** *Brit. sp. of* SEPULCHER

**sep·ul·ture** (sep′'l chər) *n.* burial; interment

**seq.** [L. *sequentes* or *sequentia*] the following: also **seqq.**

**se·quel** (sē′kwəl) *n.* [< MFr. < L. < *sequela* < *sequi*, to follow] **1.** something that follows; continuation **2.** a result or consequence **3.** any literary work complete in itself but continuing a story begun in an earlier work

**se·quence** (sē′kwəns) *n.* [< MFr. < LL. < L. *sequens*: see ff.] **1.** *a*) the following of one thing after another; succession or continuity *b*) the order in which this occurs **2.** a continuous or related series **3.** a resulting event; consequence **4.** *Math.* an ordered set of quantities or elements **5.** *Motion Pictures* the series of shots forming a single, uninterrupted episode —*vt.* **-quenced**, **-quenc·ing** to arrange in a sequence

**se·quent** (-kwənt) *adj.* [L. *sequens*, prp. of *sequi*, to follow] **1.** following in time or order; subsequent **2.** following as a result; consequent —*n.* something sequent; consequence

**se·quen·tial** (si kwen′shəl) *adj.* **1.** *same as* SEQUENT **2.** characterized by or forming a regular sequence of parts

**se·ques·ter** (si kwes′tər) *vt.* [< MFr. < LL. *sequestrare*, to remove < L. *sequester*, trustee] **1.** to set apart; separate **2.** to take possession of (property) as security for a debt, claim, etc. **3.** to confiscate; seize, esp. by authority **4.** to withdraw; seclude —**se·ques′tered** *adj.*

**se·ques·trate** (-trāt) *vt.* **-trat·ed**, **-trat·ing** *same as* SEQUESTER —**se′ques·tra′tor** *n.*

**se·ques·tra·tion** (sē′kwes trā′shən, si kwes′-) *n.* **1.** a sequestering or being sequestered; seclusion; separation **2.** *a*) the legal seizure of property for security *b*) confiscation of property, as by court action

**se·quin** (sē′kwin) *n.* [Fr. < It. *zecchino* < *zecca*, a mint < Ar. *sikkah*, a stamp] **1.** an obsolete Italian gold coin **2.** a small, shiny spangle, as a metal disk, esp. one of many sewn on fabric for decoration —*vt.* **-quined** or **-quinned**, **-quin·ing** or **-quin·ning** to adorn with sequins

**se·quoi·a** (si kwoi′ə) *n.* [ModL., genus name: after *Sequoya*, Am. Indian (c. 1760–1843) who devised the Cherokee syllabary] either of two giant evergreen trees; specif., *a*) BIG TREE *b*) REDWOOD

**se·rag·lio** (si ral′yō, -räl′-) *n., pl.* **-lios** [It. *serraglio*, enclosure (infl. by Turk. *serai*, palace), ult. < LL. *serare*, to lock < *sera*, a lock] **1.** the part of a Moslem's household where his wives or concubines live; harem **2.** the palace of a Turkish sultan Also **se·rail** (sə rī′, -rīl′, -räl′)

**se·ra·pe** (sə rä′pē) *n.* [MexSp.] a woolen blanket, often brightly colored, worn as an outer garment by men in Spanish-American countries

**ser·aph** (ser′əf) *n., pl.* **-aphs**, **-a·phim′** (-ə-fim′) [< LL. < Heb. *sĕrāphīm*, pl.] *Bible* one of the heavenly beings mentioned in Isaiah as surrounding the throne of God —**se·raph·ic** (sə raf′ik) *adj.* —**se·raph′i·cal·ly** *adv.*

**Serb** (sʉrb) *n.* **1.** a native or inhabitant of Serbia **2.** *same as* SERBIAN (*n.* 1) —*adj. same as* SERBIAN

**Ser·bi·a** (sʉr′bē ə) republic of Yugoslavia, in the E part: 21,580 sq. mi.; cap. Belgrade

**Ser·bi·an** (-ən) *adj.* of Serbia, the Serbs, or their language —*n.* **1.** Serbo-Croatian as spoken in Serbia **2.** *same as* SERB (*n.* 1)

SERAPE

**Ser·bo-Cro·a·tian** (sʉr′bō krō ā′shən) *n.* the major South Slavic language of Yugoslavia: it is generally written in the Roman alphabet in Croatia and in the

Cyrillic alphabet in Serbia —*adj.* of this language or the people who speak it

**sere¹** (sir) *n.* [< SERIES] *Ecol.* the complete series of communities occurring in succession in an area

**sere²** (sir) *adj.* [var. of SEAR] [Poet.] withered

**ser·e·nade** (ser′ə nād′) *n.* [< Fr. < It. *serenata,* ult. < L. *serenus,* clear] **1.** the act of playing or singing music outdoors at night, esp. by a lover under the window of his sweetheart **2.** a piece of music suitable for this —*vt., vi.* **-nad′ed, -nad′ing** to play or sing a serenade (to) —*ser′e-nad′er n.*

**ser·en·dip·i·ty** (ser′ən dip′ə tē) *n.* [after the princes in a Per. fairy tale, *The Three Princes of Serendip,* who make such discoveries] a seeming gift for making fortunate discoveries accidentally —*ser′en·dip′i·tous adj.*

**se·rene** (sə rēn′) *adj.* [L. *serenus*] **1.** clear; unclouded [a *serene* sky] **2.** untroubled; calm, peaceful, etc. **3.** [S-] exalted: in titles [His *Serene* Highness] —**se·rene′ly** *adv.* —**se·ren′i·ty** (-ren′ə tē), **se·rene′ness** *n.*

**serf** (surf) *n.* [OFr. < L. *servus,* a slave] **1.** a person in a slavelike condition under the feudal system, bound to his master's land and transferred with it **2.** a person treated like a slave —**serf′dom, serf′hood′** *n.*

**Serg., serg.** sergeant

**serge** (surj) *n.* [< OFr. < L. < *sericus,* silken, lit., of the *Seres,* prob. the Chinese, prob. ult. < Chin. *se,* silk] a strong, twilled fabric made of wool, silk, rayon, etc. and used for suits, coats, linings, etc. —*vt.* **serged, serg′ing** to finish off (a cut or raveling edge) with overcast stitches

**ser·geant** (sär′jənt) *n.* [< OFr. < L. *serviens,* serving < *servire,* to serve] **1.** *same as* SERGEANT-AT-ARMS **2.** *a)* a noncommissioned officer of the fifth grade, ranking just above a corporal in the U.S. Army and Marine Corps *b)* generally, any of the noncommissioned officers in the U.S. armed forces with *sergeant* as part of the title of their rank **3.** a police officer ranking next below a captain or a lieutenant —*ser′gean·cy, pl.* **-cies, ser′geant·ship′** *n.*

**ser·geant-at-arms** (-ət ärmz′) *n., pl.* **ser·geants-at-arms′** an officer appointed to keep order, as in a legislature

**sergeant first class** *U.S. Army* the seventh grade of enlisted man, ranking just below master sergeant

**sergeant major** *pl.* **sergeants major 1.** the chief administrative noncommissioned officer of a military headquarters: an occupational title, not a rank **2.** *U.S. Army & Marine Corps* the highest ranking noncommissioned officer

**se·ri·al** (sir′ē əl) *adj.* [< ModL. < L. *series,* a row, SERIES] **1.** of, arranged in, or forming a series [*serial* numbers] **2.** appearing or published in a series of continuing parts at regular intervals **3.** of a serial or serials **4.** *same as* TWELVE-TONE —*n.* a story presented in serial form, as in periodicals, movies, radio, TV, etc. —**se′ri·al·ly** *adv.*

**se·ri·al·ize** (-īz′) *vt.* **-ized′, -iz′ing** to put or publish (a story, etc.) in serial form —**se′ri·al·i·za′tion** *n.*

**serial number** any of a series of numbers given to a person (as a soldier) or thing (as an engine) for identification

**se·ri·a·tim** (sir′ē āt′im) *adv., adj.* [ML. < L. *series*] one after another in order; serial(ly)

**se·ries** (sir′ēz) *n., pl.* **-ries** [L. < *serere,* to join together] **1.** a number of similar things arranged in a row [a *series* of arches] **2.** a number of similar persons, things, or events coming one after another; sequence **3.** a number of things produced as a related group; set **4.** *Elec.* a circuit connection in which the components are joined end to end, forming a single path for the current: usually in the phrase **in series 5.** *Geol.* a subdivision of a geologic system **6.** *Math.* a sequence, often infinite, of terms to be added or subtracted —*adj. Elec.* designating or of a circuit in series

**ser·if** (ser′if) *n.* [Du. *schreef,* a stroke < *schrijven,* to write < L. *scribere*] *Printing* a fine line projecting from a main stroke of a letter

**ser·i·graph** (ser′ə graf′) *n.* [< L. *sericum,* silk + -GRAPH] a color print made by the silk-screen process and printed by the artist himself —**se·rig′ra·phy** (sə rig′rə fē) *n.*

**se·ri·o·com·ic** (sir′ē ō käm′ik) *adj.* partly serious and partly comic —**se′ri·o·com′i·cal·ly** *adv.*

**se·ri·ous** (sir′ē əs) *adj.* [< ML. *seriosus* < L. *serius*] **1.** earnest, grave, sober, or solemn [a *serious* man] **2.** *a)* meaning what one says; not joking or trifling *b)* meant in earnest **3.** concerned with grave, important matters; weighty [a *serious* novel] **4.** requiring careful consideration [a *serious* problem] **5.** giving cause for concern [a *serious* wound] —**se′ri·ous·ly** *adv.* —**se′ri·ous·ness** *n.*

**se·ri·ous-mind·ed** (-mīn′did) *adj.* having or showing earnestness of purpose, etc.; not frivolous, jocular, etc. —**se′ri·ous-mind′ed·ly** *adv.* —**se′ri·ous-mind′ed·ness** *n.*

**ser·jeant** (sär′jənt) *n.* Brit. var. of SERGEANT

**ser·mon** (sur′mən) *n.* [OFr. < LL. < L. *sermo,* a discourse] **1.** a speech, esp. by a clergyman during services,

on some religious topic or on morals **2.** any serious or boring talk on one's behavior, responsibilities, etc. —**ser·mon′ic** (-män′ik) *adj.*

**ser·mon·ize** (-nīz′) *vi., vt.* **-ized′, -iz′ing** to preach (to); lecture —**ser′mon·iz′er** *n.*

**Sermon on the Mount** the sermon given by Jesus to his disciples: Matt. 5–7, Luke 6:20–49

**se·rol·o·gy** (si räl′ə jē) *n.* [< SERUM + -LOGY] the science dealing with the properties and actions of serums —**se·ro·log·ic** (sir′ə läj′ik), **se′ro·log′i·cal** *adj.* —**se·rol′o·gist** *n.*

**se·rous** (sir′əs) *adj.* **1.** of or containing serum **2.** like serum; thin and watery

**ser·pent** (sur′pənt) *n.* [OFr. < L. < prp. of *serpere,* to creep] **1.** a snake, esp. a large or poisonous one **2.** a sly, treacherous person

**ser·pen·tine** (sur′pən tēn′, -tīn′) *adj.* of or like a serpent; esp., *a)* evilly cunning; treacherous *b)* coiled, twisted, or winding —*n.* **1.** a coil of thin paper thrown out to unwind as a streamer **2.** a green or brownish-red mineral, magnesium silicate

**ser·rate** (ser′āt, -it; *for v. usually* sə rāt′) *adj.* [L. *serratus* < *serra,* a saw] having sawlike notches along the edge, as some leaves: also **ser·rat′ed** —*vt.* **-rat′ed, -rat′ing** to make serrate

**ser·ra·tion** (sə rā′shən) *n.* **1.** the condition of being serrate **2.** a single tooth or notch in a serrate edge **3.** a formation of these Also **ser·ra·ture** (ser′ə chər)

**ser·ried** (ser′ēd) *adj.* [pp. of obs. *serry* < Fr. *serrer,* to crowd < LL. *serare:* see SERAGLIO] placed close together; compact, as soldiers in ranks

**se·rum** (sir′əm) *n., pl.* **-rums, -ra** (-ə) [L., whey] **1.** any watery animal fluid, esp. the yellowish fluid that is left after blood clots: in full, **blood serum 2.** blood serum used as an antitoxin, taken from an animal made immune to a specific disease by inoculation **3.** whey **4.** watery plant fluid

**serum albumin** the most abundant protein of blood serum, serving to regulate osmotic pressure and used in the emergency treatment of shock

**serv·ant** (sur′vənt) *n.* [OFr. < prp. of *servir* < L. *servire,* to serve] **1.** a person hired to work in another's home as a maid, cook, chauffeur, etc. **2.** a person employed by a government: cf. PUBLIC SERVANT, CIVIL SERVANT **3.** a person who works earnestly for a cause, etc.

**serve** (surv) *vt.* **served, serv′ing** [< OFr. < L. *servire,* to serve < *servus,* a slave] **1.** to work for as a servant **2.** *a)* to do services for; aid; help *b)* to give reverence to, as God **3.** to do military or naval service for **4.** to pass or spend (a term of imprisonment, military service, etc.) **5.** to carry out the duties of (a position, office, etc.) **6.** to provide (customers) with (goods or services) **7.** to prepare and offer (food, etc.) to (a person or persons) **8.** *a)* to meet the needs of [a tool to *serve* many purposes] *b)* to promote or further [to *serve* the national interest] **9.** to be used by [one hospital *serves* the town] **10.** to function for [my memory *serves* me well] **11.** to treat [she was cruelly *served*] **12.** to deliver (a summons, subpoena, etc.) to (someone) **13.** to hit (a tennis ball, etc.) to one's opponent in order to start play **14.** to operate (a large gun) **15.** to copulate with (a female): said of an animal **16.** *Naut.* to put a binding around in order to strengthen (rope) —*vi.* **1.** to work as a servant **2.** to be in service [to *serve* in the navy] **3.** to carry out the duties of an office or position **4.** to be of service; function **5.** to meet needs or satisfy requirements **6.** to wait on table **7.** to be suitable: said of weather, wind, etc. **8.** to start play by hitting the ball, etc. —*n.* the act or manner of serving the ball in tennis, etc., or one's turn to serve —**serve (someone) right** to be what (someone) deserves, as for doing something wrong

**serv·er** (sur′vər) *n.* **1.** a person who serves, as a waiter, etc. **2.** a thing used in serving, as a tray, cart, etc.

**serv·ice** (sur′vis) *n.* [< OFr. < L. *servitium* < *servus,* a slave] **1.** the occupation or condition of a servant **2.** *a)* employment, esp. public employment *b)* a branch of this, including the people in it; specif., the armed forces **3.** work done or duty performed for others [repair *service*] **4.** a religious ceremony, esp. a meeting for prayer **5.** *a)* an act of assistance *b)* the result of this; benefit *c)* [*pl.*] friendly help; also, professional aid [a fee for *services*] **6.** the act or manner of serving food **7.** a set of utensils used in serving [a tea *service*] **8.** a system or method of providing people with electric power, water, transportation, etc. **9.** installation, maintenance, repairs, etc. provided to customers by a dealer, etc. **10.** the act or manner of serving the ball in tennis, etc., or one's turn to serve **11.** *Law* notification of legal action, esp. through the serving of a writ, etc. **12.** *Naut.* any strong material, as wire or twine, used in serving (ropes) —*adj.* **1.** of, for, or in service **2.** of, for, or used by servants, tradespeople, etc. [a rear *service* entrance]

—*vt.* **-iced, -ic·ing** 1. to furnish with a service 2. to copulate with (a female): said of an animal 3. to make or keep fit for service, as by adjusting, repairing, etc. —**at one's service** 1. ready to serve one 2. ready for one's use —**in service** 1. in use; functioning 2. in the armed forces 3. working as a servant —**of service** helpful; useful

**serv·ice·a·ble** (sur′vis ə b'l) *adj.* 1. that can be of service; useful 2. that will give good service; durable —**serv′·ice·a·bil′i·ty, serv′ice·a·ble·ness** *n.* —**serv′ice·a·bly** *adv.*

**serv·ice·man** (sur′vis man′, -mən) *n., pl.* **-men′** (-men′, -mən) 1. a member of the armed forces 2. a person whose work is servicing or repairing something: also **service man**

**service mark** a symbol, word, etc. used by a supplier of services, as transportation, laundry, etc., to distinguish the services from those of competitors: usually registered and protected by law: cf. TRADEMARK

**service station** 1. a place providing maintenance, parts, etc. as for electrical equipment 2. a place providing these, and selling gas and oil, for motor vehicles

**service stripe** a stripe, or any of the parallel diagonal stripes, worn on the left sleeve of a uniform to indicate years spent in the service

**ser·vi·ette** (sur′vē et′) *n.* [Fr. < MFr. < *servir*, to serve] a table napkin

**ser·vile** (sur′v'l, -vīl) *adj.* [< L. < *servus*, a slave] 1. of a slave or slaves 2. like that of slaves or servants [*servile* employment] 3. humbly yielding or submissive; cringing —**ser′vile·ly** *adv.* —**ser·vil·i·ty** (sər vil′ə tē), *pl.* **-ties, ser′vile·ness** *n.*

**serv·ing** (-viŋ) *n.* a helping of food —*adj.* used for serving food [a *serving* spoon]

**ser·vi·tor** (sur′və tər) *n.* a servant, attendant, etc.

**ser·vi·tude** (sur′və tood′, -tyood′) *n.* [MFr. < L. < *servus*, a slave] 1. slavery or bondage 2. work imposed as punishment for crime

**ser·vo·mech·a·nism** (sur′vō mek′ə niz'm) *n.* [SERVO(MOTOR) + MECHANISM] an automatic control system in which the output is compared with the input through feedback so that any error in control is corrected

**ser·vo·mo·tor** (sur′vō mōt′ər) *n.* [< Fr. *servo-moteur* < L. *servus*, slave + Fr. *moteur*, MOTOR] a device, as an electric motor, that is controlled by an amplified signal as from a servomechanism

**ses·a·me** (ses′ə mē′) *n.* [< L. < Gr. *sésamon*, of Sem. orig.] 1. an East Indian plant whose flat seeds yield an edible oil 2. its seeds, used for flavoring bread, rolls, etc. See also OPEN SESAME

**ses·qui-** [< L. < *semis*, half + *que*, and] *a combining form meaning* one and a half [*sesquicentennial*]

**ses·qui·cen·ten·ni·al** (ses′kwi sen ten′ē əl) *adj.* of or ending a period of 150 years —*n.* a 150th anniversary or its celebration

**ses·sile** (ses′il, -īl) *adj.* [< L. pp. of *sedere*, to sit] 1. *Anat., Zool.* attached directly by its base 2. *Bot.* attached directly to the main stem

**ses·sion** (sesh′ən) *n.* [< L. *sessio* < *sedere*, to sit] 1. *a)* the sitting together or meeting of a court, legislature, council, etc. *b)* a continuous series of such meetings *c)* the period a session lasts 2. a school term or period of study, classes, etc. 3. the governing body of a Presbyterian church 4. any period of activity [a *session* of golf] —**in session** meeting —**ses′sion·al** *adj.*

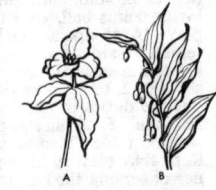

SESSILE LEAVES
(A, trillium; B, Solomon's seal)

**ses·tet** (ses tet′, ses′tet) *n.* [< It. dim. of *sesto*, sixth < L. < *sex*, six] 1. *Music* same as SEXTET 2. *a)* the final six lines of a sonnet *b)* a poem of six lines

**set** (set) *vt.* **set, set′ting** [OE. *settan*] 1. to cause to sit; seat 2. *a)* to cause (a fowl) to sit on eggs to hatch them *b)* to put (eggs) under a fowl to hatch them 3. to put in a certain or designated place or position [*set* the book on the table, *set* the wheel on the axle] 4. to bring (something) into contact with something else [to *set* a match to paper] 5. to affix (one's signature, etc.) to a document 6. to cause to be in some condition or relation 7. to cause to be in working or proper condition; arrange; fix; specif., *a)* to fix (a net, trap, etc.) to catch animals *b)* to fix (a sail) to catch the wind *c)* to adjust; regulate [to *set* a clock] *d)* to place (oneself) in readiness for action *e)* to arrange (a table) with tableware for a meal *f)* to put (a dislocated or fractured bone) into normal position 8. *a)* to put into a fixed position [he *set* his jaw] *b)* to cause (one's mind, etc.) to be fixed, determined, etc. *c)* to cause to become firm [pectin *sets* jelly] *d)* to make (a color) fast in dyeing *e)* to mount (gems) in jewelry *f)* to decorate (jewelry) with gems *g)* to arrange (hair) in a certain style with lotion,

hairpins, etc. 9. to cause to take a specified direction; direct [he *set* his face toward home] 10. to appoint; establish; specif., *a)* to station (a person) for certain duties *b)* to fix (limits or boundaries) *c)* to fix (a time) for (an event) *d)* to establish (a rule, record, etc.) *e)* to furnish (an example) for others *f)* to introduce (a fashion, etc.) *g)* to fix (a quota) for a given period *h)* to begin to apply (oneself) to a task 11. *a)* to fix (the amount of a price, fine, etc.) *b)* to fix or put as an estimate [to *set* little store by someone] 12. to point toward (game): said of dogs 13. *Baking* to put aside (leavened dough) to rise 14. *Bridge* to prevent (one's opponents) from making their bid 15. *Music* to write or fit (words *to* music or music *to* words) 16. *Printing a)* to arrange (type) for printing *b)* to put (manuscript) into type 17. *Theater a)* to place (a scene) in a given locale *b)* to arrange the scenery and properties on (the stage) —*vi.* 1. to sit on eggs: said of a fowl 2. to become firm or hard [the cement *set*] 3. to become fast, as a dye 4. *a)* to begin to move, travel, etc. (with *out, forth, on, off*, etc.) *b)* to get started [to *set* to work] 5. to have a certain direction; tend 6. *a)* to sink below the horizon *b)* to wane; decline 7. to hang or fit in a certain way [the jacket *sets* well] 8. to grow together: said of a broken bone 9. [Now Dial.] to sit 10. *Bot.* to begin to develop into a fruit —*adj.* 1. fixed in advance [a *set* time] 2. established, as by authority 3. deliberate; intentional [a *set* speech] 4. conventional [a *set* speech] 5. fixed; rigid 6. *a)* resolute *b)* obstinate 7. firm in consistency 8. ready [get *set*] 9. formed; built —*n.* 1. a setting or being set; specif., the act of a dog in setting game 2. the way or position in which a thing is set; specif., *a)* direction, as of a current *b)* tendency; inclination *c)* warp; bend *d)* the way in which an article of clothing fits *e)* the position of a part of the body [the *set* of her head] 3. something which is set; specif., *a)* a twig, slip, young bulb, etc. for planting or grafting *b)* the constructed scenery for a play, movie, etc. 4. *a)* the act or a style of arranging hair *b)* the lotion, etc. used for this: in full, **hair set** 5. a group of persons or things classed or belonging together [the social *set*, a *set* of tools, books, china, etc.] 6. assembled equipment for radio or television reception 7. *Math.* a collection of elements or objects that satisfy a given condition 8. *Tennis* a group of games of which the winner must win a specified number, usually (and at least) six —**all set** [Colloq.] prepared; ready —**set about** to begin; start doing —**set against** 1. to balance 2. to compare 3. to make hostile toward —**set aside** 1. to reserve for a purpose: also **set apart** 2. to discard; reject 3. to annul —**set back** 1. to reverse or hinder the progress of 2. [Slang] to cost (a person) a specified sum of money —**set down** 1. to put down 2. to land (an airplane) 3. to put in writing or print 4. to establish (rules, etc.) 5. to ascribe —**set forth** 1. to publish 2. to express in words —**set in** 1. to begin 2. to insert —**set off** 1. to start (a person) doing something 2. to make begin 3. to make prominent by contrast 4. to enhance 5. to cause to explode —**set on** 1. to incite to attack 2. to attack: also **set upon** —**set out** 1. to display, as for sale 2. to plant 3. to undertake —**set to** 1. to get to work; begin 2. to begin fighting —**set up** 1. to place in an upright position 2. to raise to power, a high position, etc. 3. to present as specified 4. to put together or erect (a tent, machine, etc.) 5. to establish; found 6. to make detailed plans for 7. to begin 8. to make successful, rich.

**se·ta** (sēt′ə) *n., pl.* **-tae** (-ē) [ModL. < L., a stiff hair] *Bot., Zool.* a bristle or bristlelike part or organ

**set·back** (set′bak′) *n.* 1. a reversal or check in progress; relapse 2. a steplike recessed section, as in the upper part of a wall

**Seth** (seth) [LL. < Gr. < Heb. *shēth*, lit., appointed] 1. a masculine name 2. *Bible* the third son of Adam

**set·off** (set′ôf′) *n.* 1. a thing that makes up for something else; counterbalance 2. *a)* a debt claimed by a debtor against his creditor *b)* a claim for this

**set piece** 1. an artistic composition intended to impress others 2. a scenic display of fireworks 3. any situation carefully planned beforehand

**set·screw** (set′skrōō′) *n.* a machine screw passing through one part and against or into another to prevent movement, as of a ring around a shaft

**set·tee** (se tē′) *n.* [prob. altered < SETTLE¹] 1. a seat or bench with a back 2. a small or medium-sized sofa

**set·ter** (set′ər) *n.* 1. a person who sets or a thing used in setting 2. any of several breeds of long-haired bird dog trained to find game and point it out by standing rigid: see ENGLISH SETTER, IRISH SETTER

**set·ting** (set′iŋ) *n.* 1. the act of one that sets 2. the position of something, as a dial, that has been set 3. a thing in or on which something, as a gem, has been set 4. time and place, environment, etc. of an event, story, play, etc. 5. actual physical surroundings, real or artificial 6. the music for a set of words 7. the eggs in the nest of a setting hen 8. same as PLACE SETTING

**set·tle¹** (set′'l) *n.* [OE. *setl*] a long wooden bench with a back and armrests

**set·tle²** (set′'l) *vt.* **-tled, -tling** [OE. < *setl*, a seat] **1.** to put in order; arrange as desired [to *settle* one's affairs] **2.** to set in place firmly or comfortably **3.** to establish as a resident or residents [he *settled* his family in London] **4.** to migrate to; colonize [New York was *settled* by the Dutch] **5.** to cause to sink and become more compact [the rain *settled* the dust] **6.** to clarify (a liquid) by causing the sediment to sink to the bottom **7.** to free (the mind, nerves, stomach, etc.) from disturbance **8.** to establish in business, marriage, etc. **9.** to fix definitely; decide (something in doubt) **10.** to end (a dispute) **11.** to pay (a bill, debt, etc.) **12.** to make over (property, etc.) to someone by legal action (with *on* or *upon*) **13.** to decide (a legal dispute) without court action —*vi.* **1.** to stop moving and stay in one place **2.** to cast itself, as fog over a landscape or gloom over a person **3.** to become localized in a part of the body: said of pain or disease **4.** to take up permanent residence **5.** to move downward; sink [the car *settled* in the mud] **6.** to become more dense by sinking, as sediment **7.** to become clearer by the settling of dregs **8.** to become more stable or composed **9.** *a)* to reach a decision (with *with, on,* or *upon*) *b)* to accept something less than what is hoped for [he'll *settle* for any kind of work] **10.** to pay a bill or debt —**settle down 1.** to take up permanent residence, a regular job, etc. **2.** to become less nervous, erratic, etc. **3.** to apply oneself steadily

**set·tle·ment** (-mənt) *n.* **1.** a settling or being settled **2.** a new colony **3.** a village **4.** a community established by a religious or social group **5.** an agreement, adjustment, etc. **6.** *a)* the disposition of property for the benefit of a person *b)* this property **7.** an institution, usually in a depressed neighborhood, offering social services and recreational and educational activities: also **settlement house**

**set·tler** (set′lər) *n.* **1.** a person or thing that settles **2.** one who settles in a new country

**set·tlings** (-liŋz) *n.pl.* sediment; dregs

**set-to** (set′tōō′) *n., pl.* **-tos′** (-tōōz′) [Colloq.] **1.** a fight or struggle **2.** any brisk or vigorous contest

**set·up** (set′up′) *n.* **1.** the way in which something is set up; specif., *a)* plan, makeup, etc., as of equipment, an organization, etc. *b)* details of a plan of action, etc. **2.** bodily posture; carriage **3.** the glass, ice, soda water, etc. for preparing an alcoholic drink **4.** [Colloq.] *a)* a contest deliberately arranged to result in an easy victory *b)* the contestant marked for defeat *c)* any undertaking that is, or is made, very easy *d)* a person easily tricked

**Seu·rat** (sö rä′), **Georges (Pierre)** (zhôrzh) 1859–91; Fr. painter

**Se·vas·to·pol** (sə vas′tə pōl; *Russ.* se′väs tô′pəl y′) seaport in SW Crimea, on the Black Sea: pop. 229,000

**sev·en** (sev′'n) *adj.* [OE. *seofon*] totaling one more than six —*n.* **1.** the cardinal number between six and eight; 7; VII **2.** anything having seven units or members, or numbered seven

**sev·en·fold** (-fōld′) *adj.* [see -FOLD] **1.** having seven parts **2.** having seven times as much or as many —*adv.* seven times as much or as many

**Seven Hills of Rome** seven low hills on the E bank of the Tiber, on & about which Rome was originally built

**seven seas** all the oceans of the world

**sev·en·teen** (sev′'n tēn′) *adj.* [OE. *seofentyne*] seven more than ten —*n.* the cardinal number between sixteen and eighteen; 17; XVII

**sev·en·teenth** (-tēnth′) *adj.* **1.** preceded by sixteen others in a series; 17th **2.** designating any of the seventeen equal parts of something —*n.* **1.** the one following the sixteenth **2.** any of the seventeen equal parts of something; 1/17

**sev·en·teen-year locust** (sev′'n tēn′yir′) a cicada which lives underground as a larva for from thirteen to seventeen years before emerging as an adult

**sev·enth** (sev′'nth) *adj.* [< ME. < *seoven* + -TH²] **1.** preceded by six others in a series; 7th **2.** designating any of the seven equal parts of something —*n.* **1.** the one following the sixth **2.** any of the seven equal parts of something; 1/7 **3.** *Music a)* the seventh tone of an ascending diatonic scale, or a tone six degrees above or below a given tone *b)* the interval between two such tones, or a combination of them —**sev′enth·ly** *adv.*

**seventh heaven 1.** in certain ancient cosmologies, the outermost of the spheres enclosing the earth, in which God and his angels are **2.** a state of perfect happiness

**sev·en·ti·eth** (sev′'n tē ith) *adj.* **1.** preceded by sixty-nine others in a series; 70th **2.** designating any of the seventy equal parts of something —*n.* **1.** the one following the sixty-ninth **2.** any of the seventy equal parts of something; 1/70

**sev·en·ty** (-tē) *adj.* seven times ten —*n., pl.* **-ties** the cardinal number between sixty-nine and seventy-one; 70; LXX —**the seventies** the numbers or years, as of a century, from seventy through seventy-nine

**sev·er** (sev′ər) *vt., vi.* [< OFr., ult. < L. *separare*] **1.** to separate; divide **2.** to part or break off; cut in two [to *sever* a cable, to *sever* a relationship] —**sev′er·a·ble** *adj.*

**sev·er·al** (sev′ər əl, sev′rəl) *adj.* [< Anglo-Fr. < ML. < L. *separ*, separate] **1.** separate; distinct **2.** different; respective [parted and went their *several* ways] **3.** more than two but not many; few —*n.* [*with pl. v.*] an indefinite but small number (*of* persons or things) —*pron.* [*with pl. v.*] several persons or things; a few

**sev·er·al·ly** (-ē) *adv.* **1.** separately; distinctly **2.** respectively; individually

**sev·er·ance** (sev′ər əns, sev′rəns) *n.* a severing or being severed

**severance pay** extra pay given to an employee dismissed through no fault of his own

**se·vere** (sə vir′) *adj.* **-ver′er, -ver′est** [< MFr. < OFr. < L. *severus*] **1.** harsh or strict, as in treatment; stern **2.** serious; grave [a *severe* glance, a *severe* wound] **3.** rigidly accurate or demanding **4.** extremely plain or simple [a *severe* style] **5.** keen; intense [*severe* pain] **6.** difficult; rigorous [a *severe* test] —**se·vere′ly** *adv.* —**se·vere′ness** *n.*

**se·ver·i·ty** (sə ver′ə tē) *n.* **1.** a being severe; specif., *a)* strictness; harshness *b)* seriousness; gravity *c)* rigid accuracy *d)* extreme plainness, as in style *e)* keenness, as of pain *f)* rigorousness **2.** *pl.* **-ties** something severe

**Sev·ern** (sev′ərn) river flowing from C Wales through England & into the Bristol Channel

**Se·ville** (sə vil′) city in SW Spain: pop. 622,000: Sp. name **Se·vil·la** (sā vē′lyä)

**Sè·vres** (sev′rə) *n.* [< *Sèvres*, suburb of Paris] a type of fine French porcelain

**sew** (sō) *vt.* **sewed, sewn** or **sewed, sew′ing** [OE. *siwian*] **1.** to join or fasten with stitches made with needle and thread **2.** to make, mend, etc. by such means —*vi.* to work with needle and thread or at a sewing machine —**sew up 1.** to close together the edges of with stitches **2.** [Colloq.] *a)* to get or have absolute control of *b)* to bring to a successful conclusion *c)* to make certain of success in

**sew·age** (sōō′ij, syōō′-) *n.* the waste matter carried off by sewers or drains

**Sew·ard** (sōō′ərd), **William Henry** 1801–72; U.S. statesman; secretary of state (1861–69)

**sew·er¹** (sōō′ər, syōō′-) *n.* [MFr. *esseweur*, ult. < L. *ex*, out + *aqua*, water] a pipe or drain, usually underground, for carrying off water and waste matter

**sew·er²** (sō′ər) *n.* a person or thing that sews

**sew·er·age** (sōō′ər ij, syōō′-) *n.* **1.** removal of surface water and waste matter by sewers **2.** a system of sewers **3.** *same as* SEWAGE

**sew·ing** (sō′iŋ) *n.* **1.** the act or occupation of a person who sews **2.** material for sewing; needlework

**sewing circle** a group of women who meet regularly to sew, as for some charitable purpose

**sewing machine** a machine with a mechanically driven needle used for sewing and stitching

**sewn** (sōn) alt. pp. of SEW

**sex** (seks) *n.* [L. *sexus* < ? *secare*, to divide] **1.** either of the two divisions, male or female, of persons, animals, or plants, with reference to their reproductive functions **2.** the character of being male or female **3.** anything connected with sexual gratification or reproduction; esp., the attraction of one sex for the other **4.** sexual intercourse —*adj.* [Colloq.] *same as* SEXUAL

**sex-** [< L. *sex*, six] *a combining form meaning* six

**sex·a·ge·nar·i·an** (sek′sə ji ncr′ē ən) *adj.* [< L. < *sex-ageni*, sixty each] sixty years old, or between the ages of sixty and seventy —*n.* a person of this age

**sex appeal** the physical attractiveness and erotic charm that attracts members of the opposite sex

**sex chromosome** a sex-determining chromosome in the germ cells of most animals and a few plants: in most animals, all the eggs carry an X chromosome and the spermatozoa either an X or Y chromosome, and an egg receiving an X chromosome at fertilization will develop into a female (XX) while one receiving a Y will develop into a male (XY)

**sexed** (sekst) *adj.* **1.** of or having sex **2.** having (a specified degree of) sexuality

**sex hormone** any hormone, as testosterone, estrogen, etc., having an effect upon the reproductive organs, sexual characteristics, etc.

**sex·ism** (sek′siz′m) *n.* [SEX + (RAC)ISM] the economic exploitation and social domination of members of one sex by the other, specif. of women by men —**sex′ist** *adj., n.*

**sex·less** (seks′lis) *adj.* **1.** lacking the characteristics of sex; asexual **2.** lacking in normal sexual appetite or appeal —**sex′less·ly** *adv.* —**sex′less·ness** *n.*

**sex linkage** *Genetics* the phenomenon by which inherited characters are determined by genes carried on one of the sex chromosomes —**sex′-linked′** (-liŋkt′) *adj.*

**sex·ol·o·gy** (sek säl′ə jē) *n.* the science dealing with human sexual behavior —**sex·ol′o·gist** *n.*

**sex·ploi·ta·tion** (seks′ploi tā′shən) *n.* [SEX + (EX)PLOITATION] the use of explicit sexual material, esp. in motion pictures, for promotional reasons

**sext** (sekst) *n.* [< ML. < L. *sexta* (*hora*), sixth (hour) [*often* S-] the fourth of the canonical hours, orig. set for the sixth hour of the day (counting from 6 A.M.), or noon

**sex·tant** (seks′tənt) *n.* [ModL. *sextans*, arc of a sixth part of a circle < L. < *sextus*, sixth] an instrument used by navigators for measuring the angular distance of the sun, a star, etc. from the horizon, as in finding the position of a ship

**sex·tet, sex·tette** (seks tet′) *n.* [altered < SESTET] **1.** any group of six **2.** *Music* a) a composition for six voices or instruments b) the six performers of this

**sex·til·lion** (seks til′yən) *n.* [Fr. < L. *sextus*, sixth + Fr. (*m*)*illion*] **1.** in the U.S. and France, the number represented by 1 followed by 21 zeros **2.** in Great Britain and Germany, the number represented by 1 followed by 36 zeros —*adj.* amounting to one sextillion in number

SEXTANT

**sex·ton** (seks′tən) *n.* [< OFr. < ML. *sacristanus*, SACRISTAN] **1.** a church official in charge of the maintenance of church property **2.** an official in a synagogue who manages its day-to-day affairs

**sex·tu·ple** (seks tōō′p'l, -tyōō′-, -tup′l; seks′tōō p'l) *adj.* [< L. *sextus*, sixth, after QUADRUPLE] **1.** consisting of six **2.** six times as much or as many **3.** *Music* having six beats to the measure —*n.* an amount six times as much or as many —*vt., vi.* -**pled, -pling** to multiply by six

**sex·tu·plet** (seks tup′lit, -tōō′plit, -tyōō′-; seks′tōō plit) *n.* [dim. of prec.] **1.** any of six offspring born at a single birth **2.** a group of six, usually of one kind

**sex·u·al** (sek′shōō wəl) *adj.* **1.** of or involving sex, the sexes, the organs of sex and their functions, etc. **2.** *Biol.* a) having sex b) designating or of reproduction by the union of male and female germ cells —**sex′u·al′i·ty** (-wal′ə-tē) *n.* —**sex′u·al·ly** *adv.*

**sex·y** (sek′sē) *adj.* **sex′i·er, sex′i·est** [Colloq.] exciting or intended to excite sexual desire; erotic —**sex′i·ly** *adv.* —**sex′i·ness** *n.*

**Sey·chelles** (sā shel′, -shelz′) country on a group of islands in the Indian Ocean, northeast of Madagascar: a member of the Commonwealth: 107 sq. mi.; pop. 58,000

**sfor·zan·do** (sfôr tsän′dō) *adj., adv.* [It. < *sforzare*, to force] *Music* with emphasis: abbrev. **sf., sfz.** —*n., pl.* -**dos** a sforzando note or chord Also **sfor·za′to** (-tsä′tō)

**sgraf·fi·to** (skrä fē′tō) *n., pl.* -**fi′ti** (-tē) [It. < *sgraffiare*, to scratch] **1.** the producing of a design on ceramics, stuccoed façades, etc. by incising the outer coating to reveal a ground of a different color **2.** such a design or the object bearing it

**Sgt., Sgt.** Sergeant

**sh** (sh: *a lengthened sound*) *interj.* hush!

**shab·by** (shab′ē) *adj.* -**bi·er, -bi·est** [< dial. *shab*, scab < OE. *sceabb*] **1.** run down; dilapidated **2.** a) showing much wear; threadbare: said of clothing b) wearing such clothing **3.** unworthy [*a shabby* offering] **4.** shameful [*shabby* treatment] —**shab′bi·ly** *adv.* —**shab′bi·ness** *n.*

**Sha·bu·oth** (shä vōō′ōt, shə vōō′ōs) *n. var. of* SHAVUOT

**shack** (shak) *n.* [prob. < Scot. dial. *shachle*, a shanty] a small, crudely built cabin; shanty —**shack up with** [Slang] to share living quarters with (one's lover)

**shack·le** (shak′'l) *n.* [OE. *sceacul*] **1.** a metal fastening, usually one of a linked pair, for the wrist or ankle of a prisoner; fetter; manacle **2.** [*usually pl.*] anything that keeps one from acting, thinking, or developing freely **3.** any of several devices for fastening or coupling —*vt.* -**led, -ling** to bind, fasten, or hinder with or as with shackles —**shack′ler** *n.*

**shad** (shad) *n., pl.* **shad, shads:** see PLURAL, II, D, 2 [OE. *sceadd*] **1.** any of several herringlike saltwater food fishes that spawn in rivers **2.** any of various similar fishes, esp. the **gizzard shad,** often stocked in fresh waters as food for other fish

SHACKLES

**shad·ber·ry** (-ber′ē, -bər ē) *n., pl.* -**ries** *same as* JUNEBERRY: also called **shad·bush** (-boosh′)

**shade** (shād) *n.* [OE. *sceadu*] **1.** slight darkness caused by a more or less opaque object cutting off rays of light, as from the sun **2.** an area less brightly lighted than its surroundings, as an open place sheltered from sunlight **3.** [Archaic] a) a shadow b) [*often pl.*] a secluded place **4.** a representation of darkness in a painting, etc. **5.** degree of darkness of a color **6.** a) a small difference [*shades* of opinion] b) a slight amount or degree; trace [*a shade* of humor in his voice] **7.** [Chiefly Literary] a) a ghost b) anything lacking reality **8.** a) any device used to protect or screen from light [*a window shade*] b) a partial cover for an electric lamp, etc., for diffusing or directing light: in full, **lamp shade 9.** [*pl.*] [Slang] sunglasses —*vt.* **shad′ed, shad′ing 1.** to protect or screen from light or heat **2.** to provide with a shade **3.** to hide or screen as with a shadow **4.** to darken; dim **5.** a) to represent the effects of shade in (a painting, etc.) b) to mark with gradations of light or color **6.** to change by very slight degrees or gradations **7.** to lessen (a price) slightly —*vi.* to change or vary slightly or by degrees —**in** (or **into**) **the shade 1.** in or into darkness or shadow **2.** in or into comparative obscurity —**shades of (something)!** how suggestive of (something) past! [*shades of* Prohibition!] —**the shades 1.** the increasing darkness, as of evening **2.** Hades —**shade′less** *adj.*

**shad·ing** (-iŋ) *n.* **1.** a shielding against light **2.** the representation of light or shade in a picture **3.** any small variation, as in quality

**shad·ow** (shad′ō) *n.* [< dat. & gen. of OE. *sceadu,* shade] **1.** the darkness or the dark shape cast upon a surface by something cutting off light from it **2.** [*pl.*] the growing darkness after sunset **3.** a) gloom, sadness, etc. b) anything causing gloom, doubt, etc. **4.** a dark or shaded area, as in a picture **5.** a) something imagined, not real b) a ghost; apparition **6.** a vague indication or omen **7.** a) a faint suggestion or appearance; trace [*a shadow* of hope] b) remnant; vestige **8.** a constant companion **9.** a person who trails another closely, as a spy —*vt.* **1.** to throw a shadow upon **2.** to make dark or gloomy **3.** to foreshadow (often with *forth*) **4.** to follow closely, esp. in secret —**in** (or **under**) **the shadow of 1.** very close to **2.** under the influence of —**under the shadow of 1.** *see prec. phrase* **2.** in danger of —**shad′ow·er** *n.* —**shad′ow·less** *adj.*

**shad·ow·box** (-bäks′) *vi.* to spar with an imaginary opponent, esp. in training as a boxer —**shad′ow·box′ing** *n.*

**shad·ow·y** (shad′ə wē) *adj.* **1.** that is or is like a shadow; specif., a) without reality; illusory b) dim; indistinct **2.** shaded or full of shadow —**shad′ow·i·ness** *n.*

**shad·y** (shād′ē) *adj.* **shad′i·er, shad′i·est 1.** giving shade **2.** shaded, as from the sun; full of shade **3.** [Colloq.] of questionable character or honesty —**on the shady side of** beyond (a given age) —**shad′i·ly** *adv.* —**shad′i·ness** *n.*

**shaft** (shaft) *n.* [OE. *sceaft*] **1.** a) the long stem or handle of an arrow or spear b) an arrow or spear **2.** a missile or something like a missile [*shafts* of light, wit, etc.] **3.** a long, slender part or object; specif., a) the stem of a feather b) a column or obelisk; also, the main, usually cylindrical, part between the ends of a column c) a flagpole d) a handle, as on some tools or implements e) either of the two poles between which an animal is harnessed to a vehicle f) a bar supporting, or transmitting motion to, a mechanical part [the drive *shaft* of an engine] **4.** a long, narrow opening sunk into the earth [a mine *shaft*] **5.** a vertical opening through the floors of a building **6.** a conduit for air, as in heating —*vt.* [Slang] to cheat, trick, exploit, etc. —**get the shaft** [Slang] to be cheated, tricked, etc. —**give (someone) the shaft** [Slang] to cheat or trick (someone)

**shag¹** (shag) *n.* [OE. *sceacga*] **1.** a) a long, heavy, coarse nap, as on some rugs b) fabric with such a nap **2.** any disordered, tangled mass **3.** coarse, shredded tobacco —*vt.* **shagged, shag′ging** to make shaggy or rough

**shag²** (shag) *vt.* **shagged, shag′ging** [< ?] to chase after and retrieve (baseballs hit in batting practice)

**shag·bark** (shag′bärk′) *n.* **1.** a hickory tree with gray, shredding bark **2.** its wood **3.** its edible nut

**shag·gy** (shag′ē) *adj.* -**gi·er, -gi·est 1.** covered with long, coarse hair or wool **2.** carelessly groomed; unkempt **3.** of tangled, coarse growth; straggly **4.** having a rough nap or surface —**shag′gi·ly** *adv.* —**shag′gi·ness** *n.*

**sha·green** (shə grēn′) *n.* [Fr. *chagrin* < Turk. *saghri,* hide] **1.** rawhide with a rough, granular surface, made from the skin of a horse, seal, etc. **2.** the hard, rough skin of the shark or dogfish

**shah** (shä) *n.* [Per. *shāh*] a title of the ruler of Iran

**Shak.** Shakespeare

**shake** (shāk) *vt.* **shook, shak′en, shak′ing** [OE. *sceacan*] **1.** to cause to move up and down, back and forth, or from side to side with short, quick movements **2.** to bring, force, mix, scatter, etc. by abrupt, brisk movements [*shake* the medicine before taking it, *shake* salt on the steak*]* **3.** to cause to tremble **4.** *a)* to cause to totter or become unsteady *b)* to unnerve; upset *[he was* shaken *by the news]* **5.** to brandish; wave **6.** to clasp (another's hand), as in greeting **7.** [Colloq.] to get away from or rid of *[to shake* one's pursuers*]* **8.** *Music same as* TRILL —*vi.* **1.** to move quickly up and down, back and forth, etc.; vibrate **2.** to tremble, quiver, etc., as from cold or fear **3.** to become unsteady; totter **4.** to clasp each other's hand, as in greeting **5.** *Music same as* TRILL —*n.* **1.** an act of shaking **2.** an unsteady movement; tremor **3.** a natural fissure in rock or timber **4.** a long shingle split from a log **5.** [Colloq.] an earthquake **6.** *short for* MILKSHAKE **7.** *[pl.]* [Colloq.] a convulsive trembling (usually with *the*) **8.** [Colloq.] a moment *[be back in a shake]* **9.** [Colloq.] a kind of treatment *[a fair shake]* **10.** *Music same as* TRILL —**no great shakes** [Colloq.] not outstanding or unusual —**shake down 1.** to bring down or cause to fall by shaking **2.** to cause to settle by shaking **3.** to test or condition (new equipment, etc.) **4.** [Slang] to extort money from —**shake off** to get away from or rid of —**shake out** to make fall out, empty, straighten out, etc. by shaking —**shake up 1.** to shake, esp. so as to mix or loosen **2.** to disturb or rouse by or as by shaking **3.** to jar or shock **4.** to reorganize as by shaking —**shak′a·ble, shake′a·ble** *adj.*

**shake·down** (shāk′doun′) *n.* [Colloq.] **1.** an extortion of money, as by blackmail **2.** a thorough search of a person or place —*adj.* for testing the performance, acclimating the personnel, etc. *[the shakedown cruise for a ship]*

**shak·en** (-′n) *pp. of* SHAKE

**shake·out** (-out′) *n.* **1.** any movement in the prices of securities that forces speculators to sell **2.** any drop in economic activity that eliminates marginal or unprofitable businesses, products, etc.

**shak·er** (shā′kər) *n.* **1.** a person or thing that shakes **2.** a device used in shaking *[a cocktail shaker]* **3.** [S-] [short for earlier *Shaking Quaker:* from trembling under emotional stress of devotions] a member of a former religious sect practicing celibacy, communal living, etc.

**Shake·speare** (shāk′spir), **William** 1564-1616; Eng. poet & dramatist: also sp. **Shakespere, Shakspere,** etc. —**Shake·spear′e·an, Shake·spear′i·an** *adj., n.*

**Shakespearean sonnet** a sonnet composed of three quatrains and a final couplet

**shake-up** (shāk′up′) *n.* a shaking up; specif., an extensive reorganization, as in policy or personnel

**shak·o** (shak′ō) *n., pl.* **shak′os** [< Fr. < Hung. *csákó* < ? G. *zacke,* a peak] a stiff, cylindrical military dress hat, usually with a flat top and a plume

**shak·y** (shā′kē) *adj.* **shak′i·er, shak′i·est 1.** not firm, substantial, etc.; weak, unsound, etc., as a structure, belief, etc. **2.** *a)* trembling *b)* nervous or jittery **3.** not dependable or reliable; questionable *[shaky* evidence*]* —**shak′i·ly** *adv.* —**shak′i·ness** *n.*

**shale** (shāl) *n.* [OE. *scealu,* a shell] a fine-grained rock formed largely by the hardening of clay: it splits easily into thin layers —**shal′y** *adj.* **shal′i·er, shal′i·est**

SHAKO

**shall** (shal; *unstressed* shəl) *v., pt.* **should** [OE. *sceal,* inf. *sceolan*] **1.** an auxiliary sometimes used to express the simple future in the first person *[I shall* tell him*]* and determination, obligation, etc. in the second and third persons *[you shall* obey*]:* see also WILL² **2.** an auxiliary regularly used: *a)* in questions in the first person asking for agreement *[shall* we dance?*] b)* in laws and resolutions *[the fine shall* not exceed $100*]*

**shal·lop** (shal′əp) *n.* [< Fr., prob. orig. fig. use of *chaloupe,* nutshell, ult. < OFr. *escalope,* SCALLOP] any of various earlier small open boats fitted with oars or sails or both

**shal·lot** (shə lät′) *n.* [obs. Fr. *eschalote,* altered < OFr. *eschaloigne,* scallion] **1.** a small onion whose clustered bulbs, like garlic but milder, are used for flavoring **2.** same *as* GREEN ONION

**shal·low** (shal′ō) *adj.* [ME. *shalow* < OE. hyp. *scealw*] **1.** not deep *[a shallow* lake*]* **2.** lacking depth of character or intellect; superficial —*n. [usually pl., often with sing. v.]* a shallow place in water; shoal —*vt., vi.* to make or become shallow —**shal′low·ly** *adv.* —**shal′low·ness** *n.*

**sha·lom** (shä lōm′) *n., interj.* [Heb. *shālōm,* lit., peace] a word used as the traditional Jewish greeting or farewell

**shalt** (shalt; *unstressed* shəlt) *archaic 2d pers. sing., pres. indic., of* SHALL

**sham** (sham) *n.* [prob. < a dial. var. of SHAME] **1.** *a)* an imitation that is meant to deceive *b)* a hypocritical action,

false appearance, etc. **2.** one who falsely affects a certain character **3.** *short for* PILLOW SHAM —*adj.* not genuine or real; false; fake —*vt., vi.* to fake; pretend —**sham′mer** *n.*

**sha·man** (shā′mən, shä′-; sham′ən) *n., pl.* **-mans** [Russ., ult. < Prakrit *śamana,* Buddhist monk] a priest or medicine man of shamanism —**sha·man·ic** (shə man′ik) *adj.*

**sha·man·ism** (-iz'm) *n.* **1.** a religion of northeast Asia, based on a belief in spirits who are influenced only by shamans **2.** a similar religion of some American Indians —**sha′man·ist** *n.* —**sha′man·is′tic** *adj.*

**sham·ble** (sham′b'l) *vi.* **-bled, -bling** [orig. *adj.,* in *shamble legs,* prob. < ff., in obs. sense of stool] to walk in a clumsy manner, barely lifting the feet —*n.* a shambling walk

**sham·bles** (-b'lz) *n.pl. [with sing. v.]* [OE. *scamol,* a bench, ult. < L. *scamellum,* dim. < *scamnum,* a bench] **1.** a slaughterhouse **2.** a scene of great slaughter or bloodshed **3.** any scene or condition of great destruction or disorder *[the children left the room a shambles]*

**shame** (shām) *n.* [OE. *scamu*] **1.** a painful feeling of having lost the respect of others because of the improper behavior, incompetence, etc. of oneself or another **2.** a capacity for such feeling **3.** dishonor or disgrace **4.** a person or thing that brings dishonor or disgrace **5.** something unfortunate or outrageous —*vt.* **shamed, sham′ing 1.** to cause to feel shame **2.** to dishonor or disgrace **3.** to force by a sense of shame *[shamed* into apologizing*]* —**for shame!** you ought to be ashamed! —**put to shame 1.** to cause to feel shame **2.** to do much better than; surpass

**shame·faced** (-fāst′) *adj.* [altered < OE. < *scamu,* shame + *fæst,* fast] **1.** shy or bashful **2.** showing a feeling of shame; ashamed —**shame·fac·ed·ly** (shām′fās′id lē, shām′fāst′lē) *adv.* —**shame′fac′ed·ness** *n.*

**shame·ful** (-fəl) *adj.* **1.** bringing or causing shame or disgrace; disgraceful **2.** not just, moral, or decent; offensive —**shame′ful·ly** *adv.* —**shame′ful·ness** *n.*

**shame·less** (-lis) *adj.* having or showing no shame, modesty, or decency; brazen —**shame′less·ly** *adv.* —**shame′less·ness** *n.*

**sham·my** (sham′ē) *n., pl.* **-mies;** *adj.; vt.* **-mied, -my·ing** *same as* CHAMOIS (*n., adj.* 1, *vt.*)

**sham·poo** (sham pōō′) *vt.* **-pooed′, -poo′ing** [Hindi *chāmpo,* imper. of *chāmpnā,* to press] **1.** formerly, to massage **2.** to wash (the hair and scalp), esp. with shampoo **3.** to wash the hair and scalp of **4.** to wash (a rug, upholstery, etc.) with a shampoo —*n.* **1.** the act of washing hair, a rug, etc. **2.** a special soap, or soaplike preparation, that produces suds —**sham·poo′er** *n.*

**sham·rock** (sham′räk′) *n.* [< Ir. dim. of *seamar,* clover] any of certain clovers or cloverlike plants with leaflets in groups of three: the emblem of Ireland

**Shang·hai** (shaŋ′hī′, shäŋ′-) seaport in E China, near the mouth of the Yangtze: pop. c. 10,000,000

**shang·hai** (shaŋ′hī, shaŋ hī′) *vt.* **-haied, -hai·ing** [< prec., in allusion to such kidnapping for crews on the China run] **1.** to kidnap, usually by drugging, for service aboard ship **2.** [Slang] to induce (another) to do something through force or underhanded methods —**shang′hai·er** *n.*

**Shan·gri-La** (shaŋ′grə lä′) *n.* [< the scene of J. Hilton's novel, *Lost Horizon*] any imaginary, idyllic utopia or hidden paradise

**shank** (shaŋk) *n.* [OE. *scanca*] **1.** the part of the leg between the knee and the ankle in man or a corresponding part in animals **2.** the whole leg **3.** a cut of meat from the leg of an animal **4.** a straight, narrow part between other parts, as *a)* the part of a tool between the handle and the working part *b)* the narrow part of a shoe sole **5.** a projection on some buttons by which they are sewn to fabric **6.** the body of a piece of type —**ride (or go) on shank's mare** to walk —**shank of the evening** a relatively early part of the evening

**Shan·non** (shan′ən) river in WC Ireland, flowing southwestward into the Atlantic

**shan't** (shant) shall not

**shan·tey** (shan′tē) *n., pl.* **-teys** *var. of* CHANTEY

**Shan·tung** (shan′tuŋ′, shän′dooŋ′) province of NE China, on the Yellow Sea —*n.* [*sometimes* s-] a fabric of silk, rayon, etc. with an uneven surface

**shan·ty¹** (shan′tē) *n., pl.* **-ties** [< CanadFr. *chantier,* workshop] a small, shabby dwelling; hut

**shan·ty²** (shan′tē) *n., pl.* **-ties** *var. of* CHANTEY

**shan·ty·town** (-toun′) *n.* the section of a city where there are many ramshackle houses

**shape** (shāp) *n.* [< OE. (ge)*sceap,* form, akin to *scieppan,* to create] **1.** the way a thing looks because of its outline; outer form **2.** the form of a particular person or thing, or class of things **3.** the contour of the body; figure **4.** assumed appearance; guise *[a foe in the shape of a friend]* **5.** a phantom **6.** a mold used for shaping **7.** definite or regular form [to begin to take *shape*] **8.** [Colloq.] *a)* condition; state [a patient in poor *shape*] *b)* good physical condition [exercises that keep one in *shape*] —*vt.* **shaped, shap′ing 1.** to give definite shape to; make **2.** to arrange, express, or devise (a plan, answer, etc.) in definite form **3.** to adapt [*shape* your plans to your abilities] **4.** to direct or conduct (one's life, the course of events, etc.) —*vi.* [Colloq.] to take shape —**shape up** [Colloq.] **1.** to develop to a definite form, condition, etc. **2.** to develop satisfactorily **3.** to behave as required —**take shape** to begin to have definite form —**shap′er** *n.*

**shape·less** (-lis) *adj.* **1.** without distinct or regular form **2.** without a pleasing shape; unshapely —**shape′less·ly** *adv.* —**shape′less·ness** *n.*

**shape·ly** (-lē) *adj.* **-li·er, -li·est** having a pleasing shape; well-proportioned: used esp. of a woman —**shape′li·ness** *n.*

**shard** (shärd) *n.* [OE. *sceard*] a fragment or broken piece, esp. of pottery; potsherd

**share**[1] (sher) *n.* [OE. *scearu*] **1.** a part or portion that belongs to an individual, or the part contributed by one **2.** a just or full part [to do one's *share* of work] **3.** any of the parts into which the ownership of a property is divided; esp., any of the equal parts of the capital stock of a corporation —*vt.* **shared, shar′ing 1.** to distribute in shares **2.** to receive, use, experience, etc. in common with another or others —*vi.* **1.** to have a share; participate (often with *in*) **2.** to share or divide something equally (often with *out* or *with*) —**go shares** to take part jointly, as in an enterprise —**share and share alike** with each having an equal share —**shar′er** *n.*

**share**[2] (sher) *n.* [OE. *scear*] the part of a plow or other agricultural tool that cuts the soil

**share·crop** (sher′kräp′) *vi., vt.* **-cropped′, -crop′ping** to work (land) for a share of the crop, esp. as a tenant farmer —**share′crop′per** *n.*

**share·hold·er** (sher′hōl′dər) *n.* a person who holds or owns a share or shares, esp. in a corporation

**shark**[1] (shärk) *n.* [prob. < G. *schurke*, scoundrel] **1.** a person who victimizes others, as by swindling **2.** [Slang] a person with great ability in a given activity; expert

**shark**[2] (shärk) *n.* [? akin to prec.] any of numerous, usually large, mostly marine fishes with a tough, slate-gray skin: most sharks are fish-eaters and some will attack man

**shark·skin** (-skin′) *n.* **1.** leather made from the skin of a shark **2.** a cloth of cotton, wool, rayon, etc. with a smooth, silky surface **3.** a fabric woven with a pebbly pattern

**Shar·on** (sher′ən) [? < ROSE OF SHARON] a feminine name

SHARK
(45 ft. maximum
length)

**sharp** (shärp) *adj.* [OE. *scearp*] **1.** having a very thin edge or fine point, suitable for cutting or piercing; keen **2.** having a point or edge; not rounded [a *sharp* ridge] **3.** not gradual; abrupt [a *sharp* turn] **4.** clearly defined; distinct [a *sharp* contrast] **5.** quick or acute in perception or intellect; specif., *a)* acutely sensitive in seeing, hearing, etc. *b)* clever **6.** attentive; vigilant [a *sharp* lookout] **7.** crafty; underhanded **8.** harsh, biting, or severe [*sharp* criticism] **9.** violent [a *sharp* attack] **10.** brisk; active [a *sharp* run] **11.** severe; intense [a *sharp* pain] **12.** strong; pungent, as in taste **13.** high-pitched; shrill [a *sharp* sound] **14.** cold and cutting [a *sharp* wind] **15.** [Slang] attractively dressed or groomed **16.** *Music a)* higher in pitch by a half step [C *sharp* (C♯)] *b)* above true pitch —*n.* **1.** [Colloq.] an expert **2.** [Colloq.] *same as* SHARK[1], SHARPER **3.** *Music a)* a tone one half step above another *b)* the symbol (♯) indicating this —*vt. Music* to make sharp —*vi. Music* to sing or play above true pitch —*adv.* **1.** in a sharp manner; specif., *a)* abruptly or briskly *b)* attentively or alertly *c)* so as to have a sharp point or edge *d)* keenly; piercingly *e) Music* above true pitch **2.** precisely [one o'clock *sharp*] —**sharp′ly** *adv.* —**sharp′ness** *n.*

**sharp·en** (shär′p'n) *vt., vi.* to make or become sharp or sharper —**sharp′en·er** *n.*

**sharp·er** (-pər) *n.* a person, esp. a gambler, who is dishonest in dealing with others; swindler

**sharp·ie** (shär′pē) *n.* [< SHARP] **1.** a long, narrow, flat-bottomed fishing boat with one or two masts, each with a triangular sail **2.** [Colloq.] a shrewd, cunning person

**sharp·shoot·er** (shärp′shōōt′ər) *n.* a person who shoots with great accuracy; good marksman —**sharp′shoot′ing** *n.*

**sharp-tongued** (-tuŋd′) *adj.* using or characterized by sharp or harshly critical language

**sharp-wit·ted** (-wit′id) *adj.* having or showing keen intelligence; thinking quickly and effectively —**sharp′-wit′ted·ly** *adv.* —**sharp′-wit′ted·ness** *n.*

**Shas·ta** (shas′tə), **Mount** [< a tribal name] volcanic mountain in the Cascade Range, N Calif.

**Shasta daisy** [after prec.] a daisylike chrysanthemum having large flowers

**Shatt-al-A·rab** (shat′əl ä′räb) river in SE Iraq, formed by the confluence of the Tigris & Euphrates rivers, & flowing into the Persian Gulf

**shat·ter** (shat′ər) *vt.* [ME. *schateren*, to scatter] **1.** to break into pieces suddenly, as with a blow **2.** to damage severely [to *shatter* one's health] —*vi.* to burst into pieces —*n.* [*pl.*] broken pieces: chiefly in **in** (or **into**) **shatters**

**shave** (shāv) *vt.* **shaved, shaved** or **shav′en, shav′ing** [OE. *sceafan*] **1.** to cut away thin slices from [to *shave* the edge of a door] **2.** to scrape into thin sections or slices [*shaved* ham] **3.** *a)* to cut off (hair, esp. the beard) at the surface of the skin (often with *off* or *away*) *b)* to cut the hair to the surface of [to *shave* the chin, the legs, etc.] *c)* to cut the beard of (a person) **4.** to barely touch or almost touch in passing; graze **5.** to trim (grass, etc.) closely —*vi.* to cut off hair with a razor or shaver; shave oneself —*n.* **1.** a tool used for cutting off thin slices **2.** something shaved off; shaving **3.** the act or an instance of shaving the beard

**shav·en** (shā′v'n) *alt. pp. of* SHAVE —*adj.* **1.** shaved or tonsured **2.** closely trimmed

**shav·er** (-vər) *n.* **1.** a person who shaves **2.** an instrument used in shaving; esp., a device with a small electric motor that operates a set of cutters **3.** [Colloq.] a boy; lad

**shave·tail** (shāv′tāl′) *n.* [orig., an unbroken mule] [Slang] a second lieutenant, esp. one recently appointed

**Sha·vi·an** (shā′vē ən) *adj.* [< ModL. *Shavius*, Latinized < SHAW] of or characteristic of George Bernard Shaw or his work —*n.* an admirer of Shaw or his work

**shav·ing** (shā′viŋ) *n.* **1.** the act of one that shaves **2.** a thin piece of wood, metal, etc. shaved off

**Sha·vu·ot** (shä vōō′ŏt, shə vōō′ōs) *n.* [Heb. *shābhū′oth*, lit., weeks] a Jewish holiday, orig. celebrating the spring harvest, now chiefly commemorating the revelation of the Law at Mount Sinai

**Shaw** (shô), **George Bernard** 1856–1950; Brit. dramatist & critic, born in Ireland

**shawl** (shôl) *n.* [prob. via Urdu < Per. *shāl*] an oblong or square cloth worn, esp. by women, as a covering for the head or shoulders

**shawm** (shôm) *n.* [< MFr., ult. from L. *calamus*, a reed] an early double-reed wind instrument resembling the oboe

**Shaw·nee** (shô nē′, shô′nē) *n.* [< Algonquian < *shawun*, south + *ogi*, people] **1.** *pl.* **-nees′, -nee′** any member of a tribe of N. American Indians living at various times in the East and Midwest, and now chiefly in Oklahoma **2.** their Algonquian language

**shay** (shā) *n.* [back-formation < CHAISE, assumed as pl.] [Dial.] a light carriage; chaise

**she** (shē; *unstressed* shi) *pron. for pl. see* THEY [prob. after OE. *seo*, fem. def. article, replacing OE. *heo*, she] the woman, girl, or female animal (or the object regarded as female) previously mentioned: *she* is the nominative case form of the feminine third personal pronoun —*n., pl.* **shes** a woman, girl, or female animal

**sheaf** (shēf) *n., pl.* **sheaves** [OE. *sceaf*] **1.** a bunch of cut stalks of grain, etc. bound together **2.** a collection, as of papers, bound in a bundle —*vt. same as* SHEAVE[2]

**shear** (shir) *vt.* **sheared, sheared** or **shorn, shear′ing** [OE. *scieran*] **1.** to cut as with shears **2.** *a)* to remove (the hair, wool, etc.) by cutting *b)* to cut the hair, wool, etc. from **3.** to tear (*off*) by shearing stress **4.** to move through as if cutting **5.** to strip (*of* a power, right, etc.) —*vi.* **1.** to use shears, etc. in cutting wool, metal, etc. **2.** to break under a shearing stress **3.** to move as if by cutting —*n.* **1.** *a) rare var. of* SHEARS *b)* a single blade of a pair of shears **2.** a machine used in cutting metal **3.** the act or result of shearing; specif., the shearing of wool from an animal [a sheep of three *shears*] **4.** *same as* SHEARING STRESS —**shear′er** *n.*

**sheared** (shird) *adj.* subjected to shearing: said esp. of fur trimmed to give it an even surface [*sheared* beaver]

**shearing stress** the force causing two contacting parts to slide upon each other in opposite directions parallel to their plane of contact

**shears** (shirz) *n.pl.* [*also with sing. v.*] **1.** large scissors: also called **pair of shears 2.** any of several large tools or machines with two opposed blades, used to cut metal, etc.

**shear·wa·ter** (shir′wôt′ər, -wät′-) *n.* any of various black-and-white sea birds, related to the albatrosses, that skim the water in flight

**sheath** (shēth) *n., pl.* **sheaths** (shēthz, shēths) [OE. *sceath*] **1.** a case for the blade of a knife, sword, etc. **2.** a covering resembling this, as the membrane around a muscle, etc. **3.** a woman's closefitting dress —*vt. same as* SHEATHE

**sheathe** (shēth) *vt.* **sheathed, sheath′ing 1.** to put into a sheath or scabbard **2.** to enclose in a case or covering

**sheath·ing** (shē′thiŋ) *n.* something that sheathes, as the inner covering of boards or waterproof material on the roof or outside wall of a frame house

**sheath knife** a knife carried in a sheath

**sheave**[1] (shēv, shiv) *n.* [ME. *scheve*] a wheel with a grooved rim, as in a pulley block

**sheave**[2] (shēv) *vt.* **sheaved, sheav'ing** [< SHEAF] to gather and fix (grain, papers, etc.) in a sheaf or sheaves

**sheaves**[1] (shēvz) *n. pl. of* SHEAF

**sheaves**[2] (shēvz, shivz) *n. pl. of* SHEAVE[1]

**She·ba** (shē'bə) *Biblical name of* SABA

**Sheba, Queen of** *Bible* the queen who visited King Solomon to investigate his reputed wisdom: I Kings 10:1-13

**she·bang** (shə baŋ') *n.* [Colloq.] an affair, business, contrivance, thing, etc.: chiefly in **the whole shebang**

**She·bat** (shə vät') *n.* [Heb.] the fifth month of the Jewish year: see JEWISH CALENDAR

**shed**[1] (shed) *n.* [OE. *scead*] **1.** a small, rough building or lean-to, used for shelter or storage **2.** a large, barnlike or hangarlike structure for storage

**shed**[2] (shed) *vt.* **shed, shed'ding** [OE. *sceadan*, to separate] **1.** to pour out; emit **2.** to cause to flow; let fall in drops *[to shed tears]* **3.** to send forth or spread about; radiate *[to shed confidence]* **4.** to cause to flow off without going through; repel *[oilskin sheds water]* **5.** to cast off (a natural growth or covering, as leaves, hair, etc.) *—vi.* to shed leaves, hair, etc. *—n. same as* WATERSHED **—shed blood** to kill in a violent way **—shed'der** *n.*

**she'd** (shēd) **1.** she had **2.** she would

**sheen** (shēn) *n.* [< the adj.] **1.** brightness; luster **2.** bright attire *—adj.* [OE. *sciene*, beautiful] [Archaic] of shining beauty; bright *—vi.* [Dial.] to shine; gleam

**sheep** (shēp) *n., pl.* **sheep** [OE. *sceap*] **1.** a cud-chewing mammal related to the goats, with heavy wool and edible flesh called mutton **2.** leather made from sheepskin **3.** a person who is meek, stupid, timid, etc. **—make** (or **cast**) **sheep's eyes at** to look shyly but amorously at

**sheep·cote** (-kōt') *n.* [cf. COTE] *chiefly Brit. var. of* SHEEPFOLD: also **sheep'cot'** (-kät')

**sheep-dip** (-dip') *n.* any chemical preparation used as a bath, as to free sheep from vermin or to clean the fleece

**sheep dog** any dog trained to herd and protect sheep

**sheep·fold** (-fōld') *n.* a pen or enclosure for sheep

**sheep·herd·er** (-hur'dər) *n.* a person who herds or takes care of a large flock of grazing sheep **—sheep'herd'ing** *n.*

**sheep·ish** (-ish) *adj.* **1.** *a)* embarrassed by being caught in a mistake, lie, etc. *b)* awkwardly shy or bashful **2.** meek, timid, etc. like sheep **—sheep'ish·ly** *adv.* **—sheep'ish·ness** *n.*

**sheep·man** (-man', -mən) *n., pl.* **-men** (-men', -mən) a person who raises sheep for the market

**sheep·shank** (-shaŋk') *n.* a knot used for shortening a rope

**sheeps·head** (shēps'hed') *n., pl.* **-head', -heads':** see PLURAL, II, D; **2** any of several fishes; esp., *a)* an ocean food fish of the eastern coast of the U.S. *b)* the freshwater drum of central N. America

**sheep·skin** (shēp'skin') *n.* **1.** the skin of a sheep, esp. with the fleece left on **2.** parchment or leather made from the skin of a sheep **3.** [Colloq.] *same as* DIPLOMA

**sheer**[1] (shir) *vi.* [var. of SHEAR] to turn aside from a course; swerve; deviate *—vt.* to cause to sheer *—n.* **1.** deviation from a course **2.** the oblique heading of a ship riding at a single bow anchor **3.** the upward curve of a ship's deck lines as seen from the side

**sheer**[2] (shir) *adj.* [ON. *skærr*] **1.** very thin; transparent: said of textiles **2.** not mixed with anything else; pure **3.** absolute; downright *[sheer persistence]* **4.** extremely steep, as the face of a cliff *—adv.* **1.** completely; utterly **2.** very steeply *—n.* thin, fine material, or a garment made of it **—sheer'ly** *adv.* **—sheer'ness** *n.*

**sheet**[1] (shēt) *n.* [OE. *sceat*] **1.** a large piece of cotton, linen, etc., used on a bed **2.** *a)* a single piece of paper *b)* a large piece of paper with a number of pages printed on it, to be folded into a signature for binding into a book: *usually used in pl. c)* [Colloq.] a newspaper *[a scandal sheet]* **3.** a broad, continuous surface or layer, as of flame, water, etc. **4.** a broad, thin piece, as of glass, metal, etc. **5.** a flat baking pan *[a cookie sheet]* **6.** [Chiefly Poet.] a sail *—vt.* to cover or provide with, or form into, a sheet or sheets *—adj.* in the form of a sheet *[sheet iron]* **—sheet'like'** *adj.*

**sheet**[2] (shēt) *n.* [short for OE. *sceatline*] **1.** a rope for controlling the set of a sail, attached to a lower corner **2.** [pl.] the spaces not occupied by thwarts, at the bow and stern of an open boat

**sheet anchor** a large anchor used only in emergencies

**sheet bend** *Naut.* a knot used in fastening a rope to the bight of another rope or to an eye

**sheet·ing** (shēt'iŋ) *n.* **1.** cotton or linen material used for making sheets **2.** material used in covering or lining a surface *[copper sheeting]*

**sheet metal** metal rolled thin in the form of a sheet

**sheet music** music printed on unbound sheets of paper

**Shef·field** (shef'ēld) city in Yorkshire, NC England: pop. 525,000

**sheik, sheikh** (shēk) *n.* [Ar. *shaikh*, old man] **1.** the chief of an Arab family, tribe, or village **2.** an official in the Moslem religious organization **—sheik'dom, sheikh'dom** *n.*

**Shei·la** (shē'lə) [Ir.] a feminine name

**shek·el** (shek'l) *n.* [< Heb. < *shāgal*, to weigh] **1.** among the ancient Hebrews, Babylonians, etc., a unit of weight (about half an ounce), or a gold or silver coin of this weight **2.** the monetary unit of Israel: see MONETARY UNITS, table **3.** [pl.] [Slang] money

**shel·drake** (shel'drāk') *n., pl.* **-drakes', -drake':** see PLURAL, II, D, 1 [prob. < a ME. cognate of MDu. *schillede*, variegated + *drake*, drake] **1.** a large, old-world wild duck that feeds on fish, etc. and nests in burrows: the plumage is variegated **2.** *same as* MERGANSER

**shelf** (shelf) *n., pl.* **shelves** [prob. < MLowG. *schelf*] **1.** a thin, flat length of wood, metal, etc. fixed horizontally to a wall, or in a cupboard, etc., used for holding things **2.** the contents or capacity of a shelf **3.** something like a shelf; specif., *a)* a flat ledge of rock *b)* a sand bar or reef **—on the shelf** out of use, circulation, etc. **—shelf'like'** *adj.*

**shell** (shel) *n.* [OE. *sciel*] **1.** a hard outer covering, as of a turtle, egg, nut, etc. **2.** something like a shell in being hollow, empty, a covering, etc., as the hull of a boat, an unfilled pie crust, etc. **3.** a shy or uncommunicative manner *[to come out of one's shell]* **4.** a woman's pullover, sleeveless knit blouse **5.** a light, long, narrow racing boat rowed by a team of oarsmen **6.** an explosive artillery projectile containing high explosives and sometimes shrapnel, chemicals, etc. **7.** a small-arms cartridge *—vt.* **1.** to remove the shell or covering from *[to shell peas]* **2.** to separate (kernels of corn, etc.) from the ear **3.** to fire shells at from large guns; bombard *—vi.* to separate from the shell or covering **—shell out** [Colloq.] to pay out (money) **—shell'-like'** *adj.* **—shell'y** *adj.*

**she'll** (shēl; *unstressed* shil) **1.** she shall **2.** she will

**shel·lac, shel·lack** (shə lak') *n.* [SHEL(L) + LAC, used as transl. of Fr. *laque en écailles*, lac in fine sheets] **1.** refined lac, a resin usually produced in thin, flaky layers, used in making varnish, phonograph records, etc. **2.** a thin varnish containing this resin and alcohol *—vt.* **-lacked', -lack'ing 1.** to apply shellac to; cover with shellac **2.** [Slang] to beat *b)* to defeat decisively

**shell·back** (shel'bak') *n.* [prob. referring to the shell of the sea turtle] **1.** an old, experienced sailor **2.** anyone who has crossed the equator by ship

**shell·bark** (-bärk') *n. same as* SHAGBARK

**-shelled** (sheld) *a combining form meaning* having a (specified kind of) shell *[soft-shelled crab]*

**Shel·ley** (shel'ē), Percy Bysshe (bish) 1792-1822; Eng. poet

**shell·fire** (shel'fir') *n.* the firing of large shells

**shell·fish** (-fish') *n., pl.* **-fish', -fish'es:** see FISH any aquatic animal with a shell, esp. such an animal that is edible, as the clam, lobster, etc.

**shell game 1.** a swindling game in which the victim bets that a pea is under one of three shells manipulated by sleight of hand **2.** any scheme for victimizing people

**shell·proof** (-prōōf') *adj.* proof against damage from shells or bombs

**shell shock** *an earlier term for* COMBAT FATIGUE **—shell'-shocked'** *adj.*

**shel·ter** (shel'tər) *n.* [< ? OE. *sceldtruma*, troop protected by interlocked shields < *scield*, shield + *truma*, a troop] **1.** something that covers or protects; place of protection against the elements, danger, etc. **2.** a being covered, protected, etc.; refuge *—vt.* to provide shelter or refuge for *—vi.* to find shelter or refuge **—shel'ter·less** *adj.*

**sheltered workshop** a workshop and training center for the handicapped, where they can earn wages but are free from the competitive stress of most jobs

**shelter tent** a small, portable tent that shelters two men: it is made from two sections ( **shelter halves** ), each of which is carried by a soldier in his field equipment

**shelve** (shelv) *vi.* **shelved, shelv'ing** [< SHELF] to slope gradually *—vt.* **1.** to furnish with shelves **2.** to put on a shelf or shelves **3.** *a)* to lay aside *[to shelve a discussion]* *b)* to dismiss from active service

**shelves** (shelvz) *n. pl. of* SHELF

**shelv·ing** (shel'viŋ) *n.* **1.** material for shelves **2.** shelves collectively **3.** the condition or degree of sloping

**Shem** (shem) *Bible* the eldest of Noah's sons: Gen. 5:32

**Shem·ite** (shem'īt) *n. rare var. of* SEMITE

**Shen·an·do·ah** (shen'ən dō'ə) [< AmInd., lit., ? spruce stream] river in N Va., flowing between the Blue Ridge & Allegheny mountains into the Potomac

**she·nan·i·gan** (shi nan'i g'n) *n.* [altered < ? Ir. *sionna-*

---

fat, āpe, cär, ten, ēven, is, bīte; gō, hôrn, tōōl, look; oil, out; up, fur; get; joy; yet; chin; she; thin, *then*; zh, leisure; ŋ, ring; ə for *a* in *ago*, *e* in *agent*, *i* in *sanity*, *o* in *comply*, *u* in *focus;* as in *able* (ā'b'l); Fr. bál; ë, Fr. coeur; ö, Fr. feu; ô, Fr. mon; ō, Fr. coq; ü, Fr. duc; r, Fr. cri; H, G. ich; kh, G. doch; ‡foreign; *hypothetical; < derived from. See inside front cover.

**chuighim,** I play the fox] [*usually pl.*] [Colloq.] nonsense; trickery; mischief

**Shen·yang** (shun′yäŋ′) city in NE China: pop. c. 4,000,000

**She·ol** (shē′ōl, shē ōl′) [< Heb. < *shā'al*, to dig] *Bible* a place in the earth conceived of as the dwelling of the dead

**shep·herd** (shep′ərd) *n.* [OE. *sceaphyrde*: see SHEEP & HERD²] **1.** a person who herds sheep **2.** a leader of a group; esp., a clergyman —*vt.* to herd, guard, lead, etc. as a shepherd —**shep′herd·ess** *n.fem.*

**shepherd dog** same as SHEEP DOG

**shepherd's pie** a meat pie with mashed potatoes on top

**shepherd's purse** a small weed of the mustard family, with triangular, pouchlike pods

**Sher·a·ton** (sher′ə tən) *adj.* [after T. *Sheraton* (1751–1806), Eng. cabinetmaker] designating or of a style of furniture having simplicity of form, straight lines, etc.

**sher·bet** (shur′bət) *n.* [< Turk. < Ar. *sharbah*, a drink] **1.** [Brit.] a beverage made of watered fruit juice and sugar **2.** a frozen dessert like an ice but with gelatin added

**Sher·brooke** (shur′brook) city in S Quebec, Canada: pop. 76,000

**Sher·i·dan** (sher′i d'n) **1. Philip Henry,** 1831–88; Union general in the Civil War **2. Richard Brins·ley** (brinz′lē), 1751–1816; Brit. dramatist & politician, born in Ireland

**she·rif** (shə rēf′) *n.* [Ar. *sharîf*, noble] **1.** a descendant of Mohammed through his daughter Fatima **2.** an Arab prince or chief

**sher·iff** (sher′if) *n.* [< OE. < *scir*, shire + *gerefa*, reeve] **1.** in England, esp. formerly, any of various officers of a shire, or county **2.** in the U.S., the chief law-enforcement officer of a county, charged with the keeping of the peace and the execution of court orders —**sher′iff·dom** *n.*

**Sher·man** (shur′mən), **William Tecumseh** 1820–91; Union general in the Civil War

**sher·ry** (sher′ē) *n.*, *pl.* **-ries** [< earlier *sherris* < *Xeres* (now Jerez), Spain] **1.** a strong, yellow or brownish Spanish wine **2.** any similar wine made elsewhere

**Sher·wood Forest** (shur′wood) forest in C England, near Nottingham, made famous in the Robin Hood legends

**she's** (shēz) **1.** she is **2.** she has

**Shet·land Islands** (shet′lənd) group of islands northeast of the Orkney Islands, constituting a region (**Shetland**) of Scotland

**Shetland pony** any of a breed of sturdy ponies with a rough coat and long tail and mane, orig. from the Shetland Islands

**She·vu·oth** (shə voo′ōt) *n.* [Heb.] same as SHAVUOT

**shew** (shō) *n.*, *vt.*, *vi.* **shewed, shewn** or **shewed, shew′ing** archaic sp. of SHOW

**shew·bread** (-bred′) *n.* [prec. + BREAD, transl. of Heb. *lehem pānīm*, presence bread] the unleavened bread placed at the altar in the ancient Temple as an offering every Sabbath by the priests

**SHF, S.H.F., shf, s.h.f.** superhigh frequency

**shib·bo·leth** (shib′ə ləth) *n.* [< LL. < Heb. *shibbōleth*, a stream] **1.** *Bible* the test word used by the men of Gilead to distinguish the escaping Ephraimites, who pronounced the initial (sh) as (s): Judg. 12:4-6 **2.** something said or done that is a sign or test of belonging to a certain group

**shied** (shīd) *pt. & pp.* of SHY

**shield** (shēld) *n.* [OE. *scield*] **1.** a broad piece of armor carried in the hand or worn on the forearm to ward off blows or missiles **2.** any person or thing that guards or protects **3.** anything shaped like a triangular shield, broad at the top and with curved sides, as an escutcheon, badge, etc. **4.** a safety screen or guard, as over the moving parts of machinery **5.** a pad worn at the armpit to protect a garment from perspiration: also **dress shield** —*vt.*, *vi.* to be a shield (for); defend; protect —**shield′er** *n.*

**shift** (shift) *vt.* [OE. *sciftan*, to divide] **1.** to move or transfer as from one person, place, direction, etc. to another **2.** to replace by another or others; change or exchange **3.** to change the arrangement of (gears) in driving a motor vehicle —*vi.* **1.** to change position, direction, form, etc. **2.** to get along; manage [to *shift* for oneself] **3.** to use tricky or expedient methods **4.** to change from one gear arrangement to another **5.** in typing, to change from small letters, etc. to capitals, etc. by depressing a key (**shift key**) —*n.* **1.** the act of shifting; change [a *shift* in public opinion, a *shift* in the wind] **2.** a plan of conduct, esp. for an emergency; expedient; stratagem **3.** a deceitful scheme; trick **4.** short for GEARSHIFT **5.** a group of people working in relay with other groups, or the work period involved [the night *shift*] **6.** *a)* [Now Rare] a woman's slip *b)* a loose dress that hangs straight with no waistline **7.** *Football* a regrouping of the offensive backfield shortly before the ball is put in play — **make shift** to do the best one can (*with* the means at hand) —**shift′a·ble** *adj.* —**shift′er** *n.*

**shift·less** (-lis) *adj.* lazy or careless —**shift′less·ly** *adv.* — **shift′less·ness** *n.*

**shift·y** (shif′tē) *adj.* **shift′i·er, shift′i·est** having or showing a nature that is not to be trusted; full of shifts; tricky — **shift′i·ly** *adv.* —**shift′i·ness** *n.*

**Shih·chia·chuang** (shu′jyä′jwän′) city in NE China, southwest of Peking: pop. 1,118,000

**Shih Tzu** (shē′ dzoo′) *pl.* **Shih Tzus, Shih Tzu** [< Chin. *shih*, lion + *tzu*, son] any of a Chinese breed of small dog with long, silky hair and short legs

**Shi·ko·ku** (shē′kô koo′) smallest of the four major islands of Japan, south of Honshu: c. 6,860 sq. mi.

**shill** (shil) *n.* [< ?] [Slang] the confederate of a gambler, pitchman, auctioneer, etc. who pretends to buy, bet, or bid so as to lure others

**shil·le·lagh, shil·la·lah** (shi lā′lē, -lə) *n.* [< *Shillelagh*, Irish village] a club or cudgel: also sp. **shil·le′lah**

**shil·ling** (shil′iŋ) *n.* [OE. *scylling*] **1.** *a)* a British money of account and silver coin, equal to 1/20 of a pound: symbol, /: coinage discontinued in 1971 *b)* any of several monetary units used in other countries: see MONETARY UNITS. **2.** a coin of colonial America

**shil·ly-shal·ly** (shil′ē shal′ē) *vi.* **-lied, -ly·ing** [a redupl. of *shall 1?*] to be unable to make up one's mind; show indecision; vacillate —*n.* the act of shilly-shallying

**Shi·loh** (shī′lō) [after an ancient town in Israel] region in SW Tenn.: scene of a Civil War battle (1862)

**shim** (shim) *n.* [< ?] a thin piece of wood, metal, etc. used for filling space, leveling, etc. —*vt.* **shimmed, shim′ming** to fit with a shim or shims

**shim·mer** (shim′ər) *vi.* [OE. *scymrian*] **1.** to shine with an unsteady light; glimmer **2.** to form a wavering image, as by reflection from waves of heat —*n.* a shimmering light

**shim·my** (shim′ē) *n.* [< CHEMISE] **1.** a jazz dance of the 1920's, with much shaking of the body **2.** a shaking or wobbling, as in the front wheels of an automobile —*vi.* **-mied, -my·ing** to shake or wobble

**shin** (shin) *n.* [OE. *scinu*] **1.** the front part of the leg between the knee and the ankle **2.** the lower foreleg in beef — *vt.*, *vi.* **shinned, shin′ning** to climb (a rope, pole, etc.) by gripping with both hands and legs: often with *up*

**shin·bone** (shin′bōn′) *n.* same as TIBIA

**shin·dig** (shin′dig′) *n.* [folk-etym. form of colloq. *shindy*, commotion] [Colloq.] a dance, party, or other social affair

**shine** (shīn) *vi.* **shone,** or, esp. for vt. 2, **shined, shin′ing** [OE. *scinan*] **1.** to give off or reflect light; gleam; glow **2.** to excel; be eminent **3.** to show itself clearly [love *shone* from her face] —*vt.* **1.** to direct the light of [to *shine* a flashlight] **2.** to make shiny by polishing —*n.* **1.** brightness; radiance **2.** luster; polish; gloss **3.** short for SHOE-SHINE **4.** splendor; brilliance **5.** sunshine; fair weather — **shine up to** [Slang] to curry favor with —**take a shine to** [Slang] to take a liking to (someone)

**shin·er** (-ər) *n.* **1.** a person or thing that shines **2.** *pl.* **-ers, -er:** see PLURAL, II, D, 1 any of a number of freshwater minnows with silvery scales **3.** [Slang] same as BLACK EYE

**shin·gle¹** (shiŋ′g'l) *n.* [prob. < Scand.] [Chiefly Brit.] **1.** coarse, waterworn gravel, as on a beach **2.** an area covered with this —**shin′gly** *adj.* **-gli·er, -gli·est**

**shin·gle²** (shiŋ′g'l) *n.* [prob. altered < OE. *scindel*, ult. < L. *scindula*, a shingle] **1.** a thin, wedge-shaped piece of wood, slate, etc. laid with others in a series of overlapping rows as a covering for roofs, etc. **2.** a woman's short haircut with the hair over the nape shaped close to the head **3.** [Colloq.] a small signboard, as that of a doctor or lawyer —*vt.* **-gled, -gling** to cover (a roof, etc.) with shingles

**shin·gles** (shiŋ′g'lz) *n.* [< ML. < L. *cingulum*, a girdle < *cingere*, to gird] same as HERPES ZOSTER

**shin·ing** (shīn′iŋ) *adj.* **1.** giving off or reflecting light; bright **2.** brilliant; splendid [a *shining* example]

**shin·ny¹** (shin′ē) *n.*, *pl.* **-nies** [prob. < SHIN] **1.** a simple form of hockey played by children **2.** the curved stick used in this game Also sp. **shin′ney**

**shin·ny²** (shin′ē) *vi.* **-nied, -ny·ing** same as SHIN

**shin·plas·ter** (shin′plas′tər) *n.* **1.** a plaster or poultice for use on sore shins **2.** formerly, a piece of paper money having a face value of less than a dollar

**shin·splints** (-splints′) *n.pl.* [with sing. v.] [? < SHIN + *splint*, bony growth] painful strain of extensor muscles in the lower leg, caused by running on a hard surface

**Shin·to** (shin′tō) *n.* [Jap. < Chin. *shin*, god + *tao*, way] a religion of Japan, emphasizing worship of nature and of ancestors —**Shin′to·ism** *n.* —**Shin′to·ist** *n.*, *adj.*

**shin·y** (shīn′ē) *adj.* **shin′i·er, shin′i·est 1.** bright; shining **2.** highly polished; glossy —**shin′i·ness** *n.*

**ship** (ship) *n.* [OE. *scip*] **1.** any large vessel navigating deep water **2.** a sailing vessel with a bowsprit and at least three square-rigged masts **3.** a ship's officers and crew **4.** an aircraft —*vt.* **shipped, ship′ping 1.** to put or take on board a ship **2.** to send or transport by any carrier [to *ship* coal by rail] **3.** to take in (water) over the side, as in a heavy sea **4.** to put or fix in its proper place on a ship or boat *[ship the oars]* **5.** to hire for work on a ship **6.** [Colloq.] to send (*away, out,* etc.); get rid of —*vi.* **1.** to go aboard ship; embark **2.** to be hired to serve on a ship **3.** to travel by ship —**ship over** to enlist or reenlist in the U.S. Navy —**when** (or **if,** etc.) **one's ship comes in** (or **home**) when (or if, etc.) one's fortune is made —**ship'pa·ble** *adj.*

**-ship** (ship) [OE. *-scipe*] *a suffix meaning:* **1.** the quality or state of *[friendship]* **2.** *a*) the rank or office of *[governorship]* *b*) one having the rank of *[lordship]* **3.** ability as *[leadership]* **4.** all individuals (of the specified class) collectively *[readership]*

**ship biscuit** *same as* HARDTACK

**ship·board** (ship'bôrd') *n.* a ship: chiefly in **on shipboard,** aboard a ship —*adj.* done, happening, used etc. on a ship *[a shipboard romance]*

**ship·build·er** (-bil'dər) *n.* one whose business is building ships —**ship'build'ing** *n.*

**ship canal** a canal large enough for seagoing ships

**ship·load** (-lōd') *n.* the load of a ship

**ship·mas·ter** (-mas'tər) *n.* the officer in command of a merchant ship; captain

**ship·mate** (-māt') *n.* a fellow sailor on the same ship

**ship·ment** (-mənt) *n.* **1.** the shipping or transporting of goods **2.** goods shipped

**ship of the line** formerly, a warship of the largest class, having a position in the line of battle

**ship·own·er** (-ō'nər) *n.* an owner of a ship or ships

**ship·per** (-ər) *n.* a person who ships goods

**ship·ping** (-iŋ) *n.* **1.** the act or business of transporting goods **2.** ships collectively, as of a nation or port, esp. with reference to tonnage

**ship·shape** (-shāp') *adj.* having everything neatly in place, as on board ship; trim —*adv.* in a neat and orderly manner

**ship·side** (-sīd') *n.* the area on a pier alongside a ship

**ship·worm** (-wʉrm') *n.* any of various small mollusks with wormlike bodies: they burrow into submerged wood

**ship·wreck** (-rek') *n.* **1.** the remains of a wrecked ship **2.** the loss or destruction of a ship through storm, collision, etc. **3.** any ruin or destruction —*vt.* **1.** to cause to undergo shipwreck **2.** to destroy, ruin, or wreck

**ship·wright** (-rīt') *n.* a man, esp. a carpenter, whose work is the construction and repair of ships

**ship·yard** (-yärd') *n.* a place where ships are built and repaired

**shire** (shīr) *n.* [OE. *scir,* office] **1.** any of the former districts in Great Britain coinciding generally with the modern county **2.** any of the counties of Great Britain with a name ending in *-shire*

**shirk** (shʉrk) *vt., vi.* [? akin to G. *schurke,* rascal] to neglect or evade doing (something that should be done) —**shirk'er** *n.*

**Shir·ley** (shʉr'lē) [ult. < OE. *scire,* shire + *leah,* lea] a feminine name

**shirr** (shʉr) *n.* [< ?] *same as* SHIRRING —*vt.* **1.** to make shirring in (cloth or a garment) **2.** to bake (eggs) with crumbs in small buttered dishes

**shirr·ing** (-iŋ) *n.* **1.** a gathering made in cloth by drawing the material up on parallel rows of short, running stitches **2.** any trim made by shirring

**shirt** (shʉrt) *n.* [OE. *scyrte*] **1.** *a*) the usual sleeved garment worn by men on the upper part of the body, often under a suit coat, typically having a collar and a buttoned opening down the front *b*) a similar garment for women **2.** *same as* UNDERSHIRT —**keep one's shirt on** [Slang] to remain patient or calm —**lose one's shirt** [Slang] to lose everything

**shirt·ing** (-iŋ) *n.* material for making shirts

**shirt·sleeve** (-slēv') *adj.* **1.** in, or suitable for being in, one's shirt sleeves **2.** plain; informal **3.** homespun; homely *[shirt-sleeve philosophy]*

**shirt·tail** (shʉrt'tāl') *n.* the part of a shirt extending below the waist

**shirt·waist** (-wāst') *n.* **1.** a woman's blouse tailored more or less like a shirt **2.** a dress with a bodice like a shirtwaist: also **shirtwaist dress, shirt'dress'** *n.*

**shish ke·bab** (shish' kə bäb') [< Arm., ult. < Ar. *shish,* skewer + *kabab,* kebab] a broiled dish consisting of small chunks of meat, esp. lamb, placed on skewers alternately with tomatoes, onions, etc.: also **shish' ka·bob'**

**shiv** (shiv) *n.* [prob. < Romany *chiv,* a blade] [Slang] a knife, esp. one with a narrow blade used as a weapon

**Shi·va** (shē'və) *var. of* SIVA

**shiv·a·ree** (shiv'ə rē', shiv'ə rē') *n.* [< CHARIVARI] a mock serenade, as to newlyweds, with kettles, horns, etc. —*vt.* -**reed', -ree'ing** to serenade with a shivaree

**shiv·er¹** (shiv'ər) *n.* [ME. *schivere*] a fragment or splinter of something broken, as glass —*vt., vi.* to break into many fragments or splinters; shatter —**shiv'er·y** *adj.*

**shiv·er²** (shiv'ər) *vi.* [ME. *cheveren* < ? OE. *ceafl,* a jaw] to shake, tremble, etc., as from fear or cold —*n.* a shaking, trembling, etc., as from fear or cold —**the shivers** a fit of shivering —**shiv'er·y** *adj.*

**shmaltz** (shmälts) *n.* [Slang] *var. sp.* of SCHMALTZ — **shmaltz'y** *adj.* **shmaltz'i·er, shmaltz'i·est**

**shoal¹** (shōl) *n.* [OE. *scolu*] **1.** a large group; mass; crowd **2.** a large school of fish —*vi.* to come together in or move about as a shoal

**shoal²** (shōl) *n.* [OE. *sceald,* shallow] **1.** a shallow place in a river, sea, etc. **2.** a sand bar, etc. forming a shallow place that is a danger to navigation, esp. one visible at low water —*vt., vi.* to make or become shallow —**shoal'y** *adj.* **shoal'i·er, shoal'i·est**

**shoat** (shōt) *n.* [< ?] a young hog of between about 100 and 180 lbs.

**shock¹** (shäk) *n.* [< Fr. < MFr. *choquer,* prob. < MDu. *schokken,* to collide] **1.** *a*) a sudden, powerful blow, shake, disturbance, etc. *b*) the effect of this **2.** *a*) a sudden and strong upsetting of the mind or feelings *b*) something causing this *[her accident was a shock to us]* **3.** the violent effect on the body of an electric current passed through it **4.** [Colloq.] *short for* SHOCK ABSORBER: *used in pl.* **5.** *Med.* a disorder caused by severe injury or damage to the body, loss of blood, etc., and marked by a sharp drop in blood pressure, a rapid pulse, etc. —*vt.* **1.** to disturb emotionally; astonish, horrify, etc. **2.** to affect with physical shock **3.** to produce electric shock in —*vi.* to be shocked, distressed, etc. *[one who does not shock easily]* — **shock'er** *n.*

**shock²** (shäk) *n.* [prob. via MDu. or MLowG. *schok*] a number of grain sheaves, as of corn or wheat, stacked together on end to cure and dry —*vt., vi.* to gather in shocks

**shock³** (shäk) *n.* [< ? prec.] a thick, bushy or tangled mass, as of hair

**shock absorber** a device, as on the springs of a car, that lessens or absorbs the force of shocks

**shock·ing** (shäk'iŋ) *adj.* causing great surprise, horror, disgust, etc. —**shock'ing·ly** *adv.*

**shock·proof** (-prōōf') *adj.* able to absorb shock without being damaged *[a shockproof watch]*

SHOCKS OF CORN

**shock therapy** a method of treating certain psychotic conditions by injecting certain drugs or by applying electric current to the brain, which results in convulsion or coma: also **shock treatment**

**shock troops** troops especially chosen, trained, and equipped to lead an attack

**shod** (shäd) *alt. pt. & pp. of* SHOE

**shod·den** (shäd''n) *alt. pp. of* SHOE

**shod·dy** (shäd'ē) *n., pl.* **shod'dies** [< ?] **1.** an inferior woolen yarn or cloth made from fibers of used fabrics **2.** anything of less worth than it seems to have; esp., an inferior or imitation —*adj.* **shod'di·er, shod'di·est 1.** *a*) made of shoddy *b*) made of any inferior material *c*) poorly done or made **2.** sham **3.** contemptible; low *[a shoddy trick]* —**shod'di·ly** *adv.* —**shod'di·ness** *n.*

**shoe** (shōō) *n.* [OE. *sceoh*] **1.** an outer covering for the foot, made of leather, canvas, etc. and usually having a stiff sole and a heel **2.** something like a shoe in shape or use; specif., *a*) *short for* HORSESHOE, BRAKE SHOE *b*) the metal strip along the bottom of a sled runner *c*) the casing of a pneumatic tire —*vt.* **shod** or **shoed, shod** or **shoed** or **shod'den, shoe'ing** to furnish with shoes —**fill one's shoes** to take one's place —**in another's shoes** in another's position

**shoe·black** (-blak') *n. same as* BOOTBLACK

**shoe·horn** (-hôrn') *n.* an implement of metal, horn, plastic, etc. with a troughlike blade, inserted at the back of a shoe to help in slipping the heel in —*vt.* to force or squeeze into a narrow space

**shoe·lace** (-lās') *n.* a length of cord, leather, etc. used for lacing and fastening a shoe

**shoe·mak·er** (-māk'ər) *n.* a person whose business is making or repairing shoes —**shoe'mak'ing** *n.*

**shoe·pac** (-pak') *n.* [altered (after SHOE & PAC) < AmInd. *shipak* < *paku,* shoe] *same as* PAC

**sho·er** (shōō'ər) *n.* a person who shoes horses

**shoe·shine** (-shīn') *n.* the cleaning and polishing of a pair of shoes

**shoe·string** (-striŋ') *n.* **1.** *same as* SHOELACE **2.** a small amount of money as capital *[the business was started on a shoestring]*

---

fat, āpe, cär; ten, ēven; is, bīte; gō, hôrn, tōōl, lŏŏk; oil, out; up, fʉr; get; joy; yet; chin; she; thin, then; zh, leisure; ŋ, ring; ə for a in ago, e in agent, i in sanity, o in comply, u in focus; ' as in able (ā'b'l); Fr. bal; ë, Fr. coeur; ö, Fr. feu; Fr. mon; ô, Fr. coq; ü, Fr. duc; r, Fr. cri; H, G. ich; kh, G. doch; ‡foreign; *hypothetical; < derived from. See inside front cover.

**shoestring potatoes** potatoes cut into long, very narrow strips and fried crisp in deep fat

**shoe tree** a form, as of wood or metal, put into a shoe to stretch it or preserve its shape

**sho·gun** (shō'gun', -gŏon') *n.* [Jap. < Chin. *chiang-chun,* leader of an army] any of the military governors who ruled Japan until 1868 —**sho'gun·ate** (-it, -gə nāt') *n.*

**Sho·lo·khov** (shô'lô khôf), **Mi·kha·il** (**Aleksandrovich**) (mi khä ēl') 1905– ; Russ. novelist

**Sho·lom A·leich·em** (shô'lŏm ä läkh'əm) (pseud. of *Solomon Rabinowitz*) 1859–1916; Russ. writer in Yiddish

**shone** (shōn) *pt. & pp. of* SHINE

**shoo** (shōo) *interj.* [echoic] 1. an exclamation used in driving away chickens and other animals 2. go away! get out! —*vi.* **shooed, shoo'ing** to cry "shoo" —*vt.* to drive away abruptly, by or as by crying "shoo"

**shoo-in** (shōo'in') *n.* [SHOO + IN] [Colloq.] someone or something expected to win easily in an election, a race, etc.

**shook** (shook) *pt. and dial. pp. of* SHAKE —**shook up** [Slang] upset; disturbed

**shoot** (shōot) *vt.* **shot, shoot'ing** [OE. *sceotan*] 1. *a)* to move swiftly over, by, etc. [to *shoot* the rapids in a canoe] *b)* to make move with great force [to *shoot* an elevator upward] 2. to pour, empty out, or dump, as down a chute 3. *a)* to hurl or thrust out [volcanoes *shooting* molten rock] *b)* to cast (an anchor, net, etc.) *c)* to throw away or spoil (an opportunity, etc.) *d)* [Colloq.] to use up or waste (time, money, etc.) 4. to slide (a door bolt) into or out of its fastening 5. *a)* to streak or fleck (*with* another color or substance) [blue *shot* with orange] *b)* to vary (*with* something different) [a story *shot* with humor] 6. to put forth (a branch, leaves, etc.) 7. *a)* to launch (a rocket), discharge (a bullet, arrow, etc.), or fire (a gun, bow, etc.) *b)* to discharge (rays) with force 8. to send forth (a question, fist, etc.) swiftly or with force 9. to hit, wound, kill, or destroy with a bullet, arrow, etc. 10. to take the altitude of (a star), as with a sextant 11. to photograph or film 12. to inject, as with drugs 13. *Games, Sports a)* to throw or drive (a ball, etc.) toward the objective *b)* to score (a goal, points, etc.) *c)* to play (golf, pool, craps, etc.) *d)* to make (a specified bet), as in craps —*vi.* 1. *a)* to move swiftly, as an arrow from a bow *b)* to spurt or gush 2. to be felt suddenly and keenly, as pain, etc. 3. to grow or sprout rapidly 4. to jut out; project 5. to fire a missile, gun, etc. 6. to use guns, bows and arrows, etc., as in hunting 7. *a)* to photograph a scene *b)* to start movie cameras working 8. *Sports a)* to propel a ball, etc. toward the objective *b)* to roll dice —*n.* 1. *a)* the act of shooting *b)* a shooting trip, party, or contest 2. the act of sprouting 3. a new growth; sprout or twig 4. the launching of a rocket, guided missile, etc. 5. a sloping trough; chute 6. a spasm of pain —*interj.* 1. an exclamation of disgust, disappointment, etc. 2. begin talking! —**shoot at** (or **for**) [Colloq.] to strive for —**shoot from the hip** to act or talk impetuously —**shoot off one's** (or **at the**) **mouth** [Slang] 1. to speak without caution; blab 2. to boast —**shoot'er** *n.*

**shooting star** *same as* METEOR

**shoot-out, shoot·out** (shōot'out') *n.* [Slang] a battle with handguns, etc., as between police and criminals

**shop** (shäp) *n.* [OE. *sceoppa,* booth] 1. *a)* a place where certain goods or services are offered for sale *b)* a specialized department in a large store [the gourmet *shop*] 2. a place where a particular kind of work is done [a printing *shop*] 3. in some schools, a manual-training course, class, or department —*vi.* **shopped, shop'ping** to visit shops so as to examine or buy merchandise —**set up shop** to start a business —**shop around** 1. to go from shop to shop, looking for bargains or special items 2. to search for a good or better job, idea, etc. —**talk shop** to discuss one's work

**shop·girl** (-gurl') *n.* [Chiefly Brit.] *same as* SALESWOMAN

**shop·keep·er** (shäp'kē'pər) *n.* a person who owns or operates a shop, or small store —**shop'keep'ing** *n.*

**shop·lift·er** (-lif'tər) *n.* a person who steals articles from a store during shopping hours —**shop'lift'** *vt., vi.*

**shoppe** (shäp) *n. var. of* SHOP (sense 1)

**shop·per** (shäp'ər) *n.* 1. a person who shops; esp., one hired by a store to shop for others 2. a person hired by a store to compare competitors' merchandise and prices

**shopping center** a complex of stores, restaurants, etc. with an adjoining parking lot

**shop steward** a person elected by his fellow workers in a union shop to represent them in dealing with the employer

**shop·talk** (shäp'tôk') *n.* 1. the specialized vocabulary of a particular occupation, etc. 2. conversation about one's work, esp. after hours

**shop·worn** (-wôrn') *adj.* 1. soiled, faded, etc. from having been displayed in a shop 2. drab, dull, trite, etc.

**Shor·an** (shôr'an) *n.* [*Sho(rt) Ra(nge) N(avigation)*] [*also* s-] a radar system for locating the position of a plane, etc. by signals from a pair of transponders on the ground

**shore¹** (shôr) *n.* [< OE. hyp. *score* < or akin to *scorian,* to jut out] 1. land at the edge of a body of water 2. land as opposed to water

**shore²** (shôr) *n.* [akin to MDu. *schore,* OIce. *skortha,* a prop] a beam, etc. placed under or against something as a prop —*vt.* **shored, shor'ing** to support or make stable as with shores (usually *with up*)

**shore dinner** a meal with a variety of seafood dishes

**shore leave** leave granted to a ship's crew for going ashore

**shore·line** (-līn') *n.* the edge of a body of water

**shore patrol** a detail of the U.S. Navy, Coast Guard, or Marine Corps serving as military police on shore

**shore·ward** (-wərd) *adv.* toward the shore: also **shore'wards** —*adj.* moving toward the shore

**shor·ing** (shôr'iŋ) *n.* 1. the act of supporting with shores 2. a system of shores used for support

**shorn** (shôrn) *alt. pp. of* SHEAR

**short** (shôrt) *adj.* [OE. *scort*] 1. not extending far from end to end; not long 2. not great in range or scope [a *short* journey, view, etc.] 3. low in height; not tall 4. lasting but a little time; brief 5. not retentive [a *short* memory] 6. condensed or concise 7. brief to the point of rudeness; curt 8. less than a sufficient or correct amount [*short* on money] 9. not far enough to reach the objective [the shot fell *short*] 10. having a tendency to crumble, as pastry 11. *a)* not possessing at the time of sale the commodity or security one is selling *b)* designating or of a sale of commodities or securities which the seller does not have but expects to buy later at a lower price 12. *Phonet. & Prosody* comparatively brief in duration, as sounds, syllables, etc. —*n.* 1. something short; specif., *a)* a short sound or syllable *b)* *same as* SHORT SUBJECT 2. a variation of clothing size shorter than the average 3. [*pl.*] *a)* formerly, knee breeches *b)* short trousers reaching partway to the knee *c)* a man's undergarment of similar form 4. [*pl.*] items needed to make up a shortage or deficiency 5. [*pl.*] a byproduct of wheat milling that consists of bran, germ, and coarse meal 6. *clipped form of: a)* SHORTSTOP *b)* SHORT CIRCUIT —*adv.* 1. abruptly; suddenly 2. rudely; curtly 3. briefly; concisely 4. so as to be short 5. by surprise; unawares [caught *short*] 6. by a short sale —*vt., vi.* 1. to give less than what is needed, usual, etc. 2. *clipped form of: a)* SHORTCHANGE *b)* SHORT-CIRCUIT —**fall** (or **come**) **short** 1. to be insufficient 2. to fail to reach —**in short** 1. in summing up 2. briefly —**run short** to have less than enough —**short for** being an abbreviation of —**short of** 1. less than 2. lacking 3. without actually resorting to —**the short end of the stick** the worst of a deal —**short'ish** *adj.* —**short'ness** *n.*

**short·age** (-ij) *n.* a deficiency in amount; deficit

**short·bread** (-bred') *n.* a rich, crumbly cake or cookie made with much shortening

**short·cake** (-kāk') *n.* a light biscuit or a sweet cake served with fruit, etc. as a dessert

**short·change** (-chānj') *vt., vi.* **-changed', -chang'ing** [Colloq.] 1. to give less money than is due in change 2. to cheat —**short'chang'er** *n.*

**short-cir·cuit** (-sur'kit) *vt.* 1. *Elec.* to make a short circuit in 2. to bypass (an obstruction, custom, etc.) 3. to thwart —*vi.* to develop a short circuit

**short circuit** 1. a usually accidental low-resistance connection between two points in an electric circuit that deflects the current or causes excessive current flow 2. popularly, a disrupted electric circuit resulting from this

**short·com·ing** (-kum'iŋ) *n.* a falling short of what is expected or required; defect or deficiency

**short·cut** (-kut') *n.* 1. a shorter way to get to the same place 2. any way of saving time, effort, expense, etc.

**short·en** (shôrt'n) *vt., vi.* to make or become short or shorter —**short'en·er** *n.*

**short·en·ing** (shôrt'n iŋ, shôrt'niŋ) *n.* 1. a making or becoming short or shorter 2. fat used to make pastry, etc. crisp or flaky

**short·hand** (-hand') *n.* any system of special symbols for letters, words, and phrases for taking notes, dictation, etc. rapidly —*adj.* written in or using shorthand

ß ∂ ‿ ' ⌒ ﺷ

"THIS IS A SAMPLE OF SHORTHAND WRITING"

**short-hand·ed** (-han'did) *adj.* short of workers or helpers

**short·head·ed** (shôrt'hed'id) *adj.* having a short or broad head —**short'head'ed·ness** *n.*

**short·horn** (-hôrn') *n.* any of a breed of cattle with short, curved horns: they are raised for both beef and milk

**short-lived** (-līvd', -livd') *adj.* having or tending to have a short life span or existence

**short·ly** (-lē) *adv.* 1. in a few words; briefly 2. in a short time; soon 3. abruptly and rudely; curtly

**short order** any food that can be cooked or served quickly when ordered, as at a lunch counter —**short'-or'der** *adj.*

**short-range** (shôrt′rānj′) *adj.* **1.** having a range of short distance **2.** not looking far into the future *[short-range plans]*

**short shrift** very little care or attention, as from lack of patience or sympathy —**make short shrift of** to dispose of quickly and impatiently: also **give short shrift**

**short·sight·ed** (shôrt′sīt′id) *adj.* **1.** *same as* NEARSIGHTED **2.** having or showing a lack of foresight —**short′sight′ed·ly** *adv.* —**short′sight′ed·ness** *n.*

**short·stop** (-stäp′) *n. Baseball* the infielder stationed between second and third base

**short story** a kind of story shorter than the novel or novelette and more limited in scope and number of characters

**short subject** any short film presentation shown along with the feature in a motion-picture program

**short-tem·pered** (-tem′pərd) *adj.* having a tendency to lose one's temper; easily or quickly angered

**short-term** (-turm′) *adj.* **1.** for a short time **2.** designating or of a capital gain, loan, etc. that involves a relatively short period

**short ton** a ton that is 2,000 pounds avoirdupois

**short-waist·ed** (-wās′tid) *adj.* with a high waistline

**short·wave** (-wāv′) *n.* **1.** a radio wave sixty meters or less in length **2.** a radio or radio band for broadcasting or receiving shortwaves: in full, **shortwave radio**

**short-wind·ed** (-win′did) *adj.* **1.** easily put out of breath by exertion **2.** breathing with quick, labored breaths

**short·y, short·ie** (-ē) *n., pl.* **short′ies** [Colloq.] a person or thing of less than average height or size

**Sho·sho·ne** (shō shō′nē) *n.* [< ? Shoshonean *tsosoni*, curly head] **1.** *pl.* **-sho′nes, -sho′ne** any member of a group of N. American Indians scattered over Idaho, Nevada, Utah, Wyoming, and California **2.** their Shoshonean language Also sp. **Sho·sho′ni**

**Sho·sho·ne·an** (shō shō′nē ən, shō′shə nē′ən) *n.* a branch of the Uto-Aztecan languages —*adj.* **1.** of Shoshonean **2.** of the Shoshones

**Sho·sta·ko·vich** (shô′stä kô′vich; *E.* shäs′tə kō′vich) **Dmi·tri** (d′mē′trē) 1906–75; Russ. composer

**shot**[1] (shät) *n.* [OE. *sceot*] **1.** the act of shooting; discharge of a missile, esp. from a gun **2.** *a)* the distance a missile travels *b)* range; scope **3.** an attempt to hit with a missile **4.** *a)* any attempt or try *b)* a guess **5.** a pointed, critical remark **6.** the flight or path of an object thrown, driven, etc. in any of several games **7.** *a)* a projectile to be discharged from a firearm, esp. a solid ball or bullet *b)* such projectiles collectively **8.** a small pellet or pellets of lead, used for a charge of a shotgun **9.** the ball used in the shot put: see SHOT PUT **10.** a blast **11.** a marksman *[a fair shot]* **12.** *a)* a single photograph *b)* a sequence or view taken by a single continuous run of a movie or TV camera **13.** a hypodermic injection, as of vaccine **14.** a drink of liquor **15.** [Colloq.] a bet, with reference to the odds given *[a ten-to-one shot]* —*vt.* **shot′ted, shot′ting** to load or weight with shot —**a shot in the arm** something that bolsters up, encourages, etc. —**call the shots 1.** to give orders **2.** to control what happens —**have (or take) a shot at** [Colloq.] to make a try at —**like a shot** quickly or suddenly

**shot**[2] (shät) *pt. & pp. of* SHOOT —*adj.* **1.** variegated, streaked, etc. with another color or substance **2.** varied with something different **3.** [Colloq.] ruined or worn out

**shote** (shōt) *n. var. of* SHOAT

**shot·gun** (shät′gun′) *n.* a smoothbore gun for firing a charge of small shot at short range —*vt., vi.* to shoot, force, etc. with a shotgun

**shot put** (poot′) *n.* a contest in which a heavy metal ball is propelled by an overhand thrust from the shoulder **2.** a single put of the shot —**shot′-put′ter** *n.* —**shot′-put′ting** *n.*

**should** (shood; *unstressed, often* shəd) *v.* [OE. *sceolde,* pt. of *sceal,* I am obliged] **1.** *pt. of* SHALL **2.** an auxiliary used to express: *a)* obligation, duty, etc. *[he should help her] b)* expectation or probability *[he should be here soon] c)* equivalent to *ought to c)* futurity from the standpoint of the past in indirect quotations: replaceable by *would [I said I should (or would)* be home late] *d)* futurity in polite requests or in statements implying doubt: replaceable by *would [I should (or would)* think he'd like it] *e)* a future condition *[if I should die tomorrow] f)* a past condition: replaceable by *would [I should (or would)* have gone had you asked me] In the usage of some grammarians, the distinctions between *should* and *would* are the same as those between *shall* and *will:* see WILL[2]

**shoul·der** (shōl′dər) *n.* [OE. *sculdor*] **1.** *a)* the joint connecting the arm or forelimb with the body *b)* the part of the body including this joint, extending to the base of the neck **2.** [*pl.*] the two shoulders and the part of the back be-

tween them **3.** a cut of meat consisting of the upper foreleg and attached parts **4.** the part of a garment that covers the shoulder **5.** a shoulderlike projection **6.** the strip along the edge of a paved road; berm —*vt.* **1.** to push along or through, as with the shoulder **2.** to carry upon the shoulder **3.** to assume the burden of —*vi.* to push with the shoulder —**cry on someone's shoulder** to tell one's troubles to someone in seeking sympathy —**put one's shoulder to the wheel** to set to work vigorously —**shoulder arms** to rest a rifle against the shoulder, supporting the butt with the hand —**shoulder to shoulder 1.** side by side and close together **2.** working together —**straight from the shoulder 1.** moving straight forward from the shoulder: said of a blow **2.** without reserve; frankly —**turn (or give) a cold shoulder to** to treat with disdain; avoid

**shoulder blade** either of two flat bones in the upper back

**shoulder harness** a restraining strap passing over the shoulder and body to the hip, used for safety in a car

**shoulder strap 1.** a strap, usually one of a pair, worn over the shoulder to support a garment **2.** a strap worn over the shoulder for carrying an attached purse, camera, etc. **3.** a flap of cloth on the shoulder of a uniform, coat, etc.

**should·n't** (shood′'nt) should not

**shouldst** (shoodst) *archaic 2d pers. sing. pt. of* SHALL: used with thou: also **should·est** (shood′ist)

**shout** (shout) *n.* [ME. *schoute*] a loud, sudden cry, call, or outburst —*vt., vi.* to utter in a shout or cry out loudly —**shout down** to silence by loud shouting —**shout′er** *n.*

**shove** (shuv) *vt., vi.* **shoved, shov′ing** [OE. *scufan*] **1.** to push, as along a surface **2.** to push roughly —*n.* a push or thrust —**shove off 1.** to push (a boat) away from shore **2.** [Colloq.] to start off; leave —**shov′er** *n.*

**shov·el** (shuv′'l) *n.* [OE. *scofl*] **1.** *a)* a tool with a broad scoop or blade and a long handle: used in lifting and moving loose material *b)* any machine with a shovellike device **2.** *same as* SHOVELFUL —*vt.* **-eled** or **-elled, -el·ing** or **-el·ling 1.** to lift and move with a shovel **2.** to dig out (a path, etc.) with a shovel **3.** to put in large quantities *[to shovel food in one's mouth]* —*vi.* to use a shovel

**shov·el·er, shov·el·ler** (shuv′'l ər, shuv′lər) *n.* **1.** a person or thing that shovels **2.** a freshwater duck with a long, broad, flattened bill: also **shov′el·bill′**

**shov·el·ful** (shuv′'l fool′) *n., pl.* **-fuls′** as much as a shovel will hold

**show** (shō) *vt.* **showed, shown** or **showed, show′ing** [OE. *sceawian,* to look] **1.** to bring or put in sight; make visible; exhibit; display **2.** to guide; conduct *[show* him to his room] **3.** to direct attention to; point out *[we showed* him the sights] **4.** to reveal, manifest, etc. *[to show* anger] **5.** to explain, prove, or demonstrate *[to show* how it works] **6.** to register *[a clock shows* the time] **7.** to grant or bestow (favor, mercy, etc.) —*vi.* **1.** to be or become seen; appear **2.** to be noticeable *[the scratch won't show]* **3.** to finish third or no worse than third in a horse or dog race **4.** [Colloq.] to come or arrive as expected —*n.* **1.** a showing or demonstration *[a show* of passion] **2.** a display or exhibition, esp. in public or for the public **3.** a spectacular, pompous display **4.** a trace as of metal, coal, etc. in the earth **5.** something false; pretense *[her* sorrow was mere *show]* **6.** a ridiculous spectacle **7.** a presentation of entertainment, as a TV program or a movie **8.** third position at the finish of a horse or dog race —**for show** in order to attract attention —**put (or get) the show on the road** [Slang] to start an activity, venture, etc. —**show off 1.** to make a display of **2.** to do something meant to attract attention —**show up 1.** to expose or be exposed **2.** to come; arrive **3.** [Colloq.] to surpass

**show·boat** (-bōt′) *n.* a boat with a theater in which plays are presented for people who live in river towns

**show·bread** (-bred′) *n. same as* SHEWBREAD

**show business** the theater, motion pictures, television, etc. as a business or industry: also [Colloq.] **show biz**

**show·case** (-kās′) *n.* **1.** a glass-enclosed case for protecting things on display **2.** a means of displaying to good advantage *[the revue was a showcase* for new talent] —*vt.* **-cased′, -cas′ing** to display to good advantage

**show·down** (-doun′) *n.* [Colloq.] **1.** *Poker* the laying down of the cards face up to see who wins **2.** any action that brings matters to a climax or settles them

**show·er**[1] (shō′ər) *n.* a person who shows something

**show·er**[2] (shou′ər) *n.* [OE. *scur*] **1.** a brief fall of rain, hail, sleet, or snow **2.** a sudden, abundant fall or flow, as of tears, rays, sparks, etc. **3.** a party at which gifts are presented to the guest of honor **4.** *a)* a bath in which the body is sprayed with fine streams of water from a perforated nozzle: in full, **shower bath** *b)* an apparatus, or a room or enclosure, for this —*vt.* **1.** to make wet as with a spray of water **2.** to pour forth as in a shower [*showered* with praise] —*vi.* **1.** to fall or come as a shower **2.** to bathe under a shower —**show′er·y** *adj.*

**show·girl** (shō′gʉrl′) *n. same as* CHORUS GIRL

**show·ing** (shō′iŋ) *n.* an exhibition, display, or performance

**show·man** (shō′mən) *n., pl.* **-men 1.** a person whose business is producing or presenting shows **2.** a person skilled at this or at presenting anything in a striking manner —**show′man·ship′** *n.*

**shown** (shōn) *alt. pp. of* SHOW

**show·off** (shō′ôf′) *n.* **1.** a showing off to attract attention **2.** a person who shows off

**show·piece** (-pēs′) *n.* **1.** something exhibited **2.** something that is a fine example of its kind

**show·place** (-plās′) *n.* **1.** a place that is exhibited to the public for its beauty, etc. **2.** any place that is beautiful, lavishly furnished, etc.

**show·room** (-rōōm′) *n.* a room where merchandise is displayed, as for advertising or sale

**show window** a store window for displaying goods

**show·y** (-ē) *adj.* **show′i·er, show′i·est 1.** of striking appearance **2.** attracting attention in a gaudy or flashy way —**show′i·ly** *adv.* —**show′i·ness** *n.*

**shrank** (shraŋk) *alt. pt. of* SHRINK

**shrap·nel** (shrap′n'l) *n.* [after H. *Shrapnel* (1761–1842), Brit. general who invented it] **1.** an artillery shell filled with an explosive charge and many small metal balls, set to explode in the air **2.** these metal balls or the shell fragments scattered by any exploding shell

**shred** (shred) *n.* [OE. *screade*] **1.** a long, narrow strip or piece cut or torn off **2.** a very small piece or amount; fragment [not a *shred* of truth] —*vt.* **shred′ded** or **shred, shred′ding** to cut or tear into shreds —**shred′der** *n.*

**Shreve·port** (shrēv′pôrt) [after H. M. *Shreve* (1785–1854), U.S. inventor] city in NW La.; pop. 206,000

**shrew** (shrōō) *n.* [OE. *screawa*] **1.** a small, mouselike mammal with soft, brown fur and a long snout: also **shrew′mouse′**, *pl.* **-mice′ 2.** a nagging, bad-tempered woman —**shrew′ish** *adj.* —**shrew′ish·ness** *n.*

**shrewd** (shrōōd) *adj.* [< ME. pp. of *schrewen,* to curse < *schrewe,* shrew] keen-witted, clever, or sharp in practical affairs; astute —**shrewd′ly** *adv.* —**shrewd′ness** *n.*

**shriek** (shrēk) *vi.* [prob. < ON.] to make a loud, sharp, piercing cry or sound; screech; scream —*vt.* to utter with a shriek —*n.* a loud, piercing cry or sound —**shriek′er** *n.*

**shrift** (shrift) *n.* [OE. *scrift* < *scrifan,* to shrive] [Archaic] **1.** confession to and absolution by a priest **2.** the act of shriving See also SHORT SHRIFT

**shrike** (shrīk) *n.* [OE. *scric*] any of several shrill-voiced birds with hooked beaks: most types feed on insects, some on small birds, frogs, etc., which are sometimes impaled on thorns

**shrill** (shril) *adj.* [ME. *schrille:* echoic] **1.** having or producing a high, thin, piercing tone; high-pitched **2.** characterized or accompanied by shrill sounds **3.** irritatingly insistent —*vt., vi.* to utter with or make a shrill sound —**shrill′ness** *n.* —**shril′ly** *adv.*

**shrimp** (shrimp) *n., pl.* **shrimps, shrimp:** see PLURAL, II, D, 1 [< base of OE. *scrimman,* to shrink] **1.** a small, long-tailed crustacean, valued as food **2.** [Colloq.] a small, slight person —*vi.* to fish for shrimp —**shrimp′er** *n.*

**shrine** (shrīn) *n.* [OE. *scrin* < L. *scrinium,* box] **1.** a container holding sacred relics **2.** the tomb of a saint or revered person **3.** a place of worship, usually one whose center is a sacred scene or object **4.** a place or thing hallowed or honored because of its history or associations

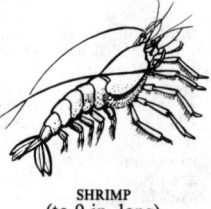
SHRIMP
(to 9 in. long)

**shrink** (shriŋk) *vi.* **shrank** or **shrunk, shrunk** or **shrunk′en, shrink′ing** [OE. *scrincan*] **1.** to contract, as from heat, cold, wetness, etc. **2.** to lessen, as in amount, worth, etc. **3.** to draw back in fear, dislike, etc.; cower or flinch —*vt.* to cause to shrink or contract —*n.* **1.** a shrinking **2.** [< (*head*)*shrink*(*er*)] [Slang] a psychiatrist: also **shrink′er**

**shrink·age** (shriŋ′kij) *n.* **1.** the act or process of shrinking, as of a fabric in washing **2.** decrease in value; depreciation **3.** the amount of shrink, decrease, etc.

**shrinking violet** a very shy or modest person

**shrink-wrap** (shriŋk′rap′) *vt.* **-wrapped′, -wrap′ping** to wrap (a commodity) in a tough, transparent plastic material which is then shrunk by heating to form a sealed, tightfitting package —*n.* a wrapping of such material

**shrive** (shrīv) *vt., vi.* **shrived** or **shrove, shriv′en** (shriv′'n) or **shrived, shriv′ing** [OE. *scrifan,* ult. < L. *scribere,* to write] [Archaic] **1.** to hear the confession of (a person) and, usu-

ally after penance, give absolution **2.** to get absolution for (oneself) by confessing and doing penance

**shriv·el** (shriv′'l) *vt., vi.* **-eled** or **-elled, -el·ing** or **-el·ling** [prob. < Scand.] **1.** to shrink and make or become wrinkled or withered **2.** to make or become helpless, useless, etc.

**shroud** (shroud) *n.* [OE. *scrud*] **1.** a cloth used to wrap a corpse for burial **2.** something that covers, protects, or screens; veil **3.** any of the ropes stretched from a ship's side to a masthead to offset lateral strain on the mast **4.** any of the lines from a parachute's canopy to the harness: in full, **shroud line** —*vt.* **1.** to wrap (a corpse) in a shroud **2.** to hide; cover; screen

**shrove** (shrōv) *alt. pt. of* SHRIVE

**Shrove·tide** (shrōv′tīd′) *n.* the three days before Ash Wednesday (**Shrove Sunday, Monday,** and **Tuesday**), formerly set aside as a period of confession and of festivity just before Lent

**shrub[1]** (shrub) *n.* [OE. *scrybb,* brushwood] a low, woody plant with several permanent stems instead of a single trunk; bush —**shrub′like′** *adj.*

**shrub[2]** (shrub) *n.* [< Ar. *sharāb,* drink] a drink made of fruit juice, sugar, and, usually, rum or brandy

**shrub·ber·y** (shrub′ər ē) *n., pl.* **-ber·ies** a group or heavy growth of shrubs, as around a house

**shrub·by** (-ē) *adj.* **-bi·er, -bi·est 1.** covered with shrubs **2.** like a shrub —**shrub′bi·ness** *n.*

**shrug** (shrug) *vt., vi.* **shrugged, shrug′ging** [ME. *schruggen,* orig., to shiver] to draw up (the shoulders), as in expressing indifference, doubt, disdain, etc. —*n.* the gesture so made —**shrug off** to dismiss in a carefree way

**shrunk** (shruŋk) *alt. pt. & pp. of* SHRINK

**shrunk·en** (-'n) *alt. pp. of* SHRINK —*adj.* contracted in size

‡**shtet·l** (shtet′'l) *n., pl.* **shtet′lach** (-läkh); E. **shtet′ls** (-'lz) [Yid., dim. of *shtat,* city < G. *stadt*] any of the former Jewish village communities of E Europe, esp. in Russia

**shtick** (shtik) *n.* [Yid., pranks, caprice] [Slang] **1.** a comic piece of business, as in a vaudeville act **2.** a characteristic talent, trait, bit of behavior, etc.

**shuck** (shuk) *n.* [< ?] **1.** a shell, pod, or husk **2.** the shell of an oyster or clam **3.** [Slang] *a)* a hoax or fraud *b)* a phony —*vt.* **1.** to remove shucks from (corn, clams, etc.) **2.** to remove like a shuck [to *shuck* one's clothes] —*vi.* [Slang] to fool or deceive —**shuck′er** *n.*

**shucks** (shuks) *interj.* an exclamation of mild disappointment, embarrassment, etc.

**shud·der** (shud′ər) *vi.* [ME. *schoderen*] to shake or tremble suddenly and violently, as in horror —*n.* a shuddering; sudden, strong tremor —**the shudders** a feeling of horror, disgust, etc. —**shud′der·ing·ly** *adv.* —**shud′der·y** *adj.*

**shuf·fle** (shuf′'l) *vt.* **-fled, -fling** [prob. < or akin to LowG. *schuffeln* < base of SHOVE] **1.** to move (the feet) with a dragging gait **2.** to mix (playing cards) so as to change their order **3.** to mix together in a jumbled mass **4.** to shift (things) about from one place to another **5.** to bring, put, or thrust (*into* or *out of*) clumsily or trickily —*vi.* **1.** to move by dragging or scraping the feet, as in walking or dancing **2.** to act in a shifty, tricky, or dishonest manner **3.** to shift repeatedly from one position or place to another **4.** to shuffle playing cards —*n.* **1.** the act of shuffling **2.** a deceptive action; evasion; trick **3.** *a)* a shuffling of the feet *b)* a gait, dance, etc. characterized by this **4.** *a)* a shuffling of playing cards *b)* one's turn at this —**lose in the shuffle** to leave out in the confusion of things —**shuffle off** to get rid of —**shuf′fler** *n.*

**shuf·fle·board** (-bôrd′) *n.* [< earlier *shovel board,* after the shape of the cues] **1.** a game in which large disks are pushed with a cue along a smooth lane toward numbered squares **2.** the surface on which it is played

**shun** (shun) *vt.* **shunned, shun′ning** [OE. *scunian*] to keep away from; avoid strictly —**shun′ner** *n.*

**shunt** (shunt) *vt., vi.* [< ? or akin to prec.] **1.** to move or turn to one side; turn aside **2.** to switch (a train, etc.) from one track to another **3.** *Elec.* to divert or be diverted by a shunt —*n.* **1.** a shunting **2.** a railroad switch **3.** *Elec.* a conductor connecting two points in a circuit and diverting part of the current from the main circuit —**shunt′er** *n.*

**shush** (shush) *interj.* [echoic] hush! be quiet! —*vt.* to say "shush" to; tell (another) to be quiet

**shut** (shut) *vt.* **shut, shut′ting** [OE. *scyttan* < base of *sceotan,* to shoot] **1.** *a)* to move (a door, window, lid, etc.) into a position that covers the opening to which it is fitted *b)* to fasten (a door, etc.) securely, as with a bolt or catch **2.** to close (an opening, container, etc.) **3.** *a)* to prevent entrance to or exit from; bar *b)* to confine or enclose (*in* a room, cage, etc.) **4.** to fold up or close the parts of (an umbrella, a book, the eyes, etc.) **5.** to stop or suspend the operation of (a school, business, etc.) —*vi.* to become shut —*adj.* closed, fastened, etc. —*n.* the act or time of shutting —**shut down 1.** to close by lowering **2.** to settle over (a place) so as to conceal, as fog or night **3.** to close (a factory, etc.), usually temporarily —**shut in** to surround or enclose —**shut off 1.** to prevent the passage of (water, electricity, etc.) **2.** to prevent passage through (a road, faucet, etc.) **3.** to separate; isolate —**shut out 1.** to deny entrance to; exclude (sound, a view, etc.) **2.** to prevent (the opposition) from scoring in a game —**shut up 1.** to enclose, confine, or imprison **2.** to close all the entrances to **3.** [Colloq.] *a)* to stop or cause to stop talking *b)* to prevent from speaking or writing freely; censor

**shut·down** (-doun′) *n.* a stoppage or suspension of work or activity, as in a factory

**shut-eye** (-ī′) *n.* [Slang] sleep

**shut-in** (-in′) *n.* a person who is too ill, weak, etc. to go out —*adj.* not able to go out

**shut-off** (-ôf′) *n.* **1.** something that shuts off a flow, as a valve **2.** a stoppage or interruption

**shut·out** (-out′) *n.* **1.** a preventing of the opposing team from scoring **2.** a game in which this occurs

**shut·ter** (shut′ər) *n.* **1.** a person or thing that shuts **2.** a movable, usually hinged cover for a window **3.** anything used to cover an opening; specif., a device for opening and closing the aperture of a camera lens to expose the film or plate —*vt.* to close or furnish with shutters

**shut·tle** (shut′'l) *n.* [OE. *scytel*, missile: from being cast back and forth] **1.** *a)* a device used to pass the woof thread back and forth between the warp threads in weaving *b)* any of several devices having a similar use or motion, as the device that carries the lower thread back and forth on a sewing machine **2.** a bus, train, helicopter, etc. making frequent trips back and forth over a short route —*vt., vi.* -tled, -tling **1.** to move rapidly to and fro **2.** to go by means of a shuttle

**shut·tle·cock** (-käk′) *n.* **1.** a rounded piece of cork having a flat end stuck with feathers: it is struck back and forth across a net by players in badminton or in battledore and shuttlecock **2.** the game of battledore and shuttlecock —*vt., vi.* to go, send, or bandy back and forth

**shy¹** (shī) *adj.* **shy′er** or **shi′er, shy′est** or **shi′est** [OE. *sceoh*] **1.** easily frightened or startled; timid **2.** not at ease with other people; bashful **3.** distrustful; wary **4.** [Slang] lacking in amount; short (*on* or *of*) —*vi.* **shied, shy′ing 1.** to move or pull back suddenly when startled; start **2.** to be or become cautious or unwilling; draw back (often with *at* or *from*) —*n., pl.* **shies** an act of shying; start, as of a horse —**fight shy of** to avoid or evade —**shy′er** *n.* —**shy′ly** *adv.* —**shy′ness** *n.*

**shy²** (shī) *vt., vi.* **shied, shy′ing** [< ? or akin to prec.] to fling, toss, etc. sidewise with a jerk [*shying* stones at a target] —*n., pl.* **shies** a shying; fling

**Shy·lock** (shī′läk′) the moneylender in Shakespeare's *Merchant of Venice* —*n.* an exacting creditor

**shy·ster** (shī′stər) *n.* [prob. altered < G. *scheisser*, defecator] [Slang] a person, esp. a lawyer, who uses unethical or tricky methods

**si** (sē) *n. Music* same as TI

‡**sí** (sē) *adv.* [Sp.] yes: also [It.] **sì**

**Si** *Chem.* silicon

**Si·am** (sī am′) *former name of* THAILAND

**Si·a·mese** (sī′ə mēz′, -mēs′) *n., pl.* **Si′a·mese′** same as THAI —*adj.* same as THAI

**Siamese cat** a breed of short-haired cat characterized by blue eyes and a fawn-colored coat shading to a darker color at the face, ears, paws, and tail

**Siamese twins** [after such a pair born in Siam] any pair of twins born joined to each other

**Si·an** (shē′än′) city in NC China: pop. c. 1,500,000

**sib** (sib) *n.* [OE. *sibb*] **1.** blood relatives; kin **2.** a blood relative **3.** a sibling —*adj.* related by blood

**Si·be·li·us** (si bā′lē oos; *E.* sə bāl′yəs), **Jean (Julius Christian)** (zhän) 1865-1957; Finn. composer

**Si·be·ri·a** (sī bir′ē ə) region in N Asia, between the Urals & the Pacific; Asiatic section of the R.S.F.S.R. —**Si·ber′i·an** *adj., n.*

**sib·i·lant** (sib′'l ənt) *adj.* [< L. < *sibilare*, to hiss] having or making a hissing sound —*n. Phonet.* a consonant characterized by a hissing sound, as (s), (z), (sh), (zh), (ch), and (j) —**sib′i·lance, sib′i·lan·cy** *n., pl.* **-cies** —**sib′i·lant·ly** *adv.*

**sib·ling** (sib′liŋ) *n.* [20th-c. readoption of OE. *sibling*, a relative] one of two or more persons born of the same parents, or, sometimes, having one parent in common; brother or sister

**Sib·yl** (sib′'l) [L. *Sibylla*: see ff.] a feminine name

**sib·yl** (sib′'l) *n.* [< L. < Gr. *sibylla*] **1.** any of certain women consulted as prophetesses or oracles by the ancient Greeks and Romans **2.** a prophetess; fortuneteller — **sib′yl·line′** (-'l in′, -ēn′, -in) *adj.*

‡**sic¹** (sik) *adv.* [L.] thus; so: used within brackets, [*sic*], to show that a quoted passage, esp. one containing some error, is shown exactly as in the original

**sic²** (sik) *vt.* [var. of SEEK] **sicked, sick′ing 1.** to pursue and attack: said esp. of or to a dog **2.** to urge to attack [to *sic* a dog on someone]

**Sic·i·ly** (sis′'l ē) island of Italy, off its S tip: with small nearby islands, 9,926 sq. mi.: It. name **Si·ci·lia** (sēchēl′yä) —**Si·cil·ian** (si sil′yən, -ē ən) *adj., n.*

**sick¹** (sik) *adj.* [OE. *seoc*] **1.** suffering from disease; physically or mentally ill **2.** having nausea; vomiting or about to vomit **3.** characteristic of sickness [a *sick* expression] **4.** of or for sick people [*sick* leave] **5.** deeply disturbed, as by grief, failure, etc. **6.** disgusted by reason of excess [*sick* of his excuses]: often **sick and tired 7.** unsound **8.** having a great longing (*for*) [*sick* for the hills] **9.** of sickly color; pale **10.** menstruating **11.** [Colloq.] sadistic, morbid, etc. [a *sick* joke] —**the sick** sick people collectively

**sick²** (sik) *vt.* same as SIC²

**sick bay** a ship's hospital or dispensary

**sick·bed** (sik′bed′) *n.* the bed of a sick person

**sick call** *Mil.* **1.** a daily formation for those who wish to receive medical attention **2.** the time for this

**sick·en** (sik′'n) *vt., vi.* to make or become sick, disgusted, etc. —**sick′en·er** *n.*

**sick·en·ing** (-iŋ) *adj.* **1.** causing sickness or nausea **2.** disgusting —**sick′en·ing·ly** *adv.*

**sick headache 1.** any headache accompanied by nausea **2.** same as MIGRAINE

**sick·ish** (sik′ish) *adj.* **1.** somewhat sick or nauseated **2.** somewhat sickening or nauseating —**sick′ish·ly** *adv.*

**sick·le** (sik′'l) *n.* [OE. *sicol*, ult. < L. *secula* < *secare*, to cut] a tool consisting of a crescent-shaped blade with a short handle, for cutting tall grass, etc.

**sick leave** leave from work granted for illness, often with pay (**sick pay**) for a limited number of days

**sickle cell anemia** an inherited chronic anemia found chiefly among Negroes, characterized by an abnormal red blood cell (**sickle cell**) containing a defective form of hemoglobin that causes the cell to become sickle-shaped when deprived of oxygen: also **sickle cell disease**

SICKLE

**sick·ly** (sik′lē) *adj.* **-li·er, -li·est 1.** in poor health; sick much of the time **2.** of or produced by sickness [a *sickly* pallor] **3.** producing illness; unhealthful **4.** sickening, as an odor **5.** faint; feeble [a *sickly* light] **6.** weak; insipid [a *sickly* smile] —*adv.* in a sick manner: also **sick′li·ly** —*vt.* **-lied, -ly·ing** to make sickly, as in color, vigor, etc. —**sick′li·ness** *n.*

**sick·ness** (-nis) *n.* **1.** a being sick or diseased; illness **2.** a particular disease or illness **3.** nausea

**sick·room** (-rōōm′) *n.* the room to which a sick person is confined

**Sid·dhar·tha Gau·ta·ma** (sid där′tə gout′ə mə, gôt′-) *see* BUDDHA

**side** (sīd) *n.* [OE.] **1.** the right or left half of a human or animal body **2.** a position beside one **3.** *a)* any of the lines or surfaces that bound something [a square has four *sides*] *b)* either of the two bounding surfaces of an object that are not the front, back, top, or bottom **4.** either of the two surfaces of paper, cloth, etc. **5.** a particular or specified surface [the inner *side* of a vase, the visible *side* of the moon] **6.** a particular part or quality of a person or thing [his cruel *side*, the bright *side* of life] **7.** the slope of a hill, bank, etc. **8.** any location, area, space, etc. with reference to a central point or line, or to the speaker **9.** the ideas, opinions, or position of one person or faction opposing another [his *side* of the argument] **10.** one of the parties in a contest, conflict, etc. **11.** line of descent through either parent **12.** any of the pages containing an actor's part in a play **13.** [Brit. Slang] superior or patronizing manner **14.** [Brit.] *Billiards* same as ENGLISH (*n.* 3) —*adj.* **1.** of, at, or on a side [a *side* door] **2.** to or from one side [a *side* glance] **3.** done, happening, etc. on the side [a *side* effect] **4.** not main; secondary [a *side* issue] —*vt.* **sid′ed, sid′ing** to furnish with sides or siding —**on the side** in addition to the main thing, part, course, etc. —**side by side** beside each other; together —**side with** to support (one of opposing factions, etc.) —**take sides** to support one of the parties in a dispute, etc.

**side arms** weapons of the kind that may be worn at the side or at the waist, as a sword, pistol, etc.

**side·board** (sīd′bôrd′) *n.* a piece of dining-room furniture for holding table linen, silver, china, etc.

**side·burns** (-burnz′) *n.pl.* [reversed < BURNSIDES] **1.** same as BURNSIDES **2.** the hair growing on a man's face just in front of the ears, esp. when the rest of the beard is cut off

---

fat, āpe, cär; ten, ēven; is, bīte; gō, hôrn, tōōl, look; oil, out; up, fur; get; joy; yet; chin; she; thin, *th*en; zh, leisure; ŋ, ring; ə for *a* in *ago, e* in *agent, i* in *sanity, o* in *comply, u* in *focus*; ′ as in *able* (ā′b'l); Fr. bâl; ë, Fr. coeur; ö, Fr. feu; Fr. mon; ô, Fr. coq; ü, Fr. duc; r, Fr. cri; H, G. ich; kh, G. doch; ‡foreign; *hypothetical; < derived from. See inside front cover.

**side·car** (-kär') *n.* a small car attached to the side of a motorcycle, for carrying a passenger, parcels, etc.

**sid·ed** (sīd'id) *adj.* having (a specified number or kind of) sides *[six-sided]*

**side dish** any food served along with the main course, usually in a separate dish

**side·kick** (-kik') *n.* [Slang] 1. a companion; close friend 2. a partner; confederate

**side·light** (-līt') *n.* 1. a light coming from the side 2. a bit of incidental information on a subject

**side·line** (-līn') *n.* a line along the side; specif., *a)* either of the two lines marking the side limits of a playing area, as in football or basketball *b)* [*pl.*] the areas just outside these lines *c)* a line, as of merchandise or work, in addition to one's main line —*vt.* **-lined', -lin'ing** to remove from active participation, as because of injury —**side'lin'er** *n.*

**side·long** (-lôŋ') *adv.* toward the side; obliquely —*adj.* 1. inclined; slanting 2. directed to the side, as a glance

**side·man** (-man') *n., pl.* **-men'** (-men') [as distinguished from the *front man,* or leader] a member of a jazz or dance band other than the leader

**side·piece** (-pēs') *n.* a piece forming, or attached to, the side of something

**si·de·re·al** (sī dir'ē əl) *adj.* [< L. < *sidus* (gen. *sideris,* a star] 1. of the stars or constellations; astral 2. with reference to the stars —**si·de're·al·ly** *adv.*

**sidereal day** the time between two successive passages of the vernal equinox over the upper meridian: it measures one rotation of the earth and is equal to 23 hours, 56 minutes, 4.091 seconds of mean solar time

**sidereal year** *see* YEAR (sense 3)

**sid·er·ite** (sid'ə rīt') *n.* [< G. < L. < Gr. < *sidēros,* iron] a yellowish to light-brown iron ore, FeCO₃ —**sid'er·it'ic** (-rit'ik) *adj.*

**side·sad·dle** (sīd'sad''l) *n.* a saddle for women wearing skirts, upon which the rider sits with both legs on the same side of the animal —*adv.* on or as if on a sidesaddle

**side·show** (-shō') *n.* 1. a small show apart from the main show, as of a circus 2. activity of minor importance

**side·slip** (-slip') *vi.* **-slipped', -slip'ping** 1. to slip sideways, as on skis 2. *Aeron.* to move in a sideslip —*vt.* to cause to sideslip —*n.* 1. a slip or skid to the side 2. *Aeron.* a sideways and downward movement toward the inside of a turn by an airplane in a sharp bank

**side·split·ting** (-split'iŋ) *adj.* 1. very hearty: said of laughter 2. causing hearty laughter

**side·step** (-step') *vt.* **-stepped', -step'ping** to avoid by or as by stepping aside; dodge —*vi.* to step to one side

**side step** a step to one side, as to avoid something, or a step taken sidewise

**side·swipe** (-swīp') *vt., vi.* **-swiped', -swip'ing** to hit along the side in passing —*n.* a glancing blow of this kind

**side·track** (-trak') *vt., vi.* 1. to switch (a train, etc.) to a siding 2. to turn away from the main issue —*n.* a railroad siding

**side·walk** (-wôk') *n.* a path for pedestrians, usually paved, along the side of a street

**side·wall** (-wôl') *n.* the side of an automobile tire between the tread and the rim of a wheel

**side·ward** (-wərd) *adv., adj.* directed or moving toward one side: also **side'wards** *adv.*

**side·ways** (-wāz') *adv.* 1. from the side 2. with one side forward 3. toward one side; obliquely —*adj.* turned or moving toward or from one side Also **side'way, side'wise'** (-wīz')

**side-wheel** (sīd'hwēl', -wēl') *adj.* designating a steamboat having a paddle wheel on each side —**side'-wheel'er** *n.*

**side whiskers** whiskers at the side of the face

**side·wind·er** (sīd'wīn'dər) *n.* 1. a small desert rattlesnake of the SW U.S. that moves by looping its body sideways 2. [S-] an air-to-air missile

**sid·ing** (sīd'iŋ) *n.* 1. shingles, boards, aluminum panels, etc. forming the outside covering of a frame building 2. a short railroad track connected with a main track by a switch and used for unloading, bypassing, etc.

**si·dle** (sī'd'l) *vi.* **-dled, -dling** [< *sideling,* sideways] to move sideways, esp. in a shy or stealthy manner —*vt.* to make go sideways —*n.* a sidling movement

**Sid·ney** (sid'nē) 1. [< the surname *Sidney,* prob. reduced from *St. Denis*] a masculine or feminine name: dim. **Sid** 2. **Sir Philip,** 1554–86; Eng. poet, soldier, & statesman

**Si·don** (sī'd'n) chief city of ancient Phoenicia, on the Mediterranean in what is now SW Lebanon

**siege** (sēj) *n.* [OFr., ult. < L. *obsidere,* to besiege < *ob-,* against + *sedere,* to sit] 1. the surrounding of a city, fort, etc. by an enemy army trying to capture it by continued blockade and attack 2. any stubborn and continued effort to win or control something 3. a long, distressing period *[a siege* of illness] 4. [Obs.] a seat; throne —*vt.* **sieged, sieg'ing** *same as* BESIEGE —**lay siege to** to subject to a siege

**Sieg·fried** (sēg'frēd, sig'-) a hero of Germanic legend who wins the treasure of the Nibelungs

**si·en·na** (sē en'ə) *n.* [It. *terra di Siena,* lit., earth of Siena, city in Italy] 1. a yellowish-brown earth pigment containing iron and manganese 2. a reddish-brown pigment made by burning this; burnt sienna 3. either of these colors

**si·er·ra** (sē er'ə) *n.* [Sp. < L. *serra,* a saw] a range of mountains with a saw-toothed appearance

**Si·er·ra Le·one** (sē er'ə lē ōn') country in W Africa, on the Atlantic, between Guinea & Liberia: a member of the Commonwealth: 27,925 sq. mi.; pop. 2,600,000

**Si·er·ra Ma·dre** (sē er'ə mä'drä; *Sp.* sye'rä mä'dre) mountain system of Mexico, consisting of three ranges bordering the central plateau

**Sierra Nevada** [Sp., lit., snowy range] mountain range in E Calif.: also called **the Si·er·ras** (sē er'əz)

**si·es·ta** (sē es'tə) *n.* [Sp. < L. *sexta* (*hora*), sixth (hour), noon] a brief nap or rest taken after the noon meal, esp. in Spain and some Latin American countries

‡**sieur** (syër) *n.* [OFr., inflected form of *sire,* SIRE] *archaic French title of respect meaning* SIR

**sieve** (siv) *n.* [OE. *sife*] a utensil having many small openings, used to strain solids from liquids or to separate fine particles from coarser ones; strainer; sifter —*vt., vi.* **sieved, siev'ing** to pass through a sieve

**sift** (sift) *vt.* [OE. *siftan*] 1. to pass through a sieve so as to separate the coarse from the fine particles, or to break up lumps, as of flour 2. to scatter by or as by the use of a sieve 3. to examine with care; weigh (evidence, etc.) 4. to separate; screen *[to sift* fact from fable] —*vi.* 1. to sift something 2. to pass as through a sieve —**sift'er** *n.*

**sift·ings** (-iŋz) *n.pl.* sifted matter

**sigh** (sī) *vi.* [OE. *sican*] 1. to take in and let out a long, deep, sounded breath, as in sorrow, relief, fatigue, etc. 2. to make a sound like a sigh *[trees sighing* in the wind] 3. to long or lament (*for*) —*vt.* to express with a sigh —*n.* the act or sound of sighing —**sigh'er** *n.*

**sight** (sīt) *n.* [OE. (ge)sihi < base of *seon,* to see] 1. *a)* something seen; view *b)* a remarkable view; spectacle *c)* a thing worth seeing: *usually used in pl.* [the *sights* of the city] 2. the act of seeing 3. a look; glimpse 4. any device used to aid the eyes in lining up a gun, optical instrument, etc. on its objective 5. aim or an observation taken as with a sextant, gun, etc. 6. the ability to see; vision; eyesight 7. range of vision 8. one's thinking or opinion *[a hero in her sight]* 9. a person or thing not pleasant to look at 10. [Dial.] a large amount; lot *[a sight* better than fighting] —*vt.* 1. to observe or examine by taking a sight 2. to catch sight of; see 3. *a)* to furnish with a sighting device *b)* to adjust the sights of 4. to aim (a gun, etc.) at (a target), using the sights —*vi.* 1. to take aim or an observation with a sight 2. to look carefully *[sight* along the line] —*adj.* 1. read, done, understood, etc. as soon as seen 2. payable when presented *[a sight* draft] —**a sight for sore eyes** [Colloq.] a welcome sight —**at** (or on) **sight** when or as soon as seen —**by sight** by recognizing but not through being acquainted —**catch sight of** to see, esp. briefly; glimpse —**lose sight of** 1. to see no longer 2. to forget —**not by a long sight** 1. not nearly 2. not at all —**out of sight** 1. not in sight 2. [Colloq.] extremely high, as in price, standards, etc. 3. [Slang] excellent; wonderful —**sight unseen** without seeing (the thing) beforehand

**sight·ed** (-id) *adj.* 1. having sight; not blind 2. having (a specified kind of) sight: used in combination *[farsighted]*

**sight·less** (-lis) *adj.* 1. blind 2. unseen —**sight'less·ly** *adv.* —**sight'less·ness** *n.*

**sight·ly** (-lē) *adj.* **-li·er, -li·est** pleasant to the sight

**sight·see·ing** (-sē'iŋ) *n.* the act of visiting places and things of interest —*adj.* for or engaged in seeing sights —**sight'se'er** *n.*

**sig·ma** (sig'mə) *n.* [Gr.] the eighteenth letter of the Greek alphabet (Σ, σ)

**sig·moid** (-moid) *adj.* having a double curve like the letter S: also **sig·moi'dal** —**sig·moi'dal·ly** *adv.*

**sigmoid flexure** *Anat.* the last curving part of the colon, ending in the rectum 2. *Zool.* an S-shaped curve

**Sig·mund** (sig'mənd) [< G. & ON.] a masculine name

**sign** (sīn) *n.* [< OFr. < L. *signum*] 1. something that indicates a fact, quality, etc. *[black is a sign* of mourning] 2. *a)* a gesture that tells something specified *[a nod is a sign* of approval] *b)* any of the gestures used in sign language 3. a mark or symbol having a specific meaning *[the sign* ¢ for cent(s)] 4. a publicly displayed board, placard, etc. bearing information, advertising, etc. 5. any visible trace or indication *[the signs* of spring] 6. an omen 7. *same as* SIGN OF THE ZODIAC —*vt.* 1. to mark with a sign, esp. of the cross as in blessing 2. to write one's name on, as in agreement, authorization, etc. 3. to write (one's name) as a signature 4. to hire by written contract —*vi.* 1. to write one's signature, as in attesting or confirming something 2. to make a sign; signal —**sign away** (or **over**) to transfer title to (something) by signing a document —**sign in** (or **out**) to sign a register on arrival (or departure) —**sign off** to stop broadcasting, as for the day —**sign on** to hire or be hired —**sign up 1.** *same as* SIGN ON **2.** to enlist in military service —**sign'er** *n.*

**sig·nal** (sig'n'l) *n.* [< OFr. < VL. *signale*, ult. < L. *signum*, a sign] **1.** any sign, event, etc. that is a call to some kind of action *[a bugle signal to attack]* **2.** *a)* a sign given by gesture, a device, etc. to convey a command, direction, warning, etc. *b)* an object or device providing such a sign **3.** *Card Games* a bid or play designed to guide one's partner **4.** *Telegraphy, Radio & TV,* etc. the electrical impulses, sound or picture elements, etc. transmitted or received —*adj.* **1.** not ordinary; notable **2.** used as a signal —*vt., vi.* **-naled** or **-nalled, -nal·ing** or **-nal·ling 1.** to make a signal or signals (to) **2.** to communicate by signals —**sig'nal·er, sig'nal·ler** *n.*

**signal corps** the part of an army in charge of communications, as by radio

**sig·nal·ize** (-īz') *vt.* **-ized', -iz'ing 1.** to make notable **2.** to draw attention to —**sig'nal·i·za'tion** *n.*

**sig·nal·ly** (-ē) *adv.* notably; remarkably

**sig·nal·man** (-mən, -man') *n., pl.* **-men** (-mən, -men') a person responsible for signaling or receiving signals

**sig·na·to·ry** (sig'nə tôr'ē) *adj.* that has or have joined in the signing of something —*n., pl.* **-ries** any of the persons, states, etc. that have signed a document

**sig·na·ture** (sig'nə chər) *n.* [< LL. < L. *signare*, to sign] **1.** a person's name written by himself **2.** the act of signing one's name **3.** an identifying characteristic or mark **4.** *Music* a sign or signs placed at the beginning of a staff to show key or time **5.** *Printing a)* a large sheet on which pages are printed in some multiple of four, and which, when folded to page size, forms one section of a book *b)* a letter or number on the first page of each sheet showing in what order that section is to be bound **6.** *Radio & TV* a theme song, picture, etc. used to identify a program

**sign·board** (sīn'bôrd') *n.* a board bearing a sign, esp. one advertising a business, product, etc.

**sig·net** (sig'nit) *n.* [MFr. dim. of *signe*, a sign] **1.** a small seal used in marking documents as official, etc. **2.** a mark made by a signet

**signet ring** a finger ring containing a signet, often in the form of an initial or a monogram

**sig·nif·i·cance** (sig nif'ə kəns) *n.* **1.** that which is signified; meaning **2.** the quality of being significant; suggestiveness; expressiveness **3.** importance; consequence

**sig·nif·i·cant** (-kənt) *adj.* [< L. prp. of *significare*, to signify] **1.** *a)* having or expressing a meaning *b)* full of meaning **2.** important; momentous **3.** having or expressing a special or hidden meaning **4.** of a difference too large to be due to chance, as in statistics Also **sig·nif'i·ca'-tive** (-kāt'iv) —**sig·nif'i·cant·ly** *adv.*

**sig·ni·fi·ca·tion** (sig'nə fi kā'shən) *n.* **1.** significance; meaning **2.** a signifying; indication

**sig·ni·fy** (sig'nə fī') *vt.* **-fied', -fy'ing** [< OFr. < L. *significare* < *signum*, a sign + *facere*, to make] **1.** to be a sign or indication of; mean **2.** to show or make known by a sign, words, etc. —*vi.* **1.** to be significant; matter **2.** [Chiefly Black Slang] to engage in verbal play involving boastful taunts, witty insults, indirect threats, etc. —**sig'ni·fi'a·ble** *adj.* —**sig'ni·fi'er** *n.*

**sign language** communication of thoughts or ideas by means of signs and gestures of the hands and arms

**sign of the zodiac** any of the twelve divisions of the zodiac, each represented by a symbol: see ZODIAC

‡**si·gnor** (sē nyôr'; *E.* sēn'yôr) *n., pl.* **si·gno'ri** (-nyô'rē); *E.* **si'gnors** [It.] **1.** [S-] Mr.: Italian title of respect, used before the name **2.** a gentleman; man

‡**si·gno·ra** (sē nyô'rä; *E.* sēn yôr'ə) *n., pl.* **si·gno're** (-re); *E.* **si·gno'ras** [It.] **1.** [S-] Mrs.; Madam: Italian title of respect **2.** a married woman

‡**si·gno·re** (sē nyô're) *n., pl.* **si·gno'ri** (-rē) [It.] **1.** [S-] sir: Italian title of respect, used in direct address without the name **2.** a gentleman; man

‡**si·gno·ri·na** (sē'nyô rē'nä; *E.* sēn'yə rē'nə) *n., pl.* **-ri'ne** (-ne); *E.* **-ri'nas** [It.] **1.** [S-] Miss: Italian title of respect **2.** an unmarried woman or girl

**sign·post** (sīn'pōst') *n.* **1.** a post with a sign on it, as for showing a route or direction **2.** a clear indication

**Si·gurd** (sig'ərd) a hero of Norse legend identified with the German SIEGFRIED

**Sikh** (sēk) *n.* [Hindi, a disciple] a member of a monotheistic Hindu religious sect that rejects the caste system —*adj.* of Sikhs —**Sikh'ism** *n.*

**si·lage** (sī'lij) *n.* [contr. (after SILO) < ENSILAGE] green fodder stored in a silo

**Si·las** (sī'ləs) [LL. < Gr. < Aram. *sh'îlâ*, lit., asked for] a masculine name: dim. *Si*

**sild** (sild) *n., pl.* **sild, silds:** see PLURAL, II, D, 2 [Norw., herring] any of several small or young herrings canned as Norwegian sardines

**si·lence** (sī'ləns) *n.* **1.** the state or fact of keeping silent or still **2.** absence of any sound or noise; stillness **3.** a withholding of knowledge or omission of mention **4.** failure to communicate, write, etc. —*vt.* **-lenced, -lenc·ing 1.** to make silent **2.** to put down; repress **3.** to put (enemy guns) out of action —*interj.* be silent!

**si·lenc·er** (sī'lən sər) *n.* **1.** one that silences **2.** a device for muffling the report of a firearm **3.** [Chiefly Brit.] a muffler for an internal-combustion engine

**si·lent** (sī'lənt) *adj.* [< L. < prp. of *silere*, to be silent] **1.** making no vocal sound; mute **2.** seldom speaking; not talkative **3.** free from sound or noise; quiet; still **4.** not spoken, expressed, etc. *[silent grief, the silent* "b" in "debt"*]* **5.** making no mention, explanation, etc. **6.** not active *[factories now silent]* **7.** designating or of films without synchronized sound —**si'lent·ly** *adv.*

**silent butler** a dish with a hinged cover and handle, in which to empty ashtrays, brush crumbs, etc.

**silent partner** a partner who shares in financing but not in managing a business, firm, etc.

**Si·le·sia** (sī lē'shə, si-; -zhə) region in E Europe, mainly in SW Poland —**Si·le'sian** *adj., n.*

**si·lex** (sī'leks) *n.* [L.] **1.** silica, esp. in the form of flint or quartz **2.** heat-resistant glass of fused quartz

**sil·hou·ette** (sil'oo wet') *n.* [Fr., after E. de *Silhouette*, 18th-c. Fr. minister of finance] **1.** *a)* a profile portrait in black or in some solid color, often a cutout mounted on a light background *b)* any dark shape seen against a light background **2.** the outline of a figure, garment, etc.; contour —*vt.* **-et'ted, -et'ting** to show or project in silhouette

**sil·i·ca** (sil'i kə) *n.* [ModL. < L. *silex*, flint] the dioxide of silicon, SiO$_2$, a hard, glassy mineral found in various forms, as in quartz, sand, opal, etc.

**sil·i·cate** (sil'i kit, -kāt') *n.* a salt or ester derived from silica or a silicic acid

SILHOUETTE

**si·li·ceous** (sə lish'əs) *adj.* **1.** of, containing, or like silica **2.** growing in soil that has much silica in it

**si·lic·ic** (sə lis'ik) *adj.* of, like, or derived from silicon

**silicic acid** any of several jellylike precipitates formed by acidifying sodium silicate solution

**sil·i·con** (sil'i kən, -kän') *n.* [ModL., ult. < L. *silex*, flint] a nonmetallic chemical element second only to oxygen in its abundance in nature and found always in combination, as in silica: symbol, Si; at. wt., 28.086; at. no., 14

**sil·i·cone** (-kōn') *n.* [SILIC(ON) + -ONE] any of a group of polymerized, organic silicon compounds highly resistant to heat, water, etc. and used in lubricants, polishes, etc.

**silicone rubber** a rubberlike polymer made from certain silicones: it keeps its elasticity over a wide temperature range and is used in gaskets, insulation, etc.

**sil·i·co·sis** (sil'ə kō'sis) *n.* [ModL.: see SILICON & -OSIS] a chronic lung disease caused in miners, stonecutters, etc. by inhaling silica dust over a long period of time

**silk** (silk) *n.* see PLURAL, II, D, 3 [OE. *seoluc*, ult. < ? L. *sericus:* see SERGE] **1.** the fine, soft, shiny fiber produced by silkworms **2.** thread or fabric made from this **3.** a garment or other article of such fabric **4.** any silklike filament or substance *[corn silk]* —*adj.* of or like silk —**hit the silk** [Slang] to parachute from an aircraft

**silk cotton** *same as* KAPOK

**silk·en** (sil'k'n) *adj.* **1.** made of silk **2.** dressed in silk **3.** like silk, as in being soft, smooth, glossy, or luxurious

**silk hat** a tall, cylindrical hat covered with silk or satin, worn by men in formal dress

**silk-screen** (silk'skrēn') *adj.* **1.** designating or of a stencil process of printing a design through a screen of silk or other fine cloth, parts of the screen being blocked as with an impermeable film **2.** designating a print made by this process —*vt.* to print by this process

**silk-stock·ing** (-stäk'iŋ) *adj.* **1.** fashionably or richly dressed **2.** wealthy or aristocratic —*n.* a member of the wealthy or aristocratic class

**silk·worm** (-wurm') *n.* any of certain moth caterpillars that produce cocoons of silk fiber

---

**silk·y** (sil′kē) *adj.* **silk′i·er, silk′i·est** **1.** of or like silk; soft, smooth, lustrous, etc. **2.** having fine, soft hairs, as some leaves —**silk′i·ly** *adv.* —**silk′i·ness** *n.*

**sill** (sil) *n.* [OE. *syll*] **1.** a heavy, horizontal timber or line of masonry supporting a house wall, etc. **2.** a horizontal piece forming the bottom frame of the opening into which a window or door is set

**sil·la·bub** (sil′ə bub′) *n. var. of* SYLLABUB

**sil·ly** (sil′ē) *adj.* **-li·er, -li·est** [OE. *sælig*, happy, blessed < *sæl*, happiness (sense development: happy → blissful → unaware of reality → foolish)] **1.** having or showing little sense or judgment; foolish, absurd, etc. **2.** frivolous or trivial **3.** [Colloq.] dazed or senseless, as from a blow —*n., pl.* **-lies** a silly person —**sil′li·ly** (or **sil′ly**) *adv.* —**sil′li·ness** *n.*

**si·lo** (sī′lō) *n., pl.* **-los** [Fr. < Sp. < L. < Gr. *siros*] **1.** an airtight pit or tower in which green fodder is stored **2.** a large, underground structure for storing and launching a long-range ballistic missile —*vt.* **-loed, -lo·ing** to store in a silo

**silt** (silt) *n.* [prob. < Scand.] earthy sediment made up of fine particles carried or laid down by moving water —*vt., vi.* to fill or choke up with silt —**sil·ta·tion** (sil tā′shən) *n.* —**silt′y** *adj.* **silt′i·er, silt′i·est**

**Si·lu·ri·an** (si loor′ē ən, sī-) *adj.* [< L. *Silures,* ancient tribe in Wales] designating or of the geological period after the Ordovician in the Paleozoic Era —**the Silurian** the Silurian Period or its rocks: see GEOLOGY, chart

**sil·va** (sil′və) *n.* [ModL. < L., a forest] **1.** the forest trees of an area **2.** *pl.* **-vas, -vae** (-vē) a book or treatise describing these

**sil·van** (sil′vən) *adj., n. same as* SYLVAN

**sil·ver** (sil′vər) *n.* [OE. *seolfer*] **1.** a white, metallic chemical element that is extremely ductile and malleable and takes a high polish: it is a precious metal and is used in coins, jewelry, etc.: symbol, Ag; at. wt., 107.868; at. no., 47 **2.** *a)* silver coin *b)* money; riches **3.** articles, esp. tableware, made of or plated with silver **4.** the lustrous, grayish-white color of silver **5.** something having this color, as the coating for a mirror —*adj.* **1.** of or containing silver; silvery **2.** of or advocating silver as a currency standard **3.** having a silvery color, tone, etc. **4.** eloquent [a *silver* tongue] **5.** marking the 25th anniversary [a *silver* wedding anniversary] —*vt.* **1.** to cover with silver **2.** to make silvery in color —*vi.* to become silvery

**silver birch** *same as* PAPER BIRCH

**silver certificate** formerly, a type of U.S. paper currency redeemable in silver

**sil·ver·fish** (-fish′) *n.* **1.** *pl.* **-fish′, -fish′es:** see FISH any of various unrelated fishes of silvery color **2.** *pl.* **-fish′** a wingless insect with silvery scales and long feelers, found in damp, dark places

**silver fox 1.** a N. American fox with white-tipped black fur **2.** this fur

**silver iodide** a yellow powder, AgI, that darkens in light: used in photography, to seed clouds, etc.

**silver lining** anything seen as hopeful or comforting in the midst of despair, misfortune, etc.

**silver nitrate** a colorless, crystalline salt, $AgNO_3$, used in silver-plating, photography, medicine, etc.

**sil·ver-plate** (-plāt′) *vt.* **-plat′ed, -plat′ing** to coat with silver, esp. by electroplating

**silver plate** tableware made of, or plated with, silver

**silver salmon** *same as* COHO

**sil·ver·side** (-sīd′) *n.* any of certain small, mostly saltwater fishes with silver stripes along the sides: also **sil′ver·sides′**

**sil·ver·smith** (-smith′) *n.* a skilled worker who makes articles of silver

**silver standard** a monetary standard in which the basic currency unit is made equal to and redeemable by a specified quantity of silver

**sil·ver·ware** (-wer′) *n.* **1.** articles, esp. tableware, made of or plated with silver **2.** any metal tableware

**sil·ver·y** (sil′vər ē) *adj.* **1.** like silver, as in color or luster **2.** covered with or containing silver **3.** soft and clear, like the sound of a silver bell —**sil′ver·i·ness** *n.*

**Sim·e·on** (sim′ē ən) *Bible* the second son of Jacob and Leah, or the tribe of Israel descended from him

**Simeon Sty·li·tes** (stī lī′tēz), **Saint** 390?–459? A.D.; Syrian monk who lived & preached on top of a pillar near Antioch, for over 30 years

**Sim·hat To·rah** (sim khät′ tō rä′, sim′khäs tō′rə) [< Heb., lit., rejoicing in the Torah] a Jewish festival in early fall marking the end of the annual cycle of Torah readings and the beginning of the next cycle: also sp. **Simchath Torah**

**sim·i·an** (sim′ē ən) *adj.* [< L. *simia,* an ape, prob. < *simus,* flat-nosed < Gr.] of or like an ape or monkey —*n.* an ape or monkey

**sim·i·lar** (sim′ə lər) *adj.* [< Fr. < L. *similis*] **1.** nearly but not exactly the same or alike **2.** *Geom.* having the same shape, but not the same size or position —**sim′i·lar·ly** *adv.*

**sim·i·lar·i·ty** (sim′ə lar′ə tē) *n.* **1.** a being similar; likeness **2.** *pl.* **-ties** a point, feature, or instance in which things are similar

**sim·i·le** (sim′ə lē) *n.* [L., a likeness < *similis,* like] a figure of speech in which one thing is likened to another, dissimilar thing by using *like, as,* etc. (Ex.: a voice like thunder): cf. METAPHOR

**si·mil·i·tude** (sə mil′ə tōōd′, -tyōōd′) *n.* [MFr. < L. *similitudo*] **1.** a person or thing resembling another; counterpart **2.** the form or likeness (*of* some person or thing) **3.** [Rare] a simile **4.** similarity; likeness

**Si·mi Valley** (sə mē′; *popularly,* sē′mē) [prob. < AmInd. *shimiji,* little white clouds] city in SW Calif., northwest of Los Angeles: pop. 78,000

**sim·mer** (sim′ər) *vi.* [of echoic origin] **1.** to remain at or just below the boiling point **2.** to be about to break out, as in anger, revolt, etc. —*vt.* **1.** to make (a liquid) simmer **2.** to cook in such a liquid —*n.* a simmering —**simmer down 1.** to simmer, as a liquid, until the volume is reduced **2.** to become calm; cool off

**Si·mon** (sī′mən) [LL. < Gr. < Heb. *shim'ōn,* lit., heard] **1.** a masculine name **2.** *Bible* one of the twelve apostles, called *Peter* or *Simon Peter*

**Simon Le·gree** (lə grē′) **1.** the villainous slave overseer in H. B. STOWE's novel *Uncle Tom's Cabin* **2.** any cruel taskmaster

**Simon Ma·gus** (mā′gəs) *Bible* a Samaritan magician who offered money for instruction in the rite of imparting the Holy Ghost: Acts 8:9–24

**si·mon-pure** (sī′mən pyoor′) *adj.* [after *Simon Pure,* a Quaker in S. Centlivre's play *A Bold Stroke for a Wife* (1718)] genuine; authentic

**si·mo·ny** (sī′mə nē, sim′ə-) *n.* [< OFr. < ML. *simonia* < SIMON MAGUS] the buying or selling of sacred or spiritual things, as church offices

**si·moom** (si mōōm′) *n.* [< Ar. < *samma,* to poison] a hot, violent, sand-laden wind of the African and Asiatic deserts: also **si·moon′** (-mōōn′)

**simp** (simp) *n. slang clipped form of* SIMPLETON

**sim·pa·ti·co** (sim pät′i kō, -pat′-) *adj.* [< It. *simpatico* or Sp. *simpático*] compatible or congenial

**sim·per** (sim′pər) *vi.* [akin to MDu. *simperlijc,* dainty, affected] to smile in a silly or affected way —*vt.* to say with a simper —*n.* a silly or affected smile —**sim′per·er** *n.* —**sim′per·ing·ly** *adv.*

**sim·ple** (sim′p'l) *adj.* **-pler, -plest** [OFr. < L. *simplex*] **1.** having only one part, feature, etc.; not compound or complex **2.** having few parts, etc.; not complicated or involved **3.** easy to do, solve, or understand, as a task, question, etc. **4.** without additions or qualifications [the *simple* facts] **5.** *a)* not ornate; unadorned [*simple* clothes] *b)* not luxurious; plain [*simple* tastes] **6.** pure; unadulterated **7.** without guile or deceit **8.** *a)* not showy or affected; natural *b)* not sophisticated; naive **9.** of low rank or position; lowly or ordinary **10.** insignificant; unimportant **11.** *a)* stupid or foolish *b)* uneducated or ignorant **12.** *Chem.* elementary or unmixed **13.** *Law* unconditional [in fee *simple*] **14.** *Zool.* not divided into parts; not compounded —*n.* **1.** an ignorant or foolish person **2.** something having only one part, substance, etc. **3.** [Archaic] a medicinal plant or herb, or a medicine made from it —**sim′ple·ness** *n.*

**simple fraction** a fraction in which both numerator and denominator are whole numbers, as 1/2

**simple fracture** a bone fracture in which the broken ends of bone do not pierce the skin

**sim·ple-heart·ed** (-härt′id) *adj.* artless or unsophisticated

**simple interest** interest computed on principal alone, not on principal plus interest

**simple machine** any of the basic mechanical devices, including the lever, wheel and axle, pulley, wedge, screw, and inclined plane, essential to any complex machine

**sim·ple-mind·ed** (-mīn′did) *adj.* **1.** artless; unsophisticated **2.** foolish; stupid; silly **3.** mentally retarded —**sim′ple-mind′ed·ly** *adv.* —**sim′ple-mind′ed·ness** *n.*

**simple sentence** a sentence having one main clause and no subordinate clauses (Ex.: The boy ran home.)

**sim·ple·ton** (sim′p'l tən) *n.* [< SIMPLE] a person who is stupid or easily deceived; fool

**sim·plic·i·ty** (sim plis′ə tē) *n., pl.* **-ties 1.** a being simple; freedom from complexity or intricacy **2.** absence of luxury, elegance, etc.; plainness **3.** freedom from affectation **4.** lack of sense; foolishness

**sim·pli·fy** (sim′plə fī′) *vt.* **-fied′, -fy′ing** to make simpler, easier, less complex, etc. —**sim′pli·fi·ca′tion** *n.* —**sim′pli·fi′er** *n.*

**sim·plist** (sim′plist) *n.* a person given to simplistic explanations, theories, etc. —*adj. same as* SIMPLISTIC —**sim′plism** *n.*

**sim·plis·tic** (sim plis′tik) *adj.* making complex problems seem to be simple; oversimplifying or oversimplified —**sim·plis′ti·cal·ly** *adv.*

**sim·ply** (sim′plē) *adv.* **1.** in a simple way **2.** merely; only [*simply* trying to help] **3.** absolutely; completely

**sim·u·la·crum** (sim'yoo lā'krəm) *n., pl.* **-cra** (-krə) [L. < *simulare:* see ff.] **1.** an image; likeness **2.** false appearance; semblance **3.** a mere pretense; sham

**sim·u·late** (sim'yoo lāt') *vt.* **-lat'ed, -lat'ing** [< L. pp. of *simulare*, to feign < *simul*, likewise] **1.** to give a false appearance of; feign [to *simulate* an interest] **2.** to look or act like [an insect *simulating* a twig] **—sim'u·la'tion** *n.* **—sim'u·la'tive** *adj.*

**sim·u·la·tor** (-lāt'ər) *n.* one that simulates; specif., a training device that duplicates artificially the conditions likely to be encountered in some operation, as in a spacecraft [a flight *simulator*]

**si·mul·cast** (sī'm'l kast') *vt.* **-cast'** or **-cast'ed, -cast'ing** [SIMUL(TANEOUS) + (BROAD)CAST] to broadcast (a program, event, etc.) simultaneously by radio and television **—** *n.* a program, etc. so broadcast

**si·mul·ta·ne·ous** (sī'm'l tā'nē əs, -tān'yəs) *adj.* [< ML., ult. < L. *simul*, at the same time] occurring, done, existing, etc. together or at the same time **—si'mul·ta·ne'i·ty** (-tə nē'ə tē), **si'mul·ta'ne·ous·ness** *n.* **—si'mul·ta'ne·ous·ly** *adv.*

**sin** (sin) *n.* [OE. *synne*] **1.** *a)* the breaking of religious or moral law, esp. through a willful act *b)* the state of committing sins **2.** any offense or fault **—** *vi.* **sinned, sin'ning** to commit a sin

**sin** sine

**Si·nai** (sī'nī; *occas.* sī'ni ī'), **Mount** *Bible* the mountain where Moses received the Law from God: Ex. 19

**Sinai Peninsula** broad peninsula in NE Egypt, between the Gulf of Suez & an E arm of the Red Sea

**since** (sins) *adv.* [< OE. *siththan*, ult. < *sith*, after + *thon*, instrumental form of *thæt*, that] **1.** from then until now [he came Monday and has been here ever *since*] **2.** at some or any time between then and now [he was ill last week but has *since* recovered] **3.** before now; ago [gone long *since*] **—prep. 1.** continuously from (the time given) until now [out walking *since* noon] **2.** during the period following [he's written twice *since* May] **—conj. 1.** after the time that [two years *since* he died] **2.** continuously from the time when [lonely ever *since* he left] **3.** inasmuch as; because [*since* you're tired, let's go home]

**sin·cere** (sin sir') *adj.* **-cer'er, -cer'est** [< MFr. < L. *sincerus*, clean] **1.** without deceit or pretense; truthful; honest **2.** genuine; real [*sincere* grief] **—sin·cere'ly** *adv.*

**sin·cer·i·ty** (sin ser'ə tē) *n., pl.* **-ties** a being sincere; honesty, genuineness, etc.

**Sin·clair** (sin klār'), **Up·ton** (**Beall, Jr.**) (up't'n) 1878–1968; U.S. novelist & socialist

**Sind** (sind) region in S Pakistan, in the Indus valley

**sine** (sīn) *n.* [ML. *sinus* (< L., a curve), used as transl. of Ar. *jaib*, bosom of a garment] *Trigonometry* the ratio between the side opposite a given acute angle in a right triangle and the hypotenuse

**‡si·ne** (sī'nē, sē'nä) *prep.* [L.] without

**si·ne·cure** (sī'nə kyoor, sin'ə-) *n.* [< ML. < L. *sine*, without + *cura*, care] **1.** a church benefice not involving spiritual care of members **2.** any position that brings profit without involving much work, responsibility, etc.

**si·ne di·e** (sī'nē dī'ē, sin'ā dē'ā) [LL.] without (a) day (being set for meeting again); for an indefinite period

**si·ne qua non** (sī'nē kwä nän', sin'ā kwä nōn') [L., without which not] something essential or indispensable

**sin·ew** (sin'yoo) *n.* [OE. *seonwe*, oblique form < nom. *seonu*] **1.** a tendon **2.** muscular power; strength **3.** [*often pl.*] any source of power **—vt.** to strengthen as with sinews

**sin·ew·y** (-yoo wē) *adj.* **1.** of or like sinew; tough **2.** having many sinews, as a cut of meat **3.** having good muscular development **4.** vigorous; powerful

**sin·ful** (sin'fəl) *adj.* full of or characterized by sin; wicked **—sin'ful·ly** *adv.* **—sin'ful·ness** *n.*

**sing** (siŋ) *vi.* **sang** or now rarely **sung, sung, sing'ing** [OE. *singan*] **1.** *a)* to produce musical sounds with the voice *b)* to perform musical selections vocally **2.** to use song in description, praise, etc. [of thee I *sing*] **3.** *a)* to make musical sounds like those of the human voice, as a songbird *b)* to whistle, buzz, hum, etc., as a teakettle, bee, etc. **4.** to admit of being sung **5.** to rejoice [his heart *sang*] **—vt. 1.** to render or utter by singing **2.** to chant **3.** to describe, proclaim, etc. in song **4.** to bring or put, as to sleep, by singing **—n. 1.** a sound of whistling, humming, etc. **2.** [Colloq.] *a)* a singing by a group gathered for the purpose *b)* the group **—sing out** [Colloq.] to speak or call out loudly **—sing'a·ble** *adj.* **—sing'er** *n.*

**sing.** singular

**sing-a·long** (siŋ'ə lôŋ') *n.* [Colloq.] an informal gathering of people to join in the singing of songs

**Sin·ga·pore** (siŋ'gə pôr', siŋ'ə-) **1.** island country off the S tip of the Malay Peninsula: a member of the Commonwealth: 225 sq. mi.; pop. 2,110,000 **2.** its capital, a seaport: pop. c.1,000,000

**singe** (sinj) *vt.* **singed, singe'ing** [OE. *sengan*] **1.** to burn superficially or slightly **2.** to expose (a carcass) to flame in removing bristles or feathers **—** *n.* a slight burn

**Sin·gha·lese** (siŋ'gə lēz', -lēs') *adj., n., pl.* **-lese'** same as SINHALESE

**sin·gle** (siŋ'g'l) *adj.* [< OFr. < L. *singulus*] **1.** *a)* one only; one and no more *b)* distinct from others of the same kind [every *single* time] **2.** without another; alone **3.** of or for one person or family, as a house **4.** between two persons only [*single* combat] **5.** unmarried **6.** having only one part; not double, compound, etc. **7.** uniform **8.** unbroken **9.** having only one set of petals **10.** sincere **—vt. -gled, -gling** to select from others (usually with *out*) **—vi.** *Baseball* to hit a single **—n. 1.** a single person or thing; specif., *a)* a hotel room, a ticket, etc. for one person *b)* [Colloq.] a one-dollar bill **2.** *Baseball* a hit by which the batter reaches first base **3.** *Cricket* a hit by which one run is scored **4.** [*pl.*] *Tennis*, etc. a match with only one player on each side **—sin'gle·ness** *n.*

**sin·gle-breast·ed** (-bres'tid) *adj.* overlapping over the breast just enough to be fastened with one button or one row of buttons, as a coat

**single entry** a system of bookkeeping in which a single account is kept, usually of cash and of debts owed to and by the concern in question

**single file 1.** a single column of persons or things, one directly behind another **2.** in such a column

**sin·gle-foot** (-foot') *n.* the gait of a horse in which the legs move in lateral pairs, each foot falling separately

**sin·gle-hand·ed** (-han'did) *adj.* **1.** having only one hand **2.** using or requiring the use of only one hand **3.** done or working alone **—adv. 1.** by means of only one hand **2.** without help **—sin'gle-hand'ed·ly** *adv.*

**sin·gle-heart·ed** (-här'tid) *adj.* honest; sincere **—sin'gle-heart'ed·ly** *adv.* **—sin'gle-heart'ed·ness** *n.*

**sin·gle-mind·ed** (-mīn'did) *adj.* **1.** same as SINGLE-HEARTED **2.** with only one aim or purpose **—sin'gle-mind'ed·ly** *adv.* **—sin'gle-mind'ed·ness** *n.*

**sin·gle-space** (-spās') *vt., vi.* **-spaced', -spac'ing** to type (copy) so as to leave no line space between lines

**single standard** a moral code with the same standard for men and women alike, esp. in matters of sex

**sin·gle·stick** (-stik') *n.* **1.** a swordlike stick formerly used for fencing **2.** the sport of fencing with such sticks

**sin·glet** (siŋ'glit) *n.* [Brit.] a man's undershirt or jersey

**single tax** **1.** a system of taxation with only one tax, as on the value of land **2.** such a tax **—sin'gle-tax'** *adj.*

**sin·gle·ton** (siŋ'g'l tən) *n.* **1.** the only playing card held by a player in a given suit **2.** a single thing, all by itself

**sin·gle·tree** (-trē') *n.* [< earlier *swingletree* < ME. *swingle*, a rod + *tre*, a tree] a pivoted crossbar at the front of a wagon, etc., to which the traces of a horse's harness are hooked

**sin·gly** (siŋ'glē) *adv.* **1.** as a single, separate person or thing; alone **2.** one by one **3.** without help; unaided

**Sing Sing** (siŋ'siŋ') a N.Y. State penitentiary at Ossining

**sing·song** (siŋ'sôŋ', -säŋ') *n.* **1.** *a)* an unvarying rise and fall of tone *b)* speech, tones, etc. marked by this **2.** *a)* monotonous rhyme or rhythm in verse *b)* verse with this **—adj.** monotonous because done in singsong

**sin·gu·lar** (siŋ'gyə lər) *adj.* [< OFr. < L. *singulus*, single] **1.** being the only one of its kind; unique **2.** extraordinary; remarkable [*singular* beauty] **3.** strange; odd [a *singular* remark] **4.** [Archaic] separate; individual **5.** *Gram.* designating or of that category of number referring to only one **—n.** *Gram.* **1.** the singular number **2.** the singular form of a word **3.** a word in singular form **—sin'gu·lar'i·ty** (-lar'ə tē) *n., pl.* **-ties** **—sin'gu·lar·ly** *adv.*

**sin·gu·lar·ize** (siŋ'gyə lə rīz') *vt.* **-ized', -iz'ing** to make singular

**Sin·ha·lese** (sin'hə lēz', sin'ə-; -lēs') *adj.* of Ceylon, its principal people, their language, etc. **—n. 1.** *pl.* **-lese'** any member of the Sinhalese people **2.** their language

**sin·is·ter** (sin'is tər) *adj.* [< L. *sinister*, left-hand or unlucky (side)] **1.** of or on the left-hand side (on a coat of arms, the right of the viewer) **2.** threatening harm, evil, etc.; ominous **3.** evil or dishonest, esp. in a dark, mysterious way [a *sinister* plot] **4.** unfortunate or disastrous [a *sinister* fate] **—sin'is·ter·ly** *adv.* **—sin'is·ter·ness** *n.*

**sin·is·tral** (sin'is trəl) *adj.* [OFr. < L.: see prec.] **1.** on the left-hand side; left **2.** left-handed

**sin·is·trorse** (sin'is trôrs') *adj.* [< ModL. < L. < *sinister,* left + pp. of *vertere,* to turn] *Bot.* twining upward to the left, as the stems of some vines

**Si·nit·ic** (si nit'ik) *n.* [see SINO-, -ITE, & -IC] a branch of Sino-Tibetan, including Chinese languages —*adj.* of China, the Chinese, their languages, etc.

**sink** (siŋk) *vi.* sank or sunk, sunk or obs. sunk'en, sink'ing [OE. *sincan*] **1.** to go beneath the surface of water, snow, etc. and be partly or completely covered **2.** *a)* to go down slowly *b)* to seem to descend, as the sun **3.** to become lower in level, as a lake **4.** to decrease in degree, volume, or strength, as wind, flames, a sound, etc. **5.** to become less in value or amount, as prices **6.** to become hollow; recede, as the cheeks **7.** to pass gradually (*into* sleep, despair, etc.) **8.** to become increasingly and dangerously ill; fail **9.** *a)* to lose social position, wealth, etc. *b)* to lose or abandon one's moral values and stoop (*to* an unworthy action) **10.** to become absorbed; penetrate —*vt.* **1.** to cause to sink; make go beneath a surface, make go down, make lower, etc. **2.** to make (a well, engraved design, etc.) by digging, drilling, or cutting **3.** *a)* to invest (money, capital, etc.) *b)* to lose by investing **4.** to hold back, suppress, or conceal (evidence, identity, etc.) **5.** to pay up (a debt) **6.** to defeat; undo; ruin **7.** *Sports* to put (a basketball) through the basket or (a golf ball) into the hole, and so score —*n.* **1.** a cesspool or sewer **2.** any place or thing considered morally filthy or corrupted **3.** a basin, as in a kitchen, with a drainpipe and, usually, a water supply **4.** *Geol. a)* an area of slightly sunken land, esp. one in which water collects *b)* same as SINKHOLE (sense 2) —**sink in** [Colloq.] to be grasped by the mind, esp. with difficulty —**sink'a·ble** *adj.*

**sink·er** (siŋ'kər) *n.* **1.** a person or thing that sinks **2.** a lead weight for fishing **3.** [Colloq.] a doughnut

**sink·hole** (siŋk'hōl') *n.* **1.** same as CESSPOOL **2.** *Geol.* a hollow into which surface water flows and sinks

**Sin·kiang** (sin'kyaŋ'; *Chin.* shin'jyäŋ') autonomous region of NW China, between Tibet & U.S.S.R.: 635,830 sq. mi.

**sinking fund** a fund made up of sums of money set aside at intervals, usually invested at interest, to pay a debt, meet expenses, etc.

**sin·less** (sin'lis) *adj.* without sin; innocent —**sin'less·ly** *adv.* —**sin'less·ness** *n.*

**sin·ner** (-ər) *n.* a person who sins; wrongdoer

**Sinn Fein** (shin' fān') [Ir., we ourselves] an early 20th-cent. Irish revolutionary movement working for independence and to revive Irish culture —**Sinn' Fein'er**

**Si·no-** [< Fr. < LL. < Gr. *Sinai,* an Oriental people] a combining form meaning: **1.** of the Chinese people or language **2.** Chinese and

**Si·nol·o·gy** (sī näl'ə jē, si-) *n.* [SINO- + -LOGY] the study of Chinese languages, customs, etc. —**Si·no·log·i·cal** (sī'nə läj'i k'l, sin'ə-) *adj.* —**Si·nol'o·gist** *n.*

**Si·no-Ti·bet·an** (sī'nō ti bet''n, sin'ō-) *adj.* designating or of a family of languages of C and SE Asia, including Sinitic, Tibetan, and Burmese —*n.* this family

**sin·u·ate** (sin'yoo wit; *also, and for v. always,* -wāt') *adj.* [< L. pp. of *sinuare,* to bend < *sinus,* a bend] **1.** same as SINUOUS **2.** *Bot.* having an indented, wavy margin, as some leaves —*vi.* **-at'ed, -at'ing** to wind in and out —**sin'u·ate·ly** *adv.* —**sin'u·a'tion** *n.*

**sin·u·ous** (sin'yoo wəs) *adj.* [< L. < *sinus,* a bend] **1.** bending or winding in and out **2.** not straightforward; devious —**sin'u·os'i·ty** (-wäs'ə tē) *n., pl.* **-ties** —**sin'u·ous·ly** *adv.*

**si·nus** (sī'nəs) *n.* [L., a bent surface] **1.** a bend or curve **2.** a cavity, hollow, or passage; specif., *Anat., Zool. a)* any air cavity in the skull opening into a nasal cavity *b)* a channel for venous blood **3.** a channel leading from a pus-filled cavity

**si·nus·i·tis** (sī'nə sīt'əs) *n.* [ModL.: see prec. & -ITIS] inflammation of a sinus or sinuses, esp. of the nasal

**si·nu·soi·dal projection** (sī'nə soi'd'l) [< ML. *sinus* < L.: see SINUS] a map projection showing the entire surface of the earth, with straight lines of latitude and curved lines of longitude

**Si·on** (sī'ən) *var. of* ZION

**-sion** (shən; *sometimes* zhən) [< L. *-sio*] a suffix meaning act, quality, condition, or result of [*discussion, confusion*]

**Siou·an** (soō'ən) *adj.* designating or of a language family of N. American Indians of the west central U.S., central Canada, etc.: it includes Dakota, Crow, etc. —*n.* this family of languages

**Sioux** (soō) *n., pl.* **Sioux** (soō, soōz) [Fr. < Ojibway dim. of *nadowe,* an adder, hence, an enemy] *same as* DAKOTA¹ (*n.* 1 & 2) —*adj. same as* DAKOTA¹ (*adj.* 1)

**Sioux City** city in W Iowa, on the Missouri River: pop. 82,000

**Sioux Falls** city in SE S.Dak.: pop. 81,000

**sip** (sip) *vt., vi.* **sipped, sip'ping** [akin to LowG. *sippen*] to drink a little at a time —*n.* **1.** a sipping **2.** a small quantity sipped —**sip'per** *n.*

**si·phon** (sī'fən) *n.* [Fr. < L. < Gr. *siphōn,* a tube] **1.** a bent tube for carrying liquid out over the edge of a container to a lower level through the atmospheric pressure on the surface of the liquid **2.** *same as* SIPHON BOTTLE **3.** a tubelike organ, as in a cuttlefish, for drawing in or ejecting liquids —*vt., vi.* to draw off, or pass, through a siphon —**si'phon·al** (-'l), **si·phon'ic** (-fän'ik) *adj.*

SIPHON

**siphon bottle** a heavy, sealed bottle with a tube inside connected at the top with a valve and nozzle used to release the pressurized, carbonated water within

**sir** (sur) *n.* [< *sire:* see ff.] **1.** [*sometimes* S-] a respectful term of address used to a man: not followed by the name: often used in the salutation of a letter **2.** [S-] the title used before the name of a knight or baronet **3.** [Archaic] a term of address used with the title of a man's office, etc. [*sir judge*]

**sire** (sīr) *n.* [< OFr., a master < L. *senior:* see SENIOR] **1.** a title of respect used in addressing a king **2.** [Poet.] a father or forefather **3.** the male parent of an animal —*vt.* **sired, sir'ing** to beget: said esp. of animals

**si·ren** (sī'rən) *n.* [< OFr., ult. < Gr. *Seirēn*] **1.** *Gr. & Rom. Myth.* any of several sea nymphs who lured sailors to their death on rocky coasts by seductive singing **2.** a seductive woman **3.** a device using steam or air driven against a rotating, perforated disk to make a loud, wailing sound, esp. as a warning signal —*adj.* of or like a siren; dangerously seductive

**Sir·i·us** (sir'ē əs) [L. < Gr. *Seirios,* lit., the scorcher] *same as* DOG STAR (sense 1)

**sir·loin** (sur'loin) *n.* [< MFr. < OFr. *sur,* over < *loigne,* loin] a choice cut, esp. of beef, from the loin end just in front of the rump

**si·roc·co** (sə räk'ō) *n., pl.* **-cos** [It. < Ar. *sharq,* the east] **1.** a hot, steady wind blowing from the Libyan deserts into S Europe **2.** any wind like this

**sir·rah, sir·ra** (sir'ə) *n.* [< SIR] [Archaic] a contemptuous term of address used to a man

**sir·ree, sir·ee** (sə rē') *interj.* [< SIR] an interjection used for emphasis after *yes* or *no*

**sis** (sis) *n. colloq.* shortened form of SISTER

**si·sal** (sī's'l) *n.* [< *Sisal,* Yucatán, a former seaport] **1.** a strong fiber obtained from a widely cultivated agave native to S Mexico, used for making rope, insulation, etc. **2.** the agave itself Also **sisal hemp**

**sis·sy** (sis'ē) *n., pl.* **-sies** [dim. of SIS] **1.** [Colloq.] *a)* an effeminate man or boy *b)* a coward **2.** [Slang] a homosexual —*adj.* [Colloq.] of or like a sissy: also **sis'si·fied'** (-ə fīd') —**sis'sy·ish** *adj.*

**sis·ter** (sis'tər) *n.* [ON. *systir*] **1.** a female as she is related to other children of her parents **2.** a close friend who is like a sister **3.** a female fellow member of the same race, creed, profession, organization, etc. **4.** a member of a female religious order; nun **5.** one of the same kind, model, etc. **6.** [Brit.] a nurse, esp. a head nurse —*adj.* related as sisters

**sis·ter·hood** (-hood') *n.* **1.** the state of being a sister or sisters **2.** an association of women united in a common interest, work, creed, etc.

**sis·ter-in-law** (-in lô') *n., pl.* **sis'ters-in-law'** **1.** the sister of one's husband or wife **2.** the wife of one's brother **3.** the wife of the brother of one's husband or wife

**sis·ter·ly** (-lē) *adj.* **1.** of or like a sister **2.** friendly, kind, affectionate, etc. —**sis'ter·li·ness** *n.*

**Sis·tine Chapel** (sis'tēn) [< It. (after Pope *Sixtus* IV)] the principal chapel in the Vatican, with frescoes by Michelangelo

**Sis·y·phus** (sis'ə fəs) *Gr. Myth.* a greedy king doomed forever in Hades to roll uphill a heavy stone which always rolled down again

**sit** (sit) *vi.* **sat, sit'ting** [OE. *sittan*] **1.** *a)* to rest the body on the buttocks, as on a chair *b)* to rest on the haunches with forelegs braced, as a dog *c)* to perch, as a bird **2.** to cover eggs for hatching **3.** *a)* to occupy a seat as a judge, legislator, etc. *b)* to be in session, as a court **4.** to pose, as for a portrait **5.** to be inactive **6.** to be located [a house *sitting* on a hill] **7.** to hang on the wearer [a coat *sitting* loosely] **8.** to rest or lie as specified [cares sit lightly on him] **9.** *same as* BABY-SIT —*vt.* **1.** to cause to sit **2.** to stay seated on (a horse, etc.) **3.** to have seating space for —*n.* [Colloq.] the time spent seated —**sit back** **1.** to relax **2.** to be passive —**sit down** to take a seat —**sit in** to take part; attend (often with *on*) —**sit on** (or **upon**) **1.** to be on (a jury, committee, etc.) **2.** to confer on **3.** [Colloq.] to suppress, squelch, etc. —**sit out** **1.** to stay until the end of **2.** to stay seated during or take no part in (a dance, game, etc.) —**sit up** **1.** to rise to a sitting position **2.** to sit erect **3.** to put off going to bed **4.** [Colloq.] to become suddenly alert —**sit well with** to be agreeable to

**si·tar** (si tär′) *n.* [Hindi *sitār*] a lutelike instrument of India with a long, fretted neck, a resonating gourd or gourds, and strings that vibrate along with those being played —**si·tar′ist** *n.*

**sit·com** (sit′käm′) *n.* [Colloq.] *short for* SITUATION COMEDY

**sit-down** (sit′doun′) *n.* **1.** a strike in which strikers stay inside a factory, etc. refusing to work until agreement is reached: in full, **sit-down strike 2.** a form of civil disobedience in which demonstrators sit down in streets, etc. and resist being moved —**sit′-down′er** *n.*

SITAR

**site** (sīt) *n.* [< L. *situs*, position < pp. of *sinere*, to put down] **1.** a piece of land considered for a certain purpose [a good *site* for a town] **2.** the place or scene of anything —*vt.* **sit′ed, sit′ing** to locate on a site

**sith** (sith) *adv., conj., prep.* [OE. *siththa*] *archaic form of* SINCE

**sit-in** (sit′in′) *n.* a sit-down inside a public place by a group demonstrating for civil rights, against war, etc.

**sit·ter** (sit′ər) *n.* one that sits; specif., *a*) *short for* BABY SITTER *b*) a brooding hen

**sit·ting** (sit′iŋ) *n.* **1.** the act or position of one that sits **2.** a session or meeting, as of a court **3.** a period of being seated at some activity **4.** *a*) a brooding upon eggs *b*) a clutch of eggs being hatched —*adj.* that sits; seated

**Sitting Bull** 1834?-90; Sioux Indian chief whose tribe annihilated the attacking troops of General Custer (1876)

**sitting room** *same as* LIVING ROOM

**sit·u·ate** (sich′ōō wāt′) *vt.* **-at′ed, -at′ing** [< ML. pp. of *situare*, to place < L. *situs*, SITE] to put in a certain place or position; place; locate

**sit·u·at·ed** (-id) *adj.* **1.** placed as to site or position; located **2.** placed as to circumstances

**sit·u·a·tion** (sich′ōō wā′shən) *n.* **1.** location; position **2.** a place; locality **3.** condition with regard to circumstances **4.** *a*) a combination of circumstances at a given time in real life or in the plot of a play, novel, etc. *b*) a difficult state of affairs **5.** a position of employment

**sit·u·a·tion·al** (-'l) *adj.* of, resulting from, or adjusted to fit a specific situation —**sit′u·a′tion·al·ly** *adv.*

**situation comedy** a comedy, esp. a comic television series, made up of contrived episodes involving stock characters

**sit-up, sit·up** (sit′up′) *n.* an exercise in which a person lying flat on the back rises to a sitting position without using the hands and keeping the legs straight

**sitz bath** (sits, zits) [< G. *sitzbad*, a sitting bath] **1.** a bath in which only the hips and buttocks are covered **2.** the tub or basin for this

**Si·va** (sē′və, shē′-) Hindu god of destruction and reproduction, a member of the supreme Hindu trinity: see BRAHMA, VISHNU —**Si′va·ism** *n.* —**Si′va·is′tic** *adj.*

**Si·van** (sē vän′, siv′ən) *n.* [Heb.] the ninth month of the Jewish year: see JEWISH CALENDAR

**six** (siks) *adj.* [OE. *sex*] totaling one more than five —*n.* **1.** the cardinal number between five and seven; 6; VI **2.** a group of six; half a dozen **3.** anything having six units or members, or numbered six —**at sixes and sevens** [Colloq.] **1.** in confusion or disorder **2.** disagreeing

**six·fold** (-fōld′) *adj.* [see -FOLD] **1.** having six parts **2.** having six times as much or as many —*adv.* six times as much or as many

**six·pence** (-pəns) *n.* **1.** the sum of six British (old) pennies **2.** a British coin of this value, discontinued (1971)

**six·pen·ny** (-pen′ē, -pə nē) *adj.* **1.** worth or costing sixpence **2.** designating a size of nails, two inches long

**six-shoot·er** (-shōōt′ər) *n.* [Colloq.] a revolver that fires six shots without reloading: also **six′-gun′**

**six·teen** (siks′tēn′) *adj.* [OE. *syxtene*] six more than ten —*n.* the cardinal number between fifteen and seventeen; 16; XVI

**six·teenth** (siks′tēnth′) *adj.* **1.** preceded by fifteen others in a series; 16th **2.** designating any of the sixteen equal parts of something —*n.* **1.** the one following the fifteenth **2.** any of the sixteen equal parts of something; 1/16

**sixteenth note** *Music* a note having one sixteenth the duration of a whole note: see NOTE, illus.

**sixth** (siksth) *adj.* [OE. *sixta*] **1.** preceded by five others in a series; 6th **2.** designating any of the six equal parts of something —*n.* **1.** the one following the fifth **2.** any of the six equal parts of something; 1/6 **3.** *Music a*) the sixth tone of an ascending diatonic scale, or a tone five degrees above or below any given tone *b*) the interval between two such tones, or a combination of them —**sixth′ly** *adv.*

**sixth sense** a power to perceive by intuition, thought of as a sense in addition to the commonly accepted five senses

**six·ti·eth** (siks′tē ith) *adj.* **1.** preceded by fifty-nine others in a series; 60th **2.** designating any of the sixty equal parts of something —*n.* **1.** the one following the fifty-ninth **2.** any of the sixty equal parts of something; 1/60

**six·ty** (siks′tē) *adj.* [OE. *sixtig*] six times ten —*n., pl.* **-ties** the cardinal number between fifty-nine and sixty-one; 60; LX —**the sixties** the numbers or years, as of a century, from sixty through sixty-nine

**six·ty-fourth note** (-fôrth′) *Music* a note having one sixty-fourth the duration of a whole note: see NOTE, illus.

**siz·a·ble** (sī′zə b'l) *adj.* quite large or bulky: also **size′a·ble** —**siz′a·ble·ness** *n.* —**siz′a·bly** *adv.*

**size**[1] (sīz) *n.* [< OFr. *sise*, short for *assise*: see ASSIZE] **1.** that quality of a thing which determines how much space it occupies; dimensions **2.** any of a series of graded classifications for goods [*size* ten shoes] **3.** *a*) extent, amount, etc. *b*) sizable amount, dimensions, etc. **4.** ability to meet needs **5.** [Colloq.] true state of affairs —*vt.* **sized, siz′ing** to make or arrange according to size —**of a size** of one or the same size —**size up** [Colloq.] to estimate; judge

**size**[2] (sīz) *n.* [ME. *syse*] any thin, pasty or gluey substance used as a glaze or filler on porous materials, as on paper or cloth —*vt.* **sized, siz′ing** to apply size to

**-sized** (sīzd) *a combining form meaning* having (a specified) size [small-*sized*] : also **-size** [life-*size*]

**siz·ing** (sī′ziŋ) *n.* **1.** *same as* SIZE[2] **2.** the act or process of applying such size

**siz·zle** (siz′'l) *vi.* **-zled, -zling** [echoic] **1.** to make a hissing sound when in contact with heat **2.** to be extremely hot **3.** to simmer with suppressed rage —*n.* a sizzling sound

**S.J.** Society of Jesus

**Skag·er·rak** (skag′ə rak′) arm of the North Sea, between Norway & Denmark

**skald** (skôld, skäld) *n.* [ON. *skāld*] any ancient Scandinavian poet, specif. of the Viking period —**skald′ic** *adj.*

**skate**[1] (skāt) *n.* [assumed sing. < Du. *schaats*, a skate < ONormFr. < OFr. *eschace*, stilt < Frank.] **1.** *a*) a bladelike metal runner in a frame to be fastened to a shoe, used for gliding on ice *b*) a shoe with this attached Also **ice skate 2.** a frame or shoe with two pairs of small wheels, for gliding on a sidewalk, etc.: also **roller skate 3.** a skating —*vi.* **skat′ed, skat′ing** to move along on skates —**skat′er** *n.*

**skate**[2] (skāt) *n., pl.* **skates, skate**: see PLURAL, II, D, 1 [ON. *skata*] any of various rays with a broad, flat body and short, spineless tail

**skate·board** (skāt′bôrd′) *n.* a short, oblong board with two wheels at each end, which one rides on, usually while standing —*vi.* **-board′ed, -board′ing** to ride on a skateboard

**ske·dad·dle** (ski dad′'l) *vi.* **-dled, -dling** [coinage of Civil War period] [Colloq.] to run off; leave fast

**skeet** (skēt) *n.* [ult. < ON. *skeyti*, a projectile] trapshooting done from different angles, usually eight

**skein** (skān) *n.* [< MFr. *escaigne*] **1.** a quantity of thread or yarn wound in a coil **2.** a coil of hair, etc.

**skel·e·ton** (skel′ə t'n) *n.* [ModL. < Gr. *skeleton* (*sōma*), dried (body) < *skeletos*, dried up] **1.** the hard framework of an animal, supporting the tissues and protecting the organs; specif., all the bones or bony framework of a human being or other vertebrate **2.** anything like a skeleton; specif., *a*) a very lean or thin person or animal *b*) a supporting framework, as of a ship *c*) an outline, as of a novel —*adj.* of or like a skeleton; greatly reduced [a *skeleton* force] —**skeleton in the closet** some fact, as about a relative, kept secret because of shame —**skel′e·tal** (-t'l) *adj.*

**skel·e·ton·ize** (-īz′) *vt.* **-ized′, -iz′ing 1.** to reduce to a skeleton **2.** to outline **3.** to reduce greatly in number or size

**skeleton key** a key with much of the bit filed away so that it can open any of various simple locks

**skep·tic** (skep′tik) *adj.* [< L. < Gr. *skeptikos*, inquiring] *var. of*

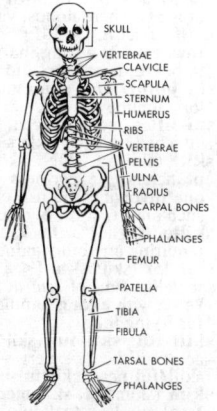

SKULL
VERTEBRAE
CLAVICLE
SCAPULA
STERNUM
HUMERUS
RIBS
VERTEBRAE
PELVIS
ULNA
RADIUS
CARPAL BONES
PHALANGES
FEMUR
PATELLA
TIBIA
FIBULA
TARSAL BONES
PHALANGES

HUMAN SKELETON

**SKEPTICAL** —*n.* **1.** [S-] a member of any of the ancient Greek philosophical schools that denied the possibility of real knowledge **2.** a believer in philosophical skepticism **3.** one who habitually doubts or questions matters generally accepted **4.** one who doubts religious doctrines
**skep·ti·cal** (skep′ti k'l) *adj.* **1.** of or characteristic of skeptics or skepticism **2.** not easily convinced; doubting; questioning **3.** doubting the fundamental doctrines of religion —**skep′ti·cal·ly** *adv.*
**skep·ti·cism** (-siz′m) *n.* **1.** [S-] the doctrines of the ancient Greek Skeptics **2.** the philosophical doctrine that the truth of all knowledge must always be in question **3.** skeptical attitude; doubt, esp. about religious doctrines
**sketch** (skech) *n.* [Du. *schets* < It. *schizzo* < L. < Gr. *schedios*, extempore] **1.** a simple, rough drawing or design, done rapidly **2.** a brief plan; outline **3.** a short, light, informal story, description, skit, etc. —*vt., vi.* to make a sketch (of) —**sketch′a·ble** *adj.* —**sketch′er** *n.*
**sketch·book** (-book′) *n.* **1.** a book of drawing paper for making sketches **2.** a book of literary sketches Also **sketch book**
**sketch·y** (-ē) *adj.* **sketch′i·er, sketch′i·est 1.** having the form of a sketch; not detailed **2.** not complete; inadequate —**sketch′i·ly** *adv.* —**sketch′i·ness** *n.*
**skew** (skyo̅o̅) *vi.* [< ONormFr. *eskiuer*, altered < OFr. < OHG.: see ESCHEW] **1.** to take a slanting course; swerve or twist **2.** to glance sideways (*at*) —*vt.* **1.** to make slanting or oblique **2.** to bias or distort —*adj.* **1.** slanting; oblique **2.** not symmetrical —*n.* **1.** a slant or twist **2.** a slanting part or movement —**skew′ness** *n.*
**skew·er** (skyo̅o̅′ər) *n.* [< ON. *skifa*, a slice] **1.** a long pin used to hold meat together while cooking or as a brochette **2.** any similar pin or rod —*vt.* to fasten or pierce as with skewers
**ski** (skē; *Brit. also* shē) *n., pl.* **skis, ski** [Norw. < ON. *skith*, snowshoe, strip of wood] **1.** either of a pair of long, thin runners of wood, metal, etc., fastened to the shoes for gliding over snow **2.** a water ski: see WATER-SKI —*vi.* **skied** (skēd), **ski′ing 1.** to glide on skis, as down snow-covered hills **2.** *short for* WATER-SKI —**ski′er** *n.*

SKEWERS

**skid** (skid) *n.* [prob. < ON. *skith*: see SKI] **1.** a plank, log, etc. used as a support or as a track to slide or roll a heavy object on **2.** a low, movable platform for holding loads or stacks **3.** [*pl.*] a protective wooden fender put against the side of a ship **4.** a runner in place of a wheel on some aircraft landing gear **5.** a sliding wedge or drag used to check a vehicle's motion by pressure against a wheel **6.** a skidding —*vt.* **skid′ded, skid′ding 1.** to brake or lock (a wheel) with a skid **2.** to support or move on skids **3.** to cause (a wheel, vehicle, etc.) to skid —*vi.* **1.** to slide without turning, as a wheel when brakes are applied on a slippery surface **2.** to slide, as a vehicle not controlled on an icy road **3.** to decline sharply, as prices —**be on** (or **hit**) **the skids** [Slang] to be on the downgrade —**put the skids on** (or **under**) [Slang] to thwart or cause to fail —**skid′der** *n.*
**skid·dy** (-ē) *adj.* **-di·er, -di·est** having a slippery surface on which vehicles are liable to skid
**skid row** [altered < *skid road*, a trail for dragging logs, hence a section of town where loggers gathered] a section of a city where hobos, vagrants, derelicts, etc. gather
**skiff** (skif) *n.* [< MFr. < It. *schifo* < Gmc.] **1.** any light rowboat **2.** a long, narrow rowboat, esp. one with a centerboard, outrigger, and a small sail
**ski jump 1.** a jump made by a skier after skiing down a long incline or track **2.** such an incline or track
**ski lift** a motor-driven, endless cable, typically with seats attached, to carry skiers up a slope
**skill** (skil) *n.* [ON. *skil*, distinction] **1.** great ability or proficiency; expertness **2.** an art, craft, or science, esp. one involving the use of the hands or body **3.** ability in such an art, craft, or science
**skilled** (skild) *adj.* **1.** having skill; skillful **2.** having or requiring an ability gained by special experience or training
**skil·let** (skil′it) *n.* [< ? OFr. dim. of *escuelle*, basin < L. *scutella*, dim. of *scutra*, a dish] **1.** [Chiefly Brit.] a pot or kettle with a long handle **2.** a shallow pan with a handle, for frying food
**skill·ful, skil·ful** (skil′fəl) *adj.* having or showing skill; accomplished; expert —**skill′ful·ly, skil′ful·ly** *adv.* —**skill′ful·ness, skil′ful·ness** *n.*
**skim** (skim) *vt.* **skimmed, skim′ming** [prob. akin to SCUM] **1.** *a)* to clear (a liquid) of floating matter *b)* to remove (floating matter) from a liquid **2.** to coat with a thin layer [a pond *skimmed* with ice] **3.** to look through (a book, etc.) hastily **4.** *a)* to glide swiftly over *b)* to throw so as to make ricochet lightly [*skim* a flat stone across water] —*vi.* **1.** to move along swiftly and lightly; glide **2.** to read hastily (*through* or *over* a book, etc.) **3.** to become

thinly coated, as with scum —*n.* **1.** something skimmed **2.** a skimming **3.** a thin coating
**skim·mer** (-ər) *n.* **1.** one that skims **2.** a utensil for skimming liquids **3.** a hat, usually of straw, with a flat crown and a wide, straight brim
**skim milk** milk from which cream has been removed: also **skimmed milk**
**skimp** (skimp) *adj.* [prob. altered < SCRIMP] [Colloq.] *same as* SCANTY —*vi.* [Colloq.] **1.** to give or allow too little; be stingy **2.** to keep expenses very low —*vt.* [Colloq.] **1.** to do poorly or carelessly **2.** to be stingy in or toward; specif., to make too small, too short, etc.
**skimp·y** (skim′pē) *adj.* **skimp′i·er, skimp′i·est** [Colloq.] barely or not quite enough; scanty —**skimp′i·ness** *n.*
**skin** (skin) *n.* [ON. *skinn*] **1.** the outer covering of the animal body **2.** this covering removed and prepared for use; pelt **3.** a skinlike outer layer, as fruit rind, a film or scum, etc. **4.** a container made of animal skin, for holding liquids **5.** [Slang] [*pl.*] a set of drums —*vt.* **skinned, skin′ning 1.** to cover as with skin **2.** to remove skin from **3.** to injure by scraping (one's knee, etc.) **4.** [Colloq.] *a)* to defraud; swindle *b)* to criticize severely **5.** [Colloq.] to urge on (a mule, ox, etc.), esp. by whipping —*vi.* [Colloq.] **1.** to climb (*up* or *down*) **2.** to move (*through*), pass (*by*), succeed, etc. by a tiny margin —**by the skin of one's teeth** by the tiniest margin; barely —**get under one's skin** [Colloq.] to anger or irritate one —**have a thick** (or **thin**) **skin** to be insensitive (or very sensitive) to criticism, etc. —**save one's skin** [Colloq.] to avoid death or injury —**skin′ner** *n.*
**skin-deep** (-dēp′) *adj.* **1.** penetrating no deeper than the skin **2.** without real significance; superficial —*adv.* so as to be skin-deep
**skin diving** underwater swimming in which the swimmer, without lines to the surface, is variously equipped with a face mask, flipperlike footgear, a snorkel or scuba equipment, etc. —**skin′-dive′** (-dīv′) *vi.* **-dived′, -div′ing** —**skin diver**
**skin·flint** (-flint′) *n.* [lit., one who would skin a flint for economy] a niggardly person; miser
**skin grafting** the surgical transplanting of skin (**skin graft**) to replace skin destroyed, as by burning
**skink** (skiŋk) *n.* [< L. < Gr. *skinkos*] a lizard with a very long, shiny body and short legs
**skin·less** (skin′lis) *adj.* without a skin, casing, etc.
**skinned** (skind) *adj.* having skin (of a specified kind) [dark-*skinned*]
**skin·ny** (skin′ē) *adj.* **-ni·er, -ni·est 1.** of or like skin **2.** without much flesh; emaciated; thin **3.** inferior; inadequate —**skin′ni·ness** *n.*
**skin·ny-dip** (-dip′) *vi.* **-dipped′, -dip′ping** [Colloq.] to swim in the nude —*n.* [Colloq.] a swim in the nude
**skin test** any test for detecting the presence of a disease or allergy from the reaction of the skin to a test substance
**skin·tight** (skin′tīt′) *adj.* clinging closely to the skin; tightfitting [a *skintight* dress]
**skip** (skip) *vi.* **skipped, skip′ping** [prob. < Scand.] **1.** to leap, jump, etc. lightly; specif., to move along by hopping lightly on one foot and then the other **2.** to be deflected from a surface; ricochet **3.** to pass from one point to another, omitting what lies between **4.** to be promoted in school beyond the next regular grade **5.** [Colloq.] to leave hurriedly; abscond —*vt.* **1.** to leap lightly over **2.** to pass over or omit **3.** to fail to attend a session of (school, church, etc.) **4.** to cause to skip or ricochet **5.** to promote to the school grade beyond the next regular one **6.** [Colloq.] to leave (a town, etc.) hurriedly —*n.* **1.** *a)* an act of skipping; leap *b)* a skipping gait alternating light hops on each foot **2.** a passing over or omitting —**skip it!** it doesn't matter!
**ski pants** pants that fit snugly at the ankles, worn for skiing and other winter sports
**skip·jack** (-jak′) *n., pl.* **-jacks′, -jack′:** see PLURAL, II, D, 1 any of several kinds of fish that play at the surface of the water
**ski·plane** (skē′plān′) *n.* an airplane with skis for landing gear, for use on snow
**ski pole** either of a pair of light poles with a sharp tip, used by skiers as a help in climbing, keeping balance, etc.
**skip·per¹** (skip′ər) *n.* **1.** a person or thing that skips **2.** any of various skipping insects
**skip·per²** (skip′ər) *n.* [MDu. *schipper* < *schip*, a ship] **1.** the captain of a ship **2.** any leader, director, or captain —*vt.* to act as skipper of
**skirl** (skurl) *vt., vi.* [prob. < Scand.] [Scot. & Dial.] to sound out in shrill, piercing tones, as a bagpipe —*n.* a shrill sound, as of a bagpipe
**skir·mish** (skur′mish) *n.* [< MFr. < It. < *schermire*, to fight < Gmc.] **1.** a brief fight between small groups, usually an incident of a battle **2.** any slight, unimportant conflict —*vi.* to take part in a skirmish —**skir′mish·er** *n.*
**skirt** (skurt) *n.* [ON. *skyrt*, shirt] **1.** that part of a dress, coat, robe, etc. that hangs below the waist **2.** a woman's

garment that hangs down from the waist **3.** something like a skirt, as a flap hanging from a saddle **4.** [*pl.*] the outer parts; outskirts, as of a city **5.** [Old Slang] a girl or woman —*vt.* **1.** to lie along or form the edge of **2.** *a*) to move along the edge of or pass around *b*) to miss narrowly **3.** to avoid (a difficult issue, problem, etc.) **4.** to border or edge with something —*vi.* to be on, or move along, the edge — **skirt′ed** *adj.* —**skirt′er** *n.*

**skit** (skit) *n.* [prob. < Scand. var. of ON. *skjota*, to shoot] **1.** a short piece of satirical or humorous writing **2.** a short, comic theatrical sketch

**ski tow** a kind of ski lift enabling skiers to glide up the slope on their skis, towed by the endless cable

**skit·ter** (skit′ər) *vi.* [freq. of dial. *skite*, to dart about < Scand.] to skip or move along quickly or lightly, esp. over water —*vt.* to cause to skitter

**skit·tish** (skit′ish) *adj.* [see SKIT & -ISH] **1.** lively or playful, esp. in a coy way **2.** easily frightened **3.** fickle; undependable —**skit′tish·ly** *adv.* —**skit′tish·ness** *n.*

**skit·tle** (skit′'l) *n.* [prob. < Scand. cognate of SHUTTLE] **1.** [*pl. with sing. v.*] a British form of ninepins in which a wooden disk or ball is used to knock down the pins **2.** any of these pins —**(not) all beer and skittles** (not) pure pleasure

**skiv·vy** (skiv′ē) *n., pl.* **-vies** [< ?] [Slang] **1.** a man's, esp. a sailor's, short-sleeved undershirt: usually **skivvy shirt 2.** [*pl.*] men's underwear

**skoal** (skōl) *interj.* [Dan. & Norw. *skaal*, a cup < ON. *skāl*, a bowl] to your health!: a toast

**Sko·pje** (skô′pye) city in SE Yugoslavia; capital of Macedonia: pop. 172,000

**Skr., Skrt., Skt.** Sanskrit

**sku·a** (skyōō′ə) *n.* [ModL., ult. < ON. *skūfr*, a tuft] any of several large, brown and white sea gulls, found in cold seas

**skul·dug·ger·y, skull·dug·ger·y** (skul dug′ər ē) *n.* [< ?] [Colloq.] sneaky, dishonest behavior; trickery

**skulk** (skulk) *vi.* [prob. < LowG. *schulken* or Dan. *skulke*] **1.** to move about in a stealthy or sinister manner; slink **2.** [Chiefly Brit.] to avoid work or responsibility; shirk —*n.* a person who skulks —**skulk′er** *n.* —**skulk′ing·ly** *adv.*

**skull** (skul) *n.* [< Scand.] **1.** the bony framework of the head, enclosing the brain **2.** the human head or mind

**skull and crossbones** a representation of two crossed thighbones under a human skull, used as a symbol of death or extreme danger

**skull·cap** (-kap′) *n.* a light, closefitting, brimless cap

**skunk** (skuŋk) *n.* [< AmInd. *segonku*] **1.** *a*) *pl.* **skunks, skunk:** see PLURAL, II, D, 1 a bushy-tailed mammal about the size of a cat: it has black fur with white stripes down its back, and ejects a foul-smelling liquid when molested *b*) its fur **2.** [Colloq.] a despicable, offensive person —*vt.* [Slang] to defeat overwhelmingly in a game or contest

**skunk cabbage** a plant having large, cabbagelike leaves and a disagreeable smell

**sky** (skī) *n., pl.* **skies** [ON., a cloud] **1.** [*often pl.*] the upper atmosphere, esp. with reference to its appearance [*blue skies,* a cloudy *sky*] **2.** the heavens, apparently arching over the earth **3.** heaven —*vt.* **skied** or **skyed, sky′ing** [Colloq.] to hit, throw, etc. high in the air —**out of a clear (blue) sky** without warning —**to the skies** without reserve

**sky blue** a blue color like that of the sky on a clear day — **sky′-blue′** *adj.*

**sky·cap** (-kap′) *n.* a porter at an air terminal

**sky diving** the sport of jumping from an airplane and executing free-fall maneuvers before opening the parachute — **sky′-dive′** (-dīv′) *vi.* **-dived′, -div′ing** —**sky diver**

**sky-high** (skī′hī′) *adj., adv.* **1.** very high **2.** so as to be completely blasted; to pieces

**sky·jack** (-jak′) *vt.* [Colloq.] to hijack (an aircraft) —**sky′-jack′er** *n.* —**sky′jack′ing** *n.*

**sky·lark** (-lärk′) *n.* a Eurasian lark, famous for the song it utters as it soars toward the sky —*vi.* [SKY + LARK²] to play about boisterously; frolic

**sky·light** (-līt′) *n.* a window in a roof or ceiling

**sky·line** (-līn′) *n.* **1.** the line along which sky and earth seem to meet **2.** the outline, as of a city, seen against the sky

**sky pilot** [Slang] a clergyman; esp., a military chaplain

**sky·rock·et** (-räk′it) *n.* a firework rocket that explodes in midair, with colored flame, sparks, etc. —*vi., vt.* to rise or cause to rise rapidly to a great height, success, etc.

**sky·sail** (skī′sāl′, -s′l) *n.* the small sail set above the royal at the top of a square-rigged mast

**sky·scrap·er** (-skrā′pər) *n.* a very tall building

**sky·ward** (-wərd) *adv., adj.* toward the sky: also **sky′wards** *adv.*

**sky·ways** (-wāz′) *n.pl.* routes of air travel

**sky·writ·ing** (-rīt′iŋ) *n.* the tracing of words, etc. in the sky by trailing smoke from an airplane in flight —**sky′write′** *vi., vt.* **-wrote′, -writ′ten, -writ′ing** —**sky′writ′er** *n.*

**slab** (slab) *n.* [ME. *sclabbe*] **1.** a piece that is flat, broad, and fairly thick [a *slab* of concrete] **2.** a rough piece cut from the outside of a log

**slack¹** (slak) *adj.* [OE. *slæc*] **1.** slow; sluggish **2.** barely moving, as a current of air **3.** not busy or active; dull [a *slack* period] **4.** loose; not tight or taut **5.** weak; lax **6.** careless or negligent [a *slack* workman] —*vt.* **1.** to make slack **2.** to slake —*vi.* **1.** to be or become slack; slacken **2.** to be idle, careless, or negligent —*adv.* in a slack manner — *n.* **1.** a part that is slack or hangs loose **2.** a lack of tension **3.** a stoppage of movement in a current **4.** a dull period; lull —**slack off** to slacken —**slack up** to go more slowly — **slack′ly** *adv.* —**slack′ness** *n.*

**slack²** (slak) *n.* [akin to Fl. *slecke*, dross, Du. *slak*] a mixture of small pieces of coal, coal dust, and dirt left from the screening of coal

**slack·en** (slak′'n) *vt., vi.* **1.** to make or become less active, intense, etc. **2.** to relax or loosen —**slack′en·er** *n.*

**slack·er** (-ər) *n.* **1.** a person who shirks his work or duty **2.** a person who evades military service in wartime

**slacks** (slaks) *n.pl.* trousers for men or women; esp., trousers that are not part of a suit

**slag** (slag) *n.* [MLowG. *slagge*] **1.** the fused refuse separated from a metal in smelting **2.** lava resembling this —*vt., vi.* **slagged, slag′ging** to form into slag

**slain** (slān) *pp. of* SLAY

**slake** (slāk) *vt.* **slaked, slak′ing** [OE. *slacian* < *slæc*, slack] **1.** to make (thirst, desire, etc.) less intense by satisfying **2.** to put out (a fire) **3.** to produce a chemical change in (lime) by combination with water —*vi.* to become slaked

**slaked lime** *same as* CALCIUM HYDROXIDE

**sla·lom** (slä′ləm) *n.* [Norw., sloping trail] a downhill skiing race over a zigzag course —*vi.* to ski in a slalom

**slam¹** (slam) *vt.* **slammed, slam′ming** [prob. < Scand.] **1.** to shut with force and noise [to *slam* a door] **2.** to hit, put, etc. with force and noise [to *slam* a baseball over the fence] **3.** [Colloq.] to criticize severely —*vi.* to shut, go into place, etc. with force and noise —*n.* **1.** the act or noise of slamming **2.** [Colloq.] a severe criticism

**slam²** (slam) *n.* [< ?] *Bridge shortened form of* GRAND SLAM or LITTLE SLAM

**slam·mer** (slam′ər) *n.* [Slang] a prison or jail

**slan·der** (slan′dər) *n.* [< Anglo-Fr. < LL. *scandalum*: see SCANDAL] **1.** the utterance of a falsehood damaging to a person's character or reputation: cf. LIBEL **2.** such a spoken falsehood —*vt.* to utter a slanderous statement about — **slan′der·er** *n.*

**slan·der·ous** (-əs) *adj.* **1.** containing slander **2.** uttering slander —**slan′der·ous·ly** *adv.*

**slang** (slaŋ) *n.* [18th-c. cant < ?] **1.** orig., the specialized vocabulary of criminals, tramps, etc.: now usually called CANT¹ **2.** the specialized vocabulary of those in the same work, way of life, etc.: now usually called SHOPTALK, ARGOT, JARGON **3.** highly informal language, usually short-lived and of a vigorous or colorful nature, that is usually avoided in formal speech and writing: it consists of both coined words and those with new meanings —*vi.* to use slang or abusive talk

**slang·y** (-ē) *adj.* **slang′i·er, slang′i·est 1.** of, like, or containing slang **2.** given to using slang —**slang′i·ly** *adv.* — **slang′i·ness** *n.*

**slant** (slant) *vt., vi.* [< Scand.] **1.** to turn or lie in a direction that is not straight up and down or straight across; slope **2.** to write or tell so as to appeal to a particular interest or to express a particular bias —*n.* **1.** *a*) a slanting surface, line, etc.; slope *b*) *same as* VIRGULE **2.** a point of view or attitude, or one that shows bias —*adj.* oblique; sloping — **slant′ing** *adj.* —**slant′ing·ly** *adv.*

**slant rhyme** rhyme in which there is close but not exact correspondence of sounds (Ex.: *lid, lad; wait, made*)

**slant·wise** (-wīz′) *adv.* so as to slant or slope; obliquely: also **slant′ways′** —*adj.* slanting; oblique

**slap** (slap) *n.* [LowG. *sklapp:* echoic] **1.** *a*) a blow with something flat, as the palm of the hand *b*) the sound of this, or a sound like it **2.** an insult; rebuff —*vt.* **slapped, slap′ping 1.** to strike with something flat **2.** to put, hit, etc. carelessly or with force —*vi.* to make a dull, sharp noise, as upon impact —*adv.* **1.** [Colloq.] straight; directly **2.** [Brit. Colloq.] abruptly —**slap down** [Colloq.] to rebuke or rebuff sharply —**slap′per** *n.*

**slap·dash** (-dash′) *n.* something done carelessly and hastily —*adv.* in a hasty, careless manner —*adj.* hasty, careless, impetuous, etc.

**slap-hap·py** (-hap′ē) *adj.* [Slang] 1. dazed, as by blows to the head 2. silly or giddy

**slap·jack** (-jak′) *n. same as* FLAPJACK

**slap·stick** (-stik′) *n.* 1. a device, formerly used by stage comedians, made of two wooden slats that slap together loudly when hit against something 2. crude comedy full of horseplay —*adj.* characterized by such comedy

**slash** (slash) *vt.* [< ? OFr. *esclachier,* to break] 1. to cut or wound with sweeping strokes, as of a knife 2. to whip viciously; lash 3. to cut slits in (a fabric, dress, etc.), esp. so as to expose underlying material 4. to reduce drastically *[to slash prices]* 5. to criticize severely —*vi.* to make a sweeping motion with or as with something sharp —*n.* 1. a sweeping stroke made as with a knife 2. a cut made by such a stroke; gash 3. *same as* VIRGULE 4. a slit in a fabric, dress, etc. 5. *a)* an open place in a forest, cluttered with branches, chips, etc. as from the cutting of timber *b)* such debris —**slash′er** *n.*

**slash·ing** (-iŋ) *adj.* 1. severe; violent 2. dashing; spirited —*n. same as* SLASH (*n.* 4 & 5) —**slash′ing·ly** *adv.*

**slat** (slat) *n.* [OFr. *esclat,* fragment] 1. a thin, narrow strip of wood, metal, etc. *[slats of a Venetian blind]* 2. *[pl.]* [Slang] *a)* the ribs *b)* the buttocks —*vt.* **slat′ted, slat′ting** to provide or make with slats

**slate** (slāt) *n.* [< OFr. fem. of *esclat:* see prec.] 1. a hard, fine-grained rock that separates easily into thin, smooth layers 2. its bluish-gray color: also **slate blue** 3. a thin piece of slate, esp. one used as a roofing tile or as a tablet for writing on with chalk 4. a list of candidates proposed for nomination or election —*vt.* **slat′ed, slat′ing** 1. to cover with slate 2. to choose or schedule, as for a list of candidates, appointments, etc. —**a clean slate** a clean record without blemish —**slat′er** *n.* —**slat′y** *adj.*

**slat·tern** (slat′ərn) *n.* [< dial. *slatter,* to slop] 1. a woman who is careless and sloppy in her habits, appearance, etc. 2. a slut —**slat′tern·li·ness** *n.* —**slat′tern·ly** *adj., adv.*

**slaugh·ter** (slôt′ər) *n.* [ON. *slātr,* lit., slain flesh] 1. the killing of animals for food; butchering 2. the brutal killing of a human being 3. the killing of people in large numbers, as in battle —*vt.* 1. to kill (animals) for food; butcher 2. to kill (people) brutally or in large numbers —**slaugh′ter·er** *n.* —**slaugh′ter·ous** *adj.*

**slaugh·ter·house** (-hous′) *n.* a place where animals are butchered for food; abattoir

**Slav** (släv, slav) *n.* a member of any of a group of Slavic-speaking peoples of E, SE, and C Europe, including the Russians, Ukrainians, Serbs, Croats, Bulgars, Czechs, Poles, Slovaks, etc. —*adj. same as* SLAVIC

**Slav.** Slavic

**slave** (slāv) *n.* [< OFr. < ML. *sclavus,* slave, orig. Slav < LGr. *Sklabos:* first applied to captive Slavs] 1. a human being who is owned as property by another and is under his absolute control 2. a person who is dominated by some influence, habit, person, etc. *[slaves to fashion]* 3. a person who slaves; drudge 4. any ant enslaved by ants of other species: also **slave ant** 5. a device actuated or controlled by another, similar device —*vi.* **slaved, slav′ing** 1. to work like a slave; drudge 2. to deal in slaves

**slave driver** 1. a person who oversees the work of slaves 2. any merciless taskmaster

**slave·hold·er** (-hōl′dər) *n.* a person who owns slaves —**slave′hold′ing** *adj., n.*

**slav·er¹** (slav′ər) *vi.* [< Scand.] to let saliva run from the mouth; drool —*n.* saliva drooling from the mouth

**slav·er²** (slā′vər) *n.* 1. a ship used in the slave trade: also **slave ship** 2. a person who deals in slaves

**slav·er·y** (slā′və rē, slāv′rē) *n.* 1. the owning of slaves as a practice or institution 2. the condition of being a slave; bondage 3. a condition of domination by some influence, habit, etc. 4. hard work or toil; drudgery

**slave trade** traffic in slaves; specif., the transportation of African Negroes to America for sale as slaves

**slav·ey** (slā′vē, slav′ē) *n., pl.* **-eys** [Brit. Colloq.] a female domestic servant who does menial work

**Slav·ic** (släv′ik, slav′-) *adj.* of the Slavs, their languages, etc. —*n.* a principal branch of the Indo-European family of languages, including Russian, Ukrainian, Byelorussian (**East Slavic**); Old Church Slavic, Bulgarian, Serbo-Croatian, Slovenian (**South Slavic**); and Polish, Sorbian, Czech, Slovak (**West Slavic**) Also **Sla·von·ic** (slə vän′ik)

**slav·ish** (slā′vish) *adj.* 1. of or like slaves; specif., *a)* servile *b)* laborious 2. blindly dependent *[slavish imitation]* —**slav′ish·ly** *adv.* —**slav′ish·ness** *n.*

**Sla·vo·ni·a** (slə vō′nē ə) region in Croatia, N Yugoslavia —**Sla·vo′ni·an** *adj., n.*

**slaw** (slô) *n. short for* COLESLAW

**slay** (slā) *vt.* **slew** for 2 **slayed, slain, slay′ing** [OE. *slean*]

1. to kill by violent means 2. [Slang] to impress, delight, amuse, etc. greatly —**slay′er** *n.*

**sleaze** (slēz) *n.* [< SLEAZY] [Slang] 1. the quality or condition of being sleazy; sleaziness 2. anything cheap, vulgar, shoddy, etc.

**slea·zy** (slē′zē) *adj.* **-zi·er, -zi·est** [< *Slesia,* var. of SILESIA] 1. flimsy or thin in substance *[a sleazy fabric]* 2. shoddy, cheap, etc. —**slea′zi·ly** *adv.* —**slea′zi·ness** *n.*

**sled** (sled) *n.* [MLowG. or MDu. *sledde*] a vehicle mounted on runners for coasting or for carrying loads on snow, ice, etc. —*vt., vi.* **sled′ded, sled′ding** to carry or ride on a sled

**sledge¹** (slej) *n., vt., vi.* **sledged, sledg′ing** [OE. *slecge* < base of *slean,* to strike] *same as* SLEDGEHAMMER

**sledge²** (slej) *n.* [MDu. *sleedse*] a large, heavy sled for carrying loads over ice, snow, etc. —*vt.* **sledged, sledg′ing** to carry by sledge

**sledge·ham·mer** (-ham′ər) *n.* [see SLEDGE¹] a long, heavy hammer, usually held with both hands —*vt., vi.* to strike as with a sledgehammer —*adj.* crushingly powerful

**sleek** (slēk) *adj.* [var. of SLICK] 1. smooth and shiny; glossy *[sleek fur]* 2. having a healthy, glowing, well-groomed appearance 3. speaking or acting in a smooth but insincere way 4. luxurious, elegant, etc. —*vt.* to make sleek: also **sleek′en** —**sleek′ly** *adv.* —**sleek′ness** *n.*

**sleep** (slēp) *n.* [OE. *slæp*] 1. *a)* a condition of rest for the body and mind at regular times, during which the eyes stay closed and there is dreaming *b)* a period of sleeping 2. any state like sleep, as a coma —*vi.* **slept, sleep′ing** 1. to be in the state of sleep; slumber 2. to be in a state like sleep, as hibernation 3. [Colloq.] to have sexual intercourse (*with*) 4. [Colloq.] to postpone a decision (*on*) —*vt.* 1. to have (a specified kind of sleep) *[to sleep the sleep of the just]* 2. to provide sleeping accommodations for —**last sleep** death —**sleep away** to spend in sleep —**sleep in** 1. to sleep at the place where one is in domestic service 2. to sleep later than usual in the morning —**sleep off** to rid oneself of by sleeping —**sleep over** [Colloq.] to spend the night at another's home

**sleep·er** (slē′pər) *n.* 1. one who sleeps, esp. as specified *[a light sleeper]* 2. a beam laid flat for supporting something 3. [Chiefly Brit.] a railroad tie 4. *same as* SLEEPING CAR 5. something that achieves an unexpected success, importance, etc. 6. *[usually pl.]* pajamas that enclose the feet

**sleeping bag** a large bag with a warm lining, for sleeping in, esp. outdoors

**sleeping car** a railroad car with berths, compartments, etc. for passengers to sleep in

**sleeping pill** a pill or capsule containing a drug, esp. a barbiturate, that helps put one to sleep

**sleeping sickness** 1. an infectious disease, esp. of tropical Africa, transmitted by the bite of the tsetse fly: it is characterized by fever, lethargy, and coma, usually ending in death 2. inflammation of the brain, caused by a virus and inducing drowsiness, etc.

**sleep·less** (slēp′lis) *adj.* 1. with little or no sleep *[a sleepless night]* 2. always alert or active —**sleep′less·ly** *adv.* —**sleep′less·ness** *n.*

**sleep·walk·ing** (slēp′wôk′iŋ) *n.* the act or practice of walking while asleep; somnambulism —**sleep′walk′** *vi.* —**sleep′walk′er** *n.*

**sleep·wear** (-wer′) *n.* clothes to be worn in bed, as pajamas

**sleep·y** (slē′pē) *adj.* **sleep′i·er, sleep′i·est** 1. ready or likely to fall asleep; drowsy 2. not very active; dull; quiet *[a sleepy little town]* 3. causing or showing drowsiness —**sleep′i·ly** *adv.* —**sleep′i·ness** *n.*

**sleet** (slēt) *n.* [< OE. hyp. *sliete*] 1. rain that freezes as it falls 2. a mixture of rain and snow 3. the icy coating formed when rain freezes on trees, streets, etc. —*vi.* to shower in the form of sleet —**sleet′y** *adj.*

**sleeve** (slēv) *n.* [OE. *sliefe*] 1. that part of a garment that covers an arm or part of an arm 2. a tube or tubelike part fitting around another part 3. an envelope for a phonograph record —*vt.* **sleeved, sleev′ing** to provide with sleeves —**up one's sleeve** hidden but ready at hand —**sleeved** *adj.* —**sleeve′less** *adj.*

**sleigh** (slā) *n.* [Du. *slee,* contr. of *slede,* sled] a carriage with runners instead of wheels, for travel over snow and ice —*vi.* to ride in or drive a sleigh —**sleigh′ing** *n.*

**sleight** (slīt) *n.* [< ON. *slægth < slægr,* crafty] 1. cunning used in deceiving 2. skill or dexterity

**sleight of hand** 1. skill in using the hands so as to confuse those watching, as in doing magic tricks 2. tricks that deceive in or as in this way

**slen·der** (slen′dər) *adj.* [< ?] 1. long and thin 2. having a slim, trim figure 3. small in amount, size, degree, etc.; slight *[slender earnings, slender hope]* —**slen′der·ly** *adv.* —**slen′der·ness** *n.*

**slen·der·ize** (-īz′) *vt.* **-ized′, -iz′ing** to make or cause to seem slender —*vi.* to become slender

**slept** (slept) *pt. & pp. of* SLEEP

**sleuth** (slo̅o̅th) *n.* [ON. *sloth*, a track, spoor] **1.** a blood-hound: in full, **sleuth′hound′ 2.** [Colloq.] a detective —*vi.* to act as a detective

**slew**[1] (slo̅o̅) *n. same as* SLOUGH[2] (sense 4)

**slew**[2] (slo̅o̅) *n., vt., vi. same as* SLUE[1]

**slew**[3] (slo̅o̅) *n.* [Ir. *sluagh*, a host] [Colloq.] a large number or amount; a lot

**slew**[4] (slo̅o̅) *pt. of* SLAY

**slice** (slīs) *n.* [OFr. *esclice*, ult. < Frank. *slizzan*, to slice] **1.** a thin, broad piece cut from something [*a slice* of cake] **2.** a part or share [*a slice* of the profits] **3.** a spatula or knife with a broad, flat blade **4.** *a*) the path of a hit ball that curves away to the right from a right-handed player or to the left from a left-handed player *b*) a ball that follows such a path —*vt. sliced, slic′ing* **1.** to cut into slices **2.** *a*) to cut as a slice (with *off, from, away,* etc.) *b*) to cut through like a knife **3.** to separate into parts or shares **4.** to hit (a ball) in a slice —*vi.* to cut (*through*) like a knife —**slic′er** *n.*

**slick** (slik) *vt.* [OE. *slician*] **1.** to make sleek or smooth **2.** [Colloq.] to make smart, neat, or tidy (with *up*) —*adj.* **1.** sleek; smooth **2.** slippery; oily, as a surface **3.** clever, skillful, or ingenious, esp. in a way considered tricky, smooth, etc. —*n.* **1.** *a*) a smooth area on the surface of water, as resulting from a film of oil *b*) such a film of oil **2.** [Colloq.] a magazine printed on paper with a glossy finish —*adv.* smoothly, cleverly, etc. —**slick′ly** *adv.* —**slick′ness** *n.*

**slick·er** (-ər) *n.* **1.** a loose, waterproof coat **2.** [Colloq.] a person with smooth, tricky ways

**slide** (slīd) *vi.* **slid, slid′ing** [OE. *slidan*] **1.** to move along in constant contact with a smooth surface, as on ice **2.** to move quietly and smoothly; glide **3.** to move stealthily or unobtrusively **4.** to slip [*it slid* from his hand] **5.** to pass gradually (*into* or *out of* some condition, habit, etc.) —*vt.* **1.** to cause to slide **2.** to move or slip quietly or stealthily (*in* or *into*) —*n.* **1.** an act of sliding **2.** a smooth, sloping track, surface, or chute down which to slide **3.** something that works by sliding **4.** a piece of film with a photograph on it, mounted for use with a viewer or projector **5.** a small glass plate on which objects are mounted for microscopic study **6.** *a*) the fall of a mass of rock, snow, etc. down a slope *b*) the mass that falls **7.** a U-shaped section of tubing which is moved to change the pitch of a trombone, etc. —**let slide** to fail to take care of (some matter) —**slid′er** *n.*

**slide fastener** a zipper or a zipperlike device having two grooved edges joined or separated by a slide

**slide rule** an instrument consisting of a ruler with a central sliding piece, both marked with logarithmic scales: used for rapid mathematical calculations

**sliding scale** a scale or schedule, as of costs, wages, etc., that varies with given conditions or standards

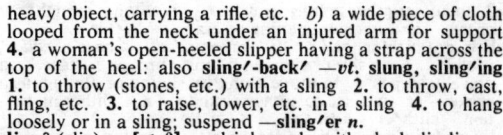

SLIDE RULE

**slight** (slīt) *adj.* [OE. *sliht*] **1.** *a*) light in build; slender *b*) frail; fragile **2.** having little weight, strength, substance, or significance **3.** small in amount or extent [*a slight* fever] —*vt.* **1.** to do carelessly or poorly; neglect **2.** to treat with disrespect or indifference **3.** to treat as unimportant —*n.* a slighting or being slighted by pointedly discourteous treatment —**slight′ing** *adj.* — **slight′ing·ly** *adv.* —**slight′ly** *adv.* —**slight′ness** *n.*

**sli·ly** (slī′lē) *adv. var. of* SLYLY

**slim** (slim) *adj.* **slim′mer, slim′mest** [Du., crafty, bad] **1.** small in girth in proportion to height or length; slender **2.** small in amount, degree, or extent; slight; scant; meager —*vt., vi.* **slimmed, slim′ming** to make or become slim —**slim′ly** *adv.* —**slim′ness** *n.*

**slime** (slīm) *n.* [OE. *slim*] any soft, moist, slippery, often sticky matter, as thin mud, the mucous coating on fish, etc.; specif., any such matter considered disgusting —*vt.* **slimed, slim′ing 1.** to cover with slime **2.** to clean slime from

**slim·y** (slī′mē) *adj.* **slim′i·er, slim′i·est 1.** of or like slime **2.** covered with slime **3.** disgusting; repulsive — **slim′i·ly** *adv.* —**slim′i·ness** *n.*

**sling**[1] (sliŋ) *n.* [ME. *slinge(n)*, prob. < ON. *slyngva*, to throw] **1.** *a*) a primitive instrument for throwing stones, etc., consisting of a piece of leather tied to cords that are whirled for releasing the missile *b*) *same as* SLINGSHOT **2.** a throwing as with a sling; cast; fling **3.** *a*) a looped or hanging band, strap, etc., used in raising or lowering a

heavy object, carrying a rifle, etc. *b*) a wide piece of cloth looped from the neck around an injured arm for support **4.** a woman's open-heeled slipper having a strap across the top of the heel: also **sling′-back′** —*vt.* **slung, sling′ing 1.** to throw (stones, etc.) with a sling **2.** to throw, cast, fling, etc. **3.** to raise, lower, etc. in a sling **4.** to hang loosely or in a sling; suspend —**sling′er** *n.*

**sling**[2] (sliŋ) *n.* [< ?] a drink made with alcoholic liquor, water, sugar, and lemon juice

**sling·shot** (sliŋ′shät′) *n.* a Y-shaped piece of wood, metal, etc. with an elastic band fastened to the upper tips for shooting stones, etc.

**slink** (sliŋk) *vi.* **slunk, slink′ing** [OE. *slincan*, to creep] to move in a fearful or sneaky way, or as if ashamed —**slink′ing·ly** *adv.*

**slink·y** (sliŋ′kē) *adj.* **slink′i·er, slink′i·est 1.** sneaky in movement **2.** [Slang] sinuous and graceful in movement, line, etc. —**slink′i·ness** *n.*

**slip**[1] (slip) *vi.* **slipped, slip′ping** [MLowG. *slippen*] **1.** to go quietly or secretly [to *slip* out of a room] **2.** *a*) to move or pass smoothly, quickly, or easily *b*) to get (*into* or *out of* clothes) quickly **3.** to pass gradually into or out of some condition, habit, etc. [to *slip* off to sleep] **4.** to escape from one's mind, power, etc. [to let a chance *slip* by] **5.** to shift or slide from position [the plate *slipped* from my hand] **6.** to slide accidentally, lose footing, etc. [to *slip* on ice] **7.** to make a mistake; err **8.** to become worse; weaken, lower, etc. [my memory is *slipping*, prices have *slipped*] —*vt.* **1.** to put or move smoothly, easily, or quickly [to *slip* a bolt into place, to *slip* one's shoes off, to *slip* in a snide remark] **2.** to escape (one's mind) **3.** to get loose from [the dog *slipped* his leash] **4.** to let loose; release **5.** to transfer (a stitch) from one needle to another without knitting it, as in forming patterns **6.** to put out of joint; dislocate —*n.* **1.** *a*) an inclined plane leading down to water, on which ships are built or repaired *b*) a water channel between piers or wharves for ship docking **2.** a leash for a dog **3.** *a*) a woman's sleeveless undergarment, suspended from shoulder straps to the hemline of the skirt *b*) a petticoat; half slip **4.** a pillowcase **5.** a slipping or falling down **6.** an error or mistake in judgment, conduct, speech, etc., esp. one made by accident in speaking, writing, etc. [a *slip* of the tongue] **7.** an accident or mishap **8.** *Cricket* a fielder placed behind the wickets on the off side **9.** *Geol.* **a**) a movement resulting in a small fault or landslide *b*) a smooth surface where such movement has taken place —**give someone the slip** to evade or escape from someone —**let slip** to say without intending to —**slip one over on** [Colloq.] to trick; hoodwink —**slip up** to make a mistake

**slip**[2] (slip) *n.* [< MDu. < *slippen*, to cut] **1.** a stem, root, twig, etc. cut off for planting or grafting **2.** a young, slim person [a *slip* of a girl] **3.** a long, narrow piece; strip **4.** a small piece of paper, esp. one for a specific use [an order *slip*] —*vt.* **slipped, slip′ping** to take a slip from (a plant) for planting or grafting

**slip**[3] (slip) *n.* [OE. *slypa*, a paste] *Ceramics* clay thinned to a watery paste for decorating, casting, or cementing

**slip·case** (-kās′) *n.* a boxlike container for a book or set of books, open at one end to expose the spine or spines

**slip·cov·er** (-kuv′ər) *n.* a removable, fitted cloth cover for an armchair, sofa, etc. —*vt.* to cover (a chair, etc.) with a slipcover

**slip·knot** (-nät′) *n.* a knot made so that it will slip along the rope, etc. around which it is tied

**slip-on** (-än′) *adj.* easily put on or taken off, as shoes without laces, or a garment to be slipped on or off over the head —*n.* a slip-on shoe or garment

**slip·o·ver** (-ō′vər) *adj., n. same as* PULLOVER

**slip·page** (slip′ij) *n.* **1.** a slipping, as of one gear past another **2.** the amount of this

**slipped disk** a herniated disk between two vertebrae, esp. in the lumbar region, often causing sciatica

**slip·per** (slip′ər) *n.* a light, low shoe easily slipped on the foot, esp. one for indoor wear —**slip′pered** *adj.*

**slip·per·y** (slip′ər ē, slip′rē) *adj.* **-per·i·er, -per·i·est** [OE. *slipur*] **1.** causing or liable to cause slipping, as a wet surface **2.** tending to slip away, as from the grasp **3.** not reliable; tricky —**slip′per·i·ness** *n.*

**slippery elm 1.** a N. American elm with sticky inner bark and hard wood **2.** the wood or bark

**slip·shod** (slip′shäd′) *adj.* [SLIP[1] + SHOD] **1.** wearing shoes with worn-down heels **2.** careless; slovenly

**slip·stream** (-strēm′) *n.* the current of air thrust backward by the spinning propeller of an aircraft

**slipt** (slipt) *archaic or poetic pt. of* SLIP[1]

**slip-up** (slip′up′) *n.* [Colloq.] an error, oversight, or mishap

**slit** (slit) *vt.* **slit, slit′ting** [akin to OE. *slitan*, to cut] **1.** to cut or split open, esp. by a straight, lengthwise incision

fat, āpe, cär; ten, ēven; is, bīte; gō, hôrn, to̅o̅l, look; oil, out; up, fur; get; joy; yet; chin; she; thin, then; zh, leisure; ŋ, ring; ə for *a* in *ago*, *e* in *agent*, *i* in *sanity*, *o* in *comply*, *u* in *focus*; ' as in *able* (ā′b'l); Fr. bal; ë, Fr. coeur; ö, Fr. feu; Fr. mon; ô, Fr. coq; ü, Fr. duc; r, Fr. cri; H, G. ich; kh, G. doch; ‡foreign; *hypothetical; < derived from. See inside front cover.

**2.** to cut lengthwise into strips —*n.* **1.** a long, straight cut or tear **2.** a narrow opening or crack —**slit′ter** *n.*

**slith·er** (sli*th*′ər) *vi.* [< OE. *sliderian*, freq. < base of *slidan*, to slide] **1.** to slip or slide on a loose, broken surface, as a gravelly slope **2.** to move along by sliding or gliding, as a snake —*vt.* to cause to slither or slide —*n.* a slithering motion —**slith′er·y** *adj.*

**sliv·er** (sliv′ər) *n.* [OE. *slifan*, to cut] **1.** a thin, sharp piece that has been cut, split, or broken off; splinter **2.** a loose, thin, continuous fiber, as of flax, ready to be drawn and twisted —*vt., vi.* to cut or break into slivers

**slob** (släb) *n.* [Ir. *slab*, mud < Scand.] [Colloq.] a sloppy, coarse, or gross person

**slob·ber** (släb′ər) *vi.* [< or akin to LowG. *slubberen*, to swig] **1.** to let saliva, food, etc. run from the mouth; slaver **2.** to speak, write, etc. in a gushy or maudlin way —*vt.* to smear or dribble on with saliva —*n.* **1.** saliva, etc. running from the mouth **2.** gushy talk or writing —**slob′ber·er** *n.* —**slob′ber·y** *adj.*

**sloe** (slō) *n.* [OE. *sla*] **1.** *same as* BLACKTHORN (sense 1) **2.** the small, blue-black, plumlike fruit of the blackthorn **3.** any of various wild plums

**sloe-eyed** (-īd′) *adj.* **1.** having large, dark eyes **2.** having almond-shaped eyes

**sloe gin** a red liqueur made of gin flavored with sloes

**slog¹** (släg) *vt., vi.* **slogged, slog′ging** [var. of SLUG⁴] to hit hard; slug —**slog′ger** *n.*

**slog²** (släg) *vt., vi.* **slogged, slog′ging** [ME. *sluggen*: see SLUGGARD] **1.** to make (one's way) with great effort; plod **2.** to work hard (*at* something); toil —**slog′ger** *n.*

**slo·gan** (slō′gən) *n.* [< Gael. < *sluagh*, a host + *gairm*, a call] **1.** orig., a battle cry of Scottish Highland and Irish clans **2.** a catchword or motto associated with a political party or other group **3.** a catch phrase used to advertise a product

**slo·gan·eer** (slō′gə nir′) *vi.* to coin or make use of slogans —*n.* a person who coins or uses slogans

**slo·gan·ize** (slō′gə nīz′) *vt.* **-ized′, -iz′ing** to express in the form of a slogan —**slo′gan·is′tic** *adj.*

**sloid, slojd** (sloid) *n. same as* SLOYD

**sloop** (sl◯p) *n.* [< Du. < LowG. < *slupen*, to glide] a fore-and-aft rigged, single-masted sailing vessel

**slop** (släp) *n.* [OE. *sloppe* (only in comp.)] **1.** watery snow or mud; slush **2.** a splash or puddle of spilled liquid **3.** liquid or semiliquid food that is unappetizing or of poor quality **4.** [*often pl.*] *a*) liquid waste of any kind *b*) kitchen swill, used for feeding pigs **5.** [Slang] a sloppy person —*vi.* **slopped, slop′ping 1.** to spill or splash **2.** to walk or splash through slush or mud —*vt.* **1.** to spill liquid on **2.** to spill **3.** to feed swill or slops to (pigs, etc.) —**slop over 1.** to overflow or spill **2.** [Colloq.] to display sentimentality; gush

SLOOP

**slope** (slōp) *n.* [< OE. pp. of *aslupan*, to slip away < *slupan*, to glide] **1.** ground that slants up or down, as a hillside **2.** any inclined line, surface, position, etc.; slant **3.** amount or degree of slant **4.** the land area that drains into a given ocean —*vi., vt.* **sloped, slop′ing** to slant or cause to slant up or down —**slop′er** *n.*

**slop·py** (släp′ē) *adj.* **-pi·er, -pi·est 1.** wet and splashy; muddy or slushy **2.** splashed or spotted with liquids **3.** *a*) very untidy; slovenly or messy *b*) careless; slipshod **4.** [Colloq.] gushingly sentimental —**slop′pi·ly** *adv.* —**slop′pi·ness** *n.*

**sloppy Joe** ground meat cooked with tomato sauce, etc. and served on a bun

**slops** (släps) *n.pl.* [< OE. *-slop*, as in *oferslop*, loose outer garment] **1.** loose-fitting outer garments, esp. coveralls **2.** clothing, bedding, etc. issued or sold to seamen **3.** cheap, ready-made clothing

**slosh** (släsh) *vt.* [var. of SLUSH] **1.** to shake or agitate (a liquid or something in it) **2.** to apply (a liquid) carelessly or lavishly —*vi.* **1.** to splash or move clumsily through water, mud, etc. **2.** to splash about: said of a liquid —*n.* **1.** *same as* SLUSH **2.** the sound of liquid splashing about — **slosh′y** *adj.*

**slot** (slät) *n.* [< OFr. *esclot*, the hollow between the breasts] **1.** a narrow notch, groove, or opening, as a slit for a coin in a vending machine **2.** [Colloq.] a position in a group, series, schedule, etc. —*vt.* **slot′ted, slot′ting 1.** to make a slot in **2.** [Colloq.] to place in a series, schedule, etc.

**sloth** (slôth, slōth, släth) *n.* [OE. *slæwth* < *slaw*, slow] **1.** the condition of not liking to work or be active; indolence; laziness **2.** any of several slow-moving mammals of Central and South America that live in trees, often hanging upside down from the branches

**sloth·ful** (-fəl) *adj.* characterized by sloth; indolent; lazy —**sloth′ful·ly** *adv.* —**sloth′ful·ness** *n.*

**slot machine** a machine, esp. a gambling device, worked by putting a coin in a slot

**slouch** (slouch) *n.* [ON. *slōkr*, lazy fellow < *slōka*, to droop] **1.** *a*) a person who is awkward or lazy *b*) [Colloq.] a person who lacks skill [he's no *slouch* at golf] **2.** *a*) a drooping or bending forward of the head and shoulders *b*) slovenly posture in general **3.** a drooping, as of a hat brim —*vi.* **1.** to sit, stand, walk, etc. in a slouch **2.** to droop, as a hat brim —*vt.* to cause to slouch

**slouch·y** (-ē) *adj.* **slouch′i·er, slouch′i·est** slouching, esp. in posture —**slouch′i·ly** *adv.* —**slouch′i·ness** *n.*

**slough¹** (sluf) *n.* [ME. *slouh*] **1.** the skin of a snake, esp. the outer, castoff layer **2.** any castoff layer, covering, etc.: often used figuratively **3.** *Med.* the dead tissue that separates from living tissue or an ulceration —*vi.* **1.** to be shed, cast off, etc. **2.** to shed skin or other covering **3.** *Med.* to separate from the surrounding tissue Often with *off* —*vt.* **1.** to shed or throw (*off*); get rid of **2.** *Bridge* to discard (a card considered valueless) —**slough over** to gloss over; minimize —**slough′y** *adv.*

**slough²** (slou; *for 4 slōō*) *n.* [OE. *sloh*] **1.** a place full of soft, deep mud **2.** [< *Slough of Despond*, a swamp in Bunyan's *Pilgrim's Progress*] deep, hopeless discouragement **3.** moral corruption **4.** a swamp, bog, etc., esp. as part of an inlet —**slough′y** *adj.*

**Slo·vak** (slō′väk, -vak) *n.* **1.** any of a Slavic people living chiefly in Slovakia **2.** their West Slavic language, related to Czech —*adj.* of Slovakia, the Slovaks, or their language

**Slo·va·ki·a** (slō vä′kē ə, -vak′ē ə) region comprising E Czechoslovakia —**Slo·va′ki·an** *adj., n.*

**slov·en** (sluv′ən) *n.* [prob. < MDu. *slof*, lax] a person who is careless in his appearance, habits, work, etc.; dirty or untidy person

**Slo·ve·ni·a** (slō vē′nē ə, -vēn′yə) republic of Yugoslavia, in the NW part: 7,896 sq. mi.; cap. Ljubljana

**Slo·ve·ni·an** (slō vē′nē ən, -vēn′yən) *n.* **1.** any of a Slavic people living chiefly in Slovenia **2.** their South Slavic language —*adj.* of Slovenia, Slovenians, or their language Also **Slo·vene** (slō′vēn, slō vēn′)

**slov·en·ly** (sluv′ən lē) *adj.* **-li·er, -li·est** of or like a sloven; careless in appearance, habits, work, etc.; untidy —*adv.* in a slovenly manner —**slov′en·li·ness** *n.*

**slow** (slō) *adj.* [OE. *slaw*] **1.** not quick or clever in understanding; dull; obtuse **2.** taking a longer time than is expected or usual **3.** marked by low speed, etc.; not fast **4.** making speed difficult [a *slow* track] **5.** showing a time that is behind the correct time: said of a timepiece **6.** *a*) passing slowly or tediously *b*) not lively; dull **7.** not active; slack [*slow* trading] **8.** lacking in energy; sluggish **9.** burning so as to give off low heat [a *slow* fire] **10.** *Photog.* adapted to a relatively long exposure time —*vt., vi.* to make or become slow or slower (often with *up* or *down*) —*adv.* in a slow manner —**slow′ly** *adv.* —**slow′ness** *n.*

**slow burn** [Slang] a gradual working up or show of anger: often in the phrase **do a slow burn**

**slow-mo·tion** (-mō′shən) *adj.* **1.** moving below usual speed **2.** designating a motion-picture or taped television sequence in which the action is made to appear much slower than the actual action

**slow·poke** (-pōk′) *n.* [Slang] a person who acts or moves slowly

**slow time** *same as* STANDARD TIME

**sloyd** (sloid) *n.* [Sw. *slöjd*, skill] a system of manual training originating in Sweden, based upon the use of hand tools in woodcarving

**slub** (slub) *n.* [< ?] **1.** a roll of fiber twisted slightly for use in spinning **2.** a thick, irregular place in yarn

**sludge** (sluj) *n.* [var. of *slutch*, mud] **1.** mud, mire, or ooze **2.** spongy lumps of drift ice **3.** any heavy, slimy deposit, sediment, or mass, as the waste resulting from oil refining, the sediment in a crankcase, etc. —**sludg′y** *adj.* **sludg′i·er, sludg′i·est**

**sludge·worm** (-wurm′) *n.* a small, freshwater worm able to live where there is little oxygen, as in polluted waters

**slue¹** (slōō) *vt., vi.* **slued, slu′ing** [< ?] to turn or swing around a fixed point —*n.* **1.** the act of sluing **2.** the position to which a thing has been slued

**slue²** (slōō) *n. same as* SLOUGH² (sense 4)

**slue³** (slōō) *n. same as* SLEW³

**slug¹** (slug) *n.* [ME. *slugge*, clumsy one < Scand.] **1.** a small mollusk resembling a land snail, but usually having only a rudimentary internal shell **2.** rarely, a larva resembling a slug **3.** a person, vehicle, etc. that moves slowly

**slug²** (slug) *n.* [prob. < prec.] **1.** a small piece of metal; specif., a bullet **2.** a piece of metal used in place of a coin in automatic coin machines **3.** *Printing a*) a strip of nonprinting metal used to space between lines *b*) a lino or type made in one piece, as by a linotype machine

**slug³** (slug) *n.* [prob. < or akin to Dan. *sluge*, to gulp] [Slang] a single drink, esp. of alcoholic liquor

**slug⁴** (slug) *vt.* **slugged, slug′ging** [ON. *slag*] [Colloq.] to hit hard, esp. with the fist or a bat —*n.* [Colloq.] a hard blow or hit —**slug′ger** *n.*

**slug·gard** (slug′ərd) *n.* [< ME. < *sluggen*, to be lazy] a habitually lazy or idle person —*adj.* lazy or idle: also **slug′·gard·ly**

**slug·gish** (-ish) *adj.* [SLUG¹ + -ISH] **1.** lacking energy or alertness; slothful **2.** slow or slow-moving **3.** below normal —**slug′gish·ly** *adv.* —**slug′gish·ness** *n.*

**sluice** (slōōs) *n.* [< OFr. *escluse* < LL. < pp. of L. *excludere*, EXCLUDE] **1.** an artificial channel for water, with a gate at its head to regulate the flow, as in a canal **2.** the water held back by such a gate **3.** such a gate: also **sluice gate 4.** any channel, esp. one for excess water **5.** a sloping trough through which water is run, as in carrying logs, etc. —*vt.* **sluiced, sluic′ing 1.** to draw off as by means of a sluice **2.** to wash with water from or as from a sluice **3.** to carry (logs, etc.) in a sluice —*vi.* to run or flow as in a sluice

**slum** (slum) *n.* [< cant: orig. sense, a room < ?] a heavily populated area of a city having much poverty, poor housing, etc. —*vi.* **slummed, slum′ming** to visit or tour slums —**slum′mer** *n.* —**slum′my** *adj.* **-mi·er, -mi·est**

**slum·ber** (slum′bər) *vi.* [< OE. < *sluma*, slumber] **1.** to sleep **2.** to be quiet or inactive —*vt.* to spend in sleeping —*n.* **1.** sleep **2.** an inactive state —**slum′ber·er** *n.*

**slum·ber·ous** (-əs) *adj.* **1.** inclined to slumber; sleepy **2.** suggestive of slumber **3.** causing sleep **4.** calm; quiet [a *slumberous* town] Also **slum′brous** (-brəs)

**slum·gul·lion** (slum′gul′yən) *n.* [< ?] [Colloq.] any inexpensive stew or hash

**slum·lord** (slum′lôrd′) *n.* [SLUM + (LAND)LORD] an absentee landlord of slum dwellings, esp. one who charges rents that are too high and fails to make repairs, etc.

**slump** (slump) *vi.* [prob. < or akin to MLowG. *slumpen*, to come about by accident] **1.** to fall or sink suddenly **2.** to decline suddenly, as in value, etc. **3.** to have a drooping posture —*n.* **1.** a sudden or sharp fall, decline, etc. **2.** a drooping posture **3.** a period during which a player, team, etc. performs below normal

**slung** (slung) *pt. & pp. of* SLING¹

**slunk** (slungk) *pt. & pp. of* SLINK

**slur** (slur) *vt.* **slurred, slur′ring** [prob. < MDu. *sleuren*, to drag] **1.** to pass (*over*) quickly and carelessly **2.** to pronounce rapidly in an unclear way **3.** to discredit or belittle **4.** *Music* a) to sing or play (successive notes) by gliding from one to another without a break b) to mark (notes) with a slur —*n.* **1.** a slurring **2.** something slurred, as a pronunciation **3.** a remark that is harmful to a person's reputation; aspersion **4.** *Music* a curved symbol (‿) or (⌒) connecting slurred notes —**slur′ring·ly** *adv.*

**slurp** (slurp) *vt., vi.* [Du. *slurpen*, to sip] [Slang] to drink or eat noisily —*n.* [Slang] a loud sipping noise

**slush** (slush) *n.* [prob. < Scand.] **1.** partly melted snow or ice **2.** soft mud; mire **3.** grease **4.** overly sentimental talk or writing —*vi.* to walk or move through slush —**slush′i·ness** *n.* —**slush′y** *adj.* **slush′i·er, slush′i·est**

**slush fund** money used for bribery, influencing politicians, voters, etc., or other corrupt purposes

**slut** (slut) *n.* [prob. akin to MLowG. *slote*, ditch] **1.** a dirty, slovenly woman; slattern **2.** a sexually promiscuous woman **3.** a female dog; bitch —**slut′tish** *adj.* —**slut′tish·ly** *adv.* —**slut′tish·ness** *n.*

**sly** (slī) *adj.* **sli′er** or **sly′er, sli′est** or **sly′est** [ON. *slœgr*] **1.** [Dial.] skillful or clever **2.** skillful at tricking or fooling others, in a secretive or underhanded way **3.** tricking or teasing in a playful way —**on the sly** secretly —**sly′ly** *adv.* —**sly′ness** *n.*

**Sm** *Chem.* samarium

**smack¹** (smak) *n.* [OE. *smæc*] **1.** a slight but distinctive taste or flavor **2.** *a*) a small amount; bit *b*) a trace; touch —*vi.* to have a smack (*of*) [actions that *smack* of treason] 

**smack²** (smak) *n.* [< ? or akin to MDu. *smack*, of echoic orig.] **1.** a sharp noise made by parting the lips suddenly **2.** a loud kiss **3.** *a*) a sharp blow with a flat object; slap *b*) the sound of this —*vt.* **1.** to part (the lips) suddenly so as to make a smack **2.** to kiss or slap loudly —*vi.* to make a loud, sharp noise, as when hitting something —*adv.* **1.** with a smack; violently **2.** directly; squarely: also [Colloq.] **smack′·dab′**

**smack³** (smak) *n.* [prob. < Du. *smak*] **1.** a small sailboat, usually rigged as a sloop **2.** a fishing boat with a well for keeping fish alive

**smack·ing** (-iŋ) *adj.* brisk; sharp; lively

**small** (smôl) *adj.* [OE. *smæl*] **1.** comparatively little in size; not large **2.** *a*) little in quantity, extent, value, duration, etc. [a *small* income] *b*) consisting of relatively few units; low in numbers [a *small* crowd] **3.** of little importance; trivial **4.** young [*small* children] **5.** having relatively little investment, capital, etc. [a *small* business] **6.** small-minded; petty **7.** of low or inferior rank **8.** gentle and low; soft, as a sound —*adv.* **1.** in small pieces **2.** in a low tone; softly **3.** in a small manner —*n.* **1.** the small or narrow part [the *small* of the back] **2.** [pl.] small articles —**feel small** to feel shame or humiliation —**small′·ish** *adj.* —**small′ness** *n.*

**small arms** firearms of small caliber, held in the hand or hands when fired, as pistols, rifles, etc.

**small·clothes** (smôl′klōz′, -klōthz′) *n.pl.* [Archaic] closefitting knee breeches of the 18th cent.

**small hours** the first few hours after midnight

**small-mind·ed** (-mīn′did) *adj.* selfish, petty, prejudiced, narrow-minded, etc. —**small′-mind′ed·ly** *adv.* —**small′-mind′ed·ness** *n.*

**small potatoes** [Colloq.] a petty or insignificant person (or people) or thing (or things)

**small·pox** (-päks′) *n.* an acute, highly contagious virus disease causing fever, vomiting, and pustular eruptions that often leave pitted scars, or pockmarks

**small-scale** (-skāl′) *adj.* **1.** drawn to a small scale **2.** of limited scope; not extensive [*small-scale* trading]

**small talk** light conversation about common, everyday things; chitchat

**small-time** (-tīm′) *adj.* [Colloq.] of little importance or significance; minor or petty

**smart** (smärt) *vi.* [OE. *smeortan*] **1.** *a*) to cause sharp, stinging pain, as a slap, wound, etc. *b*) to feel such pain **2.** to feel mental distress, as in resentment, remorse, etc. —*vt.* to cause to smart —*n.* a smarting sensation or distress —*adj.* **1.** causing sharp or stinging pain [a *smart* slap] **2.** sharp or stinging, as pain **3.** brisk; lively [a *smart* pace] **4.** *a*) intelligent, alert, clever, witty, etc. *b*) shrewd or sharp, as in one's dealings **5.** neat; trim; spruce **6.** in fashion; stylish **7.** [Colloq.] impertinent, flippant, or saucy **8.** [Dial.] quite strong, intense, etc.; considerable [a right *smart* rain] —*adv.* in a smart way —**smart′ly** *adv.* —**smart′ness** *n.*

**smart al·eck, smart al·ec** (al′ik) [SMART + *Aleck*, dim. of ALEXANDER] [Colloq.] a conceited, cocky person —**smart′-al′eck, smart′-al′eck·y** *adj.*

**smart·en** (smärt′'n) *vt.* to make smart or smarter; specif., *a*) to improve in appearance *b*) to make more alert, aware, etc. Usually with *up*

**smart set** sophisticated, fashionable people

**smart·weed** (-wēd′) *n.* a knotgrass whose bitter juice is thought to cause skin irritation

**smart·y** (smär′tē) *n., pl.* **smart′ies** [Colloq.] same as SMART ALECK: also **smart′y-pants′**

**smash** (smash) *vt.* [prob. < *s*-, intens. + MASH] **1.** to break into pieces with noise or violence **2.** to hit (a tennis ball, etc.) with a hard overhand stroke **3.** to hit with a hard, heavy blow **4.** to ruin completely; destroy —*vi.* **1.** to break into pieces **2.** to be destroyed **3.** to move or collide with force —*n.* **1.** a hard, heavy hit; specif., a hard overhand stroke, as in tennis **2.** *a*) a violent, noisy breaking *b*) the sound of this **3.** *a*) a violent collision *b*) a wreck **4.** total failure, esp. in business **5.** an overwhelming popular success —*adj.* that is a smash (*n.* 5) —**go to smash** [Colloq.] **1.** to become smashed **2.** to fail completely —**smash′er** *n.*

**smashed** (smasht) *adj.* [Slang] drunk; intoxicated

**smash·ing** (smash′iŋ) *adj.* **1.** that smashes **2.** [Colloq.] extraordinary —**smash′ing·ly** *adv.*

**smash-up** (-up′) *n.* **1.** a violent wreck or collision **2.** total failure; ruin **3.** any disaster

**smat·ter** (smat′ər) *vt.* [prob. akin to MHG. *smetern*, to chatter] [Now Rare] to speak, study, or learn superficially —*n.* same as SMATTERING

**smat·ter·ing** (-iŋ) *n.* **1.** slight or superficial knowledge **2.** a small number

**smear** (smir) *vt.* [OE. *smerian*, to anoint] **1.** to cover or soil with something greasy, sticky, etc. **2.** to apply (something greasy, sticky, etc.) **3.** to make an unwanted mark on, or to obscure, by rubbing **4.** to make a smear with (the hand, a rag, etc.) **5.** to harm the reputation of; slander **6.** [Slang] to overwhelm or defeat decisively —*vi.* to be or become smeared —*n.* **1.** a mark made by smearing **2.** a small quantity of some substance smeared on a slide for microscopic study, etc. **3.** a slandering

**smear·case** (-kās′) *n.* [< G. *schmierkäse* < *schmieren*, to spread + *käse*, cheese] same as COTTAGE CHEESE

**smear·y** (smir′ē) *adj.* **smear′i·er, smear′i·est 1.** covered with smears; smeared **2.** tending to smear, as wet ink —**smear′i·ness** *n.*

**smell** (smel) *vt.* **smelled** or **smelt, smell′ing** [ME. *smellen*] **1.** to be aware of by means of the nose and the olfactory nerves; detect the odor of **2.** to sense the presence of [to

**smell** trouble] **3.** to test by the odor; sniff [*smell* the milk to tell if it's sour] —*vi.* **1.** to use the sense of smell; sniff (often with *at* or *of*) **2.** *a)* to have a scent or odor *b)* to have an unpleasant odor **3.** to have the odor or a suggestion (*of*) [it *smells* of garlic] **4.** [Colloq.] *a)* to lack ability, worth, etc. *b)* to be foul, corrupt, etc. —*n.* **1.** that one of the five senses by which a substance is perceived through the stimulation of nerves (*olfactory nerves*) in the nasal cavity **2.** the stimulation of any specific substance upon the olfactory nerves; odor; scent **3.** an act of smelling **4.** that which suggests the presence of something; trace —**smell out** to look for or find as by smelling —**smell up** to cause to stink —**smell′er** *n.*

**smelling salts** carbonate of ammonium, inhaled to relieve faintness, headaches, etc.

**smell·y** (smel′ē) *adj.* **smell′i·er, smell′i·est** having an unpleasant smell —**smell′i·ness** *n.*

**smelt**[1] (smelt) *n., pl.* **smelts, smelt**: see PLURAL, II, D, 1 [OE.] a small, silvery, salmonlike food fish found in northern seas

**smelt**[2] (smelt) *vt.* [MDu. or MLowG. *smelten*] **1.** to melt or fuse (ore, etc.) so as to separate impurities from pure metal **2.** to refine or extract (metal) in this way —*vi.* to be smelted

**smelt·er** (smel′tər) *n.* **1.** a person engaged in the work of smelting **2.** a place where smelting is done: also **smelt′er·y,** *pl.* **-er·ies**

**smidg·en** (smij′ən) *n.* [prob. < dial. *smidge*, var. of *smitch*, a particle] [Colloq.] a small amount; a bit: also **smidg′in, smidg′eon**

**smi·lax** (smī′laks) *n.* [L. < Gr. *smilax*, bindweed] **1.** same as CAT BRIER **2.** a twining greenhouse vine of the lily family, with bright green leaves

**smile** (smīl) *vi.* **smiled, smil′ing** [ME. *smilen*] **1.** to show pleasure, amusement, affection, irony, etc. by an upward curving of the corners of the mouth and a sparkling of the eyes **2.** to regard with favor (with *on* or *upon*) —*vt.* **1.** to express with a smile **2.** to affect by smiling —*n.* **1.** the act or facial expression of smiling **2.** a favorable or agreeable appearance —**smile away** to get rid of by smiling —**smil′er** *n.* —**smil′ing·ly** *adv.*

**smirch** (smurch) *vt.* [prob. < OFr. *esmorcher*, to hurt] **1.** to soil or smear as with grime **2.** to dishonor (a reputation) —*n.* **1.** a smudge; smear **2.** a stain on a reputation

**smirk** (smurk) *vi.* [OE. *smearcian*, to smile] to smile in a conceited or self-satisfied way —*n.* such a smile —**smirk′er** *n.* —**smirk′ing·ly** *adv.*

**smite** (smīt) *vt.* **smote, smit′ten** or **smote, smit′ing** [OE. *smitan*] **1.** [Now Rare] *a)* to hit or strike hard *b)* to defeat, punish, or kill **2.** to attack with disastrous effect **3.** to affect strongly and suddenly (*with*) [*smitten* with dread] **4.** to distress [*smitten* by conscience] **5.** to impress favorably [*smitten* with her charms] —*vi.* [Now Rare] to hit or strike hard —**smit′er** *n.*

**Smith** (smith) **1. Adam,** 1723–90; Scot. economist **2. Captain John,** 1580–1631; Eng. colonist in America **3. Joseph,** 1805–44; U.S. founder of the Mormon Church

**smith** (smith) *n.* [OE.] **1.** a person who makes or repairs metal objects; metalworker: usually in combination [*silversmith*] **2.** shortened form of BLACKSMITH

**smith·er·eens** (smith′ə rēnz′) *n.pl.* [Ir. *smidirīn*] [Colloq.] small fragments; bits

**smith·y** (smith′ē; *chiefly Brit.* smith′ē) *n., pl.* **smith′ies** [OE. *smiththe*] **1.** the workshop of a smith, esp. a blacksmith **2.** same as BLACKSMITH

**smit·ten** (smit′'n) *alt. pp. of* SMITE

**smock** (smäk) *n.* [OE. *smoc* or ON. *smokkr*] a loose, shirtlike, outer garment worn to protect the clothes —*vt.* **1.** to dress in a smock **2.** to decorate with smocking

**smock·ing** (smäk′iŋ) *n.* shirred, decorative stitching used in gathering cloth, as to make it hang in even folds

**smog** (smôg, smäg) *n.* [SM(OKE) + (F)OG] a harmful mixture of fog and smoke —**smog′gy** *adj.* **-gi·er, -gi·est**

**smoke** (smōk) *n.* [OE. *smoca*] **1.** *a)* the vaporous matter, with suspended particles of carbon, arising from something burning *b)* a cloud of this **2.** any vapor, fume, etc. resembling smoke **3.** *a)* an act or period of smoking tobacco, etc. [time for a *smoke*] *b)* something to smoke, as a cigarette **4.** something fleeting, unreal, or obscuring —*vi.* **smoked, smok′ing 1.** to give off smoke or a smokelike substance **2.** to discharge smoke excessively or improperly, as a fuel, a fireplace, etc. **3.** *a)* to draw the smoke of tobacco, etc. into the mouth and blow it out again *b)* to be a habitual smoker —*vt.* **1.** to stain or color with smoke **2.** to cure (meat, fish, etc.) with smoke **3.** to fumigate as with smoke **4.** to force out with smoke [to *smoke* an animal from its lair] **5.** to use (tobacco, a pipe, etc.) in smoking —**smoke out** to force out of hiding, secrecy, etc. —**smok′a·ble, smoke′a·ble** *adj.*

**smoke·house** (-hous′) *n.* a building where meats, fish, etc. are cured or flavored with smoke

**smoke·less** (-lis) *adj.* having or making little or no smoke

**smok·er** (smō′kər) *n.* **1.** a person or thing that smokes; specif., a person who habitually smokes tobacco **2.** a railroad car or compartment reserved esp. for smoking: also **smoking car 3.** an informal party for men only

**smoke screen 1.** a cloud of smoke spread to screen the movements of troops, ships, etc. **2.** anything said or done to conceal or mislead

**smoke·stack** (smōk′stak′) *n.* a pipe for the discharge of smoke from a steamship, factory, etc.

**Smok·ies** (smō′kēz) *same as* GREAT SMOKY MOUNTAINS

**smoking jacket** a man's lounging jacket for wear at home

**smok·y** (smō′kē) *adj.* **smok′i·er, smok′i·est 1.** giving off smoke, esp. excessive smoke **2.** like, of, or as of smoke [a *smoky* haze] **3.** filled with smoke **4.** having the color of smoke **5.** flavored by smoking **6.** darkened or soiled by smoke —**smok′i·ly** *adv.* —**smok′i·ness** *n.*

**Smoky Mountains** *same as* GREAT SMOKY MOUNTAINS

**smol·der** (smōl′dər) *vi.* [ME. *smoldren* < Gmc.] **1.** to burn and smoke without flame **2.** to exist in a suppressed state **3.** to have or show suppressed anger or hate —*n.* the act or condition of smoldering

**Smol·lett** (smäl′it), **To·bi·as George** (tō bī′əs) 1721–71; Brit. novelist, born in Scotland

**smolt** (smōlt) *n.* [LME. (Scot.)] a young salmon when it first leaves fresh water and descends to the sea

**smooch**[1] (smōōch) *n.* same as SMUTCH

**smooch**[2] (smōōch) *n.* [ult. akin to SMACK[2]] [Slang] a kiss —*vi., vt.* [Slang] to kiss or pet —**smooch′y** *adj.*

**smooth** (smōōth) *adj.* [OE. *smoth*] **1.** having an even surface with no roughness or projections **2.** without lumps [a *smooth* paste] **3.** even or gentle in flow or movement [a *smooth* voyage] **4.** free from interruptions, difficulties, etc. [*smooth* progress] **5.** calm; serene [a *smooth* temper] **6.** free from hair, beard, etc. **7.** not harsh to the taste **8.** having an easy, flowing rhythm or sound **9.** suave, polished, or ingratiating, esp. in an insincere way **10.** *Phonet.* not aspirated —*vt.* **1.** to make level or even **2.** to remove the lumps from **3.** to free from interruptions, difficulties, etc. **4.** to make calm; soothe **5.** to make less crude; refine —*vi.* to become smooth —*adv.* in a smooth manner —*n.* **1.** a smooth part **2.** an act of smoothing —**smooth away** to remove (difficulties, etc.) —**smooth down** to make or become smooth, or even, calm, etc. —**smooth over** to gloss over or make light of (an unpleasant situation) —**smooth′er** *n.* —**smooth′ly** *adv.* —**smooth′ness** *n.*

**smooth·bore** (-bôr′) *adj.* not rifled or grooved inside the barrel: said of guns —*n.* a smoothbore gun

**smooth·en** (-'n) *vt., vi.* to make or become smooth

**smooth muscle** unstriated involuntary muscle, occurring in the walls of the uterus, intestines, etc.

**smooth-shav·en** (-shā′v'n) *adj.* wearing no beard or mustache

**smooth-spo·ken** (-spō′k'n) *adj.* speaking in a pleasing, persuasive, or polished manner

**smooth-tongued** (-tuŋd′) *adj.* smooth-spoken, esp. in a plausible or flattering way

**smor·gas·bord, smör·gås·bord** (smôr′gəs bôrd′, smur′-) *n.* [Sw.] **1.** a wide variety of appetizers, cheeses, fishes, meats, salads, etc., served buffet style **2.** a meal composed of these **3.** a restaurant serving smorgasbord

**smote** (smōt) *pt. & alt. pp. of* SMITE

**smoth·er** (smuth′ər) *vt.* [ME. *smorthren* < *smorther*, dense smoke] **1.** to keep from getting enough air to breathe, or kill in this way; suffocate; stifle **2.** to cover (a fire), causing it to smolder or go out **3.** to cover over thickly [liver *smothered* in onions] **4.** to hide or suppress as by covering, as a yawn —*vi.* **1.** to be kept from getting enough air to breathe, or to die in this way **2.** to be hidden or suppressed —*n.* dense, suffocating smoke, dust, etc. —**smoth′er·er** *n.* —**smoth′er·y** *adj.*

**smoul·der** (smōl′dər) *vi., n. Brit. sp. of* SMOLDER

**smudge** (smuj) *n.* [prob. < ME. *smogen*] **1.** a stain, smear, etc.; dirty spot **2.** *a)* a fire made to produce dense smoke *b)* such smoke produced by burning a substance in containers (**smudge pots**), esp. for driving away insects or protecting plants from frost —*vt.* **smudged, smudg′ing 1.** to protect (an orchard, etc.) with smudge **2.** to make dirty; soil —*vi.* **1.** to blur or smear **2.** to become smudged —**smudg′y** *adj.*

**smug** (smug) *adj.* **smug′ger, smug′gest** [prob. < LowG. *smuk*, trim] **1.** orig., neat, trim, etc. **2.** so pleased with oneself, one's opinions, etc. as to be annoying to others; too self-satisfied —**smug′ly** *adv.* —**smug′ness** *n.*

**smug·gle** (smug′'l) *vt.* **-gled, -gling** [< LowG. *smuggeln*] **1.** to bring into or take out of a country secretly or illegally **2.** to bring, take, etc. secretly —*vi.* to smuggle forbidden or taxable goods —**smug′gler** *n.*

**smut** (smut) *n.* [< or akin to LowG. *smutt*] **1.** *a)* sooty matter *b)* a particle of this **2.** a soiled spot **3.** pornographic or obscene talk, writing, etc. **4.** *Bot. a)* a plant disease in which certain fungi form masses of black spores that break up into a fine powder *b)* any fungus causing smut —*vt.*, *vi.* smut′ted, smut′ting to make or become smutty

**smutch** (smuch) *vt.* [akin to prec.] to smudge; soil —*n.* 1. a dirty mark; smudge 2. soot, dirt, etc. —**smutch′y** *adj.*

**smut·ty** (smut′ē) *adj.* -ti·er, -ti·est 1. soiled with smut 2. affected with plant smut 3. pornographic or obscene —**smut′ti·ly** *adv.* —**smut′ti·ness** *n.*

**Smyr·na** (smur′nə) *former name of* IZMIR

**Sn** [L. *stannum*] *Chem.* tin

**SN** *U.S. Navy* Seaman

**snack** (snak) *n.* [prob. < MDu. *snacken*, to snap] a light meal or refreshment taken between regular meals —*vi.* to eat a snack or snacks

**snack bar** a lunch counter, cafeteria, etc. serving snacks

**snaf·fle** (snaf′′l) *n.* [prob. < Du. < ODu. dim. of *snabbe*, bill of a bird] a bit, usually light and jointed, attached to a bridle and having no curb —*vt.* -fled, -fling to fit with or control by a snaffle

**sna·fu** (sna fōō′, snaf′ōō) *adj.* [orig. military slang for phrase *s(ituation) n(ormal), a(ll) f(ouled)*–a euphemism– *u(p)*] [Slang] in disorder or confusion; completely mixed up —*vt.* -fued′, -fu′ing [Slang] to throw into confusion

**snag** (snag) *n.* [< Scand.] 1. a sharp part, point, etc. that sticks out and may catch on things 2. an underwater tree stump or branch dangerous to navigation 3. a snag-gletooth 4. a small branch of an antler 5. a tear or a pulled, looped-out thread in fabric, made by or as by a snag 6. an unexpected or hidden difficulty —*vt.* snagged, snag′ging 1. to catch, tear, etc. on a snag 2. to hinder; impede 3. to catch quickly —*vi.* 1. to strike a snag in water 2. to develop a snag —**snag′gy** *adj.* -gi·er, -gi·est

**snag·gle·tooth** (snag′′l tōōth′) *n., pl.* -teeth′ [< prec.] 1. a tooth that sticks out beyond the others 2. a crooked or broken tooth —**snag′gle·toothed′** *adj.*

**snail** (snāl) *n.* [OE. *snægl*] 1. a slow-moving gastropod mollusk living on land or in water and having a spiral protective shell 2. any lazy, slow-moving person or animal

**snake** (snāk) *n.* [OE. *snaca*] 1. any of various limbless reptiles with a long, scaly body, lidless eyes, and a tapering tail: some species have a poisonous bite 2. a treacherous or deceitful person 3. a long, flexible rod of spiraled wire, used by a plumber to clear blocked pipes, etc. —*vi.* snaked, snak′ing to move, twist, etc. like a snake —*vt.* [Colloq.] to drag, pull, or jerk —**snake′like′** *adj.*

**snake dance** an informal parade in which the celebrants join hands in a long, winding line

**snake in the grass** a treacherous person or harmful thing that is hidden or seemingly harmless

**Snake River** [transl. (prob. erroneous) of earlier *Shoshone River*] river in NW U.S., flowing from NW Wyo. into the Columbia River in Wash.: 1,038 mi.

**snake·root** (-rōōt′, -rŏot′) *n.* 1. any of various plants reputed to be remedies for snake bites 2. the roots of any of these plants

**snake·skin** (-skin′) *n.* a snake's skin or leather from it

**snak·y** (snā′kē) *adj.* snak′i·er, snak′i·est 1. of or like a snake or snakes 2. sinuous; winding; twisting 3. cunningly treacherous or evil 4. infested with snakes

**snap** (snap) *vi., vt.* snapped, snap′ping [< MDu. or MLowG. *snappen*] 1. to bite suddenly (often with *at*) 2. to snatch or grasp quickly or eagerly (often with *at* or *up*) 3. to speak or say in a sharp, abrupt way [to *snap* out orders, to *snap* back at a person in anger] 4. to break or part suddenly, esp. with a sharp, cracking sound 5. to break down suddenly under strain, as nerves, resistance, etc. 6. to make or cause to make a sudden, sharp, cracking sound [to *snap* one's fingers] 7. to close, fasten, etc. with a sound like this, as a lock 8. to move or cause to move suddenly and smartly [to *snap* to attention, *snap* the ball to me] 9. to take a snapshot (of) —*n.* 1. a sudden bite, grasp, snatch, etc. 2. a sudden breaking or parting 3. a sudden, sharp cracking or clicking sound 4. a short, angry utterance or way of speaking 5. a brief spell of cold weather 6. any clasp or fastening that closes with a click 7. a hard, thin cookie [gingersnaps] 8. *same as* SNAPSHOT 9. [Colloq.] alertness, vigor, or energy 10. [Slang] an easy job, problem, etc. —*adj.* 1. made or done quickly without deliberation [a *snap* decision] 2. that fastens with a snap 3. [Slang] simple; easy —*adv.* with, or as with, a snap —**not a snap** not at all —**snap back** to recover quickly from an illness, disappointment, etc. —**snap one's fingers at** to show lack of concern for —**snap out of it** to recover quickly or regain one's senses

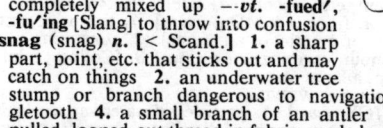
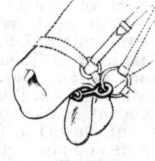
SNAFFLE

**snap bean** any of various green beans or wax beans

**snap·drag·on** (-drag′ən) *n.* [SNAP + DRAGON: from the mouth-shaped flowers] a plant with spikes of saclike two-lipped flowers in white, yellow, red, etc.

**snap·per** (-ər) *n.* 1. a person or thing that snaps 2. *pl.* -pers, -per: see PLURAL, II, D, 1 *a) same as* SNAPPING TURTLE *b)* any of various bony fishes of warm seas; esp., the red snapper

**snapping turtle** any of several large, freshwater turtles of N. America, with powerful jaws that snap with great force

**snap·pish** (snap′ish) *adj.* 1. likely to snap or bite 2. cross or irritable; sharp-tongued —**snap′pish·ly** *adv.* —**snap′pish·ness** *n.*

**snap·py** (snap′ē) *adj.* -pi·er, -pi·est 1. snappish; cross 2. that snaps; snapping 3. [Colloq.] *a)* brisk, vigorous, or lively [a *snappy* pace] *b)* sharply chilly [snappy weather] —**make it snappy** [Slang] be quick; hurry —**snap′pi·ly** *adv.* —**snap′pi·ness** *n.*

**snap·shot** (-shät′) *n.* a photograph taken with brief exposure by snapping the shutter of a hand camera

**snare** (sner) *n.* [OE. *sneare* < ON. *snara*] 1. a trap for small animals, usually consisting of a noose which jerks tight upon the release of a spring trigger 2. anything dangerous, risky, etc. that tempts or attracts; trap 3. *a)* a length of spiraled wire or of gut strung across the bottom of a snare drum for added vibration *b)* [pl.] a set of snare drums —*vt.* snared, snar′ing 1. to catch in a trap or snare 2. to lure into a situation that is dangerous, risky, etc. —**snar′er** *n.*

**snare drum** a small, double-headed drum with snares

**snarl¹** (snärl) *vi.* [< earlier *snar*, to growl] 1. to growl fiercely, baring the teeth, as a threatening dog 2. to speak sharply, as in anger —*vt.* to utter with a snarl —*n.* 1. a fierce, harsh growl 2. a harsh, angry utterance —**snarl′er** *n.* —**snarl′ing·ly** *adv.* —**snarl′y** *adj.*

SNARE DRUM

**snarl²** (snärl) *vt.* [ME. *snarlen*, akin to SNARE] 1. to make (thread, hair, etc.) knotted or tangled 2. to make disordered or confused [to *snarl* traffic] —*vi.* to become knotted or tangled —*n.* 1. a tangle or knot 2. a confused, disordered state or situation; confusion —**snarl′y** *adj.*

**snatch** (snach) *vt.* [prob. var. of ME. *snakken*, to seize] 1. to grasp or seize suddenly, eagerly, or without right, warning, etc.; grab 2. to remove abruptly or hastily 3. to take, get, etc. hastily or while there is a chance 4. [Slang] to kidnap —*vi.* to try to seize a thing suddenly; grasp (*at* something) —*n.* 1. the act of snatching 2. a short time [to sleep in *snatches*] 3. a fragment; bit [snatches of gossip] —**snatch′er** *n.*

**snatch·y** (-ē) *adj.* snatch′i·er, snatch′i·est done in snatches; not complete or continuous; disconnected

**sneak** (snēk) *vi.* sneaked or colloq. snuck, sneak′ing [prob. < OE. hyp. *snecan*, akin to *snican*, to crawl] 1. to move quietly and stealthily so as to avoid notice 2. to act in an underhanded or cowardly manner —*vt.* to give, put, take, etc. secretly or in a sneaking manner —*n.* 1. one who sneaks; sneaking, underhanded, contemptible person 2. an act of sneaking —*adj.* without warning [a *sneak* attack] —**sneak out of** to avoid (a duty, etc.) craftily

**sneak·er** (snē′kər) *n.* 1. a person or animal that sneaks 2. a cloth shoe with a heelless, soft rubber sole

**sneak·ing** (-kiŋ) *adj.* 1. cowardly, stealthy, underhanded, or furtive 2. not admitted; secret [a *sneaking* fondness for candy] —**sneaking suspicion** a slight or growing suspicion —**sneak′ing·ly** *adv.*

**sneak preview** an advance single showing of a movie, as for getting audience reaction before regular showings

**sneak thief** a person who commits thefts in a sneaking way, without the use of force or violence

**sneak·y** (snē′kē) *adj.* sneak′i·er, sneak′i·est of or like a sneak; underhanded —**sneak′i·ly** *adv.* —**sneak′i·ness** *n.*

**sneer** (snir) *vi.* [ME. *sneren*] 1. to look scornful or sarcastic, as by curling the lip 2. to express scorn, derision, etc. in speech or writing —*vt.* to utter in a sneering way —*n.* 1. an act of sneering 2. a sneering look, remark, etc. —**sneer′er** *n.* —**sneer′ing·ly** *adv.*

**sneeze** (snēz) *vi.* sneezed, sneez′ing [ME. *snesen*, altered < *fnesen* < OE. *fneosan*] to exhale breath from the nose and mouth in a sudden, uncontrolled way, as because the mucous membrane of the nose has been irritated —*n.* an act of sneezing —**not to be sneezed at** not to be disregarded —**sneez′er** *n.* —**sneez′y** *adj.*

**snell** (snel) *n.* [U.S. dial. < ?] a short length of gut, nylon, etc. used to attach a fishhook to a fish line —*vt.* to attach (a fishhook) to a snell

**snick**[1] (snik) *n.* [prob. < *snick or snee*, combat with knives] a small cut or notch; nick —*vt.* to nick

**snick**[2] (snik) *n., vt., vi.* [echoic] *same as* CLICK

**snick·er** (snik′ər) *vi.* [echoic] to laugh in a sly or partly stifled manner, as in disrespect or embarrassment —*vt.* to utter with a snicker —*n.* a snickering laugh —**snick′er·er** *n.* —**snick′er·ing·ly** *adv.*

**snide** (snīd) *adj.* [orig., counterfeit < thieves' slang, prob. of Du. dial. or G. origin] slyly malicious or derisive [a snide remark] —**snide′ly** *adv.* —**snide′ness** *n.*

**sniff** (snif) *vi.* [echoic] **1.** to draw air up the nose with enough force to be heard, as when trying to smell something **2.** to express disdain, skepticism, etc. by sniffing —*vt.* **1.** to draw (air, an inhalant, etc.) up the nose with some force **2.** to smell (a substance) by sniffing **3.** to detect, perceive, etc. as by sniffing (often with *out*) —*n.* **1.** an act or sound of sniffing **2.** something sniffed —**sniff′-er** *n.*

**snif·fle** (snif′'l) *vi.* **-fled, -fling** to sniff repeatedly, as in checking mucus running from the nose —*n.* an act or sound of sniffling —**the sniffles** [Colloq.] a head cold, etc. in which there is much sniffling —**snif′fler** *n.*

**sniff·y** (-ē) *adj.* **sniff′i·er, sniff′i·est** [Colloq.] characterized by or having a tendency to sniff: also **sniff′ish** —**sniff′i·ly** *adv.* —**sniff′i·ness** *n.*

**snif·ter** (snif′tər) *n.* a globe-shaped goblet with a small opening to concentrate the aroma, as of brandy

**snig·ger** (snig′ər) *vi., vt., n.* [echoic] *same as* SNICKER

**snip** (snip) *vt.* **snipped, snip′ping** [Du. *snippen*] **1.** to cut with scissors, etc. in a short, quick stroke or strokes **2.** to remove by such cutting —*vi.* to make a short, quick cut or cuts —*n.* **1.** a small cut made with scissors, etc. **2.** the sound of this **3.** a small piece cut off **4.** [*pl.*] heavy hand shears for cutting sheet metal, etc. **5.** [Colloq.] a young, small, or insignificant person, esp. one regarded as impudent —**snip′per** *n.*

**snipe** (snīp) *n.* [ON. *snipa*] **1.** *pl.* **snipes, snipe:** see PLURAL, II, D, 1 any of certain wading birds with a long, flexible bill, living chiefly in marshy places **2.** a shot from a hidden position —*vi.* **sniped, snip′ing** **1.** to hunt or shoot snipe **2.** to shoot from a hidden position at individuals of an enemy force **3.** to direct an attack (*at someone*) in a sly or underhanded way —**snip′er** *n.*

**snip·pet** (snip′it) *n.* [dim. of SNIP] **1.** a small scrap or fragment, specif. of information, a writing, etc. **2.** [Colloq.] *same as* SNIP (*n.* 5) —**snip′pet·y** *adj.*

**snip·py** (snip′ē) *adj.* **-pi·er, -pi·est** **1.** made up of small scraps or snips; fragmentary **2.** [Colloq.] curt, sharp, etc., esp. in a rude or insolent way —**snip′pi·ly** *adv.* —**snip′pi·ness** *n.*

**snit** (snit) *n.* [< ? SN(IPPY) + (F)IT[2]] a fit of anger, pique, etc.: usually in the phrase **in** (or **into**) **a snit**

**snitch** (snich) *vt.* [< 18th-c. thieves' slang: orig. sense "a nose"] [Slang] to steal (usually something of little value); pilfer —*vi.* [Slang] to be an informer; tattle (*on*) —*n.* [Slang] an informer: also **snitch′er**

**sniv·el** (sniv′'l) *vi.* **-eled** or **-elled, -el·ing** or **-el·ling** [akin to OE. *snofl*, mucus] **1.** to have mucus running from the nose **2.** to cry and sniffle **3.** to complain in a whining, tearful manner **4.** to make a tearful, often false display of grief, sympathy, etc. —*n.* **1.** nasal mucus **2.** a sniffling **3.** a sniveling display of grief, etc. —**sniv′el·er** *n.*

**snob** (snäb) *n.* [< ? ON. *snāpr*, dolt] **1.** a person who attaches great importance to wealth, social position, etc., having contempt for those he considers inferior **2.** a person who feels and acts smugly superior about his particular tastes or interests [an intellectual snob] —**snob′ber·y** *n., pl.* **-ber·ies** —**snob′bish** *adj.* —**snob′bish·ly** *adv.* —**snob′bish·ness** *n.* —**snob′bism** *n.*

**snood** (snood) *n.* [OE. *snod*] a baglike net worn at the back of a woman's head to hold the hair —*vt.* to bind (the hair) with a snood

**snook** (snook) *n., pl.* **snook, snooks:** see PLURAL, II, D, 2 [Du. *snoek*, pike] a pikelike fish of warm seas; esp., a game and food fish of the tropical Atlantic

**snoop** (snoop) *vi.* [Du. *snoepen*, to eat snacks on the sly] [Colloq.] to look about in a sneaking, prying way —*n.* [Colloq.] **1.** one who snoops: also **snoop′er** **2.** the act of snooping —**snoop′i·ness** *n.* —**snoop′y** *adj.* **snoop′i·er, snoop′i·est**

**snoot** (snoot) *n.* [SEE SNOUT] [Colloq.] **1.** the nose **2.** the face **3.** a grimace —*vt.* to snub

**snoot·y** (-ē) *adj.* **snoot′i·er, snoot′i·est** [prec. + -Y[2]] [Colloq.] haughty; snobbish —**snoot′i·ly** *adv.* —**snoot′i·ness** *n.*

**snooze** (snooz) *n.* [< ? LowG. *snusen*, to snore] [Colloq.] a brief sleep; nap —*vi.* **snoozed, snooz′ing** [Colloq.] to take a brief sleep; nap —**snooz′er** *n.*

**snore** (snôr) *vi.* **snored, snor′ing** [echoic] to breathe, while asleep, with harsh sounds caused by vibration of the soft palate, usually with the mouth open —*n.* the act or sound of snoring —**snor′er** *n.*

**snor·kel** (snôr′k'l) *n.* [G. *schnörkel*, spiral] **1.** a device for submarines, with air intake and exhaust tubes, permitting submergence for long periods **2.** a breathing tube extending above the surface of the water, used in swimming just below the surface —*vi.* **-keled, -kel·ing** to move or swim under water using a snorkel —**snor′kel·er** *n.*

SNORKEL

**snort** (snôrt) *vi.* [ME. *snorten*, akin to SNORE] **1.** to force breath from the nose in a sudden and noisy way **2.** to express anger, scorn, etc. by a snort **3.** to make a noise like a snort, as in laughing boisterously —*vt.* to express or utter with a snort —*n.* **1.** the act or sound of snorting **2.** [Slang] a drink of straight liquor, taken in one gulp —**snort′er** *n.* —**snort′ing·ly** *adv.*

**snot** (snät) *n.* [OE. (ge)*snot*, mucus] **1.** nasal mucus: a vulgar term **2.** [Slang] a young person who is insolent

**snot·ty** (-ē) *adj.* **-ti·er, -ti·est** **1.** of, like, or dirtied with snot **2.** [Slang] *a*) offensive; contemptible *b*) impudent, insolent, etc. —**snot′ti·ly** *adv.* —**snot′ti·ness** *n.*

**snout** (snout) *n.* [prob. < MDu. *snute*] **1.** the projecting nose and jaws, or muzzle, of an animal **2.** something like an animal's snout, as a nozzle or spout **3.** [Colloq.] a human nose, esp. a large one

**snout beetle** *same as* WEEVIL

**snow** (snō) *n.* [OE. *snaw*] **1.** particles of water vapor which when frozen in the upper air fall to earth as soft, white, crystalline flakes **2.** *a*) a falling of snow *b*) snowy weather **3.** a mass of fallen snow **4.** [Poet.] whiteness **5.** fluctuating spots appearing on a TV screen as a result of a weak signal **6.** [Slang] cocaine or heroin —*vi.* to fall as or like snow —*vt.* **1.** to shower or let fall as or like snow **2.** to cover, obstruct, etc. with or as with snow (usually with *in, under*, etc.) **3.** [Slang] to deceive, win over, etc. by glib talk, flattery, etc. —**snow under** to overwhelm as with work or defeat

**snow·ball** (-bôl′) *n.* **1.** a mass of snow packed together into a ball **2.** a cultivated European cranberry bush with round clusters of white or pinkish flowers —*vi.* **1.** to increase rapidly and out of control like a ball of snow rolling downhill **2.** to throw snowballs —*vt.* **1.** to throw snowballs at **2.** to cause to increase rapidly

**snow·bank** (-baŋk′) *n.* a large mound of snow

**snow·ber·ry** (-ber′ē) *n., pl.* **-ries** **1.** a hardy N. American plant with small, pink flowers and soft, white berries **2.** any of various other plants with white berries **3.** any of these berries

**snow·bird** (-burd′) *n.* **1.** a widely distributed N. American junco **2.** *same as* SNOW BUNTING

**snow-blind** (-blīnd′) *adj.* blinded temporarily by ultraviolet rays of the sun reflected from snow —**snow blindness**

**snow blower** a motorized, hand-guided machine on wheels, for removing snow as from walks: also **snow thrower**

**snow·bound** (-bound′) *adj.* shut in or blocked off by snow

**snow bunting** a small finch inhabiting cold regions in the Northern Hemisphere

**snow·cap** (-kap′) *n.* a cap of snow, as on a mountain, the top of a tree, etc. —**snow′capped′** *adj.*

**snow·drift** (-drift′) *n.* **1.** a smooth heap of snow blown together by the wind **2.** snow blown along by the wind

**snow·drop** (-dräp′) *n.* a low-growing, bulbous plant with small, bell-shaped white flowers

**snow·fall** (-fôl′) *n.* **1.** a fall of snow **2.** the amount of snow that falls in a given area or period of time

**snow·field** (-fēld′) *n.* a large expanse of snow

**snow·flake** (-flāk′) *n.* **1.** a single crystal of snow **2.** *same as* SNOW BUNTING **3.** a European bulbous plant with drooping white flowers

**snow goose** a white goose that breeds in the Arctic, having a red bill and black wing tips

**snow leopard** a large, whitish cat of the mountains of C Asia, having many dark blotches on its fur

**snow line** (or **limit**) the lower boundary of a high region in which snow never melts

**snow·man** (-man′) *n., pl.* **-men′** (-men′) a crude human figure made of snow packed together

**snow·mo·bile** (-mō bēl′) *n.* a motor vehicle for traveling over snow, usually with steerable runners at the front and tractor treads at the rear —*vi.* **-biled, -bil′ing** to travel by snowmobile

**snow-on-the-moun·tain** (snō′än thə moun′t'n) *n.* a widely cultivated spurge of the western U.S., with small flowers and the margins of the upper leaves white

**snow·plow** (snō′plou′) *n.* **1.** any plowlike machine used to clear snow off a road, railroad, etc. **2.** *Skiing* a stemming of both skis, as for stopping, with the tips of the skis pointed at each other —*vi.* to stem with both skis

**snow·shoe** (-shōō′) *n.* a racket-shaped frame of wood criss-crossed with strips of leather, etc., worn on the feet to prevent sinking in deep snow —*vi.* **-shoed′, -shoe′ing** to use snowshoes in walking —**snow′-sho′er** *n.*

**snowshoe hare** a hare of N. N. America that is brown in summer and white in winter: also **snowshoe rabbit**

**snow·slide** (-slīd′) *n.* an avalanche of mainly snow

**snow·storm** (-stôrm′) *n.* a storm with a heavy snowfall

**snow·suit** (-sōōt′) *n.* a heavily lined one-piece garment or set of pants and jacket, often with a hood, worn by children

SNOWSHOES

**snow tire** a tire with a deep tread, and sometimes protruding studs, for added traction on snow or ice

**snow-white** (-hwīt′, -wīt′) *adj.* white as snow

**snow·y** (snō′ē) *adj.* **snow′i·er, snow′i·est** 1. of or characterized by snow 2. covered or filled with snow 3. like snow; specif., *a)* pure; spotless *b)* white —**snow′i·ly** *adv.* —**snow′i·ness** *n.*

**snub** (snub) *vt.* **snubbed, snub′bing** [ON. *snubba,* to chide] 1. orig., to check with sharp words 2. to treat with scorn, disregard, etc.; slight 3. *a)* to check suddenly the movement of (a rope, etc.) by turning it around a post *b)* to make (a boat, etc.) fast in this way 4. to put out (a cigarette) —*n.* 1. scornful, slighting action or treatment 2. a snubbing, or checking —*adj.* short and turned up; pug: said of the nose —**snub′ber** *n.*

**snub·by** (-ē) *adj.* **-bi·er, -bi·est** turned up; snub

**snub-nosed** (-nōzd′) *adj.* having a snub nose

**snuck** (snuk) *colloq. pt. & pp. of* SNEAK

**snuff**[1] (snuf) *n.* [< ?] the charred end of a candlewick —*vt.* 1. to trim off the charred end of (a candlewick) 2. to put out (a candle) —**snuff out** 1. to put out (a candle, etc.); extinguish 2. to destroy or cause to die suddenly

**snuff**[2] (snuf) *vt.* [MDu. *snuffen*] 1. to inhale strongly through the nose; sniff 2. to smell or sniff at —*vi.* 1. to sniff or snort 2. [Rare] to use snuff —*n.* 1. the act or sound of snuffing; sniff 2. *a)* a preparation of powdered tobacco taken up into the nose by sniffing or applied to the gums *b)* a pinch of this —**up to snuff** [Colloq.] up to the usual standard —**snuff′y** *adj.* **snuff′i·er, snuff′i·est**

**snuff·box** (-bäks′) *n.* a small box for holding snuff

**snuff·er** (-ər) *n.* 1. a device with a cone on the end of a handle, for putting out a burning candle: in full, **candle snuffer** 2. [*pl.*] an instrument like shears, for snuffing a candle: also **pair of snuffers**

**snuf·fle** (snuf′'l) *vi.* **-fled, -fling** [freq. of SNUFF[2]] 1. to breathe audibly and with difficulty or by constant sniffing, as a dog in trailing; sniffle 2. to speak or sing in a nasal tone —*vt.* to utter by snuffling —*n.* 1. the act or sound of snuffling 2. a nasal tone or twang —**the snuffles** *same as* the SNIFFLES —**snuf′fler** *n.*

**snug** (snug) *adj.* **snug′ger, snug′gest** [prob. ult. < Scand.] 1. protected from the weather; warm and cozy 2. compact and convenient; neat [a *snug* cottage] 3. large enough to provide ease: said of an income 4. tight in fit [a *snug* coat] 5. well-built; seaworthy 6. hidden or concealed [to lie *snug*] —*adv.* so as to be snug —*vt.* **snugged, snug′ging** to make snug or secure —**snug′ly** *adv.* —**snug′ness** *n.*

**snug·gle** (-'l) *vi.* **-gled, -gling** [freq. of SNUG] to lie closely and comfortably; cuddle, as for warmth, in affection, etc. —*vt.* to cuddle

**so**[1] (sō) *adv.* [OE. *swa*] 1. in the way shown, expressed, understood, etc. [hold the bat just *so*] 2. *a)* to such an extent [why are you *so* late?] *b)* very [they are *so* happy] *c)* [Colloq.] very much [she *so* wants to go] 3. for the reason specified; therefore [they were tired, and *so* left] 4. more or less; approximately [fifty dollars or *so*] : in this sense often regarded as a pronoun 5. also; likewise [I'm going and *so* are you] : also used colloquially in contradicting a negative statement [I did *so* tell the truth!] 6. then [and *so* to bed] —*conj.* 1. in order that; with the purpose that: usually followed by *that* [talk louder *so* (that) all may hear] 2. [Colloq.] with the result that [he smiled, *so* I did too] 3. if only; as long as (that) [*so* that which has been specified or named [he is a friend and will remain *so*] —*interj.* an exclamation of surprise, approval, triumph, etc. —*adj.* 1. true; in reality [that's *so*] 2. in proper order [everything must be just *so*] —**and so on** (or **forth**) and the rest; et

cetera (etc.) —**so as** with the purpose or result (followed by an infinitive) —**so much** to an unspecified but limited degree, amount, etc. [paid *so much* per day] —**so much for** no more need be said about [*so much for* that] —**so what?** [Colloq.] even if so, what then?: used to express disregard, challenge, etc.

**so**[2] (sō) *n. Music same as* SOL[2]

**So.** 1. south 2. southern

**soak** (sōk) *vt.* [OE. *socian*] 1. to make thoroughly wet; drench or saturate 2. to submerge in a liquid, as for thorough wetting, softening, soothing, etc. 3. *a)* to take in (liquid) by absorbing (usually with *up*) *b)* to absorb by exposure to it [to *soak* up sunshine] 4. to take in mentally [to *soak* up knowledge] 5. [Colloq.] to overcharge —*vi.* 1. to stay immersed in liquid for wetting, softening, etc. 2. to pass (*into* or *through*) as a liquid does [rain soaking through his coat] 3. to become absorbed mentally [the fact *soaked* into his head] —*n.* 1. a soaking or being soaked 2. liquid used for soaking 3. [Slang] a drunkard

**so-and-so** (sō′ən sō′) *n., pl.* **so′-and-sos′** [Colloq.] some person or thing whose name is not specified: often used to avoid vulgar or offensive name-calling

**soap** (sōp) *n.* [OE. *sape*] 1. a substance used with water to produce suds for washing, usually produced by the action of an alkali, as caustic soda, on fats or oils 2. any metallic salt of a fatty acid 3. [Slang] *same as* SOAP OPERA: also **soap′er** —*vt.* to lather, scrub, etc. with soap —**no soap** [Slang] 1. (it is) not acceptable 2. to no avail

**soap·ber·ry** (-ber′ē) *n., pl.* **-ries** 1. any of various trees with fruits containing a soapy material 2. the globe-shaped fruit, with yellowish flesh and a large, round seed

**soap·box** (-bäks′) *n.* 1. a box for soap 2. any improvised platform used by a person (**soapbox orator**) making an informal, often impassioned speech to a street audience

**soap opera** [Colloq.] a daytime radio or TV serial drama of a melodramatic, sentimental nature: originally, many of the sponsors were soap companies

**soap·stone** (-stōn′) *n. same as* STEATITE

**soap·suds** (-sudz′) *n.pl.* 1. soapy water, esp. when stirred into a foam 2. the foam on soapy water

**soap·y** (sō′pē) *adj.* **soap′i·er, soap′i·est** 1. covered with or containing soap 2. of or like soap 3. [Slang] suave; oily —**soap′i·ly** *adv.* —**soap′i·ness** *n.*

**soar** (sôr) *vi.* [OFr. *essorer,* ult. < L. *ex-,* out + *aura,* air] 1. to rise or fly high into the air 2. to sail or glide along high in the air, as a glider does on air currents 3. to rise above the ordinary level [*soaring* prices] —*n.* 1. soaring range 2. the act of soaring —**soar′er** *n.*

**sob** (säb) *vi.* **sobbed, sob′bing** [ME. *sobben*] 1. to weep aloud with short, gasping breaths 2. to make a sound like this, as the wind —*vt.* 1. to put (oneself), as to sleep, by sobbing 2. to utter with sobs —*n.* the act or sound of sobbing —**sob′-bing·ly** *adv.*

**so·ber** (sō′bər) *adj.* [< OFr. < L. *sobrius*] 1. temperate, esp. in the use of alcoholic liquor 2. not drunk 3. serious, solemn, sedate, etc. 4. quiet; plain: said of color, clothes, etc. 5. not distorted [the *sober* truth] 6. showing mental and emotional balance —*vt., vi.* to make or become sober (often with *up* or *down*) —**so′ber·ly** *adv.* —**so′ber·ness** *n.*

**so·ber-mind·ed** (-mīn′did) *adj.* sensible and serious

**so·bri·e·ty** (sə brī′ə tē, sō-) *n.* a being sober; specif., *a)* temperance, esp. in the use of alcoholic liquor *b)* seriousness; sedateness

**so·bri·quet** (sō′brə kā′, sō′brə kā′) *n.* [Fr.] 1. a nickname 2. an assumed name

**sob story** [Colloq.] a very sad story; esp., an account of personal troubles meant to arouse sympathy

**Soc., soc.** 1. social 2. socialist 3. society

**so-called** (sō′kôld′) *adj.* 1. popularly known by this term [the *so-called* nuclear powers] 2. inaccurately regarded as such [a *so-called* liberal]

**soc·cer** (säk′ər) *n.* [alt. < (AS)SOC(IATION FOOTBALL)] a kind of football played with a round ball moved chiefly by kicking

**so·cia·ble** (sō′shə b'l) *adj.* [Fr. < L. < *socius;* see ff.] 1. enjoying or requiring the company of others; friendly; affable 2. characterized by pleasant, informal conversation and companionship —*n.* a social, esp. a church social —**so′cia·bil′i·ty** *n., pl.* **-ties** —**so′cia·bly** *adv.*

**so·cial** (sō′shəl) *adj.* [< Fr. < L. *socialis < socius,* companion] 1. of or having to do with human beings living together in a situation or group relation affecting their common welfare [*social* problems] 2. living in this way [man as a *social* being] 3. of or having to do with the ranks of society, specif. the more fashionable ranks [a *social* event] 4. getting along well with others; sociable 5. of or for companionship **6.** of or engaged in welfare work /a *social* agency/ **7.** living in groups or communities /the ant is a *social* insect/ —*n.* an informal gathering for recreation; party —**so′cial·ly** *adv.*

**social climber** a person who seeks higher social status by getting acquainted with distinguished or wealthy people

**social disease** any venereal disease

**so·cial·ism** (sō′shəl iz′m) *n.* **1.** any of various theories of the ownership and operation of the means of production and distribution by society rather than by private individuals, with all members of society sharing in the work and the products **2.** [*often* S-] *a*) a political movement for establishing such a system *b*) the doctrines, etc. of the Socialist parties **3.** the stage of society, in Marxist doctrine, coming between the capitalist stage and the communist stage (see COMMUNISM, sense 2), in which private ownership of the means of production and distribution has been eliminated

**so·cial·ist** (-ist) *n.* **1.** an advocate or supporter of socialism **2.** [S-] a member of a Socialist Party —*adj.* **1.** of or like socialism or socialists **2.** advocating or supporting socialism **3.** [S-] designating or of a political party advocating Socialism Also **so′cial·is′tic** —**so′cial·is′ti·cal·ly** *adv.*

**so·cial·ite** (sō′shə līt′) *n.* a socially prominent person

**so·ci·al·i·ty** (sō′shē al′ə tē) *n.* **1.** a being social or sociable **2.** *pl.* **-ties** the tendency to form social groups

**so·cial·ize** (sō′shə līz′) *vt.* **-ized′, -iz′ing 1.** to make social or fit for cooperative group living **2.** to adapt to the common needs of a social group **3.** to put under government ownership **4.** to cause to become socialist —*vi.* to take part in social activity —**so′cial·i·za′tion** *n.* —**so′cial·iz′er** *n.*

**socialized medicine** any system supplying complete medical and hospital care, through public funds, for all the people in a community, district, or nation

**social science 1.** the study of people living together in groups, families, etc. **2.** any of several studies, as history, economics, civics, etc., dealing with society and the activity of its members —**social scientist**

**social secretary** a secretary employed by an individual to handle his social appointments and correspondence

**social security** a Federal system of old-age, unemployment, or disability insurance, financed by a fund maintained by employees, employers, and the government

**social service** *same as* SOCIAL WORK —**so′cial-serv′ice** *adj.*

**social studies** a course of study, esp. in elementary and secondary schools, including history, civics, geography, etc.

**social welfare 1.** the welfare of society, esp. of those who are underprivileged or disadvantaged because of poverty, unemployment, etc. **2.** *same as* SOCIAL WORK

**social work** any activity designed to promote the welfare of the community and the individual, as through counseling services, recreation and rehabilitation centers, aid for the needy and aged, etc. —**social worker**

**so·ci·e·ty** (sə sī′ə tē) *n., pl.* **-ties** [< MFr. < L. *societas* < *socius,* companion] **1.** a group of persons regarded as forming a single community, esp. as forming a distinct social or economic class **2.** the system or condition of living together in such a group /an agrarian *society*/ **3.** all people, collectively, regarded as a community of mutually dependent individuals **4.** companionship **5.** one's friends or associates **6.** any organized group of people with work, interests, etc. in common /a medical *society*/ **7.** a group of persons regarded as a dominant class because of their wealth, birth, etc. —*adj.* of or involving society (*n.* 7) —**so·ci′e·tal** *adj.* —**so·ci′e·tal·ly** *adv.*

**Society Islands** group of French islands in the South Pacific: chief island, Tahiti

**Society of Friends** a Christian religious sect founded in England c. 1650 by George Fox: the Friends have no formal creed, rites, liturgy, or priesthood, and reject violence in human relations, including war

**Society of Jesus** *see* JESUIT

**so·ci·o-** (sō′sē ō′, -shē-; -ə) [Fr. < L. *socius,* companion] *a combining form meaning* social, society, sociological

**so·ci·o·bi·ol·o·gy** (sō′sē ō bī äl′ə jē, -shē-) *n.* the scientific study of the biological bases for animal and human social behavior —**so′ci·o·bi·ol′o·gist** *n.*

**so·ci·o·e·co·nom·ic** (-ē′kə näm′ik, -ek′ə-) *adj.* of or involving both social and economic factors

**so·ci·ol·o·gy** (sō′sē äl′ə jē, -shē-) *n.* [< Fr.: see SOCIO- & -LOGY] the science of human society and of social relations, organization, and change; specif., the study of the beliefs, values, etc. of groups in society —**so′ci·o·log′i·cal** (-ə läj′i k'l), **so′ci·o·log′ic** *adj.* —**so′ci·o·log′i·cal·ly** *adv.* —**so′ci·ol′o·gist** *n.*

**so·ci·o·path** (sō′sē ə path′, -shē-) *n.* [SOCIO- + (PSYCHO)PATH] a psychopathic personality whose behavior is aggressively antisocial —**so′ci·o·path′ic** *adj.*

**so·ci·o·po·lit·i·cal** (sō′sē ō pə lit′i k'l, -shē-) *adj.* of or involving both social and political factors

**sock¹** (säk) *n.* [OE. *socc* < L. *soccus,* a light, low-heeled shoe] **1.** a light shoe worn by comic characters in ancient

Greek and Roman drama **2.** comic drama **3.** *pl.* **socks, sox** a short stocking reaching only part way to the knee —**socked in** grounded (as aircraft) or closed (as an airfield) because of fog

**sock²** (säk) *vt.* [Slang] to hit with force, esp. with the fist —*n.* [Slang] a blow —*adv.* [Slang] directly; squarely —**sock away** to set aside (money)

**sock·et** (säk′it) *n.* [< Anglo-Fr., dim. < OFr. *soc,* plowshare < Gaul.] a hollow part into which something fits /an eye *socket,* the *socket* for a light bulb/

**sock·eye** (säk′ī′) *n.* [< AmInd. *suk-kegh*] a salmon of the N Pacific with red flesh, often canned

**Soc·ra·tes** (säk′rə tēz′) 470?-399 B.C.; Athenian philosopher & teacher —**So·crat·ic** (sə krat′ik, sō-) *adj., n.*

**Socratic method** a method of teaching, as used by Socrates, in which a series of questions leads the answerer to a logical conclusion foreseen by the questioner

**sod** (säd) *n.* [prob. < MDu. or MLowG. *sode*] **1.** a surface layer of earth containing grass plants with their matted roots; turf **2.** a piece of this layer —*vt.* **sod′ded, sod′ding** to cover with sod or sods

**so·da** (sō′də) *n.* [ML., ult. < Ar. *suwwād,* a plant burned to produce soda] **1.** *a*) sodium oxide, Na₂O *b*) *same as:* (1) SODIUM BICARBONATE (2) SODIUM CARBONATE (3) SODIUM HYDROXIDE **2.** *a*) *same as* SODA WATER (sense 1) *b*) [Chiefly Eastern] a drink of soda water flavored with syrup *c*) a confection of soda water flavored with syrup, fruit, etc. and served with ice cream in it

**soda ash** crude sodium carbonate (sense 1)

**soda cracker** a light, crisp cracker, usually salted, made from a dough of flour, water, and leavening, orig. baking soda and cream of tartar

**soda fountain 1.** a counter for making and serving soft drinks, sodas, sundaes, etc. **2.** an apparatus for making soda water, with faucets for drawing it off

**soda jerk** [Slang] a person who works at a soda fountain: also **soda jerk·er** (jur′kər)

**so·dal·i·ty** (sō dal′ə tē) *n., pl.* **-ties** [< L. < *sodalis,* companion] **1.** an association or brotherhood **2.** *R.C.Ch.* a devotional or charitable lay society

**soda pop** a flavored, carbonated soft drink, esp. as sold in tightly capped bottles or in cans

**soda water 1.** water charged under pressure with carbon dioxide gas, used in ice-cream sodas, as a chaser or mix, etc. **2.** *same as* SODA POP

**sod·den** (säd′'n) *obs. pp. of* SEETHE —*adj.* **1.** soaked through **2.** soggy from improper baking or cooking, as bread **3.** dull or stupefied, as from drunkenness —*vt., vi.* to make or become sodden —**sod′den·ness** *n.*

**so·di·um** (sō′dē əm) *n.* [ModL. < SODA] a silver-white, alkaline metallic chemical element, found in nature only in combined form: symbol, Na; at. wt., 22.9898; at. no., 11

**sodium benzoate** a sweet, white powder, the sodium salt of benzoic acid, used as a food preservative

**sodium bicarbonate** a white, crystalline compound, NaHCO₃, used in baking powder, as an antacid, etc.

**sodium carbonate 1.** the anhydrous sodium salt of carbonic acid, Na₂CO₃ **2.** any of the hydrated carbonates of sodium; esp., *same as* SAL SODA

**sodium chloride** common salt, NaCl

**sodium cyanide** a white, highly poisonous salt, NaCN, used in electroplating, as an insecticide, etc.

**sodium hydroxide** a white, strongly caustic substance, NaOH, used in chemistry, etc.

**sodium hyposulfite** *see* SODIUM THIOSULFATE

**sodium nitrate** a clear, crystalline salt, NaNO₃, used in manufacturing explosives, fertilizers, etc.

**sodium pentothal** *same as* THIOPENTAL SODIUM

**sodium thiosulfate** a white, crystalline salt, Na₂S₂O₃, used as a fixing agent in photography, etc.: popularly but incorrectly called (*sodium*) *hyposulfite* or *hypo*

**Sod·om** (säd′əm) *Bible* a city destroyed by fire together with a neighboring city, Gomorrah, because of the sinfulness of the people: Gen. 18-19

**Sod·om·ite** (-īt′) *n.* **1.** an inhabitant of Sodom **2.** [s-] a person who practices sodomy

**sod·om·ize** (-īz′) *vt.* **-ized′, -iz′ing** [SODOM(Y) + -IZE] to engage in sodomy with; specif., to force sodomy upon

**sod·om·y** (-ē) *n.* [< SODOM] any sexual intercourse held to be abnormal, as between a person and an animal or between two persons of the same sex

**so·ev·er** (sō ev′ər) *adv.* **1.** in any way /how dark *soever* it may be/ **2.** of any kind; at all /no rest *soever*/

**-so·ev·er** (sō ev′ər) *a combining form added for emphasis or generalization* to who, what, when, where, how, etc., *and meaning* any (person, thing, time, place, or manner) of all those possible

**so·fa** (sō′fə) *n.* [Fr. < Ar. *ṣuffah,* a cushion] an upholstered couch with fixed back and arms

**So·fi·a** (sō′fē ə, sō fē′ə; *Bulg.* sô′fē yä′) capital of Bulgaria, in the W part: pop. 868,000

**S. of Sol.** Song of Solomon

**soft** (sôft, säft) *adj.* [OE. *softe*] **1.** giving way easily under pressure, as a feather pillow or moist clay **2.** easily cut, shaped, or worn away *[a soft* wood or metal*]* **3.** not as hard as is normal, desirable, etc. *[soft* butter*]* **4.** smooth to the touch **5.** *a)* bland; not acid, sour, or sharp *b)* easy to digest because free from roughage: said of a diet **6.** nonalcoholic: said of drinks **7.** having few or none of the mineral salts that interfere with the lathering of soap: said of water **8.** mild or temperate, as a breeze, climate, etc. **9.** *a)* weak; not strong or vigorous *b)* having flabby muscles **10.** requiring little effort; easy *[a soft* job*]* **11.** *a)* kind or lenient; not severe *b)* easily influenced or imposed upon **12.** not bright; subdued: said of color or light **13.** showing little contrast or distinctness, as an etching **14.** gentle; low: said of sound **15.** *Finance* unstable and declining: said of a market, prices, etc. **16.** *Phonet.* *a)* sibilant: said of *c* and *g*, as in *cent* and *germ* *b)* voiced — *adv.* softly; gently; quietly —*n.* something soft; soft part — *interj.* [Archaic] hush! stop! —**be soft on 1.** to treat gently **2.** to feel amorous toward —**soft in the head** stupid or foolish —**soft′ish** *adj.* —**soft′ly** *adv.* —**soft′ness** *n.*

**soft·ball** (sôft′bôl′, säft′-) *n.* **1.** a game like baseball played on a smaller diamond and with a larger and softer ball **2.** the ball used

**soft-boiled** (-boild′) *adj.* boiled only a short time so that the yolk is still soft: said of an egg

**soft coal** *same as* BITUMINOUS COAL

**soft-cov·er** (-kuv′ər) *n. same as* PAPERBACK —*adj.* bound as a paperback

**soft drink** a nonalcoholic, esp. carbonated drink

**sof·ten** (sôf′'n, säf′-) *vt., vi.* **1.** to make or become soft or softer **2.** to make or become less resistant —**sof′ten·er** *n.*

**soft·goods** (sôft′goodz′) *n.pl.* goods that last a relatively short time, esp. textile products: also **soft goods**

**soft·head·ed** (-hed′id) *adj.* stupid or foolish —**soft′-head′ed·ly** *adv.* —**soft′head′ed·ness** *n.*

**soft·heart·ed** (-här′tid) *adj.* **1.** full of compassion or tenderness **2.** not strict or severe, as in discipline —**soft′-heart′ed·ly** *adv.* —**soft′heart′ed·ness** *n.*

**soft landing** a safe landing, as of a spacecraft on the moon, in which the craft and its contents remain unharmed —**soft′-land′** *vi., vt.*

**soft palate** the soft, fleshy part at the rear of the roof of the mouth; velum

**soft-ped·al** (-ped′'l) *vt.* **-aled** or **-alled, -al·ing** or **-al·ling 1.** to soften the tone of (a musical instrument) by use of a special pedal (**soft pedal**) **2.** [Colloq.] to tone down; make less emphatic, less noticeable, etc.

**soft sell** selling that relies on subtle suggestion rather than high-pressure salesmanship —**soft′-sell′** *adj.*

**soft-shell** (-shel′) *adj.* **1.** having a soft shell **2.** having an unhardened shell as the result of recent molting Also **soft′-shelled′**

**soft-shoe** (-shōō′) *adj.* designating a kind of tap dancing done without metal taps on the shoes

**soft shoulder** soft ground along the edge of a highway

**soft-soap** (-sōp′) *vt., vi.* **1.** to apply soft soap to **2.** [Colloq.] to flatter —**soft′-soap′er** *n.*

**soft soap 1.** soap in liquid or semifluid form **2.** [Colloq.] flattery or smooth talk

**soft-spo·ken** (-spō′k′n) *adj.* **1.** speaking or spoken with a soft, low voice **2.** smooth; suave

**soft touch** [Slang] a person who is easily persuaded to give or lend money

**soft·ware** (-wer′) *n.* the programs, data, routines, etc. for a computer: cf. HARDWARE (3 *b*)

**soft·wood** (-wood′) *n.* **1.** *a)* any light, easily cut wood *b)* a tree yielding such wood **2.** *Forestry* wood from a needle-bearing conifer

**soft·y, soft·ie** (sôf′tē, säf′-) *n., pl.* **soft′ies** [Colloq.] a person who is overly sentimental or trusting

**sog·gy** (säg′ē, sôg′ē) *adj.* **-gi·er, -gi·est** [prob. < or akin to ON. *sog*, lit., a sucking] **1.** saturated with moisture; soaked **2.** moist and heavy; sodden *[a soggy* cake*]* **3.** dull and boring —**sog′gi·ly** *adv.* —**sog′gi·ness** *n.*

**soil¹** (soil) *n.* [Anglo-Fr. < OFr. < L. *solum*] **1.** the surface layer of earth, supporting plant life **2.** any place for growth or development **3.** land; country *[foreign soil]* **4.** ground or earth —**the soil** life and work on a farm

**soil²** (soil) *vt.* [< OFr., ult. < L. *suculus*, dim. of *sus*, pig] **1.** to make dirty **2.** to smirch or stain **3.** to bring disgrace upon **4.** to corrupt or defile —*vi.* to become soiled —*n.* **1.** a soiled spot; stain **2.** excrement, sewage, etc. **3.** a soiling or being soiled

**soi·ree, soi·rée** (swä rä′) *n.* [< Fr. < *soir*, evening] a party or gathering in the evening

**so·journ** (sō′jurn; *also, for v.,* sō jurn′) *vi.* [< OFr. < L. *sub-*, under + *diurnus*, of a day < *dies*, day] to live some-

where temporarily; stay for a while —*n.* a brief stay; visit —**so′journ·er** *n.*

**so·kol** (sō′kôl) *n.* [Czech, lit., falcon] an organization promoting physical health, esp. through gymnastics

**Sol** (säl) [L.] **1.** *Rom. Myth.* the sun god: identified with the Greek god Helios **2.** the sun personified

**sol¹** (sōl; *Sp.* sôl) *n., pl.* **sols,** *Sp.* **so·les** (sō′les) [Sp., lit., sun] *see* MONETARY UNITS, table (Peru)

**sol²** (sōl) *n.* [< ML. *sol(ve)*: see GAMUT] *Music* a syllable representing the fifth tone of the diatonic scale

**sol³** (säl, sōl) *n.* a liquid colloidal solution

**sol·ace** (säl′is) *n.* [< OFr. < L. < *solari*, to comfort] **1.** an easing of grief, loneliness, etc. **2.** something that eases or relieves; comfort; relief Also **sol′ace·ment** —*vt.* **-aced, -ac·ing 1.** to give solace to; comfort **2.** to lessen (grief, sorrow, etc.) —**sol′ac·er** *n.*

**so·lar** (sō′lər) *adj.* [L. *solaris* < *sol*, the sun] **1.** of or having to do with the sun **2.** produced by or coming from the sun *[solar* energy*]* **3.** depending upon the sun's light or energy *[solar* heating*]* **4.** measured by the earth's motion with relation to the sun *[mean solar* time*]*

**solar battery** an assembly of devices (**solar cells**) that convert the energy of sunlight into electricity

**solar flare** a short-lived increase of intensity in the light of the sun, usually near a sunspot

**so·lar·i·um** (sō ler′ē əm, sə-) *n., pl.* **-i·a** (-ə) [L. < *sol*, the sun] a glassed-in porch, room, etc. where people sun themselves, as in treating illness

**solar plexus 1.** a network of nerves in the abdominal cavity behind the stomach **2.** [Colloq.] the area of the belly just below the sternum

**solar system** the sun and all the heavenly bodies that revolve around it

**solar wind** streams of ionized gas particles constantly emitted by the sun

**sold** (sōld) *pt. & pp.* of SELL

**sol·der** (säd′ər) *n.* [< OFr. < L. *solidare*, to make firm] **1.** a metal alloy used when melted to join or patch metal parts or surfaces **2.** anything that joins or fuses; bond —*vt., vi.* **1.** to join (things) with solder **2.** to unite or become united —**sol′der·er** *n.*

**sol·der·ing iron** (säd′ər iŋ) a pointed metal tool heated for use in melting and applying solder

**sol·dier** (sōl′jər) *n.* [< OFr. < *solde*, pay < LL. *solidus*, a coin] **1.** a member of an army **2.** an enlisted man, as distinguished from an officer **3.** a man of much military experience **4.** a person who works for a specified cause —*vi.* **1.** to serve as a soldier **2.** to shirk one's duty, as by pretending to work, to be ill, etc. —**sol′dier·li·ness** *n.* —**sol′dier·ly** *adj.*

**soldier of fortune 1.** a mercenary soldier, esp. one seeking adventure or excitement **2.** any adventurer

**sol·dier·y** (-ē) *n., pl.* **-dier·ies 1.** soldiers collectively **2.** military science: also **sol′dier·ship**

**sole¹** (sōl) *n.* [< OFr., ult. < L. *solum*, a base, bottom] **1.** the bottom surface of the foot **2.** the part of a shoe, sock, etc. corresponding to this **3.** the bottom surface of various objects, as a golf club —*vt.* **soled, sol′ing** to furnish (a shoe, etc.) with a sole, esp. a new sole

**sole²** (sōl) *adj.* [< OE. < L. *solus*] **1.** *a)* without another; single; one and only *b)* acting, working, etc. alone without help **2.** of or having to do with only one (specified) person or group **3.** not shared; exclusive *[sole* rights to a patent*]* **4.** [Archaic] alone; solitary

**sole³** (sōl) *n., pl.* **sole, soles:** see PLURAL, II, D, 2 [OFr. < L. *solea*, sole of a shoe, kind of fish: named from its shape] any of certain sea flatfishes, highly valued as food

**sol·e·cism** (säl′ə siz′m) *n.* [< L. < Gr. < *soloikos*, speaking incorrectly < dialect used in Soloi, city in Asia Minor] **1.** a violation of the conventional usage, grammar, etc. of a language (Ex.: "We done it" for "We did it") **2.** a mistake in etiquette —**sol′e·cist** *n.* —**sol′e·cis′tic** *adj.* —**sol′e·cis′-ti·cal·ly** *adv.*

**sole·ly** (sōl′lē) *adv.* **1.** without another or others; alone **2.** only, exclusively, merely, or altogether *[to read solely* for pleasure*]*

**sol·emn** (säl′əm) *adj.* [< OFr. < L. *sollemnis*, yearly < *sollus*, all + *annus*, year] **1.** *a)* observed or done according to ritual, as religious rites, etc. *b)* sacred **2.** according to strict form; formal **3.** serious; deeply earnest **4.** awe-inspiring; very impressive **5.** somber because dark in color —**sol′emn·ly** *adv.* —**sol′emn·ness** *n.*

**so·lem·ni·fy** (sə lem′nə fī′) *vt.* **-fied′, -fy′ing** to make solemn

**so·lem·ni·ty** (-tē) *n., pl.* **-ties 1.** solemn ceremony, ritual, etc. **2.** seriousness; gravity

**sol·em·nize** (säl′əm nīz′) *vt.* **-nized′, -niz′ing 1.** to celebrate formally or according to ritual **2.** to perform the ceremony of (marriage, etc.) —**sol′em·ni·za′tion** *n.*

**so·le·noid** (sō′lə noid′, säl′ə-) *n.* [< Fr. < Gr. *sōlēn*, a channel + *eidos*, a form] a coil of wire carrying an electric current and acting like a magnet —**so′le·noi′dal** *adj.*

**sole·plate** (sōl′plāt′) *n.* [SOLE¹ + PLATE] the ironing surface of a flatiron

**sol-fa** (sōl′fä′) *n.* [It. *solfa* < *sol* + *fa*: see GAMUT] **1.** the syllables *do, re, mi, fa, sol, la, ti, do,* used for the tones of a scale, regardless of key **2.** the use of these syllables in vocal exercises —*vt., vi.* **-faed′** (-fäd′), **-fa′ing** to sing (a scale, etc.) to these syllables —**sol′-fa′ist** *n.*

**sol·feg·gio** (säl fej′ō, -fej′ē ō′) *n., pl.* **-feg′gios, -feg′gi** (-fej′ē) [It. < *solfa*: see prec.] **1.** voice practice in which scales are sung to the sol-fa syllables **2.** the use of these syllables in singing

**so·lic·it** (sə lis′it) *vt.* [< MFr. < L.: see SOLICITOUS] **1.** to ask or seek earnestly; appeal to or for **2.** to entice (someone) to do wrong **3.** to approach for some immoral purpose, as a prostitute does —*vi.* to solicit someone or something —**so·lic′i·ta′tion** *n.*

**so·lic·i·tor** (-ər) *n.* **1.** a person who solicits; esp., one who seeks trade, contributions, etc. **2.** in England, a member of the legal profession who is not a barrister **3.** in the U.S., a lawyer serving as official law officer for a city, department, etc.

**solicitor general** *pl.* **solicitors general, solicitor generals 1.** a law officer (in the Department of Justice in the U.S.) ranking next below the attorney general **2.** the chief law officer in some States

**so·lic·i·tous** (sə lis′ə təs) *adj.* [L. *sollicitus* < *sollus*, whole + pp. of *ciere*, to set in motion] **1.** showing care, attention, or concern *[solicitous* for her welfare*]* **2.** showing anxious desire; eager *[solicitous* to make friends*]* **3.** full of anxiety —**so·lic′i·tous·ly** *adv.* —**so·lic′i·tous·ness** *n.*

**so·lic·i·tude** (-tōōd′, -tyōōd′) *n.* the state of being solicitous; care, concern, etc.

**sol·id** (säl′id) *adj.* [< MFr. < L. *solidus*] **1.** tending to keep its form rather than to flow or spread out like a liquid or gas; relatively firm or compact **2.** not hollow **3.** having the three dimensions of length, breadth, and thickness **4.** firm and strong; substantial; sturdy **5.** serious; not trivial **6.** complete *[solid* satisfaction*]* **7.** having no breaks or divisions **8.** with no pauses *[to talk for a solid hour]* **9.** of one or the same color, material, etc. throughout **10.** showing unity; unanimous *[a solid vote]* **11.** thick or dense, as a fog **12.** firm or dependable *[a solid friendship]* **13.** [Colloq.] having a firmly favorable relationship **14.** [Colloq.] healthful and filling *[a solid meal]* **15.** [Slang] excellent **16.** *Printing* set without leads between the lines of type —*n.* **1.** a substance that is solid, not a liquid or gas **2.** an object or figure having length, breadth, and thickness —**sol′id·ly** *adv.* —**sol′id·ness** *n.*

**sol·i·dar·i·ty** (säl′ə dar′ə tē) *n., pl.* **-ties** agreement of all elements or individuals, as of a group; complete unity

**solid fuel** a rocket fuel in solid form, consisting of both fuel and oxidizer combined or mixed

**solid geometry** geometry dealing with solid figures

**so·lid·i·fy** (sə lid′ə fī′) *vt., vi.* **-fied′, -fy′ing 1.** to make or become solid, firm, hard, etc. **2.** to crystallize **3.** to make or become solid, strong, or united —**so·lid′i·fi·ca′tion** *n.*

**so·lid·i·ty** (-tē) *n.* a being solid; firmness, hardness, etc.

**sol·id-state** (säl′id stāt′) *adj.* designating or of electronic devices, as semiconductors, that can control current without heated filaments, moving parts, etc.

**sol·i·dus** (säl′i dəs) *n., pl.* **-i·di′** (-dī′) [LL. < L.] **1.** a gold coin of the Late Roman Empire **2.** a slant line (/) used to separate shillings from pence (Ex.: 7/6) *b*) same as VIRGULE

**so·lil·o·quize** (sə lil′ə kwīz′) *vi.* **-quized′, -quiz′ing** to deliver a soliloquy; talk to oneself —*vt.* to utter in a soliloquy —**so·lil′o·quist** (-kwist) *n.*

**so·lil·o·quy** (-kwē) *n., pl.* **-quies** [< LL. < L. *solus*, alone + *loqui*, to speak] **1.** a talking to oneself **2.** lines in a drama in which a character reveals his thoughts to the audience by speaking as if to himself

**sol·ip·sism** (säl′ip siz′m) *n.* [< L. *solus*, alone + *ipse*, self + -ISM] **1.** the theory that the self can be aware only of its own experiences or states **2.** the theory that nothing exists but the self —**sol′ip·sist** *n.* —**sol′ip·sis′tic** *adj.*

**sol·i·taire** (säl′ə ter′) *n.* [< Fr. < L.: see ff.] **1.** a single gem, such as a diamond, set by itself **2.** any of many games, esp. card games, played by one person

**sol·i·tar·y** (-ter′ē) *adj.* [< OFr. < L. *solitarius* < *solus*, alone] **1.** living or being alone **2.** single; only *[a solitary example]* **3.** lacking companions; lonely **4.** with few or no people; remote *[a solitary place]* **5.** done in solitude —*n., pl.* **-tar′ies 1.** a person who lives by himself; esp., a hermit **2.** [Colloq.] *same as* SOLITARY CONFINEMENT —**sol′i·tar′i·ly** *adv.* —**sol′i·tar′i·ness** *n.*

**solitary confinement** confinement of a prisoner, usually as extra punishment, away from all others

**sol·i·tude** (säl′ə tōōd′, -tyōōd′) *n.* [< MFr. < L. *solitudo* < *solus*, alone] **1.** a being solitary, or alone; seclusion **2.** a secluded place —**sol′i·tu′di·nous** *adj.*

**sol·mi·za·tion** (säl′mi zā′shən) *n.* [< Fr. < *sol* + *mi*: see GAMUT] solfeggio, or any similar use of a system of syllables in singing

**so·lo** (sō′lō) *n., pl.* **-los;** for *n.* 1 & 3, sometimes **-li** (-lē) [It. < L. *solus*, alone] **1.** a musical piece or passage to be played or sung by one person **2.** an airplane flight made by a pilot alone **3.** any performance by one person alone **4.** any card game in which there are no partners —*adj.* **1.** for or by a single voice, person, or instrument **2.** performing a solo —*adv.* alone —*vi.* to make a solo flight —**so′lo·ist** *n.*

**Sol·o·mon** (säl′ə mən) [LL. < Gr. < Heb. *shĕlōmōh*, lit., peaceful < *shālōm*, peace] **1.** a masculine name: dim. *Sol* **2.** *Bible* king of Israel; son & successor of DAVID: noted for his wisdom —*n.* a very wise man

**Solomon Islands 1.** country on a group of islands in the SW Pacific, east of New Guinea: c. 11,500 sq. mi.; pop. 206,000 **2.** group of islands including this country and other islands belonging to Papua New Guinea

**Solomon's seal 1.** the Star of David used as a mystic symbol in the Middle Ages **2.** any of various plants with broad, waxy leaves and black or black berries

**So·lon** (sō′lən, -län) 640?-559? B.C.; Athenian statesman & lawgiver —*n.* [*sometimes* s-] a wise lawmaker

**so long** *colloq.* term for GOODBYE

**sol·stice** (säl′stis, sōl′-) *n.* [MFr. < L. *solstitium* < *sol*, sun + *sistere*, to make stand still < *stare*, to stand] **1.** either of two points on the sun's ecliptic at which it is farthest north or farthest south of the celestial equator **2.** the time of reaching either of these points: see SUMMER SOLSTICE, WINTER SOLSTICE —**sol·sti′tial** (-stish′əl) *adj.*

**sol·u·ble** (säl′yoo b′l) *adj.* [MFr. < L. *solubilis* < *solvere*: see SOLVE] **1.** that can be dissolved; able to pass into solution **2.** that can be solved —**sol′u·bil′i·ty** *n., pl.* **-ties**

**sol·ute** (säl′yōōt, sō′lōōt) *n.* the substance dissolved in a solution —*adj.* dissolved; in solution

**so·lu·tion** (sə lōō′shən) *n.* [< OFr. < L. < pp. of *solvere*: see ff.] **1.** *a*) the solving of a problem *b*) the answer to a problem *c*) an explanation, etc. *[the solution of a mystery]* **2.** *a*) the dispersion of one or more substances in another, usually a liquid, so as to form a homogeneous mixture; dissolving *b*) a being dissolved *c*) the mixture, usually a liquid, so produced **3.** a breaking up; dissolution

**solution set** *Math.* the root or values that satisfy a given equation or inequality

**solve** (sälv) *vt.* **solved, solv′ing** [< L. *solvere*, to loosen < *se-*, apart + *luere*, to let go] to find a satisfactory answer for (a problem, mystery, etc.); make clear; explain —**solv′a·bil′i·ty** *n.* —**solv′a·ble** *adj.* —**solv′er** *n.*

**sol·vent** (säl′vənt) *adj.* [< L. prp. of *solvere*: see SOLVE] **1.** able to pay all one's debts **2.** that can dissolve another substance —*n.* **1.** a substance that can dissolve another one **2.** something that solves or explains —**sol′ven·cy** *n.*

**Sol·y·man** (säl′i mən) *same as* SULEIMAN

**So·ma·li** (sō mä′lē, sə-) *n.* **1.** *pl.* **-lis, -li** a member of an Islamic, pastoral people of Somalia and nearby regions **2.** their Eastern Cushitic language

**So·ma·li·a** (sō mä′lē ə, sə-; -mäl′yə) country of E Africa, on the Indian Ocean & the Gulf of Aden: 246,201 sq. mi.; pop. 2,864,000

**so·mat·ic** (sō mat′ik) *adj.* [Gr. *sōmatikos* < *sōma*, the body] **1.** of the body; corporeal; physical **2.** of the cells (**somatic cells**) of an organism that become differentiated into the tissues, organs, etc. of the body **3.** of the outer walls of the body —**so·mat′i·cal·ly** *adv.*

**som·ber** (säm′bər) *adj.* [Fr. *sombre*, ult. < L. *sub*, under + *umbra*, shade] **1.** dark and gloomy or dull **2.** mentally depressed or depressing; melancholy **3.** solemn; grave Also, chiefly Brit. sp., **som′bre** —**som′ber·ly** *adv.* —**som′ber·ness** *n.*

**som·bre·ro** (säm brer′ō, səm-) *n., pl.* **-ros** [Sp. < *sombra*, shade: see prec.] a broad-brimmed felt or straw hat, worn in Mexico, the Southwest, etc.

**some** (sum; *unstressed* səm) *adj.* [OE. *sum*] **1.** being a certain one or ones not specified or known *[some* people smoke*]* **2.** being of a certain unspecified quantity, degree, etc. *[have some* butter*]* **3.** about *[some* ten of us*]* **4.** [Colloq.] remarkable; striking *[it was some* fight*]* —*pron.* **1.** a certain one or ones not specified or known *[some* agree*]* **2.** a certain unspecified number, quantity, etc. *[take some]* —*adv.* **1.** about

SOMBRERO

*[some* ten men*]* **2.** [Colloq.] to some extent *[slept some]* **3.** [Colloq.] to a great extent, at a great rate, etc. *[must run some* to catch up*]* —**and then some** [Colloq.] and more than that

**-some¹** (səm) [OE. *-sum] a suffix meaning* like, tending to, tending to be *[tiresome, lonesome]*

**-some²** (səm) [< ME. *sum,* SOME] *a suffix meaning* (a specified) number together *[twosome]*

**-some³** (sōm) [< Gr. *sōma,* body] *a combining form meaning* body *[chromosome]*

**some·bod·y** (sum′bud′ē, -bäd′ē, -bəd ē) *pron.* a person unknown or not named; some person; someone —*n., pl.* **-bod′-ies** a person of importance

**some·day** (-dā′) *adv.* at some future time

**some·how** (-hou′) *adv.* in a way not known, stated, or understood *[it was somehow* damaged*]* : often in **somehow or other**

**some·one** (-wun′, -wən) *pron. same as* SOMEBODY

**some·place** (-plās′) *adv.* in, to, or at some place; somewhere

**som·er·sault** (sum′ər sôlt′) *n.* [altered < MFr. *sombresault* < L. *supra,* over + *saltus,* a leap] an acrobatic stunt done by turning the body one full revolution, heels over head: often used figuratively, as of a complete reversal of opinion —*vi.* to do a somersault Also **som′er·set′** (-set′)

**Som·er·ville** (sum′ər vil′) [? after Capt. R. *Somers* (1778–1804)] city in E Mass.: suburb of Boston: pop. 77,000

**some·thing** (sum′thiŋ) *n.* **1.** a thing not definitely known, understood, etc. *[something* went wrong*]* **2.** some thing or things, definite but unspecified *[have something* to eat*]* **3.** a bit; a little *[something* over an hour*]* **4.** [Colloq.] a remarkable person or thing —*adv.* **1.** somewhat **2.** [Colloq.] really *[sounds something* awful*]* Also used after a figure to indicate a fraction beyond *[the bus leaves at six something]* —**make something of 1.** to find a use for **2.** to treat as of great importance **3.** [Colloq.] to treat as a point of dispute —**something else** [Slang] a really remarkable person or thing

**some·time** (-tīm′) *adv.* **1.** at some time not known or specified **2.** at some future time **3.** [Archaic] *a)* sometimes *b)* formerly —*adj.* **1.** former *[his sometime* friend*]* **2.** occasional *[his wit is a sometime* thing*]*

**some·times** (-tīmz′) *adv.* at times; occasionally

**some·way** (-wā′) *adv.* in some way or manner; somehow or other: also **some′ways′**

**some·what** (-hwut′, -hwät′, -wut′, -wət) *n.* some degree, amount, part, etc. *[somewhat* of a surprise*]* —*adv.* to some extent, degree, etc.

**some·where** (-hwer′, -wer′) *adv.* **1.** in, to, or at some place not known or specified **2.** at some time, degree, age, figure, etc. (with *about, around, in,* etc.) —*n.* an unspecified or undetermined place Also [Chiefly Dial.] **some′wheres′**

**Somme** (sum; *Fr.* sôm) river in N France flowing west into the English Channel

**som·me·lier** (sum′əl yā′) *n.* [Fr. < MFr., orig., person in charge of pack animals] a wine steward

**som·nam·bu·late** (säm nam′byoo lāt′, səm-) *vt.* **-lat′ed, -lat′ing** [< L. *somnus,* sleep + pp. of *ambulare,* to walk] to walk in a trancelike state while asleep —**som·nam′bu·lant** *adj.* —**som·nam′bu·la′tion** *n.* —**som·nam′bu·la′tor** *n.*

**som·nam·bu·lism** (-liz′m) *n.* [see prec.] **1.** the act or practice of sleepwalking **2.** the trancelike state of a sleepwalker —**som·nam′bu·list** *n.* —**som·nam′bu·lis′tic** *adj.*

**som·nif·er·ous** (säm nif′ər əs, səm-) *adj.* [< L. < *somnus,* sleep + *ferre,* to bring] causing sleep; soporific: also **som·nif′ic** —**som·nif′er·ous·ly** *adv.*

**som·no·lent** (säm′nə lənt) *adj.* [< MFr. < L. *somnolentus* < *somnus,* sleep] **1.** sleepy; drowsy **2.** causing drowsiness —**som′no·lence** *n.* —**som′no·lent·ly** *adv.*

**son** (sun) *n.* [OE. *sunu*] **1.** a boy or man as he is related to either or both parents: sometimes also used of animals **2.** a male descendant **3.** *a)* a son-in-law *b)* a stepson **4.** a male thought of as if in the relation of child to parent or to a formative influence *[a son* of revolution*]* **5.** a familiar form of address to a boy or younger man —**the Son** Jesus Christ, as the second person of the Trinity

**so·nant** (sō′nənt) *adj.* [< L. prp. of *sonare,* to SOUND¹] **1.** of sound **2.** having sound; sounding —**so′nance** *n.*

**so·nar** (sō′när) *n.* [so(und) n(avigation) a(nd) r(anging)] an apparatus that transmits high-frequency sound waves through water and registers the vibrations reflected back from an object: used to locate submarines, find depths, etc.

**so·na·ta** (sə nät′ə) *n.* [It. < L. *sonare,* to SOUND¹] a musical composition for one or two instruments, usually in three or four movements in different tempos, etc.

**sonde** (sänd) *n.* [Fr., a sounding line] any of various devices for measuring and usually telemetering meteorological and other physical data during ascent and descent through the atmosphere

**‡son et lu·mière** (sōn nā lü myer′) [Fr., lit., sound and light] a historical spectacle at night before a monument, etc., using special lighting effects, narration, music, etc.

**song** (sôŋ) *n.* [OE. *sang*] **1.** the act or art of singing **2.** a piece of music sung or as if for singing **3.** *a)* poetry; verse *b)* a ballad or lyric that is or can be set to music **4.** a musical sound like singing *[the song* of the lark*]* —**for a song** cheaply —**song′ful** *adj.* —**song′less** *adj.*

**song·bird** (-bʉrd′) *n.* **1.** a bird that makes vocal sounds that are like music **2.** a woman singer

**song·fest** (-fest′) *n.* [SONG + -FEST] an informal gathering of people for singing songs, esp. folk songs

**Song of Solomon** a book of the Bible consisting of a love poem, dramatic and lyrical in character: also called **Song of Songs, Canticle of Canticles**

**song sparrow** a common N. American sparrow with a striped breast, noted for its sweet song

**song·ster** (sôŋ′stər) *n.* [OE. *sangestre*] **1.** a singer **2.** a writer of songs or poems **3.** a songbird —**song′stress** *n.fem.*

**song thrush** a European songbird with brown wings and a white breast

**song·writ·er** (-rīt′ər) *n.* a person who writes words or music or both for songs, esp. popular songs

**son·ic** (sän′ik) *adj.* [< L. *sonus,* SOUND¹ + -IC] **1.** of or having to do with sound **2.** designating or of a speed equal to the speed of sound (about 1088 feet per second through air at sea level at 32° F)

**sonic barrier** the large increase in drag encountered by an aircraft approaching the speed of sound

**sonic boom** an explosive sound generated by the accumulation of pressure in a wave preceding an aircraft moving at or above the speed of sound

**sonic depth finder** *same as* FATHOMETER

**son-in-law** (sun′in lô′) *n., pl.* **sons′-in-law′** the husband of one's daughter

**son·net** (sän′it) *n.* [Fr. < It. < Pr. dim. of *son,* a song < L. *sonus,* SOUND¹] a poem normally of fourteen lines (typically in iambic pentameter) in any of several fixed verse and rhyme schemes, expressing a single theme: see SHAKESPEAREAN SONNET —*vt., vi.* to write sonnets (about): also **son′net·ize′** (-ə tīz′) **-ized′, -iz′ing**

**son·net·eer** (sän′ə tir′) *n.* a person who writes sonnets

**son·ny** (sun′ē) *n., pl.* **-nies** little son: used in addressing any young boy in a familiar way

**son·o·buoy** (sän′ō boo′ē, sō′nō-; -boi′) *n.* [< L. *sonus,* SOUND¹ + BUOY] a buoy that transmits amplified sound signals picked up under water

**so·no·rant** (sə nôr′ənt, sō-) *n.* [SONOR(OUS) + (CONSON)ANT] *Phonet.* a voiced consonant that is less sonorous than a vowel but more sonorous than an unvoiced plosive, as *l, m, n, r, y, w:* sonorants may occur as syllabics

**so·nor·i·ty** (sə nôr′ə tē, sō-) *n., pl.* **-ties** the quality or state of being sonorous; resonance

**so·no·rous** (sə nôr′əs, sän′ər əs) *adj.* [< L. < *sonor,* a sound] **1.** producing or capable of producing sound, esp. a full, deep, or rich sound; resonant **2.** full, deep, or rich: said of sound **3.** high-sounding; impressive *[sonorous* prose*]* —**so·no′rous·ly** *adv.* —**so·no′rous·ness** *n.*

**Soo** (soo) [alteration of *Sault*] region in N Mich. & S Ontario, Canada, at the cities of Sault Ste. Marie & the ship canals (**Soo Locks**) that bypass a rapids of the St. Marys River: see SAULT STE. MARIE

**soon** (soon) *adv.* [OE. *sona,* at once] **1.** in a short time; shortly *[we will soon* be there*]* **2.** promptly; quickly *[as soon* as possible*]* **3.** ahead of time; early *[he left too soon]* **4.** readily; willingly *[I would as soon* go as stay*]* —**had sooner** would rather —**sooner or later** eventually

**soot** (soot, soot) *n.* [OE. *sot*] a black substance consisting chiefly of carbon particles formed by the incomplete combustion of burning matter —*vt.* to cover, soil, or treat with soot

**sooth** (sooth) *adj.* [OE. *soth*] **1.** [Archaic] true **2.** [Poet.] soothing; smooth —*n.* [Archaic] truth —**in sooth** [Archaic] in truth —**sooth′ly** *adv.*

**soothe** (sooth) *vt.* **soothed, sooth′ing** [OE. *sothian* < *soth,* truth] **1.** to make calm or composed, as by gentleness, flattery, etc. **2.** to relieve (pain, etc.) —*vi.* to have a soothing effect —**sooth′er** *n.* —**sooth′ing** *adj.* —**sooth′ing·ly** *adv.*

**sooth·say·er** (sooth′sā′ər) *n.* a person who claims to foretell the future —**sooth′say′ing** *n.*

**soot·y** (soot′ē, soot′ē) *adj.* **soot′i·er, soot′i·est 1.** of, like, or covered with soot **2.** dark or black like soot —**soot′i·ness** *n.*

**sop** (säp) *n.* [OE. *sopp*] **1.** a piece of food, as bread, soaked in milk, gravy, etc. **2.** *a)* something given by way of appeasement, etc. *b)* a bribe —*vt.* **sopped, sop′ping 1.** to soak, steep, etc. in or with liquid 2. to take (*up*), as liquid, by absorption —*vi.* 1. to soak (*in, into,* or *through* something) 2. to be or become thoroughly wet

**SOP, S.O.P.** standing (or standard) operating procedure

**sop.** soprano

**So·phi·a** (sō fē'ə) [< Gr. *sophia,* wisdom < *sophos,* wise] a feminine name: var. *Sophie, Sophy*

**soph·ism** (säf'iz'm) *n.* [< OFr. < L. < Gr. < *sophos,* clever] clever and reasonable argument that is, however, faulty or misleading; fallacy or sophistry

**soph·ist** (-ist) *n.* [< L. < Gr. *sophistēs,* wise man] 1. [*often* S-] in ancient Greece, any of a group of teachers of rhetoric, philosophy, etc., some of whom were notorious for their clever, specious arguments 2. a learned person 3. any person practicing clever, specious reasoning

**so·phis·ti·cal** (sə fis'ti k'l) *adj.* 1. of or characteristic of sophists or sophistry 2. clever and plausible but misleading Also **so·phis'tic** —**so·phis'ti·cal·ly** *adv.*

**so·phis·ti·cate** (sə fis'tə kāt'; *for n. usually* -kit) *vt.* **-cat'ed, -cat'ing** [< ML. < L. *sophisticus,* sophistical] 1. to change from being natural, simple, naive, etc. to being artificial, worldly-wise, etc. 2. to bring to a more developed, complex, or refined form, level, etc. —*n.* a sophisticated person

**so·phis·ti·cat·ed** (-kāt'id) *adj.* 1. not simple, natural, or naive; wise in the ways of the world; knowledgeable, subtle, etc. 2. appealing to sophisticated people 3. highly complex, refined, etc.; of an advanced form, technique, etc. —**so·phis'ti·cat'ed·ly** *adv.*

**so·phis·ti·ca·tion** (sə fis'tə kā'shən) *n.* 1. the act or process of sophisticating 2. the state or quality of being sophisticated

**soph·is·try** (säf'is trē) *n., pl.* **-tries** 1. unsound or misleading but subtle argument or reasoning 2. the methods of the Sophists

**Soph·o·cles** (säf'ə klēz') 496?–406 B.C.; Gr. writer of tragedies

**soph·o·more** (säf'ə môr') *n.* [altered (after Gr. *sophos,* wise + *mōros,* foolish) < obs. *sophumer,* lit., sophist] 1: a student in his second year of college or the tenth grade at high school 2. a person in his second year of some enterprise —*adj.* of or for sophomores

**soph·o·mor·ic** (säf'ə môr'ik) *adj.* of or like sophomores, often regarded as self-assured, opinionated, etc. though immature: also **soph'o·mor'i·cal** —**soph'o·mor'i·cal·ly** *adv.*

**-so·phy** (sə fē) [< Gr. *sophia,* skill, wisdom] *a combining form meaning* knowledge [*philosophy*]

**sop·o·rif·ic** (säp'ə rif'ik, sō'pə-) *adj.* [< Fr. < L. *sopor,* sleep + -FIC] 1. causing or tending to cause sleep 2. sleepy —*n.* a drug, etc. that causes sleep

**sop·ping** (säp'iŋ) *adj.* thoroughly wet; drenched

**sop·py** (säp'ē) *adj.* **-pi·er, -pi·est** 1. very wet; sopping 2. rainy 3. [Colloq.] sentimental —**sop'pi·ness** *n.*

**so·pra·no** (sə pran'ō, -prä'nō) *n., pl.* **-nos, -ni** (-prä'nē) [It. < *sopra,* above] 1. the highest singing voice of women, girls, and young boys 2. *a)* a voice or singer with this range *b)* a musical instrument with this range *c)* a part for a soprano —*adj.* of, for, or having the range of a soprano

**so·ra** (sôr'ə) *n.* [< ? AmInd.] a small, short-billed wading bird of the rail family, living in marshes: also **sora rail**

**sor·bic acid** (sôr'bik) [ult. < L. *sorbus,* a kind of tree] a white, crystalline solid, $C_6H_8O_2$, used as a food preservative, fungicide, etc.

**sor·bi·tol** (sôr'bi tôl', -tōl') *n.* [see prec.] a white, sweet, crystalline alcohol, $C_6H_8(OH)_6$, used as a moistening agent in lotions, etc., and as a sugar substitute

**Sor·bonne** (sôr bän'; *Fr.* sôr bôn') the liberal arts college of the University of Paris

**sor·cer·er** (sôr'sər ər) *n.* a person who practices sorcery; wizard —**sor'cer·ess** *n.fem.*

**sor·cer·y** (-ē) *n., pl.* **-cer·ies** [< OFr. < *sorcier,* sorcerer < L. *sors,* lot, share] 1. the supposed use of magical power by means of charms, spells, etc., usually for an evil purpose; witchcraft; black magic 2. seemingly magical power, charm, etc. —**sor'cer·ous** *adj.* —**sor'cer·ous·ly** *adv.*

**sor·did** (sôr'did) *adj.* [< Fr. < L. < *sordes,* filth] 1. *a)* dirty; filthy *b)* squalid; depressingly wretched 2. *a)* base; ignoble *b)* meanly selfish or grasping —**sor'did·ly** *adv.* —**sor'did·ness** *n.*

**sore** (sôr) *adj.* **sor'er, sor'est** [OE. *sar*] 1. *a)* giving pain; painful [a *sore* throat] *b)* feeling pain, as from bruises, etc. 2. *a)* filled with sadness, grief, etc. [*sore* at heart] *b)* causing sadness, grief, etc. [*sore* hardships] 3. provoking irritation [a *sore* point] 4. [Colloq.] angry; offended —*n.* 1. a sore, usually infected spot on the body, as an ulcer or blister 2. a source of pain, distress, etc. —*adv.* [Archaic] sorely —**sore'ness** *n.*

**sore·head** (-hed') *n.* [Colloq.] a person who is angry, resentful, disgruntled, etc., or one easily made so

**sore·ly** (-lē) *adv.* 1. grievously; painfully [*sorely* vexed] 2. urgently; extremely [*sorely* needed]

**sor·ghum** (sôr'gəm) *n.* [< It. *sorgo*] 1. any of several tropical cereal grasses grown for grain, syrup, fodder, etc. 2. a syrup made from the sweet juices of a variety (**sorgo**) of sorghum

**so·ror·al** (sə rôr'l) *adj.* [see ff.] of or like a sister or sisters; sisterly —**so·ror'al·ly** *adv.*

**so·ror·i·ty** (sə rôr'ə tē) *n., pl.* **-ties** [< ML. < L. *soror,* sister] a group of women or girls joined together for social or professional reasons; specif., a Greek-letter college organization

**sor·rel¹** (sôr'əl, sär'-) *n.* [< OFr. < Frank. *sur,* sour] 1. any of several plants with sour, fleshy leaves; dock 2. *same as* WOOD SORREL

**sor·rel²** (sôr'əl, sär'-) *n.* [< OFr. < *sor,* light brown < ML. *saurus* < Gmc.] 1. light reddish brown 2. a horse, etc. of this color —*adj.* light reddish-brown

**sor·row** (sär'ō, sôr'ō) *n.* [OE. *sorg*] 1. mental suffering caused by loss, disappointment, etc.; sadness, grief, or regret 2. that which produces such suffering; trouble, misfortune, etc. 3. the outward expression of such suffering; mourning 4. earnest repentance —*vi.* to feel or show sorrow; grieve —**sor'row·er** *n.* —**sor'row·ing·ly** *adv.*

**sor·row·ful** (-ə fəl) *adj.* feeling, causing, or expressing sorrow; sad —**sor'row·ful·ly** *adv.* —**sor'row·ful·ness** *n.*

**sor·ry** (sär'ē, sôr'ē) *adj.* **-ri·er, -ri·est** [OE. *sarig* < *sar,* sore] 1. full of sorrow, pity, sympathy, etc.: also used in apologizing or in showing mild regret 2. *a)* inferior in worth or quality; poor *b)* wretched, pitiful, miserable, etc. —**sor'ri·ly** *adv.* —**sor'ri·ness** *n.*

**sort** (sôrt) *n.* [< MFr., ult. < L. *sors* (gen. *sortis*), a lot] 1. any group related by having something in common; kind; class 2. quality or type; nature [remarks of that *sort*] —*vt.* to arrange according to class or kind (often with *out*) —**of sorts** 1. of various kinds 2. of an inferior kind: also **of a sort** —**out of sorts** [Colloq.] cross, irritable, or ill —**sort of** [Colloq.] somewhat —**sort'a·ble** *adj.* —**sort'er** *n.*

**sor·tie** (sôr'tē) *n.* [Fr. < *sortir,* to issue] 1. a sudden attack or raid by troops from a besieged place; sally 2. one mission by a single military plane

**SOS** (es'ō'es') 1. a signal of distress in code (···---···) used internationally in wireless telegraphy, as by ships 2. [Colloq.] any urgent call for help

**so-so** (sō'sō') *adv.* indifferently; just passably —*adj.* neither too good nor too bad; just fair Also **so so**

**sos·te·nu·to** (säs'tə nōōt'ō) *n., adj., adv.* [It.] *Music* sustained or prolonged in tempo

**sot** (sät) *n.* [< Late OE. *sott* or OFr. *sot,* a fool < VL. *sottus*] a drunkard —**sot'tish** *adj.* —**sot'tish·ly** *adv.*

**sot·ted** (sät'id) *adj.* besotted; stupefied

**sot·to vo·ce** (sät'ō vō'chē) [It., under the voice] in an undertone, so as not to be overheard

**sou** (sōō) *n., pl.* **sous** (sōōz; *Fr.* sōō) [Fr. < OFr. *sol* < LL. *solidus,* SOLIDUS] any of several former French coins, esp. one equal to five centimes

**sou·brette** (sōō bret') *n.* [Fr. < Pr. < *soubret,* sly, ult. < L. *superare,* to be above] *Theater* 1. the role of a lady's maid, esp. one involved in intrigue, or of any pretty, flirtatious young woman 2. an actress who plays such roles

**sou·bri·quet** (sōō'brə kā') *n. var. of* SOBRIQUET

**souf·flé** (sōō flā', sōō'flā) *adj.* [Fr. < pp. of *souffler,* to blow] made light and puffy in cooking: also **souf·fléed'** (-flād') —*n.* a baked food made light and puffy by adding beaten egg whites before baking [a cheese *soufflé*]

**sough** (sou, suf) *n.* [< OE. *swogan,* to sound] a soft, murmuring, sighing, or rustling sound —*vi.* to make a sough

**sought** (sôt) *pt. & pp. of* SEEK

**souk** (sōōk) *n.* [Ar. *sūq*] an open-air marketplace in North Africa and the Middle East

**soul** (sōl) *n.* [OE. *sawol*] 1. the part of one's being that is thought of as the center of feeling, thinking, will, etc. apart from the body: in some religions the soul is believed to go on after death 2. the moral or emotional nature of man 3. spiritual or emotional warmth, force, etc. 4. vital or essential part, quality, etc. 5. the central or leading figure [Daniel Boone, *soul* of the frontier] 6. embodiment; personification [the *very* soul of kindness] 7. a person [a town of 1,000 *souls*] 8. [Colloq.] *a)* among U.S. Negroes, a sense of racial pride and social and cultural solidarity *b) short for* SOUL FOOD or SOUL MUSIC —*adj.* [Colloq.] of, for, like, or characteristic of U.S. Negroes —**upon my soul!** an exclamation of surprise

**soul food** [Colloq.] items of food popular orig. in the South esp. among Negroes, as chitterlings, ham hocks, yams, turnip greens, etc.

**soul·ful** (sōl'fəl) *adj.* full of or showing deep feeling —**soul'ful·ly** *adv.* —**soul'ful·ness** *n.*

**soul·less** (-lis) *adj.* lacking soul, sensitivity, or deep feeling —**soul'less·ly** *adv.* —**soul'less·ness** *n.*

**soul music** [Colloq.] *a form of* RHYTHM AND BLUES (with added elements of U.S. Negro gospel singing)

**soul-search·ing** (-sur'chiŋ) *n.* a close, honest examination of one's true feelings, motives, etc.

**sound**[1] (sound) *n.* [< OFr. *son* < L. *sonus*] **1.** *a*) vibrations in air, water, etc. that act on the nerves of the inner ear and produce the sensation of hearing *b*) the sensation that these vibrations stimulate in the ear **2.** *a*) any identifiable noise, tone, vocal utterance, etc. *[the sound* of a violin, speech *sounds] b*) such effects transmitted by or recorded for radio, television, movies, etc. **3.** the distance within which a sound may be heard; earshot **4.** the impression made by something said, etc.; drift *[the sound* of his report*]* **5.** meaningless noise *—vi.* **1.** to make a sound **2.** to seem or appear through sound or utterance *[to sound* troubled*] —vt.* **1.** *a*) to cause to sound *b*) to produce the sound of *c*) to utter distinctly *[to sound* one's r's*]* **2.** to express, signal, proclaim, etc. *[sound* the alarm, *sound* his praises*]* **3.** to examine (the chest) by percussion, etc. **—sound off 1.** to speak in turn, as in counting off **2.** [Slang] *a*) to give free voice to complaints, opinions, etc. *b*) to speak in a loud or offensive way **—sound′er** *n.*

**sound**[2] (sound) *adj.* [OE. *(ge)sund*] **1.** free from defect, damage, or decay *[sound* timber*]* **2.** normal and healthy *[a sound* body and mind*]* **3.** firm and safe; stable; secure *[a sound* bank*]* **4.** based on valid reasoning; sensible *[sound* advice*]* **5.** agreeing with established views or beliefs *[sound* doctrine*]* **6.** thorough, complete, forceful, etc. *[a sound* defeat*]* **7.** deep and undisturbed: said of sleep **8.** morally strong; honest, loyal, etc. **9.** *Law* valid *—adv.* completely; deeply *[sound* asleep*]* **—sound′ly** *adv.* **—sound′ness** *n.*

**sound**[3] (sound) *n.* [< OE. & ON. *sund*] **1.** a wide channel linking two large bodies of water or separating an island from the mainland **2.** a long arm of the sea **3.** the air bladder of certain fishes

**sound**[4] (sound) *vt.* [< MFr. *sonder* < VL. *subundare* < L. *sub*, under + *unda*, a wave] **1.** *a*) to measure the depth of (water), esp. with a weighted line (**sounding line**) *b*) to examine (the bottom of the sea, etc.) with a line that brings up particles that stick to it *c*) to probe (the atmosphere or space) so as to gain data **2.** to try to find out the opinions of (a person): often with *out* **3.** *Med.* to examine with a sound, or probe *—vi.* **1.** to sound water **2.** to dive suddenly downward through the water: said esp. of whales, etc. **3.** to try to find out something *—n. Med.* a long probe used in examining body cavities **—sound′a·ble** *adj.* **—sound′er** *n.*

**sound barrier** *same as* SONIC BARRIER

**sound effects** sounds, as of thunder, animals, etc., produced artificially or by recording as for radio, TV, etc.

**sound·ing**[1] (soun′diŋ) *adj.* **1.** giving forth sound **2.** resonant; sonorous **3.** high-sounding; bombastic

**sound·ing**[2] (soun′diŋ) *n.* **1.** *a*) the act of measuring the depth of water *b*) depth so measured *c*) *[pl.]* a place, usually less than 600 feet in depth, where a sounding line will touch bottom **2.** *a*) an examination of the atmosphere, as with a radiosonde *b*) a probe of space, as with a rocket **3.** *[pl.]* measurements or data learned by sounding **4.** *[often pl.]* a sampling, as of public opinion

**sounding board 1.** a thin plate of wood, etc. built into a musical instrument to increase its resonance: also **sound′-board′** *n.* **2.** any structure designed to reflect sound **3.** a person on whom one tests one's ideas, opinions, etc.

**sound·less** (sound′lis) *adj.* without sound; noiseless **—sound′less·ly** *adv.* **—sound′less·ness** *n.*

**sound·proof** (-prōōf′) *adj.* able to keep sound from coming through *—vt.* to make soundproof

**sound track** the area along one side of a motion-picture film, carrying the sound record of the film

**sound wave** *Physics* a pressure wave transported by an elastic medium, as air; esp., such a wave vibrating at a frequency that can be heard

**soup** (sōōp) *n.* [Fr. *soupe* < OFr., soup: of Gmc. origin] **1.** a liquid food made by cooking meat, vegetables, etc. in water, milk, etc. **2.** [Slang] a heavy fog **3.** [Slang] nitroglycerin **—in the soup** [Slang] in trouble **—soup up** [Slang] to increase the power, capacity for speed, etc. of (an engine, etc.) **—soup′y** *adj.* **soup′i·er, soup′i·est**

**soup·çon** (sōōp sôn′, sōōp′sôn′) *n.* [Fr.] **1.** a suggestion or trace, as of a flavor **2.** a tiny amount; bit

**soupe du jour** (sōōp′dōō zhōōr′) [Fr., lit., soup of the day] the featured soup on a menu for that day: also **soup du jour**

**soup kitchen** a place where hot soup or the like is given to people in dire need

**soup·spoon** (sōōp′spōōn′) *n.* a large-bowled spoon for eating soup

**sour** (sour) *adj.* [OE. *sur*] **1.** having the sharp, acid taste of lemon juice, vinegar, etc. **2.** made acid or spoiled by fermentation *[sour* milk*]* **3.** cross, bad-tempered, peevish, bitter, etc. **4.** below what is usual; poor *[his* game has gone *sour]* **5.** distasteful or unpleasant **6.** gratingly wrong or off pitch *[a sour* note*]* **7.** excessively acid: said of soil *—n.* **1.**

something sour **2.** a cocktail made with lime or lemon juice *[a* whiskey *sour] —vt., vi.* to make or become sour **—sour′ish** *adj.* **—sour′ly** *adv.* **—sour′ness** *n.*

**source** (sôrs) *n.* [< OFr. < pp. of *sourdre* < L. *surgere*, to rise] **1.** a spring, etc. from which a stream arises **2.** that from which something originates, develops, etc. **3.** *a*) that by which something is supplied *b*) a person, book, etc. that provides information **4.** the point from which light rays, sound waves, etc. come forth

**source·book** (-bŏŏk′) *n.* a collection of selections from documents giving fundamental information about a subject to be studied or written about; also, a diary, journal, etc. giving such information

**sour·dough** (sour′dō′) *n.* **1.** [Dial.] fermented dough saved from one baking to the next, for use as leaven **2.** a prospector in the western U.S. or Canada: so called from his using sourdough

**sour grapes** [from Aesop's fable in which the fox, after futile efforts to reach some grapes, scorns them as being sour] a scorning or belittling of something only because it cannot be had or done

**sour gum** a hardy tree of E N. America, having purplish fruits and foliage that turns flaming red in autumn

**sour·puss** (sour′pŏŏs′) *n.* [Slang] a gloomy or disagreeable person

**Sou·sa** (sōō′zə, -sə), **John Philip** 1854–1932; U.S. bandmaster & composer of marches

**souse** (sous) *n.* [< OFr. < OHG. *sulza*, brine] **1.** a pickled food, esp. the feet, ears, and head of a pig **2.** liquid for pickling; brine **3.** a plunging into a liquid **4.** [Slang] a drunkard *—vt., vi.* **soused, sous′ing 1.** to pickle **2.** to plunge or steep in a liquid **3.** to make or become soaking wet **4.** [Slang] to make or become intoxicated

**sou·tane** (sōō tan′, -tän′) *n.* [Fr. < It. *sottana*] *same as* CASSOCK

**south** (south) *n.* [OE. *suth*] **1.** the direction to the left of a person facing the sunset (180° on the compass, opposite north) **2.** a region or district in or toward this direction **3.** *[often* S-*]* the southern part of the earth, esp. the antarctic regions *—adj.* **1.** in, of, to, or toward the south **2.** from the south **3.** [S-] designating the southern part of a country, etc. *—adv.* in or toward the south **—the South** that part of the U.S. bounded on the north by Pennsylvania, the Ohio River, and N Missouri

**South Africa** country in southernmost Africa: 472,358 sq. mi.; pop. 21,525,000; caps. Cape Town, Pretoria **—South African**

**South African Dutch 1.** the Boers **2.** *same as* AFRIKAANS

**South America** S continent in the Western Hemisphere: c. 6,864,000 sq. mi.; pop. 190,000,000 **—South American**

**South·amp·ton** (sou thamp′tən) seaport in S England: pop. 210,000

**South Australia** state of SC Australia

**South Bend** [from its being at the southernmost bend in the St. Joseph River] city in N Ind.: pop. 110,000

**south·bound** (south′bound′) *adj.* going southward

**South Carolina** [see CAROLINA] Southern State of the U.S., on the Atlantic: 31,055 sq. mi.; pop. 3,119,000; cap. Columbia: abbrev. **S.C., SC —South Carolinian**

**South China Sea** arm of the W Pacific, touching Taiwan, the Philippines, Borneo, & SE Asia

**South Dakota** [see DAKOTA[2]] Middle Western State of the U.S.: 77,047 sq. mi.; pop. 690,000; cap. Pierre: abbrev. **S.Dak., SD —South Dakotan**

**south·east** (south′ēst′; *nautical* sou-) *n.* **1.** the direction halfway between south and east; 45° east of due south **2.** a region or district in or toward this direction *—adj.* **1.** in, of, to, or toward the southeast **2.** from the southeast, as a wind *—adv.* in, toward, or from the southeast **—the Southeast** the southeastern part of the U.S.

**south·east·er** (south′ēs′tər; *nautical* sou-) *n.* a storm or strong wind from the southeast

**south·east·er·ly** (-tər lē) *adj., adv.* **1.** in or toward the southeast **2.** from the southeast

**south·east·ern** (-tərn) *adj.* **1.** in, of, or toward the southeast **2.** from the southeast **3.** [S-] of or characteristic of the Southeast **—South′east′ern·er** *n.*

**south·east·ward** (-ēst′wərd) *adv., adj.* toward the southeast: also **south′east′wards** *adv. —n.* a southeastward direction, point, or region

**south·east·ward·ly** (-wərd lē) *adj., adv.* **1.** toward the southeast **2.** from the southeast, as a wind

**south·er** (sou′thər) *n.* a storm or wind from the south

**south·er·ly** (suth′ər lē) *adj., adv.* **1.** toward the south **2.** from the south

**south·ern** (suth′ərn) *adj.* **1.** in, of, or toward the south **2.** from the south **3.** [S-] of or characteristic of the South **—south′ern·most** *adj.*

---

**Southern Cross** a small S constellation with four bright stars in the form of a cross

**south·ern·er** (su*th*'ər nər, -ə nər) *n.* a native or inhabitant of the south, specif. [S-] of the southern part of the U.S.

**Southern Hemisphere** that half of the earth south of the equator

**southern lights** *same as* AURORA AUSTRALIS

**Southern Rhodesia** *former name of* RHODESIA

**Southern Yemen** *former name of* YEMEN (sense 2)

**Sou·they** (su*th*'ē, sou'*th*ē), **Robert** 1774–1843; Eng. poet & writer

**South·field** (south'fēld') city in SE Mich.: suburb of Detroit: pop. 76,000

**South Gate** [< *South Gate Gardens,* south of Los Angeles] city in SW Calif.: suburb of Los Angeles: pop. 67,000

**South Island** S island of the two main islands of New Zealand

**south·land** (south'land', -lənd) *n.* [*also* S-] the southern region of a country **—south'land'er** *n.*

**south·paw** (-pô') *n.* [SOUTH + PAW: in the Chicago ballpark (c. 1885) the pitcher's left arm was toward the south] [Slang] a person who is left-handed; esp., a left-handed baseball pitcher **—adj.** [Slang] left-handed

**South Pole** the southern end of the earth's axis

**South Sea Islands** islands in temperate or tropical parts of the South Pacific **—South Sea Islander**

**South Seas 1.** the South Pacific **2.** all the seas located south of the equator

**south-south·east** (south'south'ēst'; *nautical* sou'sou-) *n.* the direction halfway between due south and southeast; 22°30' east of due south **—adj., adv. 1.** in or toward this direction **2.** from this direction

**south-south·west** (-west') *n.* the direction halfway between due south and southwest; 22°30' west of due south **—adj., adv. 1.** in or toward this direction **2.** from this direction

**south·ward** (south'wərd; *nautical* su*th*'ərd) *adv., adj.* toward the south: also **south'wards** *adv.* **—n.** a southward direction, point, or region

**south·ward·ly** (-lē) *adj., adv.* **1.** toward the south **2.** from the south

**south·west** (south'west'; *nautical* sou-) *n.* **1.** the direction halfway between south and west; 45° west of due south **2.** a district or region in or toward this direction **—adj. 1.** in, of, to, or toward the southwest **2.** from the southwest **—adv.** in, toward, or from the southwest **—the Southwest** the southwestern part of the U.S., esp. Okla., Tex., N.Mex., Ariz., and S Calif.

**South West Africa** territory in S Africa, on the Atlantic, formerly held as a mandate by South Africa (mandate revoked by the UN, 1966) See NAMIBIA

**south·west·er** (south'wes'tər; *nautical* sou-) *n.* **1.** a storm or strong wind from the southwest **2.** a sailor's waterproof hat, having a broad brim in the back

**south·west·er·ly** (-tər lē) *adj., adv.* **1.** in or toward the southwest **2.** from the southwest

**south·west·ern** (-tərn) *adj.* **1.** in, of, or toward the southwest **2.** from the southwest **3.** [S-] of or characteristic of the Southwest **—South'west'ern·er** *n.*

**south·west·ward** (-west'wərd) *adv., adj.* toward the southwest: also **south'west'wards** *adv.* **—n.** a southwestward direction, point, or region

SOUTHWESTER

**south·west·ward·ly** (-lē) *adj., adv.* **1.** toward the southwest **2.** from the southwest, as a wind

**sou·ve·nir** (sōō'və nir', sōō'və nir') *n.* [Fr., orig. inf., to remember < L. *subvenire,* to come to mind] something kept as a reminder of a place, person, or occasion; keepsake; memento

**sou'·west·er** (sou wes'tər) *n. same as* SOUTHWESTER

**sov·er·eign** (säv'rən, -ər in; *occas.* suv'-) *adj.* [< OFr. *soverain,* ult. < L. *super,* above] **1.** above or superior to all others; greatest **2.** supreme in power, rank, etc. **3.** of or being a ruler; reigning **4.** independent of all others [a *sovereign* state] **5.** excellent **6.** very effectual, as a remedy **—n. 1.** a person having sovereign authority; specif., a monarch or ruler **2.** esp. formerly, a British gold coin valued at 20 shillings **—sov'er·eign·ly** *adv.*

**sov·er·eign·ty** (-tē) *n., pl.* **-ties 1.** a being sovereign **2.** the status, rule, power, etc. of a sovereign **3.** supreme and independent political authority **4.** a sovereign state

**so·vi·et** (sō'vē it, -et'; sō'vē et') *n.* [Russ., lit., council] **1.** in the Soviet Union, any of various elected governing councils, ranging from village and town soviets to the Supreme Soviet of the whole country **2.** [S-] [*pl.*] the Soviet people or their officials **—adj. 1.** of a soviet or soviets **2.** [S-] of or connected with the Soviet Union **—so'vi·et·ism** *n.*

**so·vi·et·ize** (sō'vē ə tīz') *vt.* **-ized', -iz'ing** [*often* S-] **1.** to change to a soviet form of government **2.** to make conform to the system, principles, etc. of the Soviets **—so'vi·et·i·za'tion** *n.*

**Soviet Union** *same as* UNION OF SOVIET SOCIALIST REPUBLICS: also **Soviet Russia**

**sow**[1] (sou) *n.* [OE. *sugu*] **1.** an adult female pig or hog **2.** an adult female of certain other mammals, as the bear

**sow**[2] (sō) *vt.* **sowed, sown** (sōn) or **sowed, sow'ing** [OE. *sawan*] **1.** to scatter or plant (seed) for growing **2.** to plant (a field, etc.) with seed **3.** to spread or scatter; disseminate **4.** to plant in the mind **—vi.** to sow seed **—sow'er** *n.*

**sow·bel·ly** (sou'bel'ē) *n.* [Colloq.] *same as* SALT PORK

**sow bug** (sou) any of several small crustaceans with a flat, oval body, living in damp places, as under rocks

**sox** (säks) *n. alt. pl. of* SOCK[1] (sense 3)

**soy** (soi) *n.* [Jap., colloq. for *shōyu* < Chin. < *chiang,* salted bean + *yu,* oil] **1.** a dark, salty sauce made from fermented soybeans steeped in brine, used esp. with Chinese and Japanese dishes: also **soy sauce 2.** the soybean plant or its seeds Also, chiefly Brit., **soy·a** (soi'ə)

**soy·bean** (soi'bēn') *n.* **1.** a plant of the legume family, native to China and Japan but widely grown for forage and cover and for its seeds, rich in protein and oil **2.** its seed

**SP, S.P.** Shore Patrol

**Sp. 1.** Spain **2.** Spaniard **3.** Spanish

**sp. 1.** special **2.** *pl.* **spp.** species **3.** spelling

**spa** (spä) *n.* [< *Spa,* a health resort in Belgium] **1.** a spring of mineral water, or a place with such a spring **2.** a commercial establishment with sauna, whirlpool baths, exercise rooms, etc. **3.** a large whirlpool bath with ledges for seating several people

**space** (spās) *n.* [< OFr. < L. *spatium*] **1.** *a)* the continuous, boundless expanse extending in all directions or in three dimensions, within which all things exist *b) same as* OUTER SPACE **2.** *a)* the distance, expanse, or area between, over, or within things *b)* area or room for something [*parking space*] **3.** an interval or period of time **4.** reserved accommodations, as on a ship **5.** *Music* the open area between any two lines of a staff **6.** *Printing a)* a blank piece of type metal used to separate characters, etc. *b)* the area left vacant by this on a printed or typed line **—adj.** of space **—vt.** **spaced, spac'ing** to arrange with spaces between **—space'less** *adj.* **—spac'er** *n.*

**Space Age** [*also* s- a-] the period, since 1957, in which artificial satellites and manned space vehicles have been launched **—space'-age'** *adj.*

**space bar** a bar, as on a typewriter keyboard, pressed to leave a blank space or spaces between words, etc.

**space·craft** (spās'kraft') *n., pl.* **-craft'** a spaceship or satellite for use in outer space

**space·flight** (-flīt') *n.* a flight through outer space

**space heater** a small heating unit for a room or small area

**space·man** (-man', -mən) *n., pl.* **-men'** (-men', -mən) an astronaut or any of the crew of a spaceship

**space·port** (-pôrt') *n.* a center where spacecraft are assembled, tested, and launched

**space·ship** (-ship') *n.* a rocket-propelled vehicle for travel in outer space

**space station** (or **platform**) a structure designed to orbit in space as a launching pad or as an observation center

**space·suit** (-sōōt') *n. same as* G-SUIT, esp. one modified for use in spaceflights

**space-time** (**continuum**) (-tīm') a continuum having the three dimensions of space and that of time, in which any event can be located

**space·walk** (-wôk') *n.* the act of an astronaut in moving about in space outside his spacecraft **—vi.** to engage in a spacewalk **—space'walk'er** *n.*

**spa·cial** (spā'shəl) *adj. alt. sp. of* SPATIAL

**spac·ing** (spā'siŋ) *n.* **1.** the arrangement of spaces **2.** space or spaces, as between printed words **3.** the act of a person or thing that spaces

**spa·cious** (spā'shəs) *adj.* **1.** having more than enough space or room; vast; extensive **2.** not confined or limited; large **—spa'cious·ly** *adv.* **—spa'cious·ness** *n.*

**Spack·le** (spak'l) [ult. < L. *spatula,* SPATULA] *a trademark for* a powdery substance (**spackling compound**) that is mixed with water and dries hard, to cover wall seams, nail holes, etc. **—n.** [s-] this substance **—vt.** **-led, -ling** [s-] to put spackle on

**spade**[1] (spād) *n.* [OE. *spadu*] a heavy, long-handled digging tool with a flat blade that is pressed into the ground with the foot **—vt., vi.** **spad'ed, spad'ing** to dig or cut as with a spade **—call a spade a spade** to use plain, blunt words **—spade'ful** *n.*

**spade**[2] (spād) *n.* [Sp. *espada,* sword (sign used on Spanish cards) < L. *spatha,* SPATULA] **1.** the black figure ( ♠ ) marking one of the four suits of playing cards **2.** [*pl.*] this suit **3.** a card of this suit **—in spades** [Colloq.] in an extreme or emphatic way

**spade·work** (spād'wurk') *n.* work done to get a project started, esp. when tiresome or difficult

**spa·dix** (spā′diks) *n., pl.* **-dix·es, -di·ces′** (spā′də sēz′, spā dī′sēz) [ModL. < L., a palm branch < Gr. *spadix*] a fleshy spike of tiny flowers, usually enclosed in a spathe

**spa·ghet·ti** (spə get′ē) *n.* [It., dim. pl. of *spago*, small cord] long, thin strings of pasta, cooked by boiling or steaming and served with a sauce

**Spain** (spān) country in SW Europe, on the Iberian Peninsula: 194,346 sq. mi.; pop. 34,134,000; cap. Madrid

**spake** (spāk) *archaic pt. of* SPEAK

**span¹** (span) *n.* [OE. *sponn*] **1.** a measure of length, equal to nine inches, based on the distance between the tips of the extended thumb and little finger **2.** *a)* the full amount or extent between any two limits *b)* the distance between ends or supports [the span of an arch] *c)* the full duration, as of attention **3.** a part between two supports [a bridge of four *spans*] **4.** *shortened form of* WINGSPAN **5.** [borrowed in U.S. < Du. *span*, in same sense] a team of two animals used together —*vt.* **spanned, span′ning 1.** to measure, esp. by the hand with the thumb and the little finger extended **2.** to encircle with the hand or hands, as in measuring **3.** to extend, reach, or pass over or across [a bridge *spans* the river]

**span²** (span) *archaic pt. of* SPIN

**Span. 1.** Spaniard **2.** Spanish

**span·dex** (span′deks) *n.* [< EXPAND] an elastic fiber, chiefly a polymer of polyurethane, used in girdles, etc.

**span·drel** (span′drəl) *n.* [< dim. of Anglo-Fr. *spaundre* < OFr. *espandre*, to expand] **1.** the space between the exterior or curve of an arch and a rectangular frame enclosing it **2.** any of the spaces between a series of arches and a cornice above

**spang** (spaŋ) *adv.* [< dial. *spang*, to leap] [Colloq.] abruptly, directly, or exactly

**span·gle** (spaŋ′g'l) *n.* [< dim. of ME. *spang*, a clasp < OE.] **1.** a small piece of bright metal, esp. any of those sewn on fabric for decoration **2.** any small, glittering object —*vt.* **-gled, -gling** to cover with spangles —*vi.* to glitter as with spangles —**span′gly** *adj.* **-gli·er, -gli·est**

**Span·iard** (span′yərd) *n.* a native or inhabitant of Spain

**span·iel** (span′yəl) *n.* [< MFr. *espagnol*, lit., Spanish, ult. < L. *Hispania*, Spain] **1.** any of several breeds of dog with a silky coat, drooping ears, and short legs and tail **2.** a servile, fawning person

**Span·ish** (span′ish) *adj.* of Spain, its people, their language, etc. —*n.* the Romance language of Spain and of Spanish America —**the Spanish** the people of Spain

SPRINGER SPANIEL
(18 in. high at shoulder)

**Spanish America** Mexico and those countries in Central and South America in which Spanish is the chief language

**Span·ish-A·mer·i·can** (-ə mer′ə kən) *adj.* **1.** of both Spain and America **2.** of Spanish America or its people —*n.* a native or inhabitant of Spanish America, esp. one of Spanish descent

**Spanish-American War** the war between the U.S. and Spain (1898)

**Spanish Armada** *see* ARMADA (sense 1 *b*)

**Spanish Civil War** the civil war in Spain (1936–39)

**Spanish Inquisition** the Inquisition as reorganized in Spain in 1478: notorious for its cruel and extreme practices

**Spanish Main 1.** orig., the coastal region of the Americas along the Caribbean Sea; esp., the N coast of S. America **2.** later, the Caribbean Sea itself, or that part of it adjacent to the N coast of S. America

**Spanish moss** a rootless epiphytic plant often growing in long, graceful strands from the branches of trees in the SE U.S. and tropical America

**Spanish omelet** an omelet folded around a sauce of chopped onion, green pepper, and tomato

**Spanish rice** boiled rice cooked with tomatoes and chopped onions, green peppers, etc.

**spank** (spaŋk) *vt.* [echoic] to strike with something flat, as the open hand, esp. on the buttocks, as in punishment —*vi.* to move along swiftly —*n.* a smack given in spanking

**spank·er** (spaŋ′kər) *n.* **1.** a person or thing that spanks **2.** [Colloq.] an unusually fine, large, etc. person or thing **3.** *Naut.* *a)* a fore-and-aft sail on the after mast of a square-rigged vessel *b)* the after mast and its sail on a schooner-rigged vessel of more than three masts

**spank·ing** (-kiŋ) *adj.* **1.** rapid **2.** brisk: said of a breeze **3.** [Colloq.] unusually fine, large, etc. —*adv.* [Colloq.] altogether; completely [*spanking* new] —*n.* a series of smacks given by one who spanks

**span·ner** (span′ər) *n.* **1.** one that spans **2.** *chiefly Brit. term for* WRENCH (tool for turning nuts, bolts, etc.)

**Span·sule** (span′sool, -syool) [SPAN¹ + (CAP)SULE] *a trademark for* a long-acting medicinal capsule whose tiny beads of medicine dissolve at spaced intervals —*n.* [s-] such a capsule

**Spar, SPAR** (spär) *n.* [< *s(emper) par(atus)*, (always prepared), L. motto of the Coast Guard] a woman member of the U.S. Coast Guard

**spar¹** (spär) *n.* [< MDu. or MLowG. *spar*] any shiny, crystalline mineral that cleaves easily into chips or flakes —**spar′ry** *adj.* **-ri·er, -ri·est**

**spar²** (spär) *n.* [< ON. *sparri* or MDu. *sparre*] **1.** any pole, as a mast, yard, or boom, for supporting the sails on a ship **2.** a lengthwise support for the ribs of an airplane wing —*vt.* **sparred, spar′ring** to equip with spars

**spar³** (spär) *vi.* **sparred, spar′ring** [prob. < MFr. < It. *sparare*, to kick < *parare*, to parry] **1.** to fight with the feet and spurs: said of a fighting cock **2.** to box with jabbing or feinting movements, landing few heavy blows, as in practice matches **3.** to dispute; argue —*n.* a sparring match

**spare** (sper) *vt.* **spared, spar′ing** [OE. *sparian*] **1.** to treat with mercy; refrain from killing, hurting, etc. **2.** to save or free (a person) from (something) [*spare* me the trouble] **3.** to omit, avoid using, or use frugally [*spare* no effort] **4.** to part with or give up (money, time, etc.) without trouble to oneself —*vi.* **1.** to be frugal **2.** to show mercy —*adj.* **1.** not in regular use; extra [a *spare* room] **2.** not taken up by regular work or duties; free [*spare* time] **3.** meager; scanty [*spare* rations] **4.** not fleshy; lean —*n.* **1.** an extra part, thing, etc. **2.** *Bowling* *a)* a knocking down of all the pins in two consecutive rolls of the ball *b)* a score so made —(something) to spare a surplus of (something) —**spare′ly** *adv.* —**spare′ness** *n.* —**spar′er** *n.*

**spare·ribs** (sper′ribz′) *n.pl.* [altered (after SPARE, *adj.*) < MLowG. *ribbesper*] a cut of meat, esp. pork, consisting of the thin end of the ribs with most of the meat cut away

**spar·ing** (sper′iŋ) *adj.* **1.** that spares **2.** frugal **3.** scanty; meager —**spar′ing·ly** *adv.* —**spar′ing·ness** *n.*

**spark¹** (spärk) *n.* [OE. *spearca*] **1.** a glowing bit of matter, esp. one thrown off by a fire **2.** any flash or sparkle of light like this **3.** a tiny beginning or vestige, as of life, interest, etc.; particle or trace **4.** liveliness; vivacity **5.** *Elec.* *a)* a very brief flash of light accompanying an electric discharge through air or some other insulating material *b)* such a discharge, as in a spark plug —*vi.* **1.** to make or throw off sparks **2.** to come forth as or like sparks —*vt.* to stir into action; be the force that enlivens —**spark′er** *n.*

**spark²** (spärk) *n.* [ON. *sparkr*, lively] **1.** a dashing, gallant young man **2.** a beau or lover —*vt., vi.* [Colloq.] to court, woo, pet, etc. An old-fashioned term

**spark gap** a space between two electrodes through which a spark discharge may take place

**spar·kle** (spär′k'l) *vi.* **-kled, -kling** [< ME. freq. of *sparken*, to SPARK¹] **1.** to throw off sparks **2.** to shine with flashes of light; glitter, as jewels **3.** to be brilliant and lively **4.** to bubble or effervesce, as some wines —*vt.* to make sparkle —*n.* **1.** a spark, or glowing particle **2.** a sparkling, or glittering **3.** brilliance; liveliness

**spar·kler** (-klər) *n.* one that sparkles; specif., *a)* a pencil-shaped firework that burns with bright sparks *b)* [pl.][Colloq.] bright, clear eyes *c)* [Colloq.] a diamond or similar gem

**spark plug 1.** a piece fitted into a cylinder of an internal-combustion engine to make sparks that ignite the fuel mixture within **2.** [Colloq.] a person or thing that inspires, activates, etc. —**spark′plug′** *vt.* **-plugged′, -plug′ging**

**sparring partner** any person with whom a prizefighter boxes for practice

**spar·row** (spar′ō) *n.* [OE. *spearwa*] **1.** any of several old-world weaver-birds, esp. of a genus including the ENGLISH SPARROW, now common in the U.S. **2.** any of many finches native to both the Old and New Worlds; esp., any of various American species, as the SONG SPARROW

SPARK PLUG
(cutaway model)

TERMINAL

INSULATOR

ELECTRODES

GAP

**sparrow hawk 1.** a small European hawk with short wings **2.** a small American falcon

**sparse** (spärs) *adj.* [< L. pp. of *spargere*, to scatter] thinly spread or scattered; not dense —**sparse′ly** *adv.* —**sparse′ness, spar·si·ty** (spär′sə tē) *n.*

**Spar·ta** (spär′tə) city in the S Peloponnesus, Greece, a powerful military city in ancient Laconia

**Spar·ta·cus** (spär′tə kəs) ?–71 B.C.; Thracian slave & gladiator in Rome: leader of a slave revolt

fat, āpe, cär; ten, ēven; is, bīte; gō, hôrn, tōōl, lŏŏk; ôil, out; up, fʉr; get; joy; yet; chin; she; thin, *th*en; zh, leisure; ŋ, ring; ə for *a* in *ago*, *e* in *agent*, *i* in *sanity*, *o* in *comply*, *u* in *focus*; ' as in *able* (ā′b'l); Fr. bàl; ë, Fr. coeur; ö, Fr. feu; Fr. mon; ô, Fr. coq; ü, Fr. duc; r, Fr. cri; H, G. ich; kh, G. doch; ‡foreign; *hypothetical; < derived from. See inside front cover.

**Spar·tan** (spär't'n) *adj.* **1.** of ancient Sparta, its people, or their culture **2.** like or characteristic of the Spartans; brave, stoical, frugal, highly disciplined, strict, etc. —*n.* **1.** a citizen of Sparta **2.** a person with Spartan traits —**Spar'tan·ism** *n.*

**spar varnish** a durable varnish for outdoor surfaces

**spasm** (spaz'm) *n.* [< MFr. < L. < Gr. *spasmos* < *span*, to pull] **1.** a convulsive, involuntary contraction of a muscle or muscles **2.** any short, sudden burst of activity, feeling, etc.

**spas·mod·ic** (spaz mäd'ik) *adj.* [ModL. *spasmodicus* < Gr. < *spasmos*: see prec.] of, like, or characterized by a spasm or spasms; sudden, violent, and temporary; fitful; intermittent Also **spas·mod'i·cal** —**spas·mod'i·cal·ly** *adv.*

**spas·tic** (spas'tik) *adj.* [< L. < Gr. *spastikos*, pulling < *span:* see SPASM] of, marked by, or having spasm or spastic paralysis —*n.* a person with spastic paralysis —**spas'ti·cal·ly** *adv.*

**spastic paralysis** a condition, as in cerebral palsy, in which certain muscles stay contracted and movements are more or less uncontrollable

**spat**[1] (spat) *n.* [prob. echoic] **1.** a quick, slapping sound **2.** [Colloq.] a brief, petty quarrel or dispute —*vi.* **spat'ted, spat'ting 1.** to strike with a spat **2.** [Colloq.] to have a spat, or quarrel

**spat**[2] (spat) *n.* [contr. < SPATTERDASH] a short gaiter for the instep and ankle

**spat**[3] (spat) *alt. pt. & pp.* of SPIT[2]

**spat**[4] (spat) *n.* [Anglo-Fr. < ?] **1.** the spawn of the oyster or other bivalve shellfish **2.** a young oyster or young oysters —*vi.* **spat'ted, spat'ting** to spawn: said of oysters

**spate** (spāt) *n.* [ME. < ?] **1.** [Chiefly Brit.] a sudden flood or heavy rain **2.** a large outpour, as of words

**spathe** (spāth) *n.* [< ModL. < L. < Gr. *spathē,* flat blade] a large, leaflike part or pair of such parts enclosing a flower cluster (as a spadix)

SPATHE

SPADIX

**spa·tial** (spā'shəl) *adj.* [< L. *spatium*, space] **1.** of space **2.** happening or existing in space —**spa'ti·al'i·ty** (-shē al'ə-tē) *n.* —**spa'tial·ly** *adv.*

**spat·ter** (spat'ər) *vt.* [akin to Fris. freq. of *spatten*, to splash] **1.** to scatter in drops or small blobs **2.** to splash with these **3.** to defame —*vi.* **1.** to be scattered in drops, etc., as fat in frying **2.** to fall or strike as in a shower, as raindrops or pellets —*n.* **1.** *a)* a spattering *b)* its sound **2.** a mark made by spattering

**spat·ter·dash** (-dash') *n.* [prec. + DASH] a long legging formerly worn to protect the stocking or trouser leg, as in wet weather

**spat·u·la** (spach'ə lə) *n.* [L., dim. of *spatha*, flat blade] a knifelike implement with a flat, flexible blade used for spreading or blending foods, paints, etc., for scraping, etc.

**spav·in** (spav'in) *n.* [MFr. *esparvain*] a disease of horses in which a deposit of bone (**bone spavin**) or an infusion of lymph (**bog spavin**) develops in the hock joint, usually causing lameness —**spav'ined** *adj.*

**spawn** (spôn) *vt., vi.* [< Anglo-Fr. < OFr. *espandre*, to shed < L.: see EXPAND] **1.** to produce or deposit (eggs, sperm, or young) **2.** to bring into being (esp. something regarded with contempt and produced in great quantity) —*n.* **1.** the mass of eggs or young produced by fishes, mollusks, amphibians, etc. **2.** something produced; specif., offspring or progeny: usually contemptuous

**spay** (spā) *vt.* [< Anglo-Fr. < OFr. < *espee*, sword < L. *spatha:* see SPATHE] to sterilize (a female animal) by removing the ovaries

**S.P.C.A.** Society for the Prevention of Cruelty to Animals

**speak** (spēk) *vi.* **spoke** or archaic **spake, spo'ken** or archaic **spoke, speak'ing** [OE. *specan*, earlier *sprecan*] **1.** to utter words with the ordinary voice; talk **2.** to express opinions, feelings, ideas, etc. by or as by talking **3.** to make a request or reservation (*for*): usually in the passive [a seat not yet spoken for] **4.** to make a speech; discourse **5.** to be a spokesman (*for*) **6.** to converse **7.** to give out sound —*vt.* **1.** to make known by or as by speaking **2.** to use or be able to use (a given language) in speaking **3.** to utter (words) orally —**so to speak** that is to say —**speak for itself** to be self-evident —**speak out** (or **up**) **1.** to speak audibly or clearly **2.** to speak freely or forcefully —**speak well for** to indicate something favorable about —**to speak of** worthy of mention [no gains to speak of] —**speak'a·ble** *adj.*

**speak·eas·y** (-ē'zē) *n., pl.* -eas'ies [SPEAK + EASY: so named from the secretive atmosphere] [Slang] a place selling alcoholic drinks illegally, esp. during Prohibition

**speak·er** (spē'kər) *n.* **1.** a person who speaks or makes speeches **2.** a person who serves as presiding officer of a lawmaking body; specif., [S-] the presiding officer of the U.S. House of Representatives: in full, **Speaker of the House 3.** a loudspeaker —**speak'er·ship'** *n.*

**speak·ing** (-kiŋ) *adj.* **1.** that speaks, or seems to speak;

expressive; vivid **2.** in or for speech —*n.* **1.** the act or art of one who speaks **2.** utterance; discourse

**speaking in tongues** *same as* GLOSSOLALIA

**spear** (spir) *n.* [OE. *spere*] **1.** a weapon with a long shaft and sharp head, for thrusting or throwing **2.** any spearlike, often forked implement, as one used in fishing **3.** [var. of SPIRE] a long blade or shoot, as of grass —*vt.* **1.** to pierce or stab as with a spear **2.** to catch (fish, etc.) as with a spear —*vi.* **1.** to pierce like a spear **2.** to sprout into a long stem —**spear'er** *n.*

**spear·head** (-hed') *n.* **1.** the pointed head of a spear **2.** the person or persons leading an activity, esp. a military attack —*vt.* to lead (an attack, etc.)

**spear·man** (-mən) *n., pl.* **-men** a fighting man armed with a spear

**spear·mint** (-mint') *n.* [from its flower spikes] a fragrant plant of the mint family, used for flavoring

**spec. 1.** special **2.** specification **3.** speculation

**spe·cial** (spesh'əl) *adj.* [< OFr. < L. < *species*, kind] **1.** different, distinctive, or unique **2.** exceptional; extraordinary **3.** highly regarded [a *special* friend] **4.** of or for a particular occasion, purpose, etc. [a *special* edition] **5.** not general or regular; specific [*special* legislation] —*n.* something special, as a featured item on a menu or in a sale, or a special TV program not part of a regular series —**spe'cial·ly** *adv.*

**special delivery** delivery of mail by special postal messenger, for an extra fee

**spe·cial·ist** (-ist) *n.* **1.** a person who specializes in a particular branch of study, professional work, etc. **2.** *U.S. Army* any of six grades above private first class for enlisted personnel with technical duties —*adj.* of a specialist: also **spe'cial·is'tic** —**spe'cial·ism** *n.*

**spe·ci·al·i·ty** (spesh'ē al'ə tē) *n., pl.* **-ties** chiefly Brit. var. of SPECIALTY

**spe·cial·ize** (spesh'ə līz') *vt.* **-ized', -iz'ing 1.** to make special or specific **2.** to direct toward a specific end **3.** *Biol.* to adapt (parts or organs) to a special condition, use, etc. —*vi.* **1.** to make a specialty of something; specif., to take up a special study or work in a special branch of a profession **2.** *Biol.* to become specialized —**spe'cial·i·za'tion** *n.*

**spe·cial·ty** (-əl tē) *n., pl.* **-ties 1.** a special quality, feature, etc. **2.** a special field of study, branch of a profession, etc. **3.** the state of being special **4.** a product, line of products, etc. given special attention and care to make it attractive, superior, etc. [a bakery whose *specialty* is pie]

**spe·ci·a·tion** (spē'shē ā'shən, -sē-) *n. Biol.* the process of developing new species through evolution —**spe'ci·ate'** (-āt') *vi.* **-at'ed, -at'ing**

**spe·cie** (spē'shē, -sē) *n.* [abl. of L. *species*, kind: cf. use in phr. below] coin, as distinguished from paper money —**in specie 1.** in kind **2.** in coin

**spe·cies** (-shēz, -sēz) *n., pl.* **-cies** [L., appearance, shape, kind, etc.] **1.** a distinctive kind; sort; variety; class **2.** *Biol.* a group of highly similar plants or animals that is part of a genus and that can reproduce fertile offspring only among themselves **3.** *Logic* a class of things with distinctive common attributes, grouped with similar classes in a genus **4.** *R.C.Ch. a)* the outward form of the consecrated Eucharistic bread and wine *b)* the bread or wine —**the species** the human race

**specif.** specifically

**spe·cif·ic** (spi sif'ik) *adj.* [LL. *specificus* < L. *species* (see SPECIES) + *-ficus*, -FIC] **1.** specifying or specified; precise; definite; explicit **2.** of or forming a species **3.** peculiar to or characteristic of something [*specific* traits] **4.** of a particular sort **5.** *Med. a)* specially indicated as a cure for a particular disease [a *specific* remedy] *b)* produced by a particular microorganism [a *specific* disease] **6.** *Physics* designating a constant characteristic in relation to a fixed standard —*n.* **1.** something specially suited for a given use or purpose **2.** a specific cure or remedy **3.** a distinct item or detail; particular —**spe·cif'i·cal·ly** *adv.* —**spec·i·fic·i·ty** (spes'ə fis'ə tē) *n.*

**spec·i·fi·ca·tion** (spes'ə fi kā'shən) *n.* **1.** a specifying; detailed mention **2.** [*usually pl.*] a statement of particulars as to size, materials, etc. [*specifications* for a new building] **3.** something specified; specified item, etc.

**specific gravity** the ratio of the weight or mass of a given volume of a substance to that of an equal volume of another substance (water for liquids and solids, air or hydrogen for gases) used as a standard

**spec·i·fy** (spes'ə fī') *vt.* **-fied', -fy'ing** [< OFr. < LL. *specificus,* SPECIFIC] **1.** to mention or describe in detail; state definitely or explicitly **2.** to include as an item in a set of specifications —**spec'i·fi'a·ble** *adj.* —**spec'i·fi'er** *n.*

**spec·i·men** (spes'ə mən) *n.* [L. < *specere,* to see] **1.** a part of a whole, or one individual of a group, used as a sample of the rest **2.** [Colloq.] a (specified kind of) individual or person [an odd *specimen*] **3.** *Med.* a sample, as of urine, for analysis

**spe·cious** (spē′shəs) *adj.* [< L. *speciosus* < *species*, appearance] seeming good, sound, etc., but not really so [*specious* logic] —**spe′cious·ly** *adv.* —**spe′cious·ness** *n.*

**speck** (spek) *n.* [OE. *specca*] 1. a small spot or mark 2. a tiny bit; particle —*vt.* to mark with specks

**speck·le** (spek′'l) *n.* [dim. of ME. *specke*, SPECK] a small mark of contrasting color; speck —*vt.* **-led, -ling** to mark with speckles

**specs** (speks) *n.pl.* [Colloq.] 1. eyeglasses 2. specifications: see SPECIFICATION (sense 2)

**spec·ta·cle** (spek′tə k'l) *n.* [< OFr. < L. < *spectare*, freq. of *specere*, to see] 1. something to look at, esp. a remarkable sight 2. a public show on a grand scale 3. [*pl.*] eyeglasses: old-fashioned term —**spec′ta·cled** *adj.*

**spec·tac·u·lar** (spek tak′yə lər) *adj.* of or like a spectacle; strikingly grand or unusual —**spec·tac′u·lar·ly** *adv.*

**spec·ta·tor** (spek′tāt ər, spek tāt′-) *n.* [L. < pp. of *spectare*, to behold] a person who watches something without taking part; onlooker [*spectators* at sports events]

**spec·ter** (spek′tər) *n.* [< Fr. < L. *spectrum*, appearance, apparition < *spectare*, to behold] 1. a ghost; apparition 2. any object of dread Also, Brit. sp., **spec′tre**

**spec·tra** (spek′trə) *n.* alt. pl. of SPECTRUM

**spec·tral** (-trəl) *adj.* 1. of or like a specter; ghostly 2. of a spectrum —**spec·tral′i·ty** (-tral′ə tē), **spec′tral·ness** *n.* —**spec′tral·ly** *adv.*

**spec·tro-** [< SPECTRUM] *a combining form meaning:* 1. of radiant energy as shown in a spectrum 2. of or by a spectroscope

**spec·tro·gram** (spek′trə gram′) *n.* a photograph of a spectrum

**spec·tro·graph** (-graf′) *n.* an instrument for breaking up light into a spectrum and photographing the spectrum —**spec′tro·graph′ic** *adj.* —**spec′tro·graph′i·cal·ly** *adv.*

**spec·trom·e·ter** (spek träm′ə tər) *n.* an instrument for measuring spectral wavelengths —**spec′tro·met′ric** (-trə met′rik) *adj.* —**spec·trom′e·try** (-ə trē) *n.*

**spec·tro·scope** (spek′trə skōp′) *n.* an optical instrument for breaking up light from any source into a spectrum so that it can be studied —**spec′tro·scop′ic** (-skäp′ik) *adj.* —**spec′tro·scop′i·cal·ly** *adv.*

**spec·tros·co·py** (spek träs′kə pē) *n.* the study of spectra by use of the spectroscope —**spec·tros′co·pist** *n.*

**spec·trum** (spek′trəm) *n.,* pl. **-tra** (-trə), **-trums** [ModL., special use of L. *spectrum*: see SPECTER] 1. the series of colored bands into which white light is broken up by passing through a prism, etc.: it is arranged according to wavelength, from red, the longest wave visible, to violet, the shortest 2. any like series of bands or lines formed from other kinds of radiant energy 3. a range or extent, as of opinion 4. *same as* RADIO SPECTRUM

VIOLET
INDIGO
BLUE
GREEN
YELLOW
ORANGE
RED

SPECTRUM

**spec·u·late** (spek′yə lāt′) *vi.* **-lat′ed, -lat′ing** [< L. pp. of *speculari*, to view < *specula*, watch tower < *specere*, to see] 1. to think about the various aspects of a subject; ponder; esp., to conjecture 2. to buy or sell stocks, land, etc., hoping to gain from price changes; also, to engage in any risky venture for possible huge profits —**spec′u·la′tion** *n.* —**spec′u·la′tive** (-lāt′iv, -lə tiv) *adj.* —**spec′u·la′tive·ly** *adv.* —**spec′u·la′tor** *n.*

**spec·u·lum** (spek′yə ləm) *n.,* pl. **-la** (-lə), **-lums** [L. < *specere*, to look] 1. a mirror, esp. one of polished metal used as a reflector in a telescope, etc. 2. *Med.* an instrument used to dilate a passage for easier examination —**spec′u·lar** (-lər) *adj.* —**spec′u·lar·ly** *adv.*

**sped** (sped) alt. pt. & pp. of SPEED

**speech** (spēch) *n.* [OE. *spæc, spræc* < base of *sprecan*, to speak] 1. the act of speaking 2. the power or ability to speak 3. the manner of speaking 4. what is spoken; utterance, talk, etc. 5. a talk given to an audience 6. the language or dialect used by a certain group of people 7. the study of the theory and practice of speaking

**speech·i·fy** (spē′chə fī′) *vi.* **-fied′, -fy′ing** to make a speech: used humorously or contemptuously —**speech′i·fi′er** *n.*

**speech·less** (spēch′lis) *adj.* 1. not able to speak 2. silent, as from shock 3. not expressed or expressible in words —**speech′less·ly** *adv.* —**speech′less·ness** *n.*

**speed** (spēd) *n.* [OE. *spæd,* success] 1. the act or state of moving rapidly; swiftness 2. *a)* the rate of movement; velocity *b)* the rate or rapidity of any action [*reading speed*] 3. an arrangement of gears for the drive of an en-

gine 4. [Colloq.] one's kind or level of taste, ability, etc. 5. [Slang] any of various amphetamine compounds 6. [Archaic] luck; success —*adj.* of speed —*vi.* **sped** or **speed′ed, speed′ing** 1. to go fast, esp. at a speed greater than the legal limit 2. [Archaic] *a)* to get along; fare *b)* to prosper —*vt.* 1. to help succeed; aid 2. to wish Godspeed to 3. to cause to go, move, etc. swiftly —**speed up** to go or make go faster —**speed′er** *n.*

**speed·boat** (-bōt′) *n.* a motorboat built for speed

**speed·om·e·ter** (spi däm′ə tər) *n.* [< SPEED + -METER] a device attached to a motor vehicle, etc. to indicate speed, as in miles per hour

**speed·ster** (spēd′stər) *n.* a person or thing that speeds

**speed·up** (-up′) *n.* an increase in speed; esp., an increase in the rate of output, etc., as required by an employer

**speed·way** (-wā′) *n.* 1. a track for racing cars or motorcycles 2. a road for high-speed traffic

**speed·well** (-wel′) *n.* any of various plants of the figwort family, with spikes of white or bluish flowers

**speed·y** (spēd′ē) *adj.* **speed′i·er, speed′i·est** 1. rapid; swift 2. without delay; quick; prompt [a *speedy* reply] —**speed′i·ly** *adv.* —**speed′i·ness** *n.*

**spe·le·ol·o·gy** (spē′lē äl′ə jē) *n.* [< L. < Gr. *spēlaion,* a cave + -LOGY] the scientific study and exploration of caves —**spe′le·ol′o·gist** *n.*

**spell**[1] (spel) *n.* [OE., a saying] 1. a word or formula supposed to have some magic power 2. magical power or irresistible influence; charm; fascination —**cast a spell on** to enchant —**under a spell** enchanted

**spell**[2] (spel) *vt.* **spelled** or **spelt, spell′ing** [< OFr. *espeller,* to explain < Frank. *spellōn*] 1. to name, write, or signal, esp. correctly, the letters of (a word, etc.) 2. to make up, or form (a word, etc.): said of specified letters 3. to mean [red *spells* danger] —*vi.* to spell words, etc. —**spell out** 1. to read letter by letter or with difficulty 2. to discern as if by close reading 3. to explain in detail

**spell**[3] (spel) *vt.* **spelled, spell′ing** [OE. *spelian*] [Colloq.] to work in place of (another) while he rests; relieve —*n.* 1. a turn of working in place of another 2. any period of work, duty, etc. 3. a period (*of* being in some state) [a *spell* of gloom] 4. a period of specified weather [a cold *spell*] 5. [Colloq.] a period of time that is indefinite, short, etc. 6. [Colloq.] a period of some illness 7. [Dial.] a short distance

**spell·bind** (spel′bīnd′) *vt.* **-bound′, -bind′ing** to hold or affect as by a spell; fascinate; enchant —**spell′bind′er** *n.*

**spell·down** (-doun′) *n.* a spelling contest in which each contestant who misspells a word must drop out: also **spelling bee**

**spell·er** (-ər) *n.* 1. a person who spells words [a good *speller*] 2. an exercise book used to teach spelling

**spell·ing** (-iŋ) *n.* 1. the act of one who spells words 2. the way a word is spelled

**spelt**[1] (spelt) alt. pt. & pp. of SPELL[2]

**spelt**[2] (spelt) *n.* [OE. < LL. *spelta*] a species of wheat with grains that do not thresh free of chaff

**spe·lunk·er** (spi luŋ′kər) *n.* [< obs. *spelunk,* a cave (ult. < Gr. *spēlynx*) + -ER] a person who explores caves as a hobby —**spe·lunk′ing** *n.*

**Spen·cer** (spen′sər), Herbert 1820–1903; Eng. philosopher —**Spen·ce′ri·an** (-sir′ē ən) *adj., n.*

**spend** (spend) *vt.* **spent, spend′ing** [< OE. *spendan* (in comp.) < ML. < L. *expendere,* to expend] 1. to use up, exhaust, etc. [his fury was *spent*] 2. to pay out (money) 3. to give or devote (time, effort, etc.) to something 4. to pass (time) [*spending* hours alone] 5. to waste; squander —*vi.* to pay out or use up money, etc. —**spend′a·ble** *adj.* —**spend′er** *n.*

**spend·thrift** (-thrift′) *n.* a person who spends money carelessly; squanderer —*adj.* wasteful; extravagant

**Spen·ser** (spen′sər), Edmund 1552?-99; Eng. poet —**Spen·se′ri·an** (-sir′ē ən) *adj., n.*

**spent** (spent) pt. & pp. of SPEND —*adj.* 1. tired out; physically exhausted 2. used up; worn out

**sperm**[1] (spurm) *n.* [< MFr. < LL. < Gr. *sperma,* seed < *speirein,* to sow] 1. the fluid from the male reproductive organs; semen 2. *same as* SPERMATOZOON

**sperm**[2] (spurm) *n.* shortened form of: 1. SPERMACETI 2. SPERM OIL 3. SPERM WHALE

**-sperm** (spurm) [see SPERM[1]] *a combining form meaning* seed [*gymnosperm*]

**sper·ma·ce·ti** (spur′mə set′ē, -sēt′ē) *n.* [ML. < LL. *sperma,* SPERM[1] + L. *ceti,* gen. of *cetus,* a whale] a white, waxlike substance from oil in the head of a sperm whale or dolphin, used in making cosmetics, ointments, candles, etc.

**-sper·mal** (spur′m'l) *same as* -SPERMOUS

**sper·mat·ic** (spər mat′ik) *adj.* of, like, or having to do with sperm or sperm cells

**sper·mat·o-** [< Gr. *sperma* (gen. *spermatos*), SPERM[1]] *a combining form meaning* seed or sperm

**sper·mat·o·phyte** (spər mat′ə fīt′, spur′mə tə-) *n.* [SPERMATO- + -PHYTE] any seed-bearing plant —**sper·mat·o·phyt′ic** (-fit′ik) *adj.*

**sper·mat·o·zo·on** (spər mat′ə zō′än, -ən; spur′mə tə-) *n., pl.* -**zo′a** (-ə) [ModL. < SPERMATO- + Gr. *zōion*, animal] the male germ cell, found in semen: it penetrates and fertilizes the egg of the female —**sper·mat′o·zo′al, sper·mat′o·zo′an, sper·mat·o·zo′ic** *adj.*

**sperm oil** a lubricating oil from the sperm whale

**-sper·mous** (spur′məs) *a combining form meaning* having (a specified number or kind of) seed

**sperm whale** a large, toothed whale of warm seas: a closed cavity in its roughly square head contains sperm oil

**spew** (spyōō) *vt., vi.* [OE. *spiwan*] **1.** to throw up from or as from the stomach; vomit **2.** to flow or gush forth —*n.* something spewed —**spew′er** *n.*

**sp. gr.** specific gravity

**sphag·num** (sfag′nəm) *n.* [ModL. < Gr. *sphagnos*, kind of moss] **1.** a spongelike moss found in bogs **2.** a mass of such mosses, used to improve soil, to pot plants, etc. —**sphag′nous** (-nəs) *adj.*

**sphal·er·ite** (sfal′ə rīt′) *n.* [< G. < Gr. *sphaleros*, deceptive] native zinc sulfide, ZnS, the principal ore of zinc, usually brownish with a resinous luster

**sphe·noid** (sfē′noid) *adj.* [< ModL. < Gr. < *sphēn*, a wedge + -OID] *Anat.* designating or of the wedge-shaped compound bone at the base of the skull: also **sphe·noi′dal** —*n.* the sphenoid bone

**sphere** (sfir) *n.* [< OFr. < L. < Gr. *sphaira*] **1.** any round body with a surface equally distant from the center at all points; globe; ball **2.** a star or planet **3.** the visible heavens; sky **4.** *short for* CELESTIAL SPHERE **5.** any of a series of transparent shells that ancient astronomers imagined as revolving one within another around the earth and containing the stars, planets, sun, and moon **6.** the place or range of action, knowledge, etc.; compass **7.** place in society —*vt.* **sphered, spher′ing** [Chiefly Poet.] **1.** to put in or as in a sphere **2.** to put among the heavenly spheres **3.** to form into a sphere

**-sphere** (sfir) *a combining form meaning:* **1.** of or like a sphere [*hydrosphere*] **2.** of any of the layers of gas around the earth [*ionosphere*]

**spher·i·cal** (sfer′i k'l, sfir′-) *adj.* **1.** shaped like a sphere; globular **2.** of a sphere or spheres Also **spher′ic** — **spher′i·cal·ly** *adv.* —**sphe·ric·i·ty** (sfi ris′ə tē) *n.*

**sphe·roid** (sfir′oid) *n.* a body that is almost but not quite a sphere —*adj.* of this shape: also **sphe·roi′dal**

**sphinc·ter** (sfiŋk′tər) *n.* [LL. < Gr. *sphinktēr* < *sphingein*, to draw close] *Anat.* a ring-shaped muscle that surrounds a natural opening in the body and can open or close it by expanding or contracting —**sphinc′ter·al** *adj.*

**sphinx** (sfiŋks) *n., pl.* **sphinx′es, sphin′ges** (sfin′jēz) [L. < Gr. *sphinx*, lit., the strangler] **1.** any ancient Egyptian statue having a lion's body and the head of a man, ram, or hawk; specif., [S-] a huge statue of this kind with a man's head, near Cairo, Egypt **2.** *a*) *Gr. Myth.* a winged monster with a lion's body and a woman's head and breasts; specif., [S-] such a monster at Thebes, who strangled passers-by unable to solve its riddle *b*) a person who is hard to know or understand

**sphyg·mo·ma·nom·e·ter** (sfig′mō mə näm′ə tər) *n.* [< Gr. *sphygmos*, the pulse + MANOMETER] a manometer with an attached inflatable band wrapped around an upper arm to compress the artery, used to measure blood pressure

**spi·cate** (spī′kāt) *adj.* [L. *spicatus*, spiked] *Bot., Zool.* formed or arranged like a spike or spikes

**spice** (spīs) *n.* [OFr. *espice* < L. *species*, sort] **1.** *a*) any of several vegetable substances, as clove, cinnamon, pepper, etc., used to season food *b*) such substances collectively **2.** a spicy aroma **3.** that which adds zest or interest —*vt.* **spiced, spic′ing 1.** to season or flavor with spice **2.** to add zest or interest to

**spice·bush** (-boosh′) *n.* an aromatic E N. American plant with small, yellowish flowers and red fruit

**Spice Islands** *former name of the* MOLUCCAS

**spick-and-span** (spik′'n span′) *adj.* [< *spick*, var. of SPIKE[1] + *span-new* < ON. < *spānn*, a chip + *nỹr*, new] **1.** new or fresh **2.** neat and clean

**spic·ule** (spik′yōōl) *n.* [< ModL. < ML. < L. dim. of *spica*, a point] **1.** *Bot.* a small spike **2.** *Zool.* a small, hard, needlelike piece or process, as in the skeleton of a sponge: also **spic′u·lum** (-yə ləm), *pl.* -**la** (-lə) —**spic′u·late′** (-yə lāt′), **spic′u·lar** (-lər) *adj.*

**spic·y** (spī′sē) *adj.* **spic′i·er, spic′i·est 1.** containing or full of spices **2.** having the flavor or aroma of spice **3.** lively, interesting, etc. **4.** risqué; racy —**spic′i·ly** *adv.* — **spic′i·ness** *n.*

**spi·der** (spī′dər) *n.* [ME. *spithre*, ult. < OE. *spinnan*, to spin] **1.** any of various small arachnids with a body in two parts, the front part bearing the legs and the back part hav-

ing organs that spin threads for making nests, cocoons, or webs **2.** a cast-iron frying pan, orig. one with legs **3.** any of various devices with leglike extensions —**spi′der·y** *adj.*

**spider monkey** a monkey of South and Central America with long, spidery limbs and a long tail

**spi·der·wort** (-wurt′) *n.* any of various fleshy perennial plants with grasslike leaves and showy purplish, white, or pink flowers

**spiel** (spēl) *n.* [G., play] [Slang] a talk or harangue, as in selling —*vi.* [Slang] to give a spiel —**spiel off** [Slang] to recite as by rote —**spiel′er** *n.*

**spi·er** (spī′ər) *n.* a person who spies

**spiff** (spif) *vt.* [see ff.] [Slang] to make spiffy; spruce (*up*)

**spiff·y** (-ē) *adj.* **spiff′i·er, spiff′i·est** [< dial. *spiff*, well-dressed person] [Slang] spruce, smart, or dapper

**spig·ot** (spig′ət, spik′-) *n.* [ME. *spigote*] **1.** a plug or peg used to stop the vent in a barrel, etc. **2.** a faucet

**spike**[1] (spīk) *n.* [< ON. *spīkr* or < MDu. & MLowG. *spīker*] **1.** a long, heavy nail **2.** a sharp-pointed projection, as along the top of an iron fence **3.** *a*) any of the pointed metal projections on the bottoms of shoes used in baseball, golf, etc. *b*) [*pl.*] a pair of such shoes *c*) a high, very thin heel on a woman's shoe: also **spike heel** —*vt.* **spiked, spik′ing 1.** to fasten or equip as with a spike or spikes **2.** to pierce, cut, etc. with, or impale on, a spike or spikes **3.** to thwart or block (a scheme, etc.) **4.** [Slang] to add alcoholic liquor to (a drink) —**spik′y** *adj.*

**spike**[2] (spīk) *n.* [L. *spica*] **1.** an ear of grain **2.** a long flower cluster with flowers attached directly to the stalk —**spiked** *adj.*

**spike·let** (-lit) *n.* a small spike, as in a flower cluster

**spike·nard** (-nərd, -närd) *n.* [< LL. < L. *spica*, ear of grain + *nardus*, NARD] **1.** a fragrant ointment used in ancient times **2.** the Asiatic plant from which it is made

**spile** (spīl) *n.* [MDu., a splinter] **1.** a plug or spigot, as for a barrel **2.** a tap driven into a maple tree to draw off sap **3.** a heavy stake driven into the ground as a support —*vt.* **spiled, spil′ing 1.** to furnish with spiles, or stakes **2.** to set a spile into (a tree, barrel, etc.) **3.** to plug (a hole) with a spile

SPIKES
(left, plantain;
right, common
mullein)

**spill**[1] (spil) *vt.* **spilled** or **spilt, spill′ing** [OE. *spillan*, to destroy] **1.** to let or make fall or flow over from a container, esp. without intending to **2.** to shed (blood) **3.** to lessen the pressure of (wind) on (a sail) **4.** to scatter at random from a container **5.** [Colloq.] to let (a secret) become known **6.** [Colloq.] to make (a rider, load, etc.) fall off —*vi.* to be spilled from a container —*n.* **1.** a spilling **2.** what is spilled **3.** a spillway **4.** [Colloq.] a fall; tumble —**spill over** to overflow

**spill**[2] (spil) *n.* [prob. via dial. *spil* < ON. *spila*, a splinter] **1.** a splinter **2.** a thin roll of paper, thin stick, etc. set on fire to light a pipe, candle, etc. **3.** a paper cone

**spill·way** (spil′wā′) *n.* [SPILL[1] + WAY] a channel to carry off excess water, as around a dam

**spin** (spin) *vt.* **spun** or archaic **span, spun, spin′ning** [OE. *spinnan*] **1.** *a*) to draw out and twist fibers of (wool, cotton, etc.) into thread *b*) to make (thread, yarn, etc.) thus **2.** to make (a web, cocoon, etc.) from a viscous fluid extruded from the body as a thread: said of spiders, etc. **3.** to produce in a way that suggests spinning **4.** to draw *out* (a story, etc.) to great length **5.** to make whirl [to *spin* a top] **6.** to make (wheels of a vehicle) rotate without traction, as on ice **7.** to extract water from (clothes) in a washer by swift rotation —*vi.* **1.** to spin thread, etc. **2.** to fish with a spinning reel **3.** to whirl **4.** to feel dizzy and seem to be spinning **5.** to go into a spin: said of an aircraft **6.** to move along swiftly and smoothly **7.** to rotate freely without traction —*n.* **1.** the spinning or rotating of something **2.** a moving along swiftly and smoothly **3.** a ride in a motor vehicle **4.** the descent of an airplane nose first along a spiral path **5.** any sudden, steep downward movement —**spin off 1.** to produce as a secondary development **2.** to get rid of

**spin·ach** (spin′ich, -ij) *n.* [< MFr. < OSp. *espinaca* < Ar. < Per. *aspanākh*] **1.** a plant of the goosefoot family, with large, dark-green, edible leaves **2.** the leaves

**spi·nal** (spī′n'l) *adj.* of the spine or spinal cord —*n.* a spinal anesthetic —**spi′nal·ly** *adv.*

**spinal anesthesia** anesthesia of the lower part of the body by injection of an anesthetic into the spinal cord, usually in the lumbar region —**spinal anesthetic**

**spinal column** the series of joined vertebrae forming the axial support for the skeleton; spine

**spinal cord** the thick cord of nerve tissue of the central nervous system, in the spinal column

**spin·dle** (spin′d'l) *n.* [< OE. *spinel* < *spinnan*, to spin] **1.** a slender rod or pin for twisting, winding, or holding the thread in spinning by hand, on a spinning wheel, or in a spinning machine  **2.** something spindle-shaped, as a slender, decorative rod in some chair backs  **3.** any rod, pin, or shaft that revolves or serves as an axis for a revolving part  **4.** in a lathe, a shaftlike part that rotates (**live spindle**) or does not rotate (**dead spindle**) while holding the thing to be turned  **5.** a metal spike on a base, to stick papers on for temporary filing: also **spindle file  6.** *Naut.* a metal rod or pipe topped with a lantern, etc. and fastened to a rock, shoal, etc. to warn vessels —*adj.* of or like a spindle —*vi.* **-dled, -dling** to grow in or into a long, slender shape or stem —*vt.*  **1.** to form into a spindle  **2.** to stick on a spindle (*n.* 5) for filing

**spin·dle·legs** (-legz′) *n.pl.*  **1.** thin legs  **2.** [*with sing. v.*] [Colloq.] a person with thin legs —**spin′dle-leg′ged** (-leg′id, -legd′) *adj.*

**spin·dly** (spin′dlē) *adj.* **-dli·er, -dli·est** long or tall and very thin or slender: also **spin′dling** (-dlin)

**spin·drift** (spin′drift′) *n.* [< Scot. var. of *spoondrift* < *spoon*, to scud (< ?) + DRIFT] spray blown from a rough sea or surf

**spine** (spīn) *n.* [< OFr. < L. *spina*, a thorn]  **1.** any of the short, sharp, woody projections on a cactus, etc.  **2.** *a)* a sharp process of bone  *b)* any of the sharp, stiff projections on certain animals, as a porcupine quill  *c)* anything like either of these  **3.** the spinal column; backbone  **4.** anything suggesting a backbone, as  *a)* the crest of a hill  *b)* the narrow back part of a bound book

**spi·nel** (spi nel′, spin′'l) *n.* [< MFr. < It. dim. of *spina*, spine < L. (see prec.)] a hard, crystalline mineral found in various colors: a red variety (**ruby spinel**) is used as a gem

**spine·less** (spīn′lis) *adj.*  **1.** having no backbone; invertebrate  **2.** having a weak backbone  **3.** lacking courage, willpower, etc.  **4.** having no spines or thorns —**spine′less·ly** *adv.* —**spine′less·ness** *n.*

**spin·et** (spin′it) *n.* [< MFr. < It. *spinetta*, prob. < *spina*, a thorn]  **1.** an obsolete, small harpsichord  **2.** a small upright piano or electronic organ

**spin·na·ker** (spin′ə kər) *n.* [said to be altered < *Sphinx*, name of a yacht that carried the sail] a large, triangular forward sail used on some racing yachts

**spin·ner** (spin′ər) *n.* a person or thing that spins; specif., a fishing lure having blades that revolve or flutter when drawn through the water; also, any of its blades

**spin·ner·et** (spin′ə ret′) *n.* [dim. of SPINNER]  **1.** the organ used by spiders, caterpillars, etc. to spin their silky threads  **2.** a device with tiny holes through which a solution is forced in making synthetic fibers

**spin·ning** (spin′in) *n.*  **1.** the act of making thread, etc. from fibers or filaments  **2.** fishing done with a rod that has a fixed spool, a light line, and light lures —*adj.* that spins or is used in spinning

**spinning jenny** an early spinning machine with several spindles, for spinning more than one thread at a time

**spinning wheel** a simple spinning machine with a single spindle driven by a large wheel

**spin·off** (spin′ôf′) *n.*  **1.** distribution to a corporation's shareholders of stock held in a subsidiary corporation  **2.** a secondary benefit, development, etc.

**spi·nose** (spī′nōs) *adj.* [< L. < *spina*, spine] full of or covered with spines: also **spi′nous** (-nəs) —**spi′nose·ly** *adv.* —**spi·nos′i·ty** (-näs′ə tē) *n., pl.* **-ties**

**Spi·no·za** (spi nō′zə), **Ba·ruch** (bə rook′) or **Benedict** 1632–77; Du. philosopher —**Spi·no′zism** (-ziz′m) *n.*

**spin·ster** (spin′stər) *n.* [ME. < *spinnen*, to spin + -STER]  **1.** a woman who spins thread or yarn  **2.** an unmarried woman, esp. an older one; old maid —**spin′ster·hood′** *n.* —**spin′ster·ish** *adj.*

**spin·y** (spī′nē) *adj.* **spin′i·er, spin′i·est  1.** covered with spines or thorns  **2.** full of difficulties; troublesome  **3.** spine-shaped —**spin′i·ness** *n.*

**spiny anteater** *same as* ECHIDNA

**spin·y-finned** (spī′nē find′) *adj.* having fins supported by pointed, stiff spines

**spiny lobster** a sea crustacean similar to the common lobster, but lacking large pincers and having a spiny shell

**spi·ra·cle** (spī′rə k'l, spir′ə-) *n.* [L. *spiraculum* < *spirare*, to breathe] *Zool.* an opening for breathing, as one of the tracheal openings of arthropods, or the blowhole of a whale

**spi·ral** (spī′rəl) *adj.* [< ML. < L. *spira*, a coil < Gr. *speira*]  **1.** circling or coiling around a central point in a flat curve that constantly increases (or decreases) in size  **2.** circling an axis in a curve of conical or cylindrical form; helical —*n.*  **1.** a spiral curve occurring in a single plane  **2.** a spiral curve occurring in a series of planes; helix  **3.** something having a spiral form  **4.** a spiral path or flight  **5.** a section of a spiral  **6.** a continuous, widening decrease or increase [an inflationary *spiral*] —*vi., vt.* **-raled** or **-ralled,**

**-ral·ing** or **-ral·ling** to move in or form (into) a spiral — **spi′ral·ly** *adv.*

**spi·rant** (spī′rənt) *n., adj.* [< L. prp. of *spirare*, to breathe] *same as* FRICATIVE

**spire** (spīr) *n.* [OE. *spir*]  **1.** a sprout, spike, or stalk of a plant, blade of grass, etc.  **2.** the top part of a pointed, tapering object or structure, as a mountain peak  **3.** anything that tapers to a point, as a steeple —*vi.* **spired, spir′ing** to extend upward, tapering to a point

**spi·re·a** (spī rē′ə) *n.* [< ModL. genus name < L. < Gr. < *speira*, a coil] any of several plants of the rose family, with dense clusters of small, pink or white flowers: also sp. **spi·rae′a**

**spi·ril·lum** (spī ril′əm) *n., pl.* **-la** (-ə) [ModL., dim. of L. *spira* (see SPIRAL)] a bacterium having the form of a spiral thread and moving by means of flagella

**spir·it** (spir′it) *n.* [< OFr. < L. *spiritus*, breath < *spirare*, to breathe]  **1.** the life principle or the soul, esp. in man, sometimes regarded as immortal  **2.** the thinking, feeling part of man; mind; intelligence  **3.** [*also* S-] life, will, thought, etc., regarded as separate from matter  **4.** a supernatural being, as a ghost, angel, demon, fairy, etc.  **5.** an individual person or personality [a brave *spirit*]  **6.** [*usually pl.*] disposition; mood [high *spirits*]  **7.** vivacity, courage, enthusiasm, etc.  **8.** enthusiasm and loyalty [school *spirit*]  **9.** real meaning; true intention [to follow the *spirit* if not the letter of the law]  **10.** an essential quality or prevailing tendency [the *spirit* of the Renaissance]  **11.** [*usually pl.*] distilled alcoholic liquor  **12.** [*often pl.*] any liquid produced by distillation  **13.** an alcoholic solution of a volatile substance [*spirits* of camphor] —*vt.*  **1.** to inspirit, encourage, cheer, etc.  **2.** to carry (*away, off,* etc.) secretly and swiftly —*adj.*  **1.** of spirits or spiritualism  **2.** operating by the burning of alcohol [a *spirit* lamp] —**out of spirits** sad; depressed —**the Spirit** *same as* HOLY SPIRIT —**spir′it·less** *adj.* —**spir′it·less·ly** *adv.* —**spir′it·less·ness** *n.*

**spir·it·ed** (-id) *adj.*  **1.** full of spirit; lively; vigorous; animated  **2.** having a (specified) character, mood, or disposition [low-*spirited*] —**spir′it·ed·ly** *adv.* —**spir′it·ed·ness** *n.*

**spir·it·ism** (-iz′m) *n. same as* SPIRITUALISM —**spir′it·ist** *n., adj.* —**spir′it·is′tic** *adj.*

**spirit level** *same as* LEVEL (*n.* 1)

**spir·it·ous** (spir′i təs) *adj. same as* SPIRITUOUS

**spirits of ammonia** a 10% solution of ammonia in alcohol: also **spirit of ammonia**

**spir·it·u·al** (spir′i choo wəl, -chool) *adj.*  **1.** of the spirit or soul as distinguished from the body or material matters  **2.** of or consisting of spirit; not corporeal  **3.** refined in thought or feeling  **4.** of religion or the church; sacred, devotional, etc.  **5.** spiritualistic or supernatural —*n.*  **1.** a religious folk song of U.S. Negro origin  **2.** [*pl.*] religious or church matters —**spir′it·u·al′i·ty** (-wal′ə tē), *pl.* **-ties, spir′it·u·al·ness** *n.* —**spir′it·u·al·ly** *adv.*

**spir·it·u·al·ism** (-iz′m) *n.*  **1.** the belief that the dead survive as spirits which can communicate with the living, esp. with the help of a medium  **2.** the philosophical doctrine that all reality is in essence spiritual  **3.** spiritual quality —**spir′it·u·al·ist** *n.* —**spir′it·u·al·is′tic** *adj.*

**spir·it·u·al·ize** (spir′i choo wə līz′, -choo līz′) *vt.* **-ized′, -iz′ing  1.** to make spiritual; remove worldliness from  **2.** to give a spiritual sense or meaning to —**spir′it·u·al·i·za′tion** *n.*

‡**spi·ri·tu·el** (spē rē tü el′; *E.* spir′i choo wel′) *adj.* [Fr.] having or showing a refined nature or, esp., a quick, graceful wit or mind —**spi·ri·tu·elle′** *adj. fem.*

**spir·it·u·ous** (spir′i choo wəs) *adj.* of, like, or containing alcohol: said of distilled beverages —**spir′it·u·os′i·ty** (-wäs′ə tē) *n.*

**spi·ro-** [< Gr. *speira*, a coil] *a combining form meaning* spiral or coil [*spirochete*]

**spi·ro·chete** (spī′rə kēt′) *n.* [< ModL. < Gr. *speira*, a spiral + *chaitē*, hair] any of various spiral-shaped bacteria, some of which cause disease: also sp. **spi′ro·chaete′**

**spirt** (spurt) *n., vt., vi. same as* SPURT

**spir·y** (spīr′ē) *adj.* **spir′i·er, spir′i·est  1.** of, or having the form of, a spire  **2.** having many spires

**spit**[1] (spit) *n.* [OE. *spitu*]  **1.** a thin, pointed rod on which meat is impaled for broiling or roasting over a fire or other direct heat  **2.** a narrow point of land, or a narrow reef or shoal, extending into a body of water —*vt.* **spit′ted, spit′ting** to impale as on a spit —**spit′ter** *n.*

**spit**[2] (spit) *vt.* **spit** or, esp. Brit., **spat, spit′ting** [OE. *spittan*]  **1.** to eject from the mouth  **2.** to throw (*out*), emit, or utter explosively [to *spit* out an oath] —*vi.*  **1.** to eject saliva from the mouth; expectorate  **2.** to make an explosive hissing noise, as an angry cat  **3.** to express contempt by spitting saliva (*on* or *at*)  **4.** to sputter, as frying fat —*n.*  **1.** the act of spitting  **2.** saliva  **3.** a salivalike, frothy secretion of certain insects **4.** [Colloq.] the perfect likeness, as of a person: in **spit and image** (spit'n im'ij) —**spit up** to bring up from the stomach or throat —**spit'ter** *n.*

**spit·ball** (-bôl') *n.* **1.** a piece of paper chewed up into a wad for throwing **2.** *Baseball* a pitch, now illegal, made to curve by moistening one side of the ball as with saliva

**spite** (spīt) *n.* [short for DESPITE] **1.** a mean or evil feeling toward another, along with a desire to hurt, humiliate, etc.; malice **2.** an instance of this; a grudge —*vt.* **spit'ed, spit'ing** to show one's spite for by hurting, frustrating, etc. —**in spite of** regardless of —**spite'ful** *adj.* —**spite'ful·ly** *adv.* —**spite'ful·ness** *n.*

**spit·fire** (spit'fir') *n.* a person, esp. a woman or girl, who is easily aroused to violent outbursts of temper

**Spits·ber·gen** (spits'bur'gən) group of Norw. islands in the Arctic Ocean, east of Greenland

**spit·ting im·age** (spit'n im'ij) *alteration of* SPIT AND IMAGE: see SPIT²

**spit·tle** (spit'l) *n.* [< OE. *spætl*, var. of *spatl*] saliva; spit

**spit·toon** (spi tōōn') *n.* a container to spit into

**spitz** (spits) *n.* [G. < *spitz*, pointed] a small Pomeranian dog with pointed muzzle and ears and a long, silky coat

**splash** (splash) *vt.* [intens. extension of PLASH²] **1.** to cause (a liquid) to scatter and fall in drops **2.** to dash or scatter a liquid, mud, etc. on, so as to wet or soil **3.** to cause to splash a liquid [to *splash* the oars] **4.** to make (one's way) by splashing **5.** to mark as by splashing [*splashed* with sunlight] **6.** to display conspicuously [scandal was *splashed* on the front page] —*vi.* **1.** to dash or scatter a liquid about **2.** to move, fall, strike, or scatter with a splash —*n.* **1.** the act or sound of splashing **2.** a mass of splashed water, mud, etc. **3.** a spot or mark made as by splashing **4.** a patch of color, light, etc. —**make a splash** [Colloq.] to attract great, often brief, attention —**splash'er** *n.* —**splash'i·ness** *n.* —**splash'y** *adj.*

**splash·down** (-doun') *n.* the landing of a spacecraft on water

**splat¹** (splat) *n.* [via dial. < base of SPLIT] a thin, flat piece of wood, esp. as used in the back of a chair

**splat²** (splat) *n., interj.* a splattering or wet, slapping sound

**splat·ter** (-ər) *n., vt., vi.* [< SPATTER] spatter or splash

**splay** (splā) *vt., vi.* [< ME. *displaien*, to display] **1.** to spread out or apart; extend (often with *out*) **2.** to slope —*n.* a sloping surface or angle **2.** a spreading; expansion —*adj.* **1.** sloping, spreading, or turning outward **2.** broad and flat **3.** awkward

**splay·foot** (-foot') *n., pl.* -**feet'** **1.** a foot that is flat and turned outward **2.** the condition of having such feet —*adj.* of or having splayfoot: also **splay'foot'ed**

**spleen** (splēn) *n.* [< OFr. < L. < Gr. *splen*, spleen] **1.** a large, vascular, lymphatic organ in the upper left part of the abdomen: it modifies the blood structure and was formerly regarded as the seat of certain emotions **2.** malice; spite; bad temper —**spleen'ful, spleen'ish, spleen'y** *adj.*

**splen·did** (splen'did) *adj.* [L. *splendidus* < *splendere*, to shine] **1.** having or showing splendor; specif., *a)* shining; brilliant *b)* magnificent; gorgeous **2.** worthy of high praise; grand; glorious; illustrious **3.** [Colloq.] very good; excellent —**splen'did·ly** *adv.* —**splen'did·ness** *n.*

**splen·dif·er·ous** (splen dif'ər əs) *adj.* [Colloq.] gorgeous; splendid: used jokingly —**splen·dif'er·ous·ly** *adv.* —**splen·dif'er·ous·ness** *n.*

**splen·dor** (splen'dər) *n.* [< OFr. < L. < *splendere*, to shine] **1.** great luster; brilliance **2.** magnificent richness or glory; pomp; grandeur Also, Brit. sp., **splen'dour** —**splen'dor·ous, splen'drous** *adj.*

**sple·net·ic** (spli net'ik) *adj.* [LL. *spleneticus*] **1.** of the spleen **2.** irritable; peevish; spiteful Also **sple·net'i·cal** —*n.* a spleenful person —**sple·net'i·cal·ly** *adv.*

**splen·ic** (splen'ik, splēn'-) *adj.* [< L. < Gr. *splēnikos*] **1.** of or having to do with the spleen **2.** in or near the spleen

**splice** (splīs) *vt.* **spliced, splic'ing** [MDu. *splissen*] **1.** to join (ropes or rope ends) by weaving together the end strands **2.** to join the ends of (timbers) by overlapping and binding or bolting together **3.** to fasten the ends of (wire, motion-picture film, etc.) together, as by cementing, twisting, etc. **4.** [Slang] to join in marriage —*n.* a joint or joining made by splicing —**splic'er** *n.*

**splint** (splint) *n.* [MDu. or MLowG. *splinte*] **1.** a thin strip of wood or cane woven together with others to make baskets, chair seats, etc. **2.** a thin, rigid strip of wood, metal, etc. used to keep a broken bone in place or to keep a part of the body in a fixed position —*vt.* to fit, support, or hold in place as with a splint or splints

**splin·ter** (splin'tər) *vt., vi.* [< MDu., akin to *splinte*, splint] **1.** to break or split into thin, sharp pieces **2.** to break into groups with opposing views —*n.* **1.** a

thin, sharp piece of wood, bone, etc., made by splitting or breaking **2.** a splinter group —*adj.* designating a group that separates from a main party, church, etc. because of opposing views —**splin'ter·y** *adj.*

**split** (split) *vt.* **split, split'ting** [MDu. *splitten*] **1.** to separate, cut, etc. along the grain or length into two or more parts **2.** to break or tear apart by force **3.** to divide into parts or shares **4.** to cast (one's vote) for candidates of more than one party **5.** to cause (a group, political party, etc.) to separate into factions **6.** *a)* to break (a molecule) into atoms or into smaller molecules *b)* to produce nuclear fission in (an atom) **7.** *Finance* to divide (stock) by substituting some multiple of the original shares —*vi.* **1.** to separate lengthwise into two or more parts **2.** to break apart; burst **3.** to separate because of failure to agree (often with *up*) **4.** [Slang] to leave a place; depart —*n.* **1.** the act or result of splitting; specif., *a)* a break; crack *b)* a division in a group, between persons, etc. **2.** a splinter **3.** a confection made of a split banana or other fruit with ice cream, sauces, nuts, etc. **4.** [often *pl.*] the feat of spreading the legs apart until they lie flat on the floor, the body remaining upright **5.** [Colloq.] a small bottle of wine, etc., usually about six ounces **6.** [Colloq.] a share, as of loot **7.** *Bowling* an arrangement of pins after the first bowl, so separated as to make a spare extremely difficult —*adj.* **1.** separated along the length or grain **2.** divided; separated —**split off** to break off or separate as by splitting —**split'ter** *n.*

**split infinitive** *Gram.* an infinitive with the verbal and the *to* separated by an adverb (Ex.: he decided *to gradually change* his style): despite objections to this construction, many writers use it to avoid ambiguity or wrong emphasis

**split-lev·el** (-lev'l) *adj.* designating or of a type of house with floor levels so staggered that each level is about a half story above or below the adjacent one

**split pea** a green or yellow pea that has been shelled, dried, and split: used esp. for making soup

**split personality** *a popular name for* SCHIZOPHRENIA

**split second** a fraction of a second —**split'-sec'ond** *adj.*

**split shift** a shift, or work period, separated into two parts by a period longer than the usual one for a meal or rest

**split ticket** a ballot cast for candidates of more than one party

**split·ting** (split'iŋ) *adj.* **1.** that splits **2.** *a)* aching severely: said of the head *b)* severe, as a headache

**split-up** (-up') *n.* a breaking up or separating into two or more parts, unions, groups, etc.

**splotch** (spläch) *n.* [prob. a fusion of SPOT & BLOTCH] a spot, splash, or stain, esp. one that is irregular —*vt., vi.* to mark or be marked with splotches —**splotch'y** *adj.*

**splurge** (splurj) *n.* [echoic] [Colloq.] **1.** any very showy display or effort **2.** a spell of extravagant spending —*vi.* **splurged, splurg'ing** [Colloq.] **1.** to make a splurge **2.** to spend money extravagantly —**splurg'er** *n.*

**splut·ter** (splut'ər) *vi.* [var. of SPUTTER] **1.** to make hissing or spitting sounds; sputter **2.** to speak hurriedly and confusedly, as when excited —*vt.* **1.** to utter hurriedly and confusedly **2.** to spatter —*n.* a spluttering sound or utterance —**splut'ter·er** *n.* —**splut'ter·y** *adj.*

**spoil** (spoil) *vt.* **spoiled** or **spoilt, spoil'ing** [< MFr. < L. *spoliare* < *spolium*, plunder] **1.** to damage or injure so as to make useless, valueless, etc.; destroy **2.** to impair the enjoyment, quality, etc. of [rain *spoiled* the picnic] **3.** to let (a person) have his own way so much that he demands or expects it —*vi.* to be damaged or injured so as to become useless, valueless, etc.; decay, as food —*n.* **1.** [*usually pl.*] *a)* goods, territory, etc. taken by plunder; booty *b)* public offices to which the political party that wins has the power to appoint people **2.** an object of plunder; prey —**be spoiling for a fight,** etc. to be aggressively eager for a fight, etc. —**spoil'a·ble** *adj.* —**spoil'er** *n.*

**spoil·age** (-ij) *n.* **1.** a spoiling or being spoiled **2.** something spoiled or the amount spoiled

**spoils·man** (spoilz'mən) *n., pl.* -**men** a person who aids a political party in order to share in the spoils

**spoil·sport** (spoil'spôrt') *n.* a person who behaves in such a way as to ruin the pleasure of others

**spoils system** the practice of treating public offices as the booty of the political party that wins an election, to be distributed among party workers

**Spo·kane** (spō kan') [< ? AmInd. *spokanee*, sun] city in E Wash.: pop. 171,000

**spoke¹** (spōk) *n.* [OE. *spaca*] **1.** any of the braces extending from the hub to the rim of a wheel **2.** a ladder rung **3.** any of the handholds along the rim of a ship's steering wheel —*vt.* **spoked, spok'ing** to equip with spokes

**spoke²** (spōk) *pt. & archaic pp. of* SPEAK

**spo·ken** (spō'k'n) *pp. of* SPEAK —*adj.* **1.** uttered; oral **2.** characterized by a (specified) kind of voice [soft-*spoken*]

**spoke·shave** (spōk'shāv') *n.* a planing tool consisting of a blade with a handle at either end, used for shaping rounded surfaces, as, formerly, spokes

SHORT
SPLICE

**spokes·man** (spōks'mən) *n., pl.* **-men** a person who speaks or gives information for another or for a group

**spo·li·a·tion** (spō'lē ā'shən) *n.* [L. *spoliatio*] 1. robbery; plundering 2. the act of spoiling or damaging —**spo'li·a'tive** *adj.*

**spon·dee** (spän'dē) *n.* [< L. < Gr. < *spondē*, solemn libation (one accompanied by a solemn melody)] a metrical foot consisting of two long or heavily accented syllables —**spon·da'ic** (-dā'ik) *adj.*

**sponge** (spunj) *n.* [OE. < L. < Gr. *spongia*] 1. a plantlike sea animal having a porous structure and a tough, fibrous skeleton and growing fixed to surfaces under water 2. the skeleton of such animals, light in weight and highly absorbent, used for washing surfaces, in bathing, etc. 3. any substance like this; specif., *a*) a piece of spongy plastic, cellulose, etc. *b*) a pad of gauze or cotton, as used in surgery *c*) a light, porous pudding *d*) a raised bread dough 4. [Colloq.] a person who lives upon others as a parasite —*vt.* **sponged, spong'ing** 1. to use a sponge on so as to dampen, wipe clean, etc. 2. to remove as with a damp sponge (with *out, off*, etc.) 3. to absorb with or like a sponge (often with *up*) 4. [Colloq.] to get as by begging, imposition, etc. —*vi.* 1. to gather sponges from the sea 2. to take up liquid like a sponge 3. [Colloq.] to be a parasite (often with *off* or *on*) —**throw** (or **toss**, etc.) **in the sponge** [Colloq.] to admit defeat; give up —**sponge'like'** *adj.* —**spong'er** *n.* —**spon'gi·ness** *n.* —**spon'gy** *adj.*

**sponge bath** a bath taken by using a wet sponge or cloth without getting into water or under a shower

**sponge·cake** (-kāk') *n.* a light cake of spongy texture made of flour, beaten eggs, sugar, etc., but no shortening: also **sponge cake**

**sponge rubber** rubber processed to have a spongelike texture denser than foam rubber: used for gaskets, etc.

**spon·son** (spän'sən) *n.* [altered < ? EXPANSION] 1. a structure that projects over the side of a ship or boat, as a gun platform 2. a winglike piece attached to the hull of a seaplane to give stability in the water

**spon·sor** (spän'sər) *n.* [L. < *spondere*, to promise solemnly] 1. a person or agency that acts as endorser, proponent, adviser, surety, etc. for a person, group, or activity 2. a godparent; person who answers for a child, as at baptism, making the promises prescribed 3. a business firm or other agency that alone or with others pays for a radio or TV program on which it advertises or promotes something —*vt.* to act as sponsor for —**spon·so'ri·al** (-sôr'ē əl) *adj.* —**spon'sor·ship'** *n.*

**spon·ta·ne·i·ty** (spän'tə nē'ə tē, -nā'-) *n.* 1. the state or quality of being spontaneous 2. *pl.* **-ties** spontaneous behavior, movement, action, etc.

**spon·ta·ne·ous** (spän tā'nē əs) *adj.* [< LL. < L. *sponte*, of free will] 1. moved by a natural feeling or impulse, without constraint, effort, or forethought 2. acting by internal energy, force, etc. 3. growing naturally; wild —**spon·ta'ne·ous·ly** *adv.* —**spon·ta'ne·ous·ness** *n.*

**spontaneous combustion** the process of catching fire as a result of heat generated by internal chemical action

**spontaneous generation** the theory, now discredited, that living organisms can originate from nonliving matter

**spoof** (spoof) *n.* [coined c. 1889] [Slang] 1. a hoax, joke, or deception 2. a light parody or satire —*vt., vi.* [Slang] 1. to fool; deceive 2. to satirize in a playful manner

**spook** (spook) *n.* [Du.] [Colloq.] 1. a specter; ghost 2. any person suggestive of a specter, as an eccentric, a secret agent, etc. —*vt., vi.* [Colloq.] to startle or be startled, frightened, etc. —**spook'i·ly** *adv.* —**spook'i·ness** *n.* —**spook'y** *adj.* **spook'i·er, spook'i·est**

**spool** (spool) *n.* [< MFr. < MDu. *spoele*] 1. a cylinder, often hollowed and with a rim at either end, upon which thread, wire, etc. is wound 2. something like a spool —*vt.* to wind on a spool

**spoon** (spoon) *n.* [OE. *spon*, a chip] 1. a utensil consisting of a small, shallow bowl with a handle, used for eating or stirring food or drinks 2. something shaped like a spoon, as a shiny, curved fishing lure, usually of metal —*vt.* to take up as with a spoon —*vi.* [Colloq.] to make love, as by kissing or caressing: an old-fashioned term

**spoon·bill** (-bil') *n.* 1. a wading bird with a broad, flat bill that is spoon-shaped at the tip 2. any of various other birds with a bill like this

**spoon·drift** (-drift') *n. early form of* SPINDRIFT

**spoon·er·ism** (spoon'ər iz'm) *n.* [after Rev. W. A. *Spooner* (1844-1930), of Oxford Univ.] an unintentional interchange of sounds in two or more words (Ex.: "a well-boiled icicle" for "a well-oiled bicycle")

**spoon-feed** (spoon'fēd') *vt.* **-fed', -feed'ing** 1. to feed with a spoon 2. to pamper; coddle 3. to treat, instruct, etc. so as to discourage independent thought and action

**spoon·ful** (-fool') *n., pl.* **-fuls'** as much as a spoon will hold

**spoor** (spoor, spôr) *n.* [Afrik. < MDu.] the track or trail of a wild animal hunted as game —*vt., vi.* to hunt by following a spoor

**Spo·ra·des** (spôr'ə dēz'; *Gr.* spô rä'thes) the Gr. islands along the W coast of Turkey, esp. the Dodecanese

**spo·rad·ic** (spô rad'ik, spə-) *adj.* [< ML. < Gr. *sporadikos* < *sporas*, scattered] 1. happening from time to time; not regular 2. appearing singly, apart, or in isolated instances —**spo·rad'i·cal·ly** *adv.*

**spo·ran·gi·um** (spô ran'jē əm, spə-) *n., pl.* **-gi·a** (-ə) [ModL. < *spora* (see ff.) + Gr. *angeion*, vessel] *Bot.* an organ or single cell producing spores —**spo·ran'gi·al** *adj.*

**spore** (spôr) *n.* [ModL. *spora* < Gr. *spora*, a seed] a small reproductive body, usually a single cell, produced by bacteria, mosses, ferns, certain protozoans, etc. and capable of giving rise to a new individual —*vi.* **spored, spor'ing** to develop spores

**spore case** *same as* SPORANGIUM

**spo·ro-** *a combining form meaning* spore [*sporophyte*]: also, before a vowel, **spor-**

**spo·ro·go·ni·um** (spôr'ə gō'nē əm) *n., pl.* **-ni·a** (-ə) [ModL.: see SPORO- & -GONIUM] the sporophyte in mosses and liverworts, usually a spore-bearing capsule on a stalk

**spor'o·phyll** (spôr'ə fil) *n.* [SPORO- + -PHYLL] a leaf or leaflike part producing one or more sporangia —**spo'ro·phyl'la·ry** (-fil'ə rē) *adj.*

**spo·ro·phyte** (-fīt') *n.* [SPORO- + -PHYTE] the asexual spore-bearing phase of some plants: cf. GAMETOPHYTE —**spo'ro·phyt'ic** (-fit'ik) *adj.*

**spor·ran** (spär'ən, spôr'-) *n.* [ScotGael. *sporan*] a leather pouch or purse, usually fur-covered, worn hanging from the belt in the dress costume of Scottish Highlanders

**sport** (spôrt) *n.* [short for DISPORT] 1. any recreational activity; diversion 2. such an activity requiring bodily exertion and carried on according to a set of rules, whether outdoors, as golf, or indoors, as bowling 3. fun or play 4. *a*) an object of ridicule; laughingstock *b*) a thing or person buffeted about, as though a plaything 5. [Colloq.] a gambler 6. [Colloq.] *a*) a person who is sportsmanlike [be a *sport!*] *b*) a person judged according to his ability to take defeat, teasing, etc. [a good (or poor) *sport*] 7. [Colloq.] a pleasure-loving, flashy person 8. a plant or animal showing some marked variation from the normal type —*vt.* [Colloq.] to wear or display [to *sport* a loud tie] —*vi.* 1. to play or frolic 2. *a*) to joke or jest *b*) to trifle or play (*with*) *c*) to ridicule someone or something —*adj.* 1. of or for sports 2. suitable for informal, casual wear [a *sport* coat] —**in** (or **for**) **sport** in joke or jest —**make sport of** to ridicule —**sport'er** *n.* —**sport'ful** *adj.* —**sport'ful·ly** *adv.*

**sport·ing** (-iŋ) *adj.* 1. of, interested in, or taking part in sports 2. sportsmanlike; fair 3. having to do with games, races, etc. involving gambling or betting 4. *Biol.* inclined to mutate —**sport'ing·ly** *adv.*

**sporting chance** [Colloq.] a fair or even chance

**spor·tive** (spôr'tiv) *adj.* 1. fond of or full of sport or merriment 2. done in fun or play, not in earnest —**spor'tive·ly** *adv.* —**spor'tive·ness** *n.*

**sports** (spôrts) *adj. same as* SPORT [*sports* clothes]

**sports** (or **sport**) **car** a low, small automobile, typically with seats for two and a high-compression engine

**sports·cast** (spôrts'kast') *n.* a radio or TV broadcast of sports news —**sports'cast'er** *n.*

**sports·man** (-mən) *n., pl.* **-men** 1. a man who is interested in or takes part in sports, esp. in hunting, fishing, etc. 2. a person who plays fair and can take defeat without complaint or victory without gloating —**sports'man·like'**, **sports'man·ly** *adj.* —**sports'man·ship'** *n.*

**sports·wear** (-wer') *n.* clothes worn while engaging in sports or for informal, casual wear

**sports·wom·an** (-woom'ən) *n., pl.* **-wom'en** (-wim'ən) a woman who is interested in or takes part in sports

**sports·writ·er** (-rīt'ər) *n.* a reporter who writes about sports or sports events

**sport·y** (spôr'tē) *adj.* **sport'i·er, sport'i·est** [Colloq.] 1. sportsmanlike 2. characteristic of a sport or sporting man 3. loud, flashy, or showy, as clothes —**sport'i·ly** *adv.* —**sport'i·ness** *n.*

**spor·ule** (spôr'yool) *n.* a small spore

**spot** (spät) *n.* [< or akin to MDu. *spotte*] 1. a small area differing from the surrounding area, as in color 2. a mark, stain, blot, speck, etc. 3. a flaw, as in character; fault 4. a locality; place [a good fishing *spot*] 5. *shortened form of* SPOTLIGHT 6. [Chiefly Brit. Colloq.] a small quantity; bit [a *spot* of tea] 7. [Colloq.] a position or job 8. [Colloq.] a position in a schedule —*vt.* **spot'ted, spot'ting** 1. to mark with spots 2. to stain; blemish 3. to place in or on a given spot or spots; locate **4.** to remove (spots or marks), as in dry cleaning **5.** *a)* to pick out; recognize *[to spot someone in a crowd] b)* to determine the location of (a target, the enemy, etc.) **6.** [Colloq.] to allow as a handicap *[I spotted him two points]* —*vi.* **1.** to become marked with spots **2.** to make a stain, as ink, etc. —*adj.* **1.** *a)* ready; on hand *[spot cash] b)* involving immediate payment of cash **2.** made at random or by sampling *[a spot survey]* **3.** *a)* broadcast from the place of occurrence *[spot news] b)* inserted between regular radio or TV programs *[a spot announcement]* —**hit the spot** [Colloq.] to satisfy a craving —**in a (bad) spot** [Slang] in trouble —**on the spot 1.** at the place mentioned **2.** at once **3.** [Slang] in trouble or in a demanding situation **4.** [Slang] in danger, esp. of being murdered —**spot′less** *adj.* —**spot′less·ly** *adv.* —**spot′less-ness** *n.*

**spot-check** (-chek′) *vt.* to check or examine at random or by sampling —*n.* an act or instance of such checking

**spot·light** (-līt′) *n.* **1.** a strong beam of light focused on a particular person, thing, etc., as on a stage **2.** a lamp used to project such a light, as on an automobile **3.** public notice —*vt.* to focus a spotlight on

**spot·ted** (-id) *adj.* **1.** marked with spots **2.** stained; blemished; sullied

**spotted fever** any of various diseases accompanied by fever and skin eruptions

**spot·ter** (spät′ər) *n.* a person who spots; specif., *a)* a person whose work is removing spots, etc. in dry cleaning *b)* a person hired to watch for dishonesty among employees, as in a store *c)* a person who watches for, and reports, enemy aircraft

**spot·ty** (-ē) *adj.* **-ti·er, -ti·est 1.** having, occurring in, or marked with spots **2.** not uniform or consistent, as in quality; uneven —**spot′ti·ly** *adv.* —**spot′ti·ness** *n.*

**spot welding** a process in which metal pieces are held together between two electrodes and welded by a powerful surge of current —**spot′-weld′** *vt., vi.* —**spot′-weld′er** *n.*

**spous·al** (spou′z'l) *n.* [< ESPOUSAL] *[often pl.]* [Now Rare] a marriage ceremony —*adj.* [Now Rare] of marriage

**spouse** (spous; *also, esp. for vt.,* spouz) *n.* [< OFr. < L. pp. of *spondere:* see SPONSOR] a partner in marriage —*vt.* **spoused, spous′ing** [Archaic] to marry

**spout** (spout) *n.* [ME. *spute* < *spouten,* to spout] **1.** a lip or projecting tube, as of a teapot, drinking fountain, etc., by which a liquid is poured or discharged **2.** a stream, jet, etc. as of liquid from a spout **3.** *same as: a)* DOWNSPOUT *b)* WATERSPOUT —*vt.* **1.** to shoot out (liquid, etc.) from a spout **2.** to utter in a loud, pompous manner —*vi.* **1.** to shoot out with force in a jet: said of liquid, etc. **2.** to discharge liquid, etc. as from a spout **3.** to spout words, esp. (usually **spout off**) in a hasty or rash way —**spout′er** *n.*

**sprain** (sprān) *vt.* [< ? OFr. *espreindre,* to strain < L. < *ex-,* out + *premere,* to press] to wrench or twist a ligament or muscle of (a joint, as the ankle) without dislocating the bones —*n.* **1.** an act of spraining **2.** an injury resulting from this

**sprang** (spraŋ) *alt. pt. of* SPRING

**sprat** (sprat) *n.* [OE. *sprott*] **1.** a small, sardinelike, European fish of the herring family **2.** any of several other small herrings

**sprawl** (sprôl) *vi.* [OE. *spreawlian*] **1.** *a)* to spread the limbs in a relaxed or awkward position *b)* to sit or lie in such a position **2.** to crawl awkwardly **3.** to spread out awkwardly or unevenly, as handwriting, a line of men, etc. —*vt.* to cause to sprawl —*n.* a sprawling movement or position —**sprawl′er** *n.* —**sprawl′y** *adj.*

**spray¹** (sprā) *n.* [< or akin to MDu. *spraeien,* to spray] **1.** a cloud or mist of fine liquid particles, as of water from breaking waves **2.** *a)* a jet of such particles, as from a spray gun *b)* a device for shooting out such a jet **3.** something likened to a spray *[a spray of gunfire]* —*vt., vi.* **1.** to direct a spray (upon) **2.** to shoot out in a spray —**spray′er** *n.*

**spray²** (sprā) *n.* [ME.] **1.** a small branch or sprig of a tree or plant, with leaves, berries, flowers, etc. **2.** a design or ornament like this

**spray can** a can in which gas under pressure is used to shoot out the contents as a spray

**spray gun** a device that shoots out a spray of liquid, as paint or insecticide, by air pressure

**spread** (spred) *vt.* **spread, spread′ing** [OE. *sprædan*] **1.** to open or stretch out so as to cover more space; unfold; unfurl **2.** to lay out in display **3.** to move apart (the fingers, arms, wings, etc.) **4.** *a)* to distribute over an area; scatter *b)* to distribute among a group **5.** *a)* to distribute in a thin layer; smear *b)* to cover by smearing (*with* something) **6.** to extend or prolong in time **7.** to cause to be widely or more widely known, felt, existent, etc. **8.** to cover or deck (*with* something) **9.** *a)* to set (a table) for a meal *b)* to set (food) on a table **10.** to push apart or farther apart —*vi.* **1.** to extend itself; be expanded **2.** to become distributed **3.** to be made widely or more widely known, felt, etc. **4.** to be

pushed apart or farther apart **5.** to admit of being smeared, as butter —*n.* **1.** the act of spreading; extension **2.** *a)* the extent to which something can be spread *b)* the interval between the highest and lowest figures of a set **3.** an expanse; extent **4.** *a)* two facing pages of a magazine, etc., treated as a single sheet *b)* printed matter set across a page or several columns of a newspaper, etc. **5.** a cloth cover for a table, bed, etc. **6.** any soft substance, as jam, used for spreading on bread **7.** [Colloq.] a meal, esp. one with a wide variety of food **8.** [Colloq.] a pretentious display **9.** [Western] a ranch —**spread oneself** [Colloq.] **1.** to exert oneself in order to make a good impression, etc. **2.** to show off —**spread oneself thin** to try to do too many things at once —**spread′er** *n.*

**spread-ea·gle** (spred′ē′g'l) *adj.* **1.** having the figure of an eagle with the wings and legs spread **2.** [Colloq.] boastful about the U.S. —*vt.* **-gled, -gling** to stretch out in the form of a spread eagle, as for a flogging

**spree** (sprē) *n.* [18th-c. slang for earlier *spray* < ?] **1.** a lively, noisy frolic **2.** a drinking bout **3.** a period of unrestrained activity *[a shopping spree]*

**sprig** (sprig) *n.* [ME. *sprigge*] **1.** *a)* a little twig or spray *b)* a design or ornament like this **2.** a young fellow; stripling —*vt.* **sprigged, sprig′ging** to decorate with a design of sprigs —**sprig′gy** *adj.* **-gi·er, -gi·est**

**spright·ly** (sprīt′lē) *adj.* **-li·er, -li·est** [< *spright,* var. of SPRITE + -LY¹] gay, lively, brisk, etc. —*adv.* in a sprightly manner —**spright′li·ness** *n.*

**spring** (spriŋ) *vi.* **sprang** or **sprung, sprung, spring′ing** [OE. *springan*] **1.** to move suddenly and rapidly; specif., *a)* to leap; bound *b)* to appear suddenly *c)* to be resilient; bounce **2.** to arise as from some source; specif., *a)* to grow or develop *b)* to come into existence *[towns sprang up]* **3.** to become bent, warped, split, etc. *[the door has sprung]* **4.** to rise up above surrounding objects; tower Often followed by *up* —*vt.* **1.** to cause to leap forth suddenly **2.** to cause to snap shut, as by a spring **3.** *a)* to cause to warp, bend, split, etc., as by force *b)* to stretch (a spring, etc.) too far **4.** to make known suddenly *[to spring a surprise]* **5.** [Slang] to get (someone) released from jail, as by paying bail —*n.* **1.** a springing; specif., *a)* a jump or leap, or the distance so covered *b)* a sudden darting or flying back **2.** *a)* elasticity; resilience *b)* energy or vigor, as in one's walk **3.** a device, as a coil of wire, that returns to its original form after being forced out of shape: used to absorb shock, etc. **4.** *a)* a flow of water from the ground, the source of a stream *b)* any source or origin **5.** *a)* that season of the year when plants begin to grow after lying dormant all winter *b)* any period of beginning **6.** *Naut.* a split or break, as in a mast —*adj.* **1.** of, for, appearing in, or planted in the spring **2.** of or like a spring; elastic; resilient **3.** having, or supported on, springs *[spring mattress]* **4.** coming from a spring *[spring water]* —**spring a leak** to begin to leak suddenly

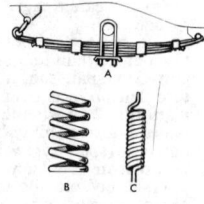

SPRINGS
(A, leaf; B, helical;
C, expansion)

**spring·board** (spriŋ′bôrd′) *n.* **1.** a flexible, springy board used by acrobats as a takeoff in leaping **2.** *same as* DIVING BOARD **3.** a starting point

**spring·bok** (-bäk′) *n., pl.* **-bok′, -boks′:** see PLURAL, II, D, 2 [Afrik. < Du. *springen,* to spring + *bok,* a buck] a South African gazelle that leaps high in the air when startled: also **spring′buck′** (-buk′)

**spring chicken 1.** a young chicken, esp. one only a few months old, used for broiling or frying **2.** [Slang] a young or inexperienced person

**spring·er** (-ər) *n.* **1.** a person or thing that springs **2.** *short for* SPRINGER SPANIEL **3.** *same as* SPRING CHICKEN

**springer spaniel** a breed of field spaniel used for flushing, or springing, game

**spring fever** the laziness and listlessness that many people feel during the first warm days of spring

**Spring·field** (spriŋ′fēld′) [sense 1 after *Springfield,* village in SE England; others prob. after sense 1] **1.** city in SW Mass.: pop. 152,000 **2.** city in SW Mo.: pop. 133,000 **3.** capital of Ill., in the C part: pop. 100,000 **4.** city in WC Ohio: pop. 73,000

**spring lock** a lock in which the bolt is snapped into place automatically by a spring

**spring tide 1.** a tide occurring at the new and the full moon, normally the highest tide of the month **2.** any great flow, rush, or flood

**spring·time** (spriŋ′tīm′) *n.* the season of spring: also **spring′tide′** (-tīd′)

**spring·y** (-ē) *adj.* **spring′i·er, spring′i·est 1.** flexible; elastic **2.** having many springs of water —**spring′i·ly** *adv.* —**spring′i·ness** *n.*

**sprin·kle** (sprin'k'l) *vt.* **-kled, -kling** [ME. *sprenklen*] **1.** to scatter (water, salt, etc.) in drops or particles **2.** *a)* to scatter drops or particles upon *b)* to dampen before ironing **3.** to distribute at random —*vi.* **1.** to scatter something in drops or particles **2.** to fall in drops or particles **3.** to rain lightly —*n.* **1.** the act of sprinkling, or a small amount sprinkled **2.** a light rain —**sprin'kler** *n.*

**sprin·kling** (-klin) *n.* **1.** a small number or amount, esp. when thinly distributed **2.** the act of one that sprinkles

**sprint** (sprint) *vi.* [< Scand.] to run or race at full speed, esp. for a short distance —*n.* **1.** the act of sprinting **2.** a short race at full speed **3.** a brief period of intense activity —**sprint'er** *n.*

**sprit** (sprit) *n.* [OE. *spreot*] a pole or spar extended diagonally upward from a mast to the topmost corner of a fore-and-aft sail

**sprite** (sprit) *n.* [< OFr. *esprit* < L. *spiritus:* see SPIRIT] **1.** an elf, pixie, fairy, or goblin **2.** an elflike person

**sprit·sail** (sprit'sāl', -s'l) *n.* a sail extended by a sprit

**spritz** (sprits; *G.* shprits) *vt., vi., n.* [ult. < MHG. *sprütze* < *sprützen,* to spray] squirt or spray

**sprock·et** (spräk'it) *n.* [< ?] **1.** any of the teeth or points, as on the rim of a wheel, arranged to fit into the links of a chain **2.** a wheel fitted with sprockets: in full, **sprocket wheel**

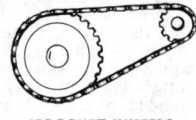

SPROCKET WHEELS

**sprout** (sprout) *vi.* [OE. *sprutan*] **1.** to begin to grow or germinate; give off shoots or buds **2.** to grow or develop rapidly —*vt.* to cause to sprout or grow —*n.* **1.** a young growth on a plant, as a stem or branch; shoot **2.** a new growth from a bud, rootstock, etc. **3.** any offshoot or scion **4.** [*pl.*] *shortened form of* BRUSSELS SPROUTS

**spruce**[1] (sproos) *n.* [< OFr. < ML. *Prussia:* prob. because first known as from Prussia] **1.** any of various evergreen trees of the pine family, having slender needles **2.** its wood

**spruce**[2] (sproos) *adj.* **spruc'er, spruc'est** [ME. *Spruce,* Prussia, esp. in phr. *Spruce leather,* fine leather imported from Prussia] neat and trim; smart; dapper —*vt., vi.* **spruced, spruc'ing** to make or become spruce (usually with *up*) —**spruce'ly** *adv.* —**spruce'ness** *n.*

**sprung** (sprun) *pp. & alt. pt.* of SPRING —*adj.* having the springs broken, overstretched, or loose

**spry** (spri) *adj.* **spri'er** or **spry'er, spri'est** or **spry'est** [< Scand.] full of life; active, brisk, and agile, esp. though elderly —**spry'ly** *adv.* —**spry'ness** *n.*

**spt.** seaport

**spud** (spud) *n.* [prob. < Scand.] **1.** a sharp spade for rooting out weeds, etc. **2.** [Colloq.] a potato —*vt., vi.* **spud'ded, spud'ding** to dig, etc. with a spud —**spud'der** *n.*

**spue** (spyoo) *vt., vi.* spued, spu'ing *same as* SPEW

**spume** (spyoom) *n.* [< MFr. < L. *spuma*] foam, froth, or scum —*vt., vi.* **spumed, spum'ing** to foam or froth —**spu'mous, spum'y** *adj.*

**spu·mo·ni** (spə mō'nē) *n.* [It.] an Italian frozen dessert of ice cream in layers of several flavors and colors, often containing bits of fruit and nuts: also sp. **spumone**

**spun** (spun) *pt. & pp.* of SPIN —*adj.* formed by or as if by spinning

**spunk** (spunk) *n.* [IrGael. *sponc,* tinder < L. *spongia,* sponge] **1.** wood or fungus that smolders when ignited; punk **2.** [Colloq.] courage; spirit

**spunk·y** (spun'kē) *adj.* **spunk'i·er, spunk'i·est** [Colloq.] having spunk; courageous; spirited —**spunk'i·ly** *adv.* —**spunk'i·ness** *n.*

**spur** (spur) *n.* [OE. *spura*] **1.** a pointed device worn on the heel by horsemen and used to urge the horse forward **2.** anything that urges or incites; stimulus to action **3.** something like a spur; specif., *a)* a spinelike process, as on the wings or legs of certain birds *b)* a spinelike outgrowth of bone, as on the human heel, resulting from injury, disease, etc. *c)* a sharp metal device attached as a weapon to the leg of a gamecock *d)* a short branch or shoot of a tree, etc. **4.** a ridge projecting from the main mass of a mountain or mountain range **5.** a short side track (**spur track**) connected with the main track of a railroad **6.** *Bot.* a slender, tubelike structure formed by an extension of one or more petals or sepals, often holding nectar —*vt.* **spurred, spur'ring 1.** to prick with spurs **2.** to urge on; incite; stimulate **3.** to provide with a spur or spurs —*vi.* **1.** to spur one's horse; to hurry; hasten —**on the spur of the moment** abruptly and impulsively —**win one's spurs** to gain distinction or honor —**spur'like'** *adj.* —**spur'rer** *n.*

**spurge** (spurj) *n.* [< MFr. < *espurger,* to purge < L. *expurgare:* see EXPURGATE] any of a genus of plants having a milky juice and tiny flowers often protected by showy, scalelike leaves —*adj.* designating a family of plants, usually with milky juice and diclinous flowers, including the poinsettia, cassava, rubber tree, etc.

**spur gear 1.** a gearwheel with radial teeth parallel to the axle: also **spur wheel 2.** gearing having this kind of gearwheel: also **spur gearing**

**spu·ri·ous** (spyoor'ē əs) *adj.* [L. *spurius*] **1.** [Now Rare] illegitimate **2.** not true or genuine; false; counterfeit —**spu'ri·ous·ly** *adv.* —**spu'ri·ous·ness** *n.*

**spurn** (spurn) *vt.* [OE. *spurnan*] **1.** to push or drive away as with the foot **2.** to reject in a scornful way —*n.* **1.** a kick **2.** scornful treatment or rejection —**spurn'er** *n.*

**spurred** (spurd) *adj.* having, wearing, or fitted with spurs or spurlike parts

**spurt** (spurt) *vt.* [OE. *spryttan* < base of *sprutan,* to sprout] to expel suddenly in a stream or gushing flow; squirt; jet —*vi.* **1.** to gush forth in a stream or jet **2.** to show a sudden, brief burst of energy or increased activity —*n.* **1.** a sudden gushing or shooting forth; jet **2.** a sudden, brief burst of energy, etc.

**sput·nik** (spoot'nik, sput'-) *n.* [Russ., lit., co-traveler] an artificial satellite of the earth; specif., [S-] any of those put into orbit by the U.S.S.R. beginning in 1957

**sput·ter** (sput'ər) *vi.* [Du. *sputteren*] **1.** to spit out bits of saliva, food, etc., as when talking excitedly; splutter **2.** to talk in an excited, confused way, spitting out one's words **3.** to make sharp, sizzling or spitting sounds, as frying fat —*vt.* **1.** to spit out (bits or drops) in an explosive manner **2.** to utter by sputtering —*n.* **1.** the act or noise of sputtering **2.** matter thrown out in sputtering **3.** hasty, confused utterance —**sput'ter·ing·ly** *adv.*

**spu·tum** (spyoot'əm) *n., pl.* **spu'ta** (-ə) [< L. < pp. of *spuere,* to SPIT[2]] saliva, usually mixed with mucus, spit out from the mouth

**spy** (spi) *vt.* **spied, spy'ing** [< OFr. < OHG. *spehōn* to examine] to catch sight of; see —*vi.* **1.** to watch closely and secretly; act as a spy **2.** to look carefully —*n., pl.* **spies 1.** a person who keeps close and secret watch on another or others **2.** a person employed by a government to get secret information about the affairs, esp. military affairs, of another government, as of an enemy in wartime —**spy out** to discover or seek to discover by looking carefully

**spy·glass** (-glas') *n.* a small telescope

**sq.** **1.** squadron **2.** square

**sq. ft., sq. in.,** etc. square foot, square inch, etc.

**squab** (skwäb, skwôb) *n.* [prob. < Scand.] **1.** a very young pigeon **2.** a short, stout person **3.** [Brit.] a stuffed cushion or couch —*adj.* short and stout: also **squab'by**

**squab·ble** (skwäb''l, swôb'-) *vi.* **-bled, -bling** [< Scand.] to quarrel noisily over a small matter; wrangle —*n.* a noisy, petty quarrel; wrangle —**squab'bler** *n.*

**squad** (skwäd, skwôd) *n.* [< Fr. < Sp. *escuadra,* or It. *squadra,* a square, both ult. < L.: see SQUARE] **1.** *a)* a small group of soldiers assembled for drill, duty, etc. *b)* the smallest military tactical unit, often part of a platoon **2.** *a)* any small group of people working together [a police squad] *b)* an athletic team —*vt.* **squad'ded, squad'ding 1.** to form into a squad **2.** to assign to a squad

**squad car** a police patrol car, usually communicating with headquarters by radiotelephone

**squad·ron** (-rən) *n.* [< It. < *squadra:* see SQUAD] **1.** a group of warships assigned to special duty **2.** a unit of cavalry consisting of from two to four troops, etc. **3.** *a)* U.S. Air Force a unit consisting of two or more flights *b)* a formation of six or more aircraft **4.** any organized group

**squal·id** (skwäl'id, skwôl'-) *adj.* [< L. < *squalere,* to be foul] **1.** foul; filthy **2.** wretched; sordid —**squa·lid'i·ty, squal'id·ness** *n.* —**squal'id·ly** *adv.*

**squall**[1] (skwôl) *n.* [< Scand.] **1.** a brief, violent windstorm, usually with rain or snow **2.** [Colloq.] trouble or disturbance —*vi.* to storm briefly —**squall'y** *adj.*

**squall**[2] (skwôl) *vi., vt.* [ON. *skvala,* to cry out] to cry or scream loudly or harshly —*n.* a harsh, shrill cry or loud scream —**squall'er** *n.*

**squal·or** (skwäl'ər, skwôl'-) *n.* [L., foulness] a being squalid; filth and wretchedness

**squa·ma** (skwā'mə) *n., pl.* **-mae** (-mē) [L., a scale] a scale or scalelike part of an animal or plant —**squa'mate** (-māt), **squa'mous** (-məs), **squa'mose** (-mōs) *adj.*

**squan·der** (skwän'dər, skwôn'-) *vt., vi.* [prob. < dial. *squander,* scatter] to spend or use (money, time, etc.) wastefully

**square** (skwer) *n.* [< OFr., ult. < L. *ex-,* out + *quadrare,* to square < *quadrus,* a square < *quattuor,* four] **1.** a plane figure having four equal sides and four right angles **2.** anything shaped like or nearly like this **3.** an area bounded by streets on four sides; also, the distance along one side of such an area; block **4.** an open area bounded by several streets, used as a park, plaza, etc. **5.** an instrument having two sides that form a 90° angle, used for drawing or testing right angles **6.** a solid piece with at least one face that is square [a cake cut into *squares*] **7.** the product of a number multiplied by itself [9 is the *square* of 3] **8.** [Slang] a person who is square (adj. 11) —*vt.* **squared, squar′ing 1.** *a*) to make into a square *b*) to make into any rectangle **2.** to test or adjust with regard to straightness or evenness **3.** to bring to or near to the form of a right angle [*square* your shoulders] **4.** *a*) to settle; adjust [to *square* accounts] *b*) to settle the accounts of **5.** to make equal [to *square* the score of a game] **6.** to bring into agreement [to *square* a statement with the facts] **7.** to mark off (a surface) in squares **8.** to bring into the correct position, as with reference to a line, course, etc. **9.** to multiply (a quantity) by itself **10.** to determine the square that is equal in area to (a figure) —*vi.* to fit; agree; accord (*with*) —*adj.* **1.** *a*) having four equal sides and four right angles *b*) more or less cubical, as a box **2.** forming a right angle, or having a rectangular part or cross section **3.** correctly adjusted; straight, level, even, etc. **4.** *a*) leaving no balance; balanced *b*) even in score; tied **5.** just; fair; honest **6.** clear; direct; straightforward [a *square* refusal] **7.** *a*) designating or of a unit of surface measure in the form of a square with sides of a specified length *b*) given or stated in terms of such measure **8.** having a shape broad for its length or height, with a solid, sturdy appearance [a *square* build] **9.** designating a number that is the product of another number multiplied by itself **10.** [Colloq.] satisfying; substantial [a *square* meal] **11.** [Slang] old-fashioned or unsophisticated —*adv.* **1.** honestly; fairly **2.** so as to be or form a square; at right angles **3.** directly; exactly **4.** so as to face **5.** firmly; solidly —**on the square 1.** at right angles **2.** [Colloq.] honest(ly), fair(ly), genuine(ly), etc. — **square away 1.** to bring a ship's yards around so as to sail before the wind **2.** *same as* SQUARE OFF —**square off** to get into position for attacking or for defending —**square oneself** [Colloq.] to make up for a wrong one has done —**square the circle 1.** to find a square equal in area to a circle: an insoluble problem **2.** to do or attempt something that seems impossible —**square up** to make a settlement, as by payment —**square′ly** *adv.* —**square′ness** *n.* —**squar′er** *n.* —**squar′ish** *adj.*

**square dance** a lively dance with various steps and figures, the couples forming squares, etc. —**square′-dance′** *vi.* **-danced′, -danc′ing**

**square deal** [Colloq.] any dealing that is honest and fair

**square knot** a double knot in which the free ends run parallel to the standing parts

**square measure** a system of measuring area, esp. the system in which 144 square inches = 1 square foot or that in which 10,000 square centimeters = 1 square meter: see TABLES OF WEIGHTS AND MEASURES in Supplements

**square-rigged** (-rigd′) *adj.* having square sails as principal sails —**square′-rig′ger** *n.*

**square root** the number that is multiplied by itself to produce a given number [3 is the *square root* of 9]

**square sail** a four-sided sail

**square shooter** [Colloq.] an honest, just person

**square-shoul·dered** (-shōl′dərd) *adj.* having shoulders jutting out squarely from the body's axis

**squash¹** (skwäsh, skwôsh) *vt.* [< OFr. *esquasser*, ult. < L. *ex-*, intens. + pp. of *quatere*, to shake] **1.** *a*) to crush into a soft or flat mass *b*) to press tightly or too tightly **2.** to suppress; quash **3.** [Colloq.] to silence (another) crushingly —*vi.* **1.** to be squashed by pressure, etc. **2.** to make a sound of squashing **3.** to force one's way; squeeze —*n.* **1.** something squashed; crushed mass **2.** the act or sound of squashing **3.** either of two games (**squash rackets, squash tennis**) played in a four-walled court with rackets and a rubber ball **4.** [Brit.] fruit juice or fruit-flavored syrup mixed with soda water —*adv.* with a squash

**squash²** (skwäsh, skwôsh) *n.* [< Algonquian] **1.** the fleshy fruit of various plants of the gourd family, cooked as a vegetable **2.** a plant, usually a vine, bearing this fruit

**squash·y** (-ē) *adj.* **-i·er, -i·est 1.** soft and wet; mushy **2.** easily squashed, as overripe fruit — **squash′i·ly** *adv.* —**squash′i·ness** *n.*

**squat** (skwät, skwôt) *vi.* **squat′ted, squat′ting** [< MFr. *esquatir*, ult. < L. *ex-*, intens. + *coactus*, pp. of *cogere*, to force] **1.** to crouch, with the knees bent and the weight on the balls of the feet **2.** to crouch close to the ground, as an animal **3.** to settle on land without any right or title to it **4.** to settle on public land under government regulation so as to get title to it —*adj.* **1.** crouched in a

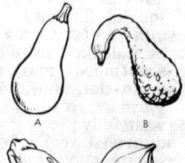

SQUASH
(A, butternut; B, crookneck; C, white bush; D, acorn)

squatting position **2.** short and thick: also **squat′ty** —*n.* the act or position of squatting —**squat′ly** *adv.* —**squat′ness** *n.* —**squat′ter** *n.*

**squaw** (skwô) *n.* [< Algonquian] a N. American Indian woman, esp. a wife: now sometimes felt to be a contemptuous term

**squawk** (skwôk) *vi.* [echoic] **1.** to utter a loud, harsh cry, as a parrot **2.** [Colloq.] to complain or protest —*vt.* to utter in a squawk —*n.* **1.** a squawking cry **2.** [Colloq.] a complaint —**squawk′er** *n.*

**squawk box** [Slang] an intercom speaker

**squaw man** a white man married to a N. American Indian woman, esp. one living with her tribe

**squeak** (skwēk) *vi.* [prob. akin to ON. *skvakka*, to gurgle] to make or utter a short, sharp, high-pitched sound or cry —*vt.* to utter with a squeak —*n.* a short, shrill sound or cry —**narrow** (or **close**) **squeak** [Colloq.] a narrow escape —**squeak through** (or **by,** etc.) [Colloq.] to barely manage to succeed, survive, etc. —**squeak′i·ly** *adv.* —**squeak′y** *adj.* **-i·er, -i·est**

**squeak·er** (-ər) *n.* **1.** one that squeaks **2.** [Colloq.] a narrow escape, victory, etc.

**squeal** (skwēl) *vi.* [prob. akin to ON. *skvala:* see SQUALL²] **1.** to make or utter a long, shrill sound or cry **2.** [Slang] to inform against, or tell on, someone —*vt.* to utter with a squeal —*n.* a long, shrill sound or cry —**squeal′er** *n.*

**squeam·ish** (skwēm′ish) *adj.* [< Anglo-Fr. *escoimous,* orig., shy] **1.** easily nauseated **2.** easily shocked or offended; prudish **3.** too fastidious —**squeam′ish·ly** *adv.* —**squeam′ish·ness** *n.*

**squee·gee** (skwē′jē) *n.* [prob. akin to SQUEEZE] a T-shaped tool with a blade of rubber, etc., for wiping liquid off a surface —*vt.* **-geed, -gee·ing** to use a squeegee on

**squeeze** (skwēz) *vt.* **squeezed, squeez′ing** [OE. *cwysan,* to squeeze] **1.** to press hard or closely, esp. from two or more sides **2.** *a*) to press so as to extract liquid, etc. [to *squeeze* oranges] *b*) to extract (liquid, etc.) by pressure **3.** to force (*into, out,* etc.) as by pressing **4.** to get or extort by force or unfair means **5.** to oppress with taxes, etc. **6.** to put pressure on (someone) to do something, as to pay money **7.** to embrace closely; hug **8.** *Baseball* to score (a run or runner) by a squeeze play —*vi.* **1.** to yield to pressure [a wet sponge *squeezes* easily] **2.** to exert pressure **3.** to force one's way by pushing or pressing (*in, out, through,* etc.) —*n.* **1.** a squeezing or being squeezed **2.** *a*) a close embrace; hug *b*) a firm handclasp **3.** the state of being closely pressed or packed; crush **4.** a difficult situation; pinch **5.** a quantity extracted by squeezing **6.** [Colloq.] pressure exerted, as in extortion: esp. in **put the squeeze on 7.** *short for* SQUEEZE PLAY —**squeeze through** (or **by,** etc.) [Colloq.] to barely manage to succeed, survive, etc. —**squeez′er** *n.*

**squeeze play 1.** *Baseball* a play in which a bunter scores a runner from third base moving at the first pitching motion **2.** pressure or coercion exerted to achieve some goal

**squelch** (skwelch) *n.* [prob. echoic] **1.** the sound of liquid, mud, etc. moving under pressure or suction, as in wet shoes **2.** [Colloq.] a suppressing or silencing; esp., a crushing retort, rebuke, etc. —*vt.* **1.** to crush as by stamping upon; squash **2.** [Colloq.] to suppress or silence completely and crushingly —*vi.* **1.** to walk heavily through mud, etc., making a splashing sound **2.** to make such a sound —**squelch′er** *n.*

**squib** (skwib) *n.* [prob. echoic] **1.** a firecracker that hisses before exploding **2.** a short, witty writing that criticizes, etc. —*vt., vi.* **squibbed, squib′bing 1.** to shoot off (a squib) **2.** to put out a squib (against); criticize

**squid** (skwid) *n., pl.* **squids, squid:** see PLURAL, II, D, 1 [prob. akin to SQUIRT] any of various cephalopod mollusks having a slender body and ten arms, two arms being much longer than the others

**squig·gle** (skwig′'l) *n.* [SQU(IRM) + (W)IGGLE] **1.** a short curved or wavy line; curlicue **2.** an illegible or meaningless scribble —*vt.* **-gled, -gling** to form into or write as a squiggle or squiggles —*vi.* **1.** to make squiggles **2.** to squirm along; wriggle —**squig′gly** *adj.*

**squil·gee** (skwē′jē; skwil′jē *is a sp. pron.*) *n., vt.* **-geed, -gee·ing** *sailors′ var. of* SQUEEGEE

**squill** (skwil) *n.* [< L. < Gr. *skilla*] **1.** *a*) the dried bulb of a plant of the lily family, formerly used in medicine *b*) this plant **2.** a strain of this plant having red bulbs that yield a powder used chiefly in rat poison

**squinch** (skwinch) *vt.* [SQU(INT) + (P)INCH] **1.** *a*) to squint (the eyes) *b*) to pucker or screw up (the face, nose, etc.) **2.** to squeeze or compress —*vi.* **1.** to squint or pucker

SQUID
(small species to 8 in. long)

**2.** to crouch down or draw oneself together **3.** to flinch
**squint** (skwint) *vi.* [see ASQUINT] **1.** to peer with the eyes partly closed, as in too strong light **2.** to look sidelong or askance **3.** to be cross-eyed **4.** to incline (*toward* a given direction, belief, etc.) —*vt.* to keep (the eyes) partly closed in peering —*n.* **1.** a squinting **2.** an inclination **3.** a being cross-eyed **4.** [Colloq.] a glance, often sidelong —*adj.* **1.** looking sidelong or askance **2.** cross-eyed — **squint′er** *n.* —**squint′y** *adj.*

**squire** (skwīr) *n.* [< OFr. *esquier:* see ESQUIRE] **1.** a young man of high birth who attended a knight **2.** in England, a country gentleman who owns much land **3.** a title of respect for a justice of the peace, etc., as in a rural district **4.** an attendant; esp., a man escorting a woman —*vt.*, *vi.* to act as a squire (to)

**squirm** (skwurm) *vi.* [prob. echoic, infl. by WORM] **1.** to twist and turn the body in a snakelike movement; wriggle; writhe **2.** to show or feel distress, as from embarrassment —*n.* a squirming —**squirm′y** *adj.* **-i·er**, **-i·est**

**squir·rel** (skwur′əl; *chiefly Brit.* skwir′-) *n.*, *pl.* **-rels**, **-rel**: see PLURAL, II, D, 1 [< OFr., ult. < L. *sciurus* < Gr. < *skia*, a shadow + *oura*, tail] **1.** *a)* any of a group of small, tree-dwelling rodents with heavy fur and a long, bushy tail *b)* any of various burrowing rodents, as chipmunks, related to these **2.** the fur or some of these animals —*vt.* **-reled** or **-relled**, **-rel·ing** or **-rel·ling** to store or hide (*away*)

**squirt** (skwurt) *vt.* [prob. < or akin to LowG. & Du. *swirtjen*, to squirt] **1.** to shoot out (a liquid) in a jet or narrow stream **2.** to wet with liquid thus shot out —*vi.* to be squirted out; spurt —*n.* **1.** a device for squirting, as a syringe **2.** a squirting **3.** a small amount of squirted liquid; jet **4.** [Colloq.] a small or young person, esp. one who is impudent —**squirt′er** *n.*

**squirt gun** a toy gun that shoots a stream of water

**squish** (skwish) *vi.* to make a soft, splashing sound when walked on, squeezed, etc. —*vt.* [Colloq.] to squeeze into a soft mass; squash —*n.* **1.** a squishing sound **2.** [Colloq.] a squashing; squash —**squish′y** *adj.*

**squoosh** (skwoosh) *vt.* [< SQUASH[1]] [Colloq.] **1.** to squeeze or crush into a soft, liquid mass **2.** *same as* SLOSH

**Sr** *Chem.* strontium

**Sr.** **1.** Senior **2.** [Sp.] *Señor* **3.** Sister

**Sra.** [Sp.] *Señora*

**Sri Lan·ka** (srē laŋ′kə) *official name of* CEYLON

**S.R.O.** standing room only

**Srta.** [Sp.] *Señorita*

**SS.** [L. *Sancti*] Saints

**ss., ss** *Baseball* shortstop

**S.S., SS, S/S** steamship

**S.S.A.** Social Security Administration

**SSE, S.S.E., s.s.e.** south-southeast

**SSgt** Staff Sergeant

**S.S.R., SSR** Soviet Socialist Republic

**SSS** Selective Service System

**SSW, S.S.W., s.s.w.** south-southwest

**-st** *same as* -EST

**St.** **1.** Saint: terms beginning with *St.* are entered in this dictionary as if spelled *St-* **2.** Strait **3.** Street

**St., st.** **1.** statute(s) **2.** stratus

**Sta.** Station

**stab** (stab) *n.* [ME. *stabbe*, prob. < var. of *stubbe*, stub] **1.** a wound made by piercing with a knife, dagger, etc. **2.** a thrust, as with a knife **3.** a sudden, sharp hurt or pain —*vt.* **stabbed**, **stab′bing** **1.** to pierce or wound as with a knife **2.** to thrust (a knife, etc.) into something **3.** to go into in a sharp, thrusting way —*vi.* **1.** to make a thrust or piercing wound as with a knife **2.** to feel like a stabbing knife: said of pain —**make** (or **take**) **a stab at** to make an attempt at —**stab in the back** to harm by treachery

**sta·bile** (stā′b'l, -bil; *also, and for n. usually,* -bēl) *adj.* [L. *stabilis:* see STABLE[1]] stable; stationary —*n.* a large stationary abstract sculpture, usually of metal, wire, wood, etc.

**sta·bil·i·ty** (stə bil′ə tē) *n.*, *pl.* **-ties** **1.** a being stable, or fixed; steadiness **2.** firmness of character, purpose, etc. **3.** resistance to change **4.** the capacity of an object to return to equilibrium

**sta·bi·lize** (stā′bə līz′) *vt.* **-lized′**, **-liz′ing** **1.** to make stable, or firm **2.** to keep from changing, as in price **3.** to give stability to (an airplane, ship, etc.) with a stabilizer —*vi.* to become stabilized —**sta′bi·li·za′tion** *n.*

**sta·bi·liz·er** (-lī′zər) *n.* a person or thing that stabilizes; specif., *a)* an airfoil to keep an airplane steady in flight, specif. the horizontal part of the tail *b)* a gyrostabilizer or other device to steady a ship in rough waters *c)* any additive used in a substance to keep it stable, retard deterioration, etc.

**sta·ble[1]** (stā′b'l) *adj.* **-bler**, **-blest** [< OFr. < L. *stabilis* < *stare*, to stand] **1.** *a)* not easily moved or put off balance;

firm; steady *b)* not likely to break down, fall apart, etc. **2.** firm in character, purpose, etc.; steadfast **3.** not likely to change or be affected adversely; enduring **4.** capable of returning to equilibrium **5.** *Chem.*, *Physics* not readily decomposing —**sta′bly** *adv.*

**sta·ble[2]** (stā′b'l) *n.* [< OFr. < L. *stabulum* < *stare*, to stand] **1.** *a)* a building in which horses or cattle are sheltered and fed *b)* a group of animals kept in such a building **2.** *a)* all the racehorses of one owner *b)* the people who take care of and train these horses **3.** [Colloq.] all the athletes, performers, etc. under one management —*vt.*, *vi.* **-bled**, **-bling** to keep or be kept in a stable

**sta·ble·boy** (-boi′) *n.* a boy who works in a stable

**stac·ca·to** (stə kät′ō) *adj.* [It., detached] **1.** *Music* with distinct breaks between successive tones **2.** made up of abrupt, distinct elements or sounds —*adv.* so as to be staccato —*n.*, *pl.* **-tos** something staccato

**stack** (stak) *n.* [ON. *stakkr*] **1.** a large pile of straw, hay, etc., esp. one neatly arranged, as in the form of a cone **2.** any somewhat orderly pile **3.** a number of arms, esp. three rifles, leaned together on end to form a cone **4.** *a)* a grouping of chimney flues *b)* *same as* SMOKESTACK **5.** [*pl.*] the main area and shelves for shelving books in a library **6.** [Colloq.] a large amount —*vt.* **1.** to pile in a stack **2.** to load with stacks **3.** to assign (aircraft) to various altitudes for circling before landing **4.** to arrange in advance underhandedly for a desired result [to *stack* a jury] —**stack up 1.** to come to as a total **2.** to stand in comparison (*with* or *against*) —**stack′a·ble** *adj.* —**stack′er** *n.*

**stacked** (stakt) *adj.* [Slang] having a full, shapely figure; curvaceous: said of a woman

**stacked** (or **stack**) **heel** a heel on a woman's shoe of several layers alternating in shade

**stack·up** (stak′up′) *n.* an arrangement of circling aircraft at various altitudes awaiting their turn to land

**sta·di·um** (stā′dē əm) *n.*, *pl.* **-di·a** (-ə); *also, and for sense 2 usually,* **-di·ums** [L. < Gr. *stadion*, fixed standard of length] **1.** in ancient Greece and Rome, a track for footraces, about 607 feet long, with tiers of seats for spectators **2.** a large, open structure for football, baseball, etc. with tiers of seats for spectators

**staff** (staf) *n.*, *pl.* **staffs**; *also, for senses 1 & 5,* **staves** [OE. *stæf*] **1.** a stick, rod, or pole used as for support, a weapon, a symbol of authority, a measure, etc. **2.** a group of people assisting a leader **3.** a group of officers serving a commanding officer as advisers and administrators **4.** a specific group of workers [a teaching *staff*] **5.** *Music* the five horizontal lines and four intermediate spaces on which music is written —*adj.* of, by, for, or on a staff —*vt.* to provide with a staff, as of workers

**staff·er** (-ər) *n.* a member of a staff

**staff officer 1.** an officer on a staff **2.** *U.S. Navy* a commissioned officer with nonmilitary duties, as a surgeon

**staff of life** bread, regarded as the basic food

**staff sergeant 1.** *U.S. Army & Marine Corps* an enlisted man ranking above sergeant **2.** *U.S. Air Force* an enlisted man ranking above airman first class

**stag** (stag) *n.*, *pl.* **stags**, **stag**: see PLURAL, II, D, 1 [OE. *stagga*] **1.** *a)* a full-grown male deer *b)* the male of various other animals **2.** a male animal castrated in maturity **3.** *a)* a man who attends a social gathering unaccompanied by a woman *b)* a social gathering for men only —*adj.* for men only —**go stag** [Colloq.] **1.** to go as a stag (sense 3 *a*) **2.** to go unescorted by a man

**stage** (stāj) *n.* [< OFr. *estage*, ult. < L. pp. of *stare*, to stand] **1.** a platform or dock **2.** a workmen's scaffold **3.** a level, floor, or story **4.** *a)* a platform on which plays, speeches, etc. are presented *b)* any area, as in an arena theater, in which actors perform *c)* the whole working section of a theater, including the acting area, the backstage area, etc. *d)* the theater as a profession (with *the*) **5.** the scene of an event or events **6.** a stopping point on a route, esp. formerly for a stagecoach **7.** the distance between two such points **8.** *shortened form of* STAGECOACH **9.** a period or degree in a process of development, change, etc. **10.** any of two or more propulsion units used in sequence as the rocket of a spacecraft, etc. **11.** *Radio* an element or part in a complex arrangement —*vt.* **staged**, **stag′ing 1.** to present as on a stage **2.** to plan and carry out [stage an attack] —*vi.* to be presented on the stage, as a play —**by easy stages** a little at a time, with many stops to rest

**stage·coach** (-kōch′) *n.* formerly, a horse-drawn coach on scheduled trips over a regular route

**stage·craft** (-kraft′) *n.* skill in writing or staging plays

**stage door** an outside door leading to the backstage part of a theater, used by actors, production staff, etc.

**stage fright** nervousness felt when appearing as a speaker or performer before an audience

**stage·hand** (-hand') *n.* a person who helps to set and remove scenery and furniture, operate the curtain, etc. for a stage performance

**stage-man·age** (-man'ij) *vt.* **-aged, -ag·ing** **1.** to be stage manager for **2.** to arrange or display with dramatic effect, esp. as if from behind scenes

**stage manager** an assistant to the director of a play, in overall charge backstage during an actual performance

**stage-struck** (-struk') *adj.* having an intense desire to act or otherwise work in the theater

**stage whisper** **1.** a loud whisper by an actor on the stage, thought of as being heard only by the audience and not by his fellow actors **2.** any similar loud whisper made at a social gathering

**stag·ger** (stag'ər) *vi.* [ON. *stakra*, to totter] **1.** to totter, sway, or reel, as from a blow, fatigue, drunkenness, etc. **2.** to waver in purpose, etc. —*vt.* **1.** to make stagger **2.** to affect strongly, as with astonishment **3.** to set alternately, as on either side of a line; make zigzag *[to stagger the teeth of a saw]* **4.** to arrange (duties, vacations, etc.) so as to avoid crowding —*n.* **1.** a staggering, tottering, etc. **2.** a staggered arrangement **3.** *[pl., with sing. v.]* a disease or toxic condition of horses, cattle, etc., marked by loss of coordination, staggering, etc. —**stag'ger·er** *n.* —**stag'ger·ing** *adj.* —**stag'ger·ing·ly** *adv.*

**stag·ing** (stā'jiŋ) *n.* **1.** a temporary structure used for support; scaffolding **2.** the business of operating stagecoaches **3.** travel by stagecoach **4.** the act or process of presenting a play on the stage

**stag·nant** (stag'nənt) *adj.* [< L. prp. of *stagnare*, to stagnate] **1.** not flowing or moving **2.** foul from lack of movement: said of water, etc. **3.** lacking activity, etc.; sluggish —**stag'nan·cy** (-nən sē) *n.* —**stag'nant·ly** *adv.*

**stag·nate** (-nāt) *vi., vt.* **-nat·ed, -nat·ing** [< L. pp. of *stagnare*, to stagnate < *stagnum*, a swamp] to become or make stagnant —**stag·na'tion** *n.*

**stag·y** (stā'jē) *adj.* **stag'i·er, stag'i·est** **1.** of the stage; theatrical **2.** affected; not real Also **stage'y** —**stag'i·ly** *adv.* —**stag'i·ness** *n.*

**staid** (stād) *archaic pt. & pp. of* STAY³ —*adj.* sober; sedate —**staid'ly** *adv.* —**staid'ness** *n.*

**stain** (stān) *vt.* [< OFr. < L. *dis-*, from + *tingere*, to color] **1.** to spoil the appearance of by discoloring or spotting **2.** to disgrace or dishonor (one's character, reputation, etc.) **3.** to change the appearance of (wood, glass, etc.) by applying a dye, pigment, etc. **4.** to treat (material for microscopic study) with a coloring matter, as to make transparent parts visible —*vi.* to impart or take a stain —*n.* **1.** a discoloration, spot, etc. resulting from staining **2.** a moral blemish; dishonor **3.** a dye, pigment, etc. for staining wood or for staining material for microscopic study —**stain'a·ble** *adj.* —**stain'er** *n.*

**stain·less** (-lis) *adj.* **1.** without a stain **2.** that resists staining, rusting, etc. **3.** made of stainless steel —*n.* flatware made of stainless steel —**stain'less·ly** *adv.*

**stainless steel** steel alloyed with chromium, etc., virtually immune to rust and corrosion

**stair** (ster) *n.* [OE. *stæger*] **1.** *[usually pl.]* a flight of steps; staircase **2.** one of a series of steps leading from one level to another

**stair·case** (-kās') *n.* a flight of stairs with a supporting structure and a handrail: also **stair'way'** (-wā')

**stair·well** (-wel') *n.* a vertical shaft (in a building) containing a staircase: also **stair well**

**stake** (stāk) *n.* [OE. *staca*] **1.** a length of wood or metal pointed at one end for driving into the ground, as for marking a boundary **2.** *a)* the post to which a person was tied for execution by burning *b)* such execution **3.** any of the posts fitted into sockets at the edge of a railway flatcar, truck bed, etc., to help hold a load **4.** *[often pl.]* something, esp. money, risked in a wager, game, or contest **5.** *[often pl.]* a prize given a winner, as in a race **6.** *[pl., with sing. v.]* a race in which a prize is offered **7.** a share or interest, as in property **8.** *[Colloq.]* a grubstake —*vt.* **staked, stak'ing** **1.** *a)* to mark the boundaries of as with stakes *b)* to establish (a claim) thus **2.** to support (a plant, etc.) by tying to a stake **3.** to tether to a stake **4.** to risk; gamble **5.** *[Colloq.]* *a)* to furnish with money or resources *b)* to grubstake —**at stake** being risked —**pull up stakes** *[Colloq.]* to change one's place of residence, business, etc. —**stake out** to station (police, etc.) in an attempt to capture a suspected criminal at (a specified place)

**stake·hold·er** (-hōl'dər) *n.* one who holds money, etc. bet by others and pays it to the winner

**stake·out** (-out') *n.* **1.** the staking out of police, etc. in an attempt to capture a suspected criminal **2.** the place where police, etc. are staked out

**Sta·kha·no·vism** (stə khä'nə viz'm) *n.* [< A. G. *Stakhanov*, Soviet miner] in the Soviet Union, a system of working in teams to get higher production through greater efficiency, with bonuses, etc. given for success —**Sta·kha'no·vite'** (-vīt') *adj., n.*

**sta·lac·tite** (stə lak'tīt; *chiefly Brit.* stal'ək tīt') *n.* [ModL. < Gr. *stalaktos*, dripping < *stalassein*, to drip] an icicle-shaped deposit hanging from the roof of a cave, formed by evaporation of dripping water full of lime —**stal·ac·tit·ic** (stal'ək tit'ik) *adj.*

STALACTITES
STALAGMITES

**sta·lag·mite** (stə lag'mīt; *chiefly Brit.* stal'əg mīt') *n.* [ModL. < Gr. *stalagmos*, a dropping < *stalassein*, to drip] a cone-shaped deposit built up on the floor of a cave by dripping water full of lime, often from a stalactite above —**stal·ag·mit·ic** (stal'əg mit'ik) *adj.*

**stale** (stāl) *adj.* **stal'er, stal'est** [prob. < LowG.] **1.** having lost freshness; specif., *a)* flat; tasteless *b)* hard and dry, as bread *c)* having little oxygen; stagnant *[stale air]* *d)* beginning to decay, as eggs **2.** no longer new or interesting; trite *[a stale joke]* **3.** ineffective, weakened, etc. from too much or too little activity —*vt., vi.* **staled, stal'ing** to make or become stale —**stale'ly** *adv.* —**stale'ness** *n.*

**stale·mate** (stāl'māt') *n.* [OFr. *estal*, a fixed location + *mate* (to checkmate)] **1.** *Chess* any situation in which a player cannot move without placing his king in check: it results in a draw **2.** a deadlock; standstill —*vt.* **-mat'ed, -mat'ing** to bring into a stalemate

**Sta·lin** (stä'lin), **Joseph** (born *Iosif Vissarionovich Dzhugashvili*) 1879–1953; premier of the U.S.S.R. (1941–53) —**Sta'lin·ism** *n.* —**Sta'lin·ist** *adj., n.*

**Sta·lin·grad** (stä'lin grät'; *E.* stä'lin grad') *former name of* VOLGOGRAD

**stalk¹** (stôk) *vi.* [OE. *stealcian* < *stealc*, steep] **1.** *a)* to walk in a stiff, haughty, or grim manner *b)* to advance or spread grimly *[plague stalks across the land]* **2.** to pursue or approach game, etc. stealthily —*vt.* **1.** to pursue or approach (game, etc.) stealthily **2.** to stalk through —*n.* **1.** a slow, stiff, or haughty stride **2.** a stalking of game, etc. —**stalk'er** *n.*

**stalk²** (stôk) *n.* [akin to OE. *stela*, stalk] **1.** any stem or stemlike part, as a slender rod or support **2.** *Bot. a)* the main stem or axis of a plant *b)* a lengthened part on which an organ grows or is supported, as the petiole of a leaf **3.** *Zool.* a lengthened support for an animal organ or for a whole body —**stalked** *adj.* —**stalk'i·ness** *n.* —**stalk'less** *adj.* —**stalk'y** *adj.* **-i·er, -i·est**

**stalk·ing-horse** (stôk'iŋ hôrs') *n.* **1.** a horse, or a figure of one, used as cover by a hunter **2.** anything used to hide intentions, schemes, etc. **3.** a person put forth as a political candidate until the candidate actually preferred is announced

**stall¹** (stôl) *n.* [OE. *steall*] **1.** *a)* formerly, a stable *b)* a compartment for one animal in a stable **2.** any of various compartments, sections, etc.; specif., *a)* a booth, etc. where goods are sold, as at a fair *b)* an enclosed seat in a church *c)* [Brit.] a theater seat near the stage *d)* a small, enclosed space, as for taking a shower *e)* any of the spaces marked off for parking cars in a garage, etc. **3.** a protective sheath for a finger; cot **4.** a stopping or standing still due to failure to work properly **5.** the tendency of an aircraft to drop or go out of control due to loss of lift and increase of drag —*vt., vi.* **1.** to put, keep, or be kept in a stall **2.** to stick fast, as in mud **3.** to stop as from failure to work properly **4.** to put (an aircraft) into a stall, or go into a stall

**stall²** (stôl) *vi.* [< obs. *stale*, a decoy < Anglo-Fr. *estale*] to act or speak evasively so as to deceive or delay —*vt.* to put off or delay by stalling (usually with *off*) —*n.* [Colloq.] any trick used in stalling

**stal·lion** (stal'yən) *n.* [OFr. *estalon* < Gmc. *stal*, a stall] an uncastrated male horse, esp. one used as a stud

**stal·wart** (stôl'wərt) *adj.* [OE. *stælwyrthe* < *stathol*, foundation + *wyrthe*, worth] **1.** sturdy; robust **2.** brave; valiant **3.** resolute; firm —*n.* **1.** a stalwart person **2.** a firm supporter of a cause, esp. that of a political party —**stal'wart·ly** *adv.* —**stal'wart·ness** *n.*

**sta·men** (stā'mən) *n., pl.* **-mens, stam·i·na** (stam'ə nə) [ModL. < L., a thread, orig., warp] a pollen-bearing organ in a flower, made up of a slender stalk (*filament*) and a pollen sac (*anther*)

**Stam·ford** (stam'fərd) [after *Stamford*, town in NE England] city in SW Conn.: pop. 102,000

**stam·i·na** (stam'ə nə) *n.* [L., pl. of STAMEN] resistance to fatigue, illness, hardship, etc.; endurance

**stam·i·nate** (stam'ə nit, -nāt') *adj.* **1.** having stamens but no pistils, as male flowers **2.** having stamens

**stam·mer** (stam'ər) *vt., vi.* [OE. *stamerian*] to speak or say with pauses that one cannot control, often with rapid repetitions of syllables or initial sounds, as because of excitement, embarrassment, or mental conflicts —*n.* the act or habit of stammering —**stam′mer·er** *n.* —**stam′mer·ing·ly** *adv.*

**stamp** (stamp) *vt.* [ME. *stampen*] **1.** to bring (the foot) down forcibly on the ground, a floor, etc. **2.** *a)* to strike down on forcibly with the foot *b)* to beat, crush, etc. by treading on heavily *c)* to remove by stamping the feet [*stamped* the snow from his boots] *d)* to pulverize (ore, etc.) by grinding or crushing **3.** *a)* to imprint or cut out (a design, lettering, etc.) by bringing a form forcibly against a material *b)* to cut out or make as by applying a die to metal [to *stamp* auto bodies] **4.** to impress or imprint with a design, etc., as to decorate, show ownership, etc. **5.** to impress distinctly or indelibly [a face *stamped* with grief] **6.** to put an official seal or a stamp on (a document, letter, etc.) **7.** to characterize or reveal distinctly, as if by imprinting —*vi.* **1.** to bring the foot down forcibly on the ground, etc. **2.** to walk with loud, heavy steps —*n.* **1.** a stamping **2.** a machine, tool, etc. for stamping or crushing ore, etc. **3.** *a)* any implement, as a die, that is brought forcibly against something to mark or shape it *b)* the mark or form so made **4.** a mark, seal, etc. used to show officially that a tax has been paid, authority given, etc. **5.** *a)* a small piece of paper, distinctively imprinted and usually gummed, sold by a government and required to be put on a letter, parcel, document, etc. to show that the prescribed fee has been paid *b)* any similar piece of paper, issued by an organization, business, etc. [trading *stamps*] **6.** a characteristic sign or impression [the *stamp* of truth] **7.** character; kind; class; type —**stamp out 1.** to crush or put out (a fire, etc.) by treading on forcibly **2.** to crush or put down (a revolt, etc.) —**stamp′er** *n.*

**stam·pede** (stam pēd′) *n.* [AmSp. *estampida* < Sp. < *estampar*, to stamp < Gmc.] **1.** a sudden, headlong running away of a herd of frightened horses, cattle, etc. **2.** a confused, headlong rush of many people **3.** any sudden, spontaneous mass movement —*vi.* **-ped′ed, -ped′ing** to move in a stampede —*vt.* to cause to stampede —**stam·ped′er** *n.*

**stamp·ing ground** (stam′piŋ) [Colloq.] a regular or favorite gathering place or resort

**stance** (stans) *n.* [< OFr., ult. < L. prp. of *stare*, to stand] **1.** a particular way of standing, esp. in regard to placing the feet **2.** an attitude adopted for dealing with a situation

**stanch** (stônch, stanch, stänch) *vt., vi., adj. see* STAUNCH

**stan·chion** (stan′chən, -shən) *n.* [< OFr. < *estance*: see STANCE] **1.** an upright bar, post, etc. used as a support **2.** a restraining device in a stall, fitted loosely about a cow's neck —*vt.* **1.** to support with stanchions **2.** to confine with a stanchion

**stand** (stand) *vi.* **stood, stand′ing** [OE. *standan*] **1.** *a)* to be or stay upright on the feet *b)* to be or stay upright on its base, bottom, etc., as a vase *c)* to grow upright: said of plants **2.** to rise to an upright position, as from sitting **3.** *a)* to take, or be in, a (specified) upright position [*stand* straight] *b)* to take, keep, or be in a (specified) position or attitude [I *stand* opposed] **4.** to have a (specified) height when standing [he *stands* six feet] **5.** *a)* to be situated *b)* to stay where situated **6.** to gather and remain: said of a liquid **7.** to remain unchanged, valid, etc. [the law still *stands*] **8.** to be in a (specified) condition [they *stood* in awe, he *stands* to lose] **9.** to be of a (specified) rank, degree, etc. [to *stand* first in grades] **10.** to remain resolute or firm **11.** to make resistance **12.** *a)* to halt *b)* to remain stationary **13.** to show the (specified) relative position of those involved [the score *stands* at 10 to 8] **14.** [Chiefly Brit.] to be a candidate, as for office; run **15.** *Naut.* to take or hold a certain course —*vt.* **1.** to make stand; put upright **2.** to put up with; endure **3.** to be unaffected by; withstand **4.** to undergo [to *stand* trial] **5.** to do the duty of [*stand* watch] **6.** [Colloq.] *a)* to bear the cost of (a meal, etc.), as when treating *b)* to treat (a person) to food, drink, etc. —*n.* **1.** a standing; esp.; a halt or stop; specif., *a)* a stopping to counterattack, resist, etc., as in retreat *b)* a halt by a touring theatrical company to give a performance; also, the place stopped at **2.** the place where one stands or is supposed to stand; position **3.** a view, opinion, etc., as on an issue **4.** a structure to stand or sit on; specif., *a)* a raised platform for a band, etc. *b)* [often *pl.*] a set of benches in tiers, as for spectators *c)* the place where a witness testifies in a courtroom **5.** *a)* a booth, stall, etc. where goods are sold *b)* a parking space reserved for taxicabs, etc. *c)* a business location **6.** a rack, small table, etc. for holding things **7.** a standing growth of trees or plants —**make a stand 1.** to take a position for defense or opposition **2.** to support a definite position, opinion, etc. —**stand a chance** to have a chance —**stand by 1.** to be near and ready to act as needed **2.** to aid or support **3.** to keep (a promise, etc.) **4.** to be

present, esp. as an onlooker **5.** *Radio & TV* to stay tuned in, as for a program to continue —**stand for 1.** to be a symbol for or sign of; represent **2.** [Colloq.] to put up with; endure —**stand in** [Colloq.] to be on good terms (usually with *with*) —**stand in for** to substitute for —**stand off 1.** to keep at a distance **2.** to put off or evade —**stand on 1.** to be founded on **2.** to insist upon (ceremony, one's rights, etc.) —**stand one's ground** to maintain one's position —**stand out 1.** to project **2.** to show up clearly **3.** to be prominent or outstanding **4.** to refuse to give in —**stand up 1.** to rise to or be in a standing position **2.** to prove valid, durable, etc. **3.** [Slang] to fail to keep an engagement with —**stand up for** to defend; support —**stand up to** to confront fearlessly —**stand′er** *n.*

**stand·ard** (stan′dərd) *n.* [OFr. *estendard*, ult. < Gmc.] **1.** a flag, banner, etc. used as an emblem or symbol of a leader, people, military unit, etc. **2.** something established as a rule or basis of comparison in measuring or judging quantity, quality, value, etc. **3.** a usage or practice that is generally accepted or followed; criterion [moral *standards*] **4.** an upright support **5.** a piece of music that has remained popular for many years **6.** a tree or shrub with a single, tall stem —*adj.* **1.** used as or conforming to an established rule, model, etc. **2.** generally accepted as reliable or authoritative [*standard* reference books] **3.** regular or typical; ordinary [*standard* procedure] **4.** suitable to speech or writing that is more or less formal; not slang, dialectal, obsolete, etc. [*standard* English]

**stand·ard-bear·er** (-ber′ər) *n.* **1.** a person carrying the standard, or flag, as of a military group **2.** a leader of a movement, political party, etc.

**standard gauge 1.** a width of 56½ inches between the rails of a railroad track **2.** such a track, or a locomotive or car for it —**stand′ard-gauge′** *adj.*

**stand·ard·ize** (stan′dər dīz′) *vt.* **-ized′, -iz′ing 1.** to make standard or uniform; make the same in all cases **2.** to test by or adjust to a standard —**stand′ard·i·za′tion** *n.* —**stand′ard·iz′er** *n.*

**standard of living** level of daily living, as of a nation, class, or person, with regard to the adequacy of necessities and comforts

**standard time** the time in any of the 24 time zones, each an hour apart, into which the earth is divided: it is based on distance east or west of Greenwich, England, and in North America, the eight zones (*Atlantic, Eastern, Central, Mountain, Pacific, Yukon, Alaska,* and *Bering*) use the mean solar times of the 60th, 75th, 90th, 105th, 120th, 135th, 150th, and 165th meridians, respectively: standard time is the official time for each zone except when daylight-saving time is in effect: see TIME, chart

**stand·by** (stand′bī′) *n., pl.* **-bys′ 1.** a person or thing that can always be depended on, or one ready to be used if needed **2.** a person waiting to board a plane, etc. if space becomes available —*adj.* of, for, or being a standby —**on standby** ready or waiting as a standby

**stand·ee** (stan dē′) *n.* [Colloq.] a person who stands, usually because no seats are vacant

**stand-in** (stand′in′) *n.* **1.** a person who stands in a performer's place in movies, etc. while lights, cameras, etc. are being adjusted **2.** any substitute for another

**stand·ing** (stan′diŋ) *n.* **1.** the act, state, or position of one that stands **2.** status, rank, or reputation **3.** the time that something lasts; duration [of long *standing*] —*adj.* **1.** that stands; upright **2.** in or from a standing position [a *standing* jump] **3.** not flowing; stagnant **4.** lasting; permanent **5.** stationary **6.** not in use

**standing army** a permanent army

**standing room** room in which to stand, esp. when there are no vacant seats, as in a theater

**Stan·dish** (stan′dish), **Miles** (or **Myles**) 1584?-1656; Eng. colonist; military leader of Plymouth Colony

**stand·off** (stand′ôf′) *n.* **1.** a standing off or being stood off **2.** an equalizing effect **3.** a tie or draw in a contest —*adj.* **1.** that stands off **2.** same as STANDOFFISH

**stand·off·ish** (stand′ôf′ish) *adj.* reserved and cool; aloof —**stand′off′ish·ly** *adv.* —**stand′off′ish·ness** *n.*

**stand·out** (stand′out′) *n.* [Colloq.] a person or thing of outstanding superiority —*adj.* [Colloq.] outstandingly superior

**stand·pat** (-pat′) *adj.* [Colloq.] sticking firmly to an opinion, policy, etc. —**stand′pat′ter** *n.* —**stand′pat′tism** *n.*

**stand·pipe** (-pīp′) *n.* a large vertical pipe or cylindrical tank for storing water

**stand·point** (-point′) *n.* the point or position from which something is seen or judged; point of view

**stand·still** (-stil′) *n.* a stop, halt, or cessation

**stand-up** (-up′) *adj.* **1.** upright; erect **2.** done, taken, etc. in a standing position **3.** designating or of a comedian who delivers monologues

**Stan·ford-Bi·net test** (stan′fərd bi nā′) a revision, wider in range, of the Binet-Simon test: developed at Stanford University (Calif.)

**stan·hope** (stan′hōp, -əp) *n.* [after F. *Stanhope*, 19th-c. Eng. clergyman] a light, open carriage with two or four wheels and usually one seat

**Stan·hope** (stan′əp), **Philip Dor·mer** (dôr′mər) *see* 4th Earl of CHESTERFIELD

**Stan·i·slav·sky** (stan′i släf′skē, stän′-), **Kon·stan·tin** (kän′stən tēn′) (born *Konstantin Sergeyevich Alekseyev*) 1863–1938; Russ. actor, director, & teacher of acting

**stank** (staŋk) *alt. pt. of* STINK

**Stan·ley** (stan′lē) **1.** [< OE. *stan leah*, stone lea] a masculine name **2.** Sir **Henry Morton**, (born *John Rowlands*) 1841–1904; Brit. journalist & explorer in Africa

**stan·nic** (stan′ik) *adj.* [< LL. *stannum*, tin + -IC] of or containing tin, specif. with a valence of four

**stan·nous** (-əs) *adj.* [< LL. *stannum*, tin + -OUS] of or containing tin, specif. with a valence of two

**Stan·ton** (stan′t′n), **Edwin Mc·Mas·ters** (mək mas′tərz) 1814–69; U.S. statesman; secretary of war (1862–68)

**stan·za** (stan′zə) *n.* [It., room, ult. < L. *stare*, to stand] a group of lines of verse, usually four or more and regular in pattern, forming one of the divisions of a poem or song —**stan·za′ic** (-zā′ik) *adj.*

**sta·pes** (stā′pēz) *n., pl.* **sta′pes, sta·pe·des** (stə pē′dēz, stā′pə dēz′) [ModL. < ML., a stirrup, prob. < Gmc.] *Anat.* a small, stirrup-shaped bone, the innermost of the three bones in the middle ear

**staph** (staf) *n. shortened form of* STAPHYLOCOCCUS

**staph·y·lo·coc·cus** (staf′ə lō käk′əs) *n., pl.* **-coc′ci** (-käk′sī) [ModL. < Gr. *staphylē*, bunch of grapes + -COC-CUS] any of a genus of spherical bacteria that generally occur in clusters or chains and cause pus to form in abscesses, etc. —**staph′y·lo·coc′cal** (-käk′′l), **staph′y·lo·coc′cic** (-käk′sik) *adj.*

**sta·ple**[1] (stā′p′l) *n.* [< OFr. < MDu. *stapel*, mart] **1.** a chief commodity made, grown, etc. in a particular place **2.** a chief item or element **3.** raw material **4.** any common, regularly stocked item of trade, as salt, flour, etc. **5.** the fiber of cotton, wool, etc. with regard to length and fineness —*adj.* **1.** regularly stocked **2.** produced or consumed regularly and in quantity **3.** chief; main *[a staple industry]* —*vt.* **-pled, -pling** to sort (wool, cotton, etc.) according to staple —**sta′pler** *n.*

**sta·ple**[2] (stā′p′l) *n.* [OE. *stapol*, a post] **1.** a U-shaped piece of metal with sharp-pointed ends, driven into a surface to hold a hook, wire, etc. in place **2.** a similar piece of thin wire driven through papers, etc. so that the ends bend over as a binding —*vt.* **-pled, -pling** to fasten with a staple or staples —**sta′pler** *n.*

**star** (stär) *n.* [OE. *steorra*] **1.** any heavenly body seen as a point of light in the night sky; specif., *Astron.* any self-luminous, gaseous, spheroidal heavenly body, as the sun, seen (except for the sun) as a fixed point of light **2.** a flat figure with usually five or six projecting points, representing a star **3.** a mark, emblem, etc. resembling such a figure, used as an award, insigne, etc. **4.** an asterisk **5.** *a*) *Astrol.* a planet, etc. regarded as influencing human fate *b*) *[often pl.]* fate; destiny **6.** a person who excels, esp. in a sport **7.** a leading actor or actress —*vt.* **starred, star′ring 1.** to decorate with stars **2.** to mark with a star or stars as a grade of quality **3.** to mark with an asterisk **4.** to present (a performer) in a leading role —*vi.* **1.** to excel, esp. in a sport **2.** to have a leading role —*adj.* **1.** excelling *[a star athlete]* **2.** of a star or stars —**star′less** *adj.* —**star′-like′** *adj.*

**star·board** (stär′bərd, -bôrd) *n.* [< OE. < *steoran*, to steer (with a large oar used on the ship's right side) + *bord*, board] the right-hand side of a ship or airplane as one faces forward, toward the bow —*adj.* of or on the starboard —*vt., vi.* to move or turn (the helm) to the starboard side

**starch** (stärch) *n.* [ult. < OE. *stearc*, stiff] **1.** a white, tasteless, odorless food substance found in potatoes, grain, etc.: it is a complex carbohydrate $(C_6H_{10}O_5)_n$ **2.** a powdered form of this, used in laundering to stiffen cloth, etc. **3.** *[pl.]* starchy foods **4.** stiff formality **5.** [Colloq.] vigor —*vt.* to stiffen as with starch —**starch′a·ble** *adj.* —**starch′-less** *adj.*

**Star Chamber 1.** a royal English court or tribunal abolished in 1641, notorious for its harsh, arbitrary, and secret procedures **2.** *[also* s- c-*]* any similar tribunal, etc.

**starch·y** (stär′chē) *adj.* **starch′i·er, starch′i·est 1.** of, containing, or like starch **2.** stiffened with starch **3.** formal; unbending —**starch′i·ly** *adv.* —**starch′i·ness** *n.*

**star-crossed** (stär′krôst′) *adj.* [see STAR (n. 5)] ill-fated

**star·dom** (-dəm) *n.* **1.** the status of a star of stage, screen, etc. **2.** such stars collectively

**stare** (ster) *vi.* **stared, star′ing** [OE. *starian*] to look with a steady, fixed gaze, eyes wide open, as in wonder, curiosity, dullness, etc. —*vt.* to inspect or affect in a given way by staring —*n.* a staring look —**stare down** to stare back at

(another) until he looks away —**stare one in the face** to be pressing or inescapable —**star′er** *n.*

**star·fish** (stär′fish′) *n., pl.* **-fish′, -fish′es:** see FISH a small sea animal with a hard, spiny skeleton and five or more arms or rays arranged like the points of a star

**star·gaze** (-gāz′) *vi.* **-gazed′, -gaz′ing 1.** to gaze at the stars **2.** to daydream —**star′gaz′er** *n.*

**stark** (stärk) *adj.* [OE. *stearc*] **1.** *a*) stiff or rigid, as a corpse *b*) harsh; severe **2.** sharply outlined or prominent *[one stark tree]* **3.** bleak; desolate **4.** *a*) emptied; stripped *[stark shelves]* *b*) totally naked **5.** grimly blunt; not softened, embellished, etc. *[stark realism]* **6.** sheer; utter *[stark terror]* —*adv.* in a stark way; esp., utterly *[stark mad]* —**stark′ly** *adv.* —**stark′ness** *n.*

**star·let** (stär′lit) *n.* **1.** a small star **2.** a young actress being promoted as a possible future star

**star·light** (-līt′) *n.* light from the stars

**star·ling** (stär′liŋ) *n.* [OE. *stærlinc*, dim. of *stær*, starling] any of a family of short-tailed, dark-colored birds, esp. the **common starling**, with iridescent plumage, brought into the U.S. from Europe

**star·lit** (stär′lit′) *adj.* lighted by the stars

**Star of David** a six-pointed star formed of two equilateral triangles: a symbol of Judaism

**star·ry** (stär′ē) *adj.* **-ri·er, -ri·est 1.** set or marked with stars **2.** shining like stars; bright **3.** star-shaped **4.** lighted by or full of stars **5.** of, from, or like stars —**star′ri·ness** *n.*

**star-eyed** (-īd′) *adj.* with the eyes sparkling in a glow of wonder, romance, visionary dreams, etc.

**Stars and Bars** the original flag (1861) of the Confederacy, with three horizontal bars and a circle of stars

STAR OF DAVID

**Stars and Stripes** the red, white, and blue flag of the United States, with 13 stripes and 50 stars

**Star-Span·gled Banner** (stär′spaŋ′g′ld) **1.** the United States flag **2.** the United States national anthem: the words are by Francis Scott Key

**start** (stärt) *vi.* [OE. *styrtan* & cognate ON. *sterta*] **1.** to make a sudden, involuntary movement, as when startled **2.** to become displaced, loose, warped, etc. **3.** to stick out or seem to stick out *[eyes starting in fear]* **4.** *a*) to go into action or motion; begin to do something or go somewhere *b*) to make or have a beginning; commence **5.** to be among the beginning entrants in a race, players in a game, etc. **6.** to spring into being, activity, etc. —*vt.* **1.** to make move suddenly; rouse or flush (game) **2.** to displace, loosen, warp, etc. **3.** *a*) to enter upon; begin doing, etc. *b*) to set into motion, action, etc. **4.** to introduce (a topic, etc.) **5.** to cause to be among those starting in a race, game, etc. —*n.* **1.** a sudden, brief shock or fright **2.** a sudden, startled movement; leap, jerk, etc. **3.** *[pl.]* brief bursts of activity: usually in *by fits and starts* **4.** *a*) a part that is loosened, warped, etc. *b*) the resulting break or gap **5.** the act of starting, or beginning **6.** *a*) the place or time of a beginning; starting point *b*) a lead or other advantage, as the beginning of a race **7.** an opportunity to begin a career, etc. —**start in** to begin a task, activity, etc. —**start out** (or **off**) to begin a journey, action, etc. —**start up 1.** to spring up **2.** to cause (a motor, etc.) to begin running

**start·er** (-ər) *n.* a person or thing that starts; specif., *a*) the first in a series *b*) one starting in a race, etc. *c*) one giving the signal to start *d*) one supervising departing trucks, etc. *e*) any of various devices for starting an internal-combustion engine

**star·tle** (stärt′′l) *vt.* **-tled, -tling** [< ME. freq. of *sterten*, to start] to surprise, frighten, or alarm suddenly; esp., to make jump, jerk, etc. as from sudden fright —*vi.* to be startled —*n.* a startled reaction —**star′tler** *n.* —**star′tling** *adj.* —**star′tling·ly** *adv.*

**starve** (stärv) *vi.* **starved, starv′ing** [OE. *steorfan*, to die] **1.** *a*) to die from lack of food *b*) to suffer or get weak from hunger *c*) [Colloq.] to be very hungry **2.** to suffer great need (with *for*) *[starving for affection]* —*vt.* **1.** to cause to starve **2.** to force by starving *[to starve an enemy into submission]* —**star·va′tion** *n.*

**starve·ling** (-liŋ) *n.* a starving person or animal —*adj.* **1.** starving **2.** impoverished

**stash** (stash) *vt.* [prob. a blend of STORE & CACHE] [Colloq.] to put or hide in a secret or safe place —*n.* [Slang] **1.** a place for hiding things **2.** something hidden away

**sta·sis** (stā′sis, stas′is) *n., pl.* **-ses** (-sēz) [ModL. < Gr., a standing] **1.** *a*) a stoppage of the flow of a bodily fluid, as of blood *b*) reduced peristalsis of the intestines **2.** a state of equilibrium or stagnancy

**-stat** (stat) [< ModL. < Gr. *-statēs*] *a combining form meaning* stationary, making stationary *[thermostat]*

**state** (stāt) *n.* [< OFr. < L. *status* < pp. of *stare*, to stand] **1.** a set of circumstances or attributes characterizing a person or thing at a given time; condition *[a state of poverty]*

**2.** a particular mental or emotional condition *[a state of bliss]* **3.** condition as regards structure, form, etc. *[liquid state]* **4.** *a)* social status; esp., high rank *b)* ceremonious display; pomp **5.** *[sometimes* S-*] a)* a body of people politically organized under one government within a definite territory *b)* the authority represented by such a body of people **6.** *[usually* S-*]* any of the political units together constituting a federal government, as in the U.S. **7.** the territory of a state (senses 5 *a* & 6) **8.** civil government *[church and state]* **9.** the sphere of highest governmental authority *[matters of state]* —*adj.* **1.** ceremonial **2.** *[sometimes* S-*]* of the government or a state —*vt.* **stat′ed, stat′ing 1.** to set or establish by specifying *[the stated hour]* **2.** to set forth or express in a specific, definite, or formal way *[to state* one's objections, *stating* a musical theme*]* —**in** (or **into**) **a state** [Colloq.] in (or into) an agitated emotional condition —**lie in state** to be displayed formally to the public before burial —**the States** the United States —**stat′a·ble** *adj.* —**state′less** *adj.*
**state·craft** (-kraft′) *n.* the ability of a statesman
**State·hood** (-hood′) *n.* the condition of being a State of the U.S. rather than a Territory
**State·house** (-hous′) *n.* the official meeting place of the legislature of a State of the U.S.: also **State House** or **State Capitol**
**state·ly** (-lē) *adj.* **-li·er, -li·est** dignified, imposing, grand, or the like —**state′li·ness** *n.*
**state·ment** (-mənt) *n.* **1.** *a)* the act of stating *b)* the thing stated or said **2.** *a)* a summary of a financial account *b)* a listing of charges for goods, etc.
**Stat·en Island** (stat′'n) [< Du. *Staaten Eylandt,* States Island, after States-General, name of the legislative assembly of the Netherlands] island between New Jersey and Long Island, forming the borough of Richmond, New York City
**state·room** (stāt′rōōm′) *n.* **1.** a private cabin on a ship **2.** a private room in a railroad car
**state's evidence** *Law* evidence given by or for the prosecution in a criminal case, esp. by a criminal against his associates —**turn state's evidence** to give such evidence for the prosecution
**state·side** (stāt′sīd′) *adj.* [Colloq.] of or having to do with the U.S. (as viewed from abroad) —*adv.* [Colloq.] in, to, or toward the U.S.
**states·man** (stāts′mən) *n., pl.* **-men** a person who shows wisdom and skill in conducting state affairs or dealing with public issues, or one experienced in the business of government —**states′man·like′, states′man·ly** *adj.* —**states′man·ship′** *n.*
**state socialism** the theory, doctrine, or practice of an economy planned and controlled by the state, based on state ownership of public utilities, basic industries, etc.
**States' rights** all the rights and powers which the Constitution neither grants to the Federal government nor denies to the State governments: also **State rights**
**state-wide** (stāt′wīd′) *adj.* extending throughout a state
**stat·ic** (stat′ik) *adj.* [< ModL. < Gr. *statikos,* causing to stand < *histanai,* to cause to stand] **1.** acting through weight only: said of the pressure exerted by a motionless body **2.** of masses, forces, etc. at rest or in equilibrium: opposed to DYNAMIC **3.** at rest; inactive; stationary **4.** *Elec.* designating, of, or producing stationary electrical charges, as from friction **5.** *Radio* of or having to do with static Also **stat′i·cal** —*n.* **1.** *a)* electrical discharges in the atmosphere that interfere with radio or TV reception, etc. *b)* interference or noises produced by such discharges **2.** [Slang] remarks showing disapproval —**stat′i·cal·ly** *adv.*
**stat·ics** (-iks) *n.pl.* [*with sing. v.*] [see prec.] the branch of mechanics dealing with bodies, masses, or forces at rest or in equilibrium
**sta·tion** (stā′shən) *n.* [< OFr. < L. < pp. of *stare,* to stand] **1.** the place where a person or thing stands or is located, esp. an assigned post, position, etc. *[a guard's station,* a police *station]* **2.** in Australia, a sheep or cattle ranch **3.** *a)* a regular stopping place, as on a bus line or railroad *b)* the building or buildings at such a place **4.** social standing or position **5.** *a)* a place equipped to transmit or receive radio waves; esp., the studios, technical installations, etc. of an establishment for radio or television transmission *b)* such an establishment, or the broadcasting frequency or channel assigned to it —*vt.* to assign to a station; post
**station agent** an official in charge of a small railroad station, or of a department in a larger station
**sta·tion·ar·y** (stā′shə ner′ē) *adj.* [< L. < *statio:* see STATION] **1.** not moving or movable; fixed **2.** unchanging in condition, value, etc. **3.** not migratory or itinerant —*n., pl.* **-ar′ies** a person or thing that is stationary
**stationary engineer** a person who operates and maintains stationary engines, such as steam boilers, turbines, etc.

**sta·tion·er** (stā′shə nər) *n.* [< ML. *stationarius* < L., STATIONARY] a person who sells office supplies, greeting cards, some books, etc.
**sta·tion·er·y** (-ner′ē) *n.* [see prec. & -ERY] writing materials; specif., paper and envelopes used for letters
**sta·tion·mas·ter** (stā′shən mas′tər) *n.* an official in charge of a large railroad station
**station wagon** an automobile with folding or removable rear seats and a tailgate that can be opened for loading luggage, packages, etc.
**stat·ism** (stāt′iz'm) *n.* the doctrine or practice of vesting economic control and planning in a centralized state government —**stat′ist** *n., adj.*
**sta·tis·tic** (stə tis′tik) *adj. rare var. of* STATISTICAL —*n.* a statistical item or element
**sta·tis·ti·cal** (-ti k'l) *adj.* of, having to do with, consisting of, or based on statistics —**sta·tis′ti·cal·ly** *adv.*
**stat·is·ti·cian** (stat′is tish′ən) *n.* an expert or specialist in statistics
**sta·tis·tics** (stə tis′tiks) *n.pl.* [< G. < ModL. *statisticus* < L. *status:* see STATE] **1.** facts or data of a numerical kind, assembled and classified so as to present significant information **2.** [*with sing. v.*] the science of compiling such facts
**sta·tor** (stāt′ər) *n.* [ModL. < L. < pp. of *stare,* to stand] the fixed part, as the housing, of a motor, dynamo, etc.
**stat·u·ar·y** (stach′ōō wer′ē) *n. -ar′ies* **1.** statues collectively **2.** the art of making statues —*adj.* of or suitable for statues
**stat·ue** (stach′ōō) *n.* [< OFr. < L. < *statuere,* to place < *stare,* to stand] the form of a person or animal carved in stone, wood, etc., modeled in clay, etc., or cast in plaster, bronze, etc., esp. when done in the round
**stat·u·esque** (stach′ōō wesk′) *adj.* like a statue; specif., *a)* tall and well-proportioned *b)* having a stately grace and dignity —**stat′u·esque′ly** *adv.* —**stat′u·esque′ness** *n.*
**stat·u·ette** (-wet′) *n.* a small statue
**stat·ure** (stach′ər) *n.* [OFr. < L. *statura < statuere:* see STATUE] **1.** the height of the body in a natural standing position **2.** growth or level of attainment, esp. as worthy of esteem *[moral stature]*
**sta·tus** (stāt′əs, stat′-) *n., pl.* **-tus·es** [L.: see STATE] **1.** condition or position with regard to law *[the status* of a minor*]* **2.** *a)* position; rank *[high status] b)* high position; prestige *[seeking status]* **3.** state or condition, as of affairs
**status quo** (kwō′) [L., lit., the state in which] the existing state of affairs: also **status in quo**
**status symbol** a possession, practice, etc. regarded as a mark of social status, esp. of high social status
**stat·ute** (stach′ōōt, -ōot) *n.* [< OFr. < LL. < L. pp. of *statuere:* see STATUE] **1.** an established rule **2.** *a)* a law passed by a legislative body and set forth in a formal document *b)* such a document
**statute law** law established by a legislative body
**statute mile** a unit of measure (5,280 feet): see MILE
**statute of limitations** a statute limiting the period within which a specific legal action may be taken
**stat·u·to·ry** (stach′ōō tôr′ē) *adj.* **1.** of, or having the nature of, a statute **2.** fixed, authorized, or established by statute **3.** declared by statute to be punishable: said of an offense
**St. Augustine** [after St. AUGUSTINE, sense 2 *a*] seaport in NE Fla.: oldest city in the U.S.: pop. 12,000
**staunch** (stônch, stänch) *vt.* [OFr. *estanchier,* ult. < L. *stans:* see STANCE] **1.** to stop or check (the flow of blood or of tears, etc.) from (a wound, opening, etc.) **2.** *a)* to stop or lessen (a drain of resources, etc.) *b)* to stop up (a source of leakage, etc.) —*vi.* to cease flowing —*adj.* **1.** watertight; seaworthy *[a staunch* ship*]* **2.** firm; steadfast *[a staunch* supporter*]* **3.** strong; solidly made Also **stanch** For the *adj.,* **staunch** is now the prevailing form; for the *v.,* usage is about evenly divided between **staunch** and **stanch** —**staunch′ly** *adv.* —**staunch′ness** *n.*
**stave** (stāv) *n.* [ME., taken as sing. of *staves,* pl. of *staf,* STAFF] **1.** *a)* any of the thin, shaped strips of wood, metal, etc. set edge to edge to form the wall of a barrel, bucket, etc. *b)* any similar slat, bar, rung, etc. **2.** a stick or staff **3.** a set of lines of a poem or song; stanza **4.** *Music* same as STAFF —*vt.* **staved** or **stove, stav′ing 1.** to puncture or smash, esp. by breaking in staves **2.** to furnish with staves —*vi.* to be or become stove in, as a boat —**stave in** to break or crush inward —**stave off** to ward off or hold off, as by force, cleverness, etc.

STAVE

**staves** (stāvz) *n.* **1.** *alt. pl. of* STAFF **2.** *pl. of* STAVE

**stay**¹ (stā) *n.* [OE. *stæg*] a heavy rope or cable, usually of wire, used as a brace, as for a mast of a ship; guy —*vt.* to brace or support with stays

**stay**² (stā) *n.* [MFr. *estaie* < Frank.] **1.** a support; prop **2.** a strip of stiffening material used in a corset, shirt collar, etc. —*vt.* **1.** to support, or prop up **2.** to comfort in spirit **3.** to cause to rest (*on, upon,* or *in*)

**stay**³ (stā) *vi.* **stayed** or archaic **staid, stay'ing** [< Anglo-Fr. < OFr. *ester* < L. *stare,* to stand] **1.** to continue in the place or condition specified; remain; keep /*to stay* at home, *to stay* healthy/ **2.** to live, dwell, or reside, esp. temporarily **3.** to stop; halt **4.** to pause; wait; delay **5.** [Colloq.] to continue or endure; last **6.** [Colloq.] to keep up (*with* another contestant in a race, etc.) —*vt.* **1.** to stop, halt, or check **2.** to hinder, impede, or detain **3.** to postpone or delay (legal action) **4.** to satisfy for a time (thirst, appetite, etc.) **5.** *a*) to remain through (often *with out*) /*to stay* the week (out)/ *b*) to be able to last through /*to stay* the distance/ —*n.* **1.** *a*) a stopping or being stopped *b*) a halt, check, or pause **2.** a postponement in legal action /*a stay* of execution/ **3.** the action of remaining, or the time spent, in a place /a long *stay* in Spain/ —**stay put** [Colloq.] to remain in place or unchanged

**staying power** ability to last or endure; endurance

**stay·sail** (-sāl', -s'l) *n.* a sail, esp. a triangular sail, fastened on a stay

**St. Cath·a·rines** (kath'rinz, -ər inz) city in SE Ontario, Canada, on the Welland Canal: pop. 123,000

**St. Clair** (kler), **Lake** [after Fr. *Sainte Claire* (St. Clare of Assisi, 1194–1253)] lake between SE Mich & Ontario, Canada

**St. Clair Shores** city in SE Mich., on Lake St. Clair: suburb of Detroit: pop. 76,000

**St. Croix** (kroi) [Fr., holy cross] largest island of the Virgin Islands of the U.S.

**Ste.** [Fr. *Sainte*] Saint (female)

**stead** (sted) *n.* [OE. *stede*] the place or position of a person or thing as filled by a substitute or successor /he came in my *stead*/ —**stand (one) in good stead** to give (one) good use, service, etc.

**stead·fast** (sted'fast', -fəst) *adj.* [OE. *stedefæste*] **1.** firm, fixed, or established **2.** not changing or wavering; constant —**stead'fast'ly** *adv.* —**stead'fast'ness** *n.*

**stead·y** (sted'ē) *adj.* **stead'i·er, stead'i·est** [see STEAD & -Y²] **1.** that does not shake, totter, etc.; firm; stable **2.** constant, regular, or continuous; not changing, faltering, etc. /a *steady* gaze/ **3.** constant in behavior, loyalty, etc. **4.** habitual or regular /a *steady* customer/ **5.** not easily excited; calm and controlled /*steady* nerves/ **6.** sober; staid; reliable **7.** staying headed in the same direction: said of a ship —*interj.* keep calm! —*vt., vi.* **stead'ied, stead'y·ing** to make or become steady —*n.* [Colloq.] one's regular sweetheart —**go steady** [Colloq.] to be sweethearts —**stead'i·ly** *adv.* —**stead'i·ness** *n.*

**stead·y-state theory** (-stāt') a theory of cosmology holding that as the universe expands, new matter is continuously created

**steak** (stāk) *n.* [ON. *steik* < base of *steikja,* to roast on a spit] a slice of meat, esp. beef, or of a large fish, cut thick for broiling or frying

**steak tar·tare** (tär tär') [*tartare,* pseudo-Fr. for TARTAR: hence, steak in Tartar style] raw sirloin or tenderloin steak ground up and mixed with chopped onion, raw egg, salt, and pepper, and eaten uncooked

**steal** (stēl) *vt.* **stole, stol'en, steal'ing** [OE. *stælan*] **1.** to take (another's property, etc.) dishonestly, esp. in a secret manner **2.** to take slyly, surreptitiously, etc. /to *steal* a look/ **3.** to gain slyly or artfully /he *stole* her heart/ **4.** to be the outstanding performer in (a scene, act, etc.), esp. in a subordinate role **5.** to move, put, or convey stealthily (*in, into, from, away,* etc.) **6.** *Baseball* to gain (a base) safely without the help of a hit, walk, or error —*vi.* **1.** to be a thief **2.** to move, pass, etc. stealthily, quietly, etc. —*n.* [Colloq.] **1.** an act of stealing **2.** something stolen **3.** something obtained at an unusually low cost —**steal'er** *n.*

**stealth** (stelth) *n.* [ME. *stelthe* < base of *stelen,* to steal] secret, furtive, or artfully sly action or behavior —**stealth'i·ly** *adv.* —**stealth'i·ness** *n.* —**stealth'y** *adj.* **stealth'i·er, stealth'i·est**

**steam** (stēm) *n.* [OE.] **1.** orig., a vapor **2.** *a*) water as converted into a vapor or gas by being heated to the boiling point: used for heating, as a source of power, etc. *b*) the power supplied by steam under pressure *c*) [Colloq.] driving force; energy **3.** condensed water vapor; mist —*adj.* **1.** using steam; heated, operated, etc. by steam **2.** containing or conducting steam —*vi.* **1.** to give off steam or a vapor **2.** to be given off as steam **3.** to become covered with condensed steam, as a window (usually *with up*) **4.** to generate steam **5.** to move by steam power **6.** [Colloq.] to seethe with anger; fume —*vt.* to expose to the action of steam, as in cooking —**let (or blow) off steam** [Colloq.] to release pent-up emotion

**steam·boat** (-bōt') *n.* a steamship, esp. a small one

**steam engine** **1.** an engine using steam under pressure to supply mechanical energy **2.** a locomotive powered by steam

**steam·er** (stē'mər) *n.* **1.** something operated by steam power, as a steamship or, formerly, a steam-powered automobile **2.** a container in which things are cooked, cleaned, etc. with steam

**steam fitter** a mechanic whose work (**steam fitting**) is installing and maintaining steam boilers, pipes, etc.

**steam heat** heat given off by steam in a closed system of pipes and radiators

**steam iron** an electric iron that releases steam through vents in the soleplate onto material being pressed

**steam·roll·er** (stēm'rōl'ər) *n.* **1.** a heavy, steam-driven roller used in building and repairing roads **2.** power which crushes opposition or forces its way relentlessly —*vt.* to crush, override, or force as if with a steamroller —*vi.* to move or act with overwhelming, crushing force Also **steam'roll'** —*adj.* relentlessly overpowering

**steam·ship** (-ship') *n.* a ship driven by steam power

**steam shovel** a large, mechanically operated digger, powered by steam

**steam table** a serving table or counter, as in restaurants, having steam-heated compartments to keep foods warm

**steam·y** (stē'mē) *adj.* **steam'i·er, steam'i·est** **1.** of or like steam **2.** filled with steam **3.** giving off steam —**steam'i·ly** *adv.* —**steam'i·ness** *n.*

**ste·ap·sin** (stē ap'sin) *n.* [< Gr. *stea(r),* fat + (PE)PSIN] the lipase present in pancreatic juice

**ste·ar·ic acid** (stē är'ik, stir'ik) [< Fr. < Gr. *stear,* tallow] a colorless, waxlike fatty acid, $C_{18}H_{36}O_2$, found in many animal and vegetable fats, and used in making candles, soaps, etc.

**ste·a·rin** (stē'ə rin, stir'in) *n.* [< Fr. < Gr.: see prec. & -INE⁴] a white, crystalline substance, ($C_{18}H_{35}O_2)_3C_3H_5$, found in the solid portion of most animal and vegetable fats: also **ste'a·rine** (-rin, -rēn')

**ste·a·tite** (stē'ə tīt') *n.* [L. *steatitis* < Gr. *stear,* tallow] a compact, massive variety of talc; soapstone —**ste'a·tit'ic** (-tit'ik) *adj.*

**sted·fast** (sted'fast', -fəst) *adj.* earlier var. of STEADFAST —**sted'fast'ly** *adv.* —**sted'fast'ness** *n.*

**steed** (stēd) *n.* [OE. *steda*] a horse; esp., a high-spirited riding horse: literary term

**steel** (stēl) *n.* see PLURAL, II, D, 3 [OE. *stiele*] **1.** a hard, tough metal composed of iron alloyed with a small percentage of carbon and often variously with other metals, as nickel, chromium, etc., to produce hardness, etc. **2.** something made of steel; specif., [Poet.] a sword or dagger **3.** great strength or hardness —*adj.* of or like steel —*vt.* **1.** to cover or edge with steel **2.** to make hard, tough, unfeeling, etc. —**steel'i·ness** *n.* —**steel'y** *adj.* **-i·er, -i·est**

**steel blue** a metallic blue color like that of tempered steel —**steel'-blue'** *adj.*

**Steele** (stēl), **Sir Richard** 1672–1729; Brit. essayist & dramatist, born in Ireland

**steel gray** a bluish-gray color —**steel'-gray'** *adj.*

**steel guitar** a type of guitar, now esp. an electric guitar, with raised metal strings, held on the lap or mounted on legs and played by plucking while sliding a steel bar across the strings to change the pitch

**steel mill** a mill where steel is made, processed, and shaped: also **steel'works'** *n.*

**steel wool** long, hairlike shavings of steel in a pad or ball, used for scouring, smoothing, and polishing

**steel·work·er** (stēl'wur'kər) *n.* a worker in a steel mill

**steel·yard** (stēl'yärd', stil'yərd) *n.* [STEEL & YARD¹ (in obs. sense of "rod")] a scale consisting of a metal arm suspended from above: the object to be weighed is hung from the shorter end and a weight is moved along the graduated longer end until the arm balances

**steen·bok** (stēn'bäk', stän'-) *n., pl.* **-bok', -boks':** see PLURAL, II, D, 2 [Afrik. < Du. *steen,* a stone + *bok,* a buck] *same as* STEINBOK: also **steen'buck'** (-buk')

**steep**¹ (stēp) *adj.* [OE. *steap,* lofty] **1.** having a sharp rise or slope; precipitous /a *steep* incline/ **2.** [Colloq.] *a*) unreasonably high or great; excessive /a *steep* price/ *b*) extreme —*n.* a steep slope —**steep'ly** *adv.* —**steep'ness** *n.*

**steep**² (stēp) *vt.* [akin to ON. *steypa*] **1.** to soak in liquid, as in order to extract the essence of **2.** to immerse, saturate, imbue, etc. /*steeped* in folklore/ —*n.* **1.** a steeping or being steeped **2.** liquid in which something is steeped —*vi.* to be steeped, as tea leaves

**steep·en** (-'n) *vt., vi.* to make or become steep or steeper

**stee·ple** (stē'p'l) *n.* [OE. *stepel*] **1.** a tower rising above the main structure of a building, esp. of a church, usually capped with a spire **2.** *same as* SPIRE —**stee'pled** *adj.*

**stee·ple·chase** (-chās') *n.* [the race orig. had as its goal a distant, visible steeple] **1.** orig., a horse race run across country **2.** a horse race run over a prepared course obstructed with ditches, hedges, etc.

**stee·ple·jack** (-jak′) *n.* a person whose work is building, painting, or repairing steeples, smokestacks, etc.

**steer**[1] (stir) *vt.* [OE. *stieran*] **1.** to guide (a ship or boat) by means of a rudder **2.** to direct the course of (an automobile, etc.) **3.** to oversee; direct *[he steered* our efforts] **4.** to set and follow (a course) —*vi.* **1.** to steer a ship, automobile, etc. **2.** to be steered *[the car steers* easily] **3.** to set and follow a course —*n.* [Colloq.] a suggestion; tip —**steer clear of** to avoid —**steer′a·ble** *adj.* —**steer′er** *n.*

**steer**[2] (stir) *n.* [OE. *steor*] **1.** a castrated male of the cattle family **2.** loosely, any male of beef cattle

**steer·age** (stir′ij) *n.* **1.** *a)* the act of steering *b)* the response of a ship to the helmsman's guidance **2.** formerly, a section in some passenger ships occupied by passengers paying the lowest fare

**steer·age·way** (-wā′) *n.* the minimum forward speed needed to make a ship respond to the helmsman's guidance

**steers·man** (stirz′mən) *n., pl.* **-men** a person who steers a ship or boat; helmsman

**Ste·fans·son** (stef′an sən), **Vil·hjal·mur** (vil′hyoul′mər) 1879–1962; U.S. arctic explorer, born in Canada

**stein** (stīn) *n.* [G.] **1.** an earthenware beer mug, or a similar mug of pewter, glass, etc. **2.** the amount that a stein will hold

**Stein** (stīn), **Gertrude** 1874–1946; U.S. writer in France

**Stein·beck** (stīn′bek′), **John (Ernst)** 1902–68; U.S. novelist & short-story writer

**stein·bok** (stīn′bäk′) *n., pl.* **-bok′, -boks′**: see PLURAL, II, D, 2 [< G.] a small, reddish antelope found in grassy areas of S and E Africa

**ste·le** (stē′lē; *also, & for 2 usually,* stēl) *n.* [< L. < Gr. *stēlē*, a slab] **1.** an upright stone slab with an inscription or design, as a grave marker **2.** a prepared surface with an inscription or design, as on a façade

**Stel·la** (stel′ə) [L. *stella*, a star] a feminine name

**stel·lar** (stel′ər) *adj.* [< LL. < L. *stella*, a star] **1.** of the stars or a star **2.** like a star, as in shape **3.** by or as by a star performer; excellent **4.** leading; chief *[a stellar* role]

**stel·late** (stel′āt, -it) *adj.* [< L. pp. of *stellare*, to cover with stars < *stella*, a star] star-shaped; coming out in rays or points from a center: also **stel′lat·ed** —**stel′late·ly** *adv.*

**stem**[1] (stem) *n.* [OE. *stemn*] **1.** the main stalk or trunk of a tree, shrub, or other plant, extending above the ground and bearing the leaves, flowers, etc. **2.** any stalk supporting leaves, flowers, or fruit **3.** a stemlike part; specif., *a)* the slender part of a tobacco pipe attached to the bowl *b)* a narrow supporting part above the foot of a wineglass, goblet, etc. *c)* the shaft projecting from a watch, with a knob for winding the spring *d)* the thick stroke of a letter, as in printing *e)* the vertical line of a musical note **4.** the prow of a ship; bow **5.** a branch of a family **6.** the part of a word to which inflectional endings are added —*vt.* **stemmed, stem′ming 1.** to remove the stem from (a fruit, etc.) **2.** to make headway against *[to row upstream, stemming* the current] —*vi.* to originate or derive —**from stem to stern 1.** from one end of a ship to another **2.** through the length of anything —**stem′less** *adj.* —**stem′like′** *adj.*

**stem**[2] (stem) *vt.* **stemmed, stem′ming** [ON. *stemma*] **1.** to stop or check; esp., to dam up (a river, etc.), or to stop or check as if by damming up **2.** to turn (a ski) in stemming —*vi.* to stop or slow down in skiing by turning the tip of the ski(s) inward

**stemmed** (stemd) *adj.* **1.** having a stem *[a thin-stemmed* goblet] **2.** with the stem or stems removed

**stem-wind·ing** (stem′wīn′diŋ) *adj.* wound, as a watch, by turning a knurled knob at the outer end of the stem —**stem′-wind′er** *n.*

**stench** (stench) *n.* [OE. *stenc*] an offensive smell; stink

**sten·cil** (sten′s'l) *vt.* **-ciled** or **-cilled, -cil·ing** or **-cil·ling** [< OFr. *estencele*, ult. < L. *scintilla*, a spark] to make, mark, or paint with a stencil —*n.* **1.** a thin sheet, as of paper or metal, perforated or cut through in such a way that when ink, paint, etc. is applied to the sheet, the patterns, designs, letters, etc. are marked on the surface beneath **2.** a pattern, design, etc. made by stenciling —**sten′cil·er, sten′cil·ler** *n.*

**Sten·dhal** (sten′däl; *Fr.* stan dàl′) (pseud. of *Marie Henri Beyle*) 1783–1842; Fr. novelist & essayist

**sten·o-** [< Gr. *stenos*, narrow] *a combining form meaning* narrow, thin, small, etc. *[stenography]*

**ste·nog·ra·pher** (stə näg′rə fər) *n.* a person skilled in stenography

**ste·nog·ra·phy** (-fē) *n.* [STENO- + -GRAPHY] shorthand writing; specif., the skill or work of writing down dictation, testimony, etc. in shorthand and later transcribing it,

as on a typewriter —**sten·o·graph·ic** (sten′ə graf′ik), **sten′o·graph′i·cal** *adj.* —**sten′o·graph′i·cal·ly** *adv.*

**sten·o·type** (sten′ə tīp′) *n.* [STENO- + -TYPE] **1.** a symbol or symbols used in stenotypy **2.** a keyboard machine used in stenotypy —*vt.* **-typed′, -typ′ing** to record by stenotype

**sten·o·typ·y** (-tī′pē) *n.* shorthand in which symbols representing sounds, words, or phrases are typed on a keyboard machine —**sten′o·typ′ist** *n.*

**Sten·tor** (sten′tôr) a Greek herald in the *Iliad* having a very loud voice —*n.* [*usually* s-] a person having a very loud voice

**sten·to·ri·an** (sten tôr′ē ən) *adj.* [< prec.] very loud

**step** (step) *n.* [OE. *stepe*] **1.** the act of moving and placing the foot, as in walking, dancing, climbing, etc. **2.** the distance covered by such a movement **3.** a short distance **4.** *a)* a manner of stepping; gait *b)* any pace or stride in marching *[the goose step] c)* a sequence of movements in dancing, usually repeated in a set pattern **5.** the sound of stepping; footfall **6.** a mark made by stepping; footprint **7.** a rest for the foot in climbing, as a stair or the rung of a ladder **8.** [*pl.*] a flight of stairs **9.** something resembling a stair step, as a raised frame supporting a mast **10.** a degree; rank; level; stage **11.** any of a series of acts, processes, etc. **12.** *Music a)* a degree of the staff or scale *b)* the interval between two consecutive degrees —*vi.* **stepped, step′ping 1.** to move by executing a step **2.** to walk, esp. a short distance **3.** to move with measured steps, as in dancing **4.** to move quickly: often with *along* **5.** to come or enter (*into* a situation, etc.) **6.** to put or press the foot down (*on* something) *[step* on the brake] —*vt.* **1.** to take (one or more strides or paces) **2.** *a)* to set (the foot) down *b)* to move across or over by foot **3.** to execute the steps of (a dance) **4.** to measure by taking steps: usually with *off [step* off ten paces] **5.** to provide with steps; specif., *a)* to cut steps in *b)* to arrange in a series of degrees or grades —**break step** to stop marching in cadence —**in step 1.** keeping to a set rhythm in marching, dancing, etc. **2.** in conformity or agreement —**keep step** to stay in step —**out of step** not in step —**step by step** by degrees; gradually —**step down 1.** to resign (*from* an office, etc.) **2.** to decrease, as in rate —**step in** to start to participate; intervene —**step on it** [Colloq.] to go faster; hurry —**step out** [Colloq.] to go out for a good time —**step up 1.** to approach **2.** to advance **3.** to increase, as in rate —**take steps** to adopt certain measures —**watch one's step** [Colloq.] to be careful

**step·broth·er** (step′bruth′ər) *n.* one's stepparent's son by a former marriage

**step·child** (-chīld′) *n., pl.* **-chil′dren** [OE. *steop-*, orphaned: orig. used of orphaned children] a child that one's husband or wife had by a former marriage

**step·daugh·ter** (-dôt′ər) *n.* a female stepchild

**step-down** (-doun′) *adj.* that steps down, or decreases, power, speed, etc., as a transformer, gear, etc. —*n.* a decrease, as in intensity, etc.

**step·fa·ther** (-fä′thər) *n.* a male stepparent

**steph·a·no·tis** (stef′ə nōt′is) *n.* [ModL. < Gr. < *stephanos*, a crown] a woody vine grown for its white, waxy, sweet-scented flowers

**Ste·phen** (stē′vən) [L. *Stephanus* < Gr. < *stephanos*, a crown] a masculine name: dim. *Steve*

**step-in** (step′in′) *adj.* put on by being stepped into —*n.* a step-in garment or [*pl.*], esp. formerly, undergarment

**step·lad·der** (-lad′ər) *n.* a four-legged ladder having broad, flat steps

**step·moth·er** (-muth′ər) *n.* a female stepparent

**step·par·ent** (-per′ənt, -par′-) *n.* [see STEPCHILD] the person who has married one's parent after the death or divorce of the other parent

**steppe** (step) *n.* [< Russ. *step′*] **1.** any of the great plains of SE Europe and Asia, having few trees **2.** any similar plain

**stepped-up** (stept′up′) *adj.* increased, as in tempo

**step·per** (step′ər) *n.* a person or animal that steps in a specified manner, as a dancer or a horse

**step·ping·stone** (step′iŋ stōn′) *n.* **1.** a stone, usually one of a series, used to step on, as in crossing a stream, etc. **2.** a means of advancement Also **stepping stone**

**step·sis·ter** (-sis′tər) *n.* one's stepparent's daughter by a former marriage

**step·son** (-sun′) *n.* a male stepchild

**step-up** (-up′) *adj.* that steps up, or increases, power, speed, etc., as a transformer, gear, etc. —*n.* an increase, as in intensity, etc.

**-ster** (stər) [OE. *-estre*, orig. a fem. agent suffix] *a suffix meaning:* **1.** a person who is, does, or creates (something specified) *[oldster, punster]*: often derogatory *[rhymester]* **2.** a person associated with (something specified) *[gangster]*

**stere** (stir) *n.* [Fr. *stère* < Gr. *stereos*, solid, cubic] a cubic meter

**ster·e·o** (ster′ē ō′, stir′-) *n., pl.* **-os′** 1. *a*) a stereophonic record player, radio, record, tape, etc. *b*) a stereophonic system 2. a stereoscope or a stereoscopic picture, etc. 3. *shortened form of: a*) STEREOTYPE *b*) STEREOTYPY —*adj.* shortened form of STEREOPHONIC

**ster·e·o-** [< Gr. *stereos*, hard, firm] *a combining form meaning* solid, firm, three-dimensional *[stereoscope]*

**ster·e·o·phon·ic** (ster′ē ə fän′ik, stir′-) *adj.* [prec. + PHONIC] designating or of sound reproduction, as in motion pictures, records, tapes, or broadcasting, using two or more channels to carry and reproduce through separate speakers a blend of sounds from separate sources —**ster′e·o·phon′i·cal·ly** *adv.*

**ster·e·op·ti·con** (-äp′ti kən, -kän′) *n.* [< Gr. *stereos*, solid + *optikon*, of sight] a kind of slide projector that allows one view to fade out while the next is fading in

**ster·e·o·scope** (ster′ē ə skōp′, stir′-) *n.* [STEREO- + -SCOPE] an instrument that gives a three-dimensional effect to photographs viewed through it: it has two eyepieces, through which two slightly different views of the same scene are viewed side by side —**ster′e·o·scop′ic** (-skäp′ik) *adj.* —**ster′e·o·scop′i·cal·ly** *adv.*

STEREOSCOPE

**ster·e·os·co·py** (ster′ē äs′kə pē, stir′-) *n.* the science of stereoscopic effects and techniques

**ster·e·o·type** (ster′ē ə tīp′, stir′-) *n.* [< Fr.: see STEREO- & -TYPE] 1. a one-piece printing plate cast in type metal from a mold (*matrix*), as of a page of set type 2. *same as* STEREOTYPY 3. a fixed idea or popular conception, as about how a certain type of person looks, acts, etc. —*vt.* **-typed′**, **-typ′ing** 1. to make a stereotype of 2. to print from stereotype plates —**ster′e·o·typ′er, ster′e·o·typ′ist** *n.*

**ster·e·o·typed** (-tīpt′) *adj.* 1. having the nature of a stereotype; esp., hackneyed; trite; not original 2. printed from stereotype plates

**ster·e·o·typ·y** (-tī′pē) *n.* the process of making or printing from stereotype plates

**ster·ile** (ster′l; *Brit. & Canad.,* usually -īl) *adj.* [L. *sterilis*] 1. incapable of producing others of its kind; barren 2. producing little or nothing *[sterile soil]* 3. lacking in interest or vitality *[a sterile style]* 4. free from living microorganisms; esp., aseptic —**ster′ile·ly** *adv.* —**ste·ril·i·ty** (stə ril′ə tē) *n.*

**ster·i·lize** (ster′ə līz′) *vt.* **-lized′**, **-liz′ing** to make sterile; specif., *a*) to make incapable of producing others of its kind *b*) to make (land) unproductive *c*) to free from living microorganisms, as by subjecting to great heat or chemical action Also *[Chiefly Brit.]* **ster′i·lise′** —**ster′i·li·za′tion** *n.* —**ster′i·liz′er** *n.*

**ster·ling** (stur′liŋ) *n.* [ME. *sterlinge*, Norman silver penny < ?] 1. sterling silver or articles made of it 2. the standard of fineness of legal British coinage: for silver, 0.500; for gold, 0.91666 3. British money —*adj.* 1. of standard quality: said of silver that is at least 92.5 percent pure 2. of or payable in British money 3. made of sterling silver 4. worthy; excellent

**Ster·ling Heights** (stur′liŋ) [? ult. after Lord *Sterling,* general in the Am. Revolutionary Army] city in SE Mich.: suburb of Detroit: pop. 109,000

**stern**[1] (sturn) *adj.* [OE. *styrne*] 1. hard; severe; strict *[stern measures]* 2. grim; forbidding *[a stern face]* 3. that cannot be changed *[stern reality]* 4. unshakable; firm *[stern determination]* —**stern′ly** *adv.* —**stern′ness** *n.*

**stern**[2] (sturn) *n.* [ON. *stjorn,* steering < *styra,* to steer] 1. the rear end of a ship, boat, etc. 2. the rear end of anything

**Sterne** (sturn), **Laurence** 1713–68; Brit. novelist, born in Ireland

**stern·most** (sturn′mōst′) *adj.* 1. nearest the stern 2. farthest astern; rearmost

**stern·post** (sturn′pōst′) *n.* the main, upright piece at the stern of a vessel, usually supporting the rudder

**ster·num** (stur′nəm) *n., pl.* **ster′nums, ster′na** (-nə) [ModL. < Gr. *sternon*] a thin, flat structure of bone and cartilage to which most of the ribs are attached in the front of the chest in most vertebrates; breastbone —**ster′nal** *adj.*

**ster·nu·ta·tion** (stur′nyoo tā′shən) *n.* [< L. < freq. of *sternuere,* to sneeze] a sneeze or the act of sneezing —**ster·nu·ta·to·ry** (stər nyoot′ə tôr′ē), **ster′nu·ta′tive** *adj.*

**stern·ward** (sturn′wərd) *adv., adj.* toward the stern; astern: also **stern′wards** *adv.*

**stern·way** (-wā′) *n.* backward movement of a ship

**stern-wheel·er** (-hwēl′ər, -wēl′ər) *n.* a steamer propelled by a paddle wheel at the stern

**ster·oid** (stir′oid, ster′-) *n.* [STER(OL) + -OID] any of a group of compounds including the sterols, sex hormones, etc.,

characteristically having the ring structure of the sterols —**ste·roi′dal** *adj.*

**ster·ol** (stir′ōl, ster′-; -ōl) *n.* [< (CHOLE)STEROL] any of a group of solid cyclic alcohols, as cholesterol, found in plant and animal tissues

**ster·to·rous** (stur′tə rəs) *adj.* [< L. *stertere,* to snore] characterized by loud, labored breathing, or snoring —**ster′to·rous·ly** *adv.* —**ster′to·rous·ness** *n.*

**stet** (stet) [L.] let it stand: a printer's term used to indicate that matter previously struck out is to remain —*vt.* **stet′ted, stet′ting** to cancel a change in or deletion of (a word, line, etc.), as by writing "stet" in the margin of a proof or manuscript

**steth·o·scope** (steth′ə skōp′) *n.* [< Fr. < Gr. *stēthos,* chest + -SCOPE] *Med.* a hearing instrument placed against the body for examining the heart, lungs, etc. by listening to the sounds they make —**steth′o·scop′ic** (-skäp′ik), **steth′o·scop′i·cal** *adj.* —**steth′o·scop′i·cal·ly** *adv.* —**ste·thos·co·py** (stə thäs′kə pē) *n.*

**Stet·son** (stet′s′n) *a trademark for* hats of various kinds —*n.* *[often* **s-**] a man's hat, worn esp. by Western cowboys, usually of felt, with a broad brim and a high crown

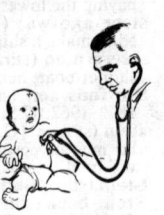
STETHOSCOPE

**Steu·ben** (stōo′b′n; *G.* shtoi′bən), Baron **Frederick William Augustus von** 1730–94; Prussian military officer: served as Am. general in the Revolutionary War

**ste·ve·dore** (stē′və dôr′) *n.* [< Sp. < *estivar,* to stow < L. *stipare,* to cram] a person employed at loading and unloading ships —*vt.,* *vi.* **-dored′, -dor′ing** to load or unload the cargo of (a ship)

**Ste·ven** (stē′vən) [see STEPHEN] a masculine name

**Ste·ven·son** (stē′vən s′n), **Robert Louis (Balfour)** 1850–94; Scot. novelist, poet, & essayist

**stew** (stōo, styōo) *vt.* [< MFr. *estuver,* ult. < L. *ex,* out + Gr. *typhos,* steam] to cook by simmering slowly for a long time —*vi.* 1. to undergo cooking in this way 2. to live in hot, overcrowded conditions 3. to fret or worry —*n.* 1. a dish, esp. of meat and vegetables, cooked by stewing 2. a state of anxiety or worry —**stew in one's own juice** to suffer from one's own actions

**stew·ard** (stōo′ərd, styōo′-) *n.* [OE. *stiweard* < *stig,* enclosure + *weard,* a keeper] 1. a person in charge of the affairs of a large household, who supervises the kitchen and servants, manages the accounts, etc. 2. one who acts as an administrator, as of finances and property, for another 3. a person variously responsible for the food and drink, the service personnel, etc. in a club, restaurant, etc. 4. a person in charge of arrangements for a ball, race, etc. 5. an attendant on a ship, airplane, etc. who looks after the passengers' comfort 6. *short for* SHOP STEWARD —*vi.* to act as a steward —**stew′ard·ship′** *n.*

**stew·ard·ess** (-ər dis) *n.* a woman steward (esp. sense 5)

**Stew·art** (stōo′ərt, styōo′-) [see STUART] a masculine name

**stewed** (stōod) *adj.* 1. cooked by stewing, as food 2. [Slang] drunk; intoxicated

**stew·pan** (stōo′pan′, styōo′-) *n.* a pan for stewing

**St. George's Channel** strait between Ireland & Wales, connecting the Irish Sea with the Atlantic

**St. He·le·na** (hə lē′nə, hel′i nə) Brit. island in the S Atlantic, c. 1,200 mi. from Africa: site of Napoleon's exile (1815–21)

**stick** (stik) *n.* [OE. *sticca*] 1. a twig or small branch broken or cut off, esp. a dead and dry one 2. a long, slender piece of wood, often shaped for a specific purpose, as a wand, staff, club, cane, rod, etc. 3. a stalk, as of celery 4. something shaped like a stick *[a stick of chewing gum]* 5. a separate article *[every stick of furniture]* 6. an implement for striking a ball, puck, etc. *[a hockey stick]* 7. a stab or thrust 8. the power of adhering or making adhere 9. [Colloq.] a dull or stupid person 10. [Slang] a marijuana cigarette 11. *Aeron.* a lever that controls the altitude and movement of an airplane: in full, **control stick** —*vt.* **stuck** or for *vt.* 8 **sticked, stick′ing** 1. to pierce or puncture, as with a pointed instrument 2. to kill by stabbing 3. to pierce something with (a knife, pin, etc.) 4. to thrust or push (*in, out,* etc.) 5. *a*) to fasten or attach by gluing, pinning, etc. *b*) to decorate with things fastened in this way 6. to transfix or impale 7. to obstruct, bog down, etc.; also, to detain, delay, etc.: usually used in the passive *[the wheels were stuck,* he was *stuck* in town*]* 8. to prop (a vine, etc.) with a stick 9. [Colloq.] to place; put; set 10. [Colloq.] to make sticky by smearing 11. [Colloq.] to puzzle; baffle 12. [Slang] *a*) to make pay excessively *b*) to impose a disagreeable task, burden, etc. upon —*vi.* 1. to be or remain fixed or embedded by a pointed end, as a nail, etc. 2. to be or remain attached by adhesion; adhere 3. *a*) to remain in the same place *[they stick at home]* *b*) to remain fixed in the memory *c*) to remain in effect [to make charges *stick*] **4.** to keep or stay close [friends *stick* together, *stick* to the trail] **5.** to persevere [to *stick* at a job] **6.** to remain firm; endure **7.** to become fixed, blocked, embedded, jammed, etc. [my shoe *stuck* in the mud, the gears *stuck*] **8.** to be puzzled **9.** to hesitate; scruple [he'll *stick* at nothing] **10.** to protrude or extend (with *out*, *up*, etc.) —**be on the stick** [Slang] to be alert, efficient, etc. —**stick around** [Slang] to stay near at hand —**stick by** (or **to**) to remain loyal to —**stick it out** [Slang] to endure something to the end —**stick to one's ribs** to be nourishing: said of food —**stick up** [Slang] to commit armed robbery upon —**stick up for** [Colloq.] to uphold; defend —**the sticks** [Colloq.] the rural districts —**stick′like′** *adj.*

**stick·ball** (stik′bôl′) *n.* a game like baseball played by children, as on city streets, with improvised equipment such as a broom handle and a soft rubber ball

**stick·er** (-ər) *n.* a person or thing that sticks; specif., *a*) a bur, barb, or thorn *b*) a gummed label *c*) [Colloq.] *same as* STICKLER *d*) [Slang] a knife used as a weapon

**stick·le** (-'l) *vi.* **-led, -ling** [prob. < ME. *stightlen*, to dispose, ult. < OE. *stihtan*, to arrange] **1.** to raise objections, haggle, etc., esp. in a stubborn way, usually about trifles **2.** to scruple (*at*)

**stick·le·back** (stik′'l bak′) *n.* [< OE. *sticel*, a prick + ME. *bak*, back] a small, scaleless fish with sharp spines: the male builds a nest for the eggs

**stick·ler** (stik′lər) *n.* [cf. STICKLE] **1.** a person who insists on strict observance of something [a *stickler* for discipline] **2.** [Colloq.] something puzzling to solve

**stick·pin** (-pin′) *n.* a pin, esp. one set with a gem, worn as an ornament in a cravat or necktie

**stick shift** a gearshift for a motor vehicle operated manually, rather than automatically, by moving a lever, esp. one on the floor

**stick-to-it·ive·ness** (stik tōō′it iv nis) *n.* [Colloq.] persistence; perseverance

**stick-up** (stik′up′) *n. slang term for* HOLDUP (sense 2)

**stick·y** (-ē) *adj.* **stick′i·er, stick′i·est 1.** that sticks; adhesive; clinging **2.** covered with an adhesive substance **3.** [Colloq.] hot and humid **4.** [Colloq.] difficult; troublesome [a *sticky* problem] **5.** [Colloq.] overly sentimental —**stick′i·ly** *adv.* —**stick′i·ness** *n.*

**sticky wicket 1.** *Cricket* a damp area between wickets, making play difficult and slow **2.** [Chiefly Brit.] a difficult or awkward situation

**stiff** (stif) *adj.* [OE. *stif*] **1.** hard to bend or stretch; rigid; firm **2.** hard to move or operate; not free or limber **3.** stretched tight; taut **4.** *a*) sore or limited in movement: said of joints or muscles *b*) having such joints or muscles **5.** not fluid or loose; thick; dense [a *stiff* sauce] **6.** moving swiftly, as a breeze **7.** containing much alcohol: said of a drink **8.** of high potency [a *stiff* dose of medicine] **9.** harsh [a *stiff* punishment] **10.** difficult [a *stiff* climb] **11.** constrained or awkward; not easy or graceful **12.** resolute or stubborn, as a person, a fight, etc. **13.** [Colloq.] high [a *stiff* price] **14.** [Slang] drunk —*adv.* **1.** to a stiff condition **2.** [Colloq.] completely [scared *stiff*] —*n.* [Slang] **1.** a corpse **2.** a drunken person **3.** an excessively formal person **4.** a rough person **5.** a hobo —*vt.* **stiffed, stiff′ing** [Slang] to cheat, as by leaving no tip or gratuity —**stiff′ish** *adj.* —**stiff′ly** *adv.* —**stiff′ness** *n.*

**stiff-arm** (-ärm′) *vt.* to push away (an opponent, etc.) with one's arm out straight —*n.* the act of stiff-arming

**stiff·en** (stif′'n) *vt., vi.* to make or become stiff or stiffer —**stiff′en·er** *n.*

**stiff-necked** (stif′nekt′) *adj.* stubborn; obstinate

**sti·fle** (stī′f'l) *vt.* **-fled, -fling** [ult. < MFr. *estouffer*, to smother] **1.** to suffocate; smother **2.** to suppress or check; stop [to *stifle* a sob] —*vi.* **1.** to die from lack of air **2.** to suffer from lack of fresh, cool air —**sti′fling** *adj.*

**stig·ma** (stig′mə) *n., pl.* **-mas;** also, and for **4, 5, & 6** usually, **stig·ma·ta** (stig mät′ə, stig′mə te) [L. < Gr., lit., a prick with a pointed instrument] **1.** formerly, a brand, as on a criminal **2.** a mark of disgrace or reproach **3.** a mark, sign, etc. indicating that something is not considered normal **4.** a small mark, scar, opening, etc., as a pore, on the surface of a plant or animal **5.** a spot on the skin, esp. one that bleeds as because of nervous tension **6.** [*pl.*] marks resembling the Crucifixion wounds of Jesus **7.** *Bot.* the upper tip of the style of a flower, on which pollen falls —**stig·mat′ic** (-mat′ik), **stig·mat′i·cal** *adj.*

**stig·ma·tize** (stig′mə tīz′) *vt.* **-tized′, -tiz′ing 1.** to mark with a stigma **2.** to mark as disgraceful —**stig′ma·ti·za′tion** *n.*

**stile** (stīl) *n.* [OE. *stigel* < *stigan*, to climb] **1.** a step or set of steps used in climbing over a fence or wall **2.** *shortened form of* TURNSTILE

**sti·let·to** (sti let′ō) *n., pl.* **-tos, -toes** [It., dim. of *stilo*, a dagger < L. *stilus*: see STYLE] a small dagger with a slender, tapering blade —*vt.* **-toed, -to·ing** to stab or kill with a stiletto

**still**[1] (stil) *adj.* [OE. *stille*] **1.** without sound; quiet; silent **2.** hushed, soft, or low in sound **3.** not moving; motionless: following *stand*, *sit*, *lie*, etc., sometimes regarded as an adverb **4.** calm; tranquil; unruffled [still water] **5.** not effervescent: said of wine **6.** *Motion Pictures* designating or of a single posed photograph or one made from a single frame of motion-picture film, for use as in publicity —*n.* **1.** silence; quiet [in the *still* of the night] **2.** a still photograph —*adv.* **1.** at or up to the time indicated, whether past, present, or future **2.** even; yet [still colder] **3.** nevertheless; yet [rich but *still* unhappy] **4.** [Archaic] ever; constantly —*conj.* nevertheless; yet —*vt.* to make still; specif., *a*) to make silent *b*) to make motionless *c*) to calm; relieve —*vi.* to become still —**still′ness** *n.*

**still**[2] (stil) *n.* [< obs. *still*, to DISTILL] **1.** an apparatus used for distilling liquids, esp. alcoholic liquors **2.** *same as* DISTILLERY —*vt., vi.* [Dial.] to distill (alcoholic liquor) illegally

**still·born** (stil′bôrn′) *adj.* **1.** dead at birth **2.** unsuccessful from the beginning; abortive —**still′birth′** *n.*

**still life 1.** an arrangement of objects, as fruit in a bowl, flowers in a vase, etc. as the subject of a painting, drawing, etc. **2.** *pl.* **still lifes** such a painting, etc. —**still′-life′** *adj.*

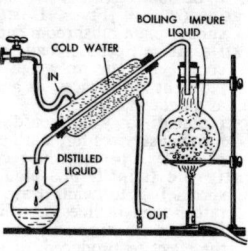

BOILING / IMPURE LIQUID / COLD WATER / IN / DISTILLED LIQUID / OUT

**STILL**

**Still·son wrench** (stil′s'n) [after its U.S. inventor (in 1869), D. *Stillson*] *a trademark for* a wrench with a jaw that moves through a collar pivoted to the shaft, used for turning pipes, etc.: the jaw tightens as pressure is applied to the handle

**still·y** (stil′ē; *for adv.* stil′lē) *adj.* **still′i·er, still′i·est** [Literary] still; silent; calm —*adv.* in a still manner; quietly

**stilt** (stilt) *n.* [prob. < MLowG. or MDu. *stelte*] **1.** either of a pair of poles, each with a footrest somewhere along its length, used for walking with the feet above the ground, as in play **2.** any of a number of long posts used to hold a building, etc. above the ground or out of the water **3.** *pl.* **stilts, stilt:** see PLURAL, II, D, 1 any of several wading birds of the avocet family

**stilt·ed** (stil′tid) *adj.* **1.** raised on or as on stilts **2.** formal or dignified in a way that is not natural; pompous —**stilt′ed·ly** *adv.* —**stilt′ed·ness** *n.*

**Stil·ton** (**cheese**) (stil′t'n) [< *Stilton*, village in EC England] a rich, crumbly cheese with veins of blue-green mold

**stim·u·lant** (stim′yə lənt) *adj.* stimulating —*n.* anything that stimulates; specif., *a*) any drug, etc. that temporarily speeds up the heartbeat or some other body process *b*) popularly, an alcoholic drink: actually alcohol is a body depressant

**stim·u·late** (-lāt′) *vt.* **-lat′ed, -lat′ing** [< L. pp. of *stimulare*, to prick < *stimulus*, a goad] **1.** to make active or more active; stir up or spur on; arouse; excite **2.** to invigorate as by an alcoholic drink **3.** *Med., Physiol.* to excite (an organ, etc.) to activity or increased activity —*vi.* to act as a stimulant or stimulus —**stim′u·lat′er, stim′u·la′tor** *n.* —**stim′u·la′tive** *adj., n.*

**stim·u·lus** (-ləs) *n., pl.* **-u·li′** (-lī′) [L., a goad] **1.** something that stirs to action or increased action; incentive **2.** *Physiol., Psychol.* any action or agent that causes or changes an activity in an organism, organ, etc.

**sti·my** (stī′mē) *n., pl.* **-mies,** *vt.* **-mied, -my·ing** *same as* STYMIE

**sting** (stiŋ) *vt.* **stung, sting′ing** [OE. *stingan*] **1.** to prick or wound with a sting: said of plants and insects **2.** to cause sharp, sudden, smarting pain to [cold wind *stings* the face] **3.** to cause to suffer mentally [his conscience *stung* him] **4.** to stimulate suddenly and sharply [*stung* into action] **5.** [Slang] to cheat; esp., to overcharge —*vi.* **1.** to use a sting **2.** to cause or feel sharp, smarting pain, either physical or mental —*n.* **1.** the act or power of stinging **2.** a pain or wound resulting from or as from stinging **3.** a thing that stimulates; goad **4.** a sharp-pointed organ, as in insects, used to prick, wound, or inject poison **5.** any of the stinging, hollow hairs on some plants, as nettles —**sting′er** *n.* —**sting′ing·ly** *adv.* —**sting′less** *adj.*

**sting·ray** (stiŋ′rā′) *n.* a large ray (fish) having having a whiplike tail with a sharp spine or spines that can inflict painful wounds: also **sting·a·ree** (stiŋ′ə rē′, stiŋ′ə rē′)

**stin·gy**[1] (stin′jē) *adj.* **stin′gi·er, stin′gi·est** [akin to STING] **1.** giving or spending grudgingly; miserly **2.** less than needed or expected —**stin′gi·ly** *adv.* —**stin′gi·ness** *n.*

**sting·y**[2] (stiŋ′ē) *adj.* stinging or capable of stinging

**stink** (stiŋk) *vi.* **stank** or **stunk, stunk, stink′ing** [OE. *stincan*] **1.** to give off a strong, bad smell **2.** to be offensive or hateful **3.** [Slang] to be no good, or of low quality —*n.* **1.** a strong, bad smell; stench **2.** [Slang] a strong public reaction, as of outrage, censure, or protest —**stink out** to drive out by a strong, bad smell —**stink up** to cause to stink —**stink′er** *n.* —**stink′ing** *adj.* —**stink′ing·ly** *adv.*

**stink bomb** a device made to burn or explode and give off an offensive smell

**stink·bug** (-bug′) *n.* any of various foul-smelling bugs

**stink·weed** (-wēd′) *n.* any of several foul-smelling plants, as the jimson weed

**stint** (stint) *vt.* [OE. *styntan*, to blunt] to limit to a certain, usually small, quantity or share —*vi.* to be sparing in giving or using —*n.* **1.** restriction; limit **2.** a task or share of work to be done —**stint′er** *n.* —**stint′ing·ly** *adv.*

**stipe** (stīp) *n.* [Fr. < L. *stipes*, tree trunk] a stalk, as that supporting a mushroom cap, fern frond, etc.

**sti·pend** (stī′pend, -pənd) *n.* [L. *stipendium* < *stips*, small coin + *pendere*, to weigh out, pay] **1.** a regular or fixed payment for services, as a salary **2.** any periodic payment, as an allowance

**sti·pen·di·ar·y** (stī pen′dē er′ē) *adj.* **1.** receiving, or performing services for, a stipend **2.** paid for by a stipend —*n.*, *pl.* **-ar′ies** a person who receives a stipend

**stip·ple** (stip′'l) *vt.* **-pled, -pling** [< Du. < *stippel*, a speckle] **1.** to paint, draw, engrave, or apply in small dots rather than in lines or solid areas **2.** to mark with dots; fleck —*n.* **1.** *a)* the art of painting, drawing, etc. in dots *b)* the effect so produced, or an effect like it, as in nature **2.** stippled work Also **stip′pling** *n.* —**stip′pler** *n.*

**stip·u·late** (stip′yə lāt′) *vt.* **-lat′ed, -lat′ing** [< L. pp. of *stipulari*, to bargain] **1.** to arrange definitely, as in a contract **2.** to specify as an essential condition of an agreement —*vi.* to make a specific demand (*for* something) as a condition of an agreement —**stip′u·la′tion** *n.* —**stip′u·la′tor** *n.* —**stip′u·la·to′ry** (-lə tôr′ē) *adj.*

**stip·ule** (stip′yōōl) *n.* [ModL. *stipula* < L., a stalk] either of a pair of small, leaflike parts at the base of some leafstalks —**stip′-u·lar** (-yōō lər) *adj.* —**stip′u·late** (-lit, -lāt′), **stip′u·lat′ed** *adj.*

**stir**[1] (stur) *vt.* **stirred, stir′ring** [OE. *styrian*] **1.** to move, shake, etc., esp. slightly **2.** to rouse from sleep, lethargy, etc. **3.** to make move or be active [*stirring* oneself to finish the work] **4.** to mix (a liquid, etc.) by moving a spoon, fork, spatula, etc. around **5.** to excite the feelings of; move deeply **6.** to incite or provoke (often with *up*) **7.** to evoke, or call up [to *stir* memories] —*vi.* **1.** to move, esp. only slightly **2.** to be busy and active **3.** to begin to show signs of activity **4.** to do or undergo mixing —*n.* **1.** a stirring, or the sound of this **2.** movement; activity **3.** excitement or commotion —**stir′rer** *n.*

**stir**[2] (stur) *n.* [prob. ult. < Romany] [Slang] a prison

**stir-cra·zy** (-krā′zē) *adj.* [see STIR[2]] [Slang] suffering nervous strain from being confined for a long time

**stir-fry** (-frī′) *vt.* **-fried′, -fry′ing** in Chinese cooking, to fry very quickly in a wok, with a little oil, while stirring constantly

**stir·ring** (stur′iŋ) *adj.* **1.** active; busy **2.** that stirs one's feelings; moving; rousing [*stirring* music]

**stir·rup** (stur′əp, stir′-) *n.* [OE. *stigrap*] **1.** a flat-bottomed ring hung by a strap from a saddle and used as a footrest **2.** any of various stirruplike supports, clamps, etc.

**stirrup (bone)** *same as* STAPES

**stitch** (stich) *n.* [OE. *stice*, a puncture] **1.** *a)* a single complete in-and-out movement of a threaded needle in sewing *b) same as* SUTURE (*n.* 3 *c*) **2.** a single loop of yarn worked off a needle in knitting, crocheting, etc. **3.** a loop, knot, etc. made by stitching **4.** a particular kind of stitch or stitching **5.** a sudden, sharp pain, as in the side **6.** a bit, as of work, or piece, as of clothing [not wearing a *stitch*] —*vi.* to make stitches; sew —*vt.* to fasten, repair, adorn, etc. with stitches; sew —**in stitches** laughing uproariously —**stitch′er** *n.*

**stitch·er·y** (-ər ē) *n.* ornamental needlework, as embroidery, crewelwork, etc.

**sti·ver** (stī′vər) *n.* [Du. *stuiver*] **1.** a former Dutch coin equal to 1/20 of a guilder **2.** a trifling sum

**St. John 1.** seaport in S New Brunswick, Canada: pop. 86,000 **2.** island of the Virgin Islands of the U.S.

**St. John's** capital of Newfoundland; seaport on the SE coast: pop. 87,000

**St. Joseph** city in NW Mo., on the Missouri River: pop. 77,000

**St-Lau·rent** (san lô rän′) city in SW Quebec, Canada: suburb of Montreal: pop. 64,000

**St. Lawrence** [< Fr. *St. Laurent,* Rom. martyr (?–285)] **1.** river flowing from Lake Ontario into the Gulf of St. Lawrence **2.** Gulf of, inlet of the Atlantic in E Canada

**St. Lawrence Seaway** inland waterway for oceangoing ships, connecting the Great Lakes with the Atlantic: it consists of the St. Lawrence River & several locks & canals

**St. Lou·is** (lōō′is, lōō′ē) city & port in E Mo., on the Mississippi: pop. 453,000 (met. area 2,345,000)

**St. Lu·ci·a** (lōō′shē ə, -shə; lōō sē′ə) country on an island in the Windward group of the West Indies: 238 sq. mi.; pop. 112,000

**St. Mo·ritz** (sänt′ mō rits′; *Fr.* san mô rēts′) mountain resort town in SE Switzerland

**stoat** (stōt) *n., pl.* **stoats, stoat:** see PLURAL, II, D, 1 [ME. *stote*] a large European weasel, esp. in its brown summer coat: see ERMINE (sense 1)

**sto·chas·tic** (stō kas′tik) *adj.* [< Gr. *stochastikos*, proceeding by guesswork, ult. < *stochos*, a target] of, pertaining to, or arising from chance; random

**stock** (stäk) *n.* [OE. *stocc*] **1.** the trunk of a tree **2.** [Archaic] *a)* a tree stump *b)* a wooden block or log **3.** anything lacking life, motion, or feeling **4.** *a)* a plant stem into which a graft is inserted *b)* a plant from which cuttings are taken **5.** a rhizome or rootstock **6.** any of certain plants of the mustard family **7.** *a)* the first of a line of descent *b)* a line of descent; ancestry or family *c)* a strain, race, or other related group of animals or plants *d)* a group of related languages or families of languages **8.** a supporting or main part, as of an implement, etc., to which the working parts are attached, as the butt of a whip, the frame of a plow, the part of a rifle holding the barrel, etc. **9.** [*pl.*] a framework; specif., *a)* a former instrument of punishment consisting of a wooden frame with holes for confining an offender's ankles and, sometimes, his wrists *b)* a frame of timbers supporting a ship during construction **10.** raw material **11.** water in which meat, fish, etc. has been boiled, used as a base for soup or gravy **12.** paper of a specified weight, kind, etc. **13.** a store or supply; specif., *a)* all the animals, equipment, etc. kept on a farm *b) short for* LIVESTOCK *c)* the total amount of goods on hand in a store, etc.; inventory **14.** *a)* the capital invested in a company or corporation by individuals through the purchase of shares *b)* the proportionate share in the ownership of a corporation held by an individual stockholder, as represented by shares of this capital in the form of stock certificates *c)* [Colloq.] a part interest in something **15.** a stock company (sense 2), or its repertoire **16.** a former type of wide, stiff cravat —*vt.* **1.** to attach to a stock [to *stock* a plow] **2.** *a)* to furnish (a farm) with stock or (a shop, etc.) with stock *b)* to supply with [to *stock* a pond with fish] **3.** to keep a supply of, as for sale or for future use —*vi.* to put in a stock, or supply (often with *up*) —*adj.* **1.** continually kept in stock [*stock* sizes] **2.** common, hackneyed, or trite [a *stock* excuse] **3.** that deals with stock [a *stock* boy] **4.** of or relating to a stock company **5.** for breeding [a *stock* mare] **6.** of, or for the raising of, livestock [*stock* farming] —**in** (or **out of**) **stock** (not) available for sale or use —**take stock 1.** to inventory the stock on hand **2.** to examine the situation before deciding or acting —**take** (or **put**) **stock in** to have faith in, regard as important, etc.

**stock·ade** (stä kād′) *n.* [< Fr. < Pr. *estacado* < *estaca,* a stake] **1.** a barrier of stakes driven into the ground side by side, for defense against attack **2.** an enclosure, as a fort, made with such stakes **3.** an enclosure for military prisoners —*vt.* **-ad′ed, -ad′ing** to surround, protect, or fortify with a stockade

**stock·bro·ker** (stäk′brō′kər) *n.* a person who acts as an agent for others in buying and selling stocks and bonds —**stock′bro′ker·age, stock′bro′king** *n.*

**stock car** a passenger automobile of standard make, modified in various ways for use in racing

**stock company 1.** a company or corporation whose capital is divided into shares **2.** a commercial theatrical company that presents a repertoire of plays, usually at one theater

**stock dividend 1.** a dividend in the form of additional shares of the same stock **2.** the payment of such a dividend

**stock exchange 1.** a place where stocks and bonds are regularly bought and sold **2.** an association of stockbrokers who meet together for buying and selling stocks and bonds according to regulations

**stock·fish** (stäk′fish′) *n., pl.* **-fish′, -fish′es:** see FISH [< MDu. < *stok,* stick + *visch,* fish] a fish split and dried without salt in the open air

**stock·hold·er** (-hōl′dər) *n.* a person owning stock or shares in a given company

**Stock·holm** (stäk′hōm′, -hōlm′; *Sw.* stôk′hôlm′) capital of Sweden, on the Baltic: pop. 768,000 (met. area 1,280,000)

**stock·i·nette, stock·i·net** (stäk′ə net′) *n.* [prob. for earlier *stocking net*] an elastic, machine-knitted cloth used for making stockings, underwear, etc.

**stock·ing** (stäk′iŋ) *n.* [< STOCK, in obs. sense of leg covering + -ING] **1.** a closefitting covering, usually knitted, for the foot and, usually, most of the leg **2.** something like this, as a patch of color on an animal's leg —**in one's stocking feet** wearing stockings or socks but no shoes

**stocking cap** a long, tapered knitted cap

**stock in trade 1.** merchandise stocked in a store **2.** tools, materials, etc. used in carrying on a trade or business **3.** any of the resources, practices, or devices always in use by a person or group

**stock·man** (-mən; *also, esp. for 2,* -man′) *n., pl.* -**men** (-mən, -men′) **1.** a man who owns or raises livestock **2.** a man who works in a stockroom or warehouse

**stock market 1.** *same as* STOCK EXCHANGE **2.** the business carried on at a stock exchange **3.** the prices quoted on stocks and bonds

**stock·pile** (-pīl′) *n.* a supply of goods, raw material, etc., stored up esp. in anticipation of future shortage or emergency —*vt., vi.* -**piled′, -pil′ing** to accumulate a stockpile (of) —**stock′pil′er** *n.*

**stock·room** (-rōōm′) *n.* a room in which a store of goods, materials, etc. is kept: also **stock room**

**stock split** the act or result of splitting stock: see SPLIT (*vt.* 7)

**stock-still** (-stil′) *adj.* perfectly motionless

**Stock·ton** (stäk′tən) [after R. F. Stockton (1795-1866), U.S. naval officer] city in C Calif.: pop. 150,000

**stock·y** (stäk′ē) *adj.* **stock′i·er, stock′i·est 1.** heavily built; sturdy; short and thickset **2.** having a strong, thick stem: said of a plant —**stock′i·ness** *n.*

**stock·yard** (stäk′yärd′) *n.* **1.** an enclosure for stock on a farm **2.** an enclosure with pens, sheds, etc. where cattle, hogs, etc. are kept just before slaughter or shipment: *usually used in pl.*

**stodg·y** (stäj′ē) *adj.* **stodg′i·er, stodg′i·est** [< dial. *stodge,* heavy food + -Y²] **1.** heavily built; bulky and slow in movement **2.** dull; uninteresting **3.** drab, unfashionable, or unattractive **4.** very old-fashioned or conventional —**stodg′i·ly** *adv.* —**stodg′i·ness** *n.*

**sto·gie, sto·gy** (stō′gē) *n., pl.* -**gies** [contr. < *Conestoga,* town in Pa.] a long, thin, inexpensive cigar

**Sto·ic** (stō′ik) *n.* [< L. < Gr. < *stoa,* colonnade: Zeno taught under a colonnade at Athens] **1.** a member of a Greek school of philosophy founded by Zeno about 308 B.C., holding that all things, properties, relations, etc. are governed by unchanging natural laws, and that the wise man should be indifferent to the external world and to passion or emotion **2.** [**s-**] a stoical person —*adj.* **1.** of the Stoics or their philosophy **2.** [**s-**] *same as* STOICAL

**sto·i·cal** (-i k′l) *adj.* **1.** showing austere indifference to joy, grief, pain, etc.; calm and unflinching under suffering, bad fortune, etc. **2.** [S-] *same as* STOIC —**sto′i·cal·ly** *adv.*

**Sto·i·cism** (-siz′m) *n.* **1.** the philosophy of the Stoics **2.** [**s-**] indifference to pleasure or pain

**stoke** (stōk) *vt., vi.* **stoked, stok′ing** [< STOKER] **1.** to stir up and feed fuel to (a fire) **2.** to tend (a furnace, boiler, etc.) **3.** to feed or eat large quantities of food; fill (*up*)

**stoke·hold** (-hōld′) *n.* **1.** the room containing the boilers on a ship **2.** *same as* STOKEHOLE (sense 2)

**stoke·hole** (-hōl′) *n.* **1.** the opening in a furnace or boiler through which the fuel is put **2.** a space in front of a furnace or boiler from which the fire is tended, as on a ship

**Stoke-on-Trent** (stōk′än trent′) city in WC England, on the Trent River: pop. 271,000

**stok·er** (stōk′ər) *n.* [Du. < *stoken,* to poke < *stok,* a stick] **1.** a man who tends a furnace, specif. of a steam boiler, as, esp. formerly, on a ship or locomotive **2.** a mechanical device that stokes a furnace

**stole¹** (stōl) *n.* [OE. < L. < Gr. *stolē,* a garment] **1.** a long, decorated strip of cloth worn like a scarf by officiating clergymen of various churches **2.** a woman's long scarf of cloth or fur worn around the shoulders, with the ends hanging in front

**stole²** (stōl) *pt. of* STEAL

**stol·en** (stō′lən) *pp. of* STEAL

**stol·id** (stäl′id) *adj.* [L. *stolidus,* slow] having or showing little or no emotion or sensitivity; unexcitable —**sto·lid·i·ty** (stə lid′ə tē), **stol′id·ness** *n.* —**stol′id·ly** *adv.*

**sto·lon** (stō′län) *n.* [ModL. *stolo* (gen. *stolonis*) < L., a shoot] *Bot.* a runner; esp., a stem running underground

**sto·ma** (stō′mə) *n., pl.* -**ma·ta** (-mə tə), STOLE -**mas** [ModL. < Gr. *stoma,* mouth] **1.** a microscopic opening in the epidermis of plants, serving for gaseous exchange **2.** *Zool.* a mouth or mouthlike opening —**sto·ma·tal** (stō′mə t′l, stäm′ə-) *adj.*

**stom·ach** (stum′ək) *n.* [< OFr. < L. < Gr. *stomachos,* gullet < *stoma,* mouth] **1.** the large, saclike organ of vertebrates into which food passes from the esophagus or gullet for storage while undergoing the early processes of digestion: in cud-chewing animals it consists of four chambers **2.** any digestive cavity **3.** the abdomen, or belly **4.** appetite for food **5.** desire or inclination of any kind —*vt.* **1.** to be able to eat or digest **2.** to tolerate; bear

**stom·ach·ache** (-āk′) *n.* pain in the stomach or abdomen

**stom·ach·er** (-ər) *n.* an ornamented, triangular piece of cloth formerly worn, esp. by women, as a covering for the chest and abdomen

**sto·mach·ic** (stə mak′ik) *adj.* **1.** of or having to do with the stomach **2.** acting as a digestive tonic Also **sto·mach′i·cal** —*n.* a digestive tonic —**sto·mach′i·cal·ly** *adv.*

**-stome** (stōm) [< Gr. *stoma,* mouth] *a combining form meaning* mouth

**-sto·mous** (stə məs) [< Gr. *stoma,* mouth] *a combining form meaning* having a (specified kind of) mouth

**stomp** (stämp) *vt., vi. var. of* STAMP; esp., to injure or kill by stamping (on) —*n.* formerly, **1.** a jazz tune with a lively rhythm and a strong beat **2.** a dance to this music

**-sto·my** (-stə mē) [< Gr. < *stoma,* mouth] *a combining form meaning* a surgical opening into (a specified part)

**stone** (stōn) *n.* [OE. *stan*] **1.** the hard, solid, nonmetallic mineral matter of which rock is composed **2.** a small piece of rock **3.** a piece of rock shaped for some purpose; specif., *a*) a building block *b*) a gravestone *c*) a milestone *d*) a grindstone **4.** *a*) the stonelike seed of certain fruits, as of a date *b*) the hard endocarp and the enclosed seed of a drupe, as of a peach **5.** *short for* PRECIOUS STONE **6.** *pl.* **stone** in Great Britain, a unit of weight equal to 14 pounds **7.** *Med. same as* CALCULUS (sense 1) —*vt.* **stoned, ston′ing 1.** to throw stones at or kill with stones **2.** to furnish, pave, line, etc. with stones **3.** to remove the stone from (a peach, etc.) —*adj.* of stone or stoneware —**cast the first stone** to be the first to censure or criticize —**leave no stone unturned** to do everything possible —**ston′er** *n.*

**stone-** [< prec., with the sense of "like a stone"] *a combining form used in hyphenated compounds, meaning* very, completely [*stone*-blind]

**Stone Age** the early period in human culture during which stone implements were used

**stone-blind** (stōn′blīnd′) *adj.* completely blind

**stone·crop** (-kräp′) *n. popular name for* SEDUM

**stone·cut·ter** (-kut′ər) *n.* a person or machine that cuts stone and makes it smooth —**stone′cut′ting** *n.*

**stoned** (stōnd) *adj.* **1.** having the stones removed [*stoned* peaches] **2.** [Slang] *a*) drunk; intoxicated *b*) under the influence of a drug

**stone-deaf** (stōn′def′) *adj.* completely deaf

**stone·fly** (-flī′) *n., pl.* -**flies** any of various soft-bodied, winged insects in an undeveloped stage that live under stones in swift streams

**Stone·henge** (stōn′henj′) [< ME. *ston,* stone + OE. *henge,* (something) hanging] a circular arrangement of prehistoric monoliths in S England

**stone·ma·son** (-mā′s′n) *n.* a person who cuts stone to shape and uses it in making walls, buildings, etc. —**stone′ma′son·ry** (-rē) *n.*

**stone's throw** a relatively short distance

**stone·ware** (stōn′wer′) *n.* a coarse, dense pottery containing much silica or sand and flint

**stone·work** (-wurk′) *n.* **1.** the art or process of working in stone **2.** something made or built in stone **3.** [*pl.*] a place where stonecutting is done

**ston·y** (stō′nē) *adj.* **ston′i·er, ston′i·est 1.** covered with or having many stones **2.** of or like stone; specif., *a*) hard *b*) unfeeling; pitiless *c*) cold; fixed; rigid Also **ston′ey** —**ston′i·ly** *adv.* —**ston′i·ness** *n.*

**stood** (stood) *pt. & pp. of* STAND

**stooge** (stōōj) *n.* [< ?] [Colloq.] **1.** an actor who aids a comedian by feeding him lines, being the victim of pranks, etc. **2.** anyone who acts as a foil, underling, etc. —*vi.* **stooged, stoog′ing** [Colloq.] to be a stooge (*for* someone)

**stool** (stōōl) *n.* [OE. *stol*] **1.** *a*) a single seat having no back or arms *b*) *same as* FOOTSTOOL **2.** a toilet, or water closet **3.** the fecal matter eliminated in a single bowel movement **4.** *a*) a root or tree stump sending out shoots *b*) a cluster of such shoots —*vi.* **1.** to put out shoots in the form of a stool **2.** [Colloq.] to act as a stool pigeon

**stool pigeon 1.** a pigeon or other bird used as a decoy **2.** a person serving as a decoy **3.** [Colloq.] a spy or informer, esp. for the police: also **stool·ie** (stōōl′ē) *n.*

**stoop¹** (stōōp) *vi.* [OE. *stupian*] **1.** to bend the body forward or in a crouch **2.** to carry the head and shoulders habitually bent forward **3.** to lower one's dignity or do something beneath one's dignity **4.** to swoop down, as a

bird of prey —*vt.* to bend (the head, etc.) forward —*n.*
**1.** the act or position of stooping the body, esp. habitually
**2.** a lowering of one's dignity **3.** a swoop, as by a hawk at prey —**stoop′er** *n.* —**stoop′ing·ly** *adv.*

**stoop²** (sto͞op) *n.* [Du. *stoep*] a small porch or platform with steps, at the door of a house

**stop** (stäp) *vt.* **stopped, stop′ping** [< OE. *-stoppian* (in comp.) < WGmc. *stoppōn*, ult. < Gr. *styppē*, tow fibers] **1.** to close by filling, shutting off, covering, etc. **2.** to staunch (a wound, etc.) **3.** to block up (a passage, pipe, etc.); obstruct: often with *up* **4.** to close (a bottle, etc.) as with a cork **5.** to cause to cease motion, activity, etc. **6.** to prevent the passage of (water, light, etc.); block **7.** to halt the progress of (a person, vehicle, etc.) **8.** *a)* to check (a blow, stroke, etc.); parry; counter *b)* to defeat (an opponent) **9.** to baffle; perplex **10.** to cease; desist from (with a gerund) [*stop* talking] **11.** to cause to end [*stop* that racket] **12.** to cause (an engine, machine, etc.) to cease operation **13.** to close (a finger hole of a wind instrument) or press down (a violin string, etc.) to produce a desired tone **14.** to keep from beginning, acting, etc.; prevent **15.** to notify one's bank to withhold payment on (one's check) —*vi.* **1.** to cease moving, walking, etc.; halt **2.** to leave off doing something; desist **3.** to cease operating or functioning **4.** to come to an end **5.** to become clogged **6.** to tarry or stay for a while (often with *at* or *in*) —*n.* **1.** a stopping or being stopped; check; cessation **2.** a finish; end **3.** a stay or brief visit **4.** a place stopped at, as on a bus route **5.** something that stops; obstruction; specif., *a)* a plug or stopper *b)* an order to withhold payment on a check *c)* a mechanical part that stops or regulates motion *d)* [Chiefly Brit.] a punctuation mark, esp. a period **6.** *a)* a stopping of a violin string, finger hole of a wind instrument, etc. to produce a desired pitch *b)* such a hole **7.** *a)* a tuned set of organ pipes, reeds, or electronic devices of the same type and tone quality *b)* a pull, lever, or key for putting such a set into or out of operation **8.** *Phonet. a)* a complete stopping of the outgoing breath, as with the lips, tongue, or velum *b)* a consonant formed in this way, as *p, b, k, g, t,* and *d* —that stops or is meant to stop [a *stop* signal] —**pull out all (the) stops 1.** to use all the stops in playing an organ **2.** to make an all-out effort —**put a stop to** to cause to cease —**stop off** to stop for a short visit on the way to a place —**stop over 1.** to visit for a while: also **stop in** (or **by**) **2.** to break a journey, as for rest

**stop·cock** (-käk′) *n.* a valve for stopping or regulating the flow of a fluid, as through a pipe

**stope** (stōp) *n.* [prob. < MLowG. *stōpe*] a steplike excavation formed by removing ore from around a mine shaft —*vt., vi.* **stoped, stop′ing** to mine in stopes

**stop·gap** (stäp′gap′) *n.* a person or thing serving as a temporary substitute —*adj.* used as a stopgap

**stop·light** (-līt′) *n.* **1.** a traffic light, esp. when red and signaling vehicles to stop **2.** a light at the rear of a vehicle, that lights up when the brakes are applied

**stop·o·ver** (-ō′vər) *n.* **1.** a brief stop or stay at a place in the course of a journey **2.** a place for such a stop Also **stop′-off′**

**stop·page** (-ij) *n.* **1.** a stopping or being stopped **2.** an obstructed condition; block

**stop·per** (-ər) *n.* **1.** a person or thing that stops **2.** something inserted to close an opening; plug —*vt.* to close with a plug or stopper

**stop·ple** (-'l) *n.* [< ME. dim. < *stoppen*, to stop] a stopper, or plug —*vt.* **-pled, -pling** to close with a stopple

**stop street** a street intersection at which vehicles must come to a complete stop before continuing

**stop·watch** (stäp′wäch′) *n.* a watch with a hand that can be started and stopped instantly so as to indicate fractions of seconds, as for timing races, etc.

**stor·age** (stôr′ij) *n.* **1.** a storing or being stored **2.** *a)* a place or space for storing goods *b)* the cost of keeping goods stored **3.** *same as* MEMORY (sense 7)

**storage battery** a battery of electrochemical cells for generating electric current: the cells can be recharged by passing a current through them in the direction opposite to the discharging flow of current

**store** (stôr) *vt.* **stored, stor′ing** [< OFr. *estorer* < L. *instaurare*, to restore] **1.** to put aside for use when needed **2.** to furnish with a supply or stock **3.** to put in a warehouse, etc. for safekeeping **4.** to be a place for the storage of **5.** to keep or put (information) in a computer memory unit —*vi.* to undergo

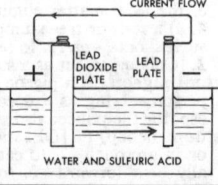

CURRENT FLOW
LEAD DIOXIDE PLATE
LEAD PLATE
WATER AND SULFURIC ACID

STORAGE BATTERY CELL
(current flow when charging)

storage in a specified manner —*n.* **1.** a supply (*of* something) for use when needed; reserve **2.** [*pl.*] supplies, esp. of food, clothing, etc. **3.** a retail establishment where goods are regularly offered for sale **4.** a storehouse; warehouse **5.** a great amount; abundance —*adj.* of a kind sold in stores —**in store** set aside for, or awaiting one in, the future —**set** (or **put** or **lay**) **store by** to value; esteem —**stor′a·ble** *adj.*

**store·front** (-frunt′) *n.* **1.** the front of a store **2.** a room at the ground front of a building, housing a retail store —*adj.* housed in a storefront [a *storefront* church]

**store·house** (-hous′) *n.* a place where things are stored; esp., a warehouse

**store·keep·er** (-kē′pər) *n.* **1.** a person in charge of stores, or supplies **2.** a retail merchant

**store·room** (-ro͞om′) *n.* a room where things are stored

**sto·rey** (stôr′ē) *n., pl.* **-reys** *Brit. sp. of* STORY²

**sto·ried¹** (stôr′ēd) *adj.* **1.** ornamented with designs showing scenes from history, a story, etc. **2.** famous in story or history

**sto·ried²** (stôr′ēd) *adj.* having stories, or floors: usually in hyphenated compounds [many-*storied*]

**stork** (stôrk) *n., pl.* **storks, stork:** see PLURAL, II, D, 1 [OE. *storc*] a large, long-legged wading bird, having a long neck and bill

**storm** (stôrm) *n.* [OE.] **1.** a disturbance of the atmosphere in which there is a strong wind usually along with rain, snow, etc. and often with thunder and lightning **2.** any heavy fall of snow, rain, etc. **3.** anything resembling a storm [a *storm* of bullets] **4.** a strong emotional outburst **5.** a strong disturbance or upheaval of a political or social nature **6.** a sudden, strong attack on a fortified place **7.** *Meteorol.* a wind whose speed is 64 to 72 miles per hour —*vi.* **1.** to blow violently, rain, snow, etc. **2.** to rage; rant **3.** to rush or move violently [to *storm* into a room] —*vt.* **1.** to attack (someone) in a vigorous or angry outburst **2.** to capture or attempt to capture (a fortified place) with a sudden, strong attack

**storm·bound** (-bound′) *adj.* halted, delayed, or cut off by storms

**storm cellar** a deep cellar for shelter during heavy windstorms

**storm door** (or **window**) an extra door (or window) placed outside the regular one as added protection against winter weather

**storm trooper** a member of Hitler's Nazi party militia, notorious for their brutal and terroristic methods

**storm·y** (stôr′mē) *adj.* **storm′i·er, storm′i·est 1.** of, characteristic of, or affected by storms **2.** having or characterized by storms **3.** violent, raging, turbulent, etc. —**storm′i·ly** *adv.* —**storm′i·ness** *n.*

**stormy petrel 1.** any of several small petrels whose presence is thought to warn of coming storms: also **storm petrel 2.** a person thought to bring trouble wherever he goes

**Stor·ting, Stor·thing** (stôr′tiŋ′) *n.* [Norw. < *stor,* great + *ting,* assembly] the parliament of Norway

**sto·ry¹** (stôr′ē) *n., pl.* **-ries** [< OFr. < L. < Gr. *historia:* see HISTORY] **1.** the telling of an event or series of events, whether true or fictitious; account; narration **2.** an anecdote or joke **3.** *a)* a fictitious literary composition shorter than a novel; narrative; tale *b)* such tales as a form of literature **4.** the plot of a novel, play, etc. **5.** *a)* a report or rumor *b)* [Colloq.] a falsehood or fib **6.** romantic legend or history **7.** a news event or a report of it, as in the newspapers —*vt.* **-ried, -ry·ing** to decorate with paintings, etc. of scenes from history or legend

**sto·ry²** (stôr′ē) *n., pl.* **-ries** [ML. *historia,* a picture (< L.: see HISTORY): prob. from use of "storied" windows or friezes marking the outside of different floors] **1.** a horizontal division of a building extending from a floor to the ceiling directly above it; floor [ten *stories* high] **2.** all the rooms on the same level of a building

**sto·ry·book** (stôr′ē book′) *n.* a book of stories, esp. one for children —*adj.* typical of romantic tales in storybooks

**sto·ry·tell·er** (-tel′ər) *n.* **1.** a person who narrates stories **2.** [Colloq.] a fibber or liar —**sto′ry·tell′ing** *n.*

**sto·tin·ka** (stô tiŋ′kä) *n., pl.* **-tin′ki** (-kē) [Bulg.] see MONETARY UNITS, table (Bulgaria)

**stoup** (sto͞op) *n.* [ON. *staup*] **1.** [Brit. Dial.] a drinking cup; tankard **2.** a basin for holy water in a church

**stout** (stout) *adj.* [OFr. *estout,* bold, prob. < Frank. *stolt*] **1.** courageous; brave **2.** *a)* strong in body; sturdy *b)* firm; substantial [a *stout* wall] **3.** powerful; forceful **4.** fat; thickset; corpulent —*n.* **1.** a fat person **2.** a garment in a size for a fat man **3.** a heavy, dark-brown brew like porter, but with a higher percentage of hops —**stout′ish** *adj.* —**stout′ly** *adv.* —**stout′ness** *n.*

**stout·heart·ed** (-här′tid) *adj.* courageous; brave —**stout′-heart′ed·ly** *adv.* —**stout′heart′ed·ness** *n.*

**stove¹** (stōv) *n.* [MDu., a heated room] an apparatus using fuel or electricity for heating, cooking, etc.

**stove²** (stōv) *alt. pt. & pp. of* STAVE

**stove·pipe** (stōv′pīp′) *n.* **1.** a metal pipe used to carry off smoke or fumes from a stove **2.** [Colloq.] a man's tall silk hat: in full, **stovepipe hat**

**stow** (stō) *vt.* [OE. *stow,* a place] **1.** to pack or store away; esp., to pack in an orderly, compact way **2.** to fill by packing thus **3.** to hold: said of a container, etc. **4.** [Slang] to stop *[stow* the chatter*]* —**stow away 1.** to put or hide away **2.** to be a stowaway **3.** to consume (food or drink), esp. in large amounts

**stow·age** (-ij) *n.* **1.** a stowing or being stowed **2.** place or room for stowing **3.** something stowed **4.** charges for stowing

**stow·a·way** (-ə wā′) *n.* a person who hides aboard a ship, airplane, etc. to get free passage, evade port officials, etc.

**Stowe** (stō), **Harriet (Elizabeth) Beecher** 1811–96; U.S. novelist: sister of Henry Ward BEECHER

**St. Paul** capital of Minn., on the Mississippi: pop. 270,000: see MINNEAPOLIS

**St. Pe·ters·burg** (pē′tərz bʉrg′) **1.** *former name of* LENINGRAD **2.** city in WC Fla., on Tampa Bay: pop. 237,000

**stra·bis·mus** (strə biz′məs) *n.* [ModL. < Gr. < *strabizein,* to squint < *strabos,* twisted] a disorder of the muscles of the eyes, as cross-eye, in which both eyes cannot be focused on the same point at the same time —**stra·bis′mal, strabis′mic** *adj.* —**stra·bis′mal·ly** *adv.*

**Strad** (strad) *n.* clipped form of STRADIVARIUS

**strad·dle** (strad′l) *vt.* -**dled,** -**dling** [freq. of STRIDE] **1.** to place oneself with a leg on either side of **2.** to spread (the legs) wide apart **3.** to take or appear to take both sides of (an issue); avoid committing oneself on —*vi.* **1.** to sit, stand, or walk with the legs wide apart **2.** to be spread apart: said of the legs **3.** to straddle an issue, etc. —*n.* **1.** the act or position of straddling **2.** a refusal to commit oneself definitely —**strad′dler** *n.*

**Stra·di·va·ri** (strä′dē vä′rē), **An·to·nio** (än tô′nyô̵) (L. name *Antonius Stradivarius*) 1644–1737; It. violin maker

**Strad·i·var·i·us** (strad′ə ver′ē əs) *n.* a string instrument, esp. a violin, made by A. Stradivari or his sons

**strafe** (strāf; *chiefly Brit.* sträf) *vt.* **strafed, straf′ing** [< G. phr. *Gott strafe England* (God punish England!) to attack with machine-gun fire from low-flying aircraft —**straf′er** *n.*

**strag·gle** (strag′l) *vi.* -**gled,** -**gling** [prob. < ME. freq. of *straken,* to roam] **1.** to stray from the course or wander from the main group **2.** to be scattered over a wide area; ramble **3.** to leave, arrive, etc. at scattered irregular intervals **4.** to hang in an untidy way, as hair, clothes, etc. —*n.* a straggly arrangement or group —**strag′gler** *n.*

**strag·gly** (-lē) *adj.* -**gli·er,** -**gli·est** spread out in a straggling, irregular way

**straight** (strāt) *adj.* [< ME. pp. of *strecchen,* to STRETCH] **1.** having the same direction throughout its length *[a straight line]* **2.** not crooked, bent, wavy, etc. *[straight hair]* **3.** upright; erect *[straight posture]* **4.** level; even *[a straight hemline]* **5.** direct; undeviating, uninterrupted, etc. *[to hold a straight course]* **6.** supporting fully the principles, candidates, etc. of a political party *[to vote a straight ticket]* **7.** following a direct course of reasoning, etc.; methodical **8.** in order; properly arranged, etc. **9.** *a)* honest; sincere *b)* reliable *[straight information]* **10.** outspoken; frank **11.** *a)* without anything added; undiluted *[a straight shot of whiskey]* *b)* not blended with neutral grain spirits **12.** not qualified, slanted, etc. *[a straight denial]* **13.** at a fixed price per unit regardless of the quantity bought *[apples at ten cents straight]* **14.** [Slang] normal or conventional; specif., not a homosexual, not a drug addict, etc. —*adv.* **1.** in a straight line or direction; unswervingly **2.** upright; erectly **3.** *a)* without detour, delay, etc. *b)* directly *[tell it straight]* *c)* without alteration, etc. *[play the role straight]* —*n.* **1.** a being straight **2.** something straight; specif., *Poker* a hand consisting of any five cards in sequence —**straight away** (or **off**) at once; without delay —**the straight and narrow (path)** a strict code of morals —**straight′ly** *adv.* —**straight′ness** *n.*

**straight angle** an angle of 180 degrees

**straight·a·way** (-ə wā′) *adj.* extending in a straight line —*n.* **1.** a race track, or part of a track, that extends in a straight line **2.** a straight and level stretch of highway

**straight chair** a chair with a back that is straight, or almost vertical, and not upholstered

**straight·edge** (-ej′) *n.* a piece of wood, etc. with a straight edge used in drawing straight lines, testing plane surfaces, etc.

**straight·en** (-'n) *vt., vi.* to make or become straight —**straighten out 1.** to make or become less confused, easier to deal with, etc. **2.** to correct or reform the behavior of —**straight′en·er** *n.*

**straight face** a facial expression showing no amusement or other emotion —**straight′-faced′** *adj.*

**straight·for·ward** (strāt′fôr′wərd) *adj.* **1.** moving or leading straight ahead; direct **2.** honest; frank; open —*adv.* in a straightforward manner: also **straight′for′wards** —**straight′for′ward·ly** *adv.* —**straight′for′ward·ness** *n.*

**straight·jack·et** (strāt′jak′it) *n.* same as STRAITJACKET

**straight-laced** (-lāst′) *adj.* same as STRAIT-LACED (sense 2)

**straight man** an actor who serves as a foil for a comedian, feeding him lines

**straight-out** (-out′) *adj.* [Colloq.] **1.** straightforward **2.** unrestrained **3.** thoroughgoing; unqualified

**straight razor** a razor with a long, unguarded blade that can be folded into the handle

**straight·way** (-wā′) *adv.* at once; without delay

**strain¹** (strān) *vt.* [ < OFr. < L. *stringere,* to draw tight] **1.** to draw or stretch tight **2.** to exert, use, or tax to the utmost *[to strain every nerve]* **3.** to injure by overexertion; wrench *[to strain a muscle]* **4.** to injure or weaken by force, pressure, etc. *[the wind strained the roof]* **5.** to stretch beyond the normal limits *[to strain a rule to one's advantage]* **6.** *a)* to pass through a screen, sieve, etc.; filter *b)* to remove by filtration, etc. **7.** to hug: now only in **to strain to one's bosom** (or **heart,** etc.) —*vi.* **1.** to make violent efforts; strive hard **2.** to be or become strained **3.** to be subjected to great stress or pressure **4.** to pull or push with force **5.** to filter, ooze, etc. —*n.* **1.** a straining or being strained **2.** great effort, exertion, etc. **3.** an injury to a part of the body as a result of overexertion *[heart strain]* **4.** stress or force **5.** a great or excessive demand on one's emotions, resources, etc. —**strained** *adj.*

**strain²** (strān) *n.* [OE. *streon,* procreation < base of *strynan,* to produce] **1.** ancestry; lineage **2.** the descendants of a common ancestor; race; stock; line **3.** a group of individuals within a species, different in one or more characters from others in the species **4.** an inherited character or tendency **5.** a trace; streak **6.** the style or tone of a speech, book, action, etc. **7.** [*often pl.*] a passage of music; tune; air

**strain·er** (-ər) *n.* a person or thing that strains; specif., a device for straining, sifting, or filtering; sieve, filter, etc.

**strait** (strāt) *adj.* [ < OFr. < L. pp. of *stringere:* see STRICT] **1.** [Archaic] *a)* narrow; tight *b)* strict; rigid **2.** [Now Rare] difficult; distressing —*n.* **1.** [*often pl.*] a narrow waterway connecting two large bodies of water **2.** [*often pl.*] difficulty; distress **3.** [Rare] an isthmus

**strait·en** (strāt′'n) *vt.* **1.** esp. formerly, *a)* to make strait or narrow *b)* to restrict or confine; hamper **2.** to bring into difficulties: usually in the phrase **in straitened circumstances,** lacking sufficient money

**strait·jack·et** (-jak′it) *n.* a coatlike device that binds the arms tight against the body: used to restrain persons in a violent state

**strait-laced** (-lāst′) *adj.* **1.** formerly, tightly laced, as a corset **2.** narrowly strict in behavior or moral views

**Straits Settlements** former Brit. crown colony in SE Asia, including Singapore, Malacca, etc.

**strake** (strāk) *n.* [akin to STRETCH] a single line of planking or plating extending along the length of a ship

**strand¹** (strand) *n.* [OE.] shore, esp. ocean shore —*vt., vi.* **1.** to run or drive aground *[a ship stranded by the storm]* **2.** to leave or be put into a difficult, helpless position *[stranded* in a strange city with no money*]*

**strand²** (strand) *n.* [ < ?] **1.** any of the threads, fibers, wires, etc. that are twisted together to form a string, rope, or cable **2.** a ropelike length of anything *[a strand of pearls, strands of hair]* **3.** any of the parts that are bound together to form a whole *[the strands of one's life]* —*vt.* to form (a rope, etc.) by twisting strands together —**strand′er** *n.*

**strange** (strānj) *adj.* **strang′er, strang′est** [ < OFr. < L. *extraneus,* foreign < *extra,* outside] **1.** foreign; alien **2.** not previously known, seen, heard, etc.; unfamiliar **3.** unusual; extraordinary **4.** peculiar; odd **5.** reserved, distant, or cold in manner **6.** lacking experience; unaccustomed *[strange* to the job*]* —*adv.* in a strange manner —**strange′ly** *adv.* —**strange′ness** *n.*

**stran·ger** (strān′jər) *n.* **1.** an outsider or newcomer **2.** a person not known or familiar to one **3.** a person unaccustomed (*to* something) *[a stranger* to hate*]*

**stran·gle** (straŋ′g'l) *vt.* -**gled,** -**gling** [ < OFr. < L. *strangulare* < Gr. < *strangalē,* halter] **1.** to kill by squeezing the throat as with the hands, a noose, etc., so as to shut off the breath **2.** to choke or suffocate in any way **3.** to suppress, stifle, or repress —*vi.* to be strangled; choke —**stran′gler** *n.*

**stran·gle·hold** (-hōld′) *n.* **1.** an illegal wrestling hold that chokes off an opponent's breath **2.** any force that restricts or suppresses freedom

**stran·gu·late** (straŋ′gyə lāt′) *vt.* -**lat′ed,** -**lat′ing** [ < L. pp. of *strangulare*] **1.** same as STRANGLE **2.** *Med.* to cause (an intestine or other tube) to become squeezed so that a flow, as of blood, is cut off —*vi. Med.* to be strangulated — **stran′gu·la′tion** *n.*

**strap** (strap) *n.* [dial. form of STROP] 1. a narrow strip of leather, plastic, cloth, etc. often with a buckle at one end, for tying or holding things together 2. any of several straplike parts or things, as a shoulder strap, a razor strop, etc. —*vt.* **strapped, strap′ping** 1. to fasten with a strap 2. to beat with a strap 3. to strop (a razor) —**strap′less** *adj.* —**strap′per** *n.*

**strapped** (strapt) *adj.* [Colloq.] hard pressed for money

**strap·ping** (strap′iŋ) *adj.* [Colloq.] tall and sturdy; robust

**Stras·bourg** (stras′bŭrg; *Fr.* strȧz bōōr′) city & port in NE France, on the Rhine: pop. 249,000

**stra·ta** (strāt′ə, strat′-) *n. alt. pl. of* STRATUM

**strat·a·gem** (strat′ə jəm) *n.* [< L. < Gr. *stratēgēma*, act of a general < *stratos*, army + *agein*, to lead] 1. a trick, scheme, or plan for deceiving an enemy in war 2. any trick or scheme for achieving some purpose

**stra·te·gic** (strə tē′jik) *adj.* 1. of or having to do with strategy 2. sound in strategy; advantageous 3. *a)* needed for carrying out military strategy or carrying on war [*strategic* materials] *b)* directed against the military and industrial installations of the enemy [*strategic* bombing] Also **stra·te′gi·cal** —**stra·te′gi·cal·ly** *adv.*

**strat·e·gist** (strat′ə jist) *n.* one skilled in strategy

**strat·e·gy** (-jē) *n., pl.* **-gies** [< Fr. < Gr. < *stratēgos*, general: see STRATAGEM] 1. *a)* the science of planning and directing large-scale military operations *b)* a plan or action based on this 2. *a)* skill in managing or planning, esp. by using stratagems *b)* a stratagem or artful means to some end Also, esp. for sense 1, **stra·te·gics** (strə tē′jiks)

**Strat·ford-on-A·von** (strat′fərd än ā′vän) town in C England, on the Avon River: birthplace & burial place of Shakespeare: pop. 19,000: also **Strat′ford-up·on-A′von**

**strat·i·fy** (strat′ə fī′) *vt.* **-fied′, -fy′ing** [< Fr. < ModL. < L. *stratum*, layer + *facere*, to make] 1. to form or arrange in layers or strata 2. to classify (people) into groups graded according to status as determined by birth, income, education, etc. —*vi.* to become stratified —**strat′i·fi·ca′tion** (-fi kā′shən) *n.*

**stra·to·cu·mu·lus** (strāt′ō kyōōm′yə ləs, strat′-) *n., pl.* **-li′** (-lī′) [ModL.: see STRATUS & CUMULUS] a cloud type arranged in horizontal patterns, with parts that are rounded, roll-shaped, etc.

**strat·o·sphere** (strat′ə sfir′) *n.* [< Fr. < ModL. *stratum*, STRATUM + Fr. *sphère*, SPHERE] the atmospheric zone extending from about six miles to about fifteen miles above the earth's surface, in which the temperature ranges from about −45°C to −75°C —**strat′o·spher′ic** (-sfer′ik, -sfir′-) *adj.*

**stra·tum** (strāt′əm, strat′-) *n., pl.* **stra′ta** (-ə), **-tums** [ModL. < L. < *stratus*, pp. of *sternere*, to spread] 1. a horizontal layer of material, esp. any of several lying one upon another; specif., *Geol.* a single layer of sedimentary rock 2. a section, level, or division, as of the atmosphere or ocean, regarded as like a stratum 3. any of the socioeconomic groups of a society as determined by birth, income, education, etc. —**stra·tal** (strāt′'l) *adj.*

**stra·tus** (-əs) *n., pl.* **stra′ti** (-ī) [L., a strewing: see prec.] a cloud type extending in a long, low, gray layer with an almost uniform base

**Strauss** (shtrous; *E.* strous) 1. **Jo·hann** (yō′hän), 1825-99; Austrian composer, esp. of waltzes 2. **Rich·ard** (riH′ärt), 1864-1949; Ger. composer & conductor

**Stra·vin·sky** (strə vin′skē; *Russ.* strȧ vēn′ski), **I·gor** (Fedorovich) (ē′gôr) 1882-1971; U.S. composer & conductor, born in Russia

**straw** (strô) *n.* [OE. *streaw*] 1. hollow stalks of grain after threshing, used for bedding, for weaving hats, baskets, etc. 2. a single one of such stalks 3. a tube used for sucking beverages 4. something, as a hat, made of straw 5. a worthless trifle —*adj.* 1. straw-colored; yellowish 2. made of straw 3. worthless; meaningless —**a straw in the wind** a sign of what may happen —**grasp** (or **clutch, catch**) **at a straw** (or **straws**) to try anything that offers even the slightest hope —**straw′y** *adj.*

**straw·ber·ry** (-ber′ē, -bər ē) *n., pl.* **-ries** [< OE. < *streaw*, straw + *berige*, berry: prob. so called from the small achenes on the fruit] 1. the small, red, fleshy fruit of a low plant of the rose family that puts out runners 2. this plant

**strawberry blonde** reddish blonde

**strawberry mark** a small, red birthmark

**straw·board** (strô′bôrd′) *n.* a coarse cardboard made of straw pulp

**straw boss** [Colloq.] 1. an assistant to a boss or foreman 2. an overseer of work with little or no authority

**straw color** a pale-yellow color —**straw′-col′ored** *adj.*

**straw·flow·er** (-flou′ər) *n.* an annual plant whose brightly colored flower heads are dried for winter bouquets

**straw-hat** (-hat′) *adj.* [from the practice, esp. formerly, of wearing straw hats in summer] designating or of a summer theater or summer theaters

**straw man** 1. a scarecrow made of straw 2. a weak argument, opponent, etc. set up by one so that he may in attacking gain an easy, showy victory 3. a person used to disguise another's activities, etc.; blind

**straw vote** an unofficial vote or poll for sampling popular opinion on candidates or on an issue

**stray** (strā) *vi.* [< OFr. *estraier*, prob. ult. < L. *extra vagari*, to wander outside] 1. to wander from a given place, course, etc.; roam 2. to go wrong; deviate [*from* what is right) 3. to wander from the subject; be inattentive or digress —*n.* a person or thing that strays; esp., a domestic animal wandering at large —*adj.* 1. having strayed; lost 2. isolated, occasional, or incidental [a few *stray* words] —**stray′er** *n.*

**streak** (strēk) *n.* [OE. *strica*] 1. a line or long, thin mark; stripe or smear 2. a ray of light or a flash, as of lightning 3. a thin layer, as of fat in meat or ore in rock 4. a tendency in one's nature [a jealous *streak*] 5. a period, spell, or run [a *streak* of victories] —*vt.* to mark with streaks —*vi.* 1. to become streaked 2. to move swiftly 3. to engage in the prank of dashing naked through a public place —**like a streak** [Colloq.] swiftly —**streak′er** *n.*

**streak·y** (-ē) *adj.* **streak′i·er, streak′i·est** marked with or occurring in streaks; uneven —**streak′i·ness** *n.*

**stream** (strēm) *n.* [OE.] 1. a current or flow of water; specif., a small river 2. a steady flow of any fluid [a *stream* of cold air] or of rays of energy [a *stream* of light] 3. a moving line of things [a *stream* of cars] 4. a trend or course [the *stream* of events] —*vi.* 1. to flow as in a stream 2. to flow (*with*) [eyes *streaming* with tears] 3. to move steadily or swiftly 4. to float or fly, as a flag in the breeze —*vt.* to cause to stream

**stream·er** (strē′mər) *n.* 1. something that streams 2. a long, narrow flag 3. any long, narrow, flowing strip of material 4. a stream of light extending up from the horizon 5. a newspaper headline across the full page

**stream·let** (strēm′lit) *n.* a small stream; rivulet

**stream·line** (-līn′) *vt.* **-lined′, -lin′ing** to make streamlined —*adj. same as* STREAMLINED

**stream·lined** (-līnd′) *adj.* 1. having a contour designed to offer the least resistance in moving through air, water, etc. 2. arranged so as to be more efficient [a *streamlined* program] 3. with no excess, as of weight, decoration, etc.; trim [a *streamlined* figure or design]

**stream of consciousness** individual conscious experience regarded as having continuity and flow: a principle made use of in novels, etc. in presenting the thoughts, inner feelings, etc. of a character in a natural, unrestrained flow

**stream·y** (strē′mē) *adj.* **stream′i·er, stream′i·est** 1. full of streams or currents 2. flowing; streaming

**street** (strēt) *n.* [OE. < L. *stræt* < L. *strata* (*via*), paved (road)] 1. a public road in a city or town; esp., a paved thoroughfare with sidewalks and buildings along the sides 2. such a road apart from its sidewalks 3. the people living, working, etc. in the buildings along a given street —*adj.* 1. of, in, on, or near the street [the *street* floor] 2. suitable for everyday wear in public [*street* clothes]

**street·car** (-kär′) *n.* a large car on rails that provides public transportation on city streets

**street·walk·er** (-wôk′ər) *n.* a prostitute who solicits customers along the streets —**street′walk′ing** *n.*

**street·wise** (-wīz′) *adj.* [Colloq.] experienced or knowledgeable in dealing with the people in urban poverty areas, esp. those areas where crime is prevalent

**strength** (streŋkth, streŋth) *n.* [OE. *strengthu*] 1. the state or quality of being strong; power; force; vigor 2. the power to resist strain, stress, etc.; toughness; durability 3. the power to resist attack 4. legal, moral, or intellectual force 5. *a)* capacity for producing an effect *b)* potency or concentration, as of drugs, liquors, etc. 6. intensity, as of sound, color, etc. 7. force as measured in numbers [an army at full *strength*] 8. vigor of feeling or expression 9. a source of strength or support —**on the strength of** based or relying on

**strength·en** (-'n) *vt., vi.* to make or become stronger —**strength′en·er** *n.*

**stren·u·ous** (stren′yōo wəs) *adj.* [L. *strenuus*] 1. requiring or characterized by great effort or energy 2. vigorous, arduous, etc. —**stren′u·ous·ly** *adv.* —**stren′u·ous·ness** *n.*

**strep** (strep) *n. shortened form of* STREPTOCOCCUS

**strep·to·coc·cus** (strep′tə käk′əs) *n., pl.* **-coc′ci** (-käk′sī) [ModL., genus name < Gr. *streptos*, twisted + COCCUS] any of a group of spherical bacteria that occur generally in chains: some species cause serious diseases —**strep′to·coc′cal** (-käk′əl), **strep′to·coc′cic** (-käk′sik) *adj.*

**strep·to·my·cin** (-mī′sin) *n.* [< Gr. *streptos*, twisted + *mykēs*, fungus] an antibiotic drug, $C_{21}H_{39}N_7O_{12}$, used in the treatment of various bacterial diseases, as tuberculosis

**stress** (stres) *n.* [< OFr., ult. < L. *strictus*, STRICT] 1. strain or straining force; specif., force exerted upon a body, that tends to strain or deform its shape 2. emphasis; importance 3. *a)* mental or physical tension or strain *b)* urgency, pressure, etc. causing this   **4.** *a)* the relative force of utterance given a syllable or word in pronunciation or, according to the meter, in verse   *b)* an accented syllable   **5.** *Music* emphasis on a note or chord —*vt.* **1.** to put stress, pressure, or strain on   **2.** to give stress or accent to   **3.** to emphasize —**stress′ful** *adj.* —**stress′ful·ly** *adv.*

**-stress** (stris) [< -STER + -ESS] *a feminine suffix corresponding to* -STER *[songstress]*

**stretch** (strech) *vt.* [OE. *streccan*] **1.** to reach out; extend *[to stretch* out a helping hand*]* **2.** to cause (the body or limbs) to reach out to full length, as in relaxing, etc.   **3.** to pull or spread out to full extent or to a greater size   **4.** to cause to extend over a given space, distance, or time *[to stretch* pipelines across a desert*]* **5.** *a)* to extend farther or too far   *b)* to strain in interpretation, scope, etc. to questionable or unreasonable limits *[to stretch* a rule*]* **6.** to make tense with effort; strain (a muscle, etc.) —*vi.* **1.** *a)* to spread out to full extent or beyond normal limits   *b)* to extend over a given space, distance, or time   **2.** *a)* to extend the body or limbs to full length, as in relaxing, etc.   *b)* to lie down at full length (usually with *out)* **3.** to become stretched to greater size, as any elastic substance —*n.* **1.** a stretching or being stretched   **2.** *a)* an unbroken period *[a stretch* of ten days*]* *b)* [Slang] a term served in prison   **3.** the extent to which something can be stretched   **4.** an unbroken length, tract, etc. *[a stretch* of beach*]* **5.** any of the sections of a race track; esp., *short for* HOMESTRETCH —*adj.* made of elasticized fabric —**stretch′a·bil′i·ty** *n.* —**stretch′a·ble** *adj.*

**stretch·er** (-ər) *n.* **1.** one that stretches; specif., *a)* a brick or stone laid lengthwise in the face of a wall   *b)* any of various devices for stretching or shaping garments, etc.   **2.** *a)* a light frame covered with canvas, etc. and used for carrying the sick, injured, or dead   *b)* any similar device, as a wheeled cot used in ambulances

**stretch·y** (-ē) *adj.* **stretch′i·er, stretch′i·est** **1.** that can be stretched; elastic   **2.** tending to stretch too far —**stretch′i·ness** *n.*

**strew** (strōō) *vt.* **strewed, strewed** or **strewn, strew′ing** [OE. *streawian*] **1.** to spread about here and there; scatter   **2.** to cover as by scattering   **3.** to be scattered over (a surface)

**stri·a** (strī′ə) *n., pl.* **stri′ae** (-ē) [L.] **1.** a narrow groove or channel   **2.** any of a number of parallel lines, stripes, furrows, etc.; specif., any of the cylindrical fibers in voluntary muscles

**stri·ate** (strī′āt; *for adj. usually* -it) *vt.* **-at·ed, -at·ing** [< L. pp. of *striare*, to groove] to mark with striae; stripe, furrow, etc. —*adj. same as* STRIATED —**stri·a′tion** *n.*

**stri·at·ed** (strī′āt id) *adj.* marked with striae, as the voluntary muscles; striped, furrowed, etc.

**strick·en** (strik′'n) *alt. pp. of* STRIKE —*adj.* **1.** struck or wounded   **2.** suffering, as from pain, trouble, etc.

**strict** (strikt) *adj.* [< L. pp. of *stringere*, to draw tight] **1.** exact or precise *[a strict* translation*]* **2.** perfect; absolute *[the strict* truth*]* **3.** *a)* enforcing rules with great care   *b)* closely enforced or rigidly maintained   *c)* disciplining severely —**strict′ly** *adv.* —**strict′ness** *n.*

**stric·ture** (strik′chər) *n.* [< L. < pp. of *stringere*, to draw tight] **1.** strong criticism; censure   **2.** a limiting or restricting condition; restriction   **3.** *Med.* an abnormal narrowing of a passage in the body —**stric′tured** *adj.*

**stride** (strīd) *vi., vt.* **strode, strid′den, strid′ing** [OE. *stridan*] **1.** to walk with long steps, esp. in a vigorous or swaggering manner   **2.** to cross with a single, long step *[he strode* over the log*]* **3.** to straddle —*n.* **1.** the act of striding   **2.** a long step   **3.** *a)* a full step in a gait, as of a horse   *b)* the distance covered by such a step   **4.** *[usually pl.]* progress; advancement *[great strides* in industry*]* —**hit one's stride** to reach one's normal level of efficiency —**take in one's stride** to cope with easily and without undue effort —**strid′er** *n.*

**stri·dent** (strīd′'nt) *adj.* [< L. prp. of *stridere*, to rasp] harsh-sounding; shrill; grating —**stri′dence, stri′den·cy** *n.* —**stri′dent·ly** *adv.*

**strid·u·late** (strij′ōō lāt′) *vi.* **-lat′ed, -lat′ing** [< ModL. pp. of *stridulare* < L. < *stridere*, to rasp] to make a shrill, grating or chirping sound by rubbing certain body parts together, as some insects do —**strid′u·la′tion** *n.*

**strid·u·lous** (-ləs) *adj.* making a shrill, grating or chirping sound: also **strid′u·lant** (-lənt)

**strife** (strīf) *n.* [OFr. *estrif*] **1.** the act of striving; contention or competition   **2.** the act or state of fighting or quarreling; struggle; conflict

**strike** (strīk) *vt.* **struck, struck** or *occas.* (but *for vt.* 12 commonly and for *vt.* 8 & 16 usually) **strick′en, strik′ing** [OE. *strican*, to go, proceed] **1.** *a)* to give a blow to; hit; smite   *b)* to give (a blow, etc.)   *c)* to remove as by a blow *[he struck* the gun from her hand*]* *d)* to make by stamping,

printing, etc. *[to strike* coins in a mint*]* *e)* to pierce or penetrate *[struck* in the head by a bullet*]* **2.** to produce (a tone or chord) by hitting (a key or keys) or touching (a string or strings) on a musical instrument   **3.** to announce (time), as with a bell: said of clocks, etc.   **4.** *a)* to cause to come into forceful contact *[to strike* one's head on a beam*]* *b)* to thrust (a weapon, etc.) in or into something   *c)* to bring forcefully into contact *[to strike* cymbals together*]* *d)* to ignite (a match) by friction   **5.** to produce (a light, etc.) by friction   **6.** to come into forceful contact with; crash into *[the stone struck* his head*]* **7.** to wound with the fangs: said of snakes   **8.** to afflict, as with disease, pain, or death   **9.** to attack   **10.** to come into contact with; specif., *a)* to fall on; shine on, as light   *b)* to reach (the eye or ear)   *c)* to come upon *[we struck* the main road*]* *d)* to make (a path, etc.) as one goes along   *e)* to notice or find suddenly   *f)* to discover, as after drilling *[to strike* oil*]* **11.** to affect as if by contact, a blow, etc.; specif., *a)* to occur to *[struck* by an idea*]* *b)* to impress (one's fancy, sense of humor, etc.)   *c)* to seem to *[it strikes* me as silly*]* *d)* to cause to become suddenly *[to be struck* dumb*]* *e)* to overcome suddenly with strong feeling *[to be struck* with amazement*]* *f)* to arouse *[to strike* terror to the heart*]* **12.** to remove *(from* a list, record, minutes, etc.)   **13.** *a)* to make and ratify (a bargain, truce, etc.)   *b)* to arrive at by figuring, etc. *[to strike* a balance*]* **14.** *a)* to lower (a sail, flag, etc.)   *b)* to take down (a tent, etc.)   *c)* to abandon (a camp) as by taking down tents   **15.** to refuse to continue to work at (a factory, company, etc.) until certain demands have been met   **16.** to level the top of (a measure of grain, etc.) as with a stick   **17.** to assume (a pose, etc.)   **18.** to put forth (roots): said of plants   **19.** *Theater a)* to dismantle (a set)   *b)* to turn (a light) down or off —*vi.* **1.** to deliver or aim a blow; hit *(at)* **2.** *a)* to attack   *b)* to take part in a fight *(for* some objective)   **3.** *a)* to make sounds as by being struck: said of a bell, clock, etc.   *b)* to be announced by the striking of a bell, etc.: said of the time   **4.** *a)* to hit; collide *(against, on,* or *upon)* *b)* to make an impression on the mind   **5.** to ignite, as a match   **6.** to seize a bait: said of a fish   **7.** to dart in an attempt to wound, as a snake   **8.** to penetrate or pierce *(to, through,* etc.)   **9.** to come suddenly *(on* or *upon)* *[we struck* on an idea*]* **10.** to run upon a reef, rock, etc.: said of a ship   **11.** *a)* to lower sail   *b)* to lower a flag in token of surrender   **12.** to refuse to continue to work until certain demands are met   **13.** to take root: said of a plant   **14.** to proceed, esp. in a new way or direction   **15.** to move or pass quickly   **16.** *U.S. Navy* to be in training *(for* a specified rating) —*n.* **1.** the act of striking; blow; specif., a military attack   **2.** *a)* a concerted refusal by employees to go on working, in an attempt to get higher wages, better working conditions, etc.   *b)* any similar refusal to do something, undertaken as a form of protest *[a hunger strike]* **3.** the discovery of a rich deposit of oil, coal, minerals, etc.   **4.** any sudden success   **5.** the pull on the line by a fish seizing bait   **6.** *Baseball* a pitched ball which is struck at but missed, delivered through the strike zone but not struck at, hit foul but not caught, etc.: three strikes put the batter out   **7.** *Bowling a)* the act of knocking down all the pins on the first bowl   *b)* the score so made —**(out) on strike** striking *(vi.* 12) —**strike dumb** to amaze; astound —**strike home** **1.** to deliver an effective blow   **2.** to have the desired effect —**strike it rich** **1.** to discover a rich deposit of ore, oil, etc.   **2.** to become rich or successful suddenly —**strike off** **1.** to remove as by a cut or blow   **2.** to print, stamp, etc. —**strike out** **1.** to remove from a record, etc.; erase   **2.** to start out   **3.** *Baseball a)* to be put out by three strikes   *b)* to put (a batter) out by pitching three strikes   **4.** to be a failure —**strike up** **1.** to begin playing, singing, etc.   **2.** to begin (a friendship, etc.)

**strike·break·er** (-brā′kər) *n.* a person who tries to break up a strike, as by supplying scabs, threatening the strikers, etc. —**strike′break′ing** *n.*

**strik·er** (strī′kər) *n.* **1.** a person who strikes; specif., a worker who is on strike   **2.** a thing that strikes, as the clapper in a bell, etc.

**strik·ing** (strī′kiŋ) *adj.* **1.** that strikes or is on strike   **2.** impressive; outstanding; remarkable —**strik′ing·ly** *adv.*

**Strind·berg** (strind′bɛrg, strin′-; *Sw.* strin′bar′y′), (**Jo·han**) **August** 1849–1912; Swed. dramatist & novelist

**string** (striŋ) *n.* [OE. *streng*] **1.** *a)* a thin length of twisted fiber or of wire, nylon, etc. used for tying, pulling, etc.   *b)* a narrow strip of leather or cloth for fastening shoes, clothing, etc.   **2.** *a)* a length of things on a string *[a string of* pearls*]* *b)* a line, row, or series of things *[a string of* houses, a *string of* victories*]* **4.** a number of business enterprises under one ownership   **5.** a group of athletes arranged according to ability: the **first string** is more skilled than the **second string**, etc.  **6.** *a)* a slender cord of wire, gut, nylon, etc., stretched on a violin, guitar, etc., and bowed, plucked, or struck to make a musical sound  *b)* [*pl.*] all the stringed instruments of an orchestra, or their players  **7.** a strong, slender, stringlike organ, structure, etc.; specif., a fiber of a plant  **8.** [Colloq.] a condition or limitation attached to a plan, offer, etc.: *usually used in pl.* —*vt.* **strung, strung** or rare **stringed, string'ing**  **1.** to provide with strings  **2.** to thread on a string  **3.** to tie, pull, hang, etc. with a string  **4.** to adjust or tune the strings of (a musical instrument)  **5.** to make nervous or keyed (*up*)  **6.** to remove the strings from (beans, etc.)  **7.** to arrange in a row or series  **8.** to extend like a string [to *string* a cable] —*vi.* **1.** to form into a string or strings  **2.** to stretch out in a line —**on a** (or **the**) **string** completely under one's control —**pull strings 1.** to get someone to use influence in one's behalf, often secretly  **2.** to direct action of others, often secretly —**string along** [Colloq.] **1.** to agree  **2.** to fool or deceive —**string up** [Colloq.] to kill by hanging —**string'less** *adj.* —**string'like'** *adj.*

**string bean** *same as* SNAP BEAN

**string·board** (-bôrd') *n.* a board placed along the side of a staircase to cover the ends of the steps

**string·course** (-kôrs') *n.* a decorative, horizontal band of brick or stone set in the wall of a building

**stringed** (striŋd) *rare pp. of* STRING — *adj.* having strings, as certain musical instruments

**strin·gent** (strin'jənt) *adj.* [< L. prp. of *stringere*, to draw tight]  **1.** strict; severe  **2.** tight in loan or investment money [a *stringent* money market]  **3.** compelling; convincing —**strin'gen·cy** *n., pl.* **-cies** —**strin'gent·ly** *adv.* —**strin'gent·ness** *n.*

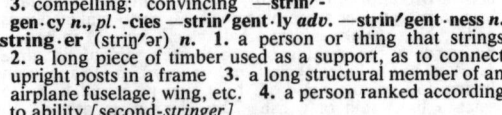

STRINGBOARD

**string·er** (striŋ'ər) *n.* **1.** a person or thing that strings  **2.** a long piece of timber used as a support, as to connect upright posts in a frame  **3.** a long structural member of an airplane fuselage, wing, etc.  **4.** a person ranked according to ability [second-*stringer*]

**string·halt** (striŋ'hôlt') *n.* a condition in horses causing the hind legs to jerk spasmodically in walking

**string·piece** (-pēs') *n.* a long, horizontal timber for supporting a framework

**string quartet** a quartet of or for players on stringed instruments, usually first and second violins, a viola, and a violoncello

**string tie** a narrow necktie, usually tied in a bow

**string·y** (striŋ'ē) *adj.* **string'i·er, string'i·est 1.** like a string or strings; long, thin, wiry, etc.  **2.** consisting of strings or fibers  **3.** having tough fibers [*stringy* meat, celery, etc.]  **4.** forming strings; ropy [*stringy* molasses] —**string'i·ness** *n.*

**strip¹** (strip) *vt.* **stripped, strip'ping** [OE. *strypan* (in comp.)]  **1.** to remove (the clothing, covering, etc.) of or from (a person); make naked  **2.** to dispossess (a person) of (honors, titles, attributes, etc.)  **3.** to plunder; rob  **4.** to peel or take off (the covering, skin, etc.) from (something)  **5.** to make bare or clear by removing fruit, growth, removable parts, etc. [to *strip* a room of furniture]  **6.** to take apart  **7.** to break or damage the thread of (a nut, bolt, etc.) or the teeth of (a gear) —*vi.* **1.** to take off all clothing; undress  **2.** to perform a striptease —**strip'per** *n.*

**strip²** (strip) *n.* [altered (after prec.) < STRIPE]  **1.** a long, narrow piece, as of land, ribbon, wood, etc.  **2.** short for COMIC STRIP  **3.** a runway for the takeoff and landing of airplanes; landing strip —*vt.* to cut or tear into strips

**stripe** (strīp) *n.* [MLowG. & MDu. *stripe*]  **1.** a long, narrow band, mark, or streak, differing as in color from the area around it  **2.** [*often pl.*] a fabric or garment with a pattern of parallel stripes  **3.** a strip of cloth or braid worn on the sleeve of a uniform to show rank, years served, etc.  **4.** type; kind; sort [a man of his *stripe*]  **5.** [Archaic] *a)* a stroke with a whip, etc.  *b)* a long welt on the skin —*vt.* **striped, strip'ing** to mark with stripes

**striped bass** (bas) a silvery game and food fish with dark stripes along the sides, found along the coasts of N. America: it goes up rivers to spawn

**strip·ling** (strip'liŋ) *n.* a grown boy; youth

**strip mining** a method of mining, esp. for coal, by laying bare a mineral deposit near the earth's surface

**stript** (stript) *rare pt. & pp. of* STRIP¹

**strip·tease** (strip'tēz') *n.* an act, as in burlesque shows, in which a woman takes off her clothes slowly, usually while music is being played —**strip'tease'** *vi.* **-teased', -teas'ing** —**strip'teas'er** *n.*

**strip·y** (strī'pē) *adj.* **strip'i·er, strip'i·est** characterized by, like, or marked with stripes

**strive** (strīv) *vi.* **strove** or **strived, striv·en** (striv''n) or **strived, striv'ing** [< OFr. < *estrif*, effort < Gmc.]  **1.** to make great efforts; try very hard [to *strive* to win]  **2.** to struggle; contend [to *strive* against tyranny] —**striv'er** *n.*

**strobe** (strōb) *n.* **1.** *shortened form of* STROBOSCOPE  **2.** an electronic tube that can emit extremely rapid, brief, and brilliant flashes of light: used in photography, the theater, etc.: also **strobe light**

**stro·bi·lus** (strō bī'ləs) *n., pl.* **-li** (-lē) [ModL. < LL. < Gr. *strobilos*, pine cone] *same as* CONE (*n.* 3): also **stro'bile** (-bīl, -bil)

**stro·bo·scope** (strō'bə skōp', sträb'ə-) *n.* [< Gr. *strobos*, a twisting round + -SCOPE]  **1.** an instrument for studying motion by illuminating a moving body, machine, etc. very briefly at frequent intervals  **2.** *same as* STROBE (*n.* 2) —**stro'bo·scop'ic** (-skäp'ik), **stro'bo·scop'i·cal** *adj.* —**stro'bo·scop'i·cal·ly** *adv.*

**strode** (strōd) *pt. of* STRIDE

**stro·ga·noff** (strô'gə nôf', strô'-) *adj.* [prob. after S. *Stroganoff*, 19th-c. Russ. gourmet] cooked with sour cream, bouillon, mushrooms, etc.: placed after the word it modifies [beef *stroganoff*]

**stroke** (strōk) *n.* [akin to OE. *strican*, to hit]  **1.** a striking of one thing against another; blow of an ax, whip, etc.  **2.** a sudden action resulting as if from a blow [a *stroke* of lightning, a *stroke* of luck]  **3.** a sudden attack, esp. of apoplexy or paralysis  **4.** *a)* a single effort to do or produce something, esp. a successful one  *b)* something accomplished by such an effort  *c)* a distinctive effect in an artistic, esp. literary, work  **5.** the sound of striking, as of a clock  **6.** *a)* a single movement, as with some tool, club, pen, etc.  *b)* any of a series of repeated rhythmic motions made against water, air, etc.  *c)* a type, manner, or rate of such a movement  **7.** a mark made by a pen, etc.  **8.** a beat of the heart  **9.** a gentle, caressing motion with the hand  **10.** *Mech.* any of the continuous, reciprocating movements of a piston, etc.  **11.** *Rowing* the rower who sits nearest the stern and sets the rate of rowing —*vt.* **stroked, strok'ing 1.** to draw one's hand, a tool, etc. gently over the surface of  **2.** to mark with strokes  **3.** to hit (a ball), as in tennis, pool, etc.  **4.** to set the rate of rowing for (a crew) —*vi.* **1.** to hit a ball in tennis, etc.  **2.** to act as stroke (*for*) in rowing —**keep stroke** to make strokes in rhythm —**strok'er** *n.*

**stroll** (strōl) *vi.* [prob. < SwissG. dial. *strolen*]  **1.** to walk in an idle, leisurely manner; saunter  **2.** to go from place to place; wander —*vt.* to stroll along or through —*n.* a strolling; leisurely walk

**stroll·er** (-ər) *n.* **1.** a person who saunters  **2.** *a)* an itinerant actor  *b)* a vagrant  **3.** a light, chairlike baby carriage

**strong** (strôŋ) *adj.* [OE. *strang*]  **1.** *a)* physically powerful; having great muscular strength; robust  *b)* healthy; sound; hale  **2.** *a)* performing well [a *strong* heart]  *b)* not easily upset [a *strong* stomach]  **3.** morally or intellectually powerful [a *strong* will or mind]  **4.** having special ability (*in a specified area*) [to be *strong* in French]  **5.** governing firmly; authoritarian  **6.** *a)* tough; firm; durable; able to resist  *b)* holding firmly [a *strong* grip]  *c)* binding tightly [*strong* glue]  **7.** having many resources; powerful in wealth, numbers, supplies, etc.  **8.** of a specified number [a force 6,000 *strong*]  **9.** having a powerful effect; drastic [*strong* measures]  **10.** having a large amount of its essential quality; not diluted [*strong* coffee]  **11.** affecting the senses powerfully [*strong* light, odor, etc.]  **12.** rancid; rank [*strong* butter]  **13.** firm and loud [a *strong* voice]  **14.** intense in degree or quality; specif., *a)* ardent; passionate  *b)* forceful; persuasive  *c)* felt deeply; decided [a *strong* opinion]  *d)* zealous [a *strong* socialist]  *e)* vigorous; forthright [*strong* language]  *f)* distinct; marked [a *strong* resemblance]  *g)* having emphasis or stress [a *strong* beat]  **15.** moving rapidly and with force [a *strong* wind]  **16.** magnifying highly [*strong* lenses]  **17.** tending toward higher prices [a *strong* market]  **18.** *Chem.* having a high ion concentration, as some acids and bases  **19.** *Gram.* expressing variation in tense by internal change of vowel rather than by inflectional endings; irregular (Ex.: swim, swam, swum) —*adv.* in a strong manner; greatly; severely —**come on strong** [Slang] to make a striking impression —**strong'ish** *adj.* —**strong'ly** *adv.*

**strong-arm** (strôŋ'ärm') *adj.* [Colloq.] using physical force —*vt.* [Colloq.] to use force upon, esp. in robbing

**strong·box** (-bäks') *n.* a heavily made box or safe for storing valuables

**strong·hold** (-hōld') *n.* **1.** a place having strong defenses; fortified place  **2.** a place where a group having certain views, attitudes, etc. is concentrated

**strong-mind·ed** (-mīn'did) *adj.* having a strong, unyielding mind or will; determined —**strong'-mind'ed·ly** *adv.* —**strong'-mind'ed·ness** *n.*

**strong-willed** (-wild') *adj.* having a strong or obstinate will

**stron·ti·um** (strän'shē əm, -shəm, -tē əm) *n.* [ModL. < *Strontian*, Scotland, where first found] a pale-yellow, metallic chemical element resembling calcium in properties and found only in combination: symbol, Sr; at. wt., 87.62; at. no., 38: a deadly radioactive isotope of strontium (**stron-**

tium 90) is present in the fallout of nuclear explosions —stron′tic *adj.*

**strop** (sträp) *n.* [OE., ult. < L. *struppus* < Gr. *strophos*, a twisted band] **1.** *same as* STRAP **2.** a device, esp. a thick leather band, used for putting a fine edge on razors —*vt.* stropped, strop′ping to sharpen on a strop —strop′per *n.*

**stro·phe** (strō′fē) *n.* [< Gr. < *strephein*, to turn] **1.** in the ancient Greek theater, *a)* a turning of the chorus from right to left *b)* that part of the song sung by the chorus during this **2.** a stanza —**stroph·ic** (sträf′ik, strō′fik), stroph′i·cal *adj.*

**strove** (strōv) *alt. pt. of* STRIVE

**strow** (strō) *vt.* strowed, strown (strōn) or strowed, strow′ing *archaic form of* STREW

**struck** (struk) *pt. & pp. of* STRIKE —*adj.* closed or affected by a labor strike

**struc·tur·al** (struk′chər əl) *adj.* **1.** of, having, or characterized by structure **2.** used in construction or building —struc′tur·al·ly *adv.*

**structural formula** a chemical formula that illustrates the arrangement of atoms and bonds in a molecule

**struc·tur·al·ist** (-ist) *n.* an advocate of structural principles, as in the analysis or application of social, economic, or linguistic theory —*adj.* of structuralists or their theories —struc′tur·al·ism *n.*

**structural linguistics** the study of a language as a coherent, uniform system without comparing it to other languages or to its forms in early periods —**structural linguist**

**struc·ture** (struk′chər) *n.* [< L. < pp. of *struere*, to arrange] **1.** manner of building, constructing, or organizing **2.** something built or constructed, as a building or dam **3.** the arrangement of all the parts of a whole [the *structure* of the atom] **4.** something composed of interrelated parts —*vt.* -tured, -tur·ing to put together according to a system; construct; organize —struc′ture·less *adj.*

**stru·del** (strōō′d'l; *G.* shtrōō′dəl) *n.* [G.] a kind of pastry made of a very thin sheet of dough filled with apple slices, cheese, etc., rolled up, and baked

**strug·gle** (strug′'l) *vi.* -gled, -gling [ME. *strogelen* < ?] **1.** to contend or fight violently with an opponent **2.** to make great efforts; strive **3.** to make one′s way with difficulty —*n.* **1.** great effort; exertion **2.** conflict; strife —strug′gler *n.* —strug′gling·ly *adv.*

**strum** (strum) *vt., vi.* strummed, strum′ming [echoic] to play (a guitar, banjo, etc.), esp. in a casual way, or without much skill —*n.* the act or sound of this —strum′mer *n.*

**strum·pet** (strum′pit) *n.* [ME. < ?] a prostitute

**strung** (strung) *pt. & alt. pp. of* STRING

**strut** (strut) *vi.* strut′ted, strut′ting [OE. *strutian*, to stand rigid] to walk in a vain, stiff, swaggering manner —*vt.* **1.** to provide with a strut or brace **2.** to make a display of —*n.* **1.** a vain, swaggering walk **2.** a brace fitted into a framework to resist pressure in the direction of its length —strut′ter *n.* —strut′ting·ly *adv.*

**strych·nine** (strik′nin, -nīn, -nēn) *n.* [Fr. < ModL. genus name < L. < Gr. *strychnos*, nightshade] a highly poisonous crystalline alkaloid, obtained from nux vomica and related plants: used in small doses as a stimulant

**St. Thomas** second largest island of the Virgin Islands of the U.S.

**Stu·art** (stōō′ərt) [< ? OE. *stigweard*, chamberlain] **1.** a masculine name **2.** ruling family of Scotland (1371–1603) & of England & Scotland (1603–1714), except during the Commonwealth (1649–60) **3. Gilbert (Charles)**, 1755–1828; U.S. portrait painter

**stub** (stub) *n.* [OE. *stybb*] **1.** a tree stump **2.** a short piece remaining after the main part has been removed or used up [a cigar *stub*] **3.** any short projection **4.** a pen with a short, blunt point **5.** a short piece of a ticket or of a leaf in a checkbook kept as a record —*vt.* stubbed, stub′bing **1.** to root out (weeds, etc.) **2.** to clear (land) of stumps **3.** to strike (one′s toe, etc.) against something by accident **4.** to put out (a cigarette, etc.) by pressing the end against a surface: often with *out*

STUB (sense 5)

**stub·ble** (stub′'l) *n.* [OFr. *estouble* < VL. < L. *stipula*, a stalk] **1.** the short stumps of grain left standing after harvesting **2.** any growth like this [a *stubble* of beard] —stub′bled *adj.* —stub′bly *adj.* -bli·er, -bli·est

**stub·born** (stub′ərn) *adj.* [prob. < OE. *stubb*, var. of *stybb*, STUB] **1.** refusing to yield, obey, or comply; resisting; resolute or obstinate **2.** done or carried on in an obstinate or persistent manner [a *stubborn* campaign] **3.** hard to handle, treat, or deal with [a *stubborn* cold] —stub′born·ly *adv.* —stub′born·ness *n.*

**stub·by** (stub′ē) *adj.* -bi·er, -bi·est **1.** covered with stubs or stubble **2.** short and heavy or dense **3.** short and thickset —stub′bi·ly *adv.* —stub′bi·ness *n.*

**stuc·co** (stuk′ō) *n., pl.* -coes, -cos [It., prob. < Gmc.] **1.** plaster or cement, either fine or coarse, used for surfacing inside or outside walls, etc. **2.** work done in this: also **stuc′co·work′** —*vt.* -coed, -co·ing to cover with stucco

**stuck** (stuk) *pt. & pp. of* STICK

**stuck-up** (stuk′up′) *adj.* [Colloq.] snobbish; conceited

**stud¹** (stud) *n.* [OE. *stud*, post] **1.** any of a series of small knobs or rounded nailheads used to ornament a surface **2.** a small, buttonlike device used as an ornament or fastener on a shirt front **3.** an upright piece in the frame of a building, to which panels, laths, etc. are nailed **4.** a metal crossbar bracing a link, as in a chain cable **5.** a projecting pin or peg used as a support, pivot, etc., or, as in an automobile tire, to increase traction on ice —*vt.* stud′ded, stud′ding **1.** to set or decorate with studs or studlike objects **2.** to be set thickly on [rocks *stud* the hillside] **3.** to scatter or cluster (something) thickly **4.** to provide (a building) with studs

**stud²** (stud) *n.* [OE. *stod*] **1.** *a)* a number of horses kept for breeding *b)* the place where these are kept **2.** *a)* same as STUDHORSE *b)* any male animal used esp. for breeding **3.** [Slang] a virile, sexually promiscuous man —*adj.* of or having to do with a stud —**at stud** available for breeding: said of male animals

**stud·book** (-book′) *n.* a register of purebred animals, esp. racehorses: also **stud book**

**stud·ding** (stud′iŋ) *n.* **1.** studs collectively, esp. for walls **2.** material used for or as studs

**stud·ding·sail** (stud′iŋ sāl′, stun′s'l) *n.* [< ?] a light, auxiliary sail set at the edge of a working sail in light weather: also **studding sail**

**stu·dent** (stōōd′'nt, styōōd′-) *n.* [< OFr. < L. prp. of *studere*, to study] **1.** a person who studies something **2.** a person who is enrolled for study in a school, college, etc. —stu′dent·ship′ *n.*

**student teacher** a student in a college or university who teaches school under supervision as a requirement for a degree in education

**stud·horse** (stud′hôrs′) *n.* a stallion kept for breeding

**stud·ied** (stud′ēd) *adj.* **1.** prepared by careful study **2.** planned beforehand; deliberate [*studied* indifference] —stud′ied·ly *adv.* —stud′ied·ness *n.*

**stu·di·o** (stōō′dē ō′, styōō′-) *n., pl.* -di·os′ [It. < L. *studium*, a study] **1.** a place where an artist or photographer does his work **2.** a place where dancing or music lessons are given **3.** a place where motion pictures are made **4.** a place where radio or television programs are produced or where recordings are made

**studio couch** a kind of couch that can be opened into a full-sized bed

**stu·di·ous** (stōō′dē əs, styōō′-) *adj.* **1.** fond of study **2.** showing close attention **3.** zealous; wholehearted —stu′di·ous·ly *adv.* —stu′di·ous·ness *n.*

**stud poker** a form of poker in which each player is dealt some cards face down and some face up

**stud·y** (stud′ē) *n., pl.* stud′ies [< OFr. < L. < *studere*, to study] **1.** the application of the mind to acquire knowledge, as by reading, investigating, etc. **2.** careful and critical examination of a subject, event, etc. **3.** a branch of learning **4.** [pl.] formal education; schooling **5.** an essay or thesis presenting results of an investigation **6.** a work of literature or art treating a subject in careful detail **7.** a first sketch for a story, picture, etc. **8.** *same as* ÉTUDE **9.** an earnest effort or intention **10.** a reverie; deep absorption **11.** a room designed for study, writing, etc. —*vt.* stud′ied, stud′y·ing **1.** to try to learn by reading, thinking, etc. **2.** *a)* to investigate carefully [to *study* the problem of crime] *b)* to look at carefully; scrutinize [to *study* a map] **3.** *a)* to read (a book, lesson, etc.) so as to know and understand it *b)* to memorize **4.** to take a course in at a school **5.** to give attention or thought to —*vi.* **1.** to study something **2.** to be a student **3.** to try hard **4.** to meditate —**study up on** [Colloq.] to make a careful study of

**stuff** (stuf) *n.* [< OFr. < *estoffer*, to cram, prob. < Frank.] **1.** the material out of which anything is or can be made **2.** basic elements; essence; character **3.** any kind of matter, unspecified **4.** cloth, esp. woolen cloth **5.** *a)* household goods *b)* personal belongings *c)* things; objects **6.** *a)* a medicine *b)* [Slang] a drug, as heroin **7.** worthless objects; junk **8.** *a)* talk or action of a specified kind *b)* foolish or worthless ideas, words, etc. [*stuff* and nonsense] **9.** [Colloq.] *a)* superior ability or special skill *b)* special control given to the ball in baseball, billiards, etc. —*vt.* **1.** to fill the inside of (something); pack; specif., *a)* to fill (a cushion, etc.) with padding *b)* to fill the skin of (a dead animal, etc.) in order to mount and preserve it *c)* to fill (a fowl, etc.) with seasoning, bread crumbs, etc. before roasting **2.** *a)* to fill too full; cram *b)* to fill to excess with food **3.** to pack or cram with **4.** to fill with information, ideas, etc. **5.** to put fraudulent votes into (a ballot box) **6.** *a)* to plug; block *b)* to choke or stop up, as with phlegm **7.** to force or push [*to stuff* money into a purse] —*vi.* to eat too much —**stuff′er** *n.*

**stuffed shirt** [Slang] a pompous, pretentious person

**stuff·ing** (-iŋ) *n.* **1.** the action of one that stuffs **2.** something used to stuff; specif., *a)* soft, springy material used as padding in cushions, etc. *b)* a seasoned mixture for stuffing fowl, etc.

**stuff·y** (stuf′ē) *adj.* **stuff′i·er, stuff′i·est 1.** poorly ventilated; having little fresh air; close **2.** having the nasal passages stopped up, as from a cold **3.** [Colloq.] *a)* dull; stodgy; old-fashioned *b)* prim; strait-laced *c)* pompous; pretentious —**stuff′i·ly** *adv.* —**stuff′i·ness** *n.*

**stul·ti·fy** (stul′tə fī′) *vt.* **-fied′, -fy′ing** [< LL. < L. *stultus,* foolish + *facere,* to make] **1.** *a)* to cause to appear foolish, stupid, absurd, etc. *b)* to make dull or sluggish **2.** to render worthless or useless —**stul′ti·fi·ca′tion** *n.*

**stum·ble** (stum′b'l) *vi.* **-bled, -bling** [< Scand.] **1.** to trip in walking, running, etc. **2.** to walk unsteadily, as when old and weak **3.** to speak, act, etc. in a confused, blundering manner **4.** to sin or err; do wrong **5.** to come by chance; happen [to *stumble* across a clue] —*vt.* **1.** to cause to stumble **2.** to perplex; confound —*n.* a stumbling —**stum′bler** *n.* —**stum′bling·ly** *adv.*

**stumbling block** an obstacle or difficulty

**stump** (stump) *n.* [prob. < or akin to MLowG. *stump*] **1.** the lower end of a tree or plant left in the ground after most of the stem or trunk has been cut off **2.** *a)* the part of an arm, leg, tooth, etc. left after the rest has been cut off or broken off *b)* a butt; stub [the *stump* of a pencil] **3.** the place where a political speech is made **4.** *a)* the sound of a heavy, tramping step *b)* such a step **5.** *Cricket* any of the three upright sticks of a wicket —*vt.* **1.** to reduce to a stump; lop **2.** to remove stumps from (land) **3.** to travel over (a district), making political speeches **4.** [Colloq.] to stub (one's toes, etc.) **5.** [Colloq.] to puzzle; baffle —*vi.* **1.** to walk heavily or clumsily, as with a wooden leg **2.** to travel about, making political speeches —**stump′er** *n.* —**stump′like′** *adj.*

**stump·y** (stum′pē) *adj.* **stump′i·er, stump′i·est 1.** covered with stumps **2.** like a stump; short and thickset; stubby —**stump′i·ness** *n.*

**stun** (stun) *vt.* **stunned, stun′ning** [< OFr. *estoner,* to stun: see ASTONISH] **1.** to make senseless or unconscious, as by a blow **2.** to shock deeply; daze; astound **3.** to overpower by a loud noise or explosion —*n.* the effect or condition of being stunned

**stung** (stuŋ) *pt. & pp. of* STING

**stunk** (stuŋk) *pp. & alt. pt. of* STINK

**stun·ner** (stun′ər) *n.* [Colloq.] a remarkably attractive, excellent, etc. person or thing

**stun·ning** (-iŋ) *adj.* **1.** that stuns **2.** [Colloq.] remarkably attractive, excellent, etc. —**stun′ning·ly** *adv.*

**stun·sail, stun·s'le** (stun′s'l) *n. same as* STUDDINGSAIL

**stunt¹** (stunt) *vt.* [OE. *stunt,* stupid] **1.** to check the growth or development of; dwarf **2.** to hinder (growth or development) —*n.* **1.** a stunting **2.** something stunted

**stunt²** (stunt) *n.* [< ?] **1.** a display of skill or daring; trick **2.** something done to attract attention, etc. —*vi.* to perform a stunt or stunts

**stunt man** a professional acrobat who takes the place of an actor when dangerous scenes involving falls, leaps, etc. are filmed

**stu·pe·fac·tion** (stōō′pə fak′shən, styōō′-) *n.* **1.** a stupefying or being stupefied **2.** stunned amazement or utter bewilderment

**stu·pe·fy** (stōō′pə fī′, styōō′-) *vt.* **-fied′, -fy′ing** [< Fr. < L. < *stupere,* to be stunned + *facere,* to make] **1.** to make dull or lethargic; stun **2.** to amaze; astonish; bewilder —**stu′pe·fi′er** *n.*

**stu·pen·dous** (stōō pen′dəs, styōō-) *adj.* [< L. gerundive of *stupere,* to be stunned] **1.** astonishing; overwhelming **2.** astonishingly great or large —**stu·pen′dous·ly** *adv.* —**stu·pen′dous·ness** *n.*

**stu·pid** (stōō′pid, styōō′-) *adj.* [L. *stupidus* < *stupere,* to be stunned] **1.** dazed; stunned; stupefied **2.** lacking normal intelligence; slow-witted; dull **3.** showing or resulting from a lack of intelligence; foolish **4.** dull and boring [a *stupid* party] —*n.* a stupid person —**stu·pid′i·ty,** *pl.* **-ties, stu′pid·ness** *n.* —**stu′pid·ly** *adv.*

**stu·por** (stōō′pər, styōō′-) *n.* [L.] **1.** a state in which the mind and senses are so dulled, as by a drug, that one can barely think, act, feel, etc. **2.** mental or moral dullness or apathy —**stu′por·ous** *adj.*

**stur·dy** (stur′dē) *adj.* **-di·er, -di·est** [OFr. *estourdi,* stunned] **1.** firm; resolute; unyielding **2.** strong; hardy **3.** strongly built —**stur′di·ly** *adv.* —**stur′di·ness** *n.*

**stur·geon** (stur′jən) *n., pl.* **stur′geons, stur′geon:** see PLURAL, II, D, 1 [OFr. *esturjon* < Frank.] any of several large food fishes having rows of spiny plates along the body and a projecting snout: valuable as a source of caviar and isinglass

**stut·ter** (stut′ər) *vt., vi.* [freq. of dial. *stut,* to stutter < ME. *stutten*] **1.** *same as* STAMMER **2.** to make (a series of repeated sounds) [*stuttering* machine guns] —*n.* the act or an instance of stuttering —**stut′ter·er** *n.*

**Stutt·gart** (stut′gärt; G. shtoot′gärt) city in S West Germany: pop. 628,000

**Stuy·ve·sant** (stī′və s'nt), **Peter** 1592–1672; Du. governor of New Netherland (1646–64)

STURGEON (to 7 ft. long)

**St. Vincent** country consisting of an island (*St. Vincent*) & a nearby island chain, in the Windward group of the West Indies: 150 sq. mi.; pop. 100,000

**sty¹** (stī) *n., pl.* **sties** [OE. *sti, stig*] **1.** a pen for pigs **2.** any foul or depraved place —*vt., vi.* **stied, sty′ing** to lodge in or as in a sty

**sty²**, **stye** (stī) *n., pl.* **sties** [< obs. dial. *styany* (taken as *sty on eye*) < dial. *styan,* rising < OE. *stigend,* prp. of *stigan,* to climb] a small, inflamed swelling of a sebaceous gland on the rim of the eyelid

**Styg·i·an** (stij′ē ən, stij′ən) *adj.* **1.** of or like the river Styx and the infernal regions **2.** [*also* s-] *a)* infernal or hellish *b)* dark or gloomy

**style** (stīl) *n.* [L. *stilus*] **1.** a pointed instrument used by the ancients in writing on wax tablets **2.** any device similar in shape or use; specif., *a)* [Obs.] a pen *b)* an etching needle *c)* a phonograph needle *d)* an engraving tool *e)* the pointer on a dial, chart, etc. *f) Bot.* the stalklike part of a carpel between the stigma and the ovary **3.** *a)* manner of expression in writing or speaking *b)* characteristic manner of expression, execution, or design, in any art, period, etc. [Gothic *style*] **4.** distinction, originality, etc. in artistic or literary expression [this author lacks *style*] **5.** the way in which anything is made or done; manner **6.** *a)* the current, fashionable way of dressing, acting, etc. *b)* something stylish *c)* a fashionable, luxurious manner [to dine in *style*] **7.** elegance of manner and bearing **8.** form of address; title [entitled to the *style* of Mayor] **9.** sort; kind; type **10.** a way of reckoning times, dates, etc.: see OLD STYLE (sense 2), NEW STYLE **11.** *Printing* a particular manner of dealing with spelling, punctuation, etc. —*vt.* **styled, styl′ing 1.** to name; call [Lincoln was *styled* the Great Emancipator] **2.** to design the style of **3.** to make conform to a particular style —**style′less** *adj.* —**styl′er** *n.*

**style·book** (-book′) *n.* a book consisting of examples or rules of style (esp. sense 11)

**styl·ish** (stī′lish) *adj.* conforming to current style, as in dress; fashionable —**styl′ish·ly** *adv.* —**styl′ish·ness** *n.*

**styl·ist** (-list) *n.* **1.** a writer, etc. whose work has style (sense 4) **2.** a person who designs, or advises on, current styles, as in dress —**sty·lis·tic** (stī lis′tik), **sty·lis′ti·cal** *adj.* —**sty·lis′ti·cal·ly** *adv.*

**styl·ize** (stī′līz) *vt.* **-ized, -iz·ing** to make conform to a given style rather than to nature; conventionalize —**styl′i·za′tion** *n.* —**styl′iz·er** *n.*

**sty·lus** (stī′ləs) *n., pl.* **-lus·es, -li** (-lī) [L., for *stilus,* pointed instrument] **1.** a style or other needlelike marking device **2.** any of various pointed tools, as for marking mimeograph stencils **3.** *a)* a sharp, pointed device for cutting the grooves of a phonograph record *b)* a phonograph needle

**sty·mie** (stī′mē) *n.* [prob. < Scot. *stymie,* a person partially blind] **1.** *Golf* the situation on a putting green when an opponent's ball lies in a direct line between the player's ball and the hole **2.** any frustrating situation —*vt.* **-mied, -mie·ing 1.** to obstruct with a stymie **2.** to block; impede Also sp. **sty′my,** *pl.* **-mies; -mied, -my·ing**

**styp·tic** (stip′tik) *adj.* [< L. < Gr. *styptikos* < *styphein,* to contract] tending to halt bleeding by contracting the tissues or blood vessels; astringent —*n.* any styptic substance

**sty·rene** (stī′rēn, stir′ēn) *n.* [< L. *styrax,* a kind of tree + -ENE] a colorless or yellowish, aromatic liquid used in the manufacture of synthetic rubber and plastics

**Sty·ro·foam** (stī′rə fōm′) *a trademark for* rigid, lightweight, cellular polystyrene, used in insulation, commercial displays, etc. —*n.* [s-] this substance

**Styx** (stiks) [L., ult. < Gr. *stygein,* to hate] *Gr. Myth.* the river encircling Hades over which Charon ferried the souls of the dead

**sua·sion** (swā′zhən) *n.* [< L. < pp. of *suadere,* to persuade] *same as* PERSUASION: now chiefly in **moral suasion,** a persuading by appealing to one's sense of morality —**sua′sive** (-siv) *adj.* —**sua′sive·ly** *adv.* —**sua′sive·ness** *n.*

**suave** (swäv; *Brit. also* swāv) *adj.* [MFr. < L. *suavis,* sweet] smoothly gracious or polite; polished; urbane —**suave′ly** *adv.* —**suave′ness** *n.* —**suav·i·ty** (swä′və tē, swav′ə-) *n.*

**sub** (sub) *n. shortened form of:* **1.** SUBMARINE **2.** SUBSCRIPTION **3.** SUBSTITUTE —*vi.* **subbed, sub′bing** [Colloq.] to be a substitute (*for* someone)

**sub-** [< L. *sub,* under] *a prefix meaning:* **1.** under, beneath [*subsoil*] **2.** lower in rank or position than [*subaltern*] **3.** to a lesser degree than, somewhat [*subtropical*] **4.** by or forming a division into smaller parts [*subsection*] **5.** *Chem.* with less than the normal amount of (the specified substance) In words of Latin origin, *sub-* is assimilated to *suc-* before *c, suf-* before *f, sug-* before *g, sum-* before *m, sup-* before *p,* and *sur-* before *r: sub-* often changes to *sus-* before *c, p,* and *t*

**sub. 1.** substitute(s) **2.** suburb(an)

**sub·ac·id** (sub as′id) *adj.* slightly acid —**sub′a·cid′i·ty** (-ə sid′ə tē) *n.* —**sub·ac′id·ly** *adv.*

**sub·al·tern** (səb ôl′tərn, sub′əl tərn) *adj.* [< Fr. < LL. < L. *sub-,* under + *alternus,* alternate] **1.** subordinate **2.** [Brit.] holding an army commission below that of captain —*n.* **1.** a subordinate **2.** [Brit.] a subaltern officer

**sub·ant·arc·tic** (sub′ant ärk′tik, -är′-) *adj.* designating or of the area surrounding the Antarctic Circle

**sub·arc·tic** (sub ärk′tik, -är′-) *adj.* designating or of the area surrounding the Arctic Circle

**sub·at·om** (sub at′əm) *n.* one of the parts that make up an atom —**sub′a·tom′ic** (-ə täm′ik) *adj.*

**sub·base·ment** (sub′bās′mənt) *n.* any floor or room below the principal basement

**sub·branch** (-branch′) *n.* a division of a branch

**sub·class** (-klas′) *n.* **1.** a division of a class; specif., *Biol.* any main natural subdivision of a class of plants or animals **2.** *Math. same as* SUBSET

**sub·clin·i·cal** (sub klin′i k'l) *adj.* without obvious clinical symptoms, as a disease in its early stages

**sub·com·mit·tee** (sub′kə mit′ē) *n.* any of the small committees with special duties into which a main committee may be divided

**sub·com·pact** (-käm′pakt) *n.* a model of automobile smaller than a compact

**sub·con·scious** (sub kän′shəs) *adj.* **1.** occurring with little or no conscious perception on the part of the individual: said of mental processes and reactions **2.** not fully conscious —**the subconscious** subconscious mental activity —**sub·con′scious·ly** *adv.* —**sub·con′scious·ness** *n.*

**sub·con·tract** (-kän′trakt; *also, for v.,* sub′kən trakt′) *n.* a secondary contract undertaking some or all of the obligations of a primary or previous contract —*vt., vi.* to make a subcontract (for) —**sub·con′trac·tor** *n.*

**sub·crit·i·cal** (-krit′i k'l) *adj.* unable to sustain a fission chain reaction: said of a nuclear reactor, etc.

**sub·cul·ture** (sub′kul′chər) *n.* **1.** a group of people of the same age, social or economic status, ethnic background, etc. and having their own interests, goals, etc. **2.** the distinct cultural patterns of such a group —**sub·cul′tur·al** *adj.*

**sub·cu·ta·ne·ous** (sub′kyoo tā′nē əs) *adj.* being, used, or introduced beneath the skin —**sub′cu·ta′ne·ous·ly** *adv.*

**sub·dea·con** (sub dē′k'n) *n.* a cleric ranking below a deacon

**sub·deb** (sub′deb′) *n.* [SUB- + DEB(UTANTE)] **1.** a girl in the years just preceding her debut into society **2.** any girl of such age —*adj.* of or suitable for a subdeb

**sub·di·vide** (sub′di vīd′, sub′di vīd′) *vt., vi.* **-vid′ed, -vid′ing 1.** to divide further after previous division **2.** to divide (land) into small parcels for sale —**sub′di·vid′er** *n.*

**sub·di·vi·sion** (sub′di vizh′ən, sub′di vizh′ən) *n.* **1.** a subdividing or being subdivided **2.** one of the parts resulting from subdividing **3.** a large tract of land subdivided into small parcels for sale

**sub·dom·i·nant** (sub däm′ə nənt) *adj.* less than or only partly dominant —*n.* **1.** something that is subdominant **2.** *Music* the fourth tone of a diatonic scale

**sub·due** (səb dōō′, -dyōō′) *vt.* **-dued′, -du′ing** [< OFr. < L. *subducere,* to remove] **1.** to win control of; conquer; vanquish **2.** to overcome, as by persuasion or training; control **3.** to make less intense; diminish; soften **4.** to repress (emotions, passions, etc.) —**sub·du′a·ble** *adj.*

**sub·em·ploy·ed** (sub′im ploid′) *adj.* designating or of those workers who are unemployed, underemployed, or employed at wages below a subsistence level

**sub·fam·i·ly** (sub′fam′ə lē) *n., pl.* **-lies 1.** any main natural subdivision of a family of plants or animals **2.** a subdivision of a language family

**sub·freez·ing** (sub′frē′ziŋ) *adj.* below freezing

**sub·gum** (sub′gum′) *adj.* [Cantonese, lit., mixed vegetables] designating any of various Chinese-American dishes, as chow mein, prepared with mushrooms, almonds, etc.

**sub·head** (sub′hed′) *n.* **1.** the title of a subdivision of a chapter, article, etc. **2.** a subordinate heading or title Also **sub′head′ing**

**sub·hu·man** (sub′hyōō′mən) *adj.* **1.** less than human **2.** nearly human

**sub·in·dex** (-in′deks) *n., pl.* **-di·ces′** (-də sēz′) *same as* SUBSCRIPT

**subj. 1.** subject **2.** subjunctive

**sub·ja·cent** (sub jā′s'nt) *adj.* [< L. prp. of *subjacere* < *sub-,* under + *jacere,* to lie] beneath; underlying —**sub·ja′cen·cy** *n.* —**sub·ja′cent·ly** *adv.*

**sub·ject** (sub′jikt; *for v.* səb jekt′) *adj.* [< OFr. < L. pp. of *subjicere* < *sub-,* under + *jacere,* to throw] **1.** under the authority or control of, or owing allegiance to, another **2.** having a disposition or tendency (*to*) [*subject* to fits of anger] **3.** liable to receive [*subject* to censure] **4.** contingent upon [*subject* to his approval] —*n.* **1.** a person under the authority or control of another; esp., a person who owes allegiance to a ruler, government, etc. **2.** someone or something undergoing a treatment, experiment, etc. **3.** something dealt with in discussion, study, writing, painting, etc.; theme **4.** the main theme of a musical composition **5.** a cause; reason **6.** a branch of learning **7.** *Gram.* the noun, noun phrase, or noun substitute in a sentence about which something is said **8.** *Philos.* the mind, or ego, that thinks or feels, as distinguished from everything outside the mind —*vt.* **1.** to bring under the authority or control of **2.** to make liable or vulnerable [*to subject* one to contempt] **3.** to cause to undergo something —**sub·jec′tion** *n.*

**sub·jec·tive** (səb jek′tiv) *adj.* **1.** of or resulting from the feelings of the subject, or person thinking; not objective; personal [*a subjective* opinion] **2.** determined by and emphasizing the ideas, feelings, etc. of the artist or writer **3.** *Gram. same as* NOMINATIVE **4.** *Med.* designating or of a symptom perceptible only to the patient —**sub·jec′tive·ly** *adv.* —**sub·jec·tiv·i·ty** (sub′jek tiv′ə tē), **sub·jec′tive·ness** *n.*

**sub·join** (səb join′) *vt.* [< MFr. < L.: see SUB- & JOIN] to add (something) at the end of a statement

**sub·ju·gate** (sub′jə gāt′) *vt.* **-gat′ed, -gat′ing** [< L. pp. of *subjugare* < *sub-,* under + *jugum,* a yoke] **1.** to bring under control or subjection; conquer **2.** to cause to become submissive —**sub′ju·ga′tion** *n.* —**sub′ju·ga′tor** *n.*

**sub·junc·tive** (səb juŋk′tiv) *adj.* [< LL. < L. pp. of *subjungere,* to SUBJOIN] designating or of that mood of a verb used to express supposition, desire, possibility, etc., rather than to state a fact [*were* in "if I *were* you" is in the *subjunctive* mood] —*n.* **1.** the subjunctive mood **2.** a verb in this mood —**sub·junc′tive·ly** *adv.*

**sub·lease** (sub′lēs′; *for v.* sub lēs′) *n.* a lease granted by a lessee to another person of all or part of the property —*vt.* **-leased′, -leas′ing** to grant, obtain, or hold a sublease of —**sub·les·see′** (-les ē′) *n.* —**sub·les·sor** (sub′les′ôr, sub′les ôr′) *n.*

**sub·let** (sub let′, sub′let′) *vt.* **-let′, -let′ting 1.** to let to another (property which one is renting) **2.** to let out (work) to a subcontractor

**sub·lieu·ten·ant** (sub′lōō ten′ənt; *Brit. & Canad.* -leften′-) *n.* [Brit. & Canad.] a naval officer ranking below a lieutenant

**sub·li·mate** (sub′lə māt′; *for adj. & n., also* -mit) *vt.* **-mat′ed, -mat′ing** [< L. pp. of *sublimare:* see ff.] **1.** to sublime (a substance) **2.** to have an ennobling effect on **3.** to express (impulses, esp. sexual impulses, regarded as unacceptable) in ways that are acceptable —*vi.* to undergo subliming —*adj.* sublimated —*n.* a substance that is the product of subliming —**sub′li·ma′tion** *n.*

**sub·lime** (sə blīm′) *adj.* [< L. < *sub-,* up to + *limen,* lintel] **1.** noble; exalted; majestic **2.** inspiring awe or admiration through grandeur, beauty, etc. —*vt.* **-limed′, -lim′ing 1.** to make sublime **2.** to purify (a solid) by heating directly to a gaseous state and condensing the vapor back into solid form —*vi.* to go through this process —**the sublime** a sublime quality or thing —**sub·lime′ly** *adv.* —**sub·lim·i·ty** (sə blim′ə tē), **sub·lime′ness** *n.*

**sub·lim·i·nal** (sub lim′ə n'l) *adj.* [< SUB- + L. *limen,* threshold + -AL] below the threshold of consciousness; specif., involving stimuli intended to take effect subconsciously through repetition —**sub·lim′i·nal·ly** *adv.*

**sub·ma·chine gun** (sub′mə shēn′) a portable, automatic or semiautomatic firearm with a short barrel and a stock, using pistol ammunition and fired from the shoulder or hip

**sub·mar·gin·al** (sub mär′ji n'l) *adj.* **1.** below minimum requirements or standards **2.** not yielding a satisfactory return [*submarginal* land] —**sub·mar′gin·al·ly** *adv.*

**sub·ma·rine** (sub′mə rēn′; *for n. & v., usually* sub′mə rēn′) *adj.* being, living, used, etc. beneath the surface of the sea —*n.* **1.** a submarine plant or animal **2.** a kind of warship, armed with torpedoes, etc., that can operate under water —*vt.* **-rined′, -rin′ing** to attack with a submarine

**submarine sandwich** *same as* HERO SANDWICH

**sub·max·il·lar·y** (sub mak′sə ler′ē) *adj.* [see SUB- & MAXILLARY] of or below the lower jaw; esp., designating or of either of two salivary glands, one on each side, beneath the lower jaw

**sub·merge** (səb murj′) *vt.* **-merged′, -merg′ing** [< L. < *sub-*, under + *mergere*, to plunge] **1.** to place under or as under water, etc. **2.** to cover over; suppress; hide **3.** to sink below a decent level of life —*vi.* to sink or plunge beneath the surface of water, etc. —**sub·mer′gence** *n.* —**sub·mer′gi·ble** *adj.*

**sub·merse** (-murs′) *vt.* **-mersed′, -mers′ing** [< L. pp. of *submergere*] *same as* SUBMERGE —**sub·mer′sion** *n.*

**sub·mers·i·ble** (-mur′sə b′l) *adj.* that can be submersed —*n.* any of various ships that can operate under water

**sub·min·i·a·ture** (sub min′ē ə chər) *adj.* designating or of a camera, electronic component, etc., smaller than one described as "miniature"

**sub·mis·sion** (səb mish′ən) *n.* [OFr. < L. < pp. of *submittere*] **1.** a submitting, yielding, or surrendering **2.** a submissive quality or state; resignation; obedience **3.** a submitting of something to another for decision, consideration, etc.

**sub·mis·sive** (-mis′iv) *adj.* having or showing a tendency to submit without resistance; docile —**sub·mis′sive·ly** *adv.* —**sub·mis′sive·ness** *n.*

**sub·mit** (-mit′) *vt.* **-mit′ted, -mit′ting** [< L. < *sub-*, under + *mittere*, to send] **1.** to present to others for decision, consideration, etc. **2.** to yield to the control, power, etc. of another; also, to allow to be subjected to treatment, analysis, etc.: often used reflexively **3.** to offer as an opinion; suggest —*vi.* **1.** *a)* to yield to the power, control, etc. of another *b)* to allow oneself to be subjected (*to* treatment, analysis, etc.) **2.** to defer to another's judgment or decision **3.** to be submissive, obedient, etc. —**sub·mit′ta·ble** *adj.* —**sub·mit′tal** *n.* —**sub·mit′ter** *n.*

**sub·nor·mal** (sub nôr′m'l) *adj.* below the normal; less than normal, esp. in intelligence —*n.* a subnormal person —**sub′nor·mal′i·ty** (-mal′ə tē) *n.* —**sub·nor′mal·ly** *adv.*

**sub·or·di·nate** (sə bôr′də nit; *for v.* -nāt′) *adj.* [< ML. pp. of *subordinare* < L. *sub-*, under + *ordinare*, to order] **1.** below another in rank, power, importance, etc.; secondary **2.** under the power or authority of another **3.** subservient or submissive **4.** *Gram.* functioning as a noun, adjective, or adverb within a sentence [a *subordinate phrase]*: cf. SUBORDINATE CLAUSE —*n.* a subordinate person or thing —*vt.* **-nat′ed, -nat′ing 1.** to place in a subordinate position **2.** to make obedient or subservient (*to*) —**sub·or′di·nate·ly** *adv.* —**sub·or′di·na′tion** *n.* —**sub·or′di·na′tive** (-nāt′iv) *adj.*

**subordinate clause** in a complex sentence, a clause that cannot function syntactically as a complete sentence by itself; dependent clause (Ex.: She will visit us *if she can*)

**subordinating conjunction** a conjunction that connects subordinate words, phrases, or clauses to some other sentence element (Ex.: *if, as, so, unless, although, when*): also **subordinate conjunction**

**sub·orn** (sə bôrn′) *vt.* [< MFr. < L. *sub-*, under + *ornare*, to furnish] **1.** to get by bribery or other illegal methods **2.** to induce or urge (another) to do something illegal, esp. to commit perjury —**sub·or·na·tion** (sub′ôr nā′shən) *n.* —**sub·or′na·tive** *adj.* —**sub·orn′er** *n.*

**sub·plot** (sub′plät′) *n.* a secondary or subordinate plot in a play, novel, etc.

**sub·poe·na** (sə pē′nə) *n.* [< ML. < L. *sub poena*, lit., under penalty: see SUB- & PAIN] a written legal order directing a person to appear in court to give testimony, etc. —*vt.* **-naed, -na·ing** to summon with such an order Also sp. **sub·pe′na**

**sub·ro·gate** (sub′rə gāt′) *vt.* **-gat′ed, -gat′ing** [< L. pp. of *subrogare, surrogare*: see SURROGATE] to substitute (one person) for another; esp., to substitute (one creditor) for another —**sub′ro·ga′tion** *n.*

**sub ro·sa** (sub rō′zə) [L., under the rose, an ancient symbol of secrecy] secretly; privately

**sub·rou·tine** (sub′rōō tēn′) *n.* a short set of instructions, often used repeatedly, that directs a digital computer in the solution of part of a problem

**sub·scribe** (səb skrib′) *vt.* **-scribed′, -scrib′ing** [L. *subscribere*: see SUB- & SCRIBE] **1.** to sign (one's name) at the end of a document, etc. **2.** to write one's signature on (a document, etc.) as an indication of consent, etc. **3.** to support; consent to **4.** to promise to contribute (money) —*vi.* **1.** to sign one's name to a document, etc. **2.** to give support or approval (*to*) **3.** to promise to contribute, or to give, a sum of money **4.** to agree to receive and pay for a periodical, theater tickets, etc. for a specified period (with *to*) —**sub·scrib′er** *n.*

**sub·script** (sub′skript) *adj.* [< L. pp. of *subscribere*, SUB-SCRIBE] written below —*n.* a figure, letter, or symbol written below and to the side of another [in $Y_3$ and $X_a$, *3* and *a* are *subscripts]*

**sub·scrip·tion** (səb skrip′shən) *n.* **1.** a subscribing **2.** something subscribed; specif., *a)* a written signature *b)* a signed document, etc. *c)* consent or sanction, esp. in writing *d)* an amount of money subscribed *e)* a formal agreement to receive and pay for a periodical, theater tickets, etc. for a specified period

**sub·se·quent** (sub′si kwənt, -kwent′) *adj.* [< L. prp. of *subsequi* < *sub-*, after + *sequi*, to follow] coming after; following in time, place, or order —**subsequent to** after; following —**sub′se·quence′** *n.* —**sub′se·quent·ly** *adv.*

**sub·serve** (səb surv′) *vt.* **-served′, -serv′ing** to be useful or helpful to (a cause, etc.); serve; aid

**sub·ser·vi·ent** (-sur′vē ənt) *adj.* **1.** that is useful or of service, esp. in a subordinate capacity **2.** submissive; obsequious —**sub·ser′vi·ence, sub·ser′vi·en·cy** *n.* —**sub·ser′vi·ent·ly** *adv.*

**sub·set** (sub′set′) *n.* a mathematical set containing some or all of the elements of a given set

**sub·side** (səb sid′) *vi.* **-sid′ed, -sid′ing** [< L. < *sub-*, under + *sidere*, to settle] **1.** to sink to the bottom; settle **2.** to sink to a lower level **3.** to become less active, intense, etc.; abate —**sub·sid′ence** (-sid′'ns, sub′si dəns) *n.*

**sub·sid·i·ar·y** (səb sid′ē er′ē) *adj.* [< L. < *subsidium:* see SUBSIDY] **1.** giving aid, service, etc.; acting as a supplement; auxiliary **2.** being in a subordinate capacity **3.** of, constituting, or maintained by a subsidy or subsidies —*n., pl.* **-ar′ies** a person or thing that is subsidiary; specif., a company (**subsidiary company**) controlled by another company that owns all or most of its shares —**sub·sid′i·ar′i·ly** *adv.*

**sub·si·dize** (sub′sə diz′) *vt.* **-dized′, -diz′ing 1.** to support with a subsidy **2.** to buy the aid of with a subsidy —**sub′si·di·za′tion** *n.* —**sub′si·diz′er** *n.*

**sub·si·dy** (sub′sə dē) *n., pl.* **-dies** [< Anglo-Fr. < L. *subsidium*, reserve troops, support] a grant of money; specif., *a)* a grant of money from one government to another *b)* a government grant to a private enterprise considered of benefit to the public

**sub·sist** (səb sist′) *vi.* [< L. < *sub-*, under + *sistere*, to stand] **1.** *a)* to continue to be or exist *b)* to continue to be in use, force, etc. **2.** to continue to live (*on* sustenance, *by* specific means, etc.) **3.** to consist (*in*) —*vt.* to maintain with sustenance

**sub·sist·ence** (-sis′təns) *n.* **1.** existence; being **2.** the act of providing sustenance **3.** means of support or livelihood; specif., the barest means needed, as just enough food, to sustain life —**sub·sist′ent** *adj.*

**sub·soil** (sub′soil′) *n.* the layer of soil beneath the surface soil —*vt.* to turn up the subsoil of —**sub′soil′er** *n.*

**sub·spe·cies** (-spē′shēz) *n.* any natural subdivision of a species that exhibits small variations in form from other subdivisions of the same species living in different regions

**sub·stance** (sub′stəns) *n.* [< OFr. < L. < *substare* < *sub-*, under + *stare*, to stand] **1.** the real or essential part of anything; essence **2.** *a)* the physical matter of which a thing consists; material *b)* matter of a particular kind or chemical composition **3.** *a)* solid quality *b)* consistency; body **4.** the real content or meaning of something said or written **5.** material possessions; property; wealth —**in substance 1.** essentially **2.** actually; really

**sub·stand·ard** (sub stan′dərd) *adj.* below standard; specif., *a)* below a legal standard *b) same as* NONSTANDARD; specif., designating or of a dialect regarded as below that used by educated speakers ["he don't" and "we ain't" are generally considered *substandard]*

**sub·stan·tial** (səb stan′shəl) *adj.* **1.** of or having substance **2.** real; actual; true **3.** strong; solid; firm **4.** ample; large **5.** of considerable value; important **6.** well-to-do **7.** with regard to essential elements —**sub·stan′ti·al′i·ty** (-shē al′ə tē), **sub·stan′tial·ness** *n.* —**sub·stan′tial·ly** *adv.*

**sub·stan·ti·ate** (səb stan′shē āt′) *vt.* **-at′ed, -at′ing 1.** to give substance to **2.** to give concrete form or body to **3.** to show to be true or real by giving evidence; prove —**sub·stan′ti·a′tion** *n.* —**sub·stan′ti·a′tive** *adj.* —**sub·stan′ti·a′tor** *n.*

**sub·stan·tive** (sub′stən tiv) *adj.* [< LL. < L. *substantia*, SUBSTANCE] **1.** existing independently **2.** of considerable amount **3.** actual; real **4.** *a)* essential *b)* having direct bearing on a matter **5.** *Gram. a)* of or expressing existence [the *substantive* verb "to be"] *b)* of or used as a substantive —*n.* **1.** something substantive **2.** a noun or any word or group of words functioning as a noun —**sub′stan·ti′val** (-tī′v'l) *adj.* —**sub′stan·ti·val·ly, sub′stan·tive·ly** *adv.* —**sub′stan·tive·ness** *n.*

**sub·sta·tion** (sub′stā′shən) *n.* a branch station

**sub·sti·tute** (sub′stə tōōt′, -tyōōt′) *n.* [< L. pp. of *substituere* < *sub-*, under + *statuere*, to put] a person or thing serving or used in place of another —*vt., vi.* **-tut′ed, -tut′ing** to put, use, or serve in place of another —*adj.* being a substitute —**sub′sti·tut′a·ble** *adj.* —**sub′sti·tu′tive** *adj.*

**sub·sti·tu·tion** (sub'stə tōō'shən, -tyōō'-) *n.* the substituting of one person or thing for another —**sub'sti·tu'-tion·al, sub'sti·tu'tion·ar'y** *adj.*

**sub·stra·tum** (sub'strāt'əm, -strat'-) *n., pl.* **-ta** (-ə), **-tums** [< L. pp. of *substernere* < *sub-*, under + *sternere*, to strew] **1.** a part, substance, etc. which lies beneath and supports another **2.** any basis or foundation **3.** loosely, *same as* SUBSOIL

**sub·struc·ture** (-struk'chər) *n.* a structure acting as a support, base, or foundation —**sub·struc'tur·al** *adj.*

**sub·sume** (səb sōōm', -syōōm') *vt.* **-sumed', -sum'ing** [< ModL. < L. *sub-*, under + *sumere*, to take] **1.** to include within a larger class, group, etc. **2.** to show (an idea, instance, etc.) to be covered by a rule, principle, etc.

**sub·sur·face** (sub'sur'fis) *adj.* lying below the surface, esp. of the earth, the oceans, etc. —*n.* a subsurface part

**sub·sys·tem** (-sis'təm) *n.* any system that is part of a larger system; component system

**sub·teen** (sub'tēn') *n.* a child nearly a teen-ager

**sub·tem·per·ate** (sub tem'pər it) *adj.* of or occurring in the colder areas of the temperate zones

**sub·ten·ant** (-ten'ənt) *n.* one who rents from a tenant; tenant of a tenant —**sub·ten'an·cy** *n.*

**sub·tend** (səb tend') *vt.* [< L. < *sub-*, under + *tendere*, to stretch] **1.** to extend under or be opposite to in position [each side of a triangle *subtends* the opposite angle] **2.** *Bot.* to enclose in an angle, as between a leaf and its stem

**sub·ter-** [L. < *subter*, below, beneath] *a prefix meaning* below, under, less than, secretly

**sub·ter·fuge** (sub'tər fyōōj') *n.* [< LL. < L. < *subter-*, below + *fugere*, to flee] any plan, action, etc. used to hide one's true objective, evade a difficult situation, etc.

**sub·ter·ra·ne·an** (sub'tə rā'nē ən) *adj.* [< L. < *sub-*, under + *terra*, earth] **1.** lying beneath the earth's surface; underground **2.** secret; hidden Also **sub'ter·ra'ne·ous** —*n.* one who lives underground —**sub'ter·ra'ne·an·ly** *adv.*

**sub·tile** (sut''l, sub'til) *adj. now rare var. of* SUBTLE —**sub'-tile·ly** *adv.* —**sub'tile·ness** *n.* —**sub'til·ty, sub·til·i·ty** (səb til'ə tē) *n., pl.* **-ties**

**sub·til·ize** (sut'''l īz', sub't'l-) *vt., vi.* **-ized', -iz'ing** to make or become subtle; esp., to discuss or argue in a subtle way —**sub'til·i·za'tion** *n.*

**sub·ti·tle** (sub'tīt''l) *n.* **1.** a secondary title of a book, play, etc. **2.** a unit of lines of dialogue or description flashed on a movie or TV screen, esp. at the bottom in translation —*vt.* **-ti'tled, -ti'tling** to add a subtitle or subtitles to

**sub·tle** (sut'''l) *adj.* **sub'tler** (-lər, -'l ər), **sub'tlest** (-list, -'l ist) [< OFr. < L. *subtilis*, orig., closely woven < *sub-*, under + *tela*, web] **1.** thin; tenuous; not dense **2.** making fine distinctions or marked by mental keenness **3.** delicately skillful; deft **4.** crafty; sly **5.** not grossly obvious [a *subtle* hint] **6.** not easily detected [a *subtle* poison] —**sub'tle·ness** *n.* —**sub'tly** *adv.*

**sub·tle·ty** (-tē) *n.* **1.** the quality or condition of being subtle **2.** *pl.* **-ties** something subtle, as a fine distinction

**sub·ton·ic** (sub tän'ik) *n. Music* the seventh tone of a diatonic scale

**sub·top·ic** (sub'täp'ik) *n.* a topic that is a division of a main topic

**sub·to·tal** (-tōt''l) *n.* a total forming part of a final, complete total —*vt., vi.* **-taled** or **-talled, -tal·ing** or **-tal·ling** to add up so as to form a subtotal

**sub·tract** (səb trakt') *vt., vi.* [< L. pp. of *subtrahere* < *sub-*, under + *trahere*, to draw] to take away or deduct (a part from a whole) or (one number or quantity from another) —**sub·tract'er** *n.* —**sub·trac'tive** *adj.*

**sub·trac·tion** (-trak'shən) *n.* a subtracting or being subtracted; esp., the mathematical process of finding the difference between two numbers or quantities

**sub·tra·hend** (sub'trə hend') *n.* [< L. gerundive of *subtrahere:* see SUBTRACT] a number or quantity to be subtracted from another

**sub·treas·ur·y** (sub'trezh'ər ē, sub trezh'-) *n., pl.* **-ur·ies** a branch treasury

**sub·trop·i·cal** (sub träp'i k'l) *adj.* designating, of, or characteristic of regions bordering on the tropical zone; nearly tropical: also **sub·trop'ic**

**sub·trop·ics** (-iks) *n.pl.* subtropical regions

**sub·urb** (sub'ərb) *n.* [< L. < *sub-*, under, near + *urbs*, town] **1.** a district on the outskirts of a city, often a separately incorporated city or town **2.** [*pl.*] a region of such districts (with *the*)

**sub·ur·ban** (sə bur'bən) *adj.* **1.** of or living in a suburb or the suburbs **2.** characteristic of the suburbs or suburbanites —**sub·ur'ban·ize'** (-īz') *vt., vi.* **-ized', -iz'ing**

**sub·ur·ban·ite** (-īt') *n.* a person living in a suburb

**sub·ur·bi·a** (sə bur'bē ə) *n.* the suburbs or suburbanites collectively: used to connote suburban values, attitudes, etc.

**sub·ven·tion** (səb ven'shən) *n.* [< OFr. < LL. < L. < *sub-*, under + *venire*, to come] a grant of money; subsidy

**sub·ver·sion** (səb vur'zhən, -shən) *n.* a subverting or being subverted; ruin; overthrow

**sub·ver·sive** (-siv) *adj.* tending or seeking to subvert —*n.* a person regarded as subversive —**sub·ver'sive·ly** *adv.* —**sub·ver'sive·ness** *n.*

**sub·vert** (səb vurt') *vt.* [< MFr. < L. < *sub-*, under + *vertere*, to turn] **1.** to overthrow or destroy (something established) **2.** to undermine or corrupt, as in morals —**sub·vert'er** *n.*

**sub·way** (sub'wā') *n.* **1.** an underground way **2.** an underground, metropolitan electric railway or the tunnel through which it runs

**suc-** *same as* SUB-: used before *c*

**suc·ceed** (sək sēd') *vi.* [L. *succedere* < *sub-*, under + *cedere*, to go] **1.** *a)* to come next after another *b)* to follow another into office, possession, etc., as by election (often with *to*) **2.** to happen or turn out as planned **3.** to accomplish something planned or tried **4.** to have success; do well; attain wealth, fame, etc. —*vt.* **1.** to follow into office, etc. **2.** to come after; follow

**suc·cess** (sək ses') *n.* [< L. < pp. of *succedere:* see prec.] **1.** *a)* a favorable outcome *b)* something having a favorable outcome **2.** the gaining of wealth, fame, etc. **3.** a successful person

**suc·cess·ful** (-fəl) *adj.* **1.** turning out to be as was hoped for **2.** having gained wealth, fame, etc. —**suc·cess'ful·ly** *adv.* —**suc·cess'ful·ness** *n.*

**suc·ces·sion** (sək sesh'ən) *n.* **1.** a succeeding or coming after another in sequence or to an office, etc. **2.** the right to succeed to an office, etc. **3.** a number of persons or things coming one after another; series; sequence **4.** *a)* a series of heirs or rightful successors *b)* the order or line of such a series —**in succession** one after another —**suc·ces'-sion·al** *adj.*

**suc·ces·sive** (sək ses'iv) *adj.* **1.** coming one after another; consecutive **2.** of succession —**suc·ces'sive·ly** *adv.* —**suc·ces'sive·ness** *n.*

**suc·ces·sor** (-ər) *n.* a person or thing that succeeds, or follows, another; esp., one who succeeds to an office, etc.

**suc·cinct** (sək sinkt') *adj.* [< L. pp. of *succingere*, to tuck up < *sub-*, under + *cingere*, to gird] **1.** clearly and briefly stated; terse **2.** concise and to the point in speaking —**suc·cinct'ly** *adv.* —**suc·cinct'ness** *n.*

**suc·cor** (suk'ər) *vt.* [< OFr. < L. *succurrere* < *sub-*, under + *currere*, to run] to aid in time of need or distress —*n.* **1.** aid; help **2.** a person or thing that succors Also, Brit. sp., **suc'cour**

**suc·co·tash** (suk'ə tash') *n.* [< AmInd.] a dish consisting of lima beans and kernels of corn cooked together

**Suc·coth** (soo kōt', sook'ōs) *n. same as* SUKKOT

**suc·cu·bus** (suk'yoo bəs) *n., pl.* **-bi** (-bī') [< ML., ult. < L. *sub-*, under + *cubare*, to lie] a female demon thought in medieval times to have sexual intercourse with sleeping men: also **suc'cu·ba** (-bə), *pl.* **-bae'** (-bē')

**suc·cu·lent** (suk'yoo lənt) *adj.* [L. *succulentus* < *sucus*, juice] **1.** juicy **2.** full of interest, vigor, etc. **3.** *Bot.* having thick, fleshy tissues for storing water, as a cactus —*n.* a succulent plant —**suc'cu·lence, suc'cu·len·cy** *n.* —**suc'cu·lent·ly** *adv.*

**suc·cumb** (sə kum') *vi.* [L. *succumbere* < *sub-*, under + *cumbere*, to lie] **1.** to give way (*to*); yield; submit **2.** to die [to *succumb* to a plague]

**such** (such) *adj.* [OE. *swilc, swelc*] **1.** *a)* of the kind mentioned or implied [one *such* as he] *b)* of the same or a similar kind [pens, pencils, and *such* supplies] **2.** certain but not specified; whatever [at *such* time as you go] **3.** so extreme; so much, etc. [*such* fun!] *Such* is used, with *as* or *that*, in making comparisons [*such* wit as his is rare] An article may occur between *such* and the noun it modifies [*such* a fool!] —*adv.* to so great a degree [*such* good news] —*pron.* such a one or ones —**as such** **1.** as being what is indicated **2.** in itself —**such as** **1.** for example **2.** like or similar to (what is specified)

**such and such** (being) something particular but not specified [he went to *such and such* a place]

**such·like** (-līk') *adj.* of such a kind; of similar kind —*pron.* persons or things of such kind

**suck** (suk) *vt.* [OE. *sucan*] **1.** *a)* to draw (liquid) into the mouth by making a vacuum with the lips, cheeks, and tongue *b)* to draw up (water, oil, etc.) by the action of a pump **2.** to take up or in as by sucking; absorb, inhale, etc. [to *suck* air into the lungs] **3.** to suck liquid from (a breast, fruit, etc.) **4.** to hold (candy, etc.) in the mouth and lick it **5.** to place (the thumb, etc.) in the mouth and draw on as if sucking *—vi.* **1.** to suck something in or up **2.** to suck milk from the breast or udder **3.** to make a sucking sound or movement *—n.* **1.** the act or sound of sucking **2.** *a)* something drawn in by sucking *b)* [Colloq.] the amount sucked at one time **—suck in 1.** to compress and pull inward *[to suck in one's belly]* **2.** [Slang] to fool, swindle, etc. **—suck up to** [Slang] to flatter or fawn upon

**suck·er** (-ər) *n.* **1.** one that sucks **2.** a carplike freshwater fish with a mouth adapted for sucking **3.** a part used for sucking; specif., *a)* a tube through which something is sucked *b)* the piston or piston valve of a suction pump *c)* an organ used by the leech, octopus, etc. for sucking or holding fast to a surface by suction **4.** a lollipop **5.** [Slang] *a)* a person easily fooled or cheated; dupe *b)* a person readily drawn to specified attractions **6.** *Bot.* a shoot from a root bud or stem bud *—vt.* **1.** to remove suckers, or shoots, from **2.** [Slang] to make a dupe of; trick *—vi.* to bear suckers, or shoots

SUCKERS

**suck·le** (suk′'l) *vt.* **-led, -ling** [prob. < ff.] **1.** to give milk to from a breast or udder; nurse **2.** to nourish; foster *—vi.* to suck milk from its mother

**suck·ling** (-liŋ) *n.* [see SUCK & -LING¹] an unweaned child or young animal

**Su·cre** (sōō′kre) city in SC Bolivia; legal capital & seat of the judiciary (cf. LA PAZ); pop. 85,000

**su·cre** (sōō′kre) *n.* [AmSp. after A.J. de Sucre, 19th-c. S. American liberator] *see* MONETARY UNITS, table (Ecuador)

**su·crose** (sōō′krōs) *n.* [< Fr. *sucre*, sugar + -OSE¹] *Chem.* pure crystalline sugar, $C_{12}H_{22}O_{11}$, extracted from sugar cane or sugar beets: it can be broken down into glucose and fructose

**suc·tion** (suk′shən) *n.* [OFr. < L. < *suctus*, pp. of *sugere*, to suck] **1.** the act or process of sucking **2.** the drawing of air out of a space to make a vacuum that will suck in surrounding air, liquid, etc. or cause something to stick to the surface **3.** the force so created *—adj.* causing or operating by suction

**suction pump** a pump that draws liquid up by suction created by pistons fitted with valves

**suc·to·ri·al** (suk tôr′ē əl) *adj.* [< ModL. < L.: see SUCTION] sucking or adapted for sucking

**Su·dan** (sōō dan′) **1.** vast plains region in NC Africa, south of the Sahara **2.** country in the E part of this region, south of Egypt: 967,500 sq. mi.; pop. 15,595,000; cap. Khartoum **—Su′da·nese′** (-də nēz′) *adj., n., pl.* **-nese′**

**Sud·bur·y** (sud′ber′ē, -bər ē) city in SE Ontario, Canada; pop. 98,000

**sud·den** (sud′'n) *adj.* [OFr. *sodain* < L. *subitaneus*, ult. < *sub-*, under + *ire*, to go] **1.** *a)* happening or coming unexpectedly; not foreseen *b)* sharp or abrupt *[a sudden turn]* **2.** done, coming, or taking place quickly or abruptly **—all of a sudden** without warning; quickly **—sud′den·ly** *adv.* **—sud′den·ness** *n.*

**sudden death** *Sports* an extra period added to a tied game, the game ending as soon as one side scores

**Su·de·ten·land** (sōō dāt′'n land′; *G.* zōō dā′tən länt′) mountainous region in N Czechoslovakia

**su·dor·if·ic** (sōō′də rif′ik, syōō′-) *adj.* [< ModL. < L. *sudor*, sweat + *facere*, to make] causing or increasing sweating *—n.* a sudorific drug, etc.

**suds** (sudz) *n.pl.* [prob. < MDu. *sudse*, marsh water] **1.** foamy, soapy water **2.** foam, froth, or lather **3.** [Slang] beer or ale *—vi.* to make suds *—vt.* [Colloq.] to wash in suds **—suds′y** *adj.* **-i·er, -i·est**

**sue** (sōō) *vt.* **sued, su′ing** [OFr. *sivre, suir*, ult. < L. *sequi*, to follow] **1.** to appeal to; petition **2.** to bring a lawsuit in court against **3.** [Archaic] to woo *—vi.* **1.** to petition; plead *(for* or *to)* **2.** [Archaic] to woo **3.** to bring legal suit **—su′er** *n.*

**suede, suède** (swād) *n.* [Fr. *Suède*, Sweden, in *gants de Suède*, Swedish gloves] **1.** tanned leather with the flesh side buffed into a nap **2.** a kind of cloth made to resemble this: also **suede cloth**

**su·et** (sōō′it, syōō′-) *n.* [dim. < Anglo-Fr. *sue* < OFr. < L. *sebum*, fat] hard fat from around the kidneys and loins of cattle and sheep: used in cooking and as a source of tallow **—su′et·y** *adj.*

**Su·ez** (sōō ez′, sōō′ez) **1.** seaport in NE Egypt, on the Suez Canal: pop. 203,000 **2. Gulf of,** NW arm of the Red Sea **3. Isthmus of,** strip of land in NE Egypt, connecting Asia & Africa

**Suez Canal** ship canal across the Isthmus of Suez, joining the Mediterranean & the Gulf of Suez

**suf-** *same as* SUB-: used before *f*

**suf·fer** (suf′ər) *vt.* [< Anglo-Fr. < OFr. < L. *sufferre* < *sub-*,

under + *ferre*, to bear] **1.** to undergo (something painful or unpleasant) **2.** to undergo (any process) **3.** to allow; tolerate **4.** to endure *—vi.* to undergo pain, harm, loss, etc. **—suf′fer·a·ble** *adj.* **—suf′fer·er** *n.* **—suf′fer·ing** *n.*

**suf·fer·ance** (suf′ər əns, suf′rəns) *n.* **1.** power or capacity to endure pain, etc. **2.** consent, toleration, etc. implied by failure to interfere or prohibit **—on sufferance** allowed or tolerated but not supported or encouraged

**suf·fice** (sə fis′, -fiz′) *vi.* **-ficed′, -fic′ing** [< OFr. < L. *sufficere* < *sub-*, under + *facere*, to make] to be enough *—vt.* [Archaic] to be enough for

**suf·fi·cien·cy** (sə fish′ən sē) *n.* **1.** sufficient means, ability, or resources; an amount that is enough **2.** a being sufficient; adequacy

**suf·fi·cient** (-′nt) *adj.* [see SUFFICE] as much as is needed; enough **—suf·fi′cient·ly** *adv.*

**suf·fix** (suf′iks; *also for v.* sə fiks′) *n.* [< ModL. < L. pp. of *suffigere* < *sub-*, under + *figere*, to fix] a syllable or group of syllables added at the end of a word or word base to change its meaning or give it grammatical function (Ex.: *-ish* in *smallish, -ed* in *walked*) *—vt.* to add as a suffix **—suf′fix·al** *adj.* **—suf·fix′ion** *n.*

**suf·fo·cate** (suf′ə kāt′) *vt.* **-cat′ed, -cat′ing** [< L. pp. of *suffocare* < *sub-*, under + *fauces*, throat] **1.** to kill by cutting off the supply of oxygen to the lungs, gills, etc. **2.** to hinder the free breathing of **3.** to smother, suppress, etc. *—vi.* **1.** to die by being suffocated **2.** to be unable to breathe freely; choke, etc. **—suf′fo·cat′ing·ly** *adv.* **—suf′fo·ca′tion** *n.* **—suf′fo·ca′tive** *adj.*

**suf·fra·gan** (suf′rə gən) *n.* [MFr. < ML. < L. *suffragari*, to support] **1.** a bishop assisting another bishop **2.** a bishop as a subordinate of his archbishop *—adj.* **1.** designating or of such a bishop **2.** subordinate to a larger see

**suf·frage** (suf′rij) *n.* [MFr. < ML. < L. *suffragium*, a vote < *sub-*, under + *fragor*, loud applause] **1.** a short prayer of supplication **2.** a vote or voting **3.** the right to vote in political elections

**suf·fra·gette** (suf′rə jet′) *n.* a woman who works for women's right to vote **—suf′fra·get′tism** *n.*

**suf·fra·gist** (suf′rə jist) *n.* a person who believes in extending the right to vote, esp. to women

**suf·fuse** (sə fyōōz′) *vt.* **-fused′, -fus′ing** [< L. pp. of *suffundere* < *sub-*, under + *fundere*, to pour] to overspread so as to fill with a glow, color, fluid, etc.: said of light, a blush, air, etc. **—suf·fu′sion** *n.* **—suf·fu′sive** (-siv) *adj.*

**sug-** *same as* SUB-: used before *g*

**sug·ar** (shoog′ər) *n.* [OFr. *sucre*, ult. < Per. *šakar* < Sans. *sarkarā*] **1.** any of a class of sweet, soluble, crystalline carbohydrates, including sucrose, lactose, maltose, glucose, fructose, etc. **2.** sucrose in crystalline or powdered form: it is the common sugar used to sweeten food **3.** a bowl for sugar, specif. as forming a set with a creamer **4.** *short for* SUGAR DIABETES **5.** [Colloq.] sweetheart **6.** [Slang] money *—vt.* **1.** to put sugar on or in **2.** to make seem pleasant or less bad *—vi.* **1.** to form sugar **2.** to boil down maple syrup to form maple sugar (usually with *off*) **—sug′ar·less** *adj.* **—sug′ar·like′** *adj.*

**sugar beet** a variety of beet with a white root from which common sugar is got

**sug·ar·bush** (-boosh′) *n.* a grove of sugar maples

**sugar cane** a very tall, tropical grass cultivated as the main source of common sugar

**sug·ar·coat** (-kōt′) *vt.* **1.** to coat with sugar **2.** to make seem less unpleasant *[to sugarcoat bad news]*

**sug·ar·cured** (-kyoord′) *adj.* treated with a pickling preparation of sugar, salt, etc., as ham

**sugar diabetes** *popular term for* DIABETES MELLITUS

**sugar loaf 1.** a conical mass of crystallized sugar **2.** a similarly shaped hill, etc.

**sugar maple** an E N. American maple valued for its hard wood and for its sap, which yields maple syrup

SUGAR CANE

**sug·ar·plum** (-plum′) *n.* a round or oval piece of sugary candy; bonbon

**sug·ar·y** (shoog′ər ē) *adj.* **1.** of, like, or containing sugar; sweet, granular, etc. **2.** too sweet or sentimental **—sug′ar·i·ness** *n.*

**sug·gest** (səg jest′; *also, & Brit. usually,* sə jest′) *vt.* [< L. pp. of *suggerere* < *sub-*, under + *gerere*, to carry] **1.** to mention as something to think over, act on, etc.: bring to the mind for consideration **2.** to call to mind through association of ideas *[objects suggested by the shapes of clouds]* **3.** to propose (someone or something) as a possibility **4.** to imply; intimate **—sug·gest′er** *n.*

**sug·gest·i·ble** (-jes′tə b'l) *adj.* easily influenced by suggestion —**sug·gest′i·bil′i·ty** *n.*

**sug·ges·tion** (-jes′chən) *n.* **1.** a suggesting or being suggested **2.** something suggested **3.** the process by which one idea leads to another through association of ideas **4.** a faint hint; trace **5.** *Psychol.* the inducing of an idea that is accepted or acted on readily without questioning

**sug·ges·tive** (-jes′tiv) *adj.* **1.** that suggests or tends to suggest ideas **2.** tending to suggest something considered improper or indecent —**sug·ges′tive·ly** *adv.* —**sug·ges′tive·ness** *n.*

**su·i·ci·dal** (s̅o̅o̅′ə sīd′əl) *adj.* **1.** of, involving, or leading to suicide **2.** having an urge to commit suicide **3.** rash to the point of being dangerous —**su′i·ci′dal·ly** *adv.*

**su·i·cide** (s̅o̅o̅′ə sīd′) *n.* [L. *sui*, of oneself + -CIDE] **1.** the intentional killing of oneself **2.** ruin of one's interests through one's own actions **3.** a person committing suicide

**su·i ge·ne·ris** (s̅o̅o̅′ē jen′ər is, s̅o̅o̅′ī) [L., lit., of his (or her or its) own kind] altogether unique

**suit** (s̅o̅o̅t) *n.* [OFr. *suite*, ult. < L. *sequi*, to follow] **1.** *a)* a set of clothes to be worn together; esp., a coat and trousers (or skirt), usually of the same material *b)* any complete outfit [a *suit* of armor] **2.** a set or series of similar things; specif., any of the four sets of thirteen playing cards each (*spades*, *clubs*, *hearts*, *diamonds*) in a pack **3.** a lawsuit **4.** a suing, pleading, or wooing —*vt.* **1.** to meet the needs of; be right for or becoming to **2.** to make fit; adapt [a dance *suited* to the music] **3.** to please; satisfy **4.** to furnish with clothes, esp. with a suit —*vi.* to be suitable, convenient, or satisfactory —**bring suit** to start legal action; sue —**follow suit 1.** to play a card of the same suit as the card led **2.** to follow the example set —**suit oneself** to do as one pleases

**suit·a·ble** (-ə b'l) *adj.* right for the purpose, occasion etc.; fitting; appropriate —**suit′a·bil′i·ty, suit′a·ble·ness** *n.* —**suit′a·bly** *adv.*

**suit·case** (-kās′) *n.* a travel case for clothes, etc., esp. a rectangular one that opens into two hinged compartments

**suite** (swēt; *for 2 b, occas.* s̅o̅o̅t) *n.* [Fr.: see SUIT] **1.** a group of attendants or servants; retinue **2.** a set or series of related things; specif., *a)* a unit of connected rooms *b)* a set of matched furniture for a room [a bedroom *suite*] **3.** *Music* an instrumental composition made up of several movements or, in earlier times, dances

**suit·ing** (s̅o̅o̅t′iŋ) *n.* cloth for making suits

**suit·or** (-ər) *n.* **1.** a person who sues, petitions, pleads, etc. **2.** a man courting or wooing a woman

**su·ki·ya·ki** (s̅o̅o̅′kē yä′kē) *n.* [Jap.] a Japanese dish of thinly sliced meat, onions, and other vegetables cooked quickly, often at table, with soy sauce, sake, sugar, etc.

**Suk·kot, Suk·koth** (s̅o̅o̅ kōt′, s̅o̅o̅k′ōs) *n.* [Heb. *sukkôth*, lit., tabernacles] a Jewish festival in early fall, celebrating the harvest and commemorating the desert wandering of the Jews during the Exodus: also **Suk′kos** (s̅o̅o̅k′ōs)

**Su·lei·man (I)** (s̅o̅o̅′lā män′) 1494?–1566; sultan of the Ottoman Empire (1520–66)

**sulf-** *a combining form meaning* of or containing sulfur

**sul·fa** (sul′fə) *adj.* designating or of a family of drugs that are sulfonamides, used in combating certain bacterial infections

**sul·fa·di·a·zine** (sul′fə dī′ə zēn′, -zin) *n.* [prec. + DI-[1] + AZ(O) + -INE[4]] a sulfa drug, $C_{10}H_{10}N_4O_2S$, used in treating certain pneumococcal, streptococcal, and staphylococcal infections

**sul·fate** (sul′fāt) *n.* a salt or ester of sulfuric acid —*vt.* **-fat·ed, -fat·ing 1.** to treat with sulfuric acid or a sulfate **2.** to convert into a sulfate **3.** to form a lead sulfate deposit on (negative storage battery plates) —*vi.* to become sulfated —**sul·fa′tion** *n.*

**sul·fide** (sul′fīd) *n.* a compound of sulfur with another element or a radical

**sul·fite** (-fīt) *n.* a salt or ester of sulfurous acid

**sul·fon·a·mide** (sul fän′ə mīd′, -mid) *n.* [< *sulfon*(*yl*), the radical SO₂ + AMIDE] a compound, as sulfadiazine, containing the univalent radical –SO₂NH₂

**sul·fur** (sul′fər) *n.* [L. *sulphur, sulfur*] **1.** a pale-yellow, nonmetallic chemical element found in crystalline or amorphous form: it burns with a blue flame and a stifling odor: symbol, S; at. wt., 32.064; at. no., 16 **2.** any of numerous butterflies with dark-bordered, yellow or orange wings **3.** a greenish-yellow color —*vt.* to sulfurize

**sul·fu·rate** (sul′fyoo rāt′, -fə-) *vt.* **-rat′ed, -rat′ing** *same as* SULFURIZE —**sul′fu·ra′tion** *n.*

**sul·fur-bot·tom** (sul′fər bät′əm) *n. same as* BLUE WHALE

**sulfur dioxide** a heavy, colorless, suffocating gas, SO₂, easily liquefied and used as a bleach, preservative, etc.

**sul·fu·re·ous** (sul fyoor′ē əs) *adj.* **1.** of, like, or containing sulfur **2.** greenish-yellow

**sul·fu·ret** (sul′fyoo ret′) *vt.* **-ret′ed** or **-ret′ted, -ret′ing** or **-ret′ting** *same as* SULFURIZE

**sul·fu·ric** (sul fyoor′ik) *adj.* **1.** of or containing sulfur, esp. sulfur with a valence of six **2.** of or derived from sulfuric acid

**sulfuric acid** an oily, colorless, corrosive liquid, H₂SO₄, used in making explosives, fertilizers, chemicals, etc.

**sul·fu·rize** (sul′fyoo rīz′, -fə-) *vt.* **-rized′, -riz′ing** to combine or treat with sulfur or a sulfur compound —**sul′fu·ri·za′tion** *n.*

**sul·fu·rous** (sul′fər əs; *for 1 usually* sul fyoor′əs) *adj.* **1.** of or containing sulfur, esp. sulfur with a valence of four **2.** like burning sulfur in odor, color, etc. **3.** of or suggesting the fires of hell **4.** violently emotional; fiery —**sul′fu·rous·ly** *adv.* —**sul′fu·rous·ness** *n.*

**sulfurous acid** a colorless acid, H₂SO₃, known only in the form of its salts or in solution in water, and used as a chemical reagent, a bleach, etc.

**sul·fur·y** (sul′fər ē) *adj.* of or like sulfur

**sulk** (sulk) *vi.* [back-formation < ff.] to be sulky —*n.* **1.** a sulky mood or state: also **the sulks 2.** a sulky person

**sulk·y** (sul′kē) *adj.* **sulk′i·er, sulk′i·est** [prob. < OE. *solcen* (in comp.), idle] sullen in a pouting or peevish way [a *sulky* child] —*n., pl.* **sulk′ies** a light, two-wheeled carriage for one person, esp., now, one used in harness races —**sulk′i·ly** *adv.* —**sulk′i·ness** *n.*

**Sul·la** (sul′ə) (*Lucius Cornelius Sulla Felix*) 138?–78 B.C.; Rom. general; dictator of Rome (82–79)

**sul·len** (sul′ən) *adj.* [ult. < L. *solus*, alone] **1.** silent and keeping to oneself because one feels angry, bitter, hurt, etc. **2.** gloomy; dismal; depressing **3.** somber; dull **4.** sluggish —**sul′len·ly** *adv.* —**sul′len·ness** *n.*

**Sul·li·van** (sul′ə vən), Sir Arthur Sey·mour (sē′môr) 1842–1900; Eng. composer: see Sir William GILBERT

**sul·ly** (sul′ē) *vt.* **-lied, -ly·ing** [prob. < OFr. *souiller*: see SOIL[2]] to soil, stain, etc., now esp. by disgracing

**sulph-** *var.*, *now esp. Brit.*, *sp. of* SULF-: for words beginning **sulph-**, see forms under **sulf-**

**sul·phur** (sul′fər) *n. var.*, *now esp. Brit.*, *sp. of* SULFUR

**sul·tan** (sul′t'n) *n.* [Fr. < Ar. *sulṭân*] a Moslem ruler; esp., [S-] formerly, the ruler of Turkey

**sul·tan·a** (sul tan′ə, -tä′nə) *n.* **1.** a sultan's wife, mother, sister, or daughter: also **sul′tan·ess** (-tən is) **2.** a small, white, seedless grape or raisin

**sul·tan·ate** (sul′t'n it, -āt′) *n.* the authority, office, reign, or dominion of a sultan

**sul·try** (sul′trē) *adj.* **-tri·er, -tri·est** [var. of *sweltry*: see SWELTER] **1.** oppressively hot and moist; sweltering **2.** fiery **3.** inflamed with passion, lust, etc. —**sul′tri·ly** *adv.* —**sul′tri·ness** *n.*

**Su·lu Archipelago** (s̅o̅o̅′l̅o̅o̅) group of islands in the Philippines, southwest of Mindanao

**sum** (sum) *n.* [< MFr. < L. *summa*, fem. of *summus*, highest] **1.** an amount of money **2.** the whole amount; totality [the *sum* of one's experiences] **3.** gist; summary: usually in **sum and substance 4.** *a)* the result gotten by adding numbers or quantities *b)* a series of numbers to be added up, or any problem in arithmetic —*vt.* **summed, sum′ming 1.** to add up **2.** to summarize —*vi.* to get, or come to, a total —**in sum** to put it briefly; in short —**sum up 1.** to add up or collect into a whole or total **2.** to summarize

**sum-** *same as* SUB-: used before *m*

**su·mac, su·mach** (shoo′mak, soo′-) *n.* [MFr. < Ar. *summāq*] **1.** *a)* any of various non-poisonous plants with compound leaves and cone-shaped clusters of hairy, red fruit *b)* the powdered leaves of some of these plants, used in tanning and dyeing **2.** any of several poisonous plants, as poison ivy

**Su·ma·tra** (soo mä′trə) large island of Indonesia, south of the Malay Peninsula: c. 165,000 sq. mi. —**Su·ma′tran** *adj., n.*

**Su·mer** (soo′mər) ancient region in the lower valley of the Euphrates River

SUMAC

**Su·mer·i·an** (soo mir′ē ən, -mer′-) *adj.* designating or of an ancient, non-Semitic people of Sumer —*n.* **1.** any of the Sumerian people **2.** the language of the Sumerians

‡**sum·ma cum lau·de** (soom′ə koom lou′de, sum′ə kum lô′dē) [L.] with the greatest praise; phrase used to signify graduation with the highest honors from a college or university

**sum·ma·rize** (sum′ə rīz′) *vt.* **-rized′, -riz′ing** to make or be a summary of —**sum′ma·ri·za′tion** *n.* —**sum′ma·riz′er** *n.*

**sum·ma·ry** (sum'ə rē) *adj.* [< ML. < L. *summa,* a sum] **1.** briefly giving the general idea; concise; condensed **2.** *a)* prompt and informal *b)* hasty and arbitrary —*n., pl.* **-ries** a brief account covering the main points; digest —**sum·mar·i·ly** (sə mer'ə lē, sum'ə rə lē) *adv.*

**sum·ma·tion** (sə mā'shən) *n.* **1.** a summing up, to find a total **2.** a total or aggregate **3.** a final summing up of arguments, as in a court trial

**sum·mer** (sum'ər) *n.* [OE. *sumor*] **1.** the warmest season of the year, following spring **2.** a year as reckoned by this season **3.** any period regarded, like summer, as a time of growth, development, etc. —*adj.* of, typical of, or suitable for summer —*vi.* to pass the summer —*vt.* to keep or feed during the summer —**sum'mer·y** *adj.*

**sum·mer·house** (-hous') *n.* a small, open structure in a garden, park, etc., for providing a shady rest

**summer house** a house or cottage, as in the country, used during the summer

**sum·mer·sault** (sum'ər sôlt') *n., vi. var. of* SOMERSAULT

**summer sausage** a type of hard, dried and smoked sausage that does not spoil easily

**summer solstice** the time in the Northern Hemisphere when the sun is farthest north of the celestial equator; June 21 or 22

**summer squash** any of various small garden squashes grown in summer and eaten before fully ripe

**sum·mer·time** (-tīm') *n.* the season of summer

**sum·mit** (sum'it) *n.* [< OFr., ult. < L. *summus,* highest] **1.** the highest point or part; top; apex **2.** the highest degree or state; acme **3.** *a)* a top level of officials; specif., in diplomacy, the level restricted to heads of government *b)* a conference at this level —*adj.* of the heads of government

**sum·mon** (sum'ən) *vt.* [< OFr., ult. < L. *summonere,* to remind secretly < *sub-,* secretly + *monere,* to warn] **1.** to call together; order to meet **2.** to call for or send for with authority **3.** to order, as by a summons, to appear in court **4.** to call upon to do something **5.** to call forth; rouse (often with *up*) [*summon* up strength] —**sum'mon·er** *n.*

**sum·mons** (-ənz) *n., pl.* **-mons·es** [< Anglo-Fr. *somonse* < OFr.: see prec.] **1.** an order to come or do something; specif., *Law* an official order to appear in court, specif. as a defendant; also, the writ containing such an order **2.** a call, knock, etc. that summons

**‡sum·mum bo·num** (soom'əm bō'nəm) [L.] the highest, or supreme, good

**su·mo** (**wrestling**) (soo'mō) [Jap. *sumō*] [*sometimes* S-] stylized Japanese wrestling engaged in by a hereditary class of large, extremely heavy men

**sump** (sump) *n.* [ME. *sompe,* a swamp] a pit, cistern, cesspool, etc. for draining or collecting liquid

**sump pump** a pump for removing liquid from a sump

**sump·tu·ar·y** (sump'choo wer'ē) *adj.* [< L. < *sumptus,* expense < pp. of *sumere,* to take] of or regulating expenses or expenditures

**sump·tu·ous** (sump'choo wəs) *adj.* [< OFr. < L. < *sumptus:* see prec.] **1.** involving great expense; costly; lavish **2.** magnificent, as in furnishings —**sump'tu·ous·ly** *adv.*

**sum total** **1.** the total arrived at by adding up a sum or sums **2.** everything involved or included

**sum·up** (sum'up') *n.* [Colloq.] a summarizing

**sun** (sun) *n.* [OE. *sunne*] **1.** *a)* the self-luminous, gaseous sphere about which the earth and other planets revolve and which furnishes light, heat, and energy for the solar system: it is about 93 million miles from earth and about 864,400 miles in diameter *b)* its heat or light **2.** any star that is the center of a planetary system **3.** something like the sun, as in warmth, brilliance, etc. **4.** [Poet.] *a)* a day *b)* a year *c)* a clime; climate —*vt., vi.* **sunned, sun'ning** to expose or be exposed to the sun so as to warm, tan, bleach, etc. —**place in the sun** a prominent or favorable position —**under the sun** on earth; in the world

**Sun.** Sunday

**sun·baked** (-bākt') *adj.* **1.** baked by the sun's heat, as bricks **2.** parched, cracked, etc. by the sun's heat

**sun bath** exposure of the body to sunlight or a sunlamp

**sun·bathe** (-bāth') *vi.* **-bathed', -bath'ing** to take a sun bath —**sun'bath'er** *n.*

**sun·beam** (-bēm') *n.* a ray or beam of sunlight

**Sun·belt** (sun'belt') *n.* that part of the U.S. comprising most of the States of the South and the Southwest: also **Sun Belt**

**sun·bon·net** (-bän'it) *n.* a large-brimmed bonnet with a back flap, worn to shade the face and neck from the sun, esp. formerly, by women and girls

**sun·burn** (-burn') *n.* an inflammation of the skin resulting from prolonged exposure to the sun's rays or a sunlamp —*vi., vt.* **-burned'** or **-burnt', -burn'ing** to get or cause to get a sunburn

**sun·burst** (-burst') *n.* **1.** a burst of sunlight, as between clouds **2.** a decoration suggesting the sun and its rays

**sun-cured** (-kyoord') *adj.* cured, as meat or fruit, by drying in the sun

**sun·dae** (sun'dē, -dā) *n.* [prob. < SUNDAY] a serving of ice cream covered with syrup, fruit, nuts, etc.

**Sun·day** (sun'dē, -dā) *n.* [OE. *sunnandæg,* lit., day of the sun] the first day of the week, observed by most Christians as a day of worship or as the Sabbath —*adj.* **1.** of or typical of Sunday **2.** done, worn, performing, etc. usually or only on Sunday

**Sunday best** [Colloq.] one's best clothes

**Sun·days** (-dēz, -dāz) *adv.* on or during every Sunday

**Sunday school** **1.** a school giving religious instruction on Sunday at a church or synagogue **2.** the teachers and pupils of such a school

**sun·der** (sun'dər) *vt., vi.* [OE. *sundrian* < *sundor,* asunder] to break apart; split —**in sunder** into parts or pieces

**Sun·der·land** (sun'dər lənd) seaport in N England, on the North Sea: pop. 218,000

**sun·di·al** (sun'dī'əl, -dīl') *n.* an instrument that shows time by the shadow of a pointer or gnomon cast by the sun on a dial marked in hours

**sun·dog** (-dôg') *n. same as* PARHELION

**sun·down** (-doun') *n. same as* SUNSET

**sun-dried** (-drīd') *adj.* dried by the sun

**sun·dries** (sun'drēz) *n.pl.* sundry items; miscellaneous things

**sun·dry** (-drē) *adj.* [OE. *syndrig,* separate < *sundor,* apart] various; miscellaneous [*sundry* articles of clothing] —*pron.* [*with pl. v.*] sundry persons or things: chiefly in **all** and **sundry** one and all

SUNDIAL

**sun·fish** (-fish') *n., pl.* **-fish', -fish'es:** see FISH **1.** any of a large family of N. American freshwater fishes including the bluegill, black bass, etc. **2.** *same as* OCEAN SUNFISH

**sun·flow·er** (-flou'ər) *n.* any of various tall plants of the composite family, with large, yellow, daisylike flowers containing edible seeds from which an oil is extracted

**sung** (suŋ) *pp. & rare pt. of* SING

**sun·glass·es** (sun'glas'iz) *n.pl.* eyeglasses with tinted lenses to protect the eyes from the sun's glare

**sunk** (suŋk) *pp. & alt. pt. of* SINK —*adj.* **1.** *same as* SUNKEN **2.** [Colloq.] utterly ruined, disgraced, etc.

**sunk·en** (-ən) *obs. pp. of* SINK —*adj.* **1.** submerged [a *sunken* ship] **2.** below the level of the surrounding or adjoining area [a *sunken* patio] **3.** fallen in; hollow [*sunken* cheeks] **4.** dejected

**sun·lamp** (sun'lamp') *n.* an electric lamp that radiates ultraviolet rays like those of sunlight

**sun·less** (-lis) *adj.* without sun or sunlight; dark

**sun·light** (-līt') *n.* the light of the sun

**sun·lit** (-lit') *adj.* lighted by the sun

**sun·ny** (sun'ē) *adj.* **-ni·er, -ni·est 1.** bright with sunlight; full of sunshine **2.** bright and cheerful **3.** of or suggestive of the sun —**on the sunny side of** somewhat younger than (a specified age) —**sun'ni·ly** *adv.* —**sun'ni·ness** *n.*

**Sun·ny·vale** (sun'ē vāl') city in W Calif.: suburb of San Jose: pop. 107,000

**sun parlor** (or **porch** or **room**) a living room or enclosed porch with large windows to let sunlight in freely

**sun·rise** (-rīz') *n.* **1.** the daily appearance of the sun above the eastern horizon **2.** the time of this **3.** the color of the sky at this time

**sun·roof** (-roof', -roof') *n.* an automobile roof with a panel that opens to let in light and air: also **sun roof**

**sun·set** (-set') *n.* **1.** the daily disappearance of the sun below the western horizon **2.** the time of this **3.** the color of the sky at this time —*adj.* designating or of a law requiring that a government agency or program end on a certain date unless it gets legislative reapproval

**sun·shade** (-shād') *n.* a parasol, awning, broad hat, etc. used for protection against the sun's rays

**sun·shine** (-shīn') *n.* **1.** the shining of the sun, or its light and heat **2.** cheerfulness, joy, etc. —*adj.* designating or of a law requiring that certain meetings, records, etc. of public bodies be open to the public —**sun'shin'y** *adj.*

**sun·spot** (-spät') *n.* any temporarily cooler region appearing from time to time as a dark spot on the sun

**sun·stroke** (-strōk') *n.* heatstroke caused by excessive exposure to the sun —**sun'struck'** (-struk') *adj.*

**sun·suit** (-soot') *n.* a garment consisting of short pants with a bib and shoulder straps, for babies and children

**sun·tan** (-tan') *n.* a darkened condition of the skin resulting from exposure to the sun or a sunlamp —**sun'-tanned'** *adj.*

**sun·up** (-up') *n. same as* SUNRISE

**Sun Valley** resort city in SC Ida.

**sun·ward** (-wərd) *adv.* toward the sun: also **sun'wards** —*adj.* facing the sun

**Sun Yat-sen** (soon' yät'sen') 1866–1925; Chin. political & revolutionary leader

**sup¹** (sup) *n., vt., vi.* **supped, sup'ping** [OE. *supan,* to drink] *same as* SIP

**sup²** (sup) *vi.* **supped, sup′ping** [< OFr. *souper* < *soupe*, soup] to have supper

**sup-** *same as* SUB-: used before *p*

**sup.** **1.** superior **2.** supplement **3.** supply

**su·per** (sōō′pər) *n.* [< ff.] **1.** *shortened form of: a)* SUPERNUMERARY *b)* SUPERINTENDENT **2.** [Colloq.] a product that is superior, extra large, etc.: a trade term —*adj.* **1.** outstanding; exceptionally fine **2.** great, extreme, or excessive

**su·per-** [L. < *super*, above] *a prefix meaning:* **1.** over, above, on top of *[superstructure]* **2.** higher in rank than, superior to *[superintendent]* **3.** *a)* surpassing *[superfine] b)* greater or better than others of its kind *[supermarket]* **4.** to a degree greater than normal *[supersaturate]* **5.** extra, additional *[supertax]*

**su·per·a·ble** (sōō′pər ə b'l) *adj.* that can be overcome; surmountable —**su′per·a·bly** *adv.*

**su·per·a·bound** (sōō′pər ə bound′) *vi.* to be greatly or excessively abundant

**su·per·a·bun·dant** (-ə bun′dənt) *adj.* overly abundant — **su′per·a·bun′dance** *n.* —**su′per·a·bun′dant·ly** *adv.*

**su·per·an·nu·ate** (-an′yōō wāt′) *vt.* **-at′ed, -at′ing** [back-formation < ff.] **1.** to set aside as old-fashioned or obsolete **2.** to retire, esp. with a pension, because of old age or infirmity —**su′per·an′nu·a′tion** *n.*

**su·per·an·nu·at·ed** (-id) *adj.* [< ML. pp. of *superannuari* < L. *super*, beyond + *annus*, year] **1.** *a)* too old for further work *b)* retired because of old age or infirmity **2.** obsolete; old-fashioned; outdated

**su·perb** (sōō purb′, sōō-) *adj.* [L. *superbus*, proud < *super*, above] **1.** noble, grand, or majestic **2.** rich; splendid **3.** excellent —**su·perb′ly** *adv.* —**su·perb′ness** *n.*

**su·per·car·go** (sōō′pər kär′gō) *n., pl.* **-goes, -gos** [< Sp. *sobrecargo* < *sobre*, over + *cargo*, CARGO] an officer on a merchant ship who has charge of the cargo, representing the shipowner

**su·per·charge** (-chärj′) *vt.* **-charged′, -charg′ing** **1.** to increase the power of (an engine), as with a supercharger **2.** *same as* PRESSURIZE (sense 1)

**su·per·charg·er** (-chär′jər) *n.* a blower or compressor used to increase the power of an internal-combustion engine by increasing the supply of air or fuel mixture to the cylinders

**su·per·cil·i·ous** (sōō′pər sil′ē əs) *adj.* [< L. < *supercilium*, eyebrow, hence (with reference to raised brows), haughtiness < *super-*, above + *cilium*, eyelid] full of or showing pride or contempt; haughty —**su′per·cil′i·ous·ly** *adv.* —**su′per·cil′i·ous·ness** *n.*

**su·per·con·duc·tiv·i·ty** (-kän′dək tiv′ə tē) *n. Physics* the ability of certain metals and alloys to conduct electricity continuously without resistance when chilled to near absolute zero: also **su′per·con·duc′tion** (-kən duk′shən) —**su′per·con·duct′ing, su′per·con·duc′tive** *adj.* —**su′per·con·duc′tor** *n.*

**su·per·cool** (-kōōl′) *vt.* to lower the temperature of (a liquid) to below its freezing point without causing solidification —*vi.* to become supercooled

**su·per·e·go** (sōō′pər ē′gō) *n., pl.* **-gos** *Psychoanalysis* that part of the psyche which is critical of the self or ego and enforces moral standards

**su·per·em·i·nent** (-em′ə nənt) *adj.* eminent beyond others —**su′per·em′i·nence** *n.* —**su′per·em′i·nent·ly** *adv.*

**su·per·er·o·ga·tion** (-er′ə gā′shən) *n.* [< LL. < pp. of *supererogare* < *super*, above + *erogare*, to pay out] the act of doing more than what is required or expected

**su·per·e·rog·a·to·ry** (-i räg′ə tôr′ē) *adj.* **1.** done beyond the degree required or expected **2.** superfluous

**su·per·fi·cial** (-fish′əl) *adj.* [< L. < *superficies*, a surface < *super-*, above + *facies*, face] **1.** *a)* of or being on the surface *b)* of surface area; plane **2.** concerned with and understanding only the easily apparent and obvious; not profound; shallow **3.** quick and cursory **4.** merely apparent —**su′per·fi′ci·al′i·ty** (-ē al′ə tē) *n., pl.* **-ties** —**su′per·fi′cial·ly** *adv.* —**su′per·fi′cial·ness** *n.*

**su·per·fine** (sōō′pər fin′, sōō′pər fin′) *adj.* **1.** too subtle, delicate, or refined **2.** of very fine quality

**su·per·flu·i·ty** (sōō′pər flōō′ə tē) *n., pl.* **-ties** **1.** a being superfluous **2.** a quantity beyond what is needed; excess **3.** something superfluous

**su·per·flu·ous** (sōō pur′flōō wəs) *adj.* [< L. < *superfluere* < *super-*, above + *fluere*, to flow] **1.** being more than is needed or wanted; excessive **2.** not needed; unnecessary —**su·per′flu·ous·ly** *adv.* —**su·per′flu·ous·ness** *n.*

**su·per·heat** (sōō′pər hēt′; *for n.* sōō′pər hēt′) *vt.* **1.** to make too hot **2.** to heat (a liquid) above its boiling point without its vaporizing. **3.** to heat (steam not in contact with water) beyond its saturation point, so that a drop in temperature will not cause it to turn back to water

**su·per·het·er·o·dyne** (sōō′pər het′ər ə dīn′) *adj.* [SUPER(SONIC) + HETERODYNE] designating or of radio reception in which some amplification is done at an intermediate supersonic frequency —*n.* a radio set for this kind of reception

**su·per·high frequency** (sōō′pər hī′) any radio frequency between 3,000 and 30,000 megahertz

**su·per·high·way** (-hī′wā′) *n. same as* EXPRESSWAY

**su·per·hu·man** (-hyōō′mən) *adj.* **1.** having a nature above that of man; divine **2.** greater than normal for a human being —**su′per·hu′man·ly** *adv.*

**su·per·im·pose** (-im pōz′) *vt.* **-posed′, -pos′ing** **1.** to put or lay on top of something else **2.** to add as a feature that dominates or does not properly fit with the rest

**su·per·in·duce** (-in dōōs′, -dyōōs′) *vt.* **-duced′, -duc′ing** to bring in as an addition —**su′per·in·duc′tion** (-duk′shən) *n.*

**su·per·in·tend** (-in tend′) *vt.* to act as superintendent of; supervise —**su′per·in·tend′ence, su′per·in·tend′en·cy** *n.*

**su·per·in·tend·ent** (-in ten′dənt) *n.* [< LL. prp. of *superintendere*: see SUPER- & INTEND] **1.** a person in charge of a department, institution, etc.; supervisor **2.** the custodian of a building, etc. —*adj.* that superintends

**Su·pe·ri·or** (sə pir′ē ər, sōō-), Lake [orig. so called from its position above Lake Huron] largest & westernmost of the Great Lakes, between Mich. & Ontario, Canada: 32,483 sq. mi.

**su·pe·ri·or** (sə pir′ē ər, sōō-) *adj.* [OFr. < L., compar. of *superus*, that is above] **1.** higher in space; placed higher up **2.** higher in order, status, rank, etc. **3.** greater in quality or value than (with *to*) **4.** above average; excellent **5.** refusing to be affected by (something painful): with *to* **6.** haughty —*n.* **1.** a superior person or thing **2.** the head of a religious community —**su·pe′ri·or′i·ty** (-ôr′ə tē) *n.*

**superl.** superlative

**su·per·la·tive** (sə pur′lə tiv, sōō-) *adj.* [< MFr. < LL. < L. < *super-*, above + *latus*, pp. of *ferre*, to carry] **1.** excelling all others; supreme **2.** excessive **3.** *Gram.* designating or of the extreme degree of comparison of adjectives and adverbs: usually indicated by the suffix *-est* (*hardest*) or by the use of *most* (*most beautiful*) —*n.* **1.** the highest degree; acme **2.** something superlative **3.** *Gram. a)* the superlative degree *b)* a word or form in this degree —**su·per′la·tive·ly** *adv.* —**su·per′la·tive·ness** *n.*

**su·per·man** (sōō′pər man′) *n., pl.* **-men′** (-men′) **1.** in Nietzsche's philosophy, a type of superior man regarded as the goal of the evolutionary struggle **2.** an apparently superhuman man

**su·per·mar·ket** (-mär′kit) *n.* a large, self-service, retail food store or market, often one of a chain

**su·per·nal** (sōō pur′n'l) *adj.* [MFr. < L. *supernus*, upper] celestial, heavenly, or divine —**su·per′nal·ly** *adv.*

**su·per·nat·u·ral** (sōō′pər nach′ər əl) *adj.* **1.** existing outside man's normal experience or the known laws of nature; specif., of or involving God or a god, or ghosts, the occult, etc. **2.** extraordinary —**the supernatural** supernatural beings, forces, happenings, etc. —**su′per·nat′u·ral·ly** *adv.*

**su·per·nat·u·ral·ism** (-iz'm) *n.* **1.** a supernatural quality or state **2.** a belief that some supernatural, or divine, force controls nature and the universe —**su′per·nat′u·ral·ist** *n., adj.* —**su′per·nat′u·ral·is′tic** *adj.*

**su·per·no·va** (-nō′və) *n., pl.* **-vae** (-vē), **-vas** [ModL.: see SUPER- & NOVA] an extremely bright nova that suddenly increases 10 million to 100 million times in brightness

**su·per·nu·mer·ar·y** (-nōō′mə rer′ē, -nyōō′-) *adj.* [< LL. < L. *super*, above + *numerus*, number] beyond the regular or needed number; extra or superfluous —*n., pl.* **-ar′ies** **1.** a supernumerary person or thing **2.** *Theater* a person with a small, nonspeaking part, as in a mob scene

**su·per·pa·tri·ot** (-pā′trē ət) *n.* a person who is or professes to be a devout patriot, often to the point of fanaticism —**su′per·pa′tri·ot′ic** (-pā′trē ät′ik) *adj.* —**su′per·pa′tri·ot·ism** *n.*

**su·per·pose** (-pōz′) *vt.* **-posed′, -pos′ing** [< Fr. < L. pp. of *superponere*: see SUPER- & POSE¹] **1.** to lay or place on, over, or above something else **2.** *Geom.* to place (one figure) on top of another that is congruent so that corresponding sides coincide —**su′per·po·si′tion** *n.*

**su·per·pow·er** (sōō′pər pou′ər) *n.* any of the few most powerful nations of the world competing for spheres of influence

**su·per·sat·u·rate** (sōō′pər sach′ə rāt′) *vt.* **-rat′ed, -rat′ing** to saturate beyond the normal point for the given temperature —**su′per·sat′u·ra′tion** *n.*

**su·per·scribe** (-skrīb′) *vt.* **-scribed′, -scrib′ing** [< L.: see SUPER- & SCRIBE] to write or mark (an inscription, name, etc.) at the top or on an outer surface of something —**su′per·scrip′tion** (-skrip′shən) *n.*

**su·per·script** (sōō′pər skript′) *adj.* written above —*n.* a figure, letter, or symbol written above and to the side of another [in y² and xⁿ, 2 and n are *superscripts*]

**su·per·sede** (sōō′pər sēd′) *vt.* **-sed′ed, -sed′ing** [< MFr. < L. *supersedere*, to preside over < *super-*, above + *sedere*, to sit] **1.** to cause to be set aside as inferior or obsolete and be replaced **2.** to take the place or office of; succeed **3.** to replace; supplant —**su′per·sed′er** *n.* —**su′per·se′dure** (-sē′jər), **su′per·sed′ence** *n.*

**su·per·sen·si·tive** (-sen′sə tiv) *adj.* highly sensitive or too sensitive —**su′per·sen′si·tiv′i·ty** *n.*

**su·per·son·ic** (-sän′ik) *adj.* [SUPER- + SONIC] **1.** designating, of, or moving at a speed in a surrounding fluid greater than that of sound in the same fluid: cf. SONIC **2.** *same as* ULTRASONIC —**su′per·son′i·cal·ly** *adv.*

**su·per·son·ics** (-sän′iks) *n.pl.* [*with sing. v.*] the science dealing with supersonic phenomena

**su·per·star** (sōō′pər stär′) *n.* a very prominent performer, as in sports, considered to have exceptional talent

**su·per·sti·tion** (sōō′pər stish′ən) *n.* [< MFr. < L. *superstitio*, ult. < *super-*, over + *stare*, to stand] **1.** any belief, based on fear or ignorance, that is not in accord with the known laws of science or with what is considered true and rational; esp., such a belief in charms, omens, the supernatural, etc. **2.** any action or practice based on such a belief **3.** such beliefs collectively

**su·per·sti·tious** (-əs) *adj.* **1.** of, characterized by, or resulting from superstition **2.** having superstitions —**su′per·sti′tious·ly** *adv.* —**su′per·sti′tious·ness** *n.*

**su·per·struc·ture** (sōō′pər struk′chər) *n.* **1.** a structure built on top of another **2.** that part of a building above the foundation **3.** that part of a ship above the main deck

**su·per·tax** (-taks′) *n.* an additional tax; esp., a surtax

**su·per·vene** (sōō′pər vēn′) *vi.* **-vened′, -ven′ing** [< L. < *super-*, over + *venire*, to come] to come or happen as something added or not expected —**su′per·ven′ient** (-vēn′yənt) *adj.* —**su′per·ven′tion** (-ven′shən), **su′per·ven′ience** (-vēn′yəns) *n.*

**su·per·vise** (sōō′pər viz′) *vt., vi.* **-vised′, -vis′ing** [< ML. pp. of *supervidere* < L. *super-*, over + *videre*, to see] to oversee, direct, or manage (work, workers, a project, etc.); superintend —**su′per·vi′sion** (-vizh′ən) *n.*

**su·per·vi·sor** (-vi′zər) *n.* **1.** a person who supervises; manager; director **2.** in certain school systems, an official in charge of the courses and teachers for a particular subject —**su′per·vi′so·ry** *adj.*

**su·pine** (sōō pīn′) *adj.* [L. *supinus*] **1.** lying on the back, face upward **2.** showing no concern or doing nothing about matters —**su·pine′ly** *adv.* —**su·pine′ness** *n.*

**supp., suppl. 1.** supplement **2.** supplementary

**sup·per** (sup′ər) *n.* [OFr. *souper*, orig. inf., to SUP²] **1.** an evening meal, as a dinner, or a late, light meal, as one eaten after the theater **2.** an evening social at which a meal is served [a church *supper*] —**sup′per·less** *adj.*

**sup·plant** (sə plant′) *vt.* [< OFr. < L. *supplantare*, to trip up < *sub-*, under + *planta*, sole of the foot] **1.** to take the place of, esp. through force or plotting **2.** to remove and replace with something else —**sup·plan·ta·tion** (sup′lan-tā′shən) *n.* —**sup·plant′er** *n.*

**sup·ple** (sup′'l) *adj.* [< OFr. < L. *supplex*, humble] **1.** bending easily; flexible **2.** lithe; limber [a *supple* body] **3.** changing easily, as under new conditions or strong influences **4.** adaptable or yielding: said of the mind, etc. — **sup′ple·ly** *adv.* —**sup′ple·ness** *n.*

**sup·ple·ment** (sup′lə mənt; *for v.* -ment′) *n.* [< L. < *supplere*: see SUPPLY¹] **1.** something added, esp. to make up for a lack **2.** a section added to a book, etc., as to give additional information **3.** a separate newspaper section containing feature stories, etc. **4.** *Math.* the number of degrees to be added to an angle or arc to make 180 degrees —*vt.* to provide a supplement to; add to —**sup′ple·men·ta′tion** *n.* —**sup′ple·ment′er** *n.*

**sup·ple·men·ta·ry** (sup′lə men′tər ē) *adj.* supplying what is lacking; additional: also **sup′ple·men′tal** —*n., pl.* **-ries** a supplementary person or thing

**supplementary angle** either of two angles that together form 180 degrees

**sup·pli·ant** (sup′lē ənt) *n.* [MFr., prp. of *supplier* < L.: see SUPPLICATE] a person who supplicates —*adj.* supplicating; beseeching —**sup′pli·ance** *n.* —**sup′pli·ant·ly** *adv.*

**sup·pli·cant** (sup′lə kənt) *adj., n. same as* SUPPLIANT

**sup·pli·cate** (sup′lə kāt′) *vt.* **-cat′ed, -cat′ing** [< L. pp. of

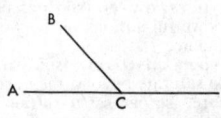

SUPPLEMENTARY ANGLES
(angle BCA and angle DCB are supplementary)

*supplicare*, to kneel down < *sub-*, under + *plicare*, to fold] **1.** to ask for humbly, as by prayer **2.** to make a humble request of —*vi.* to make a humble request, esp. in prayer —**sup′pli·ca′tion** *n.* —**sup′pli·ca′tor** *n.* —**sup′pli·ca·to′ry** (-kə tôr′ē) *adj.*

**sup·ply¹** (sə plī′) *vt.* **-plied′, -ply′ing** [< MFr. < L. *supplere*, to fill up < *sub-*, under + *plere*, to fill] **1.** to give, furnish, or provide (what is needed) **2.** to meet the needs or requirements of **3.** to make up for (a deficiency, etc.) **4.** to act as a substitute in [to *supply* another's pulpit] —*vi.* to serve as a substitute —*n., pl.* **-plies′ 1.** the act of supplying **2.** an amount available for use; stock; store **3.** [*pl.*] materials, provisions, etc. for supplying an army, a business, etc. **4.** a substitute, as for a minister **5.** *Econ.* the amount of a commodity available for purchase at a given price —*adj.* **1.** having to do with a supply or supplies **2.** serving as a substitute —**sup·pli′er** *n.*

**sup·ply²** (sup′lē) *adv.* in a supple manner; supplely

**sup·port** (sə pôrt′) *vt.* [< MFr. < LL. < L. < *sub-*, under + *portare*, to carry] **1.** *a)* to carry or bear the weight of; hold up *b)* to carry or bear (a specified weight, pressure, etc.) **2.** to give courage or faith to; help; comfort **3.** to give approval to or be in favor of; uphold **4.** to provide for (a person, institution, etc.) with money or subsistence **5.** to help prove or vindicate [evidence to *support* a claim] **6.** to bear; endure; tolerate **7.** to keep up; maintain; specif., to maintain (the price of a commodity) as by purchases **8.** *Theater* to act a subordinate role with (a specified star) —*n.* **1.** a supporting or being supported **2.** a person or thing that supports; specif., *a)* a prop, base, brace, etc. *b)* a means of subsistence *c)* an elastic device to support or bind a part of the body —**sup·port′a·ble** *adj.*

**sup·port·er** (-ər) *n.* **1.** a person who supports; advocate; adherent **2.** a thing that supports; esp., *a)* an elastic device to support the back, abdomen, etc. *b) same as* JOCK-STRAP: in full, **athletic supporter** *c) same as* GARTER

**sup·port·ive** (-iv) *adj.* that gives support, help, or approval

**sup·pose** (sə pōz′) *vt.* **-posed′, -pos′ing** [< MFr. < ML. *supponere*, ult. < L. *sub-*, under + *ponere*, to place] **1.** to take to be true, as for the sake of argument, etc. [*suppose* A equals B] **2.** to believe, think, guess, etc. **3.** to involve as a preceding condition; presuppose **4.** to consider as a suggested possibility [*suppose* he doesn't come] **5.** to expect: always in the passive [she's *supposed* to telephone] —*vi.* to think or guess; conjecture —**sup·pos′a·ble** *adj.* —**sup·pos′a·bly** *adv.* —**sup·pos′er** *n.*

**sup·posed** (sə pōzd′) *adj.* **1.** regarded as true, possible, etc., without actual knowledge **2.** merely imagined —**sup·pos′ed·ly** *adv.*

**sup·po·si·tion** (sup′ə zish′ən) *n.* **1.** the act of supposing **2.** something supposed; assumption Also **sup·pos·al** (sə-pōz′'l) —**sup′po·si′tion·al** *adj.* —**sup′po·si′tion·al·ly** *adv.*

**sup·pos·i·to·ry** (sə päz′ə tôr′ē) *n., pl.* **-ries** [< ModL. < L. < pp. of *supponere*: see SUPPOSE] a small, shaped piece of medicated substance, inserted into the rectum, vagina, etc., where it is melted and spread by the body heat

**sup·press** (sə pres′) *vt.* [< L. pp. of *supprimere* < *sub-*, under + *premere*, to press] **1.** to put down by force or authority; quell **2.** to keep from appearing or being known, published, etc. [to *suppress* a news story, a book, etc.] **3.** to keep back; restrain; check [to *suppress* a laugh, cough, etc.] **4.** to check the flow, secretion, etc. of **5.** *Electronics, Radio*, etc. to eliminate (an unwanted signal, etc.) **6.** *Psychiatry* to consciously dismiss (unacceptable ideas, impulses, etc.) from the mind —**sup·press′i·ble** *adj.* —**sup·pres′sive** *adj.* —**sup·pres′sive·ly** *adv.* —**sup·pres′sor** *n.*

**sup·pres·sion** (sə presh′ən) *n.* **1.** a suppressing or being suppressed **2.** *Psychiatry a)* the mechanism by which unacceptable ideas, impulses, etc. are suppressed *b)* something suppressed in this way

**sup·pu·rate** (sup′yoo rāt′) *vi.* **-rat′ed, -rat′ing** [< L. pp. of *suppurare* < *sub-*, under + *pus* (gen. *puris*), pus] to form or discharge pus; fester —**sup′pu·ra′tion** *n.* —**sup′pu·ra′tive** *adj.*

**su·pra-** [< L. *supra*, above, over] *a prefix meaning* above, over, beyond [*suprarenal*]

**su·pra·na·tion·al** (sōō′prə nash′ə n'l) *adj.* of, for, involving, or over all or a number of nations [*supranational* authority] —**su′pra·na′tion·al·ism** *n.*

**su·pra·re·nal** (-rē′n'l) *adj.* [< ModL.: see SUPRA- & RENAL] on or above the kidney; specif., designating or of an adrenal gland —*n.* an adrenal gland

**su·prem·a·cist** (sə prem′ə sist, soo-) *n.* a person who believes in or promotes the supremacy of a particular group [a white *supremacist*]

**su·prem·a·cy** (sə prem′ə sē, soo-) *n., pl.* **-cies 1.** the quality or state of being supreme **2.** supreme power or authority

**su·preme** (sə prēm′, soo-) *adj.* [L. *supremus*, superl. of *su-perus*, that is above] **1.** highest in rank, power, etc. **2.** highest in quality, achievement, performance, etc.; most excellent **3.** highest in degree; utmost [a *supreme* fool]

**4.** final; ultimate —**su·preme′ly** *adv.* —**su·preme′ness** *n.*
**Supreme Being** God
**Supreme Court 1.** the highest Federal court, consisting of nine judges **2.** the highest court in most States
**supreme sacrifice** the sacrifice of one's life
**Supreme Soviet** the parliament of the Soviet Union
**Supt., supt.** Superintendent
**sur-**[1] [OFr. < L. *super,* over, above] *a prefix meaning* over, upon, above, beyond [*surcharge*]
**sur-**[2] *same as* SUB-: used before *r*
**Su·ra·ba·ja** (soō′rä bä′yä) seaport in NE Java, Indonesia: pop. 1,008,000
**su·rah** (soor′ə) *n.* [< *Surat,* a seaport in India] a soft, twilled fabric of silk or rayon
**sur·cease** (sur sēs′; *for n. usually* sur′sēs) *vt., vi.* **-ceased′, -ceas′ing** [< OFr. *sursis,* pp. of *surseoir,* to pause < L. *supersedere,* to refrain from] [Archaic] to stop; end —*n.* end; cessation
**sur·charge** (sur′chärj; *also for v.* sur chärj′) *vt.* **-charged′, -charg′ing** [< OFr.: see SUR-[1] & CHARGE] **1.** to overcharge **2.** to overload **3.** to fill to excess **4.** to mark (a postage stamp) with a surcharge —*n.* **1.** *a)* an additional charge *b)* an overcharge **2.** an extra or excessive load **3.** a new face value overprinted on a postage stamp
**sur·cin·gle** (sur′siŋ′g'l) *n.* [< MFr. < *sur-,* over + L. *cingulum,* a belt] a strap passed around a horse's body to bind on a saddle, pack, etc.
**sur·coat** (-kōt′) *n.* [< MFr.: see SUR-[1] & COAT] an outer coat; esp., a short cloak worn over a knight's armor
**surd** (surd) *adj.* [L. *surdus,* deaf, mute] **1.** *Math.* IRRATIONAL **2.** *Phonet.* VOICELESS —*n.* **1.** *Math.* an irrational number or quantity, as a root that cannot be determined exactly [√ 5 is a *surd*] **2.** *Phonet.* a voiceless sound
**sure** (shoor) *adj.* **sur′er, sur′est** [< OFr. < L. *securus:* see SECURE] **1.** orig., secure or safe **2.** that will not fail; always effective [a *sure* method] **3.** that can be relied upon; trustworthy [a *sure* friend] **4.** that cannot be doubted, questioned, etc.; absolutely true **5.** having no doubt; positive; confident [to be *sure* of the facts] **6.** that can be counted on to be or happen [a *sure* defeat] **7.** bound to do, experience, etc. [*sure* to lose] **8.** never missing [a *sure* aim] —*adv.* [Colloq.] **1.** surely; inevitably **2.** certainly; indeed: used as an intensive [*sure,* I'll go] —**for sure** certain(ly); without doubt —**make sure** to be or cause to be certain —**sure enough** [Colloq.] certainly; without doubt —**to be sure** surely; certainly —**sure′ness** *n.*
**sure-fire** (-fīr′) *adj.* [Colloq.] sure to be successful or as expected; that will not fail
**sure-foot·ed** (-foot′id) *adj.* not likely to stumble, fall, or err —**sure′-foot′ed·ly** *adv.* —**sure′-foot′ed·ness** *n.*
**sure·ly** (-lē) *adv.* **1.** with confidence; in a sure, unhesitating manner **2.** without a doubt; certainly [*surely* you don't believe that!] **3.** without risk of failing: chiefly in **slowly but surely**
**sure thing** [Colloq.] **1.** something certain to win, succeed, etc. **2.** all right; O.K.: used as an interjection
**sur·e·ty** (shoor′ə tē, shoor′tē) *n., pl.* **-ties 1.** a being sure; assurance **2.** something sure; certainty **3.** something that makes sure or gives assurance, as against loss, default, etc.; security **4.** a person who makes himself responsible for another; specif., *Law* one who makes himself liable for another's debts, etc. —**sure′ty·ship′** *n.*
**surf** (surf) *n.* [earlier *suffe,* prob. var. of SOUGH] **1.** the waves of the sea breaking on the shore or a reef **2.** the foam or spray caused by this —*vi.* to engage in the sport of surfing —**surf′er** *n.*
**sur·face** (sur′fis) *n.* [Fr. < *sur-* (see SUB-) + *face,* a face] **1.** *a)* the outside or outer face of a thing *b)* any side of a thing having several sides *c)* the area of such a side **2.** outward appearance **3.** *Aeron.* an airfoil **4.** *Geom.* an extent or magnitude having length and breadth, but no thickness —*adj.* **1.** of, on, or at the surface **2.** functioning or carried on land or sea, rather than in the air or under water [*surface* forces, *surface* mail] **3.** seeming such on the surface; superficial —*vt.* **-faced, -fac·ing 1.** to treat the surface of, esp. so as to make smooth or level **2.** to give a surface to, as in paving **3.** to bring a (submarine, etc.) to the surface of the water —*vi.* **1.** to rise to the surface of the water **2.** to become known, esp. after being concealed —**sur′fac·er** *n.*
**sur·face-ac·tive** (-ak′tiv) *adj. Chem.* designating or of a substance, as a detergent, that lowers the surface tension of the solvent in which it is dissolved
**surface noise** noise produced by the friction of a phonograph needle moving in the grooves of a record
**surface tension** a property of liquids in which the surface tends to contract to the smallest possible area, so that the surface seems like a thin, elastic film under tension

**surf·board** (surf′bôrd′) *n.* a long, narrow board used in the sport of surfing —*vi.* to engage in this sport —**surf′board′er** *n.* —**surf′board′ing** *n.*
**surf·boat** (-bōt′) *n.* a sturdy, light boat used in heavy surf
**surf-cast** (-kast′) *vi.* **-cast′, -cast′-ing** to fish by casting into the ocean surf from or near the shore —**surf′-cast′er** *n.*

SURFBOARD

**sur·feit** (sur′fit) *n.* [< OFr. < *sorfaire,* to overdo < *sur-* (< L. *super*), over + *faire* (< L. *facere*), to make] **1.** too great an amount or supply; excess [a *surfeit* of compliments] **2.** an indulging in too much food, drink, etc. **3.** disgust, nausea, etc. resulting from this —*vt.* to feed or supply to excess —*vi.* [Rare] to overindulge
**surf·ing** (sur′fiŋ) *n.* the sport of riding in toward shore on the crest of a wave, esp. on a surfboard: also **surf′rid′ing**
**surf·perch** (surf′purch′) *n., pl.* **-perch′, -perch′es:** see PLURAL, II, D, 2 any of various fishes of N. American Pacific coastal waters, that bear living young
**surge** (surj) *n.* [prob. < OFr. < L. *surgere,* to rise] **1.** a large wave of water, or the swelling or rushing motion of such a wave or series of waves **2.** any sudden strong rush [a *surge* of energy, electric power, etc.; the *surge* of the crowd] —*vi.* **surged, surg′ing** to move in a surge
**sur·geon** (sur′jən) *n.* a doctor who specializes in surgery
**sur·ger·y** (sur′jər ē) *n., pl.* **-ger·ies** [< OFr. < ML. *cirurgie* < Gr. *cheirourgia,* handicraft < *cheir,* the hand + *ergein,* to work] **1.** *a)* the treatment of disease, injury, etc. by operations with the hands or instruments, as the removal of diseased parts by cutting, the setting of broken bones, etc. *b)* the branch of medicine dealing with this **2.** the operating room of a surgeon or hospital
**sur·gi·cal** (-ji k'l) *adj.* **1.** of surgeons or surgery **2.** used in or connected with surgery **3.** resulting from surgery —**sur′gi·cal·ly** *adv.*
**Su·ri·nam·e** (soor′i näm′, soor′i nam′; *Du.* soor′ə nä′mə) country on the NE coast of S. America: formerly part of the Netherlands: 55,144 sq. mi.; pop. 385,000: earlier **Su·ri·nam** (-näm′, soor′ə nam′)
**sur·ly** (sur′lē) *adj.* **-li·er, -li·est** [earlier *sirly,* imperious < *sir,* SIR] bad-tempered; sullenly rude; hostile and uncivil —**sur′li·ness** *n.*
**sur·mise** (sər mīz′; *for n. also* sur′mīz) *n.* [< OFr. pp. of *surmettre* < *sur-* (< L. *super*), upon + *mettre,* to put < L. *mittere,* to send] **1.** an idea or opinion that is only a guess; conjecture **2.** the act of surmising —*vt., vi.* **-mised′, -mis′ing** to imagine or infer (something) without conclusive evidence; guess —**sur·mis′er** *n.*
**sur·mount** (sər mount′) *vt.* [OFr. *surmonter:* see SUR-[1] & MOUNT[2]] **1.** to overcome (a difficulty) **2.** to be or lie at the top of; be or rise above **3.** to climb up and across (a height, obstacle, etc.) —**sur·mount′a·ble** *adj.*
**sur·name** (sur′nām′; *for v. also* sur′nām′) *n.* [< OFr. < *sur-* (see SUR-[1]) + *nom* < L. *nomen,* name] **1.** the family name, or last name, as distinguished from a given name **2.** a name or epithet added to a person's given name (Ex.: Ivan *the Terrible*) —*vt.* **-named′, -nam′ing** to give a surname to
**sur·pass** (sər pas′) *vt.* [< MFr. < *sur-* (see SUR-[1]) + *passer,* to PASS[2]] **1.** to be better or greater than; excel **2.** to exceed in quantity, degree, etc. **3.** to go beyond the limit, capacity, etc. of [riches *surpassing* belief] —**sur·pass′a·ble** *adj.*
**sur·pass·ing** (-iŋ) *adj.* that surpasses the average or usual; exceeding or excelling; unusually excellent —*adv.* [Archaic] exceedingly —**sur·pass′ing·ly** *adv.*
**sur·plice** (sur′plis) *n.* [< Anglo-Fr. < OFr. < ML. < L. *super-,* above + *pelliceum,* fur robe] a loose, white, wide-sleeved outer vestment worn by the clergy and choir in some churches —**sur′pliced** *adj.*
**sur·plus** (sur′plus, -pləs) *n.* [OFr. < *sur-,* above + L. *plus,* more] **1.** a quantity over and above what is needed or used; excess **2.** the excess of the assets of a business over its liabilities —*adj.* that is a surplus; excess
**sur·prise** (sər prīz′) *vt.* **-prised′, -pris′ing** [< OFr. pp. of *sorprendre* < *sur-* (see SUR-[1]) + *prendre* < L. *prehendere,* to take] **1.** to come upon suddenly or unexpectedly; take unawares **2.** to attack or capture without warning **3.** *a)* to cause to feel as-

SURPLICE

tonishment by being unexpected  *b*) to present (someone) unexpectedly with a gift, etc.  **4.**  *a*) to cause by some unexpected action to do or say something unintended: often with *into*  *b*) to bring out (something) by such means —*n.*  **1.** [Rare] a surprising  **2.** an unexpected seizure or attack  **3.** a being surprised; astonishment  **4.** something that surprises because unexpected, unusual, etc. —**take by surprise 1.** to come upon suddenly or without warning  **2.** to amaze; astound —**sur·pris'ed·ly** *adv.* —**sur·pris'er** *n.*

**sur·pris·ing** (-iŋ) *adj.* causing surprise; amazing —**sur·pris'ing·ly** *adv.*

**sur·re·al·ism** (sə rē'ə liz'm) *n.* [< Fr.: see SUR-[1] & REALISM] a modern movement in art and literature, in which an attempt is made to portray the workings of the subconscious mind, as by arranging material in unexpected, fantastic ways —**sur·re'al, sur·re'al·is'tic** *adj.* —**sur·re'al·ist** *adj., n.* —**sur·re'al·is'ti·cal·ly** *adv.*

**sur·ren·der** (sə ren'dər) *vt.* [< MFr. < *sur-* (see SUR-[1]) + *rendre*, to RENDER]  **1.** to give up possession of or power over; yield to another on compulsion  **2.** to give up or abandon [to *surrender* all hope]  **3.** to yield or resign (oneself) to an emotion, influence, etc. —*vi.*  **1.** to give oneself up, esp. as a prisoner; yield  **2.** to give in (*to*) [to *surrender* to a whim] —*n.* the act of surrendering —**sur·ren'der·er** *n.*

**sur·rep·ti·tious** (sʉr'əp tish'əs) *adj.* [< L. < pp. of *surripere* < *sub-*, under + *rapere*, to seize]  **1.** done, got, made, etc. in a secret, stealthy way; clandestine  **2.** acting in a secret, stealthy way —**sur'rep·ti'tious·ly** *adv.*

**sur·rey** (sʉr'ē) *n., pl.* -**reys** [< *Surrey*, county in England] a light pleasure carriage having four wheels, two seats, and usually a flat top

**sur·ro·gate** (sʉr'ə gāt', sʉr'-; *for n. also* -git) *n.* [< L. pp. of *surrogare* < *sub-*, in place of + *rogare*, to elect]  **1.** a deputy or substitute for another person  **2.** in some States, probate court, or a judge of this court —*vt.* -**gat'ed, -gat'ing** to put in another's place as a substitute or deputy

**sur·round** (sə round') *vt.* [< OFr. < LL. < L. *super*, over + *undare*, to rise < *unda*, a wave]  **1.** to encircle on all or nearly all sides; enclose; encompass  **2.** to cut off (a military unit, etc.) from communication or retreat by encircling —*n.* [Chiefly Brit.] something that surrounds

**sur·round·ing** (-roun'diŋ) *n.* that which surrounds; esp., [*pl.*] the things, conditions, influences, etc. that surround a given place or person; environment —*adj.* that surrounds

**sur·tax** (sʉr'taks; *for v. also* sʉr taks') *n.* an extra tax on something already taxed —*vt.* to levy a surtax on

**sur·tout** (sər tōo', -tōot') *n.* [Fr. < *sur*, over + *tout*, all] a man's long, closefitting overcoat

**sur·veil·lance** (sər vā'ləns, -vāl'yəns) *n.* [Fr. < *sur-* (see SUR-[1]) + *veiller*, to watch < L. *vigilare*, to watch]  **1.** watch kept over a person, esp. a suspect  **2.** supervision —**sur·veil'lant** *n.*

**sur·vey** (sər vā'; *also, & for n. usually* sʉr'vā) *vt.* [< Anglo-Fr. < OFr. < *sur-* (see SUR-[1]) + *veoir* < L. *videre*, to see]  **1.** to examine, inspect, or consider carefully  **2.** to look at or consider, esp. in a comprehensive way  **3.** to determine the location, form, or boundaries of (a tract of land) by measuring lines and angles with a chain, transit, etc. —*vi.* to survey land —*n., pl.* -**veys**  **1.** a detailed study made by gathering and analyzing information  **2.** a comprehensive study or examination [a *survey* of Italian art]  **3.** *a*) the process of surveying a tract of land  *b*) a plan or written description of the area surveyed

**sur·vey·ing** (sər vā'iŋ) *n.*  **1.** the act of one who surveys  **2.** the science or work of surveying land

**sur·vey·or** (-ər) *n.* a person who surveys, esp. one whose work is surveying land

**surveyor's measure** a system of measurement used in surveying, based on the chain (**surveyor's chain**) as a unit: see CHAIN (*n.* 3)

**sur·viv·al** (sər vī'v'l) *n.*  **1.** the act, state, or fact of surviving  **2.** someone or something that survives, esp. an ancient belief, custom, usage, etc.

**survival of the fittest** *popular term for* NATURAL SELECTION

**sur·vive** (sər vīv') *vt.* -**vived', -viv'ing** [< OFr. < L. < *super-*, above + *vivere*, to live]  **1.** to live or exist longer than; outlive  **2.** to continue to live after or in spite of [to *survive* a wreck] —*vi.* to continue living or existing —**sur·viv'a·bil'i·ty** *n.* —**sur·viv'a·ble** *adj.* —**sur·vi'vor** *n.*

**Su·san** (sōo'z'n) [Fr. *Susanne* < LL. < Gr. < Heb. *shōshan·nāh*, lily] a feminine name: dim. *Sue*; var. *Susanna, Susannah*

**sus·cep·ti·bil·i·ty** (sə sep'tə bil'ə tē) *n., pl.* -**ties 1.** a being susceptible  **2.** [*pl.*] sensitive feelings  **3.** a susceptible temperament

**sus·cep·ti·ble** (sə sep'tə b'l) *adj.* [< ML. < L. pp. of *suscipere*, to receive < *sus-* (see SUB-), under + *capere*, to take] easily affected emotionally; having sensitive feelings —**susceptible of** admitting; allowing [testimony *susceptible of* error] —**susceptible to** easily influenced by or affected with [*susceptible to* disease] —**sus·cep'ti·ble·ness** *n.* —**sus·cep'ti·bly** *adv.*

**su·shi** (sōo'shē) *n.* [Jap.] a Japanese dish consisting of strips of raw fish wrapped about cakes of cold cooked rice

**sus·pect** (sə spekt'; *for adj. usually, & for n. always* sus'pekt) *vt.* [< L. pp. of *suspicere* < *sus-* (see SUB-), under + *spicere*, to look]  **1.** to believe to be guilty of something specified, on little or no evidence  **2.** to believe to be bad, wrong, harmful, etc.; distrust  **3.** to think it likely; surmise; suppose —*vi.* to be suspicious —*adj.* viewed with suspicion; suspected —*n.* a person who is suspected, esp. one suspected of a crime, etc.

**sus·pend** (sə spend') *vt.* [< OFr. < L. < *sus-* (see SUB-), under + *pendere*, to hang]  **1.** to remove (someone) from a position, school, team, etc., usually for a specified time, as a punishment  **2.** to cause to become inoperative for a time  **3.** to defer or hold back (judgment, a sentence, etc.)  **4.** to hang by a support from above  **5.** to hold (dust in the air, etc.) in suspension  **6.** to keep in suspense, wonder, etc. —*vi.*  **1.** to stop temporarily  **2.** to fail to pay debts or obligations  **3.** to be suspended; hang —**sus·pend'i·ble** *adj.*

**sus·pend·ers** (sə spen'dərz) *n.pl.*  **1.** a pair of straps or bands passed over the shoulders to hold up trousers or a skirt  **2.** [Brit.] garters for holding up stockings

**sus·pense** (sə spens') *n.* [< MFr. < ML. < L. pp. of *suspendere*, to SUSPEND]  **1.** the state of being undecided  **2.** a state of usually anxious uncertainty, as in awaiting a decision  **3.** the growing excitement felt as a story, play, etc. builds to a climax

**sus·pen·sion** (sə spen'shən) *n.*  **1.** a suspending or being suspended; specif., *a*) a temporary removal from a position, school, etc.  *b*) a temporary stoppage of payment, etc.  *c*) a temporary canceling, as of rules  *d*) a deferring of action on a sentence  *e*) a holding back of a judgment, etc.  **2.** a supporting device upon or from which something is suspended  **3.** the system of springs, etc. supporting a vehicle upon its undercarriage  **4.** *Chem. a*) the condition of a substance whose particles are dispersed through a fluid but not dissolved in it  *b*) a substance in this condition  *c*) a mixture of tiny, solid particles that are suspended in a liquid and settle out on standing  **5.** *Music a*) the continuing of one or more tones of one chord into a following chord while the others are changed, creating a temporary dissonance  *b*) the tone(s) so continued

**suspension bridge** a bridge suspended from cables anchored at either end and supported by towers at intervals

**sus·pen·sive** (-siv) *adj.*  **1.** that suspends, defers, or temporarily stops something  **2.** tending to suspend judgment; undecided  **3.** of, characterized by, expressing, or in suspense —**sus·pen'sive·ly** *adv.*

**sus·pen·so·ry** (-sə rē) *adj.*  **1.** suspending, supporting, etc. [a *suspensory* muscle]  **2.** suspending or delaying, esp. so as to leave something undecided —*n., pl.* -**ries** a suspensory muscle, bandage, support, etc.: also **sus·pen'sor**

**sus·pi·cion** (sə spish'ən) *n.* [< OFr. < LL. < L. < *suspicere*, to SUSPECT]  **1.** a suspecting or being suspected  **2.** the feeling or state of mind of a person who suspects  **3.** a very small amount or degree; trace —*vt.* [Dial.] to suspect —**above suspicion** not to be suspected; honorable —**on suspicion** on the basis of suspicion —**under suspicion** suspected

**sus·pi·cious** (-əs) *adj.*  **1.** arousing or likely to arouse suspicion  **2.** showing suspicion  **3.** *a*) feeling suspicion  *b*) tending habitually to suspect evil, etc. —**sus·pi'cious·ly** *adv.* —**sus·pi'cious·ness** *n.*

**Sus·que·han·na** (sus'kwi han'ə) [< Iroquoian tribal or stream name] river flowing from C N.Y. through Pa. & Md. into Chesapeake Bay

**sus·tain** (sə stān') *vt.* [< OFr. < L. *sustinere* < *sus-* (see SUB-), under + *tenere*, to hold]  **1.** to keep in existence; maintain or prolong [to *sustain* a mood]  **2.** to provide for the support of; specif., to provide nourishment for  **3.** to support; carry the weight of  **4.** to strengthen the spirits, courage, etc. of; comfort  **5.** to endure; withstand  **6.** to undergo; suffer (an injury, loss, etc.)  **7.** to uphold the validity of [to *sustain* a verdict]  **8.** to confirm; corroborate —**sus·tain'a·ble** *adj.* —**sus·tain'er** *n.* —**sus·tain'ment** *n.*

**sus·tain·ing program** (-iŋ) any radio or TV program paid for by a station or network, not by a commercial sponsor

**sus·te·nance** (sus'ti nəns) *n.*  **1.** a sustaining or being sustained  **2.** means of livelihood; maintenance; support  **3.** that which sustains life; nourishment; food

**sut·ler** (sut'lər) *n.* [< ModDu. < *soetelen*, to do dirty work] formerly, a person following an army to sell food, liquor, etc. to its soldiers

**sut·tee** (su tē', sut'ē) *n.* [< Hindi < Sans. *satī*, virtuous wife]  **1.** a Hindu widow who threw herself alive, and was cremated, on her husband's funeral pyre  **2.** the former custom of such self-cremation: also **sut·tee'ism**

**su·ture** (sōo'chər) *n.* [< L. < pp. of *suere*, to sew]  **1.** *a*) the act of joining together by or as by sewing  *b*) the line along which such a joining is made  **2.** *Anat.* the line of junction of two bones, esp. of the skull  **3.** *Surgery a*) the stitching together of the two edges of a wound or incision *b*) the gut, thread, wire, etc. used in such stitching   *c*) any of the stitches so made —*vt.* **-tured, -tur·ing** to join together as with sutures —**su′tur·al** *adj.*

**Su·wan·nee** (sə wôn′ē, -wän′-; swô′nē, swä′-) [< AmInd. name] river flowing from S Ga. across N Fla. into the Gulf of Mexico

**su·ze·rain** (sōō′zə rin, -rān′) *n.* [Fr. < *sus*, above < L. *sursum*, upward + ending of Fr. *souverain*, SOVEREIGN] **1.** a feudal lord **2.** a state in its relation to another state over which it has political control —**su′ze·rain·ty** *n., pl.* **-ties**

**s.v.** [L. *sub verbo*] under the word (specified)

**svelte** (svelt, sfelt) *adj.* [Fr. < It., ult. < L. *evellere*, to pluck out] **1.** slender and graceful **2.** suave, polished, etc.

**Sverd·lovsk** (sferd lôfsk′) city in W R.S.F.S.R., in the Ural Mountains: pop. 1,026,000

**SW, S.W., s.w. 1.** southwest **2.** southwestern

**Sw. 1.** Sweden **2.** Swedish

**swab** (swäb) *n.* [contr. < *swabber* < ModDu. *zwabber* < *zwabben*, to do dirty work] **1.** a mop for cleaning decks, floors, etc. **2.** *a*) a small piece of cotton, sponge, etc. used to apply medicine to, or clean discharged matter from, the throat, mouth, etc. *b*) matter collected in this way **3.** a brush for cleaning the barrel of a gun **4.** [Slang] *a*) a clumsy, loutish person *b*) a sailor, esp. an enlisted man in the U.S. Navy: also **swab′bie, swab′by** (-ē) —*vt.* **swabbed, swab′bing** to clean, medicate, etc. with a swab —**swab′ber** *n.*

**Swa·bi·a** (swā′bē ə) region in SW West Germany, formerly a duchy —**Swa′bi·an** *adj., n.*

**swad·dle** (swäd′'l) *vt.* **-dled, -dling** [OE. *swethel*] **1.** to wrap (a newborn baby) in long, narrow bands of cloth (**swaddling clothes** or **bands**), as in former times **2.** to bind in or as in bandages; swathe —*n.* a cloth or bandage used for swaddling

**swag** (swag) *vi.* **swagged, swag′ging** [< or akin to Norw. *svagga*, to sway] **1.** to sway or lurch **2.** to sink down; sag —*vt.* **1.** to decorate with swags **2.** to hang in a swag —*n.* **1.** a swaying or lurching **2.** a valance, garland, chain, etc. hanging decoratively in a loop or curve **3.** [Slang] loot; plunder **4.** [Austral.] a bundle containing one's personal belongings

**swage** (swāj) *n.* [OFr. *souage*] **1.** a tool for bending or shaping metal **2.** a die or stamp for shaping metal by hammering —*vt.* **swaged, swag′ing** to shape, etc. with a swage

**swag·ger** (swag′ər) *vi.* [prob. < Norw. dial. *svagra*, freq. of *svagga*, to sway] **1.** to walk with a bold, arrogant stride; strut **2.** to boast, brag, or show off in a loud, superior manner —*n.* swaggering walk, manner, or behavior —*adj.* [Brit. Colloq.] stylish, esp. in an elegant way —**swag′ger·er** *n.* —**swag′ger·ly** *adv.*

**swagger stick** a short stick or cane as carried by some army officers, etc.: also [Brit.] **swagger cane**

**Swa·hi·li** (swä hē′lē) *n.* [< Ar. *sawāḥil*, pl. of *sāḥil*, coast + -*i*, belonging to] **1.** *pl.* **-lis, -li** any of a Bantu people of Zanzibar and the nearby mainland **2.** their Bantu language, widely used as a lingua franca in E and C Africa

**swain** (swān) *n.* [< ON. *sveinn*, boy] [Poet. or Archaic] **1.** a country youth **2.** a young rustic lover or gallant **3.** a lover —**swain′ish** *adj.* —**swain′ish·ness** *n.*

**swal·low¹** (swäl′ō) *n.* [OE. *swealwe*] **1.** any of various small, swift-flying birds with long, pointed wings and a forked tail, known for their regular migrations **2.** any of certain swifts resembling swallows —**swal′low·like′** *adj.*

**swal·low²** (swäl′ō) *vt.* [OE. *swelgan*] **1.** to pass (food, etc.) from the mouth through the esophagus into the stomach **2.** to take in; absorb; engulf (often with *up*) **3.** to take back (words said); retract **4.** to put up with; tolerate *[to swallow insults]* **5.** to refrain from expressing; suppress *[to swallow one's pride]* **6.** to utter (words) indistinctly **7.** [Colloq.] to accept as true without question —*vi.* to move the muscles of the throat as in swallowing, esp. when emotionally upset —*n.* **1.** the act of swallowing **2.** the amount swallowed at one time **3.** [Chiefly Brit.] the throat or gullet —**swal′low·er** *n.*

BARN SWALLOW
(to 7½ in. long)

**swal·low·tail** (-tāl′) *n.* **1.** something having a forked shape like that of a swallow's tail **2.** a butterfly having taillike points on the hind wings

**swal·low-tailed coat** (-tāld′) a man's full-dress coat, with long, tapering tails at the back

**swam** (swam) *pt.* of SWIM¹ & SWIM²

**swa·mi** (swä′mē) *n., pl.* **-mis** [< Hindi < Sans. *svāmin*, a

lord] **1.** master: a title of respect for a Hindu religious teacher **2.** a learned man Also sp. **swa′my** *pl.* **-mies**

**swamp** (swämp, swômp) *n.* [< dial. var. of ME. *sompe*, SUMP] a piece of wet, spongy land; marsh; bog: also **swamp′land′** —*adj.* of or native to a swamp —*vt.* **1.** to plunge in a swamp, deep water, etc. **2.** to flood with or as with water **3.** to overwhelm; ruin *[swamped by debts]* **4.** to sink (a boat) by filling with water **5.** to clear of underbrush —*vi.* to sink as in a swamp —**swamp′i·ness** *n.* —**swamp′ish** *adj.* —**swamp′y** *adj.* **swamp′i·er, swamp′i·est**

**swamp buggy** an automotive vehicle for traveling over swampy or muddy terrain

**swamp fever** *same as* MALARIA

**swan** (swän, swôn) *n.* [OE.] **1.** *pl.* **swans, swan:** see PLURAL, II, D, 1 a large-bodied water bird with webfeet, a long, graceful neck, and, usually, pure white feathers **2.** a poet or singer of great ability: cf. SWAN SONG —**swan′like′** *adj.*

**swan dive** a forward dive in which the legs are held straight and together, the back is arched, and the arms are stretched out to the sides

**Swa·nee** (swô′nē, swä′-) *same as* SUWANNEE

**swang** (swaŋ) *archaic or dial. pt.* of SWING

**swank** (swaŋk) *n.* [akin to OE. *swancor*, pliant, supple] [Colloq.] **1.** stylish display or showiness in dress, etc. **2.** swaggering, showy behavior, speech, etc. —*adj.* [Colloq.] stylish in a showy way —*vi.* [Slang] to show off; boast

**swank·y** (swaŋ′kē) *adj.* **swank′i·er, swank′i·est** [Colloq.] stylish or expensive in a showy way —**swank′i·ly** *adv.* —**swank′i·ness** *n.*

**swan's-down** (swänz′doun′, swônz′-) *n.* **1.** the soft, fine underfeathers, or down, of a swan, used for trimming clothes, etc. **2.** a soft, thick fabric of wool and silk, rayon, or cotton, used for making baby clothes, etc. **3.** a soft cotton flannel Also **swans′down′**

**Swan·sea** (swän′sē, -zē) seaport in S Wales, on Bristol Channel: pop. 171,000

**swan song 1.** the sweet song supposed in ancient legend to be sung by a dying swan **2.** the last act, final creative work, etc. of a person

**swap** (swäp, swôp) *vt., vi.* **swapped, swap′ping** [ME. *swappen*, to strike: hands were struck to conclude a bargain] [Colloq.] to exchange, trade, or barter —*n.* [Colloq.] an exchange, trade, or barter —**swap′per** *n.*

**sward** (swôrd) *n.* [OE. *sweard*, skin] grass-covered soil; turf —*vt.* to cover with sward

**sware** (swer) *archaic pt.* of SWEAR

**swarm¹** (swôrm) *n.* [OE. *swearm*] **1.** a large number of bees, led by a queen, leaving a hive to start a new colony **2.** a colony of bees in a hive **3.** a moving mass or crowd —*vi.* **1.** to fly off in a swarm: said of bees **2.** to move, collect, etc. in large numbers; throng **3.** to be filled or crowded; teem —*vt.* to crowd; throng —**swarm′er** *n.*

**swarm²** (swôrm) *vi.* [orig. nautical word < ?] to climb (a tree, mast, etc.); shin (*up*)

**swart** (swôrt) *adj.* [OE. *sweart*] *dial. var. of* SWARTHY

**swarth** (swôrth) *n. dial. var. of* SWARD —*adj. same as* SWARTHY

**swarth·y** (swôr′*th*ē, -*th*ē) *adj.* **swarth′i·er, swarth′i·est** [< dial. *swarth*, var. of SWART + -Y²] having a dark complexion; dusky —**swarth′i·ly** *adv.* —**swarth′i·ness** *n.*

**swash** (swäsh, swôsh) *vi.* [echoic] **1.** to dash, strike, wash, etc. with a splashing sound; splash **2.** to swagger —*vt.* to splash (a liquid), as in a container —*n.* **1.** a channel of water cutting through or behind a sandbank **2.** the splashing of water **3.** a swaggering action

**swash·buck·ler** (-buk′lər) *n.* [prec. + BUCKLER] a blustering, swaggering fighting man —**swash′buck′ling** *n., adj.*

**swas·ti·ka** (swäs′ti kə) *n.* [< Sans. < *svasti*, well-being] **1.** a design or ornament of ancient origin in the form of a cross with four equal arms, each bent in a right-angle extension **2.** this design with the extensions bent clockwise: used as the Nazi emblem

**swat** (swät) *vt.* **swat′ted, swat′ting** [echoic] [Colloq.] to hit with a quick, sharp blow —*n.* [Colloq.] a quick, sharp blow —**swat′ter** *n.*

**swatch** (swäch) *n.* [orig., a cloth tally < ?] **1.** a sample piece of cloth or other material **2.** a small amount or number in a cluster, bunch, or patch

**swath** (swäth, swôth) *n.* [OE. *swathu*, a track] **1.** the space covered with one cut of a scythe, etc. **2.** the strip or band of grass, wheat, etc. cut in a single trip across a lawn or field by a mower, etc. **3.** any long strip —**cut a wide swath** to make a big or showy impression

**swathe¹** (swā*th*) *vt.* **swathed, swath′ing** [OE. *swathian*] **1.** to wrap or bind up in a bandage **2.** to wrap (a bandage, etc.) around something **3.** to surround or envelop —*n.* a bandage or wrapping —**swath′er** *n.*

**swathe²** (swā*th*) *n. same as* SWATH

**sway** (swā) *vi.* [ON. *sveigja*, to bend] **1.** *a)* to swing or move from side to side or to and fro *b)* to vacillate between one opinion, etc. and another **2.** *a)* to lean or incline to one side; veer *b)* to incline in judgment or opinion —*vt.* **1.** to cause to sway, or swing to and fro, vacillate, incline to one side, etc. **2.** to change the thinking or actions of; influence in a certain direction [*swayed* by promises] **3.** [Archaic] to rule over; control —*n.* **1.** a swaying or being swayed; a swinging, leaning, etc. **2.** influence or control **3.** rule; dominion —**hold sway** to reign or prevail —**sway′er** *n.* —**sway′ing·ly** *adv.*

**sway·backed** (-bakt′) *adj.* having an abnormal sagging of the spine, usually as a result of strain or overwork, as some horses, etc. —**sway′back′** *n.*

**Swa·zi·land** (swä′zē land′) country in SE Africa, surrounded on three sides by South Africa: 6,705 sq. mi.; pop. 421,000

**swear** (swer) *vi.* **swore**, **sworn**, **swear′ing** [OE. *swerian*] **1.** to make a solemn declaration, supporting it with an appeal to God or to something held sacred [to *swear* on one's honor] **2.** to make a solemn promise; vow **3.** to use profane or vulgar, offensive language; curse **4.** *Law* to give evidence under oath —*vt.* **1.** to declare solemnly in the name of God or of something held sacred **2.** to pledge or vow on oath **3.** to assert with great emphasis **4.** to take (an oath) by swearing **5.** to administer a legal oath to — **swear by 1.** to name (something held sacred) in taking an oath **2.** to have great faith in —**swear for** to give assurance for; guarantee —**swear in** to administer an oath to (a person taking office, a witness, etc.) —**swear off** to promise to give up [to *swear off* smoking] —**swear out** to obtain (a warrant for arrest) by making a charge under oath —**swear′er** *n.*

**swear·word** (-wurd′) *n.* a word or phrase used in swearing or cursing; profane or vulgar, offensive word

**sweat** (swet) *vi.* **sweat** or **sweat′ed**, **sweat′ing** [OE. *swætan* < *swat*, sweat] **1.** to give out a salty moisture through the pores of the skin; perspire **2.** *a)* to give out moisture in droplets on its surface, as a ripening cheese *b)* to condense water in droplets on its surface [a glass of iced tea *sweats*] **3.** to ferment: said of tobacco leaves, etc. **4.** to come out in drops through pores; ooze **5.** to work hard enough to cause sweating **6.** [Colloq.] to suffer distress, anxiety, etc. —*vt.* **1.** *a)* to give out (moisture) through a porous surface *b)* to condense (moisture) on the surface **2.** to cause to perspire, as by drugs, exercise, etc. **3.** to cause to give out moisture; esp., to ferment **4.** to make wet with perspiration **5.** to heat (an alloy) so as to extract an easily fusible constituent **6.** to unite (metal parts) by heating the solder applied to the ends until it melts **7.** *a)* to cause to work so hard as to sweat *b)* to cause (employees) to work long hours at low wages under poor working conditions **8.** [Colloq.] to get information from by torture or grueling questioning **9.** [Slang] to try hard or too hard to get or achieve —*n.* **1.** the clear, salty liquid given out through the pores in the skin **2.** moisture given out or collected in droplets on a surface **3.** a sweating or being sweated **4.** a condition of eagerness, anxiety, impatience, etc. **5.** hard work; drudgery —**sweat blood** [Slang] **1.** to work very hard; overwork **2.** to be impatient, anxious, etc. —**sweat off** to get rid of (weight) by sweating —**sweat out** [Slang] **1.** to suffer through (something) **2.** to wait anxiously or impatiently for

**sweat·band** (-band′) *n.* a band of leather, etc. inside a hat to protect it against sweat from the brow

**sweat·er** (swet′ər) *n.* **1.** a person or thing that sweats **2.** a knitted outer garment for the upper part of the body, styled as a pullover or a jacket

**sweat gland** any of the many, tiny tubular glands just beneath the skin that secrete sweat

**sweat shirt** a heavy, long-sleeved cotton jersey, worn to absorb sweat during or after exercise, sometimes with loose trousers (**sweat pants**) of the same material

**sweat·shop** (-shäp′) *n.* a shop where employees work long hours at low wages under poor working conditions

**sweat·y** (-ē) *adj.* **sweat′i·er**, **sweat′i·est 1.** wet with sweat; sweating **2.** of sweat [a *sweaty* odor] **3.** causing sweat [*sweaty* work] —**sweat′i·ly** *adv.* —**sweat′i·ness** *n.*

**Swed. 1.** Sweden **2.** Swedish

**Swede** (swēd) *n.* a native or inhabitant of Sweden

**Swe·den** (swē′d'n) country in N Europe, in the E part of the Scandinavian Peninsula: 173,620 sq. mi.; pop. 8,115,000; cap. Stockholm

**Swe·den·borg** (swēd′'n bôrg′; *Sw.* sväd′'n bôr′y), **E·man·u·el** (i man′yoo wəl) (born *Emanuel Swedberg*) 1688–1772; Swed. mystic & religious philosopher —**Swe′den·bor′gi·an** (-bôr′jē ən, -gē-) *adj.*, *n.*

**Swed·ish** (swē′dish) *adj.* of Sweden, its people, their language, etc. —*n.* the North Germanic language of the Swedes —**the Swedish** the people of Sweden

**Swedish turnip** *same as* RUTABAGA

**sweep** (swēp) *vt.* **swept**, **sweep′ing** [akin to (or ? altered <) OE. *swapan*: see SWOOP] **1.** to clear or clean as by brushing with a broom [to *sweep* a floor] **2.** to remove or clear away (dirt, debris, etc.) as with a broom or brushing movement **3.** to strip, carry away, or destroy with forceful movement **4.** to carry along with a sweeping movement **5.** to touch or brush in moving across **6.** to pass swiftly over or across **7.** *a)* to drag (a river, pond, etc.) with a net, grapple, etc. *b)* to clear (waters) with a mine sweeper **8.** to rake with gunfire **9.** to win overwhelmingly [to *sweep* an election] —*vi.* **1.** to clean a surface, room, etc. as with a broom **2.** to move or progress steadily with speed, force, or gracefulness [planes *swept* across the sky] **3.** to trail, as skirts or the train of a gown **4.** to extend in a long curve or line [a road *sweeping* up the hill] —*n.* **1.** the act of sweeping, as with a broom **2.** a steady sweeping movement or stroke [the *sweep* of a scythe] **3.** a trailing, as of skirts **4.** range or scope **5.** extent or stretch [a *sweep* of meadow] **6.** a line, contour, curve, etc. that gives an impression of flow or movement **7.** a person whose work is sweeping; specif., *short for* CHIMNEY SWEEP **8.** [*usually pl.*] sweepings **9.** complete victory or success, as in a series of contests **10.** a long oar **11.** a long pole mounted on a pivot, with a bucket at one end, used for raising water **12.** *Electronics* a crossing by an electron beam of the screen of a cathode-ray tube —**sweep′er** *n.*

**sweep·ing** (-iŋ) *adj.* **1.** that sweeps **2.** extending over a wide range **3.** *a)* extensive; comprehensive *b)* complete *c)* indiscriminate —*n.* **1.** [*pl.*] things swept up, as dirt from a floor **2.** the act, work, etc. of one that sweeps —**sweep′ing·ly** *adv.*

**sweep·stakes** (-stāks′) *n.*, *pl.* **-stakes′ 1.** a lottery in which each participant puts up money in a common fund from which the money for the winners comes **2.** *a)* a contest, esp. a horse race, which determines the winners of such a lottery *b)* the prize or prizes won **3.** any of various other lotteries Also **sweep′stake′**, **sweeps**

**sweet** (swēt) *adj.* [OE. *swete*] **1.** *a)* having a taste of, or like that of, sugar *b)* containing sugar in some form [*sweet* wines] **2.** *a)* pleasant in taste, smell, sound, looks, etc. *b)* gratifying [*sweet* praise] *c)* having a friendly, pleasing disposition *d)* sentimental *e)* [Slang] good, delightful, nice, etc. **3.** *a)* not rancid, spoiled, or sour [*sweet* milk] *b)* not salty or salted: said of water or butter *c)* free from sourness or acidity: said of soil **4.** *Jazz* characterized by rather strict adherence to melody, blandness, moderate tempo, etc. —*n.* **1.** a being sweet; sweetness **2.** something sweet; specif., *a)* [Chiefly Brit.] a candy; sweetmeat *b)* [Brit.] a sweet dessert **3.** a sweetheart; darling —*adv.* in a sweet manner —**be sweet on** [Colloq.] to be in love with —**sweet′ish** *adj.* —**sweet′ly** *adv.* —**sweet′ness** *n.*

**sweet alyssum** a short garden plant with small spikes of tiny flowers

**sweet·bread** (swēt′bred′) *n.* the thymus (**heart,** or **throat, sweetbread**) or the pancreas (**stomach sweetbread**) of a calf, lamb, etc., when used as food

**sweet·bri·er, sweet·bri·ar** (-brī′ər) *n. same as* EGLANTINE

**sweet cherry 1.** an old-world cherry, widely grown for its sweet fruit **2.** its fruit

**sweet clover** any of various plants of the legume family, with small white or yellow flowers, and leaflets in groups of three: grown for hay, forage, etc.

**sweet corn** any of various strains of Indian corn with kernels rich in sugar, eaten unripe as a cooked vegetable

**sweet·en** (swēt′'n) *vt.* **1.** to make sweet with or as with sugar **2.** to make pleasant or agreeable **3.** to make less harsh, less acidic, etc. —*vi.* to become sweet

**sweet·en·er** (-ər) *n.* a sweetening agent, esp. a synthetic substance, such as saccharin

**sweet·en·ing** (-iŋ) *n.* **1.** the process of making sweet **2.** something that sweetens

**sweet flag** a perennial marsh plant with sword-shaped leaves, small, green flowers, and a sweet-scented rhizome

**sweet gum 1.** a large N. American tree with alternate maplelike leaves and spiny fruit balls **2.** the wood of this tree **3.** the aromatic balsam of this tree

**sweet·heart** (swēt′härt′) *n.* **1.** *a)* a person with whom one is in love *b)* darling; a term of endearment **2.** [Slang] a very agreeable person or an excellent thing

**sweet marjoram** *see* MARJORAM

**sweet·meat** (-mēt′) *n.* a bit of sweet food, esp. a candy, candied fruit, or the like

**sweet pea** a climbing annual plant of the legume family, with butterfly-shaped flowers

**sweet pepper 1.** a variety of the red pepper producing a large, mild fruit **2.** the fruit

**sweet potato 1.** a tropical, trailing plant with purplish flowers and a fleshy, orange or yellow, tuberlike root used as a vegetable **2.** its root **3.** [Colloq.] *same as* OCARINA

**sweet-talk** (-tôk′) *vt., vi.* [Colloq.] to talk in a flattering or blandishing way (to)

**sweet tooth** [Colloq.] a fondness or craving for sweets

**sweet william, sweet William** a perennial pink with dense, flat clusters of small flowers

**swell** (swel) *vi.* **swelled, swelled** or **swol′len, swell′ing** [OE. *swellan*] **1.** to become larger as a result of pressure from within; expand **2.** to curve out; bulge; protrude **3.** to extend above the normal level **4.** to form swells, or large waves: said of the sea **5.** to be filled (*with* pride, etc.) **6.** to increase within one [his anger *swelled*] **7.** to increase in size, force, intensity, etc. **8.** to increase in loudness —*vt.* to cause to swell; specif., *a*) to cause to increase in size, volume, etc. *b*) to cause to bulge *c*) to fill with pride, etc. *d*) to cause to increase in loudness —*n.* **1.** a part that swells; bulge; specif., *a*) a large wave that moves steadily without breaking *b*) a piece of rising ground **2.** a swelling or being swollen **3.** an increase in size, amount, degree, etc. **4.** [Colloq.] a person, esp. a man, of wealth and fashion: an old-fashioned term **5.** *Music a*) a crescendo usually followed by a decrescendo *b*) a sign (< >) indicating this *c*) a device for controlling the loudness of tones, as in an organ —*adj.* [Slang] first-rate; excellent: used in a general way to show approval

**swelled head** [Colloq.] great self-conceit

**swell·ing** (-iŋ) *n.* **1.** an increasing or being increased in size, volume, etc. **2.** a swollen part, as on the body

**swel·ter** (swel′tər) *vi.* [OE. *sweltan*, to die] to be or feel oppressively hot; sweat and wilt from great heat —*vt.* to cause to swelter —*n.* **1.** a sweltering **2.** oppressive heat

**swel·ter·ing** (-iŋ) *adj.* very hot, sweaty, sticky, etc.: also **swel′try** (-trē), **-tri·er, -tri·est** —**swel′ter·ing·ly** *adv.*

**swept** (swept) *pt. & pp. of* SWEEP

**swept·back** (swept′bak′) *adj.* having a backward slant, as the wings of an aircraft

**swept·wing** (-wiŋ′) *adj. Aeron.* having sweptback wings

**swerve** (swurv) *vi., vt.* **swerved, swerv′ing** [OE. *sweorfan*, to scour] to turn aside suddenly from a straight line, course, etc. —*n.* the act or degree of swerving —**swerv′er** *n.*

**swift** (swift) *adj.* [OE.] **1.** moving or capable of moving with great speed; fast **2.** coming, happening, or done quickly **3.** acting or responding quickly; prompt [*swift* to help] —*adv.* in a swift manner —*n.* an insect-eating, swift-flying bird resembling the swallow, as the chimney swift —**swift′ly** *adv.* —**swift′ness** *n.*

**Swift** (swift), **Jonathan** 1667–1745; Eng. satirist, born in Ireland

**swig** (swig) *vt., vi.* **swigged, swig′ging** [< ?] [Colloq.] to drink in big gulps or amounts —*n.* [Colloq.] a big gulp, esp. of liquor —**swig′ger** *n.*

**swill** (swil) *vt.* [OE. *swilian*] **1.** to flood with water so as to wash **2.** to drink greedily **3.** to feed swill to (pigs, etc.) —*vi.* to drink in large quantities —*n.* **1.** garbage, etc. mixed with liquid and fed to pigs, etc. **2.** garbage or slop **3.** the act of swilling **4.** a swig

**swim**[1] (swim) *vi.* **swam, swum, swim′ming** [OE. *swimman*] **1.** to move through water by movements of the arms and legs, or of flippers, fins, etc. **2.** to move along smoothly **3.** to float on the surface of a liquid **4.** to be immersed in a liquid **5.** to overflow [eyes *swimming* with tears] —*vt.* **1.** to move in or across (a body of water) by swimming **2.** to cause to swim **3.** to perform (a specified stroke) in swimming —*n.* an act, spell, or distance of swimming —**in the swim** conforming to the current fashions, or active in the main current of affairs —**swim′ma·ble** *adj.* —**swim′mer** *n.*

**swim**[2] (swim) *n.* [OE. *swima*] the condition of being dizzy —*vi.* **swam, swum, swim′ming 1.** to be dizzy **2.** to have a hazy, reeling, or whirling appearance

**swim bladder** a gas-filled sac in the body cavity of most bony fishes, giving buoyancy to the body

**swim·mer·et** (swim′ə ret′) *n.* any of the small abdominal appendages in certain crustaceans, used for swimming, etc.

**swimming hole** a pool or a deep place in a river, creek, etc. used for swimming

**swim·ming·ly** (swim′iŋ lē) *adv.* easily and with success

**swimming pool** a pool of water for swimming; esp., a tank specially built for the purpose

**swim·suit** (swim′sōōt′) *n.* a garment worn for swimming

**Swin·burne** (swin′bərn), **Algernon Charles** 1837–1909; Eng. poet & critic

**swin·dle** (swin′d'l) *vt.* **-dled, -dling** [< G. *schwindeln*, to cheat] **1.** to get money or property from (another) under false pretenses; cheat; defraud **2.** to get by fraud —*vi.* to engage in swindling others —*n.* an act of swindling —**swin′dler** *n.*

**swine** (swin) *n., pl.* **swine** [OE. *swin*] **1.** a pig or hog: usually used collectively **2.** a vicious, contemptible, or disgusting person

**swine·herd** (-hurd′) *n.* one who tends swine

**swing** (swiŋ) *vi.* **swung, swing′ing** [OE. *swingan*] **1.** to sway or move backward and forward, as a freely hanging object **2.** to walk, trot, etc. with freely swaying movements **3.** to

strike (*at*) **4.** to turn, as on a hinge or swivel **5.** *a*) to hang; be suspended *b*) [Colloq.] to be hanged in execution **6.** to move on a swing (*n.* 10) **7.** to have an exciting rhythmic quality [music that really *swings*] **8.** [Slang] to be very fashionable, active, etc., esp. in the pursuit of pleasure —*vt.* **1.** *a*) to move (a weapon, bat, etc.) with a sweeping motion; flourish *b*) to lift with a sweeping motion **2.** to cause (a freely hanging object) to move backward and forward **3.** to cause to turn or pivot, as on a hinge **4.** to cause to hang freely [to *swing* a scaffold from the roof] **5.** to cause to move in a curve [to *swing* a car around a corner] **6.** [Colloq.] to cause to come about successfully; manage with the desired results [to *swing* an election] **7.** to play (music) in the style of swing —*n.* **1.** the act of swinging **2.** the arc through which something swings **3.** the manner of swinging, as with a golf club, baseball bat, etc. **4.** freedom to do as one wishes **5.** a relaxed motion, as in walking **6.** a sweeping blow or stroke **7.** the course or movement of some activity, etc. **8.** the force behind something swung; impetus **9.** rhythm, as of poetry or music **10.** a seat hanging from ropes or chains, on which one can sit and swing **11.** a trip or tour [a *swing* around the country] **12.** a style of jazz music of about 1935 to 1945, characterized by large bands, improvised counterpoint, etc. —*adj.* of, in, or playing swing (music) —**in full swing** **1.** in complete and active operation **2.** going on without restraint —**swing′er** *n.*

**swin·gle** (swiŋ′g'l) *vt.* **-gled, -gling** [< MDu. < *swinghel*, a swingle] to beat and clean (flax or hemp) with a swingle —*n.* a wooden, swordlike tool for beating and cleaning

**swin·gle·tree** (-trē′) *n. same as* SINGLETREE

**swing shift** [Colloq.] the evening work shift in some factories, from midafternoon to about midnight

**swin·ish** (swin′ish) *adj.* of, like, or fit for swine; beastly, piggish, etc. —**swin′ish·ly** *adv.* —**swin′ish·ness** *n.*

**swipe** (swip) *n.* [prob. var. of SWEEP] [Colloq.] a hard, sweeping blow —*vt.* **swiped, swip′ing 1.** [Colloq.] to hit with a hard, sweeping blow **2.** [Slang] to steal —*vi.* to make a sweeping blow or stroke

**swirl** (swurl) *vi.* [ME. *swyrl*, prob. < Norw. dial. *sverra*, to whirl] **1.** to move with a whirling motion **2.** to be dizzy —*vt.* to cause to swirl —*n.* **1.** a whirl; eddy **2.** a twist; curl; whirl —**swirl′ing·ly** *adv.* —**swirl′y** *adj.*

**swish** (swish) *vi.* [echoic] **1.** to move with a sharp, hissing sound, as a cane swung through the air **2.** to rustle, as skirts —*vt.* to cause to swish —*n.* **1.** a hissing or rustling sound **2.** a movement that makes this sound —*adj.* [Slang] of, like, or for effeminate male homosexuals — **swish′y** *adj.* **swish′i·er, swish′i·est**

**Swiss** (swis) *adj.* of Switzerland, its people, or its culture —*n.* **1.** *pl.* **Swiss** a native or inhabitant of Switzerland **2.** [s-] a type of sheer fabric —**the Swiss** the people of Switzerland

**Swiss chard** *same as* CHARD

**Swiss (cheese)** a pale-yellow, hard cheese with many large holes, originally made in Switzerland

**Swiss steak** a thick cut of round steak, pounded with flour and braised, usually with tomatoes, onions, etc.

**switch** (swich) *n.* [prob. < MDu. or LowG.] **1.** a thin, flexible twig, stick, etc. used for whipping **2.** the bushy part of the tail of a cow, etc. **3.** a tress of detached hair used by women as part of a coiffure **4.** a sharp, lashing movement, as with a whip **5.** a device used to open, close, or divert an electric circuit **6.** a movable section of railroad track used in transferring a train from one track to another **7.** a shift or transference, esp. if sudden —*vt.* **1.** to whip as with a switch **2.** to jerk or swing sharply [a cow *switches* its tail] **3.** to shift; change; turn aside **4.** *a*) to operate the switch of (an electric current) *b*) to turn (an electric light, etc.) *on* or *off* in this way **5.** to transfer (a train, etc.) from one track to another by means of a switch **6.** [Colloq.] to change or exchange [to *switch* places] —*vi.* **1.** to move as from one track to another **2.** to shift; transfer **3.** to swing sharply; lash —**switch′er** *n.*

**switch·back** (-bak′) *n.* a zigzag road up a steep grade

**switch-blade knife** (-blād′) a large jackknife that snaps open when a release button on the handle is pressed

**switch·board** (-bôrd′) *n.* a panel equipped with apparatus for controlling the operation of a system of electric circuits, as in a telephone exchange

**switch-hit·ter** (-hit′ər) *n.* a baseball player who bats sometimes right-handed and sometimes left-handed

**switch·man** (-mən) *n., pl.* **-men** a railroad employee who operates switches

**switch·yard** (-yärd′) *n.* a railroad yard where cars are shifted from one track to another by means of switches

**Switz·er** (swit′sər) *n.* **1.** a Swiss **2.** a Swiss mercenary soldier

**Switz·er·land** (swit′sər lənd) country in WC Europe, in the Alps: 15,941 sq. mi.; pop. 6,270,000; cap. Bern

**swiv·el** (swiv′′l) n. [< base of OE. swifan, to revolve] a coupling device that allows free turning of the parts attached to it; specif., a chain link in two parts, one piece fitting like a collar below the bolt head of the other and turning freely about it —vt. -eled or -elled, -el·ing or -el·ling 1. to cause to turn as on a swivel 2. to fit or support with a swivel —vi. to turn as on a swivel

**swivel chair** a chair whose seat turns horizontally on a pivot in the base

**swiz·zle stick** (swiz′′l) [< ?] a small rod for stirring mixed drinks

**swob** (swäb) n., vt. swobbed, swob′bing var. sp. of SWAB

**swol·len** (swō′lən) alt. pp. of SWELL —adj. blown up; distended; bulging

**swoon** (swōōn) vi. [< OE. geswogen, unconscious] 1. to faint 2. to feel strong, esp. rapturous emotion —n. an act of swooning —swoon′er n. —swoon′ing·ly adv.

**swoop** (swōōp) vt. [OE. swapan, to sweep along] to snatch or seize suddenly: often with up —vi. to pounce or sweep (down or upon) —n. the act of swooping

**swoosh** (swoosh, swōōsh) vi., vt. [echoic intens. of SWISH] to move, pour, etc. with a sharp, rustling or whistling sound —n. such a sound

**swop** (swäp) n., vt., vi. swopped, swop′ping var. sp. of SWAP

**sword** (sôrd) n. [OE. sweord] 1. a hand weapon having a long, sharp, pointed blade, set in a hilt 2. a) power; esp., military power b) war —at swords' points ready to quarrel or fight —cross swords 1. to fight 2. to argue —put to the sword 1. to kill with a sword 2. to slaughter, esp. in war —sword′like′ adj.

**sword·fish** (-fish′) n., pl. -fish′, -fish′es: see FISH a large marine food and game fish with the upper jawbone extending in a long, flat, swordlike projection

**sword grass** any of a number of sedges or grasses with toothed or sword-shaped leaves

**sword knot** a loop of leather, ribbon, etc. attached to a sword hilt as an ornament or, orig., as a wrist support

**sword·play** (-plā′) n. the act or skill of using a sword in fencing or fighting

SWORDFISH
(to 15 ft. long)

**swords·man** (sôrdz′mən) n., pl. -men 1. a person who uses a sword in fencing or fighting 2. a person skilled in using a sword Also [Archaic] sword·man (sôrd′mən), pl. -men —swords′man·ship′ n.

**swore** (swôr) pt. of SWEAR

**sworn** (swôrn) pp. of SWEAR —adj. bound, pledged, promised, etc. by or as by an oath

**swot** (swät) n., vt. swot′ted, swot′ting var. sp. of SWAT

**swum** (swum) pp. of SWIM¹ & SWIM²

**swung** (swuŋ) pp. & pt. of SWING

**syb·a·rite** (sib′ə rīt′) n. [< Sybarite, a native of Sybaris, an ancient Greek city in S Italy, famed for its luxury] anyone very fond of luxury and self-indulgence —syb′a·rit′ic (-rit′ik) adj. —syb′a·rit′i·cal·ly adv.

**Syb·il** (sib′′l) [< SIBYL] a feminine name

**syc·a·more** (sik′ə môr′) n. [< OFr. < L. < Gr. sykomoros] 1. a shade tree native to Egypt and Asia Minor, with edible, figlike fruit 2. a maple shade tree found in Europe and Asia 3. same as PLANE¹

**syc·o·phant** (sik′ə fənt) n. [< L. < Gr. sykophantēs, informer < sykon, a fig + phainein, to show] a person who seeks favor by flattering people of wealth or influence; toady —syc′o·phan·cy n., pl. -cies —syc′o·phan′tic (-fan′tik), syc′o·phant′ish adj. —syc′o·phan′ti·cal·ly, syc′o·phant′ish·ly adv.

**Syd·ney** (sid′nē) 1. [< SIDNEY] a masculine name 2. seaport in SE Australia: pop. 2,713,000

**syl-** same as SYN-: used before l

**syl·la·bar·y** (sil′ə ber′ē) n., pl. -bar′ies [< ModL. < L. syllaba: see SYLLABLE] 1. a table of syllables 2. a set of the written characters of a language representing syllables

**syl·lab·ic** (si lab′ik) adj. 1. of a syllable or syllables 2. forming a syllable or the nucleus of a syllable; specif., standing by itself as the nucleus of a syllable without an accompanying vowel: said of a consonant, as the l in tattle 3. pronounced with the syllables distinct —n. a syllabic sound —syl·lab′i·cal·ly adv.

**syl·lab·i·cate** (si lab′ə kāt′) vt. -cat′ed, -cat′ing same as SYLLABIFY —syl·lab′i·ca′tion n.

**syl·lab·i·fy** (si lab′ə fī′) vt. -fied′, -fy′ing [< syllabification < L. syllaba, syllable + -FICATION] to form or divide into syllables —syl·lab′i·fi·ca′tion n.

**syl·la·ble** (sil′ə b′l) n. [< OFr. < L. < Gr. syllabē, ult. < syn-, together + lambanein, to hold] 1. a word or part of a word pronounced with a single, uninterrupted sounding of the voice 2. any of the parts into which a written word is divided, in fairly close relation to its spoken syllables, to show where the word can be broken at the end of a line 3. the least bit of detail, as of something said —vt., vi. -bled, -bling to pronounce in or as in syllables

**syl·la·bub** (sil′ə bub′) n. [< ?] a dessert or beverage made of sweetened milk or cream mixed with wine or cider and beaten to a froth

**syl·la·bus** (sil′ə bəs) n., pl. -bus·es, -bi′ (-bī′) [LL., a list < L. < Gr. sillybos, parchment label] a summary or outline, esp. of a course of study

**syl·lo·gism** (sil′ə jiz′m) n. [< MFr. < L. < Gr. syn-, together + logizesthai, to reason] 1. a form of reasoning in which two statements or premises are made and a logical conclusion drawn from them Ex.: All mammals are warm-blooded (major premise); whales are mammals (minor premise); therefore, whales are warmblooded (conclusion) 2. reasoning from the general to the particular —syl′lo·gis′·tic, syl′lo·gis′ti·cal adj. —syl′lo·gis′ti·cal·ly adv.

**sylph** (silf) n. [ModL. sylphus < L., a spirit < ?] 1. an imaginary being supposed to live in the air 2. a slender, graceful woman or girl —sylph′like′ adj.

**syl·van** (sil′vən) adj. [< ML. < L. silva, a wood] 1. of or characteristic of the woods or forest 2. living, found, or carried on in the woods or forest 3. wooded —n. one who lives in the woods

**Syl·vi·a** (sil′vē ə) [< L. < silva, a wood] a feminine name

**sym-** same as SYN-: used before m, p, and b

**sym·bi·o·sis** (sim′bī ō′sis, -bē-) n. [ModL. < Gr. < symbioun < syn-, together + bioun, to live] 1. Biol. the intimate living together of two kinds of organisms, esp. where such association is of mutual advantage 2. a similar relationship in which persons or groups are dependent on each other —sym′bi·ot′ic (-ät′ik) adj.

**sym·bol** (sim′b′l) n. [< Fr. < L. < Gr. symbolon, token, ult. < syn-, together + ballein, to throw] 1. an object used to represent something abstract [the dove is a symbol of peace] 2. a mark, letter, abbreviation, etc. standing for an object, quality, process, quantity, etc., as in music, chemistry, mathematics, etc. —vt. -boled or -bolled, -bol·ing or -bol·ling same as SYMBOLIZE

**sym·bol·ic** (sim bäl′ik) adj. 1. of or expressed in a symbol or symbols 2. that serves as a symbol (of something) 3. using symbolism Also sym·bol′i·cal —sym·bol′i·cal·ly adv.

**symbolic logic** a modern type of formal logic using special mathematical symbols for propositions and relationships among propositions

**sym·bol·ism** (sim′b′l iz′m) n. 1. the representation of things by use of symbols, esp. in art or literature 2. a system of symbols 3. symbolic meaning

**sym·bol·ist** (-ist) n. 1. a person who uses symbols 2. a person who practices symbolism in representing ideas, etc., esp. in art or literature —sym′bol·is′tic adj. —sym′bol·is′ti·cal·ly adv.

**sym·bol·ize** (-īz′) vt. -ized′, -iz′ing 1. to be a symbol of; typify; stand for 2. to represent by a symbol or symbols —vi. to use symbols —sym′bol·i·za′tion n. —sym′bol·iz′er n.

**sym·me·try** (sim′ə trē) n., pl. -tries [< MFr. < L. < Gr., ult. < syn-, together + metron, a measure] 1. similarity of form or arrangement on either side of a dividing line or plane; correspondence of opposite parts in size, shape, and position 2. balance or beauty of form resulting from such correspondence —sym·met·ri·cal (si met′ri k′l), sym·met′ric adj. —sym·met′ri·cal·ly adv.

**sym·pa·thet·ic** (sim′pə thet′ik) adj. 1. of, resulting from, feeling, or showing sympathy; sympathizing 2. in agreement with one's tastes, mood, etc.; congenial 3. showing favor, approval, etc. [to be sympathetic to a plan] 4. Physiol. designating or of that part of the autonomic nervous system involved in the involuntary response to alarm, as by speeding the heart rate, dilating the pupils of the eyes, etc. 5. Physics designating or of vibrations caused by other vibrations having the same period that are transmitted from a neighboring vibrating body —sym′pa·thet′i·cal·ly adv.

**sym·pa·thize** (sim′pə thīz′) vi. -thized′, -thiz′ing 1. to share or understand the feelings or ideas of another; be in sympathy 2. to feel or express sympathy, esp. in pity or compassion; commiserate 3. to be in harmony or accord —sym′pa·thiz′er n. —sym′pa·thiz′ing·ly adv.

**sym·pa·thy** (sim′pə thē) n., pl. -thies [< L. < Gr. < syn-, together + pathos, feeling] 1. sameness of feeling; affinity between persons 2. agreement in qualities; harmony; accord 3. a mutual liking or understanding arising from sameness of feeling 4. a sharing of, or the ability to share, another person's mental state, emotions, etc.; esp., [often pl.] pity or compassion felt for another's trouble, suffering, etc. 5. a feeling of approval of an idea, cause, etc.

**sympathy** (or **sympathetic**) **strike** a strike by a group of workers in support of another group on strike

**symphonic poem** a composition of program music for full symphony orchestra, interpreting particular poetic or descriptive ideas, and free in form

**sym·pho·ny** (sim′fə nē) *n., pl.* **-nies** [< OFr. < L. < Gr. *syn-*, together + *phōnē*, a sound] **1.** harmony of sounds, esp. of instruments **2.** any harmony, as of color **3.** *Music a)* an extended composition for full orchestra, having several (usually four) movements related in subject, but varying in form and execution *b)* short for SYMPHONY ORCHESTRA *c)* [Colloq.] a concert by a symphony orchestra —**sym·phon·ic** (sim fän′ik) *adj.* —**sym·phon′i·cal·ly** *adv.*

**symphony orchestra** a large orchestra of string, wind, and percussion sections for playing symphonic works

**sym·po·si·um** (sim pō′zē əm) *n., pl.* **-si·ums, -si·a** (-ə) [L. < Gr. *syn-*, together + *posis*, a drinking] **1.** any meeting or social gathering at which ideas are freely exchanged **2.** a conference organized for the discussion of some particular subject **3.** a collection of opinions, esp. a group of essays, on a given subject —**sym·po′si·ac′** (-ak′) *adj.*

**symp·tom** (simp′təm) *n.* [< ML. < LL. < Gr. *symptōma*, ult. < *syn-*, together + *piptein*, to fall] any circumstance, event, or condition that accompanies something and indicates its existence or occurrence; sign; specif., *Med.* any condition accompanying a disease or a physical disorder and serving as an aid in diagnosis —**symp′to·mat′ic** (-tə mat′ik) *adj.* —**symp′to·mat′i·cal·ly** *adv.*

**symp·tom·a·tize** (-tə mə tīz′) *vt.* **-tized′, -tiz′ing** to be a symptom or sign of: also **symp′tom·ize′**

**syn-** [Gr. < *syn*, with] *a prefix meaning* with, together with, at the same time, by means of: *syn-* is assimilated to *syl-* before *l; sym-* before *m, p, b*; and *sys-* before *s* and aspirate *h*

**syn. 1.** synonym **2.** synonymous **3.** synonymy

**syn·a·gogue** (sin′ə gäg′, -gôg′) *n.* [< OFr. < LL. < Gr. *synagōgē*, an assembly, ult. < *syn-*, together + *agein*, to bring] **1.** an assembly of Jews meeting for worship and religious study **2.** a building or place used for such an assembly **3.** the Jewish religion as organized in such local congregations Also **syn′a·gog′** —**syn′a·gog′al** (-gäg′′l, -gôg′-), **syn′a·gog′i·cal** (-gäj′i k′l) *adj.*

**syn·apse** (si naps′) *n.* [ModL. < Gr. *synapsis*, a union] the point of contact between adjacent neurons, where nerve impulses are transmitted from one to the other —**syn·ap′tic** (-nap′tik) *adj.*

**sync, synch** (siŋk) *vt., vi.* shortened form of SYNCHRONIZE

**syn·chro·mesh** (siŋ′krə mesh′) *adj.* designating or employing a device by which gears to be meshed are automatically brought to the same speed of rotation before the shift is completed —*n.* a synchromesh gear system

**syn·chro·nism** (siŋ′krə niz′m) *n.* **1.** the fact or state of being synchronous; occurrence at the same time **2.** a chronological listing of persons or events in history, showing existence or occurrence at the same time —**syn′chro·nis′tic** *adj.* —**syn′chro·nis′ti·cal·ly** *adv.*

**syn·chro·nize** (siŋ′krə nīz′) *vi.* **-nized′, -niz′ing** [< Gr. *synchronos*, contemporary < *syn-*, together + *chronos*, time] to move or occur at the same time or rate; be synchronous —*vt.* **1.** to cause to agree in time or rate of speed; regulate (clocks, action and dialogue, etc.) so as to make synchronous **2.** to assign (events, etc.) to the same date or period —**syn′chro·ni·za′tion** *n.* —**syn′chro·niz′er** *n.*

**syn·chro·nous** (-nəs) *adj.* [< LL. < Gr.: see prec.] **1.** happening at the same time; simultaneous **2.** having the same period between movements, occurrences, etc.; having the same rate and phase, as vibrations Also **syn′chro·nal** —**syn′chro·nous·ly** *adv.* —**syn′chro·nous·ness** *n.*

**syn·chro·tron** (-trän′) *n.* [SYNCHRO(NOUS) + (ELEC)TRON] a circular machine for accelerating charged particles, esp. electrons, to very high energies through the use of a low-frequency magnetic field in combination with a high-frequency electrostatic field

**syn·cline** (siŋ′klīn) *n.* [< *synclinal* < Gr. *syn-*, together + *klinein*, to incline] *Geol.* a down fold in stratified rocks from whose central axis the beds rise upward and outward in opposite directions: opposed to ANTICLINE —**syn·cli·nal** (sin klī′n′l, siŋ′klī n′l) *adj.*

**syn·co·pate** (siŋ′kə pāt′) *vt.* **-pat′ed, -pat′ing** [< ML. pp. of *syncopare*, to cut short < LL., to swoon < *syncope*: see SYNCOPE] **1.** to shorten (a word) by syncope **2.** *Music a)* to shift (the regular accent) as by beginning a tone on an unaccented beat and continuing it through the next accented beat, or on the last half of a beat and continuing it through the first half of the following beat *b)* to use such shifted accents in (a composition, etc.) —**syn′co·pa′tor** *n.*

**syn·co·pa·tion** (siŋ′kə pā′shən) *n.* **1.** a syncopating or being syncopated **2.** syncopated music, a syncopated rhythm, etc. **3.** *Gram.* same as SYNCOPE

**syn·co·pe** (siŋ′kə pē) *n.* [LL. < Gr. < *syn-*, together +

*koptein*, to cut] **1.** the dropping of sounds or letters from the middle of a word, as in *Wooster* for *Worcester* **2.** a fainting caused by an inadequate flow of blood to the brain

**syn·cre·tize** (siŋ′krə tīz′) *vt., vi.* **-tized′, -tiz′ing** [< ModL. < Gr. *synkrētizein*] to combine, unite, or reconcile

**syn·dic** (sin′dik) *n.* [Fr. < LL. < Gr. *syndikos*, advocate < *syn-*, together + *dikē*, justice] **1.** [Brit.] a business manager, esp. of a university **2.** a civil magistrate —**syn′di·cal** *adj.*

**syn·di·cal·ism** (-di k′l iz′m) *n.* a theory of trade unionism in which all means of production and distribution would be brought under the control of federations of labor unions by the use of general strikes, etc. —**syn′di·cal·ist** *adj., n.*

**syn·di·cate** (sin′də kit; *for v.* -kāt′) *n.* [Fr. *syndicat* < *syndic*, SYNDIC] **1.** a council of syndics **2.** *a)* an association of individuals or corporations formed to carry out some financial project requiring much capital *b)* any group organized to further some undertaking *c)* a group of similar organizations, as of newspapers, owned as a chain **3.** an organization that sells articles or features for publication by many newspapers —*vt.* **-cat′ed, -cat′ing** **1.** to manage as or form into a syndicate **2.** to sell (an article, etc.) through a syndicate for publication in many newspapers, etc. —*vi.* to form a syndicate —**syn′di·ca′tion** *n.* —**syn′di·ca′tor** *n.*

**syn·drome** (sin′drōm) *n.* [ModL. < Gr. < *syn-*, with + *dramein*, to run] **1.** a set of symptoms characterizing a disease **2.** any set of characteristics identifying a type, condition, etc.

**syne** (sīn) *adv., conj., prep.* [Scot.] since; ago

**syn·ec·do·che** (si nek′də kē) *n.* [< ML. < L. < Gr., ult. < *syn-*, together + *ekdechesthai*, to receive] a figure of speech in which a part is used for a whole, an individual for a class, a material for a thing, or the reverse of any of these (Ex.: *bread* for *food, the army* for *a soldier*, or *copper* for a *penny*)

**syn·er·gism** (sin′ər jiz′m) *n.* [< ModL. < Gr. < *syn-*, together + *ergon*, work] the simultaneous action of separate agencies which, together, have greater total effect than the sum of their individual effects: said esp. of drugs: also **syn′er·gy** (-jē) —**syn′er·gis′tic** *adj.*

**Synge** (siŋ), (Edmund) **John Mil·ling·ton** (mil′iŋ tən) 1871–1909; Ir. dramatist

**syn·od** (sin′əd) *n.* [OE. *sinoth*, ult. < Gr. *synodos*, lit., a meeting < *syn-*, together + *hodos*, way] **1.** a council of churches or church officials; specif., a high governing body in any of certain Christian churches **2.** any assembly or council —**syn′od·al** *adj.*

**syn·od·i·cal** (si näd′i k′l) *adj.* **1.** of a synod **2.** *Astron.* of or having to do with conjunction, esp. with the interval between two successive conjunctions of the same heavenly bodies Also **syn·od′ic** —**syn·od′i·cal·ly** *adv.*

**syn·o·nym** (sin′ə nim) *n.* [< L. < Gr. < *syn-*, together + *onyma*, a name] **1.** a word having the same or nearly the same meaning as another in the same language **2.** a word used in metonymy —**syn′o·nym′ic, syn′o·nym′i·cal** *adj.*

**syn·on·y·mous** (si nän′ə məs) *adj.* [see prec.] of the same or nearly the same meaning —**syn·on′y·mous·ly** *adv.*

**syn·on·y·my** (-mē) *n., pl.* **-mies** **1.** the study of synonyms **2.** a list or listing of synonyms, esp. one in which the terms are discriminated from one another **3.** the quality of being synonymous; sameness or near sameness of meaning

**syn·op·sis** (si näp′sis) *n., pl.* **-ses** (-sēz) [LL. < Gr. < *syn-*, together + *opsis*, a seeing] a short outline or review of the main points, as of a story; summary

**syn·op·size** (-sīz) *vt.* **-sized, -siz·ing** to make a synopsis

**syn·op·tic** (-tik) *adj.* **1.** of or giving a synopsis, summary, or general view **2.** giving an account from the same point of view: said esp. [*often* S-] of the first three Gospels Also **syn·op′ti·cal** —**syn·op′ti·cal·ly** *adv.*

**syn·o·vi·a** (si nō′vē ə) *n.* [ModL. < ?] the clear, albuminous lubricating fluid secreted by the membranes of joint cavities, tendon sheaths, etc. —**syn·o′vi·al** *adj.*

**syn·tac·tic** (sin tak′tik) *adj.* of or in accordance with syntax: also **syn·tac′ti·cal** —**syn·tac′ti·cal·ly** *adv.*

**syn·tax** (sin′taks) *n.* [< Fr. < LL. < Gr., ult. < *syn-*, together + *tassein*, to arrange] *Gram.* **1.** the arrangement of words as elements in a sentence to show their relationship to one another **2.** the organization and relationship of word groups, phrases, clauses, and sentences; sentence structure **3.** the branch of grammar dealing with this

**syn·the·sis** (sin′thə sis) *n., pl.* **-ses′** (-sēz′) [Gr. < *syn-*, together + *tithenai*, to place] **1.** the putting together of parts or elements so as to form a whole **2.** a whole formed in this way **3.** *Chem.* the formation of a complex compound by the combining of two or more simpler compounds, elements, or radicals —**syn′the·sist** *n.*

**syn·the·size** (-sīz′) *vt.* **-sized′, -siz′ing** **1.** to bring together into a whole by synthesis **2.** to form by bringing together separate parts; specif., *Chem.* to produce by synthesis rather than by extraction, refinement, etc.

**syn·the·siz·er** (-sī′zər) *n.* a person or thing that synthesizes; specif., an electronic music device that produces sounds not made by ordinary musical instruments

**syn·thet·ic** (sin thet′ik) *adj.* **1.** of, involving, or using synthesis **2.** produced by synthesis; specif., produced by chemical synthesis, rather than of natural origin **3.** not real or genuine; artificial **4.** using inflection rather than word order and separate words to express syntactic relationships /Latin is a *synthetic* language/ Also **syn·thet′i·cal** —*n.* something synthetic —**syn·thet′i·cal·ly** *adv.*

**synthetic resin** any of a large class of complex organic compounds formed from simpler molecules by polymerization, used esp. in making plastics

**syph·i·lis** (sif′ə lis) *n.* [ModL. < *Syphilus,* hero of a Latin poem (1530)] a disease, caused by a spirochete and usually passed on during sexual intercourse or gotten in the womb before birth —**syph′i·lit′ic** *adj., n.*

**sy·phon** (sī′fən) *n., vi., vt. var. sp. of* SIPHON

**Syr. 1.** Syria **2.** Syriac **3.** Syrian

**Syr·a·cuse** (sir′ə kyoos′, -kyooz′) **1.** [after ff.] city in C N.Y.: pop. 170,000 (met. area 643,000) **2.** seaport on the SE coast of Sicily: pop. 105,000

**Syr·i·a** (sir′ē ə) **1.** region of ancient times at the E end of the Mediterranean **2.** country in the NW part of this region: 71,227 sq. mi.; pop. 6,451,000; cap. Damascus

**Syr·i·ac** (sir′ē ak′) *n.* the ancient Aramaic language of Syria, used from the 3d cent. to the 13th

**Syr·i·an** (sir′ē ən) *adj.* of Syria, its people, their language, etc. —*n.* **1.** a member of the Semitic people of Syria **2.** their modern Arabic dialect

**sy·rin·ga** (sə rin′gə) *n.* [ModL., genus name < Gr. *syrinx* (see ff.): from former use in making pipes] **1.** *same as* LILAC (senses 1 & 2) **2.** *earlier name for* MOCK ORANGE

**sy·ringe** (sə rinj′, sir′inj) *n.* [< ML. < Gr. *syrinx* (gen. *syringos*), a reed, pipe] **1.** a device consisting of a narrow tube fitted at one end with a rubber bulb or piston by means of which a liquid can be drawn in and then pushed out in a stream: used to inject fluids into, or extract fluids from, body cavities, to cleanse wounds, etc. **2.** *short for* HYPODERMIC SYRINGE —*vt.* **-ringed′, -ring′ing** to cleanse, inject, etc. with a syringe

SYRINGE

**syr·inx** (sir′inks) *n., pl.* **sy·rin·ges** (sə rin′jēz), **syr′inx·es** [ModL. < Gr., a pipe] **1.** the vocal organ of songbirds, at or near the base of the trachea **2.** *same as* PANPIPE

**syr·up** (sir′əp, sur′-) *n.* [< OFr. < ML. < Ar. *sharāb,* a drink] any sweet, thick liquid; specif., *a)* a solution made by boiling sugar with water and, often, flavored *b)* any such solution used in preparing medicines *c) short for* MAPLE SYRUP, CORN SYRUP, etc. —**syr′up·y** *adj.*

**sys·tem** (sis′təm) *n.* [< LL. < Gr. *systēma,* ult. < *syn-,* together + *histanai,* to set] **1.** a group of things or parts working together or connected in some way so as to form a whole /a solar *system,* school *system, system* of highways/ **2.** a set of principles, rules, etc. linked in an orderly way to show a logical plan /an economic *system*/ **3.** a method or plan of classification or arrangement **4.** *a)* an established way of doing something; method; procedure *b)* orderliness or methodical planning in one's way of proceeding **5.** *a)* the body considered as a functioning organism *b)* a number of organs acting together to perform one of the main bodily functions /the nervous *system*/ **6.** a related series of natural objects or elements, as rivers **7.** *Geol.* a major division of stratified rocks comprising the rocks laid down during a period

**sys·tem·at·ic** (sis′tə mat′ik) *adj.* **1.** based on or forming a system **2.** according to a system, method, or plan; regular; orderly **3.** orderly in planning or doing things; methodical **4.** of or having to do with classification Also **sys′tem·at′i·cal** —**sys′tem·at′i·cal·ly** *adv.*

**sys·tem·a·tize** (sis′təm ə tīz′) *vt.* **-tized′, -tiz′ing** to form into a system; arrange according to a system; make systematic —**sys′tem·a·ti·za′tion** *n.* —**sys′tem·a·tiz′er** *n.*

**sys·tem·ic** (sis tem′ik) *adj.* of a system; specif., *Physiol.* of or affecting the entire organism or bodily system —*n.* any of a group of pesticides that are absorbed into the tissues of plants, making the plants poisonous to insects, etc. that feed on them —**sys·tem′i·cal·ly** *adv.*

**sys·tem·ize** (sis′tə mīz′) *vt.* **-ized′, -iz′ing** *same as* SYSTEMATIZE —**sys′tem·i·za′tion** *n.*

**systems analysis** an engineering technique that breaks down complex technical, social, etc. problems into basic elements whose interrelations are evaluated and programmed into a complete and integrated system —**systems analyst**

**systems engineering** a branch of engineering using computer science, facts from systems-analysis studies, etc. to design integrated operational systems for specific organizations —**systems engineer**

**sys·to·le** (sis′tə lē′) *n.* [ModL. < Gr. *systolē;* ult. < *syn-,* together + *stellein,* to send] the usual rhythmic contraction of the heart, esp. of the ventricles, during which the blood is driven onward from the chambers —**sys·tol·ic** (sis täl′ik) *adj.*

**Szcze·cin** (shche tsēn′) river port in NW Poland, on the Oder: pop. 335,000

# T

**T, t** (tē) *n., pl.* **T's, t's 1.** the twentieth letter of the English alphabet **2.** the sound of *T* or *t*

**T** (tē) *n.* an object shaped like T —*adj.* shaped like T —**to a T** to perfection; exactly

**'t** it: a contraction, as in *'twas, do't*

**-t** *var. of* -ED (in some past participles and adjectives derived from them) /slept, gilt/

**T. 1.** tablespoon(s) **2.** Territory **3.** Testament **4.** Tuesday

**t. 1.** teaspoon(s) **2.** temperature **3.** tense **4.** time **5.** ton(s) **6.** town(ship) **7.** transitive **8.** troy

**ta** (tä) *interj.* [Brit.] thank you: orig. a child's term

**Ta** *Chem.* tantalum

**tab¹** (tab) *n.* [< ?] **1.** a small, flat loop or strap fastened to something for pulling it, hanging it up, etc. **2.** an attached or projecting piece of a card or paper, useful in filing —*vt.* **tabbed, tab′bing 1.** to provide with tabs **2.** to choose or select

**tab²** (tab) *n.* [prob. < TABULATE] [Colloq.] **1.** a bill or check, as for expenses **2.** total cost or expenses —**keep tabs (or a tab) on** [Colloq.] to follow or watch every move of; check on —**pick up the tab** [Colloq.] to pay the bill or total cost

**tab³** (tab) *n. shortened form of:* **1.** TABLET **2.** TABULATOR —*vt.* **tabbed, tab′bing** *shortened form of* TABULATE

**tab.** table(s)

**tab·ard** (tab′ərd) *n.* [OFr. *tabart*] **1.** a loose, heavy jacket worn outdoors as by peasants in the Middle Ages **2.** a short-sleeved, blazoned cloak worn by a knight over his armor **3.** a herald's official coat, blazoned with his lord's arms

**Ta·bas·co** (tə bas′kō) [< *Tabasco,* a Mexican state] *a trademark for* a hot sauce made from a kind of red pepper

**tab·by** (tab′ē) *n., pl.* **-bies** [< Fr. < ML. < Ar. *'attābi,* quarter of Baghdad where it was made] **1.** a silk taffeta with wavy markings **2.** a gray or brown cat with dark stripes **3.** any pet cat, esp. a female —*adj.* having dark stripes over gray or brown

**tab·er·nac·le** (tab′ər nak′'l) *n.* [< LL. < L. *tabernaculum,* a tent, dim. of *taberna,* a hut] **1.** formerly, a temporary shelter, as a tent **2.** [T-] *a)* the portable sanctuary carried by the Jews in their wanderings from Egypt to Palestine: Ex. 25–27 *b)* later, the Jewish Temple **3.** a shrine, niche, etc. with a canopy **4.** a place of worship, esp. one seating many people **5.** a cabinetlike enclosure on an altar, for consecrated Hosts —*vi.* **-led, -ling** to dwell temporarily —*vt.* to place in a tabernacle —**tab′er·nac′u·lar** (-yə lər) *adj.*

**ta·bes dor·sa·lis** (tā′bēz dôr sā′lis, -sal′is) [ModL. < L. *tabes,* a wasting away + *dorsualis,* of the back] a chronic disease of the nervous system, usually caused by syphilis and characterized by loss of reflexes and of muscular coordination, etc.

**ta·ble** (tā′b'l) *n.* [OFr. < L. *tabula,* a board, tablet] **1.** orig., a thin slab of metal, stone, or wood, used for inscriptions; tablet **2.** *a)* a piece of furniture consisting of a flat, horizontal top set on legs *b)* such a table set with food for

**tableau** 761 **tael**

a meal *c)* food served at table *d)* the people seated at a table **3.** a large, flat-topped piece of furniture or equipment used for games, as a working surface, etc. *[pool table, examining table]* **4.** *a)* a compact, orderly list of details, contents, etc. *b)* a compact, orderly arrangement of facts, figures, etc., usually in rows and columns *[the multiplication table]* **5.** *same as* TABLELAND **6.** any of various flat surfaces, layers, or parts, as the upper, flat facet of a gem —*adj.* **1.** of, for, or on a table **2.** fit for serving at table *[table salt]* —*vt.* **-bled, -bling 1.** orig., to tabulate **2.** to put on a table **3.** to set aside the consideration of (a motion, bill, etc.) **4.** [Brit.] to put up for consideration —**at table** at a meal —**on the table** postponed or shelved: said of a bill, etc. —**the tables** laws, as the Ten Commandments, inscribed on flat stone slabs —**turn the tables** to reverse a situation completely —**under the table** [Colloq.] **1.** secretly, as a bribe **2.** drunk to the point of unconsciousness
**tab·leau** (tab′lō, ta blō′) *n., pl.* **-leaux** (-lōz, -blōz′), **-leaus** [Fr. < OFr. *tablel,* dim. of *table:* see prec.] **1.** a striking, dramatic scene or picture **2.** a representation of a scene, picture, etc. by a person or group posed in costume
**ta·ble·cloth** (tā′b'l klôth′, -kläth′) *n.* a cloth for covering a table, esp. at meals
**ta·ble d'hôte** (tä′b'l dōt′, tab′'l) *pl.* **ta′bles d'hôte′** (-b'lz, -'lz) [Fr., lit., table of the host] a complete meal with courses as specified, served at a restaurant or hotel for a set price: distinguished from ALA CARTE
**ta·ble-hop** (tā′b'l häp′) *vi.* **-hopped′, -hop′ping** to leave one's table in a restaurant, etc. and visit about at other tables —**ta′ble-hop′per** *n.*
**ta·ble·land** (-land′) *n.* a high, broad, level region; plateau
**table linen** tablecloths, napkins, etc.
**ta·ble·spoon** (-spoon′) *n.* **1.** *a)* a large spoon used for serving at table *b)* *same as* SOUPSPOON **2.** a spoon used as a measuring unit in cookery, equal to 3 teaspoonfuls or 1/2 fluid ounce **3.** *same as* TABLESPOONFUL
**ta·ble·spoon·ful** (-fool) *n., pl.* **-fuls** as much as a tablespoon will hold
**tab·let** (tab′lit) *n.* [< MFr. dim. of *table:* see TABLE] **1.** a flat, thin piece of stone, metal, etc., esp. one with an inscription **2.** a smooth, flat leaf of wood, metal, etc., used to write on **3.** a writing pad containing sheets of paper fastened at one edge **4.** a small, flat piece of some hard substance, as medicine, soap, etc.
**table tennis** a game somewhat like tennis in miniature, played on a table, with a small celluloid or plastic ball and short-handled, wooden paddles
**ta·ble·ware** (tā′b'l wer′) *n.* dishes, glassware, silverware, etc. for use at table
**Tab·loid** (tab′loid) [TABL(ET) + -OID] *a trademark for* a small tablet of medicine —*n.* **[t-]** a newspaper with pages about half the ordinary size, carrying many pictures and short, often sensational, news stories —*adj.* **[t-]** condensed; short
**ta·boo** (ta boo′, ta-) *n.* [Tongan *tabu*] **1.** *a)* among some Polynesian peoples, a sacred prohibition which makes certain people or things untouchable, unmentionable, etc. *b)* the system of such prohibitions **2.** any social restriction resulting from convention or tradition —*adj.* **1.** sacred and forbidden by taboo **2.** forbidden by tradition, etc. —*vt.* **1.** to put under taboo **2.** to prohibit or forbid
**ta·bor** (tā′bər) *n.* [OFr. *tabur* < Per. *tabīrah*] a small drum, formerly used by a fife player to beat out his own rhythmic accompaniment Also sp. **ta′bour**
**tab·o·ret** (tab′ər it, tab′ə ret′) *n.* [OFr., a stool, dim. of *tabur:* see prec.] **1.** a small tabor **2.** a stool Also sp. **tab′ou·ret**
**Ta·briz** (tä brēz′) city in NW Iran: pop. 468,000
**ta·bu** (ta boo′, ta-) *n., adj., vt. var. sp. of* TABOO
**tab·u·lar** (tab′yə lər) *adj.* [< L. < *tabula:* see TABLE] **1.** flat like a table **2.** *a)* of or arranged in tables or columns *b)* calculated by using tables —**tab′u·lar·ly** *adv.*
**tab·u·late** (tab′yə lāt′; *for adj.* -lit) *vt.* **-lat′ed, -lat′ing** [< L. *tabula* (see TABLE) + -ATE¹] to put (facts, statistics, etc.) in a table or columns; arrange systematically —*adj.* having a flat surface —**tab′u·la′tion** *n.*
**tab·u·la·tor** (-lāt′ər) *n.* a person or thing that tabulates; specif., a device or key for setting stops on a typewriter carriage, as for typing columns
**tac·a·ma·hac** (tak′ə mə hak′) *n.* [< Sp. < Nahuatl *tecomahca*] **1.** a strong-smelling gum resin used in ointments and incenses **2.** any of several trees yielding this resin
**ta·chom·e·ter** (ta käm′ə tər, tə-) *n.* [< Gr. *tachos,* speed + -METER] a device that indicates or measures the revolutions per minute of a revolving shaft —**ta·chom′e·try** *n.*
**tac·it** (tas′it) *adj.* [< Fr. < L. pp. of *tacere,* to be silent] **1.** making no sound; saying nothing **2.** unspoken; silent **3.**

not expressed openly, but implied or understood *[tacit approval]* —**tac′it·ly** *adv.* —**tac′it·ness** *n.*
**tac·i·turn** (tas′ə tʉrn′) *adj.* [< Fr. < L. < *tacere:* see prec.] almost always silent; not liking to talk —**tac′i·tur′ni·ty** *n.* —**tac′i·turn′ly** *adv.*
**Tac·i·tus** (tas′ə təs), (**Publius Cornelius**) 55?–117? A.D.; Rom. historian
**tack** (tak) *n.* [MDu. *tacke,* a twig, point] **1.** a short nail or pin with a sharp point and a somewhat large, flat head **2.** *a)* a fastening, esp. in a slight or temporary way *b)* *Sewing* a stitch for marking darts, etc. from a pattern, clipped and later removed: in full, **tailor's tack** *c)* stickiness **3.** a zigzag course, or movement in such a course **4.** a course of action or policy **5.** *Naut. a)* a rope for holding securely the forward lower corner of some sails *b)* the corner thus held *c)* the direction in which a ship is moving in relation to the position of the sails *d)* a change of direction made by changing the position of the sails *e)* a course against the wind *f)* any of a series of zigzag movements in such a course **6.** a horse's equipment, as saddles, bridles, etc. —*vt.* **1.** to fasten with tacks **2.** to attach temporarily, as with long stitches **3.** to attach as a supplement *[to tack an amendment onto a bill]* **4.** *Naut. a)* to change the course of (a ship) by turning its head to the wind *b)* to maneuver (a ship) against the wind by a series of tacks —*vi.* **1.** *a)* to tack a ship *b)* to change its course by being tacked: said of a ship **2.** to go in a zigzag course **3.** to change suddenly one's course of action —**tack′er** *n.*
**tack·le** (tak′'l; *in nautical usage, often* tā′k'l) *n.* [MDu. *takel,* pulley, rope] **1.** apparatus; equipment; gear *[fishing tackle]* **2.** a system of ropes and pulleys used to lower, raise, or move weights **3.** the act or an instance of tackling, as in football **4.** *Football* the player next to either end on the offensive or defensive line **5.** *Naut.* the running rigging and pulleys used to operate a ship's sails —*vt.* **tack′led, tack′ling 1.** to fasten by means of tackle **2.** to harness (a horse) **3.** to take hold of; seize **4.** to undertake to do, solve, or deal with *[to tackle a problem]* **5.** *Football* to stop or throw (an opponent carrying the ball) —*vi. Football* to tackle an opponent —**tack′ler** *n.*
**tack·y¹** (tak′ē) *adj.* **tack′i·er, tack′i·est** [TACK (n. 2) + -Y²] sticky, as varnish, glue, etc. before completely dry —**tack′i·ness** *n.*
**tack·y²** (tak′ē) *adj.* **tack′i·er, tack′i·est** [< *tacky,* a hillbilly < ?] [Colloq.] dowdy or shabby, as in appearance —**tack′i·ness** *n.*
**ta·co** (tä′kō) *n., pl.* **-cos** [AmSp.] a Mexican dish consisting of a fried, folded tortilla filled with chopped meat, shredded lettuce, etc.
**Ta·co·ma** (tə kō′mə) [AmInd., lit., snowy peak] seaport in W Wash., on Puget Sound: pop. 159,000
**tac·o·nite** (tak′ə nīt′) *n.* [< *Taconic* Range in Vt. and Mass., where such rock strata were first identified] a low-grade iron ore that is pelletized for blast-furnace reduction
**tact** (takt) *n.* [Fr. < L. pp. of *tangere,* to touch] a sense of the right thing to say or do without offending; skill in dealing with people
**tact·ful** (takt′fəl) *adj.* having or showing tact —**tact′ful·ly** *adv.* —**tact′ful·ness** *n.*
**tac·tic** (tak′tik) *n.* [< ModL. < Gr.: see TACTICS] **1.** *same as* TACTICS **2.** a detail or branch of tactics
**tac·ti·cal** (tak′ti k'l) *adj.* **1.** of or having to do with tactics, esp. in military or naval maneuvers **2.** characterized by or showing skill in tactics —**tac′ti·cal·ly** *adv.*
**tac·ti·cian** (tak tish′ən) *n.* an expert in tactics
**tac·tics** (tak′tiks) *n.pl.* [Gr. (*ta*) *taktika,* lit., (the) matters of arrangement < *tassein,* to arrange] **1.** *a)* [*with sing. v.*] the science of maneuvering military and naval forces in action, esp. with reference to short-range objectives *b)* actions in accord with this science **2.** any methods used to gain an end; esp., skillful methods
**tac·tile** (tak′t'l; *chiefly Brit.* -tīl) *adj.* [Fr. < L. *tactilis* < *tangere,* to touch] **1.** that can be perceived by the touch; tangible **2.** of, having, or related to the sense of touch —**tac·til′i·ty** (-til′ə tē) *n.*
**tact·less** (takt′lis) *adj.* not having or showing tact —**tact′less·ly** *adv.* —**tact′less·ness** *n.*
**tad·pole** (tad′pōl′) *n.* [ME. *tadde,* toad + *poll,* head] the larva of certain amphibians, as frogs and toads, having gills and a tail and living in water
**Ta·dzhik Soviet Socialist Republic** (tä′jik) republic of the U.S.S.R., in C Asia: 55,250 sq. mi.; pop. 2,900,000; cap. Dushanbe: also **Ta·dzhik·i·stan** (tä jek′i stän′)
**tael** (tāl) *n.* [Port. < Malay *tahil,* a weight] **1.** any of vari-

ous units of weight of E Asia **2.** formerly, a Chinese unit of money

**ta·en** (tān) [Poet.] taken

**taf·fe·ta** (taf'i tə) *n.* [< OFr., ult. < Per. < *tāftan,* to weave] a fine, rather stiff fabric of silk, nylon, acetate, etc., with a sheen —*adj.* like or made of taffeta

**taff·rail** (taf'rāl') *n.* [< Du. *tafereel,* a panel, ult. < L. *tabula:* see TABLE] the rail around a ship's stern

**taf·fy** (taf'ē) *n.* [< ?] a chewy candy made of sugar or molasses boiled down and pulled: cf. TOFFEE

**Taft** (taft), **William Howard** 1857–1930; 27th president of the U.S. (1909–13); chief justice of the U.S. (1921–30)

**tag** (tag) *n.* [prob. < Scand.] **1.** orig., a hanging end, as on a torn skirt **2.** any hanging part or loosely attached end **3.** a hard-tipped end, as of metal, on a cord or lace **4.** a card, paper, ticket, etc. attached to something as a label or for identification, etc. **5.** an epithet **6.** the sentence or sentences ending a speech, story, play, etc. **7.** a children's game in which one player, called "it," chases the others until he touches, or tags, one of them, making him "it" in turn —*vt.* **tagged, tag'ging 1.** to provide with a tag; put a tag on **2.** to identify by an epithet **3.** to choose or select **4.** to overtake and touch as in the game of tag **5.** *Baseball* to touch (a base runner) with the ball, thus putting him out **6.** [Colloq.] to follow close behind —*vi.* [Colloq.] to follow close behind a person or thing (usually with *along, after,* etc.) —**tag'ger** *n.*

**Ta·ga·log** (tä gä'läg, -lôg) *n.* **1.** *pl.* **-logs, -log** a member of a Malayan people of the Philippine Islands **2.** their Indonesian language

**Ta·gore** (tä'gôr, tə gôr'), **Sir Ra·bin·dra·nath** (rə bēn'drə nät') 1861–1941; Hindu poet

**Ta·gus** (tä'gəs) river flowing west across C Spain & Portugal into the Atlantic

**Ta·hi·ti** (tə hēt'ē, tä-) chief island of the Society Islands, in the South Pacific —**Ta·hi·ti·an** (tə hēsh'ən, tä-; -hēt'ē ən) *adj., n.*

**Ta·hoe** (tä'hō), **Lake** [< AmInd. *tah-oo,* lake] lake on the border between Calif. & Nev.: a summer resort

**Tai** (tī) *n., adj.* same as THAI

**tail¹** (tāl) *n.* [OE. *tægel*] **1.** the rear end of an animal's body, esp. when forming a distinct, flexible appendage to the trunk **2.** anything like an animal's tail in form or position [the *tail* of a shirt] **3.** a luminous train behind a comet **4.** the hind, last, bottom, or inferior part of anything **5.** [*often pl.*] the reverse side of a coin **6.** a long tress of hair **7.** *a*) the rear section of an aircraft, rocket, or missile *b*) a set of stabilizing planes at the rear of an airplane **8.** [*pl.*] [Colloq.] *a*) a swallow-tailed coat *b*) full-dress attire for men **9.** [Colloq.] a person or vehicle that follows another, esp. in surveillance —*adj.* **1.** at the rear **2.** from the rear [a *tail* wind] —*vt.* **1.** to provide with a tail **2.** to form the tail or end of, as a procession **3.** to fasten at or by the tail **4.** to fasten one end of (a brick, board, etc.) into a wall, etc. **5.** [Slang] to follow stealthily —*vi.* **1.** to become gradually smaller or fainter (with *off* or *away*) **2.** to form, or become part of, a line or tail **3.** [Colloq.] to follow close behind, as in surveillance —**on one's tail** following one closely —**turn tail** to run from danger, difficulty, etc. —**tail'less** *adj.* —**tail'like'** *adj.*

**tail²** (tāl) *n.* [< OFr. < *taillier:* see TAILOR] same as ENTAIL (*n.* 2 & 3) —*adj.* limited in a specific way as to inheritance

**tailed** (tāld) *adj.* having a (specified kind of) tail: usually in combination [*bobtailed*]

**tail·gate** (tāl'gāt') *n.* a board or gate at the back of a wagon, truck, station wagon, etc.: it can be removed or swung down for loading, etc.: also **tail'board'** —*vi., vt.* **-gat'ed, -gat'ing** to drive too closely behind (another vehicle) —**tail'gat'-er** *n.*

**tail·ing** (-iŋ) *n.* **1.** [*pl.*] refuse left in milling, mining, etc. **2.** the part of a projecting brick, stone, etc. fastened into a wall

TAILGATE

**tail·light** (tāl'līt') *n.* a light, usually red, at the rear of a vehicle to warn vehicles coming from behind

**tai·lor** (tā'lər) *n.* [< OFr. < *taillier,* to cut < LL. *taliare,* to split < L. *talea,* a twig] a person who makes, repairs, or alters clothes —*vi.* to work as a tailor —*vt.* **1.** to make (clothes) by tailor's work **2.** to make clothes for **3.** to form, alter, etc. so as to meet certain conditions [a novel *tailored* to popular taste] **4.** to fashion (women's garments) with trim, simple lines —**tai'lor·ing** *n.*

**tai·lor·bird** (-burd') *n.* any of several small Asiatic and African birds that stitch leaves together to camouflage and hold their nests

**tai·lored** (tā'lərd) *adj.* having trim, simple lines, as some women's garments, or specially fitted, as slipcovers

**tai·lor-made** (tā'lər mād') *adj.* made by or as by a tailor; specif., *a*) having trim, simple lines; tailored *b*) made-to-

order or handmade, rather than by machine in a factory

**tail·piece** (tāl'pēs') *n.* **1.** a part forming the end of something **2.** the piece of wood at the lower end of a violin, etc., to which the strings are attached **3.** a short beam with one end tailed in a wall and the other supported by a header **4.** *Printing* an ornamental design at the end of a chapter, etc.

**tail·pipe** (-pīp') *n.* **1.** an exhaust pipe at the rear of an automotive vehicle **2.** the exhaust duct of a jet engine

**tail·race** (-rās') *n.* the lower part of a millrace, through which water flows after going over a water wheel

**tail·spin** (-spin') *n.* **1.** same as SPIN (*n.* 4): also **tail spin 2.** a state of rapidly increasing depression or confusion

**tail wind** a wind blowing in the same direction as the course of a ship or aircraft

**taint** (tānt) *vt.* [prob. a merging of ME. *taynten,* to touch + Anglo-Fr. *teinter,* to color, ult. < L. *tingere,* to wet] **1.** to affect with something injurious, unpleasant, etc.; spoil; infect **2.** to make morally corrupt —*vi.* to become tainted —*n.* **1.** a trace of corruption, disgrace, etc. **2.** an infectious or contaminating trace —**taint'less** *adj.*

**Tai·pei, Tai·peh** (tī'pe') capital of Taiwan, in the N part: pop. 1,700,000

**Tai·wan** (tī'wän') island province of China, off the SE coast: seat of the Kuomintang government: 13,885 sq. mi.; pop. 14,964,000; cap. Taipei —**Tai'wan'i·an** *adj., n.*

**Tai·yü·an** (tī'yü än') city in N China: pop. 1,500,000

**Taj Ma·hal** (täzh' mə häl', täj') mausoleum at Agra, India, built (1630?–48?) by a Mogul emperor for his favorite wife

**ta·ka** (tä'kä) *n., pl.* **-ka** [< Sans. *tŏnkŏ,* silver coins] see MONETARY UNITS, table (Bangladesh)

**take** (tāk) *vt.* **took, tak'en, tak'ing** [OE. *tacan* < ON. *taka*] **1.** to get possession of by force or skill; capture, seize, etc. **2.** *a*) to win (a game, a trick at cards, etc.) *b*) to capture (an opponent's piece in chess or checkers) **3.** to get hold of; grasp or catch **4.** to affect [*taken* with a fit] **5.** to capture the fancy of **6.** to obtain, acquire, assume, etc. **7.** to get into one's hand or hold **8.** to eat, drink, etc. for nourishment or as medicine **9.** to enter into a special relationship with [to *take* a wife] **10.** to rent, lease, etc. [to *take* a cottage] **11.** to get regularly by paying for [to *take* a newspaper] **12.** to assume as a responsibility, task, etc. [to *take* a job, a vow] **13.** to assume (a symbol of duty or office, etc.) [the president *took* the chair] **14.** to join or support (one side in a contest, disagreement, etc.) **15.** to assume as if granted or due one [to *take* the blame, to *take* deductions] **16.** to get, adopt, etc. by selection or choice **17.** to use [*take* a mop to the floor] **18.** *a*) to travel by [to *take* a bus] *b*) to set out on [*take* that path] **19.** to go to for shelter, safety, etc. [*take* cover] **20.** to consider [to *take* a matter seriously] **21.** *a*) to occupy [*take* a chair] *b*) to use up [it *took* all day] **22.** to require; need [it *takes* money] **23.** to derive (a name, quality, etc.) from something or someone **24.** to extract, as for quotation [he *took* a verse from the Bible] **25.** to obtain by observation, experiment, etc. [*take* a poll] **26.** to be enrolled as a student in (a course, etc.) **27.** to write down [to *take* notes] **28.** to make (a photograph, picture, etc.) **29.** to make an impression of [*take* his fingerprints] **30.** to win (a prize, etc.) **31.** to undergo [to *take* punishment] **32.** to occupy oneself or engage in [to *take* a nap] **33.** to accept (an offer, bet, etc.) **34.** to have a specified reaction to [to *take* a joke in earnest] **35.** to confront and get over, etc. [the horse *took* the jump] **36.** to be affected by [he *took* cold] **37.** to absorb (a dye, polish, etc.) **38.** to understand **39.** to suppose [he *took* her to be a clerk] **40.** to have or feel (an emotion, etc.) [*take* pity] **41.** to make (an objection, etc.) as the result of thought **42.** to conduct; lead [this path *takes* you home] **43.** to escort [*take* a friend to lunch] **44.** to carry [to *take* a book with one] **45.** to remove as by stealing **46.** to remove by death **47.** to subtract [*take* two from four] **48.** to direct (oneself) **49.** [Colloq.] to aim (a specified action) [he *took* a jab at me] **50.** [Slang] to cheat; trick **51.** *Gram.* to be used with in construction [a transitive verb *takes* an object] —*vi.* **1.** to get possession **2.** to take root: said of a plant **3.** to catch [the fire *took* rapidly] **4.** to gain public favor; be popular **5.** to be effective in action, etc. [the vaccination *took*] **6.** to detract (*from*) [nothing *took* from the scene's beauty] **7.** to go [to *take* to the hills] **8.** [Colloq. or Dial.] to become (sick) —*n.* **1.** the act or process of taking **2.** something taken **3.** *a*) the amount taken [the day's *take* of fish] *b*) [Slang] money received; receipts **4.** a movie scene photographed with an uninterrupted run of the camera **5.** a recording or tape of a performance —**on the take** [Slang] willing or seeking to take bribes or illicit income —**take after 1.** to be, act, or look like **2.** to run after or pursue: also **take out** (or **off**) **after** —**take amiss** to become offended at (an act) as because of a misunderstanding —**take back** to retract (something said, promised, etc.) —**take down 1.** to take apart **2.** to make less conceited; humble **3.** to put in writing; record —**take five** (or **ten,** etc.) take a five (or ten, etc.) minute break, as from working —**take for** 1. to consider to be 2. to mistake for —**take in** 1. to admit; receive 2. to make smaller 3. to include 4. to understand 5. to cheat; trick 6. to visit /to *take in* the sights/ —**take it** [Slang] to withstand hardship, ridicule, etc. —**take it out on** [Colloq.] to make (another) suffer for one's own anger, irritation, etc. —**take off** 1. to go away 2. to deduct 3. to make a copy or likeness of 4. to leave the ground or water in flight: said of an aircraft 5. [Colloq.] to start 6. [Colloq.] to imitate; mimic —**take on** 1. to acquire; assume 2. to employ 3. to undertake (a task, etc.) 4. to play against; oppose 5. [Colloq.] to show violent emotion, esp. anger or sorrow —**take one's time** to be unhurried —**take out** 1. to remove 2. to apply for and get 3. [Colloq.] to escort —**take over** to begin controlling, managing, etc. —**take to** 1. to apply oneself to (work, etc.) 2. to become fond of —**take up** 1. to make tighter or shorter 2. to pay off (a mortgage, note, etc.) 3. to absorb (a liquid) 4. to accept (a challenge, etc.) 5. to become interested in (an occupation, belief, etc.) 6. to occupy (space or time) —**take upon** (or **on**) **oneself** 1. to take the responsibility for 2. to undertake Also **take upon** (or **on**) **one** —**take up with** [Colloq.] to become a friend or companion of —**tak′a·ble, take′a·ble** *adj.* —**tak′er** *n.*

**take-home pay** (tāk′hōm′) wages or salary after deductions for income tax, social security, etc. have been made

**tak·en** (tāk′'n) *pp. of* TAKE

**take·off** (-ôf′) *n.* 1. the act of leaving the ground, as in jumping or flight 2. the place from which one leaves the ground 3. the starting point or early stages of something; specif., *Econ.* the early stages of rapid, self-sustained growth and development 4. [Colloq.] an amusing or mocking imitation; burlesque Also **take′-off′**

**take·out** (-out′) *n.* a taking out —*adj.* designating or of prepared food sold by a restaurant to be eaten away from the premises Also **take′-out′**

**take·o·ver** (-ō′vər) *n.* the act of seizing power or assuming control in a nation, organization, etc.: also **take′-o′ver**

**tak·ing** (-iŋ) *adj.* attractive; winning —*n.* 1. the act of one that takes 2. something taken; catch 3. [*pl.*] earnings; profits —**tak′ing·ly** *adv.*

**talc** (talk) *n.* [Fr. < Ar. *ṭalq*] 1. a soft mineral, magnesium silicate, used to make talcum powder, lubricants, etc. 2. *shortened form of* TALCUM POWDER —*vt.* **talcked** or **talced, talck′ing** or **talc′ing** to use talc on

**tal·cum** (**powder**) (tal′kəm) a powder for the body and face made of powdered, purified talc, usually perfumed

**tale** (tāl) *n.* [OE. *talu*] 1. something told or related 2. a story of true or fictitious events; narrative 3. a piece of idle or malicious gossip 4. a falsehood; lie

**tale·bear·er** (-ber′ər) *n.* a person who spreads gossip, tells secrets, etc. —**tale′bear′ing** *adj., n.*

**tal·ent** (tal′ənt) *n.* [OE. *talente* < L. < Gr. *talanton*, a unit of money, weight] 1. any of various large units of weight or of money in ancient Greece, Rome, the Middle East, etc. 2. any natural ability or power 3. a special, superior ability in an art, science, craft, etc. 4. people who have talent —**tal′ent·ed** *adj.*

**talent scout** a person whose work is recruiting persons of superior ability in the theater, sports, etc.

**ta·ler** (tä′lər) *n., pl.* **ta′ler** [G.: see DOLLAR] a former German silver coin

**ta·les·man** (tālz′mən, tā′lēz-) *n., pl.* -**men** *Law* a person summoned to fill a vacancy in a jury when the regular jury panel lacks the proper number

**ta·li** (tā′lī) *n. alt. pl. of* TALUS[1]

**tal·i·pes** (tal′ə pēz′) *n.* [ModL. < L. *talus*, an ankle + *pes*, a foot] *same as* CLUBFOOT

**tal·i·pot** (tal′ə pät′) *n.* [Beng. *tālipāt*, palm leaf < Sans.] a palm tree of the East Indies, with gigantic leaves used for fans, umbrellas, etc., and seeds used for buttons: also **talipot palm**

**tal·is·man** (tal′is mən, -iz-) *n., pl.* -**mans** [Fr. < Ar. < MGr. *telesma*, a consecrated object] 1. a ring, stone, etc. bearing engraved figures supposed to bring good luck, keep away evil, etc. 2. anything supposed to have magic power; a charm —**tal′is·man′ic, tal′is·man′i·cal** *adj.*

**talk** (tôk) *vi.* [ME. *talken*, prob. freq. based on OE. *talian*, to reckon] 1. to put ideas into, or exchange ideas by, spoken words; speak 2. to express ideas by speech substitutes [*talk* by signs] 3. to speak trivially; chatter 4. to gossip 5. to confer; consult 6. to make noises suggestive of speech 7. to reveal secret information 8. to make a somewhat informal speech —*vt.* 1. to put into spoken words 2. to use in speaking /to *talk* Spanish, to *talk* nonsense/ 3. to discuss 4. to put into a specified condition by talking /to *talk* oneself hoarse/ —*n.* 1. *a*) the act of talking *b*) conversation 2. an informal speech 3. a conference 4. gossip 5. the subject of conversation, gossip, etc. 6. empty, frivolous dis-

cussion 7. a particular kind of speech; dialect, etc. 8. sounds, as by an animal, suggestive of speech —**big talk** [Slang] a bragging —**talk back** to answer impertinently —**talk big** [Slang] to boast —**talk down** to silence by talking louder, longer, or more effectively than —**talk down to** to talk to (a person) as if he were one's inferior in rank, intellect, etc. —**talk into** to persuade (someone) to do something —**talk out of** to dissuade (someone) from doing something —**talk over** 1. to discuss 2. to persuade (a person) by talking —**talk up** 1. to promote or praise in discussion 2. to speak loudly, boldly, etc. —**talk′er** *n.*

**talk·a·thon** (tôk′ə thän′) *n.* [TALK + (MAR)ATHON] any prolonged period of talking

**talk·a·tive** (-tiv) *adj.* talking, or fond of talking, a great deal; loquacious —**talk′a·tive·ness** *n.*

**talking book** a recording of a reading of a book, etc. for use esp. by the blind

**talking picture** *earlier name for* a motion picture with a synchronized sound track: also [Colloq.] **talk′ie** (-ē) *n.*

**talking point** a persuasive point to be emphasized, as in presenting an argument

**talk·ing-to** (tôk′iŋ tōō′) *n.* [Colloq.] a rebuke; scolding

**talk·y** (tôk′ē) *adj.* 1. talkative 2. containing too much talk, or dialogue /a *talky* novel/ —**talk′i·ness** *n.*

**tall** (tôl) *adj.* [< OE. (ge)*tæl*, swift] 1. of more than normal height or stature 2. having a specified height /five feet *tall*/ 3. [Colloq.] hard to believe; exaggerated /a *tall* tale/ 4. [Colloq.] large /a *tall* drink/ —**tall′ish** *adj.* —**tall′ness** *n.*

**Tal·la·has·see** (tal′ə has′ē) [< Creek Indian name] capital of Fla., in the N part: pop. 82,000

**Tal·ley·rand** (tal′ē rand′; *Fr.* tà lā rän′) (born *Charles Maurice de Talleyrand-Périgord*) 1754–1838; Fr. statesman

**Tal·linn** (tàl′lin) capital of the Estonian S.S.R., on the Gulf of Finland: pop. 363,000: also sp. **Tallin**

**tal·lit, tal·lith** (tä lēt′, täl′is) *n.* [< LHeb. < *ṭālal*, to cover] *Judaism* a fringed shawl worn by men during morning prayer: cf. Deut. 22:12

**tal·low** (tal′ō) *n.* [prob. < MLowG. *talg*] the pale yellow solid fat extracted from the natural fat of cattle, sheep, etc., used in making candles, soaps, lubricants, etc. —*vt.* to cover or smear with tallow —**tal′low·y** *adj.*

**tal·ly** (tal′ē) *n., pl.* -**lies** [Anglo-L. *talia* < L. *talea*, a stick] 1. *a*) orig., a stick with notches representing the amount of a debt *b*) anything used as a record for an account or score 2. an account, reckoning, or score 3. *a*) either of two corresponding parts; counterpart *b*) agreement; correspondence 4. an identifying tag or label —*vt.* -**lied, -ly·ing** 1. to put on or as on a tally 2. to count (usually with *up*) 3. to put a label or tag on —*vi.* 1. to tally something 2. to score a point or points in a game 3. to agree; correspond

**tal·ly·ho** (tal′ē hō′; *for n. & v.,* tal′ē hō′) *interj.* [altered < Fr. *taiaut*] the cry of a hunter on sighting the fox —*n., pl.* -**hos**′ 1. a cry of "tallyho" 2. a coach drawn by four horses —*vi.* to cry "tallyho"

**Tal·mud** (täl′mood, tal′-; -məd) *n.* [LHeb. *talmūdh*, lit., learning < *lāmadh*, to learn] the writings constituting the Jewish civil and religious law —**Tal·mud′ic, Tal·mud′i·cal** *adj.* —**Tal′mud·ism** *n.* —**Tal′mud·ist** *n.*

**tal·on** (tal′ən) *n.* [< OFr., ult. < L. *talus,* an ankle] 1. the claw of a bird of prey, or, sometimes, of an animal 2. a human finger or hand when like a claw in appearance or grasp —**tal′oned** *adj.*

**ta·lus**[1] (tā′ləs) *n., pl.* -**lus·es, -li** (-lī) [ModL. < L., an ankle] 1. the anklebone 2. the entire ankle

**ta·lus**[2] (tā′ləs) *n.* [Fr. < OFr. *talu* < L. *talutium*, surface indication of gold under the earth] 1. a slope 2. the sloping face of a wall in a fortification 3. a pile of rock debris at the foot of a cliff or below a rock face

**tam** (tam) *n. short for* TAM-O′-SHANTER

**ta·ma·le** (tə mä′lē) *n.* [< MexSp. < Nahuatl *tamalli*] a native Mexican food of minced meat and red peppers rolled in cornmeal, wrapped in corn husks, and cooked by baking, steaming, etc.

**tam·a·rack** (tam′ə rak′) *n.* [< Algonquian] 1. an American larch tree, usually found in swamps 2. its wood

**tam·a·rind** (tam′ə rind) *n.* [< Sp. < Ar. *tamr hindī,* date of India] 1. a tropical leguminous tree with yellow flowers and brown pods with an acid pulp 2. its fruit, used in foods, medicine, etc.

**tam·ba·la** (täm bä′lä) *n., pl.* **ma′tam·ba′la** (mä′-) [native term, lit., rooster] *see* MONETARY UNITS, table (Malawi)

**tam·bour** (tam′boor) *n.* [< MFr. < OFr. < Ar. *ṭanbūr,* stringed instrument < Per.] 1. a drum 2. an embroidery frame of two hoops, one closely fitting inside the other, that hold the cloth stretched between them 3. a door, panel, etc. as in a cabinet, made of narrow, wooden slats that glide flexibly in grooves, as around curves —*vt., vi.* to embroider on a tambour

---

fat, āpe, cär, ten, ēven, is, bīte; gō, hôrn, tōōl, look; oil, out; up, fur; get; joy; yet; chin; she; thin, then; zh, leisure; ŋ, ring; ə for *a* in *ago, e* in *agent, i* in *sanity, o* in *comply, u* in *focus;* ′ as in *able* (ā′b'l); Fr. bál; ë, Fr. coeur; ö, Fr. feu; Fr. mon; ô, Fr. coq; ü, Fr. duc; r, Fr. cri; H, G. ich; kh, G. doch; ‡foreign; *hypothetical; < derived from. See inside front cover.

**tam·bou·rine** (tam'bə rēn') *n.* [Fr., dim. of *tambour:* see TAMBOUR] a shallow, single-headed hand drum having jingling metal disks in the rim: played by shaking, hitting with the knuckles, etc. —**tam'bou·rin'ist** *n.*

**tame** (tām) *adj.* **tam'er, tam'est** [OE. *tam*] **1.** changed from a wild state, as an animal, for use by man **2.** gentle; docile **3.** crushed as by domestication; submissive **4.** without force or spirit; dull —*vt.* **tamed, tam'ing 1.** to make tame, or domestic **2.** to make gentle, docile, or spiritless **3.** to make less intense; soften —*vi.* to become tame —**tam'a·ble, tame'a·ble** *adj.* —**tame'ly** *adv.* —**tame'ness** *n.* —**tam'er** *n.*

**tame·less** (-lis) *adj.* **1.** not tamed **2.** not tamable

**Tam·er·lane** (tam'ər lān') [< *Timur lenk,* Timur the lame] 1336?–1405; Mongol warrior whose conquests extended from the Black Sea to the upper Ganges

**Tam·il** (tam''l, täm'-, tum'-) *n.* **1.** *pl.* **-ils, -il** any of a Tamil-speaking people of S India and N Ceylon **2.** the Dravidian language of the Tamils, ancient or modern

**Tam·ma·ny** (tam'ə nē) *n.* [altered < *Tamanend,* a 17th-c. Am. Indian chief] a powerful Democratic political organization of New York City, incorporated in 1789: also **Tammany Society, Tammany Hall** —*adj.* of Tammany's practices, members, etc.

**Tam·muz** (tä'mooz) *n.* [Heb.] the tenth month of the Jewish year: see JEWISH CALENDAR

**tam-o'-shan·ter** (tam'ə shan'tər) *n.* [< main character of R. Burns's poem "Tam o'Shanter"] a Scottish cap with a round, flat top and, often, a center tassel

**tamp** (tamp) *vt.* [< ? TAMPION] **1.** in blasting, to pack clay, sand, etc. around the charge in the (drill hole) **2.** to pack or pound (*down*) by a series of blows or taps

**Tam·pa** (tam'pə) [< AmInd. village name] seaport in WC Fla., on an arm (**Tampa Bay**) of the Gulf of Mexico: pop. 272,000 (met. area, incl. St. Petersburg, 1,550,000)

TAMBOURINE

TAM-O'-SHANTER

**tamp·er¹** (tam'pər) *n.* a person or thing that tamps; specif., any of various tools for tamping

**tam·per²** (tam'pər) *vi.* [var. of TEMPER] [Archaic] to plot; scheme —**tamper with 1.** to make secret, illegal arrangements with, as by bribing **2.** to meddle with, esp. so as to damage, etc. —**tam'per·er** *n.*

**Tam·pi·co** (tam pē'kō; *Sp.* täm pē'ð) seaport in E Mexico, on the Gulf of Mexico: pop. 196,000

**tam·pi·on** (tam'pē ən) *n.* [< Fr. *tapon,* a bung < Frank.] a plug or stopper put in the muzzle of a gun not in use

**tam·pon** (tam'pän) *n.* [Fr.: see prec.] a plug of cotton or other absorbent material put into a body cavity, wound, etc. to stop bleeding or absorb secretions —*vt.* to put a tampon into

**tan** (tan) *n.* [MFr. < ML. *tannum*] **1.** *same as* TANBARK **2.** tannin or a solution made from it **3.** *a*) a yellowish-brown color *b*) such a color given to fair skin as by exposure to the sun —*adj.* **tan'ner, tan'nest** yellowish-brown —*vt.* **tanned, tan'ning 1.** to change (hide) into leather by soaking in tannin **2.** to produce a tan color in, as by exposure to the sun **3.** [Colloq.] to whip severely; flog —*vi.* to become tanned

**tan** tangent

**tan·a·ger** (tan'ə jər) *n.* [ModL. *tanagra* < Port. < Tupi *tangara*] any of various small, new-world songbirds: the males usually are brilliantly colored

**tan·bark** (tan'bärk') *n.* any bark containing tannin, used to tan hides and, after the tannin has been extracted, to cover circus rings, etc.

**tan·dem** (tan'dəm) *adv.* [orig. punning use of L. *tandem,* at length (of time)] one behind another; in single file —*n.* **1.** a two-wheeled carriage drawn by horses harnessed tandem **2.** a team, as of horses, harnessed tandem **3.** a bicycle with two seats and sets of pedals placed tandem **4.** a relationship between two persons or things involving cooperative action, mutual dependence, etc. *[to work in tandem]* —*adj.* having two parts or things placed tandem

**Ta·ney** (tô'nē), **Roger B(rooke)** 1777–1864; U.S. jurist; chief justice of the U.S. (1836–64)

**tang** (taŋ) *n.* [ON. *tangi,* a sting] **1.** a projecting point or prong on a knife, file, etc. that fits into the handle **2.** a strong, penetrating taste or odor **3.** a touch or trace (*of*) **4.** a special or characteristic flavor, quality, etc. —*vt.* to provide (a knife, etc.) with a tang

**Tan·gan·yi·ka** (taŋ'gan yē'kə) **1.** mainland region of Tanzania: formerly a Brit. trust territory **2. Lake,** lake in EC Africa, between Tanganyika and Zaire

**tan·ge·lo** (tan'jə lō') *n., pl.* **-los'** [TANG(ERINE) + (*pom*)*elo,*

grapefruit] a fruit produced by crossing a tangerine with a grapefruit

**tan·gent** (tan'jənt) *adj.* [< L. prp. of *tangere,* to touch] **1.** touching **2.** *Geom.* touching and not intersecting a curved line or surface at one point only: said of a line or plane —*n.* **1.** *Geom.* a tangent line, curve, or surface **2.** *Trigonometry* the ratio of the side opposite a given acute angle in a right triangle to the adjacent side —**go (or fly) off at (or on) a tangent** to change suddenly from one line of action to another —**tan'gen·cy** *n.*

**tan·gen·tial** (tan jen'shəl) *adj.* **1.** of or like a tangent **2.** drawn as a tangent **3.** going off at a tangent **4.** merely touching on a subject —**tan·gen'tial·ly** *adv.*

**tan·ge·rine** (tan'jə rēn', tan'jə rēn') *n.* [< Fr. *Tanger,* Tangier] **1.** a variety of mandarin orange with a deep, reddish-yellow color and segments that are easily separated **2.** a deep, reddish-yellow color

**tan·gi·ble** (tan'jə b'l) *adj.* [< LL. *tangibilis* < L. *tangere,* to touch] **1.** that can be touched or felt by touch; having actual form and substance **2.** that can be appraised for value *[tangible* assets*]* **3.** definite; objective —*n.* [*pl.*] property that can be appraised for value; material things —**tan'gi·bil'i·ty, tan'gi·ble·ness** *n.* —**tan'gi·bly** *adv.*

**Tan·gier** (tan jir') seaport in N Morocco, on the Strait of Gibraltar: pop. 170,000

**tan·gle** (taŋ'g'l) *vt.* **-gled, -gling** [prob. var. of ME. *taglen,* to entangle] **1.** to hinder, obstruct, or confuse by circling, entwining, etc. **2.** to catch as in a net or snare; trap **3.** to make a snarl of; intertwist —*vi.* **1.** to become tangled **2.** [Colloq.] to quarrel or fight —*n.* **1.** an intertwisted, confused mass, as of string, branches, etc.; snarl **2.** a jumbled, confused condition **3.** a perplexed state —**tan'gler** *n.*

**tan·go** (taŋ'gō) *n., pl.* **-gos** [AmSp.] **1.** a S. American dance with long gliding steps and dips **2.** music for this —*vi.* **-goed, -go·ing** to dance the tango

**tang·y** (taŋ'ē) *adj.* **tang'i·er, tang'i·est** having a tang, or sharp flavor —**tang'i·ness** *n.*

**tank** (taŋk) *n.* [< Sp. & Port. *tanque* < *estancar,* to stop the flow of] **1.** any large container for liquid or gas *[an oil tank,* a swimming *tank]* **2.** [name chosen to conceal secret manufacture] an armored, self-propelled combat vehicle armed with guns and moving on tractor treads **3.** [Slang] a jail cell, esp. one for new prisoners —*vt.* to put or store in a tank —**tank up** [Colloq.] **1.** to supply with or get a full tank of gasoline **2.** to drink much liquor —**tank'ful'** *n., pl.* **-fuls'**

**tank·age** (taŋ'kij) *n.* **1.** the capacity of a tank or tanks **2.** *a*) the storage of fluids, gases, etc. in tanks *b*) the charge for such storage **3.** slaughterhouse waste from which the fat has been rendered in tanks

**tank·ard** (taŋ'kərd) *n.* [ME.] a large drinking cup with a handle and, often, a hinged lid

**tank car** a large tank on wheels, for carrying liquids and gases by rail

**tank·er** (taŋ'kər) *n.* **1.** a ship for carrying a cargo of oil or other liquids in large tanks **2.** a plane with a cargo of gasoline for refueling another plane in flight

**tank farming** *same as* HYDROPONICS

**tank top** [orig. worn in swimming tanks] a casual shirt like an undershirt but with wider shoulder straps

**tank town 1.** a railroad stop for locomotives to get water **2.** any small or unimportant town

**tan·ner** (tan'ər) *n.* a person whose work is tanning hides

**tan·ner·y** (-ē) *n., pl.* **-ner·ies** a place where hides are tanned

**tan·nic** (tan'ik) *adj.* of, like, or obtained from tanbark or tannin

**tannic acid** a yellowish, astringent substance, $C_{14}H_{10}O_9$, derived from oak bark, gallnuts, etc. and used in tanning, medicine, etc.

**tan·nin** (tan'in) *n. same as* TANNIC ACID

**tan·sy** (tan'zē) *n., pl.* **-sies** [OFr. *tanesie,* ult. < LL. *tanacetum* < ?] any of various strong-smelling plants with clusters of small, yellow flowers

**tan·ta·lize** (tan'tə līz') *vt.* **-lized', -liz'ing** [< TANTALUS + -IZE] to tease or disappoint by promising or showing something and then withholding it —**tan'ta·li·za'tion** *n.* —**tan'ta·liz'er** *n.* —**tan'ta·liz'ing·ly** *adv.*

**tan·ta·lum** (tan'tə ləm) *n.* [ModL. < TANTALUS: from the difficulty in extracting it from its ore] a rare, steel-blue, metallic chemical element that resists corrosion, used to make surgical instruments, parts for radio tubes, etc.: symbol, Ta; at. wt., 180.948; at. no., 73

**Tan·ta·lus** (tan'tə ləs) *Gr. Myth.* a king doomed in Hades to stand in water that always receded when he tried to drink it and under fruit branches he could never reach

**tan·ta·mount** (tan'tə mount') *adj.* [< Anglo-Fr. < OFr. *tant* (< L. *tantus,* so much) + *amonter* (see AMOUNT)] having equal value, effect, etc.; equivalent (*to*)

**tan·trum** (tan'trəm) *n.* [< ?] a violent, willful outburst of annoyance, rage, etc.; childish fit of bad temper

**Tan·za·ni·a** (tan'zə nē'ə, tän'-) country in E Africa, consisting of a mainland section (*Tanganyika*) and Zanzibar: a

member of the Commonwealth: 362,820 sq. mi.; pop. 13,634,000; cap. Dar es Salaam —Tan′za·ni′an *adj., n.*
**Tao·ism** (dou′iz′m, tou′-) *n.* [Chin. *tao*, the way + -ISM] a Chinese religion and philosophy based on the doctrines of Lao-tse and advocating simplicity, selflessness, etc. — **Tao′ist** *n., adj.* —**Tao·is′tic** *adj.*
**tap¹** (tap) *vt.* **tapped, tap′ping** [OFr. *taper*, prob. echoic] **1.** to strike lightly **2.** to strike something lightly with **3.** to make or do by tapping [*to tap* a message] **4.** to choose, as for membership in a club **5.** to repair (a shoe) by adding a thickness of leather, etc. to the heel or sole —*vi.* **1.** to strike a light, rapid blow **2.** to perform a tap dance **3.** to move with a tapping sound —*n.* **1.** a light, rapid blow, or the sound made by it **2.** the leather, etc. added in tapping a shoe **3.** a small metal plate attached to the heel or toe of a shoe, as for tap dancing —**tap′per** *n.*
**tap²** (tap) *n.* [OE. *tæppa*] **1.** a device for controlling the flow of liquid in a pipe, barrel, etc.; faucet **2.** a plug, cork, etc. for stopping a hole in a container holding a liquid **3.** liquor of a certain kind, as drawn from a certain tap **4.** a draining of liquid from a body cavity **5.** a tool used to cut threads in a female screw **6.** the act of wiretapping **7.** a place in an electrical circuit where a connection can be made —*vt.* **tapped, tap′ping 1.** to put a tap or spigot on **2.** to make a hole in for drawing off liquid **3.** to pull out the plug from **4.** to draw (liquid) from a container, cavity, etc. **5.** to make use of [*to tap* new resources] **6.** to make a connection with (an electric circuit, telephone line, etc.); specif., to wiretap (a telephone line) **7.** to cut the inner threads of (a nut, etc.) **8.** [Slang] to borrow or get money from —**on tap 1.** in a tapped cask and ready to be drawn **2.** [Colloq.] ready for consideration or action —**tap′per** *n.*
**ta·pa** (tä′pä) *n.* [< native Polynesian name] an unwoven cloth made in the Pacific islands from the treated inner bark of a mulberry tree
**tap dance** a dance performed with sharp, loud taps of the foot, toe, or heel at each step —**tap′-dance′** *vi.* **-danced′, -danc′ing** —**tap′-danc′er** *n.*
**tape** (tāp) *n.* [OE. *tæppe*, a fillet] **1.** a strong, narrow, woven strip of cotton, linen, etc. used for binding, tying, etc. **2.** a narrow strip or band of steel, paper, etc. **3.** a strip of cloth stretched above the finishing line of a race **4.** short for: *a)* TAPE MEASURE *b)* ADHESIVE TAPE, MASKING TAPE, etc. —*vt.* **taped, tap′ing 1.** to put tape on or around, as for binding, tying, etc. **2.** to measure by using a tape measure **3.** to record (sound, video material, computer data, etc.) on magnetic tape —**tap′er** *n.*
**tape deck** a simplified magnetic-tape assembly, without an amplifier or speaker but having tape reels, drive, and recording and playback heads
**tape measure** a tape with marks in inches, feet, etc. for measuring: also **tape′line′** (-līn′) *n.*
**ta·per** (tā′pər) *n.* [OE. *tapur*] **1.** a slender candle **2.** a long wick coated with wax, used for lighting candles, lamps, etc. **3.** any feeble light **4.** *a)* a gradual decrease in width or thickness [the *taper* of a pyramid] *b)* a gradual decrease in action, power, etc. —*adj.* gradually decreased in size to a point —*vt., vi.* **1.** to decrease gradually in width or thickness **2.** to lessen; diminish Often with *off*
**tape-re·cord** (tāp′ri kôrd′) *vt.* to record on magnetic tape
**tape recorder** a device for recording on magnetic tape: see MAGNETIC RECORDING
**tap·es·try** (tap′is trē) *n., pl.* **-tries** [< MFr. < OFr. *tapis*, a carpet, ult. < Gr. dim. of *tapēs*, a carpet] a heavy woven cloth with decorative designs and pictures, used as a wall hanging, furniture covering, etc. —*vt.* **-tried, -try·ing** to decorate as with a tapestry: usually in the pp.
**tape·worm** (tāp′wurm′) *n.* any of various flatworms that live as parasites in the intestines of man and other vertebrates
**tap·i·o·ca** (tap′ē ō′kə) *n.* [Port. & Sp. < Tupi < *ty*, juice + *pŷa*, heart + *oc*, to squeeze out] a starchy, granular substance prepared from the root of the cassava plant, used for puddings, etc.
**ta·pir** (tā′pər) *n., pl.* **ta′pirs, ta′pir:** see PLURAL, II, D, 1 [Sp. < Tupi *tapyra*] any of various large, hoglike mammals found mostly in tropical America: tapirs have flexible snouts
**tap·pet** (tap′it) *n.* [TAP¹ + -ET] in an engine or machine, a projection or lever that moves or is moved by recurring contact, as with a cam
**tap·room** (tap′rōōm′) *n.* same as BARROOM
**tap·root** (-rōōt′, -root′) *n.* [TAP² + ROOT¹] a main root, growing

TAPIR
(2½–3½ ft. high at shoulder)

almost vertically downward, from which branch roots spread out
**taps** (taps) *n.* [< TAP¹, because orig. a drum signal] a bugle call to put out the lights for the night, as in an army camp: also sounded at a military funeral
**tar¹** (tär) *n.* [OE. *teru*] **1.** a thick, sticky, brown to black liquid obtained by the destructive distillation of wood, coal, etc.: tars are used for protecting and preserving surfaces, in making many organic compounds, etc. **2.** loosely, any of the solids in smoke, as from tobacco —*vt.* **tarred, tar′ring** to cover or smear with or as with tar —*adj.* **1.** of or like tar **2.** tarred —**tar and feather** to cover (a person) with tar and feathers, as in punishment by mob action
**tar²** (tär) *n.* [< TAR(PAULIN)] [Colloq.] a sailor
**tar·an·tel·la** (tar′ən tel′ə) *n.* [It., dim. of ff.] **1.** a fast, whirling southern Italian dance for couples **2.** music for this
**Ta·ran·to** (tə ran′tō; *It.* tä′rän tô′) seaport in SE Italy, on an inlet (**Gulf of Taranto**) of the Ionian Sea: pop. 219,000
**ta·ran·tu·la** (tə ran′choo lə) *n., pl.* **-las, -lae** (-lē) [ML. < It. < prec.: because found nearby] **1.** a large, hairy, somewhat poisonous spider of the SW U.S. and tropical America **2.** a similar spider of S Europe
**tar·boosh** (tär bōōsh′) *n.* [Ar. *ṭarbūsh*] a brimless cap of cloth or felt shaped like a truncated cone, worn by Moslem men
**tar·dy** (tär′dē) *adj.* **-di·er, -di·est** [< OFr. < L. *tardus*, slow] **1.** slow in moving, acting, etc. **2.** late, delayed, or dilatory —**tar′di·ly** *adv.* —**tar′di·ness** *n.*
**tare¹** (ter) *n.* [< or akin to MDu. *tarwe*, wheat] **1.** any of several vetches **2.** the seed of any of these plants **3.** *Bible* a weed, perhaps the darnel
**tare²** (ter) *n.* [< MFr. < It. < Ar. *taraha*, to reject] deduction of the weight of a container, wrapper, etc. from the total weight to determine the weight of the contents —*vt.* **tared, tar′ing** to find out, allow for, or mark the tare of
**tar·get** (tär′git) *n.* [< MFr. dim. of *targe*, a shield < Frank.] **1.** orig., a small, round shield **2.** *a)* a round, flat board, straw coil, etc., marked as with concentric circles, aimed at in archery, rifle practice, etc. *b)* any object that is shot at, bombarded, etc. **3.** an objective; goal **4.** an object of attack, criticism, or ridicule —*vt.* to establish a target, or goal, for
**tar·iff** (tar′if) *n.* [< It. < Ar. *ta'rif*, information] **1.** a list or system of taxes upon exports or, esp., imports **2.** a tax of this kind, or its rate **3.** any list of prices, charges, etc. **4.** [Colloq.] any bill, charge, etc. —*vt.* **1.** to set a tariff on **2.** to fix the price of according to a tariff
**Tar·king·ton** (tär′kiŋ tən), (Newton) Booth 1869–1946; U.S. novelist
**tar·la·tan, tar·le·tan** (tär′lə tən) *n.* [Fr. *tarlatane*] a thin, stiff, open-weave muslin
**Tar·mac** (tär′mak) [< TAR¹ + MAC(ADAM)] *a trademark for* a coal-tar material used in paving —*n.* [t-] [Chiefly Brit.] a road, airport runway, etc. paved with crushed stone and tar
**tarn** (tärn) *n.* [< or akin to ON. *tjörn*] a small mountain lake
**'tar·nal** (tär′n'l) *adj. shortened dial. form of* ETERNAL: used chiefly as an intensive [a *'tarnal* fool]
**tar·na·tion** (tär nā′shən) *interj., n.* [prob. < 'TAR(NAL) + (DAM)NATION] *dial. var. of* DAMNATION: used as an intensive [what in *tarnation* is that?]
**tar·nish** (tär′nish) *vt.* [< MFr. *ternir*, to make dim, prob. < OHG. *tarnjan*, to conceal] **1.** to dull the luster of (a metal) by exposure to the air **2.** to sully (a reputation, etc.) —*vi.* **1.** to lose luster; discolor, as from oxidation **2.** to become sullied —*n.* **1.** a being tarnished; dullness **2.** the film of discoloration on a tarnished surface **3.** a stain; blemish —**tar′nish·a·ble** *adj.*
**ta·ro** (tä′rō) *n., pl.* **-ros** [Tahitian] **1.** a large, tropical Asiatic plant, cultivated for its edible tubers, the source of poi **2.** the tuber of this plant
**tar·ot** (tar′ō, -ət; ta rō′) *n.* [Fr., ult. < Ar. *taraha*, to remove] [often T-] any of a set of playing cards with pictures of symbolic figures, used in fortunetelling
**tarp** (tärp) *n.* [Colloq.] *shortened form of* TARPAULIN
**tar paper** a heavy paper impregnated with tar, used as a base for roofing, etc.
**tar·pau·lin** (tär pô′lin, tär′pə lin) *n.* [TAR¹ + -paulin, prob. < *palling* < PALL²] **1.** canvas coated with a waterproofing compound **2.** a sheet of this spread over something to keep it dry
**tar·pon** (tär′pən, -pän) *n., pl.* **-pons, -pon:** see PLURAL, II, D, 1 [< ?] a large, silvery game fish of the herring group, found in the warmer parts of the W Atlantic
**Tar·quin** (tär′kwin) (*Lucius Tarquinius Superbus*) semi-legendary Etruscan king of Rome (534?–510? B.C.)

fat, āpe, cär; ten, ēven; is, bīte; gō, hôrn, tōōl, look; oil, out; up, fur; get; joy; yet; chin; she; thin, then; zh, leisure; ŋ, ring; ə for *a* in *ago*, *e* in *agent*, *i* in *sanity*, *o* in *comply*, *u* in *focus*; ' as in *able* (ā′b'l); Fr. bal; ë, Fr. coeur; ö, Fr. feu; Fr. mon; ô, Fr. coq; ü, Fr. duc; r, Fr. cri; H, G. ich; kh, G. doch; ‡foreign; *hypothetical; < derived from. See inside front cover.

**tar·ra·gon** (tar′ə gän′) *n.* [Sp. < Ar. < Gr. *drakōn*, drag-on] **1.** an old-world wormwood whose fragrant leaves are used for seasoning **2.** these leaves

**tar·ry**[1] (tar′ē) *vi.* **-ried, -ry·ing** [prob. < OE. *tergan*, to vex, merged with OFr. *targer*, to delay < L. *tardus*, slow] **1.** to delay, linger, etc. **2.** to stay for a time, esp. longer than intended **3.** to wait —**tar′ri·er** *n.*

**tar·ry**[2] (tär′ē) *adj.* **-ri·er, -ri·est 1.** of or like tar **2.** covered or smeared with tar —**tar′ri·ness** *n.*

**tar·sal** (tär′s′l) *adj.* of the tarsus —*n.* a tarsal bone or plate

**tar·si·er** (tär′sē ər) *n.* [Fr. < *tarse*, TARSUS, from the foot structure] any of several small pri-mates of the East Indies and the Philip-pines, with very large eyes and a long tail: they live in trees and are active at night

**Tar·sus** (tär′səs) city in S Turkey, near the Mediterranean: birthplace of the Apostle Paul: pop. 57,000

**tar·sus** (-səs) *n., pl.* **-si** (-sī) [ModL. < Gr. *tarsos*, flat of the foot] **1.** the hu-man ankle, consisting of seven bones **2.** *Zool. a)* a group of bones in the ankle region of the hind limbs of verte-brates having four limbs *b)* the fifth segment from the base of an insect leg

**tart**[1] (tärt) *adj.* [OE. *teart*] **1.** sharp in taste; sour; acid **2.** sharp in meaning; cutting [a *tart* answer] —**tart′ly** *adv.* —**tart′ness** *n.*

TARSIER
(head & body
3–7 in. long;
tail 5–10 in.
long)

**tart**[2] (tärt) *n.* [MFr. *tarte*] **1.** a small shell of pastry filled with jam, jelly, etc. **2.** in England, a small pie filled with fruit or jam and often having a top crust

**tart**[3] (tärt) *n.* [< prec., orig. slang term of endearment] a prostitute or any woman of loose morals

**tar·tan** (tär′t′n) *n.* [prob. < MFr. *tiretaine*, a cloth of mixed fibers, ult. < L. *Tyrus*, TYRE] **1.** woolen cloth with a woven plaid pattern, esp. as worn in the Scottish Highlands, where each clan has its own pattern **2.** any plaid cloth or pattern **3.** a garment made of tartan —*adj.* of or made of tartan

**Tar·tar** (tär′tər) *n.* [< ML. *Tartarus* < Per. *Tātār*] **1.** same as TATAR **2.** [*usually* t-] a bad-tempered person hard to deal with —*adj.* of Tatary or the Tatars —**catch a tartar** to attack or oppose someone too strong for one

**tar·tar** (tär′tər) *n.* [< ML. < MGr. *tartaron* < ? Ar.] **1.** a potassium salt of tartaric acid forming a reddish, crustlike deposit in wine casks: in purified form called CREAM OF TAR-TAR **2.** a hard deposit on the teeth, consisting of saliva proteins, food deposits, calcium phosphate, etc.

**tartar emetic** a poisonous salt of tartaric acid used in medi-cine to cause vomiting, in dyeing as a mordant, etc.

**tar·tar·ic** (tär tar′ik, -tär′-) *adj.* of, containing, or derived from tartar or tartaric acid

**tartaric acid** a colorless, crystalline acid, $C_4H_6O_6$, found in fruit juices, etc. and obtained from tartar: it is used in dye-ing, photography, medicine, etc.

**tar·tar sauce** (tär′tər) [< Fr.] a sauce, as for seafood, consisting of mayonnaise with chopped pickles, olives, ca-pers, etc.: also sp. **tartare sauce**

**tartar steak** *same as* STEAK TARTARE

**Tar·ta·rus** (tär′tər əs) *Gr. Myth.* **1.** an infernal abyss be-low Hades **2.** Hades; hell —**Tar·tar′e·an** (-ter′ə ən) *adj.*

**Tar·ta·ry** (tär′tər ē) *same as* TATARY

**tar·trate** (tär′trāt) *n.* a salt or ester of tartaric acid

**Tar·zan** (tär′zən, -zan) *n.* [after *Tarzan*, jungle-raised hero of stories by E. R. Burroughs (1875–1950), U.S. writer] [*also* t-] a very strong, virile, and agile man: often used hu-morously

**Tash·kent** (täsh kent′) capital of the Uzbek S.S.R., in the E part: pop. 1,385,000

**task** (task) *n.* [< ONormFr. < ML. *tasca*, for *taxa*, a tax < L. *taxare*, to rate, TAX] **1.** a piece of work that one must do **2.** any piece of work **3.** any difficult undertaking —*vt.* **1.** to assign a task to **2.** to put a strain on; tax —**take to task** to reprimand or scold

**task force** a specially trained, self-contained military unit assigned a specific mission or task

**task·mas·ter** (-mas′tər) *n.* a person who assigns tasks to others, esp. when exacting or severe

**Tas·man** (täs′män; *E.* taz′mən), **A·bel Jans·zoon** (ä′bəl yän′sōn) 1603?–59; Du. navigator, esp. in the Pacific

**Tas·ma·ni·a** (taz mā′nē ə, -mān′yə) **1.** island south of Victoria, Australia **2.** state of Australia comprising this is-land & smaller nearby islands —**Tas·ma′ni·an** *adj., n.*

**Tass** (täs) [< the initial letters of the full name] a Soviet agency for gathering and distributing news

**tas·sel** (tas′l) *n.* [OFr., a knob] **1.** an ornamental tuft of threads, cords, etc. of equal length, hanging loosely from a knob or knot **2.** something resembling this; specif., a tas-sellike tuft, as of corn silk on an ear of corn —*vt.* **-seled** or **-selled, -sel·ing** or **-sel·ling** to put tassels on —*vi.* to grow tassels, as corn

**Tas·so** (täs′sō; *E.* tas′ō), **Tor·qua·to** (tôr kwä′tō) 1544–95; It. epic poet

**taste** (tāst) *vt.* **tast′ed, tast′ing** [OFr. *taster*, to touch, taste] **1.** to test the flavor of by putting a little in one's mouth **2.** to detect the flavor of by the sense of taste **3.** to eat or drink, esp. a small amount of **4.** to experience; have [to *taste* defeat] —*vi.* **1.** to tell flavors by the sense of taste **2.** to eat or drink a small amount (*of*) **3.** to have the specific flavor (*of*) [the salad *tastes* of garlic] **4.** to have a sensation or limited experience (*of* something) —*n.* **1.** the sense by which the taste buds on the tongue, when stimulat-ed by a substance, distinguish it as sweet, sour, salty, or bitter **2.** the quality perceived through this sense; flavor; savor **3.** a small amount put into the mouth to test the fla-vor **4.** a slight experience of something; sample **5.** a bit; trace; touch **6.** *a)* the ability to appreciate and judge what is beautiful, appropriate, or excellent in art, dress, etc. *b)* a specific preference [a *taste* for red ties] *c)* a style or way that shows such ability or preferences **7.** a liking; inclina-tion —**in bad, poor,** etc. (or **good, excellent,** etc.) **taste** in a form, style, or manner showing a bad (or good) sense of beauty, excellence, fitness, etc. —**in taste** in good taste —**to one's taste 1.** pleasing to one **2.** so as to please one

**taste bud** any of the cells in the epithelium of the tongue that are the sense organs of taste

**taste·ful** (tāst′fəl) *adj.* having or showing good taste [*taste-ful* décor] —**taste′ful·ly** *adv.* —**taste′ful·ness** *n.*

**taste·less** (-lis) *adj.* **1.** *a)* without taste or flavor; flat; in-sipid *b)* dull; uninteresting **2.** lacking good taste; in poor taste —**taste′less·ly** *adv.* —**taste′less·ness** *n.*

**tast·er** (tās′tər) *n.* a person who tastes; specif., one em-ployed to test the quality of wines, teas, etc. by tasting

**tast·y** (-tē) *adj.* **tast′i·er, tast′i·est 1.** that tastes good; flavorful **2.** [Now Rare] *same as* TASTEFUL —**tast′i·ly** *adv.* —**tast′i·ness** *n.*

**tat**[1] (tat) *vt.* **tat′ted, tat′ting** [< TATTING] to make by tat-ting —*vi.* to do tatting

**tat**[2] (tat) *n.* [< ? TAP[1]] *see* TIT FOR TAT

**ta·ta·mi** (tə tä′mē) *n., pl.* **-mi, -mis** [Jap.] a floor mat woven of rice straw, used traditionally in Japanese homes for sitting on, as when eating

**Ta·tar** (tät′ər) *n.* [Per.] **1.** a member of any of the Mon-golian and Turkic tribes that invaded W Asia and E Europe in the Middle Ages **2.** any of a Turkic people living in a region of EC European Russia and in parts of Asia **3.** any of their Turkic languages —*adj.* of the Tatars or their lan-guages

**Ta·ta·ry** (tät′ə rē) vast region in Europe & Asia under the control of Tatar tribes in the late Middle Ages

**'ta·ter, ta·ter** (tāt′ər) *n. dial. form of* POTATO

**tat·ter** (tat′ər) *n.* [prob. < ON. *tǫturr*, rags] **1.** a torn and hanging shred or piece, as of a garment **2.** a separate shred; rag **3.** [*pl.*] torn, ragged clothes —*vt., vi.* to reduce to tatters; make or become ragged —**tat′tered** *adj.*

**tat·ter·de·mal·ion** (tat′ər di māl′yən, -mal′-) *n.* [< prec. + ?] a person in torn, ragged clothes; ragamuffin

**tat·ting** (tat′iŋ) *n.* [prob. < Brit. dial. *tat*, to tangle] **1.** a fine lace made by looping and knotting thread that is wound on a hand shuttle **2.** the act of making this

**tat·tle** (tat′'l) *vi.* **-tled, -tling** [prob. < MDu. *tatelen*, of echoic origin] **1.** to talk idly; chatter **2.** to tell others' se-crets —*n.* idle talk; chatter —**tat′tler** *n.*

TATTING

**tat·tle·tale** (-tāl′) *n.* an in-former; talebearer: now chiefly a child's term

**tat·too**[1] (ta tōō′) *vt.* **-tooed′, -too′ing** [< Tahitian *tatau*] **1.** to puncture (the skin) with a needle and insert indelible colors so as to leave permanent marks or designs **2.** to make (marks or designs) on the skin this way —*n., pl.* **-toos′** a tattooed mark or design —**tat·too′er, tat·too′ist** *n.*

**tat·too**[2] (ta tōō′) *n., pl.* **-toos′** [< Du. < *tap toe*, shut the tap: a signal for closing barrooms] **1.** *a)* a signal on a drum, bugle, etc. summoning soldiers, etc. to their quarters at night *b)* in England, a military spectacle featuring marching, etc. **2.** any continuous drumming, rapping, etc. —*vt., vi.* **-tooed′, -too′ing** to beat or tap

**tat·ty** (tat′ē) *adj.* **-ti·er, -ti·est** [prob. akin to OE. *taetteca*, a rag] [Chiefly Brit.] shabby, decrepit, tawdry, etc. —**tat′-ti·ly** *adv.* —**tat′ti·ness** *n.*

**tau** (tô, tou) *n.* [Gr.] the nineteenth letter of the Greek al-phabet (T, τ)

**taught** (tôt) *pt. & pp. of* TEACH

**taunt** (tônt, tänt) *vt.* [< ? Fr. *tant pour tant*, tit for tat] **1.** to reproach in scornful or sarcastic language; jeer at **2.** to drive or provoke by taunting —*n.* a scornful or jeering remark; gibe —**taunt′er** *n.* —**taunt′ing·ly** *adv.*

**taupe** (tōp) *n.* [Fr. < L. *talpa*, a mole] a dark, brownish gray, the color of moleskin —*adj.* of such a color

**Tau·rus** (tôr′əs) [L., a bull] **1.** a N constellation containing the Pleiades **2.** the second sign of the zodiac: see ZODIAC, illus.

**taut** (tôt) *adj.* [ME. *toght*, tight, prob. < pp. of *togen*, to pull] **1.** tightly stretched, as a rope **2.** strained; tense *[a taut smile]* **3.** trim, tidy, etc. *[a taut ship]* —**taut′ly** *adv.* —**taut′ness** *n.*

**taut·en** (tôt′ən) *vt., vi.* to make or become taut

**tau·to-** [< Gr. < *to auto*, the same] *a combining form* meaning the same *[tautology]*

**tau·tog** (tô täg′) *n.* [< Algonquian pl. of *tautau,* a blackfish] a black or greenish food fish found off the Atlantic coast of the U.S.

**tau·tol·o·gy** (tô täl′ə jē) *n., pl.* **-gies** [< LL. < Gr.: see TAUTO- & -LOGY] **1.** needless repetition of an idea in a different word, phrase, etc.; redundancy (Ex.: "necessary essentials") **2.** an instance of this —**tau′to·log′i·cal** *adj.* —**tau′to·log′i·cal·ly** *adv.*

**tav·ern** (tav′ərn) *n.* [< OFr. < L. *taberna*] **1.** a place where liquors, beer, etc. are sold and drunk; saloon; bar **2.** an inn

**taw** (tô) *n.* **1.** a fancy marble used to shoot with in playing marbles **2.** *a)* the game of marbles *b)* the line from which the players shoot

**taw·dry** (tô′drē) *adj.* **-dri·er, -dri·est** [< St. *Audrey,* esp. in *St. Audrey laces,* sold at St. Audrey's fair, Norwich, England] cheap and showy; gaudy; sleazy —**taw′dri·ly** *adv.* —**taw′dri·ness** *n.*

**taw·ny** (tô′nē) *adj.* **-ni·er, -ni·est** [< OFr. pp. of *tanner,* to tan] brownish-yellow; tan —*n.* tawny color —**taw′ni·ness** *n.*

**tax** (taks) *vt.* [< MFr. < L. *taxare,* to appraise < base of *tangere,* to touch] **1.** orig., to determine the value of; assess **2.** to require (a person) to pay a percentage of his income, property value, etc. for the support of a government **3.** to assess a tax on (income, property, purchases, etc.) **4.** to put a burden or strain on **5.** to accuse; charge *[to be taxed with negligence]* —*n.* **1.** a compulsory payment, usually a percentage of income, property value, sales price, etc., for the support of a government **2.** a heavy demand; burden; strain —**tax′a·bil′i·ty** *n.* —**tax′a·ble** *adj.* —**tax′er** *n.*

**tax·a·tion** (tak sā′shən) *n.* **1.** a taxing or being taxed **2.** the principle of levying taxes **3.** a tax or tax levy **4.** revenue from taxes

**tax-de·duct·i·ble** (taks′di duk′tə b'l) *adj.* allowed as a deduction in computing income tax

**tax duplicate** **1.** the certification of real-estate assessments to the taxing authorities **2.** the basis on which the tax collector prepares tax bills

**tax-ex·empt** (-ig zempt′) *adj.* **1.** exempt from taxation; that may not be taxed **2.** producing nontaxable income *[tax-exempt bonds]*

**tax·i** (tak′sē) *n., pl.* **tax′is** *shortened form of* TAXICAB —*vi.* **tax′ied, tax′i·ing** or **tax′y·ing** **1.** to go in a taxi **2.** to move slowly along the ground or on water as an airplane does before taking off or after landing —*vt.* **1.** to carry in a taxi **2.** to cause (an airplane) to taxi

**tax·i·cab** (-kab′) *n.* [< *taxi(meter) cab*] an automobile in which passengers are carried for a fare shown on a meter

**tax·i·der·my** (tak′si dur′mē) *n.* [< Gr. *taxis,* arrangement + *derma,* a skin] the art of preparing, stuffing, and mounting the skins of animals so as to give a lifelike effect —**tax′i·der′mal, tax′i·der′mic** *adj.* —**tax′i·der′mist** *n.*

**tax·i·me·ter** (tak′sē mēt′ər) *n.* [Fr. *taximètre* < G. < ML. *taxa,* a tax + *-meter,* -METER] an automatic device in taxicabs that registers fares due

**taxi stand** a place where taxicabs are stationed for hire

**tax·on** (tak′sän) *n., pl.* **tax′a** (-sə) [< TAXONOMY] a taxonomic category or unit, as a species, genus, etc.

**tax·on·o·my** (tak sän′ə mē) *n.* [< Fr. < Gr. *taxis,* arrangement + *nomos,* a law] the science of classification, esp. of plants and animals into natural, related groups such as species and genera —**tax′o·nom′ic** (-sə näm′ik), **tax′o·nom′i·cal** *adj.* —**tax′o·nom′i·cal·ly** *adv.* —**tax·on′o·mist** *n.*

**tax·pay·er** (taks′pā′ər) *n.* a person who pays taxes

**tax shelter** any financial investment made for the purpose of acquiring expenses, depreciation allowances, etc., which can be used to reduce one's income tax

**tax stamp** a stamp that shows a tax has been paid

**Tay·lor** (tā′lər) [after Zachary TAYLOR] city in SE Mich.: suburb of Detroit: pop. 78,000

**Tay·lor** (tā′lər) **1.** Jer·e·my (jer′ə mē), 1613–67; Eng. bishop & theological writer **2.** Zach·a·ry (zak′ər ē), 1784–1850; U.S. general in the Mexican War; 12th president of the U.S. (1849–50)

**Tb** *Chem.* terbium

**TB, T.B., tb, t.b.** tuberculosis

**Tbi·li·si** (t'bi lē sē′) capital of the Georgian S.S.R.: pop. 889,000

**T-bone steak** (tē′bōn′) a steak from the loin, with a T-shaped bone, containing some tenderloin

**tbs., tbsp.** tablespoon; tablespoons

**Tc** *Chem.* technetium

**Tchai·kov·sky** (chī kôf′skē), **Peter Il·ich** (il′yich) 1840–93; Russ. composer: also **Pëtr Il·yich Tschai·kow·sky** (pyô′tr′ il yēch′ chī kôf′skē)

**Tchekov** *var. sp. of* CHEKHOV: also **Tchekhov**

**TD** touchdown: also **td**

**Te** *Chem.* tellurium

**tea** (tē) *n.* see PLURAL, II, D, 3 [Chin. dial. *t'e,* for Mandarin *ch'a,* tea] **1.** a white-flowered, evergreen shrub grown in warm parts of Asia for its young leaves, which are prepared by drying, etc. for use in making a common drink **2.** the dried, prepared leaves **3.** the drink made by steeping these in hot water, etc. **4.** a tealike plant, or the tealike beverage made from it or from a meat extract *[camomile tea, beef tea]* **5.** [Chiefly Brit.] a light meal, usually with tea, in the late afternoon **6.** a social gathering in the afternoon at which tea, coffee, etc. are served

**tea bag** a small, porous bag with tea leaves in it, for making an individual cup of tea

**tea ball** a hollow, perforated metal ball used to hold tea leaves in making tea

**tea·ber·ry** (-ber′ē) *n., pl.* **-ries** **1.** *same as* WINTERGREEN (sense 1) **2.** a wintergreen berry

**teach** (tēch) *vt.* **taught, teach′ing** [OE. *tæcan*] **1.** to show or help to learn how to do something; instruct **2.** to give lessons to; guide the study of **3.** to give lessons in (a subject) **4.** to give knowledge, insight, etc. to; cause to know, understand, etc. *[the accident taught her to be careful]* —*vi.* to be a teacher —**teach′a·bil′i·ty, teach′a·ble·ness** *n.* —**teach′a·ble** *adj.*

**teach·er** (tē′chər) *n.* a person who teaches, esp. in a school or college —**teach′er·ship′** *n.*

**teach·ing** (-chiŋ) *n.* **1.** the action of one who teaches; profession of a teacher **2.** something taught; precept, doctrine, etc.: *usually in pl.*

**tea·cup** (tē′kup′) *n.* **1.** a cup for drinking tea, etc. **2.** a teacupful

**tea·cup·ful** (-fool′) *n., pl.* **-fuls′** as much as a teacup will hold, about four fluid ounces

**tea·house** (tē′hous′) *n.* in the Orient, a place where tea and other refreshments are served

**teak** (tēk) *n.* [< Port. < native word *tēkka*] **1.** a large East Indian tree with hard, yellowish-brown wood used for shipbuilding, furniture, etc. **2.** its wood: also **teak′wood′**

**tea·ket·tle** (tē′ket′'l) *n.* a covered kettle with a spout and handle, used to boil water for tea, etc.

**teal** (tēl) *n.* [ME. *tele*] **1.** *pl.* **teals, teal:** see PLURAL, II, D, 1 any of several small, short-necked freshwater wild ducks **2.** a dark greenish blue: also **teal blue**

**team** (tēm) *n.* [OE., offspring] **1.** two or more horses, oxen, etc. harnessed to the same vehicle or plow **2.** a draft animal or animals and the vehicle drawn **3.** a group of people working together on a project or playing together against opponents in games —*vt., vi.* to join together in a team (often with *up*)

**team·mate** (tēm′māt′) *n.* a fellow team member

**team·ster** (-stər) *n.* one whose occupation is driving teams or trucks for hauling loads

**team teaching** teaching by several teachers working together with a group of students to explore relationships among various subject areas

**team·work** (-wurk′) *n.* the action or effort of people working together as a group

**tea party** a social gathering at which tea is served

**tea·pot** (tē′pät′) *n.* a pot with a spout, handle, and lid, for brewing and pouring tea

**tear¹** (ter) *vt.* **tore, torn, tear′ing** [OE. *teran,* to rend] **1.** to pull apart by force; rip; rend **2.** to make (a hole, etc.) by tearing **3.** to wound by tearing; lacerate **4.** to split into factions; disrupt *[ranks torn by dissension]* **5.** to divide by doubt, etc. *[torn between duty and desire]* **6.** to remove as by tearing, pulling, etc. (with *up, out, off,* etc.) —*vi.* **1.** to be torn **2.** to move with force or speed; rush —*n.* **1.** the act of tearing **2.** a torn place; rip **3.** a violent outburst **4.** [Slang] a spree —**tear at** to pull at violently in an effort to tear or remove —**tear down** to take apart; wreck, demolish, etc. —**tear into** [Colloq.] to attack or criticize violently —**tear′er** *n.*

**tear²** (tir) *n.* [OE.] **1.** a drop of the salty fluid that keeps the eyeball moist and flows from the eye in weeping **2.** any tearlike drop **3.** [*pl.*] sorrow; grief —*vi.* to shed, or fill with, tears —**in tears** weeping —**tear′less** *adj.*

**tear·drop** (tir′dräp′) *n.* a tear —*adj.* tear-shaped

**tear·ful** (-fəl) *adj.* **1.** in tears; weeping **2.** causing tears; sad —**tear′ful·ly** *adv.* —**tear′ful·ness** *n.*

**tear gas** (tir) a gas that makes the eyes sore and blinds them with tears —**tear′-gas′** *vt.* **-gassed′, -gas′sing**
**tear-jerk·er** (-jur′kər) *n.* [Slang] a play, movie, etc. that is sad in a too sentimental way —**tear′-jerk′ing** *adj.*
**tea·room** (tē′rōōm′) *n.* a restaurant that serves tea, coffee, light lunches, etc. and caters chiefly to women
**tear·y** (tir′ē) *adj.* **-i·er, -i·est** 1. tearful; crying 2. of or like tears —**tear′i·ly** *adv.* —**tear′i·ness** *n.*
**tease** (tēz) *vt.* **teased, teas′ing** [OE. *tæsan*] 1. *a)* to card or comb (flax, wool, etc.) *b)* to raise a nap on (cloth) with teasels *c)* to fluff (the hair) by brushing or combing the hair ends toward the scalp 2. to bother or annoy by mocking, poking fun, etc. 3. to pester with repeated requests 4. to tantalize —*vi.* to tease someone —*n.* 1. a teasing or being teased 2. a person who teases —**teas′er** *n.*
**tea·sel** (tē′z′l) *n.* [< OE. < base of *tæsan*, to tease] 1. a bristly plant (esp. the **fuller's teasel**) with prickly, cylindrical flower heads 2. a dried flower head of the fuller's teasel, used to raise a nap on cloth 3. any device for raising a nap on cloth —*vt.* **-seled** or **-selled, -sel·ing** or **-sel·ling** to nap (cloth) with teasels —**tea′sel·er, tea′sel·ler** *n.*
**tea·spoon** (tē′spōōn′) *n.* 1. a spoon for stirring tea, coffee, etc. and eating soft foods 2. *same as* TEASPOONFUL
**tea·spoon·ful** (-fool′) *n.*, *pl.* **-fuls′** as much as a teaspoon holds; 1/3 tablespoonful (1¹/₃ fluid drams)
**teat** (tēt, tit) *n.* [< OFr. *tete* < Gmc.] the nipple of a breast or udder
**tea·zel, tea·zle** (tē′z′l) *n.*, *vt. same as* TEASEL
**Te·bet, Te·beth** (tā vāt′, tā′vəs) *n.* [Heb.] the fourth month of the Jewish year: see JEWISH CALENDAR
**tech.** 1. technical 2. technology
**tech·ne·ti·um** (tek nē′shē əm) *n.* [ModL. < Gr. < *technē*, an art + -IUM] a metallic chemical element obtained in the fission of uranium: symbol, Tc; at. wt., 97(?); at. no., 43
**tech·nic** (tek′nik; *for n. 1 also* tek nēk′) *adj.* [< Gr. < *technē*, an art] *same as* TECHNICAL —*n.* 1. *same as* TECHNIQUE 2. [*pl.*, *with sing. or pl. v.*] the study or principles of an art
**tech·ni·cal** (tek′ni k′l) *adj.* [prec. + -AL] 1. dealing with the practical, industrial, or mechanical arts or the applied sciences 2. of, used in, or peculiar to a specific science, art, craft, etc. [*technical* terms] 3. of or showing technique [*technical* skill] 4. according to principles or rules [a *technical* difference] 5. involving or using technicalities —**tech′ni·cal·ly** *adv.*
**tech·ni·cal·i·ty** (tek′nə kal′ə tē) *n.*, *pl.* **-ties** 1. the state or quality of being technical 2. a technical point, term, method, etc. 3. a minute, formal point or detail brought to bear upon a main issue
**technical knockout** *Boxing* a victory won when the opponent, though not knocked out, is so badly hurt that the referee stops the match
**technical sergeant** *U.S. Air Force* the second grade of enlisted man, just below master sergeant
**tech·ni·cian** (tek nish′ən) *n.* a person skilled in the technicalities of some subject or in the technique of some art or science
**Tech·ni·col·or** (tek′ni kul′ər) *a trademark for* a certain process of making color motion pictures —*n.* [t-] 1. this process 2. bright colors —**tech′ni·col′ored** *adj.*
**tech·nique** (tek nēk′) *n.* [Fr. < Gr.: see TECHNIC] 1. the method of procedure (as to practical or formal details) in creating an artistic work or carrying out a scientific or mechanical operation 2. the degree of expertness shown in this 3. any method of doing a thing
**tech·no-** [< Gr. *technē*, an art] *a combining form meaning:* 1. art, science, skill 2. technical, technological [*technocracy*]
**tech·noc·ra·cy** (tek näk′rə sē) *n.* [prec. + -CRACY] government by scientists and engineers —**tech′no·crat′** (-nə-krat′) *n.* —**tech′no·crat′ic** *adj.*
**tech·no·log·i·cal** (tek′nə läj′i k′l) *adj.* 1. of technology 2. resulting from technical progress in the use of machinery and automation Also **tech′no·log′ic** —**tech′no·log′i·cal·ly** *adv.*
**tech·nol·o·gy** (tek näl′ə jē) *n.* [Gr. *technologia*, systematic treatment] 1. the science or study of the practical or industrial arts, applied sciences, etc. 2. the terms used in a science, art, etc. 3. applied science 4. a method, process, etc. for handling a specific technical problem —**tech·nol′o·gist** *n.*
**tec·ton·ic** (tek tän′ik) *adj.* [< LL. < Gr. < *tektōn*, a builder] designating, of, or pertaining to the processes that produce changes in the earth's crust
**Te·cum·seh** (ti kum′sə) 1768?-1813; chief of the Shawnee Indians
**ted** (ted) *vt.* **ted′ded, ted′ding** [prob. < ON. *tethja*, to manure] to spread or scatter (newly cut grass) for drying as hay —**ted′der** *n.*
**ted·dy bear** (ted′ē) [< *Teddy (Theodore)* Roosevelt] a child's stuffed toy made to look like a bear cub

**Te De·um** (tē dē′əm, tā dā′oom) [LL.] 1. a Christian hymn beginning *Te Deum laudamus* (We praise thee, O God) 2. music for this hymn
**te·di·ous** (tē′dē əs, tē′jəs) *adj.* full of tedium; tiresome; boring —**te′di·ous·ly** *adv.* —**te′di·ous·ness** *n.*
**te·di·um** (-dē əm) *n.* [L. *taedium* < *taedet*, it offends] the condition or quality of being tiresome, boring, or monotonous
**tee¹** (tē) *n.*, *pl.* **tees** 1. the letter T, t 2. anything shaped like a T —*adj.* shaped like a T —**to a tee** exactly
**tee²** (tē) *n.* [< prec.: the mark was orig. T-shaped] a mark aimed at in quoits, curling, etc.
**tee³** (tē) *n.* [prob. < Scot. dial. *teaz*] 1. a small, pointed holder of wood, plastic, etc. on which a golf ball is put to be driven 2. the place at each hole from which a golfer makes his first stroke —*vt.*, *vi.* **teed, tee′ing** to put (a ball) on a tee —**tee off** 1. to play a golf ball from a tee 2. to begin 3. [Slang] to make angry or disgusted

**tee-hee** (tē′hē′) *interj.*, *n.* [ME.: echoic] the sound of a titter or snicker —*vi.* **-heed′, -hee′ing** to titter or snicker
**teem¹** (tēm) *vi.* [OE. *tieman*, to bear < base of *team*, progeny] to be full; abound; swarm [a river *teeming* with fish]
**teem²** (tēm) *vt.* [ON. *taema*] to empty; pour out —*vi.* to pour [a *teeming* rain]
**teen** (tēn) *n.* [< OE. *tien*, ten] 1. [*pl.*] the years from thirteen through nineteen (of a century or a person's age) 2. *same as* TEEN-AGER —*adj. same as* TEEN-AGE
**teen-age** (-āj′) *adj.* 1. in one's teens 2. of, like, or for persons in their teens Also **teen′age′**
**teen-ag·er** (-āj′ər) *n.* a person in his teens
**tee·ny** (tē′nē) *adj.* **-ni·er, -ni·est** *colloq. var. of* TINY: also **teen′sy**
**teen·y-bop·per** (tē′nē bäp′ər) *n.* [TEEN + -Y¹ + BOP² + -ER] [Slang] a young teen-ager, esp. a girl, of the 1960's, following the latest fads
**tee·ny-wee·ny** (-wē′nē) *adj.* [Colloq.] very small; tiny: also **teen·sy-ween·sy** (tēn′sē wēn′sē)
**tee·pee** (tē′pē) *n. alt. sp. of* TEPEE
**tee shirt** *same as* T-SHIRT
**tee·ter** (tēt′ər) *vi.* [dial. *titter* < ON. *titra*, to tremble] to totter, wobble, etc. —*vt.* to cause to teeter —*n. shortened form of* TEETER-TOTTER
**tee·ter·board** (-bôrd′) *n. same as* SEESAW
**tee·ter-tot·ter** (-tät′ər, -tōt′-) *n.*, *vi. same as* SEESAW
**teeth** (tēth) *n. pl. of* TOOTH
**teethe** (tēth) *vi.* **teethed, teeth′ing** to grow teeth; cut one's teeth
**teeth·ing ring** (tē′thiŋ) a ring of ivory, plastic, etc. for teething babies to bite on
**teeth·ridge** (tēth′rij′) *n.* the ridge of gum along the inside of the upper front teeth
**tee·to·tal** (tē tōt′'l, tē′tōt′'l) *adj.* [formed by redupl. of initial letter of TOTAL] 1. [Colloq.] entire; complete 2. of or in favor of teetotalism —**tee·to′tal·er, tee·to′tal·ler** *n.* —**tee·to′tal·ly** *adv.*
**tee·to·tal·ism** (-iz'm) *n.* the principle or practice of never drinking any alcoholic liquor —**tee·to′tal·ist** *n.*
**Tef·lon** (tef′län) *a trademark for* a tough, insoluble polymer used in making nonsticking coatings for cooking utensils, etc.
**Te·gu·ci·gal·pa** (te gōo′sē gäl′pä) capital of Honduras, in the SC part: pop. 219,000
**teg·u·ment** (teg′yoo mənt) *n.* [< L. < *tegere*, to cover] *same as* INTEGUMENT
**te-hee** (tē′hē′) *interj.*, *n.*, *vi.* **-heed′, -hee′ing** *var. of* TEEHEE
**Teh·rán, Te·he·ran** (te hrän′; *E.* te ə rän′, -ran′) capital of Iran, in the NC part: pop. 3,150,000
**tek·tite** (tek′tīt) *n.* [< Gr. *tēktos*, molten < *tēkein*, to melt + -ITE] any of certain small, dark green to black glassy bodies, assumed to have come to earth from outer space
**tel-** *same as:* 1. TELE- 2. TELO-
**tel.** 1. telegram 2. telegraph 3. telephone
**Tel A·viv-Jaf·fa** (tel′ä vēv′yäf′ə, tel′ə vēv′jaf′ə) seaport in W Israel, incorporating the former cities of Tel Aviv & Jaffa: pop. 383,000: usually called **Tel Aviv**
**tel·e-** *a combining form meaning:* 1. [< Gr. < *tēle*, far off] at, over, from, or to a distance [*telegraph*] 2. [< TELE-(VISION)] of or by television [*telecast*]
**tel·e·cast** (tel′ə kast′) *vt.*, *vi.* **-cast′** or **-cast′ed, -cast′ing** [TELE- + (BROAD)CAST] to broadcast by television —*n.* a television broadcast —**tel′e·cast′er** *n.*
**tel·e·com·mu·ni·ca·tion** (tel′ə kə myōō′nə kā′shən) *n.* [*also pl.*, *with sing. or pl. v.*] communication by radio, telephone, telegraph, television, etc.
**tel·e·gram** (tel′ə gram′) *n.* [TELE- + -GRAM] a message transmitted by telegraph
**tel·e·graph** (-graf′) *n.* [< Fr.: see TELE- & -GRAPH] an ap-

paratus or system for sending messages, orig. in Morse code, by electric impulses through a wire or by means of radio waves —*vt.* 1. to send (a message) by telegraph to (someone) 2. to let another know without meaning to (something one plans to do), as by a look —*vt.* to send a telegram —**te·leg·ra·pher** (tə leg′rə fər), **te·leg′ra·phist** *n.* —**tel′e·graph′ic** *adj.* —**tel′e·graph′i·cal·ly** *adv.*

**te·leg·ra·phy** (tə leg′rə fē) *n.* 1. the operation of telegraph apparatus 2. the sending of messages by telegraph

**tel·e·ki·ne·sis** (tel′ə ki nē′sis) *n.* [ModL. < TELE- + Gr. *kinēsis*, motion] the causing of an object to move supposedly by means of psychic forces —**tel′e·ki·net′ic** (-net′ik) *adj.*

**Te·lem·a·chus** (tə lem′ə kəs) *Gr. Legend* the son of Odysseus and Penelope, who helped his father slay his mother's suitors

**Te·le·mann** (te′lə män′), **Ge·org Phi·lipp** (gā ôrk′ fē′lip) 1681-1767; Ger. composer

**tel·e·mark** (tel′ə märk′) *n.* [after *Telemark*, region in S Norway] *Skiing* a turning movement during which the outer ski is advanced and turned in at a widening angle

**tel·e·me·ter** (tel′ə mēt′ər, tə lem′ə tər) *n.* [TELE- + -METER] a device for measuring temperature, radiation, etc. at a remote point, as in outer space, and transmitting the information obtained, esp. by radio, to a distant receiver on earth —*vt., vi.* to transmit by telemeter —**tel′e·met′ric** (-met′rik) *adj.* —**tel′e·met′ri·cal·ly** *adv.* —**te·lem·e·try** (tə lem′ə trē) *n.*

**te·le·ol·o·gy** (tē′lē äl′ə jē, tel′ē-) *n.* [ModL. < Gr. *telos*, an end + *-logia* (see -LOGY)] 1. the fact or quality of having an ultimate purpose or goal 2. a belief that what happens or occurs in nature is determined by an overall design or purpose, not just by mechanical causes —**te′le·o·log′i·cal** (-ə läj′i k'l) *adj.* —**te′le·ol′o·gist** *n.*

**te·lep·a·thy** (tə lep′ə thē) *n.* [TELE- + -PATHY] supposed communication between minds by some means other than the normal functioning of the senses —**tel·e·path·ic** (tel′ə path′ik) *adj.* —**tel′e·path′i·cal·ly** *adv.* —**te·lep′a·thist** *n.*

**tel·e·phone** (tel′ə fōn′) *n.* [TELE- + -PHONE] an instrument or system for conveying speech over distances by converting sound into electric impulses sent through a wire —*vi.* -**phoned′,** -**phon′ing** to talk over a telephone —*vt.* 1. to convey (a message) by telephone 2. to speak to or reach (a person) by telephone —**tel′e·phon′er** *n.* —**tel′e·phon′ic** (-fän′ik) *adj.* —**tel′e·phon′i·cal·ly** *adv.*

**te·leph·o·ny** (tə lef′ə nē) *n.* the science of communication by telephone

**tel·e·pho·to** (tel′ə fōt′ō) *adj.* 1. telephotographic 2. designating or of a camera lens producing a large image of a distant object

**tel·e·pho·to·graph** (tel′ə fōt′ə graf′) *n.* 1. a photograph taken with a telephoto lens 2. a photograph transmitted by telephotography —*vt., vi.* 1. to take (photographs) with a telephoto lens 2. to transmit (photographs) by telephotography

**tel·e·pho·tog·ra·phy** (-fə täg′rə fē) *n.* 1. photography done with a telephoto lens 2. the science or process of transmitting photographs over distances by converting light rays into electric signals which are sent over wire or radio channels —**tel′e·pho′to·graph′ic** (-fōt′ə graf′ik) *adj.*

**tel·e·ran** (tel′ə ran′) *n.* [*tele(vision)* r(*adar*) a(*ir*) n(*avigation*)] the televised transmission to aircraft of data received by radar concerning terrain, etc., as an aid to navigation

**tel·e·scope** (tel′ə skōp′) *n.* [< It. < ModL. < Gr.: see TELE- & -SCOPE] an instrument for making distant objects, as stars, appear nearer and larger: it consists of a tube or tubes containing lenses In a *refracting telescope,* the image is focused directly on a lens; in a *reflecting telescope,* the image is focused on a concave mirror —*adj.* having parts that slide one inside another —*vi.* -**scoped′,** -**scop′ing** to slide or be forced one inside another like tubes of a collapsible telescope —*vt.* 1. to cause to telescope 2. to condense; shorten

**tel·e·scop·ic** (tel′ə skäp′ik) *adj.* 1. of a telescope 2. seen or obtained by a telescope 3. visible only through a telescope 4. farseeing 5. having sections that slide one inside another Also **tel′e·scop′i·cal** —**tel′e·scop′i·cal·ly** *adv.*

**te·les·co·py** (tə les′kə pē) *n.* the art or practice of using a telescope —**te·les′co·pist** *n.*

**tel·e·thon** (tel′ə thän′) *n.* [TELE(VISION) + (MARA)THON] a campaign, as on a lengthy telecast, asking for support for a cause, as by pledged donations made by telephone

**Tel·e·type** (tel′ə tīp′) *a trademark for* a form of teletypewriter —*n.* [*often* t-] communication by means of Teletype —*vt., vi.* -**typed′,** -**typ′ing** [*often* t-] to send (messages) by Teletype —**tel′e·typ′er, tel′e·typ′ist** *n.*

**tel·e·type·writ·er** (tel′ə tīp′rīt′ər) *n.* a form of telegraph

in which the message is typed on a keyboard that sends electric signals to a machine that prints the words

**tel·e·vise** (tel′ə vīz′) *vt., vi.* -**vised′,** -**vis′ing** to transmit by television —**tel′e·vi′sor** *n.*

**tel·e·vi·sion** (-vizh′ən) *n.* [TELE- + VISION] 1. the process of transmitting scenes or views by radio waves or, sometimes, by wire, in which light rays are converted by a camera tube into electric signals that are transmitted to a receiver that changes the signals into electron beams that are projected against the screen of a picture tube, reproducing the original image 2. television broadcasting as an industry, art, etc.; also, its facilities and related activities 3. a television receiving set —*adj.* of, in, or by television

**tel·ex** (tel′eks) *n.* [TEL(ETYPEWRITER) + EX(CHANGE)] 1. a teletypewriter with a telephone dial for making connections 2. a message sent by this —*vt.* to send (a message) by telex

**tell** (tel) *vt.* **told, tell′ing** [OE. *tellan,* lit., to calculate] 1. orig., to enumerate; count 2. to give an account of (a story, etc.) in speech or writing; narrate; relate 3. to express in words; utter [*to tell* the truth] 4. to report; announce 5. to make known; disclose 6. to recognize; distinguish [I can *tell* the difference] 7. to decide; know [he can't *tell* when to go] 8. to let know; inform 9. to request; order [*tell* him to leave] 10. to assure emphatically [it's there, I *tell* you] —*vi.* 1. to give an account or description (*of* something) 2. to be evidence or an indication (*of* something) 3. to reveal something, esp. secrets 4. to produce a result or have a marked effect —**tell off** 1. to count and separate from the total 2. [Colloq.] to rebuke severely —**tell on** 1. to make weary, worn-out, etc. 2. [Colloq.] to inform against —**tell′a·ble** *adj.*

**Tell** (tel), **William** in Swiss legend, a hero in the fight for independence from Austria, forced, on pain of death, to shoot an apple off his son's head with bow and arrow

**tell·er** (tel′ər) *n.* 1. a person who tells (a story, etc.) 2. a person who counts; specif., *a*) one who counts votes *b*) a bank clerk who pays out or receives money

**tell·ing** (tel′iŋ) *adj.* 1. having an effect; forceful; striking 2. that tells or reveals much —**tell′ing·ly** *adv.*

**tell·tale** (-tāl′) *n.* 1. a talebearer or informer 2. an outward indication of a secret 3. a device that indicates or records information —*adj.* revealing a secret

**tel·lu·ri·um** (te loor′ē əm) *n.* [ModL. < L. *tellus,* the earth] a rare, tin-white, brittle, nonmetallic chemical element: symbol, Te; at. wt., 127.60; at. no., 52

**tel·ly** (tel′ē) *n.* [Brit. Colloq.] television

**tel·o-** [< Gr. *telos,* an end] *a combining form meaning* end

**tel·pher, tel·fer** (tel′fər) *n.* [< TEL(E)- + Gr. *pherein,* to BEAR[1]] an electrically driven car suspended from and run on overhead cables —**tel′pher·age** *n.*

**Tel·star** (tel′stär′) [TEL(E)- + STAR] a satellite for relaying microwaves in communication by telephone, television, etc., first put in earth orbit in 1962

**Tel·u·gu** (tel′ə gōō′) *n.* 1. a Dravidian language of S India 2. *pl.* -**gus′,** -**gu′** a member of a Dravidian people speaking this language —*adj.* of Telugu or the Telugus Also **Tel′·e·gu′**

**tem·blor** (tem′blôr, -blər; *Sp.* tem blôr′) *n., pl.* -**blors;** *Sp.* -**blo′res** (-blô′res) [Sp. < *temblar,* to tremble] *same as* EARTHQUAKE

**te·mer·i·ty** (tə mer′ə tē) *n.* [< L. < *temere,* rashly] foolish or rash boldness; recklessness

**temp.** 1. temperature 2. temporary

**Tem·pe** (tem′pē) [after Vale of *Tempe,* river valley in E Greece] city in SC Ariz.: suburb of Phoenix: pop. 107,000

**tem·per** (tem′pər) *vt.* [< OE. & OFr., both < L. *temperare,* to regulate < *tempus,* a period] 1. to make suitable or free from excess by mingling with another thing; moderate [*temper* criticism with reason] 2. *a*) to bring to the proper texture, hardness, etc. by treating in some way [to *temper* steel by heating and sudden cooling] *b*) to toughen, as by hardship 3. *Music* to adjust the pitch of (a note, instrument, etc.) to some temperament —*vi.* to become tempered —*n.* 1. a being tempered; specif., the degree of hardness and resiliency of a metal 2. frame of mind; disposition 3. mental calm; composure: now only in **lose** (or **keep**) **one's temper** 4. a tendency to get angry 5. anger; rage 6. something used to temper a mixture, etc.

**tem·per·a** (tem′pər ə) *n.* [It. < *temperare* < L.: see prec.] 1. *a*) a way of painting that uses pigments mixed with size, casein, or egg to produce a dull finish *b*) the paint so used 2. an opaque, water-base paint used as for posters

**tem·per·a·ment** (tem′prə mənt, -pər ə mənt, -pər mənt) *n.* [L. *temperamentum,* proper mixing < *temperare:* see TEMPER] 1. one's customary frame of mind or natural disposition 2. a nature that is excitable, moody, etc. 3. *Music* a system of adjustment of the intervals between the tones of an instrument

fat, āpe, cär, ten, ēven, is, bīte; gō, hôrn, tōōl, look; oil, out; up, fur; get; joy; yet; chin; she; thin, then; zh, leisure; ŋ, ring; ə for *a* in ago, *e* in agent, *i* in sanity, *o* in comply, *u* in focus; ′ as in able (ā′b'l); Fr. bál; ë, Fr. coeur; ö, Fr. feu; Fr. mon; ô, Fr. coq; ü, Fr. duc; r, Fr. cri; H, G. ich; kh, G. doch; ‡foreign; *hypothetical; < derived from. See inside front cover.

**tem·per·a·men·tal** (tem'prə men't'l, -pər ə men't'l, -pər men't'l) *adj.* **1.** of or caused by temperament **2.** excitable by temperament; easily upset **3.** erratic in behavior —**tem'per·a·men'tal·ly** *adv.*

**tem·per·ance** (tem'pər əns, -prəns) *n.* [< MFr. < L. < prp. of *temperare:* see TEMPER] **1.** a being temperate or moderate; self-restraint **2.** moderation in drinking alcoholic liquor, or, esp., the avoiding of alcoholic liquor completely

**tem·per·ate** (tem'pər it, -prit) *adj.* [< L. pp. of *temperare*, to TEMPER] **1.** moderate in indulging the appetites; abstemious, esp. in using alcoholic liquor **2.** moderate in one's actions, speech, etc. **3.** characterized by restraint *[a temperate* reply*]* **4.** neither very hot nor very cold: said of a climate, etc. —**tem'per·ate·ly** *adv.* —**tem'per·ate·ness** *n.*

**Temperate Zone** either of two zones of the earth (**North Temperate Zone** and **South Temperate Zone**) between the tropics and the polar circles

**tem·per·a·ture** (tem'prə chər, tem'pər ə-) *n.* [< L. < *temperatus*, temperate] the degree of hotness or coldness of anything, usually as measured on a thermometer; specif., *a)* the degree of heat of a living body; also, an excess of this over the normal (about 98.6°F or 37°C in man) *b)* the degree of heat of the atmosphere

**tem·pered** (tem'pərd) *adj.* **1.** having been given the desired texture, hardness, etc. **2.** modified by other qualities, etc. **3.** having a (specified) temper *[bad-tempered]* **4.** *Music* adjusted to a temperament

**tem·pest** (tem'pist) *n.* [< OFr., ult. < L. *tempestas*, portion of time, weather < *tempus*, time] **1.** a violent storm with high winds, esp. one accompanied by rain, hail, or snow **2.** a violent outburst; tumult

**tem·pes·tu·ous** (tem pes'choo wəs) *adj.* **1.** of or like a tempest; stormy **2.** violent; turbulent —**tem·pes'tu·ous·ly** *adv.* —**tem·pes'tu·ous·ness** *n.*

**Tem·plar** (tem'plər) *n.* [from occupying quarters near the site of Solomon's Temple in Jerusalem] *same as* KNIGHT TEMPLAR

**tem·plate, tem·plet** (tem'plit) *n.* [< Fr., dim. of *temple* < L. *templum*, small timber] **1.** a pattern, usually a thin plate, for forming an accurate copy of an object or shape **2.** *Archit. a)* a short stone or timber placed under a beam to help distribute the pressure *b)* a beam for supporting joists over a doorway, etc.

**tem·ple¹** (tem'p'l) *n.* [< OE. & OFr., both < L. *templum*, orig., space marked out] **1.** a building for the worship of a god or gods **2.** [T-] any of three buildings for worshiping Jehovah, successively built by the Jews in ancient Jerusalem **3.** the synagogue of a Reform, or sometimes Conservative, congregation **4.** a Christian church **5.** a building, usually of imposing size, serving some purpose *[a Masonic temple]* —**tem'pled** *adj.*

**tem·ple²** (tem'p'l) *n.* [< OFr. < VL. < L. *tempora*, the temples, pl. of *tempus*, temple of the head] **1.** the flat area at either side of the forehead, above and behind the eye **2.** either of the sidepieces of a pair of glasses

**tem·po** (tem'pō) *n., pl.* **-pos, -pi** (-pē) [It. < L. *tempus*, time] **1.** the speed at which a piece of music is performed **2.** rate of activity; pace *[the tempo* of modern living*]*

**tem·po·ral¹** (tem'pər əl, -prəl) *adj.* [L. *temporalis* < *tempus*, time] **1.** lasting only for a time; transitory; not eternal **2.** of this world; not spiritual **3.** civil or secular; not ecclesiastical **4.** of or limited by time —*n.* a temporal thing, power, etc. —**tem'po·ral·ly** *adv.*

**tem·po·ral²** (tem'pər əl, -prəl) *adj.* [LL. *temporalis* < *tempora:* see TEMPLE²] of or near the temple or temples (of the head)

**temporal bone** either of a pair of compound bones forming the sides of the skull

**tem·po·ral·i·ty** (tem'pə ral'ə tē) *n., pl.* **-ties 1.** the quality or state of being temporal **2.** [*usually pl.*] secular properties of a church

**tem·po·rar·y** (tem'pə rer'ē) *adj.* [< L. < *tempus*, time] lasting only for a time; not permanent —**tem·po·rar·i·ly** (tem'pə rer'ə lē, tem'pə rer'ə lē) *adv.* —**tem'po·rar'i·ness** *n.*

**tem·po·rize** (tem'pə rīz') *vi.* **-rized', -riz'ing** [MFr. *temporiser* < ML. < L. *tempus*, time] **1.** to act or speak in a way one thinks is expedient, ignoring principle **2.** *a)* to put off making a decision, or to agree for a while, so as to gain time *b)* to bargain or deal (*with* a person) so as to gain time —**tem'po·ri·za'tion** *n.* —**tem'po·riz'er** *n.*

**tempt** (tempt) *vt.* [< OFr. < LL. *temptare* < L., to try the strength of] **1.** orig., to test; try **2.** to entice (a person) to do or want something that is wrong, forbidden, etc. **3.** to be inviting or enticing; attract **4.** to provoke or risk provoking (fate, etc.) —**tempt'a·ble** *adj.* —**tempt'er** *n.* —**tempt'ress** *n.fem.*

**temp·ta·tion** (temp tā'shən) *n.* **1.** a tempting or being tempted **2.** something that tempts

**tempt·ing** (temp'tiŋ) *adj.* that tempts; enticing; attractive —**tempt'ing·ly** *adv.*

**tem·pu·ra** (tem'poo rä', tem poor'ə) *n.* [Jap., lit., fried food] a Japanese dish of seafood or vegetables dipped in an egg batter and deep-fried *[shrimp tempura]*

‡**tem·pus fu·git** (tem'pəs fyoo'jit) [L.] time flies

**ten** (ten) *adj.* [OE.] totaling one more than nine —*n.* **1.** the cardinal number between 9 and 11; 10; X **2.** anything having ten units or members, or numbered ten **3.** [Colloq.] a ten-dollar bill

**ten. 1.** tenor **2.** *Music* tenuto

**ten·a·ble** (ten'ə b'l) *adj.* [Fr. < OFr. < *tenir:* see TENANT] that can be held, defended, or believed —**ten'a·bil'i·ty, ten'a·ble·ness** *n.* —**ten'a·bly** *adv.*

**te·na·cious** (tə nā'shəs) *adj.* [< L. *tenax* (gen. *tenacis*) < *tenere*, to hold] **1.** holding firmly *[a tenacious* grip*]* **2.** that retains well *[a tenacious* memory*]* **3.** holding together strongly; cohesive **4.** clinging; adhesive **5.** persistent —**te·na'cious·ly** *adv.* —**te·na'cious·ness** *n.*

**te·nac·i·ty** (tə nas'ə tē) *n.* the quality or state of being tenacious

**ten·an·cy** (ten'ən sē) *n., pl.* **-cies 1.** occupancy or duration of occupancy by a tenant **2.** any holding of property, an office, etc.

**ten·ant** (ten'ənt) *n.* [OFr., orig. prp. of *tenir*, to hold < L. *tenere*] **1.** a person who pays rent to occupy or use land, a building, etc. **2.** an occupant of or dweller in a specified place —*vt.* to occupy as a tenant —**ten'ant·a·ble** *adj.* —**ten'ant·less** *adj.*

**tenant farmer** a person who farms land owned by another and pays rent in cash or in a share of the crops

**ten·ant·ry** (ten'ən trē) *n., pl.* **-ries 1.** a body of tenants **2.** occupancy by a tenant

**ten-cent store** (ten'sent') *same as* FIVE-AND-TEN-CENT STORE

**Ten Commandments** *Bible* the ten laws forming the fundamental moral code of Israel, given to Moses by God on Mount Sinai: Ex. 20:2–17; Deut. 5:6–22

**tend¹** (tend) *vt.* [see ATTEND] **1.** to take care of; watch over; attend to **2.** to be in charge of; manage —*vi.* to pay attention; attend

**tend²** (tend) *vi.* [< OFr. < L. *tendere*, to stretch] **1.** to move or extend *[to tend* east*]* **2.** to be likely or apt; incline *[tending* to boast*]* **3.** to lead (*to* or *toward* a specified result)

**tend·en·cy** (ten'dən sē) *n., pl.* **-cies** [< ML. < L. prp. of *tendere*, to stretch] **1.** an inclination to move or act in a particular direction or way; leaning; bias **2.** a course toward some purpose, object, or result; drift **3.** a definite purpose or point of view in something said or written

**ten·den·tious** (ten den'shəs) *adj.* [< G., ult. < ML. *tendentia*, TENDENCY] showing a deliberate tendency or aim; esp., advancing a definite point of view: also sp. **ten·den'cious** —**ten·den'tious·ly** *adv.* —**ten·den'tious·ness** *n.*

**ten·der¹** (ten'dər) *adj.* [< OFr. < L. *tener*, soft] **1.** soft or delicate and easily chewed, broken, cut, etc. **2.** physically weak; frail **3.** immature; young *[the tender* age of five*]* **4.** of soft quality or delicate tone **5.** needing careful handling; ticklish *[a tender* subject*]* **6.** gentle or light, as a touch **7.** *a)* affectionate, loving, etc. *[a tender* smile*] b)* careful; considerate **8.** *a)* that is hurt or feels pain easily; sensitive *[a tender* skin*] b)* sensitive to impressions, emotions, etc. *[a tender* conscience*] c)* sensitive to others' feelings; compassionate *[a tender* heart*]* —**ten'der·ly** *adv.* —**ten'der·ness** *n.*

**ten·der²** (ten'dər) *vt.* [< Fr. < L. *tendere*, to stretch] **1.** to offer in payment of an obligation **2.** to present for acceptance; offer (an invitation, apology, etc.) —*n.* **1.** an offer of money, services, etc. made to satisfy an obligation **2.** a formal offer, as of marriage, a contract, etc. **3.** money, etc. offered in payment —**ten'der·er** *n.*

**tend·er³** (ten'dər) *n.* **1.** a person who tends, or has charge of, something **2.** *a)* a ship to supply or service another ship, a submarine, etc. *b)* a boat for carrying passengers, etc. to or from a ship close to shore **3.** the railroad car behind a steam locomotive for carrying its coal and water

**ten·der·foot** (-foot') *n., pl.* **-foots', -feet' 1.** a newcomer, specif. to the hardships of Western ranching **2.** a beginner in the Boy Scouts

**ten·der·heart·ed** (-här'tid) *adj.* having a tender heart; quick to feel pity —**ten'der·heart'ed·ly** *adv.* —**ten'der·heart'ed·ness** *n.*

**ten·der·ize** (ten'də rīz') *vt.* **-ized', -iz'ing** to make (meat) tender, as by adding a substance that softens tissues —**ten'der·iz'er** *n.*

**ten·der·loin** (ten'dər loin') *n.* **1.** the tenderest muscle of a loin of beef or pork **2.** [*usually* T-] a vice-filled district of a city: so called because viewed as choice for graft

**ten·di·ni·tis** (ten'də nīt'əs) *n.* [< ModL.: see TENDON & -ITIS] inflammation of a tendon

**ten·don** (ten'dən) *n.* [ML. *tendo* (gen. *tendinis*) < Gr. < *teinein*, to stretch] any of the cords of tough, fibrous tissue connecting muscles to bones or other parts; sinew —**ten'di·nous** (-də nəs) *adj.*

**ten·dril** (ten′drəl) *n.* [prob. < OFr. *tendrum*, ult. < L. *tener*, soft] a threadlike part of a climbing plant, serving to support it by clinging to or coiling around an object

TENDRIL

**ten·e·brous** (ten′ə brəs) *adj.* [< L. < *tenebrae*, darkness] dark; gloomy: also **te·neb·ri·ous** (tə neb′rē əs)

**ten·e·ment** (ten′ə mənt) *n.* [< OFr. < ML. < L. *tenere*, to hold] **1.** *Law* land, buildings, etc. held by tenure **2.** a dwelling house **3.** a separately tenanted room or suite **4.** *same as* TENEMENT HOUSE —**ten′e·men′tal, ten′e·men′ta·ry** *adj.*

**tenement house** an apartment building, now specif. one in the slums that is run-down and overcrowded

**ten·et** (ten′it) *n.* [L., he holds] a principle, doctrine, or belief held as a truth, as by some group

**ten·fold** (ten′fōld′) *adj.* **1.** having ten parts **2.** having ten times as much or as many —*adv.* ten times as much or as many

**ten-gal·lon hat** (ten′gal′ən) a wide-brimmed felt hat with a high, round crown, orig. worn by cowboys

**Ten·nes·see** (ten′ə sē′) [< *Tanasi*, Cherokee village name] **1.** EC State of the U.S.: 42,244 sq. mi.; pop. 4,591,000; cap. Nashville: abbrev. **Tenn.**, **TN 2.** river flowing from NE Tenn. through N Ala. & W Tenn. into the Ohio River —**Ten′nes·se′an** *adj., n.*

**Tennessee walking horse** any of a breed of saddle or light utility horse with an easy, ambling gait

**ten·nis** (ten′is) *n.* [prob. < Anglo-Fr. *tenetz*, hold (imperative) < OFr. *tenir*: see TENANT] **1.** a game (officially **lawn tennis**), usually played outdoors, in which two or four players using rackets hit a ball back and forth over a net dividing a marked rectangular area (**tennis court**) **2.** a similar but more complex old indoor game (**court tennis**), the ball being in addition bounced against walls

**tennis shoe** *same as* SNEAKER (sense 2)

**Ten·ny·son** (ten′ə s'n), **Alfred,** 1st Baron Tennyson, 1809–92; Eng. poet: called *Alfred, Lord Tennyson* —**Ten′ny·so′ni·an** (-sō′nē ən) *adj.*

**ten·on** (ten′ən) *n.* [< MFr. < *tenir*: see TENANT] a part of a piece of wood, etc. cut to stick out so that it will fit into a hole (*mortise*) in another piece to make a joint: see MORTISE, illus. —*vt., vi.* **1.** to make a tenon (on) **2.** to joint by mortise and tenon

**ten·or** (ten′ər) *n.* [< OFr. < L. < *tenere*, to hold] **1.** general course or tendency **2.** general meaning; drift **3.** general character or nature **4.** [because the tenor voice "held" the melody] *a)* the highest usual adult male voice, or its range: see also COUNTERTENOR *b)* a part for this voice *c)* a singer or instrument having this range —*adj.* of, in, or for the tenor

**tenor clef** *see* C CLEF

**ten·pen·ny** (ten′pen′ē, -pə nē) *adj.* **1.** worth ten (esp. Brit.) pennies **2.** designating a size of nails, three inches long

**ten·pins** (-pinz′) *n.pl.* **1.** [*with sing. v.*] the game of bowling in which ten pins are used **2.** the pins

**tense**[1] (tens) *adj.* **tens′er, tens′est** [< L. pp. of *tendere*, to stretch] **1.** stretched tight; strained; taut **2.** feeling, showing, or causing mental strain; anxious —*vt., vi.* **tensed, tens′ing** to make or become tense —**tense′ly** *adv.* —**tense′ness** *n.*

**tense**[2] (tens) *n.* [< OFr. < L. *tempus*, time] any form or set of forms of a verb that show the time of the action or condition

**ten·sile** (ten′s'l) *adj.* **1.** of or under tension **2.** capable of being stretched: also **ten′si·ble** (-sə b'l) —**ten·sil′i·ty** (-sil′ə tē) *n.*

**ten·sion** (ten′shən) *n.* **1.** a tensing or being tensed **2.** mental or nervous strain; tense feeling **3.** a state of strained relations **4.** a device to regulate tautness of thread, etc. **5.** *same as* VOLTAGE **6.** *a)* stress on a material by forces tending to cause extension *b)* a force exerting such stress —*vt.* to subject to tension —**ten′sion·al** *adj.*

**ten·sor** (ten′sər, -sôr) *n.* [ModL. < L. pp. of *tendere*, to stretch] any muscle that stretches a body part

**tent** (tent) *n.* [< OFr. < L. pp. of *tendere*, to stretch] **1.** a portable shelter consisting of canvas, skins, etc. stretched over poles and attached to stakes **2.** anything like a tent; specif., *short for* OXYGEN TENT —*adj.* of or like a tent —*vi.* to live in a tent —*vt.* **1.** to lodge in tents **2.** to cover as with a tent

**ten·ta·cle** (ten′tə k'l) *n.* [ModL. *tentaculum* < L. *tentare*, to touch] **1.** any of various slender, flexible growths at or near the head or mouth, as of some invertebrates, used for grasping, feeling, moving, etc. **2.** *Bot.* any of the sensitive hairs on the leaves of insect-eating plants —**ten·tac′u·lar** (-tak′yə lər) *adj.*

**ten·ta·tive** (ten′tə tiv) *adj.* [LL. *tentativus* < pp. of L. *tentare*, to try] made or done as a test or for the time being; not definite or final —**ten′ta·tive·ly** *adv.* —**ten′ta·tive·ness** *n.*

**tent caterpillar** any of the caterpillars that live in colonies in large, tentlike webs spun among the tree branches that they defoliate

**ten·ter** (ten′tər) *n.* [see TENT] a frame to stretch cloth on for even drying —*vt.* to stretch on a tenter

**ten·ter·hook** (-hook′) *n.* any of the hooked nails that hold cloth stretched on a tenter —**on tenterhooks** in suspense

**tenth** (tenth) *adj.* [OE. *teogotha*] **1.** preceded by nine others in a series; 10th **2.** designating any of the ten equal parts of something —*n.* **1.** the one following the ninth **2.** any of the ten equal parts of something; 1/10 —**tenth′ly** *adv.*

**tent stitch** [< ? TENT] an embroidery stitch forming a series of parallel slanting lines

**ten·u·ous** (ten′yoo wəs) *adj.* [< L. *tenuis*, thin + -OUS] **1.** slender or fine, as a fiber **2.** not dense; rare, as air high up **3.** not substantial; slight; flimsy *[tenuous evidence]* —**te·nu·i·ty** (tə nōō′ə tē, -nyōō′-), **ten′u·ous·ness** *n.* —**ten′u·ous·ly** *adv.*

**ten·ure** (ten′yər, -yoor) *n.* [< MFr. < *tenir:* see TENANT] **1.** the act or right of holding property, an office, etc. **2.** the period or conditions of this **3.** the holding of a position in teaching, etc. on a permanent basis after meeting specified requirements

**te·nu·to** (tə nōōt′ō) *adj.* [It., pp. of *tenere*, to hold] *Music* held for the full value, as a note

**te·pee** (tē′pē) *n.* [< Siouan < *ti*, to dwell + *pi*, used for] a cone-shaped tent of animal skins, used by the Indians of the Great Plains

**tep·id** (tep′id) *adj.* [< L. < *tepere*, to be slightly warm] slightly warm; lukewarm —**te·pid·i·ty** (tə pid′ə tē), **tep′id·ness** *n.* —**tep′id·ly** *adv.*

**te·qui·la** (tə kē′lə) *n.* [AmSp. < Nahuatl *Tequila*, a Mexican district] **1.** a strong alcoholic liquor of Mexico, distilled from pulque or mescal **2.** a Mexican agave that is a source of tequila and mescal

TEPEE

**ter. 1.** terrace **2.** territory

**ter·a-** (ter′ə) [< Gr. *teras*, monster] *a combining form meaning* one trillion *[terahertz]*

**ter·a·tism** (ter′ə tiz'm) *n.* [< Gr. *teras* (gen. *teratos*), a monster] an abnormally formed fetus; monstrosity

**ter·bi·um** (tur′bē əm) *n.* [ModL. < *Ytterby*, town in Sweden] a metallic chemical element of the rare-earth group: symbol, Tb; at. wt., 158.924; at. no., 65

**terce** (turs) *n.* [< OFr. < L. *tertia*, fem. of *tertius*, third] [*often* T-] *Eccles.* the third of the seven canonical hours

**ter·cen·te·nar·y** (tər′sen ten′ər ē, tər sen′tə ner′ē) *adj., n., pl.* **-nar·ies** [L. *ter*, three times + CENTENARY] *same as* TRICENTENNIAL: also **ter′cen·ten′ni·al** (-ten′ē əl)

**ter·cet** (tur′sit, tər set′) *n.* [Fr. < It. dim. of *terzo*, a third < L. *tertius*] a group of three lines that rhyme or are connected by rhyme with an adjacent triplet

**ter·e·binth** (ter′ə binth′) *n.* [< MFr., ult. < Gr. *terebinthos*] a small European tree whose cut bark yields a turpentine

**Ter·ence** (ter′əns) [L. *Terentius*, name of a Roman gens] **1.** a masculine name: dim. *Terry* **2.** (L. name *Publius Terentius Afer*) 190?–159? B.C.; Rom. writer of comedies

**Te·re·sa** (tə rē′sə; *Sp.* te re′sä) **1.** [var. of THERESA] a feminine name **2.** Saint, 1515–82; Sp. Carmelite nun: called **Teresa of A·vi·la** (ä′vē lä′)

**ter·gi·ver·sate** (tur′ji vər sāt′) *vi.* **-sat′ed, -sat′ing** [< L. pp. of *tergiversari* < *tergum*, the back + *versari*, to turn] **1.** to desert a cause, party, etc. **2.** to use evasions or subterfuge —**ter′gi·ver·sa′tion** *n.* —**ter′gi·ver·sa′tor** *n.*

**ter·i·ya·ki** (ter′ē yä′kē) *n.* [Jap.] meat or fish marinated or dipped in soy sauce and broiled, grilled, or barbecued: a Japanese dish

**term** (turm) *n.* [< OFr. < L. *terminus*, a limit] **1.** a set date, as for payment, termination of tenancy, etc. **2.** a set period of time; specif., *a)* a division of a school year, as a semester *b)* the period set for holding an office *c)* the normal period between conception and birth; also, the end of this period; childbirth **3.** [*pl.*] conditions of a contract, sale, etc. that limit or define it **4.** [*pl.*] personal relations *[on speaking terms]* **5.** a word or phrase having definite meaning in some science, art, etc. **6.** a word or phrase of a specified kind *[a derogatory term]* **7.** *Law a)* the time a court is in session *b)* the length of time for which an estate is granted *c*) the estate itself *d*) time allowed a debtor to pay **8.** *Logic a*) either of two concepts with a stated relation, as the subject and predicate of a proposition *b*) any one of the three parts of a syllogism **9.** *Math. a*) either of the two quantities of a fraction or ratio *b*) each quantity in a series or in an algebraic expression —*vt.* to call by a term; name —**bring to terms** to force to agree —**come to terms** to arrive at an agreement —**in terms of** regarding; concerning —**term'less** *adj.*

**ter·ma·gant** (tur'mə gənt) *n.* [< OFr. *Tervagant,* alleged Moslem deity] a quarrelsome, scolding woman; shrew

**term·er** (tur'mər) *n.* a person serving a specified term, esp. in prison *[a third-termer]*

**ter·mi·na·ble** (tur'mi nə b'l) *adj.* **1.** that can be terminated **2.** that terminates after a specified time, as a contract —**ter'mi·na·bil'i·ty, ter'mi·na·ble·ness** *n.*

**ter·mi·nal** (tur'mə n'l) *adj.* [L. *terminalis*] **1.** of, at, or forming the end or extremity of something **2.** occurring at the end of a series; concluding; final **3.** of or in the final stages of a fatal disease *[terminal* cancer] **4.** in or of a term or set period of time **5.** of, at, or forming the end of a transportation line —*n.* **1.** a terminating part; end; extremity **2.** a connective device or point on an electric circuit or conductor **3.** *a*) either end of a transportation line *b*) a station or city there or at any important point of the line **4.** a device, often with a keyboard and a cathode-ray screen, for feeding information into, or receiving information from, a computer —**ter'mi·nal·ly** *adv.*

**ter·mi·nate** (-nāt') *vt.* **-nat'ed, -nat'ing** [< L. pp. of *terminare,* to end < *terminus,* a limit] **1.** to form the end or limit of; finish or bound **2.** to put an end to; stop —*vi.* to come to an end —**ter'mi·na'tive** *adj.* —**ter'mi·na'tor** *n.*

**ter·mi·na·tion** (tur'mə nā'shən) *n.* **1.** a terminating or being terminated **2.** the end or limit **3.** *Linguis.* the end of a word; specif., an inflectional ending

**ter·mi·nol·o·gy** (tur'mə näl'ə jē) *n., pl.* **-gies** the terms or special words used in some science, art, work, etc. —**ter'·mi·no·log'i·cal** (-nə läj'i k'l) *adj.* —**ter'mi·no·log'i·cal·ly** *adv.* —**ter'mi·nol'o·gist** *n.*

**ter·mi·nus** (tur'mə nəs) *n., pl.* **-ni'** (-nī'), **-nus·es** [L., a limit] **1.** a boundary or limit **2.** a boundary stone or marker **3.** an end; final point or goal **4.** either end of a transportation line

**ter·mite** (tur'mīt) *n.* [L. *termes* (gen. *termitis*), wood-boring worm] a pale-colored, soft-bodied, antlike insect that lives in colonies and is very destructive to wooden structures

**tern** (turn) *n.* [< ON. *therna*] any of several sea birds related to the gulls, but smaller, with a more slender body and beak and a deeply forked tail

**ter·na·ry** (tur'nər ē) *adj.* [< L. < *terni,* three each] **1.** threefold; triple **2.** third in rank, etc.

**ter·nate** (tur'nāt) *adj.* [ModL., ult. < L. *terni,* three each] **1.** consisting of three **2.** arranged in threes, as some leaves —**ter'nate·ly** *adv.*

**ter·pene** (tur'pēn) *n.* [G. *terpen*] any of a series of isomeric hydrocarbons of the general formula $C_{10}H_{16}$, found in resins, etc.

**Terp·sich·o·re** (tərp sik'ə rē') *Gr. Myth.* the Muse of dancing

**terp·si·cho·re·an** (tурp'si kə rē'ən) *adj.* **1.** [T-] of Terpsichore **2.** having to do with dancing —*n.* a dancer: now only in humorous use

**ter·race** (ter'əs) *n.* [OFr., walled platform < It. *terrazzo* < L. *terra,* earth] **1.** *a*) a raised, flat mound of earth with sloping sides *b*) any of a series of flat platforms of earth with sloping sides, rising one above another, as on a hillside *c*) a geological formation of this nature **2.** an unroofed, paved area adjoining a house and overlooking a lawn or garden **3.** a gallery, portico, etc. **4.** a balcony or deck outside an apartment **5.** a flat roof, esp. of a house of Spanish architecture **6.** *a*) a row of houses on ground raised from the street *b*) a street in front of such houses —*vt.* **-raced, -rac·ing** to form into or surround with a terrace

**ter·ra cot·ta** (ter'ə kät'ə) [It., lit., baked earth < L.] **1.** a hard, brown-red, usually unglazed earthenware used for pottery, sculpture, etc. **2.** its brown-red color —**ter'ra·cot'ta** *adj.*

**terra fir·ma** (fur'mə) [L.] firm earth; solid ground

**ter·rain** (tə rān', ter'ān) *n.* [Fr. < L. < *terra,* earth] ground or a tract of ground, esp. with regard to its features or fitness for some use

**Ter·ra·my·cin** (ter'ə mī's'n) [< L. *terra,* earth + MYC(O)- + -IN[1] *a trademark for* an antibiotic derived from cultures of a soil fungus

**ter·ra·pin** (ter'ə pin) *n.* [< Algonquian] **1.** any of several American freshwater or tidewater turtles; specif., *same as* DIAMONDBACK **2.** its edible flesh

**ter·rar·i·um** (tə rer'ē əm) *n., pl.* **-i·ums, -i·a** (-ə) [ModL. < L. *terra,* earth + -*arium* as in *aquarium*] **1.** an enclosure for keeping small land animals **2.** a glass container for a garden of small plants

**ter·raz·zo** (tə raz'ō, tə rät'sō) *n.* [It., lit., TERRACE] flooring of small chips of marble set in cement and polished

**Ter·re Haute** (ter'ə hōt', hut') [Fr., lit., high land] city in W Ind., on the Wabash: pop. 61,000

**ter·res·tri·al** (tə res'trē əl) *adj.* [< L. *terrestris* < *terra,* earth] **1.** of this world; worldly; mundane **2.** of or constituting the earth **3.** consisting of land as distinguished from water **4.** living on land rather than in water, in the air, in trees, etc. **5.** growing in the ground —*n.* an inhabitant of the earth —**ter·res'tri·al·ly** *adv.*

**ter·ret** (ter'it) *n.* [< OFr. *toret,* dim. of *tour,* a turn] **1.** a ring for attaching a leash, as on a dog collar **2.** any of the rings on a harness, through which the reins pass

**ter·ri·ble** (ter'ə b'l) *adj.* [OFr. < L. *terribilis* < *terrere,* to frighten] **1.** causing terror; fearful; dreadful **2.** extreme; intense; severe **3.** [Colloq.] very bad, unpleasant, disagreeable, etc. —**ter'ri·ble·ness** *n.* —**ter'ri·bly** *adv.*

**ter·ri·er** (ter'ē ər) *n.* [MFr. *(chien) terrier,* hunting (dog) < *terrier,* hillock, ult. < L. *terra,* earth] any of various breeds of active, typically small dog, orig. bred to burrow after small game

**ter·rif·ic** (tə rif'ik) *adj.* [< L. < base of *terrere,* to frighten + -FIC] **1.** causing great fear; terrifying; dreadful **2.** [Colloq.] *a*) unusually great, intense, etc. *b*) unusually fine, enjoyable, etc. —**ter·rif'i·cal·ly** *adv.*

**ter·ri·fy** (ter'ə fī') *vi.* **-fied', -fy'ing** [L. *terrificare* < *terrificus,* TERRIFIC] to fill with terror; frighten greatly; alarm —**ter'ri·fy'ing·ly** *adv.*

**ter·ri·to·ri·al** (ter'ə tôr'ē əl) *adj.* **1.** of territory or land **2.** of or limited to a specific territory or district **3.** [T-] of a Territory or Territories **4.** *[often* T-] organized regionally for home defense —*n.* [T-] [Chiefly Brit.] a member of a Territorial force —**ter'ri·to'ri·al'i·ty** (-al'ə tē) *n.* —**ter'ri·to'ri·al·ly** *adv.*

**ter·ri·to·ry** (ter'ə tôr'ē) *n., pl.* **-ries** [L. *territorium* < *terra,* earth] **1.** the land and waters under the jurisdiction of a nation, state, ruler, etc. **2.** a part of a country or empire without the full status of a principal division; specif., *a*) [T-] formerly, a part of the U.S. without the status of a State and having an appointed governor *b*) [T-] a similar region in Canada or Australia **3.** any large tract of land; region **4.** an assigned area, as of a traveling salesman **5.** a sphere of action, existence, etc. **6.** the area occupied by an animal or pair of animals as for breeding, foraging, etc.

**ter·ror** (ter'ər) *n.* [< MFr. < L. < *terrere,* to frighten] **1.** intense fear **2.** *a*) a person or thing causing intense fear *b*) the quality of causing dread; terribleness **3.** a program of terrorism **4.** [Colloq.] a very annoying or unmanageable person, esp. a child

**ter·ror·ism** (-iz'm) *n.* **1.** the use of force and violence to intimidate, subjugate, etc., esp. as a political policy **2.** the intimidation produced in this way —**ter'ror·ist** *n., adj.* —**ter'ror·is'tic** *adj.*

**ter·ror·ize** (-īz') *vt.* **-ized', -iz'ing 1.** to fill with terror **2.** to coerce, make submit, etc. by filling with terror —**ter'·ror·i·za'tion** *n.* —**ter'ror·iz'er** *n.*

**ter·ry** (ter'ē) *n., pl.* **-ries** [prob. < Fr. pp. of *tirer,* to draw] cloth having a pile in which the loops are left uncut: also **terry cloth**

**terse** (turs) *adj.* **ters'er, ters'est** [< L. pp. of *tergere,* to wipe] free of superfluous words; concise; succinct —**terse'ly** *adv.* —**terse'ness** *n.*

**ter·tial** (tur'shəl) *adj.* [< L. < *tertius,* third] designating or of the third row of flight feathers on a bird's wing —*n.* a tertial feather

**ter·tian** (tur'shən) *adj.* [< L. < *tertius,* third] occurring every other day —*n.* a tertian fever or disease

**ter·ti·ar·y** (tur'shē er'ē, -shə rē) *adj.* [< L. < *tertius,* third] **1.** of the third rank, order, formation, etc.; third **2.** [T-] *Geol.* designating or of the first period in the Cenozoic Era **3.** *Zool. same as* TERTIAL —*n., pl.* **-ar'ies** *Zool. same as* TERTIAL —**the Tertiary** the Tertiary Period or its rocks: see GEOLOGY, chart

**tes·sel·late** (tes'ə lāt'; *for adj.* -lit) *vt.* **-lat'ed, -lat'ing** [< L. < *tessella,* little square stone] to lay out or pave in a mosaic pattern of small, square blocks —*adj.* tessellated

**test**[1] (test) *n.* [OFr., cup used in assaying < L. *testum,* earthen vessel < *testa,* shell] **1.** *a*) an examination or trial, as to prove the value or find out the nature of something *b*) a method or process, or a standard or criterion, used in this **2.** an event, situation, etc. that tries a person's qualities **3.** a set of questions, problems, etc. for determining a person's knowledge, abilities, etc.; examination **4.** *Chem. a*) a trial or reaction for identifying a substance *b*) the reagent used in the procedure *c*) a positive indication obtained by it —*vt.* to subject to a test; try —*vi.* **1.** to give or take a test for diagnosis, function, etc. *[to test* for blood sugar] **2.** to be rated as the result of a test *[to test* high] —**test'a·ble** *adj.*

**test**[2] (test) *n.* [L. *testa:* see prec.] the hard outer covering of certain invertebrate animals, as the shell of clams

**Test.** Testament

**tes·ta** (tes'tə) *n., pl.* **-tae** (-tē) [ModL. < L., a shell] *Bot.* the hard outer covering of a seed

**tes·ta·ment** (tes'tə mənt) *n.* [< OFr. < LL. < L., ult. < *testis*, a witness] **1.** orig., a covenant, esp. one between God and man **2.** [T-] *a)* either of the two parts of the Christian Bible, the *Old Testament* and the *New Testament* *b)* [Colloq.] a copy of the New Testament **3.** *a)* a testimonial *b)* an affirmation of beliefs, etc. **4.** *Law* a will: now rare except in **last will and testament** —**tes'ta·men'- ta·ry** (-men'tə rē), **tes'ta·men'tal** *adj.*

**tes·tate** (tes'tāt) *adj.* [< L. pp. of *testari*, to testify, make a will] having made and left a legally valid will —*n.* a person who has died testate

**tes·ta·tor** (tes'tāt ər, tes tāt'-) *n.* a person who has made a will, esp. one who has died leaving a valid will —**tes·ta'trix** (-tā'triks) *n.fem., pl.* **-tri·ces'** (-tri sēz')

**test ban** an agreement between or among nuclear powers to forgo tests of nuclear weapons, esp. in the atmosphere

**test case** *Law* **1.** a case that is likely to be used as a precedent **2.** a case entered into with the intention of testing the constitutionality of a particular law

**test·er**[1] (tes'tər) *n.* a person or thing that tests

**tes·ter**[2] (tes'tər) *n.* [< OFr. *testiere*, headpiece < L. *testa:* see TEST[1]] a canopy, as over a bed

**tes·ti·cle** (tes'ti k'l) *n.* [< L. dim. of *testis*, testicle] either of two oval sex glands in the male that are suspended in the scrotum and secrete spermatozoa —**tes·tic'u·lar** (-tik'yoo lər) *adj.*

**tes·ti·fy** (tes'tə fī') *vi.* **-fied'**, **-fy'ing** [< L. *testificari* < *testis*, a witness + *facere*, to make] **1.** to bear witness or give evidence, esp. under oath in court **2.** to be evidence or an indication *(his look testifies to his rage)* —*vt.* **1.** to bear witness to; affirm; give as evidence, esp. under oath in court **2.** to be evidence of; indicate —**tes'ti·fi·ca'tion** *n.* —**tes'ti·fi'er** *n.*

**tes·ti·mo·ni·al** (tes'tə mō'nē əl) *n.* **1.** a statement testifying to a person's qualifications, character, etc. or to the merits of some product, etc. **2.** something given or done as an expression of gratitude or appreciation

**tes·ti·mo·ny** (tes'tə mō'nē) *n., pl.* **-nies** [< L. < *testis*, a witness] **1.** a statement made under oath in court to establish a fact **2.** any affirmation or declaration **3.** any form of evidence; indication *(his smile was testimony of his joy)* **4.** public avowal, as of faith

**tes·tis** (tes'tis) *n., pl.* **-tes** (-tēz) [L.] *same as* TESTICLE

**tes·tos·ter·one** (tes tăs'tə rōn') *n.* [TEST(IS) + -*o*- + STER(OL) + -ONE] a male sex hormone, $C_{19}H_{28}O_2$, a crystalline steroid obtained from animal testes or synthesized: used in medicine

**test pilot** a pilot who tests new or newly designed airplanes in flight, to determine their fitness for use

**test-tube** (tes'tōōb', -tyōōb') *adj.* **1.** made in or as in a test tube; experimental **2.** produced by artificial insemination *(a test-tube baby)*

**test tube** a tube of thin, clear glass closed at one end, used in chemical experiments, etc.

**tes·tu·do** (tes tōō'dō, -tyōō'-) *n., pl.* **-di·nes'** (-də nēz') [L., tortoise (shell)] in ancient Rome, **1.** a movable, roofed shelter used by soldiers **2.** a protection formed by a group of soldiers by overlapping shields above their heads

**tes·ty** (tes'tē) *adj.* **-ti·er**, **-ti·est** [< Anglo-Fr. < OFr. *teste*, the head < L. *testa:* see TEST[1]] irritable; touchy; peevish —**tes'ti·ly** *adv.* —**tes'ti·ness** *n.*

**Tet** (tet) *n.* [Vietnamese] a three-day Asian festival in winter, celebrating the arrival of the new year

**tet·a·nus** (tet''n əs) *n.* [L. < Gr. *tetanos*, spasm, lit., stretched] an acute infectious disease, often fatal, caused by the toxin of a bacillus which usually enters the body through wounds: characterized by spasmodic contractions and rigidity of muscles; lockjaw —**te·tan·ic** (ti tan'ik) *adj.*

**tetched** (techt) *adj.* [Dial. or Humorous] touched; slightly demented

**tetch·y** (tech'ē) *adj.* **tetch'i·er**, **tetch'i·est** [prob. < OFr. *teche*, a spot + -Y[2]] touchy; irritable; peevish —**tetch'i·ly** *adv.* —**tetch'i·ness** *n.*

**tête-à-tête** (tāt'ə tāt') *n.* [Fr., lit., head-to-head] **1.** a private conversation between two people **2.** an S-shaped seat on which two people can sit facing each other —*adj.* for or of two people in private —*adv.* together privately *(to speak tête-à-tête)*

**teth·er** (teth'ər) *n.* [prob. < ON. *tjothr*] **1.** a rope or chain fastened to an animal so as to keep it within certain bounds **2.** the limit of one's abilities, resources, etc. —*vt.* to fasten with a tether —**at the end of one's tether** at the end of one's endurance, resources, etc.

**teth·er·ball** (-bôl') *n.* **1.** a game for two who hit at a ball hanging by a cord from a pole in an attempt to make the cord coil around the pole **2.** the ball used

**tet·ra** (tet'rə) *n.* [< ModL. < old genus name] a colorful tropical American fish, often kept in aquariums

**tet·ra-** [Gr. < base of *tettares*, four] *a combining form meaning* four: also, before a vowel, **tetr-**

**tet·ra·chord** (tet'rə kôrd') *n.* [< Gr.: see TETRA- & CHORD[2]] *Music* a series of four tones within the interval of a fourth —**tet'ra·chor'dal** *adj.*

**tet·ra·cy·cline** (tet'rə sī'klin, -klīn) *n.* [< TETRA- + CYCL(IC) + -INE[4]] a yellow, crystalline powder, prepared synthetically or obtained from certain microorganisms: used as an antibiotic

**tet·rad** (tet'rad) *n.* [< Gr. *tetras*, four] a group or set of four

**tet·ra·eth·yl lead** (tet'rə eth''l) a heavy, colorless, poisonous compound of lead, added to gasoline to increase power and prevent engine knock

**tet·ra·he·dron** (tet'rə hē'drən) *n., pl.* **-drons**, **-dra** (-drə) [ModL. < LGr.: see TETRA- & -HEDRON] a solid figure with four triangular faces —**tet'ra·he'dral** *adj.*

**te·tral·o·gy** (te tral'ə jē) *n., pl.* **-gies** [< Gr.: see TETRA- & -LOGY] any series of four related plays, operas, novels, etc.

**te·tram·e·ter** (te tram'ə tər) *n.* [< LL. < Gr.: see TETRA- & -METER] **1.** a line of verse containing four metrical feet **2.** verse consisting of tetrameters —*adj.* having four metrical feet

TETRAHEDRON

**te·trarch** (tē'trärk, tē'-) *n.* [< LL. < L. < Gr.: see TETRA- & -ARCH] **1.** in the ancient Roman Empire, the ruler of part (orig. a fourth part) of a province **2.** a subordinate prince, governor, etc. —**te·trarch'ic** *adj.*

**te·trarch·y** (-trär kē) *n., pl.* **-trarch·ies** **1.** the rule or territory of a tetrarch **2.** government by four persons

**tet·ra·va·lent** (tet'rə vā'lənt) *adj.* **1.** having a valence of four **2.** *same as* QUADRIVALENT (sense 1)

**te·trox·ide** (te träk'sīd) *n.* any oxide with four atoms of oxygen in each molecule

**tet·ter** (tet'ər) *n.* [OE. *teter*] any of various skin diseases, as eczema, characterized by itching

**Teut.** **1.** Teuton **2.** Teutonic

**Teu·ton** (tōōt''n, tyōōt'-) *n.* **1.** a member of the Teutones **2.** a member of any Teutonic people; esp., a German

**Teu·to·nes** (-ēz') *n.pl.* [L.] an ancient tribe, either Teutonic or Celtic, that lived in Jutland

**Teu·ton·ic** (tōō tän'ik, tyōō-) *adj.* **1.** of the ancient Teutons **2.** German **3.** designating or of a group of north European peoples including the German, Scandinavian, Dutch, English, etc. **4.** *Linguis.* earlier var. of GERMANIC —**Teu·ton'i·cal·ly** *adv.*

**Tex·as** (tek'səs) [Sp. < AmInd. *techas*, allies (against the Apaches)] SW State of the U.S., on the Gulf of Mexico & the Mexican border: 267,339 sq. mi.; pop. 14,228,000; cap. Austin: abbrev. **Tex.**, **TX** —**Tex'an** *adj., n.*

**Texas fever** an infectious disease of cattle

**Texas leaguer** *Baseball* a safely hit fly ball that falls between the infield and outfield

**Texas tower** [from its resemblance to oil rigs off the *Texas* coast] an offshore platform on foundations planted in the sea bottom, for beacons, radar installations, etc.

**text** (tekst) *n.* [< OFr. < L. *textus*, fabric < pp. of *texere*, to weave] **1.** the exact or original words of an author or speaker, as distinguished from notes, paraphrase, etc. **2.** any of the forms, versions, or editions in which a written work exists **3.** the principal matter on a printed page, as distinguished from notes, pictures, etc. **4.** the words of a song, etc. **5.** *a)* a Biblical passage used as the topic of a sermon *b)* any topic or subject dealt with **6.** *shortened form of* TEXTBOOK

**text·book** (-book') *n.* a book giving instructions in the principles of a subject of study

**tex·tile** (teks'til, -t'l, -til) *adj.* [< L. *textilis* < *textus:* see TEXT] **1.** having to do with weaving or woven fabrics **2.** that has been or can be woven —*n.* **1.** a fabric made by weaving, knitting, etc.; cloth **2.** raw material suitable for this, as cotton, wool, nylon, etc.

**tex·tu·al** (teks'choo wəl) *adj.* of, contained in, or based on a text —**tex'tu·al·ly** *adv.*

**tex·ture** (teks'chər) *n.* [< L. < *texere:* see TEXT] **1.** the character of a fabric as determined by the arrangement, size, etc. of its threads **2.** the structure or composition of anything, esp. in the way it looks or feels on the surface —*vt.* **-tured**, **-tur·ing** to cause to have a particular texture —**tex'tur·al** *adj.* —**tex'tur·al·ly** *adv.*

**-th**[1] [< OE.] *a suffix meaning:* **1.** the act of *(stealth)* **2.** the state or quality of being or having *(wealth)*

**-th**[2] [< OE.] a suffix used in forming ordinal numerals *(fourth)*: also, after a vowel, **-eth**

fat, āpe, cär, ten, ēven, is, bīte; gō, hôrn, tōōl, look; oil, out; up, fur; get; joy; yet; chin; she; thin, then; zh, leisure; ŋ, ring; ə for *a* in *ago, e* in *agent, i* in *sanity, o* in *comply, u* in *focus;* ' as in *able* (ā'b'l); Fr. bàl; ë, Fr. coeur; ö, Fr. feu; Fr. mon; ö, Fr. coq; ü, Fr. duc; r, Fr. cri; H, G. ich; kh, G. doch; ‡foreign; *hypothetical; < derived from. See inside front cover.

**-th³** [< OE.: see -ETH²] *contracted form of* -ETH² [*hath, doth*]

**Th** *Chem.* thorium

**Th.** Thursday

**Thack·er·ay** (thak′ər ē), **William Make·peace** (māk′pēs′) 1811–63; Eng. novelist

**Thai** (tī) *n.* **1.** a group of Asian languages considered to belong to the Sino-Tibetan language family **2.** the official language of Thailand **3.** *pl.* **Thais, Thai** *a*) a member of a group of Thai-speaking peoples of SE Asia *b*) a native or inhabitant of Thailand —*adj.* of Thailand, its people, etc.

**Thai·land** (tī′land, -lənd) **1.** country in SE Asia, on the Indochinese & Malay peninsulas: 198,456 sq. mi.; pop. 35,814,000; cap. Bangkok **2. Gulf of,** arm of the South China Sea between the Malay & Indochinese peninsulas

**thal·a·mus** (thal′ə məs) *n., pl.* **-mi′** (-mī′) [ModL. < L. < Gr. *thalamos*, inner room] **1.** *Anat.* a mass of gray matter at the base of the brain, involved in the transmission of certain sensations **2.** *Bot.* the receptacle of a flower —**tha·lam·ic** (thə lam′ik) *adj.*

**Tha·li·a** (thə lī′ə, thāl′yə) *Gr. Myth.* **1.** the Muse of comedy and pastoral poetry **2.** one of the three Graces

**thal·li·um** (thal′ē əm) *n.* [ModL. < Gr. *thallos*, green shoot: from its green spectrum line] a rare, bluish-white, soft, metallic chemical element: symbol, Tl; at. wt., 204.37; at. no., 81

**thal·lo·phyte** (-ə fīt′) *n.* [see ff. & -PHYTE] any of a primary division of plants including the bacteria, algae, fungi, and lichens —**thal′lo·phyt′ic** (-fit′ik) *adj.*

**thal·lus** (-əs) *n., pl.* **-li** (-ī), **-lus·es** [ModL. < Gr. *thallos*, young shoot] the plant body of a thallophyte, showing no distinction of roots, stem, or leaves —**thal′loid** (-oid) *adj.*

**Thames** (temz) river in S England, flowing east through London into the North Sea

**than** (*than, then; unstressed thən, th'n*) *conj.* [< OE. *thenne*, orig., then] a particle used: *a*) to introduce the second element in a comparison [A is taller *than* B] *b*) to express exception [none other *than* Sam] —*prep.* compared to: in *than* whom, than which [a writer *than* whom there is none finer]

**than·a·tol·o·gy** (than′ə täl′ə jē) *n.* [< Gr. *thanatos*, death + -LOGY] the study of death, esp. of the medical, psychological, and social problems associated with dying —**than′a·tol′o·gist** *n.*

**thane** (thān) *n.* [OE. *thegen*] **1.** in early England, one of a class of freemen who held land of the king or a lord in return for military services **2.** in early Scotland, a person of rank who held land of the king

**thank** (thaŋk) *vt.* [OE. *thancian*] **1.** to express appreciation to, as by saying "thank you" **2.** to hold responsible; blame: an ironic use [he can be *thanked* for our failure] —**thank you** *shortened form of* I thank you

**thank·ful** (-fəl) *adj.* feeling or expressing thanks —**thank′ful·ly** *adv.* —**thank′ful·ness** *n.*

**thank·less** (-lis) *adj.* **1.** not feeling or expressing thanks; ungrateful **2.** unappreciated [a *thankless* task] —**thank′less·ly** *adv.* —**thank′less·ness** *n.*

**thanks** (thaŋks) *n.pl.* an expression of gratitude —*interj.* I thank you —**thanks to 1.** thanks be given to **2.** on account of

**thanks·giv·ing** (thaŋks′giv′iŋ) *n.* **1.** *a*) a giving of thanks *b*) an expression of this; esp., a formal, public expression of thanks to God **2.** [T-] *a*) a U.S. holiday on the fourth Thursday of November: it commemorates the Pilgrims' celebration of the good harvest of 1621 *b*) a similar Canadian holiday on the second Monday of October In full, **Thanksgiving Day**

**Thant** (thänt, thônt), U (o͞o) 1909–74; Burmese diplomat; secretary-general of the United Nations (1962–71)

**that** (*that; unstressed thət*) *pron., pl.* **those** [OE. *thæt*] as a *demonstrative pronoun:* **1.** the person or thing mentioned or understood [*that* is John] **2.** the thing farther away [this is larger than *that* over there] **3.** something being contrasted [this possibility is more likely than *that*] **4.** [*pl.*] certain people [*those* who know] *as a relative pronoun:* **1.** who, whom, or which: generally in restrictive clauses [the road (*that*) we took] **2.** where; at which [the place *that* I saw him] **3.** when; in which [the year *that* he died] —*adj., pl.* **those 1.** designating the one mentioned or understood [*that* man is John] **2.** designating the thing farther away [*this* house is larger than *that* one] **3.** designating something being contrasted [*this* possibility is more likely than *that* one] **4.** designating a person or thing not described but well known [*that* certain feeling] —*conj.* used: **1.** to introduce a noun clause [he's gone is obvious] **2.** to introduce an adverbial clause expressing purpose [they died *that* we might live] **3.** to introduce an adverbial clause expressing result [he ran so fast that I lost him] **4.** to introduce an adverbial clause expressing cause [I'm sorry *that* I won] **5.** to introduce an incomplete sentence expressing surprise, desire, etc. [oh, *that* he were here!] —*adv.*

**1.** to that extent; so [I can't see *that* far] : also used colloquially before an adjective modified by a clause showing result [I'm *that* tired I could drop] **2.** [Colloq.] very; so very [I don't like movies *that* much] —**all that** [Colloq.] **1.** so very [he isn't *all that* rich] **2.** everything of the same sort [sex and *all that*] —**at that** [Colloq.] **1.** at that point: also **with that 2.** all things considered; even so —**that is 1.** to be specific **2.** in other words —**that's that!** that is settled!

**thatch** (thach) *n.* [OE. *thæc*] **1.** a roof or roofing of straw, rushes, palm leaves, etc. *b*) material for such a roof: also **thatch′ing 2.** any of various palms whose leaves are used for thatch: also **thatch palm 3.** a matted layer of leaves, etc. between growing vegetation and the soil **4.** the hair growing on the head —*vt.* [OE. *theccan*] to cover with or as with thatch —**thatch′y** *adj.* **thatch′i·er, thatch′i·est**

**thau·ma·tur·gy** (thô′mə tur′jē) *n.* [< Gr. < *thauma*, a wonder + *ergon*, work] the supposed working of miracles; magic —**thau′ma·tur′gic, thau′ma·tur′gi·cal** *adj.*

**thaw** (thô) *vi.* [OE. *thawian*] **1.** *a*) to melt: said of ice, snow, etc. *b*) to pass to an unfrozen state: said of frozen foods **2.** to rise in temperature above freezing, so that snow, etc. melts: with *it:* said of weather conditions [it *thawed* today] **3.** *a*) to get rid of the chill, stiffness, etc. resulting from extreme cold (often with *out*) *b*) to lose coldness or reserve of manner —*vt.* to cause to thaw —*n.* **1.** a thawing **2.** a spell of weather warm enough to allow thawing **3.** a becoming less reserved

**Th.B.** [L. *Theologiae Baccalaureus*] Bachelor of Theology

**Th.D.** [L. *Theologiae Doctor*] Doctor of Theology

**the** (*thə; before vowels* thi, thē) *adj., definite article* [OE. *se, the*] **1.** *the* (as opposed to *a, an*) refers to a particular person or thing, as *a*) that (one) being spoken of [the story ended] *b*) that (one) which is present, close, etc. [the day is hot] *c*) that (one) designated, as by a title [the Ohio (River)] *d*) that (one) considered outstanding, etc. [that's *the* hotel in town] : usually italicized in print *e*) that (one) belonging to a person previously mentioned [take me by *the* hand] *f*) that (one) considered as a unit of purchase, etc. [ten cents *the* dozen] *g*) one specified period of time [*the* fifties] *h*) [Colloq.] that (one) in a specified relationship to one [*the* wife] **2.** *the* is used to refer to that one of a number of persons or things which is identified by a modifier, as by an attributive adjective, a relative clause, a prepositional phrase, etc. **3.** *the* is used to refer to a person or thing considered generically, as *a*) one taken as the representative of the entire genus or type [the cow is a domestic animal] *b*) an adjective used as a noun [the good, the true] —*adv.* **1.** that much; to that extent [the better to see you with] **2.** by how much . . . by that much; to what extent . . . to that extent: used in a correlative construction expressing comparison [the sooner, the better]

**the·a·ter, the·a·tre** (thē′ə tər) *n.* [< OFr. < L. < Gr. *theatron* < base of *theasthai*, to view] **1.** a place or structure where plays, motion pictures, etc. are presented **2.** any place like a theater, esp. in having ascending rows of seats **3.** any scene of events [the Asian *theater* of war] **4.** *a*) the art of writing or putting on plays *b*) people engaged in putting on plays, esp. live plays on a stage

**the·a·ter-in-the-round** (-in thə round′) *n.* same as ARENA THEATER

**the·at·ri·cal** (thē at′ri k'l) *adj.* **1.** having to do with the theater, the drama, a play, etc. **2.** characteristic of the theater; dramatic; esp. (in disparagement), melodramatic or affected Also **the·at′ric** —**the·at′ri·cal·ism, the·at′ri·cal′i·ty** (-kal′ə tē) *n.* —**the·at′ri·cal·ly** *adv.*

**the·at·ri·cals** (-k'lz) *n.pl.* performances of stage plays, esp. by amateurs

**the·at·rics** (thē at′riks) *n.pl.* **1.** [*with sing. v.*] the art of the theater **2.** things done or said for theatrical effect

**Thebes** (thēbz) **1.** ancient city in S Egypt, on the Nile **2.** city in ancient Greece —**The·ban** (thē′bən) *adj., n.*

**the·ca** (thē′kə) *n., pl.* **-cae** (-sē) [ModL. < L. < Gr. *thēkē*, a case] **1.** *Bot.* a spore case, sac, or capsule **2.** *Zool., Anat.* any sac enclosing an organ or a whole organism, as the covering of an insect pupa —**the′cal** *adj.* —**the′cate** (-kit) *adj.*

**thee** (thē) *pron.* [OE. *the*] *objective case of* THOU: also used in place of *thou* by Friends (Quakers) [thee is kind]

**theft** (theft) *n.* [OE. *thiefth*] the act or an instance of stealing; larceny

**thegn** (thān) *n.* [OE.] *var. of* THANE

**the·ine** (thē′in, -ēn) *n.* [< ModL. < *thea*, tea] caffeine, esp. as found in tea

**their** (ther; *unstressed thər*) *possessive pronominal adj.* [ON. *theirra*] of, belonging to, made by, or done by them: often used colloquially after a singular subject [everyone has had *their* lunch]

**theirs** (therz) *pron.* that or those belonging to them: used with no following noun [that cat is *theirs*, *theirs* are better]: also used after *of* to indicate possession [a friend of *theirs*]

**the·ism** (thē′iz′m) *n*. [THE(O)- + -ISM] **1.** belief in a god or gods **2.** belief in one God who is creator and ruler of the universe —**the′ist** *n., adj.* —**the·is′tic, the·is′ti·cal** *adj.* —**the·is′ti·cal·ly** *adv.*

**Thel·ma** (thel′mə) [< ?] a feminine name

**them** (*them*; *unstressed th*əm, *th*′m, əm) *pron.* [ON. *theim*] objective case of THEY: also used colloquially as a predicate complement with a linking verb (Ex.: that's *them*)

**theme** (thēm) *n*. [< OFr. < L. < Gr. *thema* < base of *tithenai*, to put] **1.** *a)* a topic, as of a lecture, essay, etc. *b)* a recurring, unifying subject or idea; motif **2.** a short essay, esp. one written as a school assignment **3.** *a)* a short melody used as the subject of a musical composition *b)* a musical phrase upon which variations are developed **4.** the principal song of a movie, musical, etc., or the music used to identify a radio or television program: also **theme song** —**the·mat·ic** (thē mat′ik) *adj.* —**the·mat′i·cal·ly** *adv.*

**The·mis·to·cles** (thə mis′tə klēz′) 525?–460? B.C.; Athenian statesman & naval commander

**them·selves** (*them* selvz′, *th*əm–) *pron.* a form of the 3d pers. pl. pronoun, used: *a)* as an intensive [they went *themselves*] *b)* as a reflexive [they hurt *themselves*] *c)* as a quasi-noun meaning "their real or true selves" [they are not *themselves* today]

**then** (*th*en) *adv.* [see THAN] **1.** at that time [he was young *then*] **2.** soon afterward; next in time [he took his hat and *then* left] **3.** next in order [first comes one and *then* two] **4.** in that case; accordingly [if it rains, then I will get wet] **5.** besides; moreover [I like to walk, and *then* it's cheaper] **6.** at another time [now it's warm, *then* cold] —*adj.* being such at that time [the *then* director] —*n.* that time [by *then*, they were gone] —**but then** but on the other hand —**then and there** at that time and in that place; at once —**what then?** what would happen in that case?

**thence** (*th*ens, thens) *adv.* [OE. *thanan*] **1.** from that place **2.** from that time; thenceforth **3.** on that account; therefore

**thence·forth** (-fôrth′) *adv.* from that time onward; thereafter: also **thence′for′ward, thence′for′wards**

**the·o-** [< Gr. *theos*, god] *a combining form meaning* a god or God: also, before a vowel, **the-**

**the·oc·ra·cy** (thē äk′rə sē) *n., pl.* -cies [< Gr.: see THEO- & -CRACY] **1.** lit., the rule of a state by God or a god **2.** government by priests or clergy claiming to rule with divine authority **3.** a country so governed —**the·o·crat** (thē′ə krat′) *n.* —**the·o·crat′ic, the·o·crat′i·cal** *adj.* —**the·o·crat′i·cal·ly** *adv.*

**the·od·o·lite** (thē äd′′l īt′) *n*. [ModL. *theodelitus*] a surveying instrument used to measure vertical and horizontal angles —**the·od·o·lit′ic** (-ə lit′ik) *adj.*

**The·o·dore** (thē′ə dôr′) [< L. < Gr. < *theos*, god + *dōron*, gift] a masculine name: dim. **Ted, Teddy**

**The·od·o·ric** (thē äd′ər ik) 454?–526 A.D.; king of the Ostrogoths (474–526)

**The·o·do·si·us I** (thē′ə dō′shē əs, -shəs) (*Flavius Theodosius*) 346?–395 A.D.; Rom. general; emperor of Rome (379–395): called *the Great*

**theol. 1.** theologian **2.** theology

**the·o·lo·gi·an** (thē′ə lō′jən, -jē ən) *n.* a student of or a specialist in theology or a theology

**the·o·log·i·cal** (-läj′i k′l) *adj.* of, based on, or offering instruction in, theology or a theology: also **the·o·log′ic** —**the·o·log′i·cal·ly** *adv.*

**theological virtues** *Theol.* the three virtues (faith, hope, and charity) having God as their object

**the·ol·o·gize** (thē äl′ə jīz′) *vt.* -gized′, -giz′ing to put into theological terms —*vi.* to speculate theologically —**the·ol′o·giz′er** *n.*

**the·ol·o·gy** (thē äl′ə jē) *n., pl.* -gies [< LL. < Gr.: see THEO- & -LOGY] **1.** the study of God and of religious doctrines and matters of divinity **2.** a specific system of this study

**the·o·rem** (thē′ə rəm, thir′əm) *n.* [< Fr. < L. < Gr. *theōrēma* < *theōrein*, to view] **1.** a proposition that is not self-evident but that can be proved from accepted premises and so is established as a law or principle **2.** an expression of relations in an equation or formula **3.** *Math., Physics* a proposition embodying something to be proved —**the′o·re·mat′ic** (-rə mat′ik) *adj.*

**the·o·ret·i·cal** (thē′ə ret′i k′l) *adj.* **1.** of or constituting theory **2.** limited to or based on theory; not practi-

cal; hypothetical **3.** tending to theorize; speculative Also **the′o·ret′ic** —**the′o·ret′i·cal·ly** *adv.*

**the·o·re·ti·cian** (thē′ə rə tish′ən) *n.* a person who specializes in the theory of some art, science, etc.: also **the′o·rist** (-rist)

**the·o·rize** (thē′ə rīz′) *vi.* -rized′, -riz′ing to form a theory or theories; speculate —**the′o·ri·za′tion** *n.* —**the′o·riz′er** *n.*

**the·o·ry** (thē′ə rē, thir′ē) *n., pl.* -ries [< Fr. < LL. < Gr. < *theōrein*, to view] **1.** a speculative idea or plan as to how something might be done **2.** a systematic statement of principles involved **3.** a formulation of apparent relationships or underlying principles of certain observed phenomena which has been verified to some degree **4.** that branch of an art or science consisting in a knowledge of its principles and methods rather than in its practice **5.** popularly, a mere conjecture, or guess

**theory of games** *same as* GAME THEORY

**the·os·o·phy** (thē äs′ə fē) *n., pl.* -phies [< ML. < LGr., ult. < Gr. *theos*, god + *sophos*, wise] **1.** any of various philosophies or religions that propose to establish direct, mystical contact with divine principle through contemplation, revelation, etc. **2.** [*often* T-] the doctrines of a modern sect (**Theosophical Society**) that incorporates elements of Buddhism and Brahmanism —**the′o·soph′ic** (-ə säf′ik), **the′o·soph′i·cal** *adj.* —**the′o·soph′i·cal·ly** *adv.* —**the·os′o·phist** *n.*

**ther·a·peu·tic** (ther′ə pyoot′ik) *adj.* [ModL. < Gr., ult. < *therapeuein*, to nurse] **1.** *a)* serving to cure or heal; curative *b)* serving to preserve health [*therapeutic* abortion] **2.** of therapeutics Also **ther′a·peu′ti·cal** —**ther′a·peu′ti·cal·ly** *adv.*

**ther·a·peu·tics** (-iks) *n.pl.* [with sing. v.] the branch of medicine that deals with the treatment and cure of diseases; therapy

**ther·a·py** (ther′ə pē) *n., pl.* -pies [ModL. < Gr. < *therapeuein*, to nurse] the treatment of disease or of any physical or mental disorder by medical or physical means: often used in compounds [*hydrotherapy*] —**ther′a·pist** *n.*

**there** (*th*er) *adv.* [OE. *ther*] **1.** at or in that place: often used as an intensive [John *there* is a good boy] **2.** toward, to, or into that place [go *there*] **3.** at that point in action, speech, etc. **4.** in that matter, respect, etc. [*there* you are wrong] **5.** right now [*there* goes the whistle] *There* is also used: *a)* in interjectional phrases of approval, etc. [*there's* a fine fellow!] *b)* in impersonal constructions in which the real subject follows the verb [*there* are three men here] —*n.* that place or point [we left there at six] —*interj.* an exclamation expressing defiance, dismay, satisfaction, sympathy, etc. [*there, there!* don't worry] —**(not) all there** [Colloq.] (not) mentally sound

**there·a·bouts** (*th*er′ə bouts′) *adv.* **1.** near that place **2.** near that time **3.** near that number, amount, degree, etc. Also **there′a·bout′**

**there·af·ter** (*th*er af′tər) *adv.* **1.** after that; subsequently **2.** [Archaic] accordingly

**there·at** (-at′) *adv.* **1.** at that place; there **2.** at that time **3.** for that reason

**there·by** (-bī′) *adv.* **1.** by that means **2.** connected with that [*thereby* hangs a tale]

**there·for** (-fôr′) *adv.* for this; for that; for it

**there·fore** (*th*er′fôr′) *adv.* for this or that reason; consequently; hence: often used like a conjunction

**there·from** (*th*er frum′, -främ′) *adv.* from this; from that; from it

**there·in** (-in′) *adv.* **1.** in there; in or into that place or thing **2.** in that matter, detail, etc.

**there·in·to** (*th*er in′too) *adv.* **1.** into that place or thing **2.** into that matter, condition, etc.

**there·of** (-uv′) *adv.* **1.** of that **2.** concerning that **3.** from that as a cause, reason, etc.

**there·on** (-än′) *adv.* **1.** on that **2.** *same as* THEREUPON

**there's** (*th*erz) **1.** there is **2.** there has

**The·re·sa** (tə rē′sə) **1.** [< Fr. or Port. < L. *Therasia* < ? Gr. *therizein*, to reap] a feminine name **2.** Saint, *same as* Saint TERESA

**there·to** (*th*er too′) *adv.* **1.** to that place, thing, etc.: also **there′un′to 2.** [Archaic] besides

**there·to·fore** (*th*er′tə fôr′, *th*er′tə fôr′) *adv.* up to then; until that time; before that

**there·un·der** (*th*er un′dər) *adv.* **1.** under that; under it **2.** under the terms stated there

**there·up·on** (*th*er′ə pän′, *th*er′ə pän′) *adv.* **1.** immediately following that **2.** as a consequence of that **3.** concerning that subject, etc.

**there·with** (*th*er with′, -with′) *adv.* **1.** along with that **2.** in addition to that **3.** by that method or means **4.** immediately thereafter

**there·with·al** (_ther'with ôl'_) _adv._ **1.** in addition; besides **2.** [Obs.] along with that

**ther·mal** (thur'm'l) _adj._ [Fr. < Gr. _thermē_, heat] **1.** having to do with heat, hot springs, etc. **2.** warm or hot **3.** designating or of a loosely knitted material with air spaces to help retain body heat [_thermal_ underwear] —_n._ a rising column of warm air, caused by the uneven heating of the earth or sea by the sun —**ther'mal·ly** _adv._

**thermal barrier** the speed limit beyond which the high temperatures caused by atmospheric friction would damage or destroy a given spacecraft, rocket, etc.

**thermal spring** a spring whose water has a temperature higher than that of the air in the place where it is located

**ther·mic** (thur'mik) _adj._ of or caused by heat

**therm·i·on·ic tube** (thurm'ī än'ik, thur'mē-) [THERM(O)- + ION + -IC] an electron tube having a cathode electrically heated in order to cause electron or ion emission

**therm·is·tor** (thər mis'tər, thur'mis'-) _n._ [THERM(O)- + (RES)ISTOR] a resistor made of semiconductor material, whose resistance decreases as temperature rises: used to measure temperature, microwave power, etc.

**ther·mo-** [< Gr. _thermē_, heat] _a combining form meaning:_ **1.** heat [_thermodynamics_] **2.** thermoelectric [_thermocouple_] Also, before a vowel, **therm-**

**ther·mo·cou·ple** (thur'mə kup''l) _n._ a pair of dissimilar conductors joined together at their ends: when this junction is heated, the voltage across it is in proportion to the rise in temperature: also called **thermoelectric couple**

**ther·mo·dy·nam·ic** (thur'mō dī nam'ik) _adj._ **1.** of or having to do with thermodynamics **2.** caused or operated by heat converted into motive power —**ther'mo·dy·nam'i·cal·ly** _adv._

**ther·mo·dy·nam·ics** (-dī nam'iks) _n.pl._ [with sing. _v._] the branch of physics dealing with the reversible transformation of heat into other forms of energy, esp. mechanical energy, and with the laws governing such conversions of energy

**ther·mo·e·lec·tric** (-i lek'trik) _adj._ of or having to do with the direct relations between heat and electricity: also **ther'mo·e·lec'tri·cal** —**ther'mo·e·lec'tri·cal·ly** _adv._

**ther·mo·e·lec·tric·i·ty** (-i lek'tris'ə tē) _n._ electricity produced by heating the junction between two dissimilar conductors so as to produce an electromotive force

**ther·mo·gram** (thur'mə gram') _n._ [THERMO- + -GRAM] a record made by a thermograph

**ther·mo·graph** (-graf') _n._ [THERMO- + -GRAPH] a thermometer for recording variations in temperature automatically

**ther·mo·junc·tion** (thur'mō juŋk'shən) _n._ the point of contact between the two conductors of a thermocouple

**ther·mom·e·ter** (thər mäm'ə tər) _n._ [< Fr.: see THERMO- & -METER] an instrument for measuring temperatures, as one consisting of a sealed glass tube, marked off in degrees, in which mercury, colored alcohol, etc. rises or falls as it expands or contracts from changes in temperature: see FAHRENHEIT, CELSIUS —**ther·mo·met·ric** (thur'mə met'rik) _adj._ —**ther'mo·met'ri·cal·ly** _adv._

**ther·mo·nu·cle·ar** (thur'mō nōō'klē ər, -nyōō'-) _adj._ _Physics_ **1.** designating or of a reaction in which light atomic nuclei fuse at temperatures of millions of degrees into heavier nuclei **2.** designating, of, or employing the heat energy released in nuclear fusion

**ther·mo·pile** (thur'mə pīl') _n._ [THERMO- + PILE[1]] a device consisting of a series of thermocouples, used for measuring minute changes in temperature or for generating thermoelectric current

**ther·mo·plas·tic** (thur'mə plas'tik) _adj._ soft and moldable when subjected to heat: said of certain plastics —_n._ a thermoplastic substance

**Ther·mop·y·lae** (thər mäp'ə lē) in ancient Greece, a mountain pass on the E coast: scene of a battle (480 B.C.) in which the Persians destroyed a Spartan army

**ther·mos** (thur'məs) _n._ [Gr. _thermos_, hot] a bottle, flask, or jug with two walls enclosing a vacuum, used for keeping liquids at almost their original temperature for several hours: in full, **thermos bottle** (or **flask** or **jug**)

**ther·mo·set·ting** (thur'mō set'iŋ) _adj._ becoming permanently hard and unmoldable when once subjected to heat: said of certain plastics

**ther·mo·stat** (thur'mə stat') _n._ [THERMO- + -STAT] **1.** an apparatus for regulating temperature, esp. one that automatically controls a heating unit **2.** a device that sets off a sprinkler, etc. at a certain heat —**ther'mo·stat'ic** _adj._ —**ther'mo·stat'i·cal·ly** _adv._

**ther·mot·ro·pism** (thər mät'rə piz'm) _n._ [THERMO- + -TROPISM] _Biol._ growth or movement toward or away from a source of heat —**ther·mo·trop·ic** (thur'mə träp'ik) _adj._

**the·sau·rus** (thi sôr'əs) _n._, _pl._ **-ri** (-ī), **-rus·es** [L. < Gr. _thēsauros_, a treasure] **1.** a treasury or storehouse **2.** a book containing a store of words; specif., a book of synonyms and antonyms **3.** a classified index of terms for use in information retrieval, as from a computer

**these** (thēz) _pron._, _adj._ _pl. of_ THIS

**The·seus** (thē'sōōs, -syōōs, -sē əs) Gr. _Legend_ the principal hero of Attica, king of Athens, famed esp. for his killing of the Minotaur —**The·se·an** (thi sē'ən) _adj._

**the·sis** (thē'sis) _n._, _pl._ **the'ses** (-sēz) [L. < Gr. _thesis_, a placing < base of _tithenai_, to put] **1.** a proposition defended in argument **2.** a formal and lengthy research paper, esp. one presented as part of the requirements for a master's degree **3.** _Logic_ an unproved statement assumed as a premise

**Thes·pi·an** (thes'pē ən) _adj._ [after _Thespis_, Greek poet of 6th c. B.C.] [_often_ t-] having to do with the drama; dramatic —_n._ [_often_ t-] an actor or actress: a humorous or pretentious term

**Thes·sa·lo·ni·ans** (thes'ə lō'nē ənz) either of two books of the New Testament which were epistles from the Apostle Paul to the Christians of Thessalonica: abbrev. **Thess.**

**Thes·sa·lon·i·ca** (thes'ə län'i kə, -ə lə nī'kə) _ancient name of_ SALONIKA

**Thes·sa·ly** (thes'ə lē) division of E Greece, on the Aegean Sea —**Thes·sa·li·an** (the sā'lē ən) _adj._, _n._

**the·ta** (thāt'ə, thēt'ə) _n._ the eighth letter of the Greek alphabet (Θ, θ, ϑ,)

**thews** (thyōōz) _n.pl._, _sing._ **thew** [OE. _theaw_, custom, habit] **1.** muscular power; bodily strength **2.** muscles or sinews —**thew'y** _adj._ **thew'i·er**, **thew'i·est**

**they** (thā) _pron._ _for sing. see_ HE, SHE, IT [< ON. _their_] **1.** the persons, animals, or things previously mentioned **2.** people in general [_they_ say it's so] _They_ is the nominative case form of the third personal plural pronoun

**they'd** (thād) **1.** they had **2.** they would

**they'll** (thāl, thel) **1.** they will **2.** they shall

**they're** (ther, thā'ər) they are

**they've** (thāv) they have

**thi-** _same as_ THIO-

**thi·a·mine** (thī'ə mēn', -min) _n._ [altered < THI(O)- + (VIT)AMIN] vitamin B[1], a white, crystalline compound, $C_{12}H_{17}ON_4SCl$, found in cereal grains, egg yolk, liver, etc., or prepared synthetically: a deficiency of this vitamin results in beriberi and certain nervous disorders: also **thi'a·min** (-min)

**Thi·bet** (ti bet') _var. of_ TIBET —**Thi·bet'an** _adj._, _n._

**thick** (thik) _adj._ [OE.] **1.** of relatively great depth or extent from side to side [a _thick_ board] **2.** having large diameter in relation to length [a _thick_ pipe] **3.** measured between opposite surfaces [a wall six inches _thick_] **4.** dense; compact; specif., _a)_ marked by profuse, close growth; luxuriant [_thick_ woods] _b)_ great in number and close together [a _thick_ crowd] _c)_ having much body; not thin [_thick_ soup] _d)_ dense and heavy [_thick_ smoke] _e)_ covered [a road _thick_ with mud] _f)_ studded profusely [a sky _thick_ with stars] **5.** dark or obscure [_thick_ shadows] **6.** _a)_ slurred, muffled, or husky [_thick_ speech, a _thick_ voice] _b)_ strongly marked [a _thick_ accent] **7.** [Colloq.] stupid **8.** [Colloq.] close in friendship **9.** [Chiefly Brit. Colloq.] too much to be tolerated —_adv._ in a thick way —_n._ the thickest part or the period of greatest activity [in the _thick_ of the fight] —**through thick and thin** in good times and bad times —**thick'ish** _adj._ —**thick'ly** _adv._

**thick·en** (thik'ən) _vt._, _vi._ **1.** to make or become thick or thicker **2.** to make or become more complex or involved —**thick'en·er** _n._

**thick·en·ing** (-iŋ) _n._ **1.** the action of one that thickens **2.** a substance used to thicken **3.** the thickened part

**thick·et** (thik'it) _n._ [OE. _thiccet_ < _thicce_, thick] a thick growth of shrubs, underbrush, or small trees

**thick·head·ed** (thik'hed'id) _adj._ stupid —**thick'head'ed·ness** _n._

**thick·ness** (-nis) _n._ **1.** the quality of being thick **2.** the measure of how thick a thing is **3.** a layer [three _thicknesses_ of cloth]

**thick·set** (-set') _adj._ **1.** planted thickly or closely **2.** thick in body; stocky —_n._ [Archaic] a thicket

**thick-skinned** (-skind') _adj._ **1.** having a thick skin **2.** not easily hurt by criticism, insults, etc.

**thief** (thēf) _n._, _pl._ **thieves** (thēvz) [OE. _theof_] a person who steals, esp. secretly

**thieve** (thēv) _vt._, _vi._ **thieved**, **thiev'ing** [OE. _theofian_ < _theof_, a thief] to steal —**thiev'ish** _adj._ —**thiev'ish·ly** _adv._ —**thiev'ish·ness** _n._

**thiev·er·y** (thēv'ər ē) _n._, _pl._ **-er·ies** the act or practice of stealing or an instance of this; theft

**thigh** (thī) _n._ [OE. _theoh_] the part of the leg between the knee and the hip

**thigh·bone** (-bōn') _n._ the largest and longest bone in the body, from the hip to the knee; femur: also **thigh bone**

**thill** (thil) _n._ [OE. _thille_, a stake, pole] either of the two shafts between which a horse is hitched to a wagon

**thim·ble** (thim'b'l) _n._ [OE. _thymel_ < _thuma_, a thumb] **1.** a small cap of metal, plastic, etc. worn as a protection on the finger that pushes the needle in sewing **2.** anything like this; esp., a grooved metal ring inserted in a loop of rope, etc. to prevent wear

**thim·ble·ful** (-fŏŏl′) *n., pl.* **-fuls′** **1.** as much as a thimble will hold **2.** a very small quantity

**thim·ble·rig** (-rig′) *n. same as* SHELL GAME —*vt., vi.* **-rigged′, -rig′ging** to cheat or swindle, as in this game — **thim′ble·rig′ger** *n.*

**thin** (thin) *adj.* **thin′ner, thin′nest** [OE. *thynne*] **1.** of relatively little depth or extent from side to side *[a thin board]* **2.** having small diameter in relation to length *[thin thread]* **3.** having little fat or flesh; slender **4.** not dense or compact; specif., *a)* scanty in growth; sparse *[thin hair]* *b)* small in size or number *[thin receipts]* *c)* lacking body; watery *[thin soup]* *d)* not dense or heavy *[thin smoke]* *e)* rarefied, as air at high altitudes **5.** not deep and strong; weak *[thin colors, a thin voice]* **6.** light or sheer, as fabric **7.** easily seen through; flimsy *[a thin excuse]* **8.** slight, weak, vapid, etc. *[a thin plot, a thin argument]* —*adv.* in a thin way —*vt., vi.* **thinned, thin′ning** to make or become thin or thinner: often with *out, down,* etc. —**thin′ly** *adv.* —**thin′ness** *n.* —**thin′nish** *adj.*

**thine** (thīn) *pron.* [OE. *thin*] [Archaic or Poet.] that or those belonging to thee (you): absolute form of THY *[a friend of thine, this is thine]* —*possessive pronominal adj.* [Archaic or Poet.] thy: used before a word beginning with a vowel or unvoiced *h*

**thing**[1] (thing) *n.* [OE., a council, hence, "matter discussed, thing"] **1.** any matter, affair, or concern **2.** a happening, act, deed, incident, etc. *[to do great things]* **3.** an end to be achieved, a step in a process, etc. *[the next thing is to mix thoroughly]* **4.** an individual, distinguishable entity; specif., *a)* a tangible object, as distinguished from a quality, concept, etc. *b)* a lifeless object *c)* an item, detail, etc. *[look at each thing on the list]* *d)* the object or concept referred to by a word, symbol, or sign *e)* an object of thought; idea **5.** *a)* *[pl.]* personal belongings; also, clothes or clothing *b)* a dress, garment, etc. *[not a thing to wear]* **6.** a person or creature *[poor thing!]* **7.** something mentioned but unnamed *[where did you buy that thing?]* **8.** [Colloq.] a point of dispute; issue *[he made a thing of it]* **9.** [Colloq.] a strong, often neurotic liking, fear, aversion, etc. *[to have a thing about flying]* —**do one's (own) thing** [Colloq.] to express one's unique personality in one's own way of life, activities, etc. —**see things** [Colloq.] to have hallucinations —**the thing 1.** that which is wise, essential, etc. **2.** that which is the height of fashion

‡**thing**[2] (tiŋ; *E.* thiŋ) *n.* [ON., assembly] a Scandinavian legislative body

**thing·a·ma·bob, thing·um·a·bob** (thiŋ′ə mə bäb′) *n.* [Colloq.] *same as* THINGAMAJIG: also **thing′um·bob′**

**thing·a·ma·jig, thing·um·a·jig** (-jig′) *n.* [extension of older *thingum,* THING[1]] [Colloq.] any device or gadget: jocular substitute for a name not known or temporarily forgotten

**think**[1] (thiŋk) *vt.* **thought, think′ing** [OE. *thencan*] **1.** to form or have in the mind *[think good thoughts]* **2.** to judge; consider *[I think her charming]* **3.** to believe; surmise; expect *[I think I can go]* **4.** to determine, work out, etc. by reasoning *[to think a problem through]* **5.** [Now Rare] to intend *[thinking to do right]* **6.** *a)* to have in mind; form an idea of *[think what may be]* *b)* to recall; recollect *[think what joy was ours]* **7.** to have constantly in mind *[think success]* —*vi.* **1.** to use the mind; reflect or reason *[think before you act]* **2.** to have an opinion, belief, judgment, etc. *[I just think so, we think highly of him]* **3.** to remember (with *of* or *about*) **4.** to consider or be considerate (with *of* or *about*) **5.** to invent; conceive (*of*) —*n.* [Colloq.] the act of thinking *[give it a good think]* —*adj.* [Colloq.] having to do with thinking —**think (all) the world of** to admire or love greatly —**think better of 1.** to form a more favorable opinion of **2.** to make a more sensible decision about, after reconsidering —**think fit** to regard as proper —**think little (or nothing) of 1.** to attach little (or no) importance to **2.** to have little (or no) hesitancy about —**think on (or upon)** [Archaic] to give thought to —**think out 1.** to think about to a conclusion: also **think through 2.** to work out by thinking —**think out loud** to speak one's thoughts as they occur: also **think aloud** — **think over** to give thought to; ponder well —**think twice** to reconsider —**think up** to invent, contrive, etc. by thinking —**think′a·ble** *adj.* —**think′er** *n.*

**think**[2] (thiŋk) *v.impersonal pt.* **thought** [OE. *thyncan*] to seem: obs., except in archaic METHINKS, METHOUGHT

**think·ing** (-iŋ) *adj.* **1.** that thinks or can think; rational **2.** given to thought; reflective —*n.* thought

**think tank (or factory)** [Slang] a group of experts organized to do intensive research and problem solving, using computers, etc.

**thin·ner** (thin′ər) *n.* a person or thing that thins; esp., a substance added, as turpentine to paint, for thinning

**thin-skinned** (-skind′) *adj.* **1.** having a thin skin **2.** easily hurt by criticism, insults, etc.

**thi·o-** [< Gr. *theion,* brimstone] *a combining form meaning* sulfur, used to indicate the replacement of oxygen by sulfur

**Thi·o·kol** (thī′ə kôl′, -kōl′) [arbitrary coinage] *a trademark for* any of various synthetic rubbery compounds used as sealants and sealing adhesives

**thi·o·pen·tal (sodium)** (thī′ə pen′tal, -tôl, -t'l) [THIO- + PENT(A)- + -AL] a yellowish-white powder, $C_{11}H_{17}N_2O_2$-SNa, injected intravenously in solution as a general anesthetic and hypnotic

**thi·o·sul·fate** (thī′ō sul′fāt) *n.* a salt of thiosulfuric acid; esp., sodium thiosulfate

**thi·o·sul·fu·ric acid** (-sul fyoor′ik) [THIO- + SULFURIC] an unstable acid, $H_2S_2O_3$, whose salts are used in photography, bleaching, etc.

**third** (thurd) *adj.* [OE. *thridda*] **1.** preceded by two others in a series; 3d or 3rd **2.** next below the second in rank, value, merit, etc. **3.** designating any of the three equal parts of something —*adv.* in the third place, rank, group, etc. —*n.* **1.** the one following the second **2.** any person, thing, class, etc. that is third **3.** any of the three equal parts of something; 1/3 **4.** the third forward gear ratio of a motor vehicle **5.** *Music a)* the third tone of an ascending diatonic scale, or a tone two degrees above or below any given tone in such a scale *b)* the interval between two such tones, or a combination of them —**third′ly** *adv.*

**third base** *Baseball* the base between second base and home plate, located on the pitcher's right

**third-class** (thurd′klas′) *adj.* **1.** of the class, rank, excellence, etc. next below the second **2.** designating or of accommodations next below the second **3.** designating or of a lower-cost class of mail limited to merchandise weighing less than 16 oz. or bulk mailing of identical circulars, advertisements, etc. —*adv.* **1.** with third-class travel accommodations **2.** as or by third-class mail

**third degree** [Colloq.] harsh, grueling treatment and questioning of a prisoner in order to force a confession or information —**third′-de·gree′** *adj.*

**third dimension 1.** *a)* the dimension of depth in something *b)* the quality of having, or of seeming to have, depth, or solidity **2.** the quality of being true to life or seeming real —**third′-di·men′sion·al** *adj.*

**third party 1.** a political party competing against the two major parties in a two-party system **2.** a person other than the principals in a case or matter

**third person 1.** that form of a pronoun (as *he*) or verb (as *is*) which refers to the person or thing spoken of **2.** narration characterized by the general use of such forms

**third rail** an extra rail used in some electric railroads for supplying power

**third-rate** (-rāt′) *adj.* **1.** third in quality or other rating; third-class **2.** inferior; very poor —**third′-rat′er** *n.*

**third world** [*often* T- W-] the underdeveloped or emergent countries of the world, esp. of Africa and Asia

**thirst** (thurst) *n.* [OE. *thurst*] **1.** the discomfort or distress caused by a desire or need for water, characterized generally by dryness in the mouth and throat **2.** [Colloq.] a craving for a specific liquid, esp. for alcoholic liquor **3.** any strong desire; craving —*vi.* **1.** to be thirsty **2.** to have a strong desire or craving

**thirst·y** (thur′stē) *adj.* **thirst′i·er, thirst′i·est 1.** feeling thirst **2.** *a)* lacking water or moisture; dry *[thirsty fields]* *b)* very absorbent **3.** [Colloq.] causing thirst *[thirsty work]* **4.** having a strong desire; craving —**thirst′i·ly** *adv.* —**thirst′i·ness** *n.*

**thir·teen** (thur′tēn′) *adj.* [OE. *threotyne*] three more than ten —*n.* the cardinal number between twelve and fourteen; 13; XIII

**thir·teenth** (-tēnth′) *adj.* **1.** preceded by twelve others in a series; 13th **2.** designating any of the thirteen equal parts of something —*n.* **1.** the one following the twelfth **2.** any of the thirteen equal parts of something; 1/13

**thir·ti·eth** (thur′tē ith) *adj.* **1.** preceded by twenty-nine others in a series; 30th **2.** designating any of the thirty equal parts of something —*n.* **1.** the one following the twenty-ninth **2.** any of the thirty equal parts of something; 1/30

**thir·ty** (thur′tē) *adj.* [OE. *thritig* < *thri,* three + *-tig,* -TY[2]] three times ten —*n., pl.* **-ties 1.** the cardinal number between twenty-nine and thirty-one; 30; XXX **2.** this number used to signify the end of a dispatch, story, etc., as for a newspaper —**the thirties** the numbers or years, as of a century, from thirty through thirty-nine

**thir·ty-sec·ond note** (thur′t ē sek′ənd) *Music* a note having 1/32 the duration of a whole note: see NOTE, illus.

**this** (this) *pron., pl.* **these** [OE. *thes,* masc., *this,* neut.] **1.** the person or thing mentioned or understood *[this is

John] **2.** the thing that is nearer than another referred to as "that" [*this* is larger than that] **3.** the less remote in thought of two contrasted things [*this* is more likely than that] **4.** the fact, idea, etc. that is being, or is about to be, presented, etc. [now hear *this*] —*adj., pl.* **these 1.** designating the person or thing mentioned or understood [*this* man is John] **2.** designating the thing that is nearer than the one referred to as "that" [*this* desk is smaller than that one] **3.** designating the less remote in thought of two contrasted things [*this* possibility is more likely than that] **4.** designating something that is being, or is about to be, presented, etc. [hear *this* song] **5.** [Colloq.] designating a particular but unspecified person or thing [there's *this* lady in Iowa] —*adv.* to this extent; so [it was *this* big]

**this·tle** (this′'l) *n.* [OE. *thistel*] any of various plants of the composite family, with prickly leaves and heads of white, purple, etc. flowers; esp., the **Scotch thistle** with white down and lavender flowers —**this·tly** (this′lē) *adj.*

**this·tle·down** (-doun′) *n.* the down attached to the flower head of a thistle

**thith·er** (thith′ər, thith′-) *adv.* [OE. *thider*] to or toward that place; there —*adj.* on or toward that side; farther

**thith·er·to** (-too′; thith′ər too′, thith′-) *adv.* until that time; till then

**thith·er·ward** (-wərd) *adv.* [Rare] toward that place; thither: also **thith′er·wards**

**tho, tho'** (thō) *conj., adv.* shortened sp. *of* THOUGH

**thole** (thōl) *n.* [OE. *thol*] a pin or either of a pair of pins set vertically in the gunwale of a boat to serve as a fulcrum for an oar: also **thole′pin′** (-pin′)

**Thom·as** (täm′əs) [LL. < Gr. < Ar. *tĕ'ōma*, lit., a twin] **1.** a masculine name: dim *Tom*, *Tommy* **2.** *Bible* one of the twelve apostles, who doubted at first the resurrection of Jesus: John 20:24–29

**Tho·mism** (tō′miz'm) *n.* the theological and philosophical doctrines of Thomas Aquinas

**Thomp·son** (tämp′s'n, täm′-) **1. Benjamin,** Count Rumford, 1753–1814; Brit. scientist & statesman, born in America **2. Francis,** 1859–1907; Eng. poet

**Thompson submachine gun** [< the co-inventor, J. T. *Thompson* (1860–1940), U.S. army officer] *a trademark for* a type of submachine gun: see SUBMACHINE GUN

**thong** (thôŋ) *n.* [OE. *thwang*] **1.** a narrow strip of leather, etc. used as a lace, strap, etc. **2.** a whiplash, as of braided strips of hide

**Thor** (thôr) *Norse Myth.* the god of thunder, war, and strength, and the son of Odin

**tho·rac·ic** (thô ras′ik, thə-) *adj.* of, in, or near the thorax

**tho·ra·co-** (thôr′ə kō) *a combining form meaning* the thorax (and): also, before a vowel, **thorac-**

**tho·rax** (thôr′aks) *n., pl.* **-rax·es, -ra·ces′** (-ə sēz′) [L. < Gr. *thorax*] **1.** in man and other higher vertebrates, the part of the body between the neck and the abdomen; chest **2.** the middle one of the three main segments of an insect's body

**Tho·ra·zine** (thôr′ə zēn′) [*thor-* (< ?) + (CHLORPROM)-AZINE] *a trademark for* CHLORPROMAZINE

**Thor·eau** (thôr′ō, thə rō′), **Henry David** (born *David Henry Thoreau*) 1817–62; U.S. naturalist & writer

**tho·ri·um** (thôr′ē əm) *n.* [ModL. < THOR] a rare, grayish, radioactive chemical element, used in making electronic equipment and as a nuclear fuel; symbol, Th; at. wt., 232.038; at. no., 90 —**tho′ric** *adj.*

**thorn** (thôrn) *n.* [OE.] **1.** *a)* a very short, hard, leafless branch or stem with a sharp point *b)* any small tree or shrub bearing thorns; esp., *same as* HAWTHORN **2.** anything that keeps troubling, vexing, or irritating one: usually in the phrase **thorn in one's side** (or **flesh**) **3.** in Old English, the runic character(þ), corresponding to either the voiced or unvoiced sound of English *th*

**thorn apple 1.** *a) same as* HAWTHORN *b)* its applelike fruit **2.** a jimson weed or similar plant

**thorn·y** (thôr′nē) *adj.* **thorn′i·er, thorn′i·est 1.** full of thorns; prickly **2.** difficult or full of obstacles, vexations, pain, etc. —**thorn′i·ness** *n.*

**thor·o** (thur′ō, -ə) *adj.* shortened sp. *of* THOROUGH

**tho·ron** (thôr′än) *n.* [ModL. < THORIUM] a radioactive isotope of radon, resulting from the disintegration of thorium

**thor·ough** (thur′ō, -ə) *prep., adv.* [ME. *thoruh*, a var. of *through*, THROUGH] *obs. var. of* THROUGH —*adj.* **1.** done or proceeding through to the end; complete [a *thorough* checkup] **2.** that is completely (the thing specified); absolute [a *thorough* rascal] **3.** very exact, accurate, or painstaking, esp. about details —**thor′ough·ly** *adv.* —**thor′ough·ness** *n.*

**thor·ough·bred** (thur′ə bred′) *adj.* **1.** purebred, as a horse or dog; pedigreed **2.** thoroughly trained, cultured, etc.; well-bred **3.** excellent; first-rate —*n.* **1.** a thor-

oughbred animal; specif., [T-] any of a breed of racehorses **2.** a cultured, well-bred person

**thor·ough·fare** (-fer′) *n.* a public street open at both ends, esp. one through which there is much traffic; main road

**thor·ough·go·ing** (-gō′iŋ) *adj.* very thorough; specif., *a)* precise and painstaking *b)* absolute; out-and-out

**those** (thōz) *adj., pron.* [OE. *thas*] *pl. of* THAT

**thou** (thou) *pron.* [OE. *thu*] the nominative second person singular of the personal pronoun: formerly used in familiar address but now replaced by *you* except in poetic, religious, and some dialectal use

**though** (thō) *conj.* [< OE. *theah* & cognate ON. *tho*] **1.** in spite of the fact that; notwithstanding that [*though* it rained, he went] **2.** and yet; nevertheless; however [they will probably win, *though* no one thinks so] **3.** even if; supposing that [*though* he may fail, he will have tried] —*adv.* however; nevertheless [she sings well, *though*]

**thought**[1] (thôt) *n.* [OE. *thoht*] **1.** the act or process of thinking **2.** the power of reasoning; intellect; imagination **3.** what one thinks; idea, opinion, plan, etc. **4.** the ideas, opinions, etc. prevailing at a given time or place or among a given people [modern *thought* in education] **5.** attention; consideration [give it a moment's *thought*] **6.** intention or expectation [no *thought* of leaving] **7.** a little; trifle [be a *thought* more careful]

**thought**[2] (thôt) *pt. & pp. of* THINK

**thought·ful** (-fəl) *adj.* **1.** full of thought; meditative **2.** characterized by thought; serious **3.** heedful, careful, etc.; esp., considerate of others —**thought′ful·ly** *adv.* —**thought′ful·ness** *n.*

**thought·less** (-lis) *adj.* **1.** not stopping to think; careless **2.** not given thought; rash **3.** not considerate of others **4.** [Rare] stupid —**thought′less·ly** *adv.* —**thought′less·ness** *n.*

**thou·sand** (thou′z'nd) *n.* [OE. *thusend*] **1.** ten hundred; 1,000; M **2.** an indefinite but very large number —*adj.* amounting to one thousand in number

**thou·sand·fold** (-fōld′) *adj.* [see -FOLD] having a thousand times as much or as many —*adv.* a thousand times as much or as many: with *a*

**Thousand Island dressing** a salad dressing made of mayonnaise with ketchup, minced pickles, etc.

**Thousand Islands** group of c.1,000 islands in the St. Lawrence River at the outlet of Lake Ontario, some part of N.Y. State & some of Ontario, Canada

**thou·sandth** (thou′z'ndth) *adj.* **1.** coming last in a series of a thousand **2.** designating any of the thousand equal parts of something —*n.* **1.** the thousandth one of a series **2.** any of the thousand equal parts of something; 1/1000

**Thrace** (thrās) **1.** ancient region in the E Balkan Peninsula **2.** modern region in the SE Balkan Peninsula divided between Greece & Turkey —**Thra·cian** (thrā′shən) *adj., n.*

**thrall** (thrôl) *n.* [OE. *thræl* < ON.] **1.** orig., a slave or bondman **2.** a person under the moral or psychological domination of someone or something **3.** slavery

**thrall·dom, thral·dom** (-dəm) *n.* the condition of being a thrall; servitude; slavery

**thrash** (thrash) *vt.* [OE. *therscan*, to beat] **1.** *same as* THRESH **2.** to make move violently or wildly **3.** to give a severe beating to; flog —*vi.* **1.** *same as* THRESH **2.** to move or toss about violently [*thrashing* in agony] **3.** to make one's way by thrashing —*n.* the act of thrashing —**thrash out** to settle by much discussion —**thrash over** to go over (a problem, etc.) in great detail

**thrash·er**[1] (thrash′ər) *n.* a person or thing that thrashes

**thrash·er**[2] (thrash′ər) *n.* [E. dial. *thresher*] any of a group of gray to brownish American songbirds resembling the thrush by having a long, stiff tail and a long bill

**thread** (thred) *n.* [OE. *thræd*] **1.** *a)* a light, fine, stringlike length of two or more fibers or strands of spun cotton, silk, etc. twisted together and used in sewing *b)* a similar fine length of synthetic material, as of plastic, or of glass or metal *c)* the fine, stringy filament produced from itself by a spider, silkworm, etc. *d)* a fine, stringy length of syrup, etc. **2.** any thin line, stratum, vein, ray, etc. **3.** something like a thread in its length, sequence, etc. [the *thread* of a story] **4.** the spiral or helical ridge of a screw, bolt, nut, etc. **5.** [pl.] [Slang] a suit, or clothes generally —*vt.* **1.** *a)* to put a thread through the eye of (a needle, etc.) *b)* to arrange thread for use on (a sewing machine) **2.** to string (beads, etc.) on or as if on a thread **3.** to fashion a thread (sense 4) on or in (a screw, pipe, etc.) **4.** to interweave with or as if with threads **5.** *a)* to pass through by twisting, turning, or weaving in and out [to *thread* the streets] *b)* to make (one's way) in this fashion —*vi.* **1.** to go along in a winding way **2.** to form a thread when dropped from a spoon: said of boiling syrup beginning to thicken —**thread′er** *n.* —**thread′like′** *adj.*

**thread·bare** (-ber′) *adj.* **1.** worn down so that the threads show; having the nap worn off **2.** wearing worn-out clothes; shabby **3.** that has lost freshness or novelty; stale

**thread·y** (-ē) *adj.* **thread′i·er, thread′i·est 1.** of or like a thread; stringy; fibrous **2.** forming threads; viscid: said of liquids **3.** thin, weak, feeble, etc. *[a thready* voice*]* —**thread′i·ness** *n.*

**threat** (thret) *n.* [OE. *threat*, a throng] **1.** an expression of intention to hurt, destroy, punish, etc., as in intimidation **2.** *a)* a sign of something dangerous or harmful about to happen *[the threat of war] b)* a source of possible danger, harm, etc.

**threat·en** (thret′'n) *vt.* [OE. *threatnian*] **1.** *a)* to make threats against *b)* to express one's intention to inflict (punishment, injury, etc.) **2.** *a)* to be a sign of (danger, harm, etc.) *[clouds threatening* snow*] b)* to be a source of possible danger, harm, etc. to *[an epidemic threatens the city]* —*vi.* **1.** to make threats **2.** to be a sign or source of possible danger, etc. —**threat′en·er** *n.* —**threat′en·ing·ly** *adv.*

**three** (thrē) *adj.* [OE. *threo, thrie*] totaling one more than two —*n.* **1.** the cardinal number between two and four; 3; III **2.** anything having three units or members, or numbered three

**three-base hit** (thrē′bās′) a triple in baseball

**3-D** (thrē′dē′) *adj.* producing or designed to produce an effect of three dimensions *[a 3-D movie]* —*n.* a system or effect that adds a three-dimensional appearance to visual images, as in movies

**three-deck·er** (-dek′ər) *n.* **1.** a ship with three decks **2.** any structure with three levels **3.** [Colloq.] a sandwich made with three slices of bread

**three-di·men·sion·al** (-də men′shən 'l) *adj.* **1.** *a)* of or having three dimensions *b)* appearing to have depth or thickness in addition to height and width **2.** having a lifelike quality

**three·fold** (-fōld′) *adj.* [see -FOLD] **1.** having three parts **2.** having three times as much or as many —*adv.* three times as much or as many

**three-mile limit** (-mīl′) the outer limit of a zone of water extending three miles offshore, sometimes regarded as the limit to a country's right to control, use, etc.

**three·pence** (thrip′'ns, thrup′-, threp′-) *n.* **1.** the sum of three British pennies **2.** a British coin of this value

**three·pen·ny** (thrē′pen′ē, thrip′ə nē) *adj.* **1.** worth or costing threepence **2.** of small worth; cheap

**three-ply** (-plī′) *adj.* having three thicknesses, interwoven layers, strands, etc.

**three-quar·ter** (-kwôr′tər) *adj.* of or involving three fourths

**three·score** (thrē′skôr′) *adj.* sixty

**three·some** (-səm) *n.* a group of three persons

**thren·o·dy** (thren′ə dē) *n., pl.* **-dies** [< Gr. < *thrēnos*, lamentation + *ōidē*, song] a song of lamentation; dirge —**thre·nod·ic** (thri näd′ik) *adj.* —**thren′o·dist** *n.*

**thresh** (thresh) *vt.* [earlier form of THRASH] **1.** to beat out (grain) from its husk, as with a flail **2.** to beat grain out of (husks) **3.** to beat or strike as with a flail —*vi.* **1.** to thresh grain **2.** to toss about; thrash —**thresh out** to settle by much discussion; thrash out

**thresh·er** (-ər) *n.* **1.** a person who threshes **2.** a machine for threshing grain: also **threshing machine** **3.** a large shark with a long tail

**thresh·old** (thresh′ōld, -hōld) *n.* [OE. *therscold* < base of *therscan* (see THRASH)] **1.** *same as* DOORSILL **2.** the entrance or beginning point of something **3.** *Physiol., Psychol.* the point at which a stimulus is just strong enough to be perceived or produce a response *[the threshold of pain]*

**threw** (thrōō) *pt. of* THROW

**thrice** (thrīs) *adv.* [ME. *thries*] **1.** three times **2.** threefold **3.** greatly; highly

**thrift** (thrift) *n.* [ON. < *thrifast*, to THRIVE] **1.** orig., a thriving **2.** careful management of one's money or resources; economy; frugality **3.** a small plant with narrow leaves and small white, pink, red, or purplish flowers —**thrift′less** *adj.* —**thrift′less·ly** *adv.* —**thrift′less·ness** *n.*

**thrift·y** (-ē) *adj.* **thrift′i·er, thrift′i·est** **1.** practicing or showing thrift; economical **2.** thriving; prospering —**thrift′i·ly** *adv.* —**thrift′i·ness** *n.*

**thrill** (thril) *vi., vt.* [OE. *thyr(e)lian*, to pierce < *thyrel*, hole < *thurh*, through] **1.** to feel or cause to feel keen emotional excitement; tingle with excitement **2.** to quiver or cause to quiver; tremble; vibrate —*n.* **1.** a thrilling or being thrilled; tremor of excitement **2.** the quality of thrilling, or the ability to thrill **3.** something that causes emotional excitement **4.** a vibration; tremor; quiver

**thrill·er** (-ər) *n.* a suspenseful novel, movie, etc., esp. [Chiefly Brit.] one dealing with crime and detection

**thrive** (thrīv) *vi.* **thrived** or **throve, thrived** or **thriv·en** (thriv′'n), **thriv′ing** [< ON. *thrifast*, to prosper < *thrifa*, to grasp] **1.** to prosper or flourish; be successful, esp. by practicing thrift **2.** to grow vigorously or luxuriantly

**thro′, thro** (thrōō) *prep., adv., adj. archaic shortened sp. of* THROUGH

**throat** (thrōt) *n.* [OE. *throte*] **1.** the front part of the neck **2.** the upper part of the passage from the mouth and nose to the stomach and lungs, including the pharynx, upper larynx, trachea, and esophagus **3.** any narrow, throatlike passage or part —**jump down someone's throat** [Colloq.] to attack or criticize someone suddenly and violently —**stick in one's throat** to be hard for one to say, as from reluctance

**-throat·ed** (thrōt′id) *a combining form meaning* having a (specified kind of) throat *[ruby-throated]*

**throat·y** (-ē) *adj.* **throat′i·er, throat′i·est** **1.** produced in the throat, as some sounds or tones **2.** characterized by such sounds; husky *[a throaty* voice*]* —**throat′i·ly** *adv.* —**throat′i·ness** *n.*

**throb** (thräb) *vi.* **throbbed, throb′bing** [ME. *throbben*] **1.** to beat, pulsate, vibrate, etc. **2.** to beat strongly or fast; palpitate, as the heart under exertion **3.** to tingle or quiver with excitement —*n.* **1.** the act of throbbing **2.** a beat or pulsation, esp. a strong one of the heart —**throb′ber** *n.* —**throb′bing·ly** *adv.*

**throe** (thrō) *n.* [prob. < OE. *thrawu*, pain] a spasm or pang of pain: *usually used in pl. [the throes* of childbirth, death *throes]* —**in the throes of** in the act of struggling with (a problem, task, etc.)

**throm·bin** (thräm′bin) *n.* [< Gr. *thrombos*, a clot] the enzyme of the blood, formed from prothrombin, that causes clotting by forming fibrin

**throm·bo·sis** (thräm bō′sis) *n.* [ModL. < Gr. < *thrombos*, a clot] coagulation of the blood in the heart or a blood vessel, forming a clot —**throm·bot·ic** (-bät′ik) *adj.*

**throne** (thrōn) *n.* [< OFr. < L. < Gr. *thronos*, a seat] **1.** the chair on which a king, cardinal, etc. sits on formal or ceremonial occasions **2.** the power or rank of a king, etc.; sovereignty **3.** a sovereign ruler, etc. *[orders from the throne]* —*vt., vi.* **throned, thron′ing** to enthrone or be enthroned

**throng** (thrôŋ) *n.* [OE. *(ge)thrang* < *thringan*, to crowd] **1.** a great number of people gathered together; crowd **2.** any great number of things massed or considered together; multitude —*vi.* to gather together, move, or press in a throng; crowd —*vt.* to crowd into; fill with a multitude

**throt·tle** (thrät′'l) *n.* [prob. dim. of THROAT] **1.** [Rare] the throat or windpipe **2.** the valve that regulates the amount of fuel vapor entering an internal-combustion engine or controls the flow of steam in a steam line: also **throttle valve** **3.** the lever or pedal that controls this valve —*vt.* **-tled, -tling** **1.** to choke; strangle **2.** to stop the utterance or action of; suppress **3.** *a)* to reduce the flow of (fuel vapor, etc.) by means of a throttle *b)* to lessen the speed of (an engine, vehicle, etc.) by this or similar means —*vi.* to choke or suffocate —**throt′tler** *n.*

**through** (thrōō) *prep.* [OE. *thurh*] **1.** in one side and out the other side of; from end to end of **2.** in the midst of; among **3.** by way of **4.** over the entire extent of **5.** to various places in; around *[touring through* France*]* **6.** *a)* from the beginning to the end of *b)* up to and including *[through* Friday*]* **7.** without making a stop for *[to go through* a red light*]* **8.** past the difficulties of *[to come through* hard times*]* **9.** by means of **10.** as a result of; because of —*adv.* **1.** in one side and out the other; from end to end **2.** from the beginning to the end **3.** completely to the end *[see it through]* **4.** thoroughly; completely: also **through and through** *[soaked through]* —*adj.* **1.** extending from one place to another *[a through* street*]* **2.** traveling to the destination without stops *[a through* train*]* **3.** arrived at the end; finished **4.** at the end of one's usefulness, resources, etc. *[through* in politics*]* **5.** having no further dealings, etc. (with someone or something)

**through·out** (thrōō out′) *prep.* all the way through; in or during every part of —*adv.* **1.** in or during every part; everywhere **2.** in every respect

**through·way** (-wā′) *n. same as* EXPRESSWAY

**throve** (thrōv) *alt. pt. of* THRIVE

**throw** (thrō) *vt.* **threw, thrown, throw′ing** [OE. *thrawan*, to twist] **1.** to twist strands of (silk, etc.) into thread or yarn **2.** to cause to fly through the air by releasing from the hand while the arm is in rapid motion; cast; hurl **3.** to discharge through the air from a catapult, gun, etc. **4.** to cause to fall; upset *[thrown* by a horse*]* **5.** to move or send rapidly *[they threw* troops into the battle*]* **6.** to put suddenly and forcibly into a specified place, condition, or situation *[thrown* into confusion*]* **7.** *a)* to cast (dice) *b)* to make (a specified cast) at dice *[to throw* a five*]* **8.** to cast off; shed *[snakes throw* their skins*]* **9.** to move (the lever of a switch, clutch, etc.) or connect, disconnect, etc. by so doing **10.** *a)* to direct, cast, turn, etc. (with *at, on, upon*, etc.) *[to* *throw* a glance, a light, a shadow, etc.] *b)* to deliver (a punch) **11.** to cause (one's voice) to seem to come from some other source **12.** to put (blame *on*, obstacles *before*, etc.) **13.** [Colloq.] to lose (a game, race, etc.) deliberately **14.** [Colloq.] to give (a party, dance, etc.) **15.** [Colloq.] to have (a fit, tantrum, etc.) **16.** [Colloq.] to confuse or disconcert [the question *threw* him] **17.** *Ceramics* to shape on a potter's wheel —*vi.* to cast or hurl something —*n.* **1.** the act of one who throws; a cast **2.** the distance something is or can be thrown [*a* stone's *throw*] **3.** *a)* a spread for draping over a sofa, etc. *b)* a woman's light scarf or wrap **4.** *a)* the motion of a moving part, as a cam, eccentric, etc. *b)* the extent of such a motion —**throw a monkey wrench into** to obstruct by direct interference; sabotage —**throw away 1.** to rid oneself of; discard **2.** to waste **3.** to fail to make use of **4.** to deliver (a line or lines) in an offhand way: said of an actor or comedian —**throw back 1.** to stop from advancing **2.** to revert to the type of an ancestor —**throw cold water on** to discourage by showing no interest or by criticizing —**throw in 1.** to engage (a clutch) **2.** to add extra or free **3.** to add to others **4.** [Colloq.] to join (*with*) in cooperative action —**throw off 1.** *a)* to rid oneself of *b)* to recover from **2.** to mislead **3.** to expel, emit, etc. —**throw on** to put on (a garment) hastily —**throw oneself at** to try very hard to win the affection or love of —**throw oneself into** to engage in with great vigor —**throw oneself on** (or **upon**) to rely on for support for aid —**throw open 1.** to open completely and suddenly **2.** to remove all restrictions from —**throw out 1.** to discard **2.** to reject or remove, often with force **3.** to emit **4.** to disengage (a clutch) **5.** *Baseball* to throw the ball to a teammate who in turn retires (a runner) —**throw over 1.** to give up; abandon **2.** to jilt —**throw together 1.** to make or assemble hurriedly **2.** to cause to become acquainted —**throw up 1.** to give up or abandon **2.** to vomit **3.** to construct rapidly **4.** to mention repeatedly (*to* someone), as in reproach —**throw′er** *n.*

**throw·a·way** (thrō′ə wā′) *adj.* designed to be discarded after use [a *throwaway* bottle]

**throw·back** (-bak′) *n.* **1.** a throwing back; check or stop **2.** reversion to an ancestral type **3.** an instance of this

**throw rug** same as SCATTER RUG

**thru** (thrōō) *prep., adv., adj.* shortened sp. of THROUGH

**thrum¹** (thrum) *n.* [OE., a ligament] **1.** *a)* the row of warp thread ends left on a loom when the web is cut off *b)* any of these ends **2.** any short end thread or fringe

**thrum²** (thrum) *vt., vi.* **thrummed, thrum′ming** [echoic] **1.** to strum (a guitar, banjo, etc.) **2.** to drum (on) with the fingers —*n.* the act or sound of thrumming

**thrush¹** (thrush) *n.* [OE. *thrysce*] any of a large group of songbirds, often plain-colored, including the robin, wood thrush, blackbird, etc.

**thrush²** (thrush) *n.* [prob. akin to Dan. *trøske*] a disease, esp. of infants, caused by a fungus that forms milky white lesions on the mouth, lips, and throat

**thrust** (thrust) *vt.* **thrust, thrust′ing** [ON. *thrysta*] **1.** to push with sudden force; shove **2.** to pierce; stab **3.** to force or impose (oneself or another) upon someone else or into some position or situation —*vi.* **1.** to push or shove against something **2.** to make a stab or lunge, as with a sword **3.** to force one's way (*into, through*, etc.) **4.** to extend, as in growth —*n.* **1.** a thrusting; specif., *a)* a sudden, forceful push *b)* a stab, as with a sword *c)* any sudden attack **2.** continuous pressure of one part against another, as of a rafter against a wall **3.** *a)* the driving force of a propeller in the line of its shaft *b)* the forward force produced by the gases escaping rearward from a jet or rocket engine **4.** *a)* forward movement; impetus *b)* energy; drive **5.** the basic meaning or purpose [the *thrust* of a speech] —**thrust′er** *n.*

**thru·way** (thrōō′wā′) *n.* same as EXPRESSWAY

**Thu·cyd·i·des** (thōō sid′ə dēz′) 460?-400? B.C.; Athenian historian

**thud** (thud) *vi.* **thud′ded, thud′ding** [prob. ult. < OE. *thyddan*, to strike] to hit or fall with a dull sound —*n.* **1.** a heavy blow **2.** a dull sound, as of a heavy object dropping on a soft, solid surface

**thug** (thug) *n.* [Hindi *ṭhag* < Sans. *sthaga*, a rogue] **1.** [also T-] a member of a former religious organization in India that murdered and robbed **2.** a rough, brutal hoodlum, gangster, robber, etc. —**thug′ger·y** *n.* —**thug′gish** *adj.*

**thu·li·um** (thōō′lē əm) *n.* [ModL. < (ULTIMA) THULE] a metallic chemical element of the rare-earth group: symbol, Tm; at. wt., 168.934; at. no., 69

**thumb** (thum) *n.* [OE. *thuma*] **1.** the short, thick finger of the human hand that is nearest the wrist **2.** a corresponding part in some other animals **3.** that part of a glove, etc. which covers the thumb —*vt.* **1.** to handle, turn, soil, etc. as with the thumb **2.** [Colloq.] to ask for or get (a ride) or make (one's way) in hitchhiking by gesturing with the thumb extended —**all thumbs** clumsy; fumbling —**thumb one's nose** to raise one's thumb to the nose in a coarse ges-

ture of defiance or contempt —**thumbs down** a signal of disapproval —**thumbs up** a signal of approval —**under one's thumb** under one's influence

**thumb index** an index to the sections of a reference book, consisting of a series of rounded notches cut in the front edge of a book with a labeled tab at the base of each notch —**thumb′-in′dex** *vt.*

**thumb·nail** (-nāl′) *n.* **1.** the nail of the thumb **2.** something as small as a thumbnail —*adj.* very small or brief [a *thumbnail* sketch]

**thumb·screw** (-skrōō′) *n.* **1.** a screw with a head shaped in such a way that it can be turned with the thumb and forefinger **2.** a former instrument of torture for squeezing the thumbs

**thumb·tack** (-tak′) *n.* a tack with a wide, flat head, that can be pressed into a board, etc. with the thumb

THUMBSCREW

**thump** (thump) *n.* [echoic] **1.** a blow with something heavy and blunt **2.** the dull sound made by such a blow —*vt.* **1.** to strike with a thump or thumps **2.** to thrash; beat severely —*vi.* **1.** to hit or fall with a thump **2.** to make a dull, heavy sound; pound; throb —**thump′er** *n.*

**thump·ing** (thum′piŋ) *adj.* **1.** that thumps **2.** [Colloq.] very large; whopping —**thump′ing·ly** *adv.*

**thun·der** (thun′dər) *n.* [OE. *thunor*] **1.** the sound that is heard after a flash of lightning, caused by the sudden heating and expansion of air by electrical discharge **2.** any loud, rumbling sound like this **3.** an outburst of threatening or angry words Also used in mild oaths [yes, by *thunder!*]: also **thun′der·a′tion** —*vi.* **1.** to produce thunder [it is *thundering*] **2.** to make, or move with, a sound like thunder **3.** to make strong denunciations, etc. —*vt.* to utter, attack, etc. with a thundering sound —**steal someone's thunder** to lessen the effectiveness of someone's statement or action by anticipating him in its use —**thun′der·er** *n.*

**thun·der·bolt** (-bōlt′) *n.* **1.** a flash of lightning with the thunder heard after it **2.** something that stuns or acts with sudden force or violence

**thun·der·clap** (-klap′) *n.* **1.** a clap, or loud crash, of thunder **2.** anything like this in being sudden, startling, violent, etc.

**thun·der·cloud** (-kloud′) *n.* a storm cloud charged with electricity and producing lightning and thunder

**thun·der·head** (-hed′) *n.* a round mass of cumulus clouds coming before a thunderstorm

**thun·der·ous** (-əs) *adj.* **1.** full of or making thunder **2.** making a noise like thunder —**thun′der·ous·ly** *adv.*

**thun·der·show·er** (-shou′ər), **thun·der·squall** (-skwôl′), **thun·der·storm** (-stôrm′) *n.* a shower (or squall or storm) with thunder and lightning

**thun·der·struck** (-struk′) *adj.* amazed or shocked as if struck by a thunderbolt: also **thun′der·strick′en** (-strik′'n)

**thu·ri·ble** (thoor′ə b'l, thyoor′-) *n.* [< L. < *thus* (gen. *thuris*), incense < Gr. *thyos*, sacrifice] same as CENSER

**Thu·rin·gi·a** (thoo rin′jē ə) region of SW East Germany —**Thu·rin′gi·an** *adj., n.*

**Thurs., Thur.** Thursday

**Thurs·day** (thurz′dē, -dā) *n.* [< OE. < ON. *Thorsdagr*, Thor's day] the fifth day of the week

**Thurs·days** (-dēz, -dāz) *adv.* on or during every Thursday

**thus** (thus) *adv.* [OE.] **1.** in this or that manner; in the way just stated or in the following manner **2.** to this or that degree or extent; so **3.** consequently; therefore; hence: often used with conjunctive force **4.** for example

**thwack** (thwak) *vt.* [prob. echoic] to strike with something flat; whack —*n.* a blow with something flat

**thwart** (thwôrt) *adj.* [ON. *thvert*, transverse] lying across something else —*adv., prep.* archaic var. of ATHWART —*n.* **1.** a rower's seat extending across a boat **2.** a brace extending across a canoe —*vt.* to keep from doing or being done; block or hinder (a person, plans, etc.)

**thy** (thī) *possessive pronominal adj.* [ME. *thi*, contr. < *thin*, thy] of, belonging to, or done by thee: archaic or poet. var. of *your*: see also THINE, THOU

**thyme** (tīm) *n.* [< MFr. < L. < Gr. *thymon* < *thyein*, to offer sacrifice] any of various shrubby plants or aromatic herbs of the mint family, with white, pink, or red flowers and fragrant leaves used for seasoning —**thym′ic** *adj.*

**thy·mine** (thī′mēn, -min) *n.* [G. *thymin* < Gr. *thymos*, spirit + G. *-in*, -INE⁴] a white, crystalline base, $C_5H_6N_2O_2$, one of the substances forming the genetic code in DNA molecules

**thy·mol** (thī′môl, -mōl) *n.* [THYM(E) + -OL¹] a colorless compound, $C_{10}H_{14}O$, extracted from thyme or made synthetically: used as an antiseptic, as in mouthwashes, etc.

**thy·mus** (thī′məs) *n.* [ModL. < Gr. *thymos*] a ductless, glandlike body near the throat, that has no known function and disappears in the adult: see also SWEETBREAD: also **thymus gland** —**thy′mic** *adj.*

**thy·roid** (thī′roid) *adj.* [ModL. < Gr. < *thyreos*, door-shaped shield < *thyra*, door + *-eidēs*, -OID] **1.** designating or of a large ductless gland near the trachea, secreting the hormone thyroxine, which regulates body growth and metabolism **2.** designating or of the principal cartilage of the larynx, forming the Adam's apple —*n.* **1.** the thyroid gland **2.** the thyroid cartilage **3.** a preparation of the thyroid gland of certain animals, used in treating goiter, etc.: also **thyroid extract**

**thy·rox·ine** (thī räk′sēn, -sin) *n.* [THYR(OID) + OX(Y)-¹ + -INE⁴] a colorless, crystalline compound, $C_{15}H_{11}I_4NO_4$, the active hormone of the thyroid gland, used in treating goiter, etc.: also **thy·rox′in** (-sin)

**thyr·sus** (thur′səs) *n., pl.* **-si** (-sī) [L. < Gr. *thyrsos*] *Gr. Myth.* a staff tipped with a pine cone and sometimes entwined with ivy, carried by Dionysus, the satyrs, etc.

**thy·self** (*th*ī self′) *pron. reflexive or intensive form of* THOU: an archaic or poet. var. of *yourself*

**ti** (tē) *n.* [altered < *si:* see GAMUT, SOL-FA] *Music* a syllable representing the seventh tone of the diatonic scale

**Ti** *Chem.* titanium

**ti·ar·a** (tē er′ə, -ar′ə, -är′ə; tī-) *n.* [L. < Gr. *tiara*] **1.** an ancient Persian headdress **2.** the Pope's triple crown **3.** a woman's coronetlike headdress, often jeweled

**Ti·ber** (tī′bər) river in C Italy, flowing from the Apennines south through Rome into the Tyrrhenian Sea

**Ti·ber·i·us** (tī bir′ē əs) (*Tiberius Claudius Nero Caesar*) 42 B.C.–37 A.D.; Rom. emperor (14 A.D.–37 A.D.)

**Ti·bet** (ti bet′) autonomous region of SW China, north of the Himalayas: 471,660 sq. mi.; cap. Lhasa

**Ti·bet·an** (ti bet′'n) *adj.* of Tibet, its people, their language, etc. —*n.* **1.** a member of the Mongolic people of Tibet **2.** the Sino-Tibetan language of Tibet

**tib·i·a** (tib′ē ə) *n., pl.* **-i·ae′** (-i ē′), **-i·as** [L.] **1.** the inner and thicker of the two bones of the leg below the knee; shinbone **2.** a corresponding bone in the leg of other vertebrates —**tib′i·al** *adj.*

**tic** (tik) *n.* [Fr. < ?] a twitching of a muscle, esp. of the face, that is not consciously controlled

**tick¹** (tik) *n.* [prob. < Gmc. echoic base] **1.** a light clicking or tapping sound, as that made by a clock **2.** a mark made to check off items; check mark (✓, /, etc.) **3.** [Brit. Colloq.] a moment; instant —*vi.* **1.** to make a tick or ticks, as a clock **2.** [Colloq.] to function; work [*what makes him tick?*] —*vt.* **1.** to indicate or count by a tick or ticks **2.** [Chiefly Brit.] to check off (an item in a list, etc.) with a tick (usually *with off*)

**tick²** (tik) *n.* [OE. *ticia*] any of a large group of bloodsucking arachnids that are parasitic on man, cattle, sheep, etc., including many species that transmit diseases

**tick³** (tik) *n.* [ult. < L. < Gr. *thēkē*, a case] **1.** the cloth case that is filled with cotton, feathers, etc. to form a mattress or pillow **2.** [Colloq.] same as TICKING

**tick⁴** (tik) *n.* [contr. < TICKET] [Chiefly Brit. Colloq.] credit; trust [*to buy something on tick*]

TICK
(¼ in. long)

**tick·er** (tik′ər) *n.* a person or thing that ticks; specif., *a)* a telegraphic device that records stock market quotations, etc. on paper tape (**ticker tape**) *b)* [Old Slang] a watch *c)* [Slang] the heart

**tick·et** (tik′it) *n.* [< obs. Fr. *etiquet* (now *étiquette*), a ticket] **1.** a printed card or piece of paper that gives one a specified right, as to attend a theater, ride a bus, etc. **2.** a label or tag, as on a piece of merchandise, giving the size, price, etc. **3.** the list of candidates nominated by a political party in an election; slate **4.** [Colloq.] a summons to court for a traffic violation —*vt.* **1.** to label or tag with a ticket **2.** to issue a ticket to

**tick·et-of-leave man** (-əv lēv′) [Brit.] formerly, a person on parole from prison

**tick·ing** (tik′iŋ) *n.* [see TICK³] a strong, heavy cloth, often striped, used for casings of mattresses, pillows, etc.

**tick·le** (tik′'l) *vt.* **-led, -ling** [ME. *tikelen*] **1.** to please, gratify, etc.: often used in the passive voice with slang intensives, as **tickled pink** (or **silly, to death,** etc.) **2.** to amuse [*the joke really tickled her*] **3.** to touch or stroke lightly so as to cause twitching, laughter, etc. [*to tickle someone's ear*] —*vi.* **1.** to have a scratching or tingling sensation [*a throat that tickles*] **2.** to be ticklish —*n.* **1.** a tickling or being tickled **2.** a tickling sensation

**tick·ler** (tik′lər) *n.* **1.** a person or thing that tickles **2.** a memorandum pad, file, etc. for reminding one of things that need to be taken care of at certain future dates

**tick·lish** (-lish) *adj.* **1.** sensitive to tickling **2.** very sensitive or easily upset; touchy **3.** needing careful handling; delicate —**tick′lish·ly** *adv.* —**tick′lish·ness** *n.*

**tick-tack-toe, tic-tac-toe** (tik′tak tō′) *n.* a game in which two players take turns marking either X's or O's in an open block of nine squares, the object being to complete a line of three of one's mark first

**tick·tock** (tik′täk′) *n.* the sound made by a clock —*vi.* to make this sound

**Ti·con·der·o·ga** (tī′kän də rō′gə), **Fort** [< Iroquoian, lit., between two lakes] former fort in NE N.Y., taken from the British by Am. Revolutionary soldiers in 1775

**tid·al** (tīd′'l) *adj.* of, having, caused by, determined by, or dependent on a tide or tides —**tid′al·ly** *adv.*

**tidal wave 1.** in popular usage, an unusually great, destructive wave sent inshore by an earthquake or a very strong wind **2.** any great, widespread movement, expression of feeling, etc.

**tid·bit** (tid′bit′) *n.* [dial. *tid*, small object + BIT²] a choice bit of food, gossip, etc.

**tid·dly·winks** (tid′lē wiŋks′, tid′'l ē-) *n.* a game in which the players try to snap little colored disks into a cup by pressing their edges with a larger disk: also **tid′dle·dy·winks′** (-′l dē wiŋks′)

**tide** (tīd) *n.* [OE. *tid*, time] **1.** a period of time: now only in combination [*Eastertide*] **2.** *a)* the alternate rise and fall of the surface of oceans, seas, etc., caused by the attraction of the moon and sun: it occurs twice in each period of 24 hours and 50 minutes *b) same as* FLOOD TIDE **3.** something that rises and falls like the tide **4.** a stream, current, trend, etc. [*the tide of public opinion*] **5.** [Archaic] an opportune time —*adj. same as* TIDAL —*vi.* **tid′ed, tid′ing** to surge like a tide —*vt.* to carry as with the tide —**tide over** to help along temporarily, as through a period of difficulty —**turn the tide** to reverse a condition

**tide·land** (-land′, -lənd) *n.* **1.** land covered by water at high tide and uncovered at low tide **2.** [*pl.*] loosely, land under water just beyond this and within territorial limits

**tide·mark** (-märk′) *n.* the high-water mark or, sometimes, the low-water mark of the tide

**tide·wa·ter** (-wôt′ər, -wät′-) *n.* **1.** water, as in some streams along a coastline, that is affected by the tide **2.** an area in which water is affected by the tide —*adj.* of or along a tidewater

**ti·dings** (tī′diŋz) *n.pl.* [*sometimes with sing. v.*] [OE. *tidung*] news; information

**ti·dy** (tī′dē) *adj.* **-di·er, -di·est** [ult. < *tid*, time] **1.** neat in personal appearance, ways, etc.; orderly **2.** neat in arrangement; in order; trim **3.** [Colloq.] *a)* fairly good; satisfactory *b)* rather large; considerable [*a tidy sum*] —*vt., vi.* **-died, -dy·ing** to make (things) tidy (often *with up*) —*n., pl.* **-dies** *same as* ANTIMACASSAR —**ti′di·ly** *adv.* —**ti′di·ness** *n.*

**tie** (tī) *vt.* **tied, ty′ing** [OE. *tigan* < base of *teag*, a rope] **1.** to fasten or bind together or to something else, as with string or rope made secure by knotting, etc. **2.** to tighten and knot the laces, strings, etc. of [*to tie one's shoes*] **3.** *a)* to make (a knot or bow) *b)* to make a knot or bow in [*to tie a necktie*] **4.** to join or bind in any way [*tied by common interests*] **5.** to confine; restrict **6.** to equal (the score, record, etc.) of (opponents, a rival, etc.) **7.** *Music* to connect with a tie —*vi.* to make a tie —*n.* **1.** a string, cord, etc. used to tie things **2.** something that joins, binds, etc.; bond **3.** something that confines or restricts [*legal ties*] **4.** *short for* NECKTIE **5.** a beam, rod, etc. that holds together and strengthens parts of a building **6.** any of the parallel crossbeams to which the rails of a railroad are fastened **7.** *a)* an equality of scores, votes, etc. in a contest *b)* a contest in which scores, etc. are equal **8.** [*pl.*] low, laced shoes **9.** *Music* a curved line joining two notes of the same pitch, indicating that the tone is to be held unbroken —*adj.* that has been tied, or made equal [*a tie score*] —**tie down** to confine; restrain; restrict —**tie in 1.** to bring into or have a connection **2.** to make or be consistent, harmonious, etc. —**tie off** to close off passage through by tying with something —**tie up 1.** to tie securely **2.** to wrap up and tie with string, etc. **3.** to moor (a ship or boat) to a dock **4.** to block or hinder **5.** to cause to be already in use, committed, etc.

**tie·back** (-bak′) *n.* **1.** a sash, ribbon, tape, etc. used to tie curtains or draperies to one side **2.** a curtain with a tieback: *usually used in pl.*

**tie beam** a horizontal beam serving as a tie (*n.* 5)

**tie clasp** a decorative clasp for fastening a necktie to the shirt front: also **tie clip, tie bar**

**tie-dye** (tī′dī′) *n.* **1.** a method of dyeing designs on cloth by tightly tying bunches of it with thread, etc. so that the dye affects only exposed parts **2.** cloth so decorated or a design so made —*vt.* **-dyed′, -dye′ing** to dye in this way

**tie-in** (-in′) *adj.* designating or of a sale in which an item in demand can be bought only along with some other item or items —*n.* **1.** a tie-in sale or advertisement **2.** a connection or relationship

**tie line 1.** a direct telephone line between extensions in one or more PBX systems **2.** a line used to connect one electric power or transportation system with another

**Tien Shan** (tyen shän) mountain system in C Asia, extending across the Kirghiz S.S.R. & Sinkiang, China

**Tien·tsin** (tin′tsin′; *Chin.* tyen′jin′) seaport in NE China, on an arm of the Yellow Sea: pop. c. 4,000,000

**tie·pin** (tī′pin′) *n.* same as STICKPIN

**Tie·po·lo** (tye′pô lô), **Gio·van·ni Bat·tis·ta** (jô vän′nē bät tēs′tä) 1696–1770; Venetian painter

**tier**[1] (tir) *n.* [< MFr. *tire*, order] any of a series of layers or rows, as of seats, arranged one above or behind another —*vt., vi.* to arrange or be arranged in tiers

**ti·er**[2] (tī′ər) *n.* a person or thing that ties

**tierce** (turs) *n.* [*often* T-] same as TERCE

**Tier·ra del Fue·go** (tyer′rä del fwe′gô; *E.* tē er′ə del′ foo ā′gō) **1.** group of islands at the tip of S. America, divided between Argentina & Chile **2.** chief island of this group

**tie tack** an ornamental pin with a short point that fits into a snap, used to fasten a necktie to the shirt front

**tie-up** (tī′up′) *n.* **1.** a temporary stoppage or interruption of work, traffic, etc. **2.** connection or relation

**tiff** (tif) *n.* [< ?] **1.** a slight fit of anger or bad humor **2.** a slight quarrel; spat —*vi.* to be in or have a tiff

**tif·fin** (tif′in) *n., vi.* Anglo-Ind. *term for* LUNCH

**ti·ger** (tī′gər) *n., pl.* **-gers, -ger:** see PLURAL, II, D, 1 [< OE. & OFr., both < L. < Gr. *tigris*] **1.** a large, flesh-eating animal of the cat family, native to Asia, having a tawny coat striped with black **2.** *a)* a very energetic or persevering person *b)* a fierce, belligerent person —**have a tiger by the tail** to find oneself in a situation more difficult to handle than one expected —**ti′ger·ish** *adj.*

**tiger beetle** any of various brightly colored, often striped beetles with burrowing larvae that feed on other insects

**tiger lily** a lily having purple-spotted, orange flowers

**tiger moth** any of a group of stout-bodied moths with brightly striped or spotted wings

**tiger's eye** a semiprecious, yellow-brown stone: also **ti′ger-eye′** *n.*

**tight** (tīt) *adj.* [< OE. *-thight*, strong] **1.** made so that water, air, etc. cannot pass through *[a tight boat]* **2.** drawn, packed, spaced, etc. closely together *[a tight weave]* **3.** [Dial.] snug; trim; neat **4.** fixed securely; firm *[a tight joint]* **5.** fully stretched; taut **6.** fitting so closely as to be uncomfortable **7.** strict *[tight control]* **8.** difficult to manage: esp. in the phrase **a tight corner** (*or* **squeeze,** etc.), a difficult situation **9.** showing strain *[a tight smile]* **10.** almost even or tied *[a tight race]* **11.** sharp: said of a spiral, turn, etc. **12.** *a)* difficult to get; scarce in relation to demand *b)* characterized by such scarcity *[a tight market]* **13.** concise: said of language, style, etc. **14.** [Colloq.] stingy **15.** [Slang] drunk **16.** [Slang] intimate; friendly (usually with *with*) —*adv.* in a tight manner; esp., *a)* securely or firmly *[hold tight] b)* [Colloq.] soundly *[sleep tight]* —**sit tight** to maintain one's opinion or position —**tight′ly** *adv.* —**tight′ness** *n.*

**-tight** (tīt) [< prec.] *a combining form meaning* not letting (something specified) in or out *[watertight, airtight]*

**tight·en** (tīt′'n) *vt., vi.* to make or become tight or tighter

**tight end** *Football* an end stationed next to the tackle on the offensive line

**tight·fist·ed** (tīt′fis′tid) *adj.* stingy

**tight·fit·ting** (-fit′iŋ) *adj.* fitting very tight

**tight·knit** (-nit′) *adj.* **1.** tightly knit **2.** well organized or put together in an efficient way

**tight-lipped** (-lipt′) *adj.* **1.** having the lips closed tightly **2.** not saying much; taciturn or secretive

**tight·rope** (-rōp′) *n.* a rope stretched tight on which acrobats do balancing acts

**tights** (tīts) *n.pl.* a garment that fits tightly over the legs and the lower part of the body, worn by acrobats, dancers, etc.

**tight ship** [Colloq.] any organization or business that is highly organized and efficiently run, like a naval vessel under strict discipline

**tight·wad** (tīt′wäd′, -wôd′) *n.* [TIGHT + WAD] [Slang] a stingy person; miser

**ti·glon** (tī′glän′, -glən) *n.* [TIG(ER) + L(I)ON] the offspring of a male tiger and a female lion: also **ti′gon′** (-gän′, -gən)

**ti·gress** (tī′gris) *n.* a female tiger

**Ti·gris** (tī′gris) river flowing from EC Turkey through Iraq, joining the Euphrates to form the Shatt-al-Arab

**Ti·jua·na** (tē wä′nə, tē′ə wä′-; *Sp.* tē hwä′nä) city in Baja California, on the U.S. border: pop. 335,000

**tike** (tīk) *n.* same as TYKE

**til·bu·ry** (til′bər ē) *n., pl.* **-ries** [< *Tilbury*, a London coach builder] a light, two-wheeled carriage for two persons

**til·de** (til′də) *n.* [Sp. < L. *titulus*, title, sign] a diacritical mark (~) used in various ways, as over an *n* in Spanish to indicate a palatal nasal sound (ny), as in *señor*

**tile** (tīl) *n.* [OE. *tigele*, ult. < L. *tegula*] **1.** *a)* a thin piece of

glazed or unglazed, fired clay, stone, etc. used for roofing, flooring, decorative borders, bathroom walls, etc. *b)* a similar piece of plastic, asphalt, etc., used to cover floors, walls, etc. **2.** tiles collectively **3.** a drain of semicircular tiles or earthenware pipe **4.** burnt-clay, hollow blocks, used variously in construction **5.** any of the pieces in mah-jongg —*vt.* **tiled, til′ing** to cover with tiles —**on the tiles** [Brit. Colloq.] out carousing —**til′er** *n.*

**til·ing** (tīl′iŋ) *n.* **1.** the action of a person who tiles **2.** tiles collectively **3.** a covering of tiles

**till**[1] (til) *prep., conj.* [OE. *til*] same as UNTIL

**till**[2] (til) *vt., vi.* [OE. *tilian*, lit., to strive for] to work (land) in raising crops, as by plowing, fertilizing, etc.; cultivate —**till′a·ble** *adj.*

**till**[3] (til) *n.* [< ? ME. *tillen*, to draw] **1.** a drawer or tray, as in a store counter, for keeping money **2.** ready cash

**till·age** (til′ij) *n.* **1.** the tilling of land **2.** land that is tilled

**till·er**[1] (til′ər) *n.* [< OFr. < ML. *telarium*, weaver's beam < L. *tela*, a web] a bar or handle for turning a boat's rudder

**till·er**[2] (til′ər) *n.* a person who tills the soil

**tilt** (tilt) *vt.* [prob. < OE. *tealt*, shaky] **1.** to cause to slope or slant; tip **2.** *a)* to poise or thrust (a lance) in or as in a tilt *b)* to charge at (one's opponent) in a tilt —*vi.* **1.** to slope; incline **2.** to poise or thrust one's lance (*at* one's opponent) in a tilt **3.** to take part in a tilt or joust **4.** to dispute, argue, contend, etc. —*n.* **1.** a medieval contest in which two horsemen thrust with lances in an attempt to unseat each other **2.** any spirited contest, dispute, etc. between persons **3.** *a)* the act of tilting, or sloping *b)* a slope or slant **4.** [Colloq.] a leaning or inclination —**(at) full tilt** at full speed

**tilth** (tilth) *n.* [OE. < *tilian:* see TILL[2]] **1.** a tilling of land **2.** tilled land

**Tim.** Timothy

**tim·bal** (tim′b'l) *n.* [< Fr. < Sp. < Ar. < *al,* the + *tabl,* drum] same as KETTLEDRUM

**tim·bale** (tim′b'l) *n.* [Fr.: see prec.] **1.** a custardlike dish made with chicken, lobster, fish, etc. and baked in a small drum-shaped mold **2.** a type of fried or baked pastry shell, filled with a cooked food

**tim·ber** (tim′bər) *n.* [OE.] **1.** wood suitable for building houses, ships, etc. **2.** a large, heavy, dressed piece of wood used in building; beam **3.** [Brit.] same as LUMBER[1] (*n.* 2) **4.** trees or forests collectively **5.** personal quality or character *[a man of his timber]* **6.** a wooden rib of a ship —*vt.* to provide, build, or prop up with timbers —*adj.* of or for timber —*interj.* a warning shout by a lumberman that a cut tree is about to fall —**tim′bered** *adj.* —**tim′ber·ing** *n.*

**timber hitch** *Naut.* a knot used for tying a rope to a spar

**tim·ber·land** (tim′bər land′) *n.* land with trees suitable for timber; wooded land

**tim·ber·line** (-līn′) *n.* the line above or beyond which trees do not grow, as on mountains or in polar regions

**timber wolf** same as GRAY WOLF

**tim·bre** (tam′bər, tim′-) *n.* [Fr., earlier, sound of a bell < MFr. < OFr., ult. < Gr. *tympanon,* a drum] the quality of sound, apart from pitch or intensity, that makes one voice or musical instrument different from another

**tim·brel** (tim′brəl) *n.* [< OFr.: see prec.] an ancient type of tambourine

**Tim·buk·tu** (tim′buk too′, tim buk′too) town in C Mali, near the Niger River: pop. 9,000

**time** (tīm) *n.* [OE. *tima*] **1.** duration in which things happen in the past, present, and future; every minute there has been or ever will be **2.** a system of measuring the passing of hours *[solar time, standard time]* **3.** the period between two events or during which something exists, happens, or acts **4.** *[usually pl.]* a period of history *[medieval times, Lincoln's time]* **5.** *a)* a period characterized

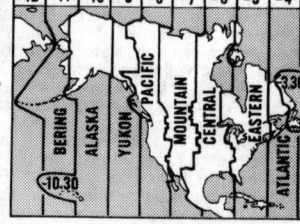

TIME ZONES

by a prevailing condition or specific experience *[a time of peace, have a good time] b)* *[usually pl.]* prevailing conditions *[times are bad]* **6.** a set period or term, as a lifetime or a term of imprisonment, apprenticeship, military service, etc. **7.** a period necessary, sufficient, measured, etc. for something *[time for play, a baking time of ten minutes]* **8.** *a)* the period worked or to be worked by an employee *b)* the hourly rate of pay for the regular working hours **9.** rate of speed in marching, driving, etc. **10.** a precise instant, minute, day, year, etc., determined by clock or calendar **11.** the point at which something happens; occasion *[the game time is 2:00 P.M.]* **12.** the usual or appointed moment for something to happen, begin, or end [*time* to get up] **13.** the suitable or proper moment [*now* is the *time* to act] **14.** any one of a series of moments at which something recurs [for the fifth *time*, *time* and *time* again] **15.** *Music a*) the grouping of rhythmic beats into measures of equal length *b*) the characteristic rhythm of a piece of music in terms of this grouping *c*) the rate of speed at which a composition is played; tempo *d*) the duration of a note or rest —*interj. Sports* a signal that a period of play or activity is ended or that play is temporarily suspended —*vt.* **timed, tim′ing 1.** to arrange the time of so as to be acceptable or suitable, opportune, etc. **2.** to adjust, set, etc. so as to coincide in time [*time* your watch with mine] **3.** to set the duration of (a syllable or musical note) as a unit of rhythm **4.** to record the pace, speed, etc. of [to *time* a runner] —*adj.* **1.** having to do with time **2.** set to explode, open, etc. at a given time [a *time* bomb] **3.** payable later [a *time* loan] **4.** designating or of any of a series of payments made over a period of time —**abreast of the times 1.** up to date **2.** informed about current matters —**against time** trying to finish in a given time —**ahead of time** sooner than due; early —**at one time 1.** together **2.** formerly —**at the same time 1.** together **2.** nonetheless; however —**at times** occasionally; sometimes —**behind the times** out of date; old-fashioned —**behind time** late —**do time** [Colloq.] to serve a prison term —**for the time being** for the present; temporarily —**from time to time** at intervals; now and then —**in good time 1.** at the proper time **2.** in a short time —**in no time** very quickly —**in time 1.** eventually **2.** before it is too late **3.** keeping the set tempo, pace, etc. —**make time** to travel, work, etc. at a fast rate of speed —**many a time** often; frequently —**on time 1.** at the appointed time; punctual(ly) **2.** to be paid for in installments over a period of time —**pass the time of day** to exchange a few words of greeting, etc. —**time after time** again and again; continually: also **time and again** —**time of one's life** [Colloq.] an experience of great pleasure for one —**time was** there was a time

**time and a half** a rate of payment one and a half times the usual rate, as for working overtime
**time capsule** a container holding articles of the present time, buried or preserved for a future age
**time clock** a clock with a mechanism for recording on a card ( **timecard** ) the time at which an employee begins and ends a work period
**time exposure 1.** a relatively long exposure of photographic film, generally for more than half a second **2.** a photograph taken in this way
**time·hon·ored** (tīm′än′ərd) *adj.* honored because in existence or usage for a long time
**time·keep·er** (-kē′pər) *n.* **1.** *same as* TIMEPIECE **2.** a person who keeps time; specif., *a*) one who keeps account of the hours worked by employees *b*) one who keeps account of the elapsed time in the periods of play in certain sports
**time-lapse** (-laps′) *adj.* of a technique of photographing a slow process on motion-picture film by exposing single frames at widely spaced intervals: the film is projected at regular speed to show the process speeded up
**time·less** (-lis) *adj.* **1.** unending **2.** eternal **3.** restricted to no specific time; always valid or true —**time′less·ly** *adv.* —**time′less·ness** *n.*
**time limit** a fixed period of time during which something must be done or ended
**time·ly** (-lē) *adj.* **-li·er, -li·est** happening, done, said, etc. at a suitable time; well-timed; opportune —**time′li·ness** *n.*
**time·out** (-out′) *n. Sports*, etc. any temporary suspension of play, as to discuss strategy, etc.
**time·piece** (-pēs′) *n.* any apparatus for measuring and recording time; esp., a clock or watch
**tim·er** (tī′mər) *n.* **1.** *same as: a*) TIMEKEEPER *b*) STOPWATCH **2.** in internal-combustion engines, a mechanism for causing the spark to be produced in the cylinder at the required instant **3.** a device for timing, or automatically starting and stopping, some mechanism
**times** (tīmz) *prep.* multiplied by: symbol, × [two *times* three is six]
**time·sav·ing** (tīm′sā′viŋ) *adj.* that saves time because of greater efficiency, etc. —**time′sav′er** *n.*
**time·serv·er** (-sur′vər) *n.* a person who seeks to advance himself by altering his principles to suit the times or to gain support or favor —**time′serv′ing** *n., adj.*
**time signature** *Music* a sign, usually like a numerical fraction, after the key signature, indicating the time, or tempo
**time study** of operational or production procedures and the time consumed by them, with the intention of increasing efficiency: in full, **time and motion study**

**time·ta·ble** (-tā′b'l) *n.* a schedule of the times for things to happen, esp. of the times of arrival and departure of planes, trains, buses, etc.
**time-test·ed** (-tes′tid) *adj.* having value proved by long use or experience
**time warp** the condition or process of being displaced from one point in time to another, as in science fiction
**time·worn** (-wôrn′) *adj.* **1.** showing signs of wear or disrepair because of long use or existence **2.** hackneyed; trite
**time zone** *see* STANDARD TIME and chart at TIME
**tim·id** (tim′id) *adj.* [< L. < *timere*, to fear] **1.** easily frightened; shy **2.** showing lack of self-confidence —**ti·mid·i·ty** (tə mid′ə tē), **tim′id·ness** *n.* —**tim′id·ly** *adv.*
**tim·ing** (tī′miŋ) *n.* **1.** *a*) the regulation of the speed with which something is performed so as to produce the most effective results *b*) the pacing of scenes, as of a play, for total effect **2.** measurement of time
**Ti·mor** (tē′môr, ti môr′) island of Indonesia, in the SE Malay Archipelago: c. 13,000 sq. mi.
**tim·or·ous** (tim′ər əs) *adj.* [< MFr. < ML. < L. *timor*, fear] **1.** full of or subject to fear; timid **2.** showing or caused by timidity —**tim′or·ous·ly** *adv.* —**tim′or·ous·ness** *n.*
**Tim·o·thy** (tim′ə thē) [< Fr. < L. < Gr. < *timē*, honor + *theos*, god] **1.** a masculine name **2.** *Bible a*) a disciple of the Apostle Paul *b*) either of the epistles from the Apostle Paul to Timothy, books of the New Testament
**tim·o·thy** (tim′ə thē) *n.* [after *Timothy* Hanson, who took the seed to the Carolinas, c. 1720] a perennial grass with dense, cylindrical spikes, widely grown for hay
**tim·pa·ni** (tim′pə nē) *n.pl., sing.* **-pa·no′** (-nō′) [It.: see TYMPANUM] kettledrums; esp., a set of kettledrums of different pitches played by one performer in an orchestra —**tim′pa·nist** *n.*
**tin** (tin) *n.* [OE.] **1.** a soft, silver-white, metallic chemical element, easily shaped at ordinary temperatures: symbol, Sn; at. wt., 118.69; at. no., 50 **2.** *same as* TIN PLATE **3.** *a*) a pan, box, etc. made of tin plate *b*) [Chiefly Brit.] a can used for preserving food; also, its contents —*vt.* **tinned, tin′ning 1.** to plate with tin **2.** [Chiefly Brit.] to put in cans for preservation
**tin·a·mou** (tin′ə mōō′) *n.* [Fr. < Carib name, *tinamu*] a bird of South and Central America resembling the partridge and quail, but related to the ostrich
**tin can 1.** a can used for preserving food **2.** [Slang] *same as* DESTROYER (sense 2)
**tinc·ture** (tiŋk′chər) *n.* [< L. *tinctura* < pp. of *tingere*, to dye] **1.** orig., a dye **2.** a light color; tint; tinge **3.** a slight trace, smattering, etc. **4.** a medicinal substance in a solution of alcohol or alcohol and water —*vt.* **-tured, -tur·ing 1.** to color lightly; tint **2.** to give a slight trace to
**tin·der** (tin′dər) *n.* [OE. *tynder*] any dry, easily flammable material, esp. as formerly used for starting a fire from a spark made by flint and steel struck together
**tin·der·box** (-bäks′) *n.* **1.** formerly, a metal box for holding tinder, flint, and steel **2.** any highly flammable object, structure, etc. **3.** any place or situation in which trouble, war, etc. is likely to flare up
**tine** (tīn) *n.* [OE. *tind*] a sharp, projecting point; prong [the *tines* of a fork] —**tined** *adj.*
**tin ear** [Colloq.] a sense of hearing that is so poorly developed that one seems deaf to certain sounds, music, etc.
**tin·foil** (tin′foil′) *n.* a very thin sheet or sheets of tin or an alloy of tin and lead, etc. used as a wrapping for food products, in insulation, etc.
**ting¹** (tiŋ) *n.* [echoic] a single, light, ringing sound, as of a small bell —*vt., vi.* to make or cause to make a ting
**‡ting²** (tiŋ) *n. same as* THING²
**ting-a-ling** (tiŋ′ə liŋ′) *n.* the sound of a small bell ringing repeatedly
**tinge** (tinj) *vt.* **tinged, tinge′ing** or **ting′ing** [L. *tingere*, to dye] **1.** to color slightly; give a tint to **2.** to give a trace, slight flavor or odor, shade, etc. to [joy *tinged* with sorrow] —*n.* **1.** a slight coloring; tint **2.** a slight trace, flavor, odor, etc.
**tin·gle** (tiŋ′g'l) *vi.* **-gled, -gling** [< ME. var. of *tinklen*, to tinkle] **1.** to have a prickling or stinging feeling, as from cold, excitement, etc. **2.** to cause this feeling —*n.* this feeling —**tin′gler** *n.* —**tin′gly** *adj.* **-gli·er, -gli·est**
**tin god** a person unworthy of the honor or respect he demands or receives
**tin·horn** (tin′hôrn′) *adj.* [Slang] cheap, showy, and phony —*n.* [Slang] a tinhorn person, esp. a gambler
**tin·ker** (tiŋ′kər) *n.* [< ?] **1.** a person who mends pots, pans, etc., usually traveling at his trade **2.** a person who can make all kinds of minor repairs **3.** a clumsy or unskill-

ful worker; bungler —*vi.* **1.** to work as a tinker **2.** to make clumsy attempts to mend something **3.** to putter aimlessly —*vt.* to mend as a tinker —**tin′ker·er** *n.*

**tinker's damn** (or **dam**) [< prec. + DAMN: with reference to the lowly status and profane speech of tinkers] something of no value: esp. in **not worth a tinker's damn**

**Tin·ker·toy** (tiŋ′kər toi′) *a trademark for* a toy set of wooden dowels, joints, wheels, etc., used by children to assemble structures —*n.* [t-] anything resembling or suggesting such a structure

**tin·kle** (tiŋ′k'l) *vi.* **-kled, -kling** [echoic] to make a series of light, clinking sounds like those of a very small bell —*vt.* **1.** to cause to tinkle **2.** to indicate, signal, etc. by tinkling —*n.* the act or sound of tinkling —**tin′kler** *n.* —**tin′kly** *adj.* **-kli·er, -kli·est**

**tin liz·zie** (liz′ē) [orig. nickname of an early model of Ford automobile] any cheap or old automobile

**tin·ner** (tin′ər) *n.* **1.** a tin miner **2.** *same as* TINSMITH

**tin·ny** (tin′ē) *adj.* **-ni·er, -ni·est 1.** of or yielding tin **2.** like tin; bright but cheap; not durable **3.** of or like the sound made in striking a tin object —**tin′ni·ly** *adv.* —**tin′ni·ness** *n.*

**Tin Pan Alley 1.** the center of popular music publishing in New York City **2.** the publishers, writers, and promoters of popular music

**tin plate** thin sheets of iron or steel plated with tin —**tin′-plate′** *vt.* **-plat′ed, -plat′ing**

**tin·sel** (tin′s'l, -z'l) *n.* [< MFr. *estincelle* < OFr.: see STENCIL] **1.** formerly, a cloth interwoven with glittering threads of gold, silver, etc. **2.** thin sheets, strips, or threads of tin, metal foil, etc., used for decoration, as on Christmas trees **3.** something that looks showy and fine but is really cheap and of little value —*adj.* **1.** of or decorated with tinsel **2.** showy; gaudy —*vt.* **-seled** or **-selled, -sel·ing** or **-sel·ling 1.** to make glitter as with tinsel **2.** to give a showy, gaudy look to —**tin′sel·ly** *adj.*

**tin·smith** (tin′smith′) *n.* a person who works in tin or tin plate; maker of tinware: also **tin′man,** *pl.* **-men**

**tint** (tint) *n.* [< L. pp. of *tingere,* to dye] **1.** a delicate color or hue; tinge **2.** a color or shading of a color, esp. with reference to its mixture with white **3.** a dye for the hair **4.** *Engraving* an even shading produced by fine parallel lines —*vt.* to give a tint to —**tint′er** *n.*

**tin·tin·nab·u·la·tion** (tin′ti nab′yoo lā′shən) *n.* [< L. *tintinnabulum,* little bell] the ringing sound of bells

**Tin·to·ret·to** (tēn′tô ret′ō; *E.* tin′tə ret′ō), **Il** (ēl) (born *Jacopo Robusti*) 1518–94; Venetian painter

**tin·type** (tin′tīp′) *n.* an old kind of photograph taken directly on a sensitized plate of enameled tin or iron

**tin·ware** (-wer′) *n.* pots, pans, etc. of tin plate

**ti·ny** (tī′nē) *adj.* **-ni·er, -ni·est** [< ME. *tine,* a little (something)] very small; diminutive —**ti′ni·ly** *adv.* —**ti′ni·ness** *n.*

**-tion** (shən) [< Fr. < OFr. < L. *-tio* (gen. *-tionis*)] *a suffix meaning:* **1.** the act of *[correction]* **2.** the state of being *[elation]* **3.** the thing that is *[creation]*

**-tious** (shəs) [< Fr. < OFr. < L. *-tiosus*] a suffix used to form adjectives from nouns ending in -TION *[cautious]*

**tip¹** (tip) *n.* [ME. *tippe*] **1.** the pointed or rounded end or top of something **2.** something attached to the end, as a cap, ferrule, etc. **3.** a top or apex, as of a mountain —*vt.* **tipped, tip′ping 1.** to make a tip on **2.** to cover the tip or tips of (*with* something) **3.** to serve as the tip of —**tip in** to insert (a map, picture, etc.) by pasting along the inner edge in bookbinding

**tip²** (tip) *vt.* **tipped, tip′ping** [akin ? to prec.] **1.** to strike lightly and sharply; tap **2.** to give a small present of money to (a waiter, porter, etc.) for some service **3.** [Colloq.] to give secret information to (often with *off*) **4.** *Baseball a)* to hit (the ball) a glancing blow *b)* to glance off (the bat, glove, etc.): said of the ball —*vi.* to give a tip or tips —*n.* **1.** a light, sharp blow; tap **2.** a piece of secret information *[a tip on the race]* **3.** a suggestion, hint, warning, etc. **4.** a small present of money given to a waiter, porter, etc. for services; gratuity —**tip one's hand** (or **mitt**) [Slang] to reveal one's plans, etc., often without intending to —**tip′per** *n.*

**tip³** (tip) *vt.* **tipped, tip′ping** [< ?] **1.** to overturn or upset (often with *over*) **2.** to cause to tilt or slant **3.** to raise (one's hat) slightly in greeting someone —*vi.* **1.** to tilt or slant **2.** to overturn or topple (often with *over*) —*n.* a tipping or being tipped; tilt; slant —**tip the scales at** to weigh (a specified amount)

**tip-off** (tip′ôf′) *n.* a giving of secret information, a hint, warning, etc.

**tip·pet** (tip′it) *n.* [prob. dim. of *tip,* TIP¹] **1.** formerly, a long, hanging part of a hood, cape, or sleeve **2.** a scarflike garment of fur, wool, etc. for the neck and shoulders, hanging down in front

**tip·ple¹** (tip′'l) *vi., vt.* **-pled, -pling** [prob. < ME. *tipelar,* tavern-keeper < ?] to drink (alcoholic liquor) habitually —*n.* alcoholic liquor —**tip′pler** *n.*

**tip·ple²** (tip′'l) *n.* [< obs. freq. of TIP³] an apparatus for emptying coal, etc. from a mine car

**tip·py** (tip′ē) *adj.* **-pi·er, -pi·est** [Colloq.] that tips easily; not steady; shaky

**tip·py-toe, tip·py·toe** (-tō′) *n., adj., adv., vi.* **-toed′, -toe′ing** *colloq. var. of* TIPTOE

**tip·ster** (tip′stər) *n.* [Colloq.] a person who sells tips, as to people betting on horse races, speculating in stocks, etc.

**tip·sy** (tip′sē) *adj.* **-si·er, -si·est 1.** that tips easily; not steady **2.** crooked; awry **3.** somewhat drunk —**tip′si·ly** *adv.* —**tip′si·ness** *n.*

**tip·toe** (tip′tō′) *n.* the tip of a toe or the tips of the toes —*vi.* **-toed′, -toe′ing** to walk stealthily or cautiously on one's tiptoes —*adj.* **1.** standing on one's tiptoes **2.** *a)* lifted up; exalted *b)* eager; alert *c)* stealthy; cautious —*adv.* on tiptoe —**on tiptoe 1.** on one's tiptoes **2.** eager or eagerly **3.** silently; stealthily

**tip·top** (-täp′) *n.* [TIP¹ + TOP¹] **1.** the highest point; very top **2.** [Colloq.] the highest in quality or excellence; best —*adj., adv.* **1.** at the highest point, or top **2.** [Colloq.] at the highest point of excellence, health, etc.

**ti·rade** (tī′rād, tī rād′) *n.* [Fr. < It. *tirata,* a volley < pp. of *tirare,* to fire] a long, vehement speech or denunciation; harangue

**Ti·ra·na** (ti rä′nə) capital of Albania, in the C part: pop. 169,000: also, Albanian **Ti·ra·në** (tē rä′nə)

**tire¹** (tīr) *vt., vi.* **tired, tir′ing** [OE. *tiorian*] **1.** to make or become weary or fatigued, as by exertion **2.** to make or become bored or impatient, as by dull talk

**tire²** (tīr) *n.* [prob. var. of ME. *atir,* equipment] a hoop of iron or rubber, or a rubber tube filled with air, fixed around the wheel of a vehicle to form a tread —*vt.* **tired, tir′ing** to furnish with tires

**tired** (tīrd) *adj.* **1.** fatigued; weary **2.** stale; hackneyed —**tired′ly** *adv.* —**tired′ness** *n.*

**tire·less** (tīr′lis) *adj.* that does not become tired —**tire′less·ly** *adv.* —**tire′less·ness** *n.*

**tire·some** (-səm) *adj.* **1.** tiring; boring **2.** annoying; irksome —**tire′some·ly** *adv.* —**tire′some·ness** *n.*

**ti·ro** (tī′rō) *n., pl.* **-ros** *var. sp. of* TYRO

**Tir·ol** (tir′äl, tī′rōl, ti rōl′) E Alpine region in W Austria & N Italy —**Ti·ro·le·an** (ti rō′lē ən) *adj., n.* —**Tir·o·lese** (tir′ə lēz′) *adj., n., pl.* **-lese′**

**'tis** (tiz) it is

**Tish·ah b'Ab** (tē shä′ bə äv′, tish′ə bôv′) a Jewish fast day commemorating the destruction of the Temple, observed on the 9th day of Ab

**Tish·ri** (tish rē′, tish′rē) *n.* the first month of the Jewish year: see JEWISH CALENDAR

**tis·sue** (tish′σ̄σ; *chiefly Brit.* tis′yōō) *n.* [< OFr. *tissu* < pp. of *tistre* < L. *texere,* to weave] **1.** cloth; esp., light, thin cloth, as gauze **2.** a tangled mass or series; mesh; network; web *[a tissue of lies]* **3.** a piece of soft, absorbent paper, used as a disposable handkerchief, as toilet paper, etc. **4.** *a) same as* TISSUE PAPER *b)* a sheet of tissue paper **5.** *Biol. a)* the substance of an organic body or organ, consisting of cells and the material between them *b)* any substance of this kind having a particular function *[epithelial tissue]* —*vt.* **-sued, -su·ing** to cover with tissue

**tissue paper** very thin, unglazed, nearly transparent paper, as for wrapping things, making tracings, etc.

**tit¹** (tit) *n.* [TIT(MOUSE)] a titmouse or other small bird

**tit²** (tit) *n.* [OE.] *same as* TEAT

**Tit.** Titus

**Ti·tan** (tīt′'n) *poetic name for* HELIOS —*n.* **1.** *Gr. Myth.* any of a race of giant deities who were overthrown by the Olympian gods **2.** [t-] any person or thing of great size or power —*adj.* [*also* t-] *same as* TITANIC —**Ti′tan·ess** *n.fem.*

**Ti·ta·ni·a** (ti tā′nē ə, tī-) in early folklore, the queen of fairyland and wife of Oberon

**Ti·tan·ic** (tī tan′ik) *adj.* **1.** of or like the Titans **2.** [t-] of great size, strength, or power —**ti·tan′i·cal·ly** *adv.*

**ti·ta·ni·um** (tī tā′nē əm, ti-) *n.* [ModL. < Gr. pl. of *Titan,* a Titan] a silvery or dark-gray, lustrous, metallic chemical element found in various minerals and used as a deoxidizing agent in molten steel: symbol, Ti; at. wt., 47.90; at. no., 22

**titanium dioxide** a compound, $TiO_2$, used esp. as a white pigment

**tit for tat** [var. of earlier *tip for tap:* see TIP²] this in return for that, as blow for blow

**tithe** (tīth) *n.* [OE. *teothe,* a tenth] **1.** one tenth of the annual produce of one's land or of one's annual income, paid as a contribution to support a church or its clergy **2.** *a)* a tenth part *b)* any small part **3.** any tax or levy —*vt., vi.* **tithed, tith′ing** to pay a tithe of (one's income, etc.) —**tith′a·ble** *adj.* —**tith′er** *n.*

**Ti·tian** (tish′ən) (It. name *Tiziano Vecellio*) 1490?–1576; Venetian painter

**ti·tian** (tish′ən) *n.* [from the hair color in many of *Titian's* portraits] reddish yellow

**Ti·ti·ca·ca** (tit′ē kä′kə; *Sp.* tē′tē kä′kä), **Lake** largest lake in S. America, on the border of SE Peru & W Bolivia

**tit·il·late** (tit'′l āt') *vt.* **-lat′ed, -lat′ing** [< L. pp. of *titillare,* to tickle] **1.** *same as* TICKLE **2.** to excite or stimulate pleasurably —**tit′il·lat′er** *n.* —**tit′il·la′tion** *n.* —**tit′il·la′tive** *adj.*

**tit·i·vate** (tit'ə vāt') *vt., vi.* **-vat′ed, -vat′ing** [prob. < TIDY, with quasi-Latin suffix] to dress up; spruce up —**tit′i·va′tion** *n.*

**tit·lark** (tit'lärk') *n.* [TIT[1] + LARK[1]] *same as* PIPIT

**ti·tle** (tīt'′l) *n.* [OFr. < L. *titulus*] **1.** the name of a book, chapter, poem, picture, piece of music, play, etc. **2.** *a) short for* TITLE PAGE *b)* a literary work having a particular title [50 new *titles* published in the fall] **3.** a descriptive name; epithet **4.** a word used to show the rank, office, occupation, etc. of a person [*"Duke," "Mayor," and "Dr."* are *titles*] **5.** a claim or right **6.** *Law a)* a right to ownership, esp. of real estate *b)* evidence of such right *c)* a document stating such a right; deed **7.** a championship, esp. in sports **8.** *Motion Pictures, TV* words shown on the screen that give credits, translations, etc. —*vt.* **-tled, -tling** to give a title to; name; entitle

**ti·tle·hold·er** (-hōl′dər) *n.* the holder of a title; specif., the winner of a championship, as in some sport

**title page** the page in the front of a book that gives the title, author, publisher, etc.

**title role** (or **part** or **character**) the character in a play, movie, etc. whose name is used as or in its title

**ti·tlist** (tīt'list) *n.* a titleholder in some sport

**tit·mouse** (tit'mous') *n., pl.* **-mice′** (-mīs') [ME. *titemose,* prob. < *tit-,* little + OE. *mase,* titmouse] a small bird found throughout the world except in S. America and Australia; esp., the **tufted titmouse,** with a crest on the head, common in the eastern U.S.

**Ti·to** (tē′tō), Marshal (born *Josip Broz*) 1892–1980; Communist party leader of Yugoslavia; president (1953–80)

**ti·trate** (tī′trāt) *vt., vi.* **-trat·ed, -trat·ing** [< Fr. *titrer* < *titre,* a standard < OFr. *title,* TITLE + -ATE[1]] to test by or be subjected to titration

**ti·tra·tion** (tī trā′shən) *n. Chem.* the process of finding out how much of a substance is in a known volume of a solution by measuring the volume of a solution of known concentration added to produce a given reaction

**tit-tat-toe** (tit'tat tō') *n. same as* TICK-TACK-TOE

**tit·ter** (tit'ər) *vi.* [echoic] to laugh in a half-suppressed way, suggestive of silliness, nervousness, etc.; giggle —*n.* the act or an instance of tittering —**tit′ter·er** *n.*

**tit·tle** (tit'′l) *n.* [ME. *title,* orig. same word as TITLE] **1.** formerly, a dot or other small mark used as a diacritic **2.** a very small particle; iota; jot

**tit·tle-tat·tle** (tit'′l tat'′l) *n., vi.* **-tled, -tling** [redupl. of *tattle*] gossip; chatter

**tit·u·lar** (tich'ə lər; *chiefly Brit.* tit'yə-) *adj.* [< L. *titulus,* title] **1.** of, or having the nature of, a title **2.** having a title **3.** existing only in title; in name only [a *titular* leader] **4.** from whom or which the title or name is taken —**tit′u·lar·ly** *adv.*

**Ti·tus** (tīt'əs) *Bible* a book of the New Testament, which was an epistle of the Apostle Paul to his disciple Titus

**tiz·zy** (tiz'ē) *n., pl.* **-zies** [< ?] [Colloq.] a state of frenzied excitement, esp. over some trivial matter

**TKO, T.K.O.** *Boxing abbrev. of* TECHNICAL KNOCKOUT

**Tl** *Chem.* thallium

**TLC, T.L.C., t.l.c.** tender, loving care

**Tm** *Chem.* thulium

**T-man** (tē′man′) *n., pl.* **T′-men′** (-men′) [< *T(reasury)-man*] [Colloq.] a law-enforcement agent of the U.S. Department of the Treasury

**TN** Tennessee

**tn.** **1.** ton(s) **2.** training

**TNT, T.N.T.** trinitrotoluene

**to** (tōō; *unstressed* too, tə) *prep.* [OE.] **1.** *a)* in the direction of; toward [turn to the left] *b)* in the direction of and reaching [he went *to* Boston] **2.** as far as [wet *to* the skin] **3.** into a condition of [a rise *to* fame] **4.** on, onto, against, at, next, etc. [tie it *to* the post] **5.** *a)* until [from noon *to* night] *b)* before [the time is ten *to* six] **6.** for the purpose of [come *to* my aid] **7.** *a)* as concerns; in respect of [open *to* attack] *b)* in the opinion of [it seems *to* me] **8.** producing or resulting in [torn *to* pieces] **9.** with; along with [add this *to* the rest] **10.** belonging with [the key *to* this house] **11.** as compared with; as against [a score of 7 *to* 0] **12.** *a)* in agreement or correspondence with [not *to* my taste] *b)* in response to [come *to* my call] **13.** constituting; in [ten *to* the peck] **14.** to the limit of [moderate *to* high prices] **15.** with (a specified person or thing) as the recipient, or indirect object, of the action [give the book *to* her] **16.** in honor of [a toast *to* you] *To* is also used as a sign of the infinitive (Ex.: it is easy *to* read) —*adv.* **1.** forward [his hat is on wrong side *to*] **2.** in the normal or desired position or direction; esp., shut or closed [the door was blown *to*] **3.** to the matter at hand [let's all fall *to*] **4.** at hand [we were close *to* when it fell] —**to and fro** back and forth

**toad** (tōd) *n.* [OE. *tade*] **1.** any of a group of tailless, leaping amphibians with a rough, warty skin, that live on moist land rather than in water, except during breeding **2.** a person regarded as loathsome, contemptible, etc.

**TOAD** (½–9 in. long)

**toad·fish** (-fish') *n., pl.* **-fish′, -fish′es:** see FISH any of various scaleless fishes with froglike heads, found in shallows off the Atlantic coast of N. America

**toad·stool** (-stōōl') *n.* a mushroom; esp., in popular usage, any poisonous mushroom

**toad·y** (tōd′ē) *n., pl.* **toad′ies** [short for *toadeater,* quack doctor's assistant who pretended to eat toads and then drank the quack's cure-all] a person who flatters and serves others in any way to gain favor: also **toad′eat′er** —*vt., vi.* **toad′ied, toad′y·ing** to be a toady (to); flatter —**toad′y·ism** *n.*

**to-and-fro** (tōō′ən frō′) *adj.* moving forward and backward; back-and-forth

**toast[1]** (tōst) *vt.* [< OFr., ult. < L. pp. of *torrere,* to parch] **1.** to brown the surface of (bread, etc.) by heating **2.** to warm thoroughly [*toast* yourself by the fire] —*vi.* to become toasted —*n.* sliced bread made brown and crisp by heat —**toast′er** *n.*

**toast[2]** (tōst) *n.* [< the toasted spiced bread formerly put in the wine] **1.** a person, thing, idea, etc. in honor of which glasses of wine, etc. are raised and drunk **2.** *a)* a proposal to drink to some person, etc. *b)* such a drink **3.** any person greatly acclaimed —*vt., vi.* to propose or drink a toast (to) —**toast′er** *n.*

**toast·mas·ter** (tōst′mas′tər) *n.* the person at a banquet who proposes toasts, introduces after-dinner speakers, etc. —**toast′mis′tress** (-mis′trəs) *n.fem.*

**toast·y** (tōs′tē) *adj.* **toast′i·er, toast′i·est 1.** of or characteristic of toast **2.** warm and comfortable or cozy

**Tob.** Tobit

**to·bac·co** (tə bak′ō) *n., pl.* **-cos** [Sp. *tabaco* < WInd., pipe in which the Indians smoked the plant] **1.** any of various plants of the nightshade family, with large leaves and white, yellow, greenish, or purple flowers, esp. a species widely cultivated for its leaves **2.** these leaves, prepared for smoking, chewing, or snuffing **3.** cigars, cigarettes, snuff, etc. **4.** the use of tobacco for smoking, etc.

**to·bac·co·nist** (tə bak′ə nist) *n.* [Chiefly Brit.] a dealer in tobacco and other smoking supplies

**To·ba·go** (tō bā′gō, tə-) island in the West Indies, northeast of Trinidad: 116 sq. mi. See TRINIDAD AND TOBAGO

**To·bit** (tō′bit) a book of the Apocrypha

**to·bog·gan** (tə bäg′ən) *n.* [CanadFr. *tabagan* < Algonquian] a long, narrow, flat sled without runners, curved back at the front end: now used for coasting downhill —*vi.* **1.** to coast, travel, etc. on a toboggan **2.** to decline rapidly —**to·bog′gan·er, to·bog′gan·ist** *n.*

**TOBOGGAN**

**To·by** (tō′bē) *n., pl.* **-bies** [< *Toby,* dim. of *Tobias,* ult. < Heb. *tōbhīyāh,* lit., the lord is good] a jug or mug for ale or beer shaped like a stout man with a three-cornered hat: also **Toby jug**

**toc·ca·ta** (tə kät′ə) *n.* [It. < pp. of *toccare,* to touch < L.] a composition in free style for the organ, piano, etc., often used as a prelude of a fugue

**to·coph·er·ol** (tō käf′ə rôl', -rōl') *n.* [< Gr. *tokos,* childbirth + *pherein,* to BEAR[1] + -OL] any of the four related oils that compose vitamin E and occur chiefly in wheat-germ oil, cottonseed oil, lettuce, etc.

**Tocque·ville** (tôk nel′; E. tōk′vil), **A·lex·is** (**Charles Henri Maurice Clérel**) **de** (à lek sē′ də) 1805–59; Fr. writer & statesman

**toc·sin** (täk′sin) *n.* [Fr. < MFr. < Pr. < *toc,* a stroke + *senh,* a bell < L. *signum,* a sign] **1.** *a)* an alarm bell *b)* its sound **2.** any alarm

**to·day** (tə dā′) *adv.* [OE. *to dæg*] **1.** on or during the present day **2.** in the present time or age; nowadays —*n.* **1.** the present day **2.** the present time or period Also, esp. formerly, **to-day**

**tod·dle** (täd′′l) *vi.* **-dled, -dling** [? freq. of TOTTER] to walk with short, uncertain steps, as a child —*n.* a toddling —**tod′dler** *n.*

**tod·dy** (täd′ē) *n., pl.* **-dies** [Anglo-Ind. < Hindi *tārī,* fermented sap < *tār,* palm tree] **1.** the sweet or fermented sap of various East Indian palms, used as a beverage **2.** a drink of brandy, whiskey, etc. mixed with hot water, sugar, etc.: also **hot toddy**

**to-do** (tə dōō′) *n.* [Colloq.] a commotion; fuss

**toe** (tō) *n.* [OE. *ta*] **1.** *a)* any of the digits of the foot *b)* the forepart of the foot *c)* that part of a shoe, sock, etc. which covers the toes **2.** anything like a toe in location, shape, or function —*vt.* **toed, toe′ing 1.** to touch, kick, etc. with the toes **2.** *a)* to drive (a nail) slantingly *b)* to fasten with nails so driven; toenail —*vi.* to stand, walk, or be formed so that the toes are in a specified position /*to toe in*/ —**on one's toes** [Colloq.] mentally or physically alert —**step** (or **tread**) **on someone's toes** to offend someone, esp. by intruding on his rights —**toe the line** (or **mark**) to follow orders, rules, etc. strictly —**toe′like′** *adj.*

**toed** (tōd) *adj.* having (a specified kind or number of) toes: usually in hyphenated compounds /*pigeon-toed*/

**toe dance** a dance performed on the tips of the toes, as in ballet —**toe′-dance′** *vi.* **-danced′, -danc′ing** —**toe′-danc′er** *n.*

**toe·hold** (tō′hōld′) *n.* **1.** a small space or ledge for supporting the toe of the foot in climbing, etc. **2.** any means of surmounting obstacles, gaining entry, etc. **3.** a slight footing or advantage **4.** *Wrestling* a hold in which one wrestler twists the other's foot

**toe·less** (-lis) *adj.* **1.** having no toe or toes **2.** having the toe open /*toeless shoes*/

**toe·nail** (-nāl′) *n.* **1.** the nail of a toe **2.** *Carpentry* a nail driven slantingly —*vt. Carpentry* to fasten with a toenail

**toff** (täf, tôf) *n.* [< *toft*, var. of TUFT] [Brit. Slang] a fashionable, upper-class person; esp., a dandy

**tof·fee, tof·fy** (tôf′ē, täf′-) *n.* [later Brit. form of TAFFY] a hard, chewy candy made with brown sugar or molasses, often with nuts; kind of taffy

**tog** (täg, tôg) *n.* [prob. ult. < L. *toga*, TOGA] [*pl.*] [Colloq.] clothes —*vt., vi.* **togged, tog′ging** [Colloq.] to dress (usually with *up* or *out*)

**to·ga** (tō′gə) *n., pl.* **-gas, -gae** (-jē) [L. < *tegere*, to cover] **1.** in ancient Rome, a loose, one-piece outer garment worn in public by citizens **2.** a robe of office —**to′gaed** (-gəd) *adj.*

**to·geth·er** (tə geth′ər) *adv.* [< OE. < *to* (see TO) + *gædre*, together < base of *gaderian*, to gather] **1.** in or into one gathering, group, or place /the family ate *together*/ **2.** in or into contact, collision, union, etc. /the cars skidded *together*/ **3.** considered collectively /he won more than all of us *together*/ **4.** *a)* with one another; in association /to live *together*/ *b)* by joint effort /*together* they lifted the sofa/ **5.** at the same time /shots fired *together*/ **6.** in succession; continuously /he worked for two days *together*/ **7.** in or into agreement, cooperation, etc. /let's get *together*/ **8.** in or into a unified whole —*adj.* [Slang] having fully developed one's abilities, ambitions, etc.

**to·geth·er·ness** (-nis) *n.* the spending of much time together, as by a family in leisure-time activities, esp. in an effort to make the family more stable and unified

**tog·ger·y** (täg′ər ē, tôg′-) *n.* [Colloq.] clothes; togs

**tog·gle** (täg′'l) *n.* [prob. < dial. *tuggle*, freq. of TUG] **1.** a rod, pin, or bolt for insertion through a loop of a rope, a link of a chain, etc. to make an attachment, prevent slipping, etc. **2.** a toggle joint or a device having one —*vt.* **-gled, -gling** to provide or fasten with a toggle

**toggle joint** a knee-shaped joint consisting of two bars pivoted together at one end: pressure put on the joint to straighten it transmits opposite, outward pressure to the open ends

**toggle switch** a switch consisting of a projecting lever moved back and forth through a small arc to open or close an electric circuit

**To·go** (tō′gō) country in W Africa, on the Atlantic, east of Ghana: 21,853 sq. mi.; pop. 1,914,000 —**To′go·lese′** (-lēz′) *adj., n., pl.* **-lese′**

**toil**[1] (toil) *vi.* [Anglo-Fr. *toiler*, to strive < OFr. < L. *tudiculare*, to stir about, ult. < *tudes*, mallet] **1.** to work hard and continuously **2.** to go or move slowly with pain or effort /to *toil* up a hill/ —*vt.* [Now Rare] to accomplish with great effort /to *toil* one's way/ —*n.* **1.** hard, exhausting work or effort **2.** a task performed by such effort —**toil′er** *n.*

**toil**[2] (toil) *n.* [OFr. *toile* < L. *tela*, a web] **1.** [Archaic] a net for trapping **2.** [*pl.*] any snare suggestive of a net

**toi·let** (toi′lit) *n.* [MFr. *toilette* < *toile*, cloth: see prec.] **1.** formerly, a dressing table **2.** the act of dressing or grooming oneself **3.** dress; attire **4.** *a)* a room, shelter, etc. for discharging wastes from the body; specif., a small room with a bowl-shaped fixture for this purpose that flushes with water *b)* such a fixture —*adj.* **1.** of or for grooming oneself **2.** for a toilet (*n.* 4b) —**make one's toilet** [Now Rare] to bathe, dress, arrange one's hair, etc.

**toilet paper** (or **tissue**) soft, absorbent paper, for cleaning oneself after discharging waste from the body

TOGGLE JOINT
(arrows indicate direction of pressure)

**toi·let·ry** (toi′lə trē) *n., pl.* **-ries** soap, lotion, cologne, etc. used in cleaning and grooming oneself

**toi·lette** (twä let′, toi-) *n.* [Fr.: see TOILET] **1.** the process of grooming oneself, including bathing, hairdressing, dressing, etc.: said of women **2.** dress or manner of dress; attire

**toilet training** the training of a young child to use a toilet when he needs to discharge bodily waste

**toilet water** a perfumed, slightly alcoholic liquid applied to the skin after bathing, shaving, etc.

**toil·some** (toil′səm) *adj.* requiring toil; laborious —**toil′-some·ly** *adv.* —**toil′some·ness** *n.*

**toil·worn** (-wôrn′) *adj.* worn out by toil

**To·kay** (tō kā′) *n.* **1.** a sweet, rich wine made in Tokay, Hungary **2.** any wine like this **3.** a large, sweet grape used for the wine

**toke** (tōk) *n.* [? < ff.] [Slang] a puff on a cigarette, esp. one of marijuana or hashish

**to·ken** (tō′k'n) *n.* [OE. *tacn*] **1.** a sign, indication, or symbol /a *token* of one's affection/ **2.** something serving as a sign of authority, identity, etc. **3.** a distinguishing mark or feature **4.** a keepsake **5.** a metal disk with a face value higher than its real value, issued as a substitute for currency, for use as fare on a bus, etc. —*vt.* to be a token of —*adj.* **1.** by way of a token, symbol, etc. **2.** merely simulated; slight or of no real account /*token* resistance/ —**by the same** (or **this**) **token** following from this —**in token of** as evidence of

**to·ken·ism** (-iz'm) *n.* a pretending to act on a principle by doing so in a very small way; specif., token integration of Negroes, as in schools, jobs, etc.

**To·ky·o** (tō′kē ō′; *Jap.* tô′kyôᵈ) capital of Japan, on the S coast of Honshu: pop. 8,907,000 (met. area 19,500,000) —**To′ky·o·ite′** (-īt′) *n.*

**told** (tōld) *pt. & pp. of* TELL —**all told** all (being) counted; in all /there were ten *all told*/

**tole** (tōl) *n.* [Fr. *tôle*, sheet iron < *table*, TABLE] a type of lacquered or enameled metalware used for trays, lamps, etc.

**To·le·do** (tə lē′dō; *also for 2, Sp.* tô lā′thô) **1.** [after ff.] port in NW Ohio, on Lake Erie: pop. 355,000 (met. area 791,000) **2.** city in C Spain: pop. 40,000 —*n., pl.* **-dos** a fine-tempered sword or sword blade made in Toledo, Spain

**tol·er·a·ble** (täl′ər ə b'l) *adj.* **1.** that can be tolerated; endurable **2.** fairly good; passable **3.** [Colloq.] in fairly good health —**tol′er·a·bil′i·ty, tol′er·a·ble·ness** *n.* —**tol′er·a·bly** *adv.*

**tol·er·ance** (-əns) *n.* **1.** a tolerating or being tolerant of others' beliefs, practices, etc. **2.** the amount of variation allowed from a standard, accuracy, etc.; specif., the difference between the allowable maximum and minimum sizes of some mechanical part **3.** *Med.* the ability to resist the effects of a drug, etc. taken over a period of time or in larger and larger doses

**tol·er·ant** (-ənt) *adj.* **1.** having or showing tolerance of others' beliefs, practices, etc. **2.** *Med.* of or having tolerance —**tol′er·ant·ly** *adv.*

**tol·er·ate** (täl′ə rāt′) *vt.* **-at′ed, -at′ing** [< L. pp. of *tolerare*, to bear] **1.** to allow; permit **2.** to recognize and respect (others' beliefs, practices, etc.) without sharing them **3.** to put up with; bear **4.** *Med.* to have tolerance for (a specific drug, etc.) —**tol′er·a′tive** *adj.* —**tol′er·a′tor** *n.*

**tol·er·a·tion** (täl′ə rā′shən) *n.* tolerance; esp., freedom to hold religious views that differ from the established ones

**toll**[1] (tōl) *n.* [OE., prob. ult. < Gr. *telos*, tax] **1.** a tax or charge for a privilege, esp. for permission to use a bridge, highway, etc. **2.** the right to demand toll **3.** a charge for some service, as for a long-distance telephone call **4.** the number lost, taken, etc. /the storm took a heavy *toll* of lives/ —*vt.* [Now Rare] **1.** to impose a toll on **2.** to gather (something) as toll

**toll**[2] (tōl) *vt.* [< ? OE. *-tillan*, to touch] **1.** to ring (a church bell, etc.) slowly with regular strokes, as for announcing a death **2.** to sound (the hour, a knell, etc.) by this **3.** to announce, summon, etc. by this —*vi.* to sound or ring slowly: said of a bell —*n.* **1.** the act or sound of tolling a bell **2.** a single stroke of the bell —**toll′er** *n.*

**toll bar** a bar, gate, etc. for stopping travel at a point where toll is taken

**toll·booth** (tōl′bōōth′) *n.* a booth at which toll is collected, as before entering a toll road

**toll bridge** a bridge at which toll is paid for passage

**toll call** a long-distance telephone call, for which there is a charge beyond the local rate

**toll·gate** (-gāt′) *n.* a gate for stopping travel at a point where toll is taken

**toll·keep·er** (-kēp′ər) *n.* a person who collects tolls at a tollgate

**toll road** a road on which toll must be paid

**Tol·stoy** (tôl stoi′; *E.* täl′stoi, tōl′-), Count Lev (E. Leo) **Ni·ko·la·ye·vich** (lyev nē′kô lä′ye vich) 1828–1910; Russ. novelist & social theorist: also sp. **Tolstoi**

**Tol·tec** (täl′tek, tōl′-) *n.* any of a group of Nahuatl Indians who were dominant in Mexico before the rise of the Aztecs —*adj.* of the Toltecs or their culture: also **Tol′tec·an**

**to·lu** (**balsam**) (tō loo′) [< Sp. < *Tolú*, seaport in Colombia] a fragrant resin obtained from a S. American tree: it is used in cough syrups, etc.

**tol·u·ene** (täl′yoo wēn′) *n.* [TOLU + (BENZ)ENE] a liquid hydrocarbon, $C_7H_8$, first obtained from tolu balsam but now from coal tar, petroleum, etc.: it is used in making dyes, explosives, etc.: also **tol′u·ol′** (-wôl′, -wōl′)

**tom** (täm) *n.* [< *Tom*, dim. of THOMAS] the male of some animals, esp. of the cat —*adj.* male [a tom turkey]

**tom·a·hawk** (täm′ə hôk′) *n.* [< Algonquian] a light ax with a head of stone, used by North American Indians as a tool and as a weapon —*vt.* to hit, cut, or kill with a tomahawk

**Tom and Jerry** (jer′ē) a hot drink made of rum, etc., beaten eggs, sugar, water or milk, and nutmeg

**to·ma·to** (tə māt′ō, -mät′ō) *n., pl.* **-toes** [< Sp. < Nahuatl *tomatl*] 1. a red or yellowish fruit with a juicy pulp, used as a vegetable: botanically it is a berry 2. the plant that it grows on

**tomb** (toom) *n.* [< Anglo-Fr. < LL. < Gr. *tymbos*] 1. a vault, chamber, or grave for the dead 2. a burial monument —**the tomb** death —**tomb′less** *adj.* —**tomb′like′** *adj.*

**tom·boy** (täm′boi′) *n.* a girl who behaves or plays like an active boy —**tom′boy′ish** *adj.* —**tom′boy′ish·ly** *adv.* —**tom′boy′ish·ness** *n.*

**tomb·stone** (toom′stōn′) *n.* a stone, usually with an inscription, marking a tomb or grave

**tom·cat** (täm′kat′) *n.* a male cat —*vi.* **-cat′ted, -cat′ting** [Slang] to be sexually promiscuous: said of a man

**Tom Collins** *see* COLLINS

**Tom, Dick, and Harry** everyone; anyone: usually preceded by *every* and used disparagingly

**tome** (tōm) *n.* [Fr. < L. < Gr. *tomos*, piece cut off] 1. orig., any volume of a work of several volumes 2. a book, esp. a large or ponderous one

**tom·fool** (täm′fool′) *n.* a foolish, stupid, or silly person —*adj.* foolish, stupid, or silly

**tom·fool·er·y** (-ər ē) *n., pl.* **-er·ies** foolish or silly behavior; nonsense

**Tom·my** (täm′ē) *n., pl.* **-mies** [< *Tommy Atkins* (for *Thomas Atkins*, fictitious name used in Brit. army sample forms)] [also t-] *epithet for* a private in the British army

**Tommy gun** alternate trademark for THOMPSON SUBMACHINE GUN —*n.* a submachine gun

**tom·my·rot** (täm′ē rät′) *n.* [Slang] nonsense; foolishness

**to·mor·row** (tə mär′ō, -môr′ō) *adv.* [OE. *to morgen*] 1. on the day after today 2. at some time in the future —*n.* 1. the day after today 2. some time in the future Also, esp. formerly, **to-morrow**

**Tom Thumb** 1. a tiny hero of English folk tales 2. any midget or small person

**tom·tit** (täm′tit′) *n.* [Chiefly Brit.] a titmouse or any of various other small birds

**tom-tom** (täm′täm′) *n.* [Hindi *tam-tam*] a simple kind of deep drum with a small head, usually beaten with the hands

**-to·my** (tə mē) [< Gr. < *temnein*, to cut] a combining form meaning: 1. a dividing [dichotomy] 2. a surgical operation [lithotomy]

**ton** (tun) *n.* [var. of TUN] 1. a unit of weight equal to 2,000 pounds avoirdupois, commonly used in the U.S., Canada, South Africa, etc.: in full, **short ton** 2. a unit of weight equal to 2,240 pounds avoirdupois, commonly used in Great Britain: in full, **long ton** 3. *same as* METRIC TON 4. a unit of internal capacity of ships, equal to 100 cubic feet: in full, **register ton** 5. a unit of carrying capacity of ships, usually equal to 40 cubic feet: in full, **measurement ton, freight ton** 6. a unit for measuring displacement of ships, equal to 35 cubic feet: it is nearly equal to the volume of a long ton of sea water: in full, **displacement ton** 7. a unit of cooling capacity of an air conditioner, equal to 12,000 B.t.u. per hour 8. [often pl.] [Colloq.] a very large amount or number Abbrev. **T., t., tn.** (*sing. & pl.*)

**ton·al** (tō′n'l) *adj.* of a tone or tonality —**ton′al·ly** *adv.*

**to·nal·i·ty** (tō nal′ə tē) *n., pl.* **-ties** 1. a quality of tone 2. *Art* the color scheme in a painting 3. *Music a)* same as KEY[1] *b)* tonal character as determined by the relationship of the tones to the keynote

**ton·do** (tän′dō) *n., pl.* **-di** (-dē), **-dos** [It., a plate] a round painting

**tone** (tōn) *n.* [< OFr. < L. < Gr. *tonos* < *teinein*, to stretch] 1. *a)* a vocal or musical sound *b)* its quality 2. an intonation, pitch, modulation, etc. of the voice that expresses a particular feeling [a *tone* of contempt] 3. a way of wording or expressing things that shows a certain attitude [the friendly *tone* of her letter] 4. normal resilience [rubber that has lost its *tone*] 5. *a)* the style, character, spirit, etc. of a place or period *b)* distinctive style; elegance 6. a

quality of color; tint or shade 7. *Linguis.* the relative height of pitch with which a syllable, word, etc. is pronounced 8. *Music a)* a sound of distinct pitch (as distinguished from a noise) that may be put into harmonic relation with other such sounds *b)* the simple tone of a musical sound as distinguished from its overtones *c)* any one of the full intervals of a diatonic scale; whole step 9. *Painting* the effect produced by the combination of light, shade, and color 10. *Physiol.* the condition of an organism, organ, muscle, etc. with reference to its normal, healthy functioning: see also TONUS —*vt.* **toned, ton′ing** 1. [Rare] *same as* INTONE 2. to give a tone to 3. to change the tone of —*vi.* to take on a tone —**tone down** 1. to make or become less bright, sharp, etc.; soften 2. to make (something written or said) less harsh —**tone in with** to harmonize with —**tone up** 1. to give a more intense tone to 2. to become strengthened or heightened —**tone′less** *adj.* —**tone′less·ly** *adv.* —**tone′less·ness** *n.* —**ton′er** *n.*

**tone arm** the pivoted arm containing the pickup on a phonograph

**tone color** *same as* TIMBRE

**tone-deaf** (-def′) *adj.* not able to distinguish accurately differences in musical pitch —**tone′-deaf′ness** *n.*

**tone poem** *same as* SYMPHONIC POEM

**tone row** (or **series**) *see* TWELVE-TONE

**tong**[1] (tôŋ, täŋ) *vt.* to seize, collect, handle, or hold with tongs —*vi.* to use tongs

**tong**[2] (tôŋ, täŋ) *n.* [Chin. *t'ang*, a meeting place] a Chinese association, society, etc.

**Ton·ga** (täŋ′gə) country on a group of islands (**Tonga Islands**) in the South Pacific, east of Fiji: a member of the Commonwealth: 270 sq. mi.; pop. 86,000

**Ton·gan** (-gən) *n.* 1. a native of Tonga 2. the Polynesian language of the Tongans

**tongs** (tôŋz, täŋz) *n.pl.* [*sometimes with sing. v.*] [OE. *tange*] a device for seizing or lifting objects, with two arms pivoted or hinged together: also called **pair of tongs**

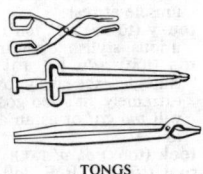

TONGS

**tongue** (tuŋ) *n.* [OE. *tunge*] 1. the movable muscular structure attached to the floor of the mouth: it is used in eating, tasting, and (in man) speaking 2. an animal's tongue used as food 3. *a)* talk; speech *b)* a manner of speaking in regard to tone, diction, etc. [a glib *tongue*] 4. a language or dialect 5. [pl.] *see* GLOSSOLALIA 6. something like a tongue in shape, position, motion, or use; specif., *a)* the flap under the laces of a shoe *b)* the clapper of a bell *c)* the pole of a wagon, etc. *d)* the projecting tenon of a tongue-and-groove joint *e)* the vibrating end of the reed in a wind instrument *f)* a narrow strip of land extending into a sea, river, etc. *g)* a long, narrow flame —*vt.* **tongued, tongu′ing** 1. [Archaic] to speak 2. to touch, lick, etc. with the tongue 3. *Music* to play by tonguing: see TONGUING —*vi.* 1. to project like a tongue 2. *Music* to use tonguing: see TONGUING —**find one's tongue** to recover the ability to talk, as after shock —**hold one's tongue** to keep from speaking —**on everyone's tongue** spoken as common gossip —**on the tip of one's** (or **the**) **tongue** almost said or remembered —**speak in tongues** to be subject to glossolalia —**tongue′less** *adj.* —**tongue′-like′** *adj.*

**tongue-and-groove joint** (tuŋ′'n groov′) a kind of joint in which a tongue or tenon on one board fits exactly into a groove in another

**tongued** (tuŋd) *adj.* having a (specified kind of) tongue: usually in compounds [sharp-*tongued*]

**tongue-lash** (tuŋ′lash′) *vt.* [Colloq.] to scold or reprove harshly —**tongue′-lash′ing** *n.*

**tongue-tie** (-tī′) *n.* limited motion of the tongue, caused by a short frenum —*vt.* **-tied′, -ty′ing** to make tongue-tied

**tongue-tied** (-tīd′) *adj.* 1. having a condition of tongue-tie 2. speechless from embarrassment, etc.

**tongue twister** a phrase or sentence hard to speak fast (Ex.: six sick sheiks)

**tongu·ing** (tuŋ′iŋ) *n.* the use of the tongue in playing a musical wind instrument, esp. for more accurate intonation of rapid notes

**ton·ic** (tän′ik) *adj.* [< Gr. < *tonos*: see TONE] 1. *a)* of or producing good muscle tone, or tension *b)* characterized by continuous muscular contraction [a *tonic* spasm] 2. invigorating to the body or mind 3. *Music* designating or based on a keynote —*n.* 1. anything that invigorates or stimulates; specif., *a)* a drug, medicine, etc. for increasing body tone *b)* a hair or scalp dressing 2. a carbonated beverage flavored with a little quinine and served in a mixed drink with gin, vodka, etc.; quinine water  3. *Music* the basic tone of a diatonic scale; keynote —**ton′i·cal·ly** *adv.*

**to·nic·i·ty** (tō nis′ə tē) *n.* the quality or condition of being tonic; esp., normal muscle tension; tonus

**to·night** (tə nīt′) *adv.* [OE. *to niht*] on or during the present or coming night —*n.* this night or the night about to come Also, esp. formerly, **to-night**

**Ton·kin** (tän′kin, tän′-) region & former Fr. state in NE Indochina: now part of North Vietnam

**ton·nage** (tun′ij) *n.* **1.** a duty or tax on ships, based on tons carried  **2.** the total shipping, in tons, of a country or port  **3.** the amount in tons a ship can carry  **4.** weight in tons

**ton·neau** (tu nō′) *n., pl.* **-neaus′, -neaux′** (-nōz′) [Fr., lit., a cask] an enclosed rear compartment for passengers in an early type of automobile

**ton·sil** (tän′s'l) *n.* [L. *tonsillae, pl.*] either of a pair of oval masses of lymphoid tissue, one on each side of the throat at the back of the mouth —**ton′sil·lar** *adj.*

**ton·sil·lec·to·my** (tän′sə lek′tə mē) *n., pl.* **-mies** the surgical removal of the tonsils

**ton·sil·li·tis** (-līt′əs) *n.* inflammation of the tonsils —**ton′sil·lit′ic** (-lit′ik) *adj.*

**ton·so·ri·al** (tän sôr′ē əl) *adj.* [< L. < *tonsor,* clipper < pp. of *tondere,* to clip] of a barber or barbering: often used humorously

**ton·sure** (tän′shər) *n.* [< MFr. < L. *tonsura* < pp. of *tondere,* to clip]  **1.** the act of shaving a man's head, esp. on top, when he becomes a priest or monk  **2.** the part of the head left bare by doing this —*vt.* **-sured, -sur·ing** to shave the head of, esp. in this way

**ton·tine** (tän′tēn, tän tēn′) *n.* [Fr. < It., after L. *Tonti,* 17th-c. banker of Naples] a fund to which a group of persons contribute, benefits finally going to the last survivor or to those surviving after a specified time

**to·nus** (tō′nəs) *n.* [ModL. < L. < Gr. *tonos:* see TONE] the slight continuous contraction characteristic of a normal muscle at rest

**ton·y** (tō′nē) *adj.* **ton′i·er, ton′i·est** [Slang] high-toned; luxurious; stylish: often ironic

**too** (tōō) *adv.* [< TO]  **1.** in addition; also  **2.** more than enough; excessively, overly, etc. *[the hat is too big]*  **3.** very; extremely *[it's too good!]* Often used only to emphasize *[I will too go]* or as an adjective with *much, many [too much to see]*

**took** (took) *pt. of* TAKE

**tool** (tōōl) *n.* [OE. *tol*]  **1.** any implement, instrument, etc. held in the hand and used for some work, as a knife, saw, or shovel  **2.** *a)* the working part of a power-driven machine, as a drill, jigsaw blade, etc. *b)* the whole machine; machine tool  **3.** anything that serves as a means to get something done *[books are tools of education]*  **4.** a person used by another to accomplish his purposes, esp. when these are illegal or unethical —*vt.* **1.** to shape or work with a tool  **2.** to provide tools or machinery for (a factory, etc.): often with *up*  **3.** to impress designs, etc. on (leather, etc.) with tools —*vi.* **1.** to use a tool or tools  **2.** to get or install the tools, equipment, etc. needed (often with *up*)  **3.** to go in a vehicle —**tool′er** *n.* —**tool′ing** *n.*

**tool·box** (-bäks′) *n.* a box or chest in which tools are kept: also **tool chest**

**tool·mak·er** (-mā′kər) *n.* a machinist who makes, maintains, and repairs machine tools —**tool′mak′ing** *n.*

**tool·room** (-rōōm′) *n.* a room, as in a machine shop, where tools are stored, kept in repair, issued to workmen, etc.

**toot** (tōōt) *vi.* [prob. via LowG. *tuten* < echoic base]  **1.** to blow a horn, whistle, etc. in short blasts  **2.** to sound in short blasts: said of a horn, etc. —*vt.* **1.** to cause to sound in short blasts  **2.** to sound (tones, etc.) as on a horn —*n.* **1.** a short blast of a horn, etc.  **2.** [Slang] a drinking spree

**tooth** (tōōth; *for v. also* tōōth) *n., pl.* **teeth** (tēth) [OE. *toth*]  **1.** *a)* any of a set of hard, bonelike structures in the jaws of most vertebrates, used for biting, tearing, and chewing *b)* any similar structure in invertebrates *c)* *[pl.]* same as DENTURE.  **2.** a toothlike part, as on a saw, comb, gearwheel, etc.  **3.** an appetite or taste for something *[a sweet tooth]*  **4.** something biting, piercing, etc. like a tooth *[the teeth of the storm]*  **5.** an effective means of enforcing something *[to put teeth into a law]* —*vt.* **1.** to provide with teeth  **2.** to make jagged; indent —*vi.* to mesh or interlock, as gears —**armed** (or **dressed) to the teeth** as armed (or dressed up) as one can be —**get** (or **sink) one's teeth into** to become fully occupied with —**in the teeth of 1.** directly against  **2.** defying —**tooth and nail** with all one's strength or resources —**tooth′less** *adj.*

**tooth·ache** (-āk′) *n.* pain in or near a tooth

**tooth·brush** (-brush′) *n.* a brush for cleaning the teeth

**toothed** (tōōtht, tōōthd) *adj.* **1.** having teeth: often used in hyphenated compounds (big-*toothed*)  **2.** notched

CROWN
DENTIN
PULP

ROOT

TOOTH

**toothed whale** any of a main division of whales, as the sperm whale, that have cone-shaped teeth

**tooth·paste** (tōōth′pāst′) *n.* a paste used in cleaning the teeth with a toothbrush

**tooth·pick** (-pik′) *n.* a very small, pointed stick for getting bits of food free from between the teeth

**tooth powder** a powder used like toothpaste

**tooth·some** (-səm) *adj.* pleasing to the taste; tasty —**tooth′some·ly** *adv.* —**tooth′some·ness** *n.*

**tooth·y** (-ē) *adj.* **tooth′i·er, tooth′i·est** showing prominent teeth —**tooth′i·ly** *adv.* —**tooth′i·ness** *n.*

**too·tle** (tōōt′l) *vi.* **-tled, -tling** [freq. of TOOT] to keep tooting softly —*n.* the act or sound of tootling

**top¹** (täp) *n.* [OE.]  **1.** the head or the crown of the head *[from top to toe]*  **2.** the highest part, point, or surface of anything  **3.** the part of a plant growing above the ground *[beet tops]*  **4.** an uppermost part or covering; specif., *a)* a lid, cap, cover, etc. *b)* a folding roof of an automobile *c)* the upper part of a two-piece garment *d)* a platform around the head of each lower mast on a sailing ship  **5.** one first in order, excellence, importance, etc.; specif., *a)* the highest degree, pitch, rank, position, etc. *b)* a person of highest rank, etc. *c)* the choicest part; pick *[the top of the crop]* *d)* the beginning, as of something being rehearsed  *e)* Baseball the first half (*of* an inning)  **6.** *Sports a)* a stroke hitting the ball near its top *b)* the forward spin given the ball by such a stroke —*adj.* of or at the top; highest, greatest, foremost, etc. —*vt.* **topped, top′ping  1.** to take off the top of (a plant, etc.)  **2.** to put a top on *[to top a cake with icing]*  **3.** to be a top for  **4.** to reach or go over the top of  **5.** to exceed in amount, height, etc. *[topped 75 pounds]*  **6.** to be better, more effective, etc. than; outdo  **7.** to be at the top of; head; lead  **8.** *Sports* to hit (a ball) near its top, giving it a forward spin —*vi.* to top someone or something —**off the top** [Slang] from gross income —**off the top of one's head** speaking offhand, without careful thought —**on top** at the top; successful —**on top of 1.** on or at the top of  **2.** resting upon  **3.** in addition to; besides  **4.** right after  **5.** controlling successfully —**over the top 1.** over the front of a trench, as in attacking  **2.** exceeding the quota or goal —**(the) tops** [Slang] the very best —**top off** to complete by adding a finishing touch —**top out** to level off

**top²** (täp) *n.* [OE.] a child's cone-shaped toy, spun on its pointed end —**sleep like a top** to sleep soundly

**to·paz** (tō′paz) *n.* [< OFr. < L. < Gr. *topazos*]  **1.** a crystalline mineral that is a silicate of aluminum and fluorine; esp., a clear, yellow variety used as a gem  **2.** a yellow variety of quartz

**top banana** [prob. from the banana-shaped soft club carried by burlesque comedians] [Slang]  **1.** a top performer in show business; specif., the star comedian in a burlesque show  **2.** the most important person in any group

**top boot** a boot reaching to just below the knee, esp. such a boot topped with a band of contrasting color

**top brass** important officials: see BRASS (sense 5)

**top·coat** (täp′kōt′) *n.* a lightweight overcoat

**top dog** [Slang] the person, company, etc. in a dominant or leading position, esp. in a competitive situation

**top-drawer** (-drôr′) *adj.* of first importance, rank, etc.

**top-dress·ing** (-dres′iŋ) *n.* material applied to a surface, as fertilizer —**top′-dress′** *vt.*

**tope** (tōp) *vt., vi.* **toped, top′ing** [Fr. *toper,* to accept a bet] [Archaic] to drink much (alcoholic liquor)

**to·pee** (tō pē′, tō′pē) *n.* [Hindi *topī*] in India, a pith helmet worn as a sunshade

**To·pe·ka** (tə pē′kə) [? Siouan, lit., good place to dig potatoes] capital of Kans., on the Kansas River: pop. 115,000

**top·er** (tō′pər) *n.* a person who topes; drunkard

**top-flight** (täp′flīt′) *adj.* [Colloq.] best; first-rate

**top·gal·lant** (täp′gal′ənt; *naut.* tə gal′-) *adj.* next above the topmast —*n.* a topgallant mast, sail, etc.

**top hat** a tall, black, cylindrical hat, usually of silk, worn by men in formal dress

**top-heav·y** (täp′hev′ē) *adj.* too heavy at the top and so likely to fall over —**top′-heav′i·ness** *n.*

**to·pi** (tō pē′, tō′pē) *n.* same as TOPEE

**to·pi·ar·y** (tō′pē er′ē) *adj.* designating or of the art of trimming and training shrubs or trees into unnatural, ornamental shapes —*n., pl.* **-ar′ies** topiary art or work

**top·ic** (täp′ik) *n.* [< L. < Gr. *ta topika,* title of work by Aristotle, ult. < *topos,* a place]  **1.** the subject of a writing, speech, discussion, etc.  **2.** a heading or item in an outline

**top·i·cal** (-i k'l) *adj.* **1.** of a particular place; local  **2.** of, using, or arranged by topics  **3.** having to do with topics of the day; of current or local interest  **4.** *Med.* of or for a particular part of the body *[a topical lotion]* —**top′i·cal′i·ty** (-kal′ə tē) *n.* —**top′i·cal·ly** *adv.*

**top kick** [Mil. Slang] same as FIRST SERGEANT

**top·knot** (täp′nät′) *n.* **1.** a knot of feathers, ribbons, etc. worn as a headdress  **2.** a tuft of hair or feathers on the crown of the head

**top·less** (-lis) *adj.* without a top; specif., designating or wearing a costume that exposes the breasts

**top-lev·el** (-lev′'l) *adj.* **1.** of or by persons of the highest office or rank **2.** in highest office or rank

**top·loft·y** (-lôf′tē) *adj.* [Colloq.] lofty in manner; haughty —**top′loft′i·ly** *adv.* —**top′loft′i·ness** *n.*

**top·mast** (täp′məst, -mast′) *n.* the second mast above the deck of a sailing ship, supported by the lower mast

**top·most** (täp′mōst′) *adj.* at the very top

**top-notch** (-näch′) *adj.* [Colloq.] first-rate; excellent

**to·pog·ra·phy** (tə päg′rə fē) *n., pl.* **-phies** [< LL. < Gr.: see TOPIC & -GRAPHY] **1.** *a)* the science of showing on maps, charts, etc. the surface features of a region, such as hills, rivers, and roads *b)* such features **2.** surveying done to discover and measure such features **3.** a study of some part or system of the body showing the relationship, size, shape, etc. of its parts **4.** a similar study of some whole, as the mind or the atom, in relation to its parts —**to·pog′ra·pher** *n.* —**top·o·graph·ic** (täp′ə graf′ik), **top′o·graph′i·cal** *adj.* —**top′o·graph′i·cal·ly** *adv.*

**to·pol·o·gy** (tə päl′ə jē) *n., pl.* **-gies** [< Gr. *topos*, a place + -LOGY] **1.** *same as* TOPOGRAPHY (senses 3 & 4) **2.** *Math.* the study of those properties of geometric figures that remain unchanged even when under distortion —**top·o·log·i·cal** (täp′ə läj′i k'l) *adj.* —**to·pol′o·gist** *n.*

**top·per** (täp′ər) *n.* **1.** a person or thing that tops **2.** [Colloq.] *a) same as* TOP HAT *b)* a woman's short topcoat **3.** [Slang] a remark, joke, etc. that tops, or surpasses, all preceding ones

**top·ping** (-iŋ) *n.* something that forms the top of, or is put on top of, something else, as a sauce on food —*adj.* [Brit. Colloq.] excellent; first-rate

**top·ple** (täp′'l) *vi.* **-pled, -pling** [< TOP[1], *v.* + freq. *-le*] **1.** to fall (*over*) from top-heaviness, etc. **2.** to totter —*vt.* **1.** to cause to topple **2.** to overthrow

**top·sail** (täp′s'l, -sāl′) *n.* **1.** in a square-rigged vessel, the square sail, or either of a pair of square sails, next above the lowest sail on a mast **2.** in a fore-and-aft-rigged vessel, the small sail set above the gaff

**top-se·cret** (-sē′krit) *adj.* designating or of the most highly restricted military or government information

**top sergeant** *colloq. var. of* FIRST SERGEANT

**top·side** (-sīd′) *n.* [*usually pl.*] the part of a ship's side above the waterline —*adv.* on or to an upper deck or the main deck of a ship

**top·soil** (-soil′) *n.* the upper layer of soil, usually darker and richer than the subsoil

**top·sy-tur·vy** (täp′sē tur′vē) *adv., adj.* [prob. < *top*, highest part + ME. *terven*, to roll] **1.** upside down; reversed **2.** in confusion or disorder —*n.* a topsy-turvy condition —**top′sy-tur′vi·ly** *adv.* —**top′sy-tur′vi·ness** *n.*

**toque** (tōk) *n.* [Fr.] a woman's small, round hat

**to·rah, to·ra** (tō′rə, tō rä′) *n.* [Heb.] *Judaism* **1.** *a)* learning, law, instruction, etc. *b)* [*also* T-] the whole of Jewish religious literature, including the Scripture, the Talmud, etc. **2.** [*usually* T-] *a)* the Pentateuch *b) pl.* **-roth, -rot** (-rəs, -rōt′) a parchment scroll containing the Pentateuch

**torch** (tôrch) *n.* [OFr. *torche*, ult. < L. *torquere*, to twist] **1.** a portable light consisting of a long piece of resinous wood, etc. flaming at one end **2.** anything viewed as enlightening, inspiring, etc. **3.** a portable device for producing a very hot flame, used in welding, etc. **4.** [Brit.] a flashlight —*vt.* [Slang] to set fire to, as in arson —**carry a** (or **the**) **torch for** [Slang] to love (someone), esp. without having one's love returned

**torch·bear·er** (-ber′ər) *n.* **1.** a person who carries a torch **2.** a person or leader who enlightens or inspires others

**torch·light** (tôrch′līt′) *n.* the light of a torch or torches —*adj.* done or carried on by torchlight

**tore** (tôr) *pt. of* TEAR[1]

**tor·e·a·dor** (tôr′ē ə dôr′) *n.* [Sp. < *torear*, to fight bulls, ult. < L. *taurus*, a bull] a bullfighter: term no longer used in bullfighting

**to·re·ro** (tə rer′ō; *Sp.* tô re′rō) *n., pl.* **-ros** (-rōz; *Sp.* -rôs) [Sp. < LL. < L. *taurus*, a bull] a bullfighter, esp. a matador

**to·ri·i** (tôr′i ē′) *n., pl.* **-ri·i′** [Jap.] a gateway at the entrance to a Shinto temple, consisting of two uprights supporting a curved horizontal beam, with a straight crosspiece just below

**To·ri·no** (tô rē′nô) *It.* name of TURIN

**tor·ment** (tôr′ment; *for v., usually* tôr ment′) *n.* [< OFr. < L. *tormentum*, a rack, torture < *torquere*, to twist] **1.** great pain, physical or mental; agony **2.** a source of pain, anxiety, or annoyance —*vt.* **1.** to make suffer greatly, in body or mind **2.** to annoy, harass, or tease —**tor·ment′ing·ly** *adv.* —**tor·men′tor, tor·ment′er** *n.*

**torn** (tôrn) *pp. of* TEAR[1]

**tor·na·do** (tôr nā′dō) *n., pl.* **-does, -dos** [< Sp. *tronada*, thunder < L. *tonare*, to thunder] **1.** a rapidly whirling column of air, usually seen as a slender, funnel-shaped cloud that usually destroys everything in its narrow path **2.** any whirlwind or hurricane —**tor·nad′ic** (-nad′ik) *adj.*

**To·ron·to** (tə rän′tō) capital of Ontario, Canada, on Lake Ontario: pop. 633,000 (met. area 2,803,000)

**tor·pe·do** (tôr pē′dō) *n., pl.* **-does** [L., numbness < *torpere*, to be stiff] **1.** *same as* ELECTRIC RAY **2.** a large, cigar-shaped, self-propelled projectile launched under water against enemy ships as from a submarine: it explodes on contact **3.** any of various other explosive devices, as an underwater mine **4.** a small firework that explodes when thrown against a hard surface —*vt.* **-doed, -do·ing** to attack, destroy, etc. as with a torpedo

**torpedo boat** a small, fast warship for attacking with torpedoes

**tor·pid** (tôr′pid) *adj.* [< L. < *torpere*, to be numb] **1.** having lost temporarily all or some ability to feel or move, as a hibernating animal; dormant **2.** sluggish or slow and dull —**tor·pid′i·ty, tor′pid·ness** *n.* —**tor′pid·ly** *adv.*

**tor·por** (tôr′pər) *n.* **1.** a state of being dormant or inactive **2.** sluggishness; dullness; apathy

**torque** (tôrk) *n.* [< L. *torques*, a twisted metal necklace] **1.** *Physics* a twisting effect exerted on a body by a force acting at a distance, equal to the force times its distance from the center of rotation **2.** popularly, any force that causes rotation

**Tor·que·ma·da** (tôr′ke mä′thä; *E.* tôr′ki mä′də), **To·más de** (tō mäs′ *the*) 1420–98; Sp. Dominican monk; first Grand Inquisitor of the Spanish Inquisition

**Tor·rance** (tôr′əns) [after J. *Torrance*, local landowner] city in SW Calif.: suburb of Los Angeles: pop. 131,000

**tor·rent** (tôr′ənt, tär′-) *n.* [Fr. < L. *torrens*, burning, rushing, prp. of *torrere*, to parch] **1.** a swift, violent stream, esp. of water **2.** a flood or rush of words, mail, etc. **3.** a very heavy fall of rain —**tor·ren·tial** (tô ren′shəl, tə-) *adj.*

**Tor·ri·cel·li** (tôr′rē chel′lē; *E.* tôr′i chel′ē), **E·van·ge·lis·ta** (e′vän je lēs′tä) 1608–47; It. physicist: discovered principle of the barometer

**tor·rid** (tôr′id, tär′-) *adj.* [< L. < *torrere*, to parch] **1.** dried by or subjected to intense heat, esp. of the sun; scorched; parched; arid **2.** so hot as to parch or scorch **3.** highly passionate, ardent, etc. —**tor·rid·i·ty** (tô rid′ə tē), **tor′rid·ness** *n.* —**tor′rid·ly** *adv.*

**Torrid Zone** the area of the earth's surface between the Tropic of Cancer & the Tropic of Capricorn and divided by the equator

**tor·sion** (tôr′shən) *n.* [< MFr. < LL. < pp. of L. *torquere*, to twist] **1.** a twisting or being twisted **2.** *Mech. a)* the stress produced in a rod, wire, etc. from having one end twisted while the other is held firm or twisted in the opposite direction *b)* the tendency of a rod, etc. so twisted to untwist again —**tor′sion·al** *adj.* —**tor′sion·al·ly** *adv.*

**tor·so** (tôr′sō) *n., pl.* **-sos, -si** (-sē) [It. < L. < Gr. *thyrsos*, a stem] **1.** the trunk of the human body **2.** a statue representing this, esp. one lacking head and limbs

**tort** (tôrt) *n.* [< OFr. < ML. < pp. of *torquere*, to twist] *Law* a wrongful act, injury, or damage (not involving a breach of contract), for which a civil action can be brought

**torte** (tôrt) *n.* [G. < It. < LL. *torta*, a twisted bread] a rich cake, variously made, as of eggs, chopped nuts, and crumbs or a little flour

**tor·til·la** (tôr tē′ə) *n.* [Sp., dim. of *torta*, a cake: see TORTE] a griddlecake of unleavened cornmeal, now sometimes of flour: a staple food throughout Mexico

**tor·toise** (tôr′təs) *n., pl.* **-tois·es, -toise:** see PLURAL, II, D, 1 [< ML. *tortuca*, ult. < ? LGr. *tartarouchos*, demon] a turtle, esp. one that lives on land: see TURTLE

**tortoise shell** **1.** the hard, mottled, yellow-and-brown shell of some turtles used, esp. formerly, in making combs, etc. **2.** a synthetic substance like this

**tor·to·ni** (tôr tō′nē) *n.* [prob. altered < It. *tortone*, lit., big tart] an ice cream made with heavy cream, maraschino cherries, almonds, etc.

**tor·tu·ous** (tôr′choo wəs) *adj.* [Anglo-Fr. < L. *tortuosus* < pp. of *torquere*, to twist] **1.** full of twists and turns; winding; crooked **2.** not straightforward; devious or deceitful —**tor′tu·os′i·ty** (-wäs′ə tē) *n., pl.* **-ties** —**tor′tu·ous·ly** *adv.* —**tor′tu·ous·ness** *n.*

**tor·ture** (tôr′chər) *n.* [Fr. < LL. *tortura* < pp. of L. *torquere*, to twist] **1.** the inflicting of severe pain, as to force information or confession **2.** a method of doing this **3.** any severe physical or mental pain, or a cause of it —*vt.* **-tured, -tur·ing** **1.** to subject to torture **2.** to cause extreme physical or mental pain to **3.** to twist or distort (meaning, language, etc.) —**tor′tur·er** *n.* —**tor′tur·ous** *adj.* —**tor′tur·ous·ly** *adv.*

**to·rus** (tôr′əs) *n., pl.* **-ri** (-ī) [L., a bulge] **1.** a large, convex molding used at the base of columns, etc. **2.** *Bot.* the receptacle of a flower stalk

**To·ry** (tôr′ē) *n., pl.* **-ries** [< Ir. *tōruidhe*, robber < *tōir*, to pursue] **1.** formerly, a member of one of the two major political parties of England: orig. opposed to Whig: changed officially c. 1830 to *Conservative* **2.** in the American Revolution, a person who showed or favored continued loyalty to Great Britain **3.** [*often* t-] any very conservative person —*adj.* [*also* t-] of or being a Tory —**To′ry·ism** *n.*

**toss** (tôs, täs) *vt.* [prob. < Scand.] **1.** to throw or pitch about; buffet [a boat *tossed* by a storm] **2.** to mix (esp. a salad) lightly **3.** to disturb; agitate **4.** to throw; specif., to throw upward lightly from the hand **5.** to throw in or bandy (ideas, remarks, etc.) **6.** to lift quickly; jerk upward [*tossed* her head in disdain] **7.** to toss up with (someone for something): see phrase below —*vi.* **1.** to be tossed or thrown about **2.** to fling oneself about in sleep, etc. **3.** to go impatiently, angrily, etc., as from a room **4.** to toss up: see phrase below —*n.* **1.** a tossing or being tossed **2.** a tossing up: see phrase below **3.** the distance that something is or can be tossed —**toss off 1.** to make, do, write, etc. quickly and casually **2.** to drink up in one draft —**toss up** to toss a coin to decide something according to which side lands uppermost —**toss′er** *n.*

**toss·up** (-up′) *n.* **1.** the act of tossing a coin to decide something according to which side lands uppermost **2.** an even chance

**tost** (tôst, täst) *archaic pt. & pp. of* TOSS

**tot**[1] (tät) *n.* [prob. < Scand.] **1.** a young child **2.** [Chiefly Brit.] a small drink of alcoholic liquor

**tot**[2] (tät) *vt., vi.* **tot′ted, tot′ting** [contr. < TOTAL] [Chiefly Brit. Colloq.] to add; total (usually with *up*)

**tot.** total

**to·tal** (tōt′'l) *adj.* [< MFr. < ML. < L. *totus*, all] **1.** constituting the (or a) whole; entire **2.** complete; utter —*n.* the whole amount or number —*vt.* **-taled** or **-talled**, **-tal·ing** or **-tal·ling 1.** to find the total of; add **2.** to equal a total of; add up to **3.** [Slang] to wreck completely —*vi.* to amount (*to*) as a whole —**to′tal·ly** *adv.*

**to·tal·i·tar·i·an** (tō tal′ə ter′ē ən, tō′tal ə-) *adj.* [TOTAL + (AUTHOR)ITARIAN] designating, of, or like a government or state in which one political group maintains complete control under a dictatorship and bans all others Also **to·tal·is·tic** (tōt′'l is′tik), **to′tal·ist** —*n.* a person favoring such a government or state —**to·tal′i·tar′i·an·ism** *n.*

**to·tal·i·ty** (tō tal′ə tē) *n., pl.* **-ties 1.** the fact or condition of being total **2.** the total amount or sum

**to·tal·i·za·tor** (tōt′'l i zāt′ər) *n.* a machine used in parimutuel betting to register bets and, usually, compute odds and payoffs while bets are being placed: also **to′tal·i·sa′tor, to′tal·iz′er**

**tote**[1] (tōt) *vt.* **tot′ed, tot′ing** [prob. < Afr. orig.] [Colloq.] **1.** to carry or haul **2.** to be armed with (a gun, etc.) —*n.* **1.** [Colloq.] *a*) a toting *b*) something toted; load **2.** *short for* TOTE BAG —**tot′er** *n.*

**tote**[2] (tōt) *vt.* **tot′ed, tot′ing** *shortened form of* TOTAL (usually with *up*)

**tote**[3] (tōt) *n. shortened form of* TOTALIZATOR

**tote bag** a large, open handbag of cloth, etc. in which women can carry shoes, small packages, etc.

**tote board** [Colloq.] a large board facing the grandstand at a race track, on which the bets, odds, and payoffs recorded by a totalizator are flashed

**to·tem** (tōt′əm) *n.* [< Algonquian] **1.** among primitive peoples, an animal or natural object considered to be related by blood to a given family or clan and taken as its symbol **2.** an image of this —**to·tem·ic** (tō tem′ik) *adj.* —**to′tem·ism** *n.* —**to′tem·ist** *n.*

**totem pole** a pole or post carved and painted with totems, often erected in front of their dwellings, by Indian tribes of northwestern N. America

**toth·er, t′oth·er, 'toth·er** (tu*th*′ər) *adj., pron.* [Chiefly Dial.] that (or the) other

**tot·ter** (tät′ər) *vi.* [prob. < Scand.] **1.** to rock or shake as if about to fall **2.** to be on the point of collapse **3.** to be unsteady on one's feet; stagger —*n.* a tottering —**tot′ter·ing** *adj.* —**tot′ter·ing·ly** *adv.* —**tot′ter·y** *adj.*

**tou·can** (tōō′kan) *n.* [Fr. < Port. < Tupi *tucana*] a brightly colored, fruit-eating bird of tropical America, with a very large beak

**touch** (tuch) *vt.* [OFr. *tochier*] **1.** to put the hand, finger, etc. on, so as to feel **2.** to bring into contact with something else [*touch* a match to kindling] **3.** to be or come into contact with **4.** to border on; adjoin **5.** to strike lightly **6.** to affect by contact [wa-

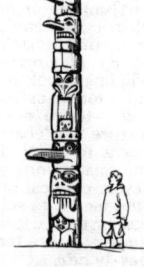

TOTEM POLE

ter won't *touch* these grease spots] **7.** to injure slightly [frost *touched* these plants] **8.** to give a light tint, aspect, etc. to [clouds *touched* with pink] **9.** to stop at (a port, etc.) in passing: said of a ship **10.** to lay hands on; handle; use **11.** to manhandle or molest **12.** to partake of [didn't *touch* his supper] **13.** to come up to; reach **14.** to compare with; equal [cooking that can't *touch* hers] **15.** to take or use wrongfully **16.** to deal with or refer to, esp. in passing **17.** to affect; concern [a subject that *touches* our welfare] **18.** to arouse an emotion in, esp. one of sympathy or gratitude **19.** to hurt the feelings of; pain [*touched* him to the quick] **20.** [Slang] to ask for, or get by asking, a loan or gift of money from **21.** *Geom.* to be tangent to —*vi.* **1.** to touch a person or thing **2.** to be or come in contact **3.** to approach; verge (*on, upon*) **4.** to pertain; bear (*on, upon*) **5.** to treat a topic slightly or in passing (with *on, upon*) **6.** to stop briefly (*at* a port, etc.) during a voyage **7.** *Geom.* to be tangent —*n.* **1.** a touching or being touched; specif., a light tap, stroke, etc. **2.** the sense by which physical objects are felt **3.** a sensation so caused; feel **4.** a special quality, skill, or manner [he lost his *touch*] **5.** an effect of being touched; specif., *a*) a mark, impression, etc. left by touching *b*) a subtle change or addition in a painting, story, etc. **6.** a very small amount, degree, etc.; specif., *a*) a trace, tinge, etc. [a *touch* of humor] *b*) a slight attack [a *touch* of the flu] **7.** formerly, a touchstone **8.** any test or criterion **9.** contact or communication [keep in *touch*] **10.** [Slang] *a*) the act of asking for a loan or gift of money, or a getting of it thus *b*) money so gotten *c*) a person with regard to how easily money can be so gotten from him **11.** *Music a*) the way that a performer strikes the keys of a piano, etc. *b*) the way that the keys of a piano, etc. respond to the fingers —**touch down** to land: said of an aircraft or spacecraft —**touch off 1.** to represent accurately or aptly **2.** to make explode; fire **3.** to produce (esp. a violent reaction, etc.) —**touch up** to improve or finish (a painting, story, etc.) by minor changes or additions —**touch′a·bil′i·ty** *n.* —**touch′a·ble** *adj.* —**touch′er** *n.*

**touch and go** an uncertain, risky, or dangerous situation —**touch-and-go** (tuch′an gō′) *adj.*

**touch·back** (-bak′) *n. Football* a play in which a player grounds the ball behind his own goal line when the ball was caused to pass the goal line by an opponent

**touch·down** (-doun′) *n.* **1.** a touching down, or landing **2.** *Football a*) a scoring play in which a player grounds the ball on or past the opponent's goal line *b*) a score of six points so made

**tou·ché** (tōō shā′) *interj.* [Fr.] *Fencing* touched: said when one's opponent scores a point by a touch: also used in congratulating someone for his witty reply, etc.

**touched** (tucht) *adj.* **1.** emotionally moved **2.** slightly unbalanced mentally: also **touched in the head**

**touch football** a kind of football in which the ball carrier is stopped by touching rather than tackling him

**touch·hole** (tuch′hōl′) *n.* in early firearms, the hole in the breech through which the charge was touched off

**touch·ing** (tuch′iŋ) *adj.* arousing tender emotion; affecting —*prep.* with regard to —**touch′ing·ly** *adv.*

**touch-me-not** (-mē nät′) *n. same as* JEWELWEED

**touch·stone** (-stōn′) *n.* **1.** a black stone formerly used to test the purity of gold or silver by the streak left on it when it was rubbed with the metal **2.** any test of genuineness

**touch-type** (-tīp′) *vi.* **-typed′, -typ′ing** to type without looking at the keys, by a system (**touch system**) in which a given key is touched with a specific finger —**touch′-typ′ist** *n.*

**touch·wood** (-wood′) *n.* dried, decayed wood or dried fungus used as tinder; punk

**touch·y** (tuch′ē) *adj.* **touch′i·er, touch′i·est** [TOUCH + -Y] **1.** easily offended or irritated; oversensitive **2.** very risky —**touch′i·ly** *adv.* —**touch′i·ness** *n.*

**tough** (tuf) *adj.* [OE. *toh*] **1.** strong but pliant; that will bend, twist, etc. without tearing or breaking **2.** not easily cut or chewed [*tough* steak] **3.** sticky; viscous [*tough* putty] **4.** *a*) physically strong; hardy *b*) mentally or morally firm **5.** hard to influence; stubborn **6.** practical and realistic **7.** overly aggressive; rough **8.** *a*) very difficult *b*) vigorous or violent [a *tough* fight] **9.** [Colloq.] unfavorable; bad [a *tough* break] **10.** [Slang] fine; excellent —*n.* a tough person; thug —**tough′ly** *adv.* —**tough′ness** *n.*

**tough·en** (-'n) *vt., vi.* to make or become tough or tougher

**tough·ie, tough·y** (-ē) *n., pl.* **-ies** [Colloq.] **1.** a tough person; ruffian **2.** a difficult problem or situation

**tough-mind·ed** (-mīn′did) *adj.* shrewd and unsentimental; practical; realistic —**tough′-mind′ed·ness** *n.*

**Tou·lon** (tōō län′; *Fr.* tōō lôn′) seaport in SE France, on the Mediterranean: pop. 175,000

**Tou·louse** (tōō lōōz′) city in S France: pop. 371,000

**Tou·louse-Lau·trec** (tōō lōōz′lō trek′), **Hen·ri** (**Marie Raymond**) **de** (än rē′ də) 1864–1901; Fr. painter

**tou·pee** (tōō pā′) *n.* [Fr. *toupet*, dim. of OFr. *toup*, tuft of hair] a man's wig, esp. one for a small bald spot

**tour** (toor) *n.* [< MFr. < OFr. < *tourner*, to TURN] **1.** a turn or shift of work; esp., a period of duty or military service at a single place: in full, **tour of duty 2.** a long trip, as for sightseeing **3.** any trip, as for inspection; round; circuit; specif., a trip, as by a theatrical company, to give performances, etc. in various cities —*vi.* to go on a tour —*vt.* **1.** to take a tour through **2.** to take (a play, etc.) on tour —**on tour** touring, as to give performances, lectures, etc.

**tour de force** (toor′ də fôrs′) *pl.* **tours′ de force′** (toor) [Fr.] an unusually skillful or ingenious production, performance, etc., sometimes a merely clever one

**touring car** an early type of open automobile, often with a folding top, seating five or more passengers

**tour·ism** (toor′iz'm) *n.* tourist travel, esp. when regarded as a business —**tour·is′tic** *adj.*

**tour·ist** (-ist) *n.* **1.** a person who makes a tour, esp. for pleasure **2.** tourist class —*adj.* **1.** of or for tourists **2.** designating or of the lowest-priced accommodations, as on a ship —*adv.* in or by means of tourist class

**tourist court** *same as* MOTEL

**tourist home** a private home in which bedrooms are rented to tourists or travelers

**tour·ma·line** (toor′mə lin, -lēn) *n.* [Fr., ult. < Sinh. *tōramalli*, a carnelian] a crystalline mineral that is a complex silicate, commonly black but also colored or transparent, used as a gemstone and in optical equipment

**tour·na·ment** (toor′nə mənt, tur′-) *n.* [< OFr. < *torneier*: see TOURNEY] **1.** in the Middle Ages, a contest in which knights on horseback tried to unseat one another with lances **2.** a series of contests in a sport, chess, or bridge, usually a competition for championship

**tour·ney** (toor′nē, tur′-) *n., pl.* **-neys** [< OFr. *torneier* < base of *tourner*: see TURN] *same as* TOURNAMENT —*vi.* to take part in a tournament; joust

**tour·ni·quet** (toor′nə kit, tur′-; -kā′) *n.* [Fr. < MFr. *turniquet*, coat of mail < OFr. *tunicle* < L. dim. of *tunica*, tunic] any device for compressing a blood vessel to stop bleeding, as a bandage twisted about a limb or a pad pressed down by a screw

**Tours** (toor; *Fr.* toor) city in WC France, on the Loire: pop. 128,000

**tou·sle** (tou′z'l) *vt.* **-sled, -sling** [freq. of ME. *tusen* (in comp.), to pull] to disorder, dishevel, rumple, etc. —*n.* a tousled condition, mass of hair, etc.

**Tous·saint L'Ou·ver·ture** (too san′ loo ver tür′) (born *Pierre François Dominique Toussaint*) 1743?-1803; Haitian Negro liberator & general

**tout** (tout) *vi., vt.* [OE. *totian*, to peep] [Colloq.] **1.** to solicit (customers, votes, etc.) **2.** to praise or recommend (a person or thing) highly **3.** *a)* esp. in England, to spy on (racehorses) to get betting tips *b)* to provide such tips on (racehorses) —*n.* [Colloq.] a person who touts —**tout′er** *n.*

**‡tout de suite** (toot swēt′) [Fr.] immediately

**tou·zle** (tou′z'l) *n., vt.* **-zled, -zling** *var. of* TOUSLE

**tow**[1] (tō) *vt.* [OE. *togian*] to pull as by a rope or chain —*n.* **1.** a towing or being towed **2.** something towed **3.** a towline —**in tow 1.** being towed **2.** as one's companion or follower **3.** under one's control

**tow**[2] (tō) *n.* [OE. *tow-*, for spinning] the coarse and broken fibers of hemp, flax, etc. before spinning

**to·ward** (tôrd; *also for prep.* tə wôrd′; *also, and for adj. usually,* tō′ərd) *prep.* [OE. *toweard*: see TO & -WARD] **1.** in the direction of **2.** facing **3.** in a way aimed at or tending to [*steps toward* peace] **4.** concerning; regarding [*my attitude toward* it] **5.** close to [*toward* noon] **6.** in order to get; for [*saving toward* a car] **7.** so as to help pay for [to contribute *toward* a new library] —*adj.* [Archaic or Rare] **1.** favorable **2.** docile **3.** at hand **4.** in progress

**to·wards** (tôrdz, tə wôrdz′) *prep. same as* TOWARD

**tow·boat** (tō′bōt′) *n. same as* TUGBOAT

**tow·el** (tou′'l, toul) *n.* [< OFr. *toaille* < Frank.] a piece of absorbent cloth or paper for wiping or drying things —*vt.* **-eled** or **-elled, -el·ing** or **-el·ling** to wipe or dry with a towel —**throw** (or **toss**, etc.) **in the towel** [Colloq.] to admit defeat —**towel off** to dry oneself, as after bathing

**tow·el·ing, tow·el·ling** (-iŋ) *n.* material for making towels

**tow·er**[1] (tou′ər) *n.* [OE. *torr* & OFr. *tur*, both < L. *turris*] **1.** a structure that is relatively high for its length and width, either standing alone or as part of another building **2.** such a structure used as a fortress or prison **3.** a person or thing like a tower in height, strength, etc. —*vi.* to rise high or stand high like a tower —**tow′ered** *adj.*

**tow·er**[2] (tō′ər) *n.* a person or thing that tows

**tow·er·ing** (tou′ər iŋ) *adj.* **1.** that towers; very high or tall **2.** very great, intense, etc. [*a towering* rage]

**tow·head** (tō′hed′) *n.* **1.** a head of pale-yellow hair **2.** a person having such hair —**tow′head′ed** *adj.*

**tow·hee** (tou′hē, tō′-) *n.* [echoic] any of various small, N. American sparrows that feed on the ground

**tow·line** (tō′lin′) *n.* a rope, chain, etc. for towing

**town** (toun) *n.* [OE. *tun*] **1.** a group of houses and buildings, larger than a village but smaller than a city **2.** a city or other thickly populated urban place **3.** *a)* in parts of the U.S., *same as* TOWNSHIP *b)* in New England and some others States, a unit of local government whose affairs are conducted by a town meeting **4.** the business center of a city **5.** the people of a town —*adj.* of or for a town —**go to town** [Slang] **1.** to go on a spree **2.** to act fast and efficiently **3.** to be very successful —**on the town** [Colloq.] out for a good time

**town clerk** an official in charge of the records, legal business, etc. of a town

**town crier** a person who formerly cried public announcements through the streets of a village or town

**town hall** a building in a town, housing the offices of public officials, the council chamber, etc.

**town house 1.** a city residence, esp. of a person who also owns a country residence **2.** a dwelling, usually two-story, that is one of a number of adjoining dwellings built as a unit

**town meeting 1.** a meeting of the people of a town **2.** esp. in New England, a meeting of the qualified voters of a town to act upon town business

**town·ship** (-ship′) *n.* **1.** orig., in England, a parish or division of a parish **2.** in parts of the U.S., a division of a county constituting a unit of local government **3.** in New England, *same as* TOWN (sense 3 b) **4.** a unit of territory in the U.S. land survey, generally six miles square **5.** in Canada, a subdivision of a province

**towns·man** (tounz′mən) *n., pl.* **-men 1.** a person who lives in, or has been reared in, a town **2.** a person who lives in the same town as one

**towns·peo·ple** (-pē′p'l) *n.pl.* **1.** the people of a town **2.** people reared in a town or city Also **towns′folk** (-fōk′)

**tow·path** (tō′path′) *n.* a path alongside a canal, for men or animals towing canalboats

**tow·rope** (-rōp′) *n.* a rope used in towing

**tow truck** a truck equipped for towing away vehicles that are disabled, illegally parked, etc.

**tox·e·mi·a** (täk sē′mē ə) *n.* [ModL.: see TOXIC & -EMIA] a condition in which poisonous substances, esp. toxins from bacteria, etc., are in the bloodstream: also sp. **tox·ae′mi·a** —**tox·e′mic** (-mik) *adj.*

**tox·ic** (täk′sik) *adj.* [< ML. < L. *toxicum*, a poison < Gr. *toxikon*, orig., poison for arrows < *toxon*, a bow] **1.** of, affected by, or caused by a toxin **2.** acting as a poison —**tox·ic′i·ty** (-sis′ə tē) *n.*

**tox·i·co-** [< Gr. *toxikon*: see prec.] *a combining form meaning* poison: also, before a vowel, **tox′ic-**

**tox·i·col·o·gy** (täk′si käl′ə jē) *n.* [< Fr.: see TOXIC & -LOGY] the science of poisons, their effects, antidotes, etc. —**tox′i·co·log′ic** (-kə läj′ik), **tox′i·co·log′i·cal** *adj.* —**tox′i·co·log′i·cal·ly** *adv.* —**tox′i·col′o·gist** *n.*

**tox·in** (täk′sin) *n.* [TOX(IC) + -IN[1]] **1.** any of various poisonous compounds produced by some microorganisms and causing certain diseases **2.** any of various similar poisons produced by certain plants or animals Toxins injected into animals or man usually cause antitoxins to form

**tox·oid** (täk′soid) *n.* [TOX(IN) + -OID] a toxin that has been treated, as with chemicals, so that its toxic qualities are removed but it can still act as an antigen

**toy** (toi) *n.* [< ? MDu. *toi*, finery] **1.** a thing of little value or importance; trifle **2.** a bauble; trinket **3.** a plaything, esp. one for children **4.** anything small; specif., a dog of a small breed —*adj.* **1.** being or like a toy **2.** of or for toys **3.** made as a toy or as a small model [*a toy* stove] —*vi.* to play or trifle (*with* a thing, idea, etc.)

**to·yon** (tō′yən) *n.* [AmSp.] a large evergreen shrub or tree of the rose family, with clusters of white flowers and bright-red berries, native to California

**toy·shop** (toi′shäp′) *n.* a shop where toys are sold

**tp.** township

**T-R** transmit-receive

**tr. 1.** trace **2.** transitive **3.** translated **4.** translation **5.** translator **6.** transpose **7.** treasurer **8.** trustee

**trace**[1] (trās) *n.* [< OFr. < *tracier*, ult. < L. pp. of *trahere*, to draw] **1.** a mark, footprint, etc. left by the passage of a person, animal, or thing **2.** a beaten path or trail **3.** a perceptible mark left by a past person, thing, or event; sign [*traces* of war] **4.** a barely perceptible amount [*a trace* of anger] **5.** something traced, drawn, recorded, etc. **6.** the visible line or spot moving across the face of a cathode-ray tube —*vt.* **traced, trac′ing 1.** [Now Rare] to move along (a path, route, etc.) **2.** to follow the trail of; track **3.** *a)* to follow the development or history of *b)* to determine (a source, date, etc.) thus **4.** to discover by investigating traces of (a prehistoric thing, etc.) **5.** to draw, outline, etc. **6.** to ornament with tracery **7.** to copy (a drawing, etc.) by following its lines on a transparent sheet placed over it **8.** to record by a curved, broken, or wavy line, as in a seismograph —*vi.* **1.** to follow a path, route, etc. **2.** to go back or date back (*to* something past) —**trace′a·bil′i·ty, trace′a·ble·ness** *n.* —**trace′a·ble** *adj.* —**trace′a·bly** *adv.*

**trace²** (trās) *n.* [< OFr. pl. of *trait:* see TRAIT] either of two straps, chains, etc. connecting a draft animal's harness to the vehicle drawn —**kick over the traces** to shake off control

**trace element 1.** a chemical element, as iron, copper, zinc, etc., essential in nutrition, but only in minute quantities **2.** any element present in minute quantities in an organism, soil, water, etc.

**trac·er** (trā′sər) *n.* **1.** one that traces; specif., *a)* a person who traces designs, etc. on transparent paper *b)* a person who traces lost or missing articles, persons, etc. *c)* an instrument for tracing designs on cloth, etc. **2.** an inquiry sent out for a letter, package, etc. missing in transport **3.** *same as* TRACER BULLET (or SHELL) **4.** an element or other substance used to follow biochemical reactions, as in an animal body, to locate diseased cells, etc.

**tracer bullet** (or **shell**) a bullet or shell that leaves a trail of smoke or fire to mark its course and help in adjusting aim

**trac·er·y** (-ē) *n., pl.* **-er·ies** [TRACE¹ + -ERY] any graceful design of lines that come together or cross in various ways, as in a stained glass window

**tra·che·a** (trā′kē ə; *chiefly Brit.* trə kē′ə) *n., pl.* **-che·ae′** (-ē′), **-che·as** [ML. < LL. < Gr. *tracheia (arteria),* rough (windpipe)] **1.** the tube through which most land vertebrates breathe, coming from the larynx and dividing into the bronchi **2.** any of the minute tubes branching through the bodies of insects, etc. and bringing in air —**tra′·che·al** *adj.*

**tra·che·o-** [< prec.] *a combining form meaning:* **1.** of the trachea **2.** the trachea and Also, before a vowel, **trache-**

**tra·che·ot·o·my** (trā′kē ät′ə mē) *n., pl.* **-mies** [see -TOMY] surgical incision of the trachea

TRACERY

**tra·cho·ma** (trə kō′mə) *n.* [< Gr. < *trachys,* rough] a contagious infection of the conjunctiva and cornea, caused by a virus and producing granulation —**tra·cho′ma·tous** (-käm′ə təs, -kō′mə-) *adj.*

**trac·ing** (trā′siŋ) *n.* **1.** the action of one that traces **2.** something made by tracing, as a copy of a drawing, or a line traced by a recording instrument

**track** (trak) *n.* [MFr. *trac,* a track] **1.** a mark or marks left by a person, animal, or thing, as a footprint or rut **2.** a trace or vestige **3.** a beaten path or trail **4.** a course or line of motion or action; route **5.** a sequence of ideas, events, etc. **6.** a path or circuit laid out for running, horse racing, etc. **7.** a pair of parallel metal rails on which trains, etc. run **8.** the distance in inches between parallel wheels, as of an automobile **9.** either of the two endless belts on tanks, some tractors, etc. on which they move **10.** *a)* athletic sports performed on a track, as running, hurdling, etc. *b)* track and field sports together **11.** *a) same as* SOUND TRACK *b)* the part of a magnetic tape or drum passing under a given recording or reading head —*vt.* **1.** *a)* to follow the track or footprints of *b)* to follow (a path, etc.) **2.** to trace by means of vestiges, evidence, etc. **3.** to plot the path of and record data from (an aircraft, spacecraft, etc.) using a telescope, radar, etc. **4.** to tread or travel **5.** *a)* to leave footprints, etc. on (often with *up*) *b)* to leave in the form of tracks [to *track* dirt over the floor] —*vi.* **1.** to be in alignment, as wheels, or a phonograph pickup in a record groove —**in one's tracks** where one is at the moment —**keep track of** to keep an account of; stay informed about —**lose track of** to fail to stay informed about —**make tracks** [Colloq.] to go or leave hurriedly —**on** (or **off**) **the track** keeping to (or straying from) the subject or goal —**track down 1.** to pursue until caught **2.** to investigate fully —**track′er** *n.* —**track′less** *adj.*

**track·age** (-ij) *n.* **1.** all the tracks of a railroad **2.** *a)* permission for a railroad to use the tracks of another *b)* a charge for this

**track·man** (-mən) *n., pl.* **-men** one whose work is laying and repairing railroad tracks: also **track′lay′er**

**track man** an athlete who competes in track or field events, as a runner, hurdler, discus thrower, etc.

**tract¹** (trakt) *n.* [< L. < pp. of *trahere,* to draw] **1.** formerly, *a)* duration of time *b)* a period of time **2.** a continuous expanse of land, etc. **3.** *Anat., Zool.* a system of parts or organs having some special function [the digestive *tract*]

**tract²** (trakt) *n.* [< LL. < L. pp. of *tractare:* see ff.] a pamphlet, esp. one on a religious or political subject

**trac·ta·ble** (trak′tə b'l) *adj.* [< L. < *tractare,* to drag, freq. of *trahere,* to draw] **1.** easily managed, taught, etc.;

docile **2.** easily worked or shaped; malleable —**trac′ta·bil′i·ty, trac′ta·ble·ness** *n.* —**trac′ta·bly** *adv.*

**trac·tion** (trak′shən) *n.* [< ML. < L. *tractus,* pp. of *trahere,* to draw] **1.** a pulling or drawing, as of a load, or a being pulled or drawn **2.** the power used by a locomotive, etc. **3.** the power, as of tires on pavement, to grip or hold to a surface while moving, without slipping —**trac′tive** *adj.*

**trac·tor** (trak′tər) *n.* [ModL. < L.: see prec.] **1.** a powerful, motor-driven vehicle with large rear wheels or endless belt treads, for pulling farm machinery, hauling loads, etc. **2.** a truck with a driver's cab and no body, for hauling one or more trailers

**trac·tor-trail·er** (-trā′lər) *n.* a combination of a tractor and a trailer or semitrailer, used in trucking

**trade** (trād) *n.* [MLowG., a track < OS. *trada,* a trail] **1.** *a)* a means of earning one's living; occupation *b)* skilled work; craft *c)* all the persons or companies in a particular line of business **2.** buying and selling, or bartering; commerce **3.** business of a specified kind [the tourist *trade*] **4.** customers; clientele **5.** a purchase or sale; deal **6.** an exchange; swap **7.** [*pl.*] the trade winds —*adj.* **1.** of trade or commerce **2.** of, by, or for the trade (*n.* 1 *c*) [a *trade* journal] **3.** of the members in the trades, or crafts, etc. [*trade* unions]: also **trades** —*vi.* **trad′ed, trad′ing 1.** to carry on a business **2.** to have business dealings (*with* someone) **3.** to make an exchange (*with* someone) **4.** [Colloq.] to be a customer (*at* a specified store, etc.) —*vt.* **1.** to exchange; barter **2.** to buy and sell (stocks, etc.) —**trade in** to give (one's used car, etc.) as part of the purchase price of a new one —**trade on** (or **upon**) to take advantage of; exploit —**trad′a·ble, trade′a·ble** *adj.*

**trade-in** (trād′in′) *n.* **1.** a used car, etc. given or taken as part payment toward a new one **2.** a deal involving such a car, etc. **3.** the amount allowed as part payment

**trade·mark** (-märk′) *n.* a symbol, design, word, etc. used by a manufacturer or dealer to distinguish his products from those of competitors: usually registered and protected by law —*vt.* **1.** to put a trademark on (a product) **2.** to register (a symbol, word, etc.) as a trademark

**trade name 1.** the name by which a commodity is commonly known in trade **2.** a name, often a trademark or service mark, used by a company to describe a product, service, etc. **3.** the name under which a company carries on business

**trad·er** (trā′dər) *n.* **1.** a person who trades; merchant **2.** a ship used in trade

**trade route** a regular route used by trading ships, caravans, etc.

**trade school** a school where a trade or trades are taught

**trades·man** (trādz′mən) *n., pl.* **-men** [Chiefly Brit.] a person engaged in trade; esp., a storekeeper —**trades′wom′an** *n.fem., pl.* **-wom′en**

**trades·peo·ple** (-pē′p'l) *n.pl.* people engaged in trade; esp., storekeepers: also **trades′folk′**

**trade union** *same as* LABOR UNION: also [Chiefly Brit.] **trades union** —**trade′-un′ion** *adj.* —**trade unionism** —**trade union-ist**

**trade wind** [earlier *trade,* adv., steadily, in phr. *to blow trade*] a wind that blows steadily toward the equator from the northeast in the tropics north of the equator and from the southeast in the tropics south of the equator

**trading post** a store or station in an outpost, settlement, etc., where trading is done, as with natives

**trading stamp** a stamp given by some merchants as a premium to customers, redeemable in merchandise

**tra·di·tion** (trə dish′ən) *n.* [< MFr. < L. < pp. of *tradere,* to deliver] **1.** *a)* the handing down orally of beliefs, customs, stories, etc. from generation to generation *b)* a belief, custom, etc. so handed down **2.** any long-established custom or practice **3.** any unwritten religious teachings regarded as coming from the founder or earliest prophet of a religion —**tra·di′tion·less** *adj.*

**tra·di·tion·al** (-'l) *adj.* of, handed down by, or conforming to tradition; conventional: also **tra·di′tion·ar′y** (-er′ē) —**tra·di′tion·al·ly** *adv.*

**tra·di·tion·al·ism** (-'l iz'm) *n.* the following of tradition or a clinging to tradition —**tra·di′tion·al·ist, tra·di′tion·ist** *n.* —**tra·di′tion·al·is′tic** *adj.*

**tra·duce** (trə dōōs′, -dyōōs′) *vt.* **-duced′, -duc′ing** [L. *traducere,* to disgrace < *tra(ns),* across + *ducere,* to lead] **1.** to say untrue or mean things about; defame **2.** to turn against; betray —**tra·duce′ment** *n.* —**tra·duc′er** *n.*

**Tra·fal·gar** (trə fal′gər; *Sp.* trä′fäl gär′), **Cape** cape on the SW coast of Spain, at the entrance of the Strait of Gibraltar: site of a naval battle (1805) in which Nelson's Brit. fleet defeated Napoleon's fleet

**traf·fic** (traf′ik) *n.* [< Fr. < It. < *trafficare,* to trade < L. *trans,* across + It. *ficcare,* to bring] **1.** buying and selling; trade, sometimes of a wrong or illegal kind [*traffic* in drugs] **2.** dealings or business (*with* someone) **3.** *a)* the movement or number of cars along a street, pedestrians along a sidewalk, etc. *b)* the cars, pedestrians, etc. **4.** the amount of business done in a given period, as measured by the number of passengers or customers, the amount of freight handled, etc. —*adj.* of traffic or its regulation —*vi.* -**ficked**, -**fick·ing** 1. to carry on traffic (*in* something) 2. to have dealings (*with* someone) —**traf′fick·er** *n.*

**traffic circle** a circular street where several streets meet, with vehicles traveling in one direction only

**traffic light** (or **signal**) a set of signal lights at intersections of streets to regulate traffic

**trag·a·canth** (trag′ə kanth′) *n.* [< Fr. < L. < Gr. < *tragos*, goat + *akantha*, thorn] 1. a tasteless gum used as a thickener and emulsifier in foodstuffs, drugs, etc. 2. any of certain Asiatic plants that yield this gum

**tra·ge·di·an** (trə jē′dē ən) *n.* an actor of tragedy

**tra·ge·di·enne** (trə jē′dē en′) *n.* an actress of tragedy

**trag·e·dy** (traj′ə dē) *n., pl.* -**dies** [< MFr. < L. < Gr. *tragōidia* < *tragos*, goat + *ōidē*, song: prob. from the goatskin dress of the performers representing satyrs] 1. a serious play having a sad or disastrous ending brought about by fate, moral weakness in a character, social pressures, etc. 2. the branch of drama consisting of such plays 3. the writing or acting of such plays 4. a novel or any narrative having a tragic theme, tone, etc. 5. the tragic element in literature or life 6. a very sad or tragic event

**trag·ic** (traj′ik) *adj.* 1. of, like, or having to do with tragedy 2. bringing great harm, suffering, etc.; very sad, disastrous, etc. 3. suitable to tragedy [a *tragic* voice] Also **trag′i·cal** —*n.* the tragic element in art or life —**trag′i·cal·ly** *adv.* —**trag′i·cal·ness** *n.*

**trag·i·com·e·dy** (traj′ə käm′ə dē) *n., pl.* -**dies** 1. a play, novel, etc. combining tragic and comic elements 2. a situation or incident in life like this —**trag′i·com′ic, trag′i·com′i·cal** *adj.* —**trag′i·com′i·cal·ly** *adv.*

**trail** (trāl) *vt.* [< MFr., ult. < L. *tragula*, sledge < *trahere*, to drag] 1. *a)* to drag or let drag behind one *b)* to bring along behind [*trailing* exhaust fumes] *c)* to pull or tow 2. *a)* to make (a path, etc.), as by treading down *b)* to make a path in (grass, etc.) 3. to follow the tracks of 4. to hunt by tracking 5. to follow or lag behind (another or others) in movement, a contest, etc. 6. *Mil.* to carry (a rifle, etc.) in one hand, with the muzzle tilted forward and the butt near the ground —*vi.* 1. to be drawn along behind one, as the train of a gown 2. to grow along the ground, etc., as some plants 3. to extend in an irregular line; straggle 4. to flow behind in a long, thin stream, wisp, etc., as smoke 5. *a)* to follow or lag behind *b)* to be losing, as in a sports contest 6. to track game: said of hounds 7. to grow gradually weaker, dimmer, etc. (with *off* or *away*) —*n.* 1. something that trails behind 2. a mark, scent, etc. left by a person, animal, or thing that has passed 3. a rough path made across country, as by repeated passage 4. a train of events, etc. following something [a *trail* of debts followed his illness] 5. a part of a gun carriage, which may be lowered to the ground to form a rear brace

**trail·blaz·er** (-blā′zər) *n.* 1. a person who blazes a trail 2. a pioneer in any field —**trail′blaz′ing** *n.*

**trail·er** (trā′lər) *n.* 1. one that trails another 2. a cart or van designed to be pulled by an automobile or truck (esp. a tractor, *n.* 2) 3. a closed vehicle designed to be pulled by a motor vehicle and equipped as a place to live or work in: see also MOBILE HOME 4. a selection of scenes from a coming motion picture, used to advertise it

**trailer park** an area, usually with piped water, electricity, etc., designed to accommodate trailers, esp. mobile homes: also **trailer camp, trailer court**

**trailing arbutus** (trā′liŋ) *same as* ARBUTUS (sense 2)

**trailing edge** *Aeron.* the rear edge of an airfoil, propeller blade, etc.

**train** (trān) *n.* [< OFr. < *trahiner*, to draw on, ult. < L. *trahere*, to pull] 1. something that drags along behind, as a part of a gown that trails 2. a group of followers or attendants in a procession; retinue 3. a group of persons, animals, vehicles, etc. moving in a line; procession; caravan 4. the persons, vehicles, etc. carrying supplies, ammunition, food, etc. for combat troops 5. a series of events that follow some happening [war brought famine in its *train*] 6. any connected sequence; series [a *train* of thought] 7. a line of gunpowder used to set off an explosive charge 8. a series of connected parts for transmitting motion [a gear *train*] 9. a line of connected railroad cars pulled or pushed by a locomotive —*vt.* 1. to guide the growth of (a plant) by tying, pruning, etc. 2. to subject to certain action, exercises, etc. so as to bring to a desired condition 3. to guide the mental, moral, etc. development of; bring up; rear 4. to teach so as to make fully skilled [to *train* airplane pilots] 5. to discipline (animals) to do tricks or obey commands 6. to make fit for some sport, as by exercise,

practice, etc. 7. to aim (a gun, binoculars, etc.) at something (usually with *on*) 8. [Colloq.] to condition (a child, puppy, etc.) to defecate and urinate in the required place —*vi.* to give or get training —**train′a·ble** *adj.* —**train′er** *n.*

**train·ee** (trā nē′) *n.* a person undergoing vocational training, military training, etc. —**train·ee′ship′** *n.*

**train·ing** (trān′iŋ) *n.* 1. the lessons, practice, drills, etc. given by one who trains or received by one who is being trained 2. the process of being trained for some sport, as by exercise, practice, etc.

**train·man** (-mən) *n., pl.* -**men** a person who works on a railroad train or in a railroad yard; esp., a brakeman

**traipse** (trāps) *vi., vt.* **traipsed, traips′ing** [< ?] [Dial. or Colloq.] to walk, wander, tramp, or gad —*n.* [Dial. or Colloq.] the act of traipsing

**trait** (trāt) *n.* [Fr., a line < L. pp. of *trahere*, to draw] a distinct quality or feature, as of personality

**trai·tor** (trāt′ər) *n.* [OFr. < < L. pp. of *tradere*, to betray] a person who betrays his country, cause, friends, etc.; one guilty of treason or treachery —**trai′tress** *n.fem.*

**trai·tor·ous** (-əs) *adj.* 1. of or like a traitor; treacherous 2. of or involving treason; treasonable —**trai′tor·ous·ly** *adv.* —**trai′tor·ous·ness** *n.*

**Tra·jan** (trā′jən) (L. name *Marcus Ulpius Trajanus*) 53?-117 A.D.; Rom. emperor (98-117), born in Spain

**tra·jec·to·ry** (trə jek′tə rē) *n., pl.* -**ries** [< ML. < L. pp. of *trajicere* < *tra(ns)*, across + *jacere*, to throw] the curved path of something hurtling through space, esp. that of a projectile

**tram** (tram) *n.* [prob. < LowG. *traam*, a beam] 1. an open railway car used in mines: also **tram′car′** 2. [Brit.] a streetcar; trolley car: also **tram′car′** *b)* a streetcar line: also **tram′line′, tram′way′** —*vt., vi.* **trammed, tram′ming** to carry or ride in a tram

**tram·mel** (tram′'l) *n.* [< MFr. < ML. *tremaculum*, kind of fishing net < L. *tres*, three + *macula*, a mesh] 1. *a)* a three-ply fishing net *b)* a fowling net Also **trammel net** 2. a shackle for a horse, esp. one to teach ambling 3. [*usually pl.*] something that hinders freedom of action 4. a device with links, etc. for hanging a pothook in a fireplace 5. an instrument for drawing ellipses —*vt.* -**meled** or -**melled, -mel·ing** or -**mel·ling** 1. to entangle as in a trammel 2. to hinder, restrain, or shackle —**tram′mel·er, tram′mel·ler** *n.*

**tramp** (tramp) *vi.* [< or akin to LowG. *trampen*, to trample] 1. *a)* to walk with heavy steps *b)* to step heavily (*on* something); stamp 2. *a)* to travel about on foot; hike *b)* to travel as or like a vagabond, hobo, etc. —*vt.* 1. to step on heavily; trample 2. to walk or ramble through —*n.* 1. a person who travels about on foot doing odd jobs or begging; hobo; vagrant 2. the sound of heavy steps 3. a journey on foot; hike 4. a freight ship that has no regular schedule, arranging for cargo, etc. as it goes along 5. [Slang] a sexually promiscuous woman —**tramp′er** *n.*

**tram·ple** (tram′p'l) *vi.* -**pled, -pling** [< ME. freq. of *trampen*: see prec.] to tread heavily —*vt.* to crush, destroy, etc. as by treading heavily on —*n.* the sound of trampling — **trample under foot** to crush or hurt by or as by trampling: also **trample on** (or **upon**) —**tram′pler** *n.*

**tram·po·line** (tram′pə lēn′, -lin; tram′pə lēn′) *n.* [< It. *trampolino*, a springboard] a sheet of strong canvas stretched tightly on a frame, used as a kind of springboard in acrobatic tumbling —**tram′po·lin′er, tram′po·lin′ist** *n.*

**trance** (trans) *n.* [< OFr. < L. *transire*, to die: see TRANSIT] 1. a state brought on by hysteria, hypnosis, etc., in which a person seems to be conscious but is unable to move or act of his own will 2. any daze, stupor, etc. 3. the condition of being completely lost in thought or meditation 4. the state a spiritualist medium is in while allegedly communicating with the dead —*vt.* **tranced, tranc′ing** *chiefly poet. var. of* ENTRANCE²

**tran·quil** (traŋ′kwəl, tran′-) *adj.* -**quil·er** or -**quil·ler, -quil·est** or -**quil·lest** [L. *tranquillus*] free from disturbance or agitation; calm, quiet, peaceful, etc. [*tranquil* waters, a *tranquil* mood] —**tran′quil·ly** *adv.*

**tran·quil·ize, tran·quil·lize** (traŋ′kwə līz′, tran′-) *vt., vi.* -**ized** or -**lized′, -iz′ing** or -**liz′ing** to make or become tranquil; specif., to calm by the use of a tranquilizer — **tran′quil·i·za′tion, tran′quil·li·za′tion** *n.*

**tran·quil·iz·er, tran·quil·liz·er** (-lī′zər) *n.* any of certain drugs used in calming persons suffering from nervous tension, anxiety, etc.

**tran·quil·li·ty, tran·quil·i·ty** (traŋ kwil′ə tē, tran-) *n.* the quality or state of being tranquil; calmness, etc.

**trans-** [L. < *trans*, across] a prefix meaning: 1. on or to the other side of, over, across, through [*transatlantic*] 2. so as to change thoroughly [*transliterate*] 3. above and beyond, transcending

---

fat, āpe, cär; ten, ēven; is, bīte; gō, hôrn, tool, look; oil, out; up, fur; get; joy; yet; chin; she; thin, then; zh, leisure; ŋ, ring; ə for *a* in *ago*, *e* in *agent*, *i* in *sanity*, *o* in *comply*, *u* in *focus*; ′ as in *able* (ā′b'l); Fr. bal; ë, Fr. coeur; ö, Fr. feu; Fr. mon; ô, Fr. coq; ü, Fr. duc; r, Fr. cri; H, G. ich; kh, G. doch; ‡foreign; *hypothetical; < derived from. See inside front cover.

**trans.** **1.** transaction(s) **2.** transitive **3.** translated **4.** translation **5.** transportation

**trans·act** (tran sakt′, -zakt′) *vt.* [< L. pp. of *transigere* < *trans-*, across + *agere*, to drive] to carry on, conduct, or complete (business, etc.) —**trans·ac′tor** *n.*

**trans·ac·tion** (-sak′shən, -zak′-) *n.* **1.** a transacting or being transacted **2.** something transacted; specif., *a)* a business deal *b)* [*pl.*] a record of the proceedings of a society, convention, etc. —**trans·ac′tion·al** *adj.*

**trans·al·pine** (trans al′pīn, tranz-; -pin) *adj.* on the other (the northern) side of the Alps, from Rome

**trans·at·lan·tic** (trans′ət lan′tik, tranz′-) *adj.* **1.** crossing or spanning the Atlantic **2.** on the other side of the Atlantic

**Trans·cau·ca·sia** (trans′kô kā′zhə, -shə) that part of the Caucasus south of the Caucasus Mountains, containing the republics of Armenia, Azerbaijan, & Georgia —**Trans′cau·ca′sian** *adj., n.*

**trans·ceiv·er** (tran sē′vər) *n.* [TRANS(MITTER) + (RE)CEIVER] an apparatus in a single housing, functioning alternately as a radio transmitter and receiver

**tran·scend** (tran send′) *vt.* [L. *transcendere* < *trans-*, over + *scandere*, to climb] **1.** to go beyond the limits of; exceed *[his story transcends belief]* **2.** to be superior to; surpass; excel —*vi.* to be transcendent

**tran·scend·ent** (-sen′dənt) *adj.* **1.** transcending; surpassing; excelling **2.** *Theol.* existing apart from the material universe —**tran·scend′ence, tran·scend′en·cy** *n.* —**transcend′ent·ly** *adv.*

**tran·scen·den·tal** (tran′sen den′t'l) *adj.* **1.** *same as: a)* TRANSCENDENT (sense 1) *b)* SUPERNATURAL **2.** abstract; metaphysical **3.** of transcendentalism —**tran′scenden′tal·ly** *adv.*

**tran·scen·den·tal·ism** (-iz'm) *n.* **1.** any of various philosophies seeking to discover the nature of reality by investigating the process of thought rather than the things that are thought about **2.** the philosophical ideas of Emerson and some other 19th-cent. New Englanders, based on a search for reality through spiritual intuition **3.** popularly, any obscure, visionary, or idealistic thought —**tran′scenden′tal·ist** *n., adj.*

**trans·con·ti·nen·tal** (trans′kän tə nen′t'l) *adj.* **1.** that crosses a (or the) continent **2.** on the other side of a (or the) continent —**trans′con·ti·nen′tal·ly** *adv.*

**tran·scribe** (tran skrīb′) *vt.* -scribed′, -scrib′ing [< L. < *trans-*, over + *scribere*, to write] **1.** to write or type out in full (shorthand notes, a speech, etc.) **2.** to translate or transliterate **3.** to arrange (a piece of music) for an instrument, etc. other than that for which it was originally written **4.** *Radio & TV* to record (a program, commercial, etc.) for broadcast later —**tran·scrib′er** *n.*

**tran·script** (tran′skript′) *n.* **1.** something made by transcribing; written, typewritten, or printed copy **2.** any copy or reproduction, esp. one that is official, as a copy of a student's record in school or college

**tran·scrip·tion** (tran skrip′shən) *n.* **1.** the act or process of transcribing **2.** a transcript; copy **3.** an arrangement of a piece of music for an instrument, voice, etc. other than that for which it was originally written **4.** a recording made for radio or television broadcasting; also, the act of using such recordings —**tran·scrip′tion·al** *adj.*

**tran·sect** (tran sekt′) *vt.* [< TRANS- + pp. of L. *secare*, to cut] to cut across —**tran·sec′tion** *n.*

**tran·sept** (tran′sept) *n.* [< ModL. < L. *trans-*, across + *septum*, enclosure] **1.** the part of a cross-shaped church at right angles to the long, main section, or nave **2.** either arm of this part, outside the nave

**trans·fer** (trans fur′; *also, & for n. always*, trans′fər) *vt.* -ferred′, -fer′ring [< L. < *trans-*, across + *ferre*, to bear] **1.** to convey, carry, send, etc. from one person or place to another **2.** to make over (title to property, etc.) to another **3.** to move (a picture, design, etc.) from one surface to another, as by making wet and pressing —*vi.* **1.** to transfer oneself or be transferred; move **2.** to change from one school, college, etc. to another **3.** to change from one bus, train, etc. to another —*n.* **1.** a transferring or being transferred **2.** one that is transferred; specif., a picture or design transferred or to be transferred from one surface to another **3.** a ticket entitling the bearer to change from one bus, train, etc. to another **4.** a document effecting a transfer **5.** a person who transfers or is transferred —**trans·fer′a·ble, trans·fer′ra·ble** *adj.* —**trans·fer′al, trans·fer′ral** *n.* —**trans·fer′ence** *n.* —**trans·fer′rer, *Law* trans·fer′or** *n.*

**trans·fer·ee** (trans′fər ē′) *n.* a person who is transferred or to whom something is transferred

**trans·fig·u·ra·tion** (trans fig′yoo rā′shən, trans′fig-) *n.* a transfiguring or being transfigured —[T-] **1.** *Bible* the change in the appearance of Jesus on the mountain: Matt. 17 **2.** a church festival (Aug. 6) commemorating this

**trans·fig·ure** (trans fig′yər) *vt.* -ured, -ur·ing [L. *transfigurare:* see TRANS- & FIGURE] **1.** to change the figure,

form, or appearance of; transform **2.** to transform so as to exalt or glorify —**trans·fig′ur·a′tion** *n.*

**trans·fix** (trans fiks′) *vt.* [< L. pp. of *transfigere* < *trans-*, through + *figere*, to fix] **1.** to pierce through as with something pointed **2.** to fasten in this way; impale **3.** to make unable to move, as if impaled *[transfixed* with horror] — **trans·fix′ion** *n.*

**trans·form** (trans fôrm′) *vt.* [L. *transformare*, ult. < *trans-*, over + *forma*, a shape] **1.** to change the form or appearance of **2.** to change the condition, character, or function of **3.** *Elec.* to change (voltage, current, etc.) by use of a transformer **4.** *Math.* to change (an algebraic expression or equation) to a different form having the same value **5.** *Physics* to change (one form of energy) into another —*vi.* [Rare] to be or become transformed —**trans·form′a·ble** *adj.* —**trans·for·ma′tion** *n.* —**trans·for·ma′tion·al** *adj.* —**trans·form′a·tive** *adj.*

**trans·form·er** (-fôr′mər) *n.* **1.** a person or thing that transforms **2.** *Elec.* a device for transferring electric energy from one alternating-current circuit to another, usually with a change in voltage, current, etc.

**trans·fuse** (trans fyo͞oz′) *vt.* -fused′, -fus′ing [< L. pp. of *transfundere* < *trans-*, across + *fundere*, to pour] **1.** to pour in or spread through; instill, imbue, infuse, permeate, etc. **2.** *Med. a)* to transfer or introduce (blood, saline solution, etc.) into a blood vessel, usually a vein *b)* to give a transfusion to —**trans·fus′er** *n.* —**trans·fus′i·ble** *adj.* —**trans·fu′sive** *adj.*

**trans·fu·sion** (-fyo͞o′zhən) *n.* a transfusing, esp. of blood

**trans·gress** (trans gres′, tranz-) *vt.* [< Fr. < L. pp. of *transgredi* < *trans-*, over + *gradi*, to step] **1.** to overstep or break (a law, commandment, etc.) **2.** to go beyond (a limit, boundary, etc.) —*vi.* to break a law, commandment, etc.; sin —**trans·gres′sive** *adj.* —**trans·gres′sor** *n.*

**trans·gres·sion** (-gresh′ən) *n.* a transgressing; breach of a law, duty, etc.; sin

**tran·ship** (tran ship′) *vt. var. sp. of* TRANSSHIP

**tran·sient** (tran′shənt) *adj.* [< L. prp. of *transire:* see TRANSIT] **1.** *a)* passing away with time; temporary; transitory *b)* passing quickly; fleeting; ephemeral **2.** staying for only a short time *[a transient* lodger] —*n.* a transient person or thing *[transients* at a hotel] —**tran′sience, tran′sien·cy** *n.* —**tran′sient·ly** *adv.*

**tran·sis·tor** (tran zis′tər, -sis′-) *n.* [TRAN(SFER) + (RE)SISTOR] a small, solid-state electronic device used instead of an electron tube

**tran·sis·tor·ize** (-tə rīz′) *vt.* -ized′, -iz′ing to equip with transistors

**trans·it** (tran′sit, -zit) *n.* [< L. pp. of *transire* < *trans-*, over + *ire*, to go] **1.** *a)* passage through or across *b)* a transition; change **2.** *a)* a carrying or being carried from one place to another *[goods in transit] b)* a system of public transportation in a city: cf. RAPID TRANSIT **3.** a surveying instrument for measuring horizontal angles: in full, **transit theodolite 4.** *Astron. a)* the apparent passage of a heavenly body across a given meridian or through the field of a telescope *b)* the apparent passage of a smaller heavenly body across the disk of a larger one —*vt., vi.* to make a transit (through or across)

**tran·si·tion** (tran zish′ən, -sish′-; *Brit.* -sizh′-) *n.* **1.** *a)* a passing from one condition, activity, place, etc. to another *b)* the period of this **2.** a word, phrase, sentence, etc. that relates one element or topic to another that follows **3.** *Music a)* a shifting from one key to another; modulation *b)* same as BRIDGE —**tran·si′tion·al** *adj.* —**tran·si′tional·ly** *adv.*

**tran·si·tive** (tran′sə tiv, -zə-) *adj.* taking a direct object to complete the meaning: said of certain verbs —*n.* a transitive verb —**tran′si·tive·ly** *adv.*

**tran·si·to·ry** (tran′sə tôr′ē, -zə-) *adj.* of a passing nature; not enduring; temporary; fleeting —**tran′si·to′ri·ly** *adv.* —**tran′si·to′ri·ness** *n.*

**transl.** **1.** translated **2.** translation

**trans·late** (trans lāt′, tranz-; trans′lāt, tranz′-) *vt.* -lat′ed, -lat′ing [< L. *translatus*, used as pp. of *transferre*, to TRANSFER] **1.** to change from one place or condition to another; specif., *Theol.* to carry up to heaven without death **2.** to put into the words of a different language **3.** to change into another medium or form *[translate* ideas into action] **4.** to put into different words; rephrase —*vi.* **1.** to make a translation into another language **2.** to be capable of being translated —**trans·lat′a·ble** *adj.* —**trans·la′tor** *n.*

**trans·la·tion** (-lā′shən) *n.* **1.** a translating or being translated **2.** writing or speech translated into another language —**trans·la′tion·al** *adj.*

**trans·lit·er·ate** (trans lit′ə rāt′, tranz-) *vt.* -at′ed, -at′ing [< TRANS- + L. *litera*, letter + -ATE¹] to write or spell (words, etc.) in corresponding characters of another alphabet —**trans·lit′er·a′tion** *n.*

**trans·lu·cent** (trans lo͞o′s'nt, tranz-) *adj.* [< L. prp. of *translucere* < *trans-*, through + *lucere*, to shine] **1.** orig., shining through **2.** letting light pass but diffusing it so that objects on the other side cannot be clearly distinguished, as frosted glass: also **trans·lu′cid** (-sid) —**trans·lu′cence, trans·lu′cen·cy** n. —**trans·lu′cent·ly** adv.

**trans·mi·grate** (-mī′grāt) vi. **-grat·ed, -grat·ing** [< L. pp. of transmigrare: see TRANS- & MIGRATE] **1.** to move from one habitation, country, etc. to another **2.** in some religions, to pass into another body at death: said of the soul —**trans′mi·gra′tion** n. —**trans·mi′gra·tor** n. —**trans·mi′gra·to′ry** (-grə tôr′ē) adj.

**trans·mis·si·ble** (trans mis′ə b'l, tranz-) adj. capable of being transmitted —**trans·mis′si·bil′i·ty** n.

**trans·mis·sion** (-mish′ən) n. **1.** a) a transmitting or being transmitted b) something transmitted **2.** the part of an automobile, etc. that transmits motive force from the engine to the wheels, as by gears **3.** the passage of radio waves through space between the transmitting station and the receiving station —**trans·mis′sive** adj.

**trans·mit** (-mit′) vt. **-mit′ted, -mit′ting** [< L. < trans-, over + mittere, to send] **1.** to send or cause to go from one person or place to another; transfer; convey **2.** to pass along (a disease, etc.) **3.** to hand down to others by heredity, inheritance, etc. **4.** to communicate (news, etc.) **5.** a) to cause (light, heat, etc.) to pass through some medium b) to conduct [water transmits sound] **6.** to convey (force, movement, etc.) from one mechanical part to another **7.** to send out (radio or television broadcasts, etc.) by electromagnetic waves —vi. to send out radio or television signals —**trans·mit′tal, trans·mit′tance, trans·mit′tan·cy** n. —**trans·mit′ti·ble, trans·mit′ta·ble** adj.

**trans·mit·ter** (trans mit′ər; for 2, often trans′mit ər, tranz′-) n. **1.** a person who transmits **2.** a thing that transmits; specif., a) the part of a telegraphic instrument by which messages are sent b) the part of a telephone, behind the mouthpiece, that converts sound into electric impulses for transmission c) the apparatus that generates, modulates, and sends out radio waves

**trans·mu·ta·tion** (trans′myoo tā′shən, tranz′-) n. **1.** a transmuting or being transmuted **2.** the conversion of base metals into gold and silver as sought in alchemy **3.** Chem. the conversion of atoms of one element into atoms of a different isotope, or element, as by nuclear bombardment —**trans′mu·ta′tion·al** adj. —**trans·mut′a·tive** (-myoot′ə-tiv) adj.

**trans·mute** (trans myoot′, tranz-) vt., vi. **-mut′ed, -mut′ing** [< L. < trans-, over + mutare, to change] to change from one form, nature, substance, etc. into another; transform —**trans·mut′a·bil′i·ty** n. —**trans·mut′a·ble** adj. —**trans·mut′a·bly** adv.

**trans·o·ce·an·ic** (trans′ō shē an′ik, tranz′-) adj. **1.** crossing or spanning the ocean **2.** from or on the other side of the ocean

**tran·som** (tran′səm) n. [prob. < L. transtrum, crossbeam] **1.** a horizontal crossbar across the top or middle of a window or the top of a door **2.** a small window directly over a door or window, usually hinged to the transom **3.** any crosspiece, as the horizontal beam of a gallows

**tran·son·ic** (tran sän′ik) adj. designating, of, or moving at a speed within the range of change from subsonic to supersonic speed

**trans·pa·cif·ic** (trans′pə sif′ik) adj. **1.** crossing or spanning the Pacific **2.** on the other side of the Pacific

**trans·par·en·cy** (trans per′ən sē, -par′-) n. **1.** a transparent state or quality: also **trans·par′ence 2.** pl. **-cies** something transparent; specif., a piece of material having a picture, etc. that is visible when light shines through it

**trans·par·ent** (-ənt) adj. [< ML. prp. of transparere < L. trans-, through + parere, to appear] **1.** transmitting light rays so that objects on the other side may be distinctly seen **2.** so fine in texture or open in mesh as to be seen through; sheer; gauzy **3.** easily understood, recognized, or detected; obvious **4.** open; frank —**trans·par′ent·ly** adv. —**trans·par′ent·ness** n.

**tran·spire** (tran spīr′) vt. **-spired′, -spir′ing** [< Fr. < ML. < L. trans, through + spirare, to breathe] to cause (vapor, moisture, etc.) to pass through tissue or other permeable substances, esp. through the pores of the skin or the surface of leaves, etc. —vi. **1.** to give off vapor, moisture, etc. as through pores **2.** to be given off, exhaled, etc. **3.** to leak out; become known **4.** to come to pass; happen: regarded by some as a loose usage —**tran′spi·ra′tion** (-spə-rā′shən) n.

**trans·plant** (trans plant′; for n. trans′plant′) vt. [< LL.: see TRANS- & PLANT] **1.** to remove from one place and plant or put in another **2.** to remove (people) from one place and resettle in another **3.** Surgery to transfer (tissue or an organ) from one individual or part of the body to another; graft —vi. to be capable of being transplanted —n. **1.** a transplanting **2.** something transplanted, as a body

organ or seedling —**trans·plant′a·ble** adj. —**trans′plan·ta′tion** n. —**trans·plant′er** n.

**tran·spon·der** (tran spän′dər) n. [TRAN(SMITTER) + (RE)SPONDER] a radio or radar transceiver that automatically transmits electrical signals when actuated by a specific signal

**trans·port** (trans pôrt′; for n. trans′pôrt) vt. [< MFr. < L. < trans-, over + portare, to carry] **1.** to carry from one place to another, esp. over long distances **2.** to carry away with emotion; enrapture **3.** to banish or deport to a penal colony, etc. —n. **1.** a transporting; transportation **2.** strong emotion, esp. of delight or joy **3.** a ship, airplane, train, etc. used for transporting soldiers, freight, etc. **4.** a transported convict —**trans·port′a·bil′i·ty** n. —**trans·port′a·ble** adj. —**trans·port′er** n.

**trans·por·ta·tion** (trans′pər tā′shən) n. **1.** a transporting or being transported **2.** a) a means or system of conveyance b) the work or business of conveying passengers or goods **3.** fare or a ticket for being transported **4.** banishment for crime, as to a penal colony

**trans·pose** (trans pōz′) vt. **-posed′, -pos′ing** [MFr. transposer: see TRANS- & POSE¹] **1.** to change the usual, relative, or respective order or position of; interchange **2.** to transfer (an algebraic term) from one side of an equation to the other, reversing the plus or minus value **3.** to rewrite or play (a musical composition) in a different key —vi. to play music in a different key —**trans·pos′a·bil′i·ty, trans·pos′a·ble·ness** n. —**trans·pos′a·ble** adj. —**trans·pos′er** n. —**trans′po·si′tion** (-pə zish′ən) n.

**trans·sex·u·al** (tran sek′shoo wəl, trans-) n. a person who tends to identify with the opposite sex, or one whose sex has been changed by means of surgery and hormone injections —**trans·sex′u·al·ism** n.

**trans·ship** (tran ship′, trans-) vt. **-shipped′, -ship′ping** to transfer from one ship, train, truck, etc. to another for reshipment —**trans·ship′ment** n.

**trans·son·ic** (-sän′ik) adj. same as TRANSONIC

**tran·sub·stan·ti·a·tion** (tran′səb stan′shē ā′shən) n. [< ML. < pp. of transubstantiare < L. trans-, over + substantia, substance] **1.** a changing of one substance into another **2.** R.C. & Orthodox Eastern Ch. the doctrine that, in the Eucharist, the whole substance of the bread and wine are changed into the body and blood of Christ, while only the appearance, taste, etc. of bread and wine remain

**trans·u·ran·ic** (trans′yoo ran′ik, tranz′-) adj. designating or of the elements, as plutonium, having atomic numbers higher than that of uranium: also **trans′u·ra′ni·um** (-rā′nē əm)

**Trans·vaal** (trans väl′, tranz-) province of South Africa, in the NE part

**trans·ver·sal** (trans vur′səl) adj. same as TRANSVERSE —n. a line that intersects two or more other lines —**trans·ver′sal·ly** adv.

**trans·verse** (trans vurs′, tranz-; also, and for n. usually, trans′vurs, tranz′-) adj. [< L. pp. of transvertere: see TRAVERSE] lying, situated, placed, etc. across; crosswise —n. a transverse part, beam, etc. —**trans·verse′ly** adv.

**transverse colon** the central portion of the large intestine, crossing the abdomen: see INTESTINE, illus.

**trans·ves·tite** (trans ves′tīt, tranz-) n. [< TRANS- + L. vestire, to clothe + -ITE] a person who derives sexual pleasure from dressing in the clothes of the opposite sex —**trans·ves′tism, trans·ves′ti·tism** n.

**Tran·syl·va·ni·a** (tran′sil vā′nē ə, -vān′yə) plateau region in C Romania —**Tran′syl·va′ni·an** adj., n.

**trap¹** (trap) n. [OE. træppe] **1.** any device for catching animals; gin, snare, etc. **2.** any stratagem or ambush designed to catch or trick unsuspecting persons **3.** any of various devices for preventing the escape of gas, offensive odors, etc., as a U-shaped part in a drainpipe **4.** an apparatus for throwing disks into the air to be shot at in trapshooting **5.** a light, two-wheeled carriage with springs **6.** same as TRAPDOOR **7.** [pl.] the cymbals, blocks, etc. attached to a set of drums, as in a jazz band **8.** [Slang] the mouth **9.** Golf same as SAND TRAP —vt. **trapped, trap′ping 1.** to catch as in a trap; entrap **2.** to hold back or seal off by a trap **3.** to furnish with a trap or traps **4.** Sports to seize (a ball) just as it bounces from the ground —vi. to set traps to catch animals, esp. for their furs

**trap²** (trap) n. [< Sw. < trappa, stair] any of several dark-colored, igneous rocks; esp., such a rock, as basalt, used in road making **2.** a geologic structure enclosing oil or gas Also **trap′rock′**

**trap³** (trap) vt. **trapped, trap′ping** [< OFr. drap, cloth] to cover with trappings; caparison —n. [pl.] [Colloq.] personal belongings, clothes, etc.

**trap·door** (trap′dôr′) n. a hinged or sliding door in a roof, ceiling, or floor

**tra·peze** (tra pēz′, trə-) *n.* [Fr. < ModL.: see ff.] a short horizontal bar, hung at a height by two ropes, on which gymnasts, acrobats, etc. swing and do stunts

**tra·pe·zi·um** (trə pē′zē əm) *n., pl.* **-zi·ums, -zi·a** (-ə) [ModL. < Gr. dim. of *trapeza*, table < *tra-*, for *tetra*, four + *peza*, a foot] **1.** a plane figure with four sides no two of which are parallel [Brit.] *same as* TRAPEZOID (sense 1) **3.** a small bone of the wrist near the base of the thumb

TRAPEZIUM

**trap·e·zoid** (trap′ə zoid′) *n.* [ModL. < Gr.: see prec. & -OID] **1.** a plane figure with four sides only two of which are parallel **2.** [Brit.] *same as* TRAPEZIUM (sense 1) **3.** a small bone of the wrist near the base of the index finger —*adj.* shaped like a trapezoid: also **trap′e·zoi′dal**

**trap·per** (trap′ər) *n.* a person who traps; esp., one who traps fur-bearing animals for their skins

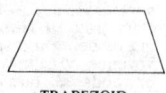

TRAPEZOID

**trap·pings** (-iŋz) *n.pl.* [see TRAP³] **1.** a highly decorated covering for a horse; caparison **2.** highly decorated clothing **3.** things accompanying something that are an outward sign of it [*trappings* of success]

**Trap·pist** (trap′ist) *n.* [< Fr. < (*La*) *Trappe*, abbey in Normandy] a monk of a branch of the Cistercian order, living under a vow of silence —*adj.* of the Trappists

**trap·shoot·ing** (trap′shoot′iŋ) *n.* the sport of shooting at clay pigeons, or disks, sprung into the air from traps — **trap′shoot′er** *n.*

**trash** (trash) *n.* [prob. < Scand.] **1.** parts that have been broken off, stripped off, etc., esp. leaves, twigs, etc. **2.** discarded or worthless things; rubbish **3.** worthless, unnecessary, offensive, or foolish matter [literary *trash*] **4.** a person or people regarded as disreputable —*vt.* [Slang] to destroy (property) by vandalism, arson, etc.

**trash·y** (-ē) *adj.* **trash′i·er, trash′i·est** containing, consisting of, or like trash; worthless —**trash′i·ness** *n.*

**‡trat·tor·i·a** (trät′tô rē′ä) *n., pl.* **-i·e** (-e) [It. < *trattore*, innkeeper] a small, inexpensive restaurant in Italy

**trau·ma** (trou′mə, trô′-) *n., pl.* **-mas, -ma·ta** (-mə tə) [ModL. < Gr.] **1.** *Med.* a bodily injury, wound, or shock **2.** *Psychiatry* an emotional shock which has a lasting effect on the mind —**trau·mat′ic** (-mat′ik) *adj.* —**trau·mat′i·cal·ly** *adv.*

**trau·ma·tize** (-tīz′) *vt.* **-tized′, -tiz′ing 1.** *Med.* to injure or wound (tissues) **2.** *Psychiatry* to subject to a trauma

**trav·ail** (trav′āl, trə vāl′) *n.* [OFr. < VL. *tripalium*, a torture device < *tria*, three + *palus*, a stake] **1.** very hard work **2.** the pains of childbirth **3.** intense pain; agony —*vi.* **1.** to toil **2.** to suffer the pains of childbirth

**trav·el** (trav′′l) *vi.* **-eled** or **-elled, -el·ing** or **-el·ling** [var. of prec.] **1.** to go from one place to another; make a journey **2.** to go from place to place as a traveling salesman **3.** to walk or run **4.** to move, pass, or be transmitted **5.** to move in a given course: said of mechanical parts, etc. **6.** to advance or progress **7.** *Basketball* to move (usually more than two steps) while holding the ball **8.** [Colloq.] to associate (*with*) **9.** [Colloq.] to move with speed —*vt.* **1.** to make a journey over or through **2.** [Colloq.] to cause to pass along —*n.* **1.** the act or process of traveling **2.** [*pl.*] trips, journeys, tours, etc. **3.** movement of any kind **4.** *a*) mechanical motion, esp. reciprocating motion *b*) the distance of a mechanical stroke, etc. —**trav′el·er, trav′el·ler** *n.*

**trav·eled, trav·elled** (-′ld) *adj.* **1.** that has traveled much **2.** much used by travelers [a *traveled* road]

**traveler's check** a check, usually one of a set, issued by a bank, etc. and sold to a traveler who signs it when it is issued and again in the presence of the one cashing it

**traveling salesman** a salesman who travels for a business firm, soliciting orders

**trav·e·logue, trav·e·log** (trav′ə lôg′, -läg′) *n.* **1.** a lecture on travels, accompanied by the showing of pictures **2.** a motion picture of travels

**trav·erse** (trav′ərs, trə-; *also, & for n. & adj.* always, trav′ərs) *vt.* **-ersed′, -ers′ing** [< OFr. < L. pp. of *transvertere* < *trans-*, over + *vertere*, to turn] **1.** *a*) to pass or extend over, across, or through *b*) to go back and forth over or along **2.** to go counter to; oppose **3.** to examine carefully **4.** to turn (a gun, etc.) laterally **5.** *Law* to deny formally (an allegation) —*vi.* **1.** to cross over **2.** to move back and forth over a place, etc. **3.** to swivel or pivot **4.** to move across a mountain slope, as in skiing, in an oblique direction —*n.* **1.** something that traverses or crosses; specif., *a*) a crossbar, crossbeam, etc. *b*) a gallery, loft, etc. crossing a building **2.** a traversing or passing across **3.** a device that causes a traversing movement **4.** a way across **5.** a zigzag course taken by a vessel —*adj.* **1.** extending across **2.** designating or of drapes hung in pairs so that they can be drawn by pulling cords at the side —**trav·ers′a·ble** *adj.* —**trav·ers′al** *n.* —**trav·ers′er** *n.*

**trav·er·tine** (trav′ər tēn′, -tin) *n.* [< It., ult. < L. (*lapis*) *Tiburtinus*, (stone) by Tibur, ancient It. city] a light-colored limestone deposited around limy springs, lakes, etc.

**trav·es·ty** (trav′is tē) *n., pl.* **-ties** [< Fr. pp. of *travestir*, to disguise < It. < L. *trans-*, over + *vestire*, to dress] **1.** a grotesque or exaggerated imitation for purposes of ridicule; burlesque **2.** a crude or ridiculous representation —*vt.* **-tied, -ty·ing** to make a travesty of

**trawl** (trôl) *n.* [< ? MDu. *traghel*, a dragnet] **1.** a large, baglike net dragged by a boat along the bottom of a fishing bank: also **trawl′net′ 2.** a long line supported by buoys, from which many short fishing lines are hung: also **trawl line** —*vt., vi.* to fish or catch with a trawl

**trawl·er** (trô′lər) *n.* a boat used in trawling

**tray** (trā) *n.* [OE. *treg*, wooden board] **1.** a flat receptacle with low sides, for holding or carrying articles **2.** a tray with its contents [a *tray* of food] **3.** a shallow, removable compartment of a trunk, cabinet, etc.

**treach·er·ous** (trech′ər əs) *adj.* **1.** full of or showing treachery; traitorous **2.** untrustworthy; unreliable [*treacherous* rocks] —**treach′er·ous·ly** *adv.* —**treach′er·ous·ness** *n.*

**treach·er·y** (-ē) *n., pl.* **-er·ies** [< OFr. < *trichier*, to trick, cheat] **1.** betrayal of trust, faith, or allegiance; disloyalty or treason **2.** an act of disloyalty or treason

**trea·cle** (trē′k′l) *n.* [< OFr. < L. < Gr. *thēriakē*, remedy for venomous bites < *thērion*, dim. of *thēr*, wild beast] [Brit.] molasses —**trea′cly** (-klē) *adj.*

**tread** (tred) *vt.* **trod, trod′den** or **trod, tread′ing** [OE. *tredan*] **1.** to walk on, in, along, over, etc. **2.** to do or follow by walking, dancing, etc. [to *tread* the measures gaily] **3.** to press or beat with the feet; trample **4.** to oppress or subdue **5.** to copulate with: said of male birds —*vi.* **1.** to move on foot; walk **2.** to set one's foot (*on, across*, etc.) **3.** to trample (*on* or *upon*) **4.** to copulate: said of birds —*n.* **1.** the act, manner, or sound of treading **2.** something on which a person or thing treads or moves, as the part of a shoe sole, wheel, etc. that touches the ground, the endless belt over cogged wheels of a tractor, etc., the horizontal surface of a stair step, etc. **3.** *a*) the thick outer layer of an automotive tire *b*) the depth or pattern of grooves in this layer —**tread the boards** to act in plays —**tread water** *pt. & pp. now usually* **tread′ed** to keep the body upright and the head above water in swimming by moving the legs up and down —**tread′er** *n.*

**trea·dle** (tred′′l) *n.* [< OE. < *tredan*: see prec.] a lever or pedal moved by the foot so as to turn a wheel —*vi.* **-dled, -dling** to work a treadle

**tread·mill** (tred′mil′) *n.* **1.** a mill wheel turned by persons treading steps built around its outer edge, or by an animal treading an endless belt **2.** any monotonous routine of duties, work, etc.

**treas. 1.** treasurer **2.** treasury

**trea·son** (trē′z′n) *n.* [< OFr. < L. < pp. of *tradere*, to deliver up < *trans-*, over + *dare*, to give] **1.** [Now Rare] betrayal of trust or faith **2.** betrayal of one's country, esp. by helping the enemy in time of war

**trea·son·a·ble** (-ə b′l) *adj.* of or involving treason; traitorous: also **trea′son·ous** —**trea′son·a·ble·ness** *n.* —**trea′son·a·bly** *adv.*

**treas·ure** (trezh′ər) *n.* [< OFr. < L. < Gr. *thēsauros*] **1.** accumulated wealth, as money, gold, jewels, etc. **2.** any person or thing considered valuable —*vt.* **-ured, -ur·ing 1.** to save up (money, etc.) for future use **2.** to value greatly; cherish

**treas·ur·er** (trezh′ər ər) *n.* a person in charge of a treasure or treasury; specif., an officer in charge of the funds of a government, corporation, society, etc. —**treas′ur·er·ship′** *n.*

**treas·ure-trove** (-trōv′) *n.* [< Anglo-Fr. < OFr. *tresor*, treasure + *trové*, pp. of *trover*, to find] **1.** treasure found hidden, the original owner of which is not known **2.** any valuable discovery

**treas·ur·y** (-ē) *n., pl.* **-ur·ies 1.** a place where treasure is kept **2.** a place where public or private funds are kept, recorded, etc. **3.** the funds or revenues of a state, corporation, etc. **4.** [T-] the governmental department in charge of revenue, taxation, etc. **5.** a collection of treasures in art, literature, etc.

**treasury note** any of the interest-bearing notes or obligations of the U.S. Treasury

**treat** (trēt) *vi.* [< OFr. *traiter* < L. *tractare*, freq. of *trahere*, to draw] **1.** to discuss terms (*with* a person or *for* a settlement) **2.** to deal with a subject; speak or write (*of*) **3.** to stand the cost of another's entertainment —*vt.* **1.** to deal with (a subject) in writing, music, etc. in a specified style **2.** to act toward (a person, animal, etc.) in a specified manner **3.** to regard in a specified way [he *treated* it as a joke] **4.** *a*) to pay for the food, drink, etc. of (another) *b*) to provide with something that pleases **5.** to subject to some process or substance, as in a chemical procedure **6.** to give medical or surgical care to (someone) or for (some disorder) —*n.* **1.** a meal, drink, etc. paid for by someone else **2.** anything that gives great pleasure **3.** *a*) the act of treating or entertaining *b*) one's turn to treat —**treat′a·bil′i·ty** *n.* —**treat′a·ble** *adj.* —**treat′er** *n.*

**trea·tise** (trēt′is) *n.* [< Anglo-Fr., ult. < OFr. *traiter:* see TREAT] a formal, systematic article or book dealing with some subject in a detailed way

**treat·ment** (-mənt) *n.* **1.** act, manner, method, etc. of treating **2.** medical or surgical care

**trea·ty** (trēt′ē) *n., pl.* **-ties** [< OFr. *traité,* ult. < pp. of L. *tractare,* to manage] a formal agreement between two or more nations, relating to peace, alliance, trade, etc.

**tre·ble** (treb′'l) *adj.* [< OFr. < L. *triplus,* triple] **1.** threefold; triple **2.** of, for, or performing the treble **3.** high-pitched or shrill —*n.* **1.** the highest part in musical harmony; soprano **2.** a singer or instrument that takes this part **3.** a high-pitched voice or sound —*vt., vi.* **-bled, -bling** to make or become threefold —**tre′bly** *adv.*

**treble clef** *Music* a sign on a staff, indicating the position of G above middle C on the second line

**tree** (trē) *n.* [OE. *treow*] **1.** a large, woody perennial plant with one main trunk which develops many branches **2.** a treelike bush or shrub **3.** a wooden beam, bar, post, etc. **4.** anything resembling a tree; specif., *short for* FAMILY TREE —*vt.* **treed, tree′ing 1.** to chase up a tree **2.** to stretch on a shoe tree —**up a tree** [Colloq.] in a situation without escape; cornered —**tree′less** *adj.* —**tree′like′** *adj.*

**tree fern** a tropical fern with a woody trunk

**tree frog** any of various frogs that live in trees: many are called *tree toads*

**tree lawn** in some cities, the strip of ground between a street and its parallel sidewalk, often planted with lawns and trees: also **tree′lawn′** *n.*

**tree·nail** (trē′nāl′; tren′′l, trun′-) *n.* [< ME. < *tre,* wood + *nayle,* nail] a dry wooden peg used to join timbers, esp. in shipbuilding: it swells when wet so as to fit tight

**tree of heaven** a fast-growing ailanthus

**tree squirrel** any of various squirrels that live in trees, as the gray squirrel, the red squirrel, etc.

**tree surgery** treatment of damaged trees as by filling cavities, pruning, etc. —**tree surgeon**

**tree toad** *see* TREE FROG

**tree·top** (trē′täp′) *n.* the topmost part of a tree

**tre·foil** (trē′foil) *n.* [< Anglo-Fr. < L. < *tri-,* three + *folium,* a leaf] **1.** a plant with leaves divided into three leaflets, as the clover **2.** any ornamental figure shaped like such a leaf

**trek** (trek) *vi.* **trekked, trek′king** [Afrik. < Du. *trekken,* to draw] **1.** in South Africa, to travel by ox wagon **2.** to travel slowly or laboriously **3.** [Colloq.] to go on foot —*n.* **1.** in South Africa, a journey made by ox wagon **2.** a journey or leg of a journey **3.** a migration **4.** [Colloq.] a short trip, esp. on foot —**trek′ker** *n.*

**trel·lis** (trel′is) *n.* [< OFr., ult. < L. *trilix,* triple-twilled] an openwork structure of thin, crossed strips, esp. of wood, on which vines are trained; lattice —*vt.* **1.** to furnish with, or train on, a trellis **2.** to cross or interweave like a trellis

**trem·a·tode** (trem′ə tōd′, trē′mə-) *n.* [< ModL. < Gr. < *trēma* (gen. *trēmatos*), a hole + *eidos,* form] any of various parasitic flatworms; fluke —*adj.* of a trematode

**trem·ble** (trem′b'l) *vi.* **-bled, -bling** [< OFr. < VL., ult. < L. < *tremere*] **1.** to shake involuntarily from cold, fear, excitement, etc.; shiver **2.** to feel great fear or anxiety **3.** to quake, totter, vibrate, etc. **4.** to quaver [a *trembling* voice] —*n.* **1.** a trembling **2.** [*sometimes pl.*] a fit or state of trembling —**trem′bler** *n.* —**trem′bling·ly** *adv.* —**trem′bly** *adj.*

**tre·men·dous** (tri men′dəs) *adj.* [< L. *tremendus* < *tremere,* to TREMBLE] **1.** such as to make one tremble; terrifying **2.** *a*) very large; great *b*) [Colloq.] wonderful, amazing, etc. —**tre·men′dous·ly** *adv.* —**tre·men′dous·ness** *n.*

**trem·o·lo** (trem′ə lō′) *n., pl.* **-los′** [It. < L.: see TREMULOUS] **1.** a trembling effect produced by rapidly repeating the same musical tone **2.** a device, as in an organ, for producing such a tone

**trem·or** (trem′ər; *occas.* trē′mər) *n.* [< OFr. < L. < *tremere,* to TREMBLE] **1.** a trembling, shaking, etc. **2.** a vibratory motion **3.** a nervous thrill; trembling sensation **4.** a trembling sound —**trem′or·ous** *adj.*

**trem·u·lous** (trem′yoo ləs) *adj.* [L. *tremulus* < *tremere,* to TREMBLE] **1.** trembling; quivering **2.** fearful; timid **3.** marked by or showing trembling or quivering Also **trem′u·lant** —**trem′u·lous·ly** *adv.* —**trem′u·lous·ness** *n.*

**tre·nail** (trē′nāl′; tren′′l, trun′-) *n.* same as TREENAIL

**trench** (trench) *vt.* [< OFr. < ? L. *truncare,* to cut off] **1.** to cut, slice, gash, etc. **2.** to dig a ditch or ditches in **3.** to surround or fortify with trenches —*vi.* **1.** to dig a ditch or ditches **2.** to infringe (*on* or *upon* another's land, rights,

etc.) **3.** to verge or border (*on*); come close —*n.* **1.** a deep furrow **2.** a long, narrow ditch with earth banked in front as a parapet, used in battle for cover, etc.

**trench·ant** (tren′chənt) *adj.* [< OFr.: see prec.] **1.** orig., cutting; sharp **2.** keen; penetrating; incisive [*trenchant* words] **3.** forceful; vigorous [a *trenchant* argument] **4.** clear-cut; distinct [a *trenchant* pattern] —**trench′an·cy** *n.* —**trench′ant·ly** *adv.*

**trench coat** a belted raincoat in a military style

**trench·er** (tren′chər) *n.* [Archaic] **1.** a wooden platter for carving and serving meat **2.** *a*) food served on a trencher *b*) a supply of food

**trench·er·man** (-mən) *n., pl.* **-men** an eater; esp., one who eats much and heartily

**trench fever** an infectious disease transmitted by body lice, in which there is remittent fever, muscular pains, etc.

**trench foot** a diseased condition of the feet from prolonged exposure to wet and cold, as of soldiers in trenches

**trench mortar** (or **gun**) any of various portable mortars for shooting projectiles at a high trajectory and short range

**trench mouth** an infectious disease of the mouth and throat in which the mucous membranes become ulcerated

**trend** (trend) *vi.* [OE. *trendan*] **1.** to extend, turn, bend, etc. in a specific direction **2.** to have a general tendency: said of events, opinions, etc. —*n.* **1.** the general direction of a river, road, etc. **2.** the general tendency or course, as of events, a discussion, etc. **3.** a vogue, or current style, as in fashions

**trend·y** (-ē) *adj.* **trend′i·er, trend′i·est** [Colloq.] of or in the latest style, or trend; faddish —**trend′i·ly** *adv.* —**trend′i·ness** *n.*

**Trent** (trent) **1.** city in N Italy: pop. 87,000: It. name **Tren·to** (tren′tō) **2.** river in C England, flowing northeast into the North Sea **3. Council of,** the council of the Roman Catholic Church held intermittently at Trent, 1545–63, to counteract the Reformation

**Tren·ton** (tren′tən) [after Wm. *Trent* (1655–1724), colonist] capital of N.J., on the Delaware River: pop. 92,000

**tre·pan** (tri pan′) *n.* [< ML. < Gr. < *trypan,* to bore] **1.** an early form of the trephine **2.** a heavy boring tool —*vt.* **-panned′, -pan′ning** *same as* TREPHINE —**trep·a·na·tion** (trep′ə nā′shən) *n.*

**tre·pang** (tri paŋ′) *n.* [Malay *tĕripang*] a boiled, smoked, and dried sea cucumber, used in the Orient for making soup

**tre·phine** (tri fīn′, -fēn′) *n.* [formed (after TREPAN) < L. *tres,* three + *fines,* ends] a type of small circular saw used in surgery to remove disks of bone from the skull —*vt.* **-phined′, -phin′ing** to operate on with a trephine —**treph·i·na·tion** (tref′ə nā′shən) *n.*

**trep·i·da·tion** (trep′ə dā′shən) *n.* [< L. < pp. of *trepidare,* to tremble < *trepidus,* disturbed] **1.** tremulous or trembling movement **2.** fearful uncertainty or anxiety

**tres·pass** (tres′pəs; *also, esp. for v.,* -pas′) *vi.* [< OFr., ult. < L. *trans-,* across + VL. hyp. *passare,* to pass] **1.** to go beyond the limits of what is considered right or moral; transgress **2.** to go on another's property without permission or right **3.** to intrude; encroach **4.** *Law* to commit a trespass —*n.* a trespassing; specif., *a*) a moral offense *b*) an encroachment; intrusion *c*) *Law* an illegal act done with force against another's person, rights, or property —**tres′pass·er** *n.*

**tress** (tres) *n.* [< OFr. < ? Frank.] **1.** orig., a braid of hair **2.** a lock of human hair **3.** [*pl.*] a woman's or girl's hair, esp. when long and falling loosely

**-tress** (tris) *a suffix meaning female* [*actress*] : see also -ESS

**tres·tle** (tres′'l) *n.* [< OFr., ult. < L. *transtrum,* a beam] **1.** a frame consisting of a horizontal beam fastened to two pairs of spreading legs, used to support planks to form a table, etc. **2.** a framework of uprights and crosspieces, supporting a bridge, etc.; also, such a bridge

**tres·tle·work** (-wurk′) *n.* a system of trestles for supporting a bridge, etc.

**trey** (trā) *n.* [< OFr. < L. *tres,* three] **1.** a playing card with three spots **2.** the side of a die bearing three spots, or a throw of the dice totaling three

TRESTLE

**tri-** [< Fr., L., or Gr.] *a combining form meaning:* **1.** having or involving three [*triangular*] **2.** triply, in three ways [*trilingual*] **3.** three times, into three [*trisect*] **4.** every third [*triannual*] **5.** *Chem.* having three atoms, groups, or equivalents of (the thing specified) [*tribasic*]

**tri·a·ble** (trī′ə b'l) *adj.* **1.** that can be tried or tested **2.** subject to trial in a law court —**tri′a·ble·ness** *n.*

**tri·ac·e·tate** (trī as′ə tāt′) *n.* a compound containing three acetate radicals in the molecule

---

**tri·ad** (trī'ad) *n.* [< LL. < Gr. < *treis*, three] **1.** a group of three persons, things, etc. **2.** a musical chord of three tones, one consisting of a root tone and its third and fifth: a triad with a major third and perfect fifth is called a *major triad;* a triad with a minor third and perfect fifth is called a *minor triad* —**tri·ad'ic** *adj.*

**tri·age** (trē äzh') *n.* [Fr. < *trier*, to sift] a system of deciding in what order battlefield casualties will receive medical treatment, according to urgency, chance of survival, etc.

**tri·al** (trī'əl, trīl) *n.* [Anglo-Fr. < *trier*, to try] **1.** *a)* a trying, testing, etc.; test *b)* a testing of qualifications, progress, etc.; probation *c)* an experiment **2.** *a)* a being tried by suffering, temptation, etc. *b)* suffering, hardship, trouble, etc., or the cause of this **3.** a formal examination of the facts of a case by a court of law to decide the validity of a charge or claim **4.** an attempt; effort —*adj.* **1.** of a trial **2.** of or for trying, testing, etc. —**on trial** in the process of being tried

**trial and error** a trying or testing over and over again until the right result is found —**tri'al-and-er'ror** *adj.*

**trial balance** a statement of the debit and credit balances of all open accounts in a double-entry bookkeeping ledger to test their equality

**trial balloon** **1.** *same as* PILOT BALLOON **2.** an action, statement, etc. made to test public opinion on an issue

**trial jury** *same as* PETIT JURY

**tri·an·gle** (trī'aŋ'g'l) *n.* [< MFr. < L.: see TRI- & ANGLE[1]] **1.** a plane figure having three angles and three sides **2.** any three-sided or three-cornered figure, area, etc. **3.** a situation involving three persons **4.** a musical instrument consisting of a steel rod bent in a triangle: it makes a high-pitched, tinkling sound when struck —**tri·an'gu·lar** (-aŋ'gyə-lər) *adj.* —**tri·an'gu·lar'i·ty** (-ler'ə tē) *n.*

TRIANGLES

**tri·an·gu·late** (trī aŋ'gyə lāt'; *for adj. usually* -lit) *vt.* -**lat'ed, -lat'ing** **1.** to divide into triangles **2.** to survey (a region) by triangulation **3.** to make triangular **4.** to measure by trigonometry —*adj.* of, like, or marked with triangles

**tri·an·gu·la·tion** (trī aŋ'gyə lā'shən) *n.* a triangulating or being triangulated; specif., *Surveying* the determining of distance between points on the earth's surface by calculations based on the division of an area into connected triangles and the measurement of their angles

**Tri·as·sic** (trī as'ik) *adj.* [< ModL. < LL. *trias*, TRIAD (because divisible into three groups) + -IC] designating or of the first period of the Mesozoic Era —**the Triassic** the Triassic Period or its rocks: see GEOLOGY, chart

**trib·al·ism** (trī'b'l iz'm) *n.* tribal organization, culture, loyalty, etc. —**trib'al·ist** *n., adj.*

**tribe** (trīb) *n.* [L. *tribus*, any of the divisions (orig. three) of the ancient Romans] **1.** a group of persons, families, or clans believed to have a common ancestor: many tribes form a close community under a leader or chief **2.** any group of people with the same occupation, ideas, etc. **3.** a subdivision of a subfamily of plants or animals **4.** loosely, any group of plants or animals classified together **5.** [Colloq.] a family —**trib'al** *adj.* —**trib'al·ly** *adv.*

**tribes·man** (trībz'mən) *n., pl.* -**men** a member of a tribe

**trib·u·la·tion** (trib'yə lā'shən) *n.* [< OFr. < LL. < *tribulare*, to afflict < L., to press < *tribulum*, threshing sledge] **1.** great misery or distress, as from oppression **2.** the cause of this; affliction; trial

**tri·bu·nal** (trī byōō'n'l, tri-) *n.* [L.: see TRIBUNE[1]] **1.** the judge's bench **2.** a court of justice **3.** any seat of judgment

**trib·une**[1] (trib'yōōn; *in a newspaper name often* tri byōōn') *n.* [< L. *tribunus* < *tribus*, tribe] **1.** in ancient Rome, *a)* any of several magistrates whose duty it was to protect the rights and interests of the plebeians *b)* any of six officers rotating command over a legion **2.** a champion of the people —**trib'une·ship'** *n.*

**trib·une**[2] (trib'yōōn) *n.* [Fr. < It. < L.: see TRIBUNAL, sense 1] a raised platform or dais for speakers

**trib·u·tar·y** (trib'yoo ter'ē) *adj.* **1.** paying tribute **2.** under another's control; subject [a tributary nation] **3.** owed or paid as tribute **4.** *a)* making additions; contributory *b)* flowing into a larger one [a tributary stream] —*n., pl.* -**tar'ies** **1.** a tributary nation or ruler **2.** a tributary stream or river

**trib·ute** (trib'yōōt) *n.* [< MFr. < L. pp. of *tribuere*, to allot, pay < *tribus*, tribe] **1.** money that one nation is forced to pay to another, more powerful nation **2.** any forced payment **3.** the obligation to pay tribute **4.** something given, done, or said to show gratitude, honor, or praise

**trice** (trīs) *vt.* **triced, tric'ing** [MDu. *trisen*, to pull < *trise*, windlass] to haul up and secure (a sail, etc.): usually with *up* —*n.* [< *at a trice*, with one pull] a very short time; instant: now only in **in a trice**

**tri·cen·ten·ni·al** (trī'sen ten'ē əl) *adj.* happening once in, or lasting for, 300 years —*n.* a 300th anniversary

**tri·ceps** (trī'seps) *n., pl.* -**ceps·es, -ceps** [ModL. < L. < *tri-*, three + *caput*, a head] a muscle having three points of origin, esp. the muscle at the back of the upper arm that extends the forearm

**tri·chi·na** (tri kī'nə) *n., pl.* -**nae** (-nē) [ModL. < Gr. *trichinos*, hairy < *thrix*, hair] a very small worm whose larvae infest the intestines and muscles of man, pigs, etc., causing trichinosis —**tri·chi'nal** *adj.*

**trich·i·no·sis** (trik'ə nō'sis) *n.* a trichinal disease marked by fever, diarrhea, muscular pains, etc. and usually acquired by eating undercooked infested pork

**trick** (trik) *n.* [ONormFr. *trique* < OFr. *trichier*, to cheat] **1.** something that is done to fool, cheat, outwit, etc.; ruse; stratagem **2.** *a)* a piece of playful mischief; prank *b)* a deception or illusion [the light played a *trick* on his eyes] **3.** a freakish, foolish, or mean act **4.** a clever or skillful act intended to amuse; specif., *a)* an act of jugglery, sleight of hand, etc. *b)* a feat done by a trained animal **5.** the art or knack of doing a thing easily, skillfully, quickly, etc. **6.** a personal mannerism **7.** a turn at work; shift **8.** *Card Games* the cards played and won in a single round —*vt.* to deceive, cheat, outwit, fool, etc. —*adj.* **1.** of, for, or using tricks [trick photography] **2.** that tricks **3.** not always working right [a trick knee] —**do** (or **turn**) **the trick** to bring about the desired result —**trick out** (or **up**) to dress up; adorn

**trick·er·y** (-ər ē) *n., pl.* -**er·ies** the use of tricks to cheat, outwit, etc.; deception; stratagem

**trick·le** (trik'l) *vi.* -**led, -ling** [prob. < freq. of ME. *striken*, to strike] **1.** to flow slowly in a thin stream or fall in drops **2.** to move little by little [the crowd *trickled* away] —*vt.* to cause to trickle —*n.* **1.** a trickling **2.** a thin flow or drip

**trick·ster** (trik'stər) *n.* a person who tricks; cheat

**trick·sy** (-sē) *adj.* -**si·er, -si·est** **1.** mischievous; prankish **2.** *same as* TRICKY —**trick'si·ness** *n.*

**trick·y** (trik'ē) *adj.* **trick'i·er, trick'i·est** **1.** given to or full of trickery **2.** intricate; difficult **3.** needing special skill or care —**trick'i·ly** *adv.* —**trick'i·ness** *n.*

**tri·clin·ic** (trī klin'ik) *adj.* [< TRI- + Gr. *klinein*, to incline + -IC] designating a crystalline form that has three unequal axes intersecting at oblique angles

**tri·col·or** (trī'kul'ər) *n.* a flag consisting of three stripes, each of a different color, esp. the flag of France —*adj.* having three colors

**tri·corn, tri·corne** (-kôrn') *adj.* [< Fr. < L. < *tri-*, three + *cornu*, horn] having three horns or corners —*n.* a tricorn hat

**tri·cot** (trē'kō) *n.* [Fr. < *tricoter*, to knit, ult. < MDu.] **1.** a thin fabric that is knitted or woven to look knitted **2.** a type of ribbed cloth for dresses

**tri·cus·pid** (trī kus'pid) *adj.* [< L.: see TRI- & CUSP] **1.** having three cusps, or points [a tricuspid tooth]: also **tri·cus'pi·date** (-pə dāt') **2.** designating or of a valve with three flaps, between the right auricle and right ventricle of the heart —*n.* a tricuspid tooth or valve

**tri·cy·cle** (trī'si k'l) *n.* [Fr.] a light, three-wheeled vehicle worked by pedals, esp. one for children

**tri·dent** (trīd'nt) *n.* [< L. < *tri-*, three + *dens* (gen. *dentis*), a tooth] a three-pronged spear

**tri·den·tate** (trī den'tāt) *adj.* having three teeth, prongs, or points

**tried** (trīd) *pt. & pp. of* TRY —*adj.* **1.** tested; proved **2.** trustworthy; faithful **3.** having endured trials and troubles

**tri·en·ni·al** (trī en'ē əl) *adj.* [< L. < *tri-*, three + *annus*, a year] **1.** happening every three years **2.** lasting three years —*n.* a triennial event —**tri·en'ni·al·ly** *adv.*

**tri·er** (trī'ər) *n.* a person or thing that tries

**Tri·este** (trē est'; *It.* trē es'te) seaport in NE Italy, on an inlet (**Gulf of Trieste**) of the Adriatic: pop. 278,000

**tri·fa·cial** (trī fā'shəl) *adj., n. same as* TRIGEMINAL

**tri·fid** (trī'fid) *adj.* [< L. < *tri-*, three + base of *findere*, to divide] divided into three lobes by deep clefts, as some leaves

**tri·fle** (trī'f'l) *n.* [< OFr. dim. of *truffe*, deception] **1.** something of little value or importance **2.** a small amount; bit **3.** a small sum of money —*vi.* -**fled, -fling** **1.** to talk or act in a joking way; deal lightly [not a person to *trifle* with] **2.** to play or toy (with something) —*vt.* to spend idly; waste [trifling time away] —**tri'fler** *n.*

**tri·fling** (-fliŋ) *adj.* **1.** frivolous; fickle **2.** trivial

**tri·fo·cal** (trī fō'k'l, trī'fō'-) *adj.* having three focal lengths —*n.* **1.** a lens with one part ground for close focus, one for intermediate focus, and one for distant focus **2.** [*pl.*] a pair of glasses with such lenses

**trig**[1] (trig) *adj.* [< ON. *tryggr*, true] [Chiefly Brit.] **1.** trim; neat **2.** in good condition —*vt.* **trigged, trig'ging** [Chiefly Brit. Dial.] to make trig (often with *out, up*)

**trig**[2] (trig) *n. shortened form of* TRIGONOMETRY

**trig., trigon.** **1.** trigonometric(al) **2.** trigonometry

**tri·gem·i·nal** (trī jem'ə n'l) *adj.* [< ModL. < L. < *tri-*, three + *geminus*, twin] designating or of either of a pair of cranial nerves, each dividing into three branches supplying the head and face —*n.* a trigeminal nerve

**trig·ger** (trig′ər) *n.* [< Du. < *trekken*, to pull] a lever, etc. which when pulled or pressed releases a catch, spring, etc.; esp., the small lever pressed back by the finger in firing a gun —*vt.* 1. to fire or set into action with a trigger 2. to set off (an action) [the fight *triggered* a riot] —**quick on the trigger** [Colloq.] 1. quick to fire a gun 2. quick to act, retort, etc.; alert

**trig·ger-hap·py** (-hap′ē) *adj.* [Colloq.] quick to resort to force, make war, etc.

**tri·glyc·er·ide** (trī glis′ər īd′) *n.* [TRI- + GLYCERIDE] any of a group of esters of fatty acids and glycerol, found in the blood and thought to be a factor in atherosclerosis

**trig·o·nom·e·try** (trig′ə näm′ə trē) *n.* [< ModL. < Gr. *trigōnon*, triangle + *-metria*, measurement] the branch of mathematics dealing with the ratios between the sides of a right triangle with reference to either acute angle (*trigonometric functions*), the relations between these ratios, and use of these facts in finding the unknown sides or angles of any triangle —**trig′o·no·met′ric** (-nə met′rik), **trig′o·no·met′ri·cal** *adj.* —**trig′o·no·met′ri·cal·ly** *adv.*

**tri·he·dral** (trī hē′drəl) *adj.* [TRI- + -HEDRAL] having three sides or faces [a *trihedral* angle] —*n.* a figure formed by three lines, each in a different plane, that intersect at a point

**trike** (trīk) *n.* [Colloq.] *same as* TRICYCLE

**tri·lat·er·al** (trī lat′ər əl) *adj.* three-sided

**tri·lin·gual** (-liŋ′gwəl) *adj.* in or using three languages

**trill** (tril) *n.* [< It. < *trillare*, of echoic origin] 1. a rapid alternation of a tone with one just above it 2. a bird's warble 3. *a)* a rapid vibration of the tongue or uvula, as in pronouncing *r* in some languages *b)* an *r*, etc. so pronounced —*vt., vi.* to sound with a trill —**trill′er** *n.*

**tril·lion** (tril′yən) *n.* [Fr. < *tri-*, TRI- + (*mi*)*llion*] 1. in the U.S. and France, the number represented by 1 followed by 12 zeros 2. in Great Britain and Germany, the number represented by 1 followed by 18 zeros —*adj.* amounting to one trillion —**tril′lionth** *adj., n.*

**tril·li·um** (tril′ē əm) *n.* [ModL., genus name < L. *tri-*, three] a plant of the lily family with an erect stem bearing a whorl of three leaves and a single, three-petaled flower

**tri·lo·bate** (trī lō′bāt) *adj.* having three lobes, as some leaves: also **tri·lo′bat·ed, tri′lobed′** (-lōbd′)

**tri·lo·bite** (trī′lə bīt′) *n.* [< ModL.: see TRI-, LOBE, & -ITE] an extinct sea arthropod with the body divided by two furrows into three parts: a common fossil in Paleozoic rocks —**tri′lo·bit′ic** (-bit′ik) *adj.*

**tril·o·gy** (tril′ə jē) *n., pl.* -gies [Gr. *trilogia*: see TRI- & -LOGY] a set of three plays, novels, etc. which form a related group, although each is a complete work

**trim** (trim) *vt.* **trimmed, trim′ming** [OE. *trymman*, to make firm < *trum*, strong] 1. to put in proper order; make neat or tidy, esp. by clipping, etc. [to *trim* hair] 2. to clip, lop, cut, etc. [to *trim* dead branches off a tree] 3. to cut (something) down to the required size or shape 4. *a)* to decorate with ornaments, colorful materials, etc. [to *trim* a Christmas tree] *b)* to arrange an attractive display of merchandise in or on [to *trim* a store window] 5. *a)* to balance (a ship) by shifting cargo, etc. *b)* to put (sails, etc.) in order for sailing 6. to balance (an aircraft in flight) by adjusting stabilizers, tabs, etc. 7. [Colloq.] *a)* to scold *b)* to beat, thrash, etc. *c)* to defeat *d)* to cheat —*vi.* 1. *a)* to take a middle position between opposing sides *b)* to change one's opinions, policy, etc. in a way that is expedient 2. to keep a ship, etc. in balance —*n.* 1. condition or order [in proper *trim*] 2. good condition or order [keep in *trim*] 3. a trimming by clipping, cutting, etc. 4. *a) same as* WINDOW DRESSING *b)* decorative molding or borders, esp. around windows and doors *c)* the interior furnishings or ornamental metalwork of an automobile *d)* any ornamental trimming 5. *a)* the condition of being ready to sail: said of a vessel *b)* the position of a vessel in relation to the horizontal *c)* correct position in the water: a ship is **in trim** if stable and floating on an even keel, **out of trim** if not *d)* the adjustment of sails, etc. in a vessel 6. something trimmed off —*adj.* **trim′mer, trim′mest** 1. orderly; neat 2. well-proportioned; smartly designed 3. in good condition —*adv.* in a trim way —**trim one's sails** to adjust

one's opinions, actions, etc. to meet changing conditions —**trim′ly** *adv.* —**trim′mer** *n.* —**trim′ness** *n.*

**tri·mes·ter** (trī mes′tər, trī′mes-) *n.* [< Fr. < L. < *tri-*, three + *mensis*, month] 1. a three-month period 2. in some colleges and universities, any of three periods into which the academic year is divided

**trim·e·ter** (trim′ə tər) *n.* [< L. < Gr.: see TRI- & METER[1]] 1. a line of verse containing three metrical feet 2. verse consisting of trimeters —*adj.* having three metrical feet

**trim·ming** (trim′iŋ) *n.* 1. the action of one that trims 2. that which trims; specif., *a)* decoration *b)* [*pl.*] side dishes or garnishes 3. [*pl.*] parts trimmed off

**tri·month·ly** (trī munth′lē) *adj.* happening or appearing every three months

**tri·nal** (trī′n'l) *adj.* [< LL. < L. *trinus*, triple < *tres*, three] threefold; triple: also **tri′na·ry** (-nər ē), **trine** (trīn)

**Trin·i·dad** (trin′ə dad′; *Sp.* trē nē *th*äth′) island in the West Indies, off the NE coast of Venezuela: see ff.: 1,864 sq. mi. —**Trin′i·dad′i·an** *adj., n.*

**Trinidad and Tobago** country in the West Indies, comprising the islands of Trinidad & Tobago: a member of the Commonwealth: 1,980 sq. mi.; pop. 1,030,000; cap. Port-of-Spain

**Trin·i·tar·i·an** (trin′ə ter′ē ən) *adj.* 1. of, about, or believing in the Trinity 2. [t-] of a trinity —*n.* one who believes in the Trinity —**Trin′i·tar′i·an·ism** *n.*

**tri·ni·tro·tol·u·ene** (trī nī′trō täl′yoo wēn′) *n.* [TRI- + NITRO- + TOLUENE] a high explosive, $CH_3C_6H_2(NO_2)_3$, derived from toluene and used for blasting, in artillery shells, etc.: also **tri·ni′tro·tol′u·ol′** (-wōl′, -wôl′): abbrev. TNT

**trin·i·ty** (trin′ə tē) *n., pl.* -ties [< OFr. < L. < *trinus*, triple] 1. a unit formed of three persons or things 2. [T-] *Christian Theol.* the union of the three divine persons (Father, Son, and Holy Spirit, or Holy Ghost) in one Godhead

**Trinity Sunday** the Sunday after Pentecost, dedicated to the Trinity

**trin·ket** (triŋ′kit) *n.* [ONormFr. *trenquet*] 1. a small piece of cheap jewelry, etc. 2. a trifle or toy

**tri·no·mi·al** (trī nō′mē əl) *adj.* [TRI- + (BI)NOMIAL] composed of three terms —*n.* 1. a mathematical expression consisting of three terms connected by plus or minus signs 2. a three-word scientific name of a plant or animal, noting the genus, species, and subspecies

**tri·o** (trē′ō) *n., pl.* **tri′os** [Fr. < It. < *tri-*, TRI- (after *duo*, DUO)] 1. a group of three 2. *Music a)* a composition for three voices or instruments *b)* the three performers of such a composition *c)* the middle section of a minuet, scherzo, etc., orig. for three parts

**tri·ode** (trī′ōd) *n.* [TRI- + (ELECTR)ODE] an electron tube containing three electrodes (an anode, cathode, and control grid)

**tri·ox·ide** (trī äk′sīd) *n.* an oxide having three oxygen atoms to the molecule

**trip** (trip) *vi.* **tripped, trip′ping** [OFr. *treper* < Gmc.] 1. to walk, run, or dance with light, rapid steps; skip; caper 2. to stumble, esp. by catching the foot 3. to make a mistake 4. to go past an escapement catch: said of an escape wheel tooth 5. [Slang] to experience a trip (*n.* 6) —*vt.* 1. to make stumble 2. to cause to make a mistake 3. to catch in a lie, error, etc. (often with *up*) 4. *a)* to release (a spring, wheel, etc.), as by moving a catch *b)* to start or operate by such action —*n.* 1. a light, quick tread 2. a going to or from a place, or to a place and returning; journey, esp. a short one 3. *a)* a stumble *b)* a maneuver to cause this 4. a mistake 5. *a)* a contrivance, as a pawl, to trip a part *b)* its action 6. [Slang] the hallucinations, sensations, etc. produced by a psychedelic drug, esp. LSD —**trip the light fantastic** to dance

**tri·par·tite** (trī pär′tīt) *adj.* [< L. < *tri-*, three + *partitus*, PARTITE] 1. divided into three parts 2. having three corresponding parts or copies 3. made or existing between three parties, as an agreement —**tri·par′tite·ly** *adv.*

**tripe** (trīp) *n.* [< MFr., prob. ult. < Ar. *tharb*, entrails, lit., fold of fat] 1. part of the stomach of an ox, etc., used as food 2. [Slang] nonsense; rubbish

**trip·ham·mer** (trip′ham′ər) *n.* a heavy, power-driven hammer with a tripping device making it alternately rise and fall: also **trip hammer**

**tri·ple** (trip′'l) *adj.* [Fr. < L. *triplus*: see the *v.*] 1. consisting of three; threefold 2. done, said, etc. three times 3. three times as much, as many, etc. 4. *Music* having three beats to the measure [*triple* time] —*n.* 1. a triple amount, number, etc. 2. *Baseball* a hit getting the batter to third base —*vt.* **tri′pled,**

TRILLIUM

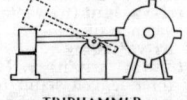

TRIPHAMMER

**tri·pling** [< ML. < L. *triplus*, threefold < *tri-*, TRI- + *-plus*, as in *duplus*, double] to make three times as much or as many —*vi.* **1.** to be tripled **2.** *Baseball* to hit a triple —**tri′ply** *adv.*

**triple play** *Baseball* a play in which three players are put out

**tri·ple-space** (-spās′) *vt., vi.* **-spaced′, -spac′ing** to type (copy) so as to leave two full spaces between lines

**tri·plet** (trip′lit) *n.* [TRIPL(E) + -ET] **1.** a group of three, usually of one kind; specif., *a*) a group of three lines of poetry, usually rhyming *b*) a group of three musical notes to be performed in the time of two of the same value **2.** any of three offspring born at a single birth

**trip·li·cate** (trip′lə kit; *for v.* -kāt′) *adj.* [< L. pp. of *triplicare*, to treble < *triplex*, threefold] **1.** threefold **2.** designating the third of identical copies —*n.* any of three identical copies —*vt.* **-cat′ed, -cat′ing** to make three identical copies of —**in triplicate** in three identical copies —**trip′·li·ca′tion** *n.*

**tri·pod** (tri′päd) *n.* [< L. < Gr. < *tri-*, three + *pous*, a foot] **1.** a three-legged caldron, stool, etc. **2.** a three-legged support for a camera, etc.

**Trip·o·li** (trip′ə lē) **1.** one of the two capitals of Libya, on the NW coast: pop. 245,000 **2.** seaport on the NW coast of Lebanon: pop. 150,000

**trip·per** (trip′ər) *n.* **1.** one that trips; specif., a device for tripping or releasing a catch, pawl, etc. **2.** [Brit. Colloq.] a tourist

**trip·ping** (-iŋ) *adj.* moving lightly and quickly —**trip′ping·ly** *adv.*

**trip·tych** (trip′tik) *n.* [< Gr. *triptychos*, threefold < *tri-*, three + *ptychē*, a fold] **1.** an ancient writing tablet of three leaves hinged together **2.** a set of three panels with pictures, carvings, etc., often hinged and used as an altarpiece

**tri·reme** (tri′rēm) *n.* [< L. < *tri-*, three + *remus*, an oar] an ancient Greek or Roman galley, usually a warship, with three banks of oars on each side

**tri·sect** (tri sekt′, tri′sekt) *vt.* [< TRI- + L. pp. of *secare*, to cut] **1.** to cut into three parts **2.** *Geom.* to divide into three equal parts —**tri·sec′tion** *n.* —**tri·sec′tor** *n.*

**tri·shaw** (tri′shô′) *n.* [< TRI- + (JINRIKI)SHA] *same as* PEDICAB

**Tris·tram** (tris′trəm) *Medieval Legend* a knight who is involved in a tragic romance with a princess, Isolde: also **Tris′tam** (-təm), **Tris′tan** (-tən)

**tri·syl·la·ble** (tri sil′ə b'l, tri′sil′-) *n.* a word of three syllables —**tri·syl·lab·ic** (tri′si lab′ik) *adj.*

**trite** (trit) *adj.* **trit′er, trit′est** [L. *tritus*, pp. of *terere*, to wear out] worn out by constant use; no longer fresh, original, etc. —**trite′ly** *adv.* —**trite′ness** *n.*

**trit·i·um** (trit′ē əm, trish′-) *n.* [ModL. < Gr. *tritos*, third] a radioactive isotope of hydrogen with an atomic weight of 3: it decays by beta-particle emission and is used in thermonuclear bombs, as a radioactive tracer, etc.

**Tri·ton** (trit′'n) **1.** *Gr. Myth.* a sea god with the head and upper body of a man and the tail of a fish **2.** the larger of Neptune's two moons —*n.* [t-] **1.** *a*) a sea snail with a long, spiral shell *b*) the shell **2.** an old-world salamander

**trit·u·rate** (trich′ə rāt′) *vt.* **-rat′ed, -rat′ing** [< LL. pp. of *triturare*, to grind < L. < *tritus:* see TRITE] to rub, crush, or grind into very fine particles; pulverize —*n.* something triturated —**trit′u·ra·ble** (-ər ə b'l) *adj.* —**trit′u·ra′tion** *n.* —**trit′u·ra′tor** *n.*

**tri·umph** (tri′əmf) *n.* [< OFr. < L. *triumphus*, akin to Gr. *thriambos*, hymn to Bacchus] **1.** in ancient Rome, a procession celebrating a victorious general's return **2.** a victory; success **3.** exultation or joy over a victory, etc. —*vi.* **1.** to be victorious, successful, etc. **2.** to rejoice or exult over victory, etc. —**tri·um′phal** (-um′f'l) *adj.*

**tri·um·phant** (tri um′fənt) *adj.* **1.** victorious; successful **2.** exulting in victory, etc. —**tri·um′phant·ly** *adv.*

**tri·um·vir** (tri um′vər) *n., pl.* **-virs, -vi·ri** (-vi ri′) [L. < *trium virum*, of three men] in ancient Rome, any of three administrators sharing authority equally —**tri·um′vi·ral** *adj.*

**tri·um·vi·rate** (-it) *n.* **1.** the office or term of a triumvir **2.** government by three men **3.** any association of three in authority **4.** any group of three

**tri·une** (tri′yōōn) *adj.* [< TRI- + L. *unus*, one] being three in one [*a triune* God] —**tri·u′ni·ty** *n.*

**tri·va·lent** (tri vā′lənt) *adj.* [TRI- + -VALENT] **1.** having a valence of three **2.** having three valences —**tri·va′lence, tri·va′len·cy** *n.*

**triv·et** (triv′it) *n.* [OE. *trefet* < L. *tripes*, tripod] **1.** a three-legged stand for holding pots, kettles, etc. over or near a fire **2.** a short-legged plate for hot dishes to rest on

**triv·i·a** (triv′ē ə) *n.pl.* [*often with sing. v.*] [ModL. < ff.] unimportant matters; trivialities

**triv·i·al** (triv′ē əl, triv′yəl) *adj.* [L. *trivialis*, of the crossroads, commonplace < *tri-*, three + *via*, a road] of little value or importance; trifling —**triv′i·al·ly** *adv.*

**triv·i·al·i·ty** (triv′ē al′ə tē) *n.* **1.** a being trivial **2.** *pl.* **-ties** a trivial thing, idea, etc.; trifle

**triv·i·al·ize** (triv′ē ə liz′) *vt., vi.* **-ized′, -iz′ing** to treat as or make seem trivial —**triv′i·al·i·za′tion** *n.*

**-trix** (triks) *pl.* **-trix·es, -tri·ces′** (tri sēz′, tri′sēz) [L.] an ending of some feminine nouns of agent

**TRM** trademark

**tro·che** (trō′kē) *n.* [< Fr. < LL. *trochiscus*, a pill < Gr. < *trochos*, a wheel] a small, usually round, medicinal lozenge

**tro·chee** (trō′kē) *n.* [< L. < Gr. *trochaios*, running < *trechein*, to run] a metrical foot of two syllables, the first accented and the other unaccented, as in English verse (Ex.: "Pēter, | Pēter, | púmpkin | éater") —**tro·cha′ic** (-kā′ik) *adj.*

**trod** (träd) *pt. & alt. pp. of* TREAD

**trod·den** (-'n) *alt. pp. of* TREAD

**trode** (trōd) *archaic pt. of* TREAD

**trog·lo·dyte** (träg′lə dit′) *n.* [< L. < Gr. < *trōglē*, a cave + *dyein*, to enter] **1.** any of the prehistoric people who lived in caves **2.** a person who lives alone in seclusion **3.** anyone who lives in a crude, primitive way —**trog′lo·dyt′ic** (-dit′ik), **trog′lo·dyt′i·cal** *adj.*

**tro·gon** (trō′gän) *n.* [ModL. < Gr. prp. of *trōgein*, to gnaw] any of various bright-colored tropical birds

**troi·ka** (troi′kə) *n.* [Russ. < *troe*, three] **1.** *a*) a Russian vehicle drawn by three horses abreast *b*) the horses **2.** any group of three; esp., an association of three in authority

**Troi·lus** (troi′ləs, trō′i ləs) *Gr. Legend* a son of King Priam: in Chaucer and Shakespeare, Troilus was the lover of the faithless Cressida

**Trois-Ri·vières** (trwä rē vyer′) city in S Quebec, Canada, on the St. Lawrence: pop. 58,000: Eng. name *Three Rivers*

**Tro·jan** (trō′jən) *adj.* of ancient Troy, its people, etc. —*n.* **1.** a native or inhabitant of ancient Troy **2.** a strong, hard-working, determined person

**Trojan horse** *Gr. Legend* a huge, hollow wooden horse filled with Greek soldiers and left at the gates of Troy: when the Trojans brought it into the city, the soldiers crept out and opened the gates to the Greek army

**Trojan War** *Gr. Legend* the ten-year war waged against Troy by the Greeks to get back Helen: see HELEN OF TROY

**troll¹** (trōl) *vt., vi.* [ME. *trollen*, to roll, wander] **1.** to roll; revolve **2.** *a*) to sing the parts of (a round, etc.) in succession *b*) to sing in a strong or full voice **3.** *a*) to fish (*for* or *in*) with a moving line, esp. with a revolving lure trailed from a moving boat *b*) to move (a lure, etc.) thus —*n.* **1.** a trolling **2.** a lure, or a lure and line, used in trolling —**troll′er** *n.*

**troll²** (trōl) *n.* [ON.] in Scandinavian folklore, any of certain supernatural beings, giants or dwarfs, living underground or in caves

**trol·ley** (träl′ē) *n., pl.* **-leys** [< TROLL¹] **1.** a wheeled carriage, basket, etc. that runs suspended from an overhead track **2.** a device, as a grooved wheel at the end of a pole, to carry electric current from an overhead wire to the motor of a streetcar, etc. **3.** a trolley car; streetcar **4.** [Brit.] a low cart —*vt., vi.* **-leyed, -ley·ing** to carry or go on a trolley

**trolley bus** an electric bus that gets its power from overhead wires by means of trolleys but does not run on tracks

**trolley car** an electric streetcar that gets its power from an overhead wire by means of a trolley

**trol·lop** (träl′əp) *n.* [prob. < G. *trolle*, a wench] a sexually promiscuous woman; specif., a prostitute

**Trol·lope** (träl′əp), **Anthony** 1815–82; Eng. novelist

**trol·ly** (träl′ē) *n., pl.* **-lies, *vt., vi.* -lied, -ly·ing** *var. of* TROLLEY

**trom·bone** (träm bōn′, träm′bōn) *n.* [It. < *tromba*, a trumpet < OHG. *trumba*] a large brass-wind instrument with a bell mouth and a long tube bent parallel to itself twice and having either a section that slides in or out (**slide trombone**) or valves (**valve trombone**) —**trom·bon′ist** *n.*

**tromp** (trämp) *vi., vt. var. of* TRAMP

**‡trompe l'oeil** (trōnp le′y′) [Fr., lit., trick of the eye] **1.** a painting, etc. so realistic that it gives the illusion of being the actual thing depicted **2.** any such illusion or effect

**-tron** (trän) [Gr. *-tron*, suffix of instrument] *a combining form meaning* instrument

TROMBONE

**troop** (trōōp) *n.* [< Fr. < OFr. < ML. *troppus*, a flock] **1.** a group of persons or animals; band, herd, etc. **2.** loosely, a great number; lot **3.** [*pl.*] *a*) a body of soldiers *b*) soldiers [45 *troops*] **4.** a subdivision of a cavalry regiment, corresponding to an infantry company **5.** a unit of Boy Scouts or Girl Scouts under an adult leader —*vi.* **1.** to gather or go as in a group **2.** to walk, go, etc. —*vt.* to form into troops

**troop·er** (trōō′pər) *n.* [prec. + -ER] **1.** an enlisted cavalryman **2.** a cavalry horse **3.** a mounted policeman **4.** [Colloq.] a member of the police force of a State

**troop·ship** (trōōp′ship′) *n.* a ship for carrying troops

**trope** (trōp) *n.* [< L. < Gr. *tropos*, a turning < *trepein*, to turn] **1.** a figure of speech **2.** the use of figures of speech

**tro·phy** (trō′fē) *n., pl.* **-phies** [< MFr. < L. < Gr. *tropaion*, token of an enemy's defeat, ult. < *trepein*, to turn] **1.** something taken from a defeated enemy and kept as a memorial of victory **2.** an animal skin, head, etc. displayed to show one's hunting prowess **3.** a prize, usually a silver cup, awarded as in a sports contest **4.** any memento

**-tro·phy** (trə fē) [Gr. *-trophia* < *trephein*, to nourish] *a combining form meaning* nutrition, growth [*hypertrophy*]

**trop·ic** (träp′ik) *n.* [< L. < Gr. *tropikos*, of a turn (of the sun at the solstices) < *tropē*, a turn] **1.** *Astron.* either of two circles of the celestial sphere (the **Tropic of Cancer**, c. 23½° north and the **Tropic of Capricorn**, c. 23½° south) parallel to the celestial equator: they are the limits of the apparent north-and-south journey of the sun **2.** *Geog. a)* either of two parallels of latitude corresponding to these, on either side of the earth's equator *b)* [*also* **T-**] [*pl.*] the region of the earth between these latitudes, noted for its hot climate —*adj.* of the tropics; tropical

**-trop·ic** (träp′ik, trō′pik) [< Gr. < *trepein*, to turn + -IC] *a combining form meaning* turning, changing, or otherwise responding to a (specified kind of) stimulus [*phototropic*] : also **-troph·ic** (träf′ik)

**trop·i·cal** (träp′i k'l) *adj.* of, in, characteristic of, or suitable for the tropics —**trop′i·cal·ly** *adv.*

**tropical fish** any of various usually brightly colored fish, orig. from the tropics, kept in an aquarium (**tropical aquarium**) maintained at a constant, warm temperature

**Tropical Zone** *same as* TORRID ZONE

**tropic bird** any of various tropical sea birds having white feathers with black markings and a pair of long tail feathers

**tro·pism** (trō′piz'm) *n.* [< ff.] the tendency of a plant or animal to grow or turn toward or away from an external stimulus such as light —**tro·pis′tic** *adj.*

**-tro·pism** (trə piz'm) [< Gr. *-tropos* (see TROPE) + -ISM] *a combining form meaning* tropism [*heliotropism*] : also **-tro·py** (trə pē)

**trop·o·sphere** (träp′ə sfir′, trō′pə-) *n.* [< Fr. < Gr. *tropos* (see TROPE) + Fr. *sphère* (see SPHERE)] the atmosphere from the earth's surface to the stratosphere, reaching from 6 to 12 miles, in which clouds form and in which temperature usually decreases as altitude increases —**trop′o·spher′ic** (-sfer′ik, -sfir′-) *adj.*

‡**trop·po** (trōp′pô) *adv.* [It.] too; too much so: a direction in music, as in *allegro non troppo*, not too fast

**trot** (trät) *vi.* **trot′ted**, **trot′ting** [< OFr. < OHG. *trottôn*, to tread] **1.** to move, ride, go, etc. at a trot **2.** to hurry; run —*vt.* to make trot —*n.* **1.** a gait of a horse, etc. in which the legs are lifted in alternating diagonal pairs **2.** a person's gait between a walk and a run **3.** a horse race for trotters **4.** [Slang] *same as* PONY (n. 3) —**trot out** [Colloq.] to bring out for others to see or admire

**troth** (trôth, trōth, träth) *n.* [ult. < OE. *treowth*, truth] [Archaic] **1.** faithfulness; loyalty **2.** truth: chiefly in **in troth**, truly; indeed **3.** one's pledged word; promise: see also PLIGHT ONE'S TROTH (at PLIGHT²) —*vt.* [Archaic] to pledge to marry

**trot·line** (trät′līn′) *n.* a strong fishing line suspended over the water and hung with short lines bearing baited hooks

**Trot·sky** (trät′skē; *Russ.* trôt′-), **Le·on** (lē′än) (born *Lev Davidovich Bronstein*) 1879–1940; Russ. revolutionist & writer: exiled (1929) —**Trot′sky·ism** *n.* —**Trot′sky·ist**, **Trot′sky·ite′** (-īt′) *adj., n.*

**trot·ter** (trät′ər) *n.* **1.** an animal that trots; esp., a horse bred and trained for trotting races **2.** the foot of a sheep or pig used as food

**trou·ba·dour** (trōō′bə dôr′) *n.* [Fr. < Pr. < *trobar*, to compose in verse] any of a class of lyric poets who lived in southern France and northern Italy in the 11th, 12th, and 13th cent. and wrote poems of love and chivalry

**trou·ble** (trub′'l) *vt.* **-bled**, **-bling** [OFr. *trubler*, ult. < LL. *turbidare*, to trouble < L. *turbidus*, turbid] **1.** to disturb or agitate [*troubled* waters] **2.** to worry; harass; perturb **3.** to cause pain or discomfort to [*troubled* by headaches] **4.** to cause difficulty or inconvenience to **5.** to annoy, tease, bother, etc. —*vi.* **1.** to take pains; bother [don't *trouble* to return it] **2.** to be distressed; worry —*n.* **1.** a state of mental distress; worry **2.** *a)* a misfortune or mishap *b)* a difficult situation *c)* a condition of needing to be repaired, fixed, etc. [tire *trouble*] **3.** a cause of annoyance, distress, etc. **4.** public disturbance **5.** bother; pains [he took the *trouble* to listen] **6.** an illness —**in trouble** [Colloq.] pregnant when unmarried —**trou′bler** *n.*

**trou·ble·mak·er** (-mā′kər) *n.* a person who habitually makes trouble for others —**trou′ble·mak′ing** *n.*

**trou·ble-shoot·er** (-shōōt′ər) *n.* a person whose work is to find and repair or eliminate mechanical breakdowns or other sources of trouble —**trou′ble-shoot′ing** *n.*

**trou·ble·some** (-səm) *adj.* full of or causing trouble —**trou′ble·some·ly** *adv.* —**trou′ble·some·ness** *n.*

**trou·blous** (trub′ləs) *adj.* [Chiefly Literary] **1.** troubled; disturbed **2.** *same as* TROUBLESOME

**trough** (trôf) *n.* [OE. *trog*] **1.** a long, narrow, open container for holding water or food for animals **2.** a vessel of similar shape, as for kneading something **3.** a gutter, esp. under the eaves of a building, for carrying off rainwater **4.** a long, narrow hollow, as between waves **5.** a low point in business activity, etc. **6.** a long, narrow area of low barometric pressure

**trounce** (trouns) *vt.* **trounced**, **trounc′ing** [< ?] **1.** to beat; thrash **2.** [Colloq.] to defeat —**trounc′er** *n.*

**troupe** (trōōp) *n.* [Fr.] a group, esp. of actors, singers, etc.; company —*vi.* **trouped**, **troup′ing** to travel as a member of a troupe —**troup′er** *n.*

**trou·sers** (trou′zərz) *n.pl.* [< obs. *trouse* < ScotGael. *triubhas*] an outer garment, esp. for men and boys, reaching from the waist usually to the ankles and divided into separate coverings for the legs; pants —**trou′ser** *adj.*

**trous·seau** (trōō′sō, trōō sō′) *n., pl.* **-seaux** (-sōz), **-seaus** [Fr. < OFr., dim. of *trousse*, a bundle] a bride's outfit of clothes, linen, etc.

**trout** (trout) *n., pl.* **trout, trouts:** see PLURAL, II, D, 2 [OE. *truht* < LL. < Gr. *trōktēs*, kind of fish < *trōgein*, to gnaw] any of various food and game fishes related to but smaller than the salmon and found chiefly in fresh water

**trove** (trōv) *n.* short for TREASURE-TROVE

**trow** (trō, trou) *vi., vt.* [OE. *treowian* < *treow*, faith] [Archaic] to believe, think, suppose, etc.

**trow·el** (trou′əl) *n.* [< MFr. < LL. < L. *trulla* < *trua*, ladle] **1.** a tool with a thin, flat, rectangular blade for smoothing plaster **2.** a tool with a thin, flat, pointed blade for applying and shaping mortar **3.** a tool with a pointed scoop for digging holes in a garden —*vt.* **-eled** or **-elled**, **-el·ing** or **-el·ling** to spread, smooth, shape, dig, etc. with a trowel

**Troy** (troi) **1.** ancient city in NW Asia Minor **2.** [after prec.] city in E N.Y., on the Hudson: pop. 57,000

**troy** (troi) *adj.* by or in troy weight

**troy weight** [< *Troyes*, a city in France] a system of weights for gold, silver, precious stones, etc.: see TABLES OF WEIGHTS AND MEASURES in Supplements

TROWELS (A, brick; B, garden)

**tru·ant** (trōō′ənt) *n.* [OFr., a beggar < Celt.] **1.** a pupil who stays away from school without permission **2.** a person who shirks his duties —*adj.* **1.** that is a truant **2.** idle; shiftless **3.** errant; straying —*vi.* to be truant —**tru′an·cy** (-ən sē) *n., pl.* **-cies** —**tru′ant·ly** *adv.*

**truant officer** a school official dealing with pupils who are truants: now usually called *attendance officer*

**truce** (trōōs) *n.* [OE. *treow*, compact, faith] **1.** a period during a war in which the nations or peoples engaged in it agree to stop fighting for a time **2.** any pause in quarreling, conflict, etc.

**truck¹** (truk) *n.* [prob. < L. < Gr. *trochos*, a wheel < *trechein*, to run] **1.** a small solid wheel, esp. for a gun carriage **2.** a small wooden disk with holes for halyards, esp. at the top of a flagpole or mast **3.** a frame with wheels at one end and handles at the other, used to carry trunks, crates, etc.: also **hand truck 4.** a low frame or platform on wheels, for carrying heavy loads **5.** an automotive vehicle for hauling loads along highways, streets, etc. **6.** a swiveling frame, with two or more pairs of wheels, under each end of a railroad car, etc. —*vt.* to carry on a truck —*vi.* **1.** to do trucking **2.** to drive a truck as one's work

**truck²** (truk) *vt., vi.* [MFr. *troquer* < ?] to exchange; barter —*n.* **1.** *same as* BARTER **2.** payment of wages in goods instead of money **3.** small commercial articles **4.** small articles of little value **5.** vegetables raised for sale in markets **6.** [Colloq.] dealings **7.** [Colloq.] rubbish

**truck·age** (truk′ij) *n.* **1.** transportation of goods by truck **2.** the charge for this

**truck·er¹** (-ər) *n.* **1.** a truck driver **2.** a person or company doing trucking Also **truck′man** (-mən), *pl.* **-men**

**truck·er²** (-ər) *n.* **1.** a truck farmer **2.** a person who sells commodities or engages in barter

**truck farm** a farm where vegetables are grown to be marketed —**truck farmer** —**truck farming**

**truck·ing** (-iŋ) *n.* the business of carrying goods by truck

**truck·le** (truk'l) *n.* [< L. *trochlea*, a pulley < Gr. < *trochos*, a wheel] **1.** orig., a small wheel **2.** *short for* TRUCKLE BED —*vi.* **-led, -ling** to give in or yield too easily (*to*)

**truckle bed** *same as* TRUNDLE BED

**truc·u·lent** (truk'yoo lənt) *adj.* [< L. < *trux* (gen. *trucis*)] **1.** fierce; savage **2.** rude; harsh; scathing **3.** ready to fight —**truc'u·lence, truc'u·len·cy** *n.* —**truc'u·lent·ly** *adv.*

**Tru·deau** (trōō dō'; *Fr.* trü dō'), **Pierre El·li·ott** (el'ē ət) 1921– ; prime minister of Canada (1968–79; 1980– )

**trudge** (truj) *vi.* **trudged, trudg'ing** [< ?] to walk, esp. wearily or laboriously —*n.* a trudging —**trudg'er** *n.*

**true** (trōō) *adj.* **tru'er, tru'est** [OE. *treowe*] **1.** faithful; loyal **2.** reliable; certain **3.** in accordance with fact; not false **4.** *a)* conforming to an original, standard, etc. *b)* exact; accurate; correct **5.** rightful; lawful *[the true heirs]* **6.** accurately fitted, placed, or shaped *[the board is true]* **7.** *a)* genuine; authentic *b)* rightly so called *[a true scholar]* **8.** [Archaic] honest, virtuous, or truthful —*adv.* truly, truthfully, accurately, etc. —*vt.* **trued, tru'ing** or **true'ing** to fit, place, or shape accurately (often with *up*) —*n.* that which is true; truth or reality (with *the*) —**come true** to happen as predicted or expected —**in** (or **out of**) **true** that is (or is not) properly set, adjusted, etc. —**true to form** behaving as might be expected —**true'ness** *n.*

**true bill** a bill of indictment endorsed by a grand jury

**true-blue** (trōō'blōō') *adj.* very loyal; staunch

**true·bred** (-bred') *adj. same as:* **1.** WELL-BRED **2.** PUREBRED

**true-false test** (trōō'fôls') a test, as of knowledge, consisting of a series of statements to be identified as either "true" or "false"

**true·heart·ed** (-här'tid) *adj.* **1.** loyal; faithful **2.** honest or sincere —**true'heart'ed·ness** *n.*

**true-life** (-līf') *adj.* like what happens in real life; true to reality *[a true-life story]*

**true·love** (-luv') *n.* (one's) sweetheart; a loved one

**truelove knot** a kind of bowknot that is hard to untie, a symbol of lasting love: also **true'-lov'er's knot**

**true ribs** ribs that are attached by cartilage directly to the breastbone; in man, the upper seven pairs of ribs

**truf·fle** (truf''l, trōō'f'l) *n.* [< Fr. < OIt. *truffa*, ult. < L. *tuber*, a knob] any of certain related fleshy, edible fungi that grow underground, esp. a European kind regarded as a delicacy

**tru·ism** (trōō'iz'm) *n.* a statement the truth of which is obvious and well known —**tru·is'tic** *adj.*

**trull** (trul) *n.* [G. *trolle*] a prostitute or trollop

**tru·ly** (trōō'lē) *adv.* **1.** in a true manner; genuinely, faithfully, rightfully, etc. **2.** really; indeed

**Tru·man** (trōō'mən), **Harry S.** 1884–1972; 33d president of the U.S. (1945–53)

**trump**[1] (trump) *n.* [altered < TRIUMPH] **1.** any playing card of a suit that ranks higher than any other suit during the playing of a hand **2.** [*occas. pl. with sing. v.*] a suit of trumps **3.** any advantage held in reserve until needed **4.** [Colloq.] a fine person —*vt.* **1.** to take (a trick, card, etc.) with a trump **2.** to outdo; surpass —*vi.* to play a trump —**trump up** to make up (a charge against someone, an excuse, etc.) in order to deceive

**trump**[2] (trump) *n., vi., vt.* [OFr. *trompe*] *archaic or poet. var. of* TRUMPET

**trump·er·y** (trum'pər ē) *n., pl.* **-er·ies** [< MFr. < *tromper*, to deceive] **1.** something showy but worthless **2.** nonsense —*adj.* showy but worthless

**trum·pet** (trum'pit) *n.* [< MFr. dim. of *trompe*, trumpet] **1.** a brass-wind instrument with a blaring tone, consisting of a tube in an oblong loop or loops, flared at the end opposite the mouthpiece **2.** something shaped like a trumpet; esp., *same as* EAR TRUMPET **3.** a sound like that of a trumpet —*vi.* **1.** to blow a trumpet **2.** to make a sound like a trumpet —*vt.* **1.** to sound on or as on a trumpet **2.** to proclaim loudly

**trumpet creeper** **1.** a vine of the southern U.S., with red, trumpet-shaped flowers **2.** a related vine of China Also **trumpet vine**

TRUMPET

**trum·pet·er** (-ər) *n.* **1.** a trumpet player **2.** a person who proclaims or heralds something **3.** a long-legged, long-necked S. American bird having a loud cry **4.** *same as* TRUMPETER SWAN **5.** a domestic pigeon with feathered feet and a rounded crest

**trumpeter swan** a N. American wild swan with a loud cry

**trumpet honeysuckle** an American honeysuckle with reddish, trumpet-shaped flowers

**trun·cate** (trun'kāt) *vt.* **-cat·ed, -cat·ing** [< L. pp. of *truncare*, to cut off < *truncus*, a stem] to shorten by cutting; lop —*adj. same as* TRUNCATED —**trun·ca'tion** *n.*

**trun·cat·ed** (-id) *adj.* **1.** cut short or appearing as if cut short **2.** having the vertex cut off by a plane

**trun·cheon** (trun'chən) *n.* [< OFr., ult. < L. *truncus*, a stem] **1.** a staff carried as a symbol of authority **2.** [Chiefly Brit.] a policeman's stick

**trun·dle** (trun'd'l) *n.* [OE. *trendel*, a circle < *trendan*, to roll] **1.** a small wheel **2.** *short for* TRUNDLE BED —*vt., vi.* **-dled, -dling** to roll along

**trundle bed** a low bed on casters, that can be rolled under a higher bed when not in use

**trunk** (truŋk) *n.* [< OFr. < L. *truncus*, trunk, orig., mutilated] **1.** the main stem of a tree **2.** a human body or animal body, not including the head and limbs **3.** the thorax of an insect **4.** the main body of a nerve, blood vessel, etc. **5.** a long, flexible snout, as of an elephant **6.** a large, reinforced box for carrying a traveler's clothes, etc. **7.** a large, long, boxlike pipe, etc. that conveys air, water, etc. **8.** [*pl.*] *same as* TRUNK HOSE **9.** [*pl.*] men's shorts worn for athletics, as boxing, swimming, etc. **10.** *short for* TRUNK LINE **11.** a compartment in an automobile, usually in the rear, for a spare tire, luggage, etc. **12.** *Archit.* the shaft of a column

**trunk·fish** (-fish') *n., pl.* **-fish', -fish'es:** see FISH a tropical fish whose body is encased in fused bony plates

**trunk hose** full, baggy breeches reaching about halfway down the thigh, worn in the 16th and 17th cent.

**trunk line** a main line of a railroad, telephone system, etc.

**trun·nion** (trun'yən) *n.* [Fr. *trognon*, a stump] either of two projecting pins on each side of a cannon, on which it pivots

**truss** (trus) *vt.* [OFr. *trousser*] **1.** orig., to tie into a bundle **2.** to tie or bind (often with *up*) **3.** to skewer or bind the wings, etc. of (a fowl) before cooking **4.** to support or strengthen with a truss —*n.* **1.** a bundle or pack **2.** an iron band around a mast, to which a yard is fastened **3.** a rigid framework of beams, struts, etc. for supporting a roof, bridge, etc. **4.** an appliance worn for supporting a hernia, usually a pad on a belt

**trust** (trust) *n.* [ON. *traust*] **1.** *a)* firm belief in the honesty, reliability, etc. of another *b)* the one trusted **2.** confident expectation, hope, etc. *[have trust in the future]* **3.** *a)* the fact of having confidence placed in one *b)* the responsibility resulting from this **4.** care; custody **5.** something entrusted to one; charge **6.** confidence in a purchaser's intention or future ability to pay for goods, etc.; credit **7.** *a)* an industrial or business combination of corporations, with control vested in a single board of trustees who are able to eliminate competition, fix prices, etc. *b) same as* CARTEL (sense 3) **8.** *Law a)* confidence placed in a person by giving him nominal ownership of property that he is to keep, use, or administer for another's benefit *b)* the property involved —*vi.* **1.** to have trust or faith; be confident **2.** to hope (*for*) **3.** to give business credit —*vt.* **1.** to have trust in; rely on, etc. **2.** to commit (*to* a person's care) **3.** to put something confidently in the charge of *[to trust a lawyer with one's case]* **4.** to allow to do something without fear of the outcome **5.** to believe or suppose **6.** to hope **7.** to grant business credit to —*adj.* **1.** relating to a trust or trusts **2.** held in trust **3.** acting as a trustee —**in trust** in the condition of being entrusted to another's care —**trust to** to rely on —**trust'a·ble** *adj.*

**trus·tee** (trus tē') *n.* **1.** a person to whom another's property or the management of another's property is entrusted **2.** a nation under whose control a trust territory is placed **3.** any of a group of persons appointed to manage the affairs of a college, hospital, etc. —*vt.* **-teed', -tee'ing** to commit (property or management) to a trustee or trustees

**trus·tee·ship** (-ship') *n.* **1.** the position or function of a trustee **2.** *a)* a commission from the United Nations to a country to administer a trust territory *b)* the state or fact of being a trust territory

**trust·ful** (trust'fəl) *adj.* full of trust or confidence in another or others; trusting —**trust'ful·ly** *adv.* —**trust'ful·ness** *n.*

**trust fund** money, stock, etc. held in trust

**trust·ing** (trus'tiŋ) *adj.* that trusts; trustful —**trust'ing·ly** *adv.* —**trust'ing·ness** *n.*

**trust territory** a territory placed by the United Nations under the control of a country that manages the affairs of the territory

**trust·wor·thy** (trust'wur'thē) *adj.* **-thi·er -thi·est** worthy of trust; dependable; reliable —**trust'wor'thi·ly** *adv.* —**trust'wor'thi·ness** *n.*

**trust·y** (trus'tē) *adj.* **trust'i·er, trust'i·est** that can be relied upon; dependable —*n., pl.* **trust'ies** a trusted person; specif., a convict granted special privileges as a trustworthy person —**trust'i·ly** *adv.* —**trust'i·ness** *n.*

**truth** (trōōth) *n., pl.* **truths** (trōōthz, trōōths) [OE. *treowth*] **1.** the quality or state of being true; specif., *a)* orig., loyalty *b)* sincerity; honesty *c)* the quality of being in agreement with reality or facts *d)* reality; actual existence *e)* agreement with a standard, rule, etc.; correctness **2.** that which is true **3.** an established or verified fact, etc. **4.** a particular belief or teaching regarded by the speaker as the true one (often with *the*) —**in truth** truly; in fact —**of a truth** certainly

**truth drug** an anesthetic or hypnotic, as thiopental sodium, regarded as tending to make a person taking it willing to answer questions: also **truth serum**

**truth·ful** (trōōth'fəl) *adj.* **1.** telling the truth; honest **2.** agreeing with fact or reality —**truth'ful·ly** *adv.* —**truth'ful·ness** *n.*

**try** (trī) *vt.* **tried, try'ing** [OFr. *trier,* ult. < ? L. pp. of *terere,* to thresh grain] **1.** to melt or render (fat, etc.) to get (the oil): usually with *out* **2.** *a)* to examine and decide (a case) in a law court *b)* to determine legally the guilt or innocence of (a person) **3.** to put to the proof; test **4.** to test the faith, patience, etc. of; afflict [he was sorely *tried*] **5.** to subject to a severe test or strain **6.** to test the effect of; experiment with [*try* this recipe] **7.** to attempt; endeavor [*try* to forget] —*vi.* **1.** to make an effort, attempt, etc. **2.** to experiment —*n., pl.* **tries** an attempt; effort; trial —**try on** to test the fit, etc. of (a garment) by putting it on —**try one's hand at** to attempt (to do something), esp. for the first time —**try out 1.** to test the quality, value, etc. of, as by using **2.** to test one's fitness, as to be on a team, act a role, etc.

**try·ing** (-iŋ) *adj.* that tries one's patience; annoying; exasperating; irksome —**try'ing·ly** *adv.*

**try·out** (trī'out') *n.* [Colloq.] **1.** a chance to prove, or a test to determine, one's fitness to be on a team, act a role, etc. **2.** a performance of a play before its official opening, as to test audience reaction

**tryp·sin** (trip'sin) *n.* [G., prob. < Gr. *tryein,* to wear away + G. *(pe)psin:* see PEPSIN] a digestive enzyme in the pancreatic juice: it changes proteins into polypeptides —**tryp'tic** *adj.*

**try·sail** (trī's'l, -sāl') *n.* [< naut. phr. *a try,* position of lying to in a storm] a small, stout, fore-and-aft sail used for keeping a vessel's head to the wind in a storm

**try square** an instrument for testing the accuracy of square work and for marking off right angles

**tryst** (trist, trīst) *n.* [OFr. *triste,* hunting station] **1.** an appointment to meet at a specified time and place, esp. one made secretly by lovers **2.** *a)* a meeting held by appointment *b)* the place of such a meeting: also **trysting place** —**tryst'er** *n.*

**tsar** (tsär, zär) *n. var. sp. of* CZAR —**tsar'dom** *n.* —**tsar'ism** *n.* —**tsar'ist** *adj., n.*

**Tschaikowsky** *see* TCHAIKOVSKY

**tset·se fly** (tset'sē, tsēt'-, set'-, sēt'-) [Afrik. < the Bantu name] any of several small flies of central and southern Africa, including the one that carries sleeping sickness

**T-shirt** (tē'shurt') *n.* [so named because T-shaped] a collarless pullover shirt with short sleeves

**Tsing·tao** (chiŋ'dou') seaport in NE China, on the Yellow Sea: pop. 1,144,000

**tsk** *interj., n.* a clicking or sucking sound made with the tongue, to express disapproval, sympathy, etc.

**tsp. 1.** teaspoon(s) **2.** teaspoonful(s)

**T square** a T-shaped ruler for drawing parallel lines

**T-strap** (tē'strap') *n.* **1.** a T-shaped strap over the instep of a shoe **2.** a woman's or girl's shoe with such a strap

**tsu·na·mi** (tsōō nä'mē) *n.* [Jap. < *tsu,* a harbor + *nami,* wave] a huge sea wave caused by a disturbance under water, as an earthquake: popularly, but inaccurately, called **tidal wave** —**tsu·na'mic** (-mik) *adj.*

**Tu.** Tuesday

**tu·a·ta·ra** (tōō'ə tä'rə) *n.* [< Maori < *tua,* back + *tara,* spine] a primitive, lizardlike reptile of islands near New Zealand, with a row of spines in the middle of the back

**tub** (tub) *n.* [MDu. *tubbe*] **1.** *a)* a round, open, wooden container, usually formed of staves and hoops fastened around a flat bottom *b)* any large, open container of metal, etc., as for washing *c)* as much as a tub will hold **2.** *a) short for* BATHTUB *b)* [Brit. Colloq.] a bath in a tub **3.** [Colloq.] a slow-moving, clumsy ship or boat —*vt., vi.* **tubbed, tub'bing 1.** [Colloq.] to wash in a tub **2.** [Brit. Colloq.] to bathe (oneself) —**tub'ba·ble** *adj.* —**tub'ber** *n.*

**tu·ba** (tōō'bə, tyōō'-) *n., pl.* **tu'bas, tu'bae** (-bē) [L., a trumpet] a large, brass-wind musical instrument having three to five valves

**tub·al** (tōō'b'l, tyōō'-) *adj.* of or in a tube, esp. a Fallopian tube [a *tubal* pregnancy]

**tub·by** (tub'ē) *adj.* **-bi·er, -bi·est 1.** shaped like a tub **2.** short and fat —**tub'bi·ness** *n.*

**tube** (tōōb, tyōōb) *n.* [Fr. < L. *tubus,* a pipe] **1.** *a)* a slender, hollow cylinder or pipe of metal, glass, rubber, etc., in which gases and liquids can flow or be kept *b)* an instrument, part, organ, etc. resembling a tube [a bronchial *tube*] **2.** a rubber casing inflated with air and used, esp. formerly, with an outer casing to form an automotive tire **3.** an enclosed, hollow cylinder of thin, pliable metal, etc. with a screw cap at one end, used for holding pastes or semiliquids **4.** *short for: a)* ELECTRON TUBE *b)* VACUUM TUBE

**5.** *a)* an underground tunnel for a railroad, subway, etc. *b)* [Brit. Colloq.] a subway —*vt.* **tubed, tub'ing 1.** to provide with, place in, or pass through a tube or tubes **2.** to make tubular —**down the tube** (or **tubes**) [Colloq.] in or into a condition of failure, defeat, loss, etc. —**the tube** [Colloq.] television —**tu'bate** *adj.* —**tube'like'** *adj.*

**tube foot** any of numerous projecting, water-filled tubes in most echinoderms, used in moving about, handling food, etc.

**tube·less tire** (-lis) a tire for an automotive vehicle, consisting of a single air-filled unit without an inner tube

**tu·ber** (tōō'bər, tyōō'-) *n.* [L., lit., a swelling] **1.** a short, thickened, fleshy part of an underground stem, as a potato **2.** a tubercle or swelling

**tu·ber·cle** (-k'l) *n.* [L. *tuberculum,* dim. of *tuber:* see prec.] **1.** a small, rounded part growing out from a bone or from the root of a plant **2.** any abnormal hard nodule or swelling; specif., the typical nodular lesion of tuberculosis

**tubercle bacillus** the bacterium causing tuberculosis

**tu·ber·cu·lar** (too bur'kyə lər, tyoo-) *adj.* **1.** of, like, or having tubercles **2.** of or having tuberculosis **3.** caused by the tubercle bacillus Also **tu·ber'cu·lous** (-ləs) —*n.* a person having tuberculosis

**tu·ber·cu·lin** (-lin) *n.* a sterile solution prepared from a culture of the tubercle bacillus and injected into the skin as a test for tuberculosis

**tu·ber·cu·lo·sis** (too bur'kyə lō'sis, tyoo-) *n.* [ModL.: see TUBERCLE & -OSIS] an infectious disease caused by the tubercle bacillus and causing tubercles to form in body tissues; specif., tuberculosis of the lungs; consumption

**tube·rose** (tōōb'rōz', tyōōb'-) *n.* [ModL. < L. *tuberosus,* TUBEROUS] a perennial Mexican plant with a tuberous rootstock and white, sweet-scented flowers

**tu·ber·ous** (tōō'bər əs, tyōō'-) *adj.* [< Fr. < L. *tuberosus:* see TUBER & -OUS] **1.** covered with rounded, wartlike swellings; knobby **2.** of, like, or having a tuber or tubers Also **tu'ber·ose'** (-ōs') —**tu'ber·os'i·ty** (-bə räs'ə tē) *n., pl.* **-ties**

**tu·bi·fex** (tōō'bə feks', tyōō'-) *n., pl.* **-fex'es, -fex'** [ModL. < L. *tubus,* a pipe + *-fex* < *facere,* to make] a small freshwater worm, found esp. in polluted waters and often used as food for aquarium fish

**tub·ing** (tōōb'iŋ, tyōōb'-) *n.* **1.** a series or system of tubes **2.** material in the form of a tube **3.** a length of tube

**tu·bu·lar** (tōō'byə lər, tyōō'-) *adj.* [< L. dim. of *tubus,* a pipe] **1.** of or shaped like a tube **2.** made with tubes Also **tu'bu·late** (-lit) —**tu'bu·lar'i·ty** (-lar'ə tē) *n.*

**tu·bule** (tōō'byool, tyōō'-) *n.* a small tube

**tuck** (tuk) *vt.* [< MDu. *tucken,* to tuck & cognate OE. *tucian,* to tug] **1.** to pull up or gather up in a fold or folds, as to make shorter **2.** to sew a fold or folds in (a garment) **3.** *a)* to thrust the edges of (a sheet, napkin, etc.) under or in, in order to make secure (usually with *up, in,* etc.) *b)* to cover or wrap snugly [*tuck* the baby in bed] **4.** to put or press snugly into a small space; cram [to *tuck* shoes in a suitcase] **5.** to put into a secluded, empty, or isolated spot —*vi.* **1.** to draw together; pucker **2.** to make tucks —*n.* a sewed fold in a garment —**tuck away 1.** to eat or drink heartily **2.** to put aside, as for future use —**tuck in 1.** to pull in or contract (one's chin, stomach, etc.) **2.** to eat or drink heartily

**tuck·er¹** (tuk'ər) *n.* **1.** a person or device that makes tucks **2.** a neck and shoulder covering formerly worn with a low-cut bodice by women **3.** [Austral. Slang] food

**tuck·er²** (tuk'ər) *vt.* [prob. < *tuck,* in obs. sense "to punish, rebuke"] [Colloq.] to tire (*out*); weary

**Tuc·son** (tōō'sän, tōō sän') [Sp. < Pima *tu-uk-so-on,* black base, after a dark stratum in a nearby mountain] city in S Ariz.: pop. 331,000 (met. area 532,000)

**Tu·dor** (tōō'dər, tyōō'-) ruling family of England (1485–1603) —*adj.* designating or of a style of architecture popular under the Tudors, characterized by shallow moldings, extensive paneling, etc.

**Tues., Tue.** Tuesday

**Tues·day** (tōōz'dē, tyōōz'-; -dā) *n.* [OE. *Tiwes dæg,* lit., day of the god of war *Tiw*] the third day of the week

**Tues·days** (-dēz, -dāz) *adv.* on or during every Tuesday

**tu·fa** (tōō'fə, tyōō'-) *n.* [It. *tufo* < L. *tofus*] a porous rock formed of calcium carbonate, etc. deposited by springs —**tu·fa'ceous** (-fā'shəs) *adj.*

**tuff** (tuf) *n.* [< Fr. < It. *tufo,* TUFA] a porous rock formed from volcanic ash, dust, etc. —**tuff·a'ceous** (-ā'shəs) *adj.*

**tuf·fet** (tuf'ət) *n.* [< TUFT] **1.** a tuft of grass **2.** [by misunderstanding of a nursery rhyme] a low stool

**tuft** (tuft) *n.* [OFr. *tufe,* prob. < L. *tufa,* helmet crest] **1.** a bunch of hairs, feathers, grass, etc. growing or tied closely together **2.** *a)* the fluffy ball forming the end of any of the clusters of threads drawn tightly through a quilt, etc. to hold the padding in place *b)* a decorative button to which a tuft is fastened —*vt.* **1.** to provide or decorate with a tuft or tufts **2.** to keep the padding of (a quilt, mattress, etc.) in place by regularly spaced tufts —*vi.* to grow in or form into tufts —**tuft′ed** *adj.* —**tuft′er** *n.* —**tuft′y** *adj.*

**tug** (tug) *vi.* **tugged, tug′ging** [prob. < ON. *toga,* to draw] **1.** to pull hard (often with *at*) **2.** to labor; toil; struggle —*vt.* **1.** to pull at with force; strain at **2.** to drag; haul **3.** to tow with a tugboat —*n.* **1.** a hard pull **2.** a great effort or a struggle, strain, etc. **3.** a rope, chain, strap, etc. used for pulling **4.** *shortened form of* TUGBOAT —**tug′ger** *n.* —**tug′ging·ly** *adv.*

**tug·boat** (-bōt′) *n.* a small, powerful boat used for towing or pushing ships, barges, etc.

**tug of war 1.** a contest in which two teams pull at opposite ends of a rope, each trying to drag the other across a central line **2.** any hard struggle

**tu·grik** (tōō′grik) *n.* [Mongol. *dughurik,* lit., wheel] *see* MONETARY UNITS, table (Mongolia)

**tu·i·tion** (tōō wish′ən, tyōō-) *n.* [ < OFr. < L. *tuitio,* protection < pp. of *tueri,* to protect] **1.** the fee for instruction, esp. at a college or private school **2.** [Now Rare] teaching; instruction —**tu·i′tion·al** *adj.*

**tu·la·re·mi·a** (tōō′lə rē′mē ə) *n.* [ModL. < *Tulare* County, California + -EMIA] an infectious disease of rodents, esp. rabbits, sometimes transmitted to man: also sp. **tu′la·rae′mi·a** —**tu′la·re′mic** *adj.*

**tu·lip** (tōō′lip, tyōō′-) *n.* [ < Fr. < Turk. *tülbend,* TURBAN: the flower resembles a turban] **1.** any of various spring-blooming bulb plants, with long, pointed leaves and a large, cup-shaped flower **2.** the flower or bulb

**tulip tree** a tree of the magnolia family with tulip-shaped, greenish-yellow flowers, and long, conelike fruit: also called **tulip poplar**

**tu·lip·wood** (-wood′) *n.* **1.** the light, soft wood of the tulip tree, used for furniture, etc. **2.** any of several woods having streaks of color

**tulle** (tōōl; *Fr.* tül) *n.* [ < *Tulle,* city in France] a thin, fine netting of silk, rayon, nylon, etc., used for veils, scarfs, etc.

**Tul·ly** (tul′ē) *Englished name of* (Marcus) Tullius (CICERO)

**Tul·sa** (tul′sə) [ < Creek Indian name] city in NE Okla., on the Arkansas River: pop. 361,000 (met. area 679,000)

**tum·ble** (tum′b'l) *vi.* **-bled, -bling** [OE. *tumbian,* to jump, dance] **1.** to do somersaults, handsprings, or similar acrobatic feats **2.** *a)* to fall suddenly or helplessly *b)* to undergo a sudden drop or downfall /prices *tumbled,* the government *tumbled]* **3.** to stumble or trip **4.** to toss or roll about **5.** to move in a hasty, disorderly manner **6.** [Colloq.] to understand suddenly (with *to*) —*vt.* **1.** to cause to tumble **2.** to put into disorder as by tossing here and there —*n.* **1.** a tumbling; specif., *a)* a somersault, handspring, etc. *b)* a fall **2.** disorder; confusion **3.** a confused heap —**give** (or **get**) **a tumble** [Colloq.] to give (or get) some favorable or affectionate notice, attention, etc.

**tum·ble·bug** (-bug′) *n.* any of various beetles that roll balls of dung, in which they deposit their eggs and in which the larvae develop

**tum·ble·down** (-doun′) *adj.* ready to tumble down; dilapidated

**tum·bler** (tum′blər) *n.* **1.** an acrobat or gymnast who does somersaults, handsprings, etc. **2.** a kind of pigeon that does somersaults in flight **3.** *a)* an ordinary drinking glass with no foot or stem *b)* its contents **4.** a part of a lock whose position must be changed by a key in order to release the bolt **5.** a device for tumbling things about

**tum·ble·weed** (tum′b'l wēd′) *n.* any of various plants which break off near the ground in autumn and are blown about by the wind

**tum·brel, tum·bril** (tum′brəl) *n.* [ < MFr. < *tomber,* to fall] **1.** a farmer's cart that can be tilted for emptying **2.** any of the carts used to carry the condemned to the guillotine during the French Revolution

**tu·me·fy** (tōō′mə fī′, tyōō′-) *vt., vi.* **-fied′, -fy′ing** [ < Fr., ult. < L. < *tumere,* to swell + *facere,* to make] to swell or cause to swell —**tu′me·fac′tion** (-fak′shən) *n.*

**tu·mes·cence** (tōō mes′'ns, tyōō-) *n.* [ < L. prp. of *tumescere,* to swell up] **1.** a swelling; distention **2.** a swollen or distended part —**tu·mes′cent** *adj.*

**tu·mid** (tōō′mid, tyōō′-) *adj.* [ < L. < *tumere,* to swell] **1.** swollen; bulging **2.** inflated; pompous —**tu·mid′i·ty, tu′mid·ness** *n.* —**tu′mid·ly** *adv.*

**tum·my** (tum′ē) *n., pl.* **-mies** stomach: a child's word

**tu·mor** (tōō′mər, tyōō′-) *n.* [L. < *tumere,* to swell] an abnormal growth of tissue in some part of the body, that is either benign or malignant: Brit. sp. **tu′mour** —**tu′mor·ous** *adj.*

**tump·line** (tump′līn) *n.* [*tump,* a tumpline < AmInd.] a broad band passed across the forehead and behind across the shoulders to support a pack on the back

**tu·mult** (tōō′mult, tyōō′-) *n.* [ < MFr. < L. *tumultus* < *tumere,* to swell] **1.** noisy commotion, as of a crowd; uproar **2.** confusion; agitation; disturbance **3.** great emotional disturbance

**tu·mul·tu·ous** (tōō mul′choo wəs) *adj.* **1.** full of or characterized by tumult; wild and noisy; uproarious **2.** making a tumult **3.** greatly disturbed —**tu·mul′tu·ous·ly** *adv.* —**tu·mul′tu·ous·ness** *n.*

**tu·mu·lus** (tōō′myə ləs, tyōō′-) *n., pl.* **-li′** (-lī′), **-lus·es** [L., a mound] an artificial mound, esp. an ancient burial mound

**tun** (tun) *n.* [OE. *tunne,* large cask & OFr. *tonne,* both < ML. *tunna* < Celt.] **1.** a large cask for liquids **2.** a measure of capacity for liquids, usually 252 wine gallons —*vt.* **tunned, tun′ning** to store in a tun or tuns

**tu·na¹** (tōō′nə, tyōō′-) *n., pl.* **tu′na, tu′nas:** see PLURAL, II, D, 2 [AmSp. < Sp. < Ar. < L. *thunnus:* see TUNNY] **1.** a large, ocean, food and game fish of the mackerel group: also called **bluefin tuna 2.** any of various related fishes, as the albacore **3.** the flesh of the tuna, often canned for food: also called **tuna fish**

**tu·na²** (tōō′nə, tyōō′-) *n.* [Sp., of WInd. origin] any of various prickly pears

**tun·a·ble** (tōōn′ə b'l, tyōōn′-) *adj.* capable of being tuned: also sp. **tune′a·ble** —**tun′a·ble·ness** *n.*

**tun·dra** (tun′drə, toon′-) *n.* [Russ.] any of the vast, nearly level, treeless plains of the arctic regions

**tune** (tōōn, tyōōn) *n.* [ME., var. of *tone,* TONE] **1.** a succession of musical tones forming a rhythmic, catchy whole; melody; air **2.** the condition of having correct musical pitch, or of being in key; also, harmony; concord: now chiefly in phrases **in tune, out of tune** —*vt.* **tuned, tun′ing 1.** to adjust (a musical instrument) to some standard of pitch **2.** to adapt (music, the voice, etc.) to some pitch, tone, etc. **3.** to adapt to some condition, mood, etc. **4.** to adjust (an electronics circuit, a motor, etc.) to the proper or desired performance —*vi.* to be in tune; harmonize —**call the tune** to be in control —**change one's tune** to change one's attitude or manner: also **sing a different tune** —**to the tune of** [Colloq.] to the amount of —**tune in 1.** to adjust a radio or television receiver to a given frequency or channel so as to receive (a specified station, program, etc.) **2.** [Slang] to become or make aware, knowing, etc. —**tune out 1.** to adjust a radio or television receiver so as to get rid of (interference, etc.) **2.** [Slang] to turn one's attention, sympathies, etc. away from —**tune up 1.** to adjust (musical instruments) to the same pitch **2.** to put (an engine) into good working condition —**tun′er** *n.*

**tune·ful** (-fəl) *adj.* full of tunes or melody; musical; melodious —**tune′ful·ly** *adv.* —**tune′ful·ness** *n.*

**tune·less** (-lis) *adj.* not musical or melodious —**tune′less·ly** *adv.* —**tune′less·ness** *n.*

**tune·up, tune-up** (-up′) *n.* an adjusting, as of an engine, to the proper condition

**tung oil** (tung) [ < Chin. *yu-t'ung* < *yu,* oil + *t'ung,* name of the tree] a fast-drying oil from the seeds of a subtropical tree (**tung tree**), used in paints, varnishes, etc.

**tung·sten** (tung′stən) *n.* [Sw. < *tung,* heavy + *sten,* stone] a hard, heavy, gray-white, metallic chemical element, used in steel, electric lamp filaments, etc.: symbol, W; at. wt., 183.85; at. no., 74 —**tung′stic** (-stik) *adj.*

**tu·nic** (tōō′nik, tyōō′-) *n.* [L. *tunica*] **1.** a loose, gownlike garment worn by men and women in ancient Greece and Rome **2.** a blouselike garment extending to the hips or lower, often belted **3.** [Chiefly Brit.] a short coat forming part of the uniform of soldiers, policemen, etc. **4.** a short vestment worn by a subdeacon **5.** *Biol.* a covering membrane or tissue

**tu·ni·cate** (tōō′ni kit, tyōō′-; -kāt′) *adj.* [ < L. pp. of *tunicare,* to put on a tunic] *Bot., Zool.* covered with or having a tunic or tunics: also **tu′ni·cat′ed** (-kāt′id) —*n.* any of several sea animals having a saclike body enclosed by a thick cellulose tunic

**tuning fork** a small steel instrument with two prongs, which when struck sounds a certain fixed tone: it is used as a guide in tuning instruments, etc.

**Tu·nis** (tōō′nis, tyōō′-) capital of Tunisia, on an inlet (**Gulf of Tunis**) of the Mediterranean: pop. 642,000

**Tu·ni·sia** (tōō nē′zhə, tyōō-; -nish′ə, -nish′ē ə) country in N Africa, on the Mediterranean: 48,332 sq. mi.; pop. 5,137,000; cap. Tunis —**Tu·ni′sian** *adj., n.*

**tun·nage** (tun′ij) *n. same as* TONNAGE

**tun·nel** (tun′'l) *n.* [MFr. *tonnelle,* vault < OFr. dim. of *tonne,* a tun] **1.** an underground or underwater passageway for automobiles, trains, etc. **2.** an animal's burrow **3.** any tunnellike passage, as one in a mine —*vt.* **-neled** or **-nelled, -nel·ing** or **-nel·ling 1.** to make a tunnel through or under **2.** to make (one's way) by digging a tunnel —*vi.* to make a tunnel —**tun′nel·er, tun′nel·ler** *n.*

**tun·ny** (tun′ē) *n., pl.* **-nies, -ny:** see PLURAL, II, D, 1 [ < MFr. < Pr. < L. < Gr. *thynnos*] *same as* TUNA¹ (senses 1 & 2)

**tu·pe·lo** (tōō′pə lō′) *n., pl.* **-los′** [ < Creek Indian *ito,* tree + *opilwa,* a swamp] **1.** any of several gum trees of the southern U.S. **2.** the fine-textured wood of any of these trees, used for mallets, furniture, etc.

**Tu·pi** (tōō pē′, tōō′pē) *n.* [Tupi, comrade] **1.** *pl.* Tu-pis', Tu·pi' any member of a group of S. American Indian tribes living chiefly along the lower Amazon 2. their language

tup·pence (tup''ns) n. same as TWOPENCE

tuque (tōōk, tyōōk) n. [CanadFr. < Fr. toque, a cap] a kind of knitted winter cap

tur·ban (tur'bən) n. [< MFr. < It. or Port. < Turk. tülbend, dial. form of dülbend < Per.] 1. a headdress of Moslem origin, consisting of a cloth wound in folds about the head, often over a cap 2. any head covering or hat made like or resembling this —tur'baned adj.

tur·bid (tur'bid) adj. [< L. < turba, a crowd] 1. muddy or cloudy from having the sediment stirred up 2. thick or dark, as clouds or smoke 3. confused or perplexed; muddled —tur·bid'i·ty, tur'bid·ness n. —tur'bid·ly adv.

TURBAN

tur·bine (tur'bin, -bīn) n. [Fr. < L. turbo, a whirl] an engine driven by the pressure of steam, water, air, etc. against the curved vanes of a wheel on a shaft

tur·bo- [< TURBINE] a combining form meaning consisting of or driven by a turbine

tur·bo·fan (tur'bō fan') n. 1. a turbojet engine in which additional thrust is obtained from the part of the air that bypasses the engine and is accelerated by a fan: in full, turbofan engine 2. a fan driven by a turbine

tur·bo·jet (-jet') n. 1. a jet engine with a turbine-driven air compressor that compresses air for fuel combustion, the resulting hot gases being used to rotate the turbine before forming the propulsive jet: in full, turbojet engine 2. an aircraft propelled by such an engine

tur·bo·prop (-präp') n. [TURBO- + PROP(ELLER)] 1. a turbojet engine whose turbine shaft drives a propeller that develops most of the thrust, some being added by a jet of the turbine exhaust gases: in full, turboprop engine 2. an aircraft propelled by such an engine

tur·bot (tur'bət) n., pl. -bot, -bots: see PLURAL, II, D, 2 [< OFr. tourbout] 1. a large European flatfish, highly regarded as food 2. any of several American flounders

tur·bu·lent (tur'byə lənt) adj. [Fr. < L. < turba, a crowd] full of commotion or wild disorder; specif., a) marked by or causing turmoil; disorderly b) violently agitated or excited c) marked by wildly irregular motion —tur'bu·lence, tur'bu·len·cy n. —tur'bu·lent·ly adv.

tu·reen (too rēn') n. [MFr. terrine, earthen vessel, ult. < L. terra, earth] a deep dish with a lid, for serving soup, etc.

turf (turf) n., pl. turfs, esp. Brit. turves (turvz) [OE.] 1. a) a surface layer of earth containing grass plants with their matted roots; sod b) a piece of this layer 2. peat 3. [Slang] one's territory —vt. to cover with turf —the turf 1. a track for horse racing 2. the sport of horse racing —turf out [Brit. Colloq.] to throw out

turf·man (-mən) n., pl. -men an owner, trainer, etc. of racehorses

Tur·ge·nev (toor gā'nyif), I·van (Sergeevich) (ē vän') 1818–83; Russ. novelist: also sp. Turgenieff, Turgeniev

tur·ges·cent (tur jes''nt) adj. [< L. prp. of turgescere, to swell up] becoming turgid or swollen —tur·ges'cence n.

tur·gid (tur'jid) adj. [< L. turgidus < turgere, to swell] 1. swollen; distended 2. bombastic; grandiloquent —tur·gid'i·ty, tur'gid·ness n. —tur'gid·ly adv.

Tu·rin (toor'in, tyoor'-; too rin', tyoo-) city in NW Italy, on the Po River: pop. 1,177,000

Turk (turk) n. 1. a native or inhabitant of Turkey; esp., a member of the Moslem people of Turkey or, formerly, of the Ottoman Empire 2. a member of any of the peoples speaking Turkic languages See also YOUNG TURK

Turk. 1. Turkey 2. Turkish

Tur·ke·stan (tur'ki stan', -stän') region in C Asia, extending from the Caspian Sea to the Gobi Desert, inhabited by Turkic-speaking peoples

Tur·key (tur'kē) country occupying Asia Minor & a SE part of the Balkan Peninsula: 301,381 sq. mi.; pop. 36,162,000; cap. Ankara

tur·key (tur'kē) n., pl. -keys, -key: see PLURAL, II, D, 1 [orig. applied to the guinea fowl, sometimes imported through Turkey and for a time identified with the Am. fowl] 1. a) a large, wild or domesticated, N. American bird with a small head and spreading tail, bred as poultry b) its flesh 2. [Slang] a failure: said esp. of a theatrical production 3. [Slang] a stupid or unpleasant person 4. Bowling three strikes in a row —talk turkey [Colloq.] to talk bluntly and directly

turkey buzzard a dark-colored vulture of temperate and tropical America, having a naked, reddish head: also called turkey vulture

Tur·ki (toor'kē, tur'-) n. 1. the Turkic languages collectively or any Turkic language 2. a member of any Turkic people —adj. designating or of the Turkic languages or the peoples who speak them

Tur·kic (tur'kik) adj. 1. designating or of a subfamily of Altaic languages, including Turkish 2. designating or of the peoples who speak any of these languages —n. the Turkic subfamily of languages

Turk·ish (tur'kish) adj. of Turkey, the Turks, their language, etc. —n. 1. the Turkic language of Turkey: in full, Ottoman-Turkish 2. loosely, same as TURKIC

Turkish bath a public bath in which the bather, after a period of heavy perspiration in a room of hot air or steam, is washed and massaged

Turkish Empire same as OTTOMAN EMPIRE

Turkish towel [also t-] a thick cotton towel of terry cloth

Tur·ki·stan (toor'ki stan', -stän') same as TURKESTAN

Turk·men Soviet Socialist Republic (turk'men) republic of the U.S.S.R., in C Asia, on the Caspian Sea: 188,400 sq. mi.; pop. 2,200,000: also Turk'men·i·stan' (-i stan', -i stän') —Turk·me·ni·an (turk mē'nē ən) adj.

Tur·ko- a combining form meaning: 1. of Turkey or the Turks 2. Turkey and 3. the Turks and Also Tur'co-

tur·mer·ic (tur'mər ik) n. [< MFr. < ML. terra merita, lit., deserving earth < ?] 1. an East Indian plant whose rhizome in powdered form is used as a yellow dye or a seasoning, and in medicine 2. its aromatic rhizome or the powder made from it

tur·moil (tur'moil) n. [tur- (< ? TURBULENT) + MOIL] a very excited or confused condition; tumult; uproar

turn (turn) vt. [< OE. turnian & OFr. tourner, both < L. tornare, to turn in a lathe, ult. < Gr. tornos, a lathe] 1. to make (a wheel, etc.) move about a center or axis; rotate; revolve 2. to move around or partly around [to turn a key, handle, etc.] 3. to do (a somersault, cartwheel, etc.) 4. to give a rounded shape to, as on a lathe 5. to give a graceful form to [to turn a pretty phrase] 6. to change the position or direction of [turn your chair around] 7. to revolve in the mind; ponder (often with over) 8. a) to bend, fold, etc. [turn the sheet back] b) to twist (one's ankle) 9. to move so that the underside is on top, and vice versa; reverse; invert [to turn pages, a collar, the soil, etc.] 10. to make topsy-turvy 11. to upset (the stomach) 12. to deflect; divert 13. a) to convert or persuade b) to prejudice 14. to go around (a corner, etc.) 15. to reach or pass (a certain age, amount, etc.) 16. to reverse the course of; repel or make recoil [to turn an attack] 17. to drive, set, let go, etc. in some way [the dog was turned loose] 18. to direct, point, aim, etc. [eyes turned ahead, thoughts turned to the past] 19. to put to a specified use; apply [he turned his hand to writing] 20. to change from one form, condition, etc. to another [to turn cream into butter] 21. to exchange for [to turn produce into hard cash] 22. to translate or paraphrase 23. to derange, distract, or infatuate 24. to make sour 25. to affect in some way [turned sick by the sight] 26. to change the color of —vi. 1. to rotate, revolve, pivot, etc. 2. to move around or partly around 3. to reel; whirl [my head is turning] 4. to become curved or bent 5. to become reversed or inverted 6. to become upset, as the stomach 7. to change or reverse one's or its course or direction [the tide turned] 8. to refer (to) 9. to go or apply (to) for help 10. to direct or shift one's attention, abilities, etc. [he turned to music] 11. to make a sudden attack (on or upon) [the dog turned on him] 12. to reverse one's feelings, allegiance, etc. [he turned against his sister] 13. to depend or hinge (on or upon) 14. to become [to turn bitter with age] 15. to change into another form [the rain turned into sleet] 16. to become rancid, sour, etc. 17. to change color, as leaves in the fall —n. 1. a turning around; rotation, as of a wheel, handle, etc. 2. a single twist, coil, winding, etc. 3. a musical ornament of four tones, with the tones above and below the principal tone alternating with it 4. a change or reversal of position, course, or direction 5. a short walk or ride around an area, as for exercise or inspection 6. the place where a change in direction occurs; bend; curve 7. a) a change in trend, events, health, etc. b) same as TURNING POINT 8. the time of change [the turn of the century] 9. a sudden, brief shock 10. an action or deed [a good turn] 11. a spell of activity 12. an attack of illness, dizziness, etc. 13. the right, duty, or chance to do something, esp. in regular order [his turn at bat] 14. an act in a variety show 15. a distinctive form, manner, detail, etc. [a quaint turn to her speech] 16. natural inclination [a curious turn of mind] —at every turn in every instance; constantly —by turns one after another in regular order —call the turn to predict successfully —**in turn** in proper sequence or succession —**out of turn 1.** not in proper sequence or order **2.** imprudently *[to talk out of turn]* —**take turns** to speak, do, etc. one after another in regular order —**to a turn** perfectly —**turn and turn about** alternately —**turn down 1.** to reject (the request, etc. of someone) **2.** to lessen the intensity or volume of —**turn in 1.** to make a turn into; enter **2.** to deliver; hand in **3.** to inform on or hand over, as to the police **4.** to give back **5.** [Colloq.] to go to bed —**turn off 1.** *a)* to leave (a road, etc.); *b)* to branch off: said of a road, etc. **2.** to shut off; stop from functioning **3.** to stop displaying suddenly *[to turn off a smile]* **4.** [Slang] to cause (someone) to become uninterested, annoyed, etc. —**turn on 1.** to start; make go on or start functioning **2.** to display suddenly *[to turn on the charm]* **3.** [Slang] to stimulate with or as with a psychedelic drug; make elated, euphoric, etc. —**turn out 1.** to put out (a light) **2.** to put outside **3.** to dismiss **4.** to come or gather *[to turn out for a picnic]* **5.** to produce **6.** to result **7.** to prove to be **8.** to become **9.** to equip, dress, etc. **10.** [Colloq.] to get out of bed —**turn over 1.** to change or reverse the position of **2.** to shift one's position **3.** to begin, or make begin, to operate, as an engine **4.** to consider; ponder **5.** to hand over; give **6.** to convert **7.** to sell and replenish (a stock of goods) **8.** to do business to the amount of —**turn to** to get to work —**turn up 1.** to fold back or over upon itself **2.** to lift up or turn face up **3.** to increase the speed, intensity, etc. of, as by turning a control **4.** to make a turn onto or into (a street, etc.) **5.** to have an upward direction **6.** to happen **7.** to make an appearance; arrive **8.** to find or be found —**turn′er** *n.*

**turn·a·bout** (turn′ə bout′) *n.* **1.** a turning about, as to face the other way **2.** a sharp change, as of opinion

**turn·buck·le** (-buk′'l) *n.* a metal loop with opposite internal threads in each end for the threaded ends of two rods or ringbolts, forming a coupling that can be turned to tighten or loosen the rods or two wires attached to the ringbolts

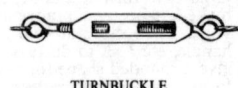

TURNBUCKLE

**turn·coat** (-kōt′) *n.* a renegade; traitor

**turn·down** (-doun′) *adj.* **1.** that can be turned down **2.** having the upper part folded down *[a turndown collar]* —*n.* **1.** a rejection **2.** a decline; downturn

**Tur·ner** (tur′nər), **J(oseph) M(allord) W(illiam)** 1775–1851; Eng. painter

**turn·ing** (tur′niŋ) *n.* **1.** the action of a person or thing that turns **2.** a place where a road, etc. turns **3.** the art or process of shaping things on a lathe

**turning point 1.** a point at which something turns or changes direction **2.** a point in time at which a decisive change occurs; crisis

**tur·nip** (tur′nip) *n.* [prob. < TURN or < Fr. *tour*, in sense of "round" + ME. *nepe* < OE. < L. *napus*, a turnip] **1.** *a)* a plant of the mustard family, with edible, hairy leaves and a roundish, light-colored root used as a vegetable *b)* same as RUTABAGA **2.** the root of either of these plants

**turn·key** (turn′kē′) *n., pl.* **-keys′** a person in charge of the keys of a prison; warder; jailer

**turn·off** (-ôf′) *n.* **1.** a turning off **2.** a place where one turns off; esp., a road or ramp leading off a highway

**turn·out** (-out′) *n.* **1.** a turning out **2.** *a)* a gathering of people, as for a meeting *b)* the number of people **3.** an amount produced **4.** *a)* a wider part of a narrow road, as for passing *b)* a railroad siding **5.** a carriage with its horse or horses **6.** *a)* equipment *b)* a set of clothes

**turn·o·ver** (-ō′vər) *n.* **1.** a turning over; specif., *a)* an upset *b)* a change from one side, opinion, etc. to another **2.** a small pie made by folding one half of the crust back over the other **3.** *a)* the selling out and replacing of a stock of goods *b)* the amount of business done during a given period in terms of the money used in buying and selling **4.** *a)* the number of workers hired as replacements during a given period *b)* the ratio of this to the average number of workers employed **5.** *Basketball, Football* loss of possession of the ball due to an error by the offensive team —*adj.* that turns over

**turn·pike** (-pīk′) *n.* [ME. *turnpyke*, a spiked barrier across a road: see TURN & PIKE⁴] **1.** same as TOLLGATE **2.** a toll road, esp. one that is an expressway

**turn·stile** (-stīl′) *n.* a post with revolving horizontal bars, often coin-operated, used at an entrance to admit persons one at a time

**turn·stone** (-stōn′) *n.* a small, ploverlike shore bird that turns over pebbles to seek food

**turn·ta·ble** (-tā′b'l) *n.* a circular rotating platform; specif., *a)* such a platform for supporting a phonograph record being played *b)* such a platform carrying tracks to turn a locomotive around

**turn·up** (turn′up′) *n.* something turned up —*adj.* that turns up or is turned up

‡**Turn·ver·ein** (toorn′fer īn′; *E.* turn′fə rīn′) *n.* [G. < *turnen*, to exercise + *verein*, a club] a club of gymnasts

**tur·pen·tine** (tur′pən tīn′) *n.* [< OFr. < L., ult. < Gr. *terebinthos*, the terebinth] **1.** an oleoresin from the terebinth **2.** any of various oleoresins obtained from pines and other conifers: in full, **gum turpentine 3.** a colorless, volatile oil distilled from such oleoresins and used in paints, in medicine, etc.: in full, **spirits (or oil) of turpentine** —*vt.* **-tined′, -tin′ing** to apply turpentine to —**tur′pen·tin′ic** (-tin′ik), **tur′pen·tin′ous** (-tī′nəs) *adj.*

**tur·pi·tude** (tur′pə tōōd′, -tyōōd′) *n.* [MFr. < L. < *turpis*, vile] the condition of being wicked, evil, or depraved

**turps** (turps) *n.pl.* [with sing. v.] same as TURPENTINE (*n.* 2)

**tur·quoise** (tur′koiz, -kwoiz) *n.* [< MFr. fem. of OFr. *turqueis*, Turkish: orig. brought to W Europe through Turkey] **1.** a greenish-blue, semiprecious stone, a hydrous phosphate of aluminum containing a small amount of copper **2.** a greenish blue —*adj.* greenish-blue Also sp. **tur′quois**

**tur·ret** (tur′it) *n.* [< OFr. dim. of *tour*: see TOWER¹] **1.** a small tower projecting from a building, usually at a corner **2.** *a)* a low, armored, usually revolving, towerlike structure for guns, as on a warship, tank, etc. *b)* a transparent dome for a gun and gunner, as on a bomber **3.** an attachment for a lathe, drill, etc., consisting of a block holding several cutting tools, which may be rotated to present any of the tools to the work: also **tur′ret·head′** —**tur′ret·ed** *adj.*

**tur·tle** (tur′t'l) *n., pl.* **-tles, -tle:** see PLURAL, II, D, 1 [altered (after TURTLEDOVE) < Fr. *tortue*, tortoise] **1.** any of various land and water reptiles having a toothless beak and a soft body encased in a hard shell into which, in most species, it can pull its head, tail, and four legs: land species are usually called *tortoise* **2.** the flesh of some turtles, used as food **3.** *archaic var. of* TURTLEDOVE —*vi.* **-tled, -tling** to hunt for turtles —**turn turtle** to turn upside down

**tur·tle·back** (-bak′) *n.* an arched structure over the deck of a ship as a protection against heavy seas

**tur·tle·dove** (-duv′) *n.* [OE. *turtle* < L. *turtur*, of echoic origin] **1.** any of several wild doves noted for their sad cooing and the devotion that the mates seem to show toward each other **2.** same as MOURNING DOVE

**tur·tle·neck** (-nek′) *n.* **1.** a high, snugly fitting, turndown collar on a pullover sweater, shirt, etc. **2.** a sweater, shirt, etc. with such a neck

**Tus·ca·loo·sa** (tus′kə lōō′sə) [< Choctaw < *taska*, warrior + *lusa*, black] city in WC Ala., near Birmingham: pop. 75,000

**Tus·ca·ny** (tus′kə nē) region of C Italy, on the Ligurian & Tyrrhenian seas: chief city, Florence —**Tus′can** *adj., n.*

**Tus·ca·ro·ra** (tus′kə rôr′ə) *n.* [< the native name, lit., hemp gatherers] **1.** *pl.* **-ras, -ra** a member of a tribe of Iroquoian Indians at one time living in Virginia and North Carolina, but later in New York and Ontario **2.** their Iroquoian language

**tush** (tush) *interj., n.* [ME. *tussch*] an exclamation expressing impatience, reproof, contempt, etc.

**tusk** (tusk) *n.* [OE. *tucs*] **1.** in elephants, wild boars, etc., a long, pointed tooth, usually one of a pair, that sticks out of the mouth **2.** any tusklike tooth or part —*vt.* to dig, gore, etc. with a tusk or tusks —**tusked** *adj.* —**tusk′like′** *adj.*

**tus·sah** (tus′ə) *n.* [< Hindi < Sans. *tasara*, lit., a shuttle] **1.** an Asiatic silkworm that produces a coarse, tough silk **2.** this silk: also **tussah silk** Also sp. **tus′sore, tus′sor** (tus′ôr)

**tus·sle** (tus′'l) *n., vi.* **-sled, -sling** [LME. freq. of *tusen*, to pull] struggle; wrestle; scuffle

**tus·sock** (tus′ək) *n.* [prob. < ME. *(to)tusen*, to rumple + -OCK] a thick tuft or clump of grass, twigs, etc. —**tus′sock·y** (-ē) *adj.*

**tut** (tut) *interj., n.* an exclamation of impatience, annoyance, rebuke, etc. —*vi.* **tut′ted, tut′ting** to utter "tuts"

**Tut·ankh·a·men** (tōōt′änk ä′mən) fl. c. 1355 B.C.; Egyptian king of the 18th dynasty: also sp. **Tutankhamon**

**tu·tee** (tōō tē′, tyōō-) *n.* [TUT(OR) + -EE] a person who is being tutored

**tu·te·lage** (tōōt′'l ij, tyōōt′-) *n.* [< L. *tutela*, protection] **1.** guardianship; care, protection, etc. **2.** teaching; instruction **3.** the condition of being under a guardian or tutor

**tu·te·lar·y** (-er′ē) *adj.* [< L. < *tutela*: see prec.] **1.** that watches over or protects **2.** of or serving as a guardian Also **tu′te·lar** (-ər) —*n., pl.* **-lar′ies** a tutelary god, spirit, etc.

**tu·tor** (tōōt′ər, tyōōt′-) *n.* [< MFr. < L. < pp. of *tueri*, to guard] **1.** a teacher who teaches one student at a time **2.** a legal guardian of a minor **3.** in English universities, an official in charge of the studies of an undergraduate **4.** in some U.S. colleges, a teacher ranking below an instructor —*vt.* **1.** to act as a tutor to; esp., to teach (students) one at a time **2.** to discipline; admonish —*vi.* **1.** to act as a tutor **2.** [Colloq.] to be tutored —**tu′tor·age, tu′tor·ship′** *n.* —**tu·to·ri·al** (tōō tôr′ē əl, tyōō-) *adj.*

**tut·ti** (tōōt′ē) *adj.* [It., ult. < L. *totus*, all] *Music* for all instruments or voices —*n., pl.* **-tis 1.** a passage played or sung by all performers **2.** the tonal effect of such a passage

**tut·ti-frut·ti** (tōōt′ē frōōt′ē) *n.* [It., all fruits] **1.** ice cream or other sweet food containing bits of candied fruits **2.** a flavoring combining a number of fruit flavors

**tu·tu** (tōō′tōō) *n.* [Fr.] a very short, full, projecting skirt worn by women ballet dancers

**Tu·tu·i·la** (tōō′tōō ē′lä) chief island of American Samoa, in the South Pacific: chief town, Pago Pago

**Tu·va·lu** (tōō′və lōō′) country consisting of a group of islands in the WC Pacific: 10 sq. mi.; pop. 6,000

**tu-whit tu-whoo** (tōō hwit′ tōō hwōō′; -wit′, -wōō′) the characteristic vocal sound made by an owl

**tux** (tuks) *n.* same as TUXEDO

**tux·e·do** (tək sē′dō) *n., pl.* **-dos** [< the name of a country club near *Tuxedo* Lake, N.Y.] **1.** a man's tailless jacket for semiformal evening wear, orig. black **2.** a suit with such a jacket, worn with a dark bow tie —*adj.* designating or of a sofa, chair, etc. with a straight back and sides at the same height

**TV** (tē′vē′) *n., pl.* **TVs, TV's** television or a television receiving set

**TVA, T.V.A.** Tennessee Valley Authority

**TV dinner** [because it can conveniently be eaten while viewing television] a frozen, precooked dinner packaged in a tray for heating and serving

**twa** (twä) *adj., n.* [OE.] *Scot. var. of* TWO

**twad·dle** (twäd′'l) *n.* [prob. akin to TATTLE] foolish, empty talk or writing; nonsense —*vt., vi.* **-dled, -dling** to talk or write in a foolish or senseless manner; prattle —**twad′dler** *n.*

**twain** (twān) *n., adj.* [OE. *twegen,* two] *archaic var. of* TWO

**Twain** (twān), **Mark** *see* Samuel Langhorne CLEMENS

**twang** (twaŋ) *n.* [echoic] **1.** a quick, sharp, vibrating sound, as of a plucked string **2.** *a*) a sharp, nasal speech sound *b*) a dialect using such sounds —*vi., vt.* **1.** to make or cause to make a twang, as a bowstring, banjo, etc. **2.** to speak or say with a twang **3.** to shoot or be released with a twang, as an arrow —**twang′y** *adj.*

**'twas** (twuz, twäz; *unstressed* twəz) it was

**twat·tle** (twät′'l) *n., vi., vt.* **-tled, -tling** *var. of* TWADDLE

**tweak** (twēk) *vt.* [OE. *twiccan,* to twitch] to give a sudden, twisting pinch to (someone's nose, ear, cheek, etc.) —*n.* such a pinch

**tweed** (twēd) *n.* [< misreading of *tweel,* Scot. form of TWILL: later assoc. with the *Tweed,* river in Scotland] **1.** a wool fabric with a rough surface, in a twill weave of two or more colors **2.** a suit, etc. of this **3.** [*pl.*] clothes of tweed

**twee·dle·dum and twee·dle·dee** (twēd′'l dum′'n twēd′'l dē′) [echoic of musical notes] two persons or things so much alike that it is hard to tell them apart

**tweed·y** (twēd′ē) *adj.* **tweed′i·er, tweed′i·est** **1.** of or like tweed **2.** having the casually tailored look, fondness of the outdoors, etc. of a person given to wearing tweeds —**tweed′i·ness** *n.*

**'tween** (twēn) *prep.* [Poet.] between

**tweet** (twēt) *n., interj.* [echoic] the thin, chirping sound of a small bird —*vi.* to make this sound

**tweet·er** (-ər) *n.* a small, high-fidelity loudspeaker for reproducing high-frequency sounds: cf. WOOFER

**tweeze** (twēz) *vt.* **tweezed, tweez′ing** [back-formation < ff.] [Colloq.] to pluck with or as with tweezers

**tweez·ers** (twē′zərz) *n.pl.* [*with sing. or pl. v.*] [< obs. *tweeze,* surgical set < Fr. pl. of *étui,* a case] small pincers for plucking out hairs, handling little objects, etc.: also **tweezer** or **pair of tweezers**

**twelfth** (twelfth) *adj.* [OE. *twelfta*] **1.** preceded by eleven others in a series; 12th **2.** designating any of the twelve equal parts of something —*n.* **1.** the one following the eleventh **2.** any of the twelve equal parts of something; 1/12

**Twelfth Day** the twelfth day (Jan. 6) after Christmas; Epiphany: the evening before, or sometimes the evening of, this day is called **Twelfth Night**

**twelve** (twelv) *adj.* [OE. *twelf*] two more than ten —*n.* **1.** the cardinal number between eleven and thirteen; 12; XII **2.** any group of twelve persons or things; dozen —**the Twelve** the Twelve Apostles

**Twelve Apostles** the twelve disciples chosen by Jesus to go forth to teach the gospel

**twelve·fold** (twelv′fōld′) *adj.* **1.** having twelve parts **2.** having twelve times as much or as many —*adv.* twelve times as much or as many

**twelve·mo** (-mō) *adj., n., pl.* **-mos** same as DUODECIMO

**twelve·month** (-munth′) *n.* a year

**twelve-tone** (-tōn′) *adj. Music* designating of a system of composition in which the twelve tones of the chromatic scale are arranged into some arbitrary, fixed succession (*tone row*) as a basis for further thematic development

**twen·ti·eth** (twen′tē ith) *adj.* **1.** preceded by nineteen others in a series; 20th **2.** designating any of the twenty equal parts of something —*n.* **1.** the one following the nineteenth **2.** any of twenty equal parts of something; 1/20

**twen·ty** (twen′tē) *adj.* [OE. *twegentig*] two times ten —*n., pl.* **-ties** **1.** the cardinal number between nineteen and twenty-one; 20; XX **2.** [Colloq.] a twenty-dollar bill —**the twenties** the numbers or years, as of a century, from twenty through twenty-nine

**twen·ty·fold** (-fōld′) *adj.* **1.** having twenty parts **2.** having twenty times as much or as many —*adv.* twenty times as much or as many

**twen·ty-one** (-wun′) *n.* a gambling game at cards in which each player's aim is to obtain from the dealer cards totaling twenty-one points or close to that total without exceeding it; blackjack

**twen·ty-twen·ty** (or 20/20) **vision** (twen′tē twen′tē) normal keenness of vision, which is the ability to see clearly at twenty feet what the normal eye can see

**'twere** (twur) [Poet.] it were

**twerp** (twurp) *n.* [< ? or akin to Dan. *tver,* perverse] [Slang] a person regarded as insignificant, contemptible, etc.

**twice** (twīs) *adv.* [OE. *twiges* < *twiga*] **1.** on two occasions or in two instances **2.** two times **3.** two times as much or as many; twofold; doubly

**twid·dle** (twid′'l) *vt.* **-dled, -dling** [prob. < TW(IST) + (D)IDDLE¹] to twirl or play with lightly —*vi.* **1.** to toy with some object **2.** to be busy about trifles —*n.* a light, twirling motion, as with the thumbs —**twiddle one's thumbs** **1.** to twirl one's thumbs idly around one another **2.** to be idle —**twid′dler** *n.* —**twid′dly** *adj.*

**twig** (twig) *n.* [OE. *twigge*] a small branch or shoot of a tree or shrub —**twigged** *adj.* —**twig′gy** *adj.* **-gi·er, -gi·est**

**twi·light** (twī′līt′) *n.* [ME. < *twi-,* two + LIGHT¹] **1.** *a*) the soft, dim light just after sunset or, sometimes, just before sunrise *b*) the period from sunset to dark **2.** any growing darkness **3.** a condition of gradual decline —*adj.* of or like twilight

**twi·lit** (twī′lit) *adj.* full of or bathed in the soft, dim light of twilight

**twill** (twil) *n.* [OE. *twilic,* woven of double thread, ult. < L. *bilix,* double-threaded] **1.** a cloth woven so as to have parallel diagonal lines or ribs **2.** the pattern of this weave —*vt.* to weave with a twill —**twilled** *adj.*

**'twill** (twil) [Poet.] it will

**twin** (twin) *adj.* [OE. *twinn* & ON. *tvinnr,* double] **1.** consisting of, or being one of a pair of, two separate but similar or closely related things; paired **2.** being two, or either of two, that have been born at the same birth [*twin* girls, a *twin* sister] —*n.* **1.** either of two born at the same birth: twins are either *identical* (produced from the same ovum) or *fraternal* (produced from separate ova) **2.** either of two persons or things very much alike in appearance, shape, etc. —*vi.* **twinned, twin′ning** **1.** to give birth to twins **2.** to be paired (with another) —*vt.* **1.** to give birth to as twins **2.** to pair or couple

**twin bill** [Colloq.] same as: **1.** DOUBLE FEATURE **2.** DOUBLE-HEADER

**twine** (twīn) *n.* [OE. *twin,* double thread] **1.** a strong thread, string, or cord of two or more strands twisted together **2.** a twining or being twined **3.** a twined thing or part; twist —*vt.* **twined, twin′ing 1.** *a*) to twist together; intertwine *b*) to form in this way **2.** to wreathe or wind (one thing) around or with another **3.** to enfold, embrace, etc. [a wreath *twining* his brow] —*vi.* **1.** to twist, interlace, etc. **2.** to twist and turn —**twin′ing·ly** *adv.*

**twin-en·gined** (twin′en′jənd) *adj.* powered by two engines: said of an airplane: also **twin′-en′gine**

**twinge** (twinj) *vt., vi.* **twinged, twing′ing** [OE. *twengan,* to squeeze] to have or cause to have a sudden, brief, darting pain or pang —*n.* **1.** a sudden, brief, darting pain or pang **2.** a sudden, brief feeling of remorse, shame, etc.; qualm

**twin·kle** (twiŋ′k'l) *vi.* **-kled, -kling** [OE. *twinclian*] **1.** to shine with quick flashes of light at intervals, as some stars; sparkle **2.** to light up, as with amusement: said of the eyes **3.** to move quickly and lightly, as a dancer's feet; flicker —*vt.* **1.** to make twinkle **2.** to emit (light) in quick flashes at intervals —*n.* **1.** a wink of the eye **2.** a quick flash of amusement, etc. in the eye **3.** a quick flash of light; sparkle **4.** the instant it takes to wink —**twin′kler** *n.*

**twin·kling** (-kliŋ) *n.* **1.** the action of a thing that twinkles **2.** *a*) the winking of an eye *b*) the very brief time it takes to wink; instant

**twirl** (twurl) *vt., vi.* [prob. < Scand.] **1.** to rotate rapidly; spin **2.** to whirl in a circle **3.** to twist or coil **4.** *Baseball* to pitch —*n.* **1.** a twirling or being twirled **2.** something twirled; specif., a twist, coil, flourish, etc. —**twirl′er** *n.*

**twist** (twist) *vt.* [< OE. *-twist,* rope (in *mæst-twist,* rope to stay a mast)] **1.** to wind (strands of cotton, silk, etc.)

around one another, as in spinning or in making thread, cord, etc. **2.** to wreathe; twine **3.** to wind (thread, rope, etc.) around something **4.** to make (one's or its way) by turning one way and then another **5.** to give spiral shape to **6.** *a)* to subject to torsion *b)* to wrench; sprain **7.** *a)* to contort or distort (the face, etc.) *b)* to cause to be malformed /fingers *twisted* with arthritis/ **8.** to confuse or disturb mentally or emotionally **9.** to distort or pervert the meaning of **10.** to cause to turn around or rotate **11.** to break off by turning the end (often with *off*) **12.** to make (a ball) go in a curve by giving it a spinning motion —*vi.* **1.** to undergo twisting and thus take on a spiral or coiled form **2.** to spiral, coil, twine, etc. (*around* or *about* something) **3.** to revolve or rotate **4.** to turn to one side **5.** to wind or meander, as a path **6.** to squirm; writhe **7.** to move in a curved path, as a ball —*n.* **1.** a strong, closely twisted silk thread **2.** a twisted roll of tobacco leaves **3.** a loaf of bread or roll made of twisted pieces of dough **4.** a knot, etc. made by twisting **5.** a sliver of peel from a lemon, lime, etc. twisted and added to a drink **6.** a twisting or being twisted **7.** a spin given to a ball in throwing or striking it **8.** stress due to torsion, or the degree of this **9.** a contortion, as of the face **10.** a wrench or sprain **11.** a turning aside; turn; bend **12.** a place at which something twists /a *twist* in the road/ **13.** a personal tendency; eccentricity; quirk **14.** distortion, as of meaning **15.** a different or unexpected meaning, method, slant, etc. /a new *twist* to an old story/

**twist·er** (twis′tər) *n.* **1.** a person or thing that twists; specif., a thrown or batted ball that has been given a twist **2.** a tornado or cyclone

**twit**[1] (twit) *vt.* **twit′ted, twit′ting** [< OE. *ætwitan* < *æt*, at + *witan*, to accuse] to reproach, tease, taunt, etc., esp. by reminding of a fault or mistake —*n.* a reproach or taunt

**twit**[2] (twit) *n.* [< TWITTER[1]] a state of nervous excitement

**twitch** (twich) *vt., vi.* [< OE. *twiccian*, to pluck] **1.** to pull (at) with a quick, slight jerk; pluck **2.** to move with a quick, slight jerk, often due to muscle spasm **3.** to ache with a sudden, sharp pain —*n.* **1.** a quick, slight jerk **2.** a sudden, quick motion, esp. one caused by muscle spasm; tic **3.** a sudden, sharp pain; twinge

**twit·ter**[1] (twit′ər) *vi.* [ME. *twiteren:* orig. echoic] **1.** to make a series of light, sharp vocal sounds; chirp, as birds do **2.** *a)* to talk in a rapid or agitated manner; chatter *b)* to giggle **3.** to tremble with excitement, etc. —*vt.* to say in a twittering manner —*n.* **1.** the act or sound of twittering **2.** a condition of trembling excitement; flutter —**twit′ter·er** *n.* —**twit′ter·y** *adj.*

**twit·ter**[2] (twit′ər) *n.* a person who twits

**'twixt** (twikst) *prep.* [Poet.] betwixt

**two** (tōō) *adj.* [OE. *twa*] totaling one more than one —*n.* **1.** the cardinal number between one and three; 2; II **2.** anything having two units or members, or numbered two —**in two** in two parts —**put two and two together** to reach an obvious conclusion by considering several facts together

**two-base hit** (tōō′bās′) a double in baseball

**two-bit** (-bit′) *adj.* **1.** [Colloq.] worth twenty-five cents **2.** [Slang] *a)* cheap; tawdry *b)* mediocre, inferior, etc.

**two bits** [Colloq.] twenty-five cents

**two-by-four** (tōō′bə fôr′, -bī-) *adj.* **1.** that measures two inches (or feet, etc.) by four inches (or feet, etc.) **2.** [Colloq.] small, narrow, cramped, etc. —*n.* any length of untrimmed lumber two inches thick and four inches wide: in the building trades, a trimmed piece 1⅝ by 3⅝ inches

**two-edged** (-ejd′) *adj.* **1.** that has two cutting edges **2.** that can have two different meanings, as a remark

**two-faced** (-fāst′) *adj.* **1.** having two faces **2.** deceitful; hypocritical —**two′-fac′ed·ly** (-fās′id lē) *adv.*

**two-fist·ed** (-fis′tid) *adj.* [Colloq.] **1.** able to use both fists **2.** vigorous; virile

**two·fold** (-fōld′) *adj.* **1.** having two parts; double **2.** having twice as much or as many —*adv.* twice as much or as many

**two-hand·ed** (-han′did) *adj.* **1.** that needs to be used or wielded with both hands **2.** worked by two people /a *two-handed* saw/ **3.** for two people, as a card game **4.** having two hands **5.** using both hands equally well

**two-leg·ged** (-leg′id, -legd′) *adj.* having two legs

**two·pence** (tup′'ns) *n.* **1.** two pence, or two British pennies **2.** a former British coin of this value

**two·pen·ny** (tup′ə nē; *also, esp. of nails,* tōō′pen′ē) *adj.* **1.** worth or costing twopence **2.** cheap; worthless **3.** designating a size of nails one inch long

**two-piece** (tōō′pēs′) *adj.* consisting of two separate parts /a *two-piece* bathing suit/

**two-ply** (-plī′) *adj.* **1.** having two thicknesses, layers, strands, etc. **2.** woven double

**two·sid·ed** (-sīd′id) *adj.* **1.** having two sides **2.** having two aspects /a *two-sided* question/

**two·some** (-səm) *n.* **1.** two people; a couple **2.** *Golf* a game involving two players

**two-step** (-step′) *n.* **1.** a ballroom dance in 2/4 time **2.** a piece of music for this dance

**two-time** (tōō′tīm′) *vt.* **-timed′, -tim′ing** [Slang] to deceive; esp., to be unfaithful to —**two′-tim′er** *n.*

**'twould** (twood) [Poet.] it would

**two-way** (tōō′wā′) *adj.* **1.** having separate lanes for vehicles going in opposite directions **2.** involving the same obligations, privileges, etc. toward each other by two parties, nations, etc. /a *two-way* cultural exchange/ **3.** involving two persons, groups, etc. /a *two-way* political race/ **4.** *a)* used for both transmitting and receiving /a *two-way* radio/ *b)* moving, operating, etc. in either of two directions

**twp.** township

**TX** Texas

**-ty**[1] (tē, ti) [< OFr. *-té* < L. *-tas*] *a suffix meaning* quality of, condition of /novelty/

**-ty**[2] (tē, ti) [OE. *-tig*] *a suffix meaning* tens, times ten /sixty/

**ty·coon** (tī kōōn′) *n.* [< Jap. < Chin. *ta*, great + *kiun*, prince] **1.** a title applied by foreigners to the former shogun of Japan **2.** a wealthy and powerful industrialist, financier, etc.

**ty·ing** (tī′iŋ) *prp. of* TIE

**tyke** (tīk) *n.* [ON. *tik*, a bitch] **1.** [Colloq.] a small child **2.** [Chiefly Brit. Dial.] a dog, esp. a mongrel or cur

**Ty·ler** (tī′lər) [after ff.] city in E Tex.: pop. 71,000

**Ty·ler** (tī′lər), **John** 1790–1862; 10th president of the U.S. (1841–45)

**tym·pa·ni** (tim′pə nē) *n.pl., sing.* **-no′** (-nō′) *var. of* TIMPANI —**tym′pa·nist** *n.*

**tym·pan·ic membrane** (tim pan′ik) a thin membrane that separates the middle ear from the external ear and vibrates when struck by sound waves; eardrum

**tym·pa·num** (tim′pə nəm) *n., pl.* **-nums, -na** (-nə) [L., a drum < Gr. *tympanon*] **1.** *Anat. same as: a)* MIDDLE EAR *b)* TYMPANIC MEMBRANE **2.** a drum or drumhead **3.** *Archit. a)* the recessed space, usually triangular, enclosed by the slanting cornices of a pediment *b)* the space enclosed by an arch and the top of the door or window below it —**tym·pan′ic** (-pan′ik) *adj.*

**Tyn·dale** (tin′d'l), **William** 1494?–1536; Eng. religious reformer & translator of the Bible: executed for heresy

**typ·al** (tīp′'l) *adj.* of, pertaining to, or serving as a type

**type** (tīp) *n.* [< LL. < L. < Gr. *typos*, a figure, model < *typtein*, to strike] **1.** a person, thing, or event that represents another, esp. another that it is thought will appear later; symbol; token; sign **2.** the characteristic form, plan, style, etc. of a particular class or group **3.** a class, group, etc. having characteristics in common /a new *type* of truck/: colloquially, *of* is often omitted **4.** a person, animal, or thing that is representative or characteristic of a class or group **5.** a perfect example; model; pattern **6.** *Biol.* a specimen designated as the one

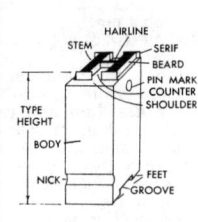

TYPE

serving as the basis for the original description and name of a taxon **7.** *Printing a)* a rectangular piece of metal or, sometimes, wood, with a raised letter, figure, etc. in reverse on its upper end *b)* such pieces collectively *c)* a printed or photographically reproduced character or characters —*vt.* **typed, typ′ing 1.** to classify according to type /to *type* a blood sample/ **2.** to write with a typewriter; typewrite —*vi.* to use a typewriter —**typ′a·ble, type′a·ble** *adj.*

**-type** (tīp) [< Gr. *typos:* see TYPE] *a combining form meaning* **1.** type, example /prototype/ **2.** stamp, print, printing type /monotype/

**type·cast** (tīp′kast′) *vt.* **-cast′, -cast′ing** to cast (an actor) repeatedly in the same type of part

**type-cast** (tīp′kast′) *vt.* **-cast′, -cast′ing** to cast (type)

**type·face** (-fās′) *n. same as* FACE (*n.* 10)

**type metal** an alloy of tin, lead, and antimony, and sometimes copper, used for making type, etc.

**type·script** (-skript′) *n.* typewritten matter or copy

**type·set** (-set′) *vt.* **-set′, -set′ting** to set in type

**type·set·ter** (-set′ər) *n.* **1.** a person who sets type; compositor **2.** a machine for setting type —**type′set′ting** *n., adj.*

**type·write** (-rīt′) *vt., vi.* **-wrote′, -writ′ten, -writ′ing** to write with a typewriter: now usually clipped to *type*

**type·writ·er** (-rīt′ər) *n.* **1.** a writing machine with a keyboard for reproducing letters, figures, etc. that resemble printed ones **2.** *earlier term for* TYPIST

**ty·phoid** (tī′foid) *n.* [TYPH(US) + -OID] **1.** orig., any typhuslike disorder **2.** an infectious disease caused by a bacillus and acquired by eating food or drinking water contaminated by excreta: it causes fever, intestinal disorders, etc.: in full, **typhoid fever** —**ty·phoi′dal** *adj.*

**ty·phoon** (tī fōōn′) *n.* [< Chin. dial. *tai-fung*, lit., great wind] any violent tropical cyclone originating in the W Pacific, esp. in the South China Sea —**ty·phon′ic** (-fän′ik) *adj.*

**ty·phus** (tī′fəs) *n.* [ModL. < Gr. *typhos*, a fever] an acute infectious disease caused by a rickettsia transmitted to man by fleas, lice, etc., and causing fever, red spots on the skin, etc.: in full, **typhus fever** —**ty′phous** (-fəs) *adj.*

**typ·i·cal** (tip′i k′l) *adj.* **1.** serving as a type; symbolic **2.** having the distinguishing characteristics, qualities, etc. of a class, group, etc.; representative **3.** belonging to a type; characteristic Also **typ′ic** —**typ′i·cal·ly** *adv.* —**typ′i·cal·ness, typ′i·cal′i·ty** (-kal′ə tē) *n.*

**typ·i·fy** (tip′ə fī′) *vt.* **-fied′, -fy′ing** [see TYPE & -FY] **1.** to be a type or emblem of; symbolize **2.** to have or show the distinctive characteristics of; be typical of —**typ′i·fi·ca′tion** *n.* —**typ′i·fi′er** *n.*

**typ·ist** (tīp′ist) *n.* a person who operates a typewriter, esp. one whose work is typing

**ty·po** (tī′pō) *n., pl.* **-pos** [Colloq.] a typographical error; mechanical mistake made in setting type or in typing

**ty·po-** [< Gr. *typos:* see TYPE] *a combining form meaning* type

**ty·pog·ra·pher** (tī päg′rə fər) *n.* a person skilled in typography; printer, compositor, etc.

**ty·po·graph·i·cal** (tī′pə graf′i k′l) *adj.* of typography; having to do with the setting of type, printing, etc.: also **ty′po·graph′ic** —**ty′po·graph′i·cal·ly** *adv.*

**ty·pog·ra·phy** (tī päg′rə fē) *n.* [< Fr. < ML.: see TYPO- & -GRAPHY] **1.** the art or process of printing from type **2.** the art or process of setting and arranging type for printing **3.** the arrangement, style, or appearance of matter printed from type

**Tyr** (tir) *Norse Myth.* the god of war and son of Odin

**ty·ran·ni·cal** (ti ran′i k′l, tī-) *adj.* **1.** of or suited to a tyrant; arbitrary; despotic **2.** harsh, cruel, unjust, etc. Also **ty·ran′nic** —**ty·ran′ni·cal·ly** *adv.*

**ty·ran·ni·cide** (ti ran′ni sīd′) *n.* **1.** the act of killing a tyrant **2.** a person who kills a tyrant

**tyr·an·nize** (tir′ə nīz′) *vi.* **-nized′, -niz′ing** **1.** to govern as a tyrant **2.** to use authority harshly or cruelly —*vt.* to treat tyrannically; oppress —**tyr′an·niz′er** *n.*

**ty·ran·no·saur** (ti ran′ə sôr′, tī-) *n.* [< ModL. < Gr. *tyrannos*, tyrant + -SAURUS] any of various huge, two-footed, flesh-eating dinosaurs of the Cretaceous Period in N. America: also **ty·ran′no·saur′us** (-əs)

**tyr·an·nous** (tir′ə nəs) *adj.* tyrannical; despotic, oppressive, unjust, etc. —**tyr′an·nous·ly** *adv.*

**tyr·an·ny** (tir′ə nē) *n., pl.* **-nies** **1.** the office, authority, government, etc. of a tyrant, or absolute ruler **2.** oppressive and unjust government; despotism **3.** very cruel and unjust use of power or authority **4.** harshness; severity **5.** a tyrannical act

**ty·rant** (tī′rənt) *n.* [< OFr. < L. < Gr. *tyrannos*] **1.** an absolute ruler **2.** a cruel, oppressive ruler; despot **3.** any person who uses his authority in an oppressive manner

**Tyre** (tīr) seaport in SW Lebanon, on the Mediterranean: center of ancient Phoenician culture: pop. 12,000 —**Tyr·i·an** (tir′ē ən) *adj., n.*

**Tyrian purple** (or **dye**) **1.** a purple or crimson dye used by the ancient Romans and Greeks: it was made from certain mollusks, orig. at Tyre **2.** bluish red

**ty·ro** (tī′rō) *n., pl.* **-ros** [ML. < L. *tiro*, recruit] a beginner in learning something; novice

**Tyr·ol** (tir′äl, tī′rōl, ti rōl′) *same as* TIROL —**Ty·ro·le·an** (ti rō′lē ən) *adj., n.* —**Tyr·o·lese** (tir′ə lēz′) *adj., n., pl.* **-lese/**

**Tyr·rhe·ni·an Sea** (ti rē′nē ən) part of the Mediterranean, between the W coast of Italy & Corsica & Sardinia

**tzar** (tsär, zär) *n. var. of* CZAR —**tzar′dom** *n.* —**tzar′ism** *n.* —**tzar′ist** *adj., n.*

**tzar·e·vitch** (tsär′ə vich, zär′-) *n. var. of* CZAREVITCH

**tza·ri·na** (tsä rē′nə, zä-) *n. var. of* CZARINA: also **tza·rit′za** (-rēt′sə)

**tzet·ze fly** (tset′sē, tsē′tsē) *var. of* TSETSE FLY

‡**tzi·gane** (tsē gän′) *n.* [Fr. < Hung.] a gypsy

# U

**U, u** (yōō) *n., pl.* **U's, u's** **1.** the twenty-first letter of the English alphabet **2.** a sound of *U* or *u*

**U** (yōō) *n.* **1.** something shaped like U **2.** *Chem.* uranium —*adj.* shaped like U

**U., U** **1.** Union **2.** United **3.** University

**U., U, u., u** unit; units

**U.A.R.** United Arab Republic

**U.A.W., UAW** United Automobile, Aerospace, and Agricultural Implement Workers of America

**U·ban·gi** (ōō bäŋ′gē, yōō baŋ′-) river in C Africa, flowing from N Zaire west & south into the Congo River

**u·biq·ui·tous** (yōō bik′wə təs) *adj.* [see ff. & -OUS] present, or seeming to be present, everywhere at the same time; omnipresent —**u·biq′ui·tous·ly** *adv.* —**u·biq′ui·tous·ness** *n.*

**u·biq·ui·ty** (-tē) *n.* [< Fr. < L. *ubique*, everywhere] the state, fact, or capacity of being, or seeming to be, everywhere at the same time; omnipresence

**U-boat** (yōō′bōt′) *n.* [< G. *U-boot*, abbrev. of *Unterseeboot*, undersea boat] a German submarine

**u.c.** *Printing* upper case

**ud·der** (ud′ər) *n.* [OE. *udr*] a mammary gland with two or more teats, as in cows

**U·fa** (ōō fä′) city in E European R.S.F.S.R., in the W foothills of the Urals: pop. 773,000

**UFO** (yōō′fō, yōō′ef ō′) *n., pl.* **UFOs, UFO's** [*u(nidentified) f(lying) o(bject)*] any of a number of unidentified objects reported, esp. since 1947, to have been seen flying at varying heights and speeds and variously regarded as hallucinations, spacecraft from another planet, etc.

**U·gan·da** (yōō gan′də, ōō gän′dä) country in EC Africa: a member of the Commonwealth: 93,981 sq. mi.; pop. 10,127,000 —**U·gan′dan** (-dən) *adj., n.*

**ugh** (ookh, uH, oo, ug, *etc.*) *interj.* [echoic] an exclamation of disgust, horror, etc.

**ug·li** (ug′lē) *n.* [altered < UGLY: from its misshapen appearance] a Jamaican citrus fruit that is a three-way cross between a grapefruit, orange, and tangerine: also called **ugli fruit**

**ug·li·fy** (ug′lə fī′) *vt.* **-fied′, -fy′ing** to make ugly; disfigure

**ug·ly** (ug′lē) *adj.* **-li·er, -li·est** [< ON. *uggligr*, fearful < *uggr*, fear] **1.** unpleasing to look at; unsightly **2.** bad, vile, repulsive, offensive, etc. [an *ugly* lie] **3.** ominous; dangerous [*ugly* storm clouds] **4.** [Colloq.] ill-tempered; cross [an *ugly* disposition] —**ug′li·ly** *adv.* —**ug′li·ness** *n.*

**ugly duckling** [from a story by H. C. Andersen] a very plain child or unpromising thing that in time becomes or could become beautiful, important, etc.

**U·gri·an** (ōō′grē ən, yōō′-) *adj.* **1.** designating or of a group of Finno-Ugric peoples of W Siberia and Hungary **2.** *same as* UGRIC (*adj.* 1) —*n.* **1.** a member of any of the Ugrian peoples **2.** *same as* UGRIC

**U·gric** (-grik) *adj.* **1.** designating or of a branch of the Finno-Ugric subfamily of languages including Hungarian (Magyar) **2.** *same as* UGRIAN (*adj.* 1) —*n.* the Ugric languages

**uh** (u, un) *interj.* **1.** *same as* HUH **2.** a prolonged sound made in speaking, as while searching for a word

**UHF, U.H.F., uhf, u.h.f.** ultrahigh frequency

**uh-huh** (ə hu′; *for 2* un′un′) *interj.* **1.** an exclamation indicating: *a)* an affirmative response *b)* that one is listening attentively **2.** *var. of* UH-UH

**uh-uh** (un′un′, -un′) *interj.* an exclamation indicating a negative response

**uit·land·er** (üt′län′dər; *E.* īt′lan′dər, āt′-) *n.* [Afrik. < Du. *uit*, out + *land*, land] [*sometimes* U-] in South Africa, a foreigner; specif., one not a Boer in the Transvaal

**U.K.** United Kingdom

**u·kase** (yōō′kās, -kāz; yōō kās′, -kāz′) *n.* [Russ. *ukaz*, edict] **1.** in Czarist Russia, an imperial order or decree **2.** any official, esp. arbitrary, decree or proclamation

**U·krain·i·an** (yōō krā′nē ən, -krī′-) *adj.* of the Ukraine, its people, their language, etc. —*n.* **1.** a native or inhabitant of the Ukraine **2.** the East Slavic language of the Ukrainians, very closely related to Russian

**Ukrainian Soviet Socialist Republic** republic of the U.S.S.R., in the SW European part: 231,990 sq. mi.; pop. 47,100,000; cap. Kiev: also called the **U·kraine** (yōō krān′)

**u·ku·le·le** (yōō/kə lā/lē; *Haw.* ōō/koo lā/lä) *n.* [Haw., lit., flea] a musical instrument with four strings, like a small guitar: also [Colloq.] **uke** (yōōk)

**UL, U.L.** Underwriters' Laboratories

**ul·cer** (ul/sər) *n.* [L. *ulcus* (gen. *ulceris*)] **1.** an open sore on the skin or some mucous membrane, that festers, damages the tissue, etc. **2.** any corrupting condition or influence

**ul·cer·ate** (ul/sə rāt/) *vt., vi.* -at'ed, -at'ing [< L. pp. of *ulcerare*] to make or become ulcerous —**ul'cer·a/tion** *n.* —**ul/cer·a/tive** *adj.*

**ul·cer·ous** (-sər əs) *adj.* **1.** having an ulcer or ulcers **2.** of or like an ulcer or ulcers

**-ule** (yōōl, yool) [< Fr. < L. *-ulus, -ula, -ulum*] *a suffix meaning* little [*sporule*]

**-u·lent** (yoo lənt) [< Fr. < L. *-ulentus*] *a suffix meaning* full of, abounding in [*fraudulent*]

**ul·na** (ul/nə) *n., pl.* **-nae** (-nē), **-nas** [ModL. < L., the elbow] **1.** the larger of the two bones of the forearm, on the side opposite the thumb **2.** a corresponding bone in the forelimb of other vertebrates —**ul/nar** (-nər) *adj.*

**-u·lose** (yoo lōs/) [< L. *-ulosus*] *a suffix meaning* characterized by, marked by [*granulose*]

**-u·lous** (yoo ləs) [< L. *-ulosus*] *a suffix meaning* tending to, characterized by [*populous*]

**Ul·ster** (ul/stər) **1.** former province of Ireland, divided to form Northern Ireland and a province (*Ulster*) of Ireland **2.** [Colloq.] Northern Ireland —**Ul'ster·man** (-mən) *n., pl.* **-men**

**ul·ster** (ul/stər) *n.* [< prec., where the fabric was orig. made] a long, loose, heavy overcoat

**ult.** **1.** ultimate **2.** ultimately **3.** ultimo

**ul·te·ri·or** (ul tir/ē ər) *adj.* [L., compar. of hyp. *ulter*, beyond] **1.** lying beyond or on the farther side **2.** later, subsequent, or future **3.** beyond what is openly said or made known [an *ulterior* motive] —**ul·te'ri·or·ly** *adv.*

**ul·ti·ma** (ul/ti mə) *n.* [L., fem. of *ultimus*, last] the last syllable of a word

**ul·ti·mate** (ul/tə mit) *adj.* [< LL. pp. of *ultimare*, to come to an end < L. *ultimus*, last] **1.** beyond which it is impossible to go; farthest; final; last **3.** most basic; fundamental; primary **4.** greatest or highest possible; maximum —*n.* something ultimate [the *ultimate* in pleasure] —**ul/ti·ma·cy** (-mə sē), **ul/ti·mate·ness** *n.* —**ul/ti·mate·ly** *adv.*

**ul·ti·ma Thu·le** (ul/ti mə thōō/lē) [L.] **1.** among the ancients, the northernmost region of the world **2.** any far-off, unknown region

**ul·ti·ma·tum** (ul/tə māt/əm) *n., pl.* **-tums, -ta** (-ə) [ModL. < LL., neut. pp.: see ULTIMATE] a final offer or demand presented to another in a dispute, esp. with a threat to break off relations, use force, etc.

**ul·ti·mo** (ul/tə mō/) *adv.* [L. *ultimo* (*mense*), (in the) last (month)] in the preceding month: an old-fashioned usage [yours of the 13th (day) *ultimo* received]

**ul·tra** (ul/trə) *adj.* [L., beyond] going beyond the usual limit; extreme —*n.* an extremist, as in opinions held

**ul·tra-** [L.] *a prefix meaning:* **1.** beyond [*ultraviolet*] **2.** to an extreme degree [*ultramodern*] **3.** beyond the range of [*ultramicroscopic*]

**ul·tra·con·serv·a·tive** (ul/trə kən sur/və tiv) *adj.* conservative to an extreme degree —*n.* an ultraconservative person

**ul·tra·high frequency** (ul/trə hī/) any radio frequency between 300 and 3,000 megahertz

**ul·tra·ma·rine** (ul/trə mə rēn/) *adj.* [< ML.: see ULTRA- & MARINE] **1.** beyond the sea **2.** deep-blue —*n.* **1.** a blue pigment orig. made from powdered lapis lazuli **2.** any similar pigment made from other substances **3.** a deep blue

**ul·tra·mi·cro·scope** (-mī/krə skōp/) *n.* an instrument for observing by dispersed light objects, as colloidal particles, too small to be seen with an ordinary microscope —**ul/tra·mi·cros/co·py** (-mī kräs/kə pē) *n.*

**ul·tra·mi·cro·scop·ic** (-mī/krə skäp/ik) *adj.* **1.** too small to be seen with an ordinary microscope **2.** of an ultramicroscope —**ul/tra·mi/cro·scop/i·cal·ly** *adv.*

**ul·tra·mod·ern** (-mäd/ərn) *adj.* modern to an extreme degree —**ul/tra·mod/ern·ism** *n.* —**ul/tra·mod/ern·ist** *n.*

**ul·tra·na·tion·al·ism** (-nash/ən 'l iz'm) *n.* nationalism that is excessive or extreme —**ul/tra·na/tion·al·ist** *adj., n.* —**ul/tra·na/tion·al·is/tic** *adj.*

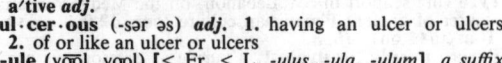

UKULELE

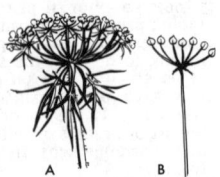

HUMERUS

ULNA    RADIUS

**ul·tra·son·ic** (-sän/ik) *adj.* [ULTRA- + SONIC] designating or of a frequency of mechanical vibrations above the range audible to the human ear, i.e., above 20,000 vibrations per second —**ul/tra·son/i·cal·ly** *adv.*

**ul·tra·son·ics** (-sän/iks) *n.pl.* [*with sing. v.*] the science dealing with ultrasonic phenomena

**ul·tra·sound** (ul/trə sound/) *n.* ultrasonic waves, used in medical diagnosis and therapy, in surgery, etc.

**ul·tra·vi·o·let** (ul/trə vī/ə lit) *adj.* **1.** lying just beyond the violet end of the visible spectrum and having wavelengths shorter than 4,000 angstroms **2.** of or producing light rays of such wavelengths —*n.* ultraviolet radiation

**ul·u·late** (yōōl/yoo lāt/, ul/-) *vi.* -lat'ed, -lat'ing [< L. pp. of *ululare*, to howl: echoic] **1.** to howl or hoot **2.** to wail or lament loudly —**ul/u·lant** (-lənt) *adj.* —**ul/u·la/tion** *n.*

**U·lys·ses** (yoo lis/ēz) [L.] *same as* ODYSSEUS

**um·bel** (um/b'l) *n.* [L. *umbella:* see UMBRELLA] a cluster of flowers with stalks of nearly equal length which spring from the same point —**um/bel·late** (-it, -āt/), **um/bel·lat/ed** *adj.* —**um/bel·late·ly** *adv.*

**um·ber** (um/bər) *n.* [< Fr. < It. (*terra d'*)*ombra*, lit., (earth of) shade, prob. < L. *umbra*, a shade] **1.** a kind of earth containing oxides of manganese and iron, used as a pigment: raw umber is yellowish-brown; burnt, or calcined, umber is reddish-brown **2.** a yellowish-brown or reddish-brown color —*adj.* of the color of raw umber or burnt umber —*vt.* to color with or as with umber

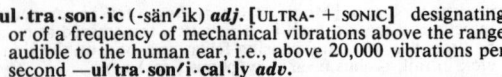

A      B

UMBEL
(A, compound;
B, simple)

**um·bil·i·cal** (um bil/i k'l) *adj.* **1.** of or like an umbilicus or an umbilical cord **2.** situated at or near the navel **3.** linked together by or as if by an umbilical cord

**umbilical cord** a cordlike structure that connects a fetus with the placenta: it is severed at birth, the navel being formed at the point where it was attached to the fetus

**um·bil·i·cus** (um bil/i kəs, um/bi li/kəs) *n., pl.* **-ci** (-sī/, -sī) [L.] **1.** *same as* NAVEL **2.** a navellike depression, as the hilum of a seed

**um·bra** (um/brə) *n., pl.* **-brae** (-brē), **-bras** [L., a shade] **1.** a shade or shadow **2.** the dark cone of shadow projecting from a planet or satellite on the side opposite the sun

**um·brage** (um/brij) *n.* [OFr. < L. < *umbra*, a shade] **1.** [Obs.] shade; shadow **2.** foliage, considered as shade-giving **3.** offense or resentment [to take *umbrage* at a remark] —**um·bra/geous** (-brā/jəs) *adj.* —**um·bra/geous·ly** *adv.*

**um·brel·la** (um brel/ə) *n.* [< It. < L. < *umbella*, parasol, dim. of *umbra*, shade] **1.** cloth, plastic, etc. stretched over a folding radial frame at the top of a stick, carried for protection against the rain or sun **2.** something that looks like this or is suggestive of this, as in its overall coverage; specif., a force of aircraft sent up to screen ground or naval forces

**umbrella tree** **1.** an American magnolia with clusters of long leaves at the ends of the branches, foul-smelling white flowers, and reddish fruit **2.** any of various trees that have an umbrellalike shape

**u·mi·ak, u·mi·ack** (ōō/mē ak/) *n.* [Esk.] an open Eskimo boat made of skins stretched on a wooden frame

**um·laut** (ōōm/lout) *n.* [G. < *um*, about + *laut*, a sound] *Linguis.* **1.** *a)* a change in sound of a vowel, caused by its assimilation to another vowel or semivowel originally in the next syllable but later generally lost *b)* a vowel resulting from such assimilation **2.** the diacritical mark (¨) placed over such a vowel, esp. in German, to indicate umlaut —*vt.* to sound or write with an umlaut

**ump** (ump) *n., vt., vi. shortened form of* UMPIRE

**um·pire** (um/pīr) *n.* [ME. *oumpere* (by faulty separation of *a noumpere*) < MFr. *nomper*, uneven, hence third person < *non*, not + *per*, even] **1.** a person chosen to give a decision in a dispute; arbiter **2.** an official who rules on the plays of a game, as in baseball —*vt., vi.* **-pired, -pir·ing** to act as umpire (in or of)

**ump·teen** (ump/tēn/) *adj.* [Slang] a great number of; very many —**ump/teenth/** *adj.*

**UMW, U.M.W.** United Mine Workers of America

**un-** (un; *unstressed, also* ən) *either of two prefixes meaning:* **1.** [OE. *un-*] not, lack of, the opposite of [*unhappy, untruth*] **2.** [OE. *un-, on-, and-*] the reverse or removal of: added to verbs to indicate a reversal of the action of the verb [*unfasten*] and to nouns to indicate a removal or release from the thing, state, etc. indicated by the noun [*unbosom*]; sometimes *un-* is merely intensive [*unloosen*] The list at the bottom of the following pages includes many of the more common compounds formed with *un-* (either prefix) that do not have special meanings

**UN, U.N.** United Nations

**un·a·ble** (un āʹbʹl) *adj.* not able; lacking the ability, means, or power to do something

**un·a·bridged** (unʹə brijdʹ) *adj.* not abridged, or shortened: often applied to a large, extensive dictionary that is not abridged from a larger work

**un·ac·count·a·ble** (unʹə kounʹtə bʹl) *adj.* 1. that cannot be explained or accounted for; strange 2. not responsible —**unʹac·countʹa·bilʹi·ty** *n.* —**unʹac·countʹa·bly** *adv.*

**un·ac·cus·tomed** (-ə kusʹtəmd) *adj.* 1. not accustomed (*to*) 2. not usual; strange [an *unaccustomed* action]

**un·ad·vised** (-əd vīzdʹ) *adj.* 1. without counsel or advice 2. thoughtlessly hasty; indiscreet —**unʹad·visʹed·ly** (-vīzʹid lē) *adv.* —**unʹad·visʹed·ness** *n.*

**un·af·fect·ed** (-ə fekʹtid) *adj.* 1. not affected, or influenced 2. without affectation; sincere and natural — **unʹaf·fectʹed·ly** *adv.* —**unʹaf·fectʹed·ness** *n.*

**un-A·mer·i·can** (-ə merʹi kən) *adj.* not American; esp., thought of as not conforming to the principles, policies, etc. of the U.S. —**unʹ-A·merʹi·can·ism** *n.*

**U·na·mu·no** (o͞oʹnä mo͞oʹnô), **Mi·guel de** (mē gelʹ *the*) 1864–1936; Sp. philosopher & writer

**u·nan·i·mous** (yo͞o nanʹə məs) *adj.* [< L. < *unus,* one + *animus,* the mind] 1. agreeing completely; united in opinion 2. showing, or based on, complete agreement — **u·na·nim·i·ty** (yo͞oʹnə nimʹə tē) *n.* —**u·nanʹi·mous·ly** *adv.*

**un·ap·proach·a·ble** (unʹə prōchʹə bʹl) *adj.* 1. not approachable or accessible, friendly, etc. 2. having no rival or equal; unmatched —**unʹap·proachʹa·bilʹi·ty** *n.* —**unʹap·proachʹa·bly** *adv.*

**un·arm** (un ärmʹ) *vt. same as* DISARM

**un·armed** (-ärmdʹ) *adj.* having no weapons, esp. firearms, or armor; defenseless

**un·as·sail·a·ble** (unʹə sālʹə bʹl) *adj.* not assailable; specif., *a*) that cannot be successfully attacked *b*) that cannot be successfully denied —**unʹas·sailʹa·ble·ness, unʹas·sailʹa·bilʹi·ty** *n.* —**unʹas·sailʹa·bly** *adv.*

**un·as·sum·ing** (-ə so͞oʹmiŋ, -syo͞oʹ-) *adj.* not assuming, pretentious, or forward; modest —**unʹas·sumʹing·ly** *adv.* —**unʹas·sumʹing·ness** *n.*

**un·at·tached** (-ə tachtʹ) *adj.* 1. not attached or fastened 2. not connected with any organization 3. not engaged or married 4. *Law* not taken as security for a judgment

**un·a·vail·ing** (-ə vāʹliŋ) *adj.* not availing; useless; futile; —**unʹa·vailʹing·ly** *adv.*

**un·a·void·a·ble** (-ə voiʹdə bʹl) *adj.* that cannot be avoided; inevitable —**unʹa·voidʹa·ble·ness** *n.* —**unʹa·voidʹa·bly** *adv.*

**un·a·ware** (-ə werʹ) *adj.* not aware or conscious [*unaware* of danger] —*adv. same as* UNAWARES —**unʹa·wareʹness** *n.*

**un·a·wares** (-ə werzʹ) *adv.* 1. without knowing or being aware 2. unexpectedly; by surprise [to sneak up on someone *unawares*]

**un·backed** (un baktʹ) *adj.* 1. without a back or backing 2. having no backers, supporters, etc.

**un·bal·ance** (-balʹəns) *vt.* **-anced, -anc·ing** 1. to throw out of balance 2. to derange (the mind) —*n.* the condition of being unbalanced

**un·bal·anced** (-balʹənst) *adj.* 1. not balanced or equal 2. not sane or normal in mind

**un·bar** (-bärʹ) *vt.* **-barredʹ, -barʹring** to unbolt or unlock

**un·bear·a·ble** (-berʹə bʹl) *adj.* that cannot be endured or tolerated —**un·bearʹa·ble·ness** *n.* —**un·bearʹa·bly** *adv.*

**un·beat·a·ble** (-bētʹə bʹl) *adj.* that cannot be defeated or surpassed

**un·beat·en** (-bētʹn) *adj.* 1. not struck, pounded, etc. 2. untrodden or untraveled 3. undefeated or unsurpassed

**un·be·com·ing** (unʹbi kumʹiŋ) *adj.* not suited to one's appearance, status, character, etc. [an *unbecoming* dress, *unbecoming* behavior] —**unʹbe·comʹing·ly** *adv.* —**unʹbe·comʹing·ness** *n.*

**un·be·known** (-bi nōnʹ) *adj.* unknown or unnoticed; without one's knowledge (usually with *to*): also **unʹbe·knownstʹ** (-nōnstʹ)

**un·be·lief** (-bə lēfʹ) *n.* a withholding or lack of belief, esp. in religion

**un·be·liev·a·ble** (-bə lēvʹə bʹl) *adj.* beyond belief; astounding; incredible —**unʹbe·lievʹa·bly** *adv.*

**un·be·liev·er** (-bə lēvʹər) *n.* 1. a person who does not believe; doubter 2. a person who does not accept any, or any particular, religious belief

**un·be·liev·ing** (-bə lēʹviŋ) *adj.* doubting; skeptical; incredulous —**unʹbe·lievʹing·ly** *adv.*

**un·bend** (un bendʹ) *vt., vi.* **-bentʹ** *or* **-bendʹed, -bendʹing** 1. to make or become less tense, less formal, etc. 2. to make or become straight again

**un·bend·ing** (-benʹdiŋ) *adj.* not bending; specif., *a*) rigid; stiff *b*) firm; resolute *c*) aloof; austere —*n.* a relaxation of restraint, severity, etc. —**un·bendʹing·ly** *adv.* —**un·bendʹing·ness** *n.*

**un·bid·den** (-bidʹ'n) *adj.* 1. not commanded 2. not invited Also **un·bidʹ**

**un·bind** (-bīndʹ) *vt.* **-boundʹ, -bindʹing** 1. to untie; unfasten 2. to release from restraints

**un·blessed, un·blest** (-blestʹ) *adj.* 1. not blessed 2. wretched; unhappy

**un·blush·ing** (-blushʹiŋ) *adj.* 1. not blushing 2. shameless —**un·blushʹing·ly** *adv.*

**un·bolt** (-bōltʹ) *vt., vi.* to draw back the bolt or bolts of (a door, etc.); unbar; open

**un·bolt·ed¹** (-bōltʹid) *adj.* not fastened with a bolt

**un·bolt·ed²** (-bōltʹid) *adj.* not bolted or sifted, as flour

**un·born** (-bôrnʹ) *adj.* 1. not born 2. still within the mother's womb 3. yet to come or be; future

**un·bos·om** (-booʹzəm, -bo͞oʹzəm) *vt., vi.* to tell or reveal (one's feelings, secrets, etc.) —**unbosom oneself** to express (oneself) openly about one's feelings, etc.

**un·bound·ed** (-bounʹdid) *adj.* 1. without bounds or limits 2. not restrained; uncontrolled

**un·bowed** (-boudʹ) *adj.* 1. not bowed or bent 2. not yielding or giving in; unsubdued

**un·bri·dled** (-brīʹdʹld) *adj.* 1. having no bridle on, as a horse 2. not controlled; unrestrained

**un·bro·ken** (-brōʹk'n) *adj.* not broken; specif., *a*) whole; intact *b*) not tamed or subdued *c*) continuous; uninterrupted *d*) not surpassed [an *unbroken* record]

**un·buck·le** (-bukʹ'l) *vt.* **-led, -ling** to unfasten the buckle or buckles of

**un·bur·den** (-burdʹ'n) *vt.* 1. to free from a burden 2. to relieve (oneself or one's mind) by disclosing (something hard to bear)

**un·but·ton** (-butʹ'n) *vt., vi.* to unfasten the buttons of

---

| | | | |
|---|---|---|---|
| unabashed | unaggressive | unarmored | unbathed |
| unabated | unaided | unartistic | unbefitting |
| unabbreviated | unaimed | unascertained | unbelted |
| unabetted | unalike | unashamed | unbiased |
| unabsolved | unallied | unasked | unblamable |
| unabsorbed | unallowable | unaspiring | unbleached |
| unacademic | unalloyed | unassigned | unblemished |
| unaccented | unalterable | unassimilated | unblinking |
| unacceptable | unaltered | unassisted | unbought |
| unacclimated | unambiguous | unassociated | unbound |
| unaccommodating | unambitious | unassorted | unbraced |
| unaccompanied | unamplified | unassured | unbraid |
| unaccomplished | unamusing | unattainable | unbranched |
| unaccounted-for | unannounced | unattempted | unbranded |
| unaccredited | unanswerable | unattended | unbreakable |
| unacknowledged | unanticipated | unattested | unbreathable |
| unacquainted | unapologetic | unattired | unbridgeable |
| unadaptable | unapparent | unattractive | unbrotherly |
| unadjustable | unappealable | unauthentic | unbruised |
| unadorned | unappealing | unauthenticated | unbrushed |
| unadulterated | unappeasable | unauthorized | unbudgeted |
| unadventurous | unappetizing | unavailable | unbuilt |
| unadvertised | unappreciated | unavenged | unburied |
| unadvisable | unappreciative | unawed | unburned |
| unaffiliated | unapproached | unbaked | unburnt |
| unafraid | unapt | unbaptized | unbusinesslike |

---

fat, āpe, cär; ten, ēven; is, bīte; gō, hôrn, to͞ol, look; oil, out; up, fur; get; joy; yet; chin; she; thin, *th*en; zh, leisure; ŋ, ring; ə for *a* in *ago*, *e* in *agent*, *i* in *sanity*, *o* in *comply*, *u* in *focus*; ʹ as in *able* (āʹbʹl); Fr. bál; ë, Fr. coeur; ö, Fr. feu; Fr. mon; ô, Fr. coq; ü, Fr. duc; r, Fr. cri; H, G. ich; kh, G. doch; ‡foreign; *hypothetical; < derived from. See inside front cover.

**un·called-for** (un kôld′fôr′) *adj.* **1.** not required **2.** unnecessary and out of place; impertinent

**un·can·ny** (-kan′ē) *adj.* **1.** mysterious in an eerie way; weird **2.** so remarkable, acute, etc. as to seem unnatural [*uncanny* vision] —**un·can′ni·ly** *adv.* —**un·can′ni·ness** *n.*

**un·cap** (-kap′) *vt.* **-capped′**, **-cap′ping 1.** to remove the cap from the head of (a person) **2.** to remove the cap from (a bottle, etc.)

**un·cared-for** (-kerd′fôr′) *adj.* not cared for or looked after; neglected

**un·cer·e·mo·ni·ous** (un′ser ə mō′nē əs) *adj.* **1.** less ceremonious than is expected; informal **2.** so curt or abrupt as to be discourteous —**un′cer·e·mo′ni·ous·ly** *adv.* —**un′cer·e·mo′ni·ous·ness** *n.*

**un·cer·tain** (un sʉrt′'n) *adj.* **1.** *a)* not surely or certainly known; questionable *b)* not sure or certain in knowledge; doubtful **2.** not definite; vague **3.** liable to change; not dependable or reliable **4.** not steady or constant; varying —**un·cer′tain·ly** *adv.* —**un·cer′tain·ness** *n.*

**un·cer·tain·ty** (-tē) *n.* **1.** lack of certainty; doubt **2.** *pl.* **-ties** something uncertain

**un·char·i·ta·ble** (-char′i tə b'l) *adj.* harsh or severe, as in opinion; unforgiving, ungenerous, or faultfinding —**un·char′i·ta·ble·ness** *n.* —**un·char′i·ta·bly** *adv.*

**un·chris·tian** (-kris′chən) *adj.* **1.** not having or practicing a Christian religion **2.** not in accord with the principles of Christianity **3.** [Colloq.] outrageous; dreadful

**un·church** (-chʉrch′) *vt.* **1.** to deprive (a person) of membership in a given church **2.** to deprive (a congregation) of its rights as a church

**un·ci·al** (un′shē əl, -shəl) *adj.* [< L. < *uncia*, an inch] designating or of a form of large, rounded letter used in the script of Greek and Latin manuscripts between 300 and 900 A.D. —*n.* **1.** an uncial letter **2.** an uncial manuscript **3.** uncial script

**un·cir·cum·cised** (un sʉr′kəm sīzd′) *adj.* **1.** not circumcised; specif., not Jewish; gentile **2.** [Archaic] heathen

**un·civ·il** (un siv′'l) *adj.* **1.** not civilized; barbarous **2.** not civil or courteous; ill-mannered —**un·civ′il·ly** *adv.*

**un·civ·i·lized** (-siv′ə līzd′) *adj.* **1.** not civilized; barbarous **2.** far from civilization

**un·clad** (-klad′) *adj.* wearing no clothes; naked

**un·clasp** (-klasp′) *vt.* **1.** to unfasten the clasp of **2.** to release from a clasp or grasp —*vi.* **1.** to become unfastened **2.** to relax the clasp or grasp

**un·cle** (uŋ′k'l) *n.* [OFr. < L. *avunculus*, one's mother's brother] **1.** the brother of one's father or mother **2.** the husband of one's aunt **3.** [Colloq.] any elderly man: a term of address —**say** (or **cry**) **uncle** to surrender or admit defeat

**un·clean** (un klēn′) *adj.* **1.** dirty; filthy; foul **2.** not pure according to religious laws **3.** morally impure; unchaste; obscene —**un·clean′ness** *n.*

**un·clean·ly** (-klēn′lē) *adj.* not cleanly; unclean; dirty —**un·clean′li·ness** *n.*

**un·clean·ly²** (-klēn′lē) *adv.* in an unclean manner

**un·clench** (-klench′) *vt., vi.* to open: said of something clenched, or clinched: also **un·clinch′** (-klinch′)

**Uncle Sam** [< abbrev. U.S.] [Colloq.] the U.S. (government or people), personified as a tall man with chin whiskers, dressed in a red, white, and blue suit

**Uncle Tom** [after an elderly Negro slave in H. B. STOWE's antislavery novel, *Uncle Tom's Cabin* (1852)] a Negro whose behavior toward whites is regarded as fawning or servile: a term of contempt —**Uncle Tom′ism**

**un·cloak** (un klōk′) *vt., vi.* **1.** to remove a cloak or other covering (from) **2.** to reveal; expose

**un·close** (-klōz′) *vt., vi.* **-closed′, -clos′ing 1.** to open **2.** to disclose or reveal

**un·clothe** (-klōth′) *vt.* **-clothed′** or **-clad′, -cloth′ing** to strip of or as of clothes; uncover; divest

**un·coil** (-koil′) *vt., vi.* to unwind or release from being coiled

**un·com·fort·a·ble** (-kumf′tər b'l, -kum′fər tə b'l) *adj.* **1.** not comfortable; feeling discomfort **2.** not pleasant; causing discomfort **3.** ill at ease —**un·com′fort·a·ble·ness** *n.* —**un·com′fort·a·bly** *adv.*

**un·com·mit·ted** (un′kə mit′id) *adj.* **1.** not committed, as a crime **2.** not bound or pledged **3.** not having taken a position **4.** not imprisoned **5.** not committed to a mental hospital

**un·com·mon** (-käm′ən) *adj.* **1.** not common; rare; not usual **2.** strange; remarkable; extraordinary —**un·com′mon·ly** *adv.* —**un·com′mon·ness** *n.*

**un·com·mu·ni·ca·tive** (un′kə myōō′nə kāt′iv, -ni kə-tiv) *adj.* not communicative; reserved; taciturn —**un′com·mu′ni·ca·tive·ly** *adv.* —**un′com·mu′ni·ca·tive·ness** *n.*

**un·com·pro·mis·ing** (un käm′prə mī′ziŋ) *adj.* not yielding or giving in at all; firm; inflexible

**un·con·cern** (un′kən sʉrn′) *n.* **1.** lack of interest; indifference **2.** lack of concern, or worry

**un·con·cerned** (-kən sʉrnd′) *adj.* not concerned; specif., *a)* not interested *b)* not solicitous or anxious —**un′con·cern′ed·ly** (-sʉr′nid lē) *adv.* —**un′con·cern′ed·ness** *n.*

**un·con·di·tion·al** (-kən dish′ən 'l) *adj.* without conditions or stipulations; absolute —**un′con·di′tion·al·ly** *adv.*

**un·con·di·tioned** (-kən dish′ənd) *adj.* **1.** *same as* UNCONDITIONAL **2.** *Psychol.* natural; inborn [an *unconditioned* reflex]

**un·con·scion·a·ble** (un kän′shən ə b'l) *adj.* **1.** not guided or restrained by conscience; unscrupulous **2.** unreasonable, excessive, etc. —**un·con′scion·a·bly** *adv.*

**un·con·scious** (-kän′shəs) *adj.* **1.** deprived of consciousness [*unconscious* from a blow on the head] **2.** not aware (*of*) **3.** not realized or intended by the person himself [*unconscious* humor] —**the unconscious** *Psychoanalysis* the sum of all memories, thoughts, feelings, etc. of which the individual is not conscious but which influence his emotions and behavior —**un·con′scious·ly** *adv.* —**un·con′scious·ness** *n.*

**un·con·sti·tu·tion·al** (un′kän stə tōō′shən 'l, -tyōō′-) *adj.* not in accordance with or permitted by a constitution, specif. the U.S. Constitution —**un′con·sti·tu′tion·al′i·ty** (-shə nal′ə tē) *n.* —**un′con·sti·tu′tion·al·ly** *adv.*

**un·con·ven·tion·al** (un′kən ven′shən 'l) *adj.* not conforming to customary, formal, or accepted practices, standards, etc. —**un′con·ven′tion·al′i·ty** (-shə nal′ə tē) *n.* —**un′con·ven′tion·al·ly** *adv.*

**un·cork** (un kôrk′) *vt.* to pull the cork out of

**un·count·ed** (-koun′tid) *adj.* **1.** not counted **2.** too many to be counted; innumerable

**un·cou·ple** (-kup′'l) *vt.* **-pled, -pling** to unfasten (things coupled); disconnect —*vi.* to become unfastened

**un·couth** (-kōōth′) *adj.* [OE. *uncuth*, unknown < *un-*, not + *cuth*, pp. of *cunnan*, to know] **1.** awkward; clumsy; ungainly **2.** uncultured; crude; boorish —**un·couth′ly** *adv.* —**un·couth′ness** *n.*

**un·cov·er** (-kuv′ər) *vt.* **1.** to make known; disclose **2.** to lay bare by removing a covering **3.** to remove the cover or protection from **4.** to remove the hat, cap, etc. from

---

| | | | |
|---|---|---|---|
| uncaged | unchivalrous | uncommissioned | unconsidered |
| uncanceled | unchosen | uncompensated | unconsoled |
| uncaring | unchristened | uncomplaining | unconsolidated |
| uncarpeted | unclaimed | uncompleted | unconstrained |
| uncataloged | unclarified | uncomplicated | unconstricted |
| uncaught | unclassifiable | uncomplimentary | unconsumed |
| unceasing | unclassified | uncomplying | uncontaminated |
| uncelebrated | uncleaned | uncompounded | uncontemplated |
| uncensored | unclear | uncomprehending | uncontested |
| uncensured | uncleared | uncompressed | uncontradictable |
| uncertified | unclipped | unconcealed | uncontrived |
| unchain | unclog | unconciliated | uncontrollable |
| unchallenged | unclouded | unconcluded | uncontrolled |
| unchangeable | uncluttered | uncondemned | unconverted |
| unchanged | uncoated | uncondensed | unconvinced |
| unchaperoned | uncocked | unconfessed | unconvincing |
| uncharacteristic | uncollectable | unconfined | uncooked |
| uncharged | uncollected | unconfirmed | uncooperative |
| uncharted | uncollectible | unconformity | uncoordinated |
| unchartered | uncolonized | unconfused | uncorrected |
| unchaste | uncolored | uncongenial | uncorroborated |
| unchastened | uncombed | unconnected | uncorrupted |
| unchecked | uncombinable | unconquerable | uncountable |
| uncherished | uncombined | unconquered | uncrate |
| unchewed | uncomely | unconscientious | uncredited |
| unchilled | uncomforted | unconsecrated | uncritical |

(the head), as in showing respect —*vi.* to bare the head, as in showing respect

**unc·tion** (uŋk′shən) *n.* [L. *unctio* < *ungere*, to anoint] **1.** *a)* the act of anointing, as in medical treatment or a religious ceremony *b)* the oil, ointment, etc. used for this **2.** anything that soothes or comforts **3.** *a)* a very earnest manner of speaking or behaving, esp. about religious matters *b)* such a manner when it is pretended or seems put on

**unc·tu·ous** (uŋk′chŏŏ wəs) *adj.* [< ML. < L. *unctum*, ointment < *ungere*, to anoint] **1.** of, like, or characteristic of an ointment; oily or greasy **2.** like oil, soap, or grease to the touch: said of certain minerals **3.** characterized by a smug, smooth pretense of spiritual feeling or earnestness, as in seeking to persuade; too suave or oily in speech or manner —**unc′tu·os′i·ty** (-wäs′ə tē), **unc′tu·ous·ness** *n.* —**unc′tu·ous·ly** *adv.*

**un·cut** (un kut′) *adj.* not cut; specif., *a)* having untrimmed margins: said of the pages of a book *b)* not ground to shape: said of a gem *c)* not abridged

**un·daunt·ed** (-dôn′tid, -dän′-) *adj.* not daunted; not afraid or discouraged —**un·daunt′ed·ly** *adv.*

**un·de·ceive** (un′di sēv′) *vt.* -**ceived′**, -**ceiv′ing** to cause to be no longer deceived, mistaken, or misled

**un·de·cid·ed** (-di sīd′id) *adj.* **1.** that is not decided or settled **2.** not having come to a decision —**un′de·cid′ed·ly** *adv.* —**un′de·cid′ed·ness** *n.*

**un·de·ni·a·ble** (-di nī′ə b′l) *adj.* **1.** that cannot be denied **2.** unquestionably good or excellent —**un′de·ni′a·bly** *adv.*

**un·der** (un′dər) *prep.* [OE.] **1.** in, at, or to a position down from; below **2.** beneath the surface of [*under* water] **3.** below and to the other side of [to drive *under* a bridge] **4.** covered or concealed by [a vest *under* a coat] **5.** *a)* lower in authority, position, etc. than *b)* lower in value, amount, etc. than *c)* lower than the required degree of [*under* age] **6.** *a)* subject to the control, government, direction, influence, etc. of *b)* bound by [*under* oath] *c)* subjected to; undergoing [*under* repair] **7.** with the character, disguise, etc. of [*under* an alias] **8.** in the (designated category) [spiders are classified *under* arachnids] **9.** during the rule of [France *under* Louis XV] **10.** being the subject of [the question *under* discussion] **11.** because of [*under* the circumstances] **12.** authorized or attested by [*under* her signature] —*adv.* **1.** in or to a lower position; beneath **2.** beneath the surface, as of water **3.** in or to a subordinate condition **4.** so as to be covered or concealed **5.** less in amount, value, etc. —*adj.* lower in position, authority, rank, amount, degree, etc.

**un·der-** [OE.] *a prefix meaning:* **1.** in, on, to, or from a lower place or state; beneath or below [*undershirt*] **2.** in an inferior or subordinate position or rank [*undergraduate*] **3.** too little, not enough, below normal [*underdeveloped*]: the list below includes some common compounds formed with *under* that can be understood if *too little* or *insufficiently* is added to the meaning of the base word

| | |
|---|---|
| underactive | undermanned |
| underbake | underprice |
| undercook | undersubscribe |
| underemphasize | undersupply |
| underexercise | undertrained |

**un·der·a·chieve** (un′dər ə chēv′) *vi.* -**chieved′**, -**chiev′-ing** to fail to do as well in school studies as might be expected from scores made on intelligence tests —**un′der·a·chieve′ment** *n.* —**un′der·a·chiev′er** *n.*

**un·der·act** (-akt′) *vt., vi.* to act (a theatrical role) with too little emphasis or too great restraint

**un·der·age** (-āj′) *adj.* **1.** not of full or mature age **2.** below the age required by law

**un·der·arm** (un′dər ärm′) *adj.* **1.** under the arm; in the armpit **2.** *same as* UNDERHAND (sense 1) —*adv. same as* UNDERHAND (sense 1)

**un·der·bel·ly** (-bel′ē) *n.* **1.** the lower, posterior part of an animal's belly **2.** any vulnerable or unprotected area or part

**un·der·bid** (un′dər bid′; *for n.* un′dər bid′) *vt., vi.* -**bid′**, -**bid′ding** **1.** to bid lower than (another person) **2.** to bid less than the worth of —*n.* a lower or inadequate bid

**un·der·bod·y** (un′dər bäd′ē) *n.* **1.** the underpart of an animal's body **2.** the undersurface of a vehicle

**un·der·brush** (-brush′) *n.* small trees, shrubs, etc. that grow beneath large trees in woods or forests

**un·der·buy** (un′dər bī′) *vt., vi.* -**bought′**, -**buy′ing** **1.** to buy at less than the real value **2.** to buy more cheaply than (another or others)

**un·der·cap·i·tal·ize** (-kap′ə tə līz′) *vt., vi.* -**ized′**, -**iz′ing** to provide (a business) with too little capital for successful operation —**un′der·cap′i·tal·i·za′tion** *n.*

**un·der·car·riage** (un′dər kar′ij) *n.* a supporting frame or structure, as of an automobile

**un·der·charge** (un′dər chärj′; *for n.* un′dər chärj′) *vt., vi.* -**charged′**, -**charg′ing** **1.** to charge too low a price (to) **2.** to provide with too little or low a charge —*n.* a charge that is too little or low

**un·der·class·man** (un′dər klas′mən) *n., pl.* -**men** a freshman or sophomore

**un·der·clothes** (un′dər klōz′, -klō*th*z′) *n.pl. same as* UNDERWEAR: also **un′der·cloth′ing** (-klō*th*′iŋ)

**un·der·coat** (-kōt′) *n.* **1.** a coating of tarlike material applied to the undersurface of a car, etc. to retard rust, etc. **2.** a coat of paint, varnish, etc. applied before the final coat Also **un′der·coat′ing** —*vt.* to apply an undercoat to

**un·der·cov·er** (-kuv′ər) *adj.* acting or done in secret

**un·der·cur·rent** (-kʉr′ənt) *n.* **1.** a current flowing below another or beneath the surface **2.** a hidden or underlying tendency, opinion, etc., usually conflicting with a more obvious one

**un·der·cut** (un′dər kut′; *for v.* un′dər kut′) *n.* **1.** a cut made below another so as to leave an overhang **2.** *Sports* an undercutting —*adj.* that is undercut —*vt.* -**cut′**, -**cut′-ting** **1.** to make an undercut (sense 1) in **2.** to cut out the underpart of **3.** to undersell or work for lower wages than **4.** to weaken the position of; undermine **5.** *Sports* to strike (a ball) with an oblique downward motion, as in golf, or to chop with an underhand stroke, as in tennis, esp. so as to impart backspin —*vi.* to undercut someone or something

**un·der·de·vel·op** (un′dər di vel′əp) *vt.* **1.** to develop to a point below what is needed **2.** *Photog.* to develop (a film, etc.) too short a time or with a weak developer

**un·der·de·vel·oped** (-əpt) *adj.* not developed to a desirable degree; specif., inadequately developed economically and industrially [*underdeveloped* nations]

**un·der·do** (-dōō′) *vt.* -**did′**, -**done′**, -**do′ing** to do less than is usual, needed, or desired

**un·der·dog** (un′dər dôg′) *n.* **1.** the one that is losing, as in a contest **2.** a person who is handicapped or a victim of injustice, discrimination, etc.

**un·der·done** (un′dər dun′) *adj.* not cooked enough, as meat

**un·der·em·ployed** (-im ploid′) *adj.* **1.** employed at less than full time **2.** working at low-skilled, poorly paid jobs when one can do more skilled work —**the underemployed** underemployed people —**un′der·em·ploy′ment** *n.*

**un·der·es·ti·mate** (-es′tə māt′; *for n.* -mit) *vt., vi.* -**mat′ed**, -**mat′ing** to set too low an estimate on or for —*n.* an estimate that is too low —**un′der·es′ti·ma′tion** *n.*

**un·der·ex·pose** (-ik spōz′) *vt.* -**posed′**, -**pos′ing** to expose (a photographic film, etc.) to inadequate light or for too short a time —**un′der·ex·po′sure** (-spō′zhər) *n.*

**un·der·feed** (-fēd′) *vt.* -**fed′**, -**feed′ing** to feed less than is needed

**un·der·foot** (un′dər foot′) *adv., adj.* **1.** under the foot or feet **2.** in the way, as of one walking

**un·der·fur** (un′dər fʉr′) *n.* the softer, finer fur under the outer coat of some animals, as beavers or seals

**un·der·gar·ment** (-gär′mənt) *n.* a piece of underwear

**un·der·gird** (un′dər gʉrd′) *vt.* -**gird′ed** or -**girt′**, -**gird′-ing** **1.** to gird or strengthen from the bottom side **2.** to supply support for

**un·der·go** (-gō′) *vt.* -**went′**, -**gone′**, -**go′ing** to experience; endure; go through

**un·der·grad·u·ate** (-graj′ōō wit) *n.* a student at a university or college who has not yet received a bachelor's degree

**un·der·ground** (un′dər ground′; *for n.* -ground′) *adj.* **1.** occurring, working, etc. beneath the surface of the earth **2.** secret; undercover **3.** designating or of noncommercial newspapers, movies, etc. that are unconventional, experi-

| | | | |
|---|---|---|---|
| uncross | uncurl | undecorated | undemanding |
| uncrowded | undamaged | undefeatable | undemocratic |
| uncrowned | undated | undefeated | undemonstrable |
| uncrystallized | undebatable | undefended | undemonstrative |
| uncultivated | undecayed | undefiled | undenied |
| uncultured | undecipherable | undefinable | undenominational |
| uncurbed | undeclared | undefined | undependable |
| uncured | undeclinable | undeliverable | undepreciated |

fat, āpe, cär; ten, ēven; is, bīte; gō, hôrn, tōōl, look; oil, out; up, fʉr; get; joy; yet; chin; she; thin, *th*en; zh, leisure; ŋ, ring; ə for *a* in *ago*, *e* in *agent*, *i* in *sanity*, *o* in *comply*, *u* in *focus*; ′ as in *able* (ā′b′l); Fr. bal; ë, Fr. coeur; ö, Fr. feu; Fr. mon; ô, Fr. coq; ü, Fr. duc; *r*, Fr. cri; H, G. ich; kh, G. doch; ‡foreign; *hypothetical; < derived from. See inside front cover.

mental, radical, etc. —*adv.* **1.** beneath the surface of the earth **2.** in or into secrecy or hiding —*n.* **1.** the entire region beneath the surface of the earth **2.** a secret movement organized to oppose the government in power or enemy forces of occupation **3.** [Brit.] a subway

**un·der·ground railroad 1.** a subway: also **underground railway 2.** [*often* U- R-] in the U.S. before the Civil War, a system set up by abolitionists to help fugitive slaves to escape to free States and Canada

**un·der·growth** (-grōth′) *n. same as* UNDERBRUSH

**un·der·hand** (un′dər hand′) *adj.* **1.** performed with the hand below the level of the elbow or shoulder **2.** *same as* UNDERHANDED (sense 1) —*adv.* **1.** with an underhand motion **2.** underhandedly

**un·der·hand·ed** (un′dər han′did) *adj.* **1.** secret, sly, deceitful, etc. **2.** lacking workers, players, etc.; shorthanded —un′der·hand′ed·ly *adv.* —un′der·hand′ed·ness *n.*

**un·der·lay** (un′dər lā′; *for n.* un′dər lā′) *vt.* -laid′, -lay′ing **1.** to cover the bottom of **2.** to raise or support with something laid underneath —*n.* something laid underneath; specif., patches of paper laid under type to raise it

**un·der·lie** (-lī′) *vt.* -lay′, -lain′, -ly′ing **1.** to lie under or beneath **2.** to form the basis or foundation of

**un·der·line** (un′dər līn′; *also, for v.,* un′dər līn′) *vt.* -lined′, -lin′ing **1.** to draw a line beneath; underscore **2.** to stress or emphasize —*n. same as* UNDERSCORE

**un·der·ling** (un′dər liŋ) *n.* [OE.: see UNDER- & -LING¹] a person who must carry out the orders of others above him; inferior: a disparaging term

**un·der·lin·ing** (-līn′iŋ) *n.* a garment lining formed of pieces cut to the shape of and attached to the sections of a garment, which are then sewed together

**un·der·ly·ing** (un′dər lī′iŋ) *adj.* **1.** lying under; placed beneath **2.** fundamental; basic

**un·der·mine** (un′dər mīn′, un′dər mīn′) *vt.* -mined′, -min′ing **1.** to dig beneath, so as to form a tunnel or mine **2.** to wear away and weaken the supports of **3.** to injure, weaken, or impair, esp. in a slow or stealthy way

**un·der·most** (un′dər mōst′) *adj., adv.* lowest in place, position, rank, etc.

**un·der·neath** (un′dər rēth′) *adv.* **1.** under; below; beneath **2.** at a lower level —*prep.* **1.** under; below; beneath **2.** under the form, guise, or authority of —*adj.* under or lower —*n.* the underpart

**un·der·nour·ish** (-nur′ish) *vt.* to provide with less food than is needed for health and growth —un′der·nour′ish·ment *n.*

**un·der·pants** (un′dər pants′) *n.pl.* an undergarment, long or short, for the lower part of the body, with a separate opening for each leg

**un·der·part** (-pärt′) *n.* the lower part or side, as of an animal's body or an airplane's fuselage

**un·der·pass** (-pas′) *n.* a passageway under something; esp., a road that runs under a railway or highway

**un·der·pay** (un′dər pā′) *vt., vi.* -paid′, -pay′ing to pay too little, or less than is right —un′der·pay′ment *n.*

**un·der·pin** (-pin′) *vt.* -pinned′, -pin′ning to support or strengthen from beneath, as with props

**un·der·pin·ning** (un′dər pin′iŋ) *n.* **1.** a supporting structure, esp. one placed beneath a wall **2.** a support or prop **3.** [*pl.*] [Colloq.] the legs

**un·der·play** (un′dər plā′) *vt., vi.* **1.** to act (a role or scene) with subtlety or little emphasis, in an intentionally restrained manner **2.** *same as* UNDERACT

**un·der·priv·i·leged** (-priv′′l ijd, -priv′lijd) *adj.* deprived of basic social rights and security through poverty, discrimination, etc. —**the underprivileged** underprivileged people

**un·der·pro·duce** (-prə dōōs′, -dyōōs′) *vt., vi.* -duced′, -duc′ing to produce in a quantity that fails to meet the need or demand —un′der·pro·duc′tion *n.*

**un·der·rate** (-rāt′) *vt.* -rat′ed, -rat′ing to rate, assess, or estimate too low

**un·der·score** (un′dər skôr′; *for n.* un′dər skôr′) *vt.* -scored′, -scor′ing *same as* UNDERLINE —*n.* a line drawn under a word, passage, etc., as for emphasis

**un·der·sea** (-sē′) *adj., adv.* beneath the surface of the sea: also **un′der·seas′** (-sēz′) *adv.*

**un·der·sec·re·tar·y** (-sek′rə ter′ē) *n., pl.* -tar′ies an assistant secretary: in U.S. government, **under secretary**

**un·der·sell** (-sel′) *vt.* -sold′, -sell′ing **1.** to sell at a lower price than (another seller) **2.** to promote in a restrained or inadequate manner

**un·der·sexed** (-sekst′) *adj.* having a weaker than normal sexual drive or interest

**un·der·shirt** (un′dər shurt′) *n.* a usually sleeveless undergarment worn under an outer shirt, esp. by men and boys

**un·der·shoot** (un′dər shōōt′) *vt.* -shot′, -shoot′ing **1.** to shoot or fall short of (a target, mark, etc.) **2.** to bring an aircraft down short of (the runway, etc.) —*vi.* to shoot or go short of the mark

**un·der·shorts** (un′dər shôrts′) *n.pl.* short underpants worn by men and boys

**un·der·shot** (-shät′) *adj.* **1.** with the lower part jutting out past the upper [an *undershot* jaw] **2.** driven by water flowing along the lower part [an *undershot* water wheel]

**un·der·side** (-sīd′) *n.* the side or surface underneath

**un·der·sign** (un′dər sīn′) *vt.* to sign one's name at the end of (a letter, document, etc.) —**the undersigned** the person or persons undersigning

UNDERSHOT WHEEL

**un·der·sized** (-sīzd′) *adj.* smaller in size than is usual, average, or proper: also **un′der·size′**

**un·der·slung** (-sluŋ′) *adj.* attached to the underside of the axles: said of an automobile frame

**un·der·staffed** (un′dər staft′) *adj.* having too small a staff; having fewer personnel than needed

**un·der·stand** (un′dər stand′) *vt.* -stood′, -stand′ing [OE. *understandan*, lit., to stand under] **1.** to get or know the meaning of **2.** to gather or assume from what is heard, known, etc.; infer **3.** to take as meant or meaning; interpret **4.** to take for granted or as a fact **5.** to supply mentally (an idea, word, etc.), as for grammatical completeness **6.** to be informed of; learn **7.** to know clearly or fully the nature, character, etc. of **8.** to have a sympathetic rapport with [no one *understands* me] —*vi.* **1.** to have understanding, comprehension, etc., either in general or with reference to something specific **2.** to be informed; believe —un′der·stand′a·ble *adj.* —un′der·stand′a·bly *adv.*

**un·der·stand·ing** (-iŋ) *n.* **1.** the act, state, or feeling of a person who understands; comprehension, knowledge, sympathetic awareness, etc. **2.** the power to think, learn, judge, etc.; intelligence; sense **3.** an explanation or interpretation [one's *understanding* of the matter] **4.** *a)* mutual comprehension, as of ideas, intentions, etc. *b)* an agreement, esp. one that settles differences or is informal —*adj.* that understands; having or showing comprehension, sympathy, etc. —un′der·stand′ing·ly *adv.*

**un·der·state** (un′dər stāt′) *vt.* -stat′ed, -stat′ing **1.** to make a weaker statement of than is warranted by truth, accuracy, or importance **2.** to express in a restrained style —un′der·state′ment *n.*

**un·der·stud·y** (un′dər stud′ē) *n., pl.* -stud′ies an actor who learns the part of another actor so that he can serve as a substitute when necessary —*vt., vi.* -stud′ied, -stud′y·ing **1.** to act as an understudy (to) **2.** to learn (a part) as an understudy

**un·der·sur·face** (-sur′fis) *n. same as* UNDERSIDE

**un·der·take** (un′dər tāk′) *vt.* -took′, -tak′en, -tak′ing **1.** to enter into or upon (a task, journey, etc.); take upon oneself; agree to do **2.** to give a promise or pledge that; contract **3.** to promise; guarantee

**un·der·tak·er** (un′dər tā′kər; *for 2* un′dər tā′kər) *n.* **1.** a person who undertakes something **2.** *earlier term for* FUNERAL DIRECTOR

**un·der·tak·ing** (un′dər tā′kiŋ; *also, & for 3 always,* un′dər tā′kiŋ) *n.* **1.** something undertaken; task; enterprise **2.** a promise; guarantee **3.** the business of an undertaker (sense 2) **4.** the act of one who undertakes a task, etc.

**un·der-the-count·er** (un′dər *thə* koun′tər) *adj.* [Colloq.] done, sold, given, etc. secretly in an unlawful or unethical way: also **un′der-the-ta′ble**

**un·der·things** (-thiŋz′) *n.pl.* women's or girls' underwear

**un·der·tone** (-tōn′) *n.* **1.** a low tone of sound or voice **2.** a subdued or background color **3.** any underlying quality, factor, element, etc. [an *undertone* of horror]

**un·der·tow** (-tō′) *n.* [UNDER- + TOW¹] a current of water moving beneath the surface water and in a different direction, as seaward under the surf

**un·der·val·ue** (un′dər val′yōō) *vt.* -ued, -u·ing **1.** to value too low, or below the real worth **2.** to regard or esteem too lightly —un′der·val′u·a′tion *n.*

**un·der·waist** (un′dər wāst′) *n.* an undergarment worn under a waist

**un·der·wa·ter** (un′dər wôt′ər, -wät′ər) *adj.* **1.** being, done, etc. beneath the surface of the water **2.** used or for use under water —*adv.* beneath the surface of the water

**un·der·way** (un′dər wā′) *adj. Naut.* not at anchor or moored or aground

**un·der·wear** (un′dər wer′) *n.* clothing worn under one's outer clothes, usually next to the skin, as undershirts, undershorts, slips, bras, etc.

**un·der·weight** (un′dər wāt′; *also for adj.,* un′dər wāt′) *adj.* below the normal, desirable, or allowed weight —*n.* less weight than is needed, desired, or allowed

**un·der·went** (un′dər went′) *pt. of* UNDERGO

**un·der·world** (un′dər wurld′) *n.* **1.** the mythical world of the dead; Hades **2.** the criminal members of society, or people living by vice or crime, regarded as a group

**un·der·write** (un′dər rīt′) *vt.* **-wrote′, -writ′ten, -writ′ing** **1.** to write under something written; subscribe to, as by signature **2.** to agree to buy (an issue of stocks, bonds, etc.) on a given date and at a fixed price, or to guarantee the purchase of (stocks or bonds to be made available to the public) **3.** to pledge to support (an undertaking, etc.) financially **4.** *a)* to sign one's name to (an insurance policy), thus assuming liability *b)* to insure *c)* to assume liability to the amount of (a specified sum) —**un′der·writ′er** *n.*

**un·de·sir·a·ble** (un′di zir′ə b'l) *adj.* not desirable; objectionable —*n.* an undesirable person —**un′de·sir′a·bil′i·ty** *n.* —**un′de·sir′a·bly** *adv.*

**un·dies** (un′dēz) *n.pl.* [Colloq.] women's or girls' underwear

**un·do** (un dōō′) *vt.* **-did′, -done′, -do′ing** **1.** *a)* to release or untie (a fastening) *b)* to open (a parcel, door, etc.) by this means **2.** to reverse or do away with (something done or its effect) **3.** to ruin or destroy **4.** to upset or perturb —**un·do′er** *n.*

**un·do·ing** (-iŋ) *n.* **1.** a reversal of something done or its effect **2.** ruin or the cause of ruin

**un·done**[1] (un dun′) *pp. of* UNDO —*adj.* **1.** ruined, disgraced, etc. **2.** emotionally upset; greatly perturbed

**un·done**[2] (un dun′) *adj.* not done; not performed, accomplished, completed, etc.

**un·doubt·ed** (-dout′id) *adj.* not doubted or called in question; certain —**un·doubt′ed·ly** *adv.*

**un·draw** (-drô′) *vt., vi.* **-drew′, -drawn′, -draw′ing** to draw (a curtain, drapes, etc.) open, back, or aside

**un·dreamed** (-drēmd′) *adj.* not even dreamed (*of*) or imagined; inconceivable: also **un·dreamt′** (-dremt′)

**un·dress** (un dres′; *for n. usually* un′dres′) *vt.* **1.** to take off the clothing of; strip **2.** to remove the dressing from (a wound) —*vi.* to take off one's clothes; strip —*n.* **1.** the state of being naked, partly clothed, in a robe, etc. **2.** ordinary or informal dress, as opposed to uniform, etc.

**Und·set** (ōōn′set), **Si·grid** (si′gri; *E.* si′grid) 1882–1949; Norw. novelist

**un·due** (un dōō′, -dyōō′) *adj.* **1.** not yet due or payable **2.** not suitable; improper [*undue* flippancy] **3.** too much; excessive [*undue* haste]

**un·du·lant** (un′joo lənt, -dyōō-; -dōō-) *adj.* moving in or as in waves; undulating

**undulant fever** a form of brucellosis, transmitted to man from domestic animals or their products, and marked by recurrent fever, sweating, and pains in the joints

**un·du·late** (-lāt′; *for adj. usually* -lit) *vt.* **-lat′ed, -lat′ing** [< L. *undulatus*, undulated, ult. < *unda*, a wave] **1.** to cause to move in waves **2.** to give a wavy form, surface, etc. to —*vi.* **1.** to move in waves **2.** to have a wavy form, surface, etc. —*adj.* having a wavy form, margin, or surface: also **un′du·lat′ed** —**un′du·la·to′ry** *adj.*

**un·du·la·tion** (un′joo lā′shən, -dyōō-, -dōō-) *n.* **1.** an undulating or undulating motion **2.** a wavy, curving form or outline, esp. one of a series **3.** *Physics* wave motion, as of light or sound, or a wave or vibration

**un·du·ly** (un dōō′lē, -dyōō′-) *adv.* beyond what is proper or right; too much [*unduly* alarmed]

**un·dy·ing** (-dī′iŋ) *adj.* not dying; immortal or eternal

**un·earned** (-urnd′) *adj.* **1.** not earned by work or service; specif., obtained as a return on an investment [*unearned* income] **2.** not deserved; unmerited

**un·earth** (-urth′) *vt.* **1.** to dig up from out of the earth **2.** to bring to light; discover or disclose

**un·earth·ly** (-urth′lē) *adj.* **1.** not, or as if not, of this earth **2.** supernatural **3.** weird; mysterious **4.** [Colloq.] fantastic, outlandish, etc. —**un·earth′li·ness** *n.*

**un·eas·y** (-ē′zē) *adj.* **-eas′i·er, -eas′i·est** **1.** having, showing, or allowing no ease of body or mind; uncomfortable **2.** awkward; constrained **3.** worried; anxious —**un·ease′, un·eas′i·ness** *n.* —**un·eas′i·ly** *adv.*

**un·ed·it·ed** (-ed′it id) *adj.* **1.** not edited for publication **2.** not assembled for presentation [an *unedited* film]

**un·em·ploy·a·ble** (un′im ploi′ə b'l) *adj.* not employable; specif., that cannot be employed because of age, physical or mental deficiency, etc. —*n.* an unemployable person

**un·em·ployed** (-im ploid′) *adj.* **1.** not employed; without work **2.** not being used; idle —**the unemployed** people who are out of work

**un·em·ploy·ment** (-im ploi′mənt) *n.* **1.** the state of being unemployed; lack of employment **2.** the number or percentage of persons in the normal labor force out of work

**un·e·qual** (un ē′kwəl) *adj.* **1.** not equal, as in size, strength, ability, value, rank, amount, etc. **2.** *a)* not balanced or symmetrical *b)* that matches unequal contestants [an *unequal* battle] **3.** not even, regular, etc.; variable **4.** not equal or adequate [*unequal* to the task] —*n.* one that is not equal to another —**un·e′qual·ly** *adv.*

**un·e·qualed, un·e·qualled** (-ē′kwəld) *adj.* not equaled; unmatched; unrivaled; supreme

**un·e·quiv·o·cal** (un′i kwiv′ə k'l) *adj.* not equivocal; not ambiguous; plain; clear —**un′e·quiv′o·cal·ly** *adv.*

**un·err·ing** (un ur′iŋ, -er′-) *adj.* **1.** free from error **2.** not missing or failing; sure; exact —**un·err′ing·ly** *adv.*

**UNESCO** (yoo nes′kō) United Nations Educational, Scientific, and Cultural Organization

**un·e·ven** (un ē′vən) *adj.* not even; specif., *a)* not level, smooth, or flat; rough; irregular *b)* not equal in size, amount, etc. *c)* not uniform; varying *d)* not equally balanced or matched *e) Math.* not evenly divisible by two —**un·e′ven·ly** *adv.* —**un·e′ven·ness** *n.*

**un·ex·am·pled** (un′ig zam′p'ld) *adj.* with nothing like it before; with no other example; unprecedented

**un·ex·cep·tion·a·ble** (-ik sep′shə nə b'l) *adj.* not exceptionable; without flaw or fault; not warranting even the slightest criticism —**un′ex·cep′tion·a·bly** *adv.*

**un·ex·cep·tion·al** (-ik sep′shən 'l) *adj.* **1.** not uncommon or unusual; ordinary **2.** not admitting of any exception **3.** *same as* UNEXCEPTIONABLE: regarded by some as a loose usage —**un′ex·cep′tion·al·ly** *adv.*

**un·ex·pect·ed** (-ik spek′tid) *adj.* not expected; unforeseen —**un′ex·pect′ed·ly** *adv.* —**un′ex·pect′ed·ness** *n.*

| | | | |
|---|---|---|---|
| undeserving | undiscriminating | undrinkable | unentertaining |
| undesignated | undiscussed | undutiful | unenthusiastic |
| undesigning | undisguised | undyed | unentitled |
| undesired | undismayed | uneatable | unenviable |
| undesirous | undispelled | uneaten | unenvious |
| undestroyed | undisposed | uneclipsed | unequipped |
| undetachable | undisputed | uneconomical | unescorted |
| undetected | undissected | unedifying | unessential |
| undeterminable | undissolved | uneducated | unestablished |
| undeterred | undistilled | uneffaced | unestimated |
| undeveloped | undistinguishable | unemancipated | unethical |
| undeviating | undistinguished | unembarrassed | uneventful |
| undevoured | undistorted | unembellished | unexacting |
| undevout | undistracted | unemotional | unexaggerated |
| undifferentiated | undistressed | unemphatic | unexamined |
| undiffused | undistributed | unemptied | unexcelled |
| undigested | undisturbed | unenclosed | unexchangeable |
| undigestible | undiversified | unencumbered | unexcitable |
| undignified | undiverted | unending | unexciting |
| undiluted | undivested | unendorsed | unexcused |
| undiminished | undivided | unendowed | unexecuted |
| undimmed | undivulged | unendurable | unexercised |
| undiplomatic | undocumented | unenforceable | unexpendable |
| undirected | undogmatic | unengaged | unexpired |
| undiscernible | undomestic | unenjoyable | unexplainable |
| undiscerning | undomesticated | unenlightened | unexplained |
| undischarged | undrained | unenriched | unexploded |
| undisciplined | undramatic | unenrolled | unexploited |
| undisclosed | undraped | unenslaved | unexplored |
| undiscouraged | undried | unentangled | unexposed |
| undiscoverable | | unenterprising | unexpressed |

**un·fail·ing** (un fāl′iŋ) *adj.* **1.** not failing **2.** never ceasing or falling short; inexhaustible **3.** always reliable; certain —**un·fail′ing·ly** *adv.*

**un·fair** (-fer′) *adj.* **1.** not just or impartial; biased; inequitable **2.** dishonest or unethical in business dealings —**unfair′ly** *adv.* —**un·fair′ness** *n.*

**un·faith·ful** (-fāth′fəl) *adj.* **1.** failing to stay loyal or to keep a vow, promise, etc.; faithless **2.** not true, accurate, etc.; untrustworthy **3.** guilty of adultery —**un·faith′ful·ly** *adv.* —**un·faith′ful·ness** *n.*

**un·fa·mil·iar** (un′fə mil′yər) *adj.* **1.** not familiar or well-known; strange *[unfamiliar* lands*]* **2.** not acquainted (*with* something) —**un′fa·mil′i·ar′i·ty** (-yar′ə tē, -ē ar′-) *n.* —**un′fa·mil′iar·ly** *adv.*

**un·fas·ten** (un fas′n) *vt.* to open or make loose; untie, unlock, undo, etc. —*vi.* to become unfastened

**un·fa·vor·a·ble** (-fā′vər ə b′l, -fāv′rə b′l) *adj.* not favorable; opposed, harmful, disadvantageous, inauspicious, etc. —**un·fa′vor·a·bly** *adv.*

**un·feel·ing** (-fēl′iŋ) *adj.* **1.** without feeling **2.** hardhearted; cruel —**un·feel′ing·ly** *adv.*

**un·feigned** (-fānd′) *adj.* genuine; real; sincere

**un·fin·ished** (-fin′isht) *adj.* **1.** not finished or completed **2.** having no finish, or final coat, as of paint

**un·fit** (-fit′) *adj.* **1.** not meeting requirements; not fit or suitable **2.** not physically or mentally fit **3.** not fitted for a given purpose —*vt.* **-fit′ted, -fit′ting** to make unfit —**un·fit′ly** *adv.* —**un·fit′ness** *n.*

**un·fix** (-fiks′) *vt.* to unfasten; loosen

**un·flap·pa·ble** (-flap′ə b′l) *adj.* [see FLAP, *n.* 4] [Colloq.] not easily excited or upset; calm

**un·fledged** (-flejd′) *adj.* **1.** not fully fledged; unfeathered, as a young bird **2.** immature; undeveloped

**un·flinch·ing** (-flin′chiŋ) *adj.* steadfast; resolute; unyielding —**un·flinch′ing·ly** *adv.*

**un·fold** (-fōld′) *vt.* **1.** to open and spread out (something folded) **2.** to lay open to view; reveal, disclose, display, or explain **3.** to open up; unwrap —*vi.* **1.** to become unfolded **2.** to develop fully

**un·for·tu·nate** (-fôr′chə nit) *adj.* **1.** *a)* having bad luck; unlucky *b)* bringing, or coming by, bad luck; unfavorable **2.** not suitable or successful —*n.* an unfortunate person —**un·for′tu·nate·ly** *adv.*

**un·found·ed** (-foun′did) *adj.* **1.** not founded on fact or truth; baseless **2.** not established

**un·freeze** (-frēz′) *vt.* **-froze′, -froz′en, -freez′ing 1.** to cause to thaw **2.** to remove financial controls from (prices, wages, etc.)

**un·friend·ed** (-fren′did) *adj.* having no friends; friendless

**un·friend·ly** (-frend′lē) *adj.* **1.** not friendly or kind; hostile **2.** not favorable or propitious —**un·friend′li·ness** *n.*

**un·frock** (-fräk′) *vt.* **1.** to remove a frock from **2.** to deprive of the rank or function of priest or minister

**un·furl** (-furl′) *vt., vi.* to open or unfold from a furled state

**un·gain·ly** (-gān′lē) *adj.* **1.** awkward; clumsy **2.** coarse and unattractive —**un·gain′li·ness** *n.*

**un·glued** (-glōōd′) *adj.* broken open; separated: said of things glued together

**un·god·ly** (-gäd′lē) *adj.* **1.** not godly or religious; impious **2.** sinful; wicked **3.** [Colloq.] outrageous; dreadful —*adv.* [Colloq.] outrageously; dreadfully —**un·god′li·ness** *n.*

**un·gov·ern·a·ble** (-guv′ər nə b′l) *adj.* that cannot be governed or controlled; unruly —**un·gov′ern·a·bly** *adv.*

**un·gra·cious** (-grā′shəs) *adj.* **1.** rude; discourteous; impolite **2.** unpleasant; unattractive —**un·gra′cious·ly** *adv.* —**un·gra′cious·ness** *n.*

**un·guard·ed** (-gärd′id) *adj.* **1.** unprotected **2.** without guile or cunning; open **3.** careless; thoughtless; imprudent —**un·guard′ed·ly** *adv.*

**un·guent** (uŋ′gwənt) *n.* [L. *unguentum* < *unguere*, to anoint] a salve or ointment —**un′guen·tar′y** (-gwən ter′ē) *adj.*

**un·guis** (uŋ′gwis) *n., pl.* **un′gues** (-gwēz) [L., a nail] a nail, claw, or hoof: also **un′gu·la** (-gyoo lə), *pl.* **-lae** (-lē′)

**un·gu·late** (-gyoo lit, -lāt′) *adj.* [< L. *ungula*, a hoof] having hoofs; of or belonging to a former group of all mammals having hoofs —*n.* a mammal having hoofs

**un·hal·lowed** (un hal′ōd) *adj.* **1.** not hallowed or consecrated; unholy **2.** wicked; profane

**un·hand** (-hand′) *vt.* to loose or release from the hand or hands or one's grasp; let go of

**un·hand·y** (-han′dē) *adj.* **-hand′i·er, -hand′i·est 1.** not handy, convenient, or easy to reach **2.** not clever with the hands; awkward —**un·hand′i·ly** *adv.* —**un·hand′i·ness** *n.*

**un·hap·py** (-hap′ē) *adj.* **-pi·er, -pi·est 1.** unlucky; unfortunate **2.** sad; wretched; sorrowful **3.** not suitable —**un·hap′pi·ly** *adv.* —**un·hap′pi·ness** *n.*

**un·health·y** (-hel′thē) *adj.* **-health′i·er, -health′i·est 1.** having or showing poor health; sickly; not well **2.** harmful to health; unwholesome **3.** harmful to morals **4.** dangerous or risky *[an unhealthy* situation*]* —**un·health′i·ly** *adv.* —**un·health′i·ness** *n.*

**un·heard** (-hurd′) *adj.* **1.** not perceived by the ear **2.** not given a hearing

**un·heard-of** (-hurd′uv′) *adj.* **1.** not heard of before; unprecedented **2.** unacceptable or outrageous *[unheard-of* behavior*]*

**un·hinge** (-hinj′) *vt.* **-hinged′, -hing′ing 1.** to remove from the hinges **2.** to dislodge or detach **3.** to throw (the mind, etc.) into confusion; unbalance or upset

**un·his·tor·ic** (un′his tôr′ik, -tär′-) *adj.* not historic or historical; specif., *Linguis.* not having a historical basis; accidental, as the *b* in *thumb:* also **un′his·tor′i·cal**

**un·hitch** (un hich′) *vt.* **1.** to free from a hitch **2.** to unfasten; release; detach

**un·ho·ly** (-hō′lē) *adj.* **-li·er, -li·est 1.** not sacred, hallowed, or consecrated **2.** wicked; profane; impious **3.** [Colloq.] outrageous; dreadful —**un·ho′li·ness** *n.*

**un·hook** (-hook′) *vt.* **1.** to remove or loosen from a hook **2.** to undo or unfasten the hook or hooks of —*vi.* to become unhooked

**un·horse** (-hôrs′) *vt.* **-horsed′, -hors′ing 1.** to throw (a rider) from a horse **2.** to overthrow

**un·hu·man** (-hyōō′mən, -yōō′-) *adj.* **1.** *rare var. of: a)* INHUMAN *b)* SUPERHUMAN **2.** not human in kind, quality, etc. —**un·hu′man·ly** *adv.*

**u·ni-** [< L. *unus*, one] *a combining form meaning* having or consisting of one only *[unicellular]*

**U·ni·ate, U·ni·at** (yōō′nē ət, -at′) *n.* [< Russ. *uniyat*, ult. < L. *unus*, one: from union with the Roman Church] a member of the Eastern Church (sense 1 *b*)

**u·ni·cam·er·al** (yōō′nə kam′ər əl) *adj.* [< UNI- + LL. *camera*, a chamber] of or having a single legislative chamber

**UNICEF** (yōō′nə sef′) United Nations International Children's Emergency Fund

**u·ni·cel·lu·lar** (yōō′nə sel′yoo lər) *adj.* having or consisting of a single cell

---

**u·ni·corn** (yōō'nə kôrn') *n.* [< OFr. < L. < *unus,* one + *cornu,* a horn] a mythical horselike animal with a single horn growing from the center of its forehead

**u·ni·cy·cle** (yōō'nə sī'k'l) *n.* a riding device with only one wheel, which is straddled by the rider

**u·ni·fi·ca·tion** (yōō'nə fi kā'shən) *n.* the act of unifying or the state of being unified

**u·ni·form** (yōō'nə fôrm') *adj.* [< MFr. < L. < *unus,* one + *-formis,* -form] **1.** always the same; not varying in form, rate, degree, manner, etc. **2.** having the same form, appearance, etc. as others of the same class **3.** consistent in action, intention, effect, etc. *[a uniform policy]* —*n.* the official or distinctive clothes worn by the members of a particular group, as policemen or soldiers —*vt.* to clothe or supply with a uniform —**uniform with** having the same form, appearance, etc. as —**u'ni·form'ly** *adv.*

**u·ni·form·i·ty** (yōō'nə fôr'mə tē) *n., pl.* **-ties** state, quality, or instance of being uniform

**u·ni·fy** (yōō'nə fī') *vt., vi.* **-fied', -fy'ing** [< MFr. < LL. *unificare:* see UNI- & -FY] to combine into one; become or make united —**u'ni·fi'a·ble** *adj.* —**u'ni·fi'er** *n.*

**u·ni·lat·er·al** (yōō'nə lat'ər əl) *adj.* **1.** of, occurring on, or affecting one side only **2.** involving one only of several parties; done by one side only *[a unilateral contract]* **3.** taking into account one side only of a matter; one-sided **4.** turned to, or having its parts on, one side —**u'ni·lat'er·al·ism** *n.* —**u'ni·lat'er·al·ly** *adv.*

**u·ni·lin·e·ar** (-lin'ē ər) *adj.* of or following a single, consistent path of development or progression

**un·im·peach·a·ble** (un'im pēch'ə b'l) *adj.* that cannot be doubted, questioned, or discredited; irreproachable —**un'im·peach'a·bly** *adv.*

**un·im·proved** (un'im prōōvd') *adj.* **1.** not bettered, improved, or developed, as land by planting, building, etc. **2.** not used to good advantage **3.** not improved in health

**un·in·hib·it·ed** (-in hib'it id) *adj.* without inhibition; esp., free from the usual social or psychological restraints

**un·ion** (yōōn'yən) *n.* [< MFr. < LL. < L. < *unus,* one] **1.** a uniting or being united; combination; junction; specif., *a)* a grouping together of nations, political groups, etc. for some specific purpose *b)* marriage **2.** something united; a whole made up of united parts; specif., *a)* an organization or confederation uniting various individuals, political units, etc. *b) short for* LABOR UNION **3.** a device symbolizing political union, used in a flag or ensign, as the white stars on a blue field in the U.S. flag **4.** a facility for social recreation on a college campus: in full, **student union 5.** a device for joining together parts; esp., a coupling for linking the ends of pipes **6.** *Math.* a set containing all the elements of two or more given sets, with no element listed more than once —**the Union** the United States of America

**Union City** [formed by the union of two older towns] city in NE N.J.: suburb of Jersey City: pop. 56,000

**un·ion·ism** (yōōn'yən iz'm) *n.* **1.** *a)* the principle of union *b)* support of this principle or of a specified union **2.** the system or principles of labor unions **3.** [U-] loyalty to the Federal union of the U.S., esp. during the Civil War —**un'ion·ist** *n.* —**un'ion·is'tic** *adj.*

**un·ion·ize** (-īz') *vt.* **-ized', -iz'ing 1.** to organize (a group of workers) into a labor union **2.** to bring into conformity with the rules, standards, etc. of a labor union —*vi.* to join or organize a labor union —**un'ion·i·za'tion** *n.*

**union jack 1.** a jack or flag consisting only of a union, esp. of the union of a national flag **2.** [U- J-] the national flag of the United Kingdom

**Union of South Africa** *former name of* SOUTH AFRICA

**Union of Soviet Socialist Republics** country in E Europe & N Asia, extending from the Baltic Sea to the Pacific: it is a union of fifteen republics: 8,603,000 sq. mi.; pop. 258,000,000; cap. Moscow

**union shop** a factory, business, etc. operating under a contract with a labor union, which requires that new workers join the union after being hired

**union suit** a suit of men's or boys' underwear uniting shirt and drawers in a single garment

**u·nique** (yōō nēk') *adj.* [Fr. < L. *unicus,* single < *unus,* one] **1.** one and only; sole **2.** having no like or equal; unparalleled **3.** highly unusual, extraordinary, etc.: a common usage still objected to by some —**u·nique'ly** *adv.* —**u·nique'ness** *n.*

**u·ni·sex** (yōō'nə seks') *adj.* [Colloq.] designating or of a fashion, as in garments, hair styles, etc., adopted by persons of either sex

**u·ni·sex·u·al** (yōō'nə sek'shoo wəl) *adj.* having one sex (male or female) only; not hermaphroditic —**u'ni·sex'u·al'i·ty** (-shoo wal'ə tē) *n.* —**u'ni·sex'u·al·ly** *adv.*

**u·ni·son** (yōō'nə sən, -zən) *n.* [MFr. < ML. < L. *unus,* one + *sonus,* a sound] **1.** identity of musical pitch, as of two or more voices or tones **2.** agreement; concord; harmony —**in unison 1.** sounding the same note at the same time **2.** with all the voices or instruments performing the same part **3.** uttering the same words, or producing the same sound, at the same time

**u·nit** (yōō'nit) *n.* [< UNITY] **1.** *a)* the smallest whole number; one *b)* the number in the position just to the left of the decimal point **2.** any fixed quantity, amount, measure, etc. used as a standard; specif., the amount of a drug, vaccine, etc. needed to produce a given result **3.** *a)* a single person or group, esp. as distinguished from others or as part of a whole *b)* a single, distinct part, esp. one used for a specific purpose *[the lens unit of a camera]*

**U·ni·tar·i·an** (yōō'nə ter'ē ən) *n.* **1.** a person who denies the doctrine of the Trinity, rejecting the divinity of Jesus and holding that God exists as one person or being **2.** a member of a Christian denomination based on these beliefs and showing tolerance of differing religious views —*adj.* **1.** of Unitarians or their beliefs **2.** [u-] *same as* UNITARY —**U'ni·tar'i·an·ism** *n.*

**u·ni·tar·y** (yōō'nə ter'ē) *adj.* **1.** of a unit or units **2.** of, based on, or characterized by unity **3.** having the nature of or used as a unit

**unit character** *Genetics* a character or trait determined by a single gene or gene pair

**u·nite** (yoo nīt') *vt., vi.* **-nit'ed, -nit'ing** [< L. pp. of *unire,* to unite < *unus,* one] **1.** to put or join together so as to make one; combine into a whole **2.** *a)* to bring or come together in common cause, interest, action, etc.; join through fellowship, legal bonds, etc. *b)* to join in marriage

**u·nit·ed** (yoo nīt'id) *adj.* **1.** combined; joined **2.** of or resulting from joint action or association **3.** in agreement —**u·nit'ed·ly** *adv.* —**u·nit'ed·ness** *n.*

**United Arab Emirates** country consisting of seven Arab sheikdoms in E Arabia: 32,300 sq. mi.; pop. 179,000

**United Arab Republic** *former name (1961–71) of* EGYPT

**United Church of Christ** a Protestant denomination formed by a merger of denominations in 1957

**United Kingdom** country in W Europe, consisting of England, Scotland, Wales, Northern Ireland, the Channel Islands, & the Isle of Man: 94,217 sq. mi.; pop. 55,730,000; cap. London: in full, **United Kingdom of Great Britain and Northern Ireland**

**United Nations** an international organization of nations pledged to promote world peace and security under a charter signed in 1945 by 50 nations: 104 additional members had been admitted by 1980

**United States of America** country made up of the N. American area extending from the Atlantic Ocean to the Pacific Ocean between Canada and Mexico, together with Alaska & Hawaii: 3,615,211 sq. mi.; pop. 226,505,000 (1980); cap. Washington: also called **United States**

---

| | | | |
|---|---|---|---|
| unidentified | unimportant | uninfluenced | unintelligible |
| unidiomatic | unimposing | uninformed | unintended |
| unilluminated | unimpregnated | uninhabitable | unintentional |
| unillustrated | unimpressed | uninhabited | uninterested |
| unimaginable | unimpressionable | uninitiated | uninteresting |
| unimaginably | unimpressive | uninjured | uninterrupted |
| unimaginative | unincorporated | uninspired | unintimidated |
| unimitated | unindulged | uninspiring | uninventive |
| unimpaired | unindustrialized | uninstructed | uninvested |
| unimpassioned | unindustrious | uninsurable | uninvited |
| unimpeded | uninfected | uninsured | uninviting |
| unimplemented | uninfested | unintegrated | uninvolved |
| unimportance | uninflected | unintelligent | unissued |

---

fat, āpe, cär, ten, ēven, is, bīte; gō, hôrn, tōōl, look; oil, out; up, fʉr; get; joy; yet; chin; she; thin, *then*; zh, leisure; ŋ, ring; ə for *a* in *ago, e* in *agent, i* in *sanity, o* in *comply, u* in *focus;* ' as in *able* (ā'b'l); Fr. bál; ë, Fr. coeur; ö, Fr. feu; Fr. mon; δ, Fr. coq; ü, Fr. duc; r, Fr. cri; H, G. ich; kh, G. doch; ‡foreign; *hypothetical; < derived from. See inside front cover.

**u·ni·tive** (yōō'nə tiv) *adj.* tending to produce unity

**u·nit·ize** (yōō'nə tīz') *vt.* **-ized', -iz'ing** to make into a single unit —**u'nit·i·za'tion** *n.*

**unit pricing** a supplementary system of pricing commodities, esp. food items, by showing the prices in terms of standard units, as of an ounce or pint

**u·ni·ty** (yōō'nə tē) *n., pl.* **-ties** [< OFr. < L. *unitas* < *unus,* one] **1.** the state of being one, or united; oneness **2.** a single, separate thing **3.** harmony; agreement; concord **4.** *a)* unification *b)* a unified group or body **5.** a complex that is a union of related parts **6.** *a)* an arrangement of parts that will produce a single, harmonious effect in an artistic or literary production *b)* an effect so produced **7.** constancy or continuity of purpose, action, etc. **8.** *Math.* any quantity, magnitude, etc. identified as a unit, or 1

**Univ.** **1.** Universalist **2.** University

**u·ni·va·lent** (yōō'nə vā'lənt, yoo niv'ə lənt) *adj. Chem.* **1.** having one valence **2.** having a valence of one —**u'ni·va'lence, u'ni·va'len·cy** *n.*

**u·ni·valve** (yōō'nə valv') *n.* **1.** a mollusk having a one-piece shell, as a snail **2.** such a one-piece shell —*adj.* **1.** having a one-piece shell **2.** having one valve only

**u·ni·ver·sal** (yōō'nə vur's'l) *adj.* [< OFr. < L.: see UNIVERSE] **1.** of the universe; present or occurring everywhere **2.** of, for, or including all or the whole; not limited **3.** entire; whole **4.** broad in knowledge, interests, etc. **5.** that can be used for all kinds, forms, sizes, etc. **6.** used, intended to be used, or understood by all **7.** *Logic* predicating something of every member of a specified class —*n.* **1.** short for UNIVERSAL JOINT **2.** *Logic* a universal proposition —**u'ni·ver'sal·ness** *n.*

**u·ni·ver·sal·ism** (-iz'm) *n.* **1.** *same as* UNIVERSALITY **2.** [U-] the theological doctrine that all souls will eventually find salvation —**U'ni·ver'sal·ist** *adj., n.*

**u·ni·ver·sal·i·ty** (yōō'nə vər sal'ə tē) *n., pl.* **-ties** **1.** quality, state, or instance of being universal **2.** unlimited range, application, occurrence, etc.; comprehensiveness

**u·ni·ver·sal·ize** (-vur'sə līz') *vt.* **-ized', -iz'ing** to make universal —**u'ni·ver'sal·i·za'tion** *n.*

**universal joint** (or **coupling**) a joint or coupling that permits a swing of limited angle in any direction, esp. one used to transmit rotary motion from one shaft to another not in line with it, as in the drive shaft of an automobile

UNIVERSAL JOINT

**u·ni·verse** (yōō'nə vurs') *n.* [L. *universum* < *unus,* one + pp. of *vertere,* to turn] **1.** the totality of all the things that exist; the cosmos **2.** the world

**u·ni·ver·si·ty** (yōō'nə vur'sə tē) *n., pl.* **-ties** [< MFr. < ML. < L. *universitas,* the whole, a society: see prec.] **1.** an educational institution of the highest level, typically having one or more undergraduate colleges and also graduate and professional schools **2.** the buildings, students, faculty, or administrators of a university

**un·joint** (un joint') *vt.* **1.** to separate (a joint) **2.** to separate the joints of

**un·just** (-just') *adj.* not just or right; unfair —**un·just'ly** *adv.* —**un·just'ness** *n.*

**un·kempt** (-kempt') *adj.* [UN- + *kempt,* pp. of dial. *kemben,* to comb] **1.** not combed **2.** not tidy, neat, or groomed —**un·kempt'ness** *n.*

**un·kind** (-kīnd') *adj.* not sympathetic to or considerate of others **2.** harsh, severe, cruel, etc. —**un·kind'ness** *n.*

**un·kind·ly** (-kīnd'lē) *adj. same as* UNKIND —*adv.* in an unkind manner —**un·kind'li·ness** *n.*

**un·known** (-nōn') *adj.* **1.** not in one's knowledge, acquaintance, etc.; unfamiliar (*to*) **2.** not discovered, identified, etc. —*n.* an unknown person, thing, or quantity

**un·lace** (-lās') *vt.* **-laced', -lac'ing** to undo or unfasten the laces of

**un·lade** (-lād') *vt., vi.* **-lad'ed, -lad'ed** or **-lad'en, -lad'ing** **1.** to unload (a ship, etc.) **2.** to discharge (a cargo, etc.)

**un·latch** (-lach') *vt., vi.* to open by release of a latch

**un·law·ful** (-lô'fəl) *adj.* **1.** against the law; illegal **2.** against ethical standards; immoral —**un·law'ful·ly** *adv.*

**un·lead·ed** (-led'id) *adj.* not mixed with tetraethyl lead: said of gasoline

**un·learn** (-lurn') *vt., vi.* to forget (something learned) by a conscious effort, as in retraining

**un·learn·ed** (-lur'nid; *for 2* -lurnd') *adj.* **1.** *a)* not learned or educated; ignorant *b)* showing a lack of learning or education **2.** known or acquired without conscious study [*unlearned* tact] —**un·learn'ed·ly** *adv.*

**un·leash** (-lēsh') *vt.* to release from or as from a leash

**un·less** (ən les') *conj.* [earlier *on lesse that,* at less than] in any case other than; except if /he won't go *unless* she does/ —*prep.* except /no one, *unless* the doctor, knows/

**un·let·tered** (un let'ərd) *adj.* **1.** *a)* uneducated *b)* illiterate **2.** not marked with letters

**un·like** (-līk') *adj.* not alike; different; dissimilar —*prep.* **1.** not like; different from **2.** not characteristic of /it's *unlike* her to cry/ —**un·like'ness** *n.*

**un·like·ly** (-līk'lē) *adj.* **1.** not likely to happen or be true; improbable **2.** not likely to succeed —*adv.* improbably —**un·like'li·hood', un·like'li·ness** *n.*

**un·lim·ber**[1] (-lim'bər) *adj.* not limber; stiff —*vi., vt.* to make or become limber

**un·lim·ber**[2] (-lim'bər) *vt., vi.* **1.** to prepare (a field gun) for use by detaching the limber **2.** to get ready for action

**un·lim·it·ed** (-lim'it id) *adj.* **1.** without limits or restrictions **2.** without boundaries

**un·load** (-lōd') *vt.* **1.** *a)* to remove (a load, cargo, etc.) *b)* to take a load, etc. from **2.** *a)* to express or tell (one's troubles, etc.) freely *b)* to relieve of something that troubles, burdens, etc. **3.** to remove the charge from (a gun) **4.** to get rid of —*vi.* to unload something

**un·lock** (-läk') *vt.* **1.** *a)* to open (a lock) *b)* to open the lock of (a door, etc.) **2.** to let loose as if by opening a lock /to *unlock* a flood of tears/ **3.** to cause to separate /to *unlock* clenched jaws/ **4.** to lay open /to *unlock* a secret/ —*vi.* to get unlocked

**un·looked-for** (-lookt'fôr') *adj.* not expected or foreseen

**un·loose** (-loos') *vt.* **-loosed', -loos'ing** to make or set loose: also **un·loos'en**

**un·luck·y** (-luk'ē) *adj.* **-luck'i·er, -luck'i·est** not lucky; having or marked by bad luck; unfortunate —**un·luck'i·ly** *adv.*

**un·make** (-māk') *vt.* **-made', -mak'ing** **1.** to cause to be as before; make revert to original condition **2.** to ruin; destroy **3.** to depose from a position or authority

**un·man** (-man') *vt.* **-manned', -man'ning** **1.** to deprive of manly courage, confidence, etc. **2.** to castrate

**un·man·ly** (-man'lē) *adj.* **-li·er, -li·est** not manly; specif., cowardly, weak, effeminate, etc. —**un·man'li·ness** *n.*

**un·manned** (-mand') *adj.* not manned; specif., without men aboard and operating by automatic or remote control

**un·man·ner·ly** (-man'ər lē) *adj.* having or showing poor manners; rude; discourteous —*adv.* rudely

**un·mask** (-mask') *vt., vi.* **1.** to remove a mask or disguise (from) **2.** to show or appear in true character

**un·mean·ing** (-mēn'iŋ) *adj.* **1.** lacking in meaning or sense **2.** showing no sense or intelligence; expressionless

**un·meet** (-mēt') *adj.* not meet, or fit; unsuitable

**un·men·tion·a·ble** (un men'shən ə b'l) *adj.* not fit to be mentioned; not nice to talk about —*n.* [*pl.*] unmentionable things; specif., underwear: a humorous usage

**un·mer·ci·ful** (-mur'si fəl) *adj.* **1.** having or showing no mercy; cruel; pitiless **2.** excessive —**un·mer'ci·ful·ly** *adv.*

**un·mind·ful** (-mīnd'fəl) *adj.* not mindful; heedless

**un·mis·tak·a·ble** (un'mis tāk'ə b'l) *adj.* that cannot be mistaken or misunderstood; clear; plain —**un'mis·tak'a·bly** *adv.*

| | | | |
|---|---|---|---|
| unjoined | unlevied | unmagnified | unmeasurable |
| unjudicial | unlicensed | unmalleable | unmeasured |
| unjustifiable | unlifelike | unmanageable | unmechanical |
| unkept | unlighted | unmanifested | unmedicated |
| unkissed | unlikable | unmanufacturable | unmeditated |
| unknit | unlikeable | unmanufactured | unmelodious |
| unknot | unlined | unmarked | unmelted |
| unknowable | unlisted | unmarketable | unmended |
| unknowing | unlit | unmarred | unmentioned |
| unlabeled | unlively | unmarried | unmercenary |
| unlabored | unlocated | unmastered | unmerited |
| unladylike | unlovable | unmatchable | unmethodical |
| unlamented | unloved | unmatched | unmilitary |
| unlaundered | unlovely | unmated | unmilled |
| unleased | unloving | unmatted | unmingled |
| unleavened | unlubricated | unmeant | unmistaken |

# unmitigated     819     unreasoningly

**un·mit·i·gat·ed** (un mit′ə gāt′id) *adj.* **1.** not lessened or eased *[unmitigated* suffering*]* **2.** out-and-out; absolute *[an unmitigated* fool*]* —**un·mit′i·gat′ed·ly** *adv.*

**un·mor·al** (-môr′l) *adj. var. of* AMORAL

**un·muz·zle** (-muz′'l) *vt.* **-zled, -zling 1.** to free (a dog, etc.) from a muzzle **2.** to stop restraining or censoring

**un·nat·u·ral** (-nach′ər əl) *adj.* not natural; specif., *a)* abnormal; strange *b)* artificial; strained *c)* abnormally evil or cruel —**un·nat′u·ral·ly** *adv.* —**un·nat′u·ral·ness** *n.*

**un·nec·es·sar·y** (-nes′ə ser′ē) *adj.* not necessary or required; needless —**un·nec′es·sar′i·ly** *adv.*

**un·nerve** (-nurv′) *vt.* **-nerved′, -nerv′ing 1.** to cause to lose one's courage, confidence, etc. **2.** to make nervous

**un·num·bered** (-num′bərd) *adj.* **1.** not counted **2.** *same as* INNUMERABLE **3.** having no identifying number

**un·oc·cu·pied** (-äk′yə pīd′) *adj.* **1.** having no occupant; vacant; empty **2.** at leisure; idle

**un·or·gan·ized** (-ôr′gə nīzd′) *adj.* **1.** having no organic structure **2.** not having or following any regular order or system **3.** not having or belonging to a labor union

**un·pack** (-pak′) *vt.* **1.** to open and remove the packed contents of **2.** to take from a crate, trunk, etc. **3.** to remove a pack or load from —*vi.* to empty a packed trunk, etc.

**un·paged** (-pājd′) *adj.* having the pages unnumbered: said of a book, etc.

**un·par·al·leled** (-par′ə leld′) *adj.* that has no parallel, equal, or counterpart; unmatched

**un·par·lia·men·ta·ry** (-pär′lə men′tər ē, -trē) *adj.* contrary to parliamentary law or usage

**un·peg** (-peg′) *vt.* **-pegged′, -peg′ging 1.** to remove a peg or pegs from **2.** to unfasten or detach in this way

**un·peo·ple** (-pē′p'l) *vt.* **-pled, -pling** to reduce the population of; depopulate

**un·pin** (-pin′) *vt.* **-pinned′, -pin′ning 1.** to remove a pin or pins from **2.** to unfasten or detach in this way

**un·pleas·ant** (-plez′'nt) *adj.* not pleasant; offensive; disagreeable —**un·pleas′ant·ly** *adv.* —**un·pleas′ant·ness** *n.*

**un·plumbed** (-plumd′) *adj.* **1.** not sounded or measured with a plumb **2.** not fully plumbed or understood

**un·polled** (-pōld′) *adj.* **1.** *a)* not canvassed in a poll *b)* not cast or registered: said of votes **2.** unshorn

**un·pop·u·lar** (-päp′yə lər) *adj.* not popular; not liked by the public or the majority —**un′pop·u·lar′i·ty** (-yə lar′ə-tē) *n.*

**un·prac·ticed** (-prak′tist) *adj.* **1.** not practiced; not regularly done, etc. **2.** not skilled or experienced

**un·prec·e·dent·ed** (-pres′ə den′tid) *adj.* having no precedent or parallel; unheard-of; novel

**un·prej·u·diced** (-prej′ə dist) *adj.* **1.** without prejudice or bias; impartial **2.** not impaired

**un·prin·ci·pled** (-prin′sə p'ld) *adj.* characterized by lack of moral principles; unscrupulous

**un·print·a·ble** (-print′ə b'l) *adj.* not printable; not fit to be printed, as because of obscenity

**un·pro·fes·sion·al** (un′prə fesh′ən 'l) *adj.* **1.** violating the ethical code of a given profession **2.** not of, typical of, or belonging to a profession —**un′pro·fes′sion·al·ly** *adv.*

**un·qual·i·fied** (un kwäl′ə fid′) *adj.* **1.** lacking the necessary qualifications; not fit **2.** not limited; absolute *[an unqualified* success*]* —**un·qual′i·fied′ly** *adv.*

**un·ques·tion·a·ble** (-kwes′chən ə b'l) *adj.* **1.** not to be questioned, doubted, or disputed; certain **2.** with no exception or qualification —**un·ques′tion·a·bly** *adv.*

**un·ques·tioned** (-kwes′chənd) *adj.* not questioned; specif., *a)* not interrogated *b)* not disputed; accepted

**un·qui·et** (-kwī′ət) *adj.* not quiet; restless, disturbed, uneasy, anxious, etc. —*n.* an unquiet state —**un·qui′et·ly** *adv.* —**un·qui′et·ness** *n.*

**un·quote** (un′kwōt′) *interj.* I end the quotation: used in speech after a quotation

**un·rav·el** (un rav′'l) *vt.* **-eled** or **-elled, -el·ing** or **-el·ling 1.** to undo (something woven, tangled, etc.); separate the threads of **2.** to make clear; solve —*vi.* to become unraveled —**un·rav′el·ment** *n.*

**un·read** (-red′) *adj.* **1.** not read, as a book **2.** having read little or nothing **3.** unlearned (*in* a subject)

**un·read·y** (-red′ē) *adj.* **1.** not ready; unprepared, as for action **2.** not prompt or alert; slow —**un·read′i·ly** *adv.* —**un·read′i·ness** *n.*

**un·real** (-rē′əl, -rēl′) *adj.* not real; imaginary, false, etc. —**un′re·al′i·ty** (-rē al′ə tē) *n., pl.* **-ties**

**un·re·al·is·tic** (un′rē ə lis′tik) *adj.* not realistic; impractical; visionary —**un′re·al·is′ti·cal·ly** *adv.*

**un·rea·son** (un rē′z'n) *n.* lack of reason; irrationality

**un·rea·son·a·ble** (-ə b'l) *adj.* not reasonable; specif., *a)* having or showing little sense *b)* excessive; immoderate —**un·rea′son·a·ble·ness** *n.* —**un·rea′son·a·bly** *adv.*

**un·rea·son·ing** (-iŋ) *adj.* lacking reason or judgment; irrational —**un·rea′son·ing·ly** *adv.*

---

| | | | |
|---|---|---|---|
| unmixed | unoffending | unpersuaded | unpriced |
| unmodified | unoffensive | unpersuasive | unprinted |
| unmoistened | unoffered | unperturbed | unprivileged |
| unmolested | unofficial | unphilosophic | unprobed |
| unmollified | unofficious | unphilosophical | unprocessed |
| unmoor | unoiled | unpicked | unprocurable |
| unmortgaged | unopen | unpierced | unproductive |
| unmotivated | unopened | unpile | unprofaned |
| unmounted | unopposed | unpitied | unprofessed |
| unmourned | unoppressed | unpitying | unprofitable |
| unmovable | unordained | unplaced | unprogressive |
| unmoved | unoriginal | unplanned | unpromising |
| unmoving | unornamental | unplanted | unprompted |
| unmown | unorthodox | unplayable | unpronounceable |
| unmuffle | unostentatious | unplayed | unpronounced |
| unmurmuring | unowned | unpleasing | unpropitious |
| unmusical | unoxidized | unpledged | unproportionate |
| unmystified | unpacified | unpliable | unproposed |
| unnail | unpaid | unploughed | unprosperous |
| unnamable | unpaid-for | unplowed | unprotected |
| unnameable | unpainful | unplucked | unproved |
| unnamed | unpainted | unplug | unproven |
| unnaturalized | unpaired | unpoetic | unprovided |
| unnavigable | unpalatable | unpoetical | unprovoked |
| unnavigated | unpardonable | unpointed | unpruned |
| unneeded | unpardoned | unpoised | unpublished |
| unneedful | unparted | unpolished | unpunctual |
| unneighborly | unpasteurized | unpolitical | unpunished |
| unnoted | unpatched | unpolluted | unpurged |
| unnoticeable | unpatented | unpopulated | unpurified |
| unnoticed | unpatriotic | unposted | unquenchable |
| unnurtured | unpaved | unpredictable | unquenched |
| unobjectionable | unpeaceful | unpremeditated | unquestioning |
| unobliged | unpenetrated | unprepared | unquotable |
| unobliging | unpensioned | unprepossessing | unquoted |
| unobscured | unperceived | unprescribed | unransomed |
| unobservant | unperceiving | unpresentable | unrated |
| unobserved | unperceptive | unpreserved | unratified |
| unobserving | unperfected | unpressed | unreachable |
| unobstructed | unperformed | unpretending | unreadable |
| unobtainable | unperplexed | unpretentious | unrealized |
| unobtrusive | unpersuadable | unpreventable | unreasoned |

---

fat, āpe, cär; ten, ēven; is, bīte; gō, hôrn, tōōl, look; oil, out; up, fur; get; joy; yet; chin; she; thin, then; zh, leisure; ŋ, ring; ə for *a* in *ago, e* in *agent, i* in *sanity, o* in *comply, u* in *focus;* ' as in *able* (ā′b'l); Fr. bal; ë, Fr. coeur; ö, Fr. feu; Fr. mon; ô, Fr. coq; ü, Fr. duc; r, Fr. cri; H, G. ich; kh, G. doch; ‡foreign; *hypothetical; < derived from. See inside front cover.

**un·re·con·struct·ed** (un'rē kən struk'tid) *adj.* 1. not reconstructed 2. holding to an outmoded practice or attitude; specif., not reconciled to the Reconstruction

**un·reel** (un rēl') *vt., vi.* to unwind as from a reel

**un·re·gen·er·ate** (un'ri jen'ər it) *adj.* 1. not spiritually reborn 2. not converted to a particular belief, etc. 3. recalcitrant or obstinate Also **un're·gen'er·at'ed**

**un·re·lent·ing** (-ri len'tiŋ) *adj.* 1. refusing to yield or relent 2. without mercy or compassion 3. not relaxing, as in effort —**un're·lent'ing·ly** *adv.*

**un·re·li·gious** (-ri lij'əs) *adj.* 1. *same as* IRRELIGIOUS 2. not involving religion; nonreligious

**un·re·mit·ting** (-ri mit'iŋ) *adj.* not stopping, relaxing, or slackening; persistent —**un're·mit'ting·ly** *adv.*

**un·re·served** (-ri zurvd') *adj.* not reserved; specif., *a)* frank; open *b)* unlimited *c)* not set aside for advance sale, as seats —**un're·serv'ed·ly** (-zur'vid lē) *adv.*

**un·rest** (un rest') *n.* a troubled or disturbed state; restlessness; specif., a state of discontent close to revolt

**un·rid·dle** (-rid'') *vt.* **-dled, -dling** to solve or explain (a riddle, mystery, etc.)

**un·rig** (-rig') *vt.* **-rigged', -rig'ging** to strip of rigging

**un·right·eous** (-ri'chəs) *adj.* 1. not righteous; wicked; sinful 2. not right; unjust; unfair —**un·right'eous·ly** *adv.* —**un·right'eous·ness** *n.*

**un·rip** (-rip') *vt.* **-ripped', -rip'ping** to rip open; take apart or detach by ripping

**un·ripe** (-rip') *adj.* 1. not ripe or mature; green 2. not yet fully developed *[unripe* plans *]* —**un·ripe'ness** *n.*

**un·ri·valed, un·ri·valled** (-ri'v'ld) *adj.* having no rival, equal, or competitor; matchless; peerless

**un·roll** (-rōl') *vt.* 1. to open or extend (something rolled up) 2. to present to view; display —*vi.* to become unrolled

**un·ruf·fled** (-ruf''ld) *adj.* not ruffled, disturbed, or agitated; calm; smooth; serene

**un·rul·y** (-rōō'lē) *adj.* **-rul'i·er, -rul'i·est** [< ME. < *un-*, not + *reuly*, orderly] hard to control, restrain, or keep in order; disobedient, disorderly, etc. —**un·rul'i·ness** *n.*

**un·sad·dle** (-sad'l) *vt.* **-dled, -dling** 1. to take the saddle off (a horse, etc.) 2. to throw from the saddle; unhorse —*vi.* to take the saddle off a horse, etc.

**un·said** (-sed') *pt. & pp. of* UNSAY —*adj.* not expressed

**un·sat·u·rat·ed** (-sach'ə rāt'id) *adj.* not saturated 2. *Chem. a)* capable of dissolving more of the solute than has been dissolved *b)* designating on organic compound with a double or triple bond between carbon atoms, capable of combining with other elements or compounds by adding on at the bond

**un·sa·vor·y** (-sā'vər ē) *adj.* 1. orig., tasteless 2. unpleasant to taste or smell 3. morally offensive —**un·sa'·vor·i·ly** *adv.* —**un·sa'vor·i·ness** *n.*

**un·say** (-sā') *vt.* **-said', -say'ing** to take back or retract (what has been said)

**un·scathed** (-skā*th*d') *adj.* not hurt; unharmed

**un·scram·ble** (-skram'b'l) *vt.* **-bled, -bling** to cause to be no longer scrambled, disordered, etc.; specif., *Electronics* to make (incoming scrambled signals) intelligible at the receiver —**un·scram'bler** *n.*

**un·screw** (-skrōō') *vt.* 1. to remove a screw or screws from 2. *a)* to remove or loosen by removing a screw or screws, or by turning *b)* to remove a threaded top, cover, etc. from (a jar, etc.) —*vi.* to be or become unscrewed

**un·scru·pu·lous** (-skrōō'pyə ləs) *adj.* not scrupulous; heedless of what is right, just, etc.; unprincipled —**un·scru'pu·lous·ly** *adv.* —**un·scru'pu·lous·ness** *n.*

**un·seal** (-sēl') *vt.* 1. to break or remove the seal of 2. to open by or as by breaking a seal

**un·seam** (-sēm') *vt.* to open the seam or seams of; rip

**un·search·a·ble** (-surch'ə b'l) *adj.* that cannot be searched into; inscrutable —**un·search'a·bly** *adv.*

**un·sea·son·a·ble** (-sē'z'n ə b'l) *adj.* 1. not usual for the season 2. coming at the wrong time; untimely; inopportune —**un·sea'son·a·ble·ness** *n.* —**un·sea'son·a·bly** *adv.*

**un·seat** (-sēt') *vt.* 1. to throw or dislodge from a seat, saddle, etc. 2. to remove from office, deprive of rank, etc.

**un·seem·ly** (-sēm'lē) *adj.* not seemly; not proper; unbecoming —*adv.* unbecomingly —**un·seem'li·ness** *n.*

**un·self·ish** (-sel'fish) *adj.* not selfish; altruistic; generous —**un·self'ish·ly** *adv.* —**un·self'ish·ness** *n.*

**un·set·tle** (-set''l) *vt.* **-tled, -tling** to make unsettled, insecure, etc.; disturb, displace, disorder, etc. —*vi.* to become unsettled —**un·set'tle·ment** *n.*

**un·set·tled** (-set''ld) *adj.* 1. not settled; not in order, not stable, not decided or determined, etc. 2. not paid or disposed of, as a debt or estate 3. having no settlers 4. not established in a place or abode —**un·set'tled·ness** *n.*

**un·sex** (-seks') *vt.* to deprive of the qualities considered characteristic of one's sex

**un·shack·le** (-shak''l) *vt.* **-led, -ling** 1. to loosen or remove the shackles from 2. to free

**un·sheathe** (-shē*th*') *vt.* **-sheathed', -sheath'ing** to remove (a sword, knife, etc.) from a sheath

**un·ship** (-ship') *vt.* **-shipped', -ship'ping** 1. to unload from a ship 2. to remove (an oar, etc.) from position

**un·sight·ly** (-sīt'lē) *adj.* not pleasant to look at; ugly —**un·sight'li·ness** *n.*

| | | | |
|---|---|---|---|
| unrebuked | unrepairable | unrhythmic | unseeded |
| unreceived | unrepaired | unrhythmical | unseeing |
| unreceptive | unrepealed | unrightful | unseen |
| unreciprocated | unrepentant | unromantic | unsegmented |
| unreclaimable | unrepenting | unroof | unsegregated |
| unreclaimed | unreplaceable | unrounded | unselected |
| unrecognizable | unreplaced | unruled | unselective |
| unrecognized | unreplenished | unsafe | unsent |
| unrecommended | unreported | unsaintly | unsentimental |
| unrecompensed | unrepresentative | unsalable | unseparated |
| unreconcilable | unrepresented | unsalaried | unserved |
| unreconciled | unrepressed | unsaleable | unserviceable |
| unrecorded | unreprieved | unsalted | unset |
| unrecoverable | unreprimanded | unsampled | unsevered |
| unrectified | unrequested | unsanctified | unsewn |
| unredeemed | unrequited | unsanctioned | unshaded |
| unrefined | unresentful | unsanitary | unshadowed |
| unreflected | unresigned | unsated | unshakable |
| unreflecting | unresistant | unsatiable | unshakeable |
| unreformed | unresisting | unsatiated | unshaken |
| unrefreshed | unresolved | unsatisfactory | unshamed |
| unregarded | unresponsive | unsatisfied | unshaped |
| unregistered | unrested | unsatisfying | unshapely |
| unregretted | unrestful | unsaved | unshared |
| unregulated | unrestrainable | unscalable | unsharpened |
| unrehearsed | unrestrained | unscaled | unshaved |
| unrelated | unrestraint | unscanned | unshaven |
| unrelaxed | unrestricted | unscarred | unshed |
| unreliability | unretarded | unscented | unshelled |
| unreliable | unretentive | unscheduled | unsheltered |
| unrelieved | unretracted | unscholarly | unshielded |
| unremedied | unretrieved | unschooled | unshod |
| unremembered | unreturned | unscientific | unshorn |
| unremorseful | unrevealed | unscorched | unshortened |
| unremovable | unrevenged | unscraped | unshrinkable |
| unremoved | unreversed | unscratched | unshrinking |
| unremunerated | unreviewed | unscreened | unshriven |
| unremunerative | unrevised | unscriptural | unshrunk |
| unrenewed | unrevoked | unsculptured | unshuffled |
| unrenowned | unrewarded | unseasoned | unshut |
| unrentable | unrewarding | unseaworthy | unshuttered |
| unrented | unrhetorical | unseconded | unsifted |
| unrepaid | unrhymed | unsecured | unsighted |

**un·skilled** (-skild′) *adj.* not skilled; specif., having, showing, or requiring no special skill or training

**un·skill·ful** (-skil′fəl) *adj.* not skillful; awkward; clumsy —**un·skill′ful·ly** *adv.* —**un·skill′ful·ness** *n.*

**un·sling** (-sliŋ′) *vt.* -**slung′**, -**sling′ing** 1. to take (a rifle, etc.) from a slung position 2. to release from slings

**un·snap** (-snap′) *vt.* -**snapped′**, -**snap′ping** to undo the snap or snaps of, so as to loosen or detach

**un·snarl** (-snärl′) *vt.* to free of snarls; untangle

**un·so·cia·ble** (-sō′shə b'l) *adj.* 1. avoiding others; not sociable 2. not conducive to sociability —**un·so′cia·bil′i·ty, un·so′cia·ble·ness** *n.* —**un·so′cia·bly** *adv.*

**un·so·cial** (-sō′shəl) *adj.* having or showing a dislike for the society of others —**un·so′cial·ly** *adv.*

**un·sol·der** (-säd′ər) *vt.* 1. to take apart (things soldered together) 2. to disunite; separate

**un·so·phis·ti·cat·ed** (un′sə fis′tə kāt′id) *adj.* not sophisticated; artless, simple, unworldly, unrefined, etc. —**un′so·phis′ti·cat′ed·ly** *adv.* —**un′so·phis′ti·ca′tion** *n.*

**un·sound** (un sound′) *adj.* not sound or free from defect; specif., *a)* not normal or healthy *b)* not safe or secure *c)* not safe and secure financially *d)* not accurate, sensible, etc. *e)* light: said of sleep —**un·sound′ly** *adv.* —**un·sound′ness** *n.*

**un·spar·ing** (-sper′iŋ) *adj.* 1. not sparing or stinting; lavish 2. not merciful; severe —**un·spar′ing·ly** *adv.*

**un·speak·a·ble** (-spēk′ə b'l) *adj.* 1. that cannot be spoken 2. marvelous, awesome, etc. beyond expression 3. indescribably bad, evil, etc. —**un·speak′a·bly** *adv.*

**un·sta·ble** (-stā′b'l) *adj.* not stable; specif., *a)* easily upset, unbalanced, disturbed, etc. *b)* changeable *c)* unreliable; fickle *d) Chem., Physics* readily decomposing —**un·sta′ble·ness** *n.* —**un·sta′bly** *adv.*

**un·stead·y** (-sted′ē) *adj.* not steady; specif., *a)* not firm or stable *b)* changeable or erratic —*vt.* -**stead′ied**, -**stead′y·ing** to make unsteady —**un·stead′i·ly** *adv.* —**un·stead′i·ness** *n.*

**un·stick** (-stik′) *vt.* -**stuck′**, -**stick′ing** to loosen or free (something stuck)

**un·stop** (-stäp′) *vt.* -**stopped′**, -**stop′ping** 1. to remove the stopper from 2. to clear (an obstructed pipe, etc.)

**un·strap** (-strap′) *vt.* -**strapped′**, -**strap′ping** to loosen or remove the strap or straps of

**un·string** (-striŋ′) *vt.* -**strung′**, -**string′ing** 1. to loosen or remove the string or strings of 2. to remove from a string 3. to make nervous, weak, upset, etc.

**un·struc·tured** (-struk′chərd) *adj.* not formally or systematically organized; loose, free, open, etc.

**un·strung** (-struŋ′) *adj.* 1. nervous, upset, etc. 2. having the string(s) loosened or detached, as a bow

**un·stud·ied** (-stud′ēd) *adj.* 1. not got by study or conscious effort 2. spontaneous; natural; unaffected 3. not having studied; unlearned or unversed (*in*)

**un·sub·stan·tial** (un′səb stan′shəl) *adj.* not substantial; specif., *a)* having no material substance *b)* flimsy; light

*c)* unreal; visionary —**un′sub·stan·ti·al′i·ty** (-stan′shē al′ə tē) *n.* —**un′sub·stan′tial·ly** *adv.*

**un·suit·a·ble** (un sōōt′ə b'l, -syōōt′-) *adj.* not suitable; unbecoming; inappropriate —**un·suit′a·bly** *adv.*

**un·sung** (-suŋ′) *adj.* 1. not sung 2. not honored or celebrated, as in song or poetry

**un·sus·pect·ed** (un′sə spek′tid) *adj.* 1. not believed guilty, bad, harmful, etc. 2. not imagined existent, probable, etc. —**un′sus·pect′ed·ly** *adv.*

**un·tan·gle** (un taŋ′g'l) *vt.* -**gled**, -**gling** 1. to free from a snarl or tangle; disentangle 2. to free from confusion; clear up; put in order

**un·taught** (-tôt′) *adj.* 1. not taught or educated 2. got without being taught; natural

**un·ten·a·ble** (-ten′ə b'l) *adj.* 1. not tenable; that cannot be defended 2. incapable of being tenanted or occupied —**un′ten·a·bil′i·ty, un·ten′a·ble·ness** *n.*

**un·thank·ful** (-thaŋk′fəl) *adj.* 1. not thankful; ungrateful 2. thankless; unappreciated —**un·thank′ful·ly** *adv.* —**un·thank′ful·ness** *n.*

**un·think·a·ble** (-thiŋk′ə b'l) *adj.* 1. beyond thought or imagination; inconceivable 2. not to be considered; impossible —**un·think′a·bly** *adv.*

**un·think·ing** (-thiŋk′iŋ) *adj.* 1. showing little or no thought or consideration; thoughtless 2. lacking the ability to think; not rational —**un·think′ing·ly** *adv.*

**un·thread** (-thred′) *vt.* 1. to draw the thread from 2. to disentangle; unravel 3. to find one's way through (a maze, etc.)

**un·throne** (-thrōn′) *vt.* -**throned′**, -**thron′ing** same as DE-THRONE —**un·throne′ment** *n.*

**un·ti·dy** (-tī′dē) *adj.* -**di·er**, -**di·est** not tidy or neat; slovenly; messy —**un·ti′di·ly** *adv.* —**un·ti′di·ness** *n.*

**un·tie** (-tī′) *vt.* -**tied′**, -**ty′ing** 1. to loosen or undo (something tied or knotted) 2. to free, as from difficulty, restraint, etc. 3. to untangle —*vi.* to become untied

**un·til** (un til′, ən-) *prep.* [ME. *untill* < *un-* (see UNTO) + *till*, till] 1. up to the time of; till [*until* payday] 2. before (a specified time) [not *until* tomorrow] —*conj.* 1. up to the time when or that [*until* I go] 2. to the point, degree, etc. that [heat water *until* it boils] 3. before [don't leave *until* he does]

**un·time·ly** (un tīm′lē) *adj.* 1. before the usual or expected time; premature [his *untimely* death] 2. at the wrong time; inopportune —*adv.* 1. prematurely 2. inopportunely —**un·time′li·ness** *n.*

**un·to** (un′tōō, -too) *prep.* [ME. *un-*, until + *to*, to] *archaic or poet. var. of:* 1. TO 2. UNTIL

**un·told** (un tōld′) *adj.* 1. not told or revealed 2. too great, numerous, etc. to be counted, measured, or described

**un·touch·a·ble** (-tuch′ə b'l) *adj.* that cannot or should not be touched —*n.* 1. an untouchable person or thing 2. in India, formerly, one whose touch was regarded as defiling to higher-caste Hindus —**un′touch·a·bil′i·ty** *n.*

**un·to·ward** (un tō′ərd, -tôrd′) *adj.* 1. inappropriate, im-

| | | | |
|---|---|---|---|
| unsigned | unspilled | unsullied | untalked-of |
| unsilenced | unspiritual | unsunk | untamable |
| unsimplified | unspoiled | unsupervised | untamed |
| unsingable | unspoken | unsupportable | untanned |
| unsinkable | unsporting | unsupported | untapped |
| unsisterly | unsportsmanlike | unsuppressed | untarnished |
| unsized | unspotted | unsure | untasted |
| unskeptical | unsprung | unsurmountable | untaxed |
| unslackened | unsquandered | unsurpassable | unteachable |
| unslaked | unstained | unsurpassed | untechnical |
| unsleeping | unstamped | unsurprised | untempered |
| unsliced | unstandardized | unsusceptible | untenanted |
| unsmiling | unstarched | unsuspecting | untended |
| unsmoked | unstarred | unsuspicious | unterrified |
| unsoftened | unstated | unsustained | untested |
| unsoiled | unstatesmanlike | unswayed | untethered |
| unsold | unstemmed | unsweetened | unthanked |
| unsoldierly | unsterilized | unswept | unthatched |
| unsolicited | unstinted | unswerving | unthawed |
| unsolidified | unstitched | unswollen | untheatrical |
| unsolvable | unstoppable | unsworn | unthoughtful |
| unsolved | unstrained | unsymmetrical | unthought-of |
| unsorted | unstratified | unsympathetic | unthrifty |
| unsought | unstressed | unsympathizing | unticketed |
| unsounded | unstriated | unsystematic | untillable |
| unsowed | unstuffed | unsystematized | untilled |
| unsown | unsubdued | untabulated | untinged |
| unspecialized | unsubmissive | untack | untired |
| unspecific | unsubsidized | untactful | untiring |
| unspecified | unsubstantiated | untagged | untitled |
| unspectacular | unsuccessful | untainted | untorn |
| unspent | unsuited | untalented | untouched |

fat, āpe, cär; ten, ēven; is, bīte; gō, hôrn, tōōl, lŏŏk; ôil, out; up, fur; get; joy; yet; chin; she; thin, *th*en; zh, leisure; ŋ, ring; ə for *a* in *ago*, *e* in *agent*, *i* in *sanity*, *o* in *comply*, *u* in *focus*; ′ as in *able* (ā′b'l); Fr. bàl; ë, Fr. coeur; ö, Fr. feu; ô, Fr. mon; ô, Fr. coq; ü, Fr. duc; r, Fr. cri; H, G. ich; kh, G. doch; ‡foreign; *hypothetical; < derived from. See inside front cover.

proper, unseemly, etc. *[an untoward remark]* **2.** not favorable or fortunate *[untoward circumstances]*

**un·true** (un trōō′) *adj.* **1.** not correct; false **2.** not agreeing with a standard or rule **3.** not faithful or loyal

**un·truth** (-trōōth′) *n.* **1.** the quality or state of being untrue **2.** an untrue statement; falsehood; lie

**un·truth·ful** (-trōōth′fəl) *adj.* **1.** not in accordance with the truth **2.** telling a lie or lies, esp. habitually —**un·truth′-ful·ly** *adv.* —**un·truth′ful·ness** *n.*

**un·tu·tored** (-tōōt′ərd, -tyōōt′-) *adj.* **1.** not tutored or taught; uneducated **2.** simple; naive; unsophisticated

**un·twine** (-twīn′) *vt.* **-twined′, -twin′ing** to undo (something twined or twisted); disentangle or unwind —*vi.* to become untwined

**un·twist** (-twist′) *vt., vi.* to turn in the opposite direction so as to loosen or separate; untwine

**un·used** (-yōōzd′) *adj.* **1.** not in use **2.** that has never been used **3.** unaccustomed (*to*)

**un·u·su·al** (-yōō′zhōō wəl) *adj.* not usual or common; rare —**un·u′su·al·ly** *adv.* —**un·u′su·al·ness** *n.*

**un·ut·ter·a·ble** (-ut′ər ə b'l) *adj.* that cannot be expressed or described —**un·ut′ter·a·bly** *adv.*

**un·var·nished** (-vär′nisht) *adj.* **1.** not varnished **2.** plain; simple; unadorned *[the unvarnished truth]*

**un·veil** (un vāl′) *vt.* to reveal as by removing a veil or covering from —*vi.* to take off a veil; reveal oneself

**un·veil·ing** (-iŋ) *n.* a formal or ceremonial removal of a covering from a new statue, tombstone, etc.

**un·voiced** (un voist′) *adj.* **1.** not uttered or expressed **2.** *Phonet.* same as VOICELESS

**un·war·y** (-wer′ē) *adj.* not wary or cautious; not alert to possible danger, trickery, etc. —**un·war′i·ly** *adv.*

**un·wea·ried** (-wir′ēd) *adj.* **1.** not weary or tired **2.** never wearying; tireless; indefatigable

**un·well** (-wel′) *adj.* not well; ailing; ill; sick

**un·wept** (-wept′) *adj.* **1.** not shed *[unwept tears]* **2.** not wept for; unmourned

**un·whole·some** (-hōl′səm) *adj.* not wholesome; specif., *a)* harmful to body or mind *b)* unhealthy or unhealthy-looking *c)* morally bad —**un·whole′some·ness** *n.*

**un·wield·y** (-wēl′dē) *adj.* hard to wield, manage, handle, etc. because of weight, shape, etc. —**un·wield′i·ness** *n.*

**un·will·ing** (-wil′iŋ) *adj.* **1.** not willing; reluctant **2.** done, given, etc. against one's will —**un·will′ing·ly** *adv.*

**un·wind** (-wīnd′) *vt.* **-wound′, -wind′ing** **1.** to wind off or undo (something wound) **2.** to uncoil **3.** to untangle **4.** to relax —*vi.* to become unwound, relaxed, etc.

**un·wise** (-wīz′) *adj.* not wise; foolish or imprudent

**un·wit·ting** (-wit′iŋ) *adj.* **1.** not knowing; unaware **2.** not intended; unintentional —**un·wit′ting·ly** *adv.*

**un·wont·ed** (-wun′tid, -wôn′-) *adj.* not common, usual, or habitual —**un·wont′ed·ly** *adv.*

**un·world·ly** (-wurld′lē) *adj.* **1.** unearthly or otherworldly **2.** not worldly-wise; unsophisticated

**un·wor·thy** (-wur′the) *adj.* **-thi·er, -thi·est** **1.** lacking merit or value; worthless **2.** not deserving (often with *of*) **3.** not fit or becoming (usually with *of*) **4.** not deserved — **un·wor′thi·ly** *adv.* —**un·wor′thi·ness** *n.*

**un·wrap** (-rap′) *vt.* **-wrapped′, -wrap′ping** to take off the wrapping of; open or undo (something wrapped) —*vi.* to become unwrapped

**un·writ·ten** (-rit′'n) *adj.* **1.** not in writing; not written or printed **2.** operating only through custom or tradition *[an unwritten rule]* **3.** not written on; blank

**unwritten law** law based on custom, usage, court decisions, etc. rather than on the action of a lawmaking body

**un·yoke** (-yōk′) *vt.* **-yoked′, -yok′ing** **1.** to release from a yoke **2.** to separate or disconnect —*vi.* **1.** to become unyoked **2.** to remove a yoke

**un·zip** (-zip′) *vt., vi.* **-zipped′, -zip′ping** **1.** to open (a zipper) **2.** to open the zipper of (a garment, etc.)

**up¹** (up) *adv.* [OE.] **1.** to a higher place **2.** in or on a higher position or level **3.** in a direction or place thought of as higher or above **4.** above the horizon **5.** to a later period *[from childhood up]* **6.** to a higher condition or rank **7.** to a higher amount, degree, etc. **8.** *a)* in or into a standing or upright position *b)* out of bed **9.** in or into action, view, consideration, etc. *[to bring a matter up]* **10.** aside; away; by *[lay up grain]* **11.** so as to be even with in space, time, degree, etc. *[keep up with the times]* **12.** so as to be tightly closed, bound, packed, etc. *[tie it up]* **13.** completely *[eat it up]* **14.** so as to stop *[to rein up a horse]* **15.** *Baseball* to one's turn at batting; at bat **16.** *Naut.* windward **17.** *Sports & Games* ahead (by a specified number of points, goals, etc.) **18.** [Colloq.] served in a cocktail glass without ice cubes The adverb *up* is also used with verbs *a)* to form combinations having special meanings (Ex.: show *up*) *b)* as an intensive (Ex.: dress *up*) *c)* as a virtually meaningless addition (Ex.: light *up* a cigarette) —*prep.* **1.** to, toward, or at a higher place, condition, rank, etc. on or in **2.** at, along, or toward a more distant part of *[up the road]* **3.** toward the source or against the flow, etc. of *[up the river]* **4.** in or toward the interior or more northerly part of (a country, territory, etc.) —*adj.* **1.** being in or directed toward a higher position, condition, etc. **2.** *a)* above the ground *b)* above the horizon **3.** higher in amount, degree, etc. *[rents are up]* **4.** *a)* standing or upright *b)* out of bed **5.** active, excited, etc. **6.** even with in space, time, etc. **7.** in the inner or higher part of a country, etc. **8.** at an end; over *[time is up]* **9.** [Colloq.] happening *[what's up?]* **10.** *Baseball* at bat —*n.* **1.** an upward slope, movement, course, etc. **2.** a train, bus, etc. headed up **3.** a period or state of prosperity, good luck, etc. —*vi.* **upped, up′ping** [Colloq.] to get up; rise: sometimes used without inflection to emphasize a second verb *[he up and left]* —*vt.* [Colloq.] to put up, lift up, or take up —**on the up and up** [Slang] honest —**up against** [Colloq.] faced with —**up against it** in difficulty, esp. financially —**up and around** (or **about**) out of bed and again active, as after an illness —**up and doing** busy; active —**up for** **1.** presented or considered for (an elective office, election, sale, auction, etc.) **2.** before a court for (trial) or on (a charge) —**up front** [Colloq.] **1.** very honest or forthright; candid **2.** in advance *[to pay for something up front]* —**up on** (or **in**) [Colloq.] well-informed about —**ups and downs** good periods and bad periods —**up to** [Colloq.] **1.** occupied with; doing; scheming *[up to mischief]* **2.** equal to (a task, etc.); capable of (doing, undertaking, etc.) **3.** as many as *[up to four]* **4.** as far as *[up to here]* **5.** dependent upon; incumbent upon —**up with!** give or restore power, favor, etc. to!

**up²** (up) *adv.* [phonetic respelling of AP(IECE)] apiece; each *[the score is seven up]*

**up-** *a combining form meaning* up *[uphill]*

**up-and-com·ing** (up′n kum′iŋ) *adj.* **1.** enterprising, alert, and promising **2.** gaining in importance or status

**up-and-down** (-doun′) *adj.* **1.** going alternately up and down, to and fro, etc. **2.** variable; changing; fluctuating

**u·pas** (yōō′pəs) *n.* [short for Malay *pohon upas*, tree of

| | | | |
|---|---|---|---|
| untraceable | unusable | unwarned | unwilling |
| untraced | unutilizable | unwarped | unwincing |
| untracked | unutilized | unwarrantable | unwinking |
| untrained | unuttered | unwarranted | unwished |
| untrammeled | unvaccinated | unwashed | unwished-for |
| untransferable | unvacillating | unwasted | unwithered |
| untransferred | unvalued | unwatched | unwithering |
| untranslatable | unvanquished | unwatchful | unwitnessed |
| untranslated | unvaried | unwatered | unwomanly |
| untransmitted | unvarying | unwavering | unwon |
| untrapped | unventilated | unwaxed | unwooded |
| untraveled | unverifiable | unweakened | unwooed |
| untraversed | unverified | unweaned | unworkable |
| untreated | unversed | unwearable | unworked |
| untried | unvexed | unweary | unworkmanlike |
| untrimmed | unvindicated | unwearying | unworn |
| untrod | unviolated | unweathered | unworried |
| untroubled | unvisited | unweave | unworshiped |
| untrustworthy | unvocalized | unwed | unwounded |
| untufted | unvulcanized | unwedded | unwoven |
| untunable | unwakened | unweeded | unwrinkled |
| untuned | unwalled | unweighed | unwrought |
| untuneful | unwaning | unwelcome | unyielding |
| unturned | unwanted | unwelded | unyouthful |
| untwilled | unwarlike | unwetted | unzealous |
| untypical | unwarmed | unwifely | unzoned |

poison] **1.** a tall Javanese tree of the mulberry family, whose whitish bark yields a poisonous juice **2.** the juice

**up·beat** (up′bēt′) *n.* **1.** an upward trend; upswing **2.** *Music* an upward stroke made by a conductor to show an unaccented beat —*adj.* lively; cheerful

**up·braid** (up brād′) *vt.* [< OE. < *up-*, up + *bregdan*, to pull, shake] to rebuke severely; censure sharply

**up·bring·ing** (up′briŋ′iŋ) *n.* the training and education received while growing up; rearing; nurture

**up·chuck** (-chuk′) *vi., vt., n.* [Slang] *same as* VOMIT

**up·com·ing** (-kum′iŋ) *adj.* coming soon; forthcoming

**up·coun·try** (-kun′trē) *adj.* of or located in the interior of a country —*n.* the interior of a country —*adv.* in or toward the interior of a country

**up·date** (up dāt′) *vt.* -dat′ed, -dat′ing to bring up to date; make conform to the most recent facts, methods, ideas, etc.

**up·draft** (up′draft′) *n.* an upward air current

**up·end** (up end′) *vt., vi.* **1.** to turn or stand on end **2.** to upset or topple

**up·grade** (up′grād′; *for v. usually* up grād′) *n.* an upward slope, esp. in a road —*adj., adv.* uphill; upward —*vt.* -grad′ed, -grad′ing **1.** to promote to a more skilled job at higher pay **2.** to raise in importance, value, etc. —**on the upgrade** advancing or improving in status, health, etc.

**up·heav·al** (up hē′v′l) *n.* **1.** an upheaving, as of the earth's crust by an earthquake **2.** a sudden, violent change

**up·heave** (-hēv′) *vt.* -heaved′ or -hove′, -heav′ing to heave or lift up —*vi.* to rise as if forced up

**up·hill** (up′hil′) *adv.* **1.** toward the top of a hill **2.** with difficulty —*adj.* **1.** going or sloping up **2.** requiring great effort

**up·hold** (up hōld′) *vt.* -held′, -hold′ing **1.** to hold up; raise **2.** to keep from falling; support **3.** to give moral support to **4.** to decide in favor of; support against opposition —**up·hold′er** *n.*

**up·hol·ster** (up hōl′stər, ə pōl′-) *vt.* [altered < ME. *upholder,* dealer in small wares < *upholden,* to repair] to fit out (furniture, etc.) with covering, padding, springs, etc. — **up·hol′ster·er** *n.*

**up·hol·ster·y** (-stər ē, -strē) *n., pl.* -ster·ies **1.** the materials used in upholstering **2.** the business or work of upholstering

**up·keep** (up′kēp′) *n.* **1.** the keeping of buildings, equipment, etc.; maintenance **2.** the cost of this **3.** state of repair

**up·land** (-lənd, -land′) *n.* land elevated above other land — *adj.* of or situated in upland

**up·lift** (up lift′; *for n.* up′lift′) *vt.* **1.** to lift up; elevate **2.** to raise to a higher moral, social, or cultural level —*n.* **1.** *a)* an uplifting *b)* any influence, movement, etc. aimed at uplifting society **2.** a brassiere designed to lift and support the breasts —**up·lift′er** *n.* —**up′lift′ment** *n.*

**up·most** (up′mōst′) *adj. same as* UPPERMOST

**up·on** (ə pän′) *prep.* on, or up and on: generally interchangeable with *on,* the choice depending on idiom, sentence rhythm, etc. —*adv.* on: used only for completing a verb *[a* canvas not painted *upon]*

**up·per** (up′ər) *adj.* **1.** higher in place or physical position **2.** farther north or farther inland **3.** higher in rank, authority, etc. **4.** [U-] *Geol.* later: used of a division of a period — *n.* the part of a shoe or boot above the sole —**on one's uppers** [Colloq.] **1.** wearing shoes with soles worn through **2.** in need; poor

**upper case** [from their being kept in the upper of two cases of type] capital-letter type used in printing, as distinguished from small letters (*lower case*) —**up′per-case′** *adj.* —**up′per-case′** *vt.* -cased′, -cas′ing

**upper class** the social class above the middle class; rich, socially prominent, or aristocratic class

**up·per·class·man** (up′ər klas′mən) *n., pl.* -men a junior or senior in a high school or college

**up·per·cut** (up′ər kut′) *n. Boxing* a short, swinging blow directed upward —*vt., vi.* -cut′, -cut′ting to hit with an uppercut

**upper hand** the position of advantage or control

**Upper House** [*often* u- h-] the smaller and less representative branch of a bicameral legislature, as the U.S. Senate

**up·per·most** (up′ər mōst′) *adj.* highest in place, power, authority, etc.; predominant; foremost —*adv.* in the highest place, rank, etc.

**Upper Vol·ta** (väl′tə) country in W Africa, north of Ghana: 108,880 sq. mi.; pop. 5,384,000

**up·pish** (up′ish) *adj.* [Colloq.] inclined to be arrogant, snobbish, etc.: also **up′pi·ty** (-ə tē) —**up′pish·ness** *n.*

**Upp·sa·la** (oop′sä′lä; *E.* up′sə le) city in EC Sweden: pop. 102,000: also sp. **Up′sa·la**

**up·raise** (up rāz′) *vt.* -raised′, -rais′ing to raise up

**up·rear** (-rir′) *vt.* **1.** to lift up **2.** to erect; build **3.** to exalt **4.** to bring up; rear —*vi.* to rise up

**up·right** (up′rīt′; *also for adv.* up rīt′) *adj.* **1.** standing or directed straight up; erect **2.** honest and just; honorable — *adv.* in an upright position —*n.* **1.** a being upright or vertical **2.** something having an upright position **3.** *short for* UPRIGHT PIANO —**up′right′ly** *adv.* —**up′right′ness** *n.*

**upright piano** a piano with a vertical rectangular body

**up·rise** (up rīz′; *for n.* up′rīz′) *vi.* -rose′, -ris′en, -ris′ing **1.** to rise; get up, move up, rise into view, swell, etc. **2.** to rise in revolt —*n.* **1.** a rising up **2.** an upward slope

**up·ris·ing** (up′rīz′iŋ) *n.* a rising up; specif., a revolt

**up·roar** (-rôr′) *n.* [Du. *oproer,* a stirring up] **1.** a violent disturbance; tumult **2.** loud, confused noise; din

**up·roar·i·ous** (up rôr′ē əs) *adj.* **1.** making, or marked by, an uproar; tumultuous **2.** *a)* loud and boisterous, as laughter *b)* causing such laughter *[an uproarious joke]* —**up·roar′i·ous·ly** *adv.* —**up·roar′i·ous·ness** *n.*

**up·root** (up rōōt′, -root′) *vt.* **1.** to tear up by the roots **2.** to destroy or remove utterly; eradicate

**up·sa·dai·sy** (up′sə dā′zē) *interj. var. of* UPSY-DAISY

**up·set** (up set′; *for n. and occas. adj.* up′set′) *vt.* -set′, -set′ting **1.** *a)* to tip over; overturn *b)* to defeat, esp. unexpectedly **2.** *a)* to disturb the functioning, fulfillment, or completion of *b)* to disturb mentally, emotionally, or physically —*vi.* to become overturned —*n.* an upsetting or being upset; specif., *a)* an overturning *b)* a defeat, esp. when unexpected *c)* a disturbance; disorder —*adj.* **1.** overturned **2.** defeated **3.** disturbed —**up·set′ter** *n.*

**up·shot** (up′shät′) *n.* [orig., the final shot in an archery match] the conclusion; result; outcome

**up·side** (-sīd′) *n.* the upper side or part

**upside down 1.** with the top side or part underneath **2.** in disorder; topsy-turvy —**up′side′-down′** *adj.*

**upside-down cake** a cake baked with a bottom layer of fruit and turned upside down before serving

**up·si·lon** (yōōp′sə län′, up′-; -lən) *n.* [Gr.] the twentieth letter of the Greek alphabet (Υ, υ)

**up·stage** (up′stāj′; *for v.* up stāj′) *adv.* toward or at the rear of a stage —*adj.* **1.** of or having to do with the rear of a stage **2.** haughty and aloof —*vt.* -staged′, -stag′ing to draw attention, as of an audience, to oneself at the expense of (another)

**up·stairs** (up′sterz′) *adv.* **1.** up the stairs **2.** on or to an upper floor or higher level —*adj.* situated on an upper floor —*n.* an upper floor or floors —**kick upstairs** [Colloq.] to promote from a position of power to a higher but less powerful position

**up·stand·ing** (up stan′diŋ) *adj.* **1.** standing straight; erect **2.** upright in character and behavior; honorable

**up·start¹** (up′stärt′) *n.* a person who has recently come into wealth, power, etc., esp. one who is aggressive; parvenu — *adj.* of or characteristic of an upstart

**up·start²** (up stärt′) *vi., vt.* to start, or spring, up or cause to spring up

**up·state** (up′stāt′) *n.* that part of a State farther to the north or away from a large city; esp., the northern part of New York —*adj., adv.* in, to, or from upstate

**up·stream** (-strēm′) *adv., adj.* in the direction against the current of a stream

**up·surge** (up surj′; *for n.* up′surj′) *vi.* -surged′, -surg′ing to surge up —*n.* a surge upward

**up·sweep** (up′swēp′; *for v.* up swēp′) *n.* **1.** a sweep or curve upward **2.** an upswept hairdo —*vt., vi.* -swept′, -sweep′ing to sweep or curve upward

**up·swept** (up′swept′) *adj.* **1.** curved upward **2.** designating or of a style of hairdo in which the hair is combed up in the back and piled on the top of the head

**up·swing** (up′swiŋ′; *for v.* up swiŋ′) *n.* a swing or trend upward; specif., an upward trend in business —*vi.* -swung′, -swing′ing **1.** to swing upward **2.** to advance

**up·sy-dai·sy** (up′sə dā′zē, up′sē-) *interj.* [baby-talk extension of UPSI] up you go: used playfully in lifting a baby

**up·take** (up′tāk′) *n.* the act of taking up; a drawing up, absorbing, etc. —**quick (or slow) on the uptake** [Colloq.] quick (or slow) to understand or comprehend

**up·thrust** (-thrust′) *n.* **1.** an upward push or thrust **2.** an upheaval of a part of the earth's crust

**up·tight, up·tight** (up′tīt′) *adj.* [Slang] **1.** very tense, nervous, anxious, etc. **2.** overly conventional or strict in attitudes **3.** in a bad way or state Also **up tight**

**up-to-date** (up′tə dāt′) *adj.* **1.** extending to the present time **2.** keeping up with what is most recent, modern, etc. —**up′-to-date′ness** *n.*

**up·town** (up'toun') *adj., adv.* of, in, like, to, or toward the upper part of a city or town —*n.* the uptown part

**up·turn** (up turn'; *for n.* up'turn') *vt., vi.* to turn up, upward, or over —*n.* an upward turn, curve, or trend —**up'turned'** *adj.*

**up·ward** (up'wərd) *adv., adj.* **1.** toward a higher place, position, degree, etc. **2.** from an earlier to a later time **3.** beyond (an indicated price, amount, etc.) *[tickets cost one dollar and upward]* Also **up'wards** *adv.* —**upwards** (or **upward**) **of** more than —**up'ward·ly** *adv.*

**up·wind** (up'wind') *adv., adj.* in the direction from which the wind is blowing or usually blows

**Ur** (ur) ancient Sumerian city on the Euphrates River, in what is now S Iraq

**u·ra·cil** (yoor'ə sil) *n.* [UR(O)- + AC(ETIC) + -IL(E)] a crystalline base, C₄H₄O₂N₂, found in ribonucleic acid

**U·ral** (yoor'əl) **1.** [*pl.*] mountain system in the W R.S.F.S.R., traditionally regarded as the boundary between Europe & Asia: also **Ural Mountains 2.** river flowing from the S section of these mountains into the Caspian Sea

**U·ral-Al·ta·ic** (-al tā'ik) *n.* the group of languages which includes, among others, the Uralic and Altaic families —*adj.* **1.** designating or of this group of languages **2.** of the peoples speaking these languages

**U·ral·ic** (yoo ral'ik, -rā'lik) *adj.* designating or of the family of languages including Finno-Ugric and Samoyed —*n.* this family of languages Also **U·ra'li·an** (-rā'lē ən)

**U·ra·ni·a** (yoo rā'nē ə) *Gr. Myth.* the Muse of astronomy

**u·ra·ni·um** (yoo rā'nē əm) *n.* [ModL. < URANUS, the planet] a very hardα, heavy, radioactive metallic chemical element: it is found only in combination, and its isotopes are important in work on atomic energy: symbol, U; at. wt., 238.03; at. no., 92

**U·ra·nus** (yoor'ə nəs, yoo rā'nəs) **1.** *Gr. Myth.* a god who personified the heavens and was the father of the Titans, Furies, and Cyclopes: he was overthrown by his son Cronus (Saturn) **2.** a planet of the solar system, seventh in distance from the sun: diameter, c. 29,500 mi.

**u·rate** (yoor'āt) *n.* a salt of uric acid

**ur·ban** (ur'bən) *adj.* [< L. < urbs, a city] **1.** of, in, or constituting a city or town **2.** characteristic of the city as distinguished from the country

**Ur·ban II** (ur'bən) 1042?-99; Pope (1088-99)

**ur·bane** (ur bān') *adj.* [< L.: see URBAN] polite and courteous in a smooth, polished way; refined —**ur·bane'ly** *adv.* —**ur·bane'ness** *n.*

**ur·ban·ism** (ur'bən iz'm) *n.* **1.** *a)* the character of life in the cities *b)* the study of this **2.** concentration of the population in the cities —**ur'ban·ist** *n., adj.*

**ur·ban·ite** (-īt') *n.* a person living in a city

**ur·ban·i·ty** (ur ban'ə tē) *n., pl.* **-ties 1.** the quality of being urbane **2.** [*pl.*] civilities, courtesies, or amenities

**ur·ban·ize** (ur'bə nīz') *vt.* **-ized', -iz'ing** to change from rural to urban —**ur'ban·i·za'tion** *n.*

**ur·ban·ol·o·gist** (ur'bə näl'ə jist) *n.* [URBAN + -o- + -LOG(Y) + -IST] a specialist in urban problems

**urban renewal** the renewal of urban areas suffering from neglect and decay, as by clearing slums and constructing new housing projects, etc.

**ur·chin** (ur'chin) *n.* [< OFr. < L. ericius, a hedgehog < er, hedgehog] **1.** *same as* SEA URCHIN **2.** a small boy, or any youngster, esp. one who is mischievous

**Ur·du** (oor'dōō) *n.* an Indic language, a variant of Hindi written with Arabic characters: an official language of Pakistan

**-ure** (ər) [Fr. < L. -ura] a suffix meaning: **1.** act or result of being *[exposure]* **2.** agent, instrument, or scope of *[legislature]* **3.** state of being *[composure]*

**u·re·a** (yoo rē'ə, yoor'ē ə) *n.* [ModL. < Fr. < Gr. ouron, urine] a soluble, crystalline solid, CO(NH₂)₂, found in the urine of mammals or produced synthetically: used in making plastics, adhesives, etc. —**u·re'al, u·re'ic** *adj.*

**u·re·mi·a** (yoo rē'mē ə, -rēm'yə) *n.* [ModL. < Gr. ouron, urine + haima, blood] a toxic condition caused by the presence in the blood of waste products normally eliminated in the urine —**u·re'mic** *adj.*

**u·re·ter** (yoo rēt'ər) *n.* [ModL. < Gr. < ourein, to urinate] a duct or tube that carries urine from a kidney to the bladder or cloaca —**u·re'ter·al, u·re·ter·ic** (yoor'ə ter'ik) *adj.*

**u·re·thra** (yoo rē'thrə) *n., pl.* **-thrae** (-thrē), **-thras** [LL. < Gr. < ouron, urine] the canal through which urine is discharged from the bladder in most mammals: in the male, semen is also discharged through the urethra —**u·re'thral** *adj.*

**U·rey** (yoor'ē), **Harold Clay·ton** (klā't'n) 1893- ; U.S. chemist

**urge** (urj) *vt.* **urged, urg'ing** [L. urgere, to press hard] **1.** *a)* to press upon the attention; speak in favor of *[to urge caution]* *b)* to entreat or plead with; exhort **2.** to stimulate or incite; provoke **3.** to drive or force onward; impel —*vi.* **1.** to make an earnest presentation of arguments, claims, charges, etc. **2.** to exert a force that impels, as to action

—*n.* **1.** the act of urging **2.** an impulse to do a certain thing —**urg'er** *n.*

**ur·gen·cy** (ur'jən sē) *n., pl.* **-cies 1.** an urgent quality or state; need for action, haste, etc. **2.** insistence; importunity **3.** something urgent

**ur·gent** (-jənt) *adj.* [MFr. < L. prp. of urgere, to urge] **1.** calling for haste, immediate action, etc.; pressing **2.** insistent —**ur'gent·ly** *adv.*

**-ur·gy** (ur'jē) [< Gr. < -ourgos, worker < ergon, work] a combining form meaning a working with or by means of (something specified) *[zymurgy]*

**-u·ri·a** (yoor'ē ə) [ModL. < Gr. < ouron, urine] a combining form meaning a (diseased) condition of the urine *[hematuria]*

**u·ric** (yoor'ik) *adj.* of, contained in, or derived from urine

**uric acid** a white, odorless, crystalline substance, C₅H₄N₄O₃, found in urine

**u·ri·nal** (yoor'ə n'l) *n.* **1.** a portable container used for urinating **2.** a place for urinating; specif., a fixture for use by men in urinating

**u·ri·nal·y·sis** (yoor'ə nal'ə sis) *n., pl.* **-ses'** (-sēz') chemical or microscopic analysis of the urine

**u·ri·nar·y** (yoor'ə ner'ē) *adj.* **1.** of urine **2.** of the organs involved in secreting and discharging urine

**u·ri·nate** (yoor'ə nāt') *vi.* **-nat'ed, -nat'ing** to discharge urine from the body —*vt.* to discharge as or with the urine —**u'ri·na'tion** *n.* —**u'ri·na'tive** *adj.*

**u·rine** (yoor'in) *n.* [OFr. < L. urina] in mammals, the yellowish fluid containing urea and other waste products, secreted from the blood by the kidneys, passed to the bladder, and periodically discharged through the urethra

**u·ri·no-** [< L. urina, urine] a combining form meaning urine, urinary tract: also, before a vowel, **urin-**

**u·ri·no·gen·i·tal** (yoor'ə nō jen'ə t'l) *adj. same as* UROGENITAL

**urn** (urn) *n.* [L. urna] **1.** *a)* a vase, esp. one with a foot or pedestal *b)* a container for the ashes of a cremated body **2.** a metal container with a faucet, used for making or serving coffee, tea, etc.

**u·ro-** [< Gr. ouron, urine] a combining form meaning urine, urination, urinary tract: also, before a vowel, **ur-**

**u·ro·gen·i·tal** (yoor'ō jen'ə t'l) *adj.* designating or of the urinary and genital organs; genitourinary

**u·rol·o·gy** (yoo räl'ə jē) *n.* the branch of medicine dealing with the urogenital or urinary system and its diseases —**u·ro·log·ic** (yoor'ə läj'ik), **u'ro·log'i·cal** *adj.* —**u·rol'o·gist** *n.*

**u·ros·co·py** (yoo räs'kə pē) *n., pl.* **-pies** examination of the urine, as for the diagnosis of disease —**u·ro·scop·ic** (yoor'ə skäp'ik) *adj.*

**Ur·sa Major** (ur'sə) [L., lit., Great Bear] the most conspicuous constellation in the northern sky: it contains the seven stars which form the Big Dipper

**Ursa Minor** [L., lit., Little Bear] the northernmost constellation: it contains the Little Dipper, with the North Star at the end of its handle

**ur·sine** (ur'sīn, -sin) *adj.* [< L. < ursus, a bear] of or like a bear or the bear family; bearlike

**Ur·su·la** (ur'sə lə) [ML., dim. of L. ursa, she-bear] **1.** a feminine name **2.** Saint, a legendary Christian Brit. princess said to have lived in the 4th cent.

**Ur·su·line** (-lin, -līn') *n.* [< ModL.: after Saint URSULA] R.C.Ch. any member of a teaching order of nuns founded c.1537 —*adj.* of this order

**ur·ti·car·i·a** (ur'tə ker'ē ə) *n.* [ModL. < L. urtica, a nettle] *same as* HIVES —**ur'ti·car'i·al** *adj.*

**U·ru·guay** (yoor'ə gwā', -gwī'; Sp. ōō'rōō gwī') **1.** country in SE S. America, on the Atlantic: 72,171 sq. mi.; pop. 2,886,000; cap. Montevideo **2.** river in SE S. America, flowing into the Río de la Plata —**U'ru·guay'an** *adj., n.*

**us** (us) *pron.* [OE.] objective case of WE: also used colloquially as a predicate complement with a linking verb (Ex.: that's us)

**U.S., US** United States

**USA, U.S.A. 1.** United States of America **2.** United States Army

**us·a·ble, use·a·ble** (yōō'zə b'l) *adj.* that can be used; fit, convenient, or available for use —**us'a·bil'i·ty, us'a·ble·ness** *n.* —**us'a·bly** *adv.*

**USAF, U.S.A.F.** United States Air Force

**us·age** (yōō'sij, -zij) *n.* **1.** the act, way, or extent of using; treatment **2.** a long-continued or established practice; custom; habit **3.** the way in which a word, phrase, etc. is used in speaking or writing, or an instance of this

**USCG, U.S.C.G.** United States Coast Guard

**USDA** United States Department of Agriculture

**use** (yōōz; *for n.* yōōs) *vt.* **used** (yōōzd; *for vt.* 6 & vi., with the following "to," yōōs'tə or yōōs'too), **us'ing** [< OFr., ult. < L. usus, pp. of uti, to use] **1.** to put or bring into action or service **2.** to practice; exercise *[use your judgment]* **3.** to behave toward; treat *[to use a friend badly]* **4.** to do away with by using; consume, expend, etc. *[to use up one's ener-*

gy] **5.** *a)* to smoke or chew (tobacco) *b)* to take or consume habitually *[to use* drugs] **6.** to accustom (used in the passive with *to)* [to become *used* to certain ways] **7.** to exploit (a person) *—vi.* to be accustomed (now only in the past tense, with an infinitive, meaning "did at one time") [he *used* to live in Iowa] *—n.* **1.** a using or being used **2.** the ability to use [he lost the *use* of his leg] **3.** the right or permission to use **4.** the need or opportunity to use [no further *use* for his services] **5.** an instance or way of using **6.** usefulness; utility **7.** the object or purpose for which something is used **8.** function, service, or benefit **9.** custom; habit; practice **10.** *Law a)* the enjoyment of property, as from occupying or employing it *b)* profit or benefit, esp. that of property held in trust by another **—have no use for 1.** to have no need of **2.** to dislike strongly **—in use** being used **—make use** of to use: also **put to use —us′er** *n.*

**used** (yoōzd) *pt. & pp. of* USE *—adj.* **1.** that has been used **2.** *same as* SECONDHAND

**use·ful** (yoōs′fəl) *adj.* that can be used; serviceable; helpful **—use′ful·ly** *adv.* **—use′ful·ness** *n.*

**use·less** (-lis) *adj.* **1.** having no use; unserviceable; worthless **2.** to no purpose; ineffectual; of no avail **—use′less·ly** *adv.* **—use′less·ness** *n.*

**U-shaped** (yoō′shāpt′) *adj.* having the shape of a U

**ush·er** (ush′ər) *n.* [OFr. *uissier* < L. *ostiarius* < *ostium,* door] **1.** an official doorkeeper **2.** a person whose duty it is to show people to their seats in a theater, church, etc. **3.** any of the groom's attendants at a wedding **4.** [Obs.] in Great Britain, an assistant teacher *—vt.* **1.** to escort or conduct (others) to seats, etc. **2.** to herald or bring (in) *—vi.* to act as an usher

**ush·er·ette** (ush′ə ret′) *n.* a woman or girl usher, as in a theater

**USIA, U.S.I.A.** United States Information Agency

**USIS, U.S.I.S.** United States Information Service

**U.S.M., USM 1.** United States Mail **2.** United States Mint

**USMC, U.S.M.C.** United States Marine Corps

**USN, U.S.N.** United States Navy

**USNG, U.S.N.G.** United States National Guard

**USO, U.S.O.** United Service Organizations

**U.S.P., U.S.Pharm.** United States Pharmacopoeia

**U.S.S.** United States Ship, Steamer, or Steamship

**U.S.S.R., USSR** Union of Soviet Socialist Republics

**u·su·al** (yoō′zhoo wəl, -zhwəl, -zhəl) *adj.* [< MFr. < LL. *usualis* < L. *usus:* see USE] such as is most often seen, heard, used, etc.; common; ordinary; customary **—as usual** in the usual way **—u′su·al·ly** *adv.* **—u′su·al·ness** *n.*

**u·su·fruct** (yoō′zyoo frukt′, -zoo-, -soo-) *n.* [< LL. < L. *usus,* a use + *fructus,* a fruit] *Law* the right to use and enjoy the advantages and profits of the property of another without altering or damaging the substance **—u′su·fruc′tu·ar′y** (-fruk′choo wer′ē) *adj., n., pl.* **-ar′ies**

**u·su·rer** (yoō′zhoo rər) *n.* a person who engages in usury

**u·su·ri·ous** (yoō zhoor′ē əs) *adj.* **1.** practicing usury **2.** of or involving usury **—u·su′ri·ous·ly** *adv.* **—u·su′ri·ous·ness** *n.*

**u·surp** (yoō surp′, -zurp′) *vt., vi.* [< MFr. < L. *usurpare* < *usus,* a use + *rapere,* to seize] to take or assume and hold (power, position, rights, etc.) by force or without right **—u·surp′er** *n.* **—u·surp′ing·ly** *adv.*

**u·sur·pa·tion** (yoō′sər pā′shən, -zər-) *n.* unlawful or violent seizure of a throne, power, etc.

**u·su·ry** (yoō′zhoo rē) *n., pl.* **-ries** [< ML. < L. *usura* < *usus:* see USE] **1.** the lending of money at interest, now specif. at a rate of interest that is excessively or unlawfully high **2.** interest at such a high rate

**usw, u.s.w.** [G. *und so weiter*] and so forth

**U·tah** (yoō′tô, -tä) [< Sp. < tribal name, lit. ? hill dwellers] Western State of the U.S.: 84,916 sq. mi.; pop. 1,461,000; cap. Salt Lake City: abbrev. **Ut., UT —U′tah·an** *adj., n.*

**Ute** (yoōt, yoō′tē) *n.* **1.** *pl.* **Utes, Ute** any member of a tribe of Shoshonean Indians living mainly in Colorado and Utah **2.** their Shoshonean language

**u·ten·sil** (yoō ten′s'l) *n.* [< MFr. < L. *utensilis,* fit for use < *uti,* to use] an implement or container used for a particular purpose, now esp. one used in a kitchen [cooking *utensils]*

**u·ter·ine** (yoōt′ər in, yoō′tə rīn′) *adj.* **1.** of the uterus **2.** having the same mother but a different father [uterine sisters]

**u·ter·us** (yoōt′ər əs) *n., pl.* **u′ter·i′** (-ī′) [L.] a hollow, muscular organ of female mammals in which the ovum is deposited and the embryo and fetus are developed; womb

**U Thant** *see* THANT

**U·ti·ca** (yoō′ti kə) [after an ancient city in N Africa] city in C N.Y., on the Mohawk River: pop. 76,000

**u·til·i·tar·i·an** (yoo til′ə ter′ē ən) *adj.* **1.** of or having utility; useful **2.** stressing usefulness over beauty, etc. **3.** of or believing in utilitarianism *—n.* a person who believes in utilitarianism

**u·til·i·tar·i·an·ism** (-iz'm) *n.* **1.** the doctrine that the value of anything is determined solely by its utility **2.** the doctrine that the purpose of all action should be to bring about the greatest happiness of the greatest number **3.** utilitarian character or quality

**u·til·i·ty** (yoo til′ə tē) *n., pl.* **-ties** [< OFr. < L. < *utilis,* useful < *uti,* to use] **1.** usefulness **2.** something useful **3.** *a)* something useful to the public, esp. the service of electricity, gas, water, etc. *b)* a company providing such a service: see also PUBLIC UTILITY **4.** *Econ.* the power to satisfy the wants of humanity *—adj.* **1.** for practical use with little attention to beauty **2.** useful or used in a number of ways **3.** *Baseball* able to substitute in several positions [utility infielder]

**utility room** a room containing various household appliances and equipment, as for heating, laundry, cleaning, etc.

**u·ti·lize** (yoōt′'l īz′) *vt.* **-lized′, -liz′ing** to put to use; make practical or profitable use of: Brit. sp. **u′ti·lise —u′ti·liz′a·ble** *adj.* **—u′ti·li·za′tion** *n.* **—u′ti·liz′er** *n.*

**ut·most** (ut′mōst′) *adj.* [OE. *utemest,* double superl. of *ut,* out] **1.** most extreme or distant; farthest **2.** of or to the greatest or highest degree, amount, number, etc.; greatest *—n.* the most or the greatest that is possible; extreme limit or degree

**U·to-Az·tec·an** (yoōt′ō az′tek ən) *adj.* designating or of a large American Indian linguistic family of the W U.S., Mexico, and Central America *—n.* the Uto-Aztecan family of languages, including Shoshone, Nahuatl, Pima, etc.

**U·to·pi·a** (yoo tō′pē ə) [ModL. < Gr. *ou,* not + *topos,* a place] an imaginary island described in a book of the same name by Sir Thomas More (1516) as having a perfect political and social system *—n.* [*often* u-] **1.** any idealized place, state, or situation of perfection **2.** any visionary scheme for an ideally perfect society

**U·to·pi·an** (-ən) *adj.* **1.** of or like Utopia **2.** [*often* u-] having or based on ideas envisioning perfection in social and political organization; idealistic; visionary *—n.* **1.** an inhabitant of Utopia **2.** [*often* u-] a person who believes in a utopia, esp. of a social or political nature; visionary **—u·to′pi·an·ism** *n.*

**U·trecht** (yoō′trekt; *Du.* ü′treHt) city in the C Netherlands: pop. 279,000

**u·tri·cle** (yoō′tri k'l) *n.* [< Fr. < L. dim. of *uter,* leather bag] a small sac, vesicle, or baglike part: also **u·tric·u·lus** (yoo trik′yə ləs), *pl.* **-li′** (-lī′) **—u·tric′u·lar** *adj.*

**U·tril·lo** (oō trē′lō; *Fr.* ōō trē lō′), **Maurice** 1883–1955; Fr. painter

**ut·ter[1]** (ut′ər) *adj.* [OE. *uttera,* compar. of *ut,* out] **1.** complete; total **2.** unqualified; absolute; unconditional **—ut′ter·ly** *adv.* **—ut′ter·ness** *n.*

**ut·ter[2]** (ut′ər) *vt.* [< ME. < *utter,* outward < *ut,* out] **1.** orig., to give out; put forth; now esp., to pass (counterfeit money, forged checks, etc.) **2.** to make or express with the voice [to *utter* a cry, to *utter* a thought] **3.** to express in any way **4.** to make known; divulge **—ut′ter·a·ble** *adj.* **—ut′ter·er** *n.*

**ut·ter·ance** (ut′ər əns, ut′rəns) *n.* **1.** the act, power, or way of uttering **2.** something uttered or said

**ut·ter·most** (ut′ər mōst′) *adj., n. same as* UTMOST

**U-turn** (yoō′turn′) *n.* a turning completely around, esp. of a vehicle within the width of a street or road, so as to head in the opposite direction

**UV, uv** ultraviolet

**u·vu·la** (yoō′vyə lə) *n., pl.* **-las, -lae′** (-lē′) [ML., dim. of L. *uva,* a grape] the small, fleshy part of the soft palate hanging down above the back of the tongue

**u·vu·lar** (-lər) *adj.* **1.** of or having to do with the uvula **2.** *Phonet.* pronounced with a vibration of the uvula, or with the back of the tongue near or touching the uvula *—n.* a uvular sound **—u′vu·lar·ly** *adv.*

**ux·o·ri·al** (ək sôr′ē əl, əg zôr′-) *adj.* [see ff.] of, befitting, or characteristic of a wife **—ux·or′i·al·ly** *adv.*

**ux·o·ri·ous** (-əs) *adj.* [< L. < *uxor,* wife] dotingly fond of or submissive to one's wife **—ux·o′ri·ous·ly** *adv.* **—ux·o′ri·ous·ness** *n.*

UVULA

**Uz·bek** (ooz′bek, uz′-) *n.* **1.** a member of a Turkic people living in the region of the Uzbek S.S.R. **2.** the Turkic language of the Uzbeks Also **Uz′beg** (-beg)

**Uzbek Soviet Socialist Republic** republic of the U.S.S.R., in C Asia: 173,546 sq. mi.; pop. 12,000,000; cap. Tashkent: also **Uz′bek·i·stan′** (-i stan′, -stän′)

---

fat, āpe, cär, ten, ēven, is, bīte; gō, hôrn, tōol, look; oil, out; up, fur; get; joy; yet; chin; she; thin, *then*; zh, leisure; ŋ, ring; ə for *a* in *ago, e* in *agent, i* in *sanity, o* in *comply, u* in *focus;* ′ as in *able* (ā′b'l); Fr. bal; ë, Fr. coeur; ö, Fr. feu; ö, Fr. mon; ǒ, Fr. coq; ü, Fr. duc; r, Fr. cri; H, G. ich; kh, G. doch; ‡foreign; *hypothetical; < derived from. See inside front cover.

# V

**V, v** (vē) *n., pl.* **V's, v's 1.** the twenty-second letter of the English alphabet **2.** the sound of *V* or *v*

**V** (vē) *n.* **1.** something shaped like V **2.** a Roman numeral for 5 **3.** [Colloq.] a five-dollar bill **4.** *Chem.* vanadium —*adj.* shaped like V

**V, v 1.** *Math.* vector **2.** velocity **3.** victory **4.** volt(s)

**v. 1.** [L. *vice*] in the place of **2.** [G. *von*] of **3.** [L. *vide*] see **4.** verb **5.** *pl.* **vv.** verse **6.** version **7.** versus **8.** vice- **9.** *pl.* **vv.** violin **10.** voice **11.** volt **12.** voltage **13.** volume

**VA, V.A.** Veterans Administration

**Va., VA** Virginia

**va·can·cy** (vā′kən sē) *n., pl.* **-cies 1.** the state of being vacant; emptiness **2.** *a)* empty space *b)* a vacant space; gap, blank, opening, etc. **3.** lack of intelligence, interest, or thought **4.** an unoccupied position or office **5.** a room, apartment, etc. available for rent

**va·cant** (vā′kənt) *adj.* [< OFr. < L. prp. of *vacare*, to be empty] **1.** having nothing in it, as a space; empty **2.** not held, filled, or occupied, as a position, a seat, a house, etc. **3.** free from work or activity [*vacant* time] **4.** without thought, interest, etc. [*a vacant* mind, stare, etc.] —**va′cant·ly** *adv.* —**va′cant·ness** *n.*

**va·cate** (vā′kāt) *vt.* **-cat·ed, -cat·ing** [< L. pp. of *vacare*, to be empty] **1.** to make vacant; specif., to leave (an office, position, etc.) or move out of (a house, room, etc.) **2.** *Law* to make void; annul —*vi.* to make an office, position, house, etc. vacant

**va·ca·tion** (və kā′shən, vā-) *n.* [< MFr. < L. *vacatio*] **1.** a rest or respite from something **2.** a period of time when one stops working, going to school, etc. in order to rest and have recreation **3.** [Rare] a vacating **4.** *Law* a formal recess between terms of court —*vi.* to take one's vacation —**va·ca′tion·er, va·ca′tion·ist** *n.*

**vac·ci·nate** (vak′sə nāt′) *vt.* **-nat′ed, -nat′ing** to inoculate with a specific vaccine in order to prevent disease, as in immunizing against smallpox —*vi.* to practice vaccination —**vac′ci·na′tor** *n.*

**vac·ci·na·tion** (vak′sə nā′shən) *n.* **1.** the act or practice of vaccinating **2.** the scar on the skin where the vaccine has been applied

**vac·cine** (vak sēn′; vak′sēn, -sin) *n.* [L. *vaccinus*, from cows < *vacca*, a cow: from use of cowpox virus in smallpox vaccine] any preparation of killed microorganisms, living weakened organisms, etc. introduced into the body to produce immunity to a specific disease by causing antibodies to be formed —**vac′ci·nal** *adj.*

**vac·il·late** (vas′ə lāt′) *vi.* **-lat′ed, -lat′ing** [< L. pp. of *vacillare*] **1.** to sway to and fro; waver **2.** to fluctuate or oscillate **3.** to waver in mind; show indecision —**vac′il·lat′ing** *adj.* —**vac′il·lat′ing·ly** *adv.* —**vac′il·la′tion** *n.*

**va·cu·i·ty** (va kyōō′ə tē) *n., pl.* **-ties** [< L. < *vacuus*, empty] **1.** a being empty; emptiness **2.** an empty space; void or vacuum **3.** lack of intelligence, interest, or thought **4.** something inane; inanity

**vac·u·ole** (vak′yoo wōl′) *n.* [Fr. < L. *vacuus*, empty] *Biol.* a fluid-filled cavity within the plasma membrane of a cell, believed to have the function of discharging excess water or wastes —**vac′u·o·lar** (-wə lər, vak′yoo wō′lər) *adj.*

**vac·u·ous** (vak′yoo wəs) *adj.* [L. *vacuus*] **1.** empty **2.** stupid; senseless; inane **3.** lacking purpose; idle —**vac′u·ous·ly** *adv.* —**vac′u·ous·ness** *n.*

**vac·u·um** (vak′yoo wəm; *also, & for adj. & v. usually,* vak′yoom) *n., pl.* **-u·ums, -u·a** (-yoo wə) [L., neut. sing. of *vacuus*, empty] **1.** a space with nothing at all in it **2.** an enclosed space, as that inside a vacuum tube, out of which most of the air or gas has been taken, as by pumping **3.** a space left empty as by the removal of something; void: often used figuratively **4.** *short for* VACUUM CLEANER —*adj.* **1.** of a vacuum **2.** used to make a vacuum **3.** having a vacuum **4.** working by suction or the creation of a partial vacuum —*vt., vi.* to clean with a vacuum cleaner: in full, **vac′u·um-clean′**

**vacuum bottle** (or **flask** or **jug**) *same as* THERMOS

**vacuum cleaner** a machine for cleaning carpets, floors, upholstery, etc. by suction: also **vacuum sweeper**

**vacuum-packed** (-pakt′) *adj.* packed in an airtight container from which most of the air was exhausted before sealing, so as to keep the contents fresh

**vacuum pump** a pump used to draw air or gas out of a sealed space

**vacuum tube** an electron tube from which the air has been evacuated to the highest possible degree

**va·de me·cum** (vā′dē mē′kəm, vä′-) [L., lit., go with me] something carried about by a person for constant use, reference, etc., as a handbook

**vag·a·bond** (vag′ə bänd′) *adj.* [< MFr. < L. *vagabundus*, strolling about < *vagari*, to wander] **1.** moving from place to place; wandering **2.** of, having to do with, or living an unsettled, drifting, irresponsible life; vagrant; shiftless **3.** aimlessly following an irregular course —*n.* **1.** a person who wanders from place to place, having no fixed abode **2.** a tramp **3.** an idle, disreputable, or shiftless person —*vi.* to wander —**vag′a·bond′age, vag′a·bond′ism** *n.*

**va·gar·y** (və ger′ē, -gar′-; vä′gər ē) *n., pl.* **-gar′ies** [< L. *vagari*, to wander] **1.** an odd, eccentric, or unexpected action **2.** an odd, whimsical, or freakish idea or notion —**va·gar′i·ous** *adj.* —**va·gar′i·ous·ly** *adv.*

**va·gi·na** (və jī′nə) *n., pl.* **-nas, -nae** (-nē) [L., a sheath] a sheath or sheathlike structure; specif., in female mammals, the canal leading from the vulva to the uterus —**vag·i·nal** (vaj′ə n'l, və jī′n'l) *adj.*

**vag·i·nate** (vaj′ə nit, -nāt′) *adj.* **1.** having a vagina or sheath; sheathed **2.** like a sheath

**va·got·o·my** (vā gät′ə mē) *n., pl.* **-mies** [VAG(US) + -TOMY] the surgical cutting of the vagus nerve

**va·gran·cy** (vā′grən sē) *n., pl.* **-cies** [< ff.] **1.** a wandering in thought or talk; digression **2.** a wandering from place to place **3.** shiftless or idle wandering without money or work, as of tramps, beggars, etc.: often a statutory offense chargeable as a misdemeanor

**va·grant** (vā′grənt) *n.* [prob. < Anglo-Fr. < OFr. *walcrer*, to wander: infl. prob. by L. *vagari*, to wander] a person who wanders from place to place; esp., one without a regular job, supporting himself by begging, etc.; vagabond, tramp, etc. —*adj.* **1.** wandering from place to place; roaming; nomadic **2.** of, characteristic of, or living the life of a vagrant **3.** following no fixed direction or course; random, wayward, etc. —**va′grant·ly** *adv.*

**vague** (vāg) *adj.* [Fr. < L. *vagus*, wandering] **1.** not clearly or precisely expressed or stated **2.** indefinite in shape or form **3.** not sharp, certain, or precise in thought or expression **4.** not known or determined; uncertain —**vague′ly** *adv.* —**vague′ness** *n.*

**va·gus** (vā′gəs) *n., pl.* **va·gi** (-jī) [ModL. < L., wandering] either of a pair of cranial nerves acting upon the larynx, lungs, heart, esophagus, and most of the abdominal organs: also **vagus nerve** —**va′gal** (-g'l) *adj.*

**vain** (vān) *adj.* [< OFr. < L. *vanus*, empty] **1.** having no real value or significance; worthless, empty, etc. [*vain* pomp] **2.** without force or effect; futile, fruitless, etc. [*a vain* attempt] **3.** having or showing an excessively high regard for one's self, looks, ability, etc.; conceited —**in vain 1.** unsuccessfully; fruitlessly **2.** lightly; profanely —**vain′ly** *adv.* —**vain′ness** *n.*

**vain·glo·ri·ous** (vān′glôr′ē əs) *adj.* [< ML.: see ff.] **1.** boastfully vain and proud of oneself **2.** characterized by boastful vanity —**vain′glo′ri·ous·ly** *adv.* —**vain′glo′ri·ous·ness** *n.*

**vain·glo·ry** (vān′glôr′ē, vān glôr′ē) *n.* [< OFr. < L. *vana gloria*, empty boasting: see VAIN & GLORY] **1.** extreme self-pride and boastfulness **2.** vain show or empty pomp

**val·ance** (val′əns, vāl′-) *n.* [< ? *Valence*, city in France] **1.** a short drapery or curtain hanging from the edge of a bed, shelf, etc., often to the floor **2.** a short drapery or facing of wood or metal across the top of a window —**val′anced** *adj.*

**vale¹** (vāl) *n.* [< OFr. < L. *vallis*] [Poet.] *same as* VALLEY

**‡va·le²** (vä′lē, wä′lā) *interj., n.* [L.] farewell

**val·e·dic·tion** (val′ə dik′shən) *n.* [< L. pp. of *valedicere* < *vale*, farewell (imper. of *valere*, to be well) + *dicere*, to say] **1.** a bidding farewell **2.** something said in parting

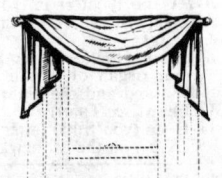

VALANCE

**val·e·dic·to·ri·an** (val′ə dik tôr′ē ən) *n.* in schools and colleges, the student, usually the one ranking highest in the class in scholarship, who delivers the valedictory

**val·e·dic·to·ry** (val′ə dik′tər ē) *adj.* said or done at parting, by way of farewell; uttered as a valediction —*n., pl.* **-ries** a farewell speech, esp. one delivered at graduation

**va·lence** (vā′ləns) *n.* [< ML., ult. < L. prp. of *valere*, to be strong] *Chem.* **1.** the combining capacity of an element or radical, as measured by the number of hydrogen or chlorine atoms which one radical or one atom of the element will combine with or replace **2.** any of the units of valence which an element may have Also **va′len·cy**, *pl.* **-cies**

**valence electrons** the mobile electrons in the outermost shell of an atom which largely determine its properties

**Va·len·ci·a** (və len′shē ə, -shə, -sē ə; *Sp.* vä len′thyä) seaport in E Spain, on the Mediterranean: pop. 624,000

**-va·lent** (vā′lənt) [< L. *valens*] *Chem. a suffix meaning:* **1.** having a specified valence **2.** having a specified number of valences

**Val·en·tine** (val′ən tīn′), Saint 3d cent. A.D.; Christian martyr of Rome

**val·en·tine** (val′ən tīn′) *n.* **1.** a sweetheart chosen or complimented on Saint Valentine's Day **2.** a greeting card or gift sent on this day

**Va·ler·i·an** (və lir′ē ən) (L. name *Publius Licinius Valerianus*) 190?-260 A.D.; Roman emperor (253-260)

**va·le·ri·an** (və lir′ē ən) *n.* [< MFr. < ML. *valeriana*] **1.** any of various plants with clusters or spikes of white, pink, red, or purplish flowers **2.** a drug made from the roots of some of these plants, formerly used as a sedative

**val·et** (val′it, val′ā; *Fr.* vá lā′) *n.* [Fr., a groom < OFr. *vaslet*, young man, page] **1.** a man's personal manservant who takes care of the man's clothes, helps him in dressing, etc. **2.** an employee, as of a hotel, who cleans or presses clothes, etc. **3.** a rack for coats, pants, etc. —*vt., vi.* to serve (a person) as a valet

**val·e·tu·di·nar·i·an** (val′ə tōō′də ner′ē ən) *n.* [< L. < *valetudo*, state of health, sickness < *valere*, to be strong] **1.** a person in poor health; invalid **2.** a person who worries constantly about his health —*adj.* **1.** in poor health; sickly **2.** anxiously concerned about one's health

**Val·hal·la** (val hal′ə) *Norse Myth.* the great hall where Odin receives and feasts the souls of heroes fallen bravely in battle: also **Val·hall′**

**val·iant** (val′yənt) *adj.* [< OFr. prp. of *valoir* < L. *valere*, to be strong] courageous; brave —**val′iance, val′ian·cy** *n.* —**val′iant·ly** *adv.*

**val·id** (val′id) *adj.* [< Fr. < L. *validus*, strong < *valere*, to be strong] **1.** having legal force; binding under law **2.** well-grounded on principles or evidence, as an argument; sound **3.** effective, cogent, etc. **4.** *Logic* correctly derived or inferred according to the rules of logic —**val′id·ly** *adv.* —**val′id·ness** *n.*

**val·i·date** (val′ə dāt′) *vt.* **-dat′ed, -dat′ing** [< ML. pp. of *validare*] **1.** to give legal force to; declare legally valid **2.** to prove to be valid —**val′i·da′tion** *n.*

**va·lid·i·ty** (və lid′ə tē) *n., pl.* **-ties** the state, quality, or fact of being valid in law or in argument, proof, etc.

**va·lise** (və lēs′) *n.* [Fr. < It. *valigia* < ?] a piece of hand luggage: an old-fashioned term

**Val·kyr·ie** (val kir′ē, val′ki rē) *n. Norse Myth.* any of the maidens of Odin who conduct the souls of heroes slain in battle to Valhalla —**Val·kyr′i·an** *adj.*

**Val·le·jo** (və lā′hō, -ō) [after M. *Vallejo* (1807-90), owner of the site] seaport in W Calif., north of Oakland: pop. 80,000

**val·ley** (val′ē) *n., pl.* **-leys** [< OFr. < L. *vallis*] **1.** a stretch of low land lying between hills or mountains **2.** the land drained or watered by a great river system [the Nile *valley*] **3.** any long dip or hollow

**Valley Forge** [after an iron *forge* on *Valley* Creek] village in SE Pa.: the place where Washington and his troops camped in the winter of 1777-78

**val·or** (val′ər) *n.* [< OFr. < LL. < L. *valere*, to be strong] great courage or bravery: also, Brit. sp., **val′our** —**val′or·ous** *adj.* —**val′or·ous·ly** *adv.* —**val′or·ous·ness** *n.*

**val·or·i·za·tion** (val′ər i zā′shən) *n.* [Port. *valorização*, ult. < LL. *valor*, VALOR] a fixing of prices, usually by government action, as by buying up a commodity at the fixed price, etc. —**val′or·ize′** (-ə rīz′) *vt., vi.* **-ized′, -iz′ing**

**Val·pa·raí·so** (val′pə rā′zō, -rī′sō) seaport in C Chile: pop. 296,000: also **Val·pa·ra·í·so** (*Sp.* väl′pä rä ē′sō)

‡**valse** (väls) *n.* [Fr.] a waltz

**val·u·a·ble** (val′yoo b′l, -yoo wə b′l) *adj.* **1.** *a)* being worth money *b)* having great value in terms of money **2.** highly regarded as precious, useful, worthy, etc. —*n.* an article of value, as a piece of jewelry —**val′u·a·ble·ness** *n.* —**val′u·a·bly** *adv.*

**val·u·ate** (val′yoo wāt′) *vt.* **-at′ed, -at′ing** to set a value on; appraise —**val′u·a′tor** *n.*

**val·u·a·tion** (val′yoo wā′shən) *n.* **1.** the act of determining the value of anything; evaluation **2.** determined or estimated value **3.** estimation of the worth, merit, etc. of anything —**val′u·a′tion·al** *adj.* —**val′u·a′tion·al·ly** *adv.*

**val·ue** (val′yōō) *n.* [< OFr. pp. of *valoir*, to be strong, to be worth < L. *valere*] **1.** a fair equivalent in money, etc. for something sold or exchanged **2.** the worth of a thing in money or goods at a certain time **3.** estimated or appraised worth **4.** purchasing power **5.** that quality of a thing that makes it more or less desirable, useful, etc. **6.** [*pl.*] the social principles, goals, or standards held by an individual, class, society, etc. **7.** precise meaning, as of a word **8.** numerical order assigned to a playing card, etc. **9.** *Art a)* relative lightness or darkness of a color *b)* the effect produced by the use of light and shade **10.** *Math.* the quantity for which a symbol stands **11.** *Music* the relative duration of a note, tone, or rest **12.** *Phonet.* the quality of a speech sound —*vt.* **-ued, -u·ing 1.** to estimate the value of; appraise **2.** to place a certain estimate of worth on in a scale of values [to *value* health above wealth] **3.** to think highly of; prize [I *value* your friendship] —**val′ue·less** *adj.* —**val′ue·less·ness** *n.* —**val′u·er** *n.*

**val·ued** (-yōōd) *adj.* **1.** estimated; appraised **2.** highly thought of; esteemed

**value judgment** an estimate made of the worth, goodness, etc. of a person, action, event, etc., esp. when such a judgment is not called for or desired

**val·vate** (val′vāt) *adj.* [L. *valvatus*, having folding doors < *valva*: see ff.] **1.** having a valve or valves **2.** *Bot. a)* meeting without overlapping, as petals, etc. *b)* opening by valves, as a pea pod

**valve** (valv) *n.* [L. *valva*, leaf of a folding door] **1.** a sluice gate **2.** *Anat.* a membranous structure which permits body fluids to flow in one direction only, or opens and closes a tube, etc. **3.** *Bot.* any of the segments into which a seed capsule separates **4.** *Mech. a)* any device in a pipe, etc. that permits a flow in one direction only, or regulates or stops the flow by means of a flap, lid, plug, etc. *b)* this flap, lid, plug, etc. **5.** *Music* a device, as in the trumpet, that opens an auxiliary to the main tube, lengthening the air column and lowering the pitch **6.** *Zool.* one of the parts making up the shell of a mollusk, clam, etc. —*vt., vi.* **valved, valv′ing 1.** to fit with a valve or valves **2.** to regulate the flow of (a fluid) by means of a valve —**valve′less** *adj.* —**valve′like′** *adj.*

VALVE
(in a faucet)

**val·vu·lar** (val′vyə lər) *adj.* **1.** having the form or function of a valve **2.** having a valve or valves **3.** of a valve or valves; esp., of the valves of the heart

**va·moose** (va mōōs′) *vi., vt.* **-moosed′, -moos′ing** [Sp. *vamos*, let us go] [Old Slang] to leave quickly; go away (from) hurriedly: also **va·mose′** (-mōs′) **-mosed′, -mos′ing**

**vamp**[1] (vamp) *n.* [< OFr. *avampié* < *avant*, before + *pié*, a foot] **1.** the part of a boot or shoe covering the instep and, in some styles, also the toes **2.** something patched up to seem new **3.** *Music* a simple, improvised introduction or interlude —*vt.* **1.** to put a vamp on (a shoe, etc.) **2.** to patch (*up*); repair **3.** to invent; fabricate **4.** *Music* to improvise —*vi. Music* to play a vamp

VAMP

**vamp**[2] (vamp) *n. shortened form of* VAMPIRE (sense 3) —*vt.* to seduce or beguile (a man) by the use of feminine charms —*vi.* to act the part of a vamp

**vam·pire** (vam′pīr) *n.* [Fr. < G. *vampir*; of Slav. orig.] **1.** *Folklore* a corpse that comes alive at night and sucks the blood of sleeping persons **2.** a person who preys on others in a dishonest, evil, or wicked way **3.** a beautiful but wicked woman who seduces men and leads them to their ruin **4.** *shortened form of* VAMPIRE BAT —**vam′pir·ism** *n.*

**vampire bat 1.** a tropical American bat that lives on the blood of animals **2.** any of various other bats mistakenly believed to be bloodsuckers

**van**[1] (van) *n.* [abbrev. < VANGUARD] **1.** the front of an army or fleet when advancing **2.** the foremost position in a line, movement, endeavor, etc., or those in this position

**van**[2] (van) *n.* [< CARAVAN] **1.** a closed truck or wagon for carrying furniture, etc. **2.** [Brit.] *a)* a closed railway car for baggage, etc. *b)* a delivery wagon or truck

**va·na·di·um** (və nā′dē əm) *n*. [ModL. < ON. *Vanadis*, a name of Freya, goddess of love] a rare, ductile metallic chemical element: cf. VANADIUM STEEL: symbol, V; at. wt., 50.942; at. no., 23

**vanadium steel** a steel alloy containing 0.15 to 0.25 percent vanadium to harden and toughen it

**Van Al·len (radiation) belt** (van al′ən) [after J. A. *Van Allen* (1914– ), U.S. physicist] a doughnut-shaped belt of high-intensity radiation encircling the earth at varying levels, starting at c. 600 mi.

**Van Bu·ren** (van byoor′ən), **Martin** 1782–1862; 8th president of the U.S. (1837–41)

**Van·cou·ver** (van koo′vər) **1.** island of British Columbia, Canada, off the SW coast **2.** seaport in SW British Columbia, opposite this island: pop. 410,000 (met. area 1,166,000)

**Van·dal** (van′d'l) *n*. **1.** a member of an East Germanic tribe that ravaged Gaul, Spain, etc. and sacked Rome (455 A.D.) **2.** [v-] a person who destroys or spoils things on purpose, esp. works of art, public property, etc. —*adj*. **1.** of the Vandals: also **Van·dal·ic** (van dal′ik) **2.** [v-] like a vandal; ruthlessly destructive

**van·dal·ism** (-iz′m) *n*. willful destruction of public or private property, esp. of that which is beautiful —**van′dal·is′·tic** *adj*.

**van·dal·ize** (-īz′) *vt*. **-ized′**, **-iz′ing** to destroy or damage (public or private property) on purpose

**Van·der·bilt** (van′dər bilt), **Cor·nel·ius** (kôr nēl′yəs) 1794–1877; U.S. capitalist & industrialist

**Van Dyck** (van dīk′), Sir **Anthony** 1599–1641; Fl. painter, in England after 1632: also sp. **Van·dyke′**

**Van·dyke (beard)** (van dīk′) a closely trimmed, pointed beard, as seen in portraits by Van Dyck

**vane** (vān) *n*. [OE. *fana*, a flag] **1.** *same as* WEATHER VANE **2.** any of several flat or curved pieces set around an axle and rotated about it by moving air, water, etc. [the *vanes* of a windmill] or mechanically rotated to move the air, water, etc. [the *vanes* of a turbine] **3.** a projecting plate or strip of metal fixed to a rocket, missile, etc. to give stability or guidance **4.** the web or flat part of a feather —**vaned** *adj*.

**van Eyck** (vän īk′), **Jan** (yän) 1385?–1441; Fl. painter

VANDYKE BEARD

**van Gogh** (van gō′, gôkh′; *Du*. vän khôkh′), **Vincent** 1853–90; Du. painter

**van·guard** (van′gärd) *n*. [< OFr. < *avant*, before + *garde*, guard] **1.** the front part of an army in an advance; the van **2.** the leading position or persons in a movement

**va·nil·la** (və nil′ə) *n*. [ModL., genus name < Sp. dim. of *vaina*, a pod < L. *vagina*, a sheath] **1.** any of various climbing tropical American orchids with fragrant flowers **2.** the podlike capsule (**vanilla bean**) of some of these plants **3.** a flavoring made from these capsules —**va·nil′lic** *adj*.

**va·nil·lin** (və nil′in, van′ə lin) *n*. a fragrant, white, crystalline substance, $C_8H_8O_3$, produced from the vanilla bean or made synthetically and used for flavoring

**van·ish** (van′ish) *vi*. [< OFr., ult. < L. *evanescere*: see EVANESCE] **1.** to go or pass suddenly from sight **2.** to cease to exist; come to an end —**van′ish·er** *n*.

**vanishing point 1.** the point where parallel lines receding from the observer seem to come together **2.** a time, place, or stage at which something disappears

**van·i·ty** (van′ə tē) *n., pl.* **-ties** [< OFr. < L. < *vanus*, vain] **1.** any thing or act that is vain, futile, or worthless **2.** a being vain, or worthless; futility **3.** a being vain, or excessively proud of oneself, one's possessions, etc. **4.** *short for* VANITY CASE **5.** *same as* DRESSING TABLE **6.** a cabinet in a bathroom with a washbowl set in the top

**vanity case** a woman's small traveling case fitted for carrying cosmetics, toilet articles, etc.

**van·quish** (vaŋ′kwish, van′-) *vt*. [< OFr. < L. *vincere*, to conquer] **1.** to conquer or defeat in battle **2.** *a*) to defeat in any conflict *b*) to overcome (a feeling, condition, etc.); suppress —**van′quish·er** *n*.

**van·tage** (van′tij) *n*. [see ADVANTAGE] **1.** a position more advantageous than that of an opponent **2.** a position that allows a clear and broad view, understanding, etc.: also **vantage point**

**Van·ua·tu** (vän wä too′) country on a group of islands in the SW Pacific: 5,700 sq. mi.; pop. 112,000

**van·ward** (van′wərd) *adj*. in the van, or front, as of an army —*adv*. toward the van

**vap·id** (vap′id) *adj*. [L. *vapidus*] **1.** having no taste or flavor **2.** lifeless; dull; boring —**vap·id·i·ty** (va pid′ə tē), *pl.* **-ties**, **vap′id·ness** *n*. —**vap′id·ly** *adv*.

**va·por** (vā′pər) *n*. [< Anglo-Fr. < MFr. < L. *vapor*] **1.** *a*) visible particles of moisture floating in the air, as fog, mist, or steam *b*) anything, as smoke, fumes, etc., given off in a cloud **2.** the gaseous form of any substance that is usually a liquid or solid **3.** [*pl.*] [Archaic] depressed spirits (often with *the*) —*vi*. **1.** to rise or pass off as vapor; evaporate **2.** to give off vapor **3.** to brag or bluster —*vt. same as* VAPORIZE —**va′por·er** *n*. —**va′por·ish** *adj*. —**va′por·like′** *adj*.

**va·por·ing** (vā′pər iŋ) *adj*. boastful, bombastic, etc. —*n*. boastful or extravagant talk or behavior

**va·por·ize** (vā′pə rīz′) *vt., vi*. **-ized′**, **-iz′ing** to change into vapor, as by heating or spraying —**va′por·iz′a·ble** *adj*. —**va′por·i·za′tion** *n*. —**va′por·iz′er** *n*.

**vapor lock** a blocking of the flow of fuel in an internal-combustion engine as the result of vaporized fuel in the fuel line, caused by excessive heat

**va·por·ous** (vā′pər əs) *adj*. **1.** giving off or forming vapor **2.** full of vapor; foggy **3.** like vapor **4.** *a*) fleeting, fanciful, etc.: said of things, ideas, etc. *b*) given to such ideas or talk Also **va′por·y** —**va′por·ous·ly** *adv*. —**va′por·ous·ness, va′por·os′i·ty** (-pə räs′ə tē) *n*.

**va·pour** (-pər) *n., vi., vt. Brit. sp. of* VAPOR

**va·que·ro** (vä ker′ō) *n., pl.* **-ros** [Sp. < *vaca*, a cow < L. *vacca*] in the Southwest, a man who herds cattle; cowboy

**var.** 1. variant(s) 2. variation 3. variety 4. various

**Va·ra·na·si** (və rän′ə sē′) city in NE India, on the Ganges: pop. 490,000

**var·i·a·ble** (ver′ē ə b'l, var′-) *adj*. **1.** apt to change or vary; changeable, inconstant, etc. **2.** that can be changed or varied **3.** *Biol*. tending to deviate in some way from the type **4.** *Math*. having no fixed value —*n*. **1.** anything changeable; thing that varies **2.** *Math. a*) a quantity that may have a number of different values *b*) a symbol for such a quantity **3.** *Naut*. a shifting wind —**var′i·a·bil′i·ty, var′i·a·ble·ness** *n*. —**var′i·a·bly** *adv*.

**variable star** a star whose brightness varies from time to time, usually in regular periods

**var·i·ance** (ver′ē əns, var′-) *n*. **1.** a varying or being variant **2.** degree of change or difference; discrepancy **3.** official permission to bypass regulations, esp. zoning laws of a city **4.** a quarrel; dispute **5.** *Accounting* the difference between actual costs of production and the expected costs —**at variance** not in agreement; conflicting

**var·i·ant** (-ənt) *adj*. varying; different; esp., different in some way from others of the same kind —*n*. anything that is variant, as a different spelling of the same word

**var·i·a·tion** (ver′ē ā′shən, var′-) *n*. **1.** *a*) the act, fact, or process of varying; change in form, condition, extent, etc. *b*) the degree or extent of such change **2.** *same as* DECLINATION (sense 3) **3.** a thing that is somewhat different from another of the same kind **4.** *Biol*. a deviation from the usual or parental type in structure or form **5.** *Music* the repetition of a melody or theme with changes in harmony, rhythm, key, etc. —**var′i·a′tion·al** *adj*.

**var·i·cel·la** (var′ə sel′ə) *n*. [ModL., dim. of *variola*: see VARIOLA] *same as* CHICKEN POX —**var′i·cel′loid** (-oid) *adj*.

**var·i·col·ored** (ver′i kui′ərd, var′-) *adj*. of several or many colors

**var·i·cose** (var′ə kōs′) *adj*. [L. *varicosus* < *varix* (gen. *varicis*), enlarged vein] **1.** abnormally and irregularly swollen [*varicose veins*] **2.** resulting from varicose veins [*varicose ulcer*] —**var′i·cos′i·ty** (-käs′ə tē) *n*.

**var·ied** (ver′ēd, var′-) *adj*. **1.** of different kinds; various **2.** variegated **3.** changed; altered —**var′ied·ly** *adv*.

**var·i·e·gate** (ver′ē ə gāt′, ver′ə gāt′; var′-) *vt*. **-gat′ed**, **-gat′ing** [< L. pp. of *variegare* < *varius*, various] **1.** to make varied in appearance by differences, as in colors **2.** to give variety to —**var′i·e·gat′ed** *adj*. —**var′i·e·ga′tion** *n*.

**va·ri·e·tal** (və rī′ə t'l) *adj*. of or being a variety

**va·ri·e·ty** (və rī′ə tē) *n., pl.* **-ties** [< Fr. < L. *varietas*] **1.** a being various or varied; absence of monotony or sameness **2.** any of the various forms of something; sort; kind [*varieties* of cloth] **3.** a number of different kinds [a *variety* of fruits, a *variety* of merchandise] **4.** a subdivision of a species; subspecies or variant; specif., *Bot.* a recognized variant of a wild plant, even though brought under cultivation —*adj*. of or in a variety show

**variety meat** meat other than flesh; specif., any of the edible organs, as the liver, kidneys, heart, etc.

**variety show** a show made up of different kinds of acts, as comic skits, songs, dances, etc.

**variety store** a retail store that sells a wide variety of relatively small and inexpensive items

**var·i·form** (ver′ə fôrm′, var′-) *adj*. having various forms

**va·ri·o·la** (və rī′ə lə) *n*. [ModL. < ML. < L. *varius*, various, mottled] any of a group of virus diseases characterized by pustular eruptions and including smallpox, cowpox, etc.

**var·i·om·e·ter** (ver′ē äm′ə tər, var′-) *n*. [VARIO(US) + -METER] **1.** a device for determining variations of magnetic force esp. at different places on the earth **2.** *Radio* a unit consisting of a coil that can be rotated within a fixed coil to vary inductance

**var·i·o·rum** (ver′ē ôr′əm, var′-) *n*. [L., of various (scholars)] **1.** an edition or text, as of a literary work, with notes by various editors, scholars, etc. **2.** an edition containing variant texts —*adj*. of or being a variorum

**var·i·ous** (ver′ē əs, var′-) *adj*. [L. *varius*, diverse] **1.** differing one from another; of several kinds **2.** *a*) several or many *[found in various parts of the country]* b) individual; distinct *[bequests to the various heirs]* **3.** many-sided; versatile **4.** characterized by variety; varied in nature or appearance —**var′i·ous·ly** *adv.*

**va·ris·tor** (və ris′tər) *n.* [VAR(IOUS) + (RES)ISTOR] a semiconductor device whose resistance drops as the voltage is increased

**var·let** (vär′lit) *n.* [OFr., var. of *vaslet:* see VALET] [Archaic] **1.** an attendant **2.** a scoundrel; knave

**var·mint, var·ment** (vär′mənt) *n.* [dial. var. of VERMIN] [Dial. or Colloq.] a person or animal regarded as troublesome or objectionable

**var·nish** (vär′nish) *n.* [< OFr. < ML. *veronix,* a resin < Gr. *Berenikē,* an ancient city] **1.** *a)* a preparation made of resinous substances dissolved in oil (**oil varnish**) or in alcohol, turpentine, etc. (**spirit varnish**), used to give a hard, glossy surface to wood, etc. *b)* any of various natural or prepared products similarly used **2.** the hard, glossy surface produced **3.** a surface gloss or smoothness, as of manner —*vt.* **1.** to cover with varnish **2.** to smooth over in a false way —**var′nish·er** *n.*

**va·room** (və rōōm′) *n., vi.* var. of VROOM

**var·si·ty** (vär′sə tē) *n., pl.* **-ties** [contr. & altered < UNIVERSITY] the main team representing a university, college, or school in some competition, esp. an athletic one —*adj.* designating or of such a team

**var·y** (ver′ē, var′-) *vt.* **var′ied, var′y·ing** [< OFr. < L. *variare* < *varius,* various] **1.** to change in form, nature, etc.; alter **2.** to make different from one another **3.** to give variety to —*vi.* **1.** to be or become different; differ or change **2.** to deviate or depart *(from)* —**var′i·er** *n.*

**vas** (vas) *n., pl.* **va·sa** (vā′sə) [L., a vessel] *Anat., Biol.* a vessel or duct —**va·sal** (vā′s'l) *adj.*

**vas·cu·lar** (vas′kyə lər) *adj.* [< ModL. < L. *vasculum,* dim. of *vas,* a vessel] **1.** *Anat., Zool.* of or consisting of vessels carrying blood or lymph **2.** *Bot.* of, consisting of, or having special cells, xylem, and phloem that carry water and food, as ferns and seed plants

**vascular bundle** a unit of the conducting system of higher plants, consisting chiefly of xylem and phloem

**vas de·fe·rens** (vas def′ə renz′) *pl.* **va·sa de·fe·ren·ti·a** (vā′sə def′ə ren′shē ə) [ModL. < L. *vas,* a vessel + *deferens,* carrying down] the duct that carries sperm from the testicle to the ejaculatory duct of the penis

**vase** (vās, vāz; *chiefly Brit.* väz) *n.* [< Fr. < L. *vas,* a vessel, dish] an open container of metal, glass, pottery, etc. used for decoration, holding flowers, etc.

**vas·ec·to·my** (vas ek′tə mē) *n., pl.* **-mies** [VAS(O)- + -ECTOMY] the cutting, tying, and removing of part of the vas deferens for the purpose of sterilizing sexually

**Vas·e·line** (vas′ə lēn′) [coinage < G. *was(ser),* water + Gr. *el(aion),* oil + -INE⁴] *a trademark for* PETROLATUM —*n.* [v-] petrolatum, or petroleum jelly

**vas·o-** [< L. *vas,* a vessel] *a combining form meaning:* **1.** blood vessels *[vasomotor]* **2.** vas deferens *[vasectomy]* **3.** vasomotor *[vasoinhibitor]* Also, before a vowel, **vas-**

**vas·o·con·stric·tor** (vas′ō kən strik′tər) *adj.* [prec. + CONSTRICTOR] *Physiol.* constricting the blood vessels —*n.* a nerve or drug doing this —**vas′o·con·stric′tion** *n.*

**vas·o·di·la·tor** (-dī′lāt′ər) *adj.* [VASO- + DILATOR] *Physiol.* dilating the blood vessels —*n.* a nerve or drug doing this —**vas′o·dil′a·ta′tion** (-dil′ə tā′shən), **vas′o·di·la′tion** *n.*

**vas·o·in·hib·i·tor** (-in hib′ə tər) *n.* [VASO- + INHIBITOR] a drug or agent inhibiting the action of the vasomotor nerves —**vas′o·in·hib′i·to′ry** (-tôr′ē) *adj.*

**vas·o·mo·tor** (-mōt′ər) *adj.* [VASO- + MOTOR] *Physiol.* regulating the diameter of blood vessels by causing contraction or dilatation, as certain nerves or nerve centers

**vas·o·pres·sin** (-pres′′n) *n.* [< VASO- + PRESS(URE) + -IN¹] a hormone of the pituitary gland that increases blood pressure

**vas·o·pres·sor** (-pres′ər) *n.* [VASO- + PRESS(URE) + -OR] a substance causing a rise in blood pressure

**vas·sal** (vas′'l) *n.* [OFr. < ML. *vassalus* < *vassus,* servant < Celt.] **1.** a person in the feudal system who held land in return for fealty, military help, etc. to an overlord **2.** a subordinate, servant, slave, etc. —*adj.* of, like, or being a vassal —**vas′sal·age** (ij) *n.*

**vast** (vast) *adj.* [L. *vastus*] very great in size, extent, amount, degree, etc. —**vast′ly** *adv.* —**vast′ness** *n.*

**Väs·te·rås** (ves′tə rôs′) city in SC Sweden: pop. 113,000

**vast·y** (vas′tē) *adj.* **-i·er, -i·est** [Archaic] vast; immense

**vat** (vat) *n.* [< OE. *fæt,* a cask] a large tank, tub, or cask for holding liquids as for use in a manufacturing process —*vt.* **vat′ted, vat′ting** to put or store in a vat

**Vat·i·can** (vat′i k'n) **1.** the papal palace, a group of buildings in Vatican City **2.** the papal government or authority —*adj.* **1.** of the Vatican **2.** designating either of

the Roman Catholic Ecumenical Councils held in Vatican City in 1869–70 (**Vatican I**) or 1962–65 (**Vatican II**)

**Vatican City** independent papal state constituted as an enclave in Rome: it includes the Vatican & St. Peter's Basilica: 108 acres: pop. c. 1,000

**vaude·ville** (vōd′vil, vôd′-; vō′də-, vô′də-) *n.* [Fr. < *Vau-de-Vire,* a valley in Normandy, famous for light, convivial songs] **1.** a stage show consisting of mixed specialty acts, including songs, dances, comic skits, acrobatics, etc. **2.** such entertainment generally —**vaude·vil′lian** (-vil′yən) *n., adj.*

**vault¹** (vôlt) *n.* [< OFr., ult. < L. *volvere,* to roll] **1.** an arched roof, ceiling, etc. of masonry **2.** an arched chamber or space, esp. when underground **3.** a cellar room used for storage **4.** *a)* a burial chamber *b)* a concrete or metal enclosure in the ground, into which the casket is lowered at burial **5.** a secure room for the safekeeping of valuables or money, as in a bank **6.** the sky as a vaultlike canopy —*vt.* **1.** to cover with a vault **2.** to build as a vault —*vi.* to curve like a vault —**vault′ed** *adj.*

GROINED VAULT

**vault²** (vôlt) *vi.* [< MFr. < OIt. *voltare,* ult. < L. *volvere,* to roll] to leap as over a barrier, esp. putting the hands on the barrier or using a long pole —*vt.* to vault over —*n.* a vaulting —**vault′er** *n.*

**vault·ing¹** (vôl′tiŋ) *n.* **1.** the arched work forming a vault **2.** a vault or vaults

**vault·ing²** (vôl′tiŋ) *adj.* **1.** that vaults or leaps **2.** reaching too far or beyond one's abilities *[vaulting ambition]*

**vaunt** (vônt, vänt) *vi., vt.* [< OFr. < LL. *vanitare* < L. *vanus,* vain] to boast or brag (of) —*n.* a boast or brag —**vaunt′ed** *adj.* —**vaunt′er** *n.*

**v.aux.** auxiliary verb

**vb. 1.** verb **2.** verbal

**VC, V.C.** Viet Cong

**V.C. 1.** Vice-Consul **2.** Victoria Cross

**VD, V.D.** venereal disease

**V-Day** (vē′dā′) *n.* Victory Day

**'ve** *contraction of* HAVE *[we've seen it]*

**Ve·a·dar** (vā′ä där′, vē′ä där′) *n.* [Heb.] a recurring extra month of the Jewish year: see JEWISH CALENDAR

**veal** (vēl) *n.* [OFr. *veel* < L. dim. of *vitulus,* a calf] **1.** the flesh of a young calf, used as food **2.** a vealer

**veal·er** (-ər) *n.* a calf, esp. as intended for food

**Veb·len** (veb′lən), **Thor·stein (Bunde)** (thôr′stīn) 1857–1929; U.S. political economist & social scientist

**vec·tor** (vek′tər) *n.* [ModL. < L., a carrier < pp. of *vehere,* to carry] **1.** *Biol.* an animal, as an insect, that transmits a disease-producing organism from one host to another **2.** *Math. a)* a physical quantity with both magnitude and direction, such as a force or velocity: distinguished from SCALAR *b)* a directed line segment representing such a quantity —**vec·to′ri·al** (-tôr′ē əl) *adj.*

**Ve·da** (vā′də, vē′-) *n.* [Sans. *veda,* knowledge] **1.** any of four ancient sacred books of Hinduism, consisting of psalms, chants, sacred formulas, etc. **2.** these books collectively —**Ve·da·ic** (vi dā′ik), **Ve′dic** *adj.*

**Ve·dan·ta** (vi dän′tə, -dan′-) *n.* [< Sans. < *veda,* knowledge + *anta,* an end] a system of Hindu monistic or pantheistic philosophy based on the Vedas —**Ve·dan′tic** *adj.* —**Ve·dan′tism** *n.*

**V-E Day** (vē′ē′) May 8, 1945, the official date of Germany's surrender ending the European phase of World War II

**Veep** (vēp) *n.* [< *veepee* (for V.P.)] *[sometimes* v-] [Colloq.] a vice-president; specif., the U.S. Vice President

**veer** (vir) *vi.* [altered < Fr. *virer,* to turn around] **1.** to change direction; shift; turn **2.** to change sides, as from one opinion to another **3.** to shift clockwise: said of the wind —*vt.* to turn or swing; change the course of —*n.* a change of direction —**veer′ing·ly** *adv.*

**veer·y** (vir′ē) *n., pl.* **veer′ies** [prob. echoic] a brown and cream-colored thrush of the eastern U.S.

**Ve·ga** (vē′gə, vā′-) [ML. < Ar.] a very bright star in the constellation Lyra

**Ve·ga** (vē′gä), **Lo·pe de** (lō′pe *the*) 1562–1635; Sp. dramatist & poet

**veg·e·ta·ble** (vej′tə b'l, vej′ə tə-) *adj.* [< ML. *vegetabilis,* vegetative < LL., animating < L. *vegetare:* see VEGETATE] **1.** of plants in general *[the vegetable kingdom]* **2.** of, like, or from vegetables *[vegetable oil]* —*n.* **1.** any plant, as distinguished from something animal or inorganic **2.** *a)* any plant that is eaten whole or in part, raw or cooked, generally with an entree or in a salad *b)* the edible part of such a plant, as the root (e.g., a carrot), tuber (a potato), seed (a pea), fruit (a tomato), stem (celery), leaf (lettuce), etc. **3.** a person thought of as vegetablelike because living in or as in a coma

**vegetable ivory** the fully ripe, ivorylike seed of a S. American palm, used to make buttons, ornaments, etc.

**vegetable oil** any of various liquid fats derived from the fruits or seeds of plants, used in food products, etc.

**veg·e·tal** (vej′ə t′l) *adj. same as:* **1.** VEGETABLE **2.** VEGETATIVE (sense 3)

**veg·e·tar·i·an** (vej′ə ter′ē ən) *n.* [VEGET(ABLE) + -ARIAN] a person who eats no meat; strictly, one who believes in a diet of only vegetables, fruits, grains, and nuts as the proper one for people —*adj.* **1.** of vegetarians, their principles, etc. **2.** consisting only of vegetables, fruits, etc. —**veg′e·tar′i·an·ism** *n.*

**veg·e·tate** (vej′ə tāt′) *vi.* -**tat′ed**, -**tat′ing** [< L. pp. of *vegetare*, to enliven < *vegetus*, lively < *vegere*, to quicken] **1.** to grow as plants **2.** to exist with little mental and physical activity; lead a dull, inactive life

**veg·e·ta·tion** (vej′ə tā′shən) *n.* **1.** the act or process of vegetating **2.** plant life in general **3.** dull, passive, unthinking existence —**veg′e·ta′tion·al** *adj.*

**veg·e·ta·tive** (vej′ə tāt′iv) *adj.* **1.** of plants or plant growth **2.** growing as plants **3.** designating or of the functions or parts of plants not related to reproduction **4.** helping plant growth *[vegetative loams]* **5.** dull and inactive *[a vegetative life]* **6.** *Zool.* of or pertaining to asexual reproduction Also **veg′e·tive** (-tiv) —**veg′e·ta′tive·ly** *adv.* —**veg′e·ta′tive·ness** *n.*

**ve·he·ment** (vē′ə mənt) *adj.* [< MFr. < L. *vehemens*, eager < *vehere*, to carry] **1.** acting or moving with great force; violent; impetuous **2.** full of or showing very strong feeling; intense, fervent, impassioned, etc. —**ve′he·mence**, **ve′he·men·cy** *n.* —**ve′he·ment·ly** *adv.*

**ve·hi·cle** (vē′ə k′l, vē′hi-) *n.* [< Fr. < L. *vehiculum*, carriage < *vehere*, to carry] **1.** a means of carrying persons or things, esp. over land or in space, as an automobile, bicycle, sled, spacecraft, etc. **2.** a means of expressing ideas **3.** a play as a means of presenting a specified actor or company **4.** *Painting* a liquid, as water or oil, with which pigments are mixed for use **5.** *Pharmacy* a substance, as a syrup, in which medicines are given —**ve·hic·u·lar** (vē hik′yoo lər) *adj.*

**veil** (vāl) *n.* [< ONormFr. < L. *vela*, pl. of *velum*, cloth] **1.** a piece of light fabric, as net or gauze, worn, esp. by women, over the face or head to hide the features or as an ornament **2.** any cloth, curtain, etc. used to conceal or separate **3.** anything that covers or conceals *[a veil of mist, a veil of silence]* **4.** *a)* a part of a nun's headdress, draped along the face and over the shoulders *b)* the state or life of a nun: chiefly in **take the veil**, to become a nun —*vt.* to cover, conceal, etc. with or as with a veil —**veiled** *adj.* —**veil′like′** *adj.*

**veil·ing** (-iŋ) *n.* **1.** a veil **2.** fabric for veils

**vein** (vān) *n.* [< OFr. < L. *vena*] **1.** any blood vessel bringing blood back to the heart from some part of the body **2.** any riblike support in an insect wing **3.** any of the fine lines, or ribs, in a leaf **4.** a layer of mineral, rock, etc. in a fissure or zone of different rock; lode **5.** a streak or marking of a color or substance different from the surrounding material, as in marble **6.** *a)* a distinctive quality or strain running through something *[a vein of humor]* *b)* course or tenor of thought, feeling, action, etc. **7.** a temporary state of mind; mood *[in a serious vein]* —*vt.* **1.** to mark as with veins **2.** to branch out through like veins

**vein·ing** (-iŋ) *n.* formation or arrangement of veins

**vein·let** (-lit) *n. same as* VENULE: also **vein′ule** (-yōōl)

**vein·y** (-ē) *adj.* **vein′i·er**, **vein′i·est** full of veins or veinlike markings

**ve·lar** (vē′lər) *adj.* **1.** of a velum; esp., of the soft palate **2.** *Phonet.* pronounced with the back of the tongue touching or near the soft palate, as the sound of *k* followed by a back vowel like (ōō) —*n.* a velar sound

**Ve·láz·quez** (ve läth′keth; *E.* və las′kes, -kwez), **Die·go** (Rodrīguez de Silva y) (dye′gồ) 1599–1660; Sp. painter: also **Ve·lás·quez** (ve läs′keth)

**Vel·cro** (vel′krồ) [arbitrary formation < VEL(VET)] *a trademark for* a nylon material made with both a surface of tiny hooks and one of pile: matching strips are used in garments, etc. as fasteners, easily pressed together or pulled apart —*n.* this material

**veld, veldt** (velt) *n.* [Afrik. < MDu. *veld*, a field] in South Africa, open grassy country

**vel·lum** (vel′əm) *n.* [MFr. *velin*, vellum < OFr. *veel*: see VEAL] **1.** a fine parchment used for writing on or for binding books **2.** a manuscript on vellum **3.** a strong paper resembling vellum —*adj.* of or like vellum

**ve·loc·i·pede** (və läs′ə pēd′) *n.* [< Fr. < L. *velox* (gen. *velocis*), swift + *pes* (gen. *pedis*), a foot] **1.** any of various early bicycles or tricycles **2.** [Now Rare] a child's tricycle

**ve·loc·i·ty** (-tē) *n., pl.* -**ties** [< Fr. < L. < *velox*: see prec.] **1.** quickness of motion or action; speed **2.** rate of

change of position, or rate of motion in a particular direction, in relation to time

**ve·lour, ve·lours** (və loor′) *n., pl.* **ve·lours′** [Fr.: see VELURE] a fabric with a soft nap like velvet, used for upholstery, draperies, hats, clothing, etc.

**ve·lum** (vē′ləm) *n., pl.* -**la** (-lə) [L., a veil] *Biol.* any of various veillike membranous partitions or coverings; specif., *same as* SOFT PALATE

**ve·lure** (və loor′) *n.* [Fr. *velours* < OFr. < LL. *villosus*, shaggy < *villus*, shaggy hair] velvet or velvetlike fabric

**vel·vet** (vel′vit) *n.* [< OFr. < VL. *villutus* < L. *villus*, shaggy hair] **1.** a rich fabric of silk, rayon, nylon, etc. with a soft, thick pile **2.** anything with a surface like that of velvet **3.** [Old Slang] extra or clear profit or gain —*adj.* **1.** made of or covered with velvet **2.** smooth or soft like velvet —**vel′vet·y** *adj.*

**velvet ant** any of various wasps that resemble ants, often covered with brightly colored hairs: females are wingless

**vel·vet·een** (vel′və tēn′) *n.* a velvetlike cotton cloth

**ve·na ca·va** (vē′nə kā′və) *pl.* **ve′nae ca′vae** (vē′nē kā′vē) [ModL. < L. *vena*, vein + *cava*, fem. of *cavus*, hollow] *Anat.* either of two large veins carrying blood to the right atrium of the heart

**ve·nal** (vē′n′l) *adj.* [L. *venalis*, salable < *venum*, sale] **1.** that can readily be bribed or corrupted **2.** characterized by bribery or corruption —**ve·nal′i·ty** (-nal′ə tē) *n., pl.* -**ties** —**ve′nal·ly** *adv.*

**ve·na·tion** (vē nā′shən) *n.* [< L. *vena*, a vein] **1.** an arrangement or system of veins, as in an insect's wing or a leaf **2.** such veins collectively

**vend** (vend) *vt., vi.* [< L. < *vendere*, contr. < *venum dare*, to offer for sale] to sell, esp. by peddling

**vend·ee** (ven′dē′) *n.* the person to whom a thing is sold

**ven·det·ta** (ven det′ə) *n.* [It. < L. *vindicta*, vengeance] **1.** a feud in which relatives of a murdered or wronged person seek vengeance on the guilty person or his family **2.** any bitter quarrel or feud —**ven·det′tist** *n.*

**vend·i·ble, vend·a·ble** (ven′də b′l) *adj.* [see VEND] capable of being sold —*n.* something vendible —**vend′i·bil′i·ty** *n.* —**vend′i·bly** *adv.*

**vending machine** a coin-operated machine for selling certain kinds of articles, refreshments, etc.

**ven·dor, vend·er** (ven′dər) *n.* **1.** one who vends, or sells; seller **2.** *same as* VENDING MACHINE

**ve·neer** (və nir′) *vt.* [G. *furnieren* < Fr. *fournir*, to furnish] **1.** to cover with a thin layer of finer material; esp., to cover (wood) with wood of a finer quality **2.** to make outwardly attractive **3.** to glue (thin wood layers) together to form plywood —*n.* **1.** a thin layer used to veneer something; also, any of the layers used in making plywood **2.** a surface appearance that hides what is below

**ve·neer·ing** (-iŋ) *n.* material used for veneer

**ven·er·a·ble** (ven′ər ə b′l, ven′rə b′l) *adj.* [see VENERATE] **1.** worthy of respect or reverence by reason of age, dignity, character, etc. **2.** impressively ancient, historic, or hallowed —**ven′er·a·bil′i·ty** *n.* —**ven′er·a·bly** *adv.*

**ven·er·ate** (ven′ə rāt′) *vt.* -**at′ed**, -**at′ing** [< L. pp. of *venerari*, to worship] to feel or show deep respect for; revere —**ven′er·a′tor** *n.*

**ven·er·a·tion** (ven′ə rā′shən) *n.* **1.** a venerating or being venerated **2.** a feeling of deep respect and reverence **3.** an act showing this

**ve·ne·re·al** (və nir′ē əl) *adj.* [< L. *venereus* < *venus* (gen. *veneris*), love] **1.** *a)* relating to sexual love or intercourse *b)* arousing sexual desire **2.** *a)* transmitted only or chiefly by sexual intercourse with an infected individual, as syphilis and gonorrhea *b)* infected with a venereal disease *c)* of or dealing with venereal disease

**ven·er·y¹** (ven′ər ē) *n.* [< L. *Venus* (gen. *Veneris*), Venus, love] [Archaic] sexual intercourse

**ven·er·y²** (ven′ər ē) *n.* [< MFr. < *vener*, to hunt < L. *venari*] [Archaic] the hunting of game; the chase

**Ve·ne·tian** (və nē′shən) *adj.* of Venice, its people, culture, etc. —*n.* a native or inhabitant of Venice

**Venetian blind** [*also* **v- b-**] a window blind made of a number of thin, horizontal slats that can be set at any angle to regulate the light and air passing through or drawn up by cords to the window top

**Ve·ne·zi·a** (ve ne′tsyä) *It. name of* VENICE

**Ven·e·zue·la** (ven′i zwā′lə, -zwē′-; *Sp.* ve′ne swe′lä) country in N S. America, on the Caribbean: 352,143 sq. mi.; pop. 10,399,000; cap. Caracas —**Ven′e·zue′lan** *adj., n.*

**venge·ance** (ven′jəns) *n.* [OFr. < *venger*, to avenge < L. *vindicare*: see VINDICATE] **1.** the return of an injury for an injury, in punishment; an avenging; revenge **2.** the desire to make such a return —**with a vengeance 1.** with great force or fury **2.** to an excessive or unusual extent

VENETIAN BLIND

**venge·ful** (venj′fəl) *adj.* **1.** desiring or seeking vengeance; vindictive **2.** arising from a desire for vengeance: said of actions or feelings **3.** inflicting vengeance —**venge′ful·ly** *adv.* —**venge′ful·ness** *n.*

**ve·ni·al** (vē′nē əl, vēn′yəl) *adj.* [OFr. < LL. *venialis* < L. *venia,* grace] **1.** that can be forgiven, pardoned, or excused, as an error or fault **2.** *R.C.Ch.* not causing spiritual death: said of sins not regarded as serious —**ve′ni·al·ly** *adv.*

**Ven·ice** (ven′is) seaport in N Italy built on more than 100 small islands in an inlet ( Gulf of Venice ) at the N end of the Adriatic: pop. 368,000

**ven·in** (ven′in) *n.* [< VEN(OM) + -IN¹] any of the specific toxic constituents of animal venoms

**ve·ni·re** (və nī′rē) *n.* [L., to come] **1.** *short for* VENIRE FACIAS **2.** a list or group of people from among whom a jury or juries will be selected

**venire fa·ci·as** (fā′shē as′) [ML., cause to come] *Law* a writ issued by a judge to a sheriff or coroner, instructing him to summon persons to serve as jurors

**ve·ni·re·man** (və nī′rē mən) *n., pl.* **-men** a member of a venire (sense 2)

**ven·i·son** (ven′i s'n, -z'n; *Brit.* ven′zən) *n.* [< OFr. < L. < pp. of *venari,* to hunt] the flesh of deer, used as food

**‡ve·ni, vi·di, vi·ci** (vā′nē vē′dē vē′chē, wā′nē wē′dē wē′kē, wē′nī vī′dī vī′sī) [L.] I came, I saw, I conquered: Julius Caesar's report to the Roman Senate of a victory

**ven·om** (ven′əm) *n.* [< OFr. < L. *venenum,* a poison] **1.** the poison secreted by some snakes, spiders, insects, etc., injected into the victim by bite or sting **2.** spite; malice

**ven·om·ous** (-əs) *adj.* **1.** full of venom; poisonous **2.** full of spite or ill will; malicious **3.** *Zool.* able to inject venom by bite or sting —**ven′om·ous·ly** *adv.* —**ven′om·ous·ness** *n.*

**ve·nous** (vē′nəs) *adj.* [L. *venosus*] **1.** *Biol. a)* of a vein or veins *b)* having veins or full of veins; veiny **2.** *Physiol.* designating blood being carried in the veins back to the heart and lungs —**ve′nous·ly** *adv.*

**vent¹** (vent) *n.* [OFr. *venter,* to blow, ult. < L. *ventus,* a wind] **1.** an issuing, as of air, or the means of this; outlet; passage; escape **2.** expression; release [giving *vent* to emotion] **3.** *a)* a small opening to let gas, etc. out *b)* a small triangular window, as in a car door, for letting air in without a direct draft **4.** the opening in a volcano through which it erupts **5.** *Zool.* the excretory opening in animals —*vt.* **1.** to make a vent in **2.** to let (steam, gas, etc.) out through an opening **3.** to give release or expression to **4.** to unburden by giving vent to feelings

**vent²** (vent) *n.* [< OFr., ult. < L. pp. of *findere,* to split] a vertical slit in a garment, esp. one put in the back or sides of a coat —*vt.* to make a vent or vents in

**ven·ti·late** (ven′t'l āt′) *vt.* **-lat′ed, -lat′ing** [< L. pp. of *ventilare,* to fan < *ventus,* a wind] **1.** *a)* to circulate fresh air in (a room, etc.) *b)* to circulate in (a room, etc.): said of fresh air **2.** to put a vent in, to let air, gas, etc. escape **3.** to examine and discuss (a grievance, etc.) openly **4.** to aerate (blood); oxygenate —**ven′ti·la′tion** *n.*

**ven·ti·la·tor** (-ər) *n.* a thing that ventilates; esp., any device used to bring in fresh air and drive out foul air

**ven·tral** (ven′trəl) *adj.* [Fr. < L. *ventralis* < *venter,* belly] of, on, or near the belly —**ven′tral·ly** *adv.*

**ven·tri·cle** (ven′tri k'l) *n.* [< L. dim. of *venter,* belly] *Anat., Zool.* a cavity; specif., *a)* either of the two lower chambers of the heart which receive blood from the atria and pump it into the arteries *b)* any of the four small continuous cavities within the brain —**ven·tric′u·lar** (-trik′yə lər) *adj.*

**ven·tril·o·quism** (ven tril′ə kwiz′m) *n.* [< L. < *venter,* belly + *loqui,* to speak + -ISM] the art or practice of speaking so that the voice seems to come from some source other than the speaker: also **ven·tril′o·quy** (-kwē) —**ven·tril′o·quist** *n.* —**ven·tril′o·quis′tic** *adj.* —**ven·tril′o·quize′** (-kwīz′) *vi., vt.* **-quized′, -quiz′ing**

**Ven·tu·ra** (ven toor′ə) [< (*San Buena)ventura* (the official name) < Sp., lit., saint of good fortune] city in SW Calif., northwest of Los Angeles: pop. 74,000

**ven·ture** (ven′chər) *n.* [< ME. *aventure:* see ADVENTURE] **1.** a risky undertaking; esp., a business enterprise in which there is danger of loss as well as chance for profit **2.** something on which a risk is taken **3.** chance; fortune: now only in **at a venture,** by mere chance —*vt.* **-tured, -tur·ing** **1.** to risk; hazard **2.** to take the risk of; brave **3.** to express (an opinion, etc.) at the risk of being criticized, etc. —*vi.* to do or go at some risk —**ven′tur·er** *n.*

**venture capital** funds invested or for investment at considerable risk in potentially very profitable enterprises

**ven·ture·some** (-səm) *adj.* **1.** inclined to venture; daring **2.** risky; hazardous —**ven′ture·some·ly** *adv.* —**ven′ture·some·ness** *n.*

**ven·tu·ri (tube)** (ven toor′ē) [after G. B. *Venturi*

(1746–1822), It. physicist] a short tube with a narrow throat that increases the velocity and lowers the pressure of a fluid flowing through it: used to measure fluid flow, to regulate the mixture in a carburetor, etc.

**ven·tur·ous** (ven′chər əs) *adj. same as* VENTURESOME —**ven′tur·ous·ly** *adv.* —**ven′tur·ous·ness** *n.*

**ven·ue** (ven′yōō, -ōō) *n.* [OFr., arrival < *venir,* to come < L. *venire*] *Law a)* the county or locality in which a cause of action or a crime occurs *b)* the county or locality in which a jury is drawn and a case tried **2.** the site of an event or activity, as of a sports contest —**change of venue** *Law* the substitution of another place of trial, as when the jury or court is likely to be prejudiced

**ven·ule** (ven′yōōl) *n.* [< L. dim. of *vena,* vein] **1.** *Anat.* a small vein **2.** *Biol.* any small branch of a vein in a leaf or in an insect wing —**ven′u·lar** (-yōō lər) *adj.*

**Ve·nus** (vē′nəs) *n.* [L., lit., love] **1.** *Rom. Myth.* the goddess of love and beauty: identified with the Greek goddess Aphrodite **2.** a planet in the solar system, second in distance from the sun: diameter, c.7,600 mi —*n.* **1.** a statue or image of Venus **2.** a very beautiful woman

**Ve·nus' fly·trap** (vē′nəs flī′trap′) a white-flowered swamp plant native to the Carolinas, having leaves with two hinged blades that snap shut and so trap insects

**Ver·a** (vir′ə) [Russ. *Vjera,* faith; also L. fem. of *verus,* true] a feminine name

**ve·ra·cious** (və rā′shəs) *adj.* [< L. < *verus,* true] **1.** habitually truthful; honest **2.** true; accurate —**ve·ra′cious·ly** *adv.* —**ve·ra′cious·ness** *n.*

**ve·rac·i·ty** (və ras′ə tē) *n., pl.* **-ties** [< ML. < L. *verus,* true] **1.** habitual truthfulness; honesty **2.** accordance with truth; accuracy of statement **3.** accuracy or precision, as of perception **4.** that which is true; truth

VENUS' FLYTRAP

**Ver·a·cruz** (ver′ə krōōz′; *Sp.* ve′rä krōōs′) seaport in E Mexico, on the Gulf of Mexico: pop. 242,000

**ve·ran·da, ve·ran·dah** (və ran′də) *n.* [Anglo-Ind. < Port. *varanda,* a balcony < *vara,* a pole < L., forked stick] an open porch, usually roofed, along the outside of a building

**verb** (vurb) *n.* [< OFr. < L. *verbum,* a word] **1.** any of a class of words expressing action, existence, or occurrence, and acting as the main part of a predicate: see also AUXILIARY VERB, LINKING VERB **2.** any phrase or construction used as a verb —*adj.* of, or functioning as, a verb

**ver·bal** (vur′b'l) *adj.* **1.** of, in, or by means of words **2.** concerned merely with words rather than with facts, ideas, or actions **3.** oral rather than written **4.** *Gram.* of, like, or derived from a verb —*n. Gram.* a verbal noun or other word derived from a verb: in English, gerunds, infinitives, and participles are verbals —**ver′bal·ly** *adv.*

**ver·bal·ism** (-iz′m) *n.* **1.** an expression in one or more words; word or word phrase **2.** words only, without any real meaning **3.** any virtually meaningless phrase

**ver·bal·ist** (-ist) *n.* **1.** a person skilled in verbal expression **2.** a person who gives more importance to words than to the facts or ideas they convey

**ver·bal·ize** (vur′bə līz′) *vi.* **-ized′, -iz′ing** **1.** to be wordy, or verbose **2.** to communicate in words —*vt.* **1.** to express in words **2.** to change (a noun, etc.) into a verb —**ver′bal·i·za′tion** *n.* —**ver′bal·iz′er** *n.*

**verbal noun** *Gram.* a noun derived from a verb and acting in some respects like a verb: in English it is either a noun ending in *-ing* (a gerund) or an infinitive (Ex.: *walking* is healthful, *to err* is human)

**ver·ba·tim** (vər bāt′əm) *adv.* [ML. < L. *verbum,* a word] word for word; in exactly the same words —*adj.* following the original, word for word [a *verbatim* account]

**ver·be·na** (vər bē′nə) *n.* [ModL., genus name < L., foliage] any of a group of ornamental plants with spikes or clusters of red, white, or purplish flowers

**ver·bi·age** (vur′bē ij) *n.* [Fr. < OFr. < L. *verbum,* a word] an excess of words beyond those needed to express concisely what is meant; wordiness

**ver·bose** (vər bōs′) *adj.* [L. *verbosus,* full of words < *verbum,* a word] using or containing too many words; wordy; long-winded —**ver·bose′ly** *adv.* —**ver·bos′i·ty** (-bäs′ə tē), **ver·bose′ness** *n.*

**‡ver·bo·ten** (fer bō′tən) *adj.* [G.] forbidden; prohibited

**ver·dant** (vur′d'nt) *adj.* [prob. < VERD(URE) + -ANT] **1.** green **2.** covered with green vegetation **3.** inexperienced; immature —**ver′dan·cy** (-d'n sē) *n.*

**Verde** (vurd), Cape peninsula on the Atlantic coast of Senegal: westernmost point of Africa

**Ver·di** (verʹdē), **Giu·sep·pe** (Fortunino Francisco) (jōō zepʹpe) 1813–1901; It. operatic composer

**ver·dict** (verʹdikt) *n.* [< Anglo-Fr. < ML. < L. *vere*, truly + *dictum*, a thing said < *dicere*, to say] **1.** *Law* the decision reached by a jury at the end of a trial **2.** any decision or judgment

**ver·di·gris** (verʹdi grēs´, -gris) *n.* [< MFr. < OFr. < *verd*, green + *de*, of + *Grece*, Greece] a green or greenish-blue coating that forms on brass, bronze, or copper

**Ver·dun** (ver dunʹ, ver-; *Fr.* ver děnʹ) **1.** city in NE France, on the Meuse River: scene of a battle of World War I **2.** city in SW Quebec, Canada: suburb of Montreal: pop. 77,000

**ver·dure** (verʹjər) *n.* [OFr. < *verd*, green] **1.** the fresh green color of growing things **2.** green vegetation **3.** vigorous or flourishing condition —**verʹdured** *adj.* —**verʹdur·ous** *adj.*

**verge**[1] (verj) *n.* [< OFr. < L. *virga*, rod] **1.** *a)* the edge, brink, or margin [the *verge* of a forest, on the *verge* of hysteria] *b)* [Brit.] a grassy border, as along a road **2.** *a)* an enclosing line or border, esp. of something circular *b)* the area enclosed **3.** a rod or staff symbolic of an office —*vi.* **verged, vergʹing** to be on the verge, brink, or border (usually with *on* or *upon*)

**verge**[2] (verj) *vi.* **verged, vergʹing** [L. *vergere*] **1.** to tend or incline (*to* or *toward*) **2.** to be in the process of change into something else; pass gradually (*into*) [dawn *verging* into daylight]

**verg·er** (verʹjər) *n.* [see VERGE[1] & -ER] **1.** a person who carries a staff of office before a bishop, etc. **2.** a church caretaker or usher

**Ver·gil** (verʹjəl) *var. of* VIRGIL —**Ver·gilʹi·an** (-jilʹē ən) *adj.*

**ver·i·est** (verʹē ist) *adj.* [superl. of VERY, *adj.*] being such to the highest degree; utter [the *veriest* nonsense]

**ver·i·fi·ca·tion** (verʹə fi kāʹshən) *n.* a verifying or being verified; establishment or confirmation of the truth or accuracy of a fact, theory, etc.

**ver·i·fy** (verʹə fī´) *vt.* **-fied´, -fyʹing** [< MFr. < ML. < L. *verus*, true + *-ficare*, -FY] **1.** to prove to be true by demonstration, evidence, etc.; confirm or substantiate **2.** to test the accuracy of, as by comparison with a standard **3.** *Law* to affirm on oath —**verʹi·fiʹa·ble** *adj.* —**verʹi·fiʹa·bly** *adv.* —**verʹi·fiʹer** *n.*

**ver·i·ly** (verʹə lē) *adv.* [Archaic] in very truth; truly

**ver·i·sim·i·lar** (verʹə simʹə lər) *adj.* [< L. < *verus*, true + *similis*, like] seeming to be true or real; likely

**ver·i·si·mil·i·tude** (verʹə si milʹə tōōd´, -tyōōd´) *n.* [< L.: see prec.] **1.** the appearance of being true or real **2.** something having the mere appearance of being true or real

**ver·i·ta·ble** (verʹi tə bʹl) *adj.* [< OFr. < L. *veritas*, truth] being such in truth or fact; actual [a *veritable* feast] —**verʹi·ta·bly** *adv.*

**ver·i·ty** (verʹə tē) *n., pl.* **-ties** [< OFr. < L. *veritas*, truth < *verus*, true] **1.** conformity to truth or fact **2.** a principle, belief, etc. taken to be fundamentally and permanently true; a truth; a reality

**ver·juice** (verʹjōōs´) *n.* [< MFr. < *vert*, green + *jus*, juice] **1.** the sour, acid juice of green, or unripe, fruit **2.** sourness of temper, looks, etc.

**Ver·laine** (ver lenʹ), **Paul** (pôl) 1844–96; Fr. poet

**Ver·meer** (ver merʹ; *E.* ver mirʹ), **Jan** (yän) 1632–75; Du. painter: also called *Jan van der Meer van Delft*

**ver·mi-** [< L. *vermis*] a combining form meaning worm

**ver·mi·cel·li** (verʹmə selʹē, -chelʹē) *n.* [It., little worms < L. dim. of *vermis*, a worm] pasta like spaghetti, but in thinner strings

**ver·mi·cide** (verʹmə sīd´) *n.* [VERMI- + -CIDE] a drug or other agent used to kill worms, esp. intestinal worms

**ver·mic·u·lar** (vər mikʹyə lər) *adj.* [< ModL. < L. dim. of *vermis*, a worm] **1.** *a)* wormlike in shape or movement *b)* having twisting lines, ridges, etc. that look like worm tracks **2.** of, made by, or caused by worms Also **ver·micʹu·late** (-lit), **ver·micʹu·latʹed** (-lātʹid)

**ver·mic·u·lite** (vər mikʹyə līt´) *n.* [< L.: see prec. & -ITE] any of various hydrous silicate minerals, usually as mica in tiny scales that expand when heated: used for insulation, water adsorption, etc.

**ver·mi·form** (verʹmə fôrm´) *adj.* [VERMI- + -FORM] shaped like a worm

**vermiform appendix** *see* APPENDIX (sense 2)

**ver·mi·fuge** (verʹmə fyōōj´) *adj.* [VERMI- + -FUGE] serving to expel worms and other parasites from the intestinal tract —*n.* a vermifuge drug

**ver·mil·ion** (vər milʹyən) *n.* [< OFr. < *vermeil*, bright-red < L. dim. of *vermis*, a worm] **1.** *a)* bright-red mercuric sulfide, used as a pigment *b)* any of several other red pigments resembling this **2.** a bright red or scarlet —*adj.* of the color vermilion

**ver·min** (verʹmin) *n., pl.* **-min** [< OFr. < L. *vermis*, a worm] **1.** *a)* any of various insects, bugs, or small animals regarded as pests because destructive, disease-carrying, etc., as flies, lice, or rats *b)* such pests collectively **2.** [Chiefly

Brit.] collectively, birds or animals that kill game on preserves **3.** *a)* a vile, loathsome person *b)* such persons collectively —**verʹmin·ous** *adj.*

**Ver·mont** (vər mäntʹ) [< Fr. *Verd Mont*, green mountain] New England State of the U.S.: 9,609 sq. mi.; pop. 511,000; cap. Montpelier: abbrev. **Vt., VT** —**Ver·montʹer** *n.*

**ver·mouth** (vər mōōthʹ) *n.* [Fr. < G. *wermut*, wormwood] a sweet or dry, fortified white wine flavored with aromatic herbs, used in cocktails and as an aperitif

**ver·nac·u·lar** (vər nakʹyə lər) *adj.* [L. *vernaculus*, native < *verna*, a homeborn slave] **1.** using the native language of a place [a *vernacular* writer] **2.** commonly spoken by the people of a particular country or place [a *vernacular* dialect] **3.** of or in the native language **4.** native to a place [*vernacular* arts] **5.** designating or of the common name, rather than the scientific Latin name, of an animal or plant —*n.* **1.** the native language or dialect of a country or place **2.** the common, everyday language of ordinary people in a particular locality **3.** the shoptalk of a profession or trade **4.** a vernacular word or term —**ver·nacʹu·lar·ism** *n.* —**ver·nacʹu·lar·ly** *adv.*

**ver·nal** (verʹnʹl) *adj.* [L. *vernalis* < *vernus* < *ver*, spring] **1.** of, relating to, or appearing or occurring in, the spring **2.** springlike; fresh, warm, and mild **3.** fresh and young; youthful —**verʹnal·ly** *adv.*

**ver·nal·ize** (-īz´) *vt.* **-ized´, -izʹing** to stimulate the growth and flowering of (a plant) by artificially shortening the dormant period —**verʹnal·i·zaʹtion** *n.*

**ver·na·tion** (vər nāʹshən) *n.* [ModL. < pp. of L. *vernare*, to flourish] *Bot.* the arrangement of leaves in a leaf bud

**Verne** (vurn; *Fr.* vern), **Jules** (jōōlz; *Fr.* zhül) 1828–1905; Fr. novelist

**ver·ni·er** (verʹnē ər, -nir) *n.* [after P. *Vernier*, 17th-c. Fr. mathematician] a short, graduated scale that slides along a longer graduated instrument and is used to indicate fractional parts of divisions: also **vernier scale**

**Ve·ro·na** (və rōʹnə; *It.* ve rôʹnä) city in N Italy: pop. 259,000 —**Ver·o·nese** (verʹə nēzʹ) *adj., n.*

**Ve·ro·ne·se** (veʹrō neʹse; *E.* verʹō nēzʹ), **Pa·o·lo** (päʹō lōʹ) (born *Paolo Cagliari*) 1528–88; Venetian painter, born in Verona

**Ve·ron·i·ca** (və ränʹi kə) [ML.] a feminine name —*n.* [v-] **1.** [ModL.] *same as* SPEEDWELL **2.** *Bullfighting* a move in which the matador holds his cape out and pivots slowly as the bull charges past him

**Ver·sailles** (vər sīʹ, -sālzʹ; *Fr.* ver säʹy´) city in NC France, near Paris: the Allies & Germany signed a peace treaty here (1919) ending World War I: pop. 95,000

**ver·sa·tile** (verʹsə tʹl; *chiefly Brit.* -tīl´) *adj.* [Fr. < L. < pp. of *versare*, freq. of *vertere*, to turn] **1.** *a)* competent in many things; able to turn easily from one subject or occupation to another *b)* adaptable to many uses or functions **2.** *Biol.* moving freely, as the anther of a flower or the antenna of an insect —**verʹsa·tile·ly** *adv.* —**verʹsa·tilʹi·ty** (-tilʹə tē) *n.*

**verse** (vurs) *n.* [< OE. & OFr. < L. *versus*, a turning, row, pp. of *vertere*, to turn] **1.** a single line of poetry **2.** *a)* poetry in general; sometimes, specif., poems of a light or amusing nature *b)* poetry of a specified kind [blank *verse*] **3.** *a)* a single poem *b)* the poetry of a particular writer, period, etc. **4.** a stanza or other short subdivision of a poem **5.** any of the single, usually numbered, short divisions of a chapter of the Bible —*vt., vi.* **versed, versʹing** [Now Rare] *same as* VERSIFY

**versed** (vurst) *adj.* [< L. pp. of *versari*, to be busy] acquainted by experience and study; skilled or learned (*in* a specified subject)

**ver·si·cle** (verʹsi kʹl) *n.* [< L. *versiculus*, dim. of *versus*, a verse] a short verse or sentence, esp. one said or sung in a religious service and followed by a response

**ver·si·fi·ca·tion** (verʹsə fi kāʹshən) *n.* **1.** the act of versifying **2.** the art, practice, or theory of poetic composition **3.** the form or metrical structure of a poem

**ver·si·fy** (verʹsə fī´) *vi.* **-fied´, -fyʹing** [< MFr. < L. < *versus*: see VERSE & -FY] to compose verses —*vt.* **1.** to tell about or describe in verse **2.** to put into verse form —**verʹsi·fiʹer** *n.*

**ver·sion** (verʹzhən, -shən) *n.* [Fr. < ML. < L. *versus*: see VERSE] **1.** *a)* a translation *b)* [often V-] a translation of the Bible **2.** an account giving one point of view [two *versions* of the accident] **3.** a particular form or variation, esp. as adapted to another art form [the movie *version* of the novel] —**verʹsion·al** *adj.*

‡**vers li·bre** (ver lēʹbr´) French term for FREE VERSE

**ver·so** (verʹsō) *n., pl.* **-sos** [ModL. (*folio*) *verso* < L., abl. of *versus*: see VERSE] *Printing* any left-hand page of a book; back of a leaf: opposed to RECTO

**verst** (vurst, verst; *Russ.* vyôrst) *n.* [< Russ. *versta*] a former Russian unit of linear measure, equal to c.3,500 feet

**ver·sus** (verʹsəs) *prep.* [ML. < L., toward < *vertere*, to turn] **1.** in contest against [our team *versus* theirs] **2.** in contrast with; as an alternative to [peace *versus* war]

**ver·te·bra** (vur'tə brə) *n., pl.* **-brae'** (-brē'), **-bras** [L., a joint < *vertere,* to turn] any of the single bones or segments of the spinal column —**ver'te·bral** *adj.*

**ver·te·brate** (-brit, -brāt') *adj.* [< L.: see prec.] **1.** having a backbone, or spinal column **2.** of or belonging to the vertebrates —*n.* any of a large group of animals, including all mammals, fishes, birds, reptiles, and amphibians, that have a backbone and a brain and cranium

**ver·tex** (vur'teks) *n., pl.* **-tex·es, -ti·ces'** (-tə sēz') [L., the top, the turning point < *vertere,* to turn] **1.** *a)* the highest point; top; apex *b) same as* ZENITH **2.** *Geom. a)* the point where the two sides of an angle intersect *b)* a corner point of a triangle, square, cube, etc.

VERTEBRAE
(A, section of spinal column; B, single vertebra)

**ver·ti·cal** (vur'ti k'l) *adj.* **1.** of or at the vertex, or highest point; directly overhead **2.** perpendicular to the plane of the horizon or to a level surface; upright; straight up or down **3.** of or including the different levels, as in the manufacture or distribution of some product **4.** *Biol.* lengthwise —*n.* **1.** a vertical line, plane, etc. **2.** upright position —**ver'ti·cal'i·ty** (-kal'ə tē) *n.* —**ver'ti·cal·ly** *adv.*

**vertical union** *same as* INDUSTRIAL UNION

**ver·ti·cil** (vur'tə sil) *n.* [L. *verticillus,* dim. of *vertex,* a whirl] *Bot.* a circle of leaves, flowers, etc. on a stem; whorl —**ver·tic·il·late** (vər tis''l it, -āt') *adj.*

**ver·tig·i·nous** (vər tij'ə nəs) *adj.* **1.** of, affected by, or causing vertigo; dizzy or dizzying **2.** whirling; spinning **3.** unstable; inconstant —**ver·tig'i·nous·ly** *adv.*

**ver·ti·go** (vur'ti gō') *n., pl.* **-goes', ver·tig·i·nes** (vər tij'ə nēz') [L. < *vertere,* to turn] *Med.* dizziness in an individual who feels as if he is whirling or as if his surroundings are

**ver·tu** (vər tōō', vur'tōō) *n. same as* VIRTU

**ver·vain** (vur'vān) *n.* [< OFr. < L. *verbena,* foliage] any of a number of verbenas

**verve** (vurv) *n.* [Fr. < OFr., caprice < L. *verba,* words] **1.** vigor and energy **2.** vivacity; spirit; dash

**ver·y** (ver'ē) *adj.* **ver'i·er, ver'i·est** [< OFr., ult. < L. *verus,* true] **1.** in the fullest sense; complete; utter *[the very* opposite of the truth] **2.** same; identical *[the very* hat he lost] **3.** exactly right, suitable, etc.; precise *[the very* one I want] **4.** even (the): used as an intensive *[the very* rafters shook] **5.** actual *[caught in the very* act] —*adv.* **1.** in a high degree; exceedingly **2.** truly; really: used as an intensive *[the very* same man]

**very high frequency** any radio frequency between 30 and 300 megahertz

**very low frequency** any radio frequency between 10 and 30 kilohertz

**Ver·y signal** (or **light**) (ver'ē, vir'ē) [after E. W. *Very,* 19th-c. U.S. ordnance expert] a colored flare fired from a special pistol (**Very pistol**) for signaling at night

**ves·i·cant** (ves'i kənt) *adj.* [< L. *vesica,* a blister] causing blisters —*n.* a vesicant agent Also **ves'i·ca·to'ry** (-kə tôr'ē) *adj., n., pl.* **-to'ries**

**ves·i·cate** (-kāt') *vt., vi.* **-cat'ed, -cat'ing** [< L. *vesica,* a bladder, blister] to blister —**ves'i·ca'tion** *n.*

**ves·i·cle** (ves'i k'l) *n.* [< Fr. < L. dim. of *vesica,* bladder] **1.** a small, membranous cavity, sac, or cyst; specif., a blister **2.** *Geol.* a small, spherical cavity in volcanic rock —**ve·sic·u·lar** (və sik'yə lər), **ve·sic'u·late** (-lit) *adj.*

**Ves·pa·si·an** (ves pā'zhē ən, -zhən) (L. name *Titus Flavius Sabinus Vespasianus*) 9–79 A.D.; Roman emperor (69–79)

**ves·per** (ves'pər) *n.* [L.] **1.** *a)* orig., evening *b)* [Poet.] [V-] *same as* EVENING STAR **2.** an evening prayer or service; specif., *[pl.] [often V-] a) R.C.Ch.* the sixth of the seven canonical hours, recited or sung in the late afternoon *b) Anglican Ch. same as* EVENSONG —*adj.* **1.** of evening **2.** of vespers

**Ves·puc·ci** (ves pōōt'chē), **A·me·ri·go** (ä'me rē'gō) (L. name *Americus Vespucius*) 1451?–1512; It. navigator

**ves·sel** (ves''l) *n.* [< OFr. < LL. dim. of L. *vas,* a vessel] **1.** a utensil for holding something, as a bowl, pot, tub, etc. **2.** a ship or large boat **3.** *a) Anat., Zool.* a tube or duct containing or circulating a body fluid *b) Bot.* a waterconducting tube in the xylem

**vest** (vest) *n.* [< Fr. < It. < L. *vestis,* a garment] **1.** *a)* a short, tightfitting, sleeveless garment worn, esp. under a suit coat, by men; waistcoat *b)* a similar, jacketlike garment worn by women *c)* a piece set into a bodice, resembling the front of a man's vest **2.** a girl's undershirt **3.** [Brit.] any undershirt —*vt.* **1.** to dress, as in church vestments; clothe

**2.** to place (some right, power, or property) in the control of a person or group (with *in*) **3.** to provide or invest (a person or group) (*with* some right, power, or property) —*vi.* **1.** to put on garments or vestments **2.** to become vested (*in* a person), as property

**Ves·ta** (ves'tə) [L.] *Rom. Myth.* the goddess of the hearth

**ves·tal** (ves't'l) *adj.* **1.** of or sacred to Vesta **2.** of the vestal virgins **3.** chaste; pure —*n.* **1.** *short for* VESTAL VIRGIN **2.** a chaste woman; specif., a virgin

**vestal virgin** in ancient Rome, any of the virgin priestesses of Vesta, who tended the sacred fire in her temple

**vest·ed interest** (ves'tid) **1.** an established right that cannot be done away with, as to some future benefit **2.** *[pl.]* the powerful persons and groups that own and control industry, business, etc.

**vest·ee** (ves tē') *n. dim. of* VEST (*n.* 1 *c*)

**ves·ti·ar·y** (ves'tē er'ē) *n., pl.* **-ar'ies** [< OFr. < L. *vestiarium:* see VESTRY] a supply room for clothing, as in a monastery

**ves·ti·bule** (ves'tə byōōl') *n.* [L. *vestibulum,* entrance hall] **1.** a small entrance hall, either to a building or a room **2.** the enclosed passage between passenger cars of a train **3.** *Anat., Zool.* any cavity or space serving as an entrance to another cavity or space

**ves·tige** (ves'tij) *n.* [Fr. < L. *vestigium,* a footprint] **1.** a trace or remaining bit of something once present or whole *[vestiges* of an ancient wall, not a *vestige* of hope] **2.** *Biol.* an organ or part not so fully developed or functional as it once was in the embryo or species: also **ves·tig·i·um** (ves tij'ē əm), *pl.* **-i·a** (-ə) —**ves·tig'i·al** (-tij'ē əl, -tij'əl) *adj.*

**vest·ment** (vest'mənt) *n.* [< OFr. < L. *vestimentum* < *vestire,* to clothe] **1.** a garment; esp., an official robe or gown **2.** *Eccles.* any of the garments worn by clergymen, etc. during religious services

**vest-pock·et** (vest'päk'it) *adj.* **1.** small enough to fit into a vest pocket *[a vest-pocket* dictionary] **2.** very small

**ves·try** (ves'trē) *n., pl.* **-tries** [< OFr. < L. *vestiarium,* a wardrobe < *vestis,* a garment] **1.** a room in a church, where vestments and sacred vessels are kept **2.** a room in a church, used for meetings, Sunday school, etc. **3.** *Anglican & Episcopal Ch.* a group of church members who manage the business affairs of the church

**ves·try·man** (-mən) *n., pl.* **-men** a member of a vestry

**ves·ture** (ves'chər) *n.* [< OFr. < VL. < L. *vestire,* to clothe] [Now Rare] **1.** clothing **2.** a covering —*vt.* **-tured, -tur·ing** [Rare or Archaic] to clothe or cover

**Ve·su·vi·us** (və sōō'vē əs) active volcano in S Italy, on the Bay of Naples (see POMPEII) —**Ve·su'vi·an** *adj.*

**vet¹** (vet) *n. shortened form of* VETERINARIAN —*vt.* **vet'ted, vet'ting** [Colloq.] **1.** to examine or treat as a veterinarian does **2.** to examine or evaluate thoroughly

**vet²** (vet) *n. shortened form of* VETERAN

**vet. 1.** veteran **2.** veterinarian **3.** veterinary

**vetch** (vech) *n.* [< ONormFr. < L. *vicia,* vetch] any of a number of leafy, climbing or trailing plants of the legume family, used chiefly as fodder or fertilizer

**vet·er·an** (vet'ər ən, vet'rən) *adj.* [L. *veteranus* < *vetus* (gen. *veteris*), old] **1.** having had long experience in some kind of work or in military service **2.** of a veteran or veterans —*n.* **1.** a person with much experience in some kind of work **2.** a person who has served in the armed forces of a country, esp. in war

**Veterans Administration** a consolidated Federal agency administering all laws on benefits for military veterans

**Veterans Day** a legal holiday in the U.S. honoring all veterans of the armed forces: observed (except 1971–77) on ARMISTICE DAY

**vet·er·i·nar·i·an** (vet'ər ə ner'ē ən, vet'rə ner'-) *n.* a person who practices veterinary medicine or surgery

**vet·er·i·nar·y** (vet'ər ə ner'ē, vet'rə-) *adj.* [< L. < *veterina,* beasts of burden] designating or of the branch of medicine dealing with the treatment of diseases and injuries in animals, esp. domestic animals —*n., pl.* **-nar'ies** *same as* VETERINARIAN

**ve·to** (vē'tō) *n., pl.* **-toes** [L., I forbid < *vetare,* to forbid] **1.** *a)* an order forbidding some proposed act; prohibition *b)* the power to prevent action thus **2.** the constitutional right or power of a ruler or legislature to reject bills passed by another branch of the government; specif., in the U.S., *a)* the power of the President to refuse to sign a bill passed by Congress *b)* a similar power held by the governors of States *c)* the exercise of this power **3.** a document or message giving the reasons of the executive for rejecting a bill: also **veto message 4.** the power of any of the five permanent members of the Security Council of the United Nations to prevent an action by casting a negative vote —*vt.*

**-toed, -to·ing 1.** to prevent (a bill) from becoming law by veto **2.** to forbid; prohibit —**ve′to·er** *n.*

**vex** (veks) *vt.* [< MFr. < L. *vexare*, to agitate] **1.** to disturb, irritate, etc., esp. in a petty, nagging way **2.** to distress or afflict **3.** to keep discussing and disputing (a matter) —**vex·ed·ly** (vek′sid lē) *adv.* —**vex′er** *n.*

**vex·a·tion** (vek sā′shən) *n.* **1.** a vexing or being vexed **2.** something that vexes; cause of annoyance or distress

**vex·a·tious** (-shəs) *adj.* characterized by or causing vexation; annoying, troublesome, etc. —**vex·a′tious·ly** *adv.*

**vex·ing** (vek′siŋ) *adj.* that vexes —**vex′ing·ly** *adv.*

**V.F.W., VFW** Veterans of Foreign Wars

**VHF, V.H.F., vhf, v.h.f.** very high frequency

**VI, V.I.** Virgin Islands (of the United States)

**vi., v.i.** intransitive verb

**v.i.** [L. *vide infra*] see below

**vi·a** (vī′ə, vē′ə) *prep.* [L., abl. sing. of *via*, a way] **1.** by way of; passing through [from Rome to London *via* Paris] **2.** by means of [*via* airmail]

**vi·a·ble** (vī′ə b'l) *adj.* [< Fr. < *vie*, life < L. *vita*] **1.** *a)* able to live; specif., developed enough to be able to live outside the uterus [a premature but *viable* infant] *b)* capable of growing [*viable* seeds] **2.** workable; likely to survive [*viable* ideas] —**vi′a·bil′i·ty** *n.* —**vi′a·bly** *adv.*

**vi·a·duct** (vī′ə dukt′) *n.* [L. *via* (see VIA) + (AQUE)DUCT] a bridge consisting of a series of short spans supported on piers or towers, usually to carry a road or railroad over a valley, gorge, etc.

**vi·al** (vī′əl) *n.* [< OFr. < OPr., ult. < Gr. *phialē*, shallow cup] a small bottle, usually of glass, for holding medicine or other liquids; phial —*vt.* **-aled** or **-alled, -al·ing** or **-al·ling** to put or keep in or as in a vial

‡**vi·a me·di·a** (vī′ə mē′dē ə, vē′ə mā′-) [L.] a middle way; course between two extremes

**vi·and** (vī′ənd) *n.* [< OFr., ult. < L. *vivenda*, neut. pl. gerundive of *vivere*, to live] **1.** an article of food **2.** [*pl.*] food; esp., choice dishes

**vi·at·i·cum** (vī at′i kəm) *n., pl.* **-ca** (-kə), **-cums** [L. < *viaticus*, of a way or road < *via*, way] **1.** money or supplies for a journey **2.** [*often* V-] the Eucharist as given to a person dying or in danger of death

**vibes** (vībz) *n.pl.* **1.** [Colloq.] a vibraphone **2.** [< VIBRATION(S)] [Slang] qualities in a person or thing that produce an emotional response in one

**vi·bra·harp** (vī′brə härp′) *n. same as* VIBRAPHONE

**vi·brant** (vī′brənt) *adj.* [< L. prp. of *vibrare*, vibrate] **1.** quivering; vibrating **2.** produced by vibration; resonant: said of sound **3.** active; lively [*vibrant* streets] **4.** energetic, sparkling, vivacious, etc. [a *vibrant* woman] —**vi′bran·cy** *n.* —**vi′brant·ly** *adv.*

**vi·bra·phone** (vī′brə fōn′) *n.* [VIBRA(TE) + -PHONE] a musical instrument resembling the marimba, but with electrically operated valves in the resonators, that produce a gentle vibrato —**vi′bra·phon′ist** *n.*

**vi·brate** (vī′brāt) *vt.* **-brat·ed, -brat·ing** [< L. pp. of *vibrare*, to vibrate] **1.** to give off (light or sound) by vibration **2.** to set in to-and-fro motion; oscillate **3.** to cause to quiver — *vi.* **1.** to swing back and forth, as a pendulum **2.** to move rapidly back and forth; quiver, as a plucked string **3.** to resound **4.** to feel very excited; thrill

**vi·bra·tile** (vī′brə til, -tīl′) *adj.* **1.** of or characterized by vibration **2.** capable of vibrating or being vibrated **3.** having a vibrating motion —**vi′bra·til′i·ty** *n.*

**vi·bra·tion** (vī brā′shən) *n.* **1.** a vibrating; esp., rapid movement back and forth; quivering **2.** *Physics a)* rapid, periodic, to-and-fro motion or oscillation of an elastic body or the particles of a fluid, as in transmitting sound *b)* a single, complete oscillation —**vi·bra′tion·al** *adj.*

**vi·bra·to** (vi brät′ō, vē-) *n., pl.* **-tos** [It.] *Music* the pulsating effect of a rapid, hardly noticeable variation in pitch, produced by a slight oscillation of the finger on a violin string, by a slight wavering of the tone in singing, etc.

**vi·bra·tor** (vī′brāt′ər) *n.* something that vibrates, as an electrical device used in massage, etc.

**vi·bra·to·ry** (vī′brə tôr′ē) *adj.* **1.** of, like, or causing vibration **2.** vibrating or capable of vibration

**vi·bur·num** (vī bur′nəm) *n.* [ModL., genus name < L., the wayfaring tree] **1.** any of various shrubs or small trees related to the honeysuckle and bearing white flowers **2.** the bark of several species, sometimes used in medicine

**vic·ar** (vik′ər) *n.* [< OFr. < L. *vicarius* < *vicis*, a change] **1.** a person who acts in place of another; deputy **2.** *Anglican Ch.* a parish priest who is not a rector and receives a stipend instead of the tithes **3.** *Protestant Episcopal Ch.* a minister in charge of one chapel in a parish **4.** *R.C.Ch.* a) a church officer acting as deputy of a bishop *b)* [V-] the Pope: in full, Vicar of Christ —**vi·car·i·al** (vī ker′ē əl, vi-) *adj.* —**vi·car′i·ate** (-it, -āt′), **vic′ar·ate** (-ər it, -ə rāt′) *n.*

**vic·ar·age** (-ij) *n.* **1.** the residence of a vicar **2.** the salary of a vicar **3.** the position or duties of a vicar

**vicar apostolic** *pl.* **vicars apostolic** *R.C.Ch.* a titular bishop in a region where no regular see has yet been organized

**vic·ar-gen·er·al** (vik′ər jen′ər əl) *n., pl.* **vic′ars-gen′er·al 1.** *Anglican Ch.* a layman serving as administrative deputy to an archbishop or bishop **2.** *R.C.Ch.* a priest, etc. acting as administrative deputy to a bishop or to the general superior of a religious order

**vi·car·i·ous** (vī ker′ē əs, vi-) *adj.* [L. *vicarius*, substituted < *vicis*, a change] **1.** *a)* taking the place of another *b)* delegated [*vicarious* powers] **2.** *a)* done or undergone by one person in place of another *b)* felt as if one were actually taking part in another's experience [a *vicarious* thrill] —**vi·car′i·ous·ly** *adv.* —**vi·car′i·ous·ness** *n.*

**vice¹** (vīs) *n.* [< OFr. < L. *vitium*] **1.** *a)* an evil or wicked action, habit, etc. *b)* depravity or corruption *c)* prostitution **2.** any fault, failing, defect, etc. —**vice′less** *adj.*

**vi·ce²** (vī′sē, -sə) *prep.* [L.: see VICE-] in the place of; as the deputy or successor of

**vice³** (vīs) *n., vt. chiefly Brit. sp. of* VISE

**vice-** [< L. *vice*, in the place of another, abl. of *vicis*: see VICAR] *a prefix meaning* one who acts in the place of; subordinate; deputy [*vice*-president]

**vice admiral** a naval officer next in rank above a rear admiral and below an admiral —**vice admiralty**

**vice-con·sul** (vīs′kän′s'l) *n.* an officer who is subordinate to or a substitute for a consul —**vice′-con′su·lar** *adj.* —**vice′-con′su·late** (-it) *n.* —**vice′-con′sul·ship′** *n.*

**vice·ge·rent** (vīs′jir′ənt) *n.* [< ML. < L. < *vice* (see VICE-) + *gerere*, to direct] a person appointed by another to exercise the latter's power and authority; deputy —*adj.* of a vicegerent: also **vice′ge′ral** —**vice′ge′ren·cy** *n.*

**vice-pres·i·dent** (vīs′prez′i dənt) *n.* **1.** *a)* an officer next in rank below a president, acting in his place during his absence or incapacity *b)* [V- P-] the elected officer of this rank in the U.S. government: he succeeds to the Presidency if the President dies or otherwise leaves office: usually written **Vice President 2.** any of several officers of a company, etc., each in charge of a department —**vice′-pres′i·den·cy** *n.* —**vice′-pres′i·den′tial** *adj.*

**vice·re·gal** (vīs′rē′g'l) *adj.* of a viceroy

**vice·re·gent** (-rē′jənt) *n.* a deputy of a regent

**vice·roy** (vīs′roi) *n.* [MFr. < *vice-* (see VICE-) + *roy*, a king < L. *rex*] a person ruling a country, province, etc. as the deputy of a sovereign —**vice′roy′al·ty**, *pl.* **-ties, vice′roy·ship′** *n.*

**vice squad** a police squad assigned to the suppression or control of prostitution, gambling, etc.

**vi·ce ver·sa** (vī′sē vur′sə, vī′sə; vīs′) [L.] the order or relation being reversed; conversely

**Vi·chy** (vish′ē, vē′shē; *Fr.* vē shē′) city in C France: capital of unoccupied France (1940–44): pop. 31,000

**vi·chy·ssoise** (vē′shē swäz′, vish′ē-) *n.* [Fr.] a thick cream soup of potatoes, etc., usually served cold

**Vichy (water) 1.** a mineral water found at Vichy **2.** a natural or processed water like this

**vic·i·nage** (vis′ə nij) *n.* [< MFr., ult. < L. *vicinus*: see ff.] **1.** *same as* VICINITY **2.** the people in a neighborhood

**vi·cin·i·ty** (və sin′ə tē) *n., pl.* **-ties** [< L. < *vicinus*, near < *vicus*, village] **1.** a being close by; nearness [two theaters in close *vicinity*] **2.** nearby region; neighborhood

**vi·cious** (vish′əs) *adj.* [< OFr. < L. < *vitium*, a vice] **1.** *a)* characterized by vice or evil; depraved *b)* debasing; corrupting **2.** ruined by defects, flaws, etc. [a *vicious* argument] **3.** having bad habits; unruly [a *vicious* horse] **4.** malicious; spiteful; mean [a *vicious* rumor] **5.** very intense, sharp, etc. —**vi′cious·ly** *adv.* —**vi′cious·ness** *n.*

**vicious circle 1.** a situation in which the solution of one problem gives rise to another, but the solution of this brings back the first, etc. **2.** *Logic* an argument which is not valid, because its conclusion rests on a premise which itself depends on the conclusion

**vi·cis·si·tude** (vi sis′ə tōōd′, -tyōōd′) *n.* [Fr. < L. *vicissitudo* < *vicis*, a turn] **1.** a condition of constant change or alternation, as a natural process **2.** [*pl.*] unpredictable changes or variations that keep occurring in life, fortune, etc.; shifting circumstances; ups and downs —**vi·cis′si·tu′di·nar′y, vi·cis′si·tu′di·nous** *adj.*

**Vicks·burg** (viks′burg) [after Rev. N. *Vick* (?-1819), early settler] city in W Miss., on the Mississippi: besieged by Grant in the Civil War (1863): pop. 25,000

**vic·tim** (vik′təm) *n.* [L. *victima*] **1.** a person or animal killed as a sacrifice to a god **2.** someone or something killed, destroyed, etc. [*victims* of war] **3.** a person who suffers some loss, esp. by being swindled; dupe

**vic·tim·ize** (vik′tə mīz′) *vt.* **-ized′, -iz′ing** to make a victim of —**vic′tim·i·za′tion** *n.* —**vic′tim·iz′er** *n.*

**vic·tim·less crime** (vik′təm lis) a statutory crime, such as prostitution or gambling, regarded as having no clearly identifiable victim

**Vic·tor** (vik′tər) [L.: see ff.] a masculine name

**vic·tor** (vik'tər) *n.* [L. < pp. of *vincere*, to conquer] the winner in a battle, struggle, etc. —*adj.* same as VICTORIOUS

**Victor Emmanuel III** 1869–1947; king of Italy (1900–46): abdicated & the monarchy dissolved (1946)

**Vic·to·ri·a**[1] (vik tôr'ē ə, -tôr'yə) **1.** [L., VICTORY] a feminine name: dim. *Vicky* **2.** (Alexandrina), 1819–1901; queen of Great Britain & Ireland (1837–1901) —*n.* [v-] **1.** a four-wheeled carriage for two passengers, with a folding top and a high seat for the coachman **2.** a S. American waterlily with large leaves and large, night-blooming flowers

VICTORIA

**Vic·to·ri·a**[2] (vik tôr'ē ə, -tôr'yə) **1.** state of Australia, in the SE part **2.** capital of Hong Kong: pop., of met. area, 2,800,000 **3.** capital of British Columbia, Canada, on Vancouver Island: pop. 63,000 **4. Lake,** lake in E Africa, bounded by Kenya, Uganda, & Tanzania

**Victoria Cross** the highest British military decoration, given for deeds of exceptional valor

**Victoria Day** a legal holiday in Canada, celebrated on the Monday immediately preceding May 25

**Vic·to·ri·an** (-ən) *adj.* **1.** of or characteristic of the time when Victoria was queen of England **2.** showing the middle-class respectability, prudery, etc. regarded as typical of Victorians —*n.* a person, esp. a British writer, of the time of Queen Victoria —**Vic·to'ri·an·ism** *n.*

**vic·to·ri·ous** (vik tôr'ē əs, -tôr'yəs) *adj.* **1.** having won a victory; winning; triumphant **2.** of, typical of, or bringing about victory

**vic·to·ry** (vik'tər ē, -trē) *n., pl.* **-ries** [< OFr. < L. *victoria* < *victor,* VICTOR] **1.** the decisive winning of a battle or war **2.** success in any contest or struggle involving the defeat of an opponent or the overcoming of obstacles

**vict·ual** (vit''l) *n.* [< MFr. < LL. < L. *victualis,* of food < *victus,* food < pp. of *vivere,* to live] **1.** [Archaic or Dial.] food or other provisions **2.** [*pl.*] [Dial. or Colloq.] articles of food —*vt.* **-ualed** or **-ualled, -ual·ing** or **-ual·ling** to supply with food —*vi.* to lay in a supply of food

**vict·ual·er, vict·ual·ler** (-ər) *n.* **1.** formerly, one who supplied victuals, as to an army **2.** [Brit.] an innkeeper

**vi·cu·ña** (vī kōōn'yə, -kōōn'ə; vi-) *n., pl.* **-ñas, -ña:** see PLURAL, II, D, 1 [Sp., of Quechuan origin] **1.** an animal found wild in the S. American Andes, related to the llama and alpaca, with soft, shaggy wool **2.** this wool **3.** a fabric made from it or in imitation of it

‡**vi·de** (vī'dē, vē'dā) [L.] see: used to direct attention to a particular page, book, etc.

‡**vide an·te** (an'tē) [L.] see before (in the book, etc.)

‡**vide in·fra** (in'frə) [L.] see below; see further on (in the book, etc.)

VICUÑA
(to 40 in. high at shoulder)

‡**vi·de·li·cet** (vi del'ə sit) *adv.* [L. < *videre licet,* it is permitted to see] that is; namely

**vid·e·o** (vid'ē ō') *adj.* [L., I see] **1.** of or used in television **2.** designating or of the picture portion of a telecast: cf. AUDIO —*n.* same as TELEVISION

**vid·e·o·cas·sette** (-ka set', -kə-) *n.* a cassette with videotape, for playing back recorded material on a TV set

**video game** an electronic device attached to a television set, that produces images on the screen, which are controlled by players competing in any of various games

**vid·e·o·phone** (vid'ē ō fōn') *n.* a telephone combined with a television receiver and transmitter so that users can see, as well as speak with, each other

**vid·e·o·tape** (vid'ē ō tāp') *n.* a magnetic tape on which a telecast can be recorded as for later broadcasting

‡**vide su·pra** (sōō'prə) [L.] see above; see earlier (in the book, etc.)

**vid·i·con** (vid'ə kän) *n.* [VID(EO) + ICON(OSCOPE)] a TV camera pickup tube in which optical images are scanned by an electron beam for transmission

**vie** (vī) *vi.* **vied, vy'ing** [< OFr. < L. *invitare,* to invite] to be a rival or rivals; compete (*with* someone) —*vi'er n.*

**Vi·en·na** (vē en'ə) capital of Austria, on the Danube: pop. 1,642,000 —*Vi·en·nese* (vē'ə nēz') *adj., n., pl.* **-nese'**

**Vien·tiane** (vyen tyän') capital of Laos, on the Mekong River: pop. c.150,000

**Vi·et Cong** (vē'et käŋ', vyet) [< Vietnamese *Viet Nam Cong San,* Vietnamese Communist] **1.** collectively, the native military force in South Vietnam, which sought national independence (1954–76) **2.** any member of this force

**Vi·et·nam** (vē'ət näm', vyet'-; -nam') country on the E coast of the Indochinese Peninsula: divided, 1954–76, into two republics (**North Vietnam** and **South Vietnam**): 129,607 sq. mi.; pop. 47,872,000; cap. Hanoi Also sp. **Viet-Nam, Viet Nam** —**Vi'et·nam·ese', Vi'et-Nam·ese'** (-nə mēz', -mēs') *adj., n., pl.* **-ese'**

**view** (vyōō) *n.* [< OFr. < L. *videre*] **1.** a seeing or looking, as in inspection **2.** sight or vision; esp., range of vision **3.** mental examination or survey [a correct *view* of the situation] **4.** *a*) a scene or prospect, as of a landscape *b*) a picture of such a scene **5.** visual appearance of something **6.** manner of regarding something; opinion **7.** an object; aim; goal [with a *view* to helping] **8.** a general survey —*vt.* **1.** to inspect; scrutinize **2.** to see; behold **3.** to survey mentally; consider **4.** to regard in a particular way —**in view 1.** in sight **2.** under consideration **3.** as an object aimed at **4.** in expectation; as a hope —**in view of** in consideration of; because of —**on view** displayed publicly —**with a view to 1.** with the purpose of **2.** with a hope of; looking forward to

**view·er** (-ər) *n.* **1.** a person who views something; spectator **2.** an optical device for individual viewing as of slides

**view·find·er** (-fīn'dər) *n.* same as FINDER (sense 2)

**view·less** (-lis) *adj.* **1.** affording no view, or prospect **2.** [Rare] invisible **3.** having or expressing no opinions

**view·point** (-point') *n.* the mental position from which things are viewed and judged; point of view

**vi·ges·i·mal** (vī jes'ə m'l) *adj.* [< L., ult. < *viginti,* twenty] **1.** of or based on the number twenty **2.** twentieth

**vig·il** (vij'əl) *n.* [< OFr. < L. < *vigil,* awake < *vigere,* to be lively] **1.** *a*) a watchful staying awake during the usual hours of sleep *b*) a watch kept, or the period of this **2.** *Eccles.* the evening or day before a festival, or the devotional services held then

**vig·i·lance** (vij'ə ləns) *n.* the quality or state of being vigilant; watchfulness

**vigilance committee** a group that sets itself up, without legal authority, to punish crime, etc. independently of the usual law-enforcement agencies

**vig·i·lant** (vij'ə lənt) *adj.* [Fr. < L. prp. of *vigilare,* to watch < *vigil,* awake] staying watchful and alert to danger or trouble —**vig'i·lant·ly** *adv.*

**vig·i·lan·te** (vij'ə lan'tē) *n.* [Sp., vigilant] a member of a vigilance committee

**vig·i·lan·tism** (vij'ə lan tiz'm) *n.* the lawless, violent methods, spirit, etc. of vigilantes —**vig'i·lan'tist** *adj.*

**vi·gnette** (vin yet') *n.* [Fr., dim. < *vigne,* a vine] **1.** an ornamental design or illustration used in a book, magazine, etc., as at the beginning or end of a chapter or section **2.** a picture or photograph shading off gradually at the edges **3.** a short, delicate literary sketch —*vt.* **-gnet'ted, -gnet'ting** to make a vignette of —**vi·gnet'tist** *n.*

**vig·or** (vig'ər) *n.* [< OFr. < L. < *vigere,* to be strong] **1.** active physical or mental force; vitality **2.** active or healthy growth **3.** intensity, force, or energy **4.** effective legal force; validity Also, Brit. sp., **vig'our**

**vig·or·ous** (vig'ər əs) *adj.* **1.** strong; robust **2.** of, characterized by, or requiring vigor **3.** forceful; energetic; powerful —**vig'or·ous·ly** *adv.* —**vig'or·ous·ness** *n.*

**vik·ing** (vī'kiŋ) *n.* [ON. *viking*] [*also* V-] any of the Scandinavian pirates who ravaged the coasts of Europe from the 8th to the 10th centuries

**vile** (vīl) *adj.* [< OFr. < L. *vilis,* cheap, base] **1.** morally evil; wicked **2.** repulsive; disgusting **3.** degrading; low **4.** very bad [*vile* weather]—**vile'ly** *adv.* —**vile'ness** *n.*

**vil·i·fy** (vil'ə fī') *vt.* **-fied', -fy'ing** [LL. *vilificare:* see VILE & -FY] to use abusive or slanderous language about; revile; defame —**vil'i·fi·ca'tion** *n.* —**vil'i·fi'er** *n.*

**vil·la** (vil'ə) *n.* [It. < L.] **1.** a country house or estate, esp. when large or luxurious and used as a retreat or summer house **2.** [Brit.] a small suburban house

**Vi·lla** (vē'yä), **Fran·cis·co** (frän sēs'kô) 1877?–1923; Mex. revolutionary leader: called *Pancho Villa*

**vil·lage** (vil'ij) *n.* [< OFr. < L. < *villa,* a country house] **1.** a group of houses in the country, larger than a hamlet and smaller than a town **2.** such a community incorporated as a municipality **3.** the people of a village, collectively —*adj.* of a village —**vil'lag·er** *n.*

**vil·lain** (vil'ən) *n.* [< OFr. < VL. *villanus,* a servant < L. *villa,* a farm] **1.** a person guilty of great crimes; evil person **2.** a wicked character in a novel, play, etc. who opposes the hero **3.** same as VILLEIN —**vil'lain·ess** *n.fem.*

**vil·lain·ous** (-əs) *adj.* **1.** of or like a villain; evil; wicked **2.** very bad or disagreeable —**vil'lain·ous·ly** *adv.*

**vil·lain·y** (-ē) *n., pl.* **-lain·ies** 1. the fact or state of being villainous 2. villainous conduct 3. a villainous act; wicked, detestable, or criminal deed

**-ville** (vil) [< Fr. *ville*, town, city] *a combining form meaning:* 1. town, city [*Evansville*] 2. place or condition characterized by: freely used in coining slang terms [*"dullsville"*]

**vil·lein** (vil′ən) *n.* [see VILLAIN] in feudal England, any of a class of serfs who by the 13th cent. had become freemen in their legal relations to all except their lord —**vil′lein·age**, **vil′len·age** *n.*

**Vil·lon** (vē yōn′), **Fran·çois** (frän swä′) (born *François de Montcorbier* or *des Loges*) 1431-?; Fr. poet

**vil·lus** (vil′əs) *n., pl.* **vil′li** (-ī) [L., shaggy hair] 1. *Anat.* any of numerous hairlike growths on certain mucous membranes of the body, as of the small intestines, serving to secrete mucus and absorb fats, etc. 2. *Bot.* any of the long, soft hairs on certain plants —**vil·los·i·ty** (vi läs′ə tē) *n., pl.* **-ties** —**vil′lous** (-əs) *adj.*

**Vil·ni·us** (vil′nē oos′) capital of the Lithuanian S.S.R.: pop. 372,000: Russ. name **Vil·na** (vēl′nä; *E.* vil′nə)

**vim** (vim) *n.* [L., acc. of *vis*, strength] energy; vigor

‡**vin** (van; *Anglicized* vin) *n.* [Fr.] wine

**vi·na·ceous** (vī nā′shəs) *adj.* [< L. < *vinum*, wine] 1. of or like wine or grapes 2. wine-colored; red

**vin·ai·grette** (vin′i gret′) *n.* [Fr. < *vinaigre*, vinegar] a small ornamental box or bottle with a perforated lid, used for holding aromatic vinegar, smelling salts, etc.

**vinaigrette sauce** a savory sauce made of vinegar, oil, herbs, etc. and used esp. on cold meats

**Vin·cent** (vin′s'nt) [< LL. < prp. of *vincere*, to conquer] a masculine name

**Vin·cent's angina** (vin′s'nts) [after J. H. *Vincent* (1862-1950), Fr. physician] *same as* TRENCH MOUTH: also called **Vincent's infection**

**Vinci, Leonardo da** *see* DA VINCI

**vin·ci·ble** (vin′sə b'l) *adj.* [< L. < *vincere*, to overcome] that can be overcome or defeated —**vin′ci·bil′i·ty** *n.*

**vin·di·ca·ble** (vin′di kə b'l) *adj.* that can be vindicated; justifiable

**vin·di·cate** (vin′də kāt′) *vt.* **-cat′ed, -cat′ing** [< L. pp. of *vindicare*, to claim < *vim*, acc. of *vis*, force + *dicere*, to say] 1. to clear from criticism, blame, suspicion, etc. 2. to defend (a cause, etc.) against opposition 3. to justify [he *vindicated* their belief in him] —**vin′di·ca′tive** (-kāt′iv, vin dik′ə tiv), **vin′di·ca′to·ry** *adj.* —**vin′di·ca′tor** *n.*

**vin·di·ca·tion** (vin′də kā′shən) *n.* 1. a vindicating or being vindicated 2. a fact or circumstance that vindicates

**vin·dic·tive** (vin dik′tiv) *adj.* [< L. *vindicta*, revenge (see VINDICATE) + -IVE] 1. revengeful in spirit 2. said or done in revenge [*vindictive* punishment] —**vin·dic′tive·ly** *adv.* —**vin·dic′tive·ness** *n.*

**vine** (vīn) *n.* [< OFr. < L. < *vinum*, wine] 1. *a)* any plant with a long, thin stem that grows along the ground or climbs a wall or other support by means of tendrils, etc. *b)* the stem of such a plant 2. *same as* GRAPEVINE (sense 1) — **vine′like′** *adj.*

**vin·e·gar** (vin′i gər) *n.* [< MFr. < *vin*, wine + *aigre*, sour < L. *acris*, acrid] 1. a sour liquid containing acetic acid, made by fermenting cider, wine, malt, etc.: it is used as a condiment and preservative 2. ill-tempered speech, character, etc. 3. forceful vigor —**vin′e·gar·y**, **vin′e·gar·ish** *adj.*

**vin·er·y** (vīn′ər ē) *n., pl.* **-er·ies** 1. an enclosed area or building in which grapevines are grown 2. vines collectively

**vine·yard** (vin′yərd) *n.* land devoted to cultivating grapevines

‡**vingt-et-un** (van tā ẽn′) *n.* [Fr., lit., twenty-one] *same as* TWENTY-ONE

**vin·i-** [< L. *vinum*, wine] *a combining form meaning* wine grapes or wine [*viniculture*]

**vin·i·cul·ture** (vin′i kul′chər) *n.* [prec. + CULTURE] the cultivation of wine grapes —**vin′i·cul′tur·al** *adj.* —**vin′i·cul′tur·ist** *n.*

**Vin·land** (vin′lənd) region, now believed to be part of N. America, discovered by Norsemen c.1000 A.D.

‡**vi·no** (vē′nō) *n.* [It. & Sp.] wine

**vi·nous** (vī′nəs) *adj.* [< L. < *vinum*, wine] 1. of, having the nature of, or characteristic of wine 2. *a)* fond of drinking wine *b)* resulting from drinking wine —**vi·nos′i·ty** (-näs′ə tē) *n.*

**Vin·son** (vin′sən), **Fred(erick) M(oore)** 1890-1953; U.S. jurist; chief justice of the U.S. (1946-53)

**vin·tage** (vin′tij) *n.* [< OFr. < L. *vindemia* < *vinum*, wine + *demere*, to remove] 1. *a)* the crop of grapes or the resultant wine of a vineyard or grape-growing region in a single season *b)* the wine, esp. a prized wine, of a particular region in a specified year 2. the act or season of gathering grapes or of making wine 3. the type or model of a particular year or period [a car of prewar *vintage*] —*adj.* 1. *a)* of choice vintage [*vintage* wine] *b)* representative of

the best 2. dating from a period long past [*vintage* clothes]

**vint·ner** (vint′nər) *n.* [< OFr. < ML. < L. *vinetum*, a vineyard] a wine merchant

**vin·y** (vī′nē) *adj.* **vin′i·er**, **vin′i·est** 1. of or like vines 2. filled or covered with vines

**vi·nyl** (vī′n'l) *n.* [< L. *vinum*, wine + -YL] the univalent radical, $CH_2$:CH-, derived from ethylene: various vinyl compounds are polymerized to form resins and plastics

**vi·ol** (vī′əl) *n.* [MFr. *viole* < OPr. *viula* < ?] any of an early family of stringed instruments, usually with six strings, frets, and a flat back: used in sizes from the treble viol to the bass viol

**vi·o·la**[1] (vē ō′lə, vī-) *n.* [It. < OPr. *viula*, viol] a stringed instrument of the violin family, slightly larger than a violin and tuned a fifth lower

**vi·o·la**[2] (vē ō′lə, vī ō′lə) *n.* [< L., a violet] any of various violets developed from a pansy

**vi·o·la·ble** (vī′ə lə b'l) *adj.* that can be, or is likely to be, violated —**vi′o·la·bil′i·ty**, **vi′o·la·ble·ness** *n.* —**vi′o·la·bly** *adv.*

**viola da gam·ba** (də gam′bə, gäm′-) [It., lit., viol for the leg] an early instrument of the viol family, held between the knees and comparable in range to the cello

**vi·o·late** (vī′ə lāt′) *vt.* **-lat′ed, -lat′ing** [< L. pp. of *violare*, to use force] 1. to break (a law, rule, promise, etc.); fail to observe; infringe on 2. to assault sexually; esp., to rape (a woman) 3. to desecrate or profane (something sacred) 4. to break in on; disturb [to *violate* one's privacy] 5. to offend, insult, etc. [to *violate* one's sense of decency] — **vi′o·la′tive** *adj.* —**vi′o·la′tor** *n.*

**vi·o·la·tion** (vī′ə lā′shən) *n.* a violating or being violated; specif., *a)* infringement or breach, as of a law *b)* rape *c)* desecration of something sacred *d)* disturbance

**vi·o·lence** (vī′ə ləns) *n.* [< MFr. < L. < *violentus*, violent] 1. physical force used so as to injure or damage 2. intense, powerful force, as of a hurricane, etc. 3. *a)* unjust or callous use of force or power, as in violating another's rights, privacy, etc. *b)* the harm done by this 4. vehemence; fury 5. a twisting of a sense, phrase, etc. so as to distort meaning 6. a violent deed or act

**vi·o·lent** (-lənt) *adj.* 1. *a)* acting with or characterized by great physical force, so as to injure, etc. *b)* acting with or characterized by unlawful force 2. caused by violence 3. *a)* furious; passionate; immoderate [*violent* language] *b)* emotionally disturbed and uncontrollable 4. extreme; intense [a *violent* storm] —**vi′o·lent·ly** *adv.*

**vi·o·let** (vī′ə lit) *n.* [< OFr. < L. *viola*, a violet] 1. *a)* any of a number of related short plants with white, blue, purple, or yellow flowers *b)* the flower of any of these plants 2. any of various similar but unrelated plants, as the African violet 3. a bluish-purple color —*adj.* bluish-purple

**violet ray** 1. the shortest ray of the visible spectrum 2. loosely, an ultraviolet ray

**vi·o·lin** (vī′ə lin′) *n.* [< It. dim. of *viola*, a viol] any instrument of the modern family of stringed instruments played with a bow and having four strings and no frets; specif., the smallest and highest-pitched instrument of this family, held horizontally under the chin

**vi·o·lin·ist** (-ist) *n.* a violin player

**vi·ol·ist** (vī′əl ist; *for 2* vē ō′list) *n.* 1. a viol player 2. a viola player

**vi·o·lon·cel·lo** (vē′ə län chel′ō, vī′ə lən-) *n., pl.* **-los** [It., dim. of *violone*, bass viol < *viola*, viol] *same as* CELLO —**vi′o·lon·cel′list** *n.*

**VIP, V.I.P.** [Colloq.] very important person

**vi·per** (vī′pər) *n.* [OFr. < L. *vipera* < ? *vivus*, living + *parere*, to bear] 1. *a)* any of a family of venomous snakes found in Europe, Africa, and Asia, including the puff adder (sense 1), etc. *b)* *same as* PIT VIPER *c)* *same as* ADDER (sense 1) 2. a malicious or treacherous person —**vi′per·ine** (-in, -īn′) *adj.*

**vi·per·ous** (-əs) *adj.* of, having the nature of, or like a viper; esp., spiteful or malicious: also **vi′per·ish** —**vi′per·ous·ly** *adv.* —**vi′per·ous·ness** *n.*

**vi·ra·go** (vi rā′gō, vī-; -rä′-) *n., pl.* **-goes, -gos** [OE. < L., a manlike maiden < *vir*, a man] a quarrelsome, shrewish woman; scold

**vi·ral** (vī′rəl) *adj.* of, involving, or caused by a virus

**vir·e·o** (vir′ē ō′) *n., pl.* **-e·os′** [L., a type of finch] any of a number of small, insect-eating, American songbirds, with olive-green or gray plumage

**vi·res·cent** (vī res′'nt, vi-) *adj.* [< L. prp. of *virescere* < *virere*, to be green] 1. turning or becoming green 2. greenish —**vi·res′cence** *n.*

VIOLIN
(A, scroll; B, pegs; C, neck; D, fingerboard; E, waist; F, tailpiece; G, chinboard)

**Vir·gil** (vur′jəl) [< L. *Vergilius*, name of the Roman gens to which the poet belonged] 1. a masculine name 2. (L. name *Publius Vergilius Maro*) 70–19 B.C.; Roman poet: author of the *Aeneid* —**Vir·gil′i·an** (-jil′ē ən) *adj.*

**vir·gin** (vur′jin) *n.* [< OFr. < L. *virgo* (gen. *virginis*), a maiden] 1. a person, esp. a woman, who has not had sexual intercourse 2. an unmarried girl or woman —[V- ] *Astron.* same as VIRGO —*adj.* 1. being a virgin 2. like a virgin; chaste; modest 3. untouched, pure, clean, etc. [*virgin* snow] 4. as yet unused, untrod, unexplored, etc. by man [a *virgin* forest] 5. being the first [a *virgin* effort] —**the Virgin** Mary, the mother of Jesus

**vir·gin·al¹** (vur′ji n′l) *adj.* 1. of or like a virgin; maidenly 2. pure; fresh; unsullied —**vir′gin·al·ly** *adv.*

**vir·gin·al²** (vur′ji n′l) *n.* [prob. akin to prec.] [*sometimes pl.*] a harpsichord; esp., a small, rectangular harpsichord of the 16th cent., placed on a table or in the lap to be played: also **pair of virginals**

**Virgin Birth** *Christian Theol.* the doctrine that Jesus was born to Mary, a virgin, and that she was his only human parent

**Vir·gin·ia** (vur jin′yə, -ē ə) 1. [L., fem. of *Virginius*, name of a Roman gens] a feminine name 2. [after ELIZABETH I, the *Virgin* Queen] Southern State of the U.S., on the Atlantic: 40,815 sq. mi.; pop. 5,346,000; cap. Richmond: abbrev. **Va., VA** —**Vir·gin′ian** *adj., n.*

**Virginia Beach** city in SE Va., on the Atlantic, near Norfolk: pop. 262,000

**Virginia cowslip** (or **bluebell**) a perennial woodland plant with clusters of blue or purple bell-shaped flowers

**Virginia creeper** same as WOODBINE (sense 2)

**Virginia deer** same as WHITE-TAILED DEER

**Virginia reel** 1. a country dance, the American variety of the reel, performed by a number of couples facing each other in two parallel lines 2. music for this dance

**Virgin Islands** group of islands in the West Indies, east of Puerto Rico: *a*) **British Virgin Islands** easternmost islands of this group, constituting a Brit. territory: 59 sq. mi.; pop. 10,000 *b*) **Virgin Islands of the United States** the islands of this group closest to Puerto Rico, constituting a territory of the U.S.: 132 sq. mi.; pop. 63,000; cap. Charlotte Amalie: abbrev. **VI, V.I.**

**vir·gin·i·ty** (vər jin′ə tē) *n.* 1. the state or fact of being a virgin; maidenhood, chastity, etc. 2. the state of being virgin, pure, clean, etc.

**Virgin Mary** Mary, the mother of Jesus

**Virgin Queen** epithet of ELIZABETH I

**vir·gin's-bow·er** (vur′jinz bou′ər) *n.* a white-flowered, rambling variety of clematis

**virgin wool** wool that has never before been processed

**Vir·go** (vur′gō) [L., lit., virgin] 1. a large constellation between Leo and Libra 2. the sixth sign of the zodiac: see ZODIAC, illus.

**vir·gule** (vur′gyōōl) *n.* [Fr. < L. dim. of *virga*, a twig] a short, diagonal line (/) placed between two words to show that either can be used (and/or), in dates or fractions (3/8), to express "per" (feet/second), etc.

**vir·i·des·cent** (vir′ə des′′nt) *adj.* [< LL., ult. < *viridis*, green] greenish —**vir′i·des′cence** *n.*

**vir·ile** (vir′əl; *chiefly Brit.* -īl) *adj.* [< L. < *vir*, a man] 1. of or characteristic of an adult man; masculine; male 2. having manly strength or vigor 3. of or capable of copulation; sexually potent —**vir′ile·ly** *adv.* —**vi·ril·i·ty** (vi ril′ə tē) *n.*

**vi·rol·o·gy** (vī räl′ə jē) *n.* [< VIR(US) + -*o*- + -LOGY] the study of viruses and virus diseases —**vi·ro·log·ic** (vī′rə läj′ik), **vi′ro·log′i·cal** *adj.* —**vi·rol′o·gist** *n.*

**vir·tu** (vər tōō′, vur′tōō) *n.* [It. < L. *virtus*, virtue] 1. a love of, or taste for, artistic objects 2. such objects, collectively 3. the quality of being so artistic, beautiful, rare, etc. as to interest a collector

**vir·tu·al** (vur′chōo wəl) *adj.* being such practically or in effect, although not in actual fact or name [a *virtual* dictator] —**vir′tu·al′i·ty** (-wal′ə tē) *n.*

**vir·tu·al·ly** (-chōo wəl ē, -chōo lē) *adv.* in effect although not in fact; for all practical purposes [*virtually* identical]

**vir·tue** (vur′chōō) *n.* [< OFr. < L. *virtus*, manliness, worth] 1. general moral excellence; goodness of character 2. a specific moral quality regarded as good 3. chastity 4. *a*) excellence in general; merit *b*) a specific excellence; good quality 5. efficacy; potency; esp., healing power, as of a medicine —**by** (or **in**) **virtue of** because of; on the grounds of —**make a virtue of necessity** to do what has to be done as if one really wanted to

**vir·tu·os·i·ty** (vur′chōo wäs′ə tē) *n., pl.* -**ties** [< ff. + -ITY] great technical skill in some fine art, esp. in the performance of music

**vir·tu·o·so** (vur′chōo wō′sō) *n., pl.* -**sos, -si** (-sē) [It.,

skilled] 1. orig., *a*) a person with a broad interest in the arts or sciences *b*) a person with highly cultivated tastes concerning art 2. a person having great technical skill in some fine art, esp. in the performance of music —*adj.* of or like that of a virtuoso: also **vir′tu·os′ic** (-wäs′ik, -wō′sik)

**vir·tu·ous** (vur′chōo wəs) *adj.* 1. having, or characterized by, moral virtue 2. chaste: said of a woman —**vir′tu·ous·ly** *adv.* —**vir′tu·ous·ness** *n.*

**vir·u·lent** (vir′yōo lənt, -oo-) *adj.* [< L. *virulentus* < *virus*, a poison] 1. *a*) extremely poisonous or injurious; deadly *b*) bitterly spiteful; full of hate and enmity 2. *Med. a*) violent and rapid in its course: said of a disease *b*) highly infectious: said of a microorganism —**vir′u·lence, vir′u·len·cy** *n.* —**vir′u·lent·ly** *adv.*

**vi·rus** (vī′rəs) *n.* [L., a poison] 1. orig., venom, as of a snake 2. *a*) any of a group of ultramicroscopic infective agents that cause various diseases in animals or plants: see also FILTERABLE VIRUS *b*) a disease caused by a virus 3. any evil or harmful influence

‡**vis** (vis) *n., pl.* **vi·res** (vī′rēz) [L.] force; strength

**vi·sa** (vē′zə) *n.* [Fr. < L. pp. of *videre*, to see] an endorsement on a passport, showing that it has been examined by the proper officials of a country and granting entry into that country —*vt.* -**saed, -sa·ing** 1. to put a visa on (a passport) 2. to give a visa to (someone)

**vis·age** (viz′ij) *n.* [< OFr. < L. *visus*, a look < pp. of *videre*, to see] 1. the face; countenance 2. appearance; aspect —**vis′aged** *adj.*

**vis-à-vis** (vē′zə vē′) *adj., adv.* [Fr.] face to face; opposite —*prep.* 1. face to face with 2. in relation to

**Visc.** 1. Viscount 2. Viscountess Also **Vis., Visct.**

**vis·cer·a** (vis′ər ə) *n.pl., sing.* **vis′cus** (-kəs) [L.] the internal organs of the body, as the heart, lungs, liver, intestines, etc.; specif., in popular usage, the intestines

**vis·cer·al** (-əl) *adj.* 1. of, like, or affecting the viscera 2. intuitive, emotional, etc. rather than intellectual —**vis′cer·al·ly** *adv.*

**vis·cid** (vis′id) *adj.* [< LL. < L. *viscum*, birdlime] being a cohesive and sticky fluid; viscous —**vis·cid·i·ty** (vi sid′ə tē) *n.* —**vis′cid·ly** *adv.*

**vis·cose** (vis′kōs) *adj.* 1. same as VISCOUS 2. of viscose —*n.* a syruplike solution made by treating cellulose with sodium hydroxide and carbon disulfide: used in making cellophane and rayon thread and fabrics (**viscose rayon**)

**vis·cos·i·ty** (vis käs′ə tē) *n., pl.* -**ties** 1. a viscous quality or state 2. *Physics* the internal friction of a fluid, caused by molecular attraction

**vis·count** (vī′kount) *n.* [< OFr. < ML. *vice comes:* see VICE- & COUNT²] a nobleman next below an earl or count and above a baron —**vis′count·cy, vis′count·y, vis′count·ship′** *n.*

**vis·count·ess** (vī′koun tis) *n.* 1. the wife of a viscount 2. a peeress having the same rank as a viscount

**vis·cous** (vis′kəs) *adj.* [< LL. < L. *viscum*, birdlime] 1. being a cohesive and sticky fluid; viscid 2. *Physics* having viscosity —**vis′cous·ly** *adv.* —**vis′cous·ness** *n.*

**vise** (vīs) *n.* [< OFr. < L. *vitis*, a vine, lit., that which winds] a device consisting of two jaws opened and closed by a screw, lever, etc., used for holding firmly an object being worked on —*vt.* **vised, vis′ing** to hold or squeeze with or as with a vise —**vise′like′** *adj.*

**vi·sé** (vē′zā, vē zā′) *n., vt.* -**séed, -sé·ing** [Fr.] same as VISA

**Vish·nu** (vish′nōō) *Hindu Theol.* the second member of the trinity (Brahma, Vishnu, and Siva), called "the Preserver": see also KRISHNA —**Vish′nu·ism** *n.*

**vis·i·bil·i·ty** (viz′ə bil′ə tē) *n., pl.* -**ties** 1. a being visible 2. *a*) the relative possibility of being seen under the conditions of distance, light, and atmosphere that exist at a certain time *b*) range of vision

**vis·i·ble** (viz′ə b′l) *adj.* [< OFr. < L. *visibilis* < pp. of *videre*, to see] 1. that can be seen 2. that can be perceived; evident; manifest 3. on hand [*visible* supply] —**vis′i·ble·ness** *n.* —**vis′i·bly** *adv.*

**Vis·i·goth** (viz′ə gäth′, -gôth′) *n.* any of the West Goths who invaded the Roman Empire late in the 4th cent. A.D. and set up a kingdom in France and Spain —**Vis′i·goth′ic** *adj.*

**vi·sion** (vizh′ən) *n.* [< OFr. < L. *visio* < pp. of *videre*, to see] 1. the act or power of seeing 2. *a*) something supposedly seen by other than normal sight, as in a dream, trance, etc. *b*) the experience of having seen something in

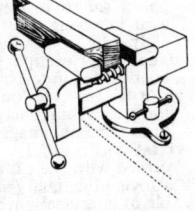

VISE

this way **3.** a mental image *[visions* of power*]* **4.** *a)* the ability to perceive something not actually visible, as through mental acuteness *b)* force or power of imagination *[a* statesman of great *vision]* **5.** something or someone of great beauty —*vt.* to see as in a vision —**vi′sion·al** *adj.*

**vi·sion·ar·y** (-er′ē) *adj.* **1.** of, having the nature of, or seen in a vision **2.** *a)* imaginary *b)* not realistic; impractical, as an idea **3.** seeing or disposed to see visions **4.** characterized by impractical ideas or schemes —*n., pl.* **-ar′ies 1.** a person who sees visions **2.** a person who has impractical ideas; dreamer

**vis·it** (viz′it) *vt.* [< OFr. < L. *visitare,* freq. < *visere,* to go to see < pp. of *videre,* to see] **1.** to go or come to see (someone) out of friendship or for business or professional reasons **2.** to stay with as a guest **3.** to go or come to (a place) as in order to inspect or look at **4.** to occur or come to *[visited* by an odd idea*]* **5.** to come upon or afflict *[a* drought *visited* the land*]* **6.** to inflict (punishment, suffering, etc.) upon (someone) —*vi.* to visit someone or something; specif., *a)* to make a social call (often with *with*) *b)* to stay with someone as a guest *c)* [Colloq.] to converse, as during a visit —*n.* a visiting; specif., *a)* a social call *b)* a stay as a guest *c)* an official call, as of a doctor, inspector, etc. *d)* [Colloq.] a friendly conversation or chat —**vis′it·a·ble** *adj.*

**vis·it·ant** (-ənt) *n.* **1.** a visitor **2.** a migratory bird in any of its temporary resting places

**vis·it·a·tion** (viz′ə tā′shən) *n.* **1.** a visiting; esp., an official visit as to inspect **2.** any trouble looked on as punishment sent by God —**the Visitation** *R.C.Ch.* **1.** the visit of the Virgin Mary to Elizabeth: Luke 1:39–56 **2.** a church feast (July 2) commemorating this —**vis′it·a′tion·al** *adj.* —**vis·it·a·to·ri·al** (viz′i tə tôr′ē əl), **vis′i·to′ri·al** *adj.*

**vis·it·ing card** (viz′i tiŋ) *same as* CALLING CARD

**visiting fireman** [Colloq.] **1.** an important visitor, esp. any of a group, given special treatment **2.** a free-spending tourist, etc.

**vis·i·tor** (viz′it ər) *n.* a person making a visit

**vi·sor** (vī′zər) *n.* [< Anglo-Fr. < OFr. < *vis,* a face] **1.** *a)* in armor, the movable part of a helmet that could be lowered to cover the upper part of the face *b)* a movable section of safety glass, that is part of a protective head covering **2.** a mask **3.** the projecting brim of a cap, for shading the eyes **4.** an adjustable shade in a car, over the windshield, for shading the eyes —**vis′ored** *adj.*

**VISTA** (vis′tə) [*V(olunteers) i(n) S(ervice) t(o) A(merica)*] a U.S. government program using volunteers who work at improving living conditions in poverty-stricken areas of the U.S.

**vis·ta** (vis′tə) *n.* [< It., ult. < L. *videre,* to see] **1.** a view, esp. one seen through a long passage, as between rows of houses or trees **2.** a comprehensive mental view of a series of events —**vis′taed** *adj.*                               VISORS

**Vis·tu·la** (vis′choo lə) river in Poland, flowing from the Carpathian Mountains into the Baltic Sea

**vis·u·al** (vizh′oo wəl) *adj.* [< LL. < L. *visus,* a sight < pp. of *videre,* to see] **1.** of, connected with, based on, or used in seeing **2.** that is or can be seen; visible —**vis′u·al·ly** *adv.*

**visual aids** motion pictures, slides, charts, etc. (but not books) used in teaching, illustrating lectures, etc.

**vis·u·al·ize** (vizh′oo wə līz′, -oo līz′) *vt.* **-ized′, -iz′ing** to form a mental image of (something not visible) —*vi.* to form a mental image —**vis′u·al·i·za′tion** *n.*

**vi·tal** (vīt′'l) *adj.* [< MFr. < L. < *vita,* life] **1.** of or concerned with life **2.** *a)* essential to life *[vital* organs*] b)* destroying life; fatal *[vital* wounds*]* **3.** *a)* essential; indispensable *b)* of crucial importance **4.** affecting the validity, truth, etc. of something *[a vital* error*]* **5.** full of life and vigor; energetic —*n.* *[pl.]* **1.** the vital organs, as the heart, brain, etc. **2.** the essential parts of anything —**vi′tal·ly** *adv.* —**vi′tal·ness** *n.*

**vi·tal·ism** (-iz'm) *n.* the doctrine that the life in living organisms is caused and sustained by a basic force (**vital force** or **principle**) that is distinct from all physical and chemical forces —**vi′tal·ist** *n., adj.* —**vi′tal·is′tic** *adj.*

**vi·tal·i·ty** (vī tal′ə tē) *n., pl.* **-ties 1.** power to live or go on living **2.** power to endure or survive **3.** mental or physical energy; vigor

**vi·tal·ize** (vīt′'l īz′) *vt.* **-ized′, -iz′ing 1.** to make vital; give life to **2.** to give vigor or animation to; make lively —**vi′tal·i·za′tion** *n.*

**Vi·tal·li·um** (vī tal′ē əm) *a trademark for* an alloy of cobalt, chromium, and molybdenum, used in bone surgery, etc.

**vital statistics** data on births, deaths, marriages, etc.

**vi·ta·min** (vīt′ə min; *Brit.* vit′-) *n.* [< L. *vita,* life + AMINE: from the orig. mistaken idea that these substances all con-

tain amino acids] any of a number of complex organic substances found variously in foods and essential for the normal functioning of the body —**vi′ta·min′ic** *adj.*

**vitamin A** a fat-soluble alcohol found in fish-liver oil, egg yolk, butter, etc. or derived from carotene in carrots and other vegetables: a deficiency of this vitamin results in night blindness: it occurs in two forms, **vitamin A₁**, and **vitamin A₂**

**vitamin B (complex)** a group of unrelated water-soluble substances, including: *a)* **vitamin B₁** (*see* THIAMINE) *b)* **vitamin B₂** (*see* RIBOFLAVIN) *c)* **vitamin B₆** (*see* PYRIDOXINE) *d)* NIACIN *e)* PANTOTHENIC ACID *f)* BIOTIN: also called **vitamin H** *g)* INOSITOL *h)* PARA-AMINOBENZOIC ACID *i)* CHOLINE *j)* FOLIC ACID *k)* **vitamin B₁₂** a complex vitamin, essential for normal growth and used esp. in treating pernicious anemia

**vitamin C** *same as* ASCORBIC ACID

**vitamin D** any of several fat-soluble vitamins occurring in fish-liver oils, milk, egg yolk, etc.: a deficiency of this vitamin tends to produce rickets: this group includes **vitamin D₂, vitamin D₃, vitamin D₄,** and **vitamin D₅**

**vitamin E** the tocopherols collectively, necessary for fertility in some animals

**vitamin H** *same as* BIOTIN

**vitamin K** a fat-soluble vitamin that promotes blood clotting: **vitamin K₁** is found chiefly in alfalfa leaves and **vitamin K₂** chiefly in fish meal: **vitamin K₃** and **vitamin K₄** are prepared synthetically

**vi·ti·ate** (vish′ē āt′) *vt.* **-at′ed, -at′ing** [< L. pp. of *vitiare* < *vitium,* a VICE!] **1.** to make imperfect or faulty; spoil **2.** to weaken morally; debase **3.** to make legally ineffective —**vi′ti·a′tion** *n.* —**vi′ti·a′tor** *n.*

**vit·i·cul·ture** (vit′ə kul′chər, vīt′-) *n.* [< L. *vitis,* a vine + CULTURE] the cultivation of grapes —**vit′i·cul′tur·al** *adj.* —**vit′i·cul′tur·ist** *n.*

**vit·re·ous** (vit′rē əs) *adj.* [< L. < *vitrum,* glass] **1.** *a)* of or like glass; glassy *b)* derived from or made of glass **2.** of the vitreous body —**vit′re·ous·ness** *n.*

**vitreous body** (or **humor**) the transparent, colorless, jelly-like substance that fills the eyeball between the retina and lens

**vit·ri·fy** (vit′rə fī′) *vt., vi.* **-fied′, -fy′ing** [< Fr. < L. *vitrum,* glass + Fr. *-fier, -FY*] to change into glass or a glass-like substance by fusion due to heat —**vit′ri·fi′a·ble** *adj.* —**vit′ri·fi·ca′tion, vit′ri·fac′tion** *n.*

**vit·rine** (vi trēn′) *n.* [Fr., ult. < L. *vitrum,* glass] a glass-paneled cabinet or glass display case for art objects, curios, etc.

**vit·ri·ol** (vit′rē əl, -ōl′) *n.* [< MFr. < ML. *vitriolum* < LL. < L. *vitreus,* glassy] **1.** *a)* any of several sulfates of metals, as of copper (*blue vitriol*), of iron (*green vitriol*), or zinc (*white vitriol*), etc. *b) same as* SULFURIC ACID: in full, **oil of vitriol 2.** sharpness or bitterness, as in speech or writing —*vt.* **-oled** or **-olled, -ol·ing** or **-ol·ling** to treat as with vitriol

**vit·ri·ol·ic** (vit′rē äl′ik) *adj.* **1.** of, like, or derived from a vitriol **2.** extremely biting or caustic *[vitriolic* talk*]*

**vit·ri·ol·ize** (vit′rē ə līz′) *vt.* **-ized′, -iz′ing 1.** to convert into vitriol **2.** to subject to the action of vitriol

**vit·tle** (vit′'l) *n., v. obs.* or *dial. var. of* VICTUAL

**vi·tu·per·ate** (vī tōō′pə rāt′, vi-; -tyōō′-) *vt.* **-at′ed, -at′ing** [< L. pp. of *vituperare* < *vitium,* a fault + *parare,* to make ready] to speak abusively to or about; berate —**vi·tu′per·a′tion** *n.* —**vi·tu′per·a′tive** *adj.* —**vi·tu′per·a′tive·ly** *adv.* —**vi·tu′per·a′tive·ness** *n.* —**vi·tu′per·a′tor** *n.*

**‡vi·va** (vē′vä) *interj.* [It., Sp.] (long) live (someone or something specified)!: an exclamation of praise

**vi·va·ce** (vi vä′chä) *adj., adv.* [It.] *Music* in a lively, spirited manner: a direction to the performer

**vi·va·cious** (vi vā′shəs, vī-) *adj.* [< L. *vivax* (gen. *vivacis*) < *vivere,* to live] full of animation; spirited; lively —**vi·va′cious·ly** *adv.* —**vi·va′cious·ness** *n.*

**vi·vac·i·ty** (vi vas′ə tē, vī-) *n.* the quality or state of being vivacious; liveliness; animation

**Vi·val·di** (vē väl′dē; *E.* vi-), **An·to·ni·o** (än tô′nyô) 1675?–1741; It. composer

**vi·var·i·um** (vī ver′ē əm) *n., pl.* **-i·ums, -i·a** (-ə) [L., ult. < *vivere,* to live] an enclosed place for animals to live as if in their natural environment

**vi·va vo·ce** (vī′və vō′sē) [ML., with living voice] by word of mouth; orally —**vi′va-vo′ce** *adj.*

**‡vive** (vēv) *interj.* [Fr.] (long) live (someone or something specified)!: an exclamation of praise

**Viv·i·an** (viv′ē ən, viv′yən) [L. *Vivianus* < *vivus,* alive] a masculine or feminine name

**viv·id** (viv′id) *adj.* [< L. < *vivere,* to live] **1.** full of life; lively; striking *[a vivid* personality*]* **2.** bright; intense: said of colors, light, etc. **3.** forming or suggesting clear or striking mental images *[a vivid* imagination, a *vivid* description*]* **4.** clearly perceived, as a recollection —**viv′id·ly** *adv.* —**viv′id·ness** *n.*

**viv·i·fy** (viv′ə fī′) *vt.* **-fied′, -fy′ing** [< Fr. < LL. < L. *vivus,* alive + *facere,* to make] **1.** to give life to; animate

2. to make more lively, active, striking, etc. —**viv′i·fi·ca′-tion** *n.* —**viv′i·fi′er** *n.*

**vi·vip·a·rous** (vī vip′ər əs) *adj.* [< L. < *vivus*, alive + *parere*, to produce] bearing living young (as most mammals and some other animals do) instead of laying eggs —**vi·vip′a·rous·ly** *adv.*

**viv·i·sect** (viv′ə sekt′) *vt., vi.* [< ff.] to practice vivisection (on) —**viv′i·sec′tor** *n.*

**viv·i·sec·tion** (viv′ə sek′shən) *n.* [< L. *vivus*, alive + SECTION] medical research consisting of surgical operations or other experiments done on living animals to study the living organs and to investigate the effects of diseases and therapy —**viv′i·sec′tion·al** *adj.*

**viv·i·sec·tion·ist** (-ist) *n.* a person who practices or favors the practice of vivisection for the good of science

**vix·en** (vik′s'n) *n.* [ME. (southern dial.) *fixen* < OE. *fyxe*, she-fox] 1. a female fox 2. an ill-tempered, shrewish woman —**vix′en·ish** *adj.* —**vix′en·ish·ly** *adv.*

**viz., viz** (viz; *often read* "namely") [ML., altered < contr. for L. *videlicet*] videlicet; that is; namely

**viz·ard** (viz′ərd) *n.* [altered < *visar*, var. of VISOR] a mask, as for disguise

**vi·zier** (vi zir′, viz′yər) *n.* [< Turk. < Ar. *wazīr*, lit., bearer of burdens < *wazara*, to bear a burden] in Moslem countries, a high officer in the government; esp., a minister of state: also sp. **vi·zir′** —**vi·zier′ate** (-it, -āt), **vi·zier′ship** *n.*

**vi·zor** (vī′zər) *n. alt. sp. of* VISOR

**V-J Day** (vē′jā′) the day on which the fighting with Japan officially ended in World War II (Aug. 15, 1945) or the day of formal surrender (Sept. 2, 1945)

**VL.** Vulgar Latin

**Vla·di·vos·tok** (vlad′i väs′täk; *Russ.* vlä′di vôs tôk′) seaport in SE R.S.F.S.R., on the Pacific: pop. 442,000

**Vla·minck** (vlà mank′), **Mau·rice de** (mô rēs′ də) 1876–1958; Fr. painter

**VLF, V.L.F., vlf, v.l.f.** very low frequency

**Vl·ta·va** (v'l′tä vä) river in W Czechoslovakia, flowing northward into the Elbe

**V-neck** (vē′nek′) *n.* a neckline V-shaped in front

**voc.** vocative

**vo·ca·ble** (vō′kə b'l) *n.* [Fr. < L. *vocabulum* < *vocare*, to call] a word; esp., a word regarded as a unit of sounds or letters rather than as a unit of meaning

**vo·cab·u·lar·y** (vō kab′yə ler′ē, və-) *n., pl.* **-lar′ies** [< ML. < L. *vocabulum*, a word: see prec.] 1. a list of words, usually arranged in alphabetical order and defined or otherwise identified, as in a dictionary or glossary 2. all the words of a language, or all those used by a particular person, class, profession, etc.

**vo·cal** (vō′k'l) *adj.* [< L. *vocalis* < *vox* (gen. *vocis*), a voice] 1. *a)* uttered by the voice; esp., spoken; oral *[vocal sounds] b)* sung or to be sung *[vocal music]* 2. having a voice; able to speak or make oral sounds 3. of, used in, connected with, or belonging to the voice *[vocal organs]* 4. full of voices 5. speaking freely or strongly —*n.* 1. a vocal sound 2. the part of a popular song that is sung, as distinguished from the parts played by the instruments —**vo′cal·ly** *adv.*

**vocal cords** either of two pairs of membranous cords or folds in the larynx, consisting of a thicker upper pair ( **false vocal cords** ) and a lower pair (**true vocal cords**): voice is produced when air from the lungs causes the lower (true) cords to vibrate

**vo·cal·ic** (vō kal′ik) *adj.* 1. *a)* of, or having the nature of, a vowel *b)* composed mainly or entirely of vowels 2. producing or involving vowel change —**vo·cal′i·cal·ly** *adv.*

**vo·cal·ist** (vō′k'l ist) *n.* a singer

**vo·cal·ize** (vō′k'l īz′) *vt.* **-ized′, -iz′ing** 1. *a)* to give utterance to; express with the voice *b)* to make capable of vocal expression 2. *Phonet. a)* to change into or use as a vowel *b)* to voice —*vi.* to make vocal sounds; speak or sing; specif., to do a singing exercise, using various vowel sounds —**vo′cal·i·za′tion** *n.* —**vo′cal·iz′er** *n.*

**vo·ca·tion** (vō kā′shən) *n.* [< LL. < L. < *vocare*, to call] 1. *a)* a call or will to carry on some work or enter a certain career, esp. a religious one *b)* the work or career toward which one believes himself to be called 2. any trade, profession, or occupation

**vo·ca·tion·al** (-'l) *adj.* 1. of a vocation, trade, occupation, etc. 2. designating or of education, training, etc. intended to prepare one for an occupation, sometimes specif. in a trade —**vo·ca′tion·al·ism** *n.* —**vo·ca′tion·al·ly** *adv.*

**vocational guidance** the work of testing and interviewing persons in order to guide them toward the choice of a suitable vocation

**voc·a·tive** (väk′ə tiv) *adj.* [< OFr. < L. < pp. of *vocare*, to call < *vox*, the voice] *Gram.* in certain inflected languages, designating or of the case indicating the person or

thing addressed —*n.* 1. the vocative case 2. a word in this case

**vo·cif·er·ate** (vō sif′ə rāt′) *vt., vi.* **-at′ed, -at′ing** [< L. pp. of *vociferari* < *vox*, voice + *ferre*, to bear] to utter or shout loudly or vehemently; bawl; clamor —**vo·cif′er·ant** (-ər ənt) *adj.* —**vo·cif′er·a′tion** *n.* —**vo·cif′er·a′tor** *n.*

**vo·cif·er·ous** (vō sif′ər əs) *adj.* loud, noisy, or vehement in making one's feelings known; clamorous —**vo·cif′er·ous·ly** *adv.* —**vo·cif′er·ous·ness** *n.*

**vod·ka** (väd′kə) *n.* [Russ., dim. of *voda*, water] a colorless alcoholic liquor distilled from wheat, rye, etc.

**vogue** (vōg) *n.* [Fr., a fashion, lit., a rowing < *voguer*, to row < MLowG.] 1. the accepted fashion at any particular time; mode: often with *the* 2. general acceptance; popularity —*adj.* in vogue: also **vogu·ish** (vō′gish)

**voice** (vois) *n.* [< OFr. < L. *vox* (gen. *vocis*)] 1. sound made through the mouth, esp. by human beings in talking, singing, etc. 2. the ability to make such sounds *[to lose one's voice]* 3. any sound, influence, etc. regarded as like vocal utterance *[the voice of the sea, the voice of one's conscience]* 4. a specified or distinctive quality of vocal sound *[an angry voice]* 5. *a)* an expressed wish, choice, opinion, etc. *[the voice of the people] b)* the right to express one's choice, opinion, etc.; vote 6. utterance or expression *[giving voice to his joy]* 7. the means by which something is expressed *[a newspaper known to be the voice of the administration]* 8. *Gram.* a form of a verb showing the connection between the subject and the verb, either as performing (**active voice**) or receiving (**passive voice**) the action 9. *Music a)* the quality of a person's singing *[a good voice] b)* a singer *c)* any of the individual parts sung or played together in a musical composition 10. *Phonet.* sound made by vibrating the vocal cords with air forced from the lungs, as in pronouncing all vowels and such consonants as (b), (d), (g), (m), etc. —*vt.* voiced, voic′ing 1. to utter or express in words 2. *Music* to regulate the tone of (organ pipes, etc.) 3. *Phonet.* to utter with voice —**in voice** with the voice in good condition, as for singing —**with one voice** unanimously —**voic′er** *n.*

**voiced** (voist) *adj.* 1. having a voice 2. having (a specified kind of) voice *[deep-voiced]* 3. expressed by the voice 4. *Phonet.* made by vibrating the vocal cords with air forced from the lungs: said of certain consonants

**voice·less** (vois′lis) *adj.* 1. having no voice; mute 2. not speaking or spoken 3. *Phonet.* uttered without voice *[p, t, k,* etc. are *voiceless* consonants] —**voice′less·ly** *adv.* —**voice′less·ness** *n.*

**voice-o·ver** (-ō′vər) *n.* the voice commenting or narrating off camera, as for a television commercial

**voice·print** (-print′) *n.* the distinctive pattern of wavy lines, etc. formed by a person's voice as recorded by an electronic device

**void** (void) *adj.* [< OFr., ult. < L. *vacivus* < *vacare*, to be empty] 1. not occupied; vacant: said of a position or office 2. *a)* having nothing in it; empty *b)* lacking; devoid (*of*) *[void of sense]* 3. useless; ineffective 4. *Law* of no legal force; not binding; invalid —*n.* 1. an empty space or vacuum 2. *a)* total absence of something normally present *b)* a feeling of emptiness or loss —*vt.* 1. *a)* to empty (the contents of something) *b)* to discharge (urine or feces) 2. to make void; annul —*vi.* to defecate or, esp., to urinate —**void′a·ble** *adj.* —**void′er** *n.*

‡**voi·là** (vwà là′) [Fr., see there] behold; there it is: often used as an interjection

**voile** (voil) *n.* [Fr., a veil] a thin, sheer fabric, as of cotton

**vol.** 1. volcano 2. *pl.* **vols.** volume 3. volunteer

**vo·lant** (vō′lənt) *adj.* [Fr. < L. prp. of *volare*, to fly] 1. flying or capable of flying 2. nimble; quick 3. *Heraldry* represented as flying

**vol·a·tile** (väl′ə t'l; *chiefly Brit.* -tīl′) *adj.* [MFr. < L. < *volare*, to fly] 1. vaporizing or evaporating quickly, as alcohol 2. *a)* unstable or explosive *[a volatile* social condition] *b)* moving capriciously from one idea, interest, etc. to another; fickle *c)* not lasting long; fleeting —**vol′a·til′i·ty** (-til′ə tē), **vol′a·tile·ness** *n.*

**vol·a·til·ize** (väl′ə t'l īz′) *vt., vi.* **-ized′, -iz′ing** to make or become volatile —**vol′a·til·i·za′tion** *n.*

**vol·can·ic** (väl kan′ik) *adj.* 1. of, from, or produced by a volcano 2. having volcanoes 3. like a volcano; likely to explode; violent —**vol·can′i·cal·ly** *adv.*

**vol·can·ism** (väl′kə niz′m) *n.* volcanic activity or phenomena

**vol·ca·no** (väl kā′nō) *n., pl.* **-noes, -nos** [It. < L. *Volcanus*, VULCAN] 1. a vent in the earth's crust through which molten rock (*lava*), rock fragments, gases, ashes, etc. erupt or burst from the earth's interior 2. a cone-shaped hill or mountain, chiefly of volcanic materials, built up around the vent, usually so as to form a crater

---

**vole** (vōl) *n.* [earlier *vole mouse* < Scand., as in Norw. *voll*, field + MOUSE] any of a number of small rodents with a stout body and short tail

**Vol·ga** (väl′gə, vôl′-; *Russ.* vôl′gä) river in western R.S.F.S.R., flowing southeastward into the Caspian Sea

**Vol·go·grad** (väl′gə grad′; *Russ.* vôl′gô grät′) city in SC European R.S.F.S.R., on the Volga: pop. 818,000

**vo·li·tion** (vō lish′ən, və-) *n.* [Fr. < ML. *volitio*, ult. < L. *velle*, to will] 1. the act or power of using the will 2. a conscious or deliberate decision —**vo·li′tion·al** *adj.*

**vol·i·tive** (väl′ə tiv) *adj.* 1. of the will 2. *Gram.* expressing a wish, as a verb, mood, etc.

**vol·ley** (väl′ē) *n., pl.* **-leys** [MFr. *volee*, ult. < L. pp. of *volare*, to fly] 1. *a*) the simultaneous discharge of a number of guns or other weapons *b*) the missiles discharged in this way 2. a burst of words or acts suggestive of this [a *volley* of curses] 3. *Sports a*) the flight of a ball, etc. before it touches the ground *b*) a return of a ball, etc. before it touches the ground *c*) loosely, any extended exchange of shots, as in tennis, esp. in warming up —*vt., vi.* **-leyed, -ley·ing** 1. to discharge or be discharged as in a volley 2. *Sports* to return (the ball, etc.) as a volley; engage in a volley —**vol′ley·er** *n.*

**vol·ley·ball** (-bôl′) *n.* 1. a game played on a court by two teams who hit a large, light, inflated ball back and forth over a high net with the hands, each team trying to return the ball before it touches the ground 2. this ball

**vol·plane** (väl′plān′) *vi.* **-planed′, -plan′ing** [Fr. *vol plané* < *voler*, to fly + *plané*, pp. of *planer*, to glide] to glide down as or in an airplane with the engine cut off —*n.* such a glide

**vols.** volumes

**volt¹** (vōlt) *n.* [< Fr. < It. < L. pp. of *volvere*, to turn about] 1. a turning movement of a horse, sideways around a center 2. *Fencing* a leap to avoid a thrust

**volt²** (vōlt) *n.* [after A. *Volta* (1745–1827), It. physicist] the mks unit of electromotive force or difference in potential between two points in an electric circuit that will send a current of one ampere through a resistance of one ohm

**volt·age** (vōl′tij) *n.* electromotive force, or difference in electrical potential, expressed in volts

**vol·ta·ic** (väl tā′ik, vōl-) *adj.* 1. designating or of electricity produced by chemical action; galvanic 2. used in so producing electricity

**voltaic battery** 1. a battery composed of voltaic cells 2. *same as* VOLTAIC CELL

**voltaic cell** a device for producing an electric current by the action of two plates of different metals in an electrolyte

**Vol·taire** (vōl ter′, väl-; *Fr.* vôl ter′) (born *François Marie Arouet*) 1694–1778; Fr. writer & philosopher

**vol·ta·me·ter** (väl tam′ə tər, vōl-) *n.* an electrolytic cell for measuring an electric current by the amount of gas liberated or metal deposited from an electrolyte

**volt·am·me·ter** (vōlt′am′mēt′ər) *n.* an instrument for measuring either voltage or amperage

**volt-am·pere** (-am′pir) *n.* a unit of electric power equal to the product of one volt and one ampere

**volt·me·ter** (vōlt′mēt′ər) *n.* an instrument for measuring voltage

**vol·u·ble** (väl′yoo b'l) *adj.* [Fr. < L. *volubilis* < pp. of *volvere*, to roll] talking very much and easily; talkative, glib, etc. —**vol′u·bil′i·ty** *n.* —**vol′u·bly** *adv.*

**vol·ume** (väl′yoom, -yəm) *n.* [MFr. < L. *volumen*, a scroll < pp. of *volvere*, to roll] 1. *a*) a collection of written or printed sheets bound together; book *b*) any of the books of a set 2. a set of the issues of a periodical over a fixed period of time, usually a year 3. the amount of space occupied in three dimensions; cubic contents 4. *a*) a quantity, bulk, mass, or amount *b*) a large quantity 5. the strength or loudness of sound 6. *Music* fullness of tone — **speak volumes** to be very meaningful

**vol·u·met·ric** (väl′yoo met′rik) *adj.* of or based on the measurement of volume: also **vol′u·met′ri·cal** —**vol′u·met′ri·cal·ly** *adv.*

**vo·lu·mi·nous** (və loo′mə nəs) *adj.* 1. writing, producing, or consisting of enough to fill many volumes 2. of great volume; large; bulky; full —**vo·lu′mi·nos′i·ty** (-näs′ə tē) *n.* —**vo·lu′mi·nous·ly** *adv.*

**vol·un·tar·y** (väl′ən ter′ē) *adj.* [< L. *voluntas*, free will, ult. < *velle*, to will] 1. brought about by one's own free choice; given or done of one's own free will 2. acting willingly or of one's own accord [a *voluntary* guide] 3. intentional [*voluntary* manslaughter] 4. controlled by the will [*voluntary* muscles] 5. having free will or the power of free choice [man is a *voluntary* agent] 6. made up of volunteers [a *voluntary* army] —*n., pl.* **-tar′ies** an organ solo played for a church service —**vol′un·tar′i·ly** (-ə lē, väl′ən ter′-) *adv.*

**vol·un·teer** (väl′ən tir′) *n.* [< obs. Fr. *volontaire*, a voluntary] 1. a person who offers to do something of his own free will 2. a person who enlists in the armed forces of his own free will —*adj.* 1. of or made up of volunteers 2. serving as a volunteer 3. *same as* VOLUNTARY —*vt.* to offer

or give of one's own free will —*vi.* to enter or offer to enter into any service of one's own free will; enlist

**vo·lup·tu·ar·y** (və lup′choo wer′ē) *n., pl.* **-ar′ies** [see ff.] a person devoted to luxurious living and sensual pleasures —*adj.* of or characterized by luxury and sensual pleasures

**vo·lup·tu·ous** (-choo wəs) *adj.* [< L. < *voluptas*, pleasure] 1. full of, producing, or characterized by sensual pleasures 2. fond of luxury, the pleasures of the senses, etc. 3. suggesting, or arising from, sensual pleasure 4. sexually attractive because of a full, shapely figure —**vo·lup′tu·ous·ly** *adv.* —**vo·lup′tu·ous·ness** *n.*

**vo·lute** (və loot′) *n.* [< L. < pp. of *volvere*, to roll] 1. a spiral or twisting form; whorl 2. *Archit.* a spiral scroll, as of an Ionic capital 3. *Zool.* any of the whorls of a spiral shell —*adj.* spiraled: also **vo·lut′ed** —**vo·lu′tion** *n.*

**vom·it** (väm′it) *n.* [< L. < pp. of *vomere*] matter thrown up from the stomach —*vi., vt.* 1. to throw up (the contents of the stomach) through the mouth 2. to throw out or be thrown out with force; belch forth —**vom′it·er** *n.*

**vom·i·tive** (-ə tiv) *adj.* of or causing vomiting; emetic

**‡von** (fôn; *E.* vän) *prep.* [G.] of; from: a prefix occurring in many names of German and Austrian families, esp. of the nobility

**voo·doo** (voo′doo) *n., pl.* **-doos** [Creole Fr. < a WAfr. word] 1. a primitive religion based on a belief in sorcery, fetishism, etc.: it originated in Africa and is still practiced, chiefly by natives of the West Indies 2. a person who practices voodoo 3. a voodoo charm, fetish, etc. —*adj.* of voodoos or their practices, beliefs, etc. —*vt.* to affect by voodoo magic —**voo′doo·ism** *n.* —**voo′doo·ist** *n.* —**voo′doo·is′tic** *adj.*

**vo·ra·cious** (vô rā′shəs, və-) *adj.* [L. *vorax* (gen. *voracis*) < *vorare*, to devour] 1. greedy in eating; ravenous; gluttonous 2. very greedy or eager in some desire or pursuit [a *voracious* reader] —**vo·ra′cious·ly** *adv.* —**vo·rac′i·ty** (-ras′ə tē), **vo·ra′cious·ness** *n.*

**Vo·ro·nezh** (vô rô′nesh) city in SC European R.S.F.S.R., near the Don: pop. 660,000

**-vo·rous** (və rəs) [< L. < *vorare*, to devour] *a combining form meaning* feeding on, eating [*omnivorous*]

**vor·tex** (vôr′teks) *n., pl.* **vor′tex·es, vor′ti·ces′** (-tə sēz′) [L. < *vertere*, to turn] 1. a whirling mass of water forming a vacuum at its center, into which anything caught in the motion is drawn; whirlpool 2. a whirl of air; whirlwind 3. any activity, situation, etc. that is like a whirl in its rush, catastrophic power, etc. —**vor′ti·cal** *adj.* —**vor′ti·cal·ly** *adv.*

**Vosges (Mountains)** (vōzh) mountain range in NE France, west of the Rhine

**vo·ta·ry** (vōt′ə rē) *n., pl.* **-ries** [< L. pp. of *vovere*, to vow + -ARY] 1. *a*) a person bound by religious vows, as a monk *b*) a devout worshiper 2. a devoted supporter; one who is devoted to some cause or interest Also **vo′ta·rist** —**vo′ta·ress** (-ris) *n.fem.*

**vote** (vōt) *n.* [L. *votum*, a vow < pp. of *vovere*, to vow] 1. a decision on a proposal, etc., or a choice between candidates for office 2. *a*) the expression of such a decision or choice *b*) the ballot, voice, etc. by which it is expressed 3. the right to exercise such a decision, etc.; suffrage 4. *a*) votes collectively *b*) a specified group of voters, or their votes [the farm *vote*] 5. [Archaic] a voter —*vi.* **vot′ed, vot′ing** to express preference in a matter by ballot, etc. —*vt.* 1. *a*) to decide, choose, enact, or authorize by vote *b*) to confer by vote *c*) to support (a specified party) in voting 2. to declare by general opinion 3. [Colloq.] to suggest —**vote down** to defeat by voting —**vote in** to elect —**vote out** to defeat (an incumbent) in an election —**vote′less** *adj.*

**vot·er** (vōt′ər) *n.* a person who has a right to vote; elector, esp. one who actually votes

**voting machine** a machine on which the votes in an election are cast, registered, and counted

**vo·tive** (vōt′iv) *adj.* [L. *votivus* < *votum:* see VOTE] given, done, etc. in fulfillment of a vow [*votive* offerings]

**vouch** (vouch) *vt.* [< OFr. < L. *vocare*, to call < *vox*, a voice] to uphold by demonstration or evidence —*vi.* 1. to give assurance, a guarantee, etc. (with *for*) [to *vouch* for his honesty] 2. to serve as evidence or assurance (*for*)

**vouch·er** (vou′chər) *n.* 1. a person who vouches, as for the truth of a statement 2. a paper giving evidence of or attesting to the expenditure or receipt of money, the accuracy of an account, etc.

**vouch·safe** (vouch sāf′) *vt.* **-safed′, -saf′ing** [< ME. *vouchen safe*, to vouch as safe] to be kind or gracious enough to give or grant —**vouch·safe′ment** *n.*

**vous·soir** (voo swär′) *n.* [Fr. < OFr., ult. < L. pp. of *volvere*, to roll] *Archit.* any of the wedge-shaped stones of which an arch or vault is built

**vow** (vou) *n.* [< OFr. < L. *votum:* see VOTE] 1. a solemn promise or pledge, as one made to God or with God as one's witness, binding oneself to an act, way of life, etc. [marriage *vows*] 2. a solemn affirmation —*vt.* 1. to promise solemnly **2.** to swear solemnly to do, get, etc. **3.** to declare in a forceful or earnest way —*vi.* to make a vow —**take vows** to enter a religious order —**vow′er** *n.*

**vow·el** (vou′əl, voul) *n.* [< MFr. < L. *vocalis* (*littera*), vocal (letter) < *vox,* a voice] **1.** any speech sound made by letting the voiced breath pass in a continuous stream through the pharynx and opened mouth **2.** a letter, as *a, e, i, o, u,* and sometimes *y,* representing such a sound —*adj.* of a vowel or vowels

‡**vox** (väks) *n., pl.* **vo·ces** (vō′sēz) [L.] voice

‡**vox po·pu·li** (päp′yoo lī′) [L.] the voice of the people; public opinion or sentiment: abbrev. **vox pop.**

**voy·age** (voi′ij) *n.* [< OFr. < L. *viaticum,* provision for a journey < *via,* way] **1.** a relatively long journey by water or, formerly, by land **2.** a journey by aircraft or spacecraft —*vi.* **-aged, -ag·ing** to make a voyage; travel —*vt.* to sail or travel over or on —**voy′ag·er** *n.*

‡**vo·ya·geur** (vwä yá zhĕr′) *n., pl.* **-geurs′** (-zhĕr′) [Fr.] in Canada, **1.** formerly, a person who transported goods and men for the fur companies **2.** any woodsman or boatman of the wilds

**vo·yeur** (vwä yur′, voi ur′) *n.* [Fr. < *voir,* to see] a person who has an exaggerated interest in viewing sexual objects or activities to obtain sexual gratification; peeping Tom —**vo′yeur′ism** *n.* —**vo′yeur·is′tic** *adj.*

**V.P., VP** Vice-President

**V.Rev.** Very Reverend

**vroom** (vroom) *n.* [echoic] the sound made by a motor vehicle in accelerating —*vi.* [Colloq.] to make, or move off with, such a sound

**vs.** versus

**v.s.** [L. *vide supra*] see above

**V-shaped** (vē′shāpt′) *adj.* shaped like the letter V

**Vt., VT** Vermont

**vt., v.t.** transitive verb

**VTOL** [*v*(*ertical*) *t*(*ake*)*o*(*ff and*) *l*(*anding*)] an aircraft, usually other than a helicopter, that can take off and land vertically

**V-type engine** (vē′tīp′) a gasoline engine in which the cylinders are set at an angle in two banks forming a V

**Vul·can** (vul′k'n) *Rom. Myth.* the god of fire and of metalworking —**Vul·ca′ni·an** (-kā′nē ən) *adj.*

**vul·can·ite** (vul′kə nīt′) *n.* [< prec. + -ITE] a hard rubber made by treating crude rubber with a large amount of sulfur and subjecting it to intense heat; ebonite: used in combs, electrical insulation, etc.

**vul·can·ize** (-nīz′) *vt., vi.* **-ized′, -iz′ing** [< VULCAN + -IZE] to treat (crude rubber) with sulfur and subject it to heat in order to increase its strength and elasticity —**vul′can·i·za′tion** *n.* —**vul′can·iz′er** *n.*

**Vulg.** Vulgate

**vul·gar** (vul′gər) *adj.* [< L. *vulgaris* < *vulgus,* the common people] **1.** of the great mass of people in general; common; popular [a *vulgar* superstition] **2.** of or in the vernacular **3.** *a*) characterized by a lack of culture, refinement, taste, etc.; crude; boorish *b*) indecent or obscene —**vul′gar·ly** *adv.* —**vul′gar·ness** *n.*

**vul·gar·i·an** (vul ger′ē ən, -gar′-) *n.* a vulgar person; esp., a rich person with coarse, showy manners or tastes

**vul·gar·ism** (vul′gər iz'm) *n.* **1.** a word, phrase, etc. that is used widely but is regarded as nonstandard, coarse, or obscene **2.** vulgar behavior, quality, etc.; vulgarity

**vul·gar·i·ty** (vul gar′ə tē) *n.* **1.** the state or quality of being vulgar, crude, etc. **2.** *pl.* **-ties** a vulgar act, habit, usage in speech, etc.

**vul·gar·ize** (vul′gə rīz′) *vt.* **-ized′, -iz′ing** to make vulgar; specif., *a*) to make coarse, crude, etc. *b*) to popularize —**vul′gar·i·za′tion** *n.* —**vul′gar·iz′er** *n.*

**Vulgar Latin** the everyday speech of the Roman people, from which the Romance languages developed

**Vul·gate** (vul′gāt, -git) *n.* [ML. *vulgata* (*editio*), popular (edition)] **1.** a Latin version of the Bible prepared in the 4th cent., serving as an authorized version of the Roman Catholic Church **2.** [v-] the vernacular, or common speech —*adj.* **1.** of or in the Vulgate **2.** [v-] of or in the vernacular

**vul·ner·a·ble** (vul′nər ə b'l) *adj.* [< LL. < L. *vulnerare,* to wound < *vulnus* (gen. *vulneris*), a wound] **1.** that can be wounded or physically injured **2.** *a*) open to, or easily hurt by, criticism or attack *b*) affected by a specified influence, etc. [*vulnerable* to political pressure] **3.** open to attack by armed forces **4.** *Bridge* open to increased penalties or increased bonuses: said of a team which has won one game —**vul′ner·a·bil′i·ty** *n.* —**vul′ner·a·bly** *adv.*

**vul·pine** (vul′pīn, -pin) *adj.* [< L. < *vulpes,* a fox] **1.** of or like a fox or foxes **2.** clever, cunning, etc.

**vul·ture** (vul′chər) *n.* [L. *vultur*] **1.** a large bird related to the eagles and hawks, with a naked head: vultures feed on carrion **2.** *same as* TURKEY BUZZARD **3.** a greedy, ruthless person who preys on others —**vul′tur·ous** *adj.*

**vul·va** (vul′və) *n., pl.* **-vae** (-vē), **-vas** [ModL. < L., womb] the external genital organs of the female —**vul′val, vul′var** *adj.* —**vul′vate** (-vāt, -vit) *adj.*

**vv. 1.** verses **2.** violins

**v.v.** vice versa

**vy·ing** (vī′iŋ) *adj.* that vies; that competes

VULTURE
(to 32 in. long;
wingspread to 6 ft.)

# W

**W, w** (dub′'l yoo, -yə) *n., pl.* **W's, w's 1.** the twenty-third letter of the English alphabet **2.** the sound of *W* or *w*

**W** *Chem.* tungsten

**W, w** watt; watts

**W., W., w, w. 1.** west **2.** western

**W. 1.** Wales **2.** Washington **3.** Wednesday **4.** Welsh

**W., w. 1.** watt(s) **2.** weight **3.** width **4.** won

**w. 1.** week(s) **2.** wide **3.** wife **4.** with

**WA** Washington (State)

**Wa·bash** (wô′bash) [< Algonquian stream and tribal name] river flowing from W Ohio across Ind. into the Ohio River

**wab·ble** (wäb′'l) *n., vt., vi.* **-bled, -bling** *var. of* WOBBLE

**Wac** (wak) *n.* a member of the Women's Army Corps

**WAC** Women's Army Corps

**wack·y** (wak′ē) *adj.* **wack′i·er, wack′i·est** [< ? WHACK + -Y²] [Slang] odd, silly, or crazy —**wack′i·ly** *adv.* —**wack′i·ness** *n.*

**Wa·co** (wā′kō) [< AmInd. tribal name] city in EC Tex.: pop. 101,000

**wad** (wäd, wôd) *n.* [ML. *wadda,* wadding < ?] **1.** a small, soft mass or ball, as a handful of cotton, crumpled paper, etc. **2.** a lump or small, compact mass [a *wad* of chewing tobacco] **3.** a mass of soft material used for padding, packing, etc. **4.** a plug stuffed against a charge to keep it firmly in place, as in a muzzleloading gun **5.** [Colloq.] a roll of paper money **6.** [Slang] a large amount, esp. of money —*vt.* **wad′ded, wad′ding 1.** to compress, or roll up, into a wad **2.** *a*) to plug with a wad *b*) to force or stuff [to *wad* oakum into a crack] **3.** to pad with wadding **4.** to hold (a charge) in place by a wad —**wad′der** *n.*

**Wad·den·zee, Wad·den Zee** (väd′ən zā′) section of the North Sea extending into the Netherlands: formerly, the N part of the Zuider Zee

**wad·ding** (wäd′iŋ, wôd′-) *n.* any soft material for use in padding, packing, stuffing, etc.; esp., cotton made up into loose, fluffy sheets

**wad·dle** (wäd′'l, wôd′-) *vi.* **-dled, -dling** [freq. of WADE] to walk with short steps, swaying from side to side, as a duck —*n.* **1.** the act of waddling **2.** a waddling gait —**wad′dler** *n.*

**wade** (wād) *vi.* **wad′ed, wad′ing** [OE. *waden,* to go] **1.** to walk through a substance, as water, mud, tall grass, etc., that slows one down **2.** to walk and splash about in shallow water in play **3.** to get through with difficulty [to *wade* through a book] **4.** [Colloq.] to start or attack with vigor (with *in* or *into*) —*vt.* to go across or through by wading —*n.* an act of wading

**wad·er** (wād′ər) *n.* **1.** a person or thing that wades **2.** *same as* WADING BIRD **3.** *a*) [*pl.*] high waterproof boots *b*) [*usually pl.*] waterproof trousers with bootlike parts for the feet, worn by fishermen

**wa·di** (wä′dē) *n., pl.* **-dis, -dies** [Ar. *wădī*] in Arabia, N Africa, etc., **1.** a valley, ravine, etc. that is dry except during the rainy season **2.** the rush of water that flows through it Also sp. **wa′dy,** *pl.* **-dies**

**wading bird** any of various unrelated, long-legged shore birds that wade the shallows and marshes for food, as the crane, heron, rail, coot, sandpiper, and snipe

**Waf** (waf) *n.* a member of the WAF

**WAF** Women in the Air Force

**wa·fer** (wā′fər) *n.* [< ONormFr. *waufre* < MDu. *wafel*] **1.** *a*) a thin, flat, crisp cracker or cookie *b*) anything resembling this, as a thin, flat disk of candy **2.** a thin cake of unleavened bread used in the Eucharist **3.** a small disk of sticky paper, used as a seal on letters, documents, etc.

**waf·fle¹** (wäf′'l, wôf′-) *n.* [Du. *wafel*] a crisp batter cake with small, square hollows, baked in a waffle iron —*adj.* having a surface like a waffle: also **waf′fled**

**waf·fle²** (wäf′'l, wôf′-) *vi.* **-fled, -fling** [orig., to yelp < echoic *waff*, to yelp] [Chiefly Brit. Colloq.] to speak or write in a wordy, vague, or indecisive manner —*n.* [Chiefly Brit. Colloq.] talk or writing of this kind

**waffle iron** a utensil or appliance for cooking waffles, having two flat, studded plates pressed together so that the waffle bakes between them

**waft** (waft, wäft) *vt.* [< obs. *wafter*, a convoy < Du. *wachter*, lit., a watcher] **1.** to carry or move (objects, sounds, etc.) lightly through the air or over water **2.** to transport as if in this manner —*vi.* **1.** to float, as in the air **2.** to blow gently: said of breezes —*n.* **1.** an odor, sound, etc. carried through the air **2.** a puff or gust of wind **3.** a wafting movement —**waft′er** *n.*

**wag¹** (wag) *vt.* **wagged, wag′ging** [prob. < ON. *vaga,* to rock] **1.** *a*) to cause to move rapidly back and forth, up and down, etc. [the dog *wagged* his tail] *b*) to shake (a finger) or nod (the head), as in reproving, etc. **2.** to move (the tongue) in talking, esp. in idle gossip —*vi.* **1.** to move rapidly back and forth, up and down, etc. **2.** to keep moving in talk: said of the tongue **3.** to walk or move with a swaying motion; waddle —*n.* the act or an instance of wagging —**wag′ger** *n.*

**wag²** (wag) *n.* [prob. < obs. *waghalter,* a gallows bird, rogue] a comical or humorous person; joker; wit

**wage** (wāj) *vt.* **waged, wag′ing** [< ONormFr. *wagier* < *wage* (OFr. *gage*), a pledge < Frank.] to engage in or carry on (a war, campaign, etc.) —*n.* **1.** [*often pl.*] money paid to an employee for work done, usually on an hourly, daily, or piecework basis **2.** [*usually pl., formerly with sing. v.*] what is given in return; recompense; requital ["The *wages* of sin is death"]

**wage earner** a person who works for wages

**wa·ger** (wā′jər) *n.* [< ONormFr.: see WAGE] *same as* BET (*n.* 1, 2) —*vt., vi. same as* BET —**wager of battle** a challenge by a defendant to prove his innocence by personal combat —**wa′ger·er** *n.*

**wag·ger·y** (wag′ər ē) *n., pl.* **-ger·ies 1.** roguish humor or merriment **2.** a joke; esp., a practical joke

**wag·gish** (-ish) *adj.* **1.** of or like a wag; roguishly merry **2.** playful; jesting [a *waggish* remark] —**wag′gish·ly** *adv.*

**wag·gle** (wag′'l) *vt.* **-gled, -gling** [freq. of WAG¹] to wag, esp. with short, quick movements —*vi.* to wobble —*n.* the act of waggling —**wag′gly** *adj.*

**wag·gon** (wag′ən) *n., vt., vi.* Brit. var. *of* WAGON

**Wag·ner** (väg′nər), (Wilhelm) **Rich·ard** (riH′ärt) 1813–83; Ger. composer

**Wag·ne·ri·an** (väg nir′ē ən) *adj.* **1.** of or like Richard Wagner or his music, theories, etc. **2.** designating or of a soprano, tenor, etc. specializing in Wagner's operas —*n.* an admirer of Wagner's music, theories, etc.

**wag·on** (wag′ən) *n.* [Du. *wagen*] **1.** *a*) a four-wheeled vehicle for hauling heavy loads *b*) a small cart used by children at play **2.** *short for:* *a*) PATROL WAGON *b*) STATION WAGON **3.** [Brit.] a railroad freight car —*vt., vi.* to carry or move (goods) in a wagon —**fix someone's wagon** [Slang] to hurt someone so as to get even with him —**hitch one's wagon to a star** to set oneself an ambitious goal —**on (or off) the wagon** [Slang] no longer (or once again) drinking alcoholic liquors

**wag·on·er** (-ər) *n.* a person who drives a wagon

**wag·on·ette** (wag′ə net′) *n.* [dim. of WAGON] a four-wheeled carriage with two seats set lengthwise facing each other behind the driver's seat

**‡wag·on-lit** (và gōn lē′) *n., pl.* **wag·ons-lits′** (-gōn lē) [Fr. < *wagon*, a car + *lit*, a bed] in Europe, a railroad sleeping car

**wag·on·load** (wag′ən lōd′) *n.* the amount a wagon holds

**wagon train** a line of wagons traveling together, as one carrying military supplies, or one in which pioneers crossed the Western plains

**wag·tail** (wag′tāl′) *n.* **1.** a small bird related to the pipits, having a long tail that wags up and down **2.** any of various similar birds

**Wah·ha·bi, Wa·ha·bi** (wä hä′bē) *n.* [Ar. *Wahhabi*] a member of a strict Moslem sect in Saudi Arabia —**Wah·ha′bism, Wa·ha′bism** *n.* —**Wah·ha′bite** (-bīt) *n., adj.*

**wa·hi·ne** (wä hē′nā) *n.* [Maori & Haw.] a Polynesian woman, esp. of Hawaii

**wa·hoo¹** (wä′hōō, wä hōō′) *n.* [< Dakota *wanhu*] a N. American shrub or small tree having red fruits and purple flowers

**wa·hoo²** (wä′hōō, wä hōō′) *n., pl.* **-hoo, -hoos:** see PLURAL, II, D, 2 [< ?] a large game and food fish, related to the mackerels and found in warm seas

**wa·hoo³** (wä hōō′, wä′hōō) *interj.* [Western] a shout expressing unrestrained enthusiasm, exhilaration, etc.

**waif** (wāf) *n.* [ONormFr., prob. < ON.] **1.** anything found that is without an owner **2.** a person without home or friends; esp., a homeless child **3.** a stray animal

**Wai·ki·ki** (wī′kē kē′, wī′kē kē′) [Haw., spurting water] famous bathing beach in Honolulu, Hawaii

**wail** (wāl) *vi.* [< ON. *væla* < *væ,* woe] **1.** to express grief or pain by long, loud cries **2.** to make a sad, crying sound [the wind *wails*] **3.** *Jazz* [Slang] to play in an intense or inspired manner —*vt.* [Archaic] **1.** to lament; mourn **2.** to cry out in mourning —*n.* **1.** a long cry of grief or pain **2.** a sound like this **3.** the act of wailing —**wail′er** *n.* —**wail′ful adj.** —**wail′ful·ly adv.**

**wain** (wān) *n.* [OE. *wægn*] [Archaic or Dial.] a wagon or cart

**wain·scot** (wān′skət, -skät′) *n.* [< MDu. *wagenschot*] **1.** a lining or paneling of wood, etc. on the walls of a room, often on the lower part only **2.** the lower part of the walls of a room when finished differently from the upper part —*vt.* **-scot·ed** or **-scot·ted, -scot·ing** or **-scot·ting** to line (a wall, etc.) with wainscoting

**wain·scot·ing, wain·scot·ting** (-iŋ) *n.* **1.** *same as* WAINSCOT **2.** material used to wainscot

**wain·wright** (wān′rīt′) *n.* [WAIN + WRIGHT] a person who builds or repairs wagons

**waist** (wāst) *n.* [< base of OE. *weaxan,* to grow] **1.** the part of the body between the ribs and the hips **2.** *a*) the part of a garment that covers the waist *b*) *same as* WAISTLINE (sense 2) *c*) the part of a garment covering the body from the shoulders to the waistline *d*) a blouse **3.** the middle, narrow part of something

**waist·band** (wāst′band′) *n.* a band encircling the waist, esp. one at the top of a skirt, trousers, etc.

**waist·coat** (wes′kət, wāst′kōt′) *n.* **1.** [Brit.] a man's vest **2.** a similar garment worn by women —**waist′coat·ed adj.**

**waist·line** (wāst′līn′) *n.* **1.** the line of the waist, between the ribs and the hips **2.** *a*) the narrow part of a woman's dress, etc., worn at the waist or above or below it as styles change *b*) the line where the waist and skirt of a dress join **3.** the distance around the waist

**wait** (wāt) *vi.* [ONormFr. *waitier* < Frank.] **1.** to stay in place or remain in readiness or in anticipation (often with *until* or *for*) **2.** to be ready [dinner is *waiting* for us] **3.** to remain undone for a time [that job will have to *wait*] **4.** to serve food (with *at* or *on*) —*vt.* **1.** to be, remain, or delay in expectation of [to *wait* orders] **2.** [Colloq.] to delay serving (a meal) as in waiting for someone [to *wait* dinner] —*n.* the act or a period of waiting —**lie in wait (for)** to wait so as to catch after planning an ambush or trap (for) —**wait on (or upon) 1.** to act as a servant to **2.** to call on or visit (esp. a superior) in order to pay one's respects, ask a favor, etc. **3.** to be a consequence of **4.** to serve (a customer, etc.) as a clerk, waiter, etc. **5.** [Dial. or Colloq.] to wait for; await —**wait out** to remain inactive during the course of —**wait table** to serve food as a waiter or servant to people at a table —**wait up 1.** to put off going to bed until someone expected arrives or something expected happens **2.** [Colloq.] to stop and wait for someone to catch up

**wait·er** (wāt′ər) *n.* **1.** a person who waits or awaits **2.** a man who waits on table, as in a restaurant **3.** a tray for carrying dishes; salver

**wait·ing** (-iŋ) *adj.* **1.** that waits **2.** of or for a wait —*n.* **1.** the act of one that waits **2.** a period of waiting —**waiting in attendance,** as on a king or other royal person

**waiting game** a delaying or postponing action until one has the advantage

**waiting list** a list of applicants, as for a vacancy or an item in short supply, in the order of their application

**waiting room** a room in which people wait, as in a railroad station, a dentist's office, etc.

WAISTLINES

**wait·ress** (wā′tris) *n.* a woman or girl who waits on table, as in a restaurant

**waive** (wāv) *vt.* **waived, waiv′ing** [< Anglo-Fr. *waiver*, to renounce < ON. *veifa*, to fluctuate] **1.** to give up or forgo (a right, claim, etc.) **2.** to refrain from insisting on or taking advantage of **3.** to postpone; defer

**waiv·er** (wā′vər) *n. Law* **1.** a waiving, or giving up voluntarily, of a right, claim, etc. **2.** a written statement of this

**wake¹** (wāk) *vi.* **woke** or **waked, waked** (or, occas. Brit., **wok′en** or **woke), wak′ing** [< OE. *wacian*, to be awake & *wacan*, to arise] **1.** to come out of sleep or a state like sleep; awake (often with *up*) **2.** to be or stay awake **3.** to become active again (often with *up*) **4.** to become alert /to *wake* to a peril/ **5.** [Chiefly Dial.] *pt. & pp.* **waked** to hold a wake —*vt.* **1.** to cause to wake from or as from sleep (often with *up*) **2.** to arouse or excite (passions, etc.) **3.** [Chiefly Dial.] *pt. & pp.* **waked** to hold a wake over (a corpse) —*n.* an all-night vigil over a corpse before burial

**wake²** (wāk) *n.* [ON. *vök*, a hole in the ice] **1.** the track left in the water by a moving boat or ship **2.** any track left behind —**in the wake of** following close behind

**wake·ful** (wāk′fəl) *adj.* **1.** keeping awake **2.** alert; watchful **3.** *a)* unable to sleep *b)* sleepless —**wake′ful·ly** *adv.* —**wake′ful·ness** *n.*

**Wake Island** (wāk) coral atoll in the N Pacific between Midway & Guam: a U.S. territory

**wake·less** (-lis) *adj.* unbroken; deep: said of sleep

**wak·en** (wāk′'n) *vi., vt.* [OE. *wacnian*] to become awake or cause to wake; wake up; rouse —**wak′en·er** *n.*

**wake-rob·in** (wāk′räb′in) *n.* **1.** *same as* TRILLIUM **2.** [Brit.] any of several plants of the arum family

**Wa·la·chi·a** (wä lā′kē ə) region in S Romania

**Wald·heim** (väld′hīm′), **Kurt** (koort) 1918- ; Austrian diplomat; secretary general of the United Nations (1972- )

**Wal·dorf salad** (wôl′dôrf) [after the old *Waldorf*-Astoria hotel in New York City] a salad made of diced raw apples, celery, and walnuts, with mayonnaise

**wale** (wāl) *n.* [OE. *walu*, a weal] **1.** a raised line made on the skin by a slash of a whip, etc.; welt **2.** *a)* a ridge on the surface of cloth, as corduroy *b)* texture of cloth **3.** [*pl.*] heavy planks fastened to the outside of the hull of a wooden ship —*vt.* **waled, wal′ing** **1.** to mark (the skin) with wales **2.** to make (cloth, etc.) with wales

**Wales** (wālz) division of the United Kingdom, occupying a peninsula of WC Great Britain, on St. George's Channel: 8,016 sq. mi.; pop. 2,662,000; chief city, Cardiff

**walk** (wôk) *vi.* [OE. *wealcan*, to roll] **1.** to move along on foot at a moderate pace by placing one foot (or, with quadrupeds, two feet) on the ground before lifting the other (or others) **2.** to appear after death as a ghost **3.** to follow a certain course, way of life, etc. /let us *walk* in peace/ **4.** *Baseball* to be advanced to first base as a result of being pitched four balls **5.** *Basketball same as* TRAVEL —*vt.* **1.** to go along, over, etc. by walking /to *walk* the deck/ **2.** to cause (a horse, dog, etc.) to walk, as for exercise **3.** to push (a bicycle, etc.) while walking alongside **4.** to go along with (a person) on a walk /I'll *walk* you home/ **5.** to bring to a specified state by walking /to *walk* oneself to exhaustion/ **6.** *Baseball a)* to advance (a batter) to first base by pitching four balls *b)* to force (a run) *in* by doing this when the bases are loaded —*n.* **1.** the act of walking **2.** a stroll or hike **3.** a route taken in walking **4.** a distance to walk /an hour's *walk* from here/ **5.** the pace of one who walks **6.** a way of walking /I knew her by her *walk*/ **7.** a particular station in life, sphere of activity, etc. /people from all *walks* of life/ **8.** a path set apart for walking **9.** an enclosure for grazing animals **10.** *Baseball* an advancing to first base on four balls —**walk (all) over** [Colloq.] **1.** to defeat decisively **2.** to domineer over —**walk away with 1.** to steal **2.** to win easily —**walk off 1.** to go away, esp. without warning **2.** to get rid of (fat, etc.) by walking —**walk off with 1.** to steal **2.** to win (something), esp. easily —**walk out** to go on strike —**walk out on** [Colloq.] to leave; desert; abandon —**walk′ing** *adj., n.*

**walk·a·way** (-ə wā′) *n.* an easily won victory

**walk·er** (-ər) *n.* **1.** a person or animal that walks **2.** a frame on wheels for babies learning to walk, or one without wheels used as a support in walking by convalescents, etc.

**walk·ie-talk·ie** (wôk′ē tôk′ē) *n.* a compact radio transmitter and receiver that can be carried by one person: also **walk′y-talk′y,** *pl.* **-talk′ies**

**walk-in** (-in′) *adj.* large enough for one to walk inside /a *walk-in* closet/ —*n.* a walk-in closet, etc.

**walking papers** [Colloq.] dismissal from a job

**walking stick 1.** a stick carried when walking; cane **2.** an insect resembling a twig: also **walk′ing·stick′** *n.*

**walk-on** (wôk′än′) *n.* a minor role in which an actor has no speaking lines or just a very few

**walk·out** (-out′) *n.* **1.** a strike of workers **2.** an abrupt departure of people as a show of protest

**walk·o·ver** (-ō′vər) *n.* an easily won victory

**walk-through** (-thrōō′) *n.* an early rehearsal of a play in which the actors begin to carry out actions on stage

**walk-up** (-up′) *n.* **1.** an upstairs apartment in a building without an elevator **2.** the building itself

**walk·way** (-wā′) *n.* a path, passage, etc. for pedestrians, esp. one that is sheltered

**wall** (wôl) *n.* [OE. *weall* < L. *vallum*, a rampart < *vallus*, a stake] **1.** an upright structure of wood, stone, etc., serving to enclose, divide, support, or protect /the *walls* of a room, building, garden, etc./ **2.** [*usually pl.*] a surrounding fortification **3.** anything like a wall in appearance or function —*adj.* of, on, in, or along a wall —*vt.* **1.** to furnish, enclose, divide, etc. with or as with a wall (often with *off, in,* etc.) **2.** to close up (an opening) with a wall (usually with *up*) —**drive** (or **push) to the wall** to place in a desperate position —**drive** (or **send,** etc.) **up the wall** [Colloq.] to make frantic, tense, etc. —**go to the wall 1.** to suffer defeat **2.** to fail in business —**off the wall** [Slang] **1.** unsound of mind; crazy **2.** very eccentric or unconventional —**walled** *adj.*

**wal·la·by** (wäl′ə bē) *n., pl.* **-bies, -by:** see PLURAL, II, D, 1 [< Australian native name] a small or medium-sized marsupial related to the kangaroo

**Wal·lace** (wôl′is, wäl′-) **1.** [ult. < Anglo-Fr. *Waleis* or ME. *Walisc*, foreign, WELSH] a masculine name: dim. *Wally* **2.** **Alfred Rus·sel** (rus′'l), 1823-1913; Eng. naturalist **3.** **Henry A(gard),** 1888-1965; U.S. politician

**Wal·la·chi·a** (wä lā′kē ə) *same as* WALACHIA

**wal·la·roo** (wäl′ə rōō′) *n.* [< Australian native name] a large kangaroo that has a stocky body and broad, thickly padded feet

**wall·board** (wôl′bôrd′) *n.* fibrous material made in thin slabs for making or covering walls and ceilings in place of plaster, etc.

**wal·let** (wôl′it, wäl′-) *n.* [ME. *walet* < ?] **1.** formerly, a knapsack **2.** a flat pocketbook, as of leather, with compartments for paper money, cards, etc.; billfold

**wall·eye** (wôl′ī′) *n.* [< ff.] **1.** an eye, as of a horse, with a whitish iris or white, opaque cornea **2.** an eye that turns outward, showing more white than is normal **3.** any of several fishes with large, staring eyes; esp., a N. American food fish of the perch family (in full, **walleyed pike**)

**wall·eyed** (-īd′) *adj.* [< ON., ult. < *vagl,* a beam + *eygr,* having eyes] **1.** having a walleye or walleyes **2.** having large, staring eyes, as some fishes

**wall·flow·er** (-flou′ər) *n.* **1.** any of a number of garden plants having racemes of yellow, orange, etc. flowers **2.** [Colloq.] a person, esp. a girl, who merely looks on at a dance from lack of a partner

**Wal·loon** (wä lōōn′) *n.* [Fr. *Wallon*] **1.** a member of a people living mostly in S and SE Belgium and nearby parts of France **2.** the French dialect of the Walloons

**wal·lop** (wäl′əp, wôl′-) *vi.* [< ONormFr. *waloper* (OFr. *galoper*), to gallop < Frank.] [Dial. or Colloq.] **1.** to move along in a rapid, reckless, awkward way **2.** to boil vigorously and noisily —*vt.* [Colloq.] **1.** to beat soundly **2.** to strike hard **3.** to defeat crushingly —*n.* [Colloq.] **1.** a hard blow **2.** the power to strike a hard blow **3.** a thrill

**wal·lop·ing** (-iŋ) *adj.* [Colloq.] impressively large; enormous —*n.* [Colloq.] **1.** a thrashing **2.** a crushing defeat

**wal·low** (wäl′ō, wôl′-) *vi.* [OE. *wealwian*, to roll around] **1.** to roll about, as in mud, dust, etc. **2.** to roll and pitch, as a ship **3.** to give oneself over to, or revel in, some feeling, way of life, etc. /to *wallow* in self-pity, to *wallow* in riches/ —*n.* **1.** a wallowing **2.** a place where animals wallow

**wall·pa·per** (wôl′pā′pər) *n.* paper for covering the walls or ceiling of a room —*vt.* to put wallpaper on or in

**Wall Street 1.** a street in lower Manhattan, New York City: main U.S. financial center **2.** U.S. financiers and their power, policies, etc., or the U.S. money market

**wall-to-wall** (wôl′tə wôl′) *adj.* **1.** that completely covers a floor /*wall-to-wall* carpeting/ **2.** [Colloq.] *a)* pervasive *b)* comprehensive; all-inclusive /*wall-to-wall* health care/

**wal·nut** (wôl′nut′, -nət) *n.* [< OE. < *wealh,* foreign + *hnutu,* a nut] **1.** any of a number of related trees, valued for their nuts and wood **2.** their edible nut, having a hard, crinkled shell and a two-lobed seed **3.** their wood, used for furniture, etc. **4.** the brown color of the heartwood of black walnut **5.** local name for SHAGBARK

**Wal·pur·gis Night** (väl poor′gis) the eve of May Day (April 30), when witches supposedly gathered for a demonic orgy

**wal·rus** (wôl′rəs, wäl′-) *n., pl.* **-rus·es, -rus:** see PLURAL, II, D, 1 [Du. < Dan. *hvalros,* prob. < ON. *hrosshvalr,* lit., horse whale] a massive sea mammal of the seal family, having two tusks jutting from the upper jaw, a thick mustache, a thick hide, and a heavy layer of blubber —*adj.* like that of a walrus *[a walrus mustache]*

**Wal·ter** (wôl′tər) [< ONormFr. < Frank. < *waldan,* to rule + *heri,* army; also < G. *Walther* < OHG.] a masculine name: dim. *Walt*

WALRUS
(to 12 ft. long & 5 ft. high)

**Wal·tham** (wôl′tham, -thəm) [? after *Waltham* Abbey, England, home of the 1st settlers] city in E Mass.: suburb of Boston: pop. 58,000

**Wal·ton** (wôl′t′n), **I·zaak** (ī′zək) 1593–1683; Eng. writer

**waltz** (wôlts, wôls) *n.* [< G. < *walzen,* to roll, dance about] **1.** a ballroom dance for couples, in 3/4 time **2.** music for this dance or in its characteristic rhythm —*adj.* of, for, or characteristic of a waltz —*vi.* **1.** to dance a waltz **2.** to move lightly and nimbly **3.** [Colloq.] to move effortlessly and successfully (usually with *through*) —*vt.* to dance with in a waltz —**waltz′er** *n.*

**Wal·vis Bay** (wôl′vis) **1.** seaport on the coast of South West Africa **2.** small exclave of South Africa surrounding this seaport

**wam·pum** (wäm′pəm) *n.* [< Algonquian] **1.** small beads made of shells and used by N. American Indians as money, for ornament, etc. **2.** [Slang] money

**wan** (wän, wôn) *adj.* **wan′ner, wan′nest** [OE. *wann,* dark] **1.** sickly pale; pallid *[a wan complexion]* **2.** suggestive of a sickly condition or great weariness; feeble *[a wan smile]* —**wan′ly** *adj.* —**wan′ness** *n.*

**wand** (wänd, wônd) *n.* [ON. *vondr*] **1.** a slender, supple switch, as of a young tree **2.** a rod carried as a symbol of authority; scepter **3.** any rod of supposed magic power

**wan·der** (wän′dər, wôn′-) *vi.* [OE. *wandrian*] **1.** to move or go about aimlessly; ramble; roam **2.** to go to a place in a casual or indirect way; idle **3.** *a)* to stray *(from a path, course, etc.) b)* to stray from home, friends, etc. (often with *off*) **4.** to go astray in mind or purpose; specif., *a)* to drift away from a subject, as in discussion *b)* to be disordered, incoherent, etc. **5.** to meander, as a river **6.** to move idly from one object to another: said of the eyes, etc. —*vt.* to roam through, in, or over —**wan′der·er** *n.* —**wan′der·ing** *adj., n.* —**wan′der·ing·ly** *adv.*

**wan·der·lust** (-lust′) *n.* [G.] an impulse, longing, or urge to wander or travel

**wane** (wān) *vi.* **waned, wan′ing** [OE. *wanian*] **1.** to grow gradually less in extent: said of the moon after it has become full **2.** to grow dim or faint: said of light, etc. **3.** to decline in power, importance, etc. **4.** to approach the end *[the day wanes]* —*n.* **1.** a waning **2.** a period of waning —**on the wane** declining, decreasing, etc.

**wan·gle** (waŋ′g′l) *vt.* **-gled, -gling** [altered < ? WAGGLE] [Colloq.] **1.** to get, make, or bring about by persuasion, influence, manipulation, etc. **2.** to falsify or juggle (accounts, etc.) —*vi.* [Colloq.] to make use of tricky and indirect methods to achieve one's aims —**wan′gler** *n.*

**Wan·kel engine** (väŋ′k′l, waŋ′-) [after F. *Wankel* (1902– ), G. engineer] a rotary combustion engine having a spinning piston and requiring fewer parts and less fuel than a comparable turbine engine

**want** (wänt, wônt) *vt.* [ON. *vanta*] **1.** to have too little of; lack **2.** to be short by (a specified amount) *[it wants two minutes of noon]* **3.** to feel the need of; crave *[to want love]* **4.** to desire or wish (followed by the infinitive) *[to want to travel]* **5.** *a)* to wish to see or speak with (someone) *[wanted on the phone] b)* to wish to apprehend, as for arrest *[wanted by the police]* **6.** [Chiefly Brit.] to require; need *Want* is also used colloquially as an auxiliary meaning *ought* or *should* *[you want to be careful]* —*vi.* **1.** to have a need or lack (usually with *for*) **2.** to be destitute or very poor —*n.* **1.** a scarcity; shortage; lack **2.** poverty; destitution **3.** a wish for something; craving **4.** something needed; need —**want′er** *n.*

**want ad** [Colloq.] a classified advertisement, as in a newspaper, stating that one wants a job, an apartment, an employee, etc.

**want·ing** (wän′tiŋ, wôn′-) *adj.* **1.** absent; lacking *[a coat with buttons wanting]* **2.** not up to some standard *[weighed and found wanting]* —*prep.* **1.** lacking (something); without **2.** minus —**wanting in** having not enough of (some quality, etc.)

**wan·ton** (wän′t′n, wôn′-) *adj.* [< OE. < *wan,* lacking + *togen,* pp. of *teon,* to bring up] **1.** orig., undisciplined *[wanton boys]* **2.** *a)* sexually loose *b)* [Poet.] frisky; playful *c)* [Poet.] capricious *[wanton winds]* **3.** senseless, unprovoked, or deliberately malicious *[wanton cruelty]* **4.**

recklessly ignoring justice, decency, morality, etc. **5.** lavish, luxurious, or extravagant —*n.* a wanton person or thing; esp., a sexually loose woman —*vi.* to be wanton —**wan′ton·ly** *adv.* —**wan′ton·ness** *n.*

**wap·i·ti** (wäp′ə tē) *n., pl.* **-tis, -ti:** see PLURAL, II, D, 1 [< Algonquian] the American elk, the largest N. American deer, with large, branching antlers and a short tail

**war** (wôr) *n.* [ONormFr. *werre,* strife < Frank.] **1.** open armed conflict between countries or between factions within the same country **2.** any active hostility, contention, or struggle *[the war against poverty]* **3.** military operations as a science —*adj.* of, used in, or resulting from war —*vi.* **warred, war′ring 1.** to carry on war **2.** to contend; strive —**at war** in a state of active armed conflict —**declare war (on) 1.** to make a formal declaration of being at war (with) **2.** to announce one's hostility (to) —**go to war 1.** to enter into a war **2.** to join the armed forces during a war

**War between the States** the U.S. Civil War (1861–65): term used by those sympathetic to the Confederacy

**war·ble** (wôr′b′l) *vt.* **-bled, -bling** [ONormFr. *werbler* < Frank.] **1.** to sing (notes, etc.) with trills, quavers, runs, etc., as a bird **2.** to express in song —*vi.* **1.** to sing melodiously, with trills, etc. **2.** to make a musical sound; babble, as a stream **3.** *same as* YODEL —*n.* **1.** an act of warbling **2.** a warbling sound; trill

**war·bler** (wôr′blər) *n.* **1.** a bird or person that warbles **2.** any of a family of small, insect-eating, new-world birds, many of which are brightly colored **3.** any of a family of small songbirds related to the thrushes

**war bonnet** a headdress with long feathers, worn by some N. American Indian warriors

**war cry 1.** a name, phrase, etc. shouted in a charge or battle **2.** a phrase or slogan adopted by a party in any conflict, contest, election, etc.

**ward** (wôrd) *vt.* [OE. *weardian,* to protect, guard] **1.** to turn aside; fend off (usually with *off*) **2.** [Rare] to guard —*n.* **1.** a guarding: now only in *watch and ward* **2.** a being under guard **3.** *a)* a child or person not able to manage his own affairs who is placed under the care of a guardian or court *b)* any person under another's care **4.** each of the divisions of a jail or prison **5.** a division of a hospital *[a maternity ward]* **6.** a division of a city or town, for purposes of administration, voting, etc. **7.** a means of defense **8.** a defensive posture, as in fencing **9.** *a)* a ridge in a lock that allows only the right key to enter *b)* the notch in a key that fits this ridge

**-ward** (wərd) [< OE. *-weard* < base of *weorthan,* to become] *a suffix meaning* in a (specified) direction or course *[backward]*

**Ward** (wôrd), **Ar·te·mus** (är′ti məs) (pseud. of *Charles Farrar Browne*) 1834–67; U.S. humorist

**war dance** a ceremonial dance performed as by some American Indian tribes before battle or after victory

**war·den** (wôr′d′n) *n.* [< ONormFr. < OFr. *gardein*] **1.** a person who guards, or has charge of, something; keeper *[a game warden]* **2.** the chief administrative official of a prison **3.** in England, a governing officer in certain hospitals, colleges, etc. **4.** in Connecticut, the chief executive of a borough **5.** *same as* CHURCHWARDEN —**war′den·ship′** *n.*

**ward·er** (wôr′dər) *n.* **1.** a watchman **2.** a person who guards an entrance **3.** [Chiefly Brit.] a warden in a jail

**ward heeler** a person who works in a ward for a political party or boss, as in getting votes: a contemptuous term

**ward·robe** (wôrd′rōb′) *n.* **1.** a closet or tall cabinet with hangers for holding clothes **2.** a room where clothes are kept, as a room in a theater for costumes **3.** one's supply of clothes

**ward·room** (wôrd′rōōm′) *n.* in a warship, a compartment used for eating and lounging by commissioned officers, except, usually, the captain

**-wards** (wərdz) *same as* -WARD

**ward·ship** (wôrd′ship′) *n.* **1.** guardianship; custody, as of a minor **2.** the condition of being a ward

**ware** (wer) *n.* [OE. *waru*] **1.** any thing or service that one has to sell: *usually used in pl.* **2.** things that are for sale, esp. a (specified) kind of merchandise *[hardware, glassware]* **3.** pottery or a specified kind of pottery

**ware·house** (wer′hous′; *for v., usually -*houz′) *n.* **1.** a building where wares, or goods, are stored **2.** [Chiefly Brit.] a wholesale store, or, sometimes, a large retail store —*vt.* **-housed′, -hous′ing** to place or store in a warehouse —**ware′house′man** (-mən) *n., pl.* **-men**

**war·fare** (wôr′fer′) *n.* **1.** the action of waging war; armed conflict **2.** conflict of any kind

**war·far·in** (wôr′fə rin) *n.* [*W(isconsin) A(lumni) R(esearch) F(oundation)* + (*coum)arin,* a chemical] **1.** a crystalline powder used as a rat poison **2.** this drug neutralized and used in medicine as an anticoagulant

**war game 1.** training in military tactics in which maps and small figures are used to represent terrain, troops, etc. **2.** *[pl.]* practice maneuvers for military troops

**war hawk** *same as* HAWK[1] (*n.* 2)

**war·head** (wôr'hed') *n.* the forward section of a self-propelled projectile, etc. containing the explosive charge

**war horse** **1.** a horse used in battle **2.** [Colloq.] a person who has engaged in many battles or struggles; veteran **3.** [Colloq.] a symphony, play, opera, etc. that has been performed so often as to seem stale and trite For 2 & 3 now usually **war'horse'** *n.*

**war·i·ly** (wer'ə lē) *adv.* in a wary manner; cautiously

**war·i·ness** (-ē nis) *n.* the quality or state of being wary

**war·like** (wôr'līk') *adj.* **1.** fit for, fond of, or ready for war **2.** of or appropriate to war **3.** threatening war

**war·lock** (wôr'läk') *n.* [OE. *wærloga*, a traitor, liar] a sorcerer or wizard: male equivalent of a *witch*

**war·lord** (wôr'lôrd') *n.* **1.** a high military officer in a warlike nation **2.** a local ruler or leader with a military following, as formerly in China

**warm** (wôrm) *adj.* [OE. *wearm*] **1.** *a)* having or giving off a moderate degree of heat [a *warm* iron] *b)* giving off pleasurable heat [a *warm* fire] *c)* hot [a *warm* night] **2.** *a)* overheated, as with exercise *b)* such as to make one heated [*warm* work] **3.** effective in keeping body heat in [*warm* clothing] **4.** marked by lively disagreement, as an argument **5.** ardent; enthusiastic [*warm* encouragement] **6.** lively, vigorous, etc. **7.** quick to anger **8.** *a)* cordial or sincere [a *warm* welcome] *b)* sympathetic or loving **9.** suggesting warmth: said of yellow, orange, or red colors **10.** newly made; fresh, as a scent or trail **11.** [Colloq.] close to discovering something **12.** [Colloq.] disagreeable [we'll make it *warm* for him] —*adv.* so as to be warm —*vt.*, *vi.* **1.** to make or become warm **2.** to make or become excited, ardent, lively, etc. **3.** to make or become friendly, affectionate, etc. —*n.* [Colloq.] a warming or being warmed —**warm up** **1.** *a)* to make or become warm *b)* to make or become warm enough to operate efficiently **2.** to reheat (cooked food, etc.): also **warm over** **3.** to make or become more animated, excited, ardent, etc. **4.** *Sports* to practice or exercise before going into a game —**warm'er** *n.* —**warm'ish** *adj.* —**warm'ly** *adv.* —**warm'ness** *n.*

**warm·blood·ed** (-blud'id) *adj.* **1.** having a relatively constant body temperature, independent of and usually warmer than that of the surroundings, as mammals and birds **2.** ardent; fervent —**warm'blood'ed·ness** *n.*

**warmed-o·ver** (wôrmd'ō'vər) *adj.* **1.** reheated [*warmed-over* hash] **2.** presented again, without significant change [*warmed-over* ideas]

**warm front** *Meteorol.* the forward edge of an advancing mass of warm air replacing colder air

**warm·heart·ed** (wôrm'här'tid) *adj.* kind, sympathetic, friendly, etc. —**warm'heart'ed·ly** *adv.* —**warm'heart'ed·ness** *n.*

**warming pan** a long-handled, covered pan for holding live coals: formerly used to warm beds

**war·mon·ger** (wôr'muŋ'gər, -mäŋ'-) *n.* a person or agency that advocates war or tries to bring about a war —**war'mon'ger·ing** *adj.*, *n.*

**warmth** (wôrmth) *n.* **1.** *a)* the state or quality of being warm *b)* mild heat **2.** *a)* excitement or vigor of feeling; enthusiasm *b)* cordial or affectionate feelings or nature *c)* slight anger **3.** a glowing effect obtained by using red, yellow, or orange

**warm-up** (wôrm'up') *n.* the act or an instance of warming up

**warn** (wôrn) *vt.* [OE. *wearnian*] **1.** to tell (a person) of a danger, coming evil, etc. **2.** to caution about certain acts [*warned* against smoking] **3.** to notify in advance **4.** to give notice to (a person) to stay or keep (*off*, *away*, etc.) —*vi.* to give warning —**warn'er** *n.*

**warn·ing** (wôr'niŋ) *n.* **1.** the act of one that warns, or the state of being warned **2.** something that serves to warn —*adj.* that warns —**warn'ing·ly** *adv.*

**War of American Independence** *Brit. name for* AMERICAN REVOLUTION

**War of 1812** a war (1812–15) between the U.S. and Great Britain

**war of nerves** a conflict or campaign using psychological means to unsettle an opponent or destroy his morale

**warp** (wôrp) *n.* [OE. *wearp*, the base of *weorpan*, to throw] **1.** *a)* a distortion, as a twist or bend in wood *b)* any similar distortion **2.** a mental twist, quirk, bias, etc. **3.** a rope run from a ship to a dock, etc., used to haul the vessel into position **4.** *a) Weaving* the threads running lengthwise in the loom and crossed by the weft or woof *b)* foundation; base —*vt.* **1.** to bend or twist out of shape **2.** to distort, pervert, bias, etc. [a *warped* mind] **3.** to move (a ship) by hauling on a line fastened to a dock, etc. —*vi.* **1.** to become bent or twisted out of shape **2.** to turn aside from the natural or right course —**warp'er** *n.*

**war paint** **1.** a pigment applied to the face and body, as by

some American Indian tribes, in preparation for war **2.** [Slang] *a)* ceremonial dress *b)* women's cosmetics

**war·path** (wôr'path') *n.* the path taken by American Indians on a warlike expedition —**on the warpath** **1.** at war, ready for war, etc. **2.** angry; ready to fight

**war·plane** (wôr'plān') *n.* any airplane for use in war

**war·rant** (wôr'ənt, wär'-) *n.* [< ONormFr. (OFr. *garant*), a warrant < Frank.] **1.** *a)* authorization, as by the law *b)* justification for some act, belief, etc. **2.** something that serves as a guarantee of some event or result **3.** a written authorization or certification for something; specif., *a)* authorization for the payment or receipt of money *b) Law* a writ authorizing an arrest, seizure, search, etc. *c) Mil.* the certificate of appointment to the grade of warrant officer —*vt.* **1.** *a)* to give (someone) authorization to do something *b)* to authorize (the doing of something) **2.** to serve as justification for (an act, belief, etc.) **3.** *a)* to guarantee the quality, quantity, etc. of (goods) to a purchaser *b)* to guarantee to (the purchaser) that goods sold are as represented **4.** [Colloq.] to state with confidence [I *warrant* he'll be late]

**war·ran·tee** (wôr'ən tē', wär'-) *n. Law* a person to whom a warranty is given

**warrant officer** a U.S. military officer ranking above an enlisted man but below a commissioned officer and holding his office on a warrant instead of a commission

**war·ran·tor** (wôr'ən tôr', wär'-; -tər) *n. Law* a person who warrants, or gives warranty: also **war'rant·er** (-tər)

**war·ran·ty** (-tē) *n.*, *pl.* **-ties** [see WARRANT] **1.** official authorization **2.** justification, as for an opinion or action **3.** *Law* a guarantee; specif., *a)* a guarantee of something in a contract, as to a purchaser that goods sold him are as represented *b)* a covenant by which the seller of real estate gives assurance of the security of the title

**War·ren¹** (wôr'ən, wär'-) **1.** [< ONormFr. < ? OHG. *Warin*, name of a people mentioned by Tacitus] a masculine name **2.** Earl, 1891–1974; U.S. jurist; chief justice of the U.S. (1953–69)

**War·ren²** (wôr'ən, wär'-) **1.** [after Dr. J. *Warren* (1741–75)] city in SE Mich.: suburb of Detroit: pop. 161,000 **2.** [after M. *Warren*, 19th-cent. U.S. surveyor] city in NE Ohio: pop. 57,000: see YOUNGSTOWN

**war·ren** (wôr'ən, wär'-) *n.* [< ONormFr. < OFr. *warir*, to preserve < Frank.] **1.** a space or limited area in which rabbits breed or are numerous **2.** any building or buildings crowded like a rabbit warren

**war·ri·or** (wôr'ē ər, wär'-; -yər) *n.* [< ONormFr. < *werrier*, to make war < *werre*, WAR] a man experienced in conflict or war; soldier

**War·saw** (wôr'sô) capital of Poland, on the Vistula River: pop. 1,284,000

**war·ship** (wôr'ship') *n.* any ship constructed or armed for combat use, as a battleship, destroyer, etc.

**wart** (wôrt) *n.* [OE. *wearte*] **1.** a small, usually hard, tumorous growth on the skin **2.** a small growth on a plant **3.** an imperfection, failing, flaw, etc. [a lovable person, *warts* and all] —**wart'y** *adj.* **wart'i·er**, **wart'i·est**

**wart hog** a wild African hog with large, incurved tusks, and a number of warts below the eyes

**war·time** (wôr'tīm') *n.* a time of war —*adj.* of or characteristic of such a time

**War·wick** (wôr'wik) [after an Earl of *Warwick* (England), friend of the founder] city on the SE coast of R.I.: suburb of Providence: pop. 87,000

**War·wick** (wôr'ik, wär'-), Earl of, (*Richard Neville*) 1428–71; Eng. statesman & military leader

**war·y** (wer'ē) *adj.* **war'i·er**, **war'i·est** [< archaic adj. *ware*, watchful + -Y²] **1.** cautious; on one's guard **2.** characterized by caution —**wary of** careful of

**was** (wuz, wäz; *unstressed* wəz) [OE. *wæs*] *1st and 3d pers. sing.*, *pt.*, *of* BE

**wash** (wôsh, wäsh) *vt.* [OE. *wæscan*] **1.** to clean by means of water or other liquid, often with soap, etc. **2.** to make clean in a religious or moral sense; purify **3.** to wet; moisten **4.** to cleanse by licking, as a cat does **5.** to flow over, past, or against: said of a sea, waves, etc. **6.** to soak (*out*), flush (*off*), or carry (*away*) by the action of water **7.** *a)* to make by flowing over and wearing away substance [rain *washed* gullies in the bank] *b)* to erode [the flood *washed* out the road] **8.** to be a cleansing agent for [soap that will *wash* silks] **9.** to cover with a thin coating of paint or metal **10.** *Chem.* to pass (a gas) over or through a liquid in order to remove soluble matter **11.** *Mining* to pass water through or over (earth, etc.) in order to separate (ore, precious stones, etc.) —*vi.* **1.** to wash oneself or one's hands, face, etc. (often with *up*) **2.** to wash clothes **3.** to undergo washing, esp. without fading, etc. **4.** to be removed by washing [the stain *washed* out] **5.** to be worn or carried away by the action of water [the bridge *washed* out] **6.** [Brit. Colloq.] to withstand a test [his story won't *wash*] —*n.* **1.** *a)* the act or an instance of washing *b)* a place where something is washed [an auto *wash*] **2.** a quantity of clothes, etc. washed, or to be washed **3.** refuse liquid food; hogwash **4.** *a)* the rush or surge of water or waves *b)* the sound of this *c)* the eddy of water caused by a propeller, oars, etc. *d)* a slipstream **5.** erosion caused by the action of water **6.** silt, mud, etc. carried and dropped by running water **7.** earth from which metals, ores, etc. may be washed **8.** *a)* low ground which is flooded part of the time and partly dry the rest *b)* a bog; marsh **9.** in the western U.S., the bed of a stream when it runs dry **10.** a thin coating of paint or metal **11.** any of various liquids for cosmetic or medicinal use [mouthwash] **12.** weak liquor or liquid food **13.** [Colloq.] water, beer, etc. drunk after strong liquor; chaser —*adj.* that can be washed without damage [a *wash* dress] —**come out in the wash** [Slang] to be revealed or explained sooner or later —**wash down 1.** to clean by washing **2.** to follow (food, a drink of whiskey, etc.) with a drink, as of water —**wash out** [Slang] to drop or be dropped from a course, esp. in military aviation, because of failure

**Wash.** Washington (State)

**wash·a·ble** (wôsh'ə b'l, wäsh'-) *adj.* that can be washed without damage —*n.* a washable fabric or garment

**wash-and-wear** (-'n wer') *adj.* designating of or fabrics or garments that need little or no ironing after washing

**wash·board** (-bôrd') *n.* **1.** a board or frame with a ridged surface of metal, glass, etc. used for scrubbing dirt out of clothes **2.** the worn surface of a paved road

**wash·bowl** (-bōl') *n.* a bowl or basin for use in washing one's hands and face, etc., esp. a bathroom fixture fitted with water faucets and a drain: also **wash'ba'sin** (-bā's'n)

**wash·cloth** (-klôth') *n.* a small cloth, usually of terry, used in washing the face or body

**wash·day** (-dā') *n.* a day when the clothes and linens of a household are washed

**washed-out** (wôsht'out', wäsht'-) *adj.* **1.** faded in color, specif. from washing **2.** [Colloq.] tired; spiritless **3.** [Colloq.] tired-looking; pale and wan

**washed-up** (-up') *adj.* **1.** cleaned up **2.** [Colloq.] tired; exhausted **3.** [Slang] finished; done for; having failed

**wash·er** (wôsh'ər, wäsh'-) *n.* **1.** a person who washes **2.** a flat disk or ring of metal, rubber, etc., used to make a seat for the head of a bolt or for a nut or faucet valve, to lock a nut in place, to provide packing, etc. **3.** a machine for washing something

**wash·er·wom·an** (-woom'ən) *n., pl.* **-wom'en** a woman whose work is washing clothes, etc. —**wash'er·man** (-mən) *n.masc., pl.* **-men**

**wash goods** washable fabrics or garments

**wash·ing** (wôsh'iŋ, wäsh'-) *n.* **1.** the act of a person or thing that washes; a cleaning, flushing, etc. in water or other liquid **2.** clothes, etc. washed or to be washed, esp. at one time **3.** matter obtained or removed by washing **4.** a thin coating, as of metal, put on in liquid form

**washing machine** a machine for washing clothes, linens, etc., now usually operated automatically; washer

**washing soda** a crystalline form of sodium carbonate

**Wash·ing·ton** (wôsh'iŋ tən, wäsh'-) [after G. WASHINGTON] **1.** NW coastal State of the U.S.: 68,192 sq. mi.; pop. 4,130,000; cap. Olympia: abbrev. **Wash., WA 2.** capital of the U.S., coextensive with the District of Columbia: pop. 638,000 (met. area 3,045,000) —**Wash'ing·to'ni·an** (-tō'nē ən) *adj., n.*

**Wash·ing·ton** (wôsh'iŋ tən, wäsh'-) **1. Book·er T**(aliaferro) (book'ər), 1856–1915; U.S. Negro educator & author **2. George,** 1732–99; 1st president of the U.S. (1789–97); commander in chief of the Continental army

**Washington's Birthday** February 22, George Washington's birthday: it is celebrated as a legal holiday in most States on the third Monday in February

**wash·out** (wôsh'out', wäsh'-) *n.* **1.** the washing away of soil, rocks, etc. by a sudden, strong flow of water **2.** a hole made by such washing away, as in a road **3.** [Slang] a complete failure

**wash·rag** (-rag') *n. same as* WASHCLOTH

**wash·room** (-rōōm') *n.* **1.** a room for washing **2.** same as RESTROOM

**wash·stand** (-stand') *n.* **1.** a table holding a bowl and pitcher, etc. for washing the face and hands **2.** a washbowl that is a bathroom fixture

**wash·tub** (-tub') *n.* a tub for washing clothes, etc.; often, a stationary metal tub fitted with water faucets and a drain

**wash·wom·an** (-woom'ən) *n., pl.* **-wom'en** same as WASHERWOMAN

**wash·y** (-ē) *adj.* **wash'i·er, wash'i·est 1.** watery; weak **2.** weak in color; pale **3.** without force or substance; insipid

**was·n't** (wuz''nt, wäz'-) was not

**WASP, Wasp** (wäsp, wôsp) *n.* a white Anglo-Saxon Protestant

**wasp** (wäsp, wôsp) *n.* [OE. *wæsp*] any of a large, worldwide group of winged insects with a slender body, biting mouthparts, and, in the females and workers, a sharp sting —**wasp'like'** *adj.* —**wasp'y** *adj.* **wasp'i·er, wasp'i·est**

**wasp·ish** (wäs'pish, wôs'-) *adj.* **1.** of or like a wasp **2.** having a slender waist **3.** bad-tempered; snappish —**wasp'ish·ly** *adv.* —**wasp'ish·ness** *n.*

**wasp waist** a very slender or tightly corseted waist

**was·sail** (wäs''l, was'-; -āl) *n.* [< ON. *ves heill,* lit., be hearty] **1.** a toast formerly given in drinking healths **2.** the spiced ale or other liquor with which such healths were drunk **3.** a celebration with much drinking, esp. at Christmas time —*vi., vt.* to drink a wassail (to) —**was'sail·er** *n.*

WASP
(1/2–3 in. long)

**Was·ser·mann test** (or **reaction**) (wäs'ər mən) [after A. von *Wassermann* (1866–1925), G. bacteriologist] a test for syphilis by determining the presence of syphilitic antibodies in the blood serum

**wast** (wäst; *unstressed* wəst) *archaic 2d pers. sing., past indic., of* BE: *used with* thou

**wast·age** (wās'tij) *n.* **1.** loss by use, decay, etc. **2.** the process of wasting **3.** anything wasted, or the amount of this; waste

**waste** (wāst) *vt.* **wast'ed, wast'ing** [ONormFr. *waster* < L. *vastare,* to lay waste] **1.** to destroy; devastate; ruin **2.** to wear away; use up **3.** to make weak or feeble [a man *wasted* by age and disease] **4.** to use up or spend without need, gain, or purpose; squander **5.** to fail to take advantage of [to *waste* an opportunity] —*vi.* **1.** to lose strength, health, flesh, etc., as by disease (often with *away*) **2.** to be used up or worn down gradually **3.** to be wasted, or not put to full or proper use —*adj.* **1.** uncultivated or uninhabited, as a desert; wild; barren; desolate **2.** left over; no longer of use [a *waste* product] **3.** excreted from the body, as feces or urine **4.** used to carry off or hold waste [a *waste* pipe, *wastebasket*] —*n.* **1.** uncultivated or uninhabited land, as a desert **2.** *a)* a desolate or devastated area *b)* a vast expanse, as of the sea **3.** a wasting or being wasted; specif., *a)* a squandering, as of money, time, etc. *b)* a failure to take advantage (*of* something) *c)* a gradual loss or decrease by use, wear, decay, etc. **4.** useless or discarded material, as ashes, garbage, etc. **5.** matter excreted from the body, as feces **6.** refuse cotton fiber or yarn, used for wiping machinery, etc. —**go to waste** to be or become wasted —**lay waste (to)** to destroy; devastate —**wast'er** *n.*

**waste·bas·ket** (wāst'bas'kit) *n.* a basket or other open container for wastepaper, bits of trash, etc.: also **wastepaper basket**

**waste·ful** (-fəl) *adj.* in the habit of wasting or characterized by waste; squandering; extravagant —**waste'ful·ly** *adv.* —**waste'ful·ness** *n.*

**waste·land** (-land') *n.* land that is uncultivated, barren, unproductive, devastated, etc.

**waste·pa·per** (-pā'pər) *n.* paper thrown away after use or as useless: also **waste paper**

**wast·ing** (wās'tiŋ) *adj.* **1.** desolating; destructive [a *wasting* war] **2.** destructive to health, as a disease —**wast'ing·ly** *adv.*

**wast·rel** (wās'trəl) *n.* **1.** a person who wastes; esp., a spendthrift **2.** a good-for-nothing

**watch** (wäch, wôch) *n.* [OE. *wæcce* < base of *wacian,* to be awake] **1.** the act or fact of keeping awake, esp. in order to protect or guard **2.** *a)* close observation for a time, as to find out something *b)* vigilant, careful guarding **3.** a person or group on duty to protect or guard **4.** [*pl.*] hours (of the night): only in **watches of the night 5.** the period of duty of a guard **6.** a small timepiece carried in the pocket, worn on the wrist, etc. **7.** *Naut. a)* any of the periods of duty (usually four hours) into which the day is divided on shipboard *b)* the part of the crew on duty during any such period —*vi.* **1.** to stay awake at night; keep vigil **2.** to be on the alert; keep guard **3.** to look; observe **4.** to be looking or waiting attentively (with *for*) [watch for your chance] —*vt.* **1.** to guard **2.** to observe carefully and constantly **3.** to keep informed about **4.** to wait for and look for [to *watch* one's chance] **5.** to keep watch over; tend —**on the watch** watching; on the lookout —**watch oneself** to be careful or cautious —**watch out** to be alert and on one's guard; be careful —**watch over** to protect from harm or danger —**watch'er** *n.*

**watch·band** (-band') *n.* a band of leather, metal, cloth, etc. for holding a watch on the wrist

**watch·case** (-kās') *n.* the metal case, or outer covering, of a watch

**watch·dog** (-dôg', -däg') *n.* **1.** a dog kept to guard property **2.** a person or group that keeps watch to prevent waste, dishonest practices, etc.

**watch fire** a fire kept burning at night as a signal or for the use of those staying awake to guard

**watch·ful** (-fəl) *adj.* **1.** watching closely; alert **2.** characterized by vigilance —**watch′ful·ly** *adv.* —**watch′ful·ness** *n.*

**watch·mak·er** (-mā′kər) *n.* a person who makes or repairs watches —**watch′mak′ing** *n.*

**watch·man** (-mən) *n., pl.* -**men** a person hired to watch or guard, esp. at night

**watch night** a religious service held on New Year's Eve: also **watch meeting** or **watch-night service**

**watch pocket** a small pocket, usually in a vest or trousers, for carrying a watch

**watch·tow·er** (-tou′ər) *n.* a high tower from which a sentinel watches for enemies, forest fires, etc.; lookout

**watch·word** (-wurd′) *n.* **1.** a password **2.** a slogan; esp., the slogan or cry of a group or party

**wa·ter** (wôt′ər, wät′-) *n.* [OE. *wæter*] **1.** the colorless, transparent liquid occurring on earth as rivers, lakes, oceans, etc., and falling as rain: chemically a compound of hydrogen and oxygen, $H_2O$, it freezes at 32° F (0° C) and boils at 212° F (100° C) **2.** [*often pl.*] a large body of water, as a river, lake, sea, etc. **3.** water with reference to its depth, its surface, its level, etc. [ten feet of *water,* under *water,* high *water*] **4.** [*pl.*] the water of mineral springs **5.** any body fluid or secretion, as urine, saliva, tears, etc. **6.** a solution of any substance, often a gas, in water [ammonia *water*] **7.** *a)* the degree of transparency and luster of a precious stone [a diamond of the first *water*] *b)* degree of quality or conformity to type [an artist of the first *water*] **8.** a wavy, lustrous finish given to linen, silk, etc., or to a metal surface **9.** *Finance* an illegal issue of watered stock —*vt.* **1.** to supply with water; specif., *a)* to give (animals) water to drink *b)* to give water to (soil, crops, etc.), as by sprinkling, irrigating, etc. *c)* to soak or moisten with water (often with *down*) *d)* to dilute with water **2.** to give a wavy luster to the finish of (silk, etc.) **3.** *Finance* to add illegally to the total face value of (stock) without increasing assets to justify this valuation —*vi.* **1.** to fill with tears: said of the eyes **2.** to secrete or fill with saliva [his mouth *watered*] **3.** to take on a supply of water **4.** to drink water: said of animals —*adj.* **1.** of or having to do with water **2.** in or on water [*water* sports] **3.** growing in or living on or near water [*water* plants, *water* birds] **4.** *a)* operated by water [a *water* wheel] *b)* derived from running water [*water* power] —**by water** by ship or boat —**hold water** to remain sound, logical, etc. [the argument won't *hold water*] —**like water** lavishly; freely: said of money spent, etc. —**make one's mouth water** to create a desire or appetite in one —**make (or pass) water** to urinate —**water down** to weaken the power or effectiveness of —**wa′ter·er** *n.* —**wa′ter·less** *adj.*

**Water Bearer** *same as* AQUARIUS

**water bed** a heavy vinyl bag filled with water and used as a bed or as a mattress in a special frame

**water beetle** any of various beetles that live in freshwater ponds and streams

**water bird** a swimming or wading bird

**water boatman** any of various water bugs that swim about by movement of their fringed, oarlike hind legs

**wa·ter·borne** (-bôrn′) *adj.* floating on or carried by water

**wa·ter·buck** (-buk′) *n., pl.* -**buck′**, -**bucks′**: see PLURAL, II, D, 2 an African antelope having lyre-shaped horns, found near rivers and streams

**water buffalo** a slow, powerful, oxlike draft animal native to S Asia, Malaya, and the Philippine Islands

**Wa·ter·bur·y** (wôt′ər ber′ē, wät′-) [from the many streams there] city in WC Conn.: pop. 103,000

**water chestnut** **1.** a Chinese sedge, growing in clumps in water **2.** its button-shaped tuber, used in cooking

**water clock** a mechanism for measuring time by the fall or flow of water; clepsydra

WATERBUCK
(2½-4 ft. high at shoulder)

**water closet** *same as* TOILET (*n.* 4)

**wa·ter·col·or** (-kul′ər) *n.* **1.** a pigment or coloring matter mixed with water for use as a paint **2.** (a) painting done with such paints —*adj.* painted with watercolors —**wa′ter·col′or·ist** *n.*

**wa·ter·cooled** (-kōōld′) *adj.* kept from overheating by having water circulated around or through it, as in pipes or a water jacket [a *water-cooled* engine] —**wa′ter·cool′** *vt.*

**water cooler** a device for cooling water, esp. by refrigeration, for drinking

**wa·ter·course** (-kôrs′) *n.* **1.** a stream of water; river, brook, etc. **2.** a channel for water, as a canal

**wa·ter·craft** (-kraft′) *n.* **1.** skill in water sports, boating, etc. **2.** *pl.* -**craft′** a boat, ship, or other water vehicle

**wa·ter·cress** (-kres′) *n.* a plant of the mustard family, growing generally in running water: its leaves are used in salads, etc.

**water cure** *same as:* **1.** HYDROPATHY **2.** HYDROTHERAPY

**wa·ter·fall** (-fôl′) *n.* a steep fall of water, as of a stream, from a height; cascade

**wa·ter·fowl** (-foul′) *n., pl.* -**fowls′**, -**fowl′**: see PLURAL, II, D, l a bird that lives on or near the water, esp. one that swims

**wa·ter·front** (-frunt′) *n.* **1.** land at the edge of a stream, harbor, etc. **2.** the part of a city or town on such land

**water gap** a break in a mountain ridge, with a stream flowing through it

**water gas** a fuel gas that is a poisonous mixture of hydrogen, carbon dioxide, carbon monoxide, and nitrogen, made by forcing steam through hot coke

**Wa·ter·gate** (-gāt′) *n.* [after *Watergate,* D.C. building housing Dem. party hdqrs., burglarized (1972) under govt. direction] a scandal that involves officials violating public trust through various crimes and abuses of power in order to maintain their positions of authority

**water gate** a gate controlling the flow of water; floodgate

**water gauge** **1.** a gauge for measuring the level or flow of water in a stream or channel **2.** a device, as a glass tube, that shows the water level in a tank, boiler, etc.

**water glass** **1.** a drinking glass; tumbler; goblet **2.** *same as* WATER GAUGE (sense 2) **3.** sodium silicate or, sometimes, potassium silicate, usually dissolved in water to form a syrupy liquid used as an adhesive, as a preservative for eggs, etc. Also **wa′ter·glass′** *n.*

**water hole** **1.** a dip or hole in the ground, in which water collects; pool; pond **2.** a hole in the ice on a body of water

**water hyacinth** a floating plant with showy lavender flowers, native to S. America: now often a hindrance to water traffic in the southern U.S., esp. Florida

**water ice** [Brit.] water and sugar flavored and frozen

**wa·ter·i·ness** (-ē nis) *n.* the state or quality of being watery

**wa·ter·ing place** (-iŋ) **1.** a place at a stream, lake, etc. where animals go to drink **2.** [Chiefly Brit.] a resort or spa with mineral springs for drinking or bathing or with a beach for swimming, water sports, etc.

**watering pot** (or **can**) a can with a spout, often having a perforated nozzle, for watering plants, etc.

**water jacket** a casing for holding water that circulates, as around the cylinders of an internal-combustion engine

**water jump** a strip, ditch, or channel of water that a horse must jump, as in a steeplechase

**water level** **1.** *a)* the surface of still water *b)* the height of this **2.** *same as* WATERLINE (senses 1 & 2)

**wa·ter·lil·y** (-lil′ē) *n., pl.* -**lil′ies** **1.** any of various water plants having large, flat, floating leaves and showy flowers in many colors **2.** the flower of such a plant

**wa·ter·line** (-līn′) *n.* **1.** the line to which the surface of the water comes on the side of a ship or boat **2.** any of several lines parallel to this, marked on the hull of a ship, indicating how far the ship has sunk in the water when it is fully or partly loaded, or unloaded **3.** a pipe, tube, etc. connected to a source of water

WATERLILY

**wa·ter·logged** (-lôgd′, -lägd′) *adj.* **1.** soaked or filled with water so as to be heavy and sluggish in movement: said of boats or floating objects **2.** soaked with water; swampy

**Wa·ter·loo** (wôt′ər lōō′, wät′-; wôt′ər lōō′, wät′-) **1.** [after ff.] city in NE Iowa: pop. 76,000 **2.** town in C Belgium: scene of Napoleon's final defeat (1815) —*n.* any disastrous or decisive defeat

**water main** a main pipe in a system of water pipes

**wa·ter·man** (wôt′ər mən, wät′-) *n., pl.* -**men** a person who works on or with boats; esp., an oarsman

**wa·ter·mark** (-märk′) *n.* **1.** a mark showing the limit to which water has risen **2.** *Papermaking a)* a faint mark in paper, produced by pressure of a projecting design, as in the mold *b)* the design —*vt.* **1.** to mark (paper) with a watermark **2.** to impress (a design) as a watermark

**wa·ter·mel·on** (-mel′ən) *n.* **1.** a large, edible fruit with a hard, green rind and juicy, pink or red pulp having many seeds **2.** the vine on which it grows

**water mill** a mill whose machinery is driven by water

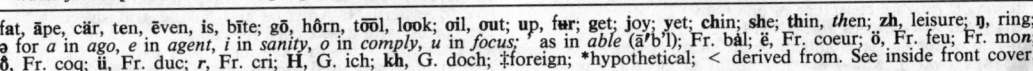

fat, āpe, cär, ten, ēven, is, bīte; gō, hôrn, tōōl, look; oil, out; up, fur; get; joy; yet; chin; she; thin, *then*; zh, leisure; ŋ, ring; ə for *a* in ago, *e* in agent, *i* in sanity, *o* in comply, *u* in focus; ′ as in able (ā′b'l); Fr. bâl; ë, Fr. coeur; ö, Fr. feu; Fr. mon; ô, Fr. coq; ü, Fr. duc; r, Fr. cri; H, G. ich; kh, G. doch; ‡foreign; *hypothetical; < derived from. See inside front cover.

**water moccasin** a large, poisonous, olive-brown pit viper found along or in rivers and swamps in the SE U.S.: often confused with various harmless water snakes

**water nymph** *Gr. & Rom. Myth.* a goddess having the form of a lovely young girl, supposed to dwell in a stream, pool, lake, etc.

**water of crystallization** water that occurs in crystalline substances and can be removed by heat: the loss of water usually results in the loss of crystalline structure

**water ouzel** any of several birds of Europe, Asia, and America; esp., the **American dipper** of western N. America that dives and swims in mountain streams

**water pipe 1.** a pipe for carrying water **2.** a smoking pipe in which the smoke is drawn through water; hookah

**water pistol** a toy gun that shoots water in a stream

**water plant** any plant living under water or with only the roots in or under water

**water polo** a water game played with a round, partly inflated ball by two teams of seven swimmers

**water power 1.** the power of running or falling water, used to drive machinery, etc. **2.** a fall of water that can be so used Also **wa′ter·pow′er** *n.*

**wa·ter·proof** (wôt′ər proof′, wät′-) *adj.* that keeps out water completely; esp., treated with rubber, plastic, etc. so that water will not penetrate —*n.* **1.** waterproof material **2.** [Chiefly Brit.] a raincoat, etc. of waterproof material —*vt.* to make waterproof —**wa′ter·proof′er** *n.*

**water rat 1.** any of various rodents that live on the banks of streams and ponds **2.** *same as* MUSKRAT

**wa·ter·re·pel·lent** (-ri pel′ənt) *adj.* that repels water but is not thoroughly waterproof

**wa·ter·shed** (-shed′) *n.* **1.** a ridge dividing the areas drained by different river systems **2.** the area drained by a river system **3.** a crucial turning point

**wa·ter·side** (-sīd′) *n.* land at the edge of a body of water —*adj.* of, at, or on the waterside

**wa·ter·ski** (-skē′) *vi.* -**skied′**, -**ski′ing** to be towed, as a sport, on skilike boards (**water skis**) by a line attached to a speedboat —**wa′ter·ski′er** *n.*

**water snake** any of numerous saltwater or freshwater snakes; esp., a thick-bodied, nonpoisonous freshwater snake that feeds on fish and amphibians

**wa·ter·soak** (-sōk′) *vt.* to soak with or in water

**water softener 1.** a chemical compound added to hard water to make it soft, or free from mineral salts **2.** a tank, etc. in which water is filtered through chemicals to make it soft

**water spaniel** either of two breeds of spaniel having a curly coat and used in hunting to retrieve waterfowl

**wa·ter·spout** (-spout′) *n.* **1.** a hole, pipe, or spout from which water runs **2.** a tornado occurring over water, appearing as a rapidly rotating column of spray

**water sprite** in folklore, a spirit, nymph, etc. dwelling in or haunting the water

**water table** the level below which the ground is saturated with water

**wa·ter·tight** (-tīt′) *adj.* **1.** so snugly put together that no water can get in or through **2.** well thought out, with no weak points: said of an argument, plan, etc. —**wa′ter·tight′ness** *n.*

**water tower 1.** an elevated tank used for water storage and for keeping equal pressure on a water system **2.** a firefighting apparatus that can be used to lift high-pressure hoses, etc. to great height

**water vapor** water in the form of mist or tiny diffused particles, esp. when below the boiling point, as in the air: distinguished from STEAM

**wa·ter·way** (-wā′) *n.* **1.** a channel through or along which water runs **2.** any body of water wide enough and deep enough for boats, ships, etc.

**water wheel 1.** a wheel with paddles turned by running water, used to give power **2.** a wheel with buckets on its rim, used for lifting water

**water wings** a device, inflated with air, used to keep one afloat while learning to swim

**wa·ter·works** (-wurks′) *n.pl.* [*often with sing. v.*] **1.** a system of reservoirs, pumps, etc. used to bring a water supply to a city, etc. **2.** a pumping station in such a system

**wa·ter·worn** (-wôrn′) *adj.* worn, smoothed, or polished by the action of running water

**wa·ter·y** (-ē) *adj.* **1.** of or like water **2.** containing or full of water **3.** thin, diluted, weak, etc. [*watery tea*] **4.** tearful **5.** in or consisting of water [a *watery* grave] **6.** soft or soggy

**Wat·ling Island** (wät′liŋ) *same as* SAN SALVADOR (island): also **Wat′lings Island**

**watt** (wät, wôt) *n.* [after ff.] the mks unit of electrical power equal to the power used by a direct current of one ampere flowing through a resistance of one ohm

**Watt** (wät, wôt), **James** 1736–1819; Scot. engineer & inventor: noted for his development of the steam engine

**watt·age** (wät′ij, wôt′-) *n.* **1.** amount of electrical power, expressed in watts **2.** the amount of watts required to operate a given appliance or device

**Wat·teau** (vá tō′; *E.* wä tō′), **(Jean) An·toine** (än twän′) 1684–1721; Fr. painter

**watt-hour** (wät′our′, wôt′-) *n.* a unit of electrical energy or work, equal to one watt acting for one hour

**wat·tle** (wät′′l, wôt′-) *n.* [OE. *watul*] **1.** a woven work of sticks intertwined with twigs or branches, used for walls, roofs, etc. **2.** [Brit. Dial.] a stick, twig, etc. **3.** in Australia, any of various acacias **4.** a fleshy, often brightly colored piece of skin that hangs from the throat of a cock, turkey, etc., or of some lizards —*adj.* made of or roofed with wattle —*vt.* -**tled**, -**tling 1.** to intertwine (sticks, twigs, etc.) so as to form an interwoven structure **2.** to construct (a fence) by intertwining twigs, etc. **3.** to build of wattle

WATTLES

**watt·me·ter** (wät′mēt′ər, wôt′-) *n.* an instrument for measuring in watts the power in an electric circuit

**Wa·tu·si** (wä tōō′sē) *n., pl.* -**sis**, -**si** any member of a tall, slender, cattle-owning people of Burundi and Rwanda: also **Wa·tut′si** (-tōōt′sē)

**Wau·ke·gan** (wô kē′gən) [< Algonquian, lit., trading place] city in NE Ill., on Lake Michigan: pop. 68,000

**waul** (wôl) *vi., n.* wail, squall, or howl

**Wau·wa·to·sa** (wô′wə tō′sə) [< AmInd. *wawatosi,* ? firefly] city in SE Wis.: suburb of Milwaukee: pop. 51,000

**Wave** (wāv) *n.* a member of the WAVES

**wave** (wāv) *vi.* **waved**, **wav′ing** [OE. *wafian*] **1.** to move up and down or back and forth in a curving motion; sway to and fro [the flag *waves*] **2.** to signal by moving a hand, arm, etc. to and fro **3.** to have the form of a series of curves [hair that *waves* naturally] —*vt.* **1.** to cause to wave or sway to and fro **2.** to brandish (a weapon) **3.** *a)* to move or swing (something) as a signal *b)* to signal (something) by doing this [to *wave* farewell] *c)* to signal to (someone) by doing this [he *waved* us on] **4.** to arrange (hair, etc.) in a series of curves —*n.* **1.** *a)* a ridge or swell moving along the surface of a body of water, etc. *b)* something that suggests this as when wind blows over a field of grain **2.** a curve or series of curves, as in the hair, etc. **3.** a motion to and fro or up and down, as that made by the hand in signaling **4.** something like a wave in action or effect; specif., an upsurge or rise [a crime *wave*] **5.** [Poet.] water; esp., the sea **6.** *Physics* a state of motion that periodically advances and retreats as it is transmitted progressively from one particle in a medium to the next in a given direction, as in the propagation of light, sound, etc. —**wave′less** *adj.* —**wave′like′** *adj.* —**wav′er** *n.*

**wave band** *Radio & TV* a specific range of wave frequencies

**wave·length** (wāv′leŋkth, -leŋth) *n. Physics* the distance, measured in the direction of the progression of a wave, from any given point to the next point characterized by the same phase: also **wave length**

**wave·let** (-lit) *n.* a little wave; ripple

**wa·ver** (wā′vər) *vi.* [< ME. < *waven,* to WAVE] **1.** to sway to and fro; flutter **2.** to show indecision; vacillate **3.** to become unsteady; falter **4.** to tremble: said of the voice, etc. **5.** to flicker: said of light —*n.* a wavering —**wa′ver·er** *n.* —**wa′ver·ing·ly** *adv.*

**WAVES** (wāvz) [orig. *W(omen) A(ppointed for) V(oluntary) E(mergency) S(ervice)*] the women's branch of the U.S. Navy

**wav·y** (wā′vē) *adj.* **wav′i·er**, **wav′i·est 1.** having waves **2.** moving in a wavelike motion **3.** having curves; forming waves and hollows **4.** like or characteristic of waves **5.** wavering; fluctuating; unsteady —**wav′i·ly** *adv.* —**wav′i·ness** *n.*

**wax¹** (waks) *n.* [OE. *weax*] **1.** an easily molded, dull-yellow substance secreted by bees for building cells; beeswax: it is used for candles, modeling, etc. **2.** any substance like this; specif., *a)* paraffin *b)* earwax *c)* sealing wax —*vt.* to rub, polish, cover, or treat with wax —*adj.* made of wax —**wax′er** *n.* —**wax′like′** *adj.*

**wax²** (waks) *vi.* **waxed**, **waxed** or archaic **wax′en, wax′ing** [OE. *weaxan,* to grow] **1.** to increase in strength, intensity, volume, etc. **2.** to become gradually full: said of the moon **3.** to become [to *wax* angry]

**wax bean 1.** a variety of kidney bean with long, narrow, yellow pods **2.** the immature pod cooked as a vegetable

**wax·ber·ry** (waks′ber′ē) *n., pl.* -**ries** *same as:* **1.** SNOWBERRY (senses 1 & 3) **2.** BAYBERRY (sense 1)

**wax·en** (wak′s'n) *adj.* **1.** made of, or covered with, wax **2.** like wax, as in being pale, soft, easily molded, etc.

**wax myrtle** *same as* BAYBERRY; esp., an evergreen shrub native to eastern N. America and having grayish-white berries coated with a wax used for candles

**wax palm 1.** *same as* CARNAUBA **2.** a palm of the Andes that yields a wax used to make candles, polishes, etc.

**wax paper** a kind of paper made moistureproof by a wax, or paraffin, coating: also **waxed paper**

**wax·wing** (waks′wiŋ′) *n.* any of a group of birds with silky-brown plumage, a showy crest, and scarlet spines, suggesting sealing wax, at the ends of the secondary quill feathers

**wax·work** (-wurk′) *n.* **1.** work, as objects, figures, etc., made of wax **2.** a human figure made of wax

**wax·works** (-wurks′) *n.pl.* [*with sing. v.*] an exhibition of wax figures made to look like famous or notorious persons: also **wax museum**

**wax·y** (wak′sē) *adj.* **wax′i·er, wax′i·est** **1.** full of, covered with, or made of wax **2.** like wax in nature or appearance —**wax′i·ness** *n.*

**way** (wā) *n.* [OE. *weg*] **1.** a road, highway, street, path, etc. **2.** room for passing; an opening, as in a crowd **3.** a course from one place to another [*highway, one-way* street] **4.** a specified route or direction [on the *way* to town] **5.** course or habits of life [to fall into evil *ways*] **6.** a method of doing something **7.** a customary or characteristic manner of living, acting, etc. [to change one's *ways*] **8.** manner; style **9.** distance [a long *way* off]: also [Colloq.] **ways** **10.** direction of movement, etc. [look this *way*] **11.** respect; point; particular [to be right in some *ways*] **12.** wish; will [to get one's *way*] **13.** range, as of experience [that never came my *way*] **14.** relationship as to those taking part [a four-*way* agreement] **15.** [Colloq.] a (specified) state or condition [he is in a bad *way*] **16.** [Colloq.] a district; locality [out our *way*] **17.** [*pl.*] a timber framework on which a ship is built and along which it slides in launching **18.** *Naut.* a ship's movement or momentum through water —*adv.* [Colloq.] away; far [*way* behind] —**by the way 1.** incidentally **2.** on or beside the way —**by way of 1.** passing through; via **2.** as a way, method, or means of —**come one's way 1.** to come to one **2.** to turn out successfully for one: also **go one's way** —**give way 1.** to withdraw; yield **2.** to break down —**give way to** to yield to —**go out of the (or one's) way** to make a special effort —**in the way** in such a position as to obstruct, hinder, etc. —**lead the way** to be a guide or example —**make one's way 1.** to proceed **2.** to succeed by one's own efforts —**make way 1.** to clear a passage **2.** to make progress —**on the way out 1.** becoming unfashionable or unpopular **2.** dying —**out of the way 1.** in a position so as not to hinder, etc. **2.** disposed of **3.** not on the right or usual route **4.** *a)* improper; amiss *b)* unusual —**the way** according to the way that [with things *the way* they are] —**under way 1.** moving; advancing **2.** *Naut. see* UNDERWAY

**way·bill** (wā′bil′) *n.* a paper giving a list of goods and shipping instructions, sent with the goods being shipped

**way·far·er** (-fer′ər) *n.* a person who travels, esp. from place to place on foot —**way′far′ing** *adj., n.*

**way·lay** (wā′lā′, wā′lā′) *vt.* **-laid′, -lay′ing** **1.** to lie in wait for and attack; ambush **2.** to wait for and accost (a person) on the way —**way′lay′er** *n.*

**Wayne** (wān) **1.** [< surname *Wayne*] a masculine name **2.** Anthony, 1745–96; Am. general in the Revolutionary War: called *Mad Anthony Wayne*

**way-out** (wā′out′) *adj.* [Colloq.] very unusual, unconventional, experimental, nonconformist, esoteric, etc.

**-ways** (wāz) [< *way* (see WAY) + adv. genit. *-s*] *a suffix meaning* in a (specified) direction, position, or manner [*endways*]: equivalent to -WISE (sense 1)

**ways and means 1.** methods and resources at the disposal of a person, company, etc. **2.** methods of raising money, as for government

**way·side** (wā′sīd′) *n.* the area close to the side of a road —*adj.* on, near, or along the side of a road —**go by the wayside** to be put aside or discarded

**way station** a small railroad station between more important ones, where through trains stop only on signal

**way·ward** (-wərd) *adj.* [see AWAY & -WARD] **1.** insistent upon having one's own way; headstrong, willful, disobedient, etc. **2.** unpredictable; erratic —**way′ward·ly** *adv.* —**way′ward·ness** *n.*

**way·worn** (-wôrn′) *adj.* tired from traveling

**W.B., W/B** waybill

**w.c. 1.** water closet **2.** without charge

**W.C.T.U.** Women's Christian Temperance Union

**we** (wē) *pron. for sing. see* I [OE.] **1.** the persons speaking or writing: sometimes used by a person in referring to two or more persons including himself and often the person or persons addressed, or by a monarch, author, editor, etc. in referring to himself **2.** you: used in direct address as to a child, invalid, etc. [shall *we* take a nap now?] *We* is the nominative case form of the first personal plural pronoun

**weak** (wēk) *adj.* [ON. *veikr*] **1.** *a)* lacking in strength of body or muscle; not physically strong *b)* lacking vitality; feeble; infirm **2.** lacking in skill or strength for combat or

competition [a *weak* team] **3.** lacking in moral strength or will power **4.** lacking in mental power **5.** *a)* lacking ruling power, or authority *b)* having few resources, little wealth, etc. [a *weak* nation] **6.** lacking in force or effectiveness **7.** *a)* not strong in material or construction; easily broken, bent, etc. *b)* not sound or secure [a *weak* fort] **8.** *a)* not functioning normally or well: said of a body organ or part [*weak* eyes] *b)* easily upset; queasy [a *weak* stomach] **9.** suggesting moral or physical lack of strength [*weak* features] **10.** lacking in volume, intensity, etc.; faint [a *weak* voice] **11.** lacking the usual or proper strength [*weak* tea] **12.** poor or deficient in something specified [*weak* in grammar] **13.** ineffective; faulty [a *weak* argument] **14.** *Chem.* having a low ion concentration, as certain acids and bases **15.** *Gram.* inflected by adding a suffix such as *-ed, -d* rather than by an internal vowel change: said of regular verbs **16.** *Phonet.* unstressed or lightly stressed **17.** *Prosody* designating or of a verse ending in which the stress falls on a word or syllable normally unstressed —**weak′ish** *adj.*

**weak·en** (-′n) *vt., vi.* to make or become weak or weaker

**weak·fish** (-fish′) *n., pl.* **-fish′, -fish′es:** see FISH [< obs. Du. < *week,* soft + *visch,* a fish] any of several ocean food fishes, esp. a species off the eastern coast of the U.S.

**weak-kneed** (wēk′nēd′) *adj.* **1.** having weak knees **2.** lacking courage, determination, resistance, etc.

**weak·ling** (-liŋ) *n.* **1.** a person or animal low in physical strength or vitality **2.** a person of weak character or intellect —*adj.* weak; feeble

**weak·ly** (-lē) *adj.* **-li·er, -li·est** sickly; feeble; weak —*adv.* in a weak way —**weak′li·ness** *n.*

**weak-mind·ed** (-mīn′did) *adj.* **1.** not firm of mind; indecisive **2.** mentally retarded **3.** showing weakness of thought —**weak′-mind′ed·ness** *n.*

**weak·ness** (-nis) *n.* **1.** a being weak **2.** a weak point; fault **3.** a liking or an unreasonable fondness (*for* something) **4.** something of which one is unreasonably fond

**weak sister** [Slang] one who is cowardly, unreliable, etc.

**weal¹** (wēl) *n.* [var. of WALE] a mark, line, or ridge raised on the skin, as by a blow; welt

**weal²** (wēl) *n.* [OE. *wela*] a prosperous state; well-being

**weald** (wēld) *n.* [OE.] [Poet.] **1.** a wooded area; forest **2.** wild, open country

**wealth** (welth) *n.* [see WEAL² & -TH¹] **1.** *a)* much money or property; riches *b)* the state of being rich; affluence **2.** a large amount; abundance [a *wealth* of ideas] **3.** valuable products, contents, or derivatives [the *wealth* of the oceans] **4.** *Econ. a)* everything having value in money or a price *b)* any useful material thing capable of being bought and sold

**wealth·y** (wel′thē) *adj.* **wealth′i·er, wealth′i·est** **1.** having wealth; rich **2.** of or suggestive of wealth **3.** abounding (in something) —**wealth′i·ly** *adv.* —**wealth′i·ness** *n.*

**wean** (wēn) *vt.* [OE. *wenian*] **1.** to accustom (a child or young animal) to food other than its mother's milk; now, often, to cause to give up drinking milk from a bottle with a nipple **2.** to withdraw (a person) by degrees (*from* a habit, object of affection, etc.) as by substituting something else —**wean′er** *n.*

**wean·ling** (-liŋ) *n.* a child or young animal that has just been weaned —*adj.* recently weaned

**weap·on** (wep′ən) *n.* [OE. *wæpen*] **1.** any instrument or device used for fighting, as specif. in warfare **2.** any organ or part (of an animal or plant) used for attacking or defending **3.** any means of attack or defense

**weap·on·ry** (-rē) *n.* **1.** the design and production of weapons **2.** weapons collectively, esp. of a nation for use in war

**wear¹** (wer) *vt.* **wore, worn, wear′ing** [OE. *werian*] **1.** *a)* to have or carry (clothing, jewelry, a weapon, etc.) on the body *b)* to hold the position symbolized by [to *wear* the heavyweight crown] **2.** to have or show in one's expression or appearance [to *wear* a smile] **3.** to damage, impair, diminish, etc. by constant use, friction, etc. (often with *away*) **4.** to bring by use to a specified state [to *wear* a coat to rags] **5.** to make by the friction of rubbing, flowing, etc. [to *wear* a hole in the rug] **6.** to tire or exhaust —*vi.* **1.** to become damaged, impaired, diminished, etc. by constant use, friction, etc. **2.** to hold up in spite of use; last [a fabric that *wears* well] **3.** to become in time; grow gradually [*courage wearing* thin] **4.** to pass away gradually: said of time [the day *wore* on] **5.** to have an irritating or exhausting effect (*on*) [noise *wearing* on his nerves] —*n.* **1.** a wearing or being worn **2.** things, esp. clothes, worn, or for wearing, on the body [men's *wear*]: often in combination [*sportswear*] **3.** damage, impairment, loss, etc. from use, friction, etc. **4.** the ability to last in spite of use [a lot of *wear* left in the tire] —**wear down 1.** to lose or cause to lose thickness or height by use, friction, etc.   **2.** to tire out; exhaust   **3.** to overcome by constant effort —**wear off** to pass away or diminish by degrees —**wear out 1.** to make or become useless from continued wear or use   **2.** to waste or consume by degrees   **3.** to tire out; exhaust —**wear′er** *n.*

**wear²** (wer) *vt.* **wore, worn, wear′ing** [altered < *veer* (to let out)]  to turn (a ship) about by swinging its bow away from the wind —*vi.* to turn about by having the bow swung away from the wind

**wear·a·ble** (wer′ə b'l) *adj.* that can be worn; suitable for wear —*n.* [*pl.*] garments; clothing —**wear′a·bil′i·ty** *n.*

**wear and tear** loss and damage resulting from use

**wear·ing** (-iŋ) *adj.* **1.** of or for wear [*wearing* apparel]   **2.** causing wear or loss ; tiring —**wear′ing·ly** *adv.*

**wea·ri·some** (wir′ē səm) *adj.* causing weariness; tiring; tiresome —**wea′ri·some·ly** *adv.* —**wea′ri·some·ness** *n.*

**wear·proof** (wer′prōōf′) *adj.* that resists wearing out

**wea·ry** (wir′ē) *adj.* **-ri·er, -ri·est** [OE. *werig*]  **1.** tired; worn out   **2.** no longer liking, patient, tolerant, etc.; bored (with *of*) [*weary* of jokes]   **3.** tiring [*weary* work]   **4.** irksome; tedious [*weary* excuses] —*vt.*, *vi.* **-ried, -ry·ing** to make or become weary —**wea′ri·ly** *adv.* —**wea′ri·ness** *n.*

**wea·sand** (wē′z'nd) *n.* [OE. *wæsend*]  the gullet; esophagus

**wea·sel** (wē′z'l) *n.*, *pl.* **-sels, -sel:** see PLURAL, II, D, 1 [OE. *wesle*]  **1.** an agile, flesh-eating mammal related to the marten, with a long, slender body, short legs, and a long, bushy tail: they feed on rats, birds, eggs, etc.   **2.** a sly or sneaky person —*vi.* **1.** to use weasel words   **2.** [Colloq.] to evade a commitment or responsibility (with *out*) —**wea′sel·ly** *adj.*

WEASEL
(6–14 in. long,
including tail)

**weasel words** words or remarks that are deliberately misleading because they can be understood in more than one way

**weath·er** (weth′ər) *n.* [OE. *weder*]  **1.** the general condition (as to temperature, moisture, cloudiness, etc.) of the atmosphere at a particular time and place   **2.** disagreeable atmospheric conditions; storm, rain, etc. —*vt.* **1.** to expose to the weather or atmosphere, as for airing, drying, seasoning, etc.   **2.** to wear away, discolor, etc. by exposure to the atmosphere   **3.** to get through safely [to *weather* a storm]   **4.** to slope (sills, etc.) so as to throw off rain, etc.   **5.** *Naut.* to pass to the windward of (a cape, reef, etc.) —*vi.* **1.** to become worn, discolored, etc. by exposure to the weather   **2.** to endure such exposure in a specified way [it *weathers* well] —*adj.* **1.** designating or of the side of a ship, etc. toward the wind; windward   **2.** exposed to the elements [*weather* deck] —**under the weather** [Colloq.] **1.** not feeling well; ailing   **2.** somewhat drunk —**weather through** to go safely through a storm, difficulty, etc.

**weath·er·beat·en** (-bēt′'n) *adj.* showing the effect of weather, as *a)* stained, damaged, or worn *b)* sunburned, roughened, etc.: said of a person, his face, etc.

**weath·er·board** (-bôrd′) *n.* a clapboard; piece of siding —*vt.* to put weatherboards on (a wall, etc.)

**weath·er·bound** (-bound′) *adj.* delayed or halted by bad weather, as a ship, airplane, etc.

**Weather Bureau** *former name of the* NATIONAL WEATHER SERVICE

**weath·er·cock** (-käk′) *n.* **1.** a weather vane in the form of a rooster   **2.** a fickle or changeable person or thing

**weather eye 1.** an eye alert to signs of changing weather   **2.** a close watch for any change

**weath·er·ing** (-iŋ) *n. Geol.* the effects of the forces of weather on rock surfaces, as in forming soil, sand, etc.

**weath·er·man** (-man′) *n.*, *pl.* **-men′** (-men′)  a person who forecasts the weather, or, esp., one who reports weather conditions and forecasts, as on television

**weather map** a map or chart showing weather conditions in a certain area at a given time by indicating barometric pressures, temperatures, wind direction, etc.

**weath·er·proof** (-prōōf′) *adj.* that can be exposed to wind, rain, snow, etc. without being damaged —*vt.* to make weatherproof

**weather station** a post or office where weather conditions are recorded and studied and forecasts are made

**weath·er·strip** (-strip′) *n.* a thin strip of metal, felt, wood, etc. used to cover the joint between a door or window and its casing, so as to keep out drafts, rain, etc.: also **weather strip** —*vt.* **-stripped′, -strip′ping** to provide with this: also **weath′er-strip′**

**weath·er·strip·ping** (-strip′iŋ) *n.* **1.** *same as* WEATHER-STRIP   **2.** weatherstrips collectively

**weather vane** a shaped piece of metal, etc., set up high to swing in the wind and show which way it is blowing

**weath·er·wise** (-wīz′) *adj.* **1.** skilled in predicting the weather   **2.** skilled in predicting shifts of opinion, feeling, etc.

**weath·er·worn** (-wôrn′) *adj. same as* WEATHER-BEATEN

**weave** (wēv) *vt.* **wove** or, chiefly for *vt.* 6 & *vi.* 3, **weaved, wo′ven** or **wove** or, chiefly for *vt.* 6 & *vi.* 3, **weaved, weav′ing** [OE. *wefan*]  **1.** *a)* to make (a fabric), esp. on a loom, by interlacing threads or yarns *b)* to form (threads) into a fabric   **2.** *a)* to construct in the mind *b)* to form (incidents, etc.) into a story, poem, etc.   **3.** *a)* to make by interlacing twigs, straw, etc. [to *weave* baskets] *b)* to interlace (twigs, straw, etc.) so as to make something   **4.** to twist (something) into, through, or among [to *weave* flowers into one's hair]   **5.** to spin (a web): said of spiders, etc.   **6.** *a)* to cause (a vehicle, etc.) to move from side to side or in and out *b)* to make (one's way) by moving thus —*vi.* **1.** to do weaving   **2.** to become interlaced   **3.** to move from side to side or in and out [*weaving* through traffic] —*n.* a method or pattern of weaving

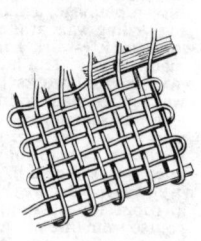

WEAVING

**weav·er** (wē′vər) *n.* **1.** a person who weaves; esp., one whose work is weaving   **2.** *same as* WEAVERBIRD

**weav·er·bird** (-burd′) *n.* any of a number of related old-world, finchlike birds that weave elaborate domed nests of sticks, grass, and other vegetation

**web** (web) *n.* [OE. *webb*]  **1.** any woven fabric; esp., a length of cloth being woven on a loom or just taken off   **2.** the network spun by a spider or by the larvae of certain insects   **3.** a carefully woven trap   **4.** anything contrived in an intricate way [a *web* of lies]   **5.** *Anat.* a tissue or membrane   **6.** *Mech.* the plate joining the flanges of a girder, rail, etc.   **7.** *Printing* a large roll of paper for continuously feeding a type of rotary press (**web press**)   **8.** *Zool. a)* the vane of a feather *b)* a membrane joining the digits of various water birds, water animals, etc. —*vt.* **webbed, web′bing 1.** to join by a web   **2.** to cover as with a web   **3.** to snare in a web —**web′like′** *adj.*

**web·bing** (-iŋ) *n.* **1.** a strong, tough fabric, as of jute, woven in strips and used for belts, in upholstery, etc.   **2.** a membrane joining the digits, as of a duck or frog   **3.** a part like this   **4.** a netlike structure of interwoven cord, etc.

**web·by** (-ē) *adj.* **web′bi·er, web′bi·est 1.** of or like a web   **2.** webbed or web-footed

**We·ber** (vā′bər), **Carl Ma·ri·a** (**Friedrich Ernst**) **von** (mä-rē′ä fôn) 1786–1826; Ger. composer

**We·bern** (vā′bərn), **An·ton** (**von**) (än′tôn) 1883–1945; Austrian composer

**web·foot** (web′foot′) *n.*, *pl.* **-feet′ 1.** a foot with the toes webbed   **2.** an animal with webfeet —**web′-foot′ed** *adj.*

**Web·ster** (web′stər) **1. Daniel,** 1782–1852; U.S. statesman & orator   **2. John,** 1580?–1625?; Eng. dramatist   **3. Noah,** 1758–1843; U.S. lexicographer —**Web·ster′i·an** (-stir′ē ən) *adj.*

**web-toed** (web′tōd′) *adj.* having webfeet

**wed** (wed) *vt.* **wed′ded, wed′ded** or **wed, wed′ding** [OE. *weddian*]  **1.** to marry; specif., *a)* to take as husband or wife *b)* to join in marriage   **2.** to join closely —*vi.* to get married

**we'd** (wēd) **1.** we had   **2.** we should   **3.** we would

**Wed.** Wednesday

**wed·ded** (wed′id) *adj.* **1.** married   **2.** devoted [*wedded* to one's work]   **3.** joined [*wedded* by common interests]

**wed·ding** (-iŋ) *n.* [OE. *weddung*]  **1.** the act or ceremony of getting married, or the festivities that go with it   **2.** a marriage anniversary   **3.** a joining together

**wedding ring** a ring put on the bride's finger by the groom during the marriage ceremony; also, a ring sometimes given to the groom by the bride during the ceremony

**wedge** (wej) *n.* [OE. *wecg*]  **1.** a piece of wood, metal, etc. tapering to a thin edge that can be driven into a narrow opening, as to split wood   **2.** anything with a wedgelike shape or part; specif., *a) Golf* an iron with much loft, as for shots out of bunkers *b)* same as WEDGIE   **3.** any action or procedure used to open the way for a change —*vt.* **wedged, wedg′ing 1.** to split as with a wedge   **2.** to fix in place by driving a wedge under, beside, etc.   **3.** to pack (*in*) or crowd together —*vi.* to push or be forced as or like a wedge —**wedge′like′** *adj.* —**wedg′y** *adj.*

WEDGE

**wedg·ie** (wej′ē) *n.* a woman's shoe having a wedgelike piece under the heel so as to form a solid sole, flat from heel to toe

**Wedg·wood** (**ware**) (wej′wood′) [after J. *Wedgwood*, 18th-c. E. potter]  *a trademark for* a fine English pottery, typically with neoclassical figures applied in relief

**wed·lock** (wed′läk′) *n.* [< OE. < *wed*, a pledge + *-lac*, offering]  the state of being married

**Wednes·day** (wenz/dē, -dā) *n.* [OE. *Wodnes dæg*, Woden's day] the fourth day of the week

**Wednes·days** (-dēz, -dāz) *adv.* on or during every Wednesday

**wee** (wē) *adj.* we/er, we/est [OE. *wege*] 1. very small; tiny 2. very early *[the wee hours]* —*n.* [Scot. & Eng. Dial.] a little bit; esp., a short time

**weed** (wēd) *n.* [OE. *weod*] 1. any undesired, uncultivated plant, esp. one growing in profusion and crowding out a desired crop, spoiling a lawn, etc. 2. [Colloq.] *a)* tobacco: with *the b)* a cigar or cigarette *c)* a marijuana cigarette 3. something useless —*vt.* 1. to remove weeds from (a garden, etc.) 2. to remove as useless, harmful, etc.: often with *out* 3. to rid of useless or harmful elements —*vi.* to remove weeds, etc. —**weed/er** *n.* —**weed/like/** *adj.*

**weed·kill·er** (-kil/ər) *n.* same as HERBICIDE

**weeds** (wēdz) *n.pl.* [< OE. *wæde,* a garment] black mourning clothes, esp. those worn by a widow

**weed·y** (wēd/ē) *adj.* weed/i·er, weed/i·est 1. full of weeds 2. of or like a weed, as in rapid growth 3. lean, lanky, ungainly, etc. —**weed/i·ness** *n.*

**week** (wēk) *n.* [OE. *wicu*] 1. a period of seven days, esp. one beginning with Sunday and ending with Saturday 2. the hours or days of work in a seven-day period *[a 40-hour week]* —**week after week** every week —**week by week** each week —**week in, week out** every week

**week·day** (-dā/) *n.* 1. any day of the week except Sunday (or, as in Judaism, Saturday) 2. any day not in the weekend —*adj.* of, for, or on a weekday

**week·days** (-dāz/) *adv.* on or during every weekday or most weekdays

**week·end, week-end** (-end/) *n.* the period from Friday night or Saturday to Monday morning: also **week end** —*adj.* of, for, or on a weekend —*vi.* to spend the weekend (at or *in* a specified place)

**week·end·er** (-en/dər) *n.* 1. a person who takes a vacation or goes for a visit on a weekend 2. a small piece of luggage for use on a weekend trip: also **weekend case** (or **bag**)

**week·ends** (-endz/) *adv.* on or during every weekend or most weekends

**week·ly** (-lē) *adj.* 1. continuing or lasting for a week 2. done, happening, appearing, etc. once a week or every week *[a weekly visit]* 3. of a week, or of each week *[a weekly wage]* —*adv.* once a week; every week —*n., pl.* -lies a periodical published once a week

**ween** (wēn) *vi., vt.* [OE. *wenan*] [Archaic] to think; suppose; imagine

**wee·nie, wee·ny¹** (wē/nē) *n., pl.* -nies [Colloq.] same as WIENER

**wee·ny²** (wē/nē) *adj.* -ni·er, -ni·est [WEE + (TI)NY] [Colloq.] small; tiny

**weep** (wēp) *vi.* wept, weep/ing [OE. *wepan*] 1. to show or express strong emotion, usually grief or sorrow, by crying, wailing, or, esp., shedding tears 2. to lament or mourn (with *for*) 3. to drip or form liquid drops, esp. of moisture condensed from the air 4. to exude liquid —*vt.* 1. to weep for; lament 2. to shed (tears, etc.) —*n.* *[often pl.]* a fit of weeping —**weep/er** *n.*

**weep·ing** (wē/piŋ) *n.* the act of one who or that which weeps —*adj.* 1. that weeps tears or other liquid 2. having graceful, drooping branches —**weep/ing·ly** *adv.*

**weeping willow** a Chinese willow widely grown as an ornamental tree for its delicate, drooping branches

**weep·y** (wē/pē) *adj.* weep/i·er, weep/i·est 1. *a)* inclined to weep; tearful *b)* exuding liquid 2. characterized by or apt to cause weeping —**weep/i·ness** *n.*

**wee·vil** (wē/v'l) *n.* [OE. *wifel*] any of numerous beetles, esp. those with projecting beaks, including many pest species that feed, esp. as larvae, on cotton, fruits, grain, etc. —**wee/vil·y, wee/vil·ly** *adj.*

**weft** (weft) *n.* [OE. *weft* < base of *wefan,* to weave] 1. in weaving, the woof 2. something woven

**weigh¹** (wā) *vt.* [OE. *wegan,* to carry] 1. to determine the weight of by means of a scale or balance 2. to have a (specified) weight *[it weighs ten pounds]:* orig., and still when used with an adverb, construed as a *vi.* 3. same as WEIGHT (*vt.* 1) 4. to lift or balance (an object) in the hand(s) in order to estimate its heaviness 5. to measure out as by weight (often with *out*) 6. *a)* to consider and choose carefully *[to weigh one's words] b)* to consider in order to make a choice *[to weigh one plan against another]* 7. *Naut.* to hoist, or lift (an anchor) —*vi.* 1. to have significance, importance, or influence 2. to be a burden (with *on* or *upon*) *[his crime weighed on his mind]* 3. *Naut.* to hoist anchor —**weigh down** 1. to make bend down as with added weight 2. to bear down on so as to oppress —**weigh in** 1. to weigh (a boxer, jockey, etc.) before or after a contest so as to verify his declared weight 2. to be so weighed —**weigh/a·ble** *adj.* —**weigh/er** *n.*

**weigh²** (wā) *n. var. of* WAY, in **under weigh,** progressing, advancing: cf. UNDERWAY

**weight** (wāt) *n.* [OE. *wiht < wegan:* see WEIGH¹] 1. a quantity weighing a specified amount 2. heaviness as a quality; specif., the force of gravity acting on a body 3. how much a thing weighs or should weigh 4. *a)* any unit of heaviness *b)* any system of such units *[troy weight]:* see TABLES OF WEIGHTS and MEASURES in Supplements *c)* a piece of metal, etc. of a specific standard heaviness, used on a balance or scale in weighing 5. any block or mass used for its heaviness; specif., *a)* one used to hold light things down *b)* one used to drive a mechanism *[clock weights] c)* one lifted for exercise 6. *a)* any heavy thing or load *b)* a burden of responsibility, sorrow, etc. 7. importance or consequence 8. influence, power, or authority 9. the relative thickness or heaviness of a fabric or article of clothing 10. *Printing* the relative thickness of the lines in fonts 11. *Sports a)* any of the classifications for boxers and wrestlers based on what they weigh *b)* how many pounds a horse must carry for a race, including the weight of the jockey, saddle, and, often, added lead weights —*vt.* 1. to add weight to 2. to load down; burden 3. to control or manipulate so as to favor a particular side *[weighted evidence]* —**by weight** as determined by weighing —**carry weight** to be important, influential, etc. —**pull one's weight** to do one's share —**throw one's weight around** to use one's authority to gain an advantage

**weight·less** (-lis) *adj.* having little or no apparent weight; specif., free of or offsetting the pull of gravity —**weight/less·ly** *adv.* —**weight/less·ness** *n.*

**weight lifting** the athletic exercise or competitive sport of lifting barbells —**weight lifter**

**weight·y** (-ē) *adj.* weight/i·er, weight/i·est 1. very heavy 2. burdensome; oppressive 3. of great significance; serious 4. of great importance —**weight/i·ness** *n.*

**Wei·ma·ra·ner** (vī/mə rän/ər, wī/-) *n.* [< *Weimar,* where the breed was developed: see ff.] any of a breed of lean, medium-sized hunting dog with a smooth, gray coat

**Wei·mar Republic** (vī/mär; *E.* wī/mär) German Republic (1919–33), created at the city of Weimar (in what is now SW East Germany) & dissolved after Hitler became chancellor

**weir** (wir) *n.* [OE. *wer*] 1. a low dam built in a river to back up or divert water, as for a mill 2. a fence built in a stream or channel to catch fish

**weird** (wird) *adj.* [ult. < OE. *wyrd,* fate] 1. of or suggestive of ghosts or other supernatural things; unearthly, mysterious, eerie, etc. 2. strikingly odd, strange, etc.; fantastic; bizarre —**weird/ly** *adv.* —**weird/ness** *n.*

**Welch** (welch, welsh) *adj., n. var. of* WELSH

**welch** (welch, welsh) *vt., vi.* [Slang] *var. of* WELSH

**wel·come** (wel/kəm) *adj.* [< OE. *wilcuma,* orig. *n.,* a welcome guest < *willa,* pleasure + *cuma,* a guest] 1. gladly received *[a welcome guest]* 2. agreeable or gratifying *[welcome news]* 3. willingly permitted or invited *[welcome to use the library]* 4. under no obligation *[you're welcome]:* used in a conventional response to thanks —*n.* an act or expression of welcoming *[a hearty welcome]* —*interj.* you are welcome: an expression of cordial greeting —*vt.* **-comed, -com·ing** 1. to greet with pleasure and hospitality 2. to receive with pleasure or satisfaction *[to welcome criticism]* 3. to meet, receive, or acknowledge in a specified way —**bid welcome** to receive with cordial greetings —**wear out one's welcome** to come too often or stay too long —**wel/com·er** *n.*

**welcome mat** a doormat: chiefly in **put out the welcome mat,** to welcome enthusiastically

**weld** (weld) *vt.* [altered < obs. *well,* to weld] 1. to unite (pieces of metal, etc.) by heating until molten and fused or until soft enough to hammer or press together 2. to unite closely —*vi.* to be welded or capable of being welded —*n.* 1. a welding or being welded 2. the joint formed by welding —**weld/a·bil/i·ty** *n.* —**weld/a·ble** *adj.* —**weld/er** *n.*

**wel·fare** (wel/fer/) *n.* [see WELL² & FARE] 1. condition of health, happiness, and comfort; well-being 2. aid by government agencies for the poor, unemployed, etc. 3. same as WELFARE WORK —**on welfare** receiving government aid because of poverty, unemployment, etc.

**welfare state** a nation in which the government assumes responsibility for the welfare of the citizens, with regard to employment, medical care, social security, etc.

**welfare work** the organized effort of a community or organization to improve the living conditions and standards of its needy members —**welfare worker**

**wel·far·ism** (wel/fer'iz'm) *n.* 1. the policies and practices of a welfare state or of public welfare agencies 2. aid given by such a state or such agencies —**wel/far'ist** *n., adj.*

**wel·kin** (wel′kin) *n.* [OE. *wolcen*] [Archaic or Poet.] the vault of heaven, the sky, or the upper air

**well**[1] (wel) *n.* [OE. *wella*, akin to *weallan*, to boil up] 1. a natural spring and pool 2. a hole sunk into the earth to get water, gas, oil, etc. 3. an abundant source 4. any shaft like a well; esp., *a)* an open shaft in a building for a staircase *b)* a shaft to let light and air into a building or between buildings *c)* an elevator shaft *d) Naut.* an enclosure for the pumps in the hold of a ship *e)* in a fishing boat, a compartment for freshly caught fish 5. any of various containers for liquid, as an inkwell 6. a depression in a platter, broiler, etc. for catching meat juices —*vi., vt.* to pour forth as from a well; gush (*up, forth, down, out,* etc.)

**well**[2] (wel) *adv.* **bet′ter, best** [OE. *wel*] 1. in a pleasing or desirable way; satisfactorily 2. in a proper or friendly way 3. skillfully 4. fittingly 5. *a)* in comfort and plenty *b)* to one's advantage 6. with good reason; in justice 7. to a considerable degree, extent, etc. 8. thoroughly 9. with certainty; definitely *[you know very well why]* 10. intimately; closely *[to know a person well]* 11. in good spirit; with good grace *Well* is also used in hyphenated compounds, to mean *properly, satisfactorily, thoroughly,* etc. *[well-defined]* —*adj.* 1. proper, right, etc. *[it is well that he came]* 2. in good health 3. in good condition —*interj.* an exclamation used to express surprise, agreement, resignation, etc., or to introduce a remark —**as well** 1. besides; in addition 2. with equal reason or effect —**as well as** 1. just as much or as good as 2. in addition to —**wish someone well** to wish someone success or good luck

**we'll** (wēl, wil) 1. we shall 2. we will

**well-ad·vised** (wel′əd vīzd′) *adj.* showing or resulting from careful consideration or sound advice; wise

**Wel·land (Ship) Canal** (wel′ənd) canal of the St. Lawrence Seaway, in Ontario, Canada, between Lake Ontario & Lake Erie

**well-ap·point·ed** (wel′ə poin′tid) *adj.* excellently furnished or equipped *[a well-appointed office]*

**well·a·way** (wel′ə wā′) *interj.* [ME. *wei la wei*, lit., woe! lo! woe!] [Archaic] alas!: also **well′a·day′** (-dā′)

**well-bal·anced** (wel′bal′ənst) *adj.* 1. carefully balanced, adjusted, etc. *[a well-balanced meal]* 2. sane; sensible

**well-be·haved** (-bi hāvd′) *adj.* behaving well; polite

**well-be·ing** (-bē′iŋ) *n.* the state of being well, happy, or prosperous; welfare

**well-be·loved** (-bi luvd′, -luv′id) *adj.* 1. deeply loved 2. highly respected: used on formal occasions

**well·born** (-bôrn′) *adj.* born into a family of high social position

**well-bred** (-bred′) *adj.* 1. showing good breeding; courteous and considerate 2. of good stock: said of animals

**well-cho·sen** (-chō′z'n) *adj.* chosen with care; proper

**well-con·tent** (-kən tent′) *adj.* thoroughly pleased or satisfied: also **well′-con·tent′ed**

**well-dis·posed** (-dis pōzd′) *adj.* 1. suitably or properly placed or arranged 2. inclined to be friendly, kindly, or favorable (*toward* a person) or receptive (*to* an idea, etc.)

**well-done** (-dun′) *adj.* 1. performed with skill and efficiency 2. thoroughly cooked: said esp. of meat —*interj.* an exclamation of approval of another's action

**well-fa·vored** (-fā′vərd) *adj.* handsome; pretty

**well-fed** (-fed′) *adj.* showing the effect of eating much good food; sleek, plump or fat

**well-fixed** (-fikst′) *adj.* [Colloq.] wealthy; well-to-do

**well-found·ed** (-foun′did) *adj.* based on facts, good evidence, or sound judgment *[a well-founded suspicion]*

**well-groomed** (-grōomd′) *adj.* 1. carefully cared for *[a well-groomed horse, a well-groomed lawn]* 2. clean and neat; carefully washed, combed, dressed, etc.

**well-ground·ed** (-groun′did) *adj.* 1. having a thorough basic knowledge of a subject 2. based on good reasons

**well·head** (wel′hed′) *n.* 1. the source of a spring of water; spring 2. any source; fountainhead

**well-heeled** (wel′hēld′) *adj.* [Slang] rich; prosperous

**well-in·formed** (-in fôrmd′) *adj.* 1. having thorough knowledge of a subject 2. having considerable knowledge of many subjects, esp. those of current interest

**Wel·ling·ton** (wel′iŋ tən) capital of New Zealand; seaport on S North Island: pop. (of urban area) 179,000

**Wel·ling·ton** (wel′iŋ tən), 1st Duke of, (*Arthur Wellesley*) 1769–1852; Brit. general & statesman, born in Ireland

**Wellington (boot)** [after prec.] [*also* w- b-] a high boot, traditionally extending just above the knee in front and just below in back, now usually just below the knee

**well-in·ten·tioned** (-in ten′shənd) *adj.* having or showing good or kindly intentions, but often with bad results

**well-knit** (-nit′) *adj.* having a strong, compact, or sturdy structure

**well-known** (-nōn′) *adj.* 1. widely or generally known; famous 2. thoroughly known

**well-made** (-mād′) *adj.* 1. skillfully and strongly built 2. skillfully contrived or plotted *[a well-made play]*

**well-man·nered** (-man′ərd) *adj.* polite; courteous

**well-mean·ing** (-mē′niŋ) *adj.* 1. having good or kindly intentions 2. said or done with good intentions, but often unwisely or with bad results: also **well′-meant′** (-ment′)

**well-nigh** (-nī′) *adv.* very nearly; almost

**well-off** (-ôf′) *adj.* 1. in a favorable or fortunate condition or circumstance 2. prosperous; well-to-do

**well-or·dered** (-ôr′dərd) *adj.* properly or carefully organized

**well-pre·served** (-pri zurvd′) *adj.* in good condition or of good appearance, in spite of age

**well-read** (-red′) *adj.* 1. having read much (*in* a subject) 2. having a wide knowledge of books through having read much

**well-round·ed** (-roun′did) *adj.* 1. well planned for proper balance *[a well-rounded program]* 2. showing interest, ability, etc. in many fields 3. shapely

**Wells** (welz), **H** (erbert) **G** (eorge) 1866–1946; Eng. novelist & historian

**well-spo·ken** (wel′spō′k'n) *adj.* 1. speaking fluently, graciously, etc. 2. properly or aptly spoken

**well·spring** (wel′spriŋ′) *n.* 1. a spring or fountainhead 2. a source of abundant supply

**well-thought-of** (wel′thôt′uv′) *adj.* having a good reputation; of good repute

**well-timed** (-tīmd′) *adj.* timely; opportune

**well-to-do** (-tə dōō′) *adj.* prosperous; well-off; wealthy

**well-turned** (-turnd′) *adj.* 1. gracefully shaped 2. expressed or worded well *[a well-turned phrase]*

**well-wish·er** (-wish′ər) *n.* a person who wishes well to another or to a cause, etc. —**well′-wish′ing** *adj., n.*

**well-worn** (-wôrn′) *adj.* 1. much worn; much used 2. overused; trite *[a well-worn joke]*

**Welsh** (welsh, welch) *adj.* of Wales, its people, their language, etc. —*n.* the Brythonic language spoken in Wales —**the Welsh** the people of Wales

**welsh** (welsh, welch) *vt., vi.* [< ?] [Slang] 1. to cheat by failing to pay a bet or other debt 2. to evade (an obligation) Often with *on* —**welsh′er** *n.*

**Welsh cor·gi** (kôr′gē) [WELSH + W. *corgi* < *corr*, dwarf + *ci*, dog] either of two breeds of short-legged dog with a fox-like head, orig. from Wales

**Welsh·man** (welsh′mən, welch′-) *n., pl.* -**men** a native or inhabitant of Wales

**Welsh rabbit** [orig., a humorous usage] a dish of melted cheese, often mixed with ale or beer, served on crackers or toast: also **Welsh rarebit**

**Welsh terrier** a wire-haired terrier closely resembling the Airedale but smaller, orig. from Wales

**welt** (welt) *n.* [ME. *welte*] 1. a strip of leather in the seam between the sole and upper of a shoe to strengthen the joining 2. a strip of material at an edge or seam of a garment, etc. to reinforce or trim it 3. *a)* a ridge raised on the skin by the blow of a whip, etc. *b)* such a blow —*vt.* 1. to furnish with a welt 2. to raise welts on (the body) 3. [Colloq.] to beat severely; thrash

**wel·ter** (wel′tər) *vi.* [MDu. *welteren*] 1. to roll about or wallow, as a pig in mud 2. to be deeply involved *[to welter in sin]* 3. to be soaked, stained, etc. *[to welter in blood]* —*n.* 1. a tossing and tumbling 2. a turmoil

**wel·ter·weight** (wel′tər wāt′) *n.* [prob. < WELT + -ER + WEIGHT] a boxer or wrestler between a lightweight and a middleweight (in boxing, 136–147 pounds)

**wen** (wen) *n.* [OE. *wenn*] a harmless skin tumor, esp. of the scalp, consisting of a sebaceous cyst

**wench** (wench) *n.* [OE. *wencel*, a child] 1. a girl or young woman: now a somewhat derogatory or jocular term 2. [Archaic] *a)* a country girl *b)* a female servant *c)* a prostitute or loose woman —*vi.* to be sexually promiscuous with prostitutes or loose women —**wench′er** *n.*

**wend** (wend) *vt.* **wend′ed** *or archaic* **went, wend′ing** [OE. *wendan*, to turn] to proceed on (one's way)

**went** (went) [old *pt.* of WEND, used to replace missing form of GO] *pt. of* GO

**wept** (wept) *pt. & pp. of* WEEP

**were** (wur; *unstressed* wər) [OE. *wæron*] *pl. & 2d pers. sing., past indic., and the past subj., of* BE

**we're** (wir) we are

**weren't** (wurnt) were not

**were·wolf** (wir′woolf′, wur′-, wer′-) *n., pl.* -**wolves′** (-woolvz′) [ < OE. < *wer*, a man + *wulf*, a wolf] Folklore a person changed into a wolf or able to take the form of a wolf at will: also sp. **wer′wolf′,** *pl.* **wer′wolves′**

**wert** (wurt; *unstressed* wərt) *archaic 2d pers. sing., past indic. & subj., of* BE: used with thou

**wes·kit** (wes′kit) *n.* [ < WAISTCOAT] a vest or waistcoat

**Wes·ley** (wes′lē, wez′-) 1. [ < the surname *Wesley*] a masculine name 2. **Charles,** 1707–88; Eng. clergyman: brother of *ff.* 3. **John,** 1703–91; Eng. clergyman & founder of the Methodist Church

**Wes·ley·an** (wes′lē ən, wez′-) *adj.* of John Wesley or the Methodist Church —*n.* a follower of John Wesley; Methodist —**Wes′ley·an·ism** *n.*

**Wes·sex** (wes′iks) former Anglo-Saxon kingdom in S England

**west** (west) *n.* [OE.] **1.** the direction to the left of a person facing north; direction in which sunset occurs (270° on the compass, opposite east) **2.** a region or district in or toward this direction **3.** [W-] the Western Hemisphere, or the Western Hemisphere and Europe; the Occident **4.** [W-] the Western Roman Empire —*adj.* **1.** in, of, to, or toward the west **2.** from the west **3.** [W-] designating the western part of a country, etc. —*adv.* in or toward the west —**the West 1.** the western part of the U.S., esp. the region west of the Mississippi **2.** the U.S. and its non-Communist allies in Europe and the Western Hemisphere

**West** (west), Benjamin 1738–1820; Am. painter in England

**West Al·lis** (al′is) [after the *Allis*-Chalmers Co. there] city in SE Wis.: suburb of Milwaukee: pop. 64,000

**West Berlin** W section of Berlin, constituting a city associated with West Germany: pop. 2,141,000: cf. BERLIN

**west·bound** (-bound′) *adj.* going westward

**West Co·vi·na** (kō vē′nə) [*Covina* said locally to mean "place of vines"] city in SW Calif.: pop. 80,000

**West End** W section of London, England

**west·er·ly** (wes′tər lē) *adj., adv.* **1.** toward the west **2.** from the west —*n., pl.* -**lies** a wind from the west

**west·ern** (-tərn) *adj.* **1.** in, of, or toward the west **2.** from the west **3.** [W-] of or characteristic of the West —*n.* a story, motion picture, etc. about cowboys or frontiersmen in the western U.S. —**west′ern·most′** (-mōst′) *adj.*

**Western Australia** state of Australia, occupying the W third of the continent

**Western Church** that part of the Catholic Church which recognizes the Pope and follows the Latin Rite; the Roman Catholic Church

**west·ern·er** (wes′tər nər) *n.* a native or inhabitant of the west, specif. [W-] of the western part of the U.S.

**Western Hemisphere** that half of the earth that includes North & South America

**west·ern·ize** (wes′tərn īz′) *vt.* -**ized′**, -**iz′ing** to make western in character, etc. —**west′ern·i·za′tion** *n.*

**Western (omelet)** an omelet prepared with diced green pepper, onion, and ham

**Western Roman Empire** the W part of the Roman Empire, from its separation (395 A.D.) to its overthrow (476)

**Western saddle** [also **w- s-**] a heavy saddle of the kind used by cowboys, with a high cantle and pommel and a horn projecting above the pommel

**Western Samoa** country in the South Pacific, consisting of two large islands & several small ones: a member of the Commonwealth: 1,130 sq. mi.; pop. 146,000

**West Germany** W section of Germany, constituting a country in NC Europe: 95,735 sq. mi.; pop. 59,974,000; cap. Bonn: cf. GERMANY

**West Haven** city in SW Conn., on Long Island Sound: suburb of New Haven: pop. 53,000

**West Indies** large group of islands between N. America & S. America: it includes the Greater Antilles, Lesser Antilles, & Bahamas —**West Indian**

**West·ing·house** (wes′tiŋ hous′), George 1846–1914; U.S. inventor & manufacturer

**West Ir·i·an** (ir′ē ən) province of Indonesia, occupying the W half of the island of New Guinea: c.160,000 sq. mi.

**West·land** (west′lənd, -land′) [from its location in the county] city in SE Mich.: suburb of Detroit: pop. 85,000

**West·min·ster Abbey** (west′min′stər) Gothic church in London where English monarchs are crowned: burial place for English monarchs and other famous persons

**west-north·west** (west′nôrth′west′; *nautical* -nôr′-) *n.* the direction halfway between due west and northwest; 22°30′ north of due west —*adj., adv.* **1.** in or toward this direction **2.** from this direction

**West Palm Beach** city in SE Fla., on a lagoon opposite Palm Beach: pop. 63,000 (met. area 552,000)

**West Point** military reservation in SE N.Y., on the west bank of the Hudson: site of the U.S. Military Academy

**west-south·west** (west′south′west′; *nautical* -sou′-) *n.* the direction halfway between due west and southwest; 22°30′ south of due west —*adj., adv.* **1.** in or toward this direction **2.** from this direction

**West Virginia** E State of the U.S., northwest of Va.: 24,181 sq. mi.; pop. 1,950,000; cap. Charleston: abbrev. **W.Va., WV** —**West Virginian**

**west·ward** (-wərd) *adv., adj.* toward the west: also **west′wards** *adv.* —*n.* a westward direction, point, or region

**west·ward·ly** (-lē) *adv., adj.* **1.** toward the west **2.** from the west

**wet** (wet) *adj.* **wet′ter, wet′test** [OE. *wæt*] **1.** covered or soaked with water or other liquid **2.** rainy; misty **3.** not yet dry [*wet* paint] **4.** preserved in liquid **5.** using, or done

with or in, water or other liquid **6.** permitting or favoring the sale of alcoholic liquors —*n.* water, rain, moisture, etc. —*vt., vi.* **wet** or **wet′ted, wet′ting 1.** to make or become wet (often with *through* or *down*) **2.** to make (a bed, oneself, etc.) wet by urination —**all wet** [Slang] wrong; in error —**wet behind the ears** [Colloq.] young and inexperienced —**wet′ly** *adv.* —**wet′ness** *n.* —**wet′ta·ble** *adj.*

**wet·back** (wet′bak′) *n.* [from the fact that many enter by swimming or wading the Rio Grande] [Colloq.] a Mexican agricultural laborer who illegally enters the U.S. to work

**wet bar** a bar or serving counter, as in a recreation room, equipped with running water

**wet blanket** a person or thing that dampens or lessens the enthusiasm or gaiety of others

**wet cell** a voltaic cell in which the electrolyte is a liquid

**weth·er** (weth′ər) *n.* [OE.] a castrated male sheep

**wet·land** (wet′land′) *n.* [*usually pl.*] swamps or marshes

**wet nurse** a woman hired to suckle another woman's child —**wet-nurse** (wet′nurs′) *vt.* -**nursed′**, -**nurs′ing**

**wet suit** a closefitting, usually one-piece suit of rubber, worn by skin divers for warmth

**we've** (wēv) we have

**wf, w.f.** *Printing* wrong font

**WGmc.** West Germanic

**whack** (hwak, wak) *vt., vi.* [echoic] [Colloq.] to strike or slap with a sharp, resounding blow —*n.* [Colloq.] a sharp, resounding blow, or its sound —**at a** (or **one**) **whack** [Colloq.] at one time and quickly or without pausing —**have** (or **take**) **a whack at** [Colloq.] **1.** to aim a blow at **2.** to make an attempt at —**out of whack** [Colloq.] not in proper condition —**whack off** [Colloq.] to separate or remove as by a chopping blow —**whack′er** *n.*

**whacked** (hwakt, wakt) *adj.* **1.** [Chiefly Brit. Colloq.] very tired; exhausted **2.** [Slang] intoxicated

**whack·ing** (hwak′iŋ, wak′-) *adj.* [Chiefly Brit. Colloq.] big; great

**whack·y** (-ē) *adj.* -**i·er**, -**i·est** [Slang] *same as* WACKY

**whale¹** (hwāl, wāl) *n., pl.* **whales, whale**: see PLURAL, II, D, 1 [OE. *hwæl*] any of various large mammals that live in the sea and have a fishlike form, with a flat, horizontal tail and with front limbs modified into flippers; esp., any of the larger mammals of this kind (up to 100 ft. in length), as distinguished from the porpoises and dolphins: see TOOTHED WHALE, WHALEBONE WHALE —*vi.* **whaled, whal′ing** to hunt whales —**a whale of a** [Colloq.] an exceptionally large, fine, etc. example of (a class of persons or things)

**whale²** (hwāl, wāl) *vt.* **whaled, whal′ing** [prob. var. of WALE] [Colloq.] to beat; whip; thrash

**whale·back** (hwāl′bak′, wāl′-) *n.* **1.** something rounded on top like a whale's back **2.** a freight steamer with the bow and upper deck rounded so water runs off

**whale·boat** (-bōt′) *n.* **1.** a long rowboat, pointed at both ends: used formerly by whalers **2.** a similar lifeboat

**whale·bone** (-bōn′) *n.* **1.** horny, elastic material hanging in fringed sheets from the upper jaw or palate of whalebone whales and straining the tiny sea animals they feed on **2.** something made of this, as a corset stay

**whalebone whale** any of a main division of whales, as the blue whale, having whalebone in the mouth and no teeth

**whal·er** (hwā′lər, wā′-) *n.* **1.** a ship used in whaling **2.** a man whose work is whaling: also **whale′man**, *pl.* -**men**

**whal·ing** (-liŋ) *n.* the work or trade of hunting and killing whales for their blubber, whalebone, etc.

**wham** (hwam, wam) *interj.* a sound imitating a heavy blow or explosion —*n.* a heavy blow or impact —*vt., vi.* **whammed, wham′ming** to strike, explode, etc. loudly

**wham·my** (-ē) *n., pl.* -**mies** [Slang] a jinx or the evil eye: usually in **put a** (or **the**) **whammy on**

**whang** (hwaŋ, waŋ) *vt.* [echoic] **1.** to strike with a resounding blow **2.** [Dial.] to thrash —*vi.* to make a loud noise by hitting —*n.* the noise or blow so made

**wharf** (hwôrf, wôrf) *n., pl.* **wharves** (hwôrvz, wôrvz), **wharfs** [OE. *hwerf*, a dam < base of *hweorfan*, to turn] a platform built along or out from the shore, where ships can dock and load or unload; pier; dock —*vt.* **1.** to bring to a wharf **2.** to unload or store on a wharf

**wharf·age** (-ij) *n.* **1.** the use of a wharf **2.** a fee charged for this **3.** wharves collectively

**Whar·ton** (hwôr′t'n, wôr′-), **Edith** (born *Edith Newbold Jones*) 1862–1937; U.S. novelist

**what** (hwut, hwät, wut, wät; *unstressed* hwət, wət) *pron.* [OE. *hwæt*, neut. of *hwa*, who] **1.** which thing, event, etc.: used in asking questions or in asking someone to repeat, explain, specify, etc. [*what* is that object? you told him *what*?] **2.** that which or those which: used as a relative pronoun [to know *what* one wants, not *what* it was] : also used elliptically for "what it is," "what to do," etc. [I'll tell you *what*] —*n.* the nature (*of* an event) [the *what* and

why of his exile] —**adj. 1.** which or which kind of: used interrogatively or relatively [*what* man told you that? I know *what* books you like] **2.** as much, or as many, as [take *what* time (or men) you need] **3.** how great, surprising, etc.: in exclamations [*what* joy!] —**adv. 1.** in what respect? to what degree? how? [*what* does it matter?] **2.** in some manner or degree; in part; partly (usually with *with*) [*what* with singing and joking, the time passed quickly] **3.** how greatly, surprisingly, etc. [*what* sad news!] —**conj.** that: in **but what**, but that [never doubt *but what* he loves you] —**interj.** an exclamation of surprise, anger, etc. [*what!* no dinner?] —**and what not** and other things of all sorts —**what about** what do you think, know, etc. concerning? —**what for 1.** why? **2.** [Slang] punishment [you'll get *what for*] —**what have you** [Colloq.] anything similar [games, toys, or *what have you*] —**what if 1.** what would happen if **2.** what difference would it make if —**what's what** [Colloq.] the true state of affairs —**what the (heck, devil, etc.) 1.** an exclamation of surprise **2.** what: used emphatically —**what though** no matter if
**what·ev·er** (hwət ev′ər, wət-) *pron.* **1.** what: used for emphasis; specif., *a*) which thing, event, etc.: used in questions [*whatever* can it be?] *b*) anything that [tell her *whatever* you like] *c*) no matter what [*whatever* you do, don't rush] **2.** [Colloq.] anything of the sort [use pen, pencil, or *whatever*] —**adj. 1.** of no matter what type, degree, etc. [make *whatever* repairs are needed] **2.** being who it may be [*whatever* man told you that, it isn't true] **3.** of any kind [no plans *whatever*] Also [Poet.] **what·e'er′** (-er′)
**what·not** (hwut′nät′, hwät′-, wut′-, wät′-) *n.* **1.** a nondescript thing **2.** a set of open shelves, as for bric-a-brac
**what's** (hwuts, hwäts, wuts, wäts) what is
**what·so·ev·er** (hwut′sō ev′ər, hwät-′, wut′-, wät′-) *pron., adj.* whatever: used for emphasis: also [Poet.] **what′so·e'er′** (-er′)
**wheal**[1] (hwēl, wēl) *n.* [akin to OE. *hwelian*, to suppurate] **1.** formerly, a pustule; pimple **2.** a small, raised patch of skin, as from an insect bite or hives
**wheal**[2] (hwēl, wēl) *n. same as* WEAL[1]
**wheat** (hwēt, wēt) *n.* see PLURAL, II, D, 3 [OE. *hwǣte*] **1.** any of a group of cereal grasses with dense spikes that grow upright and bear grains that are threshed to remove the chaff **2.** such grain, used for flour, cereals, pasta, etc.
**wheat cake** a pancake of whole-wheat flour
**wheat·en** (-'n) *adj.* **1.** made of wheat or wheat flour **2.** of the pale-yellow color of wheat
**wheat germ 1.** the wheat-kernel embryo, rich in vitamins, milled out as an oily flake **2.** the milled flakes
**whee** (hwē, wē; *with prolonged vowel*) *interj.* an exclamation expressing joy, exultation, etc.
**whee·dle** (hwē′d'l, wē′-) *vt., vi.* **-dled, -dling** [< ? G. *wedeln*, to wag the tail, hence to flatter] **1.** to influence or persuade (a person) by flattery, soothing words, coaxing, etc. **2.** to get (something) by coaxing or flattery —**whee′dler** *n.*
**wheel** (hwēl, wēl) *n.* [OE. *hweol*] **1.** a solid disk, or a circular frame connected by spokes to a central hub, capable of turning on a central axis **2.** anything like a wheel in shape, movement, etc. **3.** a device having as its main part a wheel or wheels; specif., *a*) a medieval torture instrument that was a circular frame on which a victim was painfully stretched *b*) a wheel with projecting handles, to control a ship's course *c*) *short for* POTTER'S WHEEL, SPINNING WHEEL, etc. *d*) [Colloq.] a bicycle *e*) [*pl.*] [Slang] an automobile **4.** [*usually pl.*] the moving, propelling, or controlling forces or agencies [the *wheels* of progress] **5.** a turning movement **6.** [Slang] an important or influential person: also **big wheel** —*vt., vi.* **1.** to move or roll on wheels or in a wheeled vehicle **2.** to turn round; rotate, revolve, pivot, etc. **3.** to turn so as to reverse direction, attitude, etc. (often with *about*) —**at the wheel 1.** steering a ship, motor vehicle, etc. **2.** in charge; directing activities —**wheel and deal** [Slang] to behave in an aggressive, flamboyant way, as in a business deal —**wheel of fortune** the changes, good and bad, that occur in life —**wheeled** *adj.*
**wheel and axle** a grooved wheel fixed to a shaft or drum, used for lifting weights: the turning of the wheel by a rope in the groove winds a rope on the shaft or drum
**wheel·bar·row** (-bar′ō, -ber′ō) *n.* a shallow, open box for moving small loads, having a single wheel in front, two legs in back, and two shafts with handles for raising the vehicle off its legs and pushing or pulling it
**wheel·base** (-bās′) *n.* in a motor vehicle, the distance in inches from the center of the hub of a front wheel to the center of the hub of the corresponding back wheel
**wheel·chair** (-cher′) *n.* a chair mounted on large wheels, used in moving about by persons unable to walk
**wheel·er** (-ər) *n.* **1.** a person or thing that wheels **2.** *same as* WHEEL HORSE (sense 1) **3.** something having

a specified kind or number of wheels [two-*wheeler*]
**wheel·er-deal·er** (hwēl′ər dēl′ər, wēl′-) *n.* [Slang] a person who wheels and deals: see phrase at entry WHEEL
**wheel horse 1.** the horse, or one of the horses, harnessed nearest the front wheels of a vehicle **2.** a person who works especially hard and effectively in any enterprise
**wheel·house** (-hous′) *n. same as* PILOTHOUSE
**wheel·ie** (-ē) *n.* a stunt performed on a motorcycle or bicycle, in which the front wheel is raised so that the vehicle is balanced for a moment on its rear wheel
**wheel·wright** (-rīt′) *n.* a person who makes and repairs wagon and carriage wheels
**wheeze** (hwēz, wēz) *vi.* **wheezed, wheez′ing** [ON. *hvaesa*, to hiss] **1.** to breathe hard with a whistling, breathy sound, as in asthma **2.** to make a sound like this [the old organ *wheezed*] —*vt.* to utter with a sound of wheezing —*n.* **1.** an act or sound of wheezing **2.** [Slang] a trite remark, joke, or gag —**wheez′er** *n.* —**wheez′ing·ly** *adv.*
**wheez·y** (hwē′zē, wē′-) *adj.* **wheez′i·er, wheez′i·est** wheezing or characterized by wheezing —**wheez′i·ly** *adv.*
**whelk**[1] (hwelk, welk) *n.* [OE. *wioluc*] any of various large sea snails with spiral shells, esp. those species used in Europe for food
**whelk**[2] (hwelk, welk) *n.* [OE. *hwylca*] **1.** a pimple or pustule **2.** *same as* WEAL[1]
**whelm** (hwelm, welm) *vt.* [? merging of OE. *-hwelfan*, to overwhelm, with *helmian*, to cover] **1.** to submerge or engulf **2.** to overwhelm

WHELK
(3 in. long)

**whelp** (hwelp, welp) *n.* [OE. *hwelp*] **1.** a young dog; puppy **2.** a young lion, tiger, wolf, etc.; cub **3.** a youth or child: contemptuous usage —*vt., vi.* to give birth to whelps
**when** (hwen, wen; *unstressed* hwən, wən) *adv.* [OE. *hwænne*] **1.** *a*) at what time? *b*) on what occasion or under what circumstances? *c*) at what point? [*when* shall I stop pouring?] **2.** earlier and in other circumstances [I knew him *when*] —*conj.* **1.** at the time or point that [he told us *when* we sat down] **2.** at which [a time *when* men must speak out] **3.** as soon as [come *when* I call] **4.** at whatever time that [he rested *when* he could] **5.** although [to object *when* there's no reason to do so] **6.** if [how can he help *when* they won't let him?] —*pron.* what time or which time [until *when* will you stay?] —*n.* the time or moment (*of* an event) [the *when* and where of his arrest]
**when·as** (hwen az′, wen-) *conj.* [Archaic] **1.** when **2.** inasmuch as **3.** whereas
**whence** (hwens, wens) *adv.* [OE. *hwanan*] from what place, source, cause, etc.; from where [*whence* do you come? *whence* did he get his facts?] —*conj.* **1.** to the place from which [return *whence* you came] **2.** because of which fact
**whence·so·ev·er** (hwens′sō ev′ər, wens′-) *adv., conj.* from whatever place, source, or cause
**when·ev·er** (hwen ev′ər, wen-, hwən-, wən-) *adv.* [Colloq.] when: used for emphasis [*whenever* will he learn?] —*conj.* at whatever time; on whatever occasion [visit us *whenever* you can] Also [Poet.] **when′e'er′** (-er′)
**when·so·ev·er** (hwen′sō ev′ər, wen′-) *adv., conj.* whenever: used for emphasis: also [Poet.] **when′so·e'er′** (-er′)
**where** (hwer, wer; *unstressed* hwər, wər) *adv.* [OE. *hwǣr*] **1.** in or at what place? [*where* is the car?] **2.** to or toward what place? [*where* did he go?] **3.** in what situation? [*where* will we be if we lose?] **4.** in what respect? [*where* is she to blame?] **5.** from what place or source? [*where* did you find out?] —*conj.* **1.** in or at what place [he knows *where* it is] **2.** in or at which place [we came home, *where* we ate dinner] **3.** in or at the place or situation in which [he is *where* he should be] **4.** in whatever place, situation, or respect in which [there is never peace *where* men are greedy] **5.** *a*) to or toward the place to which [he'll go *where* we go] *b*) to a place in which [send help *where* it's needed] **6.** to or toward whatever place [go *where* you please] **7.** [Colloq.] *same as* WHEREAS The use of *where* in place of *that* to introduce a noun clause is objected to by some [I see *where* taxes are going up] —*pron.* **1.** the place or situation in, at, or to which [it is a mile from *where* he lives] **2.** what or which place [*where* are you from?] —*n.* the place (*of* an event) [tell us the *where* of the party]
**where·a·bouts** (hwer′ə bouts′, wer′-) *adv.* near or at what place? where? —*n.* the place where a person or thing is [do you know his *whereabouts?*]
**where·as** (hwer az′, wer-, hwər-, wər-) *conj.* **1.** in view of the fact that: used in a formal document **2.** but on the other hand; while [she is slender, *whereas* he is stout] —*n., pl.* **-as·es** a statement beginning with "whereas"
**where·at** (-at′) *adv.* [Archaic] at what? [*whereat* was he angry?] —*conj.* [Archaic] at which point [he left, *whereat* she began to weep]
**where·by** (-bī′) *adv.* [Archaic] by what? how? [*whereby* did

you expect to profit?] —*conj.* by which; by means of which [a plan *whereby* to make money]

**where·fore** (hwer′fôr′, wer′-) *adv.* [Archaic] for what reason or purpose? why? [*wherefore* are you angry?] —*conj.* 1. for which [the reason *wherefore* we have met] 2. because of which; therefore [we won, *wherefore* rejoice] —*n.* the reason; cause

**where·from** (hwer frum′, wer-) *adv., conj.* from which

**where·in** (-in′) *adv.* [Archaic] in what way? how? [*wherein* is it wrong?] —*conj.* in which [the room *wherein* he lay]

**where·of** (-uv′) *adv., conj.* of what, which, or whom

**where·on** (-än′) *adv.* [Archaic] on what? [*whereon* do you rely?] —*conj.* on which [the hill *whereon* we stand]

**where·so·ev·er** (hwer′sō ev′ər, wer′-) *adv., conj.* wherever: used for emphasis: also [Poet.] **where′e·er′** (-er′)

**where·to** (-tōō′) *adv.* to what? toward what place, direction, or end? —*conj.* to which

**where·up·on** (hwer′ə pän′, wer′-; hwer′ə pän, wer′-) *adv.* [Archaic] upon what? whereon? —*conj.* 1. upon which [the ground *whereupon* he had fallen] 2. at which [she told a joke, *whereupon* he laughed]

**wher·ev·er** (hwer ev′ər, wer-, hwər-, wər-) *adv.* [Colloq.] where: used for emphasis [*wherever* did you hear that?] —*conj.* in, at, or to whatever place or situation [he thinks of us, *wherever* he is] Also [Poet.] **wher·e′er′** (-er′)

**where·with** (hwer with′, wer-; -with′) *adv.* [Archaic] with what? [*wherewith* shall he be saved?] —*conj.* with which [lacking the money *wherewith* to pay him] —*pron.* that with which [to have *wherewith* to build]

**where·with·al** (hwer′with ôl′, wer′-; -with-) *n.* that with which something can be done; necessary means, esp. money (usually with *the*) [the *wherewithal* to continue one's education] —*adv., conj. archaic var. of* WHEREWITH

**wher·ry** (hwer′ē, wer′-) *n., pl.* **-ries** [< ? ME. *whirren*, to whir, with idea of fast movement] 1. a light rowboat used on rivers 2. a racing scull for one person 3. [Brit.] a large, broad, but light barge —*vt.* **-ried, -ry·ing** to transport in a wherry

**whet** (hwet, wet) *vt.* **whet′ted, whet′ting** [OE. *hwettan* < *hwæt*, keen] 1. to sharpen by rubbing or grinding (the edge of a knife or tool); hone 2. to stimulate [to whet the appetite] —*n.* 1. an act of whetting 2. something that whets —**whet′ter** *n.*

**wheth·er** (hweth′ər, weth′ər) *conj.* [OE. *hwæther*] 1. if it be the case or fact that [ask *whether* she will help?] 2. in case; in either case that: used to introduce alternatives [*whether* it rains or snows] 3. either [*whether* by accident or design] —**whether or no** in any case

**whet·stone** (hwet′stōn′, wet′-) *n.* an abrasive stone for sharpening knives or other edged tools

**whew** (hyōō, hwyōō) *interj.* [echoic] an exclamation of relief, surprise, dismay, etc.

**whey** (hwā, wā) *n.* [OE. *hwæg*] the thin, watery part of milk, which separates from the thicker part (curds) after coagulation —**whey′ey** (-ē) *adj.*

**whey·face** (-fās′) *n.* 1. a pale or pallid face 2. a person having such a face —**whey′faced′** *adj.*

**which** (hwich, wich) *pron.* [OE. *hwylc*] 1. what one (or ones) of the persons, things, or events mentioned or implied? [*which* do you want?] 2. the one (or ones) that [he knows *which* he wants] 3. that: used as a relative referring to the thing or event specified in the antecedent [her hat, *which* is blue; the boat *which* sank] 4. any that; whichever [take *which* you like] 5. a thing or fact that [you are late —*which* reminds me, where is Joe?] —*adj.* 1. what one or ones (of the number mentioned or implied) [*which* man (or men) came?] 2. whatever [try *which* plan you like] 3. being the one just mentioned [he is old, *which* fact is important]

**which·ev·er** (hwich ev′ər, wich-) *pron., adj.* 1. any one (of two or more) [he may choose *whichever* (desk) he likes] 2. no matter which [*whichever* (desk) he chooses, they won't be pleased]

**which·so·ev·er** (hwich′sō ev′ər, wich′-) *pron., adj.* whichever: used for emphasis

**whick·er** (hwik′ər, wik′-) *vi.* [echoic] 1. to utter a partly stifled laugh; snicker; titter 2. to neigh or whinny

**whiff** (hwif, wif) *n.* [echoic] 1. a light puff or gust of air or wind; breath 2. a slight gust of odor [a *whiff* of garlic] 3. an inhaling or exhaling of tobacco smoke —*vt.* 1. to blow with a puff or gust; waft 2. to smoke (a pipe, etc.) —*vi.* 1. to blow or move in puffs 2. to inhale or exhale whiffs, as in smoking —**whiff′er** *n.*

**whif·fet** (-it) *n.* [dim. of prec.] 1. a little whiff 2. a small dog 3. [Colloq.] an insignificant person

**whif·fle** (-'l) *vi.* **-fled, -fling** [freq. of WHIFF] 1. to blow in gusts: said of the wind 2. to shift; veer; vacillate —*vt.* to blow or scatter with or as with a puff of wind —**whif′fler** *n.*

**whif·fle·tree** (-'l trē′) *n. var. of* WHIPPLETREE

**Whig** (hwig, wig) *n.* [< *whiggamore* (applied to Scot. Presbyterians who marched on Edinburgh in 1648) < WScot. < *whig*, a cry to urge on horses + *mare*, a horse] 1. a member of a political party in England (fl. 18th to mid-19th cent.) which championed popular rights: it later became the Liberal Party 2. in the American Revolution, a person who opposed Great Britain and supported the Revolution 3. a member of an American political party (c.1836–1856) opposing the Democratic Party —*adj.* of or being a Whig —**Whig′gish** *adj.* —**Whig′gism, Whig′ger·y** *n.*

**while** (hwīl, wīl) *n.* [OE. *hwīl*] a period of time [a short *while*] —*conj.* 1. during or throughout the time that [we talked *while* we ate] 2. at the same time that [*while* you're up, close the door] 3. *a*) although [*while* she isn't pretty, she is charming] *b*) whereas [the walls are green, *while* the ceiling is white] —*vt.* whiled, whil′ing to spend (time) in a pleasant way [to *while* away the hours] —**between whiles** at intervals —**the while** during this very time —**worth (one's) while** worth one's time; profitable

**whiles** (hwīlz, wīlz) *adv.* [Chiefly Scot.] *same as* SOMETIMES —*conj.* [Archaic or Dial.] *same as* WHILE

**whi·lom** (hwī′ləm, wī′-) *adv.* [OE. *hwilum*, dat. pl. of *hwil*, while] [Archaic] at one time; formerly —*adj.* formerly such; former [their *whilom* friends]

**whilst** (hwīlst, wīlst) *conj.* [Dial.] *same as* WHILE

**whim** (hwim, wim) *n.* [short for WHIM-WHAM] a sudden fancy; idle and passing notion; caprice

**whim·per** (hwim′pər, wim′-) *vi.* [? akin to WHINE] to cry with low, whining, broken sounds —*vt.* to utter with a whimper —*n.* a whimpering sound or cry —**whim′per·er** *n.* —**whim′per·ing·ly** *adv.*

**whim·si·cal** (hwim′zi k'l, wim′-) *adj.* 1. full of whims or whimsy; having odd notions 2. different in an odd way; freakish 3. unpredictable —**whim′si·cal′i·ty** (-kal′ə tē), *pl.* **-ties, whim′si·cal·ness** *n.* —**whim′si·cal·ly** *adv.*

**whim·sy** (hwim′zē, wim′-) *n., pl.* **-sies** [prob. < ff.] 1. an odd fancy; idle notion; whim 2. quaint or fanciful humor Also sp. **whim′sey**, *pl.* **-seys**

**whim-wham** (hwim′hwam′, wim′wam′) *n.* [< ?] 1. a bauble; trinket 2. an odd notion; whim —**the whim-whams** [Colloq.] a nervous feeling; the jitters

**whin** (hwin, win) *n.* [prob. < Scand.] *same as* FURZE

**whin·chat** (hwin′chat′, win′-) *n.* [prec. + *chat*, a warbler] a brown and buff migrating European songbird

**whine** (hwīn, wīn) *vi.* **whined, whin′ing** [OE. *hwinan*] 1. *a*) to utter a peevish, high-pitched sound, as in complaint, distress, etc. *b*) to make a drawn-out, high-pitched sound 2. to complain or beg in a childish, undignified way —*vt.* to utter with a whine —*n.* 1. the act or sound of whining 2. a complaint uttered in a whining tone —**whin′er** *n.* —**whin′i·ness** *n.* —**whin′ing·ly** *adv.* —**whin′y, whin′ey** *adj.* **whin′i·er, whin′i·est**

**whing·ding** (hwin′din′, win′-) *n.* [Slang] *same as* WINGDING

**whin·ny** (hwin′ē, win′ē) *vi.* **-nied, -ny·ing** [prob. < or akin to WHINE] to neigh in a low, gentle way: said of a horse —*vt.* to express with a whinny —*n., pl.* **-nies** the whinnying of a horse, or a similar sound

**whip** (hwip, wip) *vt.* **whipped, whip′ping** [MDu. *wippen*, to swing] 1. to move, pull, throw, etc. suddenly (usually with *out, off, up,* etc.) [to *whip* out a knife] 2. to strike, as with a strap, rod, etc.; lash; beat 3. to drive, urge, etc. by or as by whipping 4. to strike as a whip does [the rain *whipped* her face] 5. to wind (cord or thread) around (a rope, etc.), so as to prevent fraying 6. to fish (a stream, etc.) by making repeated casts 7. to beat (eggs, cream, etc.) into a froth with a fork, mixer, etc. 8. to sew (a seam, etc.) with a loose, overcasting or overhand stitch 9. [Colloq.] to defeat or outdo —*vi.* 1. to move, go, etc. quickly and suddenly [he *whipped* out the door] 2. to flap about in a whiplike manner [flags *whip* in high wind] —*n.* 1. an instrument for striking or flogging, consisting of a rod with a lash attached to one end 2. a blow, cut, etc. made with or as with a whip 3. a person who uses a whip, as a coachman 4. an officer of a political party in Congress, Parliament, etc. who enforces party discipline, attendance, etc.: also **party whip** 5. a whipping motion 6. a dessert made of sugar and whipped cream, beaten egg whites, etc., and often fruit 7. something resembling a whip in its action —**whip into shape** [Colloq.] to bring by vigorous action into a desired condition —**whip up** 1. to rouse; excite 2. [Colloq.] to prepare quickly and efficiently —**whip′like′** *adj.* —**whip′per** *n.*

**whip·cord** (-kôrd′) *n.* 1. a hard, twisted or braided cord used for whiplashes, etc. 2. a strong worsted cloth with a hard, diagonally ribbed surface

**whip hand** 1. the hand in which a driver holds his whip 2. the position of advantage or control

**whip·lash** (-lash′) *n.* **1.** the lash of a whip **2.** a sudden, severe jolting of the neck backward and then forward, as caused by the impact of a rear-end automobile collision

**whipped cream** rich sweet cream stiffened as by whipping and used as a topping on desserts, etc.: also **whip cream**

**whip·per·snap·per** (hwip′ər snap′ər, wip′-) *n.* [< *whip-snapper*, one who snaps whips] a young or unimportant person who does not seem to show proper respect for those older or more important than himself

**whip·pet** (hwip′it, wip′-) *n.* [dim. < WHIP] a swift dog resembling a small greyhound, used in racing

**whip·ping** (-iŋ) *n.* **1.** a flogging or beating, as in punishment **2.** cord, twine, etc. used to whip, or bind

WHIPPET
(18–22 in. high at shoulder)

**whipping boy** *same as* SCAPE-GOAT (sense 2)

**whipping cream** sweet cream with a high percentage of butter-fat, that can be whipped until stiff

**whipping post** a post to which offenders are tied to be whipped as a legal punishment

**whip·ple·tree** (hwip′'l trē′, wip′-) *n.* [< WHIP + TREE] *same as* SINGLETREE

**whip·poor·will** (hwip′ər wil′, wip′-) *n., pl.* **-wills′**, **-will′**: see PLURAL, II, D, 1 [echoic] a grayish bird of eastern N. America, one of the goatsuckers

**whip·saw** (hwip′sô′, wip′-) *n.* a long-bladed saw; esp., one with a handle at each end for use by two persons —*vt.* to cut with a whipsaw

**whip·stitch** (-stich′) *vt., vi. Sewing* to overcast or whip —*n.* a stitch made in this way

**whip·stock** (-stäk′) *n.* the handle of a whip

**whir, whirr** (hwur, wur) *vi., vt.* **whirred, whir′ring** [prob. < Scand.] to fly, revolve, vibrate, etc. with a whizzing or buzzing sound —*n.* a sound like this, as of a propeller

**whirl** (hwurl, wurl) *vi.* [ON. *hvirfla*] **1.** to move rapidly in a circular manner or as in an orbit **2.** to rotate or spin fast; gyrate **3.** to move, go, etc. swiftly **4.** to seem to spin; reel [my head is *whirling*] —*vt.* **1.** to cause to rotate, revolve, etc. rapidly **2.** to move, carry, etc. with a rotating motion [the wind *whirled* the leaves] —*n.* **1.** the act of whirling **2.** a whirling motion **3.** something whirling or being whirled **4.** a round of parties, etc. **5.** a tumult; uproar; stir **6.** a confused or giddy condition [my head is in a *whirl*] —**give it a whirl** [Colloq.] to make an attempt —**whirl′er** *n.*

**whirl·i·gig** (hwur′li gig′, wur′-) *n.* [see WHIRL & GIG¹] **1.** a child's toy that whirls or spins **2.** a merry-go-round **3.** a whirling motion

**whirl·pool** (hwurl′pōōl′, wurl′-) *n.* **1.** water in rapid, violent, whirling motion tending to form a circle into which floating objects are drawn; eddy of water **2.** anything like a whirlpool, as in violent motion

**whirlpool bath** a bath, as used in hydrotherapy, in which an agitating device causes a current of warm water to swirl around

**whirl·wind** (-wind′) *n.* **1.** a current of air whirling violently upward in a spiral that has a forward motion **2.** anything resembling a whirlwind, as in violent or destructive force, etc. —*adj.* carried on as fast as possible [a *whirlwind* courtship]

**whirl·y·bird** (hwur′lē burd′, wur′-) *n. colloq. term for* HELICOPTER

**whish** (hwish, wish) *vi.* [echoic] to move with a soft, rushing sound; whiz; swish —*n.* a sound so made

**whisk** (hwisk, wisk) *n.* [ON. *visk*, a brush] **1.** *a)* the act of brushing with a quick, light, sweeping motion *b)* such a motion **2.** a small bunch of straw, hair, etc. used for brushing **3.** a kitchen utensil consisting of wire loops fixed in a handle, for whipping eggs, etc. —*vt.* **1.** to move, remove, brush (*away, off, out*, etc.) with a quick, sweeping motion **2.** [Chiefly Brit.] to whip (eggs, cream, etc.) —*vi.* to move quickly, nimbly, or briskly

**whisk broom** a small, short-handled broom for brushing clothes, etc.

**whisk·er** (hwis′kər, wis′-) *n.* [see WHISK & -ER] **1.** [*pl.*] the hair growing on a man's face; esp., the beard on the cheeks **2.** *a)* a hair of a man's beard *b)* any of the long, bristly hairs growing on the upper lip of a cat, rat, etc. —**whisk′ered, whisk′er·y** *adj.*

**whis·key** (hwis′kē, wis′kē) *n., pl.* **-keys, -kies** [short for *usquebaugh* < IrGael. *uisce*, water + *beathadh*, life] **1.** a strong alcoholic liquor distilled from the fermented mash of grain, esp. of rye, wheat, corn, or barley **2.** a drink of whiskey —*adj.* of, for, or made with whiskey Also sp. **whis·ky,** *pl.* **-kies** *Note:* in the U.S. and Ireland, the usual spelling is **whiskey;** in Great Britain and Canada, it is **whisky**

**whis·per** (hwis′pər, wis′-) *vi.* [OE. *hwisprian*] **1.** to speak very softly, esp. without vibration of the vocal cords **2.** to talk in a quiet or sneaky way, as in gossiping or plotting **3.** to make a soft, rustling sound —*vt.* **1.** to say very softly, esp. by whispering **2.** to tell as a secret —*n.* **1.** a whispering; soft, low speech produced with breath but, usually, without voice **2.** something whispered; a secret, hint, rumor, etc. **3.** a soft, rustling sound —**whis′per·er** *n.* —**whis′per·ing** *adj., n.* —**whis′per·ing·ly** *adv.* —**whis′per·y** *adj.*

**whispering campaign** the spreading, by word of mouth, of nasty rumors intended to discredit a political candidate, cause, etc.

**whist¹** (hwist, wist) *interj.* [echoic] [Archaic or Dial.] hush! silence! —*vt., vi.* to be or become quiet

**whist²** (hwist, wist) *n.* [< earlier *whisk*] a card game usually played by two pairs of players, similar to, and the forerunner of, bridge

**whis·tle** (hwis′'l, wis′-) *vi.* **-tled, -tling** [OE. *hwistlian*] **1.** *a)* to make a clear, shrill sound by forcing breath between the teeth or through puckered lips *b)* to make a similar sound by sending steam through a small opening **2.** to make a clear, shrill cry: said of some birds and animals **3.** to move, pass, go, etc. with a high, shrill sound, as the wind **4.** *a)* to blow a whistle *b)* to have its whistle blown, as a train —*vt.* **1.** to produce (a tune, etc.) by whistling **2.** to summon, signal, etc. by whistling —*n.* **1.** an instrument for making whistling sounds **2.** the act or sound of whistling —**wet one's whistle** to take a drink —**whistle for** to seek or expect in vain —**whistle in the dark** to pretend to be confident —**whis′tler** *n.* —**whis′tling** *adj., n.*

**Whis·tler** (hwis′lər, wis′-), **James Ab·bott Mc·Neill** (ab′ət mək nēl′) 1834–1903; U.S. painter & etcher in England —**Whis·tle′ri·an** (-lir′ē ən) *adj.*

**whistle stop 1.** a small town, orig. one at which a train stopped only upon signal **2.** a brief stop in a small town as part of a tour, esp. in a political campaign —**whis′tle-stop′** *vi.* **-stopped′, -stop′ping**

**whit** (hwit, wit) *n.* [Early ModE. resp. of OE. *wiht*, a wight] the least bit; jot; iota: chiefly in negative constructions [not a *whit* the wiser]

**white** (hwīt, wīt) *adj.* **whit′er, whit′est** [OE. *hwit*] **1.** having the color of pure snow or milk; of the color of reflected light containing all of the visible rays of the spectrum: opposite to black: see COLOR **2.** of a light or pale color; specif., *a)* gray; silvery *b)* very blond *c)* pale; wan [a face *white* with terror] *d)* light-yellow or amber [*white* wines] *e)* blank, as a space unmarked by printing *f)* snowy **3.** colorless [*white* creme de menthe] **4.** clothed in white [the *White* Friars] **5.** pure; innocent **6.** free from evil intent; harmless [*white* magic] **7.** *a)* having a light-colored skin; Caucasoid *b)* of or controlled by Caucasoids **8.** [Slang] honest; fair —*n.* **1.** white color **2.** the state of being white; specif., *a)* fairness of complexion *b)* purity; innocence **3.** a white or light-colored part or thing, as the albumen of an egg, the white part of the eyeball, the light-colored part of meat, wood, etc., a white garment, white wine, white pigment, etc. **4.** a person with a light-colored skin; Caucasoid —*vt.* **whit′ed, whit′ing** to make white; whiten —**bleed white** to drain (a person) completely of money, resources, etc. —**white′ly** *adv.* —**white′ness** *n.*

**white ant** *popular name for* TERMITE

**white·bait** (-bāt′) *n., pl.* **-bait** **1.** any of various small, silvery European fishes, as young herring, used as food **2.** a smelt of the Pacific coast of N. America

**white bass** (bas) a silvery, freshwater, food and game fish of eastern N. America

**white birch 1.** *same as* PAPER BIRCH **2.** a European birch with silvery-white bark, widely grown in the U.S.

**white blood cell** *same as* LEUKOCYTE: also called **white blood corpuscle**

**white bread** bread of a light color, made from finely sifted wheat flour

**white bush (scallop)** a variety of summer squash having a saucer-shaped, white fruit, scalloped around the edges

**white·cap** (-kap′) *n.* a wave with its crest broken into white foam

**white cedar 1.** *a)* an evergreen tree growing in swampy land in the eastern U.S. *b)* its soft, light-colored wood, used for shingles, etc. **2.** *a)* the American arborvitae, growing in the northeastern U.S. *b)* its soft, brittle wood

**white clover** a creeping species of clover with white flower clusters, grown as a forage plant

**white-col·lar** (-käl′ər) *adj.* [from the formerly typical white shirt worn by such workers] designating or of clerical or professional workers or the like

**whited sepulcher** a hypocrite: Matt. 23:27

**white elephant 1.** an albino elephant, regarded as sacred by the Thais, Burmese, etc. **2.** something that is of little profit or use but costs a lot to maintain **3.** any object that its owner no longer wants to keep but that others may want to own or buy

**white feather** [from belief that a white feather in a gamecock's tail shows bad breeding, hence cowardice] an indication of cowardice: chiefly in **show the white feather**

**white·fish** (-fish') *n., pl.* **-fish', -fish'es:** see FISH **1.** any of various white or silvery food fishes of the salmon family, found in the lakes of the northern U.S. and Canada **2.** any of various other whitish fishes, as the **ocean whitefish** of southern California waters **3.** *same as* BELUGA (sense 2)

**white flag** a white banner or cloth hoisted as a signal of truce or surrender

**white·fly** (-flī') *n., pl.* **-flies'** any of various tiny whitish insects, often harmful to plants

**White Friar** a Carmelite friar: so called from the white mantle worn by these friars

**white gold** gold alloyed with nickel, zinc, etc., to give it a white, platinumlike appearance for use in jewelry

**white-haired** (-herd') *adj.* **1.** having white or very light hair **2.** [Colloq.] *same as* FAIR-HAIRED (sense 2)

**White·hall** (hwīt'hôl', wīt'-) a street in London, site of several government offices —*n.* the British government

**white heat 1.** the degree of intense heat (beyond red heat) at which metal, etc. glows white **2.** a state of intense emotion, excitement, etc.

**White·horse** (hwīt'hôrs', wīt'-) capital of the Yukon Territory, Canada, in the S part: pop. 13,000

**white-hot** (hwīt'hät', wīt'-) *adj.* **1.** glowing white with heat **2.** extremely angry, excited, enthusiastic, etc.

**White House, the 1.** official residence of the President of the U.S.: a white mansion in Washington, D.C. **2.** the executive branch of the U.S. government

**white lead 1.** a poisonous, heavy, white powder, basic lead carbonate, $2PbCO_3 \cdot Pb(OH)_2$, used as a paint pigment, for pottery glazes, etc. **2.** any of several white pigments containing lead, as lead sulfate

**white lie** a lie about something unimportant, often one told to spare someone's feelings

**white light** *Physics* light, as sunlight, composed of rays of all the wavelengths ranging from red to violet

**white lightning** [Slang] homemade whiskey, esp. corn whiskey, usually unaged and strong and typically colorless

**white-liv·ered** (-liv'ərd) *adj.* cowardly; craven

**white matter** whitish nerve tissue of the brain and spinal cord, consisting chiefly of nerve fibers

**white meat** any light-colored meat, as veal, pork, the breast of poultry, etc.

**White Mountains** [from the appearance of the higher peaks] range of the Appalachian system, in N N.H.

**whit·en** (hwīt''n, wīt'-) *vt., vi.* to make or become white or whiter —**whit'en·er** *n.* —**whit'en·ing** *n.*

**white oak 1.** any of a number of oaks having whitish or grayish bark and hard wood **2.** the wood of any such tree, used in barrels, furniture, etc.

**white·out** (-out') *n.* a weather condition occurring in polar regions in which the snowy ground and white sky merge so that one's sense of direction and distance disappears

**white pepper** pepper ground from the husked, dried seeds of the nearly ripe pepper berry

**white pine 1.** *a)* a pine of eastern N. America, with needles in bundles of five and soft, light wood *b)* this wood **2.** any of various pines with needles in bundles of five

**White Plains** [? after the AmInd. *quaropas,* white marshes] city in SE N.Y., near New York City: pop. 47,000

**white poplar 1.** a large old-world poplar having lobed leaves with white or gray down on the undersides, now widespread in the U.S. **2.** *same as: a)* TULIP TREE *b)* TULIP-WOOD (sense 1)

**white potato** *same as* POTATO (sense 2 *a)*

**white race** loosely, the Caucasoid group of mankind

**White Russia** *same as* BYELORUSSIAN SOVIET SOCIALIST REPUBLIC

**White Russian 1.** a native or inhabitant of White Russia; Byelorussian **2.** any of the Russians who fought against the Bolsheviks (Reds) in the Russian civil war

**white sale** a sale of sheets, towels, linens, etc. held in a store

**white sauce** a sauce for vegetables, meat, fish, etc., made of fat or butter, flour, milk or stock, and seasoning

**White Sea** arm of the Arctic Ocean, extending into NW U.S.S.R.

**white slave** a woman enticed or forced into or held in prostitution for the profit of others —**white'-slave'** *adj.* —**white slaver** —**white slavery**

**white-tailed deer** (-tāld') a common American deer having a tail that is white on the undersurface, a white-spotted red coat in summer, and a brownish-gray coat in winter: also **white'tail'** *n.*

**white tie 1.** a white bow tie, properly worn with a swallow-tailed coat **2.** a swallow-tailed coat and its accessories

**white·wall** (-wôl') *adj.* designating or of a pneumatic tire with a circular white band on the outer sidewall: also **white'-wall'** —*n.* a whitewall tire

**white·wash** (-wôsh', -wäsh') *n.* **1.** a mixture of lime, whiting, size, water, etc., for whitening walls, etc. **2.** a concealing of faults or defects as in an effort to avoid blame *b)* something said or done for this purpose **3.** [Colloq.] *Sports* a defeat in which the loser scores no points —*vt.* **1.** to cover with whitewash. **2.** to conceal the faults or defects of **3.** [Colloq.] *Sports* to defeat (an opponent) without permitting him to score —**white'wash'er** *n.* —**white'wash'ing** *n.*

**white whale** *same as* BELUGA (sense 2)

**whith·er** (hwith'ər, with'-) *adv.* [OE. *hwider*] to what place, condition, etc.? where? —*conj.* **1.** to which place, condition, etc. **2.** wherever *Where* is now almost always used in place of *whither*

**whit·ing¹** (hwīt'iŋ, wīt'-) *n., pl.* **-ings, -ing:** see PLURAL, II, D, 1 [MDu. *wijting* < *wit,* white] any of numerous unrelated ocean food fishes of N. America, Europe, and Australia, including several hakes and kingfishes

**whit·ing²** (hwīt'iŋ, wīt'-) *n.* [see WHITE, *v.* + -ING] powdered chalk used in making paints, inks, etc.

**whit·ish** (-ish) *adj.* somewhat white —**whit'ish·ness** *n.*

**whit·low** (hwit'lō, wit'-) *n.* [ME. *whitflawe:* of disputed origin] *same as* FELON²

**Whit·man** (hwit'mən, wit'-), **Walt**(er) 1819–92; U.S. poet

**Whit·ney** (hwit'nē, wit'-), **Eli** 1765–1825; U.S. inventor, esp. of the cotton gin

**Whit·ney** (hwit'nē), **Mount** [after J. *Whitney* (1819–96), U.S. geologist] mountain of the Sierra Nevada Range, EC Calif.: highest in the U.S. outside of Alas., 14,495 ft.

**Whit·sun** (hwit's'n, wit'-) *adj.* of or observed on Whitsunday or at Whitsuntide

**Whit·sun·day** (hwit'sun'dē, wit'-; -dä; -s'n dā') *n.* [OE. *Hwita Sunnandæg,* white Sunday] *same as* PENTECOST (sense 2)

**Whit·sun·tide** (-s'n tīd') *n.* the week beginning with Whitsunday, esp. the first three days of that week

**Whit·ti·er** (hwit'ē ər, wit'-) [after ff.] city in SW Calif.: suburb of Los Angeles: pop. 69,000

**Whit·ti·er** (hwit'ē ər, wit'-), **John Green·leaf** (grēn'lēf') 1807–92; U.S. poet

**whit·tle** (hwit''l, wit'-) *vt.* **-tled, -tling** [OE. *thwitan,* to cut] **1.** *a)* to cut thin shavings from (wood) with a knife *b)* to carve (an object) in this manner **2.** to reduce, destroy, etc. gradually, as if by whittling: usually with *down, away,* etc. *[to whittle down costs]* —*vi.* to whittle wood —**whit'tler** *n.*

**whit·y** (hwīt'ē, wīt'-) *adj.* **whit'i·er, whit'i·est** *same as* WHITISH

**whiz, whizz** (hwiz, wiz) *vi.* **whizzed, whiz'zing** [echoic] **1.** to make the buzzing or hissing sound of something moving swiftly through the air **2.** to speed by with or as with this sound *[the bus whizzed by him]* —*vt.* to cause to whiz —*n.* **1.** a whizzing sound or movement **2.** [Slang] a person who is very adroit or skilled at something *[a whiz at math]*

**who** (hōō) *pron.,* obj. **whom,** poss. **whose** [OE. *hwa*] **1.** what or which person or persons: used to introduce a question *[who is he? I don't know who he is]* **2.** *a)* (the, or a, person or persons) that: used to introduce a relative clause *[the man who came to dinner]* *b)* any person or persons that: used as an indefinite relative *["who steals my purse steals trash"]* The use of *who* rather than *whom* as the object of a verb or preposition *[who did you see? who was it written by?],* although widespread, is objected to by some —**who's who** who the important people are

**WHO** World Health Organization

**whoa** (hwō, wō, hō) *interj.* [for HO] stop!: used esp. in directing a horse to stand still

**who·dun·it** (hōō dun'it) *n.* [Colloq.] a mystery novel, play, etc.: cf. MYSTERY¹ (sense 2 *b)*

**who·ev·er** (-ev'ər) *pron.* **1.** any person that; whatever person **2.** no matter what person *[whoever said it, it's not so]* **3.** what person? who?: used for emphasis *[whoever told you that?]*

**whole** (hōl) *adj.* [OE. *hal*] **1.** healthy; not diseased or injured **2.** not broken, damaged, defective, etc.; intact **3.** containing all the elements or parts; complete **4.** not divided up; in a single unit **5.** constituting the entire amount, extent, etc. *[the whole week]* **6.** having both parents in common *[a whole brother]* **7.** in all aspects of one's being *[the whole man]* **8.** *Arith.* not mixed or fractional *[25 is a whole number]* —*n.* **1.** the entire amount, etc.; totality **2.** a complete organization of parts; unity, entirety, etc. —**as a whole** as a complete unit; altogether —**made out of whole cloth** completely fictitious or false —**on the whole** all things considered; in general —**whole'ness** *n.*

**whole·heart·ed** (-här'tid) *adj.* doing or done with all one's energy, enthusiasm, etc.; sincere —**whole'heart'ed·ly** *adv.* —**whole'heart'ed·ness** *n.*

**whole-hog** (hōl'hôg', -häg') *adj., adv.* [Slang] without reservation; complete(ly)

**whole milk** milk from which none of the butterfat or other elements have been removed

**whole note** *Music* a note having four times the duration of a quarter note: see NOTE, illus.

**whole number** zero or any positive or negative multiple of 1; integer /28 is a *whole number*/

**whole·sale** (hōl'sāl') *n.* the selling of goods in relatively large quantities, esp. to retailers who then sell them at higher prices to consumers —*adj.* **1.** of, connected with, or engaged in such selling **2.** extensive or sweeping [*wholesale* criticism/ —*adv.* **1.** in wholesale amounts or at wholesale prices **2.** extensively or sweepingly —*vt., vi.* **-saled', -sal'ing** to sell wholesale —**at wholesale** in wholesale quantities or at wholesale prices —**whole'sal'er** *n.*

**whole·some** (-səm) *adj.* [see WHOLE & -SOME¹] **1.** good for one's health or well-being; healthful [*wholesome* food] **2.** tending to improve the mind or character **3.** full of health and vigor **4.** suggesting health [a *wholesome* smile] —**whole'some·ly** *adv.* —**whole'some·ness** *n.*

**whole tone** *Music* an interval consisting of two adjacent semitones: also **whole step**

**whole-wheat** (-hwēt') *adj.* **1.** made of the entire cleaned kernels of wheat [*whole-wheat* flour/ **2.** made of whole-wheat flour [*whole-wheat* bread/

**who'll** (hōol) **1.** who shall **2.** who will

**whol·ly** (hō'lē, hōl'lē) *adv.* to the whole amount or extent; totally; entirely

**whom** (hōom) *pron. objective case of* WHO: see note at WHO on the use of *who* and *whom*

**whom·ev·er** (hōom ev'ər) *pron. objective case of* WHOEVER

**whomp** (hwämp) *vt.* [echoic] **1.** to beat, strike, thump, etc. **2.** to defeat decisively —*n.* the act or sound of whomping

**whom·so·ev·er** (hōom'sō ev'ər) *pron. objective case of* WHOSOEVER

**whoof** (hwoof, woof) *n.* [echoic] a deep, abrupt, breathy sound /the bear's startled *whoof*/ —*vi.* to make this sound —*interj.* an exclamation of relief, surprise, etc.

**whoop** (hōop, hwōop, wōop, woop) *n.* [OFr. *houper*, to cry out] **1.** a loud shout, cry, etc., as of excitement, joy, etc. **2.** a hoot, as of an owl **3.** the gasping sound made when a breath of air is taken in following a fit of coughing in whooping cough —*vi., vt.* to utter, or utter with, a whoop or whoops —*interj.* an exclamation of excitement, joy, etc. —**not worth a whoop** [Colloq.] worth nothing at all —**whoop it (or things) up** [Slang] **1.** to create a noisy disturbance, as in celebrating **2.** to create enthusiasm (*for*) —**whoop'er** *n.*

**whoop-de-do, whoop-de-doo** (hōop'dē dōo', hwōop'-) *n.* [extended < prec.] [Colloq.] noisy or excited activity, commotion, or fuss; hoopla, ballyhoo, to-do, etc.

**whoop·ee** (wōo'pē, hwōo'-, woo'-, hwoo'-) *interj.* [< prec.] an exclamation of great joy, gay abandonment, etc. —*n.* a shout of "whoopee!" **2.** noisy fun —**make whoopee** [Slang] to revel or have fun in a noisy way

**whoop·ing cough** (hōo'piŋ, hoo'-) an acute infectious disease, usually affecting children, in which there are repeated attacks of coughing that end in a whoop

**whooping crane** a large, white N. American crane noted for its whooping call: now nearly extinct

**whoops** (hwoops, woops, hwōops, wōops) *interj.* an exclamation uttered as in regaining one's balance after stumbling or one's composure after a slip of the tongue

**whoosh** (hwoosh, woosh) *vi., vt.* [echoic] to make or cause to make a hissing or rushing sound while moving swiftly through the air —*n.* this sound —*interj.* an exclamation imitating this or expressing surprise, fatigue, etc.

**whop** (hwäp, wäp) *vt., vi.* **whopped, whop'ping** [prob. echoic] [Colloq.] **1.** to beat, strike, etc. **2.** to defeat decisively —*n.* [Colloq.] a sharp, loud blow, thump, etc.

**whop·per** (-ər) *n.* [< prec.] [Colloq.] **1.** anything extraordinarily large **2.** a great lie

**whop·ping** (-iŋ) *adj.* [< WHOP + -ING] [Colloq.] extraordinarily large or great; colossal

**whore** (hôr) *n.* [OE. *hore* < or akin to ON. *hora*] a sexually promiscuous woman; esp., a prostitute —*vi.* **whored, whor'ing 1.** to be a whore **2.** to fornicate with whores —**whor'ish** *adj.*

**who're** (hōo'ər, hoor) who are

**whore·mon·ger** (hôr'muŋ'gər, -mäŋ'gər) *n.* a pimp; pander: also **whore'mas'ter**

**whorl** (hwôrl, wôrl, hwurl, wurl) *n.* [< dial. var. of WHIRL] anything with a coiled or spiral appearance; specif., a) any of the circular ridges that form the design of a fingerprint b) *Bot.* a circular growth of leaves, petals, etc. about the same point on a stem c) *Zool.* any of the turns in a spiral shell —**whorled** *adj.*

**whor·tle·ber·ry** (hwurt't'l ber'ē, wur'-) *n., pl.* **-ries** [< Brit. dial. form of earlier *hurtleberry* < OE. *horte*] **1.** a) a European plant having pink flowers and blue or blackish berries b) any of these berries **2.** *same as* HUCKLEBERRY

**who's** (hōoz) **1.** who is **2.** who has

**whose** (hōoz) *pron.* [OE. *hwæs*] that or those belonging to whom [*whose* is this?] —*possessive pronominal adj.* of, belonging to, made, or done by whom or which /the man *whose* car was stolen/

**who·so** (hōo'sō) *pron.* [OE. *hwa swa*] [Archaic] whoever; whosoever

**who·so·ev·er** (hōo'sō ev'ər) *pron.* whoever: used for emphasis

**whr.** watt-hour

**why** (hwī, wī) *adv.* [OE. *hwi*, instrumental case of *hwæt*, what] for what reason, cause, or purpose? [*why* did he go? he told her *why* he went] —*conj.* **1.** because of which /there is no reason *why* you should go/ **2.** the reason for which /that is *why* he went/ —*n., pl.* **whys** the reason, cause, etc. [never mind the *why*] —*interj.* an exclamation used to show surprise, impatience, etc. or to introduce a remark

**WI** Wisconsin

**Wich·i·ta** (wich'ə tô') [< AmInd.] city in S Kans., on the Arkansas River: pop. 279,000

**Wichita Falls** [see prec.] city in NC Tex.: pop. 94,000

**wick** (wik) *n.* [OE. *weoca*] a piece of cord or tape, or a thin bundle of threads, in a candle, oil lamp, etc., that absorbs the fuel and, when lighted, burns with a steady flame

**wick·ed** (wik'id) *adj.* [ME. < *wikke*, evil, akin to OE. *wicce*, witch] **1.** morally bad or wrong; acting or done with evil intent **2.** generally painful, unpleasant, etc. [a *wicked* blow on the head] **3.** naughty; mischievous **4.** [Slang] skillful [he plays a *wicked* game of golf/ —**wick'ed·ly** *adv.* —**wick'ed·ness** *n.*

**wick·er** (wik'ər) *n.* [< Scand.] **1.** a thin, flexible twig; withe **2.** a) such twigs or long, woody strips woven together, as in making baskets or furniture b) *same as* WICKERWORK (sense 1) —*adj.* made of wicker

**wick·er·work** (-wurk') *n.* **1.** things made of wicker **2.** *same as* WICKER (sense 2 a)

**wick·et** (wik'it) *n.* [ONormFr. *wiket* < Gmc.] **1.** a small door or gate, esp. one set in or near a larger one **2.** a small window or opening, as in a box office **3.** a small gate for regulating the flow of water, as to a water wheel **4.** *Cricket* a) either of two sets of three stumps each, with two bails resting on top of them b) the playing space between the two wickets c) a player's turn at bat **5.** *Croquet* any of the wire arches through which the balls must be hit; hoop

**wick·et·keep·er** (-kē'pər) *n. Cricket* the fielder stationed immediately behind the wicket

**Wick·liffe, Wic·lif** (wik'lif) *variants of* WYCLIFFE

**wide** (wīd) *adj.* [OE. *wid*] **1.** extending over a large area; esp., extending over a larger area from side to side than is usual **2.** of a specified extent from side to side [two miles *wide*] **3.** of great extent, range, etc. [a *wide* variety] **4.** roomy; ample; full [*wide* pants] **5.** opened as far as possible [eyes *wide* with fear] **6.** far from the point, issue, etc. aimed at [*wide* of the mark] —*adv.* **1.** over a relatively large area; widely **2.** to a large or full extent; fully [*wide* open] **3.** so as to miss the point, issue, etc. aimed at; astray —**wide'ly** *adv.* —**wide'ness** *n.*

**-wide** (wīd) *a combining form meaning* existing or extending throughout [nationwide]

**wide-an·gle** (wīd'aŋ'g'l) *adj.* **1.** designating or of a kind of camera lens covering a wide angle of view **2.** designating or of any of several systems using one or more movie cameras (and projectors) and a very wide, curved screen

**wide-a·wake** (-ə wāk') *adj.* **1.** completely awake **2.** alert —**wide'-a·wake'ness** *n.*

**wide-eyed** (-īd') *adj.* with the eyes wide open

**wid·en** (wīd'n) *vt., vi.* to make or become wide or wider

**wide-o·pen** (wīd'ō'p'n) *adj.* **1.** opened wide **2.** not having or enforcing laws against prostitution, gambling, liquor sales, etc. [a *wide-open* city]

**wide receiver** *Football* a player eligible to receive a pass who takes a position at some distance from the rest of the offensive team

**wide·spread** (-spred') *adj.* spread widely; esp., a) widely extended [with *widespread* arms] b) occurring over a wide area or extent [*widespread* benefits]

**widg·eon** (wij'ən) *n., pl.* **-eons, -eon:** see PLURAL, II, D, 1 [prob. < MFr. *vigeon*] any of various wild, freshwater ducks having a head with a cream-colored or white crown

**wid·get** (wij'it) *n.* [altered < GADGET] a small gadget or device, esp. one without a specific description

**wid·ow** (wid'ō) *n.* [OE. *widewe*] **1.** a woman whose husband has died and who has not remarried **2.** *Cards* a group of cards dealt to the table, typically for the use of the highest bidder **3.** *Printing* an incomplete line, as that ending a paragraph, carried over to the top of a new page or column **4.** [Colloq.] a woman whose husband is often away [a golf *widow*] —*vt.* to cause to become a widow [*widowed* by the war] —**wid'ow·hood'** *n.*

**wid·ow·er** (wid'ə wər) *n.* a man whose wife has died and who has not remarried

**widow's mite** a small gift or contribution freely given by one who can scarcely afford it: Mark 12:41–44

**widow's peak** a point formed by hair growing down in the middle of a forehead

**width** (width, witth) *n.* [< WIDE, by analogy with LENGTH] **1.** a being wide; wideness **2.** the distance from side to side **3.** a piece having a certain width *[two widths of cloth]*

**wield** (wēld) *vt.* [OE. *wealdan* & *wieldan*] **1.** to handle and use (a tool or weapon), esp. with skill and control **2.** to exercise (power, influence, etc.) —**wield'er** *n.*

**wield·y** (wēl'dē) *adj.* **wield'i·er**, **wield'i·est** that can be wielded easily; manageable

**Wien** (vēn) *Ger. name of* VIENNA

**wie·ner** (wē'nər) *n.* [short for G. *Wiener wurst*, Vienna sausage] a smoked link sausage of beef or beef and pork; frankfurter: also **wie'ner·wurst'** (-wurst')

**Wies·ba·den** (vēs'bäd''n) city in W West Germany, on the Rhine: pop. 261,000

**wife** (wīf) *n., pl.* **wives** (wīvz) [OE. *wif*] **1.** orig., a woman: still so used in *midwife, housewife,* etc. **2.** a married woman —**take to wife** to marry (a specified woman) —**wife'hood'** *n.* —**wife'less** *adj.* —**wife'ly** *adj.* **-li·er, -li·est**

**wig** (wig) *n.* [shortened < PERIWIG] **1.** *a)* a false covering of real or synthetic hair for the head, worn as part of a costume, to hide baldness, etc. *b) same as* TOUPEE **2.** [Slang] the hair, head, or mind —*vt.* **wigged, wig'ging 1.** to furnish with a wig or wigs **2.** [Slang] *a)* to annoy, upset, anger, etc. *b)* to make excited, frenzied, crazy, etc. (often with *out*) **3.** [Brit. Colloq.] to scold, rebuke, etc. —*vi.* [Slang] to be or become wigged, or upset, frenzied, etc. (often with *out*) —**wig'less** *adj.*

**wi·geon** (wij'ən) *n. var. of* WIDGEON

**wig·gle** (wig''l) *vt., vi.* **-gled, -gling** [prob. < MDu. & MLowG. *wiggelen*, freq. of *wiggen*, to move from side to side] to move with short, jerky or twisting motions from side to side —*n.* the act or an instance of wiggling

**wig·gler** (wig'lər) *n.* **1.** a person or thing that wiggles **2.** the larva of a mosquito; wriggler

**wig·gly** (-lē) *adj.* **-gli·er, -gli·est 1.** that wiggles; wiggling **2.** wavy *[a wiggly line]*

**wig·gy** (wig'ē) *adj.* **-gi·er, -gi·est** [Slang] wild, exciting, crazy, etc.

**wight** (wīt) *n.* [OE. *wiht*] [Archaic] a human being; person: now sometimes used in a patronizing way

**Wight** (wīt), **Isle of** island in the English Channel, off the S coast of England, that is an English county

**wig·let** (wig'lit) *n.* a small wig; specif., a woman's hairpiece for use along with her own hair

**wig·wag** (wig'wag') *vt., vi.* **-wagged', -wag'ging** [< obs. *wig*, to move + WAG¹] **1.** to move back and forth; wag **2.** to send (a message) by waving flags, lights, etc. back and forth in accordance with a code —*n.* **1.** the sending of messages in this way **2.** a message so sent

**wig·wam** (wig'wäm, -wôm) *n.* [< Algonquian] a dwelling made by the Indians of E and C N. America, consisting typically of a framework of arched poles covered with bark

**Wil·ber·force** (wil'bər fôrs'), **William** 1759–1833; Eng. statesman & vigorous opponent of slavery

**Wil·bur** (wil'bər) [OE. *Wilburh*: prob. < a place name meaning "willow town"] a masculine name

WIGWAM

**wil·co** (wil'kō) *interj.* [*wil(l)* *co(mply)*] I will comply with your request: used in radiotelephony

**wild** (wīld) *adj.* [OE. *wilde*] **1.** living or growing in its original, natural state; not domesticated or cultivated *[wild flowers, wild animals]* **2.** not lived in or cultivated; overgrown, waste, etc. *[wild land]* **3.** not civilized; savage *[a wild tribe]* **4.** not controlled; unruly, rough, lawless, etc. *[wild children]* **5.** lacking social or moral restraint; dissolute, orgiastic, etc. *[a wild rake, a wild party]* **6.** turbulent; stormy *[wild seas]* **7.** *a)* very excited or enthusiastic *[wild with delight]* *b)* angered, frantic, crazed, etc. *[wild with desperation]* **8.** in a state of disorder, confusion, etc. *[wild hair]* **9.** reckless, fantastic, crazy, etc. *[a wild scheme]* **10.** missing the target *[a wild shot]* **11.** *Cards* having any value specified by the holder: said of a card —*adv.* in a wild manner *[to shoot wild]* —*n.* [*usually pl.*] a wilderness or wasteland —**run wild** to grow, exist, or behave in an uncontrolled way —**wild'ly** *adv.* —**wild'ness** *n.*

**wild boar** a variety of hog living wild in Europe, Asia, and Africa, from which domestic hogs have been derived

**wild-card** (kärd) *adj. Sports* designating or of any of the teams, other than those that finish in first and sometimes second place, that qualify for a championship play-off

**wild carrot** a common weed, with finely divided leaves and white flower umbels: the ancestor of the garden carrot

**wild·cat** (wīld'kat') *n., pl.* **-cats', -cat':** see PLURAL, II, D, 1 **1.** *a)* any of various fierce, medium-sized, undomesticated animals of the cat family, as the lynx or bobcat *b)* a house cat that has escaped from domestication: in this sense, usually **wild cat 2.** a fierce, aggressive person **3.** an unsound or risky business scheme **4.** an oil well drilled in an area not known before to have oil **5.** *Naut.* a drum on a windlass, that engages chain cable links **6.** *Railroading* a locomotive and tender without cars —*adj.* **1.** unsound or financially risky **2.** *a)* operating in an illegal or unethical way *b)* not officially authorized *[a wildcat strike]* —*vi.* **-cat'-ted, -cat'ting 1.** to drill for oil in an area considered unproductive before **2.** to engage in wildcat enterprises —**wild'cat'ter** *n.*

**Wilde** (wīld), **Oscar (Fingal O'Flahertie Wills)** 1854–1900; Brit. playwright, poet, & novelist, born in Ireland

**wil·de·beest** (wil'də bēst', vil'-) *n., pl.* **-beests', -beest':** see PLURAL, II, D, 1 [Afrik. < Du. *wild*, wild + *beeste*, beast] *same as* GNU

**wil·der·ness** (wil'dər nis) *n.* [< ME. *wilderne*, wild place (< OE. < *wilde*, wild + *deor*, animal) + *-nesse, -*NESS] **1.** wasteland or overgrown land with no settlers **2.** a large, confused mass or tangle of persons or things

**wild-eyed** (wīld'īd') *adj.* **1.** staring in a wild, distracted, or demented way **2.** fantastically impractical

**wild·fire** (-fīr') *n.* a fire that spreads fast and is hard to put out *[the rumors spread like wildfire]*

**wild·flow·er** (-flou'ər) *n.* any flowering plant growing without cultivation in fields, woods, etc. Also **wild flower**

**wild·fowl** (-foul') *n., pl.* **-fowls', -fowl':** see PLURAL, II, D, 1 a wild bird, esp. a game bird: also **wild fowl**

**wild-goose chase** (-gōōs') any search or undertaking as futile as trying to catch a wild goose by chasing it

**wild·life** (wīld'līf') *n.* wild animals and birds, collectively

**wild oats** any of several wild grasses, having twisted awns and occurring as a weed in the western U.S.: also **wild oat** —**sow one's wild oats** to be sexually promiscuous in youth before settling down: usually said of a man

**wild pansy** an uncultivated pansy, esp. a European species with petals in combinations of white, yellow, and purple

**wild pitch** *Baseball* a pitch too erratic for the catcher to control, allowing a runner to advance to another base

**wild rice 1.** a tall grass of the U.S. and Canada, found in swampy borders of lakes and streams **2.** its edible grain

**wild rose** any of various wild roses growing wild, as eglantine

**Wild West** [*also* w- W-] the western U.S. in its early frontier period of lawlessness

**wild·wood** (wīld'wood') *n.* a natural woodland or forest, esp. when unfrequented by man

**wile** (wīl) *n.* [Late OE. *wil* < OE. *wigle*, magic] **1.** a sly trick; stratagem **2.** a beguiling or coquettish trick *Usually used in pl.* —*vt.* **wiled, wil'ing** to beguile; lure —**wile away** to while away (time): by confusion with *while*

**Wil·fred, Wil·frid** (wil'frid) [< OE. < *willa*, a wish, WILL¹ + *frith*, peace] a masculine name

**wil·ful** (wil'fəl) *adj. var. of* WILLFUL

**Wil·hel·mi·na** (wil'hel mē'nə; *Du.* vil'hel mē'nä) [< G. fem. of *Wilhelm:* see WILLIAM] **1.** a feminine name **2.** *(Wilhelmina Helena Pauline Maria)* 1880–1962; queen of the Netherlands (1890–1948)

**Wilkes-Bar·re** (wilks'bar'ē, -ber'ē; -ə) [after J. *Wilkes,* 18th-c. Eng. political reformer & Col. I. *Barré,* Brit. officer] city in NE Pa.: pop. 52,000

**will¹** (wil) *n.* [OE. *willa*] **1.** the power of making a reasoned choice or decision or of controlling one's own actions **2.** *a)* strong and fixed purpose; determination *[where there's a will there's a way]* *b)* energy and enthusiasm *[to work with a will]* **3.** attitude toward others *[good will]* **4.** *a)* the desire, purpose, choice, etc. of a certain person or group *[what is your will?]* *b)* a compelling command or decree *[the will of the people]* **5.** *a)* the legal statement of a person's wishes concerning the disposal of his property after death *b)* the document containing this —*vt.* **1.** to have as the object of one's will **2.** to control or influence by the power of the will **3.** to bequeath by a will —*vi.* **1.** to exert one's will **2.** to choose or prefer —**at will** when one wishes —**will'a·ble** *adj.* —**will'·less** *adj.*

**will²** (wil; *unstressed* wəl) *v., pt.* **would** [OE. *willan*] **1.** an auxiliary regularly used to express the future: in the rules of some grammarians, esp. formerly, *will* is to be used in the second and third persons for simple future and in the first person to show determination or obligation, and *shall* is to be used in the first person for simple future and in the second and third persons to show determination or obligation: in actual practice *will* and *shall* are used interchangeably, with *will* more common in all persons **2.** an auxiliary used to express: *a)* willingness *[will* you do me a favor?*]* *b)* ability or capacity *[it will* hold another quart*]* *c)* habit, custom, inclination, or inevitability *[boys will* be boys*]* *d)* expectation, surmise, etc. *[that will* be his wife with him, I suppose*]* See also SHALL —*pt., vi.* to wish; desire *[do what (or as) you will]*

**will call** the department, as of a large store, at which articles are held to be picked up, as when paid for

**willed** (wild) *adj.* having a will, esp. a specified kind of will: used in hyphenated compounds *[strong-willed]*

**will·ful** (wil'fəl) *adj.* **1.** done deliberately or intentionally **2.** always wanting one's own way; doing as one pleases; self-willed —**will'ful·ly** *adv.* —**will'ful·ness** *n.*

**Wil·liam** (wil'yəm) [ < ONormFr. < OHG. < *willeo,* WILL[1] + *helm,* protection] **1.** a masculine name **2. William I** *a)* 1027?–87; duke of Normandy who conquered England (see Battle of HASTINGS); king of England (1066–87): called *William the Conqueror b)* 1533–84; prince of Orange (1544–84); founder of the Netherlands republic: called *William the Silent* **3. William II** 1859–1941; emperor of Germany & king of Prussia (1888–1918): called *Kaiser Wilhelm* **4. William III** 1650–1702; king of England, Scotland, & Ireland (1689–1702): see MARY II

**Wil·liams** (wil'yəmz) **1. Roger,** 1603?–83; Eng. colonist in America: founder of Rhode Island **2. Tennessee,** (born *Thomas Lanier Williams*) 1914– ; U.S. playwright

**Wil·liams·burg** (wil'yəmz burg') [after WILLIAM III] city in SE Va.; colonial capital of Va., now restored to its 18th-cent. appearance

**wil·lies** (wil'ēz) *n.pl.* [ < ?] [Slang] a state of nervousness; jitters: with *the*

**will·ing** (wil'iŋ) *adj.* **1.** ready or agreeing (*to* do something) *[willing* to try*]* **2.** doing, giving, etc. or done, given, etc. readily or gladly —**will'ing·ly** *adv.* —**will'ing·ness** *n.*

**wil·li·waw, wil·ly·waw** (wil'i wô') *n.* [ < ?] a sudden, violent, cold wind blowing down from mountain passes toward the coast in far northern or southern latitudes

**will-o'-the-wisp** (wil'ə thə wisp') *n.* [earlier *Will* (personal name) *with the* wisp] **1.** a light seen moving over marshes at night: see also IGNIS FATUUS **2.** any hope or goal that leads one on but is impossible to reach

**wil·low** (wil'ō) *n.* [OE. *welig*] **1.** *a)* any of a genus of trees and shrubs bearing catkins and usually narrow leaves: the flexible twigs of certain species are used in weaving baskets, chair seats, etc. *b)* the wood of any of these **2.** [orig. made of willow] [Colloq.] a baseball bat or cricket bat

**wil·low·y** (wil'ə wē) *adj.* **1.** covered or shaded with willows **2.** like a willow; specif., slender, supple, lithe, etc.

**will·pow·er** (wil'pou'ər) *n.* strength of will, mind, or determination; self-control

**wil·ly-nil·ly** (wil'ē nil'ē) *adv.* [contr. < *will I, nill I: nill* < OE. *nyllan* < *ne,* not + *willan,* to WILL[1]] whether one wishes it or not; willingly or unwillingly —*adj.* that is or happens whether one wishes it or not

**Wil·ming·ton** (wil'miŋ tən) [after S. Compton (1673?–1743), Earl of *Wilmington*] seaport in N Del., on the Delaware River: pop. 70,000 (met. area 523,000)

**Wil·son** (wil's'n) **1. Edmund,** 1895–1972; U.S. writer & critic **2. (Thomas) Wood·row** (wood'rō), 1856–1924; 28th president of the U.S. (1913–21)

**wilt[1]** (wilt) *vi.* [var. of obs. *welk,* to wither] **1.** to become limp, as from heat or lack of water; wither; droop: said of plants **2.** to become weak or faint; languish **3.** to lose courage; quail —*vt.* to cause to wilt —*n.* a being wilted

**wilt[2]** (wilt) *archaic 2d pers. sing., pres. indic., of* WILL[2]

**Wil·ton** (wilt'n) *n.* [ < *Wilton,* England, where first made] a kind of carpet with a velvety pile of cut loops: also **Wilton carpet, Wilton rug**

**wil·y** (wī'lē) *adj.* **wil'i·er, wil'i·est** full of wiles; crafty; sly —**wil'i·ness** *n.*

**wim·ble** (wim'b'l) *n.* [ < Anglo-Fr. < MDu. *wimmel,* an auger] a tool for boring, as a gimlet, auger, etc.

**Wim·ble·don** (wim'b'l dən) city in SE England: suburb of London: scene of international lawn tennis matches

**wimp** (wimp) *n.* [ < ?] [Slang] a weak, ineffectual, or insipid person —**wimp'y** *adj.*

**wim·ple** (wim'p'l) *n.* [OE. *wimpel*] a woman's head covering of medieval times consisting of a cloth arranged about the head, cheeks, chin, and neck: now worn only by certain nuns —*vt.* **-pled, -pling 1.** to clothe as with a wimple **2.** to lay in folds **3.** to cause to ripple —*vi.* **1.** to lie in folds **2.** to ripple

**win** (win) *vi.* **won, win'ning** [OE. *winnan,* to fight] **1.** *a)* to gain a victory; be victorious; triumph (sometimes with *out*) *b)* to finish in first place in a race, contest, etc. **2.** to succeed in reaching or achieving a specified state or place (with various prepositions, adverbs, etc.) *[to win* back to health*]* —*vt.* **1.** to get by effort, struggle, etc.; specif., *a)* to gain through

WIMPLE

accomplishment *[to win* distinctions*]* *b)* to achieve (one's point, demands, etc.) *c)* to gain (a prize or award) in competition *d)* to earn (a livelihood, etc.) **2.** to be victorious in (a contest, dispute, etc.) **3.** to get to with effort *[they won* the hilltop by noon*]* **4.** to influence or persuade: often with *over [to win* someone over to one's side*]* **5.** *a)* to gain the sympathy, favor, etc. of *[to win* a supporter*]* *b)* to gain (someone's sympathy, etc.) **6.** to persuade to marry one —*n.* **1.** [Colloq.] an act of winning; victory, as in a contest **2.** *Racing* first position at the finish

**wince** (wins) *vi.* **winced, winc'ing** [ < Anglo-Fr. var. of OFr. *guenchir* < Frank.] to draw back slightly, usually grimacing, as in pain —*n.* a wincing —**winc'er** *n.*

**winch** (winch) *n.* [OE. *wince*] **1.** a crank with a handle for transmitting motion **2.** a hoisting or hauling apparatus consisting of a drum or cylinder on which is to be wound a rope or cable attached to the object to be lifted or moved —*vt.* to hoist or haul with a winch

**Win·ches·ter (rifle)** (win'ches'tər, -chis-) [after O. F. *Winchester* (1810–80), U.S. manufacturer] *a trademark for* a type of repeating rifle with a tubular magazine set horizontally under the barrel

**wind[1]** (wīnd) *vt.* **wound** or rarely **wind'ed, wind'ing** [OE. *windan*] **1.** *a)* to turn, or make revolve *[to wind* a crank*]* *b)* to move as by cranking **2.** *a)* to coil (string, ribbon, etc.) around itself or around something else *[winding* a bandage around his toe*]* *b)* to cover by encircling with something *[to wind* a spool with thread*]* **3.** *a)* to make (one's way) in a winding or twisting course *b)* to make move in such a course **4.** to introduce deviously *[winding* his prejudices throughout*]* **5.** to hoist or haul as with a winch (often with *up*) **6.** to tighten the spring of (a clock, etc.) as by turning a stem —*vi.* **1.** to move or go in a twisting or curving course **2.** to appear in a way that is circuitous, devious, etc. **3.** to coil or spiral (*about* or *around* something) **4.** to undergo winding *[this clock winds* easily*]* —*n.* **1.** the act of winding **2.** a single turn of something wound **3.** a turn; twist; bend; curve —**wind up 1.** to wind into a ball, etc. **2.** to entangle or involve **3.** to bring or come to an end; finish **4.** to make very tense, nervous, excited, etc. **5.** *Baseball* to swing the arm in getting ready to pitch the ball —**wind'er** *n.*

**wind[2]** (wind; *for n., also poet.* wīnd) *n.* [OE.] **1.** air that is moving **2.** a strong, fast-moving air current; gale **3.** an air current regarded as bearing a scent, as in hunting *[to lose (the) wind* of the fox*]* **4.** figuratively, air regarded as bearing information, indicating trends, etc. *[rumors in the wind]* **5.** breath or the power of breathing *[to get the wind* knocked out of one*]* **6.** *a)* idle or empty talk *b)* bragging; pomposity **7.** gas in the stomach or intestines **8.** [*pl.*] the wind instruments of an orchestra, or the players of these —*vt.* **1.** to expose to the wind, as for drying; air **2.** to get or follow the scent of **3.** to put out of breath *[to be winded* by a long run*]* **4.** to rest (a horse, etc.) so as to allow recovery of breath —**break wind** to expel gas from the bowels —**get (or have) wind of** to get (or have) information or a hint about —**how the wind blows** (or **lies**) what the trend of affairs, public opinion, etc. is —**in the teeth of the wind** straight against the wind: also **in the wind's eye** —**in the wind** happening or about to happen —**into the wind** in the direction from which the wind is blowing —**take the wind out of one's sails** to remove one's advantage, nullify one's argument, etc. suddenly —**wind'less** *adj.*

**wind[3]** (wīnd, wind) *vt., vi.* **wound** or rarely **wind'ed, wind'ing** [ < prec.] [Poet.] **1.** to blow (a horn, etc.) **2.** to sound (a signal, etc.), as on a horn

**wind·age** (win'dij) *n.* **1.** the disturbance of air around a moving projectile **2.** deflection of a projectile by the wind, or the degree of this

**wind·bag** (wind'bag') *n.* [Colloq.] a person who talks much and pretentiously but says little of importance

**wind·blown** (-blōn') *adj.* **1.** blown by the wind **2.** twisted in growth by the prevailing wind: said of a tree

**wind-borne** (-bôrn') *adj.* carried by the wind, as pollen

**wind·break** (-brāk') *n.* a hedge, fence, or row of trees that serves as a protection from wind

**Wind·break·er** (-brā'kər) *a trademark for* a warm sports jacket of leather, wool, etc., having a closefitting elastic waistband and cuffs —*n.* [w-] such a jacket

**wind·burn** (-burn') *n.* a roughened, reddened, sore condition of the skin, caused by overexposure to the wind

**wind chimes** (or **bells**) a cluster of small chimes or pendants of glass, ceramic, etc., hung so that they strike one another and tinkle when blown by the wind

**wind cone** *same as* WINDSOCK

**wind·fall** (-fôl') *n.* **1.** something blown down by the wind, as fruit from a tree **2.** any unexpected money or gain

**wind·flaw** (-flô') *n.* a gust of wind: see FLAW[2]

**wind·flow·er** (-flou'ər) *n. same as* ANEMONE (sense 1)

**wind·hov·er** (-huv'ər, -häv'-) *n.* [Brit.] a kestrel

**wind·i·ly** (win'də lē) *adv.* in a windy manner

**wind·i·ness** (-dē nis) *n.* a windy quality or condition

**wind·ing** (wīn′diŋ) *n.* **1.** the action or effect of a person or thing that winds; a coiling, twining, turn, bend, etc. **2.** something that winds or is wound around an object —*adj.* that winds, turns, coils, spirals, etc.

**winding sheet** a cloth in which the body of a dead person is wrapped for burial; shroud

**wind instrument** (wind) a musical instrument sounded by blowing air, esp. breath, through it, as an oboe

**wind·jam·mer** (wind′jam′ər) *n.* *Naut.* a sailing ship, esp. a large one, or one of its crew

**wind·lass** (wind′ləs) *n.* [ON. *vindass* < *vinda*, to WIND[1] + *ass*, a beam] a winch, esp. a simple one worked by a crank —*vt.*, *vi.* to hoist, etc. with a windlass

**wind·mill** (wind′mil′) *n.* a machine made to go by the wind blowing on vanes fixed like spokes of a wheel on a shaft at the top of a tower: it gives power for grinding grain, pumping water, etc. —**fight (or tilt at) windmills** to fight imaginary opponents: from Don Quixote's mistaking windmills for giants

WINDLASS

**win·dow** (win′dō) *n.* [< ON. < *vindr*, WIND[2] + *auga*, an eye] **1.** *a)* an opening in a building, vehicle, etc., to let in light or air or to look through, usually having a pane or panes of glass, etc. set in a frame that is usually movable *b)* any such pane or frame **2.** any similar opening **3.** the transparent panel of a window envelope **4.** any portion of the frequency spectrum of the earth's atmosphere through which light, heat, or radio waves can penetrate to the earth's surface —*vt.* to provide with a window or windows —**win′dow·less** *adj.*

**window box** a long, narrow box on or outside a window ledge, for growing plants

**window dressing 1.** the display of goods and trimmings in a store window to attract customers **2.** any display or attempt to make something seem better than it really is

**window envelope** an envelope with a transparent panel, through which the address on the enclosure can be seen

**win·dow·pane** (-pān′) *n.* a pane of glass in a window

**window seat** a seat built in beneath a window or windows

**window shade** a shade for a window, esp. one of stiffened cloth or heavy paper on a roller

**win·dow-shop** (-shäp′) *vi.* **-shopped′**, **-shop′ping** to look at displays of goods in store windows without entering the stores to buy —**win′dow-shop′per** *n.*

**win·dow·sill** (-sil′) *n.* the sill of a window

**wind·pipe** (wind′pīp′) *n. same as* TRACHEA (sense 1)

**wind·proof** (-prōōf′) *adj.* that the wind cannot blow through, blow out, etc. *[a windproof lighter]*

**wind·row** (-rō′) *n.* **1.** a row of hay or of grain, etc. raked together to dry **2.** a row of dry leaves, dust, etc. swept together by the wind —*vt.* to rake or sweep into windrows

**wind·shield** (-shēld′) *n.* in automobiles, etc., a transparent screen in front, as of glass, to protect the riders from wind, etc.: also, chiefly Brit., **wind′screen′**

**wind·sock** (-säk′) *n.* a long, cone-shaped cloth bag, open at both ends and attached to the top of a mast, as at an airfield, to show wind direction: also called **wind sleeve**

**Wind·sor**[1] (win′zər) ruling family of Great Britain since 1917

**Wind·sor**[2] (win′zər) **1.** city in SE England, on the Thames: site of Windsor Castle **2.** port in SE Ontario, Canada, opposite Detroit: pop. 193,000

**Windsor Castle** residence of English sovereigns since the time of William the Conqueror, located in Windsor

**Windsor chair** a style of wooden chair, esp. popular in 18th-cent. England and America, with spreading legs, a spindle back, and usually a saddlelike seat

**Windsor knot** a form of double slipknot in a four-in-hand necktie, resulting in a wider, bulkier knot

**Windsor tie** a wide necktie of silk cut on the bias, tied in a loose double bow

**wind·storm** (wind′stôrm′) *n.* a storm with a strong wind but little or no rain, hail, etc.

**wind-swept** (-swept′) *adj.* swept by or exposed to winds

**wind tee** a large T-shaped weather vane placed on a landing field to show wind direction to aircraft

**wind tunnel** a tunnellike chamber through which air is

WINDSOR chair

forced and in which scale models of airplanes, etc. are tested to determine the effects of wind pressure

**wind·up** (wind′up′) *n.* **1.** a winding up, or conclusion; close; end **2.** *Baseball* the swinging of the arm when getting ready to pitch the ball

**wind·ward** (wind′wərd; *nautical* win′dərd) *n.* the direction from which the wind blows —*adv.* toward the wind —*adj.* **1.** moving windward **2.** on the side from which the wind blows Opposed to LEEWARD

**Wind·ward Islands** (wind′wərd) S group of islands in the Lesser Antilles of the West Indies

**wind·y** (win′dē) *adj.* **wind′i·er**, **wind′i·est 1.** characterized by wind *[a windy day]* **2.** swept by strong winds *[a windy city]* **3.** violent like wind *[windy anger]* **4.** *a)* without substance; empty, flimsy, etc. *b)* long-winded, pompous, boastful, etc. **5.** *same as* FLATULENT

**wine** (wīn) *n.* [OE. *win*, ult. < L. *vinum*] **1.** the fermented juice of grapes, used as an alcoholic beverage and in cooking, etc. **2.** the fermented juice of other fruits or plants, used as a beverage *[dandelion wine]* **3.** anything that exhilarates one **4.** a dark, purplish red like that of red wine —*vt.*, *vi.* **wined**, **win′ing** to provide with or drink wine: usually in **wine and dine**, to entertain with food, drink, etc.

**wine·bib·ber** (-bib′ər) *n.* a person who drinks much wine

**wine cellar 1.** a cellar where wine is stored **2.** a stock of wine

**wine-col·ored** (-kul′ərd) *adj.* having the color of red wine; dark purplish-red

**wine gallon** the old English gallon of 231 cu. in., now the standard gallon in the U.S.

**wine·glass** (-glas′) *n.* a small glass, usually stemmed, for serving wine —**wine′glass·ful′** *n.*, *pl.* **-fuls′**

**wine·grow·ing** (-grō′iŋ) *n.* the art or process of cultivating grapes and making wine from them —**wine′grow′er** *n.*

**wine press** a vat in which grapes are trodden, or a machine for pressing them, to extract the juice for making wine

**win·er·y** (wīn′ər ē) *n.*, *pl.* **-er·ies** an establishment where wine is made

**Wine·sap** (wīn′sap′) *n.* a dark-red winter apple

**wine·skin** (wīn′skin′) *n.* in Eastern countries, a large bag for holding wine, made of the skin of an animal

**wing** (wiŋ) *n.* [< ON. pl. of *vaengr*] **1.** *a)* either of the two feathered forelimbs of a bird, developed in most birds for use in flying *b)* either of a pair of structures on a bat or an insect used for flying *c)* any of various winglike structures used by certain animals for gliding, as the pectoral fin of a flying fish **2.** either of a pair of winglike structures that angels, dragons, etc. are thought of as having **3.** something used as or like a wing; esp., a (or the) main supporting surface of an airplane **4.** something like a wing in its position or relation to the main part; esp., *a)* a distinct part of a building, often at one side or added later or having a special use *b)* either side of a theater stage out of sight of the audience *c)* any winglike part, as on some seeds **5.** a group having a winglike relation to another group; specif., *a)* the right or left section of an army, fleet, etc. *b)* a section or faction, as of a political party, viewed as radical or conservative **6.** in hockey, a position or player forward and right (or left) of center **7.** *a)* any of various air force units; specif., *U.S. Air Force*, a unit larger than a group *b)* [*pl.*] the insignia worn by pilots and crew of military aircraft **8.** a flying, or a means or way of flying: now chiefly in **give wing to, take wing** (see phrases below) **9.** [Slang] a person's arm; specif., *Baseball* a pitcher's throwing arm —*vt.* **1.** to provide with wings *b)* to cause to fly or speed as on wings *b)* to make (one's way) by flying *c)* to go through or over by flying **3.** to transport as by flight **4.** to wound, as with a bullet, in the wing, arm, etc. —*vi.* to go swiftly as on wings; fly —**give wing (or wings) to** to enable to fly or soar on or as if on wings —**on the wing 1.** flying, or while in flight **2.** in motion or while moving or traveling —**on wings of** filled with joy or rapture by *[on wings of song]* —**take wing 1.** to take flight; fly away **2.** to become joyous or enraptured —**under one's wing** under one's protection, patronage, etc. —**wing it** [Colloq.] to act, speak, etc. with little or no planning or improvise; improvise —**wing′less** *adj.*

**wing chair** an upholstered armchair with a high back from each side of which high sides, or wings, extend forward

**wing·ding** (wiŋ′diŋ′) *n.* [< ?] [Slang] an event, party, etc. that is very festive, lively, etc.

**winged** (wiŋd; *often poet.* wiŋ′id) *adj.* **1.** having wings or winglike parts **2.** moving, esp. swiftly, on or as if on wings **3.** lofty; sublime *[winged words]*

**wing nut** a nut with flared sides for turning with the thumb and forefinger

**wing·span** (wiŋ'span') *n.* the distance between the tips of an airplane's wings

**wing·spread** (-spred') *n.* **1.** the distance between the tips of a pair of fully spread wings **2.** *same as* WINGSPAN

**wing tip 1.** a man's shoe with a decorative piece of leather over the vamp, peaked toward the tongue, with perforations on it and along the sides extending back from it **2.** this piece of leather Also **wing'-tip', wing'tip'** *n.*

**wink** (wiŋk) *vi.* [OE. *wincian*] **1.** to close the eyelids and open them again quickly **2.** *a)* to close and open an eyelid quickly so as to signal, etc. *b)* to be closed and opened thus: said of the eye **3.** to shine or twinkle in flashes of light —*vt.* **1.** to make (the eyes or an eye) wink **2.** to move, remove, etc. by winking [to *wink* back tears] **3.** to signal, etc. by winking —*n.* **1.** a winking, or the instant of time it takes **2.** a tiny interval (of sleep) [didn't sleep a *wink*] **3.** a signal, etc. given by winking **4.** a twinkle —**wink at** to pretend not to notice (some wrongdoing)

**wink·er** (-ər) *n.* **1.** a person or thing that winks **2.** a blinder (for a horse) **3.** [Colloq.] an eyelash or an eye

**win·kle¹** (wiŋ'k'l) *n.* **1.** *short for* PERIWINKLE² **2.** a large whelk very destructive to oysters and clams

**win·kle²** (wiŋ'k'l) *vt.* **-kled, -kling** [< ?] [Colloq.] to pry or rout from cover, secrecy, etc. (with *out, out of,* etc.)

**win·ner** (win'ər) *n.* one that wins; esp., [Colloq.] one that seems destined to win or be successful

**win·ning** (-iŋ) *adj.* **1.** that wins; victorious **2.** attractive; charming —*n.* **1.** victory **2.** [*pl.*] something won, esp. money —**win'ning·ly** *adv.*

**Win·ni·peg** (win'ə peg') **1.** capital of Manitoba, Canada, on the Red River: pop. 561,000 (met. area 578,000) **2. Lake,** large lake in SC Manitoba

**win·now** (win'ō) *vt.* [OE. *windwian* < *wind,* WIND²] **1.** *a)* to blow the chaff from (grain) *b)* to blow off (chaff) **2.** to blow away; scatter **3.** to analyze or examine carefully so as to separate the various elements; sift **4.** *a)* to separate out (poor or useless parts) *b)* to sort out or extract (good or useful parts) —*vi.* to winnow grain —*n.* **1.** a winnowing **2.** an apparatus for winnowing —**win'now·er** *n.*

**win·o** (wī'nō) *n., pl.* **-os** [Slang] a person who habitually gets drunk on wine; esp., an alcoholic derelict who drinks only cheap wine

**win·some** (win'səm) *adj.* [OE. *wynsum,* pleasant] attractive in a sweet, engaging way; charming —**win'some·ly** *adv.* —**win'some·ness** *n.*

**Win·ston-Sa·lem** (win'stən sā'ləm) [ult. after Maj. J. *Winston* (1746–1815) & SALEM] city in north central N.C., near Greensboro: pop. 132,000

**win·ter** (win'tər) *n.* [OE.] **1.** the coldest season of the year, following autumn **2.** a year as reckoned by this season **3.** any period regarded, like winter, as a time of decline, dreariness, etc. —*adj.* **1.** of, typical of, or suitable for winter **2.** that will keep during the winter [*winter* apples] **3.** planted in the fall to be harvested in the spring [*winter* wheat] —*vi.* **1.** to pass the winter **2.** to be supplied with food and shelter in the winter —*vt.* to keep or maintain during the winter —**win'ter·er** *n.*

**win·ter·feed** (-fēd') *vt.* **-fed', -feed'ing** to feed (animals, esp. livestock) during the winter

**win·ter·green** (-grēn') *n.* **1.** an evergreen plant with small, rounded leaves, white flowers, and red, edible berries **2.** an aromatic compound (**oil of wintergreen**) made from these leaves or from birch bark or synthetically, used in medicine and as a flavoring **3.** its flavor

**win·ter·ize** (-īz') *vt.* **-ized', -iz'ing** to put into condition for winter [to *winterize* a car with antifreeze]

**win·ter·kill** (-kil') *vt., vi.* to kill or die by exposure to winter cold: said of plants

**winter solstice** the time in the Northern Hemisphere when the sun is farthest south of the celestial equator; December 21 or 22

**winter squash** any of several squashes, as the acorn squash, with a hard rind and good keeping qualities

**win·ter·time** (-tīm') *n.* the season of winter

**Win·throp** (win'thrəp), **John 1.** 1588–1649; Eng. colonist in America; 1st governor of the colony (*Massachusetts Bay Colony*) founded at Salem, Mass. **2.** 1606–76; governor of Connecticut colony (1657, 1659–76): son of *prec.*

**win·try** (win'trē) *adj.* **-tri·er, -tri·est** of or like winter; cold, bleak, etc. [a *wintry* day, a *wintry* stare] : also **win'ter·y** (-tər ē, -trē) —**win'tri·ness** (-trē nis) *n.*

**win·y** (wī'nē) *adj.* **win'i·er, win'i·est** like wine in taste, smell, color, etc.

**wipe** (wīp) *vt.* **wiped, wip'ing** [OE. *wipian*] **1.** *a)* to rub with a cloth, etc., as for cleaning or drying *b)* to clean or dry in this manner **2.** to rub or pass (a cloth, etc.) over something **3.** to apply by wiping **4.** to remove as by wiping (with *away, off,* etc.) —*n.* a wiping —**wipe out 1.** to remove; erase **2.** to kill off **3.** to destroy —**wip'er** *n.*

**wipe·out** (-out') *n.* [Slang] any fall, failure, etc.

**wire** (wīr) *n.* [OE. *wir*] **1.** metal that has been drawn into a long thread **2.** a length of this, used for conducting electric

current, etc. **3.** wire netting or other wirework **4.** anything made of wire or wirework, as a telephone cable, a snare, etc. **5.** *a)* telegraph [reply *by wire*] *b)* a telegram **6.** *Horse Racing* a wire above the finish line of a race —*adj.* made of wire or wirework —*vt.* **wired, wir'ing 1.** to furnish, connect, bind, etc. with wire **2.** to supply with a system of wires for electric current **3.** to telegraph —*vi.* to telegraph —**down to the wire** to the very last moments —**get (in) under the wire** to enter or achieve barely on time —**pull wires** to get what one wants through one's friends' influence —**wire'like'** *adj.*

**wire·draw** (-drô') *vt.* **-drew', -drawn', -draw'ing 1.** to draw (metal) into wire **2.** to reduce to the finest subtleties; strain (a point in argument)

**wire gauge** a device for measuring the diameter of wire, thickness of sheet metal, etc.: it usually consists of a disk with notches of graduated sizes along its edge

**wire·hair** (-her') *n.* a fox terrier with a wiry coat: also **wire-haired terrier**

**wire-haired** (-herd') *adj.* having coarse, or wiry, hair

**wire·less** (-lis) *adj.* **1.** without wire or wires; specif., operating with electromagnetic waves and not with conducting wire **2.** [Chiefly Brit.] *same as* RADIO —*n.* **1.** *same as: a)* WIRELESS TELEGRAPHY *b)* [Chiefly Brit.] RADIO **2.** a message sent by wireless —*vt., vi.* to communicate (with) by wireless

**wireless telegraphy** (or **telegraph**) telegraphy by radio-transmitted signals

**wireless telephone** a telephone operating by radio-transmitted signals —**wireless telephony**

**Wire·pho·to** (-fōt'ō) *a trademark for:* **1.** a system of reproducing photographs at a distance by means of electric impulses transmitted by wire **2.** a photograph so produced

**wire·pull·er** (-pool'ər) *n.* a person who gets what he wants through his friends' influence —**wire'pull'ing** *n.*

**wire service** a business organization that sends news stories, features, etc. by direct telegraph to subscribing or member newspapers and radio and television stations

**wire·tap** (-tap') *vi., vt.* **-tapped', -tap'ping** to tap (a telephone wire, etc.) to get information secretly or underhandedly —*n.* **1.** the act or an instance of wiretapping **2.** a device used in wiretapping —*adj.* of or relating to wiretapping —**wire'tap'per** *n.*

**wire·work** (-wurk') *n.* netting, mesh, etc. made of wire

**wir·ing** (wīr'iŋ) *n.* **1.** the action of a person or thing that wires **2.** a system of wires, as to provide a house with electricity —*adj.* **1.** that wires **2.** used in wiring

**wir·y** (wīr'ē) *adj.* **wir'i·er, wir'i·est 1.** of wire **2.** like wire in shape and substance; stiff **3.** lean, sinewy, and strong: said of persons and animals **4.** produced by or as if by a vibrating wire [a *wiry* sound] —**wir'i·ness** *n.*

**wis** (wis) *vt.* [ < ME. *iwis,* certainly: erroneously understood as "I know"] [Archaic] to suppose; imagine; deem

**Wis·con·sin** (wis kän's'n) [ < Fr. < Algonquian] Middle Western State of the U.S.: 56,154 sq. mi.; pop. 4,705,000; cap. Madison: abbrev. **Wis., WI** —**Wis·con'sin·ite'** (-īt') *n.*

**wis·dom** (wiz'dəm) *n.* [OE. < *wis,* WISE¹ + *-dom,* -DOM] **1.** the quality of being wise; good judgment, based on knowledge, etc.; sagacity **2.** learning; knowledge; erudition **3.** wise teaching **4.** a wise plan or course of action

**Wisdom of Solomon** one of the books of the Apocrypha: called **Wisdom** in the Douay Bible

**wisdom tooth** the back tooth on each side of each jaw in human beings, appearing usually between the ages of 17 and 25

**wise¹** (wīz) *adj.* **wis'er, wis'est** [OE. *wis*] **1.** having or showing good judgment; sagacious **2.** judicious; sound [a *wise* saying] **3.** informed [none the *wiser*] **4.** learned; erudite **5.** shrewd; cunning. **6.** [Slang] conceited, impudent, fresh —**be** (or **get**) **wise to** [Slang] to be (or become) aware of —**get wise** [Slang] **1.** to become aware of the true facts **2.** to become impudent —**put wise (to)** [Slang] to give (someone) information, etc. (about) —**wise up** [Slang] to make or become informed —**wise'ly** *adv.* —**wise'ness** *n.*

**wise²** (wīz) *n.* [OE.] way; manner: used chiefly in phrases, as **in no wise, in this wise,** etc.

**-wise** (wīz) [ < *prec.*] a suffix meaning: **1.** in a (specified) direction, position, or manner [*sidewise*] **2.** in the same way or direction as [*clockwise*] **3.** with regard to; in connection with [*weatherwise, budgetwise*]

**wise·a·cre** (wīz'ā'kər) *n.* [ < MDu. < OHG. *wizzago,* a prophet] a person who acts as though he were much wiser than he really is

**wise·crack** (-krak') *n.* [Slang] a flippant or joking remark, often a gibe or retort —*vi.* [Slang] to make wisecracks —*vt.* [Slang] to say as a wisecrack —**wise'crack'er** *n.*

**wise guy** [Slang] a person who is brashly and annoyingly conceited, knowing, etc.; smart aleck

**wish** (wish) *vt.* [OE. *wyscan*] **1.** to have a longing for; want; desire **2.** to have or express a desire concerning [to *wish* the day were over, to *wish* her good luck] **3.** to bid [to *wish* a person good morning] **4.** to request [he *wishes* her to leave] **5.** to impose (with *on*) [he *wished* hard jobs on me*] —vi.* **1.** to long; yearn **2.** to make a wish —*n.* **1.** a wishing; desire for something **2.** something wished for *[he got his wish]* **3.** a polite request with some of the force of an order **4.** *[pl.]* expressed desire for a person's health, etc. *[to offer one's best wishes]* —**wish′er** *n.*

**wish·bone** (-bōn′) *n.* the forked bone in front of the breastbone of most birds

**wish·ful** (-fəl) *adj.* having or showing a wish; desirous; longing —**wish′ful·ly** *adv.* —**wish′ful·ness** *n.*

**wishful thinking** thinking in which one interprets facts in terms of what he would like to believe

**wish·y-wash·y** (wish′ē wôsh′ē, -wäsh′ē) *adj.* [redupl. of WASHY] [Colloq.] **1.** watery; insipid; thin **2.** not strong or decisive in character; weak —**wish′y-wash′i·ly** *adv.*

**wisp** (wisp) *n.* [prob. < Scand.] **1.** a small bunch or tuft *[a wisp of straw, hair, etc.]* **2.** a thin, filmy bit or puff *[a wisp of smoke]* **3.** something delicate, frail, etc. *[a wisp of a girl]* **4.** *same as* WILL-O′-THE-WISP —*vt.* to roll into a wisp —**wisp′y** *adj.* **wisp′i·er, wisp′i·est**

**wist** (wist) *pt. & pp. of* WIT²

**wis·ter·i·a** (wis tir′ē ə) *n.* [ModL., after C. *Wistar* (1761–1818), U.S. anatomist] a twining shrub of the legume family, with showy clusters of bluish, white, pink, or purple flowers: also **wis·tar′i·a** (-ter′-)

**wist·ful** (wist′fəl) *adj.* [altered (after WISHFUL) < earlier *wistly,* attentive] showing or expressing vague yearnings or pensive longing —**wist′ful·ly** *adv.* —**wist′ful·ness** *n.*

**wit¹** (wit) *n.* [OE.] **1.** *[pl.]* powers of thinking and reasoning, esp. in a normal, effective way **2.** alert, practical intelligence; good sense **3.** *a)* the ability to make lively, clever remarks expressed in a surprising, epigrammatic, or ironic way *b)* a person having this ability, or speech or writing in which it is expressed —**at one's wits' end** at a loss as to what to do —**keep** (or **have**) **one's wits about one** to remain mentally alert, as in an emergency —**live by one's wits** to live by trickery or craftiness

**wit²** (wit) *vt., vi.* **wist, wit′ting** [OE. *witan*] [Archaic] to know or learn *Wit* is conjugated in the present indicative: (I) *wot,* (thou) *wost* or *wot(t)est,* (he, she, it) *wot* or *wot(t)eth,* (we, ye, they) *wite* or *witen* —**to wit** that is to say; namely

**witch** (wich) *n.* [OE. *wicce,* fem. of *wicca,* sorcerer] **1.** a person, now specif. a woman, who is supposed to have magic power, esp. with the help of evil spirits: cf. WARLOCK **2.** an ugly and ill-tempered old woman **3.** [Colloq.] a bewitching or fascinating woman or girl —*vt.* **1.** to put a magic spell on **2.** to charm; fascinate

**witch·craft** (-kraft′) *n.* **1.** *a)* the power or practices of witches; black magic; sorcery *b)* an instance of this **2.** bewitching attraction or charm

**witch doctor** among certain tribes, esp. in Africa, a person who practices a type of primitive medicine involving the use of magic, witchcraft, etc.

**witch·er·y** (wich′ər ē) *n., pl.* **-er·ies** **1.** witchcraft; sorcery **2.** bewitching charm; fascination

**witch hazel** [OE. *wice*] **1.** a shrub with yellow flowers and woody fruit **2.** an alcoholic lotion containing an extract from the leaves and bark of this shrub

**witch hunt** [after the cruel treatment of persons once imagined to be witches] an investigation usually carried on with much publicity, supposedly to uncover activities aimed at overthrowing the government but really to harass and weaken political opposition —**witch hunter**

**witch·ing** (wich′iŋ) *n.* witchcraft —*adj.* that witches; bewitching —**witch′ing·ly** *adv.*

**with** (with, with) *prep.* [OE., orig., against] **1.** against *[to argue with a friend]* **2.** *a)* alongside of; near to *b)* in the company of *c)* into; among *[mix blue with red]* **3.** as an associate, or companion, of *[he played golf with me]* **4.** *a)* as a member of *[to sing with a quartet]* *b)* working for *[with the firm 20 years]* **5.** in regard to; concerning *[pleased with her gift]* **6.** in the same terms as; compared to *[having equal standing with the others]* **7.** as well as *[he can run with the best]* **8.** of the same opinions as *[I'm with you]* **9.** on the side of *[he voted with the Tories]* **10.** in the opinion of *[it's all right with me]* **11.** as a result of *[faint with hunger]* **12.** *a)* by means of; using *[stir with a spoon]* *b)* by *[filled with air]* **13.** having received *[with your permission, he'll go]* **14.** having or showing *[a boy with red hair, to enter with confidence, to play with skill]* **15.** in the keeping, care, etc. of *[leave the baby with me]* **16.** *a)* added to *[the boy, with his friend, arrived]* *b)* including *[with the newcomers, the class is large]* **17.** in spite of *[with all her faults, I love her still]* **18.** *a)* at the same time as *[to rise with the chickens]* *b)* in the same direction as *[to travel with the sun]* *c)* in proportion to *[wages varying with skills]* *d)* in the course of *[grief lessens with time]* **19.** to; onto *[join one end with the other]*

**20.** from *[to part with money]* **21.** after *[with that remark, he left]* —**with that** after that

**with-** [OE. < prec.] *a combining form meaning:* **1.** away, back *[withdraw]* **2.** against, from *[withhold]*

**with·al** (with ôl′, with-) *adv.* **1.** besides **2.** despite that; notwithstanding **3.** [Archaic] with that; therewith —*prep.* [Archaic] with: used following its object

**with·draw** (-drô′) *vt.* **-drew′, -drawn′, -draw′ing 1.** to take back or draw back; remove **2.** to take back (something said, offered, etc.) —*vi.* **1.** to move back; go away; retreat **2.** to remove oneself *[from an organization, activity, association with other people, etc.)* —**with·draw′er** *n.*

**with·draw·al** (-drô′əl) *n.* **1.** the act of withdrawing **2.** a giving up the use of a narcotic drug to which one has become addicted, typically accompanied by distress of body and mind (**withdrawal symptoms**)

**with·drawn** (-drôn′) *pp. of* WITHDRAW —*adj.* withdrawing within oneself; shy, reserved, unsociable, etc.

**withe** (with, with, wīth) *n.* [OE. *withthe*] a tough, flexible twig of willow, etc., used for binding things —*vt.* **withed, with′ing** to bind with withes

**with·er** (with′ər) *vi.* [< ME. var. of *wederen,* lit., to weather] **1.** to dry up; shrivel *[plants withering in the heat, a face withering with age]* **2.** to lose strength; weaken *[our hopes soon withered]* —*vt.* **1.** to cause to wither **2.** to make feel abashed, as by a scornful glance

**with·ers** (with′ərz) *n.pl.* [OE. *withre,* resistance < *wither,* against] the highest part of the back of a horse, etc., between the shoulder blades

**with·hold** (with hōld′, with-) *vt.* **-held′, -hold′ing 1.** *a)* to hold back; restrain *b)* to take out or deduct (taxes, etc.) from wages or salary **2.** to keep from giving; refuse *[to withhold approval]* —*vi.* to refrain; forbear

**withholding tax** the amount of income tax withheld from employees' wages or salaries

**with·in** (with in′, with-) *adv.* [OE. *withinnan*] **1.** on or to the inside **2.** indoors **3.** inside the body, mind, spirit, etc. —*prep.* **1.** in the inner part of; inside **2.** not more than; not beyond *[within a mile of home]* **3.** inside the limits of *[within the law]* —*n.* the inside or the interior

**with·out** (-out′) *adv.* [OE. *withutan*] **1.** on or to the outside **2.** outdoors —*prep.* **1.** at, on, or to the outside of **2.** beyond the limits of **3.** not with; lacking *[shoes without laces]* **4.** free from *[a man without fear]* **5.** with avoidance of *[to pass by without speaking]* —*n.* the outside or the exterior *[Dial.]* unless —*go* (or **do**) *without* to manage although lacking something

**with·stand** (with stand′, with-) *vt., vi.* **-stood′, -stand′ing** to oppose, resist, or endure, esp. in a successful way

**with·y** (with′ē, with′ē) *n., pl.* **with′ies** [OE. *withig*] a tough, flexible twig of willow, etc.; withe

**wit·less** (wit′lis) *adj.* lacking wit or intelligence; foolish —**wit′less·ly** *adv.* —**wit′less·ness** *n.*

**wit·ling** (wit′liŋ) *n.* one who fancies himself a wit

**wit·ness** (wit′nis) *n.* [OE. *gewitnes,* knowledge, testimony] **1.** evidence; testimony **2.** a person who saw, or can give a firsthand account of, something **3.** a person who testifies in court **4.** a person who watches a contract, will, etc. being signed and then, as proof that he did, signs it himself **5.** something serving as evidence —*vt.* **1.** to testify to **2.** to serve as evidence of **3.** to act as witness of (a contract, will, etc.) **4.** to be present at; see personally **5.** to be the scene of *[this field witnessed a battle]* —*vi.* **1.** to give, or serve as, evidence **2.** to testify to religious beliefs or faith —**bear witness** to be or give evidence

**witness stand** the place from which a witness gives his testimony in a law court: also, Brit., **wit′ness-box′** *n.*

**wit·ted** (wit′id) *adj.* having (a specified kind of) wit: used in hyphenated compounds *[slow-witted]*

**wit·ti·cism** (wit′ə siz'm) *n.* [< WITTY + -*cism,* as in CRITICISM] a witty remark

**wit·ting** (wit′iŋ) *adj.* [ME. *wytting]* done knowingly; intentional —**wit′ting·ly** *adv.*

**wit·ty** (wit′ē) *adj.* **-ti·er, -ti·est** [OE. *wittig*] having or showing wit; cleverly amusing —**wit′ti·ly** *adv.* —**wit′ti·ness** *n.*

**Wit·wa·ters·rand** (wit wôt′ərz rand′, -wät′-; -ränt′) region in NE South Africa, containing rich gold fields

**wive** (wīv) *vi., vt.* **wived, wiv′ing** [OE. *wifian*] [Archaic] to marry (a woman)

**wives** (wīvz) *n. pl. of* WIFE

**wiz** (wiz) *n.* shortened form of WIZARD (*n.* 2)

**wiz·ard** (wiz′ərd) *n.* [ME. *wisard,* prob. < *wis,* WISE¹ + *-ard,* -ARD] **1.** a magician; sorcerer **2.** [Colloq.] a person exceptionally gifted or clever at a specified activity —*adj.* **1.** of wizards or wizardry **2.** magic **3.** [Chiefly Brit.] outstanding; excellent —**wiz′ard·ly** *adv.*

**wiz·ard·ry** (-rē) *n.* witchcraft; magic; sorcery

**wiz·en** (wiz′'n, wēz′-) *vt.*, *vi.* [OE. *wisnian*] to dry up; wither; shrivel —*adj. same as* WIZENED

**wiz·ened** (-'nd) *adj.* dried up; withered; shriveled

**wk.** *pl.* **wks.** 1. week 2. work

**WL, w.l.** 1. waterline 2. wavelength

**Wm.** William

**WNW, W.N.W., w.n.w.** west-northwest

**WO, W.O.** Warrant Officer

**woad** (wōd) *n.* [OE. *wad*] any of a group of plants of the mustard family, esp. a plant (**dyer's woad**) with yellow flowers and leaves that yield a blue dye

**wob·ble** (wäb′'l) *vi.* **-bled, -bling** [prob. < LowG. *wabbeln*] 1. to move from side to side in an unsteady way 2. to shake as jelly does 3. to waver in mind —*vt.* to cause to wobble —*n.* a wobbling motion —**wob′bler** *n.* —**wob′bli·ness** *n.* —**wob′bly** *adj.* **-bli·er, -bli·est**

**Wo·den, Wo·dan** (wōd′'n) the chief Germanic god, identified with the Norse god Odin

**woe** (wō) *n.* [OE. *wa*] 1. great sorrow; grief 2. a cause of sorrow; trouble —*interj.* alas! Also [Archaic] **wo**

**woe·be·gone** (wō′bi gôn′, -gän′) *adj.* 1. [Archaic] woeful 2. showing woe; looking sad or mournful

**woe·ful** (-fəl) *adj.* 1. full of woe; sad; mournful 2. of, causing, or involving woe 3. pitiful; wretched; miserable —**woe′ful·ly** *adv.* —**woe′ful·ness** *n.*

**wok** (wäk) *n.* [Chin.] a metal cooking pan with a convex bottom, often used with a ringlike stand

**woke** (wōk) *alt. pt. & occas. Brit. pp. of* WAKE[1]

**wok·en** (wō′k'n) *occas. Brit. pp. of* WAKE[1]

**wold** (wōld) *n.* [OE. *wald*] a treeless, rolling plain, esp. a high one

**wolf** (woolf) *n.*, *pl.* **wolves** [OE. *wulf*] 1. *a*) any of a group of wild, flesh-eating, doglike mammals, esp. the gray wolf, found throughout the Northern Hemisphere *b*) the fur of a wolf 2. *a*) a fierce, cruel, or greedy person *b*) [Slang] a man who boldly approaches women for sexual purposes —*vt.* to eat greedily (often with *down*) —**cry wolf** to give a false alarm —**keep the wolf from the door** to provide the necessities of life —**wolf′ish** *adj.* —**wolf′ish·ly** *adv.* —**wolf′ish·ness** *n.*

**wolf·ber·ry** (-ber′ē) *n.*, *pl.* **-ries** a hardy plant with pink flowers and white, spongy berries

**Wolfe** (woolf) 1. **James**, 1727–59; Eng. general: defeated the Fr. forces under Montcalm at Quebec (1759) 2. **Thomas** (Clayton), 1900–38; U.S. novelist

**wolf·hound** (woolf′hound′) *n.* a large dog of any of several breeds formerly used for hunting wolves: see IRISH WOLFHOUND, BORZOI (*Russian wolfhound*)

**wolf·ram** (wool′frəm) *n.* [G. < *wolf*, wolf + MHG. *ram*, dirt] *same as* TUNGSTEN

**wolf·ram·ite** (-frə mīt′) *n.* [< G.: see prec.] a brownish or blackish mineral, a compound of tungsten (wolfram), iron, and manganese: the principal ore of tungsten

**wolfs·bane** (woolfs′bān′) *n. same as* ACONITE (sense 1)

**Wol·sey** (wool′zē), **Thomas** 1475?–1530; Eng. statesman & cardinal; chief Chancellor (1515–29) under Henry VIII

**Wol·ver·hamp·ton** (wool′vər hamp′tən) city in WC England, near Birmingham: pop. 264,000

**wol·ver·ine** (wool′və rēn′, wool′və rēn′) *n.*, *pl.* **-ines′, -ine′**: see PLURAL, II, D, 1 [irreg. dim. < WOLF] 1. a stocky, ferocious, flesh-eating mammal with thick fur, found in the northern U.S., northern Eurasia, and Canada: the European variety is the GLUTTON (sense 3) 2. its fur Also, Brit. sp., **wol′ver·ene′**

**wolves** (woolvz) *n. pl. of* WOLF

**wom·an** (woom′ən) *n.*, *pl.* **wom′en** (wim′in) [OE. *wifmann* < *wif*, a female + *mann*, a human being] 1. an adult, female human being 2. women as a group ["*Woman's* work is never done"] 3. a female servant 4. *a*) [Dial.] a wife *b*) a sweetheart or a mistress 5. womanly qualities [it's the *woman* in her] —*adj.* female

**wom·an·hood** (-hood′) *n.* 1. the condition of being a woman 2. womanly qualities 3. women; womankind

**wom·an·ish** (-ish) *adj.* like, characteristic of, or suitable to a woman; feminine or effeminate —**wom′an·ish·ly** *adv.* —**wom′an·ish·ness** *n.*

**wom·an·ize** (-īz′) *vt.* **-ized′, -iz′ing** to make effeminate —*vi.* [Colloq.] to be sexually promiscuous with women —**wom′an·iz′er** *n.*

**wom·an·kind** (-kīnd′) *n.* women in general

**wom·an·like** (-līk′) *adj.* womanly

**wom·an·ly** (-lē) *adj.* 1. like a woman; womanish 2. characteristic of or fit for a woman —**wom′an·li·ness** *n.*

**woman suffrage** the right of women to vote in governmental elections —**wom′an-suf′fra·gist** *n.*

**womb** (wōōm) *n.* [OE. *wamb*] 1. *same as* UTERUS 2. any place in which something is contained, developed, etc.

**wom·bat** (wäm′bat) *n.* [altered < Australian native name] a burrowing marsupial that looks like a small bear, found in Australia, Tasmania, and several Pacific islands

**wom·en** (wim′in) *n. pl. of* WOMAN

**wom·en·folk** (-fōk′) *n.pl.* [Dial. or Colloq.] women; womankind: also **wom′en·folks′**

**women's rights** the rights claimed by and for women of equal privileges and opportunities with men: cf. FEMINISM: also **woman's rights**

**won**[1] (wun) *pt. & pp. of* WIN

**won**[2] (wän) *n.*, *pl.* **won** [Korean < Chin. *yüan*, round] the monetary unit of North Korea and South Korea: see MONETARY UNITS, table

**won·der** (wun′dər) *n.* [OE. *wundor*] 1. a person, thing, or event so unusual as to cause surprise, amazement, etc.; marvel 2. the feeling of surprise, amazement, etc. caused by something strange, remarkable, etc. 3. a miracle —*vi.* 1. to feel wonder; marvel 2. to have curiosity, sometimes mixed with doubt —*vt.* to have curiosity or doubt about; want to know [I *wonder* what he meant] —**do wonders for** to make a remarkable improvement in —**no wonder!** now I know why! —**won′der·er** *n.*

**won·der·ful** (-fəl) *adj.* 1. that causes wonder; marvelous; amazing 2. [Colloq.] very good; excellent —**won′der·ful·ly** *adv.* —**won′der·ful·ness** *n.*

**won·der·land** (-land′) *n.* an imaginary land or place full of wonders, or a real place like this

**won·der·ment** (-mənt) *n.* wonder or amazement

**won·der-struck** (-struk′) *adj.* struck with wonder, surprise, admiration, etc.: also **won′der-strick′en** (-strik′'n)

**won·der·work** (-wurk′) *n.* 1. a wonderful work; wonder 2. a miraculous act; miracle —**won′der·work′er** *n.*

**won·drous** (wun′drəs) *adj.* [Now Rare] wonderful —*adv.* [Now Rare] wonderfully; remarkably —**won′drous·ly** *adv.*

**wont** (wônt, wōnt, wunt, wänt) *adj.* [ult. < OE. *wunian*, to be used to] accustomed [he was *wont* to rise early] —*n.* usual practice; habit

**won't** (wōnt) [contr. < ME. *wol not*] will not

**wont·ed** (wôn′tid, wôn′-, *etc.*) *adj.* customary; accustomed

**won ton** (wän′ tän′) a Chinese dish consisting of casings of noodle dough filled with ground meat and boiled: served in a broth (**won-ton soup**) or fried

**woo** (wōō) *vt.* [OE. *wogian*] 1. to try to get the love of; seek as a mate; court 2. to try to get; seek [to *woo* fame] 3. to entreat; coax; urge —*vi.* 1. to court a person 2. to make entreaty —**woo′er** *n.*

**wood** (wood) *n.* [OE. *wudu*] 1. [*usually pl.*] a thick growth of trees; forest or grove 2. the hard, fibrous substance beneath the bark of trees and shrubs 3. lumber or timber 4. wood used as fuel; firewood 5. something made of wood; specif., *a*) a wooden cask [whiskey aged in *wood*] *b*) [*pl.*] woodwind instruments *c*) Golf any of a set of numbered clubs with wooden heads having various lofts —*adj.* 1. made of wood; wooden 2. for cutting, shaping, or holding wood 3. growing or living in woods —*vt.* 1. to plant trees thickly over 2. to furnish with wood, esp. for fuel —*vi.* to get a supply of wood —**out of the woods** [Colloq.] out of difficulty, danger, etc.

**wood alcohol** *same as* METHANOL

**wood·bine** (wood′bīn′) *n.* [OE. *wudubinde*: see WOOD & BIND] 1. a European climbing honeysuckle 2. a tendril-climbing vine growing in eastern N. America, with green flower clusters and dark-blue, inedible berries

**wood block** a block of wood, esp. one used in making a woodcut —**wood′block′** *adj.*

**wood·carv·ing** (-kär′viŋ) *n.* 1. the art or craft of carving wood by hand to make art objects, decorative moldings, etc. 2. an object so made —**wood′carv′er** *n.*

**wood·chuck** (-chuk′) *n.* [altered < Algonquian name] a common N. American marmot, an animal that burrows in the ground and sleeps all winter; groundhog

**wood·cock** (-käk′) *n.*, *pl.* **-cocks′, -cock′**: see PLURAL, II, D, 1 1. a widespread, European, migratory game bird with short legs and a long bill 2. a smaller, related game bird of eastern N. America

**wood·craft** (-kraft′) *n.* 1. matters relating to the woods, as camping, hunting, etc. 2. *same as: a*) WOODWORKING *b*) WOODCARVING 3. skill in any of these

**wood·cut** (-kut′) *n.* 1. a wooden block engraved with a design, etc. 2. a print made from this

**wood·cut·ter** (-kut′ər) *n.* a person who fells trees, cuts wood, etc. —**wood′cut′ting** *n.*

**wood·ed** (-id) *adj.* covered with trees or woods

**wood·en** (wood′'n) *adj.* 1. made of wood 2. stiff, clum-

WOLVERINE
(2½–3½ ft. long,
including tail;
12–16 in. high
at shoulder)

WOODCHUCK
(head & body
to 15 in. long;
tail to 6 in.
long)

sy, or lifeless **3.** dull; insensitive —**wood'en·ly** *adv.* —**wood'en·ness** *n.*

**wood engraving 1.** the art or process of engraving on wood **2.** *same as* WOODCUT —**wood engraver**

**wood·en·head·ed** (wŏŏd''n hed'id) *adj.* [Colloq.] dull; stupid —**wood'en·head'ed·ness** *n.*

**wooden horse** *same as* TROJAN HORSE

**wood·en·ware** (-wer') *n.* bowls, dishes, etc. made of wood

**wood·land** (wŏŏd'land'; *also, and for adj. always,* -lənd) *n.* land covered with woods or trees —*adj.* of, living in, or relating to the woods —**wood'land·er** *n.*

**wood louse** *same as* SOW BUG

**wood·man** (-mən) *n., pl.* -**men** *same as* WOODSMAN

**wood·note** (-nōt') *n.* a sound of a forest bird or animal

**wood nymph** a nymph that lives in the woods; dryad

**wood·peck·er** (-pek'ər) *n.* any of various tree-climbing birds that have a strong, pointed bill used to drill holes in bark to get insects

**wood·pile** (-pīl') *n.* a pile of wood, esp. of firewood

**wood pulp** pulp from wood fiber, used in making paper

**wood·ruff** (-ruf') *n.* [OE. *wudurofe*] a plant with small white, pink, or blue, lily-shaped flowers

**wood screw** a metal screw with a sharp point and a coarse thread, for use in wood

**wood·shed** (-shed') *n.* a shed for storing firewood

**woods·man** (wŏŏdz'mən) *n., pl.* -**men 1.** a person who lives or works in the woods, as a hunter, woodcutter, etc. **2.** a person at home in the woods or skilled in woodcraft

**wood sorrel** any of a group of creeping plants with white, pink, red, or yellow, five-petaled flowers

**wood·sy** (wŏŏd'zē) *adj.* -**si·er,** -**si·est** of, characteristic of, or like the woods —**wood'si·ness** *n.*

**wood tar** a dark, sticky, syruplike substance obtained by the destructive distillation of wood

**wood thrush** a large, brown thrush of eastern N. America, having a sweet, clear song: also called **wood robin**

**wood turning** the art or process of turning, or shaping, wood on a lathe —**wood'·turn'er** *n.* —**wood'·turn'ing** *n.*

**wood·wind** (-wind') *n.* **1.** [*pl.*] the wind instruments of an orchestra made, esp. originally, of wood: clarinets, oboes, bassoons, flutes, and English horns **2.** any of these instruments —*adj.* of or for such instruments

**wood·work** (-wurk') *n.* **1.** work done in wood **2.** things made of wood, esp. interior moldings, doors, stairs, etc.

**wood·work·ing** (-wur'kiŋ) *n.* the art or work of making things out of wood —*adj.* of woodworking —**wood'work'er** *n.*

**wood·worm** (-wurm') *n.* any of a number of insect larvae that live on and burrow in wood

**wood·y** (wŏŏd'ē) *adj.* **wood'i·er, wood'i·est 1.** covered with trees; wooded **2.** consisting of or forming wood [a *woody* plant] **3.** like wood —**wood'i·ness** *n.*

**woof**[1] (wŏŏf, wŏŏf) *n.* [OE. *owef < o-* (*< on*) + *-wef <* base of *wefan,* to weave] **1.** the horizontal threads crossing the warp in a woven fabric; weft **2.** a woven fabric

**woof**[2] (wŏŏf) *n.* a gruff barking sound of or like that of a dog —*vi.* to make such a sound

**woof·er** (wŏŏf'ər) *n.* [prec. + -ER] in an assembly of two or more loudspeakers, a large speaker for reproducing low-frequency sounds: cf. TWEETER

**wool** (wŏŏl) *n.* see PLURAL, II, D, 3 [OE. *wull*] **1.** *a)* the soft, curly hair of sheep *b)* the hair of some other animals, as the goat, llama, or alpaca **2.** *a)* yarn spun from the fibers of such hair *b)* cloth, clothing, etc. made of this yarn **3.** anything that looks or feels like wool —*adj.* of wool or woolen goods —**all wool and a yard wide** genuine —**pull the wool over someone's eyes** to deceive or trick someone —**wool'like'** *adj.*

**wool·en** (-ən) *adj.* **1.** made of wool **2.** of or relating to wool or woolen cloth —*n.* [*pl.*] woolen goods or clothing Also, chiefly Brit. sp., **wool'len**

**wool·gath·er·ing** (-gath'ər iŋ) *n.* absent-mindedness or daydreaming —**wool'gath'er·er** *n.*

**wool·grow·er** (-grō'ər) *n.* a person who raises sheep for wool —**wool'grow'ing** *n.*

**wool·ly** (wŏŏl'ē) *adj.* -**li·er,** -**li·est 1.** of or like wool **2.** bearing wool **3.** covered with wool or something like wool in texture **4.** rough and uncivilized: chiefly in **wild and woolly 5.** confused; fuzzy [*woolly* ideas] —*n., pl.* -**lies 1.** [Western] a sheep **2.** a woolen garment; specif., [*pl.*] long underwear —**wool'li·ness** *n.*

**wool·sack** (wŏŏl'sak') *n.* **1.** a sack of wool **2.** a cushion stuffed with wool, on which the British Lord Chancellor sits in the House of Lords

**wool·y** (wŏŏl'ē) *adj.* **wool'i·er, wool'i·est,** *n., pl.* **wool'ies** *same as* WOOLLY —**wool'i·ness** *n.*

**wooz·y** (wŏŏ'zē, wŏŏz'ē) *adj.* **wooz'i·er, wooz'i·est** [prob. < *wooze,* var. of OOZE[1]] [Colloq.] **1.** dizzy, faint, and sick-

ish **2.** befuddled, as from drink —**wooz'i·ly** *adv.* —**wooz'i·ness** *n.*

**Worces·ter** (wŏŏs'tər) [after *Worcester,* city in E England] city in C Mass.: pop. 162,000

**Worces·ter·shire sauce** (wŏŏs'tər shir') [orig. made in *Worcester,* England] a spicy sauce for meats, poultry, etc., containing soy, vinegar, etc.

**word** (wurd) *n.* [OE.] **1.** *a)* a speech sound, or series of speech sounds, serving to communicate meaning; unit of language consisting of a single morpheme or a group of morphemes *b)* a letter or group of letters, written or printed, representing such a unit of language **2.** a brief expression; remark [a *word* of advice] **3.** a promise [he gave his *word*] **4.** news; information [no *word* from home] **5.** *a)* a password or signal *b)* a command; order **6.** [*usually pl.*] *a)* talk; speech *b)* lyrics; text; libretto **7.** [*pl.*] a quarrel; dispute **8.** an ordered combination of characters with meaning, regarded as a unit and stored in a computer —*vt.* to express in words; phrase —**a good word** a favorable comment, or commendation —**by word of mouth** by speech; orally —**have a word with** to have a brief conversation with —**have no words for** to be incapable of describing —**have words with** to argue angrily with —**in a word** in short; briefly —**in so many words** precisely; succinctly —**man (or woman) of his (or her) word** one who keeps his promises —**of many (or few) words** talkative (or untalkative) —**take the words out of one's mouth** to say what one was about to say oneself —**the Word 1.** the Bible: also **Word of God 2.** the spirit of God as revealed in Jesus: John 1:1 **3.** *same as* GOSPEL (sense 1) —**(upon) my word!** indeed! really! —**word for word** in precisely the same words —**word'less** *adj.* —**word'less·ly** *adv.* —**word'less·ness** *n.*

**word·age** (-ij) *n.* **1.** words collectively, or the number of words (*of* a story, novel, etc.) **2.** wordiness **3.** wording

**word·book** (-book') *n.* a dictionary, lexicon, or vocabulary

**word-for-word** (-fər wurd') *adj.* in exactly the same words

**word·ing** (-iŋ) *n.* choice and arrangement of words; diction

**word of honor** pledged word; solemn promise

**word order** the arrangement of words in a phrase, clause, or sentence

**word processing** an automated, computerized system in which letters, records, etc. are prepared, stored, or reproduced, as by using an electronic typewriter

**word square** a square made of letters so arranged that they spell the same words horizontally and vertically

**Words·worth** (wurdz'wərth), **William** 1770-1850; Eng. poet

**word·y** (wur'dē) *adj.* **word'i·er, word'i·est** containing or using many or too many words; verbose —**word'i·ly** *adv.* —**word'i·ness** *n.*

**wore** (wôr) *pt. of* WEAR[1]

**work** (wurk) *n.* [OE. *weorc*] **1.** physical or mental effort exerted to do or make something; labor; toil **2.** employment at a job [out of *work*] **3.** occupation, profession, business, trade, craft, etc. **4.** *a)* something one is making, doing, or acting upon; task [to take *work* home] *b)* the amount of this [a day's *work*] **5.** something that has been made or done; specif., *a)* an act; deed: *usually used in pl.* [good *works*] *b)* [*pl.*] collected writings *c)* [*pl.*] engineering structures, as bridges, dams, etc. *d)* a fortification *e)* needlework; embroidery *f)* *same as* WORK OF ART **6.** [*pl., with sing. v.*] a place where work is done, as a factory **7.** workmanship **8.** the action of, or effect produced by, natural forces **9.** *Mech.* transference of force from one body or system to another, measured by the product of the force and the amount of displacement in the line of force —*adj.* of, for, or used in work —*vi.* **worked** or **wrought, work'ing 1.** to do work; labor; toil **2.** to be employed **3.** *a)* to perform its function; operate; act *b)* to operate effectively **4.** to undergo fermentation **5.** to produce results or exert an influence [let it *work* in his mind] **6.** to be manipulated, kneaded, etc. [putty that *works* easily] **7.** to move, proceed, etc. slowly and with or as with difficulty **8.** to move, twitch, etc. as from agitation [his face *worked* with emotion] **9.** to change into a specified condition, as by repeated movement [the handle *worked* loose] —*vt.* **1.** to cause; bring about [his idea *worked* wonders] **2.** to mold; shape [to *work* silver] **3.** to sew, embroider, etc. [to *work* a sampler] **4.** to solve (a mathematical problem or a puzzle) **5.** to manipulate; knead [to *work* dough] **6.** to bring into a specified condition, as by moving back and forth [to *work* a nail loose] **7.** to cultivate (soil) **8.** to cause to function; operate; use **9.** to cause fermentation in **10.** to cause to work [to *work* a crew hard] **11.** to influence; persuade [*work* him to your ideas] **12.** to make (one's way, etc.) by work or effort **13.** to provoke; rouse [to *work* oneself into a rage] **14.** to carry on activity in, along, etc.; cover [a salesman who has been successfully *working* this territory] **15.**

[Colloq.] to make use of, esp. by clever dealing /work your connections/ —at work working —get (or give one) the works [Slang] to be (or cause one to be) the victim of an ordeal —in the works [Colloq.] in the process of being planned or done —make short (or quick) work of to deal with or dispose of quickly —out of work unemployed —shoot the works [Slang] 1. to risk everything on one chance 2. to make a supreme effort —the works 1. the working parts (of a watch, clock, etc.) 2. [Colloq.] everything —work in to insert or be inserted —work off 1. to get rid of, as by exertion 2. to pay (a debt or obligation) by work instead of money —work on (or upon) 1. to influence 2. to try to persuade —work out 1. to make its way out, as from being embedded 2. to exhaust (a mine, etc.) 3. same as WORK OFF (sense 2) 4. to accomplish 5. to solve 6. to result in some way 7. to develop; elaborate 8. to engage in a workout —work over [Colloq.] to subject to harsh or cruel treatment —work up 1. to advance; rise 2. to develop; elaborate 3. to arouse; excite

**work·a·ble** (wur'kə b'l) *adj.* 1. that can be worked 2. practicable; feasible —work'a·bil'i·ty *n.*

**work·a·day** (wur'kə dā') *adj.* 1. of or suitable for working days; everyday 2. commonplace; ordinary

**work·a·hol·ic** (wur'kə hôl'ik, -häl'-) *n.* [WORK + -a- + (ALCO)HOLIC] a person having a compulsive need to work

**work·bench** (wurk'bench') *n.* a table at which work is done, as by a mechanic, carpenter, etc.

**work·book** (-book') *n.* 1. a book containing questions and exercises to be worked by students 2. a book of operating instructions 3. a book containing a record of work planned or done

**work·day** (-dā') *n.* 1. a day on which work is done; working day 2. the part of a day during which work is done /a 7-hour workday/ —adj. same as WORKADAY

**work·er** (wur'kər) *n.* 1. a person, animal, or thing that works; specif., a person who works for a living 2. a person who works for a cause, etc. 3. any of various sterile female ants, bees, etc. that do work for the colony

**work force** the total number of workers actively employed in, or available for work in, a nation, region, plant, etc.

**work·horse** (wurk'hôrs') *n.* 1. a horse used for working, as for pulling a plow 2. a steady, responsible worker with a heavy workload 3. a durable machine, vehicle, etc.

**work·house** (-hous') *n.* 1. in England, formerly, a poorhouse 2. a kind of prison where petty offenders are confined and made to work

**work·ing** (wur'kiŋ) *adj.* 1. that works 2. of, for, or used in work 3. sufficient to get work done /a working majority/ 4. on which further work may be based /a working hypothesis/ —n. 1. the act or process of a person or thing that works 2. [usually pl.] a part of a mine, quarry, etc. where work is or has been done

**working capital** the part of a company's capital that can be converted readily into cash

**working class** workers as a class; esp., industrial or manual workers as a class; proletariat —work'ing-class' *adj.*

**working day** 1. a day on which work is done, esp. as distinguished from a Sunday, holiday, etc. 2. the part of a day during which work is done; specif., the number of hours each day that an employee is required to work

**work·ing·man** (-man') *n.*, *pl.* **-men** (-men') a worker; esp., an industrial or manual worker; wage earner; laborer

**work·ing·wom·an** (-woom'ən) *n.*, *pl.* **-wom'en** a woman worker; esp., a woman industrial or manual worker

**work·load** (wurk'lōd') *n.* the amount of work assigned to be completed within a given period of time

**work·man** (wurk'mən) *n.*, *pl.* **-men** 1. same as WORKING-MAN 2. a craftsman

**work·man·like** (-līk') *adj.* characteristic of a good workman; skillful: also **work'man·ly**

**work·man·ship** (-ship') *n.* 1. skill of a workman; craftsmanship 2. something produced by this skill

**work of art** 1. something produced in one of the fine arts, as a painting, sculpture, etc. 2. anything made, performed, etc. with great skill and beauty

**work·out** (wurk'out') *n.* 1. a period of doing exercises intended to develop physical fitness or athletic skill 2. any exercise, work, etc. requiring great effort

**work·room** (-rōōm') *n.* a room in which work is done

**work·shop** (-shäp') *n.* 1. a room or building where work is done 2. a seminar or series of meetings for intensive study, work, etc. in some field /a writers' workshop/

**work song** a folk song sung by laborers, as in the fields, with a marked rhythm matching the rhythm of their work

**work·week** (-wēk') *n.* the total number of hours or days worked in a week for the regular wage or salary

**work·wom·an** (-woom'ən) *n.*, *pl.* **-wom'en** same as WORK-INGWOMAN

**world** (wurld) *n.* [OE. werold] 1. *a)* the planet earth *b)* the whole universe *c)* any heavenly body imagined as being in-

habited 2. the earth and its inhabitants 3. *a)* mankind *b)* people generally /the news startled the world/ 4. *a)* [also W-] some part of the earth /the Old World/ *b)* some period of history, its society, etc. /the ancient world/ *c)* any sphere or domain /the animal world/ *d)* any sphere of human activity /the world of music/ 5. individual experience, outlook, etc. /his world is narrow/ 6. *a)* the usual social life of people, as apart from a life devoted to religious or spiritual matters *b)* people leading the usual social life 7. [often pl.] a large amount; great deal /to do a world (or worlds) of good/ —bring into the world to give birth to —come into the world to be born —for all the world 1. for any reason or consideration at all 2. in every respect; exactly —in the world 1. on earth or in the universe; anywhere 2. at all; ever

**world·beat·er** (-bēt'ər) *n.* [Colloq.] one that is, or has the qualities needed to become, a great success

**world·ling** (-liŋ) *n.* a worldly person

**world·ly** (wurld'lē) *adj.* **-li·er, -li·est** 1. of or limited to this world; temporal or secular 2. devoted to or concerned with the affairs, pleasures, interests, etc. of this world: also **world'ly-mind'ed** 3. worldly-wise —**world'li·ness** *n.*

**world·ly-wise** (-wīz') *adj.* wise in the ways or affairs of the world; sophisticated

**world power** a nation or organization large or powerful enough to have a worldwide influence

**World Series** [also w- s-] an annual series of games between the winning teams of the two major U.S. baseball leagues to decide the championship

**world-shak·ing** (wurld'shā'kiŋ) *adj.* of great importance, effect, or influence; momentous

**World War I** the war (1914–18) between the Allies (Great Britain, France, Russia, the U.S., Italy, Japan, etc.) and the Central Powers (Germany, Austria-Hungary, etc.)

**World War II** the war (1939–45) between the United Nations (Great Britain, France, the Soviet Union, the U.S., etc.) and the Axis (Germany, Italy, Japan, etc.)

**world-wea·ry** (wurld'wir'ē) *adj.* weary of the world; bored

**world·wide** (-wīd') *adj.* extending throughout the world

**worm** (wurm) *n.* [OE. *wyrm*, serpent] 1. any of many long, slender, soft-bodied, creeping animals, as the annelids, roundworms, etc. 2. popularly, *a)* an insect larva, as a grub *b)* any of several mollusks, as the shipworms *c)* any of various wormlike animals, as the rotifer 3. a person looked down on as being too meek, wretched, etc. 4. something thought of as being wormlike because of its spiral shape; specif., a short, rotating screw that meshes with the teeth of a worm wheel or a rack 5. [pl.] Med. any disease or disorder caused by parasitic worms in the intestines, etc. —vi. to move, proceed, etc. like a worm, in a winding, creeping, or roundabout manner —vt. 1. to bring about, get, make, etc. in a winding, creeping, or roundabout manner 2. to rid of worms; esp., to purge of intestinal worms —worm'er *n.* —worm'like' *adj.*

**worm-eat·en** (-ēt'n) *adj.* 1. eaten into by worms, termites, etc. 2. worn-out, out-of-date, etc.

**worm gear** 1. same as WORM WHEEL 2. a gear consisting of a worm and worm wheel

**worm·hole** (-hōl') *n.* a hole made, as in wood, by a worm, termite, etc.

**Worms** (vôrmz; *E.* wurmz) city in West Germany, on the Rhine: scene of an assembly (*Diet of Worms*), 1521, at which Martin Luther was condemned for heresy

**worm wheel** a toothed wheel designed to gear with the thread of a worm

**worm·wood** (wurm'wood') *n.* [altered by folk etym. < OE. *wermod*] 1. any of various strong-smelling plants; esp., a Eurasian perennial that yields a bitter-tasting, dark-green oil (**wormwood oil**) used in making absinthe 2. a bitter experience

WORM GEAR

**worm·y** (wur'mē) *adj.* **worm'i·er, worm'i·est** 1. containing a worm or worms; worm-infested 2. same as WORM-EATEN 3. like a worm 4. debased; groveling —**worm'i·ness** *n.*

**worn** (wôrn) *pp. of* WEAR¹ —*adj.* 1. showing the effects of use, wear, etc. 2. damaged by use or wear 3. showing the effects of worry or anxiety 4. exhausted; spent

**worn-out** (-out') *adj.* 1. used or worn until no longer effective, usable, or serviceable 2. exhausted; tired out

**wor·ri·ment** (wur'ē mənt) *n.* 1. a worrying or being worried; mental disturbance; anxiety 2. a cause of worry

**wor·ri·some** (-səm) *adj.* 1. causing worry or anxiety 2. having a tendency to worry —**wor'ri·some·ly** *adv.*

**wor·ry** (wur'ē) *vt.* **-ried, -ry·ing** [OE. *wyrgan*, to strangle] 1. *a)* to treat roughly, as with continual biting /a dog *worrying* a bone/ *b)* to pluck at, touch, etc. repeatedly in a nervous way /to *worry* a loose tooth with the tongue/ 2. to annoy; bother 3. to cause to feel troubled or uneasy —*vi.* 1. to bite, pull, or tear (*at* an object) with the teeth 2. to be anxious, troubled, etc. **3.** to manage to get (*along* or *through*) in the face of difficulties —*n.*, *pl.* **-ries 1.** the act of worrying **2.** a troubled state of mind; anxiety **3.** something that causes anxiety —**wor′ri·er** *n.*

**wor·ry·wart** (-wôrt′) *n.* [WORRY + WART] [Colloq.] a person who tends to worry, esp. over trivial details

**worse** (wurs) *adj. compar. of* BAD¹ & ILL [OE. *wiersa*] **1.** *a*) bad, evil, harmful, etc. in a greater degree *b*) of inferior quality or condition **2.** in poorer health; more ill **3.** in a less satisfactory situation —*adv. compar. of* BADLY & ILL in a worse manner; to a worse extent —*n.* that which is worse —**for the worse** to a worse condition

**wors·en** (wur′s′n) *vt.*, *vi.* [orig., a dial. word < prec. + -EN] to make or become worse

**wor·ship** (wur′ship) *n.* [< OE.: see WORTH & -SHIP] **1.** *a*) reverence or devotion for a deity; veneration *b*) a church service or other rite showing this **2.** intense love or admiration of any kind **3.** something worshiped **4.** [Chiefly Brit.] a title of honor (preceded by *your* or *his*) used in addressing magistrates, etc. —*vt.* **-shiped** or **-shipped**, **-ship·ing** or **-ship·ping 1.** to show religious reverence for **2.** to have intense love or admiration for —*vi.* to engage in worship —**wor′ship·er**, **wor′ship·per** *n.*

**wor·ship·ful** (-fəl) *adj.* **1.** [Chiefly Brit.] honorable; respected: used as a title of respect **2.** feeling or offering great devotion or respect —**wor′ship·ful·ly** *adv.* —**wor′ship·ful·ness** *n.*

**worst** (wurst) *adj. superl. of* BAD¹ & ILL [OE. *wyrsta*] **1.** *a*) bad, evil, harmful, etc. in the greatest degree *b*) of the lowest quality or condition **2.** in the least satisfactory situation —*adv. superl. of* BADLY & ILL in the worst manner; to the worst extent —*n.* that which is worst —*vt.* to get the better of; defeat —**at worst** under the worst circumstances —**if (the) worst comes to (the) worst** if the worst possible thing happens —**(in) the worst way** [Slang] very much; greatly —**make the worst of** to be pessimistic about

**wor·sted** (woos′tid, wur′stid) *n.* [after *Worsted*, now *Worstead*, England, where first made] **1.** a smooth, hardtwisted thread or yarn made from long-staple wool **2.** fabric made from this —*adj.* made of worsted

**wort¹** (wurt) *n.* [< OE. *wyrt* (in compounds)] a liquid prepared with malt which, after fermenting, becomes beer, ale, etc.

**wort²** (wurt) *n.* [OE. *wyrt*, a root] a plant or herb: now usually in compounds [*liverwort*]

**worth** (wurth) *n.* [OE. *weorth*] **1.** material value, esp. as expressed in terms of money **2.** the esteem in which a person or thing is held; importance, value, etc. **3.** the quantity of something that may be had for a given sum [a dime's *worth* of nuts] **4.** wealth; possessions —*adj.* [*with prepositional force*] **1.** deserving or worthy of; meriting **2.** equal in value to (something specified) **3.** having wealth amounting to —**for all one is worth** to the utmost —**put in one's two cents' worth** to give one's opinion

**worth·less** (-lis) *adj.* without worth or merit; useless, valueless, etc. —**worth′less·ly** *adv.* —**worth′less·ness** *n.*

**worth·while** (-hwil′, -wil′) *adj.* important or valuable enough to repay time or effort spent; of true value

**wor·thy** (wur′thē) *adj.* **-thi·er**, **-thi·est 1.** having worth, value, or merit **2.** deserving; meriting (often with *of* or an infinitive) —*n.*, *pl.* **-thies** a person of outstanding worth or importance: often used humorously —**wor′thi·ly** *adv.* —**wor′thi·ness** *n.*

**wot** (wät) *1st* & *3d pers. sing.*, *pres. indic., of* WIT²

**would** (wood; *unstressed* wəd) *v.* [OE. *wolde*, pt. of *willan*, to will] **1.** *pt. of* WILL² **2.** an auxiliary used: *a*) to express condition [he *would* go if you *would*] *b*) in indirect discourse to express futurity [he said he *would* come] *c*) to express habitual action [Sundays he *would* sleep late] *d*) to soften a request [*would* you please leave?] **3.** I wish [*would* that she were here] See also SHOULD

**would-be** (wood′bē′) *adj.* **1.** wishing or pretending to be [a *would-be* expert] **2.** intended to be [a *would-be* help]

**would·n't** (wood′n't) would not

**wouldst** (woodst) *archaic 2d pers. sing. of* WILL²: *used with* thou: also would·est (wood′ist)

**wound¹** (woond) *n.* [OE. *wund*] **1.** an injury in which the skin or other tissue is broken, cut, torn, etc. **2.** any hurt to the feelings, honor, etc. —*vt.*, *vi.* to inflict a wound (*on* or *upon*); injure —**the wounded** persons wounded, esp. in warfare

**wound²** (wound) **1.** *pt.* & *pp. of* WIND¹ **2.** *pt.* & *pp. of* WIND³

**wove** (wōv) *pt.* & *alt. pp. of* WEAVE

**wo·ven** (-'n) *alt. pp. of* WEAVE

**wow¹** (wou) *interj.* an exclamation of surprise, pleasure, pain, etc. —*n.* [Slang] a remarkable, successful, exciting, etc. person or thing —*vt.* [Slang] to be a great success with

**wow²** (wou) *n.* [echoic] a distortion in reproduced sound, caused by variations in speed of the turntable, tape, etc. either in recording or playing

**WPA, W.P.A.** Works Progress (later, Work Projects) Administration

**wpm** words per minute

**wrack¹** (rak) *n.* [< OE. *wræc*, misery & MDu. *wrak*, a wreck] **1.** ruin; destruction: now chiefly in **wrack and ruin 2.** seaweed, etc. cast up on shore

**wrack²** (rak) *vt.* [< RACK¹] *same as* RACK¹; esp., to subject to extreme mental or physical suffering; torture

**wraith** (rāth) *n.* [Scot., ult. < ON. *vorthr*, guardian < *vartha*, to guard] **1.** a ghost **2.** a ghostlike figure of a person supposedly seen just before his death

**wran·gle¹** (raŋ′g'l) *vi.* **-gled**, **-gling** [< ME. freq. of *wringen*, to WRING] **1.** to quarrel angrily and noisily **2.** to argue; dispute —*vt.* to argue (a person) *into* or *out of* something —*n.* an angry, noisy dispute or quarrel

**wran·gle²** (raŋ′g'l) *vt.* **-gled**, **-gling** [< WRANGLER²] to herd (livestock, esp. saddle horses)

**wran·gler¹** (raŋ′glər) *n.* [WRANGLE¹ + -ER] a person who wrangles, or argues, esp. in a noisy or angry way

**wran·gler²** (raŋ′glər) *n.* [< (*horse*) *wrangler*, partial transl. of AmSp. *caballerango*, a groom] a cowboy who herds livestock, esp. saddle horses

**wrap** (rap) *vt.* **wrapped** or **wrapt**, **wrap′ping** [ME. *wrappen*] **1.** *a*) to wind or fold (a covering) around something *b*) to cover by this means **2.** to envelop; hide; conceal [a town *wrapped* in fog] **3.** to enclose and fasten in a wrapper of paper, etc. **4.** to wind or fold [to *wrap* one's arms around someone] —*vi.* to twine, extend, coil, etc. (usually with *over*, *around*, etc.) —*n.* **1.** an outer covering; esp., an outer garment worn by being wrapped around the body **2.** [*pl.*] secrecy; censorship [plans kept under *wraps*] —**wrapped up in 1.** devoted to; absorbed in (work, etc.) **2.** involved in —**wrap up 1.** to enfold in a covering **2.** to put on warm clothing **3.** [Colloq.] *a*) to bring to an end *b*) to give a concluding report, etc.

**wrap·a·round** (rap′ə round′) *adj.* **1.** that has a full-length opening and is wrapped around the body [a *wraparound* skirt] **2.** molded, etc. so as to curve [a *wraparound* windshield] —*n.* a wraparound garment, esp. a skirt

**wrap·per** (-ər) *n.* **1.** a person or thing that wraps **2.** that in which something is wrapped; covering; cover **3.** a woman's dressing gown **4.** a baby's robe

**wrap·ping** (-iŋ) *n.* [*often pl.*] the material, as paper, in which something is wrapped

**wrap-up** (-up′) *adj.* [Colloq.] **1.** making final; concluding **2.** that comes at the end and summarizes —*n.* **1.** [Colloq.] *a*) the concluding event, action, etc. in a sequence *b*) a concluding, summarizing report, etc. **2.** [Slang] a quick, easy sale or the customer to whom the sale is made

**wrasse** (ras) *n.*, *pl.* **wrass′es**, **wrasse**: see PLURAL, II, D, 1 [Corn. *wrach*] any of various fishes with spiny fins and bright coloring, found esp. in tropical seas

**wras·tle** (ras′'l) *n.*, *vi.*, *vt.* **-tled**, **-tling** *dial. or colloq. var. of* WRESTLE: also **wras′sle** **-sled**, **-sling**

**wrath** (rath; *chiefly Brit.* rôth) *n.* [OE. *wræththo* < *wrath*, wroth] **1.** intense anger; rage **2.** any action carried out in great anger, esp. for punishment or vengeance

**wrath·ful** (-fəl) *adj.* **1.** full of wrath **2.** resulting from or expressing wrath —**wrath′ful·ly** *adv.* —**wrath′ful·ness** *n.*

**wreak** (rēk) *vt.* [OE. *wrecan*, to revenge] **1.** to give vent or free play to (anger, malice, etc.) **2.** to inflict (vengeance), cause (havoc), etc. —**wreak′er** *n.*

**wreath** (rēth) *n.*, *pl.* **wreaths** (rēthz) [OE. *writha*, a ring < *writhan*, to twist] **1.** a twisted band or ring of leaves, flowers, etc. **2.** something suggesting this in shape [*wreaths* of smoke] —**wreath′like′** *adj.*

**wreathe** (rēth) *vt.* **wreathed**, **wreath′ing 1.** to coil, twist, or entwine, esp. so as to form a wreath **2.** to coil, twist, or entwine around; encircle [clouds *wreathe* the hills] **3.** to decorate with wreaths **4.** to cover or envelop [a face *wreathed* in smiles] —*vi.* **1.** to have a twisting or coiling movement **2.** to form a wreath

**wreck** (rek) *n.* [Anglo-Fr. *wrec* < ON. *vrek*, driftwood, wreckage] **1.** goods or wreckage cast ashore after a shipwreck **2.** *a*) the disabling or destruction of a ship by a storm or other disaster; shipwreck *b*) a ship thus disabled or destroyed **3.** the remains of anything that has been destroyed or badly damaged **4.** a person in very poor health **5.** a wrecking or being wrecked; ruin —*vt.* **1.** to destroy or damage badly **2.** to tear down (a building, etc.) **3.** to overthrow; thwart **4.** to destroy the health of —*vi.* **1.** to be wrecked **2.** to work as a wrecker

**wreck·age** (-ij) *n.* **1.** a wrecking or being wrecked **2.** the remains of something that has been wrecked

**wreck·er** (-ər) *n.* **1.** a person or thing that wrecks **2.** a person who causes ruin, obstruction, etc.  **3.** a person, car, train, etc. that salvages or clears away wrecks; specif., a truck equipped to tow away wrecked or disabled automobiles  **4.** a person whose work is tearing down and salvaging buildings, etc.

**wreck·ing** (-iŋ) *n.* the act or work of a wrecker —*adj.* engaged or used in dismantling or salvaging wrecks

**wrecking bar** a crowbar with a chisellike point at one end and a curved claw at the other

**wren** (ren) *n.* [OE. *wrenna*] any of various small, insect-eating songbirds having a long bill, rounded wings, and a stubby, erect tail

**Wren** (ren), Sir **Christopher** 1632–1723; Eng. architect

**wrench** (rench) *n.* [OE. *wrenc*, a trick]  **1.** a sudden, sharp twist or pull  **2.** an injury caused by a twist or jerk, as to the back  **3.** a sudden feeling of anguish, grief, etc., as at parting with someone  **4.** any of a number of tools used for holding and turning nuts, bolts, pipes, etc. —*vt.* **1.** to twist, pull, or jerk violently  **2.** to injure (a part of the body) with a twist or wrench  **3.** to distort (a meaning, statement, etc.) —*vi.* to pull or tug (*at* something) with a wrenching movement

**wrest** (rest) *vt.* [OE. *wræstan*]  **1.** to pull or force away violently with a twisting motion  **2.** to take by force; usurp  **3.** to distort or change the true meaning, purpose, etc. of —*n.* a wresting; a twist; wrench

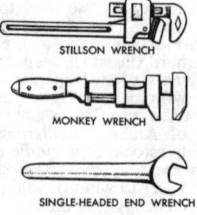

STILLSON WRENCH

MONKEY WRENCH

SINGLE-HEADED END WRENCH

TYPES OF WRENCH

**wres·tle** (res′'l) *vi., vt.* -tled, -tling [< OE. freq. of *wræstan*, to twist]  **1.** to struggle hand to hand with (an opponent) in an attempt to throw or force him to the ground without striking blows  **2.** to struggle hard (*with* a problem, etc.) or struggle to move or lift (something) —*n.* **1.** a wrestling; wrestling bout  **2.** a struggle or contest —**wres′-tler** *n.*

**wres·tling** (-liŋ) *n.* a form of sport in which the opponents wrestle, or struggle hand to hand

**wretch** (rech) *n.* [OE. *wrecca*, an outcast]  **1.** a miserable or unhappy person  **2.** a person who is despised or scorned

**wretch·ed** (-id) *adj.* [OE. *wræcc*]  **1.** very unhappy; miserable; unfortunate  **2.** causing misery [*wretched* slums]  **3.** very inferior [a *wretched* meal]  **4.** deserving to be despised —**wretch′ed·ly** *adv.* —**wretch′ed·ness** *n.*

**wrig·gle** (rig′'l) *vi.* -gled, -gling [MLowG. *wriggeln*]  **1.** to twist and turn to and fro; squirm  **2.** to move along with a twisting, writhing motion  **3.** to make one's way by subtle or shifty means; dodge —*vt.* **1.** to cause to wriggle  **2.** to bring into a specified condition by wriggling —*n.* a wriggling —**wrig′gly** *adj.* -gli·er, -gli·est

**wrig·gler** (-lər) *n.* **1.** a person or thing that wriggles  **2.** the larva of a mosquito; wiggler

**wright** (rīt) *n.* [OE. *wyrhta* < *wyrcan*, to work] a person who makes, constructs, or repairs: used chiefly in compounds [shipwright]

**Wright** (rīt)  **1. Frank Lloyd**, 1869–1959; U.S. architect  **2. Or·ville** (ôr′vil), 1871–1948 & his brother **Wilbur**, 1867–1912; U.S. airplane inventors

**wring** (riŋ) *vt.* **wrung** or rare **wringed**, **wring′ing** [OE. *wringan*]  **1.** *a)* to squeeze, press, or twist, esp. so as to force out water or other liquid  *b)* to force out (water, etc.) by this means (usually with *out*)  **2.** to clasp and twist (the hands) together as an expression of distress  **3.** to clasp (another's hand) forcefully in greeting  **4.** to wrench or twist forcibly  **5.** to get or extract by force, threats, persistence, etc.  **6.** to afflict with anguish, pity, etc. [the story *wrung* her heart] —*vi.* to squirm or twist with force or great effort —*n.* a wringing

**wring·er** (-ər) *n.* **1.** a person or thing that wrings  **2.** a device with two rollers close together between which wet clothes are run to squeeze out the water

**wrin·kle**[1] (riŋ′k'l) *n.* [prob. < OE. (*ge*)*wrinclod*, pp. of (*ge*)*wrinclian*, to wind about]  **1.** a small ridge or furrow in a normally smooth surface, caused by contraction, folding, etc.  **2.** a crease or pucker in the skin —*vt., vi.* -kled, -kling to contract or pucker into small ridges or creases —**wrin′kly** *adj.* -kli·er, -kli·est

**wrin·kle**[2] (riŋ′k'l) *n.* [prob. ult. < OE. *wrenc*, a trick] [Colloq.] a clever or novel trick, idea, or device

**wrist** (rist) *n.* [OE.]  **1.** the joint or part of the arm between the hand and the forearm; carpus  **2.** the corresponding part in an animal —**a slap** (or **tap**) **on the wrist** a token punishment, less severe than seems called for

**wrist·band** (rist′band′) *n.* a band that goes around the wrist, as on the cuff of a sleeve

**wrist·let** (-lit) *n.* **1.** a closefitting band or strip of material worn around the wrist, as for warmth  **2.** a bracelet

**wrist pin** the stud or pin by which the connecting rod is attached to a wheel, crank, etc.

**wrist·watch** (-wäch′, -wôch′) *n.* a watch worn on a strap or band that fits around the wrist

**writ** (rit) *n.* [OE. < *writan*, to write]  **1.** [Rare or Archaic] something written  **2.** a formal legal document ordering or prohibiting some action

**write** (rīt) *vt.* **wrote**, **writ′ten**, **writ′ing**; archaic pt. & pp. **writ** [OE. *writan*, to scratch, write]  **1.** *a)* to form (words, letters, etc.) on a surface, esp. with a pen or pencil  *b)* to form the words, letters, etc. of [*write* your name]  **2.** to spell (a word, etc.) [words *written* the same are often pronounced differently]  **3.** to know (a specific language, etc.) well enough to communicate in writing  **4.** to be the author or composer of (literary or musical material)  **5.** to fill in (a check, form, etc.) with the writing required  **6.** to cover with writing [he *wrote* 10 pages]  **7.** to communicate in writing [he *wrote* that he was ill]  **8.** to communicate with in writing [*write* me every day]  **9.** to record (information) in a computer's memory or on a tape, etc. for use by a computer  **10.** to leave signs or evidence of [greed was *written* on his face] —*vi.* **1.** to form words, letters, etc. on a surface, esp. with a pen or pencil  **2.** to write books or other literary matter  **3.** to write a letter  **4.** to produce writing of a specified kind [to *write* legibly] —**write down  1.** to put into written form  **2.** to discredit in writing —**write in** to vote for (someone not officially on a ballot) by inserting his name on the ballot —**write off  1.** to cancel or remove from accounts (bad debts, etc.)  **2.** to drop from consideration —**write out  1.** to put into writing  **2.** to write in full —**write up  1.** to write an account of  **2.** to praise in writing

**writ·er** (rīt′ər) *n.* a person who writes, esp. as a business or occupation; author, journalist, etc.

**write-up** (rīt′up′) *n.* [Colloq.] a written report or description, often a favorable account, as for publicity

**writhe** (rīth) *vt.* **writhed**, **writh′ing** [OE. *writhan*, to twist] to cause to twist or turn; contort —*vi.* **1.** to make twisting or turning movements; squirm  **2.** to suffer great emotional distress —*n.* a writhing movement

**writ·ing** (rīt′iŋ) *n.* **1.** the act of a person who writes  **2.** something written, as a letter, document, etc.  **3.** written form  **4.** *short for* HANDWRITING  **5.** a literary work  **6.** the profession or occupation of a writer  **7.** the art, style, etc. of literary composition —*adj.* **1.** that writes  **2.** used in writing

**writ·ten** (rit′'n) *pp. of* WRITE —*adj.* put down in a form to be read; not spoken or oral

**Wroc·ław** (vrōts′läf) city in SW Poland, on the Oder River: pop. 514,000

**wrong** (rôŋ) *adj.* [OE. *wrang* < ON. *rangr*, twisted]  **1.** not just, moral, etc.; unlawful, immoral, or improper  **2.** not in accordance with an established standard, etc. [the *wrong* method]  **3.** not suitable or appropriate [the *wrong* thing to say]  **4.** *a)* contrary to fact, reason, etc.; incorrect  *b)* acting, believing, etc. incorrectly; mistaken  **5.** in an unsatisfactory or bad condition  **6.** not functioning properly [what's *wrong* with the light?]  **7.** designating the unfinished, inner, or under side [the *wrong* side of a fabric] —*adv.* in a wrong manner, direction, etc.; incorrectly —*n.* **1.** something wrong, esp. an unjust or immoral act  **2.** *Law* a violation of a legal right —*vt.* **1.** to treat badly or unjustly; injure  **2.** to think badly of without real justification —**get** (**someone** or **something**) **wrong** [Colloq.] to fail to understand (someone or something) properly —**go wrong  1.** to turn out badly  **2.** to change from good behavior to bad —**in the wrong** not on the side supported by truth, justice, etc. —**wrong′er** *n.* —**wrong′ly** *adv.* —**wrong′ness** *n.*

**wrong·do·ing** (-dōō′iŋ) *n.* any act or behavior that is wrong; transgression —**wrong′do′er** *n.*

**wrong·ful** (-fəl) *adj.* **1.** full of wrong; unjust, unfair, or injurious  **2.** without legal right; unlawful —**wrong′ful·ly** *adv.* —**wrong′ful·ness** *n.*

**wrong·head·ed** (-hed′id) *adj.* stubborn in sticking to wrong opinions, ideas, etc.; perverse —**wrong′head′ed·ly** *adv.* —**wrong′head′ed·ness** *n.*

**wrong number** a telephone number reached through error, as by dialing incorrectly, or the person reached

**wrote** (rōt) *pt. of* WRITE

**wroth** (rôth; *chiefly Brit.* rōth) *adj.* [OE. *wrath*] angry; wrathful; incensed

**wrought** (rôt) *alt. pt. & pp. of* WORK —*adj.* **1.** formed; fashioned  **2.** shaped by hammering or beating: said of metals  **3.** elaborated with care  **4.** decorated; ornamented

**wrought iron** a kind of iron that contains some slag and very little carbon: it is tough but easy to work or shape —**wrought′-i′ron** *adj.*

**wrought-up** (rôt′up′) *adj.* very disturbed or excited

**wrung** (ruŋ) *pt. & pp. of* WRING

**wry** (rī) *vt., vi.* **wried**, **wry′ing** [OE. *wrigian*, to turn] to writhe or twist —*adj.* **wri′er**, **wri′est  1.** turned or bent to one side; twisted; distorted  **2.** made by twisting or distorting the features *[a wry face]* **3.** perverse; ironic *[wry humor]* —**wry′ly** *adv.* —**wry′ness** *n.*

**wry·neck** (-nek′) *n.* **1.** a condition in which the neck is twisted by a muscle spasm **2.** a bird related to the woodpecker, noted for its habit of twisting its neck

**WSW, W.S.W., w.s.w.** west-southwest

**wt.** weight

**Wu·han** (wōō′hän′) city in EC China, on the Yangtze: pop. 2,500,000

‡**Wun·der·kind** (voon′dər kint′) *n., pl.* **-kin′der** (-kin′dər) [G. < *wunder,* wonder + *kind,* child] a child prodigy

**Wup·per·tal** (voop′ər täl′) city in the Ruhr Basin of West Germany: pop. 414,000

**wurst** (wurst, woorst; *G.* voorsht) *n.* [G.] sausage: often used in combination *[bratwurst, knackwurst]*

**W.Va., WV** West Virginia

**Wy·an·dotte** (wī′ən dät′) *n.* [< Iroquoian < ?] any of a breed of American chickens

**Wy·att** (wī′ət), Sir **Thomas** 1503?–42; Eng. poet

**wych-elm** (wich′elm′) *n.* [< OE. *wice,* applied to trees with pliant branches + ELM] **1.** a small variety of elm native to Europe and N Asia **2.** its wood

**Wych·er·ley** (wich′ər lē), **William** 1640?–1716; Eng. dramatist

**Wyc·liffe** (or **Wyc·lif**) (wik′lif), **John** 1324?–84; Eng. religious reformer: made the first complete translation of the Bible into English

**Wy·o·ming** (wī ō′miŋ) [< Algonquian, lit., large plains] **1.** Western State of the U.S.: 97,914 sq. mi.; pop. 471,000; cap. Cheyenne: abbrev. **Wyo., WY 2.** city in SW Mich.: suburb of Grand Rapids: pop. 60,000 —**Wy·o′ming·ite′** (-īt′) *n.*

# X

**X, x** (eks) *n., pl.* **X's, x's 1.** the twenty-fourth letter of the English alphabet **2.** a sound of *X* or *x*

**X** (eks) *n.* **1.** a mark shaped like X, used to represent the signature of a person who cannot write, to mark a particular point on a map or diagram, etc. **2.** the Roman numeral for 10 **3.** a person or thing unknown or unrevealed —*adj.* shaped like X

**X** a motion-picture rating meaning that no one under the age of seventeen is to be admitted

**x** *a symbol for:* **1.** *Math. a)* an unknown quantity *b)* times (in multiplication) *[3 × 3 = 9] c)* an abscissa **2.** *a)* by *[3 ft. × 4 ft.] b)* power of magnification (in optical instruments) *c)* one's choice or answer (on a ballot, test, etc.)

**x** (eks) *vt.* **x-ed** or **x'd, x-ing** or **x'ing 1.** to indicate (one's choice, etc.) by marking with an X **2.** to cross (*out*) words or letters with an X or X's

**xan·the·in** (zan′thē in) *n.* [Fr. *xanthéine*] the water-soluble part of the yellow pigment in some plants

**xan·thic** (zan′thik) *adj.* [< Fr.: see XANTHO- & -IC] **1.** yellow **2.** of or having to do with xanthine

**xan·thine** (-thēn, -thin) *n.* [Fr.: cf. XANTHO- & -IN¹] a white, crystalline nitrogenous compound present in blood, urine, and certain plants

**Xan·thip·pe** (zan tip′ē) 5th cent. B.C.; wife of Socrates: her name has become proverbial for the nagging wife

**xan·tho-** (zan′thō-, -thə) [< Gr. *xanthos,* yellow] *a combining form meaning* yellow: also, before a vowel, **xanth-**

**xan·thous** (zan′thəs) *adj.* [Gr. *xanthos*] yellow

**Xa·vi·er** (zā′vē ər, zav′ē-; zāv′yər), Saint **Francis** 1506–52; Sp. Jesuit missionary

**x-ax·is** (eks′ak′sis) *n., pl.* **x′-ax′es** (-sēz) *Math.* the horizontal axis along which the abscissa is measured

**X chromosome** *Genetics* one of the sex chromosomes: see SEX CHROMOSOME

**Xe** *Chem.* xenon

**xe·bec** (zē′bek) *n.* [< Fr. *chébec,* ult. < Ar. *shabbāk*] a small, three-masted ship with overhanging bow and stern: once common in the Mediterranean

**xen·o-** [< Gr. *xenos*] *a combining form meaning:* **1.** stranger, foreigner *[xenophobia]* **2.** strange, foreign Also, before a vowel, **xen-**

**xe·non** (zē′nän, zen′än) *n.* [Gr., neut. of *xenos,* strange] a heavy, colorless, gaseous chemical element present in the air in minute quantities: used in electron tubes, lasers, etc.: symbol, Xe; at. wt., 131.30; at. no., 54

**xen·o·pho·bi·a** (zen′ə fō′bē ə) *n.* [ModL.: see XENO- & -PHOBIA] fear or hatred of strangers or foreigners —**xen′o·phobe′** (-fōb′) *n.* —**xen′o·pho′bic** (-fō′bik) *adj.*

**Xen·o·phon** (zen′ə fən) 430?–355? B.C.; Gr. historian, essayist, & military leader

**xe·rog·ra·phy** (zi räg′rə fē) *n.* [< Gr. *xēros,* dry +

-GRAPHY] a process for copying printed or written material, etc., in which an image of the material is electrically charged on a surface and attracts oppositely charged dry ink particles, which are then fused in place —**xe·ro·graph′ic** (zir′ə graf′ik) *adj.*

**xe·roph·i·lous** (zi räf′ə ləs) *adj.* [< Gr. *xēros,* dry + -PHILOUS] thriving in a hot, dry climate —**xe·roph′i·ly** *n.*

**xe·ro·phyte** (zir′ə fīt′) *n.* [< Gr. *xēros,* dry + -PHYTE] a plant adapted to grow under very dry or desert conditions —**xe′ro·phyt′ic** (-fit′ik) *adj.*

**Xe·rox** (zir′äks) *a trademark for* a device for copying printed or written material, etc. by xerography —*n.* a copy made by such a device —*vt., vi.* to reproduce by such a device

**Xer·xes I** (zurk′sēz) 519?–465? B.C.; king of Persia (486?–465?): son of DARIUS I: called *the Great*

**Xho·sa** (kō′sä, -zä; *the k is actually a click*) *n.* **1.** *pl.* **Xho′sas, Xho′sa** any member of a people living in Cape Province, South Africa **2.** their Bantu language, characterized by clicks Also sp. **Xo′sa**

**xi** (zī, sī; *Gr.* ksē) *n.* [Gr.] the fourteenth letter of the Greek alphabet (Ξ, ξ)

**Xmas** (kris′məs; *popularly* eks′məs) *n.* [X (chi), 1st letter in Gr. *Christos,* Christ + -MAS] *same as* CHRISTMAS

**X-ray** (eks′rā′) *n.* **1.** an electromagnetic ray or radiation of very short wavelength produced by the bombardment of a metal by a stream of electrons, as in a vacuum tube: X-rays can penetrate solid substances and are widely used in medicine to study the bones, organs, etc. inside the body and to diagnose and treat certain disorders **2.** a photograph made by means of X-rays —*adj.* of, by, or having to do with X-rays —*vt.* to examine, treat, or photograph with X-rays Also **X ray, x-ray, x ray**

**xy·lem** (zī′ləm, -lem) *n.* [G. < Gr. *xylon,* wood] the woody tissue of a plant, which gives support to softer tissues and contains vessels or cells that conduct water, minerals, etc.

**xy·lo-** [< Gr. *xylon*] *a combining form meaning* wood *[xylophone]* : also, before a vowel, **xyl-**

**xy·lo·phone** (zī′lə fōn′) *n.* [XYLO- + -PHONE] a musical instrument consisting of a series of wooden bars graduated in length so as to sound the notes of the scale when struck with small wooden hammers —**xy′lo·phon′ist** (-fō′nist, zī läf′ə nist) *n.*

**xy·lose** (zī′lōs) *n.* [XYL(O)- + -OSE¹] a colorless sugar derived from wood, straw, corncobs, etc. and used in dyeing, diabetic foods, etc.

XYLOPHONE

# Y

**Y, y** (wī) *n., pl.* **Y's, y's** 1. the twenty-fifth letter of the English alphabet 2. a sound of *Y* or *y*

**Y** (wī) *n.* 1. something shaped like Y 2. *Chem.* yttrium —*adj.* shaped like Y

**y** *Math.* a symbol for: 1. the second of a set of unknown quantities, *x* usually being the first 2. an ordinate

**-y¹** (ē, i) [ME. *-y, -i, -ie,* prob. < OFr.] *a suffix meaning* little, dear: used in forming diminutives, nicknames, and terms of endearment *[kitty, Billy]*

**-y²** (ē, i) [OE. *-ig*] *a suffix meaning:* 1. having, full of, or characterized by *[dirty]* 2. somewhat; rather *[chilly]* 3. tending to *[sticky]* 4. suggestive of, somewhat like *[wavy]* In some words, *-y* simply adds force without changing the meaning *[vasty]*

**-y³** (ē, i) [< OFr. *-ie* < L. *-ia* < or akin to Gr. *-ia*] *a suffix meaning:* 1. quality or condition of (being) *[jealousy]* 2. a shop or goods of a specified kind *[bakery]* 3. a collective body of a specified kind *[soldiery]*

**-y⁴** (ē, i) [< Anglo-Fr. *-ie* < L. *-ium*] *a suffix meaning* action of *[inquiry, entreaty]*

**Y, Y.** *short for* YMCA *or* YWCA

**y.** 1. yard(s) 2. year(s)

**yacht** (yät) *n.* [Du. *jacht,* short for *jaghtschip,* pursuit ship] a large boat or small ship for pleasure cruises, races, etc. —*vi.* to sail in a yacht —**yacht′ing** *n.*

**yachts·man** (yäts′mən) *n., pl.* **-men** a person who owns or sails a yacht —**yachts′man·ship′** *n.*

**yack** (yak) *vi., n. var. of* YAK²

**yah** (yä, ya) *interj.* a shout of scorn, defiance, etc.

**Ya·hoo** (yä′hōō) *n.* 1. in Swift's *Gulliver's Travels,* any of a race of coarse, brutish creatures having the form and vices of man 2. [y-] a vicious, coarse person

**Yah·weh, Yah·we** (yä′we) [Heb.: see JEHOVAH] God: a form of the Hebrew name in the Scriptures: also **Yah·ve, Yah·veh** (yä′ve)

**yak¹** (yak) *n., pl.* **yaks, yak:** see PLURAL, II, D, 1 [Tibet. *gyak*] a stocky, long-haired wild ox of Tibet and C Asia, often used as a beast of burden

**yak²** (yak; *also, for n.* 2, yäk) *vi.* **yakked, yak′king** [echoic] [Slang] to talk much or idly; chatter —*n.* [Slang] 1. idle talk or chatter 2. *a)* a loud laugh, esp. as audience response to comedy *b)* a joke or comic bit that gets such a laugh Also, *for vi. & n.* (sense 1), **yak′-yak′, yak·e·ty-yak** (yak′ə tē yak′) —**yak′ker** *n.*

**Ya·lu** (yä′lōō′; *Chin.* yä′lü′) river flowing along the Manchuria–North Korea border into the Yellow Sea

**yam** (yam) *n.* [Port. *inhame,* prob. < WAfr. name] 1. *a)* the edible, starchy root of a climbing plant grown in tropical regions *b)* this plant 2. [South] the sweet potato

**ya·mal·ka, ya·mul·ka** (yäm′əl kə) *n. var. of* YARMULKE

**yang** (yäŋ, yaŋ) *n.* [< Chin. dial.] in Chinese philosophy, the active, positive, masculine force or principle in the universe, complementary to the *yin:* see YIN

**Yang·tze** (yaŋ′sē; *Chin.* yäŋ′tse′) river in C China, flowing from Tibet into the East China Sea: c. 3,400 mi.

**Yank** (yaŋk) *n.* [Slang] a Yankee; esp., a U.S. soldier in World Wars I and II —*adj.* of or like a Yank or Yanks

**yank** (yaŋk) *n.* [< ?] [Colloq.] a sudden, strong pull; jerk —*vt., vi.* [Colloq.] to jerk

**Yan·kee** (yaŋ′kē) *n.* [< ? Du. *Jan Kees* (taken as pl.) < *Jan,* John + *Kees* < *kaas,* cheese: a disparaging nickname applied by Dutch colonists in America to English settlers] 1. a native or inhabitant of New England 2. *a)* a native or inhabitant of a Northern State; Northerner *b)* a Union soldier in the Civil War 3. a native or inhabitant of the U.S. —*adj.* of or like Yankees —**Yan′kee·dom** *n.*

**Yankee Doo·dle** (dōō′d'l) an old American song, popular during the Revolutionary War

‡**Yan·qui** (yäŋ′kē) *n., pl.* **-quis** (-kēs) *American Spanish respelling of* YANKEE (sense 3)

**yap** (yap) *vi.* **yapped, yap′ping** [echoic] 1. to make a sharp, shrill bark or yelp 2. [Slang] to talk noisily and stupidly —*n.* 1. a sharp, shrill bark or yelp 2. [Slang] *a)* noisy, stupid talk *b)* a crude, noisy person *c)* the mouth —**yap′per** *n.* —**yap′ping·ly** *adv.*

**yard¹** (yärd) *n.* [OE. *gierd,* a rod] 1. *a)* a measure of length, equal to 3 feet, or 36 inches 2. a cubic yard *[a yard of topsoil]* 2. *Naut.* a slender rod or spar fastened across a mast to support a sail or to hold signal flags, lights, etc.

3. [Slang] one hundred dollars or, sometimes, one thousand dollars

**yard²** (yärd) *n.* [OE. *geard,* enclosure] 1. the ground around or next to a house or other building 2. a pen, etc. for livestock or poultry 3. a place in the open used for a particular purpose, work, etc. *[a navy yard, a lumberyard]* 4. a railroad center where trains are made up, serviced, switched, etc. —*vt.* to put, keep, or enclose in a yard (often with *up*)

**yard·age** (yär′dij) *n.* 1. measurement in yards 2. the extent of something so measured 3. distance covered in advancing a football

**yard·arm** (yärd′ärm′) *n. Naut.* either end of a yard supporting a square sail, signal lights, etc.

**yard·bird** (-burd′) *n.* [Slang] 1. a military recruit, esp. a rookie assigned to menial duties 2. a convict

**yard goods** textiles made in standard width, usually sold by the yard

**yard·man** (-mən) *n., pl.* **-men** a man who works in a yard

**yard·mas·ter** (-mas′tər) *n.* a man in charge of a railroad yard

**yard·stick** (-stik′) *n.* 1. a measuring stick one yard long 2. any standard used in judging, comparing, etc.

**yar·mul·ke** (yär′məl kə) *n.* [Yid. < Pol. *yarmutka*] a skullcap often worn by Jewish men and boys at prayer or study, at meals, etc.: also **yar′mal·ke, yar′mel·ke**

**yarn** (yärn) *n.* [OE. *gearn*] 1. a continuous strand or thread of spun wool, silk, cotton, nylon, glass, etc., for weaving, knitting, rope-making, etc. 2. [Colloq.] a tale or story, esp. one that seems exaggerated —*vi.* [Old Colloq.] to tell yarns —**spin a yarn** [Colloq.] to tell a yarn

**Ya·ro·slavl, Ya·ro·slavl'** (yä′rō släv′l') city in W European R.S.F.S.R., on the Volga: pop. 517,000

**yar·row** (yar′ō) *n.* [OE. *gæruwe*] a plant of the composite family, having a strong smell, finely divided leaves, and clusters of small, pink or white flower heads

**yat·a·ghan, yat·a·gan** (yat′ə gan′, -gən) *n.* [Turk. *yataghan*] a type of Turkish short saber with a double-curved blade and a handle without a guard

**yat·ter** (yat′ər) *n.* [prob. < YA(K)² + (CHA)TTER] [Slang] to talk idly about trivial things —*n.* [Slang] a yattering

**yaw** (yô) *vi.* [ON. *jaga,* to sway] 1. to swing back and forth across its course, as a ship pushed by high waves 2. to rotate or swing about the vertical axis, as an aircraft, spacecraft, etc. —*vt.* to cause to yaw —*n.* a yawing

**yawl** (yôl) *n.* [< MLowG. *jolle* or Du. *jol*] 1. a ship's boat 2. a sailboat like a ketch, but with the short mizzenmast behind the rudderpost

**yawn** (yôn) *vi.* [prob. merging of OE. *ginian* & *ganian,* to gape] 1. to open the mouth wide and breathe in deeply, as one often does automatically when sleepy or tired 2. to open wide; gape *[a yawning chasm]* —*vt.* to express with a yawn —*n.* a yawning —**yawn′er** *n.*

**yawp** (yôp) *vi.* [ME. *yolpen*] 1. to utter a loud, harsh call or cry 2. [Slang] to talk noisily and stupidly —*n.* the act or sound of yawping —**yawp′er** *n.*

**yaws** (yôz) *n.pl.* [*with sing. v.*] [of Carib origin] a tropical infectious disease caused by a spirochete and characterized by raspberrylike skin eruptions followed by destructive lesions

**y-ax·is** (wī′ak′sis) *n., pl.* **y′-ax′es** (-sēz) *Math.* the vertical axis along which the ordinate is measured

**Yb** *Chem.* ytterbium

**Y chromosome** *Genetics* one of the sex chromosomes: see SEX CHROMOSOME

**y·clept, y·cleped** (i klept′) *pp.* [OE. *geclypod,* pp. of *clipian,* to call] [Archaic] called; named

**yd.** *pl.* **yds.** yard

**ye¹** (t͟hə, t͟hi, t͟hē; *now often* yē) *adj.* archaic form of THE: *y* was substituted for the thorn (þ), the Old and Middle English character representing the sound (*th*)

**ye²** (yē; *unstressed* yi) *pron.* [OE. *ge*] [Archaic] you

**yea** (yā) *adv.* [OE. *gea*] 1. yes: used to express affirmation 2. indeed; truly —*n.* an answer or vote of "yes" —*interj.* a cry used in cheering on an athletic team

**yeah** (ya, ye, ye′ə, *etc.*) *adv.* [Colloq.] yes

**yean** (yēn) *vt., vi.* [< OE. hyp. *ge-eanian*] to bring forth (young): said of a sheep or goat

**yean·ling** (-liŋ) *n.* a lamb or kid —*adj.* newborn

**year** (yir) *n.* [OE. *gear*] **1.** a period of 365 days (in leap year, 366 days) divided into 12 months (from Jan. 1 through Dec. 31) **2.** the period (365 days, 5 hours, 48 minutes, and 46 seconds) spent by the sun in its apparent passage from vernal equinox to vernal equinox: the year of the seasons: also **tropical** or **solar year 3.** the period (365 days, 6 hours, 9 minutes, and 9.54 seconds) spent by the sun in its apparent passage from a fixed star and back to the same position again: also **sidereal year 4.** a period of 12 lunar months, as in the Jewish calendar: also **lunar year 5.** the period of time in which any planet makes its revolution around the sun **6.** a period of 12 calendar months starting from any date *[six years ago]* **7.** a calendar year of a specified number in an era *[the year 500 B.C.]* **8.** a particular annual period of less than 365 days *[a school year]* **9.** *[pl.] a)* age *[old for his years] b)* time: esp., a long time *[years ago]* **—year after year** every year **—year by year** each year **—year in, year out** every year
**year·book** (-book') *n.* a book published each year, as one with statistics and data of the past year, one with pictures and reports of a school's graduating class, etc.
**year·ling** (yir'liŋ, yur'-) *n.* an animal one year old or in its second year **—adj.** being a year old
**year·long** (yir'lôŋ') *adj.* continuing for a full year
**year·ly** (-lē) *adj.* **1.** lasting a year **2.** done, happening, etc. once a year, or every year **3.** of a year, or each year **—adv.** annually; every year
**yearn** (yurn) *vi.* [OE. *gyrnan* < *georn*, eager] **1.** to be filled with longing or desire **2.** to feel tenderness or sympathy **—yearn'er** *n.* **—yearn'ing** *n., adj.* **—yearn'ing·ly** *adv.*
**year-round** (yir'round') *adj.* open, in use, operating, etc. throughout the year
**yea·say·er** (yā'sā'ər) *n.* [YEA + SAY + -ER] a person who is affirmative, positive, etc. in his attitude toward life
**yeast** (yēst) *n.* [OE. *gist*] **1.** any of various single-celled fungi that live on sugary solutions, ferment sugars to form alcohol and carbon dioxide, and are used in making beer, whiskey, etc. and as a leavening in baking: also **yeast plant 2.** *a)* the yellowish, moist mass of yeast plants occurring as a froth on fermenting solutions *b)* this substance dried in flakes or granules or compressed into cakes **3.** foam; froth **4.** *a)* something that agitates or causes ferment: leaven *b)* ferment; agitation **—yeast'like'** *adj.*
**yeast·y** (yēs'tē) *adj.* **yeast'i·er, yeast'i·est 1.** of, like, or containing yeast **2.** frothy; foamy **3.** light; frivolous **4.** in a ferment; restless **—yeast'i·ness** *n.*
**Yeats** (yāts), **William Butler** 1865–1939; Ir. poet, playwright, & essayist
**yegg** (yeg) *n.* [Old Slang] a safecracker or burglar
**yell** (yel) *vi.* [OE. *giellan*] to cry out loudly; shout; scream **—vt.** to utter by yelling **—n. 1.** a loud outcry or shout; scream **2.** a rhythmic cheer given in unison, as by students at a football game **—yell'er** *n.*
**yel·low** (yel'ō) *adj.* [OE. *geolu*] **1.** of the color of gold, butter, or ripe lemons **2.** having a yellowish skin; Mongoloid **3.** [Colloq.] cowardly **4.** cheaply sensational *[yellow journalism]* **—n. 1.** a yellow color; color between orange and green in the spectrum **2.** a yellow pigment or dye **3.** the yolk of an egg **—vt., vi.** to make or become yellow **—yel'low·ish** *adj.* **—yel'low·ness** *n.*
**yel·low-bel·ly** (-bel'ē) *n., pl.* **-lies** [Slang] a contemptible coward **—yel'low-bel'lied** *adj.*
**yel·low·bird** (-burd') *n.* a bird yellow in color, as the yellow warbler, the American goldfinch, etc.
**yel·low-dog contract** (-dôg') a contract, now illegal, by which a new employee agrees not to join a labor union
**yellow fever** a tropical disease caused by a virus carried to man by the bite of the **yellow-fever mosquito**, and marked by fever, jaundice, vomiting, etc.
**yel·low·ham·mer** (-ham'ər) *n.* [ult. < OE. *geolu*, yellow + *amore*, kind of finch] **1.** a small European finch having a yellow head, neck, and breast: also called **yellow bunting 2.** the golden-winged flicker
**yellow jack 1.** *same as* YELLOW FEVER **2.** a yellow flag used as a signal of quarantine
**yellow jacket** any of several social wasps or hornets having bright-yellow markings
**Yel·low·knife** (yel'ō nīf') town on Great Slave Lake, NW Canada; capital of Northwest Territories: pop. 8,000
**yellow metal 1.** gold **2.** brass that is 60 parts copper and 40 parts zinc
**Yellow Pages** *[also* y- p-*]* the section or volume of a telephone directory, on yellow paper, containing classified listings of subscribers according to business, profession, etc.
**yellow pine 1.** any of several N. American pines having yellowish wood **2.** this wood

**Yellow River** *same as* HWANG HO
**Yellow Sea** arm of the East China Sea, between China & Korea
**Yel·low·stone** (yel'ō stōn') [ult. ? Fr. transl. of native name] river flowing from NW Wyo. through Mont. into the Missouri River
**Yellowstone National Park** national park mostly in NW Wyo., containing geysers, boiling springs, etc.
**yellow streak** a tendency to be cowardly
**yellow warbler** a small, bright-yellow N. American warbler
**yel·low·wood** (-wood') *n.* **1.** any of several trees with yellow wood, esp. one of the southeastern U.S. **2.** its wood
**yel·low·y** (yel'ə wē) *adj.* somewhat yellow
**yelp** (yelp) *vi.* [OE. *gielpan*, to boast] **1.** to utter a short, sharp cry or bark, as a dog **2.** to cry out sharply, as in pain **—vt.** to express by yelping **—n.** a short, sharp cry or bark
**Yem·en** (yem'ən) **1.** country in S Arabia, on the Red Sea: c. 75,000 sq. mi.; pop. 5,000,000: in full, **Yemen Arab Republic 2.** country in S Arabia, on the Arabian Sea, east of Yemen (sense 1): c. 110,000 sq. mi.; pop. 1,475,000: in full, **People's Democratic Republic of Yemen —Yem'en·ite'** (-ə nīt'), **Yem'e·ni** (-ə nē) *adj., n.*
**yen**[1] (yen) *n., pl.* **yen** [Jap. < Chin. *yüan*, round] the monetary unit of Japan: see MONETARY UNITS, table
**yen**[2] (yen) *n.* [Chin. *yan*, opium] [Colloq.] a strong longing or desire **—vi. yenned, yen'ning** [Colloq.] to have a yen (*for*); long; yearn
**Ye·ni·sei, Ye·ni·sey** (ye'ni sā') river in C Siberian R.S.F.S.R., flowing north into the Arctic Ocean: c. 2,600 mi.
**yen·ta, yen·te** (yen'tə) *n.* [Yid.] a woman gossip or busybody
**yeo·man** (yō'mən) *n., pl.* **-men** [ME. *yeman*, prob. contr. < *yung man*, young man] **1.** orig., *a)* a manservant in a royal or noble household *b)* a freeholder of a class below the gentry **2.** [Brit.] *a)* a small landowner *b) same as* YEOMAN OF THE GUARD *c)* a member of the yeomanry (sense 2) **3.** *U.S. Navy* a petty officer assigned to clerical duty **—adj.** of or like yeomen: see also YEOMAN'S SERVICE
**yeo·man·ly** (-lē) *adj.* **1.** of, like, or befitting a yeoman **2.** brave; sturdy **—adv.** in a yeomanly manner
**yeoman of the (royal) guard** any of the 100 men forming a ceremonial guard for the English royal family
**yeo·man·ry** (-rē) *n.* **1.** yeomen collectively **2.** a British volunteer cavalry force, orig. a home guard, but now part of the Territorial Army
**yeoman's service** very good, useful, or loyal service or assistance: also **yeoman service**
**yep** (yep) *adv.* [Slang] yes: an affirmative reply
**-yer** (yər) *same as* -IER: usually after *w,* as in *lawyer*
**Ye·re·van** (ye re vän') capital of the Armenian S.S.R., at the foot of Mt. Ararat: pop. 767,000
**yes** (yes) *adv.* [OE. *gese*, prob. < *gea,* yea + *si,* be it so] **1.** aye; yea; it is so: the opposite of NO, used to express agreement, consent, affirmation, etc. **2.** not only that, but more; moreover *[ready, yes,* eager to help*] Yes* is sometimes used alone in inquiry to signify "What is it?" or as a polite expression of interest **—n., pl. yes'es 1.** the act of saying yes **2.** an affirmative vote, voter, etc. **—vt., vi. yessed, yes'sing** to say *yes* (to)
**yes man** [Slang] a person who indicates approval of every suggestion or opinion offered by his superior
**yes·ter** (yes'tər) *adj.* [< ff.] **1.** of yesterday **2.** previous to this Usually in combination *[yestereve, yesteryear]*
**yes·ter·day** (yes'tər dē, -dā') *n.* [< OE. < *geostran,* yesterday + *dæg,* day] **1.** the day before today **2.** a recent day or time **3.** *[usually pl.]* time gone by **—adv. 1.** on the day before today **2.** recently **—adj.** of yesterday
**yes·ter·year** (-yir') *n., adv.* [Poet.] **1.** last year **2.** (in) recent years
**yet** (yet) *adv.* [OE. *giet*] **1.** up to now or to the time specified; thus far *[he hasn't gone yet]* **2.** at the present time; now *[we can't leave yet]* **3.** still; even now *[there is yet a chance for peace]* **4.** at some future time; sooner or later *[she will thank you yet]* **5.** now or at a particular time, as continuing from a preceding time *[we could hear her yet]* **6.** in addition; still *[he was yet more kind]* **7.** as much as; even *[he did not come, nor yet write]* **8.** now, after all the time that has elapsed *[hasn't he finished yet?]* **9.** nevertheless *[he was rich, yet lonely]* **—conj.** nevertheless; however *[she seems happy, yet she is troubled]* **—as yet** up to now
**ye·ti** (yet'ē) *n.* [Tibet.] *[often* Y-] *same as* ABOMINABLE SNOWMAN
**yew** (yōō) *n.* [OE. *iw*] **1.** an evergreen shrub or tree with red, waxy cones and a fine-grained, elastic wood **2.** the wood, used esp. for making archers' bows

**Yid·dish** (yid′ish) *n.* [Yid. *yidish* < G. *jüdisch*, Jewish, ult. < L. *Judaeus*, a Jew] a language derived from medieval High German, spoken by East European Jews and their descendants in other countries: it is written in the Hebrew alphabet and contains vocabulary borrowings from Hebrew, Russian, Polish, English, etc.: abbrev. **Yid.** —*adj.* of or in this language

**yield** (yēld) *vt.* [OE. *gieldan*, to pay] **1.** to produce; specif., *a)* to give or furnish as a natural process [the orchard *yields* a good crop] *b)* to give in return; produce as a result, profit, etc. **2.** to give up under pressure; surrender **3.** to concede; grant —*vi.* **1.** to produce or bear **2.** to give up; surrender **3.** to give way to physical force **4.** to give place; lose precedence, etc. (often with *to*); specif., *a)* to let another (motorist) have the right of way *b)* to give up willingly a right, etc. —*n.* **1.** the amount yielded or produced **2.** the earnings received from investment in stocks, bonds, etc. **3.** the force in kilotons or megatons of a nuclear or thermonuclear explosion —**yield′er** *n.*

**yield·ing** (yēl′diŋ) *adj.* **1.** producing a good yield; productive **2.** bending easily; flexible **3.** submissive

**yin** (yin) *n.* [< Chin. dial.] in Chinese philosophy, the passive, negative, feminine force or principle in the universe, complementary to the *yang:* see YANG

**yip** (yip) *n.* [echoic] [Colloq.] a yelp, or bark —*vi.* **yipped**, **yip′ping** [Colloq.] to yelp, or bark

**yipe** (yīp) *interj.* an exclamation of pain, dismay, alarm, etc.

**yip·pee** (yip′ē) *interj.* an exclamation of joy, delight, etc.

**-yl** (il; *now rarely* ēl) [< Gr. *hylē*, wood] *Chem. a combining form meaning:* **1.** a univalent hydrocarbon radical [*ethyl*] **2.** a radical containing oxygen [*hydroxyl*]

**YMCA, Y.M.C.A.** Young Men's Christian Association

**YMHA, Y.M.H.A.** Young Men's Hebrew Association

**yob** (yäb) *n.* [inversion of BOY] [Brit. Slang] a hoodlum or lout: also **yob·bo** (yä′bō)

**yock** (yäk) *n.* [var. of YAK²] [Slang] a loud laugh or something evoking loud laughter; yak: also sp. **yok**

**yo·del** (yō′d'l) *vt., vi.* **-deled** or **-delled**, **-del·ing** or **-del·ling** [G. *jodeln*] to sing with sudden changes back and forth between the normal chest voice and the falsetto —*n.* **1.** the act or sound of yodeling **2.** a song sung in this way —**yo′del·er, yo′del·ler** *n.*

**yo·ga** (yō′gə) *n.* [Sans., union] **1.** *Hinduism* a discipline by which one seeks to achieve union with the universal soul through deep meditation, prescribed postures, controlled breathing, etc. **2.** a system of exercising involving such postures, breathing, etc. —**yo′gic** (-gik) *adj.*

**yo·gi** (yō′gē) *n., pl.* **-gis** a person who practices yoga: also **yo′gin** (-gin)

**yo·gurt** (yō′gərt) *n.* [Turk. *yōghurt*] a thick, semisolid food made from milk fermented by a bacterium, believed to have a beneficial effect on the intestines: often prepared with various flavors: also sp. **yo′ghurt, yo′ghourt**

**yo-heave-ho** (yō′hēv′hō′) *interj.* a chant formerly used by sailors while pulling or lifting together in rhythm

**yoicks** (yoiks) *interj.* [earlier *hoik, hike*, also *yoaks*] [Brit.] a cry used for urging on the hounds in fox hunting

**yoke** (yōk) *n., pl.* **yokes;** for 2, usually **yoke** [OE. *geoc*] **1.** a wooden frame with bows at either end, fitted around the necks of a pair of oxen, etc. to harness them **2.** a pair of animals harnessed together **3.** the condition of being under another's power or control; bondage **4.** something that binds, unites, etc. **5.** something like a yoke, as a frame fitting over the shoulders for carrying pails, etc. **6.** a part of a garment fitted closely around the shoulders or hips to support the gathered parts below —*vt.* **yoked, yok′ing 1.** to put a yoke on **2.** to harness (an animal) to (a plow, etc.) **3.** to join together —*vi.* to be joined together

YOKE (on pair of oxen)

**yo·kel** (yō′k'l) *n.* [prob. < dial. *yokel*, green woodpecker] a country person; rustic: a contemptuous term

**Yo·ko·ha·ma** (yō′kə hä′mə; *Jap.* yô′kô hä′mä) seaport on the S coast of Honshu, Japan: pop. 1,789,000

**yolk** (yōk) *n.* [OE. *geolca*] the yellow, principal substance of an egg —**yolked, yolk′y** *adj.*

**yolk sac** a sac containing yolk that is attached to and supplies nourishment for the embryos of birds, fishes, and reptiles

**Yom Kip·pur** (yäm kip′ər, yôm-; *Heb.* yôm′ kē pōōr′) a Jewish holiday, the Day of Atonement, a fast day observed on the 10th day of Tishri

**yon** (yän) *adj., adv.* [OE. *geon*] [Archaic or Dial.] yonder

**yon·der** (yän′dər) *adj.* [ME.] **1.** farther; more distant (with *the*) **2.** being at a distance, but within, or as within, sight —*adv.* at or in that place; over there

**Yon·kers** (yäŋ′kərz) [< Du. *De Jonkers* (*Land*), the young nobleman's (land)] city in SE N.Y., on the Hudson: suburb of New York City: pop. 195,000

**yoo-hoo** (yōō′hōō′) *interj., n.* a shout or call used to attract someone's attention

**yore** (yôr) *adv.* [OE. *geara*] [Obs.] long ago —*n.* time long past: now only in **of yore**, formerly

**York¹** (yôrk) ruling family of England (1461–85)

**York²** (yôrk) [after ff.] city in SE Pa.: pop. 45,000

**York·shire** (yôrk′shir) former county of N England, on the North Sea: now divided into three counties (*North Yorkshire, South Yorkshire,* and *West Yorkshire*)

**Yorkshire pudding** a batter of flour, eggs, and milk baked in the drippings of roasting meat

**Yorkshire terrier** a long-haired toy terrier of a breed originating in Yorkshire, England

**York·town** (yôrk′toun′) [after the Duke of *York,* later CHARLES I] town in SE Va.: scene of the surrender of Cornwallis to Washington (1781)

**Yo·sem·i·te National Park** (yō sem′ə tē) [< AmInd., lit., grizzly bears, killers] national park in EC Calif., in the Sierra Nevadas: notable for its steep-walled valley (**Yosemite Valley**) & its high waterfalls (**Yosemite Falls**)

**you** (yōō; *unstressed* yoo, yə) *pron.* [OE. *eow*, dat. & acc. pl. of *ge,* YE²] **1.** the person or persons to whom one is speaking or writing: *you* is the nominative and objective form (sing. & pl.) of the second personal pronoun **2.** a person or people generally [*you* never can tell!]

**you-all** (yōō ôl′, yôl) *pron. Southern colloq. for* YOU: chiefly used as a pl. form

**you'd** (yōōd; *unstressed* yood, yəd) **1.** you had **2.** you would

**you'll** (yōōl; *unstressed* yool, yəl) **1.** you will **2.** you shall

**young** (yuŋ) *adj.* [OE. *geong*] **1.** being in an early period of life or growth **2.** characteristic of youth in quality, appearance, etc.; fresh; vigorous **3.** representing or embodying a new tendency, social movement, etc. **4.** of youth or early life **5.** lately begun; in an early stage **6.** lacking experience or practice; immature; green **7.** younger than another of the same name or family —*n.* **1.** young people **2.** offspring, esp. young offspring, collectively [a bear and her *young*] —**with young** pregnant

**Young** (yuŋ), **Brig·ham** (brig′əm) 1801–77; U.S. Mormon leader

**young·ber·ry** (yuŋ′ber′ē) *n., pl.* **-ries** [after B. *Young,* 19th-c. U.S. horticulturist] **1.** a large, sweet, dark-purple berry, a cross between a blackberry and a dewberry **2.** the trailing bramble bearing this fruit

**young blood 1.** young people **2.** youthful vigor, ideas, etc.

**young·ish** (yuŋ′ish) *adj.* rather young

**young·ling** (-liŋ) *n.* **1.** a young person; youth **2.** a young animal or plant —*adj.* young

**young·ster** (-stər) *n.* **1.** a child **2.** a youth **3.** a young animal

**Youngs·town** (yuŋz′toun′) [after J. *Young*, an early (c. 1800) settler] city in NE Ohio: pop. 115,000 (met. area, with Warren, 530,000)

**Young Turk** [orig., member of early 20th-c. revolutionary party in Turkey] [*also* y- T-] any of a group of younger people seeking to take control of an organization, political party, etc. from the older, usually conservative, people in power

**your** (yoor, yôr; *unstressed* yər) *possessive pronominal adj.* [OE. *eower*] of, belonging to, or done by you: also used before some titles [*your* Honor]

**you're** (yoor, yōōr; *unstressed* yər) you are

**yours** (yoorz, yôrz) *pron.* that or those belonging to you: the absolute form of *your,* used without a following noun [that book is *yours, yours* are better] : also used after *of* to indicate possession [a friend of *yours*]

**your·self** (yər self′, yoor-) *pron., pl.* **-selves′** (-selvz′) **1.** a form of the 2d pers. sing. pronoun, used: *a)* as an intensive [you *yourself* went] *b)* as a reflexive [you hurt *yourself*] *c)* as a quasi-noun meaning "your real or true self" [you are not *yourself* today] **2.** *same as* ONESELF [it is best to do it *yourself*]

**yours truly 1.** a phrase used before the signature in ending a letter **2.** [Colloq.] I or me

**youth** (yōōth) *n., pl.* **youths** (yōōths, yōōthz) [OE. *geoguthe*] **1.** the state or quality of being young **2.** the period of life coming between childhood and maturity; adolescence **3.** an early stage of growth or existence **4.** young people collectively **5.** a young person; esp., a young man

**youth·ful** (-fəl) *adj.* **1.** young; possessing youth **2.** of, characteristic of, or suitable for youth **3.** fresh; vigorous **4.** new; early; in an early stage —**youth′ful·ly** *adv.* —**youth′ful·ness** *n.*

**youth hostel** any of a system of supervised shelters providing cheap lodging on a cooperative basis for young people on bicycle tours, hikes, etc.

**you've** (yōōv; *unstressed* yoov, yəv) you have

**yow** (you) *interj.* an exclamation of pain, surprise, etc.

**yowl** (youl) *vi.* [< ON. *gaula*] to utter a long, mournful cry; howl —*n.* such a cry

**yo-yo** (yō′yō′) *n.* [< Tagalog name: the toy came to the U.S. from the Philippines] **1.** a spoollike toy attached to one end of a string upon which it may be made to spin up and down 2. [Slang] a person who is dull or stupid

**Y·pres** (ē′pr′) town in NW Belgium, near the Fr. border: center of heavy fighting in World War I

**yr.** 1. year(s) 2. younger 3. your

**yrs.** 1. years 2. yours

**yt·ter·bi·um** (i tər′bē əm) *n.* [ModL. < *Ytterby*, Sweden] a scarce, silvery, metallic chemical element of the rare-earth group: symbol, Yb; at. wt., 173.04; at. no., 70

**yt·tri·um** (it′rē əm) *n.* [ModL. < *Ytterby*, Sweden] a rare, silvery, metallic chemical element: symbol, Y; at. wt., 88.905; at. no., 39

**yu·an** (yōō än′) *n.* [Chin. *yüan*, round] *see* MONETARY UNITS, table (China)

**Yu·ca·tán, Yu·ca·tan** (yōō′kä tän′; *E.* yōō′kə tan′) peninsula comprising SE Mexico, British Honduras, & part of W Guatemala: it extends north into the Gulf of Mexico

**yuc·ca** (yuk′ə) *n.* [ModL., genus name < Sp. *yuca*] 1. a plant of the U.S. and Latin America, having stiff, sword-shaped leaves and white flowers in an erect raceme 2. its flower

**yuck·y** (yuk′ē) *adj.* **-i·er, -i·est** [Slang] unpleasant, disgusting, etc.

**Yu·go·slav** (yōō′gō släv′, -gə-) *adj.* of Yugoslavia or its people: also **Yu′go·slav′ic** —*n.* a member of a Slavic peo-ple, including Serbs, Croats, and Slovenes, who live in Yugoslavia Also **Yu′go·sla′vi·an**

**Yu·go·sla·vi·a** (yōō′gō släv′vē ə, -gə släv′yə) country in the NW Balkan Peninsula, on the Adriatic: 98,766 sq. mi.; pop. 20,672,000; cap. Belgrade

**yuk** (yuk) *n.* [echoic] [Slang] a loud laugh of amusement, or something evoking such a laugh —*vi.* yukked, yuk′king [Slang] to laugh loudly Also sp. **yuck**

**Yu·kon** (yōō′kän) 1. territory of NW Canada, east of Alas.: 207,076 sq. mi.; pop. 22,000; cap. Whitehorse: in full, **Yukon Territory:** abbrev. **Y.T.** 2. river flowing through this territory & Alas. into the Bering Sea

**Yukon Standard Time** *see* STANDARD TIME

**yule** (yōōl) *n.* [OE. *geol*] Christmas or the Christmas season

**yule log** a large log formerly used as a foundation for the ceremonial Christmas Eve fire

**yule·tide** (-tīd′) *n.* Christmas time

**yum** (yum) *interj.* [echoic] delicious; excellent

**yum·my** (yum′ē) *adj.* **-mi·er, -mi·est** [echoic] [Colloq.] very tasty; delectable; delicious

**yup** (yup) *adv.* [Slang] yes: an affirmative reply

**yurt** (yoort) *n.* [< Russ. *yurta*, lit., dwelling] a circular tent on a framework of poles, used by the nomads of Mongolia

**YWCA, Y.W.C.A.** Young Women's Christian Association

**YWHA, Y.W.H.A.** Young Women's Hebrew Association

# Z

**Z, z** (zē; *Brit. & Canad.* zed) *n., pl.* **Z's, z's** 1. the twenty-sixth and last letter of the English alphabet 2. the sound of Z or z 3. *a symbol for* the last in a sequence or group

**Z** (zē; *Brit. & Canad.* zed) *n.* an object shaped like Z —*adj.* shaped like Z

**z** *Math.* a symbol for: 1. the third in a set of unknown quantities, *x* and *y* usually being the first two 2. a variable

**Z., z.** 1. zero 2. zone

**Za·greb** (zä′greb) city in NW Yugoslavia; capital of Croatia: pop. 457,000

**Za·ire, Za·ïre** (zä ir′) 1. country in C Africa, on the equator: a former Belgian colony: 905,563 sq. mi.; pop. 22,477,000; cap. Kinshasa 2. *same as* CONGO (River)

**za·ire** (zä ir′) *n., pl.* **-ire′** [< Port., prob. < Bantu *nzadi*, big river] *see* MONETARY UNITS, table (Zaire)

**Zam·be·zi** (zam bē′zē) river in S Africa, flowing through Zambia & Mozambique into the Indian Ocean: c. 1,600 mi.

**Zam·bi·a** (zam′bē ə) country in S Africa: a member of the Commonwealth: 290,323 sq. mi.; pop. 4,336,000

**za·ny** (zā′nē) *n., pl.* **-nies** [< Fr. < It. *zanni*, orig., an abbrev. pronun. of *Giovanni*, John] 1. a clown or buffoon 2. a silly or foolish person; simpleton —*adj.* **-ni·er, -ni·est** of or like a zany; specif., *a)* comical in a crazy way *b)* foolish or crazy —**za′ni·ly** *adv.* —**za′ni·ness** *n.*

**Zan·zi·bar** (zan′zə bär′) 1. group of islands off the E coast of Africa, constituting a part of Tanzania 2. largest island of this group: 640 sq. mi.

**zap** (zap) *vt., vi.* **zapped, zap′ping** [echoic] [Slang] to move, strike, stun, kill, etc. with sudden speed and force —*n.* [Slang] energy, verve, pep, etc. —*interj.* an exclamation used to express sudden, swift action

**Za·po·rozh·e, Za·po·rozh·ye** (zä′pô rôzh′ye) city in the SE Ukrainian S.S.R., on the Dnepr: pop. 658,000

**Za·ra·go·za** (thä′rä gô′thä) city in NE Spain: pop. 657,000

**Zar·a·thus·tra** (zar′ə thōōs′trə) *Persian name of* ZOROASTER

**zarf** (zärf) *n.* [Ar. *zarf*, a saucer] a small, cuplike holder, used in the Levant for a hot coffee cup

**zeal** (zēl) *n.* [< LL. *zelus* < Gr. *zēlos*] intense enthusiasm; ardent endeavor or devotion; fervor

**Zea·land** (zē′lənd) largest island of Denmark, between Jutland & Sweden: 2,912 sq. mi.; chief city, Copenhagen

**zeal·ot** (zel′ət) *n.* [< LL. < Gr. *zēlōtēs* < *zēlos*, zeal] a person who is zealous, esp. to an extreme or excessive degree; fanatic —**zeal′ot·ry** *n.*

**zeal·ous** (zel′əs) *adj.* full of or showing zeal; fervent; enthusiastic —**zeal′ous·ly** *adv.* —**zeal′ous·ness** *n.*

**ze·bec, ze·beck** (zē′bek) *n. same as* XEBEC

**ze·bra** (zē′brə; *Brit. & Canad.* zeb′rə) *n., pl.* **-bras, -bra:** see PLURAL, II, D, 1 [Port., prob. ult. < L. *equiferus*, a wild horse] any of several swift African mammals related to and resembling the horse but with dark stripes on a white or tawny body

**zebra fish** any of a number of unrelated fishes with barred, zebralike markings, often kept in aquariums

**ze·bu** (zē′byōō) *n., pl.* **-bus, -bu:** see PLURAL, II, D, 1 [Fr. *zébu* < ?] an oxlike domestic animal of Asia and Africa: it has a large hump and short, curving horns: see BRAHMAN (sense 2)

**Zech·a·ri·ah** (zek′ə rī′ə) *Bible* 1. a Hebrew prophet of the 6th cent. B.C. 2. the book containing his prophecies: abbrev. **Zech.**

**zed** (zed) *n.* [< MFr. < LL. < Gr. *zēta*] *Brit. & usual Canad.* name for the letter Z, z

**zee** (zē) *n., pl.* zees the letter Z, z

**‡Zeit·geist** (tsīt′gīst′) *n.* [G., time spirit] the trend of thought and feeling in a period of history

**Zen** (zen) *n.* [Jap. < Chin., ult. < Sans. *dhyāna*, meditation] 1. a Japanese Buddhist sect that seeks enlightenment through meditation and intuition rather than in traditional scripture 2. the beliefs and practices of this sect

**Zend** (zend) *n.* [Per., interpretation] the Middle Persian translation of and commentary on the Zoroastrian Avesta

**Zend-A·ves·ta** (-ə ves′tə) *n.* the sacred writings of the Zoroastrians

**ze·nith** (zē′nith; *Brit.* zen′ith) *n.* [< MFr. < ML. *cenit* < Ar. *semt*, road < L. *semita*, path] 1. the point in the sky directly overhead: that point of the celestial sphere directly opposite to the nadir 2. the highest point; peak

**Ze·no** (zē′nō) 334?–261? B.C.; Gr. philosopher: founder of Stoicism

**Zeph·a·ni·ah** (zef′ə nī′ə) *Bible* 1. a Hebrew prophet of the 7th cent. B.C. 2. the book containing his prophecies: abbrev. **Zeph.**

**zeph·yr** (zef′ər) *n.* [< L. < Gr. *zephyros*] 1. the west wind 2. a soft, gentle breeze 3. a fine, soft, lightweight yarn, cloth, or garment

**zep·pe·lin** (zep′ə lin, zep′lin) *n.* [after F. von *Zeppelin* (1838–1917), G. inventor] [often Z-] a type of dirigible airship designed around 1900

**ze·ro** (zir′ō, zē′rō) *n., pl.* **-ros, -roes** [Fr. *zéro* < It. < Ar. *sifr*, CIPHER] 1. the symbol or numeral 0; cipher; naught 2. the point, marked 0, from which positive or negative quantities are reckoned on a graduated scale, as on thermometers 3. a temperature that causes a thermometer to register zero 4. nothing 5. the lowest point [his chances sank to *zero*] —*adj.* 1. of or at zero 2. without measurable value 3. designating or of visibility, as in flying, thought to extend no farther than a few feet —*vt.* **-roed, -ro·ing** to adjust (an instrument, etc.) to a zero point from which all positive or negative readings are to be made —**zero in 1.** to adjust the sight settings of (a rifle) by calibrated firing on a standard range **2.** to aim (a gun or guns) directly at (a target) —**zero in on 1.** to adjust gunfire so as to be aiming directly at (a target) **2.** to concentrate attention on

**ze·ro-base** (-bās′) *adj.* [from the idea of starting at zero] designating or of budgeting in which each item is evaluated on its merits without considering previous budgets: also **ze′ro-based′**

**zero gravity** a condition of weightlessness

**zero hour 1.** the time set for the beginning of an attack or other military operation **2.** any critical point

**zero (population) growth** a condition in a given population in which the birthrate equals the death rate so that the population remains constant

**ze·ro-sum** (-sum′) *adj.* in game theory, designating or of a situation, competition, etc. in which a gain for one must result in a loss for another or others

**zest** (zest) *n.* [Fr. *zeste,* orange peel used to give flavor] **1.** stimulating or exciting quality; flavor; relish **2.** keen enjoyment; gusto (often with *for*) [a zest for life] —**zest′ful** *adj.* —**zest′ful·ly** *adv.* —**zest′ful·ness** *n.* —**zest′y** *adj.*

**ze·ta** (zāt′ə, zēt′ə) *n.* [Gr.] the sixth letter of the Greek alphabet (Z, ζ)

**Zeus** (zōōs) the supreme deity of the ancient Greeks, son of Cronus and Rhea: identified with the Roman god Jupiter

**zig·gu·rat** (zig′ōō rat) *n.* [Assyr. *ziqquratu,* height] an ancient Assyrian or Babylonian temple built as a pyramid with steplike stories

**zig·zag** (zig′zag′) *n.* [Fr.] **1.** a series of short, sharp angles or turns in alternate directions, as in a line or course **2.** a design, path, etc. having a series of such angles or turns —*adj.* having the form of a zigzag —*adv.* in a zigzag course —*vt., vi.* **-zagged′, -zag′ging** to move or form in a zigzag

**zilch** (zilch) *n.* [nonsense syllable, orig. used in the 1930's as name of a magazine character] [Slang] nothing; zero

**zil·lion** (zil′yən) *n.* [arbitrary coinage, after MILLION] [Colloq.] a very large, indefinite number

**Zim·ba·bwe** (zim bä′bwe) country in S Africa, north of South Africa: 150,333 sq. mi.; pop. 6,930,000; cap. Salisbury

**zinc** (ziŋk) *n.* [G. *zink*] a bluish-white, metallic chemical element, used as a protective coating for iron, in electric batteries and in alloys, and, in the form of salts, in medicines: symbol, Zn; at. wt., 65.37; at. no., 30 —*vt.* **zincked** or **zinced, zinck′ing** or **zinc′ing** to coat or treat with zinc; galvanize —**zinc′ic** (-ik), **zinck′y, zink′y, zinc′y** *adj.*

**zinc ointment** an ointment containing zinc oxide

**zinc oxide** a white powder, ZnO, used as a pigment and in making glass, cosmetics, ointments, etc.

**zinc white** zinc oxide used as a white pigment

**zing** (ziŋ) *n.* [echoic] [Slang] **1.** a shrill, high-pitched sound, as of something moving at high speed **2.** vitality, vigor, zest, etc. —*vi.* [Slang] to make a shrill, high-pitched sound —**zing′y** *adj.* **zing′i·er, zing′i·est**

**zing·er** (ziŋ′ər) *n.* [Slang] something said or done that has zing, as a retort, punch line, etc.

**zin·ni·a** (zin′ē ə, zin′yə) *n.* [ModL., after J. G. Zinn, 18th-c. G. botanist] a plant of the composite family, having colorful flowers, native to N. and S. America

**Zi·on** (zī′ən) **1.** the hill in Jerusalem on which the Temple was built: a symbol of the center of Jewish national life **2.** *a)* Jerusalem *b)* the land of Israel **3.** the Jewish people **4.** heaven **5.** the theocracy of God

**Zi·on·ism** (-iz′m) *n.* a movement formerly for reestablishing, now for supporting, the Jewish national state of Israel —**Zi′on·ist** *n., adj.* —**Zi′on·is′tic** *adj.*

**zip** (zip) *n.* [echoic] **1.** a short, sharp hissing sound, as of a passing bullet **2.** [Colloq.] energy; vim **3.** [Slang] a score of zero —*vi.* **zipped, zip′ping 1.** to make, or move with, a zip **2.** [Colloq.] to act or move with speed or energy **3.** to become fastened or unfastened by means of a zipper —*vt.* to fasten or unfasten with a zipper

**ZIP code** (zip) [z(*oning*) i(*mprovement*) p(*lan*)] a system devised to speed mail deliveries, under which the post office assigns a code number to individual areas and places

**zip·per** (zip′ər) *n.* **1.** a person or thing that zips **2.** a device used to fasten and unfasten two edges of material: it consists of two rows of interlocking tabs worked by a part that slides up or down —*vt., vi.* to fasten with a zipper

**zip·py** (-ē) *adj.* **-pi·er, -pi·est** [< ZIP + -Y²] [Colloq.] full of vim and energy; brisk

**zir·con** (zur′kän) *n.* [G. *zirkon,* ult. < Per. *zargūn,* gold-colored < *zar,* gold] a crystalline silicate of zirconium, ZrSiO₄, colored yellow, brown, red, etc.: transparent varieties are used as gems

**zir·co·ni·um** (zər kō′nē əm) *n.* [ModL.: see prec.] a soft, gray or black metallic chemical element used in alloys, ceramics, etc.: symbol, Zr; at. wt., 91.22; at. no., 40

**zit** (zit) *n.* [< ?] a pimple, esp. one on the face

**zith·er** (zith′ər, zith′-) *n.* [G. < L. < Gr. *kithara,* a lute] a

musical instrument having from thirty to forty strings stretched across a flat soundboard and played with a plectrum and the fingers

**zlo·ty** (zlô′tē) *n., pl.* **-tys** [Pol., lit., golden] *see* MONETARY UNITS, table (Poland)

**Zn** *Chem.* zinc

**zo-** *same as* ZOO-: used before a vowel

**-zo·a** (zō′ə) [ModL. < Gr. *zōia,* pl. of *zōion,* an animal] a combining form used in zoology to form names of groups [Protozoa]

**zo·di·ac** (zō′dē ak′) *n.* [< MFr. < L. < Gr. *zōidiakos (kyklos),* lit., (circle) of animals < *zōidion,* dim. of *zōion,* animal] **1.** an imaginary belt in the heavens extending on either side of the apparent path of the sun and including the paths of the moon and the planets: it is divided into twelve equal parts, or signs, each named for a different constellation **2.** a diagram representing the zodiac and its signs: used in astrology —**zo·di·a·cal** (-dī′ə k'l) *adj.*

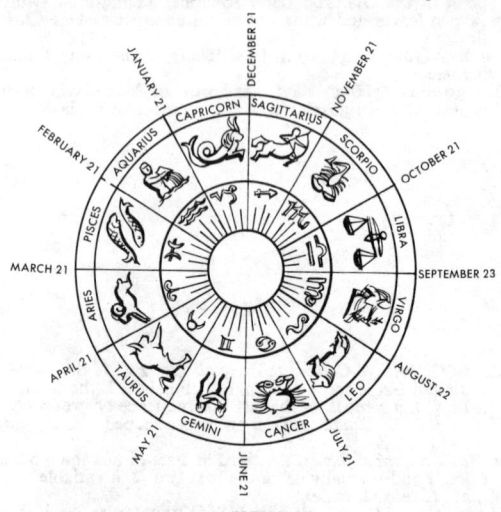

ZODIAC

**Zo·la** (zō lä′; *E.* zō′lə), **É·mile** (**Édouard Charles Antoine**) (ā mēl′) 1840–1902; Fr. novelist

**zom·bie** (zäm′bē) *n.* [of Afr. origin] **1.** in West Indian superstition, a dead person supposedly brought back by magic power to a form of life in which he can be made to move or act as he is ordered: also **zom′bi 2.** [Slang] *a)* a person like a zombie as in seeming to be half dead, to move automatically, etc. *b)* an eccentric person

**zone** (zōn) *n.* [Fr. < L. < Gr. *zōnē* < *zōnnynai,* to gird] **1.** *a)* an encircling band, stripe, etc. distinct in color, structure, etc. from what surrounds it *b)* formerly, a belt or girdle **2.** any of the five great divisions into which the earth's surface is marked off by imaginary lines: see TORRID ZONE, TEMPERATE ZONE, and FRIGID ZONE **3.** any region considered with reference to its particular use, crops, geological features, etc. [a canal *zone,* cotton *zone]* **4.** *a)* any area of a city restricted by law for a particular use, as for homes, businesses, etc. *b)* any space along a street or road restricted by traffic regulations [no parking *zone]* **5.** *a)* any of the numbered sections into which a metropolitan area is divided to make mail delivery easier *b)* any of a series of concentric areas about a given point, each having a different postage rate **6.** *short for* TIME ZONE **7.** *Sports* any of the areas into which a football field, basketball court, etc. is divided —*vt.* **zoned, zon′ing 1.** to mark off into zones; specif., *a)* to divide (a city, etc.) into zones for particular uses *b)* to limit (an area of a city, etc.) as a zone for a particular use **2.** to encircle —**zon′al** *adj.*

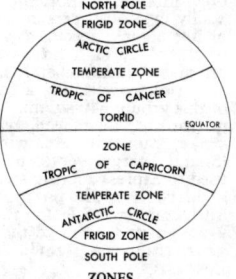

ZONES

**zonked** (zäŋkt) *adj.* [pp. of *zonk,* to strike, beat] [Slang] highly intoxicated or under the influence of a drug

**zoo** (zōō) *n.* [< ZOO(LOGICAL GARDEN)] a place where a collection of wild animals is kept for public showing

**zo·o-** [< Gr. *zōion,* animal] a combining form meaning: **1.**

animal, animals **2.** zoology and *[zoogeography]* Words beginning with *zoo-* are sometimes written **zoö-**

**zo·o·ge·og·ra·phy** (zō′ə jē äg′rə fē) *n.* the science dealing with the geographical distribution of animals —**zo′o·ge′o·graph′ic** (-jē′ə graf′ik), **zo′o·ge′o·graph′i·cal** *adj.*

**zo·og·ra·phy** (zō äg′rə fē) *n.* [ZOO- + -GRAPHY] the branch of zoology concerned with the description of animals, their habits, etc. —**zo·og′ra·pher** *n.* —**zo·o·graph·ic** (zō′ə graf′ik), **zo′o·graph′i·cal** *adj.*

**zo·oid** (zō′oid) *n.* [ZO(O)- + -OID] **1.** a comparatively independent animal organism produced by fission, gemmation, etc. rather than by sexual means **2.** any of the individual members of a colonial or compound organism, as a coral or hydroid —*adj.* of, or having the nature of, an animal: also **zo·oi′dal**

**zool. 1.** zoological **2.** zoology

**zoological garden** *same as* ZOO (sense 1)

**zo·ol·o·gy** (zō äl′ə jē) *n.* [ < ModL.: see ZOO- & -LOGY] **1.** the branch of biology that deals with animals, their life, growth, classification, etc. **2.** the animal life of an area; fauna **3.** the characteristics of an animal or an animal group —**zo′o·log′i·cal** (-ə läj′i k'l), **zo′o·log′ic** *adj.* —**zo′·o·log′i·cal·ly** *adv.* —**zo·ol′o·gist** *n.*

**zoom** (zōōm) *vi.* [echoic] **1.** to make a loud, low-pitched, buzzing or humming sound **2.** to move with a zooming sound **3.** to climb suddenly and sharply: said of an airplane **4.** to rise rapidly *[prices zoomed]* **5.** to focus a camera by using a zoom lens —*vt.* to cause to zoom —*n.* **1.** a zooming or a zooming sound **2.** *same as* ZOOM LENS —*adj.* equipped with a zoom lens

**zoom lens** a system of lenses, as in a movie or TV camera, that can be rapidly adjusted for close-up shots or distance views while keeping the image in focus

**zo·oph·i·lism** (zō äf′ə liz′m) *n.* [ZOO- + PHIL(O)- + -ISM] extreme love for animals; specif., abnormal sexual attraction to animals: also **zo·oph′i·ly**

**zo·o·phyte** (zō′ə fīt′) *n.* [ < ModL. < Gr.: see ZOO- & -PHYTE] any animal, as a coral, sponge, etc., that looks and grows somewhat like a plant —**zo′o·phyt′ic** (-fit′ik), **zo′o·phyt′i·cal** *adj.*

**zo·o·plank·ton** (zō′ə plaŋk′tən) *n.* plankton consisting of animals, as protozoans

**zo·o·spore** (zō′ə spôr′) *n. Bot.* an asexual spore, esp. of certain fungi or algae, capable of independent motion usually by means of cilia or flagella —**zo′o·spor′ic**, **zo·os′po·rous** (-äs′pə rəs) *adj.*

**zo·ri** (zôr′ē) *n., pl.* **zo′ris**, **zo′ri** [Jap.] a sandal of a Japanese style, consisting of a flat sole held on the foot with a thong between the big toe and the toe next to it

**Zo·ro·as·ter** (zō′rō as′tər, zôr′ō as′-) ? 6th or 7th cent. B.C.; Per. religious leader: founder of Zoroastrianism —**Zo′ro·as′tri·an** (-trē ən) *adj., n.*

**Zo·ro·as·tri·an·ism** (-trē ən iz′m) *n.* the religious system of the ancient Persians, teaching the eventual triumph of the spirit of good over the spirit of evil

**Zou·ave** (zōō äv′, zwäv) *n.* [Fr. < Ar. *Zwāwa*, an Algerian tribe] **1.** a member of a former infantry unit in the French army that wore a colorful Oriental uniform **2.** a member of any military group wearing a similar colorful uniform

**zounds** (zoundz) *interj.* [altered < the oath *(by) God's wounds*] [Archaic] a mild oath expressing surprise or anger

**zow·ie** (zou′ē) *interj.* an exclamation expressing excitement, enthusiasm, admiration, etc.

**zoy·si·a** (zoi′sē ə) *n.* [ModL., after Karl von *Zois,* 18th-c. G. botanist] a creeping, wiry grass used for lawns in warm, dry regions

**Zr** *Chem.* zirconium

**zuc·chet·to** (zōō ket′ō, -ə; *It.* tsōō ket′tô) *n., pl.* **-tos**; *It.* **-ti** (-tē) [ < *It.* < *zucca,* a gourd] *R.C.Ch.* a skullcap worn by clergymen: a priest's is black, a bishop's purple, a cardinal's red, and the Pope's white

**zuc·chi·ni** (zōō kē′nē) *n., pl.* **-ni, -nis** [It., pl. of *zucchino,* dim. of *zucca,* a gourd] a variety of summer squash that is green-skinned and shaped somewhat like a cucumber

**Zui·der Zee, Zuy·der Zee** (zī′dər zē′; *Du.* zöi′dər zā′) former arm of the North Sea, which extended into the Netherlands: the S section (now called IJSSELMEER) was shut off from the North Sea by dikes: cf. WADDENZEE

**Zu·lu** (zōō′lōō) *n.* **1.** *pl.* **-lus, -lu** any member of a cattle-owning people living in Natal, South Africa **2.** their Bantu language —*adj.* of the Zulus, their language, etc.

**Zu·lu·land** (zōō′lōō land′) region, formerly a Zulu kingdom, in Natal province, South Africa, on the Indian Ocean

**Zu·ñi** (zōōn′yē) *n.* [AmSp. < AmInd.] **1.** *pl.* **-ñis, -ñi** any member of a tribe of American Indians living in a pueblo in W New Mexico **2.** their language —**Zu′ñi·an** *adj., n.*

**Zur·ba·rán** (thōōr′bä rän′), **Fran·cis·co de** (frän thēs′kô the) 1598–1664; Sp. painter

**Zur·ich** (zoor′ik) city in N Switzerland: pop. 428,000: also written **Zür·ich** (*G.* tsü′riH)

**zwie·back** (swē′bak, swī′-, tswē′-, zwī′-; -bäk; *G.* tsvē′bäk′) *n.* [G. < *zwie-,* twice + *backen,* to bake] a kind of rusk or biscuit that is sliced and toasted after baking

**Zwing·li** (tsviṅ′lē; *E.* zwiṅ′glē, swiṅ′-), **Ul·rich** (ool′riH) or **Hul·dreich** (hool′drīH) 1484–1531; Swiss Protestant reformer —**Zwing′li·an** *adj., n.*

**zy·gote** (zī′gōt, zig′ōt) *n.* [ < Gr. *zygōtos,* yoked < *zygon,* a yoke] a cell formed by the union of male and female gametes; fertilized egg cell before cleavage —**zy·got′ic** (-gät′ik) *adj.* —**zy·got′i·cal·ly** *adv.*

**zy·mase** (zī′mās) *n.* [Fr.: see ff. & -ASE] an enzyme, present in yeast, that promotes fermentation by breaking down glucose and some other carbohydrates into alcohol and carbon dioxide

**zyme** (zīm) *n.* [Gr. *zymē,* a leaven] [Obs.] a ferment or enzyme

**zy·mo-** [ < Gr. *zymē,* a leaven] *a combining form meaning* fermentation *[zymology]* : also, before a vowel, **zym-**

**zy·mo·gen** (zī′mə jən) *n. Biochem.* an inactive form of an enzyme that can be made active

**zy·mol·o·gy** (zī mäl′ə jē) *n.* [ZYMO- + -LOGY] the science dealing with fermentation —**zy′mo·log′ic** (-mə läj′ik), **zy′·mo·log′i·cal** *adj.* —**zy·mol′o·gist** *n.*

**zy·mur·gy** (zī′mər jē) *n.* [ZYM(O)- + -URGY] the branch of chemistry dealing with fermentation, as applied in wine making, brewing, etc.

---

# TABLES OF WEIGHTS AND MEASURES

## Linear Measure

| | | | | |
|---|---|---|---|---|
| 1 mil | = | 0.001 inch | = | 0.0254 millimeter |
| 1 inch | = | 1,000 mils | = | 2.54 centimeters |
| 12 inches | = | 1 foot | = | 0.3048 meter |
| 3 feet | = | 1 yard | = | 0.9144 meter |
| 5½ yards or 16½ feet | = | 1 rod (or pole or perch) | = | 5.029 meters |
| 40 rods | = | 1 furlong | = | 201.168 meters |
| 8 furlongs or 1,760 yards or 5,280 feet | = | 1 (statute) mile | = | 1.6093 kilometers |
| 3 miles | = | 1 (land) league | = | 4.83 kilometers |

## Square Measure

| | | | | |
|---|---|---|---|---|
| | | 1 square inch | = | 6.452 square centimeters |
| 144 square inches | = | 1 square foot | = | 929.03 square centimeters |
| 9 square feet | = | 1 square yard | = | 0.8361 square meter |
| 30¼ square yards | = | 1 square rod (or square pole or square perch) | = | 25.292 square meters |
| 160 square rods or 4,840 square yards or 43,560 square feet | = | 1 acre | = | 0.4047 hectare |
| 640 acres | = | 1 square mile | = | 259.00 hectares or 2.590 square kilometers |

## Cubic Measure

| | | | | |
|---|---|---|---|---|
| | | 1 cubic inch | = | 16.387 cubic centimeters |
| 1,728 cubic inches | = | 1 cubic foot | = | 0.0283 cubic meter |
| 27 cubic feet | = | 1 cubic yard | = | 0.7646 cubic meter |
| | | (in units for cordwood, etc.) | | |
| 16 cubic feet | = | 1 cord foot | = | 0.453 cubic meter |
| 128 cubic feet or 8 cord feet | = | 1 cord | = | 3.625 cubic meters |

## Nautical Measure

| | | | | |
|---|---|---|---|---|
| 6 feet | = | 1 fathom | = | 1.829 meters |
| 100 fathoms | = | 1 cable's length (ordinary) | | |

(In the U.S. Navy 120 fathoms or 720 feet, or 219.456 meters, = 1 cable's length; in the British Navy, 608 feet, or 185.319 meters, = 1 cable's length.)

| | | | | |
|---|---|---|---|---|
| 10 cables' length | = | 1 international nautical mile | = | 1.852 kilometers (exactly) |

(6,076.11549 feet, by international agreement)

1 international nautical mile = 1.150779 statute miles (the length of a minute of longitude at the equator)

| | | | | |
|---|---|---|---|---|
| 3 nautical miles | = | 1 marine league (3.45 statute miles) | = | 5.56 kilometers |
| 60 nautical miles | = | 1 degree of a great circle of the earth = 69.047 statute miles | | |

## Dry Measure

| | | | | | | |
|---|---|---|---|---|---|---|
| | | 1 pint | = | 33.60 cubic inches | = | 0.5506 liter |
| 2 pints | = | 1 quart | = | 67.20 cubic inches | = | 1.1012 liters |
| 8 quarts | = | 1 peck | = | 537.61 cubic inches | = | 8.8098 liters |
| 4 pecks | = | 1 bushel | = | 2,150.42 cubic inches | = | 35.2390 liters |

According to United States government standards, the following are the weights avoirdupois for single bushels of the specified grains: for wheat, 60 pounds; for barley, 48 pounds; for oats, 32 pounds; for rye, 56 pounds; for shelled corn, 56 pounds. Some States have specifications varying from these.

The British dry quart = 1.032 U.S. dry quarts

## Liquid Measure

| | | | | | | |
|---|---|---|---|---|---|---|
| 1 gill | = | 4 fluid ounces | = | 7.219 cubic inches | = | 0.1183 liter |
| | | (see next table) | | | | |
| 4 gills | = | 1 pint | = | 28.875 cubic inches | = | 0.4732 liter |
| 2 pints | = | 1 quart | = | 57.75 cubic inches | = | 0.9464 liter |
| 4 quarts | = | 1 gallon | = | 231 cubic inches | = | 3.7854 liters |

The British imperial gallon (4 imperial quarts) = 277.42 cubic inches = 4.546 liters. The barrel in Great Britain equals 36 imperial gallons, in the United States, usually 31½ gallons.

## Apothecaries' Fluid Measure

| | | | | | | |
|---|---|---|---|---|---|---|
| | | 1 minim | = | 0.0038 cubic inch | = | 0.0616 milliliter |
| 60 minims | = | 1 fluid dram | = | 0.2256 cubic inch | = | 3.6966 milliliters |
| 8 fluid drams | = | 1 fluid ounce | = | 1.8047 cubic inches | = | 0.0296 liter |
| 16 fluid ounces | = | 1 pint | = | 28.875 cubic inches | = | 0.4732 liter |

See table immediately preceding for quart and gallon equivalents.
The British pint = 20 fluid ounces.

## Circular (or Angular) Measure

| | | |
|---|---|---|
| 60 seconds (") | = | 1 minute (') |
| 60 minutes | = | 1 degree (°) |
| 90 degrees | = | 1 quadrant or 1 right angle |
| 180 degrees | = | 2 quadrants or 1 straight angle |
| 4 quadrants or 360 degrees | = | 1 circle |

## Avoirdupois Weight

(The grain, equal to 0.0648 gram, is the same in all three tables of weight.)

| | | | | |
|---|---|---|---|---|
| 1 dram or 27.34 grains | | | = | 1.772 grams |
| 16 drams or 437.5 grains | = | 1 ounce | = | 28.3495 grams |
| 16 ounces or 7,000 grains | = | 1 pound | = | 453.59 grams |
| 100 pounds | = | 1 hundredweight | = | 45.36 kilograms |
| 2,000 pounds | = | 1 ton | = | 907.18 kilograms |

In Great Britain, 14 pounds (6.35 kilograms) = 1 stone, 112 pounds (50.80 kilograms) = 1 hundredweight, and 2,240 pounds (1,016.05 kilograms) = 1 long ton.

### Troy Weight
(The grain, equal to 0.0648 gram, is the same in all three tables of weight.)

|  |  |  |  |  |  |
|---|---|---|---|---|---|
| | 3.086 | grains | = 1 carat | = 200.00 | milligrams |
| | 24 | grains | = 1 pennyweight | = 1.5552 | grams |
| 20 pennyweights or | 480 | grains | = 1 ounce | = 31.1035 | grams |
| 12 ounces or 5,760 | grains | | = 1 pound | = 373.24 | grams |

### Apothecaries' Weight
(The grain, equal to 0.0648 gram, is the same in all three tables of weight.)

|  |  |  |  |
|---|---|---|---|
| 20 grains | = 1 scruple | = | 1.296 grams |
| 3 scruples | = 1 dram | = | 3.888 grams |
| 8 drams or 480 grains | = 1 ounce | = | 31.1035 grams |
| 12 ounces or 5,760 grains | = 1 pound | = | 373.24 grams |

## THE METRIC SYSTEM
### Linear Measure

|  |  |  |  |
|---|---|---|---|
| | 1 millimeter | = | 0.03937 inch |
| 10 millimeters | = 1 centimeter | = | 0.3937 inch |
| 10 centimeters | = 1 decimeter | = | 3.937 inches |
| 10 decimeters | = 1 meter | = | 39.37 inches or 3.2808 feet |
| 10 meters | = 1 decameter | = | 393.7 inches |
| 10 decameters | = 1 hectometer | = | 328.08 feet |
| 10 hectometers | = 1 kilometer | = | 0.621 mile or 3,280.8 feet |
| 10 kilometers | = 1 myriameter | = | 6.21 miles |

### Square Measure

|  |  |  |  |
|---|---|---|---|
| | 1 square millimeter | = | 0.00155 square inch |
| 100 square millimeters | = 1 square centimeter | = | 0.15499 square inch |
| 100 square centimeters | = 1 square decimeter | = | 15.499 square inches |
| 100 square decimeters | = 1 square meter | = | 1,549.9 square inches or 1.196 square yards |
| 100 square meters | = 1 square decameter | = | 119.6 square yards |
| 100 square decameters | = 1 square hectometer | = | 2.471 acres |
| 100 square hectometers | = 1 square kilometer | = | 0.386 square mile or 247.1 acres |

### Land Measure

|  |  |  |  |
|---|---|---|---|
| 1 square meter | = 1 centiare | = | 1,549.9 square inches |
| 100 centiares | = 1 are | = | 119.6 square yards |
| 100 ares | = 1 hectare | = | 2.471 acres |
| 100 hectares | = 1 square kilometer | = | 0.386 square mile or 247.1 acres |

### Volume Measure

|  |  |  |  |
|---|---|---|---|
| 1,000 cubic millimeters | = 1 cubic centimeter | = | 0.06102 cubic inch |
| 1,000 cubic centimeters | = 1 cubic decimeter | = | 61.023 cubic inches or 0.0353 cubic foot |
| 1,000 cubic decimeters | = 1 cubic meter | = | 35.314 cubic feet or 1.308 cubic yards |

(the unit is called a *stere* in measuring firewood)

### Capacity Measure

|  |  |  |  |
|---|---|---|---|
| 10 milliliters | = 1 centiliter | = | 0.338 fluid ounce |
| 10 centiliters | = 1 deciliter | = | 3.38 fluid ounces or 0.1057 liquid quart |
| 10 deciliters | = 1 liter | = | 1.0567 liquid quarts or 0.9081 dry quart |
| 10 liters | = 1 decaliter | = | 2.64 gallons or 0.284 bushel |
| 10 decaliters | = 1 hectoliter | = | 26.418 gallons or 2.838 bushels |
| 10 hectoliters | = 1 kiloliter | = | 264.18 gallons or 35.315 cubic feet |

### Weights

|  |  |  |  |
|---|---|---|---|
| 10 milligrams | = 1 centigram | = | 0.1543 grain or 0.000353 ounce (avdp.) |
| 10 centigrams | = 1 decigram | = | 1.5432 grains |
| 10 decigrams | = 1 gram | = | 15.432 grains or 0.035274 ounce (avdp.) |
| 10 grams | = 1 decagram | = | 0.3527 ounce |
| 10 decagrams | = 1 hectogram | = | 3.5274 ounces |
| 10 hectograms | = 1 kilogram | = | 2.2046 pounds |
| 10 kilograms | = 1 myriagram | = | 22.046 pounds |
| 10 myriagrams | = 1 quintal | = | 220.46 pounds |
| 10 quintals | = 1 metric ton | = | 2,204.6 pounds |

## MARKS OF PUNCTUATION

### The Period [ . ]

1. Use a period at the end of declarative sentences, indirect questions, and most imperative sentences.
    This book is very helpful. (*declarative sentence*)
    He asked what the score was. (*indirect question*)
    Write your name at the top of each sheet. (*imperative sentence*)
2. Use a period after most abbreviations. (See the section on abbreviations, p. 881)
3. Use three periods (called *suspension points* or *ellipsis marks*) to show that material has been omitted from a quotation. Use four periods when the omission comes at the end of a sentence.
    "There are four ways . . . to remedy the situation."
    *Original*: "There are four ways, none of which has been mentioned by my opponent, to remedy the situation."
4. A period may be used after a polite request phrased as a question.
    Would you please send me a copy of your catalog.
5. Do *not* use a period at the end of the title of a book, magazine, article, poem, or essay.
6. In a typed manuscript there should be two spaces between a period and the beginning of the next sentence.
7. In a typed manuscript, abbreviations do not have internal spacing.
    U.S.A.
    Ph.D.
    e.g.

### The Question Mark [ ? ]

1. Use a question mark at the end of a direct question.
    Do you have the money?
    "Do you have the money?" he asked. (Note that a comma is not used after the question mark.)
2. Use a question mark after each query in a series if you wish to emphasize each element.
    Have you heard the candidate give her views on civil rights? the war? urban problems? or the farm problem?
3. Use a question mark enclosed in parentheses to show uncertainty about a word, fact, or number.
    He was born in 1572(?) and died in 1622.
4. In a typed manuscript there should be two spaces between a question mark and the beginning of the next sentence.

### The Exclamation Mark [ ! ]

1. Use the exclamation mark after a forceful interjection or imperative sentence.
    Help!
    Please! Don't leave now!
2. In a typed manuscript there should be two spaces between an exclamation mark and the beginning of the next sentence.

### The Comma [ , ]

1. Use a comma before the conjunctions *and, but, for, or, yet,* and *nor* when they join the clauses of a compound sentence.
    We inquired for him at the address she gave us, but no one there had ever heard of a person by that name.
    *Note*: Between most short clauses and between many long ones when the meaning is clear, the comma is omitted.
    First he stopped at the bank and then he went home.
2. Use a comma to separate an introductory clause or phrase from a main clause.
    When he had tired of the mad pace of New York, he moved to Dubuque.
    In the beginning, he liked the work.
    *Note*: If the introductory clause or phrase is short, or if there is no danger of ambiguity, the comma may be omitted. The following examples require commas because their omission slows up comprehension.
    In spite of all that, she got a passing grade.
    If the police shoot, the woman may be wounded.
3. Use a comma to set off introductory *yes* and *no*, mild exclamations, words of direct address, and introductory words that serve as a transition (*however, anyway*, etc.)
    Yes, I am going too.
    Jane, bring the book with you.
    Nevertheless, he was there when the trouble started.
4. Use a comma to set off a question at the end of a statement.
    You are coming too, aren't you?
5. Use a comma to set off dates, addresses, and titles.
    The letter was dated June 20, 1973, and was sent airmail.
    He lived at 21 Baker Street, Elyria, Ohio, for twenty years.
    Dr. Mary Harris, Director of Admissions.

6. Use a comma to set off contrasted sentence elements.
    Fred, not Jim, was first in his class.
7. Use a comma to indicate an omitted word or words in parallel constructions within a sentence.
    Irene is studying hard; Susan, scarcely at all.
8. Use a comma to set off sentence elements out of natural order.
    That he would accept the money, none of us seriously doubted.
9. Use a comma to separate words, phrases, and clauses in a series.
    The menu offered the usual choice of steak, chops, or chicken.
    If he studies hard, if he takes good notes, and if he participates in class discussion, he will probably pass.
    *Note*: In the style of some individuals and publications, the final comma before the conjunction is omitted.
    The daffodils, hyacinths, tulips and lilacs were in bloom.
10. Use a comma to set off absolute and parenthetical elements in the sentence.
    We finished within the allotted time, however.
    He did not say that, as you will realize when we play the recording, but he did imply it.
11. Use a comma to separate coordinate adjectives modifying the same noun. (If you can substitute *and* for the comma, the adjectives are coordinate.)
    It was a quaint, old-fashioned, vine-covered cottage.
    She had bright, mischievous, laughing brown eyes.
    But do not use a comma to separate noncoordinate adjectives modifying the same noun.
    Professor Jones is a kind old gentleman.
12. Use a comma or commas to set off nonrestrictive phrases or clauses from the rest of the sentence. (A nonrestrictive phrase or clause is one not essential to the meaning of the sentence.)
    My gun, which is now over the mantlepiece, hasn't been used for years.
    He found the paper on the roof, where the newsboy had thrown it.
13. Use a comma to set off direct quotations from such expressions as *he said, she replied*, etc.
    He said, "I'll never believe you again."
    "I know you can pass this course," he said, "if you will only try."
    *But note*: If the *he said* (or similar expression) comes between two independent clauses, then it must be followed by a period or semicolon, not by a comma.
    "Try this book," he said. "I think you will like it."
14. Use a comma following the salutation of a personal letter and following the closing phrase of every letter.
    Dear Jean,
    Very truly yours,
15. Use a comma before and after a dependent clause that comes in the middle of a sentence.
    The apples, although they had been freshly picked, became spoiled in shipment.
16. Use a comma after terms (*e.g., i.e., namely*) that introduce a series or an example.
    Some of our presidents, e.g., Jefferson, J. Q. Adams, and Buchanan, had previously been secretaries of state.
    *But note*: "Such as" should not have a comma preceding or following it.
    I enjoy sports such as football, basketball, and track.
17. Use a comma to set off the one spoken to in direct address.
    "John, you're the troublemaker in this class."
    "Yes, sir, I guess I am."
18. Use a comma to separate thousands in numbers of one thousand or over.
    The area of the earth is approximately 196,950,000 sq. mi.
19. Use a comma to separate inverted names, phrases, etc., as in a bibliography, index, or catalog.
    Jones, Harold T.
    Persia, architecture of
    radios, portable
20. In a typed manuscript a comma is followed by one space.

### Misused and Unnecessary Commas

1. Do not use a comma to separate independent clauses not joined by a conjunction. This error is called the *comma splice* or *comma fault*.
    Evanston is by no means a resort city; however, its recreation facilities are of the finest. (*not* . . . a resort city, however, . . .)
    John told me he was an officer in the army; that isn't what I heard from others, however. (*not* . . . in the army, that isn't what . . .)

2. Do not use a comma or commas to set off restrictive phrases or clauses—that is, phrases or clauses necessary to the proper identification of the words they modify.

The book which I am reading is a history text.

3. Do not use a comma to separate a verb from a noun clause used as its subject or as its object.

That the professor enjoyed his subject was evident.
(*not* That the professor enjoyed his subject, was evident.)
I cannot imagine what made me do it. (*not* I cannot imagine, what made me do it.)

4. Do not use a comma between a noun and an adjective that comes directly before it.

It was a cold, wet, miserable day. (*not* . . . a cold, wet, miserable, day.)

5. Do not use a comma before *that* introducing an indirect statement.

He said that he would be there. (*not* He said, that he would be there.)

## The Semicolon  [ ; ]

1. Use a semicolon between two independent clauses when they are not joined by a coordinating conjunction and the ideas expressed are very closely connected.

Good English requires more than correctness; it demands clarity, precision, and smoothness.

2. Use a semicolon to separate independent clauses joined only by conjunctive adverbs (*however, furthermore, nevertheless, consequently, also, besides, thus, otherwise, accordingly, hence, moreover, than,* etc.)

The bill was sent to the Senate; however, it was buried there in committee.

3. Use a semicolon with a coordinating conjunction if the independent clauses themselves contain commas.

The war, which was an abomination, had ended; and the battle for peace was to begin, at long last.

4. Use a semicolon to separate elements of a series when the elements themselves contain internal punctuation.

The participants came from Albany, New York; Cleveland, Ohio; and London, England.

5. Do *not* use a semicolon as the equivalent of a colon. Although a semicolon is often interchangeable with a period, it is never interchangeable with a colon.

6. Do *not* use a semicolon as the equivalent of a comma. Except for the special uses described in 3 and 4 above, the semicolon should never be used as a substitute for the comma.

7. In a typed manuscript a semicolon is followed by one space.

## The Colon  [ : ]

1. Use a colon before a long, formal quotation, formal statement, or list of items.

Lincoln arose and spoke as follows: "Fourscore and seven years ago . . . ."
The court's rules were simply stated: no television, no photographs, no demonstrations.
The following materials will be needed: pen, pencil, notebook, paper, and typewriter.

2. Use a colon after a main clause when the succeeding clause or clauses explain the first clause.

English usage is like table etiquette: it is conventional and its sanction is a social one.

3. Use a colon following the salutation of a formal letter. In informal letters a comma may be used.

Dear Ms. Brown:
Dear Sir:
Dear Bob,

4. Use a colon to separate chapter and verse of a Biblical citation, volume and page numbers in references, numerals designating hours and minutes, and the parts of a ratio.

Exodus 4:6
*U.S. Encyclopedia* 12:587
10:45 A.M.
11:10 odds

5. In a typed manuscript a colon is followed by one space.

## The Dash  [ — ]

1. Use a dash to indicate an abrupt break in the structure of the sentence or an unfinished statement.

He is—how shall I say it?—an officious zealot.
He said, "I am at a loss to understand—"
*Note:* When the dash comes at the end of the sentence, it is not followed by a period.

2. Use a dash to set off a summary or a long appositive.

Behind his apparent solicitude for her health, comfort, and happiness, one motive was evident to us—his eagerness for a bequest in her will.

3. Use a dash to set off strongly parenthetical expressions.

I was offended—no, enraged would be more accurate—by his actions.

4. Use a dash between numbers, dates, times, places, etc. that mark limits.

Look at pages 17—34.
Franklin lived 1706—90.
The office hours are 8:00—5:00 daily.
He will arrive on the New York—Chicago express.

5. Do not use dashes indiscriminately as a substitute for other marks of punctuation.

6. A dash is made in typing by using two hyphens with no space between them and the preceding and following words.

## Parentheses  [ ( ) ]

1. Use parentheses to enclose material that serves as an explanation, supplement, or example.

He ran 1500 meters (a little less than a mile).

2. Use parentheses to enclose figures and letters in the text of a piece of writing to indicate order of enumeration.

The subjects for this course are (1) English, (2) shorthand, (3) bookkeeping, (4) typewriting.

3. Use parentheses to enclose cross-references.

The amount of this yearly increase is astonishing (see Appendix A).
"Unexceptionable" is not to be confused with "unexceptional" (consult the dictionary).

4. Use parentheses in formal business writing to confirm a sum previously given in words.

I enclose my check for five hundred dollars ($500.00) to cover payment in full.

5. The conventions governing the use of parentheses with other marks of punctuation are as follows:

a. When a complete sentence within parentheses stands alone (that is, not as part of another sentence), the terminal punctuation is enclosed within parentheses.

He said that knowledge is sometimes useful. (That must be the unexceptionable statement of the century.)

b. When a complete sentence within parentheses is part of another sentence:
• It does not begin with a capital letter unless the first word is a proper noun.
• No period is used within the parentheses.
• If it is a question, a question mark is used within the parentheses.

Later in his analysis he stated that quality control was uneconomical (does he think this true for all lines?) and that its enforcement was ineffective.

c. When a word, phrase, or clause within parentheses is part of a sentence:
• A comma, semicolon, or period is never used after the last word in the parentheses.
• A comma, semicolon, or period is used following the second parenthesis only if the sentence without the parenthetical material requires punctuation at that point.
• A question mark or exclamation mark is used within the parentheses if it applies to the material within the parentheses.

He considered reporting Jim's threat (could it have been just so much bluster?) but then decided to have a heart-to-heart talk with him first.

6. In a typed manuscript matter in parentheses within a sentence is separated from the words on either side of the parentheses by a single space. A sentence standing by itself within parentheses is separated from the preceding and following sentences by two spaces.

## Quotation Marks  [ " " ]

1. Use quotation marks to enclose all direct quotations.

"Are you," she asked, "the man who helped my son?"
"Yes," he said, "I helped him. I didn't do much, though."

2. Use single quotation marks to enclose a quotation within another quotation.

The teacher said, "William Hazlitt's dying words were 'It was a happy life.' "

3. Use quotation marks to enclose titles of articles, chapters of a book, essays, short stories, short poems, and musical compositions.

The third chapter, "Some Solutions to the Problem," perhaps the most valuable in the book.
One of Emerson's characteristic essays is "Self Reliance."
I enjoyed Steinbeck's short story "The Leader of the People."
She made us memorize the poem "Dover Beach," none of us liked.
She sang "Over the Bounding Waves" loudly with appropriate gestures.

4. Use quotation marks to enclose words specially, words used in special senses, or words referred to. (Italics may also be used in such cases.)

Such words as "good," "bad," "beautiful" are merely judgment words.
What was the "real" meaning of her question?

5. A long quotation of a number of lines is usually placed in a paragraph that is indented on both sides, single-spaced, and without quotation marks.
6. Generally speaking, do not use quotation marks to redeem slang. If the slang expression is the best and most exact expression for the context, then use it without the apology of quotation marks; if it is not, putting it in quotation marks probably will not improve it or make it acceptable.
7. The conventions governing the use of quotation marks with other forms of punctuation are as follows:
  **a.** The comma and the period are *always* enclosed within quotation marks.
"I'm sorry," he said, "but I don't believe you."
  **b.** The colon and semicolon are *never* enclosed within quotation marks.
I had not read Francis Bacon's essay, "Of Truth"; in fact, I had never heard of it.
  **c.** The dash, question mark, and exclamation mark are enclosed within quotation marks if they apply to the quoted material. They are placed after the quotation marks if they apply to the whole sentence.
"Am I going too?" she asked.
Did she say, "I am going too"?

## Brackets [ ]

1. Use brackets to enclose matter which you insert in the text of a quoted passage to explain, comment, or correct.
"He was born in 1805 [actually in 1802] in . . . ."
According to *Time* magazine, "It [*Rabbit, Run*] was a flawlessly turned portrait of a social cripple who understood somehow that, running, he was more alive than he would be standing still."
2. Use brackets to enclose the Latin word *sic*, meaning "thus," when you insert it into a quotation following a mistake in fact, spelling, grammar, etc. to indicate to the reader that you are quoting verbatim from your source and that the mistake was in your source and was not yours.
"Andrew Johnson never attended school and was scarcely able to read when he met Eliza McCardle, whom he married on May 5, 1927 [sic]."
3. In a typed manuscript insert brackets in ink if your typewriter lacks these characters.

## Apostrophe [ ' ]

1. Use the apostrophe to indicate the possessive case of the noun or pronoun.
the student's book
John's golf clubs
one's obligation
2. **a.** For nouns not ending in *s* add the apostrophe followed by *s*.
children's shoes
dog's collar
men's suits
  **b.** For singular nouns ending in an *s*, *sh*, or *z* sound, the possessive is formed either by adding the apostrophe to the final *s* or by adding the apostrophe and another *s*.
James' book *or* James's book
conscience' sake *or* conscience's sake
  **c.** For plural nouns ending in an *s*, *sh*, or *z* sound, use the apostrophe alone.
the Joneses' house
dogs' collars
the ladies' purses
  **d.** In compound constructions place the apostrophe and *s* on the word standing immediately before the word being modified.
King of England's daughter
else's opinion
law's cousin
possession is shown by adding the apostrophe last name only or to all the names.
and Christopher's home
and Christopher's home
hip is denoted by the apostrophe and the plural form of the modified word.
Christopher's homes
ewriters
dicate the omission of letters
the plurals of figures,
your sentence.
with the personal pronouns
ur's?)
It's color is faded.)

6. The apostrophe is often omitted in the names of organizations.
Teachers College
Citizens Bank
Lions International
Veterans Administration

## Italics

Italics (slanted type in printing) are indicated in a typed or handwritten manuscript by underlining.
1. Use italics for titles of books, magazines, plays, movies, long musical compositions, and names of trains, planes, and ships.
I read Austin Warren's *Rage for Order*.
*Esquire* is one of my favorite magazines.
We saw Alec Guinness in *The Horse's Mouth*.
We sailed on the *Cristoforo Colombo*.
Jim Frantz gave us Menotti's *The Medium* for Christmas.
Mort Walker directed García Lorca's *Blood Wedding*.
2. Use italics to emphasize a word or larger element in a sentence or to refer to a word as a word.
*Moderation* and *pragmatism* are the key terms to describe his fiscal policies.
The dictionary under the word *run* lists dozens of meanings.
*Note*: Do not overuse italics for emphasis.
3. Use italics to indicate a foreign word or phrase which has not been fully adopted as an English word. Check the dictionary to see whether the foreign word or phrase you want to use is so regarded.
His motto was *ars gratia artis*, which means "art for art's sake."
I thought the bullfighter would never deliver the *coup de grâce*.
He received a per diem allowance while on the trip.
(Note that the phrase "per diem," a Latin phrase, is now a fully naturalized English term and, hence, is not italicized.)

## The Hyphen [ - ]

1. Use a hyphen to divide a word at the end of a line.
*But note*:
• Words of one syllable cannot be divided (this includes verbs such as "worked").
• Words of more than one syllable can be divided only between syllables. (Consult the dictionary.)
• Suffixes of fewer than three letters should not be separated from the rest of the word.
• Never divide a word so that only one letter stands at the end of the line.
• Hyphenated words should be divided only at the hyphen.
2. Use a hyphen between parts of a compound modifier preceding a noun except when the compound includes an adverb ending in *ly*. Compound modifiers following a noun are usually not hyphenated.
It was their twenty-fifth anniversary.
(All compound numerical modifiers between twenty-one and ninety-nine are hyphenated.)
She was a well-dressed woman.
The woman was well dressed.
(Here the compound follows the noun.)
She was a smartly dressed woman.
(Here the compound includes an adverb ending in *ly*.)
3. Use the dictionary to check on the hyphenation of other compound words. The practice of hyphenating words varies, and dictionaries seek to show the prevailing current practices. The main thing is to be consistent in one's treatment of any particular compound word.

## NUMBERS

1. Use figures to express dates, hours, street numbers, decimals, measures, percentages, and volume, chapter, and page numbers.

| | |
|---|---|
| April 22, 1969 | Vol. II |
| 12:05 P.M. or p.m. | Chapter V |
| 21 Baker Street | p. 83 |
| .3715 | 73% or 73 percent |
| 16 pounds | 80° or 80 degrees |

2. Use figures to record uneven sums of money, and numbers over one hundred except when the numbers can be written as two words.
$4.19
122 *but* five thousand
3. Be consistent in your use of numbers within any piece of writing; do not, for example, spell out a number which can be expressed in two words (fifteen thousand) and later use figures for the same kind of number (20,000).
4. Usually spell out ordinal numbers.

| | |
|---|---|
| Third Reich | Tenth Street |
| eighteenth century | Twenty-third Psalm |

5. Do not begin a sentence with a figure. If spelling out the

number, however, would be awkward, recast the sentence so that it does not begin with a number.

Nine hundred and sixty students attended the rally.

He received 2,694,386 votes. (*not* Two million six hundred and ninety-four thousand three hundred and eighty-six votes were cast for him.)

## CAPITALIZATION

1. Capitalize the first word of a sentence.
2. Capitalize the pronoun *I* and the interjection *O.*
3. Capitalize the first word in a quotation.
   He asked, "Are you going too?"
4. Capitalize the first word of a direct question falling within a sentence.
   This story answers the question, Where does true happiness really lie?
5. Capitalize all nouns referring to the deity and to the Bible and other sacred books and persons. Pronouns referring to the deity are capitalized by many, but not all, writers.

| | |
|---|---|
| God | The Ten Commandments  the Holy Bible |
| Christ | The Blessed Virgin  the Koran |
| The Holy Spirit | the Incarnate Word |

6. Capitalize the names of gods and goddesses of polytheistic religions.
   Zeus, Thor, Venus
7. Use a capital letter for *President* and *Presidency* when these refer to the office of President of the United States.
   The President will speak 9:00 P.M.
   *But note:* The president [of a company] will address the luncheon.
8. Use a capital letter for official titles before the names of officials.
   Mayor Davis, President Kennedy, Governor Blair
   *But note:* Mr. Williams was governor of Michigan.
9. Capitalize proper nouns, and adjectives formed from proper nouns. (Consult the dictionary when in doubt.)

| | | |
|---|---|---|
| Michael Mardikes | Germany | Catholicism  Fifth Avenue |
| London | Maine | Protestant  Shakespearean |

10. Capitalize every word except conjunctions, articles, and short prepositions in the titles of books and magazines, music and art, etc. The first word of the title is always capitalized.
    *The Decline and Fall of the Roman Empire*
    *The Taming of the Shrew*
    *The Atlantic Monthly*
    *The Magic Flute*
11. Capitalize every word except conjunctions, articles, and short prepositions in the names (or derived adjectives, verbs, etc.) of organizations, institutions, businesses, agencies, movements, religions, holidays, holy days, etc. Sometimes the initial article is capitalized as part of the official name.

| | |
|---|---|
| The World Publishing Company | Memorial Day |
| the Boy Scouts of America | Corpus Christi |
| Internal Revenue Service | Buddhism |
| Yom Kippur | Library of Congress |

12. Capitalize the names of nationalities, languages, and the anthropological terms for major groups of mankind.

| | |
|---|---|
| Italian | Mongoloid |
| English | Negroid |
| Latin | Caucasoid |

*But note:* Do not capitalize *white, black, yellow,* or *red* when referring to groups of mankind.
13. Capitalize the names of all heavenly bodies.

| | |
|---|---|
| Mars | Virgo |
| Sirius | Big Dipper |

*But note: Earth, sun,* and *moon* are not capitalized except when cited along with other heavenly bodies. The moon shines by means of light reflected from the sun. (*But:* Mercury is the planet closest to the Sun.)
14. Capitalize a title, rank, etc. followed by a proper name or of an epithet used with or in place of a proper name.

| | |
|---|---|
| Lord Byron | General MacArthur |
| The Great Emancipator | Catherine the Great |

15. Capitalize the names of trademarks.
    Dacron, Vaseline
16. Capitalize compass directions and adjectives derived from them when they refer to a specific geographical area.
    He lives in the East.
    She lives in the Middle West.
    He is a Southern congressman.
    *But note:* Chicago is east of Kansas City.
17. Capitalize words denoting family relationships only when they precede the name of a person or when they stand unmodified as a substitute for a person's name.
    I wrote to Grandfather Smith.
    I wrote Mother a letter.
    I wrote my mother a letter.
18. Capitalize the names of abstract or inanimate things that are personified.
    It has been said that Justice is lame as well as blind.
    It was the work of Fate.
    And now Spring came scattering her vexatious dandelions.

19. Capitalize geographical terms when they are part of a proper name.

| | |
|---|---|
| Long Island Sound | the Gobi Desert |
| the Great Lakes | Mount Hood |
| the Dead Sea | the Straits of Mackinac |

*But note:* Do not capitalize geographical terms when they are used with two or more proper names (e.g., the Missouri River, *but* the Missouri and Mississippi rivers).
20. Capitalize government departments and offices.

| | |
|---|---|
| Senate | Supreme Court |
| House of Representatives | Court of Appeals |

## ABBREVIATIONS

In general, do not use abbreviations in formal or informal writing (including business letters), except for the universally recognized cases given below.
1. Use abbreviations for the titles *Mr., Ms., Mrs., Dr.* These are never spelled out.
2. You may use abbreviations for the titles of college faculty, clergy, government officials, military personnel, etc. if the title is followed by a full name (first name and surname); if only the surname is used, the title must be written out.

| | |
|---|---|
| Prof. Ralph King, Jr. *but* | Professor King (*never* Professor King, Jr. Use *Jr.* and *Sr.* only with full names) |
| Rev. William Clancy *but* | The Reverend Dr. *or* Mr. *or* Father Clancy (*never* Reverend Clancy) |
| Gov. Warren Hearnes *but* | Governor Hearnes |
| Hon. Warren Hearnes *but* | The Honorable Warren Hearnes or The Honorable Mr. Hearnes |
| Col. John Daniel | *but* Colonel Daniel |

3. Use abbreviations for titles of religious orders, following the full name and a comma. Women's names are preceded by their title and followed by a surname if that is the custom of the order. Men's names may or may not be preceded by a title, according to one's choice.
   Sister Bede Sullivan, O.S.B.
   Mother Angela Therese, I.H.M.
   Father James Agattas, S.J. *or* Fr. James Agattas, S.J. *or* James Agattas, S.J. *or* Rev. James Agattas, S.J. (the last form is now the most usual)
4. Abbreviate the names of organizations when the full names the abbreviations stand for are universally known.

| | |
|---|---|
| AFL-CIO | NAACP |
| DAR | UNESCO |

5. Abbreviate the names of government agencies and military services and terms when the abbreviations are universally used. These abbreviations do not usually have periods (consult the dictionary entry for an abbreviation when in doubt about the use of periods with it).

| | |
|---|---|
| CIA | USN |
| FBI | USAF |
| NATO | MP |
| HEW | PX |

6. Abbreviate certain foreign terms in frequent use. etc., e.g., i.e.
7. Do *not* abbreviate in formal writing, except in footnotes or bibliographies, the days of the week, months of the year, States, countries (except U.S. and U.S.S.R.), weights and measures, or the words *street* and *avenue.*

## SPELLING

The general principles or rules given here apply primarily to American usage. They are not complete but should provide practical helps for the spelling of many common words.

## Words Ending in -e

Words that end in a silent *-e* usually drop the *-e* when a suffix beginning with a vowel is added.

| | |
|---|---|
| assume — assuming | sense — sensible |
| grope — groping | style — stylish |
| purple — purplish | rogue — roguish |

However, the *-e* is kept in a few words, as in these common exceptions.

| | | |
|---|---|---|
| shoeing | hoeing | toeing |
| dyeing | singeing | mileage |

Words that end in a silent *-e* usually keep the *-e* when suffix beginning with a consonant is added.

| | |
|---|---|
| awe — awesome | improve — improve |
| fate — fateful | time — timely |

However, many words that end in a silent *-e* imme preceded by a vowel other than *-e* drop the *-e* when is added.

| | |
|---|---|
| true — truly | argue — argum |
| value — valuation | pursue — pursu |

Other exceptions:

| | | |
|---|---|---|
| awful | wisdom | ninth |

## Words Ending in -ce or -ge

Words that end in -ce or -ge retain the -e when suffixes that begin with a, o, or u are added, so that the c or g will not be pronounced with the hard sound.

| | |
|---|---|
| peace — peaceable | advantage — advantageous |
| service — serviceable | change — changeable |
| notice — noticeable | courage — courageous |

## Words Ending in a Consonant

Words that end in a single consonant preceded by a single vowel usually double that consonant when a suffix beginning with a vowel is added. This rule applies to words of one syllable as well as to words of more than one syllable that are accented on the last syllable.

| | |
|---|---|
| spin — spinning | propel — propellant |
| big — biggest | recur — recurrence |
| trot — trotter | permit — permitted |
| abet — abetted | regret — regrettable |

When the addition of the suffix shifts the accent from the last syllable to a prior syllable, the consonant is not doubled.

| | |
|---|---|
| prefer — preference | refer — reference |

Words that end in two or more consonants, words that end in a single consonant preceded by more than one vowel, and words that are not accented on the last syllable usually do not double the final consonant when a suffix beginning with a vowel is added.

| | |
|---|---|
| hurl — hurling | sprout — sprouted |
| count — counter | profit — profiteer |
| return — returned | benefit — benefited |
| conceal — concealed | prosper — prosperous |
| prevail — prevailing | combat — combative |

## Words Ending in -y

Words that end in -y preceded by a consonant usually change the y to an i when a suffix that does not begin with an i is added.

| | |
|---|---|
| charity — charities | duty — dutiful |
| dizzy — dizziness | ply — plies |
| marry — married | study — studious |
| marrying | studying |

Words that end in -y preceded by a vowel usually remain unchanged when a suffix is added.

| | |
|---|---|
| convey — conveyance | boy — boyish |
| enjoy — enjoying | play — playing |

Exceptions:

| | | |
|---|---|---|
| paid | said | laid |
| daily | gaiety | slain |

## Words Ending in -ie

Words that end in -ie change the -ie to y when the suffix -ing is added.

| | | |
|---|---|---|
| lie — lying | die — dying | vie — vying |

## Words Ending in -c

Words that end in -c usually take on a k when a suffix beginning with i, e, or y is added.

| | |
|---|---|
| picnic — picnicker | shellac — shellacked |
| mimic — mimicking | panic — panicky |
| colic — colicky | rollic — rollicking |

## Words Containing ie or ei

Words that contain ie or ei usually are spelled with the i before the e when the combination represents the sound (ē), except after the letter c where the e usually precedes the i.

| | | |
|---|---|---|
| grief | believe | perceive | ceiling |
| piece | siege | receipt | conceit |
| brief | hygiene | deceive | receive |
| field | achieve | | |

Exceptions:

| | | |
|---|---|---|
| ither | neither | leisure |
| ze | weird | financier |

e words in which ie and ei have the sounds (ā), (e), the spelling ei is usually found.

| | |
|---|---|
| heifer | forfeit |
| foreign | counterfeit |
| sovereign | height |
| heir | sleight |

| | |
|---|---|
| friend | sieve |
| kerchief | |

the ie and ei combinations have lling corresponds with the pro-

| |
|---|
| society |
| de-ice |

ed as a suffix drops one l.

| | | |
|---|---|---|
| cupful | spoonful | eyeful |

## The Endings -ceed, -sede, -cede

Three words end in -ceed. One ends in -sede. The other verbs with the final sound (sēd) end in -cede.

| | | |
|---|---|---|
| exceed | supersede | recede |
| proceed | | intercede |
| succeed | | precede, etc. |

## FORMATION OF PLURALS

Most nouns in English form the plural by adding -s or -es. When the singular noun ends in a sound that allows -s to be added and pronounced without the formation of a new syllable, -s is used. When the singular noun ends in such a sound that -s cannot be joined to it and pronounced without the formation of an additional syllable, -es is used.

| | |
|---|---|
| book — books | torch — torches |
| cake — cakes | kiss — kisses |
| doctor — doctors | tax — taxes |
| room — rooms | bush — bushes |

## Nouns Ending in -o

Nouns that end in -o preceded by a vowel form the plural by adding -s to the singular.

| | |
|---|---|
| radio — radios | tattoo — tattoos |
| folio — folios | vireo — vireos |

Most nouns that end in -o preceded by a consonant form the plural by adding -es to the singular. Some, however, add -s only. There is no fixed rule that deals with this distinction.

| | |
|---|---|
| hero — heroes | solo — solos |
| potato — potatoes | piano — pianos |
| tomato — tomatoes | octavo — octavos |

## Nouns Ending in -f

Most nouns that end in -f or the sound of -f form their plurals regularly, but some common words drop the -f and add -ves. A few nouns have both forms.

| | |
|---|---|
| calf — calves | life — lives |
| knife — knives | loaf — loaves |
| leaf — leaves | thief — thieves |
| shelf — shelves | wife — wives |
| hoof — hoofs, hooves | wharf — wharfs, wharves |

## Nouns Ending in -y

Nouns that end in -y preceded by a consonant usually form the plural by dropping the -y and adding -ies.

| | |
|---|---|
| lady — ladies | story — stories |
| army — armies | study — studies |
| fly — flies | library — libraries |

However, the plural of proper nouns ending in -y is formed by adding -s: both Harrys, the three McNallys.

Nouns that end in -y preceded by a vowel form the plural regularly, by adding -s.

| | |
|---|---|
| boy — boys | quay — quays |
| tray — trays | toy — toys |
| key — keys | buy — buys |

## Change of Vowel

Some nouns form the plural by a vowel change.

| | |
|---|---|
| man — men | goose — geese |
| mouse — mice | foot — feet |
| tooth — teeth | woman — women |

Compounds that end with these words form the plural by the same vowel change.

| | |
|---|---|
| postman — postmen | dormouse — dormice |
| bucktooth — buckteeth | splayfoot—splayfeet |

Nouns that end in -man but are not compounds form the plural regularly, by adding -s.

| | |
|---|---|
| human — humans | German — Germans |
| cayman — caymans | Norman — Normans |
| talisman — talismans | Ottoman — Ottomans |

Similarly the noun mongoose is not a compound of goose and has the plural mongooses, while goose in the sense of a tailor's pressing iron has the plural gooses.

## Nouns from Foreign Languages

Nouns derived from foreign languages often keep their original plurals.

| | |
|---|---|
| alumna — alumnae | datum — data |
| alumnus — alumni | kibbutz — kibbutzim |
| analysis — analyses | monsieur — messieurs |
| basis — bases | phylum — phyla |

Many such nouns, however, have an Anglicized plural as well as the original plural. Either is correct.

appendix — appendices, appendixes
cherub — cherubim, cherubs
criterion — criteria, criterions
focus — foci, focuses
index — indices, indexes
radius — radii, radiuses